- pronunciation given in IPA
  Aussprache in internationaler Lautschrift
- compound block with a swung dash representing the first element of each compound
  Kompositablock mit Tilde für den ersten Teil jeder Zusammensetzung
- cross-reference to a synonymous headword
  Verweis auf synonymes Stichwort
- sense indicator
  Indikator
- usage example
  Anwendungsbeispiel
- style labels (also given for translation)
  Stilschichtangaben (auch für Übersetzungen)
- information on syntax
  syntaktische Angabe
- subject label
  Bereichsangabe
- phrasal verbs listed under main verb
  Verben in festen Verbindungen mit Präpositionen oder Adverbien (Phrasal verbs) *im Anschluß an das jeweilige einfache Verb*
- semantic categories
  Gliederung nach Bedeutungsunterschieden
- stress mark
  Betonungszeichen

bailiff ['beɪlɪf] *n.* **a)** ≈ Justizbeamte, *der;* Büttel, *der (veralt.); (performing distraints)* Gerichtsvollzieher, *der; (serving writs)* Gerichtsbote, *der (veralt.);* **b)** *(agent of landlord)* Verwalter, *der;* Vogt, *der (hist.);* **c)** *(Amer. Admin.: court official)* ≈ Gerichtsbeamte, *der*

bairn [beən] *n. (Scot./N.Engl./literary)* Kind, *das*

ball: ~park *n. (Amer.)* Baseballfeld, *das;* **your estimate is not in the right ~park** *(fig.)* mit deiner Schätzung liegst du völlig falsch *(ugs.);* **~-pen, ~-point, ~-point 'pen** *ns.* Kugelschreiber, *der;* **~room** *n.* Tanzsaal, *der*

basketful ['bɑːskɪtfʊl] *see* **basket b**

'**bawdy-house** *n. (arch.)* Bordell, *das*

beat [biːt] **1.** *v.t.,* **beat, beaten** ['biːtn] **a)** *(strike repeatedly)* schlagen ‹*Trommel, Rhythmus, Eier, Teig*›; klopfen ‹*Teppich*›; hämmern ‹*Gold, Silber usw.*›; **~ the dust out of a carpet/cushion** einen Teppich/ein Polster ausklopfen; **~ a path through sth.** sich *(Dat.)* einen Weg durch etw. bahnen; **~ one's breast** *(lit. or fig.)* sich *(Dat.)* an die Brust schlagen

beggar ['begə(r)] **1.** *n.* **a)** Bettler, *der*/Bettlerin, *die;* **~s can't be choosers** *(prov.)* man kann es sich *(Dat.)* eben nicht immer aussuchen; **b)** *(coll.: person)* Arme, *der/die*

berk [bɜːk] *n. (Brit. sl.)* Dussel, *der (ugs.);* Spinner, *der (ugs.);* Blödmann, *der (salopp)*

Berlin [bɜː'lɪn] **1.** *pr. n.* Berlin *(das).* **2.** *attrib. adj.* Berliner; *(Ling.)* berlinisch

blazon ['bleɪzn] *v.t.* **a)** *(Her.) (describe) nach den Regeln der Heraldik beschreiben*

break [breɪk] **1.** *v.t.,* **broke** [brəʊk], **broken** ['brəʊkn] **a)** brechen

~ a'way 1. *v.t.* **~ sth. away [from sth.]** etw. [von etw.] losbrechen *od.* abbrechen. **2.** *v.i.* **a) ~ away [from sth.]** [von etw.] losbrechen *od.* abbrechen; *(separate itself/oneself)* sich [von etw.] lösen; *(escape)* [aus etw.] entkommen; **he broke away from them** er distanzierte sich von ihnen; *(escaped)* er entkam ihnen; **b)** *(Footb.)* sich freilaufen

~ 'down 1. *v.i.* **a)** *(fail)* zusammenbrechen; ‹*Verhandlungen:*› scheitern; **b)** *(cease to function)* ‹*Auto:*› eine Panne haben; ‹*Telefonnetz:*› zusammenbrechen; **the machine has broken down** die Maschine funktioniert nicht mehr; **c)** *(be overcome by emotion)* zusammenbrechen; **d)** *(Chem.)* aufspalten. **2.** *v.t.* **a)** *(demolish)* aufbrechen ‹*Tür*›; zum Einsturz bringen ‹*Mauer*›; umknicken ‹*Baum*›; **b)** *(suppress)* brechen ‹*Widerstand*›; niederreißen ‹*Barriere, Schranke*›; **c)** *(analyse)* aufgliedern. *See also* **breakdown; broken-down**

~ 'in 1. *v.i.* **a)** *(intrude forcibly)* einbrechen; *see also* **break-in; b)** *(interrupt)* **~ in [on sb./sth.]** [jmdn./etw.] unterbrechen. **2.** *v.t.* **a)** *(accustom to habit)* eingewöhnen; einarbeiten ‹*Lehrling etc.*›; *(tame)* zureiten ‹*Pferd*›; abrichten ‹*Hund*›; *(discipline)* zur Disziplin erziehen; **b)** *(wear etc. until comfortable)* einlaufen ‹*Schuhe*›; sich gewöhnen an (+ *Akk.*) ‹*Brille, Gebiß*›

- indication of approximate equivalence
  Angabe ungefährer Entsprechungen
- regional and national labels
  räumliche Zuordnungen
- idiomatic phrase
  feste Wendung
- indication of archaic usage
  zeitliche Zuordnung
- swung dash representing the headword
  die Tilde vertritt das Stichwort
- label to indicate specific aspect of usage
  Hinweis auf besondere Gebrauchsweise
- proverb
  Sprichwort
- gloss where no translation is possible
  Umschreibung, wenn eine Übersetzung nicht möglich ist
- grammatical information
  grammatische Angaben
- grammatical categories
  Gliederung nach grammatischen Gesichtspunkten
- cross-reference for additional information
  Verweis auf zusätzliche Informationen
- collocators
  Kollokatoren

The Oxford–Duden German Dictionary

The Oxford-Duden German Dictionary

Revised Edition

German–English / English–German

Edited by the Dudenredaktion and the
German Section of the Oxford University Press Dictionary Department

Chief Editors

W. Scholze-Stubenrecht · J. B. Sykes

CLARENDON PRESS · OXFORD

Oxford University Press, Great Clarendon Street, Oxford OX2 6DP
Oxford New York
Athens Auckland Bangkok Bogota Bombay
Buenos Aires Calcutta Cape Town Dar es Salaam
Delhi Florence Hong Kong Istanbul Karachi
Kuala Lumpur Madras Madrid Melbourne
Mexico City Nairobi Paris Singapore
Taipei Tokyo Toronto Warsaw
and associated companies in
Berlin Ibadan

Oxford is a trade mark of Oxford University Press

Published in the United States by
Oxford University Press Inc., New York

First published 1990
Reprinted in enlarged format 1994
Revised edition 1997

British Library Cataloguing in Publication Data
Data available

Library of Congress Cataloging in Publication Data
Data available
ISBN 0–19–860130–1
ISBN 0–19–860132–8 (Thumb index ed.)

3 5 7 9 10 8 6 4 2

Printed in the United States of America

Foreword

The Oxford–Duden German Dictionary is the product of nearly ten years of joint work by two of the world's foremost dictionary publishers, Oxford University Press and the Dudenredaktion of the Bibliographisches Institut, Mannheim. Members of the editorial team were based in their own countries and thus in constant contact with their own language, making use of the unparalleled databases maintained and continually expanded by the two publishers for their celebrated native-speaker dictionaries such as the *Concise Oxford Dictionary* and *Das Grosse Wörterbuch der Deutschen Sprache*. German and English editors met regularly in order to discuss the text in detail, ensure consistency, and achieve precise meshing together of the two languages.

The vocabulary is up to date, and regional language has been extensively covered. Meanings are precisely classified and differentiated to guide the reader to the correct translation; general translations have been carefully chosen for maximum usefulness; many phrases and sentences are translated in their entirety where guidance is needed on style, usage, or word order. Extensive appendices give help with grammar, punctuation, letter writing, and numerical expressions such as those for time and money.

This is the first bilingual dictionary ever to be produced by a team based in both language areas. We are confident that it will make a significant contribution in an age when the language barrier is coming to be the only one remaining between nations of the European Community, and that it will meet the needs of translators, business people, teachers, and secondary-school, high-school, college, and university students in the 1990s.

JOHN SYKES

Oxford University Press

The principal members of the team have been

in Oxford	**in Mannheim**
John Sykes	Werner Scholze-Stubenrecht
Michael Clark	Roland Breitsprecher
Robin Sawers	Olaf Thyen
Vineeta Gupta	Brigitte Alsleben
Bernadette Mohan	Eckhard Böhle
Colin Hope	Maria Dose
Maurice Waite	Gabriele Gassen
John Pheby	Wolfgang Eckey
Eva Vennebusch	Eva Krampe
Clare Rütsch	Susanne Lücking
Judith Cunningham	Marion Trunk-Nußbaumer
Valerie Langrish	
Christopher Burton	
Timothy Connell	

Compilers

Christine Ayorinde
Cyprian Blamires
Ann Clark
John Craddock
Peter Dyer
Stuart Fortey
Susan Ghanouni
Lilian Hall
Fergus McGauran
Neil Morris
Ewald Osers
Ray Perkins
Gunhild Prowe
Eva Sawers
Amanda Thorndike
Richard Toms

in the Institut für Anglistik und Amerikanistik der Universität Mainz in Germersheim

Horst W. Drescher
Dagmar Steffen

Fee Engemann
Lothar Görke
Cosima Heise
Carola Jansen
Ferdinand Kiefer
Ulrike Kraus
Karina Nehl
Lotte Neiffer
Michael Petersen
Ulrike Röhrenbeck
Joachim Schwend
Magdalena Seubel
Annemarie Thiemann

In Oxford considerable help was also given by

Lisa Bennett
Kathryn Buck
Doris Clifton
Shân Fermor
Harry Ferrar
Ursula Lang
Fred McDonald
Victoria Paleit
Jean Pheby
Cora Schenberg Komisar
Joan Spencer
Trish Stableford

Contents

Proprietary names

Guide to the use of the Dictionary

Hinweise für die Benutzung des Wörterbuchs

1. Order of entries

1. Anordnung der Artikel

a) Headwords

a) Alphabetische Ordnung der Stichwörter

Headwords (with the exception of phrasal verbs - see below) are entered in strict alphabetical order, ignoring hyphens, apostrophes, and spaces.

Die Stichwörter sind (mit Ausnahme der *Phrasal verbs* im englisch-deutschen Teil; s.u.) alphabetisch angeordnet, wobei Bindestriche, Apostrophe und Wortzwischenräume keine Rolle spielen.

Examples/Beispiele:

liberal
liberal arts
liberalism

Pinte
Pin-up-Girl
Pinzette

Abbreviations are also entered in alphabetical order in the main Dictionary.

Abkürzungen sind ebenfalls an ihrer entsprechenden Stelle im Alphabet zu finden.

Examples/Beispiele:

clutter
cm. *abbr.*
CND *abbr.*

Nockerl
NOK ... *Abk.*
nölen

Headwords spelt the same but with unrelated meanings are entered separately with a raised number in front of each.

Stichwörter mit hochgestellten Ziffern vor den Anfangsbuchstaben werden zwar gleich geschrieben, haben aber völlig unterschiedliche Bedeutungen.

Examples/Beispiele:

¹dam ... [Stau]damm, *der*
²dam ... Muttertier, *das*

¹Bank ... bench
²Bank ... bank

For the purpose of alphabetical ordering, capital letters are treated as small letters, accented letters as unaccented letters, and the German character *ß* as *ss*.

Umlaute werden wie die entsprechenden nicht umgelauteten Vokale eingeordnet. Entsprechendes gilt für Akzente, und der Buchstabe ß wird wie ss eingeordnet.

Examples/Beispiele:

knurled	**elaboration**
KO	**élan**
koala	**eland**
Buchladen	**Fasnacht**
Büchlein	**Faß**
Buchmacher	**Fassade**

Each English phrasal verb is entered on a new line immediately following the entry for its first element, which is indicated by a swung dash.

Im englisch-deutschen Teil werden die *Phrasal verbs* auf einer neuen Zeile unmittelbar an das Grundwort angeschlossen, wobei dieses durch eine Tilde repräsentiert wird.

Examples/Beispiele: **track**
~ 'down
tracker

¹plump
~ 'out
~ 'up
²plump

b) Compounds

Hyphenated English compounds and all German compounds are entered in their alphabetical place in the Dictionary, as are English compounds written as two or more words if they are regarded as having independent status in the language, e.g. **love affair.** Those not so regarded are given as phrases in the entry for their first word, so for example **love game** is given as **~ game** under **love.** Where two or more compounds with the same first element occur consecutively, they are given in paragraph-like blocks. The first element is given only once at the beginning of the block and is thereafter represented by a swung dash (~).

b) Einordnung von Komposita

Die im Englischen häufig getrennt geschriebenen Komposita werden als selbständige Stichwörter behandelt, wenn sie als eigenständige Wörter gelten können; z. B. wird **love affair** als Stichwort an der entsprechenden Stelle im Alphabet aufgeführt. Wenn ein Kompositum als weniger eigenständig oder nur als Anwendungsbeispiel betrachtet wird, erscheint es unter dem Stichwort, das den ersten Bestandteil bildet, z. B. findet sich unter dem Stichwort **love** als Anwendungsbeispiel **love game.** Mehrere aufeinanderfolgende als Stichwörter aufgeführte Komposita mit gemeinsamem ersten Element sind im Wörterbuch zu Absätzen zusammengefaßt. Dabei steht das erste Element nur am Anfang des Absatzes; es wird innerhalb des Absatzes durch eine Tilde repräsentiert.

In the English-German section, a compound in a block is spelt with the same initial letter – capital or small – as the first element at the beginning of the block, unless the opposite is shown.

Wenn im englisch-deutschen Teil in einem Kompositablock sowohl groß als auch klein geschriebene Stichwörter vorkommen, so erscheint das erste Element zu Beginn des Absatzes entweder in Groß- oder in Kleinschreibung. Bei davon abweichender Schreibung im selben Block steht dann vor der Tilde der zu verwendende Buchstabe.

Examples/Beispiele: **grand: ~niece ... G~ Prix**
Great: ~ Bear ... g~coat

In the German-English section, the first element of a block of compounds has a capital letter if the block contains only nouns, and a small letter if it contains no nouns. If the block contains nouns and other parts of speech, both forms of the first element are given.

Wenn im deutsch-englischen Teil das erste Element sowohl in Groß- als auch in Kleinschreibung gezeigt wird, gilt die Großschreibung für alle Substantive und die Kleinschreibung für die anderen Wortarten.

Examples/Beispiele: **Stech-: ~fliege ... ~zirkel**
kurz-: ~|treten ... ~um
englisch-, Englisch-: ~horn ... ~sprachig

With compounds written as one word, the swung dash is followed immediately by the second element.

Bei Komposita, die zusammengeschrieben werden, steht das zweite Element direkt nach der Tilde.

Examples/Beispiele: **farm: ~stead**
Tipp-: ~fehler

With hyphenated compounds, the hyphen appears between the swung dash and the second element.

Bei Komposita, die mit Bindestrich geschrieben werden, erscheint der Bindestrich zwischen der Tilde und dem zweiten Element.

Examples/Beispiele: **awe: ~-stricken**
Kaffee-: ... ~-Ersatz

With English compounds written as two (or more) words there is a space between the swung dash and the second element.

Bei englischen Komposita, die getrennt geschrieben werden, erscheint ein Zwischenraum zwischen der Tilde und dem zweiten Element

Example/Beispiel: **bank: ~ manager**

c) Phrases

Idioms, fixed phrases, proverbs, and quotations are usually entered under only one word, and cross-references, starting with *see also* or *s. auch*, are given at other words under which the user might look. At **ask 2,** for example, there is the cross-reference *see also* **trouble 1 a,** because the expressions **you are asking for trouble** and **that's asking for trouble** are entered under **trouble,** and at **Stamm a)** there is the cross-reference *s. auch* **Apfel,** because the expression **der Apfel fällt nicht weit vom Stamm** is entered under **Apfel.**

c) Einordnung von festen Wendungen

Aus mehreren Wörtern bestehende feste Wendungen, idiomatische Ausdrücke, Sprichwörter, Zitate und dergleichen sind gewöhnlich nur unter einem Stichwort verzeichnet. Das Wörterbuch gibt, wo es den Bearbeitern nützlich erschien, Verweise auf Fundstellen. Solche Verweise haben die Form *see also* ... bzw. *s. auch* ... und stehen am Schluß eines Artikels bzw. eines Gliederungspunkts. So findet sich etwa unter **ask 2** der Hinweis *see also* **trouble 1 a,** weil unter dem Stichwort **trouble** die Beispiele **you are asking for trouble** und **that's asking for trouble** zu finden sind, und unter **Stamm a)** der Hinweis *s. auch* **Apfel,** weil unter **Apfel** die Redensart **der Apfel fällt nicht weit vom Stamm** behandelt ist.

2. Division of entries

a) Numbered categories

When a word can be used as different parts of speech, these are numbered.

2. Untergliederung der Artikel

a) Untergliederung durch Ziffern

Wenn ein Stichwort mehreren Wortarten angehören kann, steht vor jeder Wortartangabe eine Ziffer.

Examples/Beispiele: **blame** ... **1.** *v. t.* ... **2.** *n.*

entgegen 1. *Adv.* ... **2.** *Präp.*

Adverbial use of a German adjective is given in a separate numbered section.

Bei deutschen Adjektiven erhält der adverbiale Gebrauch eine eigene Ziffer (**1.** *Adj.* ... **2.** *adv.* ...). Unter dieser Ziffer wird gegebenenfalls auch die Verwendung als Attribut zu Adverbien oder anderen Adjektiven behandelt.

Example/Beispiel: **gemütlich 1.** *Adj.* ... **2.** *adv.*

In verb entries, transitive, intransitive, and reflexive uses are also numbered.

Bei Verben unterscheiden die Ziffern außerdem den transitiven, intransitiven und reflexiven Gebrauch des Verbs.

Examples/Beispiele: **freeze** ... **1.** *v. i.* ... **2.** *v. t.*

beschäftigen 1. *refl. V.* ... **2.** *tr. V.*

Entries for German prepositions are divided into numbered sections if they can take more than one case.

Bei deutschen Präpositionen dienen die Ziffern zur Untergliederung nach den Kasus, mit denen die Präposition stehen kann.

Example/Beispiel: **an** ... **1.** *Präp. mit Dat.* ... **2.** *Präp. mit Akk.*

b) Letter categories

When a word has more than one sense (as a particular part of speech) the different senses are distinguished by letters and usually arranged in order of frequency.

b) Untergliederung durch Buchstaben

Wenn ein Stichwort mehrere Bedeutungen haben kann, werden diese mit Buchstaben unterschieden. Dabei steht normalerweise die häufigste Bedeutung an erster Stelle.

Examples/Beispiele: **alien** ... **1.** *adj.* ... **a)** *(strange)* ... **b)** *(foreign)* ... **c)** *(different)* ... **d)** *(repugnant)* ... **e)** *(contrary)*

gemütlich 1. *Adj.* **a)** *(behaglich)* ... **b)** *(ungezwungen)* ... **c)** *(umgänglich)* ... **d)** *(gemächlich)*

3. The headword

a) Form of the headword

The headword appears in bold type at the beginning of the entry.
Verbs are given as infinitives (without *to* in English).
Nouns are given in the nominative singular, but those which occur only in the plural are given in the nominative plural.

3. Das Stichwort

a) Form des Stichworts

Das Stichwort erscheint fett gedruckt am Anfang des Artikels.
Verben erscheinen im Infinitiv. (Im Englischen ohne *to*.)
Substantive erscheinen im Nominativ Singular. Substantive, die nur als Plural vorkommen, erscheinen im Nominativ Plural.

Examples/Beispiele: **trousers** ... *n. pl.*

Kosten *Pl.*

German adjectives (and pronouns declined like adjectives) are given without endings, and adjectives which strictly speaking have no undeclined form are given with an ellipsis instead of any ending.

Deutsche Adjektive (und Pronomen, die wie Adjektive dekliniert werden) erscheinen in endungsloser Form. Auch Adjektive, die eigentlich keine endungslose Form haben, erscheinen ohne Endung, mit Auslassungspunkten.

Example/Beispiel: **äußer...**

Separate entries are given for all forms of the German definite article and of German pronouns which are not declined like adjectives. So, for example, **der, den, dem, die,** etc., **euch,** and **ihr** are all entered as headwords. In the same way, all forms of English pronouns are headwords – **her,** for example, as well as **she.**
German demonstrative pronouns are treated under the masculine nominative singular, e.g. **derjenige.**
Inflected forms are entered as headwords with cross-references to their root forms if these are not easily identifiable.

Examples/Beispiele:
did *see* **'do**
apices *pl. of* **apex**
höher ... *s.* **hoch**
dasjenige *s.* **derjenige**
zog *1. u. 3. Pers. Sg. Prät. v.* **ziehen**

Deutsche Pronomen, die nicht wie Adjektive dekliniert werden, und die bestimmten Artikel erscheinen in allen Formen als selbständige Stichwörter. Es erscheint also z. B. nicht nur **der,** sondern auch **des, dem, den** usw. als Stichwort, und die Form **euch** wird nicht unter **ihr** abgehandelt, sondern ist selbst Stichwort. Ebenso werden englische Pronomen in allen Formen als Stichwörter aufgeführt, also erscheint z. B. nicht nur **she,** sondern auch **her** als Stichwort.
Deutsche Demonstrativpronomen werden an der alphabetischen Stelle der maskulinen Form behandelt, also erscheinen z. B. **diejenige** und **dasjenige** unter dem Stichwort **derjenige.**
Als Stichwörter erscheinen auch bestimmte Flexionsformen, die sich nicht ohne weiteres auf ihre Grundform zurückführen lassen. Ein Verweis führt zur Grundform.

b) Symbols used with headwords

With English headwords:

' shows stress on the following syllable (for more information see 4).

b) Zeichen am Stichwort

Am englischen Stichwort kann das folgende Zeichen auftreten:

' Betonungszeichen vor der zu betonenden Silbe. (Näheres siehe unter 4.)

With German headwords:

Am deutschen Stichwort können die folgenden Zeichen auftreten:

_ indicates a long vowel or a diphthong, stressed in words of more than one syllable.

_ Betonungszeichen in Form eines Strichs unter betonten langen Vokalen.

Examples/Beispiele: **Hi̱e̱b, Bla̱u̱, Hörer, amti̱e̱ren**

. indicates a short vowel, stressed in words of more than one syllable:

. Betonungszeichen in Form eines Punktes unter betonten kurzen Vokalen.

Examples/Beispiele: **Rẹcht, bịtter**

· shows the juncture of elements forming a word.

· Punkt, der bei zusammengesetzten Wörtern die Kompositionsfuge markiert.

Examples/Beispiele: **Kẹrn·kraft, um·brạnden**

| shows the juncture of elements forming a compound verb and indicates that the verb is separable (for more information see Outline of German grammatical forms on p. 1658).

| senkrechter Strich, der bei zusammengesetzten Verben die Kompositionsfuge markiert und gleichzeitig anzeigt, daß das Verb unfest zusammengesetzt ist.

Examples/Beispiele: **vo̱r|haben, ụm|werfen**

4. Pronunciation

The pronunciation of a headword is given in square brackets immediately after it, in the International Phonetic Alphabet (IPA), which is explained on the inside back cover. German pronunciations are based on the DUDEN-Aussprachewörterbuch, while English pronunciations are those common in educated Southern British English.

A *simple headword* without a pronunciation given is pronounced in the same way as the headword immediately before it.

The pronunciation of a *German derivative* with none given can be deduced from that of its root word. The stress, however, is always shown, by _ or . (see 3 b).

Abbreviations without pronunciations given are pronounced as their full forms, except for English ones consisting of two or more capital letters, which are pronounced as individual letters, with the stress on the last, e.g. **BBC** is pronounced [bi:bi:'si:].

The pronunciation of a *compound* with none given can be derived from the pronunciations of its elements, and, unless the compound is in a block, the stress is always shown by the symbol ', _, or . (see 3 b), e.g. **'doughnut** is pronounced as **dough + nut,** with the stress on **dough,** and **ba̱u̱·sparen** is pronounced as **Bau + sparen,** with the stress on **bau.** With German compounds, juncture between elements is shown either by · in the headword (as in 3 b) or, within a block of compounds, by the point where the compound is divided.

4. Angaben zur Aussprache

Die Aussprache des Stichworts ist in Lautschrift in eckigen Klammern unmittelbar nach dem Stichwort angegeben. Die Ausspracheangaben für das Deutsche richten sich nach dem DUDEN-Aussprachewörterbuch, für das Englische nach der *Received Pronunciation* in Südengland. Die dabei verwendeten Zeichen der internationalen Lautschrift der *International Phonetic Association* (IPA) sind im hinteren Buchinnendeckel verzeichnet und erklärt.

Bei mehreren *gleichlautenden Stichwörtern* ist die Aussprache beim ersten Stichwort zu finden.

Bei deutschen *Ableitungen* ohne Ausspracheangabe kann die Aussprache vom Grundwort abgeleitet werden. Bei ihnen wird daher nur die Betonung angegeben, und zwar durch Zeichen am Stichwort selbst (s. 3 b).

Abkürzungen ohne Ausspracheangabe werden wie ihre vollen Formen ausgesprochen. Dies gilt jedoch nicht für die aus mindestens zwei Großbuchstaben bestehenden englischen Abkürzungen, die wie die einzelnen Buchstaben mit Betonung des letzten gesprochen werden (**BBC** also z. B. wie [bi:bi:'si:]).

Bei *Komposita* ohne Ausspracheangabe ergibt sich die Aussprache aus der der einzelnen Bestandteile. Bei ihnen ist daher nur die Betonung angegeben, und zwar durch Zeichen am Stichwort selbst (s. 3 b): **'doughnut** wird wie **dough + nut** ausgesprochen, die Betonung liegt auf **dough, ba̱u̱·sparen** wird wie **Bau + sparen** ausgesprochen, die Betonung liegt auf **bau.** Bei deutschen Komposita wird die Kompositionsfuge entweder durch einen in das Stichwort gesetzten Punkt (siehe auch 3 b) oder durch die Eingliederung des Stichworts in einen Block von Komposita (siehe auch 1 b) deutlich.

If part of a German compound is not in the Dictionary as a headword, then just that part is given a pronunciation, with a hyphen standing for the rest.

Ist ein Bestandteil eines deutschen Kompositums nicht im Wörterbuch als Stichwort verzeichnet, wird die Aussprache nur für diesen Teil in Lautschrift angegeben, wobei für den anderen Teil ein Bindestrich steht.

Example/Beispiel: **Schaussteller** [-ʃtɛlɐ]

If stress alone needs to be shown in square brackets, each syllable is represented by a hyphen.

Wenn in einer Ausspracheklammer nur die Betonung angegeben werden soll, steht für jede Silbe ein waagerechter Strich.

Example/Beispiel: **come to 1.** ['--] *v. t.* ... **2.** [-'-] *v. i.*

In blocks of compounds, stress is given as follows:

In Kompositablöcken ist die Betonung folgendermaßen angegeben:

In the English-German section:

Im englisch-deutschen Teil:

If no stress is shown (by the IPA stress mark), it falls on the first element.

Das erste Element ist normalerweise das betonte Element und nicht weiter gekennzeichnet. Ist ein anderes als das erste Element betont, so wird dies durch das IPA-Betonungszeichen gezeigt.

Example/Beispiel: **country: ~folk** ... ~ **'gentleman**

In the German-English section:

Im deutsch-englischen Teil:

When the first element at the beginning of the block has a stress mark, this stress applies to all compounds in the block.

Wenn das erste Element zu Beginn des Blocks durch einen untergesetzten Punkt oder Strich als betont markiert ist, gilt dies für alle Komposita im Block.

Example/Beispiel: **Vanille-: ~eis** ... **~geschmack** ... **~pudding**

Exceptions are given in square brackets, with a hyphen standing for each syllable.

Ausnahmen davon werden in eckigen Klammern angegeben, wobei für jede Silbe ein waagerechter Strich steht.

Example/Beispiel: **drei-, Drei-:** ... **~käsehoch** [-'---]

When no stress is shown for the first element at the beginning of a block, the stress of each compound is given individually.

Wenn das erste Element zu Beginn des Blocks nicht als betont markiert ist, wird bei jedem Kompositum im Block die Betonung angegeben.

Example/Beispiel: **nord-, Nord-: ~seite** ['---] ... **~stern** ['--] ... **~-Süd-Dialog** ... **~-Süd-Gefälle** ... **~südlich**

5. Grammatical information

Grammatical information on a headword immediately follows the headword or its pronunciation. The part of speech comes first; if the word can be more than one part of speech, each is listed in a separate numbered section (see also 2 a).

The following grammatical information is given:

5. Grammatische Angaben

Unmittelbar nach dem Stichwort bzw. der Ausspracheklammer folgen die grammatischen Angaben zum Stichwort. Die Wortart wird an erster Stelle angegeben. Wenn das Stichwort mehreren Wortarten angehören kann, steht vor jeder Wortartangabe eine Ziffer (siehe auch 2 a).
Die folgenden grammatischen Angaben werden gemacht:

a) Nouns

In the English-German section, nouns are labelled with the abbreviation *n.* and proper nouns with *pr. n.* Irregular plurals are always given.

a) Bei Substantiven

Im englisch-deutschen Teil werden Substantive durch die Angabe *n.* gekennzeichnet. Eigennamen werden mit *pr. n.* gekennzeichnet; unregelmäßige Pluralformen werden angegeben.

Examples/Beispiele: **boy** ... *n.*
Australia ... *pr. n.*
bijou ... *n., pl.* ~x
mouse ... *n., pl.* mice
haddock ... *n., pl. same*

In the German-English section, nouns are denoted by the inclusion of a definite article.

Im deutsch-englischen Teil werden Substantive durch die Angabe des bestimmten Artikels gekennzeichnet.

Example/Beispiel: **Tante** ... die

If this article is in parentheses, the word is a proper noun and the article is used only in certain circumstances.

Steht der Artikel in runden Klammern, handelt es sich bei dem Substantiv um einen Eigennamen, der nur unter gewissen Umständen mit dem bestimmten Artikel gebraucht wird.

Examples/Beispiele: **Belgien** ... (das)
Karl ... (der)

The definite article is followed by the genitive and plural endings for the noun with the headword represented by a swung dash.

Auf den Artikel folgen die Genitiv- und die Pluralendung des Substantivs. Dabei steht für das Stichwort die Tilde.

Example/Beispiel: **Tante** ... die; ~n, ~n

If only one ending is given, it is the genitive, and the word has no plural.

Wird nur eine Endung angegeben, so handelt es sich um die Genitivendung, das Stichwort hat in diesem Fall keinen Plural.

Example/Beispiel: **Schlaf** ... der; ~[e]s

The label *n. pl.* or *Pl.* indicates that the noun exists only in the plural.

Die Angabe *n. pl.* im Englischen bzw. *Pl.* im Deutschen weist darauf hin, daß das Wort nur im Plural vorkommt.

Examples/Beispiele: **pants** ... *n. pl.*
police ... *n. pl.*
Ferien ... *Pl.*
Niederlande *Pl.*

The label *no. pl.* or *o. Pl.* indicates that the noun (sometimes only in a particular sense) has no plural.

Die Angabe *no pl.* im Englischen bzw. *o. Pl.* im Deutschen weist darauf hin, daß das Stichwort bzw. die betreffende Bedeutung des Stichworts keinen Plural hat.

Examples/Beispiele: **artificiality** ... *n., no pl.*
decision ... *n.* a) ... b) *no pl.*
Eherecht das; *o. Pl.*
Dummheit die; ~, ~en a) *o. Pl.*

German nouns are not labelled *o. Pl.* if it is clear from the absence of a plural ending that they have no plural.

Zum deutschen Stichwort wird die Angabe *o. Pl.* nicht gemacht, wenn schon an der fehlenden Pluralendung zu erkennen ist, daß das Wort keinen Plural hat.

The label *no art.* or *o. Art.* indicates that the noun (sometimes only in a particular sense) cannot be used with an article.

Die Angabe *no art.* im Englischen bzw. *o. Art.* im Deutschen steht bei einem Substantiv, das (manchmal nur in einer bestimmten Bedeutung) nicht mit dem Artikel verbunden werden kann.

Examples/Beispiele: **Christianity** ... *no art.*
[1]Nord ... *o. Art.*

English nouns labelled *no indef. art.* or *no def. art.* cannot be used with the indefinite article and the definite article respectively (again, sometimes only in particular senses).

Im Englischen wird oft weiter differenziert zwischen *no indef. art.* (= das Substantiv kann nicht mit dem unbestimmten Artikel verbunden werden) und *no def. art.* (= das Substantiv kann nicht mit dem bestimmten Artikel verbunden werden).

Example/Beispiel: **humour** ... *n.* a) *no pl., no indef. art.*

b) Verbs

Verbs are labelled as transitive, intransitive, or reflexive.

b) Bei Verben

Verben werden als transitive, intransitive oder reflexive Verben gekennzeichnet.

Examples/Beispiele: **engrave** ... *v. t.*
creep ... *v. i.*
behave ... *v. refl.*

ehren *tr. V.*
leuchten *itr. V.*
freuen ... *refl. V.*

In the English-German section the following additional information is given:

The entries for irregular verbs give their past tense, past participle, and any other forms necessary. Identical forms are given only once.

Im englisch-deutschen Teil werden folgende Angaben gemacht:

Bei unregelmäßigen Verben werden die Stammformen (Präteritum und 2. Partizip) angegeben, wobei gleichlautende Formen nur einmal genannt werden.

Examples/Beispiele: [1]**hide** ... **hid** ... **hidden**
[1]**die** ... **dying**
make ... **made**

The doubling of a final consonant before **-ed** or **-ing** is also shown.

Wenn der Endkonsonant eines Verbs bei der Bildung einer Form auf **-ed** oder **-ing** verdoppelt wird, wird das ebenfalls angegeben.

Example/Beispiel: [4]**bat** *v. t.*, **-tt-**

In the German-English section, the following additional information is given:

Irregular verbs are labelled *unr.*, and their parts (present, preterite, and past participle) are given on pp. 1665–1667.

Im deutsch-englischen Teil werden darüber hinaus folgende Angaben gemacht:

Unregelmäßige Verben werden mit *unr.* bezeichnet, ihre Stammformen (Präsens, Präteritum und Partizip Perfekt) können auf S. 1665–1667 nachgeschlagen werden.

Examples/Beispiele: **klingen** *unr. itr. V.*
leihen ... *unr. tr. V.*

Verbs which are always or sometimes conjugated with *sein* rather than *haben* are labelled accordingly.

Verben, die nicht oder nicht immer mit *haben* konjugiert werden, sind mit einem entsprechenden Hinweis versehen.

Examples/Beispiele: **sterben** ... *mit sein*
robben ... *meist, mit Richtungsangabe nur, mit sein*

Separable compound verbs are indicated by a vertical line at the point where the word is split.

Bei unfest zusammengesetzten Verben zeigt ein ins Wort hineingesetzter senkrechter Strich, wo das Verb gegebenenfalls getrennt wird.

Example/Beispiel: **auf|stehen**

c) Adjectives and adverbs

Irregular and, in the German-English section, umlauted comparative and superlative forms are given.

c) Bei Adjektiven und Adverbien

Zu Adjektiven und Adverbien werden unregelmäßige und – im deutsch-englischen Teil – umlautende Steigerungsformen angegeben:

Examples/Beispiele: **bad** ... **worse** ... **worst**
gut ... **besser** ... **best...**
kalt ... **kälter** ... **kältest...**

The indication *attrib.* or *nicht präd.* indicates that an adjective is used attributively and not predicatively.

Der Hinweis *attrib.* bzw. *nicht präd.* bei einem Adjektiv weist darauf hin, daß das Adjektiv nur als Attribut und nicht als Prädikatsteil verwendet wird.

Examples/Beispiele: **giant** ... *attrib. adj.*
heutig *Adj.; nicht präd.*

The indication *pred.* or *nicht attrib.* indicates that an adjective is used predicatively and not attributively.

Der Hinweis *pred.* bzw. *nicht attrib.* weist darauf hin, daß das Adjektiv nur als Prädikatsteil und nicht als Attribut verwendet wird.

Examples/Beispiele: **afraid** ... *pred. adj.*
hops ... *Adj.; nicht attr.*

d) Prepositions

The entry for each German preposition indicates with which case or cases it is used.

d) Bei Präpositionen

Für jede deutsche Präposition wird der Kasus bzw. werden die Kasus angegeben, mit dem die Präposition steht.

Examples/Beispiele: **um** ... *Präp. mit Akk.*
vor ... **1.** *Präp. mit Dat.* ... **2.** *Präp. mit Akk.*

Contractions of a preposition and a definite article are shown thus:

Präpositionen, die mit dem bestimmten Artikel zusammengezogen sind, werden so gekennzeichnet:

Example/Beispiel: **vom** ... *Präp. + Art.*

e) Compounds

Compounds are always labelled with their part of speech or gender, but any further grammatical information is given at the entry for the second element.

e) Bei Komposita

Bei Komposita wird stets die Wortart angegeben. Wenn keine weiteren grammatischen Angaben gemacht werden, können diese dem Eintrag für das zweite Element des Kompositums entnommen werden.

Examples/Beispiele: **half-life** *n.*
life ... *n., pl.* **lives**
Radau·bruder der
Bruder ... der; ~s, Brüder

6. Labels

After the grammatical information comes any necessary information on the style, usage, regional restrictions, or subject fields of a word, printed in italics within parentheses. Many labels are abbreviations, which are explained on pp. 29–33.
A label placed at the start of an entry or of a numbered or letter category applies to the whole of that entry or category.

6. Kennzeichnungen

Im Anschluß an die grammatischen Angaben wird der Benutzer auf die stilistische, zeitliche, regionale und fachliche Zuordnung des Stichworts hingewiesen. Diese Angaben stehen in Kursivschrift in runden Klammern. Sie sind häufig abgekürzt, eine Liste der verwendeten Abkürzungen befindet sich auf S. 29–33.
Wenn eine derartige Angabe am Anfang eines Artikels oder eines Gliederungspunktes steht, gilt sie für den ganzen Artikel oder Punkt.

a) Style and usage labels

Labels are used to mark all words and expressions which are not neutral in style. Both headwords and their translations are labelled to help the user to understand the headwords and to use the translations correctly in context.

a) Angaben zur stilistischen Bewertung

Wörter und Wendungen, die nicht der normalsprachlichen Stilschicht angehören, werden sowohl in der Ausgangs- als auch in der Zielsprache mit Angaben zu ihrer stilistischen und zeitlichen Einordnung versehen. Der Benutzer kann somit die Stichwörter richtig verstehen und die Übersetzungen im korrekten Zusammenhang verwenden.

The following style and usage labels are used to describe English:		Für das Englische werden zur stilistischen Bewertung und zeitlichen Zuordnung die folgenden Angaben verwendet:
(poet.)	poetic (e.g. **beauteous, the deep**).	in dichterischer, poetischer Sprache verwendet (z. B. **beauteous, the deep**).
(literary)	literary or elevated (e.g. **bed of sickness, countenance, valorous**).	für einen gehobenen, literarischen Stil charakteristisch (z. B. **bed of sickness, countenance, valorous**).
(rhet.)	used for deliberate impressive or persuasive effect (e.g. **bounteous, plenteous**).	bewußt dazu eingesetzt, andere zu beeindrucken oder zu überzeugen (z. B. **bounteous, plenteous**).
(formal)	used only in formal speeches and writing (e.g. **hereafter, partake, proceed**).	bei offiziellen und formellen Gelegenheiten unter Menschen, die sich nicht gut kennen, verwendet (z. B. **hereafter, partake, proceed**).
(coll.)	everyday, conversational language; not generally written, but would not cause offence or ridicule (e.g. **Aussie, come a cropper, loo**).	gesprochene Alltagssprache, die in schriftlichen Texten im allgemeinen nicht verwendet wird (z. B. **Aussie, come a cropper, loo**).
(child lang.)	used only by or to small children (e.g. **bow-wow, choo-choo, potty**).	nur von kleinen Kindern oder im Umgang mit ihnen verwendet (z. B. **bow-wow, choo-choo, potty**).
(sl.)	especially colloquial and expressive; often used only by particular groups (e.g. **guv, kick the bucket, scarper**).	besonders umgangssprachlich, oft nur von bestimmten Personengruppen verwendet (z. B. **guv, kick the bucket, scarper**).
(coarse)	coarse and offensive (e.g. **bollocks, fuck, piss**).	im allgemeinen als anstößig empfunden (z. B. **bollocks, fuck, piss**).
(dated)	somewhat old-fashioned; used particularly by older people (e.g. **by Jove, ripping, top-hole**).	zwar noch gelegentlich von älteren Leuten verwendet, aber altmodisch klingend (z. B. **by Jove, ripping, top-hole**).
(arch.)	found only in literature but still used jocularly, ironically, or for a deliberately old-fashioned effect (e.g. **forsooth, peradventure, thou**).	heute nur noch gelegentlich in scherzhafter oder altertümelnder Weise verwendet (z. B. **forsooth, peradventure, thou**).
(Hist.)	current term for an obsolete thing (e.g. **ducking-stool, oubliette**).	bedeutet, daß die bezeichnete Sache, Einrichtung usw. heute nicht mehr existiert; das so gekennzeichnete Wort ist aber nicht veraltet (z. B. **ducking-stool, oubliette**).

The following style and usage labels are used to describe German:		Für das Deutsche werden zur stilistischen Bewertung und zeitlichen Zuordnung die folgenden Angaben verwendet:
(dichter.)	poetic (e.g. **Aar, Odem**).	in dichterischer, poetischer Sprache verwendet (z. B. **Aar, Odem**).
(geh.)	formal, cultivated, or elevated; sometimes considered solemn or affected (e.g. **Antlitz, signifikant, dergestalt**).	für einen feierlichen, gehobenen oder gewählten Stil charakteristisch (z. B. **Antlitz, signifikant, dergestalt**).
(Papierdt.)	formal and stilted; mainly written (e.g. **seitens, in Wegfall kommen**).	für einen unlebendigen, formellen und gespreizten Stil charakteristisch (z. B. **seitens, in Wegfall kommen**).
(ugs.)	everyday, conversational language; not generally written, but would not cause offence or ridicule (e.g. **Stunk, jmdm. über den Kopf wachsen**).	gesprochene Alltagssprache, die in schriftlichen Texten im allgemeinen nicht verwendet wird (z. B. **Stunk, jmdm. über den Kopf wachsen**).
(fam.)	used only between people on very familiar terms; otherwise considered silly or ridiculous (e.g. **Popo, Beißerchen**).	nur unter miteinander sehr vertrauten Menschen gebräuchlich; kann sonst als albern empfunden werden (z. B. **Popo, Beißerchen**).
(Kinderspr.)	used only by and to small children (e.g. **Wauwau, heia**).	nur von kleinen Kindern oder im Umgang mit ihnen verwendet (z. B. **Wauwau, heia**).
(salopp)	especially colloquial and expressive; often used only by particular groups (e.g. **Sauferei, ins Gras beißen müssen**).	besonders umgangssprachlich, oft nur von bestimmten Personengruppen verwendet (z. B. **Sauferei, ins Gras beißen müssen**).

(derb)	coarse and offensive (e.g. **Fresse, abkratzen**).	im allgemeinen als grob und anstößig empfunden (z. B. **Fresse, abkratzen**).
(vulg.)	especially coarse and offensive, mainly sexual terms (e.g. **ficken, Fotze**).	als besonders anstößig und vulgär empfunden; vor allem aus dem Bereich der Sexualität (z. B. **ficken, Fotze**).
(volkst.)	avoided by specialists as potentially misleading or insufficiently scientific; mainly names of plants, animals, and illnesses (e.g. **Karfunkel, Schusterpalme**).	von Fachleuten meist vermieden, weil mißverständlich oder zu unspezifisch, vor allem Bezeichnungen für Pflanzen, Tiere und Krankheiten (z. B. **Karfunkel, Schusterpalme**).
(veralt.)	either dated or found only in literature but still used jocularly, ironically, or for a deliberately old-fashioned effect (e.g. **Schwindsucht, Spezerei**).	heute nicht mehr oder kaum noch gebraucht, aber in älterer Literatur zu finden oder heute noch in scherzhafter, ironischer oder altertümelnder Weise verwendet (z. B. **Schwindsucht, Spezerei**).

b) Regional labels

Words and expressions restricted to particular areas of the English- and German-speaking worlds are labelled accordingly. For English, the most common labels are *(Brit.)*, *(Amer.)*, *(Austral.)*, and *(Scot.)*. German items may be labelled *(DDR)*, *(österr.)*, *(schweiz.)*, *(nordd.)*, *(südd.)*, *(berlin.)*, etc.

The label *(dial.)* or *(landsch.)* indicates that a word is used in a number of regions or dialects.

b) Angaben zur regionalen Zuordnung

Wörter und Wendungen, die nicht im gesamten englischen bzw. deutschen Sprachraum üblich sind, werden entsprechend gekennzeichnet. Für englische Stichwörter werden vor allem die Angaben *(Brit.)*, *(Amer.)*, *(Austral.)*, *(Scot.)* usw. gemacht. Deutsche Stichwörter können mit *(DDR)*, *(österr.)*, *(schweiz.)*, *(nordd.)*, *(südd.)*, *(berlin.)* usw. markiert sein.

Die Angabe *(dial.)* bzw. *(landsch.)* weist darauf hin, daß ein Wort in mehreren Regionen oder Mundarten gebräuchlich ist.

c) Subject-field labels

Terms used in specialist or technical fields are labelled accordingly.

c) Bereichsangaben

Wörter, die bestimmten Sachgebieten, Fachbereichen, Fach- oder Sondersprachen zuzuordnen sind, werden ebenfalls gekennzeichnet.

Examples/Beispiele: **colonnade** ... *(Archit.)*
entr'acte ... *(Theatre)*
Gelbfieber ... *(Med.)*
Hirschfänger ... *(Jägerspr.)*

German terms used in a number of fields but requiring only one translation are often simply labelled *(fachspr.)*.

Deutsche Stichwörter, die mehreren Fachbereichen zugehören, aber nur eine Übersetzung haben, werden gelegentlich nur mit *(fachspr.)* gekennzeichnet.

Example/Beispiel: **binär** ... *(fachspr.)* binary

d) Further usage labels

Figurative, derogatory, euphemistic, etc. use is indicated with appropriate labels.

d) Weitere Kennzeichnungen

Bildlicher, abwertender, verhüllender usw. Gebrauch wird durch entsprechende Angaben markiert.

Examples/Beispiele: **assail** ... *(fig.)*
intimate ... *(euphem.)*
hochkarätig ... *(fig.)*
Quatsch ... *(abwertend)*

e) Combinations of labels

Labels combined within parentheses, with no separating punctuation, apply simultaneously: *(südd. ugs.)* means that the word is used in southern Germany and is colloquial; *(fig. coll.)* means that in the

e) Kombination von mehreren Kennzeichnungen

Stehen in einer Klammer mehrere Kennzeichnungen nebeneinander, so gelten sie gleichermaßen: *(südd. ugs.)* bedeutet, daß das Wort in Süddeutschland gebräuchlich und umgangssprachlich ist; *(fig.*

sense or context in question the word is used figuratively and is colloquial.
Labels separated by commas or slashes cannot apply simultaneously: *(Phys., Biol.)* means that the word occurs in the fields of both physics and biology; *(arch./joc.)* means that the word occurs either in older texts or in jocular use.

coll.) bedeutet, daß das Wort hier bildlich gebraucht wird und umgangssprachlich ist.
Werden die Kennzeichnungen durch Komma oder Schrägstrich getrennt, dann gelten sie unabhängig voneinander: *(Phys., Biol.)* bedeutet, daß das Wort zu den Fachbereichen Physik und Biologie gehört; *(arch./joc.)* bedeutet, daß das Wort entweder veraltet ist oder scherzhaft gebraucht wird.

7. Indicators

Indicators, printed in italics in parentheses before translations, distinguish between the various senses of a headword and, together with subject-field labels, tell the reader which sense is being translated. They should not be mistaken for full definitions such as are found in a monolingual dictionary.

7. Indikatoren

Indikatoren sind kurze Hinweise, die angeben, welche Bedeutung des Stichworts gerade übersetzt wird. Sie stehen in Kursivschrift in runden Klammern vor der Übersetzung.

Examples/Beispiele:

flapjack ... *(oatcake)* ... *(pancake)*
below ... *(position)* ... *(direction)* ... *(later in text)*

Kanadier ... *(Einwohner Kanadas)* ... *(Boot)*
Luke ... *(Dach~)* ... *(bei Schiffen)*

Indicators may be combined with the labels described in 6 above.

Indikatoren können in einer Klammer mit den oben unter 6. beschriebenen Kennzeichnungen kombiniert werden.

Examples/Beispiele:

[3]chuck ... *(Amer. coll.: food)*
Schmelze ... *(Technik: verflüssigtes Metall)*

8. Translations and collocators

a) Translations

Normally, one general translation is given for each word or sense of a word. If two or more are given, separated by semi-colons, they are synonymous and interchangeable.

8. Übersetzungen und Kollokatoren

a) Die Übersetzung

Im Normalfall wird für jedes Stichwort bzw. jede Bedeutung eines Stichworts zuerst eine allgemeine Übersetzung gegeben; selten auch zwei oder mehrere gleichwertige und gegeneinander austauschbare Übersetzungen, die mit Semikolons aneinandergereiht sind.

Examples/Beispiele:

engrossing ... fesselnd
anchovy ... An[s]chovis, *die;* Sardelle, *die*

entzückt ... delighted
Elitedenken ... élitist thinking; élitism

Unless qualified by labels, indicators, or collocators, a translation can be regarded as adequate in practically all contexts. Where necessary, a translation is labelled for style, region, etc. in a similar way to headwords, but in the same language as the translation.

Die angegebene Übersetzung, sofern sie nicht durch Zusätze (Kennzeichnungen, Indikatoren, Kollokatoren) eingeschränkt ist, kann als adäquate Übersetzung für nahezu alle Kontexte angesehen werden. Die Übersetzungen werden ähnlich wie die Stichwörter (jedoch in der Zielsprache) nötigenfalls mit Kennzeichnungen zur stilistischen Bewertung, zur regionalen Zuordnung usw. versehen.

Examples/Beispiele:

alongside ... längsseits *(Seemannsspr.)*
grub ... Fressen, *das (salopp)*

hoppnehmen ... nab *(sl.)*
Hornhautentzündung ... keratitis *(Med.)*

Specialist terms are often given two translations: a general or popular one and a specialist one, which is labelled *(fachspr.)* or *(as tech. term)*.

Für Fachausdrücke werden oft zwei Übersetzungen gegeben, eine allgemeinsprachliche und eine fachsprachliche; die fachsprachliche Übersetzung ist dann mit *(fachspr.)* bzw. *(as tech. term)* gekennzeichnet.

Examples/Beispiele: **bilingual** ... zweisprachig; bilingual *(fachspr.)*
Schote ... pod; siliqua *(as tech. term)*

English nouns which can signify a person of either sex are generally given a translation for each.

Bei englischen Substantiven, die Menschen beiderlei Geschlechts bezeichnen können, wird als Übersetzung im allgemeinen sowohl die männliche als auch die weibliche Form angegeben.

Examples/Beispiele: **European** ... Europäer, *der*/Europäerin, *die*
buyer ... Käufer, *der*/Käuferin, *die*
client ... Auftraggeber, *der*/-geberin, *die*

Words which are untranslatable because they have no equivalent in the other language (mainly the names of institutions, customs, foods, etc.) are given a short explanation (gloss) in italic type.

Stichwörter, die nicht übersetzt werden können, weil sie in der Zielsprache kein Äquivalent haben (meist Bezeichnungen für Institutionen, Bräuche, Eßwaren u. ä.), sind mit einer kurzen Erklärung (Glosse) in Kursivschrift versehen.

Examples/Beispiele: **gerrymander** ... *willkürlich in Wahlbezirke aufteilen, um einer politischen Partei Vorteile zu verschaffen*
Christmas stocking ... *von den Kindern am Heiligabend aufgehängter Strumpf, den der Weihnachtsmann mit Geschenken füllen soll*
Einwohnermeldeamt ... *local government office for registration of residents*
Schützenfest ... *shooting competition with fair*

A gloss is occasionally added to a translation to aid understanding of the headword.

Glossen dieser Art werden gelegentlich auch zusätzlich zu einer Übersetzung gegeben, um die Bedeutung des Stichworts zu erläutern.

Examples/Beispiele: **clambake** *n. (Amer.)* Picknick, *das (bes. am Strand, bei dem Muscheln und Fisch auf heißen Steinen gebacken werden)*
Bestarbeiter der *(DDR)* best worker *(worker receiving an award as being the most efficient in his department, factory, etc.)*

The symbol ≈ indicates that the translation given is to be taken only as an approximate equivalent.

Das Symbol ≈ zeigt an, daß die vorgeschlagene Übersetzung nur als ungefähres Äquivalent des Stichworts zu verstehen ist.

Examples/Beispiele: **A level** ... ≈ Abitur, *das*
Finanzamt ... ≈ Inland Revenue

A cross-reference of the form *see* or *s.* indicates that a translation can be found under the entry referred to (see also 10).

Ein Verweis mit *see* bzw. *s.* auf ein anderes Stichwort zeigt, daß die Übersetzung dort nachgeschlagen werden kann (siehe auch 10).

b) Collocators

As the choice of the correct translation often depends on the context in which it is to be used, collocators (words with which a translation typically occurs) are frequently supplied for translations of verbs, adjectives, adverbs, and combining forms. They are printed in italics in angle brackets.

b) Kollokatoren

Oft hängt die Wahl der richtigen Übersetzung davon ab, mit welchen anderen Wörtern die Übersetzung im Satz verbunden werden soll. Zu vielen Übersetzungen von Verben, Adjektiven, Adverbien und Wortbildungselementen sind deshalb einige typischerweise mit der Übersetzung verbundene

Wörter, sogenannte Kollokatoren, angegeben. Sie stehen in Kursivschrift in Winkelklammern.

Examples/Beispiele: **acquire** ... erwerben ⟨*Land, Besitz, Wohlstand, Kenntnisse*⟩; sammeln ⟨*Erfahrungen*⟩; ernten ⟨*Lob*⟩

flink ... nimble ⟨*fingers*⟩; sharp ⟨*eyes*⟩; quick ⟨*hands*⟩

If a collocator goes with more than one translation, the translations concerned are separated by commas instead of semi-colons.

Wenn Kollokatoren sich auf mehrere gleichwertige Übersetzungen beziehen, sind diese Übersetzungen mit Kommas statt mit Semikolons aneinandergereiht.

Examples/Beispiele: **achieve** ... herstellen, herbeiführen ⟨*Frieden, Harmonie*⟩

kürzen ... shorten, take up ⟨*garment*⟩; ... shorten, abridge ⟨*article, book*⟩; ... reduce, cut ⟨*pension, budget, etc.*⟩

With verbs, typical subjects and objects are given as collocators. Subjects are placed before the translation.

Kollokatoren zu Verben sind Substantive, die typischerweise entweder als Subjekte oder als Objekte des Verbs fungieren. Ist der Kollokator das Subjekt des Verbs, steht er vor der Übersetzung.

Examples/Beispiele: **hiss** ... ⟨*Katze, Lokomotive:*⟩ fauchen

schwenken ... ⟨*marching column*⟩ swing, wheel; ⟨*camera*⟩ pan; ⟨*path, road, car*⟩ swing

Objects are placed after the translation.

Ist der Kollokator das Objekt des Verbs, steht er hinter der Übersetzung.

Examples/Beispiele: **comb** ... kämmen ⟨*Haare, Flachs, Wolle*⟩ ... striegeln ⟨*Pferd*⟩ ... durchkämmen ⟨*Gelände, Wald*⟩

herunterreißen ... pull off ⟨*plaster, wallpaper*⟩; tear down ⟨*poster*⟩

With English translations consisting of more than one word, collocators are placed at the appropriate point.

Bei mehrteiligen englischen Übersetzungen steht der Kollokator an der Stelle, wo er auch im Satz stehen müßte.

Example/Beispiel: **verheizen** ... use ⟨*troops*⟩ as cannon-fodder; ... run ⟨*employee, subordinate, etc.*⟩ into the ground

With adjectives, collocators are nouns which the translations typically qualify. They are normally placed after the translation.

Kollokatoren zu Adjektiven sind Substantive, mit denen das Adjektiv typischerweise verwendet wird. Sie stehen normalerweise nach der Übersetzung.

Examples/Beispiele: **coated** ... gestrichen ⟨*Papier*⟩; belegt ⟨*Zunge*⟩; imprägniert ⟨*Stoff*⟩; getönt ⟨*Glas, Linsen*⟩

grimmig ... furious ⟨*person*⟩; grim ⟨*face, expression*⟩; fierce, ferocious ⟨*enemy, lion, etc.*⟩

Where a collocator for an adjective is placed before the translation, the translation is postpositive – it must be used after the noun it qualifies.

Wenn ein Kollokator zu einem Adjektiv vor der Übersetzung steht, bedeutet dies, daß die Übersetzung nachgestellt werden muß.

Examples/Beispiele: **flowery** ... ⟨*Wiese*⟩ voller Blumen

eisenhaltig ... ⟨*food*⟩ containing iron

With a translation that is used in compounds, other elements with which it typically combines are given as collocators.

Bei Übersetzungen, die ein Wortbildungselement darstellen, werden als Kollokatoren solche Elemente angeführt, mit denen die Übersetzung typischerweise kombiniert wird.

Examples/Beispiele: **marine** ... See⟨*versicherung, -recht, -schiffahrt*⟩

-süchtig ... ⟨*drug-, heroin-, morphine-, etc.*⟩addicted

(Thus, **marine law** is translated as **Seerecht,** and **drogensüchtig** as **drug-addicted.** / Die Verbindung **marine law** wird also mit **Seerecht** übersetzt, **drogensüchtig** mit **drug-addicted.**)

With adverbs, collocators are verbs and adjectives which the translations typically qualify. Verbs are shown before the translation in the German-English section, but after it in the English-German, while adjectives and participles are always placed after, as in connected language.

Kollokatoren zu Adverbien sind Verben oder Adjektive oder adjektivisch gebrauchte Partizipien, mit denen das Adverb typischerweise verbunden wird. Dabei stehen im deutsch-englischen Teil Verben vor der Übersetzung, im englisch-deutschen Teil dahinter; Adjektive und Partizipien stehen immer hinter der Übersetzung, entsprechend ihrer Stellung im Satz.

Examples/Beispiele: **excessively** ... unmäßig ⟨*trinken, essen*⟩
flimsily ... hastig ⟨*errichtet*⟩; schlecht ⟨*gebunden, verpackt*⟩
probeweise ... ⟨*employ*⟩ on a trial basis
schwer ... seriously ⟨*injured*⟩; greatly, deeply ⟨*disappointed*⟩; ⟨*punish*⟩ severely, heavily

c) Translation of abbreviations

c) Die Übersetzung von Abkürzungen

Abbreviations are normally translated by the corresponding abbreviation in the other language.

Abkürzungen erhalten normalerweise die entsprechende Abkürzung in der Zielsprache als Übersetzung.

Examples/Beispiele: **e.g.** ... z. B.
GDR ... DDR, *die*
WEZ ... GMT
usw. ... etc.

Where an abbreviation is best translated by one or more complete words, then they are given.

Wenn die gebräuchlichste zielsprachliche Entsprechung einer ausgangssprachlichen Abkürzung jedoch keine Abkürzung ist, wird als Übersetzung statt einer zielsprachlichen Abkürzung diese Entsprechung angegeben.

Examples/Beispiele: **s.a.e.** ... addressierter Freiumschlag
GPO ... Post, *die*
Pkw ... car
WC ... toilet

If there is no corresponding abbreviation in the other language, the full form is translated or explained if not itself entered in the Dictionary.

Gibt es zu einer Abkürzung keine entsprechende Abkürzung in der Zielsprache, wird die volle Form angegeben und mit einer Übersetzung oder Erklärung versehen, sofern diese Vollform nicht selbst im Wörterverzeichnis zu finden ist.

Examples/Beispiele: **GCSE** ... **General Certificate of Secondary Education**
FA ... **Football Association** *(Britischer Fußballverband)*
MA ... **Mittelalter**
ZDF ... **Zweites Deutsches Fernsehen** Second German Television Channel

d) Further information given with translations

d) Zusätzliche Angaben bei Übersetzungen

Where necessary, translations are accompanied by information on usage, word order, etc.

The prepositions typically following verbs are given and translated.

Wo es nötig ist, sind die Übersetzungen mit Hinweisen zu ihrer Gebrauchsweise, ihrer Stellung im Satz usw. versehen.
Bei Verben wird der präpositionale Anschluß des Stichworts angegeben und übersetzt.

Examples/Beispiele: **conceal** ... verbergen (**from** vor + *Dat.*)
sinnieren ... ponder (**über** + *Akk.* over); muse (**über** + *Akk.* [up]on)

Where a German verb takes a case other than the accusative, this is shown, together with any English preposition used to 'translate' it.

Ebenso wird bei deutschen Verben der zum Anschluß an das Stichwort verwendete Kasus samt der entsprechenden englischen Präposition angegeben, sofern es sich nicht um den bei transitiven Verben stets erforderlichen Akkusativ handelt.

Example/Beispiel: **verdächtigen** ... suspect (*Gen.* of)

The indication *nachgestellt* or *postpos.* means that a translation of an adjective always follows its noun. (This is not shown when the fact is clear from the position of a collocator, as described in 8 b.)

Bei Übersetzungen von Adjektiven besagt der Hinweis *nachgestellt* bzw. *postpos.*, daß die angegebene Übersetzung dem Substantiv nachgestellt werden muß. (Dieser Hinweis entfällt, wenn die Stellung eines Kollokators dies schon, wie unter 8 b beschrieben, zeigt.)

Examples/Beispiele: **friendless** ... ohne Freund[e] *nachgestellt*
stahlhart ... as hard as steel *postpos.*

English translations marked *postpos.* can also be used predicatively, e.g. **she is as hard as steel.**

Mit *postpos.* markierte englische Übersetzungen können auch prädikativ gebraucht werden (also: **she is as hard as steel**).

The indication *attr.* or *attrib.* means that a translation can be used attributively and not predicatively.

Die Angabe *attr.* bzw. *attrib.* weist darauf hin, daß die angegebene Übersetzung nur als Attribut und nicht als Prädikatsteil verwendet werden darf.

Examples/Beispiele: **preferable** ... vorzuziehend *attr.*
achtseitig ... eight-page *attrib.*

The indication *präd.* or *pred.* means that a translation can be used predicatively and not attributively.

Die Angabe *präd.* bzw. *pred.* weist umgekehrt darauf hin, daß die angegebene Übersetzung nur als Prädikatsteil und nicht als Attribut verwendet werden darf.

Examples/Beispiele: **preferable** ... vorzuziehen *präd.*
irreparabel ... beyond repair *pred.*

The indication *Pl.* or *pl.* means that a translation of a noun exists only in the plural (in that sense).

Bei Übersetzungen von Substantiven bedeutet der Hinweis *Pl.* bzw. *pl.*, daß die angegebene Übersetzung ein Pluraletantum ist.

Examples/Beispiele: **measles** ... Masern *Pl.*
cost ... Kosten *Pl.*
Brille ... glasses *pl.*
Polizei ... police *pl.*

In the English-German section, German nouns are given the appropriate definite article. If this is in parentheses, the noun is a proper noun which is used with the article only in certain circumstances.

Im englisch-deutschen Teil erhalten als Übersetzungen angegebene deutsche Substantive den bestimmten Artikel. Steht der Artikel in runden Klammern, handelt es sich bei dem Substantiv um einen Eigennamen, der nur unter gewissen Umständen mit dem Artikel verbunden wird.

Examples/Beispiele: **¹cow** ... Kuh, *die*
table ... Tisch, *der*
Italy ... Italien *(das)*
Eve ... Eva *(die)*

The indication *no art.* means that an English noun translation cannot be used with an article; *no def. art.* and *no indef. art.* mean that it cannot be used with a definite article and an indefinite article respectively.

Wenn Übersetzungen von deutschen Substantiven mit dem Hinweis *no art.* versehen sind, können sie nicht mit dem Artikel verbunden werden. Oft wird weiter differenziert zwischen *no def. art.* und *no indef. art.*

Example/Beispiel: **Ostermontag** ... Easter Monday *no def. art.*

Attributive use of an English noun is indicated by *attrib.* when it needs a separate translation.

Für den attributiven Gebrauch von englischen Substantiven wird oft eine eigene Übersetzung angegeben. Vor dieser Übersetzung steht dann der Hinweis *attrib.*

Examples/Beispiele: **marble** ... *attrib.* marmorn
mountain ... *attrib.* Gebirgs-

9. Phrases

Following the general translation(s) of a headword are phrases in which the general translation(s) cannot be used. These include typical uses, fixed phrases, idioms, and proverbs. All are printed in medium bold type and are translated in their entirety. A swung dash is used to represent the headword.

9. Anwendungsbeispiele

Im Anschluß an die allgemeine[n] Übersetzung[en] des Stichworts werden Anwendungsbeispiele für Fälle gegeben, in denen die allgemeine Übersetzung nicht verwendbar ist. Außerdem werden typische Verwendungen des Stichworts, feste Wendungen, Redensarten und Sprichwörter gezeigt. Die Anwendungsbeispiele sind halbfett gedruckt und werden immer als Ganzes übersetzt. Innerhalb der Beispiele repräsentiert die Tilde das Stichwort.

Examples/Beispiele: **giggle** ... **have a ~ about sth.** ... **[a fit of] the ~s**
knistern ... **mit etw. ~** ... **eine ~de Atmosphäre**

In blocks of compounds, the swung dash in a phrase represents only the first element of the compound.

In Kompositablöcken steht auch in den Anwendungsbeispielen die Tilde immer nur für den ersten Bestandteil des Kompositums.

Examples/Beispiele: **apple:** ... **~cart** ... **upset the ~cart**
selbst-, Selbst-: ... **~bedienung** ... **hier ist ~bedienung**

Phrases and their translations can be given any of the labels mentioned in 6.

Die Anwendungsbeispiele und deren Übersetzungen werden gegebenenfalls mit den unter 6 erläuterten Kennzeichnungen versehen.

Examples/Beispiele: **corner** ... **cut ~s** *(fig.)*
edge ... **have/get the ~ [on sb./sth.]** *(coll.)*
Strang ... **über die Stränge schlagen** *(ugs.)*
Kapitel ... **das ist ein ~ für sich** *(fig.)*

In addition, any label attaching to a headword also applies to all phrases in that entry.

Außerdem gelten bereits für das Stichwort angegebene Kennzeichnungen auch für das Beispiel.

Examples/Beispiele: **beddy-byes** ... *(child lang.)* ... **off to ~**
Schmäh ... *(österr. ugs.)* ... **einen ~ führen**

To save space, phrases may be combined.

Aus Platzgründen werden oft mehrere Beispiele zusammengefaßt.

- Two complete phrases separated by a comma are synonymous and share a translation.

- Wenn zwei vollständige Beispiele mit Komma aneinandergereiht sind, sind sie synonym und haben eine gemeinsame Übersetzung.

Examples/Beispiele: **cash** ... **pay [in] ~, pay ~ down bar zahlen**
ausrasten ... **er rastete aus, es rastete bei ihm aus** ... **something snapped in him**

– Where portions of a phrase or translation are separated by *or* or *od.*, they are synonymous and interchangeable.

– Wenn Teile eines Beispiels oder einer Übersetzung mit *or* bzw. *od.* aneinandergereiht sind, haben sie die gleiche Bedeutung und sind beliebig austauschbar.

Examples/Beispiele: **decision** ... **come to** *or* **arrive at** *or* **reach a ~**: zu einer Entscheidung kommen

Bankrott ... **seinen ~ anmelden** *od.* **ansagen** *od.* **erklären** declare oneself bankrupt

– Where portions of a phrase or translation are separated by an oblique, they are syntactically interchangeable but have different meanings.

– Wenn Teile eines Beispiels bzw. seiner Übersetzung mit Schrägstrich aneinandergereiht sind, sind sie zwar syntaktisch austauschbar, haben aber nicht die gleiche Bedeutung.

Examples/Beispiele: **beginning** ... **at the ~ of February/the month** Anfang Februar/des Monats

durchschaubar ... **leicht/schwer ~ sein** be easy/difficult to see through

– Portions of a phrase and its translation in square brackets may be omitted, but always together, i.e. both phrase and translation are to be read either with or without the bracketed portions.

– Wenn Teile eines Beispiels und Teile seiner Übersetzung in eckigen Klammern stehen, stellen sie einen auslaßbaren Zusatz zu dem Beispiel dar. Beispiel und Übersetzung müssen also beide entweder mit oder ohne den eingeklammerten Teil gelesen werden.

Examples/Beispiele: **clear** ... **make it ~ [to sb.] that** ... [jmdm.] klar und deutlich sagen, daß ...

verpflichten ... **sich verpflichtet fühlen[, etw. zu tun]** feel obliged [to do sth.]

NB: Square brackets are also used generally to enclose optional elements of words and phrases, e.g. **choos[e]y; cost sb. dear[ly]; Wach[t]·turm; er vermochte [es] nicht, mich zu überzeugen.**

NB: Eckige Klammern werden außerdem generell dazu verwendet, beliebig auslaßbare Teile von Wörtern und Sätzen einzuklammern, z. B. **choos[e]y; cost sb. dear[ly]; Wach[t] · turm; er vermochte [es] nicht, mich zu überzeugen.**

In phrases and their translations, *jmd., jmds., jmdm., jmdn., sb.* and *sb.'s* stand for any noun or pronoun indicating one or more persons, and *etw., einer Sache* (genitive or dative), *sth.,* or *sth.'s* stand for any noun or pronoun indicating one or more things.

In den Anwendungsbeispielen und ihren Übersetzungen werden Substantive und Pronomen, die Personen im weitesten Sinne bezeichnen, durch die Abkürzungen *jmd., jmds., jmdm., jmdn.* auf der deutschen und *sb., sb.'s* auf der englischen Seite vertreten. Substantive und Pronomen, die Sachen im weitesten Sinne bezeichnen, werden durch die Abkürzungen *etw.* (oder auch *einer Sache* im Genitiv und Dativ) auf der deutschen und *sth., sth.'s* auf der englischen Seite vertreten.

Example/Beispiel: **Ohr** ... **jmdm. etw. ins ~ flüstern** whisper sth. in sb.'s ear

In German phrases and translations, the reflexive pronoun *sich* is accusative unless it is marked *(Dat.)* (= dative) or could only be dative, e. g. **etw. von sich geben; sich/jmdm. Luft zufächeln.**

In deutschen Anwendungsbeispielen und Übersetzungen ist das Wort *sich* ein Akkusativ, wenn es nicht mit *(Dat.)* gekennzeichnet ist oder auf Grund des Kontextes eindeutig Dativ ist (wie etwa in **etw. von sich geben; sich/jmdm. Luft zufächeln**).

In phrases and their translations, stress which is unusual or affects meaning is shown using the symbols explained in 4.

Ungewöhnliche oder bedeutungsverändernde Betonungen werden bei Anwendungsbeispielen und deren Übersetzungen mit Hilfe der unter 4 erklärten Betonungszeichen angegeben.

Examples/Beispiele: **that** ... **he is 'like ~**

somit ... **und somit kommen wir zu Punkt 2**

In English phrases, *you, your, yourself,* etc. are generally translated as the 'familiar' *du, dich, dein,* etc. The more formal *Sie, Ihnen, Ihr,* etc. are used only when they are more appropriate for a given example. Similarly, the English colloquial contractions *can't, won't,* etc. are frequently used. In all cases it is up to the reader to decide which forms are required by the context being translated.

Bei der Übersetzung von englischen Beispielsätzen ins Deutsche werden die Anrede *you* und ihre Formen im allgemeinen durch das vertraulichere *du* und seine Formen wiedergegeben. Das förmlichere *Sie* wird nur verwendet, wenn das jeweilige Beispiel dies nahelegt. Ähnlich wird im Englischen häufig die umgangssprachliche Kurzform (z.B. *can't, won't, hasn't*) verwendet. Grundsätzlich bleibt es dem Benutzer überlassen, die Form dem Zweck und Kontext entsprechend zu wählen, für den die Übersetzung benötigt wird.

10. Cross-references

Cross-references beginning with *see* or *s.* which take the place of a translation refer to a headword at which the translation is to be found. This kind of cross-reference occurs mainly in the following circumstances:

- with synonyms

- with variant spellings

- with masculine and feminine forms of a German noun which have the same translation.

10. Verweise

Verweise mit *see* bzw. *s.* anstelle einer Übersetzung weisen auf ein anderes Stichwort, unter dem die Übersetzung zu finden ist. Diese Art von Verweis findet sich vor allem in den folgenden Fällen:

- bei Synonymen

Examples/Beispiele: **false move** *see* **false step**

fortbringen ... *s.* **wegbringen**

- bei Wörtern mit mehreren Schreibweisen

Examples/Beispiele: **beduin** *see* **bedouin**

winklig ... *s.* **winkelig**

- bei weiblichen und männlichen Formen eines deutschen Substantivs, die im Englischen die gleiche Übersetzung haben.

Example/Beispiel: **Primanerin** ... *s.* **Primaner**

Cross-references beginning with *see* or *s.* which are followed by a colon and a list of translations occasionally occur at derivatives, such as nouns and adverbs derived from adjectives. They refer the user to the entry containing the indicators and collocators necessary for distinguishing the translations.

Verweise mit *see* bzw. *s.*, die vor einer Reihe von Übersetzungen stehen, treten gelegentlich bei Ableitungen auf, z.B. bei Substantiven oder Adverbien, die von einem Adjektiv abgeleitet sind. Sie zeigen, wo die Indikatoren und Kollokatoren, die zur Unterscheidung der Übersetzungen nötig sind, zu finden sind.

Examples/Beispiele: **cogent** ... *adj. (convincing)* überzeugend ⟨*Argument, Grund*⟩; zwingend ⟨*Grund*⟩; *(valid)* stichhaltig ⟨*Kritik, Analyse*⟩

cogently ... *adv. see* **cogent:** überzeugend; zwingend; stichhaltig

verbreiten 1. *tr. V.* **a)** *(bekannt machen)* spread ⟨*rumour, lies, etc.*⟩; ... **b)** *(weitertragen)* spread ⟨*disease, illness, etc.*⟩; disperse ⟨*seeds, spores, etc.*⟩; **c)** *(erwecken)* radiate ⟨*optimism, happiness, calm, etc.*⟩; spread ⟨*fear*⟩

Verbreitung die; ~, ~en a) *s.* **verbreiten 1 a, b, c:** spreading; ... dispersal; radiation

Cross-references beginning with *see also* or *s. auch* refer to headwords at which further information may be found. They either help the user to find a phrase or idiom (see also 1 c) or refer to an entry which serves as a model for a set of words because it is treated more comprehensively.

Verweise mit *see also* bzw. *s. auch* weisen auf ein Stichwort hin, unter dem zusätzliche Informationen gefunden werden können. Diese Art von Verweis dient entweder zum Auffinden von festen Wendungen usw. (vgl. 1 c) oder weist auf ein Stichwort hin, das als Muster für einen bestimmten Typ besonders ausführlich behandelt wurde.

Examples/Beispiele: **Taurus** ... *see also* **Aries**

Französisch ... *s. auch* **Deutsch**

English abbreviations used in the Dictionary / Im Wörterverzeichnis verwendete englische Abkürzungen

abbr(s).	abbreviation(s)
abs.	absolute
adj(s).	adjective(s)
Admin.	Administration, Administrative
adv.	adverb
Aeronaut.	Aeronautics
Agric.	Agriculture
Alch.	Alchemy
Amer.	American, America
Anat.	Anatomy
Anglican Ch.	Anglican Church
Anglo-Ind.	Anglo-Indian
Ant.	Antiquity
Anthrop.	Anthropology
arch.	archaic
Archaeol.	Archaeology
Archit.	Architecture
art.	article
Astrol.	Astrology
Astron.	Astronomy
Astronaut.	Astronautics
attrib.	attributive
Austral.	Australian, Australia
Bacteriol.	Bacteriology
Bibliog.	Bibliography
Biochem.	Biochemistry
Biol.	Biology
Bookk.	Bookkeeping
Bot.	Botany
Brit.	British, Britain
Can.	Canadian, Canada
Chem.	Chemistry
Cinemat.	Cinematography
coll.	colloquial
collect.	collective
comb.	combination
Commerc.	Commerce, Commercial
Communication Res.	Communication Research
compar.	comparative
condit.	conditional
conj.	conjunction
Constr.	Construction
constr.	construed
contr.	contracted form
def.	definite
Dent.	Dentistry
derog.	derogatory
dial.	dialect
Diplom.	Diplomacy
Dressm.	Dressmaking
Eccl.	Ecclesiastical
Ecol.	Ecology
Econ.	Economics
Educ.	Education
Electr.	Electricity
ellipt.	elliptical
emphat.	emphatic
esp.	especially
Ethnol.	Ethnology
Ethol.	Ethology
euphem.	euphemistic
excl.	exclamation, exclamatory
expr.	expressing
fem.	feminine
fig.	figurative
Footb.	Football
Gastr.	Gastronomy
Geneal.	Genealogy
Geog.	Geography
Geol.	Geology
Geom.	Geometry
Graph. Arts	Graphic Arts
Her.	Heraldry
Hist.	History, Historical
Horol.	Horology
Hort.	Horticulture
Hydraulic Engin.	Hydraulic Engineering
imper.	imperative
impers.	impersonal
Ind.	Indian, India
indef.	indefinite
Information Sci.	Information Science
int.	interjection
interrog.	interrogative
Int. Law	International Law
Ir.	Irish, Ireland
iron.	ironical
joc.	jocular
Journ.	Journalism
lang.	language
Ling.	Linguistics
Lit.	Literature
lit.	literal
Magn.	Magnetism
Managem.	Management
masc.	masculine
Math.	Mathematics
Mech.	Mechanics
Mech. Engin.	Mechanical Engineering
Med.	Medicine
Metalw.	Metalwork
Metaph.	Metaphysics
Meteorol.	Meteorology
Mil.	Military
Min.	Mineralogy
Motor Veh.	Motor Vehicles
Mount.	Mountaineering
Mus.	Music
Mythol.	Mythology
n.	noun
Nat. Sci.	Natural Science
Naut.	Nautical
neg.	negative
N. Engl.	Northern English
ns.	nouns
Nucl. Engin.	Nuclear Engineering
Nucl. Phys.	Nuclear Physics
Num.	Numismatics
N. Z.	New Zealand
obj.	object
Oceanog.	Oceanography
Ornith.	Ornithology
P	Proprietary name
Palaeont.	Palaeontology
Parapsych.	Parapsychology
Parl.	Parliament
pass.	passive
Pharm.	Pharmacy
Philat.	Philately
Philos.	Philosophy

Phonet.	Phonetics
Photog.	Photography
phr(s).	phrase(s)
Phys.	Physics
Physiol.	Physiology
pl.	plural
poet.	poetical
Polit.	Politics
poss.	possessive
postpos.	postpositive
p.p.	past participle
pred.	predicative
pref.	prefix
Prehist.	Prehistory
prep.	preposition
pres.	present
pres. p.	present participle
pr. n.	proper noun
pron.	pronoun
Pros.	Prosody
prov.	proverbial
Psych.	Psychology
p.t.	past tense
Railw.	Railways
RC Ch.	Roman Catholic Church
refl.	reflexive
rel.	relative
Relig.	Religion
Res.	Research
Rhet.	Rhetoric
rhet.	rhetorical
S. Afr.	South African, South Africa

sb.	somebody
Sch.	School
Sci.	Science
Scot.	Scottish, Scotland
Shipb.	Shipbuilding
sing.	singular
sl.	slang
Sociol.	Sociology
Soc. Serv.	Social Services
Soil Sci.	Soil Science
St. Exch.	Stock Exchange
sth.	something
suf.	suffix
superl.	superlative
Surv.	Surveying
symb.	symbol
tech.	technical
Teleph.	Telephony
Telev.	Television
Theol.	Theology
Univ.	University
usu.	usually
v. aux.	auxiliary verb
Vet. Med.	Veterinary Medicine
v.i.	intransitive verb
voc.	vocative
v. refl.	reflexive verb
v.t.	transitive verb
v.t. & i.	transitive and intransitive verb
W. Ind.	West Indian, West Indies
Woodw.	Woodwork
Zool.	Zoology

German abbreviations used in the Dictionary / Im Wörterverzeichnis verwendete deutsche Abkürzungen

a.	anderes; andere
ä.	ähnliches; ähnliche
Abk.	Abkürzung
adj.	adjektivisch
Adj.	Adjektiv
adv.	adverbial
Adv.	Adverb
Akk.	Akkusativ
amerik.	amerikanisch
Amtsspr.	Amtssprache
Anat.	Anatomie
Anthrop.	Anthropologie
Archäol.	Archäologie
Archit.	Architektur
Art.	Artikel
Astrol.	Astrologie
Astron.	Astronomie
A. T.	Altes Testament
attr.	attributiv
Ausspr.	Aussprache
Bauw.	Bauwesen
Bergmannsspr.	Bergmannssprache
berlin.	berlinisch
bes.	besonders
Bez.	Bezeichnung
bibl.	biblisch
bild. Kunst	bildende Kunst
Biol.	Biologie
Bodenk.	Bodenkunde
Börsenw.	Börsenwesen
Bot.	Botanik
BRD	Bundesrepublik Deutschland
brit.	britisch
Bruchz.	Bruchzahl
Buchf.	Buchführung
Buchw.	Buchwesen
Bürow.	Bürowesen
chem.	chemisch
christl.	christlich
Dat.	Dativ
DDR	Deutsche Demokratische Republik
Dekl.	Deklination
Demonstrativpron.	Demonstrativpronomen
d. h.	das heißt
dichter.	dichterisch
Druckerspr.	Druckersprache
Druckw.	Druckwesen
dt.	deutsch
DV	Datenverarbeitung
Eisenb.	Eisenbahn
elektr.	elektrisch
Elektrot.	Elektrotechnik
Energievers.	Energieversorgung
Energiewirtsch.	Energiewirtschaft
engl.	englisch
etw.	etwas
ev.	evangelisch
fachspr.	fachsprachlich
fam.	familiär
Fem.	Femininum
Ferns.	Fernsehen
Fernspr.	Fernsprechwesen
fig.	figurativ
Finanzw.	Finanzwesen
Fischereiw.	Fischereiwesen

Fliegerspr.	Fliegersprache
Flugw.	Flugwesen
Forstw.	Forstwesen
Fot.	Fotografie
Frachtw.	Frachtwesen
Funkw.	Funkwesen
Gastr.	Gastronomie
Gattungsz.	Gattungszahl
Gaunerspr.	Gaunersprache
geh.	gehoben
Gen.	Genitiv
Geneal.	Genealogie
Geogr.	Geographie
Geol.	Geologie
Geom.	Geometrie
Handarb.	Handarbeit
Handw.	Handwerk
Hausw.	Hauswirtschaft
Her.	Heraldik
hess.	hessisch
Hilfsv.	Hilfsverb
hist.	historisch
Hochschulw.	Hochschulwesen
Holzverarb.	Holzverarbeitung
Imkerspr.	Imkersprache
Indefinitpron.	Indefinitpronomen
indekl.	indeklinabel
Indik.	Indikativ
Inf.	Infinitiv
Informationst.	Informationstechnik
Interj.	Interjektion
iron.	ironisch
itr.	intransitiv
Jagdw.	Jagdwesen
Jägerspr.	Jägersprache
jmd.	jemand
jmdm.	jemandem
jmdn.	jemanden
jmds.	jemandes
Jugendspr.	Jugendsprache
jur.	juristisch
Kardinalz.	Kardinalzahl
kath.	katholisch
Kaufmannsspr.	Kaufmannssprache
Kfz-W.	Kraftfahrzeugwesen
Kinderspr.	Kindersprache
Kochk.	Kochkunst
Konj.	Konjunktion
Kosew.	Kosewort
Kunstwiss.	Kunstwissenschaft
Kurzf.	Kurzform
Kurzw.	Kurzwort
landsch.	landschaftlich
Landw.	Landwirtschaft
Literaturw.	Literaturwissenschaft
Luftf.	Luftfahrt
ma.	mittelalterlich
MA.	Mittelalter
marx.	marxistisch
Mask.	Maskulinum
Math.	Mathematik
Mech.	Mechanik
Med.	Medizin
Meeresk.	Meereskunde
Met.	Meteorologie

Metall.	Metallurgie
Metallbearb.	Metallbearbeitung
Milit.	Militär
Mineral.	Mineralogie
Modalv.	Modalverb
Münzk.	Münzkunde
Mus.	Musik
Mythol.	Mythologie
Naturw.	Naturwissenschaft
Neutr.	Neutrum
niederdt.	niederdeutsch
Nom.	Nominativ
nordamerik.	nordamerikanisch
nordd.	norddeutsch
nordostd.	nordostdeutsch
nordwestd.	nordwestdeutsch
ns.	nationalsozialistisch
N. T.	Neues Testament
o.	ohne; oben
o. ä.	oder ähnliches; oder ähnliche
od.	oder
Ordinalz.	Ordinalzahl
orth.	orthodox
ostd.	ostdeutsch
österr.	österreichisch
Päd.	Pädagogik
Paläont.	Paläontologie
Papierdt.	Papierdeutsch
Parapsych.	Parapsychologie
Parl.	Parlament
Part.	Partizip
Perf.	Perfekt
Pers.	Person
pfälz.	pfälzisch
Pharm.	Pharmazie
Philat.	Philatelie
Philos.	Philosophie
Physiol.	Physiologie
Pl.	Plural
Plusq.	Plusquamperfekt
Polizeiw.	Polizeiwesen
Postw.	Postwesen
präd.	prädikativ
Prähist.	Prähistorie
Präp.	Präposition
Präs.	Präsens
Prät.	Präteritum
Pron.	Pronomen
Psych.	Psychologie
Raumf.	Raumfahrt
Rechtsspr.	Rechtssprache
Rechtsw.	Rechtswesen
refl.	reflexiv
regelm.	regelmäßig
Rel.	Religion
Relativpron.	Relativpronomen
rhein.	rheinisch
Rhet.	Rhetorik
röm.	römisch
röm.-kath.	römisch-katholisch
Rundf.	Rundfunk
s.	siehe
S.	Seite
scherzh.	scherzhaft
schles.	schlesisch
schott.	schottisch
Schülerspr.	Schülersprache
Schulw.	Schulwesen
schwäb.	schwäbisch
schweiz.	schweizerisch
Seemannsspr.	Seemannssprache
Seew.	Seewesen
Sexualk.	Sexualkunde
Sg.	Singular
s. o.	siehe oben
Soldatenspr.	Soldatensprache
Sozialpsych.	Sozialpsychologie
Sozialvers.	Sozialversicherung
Soziol.	Soziologie
spött.	spöttisch
Spr.	Sprichwort
Sprachw.	Sprachwissenschaft
Steuerw.	Steuerwesen
Studentenspr.	Studentensprache
s. u.	siehe unten
Subj.	Subjekt
subst.	substantivisch; substantiviert
Subst.	Substantiv
südd.	süddeutsch
südwestd.	südwestdeutsch
Suff.	Suffix
Textilw.	Textilwesen
Theol.	Theologie
thüring.	thüringisch
Tiermed.	Tiermedizin
tirol.	tirolisch
tr.	transitiv
Trenn.	Trennung
u.	und
u. a.	und andere[s]
u. ä.	und ähnliches
ugs.	umgangssprachlich
unbest.	unbestimmt
unpers.	unpersönlich
unr.	unregelmäßig
usw.	und so weiter
v.	von
V.	Verb
verächtl.	verächtlich
veralt.	veraltet; veraltend
Verhaltensf.	Verhaltensforschung
verhüll.	verhüllend
Verkehrsw.	Verkehrswesen
Vermessungsw.	Vermessungswesen
Versicherungsw.	Versicherungswesen
vgl.	vergleiche
Vkl.	Verkleinerungsform
Völkerk.	Völkerkunde
Völkerr.	Völkerrecht
Volksk.	Volkskunde
volkst.	volkstümlich
vulg.	vulgär
Werbespr.	Werbesprache
westd.	westdeutsch
westfäl.	westfälisch
Wiederholungsz.	Wiederholungszahlwort
wiener.	wienerisch
Winzerspr.	Winzersprache
Wirtsch.	Wirtschaft
Wissensch.	Wissenschaft
Wz.	Warenzeichen
Zahnmed.	Zahnmedizin
z. B.	zum Beispiel
Zeitungsw.	Zeitungswesen
Zollw.	Zollwesen
Zool.	Zoologie
Zus.	Zusammensetzung
Zusschr.	Zusammenschreibung

A

a, A [a:] **das; ~, ~ a)** *(Buchstabe)* a/A; **kleines a** small a; **großes A** capital A; **das A und O** *(fig.)* the essential thing/things (*Gen.* for); **von A bis Z** *(fig. ugs.)* from beginning to end; **wer A sagt, muß auch B sagen** *(fig.)* if one starts a thing, one must go through with it; **b)** *(Musik)* [key of] A

ä, Ä [ɛ:] **das; ~, ~:** a umlaut

a *Abk.* Ar, Are

à [a] *Präp. mit Nom., Akk. (Kaufmannsspr.)* **zehn Marken à 50 Pfennig** ten stamps at 50 pfennigs each; **zehn Kisten à zwölf Flaschen** ten cases of twelve bottles each

A *Abk.* **a) Autobahn** ≈ M; **b)** *(Phys.)* **Ampere** A

Aa [a'|a] **das;** ~ *(Kinderspr.)* poo[-poo] *(child lang.)*; **Aa machen** do poo-poo *or* big jobs *(child lang.)*; do a big job *(Amer. child lang.)*

[1]AA *Abk.* **Anonyme Alkoholiker** AA

[2]AA [a:'|a:] **das;** ~ *Abk.* **Auswärtiges Amt**

Aachen ['a:xn̩] **(das);** ~s Aix-la-Chapelle; Aachen

Aal [a:l] **der; ~[e]s, ~e** eel; ~ **grün** *(Kochk.)* green eels; stewed eels; ~ **blau** *(Kochk.)* blue eel; **glatt wie ein ~ sein** be as slippery as an eel; **sich [drehen und] winden** *od.* **krümmen wie ein ~:** twist and turn like an eel

aalen *refl. V. (ugs.)* stretch out; **sich in der Sonne/auf der Wiese** *usw.* **~:** lie stretched out in the sun/in the meadow *etc.*

aal-, Aal-: ~glatt *(abwertend)* **1.** *Adj.* slippery; **~glatt sein** be as slippery as an eel; **2.** *adv.* smoothly; **sich ~glatt herausreden** glibly talk one's way out; **~kasten der** eeltrap; **~suppe die** eel soup

a. a. O. *Abk.* **am angegebenen Ort** loc. cit.

Aar [a:ɐ̯] **der; ~[e]s, ~e** *(dichter. veralt.)* eagle

Aas [a:s] **das; ~es, ~e** *od.* **Äser** ['ɛ:zɐ] **a)** *Pl.* ~e *(Kadaver)* carrion *no pl., no indef. art.*; rotten carcass; **~ fressen** eat carrion; **b)** *Pl.* Äser *(salopp) (abwertend)* swine; *(mit Anerkennung)* devil; **ein raffiniertes/kleines ~:** a cunning/little devil; **kein ~:** not one damned person

Aas·blume die *(Bot.)* carrion flower

aasen *itr. V. (ugs., bes. nordd.)* **mit etw. ~:** be wasteful with sth.; **mit dem Geld ~:** throw [one's] money around

aas, Aas-: ~fliege die *(Zool.) (Calliphorinae)* blowfly; *(Sarcophaginae)* flesh-fly; **~fresser der** *(Zool.)* carrion-eater; scavenger; **~geier der** vulture; **wie [die] ~geier** *(abwertend)* like vultures

aasig 1. *Adv. (ugs.)* **~ frieren** be absolutely frozen; **~ kalt** damned cold; **es tut ~ weh** it hurts like mad *(sl.)*. **2.** *Adj.* malicious; mean

Aas-: ~käfer der carrion-beetle; **~seite die** *(Gerberei)* flesh side

ab [ap] **1.** *Präp. mit Dat.* **a)** *(zeitlich)* from; **ab 1980** as from 1980; **Jugendliche ab 16 Jahren** young people over the age of 16; **ab [dem] 3. April** from the 3rd of April; **ab wann?** from when?; from what time?; **b)** *(bes. Kaufmannsspr.: räumlich)* ex; **ab Werk** ex works; **ab [unserem] Lager** ex store; ex warehouse *(Amer.)*; **ab Frankfurt fliegen** fly from Frankfurt; **ab Köln führt der Zug einen Speisewagen** from Cologne onwards the train has a dining-car; **c)** *([Rang]folge)* from ... on[wards]; **ab nächster Ausgabe** from the next edition onwards; **ab zweitausend Stück aufwärts** from two thousand items onwards; **ab 20 DM** from 20 DM [upwards]. **2.** *Adv.* **a)** *(weg)* off; away; **nicht weit ab vom Weg** not far [away] from the path; **an der Kreuzung links ab** turn off left at the junction; **b)** *(ugs.: Aufforderung)* off; away; **ab nach Hause** get off home; **ab die Post** *(fig.)* off you/we *etc.* go; **ab nach Kassel** *(fig.)* it's off and away; **X ab/X und Y ab** *(Theater)* exit X/exeunt X and Y; **Film/Ton ab!** *(Film)* camera!/sound!; **Film ab!** *(im Vorführraum)* film, please!; **c)** *(milit. Kommando)* **Gewehr ab!** order arms!; *s. auch* **[1]Helm a; d) ab und zu** *od. (nordd.)* **an** now and then; from time to time; *s. auch* **absein**; **auf 3e, f; von 1a, b**

Abakus ['a(:)bakʊs] **der; ~, ~:** abacus

ạbänderbar, ạbänderlich *Adj.* alterable

ạb|ändern 1. *tr. V.* alter; change; amend ⟨*text*⟩. **2.** *itr. V. (Biol.)* mutate

Ạb·änderung die alteration; *(eines Paragraphen)* amendment

Ạbänderungs-: ~antrag der *s.* **Änderungsantrag; ~klage die** *(Rechtsw.)* application for a variation *(of periodical payments)*

Abandon [abã'dõ:] **der; ~s, ~s** *(Rechtsw.)* abandonment

abandonnieren [abãdɔ'ni:rən] *tr., itr. V. (Rechtsw.)* abandon

ạb|arbeiten 1. *tr. V.* **a)** *(abgelten)* work for ⟨*meal*⟩; work off ⟨*debt, amount*⟩; **seine Überfahrt ~:** work one's passage; **b)** *(abnutzen)* wear out [with work]; **abgearbeitete Hände** work-worn hands; **c)** *(beseitigen)* remove; *(abfeilen)* file off. **2.** *refl. V.* slave [away]; work like a slave

Ạb·art die variety

ạb·artig *Adj.* deviant; abnormal

Ạb·artigkeit die a) *(Eigenschaft)* abnormality; deviancy; **b)** *(Handlung)* abnormal act

ạb|äsen *tr. V. (Jägerspr.)* crop

ạb|asten *refl. V. (ugs.)* slave [away]; **sich mit etw. ~:** heave sth. around; **sich** *(Dat.)* **[mit etw.] einen ~** *(salopp)* slave away [heaving sth. around]

ạb|ätzen *tr. V.* **a)** *(reinigen)* clean [with corrosive]; **b)** *(entfernen)* remove [with corrosive]; *(Med.)* cauterize

Abb. *Abk.* **Abbildung** Fig.

ạb|backen *unr. itr. V.; mit sein (Kochk.)* ⟨*dough etc.*⟩ come away

ạb|baken ['apba:kn̩] *tr. V. (Seew.)* mark [with buoys]; buoy

ạb|balgen *tr. V. (Jägerspr.)* skin ⟨*animal*⟩

Ạb·bau der a) *(Zerlegung)* dismantling; *(von Zelten, Lagern)* striking; **b)** *(Senkung)* reduction; **c)** *s.* **abbauen 1d:** cutback (*Gen.* in); pruning; **der ~ von Beamten** the cutback in civil service jobs; **der ~ von Vorurteilen** the breaking down of prejudices; **d)** *(Chemie, Biol.)* breakdown; **e)** *(Bergbau)* mining; *(im Steinbruch)* quarrying; *(von Flözen)* working; **f)** *(Landw.)* reduced yield; **einem ~ unterliegen** ⟨*crop variety*⟩ yield less

ạb|bauen 1. *tr. V.* **a)** *(zerlegen)* dismantle; strike ⟨*tent, camp*⟩; dismantle, take down ⟨*scaffolding*⟩; **b)** *(senken)* reduce ⟨*wages*⟩; **c)** *(beseitigen)* gradually remove; break down ⟨*prejudices, inhibitions*⟩; **etw. planmäßig ~:** phase sth. out; **d)** *(verringern)* cut back ⟨*staff*⟩; prune ⟨*jobs*⟩; **e)** *(Chemie, Biol.)* break down ⟨*carbohydrates, alcohol*⟩; **f)** *(Bergbau)* mine ⟨*coal, gold*⟩; quarry ⟨*stone*⟩; work ⟨*seam*⟩. **2.** *itr. V.* **a)** *(nachlassen)* fade; slow down; **kurz vor dem Ziel baute er stark ab** he faded badly just before the finish; **körperlich ~:** decay physically; **b)** *(Landw.)* ⟨*crop variety*⟩ decline in yield

Ạbbau·produkt das *(Chemie)* decomposition product; *(Biol.)* product of catabolism

ạbbau·würdig *Adj. (Bergbau)* workable

ạb|bedingen *unr. tr. V. (Rechtsspr.)* waive

ạb|beißen 1. *unr. tr. V.* bite off; **eine Zigarre ~:** bite the end off a cigar. **2.** *unr. itr. V.* have a bite; **laß deinen Bruder [von der Banane] ~!** let your brother have a bite [of the banana]!

ạb|beizen *tr. V. (Handw.)* strip ⟨*wooden object*⟩; **die alte Farbe [von etw.] ~:** strip the old paint off [sth.]

ạb|bekommen *unr. tr. V.* **a)** *(bekommen)* get; **sie hat keinen Mann ~** *(ugs.)* she didn't catch herself a husband; **b)** *(hinnehmen müssen)* **einen Schlag/ein paar Kratzer ~:** get hit/get a few scratches; **den ganzen Segen ~** *(ugs. iron.)* get the full benefit *(iron.)*; **etwas ~:** *(getroffen werden)* get *or* be hit; *(verletzt werden)* get *or* be hurt; **er hat im Krieg etwas ~** *(ugs.)* he was injured in the war; **der Wagen hat nichts ~:** the car wasn't damaged; **c)** *(entfernen können)* get ⟨*paint, lid, chain*⟩ off

ạb|berufen *unr. tr. V.* recall ⟨*ambassador, envoy*⟩ **(aus, von** from); **Gott hat ihn aus diesem Leben ~** *(verhüll.)* God has taken him from us

Ạb·berufung die recall

ạb|bestellen *tr. V.* cancel ⟨*newspaper, hotel room, plumber, etc.*⟩; ask to have ⟨*telephone*⟩ disconnected; **jmdn. ~:** cancel sb.'s appointment

Ạb·bestellung die cancellation

ạb|betteln *tr. V. (ugs.)* **jmdm. etw. ~:** beg sth. from sb.

ạb|bezahlen *tr. V.* pay off ⟨*debts, television set, etc.*⟩

ạb|biegen 1. *unr. itr. V.; mit sein* turn off; **links/rechts/an der Kreuzung ~:** turn [off] left/right/at the junction. **2.** *unr. tr. V.* **a)** bend ⟨*rod, metal sheet, etc.*⟩; **b)** *(ugs.: abwenden)* get out of *(coll.)* ⟨*obligation*⟩; head off *(coll.)* ⟨*row*⟩; **sie hat die Sache noch einmal abgebogen** she just managed to stop things going too far

Ạbbieger der; ~s, ~ *(Verkehrsw.)* motorist/cyclist/car *etc.* turning off

Ạbbiege·spur die turning-off lane

Ạb·biegung die bend

Ạb·bild das *(eines Menschen)* likeness; *(eines Gegenstandes)* copy; *(im Spiegel)* reflection; *(fig.)* portrayal

ạb|bilden *tr. V.* copy; reproduce ⟨*object, picture*⟩; portray, depict ⟨*person*⟩; depict ⟨*landscape*⟩; *(fig.)* portray; depict; **auf dem Foto ist ein Haus abgebildet** the photograph shows a house; **jmdn./einen Gegenstand/die Landschaft naturgetreu ~:** depict sb./copy *or* reproduce an object/depict the scenery faithfully

Ạb·bildung die a) *(Bild)* illustration; *(Schaubild)* diagram; **die ~ einer unbekleideten Dame** a/the picture of a nude woman; **b)** *o. Pl. (das Abbilden)* reproduction; *(fig.)* portrayal

Ạbbildungs·fehler der *(Optik)* aberration; image defect

ạb|bimsen *tr., itr. V. (ugs.)* crib ⟨*exercises*⟩

ạb|binden 1. *unr. tr. V.* **a)** *(losbinden)* untie; undo; **die Schürze/Krawatte ~:** undo *or* untie one's apron/tie; **eine Schnur ~:** untie a piece of string; **b)** *(abschnüren)* put a tourniquet on ⟨*artery, arm, leg, etc.*⟩; tie ⟨*umbilical cord*⟩; **c)** *(Kochk.)* thicken ⟨*sauce, gravy*⟩; bind ⟨*rissole etc.*⟩; **d)** *(Zimmerei)* make trial assembly of; **e)** *(Landw.)* wean ⟨*calf*⟩. **2.** *unr. itr. V. (Bauw.)* ⟨*concrete*⟩ set

Ạb·bitte die *(geh.)* **jmdm. ~ leisten** *od.* **tun** ask sb.'s pardon

ạb|bitten *unr. tr. V. (geh.)* **jmdm. etwas/vieles abzubitten haben** have something/a lot to apologize to sb. for

ạb|blasen *unr. tr. V.* **a)** *(ugs.: absagen)* call off ⟨*enterprise, party*⟩; **b)** *(Technik)* discharge ⟨*fumes*⟩; **c)** *(Milit.)* **das Manöver/den Angriff/das Gefecht ~:** sound the retreat; **d)** *(Jägerspr.)* **die Jagd ~:** call off the hounds/beaters *etc.*

ạb|blassen *itr. V.; mit sein* fade

ạb|blättern *itr. V.; mit sein* flake off

ạb|bleiben *unr. itr. V.; mit sein (ugs., bes. nordd.)* **wo ist er/es nur abgeblieben?** where has he/it got to *(Brit.) or* gone *(Amer.)*?; where can he/it be?

ạbblendbar *Adj.* **~er Innenspiegel** *od.* **Rückspiegel** anti-dazzle rear-view mirror

Ạb·blende die *(Film)* fade[-out]

ạb|blenden 1. *tr., itr. V.* black out ⟨*window, lights*⟩; dip *(Brit.)*, dim *(Amer.)* ⟨*headlights*⟩; **bei Gegenverkehr frühzeitig ~:** dip *or (Amer.)* dim headlights promptly when there is oncoming traffic. **2.** *itr. V.* **a)** *(Film)* fade [out]; **b)** *(Fot.)* stop down

Ạbblend-: ~licht das; *o. Pl.* dipped *(Brit.) or (Amer.)* dimmed beam; **mit ~licht fahren** drive on dipped *or* dimmed headlights; **~schalter der** dip-switch *(Brit.)*; dimmer switch *(Amer.)*

ạb|blitzen *itr. V.; mit sein (ugs.)* **sie ließ alle Verehrer ~:** she gave all her admirers the brush-off; **bei jmdm. [mit etw.] ~:** fail to get anywhere [with sth.] with sb. *(coll.)*

ạb|blocken *tr. V. (Sport; auch fig.)* block

ạb|blühen *itr. V.; mit haben od. sein (auch fig.)* fade

ạb|bohren *tr. V. (Bergbau)* drill out

Ạb·brand der a) *(Kerntechnik)* burn-up; **b)** *(Metall.)* melting loss

ạb|brausen 1. *tr. V. s.* **abduschen. 2.** *itr. V.; mit sein (ugs.)* roar off

ạb|brechen 1. *unr. tr. V.* **a)** *(abtrennen)* break off; break ⟨*needle, pencil*⟩; **sich** *(Dat.)* **einen Fingernagel/Zahn ~:** break a fingernail/a tooth; **b)** *(zerlegen)* strike ⟨*tent, camp*⟩; **c)** *(abreißen)* demolish, pull down ⟨*building, tower*⟩; **d)** *(beenden)* break off ⟨*negotiations, [diplomatic] relations, discussion, conversation, connection, activity, training*⟩; call off ⟨*strike*⟩; *(vorzeitig, wider Erwarten)* cut short ⟨*conversation, studies, holiday, activity*⟩; **den Kampf ~** *(Boxen)* stop the fight; **ein abgebrochenes Studium** an unfinished course of studies; **abgebrochene Sätze** fragmentary sentences; *s. auch* **abgebrochen 2. 2.** *unr. itr. V.* **a)** *mit sein (entzweigehen)* break [off]; **die Armlehne von dem Sessel ist mir abgebrochen, als ich ...:** the arm broke off the armchair when I ...; **b)** *(aufhören)* break off; **c)** *mit sein (beendet werden)* **die Verbindung brach ab** the connection was cut off; **d)** *mit sein (steil abfallen)* fall away [steeply]. **3.** *unr. refl. V.* **sich** *(Dat.)* **einen/keinen ~** *(salopp)* put/not put oneself out

ạb|bremsen 1. *tr. V.* **a)** brake; **vor der Kurve den Wagen ~:** slow the car down before the bend; **b)** retard ⟨*motion*⟩; break ⟨*fall*⟩; *(fig.)* curb ⟨*zeal*⟩. **2.** *itr. V.* brake; apply the brakes; **stark/auf 40 ~:** brake hard/to 40

ạb|brennen 1. *unr. itr. V.; mit sein* **a)** *(zerstört werden)* be burned down; ⟨*farm*⟩ be burned out; **das Haus ist abgebrannt** the house has burned down; **wir sind schon zweimal abgebrannt** we've been burned out twice already; **dreimal umgezogen ist [so gut wie] einmal abgebrannt** *(Spr.)* you can lose just as much moving [house] three times as you can if your house burns down; *s. auch* **abgebrannt 2; Grundmauer; b)** *(sich aufbrauchen)* ⟨*fuse*⟩ burn away; ⟨*candle*⟩ burn down; **abgebrannte Streichhölzer** used *or* burnt matches. **2.** *unr. tr. V.* **a)** let off ⟨*firework*⟩; **b)** *(zerstören)* burn down ⟨*building*⟩

Abbreviatur [abrevi̯a'tu:ɐ̯] **die; ~, ~en** *(Druckw., Mus.)* abbreviation

ạb|bringen *unr. tr. V.* **a) jmdn. von etw. ~** make sb. give up sth.; **jmdn. vom Kurs ~:** make sb. change course; **jmdn. von der Fährte ~:** throw sb. off the scent; **jmdn. davon ~, etw. zu tun** stop sb. doing sth.; *(abraten)* dissuade sb. from doing sth.; **er läßt sich von seinem Plan nicht ~** he can't be persuaded to give up *or* drop his plan; **jmdn. vom Thema ~:** get sb. away from the subject; **b)** *(ugs.: lösen)* **etw. [von etw.] ~:** get sth. off [sth.]

ạb|bröckeln *itr. V.; mit sein (auch fig.)* crumble away; *(Börsenw.)* ⟨*price, exchange rate*⟩ decline gradually

Ạb·bruch der a) *o. Pl.* demolition; pulling down; **etw. auf ~ verkaufen** sell sth. at demolition value; **b)** *(Beendigung)* breaking-off; *(Sport)* abandonment; *(Boxen)* stopping; **Sieger durch ~** *(Boxen)* winner when the fight was stopped; **c) einer Sache** *(Dat.)* **[keinen] ~ tun** do [no] harm to sth.; **das tut der Liebe keinen ~** *(ugs. scherzh.)* never mind *(coll.)*; **d)** *o. Pl. (eines Zeltes, Lagers)* striking

ạbbruch-, Ạbbruch-: ~arbeit die demolition work; **~firma die** demolition firm; **~haus das** condemned house; **~reif** *Adj.* ripe for demolition *postpos.*; **~sieg der** *(Boxen)* win when the fight was stopped; **~unternehmen das** demolition firm

ạb|brühen *tr. V. (Kochk.)* blanch; *s. auch* **abgebrüht 2**

ạb|brummen *tr. V. (ugs.)* do *(coll.)*; **er muß noch drei Jahre ~:** he has got another three years to do

ạb|buchen *tr. V.* ⟨*bank*⟩ debit **(von** to); ⟨*creditor*⟩ claim by direct debit **(von** to); *(fig.: als verloren betrachten)* write off; **etw. ~ lassen** *(durch die Bank)* pay sth. by standing order; *(durch Gläubiger)* pay sth. by direct debit

Ạb·buchung die debiting; **~ per Dauerauftrag** payment by standing order/direct debit

ạb|bummeln *tr. V. (ugs.)* take time off in lieu for

ạb|bürsten *tr. V.* **a)** brush off; **jmdm. die Haare/den Schmutz ~:** brush the hairs/the dirt off sb.; **die Haare/den Schmutz von etw. ~:** brush the hairs/the dirt off sth.; **b)** *(säubern)* brush ⟨*garment*⟩; **c)** *(ugs.: zurechtweisen)* **jmdn. ~:** give sb. a dressing down

ạb|busseln *tr. V. (österr.) s.* **abküssen**

ạb|büßen *tr. V.* **a)** serve [out] ⟨*prison sentence*⟩; **b)** *(Rel.)* atone for; do penance for

Ạbbüßung die; ~: nach ~ seiner Strafe after serving [out] his sentence

Abc [a(:)be(:)'tse:] **das; ~: a)** ABC; **nach dem ~ ordnen** arrange alphabetically; **b)** *(fig.: Grundlagen)* ABC; fundamentals *pl.*

Abc-Buch das *(veralt.) s.* **Fibel a**

ạb|checken *tr. V.* check; check through ⟨*list*⟩; check off ⟨*names etc.*⟩

Abc-Schütze der child just starting school

ABC-: ~-Staaten *Pl.* **die ~-Staaten** Argentina, Brazil, and Chile; **~-Waffen** *Pl.* ABC weapons

ạb|dachen ['apdaxn̩] *refl. V. (Geogr.)* slope down

Ạbdachung die; ~, ~en *(Geogr.)* downward slope *or* incline

ạb|dämmen *tr. V.* **a)** dam up ⟨*river, pond, lake*⟩; dam off ⟨*meadow, land*⟩; **b)** *(isolieren)* insulate

Ạbdämmung die; ~, ~en a) dam; *(am Ufer)* dyke; *(Verfahren)* damming; **b)** *(Isolierung)* insulation

Ạb·dampf der *(Technik)* exhaust steam

ạb|dampfen 1. *itr. V.; mit sein* steam away; *(ugs.: abfahren)* set off. **2.** *tr. V. (Chemie)* evaporate

ạb|dämpfen *tr. V.* damp, muffle ⟨*sound*⟩; dim ⟨*light*⟩

Ạbdampf-: ~heizung die exhaust-steam heating; **~rück·stand der** residue from evaporation; **~turbine die** exhaust-steam turbine

ạb|danken *itr. V.* ⟨*ruler*⟩ abdicate; ⟨*government, minister*⟩ resign; *s. auch* **abgedankt 2**

Ạbdankung die; ~, ~en a) *(eines Herrschers)* abdication; *(eines Ministers, einer Regierung)* resignation; **b)** *(veralt.: Entlassung)* retirement; **c)** *(bes. schweiz.: Trauerfeier)* funeral service

ạb|darben *refl. V.* **sich** *(Dat.)* **etw. [vom Munde] ~** *(geh.)* stint oneself to save sth.

Ạbdeck·band das; *Pl.* **~bänder** masking tape

ạb|decken 1. *tr. V.* **a)** open up; uncover ⟨*container*⟩; **der Orkan hat viele Häuser abgedeckt** the hurricane blew the roofs off many houses; **das Bett ~:** pull back the bedspread/bedclothes; **b)** *(herunternehmen, -reißen)* take off; remove; **Bretter von einer Grube ~:** take planks off a trench; **der Sturm deckte das Dach ab** the storm blew the roof off; **c)** *(abräumen)* clear ⟨*table*⟩; clear away ⟨*dishes*⟩; **d)** *(zudecken)* cover [up] ⟨*trench, grave*⟩; **etw. mit Plastikfolie ~:** cover sth. [up] with plastic film; **e)** *(schützen)* cover ⟨*person*⟩; *(Schach)* defend; **f)** *(Sport)* mark ⟨*player*⟩; **g)** *(bezahlen, ausgleichen, berücksichtigen)* cover; meet ⟨*need, demand*⟩; deal with ⟨*problem*⟩; **h)** *(veralt.: abhäuten)* skin; flay. **2.** *itr. V. (den Tisch ~)* clear the table

Ạbdecker der; ~s, ~ *(veralt.)* knacker *(Brit.)*; *(der Tiere abhäutet)* skinner

Abdeckerei die; ~, ~en *(veralt.)* knacker's yard; *(wo Tiere abgehäutet werden)* skinnery *(arch.)*

Ạbdeck-: ~plane die canvas; tarpaulin; **~platte die** *(Bauw.)* coping stone

Ạb·deckung die a) *(Bedeckung)* covering; **b)** *(Ausgleich, Bezahlung, Berücksichtigung)* covering; *(von Bedürfnissen, Forderungen)* meeting; **zur ~ des Risikos** to cover the risk

ạb|dichten *tr. V.* seal, stop up ⟨*hole, crack, gap*⟩; seal ⟨*pipe, container*⟩; plug ⟨*leak*⟩; **das Fenster/die Tür ~:** draughtproof the window/the door

Ạb·dichtung die a) seal; *(von Fenstern, Türen)* draught-proofing; **b)** *o. Pl. (Vorgang)* sealing/draught-proofing

ạb|dienen *tr. V.* serve [out]

ạbdingbar *Adj. (Rechtsspr.)* alterable by mutual consent

ạb|dorren *itr. V.; mit sein (geh.)* dry up and wither away

ạb|drängen *tr. V.* push away; force away; drive ⟨*animal*⟩ away; **jmdn. von etw. ~:** push sb. away from sth.; **einen Spieler vom Ball ~** *(Fußball)* force a player off the ball; **das Auto wurde von der Straße abgedrängt** the car was forced off the road; **ein Schiff vom Kurs ~:** force a ship off course

ạb|drehen 1. *tr. V.* **a)** *(ausschalten)* turn off; turn *or* switch off ⟨*light, lamp, electricity, fire, radio*⟩; **den Hahn ~** *(fig.)* turn off the supply; **b)** *(Film)* finish shooting ⟨*scene, film*⟩; **c)** *(abtrennen)* twist off; **einem Huhn den Hals** *od.* **Kopf ~:** wring a chicken's neck; *s. auch* **Gurgel; d)** *(abschrauben)* screw off ⟨*lid, top*⟩. **2.** *itr. V.; meist mit sein (die Richtung ändern)* turn off; **nach Süden ~:** turn [off] southwards

Ạb·drift die *(Seew.)* leeway

ạb|driften *itr. V.; mit sein* **a)** *(Seew.)* be blown; make leeway *(Naut.)*; **nach rechts/links/ins Drogenmilieu ~** *(fig.)* drift to the Right/Left/into the world of drug addicts

ạb|drosseln *tr. V. (Technik)* reduce ⟨*fuel or power supply*⟩; throttle back ⟨*motor, engine*⟩; *(stoppen)* cut ⟨*motor, engine*⟩; *(fig.: verringern)* cut back; curb

¹Ạb·druck der; *Pl.* **Ạbdrücke** mark; imprint; *(Finger~)* fingermark; *(Fuß~)* footprint; footmark; *(Wachs~)* impression; *(Gips~)* cast; **einen ~ nehmen** *od.* **machen** make a cast/impression

²Ạb·druck der; *Pl.* **~e a)** *o. Pl. (Vorgang)* printing; *(Wieder~)* reprinting; **vor dem ~:** before printing; **b)** *(Ergebnis) (einer Graphik)* print; *(eines Buchs, Artikels)* [printed] text

ạb|drucken *tr. V.* print; *(veröffentlichen)* publish

ạb|drücken 1. *itr. V. (schießen)* pull the trigger; shoot; **auf jmdn./etw. ~:** shoot *or* fire at sb./sth. **2.** *tr. V.* **a)** *(abfeuern)* fire ⟨*revolver, gun*⟩; **b)** *(zudrücken)* constrict; **c) jmdm. die Luft ~:** stop sb. breathing; **d) jmdm. das Herz ~:** burden sb.'s heart; **e)** *(ugs.: umarmen)* hug. **3.** *refl. V.* **a) sich [in etw.** *(Dat.)***] ~:** make marks [in sth.]; ⟨*track*⟩ be imprinted [in sth.]; **b) sich [mit dem Fuß] ~:** push oneself away with one's foot

ạb|ducken *tr., itr. V. (Boxen)* duck ⟨*punch*⟩

ạb|dunkeln *tr. V.* **a)** *(verdunkeln)* darken ⟨*room*⟩; dim ⟨*light*⟩; **b)** *(abtönen)* tone down

ạb|duschen *tr. V.* **a) sich/jmdn. [kalt/warm] ~:** take/give sb. a [cold/hot] shower; **sich/jmdm. den Rücken ~:** shower one's/sb.'s back; **b)** *(entfernen)* shower off

ạb|ebben *itr. V.; mit sein* recede; abate

abend ['a:bn̩t] *Adv.* **heute/morgen/gestern ~:** this/tomorrow/yesterday evening; tonight/tomorrow night/last night *(coll.)*; **Sonntag ~:** [on] Sunday evening *or (coll.)* night; **seit Sonntag ~:** since Sunday evening/night; **was gibt es heute ~ [zu essen]?** what's for dinner/supper?

Ạbend der; ~s, ~e a) evening; **es wird ~:** evening is drawing in; **als es ~ wurde** when evening came; **diesen ~:** that evening *or (coll.)* night; *(heute)* this evening; tonight *(coll.)*; **guten ~!** good evening; **des ~s** *(geh.)* of an evening; in the evenings; **eines [schönen] ~s** one evening; **am [frühen/späten] ~:** [early/late] in the evening; **am ~ vorher** *od.* **zuvor** the evening *or (coll.)* night before; the previous evening; **bis zum [späten] ~:** until [late in the] evening; *(als Frist)* by [late] evening; **am selben/nächsten ~:** the same/following evening *or (coll.)* night; **am ~ des 1. Mai** on the evening *or (coll.)* night of 1 May; **~ für ~, jeden ~:** every [single] evening *or (coll.)* night; **gegen ~** towards evening; **während des ~s** during the evening; **während des ganzen ~s** throughout the [entire] evening; **zu ~ essen** have dinner; *(allgemeiner)* have one's evening meal; **was essen wir zu ~?** what are we having this evening?; what is there for dinner/supper?; **was machen wir jetzt mit dem angebrochenen ~?** *(ugs.)* what shall we do with the rest of the evening?; **je später der ~, desto schöner die Gäste** *(scherzh.)* we're the happier to see you now you 'have come; **du kannst mich [mal] am ~ besuchen** *(ugs. verhüll.)* you know what 'you can do *(coll.)*; *s. auch* **heilig b; Tag a; b)** *(Geselligkeit)* evening; *(Kultur~)* soirée; **ein bunter ~:** a social [evening] *or (coll.)* night; **c)** *(veralt.: Westen)* the Occident *(literary)*; **gen ~:** to the west *or (literary)* Occident; **d)** *(geh.: Ende)* evening

Ạbend-: ~abitur das 'Abitur' through evening classes; **~akademie die** evening school; **~andacht die** evening service; **~an·zug der** dinner dress; evening suit; **~aus·gabe die** evening edition; **~blatt das** evening [news] paper; **~brot das** evening meal; supper; **~brot essen** have one's evening meal; have supper; **wann gibt es ~brot?** when's supper?; **was gibt es zum ~brot?** what's for supper?; **~dämmerung die** [evening] twilight

ạbende·lang 1. *Adj.* lasting whole evenings *postpos., not pred.* **2.** *adv.* for whole evenings

ạbend-, Ạbend-: ~essen das dinner; **das ~essen einnehmen** *(geh.)* have dinner; **nach dem ~essen** after dinner; **was gibt es zum ~essen?** what's for dinner?; **~füllend** *Adj.* occupying a whole evening *postpos., not pred.*; **ein ~füllendes Programm** a full evening's programme; **~gage die** evening's fee; **~gebet das** evening prayers *pl.*; *(von Kindern)* bedtime prayers *pl.*; **das ~gebet sprechen** say one's evening/bedtime prayers; **~gottes·dienst der** evening service; *(kath. Rel.)* evening mass; **~gymnasium das** night school, evening classes *pl. (leading to the 'Abitur')*; **~himmel der** sunset sky; **~karte die** *(Gastron.)* evening menu; **~kasse die** box-office *(open on the evening of the performance)*; **~kleid das** evening dress *or* gown; **~kurs[us] der** evening class *or* course; **etw. in ~en lernen** learn sth. at night school; **~land das;** *o. Pl.* West; Occident *(literary)*; **~ländisch** [-lɛndɪʃ] *Adj.* Western; Occidental *(literary)*

ạbendlich 1. *Adj.; nicht präd.* evening ⟨*quiet, coolness*⟩ of the evening; **die ~en Straßen der Stadt** the streets of the town at evening. **2.** *adv.* **es war ~ still geworden** the stillness of evening had descended; **der Himmel ist ~ gerötet** the sky is showing the red colours of evening

Ạbend·mahl das a) *(im Gottesdienst)* Communion; **das ~ nehmen** receive Communion; **b)** *o. Pl. (N.T.)* Last Supper; **c)** *(bes. südd.) s.* **Abendessen**

Ạbendmahls-: ~gottes·dienst der Communion service; **~kelch der** Communion cup; **~wein der** Communion wine

Ạbend-: ~mahl·zeit die dinner; evening meal; **die ~mahlzeit einnehmen** *(geh.)* have dinner *or* one's evening meal; **~messe die** *(kath. Rel.)* evening mass; **~nachrichten** *Pl.* evening news *sing.*; **~programm das** evening programmes *pl.*; **was gibt's im ~programm?** what's on this evening?; **damit ist das heutige ~programm beendet** that is the end of our programmes for today; **~rot das: ein/das ~rot** the redness of the sunset sky; **gestern war ~rot** there was a red sunset last night; **~röte die** *(geh.) s.* **Abendrot**

ạbends *Adv.* in the evenings; **um sechs Uhr ~:** at six o'clock in the evening; **Montag** *od.* **montags ~:** [on] Monday evenings; **von morgens bis ~:** from morning to night; **spät ~:** late in the evening

Ạbend-: ~schule die night school; evening classes *pl.*; **~schüler der** student at evening classes; **~sonne die** evening sun; **~stern der** evening star; **~stille die** evening stillness; **die ländliche ~stille** the evening stillness of the countryside; **~studium das** *(DDR) course of evening classes leading to a degree or diploma*; **~stunde die** evening hour; **in den frühen/späten ~stunden** early/late in the evening; **bis in die späten ~stunden** till late in the evening; **~toilette die** evening dress; **in großer ~toilette** *(geh.)* in full evening dress; **~vorstellung die** evening performance; **~wind der** evening breeze; **~zeit die: zur ~zeit** in the evening; **~zeitung die** *s.* **~blatt; ~zug der** evening train

Ạbenteuer ['a:bn̩tɔyɐ] **das; ~s, ~ a)** *(auch fig.)* adventure; **auf ~ ausgehen** go off in search of adventure; **b)** *(Unternehmen)* venture; **c)** *(Liebesaffäre)* affair

Ạbenteuer-: ~buch das adventure book; **~geschichte die** adventure story

Ạbenteuerin *s.* **Abenteurerin**

ạbenteuerlich 1. *Adj.* **a)** *(riskant)* risky; hazardous; **b)** *(bizarr)* bizarre. **2.** *adv. (bizarr)* bizarrely; bizarrely, fantastically ⟨*dressed*⟩

Ạbenteuerlichkeit die; ~ a) *(Gewagtheit)* riskiness; hazardousness; **b)** *(Bizarrheit)* bizarreness

ạbenteuer-, Ạbenteuer-: ~lust die thirst for adventure; **~lustig** *Adj.* adventurous; **~lustig sein** have a thirst for adventure; **~roman der** adventure novel; **~spielplatz der** adventure playground

Ạbenteurer ['a:bn̩tɔyrɐ] **der; ~s, ~:** adventurer

Ạbenteurerin die; ~, ~nen adventuress

Ạbenteurer-: ~leben das adventurer's life; **~natur die a)** *o. Pl. (Neigung)* adventurous nature; **b)** *(Mensch)* adventurous person

aber ['a:bɐ] **1.** *Konj.* **a)** *(jedoch)* but; **wir ~ ...:** we, however, ...; **~ trotzdem** but in spite of that; **da er das ~ nicht wußte** but *or* however, since he didn't know that; **oder ~ [auch]** or else; **b)** *(Einwand)* but; **~ warum denn?** but why?; **das stimmt ~ nicht** but that's not right; **c)** *(veralt.: Anknüpfung)* but; **als er ~ nicht kam ...:** but when he didn't come ... **2.** *Adv. (veralt.: wieder)* **~ und abermals** again and again; time and again; **tausend und ~ tausend** thousands upon thousands. **3.** *Partikel* **das ist ~ schön!** why, isn't that nice!; **~ ja/nein!** why, yes/no! **~ natürlich!** but *or* why of course!; **alles, ~ auch alles** everything, but everything; **~ immer!** *(ugs.)* why, certainly!; **das hat ~ geschmeckt** that really tasted good; **das ist ~ auch zu dumm** it's just 'too stupid *or (Amer.)* dumb; **das dauert ~** *(ugs.)* what a time it's taking!; **du bist ~ groß!** aren't you tall!; **hat der ~ eine große Nase!** hasn't he got a big nose!; **Sie kommen ~ spät heute** you 'are late today; **~, ~, meine Herrschaften!** now, now, [ladies and] gentlemen

Ạber das; ~s, ~: ich dulde kein ~: it's no use your objecting; *s. auch* **Wenn**

Ạber·glaube[n] der a) *(Irrglaube)* superstition; **b)** *(Vorurteil)* myth

ạber·gläubig *(veralt.)*, **ạber·gläubisch** [-glɔybɪʃ] *Adj.* superstitious

ạber·hundert *unbest. Zahlw. (geh.)* hundreds [upon hundreds] of

Ạber·hunderte *Pl. (geh.)* hundreds [upon hundreds]

ạb|erkennen *unr. tr. V.* **jmdm. ein Recht ~:** revoke sb.'s right (**auf** + *Akk.* to); *(Sport)* **jmdm. den Sieg/Titel ~:** disallow sb.'s victory/strip sb. of his/her title

Ạberkennung die; ~, ~en revocation; *(Sport)* **die ~ ihres Sieges/Titels** disallowing her victory/stripping her of her title

ạbermalig *Adj.; nicht präd. (wiederholt)* repeated; *(nochmalig)* renewed

abermals ['a:bɐma:ls] *Adv.* once again; once more

ab|ernten *tr. V.* finish the harvesting of; finish harvesting *or* picking ‹*fruit*›; **das Getreide ist abgeerntet** the corn is all in; **die Apfelbäume waren fast abgeerntet** nearly all the fruit had been picked from the apple-trees; **abgeerntete Felder** empty fields
Aberration [ap|era'tsio:n] **die; ~, ~en** *(Astron., Optik)* aberration
aber·tausend *unbest. Zahlw. (geh.)* thousands [upon thousands] of
Aber·tausende *Pl. (geh.)* thousands [upon thousands]
Aber·witz der; *o. Pl. (geh.)* lunacy; **ein ~:** a piece of lunacy
aber·witzig *Adj.* crazy
ab|essen *unr. tr. V.* **a)** *(wegessen)* **etw. [von etw.] ~:** eat sth. off [sth.]; **b)** *(leer essen)* clear ‹*plate, table*›; **abgegessene Teller** empty plates; **abgegessenes Geschirr** dirty dishes
Abessinien [abɛ'si:ni̯ən] **(das); ~s** *(veralt.)* **a)** Abyssinia; **b)** *(scherzh.: FKK-Strand)* nudist beach
Abessinier der; ~s, ~ *(veralt.)* Abyssinian
Abf. *Abk.* **Abfahrt** dep.
ab|fackeln *tr. V. (Technik)* flare [off]
abfahr·bereit *Adj.* ready to go *or* leave *pred.*; **die ~en Fahrzeuge** the vehicles which are/were ready to leave
ab|fahren 1. *unr. itr. V.; mit sein* **a)** *(wegfahren)* leave; depart; **wo fährt der Zug nach Paris ab?** where does the Paris train leave from?; **b)** *(hinunterfahren)* drive down; *(Skisport)* ski *or* go down; **c)** *(salopp: sich begeistern)* **auf jmdn./etw. [voll] ~:** be mad about sb./sth.; **d)** *(salopp: abgewiesen werden)* **jmdn. ~ lassen** tell sb. where he/she can go *(sl.)*; **bei jmdm. ganz schön ~:** get absolutely nowhere with sb. *(coll.)*. **2.** *unr. tr. V.* **a)** *(abtransportieren)* take away; **b)** *(abnutzen)* wear out; **abgefahrene Reifen** worn tyres; **c)** *auch mit sein (entlangfahren)* drive the whole length of ‹*street, route*›; drive through ‹*district*›; **d)** *(ugs.: abtrennen)* **jmdm. ein Bein ~:** run over sb. and sever his/her leg; **e)** *(Film, Ferns.)* start. **3.** *unr. refl. V. (sich abnutzen)* wear out
Ab·fahrt die a) departure; **b)** *(Skisport)* descent; *(Strecke)* run; *s. auch* **Abfahrtslauf; c)** *(Autobahn~) s.* **Ausfahrt a**
abfahrt·bereit *s.* **abfahrbereit**
Abfahrts-: ~lauf der *(Skisport)* downhill [racing]; **~läufer der** *(Skisport)* downhill racer; **~rennen das** *(Skisport)* downhill [racing]
Abfahrt[s]·zeit die time of departure; departure time
Ab·fall der a) *(Küchen~ o.ä.)* rubbish, *(Amer.)* garbage *or* trash *no indef. art., no pl.*; *(Fleisch~)* offal *no indef. art., no pl.*; *(Industrie~)* waste *no indef. art.*; *(auf der Straße)* litter *no indef. art., no pl.*; **den ~ runtertragen** *(ugs.)* empty the rubbish; **b)** *o. Pl. (Rückgang)* drop *(Gen.,* **in** + *Dat.* in); **c)** *o. Pl. (Abtrünnigkeit) (vom Glauben)* apostasy; *(eines Landes)* secession **(von** from)
Abfall-: ~beseitigung die refuse disposal; *(industriell)* waste disposal; **~eimer der** rubbish *or* waste bin; trash *or* garbage can *(Amer.)*; *(auf der Straße)* litter bin; trash *or* litter basket *or* can *(Amer.)*
ab|fallen *unr. itr. V.; mit sein* **a)** *(ugs.: herausspringen)* **wieviel fällt für jeden ab?** what will each person's share be?; **für dich wird auch eine Kleinigkeit ~:** you'll get something out of it too; **dabei fällt nicht viel ab** not much will come out of it; **b)** *(übrigbleiben)* be left [over]; **c)** *(herunterfallen)* fall off; **d)** *(verschwinden)* **von jmdm. ~:** leave sb.; **alle Unsicherheit fiel von ihm ab** he shed all his diffidence; **e)** *(sich lossagen)* ‹*country*› secede; **vom Glauben ~:** desert the faith; **seine Anhänger fielen von ihm ab** his followers deserted him; **f)** *(nachlassen)* drop; **g)** *(bes. Sport: zurückfallen)* drop *or* fall back; **h)** *(sich senken)* ‹*land, hillside, road*› drop away; slope; **i)** *(im Vergleich)* **gegenüber jmdm./etw.** *od.* **gegen jmdn./etw. stark ~:** be markedly inferior to sb./sth.; **j)** *(Seemannsspr.)* cast
Abfall·haufen der rubbish-heap; *(in einer Werkstatt usw.)* waste-pile
ab·fällig 1. *Adj.* disparaging; derogatory. **2.** *adv.* **sich ~ über jmdn. äußern** make disparaging *or* derogatory remarks about sb.
Abfall-: ~produkt das *(auch fig.)* by-product; *(Sekundärstoff)* secondary product; **~verwertung die** recycling of waste
ab|fälschen *tr. V. (Ballspiele)* deflect
ab|fangen *unr. tr. V.* **a)** intercept ‹*agent, message, aircraft*›; **b)** *(auf-, anhalten)* catch; **c)** *(Sport: einholen)* **jmdn. ~:** catch sb. up; catch up with sb.; **d)** *(abwehren)* repel ‹*charge, assault*›; ward off ‹*blow, attack*›; *(fig.)* stop ‹*development*›; cushion ‹*impact*›; **e)** *(Bauw.)* shore up; **f)** *(unter Kontrolle bringen)* get ‹*vehicle, aircraft*› under control
Abfang·jäger der *(Luftwaffe)* interceptor
ab|färben *itr. V.* **a)** ‹*colour, garment, etc.*› run; ‹*wet paint etc.*› leave marks; **b)** *(beeinflussen)* **auf jmdn./etw. ~:** rub off on sb./sth.
ab|fasen *tr. V. (Technik)* bevel ‹*edge*›
ab|fassen *tr. V.* write ‹*report, letter, etc.*›; draw up ‹*will*›
Ab·fassung die writing; *(eines Testaments)* drawing up
ab|faulen *itr. V.; mit sein* rot off
ab|federn 1. *tr. V.* **a)** *(federnd abfangen)* absorb; **b)** *(Technik)* spring ‹*axle etc.*›. **2.** *itr. V.* bend at the knees on landing [to absorb the shock]; *(beim Absprung)* push off
ab|fegen *tr. V. s.* [2]**abkehren**
ab|feiern *tr. V.* use up ‹*excess hours worked*› *(by taking time off)*
ab|feilen *tr. V.* **a)** *(entfernen)* file off; **etw. von etw. ~:** file sth. off sth.; **b)** *(verkürzen, glätten)* file down
ab|fertigen *tr. V.* **a)** handle, dispatch ‹*mail*›; deal with ‹*applicant, application*›; deal with, handle ‹*passengers*›; serve ‹*customer*›; clear ‹*ship*› for sailing; clear ‹*aircraft*› for take-off; clear ‹*lorry*› for departure; *(vorbereiten)* prepare ‹*ship etc.*› for departure; prepare ‹*mail*› for dispatch; *(kontrollieren)* clear; check; **der Zoll hat zügig abgefertigt** customs clearance was quick; **b)** *(ugs.: unfreundlich behandeln)* **jmdn. [grob/barsch] ~:** [roughly/rudely] turn sb. away; **er hat mich ganz kurz abgefertigt** he was very short with me; **c)** *(Sport)* trounce; **der Gegner wurde [mit] 5:1 abgefertigt** the opponent was trounced 5:1
Ab·fertigung die a) *s.* **abfertigen a:** handling; dispatching; serving; clearing for sailing/take-off/departure; preparing for departure/dispatch; *(Kontrolle)* clearance; checking; **die unfreundliche ~ am Flughafen/im Laden** the unfriendly service at the airport/in the shop; **b)** *(Abteilung)* dispatch office; **c)** *(österr.) s.* **Abfindung**
Abfertigungs·schalter der *(am Flughafen)* check-in desk; *(beim Zoll)* customs desk
ab|feuern *tr. V.* fire; **Schüsse/eine Kanone [auf jmdn./etw.] ~:** fire shots/a cannon [at sb./sth.]; **das ganze Magazin ~:** fire off the whole magazine
ab|filtern, ab|filtrieren *tr. V. (fachspr.)* filter out
ab|finden 1. *unr. tr. V.* **a)** *(entschädigen)* **jmdn. mit etw. ~:** compensate sb. with sth.; **seine Gläubiger ~:** settle with one's creditors; **er wurde großzügig abgefunden** he received a generous settlement. **2.** *unr. refl. V.* **sich ~:** resign oneself; **sich ~ mit** come to terms with; learn to live with ‹*noise, heat*›; **sich damit ~, daß ...:** come to terms with the fact that ...
Abfindung die; ~, ~en a) *(Summe)* settlement; **eine ~ in Höhe von ... zahlen** make a settlement of ...; **b)** *(Vorgang) (Entschädigung)* compensation; *(von Gläubigern)* paying-off
Abfindungs·summe die *s.* **Abfindung a**
ab|fischen *tr. V.* fish out
ab|flachen ['apflaxn̩] **1.** *tr. V. (flacher machen)* flatten [out]. **2.** *refl. V.* **a)** *(flacher werden)* flatten out; become flatter; **b)** *(nachlassen)* drop off
Abflachung die; ~, ~en a) flattening; **b)** *(Nachlassen)* dropping off
ab|flauen *itr. V.; mit sein* die down; subside; ‹*interest, conversation*› flag; ‹*business*› become slack; ‹*noise*› abate; **die Konjunktur flaut ab** the economy is running down
ab|fliegen 1. *unr. itr. V.; mit sein* ‹*person*› leave [by aeroplane]; ‹*aircraft*› take off; ‹*bird*› fly off *or* away; **die Maschine nach Brüssel fliegt um 13[30] Uhr ab** the plane for Brussels leaves at 13.30. **2.** *unr. tr. V.* **a)** *(wegbringen)* fly out **(aus** of); **b)** *(kontrollieren)* fly over ‹*district*›; fly along ‹*road*›
ab|fließen *unr. itr. V.; mit sein* **a)** flow off; *(wegfließen)* flow away; **aus etw. ~:** drain away from sth.; **von etw. ~** run off sth.; **sämtliche Gewinne fließen ins Ausland ab** *(fig.)* all profits are siphoned off abroad; **b)** *(sich leeren)* **die Wanne fließt nicht ab** the bath won't empty
Ab·flug der departure
Abflug-: ~hafen der *(Flugw.)* airport of departure; **die Maschine kehrte zum ~hafen zurück** the aircraft returned to the airport it had started from; **~zeit die** departure time
Ab·fluß der a) drain; *(von Gewässern)* outlet; *(Rohr)* drain-pipe; *(für Abwasser)* waste-pipe; **b)** *o. Pl. (das Abfließen)* draining away; **der ~ von Kapital ins Ausland** *(fig.)* the flow of capital abroad
Abfluß-: ~graben der drainage ditch; **~hahn der** outlet cock *or (Amer.)* faucet; **~rohr das** outlet pipe
Ab·folge die sequence; **die ~ der Jahreszeiten** the cycle of the seasons
ab|fordern *tr. V.* **jmdm. etw. ~:** demand sth. of sb.
ab|fotografieren *tr. V.* take pictures of
ab|fragen *tr. V.* **a)** test; **jmdn.** *od.* **jmdm. die Vokabeln ~:** test sb. on his/her vocabulary; **b)** *(DV)* retrieve, read out ‹*data*›; interrogate ‹*measuring-instrument, store*›
ab|fressen *unr. tr. V.* **a)** *(wegfressen)* **etw. [von etw.] ~:** eat sth. off [sth.]; **b)** *(leer fressen)* strip ‹*tree, stem, etc.*› bare
ab|frieren 1. *unr. itr. V.; mit sein* **die Ohren froren ihm ab** he lost his ears through frostbite. **2.** *unr. refl. V.* **sich** *(Dat.)* **etw. ~:** lose sth. by frostbite; **sich** *(Dat.)* **einen ~** *(ugs.)* freeze to death *(coll.)*
ab|frottieren *tr. V.* rub down [thoroughly]
ab|fühlen *tr. V.* feel; palpate *(Med.)*
Abfuhr die; ~, ~en a) *(Abtransport)* removal; **b)** *(Zurückweisung)* **jmdm. eine ~ erteilen** rebuff sb.; turn sb. down; **sich eine ~ holen** be rebuffed *or* turned down; **die Mannschaft holte sich eine deutliche ~:** the team was soundly trounced
ab|führen 1. *tr. V.* **a)** *(nach Festnahme)* take away; **b)** *(zahlen)* pay out; **Steuern ans Finanzamt ~:** pay taxes to the Inland Revenue; **c)** *auch itr. (abbringen)* take away; **jmdn. vom Thema ~:** take sb. away from the subject. **2.** *itr. V.* **a)** *(für Stuhlgang sorgen)* be a laxative; have a laxative effect; **ein ~des Mittel** a laxative; **ein stark ~des Mittel** a purgative; **b)** *(den Darm leeren)* move one's bowels; **c)** *(abzweigen)* ‹*road*› branch off
Abführ-: ~mittel das laxative; *(stärker)* purgative; **~pille die** laxative pill
Abfüll-: ~an·lage die bottling/canning plant; **~datum das** bottling/canning date
ab|füllen *tr. V.* fill ‹*sack, bottle, barrel*›;

Wein in Flaschen ~: bottle wine; **Bier in Dosen ~:** can beer

[1]**ạb|füttern** *tr., itr. V.* feed ⟨*animals*⟩

[2]**ạb|füttern** *tr. V.* line ⟨*coat, jacket*⟩

Ạb·gabe die a) handing in; *(eines Briefes, Pakets, Telegramms)* delivery; *(eines Gesuchs, Antrags)* submission; **gegen ~ des Coupons erhalten Sie ...:** on handing in *or* producing the coupon you will receive ...; **b)** *(Steuer, Gebühr)* tax; *(auf Produkte)* duty; *(Gemeinde~)* rate; *(Beitrag)* contribution; **c)** *(Ausstrahlung)* release; emission; **eine ~ von 60 Watt** an output of 60 watts; **d)** *(Sport: Abspiel)* pass; **e)** *o. Pl. (das Abfeuern)* firing; **f)** *(das Äußern) (von Erklärungen)* giving; *(von Urteilen, Aussagen)* making; *(Stimm~)* casting; **g)** *(Verlust)* loss; *(Sport: von Punkten)* dropping; **h)** *(Verkauf)* selling; **„~ nur in Kisten"** 'sold only by the crate'

ạbgaben·frei 1. *Adj.* ⟨*business, trade, product*⟩ free from tax; *(zollfrei)* duty-free. **2.** *adv.* without paying taxes

Ạbgaben·ordnung die *(Finanzw.)* tax law

ạbgabe[n]·pflichtig *Adj.* ⟨*person, business, trade*⟩ liable to tax; ⟨*product*⟩ subject to duty

Abgabe·zug der *(Schach)* sealed move

Ạb·gang der a) *(das Weggehen)* leaving; departure; *(eines Zuges, Schiffes)* departure *(Theater)* exit; *(fig.)* departure; **sich einen guten ~ verschaffen** *(fig.)* make a good exit; **b)** *(jmd., der ausscheidet)* departure; *(Schule)* leaver; **c)** *(bes. Amtsspr.: Todesfall)* death; **den ~ machen** *(salopp)* kick the bucket *(sl.)*; croak *(sl.)*; **d)** *(Turnen)* dismount; **e)** *o. Pl. (Ausscheidung)* passing; *(von Eiter, Würmern)* discharge; **durch [einen] natürlichen ~:** by being passed naturally; **f)** *(Med.: Fehlgeburt)* miscarriage; **g)** *o. Pl. (Absendung)* dispatch; **nach ~ des Briefes** after posting off *or* sending the letter; **h)** *o. Pl. (Kaufmannsspr.)* **die Ware findet reißenden ~:** the product is a best seller

ạb·gängig *Adj. (bes. österr.)* missing

Ạbgängigkeits·anzeige die *(österr.) s.* **Vermißtenanzeige**

Ạbgangs·zeugnis das *(Schulw.)* ≈ leaving certificate

Ạb·gas das exhaust; *(in geschlossenem Raum)* exhaust fumes *pl.*; **~e** exhaust fumes; **industrielle ~e** waste gases

ạbgas-, Ạbgas-: ~entgiftung die *(Kfz-W.)* emission control; **~frei 1.** *Adj.* exhaust-free ⟨*engine*⟩; **2.** *adv.* **das Auto fährt ~:** the car produces no exhaust fumes; **~katalysator der** *(Kfz-W.)* catalytic converter; **~sonder·untersuchung die** *(Kfz-W.)* exhaust-emission check; **~turbine die** *(Technik)* exhaust-driven turbine; **~verwertung die** *(Technik)* utilization of exhaust-gas heat; **~wolke die** cloud of exhaust fumes

ạb|gaunern *tr. V. (ugs.)* **jmdm. etw. ~:** con sb. out of sth. *(coll.)*

ạbgearbeitet *s.* **abarbeiten b**

ạb|geben 1. *unr. tr. V.* **a)** *(aushändigen)* hand over; deliver ⟨*letter, parcel, telegram*⟩; hand in, submit ⟨*application*⟩; hand in ⟨*school work*⟩; **etw. bei jmdm. ~:** deliver sth. *or* hand sth. over to sb.; **etw. für jmdn. ~:** leave sth. for sb.; **den Mantel in der Garderobe ~:** leave one's coat in the cloakroom; **b)** *(abtreten)* **jmdm. [etwas] von etw. ~:** let sb. have some of sth.; **den Vorsitz/die Spitze ~:** give up the chair/the leadership; **einen Punkt/Satz/eine Runde ~** *(Sport)* drop a point/set/round; **c)** *(abfeuern)* fire; **einen Schuß [auf jmdn./etw.] ~:** fire a shot [at sb./sth.]; **d)** *(ausstrahlen)* emit ⟨*radiation*⟩; radiate ⟨*heat*⟩; give off ⟨*gas*⟩; transmit ⟨*radio message*⟩; **e)** *(äußern)* make ⟨*judgement, statement*⟩; cast ⟨*vote*⟩; **seine Stimme für jmdn. ~:** cast one's vote in favour of sb.; vote for sb.; **f)** *(fungieren als)* make; **eine traurige Figur ~:** cut a sorry figure; **g)** *(verkaufen)* sell; *(zu niedrigem Preis)* sell off; **gebrauchte Skier billig abzugeben** second-hand skis for sale cheap; **h)** *auch itr. (Sport: abspielen)* pass. **2.** *unr. refl. V. (sich befassen)* **sich mit jmdm./etw. ~:** spend time on sb./sth.; *(geringschätzig)* waste one's time on sb./sth

ạb·gebrannt 1. *2. Part. v.* **abbrennen. 2.** *Adj.; nicht attr. (ugs.)* broke *(coll.)*

ạb·gebrochen 1. *2. Part. v.* **abbrechen. 2.** *Adj. (ugs. scherzh.)* **a) ein ~er Mediziner** *usw.: a former medical etc. student who never completed his training;* **b) ein ~er Riese** a midget

ạbgebrüht 1. *2. Part. v.* **abbrühen. 2.** *Adj. (ugs.)* hardened

ạbgedankt 1. *2. Part. v.* **abdanken. 2.** *Adj.* retired

ạb·gedroschen *Adj. (ugs.)* hackneyed; well-worn; trite

Ạbgedroschenheit die; ~ *(ugs.)* triteness; hackneyedness

abgefeimt ['apgəfaimt] *Adj.* infernally cunning ⟨*villain, rogue*⟩; villainous ⟨*scheme*⟩

Ạbgefeimtheit die; ~, ~en *(Handlung)* piece of villainy; *(Charakter)* infernal cunning; **seine ~en** his villainy *sing.*

ạb·gegriffen 1. *2. Part. v.* **abgreifen. 2.** *Adj.* **a)** *(abgenutzt)* battered; **b)** *(fig.: abgedroschen)* hackneyed; well-worn

ạbgehackt 1. *2. Part. v.* **abhacken. 2.** *Adj.* broken ⟨*voice*⟩; clipped ⟨*speech*⟩; fragmentary ⟨*sentence*⟩. **3.** *adv.* in short bursts

ạb·gehangen 1. *2. Part. v.* [1]**abhängen. 2.** *Adj.* hung; **ein gut ~es Steak** a well-hung steak

ạbgehärmt 1. *2. Part. v.* **abhärmen. 2.** *Adj.* careworn; haggard

ạbgehärtet 1. *2. Part. v.* **abhärten. 2.** *Adj. (körperlich)* tough; *(seelisch)* callous

ạb|gehen 1. *unr. itr. V.; mit sein* **a)** *(sich entfernen)* leave; go away *or* off; *(Theater)* exit; go off; **von der Bühne ~:** leave the stage; **nach hinten ~:** go out at the back; **b)** *(ausscheiden)* leave; **von der Schule ~:** leave school; **c)** *(abfahren)* ⟨*train, ship, bus*⟩ leave, depart; **d)** *(abgeschickt werden)* ⟨*message, letter*⟩ be sent [off]; **e)** *(abzweigen)* branch off; *(in andere Richtung)* turn off; **f)** *(sich lösen)* come off; ⟨*spot, stain*⟩ come out; ⟨*avalanche*⟩ come down; **g)** *(Turnen)* dismount; **h)** *(abgerechnet werden)* **von etw. [an jmdn.] ~:** have to be deducted from sth. [and paid to sb.]; **i)** *(fehlen)* **jmdm. geht etw. [völlig] ab** sb. is [totally] lacking in sth.; **mir geht jedes Interesse daran ab** it does not interest me in the slightest; **sich** *(Dat.)* **nichts ~ lassen** never stint oneself; **j)** *(ausgehen)* go off; **k)** *(ausgeschieden werden)* ⟨*pus, worms*⟩ be discharged; *(mit normalen Ausscheidungen)* be passed; **jmdm. geht Kot ab** sb. has a motion *or (Amer.)* movement; **eine Blähung ~ lassen** break wind; **ihm ging einer ab** *(derb)* he shot his load *(coarse)*; **l)** *(aufgeben)* **~ von** abandon ⟨*demand, agreement, principle*⟩; give up ⟨*habit*⟩. **2.** *unr. tr. V.; auch mit sein* walk all along; go over ⟨*area*⟩ on foot

ạbgehetzt 1. *2. Part. v.* **abhetzen. 2.** *Adj.* exhausted; *(außer Atem)* breathless

ạbgekämpft *Adj.* worn out; exhausted; combat-weary ⟨*troops*⟩

ạbgekartet *Adj. (ugs.)* pre-arranged; **von vornherein ~:** set up in advance; **eine ~e Sache** *od.* **ein abgekartetes Spiel sein** be rigged in advance

ạbgeklappert 1. *2. Part. v.* **abklappern. 2.** *Adj. (abwertend)* beat-up, *(Brit. sl.)* clapped-out ⟨*machine, bicycle, horse, etc.*⟩; hackneyed, well-worn, trite ⟨*expression*⟩

ạbgeklärt 1. *2. Part. v.* **abklären. 2.** *Adj.* serene

Ạbgeklärtheit die; ~: serenity

ạbgelagert 1. *2. Part. v.* **ablagern. 2.** *Adj.* mature ⟨*wine*⟩; seasoned ⟨*timber, tobacco*⟩; **gut ~es Holz** well-seasoned timber

ạbgelebt 1. *2. Part. v.* **ableben. 2.** *Adj.* [old and] weary ⟨*person*⟩; worn ⟨*face*⟩

ạb·gelegen *Adj.* remote; *(einsam)* isolated; out-of-the-way ⟨*district*⟩; *(abgeschieden)* secluded; *(fig.)* recondite

Ạb·gelegenheit die; ~: remoteness; *(einsame Lage)* isolation

ạb|gelten *unr. tr. V.* satisfy, settle ⟨*claim*⟩

Ạb·geltung die; ~, ~en settlement

ạbgemagert 1. *2. Part. v.* **abmagern. 2.** *Adj.* emaciated; wasted

ab·gemessen 1. *2. Part. v.* **abmessen. 2.** *Adj. (geh.)* measured. **3.** *adv. (geh.)* in a measured fashion

ạb·geneigt *Adj.* **einer Sache** *(Dat.)* **~ sein** be averse to sth.; **ein stiller, jeder Publicity ~er Mensch** a quiet person averse to public notice; **die jeder Reform ~en Politiker** the politicians opposed to any reform; **jmdm. ~ sein** be ill-disposed towards sb.; **[nicht] ~ sein, etw. zu tun** [not] be averse to doing sth.

ạbgenutzt 1. *2. Part. v.* **abnutzen. 2.** *Adj.* worn ⟨*tyre, chair, handle*⟩; well-used ⟨*implement*⟩; well-worn ⟨*phrase*⟩

Ạbgeordnete der/die; *adj. Dekl.* member [of parliament]; *(in West-Berlin, Frankreich)* deputy; **Herr ~r [Schmidt]/Frau ~ [Müller]** *(im Parlament)* the honourable Member; **der [Herr] ~ Meier** Mr Meier

Ạbgeordneten·haus das parliament; *(in West-Berlin, Frankreich)* Chamber of Deputies

ạb|geraten *unr. itr. V.; mit sein (veralt.)* **vom Weg ~:** lose one's way; stray from one's path

ạb·gerissen 1. *2. Part. v.* **abreißen. 2.** *Adj.* **a)** *(zerlumpt)* ragged; **b)** *(zusammenhanglos)* disconnected; fragmentary

Ạb·gesandte der/die *(veralt.)* ambassador; *(fig.)* emissary

Ạb·gesang der a) *(Abschied)* **ein ~ auf etw.** *(Akk.)* a farewell to sth.; **b)** *(geh.: letztes Werk)* swan song; **c)** *(Verslehre)* abgesang *(final part of Minnesang strophe)*

ạbgeschabt 1. *2. Part. v.* **abschaben. 2.** *Adj.* shabby; worn

ạb·geschieden 1. *2. Part. v.* **abscheiden. 2.** *Adj.* **a)** secluded; *(abgelegen)* isolated; **b)** *(geh.: tot)* departed. **3.** *adv.* ⟨*live*⟩ in seclusion

Ạbgeschiedenheit die; ~: seclusion; *(Abgelegenheit)* isolation

ạb·geschlagen 1. *2. Part. v.* **abschlagen. 2.** *Adj.* **a)** *(Sport)* [well] beaten; **~ auf dem neunten Tabellenplatz** in lowly ninth place; **b)** *(erschöpft)* exhausted; tired out

ạb·geschlossen 1. *2. Part. v.* **abschließen. 2.** *Adj.* **a)** *(abgesondert)* secluded; solitary; **b)** *(in sich geschlossen)* enclosed; self-contained ⟨*flat*⟩. **3.** *adv.* ⟨*live*⟩ in seclusion

Ạb·geschlossenheit die; ~: seclusion; *(Abgelegenheit)* a isolation

abgeschmackt ['apgəʃmakt] *Adj.* tasteless

ạb·geschnitten 1. *2. Part. v.* **abschneiden. 2.** *Adj.* isolated; **von der Außenwelt ~:** cut off from the outside world

ạb·gesehen 1. *2. Part. v.* **absehen. 2.** *Adv.* **~ von jmdm./etw.** apart from sb./sth.; **~ davon, daß ...:** apart from the fact that ...

ạb·gesessen 1. *2. Part. v.* **absitzen. 2.** *Adj.* worn

ạb·gespannt 1. *2. Part. v.* **abspannen. 2.** *Adj.* weary; exhausted

Ạb·gespanntheit die; ~: weariness; exhaustion

ạbgespielt 1. *2. Part. v.* **abspielen. 2.** *Adj.* ⟨*record etc.*⟩ worn out with repeated playing

ab·gestanden 1. *2. Part. v.* **abstehen. 2.** *Adj.* **a)** *(schal)* flat; *(fig.)* trite; **b)** *(verbraucht)* stale

ạb·gestorben 1. *2. Part. v.* **absterben. 2.** *Adj.* dead ⟨*branch, tree*⟩; numb ⟨*fingers, legs, etc.*⟩

ạbgestumpft **1.** *2. Part. v.* **abstumpfen. 2.** *Adj.* apathetic and insensitive ‹*person*›; deadened ‹*conscience, perception*›; **gegenüber einer Sache ~ sein** be hardened to sth.
Ạbgestumpftheit die; ~: apathy and insensitivity
ạbgetakelt **1.** *2. Part. v.* **abtakeln. 2.** *Adj. (salopp: heruntergekommen)* faded
ạb·getragen **1.** *2. Part. v.* **abtragen. 2.** *Adj.* well-worn
ạb·getreten **1.** *2. Part. v.* **abtreten. 2.** *Adj.* worn down
ạbgewetzt **1.** *2. Part. v.* **abwetzen. 2.** *Adj.* well-worn; battered ‹*case etc.*›
ạb|gewinnen *unr. tr. V.* **a)** *(beim Spiel)* **jmdm. Geld ~:** win money from sb.; **b)** *(erlangen von)* **jmdm. etw. ~:** get sth. out of sb.; win sth. from sb.; **einer Sache** *(Dat.)* **etw. ~:** win *or* gain sth. from sth.; **c)** *(fig.)* **ich kann ihm/dem nichts ~:** he/it does not do anything for me *(coll.)*; *s. auch* **Geschmack a**
ạbgewirtschaftet **1.** *2. Part. v.* **abwirtschaften. 2.** *Adj.* run down
ạb·gewogen **1.** *2. Part. v.* **abwägen, abwiegen. 2.** *Adj.* carefully weighed; balanced ‹*judgement*›; carefully considered ‹*account*›
ab|gewöhnen *tr. V.*: **jmdm. etw. ~:** make sb. give up *or* stop sth.; **sich** *(Dat.)* **etw. ~:** give up *or* stop sth.; **noch einen zum Abgewöhnen trinken/eine zum Abgewöhnen rauchen** *(ugs.)* have just one more *(coll.)*; **zum Abgewöhnen [sein]** *(ugs.)* [be] awful
ạbgewrackt **1.** *2. Part. v.* **abwracken. 2.** *Adj. (abwertend)* superannuated
ạbgezehrt *Adj.* emaciated
ạbgezirkelt **1.** *2. Part. v.* **abzirkeln. 2.** *Adj.* measured out ‹*flower-beds*›; carefully weighed ‹*words*›; **ein exakt ~er Paß** *(Sport)* a precisely calculated pass. **3.** *adv.* with calculated precision
ạb|gießen *unr. tr. V.* **a)** pour away ‹*liquid*›; drain ‹*potatoes*›; **den Eimer ~:** pour some water *etc.* out of the bucket; **b)** *(bild. Kunst; Gießerei)* **etw. [in Bronze] ~:** cast sth. [in bronze]
Ạb·glanz der **a)** *(Reflex)* reflection; **b)** *(Nachklang)* distant echo; pale reflection
ạb|gleichen *unr. tr. V. (Funkw., Elektronik)* balance
ạb|gleiten *unr. itr. V.*; *mit sein (geh.)* **a)** *(abrutschen)* slide *or* slip off; **von/an etw.** *(Dat.)* **~:** slip *or* slide off sth.; **b)** *(absinken)* **in etw.** *(Akk.)* **~:** slip down into sth.
Ạb·gott der idol
Abgötterei [apgœtəˈrai̯] **die; ~:** idolatry
abgöttisch [ˈapgœtɪʃ] **1.** *Adj.* idolatrous. **2.** *adv.* **jmdn. ~ verehren/lieben** idolize sb.
ạb|graben *unr. tr. V.* dig out; *s. auch* **Wasser a**
ạb|grasen *tr. V.* **a)** graze away ‹*pasture*›; **b)** *(ugs.: absuchen)* **etw. nach etw. ~:** comb *or* scour sth. for sth.
ạb|greifen *unr. tr. V.* **a)** measure *(with one's hand)*; **eine Strecke mit dem Zirkel ~:** measure a distance with compasses; *s. auch* **abgegriffen 2**; **b)** *(Elektrot.)* pick up
ạb|grenzen *tr. V.* **a)** bound; **etw. nach allen Seiten ~:** enclose sth.; **etw. gegen** *od.* **von etw. ~:** separate sth. from sth.; **b)** *(unterscheiden)* differentiate; distinguish; *(festlegen)* demarcate; **zwei Theorien gegeneinander** *od.* **voneinander ~:** differentiate between two theories; **sich von jmdm. ~:** differentiate oneself from sb.
Ạbgrenzung die; ~, ~en **a)** boundary; **~ nach allen Seiten** enclosure; **b)** *(Unterscheidung)* differentiation; *(Festlegung)* demarcation; **Politik der ~:** policy of demarcation *(by the GDR from the Federal Republic)*
Ạb·grund der **a)** *(Schlucht)* abyss; chasm; *(Abhang)* precipice; **b)** *(fig. geh.)* dark abyss; **die Abgründe der menschlichen Seele** the depths of the human soul; **ein ~ von Verzweiflung** an abyss of despair
abgründig [ˈapgrʏndɪç] *(geh.)* **1.** *Adj.* **a)** *(rätselhaft)* inscrutable ‹*smile*›; hidden ‹*meaning*›; dark ‹*secret*›; **b)** *(unermeßlich)* unbounded. **2.** *adv.* **a)** *(rätselhaft)* ‹*smile*› inscrutably; **b)** *(sehr)* thoroughly
ạbgrund·tief *Adj.* out and out
Ạb·gruppierung die salary downgrading
ạb|gucken *(ugs.)* **1.** *tr. V.* **a) [bei** *od.* **von] jmdm. etw. ~:** learn sth. by watching sb.; **b) ich guck' dir nichts ab!** *(fam.)* you needn't be self-conscious just because I'm watching you. **2.** *itr. V. (abschreiben)* **[bei jmdm.] ~:** copy [from sb.]; copy [sb. else's] work
Ạb·guß der *(bild. Kunst, Gießerei) (Verfahren)* casting; *(Ergebnis)* cast; **ein ~ in Bronze** a bronze [cast]
ạb|haben *(ugs.) unr. tr. V.* **a)** *auch itr. (erhalten)* **etwas/ein Stück usw. [von etw.] ~:** have some/a piece *etc.* [of sth.]. **du kannst gerne davon ~:** you're welcome to have some; **b)** *(abgenommen haben)* have off; **du hast die Mütze ja schon wieder ab!** why, you've got your cap off again!; **c)** *(entfernt haben)* have got off
ạb|hacken *tr. V.* chop off; **jmdm. die Hand** *usw.* **~:** chop sb.'s hand *etc.* off; *s. auch* **abgehackt 2, 3**
ạb|haken *tr. V.* **a)** *(mit Haken versehen)* tick off; check off *(Amer.)*; *(fig.: erledigen)* deal with; **b)** *(vom Haken abnehmen)* unclip
ạb|halftern *tr. V.* **a)** *(ugs.: entlassen)* sack *(coll.)*; **b)** *(das Halfter abnehmen von)* **ein Pferd ~:** take the halter off a horse
ạb|halten *unr. tr. V.* **a)** *(fernhalten)* **[von jmdm./etw.] ~:** keep ‹*person, wind, cold, flies, etc.*› off [sb./sth.]; keep ‹*trouble*› away [from sb.]; **b)** *(hindern)* **jmdn. davon ~, etw. zu tun** stop sb. doing sth.; prevent sb. from doing sth.; **c)** *(durchführen)* hold ‹*elections, meeting, referendum*›; **d)** *(bei der Notdurft)* hold ‹*child*› out; **e)** *(weghalten)* hold away; **etw. ein Stück von sich ~:** hold sth. away from oneself
Ạb·haltung die **a)** *(Verhinderung)* **eine [dringende] ~ haben** be [unavoidably] held up; **b)** *o. Pl. (Durchführung)* holding
ạb|handeln *tr. V.* **a)** *(abkaufen)* **jmdm. etw. ~:** do a deal with sb. for sth.; **b)** *(herunterhandeln)* **jmdm. zehn Mark ~:** beat sb. down by ten marks; *(fig.)* **sich** *(Dat.)* **von etw. nichts ~ lassen** not be persuaded to part with any of sth.; **c)** *(darstellen)* treat; deal with
abhanden [apˈhandn̩] *Adv.* *in* **~ kommen** get lost; go astray; **etw. kommt jmdm. ~:** sb. mislays *or* loses sth.
Ạb·handlung die **a)** *(Aufsatz)* treatise **(über** + *Akk.* on); **b)** *(das Abhandeln)* treatment
Ạb·hang der slope; incline
[1]**ạb|hängen** *unr. itr. V.* **a)** *(abhängig sein)* **[ganz allein] von jmdm./etw. ~:** depend [entirely] on sb./sth.; **davon hängt sehr viel für mich ab** a lot depends on it for me; **von jmdm./etw. ~** *(angewiesen sein)* be dependent on sb./sth.; **b)** *(hängen)* hang; *s. auch* **abgehangen 2**
[2]**ạb|hängen** **1.** *tr. V.* **a)** *(abnehmen)* take down; **ein Bild von der Wand ~:** take a picture [down] off the wall; **b)** *(Eisenb.: abkuppeln)* uncouple; **c)** *(ugs.: abschütteln)* shake off *(coll.)* ‹*pursuer, competitor*›. **2.** *itr. V. (den Hörer auflegen)* hang up
abhängig [ˈaphɛŋɪç] *Adj.* **a) von jmdm./etw. ~ sein** *(bedingt)* depend on sb./sth.; *(angewiesen)* be dependent on sb./sth.; **von einer Droge ~ sein** be addicted to *or* dependent on a drug; **etw. von etw. ~ machen** make sth. conditional upon sth.; **b)** *(Sprachw.)* indirect *or* reported ‹*speech*›; subordinate ‹*clause*›; oblique ‹*case*›
-abhängig *Adj.* dependent on ...
Ạbhängige der/die; *adj. Dekl. (Rechtspr.)* dependant; *(Untergebene)* subordinate
Ạbhängigkeit die; ~, ~en dependence; **~ von Drogen** addiction to *or* dependence on drugs; **in ~ von jmdm./etw. geraten** become dependent on sb./sth.
-ạbhängigkeit die dependence on ...
Ạbhängigkeits·verhältnis das relationship of dependence **(zu** on)
ạb|härmen *refl. V.* **sich [um jmdn.] ~:** pine away with grief [over sb.]; *s. auch* **abgehärmt 2**
ạb|härten *tr. V.* harden; **sich/seinen Körper durch Sport ~:** harden oneself/one's body with sporting activity; *s. auch* **abgehärtet 2**
Ạb·härtung die; ~: hardening; **zur ~:** to harden oneself
ạb|haspeln *tr. V.* **a)** *(abwickeln)* unwind; *(von einer Spule)* unreel; **b)** *(hastig vortragen)* reel off
ạb|hauen **1.** *unr. tr. V.* **a)** *(abtrennen)* chop off; **jmdm. den Arm** *usw.* **~:** cut sb.'s arm *etc.* off. **b)** *Prät. nur* haute ab *(abschlagen)* knock off. **2.** *unr. itr. V.*; *mit sein*; *Prät. nur* haute ab *(salopp: verschwinden)* beat it *(sl.)*; **hau ab!** get lost! *(sl.)*
ạb|häuten *tr. V.* skin
ạb|heben **1.** *unr. tr. V.* **a)** lift off ‹*lid, cover, etc.*›; **[den Hörer] ~:** answer [the telephone]; **b)** *(Kartenspiel) (in zwei Hälften teilen)* cut [the pack]; *(nehmen)* draw ‹*card*›; **c)** *(von einem Konto)* withdraw ‹*money*›; **ich möchte gern [Geld] ~:** I would like to make a withdrawal. **2.** *unr. itr. V.* **a)** *(in die Luft)* ‹*balloon*› rise; ‹*aircraft, bird*› take off; ‹*rocket*› lift off; **nachdem das Flugzeug abgehoben hatte** after take-off; **b) auf etw.** *(Akk.)* **~:** lay emphasis on sth.; stress sth.; **c)** *(ugs.: unrealistisch werden)* lose touch with the real world; **der hat abgehoben** *(ist verrückt geworden)* he's cracked *(coll.)*. **3.** *unr. refl. V. (sich abzeichnen)* stand out; contrast; **sich von** *od.* **gegen etw./von jmdm. ~:** stand out against *or* contrast with sth./sb.
Ạb·hebung die withdrawal
ạb|heften *tr. V.* file; **etw. in einem** *od.* **einen Ordner ~:** file sth.
ạb|heilen *itr. V.*; *mit sein* heal up
ạb|helfen *unr. itr. V.* **einem Bedürfnis ~:** meet a need; **einem Mißstand ~:** put an end to an abuse; **einem Übelstand ~:** remedy an evil; **dem ist leicht abzuhelfen** that is easily remedied
ạb|hetzen **1.** *tr. V.* ride ‹*horse etc.*› to exhaustion. **2.** *refl. V.* rush *or* dash [around]; **hetz dich doch nicht so ab!** don't rush around so much!; *s. auch* **abgehetzt 2**
ab|heuern [ˈaphɔy̯ɐn] *(Seemannsspr.)* **1.** *tr. V.* pay off. **2.** *itr. V.* be paid off
Ạb·hilfe die; *o. Pl.* action to improve matters; **~ schaffen** find a remedy; put things right; **baldige/schnellste ~:** speedy/immediate action
ạb|hobeln *tr. V.* **a)** plane down; **b)** *(entfernen)* plane off
ạbhol·bereit *Adj.* ready for collection *postpos.*
ạb·hold *Adj.* *in* **einer Sache** *(Dat.)* **~ sein** *(geh.)* be averse to sth.
ạb|holen *tr. V.* **a)** collect, pick up ‹*parcel, book, tickets, etc.*›; pick up, fetch ‹*person*›; **ein Paket auf der Post ~:** collect a parcel at the post office; **ich hole Sie am Bahnhof ab** I'll pick you up at the station; **jmdn. zum Essen ~:** call for sb. and go for a meal; **b)** *(ugs. verhüll.: verhaften)* take away
Ạbholer der; ~s, ~ *(Postw.) addressee who collects mail from the post office instead of having it delivered*
Ạbholung die; ~, ~en collection
ạb|holzen *tr. V.* fell ‹*trees*›; clear ‹*area*› [of trees]
Ạbhör·anlage die listening *or (coll.)* bugging system
ạb|horchen *tr. V.* listen to; **sich ~ lassen** *(beim Arzt)* have one's lungs/chest sounded
ạb|hören *tr. V.* **a)** *(abfragen)* **jmdm.** *od.*

jmdn. Vokabeln ~: test sb.'s vocabulary [orally]; das Einmaleins ~: ask questions on the multiplication table; b) (anhören, heimlich hören) listen to; c) (überwachen) tap ‹telephone, telephone conversation›; bug (coll.)‹conversation, premises›; jmdn. ~: tap sb.'s telephone; d) s. abhorchen

Abhör·gerät das listening device; bug (coll.)

abhör·sicher Adj. bug-proof (coll.); tap-proof ‹telephone›

ab|hungern tr. V. a) (verlieren) take off, lose ‹weight›; b) (sparen) sich (Dat.) das Geld für die Reise ~: go or (Amer.) do without to save the money for the trip

Abi ['abi] das; ~s, ~s (Schülerspr.) s. Abitur

ab|irren itr. V.; mit sein (geh.) stray; vom Weg ~: stray from one's path; (fig.) stray; err

ab|isolieren tr. V. (Elektrot.) strip the insulation off

Abisolier·zange die wire-strippers pl.

Abitur [abi'tu:ɐ̯] das; ~s, ~e Abitur (school-leaving examination at grammar school needed for entry to higher education); ≈ A levels (Brit.); sein od. das ~ machen do or take one's Abitur; haben Sie ~? have you got your Abitur?

Abiturient [abitu'ri̯ɛnt] der; ~en, ~en sb. who is taking/has passed the 'Abitur'

Abiturienten·klasse die class of pupils in last year at grammar school; ≈ upper sixth or A-level class (Brit.)

Abiturientin die; ~, ~nen s. Abiturient

Abitur·zeugnis das Abitur certificate

ab|jagen 1. tr. V. (abnehmen) jmdm. etw. ~: finally get sth. away from sb. 2. refl. V. s. abhetzen 2

Abk. Abk. Abkürzung abbr.

ab|kämmen tr. V. a) (entfernen) comb out; b) (absuchen) comb, scour (nach for)

ab|kanten tr. V. (Technik) fold (near the edge)

ab|kanzeln tr. V. (ugs.) jmdn. ~: give sb. a dressing down; reprimand sb.

ab|kapiteln tr. V. (veralt.) jmdn. ~: read sb. a lesson; chide sb. (dated)

ab|kapseln tr. V. encapsulate; sich gegen die Umwelt ~ (fig.) isolate oneself from one's surroundings

ab|karten tr. V. s. abgekartet

ab|kassieren tr., itr. V. a) (kassieren) jmdn. od. bei jmdm. ~ (im Restaurant) give sb. his/her bill; (ohne Rechnung) settle up with sb.; (im Bus usw.) die Fahrgäste ~: take the fares; b) (ugs.) s. kassieren 2 b

ab|kauen tr. V. chew ‹pencil›; bite ‹fingernails›

ab|kaufen tr. V. a) jmdm. etw. ~: buy sth. from sb.; b) (ugs.: glauben) das kaufe ich dir nicht ab I'm not buying that story (coll.)

Abkehr die; ~: eine ~ von alten Traditionen a rejection of or turning away from ancient traditions

¹ab|kehren tr. V. (abwenden) turn away; sein Gesicht ~: turn one's face away; sich [von jmdm./etw.] ~: turn away [from sb./sth.]; sich von der Welt ~ (fig.) turn one's back on the world; die uns abgekehrte Seite des Mondes/des Schiffes the far side of the moon/the ship

²ab|kehren tr. V. a) (entfernen) brush off; den Schmutz von etw. ~: brush the dirt off sth.; b) (säubern) etw. ~: brush sth. clean

ab|ketteln, ab|ketten tr. (auch itr.) V. (Handarb.) cast off

ab|kippen 1. tr. (auch itr.) V. (abladen) tip out; dump ‹refuse›. 2. itr. V.; mit sein (herunterfallen) tip over

ab|klappern tr. V. (ugs.) trudge round ‹town, district›; alle Läden nach etw. ~: do the rounds of all the shops looking for sth.; s. auch abgeklappert 2

ab|klären tr. V. clear up; sort out (coll.); s. auch abgeklärt 2

Ab·klatsch der (abwertend) pale imitation; poor copy

ab|klatschen tr. V. a) (beim Tanzen) jmdn. ~ (clap one's hands and) cut in to dance with sb.; beim nächsten Tanz darf abgeklatscht werden an excuse-me dance comes next; b) (Ballspiele) palm away ‹ball, shot›

ab|klemmen tr. V. a) (zusammenpressen) clamp; b) (lösen) disconnect; c) (abtrennen) sever

ab|klingen unr. itr. V.; mit sein a) (leiser werden) grow fainter; b) (nachlassen) subside; die away

ab|klopfen 1. tr. V. a) (entfernen) knock or tap off; jmdm. etw. [von der Jacke] ~: tap sth. off sb.['s jacket]; b) (säubern) knock/tap the dirt/snow/crumbs etc. off; sich (Dat.) die Hände ~: clap one's hands together to knock the flour/powder etc. off; c) (untersuchen) tap; etw. auf seine Zuverlässigkeit hin ~ (fig.) check the reliability of sth. 2. itr., tr. V. (Musik) tap one's baton to stop

ab|knabbern tr. V. nibble off; gnaw off

ab|knallen tr. V. (salopp) shoot down; gun down

ab|knapsen tr. V. (ugs.) a) (wegnehmen) pinch (coll.); jmdm. etwas/ein Drittel von seinem Lohn ~: take some/a third of sb.'s wages; b) s. abzwacken a

ab|kneifen unr. tr. V. nip off; pinch off

ab|knicken 1. tr. V. a) (abbrechen) snap or break off; b) (knicken) bend. 2. itr. V.; mit sein a) (abbrechen) snap; break; b) (einknicken) bend over; in der Hüfte ~: bend at the hips; c) (Verkehrsw.) ~de Vorfahrt priority for traffic turning right/left

ab|knipsen tr. V. (ugs.) snip off

ab|knöpfen tr. V. a) unbutton; b) (salopp) jmdm. Geld ~: get money out of sb.

ab|knutschen tr. V. (ugs.) a) kiss and fondle; b) (sexuell) jmdn. ~/sich mit jmdm. ~: smooch (coll.) or (sl.) neck with sb.; sich ~: smooch (coll.); neck (sl.)

ab|kochen 1. tr. V. a) (keimfrei machen) boil; b) (salopp: schröpfen) rip off (sl.); fleece (coll.). 2. itr. V. (im Freien kochen) cook in the open air

ab|kommandieren tr. V. detail; (fig.) detail; send; jmdn. zum Dienst/zu einer Einheit ~: detail sb. for duty/to a unit; jmdn. an die Front ~: send sb. to the front

Abkomme der; ~n, ~n (geh.) s. Nachkomme

ab|kommen unr. itr. V.; mit sein a) (abweichen) vom Weg ~: lose one's way; immer mehr vom Weg ~: go further and further astray; vom Kurs ~: go off course; von der Fahrbahn ~: leave the road; vom rechten Weg ~ (fig. geh.) stray from the straight and narrow; b) (abschweifen) digress; vom Thema ~: stray from the topic; digress; c) (aufgeben) von einem Plan ~: abandon or give up a plan; d) (Sport) der Läufer ist gut/schlecht abgekommen the runner got a good/bad start; der Springer ist gut/schlecht abgekommen the jumper made a good/bad take-off; e) (Schießen) aim

Ab·kommen das; ~s, ~: agreement; ein ~ [über etw. (Akk.)] treffen od. schließen come to an agreement [on sth.]

abkömmlich ['apkœmlɪç] Adj. free; available

Abkömmling ['apkœmlɪŋ] der; ~s, ~e a) (Nachkomme) descendant; b) (Chemie) derivative

ab|können unr. tr. V. a) (nordd.: mögen) stand; (vertragen) take; b) (ugs.: abgemacht werden dürfen) das Bild kann ab that picture can go

ab|konterfeien tr. V. (veralt.) jmdn. ~: (zeichnen) draw a good likeness of sb.; (fotografieren) take sb.'s photograph

ab|koppeln tr. V. uncouple; (fig.) separate; dissociate

ab|kratzen 1. tr. V. a) (entfernen) (mit den Fingern) scratch off; (mit einem Werkzeug) scrape off; b) (säubern) scrape [clean]. 2. itr. V.; mit sein (derb) croak (sl.); snuff it (sl.)

ab|kriegen tr. V. (ugs.) s. abbekommen

ab|kucken tr., itr. V. (nordd.) s. abgucken

ab|kühlen 1. tr. V. (kühlen) cool down; jmds. Eifer ~ (fig.) dampen sb.'s ardour; jmdn. ~ (fig.) cool sb. off. 2. itr. V.; meist mit sein (kühler werden) cool down; get cooler; es hat stark abgekühlt it has become a lot cooler; die Begeisterung kühlte ab (fig.) enthusiasm waned. 3. refl. V. (kühler werden) cool down; get cooler

Ab·kühlung die cooling; (fig.) cooling [off]

Abkunft ['apkʊnft] die; ~ (geh.) descent; ein Mädchen bürgerlicher ~: a girl of bourgeois family

ab|kupfern tr. V. (ugs.) copy mechanically (bei from)

ab|kuppeln tr. V. s. abkoppeln

ab|kürzen tr., itr. V. a) (räumlich); eine Strecke um 5 km ~: shorten a distance by 5 km; den Weg ~: take a shorter route; wir haben abgekürzt, indem wir durch die Gärten gegangen sind we took a short cut through the gardens; b) (zeitlich) cut short; c) (kürzer schreiben) abbreviate (mit to); sich [mit] H. S. ~: have the initials H. S.

Ab·kürzung die a) (Weg) short cut; b) (Wort) abbreviation; c) (das Abkürzen) cutting short; zur ~ des Verfahrens to shorten the procedure

Abkürzungs-: ~liste die s. ~verzeichnis; ~punkt der (Schriftw.) full stop; ~verzeichnis das list of abbreviations

ab|küssen tr. V. cover with kisses

Abl. Abk. Ableitung

ab|laden unr. tr., itr. V. a) unload, off-load ‹case, sack, barrel, goods, vehicle›; dump, unload ‹gravel, sand, rubble›; seine Sorgen bei jmdm. ~ (fig.) unburden oneself to sb.; b) (Seew.: beladen) load ‹ship›

Ablader der; ~s, ~ (Seew.) shipping agent

Ab·lage die a) (Vorrichtung) storage place; b) (Raum) storage room; c) (Bürow.) filing; d) (von Eiern) laying; e) (schweiz.) s. Annahmestelle, Zweigstelle

ab|lagern 1. tr. V. a) (absetzen) deposit; b) (deponieren) dump. 2. refl. V. be deposited. 3. itr. V.; meist mit sein (reifen) season; s. auch abgelagert 2

Ab·lagerung die a) deposit; b) (das Absetzen) deposition; bei der ~ von Mineralien when minerals have been deposited; c) (das Deponieren) dumping; d) (das Reifen) seasoning

ablandig Adj. (Seemannsspr.) offshore

Ablaß ['aplas] der; Ablasses, Ablässe (kath. Rel.) indulgence

Ablaß·brief der (hist.) letter of indulgence

ab|lassen 1. unr. tr. V. a) (ablaufen lassen) let out (aus of); sein Wasser ~: pass water; b) (ausströmen lassen) let off ‹steam›; let out ‹air›; eine Blähung ~: break wind; c) (leeren) empty; d) (abgeben) jmdm. etw. ~: let sb. have sth.; e) (nachlassen) [jmdm.] vom Preis 20 % ~: give [sb.] a 20 % discount; f) (ugs.: nicht anziehen, befestigen) leave ‹tie, hat, badge, etc.› off; g) (salopp: äußern) come out with. 2. unr. itr. V. a) (aufgeben) von etw. ~: give sth. up; b) (sich nicht mehr befassen) von jmdm./etw. ~: leave sb./sth. alone

Ablaß-: ~prediger der (hist.) pardoner; ~ventil das (Technik) outlet valve

Ablativ ['ablati:f] der; ~s, ~e (Sprachw.) ablative

Ab·lauf der a) (Verlauf) course; der ~ der Ereignisse the course of events; der ~ des Überfalls/des Programms/der Handlung the sequence of events during the raid/the order of events on the programme/the development of the plot; b) (das Stattfinden) passing or going off; für den reibungslosen

~ **einer Veranstaltung sorgen** ensure that an event passes *or* goes off smoothly; **c)** *(Prozeß)* process; **d)** *o. Pl. (Ende)* **nach ~ eines Jahres** after a year; **nach ~ einer Frist** at the end of a period of time; **mit ~ des Kalenderjahres** at the end of one calendar year; **e)** *(Abfluß)* outlet

ab|laufen 1. *unr. itr. V.; mit sein* **a)** *(abfließen)* flow away; *(aus einem Behälter)* run *or* flow out; *(sich leeren)* empty; **das Badewasser ~ lassen** let the bathwater out; **b)** *(herabfließen)* run down; **von/an etw.** *(Dat.)* **~:** run off sth.; **an ihm läuft alles ab** *(fig.)* it's like water off a duck's back [with him]; **jmdn. ~ lassen** *(ugs.)* send sb. packing; **das Geschirr ~ lassen** let the dishes drain; **c)** *(verlaufen)* pass *or* go off; **gut/glimpflich abgelaufen sein** have gone *or* passed off well/smoothly; **d)** *(stehengeblieben sein)* ‹*alarm clock*› run down; ‹*parking meter*› expire; **e)** *(aufhören, ungültig werden)* ‹*period, contract, passport*› expire; **f)** *(abspulen)* **~ lassen** play ‹*tape*›; run ‹*film*› through; **g)** *(abrollen)* run out ‹*rope etc.*›; **h)** *(Seemannsspr.)* be launched. **2.** *unr. tr. V.* **a)** *auch mit sein (entlanglaufen)* walk all along; go over ‹*area*› on foot; *(schnell)* run all along; **b)** *(abnutzen)* wear down; *s. auch* **Bein a; Fuß b; Schuhsohle**

ab|lauschen *tr. V. (geh.)* **jmdm. etw. ~:** learn sth. by listening to sb.

Ab·laut der *(Sprachw.)* ablaut

ab|lauten *itr. V. (Sprachw.)* undergo ablaut; **das sind ~de Verben** these verbs undergo ablaut

ab|läuten *itr. V.* **a)** ring the bell [to start]; **b)** *(veralt.: beim Telefon)* ring off

ab|leben *itr. V.; mit sein (geh.)* pass away; *s. auch* **abgelebt 2**

Ab·leben das; *o. Pl. (geh.)* decease; demise

ab|lecken *tr. V.* **a)** *(entfernen)* lick off; **b)** *(säubern)* lick clean; **sich** *(Dat.)* **die Finger ~:** lick one's fingers

ab|ledern *tr. V.* leather down

ab|legen 1. *tr. V.* **a)** *(niederlegen)* lay *or* put down; lay ‹*egg*›; **b)** *(Bürow.)* file; **c)** *(nicht mehr tragen)* stop wearing; **abgelegte Kleidung** old clothes *pl.*; cast-offs *pl.*; **d)** *(aufgeben)* give up ‹*habit*›; lose ‹*shyness*›; put aside ‹*arrogance*›; **e)** *(machen, leisten)* swear ‹*oath*›; sit ‹*examination*›; give ‹*account*›; make ‹*confession*›; *s. auch* **Bekenntnis a; f)** *(geh.: beabsichtigen)* **es auf etw.** *(Akk.)* **~:** want sth. **2.** *tr., itr. V.* **a)** *(ausziehen)* take off; **möchten Sie ~?** would you like to take your coat off?; **b)** *(Kartenspiel) (abwerfen)* discard; *(auflegen)* put down. **3.** *itr. V. (Seemannsspr.: losfahren)* **[vom Kai] ~:** cast off

Ableger der; ~s, ~: a) *(Bot.)* layer; **b)** *(Steckling)* cutting; *(fig. ugs.: Sohn)* offspring; *(fig.: Filiale)* offshoot

ab|lehnen 1. *tr. V.* **a)** *(zurückweisen)* decline; decline, turn down ‹*money, invitation, position*›; reject ‹*suggestion, applicant*›; **b)** *(nicht genehmigen)* turn down; reject; reject, throw out ‹*bill*›; **c)** *(verweigern)* **es ~, etw. zu tun** refuse to do sth.; **d)** *(mißbilligen)* disapprove of; reject. **2.** *itr. V.* decline; **sie haben ohne Begründung abgelehnt** *(nicht genehmigt)* they rejected it/them without giving any reason

ablehnend 1. *Adj.* negative ‹*reply, attitude*›; **ein ~er Bescheid** a rejection. **2.** *adv.* **einer Sache** *(Dat.)* **~ gegenüberstehen** take a negative view of sth.; **sich ~ zu etw. äußern** voice one's opposition to sth.

Ablehnung die; ~, ~en a) *(Zurückweisung)* rejection; **auf ~ stoßen** meet with opposition; **b)** *(Mißbilligung)* disapproval; **auf ~ stoßen** meet with disapproval; **c)** *(Weigerung)* refusal

ab|leisten *tr. V.* serve out

ab|leiten 1. *tr. V.* **a)** divert; **b)** *(herleiten; auch Sprachw., Math.)* **etw. aus/von etw. ~:** derive sth. from sth.; **das Wort ist aus dem Spanischen abgeleitet** the word is derived from Spanish; **c)** *(Math.: differenzieren)* differentiate ‹*function*›. **2.** *refl. V. (sich herleiten)* **sich aus/von etw. ~:** derive *or* be derived from sth.

Ab·leitung die a) *(das Ableiten; auch Math., Sprachw.)* derivation; **b)** *(Sprachw.: Wort; Math.: Ergebnis des Differenzierens)* derivative

Ableitungs·silbe die *(Sprachw.)* affix

ab|lenken 1. *tr. V.* **a)** *(Richtung ändern)* deflect; **einen Verdacht von sich ~** *(fig.)* divert suspicion from oneself; **b)** *auch itr. (abbringen)* **jmdn. von etw. ~:** distract sb. from sth.; **alles, was ablenkt** everything that is distracting; **c)** *auch itr. (zerstreuen)* divert; **sich ~:** amuse *or* divert oneself; **das lenkt dich davon ab** that'll take your mind off it; **das lenkt ab** it's amusing *or* diverting. **2.** *itr. V. (ausweichen)* **[vom Thema] ~:** change the subject

Ab·lenkung die a) *(Richtungsänderung)* deflection; **b)** *(Störung)* distraction; **c)** *(Zerstreuung)* diversion

Ablenkungs·manöver das diversion[ary tactic]

ablesbar *Adj.* **~ sein** ‹*scale, dial*› be readable; **an etw.** *(Dat.)* **~ sein** *(fig.)* be detectable from sth.

[1]ab|lesen *unr. tr. V.* **a)** *(wegnehmen)* pick off; **b)** *(säubern)* pick clean; groom ‹*coat*›

[2]ab|lesen 1. *unr. tr., itr. V.* **a)** read ‹*speech, lecture*›; **werden Sie frei sprechen oder ~?** will you be talking from notes or reading your speech?; **b)** *(feststellen, prüfen)* check ‹*time, speed, temperature*›; **[das Gas/den Strom] ~:** read the gas/electricity meter; **die Temperatur auf dem** *od.* **am Thermometer ~:** read off the temperature on the thermometer; **das Thermometer/den Tacho ~:** read the thermometer/speedo. **2.** *unr. tr. V. (erkennen)* see; gauge ‹*significance*›; **etw. an etw.** *(Dat.)* **~:** see sth. from sth.; **jmdm. jeden Wunsch von den Augen ~:** read sb.'s every wish in his/her eyes

ab|leuchten *tr. V.* shine a light all over

ab|leugnen *tr., itr. V.* deny ‹*involvement, guilt*›; deny any involvement in ‹*crime*›; **sie leugnet stur ab** she flatly denies it

ab|lichten *tr. V.* **a)** *(fotokopieren)* photocopy; **b)** *(fotografieren)* take a photograph of

ab|liefern *tr., itr. V.* deliver ‹*goods*›; hand in ‹*manuscript, examination paper, weapon, etc.*›; *(fig. ugs.)* take/bring ‹*person*› **(in/auf + Dat., bei to)**; **er hat pünktlich abgeliefert** he delivered it/handed it in on time

Ab·lieferung die *(von Waren)* delivery; *(von Manuskripten usw.)* handing in

ab|liegen *unr. itr. V.* be out of the way; *s. auch* **abgelegen**

ab|listen ['aplɪstn̩] *tr. V.* **jmdm. etw. ~:** *(durch Betrug)* swindle sb. out of sth.; *(durch Charme)* cajole sb. into giving sth.

ab|locken *tr. V.* **jmdm. etw. ~:** coax sth. out of sb.

ablösbar *Adj.* **a)** removable; **b)** *(Finanzw.)* redeemable

ab|löschen 1. *tr. V.* **a)** *(trocknen)* blot ‹*ink, letter, etc.*›; **b)** *(abwischen)* wipe ‹*blackboard*›; wipe out ‹*writing*›; **c)** *(Kochk.)* **etw. mit Rotwein** *usw.* **~:** add red wine *etc.* to sth.; **d)** *(löschen)* extinguish; put out. **2.** *itr. V.* **a)** *(trocknen)* blot it/them; **b)** *(abwischen)* wipe [the blackboard]; **c)** *(Kochk.)* **mit Rotwein** *usw.* **~:** add red wine *etc.*

Ablöse die; ~, ~n a) *s.* **Ablösesumme; b)** *(österr.) single payment made by tenant at start of tenancy*

ab|lösen 1. *tr. V.* **a)** *(lösen)* **etw. [von etw.] ~:** get sth. off [sth.]; remove sth. [from sth.]; **b)** *(abwechseln)* relieve; take over from; *(fig.: ersetzen)* replace; **sich** *od.* **einander ~:** take turns; **c)** *(verhüll.: entlassen)* remove from office; **d)** *(Finanzw.: tilgen)* redeem. **2.** *refl. V. (sich lösen)* ‹*retina*› become detached; **sich von etw. ~:** come off sth.

Ablöse·summe die *(Sport)* transfer fee

Ab·lösung die a) *(eines Postens)* changing; *(fig.: Verdrängung, Ersetzung)* replacement; **ich schicke Ihnen jemanden zur ~:** I'll send someone to relieve you; **b)** *(Ersatz)* relief; **c)** *(das Ablösen)* detaching; *(der Netzhaut)* detachment; **d)** *(verhüll.: Entlassung)* removal; **e)** *(Finanzw.: Tilgung)* redemption; **f)** *(Psych.)* dissolution of an emotional tie/ emotional ties; **die ~ von seinen Eltern** breaking away emotionally from his parents

ab|luchsen ['aplʊksn̩] *tr. V. (salopp)* **jmdm. etw. ~:** get *or (sl.)* wangle sth. out of sb.

Ab·luft die *(Technik)* vitiated air

ab|lutschen *tr. V.* **a)** suck off; *(säubern)* suck clean; **die Marmelade von den Fingern ~:** suck the jam off one's fingers; **ein abgelutschter Bonbon** a half-sucked sweet; **b)** *(vulg.)* **jmdm. einen ~:** suck sb. off *(sl.)*

ab|machen *tr. V.* **a)** *(ugs.: entfernen)* take off; take down ‹*sign, rope*›; **etw. von etw. ~:** take sth. off sth.; **b)** *(vereinbaren)* agree; arrange; **abgemacht, wir kommen mit!** all right, we'll come; **c)** *(klären)* sort out; **das muß er mit sich selbst ~:** that's something he'll have to sort out by himself

Abmachung die; ~, ~en agreement; arrangement; **eine ~ [mit jmdm.] treffen** come to an agreement *or* arrangement [with sb.]

ab|magern 1. *itr. V.; mit sein* become thin; *(absichtlich)* slim; **bis auf die Knochen ~:** become a mere skeleton; *s. auch* **abgemagert 2. 2.** *tr. V.* **a)** *(Technik)* **das Gemisch ~:** make the mixture leaner; **b)** *(verringern)* cut back on; *(leichter machen)* make lighter

Abmagerung die; ~, ~en *(Vorgang)* weight loss; *(Zustand)* emaciation

Abmagerungs·kur die reducing diet; **eine ~ machen** go on a diet; **er macht gerade eine ~:** he's dieting at the moment

ab|mähen *tr. V.* mow

ab|mahnen *tr. V. s.* **verwarnen**

Ab·mahnung die *s.* **Verwarnung**

ab|malen *tr. V.* paint a picture of **(aus, von** from)

Ab·marsch der departure; **im ~ sein** be marching off; **~!** forward march!

abmarsch·bereit *Adj.* ready to depart; *(Milit.)* ready to march

ab|marschieren *itr. V.; mit sein* depart; *(Milit.)* march off

ab|matten ['apmatn̩] *tr. V. (geh.)* fatigue

ab|meißeln *tr. V.* chisel *or* carve off

Abmelde·bestätigung die *document confirming that one has notified the authorities of one's intention to move from an address*

ab|melden *tr. V.* **a)** *(das Weggehen melden)* **sich/jmdn. ~:** report that one/sb. is leaving; **sich [bei jmdm.] vom Dienst ~:** report absent from duty [to sb.]; **b)** *(Umzug melden) notify the authorities that one is moving from an address;* **abgemeldet sein** have given notice of moving away; **c) ein Auto ~:** cancel a car's registration; **ein abgemeldetes Auto** a car of which the registration has been cancelled; **sein Telefon ~:** have one's phone disconnected; **seinen Fernseher ~:** cancel one's TV licence; **d)** *(Sportjargon: beherrschen)* **jmdn. ~:** shut sb. out of the game/ race *etc.*; **abgemeldet sein** be kept out of the game/race *etc.*; **e)** *(ugs.)* **[bei jmdm.] abgemeldet sein** no longer be of interest [to sb.]; **er ist jetzt bei mir abgemeldet** I want nothing more to do with him

Ab·meldung die a) *(beim Weggehen)* report that one is leaving; **b)** *(beim Umzug) registration of a move with the authorities at one's old address;* **c)** *(des Telefons)* disconnection; **d) ~ eines Autos/eines Fernsehers** cancellation of a car's registration/a television licence; **e)** *s.* **Abmeldebestätigung**

ab|messen *unr. tr. V.* **a)** measure; *(fig.)* measure; assess; **b)** *(abteilen)* measure off; *s. auch* **abgemessen 2, 3**
Ab·messung die a) *meist Pl. (Dimension)* dimension; measurement; **b)** *(das Abmessen)* measuring
ab|mildern *tr. V.* **a)** *(dämpfen)* break, cushion ⟨*fall, impact*⟩; **b)** *(abschwächen)* tone down; take the edge off
ab|montieren 1. *tr. V. (entfernen)* take off, remove ⟨*part, wheel*⟩; dismantle ⟨*machine, equipment*⟩. **2.** *itr. V. (Fliegerspr.: sich lösen)* come off
ab|mühen *refl. V.* **sich [mit jmdm./etw.] ~:** toil [for sb.'s benefit/with sth.]; **sie mühte sich mit dem schweren Koffer ab** she struggled with the heavy suitcase
ab|murksen *tr. V. (salopp)* do in *(sl.)*
ab|müssen *unr. itr. V. (ugs.)* **das muß ab** it will have to come off; **der Baum/das Plakat muß ab** the tree/poster will have to come down
ab|mustern *(Seemannsspr.)* **1.** *tr. V. (entlassen)* discharge. **2.** *itr. V.* sign off; **von einem Schiff ~:** leave a ship
ab|nabeln *tr. V.* **ein Kind ~:** cut a child's cord; **sich vom Elternhaus ~** *(fig.)* break away from the parental home
ab|nagen *tr. V.* gnaw off; **etw. von etw. ~** gnaw sth. off sth.; **ein abgenagter Knochen** a gnawed bone
ab|nähen *tr. V.* take in ⟨*skirt, jacket, etc.*⟩
Abnäher ['apnɛ:ɐ] **der; ~s, ~:** tuck
Abnahme ['apna:mə] **die; ~, ~n a)** *o. Pl. (das Entfernen)* removal; **vor/bei/nach der ~ des Verbandes** before/when/after the bandage was/is removed; **b)** *(Verminderung)* decrease; decline; **c)** *(Kauf)* purchasing; **bei ~ größerer Mengen** when large quantities are purchased; **d)** *(Prüfung) (eines Gebäudes, einer Strecke)* inspection and approval; *(eines Fahrzeugs)* testing and passing; *(Freigabe)* passing; **e)** *(Entgegennahme) (eines Eides)* administration; *(eines Versprechens)* extraction; *(einer Parade)* taking the salute (*Gen.* at)
Abnahme·garantie die guaranteed purchase; firm order
abnehmbar *Adj.* detachable; removable
ab|nehmen 1. *unr. tr. V.* **a)** *(entfernen)* take off; remove; take down ⟨*picture, curtain, lamp*⟩; **jmdm. das Bein ~:** take sb.'s leg off; **sich** *(Dat.)* **den Bart ~:** shave one's beard off; **b)** *(übernehmen)* take; **jmdm. den Koffer ~:** take sb.'s suitcase [from him/her]; **kann/darf ich Ihnen etwas ~?** can/may I carry something for you?; **jmdm. einen Weg/eine Arbeit ~:** save sb. a journey/a job; **jmdm. seine Sorgen ~:** relieve sb. of his/her worries; **c)** *(entgegennehmen)* **jmdm. ein Versprechen/einen Eid ~:** make sb. give a promise/swear an oath; **jmdm. die Beichte ~:** hear sb.'s confession; **eine Parade ~:** take the salute at a parade; **eine Prüfung ~:** conduct an examination; **d)** *(prüfen)* inspect and approve; test and pass ⟨*vehicle*⟩; **e)** *(stehlen)* take; *(beschlagnahmen)* take away ⟨*driving licence, passport*⟩; *(abgewinnen)* **jmdm. etw. ~:** take sth. off sb.; **jmdm. ein paar Meter ~:** gain a few metres over sb.; **f)** *(abverlangen)* **jmdm. etw. ~:** charge sb. sth.; **g)** *(abkaufen)* **jmdm. etw. ~:** buy sth. from sb.; **h)** *(ugs.: glauben)* buy *(coll.)*; **diese Geschichte nehme ich dir nicht ab** I'm not buying that story *(coll.)*; **i)** *(übertragen)* take ⟨*fingerprint*⟩. **2.** *unr. itr. V.* **a)** *auch tr. (beim Telefon)* answer; **den Hörer ~:** pick up the receiver; **b)** *auch tr. (Handarb.)* decrease; **c)** *(Gewicht verlieren)* lose weight; **sechs Kilo ~:** lose six kilos; **d)** *(sich verringern)* decrease; drop; ⟨*attention, interest*⟩ flag; ⟨*brightness*⟩ diminish; **die Tage nehmen ab** the days are getting shorter; **wir haben ~den Mond** there is a waning moon
Abnehmer der; ~s, ~: buyer
Ab·neigung die dislike (**gegen** for); aversion (**gegen** to)
abnorm [ap'nɔrm] **1.** *Adj.* abnormal; *(ungewöhnlich)* exceptional. **2.** *adv.* abnormally; *(ungewöhnlich)* unusually
ab·normal *Adj., adv. (bes. österr. u. schweiz.) s.* **anormal**
Abnormität [apnɔrmi'tɛ:t] **die; ~, ~en a)** *(Mißbildung)* deformity; **b)** *(Mißgeburt)* freak
ab|nötigen *tr. V. (geh.)* **jmdm. Respekt ~:** compel sb.'s respect; **jmdm. ein Geständnis/die Zustimmung ~:** extract a confession/agreement from sb.
ab|nutzen, *(landsch.:)* **ab|nützen 1.** *tr. V.* wear out. **2.** *refl. V.* wear out; become worn; ⟨*expressions, arguments*⟩ become hackneyed; **das Material nutzt sich rasch ab** the material wears very quickly; *s. auch* **abgenutzt 2**
Ab·nutzung, *(landsch.:)* **Ab·nützung die** wear [and tear] *no indef. art.*
Abnutzungs·erscheinung die sign of wear and tear; *(fig.)* sign of disenchantment
Abonnement [abɔnə'mã:] **das; ~s, ~s** subscription (+ *Gen.* to); *(Theater, Oper)* subscription ticket; **eine Zeitschrift im ~ beziehen** subscribe to *or* have a subscription to a magazine
Abonnement[s]-: ~karte die subscription ticket; **~konzert das** subscription concert
Abonnent [abɔ'nɛnt] **der; ~en, ~en, Abonnentin die; ~, ~nen** subscriber (+ *Gen.* to); *(Theater, Oper)* season-ticket holder
abonnieren [abɔ'ni:rən] **1.** *tr. V.* subscribe to; have a subscription to; *(Theater, Oper)* have a season ticket for. **2.** *itr. V. (bes. schweiz.)* **abonniert sein auf** (+ *Akk.*) have a subscription to ⟨*newspaper, magazine, concerts*⟩; *(Theater, Oper)* have a season ticket for; *(fig.)* get as a matter of course
ab|ordnen *tr. V.* send; **jmdn. als Delegierten ~:** delegate sb.; **jmdn. zu einer Konferenz ~:** delegate sb. to a conference; **jmdn. nach Wien ~:** send sb. to Vienna
Ab·ordnung die delegation
¹Abort [a'bɔrt] **der; ~[e]s, ~e** *(veralt., noch fachspr.)* lavatory
²Abort der; ~s, ~e *(Med.)* **a)** *(Fehlgeburt)* miscarriage; **b)** *(Abtreibung)* abortion
Abort·grube die cesspool
ab|packen *tr. V.* pack; wrap ⟨*bread*⟩; **abgepacktes Obst/abgepackte Fleischportionen** packaged fruit/pieces of meat
ab|passen *tr. V.* **a)** *(abwarten)* wait for; **b)** *(aufhalten)* catch
ab|pausen *tr., itr. V.* trace
ab|pellen *tr. V. (nordd.)* peel; peel the skin off ⟨*sausage*⟩
ab|perlen *itr. V.; mit sein* **von etw. ~:** roll off sth.
ab|pfeifen *(Sport)* **1.** *itr. V.* blow the whistle; **der Schiedsrichter hatte abgepfiffen** the whistle had gone. **2.** *tr. V.* **a)** *(unterbrechen)* [blow the whistle to] stop; **b)** *(beenden)* blow the whistle for the end of ⟨*match, game, half*⟩
Ab·pfiff der *(Sport)* final whistle; *(Halbzeit~)* half-time whistle
ab|pflücken *tr. V.* **a)** pick; **sich** *(Dat.)* **etw. ~:** pick oneself sth.; **b)** *(leer pflücken)* pick clean
ab|placken *(ugs.),* **ab|plagen** *refl. V.* slave away; flog oneself to death *(coll.)*; **sich mit etw./jmdm. ~:** slave away at sth./for sb.'s benefit; **sich mit einem Problem ~:** wrestle with a problem
ab|platten ['applatn̩] *tr. V.* flatten [out]
ab|platzen *itr. V.; mit sein* ⟨*lacquer, enamel, plaster*⟩ flake off; ⟨*button*⟩ fly off
ab|prägen 1. *refl. V.* **sich in etw.** *(Dat.)* **~:** leave an impression in sth.; *(fig.)* leave its/their mark on sth. **2.** *tr. V. (Technik)* take ⟨*cast*⟩; make ⟨*mould*⟩
ab|prallen *itr. V.; mit sein* rebound; bounce off; ⟨*missile*⟩ ricochet; **an** *od.* **von etw.** *(Dat.)* **~:** rebound/ricochet off sth.; **an jmdm. ~** *(fig.)* bounce off sb.
Abpraller der; ~s, ~ *(Sport)* rebound; *(ugs.: eines Geschosses)* ricochet
ab|pressen *tr. V.* **a)** *(abnötigen)* **jmdm. etw. ~:** extort sth. from sb.; **b)** *(abschnüren)* **das preßte uns den Atem ab** it took our breath away
Ab·produkt das *(bes. DDR)* waste product
ab|protzen 1. *tr. V. (Milit.)* unlimber. **2.** *itr. V. (derb)* have *or (Amer.)* take a crap *(vulg.)*; crap *(vulg.)*
ab|pumpen *tr. V.* pump out; extract ⟨*milk*⟩ by breast-pump
ab|putzen *tr. V. (ugs.)* **a)** wipe; **jmdm./sich das Gesicht** *usw.* **~:** clean sb.'s/one's face *etc.*; **b)** *(entfernen)* **etw. von jmdm./etw. ~:** wipe sth. off sb./sth.
ab|quälen *refl. V.* **sich [mit etw.] ~:** struggle [with sth.]; **sich** *(Dat.)* **einen Brief ~:** force oneself to write a letter; **da hat er sich was abgequält** he must have had a struggle to get that out
ab|qualifizieren *tr. V.* denigrate; **jmdn./etw. als etw. ~:** dismiss sb./sth. as sth.; **sich selbst ~:** show oneself up
ab|quetschen 1. *tr. V.* **jmdm. einen Arm/ein Bein ~:** crush sb.'s arm/leg. **2.** *refl. V. (ugs.: hervorbringen)* **sich** *(Dat.)* **etw. ~:** force out ⟨*words, smile*⟩; **sich** *(Dat.)* **ein paar Tränen ~:** squeeze out a few tears
ab|rackern *refl. V. (ugs.)* slave [away]; flog oneself to death *(coll.)*; **sich mit etw. ~:** slave away at sth.
Abraham ['a:braham] **(der) a)** Abraham; **b)** *in* **[sicher] wie in ~s Schoß** *(ugs.)* as safe as houses *(coll.)*
Abrakadabra [a:braka'da:bra] **das; ~s a)** *(Zauberwort)* abracadabra; **b)** *(unsinniges Gerede)* blitherings *pl.*
ab|rasieren *tr. V.* shave off; **jmdm./sich den Bart ~:** shave off sb.'s/one's beard
ab|raten *unr. itr., tr. V.* **jmdm. von etw. ~:** advise sb. against sth.; **jmdm. [davon] ~, etw. zu tun** advise sb. not to do sth. *or* against doing sth.; **da kann ich nur abraten** I can only advise you against it
Ab·raum der; *o. Pl. (Bergbau)* overburden
ab|räumen 1. *tr. V.* **a)** clear away; **b)** *(leer machen)* clear ⟨*table*⟩; **c)** *(Bergbau)* remove ⟨*overburden*⟩. **2.** *itr. V.* **a)** clear away; **b)** *(vom Tisch)* clear the table; **c)** *(Bergbau)* remove the overburden
ab|rauschen *itr. V.; mit sein (ugs.)* *(schnell)* rush off; *(auffällig)* sweep off
ab|reagieren 1. *tr. V.* work off; **seine Wut an jmdm. ~:** take one's anger out on sb. **2.** *refl. V.* work off one's feelings
ab|rechnen 1. *itr. V.* **a)** cash up; **b)** *(fig.)* **mit jmdm. ~:** call sb. to account. **2.** *tr. V.* **a)** **die Kasse ~:** reckon up the till; total the cash *or* register *(Amer.)*; **seine Einnahmen ~:** agree one's takings; **seine Spesen ~:** claim one's expenses; **b)** *(abziehen)* deduct
Ab·rechnung die a) *(Schlußrechnung)* cashing up *no art.*; **die Kellnerin machte die ~:** the waitress was cashing up; **b)** *(Aufstellung)* statement; *(Kaufmannsspr.: Bilanz)* balance; *(Dokument)* balance-sheet; **der Tag der ~:** the day of reckoning; **c)** *(Vergeltung)* reckoning; **d)** *(Abzug)* deduction; **nach ~ der Unkosten** after deducting expenses; **etw. in ~ bringen** *(Amtsspr.)* deduct sth.; **in ~ kommen** *(Amtsspr.)* be deducted
Abrechnungs-: ~stelle die *(Finanzw.)* clearing-house; **~verkehr der** *(Finanzw.)* clearing
Ab·rede die a) arrangement; agreement; **b)** **etw. in ~ stellen** deny sth.
ab|regen *refl. V. (ugs.)* calm down; **reg dich ab!** cool it! *(coll.)*; calm down!
ab|reiben *unr. tr. V.* **a)** *(entfernen)* rub off; *(Kochk.)* grate; **etw. von etw. ~:** rub/grate

sth. off sth.; **abgeriebene Zitronenschale** grated lemon peel; **b)** *(säubern)* rub; **[sich** *(Dat.)*] **die Hände an der Hose ~**: rub one's hands on one's trousers; **c)** *(frottieren)* rub down; **jmds. Hände mit Schnee ~**: rub sb.'s hands with snow

Ab·reibung die a) *(ugs.: Prügel)* hiding *(coll.) or (Amer.)* licking; **jmdm. eine ~ verpassen** give sb. a good hiding; **b)** *(Med.)* rubbing

Ab·reise die departure (**nach** for); **bei meiner ~**: when I left/leave

ab|reisen *itr. V.; mit sein* leave (**nach** for)

Abreiß·block der; ~s, ~s *od.* **Abreißblöcke** tear-off notebook

ab|reißen 1. *unr. tr. V.* **a)** *(entfernen)* tear off; tear down ‹*poster, notice*›; pull off ‹*button*›; break off ‹*thread*›; *s. auch* **Kopf a; b)** *(niederreißen)* demolish, pull down ‹*building*›; demolish ‹*area*›; **c)** *(salopp: ableisten)* get through; stick out *(coll.)*; *s. auch* **abgerissen 2. 2.** *unr. itr. V.; mit sein* **a)** *(sich lösen)* fly off; ‹*shoe-lace*› break off; **b)** *(aufhören)* come to an end; ‹*connection, contact*› be broken off; **in nicht ~der Folge** in a never-ending procession

Abreiß·kalender der tear-off calendar

ab|reiten 1. *unr. itr. V.; mit sein (wegreiten)* ride off *or* away. **2.** *unr. tr. V.* **a)** *mit sein od. haben (entlangreiten)* ride the whole length of; ride over ‹*district*›; **b)** *(Pferdesport: vorbereiten)* supple; **c)** *(müde reiten)* ride to exhaustion; **d)** *(Seemannsspr.)* ride out ‹*storm*›

Abreite·platz, Abreit·platz der *(Pferdesport)* warming-up arena

ab|richten *tr. V.* train

Ab·richter der trainer

Ab·richtung die; ~: training

ab|riegeln *tr., itr. V.* **a)** *(zusperren)* **[die Tür] ~**: bolt the door; **b)** *(absperren)* seal *or* cordon off ‹*area*›

Abrieg[e]lung die; ~, ~en sealing *or* cordoning off

ab|ringen *unr. tr. V.* **a)** *(abnötigen)* **jmdm. etw. ~**: extract sth. from sb.; **sich** *(Dat.)* **ein Lächeln ~**: force a smile; **b)** *(entreißen)* **jmdm./einer Sache etw. ~**: wrest sth. from sb./sth.

Ab·riß der a) *o. Pl.: s.* **abreißen 1 b**: demolition; pulling down; **auf ~ stehen** *(ugs.)* be scheduled for demolition; **b)** *(von Eintrittskarten)* tear-off section; **c)** *(knappe Darstellung)* outline

Abriß·arbeiten *Pl. s.* **Abbrucharbeit**

ab|rollen 1. *tr. V.* unwind; **sich ~**: unwind [itself]. **2.** *itr. V.; mit sein* **a)** unwind [itself]; **b)** *(vonstatten gehen)* go off; ‹*events*› unfold; **sein Leben rollte vor seinen Augen ab** his life passed before his eyes; **c)** *(Sport)* roll over (**über** + *Akk.* on to)

ab|rubbeln *tr. V. (bes. nordd.)* **jmdn./sich ~**: dry sb./oneself by rubbing; rub sb./oneself down; **jmdm./sich den Rücken ~**: dry sb.'s/one's back by rubbing

ab|rücken 1. *tr. V. (wegschicken)* move away. **2.** *itr. V.; mit sein* **a)** move away; **von jmdm./etw. ~**: move away from sb./sth.; **b)** *(Milit.) (abmarschieren)* move out; *(zurückmarschieren)* march back; **c)** *(ugs.: sich entfernen)* clear out *(coll.)*

Ab·ruf der a) auf ~: on call; *(DV)* in retrievable form; **sich auf ~ bereithalten** be on call; **b)** *(Kaufmannsspr.)* request for delivery; **etw. auf ~ kaufen** buy sth. on call purchase

abrufbar a) *(DV)* retrievable; **b)** *(Finanzw.)* withdrawable

abruf·bereit *Adj.* **a)** on call *postpos.*; **b)** *(Kaufmannsspr.)* ready for delivery on demand *postpos.*

ab|rufen *unr. tr. V.* **a)** summon, call ‹*person*›; **er wurde ins Jenseits/aus diesem Leben abgerufen** *(geh. verhüll.)* he was taken from us; **b)** *(DV)* retrieve; **c)** *(Kaufmannsspr.)* **etw. ~**: ask for sth. to be delivered; **d)** *(Finanzw.)* withdraw

ab|runden *tr. V.* **a)** round off; **abgerundete Ecken** rounded corners; **b)** *(auf eine runde Zahl bringen)* round up/down (**auf** + *Akk.* to); **etw. nach oben/unten ~**: round sth. up/down; **ein Betrag von abgerundet 27,50 Mark** a rounded [up/down] sum of 27.50 marks; **c)** *(vervollkommnen)* round off; complete

Ab·rundung die a) rounding off; **b)** *(von Zahlen)* rounding up/down; **c)** *(Vervollkommnung)* rounding off; **zur ~ des Geschmacks** to round off the taste

ab|rupfen *tr. V.* pull off

abrupt [ap'rʊpt] **1.** *Adj.* abrupt. **2.** *adv.* abruptly

ab|rüsten *itr., tr. V.* disarm

Ab·rüstung die; ~: disarmament

Abrüstungs-: ~konferenz die disarmament conference; **~verhandlungen** *Pl.* disarmament negotiations

ab|rutschen *itr. V.; mit sein* **a)** *(abgleiten)* slip; **von etw. ~**: slip off sth.; **das Pferd rutschte mit den Hinterbeinen ab** the horse's hind feet slipped; **sie ist mit dem Messer abgerutscht** her knife slipped; **b)** *(nach unten rutschen)* slide down; ‹*earth*› subside; ‹*snow*› give way; ‹*aircraft*› side-slip; *(fig.)* ‹*pupil, competitor, etc.*› slip (**auf** + *Akk.* to); **c)** *(moralisch absinken)* go downhill

ABS *Abk.* **Antiblockiersystem**

Abs. *Abk.* **a) Absender; b) Absatz**

ab|säbeln *tr. V. (ugs.)* hack off

[1]ab|sacken *itr. V.; mit sein (ugs.)* **a)** *(nach unten sinken)* fall; ‹*ground*› subside; ‹*aircraft*› lose altitude; **b)** *(moralisch absinken)* go downhill

[2]ab|sacken *tr. V.* sack ‹*grain, sugar, etc.*›

Ab·sage die a) *(auf eine Einladung)* refusal; *(auf eine Bewerbung)* rejection; **jmdm. eine ~ erteilen** reject sb.; **eine ~ an jede Form totalitärer Politik** a rejection of all forms of totalitarian politics; **b)** *(Rundf.)* closing announcement

ab|sagen 1. *tr. V.* cancel; withdraw ‹*participation, co-operation*›. **2.** *itr. V.* **a)** cry off; **jmdm. ~**: tell sb. one cannot come; put sb. off *(coll.)*; **telefonisch ~**: ring to say one cannot come; **ich muß Ihnen für Donnerstag ~**: I must cancel our meeting/visit/appointment *etc.* on Thursday; **b) dem Bewerber wurde abgesagt** the applicant was rejected; **c)** *(Rundf.)* make the closing announcement

ab|sägen *tr. V.* **a)** saw off; **b)** *(ugs.)* **jmdn. ~**: get rid of sb.

ab|sahnen 1. *itr. V. (ugs.)* make a killing *(coll.)*. **2.** *tr. V.* **a)** *(ugs.)* **100 000 Mark ~**: pocket 100,000 marks; **b)** *(Rahm entfernen von)* cream ‹*milk*›

ab|satteln *tr., itr. V.* unsaddle

Ab·satz der a) *(am Schuh)* heel; **auf dem ~ kehrtmachen, sich auf dem ~ herumdrehen** turn on one's heel; **b)** *(Textunterbrechung)* break; **einen ~ machen** make a break; start a new line; **c)** *(Abschnitt)* paragraph; **d)** *(Kaufmannsspr.)* sales *pl.*; **guten/keinen ~ finden** sell well/not sell at all; *s. auch* **reißend; e)** *(einer Innentreppe)* landing; *(zwischen Geschossen)* half-landing; *(Mauer~)* ledge

absatz-, Absatz-: ~chance die *(Kaufmannsspr.)* sales prospect; **~flaute die** *(Kaufmannsspr.)* drop in sales; **~förderung die** *(Kaufmannsspr.)* sales promotion; **~gebiet das** *(Kaufmannsspr.)* sales territory; *(von Produkten)* market area; **~kick der** *(Fußball)* back-heel; **~markt der** *(Kaufmannsspr.)* market; **~schwierigkeiten** *Pl. (Kaufmannsspr.)* sales problems; *(beim Vertrieb)* marketing difficulties; **~steigerung die** *(Kaufmannsspr.)* increase in sales; **~trick der** *(Fußball)* clever back-heel; **~weise** *Adv.* paragraph by paragraph

ab|saufen *unr. itr. V.; mit sein* **a)** *(salopp: untergehen)* go to the bottom; **b)** *(derb: ertrinken)* drown; **c)** *(ugs.)* ‹*engine, car*› flood; **d)** *(salopp: sich mit Wasser füllen)* flood; **abgesoffen sein** be under water; be flooded

ab|saugen *tr. V.* **a)** *(entfernen)* suck away; **etw. aus/von etw. ~**: suck sth. out of/off sth.; **b)** *(säubern)* hoover *(Brit. coll.)*; vacuum

ab|schaben *tr. V.* **a)** *(entfernen)* scrape off; **sich** *(Dat.)* **den Bart ~** *(scherzh.)* have a shave; **b)** *(säubern)* scrape [clean]; *s. auch* **abgeschabt 2**

ab|schaffen 1. *tr. V.* **a)** *(beseitigen)* abolish ‹*capital punishment, regulation, customs duty, institution*›; repeal ‹*law*›; put an end to ‹*injustice, abuse*›; **er möchte alle Flugzeuge ~**: he'd like to do away with aeroplanes completely; **b)** *(aufgeben)* get rid of. **2.** *refl. V. (südd., schweiz.) (sich abarbeiten)* slave away; work oneself hard; *(sich anstrengen)* go at it

Ab·schaffung die a) abolition; *(von Gesetzen)* repeal; *(von Unrecht, Mißstand)* ending; **b)** *(Aufgabe)* **er sah sich zur ~ seines Autos/Hundes gezwungen** he was forced to get rid of *or* give up his car/dog

ab|schälen 1. *tr. V.* **a)** *(lösen)* peel off; **etw. von etw. ~**: peel sth. off sth.; **b)** *(befreien von)* bark ‹*tree*›. **2.** *refl. V. (sich lösen)* peel off; **die Haut schält sich ab** the skin is peeling

abschaltbar *Adj.* which can be switched off *postpos., not pred.*; **das ist ~**: it can be switched off

ab|schalten 1. *tr., itr. V. (ausschalten)* switch off; turn off; shut down ‹*power-station*›. **2.** *itr. V. (ugs.: nicht zuhören; Abstand gewinnen)* switch off

Ab·schaltung die switching off; *(eines Kraftwerks)* shut-down

Abschattung ['ap-ʃatʊŋ] **die; ~, ~en** shade; hue; *(fig.)* shade; nuance

ab|schätzen *tr. V.* estimate; size up ‹*person, possibilities*›; **jmdn. ~d betrachten** look at sb. appraisingly

abschätzig ['ap-ʃɛtsɪç] **1.** *Adj.* derogatory; disparaging. **2.** *adv.* derogatorily; disparagingly

Abschätzigkeit die derogatoriness; disparagement

ab|schauen *s.* **abgucken**

Ab·schaum der; *o. Pl. (abwertend)* scum; dregs *pl.*

ab|scheiden *unr. tr. V.* **a)** *(Chemie)* precipitate; *(Physiol.)* secrete; **b)** *(geh.: abtrennen)* separate; *(fig.)* isolate; *s. auch* **abgeschieden 2**

Abscheider der; ~s, ~ *(Technik)* separator

[1]ab|scheren *unr. tr. V.* shear off ‹*hair, wool*›; shear ‹*sheep, head*›

[2]ab|scheren *(Technik)* **1.** *tr. V. (abtrennen)* shear. **2.** *itr. V. (sich lösen)* shear off

Ab·scheu der; ~s, *(selten:)* **die; ~**: detestation; abhorrence; **einen ~ vor jmdm./etw. haben** detest *or* abhor sb./sth.; **jmds. ~ erregen** arouse repugnance in sb.; repel sb.

ab|scheuern *tr. V.* **a)** *(entfernen)* scrub off; **etw. von etw. ~**: scrub sth. off sth.; **b)** *(säubern)* scrub; **c)** *(beschädigen)* graze ‹*skin*›; wear away ‹*cloth*›; **ein abgescheuerter Kragen** a badly worn collar

abscheu·erregend *Adj. s.* **abscheulich 1 b**

abscheulich [ap'ʃɔylɪç] **1.** *Adj.* **a)** *(widerwärtig)* disgusting, awful ‹*smell, taste*›; repulsive, awful ‹*sight*›; **b)** *(verwerflich, schändlich)* disgraceful ‹*behaviour*›; abominable ‹*crime*›. **2.** *adv.* **a)** disgracefully; abominably; **b)** *(ugs.: sehr)* **~ frieren** freeze [half] to death *(coll.)*; **das schmerzt ganz ~**: it hurts like hell *(coll.)*; **~ kalt/scharf** terribly cold/sharp *(coll.)*

Abscheulichkeit die; ~, ~en *s.* **abscheu-**

lich 1: disgustingness; awfulness; repulsiveness; disgracefulness; abominableness

ab|schicken *tr. V.* send [off], post ‹*letter, parcel*›; dispatch, send [off], post ‹*goods, money*›; send ‹*messenger*›

ab|schieben 1. *unr. tr. V.* **a)** push *or* shove away; **das Bett von der Wand ~:** push *or* shove the bed away from the wall; **b)** *(abwälzen)* shift; **die Verantwortung/Schuld auf jmdn. ~:** shift [the] responsibility/the blame on to sb.; **c)** *(Rechtsw.: ausweisen)* deport; **jmdn. über die Grenze ~:** put sb. over the border; **d)** *(ugs.: entfernen)* get rid of; **jmdn. in ein Heim ~:** shove sb. into a home *(coll.)*. **2.** *unr. itr. V.; mit sein (salopp: weggehen)* push off *(sl.)*; shove off *(coll.)*

Ab·schiebung die *(Rechtsw.)* deportation

Abschiebungs·haft die *(Rechtsw.)* detention prior to deportation

Abschied ['ap-ʃi:t] **der; ~[e]s, ~e a)** *(Trennung)* parting (**von** from); farewell (**von** to); **[von jmdm./etw.] ~ nehmen** say goodbye [to sb./sth.]; take one's leave [of sb./sth.]; **von einer Gewohnheit ~ nehmen** give up a habit; **beim ~:** at parting; when saying goodbye; **sich zum ~ die Hände schütteln** shake hands on parting; **zum ~ Blumen schenken** give flowers as a parting gift; **jmdm. zum ~ zuwinken** wave goodbye to sb.; **b)** *(geh.: Entlassung)* resignation; **seinen ~ nehmen** resign; ‹*officer*› resign one's commission; **den ~ erhalten** *(veralt.)* be discharged

Abschieds-: ~besuch der farewell visit; **~brief der** farewell letter; **~essen das** farewell dinner; **~feier die** *(Zeremonie)* farewell ceremony; *(Party)* farewell *or* leaving party; **~geschenk das** farewell *or* parting gift; *(einer Firma usw.)* leaving present; **~gesuch das** *(geh.)* letter of resignation; **sein ~gesuch einreichen** tender one's resignation; ‹*officer*› resign one's commission; **~gruß der** goodbye; farewell; **~kuß der** goodbye *or* parting kiss; **~rede die** farewell speech; **~schmerz der;** *o. Pl.* sorrow at parting; **~spiel das** *(Fußball)* farewell appearance; **~szene die** scene of sentimental farewells; **~vorstellung die** farewell performance

ab|schießen *unr. tr. V.* **a)** loose, fire ‹*arrow*›; fire ‹*rifle, pistol, rocket, cannon*›; launch ‹*spacecraft*›; **b)** *(töten)* take; *(salopp)* shoot down ‹*person*›; **c)** *(ugs.: entfernen)* kick *or* throw ‹*person*› out; **d)** *(von sich geben)* fire off ‹*question*›; shoot ‹*glance*›; **e)** *(zerstören)* shoot down ‹*aeroplane*›; put ‹*tank*› out of action; **f)** *(wegreißen)* shoot off ‹*arm, leg, etc.*›

ab|schilfern *itr. V.; mit sein* peel

ab|schinden *unr. refl. V.* **sich ~:** work *or* *(Brit. coll.)* flog oneself to death; **sich mit etw. ~:** struggle along with sth.

Abschirm·dienst der *(Milit.)* counter-espionage service

ab|schirmen *tr. V.* **a)** *(schützen)* shield; **jmdn./sich von der** *od.* **gegen die Umwelt ~:** screen sb./oneself off from the outside world; **b)** *(abdecken)* cover ‹*lamp*›; screen off ‹*light, radiation, radio station*›

Abschirmung die; ~, ~en a) *(Schutz)* shielding; *(von der Umwelt usw.)* screening off; **b)** *(von Licht, Strahlung)* screening off

ab|schirren *tr. V.* unharness ‹*horse*›; unyoke ‹*cattle*›

ab|schlachten *tr. V.* slaughter

ab|schlaffen ['ap-ʃlafn̩] *(ugs.)* **1.** *tr., itr. V.* *(schlaff machen)* take it out of; **das schlafft ab** it takes it out of you; **ein abgeschlaffter Typ** a lackadaisical fellow; **er saß abgeschlafft im Sessel** he sat limply in his chair. **2.** *itr. V.; mit sein (schlaff werden)* wilt; sag; **geistig ~:** lose one's intellectual vigour

Ab·schlag der a) *(Kaufmannsspr.)* reduction; discount; **b)** *(Teilzahlung)* interim payment; *(Vorschuß)* advance; **c)** *(Fußball)* goalkeeper's kick out; **d)** *(Hockey) s.* **Bully; e)** *(Golf)* tee; *(Schlag)* drive; **f)** *(Finanzw.) s.* **Disagio**

ab|schlagen 1. *unr. tr. V.* **a)** knock off; *(mit dem Beil, Schwert usw.)* chop off; **jmdm. den Kopf ~:** chop off sb.'s head; **b)** *(ablehnen)* refuse; **jmdm. etw. ~:** refuse *or* deny sb. sth.; **c)** *(abwehren)* beat *or* fend off; **d)** *(zerlegen)* dismantle; strike ‹*tent*›; **e)** *(Seemannsspr.)* unbend. **2.** *unr. itr. V.* **a)** *auch tr.* *(Fußball)* **[den Ball] ~:** kick the ball out; **b)** *(Hockey)* take a 15-metre hit. **3.** *unr. refl. V.* *(kondensieren)* **sich an etw.** *(Dat.)* **~:** condense on sth.; *s. auch* **abgeschlagen 2; Wasser e**

abschlägig ['apʃlɛ:gɪç] *(Amtsspr.)* **1.** *Adj.* negative; **ein ~er Bescheid** a refusal *or* rejection. **2.** *adv.* **jmdn. ~ bescheiden** refuse sb.; **jmds. Gesuch** *(Akk.)* **~ bescheiden** reject sb.'s application

Abschlag[s]·zahlung die *s.* **Abschlag b**

ab|schlecken *tr. V.* *(österr., südd.) s.* **ablecken**

ab|schleifen 1. *unr. tr. V.* **a)** *(entfernen)* *(von Holz)* sand off; *(von Metall, Glas usw.)* grind off; **b)** *(glätten)* sand down ‹*wood*›; grind down ‹*metal, glass, etc.*›; smooth down ‹*broken tooth*›. **2.** *unr. refl. V.* *(sich abnutzen)* wear away; **das schleift sich noch ab** *(fig.)* that will wear off in time

Abschlepp·dienst der *(Kfz-W.)* breakdown recovery service; tow[ing] service *(Amer.)*

ab|schleppen 1. *tr. V.* **a)** tow away; take ‹*ship*› in tow; **ein Auto zur Werkstatt ~:** tow a car to the garage; **b)** *(salopp: mitnehmen)* **jmdn. ~:** drag sb. off. **2.** *refl. V.* *(ugs.: schwer tragen)* **sich mit/an etw.** *(Dat.)* **~:** break one's back carrying sth. *(fig.)*

Abschlepp-: ~seil das tow-rope; *(aus Draht)* towing cable; **~stange die** tow-bar; **~wagen der** breakdown vehicle; tow truck *(Amer.)*; *(der Polizei)* tow-away vehicle

abschließbar *Adj.* lockable; **es ist nicht ~:** it cannot be locked

ab|schließen 1. *unr. tr. V.* **a)** *auch itr.* *(zuschließen)* lock ‹*door, gate, cupboard*›; lock [up] ‹*house, flat, room, park*›; **vergiß nicht, abzuschließen!** don't forget to lock up!; **b)** *(absondern, trennen)* **etw. luftdicht ~:** seal sth. hermetically; **sich ganz [von der Welt] ~:** cut oneself off [from the world] completely; **c)** *(begrenzen)* border; **d)** *(zum Abschluß bringen)* bring to an end; conclude; **die Bücher ~:** balance the books; **sein Studium ~:** finish one's studies; **Bewerber mit abgeschlossenem Universitätsstudium** applicants with a degree; **e)** *(vereinbaren)* strike ‹*bargain, deal*›; make ‹*purchase*›; enter into ‹*agreement*›; **Geschäfte ~:** conclude deals; *(im Handel)* do business; *s. auch* **abgeschlossen 2; Versicherung b; Wette. 2.** *unr. itr. V.* **a)** *(begrenzt sein)* be bordered (**mit** by); **b)** *(aufhören, enden)* end; **~d sagte er ...:** in conclusion he said ...; **seine ~den Worte waren ...:** his concluding words were ...; **mit [einem] Gewinn/Verlust ~** *(Kaufmannsspr.)* show a profit/deficit; **c)** **mit jmdm./etw. abgeschlossen haben** have finished with sb./sth.; **d)** *(Kaufmannsspr.)* **die Vertragspartner wollen morgen ~:** the parties [to the contract] want to close tomorrow

Ab·schluß der a) *(Verschluß)* seal; **ein luftdichter ~:** an airtight seal; **b)** *(abschließender Teil)* edge; **c)** *(Beendigung)* conclusion; end; **vor ~ der Arbeiten** before the completion of the work; **zum ~ noch eine Frage** one final question; **sich dem ~ nähern** be drawing to a conclusion; **kurz vor dem ~ stehen** be nearly finished *or* at an end; **etw. zum ~ bringen** finish sth.; bring sth. to an end *or* conclusion; **zum ~ kommen** *od.* **gelangen** be completed; **wir müssen mit unseren Verhandlungen zum ~ kommen** we must bring our negotiations to a close; **zum ~ unseres Programms** to end our programme; **d)** *(ugs.: ~zeugnis)* **einen/keinen ~ haben** *(Hochschulw.)* ≈ have a/have no degree *or* *(Amer.)* diploma; *(Schulw.)* ≈ have some/no GCSE passes *(Brit.)*; *(Lehre)* have/not have finished one's apprenticeship; **ohne ~** without gaining a degree *or* *(Amer.)* diploma/any GCSE passes *(Brit.)*/finishing one's apprenticeship; **e)** *(Kaufmannsspr.: Schlußrechnung)* balancing; **f)** *(Kaufmannsspr.: geschäftliche Vereinbarung)* business deal; **einen ~ über 2 Millionen Tonnen Getreide tätigen** make a deal for 2 million tons of grain; **g)** *(eines Geschäfts, Vertrags)* conclusion; **durch den ~ einer Versicherung** by taking out an insurance policy; **h)** *(Fußball)* finishing move

Abschluß-: ~ball der final dance; **~examen das** final examination; **~feier die** *(Schulw.)* leaving party; **~klasse die** *(Schulw.)* final year; **~kundgebung die** final rally; **~prüfung die a)** *(Schulw.)* leaving *or* *(Amer.)* final examination; *(Hochschulw.)* final examination; finals *pl.*; **b)** *(Wirtsch.)* audit; **~veranstaltung die** final event; **~zeugnis das** *(Schulw.)* ≈ leaving certificate *(Brit.)*; ≈ diploma *(Amer.)*

ab|schmatzen *tr. V.* *(ugs.)* **jmdn. ~:** kiss sb. noisily

ab|schmecken *tr. V.* **a)** *(kosten)* taste; try; **b)** *(würzen)* season

ab|schmeicheln *tr. V.* **jmdm. etw. ~:** wheedle sth. out of sb.

ab|schmelzen 1. *unr. itr. V.; mit sein* melt away. **2.** *unr. tr. V.* melt; *(fig.: verringern)* reduce [the size of] ‹*assets, reserves*›

ab|schmettern *tr. V.* *(ugs.)* throw out; **jmdn. ~:** turn a deaf ear to sb.

ab|schmieren 1. *tr. V.* **a)** *(Technik)* grease; **b)** *(ugs.: abschreiben)* scribble down; *(unerlaubt)* copy; ‹*child in school*› crib (**von, bei** from). **2.** *itr. V.* **a)** *(ugs.)* crib (**von, bei** from); **b)** *(Fliegerspr.)* side-slip

Abschmier·presse die *(Kfz-W.)* grease-gun

ab|schminken *tr. V.* **a)** **jmdn./sich ~:** remove sb.'s/one's make-up; **sich** *(Dat.)* **das Gesicht/die Augen ~:** remove the make-up from one's face/eyes; **als ich sie abgeschminkt sah** when I saw her without her make-up; **b)** *(salopp)* **sich** *(Dat.)* **etw. ~:** get sth. out of one's head

ab|schmirgeln *tr. V.;* **a)** *(polieren)* rub down with emery; *(mit Sandpapier)* sand down; **b)** *(entfernen)* rub off with emery; *(mit Sandpapier)* sand off

ab|schmücken *tr. V.* take the decorations off ‹*Christmas tree*›

ab|schnacken *tr. V.* *(nordd.) s.* **abschwatzen**

ab|schnallen 1. *tr. V.* **a)** *(abnehmen)* unfasten; **[sich** *(Dat.)***] den Tornister/das Holzbein ~:** take off one's knapsack/wooden leg; **b)** *(losschnallen)* unfasten; **sich ~:** unfasten one's seat-belt. **2.** *itr. V.* *(salopp)* **a)** *(nicht mehr folgen können)* switch off; **b)** *(fassungslos sein)* be flabbergasted; **da schnallst du [echt] ab** you'll be flabbergasted

ab|schneiden 1. *unr. tr. V.* **a)** *(abtrennen)* cut off; cut down ‹*sth. hanging*›; **etw. von etw. ~:** cut sth. off sth.; **sich** *(Dat.)* **den Finger ~:** cut one's finger off; **sich** *(Dat.)* **eine Scheibe Brot/Fleisch ~:** cut oneself a slice of bread/meat; *s. auch* **Scheibe b; b)** *(kürzer schneiden)* cut; **jmdm./sich die Haare/Fingernägel ~:** cut sb.'s/one's hair/fingernails; **ein Kleid/einen Rock [ein Stück] ~:** cut [a piece] off a dress/a skirt; **eine Zigarre ~:** cut the end off a cigar; **c)** **jmdm. den Weg ~:** take a short cut to get ahead of sb.; **d)** *(trennen, isolieren)* cut off; **die Truppen vom Nachschub ~:** cut off troops from reinforcements; *s. auch* **abgeschnitten 2; e)** *(un-*

terbinden) **einen Einwurf/Einwand ~:** cut short an interjection/a protest. **2.** *unr. itr. V.* **a)** *(ver-, abkürzen)* ⟨*path, road*⟩ be a short cut; ⟨*pedestrian, driver*⟩ take a short cut; **b) bei etw. gut/schlecht ~:** do well/badly in sth.

ạb|schnellen *refl. V.* **sich [vom Boden] ~:** take off

ạb|schnippeln *tr. V. (ugs.)* **Stückchen von etw. ~:** cut little bits off sth.; *(mit der Schere)* snip bits off sth.

Ạb·schnitt der a) *(Kapitel)* section; **b)** *(Milit.: Gebiet, Gelände)* sector; *(DDR: Wohnbereich)* district; *(DDR: Handelsbereich)* section *(comprising ten retail shops belonging to a manufacturing co-operative)*; **c)** *(Zeitspanne)* phase; **d)** *(Kontroll~)* [detachable] portion; *(eines Schecks)* stub, counterfoil; **die Lebensmittelkarte hatte ~e für Butter, Brot, Zucker usw.** the ration card had coupons for butter, bread, sugar, etc.; **e)** *(Math.: eines Kreises)* segment

Ạbschnitts·bevollmächtigte der *(DDR)* ≈ community policeman

ạbschnitt[s]·weise 1. *Adv.* in sections; **etw. ~ lesen** read sth. section by section. **2.** *adj.* sectionalized

ạb|schnüren *tr. V.* **a)** apply a tourniquet to; **jmdm. die Luft/das Blut ~:** stop sb. from breathing/restrict sb.'s circulation; **einem Konkurrenten die Luft ~** *(fig.)* ruin a competitor; **b)** *(blockieren)* seal off

ạb|schöpfen *tr. V.* skim off; *(fig.)* **den Rahm ~** *(am meisten bekommen)* take the lion's share; *(das Beste bekommen)* cream off the best; **den Gewinn** *od.* **Profit ~:** siphon off the profits; **überschüssige Kaufkraft ~:** absorb excess spending power

ạb|schotten *tr. V.* **a)** *(Schiffbau)* separate by a bulkhead/bulkheads; **b)** *(fig.)* **etw. [von etw.] ~:** seal sth. off [from sth.]; **sich jmdm. gegenüber ~:** seal oneself off from sb.

ạb|schrägen *tr. V.* **einen Balken/ein Brett ~:** bevel a beam/the edges of a plank

ạb|schrammen 1. *tr. V. (abschürfen)* graze; **sich** *(Dat.)* **das Knie/die Haut ~:** graze one's knee/one's skin. **2.** *itr. V.* **a)** *(nordd. salopp: weggehen)* push off *(sl.)*; **b)** *(salopp: sterben)* croak *(sl.)*; snuff it *(sl.)*

ạbschraubbar *Adj.* unscrewable

ạb|schrauben *tr. V.* unscrew [and remove]; **etw. läßt sich ~:** sth. can be unscrewed

ạb|schrecken 1. *tr. V.* **a)** *(abhalten)* deter; **sein Aussehen schreckt viele ab** many people are put off by his appearance; **b)** *(fernhalten)* scare off; **c)** *(Metall.)* quench; **d)** *(Kochk.)* pour cold water over; put ⟨*boiled eggs*⟩ into cold water. **2.** *itr. V. (eine ~de Wirkung haben)* act as a deterrent; **das schreckt eher ab** it's more likely to put people off

ạbschreckend 1. *Adj.* **a)** *(warnend)* deterrent; **ein ~es Beispiel für alle Raucher** a warning to all smokers; **b)** *(abstoßend)* repulsive. **2.** *adv.* **~ wirken** have a deterrent effect; **~ häßlich** repulsively ugly

Ạbschreckung die; ~, ~en a) deterrence; **der ~** *(Dat.)* **dienen** serve as a deterrent; **b)** *(Mittel zur ~)* deterrent

Ạbschreckungs-: ~politik die policy of deterrence; **~potential das** deterrent potential; **~theorie die** *(Rechtsw.)* theory of the deterrent value of punishment; **~waffe die** deterrent [weapon]

ạb|schreiben 1. *unr. tr. V.* **a)** *(kopieren)* copy out; **sich** *(Dat.)* **etw. ~:** copy sth. down; *(aus einem Buch, einer Zeitung usw.)* copy sth. out; **b) etw. von jmdm. ~** *(in der Schule)* copy sth. from *or* off sb.; *(als Plagiator)* plagiarize sth. from sb.; **c)** *(Wirtsch.)* amortize, write down **(mit** by**)**; **d)** *(ugs.: verlorengeben)* write off; **jmdn. abgeschrieben haben** have written sb. off; **e)** *(abnutzen)* use up ⟨*pencil, crayon, ball-point or felt pen*⟩; wear out ⟨*pen-nib*⟩. **2.** *unr. itr. V.* **a)** **bei** *od.* **von jmdm. ~** *(in der Schule)* copy off sb.; *(als Plagiator)* copy from sb.; **b)** *(brieflich absagen)* **jmdm. ~:** write to sb. and say one cannot come

Ạb·schreibung die *(Wirtsch.)* **a)** *(das Abschreiben)* amortization; **b)** *(Betrag)* depreciation provision

Ạbschreibungs-: ~möglichkeit die *(Wirtsch.) possibility of setting off items against taxable income;* **~ruine die** *(salopp) building erected not for occupation, but for purposes of offsetting depreciation against tax*

ạb|schreiten *unr. tr. V. (geh.)* **a)** *mit sein od. haben (entlanggehen an)* inspect ⟨*troops*⟩; pace ⟨*distance*⟩; **b)** *(schreitend abmessen)* pace out

Ạb·schrift die copy

ạb|schrubben *tr. V. (ugs.)* **a)** scrub; **sich/jmdm. den Rücken ~:** scrub one's/sb.'s back [down]; **sich/jmdn. ~:** scrub oneself/sb. [down]; **b)** *(schrubbend entfernen)* scrub away *or* off; **sich/jmdm. den Schmutz ~:** scrub the dirt off oneself/sb.

ạb|schuften *refl. V. (ugs.)* work like a slave; **sosehr man sich auch abschuftet** however hard you slave *or (Brit. sl.)* graft

ạb|schuppen 1. *tr. V.* scale. **2.** *refl. V.* **die Haut schuppt sich ab** the skin flakes off

ạb|schürfen *tr. V.* **sich** *(Dat.)* **die Knie/die Ellenbogen ~:** graze one's knees/one's elbows; **sich** *(Dat.)* **die Haut ~:** chafe the skin

Ạb·schürfung die a) *(das Abschürfen)* grazing; **b)** *(Schürfwunde)* graze

Ạb·schuß der a) *(eines Flugzeugs)* shooting down; *(eines Panzers)* putting out of action; **der Pilot hatte 50 Abschüsse** the pilot had 50 kills; **b)** *(von Wild)* shooting; *(fig. salopp: Eroberung)* lay *(coll.)*; **Tiere zum ~ freigeben** permit the shooting of animals; **jmdn. zum ~ freigeben** *(fig. ugs.)* throw sb. to the wolves *(fig.)*; **c)** *(das Abfeuern) (von Geschossen, Torpedos)* firing; *(von Raketen in den Weltraum)* launching

Ạbschuß·basis die launch[ing] site

abschüssig ['ap-ʃysɪç] *Adj.* downward sloping ⟨*land*⟩; **die Straße ist ~:** the road goes steeply downhill

Ạbschuß-: ~liste die *(fig. ugs.)* **er steht auf meiner ~liste** I've got it in for him *(coll.)*; **auf der/jmds. ~liste stehen** be on the/sb.'s blacklist; **~prämie die** bounty *(for shot animals)*; **~rampe die** launch[ing] pad

ạb|schütteln *tr. V.* **a)** *(herunterschütteln)* shake down ⟨*fruit*⟩; **[sich** *(Dat.)***] den Staub/den Schnee [vom Mantel] ~:** shake off the dust/the snow [from one's coat]; *s. auch* **Joch a; b) ein Tischtuch ~:** shake [out] a tablecloth; **c)** *(fig.: überwinden, loswerden)* shake off

ạb|schütten *tr. V. s.* **abgießen a**

ạb|schwächen 1. *tr. V.* **a)** *(mildern)* tone down, moderate ⟨*statement, criticism*⟩; **b)** *(verringern)* lessen ⟨*effect, impression*⟩; cushion ⟨*blow, impact*⟩; **c)** *(Fot.)* reduce. **2.** *refl. V. (nachlassen)* ⟨*interest, demand*⟩ wane; ⟨*noise, storm*⟩ abate; **das Tief/Hoch schwächt sich ab** *(Met.)* the low/high-pressure area is weakening; **der Preisauftrieb schwächt sich ab** price increases are slowing down

Ạb·schwächung die; ~, ~en a) *(Milderung)* toning down, moderation; *(abgemilderte Form)* attenuation; **b)** *(eines Aufpralls, Stoßes usw.)* cushioning; **c)** *(Fot.)* reduction; **d)** *(das Nachlassen)* waning; *(eines Hochs, Tiefs)* weakening; *(zahlenmäßig)* drop *(Gen.* in*)*

ạb|schwatzen, *(bes. südd.)* **ạb|schwätzen** *tr. V.* **jmdm. etw. ~:** talk sb. into giving one sth.; **sich** *(Dat.)* **etw. von jmdm. ~ lassen** let oneself be talked into giving sb. sth.

ạb|schweifen *itr. V.; mit sein;* **a)** digress; **ihr Blick schweifte ab** her gaze wandered; **b)** *(geh.: vom Weg abgehen)* stray

Ạbschweifung die; ~, ~en digression

ạb|schwellen *unr. itr. V.; mit sein* **a)** go down; **b)** *(geh.: zurückgehen)* ⟨*flood*⟩ subside; ⟨*noise*⟩ die away; ⟨*music*⟩ fade [away]

ạb|schwemmen *tr. V.* **a)** wash away; **b)** *(durch Schwemmen reinigen)* wash down

Ạbschwemmung die; ~, ~en wash-out

ạb|schwenken 1. *itr. V.; mit sein* turn aside; **links/rechts ~:** *(abbiegen)* turn left/right; *(die Richtung allmählich ändern)* bear to the left/right. **2.** *tr. V.* **die Tropfen vom Glas ~:** shake the drops off the glass; **die Gläser ~:** rinse the glasses and shake the drops off them

ạb|schwindeln *tr. V.* **jmdm. etw. ~:** trick sb. out of sth.

ạb|schwirren *itr. V.; mit sein* **a)** ⟨*bird, dragon-fly*⟩ whirr away; ⟨*bee, beetle, fly, wasp*⟩ buzz away; **b)** *(ugs.: weggehen)* buzz off *(sl.)*

ạb|schwitzen *tr. V.* sweat off

ạb|schwören *unr. itr. V.* **dem Teufel/seinem Glauben ~:** renounce the Devil/one's faith; **dem Alkohol/Laster ~:** forswear *or* swear off alcohol/vice

Ạb·schwung der a) *(Turnen)* dismount; **beim ~:** when dismounting; **b)** *(Wirtsch.: Rezession)* downward trend; **ein ~ der Konjunktur** a recession

ạb|segeln 1. *itr. V.* **a)** *mit sein (lossegeln)* sail away; **von Kiel ~:** sail from Kiel; **b)** *(die Saison beenden)* have the last sail of the season. **2.** *tr. V.* **die Küste ~:** sail along the coast

ạb|segnen *tr. V. (ugs. scherzh.)* sanction

ạbsehbar *Adj.* foreseeable; **in ~er Zeit** within the foreseeable future; **etw. ist noch gar nicht ~:** sth. cannot yet be predicted; **auf** *od.* **für ~e Zeit** for the foreseeable future; **nicht ~:** unforeseeable

ạb|sehen 1. *unr. tr. V.* **a)** *(voraussehen)* predict; foresee ⟨*event*⟩; **b)** *(abzielen)* **er hat es darauf abgesehen, uns zu ärgern** he's out to annoy us; **c)** *(haben wollen)* **es auf etw.** *(Akk.)* **abgesehen haben** be after sth.; **sie hat es bloß auf sein Geld abgesehen** she's only after his money; **er hat es auf sie abgesehen** he's got his eye on her; **d)** *(schikanieren)* **der Chef hat es auf ihn abgesehen** the boss has got it in for him; **e)** *s.* **abgucken 1. 2.** *unr. itr. V.* **a)** *(nicht beachten)* **von etw. ~:** leave aside *or* ignore sth.; *s. auch* **abgesehen 2; b)** *(verzichten)* **von etw. ~:** refrain from sth.; **von einer Anzeige/Klage ~:** not report sth./not press charges; **c)** *s.* **abgucken 2**

ạb|seifen *tr. V.* wash down [with soap]; **jmdn./sich ~:** soap sb./oneself down

ạb|seilen 1. *tr. V.* lower [with a rope]. **2.** *refl. V.* **a)** *(Bergsteigen)* abseil; **b)** *(salopp: sich davonmachen)* push *or* buzz off *(sl.)*

Ạbseil·haken der *(Bergsteigen)* abseil piton

ạb|sein *unr. itr. V.; mit sein (Zusschr. nur im Inf. u. Part.)* **[an etw.** *(Dat.)***] ~:** *(abgegangen sein)* have come off [sth.]; *(fehlen)* be missing [from sth.]; **seit dem Krieg ist sein linkes Bein ab** since the war he has been without his left leg

Ạb·seite die *(Textilw.)* wrong side

ạbseitig *Adj.* **a)** *(geh.: abseits gelegen)* remote; **b)** *(ausgefallen, abwegig)* esoteric; **c)** *s.* **abartig**

abseits ['apzaits] **1.** *Präp. mit Gen.* away from. **2.** *Adv.* **a)** *(entfernt)* far away; **etwas ~:** a little way away; **b)** *(Ballspiele)* **~ sein** *od.* **stehen** be offside

Ạbseits das; ~, ~ a) *(Sport)* **das war ein klares ~:** that was clearly offside; **im ~ stehen** be offside; **der Spieler lief ins ~:** the player put himself offside; **b)** *(fig.)* **im ~ stehen** have been pushed out into the cold; **ins ~ geraten** be pushed out into the cold

ạbseits-, Ạbseits-: ~falle die *(Sport)* offside trap; **~position die, ~stellung die** *(Sport)* offside position; **sich in ~stellung**

befinden be in an offside position; **~tor** *(Sport)* **das** offside goal; **~verdächtig** *Adj.* *(Sport)* which may have been offside *postpos.*; **[stark] ~ sein** look [very much] like offside

ab|senden *unr. od. regelm. tr. V.* dispatch

Ab·sender der sender; *(~angabe)* sender's address

Ab·sendung die dispatch

ab|sengen *tr. V.* singe off; singe ⟨*poultry*⟩

ab|senken 1. *refl. V.* **sich [zum See/Fluß hin] ~:** slope [down to the lake/river]. **2.** *tr. V.* **a)** *(Tiefbau)* lower; **b)** *(versenken)* sink; **c)** *(Gartenbau)* **Erdbeeren/Weinstöcke ~:** set strawberries/vines

Absenker der; ~s, ~ *(Gartenbau)* runner; set

absentieren [apzɛn'ti:rən] *refl. V.* *(geh., veralt.)* withdraw

Absenz [ap'zɛnts] **die; ~, ~en a)** absence [of mind]; **b)** *(bes. österr., schweiz.)* absence *(from school)*

ab|servieren 1. *itr. V.* clear away. **2.** *tr. V.* **a) ein Gedeck/den Tisch ~:** clear away a cover/clear the table; **b)** *(salopp: absetzen, kaltstellen)* throw out; **c)** *(salopp: töten)* **jmdn. ~:** bump sb. off *(sl.)*

absetzbar *Adj.* **a)** *(Steuerw.)* **[steuerlich] ~:** [tax-]deductible; **b)** *(verkäuflich)* saleable; **c)** *s.* **absetzen 1d: er ist nicht ~:** he cannot be dismissed/be removed from office

ab|setzen 1. *tr. V.* **a)** *(abnehmen)* take off; **b)** *(hinstellen)* put down ⟨*glass, bag, suitcase*⟩; **c)** *(aussteigen lassen)* **jmdn. ~** *(im öffentlichen Verkehr)* put sb. down; let sb. out *(Amer.)*; *(im privaten Verkehr)* drop sb. [off]; **d)** *(entlassen)* dismiss ⟨*minister, official*⟩; remove ⟨*chancellor, judge*⟩ from office; depose ⟨*king, emperor*⟩; **e)** *(ablagern)* deposit; **f)** *(absagen)* drop; call off ⟨*strike, football match*⟩; **einen Punkt von der Tagesordnung ~:** delete an item from the agenda; **g)** *(nicht mehr anwenden)* discontinue ⟨*treatment, therapy*⟩; stop taking ⟨*medicine, drug*⟩; **h)** *(von den Lippen nehmen)* take ⟨*glass, trumpet*⟩ from one's lips; *(nicht mehr schreiben mit)* lift ⟨*pen*⟩ from the paper; **i)** *(verkaufen)* sell; **j)** *(Steuerw.)* **etw. [von der Steuer] ~:** deduct sth. [from tax]; **k)** *(abwerfen)* throw ⟨*rider*⟩; **l)** *(Druckw.: als neue Zeile beginnen)* start ⟨*section*⟩ on a new line; **die folgenden Zeilen ~:** treat the subsequent lines as a new paragraph; **m)** *(Druckw.: setzen)* compose; **einen Text/ein Manuskript ~:** set [up] a text/manuscript; **n)** *(Seemannsspr.)* **ein Boot [vom Ufer] ~:** push a boat off [from the shore]; **o)** *(hervorheben)* **farblich abgesetzt** of contrasting colour *postpos.*; **wir wollen den Saum farblich ~:** we want to use a contrasting colour for the hem; **den Saum mit Samt ~:** trim the hem with velvet. **2.** *refl. V.* **a)** *(sich ablagern)* be deposited ⟨*dust*⟩ settle; ⟨*particles in suspension*⟩ settle out; **b)** *(sich distanzieren)* **sich von etw. ~:** distance oneself from sth.; **c)** *(sich unterscheiden) s.* **abheben 4; d)** *(ugs.: sich davonmachen)* get away; **e)** *(Milit.)* withdraw

Absetzung die; ~, ~en a) *s.* **absetzen 1d:** dismissal; removal from office; deposition; **b)** *(Steuerw.)* deduction; **c)** *(Absage)* cancellation; *(eines Streiks, Fußballspiels usw.)* calling off; **d)** *(Abbruch)* discontinuation

ab|sichern 1. *tr. V.* **a)** make safe; **b)** *(fig.)* substantiate ⟨*argument, conclusions*⟩; validate ⟨*result*⟩; **etw. rechtlich/vertraglich ~:** protect sth. legally/by contract; **tariflich abgesichert** protected by agreement *postpos.* **2.** *refl. V.* safeguard oneself; **sich vertraglich ~:** protect oneself by contract; **sich gegenseitig ~:** keep each other safe; **er will sich ~ für den Fall, daß ...:** he wants to cover himself against the possiblity that ...; **sich nach allen Seiten ~:** guard against all eventualities; *(gegen Einwände)* forestall criticism

Ab·sicherung die a) *(das Sichermachen)* making safe; **die Polizei ist für die ~ des Geländes verantwortlich** the police are responsible for making the site safe; **b)** *(fig.)* substantiation; *(von Ergebnissen)* validation; **zur rechtlichen/vertraglichen ~ einer Sache** *(Gen.)* to protect sth. legally/by contract

Ab·sicht die; ~, ~en a) intention; **die ~ haben, etw. zu tun** plan *or* intend to do sth.; **etw. mit** *od.* **aus ~ tun** do sth. intentionally *or* deliberately; **etw. ohne** *od.* **nicht mit ~ tun** do sth. unintentionally; **das ist ~:** that's intentional; **in der besten ~:** with the best of intentions; **aus** *od.* **in politischer/therapeutischer ~:** with a political/therapeutic purpose; **b)** *(Rechtsw.)* intent; **in betrügerischer ~ handeln** act with intent to deceive

ab·sichtlich 1. *Adj.* intentional; deliberate. **2.** *adv.* intentionally; deliberately

Absichts·erklärung die declaration of intent

absichtslos 1. *Adj* unintentional. **2.** *adv.* unintentionally

Ab·siedlung die *(Med.)* dissemination

ab|singen *unr. tr. V.* **a)** *auch itr.* **[etw.] vom Blatt ~:** sing [sth.] at sight; **b) unter Absingen der Nationalhymne/schmutziger Lieder** singing the national anthem/dirty songs

ab|sinken *unr. itr. V.; mit sein* **a)** sink; *(fig.: im Niveau)* decline; **b)** ⟨*temperature, blood pressure*⟩ drop; ⟨*interest, performance*⟩ decline; **in seinen Leistungen ~:** do *or* perform less well

Absinth [ap'zɪnt] **der; ~[e]s, ~e** absinth[e]

ab|sitzen 1. *unr. tr. V.* **a)** *(hinter sich bringen)* sit through; sit out ⟨*hours of duty etc.*⟩; *(im Gefängnis)* serve; **zehn Jahre ~:** serve *or* *(coll.)* do ten years; **seine Jahre ~:** serve one's full sentence; **b)** *s.* **abgesessen 2. 2.** *unr. itr. V. mit sein* **[vom Pferd] ~:** dismount [from one's horse]

absolut [apzo'lu:t] **1.** *Adj.* *(auch Chemie, Physik)* absolute; pure ⟨*lyricism, art*⟩; **der ~e Knüller** *(ugs.)* the high spot; **der ~e Nullpunkt** *(Physik)* absolute zero; **der ~e Ablativ** *(Sprachw.)* the ablative absolute; **die ~e Mehrheit** *(Pol.)* an absolute majority. **2.** *adv.* absolutely

Absolutheit die; ~, ~en absoluteness

Absolution [apzolu'tsio:n] **die; ~, ~en** *(kath. Rel.)* absolution; **jmdm. die ~ erteilen** give sb. absolution

Absolutismus der; ~ *(hist.)* absolutism *no art.*

absolutistisch 1. *Adj.* absolutist. **2.** *adv.* in an absolutist manner

Absolvent [apzɔl'vɛnt] **der; ~en, ~en, Absolventin die; ~, ~nen** *(einer Schule)* one who has taken the leaving *or* *(Amer.)* final examination; *(einer Akademie)* graduate; **die ~en der Handelsschule/eines Lehrgangs** those who have/had attended a commercial college/completed a course of training; **er ist ~ einer Abendschule** he has attended an evening school; *s. auch* **-in**

absolvieren [apzɔl'vi:rən] *tr. V.* **a)** complete; **das Gymnasium ~:** complete a grammar-school education; **b)** *(erledigen, verrichten)* put in ⟨*hours*⟩; do ⟨*performance, route, task*⟩; make ⟨*visit*⟩; do *(coll.)* ⟨*sights*⟩; **c)** *(kath. Rel.)* absolve

Absolvierung die; ~: completion; **nach [der] ~ einiger Besuche/seines Studiums** having paid some visits/finished one's studies

ab·sonderlich *Adj.* strange; odd

Absonderlichkeit die; ~, ~en strangeness; oddness

ab|sondern 1. *tr. V.* **a)** isolate ⟨*patient*⟩; separate ⟨*prisoner*⟩; **b)** *(Biol., Physiol.)* secrete; exude ⟨*resin*⟩; discharge ⟨*pus*⟩; *(fig. abwertend)* emit. **2.** *refl. V.* **sich [von anderen] ~:** isolate oneself [from others]

Absonderung die; ~, ~en a) isolation; **b)** *(Biol., Med.)* secretion; **c)** *(österr.: Einzelhaft)* solitary confinement

Absorbens [ap'zɔrbɛns] **das; ~, Absorbenzien** *od.* **Absorbentia** *(Chemie, Physik)* absorbent

Absorber der; ~s, ~ a) *s.* **Absorbens; b)** *(bei Kältemaschinen usw.)* absorber

absorbieren *tr. V.* **a)** *(Chemie, Physik, Physiol.)* absorb; **~d** absorbent; **b)** *(fig.)* absorb, engage ⟨*attention*⟩

Absorption [apzɔrp'tsio:n] **die; ~:** *(Chemie, Physik, Physiol.)* absorption

Absorptions·vermögen das *(Chemie, Physik, Physiol.)* absorbency

ab|spalten 1. *unr. od. regelm. tr. V.* **a)** *(abschlagen, fig.: trennen)* split off; **b)** *(Chemie)* release. **2.** *unr. od. regelm. refl. V.* split off *or* away **(aus** from); **sich von jmdm./etw. ~:** split with sb./sth.

Ab·spaltung die a) *(das Abschlagen, fig.: Trennung)* splitting-off; **b)** *(Chemie)* separation

Ab·spann der *(Ferns.)* final credits

ab|spannen *tr. V.* **a)** *(ausspannen)* unhitch ⟨*wagon*⟩; unharness ⟨*horse*⟩; unyoke ⟨*oxen*⟩; **b)** *(Technik: mit Seilen)* anchor ⟨*pole, mast*⟩; *s. auch* **abgespannt 2**

Abspann·seil das *(Brückenbau)* inclined tension cable

Abspannung die; ~, ~en a) *(Ermüdung)* weariness; fatigue; **b)** *(Technik)* anchoring; *(Abspannseil)* anchoring cable

ab|sparen *refl. V.* **sich** *(Dat.)* **etw. von seinem Lohn/Taschengeld ~:** save for sth. out of one's wages/pocket-money; **er hatte sich** *(Dat.)* **ein paar Mark abgespart** he had managed to save a few marks; *s. auch* **Mund**

ab|specken *(salopp)* **1.** *tr. V.* shed. **2.** *itr. V.* **a)** *(Gewicht verlieren)* lose weight; slim [down]; **b)** *(fig.: schrumpfen)* slim down

ab|speichern *tr. V.* *(DV)* store

ab|speisen *tr. V.* **a)** *(vertrösten)* **jmdn. mit etw. ~:** fob sb. off with sth.; **b)** *(oft abwertend: beköstigen)* feed

abspenstig ['ap-ʃpɛnstɪç] *Adj.; nicht attr.* **jmdm. etw. ~ machen** get sb. to part with sth.; **jmdm. die Kunden/die Patienten/das Personal ~ machen** lure away sb.'s customers/patients/staff; **jmdm. den Freund/die Freundin ~ machen** steal sb.'s boy-/girlfriend

ab|sperren 1. *tr. V.* **a)** *(blockieren)* seal off; close off; **b) jmdm. das Gas/das Wasser/den Strom ~:** cut off sb.'s gas/water/electricity; **c)** *(österr., südd.: abschließen)* lock ⟨*door*⟩. **2.** *itr. V.* *(österr., südd.)* lock up

Absperr-: ~gitter das barrier; **~hahn der** *(Technik)* stopcock; **~kette die** cordon

Ab·sperrung die a) *(Blockierung)* sealing off; closing off; **b)** *(Sperre)* barrier

Absperr·ventil das *(Technik)* stop valve

Ab·spiel das *(Ballspiele)* **a)** *(das Abspielen)* passing; **b)** *(Schuß)* pass

ab|spielen 1. *tr. V.* **a)** *(ablaufen lassen)* **etw. ~:** play sth. through; **b) die Nationalhymne/Internationale ~:** play the national anthem/Internationale; **ein Musikstück vom Blatt ~:** play a piece of music at sight; **c)** *(Ballspiele)* pass; *s. auch* **abgespielt 2. 2.** *refl. V.* **a)** *(stattfinden)* take place; **b)** *(sich ereignen)* happen; take place; ⟨*course of events*⟩ proceed; ⟨*war*⟩ be waged; **da spielt sich [bei mir/ihm] nichts ab!** *(salopp)* nothing doing [as far as I'm/he's concerned] *(coll.)*. **3.** *itr. V.* *(Ballspiele)* pass; **an jmdn. ~:** pass [the ball] to sb.

ab|splittern 1. *itr. V.; mit sein* ⟨*wood*⟩ splinter off; ⟨*lacquer, paint*⟩ flake off. **2.** *refl. V.* *(fig.)* **sich von einer Gruppe/Partei ~:** split away from a group/party

Ab·sprache die agreement; arrangement; **eine ~ mit jmdm. treffen** come to an agreement *or* make an arrangement with sb.;

nach ~ mit by arrangement with; nach vorheriger/ohne vorherige ~: after/without prior consultation

absprache·gemäß *Adv.* as arranged *or* agreed

ab|sprechen 1. *unr. tr. V.* a) *(aberkennen)* jmdm. etw. ~: deprive sb. of sth.; b) *(ableugnen)* jmdm. etw. ~: deny that sb. has sth.; jmdm. das Recht auf etw. *(Akk.)* ~: deny sb.'s right to sth.; jmdm. das Recht ~, etw. zu tun deny sb. the right to do sth.; c) *(vereinbaren)* arrange; etw. miteinander ~: arrange sth. together. 2. *unr. refl. V. (sich einigen)* sich [mit jmdm.] [über etw. *(Akk.)*] ~: come to *or* reach an agreement [with sb.] [about sth.]

ab|spreizen *tr. V.* stretch out ⟨*arm, leg*⟩ sideways; splay out ⟨*fingers, toes*⟩; spread out ⟨*hands*⟩; extend ⟨*finger*⟩

ab|sprengen *tr. V.* a) *(lossprengen)* split off; *(Raumf.)* jettison ⟨*stage*⟩; b) *(fig.)* separate ⟨*troops*⟩; abgesprengte Truppenteile isolated detachments of troops

ab|springen *unr. itr. V.; mit sein* a) *(losspringen)* jump off; [mit dem rechten/linken Bein] ~: ⟨*jumper*⟩ take off [on the right/left leg]; b) *(herunterspringen)* jump down; vom Fahrrad/Pferd ~: jump off one's bicycle/horse; aus dem Flugzeug ~: jump out of the aeroplane; mit dem Fallschirm ~: jump [with a parachute]; *(bei Gefahr)* bail out; „Abspringen während der Fahrt verboten" 'do not alight while the vehicle is in motion'; c) *(abplatzen)* come off; ⟨*paint*⟩ flake off; ⟨*enamel*⟩ splinter off; d) *(sich lösen)* fly off; ⟨*bicycle-chain*⟩ jump off; e) *(abprallen)* rebound; f) *(ugs.: sich zurückziehen)* drop out; *(von einem Abkommen)* back out; Kunden/Leser springen uns ab we are losing customers/readers

ab|spritzen 1. *tr. V.* a) *(reinigen)* spray [down]; b) *(entfernen)* spray off; einer Kuh *(Dat.)* den Kot ~: spray the muck off a cow; c) *(ns. verhüll.: ermorden)* jmdn. ~: give sb. a lethal injection. 2. *itr. V.* a) *(vulgär: ejakulieren)* come *(coarse)*; b) *mit sein (veralt.: weggehen)* race off; c) *mit sein (spritzend abprallen)* ⟨*liquid*⟩ splash off; ⟨*mud, mortar, etc.*⟩ splatter off

Ab·sprung der a) *(das Losspringen)* take-off; b) *(das Herunterspringen)* jump; c) *(fig.)* break; den ~ wagen risk making the break; den ~ schaffen make the break; den ~ verpassen miss the boat

Absprung·balken der *(Leichtathletik)* take-off board

ab|spulen *tr. V.* a) *(abwickeln)* unwind; sich ~: come unwound; b) *(filmen)* shoot; c) *(vorführen)* show; d) *(salopp: herunterleiern)* reel off; e) *(salopp: fahren)* cover

ab|spülen 1. *tr. V.* a) *(wegspülen)* wash off ⟨*dirt, dust*⟩; b) *(reinigen)* rinse off; sich *(Dat.)* die Hände *usw.* ~: rinse one's hands *etc.*; c) *(bes. südd.)* das Geschirr ~: wash the dishes. 2. *itr. V. (bes. südd.)* wash up

ab|stammen *itr. V.* von jmdm./vom Affen ~: be descended from sb./the apes

Abstammung die; ~, ~en descent; seiner ~ nach ist er Deutscher he is German by descent

Abstammungs·lehre die theory of evolution

Ab·stand der a) *(Zwischenraum)* distance; in 20 Meter ~: at a distance of 20 metres; im ~ von 10 Metern 10 metres apart; ~ halten keep one's distance; b) *(Punktunterschied)* gap; difference; *(Rangunterschied)* social distinction; mit ~: by far; far and away; c) *(Zeitspanne)* interval; *(kürzer)* gap; in Abständen von 20 Minuten at 20-minute intervals; [von etw.] ~ gewinnen *(fig.)* have time to recover [from sth.]; mir fehlt noch der innere ~ zu den Geschehnissen these events are still too close to me; d) *(Zurückhaltung, Distanz)* ~ halten keep one's distance; den [gebührenden/nötigen] ~ wahren keep the proper/necessary distance; e) *(geh.: Verzicht)* von etw. ~ nehmen refrain from sth.; von einer Intervention ~ nehmen refrain from intervening; davon ~ nehmen, etw. zu tun refrain from doing sth.; von einer Idee ~ nehmen abandon an idea; f) *(Entschädigung)* compensation; *(bei Übernahme einer Wohnung) payment for furniture and fittings left by previous tenant*

Abstands·summe die *s.* Abstand f

ab|statten ['ap-ʃtatn̩] *tr. V. (geh.)* jmdm. einen Besuch ~: pay sb. a visit; jmdm. Bericht ~: present one's *or* a report to sb.; jmdm. seinen Dank ~: convey one's thanks *or* express one's gratitude to sb.

ab|stauben *tr., itr. V.* a) dust; b) *(ugs.) (stehlen)* etw. ~: pinch *(sl.) or* nick *(Brit. sl.) or (Amer. coll.)* lift sth.; *(schnorren)* etw. bei jmdm. ~: sponge sth. from sb.; sie haben ordentlich abgestaubt they've been pinching things left, right, and centre *(sl.)*/sponging from all over the place; c) *(Fußballjargon)* ein Tor ~: steal a goal

Abstauber der; ~s, ~ a) *s.* Abstaubertor; b) *(Fußballjargon)* goal-hanger

Abstauber·tor das *(Fußballjargon)* opportunist goal

ab|stechen 1. *unr. tr. V.* a) slaughter ⟨*animal*⟩ *(by cutting its throat)*; jmdn. ~ *(derb)* slit sb.'s throat; *s. auch* Kalb a; b) *(ab-, herauslösen)* slice off; cut edge of ⟨*lawn*⟩; cut ⟨*peat*⟩; Teig/Klöße [mit dem Löffel] ~: cut up dough/cut out dumplings [with a spoon]; c) *(ablaufen lassen)* tap ⟨*beer, wine*⟩; einen Hochofen ~: tap a blast-furnace. 2. *unr. itr. V.* von etw./jmdm. ~: contrast with sth./sb.; gegen etw. ~: stand out against sth.

Abstecher der; ~s, ~: side-trip; *(fig.: Abschweifung)* digression

ab|stecken *tr. V.* a) *(abgrenzen)* mark out; *(fig.)* define; ein Gelände mit Pfählen/Pflöcken/Fähnchen ~: mark out an area with stakes/pegs/flags; b) *(Schneiderei)* pin up ⟨*hem*⟩; ein Kleid ~: fit a dress [by pinning]

ab|stehen *unr. itr. V.* a) *(nicht anliegen)* ⟨*hair*⟩ stand up, stick out; ⟨*pigtail[s]*⟩ stick out; ⟨*beard*⟩ grow out; ~de Ohren protruding ears; b) *(wegstehen)* 40 cm/zu weit von etw. ~: be 40 cm. away/too far away from sth.; c) *(geh.: Abstand nehmen)* von einem Plan ~: abandon a plan; davon ~, etw. zu tun refrain from doing sth.; d) Wasser ~ lassen let water stand; *s. auch* abgestanden 2; Bein a

Ab·steige die; ~, ~n *(ugs. abwertend)* cheap and crummy hotel *(sl.)*; *(Stundenhotel)* sleazy hotel

ab|steigen *unr. itr. V.; mit sein* a) *(heruntersteigen)* [vom Pferd/Fahrrad] ~: get off [one's horse/bicycle]; vom Karren ~: get down from the cart; „Radfahrer ~": 'no cycling'; 'cycling prohibited'; b) *(abwärts gehen)* go down; descend; ~d descending ⟨*pipe, branch*⟩; vom Gipfel/ins Tal ~: climb down *or* descend from the summit/into the valley; gesellschaftlich ~ *(fig.)* decline in social status; die ~de Linie *(Geneal.)* the line of descent; *s. auch* Ast a; c) *(Sport)* be relegated; d) *(übernachten, wohnen)* in einem Hotel ~: put up at a hotel

Absteige·quartier das a) *(veralt.)* stopping-place; b) *(ugs. abwertend) s.* Absteige

Ab·steiger der; ~s, ~ *(Sport) (vor dem Abstieg stehend)* team threatened with *or* facing relegation; *(abgestiegen)* relegated team; ein gesellschaftlicher ~ *(fig.)* one who has declined in social status

Abstell·bahn·hof der [rail] sidings *pl.*

ab|stellen 1. *tr. V.* a) *(absetzen)* put down; b) *(unterbringen, hinstellen)* put; *(parken)* park; c) *(ausschalten, abdrehen)*; turn *or* switch off; turn off ⟨*gas, water*⟩; jmdm. das Gas/den Strom ~: cut sb.'s gas/electricity off; jmdm. das Telefon ~: disconnect sb.'s telephone; d) *(unterbinden)* put a stop to; e) *(sein lassen)* stop; *(aufgeben)* give up; f) *(beordern)* assign; detail [off] ⟨*soldiers*⟩; g) etw. [weiter] von etw. ~ *(abrücken)* move sth. [further] away from sth.; *(entfernt stellen)* put sth. at a [greater] distance from sth.; h) *(ausrichten)* etw. auf etw. *(Akk.)* ~: gear sth. to sth. 2. *itr. V.* auf etw. *(Akk.)* ~: take account of sth.; take sth. into account; darauf ~, daß ...: take account of *or* take into account the fact that ...

Abstell-: ~gleis das siding; jmdn. aufs ~ schieben *(fig. ugs.)* put sb. out of harm's way; ~kammer die lumber-room; ~raum der store-room

ab|stemmen 1. *tr. V. (abmeißeln)* chisel off. 2. *refl. V.* push with one's feet; sich mit den Armen vom Boden ~: push oneself up from the floor with one's arms

ab|stempeln *tr. V.* a) frank ⟨*letter*⟩; cancel ⟨*stamp*⟩; der Brief war in Hamburg abgestempelt the letter had a Hamburg postmark; b) *(fig.)* jmdn. als *od.* zum Verbrecher/als geisteskrank ~: label *or* brand sb. as a criminal/as insane

ab|steppen *tr. V.* back-stitch

ab|sterben *unr. itr. V.; mit sein* a) *(eingehen, verfallen)* [gradually] die; *s. auch* abgestorben 2; b) *(gefühllos werden)* go numb; mir sind die Finger abgestorben my fingers have gone numb; c) *(verschwinden)* ⟨*custom, tradition*⟩ die out; ⟨*state, social order*⟩ wither away; d) *(ugs.: ausgehen)* ⟨*engine*⟩ die

Ab·stich der; *o. Pl.* a) *(das Abstechen)* cutting; b) *(Metall.)* tapping

Abstich-: ~loch das *(Metall.)* tapping hole; ~rinne die *(Metall.)* tapping spout

Ab·stieg der; ~[e]s, ~e a) descent; b) *(Niedergang)* decline; [sozialer *od.* gesellschaftlicher] ~: fall *or* drop in [social] status; c) *(Sport)* relegation; d) *(Weg abwärts)* way down

abstiegs·gefährdet *Adj. (Sport)* threatened with *or* facing relegation *postpos.*

Abstiegs·kandidat der *(Sportjargon)* candidate for relegation

ab|stillen 1. *tr. V.* wean. 2. *itr. V.* stop breast-feeding

ab|stimmen 1. *itr. V.* vote; es wird abgestimmt a vote is taken; geheim/namentlich/durch Handzeichen/durch Akklamation ~: vote by secret ballot/by roll-call/by a show of hands/by acclamation; über etw. *(Akk.)* ~: vote on sth.; über etw. *(Akk.)* ~ lassen put sth. to the vote. 2. *tr. V.* a) *(vereinbaren)*; etw. [miteinander] ~: discuss and agree on sth. [with each other]; etw. mit jmdm. ~: discuss and agree sth. with sb.; b) *(harmonisieren)* etw. auf etw. *(Akk.)* ~: suit sth. to sth.; *(Mode)* match sth. to sth.; etw. auf jmdn. ~: pitch sth. at sb.'s level; eine fein abgestimmte Mischung a finely balanced blend; zwei/mehrere Dinge aufeinander ~: make two/several things consistent with each other; Zeitpläne/Programme aufeinander ~: coordinate timetables/programmes; c) *(Rundf., Ferns.: einstellen)* tune; d) *(Kfz-W.)* tune [up]; adjust ⟨*carburettor*⟩. 3. *refl. V.* sich über etw. *(Akk.)* ~: discuss and agree on sth.

Ab·stimmung die a) *(Stimmabgabe)* vote; ballot; eine geheime ~: a secret ballot; zur ~ schreiten *(geh.) od.* kommen come to the vote; eine ~ [über etw. *(Akk.)*] durchführen take a vote [on sth.]; bei der ~: in the vote; *(während der ~)* during the voting; b) *(Absprache)* agreement; c) *(Harmonisierung)* coordination; d) *(Rundf., Ferns.)* tuning

Abstimmungs-: ~ergebnis das result of a/the vote; ~nieder·lage die defeat [in a/the vote]; ~sieg der victory [in a/the vote]

abstinent [apsti'nɛnt] *Adj.* **a)** teetotal; **~ sein** be a non-drinker *or* teetotaller; **b) sexuell ~:** sexually abstinent; continent; **politisch ~ sein** *(fig.)* abstain from politics
Abstinenz [apsti'nɛnts] **die; ~: a)** teetotalism; **~ üben** be teetotal; **b) sexuelle ~:** sexual abstinence; continence; **politische ~** *(fig.)* political abstinence
Abstinẹnzler der; ~s, ~: teetotaller; non-drinker
Abstinẹnzlertum das; ~s temperance
ạb|stoppen 1. *tr. V.* **a)** *(zum Stillstand bringen)* halt; stop; check ‹*advance*›; stop ‹*machine*›; **b)** *(mit der Stoppuhr)* **einen Läufer ~:** time a runner with a stop-watch; **die Zeit ~:** measure the time with a stop-watch. **2.** *itr. V.* come to a halt; ‹*person*› stop
Ạb·stoß der a) *(Fußball)* goal-kick; **den ~ ausführen** take the goal-kick; **b)** *(Sport: beim Springen)* take-off
ạb|stoßen 1. *unr. tr. V.* **a)** *(wegstoßen)* push off *or* away; **das Boot [vom Ufer] ~:** push the boat out [from the bank]; **b)** *(beschädigen)* chip ‹*crockery, paintwork, stucco, plaster*›; batter ‹*furniture*›; scuff ‹*shoes*›; *s. auch* **Horn; c)** *(verkaufen)* sell off; **d)** *(zurückweisen)* reject; **e)** *(Physik)* repel; **f)** *(anwidern)* repel; put off; **sich von jmdm./etw. abgestoßen fühlen** find sb./sth. repulsive. **2.** *unr. itr. V.* **a)** *mit sein od. haben (sich entfernen)* be pushed off; **b)** *(anwidern)* be repulsive. **3.** *refl. V.* **sich [vom Boden] ~:** push oneself off; *(beim Sprung)* take off
ạbstoßend *Adj.* repulsive
Ạbstoßung die; ~, ~en a) *(Physik, auch fig.)* repulsion; **b)** *(Verkauf)* sale; **c)** *(Med., Physiol.)* rejection
ạb|stottern *tr. V. (ugs.)* pay for in instalments; pay off ‹*debt*› by instalments; **er muß jeden Monat 400 DM ~:** he has to pay out 400 DM in instalments every month
ạb|strafen *tr. V.* punish
Ạbstrafung die; ~, ~en punishment
ạbstrahieren [apstra'hi:rən] **1.** *itr. V. (absehen)* **von etw. ~:** ignore sth.; leave sth. out of account. **2.** *tr., itr. V. (verallgemeinern)* abstract **(aus** from)
ạb|strahlen 1. *tr. V. (Physik)* radiate; *(Funkw., Elektrot.)* emit ‹*wave, frequency*›. **2.** *itr. V. (fig.)* **auf jmdn./etw. ~:** influence *or* affect sb./sth.
Ạb·strahlung die; ~ *(Physik)* radiation; *(Funkw., Elektrot.)* emission
abstrakt [ap'strakt] **1.** *Adj.* abstract. **2.** *adv.* abstractly; **~ denken** think in the abstract
Abstrạktheit die; ~: abstractness
Abstraktion [apstrak'tsio:n] **die; ~, ~en** abstraction
Abstraktiọns·vermögen das capacity for abstraction
Abstraktum [ap'straktʊm] **das; ~s, Abstrạkta a)** *(Philos.)* abstract[ion]; **b)** *(Sprachw.)* abstract noun
ạb|strampeln *refl. V. (ugs.)* **a)** *(beim Radfahren)* pedal; **sich** *(Dat.)* **einige Pfunde ~:** pedal off a few pounds; **b)** *s.* **abplacken**
ạb|streichen 1. *unr. tr. V.* **a)** *(abstreifen)* wipe; *(durch Streichen entfernen)* wipe off; **b)** *(ausstreichen)* cross off; **c)** *(abziehen)* knock off; **davon muß man die Hälfte ~** *(fig.)* you have to take it with a pinch *or* grain of salt; **d)** *(absuchen)* sweep ‹*horizon*›; comb ‹*terrain*›. **2.** *unr. itr. V.; mit sein (Jägerspr.)* fly away
Ạb·streicher der *s.* **Abtreter**
ạb|streifen *tr. V.* **a)** pull off; strip off ‹*berries*›; **sich** *(Dat.)* **die Handschuhe/den Ring ~:** take off *or* remove one's gloves/ring; **sich/jmdm. die Kleidung ~:** take off one's/sb.'s clothes; **die Asche [von der Zigarette/Zigarre] ~:** remove the ash [from one's cigarette/cigar]; **b)** *(abwischen)* wipe; *(durch Streifen entfernen)* wipe off; **seine** *od.* **sich** *(Dat.)* **die Schuhe/Sohlen ~:** wipe one's feet; **c)** *(absuchen)* comb **(nach** for)
Ạbstreifer der; ~s, ~ *s.* **Abtreter**
Ạbstreif·gitter das grille *(for removing excess paint from paint-roller)*
ạb|streiten *unr. tr. V.* deny; **~, etw. getan zu haben** deny that one has done sth.; **das läßt sich nicht ~:** there's no denying that; that cannot be denied; **das kann ihm keiner ~:** you cannot deny him that
Ạb·strich der a) *(Med.)* taking of a swab; **einen ~ machen** take a swab; **b)** *(Streichung, Kürzung)* cut; **~e [an etw.** *(Dat.)***] machen** make cuts [in sth.]; *(Einschränkungen machen)* make concessions [as regards sth.]; **c)** *(Musik)* down-stroke
ạb|strömen *itr. V.; mit sein* ‹*water*› flow away; ‹*air mass*› move away
abstrus [ap'stru:s] *Adj. (geh.)* abstruse; *(absurd)* absurd
ạb|stufen *tr. V.* **a)** *(in Stufen anlegen)* terrace ‹*slope, hill*›; layer ‹*hair*›; **b)** *(staffeln)* grade; **abgestufte Abschreckung** *(Milit.)* graduated deterrence; **c)** *(nuancieren)* differentiate; *(Kunstwiss.)* nuance
Ạb·stufung die; ~, ~en a) *(im Gelände)* terrace; **b)** *(Staffelung)* gradation; **die soziale ~:** the social hierarchy; **c)** *(Nuance)* shade; *(Nuancierung)* variety
ạb|stumpfen 1. *tr. V. (gefühllos machen)* deaden; *s. auch* **abgestumpft 2. 2.** *itr. V.; mit sein (gefühllos werden)* **man stumpft ab** one's mind becomes deadened; **gegen etw. ~:** become dead to sth.; **der Gerechtigkeitssinn stumpft ab** one's sense of justice becomes blunted
Ạb·sturz der a) fall; **b)** *(eines Flugzeugs)* crash; **ein Flugzeug zum ~ bringen** cause a plane to crash; **c)** *(Steilhang)* precipice
ạb|stürzen *itr. V.; mit sein* **a)** fall; ‹*aircraft, pilot, passenger*› crash; **tödlich ~:** fall/crash to one's death; **b)** *(geh.: abfallen)* ‹*cliff*› plunge
Ạbsturz·stelle die site of the [aircraft] crash
ạb|stützen 1. *refl. V.* support oneself **(mit** on, **an** + *Dat.* against); **sich von etw. ~:** push oneself away from sth. **2.** *tr. V.* support; *(Bauw.: gegen Einsturz)* shore up; *(fig.: untermauern)* support; back up
Ạb·stützung die *(Bauw.)* shores *pl.*
ạb|suchen *tr. V.* **a)** search **(nach** for); *(durchkämmen)* comb **(nach** for); drag ‹*pond, river, etc.*› **(nach** for); **den Himmel/Horizont ~:** scan the sky/horizon **(nach** for); **b)** *(absammeln)* **etw. von etw. ~:** pick sth. off sth.; **jmdm. die Läuse ~:** look for lice on sb.
Ạb·sud ['apzu:t] **der; ~[e]s, ~e** *(veralt.)* decoction
absurd [ap'zʊrt] *Adj.* absurd; **~es Theater** Theatre of the Absurd
absụrderweise *Adv.* absurdly enough
Absurdität [apzʊrdi'tɛ:t] **die; ~, ~en** absurdity; *(Ungereimtheit)* inconsistency
Abszeß [aps'tsɛs] **der** *(österr. auch:* **das**); **Abszẹsses, Abszẹsse a)** *(Med.)* abscess; **b)** *(Geschwür)* ulcer
Abszisse [aps'tsɪsə] **die; ~, ~en** *(Math.)* abscissa
Abszịssen·achse die *(Math.)* axis of abscissae
Abt [apt] **der; ~[e]s, Äbte** ['ɛptə] abbot
Abt. *Abk.* **Abteilung**
ab|takeln ['apta:kl̩n] *tr. V. (Seemannsspr.)* unrig ‹*ship*›; *s. auch* **abgetakelt 2**
ạb|tasten *tr. V.* **etw. ~:** feel sth. all over; **jmdn. auf Waffen** *(Akk.)* **~:** frisk sb. for weapons
Ạbtast·nadel die, Ạbtast·stift der stylus
Ạbtau·automatik die *(Elektrot.)* automatic defrost
ạb|tauchen *itr. V.* **a)** *(Seemannsspr.)* submerge; **b)** *(ugs.)* **[in die Illegalität** *od.* **in den Untergrund] ~:** go underground
ạb|tauen 1. *itr. V.; mit sein (wegschmelzen)* melt away; *(eis-/schneefrei werden)* become clear of ice/snow; ‹*refrigerator*› defrost. **2.** *tr. V. (schnee-/eisfrei machen)* melt; thaw; de-ice ‹*vehicle windows*›; **den Schnee/das Eis von etw. ~:** melt the snow/ice off sth.; **einen Kühlschrank ~:** defrost a refrigerator
Ạb·tausch der; *o. Pl.* **a)** *(Schach)* exchange; **b)** *s.* **Schlagabtausch; c)** *(schweiz.) s.* **Tausch**
ạb|tauschen *tr. V.* **a)** *(Schach)* exchange; **b) jmdm. etw. ~:** get sth. from sb. by swapping; **c)** *(schweiz.) s.* **tauschen**
Abtei [ap'tai] **die; ~, ~en** abbey
Abtei·kirche die abbey[-church]
Abteil das; ~[e]s, ~e compartment; *(eines Regals)* shelf; **ein ~ erster/zweiter Klasse** a first/second-class compartment
ạb|teilen *tr. V.* **a)** *(aufteilen)* divide [up]; **b)** *(abtrennen)* divide off
Abteil-: ~fenster das compartment window; **~tür die** compartment door
[1]**Ab·teilung die;** *o. Pl.* dividing off
[2]**Ab·teilung die a)** department; *(einer Behörde)* department; section; **die ~ für Vor- und Frühgeschichte** the department of prehistory and early history; **b)** *(Zool.)* phylum; *(Bot.)* division; **c)** *(Milit.)* unit, **d)** *(veralt.: Teil)* part
-abteilung die ... department
Abteilungs·leiter der head of department/section; departmental manager
ạb|telefonieren *itr. V.* **[jmdm.] ~:** phone [sb.] to say one cannot come
ạb|telegrafieren *itr. V.* **[jmdm.] ~:** send [sb.] a telegram to say one cannot come
ạb|teufen *tr. V. (Bergbau)* sink
ạb|tippen *tr. V. (ugs.)* type out
Äbtissin [ɛp'tɪsɪn] **die; ~, ~nen** abbess
ạb|tönen *tr. V.* tint; *(Sprachw.)* shift
Ạbtön·farbe die tinting colour
Ạb·tönung die a) *o. Pl. (das Abtönen)* tinting; *(Sprachw.)* vowel-shift; **b)** *(Farbton)* tone; shade
Ạbtönungs·partikel die *(Sprachw.)* modal particle
ạb|töten *tr. V.* destroy ‹*parasites, germs*›; deaden ‹*nerve, feeling*›; mortify ‹*desire*›
Ạb·tötung die; ~ *s.* **abtöten:** destruction; deadening; mortification
ạb|traben *itr. V.; mit sein* trot off *or* away
Abtrag ['aptra:k] **der; ~[e]s** *(geh., veralt.)* **einer Sache** *(Dat.)* **~ tun** be detrimental to sth.
ạb|tragen *unr. tr. V.* **a)** *(abnutzen)* wear out; *s. auch* **abgetragen 2; b)** *(geh.: abräumen)* clear away; **c)** *(einebnen)* level; *(Geol.)* erode; **d)** *(abbauen)* demolish; *(zum Wiederaufbau)* take down; **e)** *(geh.: abbezahlen)* discharge ‹*debt*›; pay off ‹*loan*›; **f)** *(Med.) (entfernen)* remove; *(abbauen)* disperse
abträgig ['aptrɛ:gɪç] *(schweiz.),* **abträglich** ['aptrɛ:klɪç] *Adj. (geh.)* detrimental; harmful; *(nachteilig)* unfavourable; **einer Sache** *(Dat.)* **~ sein** be detrimental *or* harmful to sth.; **~e Kritik** unfavourable criticism
Ạbtragung die; ~, ~en a) *(das Einebnen)* levelling; *(Geol.)* erosion; **b)** *(das Abbauen)* demolition; *(zum Wiederaufbau)* taking down; **d)** *(geh.: das Abbezahlen)* discharge; **e)** *(Med.: Entfernung)* removal; *(Abbau)* dispersal
ạb|trainieren 1. *itr. V.* gradually reduce one's training schedule. **2.** *tr. V.* **Fett/Pfunde ~:** get rid of fat/pounds
Ạb·transport der *s.* **abtransportieren:** taking away; removal; dispatch
ạb|transportieren *tr. V.* take away; remove ‹*dead, injured*›; *(befördern)* dispatch ‹*goods*›
ạb|treiben 1. *unr. tr. V.* **a)** *(wegtreiben)* carry away; **jmdn./ein Schiff vom Kurs ~:** drive *or* carry sb./a ship off course; **der Wind hat den Ballon nach Westen abgetrieben** the wind carried the balloon westwards; **b)** abort ‹*foetus*›; **ein Kind ~ lassen** have an abortion; **c)** *(zu Tal treiben)* bring

down; **d)** *(Med.: abgehen lassen)* expel; **e)** *(österr. Kochk.: rühren)* beat. **2.** *unr. itr. V.* **a)** *mit sein (weggetrieben werden)* be carried away; ‹*ship*› be carried off course; **b)** *(einen Abort vornehmen lassen)* have an abortion; *(Aborte vornehmen)* carry out *or* perform abortions

Ạbtreibung die; ~, ~en abortion

Ạbtreibungs-: ~paragraph der abortion law *(Section 218 of the West German criminal code);* ≈ Abortion Act; **~tourismus der** *travelling to another country or state in order to obtain an abortion;* **~verbot das** ban on abortion; **~versuch der** attempted abortion

ạb|trennen *tr. V.* **a)** detach; sever ‹*arm, leg, etc.*›; cut off ‹*button, collar, etc.*›; detach, tear off ‹*paper, voucher*›; **b)** *(abteilen, absondern)* divide off; **c)** *(Rechtsw.)* **ein Verfahren ~:** decide to handle a prosecution separately

ạbtretbar *Adj. (Rechtsw.)* transferable; cedable ‹*territory*›

ạb|treten 1. *unr. tr. V.* **a) sich** *(Dat.)* **die Füße/Schuhe ~:** wipe one's feet; **sich** *(Dat.)* **den Schnee/den Schmutz von den Schuhen ~:** wipe the snow/dirt off one's feet; **b)** *(überlassen)* **jmdm. etw. ~:** let sb. have sth.; **c)** *(Rechtsw.)* transfer; cede ‹*territory*›; **d)** *(abnutzen)* wear down. **2.** *unr. itr. V.; mit sein* **a)** *(Milit.)* dismiss; **b)** *(Theater, auch fig.)* exit; make one's exit; **XY tritt ab/die Arbeiter treten ab** exit XY/exeunt workers; **von der Bühne ~** *(fig.)* step down; leave the arena; **c)** *(zurücktreten)* step down; ‹*monarch*› abdicate; **d)** *(verhüll.: sterben)* make one's exit. **3.** *unr. refl. V. (sich abnutzen)* become worn; **sich leicht/schnell ~:** wear [out] easily/quickly

Ạbtreter der; ~s, ~: doormat

Ạbtretung die; ~, ~en *(Rechtsw.)* transfer; *(eines Staatsgebiets)* cession; **Deutschland wurde zur ~ Westpreußens gezwungen** Germany was forced to cede West Prussia

Ạb·trieb der a) *(Vieh~)* bringing down of cattle; **beim ~:** when bringing the cattle down; **b)** *(österr. Kochk.)* mixture

Ạb·trift die; ~, ~en *s.* **Abdrift**

ạb|trinken 1. *unr. tr. V.* drink off; **einen Schluck ~:** take a sip *(from a full glass).* **2.** *unr. itr. V.* take a sip *(from a full glass)*

Ạb·tritt der a) *(Theater)* exit; **b)** *(Rücktritt)* resignation; **c)** *(veralt.: Toilette)* privy *(arch.)*

Ạbtrocken·tuch das; *Pl.* **-tücher** tea-towel

ạb|trocknen 1. *tr. V.* dry; **das Geschirr ~:** dry the dishes; **sich** *(Dat.)* **die Hände/das Gesicht/die Tränen ~:** dry one's hands/face/tears; **ich muß noch [das Geschirr] ~:** I still have to dry the dishes. **2.** *itr. V.; mit sein (trocken werden)* dry off

Ạbtropf·brett das draining-board *(Brit.);* drainboard *(Amer.)*

ạb|tropfen *itr. V.; mit sein* drip off; ‹*lettuce, dishes*› drain; ‹*clothing*› drip-dry; **von etw. ~:** drip off sth.

ạb|trotzen *tr. V.* **jmdm. etw. ~:** wrest sth. from sb.

ạb|trudeln *itr. V.* **a)** *(Fliegerspr.)* go down in a spin; **b)** *(ugs.: weggehen)* push off *or* along *(coll.)*

ạbtrünnig *Adj. (einer Partei)* renegade; *(einer Religion, Sekte)* apostate; **ein ~er Vasall** a disloyal vassal; **der Kirche/dem Glauben ~ werden** desert the Church/the faith

Ạbtrünnige der/die; *adj. Dekl. (einer Partei)* renegade; deserter; *(einer Religion, Sekte)* apostate; turncoat

Ạbtrünnigkeit die; ~: apostasy; *(Treulosigkeit)* disloyalty **(von** to)

ạb|tun *unr. tr. V.* **a)** *(beiseite schieben)* dismiss; **etw. mit einer Handbewegung ~:** wave sth. aside; **b)** *(erledigen)* **damit ist die Sache abgetan** that's the end of the matter

ạb|tupfen *tr. V.* dab away; **sich/jmdm. die Tränen ~:** dab away one's/sb.'s tears; **sich** *(Dat.)* **die Stirn/Mundwinkel ~:** dab one's brow/the corners of one's mouth

ạb|urteilen *tr. V.* pass judgement on; *(fig.)* condemn

Ạburteilung die; ~, ~en passing of judgement (+ *Gen.* on); condemnation; *(fig.)* condemnation

ABV [a:be:ˈfau̯] **der;** ~[s], ~[s] *(DDR) s.* **Abschnittsbevollmächtigte**

Ạb·verkauf der *(österr., südd.)* sale

ạb|verkaufen *tr. V. (österr., südd.)* sell off

ạb|verlangen *tr. V.* **jmdm. etw. ~:** demand sth. of sb.; **jmdm. Geld ~:** demand money from sb.; **es wird Ihnen einige Mühe ~:** it will cost you some effort

ạb|wägen *unr. od. regelm. tr., itr. V.* **a)** weigh up; **zwei Dinge gegeneinander ~:** weigh two things against each other; **die Vor- und Nachteile gegeneinander ~:** weigh the advantages and disadvantages; **lange ~:** weigh things/the problem *etc.* up for a long time; *s. auch* **abgewogen 2; b)** *(veralt.) s.* **abwiegen**

ạbwägend 1. *Adj.* appraising. **2.** *adv.* appraisingly; **er sah mich kritisch-~ an** he looked at me, sizing me up critically

Ạb·wahl die voting out; **seit seiner ~:** since he was voted out

ạbwählbar *Adj.* **er/dieses Fach ist [nicht] ~:** he can[not] be voted out/this subject can[not] be dropped

ạb|wählen *tr. V.* vote out; drop ‹*school subject*›; **sechs Leute wurden aus dem Ausschuß abgewählt** six members of the committee were not re-elected

ạb|wälzen *tr. V.* pass on **(auf** + *Akk.* to); shift ‹*blame, responsibility*› **(auf** + *Akk.* on to)

ạbwandelbar *Adj.* **a)** *(variierbar)* modifiable; **ein unendlich ~es Motiv/Thema** a motif/theme capable of infinite variation; **b)** *(Sprachw. veralt.) s.* **flektierbar**

ạb|wandeln *tr. V.* **a)** *(variieren)* adapt; modify; **b)** *(Sprachw. veralt.) s.* **flektieren**

ạb|wandern 1. *itr. V.; mit sein* **a)** migrate **(aus** from, **in** + *Akk.* to); *(in ein anderes Land)* emigrate **(aus** from, **in** + *Akk.* to); **b)** *(fig.)* move over; ‹*capital*› be transferred; **in einen anderen Beruf ~:** move into a different job; **viele Spieler wandern aus der Liga ab** many players are leaving the league; **c)** *(Met.)* move away. **2.** *tr. V.; mit sein od. haben (wandernd zurücklegen)* walk *or* hike over; walk ‹*route*›

Ạb·wanderung die a) migration **(aus** from, **in** + *Akk.* to); *(in ein anderes Land)* emigration **(aus** from, **in** + *Akk.* to); **b)** *(fig.)* moving over; **~ in einen anderen Beruf** movement into a different job; **~ des Kapitals** transfer of capital; **die ~ der Spieler aus der Liga** the departure of players from the league

Ạbwanderungs·verlust der *(Soziol.)* population drain

Ạb·wandlung die adaptation; modification; *(Variante)* variation; **in ~ eines Wortes von Goethe** adapting a saying of Goethe's

Ạb·wärme die *(Technik)* waste heat

Ạb·wart der; ~s, ~e *(schweiz.)* caretaker

ạb|warten 1. *itr. V.* wait; **sie warteten ab** they awaited events; **warte ab!** wait and see; *(als Drohung)* just you wait!; **warten wir [erst mal] ab** let's wait and see; **sich ~d verhalten** adopt an attitude of 'wait and see'; **eine ~de Haltung einnehmen** decide to await events; **~ und Tee trinken** *(ugs. scherzh.)* wait and see what happens. **2.** *tr. V.* **a)** *(warten auf)* wait for; **wir müssen die Entwicklung der Dinge ~:** we must wait and see how things develop; **das bleibt [noch] abzuwarten** only time will tell; **b)** *(warten auf das Ende von)* **etw. ~:** wait for sth. to end

ạbwärts [ˈapvɛrts] *Adv.* downwards; *(den Berg hinunter)* downhill; *(den Fluß hinunter)* downstream; **der Fahrstuhl fährt ~:** the lift is going down; „~" 'going down'; **vom Major [an] ~:** from the major down

-abwärts *Adv.* **[weiter] rhein~/mosel~:** further down the Rhine/Mosel; **rhein~/mosel~ segeln** sail down the Rhine/Moselle

ạbwärts-, Ạbwärts-: ~entwicklung die deterioration; **die anhaltende ~entwicklung** the downward slide; **~|gehen** *unr. itr. V.; mit sein* **mit ihm/dem Land/ihrer Gesundheit geht es ~:** he/the country is going downhill/her health is deteriorating; **seit damals ging es eigentlich immer nur ~:** from that time on things really only got worse; **~trend der** downward trend

[1]**Abwasch** [ˈapvaʃ] **der;** ~[e]s **a)** *(das Geschirrspülen)* washing-up *(Brit.);* washing dishes *(Amer.);* **den ~ machen** do the washing-up/wash the dishes; **wir erledigen das gleichzeitig, das ist dann ein ~** *(ugs.)* we'll deal with that at the same time, and so kill two birds with one stone; **b)** *(schmutziges Geschirr)* dirty dishes *pl.*

[2]**Ạbwasch die;** ~, ~en *(österr.)* sink

ạbwaschbar *Adj.* washable

Ạbwasch·becken das sink

ạb|waschen 1. *unr. tr. V.* wash off; wash [up] ‹*dishes*›; wash down ‹*surface*›; **etw. von etw. ~:** wash sth. off sth.; **sich** *(Dat.)* **den Schmutz/das Blut ~:** wash the dirt/blood off oneself; **sich** *(Dat.)* **die Hände/sein Gesicht ~:** wash one's hands/face; **eine Schmach ~** *(fig.)* wipe out a disgrace. **2.** *unr. itr. V.* wash up, do the washing-up *(Brit.);* wash the dishes *(Amer.)*

Ạbwasch-: ~lappen der dishcloth; **~mittel das** *s.* **Spülmittel; ~tuch das** *s.* **~lappen; ~wasser das** *s.* **Spülwasser b**

Ạb·wasser das; *Pl.* **-wässer** sewage; **industrielle Abwässer** industrial effluent *sing.*

Ạbwasser-: ~auf·bereitung die sewage treatment; **~beseitigung die** disposal of sewage; **~kanal der** sewer; **~reinigung die** sewage purification

ạb|wechseln *refl., itr. V.* alternate; **die beiden wechselten sich ab** the two of them took turns; **ich wechsle mich mit ihr beim Geschirrspülen ab** she and I take it in turns to do the dishes; **Regen und Sonne wechselten miteinander ab** it rained and was sunny by turns

ạbwechselnd *Adv.* alternately

Ạbwechslung die; ~, ~en *(Wechsel)* change; *(Zerstreuung)* **etwas/wenig ~:** some/not much variety; **zur ~:** for a change; **die ~ lieben** *(verhüll.)* like a bit of variety

ạbwechslungs-: ~arm 1. *Adj.* monotonous; **2.** *adv.* monotonously; **~halber** *Adv.* for a change; **~los 1.** *Adj.* unvaried; **~los sein** lack variety; **2.** *adv.* monotonously; **~reich 1.** *Adj.* varied; **2.** *adv.* **der Urlaub verlief sehr ~reich** the holiday *or (Amer.)* vacation was full of variety; **sich ~reich ernähren** eat a varied diet; **nicht sonderlich ~reich** without much variety; **~weise** *Adv. s.* **abwechselnd**

Ạb·weg der error; **auf ~e kommen** *od.* **geraten** go astray; **jmdn. auf ~e führen** lead sb. astray

ạbwegig *Adj. (irrig, unzutreffend)* erroneous; false ‹*suspicion*›; *(falsch, abzulehnen)* mistaken; wrong; *(ungewöhnlich)* outlandish; exceptional ‹*case*›

Ạbwegigkeit die; ~, ~en *s.* **abwegig:** erroneousness; falseness; mistakenness; wrongness; outlandishness; exceptionalness

Ạb·wehr die; ~ **a)** *(Ablehnung)* hostility; **b)** *(Zurückweisung)* repulsion; *(von Schlägen)* fending off; **c)** *(Widerstand)* resistance; **d)** *(Milit.: Geheimdienst)* counter-intelligence; **er ist bei der ~:** he is in counter-intelligence; **e)** *(Sport) (Hintermannschaft)*

defence; *(~aktion)* clearance; clearing *(Amer.)*

ạbwehr-, Ạbwehr-: ~bereit *Adj.* ready to take defensive action *postpos.*; **~bereitschaft die** readiness to take defensive action; **~dienst der** counter-intelligence service

ạb|wehren 1. *tr. V.* **a)** *(zurückschlagen)* repulse; fend off, parry ⟨*blow*⟩; *(Sport)* clear ⟨*ball, shot*⟩; save ⟨*match point*⟩; **b)** *(abwenden)* avert ⟨*danger, consequences*⟩; **c)** *(von sich weisen)* avert ⟨*suspicion*⟩; deny ⟨*rumour*⟩; decline ⟨*thanks*⟩; **d)** *(fernhalten)* deter; **um die Blicke Neugieriger abzuwehren** [in order] to give protection from the stares of inquisitive people. **2.** *itr. V.* **a)** *(Sport)* clear; **zur Ecke ~:** clear the ball and give away *or* concede a corner; **b)** *(ablehnend reagieren)* demur; **eine ~de Geste** *od.* **Handbewegung** a deprecatory gesture

Ạbwehr-: ~kampf der defensive action; *(über längere Zeit)* defence; **~kraft die** power of resistance; **~mechanismus der** *(Psychoanalyse, Physiol.)* defence mechanism; **~reaktion die** *(Physiol., fig.)* defensive reaction; **~spieler der** *(Sport)* defender

¹ạb|weichen *unr. itr. V.; mit sein* **a)** deviate; **b)** *(sich unterscheiden)* differ; **voneinander ~:** differ from each other; **~des Verhalten** *(Soziol.)* deviant behaviour

²ạb|weichen 1. *itr. V.; mit sein* soften and come off. **2.** *tr. V.* soak off

Abweichler ['apvaịçlɐ] **der; ~s, ~** *(Politik)* deviationist

ạbweichlerisch *Adj. (Politik)* deviationist

Ạbweichlertum das; ~s *(Politik)* deviationism *no art*

Ạbweichung die; ~, ~en a) deviation; **~en von der Geschäftsordnung** departures from the standing orders; **in ~** *(Dat.)* **von** in contrast with; **die ~ der Magnetnadel** the variation of the compass needle; **b)** *(Unterschied)* difference

ạb|weiden *tr. V.* crop; browse ⟨*twigs, leaves*⟩; *(abgrasen)* graze

ạb|weisen *unr. tr. V.* **a)** turn away; turn down ⟨*applicant, suitor*⟩; **b)** *(ablehnen)* reject; dismiss ⟨*action, case, complaint*⟩; disallow ⟨*claim*⟩

ạbweisend 1. *Adj.* cold ⟨*look, tone of voice*⟩; negative ⟨*reply*⟩; **in ~em Ton** coldly. **2.** *adv.* coldly

Ạb·weisung die; ~, ~en *s.* **abweisen:** turning away; turning down; rejection; dismissal; disallowance

ạb|wenden 1. *unr. od. regelm. tr. V.* **a)** *(wegwenden)* turn away; **den Blick ~:** look away; avert one's gaze; **die Augen von etw. nicht ~ können** not be able to take one's eyes off sth.; **mit abgewendetem Kopf** with his/her head turned away; **b)** *nur regelm. (verhindern)* avert; **etw. von jmdm. ~:** protect sb. from sth. **2.** *unr. od. regelm. refl. V.* **a)** turn away; **b)** *(fig.)* **sich von jmdm. ~:** turn one's back on sb.; *(sich jmdm. allmählich entfremden)* become estranged from sb.

Ạb·wendung die a) *(Abkehr)* **seit seiner ~ vom Sozialismus** since he turned away from socialism; **die ~ von der bisherigen Politik** turning away from previous policy; **b)** *(Verhinderung)* **zur ~ einer Sache** *(Gen.)* in order to avert sth.

ạb|werben *unr. tr. V.* lure away; entice away; **jmdn. jmdm. ~:** lure *or* entice sb. away from sb.

Ạbwerber der; ~s, ~, Ạbwerberin die; ~, ~nen recruiter *(enticing people away from their existing employment)*

Ạb·werbung die enticement (bei from)

ạb|werfen *unr. tr. V.* **a)** *(herunterwerfen)* drop; ⟨*tree*⟩ shed ⟨*leaves, needles*⟩; ⟨*stag*⟩ shed ⟨*antlers*⟩; throw off ⟨*clothing*⟩; jettison ⟨*ballast*⟩; throw ⟨*rider*⟩; *(Kartenspiel)* discard; **das Joch der Knechtschaft/Tyrannei** *usw.* **~** *(fig. geh.)* throw or cast off the yoke of bondage/tyranny *etc.*; *s. auch* **Maske a; b)** *(herunterstoßen)* knock down; **c)** *(ins Spielfeld werfen)* throw out ⟨*ball*⟩; **d)** *(einbringen)* bring in; **Profit ~:** make a profit; **viel/wenig ~:** show a big/only a small profit. **2.** *unr. itr. V. (Sport)* throw the ball out

ạb|werten 1. *tr., itr. V.* devalue. **2.** *tr. V. (fig.: herabwürdigen)* run down; belittle

ạbwertend 1. *Adj.* derogatory. **2.** *adv.* derogatorily; in a derogatory way

Ạb·wertung die a) devaluation; **b)** *(fig.: Herabwürdigung)* reduction in status; *(eines Begriffs)* debasement; **eine ~ erfahren** lose status; **das soll keine ~ sein** that wasn't meant in any derogatory sense

ạbwesend 1. *Adj.* **a)** *(nicht zugegen)* absent; **b)** *(zerstreut)* absent-minded. **2.** *adv.* absent-mindedly

Ạbwesende der/die; *adj. Dekl.* absentee

Ạbwesenheit die; ~ a) *(Fehlen)* absence; **in ~** *(Rechtsw.)* in his/her/their absence; **durch ~ glänzen** *(iron.)* be conspicuous by one's absence; **b)** *(fig.: Zerstreutheit)* absent-mindedness

Ạb·wetter *Pl. (Bergbau)* foul air

ạb|wettern *tr. V. (Seemannsspr., auch fig.)* weather

ạb|wetzen 1. *tr. V., refl. V.* wear away; *s. auch* **abgewetzt 2. 2.** *itr. V.; mit sein (ugs.: weglaufen)* bolt; scarper *(Brit. sl.)*

ạb|wichsen *tr. V. (derb)* **sich** *(Dat.)* **einen ~:** wank *(Brit. coarse)*; jerk [oneself] off *(coarse)*; **jmdm. einen ~:** jerk sb. off *(coarse)*; wank sb. *(Brit. coarse)*

ạb|wickeln 1. *tr. V.* **a)** *(herunterwickeln)* unwind; **b)** *(erledigen)* deal with ⟨*case*⟩; do ⟨*business*⟩; *(im Auftrag)* handle ⟨*correspondence*⟩; conduct, handle ⟨*transaction, negotiations*⟩; **c)** *(organisieren)* stage. **2.** *refl. V.* **a)** *(sich abspulen)* unwind [itself]; **b)** *(durchgeführt werden)* take place; *(mit Erfolg)* go off

Ạbwicklung die; ~, ~en a) *s.* **abwickeln 1 b:** dealing (*Gen.* with); doing; handling; conducting; **b)** *(Organisation)* staging; **für eine reibungslose ~ der Veranstaltung sorgen** see to it that the function goes off smoothly; **c)** *(Kaufmannsspr., Rechtsw.: Liquidation)* liquidation

ạb|wiegeln 1. *tr. V.* **a)** pacify; calm down ⟨*crowd*⟩; **b)** *(abwertend)* appease. **2.** *itr. V.* **a)** calm things down; **b)** *(etw. herunterspielen)* play down the issue

ạb|wiegen *unr. tr. V.* weigh out; weigh ⟨*single item*⟩

Ạbwiegler der; ~s, ~: a) peacemaker; **b)** *(abwertend)* appeaser

Ạbwieglung die; ~, ~en a) conciliation; **b)** *(abwertend)* appeasement

ạb|wimmeln *tr. V. (ugs.)* get rid of ⟨*person*⟩; get out of ⟨*duty, responsibility, etc.*⟩

Ạb·wind der a) *(Met.)* katabatic wind; **b)** *(Flugw.)* downwash

ạb|winkeln *unr. tr. V.* bend; **mit abgewinkelten** *(in die Hüfte gestützten)* **Armen** with arms akimbo

ạb|winken 1. *itr. V. (2. Part. landsch. od. scherzh.: abgewunken)* **apathisch/uninteressiert ~:** wave it/them aside apathetically/uninterestedly; **2.** *tr. V. (Motorsport)* **ein Rennen ~:** wave the chequered flag; *(bei einer Unterbrechung)* stop a race; **einen Fahrer ~:** wave *or* flag down a driver

ạb|wirtschaften *itr. V.* **endgültig abgewirtschaftet haben** have gone to the wall; be finished for good; *s. auch* **abgewirtschaftet 2**

ạb|wischen *tr. V.* **a)** *(wegwischen)* wipe away; **sich/jmdm. etw. ~:** wipe sth. off oneself/sb.; **sich/jmdm. den Schweiß von der Stirn ~:** wipe off the sweat from one's/sb.'s forehead; **Staub von den Regalen ~:** wipe off dust from the shelves; **sich/jmdm. die Tränen ~:** dry one's/sb.'s tears; **b)** *(säubern)* wipe; **sich/jmdm. die Nase/die Hände** *usw.* **~:** wipe one's/sb.'s nose/hands *etc.* (an + *Dat.* on); **damit können Sie sich den Hintern** *od.* **den Arsch ~** *(derb)* you know where you can stick that *(sl.)*; *(es ist wertlos)* you might as well wipe your arse *(Brit.) or (Amer.)* ass with it *(coarse)*

ạb|wohnen *tr. V.* **a)** wear out ⟨*furniture*⟩; make ⟨*flat, house, room*⟩ shabby; **abgewohnt** shabby; **b)** use up ⟨*rent*⟩

ạb|wracken ['apvrakn̩] *tr. V.* scrap; *s. auch* **abgewrackt 2**

Ạb·wurf der a) dropping; *(von Ballast)* jettisoning; **nach zwei Abwürfen wollte er nicht mehr reiten** after being thrown twice he didn't want to do any more riding; **b)** *(Fußball)* **beim ~ stolperte der Torwart** the goalkeeper stumbled as he threw the ball out; **c)** *(Handball, Wasserball)* goal throw; **d)** *(Speer-, Diskus-, Hammerwurf)* delivery; **e)** *(Hochsprung)* failure; **f)** *(Springreiten)* fault

ạb|würgen *tr. V. (ugs.)* stifle; choke off; squash ⟨*proposal*⟩; stall ⟨*car, engine*⟩

ạb|zahlen *tr. V.* pay off ⟨*debt, loan*⟩; pay for ⟨*home, car, etc.*⟩

ạb|zählen 1. *tr. V.* count; **„bitte das Fahrgeld abgezählt bereithalten!"** 'please tender exact fare'. **2.** *itr. V.* **a)** *(Sport, Milit.)* number off; **zu zweien/vieren ~:** number off in twos/fours; **b)** *(mit Abzählreim)* count out

Abzähl·reim der counting-out rhyme

Ạb·zahlung die; ~, ~en paying off; repayment; **etw. auf ~ kaufen/verkaufen** buy/sell sth. on easy terms *or (Brit.)* on HP

Ạbzahlungs-: ~kauf der credit *or* hire purchase; **~rate die** repayment; instalment

Ạbzähl·vers der *s.* **Abzählreim**

ạb|zapfen *tr. V.* tap ⟨*beer, wine*⟩; let, draw off ⟨*blood*⟩; draw off ⟨*petrol*⟩; **Strom ~:** tap the electricity supply; **jmdm. Geld ~** *(ugs.)* touch sb. for some money *(sl.)*

ạb|zappeln *refl. V. (fig. ugs.)* flog oneself; slave away

ạb|zäumen *tr. V.* unbridle

ạb|zäunen *tr. V.* fence off

Ạbzäunung die; ~, ~en a) *o. Pl.* fencing off; **b)** *(Zaun)* fencing

Ạbzehrung die; ~, ~en *(veralt.)* wasting away; cachexia *(Med.)*; **er starb an ~:** he wasted away and died

Ạb·zeichen das a) *(Kennzeichen)* emblem; *(fig.)* badge; **militärische ~:** military insignia; **b)** *(Anstecknadel, Plakette)* badge

ạb|zeichnen 1. *tr. V.* **a)** *(nachzeichnen, kopieren)* copy; **b)** *(signieren)* initial. **2.** *refl. V.* stand out; *(fig.)* begin to emerge; *(drohend)* loom

Ạbzieh·bild das transfer

ạb|ziehen 1. *unr. tr. V.* **a)** pull off; peel off ⟨*skin*⟩; strip ⟨*bed*⟩; **ein Laken/das Bettzeug ~:** pull off a sheet/the bedclothes; **b)** *(Fot.)* make a print/prints of; **zweimal ~:** make two prints of; **c)** *(Druckw.)* run off; **etw. 50mal ~:** run off 50 copies of sth.; **d)** *(Milit., auch fig.)* withdraw; **e)** *(subtrahieren)* subtract; take away *(abrechnen)* deduct; *(kassieren)* charge for; **jmdm. zuviel ~:** overcharge sb.; **davon kannst du die Hälfte/das meiste ~** *(ugs.)* you have to take it with a pinch of salt; **f)** *(ugs.: abnehmen, ausziehen)* take off; **g)** *(schälen)* peel ⟨*peach, almond, tomato*⟩; string ⟨*runner bean*⟩; **h)** *(häuten)* skin; **i) eine Handgranate ~:** pull the pin of a hand-grenade; **j)** *(herausziehen)* take out ⟨*key*⟩; **k)** *(abfüllen)* **Wein auf Flaschen ~:** bottle wine; **l)** *(glätten)* **Parkett ~:** sand [down] parquet flooring; **ein Messer/Rasiermesser ~:** sharpen a knife/razor; **m)** *(Kochk.)* thicken; **n)** *(salopp: veranstalten)* throw ⟨*party*⟩; crack ⟨*joke*⟩; *s. auch* **Schau b. 2.** *unr. itr. V.* **a)** *mit sein (sich verflüchtigen)* escape; *(Met.)* move away; **b)** *mit sein (Milit.)* withdraw; **c)** *mit sein (ugs.: weggehen)* push off *(sl.)*; go away; **d)** *mit sein (ugs.: beschleunigen)* **der**

Wagen zieht vielleicht ab the car really takes off; **e)** *(abdrücken)* fire

Abzieher der; ~s, ~ *(Druckw.)* proof-puller

Abzieh·presse die *(Druckw.)* proof[ing]-press

ab|zielen *itr. V.* **auf etw.** *(Akk.)* **~:** be aimed at *or* directed towards sth.

ab|zirkeln *tr. V.* measure off ‹*area, section*›; *(fig.)* delineate; measure ‹*words*›; *s. auch* **abgezirkelt 2, 3**

ab|zischen *itr. V.; mit sein (salopp)* shoot off; **zisch ab!** *(verschwinde!)* beat it! *(sl.)*; push off! *(sl.)*

ab|zittern *itr. V.; mit sein (salopp)* beat it *(sl.)*; push off *(sl.)*

ab|zotteln *itr. V.; mit sein (ugs.)* trot off *or* away

Ab·zug der a) *(an einer Schußwaffe)* trigger; **die Hand** *od.* **den Finger am ~ haben** *(auch fig.)* have one's finger on the trigger; **b)** *(Fot.)* print; **c)** *(Druckw.)* proof; **d)** *(Verminderung, Abgabe)* deduction; **etw. in ~ bringen** deduct sth.; **e)** *o. Pl. (Abmarsch, auch fig.)* withdrawal; **jmdm. freien ~ gewähren** give sb. free passage; **f)** *(Öffnung für Rauch usw.)* vent; **g)** *o. Pl. (von Rauch usw.)* escape

abzüglich ['aptsy:klɪç] *Präp. mit Gen. (Kaufmannsspr.)* less; **~ 3% Rabatt** *od.* **Rabatt von 3%** less 3% discount

abzugs-, Abzugs-: ~fähig *Adj. (Steuerw.)* [tax-]deductible; **~frei** *Adj. (Steuerw.)* tax-free; **~graben der** drainage ditch; **~rohr das** flue; **~schach das** *(Schach)* discovered check

ab|zupfen *tr. V.* pluck off

ab|zwacken *tr. V. (ugs.)* **a) [sich** *(Dat.)***] das Geld/die Zeit ~:** scrape the money together/spare the time; **b)** *s.* **abzwicken**

Ab·zweig der *(Verkehrsw.)* turn-off

Abzweig·dose die *(Elektrot.)* junction-box

ab|zweigen 1. *itr. V.; mit sein* branch off. **2.** *tr. V.* **a)** *(bereitstellen)* set *or* put aside; **Geld für einen Plattenspieler ~:** put aside *or* put by money to buy a record-player; **b)** *(verhüll.: sich heimlich aneignen)* appropriate

Abzweigung die; ~, ~en a) turn-off; *(einer Pipeline)* branch; *(Gabelung)* fork; **die rechte ~ fahren** take the right fork; **b)** *(Nebenlinie)* branch-line

ab|zwicken *tr. V.* pinch *or* nip off

ab|zwingen *unr. tr. V.* **jmdm. ein Geständnis ~:** force a confession out of sb.; **sich** *(Dat.)* **ein Lächeln ~:** force oneself to smile

ab|zwitschern *itr. V.; mit sein (ugs.)* clear off *(coll.)*; push off *(sl.)*

a cappella [a ka'pɛla] *Adv.* a cappella

Accent aigu [aksãtɛ'gy] **der; ~ ~, ~s ~s** [aksãzɛ'gy] acute [accent]

Accent circonflexe [aksãsirkõ'flɛks] **der; ~ ~, ~s ~s** circumflex [accent]

Accent grave [aksã'gra:v] **der; ~ ~, ~s ~s** [aksã'gra:v] grave [accent]

Accessoire [aksɛ'soa:ɐ̯] **das; ~s, ~s** *(geh.)* accessory

Acetat [atse'ta:t] **das; ~s, ~e** *(Chemie)* acetate

Aceton das; ~s *(Chemie)* acetone

Acetylen [atsety'le:n] **das; ~s** *(Chemie)* acetylene

Acetylen-: ~brenner der oxy-acetylene torch; **~gas das** acetylene

ach [ax] **1.** *Interj.* **a)** *(betroffen, mitleidig)* oh [dear]; **~ Gott** o dear; **b)** *(bedauernd, unwirsch)* oh; **c)** *(klagend)* ah; alas *(dated)*; **~ und weh schreien** scream blue *or (Amer.)* bloody murder; **d)** *(erstaunt)* oh; **~, wirklich?** no, really?; **~, der!** oh, him!; **~, ist das schön!** oh, how lovely!; **e) ~ so!** oh, I see; **~ nein** no, no; **~ was** *od.* **wo!** of course not. **2.** *Adv. (meist iron.)* **unser ~ so edler Held** our oh-so-noble hero

Ach das; ~s *in:* **mit ~ und Krach** *(ugs.)* by the skin of one's teeth; **mit ~ und Weh** with a lot of weeping and wailing

Achat [a'xa:t] **der; ~[e]s, ~e** *(Min.)* agate

achaten *Adj.; nicht präd.* agate

Achill [a'xɪl], **Achilles** [a'xɪlɛs] **(der)** Achilles

Achilles-: ~ferse die Achilles' heel; **~sehne die** *(Anat.)* Achilles tendon

Achilleus [a'xɪlɔ̯ys] **(der)** *s.* **Achill**

Ach-Laut der velar fricative; ach-laut

achromatisch *Adj. (Optik)* achromatic

Achs-: ~abstand der *s.* **Radstand; ~bruch der** *s.* **Achsenbruch**

Achse ['aksə] **die; ~, ~n a)** *(Rad~)* axle; **auf [der] ~ sein** *(ugs.)* be on the road *or* move; **b)** *(Dreh~, Astron.)* axis; **sich um die od. um seine eigene ~ drehen** turn on one's/its own axis; **c)** *(Math.)* axis ; **d) die ~ Berlin-Rom** *(hist.)* the Berlin-Rome axis

Achsel ['aksl] **die; ~, ~n** *(Schulter)* shoulder; *(~höhle)* armpit; **jmdn. über die ~ ansehen** look down on sb.; look down one's nose at sb.; **die** *od.* **mit den ~n zucken** shrug one's shoulders; **jmdn. unter den ~ packen** seize sb. under the arms; **etw. unter die ~ klemmen** tuck sth. under one's arm

achsel-, Achsel-: ~griff der a) *(Rettungsgriff)* underarm grip; **b)** *(Ringen)* nelson; **~grube die** *s.* **~höhle; ~haare** *Pl.* hair *sing.* under one's arms; armpit hair *sing.*; **~höhle die** armpit; **~klappe die** epaulette; **~schnur die** *(Milit.)* aiguillette; **~schweiß der** underarm perspiration; **~stück das** *meist Pl. (Milit.) s.* **~klappe; ~zucken das** shrug [of the shoulders]; **sein dauerndes ~zucken** his continual shoulder-shrugging; **~zuckend** *Adj.* shrugging; **er ging ~zuckend hinaus** he went out with a shrug [of the shoulders]

achsen-, Achsen-: ~ab·stand der *s.* **Radstand; ~bruch der** broken axle; **~kreuz das** *(Math.)* axes *pl.* of coordinates; **~mächte** *Pl. (hist.)* Axis Powers; **~symmetrisch** *Adj. (Math.)* **~symmetrisch sein** have axial symmetry; **eine ~symmetrische Kurve** a curve with axial symmetry; an axially symmetric curve

-achser der; ~s, ~: ein Drei-/Sechs~: a three-/six-axle vehicle *etc.*

-achsig *Adj.* **drei-/sechs~:** three-/six-axle

Achs-: ~lager das axle-bearing; **~last die** *(Technik)* axle-weight; **~schenkel der** *(Kfz-W.)* stub-axle; **~stand der** *s.* **Radstand; ~welle die** *(Technik)* axle-shaft

[1]acht [axt] *Kardinalz.* eight; **~ mal ~ ist 64** eight eights are *or* eight times eight makes 64; **wir waren ~** *od. (geh.)* **unser ~:** we were eight; **je ~ bildeten eine Gruppe** they formed into groups of eight; **die ersten/letzten ~:** the first/last eight; **er ist ~ [Jahre]** he is eight [years old]; **mit ~ [Jahren]** as an eight-year-old; at eight years of age; **es ist ~ Uhr** it is eight o'clock; **um ~ Uhr zehn** at ten past eight; **um ~ [Uhr]** at eight [o'clock]; **um ~ herum, gegen ~:** [at] around *or* about eight [o'clock]; **um halb ~:** at half past seven; **~ Minuten vor/nach halb ~:** twenty-two minutes past seven/twenty-two minutes to eight; **dreiviertel ~** *od.* **Viertel vor ~:** [a] quarter to eight; **in ~ Tagen** in a week's time; a week from now; **Freitag/morgen in ~ Tagen** a week on Friday/a week tomorrow; **[heute] vor ~ Tagen** a week ago [today]; **gestern vor ~ Tagen** a week ago yesterday; **im Jahre ~ nach/vor Christi Geburt** in the year AD 8/8 BC; **die Linie ~ [des Busses/der Straßenbahn]** the number eight [bus/tram]; **es steht ~ zu ~/~ zu 2** *(Sport)* the score is eight all/eight to two; **ein Vater von ~ Kindern** a father of eight; *s. auch* **[1]Acht**

[2]acht *in* **wir waren zu ~:** there were eight of us; **wir rückten ihm zu ~ auf die Bude** *(ugs.)* eight of us dropped in on him; **wir haben zu ~ ein Haus gemietet** the eight of us rented a house; **sie kamen zu ~:** eight of them came; **stellt euch zu ~ auf** make lines of eight

acht... *Ordinalz.* eighth; **der ~e** *od.* **8. September** the eighth of September; *(im Brief auch)* 8 September; **am ~en** *od.* **8. September** on the eighth of September; *(im Brief auch)* 8 September; **München, [den] 8. Mai 1984** Munich, 8 May 1984; **das ~e Kapitel/der ~e Abschnitt** chapter/section eight; **sie ging als ~e durchs Ziel** she came [in] *or* finished eighth; **jede ~e [Person/Kiste** *usw.***]** one out of every eight [persons/crates *etc.*]; one [person/crate *etc.*] in eight

[1]Acht die; ~, ~en a) *(Zahl)* eight; **eine arabische/römische ~:** an arabic/Roman eight; **die ~ ist seine Glückszahl** eight is his lucky number; **b)** *(Figur)* figure eight; **c)** *(Verbiegung)* buckle; **mein Rad hat eine ~:** my wheel is buckled; **d)** *(Spielkarte)* eight; **e)** *(ugs.: Bus-, Bahnlinie)* [number] eight; **f)** *(ugs.: Handschellen)* cuffs *pl. (coll.)*; **g)** *(auf der Speise-, Weinkarte)* **ich nehme die ~:** I'll have number eight

[2]Acht die; ~ *(hist.)* outlawry; **über jmdn. die ~ verhängen, jmdn. mit der ~ belegen** outlaw sb.; **jmdn. in ~ und Bann tun** *(kirchlich)* anathematize *or* put the ban on sb.; *(fig.)* ostracize sb.

[3]Acht die; ~ *(veralt.)* **in etw. außer acht** *od.* **außer aller ~ lassen** disregard *or* ignore sth.; **sich in acht nehmen** take care; be careful; **sich vor jmdm./etw. in acht nehmen** be wary of sb./sth.

-acht die *(Kartenspiel)* eight of ...

acht, Acht: ~ad[e]rig *Adj. (Elektrot.)* eight-core; **~armig** *Adj.* eight-armed; **~armig sein** have eight arms; **~bänder** [-bɛndɐ] **der; ~s, ~** *(Verlagsw.)* eight-volume set; **~bändig** *Adj.* eight-volume; **~bändig sein/~bändig herausgebracht werden** be in/be published in eight volumes

achtbar *Adj. (geh.)* respectable; upright ‹*principles*›; **eine ~e Leistung** a creditable performance

Achtbarkeit die; ~ *(geh.)* respectability; *(einer Gesinnung)* uprightness

acht·beinig *Adj.* eight-legged; **~ sein** have eight legs

Achte der/die; *adj. Dekl.* eighth; **er war [in der Leistung] der ~:** he came eighth; **der ~ [des Monats]** the eighth [of the month]; **Heinrich der ~:** Henry the Eighth

acht-, Acht-: ~eck das; ~s, ~e octagon; **~eckig** *Adj.* octagonal; **ein Würfel ist ~eckig** a cube has eight corners; **ein Gebäude ~eckig bauen** make a building octagonal; **ein ~eckiger Hut** an eight-sided hat; **~einhalb** *Bruchz.* eight and a half

achtel ['axtḷ] *Bruchz.* eighth; **ein ~ Kilo** an eighth of a kilo; **drei ~ Liter** three eighths of a litre

Achtel das *(schweiz. meist* **der***)*; **~s, ~ a)** eighth; **b)** *(ugs.: ~pfund)* eighth of a pound; ≈ two ounces; **c)** *(ugs.: ~liter)* eighth of a litre *(of wine)*; **d)** *(Musik) s.* **Achtelnote**

Achtel-: ~finale das *(Sport)* last sixteen; **~final·spiel das** *(Sport) match in the round before the quarter-finals*; **~liter der** eighth of a litre; **~los das** lottery ticket which has one eighth of the value of a whole ticket

achteln *tr. V.* **etw. ~:** divide/cut sth. up into eight pieces

Achtel-: ~note die *(Musik)* quaver; eighth note *(Amer.)*; **~pause die** *(Musik)* quaver rest; eighth rest *(Amer.)*; **~pfund das** eighth of a pound

achte·mal *Adv.* **das ~:** for the eighth time; **das ~ wurde er gefaßt** the eighth time, he was caught

achten 1. *tr. V.* respect; observe, respect ‹*laws, commandments*›. **2.** *itr. V.* **a) auf etw.** *(Akk.)* **[nicht] ~** *([nicht] auf etw. aufpassen)* [not] mind *or* look after sth.; *(von etw. [keine] Notiz nehmen)* pay [no] attention *or* heed to sth.; **es ist [besonders] darauf zu ~, daß ...:** your attention is [particularly] drawn to the fact that ...; **auf jmdn. ~:** look out for sb.; *(aufpassen)* look after *or* keep an eye on sb.; **b)** *(geh., veralt.)* *s.* **erachten**

ächten ['ɛxtn̩] *tr. V.* **a)** *(hist.: die Acht verhängen über)* outlaw; *(kirchlich)* anathematize; **b)** *(gesellschaftlich)* ostracize; **sich geächtet fühlen** feel like an outcast; **c)** *(verdammen)* ban ‹*war, torture*›

Acht·ender der; ~s, ~ *(Jägerspr.)* eight-pointer

achten·mal *Adv.* **beim ~:** the eighth time; at the eighth attempt *etc.*; **zum ~:** for the eighth time

achtens ['axtn̩s] *Adv.* eighthly

achtens·wert *Adj.* respectable ‹*person*›; worthy, commendable ‹*motive*›

Achter ['axtɐ] **der;** ~s, ~ **a)** *(Rudern)* eight; **b)** *s.* **[1]Acht a, b, c; c)** *(ugs.: Autobus)* number eight; **d)** *(ugs.: Schraube, Dübel usw.)* [number] eight

achter-, Achter-: **~aus** *Adv.* *(Seemannsspr.)* astern; **~bahn die** roller-coaster; **~bahn fahren** go *or* ride on the roller-coaster; **~deck das** *(Seemannsspr.)* afterdeck; **~gruppe die** group of eight; **~lastig** [~lastɪç] *Adj.* *(Seemannsspr.)* stern-heavy

achterlei *Gattungsz.; indekl.* **a)** *attr.* eight kinds *or* sorts of; eight different ‹*sorts, kinds, sizes, possibilities*›; **b)** *subst.* eight [different] things

achterlich *Adj.* *(Seemannsspr.)* stern *attrib.*; **~ sein** be astern

achtern *Adv.* *(Seemannsspr.)* astern; aft; **nach ~ gehen** go astern; **nach ~ drehen** ‹*wind*› move astern; **von ~:** from astern

Achter-: **~reihe die** row *or* line of eight; **~rennen das** *(Rudern)* eights race; **~schiff das** *(Seemannsspr.)* stern; **~steven der** *(Seemannsspr.)* stern-post

acht-, Acht-: **~fach** *Vervielfältigungsz.* eightfold; **die ~fache Menge** eight times the quantity; **die ~- bis zehnfache Dosis** eight to ten times the [correct] dose; **etw. in ~facher Ausfertigung schicken** send eight copies of sth.; **~fach vergrößert/verkleinert, in ~facher Vergrößerung/Verkleinerung** magnified *or* enlarged/reduced eight times; **das Produkt ist ~fach geprüft worden** the product went through eight tests; **~fache das;** *adj. Dekl.* **das ~fache von 4 ist 32** eight fours are *or* eight times four makes 32; **er verdient das ~fache von mir** he earns eight times as much as I do; **um das ~fache steigen/steigern** increase ninefold *or* nine times; **~fältig** *(veralt.)* *s.* **~fach; ~flach das;** ~s, ~e, **~flächner der;** ~s, ~: octahedron; **~füßer der;** ~s, ~ *(Biol.)* octopod; **~füßig** *Adj.* eight-footed; *(Verslehre)* eight-foot, octonarian ‹*line*›; **~ sein** have eight feet

acht|geben *unr. itr. V.* **a)** *(aufpassen)* **auf jmdn./etw. ~:** mind *or* take care of sb./sth.; **[auf jmds. Worte] ~:** pay attention [to what sb. says]; **~ müssen, daß ...:** have to be careful that ...; **er gab nicht sonderlich acht darauf** he did not pay any particular attention to it; **in der Schule besser ~:** pay more attention at school; **b)** *(vorsichtig sein)* be careful; watch out; **gib acht!** look out!; watch out!; **auf sich** *(Akk.)* **~:** be careful

acht, Acht-: **~geschossig,** *Adj. s.* **~stöckig; ~gliedrig** *Adj.* eight-membered; **~groschen·junge der** *(abwertend)* **a)** *(Denunziant, Spitzel)* informer; nark *(Brit. sl.)*; **b)** *(käufliches Subjekt)* hireling

acht|haben *unr. itr. V.* *(veralt.)* *s.* **achtgeben**

acht-, Acht-: **~hebig** *Adj.* *(Verslehre)* *s.* **~füßig; ~hundert** *Kardinalz.* eight hundred; **~hundertjahr·feier die** octocentenary [celebrations *pl.*]; **~hundertst...** *Ordinalz.* eight-hundredth; **~hunderttausend** *Kardinalz.* eight hundred thousand; **~jährig** *Adj.* *(8 Jahre alt)* eight-year-old *attrib.*; eight years old *pred.*; *(8 Jahre dauernd)* eight-year *attrib.*; **nach ~jährigem Studium** after eight years of study; **~jährig sterben** die at [the age of] eight; **seine ~jährige Tätigkeit an dem Institut** his eight years at the institute; **mit ~jähriger Verspätung** with a delay of eight years; eight years late; **~jährige der/die;** *adj. Dekl.* eight-year-old; **als ~jähriger** when one *etc.* is/was *etc.* eight years old; **~jährlich 1.** *Adj.* eight-yearly; **in ~jährlichem Turnus** in an eight-year cycle; **2.** *adv.* every eight years; **~kampf der** *(Turnen)* eight-exercise gymnastic competition; **~kantig 1.** *Adj.* *(Technik)* eight-sided; **2.** *adv.* *(salopp)* **~kantig rausfliegen** get kicked *or* *(sl.)* booted out; **jmdn. ~kantig rausschmeißen** throw sb. out on his/her ear *(coll.)*; **~klassig** *Adj.* with eight classes; **~köpfig** *Adj.* eight-headed ‹*monster*›; ‹*family, committee*› of eight

Achtling ['axtlɪŋ] **der;** ~s, ~e octuplet

acht·los 1. *Adj.; nicht präd.* heedless. **2.** *adv.* heedlessly

Achtlosigkeit die; ~: heedlessness

acht-, Acht-: **~mal** *Adv.* eight times; **~mal so groß/soviel/so viele** eight times as big/as much/as many; **~malig** *Adj.; nicht präd.* **nach ~maliger Wiederholung bestand er die Prüfung** he passed the test at the ninth attempt; **nach ~maliger Aufforderung** at the eighth request; after being asked eight times; **trotz ~maligen Klingelns** in spite of ringing eight times; **~millionen·mal** *Adv.* eight million times; **~minuten·takt** [-'---] **der** *(Fernspr.)* *system whereby telephone calls are charged at so much per eight minutes or part thereof;* **~minütig** *Adj.* eight-minute *attrib.*; lasting eight minutes *pred.*; **mit ~minütiger Verspätung** eight minutes late; **nach ~minütiger Sonnenbestrahlung** after eight minutes' exposure to the sun; **~monatig** *Adj.* *(8 Monate alt)* eight-month-old *attrib.*; eight months old *pred.*; *(8 Monate dauernd)* eight-month *attrib.*; lasting eight months *postpos.*; *s. auch* **~jährig; ~monatlich 1.** *Adj.* eight-monthly; **im ~monatlichen Turnus** rotating every eight months; **2.** *adv.* every eight months; **~monats·kind das** child born a month prematurely; **~pfennig·marke die** eight-pfennig stamp; **~pfünder** [~pfʏndɐ] **der;** ~s, ~: eight-pounder; **~pfündig** *Adj.; nicht präd.* eight-pound; **~polig** *Adj.* *(Elektrot.)* eight-pin; eight-core ‹*cable*›; **~punkt·schrift die** *(Druckw.)* eight-point type; **~prozentig** *Adj.* eight per cent; **~räd[e]rig** *Adj.* eight-wheeled; **~räd[e]rig sein** have eight wheels

achtsam 1. *Adj.* *(geh.)* attentive. **2.** *adv.* *(sorgsam)* carefully; with care; **mit etw. [äußerst] ~ umgehen** handle sth. with [extreme] care

Achtsamkeit die; ~: attentiveness; *(Sorgsamkeit)* care

acht-, Acht-: **~seitig** *Adj.* eight-page *attrib.* ‹*letter, article*›; **ein ~seitiges Vieleck** an eight-sided polygon; **~silber der;** ~s, ~ *s.* **~silbler; ~silbig** *Adj.* eight-syllable *attrib.*; octosyllabic; **~silbler der;** ~s, ~ *(Verslehre)* octosyllabic verse *or* line; **~sitzer der;** ~s, ~: eight-seater; **~sitzig** *Adj.* eight-seater *attrib.*; **~sitzig sein** have eight seats; **~spaltig** *(Druckw.)* **1.** *Adj.* **~spaltiger Artikel** eight-column article; **~spaltig sein** have eight columns; **2.** *adv.* **~spaltig setzen** print in eight columns; **~spänner der;** ~s, ~: eight-in-hand; **~spännig** *Adj.* eight-horse; *s. auch* **vierspännig; ~sprachig** *Adj.* in eight languages *postpos.*; *s. auch* **zweisprachig; ~sprossig** *Adj.* ‹*ladder*› with eight rungs; **~sprossig sein** have eight rungs; **~spurig** *Adj.* eight-lane ‹*road, motorway*›; eight-track ‹*cassette*›; **~stellig** *Adj.* eight-figure *attrib.*; **~stellig sein** have eight figures *or* digits; **~stimmig 1.** *Adj.* for eight-part; **2.** *adv.* in eight parts; **~stöckig 1.** *Adj.* eight-storey *attrib.*; **~stöckig sein** have eight storeys *or* floors; be eight storeys high; **2.** *adv.* **~stöckig bauen** build to eight storeys; **~strophig** [~ʃtro:fɪç] *Adj.* with eight verses *postpos., not pred.*; **~strophig sein** have eight verses; **~stufig** *Adj.* with eight steps *postpos., not pred.*; **~stufig sein** have eight steps; **~stunden·rhythmus** [-'----] **der** eight-hour rhythm; **~stunden·tag** [-'---] **der** eight-hour day; **~stündig** *Adj.* eight-hour *attrib.*; lasting eight hours *postpos., not pred.*; **mit ~stündiger Verspätung** eight hours late; **nach ~stündigem Warten** after waiting for eight hours; **~stündlich 1.** *Adj.* eight-hourly; **2.** *adv.* every eight hours; **~tägig** *Adj.* *(8 Tage alt)* eight-day-old *attrib.*; *(8 Tage dauernd)* eight-day[-long] *attrib.*; **mit ~tägiger Verspätung** eight days late; **nach ~tägiger Dauer** after lasting for eight days; **sie sind meist ~tägig** they mostly last eight days; **~täglich 1.** *Adj.* **in ~täglichem Wechsel** on an eight-day rota; **2.** *adv.* every eight days; **~tausend** *Kardinalz.* eight thousand; **~tausender der** *mountain over eight thousand metres high;* **~teiler der** *(Rundf., Ferns.)* eight-part series/serial; **~teilig** *Adj.* eight-piece ‹*tea-service, toolset, etc.*›; eight-part ‹*series, serial*›; **~teilig sein** have eight pieces; *(Rundf., Ferns.)* be in eight parts; **~tonner der;** ~s, ~: eight-tonner

Acht·uhr-: eight o'clock ‹*news, train, performance, etc.*›

acht-, Acht-: **~und·ein·halb** *Bruchz.* eight and a half; **~und·vierziger der;** ~s, ~ *(hist.)* forty-eighter *(one who took part in or sympathized with the 1848 revolution)*, **~und·vierzig·stunden·woche die** forty-eight-hour week; **~und·zwanzig** *Kardinalz.* twenty-eight

Achtung die; ~ **a)** *(Wertschätzung)* respect (**vor** + *Dat.* for); **gegenseitige ~:** mutual respect; **~ vor sich** *(Dat.)* **selbst** self respect; **alle ~!** well done!; **b)** *(Respektierung)* respect (*Gen.* for); **c)** *(Aufmerksamkeit)* attention; **~!** watch out!; **~! Stillgestanden!** *(Milit.)* attention!; **~, ~!** your attention, please!; **„~, Stufe!"** 'mind the step'; **„~, Hochspannung"** 'danger high voltage'; **~, fertig, los!** on your marks, get set, go!

Ächtung die; ~, ~en **a)** *(hist.)* outlawing; *(kirchlich)* anathematization; **b)** *(gesellschaftliche ~)* ostracism; **c)** *(Verdammung)* banning

achtung·gebietend *Adj.* *(geh.)* awe-inspiring

achtungs-, Achtungs-: **~applaus der** polite applause; **~erfolg der** reasonable success; **~voll 1.** *Adj.* respectful; **2.** *adv.* respectfully

acht-: **~wöchentlich 1.** *Adj.* eight-weekly; **im ~wöchentlichen Turnus/Wechsel** every eight weeks; **2.** *adv.* every eight weeks; **~wöchig** *Adj.* *(8 Wochen alt)* eight-week-old *attrib.*; *(8 Wochen dauernd)* eight-week[-long] *attrib.*; *s. auch* **~jährig; ~zackig** *Adj.* eight-pointed

acht·zehn *Kardinalz.* eighteen; **mit ~ [Jahren] wird man volljährig** one reaches the age of majority at eighteen; **18 Uhr** 6 p.m.; *(auf der 24-Stunden-Uhr)* eighteen hundred hours; 1800; **18 Uhr 33** 6.33 p.m.; *(auf der 24-Stunden-Uhr)* 1833

achtzehn, Achtzehn-: **~ender der;** ~s, ~ *(Jägerspr.)* eighteen-pointer; **~hundert** *Kardinalz.* eighteen hundred; **das war [im Jahre] ~hundert** *od.* **1800** that was in [the year] eighteen hundred *or* 1800; **~hundert** *od.* **1800 DM pro Hektoliter** eighteen hundred *or* 1,800 DM per hectolitre; **~jährig** *Adj.* *(18 Jahre alt)* eighteen-year-old *attrib.*; eighteen years old *pred.*; *(18 Jahre dauernd)* eighteen-year *attrib.*; *s. auch* **achtjährig; ~jährige der/die;** *adj.*

Dekl. eighteen-year-old; **als ~jähriger** when one *etc.* is/was *etc.* eighteen years old
achtzehnt... *Ordinalz.* eighteenth; *s. auch* **acht...**
Acht·zehntel das eighteenth
acht·zeilig *Adj.* eight-line *attrib.*; **~ sein** have eight lines
achtzig ['axtsɪç] *Kardinalz.* eighty; **mit ~ [km/h] fahren** drive at *or (coll.)* do eighty [k.p.h.]; **über/etwa ~ [Jahre alt] sein** be over/about eighty [years old]; **Mitte [der] Achtzig sein** be in one's mid-eighties; **in die Achtzig kommen** reach one's eighties; **mit ~ [Jahren]** *od.* **Achtzig** at eighty [years of age]; **im Jahre ~ vor/nach Christi Geburt** in the year 80 BC/AD 80; **auf ~ sein** *(fig. ugs.)* be hopping mad *(coll.)*
Achtzig die; ~ a) *(Zahl)* eighty; *s. auch* **¹Acht e; b)** *s.* **achtzig**
achtziger *indekl. Adj.; nicht präd.* **ein ~ Jahrgang** an '80 vintage; **die ~ Jahre** the eighties
¹Achtziger der; ~s, ~ a) *(80jähriger)* eighty-year-old [man]; octogenarian; **b)** *(ugs.: Autobus)* number eighty; **c)** *(Wein)* '80 vintage
²Achtziger die; ~, ~ *(ugs.)* **a)** *(Briefmarke)* eighty-pfennig/schilling *etc.* stamp; **b)** *(Zigarre)* eighty-pfennig cigar
³Achtziger *Pl.* eighties; **in den ~n sein** be in one's eighties
Achtzigerin die; ~, ~nen eighty-year-old [woman]; octogenarian
Achtziger·jahre *Pl.* eighties *pl.*
achtzig-, Achtzig-: ~jährig *Adj.* *(80 Jahre alt)* eighty-year-old *attrib.*; eighty years old *pred.*; *(80 Jahre dauernd)* eighty-year *attrib.*; *s. auch* **achtjährig; ~jährige der/die**; *adj. Dekl.* eighty-year-old; **~pfennig·marke die** eighty-pfennig stamp
achtzigst... ['axtsɪçst] *Ordinalz.* eightieth; **zum Achtzigsten herzlichen Glückwunsch** best wishes on your eightieth birthday; *s. auch* **acht...**
Achtzigstel das; ~s, ~: eightieth
acht-, Acht-: ~zimmer·wohnung die eight-roomed flat; **~zöllig** *Adj.* eight-inch[-long] *attrib.*; eight-inch *attrib.* ‹*pipe*›; **~zöllig sein** be eight inches long; ‹*pipe*› be eight inches in diameter; **~zylinder der** *(ugs.)* eight-cylinder [engine/car]; **~zylinder·motor der** eight-cylinder engine; **~zylindrig** *Adj.* eight-cylinder *attrib.*; **~ sein** have eight cylinders
ächzen ['ɛçtsn̩] *itr. V.* **a)** *(schwer stöhnen)* groan; **~ und stöhnen** grunt and groan; **b)** *(knarren)* creak
Ächzer der; ~s, ~ *(ugs.)* groan
Acker ['akɐ] **der; ~s, Äcker** ['ɛkɐ] **a)** field; **auf dem ~:** in the field; *(bei der Feldarbeit)* in the fields; **den ~ bestellen** till the field; **b)** *Pl.* **~** *(altes Feldmaß)* ≈ half acre *(usually about 2,500 sq.m.)*; **vier ~ Land/Wald** ≈ two acres of land/woodland
acker-, Acker-: ~bau der; *o. Pl.* agriculture *no indef. art.*; farming *no indef. art.*; **~bau treiben** farm; **~bau und Viehzucht** farming and stock-breeding; **~bauer der** farmer; **~bau·treibend** *Adj.* farming *attrib.*; **~boden der** soil [for cultivation]; **~bürger der** *(hist.) citizen who farmed land within the city area;* **~furche die** furrow; **~gaul der** *(ugs. abwertend)* cart-horse; old nag *(derog.)*; **aus einem ~gaul kann man kein Rennpferd machen** *(Spr.)* you can't make a silk purse out of a sow's ear *(prov.)*; **~gerät das** farm implement; **~krume die** topsoil; **~land das;** *o. Pl.* farmland; **~mann der** *(veralt.) s.* **Ackersmann**
ackern *itr. V. (salopp)* **a)** *(schwer arbeiten)* slog one's guts out *(coll.)*; **b)** *(sich anstrengen)* put one's back into it *(coll.)*; work like hell *(coll.)*; **c)** *(veralt.: pflügen)* plough
Acker-: ~schädling der field pest; **~scholle die** clod [of earth]

Ackers·mann der; *Pl.* **~leute** *(veralt.)* husbandman *(arch.)*
Acker·winde die *(Bot.)* field bindweed
a conto [a 'kɔnto] *(Bankw.)* on account
Acryl-: ~faser die acrylic fibre; **~harz das** acrylic resin
Action ['ækʃən] **die; ~:** action
a. D. [a:'de:] *Abk.* **außer Dienst** retd.
A. D. *Abk.* **Anno Domini** AD
Adabei der; ~s, ~s *(österr. ugs.)* hanger-on
ad absurdum [at ap'zʊrdʊm] *in etw.* **~ ~ führen** demonstrate the absurdity of sth.
ADAC [a:de:a:'tse:] **der; ~** *Abk.* **Allgemeiner Deutscher Automobilclub** *automobile association in the FRG*
ad acta [at 'akta] *in etw.* **~ ~ legen** shelve sth.
Adagio [a'da:dʒo] **das; ~s, ~s** *(Musik)* adagio
¹Adam ['a:dam] **(der)** Adam; **seit ~s Zeiten** since the beginning of time; **bei ~ und Eva anfangen** *(ugs.)* begin from the beginning; **der alte ~:** the old Adam
²Adam der; ~s, ~s *(ugs. scherzh.: Mann)* the male of the species
Adam Riese *in* **das macht nach ~ ~ 4,50 Mark** *(ugs. scherzh.)* my arithmetic makes it 4.50 marks *(coll. joc.)*
Adams-: ~apfel der *(ugs. scherzh.)* Adam's apple; **~kostüm das** *(ugs. scherzh.)* **im ~kostüm** in one's birthday suit
Adaptation [adapta'tsio:n] **die; ~, ~en** adaptation
adaptieren [adap'ti:rən] *tr. V.* **a)** adapt; **für den Bildschirm/Film ~:** adapt for television/the screen; **b)** *(österr.: herrichten)* fit out
Adaptierung die; ~, ~en a) *s.* **Adaptation; b)** *(österr.: Herrichtung)* fitting-out
Adaption [adap'tsio:n] **die; ~, ~en** *s.* **Adaptation**
adaptiv [adap'ti:f] *Adj.* adaptive
adäquat [atlɛ'kva:t] **1.** *Adj. (passend)* appropriate (*Dat.* to); suitable (*Dat.* for); *(angemessen)* adequate ‹*reward, payment*›; appropriate, suitable ‹*measures, means*›. **2.** *adv. (passend)* suitably; appropriately; *(angemessen)* adequately
addieren [a'di:rən] **1.** *tr. V.* add [up]. **2.** *itr. V.* add. **3.** *refl. V.* add up
Addier·maschine die adding-machine
Addition [adi'tsio:n] **die; ~, ~en** addition
additiv [adi'ti:f] *Adj.* additive
Additiv das; ~s, ~e *(Chemie)* additive
ade [a'de:] *Adv. (veralt.)* farewell; **jmdm. ~ sagen** bid farewell to sb.; take one's leave of sb.; **einer Sache** *(Dat.)* **~ sagen** *(fig.)* bid farewell to sth.
Adebar ['a:dəbar] **der; ~s, ~e** *(scherzh., bes. nordd.)* stork
Adel ['a:dl̩] **der; ~s a)** nobility; **der niedere ~:** the lesser nobility *or* nobles; **der hohe ~:** the higher nobility; the aristocracy; **von ~ sein** be of noble blood; **~ verpflichtet** noblesse oblige; **er stammt aus altem ~:** he belongs to an old noble family; **b)** *(Titel)* **der erbliche/persönliche ~:** a hereditary/non-hereditary title; *(hoher ~)* a hereditary/life peerage; **c)** *(geh.: edle Gesinnung)* nobility
adelig *s.* **adlig**
Adelige *s.* **Adlige**
adeln 1. *tr. V.* **jmdn. ~:** give sb. a title; *(in den hohen Adel erheben)* raise sb. to the peerage; *(fig.)* ennoble sb. **2.** *itr. V. (geh.)* ennoble
Adels-: ~brief der patent of nobility; **~familie die, ~geschlecht das** noble family; **~krone die** *coronet of the untitled lowest rank of nobility;* **~prädikat das** title of nobility; **~stand der** nobility; *(hoher Adel)* nobility; peerage; **jmdn. in den ~stand erheben** give sb. a title/raise sb. to the peerage; **~titel der** title of nobility
Adelung die; ~, ~en conferral of a title; *(in den hohen Adel)* ennoblement

Adept [a'dɛpt] **der; ~en, ~en a)** *(hist.)* initiate; **b)** *(scherzh.)* adherent; disciple
Ader ['a:dɐ] **die; ~, ~n a)** *(Anat., Zool.)* blood-vessel; vein; *(Schlagader)* artery; **in seinen ~n fließt Bauernblut** there is peasant blood in his veins; **sich** *(Dat.)* **die ~n öffnen** *(geh.)* slash one's wrists; **jmdn. zur ~ lassen** *(veralt.)* bleed sb.; *(fig.)* milk sb.; *s. auch* **Blut; b)** *o. Pl. (Anlage, Begabung)* streak; **c)** *(Bot., Geol.)* vein; **d)** *(Elektrot.)* core
Äderchen ['ɛ:dɐçən] **das; ~s, ~:** small blood-vessel *or* vein; *(Bot.)* small vein
Aderlaß ['a:dɐlas] **der; Aderlasses, Aderlässe** [-lɛsə] **a)** *(Med.: Blutentnahme)* bleeding; **b)** *(fig.)* drain; *(finanziell)* squeeze
Aderung ['a:dərʊŋ], **Äderung** ['ɛ:dərʊŋ] **die; ~, ~en** veining
Adhäsion [athɛ'zio:n] **die; ~, ~en** *(Phys., Med., Bot.)* adhesion
Adhäsions-: ~kraft die *(Physik)* power of adhesion; **~verschluß der** resealable closure
ad hoc [at 'hɔk] *Adv.* **a)** *(zu diesem Zweck)* ad hoc; **b)** *(spontan)* on the spur of the moment
Ad-hoc-: ~-Bildung die *s.* **~-Prägung; ~-Maßnahme die** ad hoc measure; **~-Prägung die** ad hoc coinage *or* formulation
adieu [a'diø:] *Adv. (veralt.)* adieu; farewell; **jmdm. ~ sagen** bid sb. adieu *or* farewell
Adieu das; ~s, ~s *(veralt.)* adieu
Adjektiv ['atjɛkti:f] **das; ~s, ~e** *(Sprachw.)* adjective
adjektivisch ['atjɛkti:vɪʃ] *(Sprachw.)* **1.** *Adj.* adjectival. **2.** *Adv.* adjectivally
Adjunkt [at'jʊŋkt] **der; ~en, ~en** *(veralt.)* low-grade civil servant
adjustieren [atjʊs'ti:rən] *tr. V.* **a)** *(Technik) s.* **justieren a; b)** *(österr. Amtsspr.)* provide with a uniform; kit out *(Brit.)*
Adjustierung die; ~, ~en a) *s.* **Justierung a; b)** *(österr. Amtsspr.)* uniform
Adjutant [atju'tant] **der; ~en, ~en** adjutant; aide-de-camp
Adjutum [at'ju:tʊm] **das; ~s, Adjuten** *(österr. Amtsspr.)* grant
Adlatus [at'la:tʊs] **der; ~, Adlaten** *od.* **Adlati** *(scherzh.)* loyal assistant
Adler ['a:dlɐ] **der; ~s, ~:** eagle; **der ~** *(Astron.)* Aquila; the Eagle
adler-, Adler-: ~auge das *(fig.)* eagle eye; **~äugig** *Adj. (fig.)* eagle-eyed; **~blick der** eagle eye; **~farn der** *(Bot.)* eagle fern; bracken; **~horst der** eyrie; **~nase die** aquiline nose
adlig ['a:dlɪç] *Adj.* noble; **~ sein** be a noble [man/woman]
Adlige der/die *adj. Dekl.* noble [man/woman]
Administration [atmɪnɪstra'tsio:n] **die; ~, ~en** administration
administrativ [atmɪnɪstra'ti:f] **1.** *Adj.* administrative. **2.** *adv.* administratively
Administrator [atmɪnɪs'tra:tɔr] **der; ~s, ~en** [-tra'to:rən] administrator
administrieren *itr. V.* administer
Admiral [atmi'ra:l] **der; ~s, ~e** *od.* **Admiräle** [atmi'rɛ:lə] **a)** admiral; **b)** *(Schmetterling)* red admiral
Admiralität [atmirali'tɛ:t] **die; ~, ~en** admirals *pl.*; *(Marineführung)* admiralty
Admirals·rang der rank of admiral; **im ~ stehen** hold the rank of admiral
ADN [a:de:'|ɛn] *Abk. (DDR)* **Allgemeiner Deutscher Nachrichtendienst** *GDR press agency*
Adoleszenz [adolɛs'tsɛnts] **die; ~** *(bes. Med., Psych.)* adolescence
Adonis [a'do:nɪs] **der; ~, ~se** Adonis
Adonis·röschen das *(Bot.)* adonis; *(Adonis annua)* pheasant's eye
adoptieren [adɔp'ti:rən] *tr. V.* adopt
Adoption [adɔp'tsio:n] **die; ~, ~en** adoption

Adoptiv- [adɔp'ti:f-]: **~bruder der** adoptive brother; brother by adoption; **~eltern** *Pl.* adoptive parents; **~kind das** adoptive *or* adopted child; **~mutter die** adoptive mother; **~schwester die** adoptive sister; sister by adoption; **~sohn der** adoptive *or* adopted son; **~tochter die** adoptive *or* adopted daughter; **~vater der** adoptive father

Adrenalin [adrena'li:n] **das; ~s** *(Physiol., Med.)* adrenalin

Adreß·änderung die *(schweiz.)* change of address

Adressat [adrɛ'sa:t] **der; ~en, ~en, Adressatin die; ~, ~nen** addressee; *(einer Rede)* hearer; *(eines Buches)* reader; *(einer Sendung)* listener/viewer; *(nicht direkt angesprochen)* implied target

Adreß·buch das: ~ [der Stadt] [town/city] directory

Adresse [a'drɛsə] **die; ~, ~n a)** *(auch DV)* address; *(fig.: Unternehmen)* establishment; **unter folgender ~:** at the following address; **eine Warnung an jmds. ~** *(Akk.)* **richten** *(fig.)* address a warning to sb.; **sich an die richtige ~ wenden** go to the right quarters *(fig.)*; **bei jmdm. an die falsche ~ kommen** *od.* **geraten** *(ugs.)* come to the wrong address *(fig.)*; **bei jmdm. an der falschen ~ sein** *(ugs.)* have come to the wrong place *(fig.)*; **b)** *(geh.: Botschaft)* message; *(Meinungsäußerung)* address

Adressen-: ~änderung die change of address; **~büro das** mailing-list broker; **~liste die** address-list; **~verzeichnis das** directory of addresses

adressieren *tr. V.* address

Adressier·maschine die addressing-machine; Addressograph (P)

adrett [a'drɛt] **1.** *Adj.* smart. **2.** *adv.* smartly

Adria ['a:dria] **die; ~:** Adriatic

adriatisch [adri'a:tɪʃ] *Adj.* **das Adriatische Meer** the Adriatic [Sea]

adrig, ädrig *Adj. s.* **aderig, äderig**

Adsorbens [at'zɔrbɛns] **das; ~, Adsorbenzien** *od.* **Adsorbentia** *(Chemie, Physik)* adsorbent

adsorbieren *tr. V. (Chemie, Physik)* adsorb

Adsorption [atzɔrp'tsio:n] **die; ~, ~en** *(Chemie, Physik)* adsorption

A-Dur das; ~ *(Musik)* A major; **Sonate/Etüde in ~:** sonata/study in A major; **die ~-Etüde** the A major study

Advent [at'vɛnt] **der; ~s a)** Advent; **b)** *(Adventssonntag)* Sunday in Advent

Adventist der; ~en, ~en *(Rel.)* Adventist

Advents-: ~kalender der Advent calendar; **~kranz der** *garland of evergreens with four candles for the Sundays in Advent;* **~sonntag der** Sunday in Advent

Adverb [at'vɛrp] **das; ~s, ~ien** *(Sprachw.)* adverb

adverbial [atvɛr'bia:l] *(Sprachw.)* **1.** *Adj.* adverbial; **~e Bestimmung** adverbial qualification. **2.** *adv.* adverbially; as an adverb

Adverbial·satz der adverbial clause

adversativ [atvɛrza'ti:f] *(Sprachw.)* **1.** *Adj.* adversative. **2.** *adv.* adversatively

Advocatus Diaboli [atvo'ka:tʊs di'a:boli] **der; ~ ~, Advocati ~** *(kath. Kirche, fig.)* devil's advocate

Advokat [atvo'ka:t] **der; ~en, ~en** *(österr., schweiz., sonst veralt.)* lawyer; advocate *(arch.)*; *(fig.: Fürsprecher)* advocate

Advokatur [atvoka'tu:ɐ̯] **die; ~, ~en** legal profession; *(Anwaltsbüro)* legal practice

Advokatur·büro das *(schweiz.)*, **Advokaturs·kanzlei die** *(österr.)* legal practice

aerob [ae'ro:p] *Adj. (Biol.)* aerobic

Aerobic [ɛ'ro:bɪk] **das; ~s;** *meist o. Art.* aerobics *sing.*

aero-, Aero- [aero- *od.* ɛ:ro-]: **~dynamik die** aerodynamics *sing.*; **~dynamisch** *Adj.* aerodynamic; **~gramm das** air[-mail] letter; **~sol** [~'zo:l] **das; ~s, ~e** aerosol

Affaire *(veralt., österr.)*, **Affäre die; ~, ~n** affair; *(Angelegenheit)* affair; business; **die ~ Dreyfus** the Dreyfus affair; **sich aus der ~ ziehen** *(ugs.)* get out of it; **eine ~ von ein paar Stunden/Mark** *(ugs.)* a matter of a few hours/marks

Äffchen ['ɛfçən] **das; ~s, ~:** little ape/monkey

Affe ['afə] **der; ~n, ~n a)** monkey; *(Menschen~)* ape; *(fig.)* **du bist wohl vom wilden ~n gebissen!** *(salopp)* you're off your head *(coll.)* or *(sl.)* rocker!; **seinem ~n Zucker geben** *(ugs.)* really let oneself go; **jmdn. zum ~n machen** *(ugs.)* make a monkey out of sb.; *s. auch* **lausen; Schleifstein; b)** *(derb: dummer Kerl)* oaf; clot *(Brit. sl.)*; **c)** *(derb: Geck)* dandy; **ein eingebildeter ~:** a conceited so-and-so *(coll.)*; **d)** *(Milit. ugs.)* knapsack; **e)** *(salopp: Rausch)* **einen ~n [sitzen] haben** be plastered *(sl.)*

Affekt [a'fɛkt] **der; ~[e]s, ~e a)** *(Gemütsbewegung)* feeling; emotion; affect *(Psych.)*; **im ~:** in the heat of the moment; **b)** *Pl. (Leidenschaften)* passions

affekt·geladen *Adj.* emotive

Affekt·handlung die emotive act

affektiert [afɛk'ti:ɐ̯t] *(abwertend)* **1.** *Adj.* affected. **2.** *adv.* affectedly

Affektiertheit die; ~, ~en affectedness; affectation

affektiv [afɛk'ti:f] *(Psych.)* **1.** *Adj.* affective. **2.** *adv.* affectively

Affekt·stauung die *(Psych.)* emotional block

affen-, Affen-: ~arsch der *(derb)* stupid bugger *(coarse)*; **das sind doch alles ~ärsche** they are a stupid lot of buggers *(coarse)*; **~artig** *Adj. (wie Menschenaffen)* apelike; **mit ~artiger Geschwindigkeit** *(ugs.)* like a bat out of hell *(coll.)*; **~brot·baum der** *(Bot.)* baobab *or* monkey-bread tree; **~haus das** monkey-house; **~hitze die** *(salopp)* blazing heat; **es herrschte gestern eine ~hitze** yesterday was a real scorcher; **~jacke die, ~jäckchen das** *(Soldatenspr. scherzh.)* monkey-jacket; **~käfig der** monkey-cage; **~liebe die** *(ugs.)* infatuation (**zu** with); **~mensch der** ape-man; **~pinscher der** affenpinscher; **~schande die** *(salopp)* **es ist eine ~schande** it's monstrous; **~schaukel die** *(ugs. scherzh.)* **a)** *(Milit.)* aiguillette; **b)** *(meist Pl.: Zopf)* looped plait; **~stall der** *(salopp)* dump *(coll.)*; hole *(coll.)*; **hier stinkt es wie in einem ~stall** *(derb)* this place smells like a pigsty *(sl.)*; **~tanz der** *(salopp) s.* **~theater; ~tempo das** *(salopp)* **mit einem ~tempo** like mad; like the clappers *(Brit. sl.)*; **ein ~tempo anschlagen** move like hell *(coll.)*; **~theater das** *(salopp)* farce; **~weibchen das** female ape; **~zahn der** *(salopp) s.* **~tempo; ~zirkus der** *(salopp) s.* **~theater**

affig *(ugs. abwertend)* **1.** *Adj.* dandyish; *(lächerlich)* ludicrous; *(affektiert)* affected. **2.** *adv.* **~ gekleidet** dressed in a dandyish/ludicrous/affected way

Affigkeit die; ~ *(ugs. abwertend) s.* **affig:** dandyishness; ludicrousness; affectation

Äffin ['ɛfɪn] **die; ~, ~nen** female ape

Affinität [afini'tɛ:t] **die; ~, ~en** affinity (**zu** for)

Affirmation [afɪrma'tsio:n] **die; ~, ~en** *(geh.)* affirmation

affirmativ [afɪrma'ti:f] *Adj.* affirmative

affizieren [afi'tsi:rən] *tr. V. (geh.)* influence; affect

Affront [a'frõ:] **der; ~s, ~s** affront

Afghane [af'ga:nə] **der; ~n, ~n a)** Afghan; **b)** *(Hund)* Afghan hound

Afghanin die; ~, ~nen Afghan; *s. auch* **-in**

afghanisch *Adj.* Afghan

Afghanistan [af'ga:nɪsta:n] **(das); ~s** Afghanistan

Afrika ['a:frika] **(das); ~s** Africa

Afrikaans [afri'ka:ns] **das; ~** Afrikaans

Afrika·forscher der African explorer

Afrikaner [afri'ka:nɐ] **der; ~s, ~, Afrikanerin die; ~, ~nen** African; *s. auch* **-in**

afrikanisch *Adj.* African

Afrikanistik die; ~: African studies *pl., no art.*

afro-, Afro-: ~amerikaner der Afro-American; **~amerikanisch** *Adj.* Afro-American; **~-asiatisch** *Adj.* Afro-Asian; **~kubanisch** *Adj.* Afro-Cuban; **~-Look der** Afro look

After ['aftɐ] **der; ~s, ~:** anus

After-: ~furche die *(Anat.)* anal cleft; **~mieter der** *(veralt.)* subtenant; **~wissenschaft die** *(veralt. abwertend)* pseudo-science

AG [a:'ge:] *Abk.* **die; ~, ~s a) Aktiengesellschaft** PLC *(Brit.)*; Ltd. *(private company) (Brit.)*; Inc. *(Amer.)*; **b) Arbeitsgemeinschaft**

Ägäis [ɛ'gɛ:ɪs] **die; ~** Aegean

ägäisch *Adj.* Aegean

Agave [a'ga:və] **die; ~, ~n** *(Bot.)* agave

Agende [a'gɛndə] **die; ~, ~n** *(ev. Kirche)* liturgy

Agens ['a:gɛns] **das; ~, Agenzien** [a'gɛntsiən] driving force; *(Philos., Sprachw.)* agent

Agent [a'gɛnt] **der; ~en, ~en** agent

Agenten-: ~aus·tausch der exchange of [captured] agents; **~netz das** network of agents; **~ring der** spy ring; **~tätigkeit die** activity as a spy

Agentin die; ~, ~nen [female] agent

Agent provocateur [a'ʒã: provoka'tø:ɐ̯] **der; ~ ~, ~s ~s** agent provocateur

Agentur [agɛn'tu:ɐ̯] **die; ~, ~en** agency

Agentur·bericht der, Agentur·meldung die agency report

Agglomerat [aglome'ra:t] **das; ~[e]s, ~e a)** *(geh.: Anhäufung)* conglomeration; **b)** *(Geol.)* agglomerate

Agglomeration [aglomera'tsio:n] **die; ~, ~en** *(Soziol.)* agglomeration

Agglutination [aglutina'tsio:n] **die; ~, ~en** *(Sprachw.)* agglutination

agglutinierend [agluti'ni:rənt] *Adj. (Sprachw.)* agglutinative

Aggregat [agre'ga:t] **das; ~[e]s, ~e** *(Technik)* unit; *(Elektrot.)* set

Aggregat·zustand der *(Chemie)* state

Aggression [agrɛ'sio:n] **die; ~, ~en** aggression; **starke ~en haben** have strong feelings of aggression

Aggressions-: ~krieg der war of aggression; **~politik die** policy of aggression; **~trieb der** aggressive drive

aggressiv [agrɛ'si:f] **1.** *Adj.* aggressive. **2.** *adv.* aggressively

Aggressivität die; ~: aggressiveness

Aggressor [a'grɛsɔr] **der; ~s, ~en** [-'so:ren] aggressor

Ägide [ɛ'gi:də] *(geh.) in* **unter jmds. ~** *(Dat.)* under sb.'s aegis

agieren [a'gi:rən] *itr. V. (auch Theater, fig.)* act; **als jmd. ~:** play sb.

agil [a'gi:l] *Adj. (beweglich)* agile; *(geistig rege)* mentally alert

Agilität [agili'tɛ:t] **die; ~:** agility; *(geistige Regsamkeit)* mental alertness

Agitation [agita'tsio:n] **die; ~** *(Politik)* agitation; **~ betreiben** agitate

Agitator [agi'ta:tɔr] **der; ~s, ~en** [-ta'to:rən] agitator

agitatorisch 1. *Adj.* agitative; inflammatory ⟨*speech*⟩. **2.** *adv.* for purposes of agitation

agitieren 1. *itr. V.* agitate. **2.** *tr. V.* stir up

Agitprop [agɪt'prɔp] **die; ~** *(Politik)* agitprop

Agnostiker [a'gnɔstɪkɐ] **der; ~s, ~:** *(Philos.)* agnostic

Agnostizismus [agnɔsti'tsɪsmʊs] **der; ~** *(Philos.)* agnosticism *no art.*

Agonie [ago'ni:] **die; ~, ~n: [die] ~:** the throes *pl.* of death; **in ~ liegen** be in the throes of death

Agrar- [a'gra:ɐ]: **~erzeugnis das** agricultural *or* farm product; **~erzeugnisse** agricultural *or* farm produce *or* products; **~gesellschaft die** agrarian society

Agrarier [a'gra:riɐ] **der; ~s, ~** *(veralt.)* landowner

agrarisch *Adj.* agrarian; agricultural

Agrar-: ~land das; *Pl.* **~länder** agrarian country; **~markt der** agrarian *or* agricultural products market; **~politik die** agricultural policy; **~produkt das** *s.* **~erzeugnis; ~wissenschaft die** *s.* **Agronomie; ~zoll der** import tariff *(on agricultural produce)*

Agrément [a'gre'mã:] **das; ~s, ~s** *(Diplomatie)* **jmdm. das ~ erteilen/verweigern** accord/refuse an agrément to sb.

Agri·kultur [agri-] **die;** *o. Pl. (geh.)* agriculture *no art.*

Agrikultur·chemie die, Agro·chemie ['a:gro-] **die** *(DDR)* agricultural chemistry *no art.*

Agronom [agro'no:m] **der; ~en, ~en** agronomist

Agronomie [agrono'mi:] **die; ~:** agronomy *no art.*

Agro·technik die *(DDR)* agricultural technology *no art.*

Ägypten [ɛ'gʏptn̩] **(das); ~s** Egypt; **die Flucht nach ~:** the flight into Egypt

Ägypter der; ~s, ~, Ägypterin die; ~, ~nen Egyptian

ägyptisch *Adj.* Egyptian; *s. auch* **Finsternis a**

Ägyptologe [ɛgʏpto'lo:gə] **der; ~n, ~n** Egyptologist

Ägyptologie [ɛgʏptolo'gi:] **die; ~:** Egyptology *no art.*

ah [a:] *Interj. (verwundert)* oh; *(freudig, genießerisch)* ah; *(verstehend)* oh; ah

äh [ɛ(:)] *Interj.* **a)** *(angeekelt)* ugh; **b)** *(stotternd)* er; hum

aha [a'ha(:)] *Interj. (verstehend)* oh[, I see]; *(triumphierend)* aha

Aha-Erlebnis das *(Psych.)* aha experience

ahd. *Abk.* **althochdeutsch** OHG

ahistorisch 1. *Adj.* ahistorical. **2.** *adv.* ahistorically

Ahle ['a:lə] **die; ~, ~n** awl; *(des Schriftsetzers)* bodkin

Ahn [a:n] **der; ~[e]s,** *od.* **~en, ~en** *(geh.)* forebear; ancestor; *(fig.)* father

ahnden ['a:ndn̩] *tr. V. (geh.)* punish

Ahndung die; ~: punishment

[1]Ahne der; ~n, ~n *s.* **Ahn**

[2]Ahne die; ~, ~n *(geh.)* ancestress; forebear; *(fig.)* spiritual forebear

ähneln ['ɛ:nl̩n] *itr. V.* **jmdm. ~:** resemble *or* be like sb.; bear a resemblance to sb.; **jmdm. sehr/wenig ~:** strongly resemble *or* be very like sb./bear little resemblance to sb.; **das Mädchen ähnelt seiner Mutter** the girl takes after her mother; **jmdm. frappierend ~:** bear a striking resemblance to sb.; **einer Sache** *(Dat.)* **~:** be similar to sth.; be like sth.; **sich** *od. (geh.)* **einander ~:** resemble one another; be alike; **sich sehr/wenig ~:** resemble each other very strongly *or* be very much alike/bear little resemblance to each other

ahnen ['a:nən] **1.** *tr. V.* **a)** *(im voraus fühlen)* have a presentiment *or* premonition of; **etw. dumpf** *od.* **dunkel ~:** have a vague presentiment *or* premonition of sth.; sense sth. dimly; **b)** *(vermuten)* suspect; *(erraten)* guess; **wer soll denn ~, daß ...:** who would know that ...; how are you supposed to know that ...; **das konnte ich doch nicht ~!** I had no way of knowing that; **du ahnst es nicht, wen/wo/wie ...** you'll never guess whom/where/how ...; **ach, du ahnst es nicht!** *(salopp)* oh heck *(coll.)*; oh Lord *(coll.)*; **davon haben wir überhaupt nichts geahnt** we didn't suspect it for one moment; **nichts Böses ~:** be unsuspecting; **ohne es zu ~:** without suspecting *or* realizing [it]; **c)** *(vage erkennen)* just make out; **die Wagen waren in der Dunkelheit mehr zu ~ als zu sehen** one could sense the cars in the darkness, rather than see them. **2.** *itr. V. (geh.)* **mir ahnt nichts Gutes** I fear the worst; **es ahnte mir, daß ...:** I suspected that ...; **ihm ahnte Schreckliches** he was filled with *or* had a dreadful [sense of] foreboding

Ahnen-: ~bild das a) *(~porträt)* ancestral portrait; **b)** *(Völkerk.) s.* **~figur; ~figur die** *(Völkerk.)* figure *or* effigy of an ancestor; **~forschung die** genealogy; **~galerie die** gallery of ancestral portraits; **~kult der** ancestor-worship; **ein javanischer ~kult** a Javanese ancestor cult; **~paß der** *(ns.)* proof of ancestry *(proving Aryan descent)*; **~tafel die** genealogical table; **~verehrung die** ancestor-worship

Ahn-: ~frau die *(geh. veralt.)* [first] ancestress; *(fig.)* spiritual forebear; **~herr der** *(geh. veralt.)* [first] ancestor; *(fig.)* father

ähnlich ['ɛ:nlɪç] **1.** *Adj.* similar; **jmdm. ~ sein** be similar to *or* be like sb.; *(~ aussehen)* resemble sb.; be like sb.; **das Kind ist seinem Vater ~:** the child takes after his father; **sich** *(Dat.) od. (geh.)* **einander ~ sein** be similar to one another; be alike; *(~ aussehen)* resemble one another; be alike; **~ wie er/wir** like him/us; **~ wie etw. aussehen/klingen** look/sound like sth.; **ein einer Ratte ~es Tier** an animal similar to a rat; **das sieht dir/ihm ~!** *(ugs.)* that's you/him all over; that's just like you/him; **[etwas] Ähnliches** something similar. **2.** *adv.* similarly; ⟨*answer, react*⟩ in a similar way *or* manner; **~ dumm/naiv** *usw.* **argumentieren** argue in a similarly stupid/naïve *etc.* way *or* manner; **~ dumm/naiv sein** be similarly stupid/naïve; **uns geht es ~:** it is/will be much the same for us; *(wir denken, fühlen ~)* we feel much the same. **3.** *Präp. mit Dat.* like

Ähnlichkeit die; ~, ~en similarity; *(ähnliches Aussehen)* similarity; resemblance; **mit jmdm. ~ haben** be similar to *or* be like sb.; *(ähnlich aussehen)* bear a resemblance to *or* be like sb.; **mit etw. ~ haben** bear a similarity to sth.

Ahnung die; ~, ~en a) *(Vorgefühl)* presentiment; premonition; **eine ~ haben, daß ...:** have a feeling *or* hunch that ...; **b)** *(Befürchtung)* foreboding; **c)** *(ugs.: Kenntnisse)* knowledge; **von etw. [viel] ~ haben** know [a lot] about sth.; **keine ~!** [I've] no idea; [I] haven't a clue; **du hast doch keine ~:** you don't know the first thing about it; **nicht die geringste** *od.* **keine blasse ~ [von etw.] haben** not have the faintest idea [about sth.]; **haben Sie eine ~, wer/wie ...?** have you any idea who/how ...?; **von Tuten und Blasen keine ~ haben, keine ~ von Ackerbau und Viehzucht haben** *(salopp)* not know the first thing about it; **hast du 'ne ~!** *(ugs.)* that's what you think!

ahnungs·los 1. *Adj. (nichts ahnend)* unsuspecting; *(naiv, unschuldig)* naïve; innocent; *(unwissend)* naïve; **sich ~ stellen** play the innocent. **2.** *adv. (nichts ahnend)* unsuspectingly; all unawares; *(naiv, unschuldig)* naïvely; innocently; *(unwissend)* naïvely

Ahnungslosigkeit die; ~ *(Naivität, Unschuld)* naïvety; innocence; *(Unwissenheit)* naïvety

ahnungs·voll *Adj. (geh.)* full of presentiment *postpos.*; *(geheimnisvoll)* mysterious; *(Böses ahnend)* full of foreboding *postpos.*

ahoi [a'hɔy] *Interj.* **a)** *(Seemannsspr.)* **Boot/Schiff** *usw.* **~!** boat/ship *etc.* ahoy!; **b)** *s.* **helau**

Ahorn ['a:hɔrn] **der; ~s, ~e** maple

Ahorn-: ~blatt das maple-leaf; **~sirup der** maple syrup

Ähre ['ɛ:rə] **die; ~, ~n** *(von Getreide)* ear; head; *(von Gräsern)* head; *(Bot.: von Blüten)* spike; **~n lesen** glean

Ähren-: ~feld das *(geh.)* field of [ripening/ripe] corn; **~kranz der** wreath of wheat-ears; **~lese die** *o. Pl.* gleaning

Air [ɛ:ɐ] **das; ~s, ~s a)** air; aura; **b)** *(Musik)* air

Aids [e:ts] **das; ~:** AIDS

Aids-: ~kranke der/die person suffering from AIDS; **~test der** AIDS test

Air·bus ['ɛ:ɐ-] **der** *(Flugw.)* airbus

Airedale ['ɛ:ɐde:l] **der; ~s, ~s** Airedale

Airedale·terrier der Airedale terrier

ais, Ais ['a:ɪs] **das; ~, ~** *(Mus.)* A sharp

Akademie [akade'mi:] **die; ~, ~n a)** academy; **b)** *(Fachhochschule)* academy; *(Bergbau, Forst~, Bau~)* school; college; **c)** *(österr.: künstlerische Veranstaltung)* cultural function

Akademie·mitglied das member of the/an academy; academician

Akademiker [aka'de:mikɐ] **der; ~s, ~, Akademikerin die; ~, ~nen a)** *(Hochschulabsolvent)* [university/college] graduate; **b)** *s.* **Akademiemitglied**

akademisch 1. *Adj.; nicht präd.* academic; **~er Rat** [university] lecturer; **~er Oberrat** senior [university] lecturer; **der ~e Mittelbau** *the non-professional teaching staff;* **das ~e Proletariat** *the mass of jobless graduates and graduates working in jobs for which they are over-qualified;* **~er Lehrer** university teacher; **das ~e Viertel** *the 15 minutes' grace between the announced start and actual beginning of a lecture.* **2.** *adv.* academically; **~ [aus]gebildet sein** have [had] a university education; be university-educated; **dieses Problem stellt sich rein ~:** this problem is purely academic

Akademisierung die; ~: die ~ des Bundestages schreitet weiter fort the Bundestag is becoming increasingly peopled with [university] graduates

Akanthus [a'kantʊs] **der; ~, ~** *(Bot., Kunstwiss.)* acanthus

akausal *(Philos.)* **1.** *Adj.* acausal. **2.** *adv.* acausally

Akazie [a'ka:tsiə] **die; ~, ~n** *(auch volkst.: Robinie)* acacia

Akelei [akə'lai] **die; ~, ~en** aquilegia; columbine

Akklamation [aklama'tsio:n] **die; ~, ~en a)** *(Abstimmung durch Zuruf)* acclamation; **durch** *od.* **per ~:** by acclamation; **b)** *(selten: Beifall)* acclamation *no pl.*; acclaim *no pl.*

akklamieren [akla'mi:rən] *(geh.)* **1.** *itr. V. (zustimmen)* applaud. **2.** *tr. V. (durch Beifall)* acclaim

Akklimatisation [aklimatiza'tsio:n] **die; ~, ~en** acclimatization

akklimatisieren *refl. V.* become *or* get acclimatized

Akklimatisierung die; ~, ~en *s.* **Akklimatisation**

Akkolade [ako'la:də] **die; ~, ~n a)** *(Hist., Musik)* accolade; **b)** *(Druckw.)* brace

Akkord [a'kɔrt] **der; ~[e]s, ~e a)** *(Musik)* chord; **b)** *(Wirtsch.)* *(~arbeit)* piece-work; *(~lohn)* piece-work pay *no indef. art., no pl.*; *(~satz)* piece-rate; **im ~ sein** *od.* **arbeiten** be on piece-work; **etw. im ~ tun** do sth. piece-work; **im ~ hergestellt werden** be manufactured by piece-workers; **c)** *(geh.: Übereinstimmung)* accord; **d)** *(Rechtsspr.: Einigung)* settlement

Akkord-: ~arbeit die piece-work; **in ~arbeit hergestellt werden** be manufactured by piece-workers; **~arbeiter der** piece-worker

Akkordeon [a'kɔrdeɔn] **das; ~s, ~s** accordion

Akkordeonist der; ~en, ~en, Akkordeon·spieler der accordionist

Akkord-: ~lohn der *(Wirtsch.)* piece-work pay *no indef. art., no pl.*; **~satz der** *(Wirtsch.)* piece-rate; **~zuschlag der** *(Wirtsch.)* piece-rate bonus

akkreditieren [akredi'ti:rən] *tr. V.* **a)** *(bes. Dipl.)* accredit (**bei** to); **b)** *(Finanzw.)* **jmdn. ~:** grant sb. credit facilities; **akkreditiert sein** have credit facilities

Akkreditierung die; ~, ~en a) *(bes. Dipl.)* accreditation (**bei** to); **b)** *(Finanzw.)* **meine ~ bei der Bank** my credit facilities *pl. or* credit arrangement at the bank; **eine ~ von DM 10 000,–:** provision of 10,000 DM of credit

Akkreditiv [akredi'ti:f] **das; ~s, ~e a)** *(Dipl.)* credentials *pl.*; **b)** *(Finanzw.)* letter of credit

Akku ['aku] **der; ~s, ~s** *(ugs.) s.* **Akkumulator a**

Akkulturation [akʊltura'tsio:n] **die; ~, ~en** *(Völkerk., Sozialpsych.)* acculturation

akkulturieren *tr. V. (Völkerk., Sozialpsych.)* acculturate

Akkumulation [akumula'tsio:n] **die; ~, ~en** *(geh., Wirtsch.)* accumulation

Akkumulator [akumu'la:tɔr] **der; ~s, ~en** [-la'to:rən] *(Technik)* **a)** *(Stromspeicher)* accumulator *(Brit.)*; storage battery *or* cell; **b)** *(Druckspeicher, DV)* accumulator

akkumulieren *tr., itr., refl. V. (geh., Wirtsch., Soziol.)* accumulate

akkurat [aku'ra:t] **1.** *Adj.* **a)** *(sorgfältig)* meticulous; *(sauber)* neat; **b)** *(exakt, genau)* precise; exact. **2.** *adv.* **a)** *(sorgfältig)* meticulously; *(sauber)* neatly; **b)** *(exakt, genau)* precisely; exactly

Akkuratesse [akura'tɛsə] **die; ~ a)** *(Sorgfalt)* meticulousness; *(Sauberkeit)* neatness; **b)** *(Exaktheit, Genauigkeit)* precision

Akkusativ ['akuzati:f] **der; ~s, ~e** *(Sprachw.)* accusative [case]; *(Wort im ~)* accusative [form]; **im/mit dem ~ stehen** be in/take the accusative [case]

Akkusativ·objekt das *(Sprachw.)* accusative *or* direct object

Akne ['aknə] **die; ~, ~n** *(Med.)* acne

Akonto [a'kɔnto] **das; ~s, ~s** *od.* **Akonten** *(österr.),* **Akonto·zahlung die** *s.* **Anzahlung**

akquirieren [akvi'ri:rən] *itr. V. (Wirtsch.)* canvass [new] business

Akquisiteur [akvizi'tø:ɐ̯] **der; ~s, ~e** *(Wirtsch.)* canvasser

Akquisition [akvizi'tsio:n] **die; ~, ~en** *(Wirtsch.)* canvassing *no art.* for [new] business

Akquisitor [akvi'zi:tɔr] **der; ~s, ~en** [-zi'to:rən] *(österr.)* canvasser

Akribie [akri'bi:] **die; ~** *(geh.)* meticulousness; meticulous precision

akribisch [a'kri:bɪʃ] **1.** *Adj.* meticulous; meticulously precise. **2.** *adv.* meticulously; with meticulous precision; **~ genau** meticulously accurate

Akrobat [akro'ba:t] **der; ~en, ~en** acrobat

Akrobaten·truppe die troupe of acrobats

Akrobatik die; ~ a) *(Körperbeherrschung)* acrobatic skill; **b)** *(akrobatische Übungen)* acrobatics *pl.*

Akrobatin die; ~, ~nen acrobat

akrobatisch 1. *Adj.* acrobatic. **2.** *adv.* acrobatically

Akronym [akro'ny:m] **das; ~s, ~e** *(Sprachw.)* acronym

[1]**Akt** [akt] **der; ~[e]s, ~e a)** *(auch Theater, Zirkus~, Varieté~)* act; **b)** *(Zeremonie)* ceremony; ceremonial act; **c)** *(Geschlechts~)* sexual act; **d)** *(~bild)* nude; **e)** *(Amtshandlung)* action

[2]**Akt der; ~[e]s, ~en** *(bes. südd., österr.) s.* **Akte**

Akt-: ~aufnahme die nude photograph; **~bild das** nude [picture]

Akte die; ~, ~n file; **die ~ Schulze** the Schulze file; **das kommt in die ~n** it goes on file; **~n über jmdn./etw. führen** keep a file on sb./sth.; **etw. zu den ~n legen** file sth. away; *(fig.)* lay sth. to rest; **über etw.** *(Akk.)* **die ~n schließen** close the file on sth.

akten-, Akten-: ~berg der *(ugs.)* mountain of files; **~deckel der** folder; **~einsicht die** *(Amtsspr.)* **~einsicht nehmen** examine the files; **jmdm. ~einsicht gewähren** allow sb. to examine the files; **~koffer der,** *(iron.)* **~köfferchen das** attaché case; **~kundig** *Adj.; nicht attr.* on record; **~kundig werden** go on file; be recorded; **~mappe die a)** *(~tasche)* brief-case; **b)** *(~deckel)* folder; **~notiz die a)** note [for the files]; **sich** *(Dat.)* **eine kurze ~notiz von etw. machen** make a brief note of sth. [for the files]; **b)** *(längeres Schreiben)* memorandum; **~ordner der** file; **~schrank der** filing cabinet; **~stoß der** stack *or* pile of files; **~tasche die** brief-case; **~vermerk der** *s.* **~notiz a**; **~wolf der** [paper-]shredder; **~zeichen das** reference

Akteur [ak'tø:ɐ̯] **der; ~s, ~e** person involved; *(Theater)* member of the cast; *(Varieté)* performer; *(Sportjargon)* player; *(Boxen, Ringen)* contestant

Akt-: ~foto das nude photo; **~fotografie die a)** *o. Pl.* nude photography *no art.*; **b)** *(Bild)* nude photograph; **~gemälde das** nude [painting]

Aktie ['aktsiə] **die; ~, ~n** *(Wirtsch.)* share; **~n** shares *(Brit.)*; stock *(Amer.)*; **sein Geld in ~n anlegen** invest one's money in shares *(Brit.) or (Amer.)* stocks; **die ~n fallen/steigen** share *or* stock prices are falling/rising; **junge ~n** new-issue shares *or* stocks; **wie stehen die ~n?** *(ugs. scherzh.) (wie geht's)* how are things?; *(wie sind die Chancen)* what are the prospects?; **seine/meine** *usw.* **~n steigen** *(fig. ugs.)* his/my *etc.* prospects are improving

Aktien-: ~besitz der shareholdings *pl.*; **~besitzer der** shareholder; **~gesellschaft die** joint-stock company; **~index der** share index; **~kapital das** share capital; **~kurs der** share price; **~markt der** stock market; **~mehrheit die** majority shareholding (*Gen.* in); **~paket das** block of shares; **~urkunde die** share certificate *(Brit.)*; stock certificate *(Amer.)*

Aktion [ak'tsio:n] **die; ~, ~en a)** *(Unternehmung)* action *no indef. art.*; *(militärisch)* operation; **revolutionäre/politische ~en** revolutionary/political action *sing.*; **b)** *(Kampagne)* campaign; **~ saubere Umwelt** campaign to clean up the environment; *s. auch* **konzertiert**; **c)** *o. Pl. (das Handeln)* action; **in ~ treten** go into action; ‹*safety device*› come into action; **d)** *(Kaufmannsspr.: Verkauf zu Sonderpreisen)* sale

Aktionär [aktsio'nɛ:ɐ̯] **der; ~s, ~e, Aktionärin die; ~, ~nen** shareholder

Aktionärs·versammlung die shareholders' meeting

Aktionismus der; ~: actionism *no art.*

Aktionist der; ~en, ~en, Aktionistin die; ~, ~nen actionist

aktionistisch 1. *Adj.* actionist[ic]. **2.** *adv.* actionistically

aktions-, Aktions-: ~art die *(Sprachw.)* aspect; **~ausschuß der** action committee; **~bereich der** *s.* **~radius**; **~einheit die** united action *no art.* (*Gen.* by); **~fähig** *Adj.* capable of action *postpos.*; **~fähigkeit die** ability to act; **~gemeinschaft die: eine ~gemeinschaft herstellen/fordern** bring about/demand united action (**von** by); **~gruppe die** action group; **~komitee das** action committee; **~preis der** *(Kaufmannsspr.)* sale price; **zum ~preis** at sale price; **~programm das** programme for action; **~radius der a)** *(Luftwaffe, Seew.)* radius of action; **b)** *(Wirkungsbereich)* range of activity; **~unfähig** *Adj.* incapable of action *postpos.*; **~zentrum das a)** *(Mittelpunkt)* centre *or* focus for action; **b)** *(Met.)* centre of action

aktiv [ak'ti:f] **1.** *Adj.* **a)** *(auch Chemie)* active; **b)** *(Milit.)* serving *attrib.* ‹*officer, soldier*›; **er ist Soldat im ~en Dienst** he is a serving soldier; **er war in Vietnam ~:** he served in Vietnam; **c) ~e Bestechung** offering of a bribe/bribes to an official; **~e Handelsbilanz** favourable balance of trade; **~er Wortschatz** active vocabulary. **2.** *adv.* actively; **sich ~ verhalten** be active

[1]**Aktiv** ['akti:f] **das; ~s, ~e** *(Sprachw.)* active; **im ~ stehen** be in the active

[2]**Aktiv** [ak'ti:f] **das; ~s, ~e** *od.* **~s** *(bes. DDR)* committee

[1]**-aktiv** *Adj. (Werbespr.)* **saug~:** extra-absorbent; **wasch~ Substanzen** substances with a strong cleansing action; **atmungs~es Gewebe** fabric which allows the skin to breathe

[2]**-aktiv das; ~s, ~e** *od.* **~s** *(bes. DDR)* **Verkehrssicherheits~/Bezirks~/Eltern~** *usw.* traffic safety/district/parents *etc.* committee

Aktiva [ak'ti:va] *Pl. (Wirtsch.)* assets

Aktiv·bürger der *(schweiz.) citizen with full political and civil rights*

[1]**Aktive** [ak'ti:və] **der/die;** *adj. Dekl. (Sport)* participant; *(eines Vereins, einer Gewerkschaft)* active member; *(der Feuerwehr)* regular

[2]**Aktive die; ~n, ~n** *(salopp) (nicht selbstgedrehte Zigarette)* real fag *(Brit. sl.)*; store-bought cigarette *(Amer.)*; *(filterlose Zigarette)* plain fag *(sl.)*; non-filter

Aktiven *Pl.: s.* **Aktiva**

Aktiv·geschäft das *(Finanzw.)* lending and investment business

aktivierbar *Adj.* **er ist/sie sind** *usw.* **[politisch] ~:** he/they *etc.* can be [politically] mobilized

aktivieren *tr. V.* **a)** mobilize ‹*party members, group, class, etc.*›; intensify, step up ‹*work, campaign*›; **den Kreislauf ~:** stimulate the circulation; **alte Freundschaften ~:** revive old friendships; **Beziehungen ~:** reactivate connections; **b)** *(Chemie)* activate; **c)** *(Finanzw.)* **etw. ~:** enter sth. on the assets side

Aktivierung die; ~, ~en a) *(von Parteimitgliedern, einer Gruppe, Klasse)* mobilization; *(einer Arbeit, Kampagne)* intensification; *(von Beziehungen)* reactivation; **die ~ des Kreislaufs/alter Freundschaften** stimulation of the circulation/reviving old friendships; **b)** *(Chemie)* activation; **c)** *(Finanzw.)* entry on the assets side; **die ~ von etw.** entering sth. on the assets side

aktivisch *(Sprachw.)* **1.** *Adj.* active. **2.** *adv.* actively; in the active form

Aktivismus der; ~ *(Politik)* activism *no art.*

Aktivist der; ~en, ~en activist

Aktivisten-: ~bewegung die *(DDR)* activists' movement; **~schule die** *(DDR)* school for activists

Aktivistin die; ~, ~nen activist

aktivistisch *(Politik) Adj.* activist

Aktivität [aktivi'tɛ:t] **die; ~, ~en** *(auch Chemie, Radio~)* activity

Aktiv-: ~kohle die activated carbon *or* charcoal; **~posten der** *(Kaufmannsspr., fig.)* asset; **~saldo der** *(Kaufmannsspr.)* credit balance; **~seite die** *(Kaufmannsspr.)* assets side; **~urlaub der** *(Werbespr.)* activity holiday; **~vermögen das** *(Kaufmannsspr.)* realizable assets *pl.*; **~zinsen** *Pl. (Kaufmannsspr.)* interest *sing.* receivable

Akt-: ~malerei die nude painting *no art.*; **~modell das** nude model

Aktrice [ak'tri:sə] **die; ~, ~n** actress

Akt·studie die nude study

aktualisieren [aktuali'zi:rən] **1.** *tr. V.* update. **2.** *refl. V. (sich manifestieren)* be evident *or* clearly visible

Aktualisierung die; ~, ~en updating; **er sorgte für die ~ des Themas** he ensured that the subject was made topical

Aktualität [aktuali'tɛ:t] **die;** ~, ~**en a)** *(Gegenwartsbezug)* relevance [to the present]; **b)** *(von Nachrichten usw.)* topicality; **c)** *(Mode, Werbespr.)* up-to-the-minute style
Aktuar [ak'tu̯a:ɐ̯] **der;** ~**s,** ~**e a)** *(schweiz.: Schriftführer)* secretary; **b)** *(veralt.) s.* **Gerichtsschreiber**
aktuell [ak'tu̯ɛl] **1.** *Adj.* **a)** *(gegenwartsbezogen)* topical; *(gegenwärtig)* current; **von** ~**er Bedeutung** of relevance to the present *or* current situation; **dieses Problem ist nicht mehr** ~: this is no longer a problem; **b)** *(neu)* up-to-the-minute; **das Aktuellste von den Olympischen Spielen** the latest from the Olympics; **eine** ~**e Sendung** *(Ferns., Rundf.)* a [news and] current affairs programme; **c)** *(geh.: real)* real; **d)** *(Mode, Werbespr.)* fashionable; **in den** ~**en Farben** in the latest colours. **2.** *adv.* currently
Akt-: ~**zeichnen das** nude drawing *no art.;* ~**zeichnung die** nude drawing
Akupressur [akuprɛ'su:ɐ̯] **die;** ~, ~**en** *(Med.)* acupressure
Akupunkteur [akupʊŋk'tø:ɐ̯] **der;** ~**s,** ~**e** *(Med.)* acupuncturist
akupunktieren *(Med.)* **1.** *tr. V.* perform acupuncture on; **sich** ~ **lassen** have acupuncture. **2.** *itr. V.* perform acupuncture
Akupunktur [akupʊŋk'tu:ɐ̯] **die;** ~, ~**en** *(Med.)* acupuncture
Akustik [a'kʊstɪk] **die;** ~ **a)** *(Lehre vom Schall)* acoustics *sing., no art.;* **b)** *(Schallverhältnisse)* acoustics *pl.*
akustisch 1. *Adj.* acoustic. **2.** *adv.* acoustically; **ich habe Sie** ~ **nicht verstanden** I didn't hear *or* catch what you said
akut [a'ku:t] **1.** *Adj.* **a)** *(vordringlich)* acute; pressing, urgent ‹*question, issue*›; **b)** *(Med.)* acute. **2.** *adv. (Med.)* in an acute form; ~ **auftretende Asthmaanfälle** acute attacks of asthma
Akut der; ~**[e]s,** ~**e** *(Schriftw.)* acute [accent]
AKW [a:ka:'ve:] **das;** ~**[s],** ~**s** *Abk.* **Atomkraftwerk**
Akzeleration [aktselera'tsi̯o:n] **die;** ~, ~**en** *(Anthrop., Astron.)* acceleration
Akzelerator [aktsele'ra:tɔr] **der;** ~**s,** ~**en** [-ra'to:rən] *(Kerntechnik)* accelerator
Akzent [ak'tsɛnt] **der;** ~**[e]s,** ~**e a)** *(Sprachw.) (Betonung)* accent; stress; *(Betonungszeichen)* accent; **b)** *(Sprachmelodie, Aussprache)* accent; **mit starkem koreanischem** ~: with a strong Korean accent; **c)** *(Nachdruck, Gewicht)* emphasis; stress; *(in der Mode)* accent; **den** ~ **[besonders] auf etw.** *(Akk.)* **legen** lay *or* put [particular] emphasis *or* stress on sth.; **die** ~**e werden verschoben** the emphasis *or* stress is shifted; **neue** ~**e setzen** set new directions; **diesen Herbst liegen die [modischen]** ~**e bei ...:** this autumn the accent is on ...; **1969 hat neue** ~**e gesetzt** 1969 saw the beginning of new trends
akzent·frei 1. *Adj.* without an *or* any accent *postpos.* **2.** *adv.* without an *or* any accent
akzentuieren [aktsɛntu'i:rən] *tr. V.* **a)** *(deutlich aussprechen)* enunciate; articulate; *(betonen)* accentuate; stress; **b)** *(fig.: hervorheben, auch Mode)* accentuate
Akzent·verschiebung die a) *(Sprachw.)* stress shift; **b)** *(fig.)* shift of emphasis
Akzept [ak'tsɛpt] **das;** ~**[e]s,** ~**e** *(Finanzw.)* acceptance
akzeptabel [aktsɛp'ta:bl] **1.** *Adj.* acceptable. **2.** *adv.* acceptably
Akzeptanz [aktsɛp'tants] **die** *(bes. Werbespr.)* acceptance
akzeptieren *tr. V.* accept
Akzidens ['aktsidɛns] **das;** ~, **Akzidenzien a)** *(Philos.)* accident; accidental property; **b)** *(Musik)* accidental
akzidentell [aktsidɛn'tɛl], **akzidentiell** [-'tsi̯ɛl] *Adj.* **a)** *(Philos., geh.)* accidental (*Dat.* to); **b)** *(Med.)* accidental
Akzidenz [aktsi'dɛnts] **die;** ~, ~**en** *(Druckw.)* job; ~**en** job-work *sing.;* job printing *sing.*
à la [a la] *(Gastr., ugs.: im Stile von)* à la
alaaf [a'la:f] *Interj. (rhein.)* hurrah; hurray; **Kölle** ~! hurrah, Cologne!
Alabaster [ala'bastɐ] **der;** ~**s,** ~: alabaster
alabastern *Adj. (geh.)* alabaster
à la carte [ala'kart] *(Gastr.)* à la carte
Alarm [a'larm] **der;** ~**[e]s,** ~**e a)** *(Warnung)* alarm; *(Flieger~)* air-raid warning; ~ **geben** raise *or* sound *or* give the alarm; **blinder** ~: false alarm; ~ **schlagen** *(ugs.)* raise *or* sound the alarm; **bei** ~: if there is an alarm; **b)** *(~zustand)* alert; **da war ständig** ~: there was a permanent state of alert
alarm-, Alarm-: ~**anlage die** alarm system; ~**bereit** *Adj.* on alert *postpos.;* ‹*fire crew, police*› on stand-by *postpos.*, standing by *pred.;* ~**bereitschaft die** *s.* ~**bereit:** alert; **in [ständiger]** ~**bereitschaft** on [permanent] alert/stand-by; **jmdn./etw. in** ~**bereitschaft versetzen** place *or* put sb./sth. on alert/stand-by; ~**fall der** alert; **im** ~**fall** in case of alert; in the event of an alert; ~**glocke die** alarm bell
alarmieren *tr. V.* **a)** *(zu Hilfe rufen)* call [out] ‹*doctor, police, fire brigade, etc.*›; **b)** *(warnen)* alarm; ~**d** alarming; **nichts Alarmierendes** nothing alarming
Alarmierung die; ~: **bei rechtzeitiger** ~ **der Bergwacht** *usw.* if the mountain rescue service *etc.* is/had been called [out] in time; **eine sofortige** ~ **der Feuerwehr wäre geboten gewesen** the fire service *or (Amer.)* department should have been called [out] immediately; **zur** ~ **aller Demokraten führen** cause alarm on the part of all democrats
Alarm-: ~**klingel die** alarm bell; ~**pikett das** *(schweiz.) s.* **Überfallkommando;** ~**ruf der** *(fig.)* warning cry; ~**signal das** *(auch fig.)* warning signal; ~**sirene die** alarm *or* warning siren; ~**stufe die** alert stage; **höchste** ~**stufe** maximum alert; ~**stufe eins/zwei/drei** stage one/two/three alert; ~**übung die** practice drill; *(Milit.)* practice alert; ~**vor·richtung die** alarm [device]; ~**zeichen das** *(fig.)* warning signal; ~**zustand der** state of alert; **sich im** ~**zustand befinden** ‹*troops*› be on alert; ‹*fire service, police*› be on stand-by; ‹*country, province*› be on a state of alert; **in den** ~**zustand versetzen** put ‹*troops*› on alert; place *or* put ‹*fire service, police*› on stand-by; place *or* put ‹*country, province*› on a state of alert
Alaska [a'laska] **(das);** ~**s** Alaska
Alaun [a'laun] **der;** ~**s,** ~**e** alum
Alaun·stift der styptic pencil
A-Laut der A-sound
Alb [alp] **der;** ~**[e]s,** ~**en** *(Myth.)* elf
Albaner [al'ba:nɐ] **der;** ~**s,** ~, **Albanerin die;** ~, ~**nen** Albanian
Albanien [al'ba:ni̯ən] **(das);** ~**s** Albania
albanisch *Adj.* Albanian; *s. auch* **deutsch**
Albanisch das; ~**s** Albanian; *s. auch* **Deutsch**
Albatros ['albatrɔs] **der;** ~, ~**se** *(Zool.)* albatross
Alb·druck *s.* **Alpdruck**
Albe ['albə] **die;** ~, ~**n** *(christl. Kirchen)* alb
Alben *s.* **Alb, Albe, Album**
Alberei die; ~, ~**en** *s.* **Albernheit b**
[1]albern *itr. V.* fool about *or* around
[2]albern *Adj.* **a)** *(kindisch, töricht)* silly; foolish; ~**es Zeug reden** talk silly *or* foolish nonsense; **stell dich nicht so** ~ **an** don't be so silly; **sich** ~ **benehmen** act silly; **sich** *(Dat.)* ~ **vorkommen** feel silly; feel a fool; **b)** *(ugs.: nebensächlich)* silly; stupid
Albernheit die; ~, ~**en a)** *o. Pl. (albernes Verhalten)* silliness,; foolishness; **b)** *(alberne Handlung)* silliness; *(alberne Bemerkung/alberner Witz)* silly remark/joke; **diese** ~**en** this silliness *sing.*
Albinismus [albi'nɪsmʊs] **der;** ~ albinism
Albino [al'bi:no] **der;** ~**s,** ~**s** albino
Alb·traum *s.* **Alptraum**
Album ['albʊm] **das;** ~**s, Alben** album
Albumin [albu'mi:n] **das;** ~**s,** ~**e** *(Biol.)* albumin
Alchemie [alçe'mi:] **die;** ~ *(bes. österr.),* **Alchimie** [alçi'mi:] **die;** ~: alchemy *no art.*
Alchemist der; ~**en,** ~**en** *(bes. österr.),* **Alchemistin die;** ~, ~**nen** *(bes. österr.),* **Alchimist der;** ~**en,** ~**en, Alchimistin die;** ~, ~**nen** alchemist
Alchimisten·küche die alchemist's laboratory
alchimistisch 1. *Adj.* alchemical; alchemistic. **2.** *adv.* alchemistically; ~ **beeinflußt** influenced by alchemy
Aldehyd [alde'hy:t] **der;** ~**s,** ~**e** *(Chem.)* aldehyde
Alemanne [alə'manə] **der;** ~**n,** ~**n, Alemannin die;** ~, ~**nen** Alemannian; **die** ~**n** Alemannians; *(Hist.)* the Alemanni
alemannisch *Adj.* Alemannic
alert [a'lɛrt] *Adj. (ugs.)* dynamic
Aleuten [ale'u:tn̩] *Pl.* **die** ~: the Aleutian Islands; the Aleutians
Alexandriner [alɛksan'dri:nɐ] **der;** ~**s,** ~ *(Verslehre)* alexandrine
Alfa·gras ['alfa-] **das** alfa grass
Alge ['algə] **die;** ~, ~**n** alga
Algebra ['algebra, *österr.:* al'ge:bra] **die;** ~, *(fachspr.)* **Algebren** algebra
Algebraiker der; ~**s,** ~, **Algebraikerin die;** ~, ~**nen** algebraist
algebraisch 1. *Adj.* algebraic. **2.** *adv.* algebraically
Algen-: ~**pest die** seaweed plague; ~**pilz der** comycete
Algerien [al'ge:ri̯ən] **(das);** ~**s** Algeria
Algerier der; ~**s,** ~, **Algerierin die;** ~, ~**nen** Algerian
algerisch *Adj.* Algerian
Algier ['alʒi:ɐ̯] **(das);** ~**s** Algiers
Algorithmus [algo'rɪtmʊs] **der;** ~, **Algorithmen** *(Math., DV)* algorithm
alias ['a:li̯as] *Adv.* alias
Alibi ['a:libi] **das;** ~**s,** ~**s a)** *(Rechtsw.)* alibi; **b)** *(Ausrede)* alibi *(coll.);* excuse
Alibi-: ~**frau die** token woman; ~**funktion die** use as an alibi *(coll.) or* excuse; ~**funktion haben** serve as an alibi *(coll.) or* excuse
Alimente [ali'mɛntə] *Pl. (veralt., noch ugs.)* maintenance *sing. (esp. for illegitimate child);* **jmdn. auf** ~ **verklagen** sue sb. for maintenance
Alk [alk] **der;** ~**[e]s,** ~**en** *(Zool.)* auk
alkäisch [al'kɛ:ɪʃ] *Adj. (Verslehre)* alcaic
Alkali [al'ka:li] **das;** ~**s, Alkalien** alkali
alkali·frei *Adj. (Werbespr.)* non-alkaline
alkalisch *Adj. (Chemie)* alkaline
Alkaloid [alkalo'i:t] **das;** ~**[e]s,** ~**e** *(Chemie)* alkaloid
Alki ['alki] **der;** ~**s,** ~**s** *(salopp)* wino *(sl.)*
Alkohol ['alkoho:l] **der;** ~**s,** ~**e** alcohol; **unter** ~ **stehen** *(ugs.)* be under the influence *(coll.);* **jmdn. unter** ~ **setzen** *(ugs.)* get sb. drunk; *s. auch* **ertränken**
alkohol-, Alkohol-: ~**abhängig** *Adj.* dependent on alcohol *postpos.;* ~**abhängigkeit die** dependence on alcohol; alcohol dependence; ~**arm** *Adj.* low in alcohol *pred.;* ~**ausschank der** sale of alcohol[ic drinks]; **Kiosken ist der** ~**ausschank verboten** kiosks are forbidden to sell alcohol; „**kein** ~**ausschank an Jugendliche**" 'no alcohol may be sold to persons under 18'; ~**ein·fluß der,** ~**ein·wirkung die** influence of alcohol *or* drink; **unter** ~**einfluß** *od.* ~**einwirkung [stehen]** [be] under the influence of alcohol *or* drink; ~**fahne die** smell of alcohol [on one's breath]; **eine** ~**fahne haben** smell of alcohol; **jmds.** ~**fahne riechen** smell the alcohol on sb.'s breath; ~**frei** *Adj.* **a)** *(ohne ~gehalt)* non-alcoholic;

~**freie Getränke** soft *or* non-alcoholic drinks; **b)** *(ohne ~ausschank)* dry ‹*country, state, etc.*›; **c)** *(ohne ~genuß)* ‹*day, week, etc.*› without alcohol; **einen ~freien Tag einlegen** spend a day without drinking alcohol; ~**gegner der** opponent of alcohol; ~**gehalt der** alcohol content; ~**genuß der**; *o. Pl.* consumption of alcohol; **infolge ~genusses** as a result of consuming alcohol; ~**haltig** *Adj.* containing alcohol *postpos., not pred.*; ~**haltige Getränke** alcoholic drinks; **wenig/stark ~haltig sein** have a low/high alcohol content

Alkoholika [alko'ho:lika] *Pl.* alcoholic drinks

Alkoholiker der; ~s, ~, **Alkoholikerin die**; ~, ~nen alcoholic

alkoholisch *Adj.* alcoholic

alkoholisieren *tr. V.* **a)** *(mit Alkohol versetzen)* alcoholize; **b)** *(scherzh.: betrunken machen)* **jmdn.** ~: get sb. drunk

alkoholisiert *Adj.* inebriated; **in ~em Zustand** in a state of inebriation

Alkoholismus der; ~: alcoholism *no art.*

alkohol-, Alkohol-: ~**konsum der** consumption of alcohol; **er hat in letzter Zeit einen beträchtlichen ~konsum** *(ugs.)* he has recently been hitting the bottle *(coll.)*; ~**krank** *Adj. (Med.)* alcoholic; ~**mißbrauch der** alcohol abuse; ~**pegel der** *(scherzh.)* level of alcohol in one's blood; **sein ~pegel war schon ganz beträchtlich** he was already well primed; ~**reich** *Adj.* ‹*drink, wine, etc.*› with a high alcohol content; ~**reich sein** have a high alcohol content; ~**schmuggler der** bootlegger; ~**spiegel der** level of alcohol in one's blood; ~**steuer die** duty *or* tax on alcohol; ~**sucht die** alcohol addiction; alcoholism; ~**süchtig** *Adj.* addicted to alcohol *postpos.*; alcoholic; ~**süchtige der/die**; *adj. Dekl.* alcoholic; ~**sünder der** *(ugs.)* drunk[en] driver; ~**verbot das** ban on alcohol; **es herrschte ~verbot** alcohol was banned; ~**vergiftung die** alcohol[ic] poisoning

Alkoven [al'ko:vn̩] **der**; ~s, ~ alcove; *(Bettnische)* bed-recess

all [al] *Indefinitpron. u. unbest. Zahlw.* **1.** *attr. (ganz, gesamt...)* all; **in ~er Deutlichkeit** in all clarity; ~**e Freude, die sie empfunden hat** all the joy she felt; ~**es Geld, das ich noch habe** all the money I have left; ~**er Eifer nützte ihm nichts** all his zeal was to no avail; **ich kann diese Leute ~e nicht leiden** I can't stand any of these people; **ich will euch ~e nicht mehr sehen** I don't want to see any of you again; **die Ärzte verdienen ~e sehr viel** doctors all earn a great deal; ~**es Geld spendete sie dem Roten Kreuz** she donated all her money to the Red Cross; ~**es Leid der Welt** all the suffering in the world; ~ **unser/mein** *usw.* **...**: all our/my *etc.* ...; ~**es andere/Weitere/übrige** everything else; ~**es übrige hat sich nicht geändert** nothing else has changed; ~**es Schöne/Neue/Fremde** everything *or* all that is beautiful/new/strange; ~**es Gute!** all the best!; ~**e Fenster schließen** close all the windows; **sie gaben ~e Waffen ab** they handed in all their weapons; **wir/ihr/sie ~e** all of us/you/them; we/you/they all; **das sagen sie ~e** *(ugs.)* that's what they all say; ~**e Beteiligten/Anwesenden** all those involved/present; **trotz ~er Vorbehalte werde ich ...**: in spite of all my reservations I shall ...; ~**e beide/~e zehn** both of them/all ten of them; ~**e Männer/Frauen/Kinder** all men/women/children; ~**e Mädchen über zwölf Jahre** all girls over twelve; ~**e Mädchen in der Schule** all the girls in the school; ~**e Bewohner der Stadt** all the inhabitants of the town; **ohne ~en Anlaß** for no reason [at all]; without any reason [at all]; **gegen ~e Erwartungen** contrary to all expectations; ~**e Jahre wieder** every year; ~**e fünf Minuten/Meter** every five minutes/metres; **Bücher ~er Art** books of all kinds; all kinds of books; **in ~er Eile** with all haste; **in ~er Ruhe** in peace and quiet; **trotz ~er Versuche/Anstrengungen** despite all [his/her/their/*etc.*] attempts/efforts. **2.** *alleinstehend* **a)** *(gesamt..., sämtlich)* everything; ~**es geht vorüber** everything passes [in time]; ~**es für die Braut/den Bastler** everything for the bride/handicraft enthusiast; **das ~es** all that; **ich weiß nicht, was das ~es soll** I don't know what all that is supposed to mean; **das ist ~es Unsinn** that is all nonsense; **von ~em etwas verstehen/wissen** understand/know a bit about everything; **wer ~es war** *od.* **wer war ~es dort** who was there?; **wen ~es habt ihr getroffen?** who did you meet?; **das sind ~es Gauner** they're all scoundrels; **was gab es dort ~es zu sehen?** what was there to see?; **was es nicht ~es gibt!** well, would you believe it!; well, I never!; ~**[es] und jedes** everything; *(wahllos)* anything and everything; **trotz ~em** in spite of *or* despite everything; **sie liebt ihren Hund über ~es** she loves her dog more than anything else; **zu ~em fähig sein** *(fig.)* be capable of anything; ~**es schon mal dagewesen** *(ugs.)* it's all happened before; **das kenne ich ~es schon** I've heard it all before; ~**es in ~em** all in all; **vor ~em** above all; ~**es klar** *od.* **in Ordnung** *(ugs.)* everything's fine *or (coll.)* OK; ~**es klar?** everything all right *or (coll.)* OK?; **dann treffen wir uns um 5⁰⁰ Uhr, ~es klar?** we'll meet at 5 o'clock then, all right *or (coll.)* OK?; **das ist ~es** that's all *or (coll.)* it; **ist das ~es?** is that all *or (coll.)* it?; **nach ~em, was man hört/weiß** to judge from everything *or* all one hears/knows; **b)** *(jeder einzelne)* all; ~**e miteinander** all together; **ihr seid/wir sind/sie sind ..., ~e miteinander** you/we/they are ..., all of you/us/them; ~**e auf einmal** all at once; **sprecht nicht ~e auf einmal!** don't all speak at once; **am besten, wir gehen ~e auf einmal zum Chef** the best thing would be for us all to go and see the boss together; ~**e, die ...**: all those who ...; **der Kampf ~er gegen ~e** unfettered competition; **in ~em einverstanden sein** agree *or* be agreed on everything; **von ~em etwas nehmen** take a bit of everything; **er ist bei ~em, was er tut, sehr genau** he is very precise in everything he does; **sie ist in ~em sehr empfindlich** she is very sensitive about everything; **c)** *(Neutr. Sg.: ~e Beteiligten)* ~**es mal herhören!** *(ugs.)* listen everybody!; *(stärker befehlend)* everybody listen!; ~**es war nach Hause gegangen** *(ugs.)* everyone *or* everybody had gone home; ~**es aussteigen!** *(ugs.)* everyone *or* all out!; *(vom Schaffner gesagt)* all change!

All das; ~s space *no art.*; *(Universum)* universe

all-: ~**abendlich 1.** *Adj.; nicht präd.* regular evening; **2.** *adv.* every evening; ~**bekannt** *Adj. (geh.)* universally known; ~**da** *Adv. (veralt.)* there; ~**dem** *s.* **alledem**; ~**dieweil[en] 1.** *Konj. (veralt.)* since; because; **2.** *Adv.* all the while

alle *Adj.; nicht attr.* **a)** *(ugs.: verbraucht, verkauft usw.)* ~ **sein** be all gone; ~ **werden** run out; **etw. ~ machen** finish sth. off; **b)** *(salopp: erschöpft)* all in *pred.*; **c) jmdn. ~ machen** *(salopp)* do sb. in *(sl.)*

alle·dem *Pron. in* **trotz ~**: in spite of *or* despite all that; **von ~ wußte er nichts** he knew nothing about all that; **an ~ ist nichts wahr** there's no truth in any of it; **nichts von ~**: nothing of the sort *or* kind; **bei ~**: for all that; **zu ~**: in addition to *or* on top of all that

Allee [a'le:] **die**; ~, ~n avenue

Allee·baum der avenue tree

Allegorie [alego'ri:] **die**; ~, ~n allegory

Allegorik [ale'go:rɪk] **die**; ~: allegory

allegorisch 1. *Adj.* allegorical. **2.** *adv.* allegorically

Allegretto [ale'grɛto] **das**; ~s, ~s *od.* **Allegretti** allegretto

Allegro [a'le:gro] **das**; ~s, ~s *od.* **Allegri** allegro

allein [a'lain] **1.** *Adj.; nicht attr.* **a)** *(ohne andere, für sich)* alone; on one's/its own; by oneself/itself; **sie waren ~ im Zimmer** they were alone in the room; **ganz ~**: all on one's/its own; **jmdn. ~ lassen** leave sb. alone *or* on his/her own; ~ **über den Atlantik segeln** sail alone across the Atlantic; **b)** *(einsam)* alone. **2.** *adv. (ohne Hilfe)* by oneself/itself; on one's/its own; **sie kann ~ schwimmen** she can swim by herself *or* on her own; **etw. ~ machen** *(herstellen)* make sth. oneself; *(tun)* do sth. oneself; **von ~** *(ugs.)* by oneself/itself; **das müßtet ihr von ~ wissen** you shouldn't have to be told [that]. **3.** *Adv.* **a)** *(geh.: ausschließlich)* alone; **er ~ trägt die Verantwortung** he alone bears responsibility; it is his responsibility alone; **sie denkt ~ an sich** she thinks solely *or* only of herself; ~ **durch den Glauben** by faith alone; only by faith; **nicht ~ ..., sondern auch ...**: not only ..., but also ...; **b)** *(von allem anderen abgesehen)* **[schon] ~ der Gedanke/[schon] der Gedanke ~**: the mere *or* very thought [of it]; ~ **die Nebenkosten** the additional costs alone. **4.** *Konj. (veralt.)* however; but; ~, **es war zu spät** however, it was too late; it was too late, however

Allein-: ~**besitz der** sole *or* exclusive property; **im ~besitz von jmdm./in jmds. ~besitz sein** be sb.'s sole *or* exclusive property; ~**besitzer der** sole owner

alleine *(ugs.) s.* **allein**

allein-, Allein-: ~**erbe der**, ~**erbin die** sole heir; ~**erziehend** *Adj.; nicht präd.* single ‹*mother, father, parent*›; ~**erziehende der/die**; *adj. Dekl.* single parent; ~**flug der** *(Flugw.)* solo flight; ~**gang der a)** *(fig.: Tat)* independent initiative; **etw. im ~gang tun** do sth. off one's own bat; **b)** *(Sport)* solo run; *(Radfahren)* solo ride; **die Etappe praktisch im ~gang fahren** be out on one's own for practically the whole stage; **ein Tor im ~gang erzielen** score a goal from a solo run; **c)** *(Alpinistik)* solo ascent *or* climb; ~**gesellschafter der** *(Rechtsw.)* sole proprietor; ~**herrschaft die**; *o. Pl.* autocratic rule; *(Diktatur)* dictatorship; ~**herrscher der** *(auch fig.)* autocrat; *(Diktator, auch fig.)* dictator

alleinig *Adj.; nicht präd.* sole; sole, exclusive ‹*distribution rights*›

allein-, Allein-: ~**inhaber der** *(Wirtsch.)* sole owner; ~**reisende der/die** person travelling alone; ~**schuld die**; *o. Pl.* sole blame *or* responsibility *no indef. art.*; ~**sein das a)** *(das Verlassensein)* loneliness; **b)** *(das Ungestörtsein)* privacy; ~**selig·machend** *Adj. (kath. Rel.)* **die ~seligmachende Kirche/***(fig.)* **das ~seligmachende Prinzip** *usw.* the true church/principle *etc.* in which alone salvation is to be found; ~**stehend** *Adj.* ‹*person*› living on his/her own *or* alone; *(ledig)* single ‹*person*›; **ich bin ~stehend** I live on my own *or* alone/am single; ~**stehende der/die**; *adj. Dekl.* person living on his/her own *or* alone; *(Ledige[r])* single person; **ich als ~stehender ...**: living on my own I .../as a single person I ...; ~**unter·halter der** solo entertainer; ~**verdiener der** sole earner; ~**verschulden das** *s.* ~**schuld**; ~**vertretung die** *(Wirtsch.)* sole agency; *(Politik)* sole representation; ~**vertretungs·anspruch der** *(Politik)* claim to be the sole legitimate representative; ~**vertrieb der**: **den ~vertrieb von etw. haben/übernehmen** be/become the sole *or* exclusive distributor of sth.; have acquired sole *or* exclusive distribution rights to sth.

ạlle·mal *Adv.* **a)** *(ugs.: bestimmt)* any time *(coll.)*; **was der kann, das kann ich doch ~:** anything he can do, I can do too; **b)** *(jedesmal)* every time; always; *s. auch* 'ein 1

ạllen·fạlls *Adv.* **a)** *(höchstens)* at [the] most; at the outside; **~ 40 Leute** 40 people at most *or* at the outside; at most 40 people; **b)** *(nötigenfalls)* if need be; if necessary; **c)** *(bestenfalls)* at best

allenthalben ['alənt'halbn̩] *Adv.* *(geh.)* everywhere

ạller-: ~art *indekl. unbest. Gattungsz.; attr. (veralt.)* all kinds *or* sorts of; **~äußerst...** *Adj.* **a)** *(entferntest)* farthest; **b)** *(größt...)* extreme; utmost; **mit ~äußerster Vorsicht** with extreme *or* [the] utmost caution; **c)** *(schlimmst...)* worst; **im ~äußersten Fall** if the worst comes/came to the worst; **~best... 1.** *Adj.* very best; **~besten Dank** thank you very much indeed; **der/die/das Allerbeste sein** be the best of all; **es wäre das ~beste, wenn du ihn selbst fragst** the best thing [of all] would be for you to ask him yourself; **das ist das Allerbeste, was du tun kannst** that's the best thing you can do; **jmdm. das Allerbeste wünschen** wish sb. all the [very] best; **du bist mein Allerbester** you are my darling; **2.** *adv.* **am ~besten** best of all; **am ~besten wäre es, wenn ...:** the best thing [of all] would be if ...; **~dings 1.** *Adv.* **a)** *(einschränkend)* though; **es stimmt ~dings, daß ...:** it's true though that ...; **b)** *(zustimmend)* [yes,] certainly; **Habe ich dich geweckt? – Allerdings!** Did I wake you up? – You certainly did!; **2.** *Partikel (anteilnehmend)* to be sure; **das war ~dings Pech** that was bad luck, to be sure; **~erst...** *Adj.; nicht präd.* **a)** *(verstärkend: erst...)* very first; **der/die/das ~erste** the very first; **als ~erste[r] etw. tun** be the very first to do sth.; **das ~erste, was ich tun muß** the very first thing I must do; **b)** *(best...)* very best; **~frühest... 1.** *Adj.* very earliest; **2.** *adv.* **am ~frühesten** earliest of all; **~frühestens** *Adv.* at the very earliest

Allergen [alɛr'ge:n] **das; ~s, ~e** *(Med.)* allergen

Allergie [alɛr'gi:] **die; ~, ~n** *(Med.)* allergy

Allergiker [a'lɛrgikɐ] **der; ~s, ~, Allẹrgikerin die; ~, ~nen** *(Med.)* allergy sufferer

allẹrgisch 1. *Adj. (Med.)* allergic; **eine ~e Reaktion auf etw.** *(Akk.) (auch fig.)* an allergic reaction to sth.; **gegen etw. ~ sein** *(auch fig.)* be allergic to sth. **2.** *adv.* **auf etw.** *(Akk.)* **~ reagieren** have an allergic reaction to sth.; **~ auf jmdn./etw. reagieren** *(fig.)* be allergic to sb./sth.

ạller-, Ạller-: ~größt... *Adj.* utmost ⟨*trouble, care, etc.*⟩; biggest *or* largest ⟨*car, house, town, etc.*⟩ of all; tallest ⟨*person*⟩ of all; **am ~größten sein** be [the] biggest *or* largest/tallest of all; **~hạnd** *indekl. unbest. Gattungsz. (ugs.)* **a)** *attr.* all kinds *or* sorts of; **b)** *alleinstehend* all kinds *or* sorts of things; **das ist ~hand!** *(viel)* that's a lot; *(sehr gut)* that's quite something; **das ist ja** *od.* **doch ~hand!** that's just not on *(Brit. coll.)*; that really is the limit *(coll.)*; **~heiligen das; ~** *(bes. kath. Kirche)* All Saints' Day; All Hallows; **~heiligste das; ~n a)** *(Tempelinneres)* inner sanctum; *(jüdisch, orth.)* holy of holies; *(fig.)* holy of holies; inner sanctum; **b)** *(kath. Rel.)* Blessed Sacrament; **~hẹrzlichst 1.** *Adj.; nicht präd.* warmest ⟨*thanks, greetings, congratulations*⟩; most cordial ⟨*reception, welcome, invitation*⟩; **2.** *adv.* ⟨*thank, greet, congratulate*⟩ most warmly; ⟨*welcome*⟩ most warmly *or* cordially; **Sie sind ~herzlichst eingeladen ...:** you are most cordially invited ...; **~höchst... 1.** *Adj.* highest ... of all; **der ~höchste Gipfel** the highest peak of all; the topmost peak; **der ~höchste Berg der Welt** the highest mountain in the world; **es ist ~höchste Zeit, daß ...:** it really is high time that ...; **am ~höchsten sein** be the highest of all; **die ~höchsten Kreise** the very highest circles; **auf ~höchste Anordnung** on orders from the very top; **der Allerhöchste** *(dichter.)* the Most High; **2.** *adv.* **am ~höchsten** ⟨*fly, jump, etc.*⟩ the highest of all; **~höchstens** *Adv.* at the very most

ạllerlei *indekl. unbest. Gattungsz.: attr.* all kinds *or* sorts of; *alleinstehend* all kinds *or* sorts of things

Ạllerlei das; ~s, ~s *(Gemisch)* pot-pourri; *(Durcheinander)* jumble; **Leipziger ~:** 'Leipzig-style' mixed vegetables *(carrots, green beans, peas, celery, kohlrabi, and asparagus)*

ạller-, Ạller-: ~lẹtzt... *Adj.; nicht präd.* **a)** *(verstärkend)* very last; **der/die/das ~letzte** the very last [one]; **b)** *(drückt Ablehnung aus)* most dreadful *or* awful *(coll.)*; **das ist [ja** *od.* **wirklich] das Allerletzte** *(ugs.)* that [really] is the absolute limit; **c)** *(~neuest...)* very latest; **~liebst** *Adj.* **a)** *(verstärkend)* most favourite; **am ~liebsten besuchte er die Großmutter** best of all he liked to go and see his grandmother; **es wäre mir das ~liebste** *od.* **am ~liebsten, wenn ...:** I should like it best of all if ...; **das Allerliebste, was ich habe** my most favourite *or* treasured possession; **ihr Allerliebster/seine Allerliebste** her/his beloved; **b)** *(reizend)* enchanting; delightful; **~meist** *Adv.* mostly; for the most part; **~meist... 1.** *Indefinitpron. u. unbest. Zahlw.* **a)** *(die größte Menge)* by far the most *attrib.*; **das ~meiste/am ~meisten** most of all/by far the most; **b)** *(der größte Teil)* **die ~meisten Gäste** the vast majority of the guests; **die ~meiste Zeit** by far the greatest part of the time; **die ~meisten [der Arbeiter** *usw.*] the vast majority [of the workers *etc.*]; **2.** *Adv.* **am ~meisten** most of all; **die am ~meisten befahrene Straße** by far the most travelled road; **~mindest...** *Adj.; nicht präd.* slightest; least; **das ~mindeste** the very least; **nicht das ~mindeste** absolutely nothing; **nicht im ~mindesten** not in the least *or* slightest; **zum ~mindesten** at the very least; **~nächst... 1.** *Adj.* very nearest *attrib.*; *(räumliche od. zeitliche Reihenfolge ausdrückend)* very next *attrib.*; very closest ⟨*relatives*⟩; **in ~nächster Zeit** in the very near future; **am ~nächsten sein** be the nearest of all; **2.** *adv.* **am ~nächsten** nearest of all; **~neu[e]st...** *Adj.* very latest *attrib.*; **das Allerneu[e]ste** the very latest; **~nötigst..., ~notwẹndigst... 1.** *Adj.* absolutely necessary; **ich habe nur die ~nötigsten** *od.* **~notwendigsten Kleider gepackt** I only packed the clothes that are/were absolutely necessary; **am ~nötigsten** *od.* **~notwendigsten hätte ich ...:** what I'm most badly in need of is/are ....; **es am ~nötigsten** *od.* **~notwendigsten haben, etw. zu tun** be most in need of doing sth.; **der hat es am ~nötigsten** *od.* **~notwendigsten!** *(ugs.)* he's a fine one to talk; **das Allernötigste** what is/was absolutely necessary; **2.** *adv.* **am ~nötigsten** ⟨*need etc.*⟩ most badly; **~ọrten** *(veralt.)*, **~ọrts** *(geh.)* *Adv.* everywhere; **~schlịmmst... 1.** *Adj.* very worst *attrib.*; **der/die/das ~schlimmste** *od.* **am ~schlimmsten sein** be the worst of all; **das Allerschlimmste** the worst of all; **sich auf das Allerschlimmste gefaßt machen** prepare oneself for the very worst; **2.** *adv.* **am ~schlimmsten** worst of all; **~schönst... 1.** *Adj.* most beautiful *attrib.*; loveliest *attrib.*; *(angenehmst...)* very nicest *attrib.*; **in ~schönster Harmonie** in perfect harmony; **am ~schönsten war, daß ...** *(auch iron.)*; **das Allerschönste, was ich je gesehen habe** the loveliest thing I have ever seen; **das wäre ja noch das Allerschönste** that would beat everything; **2.** *adv.* **am ~schönsten war, daß ...:** the best thing of all was that ...; **da werden alle Vorurteile aufs ~schönste bestärkt** *(iron.)* that's the best possible way of reinforcing everyone's prejudices; **~seelen das; ~** *(kath. Kirche)* All Souls' Day; **~seits** *Adv.* **a)** *(alle zusammen)* **guten Morgen ~seits!** good morning everyone *or* everybody; **b)** *(überall)* on all sides; on every side; **~seits sehr geschätzt sein** be highly regarded by everyone; **~spätestens** *Adv.* at the very latest

Ạllerwẹlts-: ~gesicht/~wort/~mittel nondescript face/hackneyed word/cure-all

Ạllerwẹlts·kẹrl der Jack of all trades

ạller, Ạller-: ~wenigst... 1. *Adj.; nicht präd.* least ... of all; *Pl.* fewest ... of all; **er hat von allen das ~wenigste Geld** *od.* **am ~wenigsten Geld** he has the least money of all; **die ~wenigsten [Menschen] wissen das** very few [people] know that; **das Allerwenigste, was er hätte tun können** the very least he could have done; **2.** *adv.* **am ~wenigsten abbekommen/arbeiten** get/work [the] least of all; **das hätte ich von ihm am ~wenigsten erwartet** he's the very last person I would have expected that of; **das am ~wenigsten!** anything but that!; **~wenigstens** *Adv.* at the very least; **~werteste der;** *adj. Dekl. (ugs. scherzh.)* posterior

ạlles *s.* **all**

ạlle·sạmt *Indefinitpron. u. unbest. Zahlw. (ugs.)* all [of you/us/them]; **wir ~:** all of us; we all

Ạlles-: ~brenner der multi-fuel stove; **~fresser der** omnivore; **~kleber der** all-purpose adhesive *or* glue; **~könner der** all-rounder; **~wisser der** *(abwertend)* know-all

ạlle·zeit *Adv. (veralt.) s.* **allzeit**

ạll-, Ạll-: ~fällig *(bes. österr., schweiz.)* **1.** *Adj.* possible; **~fällige Verluste** any losses which may occur; **Allfälliges** miscellaneous; *(Tagesordnungspunkt)* any other business; **2.** *adv.* **~fällig anfallende Portokosten/~fällig vorkommende Ausnahmen** any postal charges/exceptions which may arise; **~gegenwart die** *(christl. Theol., fig.)* omnipresence; **~gegenwärtig** *Adj. (christl. Theol., fig.)* omnipresent

ạll·gemein 1. *Adj.* general; universal ⟨*conscription, suffrage*⟩; universally applicable ⟨*law, rule*⟩; **auf ~en Wunsch** by popular *or* general request; **zur ~en Überraschung** to everyone's *or* everybody's surprise; **das ~e Wohl** the common good; **im ~en Interesse** in the common interest; in everybody's interest; **~e Redensarten** common expressions; **vom Allgemeinen auf das Besondere schließen** infer the particular from the general; **im ~en** in general; generally. **2.** *adv.* **a)** *(überall, allerseits, von allen)* generally; *(generell, ausnahmslos)* universally; **es ist ~ üblich, das zu tun** it is [the] common practice to do it; **~ verbreitet** widespread; **es ist ~ bekannt, daß ...:** it is common knowledge that ...; **~ gängig** common; **~ zugänglich** open to all *or* everybody; **es wird ~ diskutiert** it is being discussed by people at large; **wird das ~ gewünscht?** is that the general wish?; **b)** *(nicht speziell, oft abwertend: unverbindlich)* ⟨*write, talk, discuss, examine, be worded*⟩ in general terms; **eine ~ gehaltene Einführung** a general introduction; **das kann man nicht so ~ behaupten** one cannot generalize like that; **c)** *(umfassend)*; **~ belesen/beschlagen sein** be well read/be knowledgeable about a wide range of subjects; **~ interessiert sein** have a wide range of interests

allgemein-, Allgemein-: ~befinden das *(Med.)* general state of health; general condition; **~begriff der** *(Philos., Sprachw.)* general concept; **~besitz der** *(auch fig.)* common property; **~bildend** *Adj.* ⟨*school, course, etc.*⟩ providing a general *or* an all-round *or (Amer.)* all-around education; **das Zeitunglesen für ~bildend halten** hold that reading newspapers is of general educational value; **~bildende polytechnische Oberschule** *(DDR)* general polytechnical secondary school; **~bildung die;** *o. Pl.* general *or* all-round *or (Amer.)* all-around education; **~gültig 1.** *Adj.; nicht präd.* universally *or* generally applicable ‹*law, rule*›; universally *or* generally valid ‹*law of nature, definition, thesis*›; **2.** *adv.* **etw. ~gültig formulieren/festlegen** formulate sth./set sth. down in universally *or* generally applicable terms; **~gültigkeit die** *s.* **~gültig 1:** universal *or* general applicability/validity; **~gut das** *(fig.)* common knowledge

Allgemeinheit die; ~, ~en a) *o. Pl. (Öffentlichkeit)* general public; public at large; **b)** *o. Pl. (Unverbindlichkeit)* generality; **c)** *Pl. (Äußerungen)* generalities

allgemein-, Allgemein-: ~interesse das public interest; **~medizin die;** *o. Pl.* general medicine; **~mediziner der** general practitioner; GP; **~platz der** platitude; commonplace; **~verbindlich 1.** *Adj.; nicht präd.* universally binding; **2.** *adv.* in universally binding terms; **~verständlich 1.** *Adj.; nicht präd.* comprehensible *or* intelligible to all *postpos.;* readily comprehensible *or* intelligible; **2.** *adv.* in a way comprehensible *or* intelligible to all; in a readily comprehensible *or* intelligible manner; **~wissen das** general knowledge; **~wohl das** public welfare *or* good

all-, All-: ~gewalt die *(geh.)* omnipotence; **~gewaltig** *(geh.) Adj.* omnipotent; all-powerful; **der Allgewaltige** the Almighty; **~gütig** *Adj.* all-gracious; **~heil·mittel das** *(auch fig.)* cure-all; panacea; universal remedy

Allianz [a'li̯ant͜s] **die; ~, ~en** alliance

Alligator [ali'ga:tɔr] **der; ~s, ~en** [...ga'to:rən] alligator

alliieren [ali'i:rən] *refl. V.* form an alliance; **sich mit jmdm. ~:** ally oneself with sb.

alliiert *Adj.; nicht präd.* allied

Alliierte der; *adj. Dekl.* ally; **die ~n** the Allies

Alliteration [alıtera't͜si̯o:n] **die; ~, ~en** *(Verslehre)* alliteration

all, All-: ~jährlich 1. *Adj.* annual; yearly; **2.** *adv.* annually; every year; **~macht die;** *o. Pl. (geh.)* omnipotence; **~mächtig** *Adj.* omnipotent; all-powerful; **der ~mächtige Gott** Almighty God; **~mächtiger Gott!** *(ugs.)* good God!; heavens above!; **~mächtige der;** *adj. Dekl.* **der ~mächtige** Almighty God; the Almighty; **~mächtiger!** good God!; heavens above!

all·mählich 1. *Adv.* gradually; **es wird ~ Zeit** it's about time; **ich werde ~ müde** I'm beginning to get tired; **wir sollten ~ gehen** it's time we got going. **2.** *adj.; nicht präd.* gradual

Allmende [al'mɛndə] **die; ~, ~n** common land

all-: ~monatlich 1. *Adj.* monthly; **2.** *adv.* monthly; every month; **~morgendlich 1.** *Adj.; nicht präd.* regular morning; **2.** *adv.* every morning; **~nächtlich 1.** *Adj.; nicht präd.* nightly; **2.** *adv.* nightly; every night

Allonge·perücke [a'lõ:ʒə-] **die** full-bottomed wig

allo- [alo-], **Allo-: ~path** [~'pa:t] **der; ~en, ~en** allopath; **~pathie** [~pa'ti:] **die; ~:** allopathy; **~pathisch 1.** *Adj.* allopathic; **2.** *adv.* allopathically; **~phon das; ~s, ~e** *(Sprachw.)* allophone

Allotria [a'lo:tria] **das; ~[s], ~:** skylarking; **~ treiben** skylark; lark about *(coll.)*

All-: ~parteien·regierung die all-party government; **~rad·antrieb der** *(Kfz-W.)* all-wheel drive

Allround- ['ɔ:l'raʊnd-] all-round; all-around *(Amer.)*

Allround·man ['ɔ:l'raʊndmən] **der; ~s, Allroundmen** all-rounder

all, All-: ~seitig 1. *Adj.* **a)** *(allgemein)* general; all-round, *(Amer.)* all-around *attrib.;* **zur ~seitigen Zufriedenheit** to the satisfaction of all *or* everyone; **b)** *(umfassend)* comprehensive; **eine ~seitige Ausbildung** an all-round *or (Amer.)* all-around education; **2.** *adv.* **a)** *(allgemein)* generally; **man war ~seitig einverstanden** there was agreement on all sides *or* general agreement; **~seitig geachtet** highly regarded by everyone; **b)** *(umfassend)* comprehensively; **~seitig gebildet sein** have had an all-round *or (Amer.)* all-around education; **~seitig begabt/interessiert sein** have all-round *or (Amer.)* all-around talents/interests; **~seits** *Adv.* everywhere; on all sides; *(in jeder Hinsicht)* in all respects; in every respect; **~seits geschätzt** highly regarded by everyone; **~strom·gerät das** *(Elektrot.)* AC/DC appliance; **~stündlich 1.** *Adj.; nicht präd.* hourly; **2.** *adv.* hourly; every hour

All·tag der a) *(Werktag)* weekday; **ein Mantel für den ~:** a coat for everyday wear; **zum ~ gehören** *(fig.)* be part of everyday life; **b)** *o. Pl. (Einerlei)* daily routine; **der graue ~:** the dull routine of everyday life; **der ~ der Ehe** the day-to-day realities of married life; **morgen geht der graue ~ wieder los** it's back to the daily grind tomorrow

all·täglich 1. *Adj.* **a)** ['-'--] *(gewöhnlich)* ordinary ‹*face, person, appearance, etc.*›; everyday ‹*topic, event, sight*›; commonplace ‹*remark*›; **ein nicht ~er Anblick** a sight one doesn't see every day; **etw. Alltägliches sein** be an everyday occurrence; **es ist nichts Alltägliches, wenn ...:** it's not every day that ...; it doesn't happen every day that ...; **b)** *(werktäglich)* everyday, workaday *attrib.* ‹*clothes*›; **c)** ['-'--] *(täglich)* daily. **2.** *adv.* **a)** *(werktäglich)* [on] weekdays; **b)** ['-'--] *(täglich)* daily; every day

Alltäglichkeit die; ~, ~en a) *o. Pl. (das Alltäglichsein)* ordinariness; **b)** *o. Pl. (Gewohnheit)* **eine ~ sein/zur ~ werden** be/become routine *or* commonplace; **c)** *(alltäglicher Vorgang)* everyday occurrence

all·tags *Adv.* [on] weekdays

Alltags- everyday *attrib.;* of everyday life *postpos., not pred.;* **~pflicht** daily duty

Alltags-: ~kleidung die everyday *or* workaday clothes *pl.;* **~mensch der** ordinary person; **~sprache die** *(Sprachw.)* everyday language; **~trott der** *(abwertend)* daily round *or* grind; **jetzt geht der ~trott wieder los** now it's back to the daily grind

all·um·fassend 1. *Adj.* all-embracing; encyclopaedic ‹*knowledge*›. **2.** *adv.* ‹*plan, inform*› in comprehensive detail; **~ gebildet sein** have had an all-round *or (Amer.)* all-around education

Allüren [a'ly:rən] *Pl. (meist abwertend)* behaviour *sing.; (geziertes Benehmen)* affectations; airs and graces

Alluvium [a'lu:vi̯ʊm] **das; ~s** *(Geol.)* Holocene epoch

all, All: ~wetter·straße die all-weather road; **~wissend** *Adj.* omniscient; **er tut, als wäre er ~wissend** he acts as if he knew everything; **~wissenheit die; ~:** omniscience; **~wöchentlich 1.** *Adj.* weekly; **2.** *adv.* weekly; every week; **~zeit** *Adv. (veralt.)* always; **~zeit bereit!** be prepared!

all·zu *Adv.* all too; **er war nicht ~ begeistert** he was not too *or* not all that enthusiastic; **nicht ~ viele** not all that many *(coll.);* not too many; **kein ~ großes Gewicht** not too heavy a weight; **~ viele Fehler** far too many mistakes

allzu-: ~bald *Adv.* all too soon; **~früh** *Adv.* all too early; *(~bald)* all too soon; **nicht ~früh** not too early; **~gern** *Adv.* ‹*like*› only too much; *(bereitwillig)* only too willingly; **ich möchte es doch ~gern machen** I would be only too pleased *or* delighted to do it; **ich esse zwar Fisch, aber nicht ~gern** I'll eat fish but I'm not all that fond *(coll.) or* not overfond of it; **~lang[e]** *Adv.* too long; **~menschlich** *Adv.* in an all too human way *or* manner; **~oft** *Adv.* too often; **nicht ~oft** not too often; not all that often *(coll.);* **~sehr** *Adv.* too much; **~sehr enttäuscht/begeistert** only too disappointed/enthusiastic; **nicht ~sehr** not too much; not all that much *(coll.);* **etw. ~sehr/nicht ~sehr mögen** like sth. all too much/not like sth. too much *or (coll.)* all that much; **nicht ~sehr interessiert** not too *or (coll.)* not all that interested; **ich habe mich ~sehr/nicht ~sehr bemüht** I tried only too hard/did not try too hard; **~viel** *Adv.* too much; **~ ist ungesund** one should never overdo things; you can have too much of a good thing

All·zweck- multi-purpose

All·zweck-: ~halle die multi-purpose hall; **~tuch das;** *Pl.* **~tücher** multi-purpose *or* all-purpose cloth

Alm [alm] **die; ~, ~en** mountain pasture; Alpine pasture

Alm·ab·trieb der *driving of the cattle down from the mountain pastures in autumn*

Almanach ['almanax] **der; ~s, ~e** *(Buchw.) (hist.)* almanac; *(eines Verlages)* yearbook *(containing a selection from the firm's publications during the year)*

Alm-: ~auf·trieb der *driving of the cattle up to the mountain pastures in spring;* **~hütte die** Alpine hut

Almosen ['almo:zn̩] **das; ~s, ~ a)** *(veralt.: Spende)* alms *pl.;* **von ~ leben** live on charity; **b)** *(abwertend: dürftiges Entgelt)* pittance

Alm-: ~rausch der; *o. Pl. (österr., südd.)* Alpine rose; alpenrose; **~wirtschaft die;** *o. Pl.* Alpine farming *no art.*

Aloe ['a:loe] **die; ~, ~n** aloe

[1]Alp [alp] **die; ~, ~en** *(bes. schweiz.) s.* **Alm**

[2]Alp der; ~[e]s, ~e *(veralt.: Kobold) goblin believed to give sleeping people nightmares by sitting on their chests at night;* ≈ incubus; **wie ein ~ auf der Brust lasten** *(geh.)* lie *or* weigh heavily on sb.; **ein ~ plagte ihn** he had nightmares

[1]Alpaka [al'paka] **das; ~s, ~s** *(Lama, Wolle)* alpaca

[2]Alpaka der; ~s *(Gewebe)* alpaca

[3]Alpaka das; ~s *(veralt.: Neusilber)* German silver; nickel silver

Alpaka·wolle die alpaca wool

Alp-: ~druck der; *o. Pl.* nightmare; **~drücken das; ~s** nightmares *pl.*

Alpen *Pl.* **die ~:** the Alps

Alpen- Alpine

alpen-, Alpen-: ~dollar der *(scherzh.)* [Austrian] schilling; **~glühen das; ~s** alpenglow; **~jäger** *Pl. (Milit.)* Alpine Troops; **~land das;** *o. Pl.* Alpine country *or* region; **~ländisch** [~lɛndıʃ] *Adj.* ‹*music, customs, dances*› of the Alpine region; ‹*goods*› from the Alpine region; **~paß der** Alpine pass; **~republik die** *(ugs.)* Alpine Republic *(Austria or Switzerland);* **~rose die** rhododendron; Alpine rose; **~veilchen das** cyclamen; **~vorland das;** *o. Pl.* foothills *pl.* of the Alps

Alpha ['alfa] **das; ~[s], ~[s]** alpha

Alphabet [alfa'be:t] **das; ~[e]s, ~e** alphabet

alphabetisch 1. *Adj.* alphabetical. **2.** *adv.* alphabetically; **etw. ~ ordnen** arrange sth. in alphabetical order *or* alphabetically

alphabetisieren *tr. V.* **a)** *(ordnen)* arrange in alphabetical order *or* alphabetically; alphabetize; **b)** *(lesen u. schreiben lehren)* **jmdn. ~:** teach sb. to read and write

Alphabetisierung die; ~ a) *(das Ordnen)* alphabetization; **b)** *(das Lehren)* teaching literacy skills; **eine Kampagne zur ~ der Bevölkerung** a campaign against illiteracy in the population

ạlpha·numẹrisch *(DV)* **1.** *Adj.* alphanumeric. **2.** *adv.* alphanumerically
Ạlpha-: **~strahlen** *Pl. (Kernphysik)* alpha rays; **~teilchen das** *(Kernphysik)* alpha particle
Ạlp·horn das; *Pl.* Alphörner alpenhorn
alpin [al'pi:n] *Adj.* **a)** Alpine; **~e Kombination** *(Ski)* Alpine combined [event]; **b)** *nicht präd. (Bergsteigen)* mountaineering
Alpinịsmus der; ~: Alpinism *no art.*
Alpinịst der; ~en, ~en Alpinist
Alpinịstik die; ~: Alpinism *no art.*
Alpinịstin die; ~, ~nen Alpinist
alpinịstisch *Adj.* mountaineering *attrib.*
Älpler ['ɛlplɐ] **der; ~s, ~, Ạ̈lplerin die; ~, ~nen** inhabitant of the Alps
Ạlp·traum der nightmare
Alraune [al'raunə] **die; ~, ~n** mandrake
¹als *Konj.* **a)** *(zeitlich)* when; *(während)* as; **~ wir zu Hause ankamen, [da] fing es an zu regnen** when *or* after we had arrived home, it started to rain; **gleich ~:** as soon as; **damals, ~:** [in the days] when; **gerade ~:** just as; **gerade ~ Tante Ida hier war** just when Aunt Ida was here; **b)** *(nach Komp.)* than; **mehr/weniger ~:** more/less than; **mehr ~ arbeiten kann ich nicht** I can't do more than work; **c)** *(bei Vergleichen)* **niemand/nirgends anders ~:** nobody/nowhere but; **mir fehlt nichts weiter, ~ daß ...:** there is nothing wrong with me other than that ...; **sie arbeiten mit anderen Methoden ~ wir** they work with different methods from ours; **alles andere ~:** anything but; **kein anderer** *od.* **niemand anderes ~ Karl** none other than Karl; **anders ~ wir sein/leben** be different/live differently from us; **soviel/soweit ~ möglich** as much/as far as possible; **so bald/schnell ~ möglich** as soon/as quickly as possible; *s. auch* **sowohl; d)** *(bei Modalsätzen)* as if; as though; **~ ob** *od.* **wenn** as if; as though; **~ ob ich das nicht wüßte!** as if I didn't know; **~ ob das neu wäre!** as if that were something new; **e)** *(in der Eigenschaft)* as; **~ Rentner/Arzt** as a pensioner/a doctor; **sich ~ Held fühlen** feel oneself [to be] a hero; **sich ~ wahr/falsch erweisen** prove [to be] true/false; **in seiner/ihrer Eigenschaft ~ ...:** in his/her capacity as ...; **f)** *(eine Folge ausdrückend)* **die Kinder sind zu klein, ~ daß sie das verstehen könnten** the children are too young to understand that; **die Zeit war zu kurz, ~ daß wir ...:** time was too short for us to ...; **g)** *(einen Grund ausdrückend)* **um so ..., ~ ...:** all the more ... since *or* in that ...; **h)** *(veralt.: vor Aufzählungen)* **~ [da sind]** to wit; namely; *s. auch* **insofern**
²ạls *Adv. (westmd.)* **a)** *(immer)* **~ etw. tun** keep on doing sth.; **gehen Sie ~ geradeaus** keep going straight on *or* ahead; **b)** *(manchmal)* sometimes
als-: **~bạld** *Adv. (geh. veralt.) (sogleich)* immediately; at once; *(kurz danach)* soon; **~bạldig** *Adj.; nicht präd. (Papierdt.)* immediate; **„zum ~baldigen Verbrauch bestimmt"** 'for immediate consumption'; **~dạnn** *Adv. (geh. veralt.)* then
also ['alzo] **1.** *Adv.* **a)** *(folglich)* so; therefore; **~ kommst du mit?** so you're coming too?; you're coming too, then?; **b)** *(veralt.: so)* thus. **2.** *Partikel* **a)** *(das heißt)* that is; **b)** *(nach Unterbrechung)* well [then]; **~, wie ich schon sagte** well [then], as I was saying; **c)** *(verstärkend);* **~, kommst du jetzt oder nicht?** well, are you coming now or not?; **na ~!** there you are[, you see]; **~ schön** well all right then; **~ so was/nun!** well, I don't know; well, really; **~, so eine Frechheit** well, what a cheek; **~, gute Nacht** good-night then; **~ dann** right then
Als-ọb das; ~ *(Philos.)* **die Philosophie des ~:** the philosophy of 'as-if'
alt [alt]; **älter** ['ɛltɐ], **ältest...** ['ɛltəst...] *Adj.* **a)** old; **~ und jung** old and young; **seine ~en Eltern** his aged parents; **hier werde ich nicht ~** *(fig. ugs.)* I won't be staying here long; **das Alte Testament** the Old Testament; **die Alte Welt** the Old World; **~ aussehen** *(fig. salopp)* be in the cart *(sl.)*; **eine drei Jahre ~e Tochter** a three-year-old daughter; **wie ~ bist du?** how old are you?; **man ist so ~, wie man sich fühlt** you're only as old as you feel; **aus ~ mach neu** give your coat/furniture *etc.* a new lease of life; **immer die ~e Platte** *od.* **Leier** it's always the same old story; *s. auch* **Dame; Eisen; Hase; Herr; b)** *(nicht mehr frisch)* old; **~es Brot** stale bread; **c)** *(vom letzten Jahr)* old; **~e Äpfel/Kartoffeln** last year's apples/potatoes; **im ~en Jahr** *(dieses Jahr)* this year; *(letztes Jahr)* last year; **d)** *(seit langem bestehend)* ancient; old; **ein ~es Volk/ein ~er Brauch** an ancient people/an ancient *or* old custom; **eine ~e Freundschaft** a long-standing friendship; **in ~er Freundschaft, Dein ...** yours, as ever, ...; **e)** *(langjährig)* long-standing ⟨*acquaintance*⟩; long-serving ⟨*employee*⟩; **f)** *(antik, klassisch)* ancient; **g)** *(vertraut)* old familiar ⟨*streets, sights, etc.*⟩; **ganz der/die ~e sein** be just the same; **es bleibt alles beim ~en** things will stay as they were; **das ist nicht das ~e Prag** it's not the old Prague I/we *etc.* knew; **alles geht seinen ~en Gang** everything goes on just as before; **h)** *(ugs.) (vertraulich)* **~er Freund/~es Haus!** old friend/pal *(coll.)*; *(bewundernd)* **ein ~er Fuchs/Gauner** an old fox/rascal; *(verstärkend)* **die ~e Hexe/der ~e Geizkragen** the old witch/skinflint
¹Ạlt der; ~s, ~e *(Musik)* **a)** *(Stimmlage)* alto; *(Frauenstimme)* contralto; alto; **b)** *o. Pl. (im Chor)* altos *pl.*; contraltos *pl.*; **c)** *(Sängerin)* contralto; alto
²Ạlt das; ~[s], ~: *top fermented, dark beer*
Altan [al'ta:n] **der; ~[e]s, ~e** *(Archit.)* balcony
Altar [al'ta:ɐ̯] **der; ~[e]s, Altäre** [al'tɛ:rə] altar; **eine Frau zum ~ führen** *(geh.)* lead a woman to the altar; **jmdn./etw. auf dem ~ des Vaterlands opfern** *(fig.)* sacrifice sb./sth. for one's country
Altạr-: **~bild das** altar-piece; **~gerät das** altar furniture; **~raum der** chancel
ạlt-, Ạlt-: **~backen** *Adj.* **a)** *(trocken)* stale ⟨*bread, roll, etc.*⟩; **b)** *(abwertend: altmodisch)* outdated ⟨*ideas, views, policies*⟩; old-fashioned ⟨*clothes*⟩; **~bau der;** *Pl.* **~bauten** old building; **~bauer der** old farmer; **~bau·wohnung die** flat *(Brit.)* or *(Amer.)* apartment in an old building; old flat *(Brit.)* *or (Amer.)* apartment; **~bekạnnt** *Adj.* well-known; **~bewạ̈hrt** *Adj.* well-tried; long-standing ⟨*tradition, acquaintanceship*⟩; **~bier das** *top fermented, dark beer;* **~bundes·kanzler der** former Federal Chancellor; **~bundes·präsident der** former Federal President; **~christlich** *Adj.* early Christian; **~deutsch** *Adj.* old German; German Renaissance ⟨*painting, art, etc.*⟩
¹Alte der; *adj. Dekl.* **a)** *(alter Mann)* old man; **komischer ~r** *(Theater)* comic old man; **b)** *(salopp) (Vater, Ehemann)* old man *(coll.)*; *(Chef)* governor *(sl.)*; boss *(coll.)*; **c)** *(österr.: Wein) fully fermented wine*
²Ạlte die; *adj. Dekl.* **a)** *(alte Frau)* old woman; **komische ~** *(Theater)* comic old woman; **b)** *(salopp) (Mutter)* old woman *(coll.)*; *(Ehefrau)* missis *(sl.)*; old woman *(coll.)*; *(Chefin)* boss *(coll.)*
³Ạlte das; *adj. Dekl.; o. Pl.* **am ~n hängen** cling to the past; **~es und Neues** the old and the new; **er kann nichts ~s wegwerfen** he cannot throw anything old away
⁴Ạlte *Pl.; adj. Dekl.* **a)** *(alte Menschen)* old people; **b) die ~n** *(salopp: Eltern)* my/his *etc.* old man and old woman *(coll.)*; *(Zool.: Tiereltern)* the parents; *(geh.: Menschen der Antike)* the ancients
ạlt; Ạlt: **~ehrwürdig** *Adj. (geh.)* venerable; time-honoured ⟨*customs*⟩; **~eingeführt** *Adj.* old-established; **~eingesessen** *Adj.* old-established; **~eingesessene der/die;** *adj. Dekl.* old-established inhabitant; **~eisen das;** *o. Pl.* scrap iron; **~englisch** *Adj.* Old English
Ạlten-: **~heim das** old people's home; old-age home *(Amer.)*; **~pfleger der** geriatric nurse; **~tages·stätte die** old people's day centre; **~teil das** *portion of farm property and certain rights retained by a farmer on handing over to his successor;* **sich aufs ~teil zurückziehen** *(fig.)* retire; **jmdn. aufs ~teil setzen** *(fig.)* send sb. into retirement; **~wohn·heim das** old people's home
Ạlter das; ~s, ~ a) age; *(hohes ~)* old age; **im ~:** in one's old age; **mit dem ~:** with age; **er ist in meinem ~:** he is my age; **in meinem ~ wirst du sehen, daß ...:** when you are my age you will see that ...; **im ~ von** at the age of; **eine Frau mittleren ~s** a middle-aged woman; **Kinder in diesem ~:** children of this age; **~ schützt vor Torheit nicht** *(Spr.)* there's no fool like an old fool *(prov.)*; **b)** *(alte Menschen)* old people *no art.*; **c)** *(Menschen einer Altersstufe)* age-group
älter ['ɛltɐ] **1.** *s.* **alt. 2.** *Adj. (nicht mehr jung)* elderly; **eine Melodie für unsere ~en Hörer** a tune for our older listeners; *s. auch* **Mitbürger**
Ạlterchen das; ~s, ~ *(ugs.)* grandad *(coll.)*
Ạ̈ltere der/die; *adj. Dekl.* **a)** *(älterer Mensch)* older person/man/woman; **für uns ~:** for us older people; **b)** *(bei Namen)* elder; **Hans Holbein der ~:** Hans Holbein the Elder
Alter ego ['altɐ 'e:go] **das; ~ ~** *(Psych.; geh.: Freund)* alter ego
ạltern 1. *itr. V.; mit sein* **a)** *(älter werden)* age; **b)** *(reifen)* mature. **2.** *tr. V. (alt machen)* age, mature ⟨*wine, spirits*⟩
alternativ [altɛrna'ti:f] **1.** *Adj. (auch: Industriekultur usw. ablehnend)* alternative. **2.** *adv.* **a)** *(die Wahl lassend)* alternatively; **b)** *(Industriekultur ablehnend)* ⟨*work, farm*⟩ using alternative methods; **~ leben/einkaufen** adopt an alternative life style/do one's shopping in alternative shops
Alternatịv·bewegung die alternative movement
¹Alternatịve die; ~, ~n alternative; **jmdn. vor die ~ stellen, mehr Miete zu zahlen oder auszuziehen** give sb. the alternative of either paying more rent or moving out
²Alternatịve der/die; *adj. Dekl.* supporter of the alternative society
Alternatịv-: **~energie die** alternative energy; **~kultur die** alternative culture
alterniẹren *itr. V.* alternate
ạlt·erprobt *Adj.* well-tried
ạlters *in* **seit ~, von ~ her** *(geh.)* from time immemorial
ạlters-, Ạlters-: **~ab·stand der** age difference; **~an·gabe die** details *pl.* of one's age; **[nicht] zur ~angabe verpflichtet sein** [not] be obliged to give one's age; **~aufbau der;** *o. Pl.* age structure; **~bedingt 1.** *Adj.* occurring at a particular age *postpos., not pred.*; *(im hohen Alter)* due to *or* caused by old age *postpos.*; **2.** *adv.* in relation to [one's/its] age; *(durch hohes Alter)* as a result of old age; **~beschwerden** *Pl.* complaints of old age; **~erscheinung die** sign of old age; **~fleck der** age spot; liver spot; **~gemäß 1.** *Adj.* ⟨*behaviour, education, etc.*⟩ appropriate to one's/its age; **2.** *adv.* in a manner appropriate to one's/its age; **das Kind entwickelt sich/spielt ~gemäß** the child is developing/playing as it should at its age; **~genosse der, ~genossin die** contemporary; person/child of the same age; **meine ~genossen** my contemporaries; people of my age; **er ist ein ~genosse von mir** he is the same age as I am; he is my age;

~**grenze die** age limit; *(für Rente)* retirement age; ~**gründe** *Pl.* reasons of age; ~**gruppe die** age-group; ~**heim das** old people's home; old-age home *(Amer.)*; ~**herz das** *(Med.) heart which has undergone physiological changes due to old age;* ~**jahr das** *(schweiz.) s.* **Lebensjahr;** ~**klasse die** *(bes. Sport)* age-group; ~**leiden das** complaint of old age; ~**los** *Adj.* ageless; ~**mäßig 1.** *Adj.* according to age *postpos., not pred.;* **2.** *adv. (dem Alter nach)* according to age; *(in bezug auf das Alter)* as far as age is concerned; ~**präsident der** president by seniority; **der** ~**präsident des Bundestages** the oldest member of the Bundestag, acting as president; ~**rente die** old-age pension; ~**ruhe·geld das** retirement pension; ~**schwach** *Adj.* old and infirm ‹*person*›; old and weak ‹*animal*›; [old and] decrepit ‹*object*›; ~**schwäche die;** *o. Pl. (bei Menschen)* [old] age and infirmity; *(bei Tieren)* [old] age and weakness; *(von Dingen)* [age and] decrepitude; ~**sicherung die** provision for one's old age; ~**sichtig** *Adj.* presbyopic *(Med.)*; ~**sichtigkeit die;** *o. Pl.* presbyopia *(Med.)*; ~**sitz der** retirement home; **er wählte Genf als seinen** ~**sitz** he chose to spend his retirement in Geneva; ~**starrsin der** obstinacy of old age; ~**stil der** later style; ~**stufe die** age; ~**unterschied der** age difference; ~**versorgung die** provision for one's old age; **gibt es hier eine betriebliche** ~**versorgung?** do you have a pension scheme here?; ~**werk das** later work; *(Gesamtheit)* later works *pl.*

A̩ltertum das; ~**s, A̩ltertümer** [-ty:mɐ] **a)** *o. Pl.* antiquity *no art.;* **das deutsche** ~: early German history; **b)** *Pl. (antike Kunstgegenstände)* antiquities

Altertümel<u>ei</u> die; ~, ~**en** archaism

altertümeln ['altɐty:m l̩n] *itr. V.* archaize

a̩ltertümlich 1. *Adj.* ancient ‹*building, monument, etc.*›; old-fashioned ‹*dress, handwriting, etc.*›; antiquated, old-fashioned ‹*appliance, device, vehicle, etc.*›. **2.** *adv.* ‹*dress, furnish, decorate*› in an old-fashioned style; ‹*work, function, etc.*› in an antiquated manner

A̩ltertümlichkeit die; ~ *s.* **altertümlich:** ancientness; old-fashionedness; antiquatedness

A̩ltertums-: ~**forscher der** archaeologist; ~**forschung die;** *o. Pl.,* ~**kunde die** archaeology *no art.;* ~**wert der** *in* ~**wert haben** have antique value

A̩lterung die; ~, ~**en a)** *(das Altwerden)* ageing; **b)** *(von Werkstoffen)* ageing; *(von Legierungen)* ageing; age-hardening; **c)** *(von Wein usw.)* ageing; maturing

A̩lterungs·prozeß der ageing process

Älteste ['ɛltəstə] **der/die;** *adj. Dekl.* **a)** *(Dorf~, Vereins~, Kirchen~ usw.)* elder; **b)** *(Sohn, Tochter)* eldest

Ältesten·rat der a) *(Bundesrepublik Deutschland) all-party parliamentary committee, which assists the Bundestag President in carrying out his duties and in regulating parliamentary business;* **b)** *(Völkerk.)* council of elders

a̩lt-, A̩lt-: ~**flöte die** *(Querflöte)* alto *or* bass flute; *(Blockflöte)* alto *or* treble recorder; ~**fränkisch** *(ugs. scherzh.)* **1.** *Adj.* old-fashioned; **2.** *adv.* in an old-fashioned way; ~**französisch das** Old French; ~**ged<u>ie</u>nt** *Adj.* long-serving; ~**glas·behälter der** bottle bank; ~**gold das** old gold; ~**griechisch** *Adj.* ancient Greek; *(Ling.)* classical *or* ancient Greek; *s. auch* **deutsch, Deutsch, ²Deutsche;** ~**griechisch das** classical *or* ancient Greek; ~**handel der** second-hand trade; ~**h<u>e</u>r·gebracht** *Adj.* traditional; ~**h<u>e</u>rren·mannschaft die** *(Sport); team of players over thirty-two;* ≈ over-thirties' team; ~**hoch·deutsch** *Adj.* Old High German; ~**hoch·deutsch das** Old High German

Alti̩st der; ~**en,** ~**en** *(Musik)* alto

Alti̩stin die; ~, ~**nen** *(Musik)* alto; contralto

a̩lt, A̩lt-: ~**jüngferlich** [~jʏŋfɐlɪç] **1.** *Adj.* old-maidish; **2.** *adv.* like an old maid/old maids; ~**kanzler der** former Chancellor; ex-Chancellor; ~**katholik der** Old Catholic; ~**katholisch** *Adj.* Old Catholic; ~**kleider·sammlung die** collection of old clothes; ~**klug;** ~**kluger,** ~**klugst... 1.** *Adj.* precocious; **2.** *adv.* precociously; ~**klugheit die** precociousness; ~**lage die** *(Musik)* alto range; **in der** ~**lage singen** be an alto; ~**last die a)** *(Ökologie)* old, improperly disposed of harmful waste *no indef. art.;* **b)** *(fig.)* inherited problem; **eine** ~**last aus den 60er Jahren** a hangover from the sixties

ältlich ['ɛltlɪç] *Adj.* rather elderly; oldish

a̩lt, A̩lt: ~**material das** scrap; ~**meister der a)** *(Vorbild)* doyen; **b)** *(Sport)* ex-champion; former champion; ~**meisterin die a)** *(Vorbild)* doyenne; **b)** *(Sport)* ex-champion; former champion; ~**metall das** scrap metal; ~**modisch 1.** *Adj.* old-fashioned; **2.** *adv.* in an old-fashioned way; ~**öl das** used oil; ~**papier das** waste paper; ~**partie die** *(Musik)* alto part; ~**philologe der** classical scholar; ~**philologie die** classical studies *pl., no art.;* ~**philologisch** *Adj.* classical; ~**römisch** *Adj.* ancient Roman; ~**rosa** *Adj.* old rose

Altruismus [altru'ɪsmus] **der;** ~ *(geh.)* altruism

Altrui̩st der; ~**en,** ~**en, Altrui̩stin die;** ~, ~**nen** *(geh.)* altruist

altrui̩stisch *(geh.)* **1.** *Adj.* altruistic. **2.** *adv.* altruistically

a̩lt-, A̩lt-: ~**sänger der** alto; ~**sängerin die** alto; contralto; ~**saxophon das** alto saxophone; ~**schlüssel der** *(Musik)* alto clef; ~**schnee der** old snow; ~**schnee·decke die** layer *or* covering of old snow; ~**silber das a)** *(veralt.: bereits verarbeitet)* old silver; **b)** *(Silberart)* oxidized silver; ~**sprachler** [~ʃpra:xlɐ] **der;** ~**s,** ~: classicist; ~**sprachlich** *Adj.* classical; ~**sprachliches Gymnasium** *grammar school concentrating on classical rather than modern languages;* ~**stadt die** old [part of the] town; **die Düsseldorfer** ~**stadt** the old part of Düsseldorf; ~**stadt·sanierung die** renovation of the old part of a/the town; ~**stein·zeit die** Old Stone Age; Palaeolithic Age; ~**stein·zeitlich** *Adj.* Palaeolithic; ~**stimme die** alto voice; *(von Frau)* alto *or* contralto voice; ~**testamentarisch,** ~**testamentlich** *Adj.* Old Testament *attrib.;* ~**überl<u>ie</u>fert** *Adj.* traditional; ~**väterisch** [~fɛ:tərɪʃ] **1.** *Adj.* old-fashioned; **2.** *adv.* in an old-fashioned way; ~**vertr<u>au</u>t** *Adj.* old familiar *attrib.;* ~**vordern** [~fɔrdɐn] *Pl. (veralt.)* forbears; forefathers; ancestors; ~**waren·händler der** second-hand dealer; ~**wasser das;** *Pl.* ~**wasser** dead arm of a/the river; ~**w<u>ei</u>ber·geschwätz,** ~**w<u>ei</u>ber·gewäsch das** *(abwertend)* empty chatter; ~**w<u>ei</u>ber·sommer der a)** Indian summer; **b)** *o. Pl. (Spinnfäden)* gossamer

¹Alu ['a:lu] **das;** ~**s** *(ugs.)* aluminium

²A̩lu die; ~ *(ugs.) Abk.:* **Arbeitslosenunterstützung** dole [money] *(Brit.);* unemployment pay

A̩lu·folie die aluminium foil

Aluminium [alu'mi:ni̯um] **das;** ~**s** aluminium

Alumi̩nium·folie die aluminium foil

Alumnat [alʊm'na:t] **das;** ~**[e]s,** ~**e** boarding-school

Alveolar [alveo'la:ɐ̯] **der;** ~**s,** ~**e** *(Sprachw.)* alveolar [consonant]

Alweg·bahn ['alve:k-] *type of overhead, high-speed monorail system*

am [am] *Präp.* + *Art.* **a)** = **an dem; b)** *(räumlich)* **am Boden** on the floor; **Frankfurt am Main** Frankfurt on [the] Main; **am Rande** on the edge; **am Institut für ...:** at the Institute for ...; **am Marktplatz** on the market square *or* place; **am Baum lehnen** lean against the tree; **am Meer/Fluß** by the sea/ on *or* by the river; **am Atlantik** on the Atlantic; **am Anfang/Ende** at the beginning/ end; **es am Herzen haben** *(ugs.)* have heart trouble; **sich am Kopf stoßen** bang one's head; **c)** *(österr.: auf dem)* on the; **d)** *(zeitlich)* on; **am Freitag** on Friday; **am 19. November** on 19 November; **am Anfang/Ende** at the beginning/end; **am letzten Freitag** last Friday; **am Morgen/Nachmittag** in the morning/afternoon; **e)** *(zur Bildung des Superlativs)* **das Rote gefällt mir am besten** I like the red one [the] best; **am gescheitesten/ schönsten sein** be the cleverest/most beautiful; **am schnellsten laufen** run [the] fastest; **das machen wir am besten nachher** it's best if we do it afterwards; **f)** *(nach bestimmten Verben)* **am Gelingen eines Planes** *usw.* **zweifeln** have doubts about *or* doubt the success of a plan *etc.;* **schuld am Scheitern eines Planes** *usw.* **sein** be to blame for the failure of a plan *etc.;* **am Wettbewerb teilnehmen** take part in the contest; **g)** *(zur Bildung der Verlaufsform)* **am Verwelken/Verfallen sein** be wilting/decaying; **h)** *(ugs.: bes. westf., rhein.)* **ich bin gerade am Kochen** I'm right in the middle of cooking; **er ist sein Auto am Putzen** he's cleaning his car

Amalgam [amal'ga:m] **das;** ~**s,** ~**e** *(Chemie, auch fig.)* amalgam

Amalg<u>a</u>m·füllung die *(Zahnmed.)* amalgam filling

amalgam<u>ie</u>ren *(Technik) tr., refl. V. (auch fig.)* amalgamate

Amalgam<u>ie</u>rung die; ~, ~**en** *(auch fig.)* amalgamation

Amaryllis [ama'rʏlɪs] **die;** ~, **Amary̩llen** amaryllis

Amateur [ama'tø:ɐ̯] **der;** ~**s,** ~**e** *(auch abwertend)* amateur

Amat<u>eu</u>r- amateur

-amateur der amateur ...

Amat<u>eu</u>r-: ~**funk der** amateur radio operating; ~**funker der** amateur radio operator

amat<u>eu</u>rhaft 1. *Adj.* amateurish. **2.** *adv.* amateurishly

Amat<u>eu</u>r-: ~**status der;** *o. Pl. (Sport)* amateur status; ~**theater das** amateur theatre

Amazonas [ama'ts̮o:nas] **der;** ~: Amazon

Amazone [ama'ts̮o:nə] **die;** ~, ~**n a)** *(Myth.)* Amazon; **b)** *(Reiterin)* woman rider; equestrienne; **c)** *(Fahrerin)* [woman] racing driver; **d)** *(veralt.: männlich wirkende Frau)* amazon

Amaz<u>o</u>nen·springen das *(Reiten)* women's show-jumping; *(Veranstaltung)* women's show-jumping competition

Amazonien [ama'ts̮o:ni̯ən] **(das);** ~**s** Amazonia

Amber ['ambɐ] **der;** ~**s,** ~**[n]** ambergris

Ambiente [am'bi̯ɛntə] **das;** ~ *(geh.)* ambience

Ambition [ambi'ts̮i̯o:n] **die;** ~, ~**en** *(geh.)* ambition; ~**en auf etw.** *(Akk.)* **haben** have ambitions of getting sth.

ambitioni̩ert [ambits̮i̯o'ni:ɐ̯t] *Adj.* *(geh.)* ambitious

ambivalent [ambiva'lɛnt] *(geh.)* **1.** *Adj.* ambivalent. **2.** *adv.* ambivalently

Ambivalenz [ambiva'lɛnts̮] *(geh.)* **die;** ~, ~**en** ambivalence

Amboß ['ambɔs] **der; A̩mbosses, A̩mbosse a)** anvil; **b)** *(Anat.)* anvil; incus

Ambra ['ambra] **die;** ~, ~**s** ambergris

Ambrosia [am'bro:zi̯a] **die;** ~ *(Myth.)* ambrosia

ambr<u>o</u>sisch *Adj. (veralt., geh.)* ambrosial

ambulant [ambu'lant] **1.** *Adj.* **a)** *(Med.)* out-patient *attrib.* ‹*treatment, therapy, etc.*›; **ein ~er Patient** an out-patient; **b)** *(umherziehend)* itinerant. **2.** *adv.* **a)** *(Med.)* **jmdn. ~ behandeln/versorgen** treat sb. as an out-patient *or* give sb. out-patient treatment/look after sb. as an out-patient; **b)** *(umherziehend)* **~ mit etw. handeln** travel around selling sth.

Ambulanz [ambu'lants] **die; ~, ~en a)** *(Feldlazarett)* field hospital; **b)** *(in Kliniken)* out-patient[s'] department; **c)** *(in Betrieben)* first-aid station; **d)** *(Krankenwagen)* ambulance

Ambulatorium [ambula'to:riʊm] **das; ~s, Ambulatorien** *(bes. DDR)* out-patient[s'] department

Ameise ['a:maizə] **die; ~, ~n** ant

Ameisen·bär der ant-eater

Ameisen-: ~haufen der anthill; **~pfad der** *(Zool.)* ant run; **~säure die;** *o. Pl.* formic acid; **~staat der** ant colony

amen ['a:mɛn] *Adv.* amen; **zu allem ja und ~ sagen** *(ugs.)* agree to anything

Amen das; ~s, ~: Amen; **das ist so sicher wie das ~ in der Kirche** *(ugs.)* you can bet your bottom dollar on it; **sein ~ zu etw. geben** *(fig.)* give one's blessing to sth.

Amerika [a'me:rika] **(das); ~s** America

Amerikaner [ameri'ka:nɐ] **der; ~s, ~ a)** American; **b)** *(Gebäck) small, flat iced cake*

Amerikanerin die; ~, ~nen American

amerikanisch *Adj.* American *s. auch* **deutsch, Deutsch, ²Deutsche**

amerikanisieren *tr. V.* Americanize

Amerikanisierung die; ~: Americanization

Amerikanismus der; ~, Amerikanismen Americanism

Amerikanist der; ~en, ~en specialist in American studies *pl.*

Amerikanistik die; ~: American studies *pl., no art.*

amerikanistisch *Adj.* American ‹*studies*›

Amethyst [ame'tʏst] **der; ~[e]s, ~e** amethyst

Ami ['ami] **der; ~[s], ~[s]** *(ugs.)* Yank *(coll.)*

Amigo der; ~s, ~s *(Jargon)* buddy *(coll.)*

Amino·säure [a'mi:no-] **die** *(Chemie)* amino acid

Ammann ['aman] **der; ~[e]s, Ammänner** *(schweiz.)* *(Gemeinde~, Bezirks~)* ≈ mayor; *(Land~)* cantonal president

Amme ['amə] **die; ~, ~n** *(Mensch)* wet-nurse; *(Tier)* foster-mother

Ammen·märchen das fairy tale *or* story

Ammer ['amɐ] **die; ~, ~n** bunting

Ammoniak [amo'niak] **das; ~s** *(Chemie)* ammonia

Ammonit [amo'ni:t] **der; ~en, ~en** *(Paläont.)* ammonite

Amnesie [amne'zi:] **die; ~, ~n** *(Med., Psych.)* amnesia

Amnestie [amnɛs'ti:] **die; ~, ~n** amnesty

amnestieren *tr. V.* grant an amnesty to; amnesty

Amnestierung die; ~, ~en: eine ~ politischer Gefangener an amnesty for political prisoners

Amöbe [a'mø:bə] **die; ~, ~n** *(Biol.)* amoeba

Amöben·ruhr die *(Med.)* amoebic dysentery

Amok ['a:mɔk] **der; ~s** *in* **~ laufen** run amok; *(ugs.: wütend werden)* go wild *(coll.)*; **~ fahren** go berserk at the wheel

Amok-: ~fahrer der berserk driver; **~fahrt die** crazed drive; **~lauf der** crazed rampage; **~läufer der** madman; **der ~läufer, der mehrere Menschen erschossen hatte** the man who had gone berserk and shot several people; **~schütze der** crazed gunman

a-Moll das; ~: A minor; **Sonate/Etüde in ~:** sonata/étude in A minor

a-Moll-: ~-Drei·klang der A minor triad; **~-Etüde die** study *or* étude in A minor; **~-Sonate die** sonata in A minor; **~-Ton·leiter die** scale of A minor

Amor ['a:mɔr] **(der)** Cupid; **~s Pfeil** *(dichter.)* Cupid's arrow *or* dart

amoralisch *(geh.)* **1.** *Adj.* immoral. **2.** *adv.* immorally

Amoralität die; ~ *(geh.)* immorality

Amorette [amo'rɛtə] **die; ~, ~n** *(Kunstwiss.)* amoretto; [little] cupid

amorph [a'mɔrf] *Adj.* *(geh.)* amorphous

Amortisation [amɔrtiza'tsio:n] **die; ~, ~en** *(Wirtsch.)* **a)** *(Schuldentilgung)* amortization; **b)** *(Kostendeckung)* **die Berechnung der ~ der Maschine** calculating how long the machine will take to pay for itself

amortisieren *(Wirtsch.)* **1.** *tr. V.* **a)** *(tilgen)* amortize; pay off; **b)** *(einbringen)* repay ‹*initial investment, acquisition costs*›. **2.** *refl. V.* *(sich bezahlt machen)* pay for itself

Amouren [a'mu:rən] *Pl.* *(veralt., noch scherzh.)* amours

amourös [amu'rø:s] *Adj.* amorous

Ampel ['ampl̩] **die; ~, ~n a)** *(Verkehrs~)* traffic lights *pl.*; **die ~ sprang auf Rot** the traffic lights turned to red; **halten Sie an der nächsten ~:** stop at the next set of traffic lights; **eine ~ umfahren** knock over a traffic light; **b)** *(Hängelampe)* hanging lamp; **c)** *(für Pflanzen)* hanging flowerpot

Ampel-: ~anlage die set of traffic lights; **~koalition die** *(ugs.) coalition between the SPD, FDP, and the Green Party*

Ampere [am'pɛ:ɐ] **das; ~[s], ~:** ampere; amp *(coll.)*

Ampere-: ~meter das ammeter; **~stunde die** ampere-hour

Ampfer ['ampfɐ] **der; ~s, ~** *(Bot.)* dock

Amphibie [am'fi:biə] **die; ~, ~n** *(Zool.)* amphibian

Amphibien·fahrzeug das amphibious vehicle

amphibisch *(Zool., Milit.)* **1.** *Adj.* amphibious. **2.** *adv.* amphibiously

Amphi·theater [am'fi:-] **das** amphitheatre

Amphore [am'fo:rə] **die; ~, ~n** amphora

Amplitude [ampli'tu:də] **die; ~, ~n** *(Math., Physik)* amplitude

Ampulle [am'pʊlə] **die; ~, ~n** *(Med.)* ampoule

Amputation [amputa'tsio:n] **die; ~, ~en** *(Med.)* amputation

amputieren *tr. (auch itr.) V.* amputate; **amputiert werden** ‹*person*› have an amputation; **jmdm. das Bein/den Arm ~:** amputate sb.'s leg/arm

Amputierte der/die; *adj. Dekl.* amputee

Amsel ['amzl̩] **die; ~, ~n** blackbird

Amt [amt] **das; ~[e]s, Ämter** ['ɛmtɐ] **a)** *(Stellung)* post; position; *(hohes politisches od. kirchliches ~)* office; **sein ~ antreten** take up one's post/take up office; **im ~ sein** be in office; **in ~ und Würden sein** be a man/woman of position and authority; **jmdn. aus dem ~ entfernen** remove sb. from his/her post/from office; **für ein ~ kandidieren** be a candidate for a post *or* position/an office; **von ~s wegen** because of one's profession *or* job; **kraft seines ~es** *(geh.)* by virtue of one's office; **b)** *(Aufgabe)* task; job; *(Obliegenheit)* duty; **seines ~es walten** *(geh.)* discharge the duties of one's office; **Scharfrichter, walte deines ~es!** executioner, do your duty!; **c)** *(Behörde) (Paß~, Finanz~, ~ für Statistik)* office; *(Sozial~, Fürsorge~, ~ für Denkmalpflege, Vermessungswesen)* department; **jmdn. dem zuständigen ~ melden** report sb. to the appropriate authorities; **von ~s wegen** by order of the authorities; *s. auch* **auswärtig c; d)** *(Gebäude usw.)* office; **e)** *(Fernsprechvermittlung)* exchange; **das Fräulein vom ~** *(veralt.)* the operator; **vom ~ vermittelt werden** be put through by the operator; **f)** *(kath. Rel.)* [sung] mass

Ämtchen ['ɛmtçən] **das; ~s, ~** *(abwertend)* petty little job

Ämter·patronage die [political] patronage in the distribution of posts/offices

Amt·frau die *s.* **Amtmann**

amtieren *itr. V.* **a)** hold office; **der ~de Generalsekretär** the incumbent Secretary-General; **der seit zwei Jahren ~de Generalsekretär** the Secretary-General who has been in *or* has held office for two years; **als Bürgermeister ~:** hold the office of mayor; **b)** *(vorübergehend)* act **(als** as)

amtlich 1. *Adj.* **a)** *nicht präd.* official; **~es Kennzeichen** registration number; *(ugs.: sicher)* definite; certain. **2.** *adv.* officially

amtlicher·seits *Adv.* officially

Amt·mann der; *Pl.* **...männer** *od.* **...leute, Amt·männin** [-mɛnɪn] **die; ~, ~nen** *senior civil servant*

amts-, Amts-: ~anmaßung die *(Rechtsw.)* unauthorized assumption of authority; **~an·tritt der** assumption of office; **bei ~antritt** on assuming office; **~an·walt der** *public prosecutor at a local court;* **~apparat der** machinery of officialdom; **~arzt der** medical officer; **~ärztlich 1.** *Adj.* **~ärztliche Gesundheits-/Impfbescheinigung** certificate of health/vaccination issued by the medical officer; **~ärztliche Untersuchung** examination by the medical officer; **2.** *adv.* ‹*authorized, certified*› by the medical officer; **sich ~ärztlich untersuchen lassen** have an official medical examination; **~blatt das** official gazette; **~bruder der** fellow clergyman; **~deutsch das** *(abwertend)* officialese; **~eid der** oath of office; **~einsetzung die** installation; **~enthebung die,** *(bes. österr. u. schweiz.)* **~entsetzung die** removal *or* dismissal from office; **~führung die;** *o. Pl.* discharge of one's office; **~geheimnis das a)** *o. Pl. (Schweigepflicht)* official secrecy *no art.*; **dem ~geheimnis unterliegen** be bound by official secrecy; **b)** *(geheime Sache)* official secret; **~gericht das a)** *(Instanz)* local *or* district court; **b)** *(Gebäude)* local *or* district court building; **~geschäfte** *Pl.* official duties; **~handlung die** official act *or* duty; **~hilfe die** official assistance *(given by one authority to another)*; **~kette die** chain of office; **~leitung die** exchange line; **~miene die** *(meist iron.)* official air; **~mißbrauch der** abuse of authority *or* one's position; **~müde** *Adj.* tired of office *postpos.*; **~nachfolger der** successor in office; **~person die** official; **~pflicht die** official duty; duty of one's office; **~richter der** *(veralt.)* local *or* district court judge; **~schimmel der;** *o. Pl. (scherzh.)* officialism; bureaucracy; **der ~schimmel wiehert** that's bureaucracy for you; **~siegel das** official seal; *(Dienststempel)* official stamp; **~sitz der a)** *(Ort)* [official] seat; **b)** *(Gebäude)* official residence; **~sprache die a)** *o. Pl. (~deutsch)* official language; officialese *(derog.)*; **in der ~sprache** in official language/officialese; **b)** *(eines Landes, einer Organisation)* official language; **~stube die** *(veralt.)* office; **~stunden** *Pl.* office hours; **~tracht die** robes *pl.* of office; official dress; *(eines Geistlichen)* vestments *pl.*; **~verweser der** *(geh.)* deputy; *(eines Herrschers)* regent; **~vorsteher der** head *or* chief [of a/the department]; **~vorsteher der Paßstelle/des Zollamtes** head of the passport/customs office; **~zeit die** period *or* term of office; **~zimmer das** office

Amulett [amu'lɛt] **das; ~[e]s, ~e** amulet; charm

amüsant [amy'zant] **1.** *Adj.* amusing; entertaining. **2.** *adv.* in an amusing *or* entertaining way

Amüsement [amyzə'mã:] **das; ~s, ~s** amusement

Amüsier·betrieb der *(oft abwertend)* night-club; *(Spielhalle)* amusement arcade; arcade room *(Amer.)*

amüsieren **1.** *refl. V.* **a)** *(sich vergnügen)* enjoy oneself; have a good time; **amüsier dich gut!** enjoy yourself!; have a good time!; **sich mit etw. ~** *(auch iron.)* have fun with sth.; **sich mit jmdm. ~:** have fun *or* a good time with sb.; **b)** *(sich lustig machen)* be amused; **sich über jmdn./etw. ~:** find sb./sth. funny; *(über jmdn./etw. lachen)* laugh at sb./sth.; *(jmdn. verspotten)* make fun of sb./sth. **2.** *tr. V.* amuse; **amüsiert zusehen** look on with amusement; **was amüsiert dich denn so?** what do you find so amusing *or* funny?

Amüsier·viertel das night-club district

amusisch *(geh.) Adj.* with no feeling for art *postpos., not pred.*; **[völlig] ~ sein** have no feeling [at all] for art.

an [an] **1.** *Präp. mit Dat.* **a)** *(räumlich)* at; *(auf)* on; **an einem Ort** at a place; **an der Tür/Wand** on the door/wall; **an der Wand stehen** stand by *or* against the wall; **eine Blase an der Ferse haben** have a blister on one's heel; **an der Mosel/Donau liegen** be [situated] on the Moselle/Danube; **Frankfurt an der Oder** Frankfurt on [the] Oder; **ein Lehrer an dieser Schule** a teacher at this school; **an etw. lehnen** lean against sth.; **nah an etw. stehen** stand close to sth.; **jmdn. an der Hand nehmen** take sb. by the hand; **Tür an Tür** next door to one another; **Laden an Laden** shop after shop; one shop after the other; **an jmdm. vorbeigehen/-sehen** go/look past sb.; **an etw. vorbeiplanen/vorbeibauen** plan/build without regard for sth.; *s. auch* **[2]Bord; Land a; b)** *(zeitlich)* on; **an jedem Sonntag** every Sunday; **an dem Abend, als er ...:** [on] the evening he ...; **das war an dem Tag, als er ...:** that was the day he ...; **an Ostern** *(bes. südd.)* at Easter; **c)** *(nach bestimmten Substantiven, Adjektiven und Verben)* in; **acht an der Zahl** eight in number; **arm/reich an Vitaminen** low/rich in vitamins; **jung an Jahren** young in years; **jmdn. an etw. erkennen** recognize sb. by sth.; **das Beste an etw.** the best thing about sth.; **ein Mangel an etw.** a shortage of sth.; **an etw. arbeiten** be working on sth.; **an etw. leiden** suffer from sth.; **was haben Sie an Zeitungen?** what newspapers have you got?; **es an der Leber bekommen/haben** get/have liver trouble; **an einer Krankheit sterben** die of a disease; **was mir an der Sache nicht gefällt** what I don't like about it; **es ist an ihm, das zu tun** it is up to him to do it; **er/sie hat etwas an sich** there ist sth. about him/her; **was er an Rente bekam** what he received by way of a pension; **an [und für] sich** actually; **die Idee ist an [und für] sich ausgezeichnet** the idea ist excellent in itself. **2.** *Präp. mit Akk.* **a)** to; *(auf, gegen)* on; **etw. an jmdn. schicken** send sth. to sb.; **etw. an etw. hängen** hang sth. on sth.; **an die Tafel schreiben** write on the blackboard; **etw. an etw. lehnen** lean sth. against sth.; **[bis] an die Decke reichen** reach [up] to the ceiling; *s. auch* **bis; [2]Bord; Land; b)** *(nach bestimmten Substantiven, Adjektiven und Verben)* **an etw./jmdn. glauben** believe in sth./sb.; **an etw. denken** think of sth.; **sich an etw. erinnern** remember *or* recall sth.; **an die Arbeit gehen** get down to work; **eine Bitte/Frage an jmdn. haben** have a request to make of sb./a question to ask sb.; **an etw. appellieren** appeal to sth.; **einen Gruß an jmdn. ausrichten lassen** send greetings to sb.; **ich konnte kaum an mich halten vor Lachen/Ärger** I could hardly contain myself for laughing/hardly contain my anger. **3.** *Adv.* **a)** *(Verkehrsw.)* **Köln an: 9.15** arriving Cologne 09.15; **b)** *(ugs.: in Betrieb)* on; **die Waschmaschine/der Fernseher ist an** the washing-machine/television is on; *s. auch* **ansein; c)** *(als Aufforderung)* **Scheinwerfer an!** spotlights on!; **d)** *(ugs.: ungefähr)* around; about; **an [die] 20 000 DM** around *or* about 20,000 DM; **e)** *in* **ohne [et]was an** *(ugs.)* with nothing on; without anything on; *s. auch* **ab 2 d; von 1 a, b**

Anabolikum [ana'bo:likʊm] **das; ~s, Anabolika** *(Med.)* anabolic steroid

Anachronismus [anakro'nɪsmʊs] **der; ~, Anachronismen** anachronism

anachronistisch **1.** *Adj.* anachronistic. **2.** *adv.* anachronistically

anaerob [an|ae'ro:p] *Adj. (Biol.)* anaerobic

Anagramm [ana'gram] **das; ~s, ~e** anagram

Anakoluth [anako'lu:t] **das** *od.* **der; ~s, ~e** *(Sprachw.)* anacoluthon

Anakonda [ana'kɔnda] **die; ~, ~s** anaconda

Anakreontik [anakre'ɔntɪk] **die; ~** *(Literaturw.)* anacreontic verse

anal [a'na:l] *(Anat., Psych.)* **1.** *Adj.* anal. **2.** *adv.* anally; **~ verkehren** have anal intercourse

Analeptikum [ana'lɛptɪkʊm] **das; ~s, Analeptika** *(Med.)* analeptic

Anal·erotik die; ~: anal eroticism

Analgetikum [anal'ge:tikʊm] **das; ~s, Analgetika** *(Med.)* analgesic

analog [ana'lo:k] **1.** *Adj.* **a)** *(gleichartig)* analogous; **~ [zu] diesem Fall** analogous to this case; **b)** *(Technik, DV)* analogue. **2.** *adv.* **a)** *(gleichartig)* analogously; **b)** *(Technik, DV)* ⟨*display, reproduce*⟩ in analogue form; **~ arbeitende Geräte** analogue devices

Analogie die; ~, ~n *(Entsprechung, auch Rechtsw., Biol., Sprachw.)* analogy; **in ~ zu etw.** in analogy to sth.

Analog-: ~rechner der *(DV)* analogue computer; **~uhr die** analogue clock; *(Armbanduhr)* analogue watch

An·alphabet der; ~en, ~en a) illiterate [person]; **~ sein** be illiterate; **b)** *(fig. abwertend)* ignoramus; **ein politischer ~ sein** be politically illiterate

Analphabetentum das; ~s illiteracy

Anal·verkehr der anal intercourse

Analysand [analy'zant] **der; ~en, ~en** *(Psychoanalyse)* analysand

Analyse [ana'ly:zə] **die; ~, ~n** *(auch: Psycho~)* analysis

analysieren *tr. V.* analyse

Analysis [a'na:lyzɪs] **die; ~** *(Math.)* analysis

Analytiker der; ~s, ~ analyst

analytisch **1.** *Adj.* analytical; **~e Geometrie** analytical geometry. **2.** *adv.* analytically

Anämie [anɛ'mi:] **die; ~, ~n** *(Med.)* anaemia

anämisch [a'nɛ:mɪʃ] *Adj. (Med., auch fig. abwertend)* anaemic

Anamnese [anam'ne:zə] **die; ~, ~n** *(Med.)* anamnesis

Ananas ['ananas] **die; ~, ~** *od.* **~se** pineapple

Anapäst [ana'pɛ:st] **der; ~[e]s, ~e** *(Verslehre)* anapaest

Anapher [a'nafɐ] **die; ~, ~n** *(Stilk.)* anaphora

Anarchie [anar'çi:] **die; ~, ~n** anarchy

anarchisch *Adj.* anarchic

Anarchismus der; ~: anarchism

Anarchist der; ~en, ~en, Anarchistin die; ~, ~nen anarchist

anarchistisch *Adj.* anarchistic

Anarcho·szene die *(ugs.)* anarchist scene

Anästhesie [an|ɛste'zi:] **die; ~, ~n** *(Med.)* anaesthesia

anästhesieren *tr. V. (Med.)* anaesthetize

Anästhesist der; ~en, ~en, Anästhesistin die; ~, ~nen *(Med.)* anaesthetist

Anatolien [ana'to:li̯ən] **(das); ~s** Anatolia

Anatom [ana'to:m] **der; ~en, ~en** *(Med.)* anatomist

Anatomie [anato'mi:] **die; ~, ~n** *(Med.)* **a)** anatomy; **b)** *(Institut)* anatomical institute

Anatomie·saal der *(Med.)* anatomy lecture theatre

anatomisch [ana'to:mɪʃ] *(Med.)* **1.** *Adj.* anatomical. **2.** *adv.* anatomically

[1]an|backen **1.** *unr. tr. V.* **etw. [kurz] ~:** bake sth. for a short time. **2.** *unr. itr. V.; mit sein (festbacken)* become baked on **(an + *Dat.*** to); stick **(an + *Dat.*** on to)

[2]an|backen *itr. V.; mit sein (nordd.: sich festsetzen)* stick **(an + *Dat.*** to)

an|bahnen **1.** *tr. V.* initiate ⟨*negotiations, talks, process, etc.*⟩; develop ⟨*relationship, connection*⟩. **2.** *refl. V.* ⟨*development*⟩ be in the offing; ⟨*friendship, relationship*⟩ start to develop; **zwischen den beiden bahnt sich etwas an** there is something going on between those two

Anbahnung die; ~, ~en *s.* **anbahnen 1:** initiation; development

an|bandeln ['anbandl̩n] *(südd., österr.),* **an|bändeln** ['anbɛndl̩n] *itr. V. (ugs.)* **mit jmdm. ~** *(flirten)* get off with sb. *(Brit. coll.)*; pick sb. up; *(Streit anfangen)* pick a quarrel with sb.

An·bau der; *Pl.* Anbauten a) *o. Pl.* building; **die Genehmigung für den ~ einer Garage an ein Haus bekommen** receive permission to build a garage on to a house; **b)** *(Gebäude)* extension; **c)** *o. Pl. (das Anpflanzen)* cultivation; growing

-anbau der; *o. Pl.* **Flachs~/Hopfen~/Futter~:** cultivation of flax/hop/fodder plants

an|bauen **1.** *tr. V.* **a)** build on; add; **eine Garage ans Haus ~:** build a garage on to the house; **b)** *(anpflanzen)* cultivate; grow. **2.** *itr. V. (das Haus vergrößern)* build an extension; *(~ lassen)* have an extension built

Anbau-: ~fläche die area of arable land; *(bebaute Fläche)* area under cultivation; **~gebiet das: die besten ~gebiete für Getreide** the best cereal-growing *or* grain-growing areas; **die wichtigsten ~gebiete für Rotwein** the principal red-wine-growing areas *or* areas for red wine; **~küche die** fitted kitchen; unit kitchen *(Amer.)*; **~möbel das** unit furniture; **~schrank der** cupboard unit

an|befehlen *unr. tr. V. (geh.)* **a)** *(befehlen)* **jmdm. etw. ~:** urge sth. on sb.; **b)** *(anvertrauen)* **jmdm. etw. ~:** commend sth. to sb.; **jmdm. ein Kind ~:** commend a child to sb.'s care

An·beginn der *(geh.)* beginning; **von ~ [an]** right from the beginning

an|behalten *unr. tr. V. (ugs.)* **etw. ~:** keep sth. on

an·bei *Adv. (Amtsspr.)* herewith; **Rückporto ~:** return postage enclosed

an|beißen **1.** *unr. tr. V.* bite into; take a bite of; **er hat die Banane nur angebissen** he only took one bite of the banana; **zum Anbeißen sein** *od.* **aussehen** *(ugs.)* look good enough to eat. **2.** *unr. itr. V. (auch fig. ugs.)* bite; **bei ihr hat noch keiner angebissen** *(fig. ugs.)* she hasn't managed to hook anybody yet

an|bekommen *unr. tr. V. (ugs.)* **a)** *(anziehen können)* **etw. ~:** manage to get sth. on; **b)** *(anzünden od. starten können)* **ein Feuer/Streichholz ~:** manage to get a fire going/a match to light; **einen Motor ~:** manage to get an engine going *or* to start

an|belangen *tr. V. in* **was mich/diese Sache** *usw.* **anbelangt** as far as I am/this matter is *etc.* concerned

an|bellen *tr. V.* bark at

an|bequemen *refl. V. (geh.)* **sich einer Sache** *(Dat.)* **~:** adapt [oneself] to sth.

an|beraumen ['anbəraumən] *tr. V. (Amtsspr.)* arrange, fix ⟨*meeting*⟩; arrange, set, fix ⟨*date*⟩

Anberaumung die; ~, ~en *(Amtsspr.) s.* **anberaumen:** arrangement; fixing; setting; **wir bitten um ~ eines neuen Termins** we should like a new date to be arranged *or* set

an|beten *tr. V. (auch fig.)* worship

Anbeter der; ~s, ~ *(auch fig.)* worshipper; *(fig.: Verehrer)* admirer

An·betracht der *in* in ~ einer Sache *(Gen.)* in consideration *or* view of sth.; in ~ dessen, daß ...: in view of the fact that ...

an|betreffen *unr. tr. V. in* was mich/diese Sache *usw.* anbetrifft as far as I am/this matter *etc.* is concerned

an|betteln *tr. V.* jmdn. ~: beg from sb.; jmdn. um etw. ~: beg sb. for sth.; [auf der Straße] angebettelt werden be stopped [in the street] by a beggar and asked for money

Anbetung die; ~, ~en *(auch fig.)* worship; *(fig.: Verehrung)* adoration

anbetungs·würdig *Adj.* adorable

an|bezahlen *tr. V.* make a down payment on; pay a deposit on

an|biedern ['anbi:dɐn] *refl. V. (abwertend)* sich [bei jmdm.] ~: curry favour [with sb.]

Anbiederung die; ~, ~en *(abwertend)* currying favour (an + *Akk.* with)

Anbiederungs·versuch der *(abwertend)* attempt to curry favour

an|bieten 1. *unr. tr. V.* offer; offer, tender ‹*resignation*›; jmdm. etw. ~: offer sb. sth.; jmdm. seine Begleitung ~: offer to accompany sb.; jmdm. ~, etw. zu tun offer to do sth. for sb.; ich habe dir immer wieder angeboten, dir zu helfen I offered time and again to help you; Verhandlungen ~: offer to negotiate; ich habe nichts anzubieten *od.* zum Anbieten I have nothing to offer you/them; sich auf der Straße ~: offer oneself on the streets; jmdm. Schläge ~ *(iron.)* threaten to hit sb. 2. *unr. refl. V.* a) offer one's services (als as); sich ~, etw. zu tun offer to do sth.; sich fürs *od.* zum Geschirrspülen *usw.* ~: offer to do the dishes-; b) *(naheliegen)* ‹*opportunity*› present itself; ‹*possibility, solution*› suggest *or* present itself; es bietet sich an, das zu tun it would seem to be the thing to do; c) *(geeignet sein)* sich für etw. ~: be suitable for sth.; dieses Tal bietet sich für die Einrichtung eines Sanatoriums geradezu an this valley is an obvious place to build a sanatorium

An·bieter der *(Wirtsch.)* supplier

an|binden 1. *unr. tr. V.* a) *(befestigen)* tie [up] (an + *Dat. od. Akk.* to); tie up, moor ‹*boat*› (an + *Dat. od. Akk.* to); tether ‹*animal*› (an + *Dat. od. Akk.* to); er läßt sich nicht ~ *(fig.)* he won't be tied down; man kann Kinder nicht ~ *(fig.)* you can't keep children on a lead; *s. auch* angebunden 2; b) *(verbinden, anschließen)* link (an + *Akk.* to); c) *(Landw.)* rear. 2. *unr. itr. V. (geh.)* mit jmdm. ~ *(Streit anfangen)* pick a quarrel with sb.; *(flirten)* flirt with sb.

An·bindung die linking (an + *Akk.* to); *(psychische ~)* involvement (an + *Akk.* in)

an|blaffen *tr. V. (ugs., auch fig.)* bark at

an|blasen *unr. tr. V.* a) blow at; jmdn. mit Rauch ~: blow smoke at sb.; b) *(anfachen)* blow on; einen Hochofen ~ *(Technik)* blow in a blast-furnace; c) *(salopp: zurechtweisen)* jmdn. ~: bawl sb. out *(coll.)*; d) die Jagd ~: sound the horn for the start of the hunt; e) *(Musik)* sound ‹*note*›; blow ‹*instrument*›

an|blecken *tr. V.* bare its/their teeth at; *(fig.)* bare his/her/their *etc.* teeth at

an|bleiben *unr. itr. V.; mit sein (ugs.)* stay on

an|blenden *tr. V.* flash [at]; jmdn. mit einer Taschenlampe ~: flash a torch at sb. *(Brit.)*; shine a flashlight at sb. *(Amer.)*

An·blick der sight; einen erfreulichen/traurigen ~ bieten be a welcome/sad sight; ihm wurde beim bloßen ~ schon schlecht the mere sight of it made him sick; beim ~ der Pyramiden at the sight of the Pyramids; es war ein ~ für Götter, als du ...: you looked a [real] sight when you ...

an|blicken *tr. V.* look at; jmdn. mit großen Augen ~: look at sb. wide-eyed; jmdn. flüchtig/starr ~: glance/stare at sb.

an|blinken *tr. V. s.* anblenden

an|blinzeln *tr. V.* a) blink at; b) *(zuzwinkern)* wink at

an|bohren *tr. V.* a) bore into; *(mit der Bohrmaschine)* bore *or* drill into-; Saboteure hatten sämtliche Benzinfässer angebohrt saboteurs had drilled holes in all the petrol drums ; b) *(erschließen)* tap [by drilling]; *(fig. ugs.: befragen)* pump

an|branden *itr. V.; mit sein (auch fig.)* surge

an|brassen *tr. V. (Seemannsspr.)* brace up

an|braten *unr. tr. V. (Kochk.)* brown; scharf ~: sear

an|brauchen *tr. V. (ugs.)* start [using]; eine angebrauchte Tube Senf a half-used tube of mustard

an|bräunen 1. *tr. V. (Kochk.)* brown [lightly]. 2. *itr. V.; mit sein (ugs.: von der Sonne braun werden)* tan [lightly]

an|brausen *itr. V.; mit sein* roar up; angebraust kommen come roaring along; *(auf einen zu)* come roaring up

an|brechen 1. *unr. tr. V.* a) crack; sich *(Dat.)* einen Knochen ~: crack a bone; b) *(öffnen)* open; start; eine angebrochene Flasche an opened bottle; c) *(zu verbrauchen beginnen)* break into ‹*supplies, reserves*›; einen Hundertmarkschein ~: break into *or (Amer.)* break a hundred mark note; was machen wir mit dem angebrochenen Abend? *(fig. ugs.)* what shall we do for the rest of the evening? 2. *unr. itr. V.; mit sein (geh.: beginnen)* ‹*dawn*› break; ‹*day*› dawn, break; ‹*darkness, night*› come down, fall; ‹*age, epoch*› dawn; ‹*autumn, winter*› set in; ‹*spring, summer*› begin

an|brennen 1. *unr. tr. V. (anzünden)* light. 2. *unr. itr. V.; mit sein* a) burn; jmdm. ist das Essen angebrannt sb. has burnt the food; nichts ~ lassen *(fig. ugs.)* not miss out on anything; der Torwart ließ nichts ~ *(Sportjargon)* the goalkeeper kept a clean sheet; b) *(zu brennen beginnen)* ‹*wood, coal, etc.*› catch

an|bringen *unr. tr. V.* a) *(befestigen)* put up ‹*sign, aerial, curtain, plaque*› (an + *Dat.* on); fix ‹*lamp, camera*› (an + *Dat.* [on] to); an etw. *(Dat.)* angebracht sein be fixed [on] to sth.-; b) *(äußern)* make ‹*request, complaint, comment, reference*›; c) *(zeigen)* display, demonstrate ‹*knowledge, experience*›; d) *(ugs.: herbeibringen)* bring; *(nach Hause)* bring home; e) *(ugs.: verkaufen)* sell; move

Anbringung die; ~ *s.* anbringen a: putting up; fixing

An·bruch der a) *o. Pl. (geh.: Beginn)* dawn[ing]; der ~ des Tages dawn; daybreak; vor/nach/bei *od.* mit ~ der Nacht before/after/at nightfall; vor ~ der Dunkelheit before darkness closes in; b) *(Bergbau)* lode; vein

an·brüchig *Adj. (Jägerspr.)* rotting

an|brühen *tr. V.* brew, make ‹*tea, coffee*›; blanch ‹*tomatoes, almonds, etc.*›

an|brüllen 1. *tr. V.* a) ‹*tiger, lion, etc.*› roar at; ‹*cow, bull, etc.*› bellow at; b) *(ugs.: anschreien)* bellow *or* bawl at. 2. *itr. V. (ugs.: zu übertönen versuchen)* gegen etw. ~: try to shout above [the noise of] sth.

an|brummen 1. *tr. V. (auch ugs.: unfreundlich anreden)* growl at. 2. *itr. V.; mit sein* angebrummt kommen come roaring along; *(auf einen zu)* come roaring up

an|brüten *tr. V.* begin to sit on ‹*eggs*›; angebrütete Eier eggs that have been sat on

Anchovis *s.* Anschovis

Anciennitäts·prinzip [ãsi̯eni'tɛ:ts-] das principle of seniority; nach dem ~: according to [the principle of] seniority

Andacht ['andaxt] die; ~, ~en a) *o. Pl. (Sammlung im Gebet)* silent prayer *or* worship; in tiefer ~: in deep devotion; in ~ versunken sunk in silent prayer *or* worship *or* in one's devotions; b) *o. Pl. (innere Sammlung)* rapt attention; mit großer ~: with rapt attention; c) *(Gottesdienst)* prayers *pl.*; eine ~ halten hold a [short] service; zur ~ gehen go to prayers *or* to the service

andächtig ['andɛçtɪç] 1. *Adj.* a) *(ins Gebet versunken)* devout; reverent; b) *(innerlich gesammelt)* rapt; c) *nicht präd. (feierlich)* reverent. 2. *adv.* a) *(ins Gebet versunken)* devoutly; reverently; b) *(innerlich gesammelt)* with rapt attention; raptly

Andachts·bild das *(Kunst, Rel.)* devotional picture

andachts·voll *(geh.) s.* andächtig

Andalusien [anda'lu:zi̯ən] (das); ~s Andalusia

an|dampfen *itr. V.; mit sein* angedampft kommen *(ugs.)* come steaming along; *(auf einen zu)* come steaming up; *(fig. scherzh.)* come charging along, puffing and blowing; *(auf einen zu)* come charging up, puffing and blowing

Andante [an'dantə] das; ~[s], ~s *(Musik)* andante

an|dauen ['andau̯ən] *tr. V. (Med.)* angedaute Nahrung partially digested food

An·dauer die continuance; bei längerer ~ des Fiebers/des schlechten Wetters if the fever continues *or* persists/the bad weather lasts for a long time

an|dauern *itr. V.* ‹*negotiations*› continue, go on; ‹*weather, rain*› last, continue

andauernd 1. *s.* andauern. 2. *Adj.; nicht präd.* continual; constant. 3. *adv.* continually; constantly; warum fragst du denn ~ dasselbe? why do you keep on asking the same thing?

Anden ['andn̩] *Pl.* die ~: the Andes

An·denken das; ~s, ~ a) *o. Pl.* memory; jmds. ~ bewahren/in Ehren halten keep/honour sb.'s memory; jmdm. ein liebevolles ~ bewahren keep fond memories of sb.; zum ~ an jmdn./etw. to remind you/us *etc.* of sb./sth.; das schenke ich dir zum ~: I'll give you that to remember me/us by; b) *(Erinnerungsstück)* memento, souvenir (an + *Akk.* of); *(Reise~)* souvenir (an + *Akk.* of)

Andenken·jäger der souvenir hunter

Anden·staat der Andean country

ander... ['andɐ...] *Indefinitpron.* 1. *attr.* a) *(zweit..., weiter...)* other; ein ~er Mann/eine ~e Frau/ein ~es Haus another man/woman/house; zum ~n Mal *(veralt.)* [for] a second time; eine ~e Frage another *or* a further question; ~e Fragen other *or* further questions; das Kleid gefällt mir nicht, haben Sie noch ~e/ein ~es? I don't like that dress, do you have any others/another?; b) am/bis zum ~[e]n Tag [on] the/by the next *or* following day; von einem Tag zum ~n from one day to the next; c) *(verschieden)* different; wir ~n the rest of us; ~er Meinung sein be of a different opinion; take a different view; das ~e Geschlecht the opposite sex; bei ~er Gelegenheit another time; statt dieses Wagens hätte ich gern einen ~en instead of that car I would like a different one; *s. auch* Land; Städtchen; d) *(neu)* einen ~en Arbeitsplatz finden find another job; er ist ein ~er Mensch geworden he is a changed man. 2. *alleinstehend* a) *(Person)* ein ~r/eine ~e: another [one]; die ~n the others; alle ~n all the others; everyone else; jeder/jede ~e anyone *or* anybody else; kein ~er/keine ~e nobody *or* no one else; was ist mit den ~n? what about the others *or* the rest?; ich will weder den einen noch den ~n heiraten I don't want to marry either of them; niemand ~er als ...: nobody *or* no one but ...; da muß ein ~r kommen *(fig.)* it will take more than you/him *etc.*; einen ~[e]n/eine ~e haben *(fig. ugs.)* have found somebody *or* someone else; auf ~e hören listen to others; eine war schöner als die ~e one was more beautiful than the other; einer hinter dem ~[e]n one after another *or* the other; nicht drängeln, einer nach dem ~n don't push, one after the other; der eine oder [der] ~e one or two *or* a few people; wenn der eine oder [der] ~e von Ihnen etwas Genaueres wissen möchte if any of you would like further details; *s. auch* recht c; b) *(Sache)* ein ~er/eine ~e/ein ~es another [one]; alles ~e everything else; ein[e]s nach dem ~[e]n first things first; das ~e schaffen wir schon allein we can manage the rest on our own; wir haben noch zwei ~e we have two others; es bleibt uns nichts ~es übrig there's nothing else we can do; sich eines ~n besinnen change one's mind; ich will weder das eine noch das ~e I don't want either; *(will beides nicht tun)* I don't want to do either; Möchtest du Tee oder Kaffee? – Weder das eine noch das ~e Would you like tea or coffee? – Neither; und ~es/vieles ~e mehr and more/much more besides; unter ~[e]m among[st] other things; so kam eins zum ~[e]n what with one thing on top of the other; das ist etwas [ganz] ~es that's [something quite] different; von etwas ~em sprechen talk about something else; *(um das bisherige Thema zu vermeiden)* change the subject; das bedeutet doch nichts ~es, als daß wir noch einmal ganz von vorn anfangen müssen that means only one thing, that we must start all over again from the beginning; ich habe nichts ~es erwartet I didn't expect anything else; dem hätte ich etwas ~es erzählt *(fig. ugs.)* I would have given him a piece of my mind; alles ~e als ...: anything but ...; das ist alles ~e als das, was ich mir vorgestellt hatte it's not at all what I had imagined; ~es zu tun haben have other things to do

änderbar *Adj.* alterable

anderen·falls *Adv.* otherwise

anderen·orts *Adv. (geh.)* elsewhere

anderen·tags *Adv. (geh.)* [on] the next *or* following day

anderen·teils *Adv. s.* einesteils

anderer·seits *Adv.* on the other hand

Ander·konto das *(Finanzw.)* trust account; client account

ander·mal *Adv.*: ein ~: another time

andern- *s.* anderen-

ändern ['ɛndɐn] 1. *tr. V.* change; alter; alter ‹*garment*›; change ‹*person*›; etw. an etw. *(Dat.)* ~: change *or* alter sth. in sth.; wenn ich an dem Kleid etwas ~ würde if I was going to change anything about the dress; daran kann man nichts ~: nothing can be done *or* there's nothing you/we *etc.* can do about it; das alles ändert nichts an der Tatsache, daß ...: none of that alters the fact that ... 2. *refl. V.* change; alter; ‹*person, weather*› change; daran hat sich nichts geändert nothing about it has changed *or* altered

ander·orts *s.* anderenorts

anders ['andɐs] *Adv.* a) *(verschieden)* ‹*think, act, feel, do*› differently (als from *or esp. Brit.* to); ‹*be, look, sound, taste*› different (als from *or esp. Brit.* to); es war alles ganz ~: it was all quite different; er ist irgendwie ~: there is something different about him; he has changed somehow; wie könnte es ~ sein! *(iron.)* surprise, surprise! *(iron.)*; mir wird ganz ~ *(ugs.)* I feel weak at the knees; es wäre alles ~ gekommen it would all have been different *or* would have turned out differently; es kommt immer ~, als man denkt things never turn out the way you think they will; es kam ~, als wir dachten things didn't turn out the way we expected; wir haben es uns ~ überlegt we've changed our minds; ich kann auch ~ *(ugs.)* you'd/he'd *etc.* better watch it *(coll.)*; das hört sich schon ~ an *(ugs.)* that's more like it; so und nicht ~: this way and no other; exactly like that; das kennt er nicht ~: he's never known any different; das kennen wir gar nicht ~ von ihm we wouldn't expect anything else from him; ich konnte nicht ~: I couldn't help it; *(ich wurde gezwungen)* I had no choice; das habe ich nicht ~ erwartet I didn't expect anything else; that was just what I expected; wie nicht ~ zu erwarten as [was to be] expected; wenn es nicht ~ geht if there is no other way; b) *(sonst)* else; irgendwo/nirgendwo ~: somewhere/nowhere else; niemand ~: nobody else; jemand ~: someone else; *(verneint, in Fragen)* anyone else; c) *(ugs.: andernfalls)* otherwise; or else

anders, Anders: ~artig *Adj.* different; ~artigkeit die; *o. Pl.* different nature; das Bewußtsein seiner ~artigkeit his consciousness that he was different; ~denkend *Adj.*; *nicht präd.* dissident; dissenting; ~denkende der/die; *adj. Dekl.* dissident; dissenter

anderseits *s.* andererseits

anders-, Anders-: ~farbig 1. *Adj.* different-coloured *attrib.*; of a different colour *postpos.*; 2. *adv.* ‹*decorated*› in a different colour; ~farbig bezogen covered in material of a different colour; ~farbige der/die person of a different colour; ~geartet *Adj.* different; of a different nature *postpos.*; ~gegengeschlechtlich *Adj.* of the opposite sex *postpos.*; ~gesinnte [~gəˈzɪntə] der/die; *adj. Dekl.* person of a different opinion; die ~gesinnten those with *or* of different opinions; ~gläubig *Adj.* of a different faith *or* religion *postpos.*; ~gläubige der/die person of a different faith *or* religion; die ~gläubigen those of different faiths *or* religions; ~herum 1. *Adv.* the other way round *or (Amer.)* around; etw. ~herum drehen turn sth. the other way; ~herum gehen/fahren go/drive round *or (Amer.)* around the other way; 2. *Adj. s.* ~rum 2; ~lautend [~lautn̩t] *Adj.*; *nicht präd.* to the contrary *postpos.*; ~rum *(ugs.)* 1. *Adv. s.* ~herum 1; 2. *Adj.*; *nicht attr.* ~rum sein be a poof *(Brit. coll.) or* a fairy *(sl.)*; be queer *(sl.)*; ~sein das *(geh.)* sein ~sein akzeptieren accept that one is different; ~wie *Adv. (ugs.)* some other way; ~wo *Adv. (ugs.)* elsewhere; mach das doch ~wo do it somewhere else *or* elsewhere; weder dort noch ~wo neither there nor anywhere else; ~woher *Adv. (ugs.)* from elsewhere; from somewhere else; kann man das ~woher beziehen? can you get that [from] anywhere else?; ~wohin *Adv. (ugs.)* elsewhere; somewhere else; warum fahren wir nie ~wohin? why do we never go somewhere else?; wir fahren immer in die Berge, nie ~wohin we always go up into the mountains, never anywhere else

anderthalb [ˈandɐtˈhalp] *Bruchz.* one and a half; ~ Pfund Mehl a pound and a half of flour; ~ Stunden an hour and a half; ~ Jahre [alt] sein be eighteen months [old]

anderthalb·fach *Vervielfältigungsz.* one and a half times; einen ~en Salto machen do a one-and-a-half somersault; den ~en Preis verlangen demand half as much again

anderthalb·mal *Adv.* one and a half times; ~ so viel Geld half as much money again; ~ so viele Besucher half as many visitors again; ~ so groß wie ...: half as big again as ...

Änderung die; ~, ~en change (+ *Gen.* in); alteration (+ *Gen.* to); *(an einem Kleidungsstück)* alteration (an + *Dat.* to); *(in einem Menschen)* change (in + *Dat.* in); eine ~ vornehmen make a change *or* an alteration; eine ~ zum Besseren a change for the better; eine ~ des Programms a change of programme; das hat uns zu einer ~ des Programms veranlaßt it has caused us to change *or* alter the programme; „~en vorbehalten" 'subject to alteration'

Änderungs-: ~antrag der *(Politik)* amendment; ~kündigung die *(Arbeitswelt) notice of intention to terminate agreement on terms and conditions of employment if changes to the agreement are not accepted*; ~schneiderei die tailor's [that does alterations]; ~vor·schlag der suggested amendment *or* change; ~wunsch der request for changes *or* alterations; haben Sie irgendwelche ~wünsche? are there any changes *or* alterations you would like to see?

anderwärts [-vɛrts] *Adv. (geh.)* elsewhere

anderweitig [-vaitɪç] 1. *Adj.*; *nicht präd. (sonstig)* other. 2. *adv.* a) *(auf andere Weise)* in another way; ~ beschäftigt sein be otherwise engaged; b) *(an jmd. anderen)* to somebody else

an|deuten 1. *tr. V.* a) *(zu verstehen geben)* intimate; hint; jmdm. etw. ~: intimate *or* hint sth. to sb.; b) *(nicht ausführen)* outline; *(kurz erwähnen)* indicate. 2. *refl. V. (sich abzeichnen)* be indicated; sobald sich die ersten wärmeren Sommertage andeuteten as soon as there was a suggestion of the first warm days of summer

An·deutung die a) *(Anspielung)* hint; eine ~ machen give *or* drop a hint (über + *Akk.* about); in ~en sprechen talk in hints; b) *(schwaches Anzeichen)* suggestion; hint

andeutungs·weise *Adv.* in the form of a hint *or* suggestion/hints *or* suggestions; davon war nur ~ die Rede it was only hinted at

an|dichten *tr. V.* jmdm. etw. ~: impute sth. to sb.; man hatte ihm Wunderkräfte angedichtet he had been credited with miraculous powers; sie hatten ihm eine Affäre mit seiner Sekretärin angedichtet they claimed that he'd had an affair with his secretary

an|dicken [ˈandɪkn̩] *tr. V. (Kochk.)* thicken

an|dienen 1. *tr. V.* a) jmdm. etw. ~: offer sth. to sb.; *(aufdringlich)* press sth. on sb. 2. *refl. V.* sich jmdm. ~: offer oneself *or* one's services to sb.; *(aufdringlich)* press oneself *or* one's services on sb.

an|diskutieren *tr. V.* [begin to] discuss briefly

an|docken *tr., itr. V. (Raumf.)* an etw. *(Dat.)* ~: dock with sth.

an|donnern *itr. V. (ugs.)* angedonnert kommen come roaring *or* thundering along; *(auf einen zu)* come roaring *or* thundering up

An·drang der; *o. Pl.* a) crowd; *(Gedränge)* crush; es herrschte großer ~: there was a large crowd/great crush; b) *(von Blut, Milch)* rush; *(von Wasser)* surge

an|drängen *itr. V.*; *mit sein* surge (gegen against); ‹*crowd*› surge forward; ‹*army*› push forward; gegen das Tor ~ *(Sport)* surge towards goal; die ~de Flut/Menschenmenge the surging tide/crowd

andre... *s.* ander...

Andreas [anˈdreːas] (der) Andrew

Andreas·kreuz das a) St Andrew's cross; b) *(Verkehrsw.)* diagonal cross

an|drehen *tr. V.* a) *(einschalten)* turn on; b) *(ugs.: verkaufen)* jmdm. etw. ~: palm sb. off with sth.; palm sth. off on sb.; laß dir bloß keinen von diesen Äpfeln ~: don't let yourself be palmed off with any of those apples; c) *(befestigen)* screw ‹*nut*› on; screw ‹*screw*› in; d) *(salopp)* jmdm. ein Kind ~: knock sb. up *(sl.)*; put sb. in the club *(Brit. sl.)*

andrerseits *s.* andererseits

an|dressieren *tr. V.* a) einem Tier ein Kunststück/artfremdes Verhalten ~: train an animal to perform a trick/to exhibit behaviour [patterns] foreign to the species; andressiertes Verhalten behaviour that is the result of training; b) *(fig. abwertend)* train; drill

an|dringen *unr. itr. V.*; *mit sein (geh.)* surge (gegen against); der ~de Feind the enemy surging forward

Androgen [androˈgeːn] das; ~s, ~e *(Med.)* androgen

androgyn [androˈgyːn] *Adj. (Psych., Bot.)* androgynous

ạn|drohen *tr. V.* **jmdm. etw. ~:** threaten sb. with sth.; **er hat mir Prügel angedroht** he threatened to beat me
Ạn·drohung die threat; **unter ~ von Gewalt** with the *or* under threat of violence; **durch die ~ seines Rücktritts** by threatening to resign
Android [andro'i:t] **der; ~en, ~en, Androide** [andro'i:də] **der; ~n, ~n** android
Androloge [andro'lo:gə] **der; ~n, ~n** *(Med.)* andrologist
Ạn·druck der; ~[e]s, ~e *(Druckw.)* **a)** *(Probe)* proof; **bereit für den ~:** ready for proofing; **b)** *(Beginn)* going to press; **lange vor dem ~:** long before going to press
ạn|drucken *(Druckw.)* **1.** *tr. V.* **a)** *(beginnen)* start printing; **b)** *(zur Probe)* proof; pull proofs of. **2.** *itr. V.* **a)** *(beginnen)* start printing; go to press; **wir können ~ lassen** we can go to press; **b)** *(zur Probe)* pull proofs
ạn|drücken *tr. V.* **a)** press down; **den Bleistift leicht ~:** press lightly with the pencil; **b)** *(einschalten)* switch on
Ạndruck·exemplar das *(Druckw.)* **a)** printed copy; **b)** *(Probe)* proof copy
ạn|dudeln *tr. V.* *in* **sich** *(Dat.)* **einen ~** *(salopp)* get plastered *(sl.)*
ạn|dünsten *tr. V.* *(Kochk.)* braise lightly
Äneas [ɛ'ne:as] **(der)** Aeneas
ạn|ecken *itr. V.; mit sein* **a)** *(anstoßen)* **an etw.** *(Dat.)* **~:** hit sth.; **b)** *(ugs.: Ärger erregen)* **bei jmdm. ~:** rub sb. [up *(Brit.)*] the wrong way
ạn|eifern *tr. V.* *(südd., österr.)* spur on
ạn|eignen *refl. V.* **a)** *(nehmen)* appropriate; **sich** *(Dat.)* **etw. widerrechtlich ~:** misappropriate sth.; **b)** *(lernen)* acquire; learn; **c)** *(angewöhnen)* acquire; pick up
Ạn·eignung die a) appropriation; **widerrechtliche ~:** misappropriation; **b)** *(Lernen)* acquisition; learning; **c)** *(Rechtsw.)* acquisition of title (*Gen.* to)
an·einạnder *Adv.* **~ denken** think of each other *or* one another; **~ vorbeigehen** pass each other *or* one another; go past each other *or* one another; **sich ~ gewöhnen** get used to each other *or* one another; **~ vorbeireden** talk at cross purposes; **sich ~ festhalten** hold each other *or* one another
aneinạnder, Aneinạnder: ~|bauen *tr. V.* build on to each other; **dicht ~gebaut** built very close together; **~|binden** *unr. tr. V.* tie together; hitch ‹*horses*› together; **~|drängen 1.** *tr. V.* push *or* press together; **2.** *refl. V.* press together; **~|drücken** *tr. V.* press together; **~|fesseln** *tr. V.* tie together; *(mit Ketten)* chain together; **man hatte uns Hände und Füße ~gefesselt** our hands and feet had been tied together; **~|fügen 1.** *tr. V.* fit together; **2.** *refl. V.* fit together; **~|geraten** *unr. itr. V.; mit sein* **mit jmdm. ~geraten** *(sich prügeln)* come to blows with sb.; *(sich streiten)* quarrel with sb.; **~|grenzen** *itr. V.* ‹*properties, rooms, etc.*› adjoin [each other *or* one another]; ‹*countries*› border on each other *or* one another; **~|halten** *unr. tr. V.* hold next to each other *or* one another; **~|hängen 1.** *tr. V.* link ‹*chains, garlands*› together; couple ‹*carriages*› together; fasten ‹*papers*› together; **2.** *unr. itr. V.* ‹*chains, garlands*› be linked together; ‹*carriages*› be coupled together; ‹*insects*› cling together; **~|klammern 1.** *tr. V.* clip ‹*papers*› together; clamp ‹*boards*› together; **2.** *refl. V.* cling together *or* to each other; **~|kleben** *tr., itr. V.* stick together; **~|knoten** *tr. V.* knot *or* tie together; **~|koppeln** *tr. V.* couple ‹*carriages*› together; link up ‹*spacecraft*›; **~|kuscheln** *refl. V.* snuggle *or* cuddle up [together *or* to each other *or* to one another]; **sie lagen ~gekuschelt** they lay snuggled *or* cuddled up [together]; **~|legen 1.** *tr. V.* put *or* place next to each other *or* one another; **2.** *refl. V.* lie next to each other *or* together; **wenn man den Hebel zieht, legen sich zwei Metallklötze ~:** when the handle is pulled, two metal blocks are brought together; **~|lehnen 1.** *tr. V.* lean against each other *or* one another; **2.** *refl. V.* lean on *or* against each other *or* one another; **~|liegen** *unr. itr. V.* ‹*properties*› adjoin [each other *or* one another]; be adjacent [to each other *or* one another]; **~liegende Steine** stones lying next to each other; **~|prallen** *itr. V.; mit sein* collide; **~|pressen** *tr. V.* press together; **~|reihen 1.** *tr. V.* string ‹*facts, anecdotes*› together; line up [next to each other *or* one another]; **Perlen auf einer Schnur ~reihen** thread pearls on a string; **2.** *refl. V.* ‹*days, nights, minutes, etc.*› follow one another; **~reihung die** stringing together; **eine bloße ~reihung von Tatsachen** a series of facts just strung together; **~|rücken 1.** *tr. V.* move *or* put ‹*chairs etc.*› together; **2.** *itr. V.; mit sein* move [up] closer together; **~|schlagen 1.** *unr. tr. V.* strike together; **2.** *unr. itr. V.; mit sein* strike each other *or* one another; **~|schmieden** *tr. V.* forge together; **~|schmiegen** *refl. V.* snuggle *or* cuddle up [together *or* to each other *or* to one another]; **~|schrauben** *tr. V.* screw together; **~|schweißen** *tr. V.* weld together; **~|setzen** *tr. V.* put together; put ‹*dominoes*› next to each other; **~|stellen 1.** *tr. V.* put together *or* next to each other; **2.** *refl. V.* stand together *or* next to each other; **stellt euch mal mit dem Rücken ~:** stand back to back; **~|stoßen 1.** *unr. tr. V.* knock together; **2.** *unr. itr. V.; mit sein* **a)** strike each other; ‹*heads, vehicles*› collide; **sie stießen mit den Köpfen ~:** their heads collided; **b)** *(~grenzen)* meet
Äneis [ɛ'ne:ɪs] **die; ~:** Aeneid
Anekdote [anɛk'do:tə] **die; ~, ~n** anecdote
anekdọten·haft 1. *Adj.* anecdotal. **2.** *adv.* ‹*relate*› in anecdotes
anekdọtisch 1. *Adj.* anecdotal. **2.** *adv.* **ein ~ gewürzter Vortrag** a lecture enlivened with anecdotes
ạn|ekeln *tr. V.* disgust; nauseate; **du ekelst mich an** you make me sick; **sich angeekelt abwenden** turn away in disgust
Anemo·mẹter [anemo-] **das** *(Met.)* anemometer
Anemone [ane'mo:nə] **die; ~, ~n** anemone
ạn|empfehlen *unr. tr. V.* *(geh.)* recommend (*Dat.* to)
ạn|erbieten *unr. refl. V.* *(geh.)* offer one's services; **sich ~, etw. zu tun** offer to do sth.
Ạnerbieten das; ~s, ~ *(geh.)* offer
ạnerkannt *Adj.* recognized; recognized, acknowledged ‹*authority, expert*›; recognized, accepted, established ‹*fact*›
ạnerkanntermaßen *Adv.* **er gehört ~ zu den besten Spielern** he is generally recognized *or* acknowledged to be one of the best players
ạnerkennen[1] *unr. tr. V.* **a)** recognize ‹*country, record, verdict, qualification, document*›; acknowledge ‹*debt*›; accept ‹*demand, bill, conditions, rules*›; allow ‹*claim, goal*›; **ein Kind ~:** acknowledge a child as one's own; **jmdn. als gleichberechtigten Partner ~:** accept sb. as an equal partner; **b)** *(nicht leugnen)* acknowledge; **c)** *(würdigen)* acknowledge, appreciate ‹*achievement, efforts*›; appreciate ‹*person*›; respect ‹*viewpoint, opinion*›; **ein ~der Blick** an appreciative look; **~d nicken** nod appreciatively; **einige ~de Worte** a few words of appreciation
ạnerkennens·wert *Adj.* commendable
ạnerkennenswerter·wẹise *Adv.* commendably

[1] *ich erkenne an (od. seltener: anerkenne), anerkannt, anzuerkennen*

Ạn·erkenntnis das; ~ses, ~se acknowledgement
Ạnerkennung die; ~, ~en a) *s.* **anerkennen a:** recognition; acknowledgement; acceptance; allowance; **b)** *(Zugeständnis)* acknowledgement; **c)** *(Würdigung) s.* **anerkennen c:** acknowledgement; appreciation; respect (*Gen.* for)
ạn|erziehen *unr. tr. V.* **jmdm. etw. ~:** instil sth. into sb.; **Kindern Pünktlichkeit ~:** bring children up to be punctual
ạn|essen *unr. refl. V.* *in* **sich** *(Dat.)* **einen Bauch ~:** develop a paunch
ạn|fachen *tr. V.* fan; *(fig.)* arouse ‹*anger, curiosity, enthusiasm*›; arouse, inflame ‹*passion*›; inspire, stir up ‹*hatred*›; inspire ‹*hope*›; ferment ‹*discord, war*›
ạn|fahren 1. *unr. tr. V.* **a)** run into; hit; **b)** *(herbeifahren)* deliver; **c)** *(ansteuern)* stop *or* call at ‹*village etc.*›; ‹*ship*› put in at ‹*port*›; **das Schiff fährt die Insel einmal wöchentlich an** the boat calls at the island once a week; **d)** *(zurechtweisen)* shout at; **e)** *(in Betrieb nehmen)* commission ‹*powerstation, blast furnace*›. **2.** *unr. itr. V.; mit sein* **a)** *(starten)* start off; **das Anfahren am Berg** hill-starting; **b)** *(heranfahren)* drive up; *(mit dem Fahrrad, Motorrad)* ride up; **angefahren kommen** come driving/riding up
Ạn·fahrt die a) *(das Anfahren)* journey; *(als Autofahrer)* drive; *(Ankunft)* arrival; **b)** *(Weg)* approach; *(Einfahrt)* entrance
Ạnfahrts-: ~weg der journey; *(als Autofahrer)* drive; **~zeit die** travelling time; **~zeiten als Arbeitszeit berechnen** count travelling time *sing.* as working time
Ạn·fall der a) *(Attacke)* attack; *(epileptischer ~, fig.)* fit; **einen ~ bekommen** *od.* *(ugs.)* **kriegen** have an attack/a fit; **in einem ~ von ...** *(fig.)* in a fit of ...; **b)** *o. Pl.* *(Anfallendes)* amount **(an** + *Dat.* of); *(Ertrag)* yield **(an** + *Dat.* of)
ạnfall·artig 1. *Adj.* **~es Husten** fits *pl.* of coughing; coughing fits *pl.*; **~e Schmerzen** spasms *pl.* of pain. **2.** *adv.* **plötzlich und ~ auftretende Zuckungen/Schmerzen** a sudden fit/sudden fits of twitching/a sudden spasm/sudden spasms of pain; **die Schmerzen kommen ~:** the pain comes in spasms
ạn·fallen 1. *unr. tr. V.* **a)** *(angreifen)* attack; **b)** *(geh.: befallen);* **Zweifel/Angst fiel mich an** I was assailed by doubt/fear; **Heimweh/Wut/Entsetzen fiel mich an** I was filled with homesickness/rage/horror; **Müdigkeit fiel mich an** I was overcome with tiredness. **2.** *unr. itr V.; mit sein* ‹*costs*› arise, be incurred; ‹*interest*› accrue; ‹*work*› come up; ‹*parcels etc.*› accumulate; **als Nebenprodukt/Nebenkosten ~:** be obtained as a by-product/be costs incurred; **alle ~den Reparaturen** any repairs that become necessary
ạn·fällig *Adj.* delicate ‹*child*›; temperamental ‹*engine*›; **gegen** *od.* **für etw. ~ sein** be susceptible to sth.; **für eine Krankheit ~ sein** be prone to an illness
Ạn·fälligkeit die; ~, ~en *(eines Kindes usw.)* delicateness; *(eines Motors usw.)* temperamental nature; **~ gegen** *od.* **für etw.** susceptibility to sth.; **~ für eine Krankheit** proneness to an illness
ạnfalls·weise *Adv.* **die Schmerzen kommen ~:** the pain comes in spasms
Ạn·fang der beginning; start; *(erster Abschnitt)* beginning; **ohne ~ und Ende** without a beginning *or* an end; **[ganz] am ~ der Straße** [right] at the start of the street; **von den Anfängen** from the beginnings; **am** *od.* **zu ~:** at first; to begin with; **am ~ schuf Gott ...:** in the beginning God created ...; **du hättest ihm gleich zu ~ sagen sollen, daß ...:** you should have told him right at the beginning *or* outset that ...; **von ~ an** from the beginning *or* outset; **~ 1984/der achtziger Jahre/Mai/der Woche** *usw.* at the beginning of 1984/the eighties/May/the week

etc.; **von ~ bis Ende** from beginning to end *or* start to finish; **der ~ vom Ende** the beginning of the end; **im ~ war das Wort** *(bibl.)* in the beginning was the Word; **einen ~ machen** make a start; **ein ~ ist gemacht** it's a start; we've/they've *etc.* made a start; **den ~ machen** make a start; start; *(nach einem Zerwürfnis o. ä.)* make the first move; **einen/keinen ~ finden** know/not know how to begin *or* start; **einen neuen ~ machen** make a new *or* fresh start; **aller ~ ist schwer** *(Spr.)* it's always difficult at the beginning; **seinen ~ nehmen** *(geh.)* begin; start; **in den** *od.* **seinen Anfängen stecken** be in its infancy; **wehret den Anfängen!** these things must be stopped at the outset; **aus bescheidenen Anfängen** from small *or* humble beginnings

ạn·fangen 1. *unr. itr. V.* **a)** begin; start; **das fängt ja gut an!** *(ugs. iron.)* that's a good start! *(iron.)*; **mit dreißig fängt das Leben erst an** life begins at thirty; **der Monat fing mit einem Donnerstag an** the first day of the month was a Thursday; **wer fängt an?** who is going to start?; **habt ihr schon angefangen?** have you already started?; **fangt doch bitte schon an** do please start; **er hat ganz klein/als ganz kleiner Angestellter angefangen** he started small/started [out] as a minor employee; **mit etw. ~:** start [on] sth.; **fang nicht wieder damit an!** don't start [all] that again!; **~, etw. zu tun** start to do sth.; **es fängt an zu schneien** *od.* **zu schneien an** it's starting *or* beginning to snow; **fang doch nicht gleich an zu weinen** don't start crying; **angefangen bei** *od.* **mit** *od.* **von ...:** starting *or* beginning with ...; **Weiß fängt an** white starts; **er hat angefangen** *(mit dem Streit o. ä.)* he started it; **[noch mal] von vorne ~:** start [again] from the beginning; start all over again; **b)** *(zu sprechen ~)* begin; **von etw. ~:** start on about sth.; **c)** *(eine Stelle antreten)* start; **bei einer Firma ~:** start working for a firm; start with a firm. **2.** *unr. tr. V.* **a)** begin; start; *(anbrechen)* start; **das Rauchen ~:** start smoking; **ich glaube, er will mit seiner Sekretärin was ~** *(ugs.)* I think he's trying to start something with his secretary; **auf seinem Schreibtisch lag ein angefangener Brief** on his desk lay a letter which he had started to write; **b)** *(machen)* do; **damit kann ich nichts/nicht viel ~:** that's no/not much good to me; *(das verstehe ich nicht/kaum)* that doesn't mean anything/much to me; **kannst du noch etwas damit ~?** is it any good *or* use to you?; **mit ihm ist heute nichts anzufangen** he is just not with it today; **mit ihm kann ich wenig ~:** he isn't my type of person; **er weiß nichts mit sich anzufangen** he doesn't know what to do with himself; **wie hast du das nun wieder angefangen?** how did you manage that?; **du mußt etwas Solides ~:** you must get yourself a proper job/training *etc.*; **du hättest es ganz anders ~ müssen** you should have gone about it quite differently

Ạn·fänger der; ~s, ~, Ạn·fängerin die; ~, ~nen beginner; *(abwertend: Stümper)* amateur; *(am Heck eines Autos)* „~" 'learner'

Ạnfänger·kurs der beginners' course; course for beginners

anfänglich ['anfɛŋlɪç] **1.** *Adj.* initial. **2.** *adv.* at first; initially

ạnfangs *Adv.* at first; initially; **gleich ~:** right at the beginning *or* outset

Ạnfangs-: ~buchstabe der initial [letter]; first letter; **~drittel das** *(Eishockey)* first period; **~erfolg der** initial success; **~gehalt das** starting salary; **~geschwindigkeit die** *(Physik)* initial velocity; **~gründe** *Pl.* rudiments; **~kapital das** starting capital; **~phase die** first *or* initial phase; **~reim der** initial *or* beginning rhyme; **~schwierigkeit die;** *meist Pl.* initial difficulty; **~silbe die** first *or* initial syllable; **~stadium das** initial stage; **im ~stadium sein** be in its/their initial stages *pl.*; **~unterricht der** elementary instruction; **ein Englischbuch für den ~unterricht** an elementary-level English book; **~zeit die** starting time

ạn|fassen 1. *tr. V.* **a)** *(fassen, halten)* take hold of; **die Kinder fassen jeden Dreck an** the children will pick up any bit of dirt; **b)** *(berühren)* touch; **faß mal meine Stirn an** feel my forehead; **nicht ~!** don't touch!; **Geschichte zum Anfassen** *(fig.)* history brought to life; **ich fasse nie wieder eine Spielkarte an** I'll never touch a pack of cards again; **c)** *(bei der Hand nehmen)* **jmdn. ~:** take sb.'s hand; **faßt euch an** take each other's hand; **d)** *(angehen)* approach, tackle ⟨*problem, task, etc.*⟩; **e)** *(behandeln)* treat ⟨*person*⟩; **f)** *(geh.: befallen)* **Ekel/Sehnsucht/Mitleid faßte mich an** I was seized with revulsion/filled with longing/pity. **2.** *itr. V. (mithelfen)* **[mit] ~:** lend a hand. **3.** *refl. V. (sich anfühlen)* feel; **das faßt sich wie Wolle an** it feels like wool

ạn|fauchen *tr. V.* **a)** ⟨*cat*⟩ spit at; **b)** *(fig.)* snap at

ạn|faulen *itr. V.; mit sein* ⟨*fruit*⟩ start to go bad; ⟨*wood*⟩ start to rot; **ein angefaulter Apfel/Balken** a bad apple/rotting beam

ạnfechtbar *Adj.* **a)** *(bes. Rechtsw.)* contestable; **b)** *(kritisierbar, bestreitbar)* disputable ⟨*statement, decision*⟩; ⟨*book*⟩ open to criticism

Ạnfechtbarkeit die; ~ *s.* **anfechtbar: a)** contestable nature; **b)** disputable nature

ạn|fechten *unr. tr. V.* **a)** *(bes. Rechtsw.)* challenge, dispute ⟨*validity, authenticity, statement*⟩; contest ⟨*will*⟩; contest, challenge ⟨*decision*⟩; dispute ⟨*contract*⟩; challenge ⟨*law, opinion*⟩; **b)** *(beunruhigen)* trouble; bother; **was ficht dich an?** *(geh.)* what is wrong *or* the matter with you?

Ạnfechtung die; ~, ~en a) *(bes. Rechtsw.) s.* **anfechten a:** challenging; disputing; contesting; **b)** *(geh.: Versuchung)* temptation

Ạnfechtungs·klage die *(Rechtsw.)* action for nullification

ạn|fegen *itr. V.; mit sein* **angefegt kommen** *(ugs.)* come belting along *(sl.)*; *(auf einen zu)* come belting up *(sl.)*

ạn|feinden *tr. V.* treat with hostility

Ạnfeindung die; ~, ~en hostility; **trotz aller ~en** despite all the hostility *sing.* shown towards him/her *etc.*; **~en ausgesetzt sein** be exposed to hostility *sing.*

ạn|fertigen *tr. V.* make; do ⟨*homework, translation*⟩; make up ⟨*medicament, preparation*⟩; prepare, draw up ⟨*report*⟩; cut, make ⟨*key*⟩; **Kleider/einen Schlüssel ~ lassen** have clothes made/a key cut

Ạn·fertigung die a) *s.* **anfertigen:** making; doing; making up; preparing; drawing up; cutting; **b)** *(Erzeugnis)* **das Regal ist eine eigene ~ [von mir]** I made the shelves myself; **eine spezielle ~ sein** be specially made

ạn|feuchten *tr. V.* moisten ⟨*lips, stamp*⟩; dampen, wet ⟨*ironing, cloth, etc.*⟩

ạn|feuern *tr. V.* spur on; **~de Rufe/Gesten** shouts of encouragement/rousing gestures

Ạn·feuerung die spurring on; **~ und Beifall** cheers and applause

Ạnfeuerungs·ruf der cheer

ạn|finden *unr. refl. V.* be found [again]; turn up

ạn|flachsen *tr. V. (ugs.)* tease; kid *(sl.)*

an|flanschen ['anflanʃn̩] *tr. V. (Technik)* flange sth. on (**an** + *Dat. od. Akk.* to)

ạn|flattern *itr. V.; mit sein* **angeflattert kommen** come fluttering along; *(auf einen zu)* come fluttering up

ạn|flehen *tr. V.* beseech; implore; **jmdn. um etw. ~:** beg sb. for sth.

ạn|fliegen 1. *unr. itr. V.; mit sein* ⟨*aircraft*⟩ fly in; *(beim Landen)* approach; come in to land; ⟨*bird etc.*⟩ fly in; **angeflogen kommen** come flying in; *(auf einen zu)* ⟨*bird*⟩ come flying up; **gegen den Wind ~:** fly into the wind. **2.** *unr. tr. V.* **a)** fly to ⟨*city, country, airport*⟩; *(beim Landen)* approach ⟨*airport*⟩; land on ⟨*runway etc.*⟩; **b)** *(ansteuern)* ⟨*aircraft*⟩ approach; ⟨*bird*⟩ fly towards, approach

ạn|flitzen *itr. V.; mit sein* **angeflitzt kommen** *(ugs.)* come racing along; *(auf einen zu)* come racing up

Ạn·flug der a) approach; **die Maschine befindet sich im ~ auf Berlin** the plane is now approaching Berlin; **b)** *(Hauch)* hint; trace; **ein humoristischer ~:** a hint *or* trace of humour; **c)** *(Anwandlung)* fit; **in einem ~ von Großzügigkeit** in a fit of generosity; **d)** *(Weg, Strecke)* flight

ạn|flunkern *tr. V. (ugs.)* tell fibs to

ạn|fordern *tr. V.* request, ask for ⟨*help*⟩; ask for ⟨*catalogue*⟩; order ⟨*goods, materials*⟩; send for ⟨*ambulance*⟩

Ạn·forderung die a) *o. Pl. (das Anfordern)* request (*Gen.* for); **die ~ von Waren/Materialien** ordering goods/materials; **b)** *(Anspruch)* demand; **große/hohe ~en an jmdn./etw. stellen** make great demands on sb./sth.; **den ~en nicht gewachsen sein** not be up to the demands

Ạn·frage die inquiry; *(Parl.)* question; **große/kleine ~** *(Parl.)* oral/written question

ạn|fragen 1. *itr. V.* inquire; ask; **bei jmdm. um etw. ~:** ask sb. for sth. **2.** *tr. V. (schweiz.)* ask

ạn|fressen 1. *unr. tr. V.* **a)** nibble [at]; ⟨*bird*⟩ peck [at]; **b)** *(zersetzen)* eat away [at]; **ein von Rost angefressenes altes Auto** a rusty old car. **2.** *unr. refl. V.* **sich** *(Dat.)* **einen Bauch ~** *(salopp)* develop a paunch; **die Tiere fressen sich einen Winterspeck an** the animals [eat to] put on winter fat

ạn|freunden *refl. V.* **a)** make *or* become friends; **sich mit jmdm./miteinander ~:** make *or* become friends with sb./become friends; **b)** *(fig.)* **sich mit einer Sache ~:** get to like sth.

ạn|frieren *unr. itr. V.; mit sein* **an etw.** *(Dat.)* **~:** freeze to sth.

ạn|fügen *tr. V.* add

Ạn·fügung die addition

ạn|fühlen 1. *refl. V.* feel; **sich hart/weich ~:** feel hard/soft; be hard/soft to the touch. **2.** *tr. V. (befühlen)* feel

Ạnfuhr die; ~, ~en transport[ation]

ạn|führen *tr. V.* **a)** lead; lead, head ⟨*procession*⟩; **unsere Mannschaft führt die Tabelle an** our team heads the table *or* is [at the] top of the table; **b)** *(zitieren)* quote; **c)** *(nennen)* quote, give, offer ⟨*example*⟩; give, offer ⟨*reason, details, proof*⟩; **zu meiner Entschuldigung möchte ich auch noch ~, daß ...:** I should also like to mention in my defence that ...; **d)** *(benennen)* name; cite; **e)** *(ugs.: hereinlegen)* have on *(Brit. coll.)*; dupe; **laß dich doch von ihm nicht ~:** don't be had on *(Brit.) or* taken in by him *(coll.)*; **f)** *(Druckw.: mit Anführungszeichen versehen)* mark with opening quotation-marks *or (Brit.)* inverted commas; **Buchtitel werden an- und abgeführt** book titles are put in quotation-marks *or (Brit.)* inverted commas

Ạn·führer der a) *(Führer)* leader; **b)** *(Rädelsführer)* ringleader

Ạn·führung die a) leadership; **unter [der] ~** (+ *Gen.*) under the leadership of; **b)** *(das Zitieren, Zitat)* quotation; **c)** *(Nennung) s.* **anführen c:** quotation; giving; offering; **ich beschränke mich auf die ~ einiger Beispiele** I will confine myself to quoting *or* giving *or* offering just a few examples; **d)** *(Benennung)* naming; citing; **e)** *(Druckw.: Anführungszeichen)* opening quotation-mark

Ạnführungs-: ~strich der, ~zeichen das quotation-mark; inverted comma *(Brit.)*; **ein Wort mit ~strichen** *od.* **~zeichen versehen** put a word in quotation-marks *or (Brit.)*

inverted commas; **~striche** *od.* **~zeichen unten/oben** *(beim Diktieren o. ä.)* quote/unquote; **halbe ~striche** *od.* **~zeichen** single quotation-marks *or (coll.)* quotes

an|füllen 1. *tr. V.* fill [up]; **mit etw. angefüllt sein** be filled *or* full with sth. **2.** *refl. V.* fill [up]

an|funkeln *tr. V.* flash one's eyes at

an|futtern *refl. V.* **in sich** *(Dat.)* **einen Bauch/ein Bäuchlein ~** *(ugs.)* develop a paunch/*(coll.)* a bit of a tummy

An·gabe die a) *(das Mitteilen)* giving; **ohne ~ von Gründen** without giving [any] reasons; **zur ~ dieser Daten bist du verpflichtet** you are obliged to give this information; **b)** *(Auskunft, Aussage)* **~n** information *sing.*; **jede einzelne ~ wurde überprüft** every piece of information has been checked; **c)** *(Anweisung)* instruction; **d)** *o. Pl. (Prahlerei)* boasting; bragging; *(angeberisches Benehmen)* showing-off; **das ist doch nur ~!** he is/they are *etc.* only boasting; **e)** *(Ballspiele)* service; serve; **[eine] ~ machen** serve; **ich habe [die] ~:** it's my serve

an|gaffen *tr. V. (abwertend)* gape at

an|gähnen *tr. V.* yawn at

an|galoppieren *itr. V.; mit sein* **angaloppiert kommen** come galloping along; *(auf einen zu)* come galloping up

an·gängig *Adj.* permissible

an|geben 1. *unr. tr. V.* **a)** give ⟨*reason*⟩; declare ⟨*income, dutiable goods*⟩; name, cite ⟨*witness*⟩; **welche Haarfarbe er hatte, kann ich nicht [genau] ~:** I cannot say *or* state [exactly] what colour hair he had; **zur angegebenen Zeit** at the appointed time; **wie oben angegeben** as stated *or* mentioned above; **der Zeuge gab an, er habe drei Schüsse gehört** the witness stated *or* maintained that he heard three shots; **b)** *(bestimmen)* set ⟨*course, direction*⟩; **den Takt ~:** keep time; **c)** *(veralt.: anzeigen, melden)* report ⟨*theft etc.*⟩; give away ⟨*accomplice etc.*⟩; **jmdn./einen Diebstahl bei der Polizei ~:** report sb./a theft to the police; **das geb' ich an!** I'm going to report that! **2.** *unr. itr. V.* **a)** *(prahlen)* boast; brag; *(sich angeberisch benehmen)* show off; **er gibt vor den Mädchen damit an, daß ...:** he boasts to all the girls that ...; **Väter geben mit ihren Kindern an** fathers boast *or* brag about their children; **~ wie eine Tüte [voll] Mücken** *(ugs.)* be just a big show-off *(coll.)*; **b)** *(Ballspiele)* serve; **wer gibt an?** whose serve is it?; whose turn is it to serve?

Angeber der; ~s, ~ a) *(Prahler)* boaster; braggart; *(sich angeberisch Benehmender)* show-off; **b)** *(veralt.: Denunziant)* informer

Angeberei die; ~, ~en a) *o. Pl. (das Angeben)* boasting; bragging; *(angeberisches Benehmen)* showing-off; **das ist doch nichts als ~:** he's/they are *etc.* only boasting/showing off; **b)** *(Handlung)* piece of showing-off; *(Äußerung)* boast; **mit seinen dummen ~en** with his stupid showing off/boasting

angeberisch *(ugs.)* **1.** *Adj.* boastful ⟨*person*⟩; pretentious, showy ⟨*glasses, car, jacket*⟩; *(im Benehmen)* ⟨*person*⟩ given to showing off; **~es Getue** *od.* **Verhalten** showing-off. **2.** *adv.* boastfully

Angebetete der/die; *adj. Dekl. (meist scherzh.)* beloved; *(Idol)* idol

An·gebinde das *(geh. veralt.)* gift; present

angeblich 1. *Adj.* alleged. **2.** *adv.* supposedly; allegedly; **er ist ~ krank** he is supposed to be ill; *(er sagt, er sei krank)* he says he's ill

an·geboren *Adj.* innate ⟨*characteristic*⟩; congenital ⟨*disease*⟩; **die Schüchternheit ist ihm ~:** he is shy by nature *or* naturally shy

An·gebot das a) offer; **b)** *(Wirtsch.: Waren~)* range; **das ~ an** *od.* **von Gemüse ist immer saisonabhängig** the selection of vegetables available always depends on the season; **das Verhältnis von ~ und Nachfrage** the relationship between supply and demand; **c)** *(Kaufmannsspr.: Sonder~)* [special] offer; **im ~:** on [special] offer; **~ der Woche** bargain of the week

an·gebracht 1. *2. Part. v.* **anbringen. 2.** *Adj.* appropriate

an·gebunden 1. *2. Part. v.* **anbinden. 2.** *Adj.* **a)** tied down; **b)** *in* **kurz ~** *(ugs.)* short; abrupt

an·gedeihen *unr. itr. V. in* **jmdm. etw. ~ lassen** *(geh.)* provide sb. with sth.; grant sb. sth.

An·gedenken das remembrance; **jmdm. ein treues ~ bewahren** keep sb. in fond remembrance; **mein Großvater seligen ~s** *(geh.)* my grandfather of blessed memory; **eine Zeit unseligen ~s** *(geh.)* a notorious period

an·gegangen 1. *2. Part. v.* **angehen. 2.** *Adj. (bes. ostmd.)* ⟨*food*⟩ that has gone off; **~ sein** have gone off

angegilbt ['angəgɪlpt] *Adj.* yellowing; slightly yellowed

an·gegossen *Adj. in* **wie ~ sitzen/passen** *(ugs.)* fit like a glove

angegraut ['angəgraut] *Adj.* greying

an·gegriffen 1. *2. Part. v.* **angreifen. 2.** *Adj.* weakened ⟨*health, stomach*⟩; strained ⟨*nerves, voice*⟩; *(erschöpft)* exhausted; *(nervlich)* strained

angehaucht 1. *2. Part. v.* **anhauchen. 2.** *Adj.* **links/rechts/sozialistisch** *usw.* **~ sein** have left-wing/right-wing/socialist *etc.* leanings

an·geheiratet *Adj.* **ein ~er Onkel/Vetter** *usw.* an uncle/a cousin *etc.* by marriage; **~ sein** be related by marriage

angeheitert ['angəhaitɐt] *Adj.* tipsy; merry *(coll.)*

an|gehen 1. *unr. itr. V.; mit sein* **a)** *(sich einschalten, entzünden)* ⟨*radio, light, heating*⟩ come on; ⟨*fire*⟩ catch, start burning; **b)** *(sich einschalten, entzünden lassen)* ⟨*radio, light*⟩ go on; ⟨*fire*⟩ light, catch; **c)** *(ugs.: beginnen)* start; **d)** *(anwachsen, wachsen)* ⟨*plant*⟩ take root; ⟨*vaccination*⟩ take; ⟨*bacteria*⟩ grow; **e)** *(geschehen dürfen)* **es mag noch ~:** it's [just about] acceptable; **es geht nicht an, daß radikale Elemente die Partei unterwandern** radical elements must not be allowed to infiltrate the party; **f)** *(bes. nordd.: wahr sein)* **das kann doch wohl nicht ~!** that can't be true!; **das kann [wohl] ~:** that could be true; **g) gegen etw./jmdn. ~:** fight sth./sb. **2.** *unr. tr. V.* **a)** *(angreifen)* attack; *(Sport)* tackle; challenge; **b)** *(in Angriff nehmen)* tackle ⟨*problem, difficulty*⟩; take ⟨*fence, bend*⟩; **c)** *(bitten)* ask; **jmdn. um etw. ~:** ask sb. for sth.; **d)** *(betreffen)* concern; **was geht dich das an?** what's it got to do with you?; **das geht dich nichts an** it's none of your business; **was das/mich angeht, [so] ...:** as far as that is/I am concerned ...

angehend *Adj.* budding ⟨*actor, artist, etc.*⟩; prospective ⟨*teacher, husband, etc.*⟩

an|gehören *itr. V.* **jmdm./einer Sache ~:** belong to sb./sth.; **der Regierung/einer Familie/Kommission ~:** be a member of the government/a family/committee; **einander ~** *(geh.)* belong to each other; **einer Nation ~:** be a national of a country

an·gehörig *Adj.* belonging (*Dat.* to); **dem Bündnis ~e Staaten** states belonging to the alliance

Angehörige der/die; *adj. Dekl.* **a)** *(Verwandte)* relative; relation; **der nächste ~:** the next of kin; **b)** *(Mitglied)* member

Angeklagte ['angəkla:ktə] **der/die;** *adj. Dekl.* accused; defendant

angeknackst *(ugs.)* **1.** *2. Part. v.* **anknacksen. 2.** *Adj.* weakened ⟨*trust, confidence*⟩; weakened ⟨*health*⟩; **ihre Gesundheit ist ~:** she's not in the best of health *or (coll.)* not all that great

angekränkelt ['angəkrɛŋkl̩t] *Adj.* sickly; **von Eitelkeit ~:** afflicted with vanity

Angel ['aŋl̩] **die; ~, ~n a)** fishing-rod; rod and line; **die ~ auswerfen/einziehen** cast/pull in the line; **b)** *(Tür~, Fenster~ usw.)* hinge; **etw. aus den ~n heben** lift sth. off its hinges; *(fig.)* turn sth. upside down

an·gelegen 1. *2. Part. v.* **anliegen. 2.** *Adj. in* **sich** *(Dat.)* **etw. ~ sein lassen** concern oneself with sth.

An·gelegenheit die matter; *(Aufgabe, Problem)* affair; concern; **öffentliche/kulturelle ~en** public/cultural affairs; **das ist meine/nicht meine ~:** that is my affair *or* business/not my concern *or* business; **kümmere dich um deine eigenen ~en!** mind your own business; **sich in jmds. ~en mischen** meddle in sb.'s affairs; **in welcher ~?** in what connection?; **in eigener/in einer privaten ~:** on a personal/private matter

an·gelegentlich *(geh.)* **1.** *Adj.* pressing ⟨*question, request*⟩; earnest ⟨*conversation, warning*⟩. **2.** *adv.* ⟨*look*⟩ very closely, thoroughly; ⟨*ask, inquire*⟩ particularly; **sich mit einer Sache ~ beschäftigen** be intensively occupied with sth.; **jmdm. ~ empfehlen, nicht mehr zu rauchen** earnestly recommend sb. to give up smoking

angelegt 1. *2. Part. v.* **anlegen. 2.** *Adj.* **auf Verteidigung/Entspannung** *(Akk.)* **~ sein** be intended for defence/be intended to promote détente

Angel-: ~gerät das a) fishing-rod; rod and line; **b)** *o. Pl.* fishing-tackle; **~haken der** fish-hook; **~leine die** fishing-line

angeln 1. *tr. V. (zu fangen suchen)* fish for; *(fangen)* catch; **er angelt sich immer die Fleischstücke aus der Suppe** *(fig.)* he always fishes the pieces of meat out of the soup; **sie hat sich einen reichen Mann geangelt** *(fig.)* she has hooked a rich husband. **2.** *itr. V.* angle; fish; **auf Hechte ~:** fish for pike; **nach etw. ~** *(fig.)* fish for sth.

an|geloben *tr. V. (österr.) s.* **vereidigen**

Angel-: ~punkt der crucial point; *(eines Problems)* crux; *(zentrales Thema)* central issue; **~rute die** fishing-rod; **~sachse der a)** *(hist.)* Anglo-Saxon; **b)** *(Engländer)* Englishman; **die ~sachsen** the English; *(Engländer u. Amerikaner)* the Anglo-Saxons; **~sächsisch** *Adj.* **a)** *(hist.)* Anglo-Saxon; **b)** *(englisch)* English; **die ~sächsischen Länder** the Anglo-Saxon countries; **~schein der** fishing permit *or* licence; **~schnur die** fishing-line; **~sport der** angling *no art.*

an·gemessen 1. *2. Part. v.* **anmessen. 2.** *Adj.* appropriate; reasonable, fair ⟨*price, fee*⟩; **den Umständen ~ sein** be appropriate to the circumstances. **3.** *adv.* ⟨*behave*⟩ appropriately; ⟨*reward*⟩ adequately; ⟨*recompense*⟩ reasonably, fairly

an·genehm 1. *Adj.* pleasant; agreeable; **ist Ihnen die Temperatur/ist es so ~?** is the temperature all right for you/is it all right like that?; **es ist mir gar nicht ~, daß ...:** I don't at all like it that ...; **wenn Ihnen das ~er ist** if you [would] prefer; **~e Reise/Ruhe!** [have a] pleasant journey/have a good rest; **[sehr] ~!** delighted to meet you; **das Angenehme mit dem Nützlichen verbinden** combine business with pleasure. **2.** *adv.* pleasantly; agreeably

angepaßt 1. *2. Part. v.* **anpassen. 2.** *Adj.* conformist

Angepaßtheit die; ~: conformism

Anger ['aŋɐ] **der; ~s, ~:** [village] green

angeregt 1. *2. Part. v.* **anregen. 2.** *Adj.* lively; animated. **3.** *adv.* **sich ~ unterhalten/~ diskutieren** have a lively *or* an animated conversation/discussion

angesäuselt *(ugs.)* **1.** *2. Part. v.* **ansäuseln. 2.** *Adj.* tipsy; merry *(coll.)*

an·geschlagen 1. *2. Part. v.* **anschlagen. 2.** *Adj.* groggy; poor, weakened ⟨*health*⟩

angeschmutzt ['angəʃmʊtst] *Adj.* slightly soiled

Angeschuldigte der/die; *adj. Dekl.* suspect

angesehen 1. *2. Part. v.* **ansehen. 2.** *Adj.* respected

An·gesicht das; ~[e]s, ~er, *österr. auch* **~e** *(geh.)* **a)** *(Gesicht)* face; **von ~ zu ~:** face to face; **jmdm. von ~ zu ~ gegenüberstehen** stand facing sb. *or* face to face with sb.; **jmdn. von ~ kennen** know sb. by sight; **b)** *in* **im ~** (+ *Gen.*) *s.* **angesichts a**

angesichts *Präp. mit Gen. (geh.)* **a) ~ des Feindes/der Gefahr/des Todes/der Stadt/der Küste** in the face of the enemy/of danger/death/in sight of the town/coast; **b)** *(fig.: in Anbetracht)* in view of

an·gespannt 1. *2. Part. v.* **anspannen. 2.** *Adj.* **a)** *(angestrengt)* close ⟨*attention*⟩; taut ⟨*nerves*⟩; **b)** *(kritisch)* tense ⟨*situation*⟩; tight ⟨*market, economic situation*⟩. **3.** *adv.* ⟨*work*⟩ concentratedly; ⟨*listen*⟩ with concentrated attention

Angespanntheit die; ~ a) *(Angestrengtheit)* attentiveness; **b)** *(kritischer Zustand) s.* **angespannt b:** tenseness; tightness

angestammt ['angəʃtamt] *Adj.* hereditary ⟨*right*⟩; inherited ⟨*property*⟩; *(scherzh.: altgewohnt)* usual ⟨*seat, place*⟩

angestaubt 1. *2. Part. v.* **anstauben. 2.** *Adj.* outdated

angestellt 1. *2. Part. v.* **anstellen. 2.** *Adj.* **bei jmdm. ~ sein** be employed by sb.; work for sb.; **fest ~ sein** have a permanent position

Angestellte der/die; *adj. Dekl.* [salaried] employee; **die ~n des öffentlichen Dienstes** salaried public employees; **Arbeiter und ~:** workers and salaried staff; blue- and white-collar workers; **die leitenden ~n** the managerial staff; the managers; **sie ist ~ bei der Stadt** she works for the town council; *(im Gegensatz zur Beamtin/Arbeiterin)* she has a salaried position with the town council

Angestellten-: ~gewerkschaft die white-collar union; **~verhältnis das** employment *no indef. art.* on a [monthly] salary; **im ~verhältnis stehen** be a salaried employee; *(kein Beamter sein)* not have guaranteed employment for life; **~versicherung die** [salaried] employees' insurance

angestrengt 1. *2. Part. v.* **anstrengen. 2.** *Adj.* close ⟨*attention*⟩; concentrated ⟨*work, study, thought*⟩; forced ⟨*joke*⟩. **3.** *adv.* ⟨*work, think, search*⟩ concentratedly

Angestrengtheit die; ~: *s.* **angestrengt 2:** closeness; concentratedness; forcedness

an·getan 1. *2. Part. v.* **antun. 2.** *Adj. in* **von jmdm./etw. ~ sein** be taken with sb./sth.; **dazu** *od.* **danach ~ sein, etw. zu tun** *(geh.)* be suitable for doing sth.

Angetraute ['angətrautə] **der/die;** *adj. Dekl. (scherzh.)* better half *(joc.)*

an·getrunken 1. *2. Part. v.* **antrinken. 2.** *Adj.* [slightly] drunk

an·gewandt 1. *2. Part. v.* **anwenden. 2.** *Adj.; nicht präd.* applied

an·gewiesen 1. *2. Part. v.* **anweisen. 2.** *Adj. in* **auf etw.** *(Akk.)* **~ sein** have to rely on sth.; **auf jmdn./jmds. Unterstützung ~ sein** be dependent on *or* have to rely on sb./sb.'s support; **auf sich selbst ~ sein** be thrown back upon one's own resources; **ich war auf jeden Pfennig ~:** I needed every pfennig

an|gewöhnen *tr. V.* **jmdm. etw. ~:** get sb. used to sth.; accustom sb. to sth.; **jmdm. ~, etw. zu tun** get sb. used to *or* accustom sb. to doing sth.; **sich** *(Dat.)* **etw. ~:** get into the habit of sth.; **sich** *(Dat.)* **schlechte Manieren ~:** become ill-mannered; **[es] sich** *(Dat.)* **~, etw. zu tun** get into the habit of doing sth.; **sich** *(Dat.)* **das Rauchen ~:** take up smoking

An·gewohnheit die habit

angezeigt 1. *2. Part. v.* **anzeigen. 2.** *Adj.; nicht attr. (geh.)* advisable

an|giften ['angıftn̩] *tr. V. (ugs.)* lay into *(coll.)*; let fly at

Angina [aŋ'gi:na] **die; ~, Anginen** angina

Angina pectoris [- 'pɛktorıs] **die; ~ ~** *(Med.)* angina [pectoris]

an|gleichen 1. *unr. tr. V.* **etw. einer Sache** *(Dat.) od.* **an etw.** *(Akk.)* **~:** bring sth. into line with sth.; **Systeme einander ~:** bring systems into line with each other. **2.** *unr. refl. V.* **sich jmdm./etw. ~** *od.* **sich an jmdn./etw. ~:** become like sb./sth.; **sich [einander** *od.* **aneinander] ~:** become like each other *or* alike

An·gleichung die: die ~ der Löhne an die Preise bringing wages into line with prices

Angler der; ~s, ~, Anglerin die; ~, ~nen angler

Anglikaner [aŋgli'ka:nɐ] **der; ~s, ~, Anglikanerin die; ~, ~nen** Anglican

anglikanisch 1. *Adj.* Anglican. **2.** *adv.* **~ beeinflußt sein** be influenced by Anglicanism

Anglikanismus der; ~: Anglicanism *no art.*

anglisieren *tr. V.* Anglicize

Anglist der; ~en, ~en English specialist *or* scholar; Anglicist; *(Student)* English student

Anglistik die; ~: Anglistics *sing.*; English [language and literature]; English studies *pl., no art.*

Anglistin die; ~, ~nen *s.* **Anglist**

anglistisch *Adj.; nicht präd.* Anglistics *attrib.*, English studies *attrib.* ⟨*seminar, journal*⟩

Anglizismus der; ~, Anglizismen Anglicism

Anglo·amerikaner [aŋglo|ameri'ka:nɐ] **der** Anglo-American

Anglo-Amerikaner der Anglo-Saxon; **die ~:** the British and the Americans

anglophil [aŋglo'fi:l] *Adj.* Anglophile

an|glotzen *tr. V. (ugs.)* gawp at *(coll.)*

Angola [aŋ'go:la] **(das); ~s** Angola

Angolaner der; ~s, ~: Angolan

Angora- [aŋ'go:ra]**: ~kaninchen das** angora rabbit; **~katze die** angora cat; **~wolle die** angora [wool]; **~ziege die** angora goat

angreifbar *Adj.* contestable

an|greifen 1. *unr. tr. V.* **a)** *(attackieren; auch fig.)* attack; **b)** *(schwächen)* weaken, affect ⟨*health, heart*⟩; affect ⟨*stomach, intestine, voice*⟩; weaken ⟨*person*⟩; **die Nerven ~:** be a strain on the nerves; **die Fahrt hat mich sehr angegriffen** I was exhausted by the journey; **c)** *([be]schädigen)* attack ⟨*metal*⟩; harm ⟨*hands*⟩; **d)** *(anbrechen)* break into ⟨*supplies, savings, etc.*⟩; **e)** *(ugs.: anfassen)* touch. **2.** *unr. itr. V. (einen Angriff machen; auch fig.)* attack

An·greifer der *(auch fig.)* attacker

an|grenzen *itr. V.* **an etw.** *(Akk.)* **~:** border on *or* adjoin sth.; **die ~den Grundstücke** the adjoining properties

An·griff der attack; **einen ~ fliegen** make *or* carry out an attack *or* an air-raid; **zum ~ übergehen** go over to the attack; take the offensive; **zum ~ blasen** *(auch fig.)* sound the charge *or* attack; **etw. in ~ nehmen** set about *or* tackle sth.; **~ ist die beste Verteidigung** *(Spr.)* attack is the best form of defence

angriffs-, Angriffs-: ~drittel das *(Eishockey)* attacking zone; **~fläche die: das Segel bot dem Wind eine große ~fläche** the sail presented a large area to the wind; **seinem Gegner eine ~fläche bieten** *(fig.)* leave oneself open to attack by one's opponent; **~fuß·ball der;** *o. Pl.* attacking football; **~krieg der** war of aggression; **~lust die** aggression; aggressiveness; **~lustig 1.** *Adj.* aggressive; **2.** *adv.* aggressively; **~punkt der** target; **~spieler der** *(Sport)* **a)** *(offensiver Spieler)* attacking player; **b)** *(Stürmer)* forward; **~waffe die** offensive weapon

an|grinsen *tr. V.* grin at

angst [aŋst] *Adj. in* **jmdm. ist/wird [es] ~ [und bange]** sb. is/becomes afraid *or* frightened; *(jmd. sorgt sich)* sb. is/becomes very worried *or* anxious; **jmdm. ~ [und bange] machen** frighten *or* scare sb.; *(jmdn. unruhig machen)* make sb. very worried *or* anxious

Angst die; ~, Ängste ['ɛŋstə] **a)** *(Furcht)* fear; *(Psych.)* anxiety; **~ bekommen** *od. (ugs.)* **kriegen** become *or* get frightened *or* scared; **~ [vor jmdm./etw.] haben** be afraid *or* frightened [of sb./sth.]; **eine existentielle ~:** existential fear; angst; **jmdn. in ~ und Schrecken versetzen** worry and frighten sb.; **es mit der ~ [zu tun] bekommen** *od. (ugs.)* **kriegen** become *or* get frightened *or* scared; **jmdm. ~ einflößen/einjagen/machen** frighten *or* scare sb.; **keine ~!** don't be afraid; **aus ~ [vor etw./jmdm.] sich verstekken** hide in fear [of sth./sb.]; **aus ~, sich zu verraten, sagte er kein einziges Wort** he didn't say a word for fear of betraying himself; **in ständiger ~ vor etw.** *(Dat.)* **leben** live in constant fear of sth.; **er hat mehr ~ als Vaterlandsliebe** *(ugs. scherzh.)* he's a scaredy-cat *(coll.)*; he's chicken *(sl.)*; **~ vor der eigenen Courage haben/bekommen** have got/get cold feet *(fig.)*; **b)** *(Sorge)* worry; anxiety; **~ [um jmdn./etw.] haben** be worried *or* anxious [about sb./sth.]; **sie hat ~, ihn zu verletzen/enttäuschen** she is worried about hurting/disappointing him; **keine ~, ich vergesse es schon nicht!** don't worry, I won't forget [it]!; **keine ~, die Rechnung wird schon noch kommen!** the bill will come all right, don't [you] worry!; **in tausend Ängsten schweben** be terribly worried

angst-, Angst-: ~erfüllt *Adj. (geh.)* frightened; terrified; **~frei 1.** *Adj.* anxiety-free ⟨*atmosphere*⟩; ⟨*school*⟩ with an anxiety-free atmosphere; ⟨*learning*⟩ without tears; **2.** *adv.* ⟨*live*⟩ without anxiety; ⟨*learn*⟩ without tears; **~gefühl das** feeling of anxiety; **~gegner der** *(Sport)* bogy opponent; *(Mannschaft)* bogy team; **~hase der** *(ugs. abwertend)* scaredy-cat *(coll.)*

ängstigen ['ɛŋstıgn̩] **1.** *tr. V.* frighten; scare; *(beunruhigen)* worry. **2.** *refl. V.* be frightened *or* afraid; *(sich sorgen)* worry; **sich vor etw.** *(Dat.)***/um jmdn. ~:** be frightened *or* afraid of sth./worried about sb.

ängstlich ['ɛŋstlıç] **1.** *Adj.* **a)** *(verängstigt)* anxious; apprehensive; **b)** *(furchtsam, schüchtern)* timorous; timid; **c)** *(übertrieben)* **mit ~er Genauigkeit** with painful meticulousness; **d)** *(besorgt)* worried; anxious; **mit ~er Spannung** anxiously. **2.** *adv.* **a)** *(verängstigt)* anxiously; apprehensively; **b)** *(besorgt)* anxiously; **~ gespannt** anxiously; **c)** *(übermäßig genau)* meticulously; **~ bemüht** *od.* **darauf bedacht sein, etw. zu tun** be at great pains to do sth.

Ängstlichkeit die; ~ a) *(Furchtsamkeit)* timorousness; timidity; **b)** *(Schüchternheit)* timidity; **c)** *(übertriebene Genauigkeit)* **die ~, mit der er die Vorschriften befolgt** the painful meticulousness with which he follows regulations; **d)** *(Besorgnis)* anxiety

Angst-: ~neurose die anxiety neurosis; **~psychose die** anxiety psychosis; **~röhre die** *(ugs. scherzh.)* topper *(coll.)*; top hat

Ångström ['ɔŋstrø:m] **das; ~[s], ~** *(veralt.)* ångström

angst-, Angst-: ~schrei der cry of fear; terrified cry; **~schweiß der** cold sweat; **der ~schweiß brach ihm aus** he broke out in a cold sweat; **~traum der** nightmare; **~verzerrt** *Adj.* ⟨*face*⟩ twisted in fear; **~voll 1.** *Adj.* anxious; apprehensive; **2.** *adv.* anxiously; apprehensively; **~zustand der** [state of] panic; **~zustände haben/bekommen** *od. (ugs.)* **kriegen** be in a/get into a [state of] panic

an|gucken *tr. V. (ugs.)* look at; **sich** *(Dat.)* **etw./jmdn. ~:** look *or* have a look at sth./

sb.; **guck dir das/den an!** [just] look at that/ him!

ạn|gurten *tr. V.* strap in; **sich ~:** put on one's seat-belt; *(im Flugzeug)* fasten one's seat-belt

Anh. *Abk.* Anhang app.

ạn|haben *unr. tr. V.* **a)** *(ugs.: am Körper tragen)* have on; **b) jmdm./einer Sache etwas ~ können** be able to harm sb./harm *or* damage sth.; **er sorgte dafür, daß niemand ihm etwas ~ konnte** he made sure that no one could touch him; **c)** *(ugs.: in Betrieb haben)* have on

ạn|haften *itr. V. (geh.)* **ein Nachteil/Risiko haftet einer Sache** *(Dat.)* **an** there is a disadvantage/risk in *or* attached to sth.; **die Schmach haftet ihr noch heute an** the disgrace remains with her even today

ạn|häkeln *tr. V.* crochet on (**an** + *Akk.* to)

Ạn·halt der clue (**für** to); *(für eine Vermutung)* grounds *pl.* (**für** for)

ạn|halten 1. *unr. tr. V.* **a)** stop; **den Atem ~:** hold one's breath; **b)** *(auffordern)* urge; **c)** *(an etw. halten)* **etw. an etw.** *(Akk.)* **~:** hold sth. up against sth.; **jmdm./sich ein Kleidungsstück ~:** hold a garment up against sb./oneself. **2.** *unr. itr. V.* **a)** stop; **b)** *(andauern)* go on; last; **c) er hat [bei ihren Eltern] um sie** *od.* **um ihre Hand angehalten** he asked [her parents] for her hand [in marriage]

ạnhaltend 1. *Adj.* constant; continuous. **2.** *adv.* constantly; continuously

Ạn·halter der hitch-hiker; **per ~ fahren** hitch[-hike]

Ạn·halterin die hitch-hiker

Ạnhalte·weg der *(Kfz-W.)* [overall] stopping distance

Ạnhalts·punkt der clue (**für** to); *(für eine Vermutung)* grounds *pl.* (**für** for)

an·hạnd 1. *Präp. mit Gen.* with the help of; on the basis of ⟨*current developments*⟩. **2.** *Adv.* **~ von** with the help of; on the basis of ⟨*current developments*⟩

Ạn·hang der a) *(eines Buches)* appendix; **b)** *(Anhängerschaft)* following; **der Minister und sein ~:** the minister and his followers; **hoffentlich bringt er nicht seinen ganzen ~ mit** let's hope he doesn't bring his whole gang along; **c)** *(Verwandtschaft)* family; *(in Heiratsanzeigen)* **Witwe ohne ~:** widow, no family *or* dependants

¹ạn|hängen *(geh.) unr. itr. V.* **a)** *(verbunden sein mit)* be attached to; **b)** *(glauben an)* subscribe to ⟨*belief, idea, theory, etc.*⟩; **einer Sekte ~:** be an adherent *or* follower of a sect; **c)** *(verehren)* be devoted to

²ạn|hängen 1. *tr. V.* **a)** hang up (**an** + *Akk.* on); **b)** *(ankuppeln)* couple on (**an** + *Akk.* to); hitch up ⟨*trailer*⟩ (**an** + *Akk.* to); **c)** *(anfügen)* add (**an** + *Akk.* to); **d)** *(ugs.: zuschreiben, anlasten)* **jmdm. etw. ~:** blame sb. for sth.; blame sth. on sb.; **er will mir nur was ~:** he just wants to pin something on me; **e)** *(ugs.: geben)* **jmdm. etw. ~:** give sb. sth.; **jmdm. einen Prozeß ~:** bring an action against sb.; take sb. to court; **laß dir keine vergammelten Tomaten ~!** don't let yourself be palmed off with bad tomatoes. **2.** *refl. V.* **a)** hang on (**an** + *Akk.* to); **b)** *(ugs.: sich anschließen)* **sich [an jmdn.** *od.* **bei jmdm.] ~:** tag along [with sb.] *(coll.)*

Ạn·hänger der a) *(Mensch)* supporter; *(einer Sekte)* adherent; follower; **b)** *(Wagen)* trailer; **eine Straßenbahn mit zwei ~n** a tram *(Brit.)* or *(Amer.)* trolley with two extra cars; **c)** *(Schmuckstück)* pendant; **d)** *(Schildchen)* label; tag

-anhänger der *(eines Sportvereins, einer politischen Richtung o. ä.)* ... supporter

Ạnhänger·kupplung die tow-bar

Ạnhängerschaft die; ~, ~en supporters *pl.*; *(einer Sekte)* followers *pl.*; adherents *pl.*; **eine breite ~ gewinnen** gain a wide following

ạnhängig *Adj. (Rechtsw.)* pending ⟨*action*⟩; **etw. ~ machen** start legal proceedings over sth.

ạnhänglich *Adj.* devoted ⟨*dog, friend*⟩; devoted, affectionate ⟨*child*⟩

Ạnhänglichkeit die; ~: devotion (**an** + *Akk.* to); **aus alter ~** *(Nostalgie)* out of old affection

Anhängsel ['anhɛŋzl] **das; ~s, ~ a)** *(Überflüssiges)* appendage (*Gen.* to); **b)** *(veralt.: Anhänger)* pendant; *(am Armband)* charm

Ạn·hauch der *(geh., auch fig.)* breath; *(Anflug)* trace; touch

ạn|hauchen *tr. V.* breathe on ⟨*mirror, glasses*⟩; blow on ⟨*fingers, hands*⟩

ạn|hauen *tr. V. (salopp)* accost; **jmdn. um 50 Mark ~:** touch *(sl.) or* tap sb. for 50 marks

ạn|häufen 1. *tr. V.* accumulate; amass; *(hamstern)* hoard. **2.** *refl. V.* accumulate; pile up

Ạn·häufung die a) *(das Anhäufen)* accumulation; amassing; *(das Hamstern)* hoarding; **b)** *(Haufen)* accumulation; *(von Hütten)* cluster

¹ạn|heben *unr. tr. V.* **a)** *(hochheben)* lift [up] ⟨*cupboard, carpet*⟩; raise ⟨*glass*⟩; **b)** *(erhöhen)* raise ⟨*prices, wages, etc.*⟩

²ạn|heben *unr. itr. V. (geh.)* commence; begin; **zu weinen/sprechen ~:** start *or* begin to cry/speak; start *or* begin crying/speaking

Ạn·hebung die increase (*Gen.* in); raising (*Gen.* of)

ạn|heften *tr. V.* tack [on] ⟨*hem, sleeve, etc.*⟩; attach ⟨*label, list*⟩; put up ⟨*sign, notice*⟩; **etw. mit Büroklammern/Reißnägeln/Heftklammern ~:** [paper-]clip/pin/staple sth. (**an** + *Akk.* to); **jmdm. einen Orden ~:** pin a medal on sb.

ạnheimelnd *Adj.* homely; cosy

anhe̱im-: ~|fallen *unr. itr. V.; mit sein (geh.)* **jmdm./dem Staate ~fallen** ⟨*wealth, property*⟩ pass to sb./the state; **der Vergessenheit/der Zerstörung/einem Betrug ~fallen** sink into oblivion/fall prey to destruction/fall victim to a fraud ; **~|geben** *(geh.)* **1.** *unr. tr. V.* **etw. den Flammen/dem Feuer ~geben** commit sth. to the flames/fire; **jmds. Obhut ~gegeben werden** be entrusted to sb.'s care; **2.** *unr. refl. V.* entrust oneself (*Dat.* to); **sich Gott ~geben** put one's trust in God; **~|stellen** *(geh.) tr. V.* **[es] jmdm. ~stellen, etw. zu tun** leave it to sb. to do sth. **; es bleibt/ist dir ~gestellt, dich zu beschweren** it is up to you to complain

anheischig ['anha̱iʃɪç] *Adj. (geh.)* **in sich ~ machen, etw. zu tun** undertake to do sth.; **jetzt macht er sich auch noch ~, mich über meine Pflichten zu belehren** now he even takes it upon himself to tell me what my duties are

ạn|heizen 1. *tr. V.* **a)** fire up ⟨*stove, boiler, etc.*⟩; **b)** *(fig. ugs.)* stimulate ⟨*interest*⟩. **2.** *itr. V.* put the heating on; *(bei einer Lokomotive)* fire up

ạn|herrschen *tr. V. (geh.)* bark at

ạn|hetzen *itr. V.; mit sein* **angehetzt kommen** *(ugs.)* come rushing *or* tearing along; *(auf einen zu)* come rushing *or* tearing up

an|heuern ['anhɔy̯ɐn] **1.** *tr. V.* **a)** *(Seemannsspr.)* sign on; **b)** *(fig. ugs.: einstellen)* sign on *or* up; *(um Hilfe bitten)* rope in. **2.** *itr. V. (Seemannsspr.)* sign on

Ạn·hieb der: auf [den ersten] ~ *(ugs.)* straight off; first go

ạn|himmeln *tr. V. (ugs.)* **a)** *(verehren)* idolize; worship; **b)** *(ansehen)* gaze adoringly at

Ạn·höhe die rise; elevation; *(Hügel)* hill

ạn|hören 1. *tr. V.* **a)** listen to; **etw. [zufällig] mit ~:** overhear sth.; **er wurde verurteilt, ohne vorher auch nur angehört worden zu sein** he was sentenced without even being given a hearing; **sich** *(Dat.)* **jmdn./etw. ~:** listen to sb./sth.; **ich kann das nicht länger** *od.* **mehr mit ~!** I can't listen to that any longer; **b)** *(anmerken)* **man hörte ihr die Verzweiflung an** one could hear the despair in her voice. **2.** *refl. V.* sound; **[das] hört sich nicht schlecht an** *(ugs.)* [that] doesn't sound bad

Ạnhörung die; ~, ~en hearing

Ạnhörungs·verfahren das hearing

ạn|hupen *tr. V.* hoot at

ạn|husten *tr. V.* cough over; **jmdn. ~:** cough over sb. *or* in sb.'s face

Anhydrid [anhy'dri:t] **das; ~s, ~e** *(Chemie)* anhydride

Änigma [ɛ'nɪgma] **das; ~s, ~ta** *u.* **Änigmen** *(geh.)* enigma

änigma̱tisch *Adj. (geh.)* enigmatic

Anilin [ani'li:n] **das; ~s** *(Chemie)* aniline

Anili̱n·leder das aniline leather

animalisch [ani'ma:lɪʃ] *Adj.* **a)** animal; **b)** *(abwertend: triebhaft)* animal; bestial

Animateur [anima'tø:ɐ̯] **der; ~s, ~e** host

Animate̱u̱rin die; ~, ~nen hostess

Animation [anima'tsi̯o:n] **die; ~, ~en** animation

Animi̱e̱r·dame die hostess

animieren [ani'mi:rən] *tr. (auch itr.) V.* **a)** encourage; **das soll zum Kaufen ~:** that's to encourage people to buy; **er fühlte sich [durch mein Beispiel] animiert** he felt prompted [by my example]; **b)** *(Film)* animate

Animi̱e̱r-: ~lokal das hostess bar; *(Nachtklub)* hostess night-club; **~mädchen das** hostess

Animosität [animozi'tɛ:t] **die; ~, ~en a)** *o. Pl.* animosity; **b)** *(Äußerung)* hostile remark

Animus ['a:nimʊs] **der; ~ a)** *(Psych.)* animus; **b)** *(ugs.: Ahnung)* **ich habe so einen ~, daß ...:** I have a feeling *or* hunch that ...

Ạn·ion das *(Chemie)* anion

Anis [a'ni:s] **der; ~[es], ~e a)** *(Pflanze)* anise; **b)** *(Gewürz)* aniseed; **c)** *(Branntwein)* aniseed brandy

Anisette [ani'zɛt] **der; ~s, ~s** anisette

Anis-: ~likör der aniseed liqueur; **~plätzchen das** aniseed biscuit; **~schnaps der** aniseed brandy

Ank. *Abk.* **Ankunft** arr.

ạn|kämpfen *itr. V.* **gegen jmdn./etw. ~:** fight [against] sb./sth.; **gegen den Strom/ Wind/die Elemente ~:** battle against the current/the wind/the elements

ạn|karren *tr. V. (ugs.)* cart along; bring along ⟨*supporters, followers*⟩

Ạn·kathete die *(Geom.)* adjacent side

Ạn·kauf der purchase; **„Heinrich Meyer, An- und Verkauf"** 'Heinrich Meyer, second-hand dealer'; **„An- und Verkauf von ..."** 'we buy and sell ...'; **durch den ~ einer Sache** *(Gen.)* by purchasing *or* buying sth.; by the purchase of sth.

ạn|kaufen *tr. V.* purchase; buy

ạn|keifen *tr. V.* scream at

Anker ['aŋkɐ] **der; ~s, ~ a)** *(eines Schiffs)* anchor; *(fig.)* support; **vor ~ gehen/liegen** *od.* **treiben** drop anchor/lie at anchor; **~ werfen** drop anchor; **b)** *(Elektrot.)* armature; **c)** *(Uhrmacherei)* anchor

Ạnker-: ~boje die anchor buoy; **~kette die** anchor cable; **~klüse die; ~, ~n** hawse-hole; *(Rohr)* hawse-pipe

ạnkern *itr. V.* **a)** *(vor Anker gehen)* anchor; drop anchor; **b)** *(vor Anker liegen)* be anchored; lie at anchor

Ạnker-: ~platz der anchorage; **~wicklung die** *(Elektrot.)* armature winding; **~winde die** windlass

ạn|ketten *tr. V.* chain up (*Dat.*, **an** + *Akk.* to)

ạn|kläffen *tr. V.* yap at

Ạn·klage die a) charge; **der Staatsanwalt hat ~ [wegen Mordes gegen ihn] erhoben** the public prosecutor brought a charge [of murder against him]; **unter ~ stehen** have been charged (**wegen** with); **jmdn. unter ~ stellen** charge sb. (**wegen** with); **b)** *(~vertre-*

tung) prosecution; **der Vertreter der ~:** counsel for the prosecution; prosecuting counsel; **c)** *(geh.: Vorwurf)* accusation

Ạnklage-: ~bank die; *Pl.* **~bänke** dock; **auf der ~bank sitzen** *(auch fig.)* be in the dock; **~erhebung die** preferral of charges; **für eine ~erhebung hinreichend sein** be sufficient to justify preferring charges

ạn|klagen 1. *tr. V.* **a)** *(Rechtsw.)* charge; accuse; **jmdn. einer Sache** *(Gen.)* *od.* **wegen etw. ~:** charge sb. with *or* accuse sb. of sth.; **b)** *(geh.: beschuldigen)* accuse; **jmdn./sich einer Sache** *(Gen.)* **~:** accuse sb./oneself of sth.; **jmdn./sich ~, etw. zu tun** accuse sb./oneself of doing sth.; **sich als etw.** *(Nom. od. Akk.)* **~:** accuse oneself of being sth. **2.** *itr. V.* cry out in accusation; **ein ~des Buch** a book that cries out in accusation; **jmdn. ~d ansehen** look at sb. accusingly

Ạn·kläger der prosecutor

Ạnklage-: ~schrift die indictment; **~vertreter der** prosecuting counsel; counsel for the prosecution; **~vertretung die** *(Vorgang, Partei)* prosecution

ạn|klammern 1. *tr. V.* peg *(Brit.)*, pin *(Amer.)* ‹*clothes, washing*› up **(an** + *Akk.* to); clip ‹*copy, sheet, etc.*› **(an** + *Akk.* to); *(mit Heftklammern)* staple ‹*copy, sheet, etc.*› **(an** + *Akk.* on). **2.** *refl. V.* **sich an jmdn./etw. ~:** cling to *or* hang on to sb./sth.

Ạn·klang der a) *o. Pl.* **in [bei jmdm.] ~ finden** meet with [sb.'s] approval; find favour [with sb.]; **mit dem Vorschlag wirst du keinen großen ~ finden** you won't find any great support for that proposal; **wenig/keinen/großen ~ finden** be poorly/badly/well received **(bei** by); **b)** *(Ähnlichkeit)* echo **(an** + *Akk.* of); **Anklänge an etw.** *(Akk.)* **enthalten** be reminiscent of sth.

ạn|klatschen *tr. V. (ugs.)* slap ‹*poster, wallpaper, etc.*› up *or* on **(an** + *Akk.* to); plaster ‹*hair*› down

ạn|kleben 1. *tr. (auch itr.) V.* stick up ‹*poster, etc.*› **(an** + *Akk.* on); **„Ankleben verboten"** 'stick *(Brit.) or* post no bills'; 'bill-posting prohibited'; **sich** *(Dat.)* **einen falschen Bart ~:** stick on a false beard. **2.** *itr. V.; mit sein* stick **(an** + *Dat.* to)

ạn|kleckern *itr. V.; mit sein* **angekleckert kommen** *(ugs.) (immer wieder kommen)* come trotting along *(coll.)*; *(auf einen zu)* come trotting up *(coll.)*; *(nach und nach eintreffen)* come drifting along *or* in

Ạnkleide·kabine die changing cubicle

ạn|kleiden *tr. V. (geh.)* dress; **sich ~:** get dressed; dress [oneself]

Ạnkleide·raum der dressing-room

ạn·klicken *tr. V. (DV)* click on

ạn|klingeln *tr., itr. V. (ugs.)* **jmdn.** *od.* **bei jmdm. ~:** ring *or* call sb. [up]

ạn|klingen *unr. itr. V.* **a)** *(erinnern)* be reminiscent **(an** + *Akk.* of); **b)** *auch mit sein (wahrnehmbar sein)* be discernible; **ein Thema ~ lassen** touch on a theme

ạn|klopfen *itr. V.* knock **(an** + *Akk. od. Dat.* at *or* on); **bei jmdm. um etw. ~** *(ugs.)* try to touch *(sl.) or* tap sb. for sth.

ạn|knabbern *tr. V. (ugs.)* nibble [at]; **der Staat muß seine Goldreserven ~** *(fig.)* the state is having to dig into its gold reserves; **zum Anknabbern aussehen** *(fig.)* look good enough to eat

ạn|knacksen *tr. V. (ugs.)* crack ‹*bone, rib*›; *(fig.)* injure ‹*pride*›; badly affect ‹*health*›

ạn|knipsen *tr. V. (ugs.)* switch *or* put on

ạn|knüpfen 1. *tr. V.* **a)** tie on **(an** + *Akk.* to); **b)** *(beginnen)* start up ‹*conversation*›; open, start ‹*negotiations*›; establish ‹*relations, business links*›; form ‹*relationship*›; **eine Bekanntschaft mit jmdm. ~:** strike up an acquaintance with sb. **2.** *itr. V.* **an etw.** *(Akk.)* **~:** take sth. up; **ich knüpfe dort an, wo wir vorige Woche aufgehört haben** I'll pick up where we left off last week

Ạnknüpfung die; ~, ~en a) *s.* **anknüpfen b:** starting up; opening; starting; establishment; forming; **b) die ~ an etw.** *(Akk.)* taking sth. up; **unter [bewußter] ~ an etw.** *(Akk.)* with [conscious] reference to sth.

Ạnknüpfungs·punkt der starting-point [for a/the conversation]

ạn|knurren *tr. V.* growl at; **sich [gegenseitig] ~** *(auch fig.)* growl at one another

ạn|kohlen *tr. V. (ugs.)* kid *(coll.)*

ạn|kommen 1. *unr. itr. V.; mit sein* **a)** *(eintreffen)* arrive; ‹*letter, parcel*› come, arrive; ‹*bus, train, plane*› arrive, get in; **seid ihr gut angekommen?** did you arrive safely *or* get there all right?; **ich bin beim 6. Kapitel angekommen** I have reached *or* got to the sixth chapter; **wann sollen die Zwillinge denn ~?** *(ugs.: geboren werden)* when are the twins due [to arrive]?; **bei ihr ist kürzlich das vierte Kind angekommen** *(ugs.: geboren worden)* she has just had her fourth child; **b)** *(ugs.: Anklang finden)* **[bei jmdm.] [gut] ~:** go down [very] well [with sb.]; **damit kommt er bei mir nicht an** he won't get anywhere with me with that; **er ist ein Typ, der bei den Frauen ankommt** he is the sort who is a success with women; **c) gegen jmdn./etw. ~:** be able to cope *or* deal with sb./fight sth.; **d)** *(unpers.: abhängen)* **auf uns/auf das Wetter kommt es dabei nicht an** it doesn't depend on us/the weather; **es kommt [ganz] darauf an, ob ...:** it [all] depends whether ...; **es kommt [ganz] darauf** *od.* **drauf an** *(ugs.)* it [all] depends; **es darauf** *od.* **drauf ~ lassen** *(ugs.)* take a chance; chance it; **es auf etw.** *(Akk.)* **~ lassen** [be prepared to] risk sth.; **man könnte es ja mal auf einen Versuch ~ lassen** one could at least give it a try; **e)** *(unpers.: entscheidend, wichtig sein)* **es kommt auf etw.** *(Akk.)* **an** sth. matters; **auf die paar Mark/Minuten kommt es [mir] nicht an/soll es mir nicht ~:** a few marks/minutes don't matter [to me]; **es kommt auf jede Minute/jeden Pfennig an** every minute/pfennig counts; **es käme auf einen Versuch an** it's *or* it would be worth a try; **da kommt es auf drei Leute mehr auch nicht mehr an** three more people won't make any difference; **es kommt nicht darauf an, was er sagt** it's not what he says that matters; **darauf kommt es mir nicht so sehr an** that doesn't matter so much to me; **f)** *(herankommen)* come along; **mit etw. ~** *(ugs.: etw. dauernd betonen)* harp on about sth.; **g)** *(ugs.: Erfolg haben)* **er ist mit seinem Manuskript bisher noch bei keinem Verlag angekommen** up to now he hasn't had any success with publishers with his manuscript; **ohne Beziehungen kommt man heute nirgends mehr an** you won't *or* don't get anywhere these days without connections. **2.** *tr. V. (geh.)* **a)** *(überkommen)* ‹*fear, desire, etc.*› come over; **b) jmdn. hart/schwer** *usw.* **~:** be hard/difficult *etc.* for sb.

Ankömmling ['ankœmlɪŋ] **der; ~s, ~e** newcomer; *(ugs.: Neugeborenes)* new arrival

ạn|können *unr. itr. V.* **a) gegen jmdn./etw. ~:** be able to fight sb./sth.; **b)** *(ugs.: ansein dürfen)* **das Licht/Radio/die Heizung kann jetzt wieder an** you/he *etc.* can put the light/radio/heating on again now

ạn|koppeln 1. *tr. V.* couple ‹*carriage*› up **(an** + *Akk.* to); hitch ‹*trailer*› up **(an** + *Akk.* to); dock ‹*spacecraft*› **(an** + *Akk.* with). **2.** *itr. V.* ‹*spacecraft*› dock **(an** + *Akk.* with)

ạn|kotzen *tr. V. (salopp)* **a)** throw up over; puke over *(coarse)*; **b)** *(fig.: anwidern)* **jmdn. ~:** make sb. sick

ạn|krallen *refl. V.* cling **(an** + *Akk. od. Dat.* at)

ạn|kratzen *tr. V.* scratch; *(fig. ugs.)* dent

ạn|kreiden *tr. V. (ugs.)* **jmdm. etw. ~:** hold sth. against sb.; **man kreidet ihm sein Verhalten als Schwäche an** his behaviour is seen *or* regarded as weakness; **das muß man ihm dick ~:** you've really got to hold that against him

Ạn·kreis der *(Geom.)* escribed circle; excircle

ạn|kreuzen 1. *tr. V.* mark with a cross; put a cross beside. **2.** *itr. V.; meist mit sein* **gegen den Wind ~** *(Segeln)* sail against *or* into the wind

ạn|kriechen *unr. itr. V.; mit sein* **angekrochen kommen** come creeping *or* crawling along; *(auf einen zu)* come creeping *or* crawling up

ạn|kündigen 1. *tr. V.* announce; **kündige dich bitte vorher an** please let me/us *etc.* know in advance that you are coming *or* give me/us *etc.* advance notice; **ein Gewitter ~:** herald a storm; **eine angekündigte/nicht angekündigte Klassenarbeit** a class test announced in advance/a surprise test. **2.** *refl. V.* ‹*spring, storm*› announce itself; ‹*illness*› show itself

Ạn·kündigung die announcement; **er besuchte uns ohne vorherige ~:** he visited us without letting us know in advance *or* with no advance notice

Ankunft ['ankʊnft] **die; ~, Ankünfte** arrival; **„~"** 'arrivals'

Ạnkunfts-: ~halle die *(Flugw.)* arrival[s] hall; **~tafel die** arrivals board

ạn|kuppeln *tr. V. s.* **ankoppeln 1**

ạn|kurbeln *tr. V.* **a)** crank [up]; **b)** *(fig.)* boost ‹*economy, production, etc.*›

Ạnkurb[e]lung die; ~, ~en boosting; **Maßnahmen zur ~ der Wirtschaft** measures to boost the economy

ạn|kuscheln *refl. V.* **sich an jmdn.** *od.* **bei jmdm./an etw.** *(Akk.)* **~:** snuggle *or* cuddle up to sb./sth.

Anl. *Abk.* **Anlage** encl.

ạn|lächeln *tr. V.* smile at; **jmdn. freundlich ~:** give a friendly smile to sb.

ạn|lachen 1. *tr. V.* smile at; **ich habe dich angelacht, nicht ausgelacht** I was laughing with you, not at you. **2.** *refl. V.* **sich** *(Dat.)* **jmdn. ~** *(ugs.)* get off with sb. *(Brit. coll.)*; pick sb. up

Ạn·lage die a) *o. Pl. (das Anlegen) (einer Kartei)* establishment; *(eines Parks, Gartens usw.)* laying out; construction; *(eines Parkplatzes, Stausees)* construction; **b)** *(Grün~)* park; *(um ein Schloß, einen Palast usw. herum)* grounds *pl.*; **die öffentlichen/städtischen ~n** public/municipal parks and gardens; **c)** *(Angelegtes, Komplex)* complex; **d)** *(Einrichtung)* facilities *pl.*; **sanitäre/militärische ~n** sanitary facilities/military installations; **die elektrische ~:** the electrical equipment; **e)** *(Werk)* plant; **f)** *(Musik~, Lautsprecher~ usw.)* equipment; system; **g)** *(Geld~)* investment; **h)** *(Konzeption)* conception; *(Struktur)* structure; **i)** *(Veranlagung)* aptitude, gift, talent **(zu** for); *(Neigung)* tendency, predisposition **(zu** to); **j)** *(Beilage zu einem Brief)* enclosure; **als ~ sende ich Ihnen/erhalten Sie ein ärztliches Attest** please find enclosed *or* I enclose a medical certificate

ạnlage-, Ạnlage-: ~bedingt 1. *Adj.* constitutional; **2.** *adv.* constitutionally; **~berater der** investment advisor; **~kapital das** investment capital

ạn|lagern *(Chemie)* **1.** *tr. V.* take up. **2.** *refl. V.* be taken up **(an** + *Akk.* by)

Ạnlage·vermögen das fixed assets *pl. or* capital

ạn|landen *tr. V.* land

ạn|langen 1. *itr. V.; mit sein* arrive; **bei/auf/an etw.** *(Dat.)* **~:** arrive at *or* reach sth.; **bei Kapitel 3 ~:** reach *or* get to chapter 3. **2.** *tr. V.* **a)** *(südd.: anfassen)* touch; **b)** *s.* **anbelangen**

Anlaß ['anlas] **der; Ạnlasses, Anlässe** ['anlɛsə] **a)** *(Ausgangspunkt, Grund)* cause **(zu** for); **der ~ des Streites** the cause of the dispute; **etw. zum ~ nehmen, etw. zu tun** use *or* take sth. as an opportunity to do sth.; **ich möchte aus gegebenem ~ darauf hinweisen, daß ...:** I would like to take this opportunity to point out that ...; **aus ~ seines Geburtstags** on the occasion of *or* to celebrate his birthday; **jmdm. ~ zu Beschwerden geben** give sb. cause for complaint; **~ zur Sorge/Beunruhigung/Klage geben** give cause for concern/unease/complaint; **beim geringsten/kleinsten ~:** for the slightest reason; **aus aktuellem ~:** because of current events; **b)** *(Gelegenheit)* occasion; **bei festlichen Anlässen** on festive occasions

an|lassen 1. *unr. tr. V.* **a)** *(in Betrieb lassen)* leave ⟨*light, radio, heating, etc.*⟩ on; leave ⟨*engine, tap*⟩ on *or* running; leave ⟨*candle*⟩ burning; **b)** *(anbehalten)* keep ⟨*coat, gloves, etc.*⟩ on; **c)** *(in Gang setzen)* start [up]. **2.** *unr. refl. V.* **sich gut/schlecht ~:** make a *or* get off to a good/bad *or* poor start; **wie läßt sich der neue Mitarbeiter denn an?** how is your new colleague getting on?

Anlasser der; **~s, ~** *(Kfz-W.)* starter

an·läßlich *Präp. mit Gen.* on the occasion of

an|lasten *tr. V.* **jmdm. ein Verbrechen ~:** accuse sb. of a crime; **jmdm. die Schuld an etw.** *(Dat.)* **~:** blame sb. for sth.; **jmdm. etw. als Versagen ~:** regard sth. as a failure on sb.'s part

an|latschen *itr. V.; mit sein (ugs.)* **angelatscht kommen** come trudging along; *(auf einen zu)* come trudging up; *(schlurfend)* come slouching along/up

An·lauf der a) run-up; **[mehr] ~ nehmen** take [more of] a run-up; **mit/ohne ~:** with/without a run-up; **er sprang mit/ohne ~:** he did a running/standing jump; **ein Sprung mit/ohne ~:** a running/standing jump; **b)** *(Versuch)* attempt; **beim** *od.* **im ersten/dritten ~:** at the first/third attempt *or (coll.)* go; **einen [neuen] ~ nehmen** make another attempt; have another go *(coll.)*; **c)** *(Sport) (Bahn)* runway; *(Strecke)* run-up

Anlauf·adresse die *s.* **Anlaufstelle**

an|laufen 1. *unr. itr. V.; mit sein* **a) angelaufen kommen** come running along; *(auf einen zu)* come running up; **b) gegen jmdn./etw. ~:** run at sb./sth.; **gegen etw. ~** *(fig.)* fight against sth.; **c)** *(Anlauf nehmen)* take a run-up; **d)** *(zu laufen beginnen)* ⟨*engine*⟩ start [up]; *(fig.)* ⟨*film*⟩ open; ⟨*production, campaign, search*⟩ start; **e)** *(sich färben)* turn; go; **f)** *(beschlagen)* mist *or* steam up. **2.** *unr. tr. V.* put in at ⟨*port*⟩

Anlauf-: ~stelle die [place of] refuge; place to go; **~stelle für solche Reiserufe** the place to which to send such SOS messages; **~zeit die: der Motor braucht einige Minuten ~zeit** the engine needs a few minutes to warm up; **morgens braucht sie immer eine gewisse ~zeit** it always takes her a certain amount of time to get going in the mornings

An·laut der *(Sprachw.)* initial sound; **der Konsonant wird im ~ stimmhaft gesprochen** the consonant is voiced when in initial position

an|lauten *itr. V. (Sprachw.)* begin **(mit** with); **der ~de Vokal** the initial vowel

an|läuten *tr., itr. V. (bes. südd.) s.* **anrufen 1c, 2a**

an|legen 1. *tr. V.* **a)** *(an etw. legen)* put *or* lay ⟨*domino, card*⟩ [down] **(an** + *Akk.* next to); place, position ⟨*ruler, protractor*⟩ **(an** + *Akk.* on); put ⟨*ladder*⟩ up **(an** + *Akk.* against); **ein Gewehr auf jmdn./etw. ~:** level a gun at sb./sth.; **sie legte das Baby an** she put the baby to her breast; **einen strengen Maßstab [an etw.** *(Akk.)***] ~:** apply strict standards [to sth.]; **b)** *(an den Körper legen)* **die Flügel/Ohren ~:** close its wings/lay its ears back; **die Arme ~:** put one's arms to one's sides; **c)** *(geh.: anziehen, umlegen)* don; put on; **d)** *(schaffen, erstellen)* lay out ⟨*town, garden, plantation, street*⟩; start ⟨*file, album*⟩; compile ⟨*statistics, index*⟩; **e)** *(gestalten, entwerfen)* structure ⟨*story, novel*⟩; **f)** *(investieren)* invest; **g)** *(ausgeben)* spend **(für** on); **h) er legt es auf einen Streit an** he is determined to have a fight; **es darauf ~, etw. zu tun** be determined to do sth.; **i)** *(nachlegen)* put on. **2.** *itr. V.* **a)** *(festmachen, landen)* moor; *(am Liegeplatz)* berth; **b)** *(Kartenspiel)* lay a card/cards; **bei jmdm. ~:** lay a card/cards on sb.'s hand; **ich kann nirgends/nicht ~:** I can't go; **c)** *(Domino)* play [a domino/dominoes]; **d)** *(das Gewehr anlegen)* aim **(auf** + *Akk.* at). **3.** *refl. V.* **sich mit jmdm. ~:** pick an argument *or* a quarrel with sb.

Anlege·platz der berth

Anleger der; **~s, ~ a)** *(Schiffahrt)* jetty; landing-pier; **b)** *(Investor)* investor

Anlege-: ~steg der jetty; landing-stage; **~stelle die** mooring

an|lehnen 1. *tr. V.* **a)** *(an etw. lehnen)* lean **(an** + *Akk. od. Dat.* against); **b)** leave ⟨*door*⟩ slightly open *or* ajar; leave ⟨*window*⟩ slightly open; **die Tür war angelehnt** the door was [left] slightly open *or* ajar. **2.** *refl. V.* **sich [an jmdn.** *od.* **jmdm./etw.] ~:** lean [on sb./against sth.]; **er lehnte sich mit dem Rücken/der Schulter an die** *od.* **der Wand an** he leaned back *or* leaned his back/leaned [with] his shoulder against the wall; **sich an ein Vorbild ~** *(fig.)* follow an example

Anlehnung die; **~, ~en a)** dependence **(an** + *Akk.* on); *(Halt, Stütze)* support; **~ an jmdn./etw. suchen/finden** look for/find support from sb./sth.; **b)** *(Nachahmung)* **in ~ an jmdn./etw.** following *or* in imitation of sb./sth.

Anlehnungs·bedürfnis das need for love and affection

anlehnungs·bedürftig *Adj.* in need of love and affection *postpos.*; **je mehr sie trank, desto ~er wurde sie** *(scherzh.)* the more she drank, the more amorous and affectionate she became

Anleihe die; **~, ~n a)** *(Darlehen)* loan; **b)** *(fig.)* borrowing; **eine ~ bei Goethe/Picasso machen** borrow from Goethe/Picasso

an|leimen *tr. V.* stick *or* glue on **(an** + *Akk. od. Dat.* to)

an|leinen *tr. V.* put ⟨*dog*⟩ on the lead; **Hunde sind anzuleinen** dogs must be kept on a lead; **der Hund war nicht angeleint** the dog was not on a lead

an|leiten *tr. V.* **a)** *(unterweisen)* instruct; teach; **jmdn. bei der Arbeit ~:** instruct sb. in the work; teach sb. the work; **b)** *(anhalten, erziehen)* teach; **die Kinder zur Selbständigkeit/Pünktlichkeit ~:** teach the children to be independent/punctual

An·leitung die instructions *pl.*

Anlern·beruf der semi-skilled occupation *or* job

an|lernen 1. *tr. V.* train; **ein angelernter Arbeiter** a semi-skilled worker. **2.** *refl. V.* **sich** *(Dat.)* **etw. ~:** learn sth. up; **eine bloß angelernte Bildung** a superficially acquired education

Anlernling ['anlɛrnlɪŋ] **der;** **~s, ~e** *(veralt.)* trainee; **~ sein** be a trainee

an|lesen 1. *unr. tr. V.* begin *or* start reading *or* to read. **2.** *unr. refl. V.* **sich** *(Dat.)* **etw. ~:** learn sth. by reading *or* from books; **eine nur angelesene Kenntnis** knowledge which comes straight out of books

an|leuchten *tr. V.* **jmdn./etw. ~:** shine a light on sb./light sth. up; **den Dieb mit der Taschenlampe ~:** shine a torch *(Brit.) or (Amer.)* flashlight on the thief

an|liefern *tr. V.* deliver

An·lieferung die delivery

an|liegen *unr. itr. V.* **a)** *(an etw. liegen)* ⟨*pullover etc.*⟩ fit tightly *or* closely; ⟨*hair, ears*⟩ lie flat; **ein eng ~der Pullover** a tight- *or* close-fitting pullover; **b)** *(ugs.: vorliegen)* be on; *(zu erledigen sein)* to be done; **was liegt an?** *(was kann ich für dich tun?)* what's up? *(coll.)*

An·liegen das; **~s, ~** *(Bitte)* request; *(Angelegenheit)* matter; **etw. zu seinem persönlichen ~ machen** take a personal interest in sth.

anliegend *Adj.* **a)** *nicht präd. (angrenzend)* adjacent; **b)** *(beiliegend)* enclosed

Anlieger der; **~s, ~:** resident; **„~ frei", „frei für ~"** 'access only'

Anlieger-: ~staat der: die ~staaten des Mittelmeers *usw.* the countries bordering the Mediterranean *etc.*; **~verkehr der** residents' vehicles *pl.*; **die Straße ist nur noch für den ~verkehr frei** the street is only open to residents; **„~verkehr frei"** 'residents only'

an|locken *tr. V.* attract ⟨*customers, tourists, etc.*⟩; lure ⟨*bird, animal*⟩

an|löten *tr. V.* solder on **(an** + *Akk. od. Dat.* to)

an|lügen *tr. V.* lie to

Anm. *Abk.* **Anmerkung**

an|machen *tr. V.* **a)** *(anschalten, -zünden usw.)* put *or* turn ⟨*light, radio, heating*⟩ on; light ⟨*fire*⟩; **b)** *(bereiten)* mix ⟨*cement, plaster, paint, etc.*⟩; dress ⟨*salad*⟩; **c)** *(ugs.: anbringen)* put ⟨*curtain, sign*⟩ up; **ein Schild an der Tür ~:** put a sign up on the door; **dem Hund das Halsband ~:** put the collar on the dog; **d)** *(ugs.: ansprechen)* ⟨*woman, girl*⟩ give ⟨*man, boy*⟩ the come-on *(sl.)*; ⟨*man, boy*⟩ chat ⟨*woman, girl*⟩ up *(Brit. coll.)*; **e)** *(ugs.: begeistern, erregen)* get ⟨*audience etc.*⟩ going; **das macht mich ungeheuer/nicht an** it really turns me on *(coll.)*/does nothing for me *(coll.)*; **f)** *(provozieren)* **mach mich nicht an!** leave me alone!

an|mahnen *tr. V.* send a reminder about; **er hat den angemahnten Betrag sofort überwiesen** he paid the outstanding amount as soon as he received a reminder

An·mahnung die reminder; **trotz mehrfacher ~:** despite repeated reminders *pl.*

an|malen *tr. V.* **a)** *(ugs.: bemalen)* paint; **etw. rot ~:** paint sth. red; **b)** *(ugs.: schminken)* paint; **sich ~:** paint one's face; **c)** *(auf etw. malen)* paint **(an** + *Akk.* on); *(auf etw. zeichnen)* draw **(an** + *Akk.* on); **jmdm./sich einen Bart ~:** paint *or* draw a beard on sb.'s/one's face *or* on sb./oneself

An·marsch der a) *o. Pl. (das Anmarschieren)* advance; **im ~ sein** *(anrücken)* be advancing; *(ugs. scherzh.: unterwegs sein)* be on one's way; **b)** *(ugs.: Weg)* walk

an|marschieren *itr. V.; mit sein* advance; **anmarschiert kommen** *(ugs.)* come marching along; *(auf einen zu)* come marching up

Anmarsch·weg der walk

an|maßen *refl. V.* **sich** *(Dat.)* **etw. ~:** claim sth. [for oneself]; arrogate sth. to oneself; **was maßt du dir an?** who do you think you are?; what do you think you are doing?; **sich ~, etw. zu tun** presume to do sth.; **darüber kannst du dir gar kein Urteil ~:** you have no right *or* it's not your place to pass judgement on that

an·maßend 1. *Adj.* presumptuous; *(arrogant)* arrogant. **2.** *adv.* presumptuously; *(arrogant)* arrogantly

Anmaßung die; **~, ~en** presumptuousness; presumption; *(Arroganz)* arrogance; **so eine [freche] ~!** what presumptuousness *or* presumption/arrogance!; **es ist eine ~ zu behaupten, daß ...:** it is presumptuous to assert that ...

an|meckern *tr. V. (ugs.)* **jmdn. ~:** have a go at sb.

Anmelde·formular das a) application form; **b)** *(einer Meldebehörde)* registration form

an|melden *tr. V.* **a)** *(als Teilnehmer)* enrol; **jmdn./sich zu einem Kursus/in** *od.* **bei einer Schule ~:** enrol sb./enrol for a course/at a school; **sich schriftlich ~:** register [in writing]; **jmdn. zu einer Impfung ~:** make an appointment for sb. to be vaccinated; **b)** *(melden, anzeigen)* license, get a licence for ‹*television, radio*›; apply for ‹*patent*›; register ‹*domicile, change of address, car, trade mark*›; **die Demonstration war nicht angemeldet** no notification had been given of the demonstration; **sich/seinen neuen Wohnsitz ~:** register one's new address; **jmdn./sich polizeilich** *od.* **bei der Polizei ~:** register sb./register with the police; *s. auch* **Konkurs; c)** *(ankündigen)* announce; *(einen Termin vereinbaren)* **sind Sie angemeldet?** do you have an appointment?; **sich beim Arzt ~:** make an appointment to see the doctor; **d)** *(geltend machen)* express, make known ‹*reservation, doubt, wish*›; put forward ‹*demand*›; assert ‹*right*›; **e)** *(Kartenspiele: ansagen)* bid; **f)** *(Fernspr.)* book; **ein Gespräch nach Übersee ~:** book an overseas call

Anmelde·pflicht die *(für den Wohnsitz)* obligation to register one's address; *(für Fernsehen, Radio)* obligation to obtain a licence; *(für das Auto)* obligation to register a/the vehicle; **für Demonstrationen besteht ~:** it is mandatory to notify the police in advance of demonstrations

anmelde·pflichtig *Adj.* **~ sein** ‹*television, radio*› need a licence; ‹*car*› have to be registered; ‹*demonstration*› have to be notified; **jeder Wohnungswechsel ist ~:** every change of address must be registered

An·meldung die a) *(zur Teilnahme)* enrolment; **b)** *s.* **anmelden b:** licensing; registration; notification; **die ~ eines Patents** the application for a patent; **c)** *(Ankündigung)* announcement; *(beim Arzt, Rechtsanwalt usw.)* making an appointment; **d)** *s.* **anmelden d:** expression; putting forward; assertion; **e)** *(Fernspr.)* booking; **die ~ eines Gesprächs** booking a call; **f)** *(Formular, Schreiben)* registration [form]; **g)** *(Büro, Schalter usw.)* reception; **sie müssen zuerst zur/in die ~ [gehen]** you must go to reception first

an|merken *tr. V.* **a) jmdm. seinen Ärger/seine Verlegenheit** *usw.* **~:** notice that sb. is annoyed/embarrassed *etc.*; notice sb.'s annoyance/embarrassment *etc.*; **man merkt ihm [nicht] an, daß er krank ist** you can[not] tell that he is ill; **sich nichts ~ lassen** not let it show; **b)** *(geh.: bemerken)* note; **c)** *(geh.: anstreichen)* mark

Anmerkung die; ~, ~en a) *(Fußnote)* note; **b)** *(geh.: Bemerkung)* comment; remark; **wenn ich dazu eine ~ machen darf** if I may comment on that

an|mieten *tr. V.* rent; hire, rent ‹*car, van*›

an·mit *Adv. (schweiz. Papierdt.)* herewith

an|montieren *tr. V.* fix on **(an + *Akk. od. Dat.*** to)

an|müssen *unr. itr. V.* have to be put on

an|mustern *(Seemannsspr.) tr., itr. V.* sign on

An·mut die; ~ *(geh.)* grace; *(Liebreiz, auch fig.: einer Landschaft usw.)* charm; *(fig.: eines Ausdrucks)* elegance; gracefulness; **mit ~:** gracefully

an|muten *tr. (auch itr.) V. (geh.)* **etw. mutet [jmdn.] fremd** *usw.* **an** sth. seems strange *etc.* [to sb.]; **alles mutete ihn wie ein Traum an** everything seemed like a dream to him; **ein seltsam ~der Anblick** a sight that seems strange to me/him *etc.*

an·mutig *(geh.)* **1.** *Adj.* graceful ‹*girl, gesture, movement, dance*›; charming, delightful ‹*girl, smile, picture, landscape*›. **2.** *adv.* ‹*move, dance*› gracefully; ‹*smile, greet*› charmingly, delightfully

anmuts·voll *(geh.) s.* **anmutig**

an|nageln *tr. V.* nail on **(an + *Akk. od. Dat.*** to); nail up ‹*notice, picture*› **(an + *Akk. od. Dat.*** on); **wie angenagelt dastehen** *(ugs.)* stand [there] rooted to the spot

an|nagen *tr. V.* gnaw [at]; *(fig. geh.)* gnaw *or* nibble away at

an|nähen *tr. V.* sew on **(an + *Akk.*** to)

an|nähern 1. *refl. V.* **a)** approach; **die Straße nähert sich der Küste allmählich immer weiter an** the road gradually gets closer and closer to the coast; **sich einem Grenzwert ~** *(Math.)* converge towards a limit; **b)** *(fig.: [menschlich] näherkommen)* **sich jmdm. ~:** come *or* get closer to sb.; **c)** *(sich angleichen)* **sich einer Sache** *(Dat.)* **~:** come *or* get closer to sth. **2.** *tr. V. (angleichen)* bring closer (*Dat.* to); **verschiedene Standpunkte einander ~:** bring differing points of view closer together; **etw. einem Vorbild ~:** make sth. more like a model

annähernd 1. *Adv. (ungefähr)* approximately; roughly; *(fast)* almost; nearly; **nicht ~ so teuer** not nearly as *or* nowhere near as expensive. **2.** *adj.; nicht präd.* approximate; rough; **mit ~er Sicherheit** with a rough degree of certainty

Annäherung die; ~, ~en a) *(das Sichannähern)* approach **(an + *Akk.*** to); **bei ~ des Zuges** as the train approaches/approached; **b)** *(fig.)* **es kam zu einer ~ der beiden Parteien** the two parties came *or* moved closer together; **eine ~ zwischen zwei Staaten herbeiführen** bring two states closer together; **c)** *(Angleichung)* **eine ~ der gegenseitigen Standpunkte** bringing the points of view on each side closer together

annäherungs-, Annäherungs-: ~versuch der advance; *(im politischen Bereich)* attempted rapprochement; **immer wieder plumpe ~versuche machen** keep making [very] obvious advances; **~weise** *Adv.* approximately; roughly; **~wert der** *s.* **Näherungswert**

Annahme ['anna:mə] **die; ~, ~n a)** *(das Annehmen)* acceptance; **die ~ eines Pakets verweigern** refuse to accept [delivery of] a parcel; **b)** *(Vermutung)* assumption; **ich war der ~, daß ...:** I assumed that ...; **in der ~, daß ...:** on the assumption that ...; **gehe ich recht in der ~, daß ...?** am I right in assuming that ...?; **ich gehe einmal von der ~ aus, daß ...:** I am working *or* going on the assumption that ...; **c)** *s.* **Annahmestelle; d)** *(Billigung)* approval; *(einer Dissertation)* acceptance; **e)** *(einer Gewohnheit)* adoption; *(eines Namens)* adoption; assumption; **f)** *(Aufnahme)* taking on; **über jmds. ~ entscheiden** decide if sb. should be taken on; **~ an Kindes Statt** *(veralt.)* adoption

Annahme-: ~schluß der deadline [for acceptance]; **wann ist ~schluß?** when is the deadline [for acceptance]?; **freitags ist für Lottoscheine ~schluß** Friday is the last day of the week for lottery coupons; **~stelle die** *(für Lotto/Wetten usw.)* place where coupons/bets are accepted; *(einer Reinigung)* branch; *(für Reparaturen)* repairs counter/department; *(für Telegramme, Pakete usw.)* telegrams/parcels counter; *(für Lieferungen)* delivery point

Annalen [a'na:lən] *Pl.* annals; **in die ~ der Firma eingehen** go down in the annals of the firm

annehmbar 1. *Adj.* **a)** *(akzeptabel)* acceptable; **b)** *(recht gut)* reasonable. **2.** *adv.* reasonably [well]

an|nehmen 1. *unr. tr. V.* **a)** accept; take; accept ‹*alms, invitation, condition, help*›; take ‹*food, telephone call*›; accept, take [on] ‹*task, job, repairs*›; accept, take up ‹*offer, invitation, challenge*›; **die** *od.* **seine Wahl ~:** accept one's election; **b)** *(Sport)* take; **er nahm den Ball mit dem Kopf an** he headed the ball down; **c)** *(billigen)* approve; accept ‹*dissertation*›; pass ‹*law*›; approve, adopt ‹*resolution*›; **d)** *(aufnehmen)* take on ‹*worker, patient, pupil*›; **e)** *(hinnehmen)* accept ‹*fate, verdict, punishment*›; **f)** *(adoptieren)* adopt; **jmdn. an Kindes Statt ~** *(veralt.)* adopt sb.; **g)** *(haften lassen)* take ‹*dye, ink*›; **kein Wasser ~:** repel water; be water-repellent; **Feuchtigkeit gut ~:** absorb moisture easily; **h)** *(sich aneignen)* adopt ‹*habit, mannerism*›; adopt, assume ‹*name, attitude*›; put on ‹*airs and graces*›; **i)** *(bekommen)* take on ‹*look, appearance, form, tone, dimension*›; **j)** *(vermuten)* assume; presume; **ich nehme es an/nicht an** I assume *or* presume so/not; **das ist/ist nicht anzunehmen** that can/cannot be assumed; **k)** *(voraussetzen)* assume; **etw. als gegeben** *od.* **Tatsache ~:** take sth. for granted *or* as read; **nehmen wir an, daß ...:** let us assume that ...; **angenommen, [daß] ...:** assuming [that] ...; **das kannst du ~!** *(ugs.)* you bet! *(coll.)*; **l)** *(Jägerspr.: angreifen)* attack; go for; **m)** *(Jägerspr.: aufnehmen)* **eine/die Fährte ~:** take up a/the scent. **2.** *unr. refl. V. (geh.)* **sich jmds./einer Sache ~:** look after sb./sth.

Annehmlichkeit die; ~, ~en comfort; *(Vorteil)* advantage

annektieren [anɛk'ti:rən] *tr. V.* annex

Annektierung die; ~, ~en, Annexion [anɛ'ksio:n] **die; ~, ~en** annexation

an|niesen *tr. V.* sneeze over

an|nieten *tr. V.* rivet on **(an + *Akk. od. Dat.*** to)

anno ['ano], **Anno** *in* **~ 1910/68** *usw.* *(veralt.)* in [the year] 1910/'68 *etc.*; **ein Auto von ~ 1932** *(veralt.)* a 1932 car; **~ dazumal** *od.* **dunnemals** *od.* **Tobak** *(ugs. scherzh.)* the year dot *(Brit. coll.)*; long ago; **~ Domini 1656** *(veralt.)* in the year of our Lord 1656

Annonce [a'nõ:sə] **die; ~, ~n** advertisement; ad *(coll.)*; advert *(Brit. coll.)*

Annoncen·teil der advertisement section

annoncieren 1. *itr. V.* advertise. **2.** *tr. V.* *(ankündigen)* announce

annullieren [anʊ'li:rən] *tr. V.* annul

Annullierung die; ~, ~en annulment

Anode [a'no:də] **die; ~, ~n** *(Physik)* anode

an|öden *tr. V. (ugs.)* bore stiff *(coll.)* *or* to death *(coll.)*

anomal ['anoma:l] **1.** *Adj.* anomalous; abnormal. **2.** *adv.* anomalously; abnormally

Anomalie die; ~, ~n a) anomaly; abnormality; **b)** *(Med.: Mißbildung)* abnormality

anonym [ano'ny:m] **1.** *Adj.* anonymous; **die Anonymen Alkoholiker** Alcoholics Anonymous. **2.** *adv.* anonymously

Anonymität [anonymi'tɛ:t] **die; ~:** anonymity

Anonymus [a'no:nymʊs] **der; ~, Anonymi** *(geh.)* anonymous writer/composer/artist *etc.*

Anopheles [a'no:felɛs] **die; ~, ~** *(Zool.)* anopheles

Anorak ['anorak] **der; ~s, ~s** anorak

an|ordnen *tr. V.* **a)** *(arrangieren)* arrange; **b)** *(befehlen)* order

An·ordnung die a) *(Ordnung, Aufstellung)* arrangement; **in alphabetischer ~:** in alphabetical order; **b)** *(Weisung)* order; **haben Sie die nötigen ~en getroffen?** have you given all the necessary orders?; **auf meine ~/auf ~ des Arztes** on my/doctor's orders *pl.*

an·organisch *Adj.* inorganic

anormal 1. *Adj.* abnormal. **2.** *adv.* abnormally

an|packen 1. *tr. V.* **a)** *(ugs.: greifen, anfassen)* grab hold of; **jmdn. am Arm ~:** grab [hold of] sb. by the arm; **mußt du das Buch mit deinen Dreckpfoten ~?** must you touch the book with your dirty hands?; **b)** *(beginnen, angehen)* tackle; **packen wir's an!** let's get down to it; **c)** *(ugs.: behandeln)* treat. **2.** *itr. V. (ugs.: mithelfen)* **[mit] ~:** lend a hand

an|pappen *(ugs.)* **1.** *tr. V.* **etw. ~:** stick sth. on **(an + *Dat.*** to). **2.** *itr. V.; mit sein* stick **(an + *Dat.*** to)

an|passen 1. *tr. V.* **a)** *(passend machen)* fit; **jmdm. einen Anzug ~:** fit sb. for a suit; **Bauteile einander ~:** fit components together;

b) *(abstimmen)* suit *(Dat.* to); **die Renten wurden am 1. Januar angepaßt** pensions were adjusted on 1 January. **2.** *refl. V.* adapt [oneself] *(Dat.* to); ‹*animal*› adapt; *(gesellschaftlich)* conform; **die am besten angepaßten Arten** the species which have adapted best; *s. auch* **angepaßt 2**

Anpassung die; ~, ~**en** adaptation **(an** + *Akk.* to); *(der Renten, Löhne usw.)* adjustment **(an** + *Akk.* to); *(an die Gesellschaft)* conformity

anpassungs·fähig *Adj.* adaptable

Anpassungs-: ~fähigkeit die; *o. Pl.* adaptability **(an** + *Akk.* to); **~schwierigkeiten** *Pl.* difficulties in adapting **(an** + *Akk.* to)

an|peilen *tr. V.* **a)** *(Funkw.)* take a bearing on; **b)** *(fig. ugs.: anstreben)* aim at; **c)** *(anvisieren)* take a sight on

an|peitschen *tr. V.* drive on

an|pesen *itr. V.; mit sein (nordd. ugs.)* **angepest kommen** come tearing *or (sl.)* belting along; *(auf einen zu)* come tearing *or (sl.)* belting up

an|pfeifen 1. *unr. tr. V.* **a) das Spiel/die zweite Halbzeit ~:** blow the whistle to start the game/the second half; **b)** *(salopp: zurechtweisen)* bawl out *(coll.).* **2.** *unr. itr. V.* blow the whistle

An·pfiff der a) *(Sport)* whistle for the start of play; **der ~ zur zweiten Halbzeit** the whistle for the start of the second half; **b)** *(salopp: Zurechtweisung)* bawling-out *(coll.)*

an|pflanzen *tr. V.* **a)** *(pflanzen, bepflanzen)* plant; **b)** *(anbauen)* grow; cultivate

An·pflanzung die a) planting; **b)** *(bepflanzte Fläche)* cultivated area; **eine ~ anlegen** lay out an area for cultivation

an|pflaumen *tr. V. (ugs.)* **a)** tease; take the mickey out of *(Brit. sl.);* **b)** *s.* **anmeckern**

Anpflaumerei die; ~, ~**en** *(ugs.)* teasing; mickey-taking *(Brit. sl.);* **laß doch deine ~en** stop teasing *or (Brit. sl.)* taking the mickey

an|pflocken *tr. V.* tie ‹*boat*› up; tether ‹*animal*›

[1]**an|picken** *tr. V.* peck at

[2]**an|picken** *(österr. ugs.)* **1.** *tr. V.* stick on. **2.** *itr. V.; mit sein* be stuck on

an|pinkeln *tr. V. (ugs.)* pee on *(coll.)*

an|pinnen *tr. V. (nordd.)* pin up **(an** + *Akk.* on)

an|pinseln *tr. V. (ugs.)* **a)** *(anstreichen)* paint; **b)** *(an etw. pinseln)* paint **(an** + *Akk.* on)

an|pirschen *refl. V.* creep up **(an** + *Akk.* on)

an|pissen *tr. V. (derb)* piss on *(coarse)*

An·pöbelei die *(ugs.)* abuse; **~en** abuse *sing.*

an|pöbeln *tr. V. (ugs.)* abuse

an|pochen *itr. V. (südd.) s.* **anklopfen**

An·prall der; ~**[e]s** impact **(auf, an** + *Akk.* with, **gegen** against)

an|prallen *itr. V.; mit sein* crash; **gegen** *od.* **an etw. ~:** crash into sb./against sth.

an|prangern *tr. V.* denounce **(als** as)

an|preisen *unr. tr. V.* extol; **etw. als etw. ~:** extol sth. as being sth.; **jmdn./etw. jmdm. ~:** extol the virtues of sb./sth. to sb.; recommend sb./sth. highly to sb.

an|preschen *itr. V.; mit sein* **angeprescht kommen** *(ugs.)* come racing along; *(auf einen zu)* come racing up

an|pressen *tr. V.* press on **(an** + *Akk.* to)

An·probe die a) fitting; **zur ~ kommen** come for a fitting; **b)** *(Raum) (beim Schneider)* fitting-room; *(im Kaufhaus)* changing-room *(Brit.);* dressing-room *(Amer.)*

an|probieren 1. *tr. V.* try on; **jmdm. etw. ~:** try sth. on sb. **2.** *itr. V.* **~ kommen** *(ugs.)* come for a fitting

an|pumpen *tr. V. (ugs.)* borrow money from; **jmdn. um 20 Mark ~:** touch *(sl.) or* tap sb. for 20 marks

an|pusten *tr. V. (ugs.)* blow on

an|quasseln *tr. V. (salopp),* **an|quatschen** *tr. V. (salopp)* speak to

Anrainer ['anrainɐ] **der;** ~**s,** ~ **a)** *(Nachbar)* neighbour; **als ~ des Sees habe ich ...:** as I live on *or* by the lake, I have ...; **b)** *(bes. österr.: Anlieger)* resident; **c)** *s.* **Anrainerstaat**

Anrainer-: ~grundstück das neighbouring property; **die ~grundstücke des Sees** the properties on *or* by the lake; **~staat der: die ~staaten des Bodensees** the countries bordering on Lake Constance

an|ranzen *tr. V. (salopp)* bawl out *(coll.)*

Anranzer der; ~**s,** ~ *(salopp)* bawling-out *(coll.)*

an|rasen *itr. V.; mit sein (ugs.)* race up; **gegen etw. ~:** crash into sth.; **angerast kommen** come racing along; *(auf einen zu)* come racing up

an|raten *unr. tr. V.* **jmdm. etw. ~:** recommend sth. to sb.; **jmdm. Vorsicht ~:** advise sb. to be careful; **auf Anraten des Arztes** on the *or* one's doctor's advice

an|rattern *itr. V.; mit sein (ugs.)* **angerattert kommen** come rattling along; *(auf einen zu)* come rattling up

an|rauchen *tr. V.* light up; **jmdm. eine Zigarette ~:** light up a cigarette for sb.; **eine angerauchte Zigarre** a partly smoked *or* half-smoked cigar

an|räuchern *tr. V.* lightly smoke

an|rauhen *tr. V.* roughen

an|raunzen *tr. V. (salopp) s.* **anranzen**

Anraunzer der; ~**s,** ~ *(salopp) s.* **Anranzer**

an|rauschen *itr. V.; mit sein (ugs.)* **angerauscht kommen** come sweeping along; *(auf einen zu)* come sweeping up; ‹*vehicle*› come roaring along; *(auf einen zu)* come roaring up

anrechenbar *Adj.* **[auf etw.** *(Akk.)***] ~ sein** count [towards sth.]

an|rechnen *tr. V.* **a)** *(gutschreiben, verbuchen)* count; take into account; **jmdm. einen Betrag/seine Überstunden ~:** credit sb. with an amount/his/her overtime; **die Untersuchungshaft kann auf die Gefängnisstrafe angerechnet werden** time spent in custody can be counted as part of *or* taken into account in the prison sentence; **er bekam einen Pluspunkt angerechnet** he was given an extra mark; **jmdm. etw. als Verdienst/Fehler ~:** count sth. to sb.'s credit/as sb.'s mistake; **sich** *(Dat.)* **etw. zur Ehre ~** *(geh.)* consider sth. an honour; **jmdm. etw. hoch ~:** think highly of sb. for sth.; **b)** *(in Rechnung stellen)* **jmdm. etw. ~:** charge sb. for sth.; **das Porto wird dem Kunden angerechnet** postage is charged to the customer; **jmdm. zuviel ~:** overcharge sb.

An·rechnung die; *o. Pl.* **a) unter ~ der Untersuchungshaft** counting *or* taking into account time spent in custody; **eine ~ der Untersuchungshaft/des Praktikums ist nicht möglich** it is not possible to take time spent in custody/practical work into account; **b)** *(Berechnung)* charge; **eine ~ der Transportkosten erfolgt nicht** transport costs *(Brit.) or (Amer.)* transportation costs are not charged; **etw. in ~ bringen** *(Papierdt.)* charge for sth.

anrechnungs·fähig *Adj. (Papierdt.) s.* **anrechenbar**

An·recht das a) right; **ein ~ auf etw.** *(Akk.)* **haben** *od.* **besitzen** have a right to *or* be entitled to sth.; **b)** *(Abonnement)* subscription

An·rede die form of address; *(Brief~)* form of address; salutation; **wie ist die ~ eines Kardinals** *od.* **für einen Kardinal?** what is the correct form of address for a cardinal?

Anrede-: ~fall der *s.* **~kasus; ~für·wort das** *s.* **~pronomen; ~kasus der** vocative [case]

an|reden *tr. V.* **a)** address; **jmdn. mit „du" ~:** address sb. as 'du'; use 'du' to sb.; **jmdn. mit dem Vornamen ~:** address *or* call sb. by his/her Christian name; **b) gegen den Lärm ~:** talk above the noise; **gegen etw. ~** *(widersprechen)* argue [against sth.]

Anrede·pronomen das personal pronoun used as form of address

an|regen 1. *tr. V.* **a)** *(ermuntern)* prompt; **jmdn. zum Nachdenken ~:** make sb. think; **b)** *(vorschlagen)* propose; suggest; raise ‹*question*›; **~, etw. zu tun** propose *or* suggest doing sth.; **c)** *(Physik)* excite. **2.** *tr. (auch itr.) V.* stimulate ‹*imagination, digestion*›; sharpen, whet, stimulate ‹*appetite*›; **Kaffee regt an** coffee acts as a stimulant; *s. auch* **angeregt 2**

anregend *Adj.* stimulating; **ein ~es Mittel** a stimulant; **Kaffee wirkt/ist ~:** coffee acts as a stimulant

An·regung die a) *(das Anregen) s.* **anregen 2:** stimulation; whetting; sharpening; **zur ~ der Verdauung/des Appetits** to stimulate the digestion/whet *etc.* the appetite; **b)** *(Denkanstoß, Idee)* stimulus; **c)** *(Vorschlag)* proposal; suggestion; **d)** *(Physik)* excitation

Anregungs·mittel das stimulant

an|reichen *s.* **zureichen**

an|reichern ['anraiçɐn] **1.** *tr. V.* **a)** *(gehaltvoller machen)* enrich; **Trinkwasser mit Fluor ~:** add fluoride to drinking water; **b)** *(akkumulieren)* accumulate; **c)** *(Kerntechnik)* enrich. **2.** *refl. V.* **a)** *(sich ansammeln)* accumulate; **b)** *(seinen Gehalt an etw. erhöhen)* be enriched

Anreicherung die; ~, ~**en a)** enrichment; **die ~ von Trinkwasser mit Fluor** the addition of fluoride to drinking water; **b)** *(Akkumulation)* accumulation; **c)** *(Kerntechnik)* enrichment

an|reihen 1. *tr. V.* add **(an** + *Akk.* to). **2.** *refl. V.* **sich hinten [an die Schlange] ~:** join the end of the queue *(Brit.);* get on the end of the line *(Amer.)*

An·reise die a) journey [there/here]; **die ~ dauert 10 Stunden** the journey there/here takes ten hours; it takes 10 hours to get there/here; **b)** *(Ankunft)* arrival

an|reisen *itr. V.; mit sein* **a)** travel there/here; **mit der Bahn ~:** go/come by train; travel there/here by train; **die aus dem ganzen Land anreisenden Besucher** the visitors travelling there/here from all over the country; **angereist kommen** come; **b)** *(ankommen)* arrive

Anreise·tag der day of arrival; **für den An- und den Abreisetag bekommen Sie Spesen** your expenses will be paid for the days of the journey there and the journey back

an|reißen *unr. tr. V.* **a)** *(durchzureißen beginnen)* partly tear; **b)** *(in Gang setzen)* start [up]; **c)** *(anzünden)* strike ‹*match*›; **d)** *(Technik)* mark [out]; **e)** *(kurz ansprechen)* touch on; **f)** *(ugs.: anbrechen)* start; open; **g)** *(ugs. abwertend: anlocken)* lure

An·reißer der a) *(ugs. abwertend: Werber)* tout; **b)** *(ugs.: Ware)* big attraction; **c)** *(Berufsbez.)* marker-out

an·reißerisch *(ugs. abwertend)* **1.** *Adj.* flashily commercial; gimmicky *(coll.)* ‹*advertisement*›. **2.** *adv.* **das Buch/die Reklame ist mir zu ~ aufgemacht** the book is too flashily commercial/the ad is too gimmicky for my liking *(coll.)*

an|reiten *unr. itr. V.; mit sein* **a) angeritten kommen** come riding along; *(auf einen zu)* come riding up; **gegen den Feind ~:** charge the enemy; **b)** *(ansteuern)* ride at ‹*obstacle*›; **c)** *(zureiten)* break in ‹*horse*›

An·reiz der incentive; **ein ~ zum Sparen** an incentive to save

an|reizen *tr. (auch itr.) V.* **a)** *(anspornen)* stimulate; encourage; **Steuerermäßigungen sollen zum Sparen ~:** tax reductions are supposed to stimulate *or* act as an incentive to saving; **b)** *(anregen, erregen)* stimulate

an|rempeln *tr. V.* barge into; *(absichtlich)* jostle

ạn|rennen 1. *unr. itr. V.; mit sein* **a) angerannt kommen** come running along; *(auf einen zu)* come running up; **er kommt wegen jeder Kleinigkeit bei mir angerannt** he comes running to me about every little thing; **b) gegen den Sturm/feindliche Stellungen ~:** run into *or* against the storm/storm enemy positions; **gegen jmdn./etw. ~** *(fig.)* fight against sb./sth. **2.** *unr. refl. V. (ugs.)* **sich** *(Dat.)* **das Knie/den Kopf an etw.** *(Dat.)* **~:** bump one's knee/head on sth.

Ạnrichte die; ~, ~n a) *(Möbel)* sideboard; **b)** *(Raum)* pantry

ạn|richten *tr. V.* **a)** *(auch itr.)* arrange ⟨*food*⟩; *(servieren)* serve; **es ist angerichtet** *(geh.)* dinner is served; **b)** cause ⟨*disaster, confusion, devastation, etc.*⟩; **was hast du wieder alles angerichtet!** what have you gone and done now? *(coll.)*

ạn|ritzen *tr. V.* scratch

ạn|rollen 1. *itr. V.; mit sein* **a)** *(zu rollen beginnen)* ⟨*vehicle, column, etc.*⟩ start moving; *(fig.)* ⟨*campaign, search operation*⟩ start; **b)** *(heranrollen)* roll up; ⟨*aircraft*⟩ taxi up; **angerollt kommen** come rolling along; *(auf einen zu)* come rolling up; **c) die Wellen rollten gegen den Deich an** the waves rolled in against the dike. **2.** *tr. V.* roll up ⟨*barrel*⟩; *(auf einem Wagen o. ä.)* wheel up

ạn|rosten *itr. V.; mit sein* start to rust; get [a bit] rusty; **ein angerostetes Messer** a rusting knife; a knife that has started to rust

ạn|rösten *tr. V.* roast lightly; toast ⟨*bread*⟩ lightly

anrüchig ['anrʏçɪç] *Adj.* **a)** *(berüchtigt)* disreputable; **b)** *(unanständig)* indecent; *(obszön)* offensive

Ạnrüchigkeit die; ~ a) *(schlechter Ruf)* disreputableness; **b)** *(Unanständigkeit)* indecency; *(Obszönität)* offensiveness

ạn|rücken 1. *itr. V.; mit sein* ⟨*troops*⟩ advance; move forward; ⟨*firemen, police*⟩ move in; **morgen rücken meine Verwandten an** *(ugs. scherzh.)* my relatives are descending on me/us tomorrow. **2.** *tr. V.* push **(an + Akk.** against); *(ziehen)* pull **(an + Akk.** against)

Ạn·ruf der a) *(telefonischer ~)* call; **danke für den ~:** thanks for ringing *(Brit.) or* calling; **b)** *(Zuruf)* call; *(eines Wachtpostens)* challenge; **auf ~:** when called/challenged; **ohne ~ schießen** shoot without warning

Ạnruf·beantworter der; ~s, ~: [telephone-]answering machine

ạn|rufen 1. *unr. tr. V.* **a)** call *or* shout to ⟨*friend, passer-by*⟩; call ⟨*sleeping person*⟩; hail ⟨*ship*⟩; ⟨*sentry*⟩ challenge; **b)** *(geh.: angehen, bitten)* appeal to ⟨*person, court*⟩ **(um** for); call upon ⟨*God*⟩; **Gott um Gnade ~:** implore God's mercy; **c)** *(telefonisch ~)* ring *(Brit.)*; call; **d)** *(geh.: begehren)* implore, beg ⟨*sb.'s mercy, help, protection, etc.*⟩. **2.** *unr. itr. V.* **a)** *(antelefonieren)* ring *(Brit.)*; call; **bei jmdm. ~:** ring *(Brit.) or* call sb.; **ruf doch mal in Köln an** ring *(Brit.) or* call Cologne; **im Büro ~:** ring *(Brit.) or* call the office; **b)** *(ugs., bes. südd.: telefonieren)* make a phone call *(coll.)*; **ich muß nur mal kurz ~:** I must just make a quick phone call *(coll.)*; **kann ich bei Ihnen/in Ihrem Büro mal ~?** can I just use your telephone *or (coll.)* phone/telephone from your office *or* use your office telephone?

Ạnrufer der; ~s, ~: caller

Ạnrufung die; ~, ~en a) *(einer Gottheit o. ä.)* invocation; **b)** *(eines Gerichts)* appeal (*Gen.* to)

ạn|rühren *tr. V.* **a)** touch; **keine Zigaretten/kein Buch ~:** never touch cigarettes/never pick up a book; **b)** *(bereiten)* mix; **c)** *(geh.: beeindrucken)* move; touch

ạns *Präp. + Art.* **a) = an das; b)** *(mit subst. Inf.)* **sich ~ Arbeiten machen** set to work; **wenn es ~ Bezahlen geht** when it comes to paying

ạn|säen *tr. V.* sow ⟨*grass, grain*⟩

Ạn·sage die a) *(Ankündigung)* announcement; **b)** *(Kartenspiel)* bid; **du hast die ~:** it's your bid

ạn|sagen 1. *tr. V.* **a)** *(ankündigen)* announce; *s. auch* **Bankrott a; Kampf d; b)** *(Kartenspiel)* bid; *s. auch* **Schneider c; c)** *(Büro.: diktieren)* dictate; **d)** *(veralt.: mitteilen)* **sagt an, was ...:** pray tell me/us what ... *(arch.)*. **2.** *refl. V.* say that one is coming; **sich zum nächsten Wochenende/für Dienstag abend/bei jmdm. ~:** say that one is coming next weekend/Tuesday evening/to see sb.

ạn|sägen *tr. V.* make a saw-cut in; start to saw through

Ạnsager der; ~s, ~, Ạnsagerin die; ~, ~nen a) *(Radio, Fernsehen)* announcer; **b)** *(im Kabarett usw.)* master of ceremonies; *(Brit.)* compère

ạn|sammeln 1. *tr. V.* *(anhäufen)* accumulate; amass ⟨*riches, treasure*⟩. **2.** *refl. V.* **a)** *(zusammenströmen)* gather; **b)** *(sich anhäufen)* accumulate; *(fig.)* ⟨*anger, excitement*⟩ build up

Ạn·sammlung die a) *(von Gegenständen)* collection; *(Haufen)* pile, heap; *(von Wasser)* pool; **b)** *(Auflauf)* crowd

ansässig ['anzɛsɪç] *Adj.* resident; **eine in London ~e Firma** a firm with its registered office in London; **sich in Bayern ~ machen** settle in Bavaria

Ạn·satz der a) *(erstes Zeichen, Beginn)* beginnings *pl.*; **einen ~ zum Bauch haben** have the beginnings of a paunch; **Ansätze zur Besserung zeigen** show the first signs of improvement; **etw. im ~ unterdrücken** nip sth. in the bud; **die ersten Ansätze** the initial stages; **gute Ansätze zeigen** make a good start; **im ~** *(ansatzweise)* to some extent; **b)** *(eines Körperteils)* base; **c)** *(Musik) (Lippenstellung)* embouchure; *(Tonerzeugung)* attack; **d)** *(Math.)* statement; **e)** *(bes. Philos.: Lösungsversuch)* approach; **f)** *(von Rost, Kalk usw.)* formation; *(Schicht)* coating; **g)** *(Wirtsch.: Voranschlag)* estimate; *(im Staatsbudget)* amount budgeted; appropriation; **etw. für etw. in ~ bringen** *(Amtsspr.)* earmark sth. for sth.; **außer ~ bleiben** *(Amtsspr.)* be left out of account; be excluded; **h)** *(Chemie: eines Versuchs)* setting up; **i)** *(Technik) (Verlängerungsstück)* extension; *(Nahtstelle)* join

ạnsatz-, Ạnsatz-: ~punkt der starting-point; point of departure; **~stück das** *(Technik)* extension; **~weise** *Adv.* to some extent

ạn|saufen *unr. refl. V. (salopp)* **sich** *(Dat.)* **einen [Rausch] ~:** get plastered *(sl.)*; **sich** *(Dat.)* **einen Bierbauch ~:** get a beer belly

ạn|saugen 1. *tr. V. (geh. auch unr.)* suck in *or* up. **2.** *refl. V. (geh. auch unr.) (sich festsetzen)* ⟨*leech etc.*⟩ attach itself *(by suction)*

Ạnsaug·rohr das *(Kfz-W.)* intake manifold; *(beim Einzylindermotor)* inlet pipe

ạn|säuseln *refl. V.* **sich** *(Dat.)* **einen ~** *(ugs.)* get tipsy; *s. auch* **angesäuselt 2**

Ạnschaffe ['anʃafə] **die; ~** *(salopp)* **auf [die] ~ gehen** *(sich prostituieren)* go on the game *(Brit. sl.)*; walk the streets *(Amer.)*; *(stehlen)* go out thieving

ạn|schaffen 1. *tr. V.* **a)** *(kaufen)* **[sich** *(Dat.)***] etw. ~** *(auch fig. ugs.)* get [oneself] sth.; **sich** *(Dat.)* **Kinder ~** *(fig. ugs.)* have children *or (coll.)* kids; **b)** *(südd., österr.: befehlen)* **jmdm. ~, daß er etw. tut** order sb. to do sth.; **c)** *(salopp: stehlen)* pinch *(sl.)*. **2.** *itr. V.* **a)** *(salopp: Prostitution betreiben)* **~ [gehen]** be on the game *(Brit. sl.)*; be walking the streets *(Amer.)*; **für jmdn. ~:** work as a prostitute for sb.; **b)** *(südd., österr.: befehlen)* **[jmdm.] ~:** give [sb.] orders

Ạn·schaffung die purchase; **~en machen** make purchases; **sich zur ~ eines Autos entschließen** decide to get *or* buy a car

Ạnschaffungs-: ~kosten *Pl.* original *or* initial cost *sing.*; acquisition cost *sing.*; **~wert der** value at the time of purchase

ạn|schalten *tr. V.* switch on

ạn|schauen *(bes. südd., österr., schweiz.) s.* **ansehen**

ạnschaulich 1. *Adj. (deutlich)* clear; *(bildhaft, lebendig)* vivid, graphic ⟨*style, description*⟩; **etw. ~ machen** make sth. vivid; bring sth. to life; **etw. durch Beispiele ~ machen** illustrate sth. by examples; **ein ~er Unterricht** teaching that makes the subject come alive. **2.** *adv. (deutlich)* clearly; *(bildhaft, lebendig)* vividly; ⟨*describe*⟩ vividly, graphically

Ạnschaulichkeit die; ~ *s.* **anschaulich:** clarity; vividness; graphicness

Ạnschauung die; ~, ~en a) *(Auffassung)* view; *(bestimmte Meinung)* opinion; **b)** *(Eindruck, Erfahrung)* experience; **aus eigener ~:** from personal *or* one's own experience; **c)** *o. Pl. (das Betrachten)* contemplation

Ạnschauungs-: ~material das illustrative material; *(für den Unterricht)* visual aids *pl.*; **~unterricht der** visual instruction; *(fig.)* object lesson; **~weise die** view

Ạn·schein der appearance; **allem** *od.* **dem ~ nach** to all appearances; **es hat den ~, als ob ...:** it appears *or* looks as if ...; **sich** *(Dat.)* **den ~ geben, als ob man etw. glaubt** pretend to believe sth.; **den ~ erwecken, etw. zu sein** give the impression of being sth.

ạn·scheinend *Adv.* apparently; seemingly

ạn|scheißen *(derb)* **1.** *unr. tr. V.* **a)** *(betrügen)* con *(sl.)*; diddle *(sl.)*; **b)** *(zurechtweisen)* **jmdn. ~:** give sb. a bollocking *(Brit. coarse)*; bawl sb. out *(coll.)*. **2.** *unr. itr. V.; mit sein* **da kommt er schon wieder angeschissen** there he is, come to make a bloody nuisance of himself again *(Brit. sl.)*

ạn|schesen *itr. V.; mit sein (nordd.)* **angeschest kommen** come rushing along; *(auf einen zu)* come rushing up

ạn|schicken *refl. V. (geh.)* **sich ~, etw. zu tun** *(sich bereit machen)* get ready *or* prepare to do sth.; *(anfangen, im Begriff sein)* be about to do sth.; be on the point of doing sth.

ạn|schieben *unr. tr. V.* push ⟨*vehicle*⟩; **könnt ihr mich mal ~?** could you give me a push?

ạn|schießen 1. *unr. tr. V.* **a)** *(durch Schuß verletzen)* shoot and wound; **das Reh war nicht tot, nur angeschossen** the deer was not dead, only wounded; **b)** *(bes. Fußball)* kick the ball against ⟨*player*⟩; shoot straight at ⟨*goalkeeper*⟩; **c)** *(ugs.: kritisieren)*; **jmdn. ~:** give sb. some stick *(sl.)*; **d)** *(Milit., Jagdw.: prüfen)* test. **2.** *unr. itr. V.; mit sein* **angeschossen kommen** come tearing *or* racing along; *(auf einen zu)* come tearing *or* racing up

ạn|schimmeln *itr. V.; mit sein* start to go mouldy; **angeschimmeltes Brot** bread that has started to go mouldy

ạn|schirren *tr. V.* harness ⟨*horse*⟩

Ạn·schiß der *(salopp)* bollocking *(Brit. coarse)*; bawling-out *(coll.)*; **einen ~ kriegen** get a bollocking *(Brit. coarse)*; get bawled out *(coll.)*

Ạn·schlag der a) *(Bekanntmachung)* notice; *(Plakat)* poster; **einen ~ machen** put up a notice/poster; **b)** *(Attentat)* assassination attempt; *(auf ein Gebäude, einen Zug o. ä.)* attack; **einen ~ auf jmdn. verüben** make an attempt on sb.'s life; **einem ~ zum Opfer fallen** be assassinated; **c)** *(Texterfassung)* keystroke; **200 Anschläge pro Minute [schreiben] ≈** [have a typing speed of] 40 words a minute; **d)** *(Musik)* touch; **e)** *(Technik)* stop; **etw. bis zum ~ niederdrücken/aufdrehen** push sth. right down/turn sth. on as far as it will go; **f)** *(Häkeln, Stricken)* first line of stitches; *(Vorgang)* casting on; **„~ 50 Maschen"** 'cast on 50 stitches'; **g)** *(Milit.*,

Jagdw.) aiming position; **mit dem Gewehr im ~**: with rifle/rifles levelled; **in ~ bringen** level ⟨*gun*⟩; **h)** *(Kaufmannsspr.)* estimate; **etw. in ~ bringen** take sth. into account *or* consideration

Anschlag·brett das notice-board *(Brit.)*; bulletin board *(Amer.)*

an|schlagen 1. *unr. tr. V.* **a)** *(aushängen)* put up, post ⟨*notice, announcement, message*⟩ **(an + *Akk.*** on); **b)** *(Häkeln, Stricken)* cast on; **c)** *(beim Versteckspiel)* tag; **d)** *(beschädigen)* chip; **e)** *(bei Musikinstrumenten)* strike ⟨*string, key, etc.*⟩; strike, sound ⟨*gong*⟩; **f)** *(erklingen lassen)* play ⟨*note, melody, etc.*⟩; **einen anderen/ernsthaften Ton ~** *(fig.)* adopt a different/serious tone; **g)** *(beginnen)* **ein rascheres Tempo/eine schnellere Gangart ~**: increase one's pace; speed up; **h)** *(befestigen)* fix on **(an + *Akk.*** to); *(mit Nägeln)* nail on **(an + *Akk.*** to); **i)** *(beim Maschinenschreiben)* press, hit ⟨*key*⟩; **j)** *(Seemannsspr.: festbinden)* bend **(an + *Dat.*** to); **k)** *(markieren)* **einen Baum ~**: mark a tree with a notch; **l)** *(Milit., Jagdw. veralt.)* level ⟨*gun*⟩; **m)** *(österr.: anstechen)* tap ⟨*barrel*⟩. **2.** *unr. itr. V.* **a)** *mit sein (anstoßen)* **an etw.** *(Akk.)* **~**: knock against sth.; **mit dem Knie/Kopf an etw.** *(Akk.)* **~**: knock one's knee/head on sth.; **b)** *(Schwimmen)* touch; **c)** *(Tasten niederdrücken)* press *or* hit the keys; **d)** *(wirken)* work; **e)** *(ugs.: dick machen)* be fattening; **bei jmdm. ~**: make sb. put on weight; **f)** *(bellen)* bark. **3.** *unr. refl. V. (stoßen)* **sich** *(Dat.)* **das Knie** *usw.* **~**: knock one's knee *etc.* **(an + *Dat.*** on)

Anschlag·säule die advertising column

an|schleichen 1. *unr. itr. V.; mit sein* creep up; **angeschlichen kommen** come creeping along; *(auf einen zu)* come creeping up. **2.** *unr. refl. V.* **sich an jmdn./etw. ~**: creep up on sb./sth.

¹an|schleifen *unr. tr. V.* grind; cut ⟨*precious stone*⟩

²an|schleifen *tr. V. (ugs.)* drag along

an|schlendern *itr. V.; mit sein* **angeschlendert kommen** come strolling along; *(auf einen zu)* come strolling up

an|schleppen *tr. V.* **a)** *(herbeibringen)* drag along; **b)** *(zum Starten)* tow-start

an|schließen 1. *unr. tr. V.* **a)** *(befestigen)* lock, secure **(an + *Akk. od. Dat.*** to); **b)** *(verbinden)* connect **(an + *Akk. od. Dat.*** to); connect up ⟨*electrical device*⟩; *(mit Stecker und Steckdose)* plug in; **angeschlossene Sender** *(Rundf., Ferns.)* linked stations; **c)** *(anfügen)* add. **2.** *unr. refl. V.* **a)** *(sich beteiligen)*; **sich jmdm./einer Sache ~**: join sb./sth.; **b) sich an etw.** *(Akk.) od.* **sich einer Sache** *(Dat.)* **~** *(zeitlich)* follow sth.; *(angrenzen an)* adjoin sth.; **an den Vortrag schloß sich eine Diskussion an** the lecture was followed by a discussion; **an das Haus schließen sich Stallungen an** stables adjoin the house; **c)** *(beipflichten)* endorse; **ich schließe mich meinem Vorredner voll und ganz an** I endorse completely the remarks of the previous speaker; **d)** *(sich zuwenden)* follow ⟨*example*⟩; grow close to ⟨*person*⟩; **sich leicht/schwer an andere ~**: make/not make friends easily. **3.** *unr. itr. V.* **an etw.** *(Akk.)* **~**: *s.* **2b**

anschließend 1. *Adv.* afterwards; **~ an etw.** *(Akk.)* after sth. **2.** *adj.* subsequent; **ein Vortrag mit ~em Theaterbesuch** a lecture followed by a visit to the theatre

An·schluß der a) *(Netz~)* connection; *(Kabel)* cable; **~ an etw.** *(Akk.)* **erhalten/haben** be connected [up] to sth.; **elektrischen ~ erhalten/haben** be connected up to the mains; **b)** *(telefonische Verbindung)* connection; **[keinen] ~ bekommen** [not] get through; **auf den ~ warten** wait to be connected; **c)** *(Verkehrs~)* connection; *(Flugw.)* connecting flight; **Sie haben ~ nach ...**: there is a connection to ...; **den ~ verpaßt haben** have missed one's connection; *(fig. ugs.) (keinen Ehepartner gefunden haben)* have got left on the shelf; *(nicht Schritt gehalten haben)* have got left behind; **d)** *(Fernsprecher)* telephone; **kein ~ unter dieser Nummer** number unobtainable; **e)** *o. Pl. (Kontakt)*; **~ finden** make friends; **~ suchen** want to meet and get to know people; **f)** *(Verbindung nach vorn)* contact **(an + *Akk.*** with); **den ~ verlieren** lose contact **(an + *Akk.*** with); **im ~ an** following; after; **im ~ an unseren Brief vom ...**: further to our letter of ...; **g)** *(Sport) s.* **~tor**; **h)** *(Politik) (Vereinigung)* union **(an + *Akk.*** with); *(verhüll.: Annexion)* anschluss **(an + *Akk.*** with)

Anschluß-: ~kabel das connecting cable *or (esp. Brit.)* lead; *(zur Verlängerung)* extension cable *or (esp. Brit.)* lead; **~tor das, ~treffer der** *(Sport)* goal which leaves/left the side only one down; **ihm gelang das ~tor** he pulled one back to leave the side only a goal down; **~zug der** connecting train; **den ~zug verpassen** miss one's connection

an|schmieden *tr. V.* forge on **(an + *Akk.*** to); **jmdn. an etw. ~** *(anketten)* chain sb. to sth.

an|schmiegen 1. *tr. V.* nestle **(an + *Akk.*** against). **2.** *refl. V.* nestle up, snuggle up **(an + *Akk.*** to, against); **sich an den Körper ~** *(fig.)* ⟨*fabric, material*⟩ cling to the body

an·schmiegsam *Adj.* affectionate ⟨*child*⟩; soft and smooth ⟨*material*⟩

an|schmieren *tr. V.* **a)** *(ugs.: täuschen)* con *(sl.)*; diddle *(sl.)*; **b)** *(beschmutzen)* smear; **jmdn./sich/etw. mit etw. ~**: get *or* smear sth. all over sb./oneself/sth.

an|schnallen *tr. V.* strap on ⟨*rucksack*⟩; put on ⟨*skis, skates*⟩; **jmdn. ~** *(im Auto)* strap sb. in; **sich ~** *(im Auto)* put on one's seat-belt; *(im Flugzeug)* fasten one's seat-belt; **„bitte ~!"** 'fasten your seat-belts, please'

Anschnall-: ~gurt der seat-belt; **~pflicht die**; *o. Pl.* compulsory wearing of seat-belts

an|schnauzen *tr. V. (ugs.)* shout at

An·schnauzer der *(ugs.)* **einen ~ [ab]kriegen** get shouted at

an|schneiden *unr. tr. V.* **a)** cut [the first slice of]; **einen frischen Laib ~**: start a fresh loaf; **b)** *(ansprechen)* raise; broach; *(gesprächsweise berühren)* touch on; **c)** trim ⟨*flower*⟩; **d)** *(Schneiderei)* **etw. an etw.** *(Akk.)* **~**: cut sth. in one piece with sth.; **angeschnittene Ärmel** sleeves cut in one piece with the garment; **e)** *(Verkehrsw., Motorsport)* cut ⟨*corner*⟩

An·schnitt der a) *(Schnittfläche)* cut end; **b)** *(erstes Stück)* first slice; end piece

an|schnorren *tr. V. (salopp)* **jmdn. [um etw.] ~**: tap sb. [for sth.] *(coll.)*

Anschovis [anˈʃoːvɪs] **die; ~, ~**: anchovy

an|schrauben *tr. V.* screw on **(an + *Akk.*** to)

an|schreiben 1. *unr. tr. V.* **a)** *(hinschreiben)* write up **(an + *Akk.*** on); *(mit Kreide)* chalk up; **angeschrieben stehen** be written/chalked up; **b)** *(ugs.: stunden)* **[jmdm.] etw. ~**: chalk sth. up [to sb.'s account]; **bei jmdm. gut/schlecht angeschrieben sein** *(ugs.)* be in sb.'s good/bad books; be on sb.'s good/black list *(Amer.)*; **c)** *(schriftlich benachrichtigen)* write to; **vierzig Prozent der angeschriebenen Studenten** forty per cent of the students written to. **2.** *unr. itr. V. (ugs.: Kredit geben)* give credit; **er läßt immer ~**: he always buys on tick *(coll.)*

An·schreiben das covering letter

an|schreien *unr. tr. V.* shout at

An·schrift die address

an|schuldigen [ˈanʃʊldɪgn̩] *tr. V. (geh.)* accuse **(*Gen.*, wegen** of); **der Angeschuldigte/die Angeschuldigten** the accused

Anschuldigung die; ~, ~en accusation

an|schwärmen 1. *itr. V.; mit sein* ⟨*bees*⟩ swarm in. **2.** *tr. V. (verehren)* idolize; adore

an|schwärzen *tr. V. (ugs.)* **jmdn. ~**: *(in Mißkredit bringen)* blacken sb.'s name; *(schlechtmachen)* run sb. down **(bei** to); *(denunzieren)* inform *or (Brit. sl.)* grass on sb. **(bei** to)

an|schweigen *unr. tr. V.* **sich [gegenseitig]/jmdn. ~**: not speak *or* talk to each other/sb.

an|schweißen *tr. V. (Technik)* weld on **(an + *Akk. od. Dat.*** to)

an|schwellen *unr. itr. V.; mit sein* **a)** *(dicker werden)* swell [up]; **stark angeschwollen** very swollen; **b)** *(lauter werden)* grow louder; ⟨*noise*⟩ rise; **c)** *(zunehmen; auch fig.)* swell, grow; ⟨*water, river*⟩ rise

An·schwellung die swelling

an|schwemmen *tr. V.* wash up *or* ashore

an|schwimmen *unr. itr. V.; mit sein* **angeschwommen kommen** come swimming along; *(auf einen zu)* come swimming up; **gegen die Strömung/Flut ~**: swim against the current/tide

an|schwindeln *tr. V. (ugs.)* **jmdn. ~**: tell sb. fibs

an|schwirren *itr. V.; mit sein (heranfliegen)* **angeschwirrt kommen** come whirring *or* buzzing along; *(fig. ugs.)* come buzzing along; *(auf einen zu)* come buzzing up

an|schwitzen *tr. V. (Kochk.)* brown lightly *(in hot fat)*

an|segeln 1. *itr. V.* **a)** *mit sein* **angesegelt kommen** come sailing along; *(auf einen zu)* come sailing up; **b)** *(Saison eröffnen)* open the sailing season. **2.** *tr. V.* make *or* head for

an|sehen 1. *unr. tr. V.* **a)** *(anblicken)* look at; **jmdn. groß/böse ~**: stare at sb./give sb. an angry look; **hübsch** *usw.* **anzusehen sein** be pretty *etc.* to look at; **b)** *(betrachten)* look at; view, look at ⟨*flat, house*⟩; watch ⟨*television programme*⟩; see ⟨*play, film*⟩; **sieh [mal] [einer] an!** *(ugs.)* well, I never! *(coll.)*; **c)** *(erkennen)* **man sieht ihm sein Alter nicht an** he does not look his age; **man sieht ihr die Strapazen an** she's showing the strain; **man sieht ihr nicht an, daß sie krank ist** there is nothing to show that she is ill; **das sah man ihm nicht an** one would not have thought so to look at him; *s. auch* **Nasenspitze**; **d)** *(zusehen)* **etw. [mit] ~**: watch sth.; **das kann man doch nicht [mit] ~**: I/you can't just stand by and watch that; **das habe ich lange genug angesehen** I've had *or* seen enough of that; **ich kann das nicht länger [mit] ~**: I can't stand this any longer; **e)** *(beurteilen)* see; **f)** *(auffassen)* regard; consider; **jmdn. als seinen Freund/als Betrüger ~**: regard sb. as a friend/a cheat; consider sb. [to be] a friend/a cheat; **etw. als/für seine Pflicht ~**: consider sth. one's duty. **2.** *unr. refl. V.* **a) sich** *(Dat.)* **etw. ~**: look at sth.; **sich** *(Dat.)* **ein Haus/Fernsehprogramm/Schauspiel/einen Film ~**: look at *or* view a house/watch a television programme/see a play/film; **das sehe sich einer an!** *(ugs.)* just look at that!; **b) das sieht sich hübsch/furchtbar** *usw.* **an** it looks pretty/terrible *etc.*

Ansehen das; ~s a) *(Wertschätzung)* [high] standing *or* reputation; **hohes ~ genießen** enjoy high standing *or* a good reputation; **[bei jmdm.] in hohem ~ stehen** be held in high esteem *or* high regard [by sb.]; **b)** *(geh.: Aussehen)* appearance; **[nur] von** *od.* **vom ~**: [only] by sight; **von** *od.* **vom ~ über jmdn. urteilen** judge sb. by appearances; **ohne ~ der Person** *(Rechtsw.)* without respect of persons

an·sehnlich *Adj.* **a)** *(beträchtlich)* considerable; **b)** *(gut aussehend, stattlich)* handsome; **er hat sich** *(Dat.)* **einen ~en Bauch angefuttert** he's developed quite a stomach

an|seilen *tr. V.* rope [up]; **sich ~:** rope up
an|sein *unr. itr. V.; mit sein; nur im Inf. u. Part. zusammengeschrieben (ugs.)* ⟨*light, gas, etc.*⟩ be on
an|sengen *tr. V.* singe [slightly]; **es riecht angesengt** there's a smell of something singeing
an|setzen 1. *tr. V.* **a)** *(in die richtige Stellung bringen)* position ⟨*ladder, jack, drill, saw*⟩; **die Feder/das Glas ~:** put pen to paper/the glass to one's lips; **den Geigenbogen/die Trompete ~:** put *or* place the violin bow in the bowing position/put the trumpet to one's lips; *s. auch* **Hebel; b)** *(anfügen)* attach, put on **(an** + *Akk. od. Dat.* to); fit **(an** + *Akk. od. Dat.* on to); **c)** *(festlegen)* fix ⟨*meeting etc.*⟩ **(für, auf** + *Akk.* for); fix, set ⟨*deadline, date, price*⟩; **d)** *(veranschlagen)* estimate; **die Kosten mit drei Millionen ~:** estimate the cost at three million; **etw. zu niedrig/hoch ~:** underestimate/overestimate sth.; **e)** *(anrühren)* mix; prepare; **f)** *(ausbilden)* **Rost/Grünspan ~:** go rusty/become covered with verdigris; **Fett ~:** put on weight; **Knospen/Früchte ~:** form buds/set fruit; **g)** *(einsetzen)* **jmdn. auf einen Erpresser** *usw.***/ein Projekt** *usw.* **~:** set *or* put sb. on to a blackmailer *etc.*/put sb. on [to] a project; **Hunde [auf eine Spur]/auf jmdn. ~:** set dogs on sb.'s/an animal's trail/on sb. **2.** *itr. V.* **a)** *(beginnen)* **zum Reden/Trinken ~:** open one's mouth to speak/raise the glass *etc.* to one's lips; **er setzte mehrmals [zum Sprechen] an, aber ...:** he kept opening his mouth to speak, but ...; **zur Landung ~:** come in to land; **zum Sprung/Überholen ~:** get ready *or* prepare to jump/overtake; **hier muß die Diskussion/Kritik ~:** this is where the discussion/criticsm must start; **b)** ⟨*nose, tail, hair, etc.*⟩ start; **c)** *(sich festsetzen)* stick
An·sicht die a) *(Meinung)* opinion; view; **meiner ~ nach** in my opinion *or* view; **nach [der] ~ der Fachleute** in the opinion of the experts; **anderer/der gleichen ~ sein** be of a different/the same opinion; **der ~ sein, daß ...:** be of the opinion that ...; **ich bin ganz Ihrer ~:** I entirely agree with you; **da bin ich anderer ~:** I disagree with you there; **die ~en sind geteilt** opinion is divided; **b)** *(Bild)* view; **Ludwigshafen in alten ~en** old views of Ludwigshafen; **c)** *(Kaufmannsspr.)* **zur ~:** on approval
ansichtig *Adj.* **jmds./einer Sache ~ werden** *(geh.)* catch sight of sb./sth.
Ansichts-: ~karte die, ~post·karte die picture postcard; **~sache die** *in* **~sache sein** be a matter of opinion; **~sendung die** article/articles [sent] on approval
an|siedeln 1. *refl. V. (ansässig werden)* settle; ⟨*industry, bacteria*⟩ become established; **auf dieser Insel haben sich seltene Vogelarten angesiedelt** rare species of birds have colonized this island. **2.** *tr. V. (ansässig machen)* settle ⟨*immigrant, refugee, etc.*⟩; establish ⟨*industry, species, variety, bacteria*⟩; **die Attentäter sind rechts anzusiedeln** *(fig.)* it can be assumed that the assassins are rightists; **etw. in einem exotischen Milieu ~** *(fig.)* give sth. an exotic setting
Ansiedelung *s.* **Ansiedlung**
An·siedler der settler
An·siedlung die a) *(das Ansiedeln) s.* **ansiedeln 2:** settlement; establishment; **b)** *(Ort)* settlement
An·sinnen das; ~s, ~: [unreasonable] request; **ein freches/seltsames** *usw.* **~:** an impudent/a strange *etc.* request
An·sitz der a) *(Jägerspr.)* hide *(Brit.)*; blind *(Amer.)*; *(Hochsitz)* raised hide *(Brit.) or (Amer.)* blind; **b)** *(österr.: Haus)* residence
an·sonst *Konj. (österr., schweiz.)* otherwise
ansonsten *Adv. (ugs.)* **a)** *(außerdem)* **der Verlag produziert ... und ~ noch Kinderbücher** the publishing house produces ... and, in addition, children's books; **aber ~ ist nichts Besonderes passiert** but apart from that *or* otherwise nothing particular has happened; **b)** *(andernfalls)* otherwise
an|spannen 1. *tr. V.* **a)** *(einspannen)* harness, hitch up ⟨*horse etc.*⟩ **(an** + *Akk.* to); hitch up, yoke up ⟨*oxen*⟩ **(an** + *Akk.* to); hitch up ⟨*carriage, cart, etc.*⟩ **(an** + *Akk.* to); **b)** *(anstrengen)* strain; **seine ganze Kraft ~:** exert all one's energies. **2.** *itr. V.* hitch up; **~ lassen** have the carriage made ready
An·spannung die strain; **unter ~ aller seiner Kräfte/Gedanken** by exerting all one's energies/by intense mental effort
an|spazieren *itr. V.; mit sein (ugs.)* **anspaziert kommen** come strolling along; *(auf einen zu)* come strolling up
An·spiel das a) *(Sport: Zuspiel)* pass; **b)** *(Spielbeginn) (Schach)* **das ~ haben** make the first move; *(Kartenspiel)* **ich habe das ~:** it's my lead; *(Fußball) s.* **Anstoß c**
an|spielen 1. *itr. V.* **a)** *(hinweisen)* **auf jmdn./etw. ~:** allude to sb./sth.; **worauf wollen Sie ~?** what are you hinting at?; **b)** *(Spiel beginnen)* start; *(Fußball)* kick off; *(Kartenspiel)* lead; *(Schach)* make the first move. **2.** *tr. V.* **a)** *(Sport: zuspielen)* **jmdn. ~:** pass to sb.; **b)** *(Kartenspiel: ins Spiel bringen)* lead
Anspielung die; ~, ~en allusion **(auf** + *Akk.* to); *(verächtlich, böse)* insinuation **(auf** + *Akk.* about)
an|spinnen 1. *unr. tr. V. (beginnen)* [gradually] start ⟨*conversation*⟩; start having ⟨*affair*⟩; start hatching ⟨*intrigue, plot*⟩. **2.** *unr. refl. V.* develop; **zwischen den beiden spinnt sich etwas an** there's something going on between those two
an|spitzen *tr. V.* **a)** *(spitz machen)* sharpen ⟨*pencil*⟩; shape ⟨*stake, post*⟩ to a point; **b)** *(ugs.: antreiben)* **jmdn. ~:** give sb. a prod; **jmdn. ~, etw. zu tun** *od.* **daß er etw. tut** prod sb. into doing sth.
An·sporn der incentive
an|spornen *tr. V.* **a)** *(anfeuern)* spur on; encourage; **b)** *(die Sporen geben)* spur ⟨*horse*⟩
An·sprache die a) *(Rede)* speech; address; **eine ~ halten** make a speech; give an address; **b)** *(Kontakt)* **~ suchen/haben** look for/have sb. to talk to
ansprechbar *Adj.* **a) ich bin jetzt beschäftigt und daher nicht ~:** you can't talk to me now, I'm too busy; **sie ist vor Müdigkeit nicht ~:** she's too tired to listen to anyone; **b)** *(zugänglich)* amenable; **c)** *(fähig zu reagieren)* responsive
an|sprechen 1. *unr. tr. V.* **a)** speak to; *(zudringlich)* accost; **jmdn. mit „Herr Doktor" ~:** address sb. as 'doctor'; **jmdn. mit seinem Vornamen ~:** use sb.'s first name; **jmdn. auf etw./jmdn./um etw. ~:** speak to sb. about sth./sb./approach *or* ask sb. for sth.; **b)** *(gefallen)* appeal to; **c)** *(zur Sprache bringen)* mention; *(kurz, oberflächlich)* touch on; **d)** *(Jagdw., Milit.)* identify. **2.** *unr. itr. V.* **a)** *(gefallen)* **[gut] ~:** go down well **(bei** with); be well received **(bei** by); **b)** *(reagieren)* ⟨*patient, brake, clutch, etc.*⟩ respond **(auf** + *Akk.* to); **c)** *(wirken)* work; **bei jmdm. gut/nicht ~:** have/not have the desired effect on sb.; **d)** *(Musik)* **gut** *od.* **leicht ~:** ⟨*instrument*⟩ be easy to play
ansprechend 1. *Adj.* attractive; attractive, appealing ⟨*personality*⟩. **2.** *adv.* attractively
Ansprech·partner der contact
an|springen 1. *unr. itr. V.; mit sein* **a)** *(in Gang kommen)* start; **b)** *(sich nähern)* **angesprungen kommen** come bounding along; *(auf einen zu)* come bounding up; **c)** *(ugs.)* **auf ein Angebot/Geschäft ~:** take up an offer/agree to a deal; **sofort auf etw.** *(Akk.)* **~:** jump at sth. [straight away]. **2.** *unr. tr. V.* **a)** *(anfallen)* pounce on; **b)** *(an jmdm. hochspringen)* jump up at; **c)** *(Turnen)* mount ⟨*box, horse, beam*⟩ with a jump
an|spritzen 1. *tr. V.* splash; *(mit Gartenschlauch, Zerstäuber, Wasserpistole)* spray. **2.** *itr. V.; mit sein (ugs.: sich nähern)* **angespritzt kommen** come rushing along; *(auf einen zu)* come rushing up
An·spruch der a) claim; *(Forderung)* demand; **hohe Ansprüche [an jmdn.] haben** *od.* **stellen** demand a great deal [of sb.]; **~ auf etw.** *(Akk.)* **erheben** lay claim to sth.; **[keine] Ansprüche stellen** make [no] demands; **in ~ nehmen** *(Gebrauch machen von)* take up, take advantage of ⟨*offer*⟩; exercise ⟨*right*⟩; *(beanspruchen)* take up ⟨*time*⟩; **jmds. Zeit/Hilfe in ~ nehmen** make demands on sb.'s time/enlist sb.'s aid; **jmdn. [stark] in ~ nehmen** make [heavy] demands on sb.; **jmdn. völlig in ~ nehmen** take up all [of] sb.'s time; **b)** *(bes. Rechtsspr.: Anrecht)* claim; **[einen] ~/keinen ~ auf etw.** *(Akk.)* **haben** be/not be entitled to sth.; **auf etw.** *(Akk.)* **~ erheben** assert one's entitlement to sth.
an·spruchs-, An·spruchs-: ~denken das; ~s *(abwertend) attitude that everything one wants should be provided by the State;* **~los 1.** *Adj.* **a)** *(genügsam)* undemanding; **b)** *(schlicht)* unpretentious; simple; **2.** *adv.* **a)** *(genügsam)* undemandingly; ⟨*live*⟩ modestly, simply; **b)** *(schlicht)* unpretentiously; simply; **~losigkeit die; ~:** *s.* **~los 1:** undemanding nature; unpretentiousness; simplicity; **~voll 1.** *Adj.* **a)** *(wählerisch);* demanding, discriminating ⟨*reader, audience, gourmet*⟩; *(hohe Anforderungen stellend)* demanding; ambitious ⟨*subject*⟩; **b)** *(Werbespr.)* exquisite; **eine ~volle Zigarette/ein ~voller Sekt** a cigarette for the discriminating smoker/champagne for the discriminating drinker; **die Cremeseife für Anspruchsvolle** the cream soap for people with discriminating taste; **2.** *adv. (Werbespr.)* exquisitely
an|spucken *tr. V.* spit at
an|spülen *tr. V.* wash up *or* ashore
an|stacheln *tr. V.* spur on **(zu** to); **jmds. Ehrgeiz/Eifer ~:** fire sb.'s ambition/enthusiasm
Anstalt ['anʃtalt] **die; ~, ~en** *(auch verhüll.)* institution; **eine ~ des öffentlichen Rechts** a public institution
Anstalten *Pl.* preparations; **[keine] ~ machen** *od. (geh.)* **treffen** make [no] preparations **(für** for); **~ machen/keine ~ machen, etw. zu tun** make a move/make no move to do sth.
Anstalts-: ~geistliche der [resident] chaplain; **~kleidung die** institutional clothing; **~leiter der** *(einer Schule)* head; *(eines Erziehungsheims)* superintendent
¹An·stand der *(Jägerspr.) s.* **Ansitz a**
²An·stand der a) *o. Pl. (Schicklichkeit)* decency; **keinen ~ haben** have no sense of decency; **gegen jeden/den ~ verstoßen** offend against common decency; **sich mit ~ aus der Affäre ziehen** emerge from the affair with no damage to one's reputation; **b)** *o. Pl. (veralt.: Benehmen)* good manners *pl.*; **dir werde ich ~ beibringen** I'll give you a lesson in manners; **c)** *(südd., österr.: Ärger)* trouble; **[keinen] ~ an etw.** *(Dat.)* **nehmen** [not] object to sth.; **keinen ~ nehmen[, etw. zu tun]** *(nicht zögern)* not hesitate [to do sth.]
an·ständig 1. *Adj.* **a)** *(sittlich einwandfrei, rücksichtsvoll)* decent; decent, clean ⟨*joke*⟩; *(ehrbar)* respectable; *(gut angesehen)* decent, respectable ⟨*job*⟩; **bleib ~!** *(auch scherzh.)* behave yourself!; be good!; **b)** *(ugs.: zufriedenstellend)* decent; respectable ⟨*result, marks*⟩; **c)** *(ugs.: beträchtlich)* sizeable ⟨*sum, amount, debts*⟩; **eine ~e Tracht Prügel** a good hiding *(coll.)*; **ein ~es Stück gefahren sein** have come a tidy old *(coll.) or* pretty long way *(coll.)*. **2.** *adv.* **a)** *(sittlich einwandfrei)* decently; *(ordentlich)* properly; **b)** *(ugs.: zufriedenstellend)* **jmdn. ~ bezahlen** pay sb. pretty well; **ganz ~ abschneiden** do quite well; **~ arbeiten** do good

work; **c)** *(ugs.: ziemlich)* ~ **ausschlafen** have a decent sleep; **es regnet ganz** ~: it's raining pretty hard; **jmdn.** ~ **eine knallen** really belt sb. one *(coll.)*

ạnständigerwẹise *Adv.* out of decency

Ạnständigkeit die; ~: decency

ạnstands-, Ạnstands-: ~besuch der formal courtesy call (**bei** on); formal courtesy visit (**bei** to); **~dame die** *(veralt.)* chaperon; **~halber** *Adv.* out of politeness; for the sake of politeness; **~happen der** *(ugs.)* **einen ~happen übriglassen** leave the last piece out of politeness; **~los** *Adv. (ohne Bedenken)* readily; without [any] hesitation; *(ohne Schwierigkeiten zu machen)* without [any] objection; **~unterricht der** lessons *pl.* in deportment *or* manners; **~wau·wau der** *(ugs. scherzh.)* chaperon

ạn|stänkern *tr. V. (salopp)* **jmdn.** ~: lay into sb. *(coll.)*

ạn|starren *tr. V.* stare at

an·stạtt 1. *Konj.* ~ **zu arbeiten/~, daß er arbeitet** instead of working. **2.** *Präp. mit Gen.* instead of

ạn|stauben *itr. V.; mit sein* get dusty; **leicht angestaubte Ware** slightly shop-worn *or (Brit.)* shop-soiled goods *pl.*

ạn|stauen 1. *tr. V.* dam up; *(fig.)* bottle up ⟨*feelings*⟩. **2.** *refl. V.* ⟨*water*⟩ accumulate; *(fig.)* ⟨*feelings*⟩ build up

ạn|staunen *tr. V.* **jmdn./etw.** ~: gaze *or* stare in wonder at sb./sth.; **jmdn./etw. mit offenem Mund** ~: gape at sb./sth. in wonder

ạn|stechen 1. *unr. tr. V.* **a)** prick; puncture ⟨*tyre*⟩; **wie ein angestochenes Schwein, wie angestochen** *(derb)* like a wild thing; **b)** *(anzapfen)* tap ⟨*barrel*⟩. **2.** *unr. itr. V. (anzapfen)* tap a/the barrel

ạn|stecken 1. *tr. V.* **a)** *(feststecken)* pin on ⟨*badge, brooch*⟩; *(am Finger)* put *or* slip ⟨*ring*⟩; **jmdm. eine Brosche/einen Ring** ~: pin a brooch on sb./put *or* slip a ring on sb.'s finger; **b)** *(infizieren, auch fig.)* infect; **ich will dich nicht** ~: I don't want to give you my cold/germs *etc.*; **c)** *(bes. nordd., mitteld.: anzünden)* light; *(in Brand setzen)* set fire to. **2.** *itr. V. (sich übertragen)* be infectious *or* catching; *(durch Berührung)* be contagious; *(fig.)* be infectious *or* contagious

ạnsteckend *Adj.* infectious; *(durch Berührung)* contagious; *(fig.)* infectious; contagious

Ạnsteck·nadel die *(Brosche)* pin; *(Plakette)* badge

Ạnsteckung die; ~, **~en** infection; *(durch Berührung)* contagion

Ạnsteckungs-: ~gefahr die risk *or* danger of infection; **~herd der** source of [the/an] infection

ạn|stehen *unr. itr. V.* **a)** *(warten)* queue [up], *(Amer.)* stand in line (**nach** for); **b)** *südd. mit sein (geh.: sich ziemen)* **jmdm. [wohl/übel]** ~: [well/ill] become sb.; **c)** *(zu erledigen sein)* be waiting to be dealt with; *(zur Beratung* ~*)* be on the agenda; **die ~den Probleme** the problems to be dealt with; **etw.** ~ **lassen** defer sth.; **d)** *(Rechtsspr.: festgesetzt sein)* be fixed *or* set (**auf** + *Akk.* for); **e)** *in* **nicht** ~, **etw. zu tun** *(geh.)* have no hesitation in doing sth.; not hesitate to do sth.; **f)** *(Geol.)* outcrop; crop out

ạn|steigen *unr. itr. V.; mit sein* **a)** *(bergan führen)* ⟨*hill*⟩ rise; ⟨*person, road, path*⟩ climb, ascend; ⟨*garden, ground*⟩ slope up, rise; **b)** *(höher werden)* ⟨*water level, temperature, etc.*⟩ rise; *(fig.)* ⟨*price, cost, rent, etc.*⟩ rise, go up, increase

an·stẹlle 1. *Präp. mit Gen.* instead of. **2.** *Adv.* ~ **von** instead of; *s. auch* **Stelle a**

ạn|stellen 1. *refl. V.* **a)** *(warten)* queue [up], *(Amer.)* stand in line (**nach** for); **b)** *(ugs.: sich verhalten)* act; behave; **sich dumm/ungeschickt** ~: act *or* behave stupidly/be clumsy; **sich dumm/ungeschickt bei etw.** ~: go about sth. stupidly/clumsily; **sich geschickt** ~: go about it well; **stell dich nicht [so] an!** don't make [such] a fuss! **2.** *tr. V.* **a)** *(aufdrehen)* turn on; **b)** *(einschalten)* switch on; turn on, switch on ⟨*radio, television*⟩; start ⟨*engine*⟩; **c)** *(einstellen)* employ (**als** as); **bei jmdm. angestellt sein** be employed by sb.; **d)** *(ugs.: beschäftigen)* **jmdn. zum Kartoffelschälen** *usw.* ~: get sb. to peel the potatoes *etc.*; **e)** *(anlehnen)* **etw. an etw.** *(Akk.)* ~: put *or* place sth. against sth.; **f)** *(anrichten)* **etwas/Unfug** ~: get up to something/to mischief; **was hast du nun wieder angestellt?** what have you been up to this time?; **sieh, was du angestellt hast** see what you've done; **g)** *(ugs.: fertigbringen)* manage; **wie soll ich es** ~, **daß er nichts merkt/daß ich rechtzeitig hinkomme?** how do I stop him noticing anything?/make sure of getting there in time?; **h)** *(ugs.: versuchen)* try; **i)** *(vornehmen)* do ⟨*calculation*⟩; draw, make ⟨*comparison*⟩; carry out ⟨*experiment, investigation*⟩; make ⟨*assumption*⟩; **Überlegungen** ~, **wie ...:** consider how ...

ạnstellig *Adj.* clever; skilful

Ạnstelligkeit die; ~: ability; skill

Ạn·stellung die a) *o. Pl. (das Einstellen)* employment; **b)** *(Stellung)* job; **ohne** ~: without a job; unemployed

Ạnstellungs-: ~verhältnis das employment *no indef. art.*; ~ **auf Zeit** temporary employment; **~vertrag der** contract of employment

ạn|steuern *tr. V. (auch fig.)* head *or* make for; **ein Thema** ~ *(fig.)* steer the conversation towards a subject

Ạn·stich der a) *(das Anstechen)* tapping; broaching; **nach dem** ~: after tapping *or* broaching the barrel; **b)** *(Getränk)* **[frischer]** ~: newly tapped beer/wine

ạn|stiefeln *itr. V.; mit sein* **angestiefelt kommen** come marching along; *(auf einen zu)* come marching up

Ạnstieg der; ~**[e]s,** ~**e a)** *o. Pl. (Zunahme, Erhöhung)* rise, increase (+ *Gen.* in); **b)** *o. Pl. (Steigung)* gradient; **c)** *(Aufstieg)* climb; ascent; *(Weg)* way up; *(für Bergsteiger)* ascent route

ạn|stieren *tr. V. (ugs.)* stare at

ạn|stiften *tr. V.* **a)** *(in Gang setzen)* instigate; *(verursachen)* cause, bring about ⟨*disaster, confusion*⟩; **b)** *(verleiten)* **jmdn. [dazu]** ~, **etw. zu tun** incite sb. to do sth.; **jmdn. zum Betrug/Mord/zu einem Verbrechen** ~: incite sb. to deception/to murder/to commit a crime; **jmdn. zu dummen Streichen** ~: put sb. up to silly tricks

Ạn·stifter der, Ạn·stifterin die instigator

Ạn·stiftung die incitement (**zu** to); ~ **zu einer Straftat** incitement to commit a serious offence

ạn|stimmen *tr. V.* **a)** *(Musik)* start singing ⟨*song*⟩; start playing ⟨*waltz, march, etc.*⟩; play ⟨*note*⟩; ⟨*band*⟩ strike up ⟨*waltz, march, etc.*⟩; **b)** *(ausbrechen in)* **Proteste/ein Geschrei** ~: start protesting/shouting; **ein Freudengeheul** ~: burst into shouts of joy

ạn|stinken *(ugs.)* **1.** *unr. tr. V. (anwidern)* **jmdn.** ~: make sb. sick. **2.** *unr. itr. V. in* **gegen jmdn./etw. nicht** ~ **können** be powerless against sb./sth.

ạn|stolzieren *itr. V.; mit sein* **anstolziert kommen** come strutting along; *(auf einen zu)* come strutting up

Ạn·stoß der a) *(Impuls)* stimulus (**zu** for); **den [ersten]** ~ **zu etw. geben** initiate sth.; **der** ~ **ging von ihr aus** she was the one who initiated things *or* [first] got things going; **es bedurfte eines neuen ~es** a fresh impetus was needed; **b)** ~ **erregen** cause *or* give offence (**bei** to); **[keinen]** ~ **an etw.** *(Dat.)* **nehmen** [not] object to sth.; *(sich [nicht] beleidigt fühlen)* [not] take offence at sth.; *s. auch* **Stein b**; **c)** *(Fußball)* kick-off; **den** ~ **ausführen** kick off; **welche Mannschaft hat** ~**?** which side will kick off?; **d)** *(Aufprall)* impact

ạn|stoßen 1. *unr. itr. V.* **a)** *mit sein* **an etw.** *(Akk.)* ~: bump into sth.; **mit dem Kopf** ~: knock *or* bump one's head; **mit dem Koffer dauernd/überall** ~: keep bumping the case against things; **b)** *(auf etw. trinken)* **[mit den Gläsern]** ~: clink glasses; **auf jmdn./etw.** ~: drink to sb./sth.; **c)** *(Fußball)* kick off; **d)** *auch mit sein (lispeln)* **[mit der Zunge]** ~: lisp; **e)** *mit sein (Anstoß erregen)* give *or* cause offence (**bei** to); **man stößt leicht bei ihm an** he easily takes offence; **f)** *(angrenzen)* **an etw.** *(Akk.)* ~: adjoin sth. **2.** *unr. tr. V. (einen Stoß geben)* **jmdn./etw.** ~: give sb./sth. a push; **jmdn. aus Versehen** ~: knock into sb. inadvertently; **jmdn. mit dem Ellenbogen/Fuß** ~ *(als Zeichen)* nudge/kick sb.; **sich** *(Dat.)* **den Kopf/die Zehe** ~: knock *or* bang one's head/stub one's toe

anstößig ['anʃtø:sɪç] **1.** *Adj.* offensive; offensive, objectionable ⟨*behaviour*⟩. **2.** *adv.* offensively; ⟨*behave*⟩ offensively, objectionably

Ạnstößigkeit die; ~, **~en a)** *o. Pl.* offensiveness; *(einer Handlung)* offensiveness, objectionableness; **b)** *(Handlung)* piece of offensive *or* objectionable behaviour; **~en** offensive *or* objectionable behaviour *sing.*

ạn|strahlen *tr. V.* **a)** illuminate; *(mit Scheinwerfer)* floodlight; *(im Theater)* spotlight; **ein Gebäude rot** ~: illuminate a building with red light; **b)** *(anblicken)* beam at; **ihre Augen strahlten ihn an** she beamed at him

ạn|streben *tr. V. (geh.)* aspire to; *(mit großer Anstrengung)* strive for

ạnstrebens·wert *Adj. s.* **anstreben:** worth aspiring to/striving for *postpos.*

ạn|streichen *unr. tr. V.* **a)** *(mit Farbe)* paint; *(mit Tünche)* whitewash; **b)** *(hervorheben)* mark (**als** as); **etw. rot** ~: mark sth. in red; **c)** *(anzünden)* strike, light ⟨*match*⟩

Ạn·streicher der *(ugs.)* [house-]painter

ạn|strengen 1. *refl. V. (sich einsetzen)* make an effort; exert oneself; *(körperlich)* exert oneself; **sich** ~, **etw. zu tun** make an effort to do sth.; **sich mehr/sehr** ~: make more of an effort/a great effort; **sich übermäßig** *od.* **zu sehr** ~: overexert oneself; **da hat er sich aber angestrengt** he has made a special effort *or* gone to a lot of trouble [there]. **2.** *tr. V.* **a)** *(anspannen)* strain ⟨*eyes, ears, voice*⟩; **alle seine Kräfte** ~: make every effort; *(körperlich)* use all one's strength; **seinen Verstand** ~: think hard; **seine Phantasie** ~: exercise one's imagination; **b)** *(strapazieren)* strain, put a strain on ⟨*eyes*⟩; be a strain on ⟨*person*⟩; **jmdn. zu sehr** ~: be too much of a strain on sb.; **c)** *(Rechtsw.: einleiten)* **eine Klage/einen Prozeß** ~: lay a charge/start proceedings (**gegen** against)

ạnstrengend *Adj. (körperlich)* strenuous; *(geistig)* demanding; ~ **zu lesen/für die Augen sein** be a strain to read/on the eyes; **Nachtfahrten finde ich** ~: I find travelling at night a strain; **es war** ~, **dem Vortrag zu folgen** following the lecture was a strain

Ạnstrengung die; ~, **~en a)** *(Einsatz)* effort; **~en machen** *od. (geh.)* **unternehmen** make an effort; **große ~en machen, etw. zu tun** make every effort to do sth.; **mit letzter/äußerster** ~: with one last/a supreme effort; **b)** *(Strapaze)* strain

Ạn·strich der a) *o. Pl. (das Anstreichen)* painting; *(mit Tünche)* whitewashing; **b)** *(Farbe)* paint; *(Tünche)* whitewash; **der erste/zweite** ~: the first/second coat; **c)** *o. Pl. (Note)* touch; *(Aussehen)* air; **einer Sache** *(Dat.)* **einen bestimmten** ~ **geben** lend sth. a certain air; **d)** *(beim Schreiben)* up-stroke

ạn|stricken *tr. V.* **etw. an etw.** *(Akk.)* ~: knit sth. on to sth.

ạn|strömen *itr. V.; mit sein* **a)** *(heranfließen)* ⟨*water*⟩ flow in; ⟨*air*⟩ stream in; **von**

Westen **~de Kaltluft** a stream of cold air from the west; **b)** *(herbeikommen)* pour *or* stream in; **angeströmt kommen** come pouring *or* streaming in

ạn|stückeln, ạn|stücken *tr. V.* add a piece to ‹*carpet etc.*›; **ein Kleid/Hemd ~:** lengthen a dress/shirt [by adding a piece on]; **etw. an etw.** *(Akk.)* **~:** attach sth. to sth.

Ạn·sturm der a) *(das Anstürmen)* onslaught; **b)** *(Andrang) (auf Kaufhäuser, Schwimmbäder)* rush **(auf +** *Akk.* to); *(auf Banken, Waren)* run **(auf +** *Akk.* on)

ạn|stürmen *itr. V.; mit sein* **a)** *(gegen etw. drängen)* **gegen etw. ~:** ‹*waves, wind*› pound sth.; *(Milit.)* storm sth.; **b) angestürmt kommen** come charging *or* rushing along; *(auf einen zu)* come charging *or* rushing up

ạn|stürzen *itr. V.; mit sein* **angestürzt kommen** come tearing *or* dashing along; *(auf einen zu)* come tearing *or* dashing up

ạn|suchen *itr. V. (österr., sonst veralt.)* **[bei jmdm.] um etw. ~** *(beantragen)* apply [to sb.] for sth.; *(bitten)* ask [sb.] for sth.

Ạnsuchen das; ~s, ~ *(österr., sonst veralt.) (Gesuch)* application **(auf +** *Akk.* for); *(Bitte)* request **(auf +** *Akk.* for); **auf jmds. ~** *(Akk.)* at sb.'s request

ạn|sülzen *tr. V. (salopp)* blether at

Antagonismus [antago'nɪsmʊs] **der; ~, Antagonịsmen** antagonism (*Gen.,* **zwischen** between)

Antagonịst der; ~en, ~en, Antagonịstin die; ~, ~nen antagonist

antagonịstisch 1. *Adj.* antagonistic. **2.** *adv.* antagonistically

ạn|tanzen *itr. V.; mit sein (ugs.)* show up *(coll.);* **angetanzt kommen** turn up

Antarktis [ant'|arktɪs] **die; ~** *(Geogr.)* **die ~:** the Antarctic

antạrktisch *Adj.* Antarctic

ạn|tasten *tr. V.* **a)** *(verbrauchen)* break into ‹*savings, provisions*›; **das Geld taste ich nicht an** I shall not touch the money; **b)** *(beeinträchtigen)* infringe, encroach on ‹*right, freedom, privilege*›; encroach on ‹*property, private life*›; **jmds. Ehre ~:** cast a slur on *or* impugn sb.'s honour; **c)** *(berühren)* touch; *(fig.)* touch on ‹*subject*›

ạn|tauchen *itr. V. (österr.)* **a)** *(anschieben)* push; **b)** *(sich mehr anstrengen)* make more effort; try harder

ạn|tauen 1. *itr. V.; mit sein (zu tauen beginnen)* ‹*ice, snow*› begin to melt *or* thaw; ‹*foodstuff*› begin to thaw. **2.** *tr. V. (tauen lassen)* **etw. ~:** allow sth. to thaw slightly

ạn|täuschen 1. *tr. V. (Boxen)* **einen linken Haken ~ und mit der Rechten zuschlagen** feint with the left and throw a right. **2.** *itr. V. (Fußball, Rugby)* **[links/rechts] ~:** dummy *(Brit.) or (Amer.)* fake [to the left/right]

Ạn·teil der a) *(jmdm. zustehender Teil)* share (**an +** *Dat.* of); **~ an etw.** *(Dat.)* **haben** share in sth.; *(zu etw. beitragen)* play *or* have a part in sth.; **b)** *(Wirtsch.)* share; **c)** *o. Pl. (Interesse)* interest (**an +** *Dat.* in); **~ an jmdm./etw. nehmen** *od. (geh.)* **bekunden** take/show an interest in sb./sth.; **an jmds. Leid/Freude ~ nehmen** sympathize with sb. in his/her suffering/share in sb.'s joy; **viele Menschen nahmen ~ am Tod seiner Frau** many people felt for him when his wife died

ạnteilig, ạnteil·mäßig 1. *Adj.* proportional; proportionate. **2.** *adv.* proportionally; proportionately

Ạn·teilnahme die a) *(Beteiligung)* participation; **unter reger ~ der Bevölkerung** with the active participation of the public; **b)** *(Interesse)* interest (**an +** *Dat.* in); **c)** *(Mitgefühl)* sympathy (**an +** *Dat.* with); **mit ~ zuhören** listen sympathetically

Ạnteil·schein der *(Wirtsch.)* share certificate

Ạnteils·eigner der *(Wirtsch.)* shareholder

ạn|telefonieren *tr. V. (ugs.)* phone *(coll.);* call; ring *(Brit.)*

Antẹnne die; ~, ~n a) aerial; antenna *(Amer.);* **eine/keine ~ für etw. haben** *(fig. ugs.)* have a/no feeling for sth.; **b)** *(Zool.)* antenna

Anthologie [antolo'gi:] **die; ~, ~n** anthology

anthrazit [antra'tsi:t] *Adj.; nicht attr.* anthracite[-grey]

Anthrazit der; ~s, ~e anthracite

anthrazit-: ~farben, ~farbig *Adj.* anthracite[-coloured]; **~grau** *Adj.* anthracite-grey

Anthropologe [antropo'lo:gə] **der; ~n, ~n** anthropologist

Anthropologie die; ~, ~n anthropology *no art.*

Anthropologin die; ~, ~nen anthropologist; *s. auch* **-in**

anthropologisch 1. *Adj.* anthropological. **2.** *adv.* anthropologically

anthropomorph [antropo'mɔrf] *Adj.* anthropomorphic

Anthropomorphismus der; ~, Anthropomorphịsmen a) *o. Pl. (Übertragung)* anthropomorphism; **b)** *(Eigenschaft)* anthropomorphic feature

Anthroposoph [antropo'zo:f] **der; ~en, ~en** anthroposophist

Anthroposophie die; ~: anthroposophy *no art.*

Anthroposophin die; ~, ~nen anthroposophist; *s. auch* **-in**

anthroposophisch *Adj.* anthroposophical

anthropozentrisch [antropo'tsɛntrɪʃ] **1.** *Adj.* anthropocentric. **2.** *adv* anthropocentrically

anti-, Anti- [anti-]: anti-

anti-, Anti-: ~alkoholiker der teetotaller; **~autoritär 1.** *Adj.* anti-authoritarian; **2.** *adv.* in an anti-authoritarian manner; **~autoritär eingestellt sein** take an anti-authoritarian view; **~baby·pille die** *(ugs.)* contraceptive pill; **~bakteriẹll 1.** *Adj.* antibacterial; **2.** *adv.* **~bakteriell wirken** have an antibacterial action

Antibiotikum [anti'bio:tikʊm] **das; ~s, Antibiọtika** *(Med.)* antibiotic

antichambrieren [antiʃam'bri:rən] *itr. V.* **a)** *(veralt.: warten)* wait in the antechamber; **b)** *(geh. abwertend: dienern)* bow and scrape **(bei** to)

anti, Anti-: ~blockier·system das *(Kfz-W.)* anti-lock braking system; **[1]~christ** ['---] **der; ~[s]** Antichrist; **[2]~christ** ['---] **der; ~en, ~en** antichristian; **~christlich** ['----] **1.** *Adj.* antichristian; **2.** *adv.* **~christlich eingestellt/gesinnt sein** be antichristian [in one's views]; **~demokratisch 1.** *Adj.* anti-democratic; **2.** *adv.* **~demokratisch eingestellt/gesinnt sein** be anti-democratic [in one's views]; **~faschịsmus der** antifascism *no art.*; **~faschịst der** anti-fascist; **~faschịstisch 1.** *Adj.* anti-fascist; **2.** *adv.* **~faschistisch eingestellt/gesinnt sein** be anti-fascist [in one's views]; **~gen das** *(Med., Biol.)* antigen; **~haft·beschichtung die** non-stick coating; **~held** ['---] **der** anti-hero; **~heldin** ['----] **die** anti-heroine

antik [an'ti:k] **1.** *Adj.* **a)** *(des klassischen Altertums)* classical; **b)** *(altertümelnd)* antique-style ‹*furniture, fittings, etc.*›; **c)** *(aus vergangenen Zeiten)* antique. **2.** *adv. (altertümelnd)* ‹*make, furnish, etc.*› in antique style

Antike [an'ti:kə] **die; ~, ~n a)** *(Epoche)* classical antiquity *no art.*; **b)** *(Kunstwerk)* classical work of art

antikisieren *itr. V.* imitate classical forms

anti, Anti-: ~klerikal 1. *Adj.* anticlerical; **2.** *adv.* **~klerikal gesinnt/eingestellt sein** be anticlerical [in one's view]; **~klerikal denken/handeln** think/act anticlerically; **~klerikalịsmus der** anticlericalism; **~klopf·mittel das** *(Kfz-W.)* antiknock [agent]; **~kommunịsmus der** anticommunism; **~kommunịst der** anticommunist; **~kommunịstisch 1.** *Adj.* anticommunist; **2.** *adv.* **~kommunistisch eingestellt/gesinnt sein** be anticommunist [in one's views]; **~körper** ['----] **der** *(Med.)* antibody

Antillen [an'tɪlən] *Pl.;* **die [Großen/Kleinen] ~:** the [Greater/Lesser] Antilles

Antilope [anti'lo:pə] **die; ~, ~n** antelope

anti, Anti-: ~militarịsmus der antimilitarism; **~militarịst der** antimilitarist; **~militarịstisch 1.** *Adj.* antimilitaristic; **2.** *adv.* ‹*argue*› along antimilitaristic lines; **~militaristisch gesinnt/eingestellt sein** be antimilitaristic [in one's views]

Antimon [anti'mo:n] **das; ~s** *(Chem.)* antimony

Antinomie [antino'mi:] **die; ~, ~n** *(Philos., Rechtsspr.)* antinomy

Antipathie [antipa'ti:] **die; ~, ~n** antipathy; **eine ~ gegen jmdn./etw. haben** have an antipathy to sb./sth

Antipode [anti'po:də] **der; ~n, ~n a)** *(Geogr.)* antipodean; **b)** *(geh.)* antipode; exact opposite

ạn|tippen *tr. V. (berühren)* give ‹*person, thing*› a [light] tap; touch ‹*accelerator, brake, etc.*›; *(fig.)* touch on ‹*point, question*›

Antiqua [an'ti:kva] **die; ~** *(Druckw.)* roman [type]

Antiquar [anti'kva:ɐ̯] **der; ~s, ~e** antiquarian bookseller; *(mit neueren gebrauchten Büchern)* second-hand bookseller

Antiquariat [antikva'ria:t] **a)** *o. Pl. (Handel)* antiquarian book trade; *(mit neueren gebrauchten Büchern)* second-hand book trade; **b)** *(Laden/Abteilung)* antiquarian bookshop/department; *(mit neueren gebrauchten Büchern)* second-hand bookshop/department; **modernes ~:** *shop/department selling remainders, defective copies, cheap editions, reprints, etc.*

antiquarisch 1. *Adj.* antique; *(Buchw.)* antiquarian; *(von neueren gebrauchten Büchern)* second-hand. **2.** *adv.* **ein Buch ~ kaufen** buy a book second-hand

antiquiert [anti'kvi:ɐ̯t] *(abwertend)* **1.** *Adj.* antiquated. **2.** *adv.* in an antiquated way

Antiquität die; ~, ~en antique

Antiquitäten-: ~händler der antique-dealer; **~laden der** antique shop; **~sammler der** collector of antiques; **~sammlung die** collection of antiques

anti, Anti: ~rakete ['-----], **~raketen·rakete die** anti-missile missile; **~semit der** anti-Semite; **~semitisch 1.** *Adj.* anti-Semitic; anti-Semite; **2.** *adv.* anti-Semitically; **~semitisch eingestellt/gesinnt sein** be anti-Semitic [in one's views]; **~semitịsmus der** anti-Semitism; **~sẹptisch** *Adj.* *(Med.)* antiseptic; **~statisch 1.** *Adj.* *(Physik)* antistatic; **2.** *adv.* **~statisch wirken** have an antistatic action; **~teilchen** ['----] **das** *(Kernphysik)* antiparticle; **~these** ['----] **die** antithesis

antithetisch 1. *Adj.* antithetical. **2.** *adv.* antithetically

Antizipation [antitsipa'tsio:n] **die; ~, ~en** *(geh.)* anticipation

antizipieren *tr. V. (geh.)* anticipate

anti·zyklisch 1. *Adj.* **a)** *(in unregelmäßiger Folge)* irregular; **b)** *(Wirtsch.)* countercyclical. **2.** *adv.* **a)** *(unregelmäßig)* irregularly; at irregular intervals; **b)** *(Wirtsch.)* in a counter-cyclical way

Antlitz ['antlɪts] **das; ~es, ~e** *(dichter., geh.)* countenance *(literary);* face

Antonym [anto'ny:m] **das; ~s, ~e** *(Sprachw.)* antonym

ạn|törnen ['antœrnən] *s.* **[1]anturnen**

ạn|traben *itr. V.* **a)** *mit sein (sich nähern)*

come trotting along; **angetrabt kommen** come trotting along; *(auf einen zu)* come trotting up; **jmdn. ~ lassen** *(ugs.: kommen lassen)* get sb. to come along promptly; **b)** start trotting; break into a trot; *(aus dem Stillstand)* set off at a trot

Antrag ['antra:k] **der; ~[e]s, Ạnträge a)** *(Gesuch)* application, request **(auf** + *Akk.* for); *(Rechtsw.: schriftlich)* petition; **einen ~ auf etw.** *(Akk.)* **stellen** make an application for sth.; apply for sth.; *(Rechtsw.: schriftlich)* enter a petition for sth.; **einem ~ stattgeben** grant an application/a petition; **auf jmds. ~:** at sb.'s request; *(Rechtsw.: schriftlich)* in response to sb.'s petition; **b)** *(Formular)* application form; **c)** *(Heirats~)* proposal of marriage; **jmdm. einen ~ machen** propose to sb.; **d)** *(Parl.)* motion; **einen ~ auf etw.** *(Akk.)* **stellen** *od.* **einbringen** table *or* put forward a motion for sth.; **e) jmdm. unzüchtige Anträge machen** make improper suggestions to sb.

ạn|tragen *unr. tr. V. (geh.)* offer; **jmdm. ~, etw. zu tun** put it to sb. that he/she should do sth.

Ạntrags·formular das application form

ạntrags·gemäß *adv.* in accordance with the/your/his *etc.* request

Ạntrag·steller der; ~s, ~: applicant

ạn|trainieren *tr. V.* **jmdm./sich Muskeln ~:** develop sb.'s/one's muscles; **Pünktlichkeit läßt sich ~:** you can train yourself to be punctual

ạn|trauen *tr. V. (veralt.)* **jmdn. jmdm. ~:** marry sb. to sb.; **meine [mir] angetraute Gattin** my wedded wife

ạn|treffen *unr. tr. V.* find; *(zufällig)* come across; **er trifft mich nie zu Hause an** he never catches me in

ạn|treiben 1. *unr. tr. V.* **a)** *(vorwärts treiben)* drive ⟨*animals, column of prisoners*⟩ on *or* along; *(fig.)* urge; **jmdn. zur Eile/zu immer besseren Leistungen ~** *(fig.)* urge sb. to hurry up/urge *or* drive sb. on to better and better performances; **b)** *(in Bewegung setzen)* drive; power ⟨*ship, aircraft*⟩; **c)** *(veranlassen)* drive; **jmdn. [dazu] ~, etw. zu tun** drive sb. to do sth.; **d)** *(anschwemmen)* **etw. ~:** wash sth. up **(an** + *Akk.* on to); **etw. an den Strand ~:** wash sth. ashore *or* up; **e)** *(Gartenbau)* force. **2.** *unr. itr. V.; mit sein (herantreiben)* drift *or* float ashore

Ạn·treiber der *(abwertend)* slave-driver

ạn|treten 1. *unr. itr. V.; mit sein* **a)** *(sich aufstellen)* form up; *(in Linie)* line up; *(Milit.)* fall in; **in Reih und Glied ~:** form up in rank and file; fall in; **b)** *(sich stellen)* meet one's opponent; *(als Mannschaft)* line up; **~ gegen** meet; *(als Mannschaft)* line up against; **zum Rückspiel ~:** line up for the return match; **c)** *(sich einfinden)* report **(bei** to); **zum Dienst/zur Arbeit ~:** report for duty/work. **2.** *unr. tr. V.* **a)** start ⟨*job, apprenticeship*⟩; take up ⟨*position, appointment*⟩; start, set out on ⟨*journey*⟩; begin ⟨*prison sentence*⟩; come into ⟨*inheritance*⟩; **jmds. Nachfolge ~:** succeed sb.; **den Urlaub ~:** go on holiday; **b)** *(festtreten)* tread down ⟨*soil*⟩

Ạn·trieb der a) *(Triebkraft)* drive; **ein Fahrzeug mit elektrischem ~:** an electrically powered *or* driven vehicle; **b)** *(Anreiz)* impulse; *(Psych.)* drive; impulse; **jmdm. neuen ~ geben** give sb. fresh impetus; **aus eigenem** *od.* **freiem** *od.* **persönlichem ~:** of one's own accord; on one's own initiative

Ạntriebs-: ~achse die *(Technik)* driving axle; **~kraft die** *(Technik)* motive *or* driving power; **~rad das** *(Technik)* drive wheel; **~welle die** *(Technik)* drive shaft

ạn|trinken 1. *unr. refl. V.* **sich** *(Dat.)* **einen Rausch/Schwips ~:** get drunk/tipsy; **sich** *(Dat.)* **einen ~** *(ugs.)* get sloshed *(coll.)*; **sich** *(Dat.)* **Mut ~:** give oneself Dutch courage. **2.** *unr. tr. V.* start drinking ⟨*wine, coffee, etc.*⟩; start drinking from ⟨*glass*⟩; start drinking out of ⟨*bottle*⟩; **eine schon angetrunkene Flasche Wein** a bottle of wine that has/had already been started

Ạn·tritt der a) beginning; **bei ~ seiner Stellung** on taking up his post; **vor ~ Ihres Urlaubs** before you go *or* before going on holiday *(Brit.) or (Amer.)* vacation; **vor ~ der Reise** before setting out on the journey; **bei ~ des Erbes/Amtes** on coming into the inheritance/taking up office; **b)** *(Sport)* acceleration *no indef. art.*

Ạntritts-: ~besuch der [formal] first visit; **seinen ~besuch bei jmdm. machen** pay one's [formal] first visit to sb.; **~rede die** inaugural speech; **~vor·lesung die** inaugural lecture

ạn|trocknen *itr. V.; mit sein* **a)** *(festkleben)* **an etw.** *(Dat.)* **~:** dry and stick to sth.; **b)** *(ein wenig trocknen)* start *or* begin to dry

ạn|tuckern *itr. V.; mit sein (ugs.)* **angetuckert kommen** come chugging along; *(auf einen zu)* come chugging up

ạn|tun *unr. tr. V.* **a) sich** *(Dat.)* **etw. Gutes ~:** give oneself a treat; treat oneself; **jmdm. ein Leid ~:** hurt sb.; **jmdm. etwas Böses/ein Unrecht ~:** do sb. harm/an injustice; **tu mir das nicht an!** don't do that to me!; **tu dir keinen Zwang an!** *(ugs.)* don't stand on ceremony!; **sich** *(Dat.)* **etw. ~** *(ugs. verhüll.)* do away with oneself; **b) das/er** *usw.* **hat es ihr angetan** she was taken with it/him *etc.*; *s. auch* **angetan 2; c)** *(geh.: anziehen)* **[sich** *(Dat.)***] etw. ~:** put sth. on; don sth.

¹ạn|turnen ['antœrnən] *(ugs.)* **1.** *tr. V.* **jmdn. ~:** ⟨*drugs, music, etc.*⟩ turn sb. on *(coll.)*. **2.** *itr. V.* turn people on *(coll.)*

²ạn|turnen *itr. V.; mit sein (ugs.)* **angeturnt kommen** come romping along; *(auf einen zu)* come romping up

Antwerpen [ant'vɛrpn̩] **(das); ~s** Antwerp

Antwort ['antvɔrt] **die; ~, ~en a)** *(Erwiderung)* answer; reply; *(bei Examen usw.)* answer; **er gab mir keine ~:** he didn't answer [me] *or* reply; he made no answer *or* reply; **er gab mir keine ~ auf meine Frage** he did not reply to *or* answer my question; **wer viel fragt, bekommt viel Antwort[en]** *(Spr.)* you'll have to make up your own mind; **keine ~ ist auch eine ~:** your/her *etc.* silence speaks for itself; **in ~ auf etw.** *(Akk.)* *(Amtsspr.)* in reply to sth.; **um ~ wird gebeten** *(auf Einladungskarten)* RSVP; **b)** *(Reaktion)* response; **als ~ auf etw.** *(Akk.)* in response to sth.

ạntworten *itr. V.* **a)** *(erwidern)* answer; reply; **auf etw.** *(Akk.)* **~:** answer sth.; reply to sth.; **jmdm. ~:** answer sb.; reply to sb.; **jmdm. auf seine Frage ~:** reply to *or* answer sb.'s question; **wie/was soll ich ihm ~?** what answer shall I give him?/what shall I tell him?; **mit Ja/Nein ~:** answer yes/no; **b)** *(reagieren)* respond **(auf** + *Akk.* to)

Ạntwort-: ~post·karte die *(Postw.)* reply card; **~schein der: internationaler ~schein** *(Postw.)* international reply coupon; **~schreiben das** reply **(auf** + *Akk.* to)

ạn|vertrauen 1. *tr. V.* **a)** *(übergeben)* **jmdm. etw. ~:** entrust sth. to sb.; entrust sb. with sth.; **sein Kind jmdm. ~:** entrust one's child to sb.'s care; **b)** *(mitteilen)* **jmdm./seinem Tagebuch etw. ~:** confide sth. to sb./one's diary. **2.** *refl. V.* **a)** *(sich mitteilen)* **sich jmdm. ~:** confide in sb.; **b)** *(sich schützen lassen)* **sich jmdm./einer Sache ~:** put one's trust in sb./sth.

ạn·verwandt *Adj. (geh.)* related

Ạn·verwandte der/die *(geh.)* relation

ạn|visieren *tr. V.* **a)** *(Milit.)* align the *or* one's sights on; **b)** *(anstreben)* aim at

ạn|wachsen *unr. itr. V.; mit sein* **a)** *(festwachsen)* grow on; **wieder ~** ⟨*finger, toe*⟩ grow back on; **die transplantierte Haut ist angewachsen** the skin graft has/skin grafts have taken; **angewachsene Ohrläppchen** earlobes attached to the sides of one's head; **b)** *(Wurzeln schlagen)* take root; **steh nicht da wie angewachsen** *(ugs.)* don't just stand there like a stuffed dummy; **c)** *(zunehmen)* increase; grow

ạn|wackeln *itr. V.; mit sein (ugs.)* **angewackelt kommen** come waddling along; *(auf einen zu)* come waddling up

ạn|wählen *tr. V.* dial; **jmdn. ~:** dial sb.'s number

Anwalt ['anvalt] **der; ~[e]s, Anwälte** ['anvɛltə], **Anwältin die; ~, ~nen a)** *(Rechts~)* lawyer; solicitor *(Brit.)*; attorney *(Amer.)*; *(vor Gericht)* barrister *(Brit.)*; attorney[-at-law] *(Amer.)*; advocate *(Scot.)*; **einen ~ nehmen** get a lawyer *or (Amer.)* an attorney; **b)** *(Fürsprecher)* advocate; champion

Ạnwalts·büro das a) *(Räume)* lawyer's office; solicitor's office *(Brit.)*; **b)** *(Sozietät)* firm of solicitors *(Brit.)*; law firm *(Amer.)*

Ạnwaltschaft die; ~, ~en a) *(Gesamtheit der Anwälte)* legal profession; **b)** *(Amt) s.* **Anwalt a:** profession of lawyer/solicitor/attorney/barrister/advocate; **c)** *o. Pl. (Vertretung)* **die ~ in einer Sache übernehmen/ablehnen** take on/refuse to take on a case

Ạnwalts-: ~kammer die *(Rechtsw.)* *professional association of lawyers;* **~kanzlei die** *s.* **~büro**

ạn|wandeln *tr. V. (geh.)* come over

Ạnwandelung, Ạn·wandlung die *(Laune)* mood; *(leichter Anfall)* fit; **in einer ~ von Großzügigkeit** *usw.* in a fit of generosity *etc.*; **dann bekommt er wieder seine ~en** then he gets one of his moods again; **eine ~ von Furcht/Schwermütigkeit** a sudden feeling of fear/a fit of melancholy

ạn|wärmen *tr. V.* warm up; warm ⟨*hands, feet*⟩

Ạn·wärter der a) candidate **(auf** + *Akk.* for); *(Sport)* contender **(auf** + *Akk.* for); **b)** *(auf den Thron)* claimant; *(Thronerbe)* heir **(auf** + *Akk.* to)

Ạn·wärterin die a) *s.* **Anwärter a; b)** *(auf den Thron)* claimant; *(Thronerbin)* heiress **(auf** + *Akk.* to)

Ạnwartschaft die; ~, ~en candidacy, candidature **(auf** + *Akk.* for); *(Sport)* being in contention **(auf** + *Akk.* for); *(auf den Thron, einen Titel)* claim **(auf** + *Akk.* to)

ạn|watscheln *itr. V.; mit sein (ugs.)* **angewatschelt kommen** come waddling along; *(auf einen zu)* come waddling up

ạn|wehen 1. *tr. V.* **a)** *(geh.: gegen jmdn. wehen)* ⟨*wind, breeze*⟩ blow [up]on; **b)** *(anhäufen)* drift ⟨*snow, sand, etc.*⟩. **2.** *itr. V.; mit sein (sich anhäufen)* drift

ạn|weisen *unr. tr. V.* **a)** *(beauftragen)* **jmdn. ~:** give sb. instructions; **jmdn. ~, etw. zu tun** instruct *or* direct sb. to do sth.; **b)** *(zuweisen)* **jmdm. etw. ~:** allocate sth. to sb.; **c)** *(anleiten)* instruct; **d)** *(überweisen)* remit; *(die Auszahlung veranlassen)* order the payment of; *s. auch* **angewiesen 2**

Ạn·weisung die a) *(Anordnung)* instruction; **~ haben, etw. zu tun** have instructions to do sth.; **auf ~ der Behörde** by order of *or* on instructions *pl.* from the authorities; **b)** *(das Zuteilen)* allocation; **c)** *(Gebrauchs~)* instructions *pl.*; **d)** *(Überweisung)* remittance; *(Anordnung zur Auszahlung)* **die ~ erfolgt demnächst** payment will be ordered shortly; **e)** *(Bankw.: Formular)* payment order

ạnwendbar *Adj.* applicable **(auf** + *Akk.* to); **schwer ~:** difficult to apply; **die Regel ist hier nicht ~:** the rule doesn't apply here

Ạnwendbarkeit die; ~: applicability **(auf** + *Akk.* to)

ạn|wenden *unr. (auch regelm.) tr. V.* use, employ ⟨*process, trick, method, violence, force*⟩; use ⟨*medicine, money, time*⟩; take ⟨*care, trouble*⟩ **(auf** + *Akk.* over); apply ⟨*rule, paragraph, proverb, etc.*⟩ **(auf** + *Akk.* to); **sich auf etw.** *(Akk.)* **~ lassen** be applicable to sth.; apply to sth.

Anwender der; ~s, ~ *(DV)* user
An·wendung die a) *s.* **anwenden**: use; employment; taking; application; **etw. in ~** *(Akk.) od.* **zur ~ bringen** *(Amtsspr.)* apply sth.; **zur ~ kommen** *od.* **gelangen, ~ finden** *(Amtsspr.)* ‹*rule, paragraph, etc.*› apply, be applicable; **b)** *(Med.)* application
Anwendungs-: ~bereich der, ~gebiet das range of application; *(eines Gesetzes, einer Regel)* scope; **~möglichkeit die** possible use *or* application
an|werben *unr. tr. V.* recruit (**für** to); *(Milit.)* enlist, recruit; **sich ~ lassen** be recruited; *(Milit.)* enlist (**für** in)
An·werbung die *s.* **anwerben**: recruitment (**für** to); enrolment (**für** in)
an|werfen *unr. tr. V.* **a)** *(ugs.: in Gang bringen)* start [up] ‹*machine, engine, vehicle*›; swing ‹*propeller*›; put *or* switch on ‹*electrical device*›; **b)** *(an etw. werfen)* **Kalk/Mörtel** *usw.* **an eine Wand ~**: rough-cast a wall [with lime/plaster *etc.*]
An·wesen das property
anwesend *Adj.* present; **die nicht ~en Mitglieder** the members [who are/were] not present; **bei etw. ~ sein** be present at sth.; **ich war nicht ganz ~** *(fig. ugs. scherzh.)* I wasn't quite with it *(coll.)*
Anwesende der/die; *adj. Dekl.* **die ~n** those present; **jeder ~/einige ~/alle ~n** everyone/some of those/all those present; **~ natürlich ausgenommen** present company excepted, of course
Anwesenheit die; ~: presence; **in ~**: in the presence (*Gen. od.* **von** of)
Anwesenheits·liste die attendance list
an|wetzen *itr. V.; mit sein (ugs.)* **angewetzt kommen** come rushing *or* tearing along; *(auf einen zu)* come rushing *or* tearing up
an|widern ['anvi:dɐn] *tr. V.* nauseate
an|winkeln *tr. V.* bend ‹*knee, arm, etc.*›
an|winseln *tr. V.* whimper at; **jmdn. um Hilfe ~**: come whining to sb. for help
Anwohner ['anvo:nɐ] **der**; ~s, ~: resident; **Parken nur für ~**: residents-only parking
Anwohnerschaft die residents *pl.*
An·wurf der a) *(Vorwurf) (esp. unjustified)* reproach; *(Beschuldigung) (esp. false)* accusation; **b)** *o. Pl. (Handball)* throw-off; *(Korbball)* centre pass
an|wurzeln *itr. V.; mit sein* take root; **wie angewurzelt [da] stehen/stehenbleiben** stand rooted to the spot
An·zahl die; *o. Pl.* number; **eine ganze ~**: a whole lot
an|zahlen *tr. V.* put down *or* pay a deposit on; *(bei Ratenzahlung)* make a down payment on; **50 DM ~**: put down 50 marks as a deposit/make a down payment of 50 marks
an|zählen *tr. V. (Boxen)* **jmdn. ~**: start to give sb. the count
An·zahlung die deposit; *(bei Ratenzahlung)* down payment; **eine ~ auf etw.** *(Akk.)* **machen** *od.* **leisten** put down *or* pay a deposit on sth./make a down payment on sth.
an|zapfen 1. *tr. V.* **a)** tap ‹*barrel, tree*›; **b)** *(ugs.: zum Abhören)* tap ‹*telephone line, wire*›; **c)** *(ugs.) s.* **anpumpen. 2.** *itr. V.* tap a/the barrel; **frisch ~**: tap a/the new barrel
An·zeichen das sign; indication; *(Med.)* symptom; **alle ~ deuten darauf hin, daß ...**: all the signs *or* indications are that ...
an|zeichnen *tr. V.* **a)** *(an etw. zeichnen)* draw (**an** + *Akk.* on); **b)** *(markieren)* mark
Anzeige ['antsaigə] **die**; ~, ~n **a)** *(Straf~)* report; **gegen jmdn. [eine] ~ [wegen etw.] erstatten** report sb. to the police/the authorities [for sth.]; **jmdn./etw. zur ~ bringen** *(Amtsspr.)* report sb./sth. to the police/the authorities; **b)** *(Inserat)* advertisement; **eine ~ in einer Zeitung aufgeben** place an advertisement in a newspaper; **c)** *(Bekanntmachung)* announcement; **d)** *(ablesbarer Stand)* display; *(eines Meßinstruments)* reading; **e)** *(Gerät)* display unit
an|zeigen *tr. V.* **a)** *(Strafanzeige erstatten)* **jmdn./etw. ~**: report sb./sth. to the police/the authorities; **sich selbst ~**: voluntarily admit an/the offence; **b)** *(zeigen)* show; indicate; show ‹*time, date*›; **c)** *(bekanntgeben)* announce; **d)** *(wissen lassen, geh.: ankündigen)* **jmdm. etw. ~**: inform *or* notify sb. of sth.; **jmdm. ~, daß ...**: inform *or* notify sb. [of the fact] that ...
Anzeigen-: ~blatt das advertiser; **~teil der** advertisement section *or* pages *pl.*; **~werbung die** newspaper and magazine advertising
Anzeige·pflicht die; *o. Pl.* **a)** statutory obligation to report a/the birth/death/[criminal] offence *etc.*; **b)** *s.* **Meldepflicht a**
An·zeiger der a) indicator; **b)** *(Zeitung)* advertiser
Anzeige·tafel die *(Sport)* scoreboard
an|zetteln *tr. V. (abwertend)* hatch ‹*plot, intrigue*›; instigate ‹*revolt*›; foment ‹*war*›
an|ziehen 1. *unr. tr. V.* **a)** *(an sich ziehen)* draw up ‹*knees, feet, etc.*›; **b)** *(anlocken)* attract; draw; *(durch Schönheit, freundliches Betragen usw.)* attract; **sich von jmdm. angezogen fühlen** feel attracted to sb.; **c)** *(anspannen)* tighten, pull tight ‹*rope, wire, chain*›; tighten ‹*guitar-string*›; **d)** *(festziehen)* tighten ‹*screw, knot, belt, etc.*›; put on, pull on ‹*handbrake*›; **e)** *(Kleidung anlegen)* dress; **sich ~**: get dressed; **f)** put on ‹*clothes*›; **sich** *(Dat.)* **etw. ~**: put sth. on; **jmdm. etw. ~**: put sth. on sb.; *(als Hilfeleistung)* put sth. on for sb.; **g)** *(aufnehmen)* absorb ‹*moisture*›; take on ‹*taste, smell*›; **h)** *(Physik)* ‹*magnet, body, etc.*› attract. **2.** *unr. itr. V.* **a)** *(Tempo beschleunigen)* accelerate; **b)** *(sich in Bewegung setzen)* ‹*car, train*› pull away, move off; ‹*horse*› move off; **c)** *(Brettspiel)* make the first move; move *or* go first; **d)** *(Börsenw., Kaufmannsspr.)* ‹*prices, costs*› rise, increase; ‹*shares, securities, commodities*› advance, move ahead
anziehend *Adj.* attractive; engaging ‹*manner, smile*›
An·ziehung die attraction
Anziehungs·kraft die a) *(Physik)* attractive force; force of attraction; **b)** *o. Pl. (Reiz)* attraction
an|zischen 1. *tr. V.* **a)** hiss at; **b)** *(ugs.: anfahren)* snarl at. **2.** *itr. V.; mit sein (ugs.: sich nähern)* **angezischt kommen** come whizzing along; *(auf einen zu)* come whizzing up
an|zockeln *itr. V.; mit sein (ugs.)* **angezockelt kommen** come jogging along; *(auf einen zu)* come jogging up; ‹*cart*› come trundling along/up
An·zug der a) *(Herren~)* suit; **jmdn. aus dem ~ stoßen** *od.* **boxen** *(salopp)* beat *or* knock the living daylights *(sl.) or* the hell *(coll.)* out of sb.; **b) im ~ sein** ‹*danger*› be imminent; ‹*storm*› be approaching; ‹*fever, illness*› be coming on; ‹*enemy*› be advancing; **c)** *(Beschleunigung)* acceleration; **d)** *(Brettspiele)* first move; **~ haben** have the first move
anzüglich ['antsy:klɪç] **1.** *Adj.* **a)** insinuating ‹*remark, question*›; **werde bloß nicht ~!** just don't start making insinuating remarks; **b)** *(anstößig)* offensive ‹*joke, remark*›. **2.** *adv.* **a)** in an insinuating way; **b)** *(anstößig)* offensively
Anzüglichkeit die *s.* **anzüglich a, b: a)** *o. Pl. (Art)* insinuating nature; offensiveness; **b)** *(Bemerkung)* insinuating remark; offensive remark/joke
Anzug·stoff der suiting
Anzugs·vermögen das acceleration
an|zünden *tr. V.* light; **ein Gebäude** *usw.* **~**: set fire to a building *etc.*; set a building *etc.* on fire
An·zünder der *(Gas~)* gas lighter; *(Feuer~)* fire-lighter *(Brit.)*
an|zweifeln *tr. V.* doubt; question
an|zwinkern *tr. V.* wink at
an|zwitschern *refl. V. (ugs.)* **in sich** *(Dat.)* **einen ~**: get sloshed *(coll.)*
AOK [a:|o:'ka:] **die**; ~ *Abk.* **Allgemeine Ortskrankenkasse**
Äols·harfe ['ɛ:ɔls-] **die** aeolian harp
Äon [ɛ'o:n] **der**; ~s, ~en *(geh.)* aeon
Aorta [a'ɔrta] **die**; ~, **Aorten** *(Med.)* aorta
Apanage [apa'na:ʒə] **die**; ~, ~n apanage; *(fig.)* subsidy
apart [a'part] **1.** *Adj.* individual *attrib.*; **~ sein** be individual in style. **2.** *adv.* **a)** in an individual style; **b)** *(Buchhandel: einzeln)* individually
Apartheid [a'pa:ɐthait] **die**; ~: apartheid *no art.*
Apartheid·politik die policy of apartheid
Apartheit die; ~: individuality
Apartment [a'partmənt] **das**; ~s, ~s studio flat *(Brit.)*; flatlet *(Brit.)*; small flat *(Brit.)*; studio apartment *(Amer.)*
Apartment·haus das block of studio flats *(Brit.) or (Amer.)* studio apartments
Apathie [apa'ti:] **die**; ~, ~n apathy
apathisch [a'pa:tɪʃ] **1.** *Adj.* apathetic. **2.** *adv.* apathetically
Apenninen [apɛ'ni:nən] *Pl.* **die ~**: the Apennines
Apennin[en]·halbinsel die *o. Pl.* Apennine peninsula
aper ['a:pɐ] *Adj. (südd., österr., schweiz.)* snowless; bare of snow *pred.*; ‹*street*› clear of snow *pred.*
Aperçu [apɛr'sy:] **das**; ~s, ~s *(geh.)* bon mot
Aperitif [aperi'ti:f] **der**; ~s, ~s aperitif
apern ['a:pɐn] *itr. V. (südd., österr., schweiz.)* **es apert** the snow is going; **die Hänge/Straßen ~**: the snow on the slopes is going/the streets are becoming clear of snow
Apex ['a:pɛks] **der**; ~, **Apizes** ['a:pitse:s] **a)** *(Astron.)* apex; **b)** *(Sprachw.) (Längezeichen)* length mark; *(Betonungszeichen)* stress mark
Apfel ['apfl] **der**; ~s, **Äpfel** ['ɛpfl] **a)** apple; **der ~ fällt nicht weit vom Stamm** *od. (ugs. scherzh.)* **Pferd** *(Spr.)* it's in the blood; **~ im Schlafrock** *(Kochk.)* apple dumpling; **Äpfel und Birnen zusammenzählen, Äpfel mit Birnen addieren** *(ugs.)* lump together totally different things; **[etw.] für einen ~ und ein Ei [kaufen]** [buy sth.] for a song; **in den sauren ~ beißen [und etw. tun]** *(ugs.)* grasp the nettle [and do sth.]; **b)** *(~baum)* apple-tree
Apfel-: ~baum der apple-tree; **~blüte die a)** apple-blossom; **b)** *(das Blühen)* blossoming of the apple-trees; **während der ~blüte** while the apple-trees are/were in blossom
Äpfelchen das; ~s, ~: little apple
apfel, Apfel-: ~grün apple-green; **~korn der** apple-flavoured schnapps; **~kuchen der** apple-cake; *(mit Äpfeln belegt)* apple flan; **gedeckter ~kuchen** apple pie; **~most der a)** (~saft) apple-juice; **b)** *(südd.: gegorener ~saft)* cider; **~mus das** apple purée; *(zu Fleisch)* apple sauce; **~saft der** apple-juice; **~schimmel der** dapple-grey [horse]
Apfelsine [apfl'zi:nə] **die**; ~, ~n **a)** orange; **b)** *(Baum)* orange-tree
Apfel-: ~strudel der apfelstrudel; **~tasche die** apple turnover *or* puff; **~wein der** cider; **~wickler der** *(Zool.)* codling moth
Aphorismus [afo'rɪsmʊs] **der**; ~, **Aphorismen** *(geh.)* aphorism
aphoristisch *(geh.)* **1.** *Adj.* aphoristic. **2.** *adv.* aphoristically
Aphrodisiakum [afrodi'zi:akʊm] **das**; ~s, **Aphrodisiaka** *(Med.)* aphrodisiac
Aplomb [a'plõ:] **der**; ~s *(geh.)* aplomb
APO, Apo ['a:po] **die**; ~ *Abk.* **außerparlamentarische Opposition**
apodiktisch [apo'dɪktɪʃ] *Adj. (Philos., geh.)* apodictic
Apokalypse [apoka'lʏpsə] **die**; ~, ~n apocalypse

apokalyptisch [apoka'lʏptɪʃ] *(Rel., fig.)* **1.** *Adj.* apocalyptic; **die Apokalyptischen Reiter** the Four Horsemen of the Apocalypse. **2.** *adv.* apocalyptically

apokryph [apo'kry:f] *Adj. (Rel., fig.)* apocryphal; **die Apokryphen** the Apocrypha *sing.*

ạpolitisch 1. *Adj.* apolitical. **2.** *adv.* apolitically

Apoll [a'pɔl] **der; ~s, ~s** *(geh.)* Apollo

apollinisch [apɔ'li:nɪʃ] *Adj. (bes. Philos.)* apollonian

Apollo [a'pɔlo] **der; ~s, ~s** *(Myth., geh.)* Apollo

Apologet [apolo'ge:t] **der; ~en, ~en** apologist

Apologetik [apolo'ge:tɪk] **die; ~, ~en a)** *(geh.: Rechtfertigung)* apologia (*Gen.* for); **b)** *o. Pl. (Theol.)* apologetics *sing.*

Apologetin die; ~, ~nen apologist

Apologie [apolo'gi:] **die; ~, ~n** *(geh.)* apologia (*Gen.* for)

Aporie [apo'ri:] **die; ~, ~n** *(Philos., geh.)* aporia

Apostel [a'pɔstl̩] **der; ~s, ~:** apostle; **die zwölf ~:** the twelve Apostles

-apostel der *(meist iron.)* apostle of ‹*economic growth, world peace, etc.*›; **ein Frischluft~/Gesundheits~:** a fresh air/health fanatic; **ein Spar~/Abnehm~:** an enthusiastic advocate of saving/slimming

Apọstel-: ~brief der epistle; **~geschichte die a)** *(apokryphe Geschichte)* Apocryphal New Testament story; **b)** *o. Pl. (Buch des N. T.)* Acts of the Apostles *constr. as sing.*

a posteriori [a: pɔste'rio:ri] *(Philos.)* a posteriori

aposteriorisch *(Philos.) Adj., adv.* a posteriori

apostolisch [apɔs'to:lɪʃ] *Adj. (Theol.)* **a)** apostolic; **das Apostolische Glaubensbekenntnis** the Apostles' Creed; **b)** *(päpstlich)* apostolic; **~er Segen** apostolic blessing; **Apostolischer Nuntius** Apostolic Nuncio; **Apostolischer Stuhl** Holy See

Apostroph [apo'stro:f] **der; ~s, ~e** *(Sprachw.)* apostrophe

apostrophieren *tr. V.* **a)** *(Sprachw.: mit Apostroph versehen)* apostrophize; **b) jmdn./etw. als etw. ~:** refer to sb./sth. as sth.; describe sb./sth. as sth.

Apotheke [apo'te:kə] **die; ~, ~n a)** chemist's [shop] *(Brit.)*; drugstore *(Amer.)*; *(im Krankenhaus)* dispensary; **b)** *(Haus~)* medicine cabinet; *(Reise~, Bord~)* first-aid kit; **c)** *(ugs. abwertend: teures Geschäft)* expensive shop; **das ist eine richtige ~:** they charge an arm and a leg there *(coll.)*

apotheken·pflichtig *Adj.* obtainable only at a chemist's [shop] *(Brit.) or (Amer.)* drugstore *postpos.*

Apotheker der; ~s, ~, Apothekerin die; ~, ~nen [dispensing] chemist *(Brit.)*; druggist

Apotheker·preise *Pl. (fig. ugs.)* fancy prices *(coll.)*

Apotheose [apote'o:zə] **die; ~, ~n** *(geh.)* apotheosis

App. *Abk.* **a) Apparat** ext.; **b) Appartement** Apt.

Apparat [apa'ra:t] **der; ~[e]s, ~e a)** *(Technik)* apparatus *no pl.*; *(Haushaltsgerät)* appliance; *(kleiner)* gadget; **b)** *(Radio~)* radio; *(Fernseh~)* television; *(Rasier~)* razor; *(elektrisch)* shaver; *(Foto~)* camera; **wir haben einen neuen Fernseher gekauft, der alte ~ war 15 Jahre alt** we've bought a new television – our old set was fifteen years old; **c)** *(Telefon)* telephone; *(Nebenstelle)* extension; **am ~ verlangt werden** be wanted on the telephone; **am ~!** speaking!; **bleiben Sie am ~!** hold the line; **wer war am ~?** who answered?; who did you speak to?; **d)** *(Personen und Hilfsmittel)* organization; *(Verwaltungs~)* system; **e)** *(ugs.: etwas Ausgefallenes, Riesiges)* whopper *(sl.)*; *(dicker Mensch)* heavyweight; **f)** *(Hochschulw.: Bücher) reference collection of books for a particular course;* **g)** *(Lesarten)* apparatus; **[text]kritischer ~:** apparatus criticus; critical apparatus

Apparate·bau der; *o. Pl. (Technik)* design and manufacture of apparatus

Apparate·medizin die; *o. Pl. (oft abwertend)* high-technology medicine

apparativ [apara'ti:f] **1.** *Adj.* **a)** *(Technik)* **~e Einrichtungen** technical equipment *sing.*; **~e Lehrmittel** machine aids in the classroom; **~e Diagnostik** machine-aided diagnosis; **b)** *(Verwaltung)* **der ~e Ausbau der Organisation** the expansion of the organization's administrative system. **2.** *adv.* **a)** *(Technik)* with the aid of machines *or* technical equipment; **~ am Leben erhalten werden** be kept alive by life-support systems; **b)** *(Verwaltung)* organizationally

Apparatschik [apa'ratʃɪk] **der; ~s, ~s** *(abwertend)* apparatchik

Apparatur [apara'tu:ɐ̯] **die; ~, ~en** apparatus *no pl.*; equipment *no indef. art., no pl.*; *(fig.)* apparatus *no pl*; **~en** *(Kontrollinstrumente usw.)* instruments and controls

Apparillo [apa'rɪlo] **der; ~s, ~s** *(ugs. scherzh.)* contraption *(coll.)*; **Der Karpfen wiegt 6 Kilo. – Mann, ist das ein ~!** The carp weighs 6 kilos – That's 'some 'fish!

Appartement [apartə'mã:, schweiz. auch: -'mɛnt] **das; ~s, ~s** *(schweiz. auch: ~e)* **a)** *s.* **Apartment; b)** *(Hotelsuite)* suite

Appeal [ə'pi:l] **der; ~s** appeal

Appeasement [ə'pi:zmənt] **das; ~s** *(Politik, meist abwertend)* appeasement

Appell [a'pɛl] **der; ~s, ~e a)** *(Mahnung)* appeal (**zu** for, **an** + *Akk.* to); **einen ~ an jmdn. richten** make an appeal to sb.; appeal to sb.; **b)** *(Milit.)* muster; *(Anwesenheits~)* roll-call; *(Besichtigung)* inspection; **zum ~ antreten** fall in for roll-call inspection; **c)** *(Jagdw.)* obedience; **~/keinen ~ haben** be/not be obedient

Appellation [apɛla'tsio:n] **die; ~, ~en** *(Rechtsw., schweiz. sonst veralt.)* appeal

Appellativ [apɛla'ti:f] **das; ~s, ~e, Appellativum** [apɛla'ti:vʊm] **das; ~s, Appellativa** *(Sprachw.)* appellative; common noun

appellieren *itr. V.* appeal (**an** + *Akk.* to)

[1]Appendix [a'pɛndɪks] **der; ~, Appendizes** [-dɪtse:s] *od.* **~es, ~e a)** *(geh.: Anhängsel)* appendage; **b)** *(Buchw.)* appendix

[2]Appendix der *od. (fachspr.:)* **die; ~, Appendizes** *(Anat.)* appendix

Apperzeption [apɛrtsɛp'tsio:n] **die; ~, ~en** *(Philos., Psych.)* apperception

Appetit [ape'ti:t] **der; ~[e]s, ~e** *(auch fig.)* appetite (**auf** + *Akk.* for); **~ auf etw. haben/bekommen** fancy sth.; **ich hätte so richtig ~ auf ...:** I could just fancy *or* eat ...; I could really go for ... *(Amer.)*; **guten ~!** enjoy your meal!; **jmdm. den ~ verderben** spoil sb.'s appetite; **das verschlug uns/ihnen** *usw.* **den ~:** that took away our/their *etc.* appetite; **mit ~ essen** enjoy one's food; **der ~ kommt beim** *od.* **mit dem Essen** appetite comes with eating *(prov.)*

appetit·anregend *Adj.* **a)** *(appetitlich)* appetizing; **b)** *(den Appetit fördernd)* ‹*medicine etc.*› that stimulates the appetite; **~ wirken** stimulate the appetite; **ein ~es Mittel** an appetite-stimulant

Appetit-: ~happen der canapé; **~hemmer der; ~s, ~:** *s.* **~zügler**

appetitlich 1. *Adj.* **a)** *(appetitanregend)* appetizing; **b)** *(sauber, ansprechend)* attractive and hygienic; **c)** *(adrett)* attractive. **2.** *adv.* **a)** *(appetitanregend)* appetizingly; **b)** *(sauber, ansprechend)* attractively and hygienically ‹*packed*›; **ein ~ gedeckter Tisch** an attractively laid table

appetit-, Appetit-: ~los 1. *Adj.* without any appetite *postpos.*; **~los sein** have lost one's appetite; **immer noch ~los sein** still have no appetite; **2.** *adv.* without any appetite; **~losigkeit die; ~:** lack of appetite; **~zügler der** appetite suppressant

Appetizer ['æpɪtaɪzə] **der; ~s, ~** *(Pharm.)* appetite stimulant

applanieren *tr. V. (österr.)* smooth over; settle

applaudieren [aplau'di:rən] *itr. (veralt. auch tr.) V.* applaud; **jmdm./einer Sache ~:** applaud sb./sth.

Applaus [a'plaus] **der; ~es, ~e** applause

applikabel [apli'ka:bl̩] *Adj. (geh.)* applicable

Applikation [aplika'tsio:n] **die; ~, ~en a)** *(Med.: Verabreichung)* administration; *(äußerlich)* application; **b)** *(Textilw.)* appliqué

applizieren [apli'tsi:rən] *tr. V.* **a)** *(Med.)* administer; *(äußerlich)* apply; **b)** *(Textilw.)* appliqué

apportieren [apɔr'ti:rən] *tr. (auch itr.) V. (Jägerspr.)* retrieve; fetch

Apportier·hund der retriever

Apposition die *(Sprachw.)* apposition

appretieren [apre'ti:rən] *tr. V. (bes. Textilind.)* dress, finish ‹*fabric, linen*›

Appretur [apre'tu:ɐ̯] **die; ~, ~en** *(bes. Textilind.)* dressing; finishing

Approbation [aproba'tsio:n] **die; ~, ~en** licence to practise *(as a doctor, dentist, chemist)*

approbieren [apro'bi:rən] *tr. V. (österr., sonst veralt.)* approve

approbiert *Adj.* registered ‹*doctor, dentist, chemist*›

Apr. *Abk.* **April** Apr.

Après-Ski [aprɛ'ʃi:] **das; ~ a)** *(Kleidung)* après-ski outfit; **b)** *(Unterhaltung)* après-ski [entertainment]

Aprikose [apri'ko:zə] **die; ~, ~n a)** *(Frucht)* apricot; **b)** *(Baum)* apricot-tree

Aprikosen·marmelade die apricot jam

April [a'prɪl] **der; ~[s], ~e** April; **der ~:** April; **~, ~!** April fool!; **der 1. ~:** the first of April; *(in bezug auf Aprilscherze)* April Fool's *or* All Fools' Day; **jmdn. in den ~ schicken** make an April fool of sb.

April-: ~scherz der April-fool trick; **das ist doch wohl ein ~scherz!** *(fig.)* you/they *etc.* can't be serious!; you/they *etc.* must be joking!; **~wetter das;** *o. Pl.* April weather

a priori [a:pri'o:ri] *(Philos.)* a priori

apriorisch *(Philos.) Adj., adv.* a priori

apropos [apro'po:] *Adv.* apropos; by the way; incidentally

Aquädukt [akvɛ'dʊkt] **der** *od.* **das; ~[e]s, ~e** aqueduct

aquamarin [akvama'ri:n] *s.* **~blau**

Aquamarin der; ~s, ~e aquamarine

aquamarin·blau *Adj.* aquamarine

Aquanaut [akva'naut] **der; ~en, ~en** aquanaut

Aquaplaning [akva'pla:nɪŋ] **das; ~[s]** aquaplaning

Aquarell [akva'rɛl] **das; ~s, ~e** *(Malerei)* water-colour [painting]

Aquarell·farbe die water-colour

aquarellieren *itr. V.* paint in water-colours

Aquarell-: ~maler der water-colour painter; water-colourist; **~malerei die a)** *o. Pl. (Maltechnik)* water-colour painting; **in ~malerei** in water-colour; **b)** *(Bild)* water-colour

Aquarien [a'kva:riən] *s.* **Aquarium**

Aquarien-: ~fisch der aquarium fish; **~haus das** aquarium

Aquarium [a'kva:riʊm] **das; ~s, Aquarien** aquarium

Aquatinta [akva'tɪnta] **die; ~, Aquatinten** *(bild. Kunst)* aquatint

Äquator [ɛ'kva:tɔr] **der; ~s; ~en** [-'to:rən] *(Erd~, Math.)* equator

äquatorial [ɛkvato'ria:l] *Adj.* equatorial

Äquator·taufe die crossing-the-line ceremony

Aquavit [akva'vi:t] **der; ~s, ~e** aquavit

Äquilibrist [ɛkvili'brɪst] **der; ~en, ~en** equilibrist

Äquinoktium [ɛkvi'nɔktsi̯ʊm] **das; ~s, Äquinoktien** *(Geogr.)* equinox

äquivalent [ɛkviva'lɛnt] *Adj.* equivalent

Äquivalent das; ~[e]s, ~e equivalent; *(Ersatz)* appropriate replacement; *(Entschädigung)* appropriate compensation

Äquivalenz [ɛkviva'lɛnts] **die; ~, ~en** *(auch Math., Logik)* equivalence

Ar [a:ɐ̯] **das** *od.* **der; ~s, ~e** are

Ära ['ɛ:ra] **die; ~, Ären** era; **die ~ Kreisky** the Kreisky era

Araber ['a:rabɐ] **der; ~s, ~** *(auch Pferd)* Arab; Arabian

Arabeske [ara'bɛskə] **die; ~, ~n** *(bild. Kunst, Musik)* arabesque

Arabien [a'ra:bi̯ən] **(das); ~s** Arabia

arabisch *Adj.* Arabian; Arab; Arabic ⟨*language, numeral, dialect, alphabet, literature*⟩; **die Arabische Halbinsel** the Arabian Peninsula; **das Arabische** Arabic; *s. auch* **deutsch, ²Deutsche**

Arabisch das; ~[s] Arabic *s. auch* **Deutsch**

Arabistik [ara'bɪstɪk] **die; ~:** Arabic studies *pl., no art.*

Aralie [a'ra:li̯ə] **die; ~, ~n** *(Bot.)* aralia

aramäisch [ara'mɛ:ɪʃ] *Adj.* Aramaic; **das Aramäische** Aramaic; *s. auch* **deutsch, Deutsch, ²Deutsche**

Arancini [aran'tʃi:ni], **Aranzini** [aran'tsi:ni] *Pl. (bes. österr.) sugar- or chocolate-coated candied orange peel*

Aräo·meter [arɛo-] **das** *(Physik)* hydrometer

Arbeit ['arbai̯t] **die; ~, ~en a)** *(auch Sport, Jagdw., Physik)* work *no indef. art.*; *(Politik, Soziol.: Arbeitskraft)* labour *no indef. art.*; **die ~[en] am Staudamm** [the] work on the dam; **an die ~ gehen, sich an die ~ machen** get down to work; **die ~ mit Asbest ist gesundheitsschädigend** working with asbestos is injurious to health; **eine widerliche ~ sein** be a revolting job *or* task; **die ~ läuft uns nicht davon** *(scherzh.)* the work can wait; **ganze** *od.* **gründliche ~ leisten** *od.* **tun** *od.* **machen** *(auch fig. iron.)* make a good job of it; **nur halbe ~ machen** leave the job half-done; only half do the job; **Tag der ~:** Labour Day; **an** *od.* **bei der ~ sein** be at work; **jmdm. bei der ~ zusehen** watch sb. working *or* at work; **mit der ~ beginnen** start work; **bei der ~ mit Chemikalien** when working with chemicals; **viel ~ haben** have a lot of work [to do]; **seine ~ tun** *od.* **machen** do one's job; **gute ~ leisten** do good work; work well; **[wieder] an die ~!** [back] to work!; **die ~ niederlegen** stop work; *(bei manueller ~)* down tools; **der/die hat die ~ nicht erfunden** *(scherzh.)* he/she is not the world's hardest worker; **etw. in ~ geben** have sth. made; **jmdm. etw. in ~ geben** get sb. to make sth.; **etw. in ~ haben** be working on sth.; **~ schändet nicht** work's no disgrace; **erst die ~, dann das Vergnügen** business before pleasure; **b)** *o. Pl. (Mühe)* trouble; **~ machen** cause bother *or* trouble; **jmdm. ~ machen** make work for sb.; **machen Sie sich keine ~!** don't go to *or* put yourself to any trouble; **sich** *(Dat.)* **~ [mit etw.] machen** take trouble [over sth.]; **viel ~ machen** *od.* **kosten** cost a lot of effort *or* hard work; **das war eine ~!** what a job that was!; **c)** *o. Pl. (~splatz, ~sstätte)* work *no indef. art.*; *(Stellung)* job; **eine ~ suchen/finden** look for/find work *or* a job; **eine ~ als ...:** work *or* a job as ...; **zur** *od.* *(ugs.)* **auf ~ gehen** go to work; **auf ~ sein** *(ugs.)* be at work; **auf ~ gehen** *(ugs.: berufstätig sein)* work; have a job; **ohne ~ sein** be out of work; be unemployed; **bei jmdm. in ~ stehen** *od.* **sein** work for sb.; be employed by sb.; **vor/nach der ~** *(ugs.)* before/after work; **d)** *(Aufträge)* work *no indef. art.*; **e)** *(Produkt, Ausführung)* work; *(handwerkliche ~)* piece of work; *(kurze schriftliche ~)* article; *(Dissertation)* dissertation; **f)** *(Klassen~)* test; **eine ~ schreiben/schreiben lassen** do/set a test

arbeiten 1. *itr. V.* **a)** *(Arbeit leisten)* work; **zu ~ haben** have work to do; **~ wie ein Pferd/** *(ugs.)* **ein Wilder** work like a slave *or* a Trojan/like mad; **er arbeitet für zwei** he does the work of two; **an etw.** *(Dat.)* **~:** work on sth.; **an sich** *(Dat.)* **~:** work to improve one's abilities; **mit Silber/Akrylfarben ~:** work in silver/acrylic paints; **mit Behinderten/Taubstummen ~:** work with the disabled/the deaf-and-dumb; **sein Geld ~ lassen** *(fig.)* make one's money work for one; **b)** *(beruflich tätig sein)* work; **seine Frau arbeitet** his wife has a job *or* works; **40 Stunden in der Woche ~:** work 40 hours a week *or* a 40-hour week; **das Büro arbeitet freitags nur bis 14⁰⁰** *(fig.)* the office closes at 2 p.m. on Fridays; **bei der Bahn/einer Firma ~:** work on the railways *(Brit.)* *or* *(Amer.)* at the railroad/for a firm; **c) über jmdn./etw. ~** *(sich befassen mit)* work on sb./sth.; **d)** *(wirksam sein)*; **für/gegen jmdn./etw. ~:** work for/against sb./sth.; **die Zeit arbeitet für/gegen uns** time is on our side/against us; **an jmds. Untergang** *(Dat.)* **~:** work to bring about sb.'s downfall; **e)** *(funktionieren)* ⟨*heart, lungs, etc.*⟩ work, function; ⟨*machine*⟩ work, operate; **mit Gas/Sonnenenergie ~:** run on gas/solar energy; **automatisch ~:** be automatic; **in meinem Magen arbeitet es** *(fig.)* my stomach is grumbling; **f)** *(ankämpfen)* work hard **(gegen** against); **g)** *(sich verändern)* ⟨*wood*⟩ warp; ⟨*must*⟩ ferment; ⟨*dough*⟩ rise; **h)** *(Sport)* work **(mit** with); **i)** *(schneidern)* **wo/bei wem lassen Sie ~?** where do you have *or* get your clothes made?; who makes your clothes?. **2.** *tr. V.* **a)** *(herstellen)* make; *(in Ton, Silber, usw.)* work; make; fashion; **b)** *(tun)* do; **was ~ Sie?** what are you doing?; *(beruflich)* what do you do for a living?; what's your job? **3.** *refl. V.* **a) sich müde/krank ~:** tire oneself out/make oneself ill with work; **sich zu Tode ~:** work oneself to death; **b)** *(Strecke zurücklegen)*; **sich durch etw./in etw.** *(Akk.)* **~:** work one's way through/into sth.; **sich nach oben ~** *(fig.)* work one's way up; **c) sich** *(Dat.)* **die Hände wund ~:** work one's fingers to the bone; **d)** *unpers.* **hier arbeitet es sich gut** this is a good place to work; **mit dieser Maschine arbeitet es sich gut/schneller** this machine is easy to work with/the work goes faster with this machine; **mit ihm arbeitet es sich angenehm** it's nice working with him; he's pleasant to work with

Arbeiter der; ~s, ~: worker; *(Bau~, Land~)* labourer; *(beim Straßenbau)* workman; **der ~ Karl Müller** the factory worker/labourer/workman Karl Müller; **wir suchen ~ und Arbeiterinnen für folgende Bereiche** we are looking for men and women to work in the following areas; **~ und Arbeiterinnen werden oft ...:** male and female workers are often ...; **die ~:** *(als Klasse)* the workers

arbeiter-, Arbeiter-: ~auf·stand der workers' rebellion *or* revolt; **~bewegung die** *(Politik)* labour movement; **~biene die** *(Zool.)* worker [bee]; **~denkmal das a)** workers' monument; monument to the working classes; **b)** *(ugs. scherzh.)* monument to inactivity *(joc.)*; **~dichter der** poet of the working class; **~familie die** working-class family; **~feindlich** *Adj.* anti-working-class; **~freundlich** *Adj.* favouring the workers *postpos.*; **~führer der** workers' leader; **~gewerkschaft die** trade union *(Brit.)*; labor union *(Amer.)*

Arbeiterin die; ~, ~nen *(auch Zool.)* worker; *s. auch* **Arbeiter**

Arbeiter-: ~jugend die young working people; *(Organisation)* labour youth movement *or* organization; **~kampf·lied das** workers' [rallying] song; **~kind das** working-class child; **~klasse die;** *o. Pl.* working class[es *pl.*]; **~kontrolle die** *(bes. DDR)* worker control; **~lied das** workers' song; **~massen** *Pl.* working masses; **~milieu das** working-class environment; **aus dem ~milieu stammen** come from a working-class environment *or* background; **~organisation die** labour organization; **~partei die** workers' party; **~priester der** worker-priest; **~rat der** workers' council

Arbeiterschaft die; ~: workers *pl.*; **aus der ~:** from among the workers

Arbeiter-: ~schriftsteller der worker-writer; working-class writer; **~selbst·verwaltung die** workers' control *no indef. art.*; *(Gremium)* workers' management committee; **in ~selbstverwaltung arbeiten** be under workers' control; **~siedlung die** workers' housing-estate *(Brit.)* *or* *(Amer.)* housing development; **~stadt die** workers' town; *(ugs.: Industriestadt, in der viele Arbeiter leben)* working-class town; **~student der** *(DDR)* worker-student; **~-und-Bauern-Fakultät die** *(DDR)* workers and farmers' faculty *(preparing young workers for university study)*; **~-und-Bauern-Inspektion die** *(DDR)* body charged with *monitoring the implementation of party and Government policy in economic and social affairs*; **~-und-Bauern-Staat der** *(DDR)* workers' and farmers' state; **~-und-Soldaten-Rat der** *(hist.)* workers' and soldiers' council; **~unruhen** *Pl.* unrest *sing.* among the workers; **~verein der** workers' association; **~verräter der** *(Politik abwertend)* traitor to the working class; **~viertel das** working-class district *or* area; **~wohl·fahrt die;** *o. Pl.* workers' welfare association

Arbeit·geber der employer

Arbeitgeber·anteil der employer's contribution

Arbeitgeberin die; ~, ~nen [female] employer; *s. auch* **-in**

Arbeitgeber-: ~seite die employers' side; **~verband der** employers' association *or* organization

Arbeitnehmer der; ~s, ~: employee

Arbeitnehmer·anteil der employee's contribution

Arbeitnehmerin die; ~, ~nen [female] employee; *s. auch* **-in**

Arbeitnehmer-: ~organisation die workers' organization; **~seite die** employees' side

Arbeits·ab·lauf der programme of work

arbeitsam *Adj. (geh. veralt.)* **a)** *(fleißig)* industrious; hard-working; **b)** *(von Arbeit erfüllt)* **ein ~es Leben** a life of hard work; **ein paar ~e Monate vor sich haben** have a few months of hard work ahead of one

arbeits-, Arbeits-: ~amt das job centre *(Brit.)*; employment exchange; labour exchange *(Brit. dated)*; **~an·fall der** volume of work; **~an·fang der** starting-time [at work]; **~anfang ist um 6 Uhr** work starts at 6 a.m.; **~an·leitung die** instructions *pl.*; **~an·tritt der vor ~antritt** before starting work *or* the/a job; **bei ~antritt** when you start/he starts *etc.* work; **~an·zug der** working clothes *pl.*; **blauer ~anzug** blue overalls *pl.*; **~atmosphäre die** working atmosphere; **~auf·fassung die** attitude to one's work; **~aufwand der: mit großem ~aufwand** with a great deal of work; **das wäre mir zuviel ~aufwand** it would be *or* involve too much work [for me]; **~auf·wendig 1.** *Adj.* requiring a great deal of work *postpos., not pred.*; **[sehr] ~aufwendig sein** require a great deal of work; **2.** *adv.* in a way that requires/required a great deal of work; **~aus·fall der** loss of working hours; **ein ~ausfall von einigen Wochen** a loss of several working weeks; **~bedingungen** *Pl.* working conditions; **~beginn der** *s.* **~anfang; ~belastung die** work-load; **~bereich der a)** *(Tätigkeit)* area of work; *(~gebiet)* field of work; **das gehört nicht in meinen ~bereich** that's not part of my job; **b)** *(im Raum)* working area; **c)** *(eines Krans)* working radius; **~beschaffung die** job creation; creation of employment; **~beschaffungs·maßnahme die** job-creation measure; **~beschaffungs·programm das** job-creation programme; **~bescheinigung die** certificate of employment *(issued to employee on leaving job, and listing responsibilities, length of service, etc.)*; **~biene die a)** *(Zool.)* worker bee; **b)** *(ugs.: emsige Frau)* busy bee; **~dienst der a)** *(Arbeit) (low-paid)* community-service work; **b)** *(Organisation)* community service agency; **c)** *s.* **Reichsarbeitsdienst; ~direktor der** personnel director *(with special responsibility for safeguarding the interests of the employees within the framework of codetermination)*; **~disziplin die** discipline in one's approach to work; **~eifer der** enthusiasm for one's work; **~ende das** finishing-time [at work]; **nach/bei ~ende** after work/when it's time to go; **um fünf Uhr haben wir** *od.* **ist bei uns ~ende** we finish work at five o'clock; **~erlaubnis die** work permit; **~erleichternd 1.** *Adj.* labour-saving; **2.** *adv.* in a labour-saving way; **~erleichterung die** saving of labour; **eine große ~erleichterung für jmdn. sein** make sb.'s work a great deal easier; save sb. a great deal of work; **~essen das** *(bes. Politik)* working lunch/dinner; **~ethos das** work ethic; **~fähig** *Adj.* fit for work *postpos.; (grundsätzlich)* able to work *postpos.;* viable ⟨*government*⟩; **~fähigkeit die;** *o. Pl.* fitness for work; *(grundsätzlich)* ability to work; **~feld das** *(geh.)* field of work; **~frei** *Adj.* **ein paar Tage/eine Woche ~frei** a few days/a week off; **Montag ist/haben wir ~frei** we've got Monday off; **~freude die** enthusiasm for one's work; **~friede** *(geh.)*, **~frieden der** industrial peace; peaceful labour *or* industrial relations *pl.;* **~früh·stück das** working breakfast; **~gang der a)** *(einzelne Operation)* operation; **b)** *(Ablauf)* process; **~gebiet das** field of work; **~gemeinschaft die** team; *(Hochschulw.)* study group; **~genehmigung die** work permit; **~gerät das a)** *(Gegenstand)* tool; **b)** *o. Pl. (Gesamtheit)* tools *pl.;* equipment *no indef. art., no pl.;* **~gericht das** industrial tribunal; **~gruppe die** study group; **~haus das** *(hist.) correctional institution for minor offenders where prisoners are required to work;* workhouse *(Amer.)*; **~hypothese die** working hypothesis; **~intensiv** *(Wirtsch.)* **1.** *Adj.* labour-intensive; **2.** *adv.* labour-intensively; **~kampf der** industrial action; **~kampfmaßnahme die** form of industrial action; **~kleidung die** work clothes *pl.;* **~klima das;** *o. Pl.* working atmosphere; **~kollege der** *(bei Arbeitern)* workmate *(Brit.);* fellow worker; *(bei Angestellten, Beamten)* colleague; **~kraft die a)** *(Vermögen zu arbeiten)* capacity for work; **seine ~kraft verkaufen** sell one's labour; **die menschliche ~kraft wird durch Roboter ersetzt** human labour is being replaced by robots; **b)** *(Mensch)* worker; **~kreis der** study group; **~lager das** labour camp; **~last die** burden of work; **~leben das;** *o. Pl.* **a)** *(Berufstätigkeit)* working life; **b)** *(Arbeitswelt)* world of work; working life *no art.;* **~leistung die** rate of output; **~lohn der** wage; wages *pl.; (auf einer Rechnung)* labour [costs *pl.*]; **~los** *Adj.* **a)** unemployed; out of work *postpos.;* **b)** *in* **~loses Einkommen** unearned income

Ạrbeitslose der/die; *adj. Dekl.* unemployed person/man/woman *etc.;* **die ~n** the unemployed *or* jobless; **es gab 2 Mio. ~:** there were 2 million [people] unemployed *or* out of work; **viele ~:** many unemployed people; many people who are/were unemployed *or* out of work

Ạrbeitslosen-: ~geld das; *o. Pl. (full-rate)* earnings-related unemployment benefit; **~heer das** army of unemployed; **~hilfe die;** *o. Pl.* **a)** *(Geld)* reduced-rate unemployment benefit; **b)** *(Institution)* reduced-rate unemployment benefit system; **~unterstützung die** *(volkst.)* unemployment benefit *or* pay; **~versicherung die;** *o. Pl.* unemployment insurance; **~ziffer die** unemployment figures *pl.*

ạrbeits-, Ạrbeits-: ~losigkeit die; ~: unemployment *no indef. art.;* **eine ~losigkeit von 0,5%** a level of unemployment of 0.5%; **~mangel der** lack of work; **~markt der** labour market; **~material das** materials *pl.; (einschließlich Werkzeugen)* materials [and equipment *or* tools]; *(für den Unterricht)* teaching aids *pl.;* **~medizin die** occupational medicine and health care; **~methode die** working method; method of working; **~minister der** minister for employment; Secretary for Employment *(Brit.);* Secretary of Labor *(Amer.);* **~ministerium das** ministry for employment; Department of Employment *(Brit.);* Department of Labor *(Amer.);* **~mittel das** material; *(Werkzeug, Wörterbuch usw.)* tool; **~mittel** *Pl.* materials/tools; *(Schreibzeug)* materials; **~moral die** morale of the workers/staff; **~nachweis der a)** *(das Nachweisen)* information *no indef. art.* about situations vacant; **b)** *(Stelle)* employment office; **~niederlegung die** walk-out; **mit ~niederlegungen drohen** threaten walk-outs; **~ordnung die a)** *(Einteilung)* organization of the work; **b)** *(Regelung des Betriebsablaufs)* [office/factory/shop] regulations *pl.;* **~organisation die** organization of the/one's work; **~ort der** place of work; **~papier das a)** *(Thesenblatt)* working paper; **b)** *Pl. (das Arbeitsverhältnis betreffende Papiere)* employment papers

ạrbeit·sparend 1. *Adj.* labour-saving. **2.** in a labour-saving way

Ạrbeits-: ~pause die break; **eine ~pause machen** take a break; **~pensum das** work quota; **~pferd das** *(auch fig.)* workhorse; **~plan der** work plan *or* schedule; **~platz der a)** *(Platz im Betrieb)* work-place; **am ~platz** at one's work-place; **b)** *(~stätte)* place of work; **den ~platz wechseln** change one's place of work; **c)** *(~verhältnis)* job; **~platz·sicherung die** safeguarding of jobs; **zur ~platzsicherung** to safeguard jobs; **~platz·studie die** job study; **~platz·wechsel der** change of job; **~probe die** sample of one's work; **~prozeß der a)** *o. Pl. (Berufstätigkeit)* **im ~prozeß stehen** be in employment; have a job; **jmdn. wieder in den ~prozeß eingliedern** get sb. back to work; **b)** *(~ablauf)* work process; **~raum der a)** workroom; *(Büroraum)* office; **b)** *s.* **Arbeitszimmer; ~recht das;** *o. Pl.* labour law; **~rechtlich** *Adj.* **~rechtliche Fragen/Literatur** issues relating to/literature on labour law; **ein ~rechtlicher Streitfall** a dispute concerning labour law; **~reich** *Adj.* ⟨*life, week, etc.*⟩ full of hard work; **~richter der** *judge on an industrial tribunal;* **~ruhe die** break [from work]; **gestern herrschte in ganz Italien ~ruhe** commerce and industry was at a standstill throughout Italy yesterday; **~sache die a)** *Pl.* work things; **b)** *Pl. (Kleidung)* work[ing] things *or* clothes; **c)** *(Rechtsw.)* labour law dispute; **~scheu** *Adj.* work-shy; **~schluß der** *s.* **~ende; ~schutz der** protection of health and safety standards at work; **~schutz·bestimmung die** regulation concerning [the protection of] health and safety at work; **~sitzung die** working session; **~sklave der** slave labourer; **als ~sklaven verkauft werden** be sold as slave labour; **~soziologie die** occupational sociology; **~stätte die a)** *(geh.)* **das war Beethovens/Schillers ~stätte** this is [the place] where Beethoven/Schiller worked *or* did his work; **b)** *(Stätte beruflicher Tätigkeit)* place of work; **~stelle die a)** *s.* **Arbeitsstätte b; b)** *(Job) s.* **Stelle g; c)** *(Abteilung)* department; **~stil der** style of working; **~studie die** work study; **~stunde die** hour of work; **2 ~stunden** *(bei Reparaturen usw.)* two hours' labour; **die Herstellung erfordert 2 000 ~stunden** manufacture takes 2,000 man-hours; **~suche die** search for a job *or* for work; **auf ~suche sein** be looking for a job; **~süchtig** *Adj.* **~süchtig sein** be a compulsive worker *or (coll.)* a workaholic; **~tag der** working day; **mein erster ~tag nach dem Urlaub** my first day back at work after the holiday *(Brit.) or (Amer.)* vacation; **das war ein harter ~tag** that was a hard day's work; **~tagung die** conference; **~takt der** *(Technik)* power stroke; **~team das** team; **~technik die** work[ing] technique; **~teilig 1.** *Adj.* ⟨*society, mode of production, etc.*⟩ based on the division of labour; **2.** *adv.* **die Produktion ~teilig gestalten** base production on the principle of the division of labour; **~teilung die** division of labour; **~tempo das** rate of work; work rate; **~therapie die** occupational therapy; **~tier das a)** work animal; **b)** *(Arbeitssüchtiger)* compulsive worker; workaholic *(coll.);* **~tisch der** work-table; *(für Schreibarbeiten)* desk; *(für technische Arbeiten)* [work-] bench; **~titel der** working title; **~überlastung die** overwork; **er klagt über ~überlastung** he complains that he's overworked

Ạrbeit-: ~suche die *s.* **Arbeitssuche; ~suchende der/die;** *adj. Dekl.* person/man/woman looking for work; **die ~suchenden** those looking for work

ạrbeits-, Ạrbeits-: ~unfähig *Adj.* unable to work *postpos.; (krankheitsbedingt)* unfit for work *postpos.;* **die Arbeitsunfähigen** those unable to work/unfit for work; **~unfähigkeit die** *s.* **~unfähig:** inability to work; unfitness for work; **~un·fall der** industrial accident; **er hatte einen ~unfall** he had an accident at work; **~un·lust die** disinclination to work; **~unter·lage die;** *meist Pl.* work paper; **das benutzt er als ~unterlage** he works from that; **~un·willig** *Adj.* unwilling to work *postpos.;* **~verfahren das** work process; **~verhältnis das a)** *contractual relationship between employer and employee;* **ein ~verhältnis eingehen** enter employment; **in einem ~verhältnis stehen** be in employment; **b)** *Pl.* working conditions; conditions of work; **~vermittlung die a)** *(Tätigkeit)* arranging employment; **b)** *(Stelle)* employment exchange; job centre *(Brit.); (Firma)* employment agency; **~verteilung die** allocation of [the] work; **~vertrag der** contract of employment; **~verweigerung die** refusal to work; **~vor·gang der** work process; **~vor·lage die: eine Skizze als ~vorlage benutzen** work from a sketch; **dieses Buch hat ihm als ~vorlage gedient** he worked from that book; **~weise die a)** way *or* method of working; **b)** *(Funktionsweise)* mode of operation; **~welt die** world of work; **~willig** *Adj.* **~willig sein** be willing to work; **~willige Kollegen** fellow employees who are willing to work; **~wissenschaft die** ergonomics *sing.;* **~woche die a)** week's work; **während seiner ersten ~woche** during his first week at work; **b)** *(wöchentliche ~zeit)* working week;

~wut die fit of work-mania; **~wütig** *Adj.* **~wütig sein** suffer from work-mania; **~zeit die a)** working hours *pl.*; **während der ~zeit** during working hours; **die ~zeit beginnt um 8 Uhr** work starts at 8 o'clock; **b)** working time; **die tägliche/wöchentliche ~zeit** the working day/week; **c)** *(als Ware)* labour time; **2 Stunden ~zeit** two hours' labour; **wir berechnen keine ~zeit** we don't charge for labour; **ich lasse mir die ~zeit bezahlen** I charge for my time; **~zeit·verkürzung** die reduction in working hours; **~zeug das**; *o. Pl.* **a)** work things *pl.*; **b)** *(Kleidung)* work[ing] things *pl. or* clothes *pl.*; **~zeugnis das** reference [from one's employer]; **~zimmer das** study

arbiträr [arbi'trɛ:ɐ̯] *(geh.)* **1.** *Adj.* arbitrary. **2.** *adv.* in an arbitrary way; arbitrarily

archaisch [ar'ça:ɪʃ] **1.** *Adj.* archaic. **2.** *adv.* in an archaic way; archaically

archaisieren *itr. V. (geh.)* archaize; **eine ~de Sprache verwenden** use *or* employ an archaistic *or* a deliberately archaic style

Archaismus der; **~, Archaismen** *(Sprachw., Stilk., Kunstw.)* archaism

Archäologe [arçɛo'lo:gə] **der**; **~n, ~n** archaeologist

Archäologie die; **~:** archaeology *no art.*

archäologisch 1. *Adj.* archaeological. **2.** *adv.* archaeologically

Archäologin die; **~, ~nen** archaeologist

Arche ['arçə] **die**; **~, ~n** ark; **die ~ Noah** Noah's Ark

Arche·typ der *(Psych., Philos.)* archetype

arche·typisch *(Psych., Philos.)* **1.** *Adj.* archetypal. **2.** *adv.* archetypally

Arche·typus der *s.* **Archetyp**

Archimedes [arçi'me:dɛs] **(der)** Archimedes

archimedisch *Adj.; nicht präd.* Archimedean; **das Archimedische Prinzip** Archimedes' Principle

Archipel [arçi'pe:l] **der**; **~s, ~e** archipelago; **„der ~ Gulag"** 'the Gulag archipelago'

Architekt [arçi'tɛkt] **der**; **~en, ~en** architect

Architekten·büro das a) architect's office; **b)** *(Firma)* firm of architects

Architektin die; **~, ~nen** architect

Architektonik [arçitɛk'to:nɪk] **die**; **~, ~en** architectonics *sing., no art.*

architektonisch 1. *Adj.* architectonic. **2.** *adv.* architectonically

Architektur [arçitɛk'tu:ɐ̯] **die**; **~, ~en a)** *o. Pl.* architecture; **b)** *(Bauwerk)* edifice

Archiv [ar'çi:f] **das**; **~s, ~e** archives *pl.*; archive

Archivalien [arçi'va:li̯ən] *Pl.* papers and documents in/from the archives

Archivar [arçi'va:ɐ̯] **der**; **~s, ~e, Archivarin die**; **~, ~nen** archivist

Archiv·bild das archive picture *or* photograph

archivieren *tr. V.* **etw. ~:** archive sth.; put sth. in the archives

Archivierung die; **~, ~en** archiving

ARD [a:|ɛr'de:] **die**; **~** *Abk.* **Arbeitsgemeinschaft der öffentlich-rechtlichen Rundfunkanstalten der Bundesrepublik Deutschland** *national radio and television network in the FRG*

Ardennen [ar'dɛnən] *Pl.* **die ~:** the Ardennes

Ardennen·offensive die *(hist.)* Ardennes offensive

Are ['a:rə] **die**; **~, ~n** *(schweiz.) s.* **Ar**

Areal [are'a:l] **das**; **~s, ~e a)** area; **b)** *(Grundstück)* grounds *pl.*; **c)** *(Biol.)* range

areligiös *Adj.* areligious

Aren *s.* **Ära**

Arena [a're:na] **die**; **~, Arenen a)** *(hist., Sport, fig.)* arena; **b)** *(Stierkampf~)* bullring; **c)** *(Manege)* [circus-]ring

Areopag [areo'pa:k] **der**; **~s** *(hist.)* Areopagus

arg [ark], **ärger** ['ɛrgɐ], **ärgst...** ['ɛrgst...] **1.** *Adj.* **a)** *(geh., landsch.: schlimm)* bad ⟨*weather, condition, state*⟩; serious ⟨*situation, wound*⟩; hard ⟨*times*⟩; extremely hackneyed ⟨*cliché*⟩; **etw. noch ärger machen** make sth. worse; **an nichts Arges denken** be completely unsuspecting; **das Ärgste befürchten** fear the worst; **wenn es zum Ärgsten kommt** if the worst comes to the worst; **im ~en liegen** be in a sorry state; **b)** *(geh. veralt.: böse)* wicked; evil; **es ist nichts Arges an ihm** there is no malice in him; **c)** *(geh., landsch.: unangenehm groß, stark)* severe ⟨*pain, hunger, shock*⟩; severe, bitter ⟨*disappointment*⟩; serious ⟨*dilemma, error*⟩; extreme, *(coll.)* terrible ⟨*embarrassment*⟩; gross ⟨*exaggeration, injustice*⟩; heavy ⟨*drinker*⟩; **in ~er Bedrängnis/Not sein** be in desperate straits; **mein ärgster Feind** my worst enemy *or* arch-enemy; **unser ärgster Konkurrent** our most dangerous competitor; **es herrschte ein ~es Gedränge** there was a dreadful crush *(coll.)*. **2.** *adv. (geh., landsch.)* extremely, *(coll.)* awfully, *(coll.)* terribly ⟨*painful, cold, steep, expensive, heavy, etc.*⟩; severely, bitterly ⟨*disappointed*⟩; extremely, *(coll.)* terribly ⟨*embarassed*⟩; ⟨*suffer, weaken*⟩ severely; ⟨*offend*⟩ deeply; ⟨*deceive*⟩ badly; ⟨*rain, pull, punch*⟩ hard; ⟨*hurt*⟩ a great deal; **der Garten ist ~ verwahrlost** the garden is badly neglected; **sich ~ blamieren** make a complete fool of oneself; **ihr treibt es gar zu ~!** you're going too far!; **etwas ~ laut** a bit too loud; **ich hab' ihn ~ gern** I like him very much *or (coll.)* an awful lot; **hast du es ~ eilig?** are you in a great *or (coll.)* terrible hurry?; **es geht ihm ~ schlecht/gut** things are going really badly/ well for him; **Schmeckt dir das Bier? – Nicht so ~:** Do you like the beer? – Not that much

Arg das; **~s** *(geh. veralt.)* malice; **kein ~ an der Sache finden** see no harm in it

Argentinien [argɛn'ti:ni̯ən] **(das)**; **~s** Argentina; the Argentine

Argentinier der; **~s, ~, Argentinierin die**; **~, ~nen** Argentinian; Argentine; *s. auch* **-in**

argentinisch *Adj.* Argentinian; Argentine

ärger *s.* **arg**

Ärger ['ɛrgɐ] **der**; **~s a)** annoyance; *(Zorn)* anger; **etw. erregt jmds. ~:** sth. annoys sb.; **seinem ~ Luft machen** vent one's anger; **seinen ~ an jmdm. auslassen** vent one's anger on sb.; **b)** *(Unannehmlichkeiten)* trouble; **häuslicher/beruflicher ~:** domestic problems *pl.*/problems *pl.* at work; **[jmdm.] ~ machen** cause [sb.] trouble; make trouble [for sb.]; **so ein ~!** how annoying!; **~ bekommen** get into trouble; **sonst gibt es ~:** otherwise there'll be trouble!

ärgerlich 1. *Adj.* annoyed; *(zornig)* angry; **ein ~es Gesicht machen** look annoyed/ angry; **~ über jmdn. sein** be annoyed at/ angry with sb.; **~ über etw.** *(Akk.)* **sein** be annoyed/angry about sth.; **~ über sich selbst** annoyed/angry at oneself; **~ werden** get angry/annoyed; **b)** *(Ärger erregend)* annoying; irritating; **wie ~!** how annoying! **2.** *adv.* **a)** with annoyance; *(zornig)* angrily; **b)** *(Ärger erregend)* annoyingly; irritatingly

Ärgerlichkeit die; **~ a)** annoyance; *(Zorn)* anger; **b)** *(einer Sache)* troublesomeness; **bei aller ~ war es doch von Vorteil** even though it was annoying, it was still an advantage

ärgern 1. *tr. V.* **a) jmdn. ~:** annoy sb.; *(zornig machen)* make sb. angry; **so was ärgert einen natürlich** that sort of thing is annoying, of course; **b)** *(reizen, necken)* tease. **2.** *refl. V.* get annoyed; *(zornig werden)* get angry; *(verärgert sein)* be annoyed/angry; **sich über jmdn. ~:** get annoyed/angry at sb.; **sich zu Tode ~** *(fig.)* be annoyed/angry to the point of distraction; **sich schwarz** *od.* **grün und blau ~:** fret and fume; **nicht ~, nur wundern!** *(ugs.)* there's no point in getting worked *or (sl.)* het up about it

Ärgernis das; **~ses, ~se a)** *o. Pl.* offence; **Erregung öffentlichen ~ses** *(Rechtsspr.)* creating a public nuisance; **b)** *(etw. Ärgerliches)* annoyance; irritation; **häusliche/berufliche ~se** minor domestic troubles/irritations and annoyances at work; **c)** *(etw. Anstößiges)* nuisance; *(etw. Skandalöses)* scandal; outrage

arg-, Arg-: ~list die; *o. Pl. (geh.) (Hinterlist)* guile; deceit; *(Heimtücke, Rechtsw.)* malice; **~listig 1.** *Adj. (hinterlistig)* guileful; deceitful; deceitful ⟨*plan*⟩; *(heimtückisch)* malicious; crafty ⟨*smile*⟩; **~listige Täuschung** *(Rechtsspr.)* malicious deception; **2.** *adv. (hinterlistig)* guilefully; deceitfully; *(heimtückisch)* maliciously; ⟨*smile*⟩ craftily; **~listigkeit die**; **~, ~en a)** *o. Pl. (Hinterlistigkeit)* guilefulness; deceitfulness; *(eines Plans, einer Absicht)* deceitfulness; *(Heimtücke)* malice; **b)** *(arglistige Handlung) s.* **arglistig a:** guileful *or* deceitful/malicious act; **~los 1.** *Adj.* **a)** guileless ⟨*person*⟩, guileless, innocent ⟨*question, remark*⟩; **b)** *(ohne Argwohn)* unsuspecting; **~los, wie ich war ...:** all unsuspecting as I was ...; **wie kannst du nur so ~los sein?** how can you be so naïve?; **2.** *adv.* **a)** guilelessly; innocently; **b)** *(ohne Argwohn)* unsuspectingly; **~losigkeit die**; **~ a)** *(eines Menschen)* guilelessness; *(einer Äußerung, Absicht)* innocence; **ich bin von seiner ~losigkeit überzeugt** I'm convinced he is not being deceitful/malicious; **b)** *(Vertrauensseligkeit)* unsuspecting nature

Argon ['argɔn] **das**; **~s** *(Chemie)* argon

ärgst... *s.* **arg**

Argument [argu'mɛnt] **das**; **~[e]s, ~e** *(auch Math.)* argument

Argumentation [argumɛnta'tsi̯o:n] **die**; **~, ~en** argumentation

argumentativ [argumɛnta'ti:f] **1.** *Adj.* **ein ~er Wahlkampf** an election campaign marked by reasoned argument; **eine rein ~e Auseinandersetzung** a conflict based solely on reasoned argument. **2.** *adv.* by [reasoned] argument; **er ist ihr ~ überlegen** he is superior to her in argument

argumentieren *itr. V.* argue; **damit kannst du nicht ~!** you can't use that as an argument

Argus·augen ['argʊs-] *Pl. (geh.)* eagle eye *sing.*; **jmdn. mit ~ beobachten** watch sb. like a hawk

Argwohn ['arkwo:n] **der**; **~[e]s** suspicion; **jmds. ~ erregen/zerstreuen** arouse/allay sb.'s suspicions *pl.*; **~ gegen jmdn. hegen** be suspicious of sb.; *s. auch* **schöpfen 1 c**

argwöhnen ['arkwø:nən] *tr. V. (geh.)* suspect; **sie argwöhnten einen Verräter in ihm** they suspected him of being a traitor

argwöhnisch *(geh.)* **1.** *Adj.* suspicious. **2.** *adv.* suspiciously

Aridität [aridi'tɛ:t] **die**; **~** *(Geogr.)* aridity

Arie ['a:ri̯ə] **die**; **~, ~n** aria

Arier ['a:ri̯ɐ] **der**; **~s, ~** *(Völkerk., Sprachw., ns.)* Aryan

arisch *Adj. (Völkerk., Sprachw., ns.)* Aryan

arisieren *tr. V. (ns.)* Aryanize

Aristokrat [arɪsto'kra:t] **der**; **~en, ~en** aristocrat

Aristokratie [arɪstokra'ti:] **die**; **~, ~n** aristocracy

Aristokratin die; **~, ~nen** aristocrat

aristokratisch 1. *Adj.* aristocratic. **2.** *adv.* aristocratically

Aristoteles [arɪs'to:telɛs] **(der)** Aristotle

Aristoteliker [arɪsto'te:likɐ] **der**; **~s, ~:** Aristotelian

aristotelisch *Adj.; nicht präd.* Aristotelian

Arithmetik [arɪt'me:tɪk] **die**; **~, ~en a)** *o. Pl.* arithmetic *no art.*; **b)** *(Buch)* textbook on arithmetic

arithmetisch 1. *Adj.* arithmetical. **2.** *adv.* arithmetically
Arkade [ar'ka:də] **die; ~, ~n a)** arch; **in** *od.* **unter den ~n** under the arcade; **b)** *(Bogenreihe, Gang)* arcade
arkadisch *(dichter.) Adj.* Arcadian
Arktis ['arktɪs] **die; ~** *(Geogr.)* **die ~:** the Arctic
arktisch 1. *Adj. (auch fig.)* arctic. **2.** *adv.* **das Klima ist ~ beeinflußt** the climate is influenced by the Arctic
Arkus ['arkʊs] **der; ~, ~** ['arku:s] *(Geom.)* arc
arm [arm], **ärmer** ['ɛrmɐ], **ärmst...** ['ɛrmst...] *Adj. (auch fig.)* poor; **wir sind um 100 Mark ärmer** we are 100 marks worse off *or* [the] poorer; **~ und reich** *(veralt.)* rich and poor [alike]; **die Gegensätze zwischen Arm und Reich** the differences between rich and poor; **selig sind, die da geistlich ~ sind** *(bibl.)* blessed are the poor in spirit; **um etw. ärmer sein/werden** have lost/lose sth.; **~ an Bodenschätzen/Nährstoffen** poor in mineral resources/nutrients; **das Gebiet ist ~ an Wasser** the area is short of water; **~ an Vitaminen sein** ‹*food*› be lacking in *or* low in vitamins; **der/die Ärmste** *od.* **Arme** the poor man/boy/woman/girl; **ach, du Armer** *od.* **Ärmster!** *(meist iron.)* oh, you poor thing!; **ich Armer!** *(dichter. veralt.)* woe is me!; *s. auch* **dran b**
Arm der; ~[e]s, ~e a) arm; **jmdn. am ~ führen** lead sb. by the arm; **er nahm** *od.* *(geh.)* **schloß sie in die ~e** he took her in his arms; **jmdm. in die ~e fallen** *od.* *(geh.)* **sinken** fall *or* sink into sb.'s arms; **nimm mich auf den ~!** carry me!; **etw. unter den ~ nehmen** put sth. under one's arm; **einen Mantel über dem ~ tragen** carry a coat over one's arm; **jmds. ~ nehmen** take sb.'s arm; take sb. by the arm; **jmdm. den ~ bieten** *(geh.)* offer sb. one's arm; **jmdn. im ~ halten** embrace sb.; **sich** *(Dat.)* **in den ~en liegen** lie in each other's *or* one another's arms; **sich aus jmds. ~en lösen** *(geh.)* free oneself from sb.'s embrace; **er hat einen langen ~** *(fig.)* his power and influence extend a long way; **den längeren ~ haben** *(fig. ugs.)* have more clout *(coll.)*; **jmds. verlängerter ~ sein** *(fig.)* be sb.'s tool *or* instrument; **jmdn. auf den ~ nehmen** *(fig. ugs.)* have sb. on *(Brit. coll.)*; pull sb.'s leg; **jmdm. in den ~ fallen** *(fig.)* stay sb.'s hand; **jmdm. in die ~e laufen** bump *or* run into sb.; **er ist mir in die ~e gelaufen** I bumped *or* ran into him; **jmdn. jmdm. in die ~e treiben** drive sb. into sb.'s arms; **jmdn. dem Alkoholismus/Terrorismus in die ~e treiben** drive sb. to alcoholism/to adopt terrorist tactics; **sich jmdm. in die ~e werfen** throw oneself into sb.'s arms; **jmdn. mit offenen ~en aufnehmen** *od.* **empfangen** welcome sb. with open arms; **jmdm. [mit etw.] unter die ~e greifen** help sb. out [with sth.]; **jmdn. am steifen ~ verhungern lassen** *(salopp)* put the screws *(coll.) or (sl.)* squeeze on sb.; *s. auch* **Bein a; b)** *(armartiger Teil)* arm; *(einer Waage)* beam; **c)** *(Ärmel)* arm; sleeve; **ein Hemd/eine Bluse mit halbem ~:** a short-sleeved shirt/blouse
Armada [ar'ma:da] **die; ~, Armaden** *u.* **~s** *(auch fig.)* armada
arm·amputiert *Adj.* ‹*person*› with an *or* one arm/both [his/her] arms amputated; **er ist ~:** he has had an arm/both [his] arms amputated
Armatur [arma'tu:ɐ] **die; ~, ~en** *(Technik)* **a)** fitting; **b)** *meist Pl. (im Kfz)* instrument
Armaturen·brett das instrument panel; *(im Kfz)* dashboard
Arm-: ~band das bracelet; *(Uhr~)* strap; **~band·uhr die** wrist-watch; **~beuge die a)** inside of the/one's elbow; crook of the/one's arm; **b)** *(Turnen)* press-up *(Brit.)*; push-up; **~bewegung die** arm movement; **~binde die a)** armband; **b)** *(Med.)* sling; **~bruch der** fracture of the arm; **er wurde mit einem ~bruch ins Krankenhaus gebracht** he was taken to hospital with a fractured arm; **~brust die** crossbow
Ärmchen ['ɛrmçən] **das; ~s, ~:** [little] arm
Arme der/die; *adj. Dekl.* poor man/woman; pauper; **die ~n** the poor *pl*; *s. auch* **arm**
Armee [ar'me:] **die; ~, ~n a)** *(Streitkräfte)* armed forces *pl.*; **b)** *(Landstreitkräfte, Verband, fig.)* army
Armee-: ~fahrzeug das army vehicle; **~korps das** army corps
Ärmel ['ɛrməl] **der; ~s, ~:** sleeve; **die ~ hochkrempeln** *(fig. ugs.)* roll up one's sleeves; **[sich** *(Dat.)*] **etw. aus dem ~ schütteln** *(ugs.)* produce sth. just like that; **leck mich am ~!** *(salopp verhüll.)* get stuffed *(Brit. sl.)*
Ärmel·auf·schlag der cuff
Armeleute-: ~essen das poor man's food; **~geruch der** smell of poverty; **~viertel das** poor district
Ärmel·halter der sleeve-band
Ärmel·kanal der *(Geogr.)* **der ~:** the [English] Channel
Ärmel·schoner der; ~s, ~, Ärmel·schützer der; ~s, ~: oversleeve
Armen-: ~haus das *(hist., fig.)* poorhouse; **Irland war das ~haus Europas** *(fig.)* Ireland was the poor man of Europe; **~häusler der** *(hist.)* inmate of the poorhouse
Armenien [ar'me:niən] **(das); ~s** Armenia
Armenier der; ~s, ~, Armenierin die; ~, ~nen Armenian
armenisch *Adj.* Armenian; *s. auch* **deutsch, Deutsch**
Armen-: ~kasse die poor-relief fund; **~recht das;** *o. Pl. (Rechtsw.)* right to legal aid; **~viertel das** poor district
Armensünder- *(österr.) s.* **Armsünder-**
ärmer *s.* **arm**
Arme·sünder der; des Armensünders, die Armensünder (ein Armersünder, zwei Armesünder) *(veralt.)* condemned man; **wie ein Armersünder dasitzen** *(ugs.)* sit there looking a picture of misery and remorse
Armesünder·glocke die *s.* **Armsünderglocke**
armieren *tr. V.* **a)** *(Milit. veralt.)* arm; **b)** *(Technik)* reinforce ‹*concrete*›; armour, sheathe ‹*cable*›
-armig *adj.* -armed; **sieben~:** seven-armed ‹*candelabrum*›; **dick~:** ‹*person*› with fat arms
Arm-: ~länge die arm length; *(Abstand)* arm's length; **ein Stück von ~länge** a piece the length of an *or* one's arm; **~lehne die** armrest; **~leuchter der a)** candelabra; **b)** *(ugs. verhüll.)* berk *(Brit. sl.)*; jerk *(sl.)*
ärmlich ['ɛrmlɪç] **1.** *Adj.* cheap ‹*clothing*›; shabby ‹*flat, office*›; meagre ‹*meal*›; **in ~en Verhältnissen leben** live in impoverished circumstances; **aus ~en Verhältnissen** from a poor family. **2.** *adv.* cheaply ‹*dressed, furnished*›; **~ leben/wohnen** live in impoverished circumstances
Ärmlichkeit die; ~ a) *s.* **ärmlich a:** cheapness; shabbiness; meagreness; **b)** *(Armut)* poverty
Ärmling ['ɛrmlɪŋ] **der; ~s, ~e** oversleeve
Arm-: ~loch das a) armhole; **b)** *(salopp verhüll.)* berk *(Brit. sl.)*; jerk *(sl.)*; **~muskel der** arm muscle; **~prothese die** artificial arm; arm prosthesis *(Med.)*; **~reif der** armlet; **~schiene die a)** *(hist.) (für den Oberarm)* brassard; *(für den Unterarm)* vambrace; **b)** *(Med.)* arm-splint
arm·selig 1. *Adj.* **a)** *(sehr arm, dürftig, unbefriedigend)* miserable; miserable, wretched ‹*dwelling*›; pathetic ‹*result, figure*›; meagre ‹*meal, food*›; paltry ‹*return, salary, sum, fee*›; **~e 10 Mark** a paltry 10 marks; **b)** *(abwertend: erbärmlich)* miserable, wretched ‹*swindler, quack*›; pathetic, miserable, wretched ‹*coward*›; pathetic, miserable ‹*amateur, bungler*›. **2.** *adv.* **~ leben** lead *or* live a miserable life; **~ eingerichtet** miserably *or* wretchedly furnished
Armseligkeit die; ~ *s.* **armselig 1:** miserableness; wretchedness; patheticness; meagreness; paltriness
Arm·sessel der armchair
ärmst... *s.* **arm**
Arm-: ~stuhl der armchair; **~stumpf der** stump of the/one's arm
Armsünder-: ~glocke die *(hist.)* bell tolled during an execution; **~miene die** *(scherzh.)* expression of misery and remorse
Armut ['armu:t] **die; ~** *(auch fig.)* poverty; **die ~ des Landes an Rohstoffen** *(fig.)* the country's lack of raw materials; **geistige ~** *(fig.)* lack of culture; cultural poverty
Armuts·zeugnis das *in* **ein ~ sein** be a sign of inadequacy; **jmdm. ein ~ ausstellen** expose sb.'s inadequacy
Armvoll der; ~, ~: armful; **zwei ~ Reisig** two armfuls of brushwood
Arnika ['arnika] **die; ~, ~s** arnica
Arom [a'ro:m] **das; ~s, ~e** *(dichter.) s.* **Aroma a**
Aroma [a'ro:ma] **das; ~s, Aromen** *od.* *(veralt.)* **Aromata a)** *(Duft)* aroma; *(Geschmack)* flavour; taste; **b)** *(Substanz, Essenz)* flavouring
aromatisch [aro'ma:tɪʃ] *Adj.* **a)** *(duftend)* aromatic; **~ duften** give off an aromatic fragrance; **b)** *(wohlschmeckend)* distinctive ‹*taste*›; **sehr ~ schmecken** have a very distinctive taste
aromatisieren *tr. V. (wohlriechend machen)* aromatize; *(wohlschmeckend machen)* flavour ‹*tea, ice-cream, chewing-gum, etc.*›
Aron[s]·stab ['a:rɔn(s)-] **der** arum; **Gefleckter ~:** cuckoo-pint; lords-and-ladies
Arrak ['arak] **der; ~s, ~e** *od.* **~s** arrack
Arrangement [arɑ̃ʒə'mɑ̃:] **das; ~s, ~s** *(geh., Mus.)* arrangement; **ein ~ treffen** come to an arrangement; **~: Gil Evans** arranger: Gil Evans
Arrangeur [arɑ̃'ʒø:ɐ] **der; ~s, ~e** *(Musik)* arranger
arrangieren [arɑ̃'ʒi:rən] **1.** *tr. V. (geh., Musik)* arrange. **2.** *itr. V. (Musik)* **er kann gut ~:** he's a good arranger. **3.** *refl. V.* **sich ~:** adapt, adjust; **sich mit jmdm. ~:** come to an accommodation with sb.; **sich mit etw. ~:** come to terms with sth.
Arrest [a'rɛst] **der; ~[e]s, ~e a)** *(Milit., Rechtsw., Schule)* detention; **einen Schüler mit ~ bestrafen** *(veralt.)* punish a pupil by putting him in detention; **b)** *(Zivilrecht)* **persönlicher ~:** attachment; **dinglicher ~:** attachment; distraint; **etw. unter ~ stellen** *od.* **mit ~ belegen** attach sth.
Arrestant [arɛs'tant] **der; ~en, ~en** detainee
Arrest·zelle die detention cell
arretieren [are'ti:rən] *tr. V.* **a)** *auch itr.* lock; **b)** *(veralt.: festnehmen)* detain; arrest
Arretierung die; ~, ~en a) locking; **b)** *(Vorrichtung)* latch; **c)** *(veralt.: Festnahme)* detention; arrest
Arrhythmie [aryt'mi:] **die; ~, ~n** *(Med.)* arrhythmia
arrivieren [ari'vi:rən] *itr. V.; mit sein (geh.)* arrive; **zum Superstar/zum Staatsfeind Nummer eins ~:** achieve superstar status/become public enemy number one; **ein arrivierter Schriftsteller** a successful writer; *(abwertend)* a parvenu writer
Arrivierte der/die; *adj. Dekl. (geh.)* man/woman who has/had arrived; *(abwertend: Emporkömmling)* parvenu
arrogant [aro'gant] *(abwertend)* **1.** *Adj.* arrogant. **2.** *adv.* arrogantly
Arroganz [aro'gants] **die; ~** *(abwertend)* arrogance
arrondieren [arɔn'di:rən] *tr. V. (geh.)* round off ‹*property, territory, etc.*›
Arsch [arʃ] **der; ~[e]s, Ärsche** ['ɛrʃə] *(derb)* **a)**

arse *(Brit. coarse);* bum *(Brit. sl.);* ass *(Amer. sl.);* **den ~ voll kriegen** get a bloody good hiding *(Brit. sl.);* **der ~ der Welt** *(fig.)* the back of beyond; **ihm geht der ~ mit Grundeis** *(fig.)* he is scared shitless *(coarse);* he is shitting himself *(coarse);* **den ~ offen haben** *(fig.)* be round the bloody twist *(Brit. sl.);* be crazy; **den ~ zukneifen** *(fig.)* kick the bucket *(sl.);* croak *(sl.);* **jmdm. den ~ aufreißen** *(fig.)* make sb. sweat blood; **jmdn. am ~ haben** *(fig.)* have sb. by the short and curlies *(Brit. sl.);* have sb. by the balls *(coarse);* **leck mich am ~!** *(fig.)* piss off *(coarse);* get stuffed *(Brit. sl.); (verflucht noch mal!; na, so was!)* bugger me! *(Brit. coarse);* **er kann mich [mal] am ~ lecken** *(fig.)* he can piss off *(coarse);* he can kiss my arse *(Brit. coarse) or* ass *(Amer. sl.);* **auf den ~ fallen** *(fig.)* come unstuck *(coll.);* **sich auf den ~ setzen** *(fig.) (fleißig arbeiten)* get *or* pull one's finger out *(sl.); (perplex sein)* freak *(sl.);* **jmdm. in den ~ kriechen** *(fig.)* kiss sb.'s arse *(Brit. coarse) or* ass *(Amer. sl.);* **das kannst du dir in den ~ stecken** *(fig.)* you can shove it up your arse *(Brit. coarse) or* ass *(Amer. sl.);* **ich könnte mir in den ~ beißen** I could kick myself; **jmdm. in den ~ treten** kick sb. *or* give sb. a kick up the arse *(Brit. coarse) or* kick in the ass *(Amer. sl.); (fig.)* give sb. a kick up the backside; **im ~ sein** *(fig.)* be buggered *(coarse);* **ein [ganzer] ~ voll** *(fig.)* a hell of a lot; **b)** *(widerlicher Mensch)* arsehole *(Brit. coarse);* ass-hole *(Amer. sl.);* **~ mit Ohren** arse-hole *(Brit. coarse);* ass-hole *(Amer. sl.);* **c)** *(nichts geltender Mensch)* piece of dirt; **wir sind die Ärsche hier** we are just so much dirt here

arsch-, Arsch-: ~backe die *(derb)* cheek *(sl.)* [of the/one's arse *(Brit. coarse) or* bum *(Brit. sl.) or* ass *(Amer. sl.)*]; **~ficker der** *(vulg.)* arse-fucker *(Brit. coarse);* bum-fucker *(Brit. coarse);* butt-fucker *(Amer. coarse);* **~geige die** *(derb abwertend)* arsehole *(Brit. coarse);* **~klar** *Adj. (derb)* bloody *(Brit. sl.) or* damned obvious; **Ich mache mit. Ist doch ~klar** I'm game. 'Course I bloody am *(Brit. sl.);* **~kriecher der** *(derb abwertend)* arse-licker *(Brit. coarse);* ass-licker *(Amer. sl.);* **~kriecherei die** *(derb abwertend)* arse-licking *(Brit. coarse);* ass-licking Brit.; **~loch das** *(derb)* **a)** *(widerlicher Mensch)* arse-hole *(Brit. coarse);* ass-hole *(Amer. sl.);* **Mensch, ich bin doch ein ~loch** what a stupid arse *(Brit. coarse) or (Amer. sl.)* ass I am; **b)** *(bedauernswerter Mensch)* poor bloody sod *(Brit. sl.);* poor bastard; **~-und-Titten-Presse die;** *o. Pl. (salopp)* tit-and-bum press *(Brit. sl.);* tit-and-ass press *(Amer. sl.);* **~wisch der** *(derb abwertend)* useless piece of paper

Arsen [ar'ze:n] **das; ~s** arsenic

Arsenal [arze'na:l] **das; ~s, ~e** arsenal

arsen·haltig *Adj.* containing arsenic *postpos., not pred.;* arsenical; **~/stark ~ sein** contain arsenic/have a high arsenic content

Arsenik [ar'ze:nɪk] **das; ~s** arsenic; arsenic trioxide

Art [a:ɐ̯t] **die; ~, ~en a)** *(Sorte)* kind; sort; *(Biol.: Spezies)* species; **Tische/Bücher aller ~:** tables/books of all kinds *or* sorts; all kinds *or* sorts of tables/books; **einzig in seiner ~:** unique of its kind; **ein Verbrecher übelster ~:** the worst sort *or* kind of criminal; **jede ~ von Gewalt ablehnen** reject all forms of violence; **diese ~ [von] Menschen** that kind *or* sort of person; people like that; **[so] eine ~ ...:** a sort *or* kind of ...; **aus der ~ schlagen** not be true to type; *(in einer Familie)* be different from all the rest of the family; **in der ~ eines Gorillas** like a gorilla; **b)** *o. Pl. (Wesen)* nature; *(Verhaltensweise)* manner; way; **es liegt nicht in ihrer ~** *od.* **ist nicht ihre ~, das zu tun** it's not [in] her nature to do that; **das entspricht nicht seiner ~:** it's not [in] his nature; that's not his way; **c)** *o. Pl. (gutes Benehmen)* behaviour; **das ist doch keine ~!** that's no way to behave!; **was ist denn das für eine ~?** what sort of behaviour is that?; **die feine englische ~** *(ugs.)* the proper way to behave; **d)** *(Weise)* way; **auf diese ~:** in this way; **auf verschiedene ~en** in various ways; **auf welche ~?** in what way?; **auf grausamste ~:** in the cruellest way; **in einer ~:** in a way; **die richtige ~, darauf zu reagieren** the right way to react to it; **auf die eine oder andere ~:** in one way or another; **~ und Weise** way; **seine ~ und Weise zu arbeiten** his way of working; **Schweinesteak nach ~ des Hauses** *(Kochk.)* pork steak à la maison; **nach Schweizer** *od.* **auf schweizerische ~** *(Kochk.)* Swiss style; **daß es eine ~ hat/hatte** *(veralt.)* with a vengeance

Art·angabe die *(Sprachw.)* adverb of manner; *(Phrase)* adverbial phrase of manner

Artefakt [arte'fakt] **das; ~[e]s, ~e** *(geh.)* artefact

art·eigen *Adj. (Biol.)* species-specific

arten·reich *Adj. (Biol.)* species-rich

Arten·reichtum der *(Biol.)* species-richness

art·erhaltend *(Biol., Verhaltensf.) Adj.* species-preserving

Art·erhaltung die *(Biol., Verhaltensf.)* preservation of the species

Arterie [ar'te:ri̯ə] **die; ~, ~n** artery

arteriell [arte'ri̯ɛl] *Adj. (Anat.)* arterial

Arterien·verkalkung die hardening of the arteries; arteriosclerosis *(Med.)*

Arterio·sklerose [arteri̯o-] **die** *(Med.)* arteriosclerosis

artesisch [ar'te:zɪʃ] *Adj.* **in ~er Brunnen** artesian well

art-, Art-: ~fremd *Adj. (Biol.)* foreign [to a/the species]; **~genosse der** conspecific; creature of the same species; **~gleich** *Adj. (Biol.)* ⟨*animal, individual*⟩ of the same species

Arthritis [ar'tri:tɪs] **die; ~, Arthritiden** *(Med.)* arthritis

arthritisch *(Med.) Adj.* arthritic

Arthrose [ar'tro:zə] **die; ~, ~n** *(Med.)* arthrosis

artifiziell [artifi'tsi̯ɛl] *(geh.)* **1.** *Adj.* artificial. **2.** *adv.* artificially

artig 1. *Adj.* **a)** well-behaved; good; **sei ~:** be good; be a good boy/girl/dog *etc.;* **b)** *(geh. veralt.: höflich)* courteous; **c)** *(veralt.: nett)* charming. **2.** *adv.* **a) sich ~ benehmen** be good; behave well; **b)** *(geh. veralt.: höflich)* courteously; **c)** *(veralt.: nett)* charmingly

-artig 1. *Adj.* **marmor~/gold~** marble-like/gold-like. **2.** *adv.* **sich explosions~ vermehren** increase explosively; **sich kegel~ verjüngen** taper like a cone

Artigkeit die; ~, ~en a) *o. Pl. (geh. veralt.)* courteousness; **b)** *(Redensart)* pleasantry; *(Kompliment)* compliment; **jmdm. ~en sagen** say nice things to sb./pay sb. compliments

Artikel [ar'ti:kl̩] **der; ~s, ~ a)** article; **b)** *(Ware)* article; item

Artikulation [artikula'tsi̯o:n] **die; ~, ~en** articulation

artikulieren 1. *tr., itr. V.* articulate; enunciate; *(Sprachw., geh.: zum Ausdruck bringen)* articulate. **2.** *refl. V.* **a)** *(sich ausdrücken)* express oneself; **b)** *(zum Ausdruck kommen)* express itself; be expressed

Artillerie [artɪlə'ri:] **die; ~, ~n** artillery

Artillerie·beschuß der artillery fire

Artillerist der; ~en, ~en artilleryman

artilleristisch *(Milit.)* **1.** *Adj.* **~e Unterstützung** artillery support. **2.** *adv.* **~ unterstützt werden** have artillery support

Artischocke [arti'ʃɔkə] **die; ~, ~n** artichoke

Artischocken·boden der artichoke bottom

Artist [ar'tɪst] **der; ~en, ~en a)** [variety/circus] artiste *or* performer; **b)** *(geh.: Virtuose)* artist

Artistik die; ~ a) circus/variety performance *no art.;* **b)** *(Geschicklichkeit)* skill; **c)** *(geh.: formale Könnerschaft)* artistry

Artistin die; ~, ~nen *s.* **Artist**

artistisch 1. *Adj.* **a) eine ~e Glanzleistung** a superb circus/variety performance; **sein ~es Können** his skill as a [circus/variety] artiste; **b)** *(geschickt)* masterly; **c)** *(geh.: technisch perfekt)* virtuoso *attrib.* **2.** *adv.* **a) eine ~ anspruchsvolle Nummer** a circus/variety act of great virtuosity; **b)** *(geschickt)* in a masterly way *or* fashion; **c)** *(geh.: technisch perfekt)* with great artistry *or* virtuosity

Artothek [arto'te:k] **die; ~, ~en** art lending library

Artus ['artʊs] **(der)** [King] Arthur

art·verwandt *Adj.* related

Arznei [a:ɐ̯ts'nai̯] **die; ~, ~en** *(veralt.)* medicine; medicament; *(zur äußeren Anwendung)* medicament; **eine bittere/heilsame ~ für jmdn. sein** *(fig. ugs.)* be a painful/salutary lesson for sb.

Arznei-: ~buch das pharmacopoeia; **~kunde, ~lehre die** pharmacology; **~mittel das** medicine; medicament; *(zur äußeren Anwendung)* medicament; **~mittel·gesetz das** *law relating to the manufacture and distribution of medicines;* **~mittel·mißbrauch der** abuse of medicines; **~mittel·sucht die** addiction to medicines; pharmacomania *(Med.);* **~schränkchen das** medicine cabinet

Arzt [a:ɐ̯tst] **der; ~es, Ärzte** ['ɛ:ɐ̯tstə] doctor; physician *(arch./formal);* **zum ~ gehen** go to the doctor['s]; **Sie sollten mal zum ~ gehen** you ought to see a/the doctor; **praktischer ~,** *(fachspr.)* **~ für Allgemeinmedizin** general practitioner; GP; **..., wie vom ~ verordnet** ... as directed by a physician; **ein ~ für Kinder-/Frauenkrankheiten** a paediatrician/gynaecologist

Arzt·beruf der; *o. Pl.* job of doctor; **in den ~ drängen** crowd into the medical profession; **den ~ ergreifen** become a doctor

Ärzte-: ~kammer die: *professional body of doctors;* ≈ General Medical Council *(Brit.);* **~muster das** medical sample

Ärzteschaft die; ~: medical profession

Arzt-: ~frau die doctor's wife; **~helferin die** doctor's receptionist

Ärztin ['ɛ:ɐ̯tstɪn] **die; ~, ~nen** doctor; physician *(formal); s. auch* **Arzt; -in**

ärztlich ['ɛ:ɐ̯tstlɪç] **1.** *Adj.* medical; **auf ~e Verordnung** on doctor's orders; **alle ~e Kunst** all the doctor's/doctors' skill. **2.** *adv.* **sich ~ behandeln lassen** have medical treatment; **„~ empfohlen"** 'recommended by doctors'

Arzt-: ~praxis die doctor's surgery *(Brit.) or* practice; **~rechnung die** doctor's bill; **~wahl die: das Recht der freien ~wahl** the right to choose one's doctor

as, [1]As [as] **das; ~, ~** *(Musik)* [key of] A flat

[2]As das; ~ses, ~se ace

A-Saite die *(Musik)* A-string

Asbest [as'bɛst] **der; ~[e]s, ~e** asbestos

Asbest-: ~anzug der asbestos suit; **~platte die** *(für Töpfe)* asbestos mat; *(für Bügeleisen)* asbestos stand

Asch·becher der *s.* **Aschenbecher**

asch·blond *Adj.* ash blond

Asche ['aʃə] **die; ~, ~n** ash[es *pl.*]; *(sterbliche Reste)* ashes *pl.;* **in ~ liegen/legen** *(fig. geh.)* lie/lay in ashes; **sich** *(Dat.)* **~ aufs Haupt streuen** *(fig. geh.)* wear sackcloth and ashes

Asch·eimer der *(nordd.)* rubbish *or* waste bin

Aschen-: ~bahn die *(Sport)* cinder-track; **~becher der** ashtray

Aschen·brödel [-brø:dl̩] **das; ~s, ~** *(auch fig.)* Cinderella

Aschen-: ~**eimer der** *(nordd.) s.* **Mülleimer**; ~**platz der** *(Tennis)* cinder-court

Aschen·puttel [-pʊtl̩] **das;** ~**s,** ~ *s.* **Aschenbrödel**

Aschen·regen der rain of ash

Ascher der; ~**s,** ~ *(ugs.)* ashtray

Ascher·mittwoch der Ash Wednesday

asch-: ~**fahl** *Adj.* ashen; ~**grau** *Adj.* ash-grey; *(~fahl)* ashen

Ascorbin·säure [askɔr'bi:n-] **die** ascorbic acid

As-Dur das *(Musik)* A flat major; *s. auch* **A-Dur**

Ase ['a:zə] **der;** ~**n,** ~**n** *(germ. Myth.)* one of the Aesir; **die** ~**n** the Aesir

äsen [ɛ:zn̩] *itr. V. (Jägerspr.)* browse; *(weiden)* graze

aseptisch *(Med.)* **1.** *Adj.* aseptic. **2.** *adv.* aseptically

Äser *s.* **Aas**

asexuell 1. *Adj.* asexual. **2.** *adv.* asexually

Asiat [a'zi̯a:t] **der;** ~**en,** ~**en, Asiatin die;** ~**,** ~**nen** Asian

asiatisch *Adj.* Asian; *(ost~)* Asian; oriental; ~ **aussehen** have an Asiatic look about one

Asien ['a:zi̯ən] **(das);** ~**s** Asia

Askese [as'ke:zə] **die;** ~: asceticism

Asket [as'ke:t] **der;** ~**en,** ~**en** ascetic

asketisch 1. *Adj.* ascetic. **2.** *adv.* ascetically

Äskulap·stab [ɛsku'la:p-] **der** staff of Aesculapius

as-Moll das *(Musik)* A flat minor

Äsop [ɛ'zo:p] **(der)** Aesop

asozial 1. *Adj.* asocial; *(gegen die Gesellschaft gerichtet)* antisocial; **ein** ~**er Mensch** a social misfit. **2.** *adv.* asocially; antisocially

Asoziale der/die; *adj. Dekl.* social misfit

Asparagus [as'pa:ragʊs] **der;** ~ **a)** *(Bot.)* asparagus; **b)** *(Grün)* asparagus fern

Aspekt [as'pɛkt] **der;** ~**[e]s,** ~**e** aspect

Asphalt [as'falt] **der;** ~**[e]s,** ~**e** asphalt

Asphalt·decke die *(Straßenbau)* asphalt surface

asphaltieren *tr. V.* asphalt

Asphalt-: ~**literat der** *(ns. abwertend) writer associated with urban rootlessness and decadence;* ~**straße die** asphalt road

Aspik [as'pi:k] **der** *(österr. auch* **das**); ~**s,** ~**e** aspic

Aspirant [aspi'rant] **der;** ~**en,** ~**en, Aspirantin die;** ~**,** ~**nen a)** *(Anwärter)* candidate; **b)** *(DDR: Wissenschaftler)* research student *(with some teaching responsibilities)*

Aspiration [aspira'tsi̯o:n] **die;** ~**,** ~**en** *(Sprachw.)* aspiration

aspirieren 1. *tr. V. (Sprachw.)* aspirate. **2.** *itr. V. (österr. geh.)* **auf etw.** *(Akk.)* ~: be a candidate for sth.

aß [a:s] *1. u. 3. Pers. Sg. Prät. v.* **essen**

[1]**Aß** [as] **das; Asses, Asse** *(österr.) s.* [2]**As**

[2]**Aß das; Asses, Asse** *(österr. ugs.: Abszeß)* boil

assanieren [asa'ni:rən] *tr. V. (österr.)* clean up

äße ['ɛ:sə] *1. u. 3. Pers. Sg. Konjunktiv II v.* **essen**

Assekuranz [aseku'rants] **die;** ~**,** ~**en** *(Wirtsch.)* assurance *(Brit.)*; insurance

Assel ['asl̩] **die;** ~**,** ~**n a)** *(Zool.)* isopod; **b)** *(Keller~, Mauer~)* woodlouse

Asservat [asɛr'va:t] **das;** ~**[e]s,** ~**e** *(Rechtw.)* exhibit

Assessor [a'sɛsɔr] **der;** ~**s,** ~**en** [asɛ'so:rən], **Assessorin die;** ~**,** ~**nen** *holder of a higher civil service post, e.g. teacher or lawyer, who has passed the necessary examinations but has not yet completed his/her probationary period; s. auch* **-in**

Assimilation [asimila'tsi̯o:n] **die;** ~**,** ~**en** *(auch fachspr.)* assimilation **(an** + *Akk.* to)

assimilieren *(auch fachspr.)* **1.** *tr. V.* assimilate. **2.** *refl. V.* assimilate **(an** + *Akk.* to)

Assistent [asɪs'tɛnt] **der,** ~**en,** ~**en, Assistentin die;** ~**,** ~**nen** assistant; *s. auch* **wissenschaftlich; -in**

Assistenz [asɪs'tɛnts] **die;** ~**,** ~**en** assistance

Assistenz-: ~**arzt der** junior doctor; ~**professor der** assistant professor; reader *(Brit.)*

assistieren *itr. V.* **[jmdm.]** ~: assist [sb.] **(bei** at)

Assonanz [aso'nants] **die;** ~**,** ~**en** *(Verslehre)* assonance

Assoziation [asotsi̯a'tsi̯o:n] **die;** ~**,** ~**en** association

Assoziations·freiheit die *(Rechtsw.)* freedom of association

assoziativ [asotsi̯a'ti:f] **1.** *Adj.* associative. **2.** *adv.* associatively

assoziieren 1. *tr. V. (bes. Psych., geh.)* associate; **bei einem Namen** *usw.* **etw.** ~: associate sth. with a name *etc.* **2.** *itr. V.* make associations; **frei** ~: free-associate. **3.** *refl. V. (sich an-, zusammenschließen)* form an association; **der Sudan ist der EG assoziiert** the Sudan is associated with the EEC

Ast [ast] **der;** ~**[e]s, Äste** ['ɛstə] **a)** branch; bough; **den** ~ **absägen, auf dem man sitzt** *(fig. ugs.)* saw off the branch one is sitting on; **auf dem absteigenden** ~ **sein** *(fig. ugs.)* be going downhill; **b)** *(in Holz)* knot; **c)** *(landsch.) (Rücken)* back; *(Buckel)* hunchback; humpback; **sich** *(Dat.)* **einen** ~ **lachen** *(ugs.)* split one's sides [with laughter]

AStA ['asta] **der;** ~**[s],** ~**[s]** *od.* **Asten** *Abk.* **Allgemeiner Studentenausschuß** ≈ Students' Union

Ästchen ['ɛstçən] **das;** ~**s,** ~ [small] branch

Aster ['astɐ] **die;** ~**,** ~**n** aster; *(Herbst~)* Michaelmas daisy

Ast·gabel die *(zwischen Stamm und Ast)* fork of a/the tree; *(zwischen Ast und Zweig)* fork of a/the branch

Ästhet [ɛs'te:t] **der;** ~**en,** ~**en** aesthete

Ästhetik [ɛs'te:tɪk] **die;** ~**,** ~**en a)** aesthetics *sing.*; **b)** *(Buch)* [book on] aesthetics; **c)** *(das Ästhetische)* aesthetics *pl*; *(Schönheitssinn)* aesthetic sense; **er hat keinen Sinn für** ~: he has no aesthetic sense

ästhetisch 1. *Adj.* aesthetic. **2.** *adv.* aesthetically

ästhetisieren *tr. (auch itr.) V. (geh.)* aestheticize

Ästhetizismus der; ~ *(geh.)* aestheticism

ästhetizistisch *(geh.) Adj.* aestheticist; aestheticizing *attrib.*

Asthma ['astma] **das;** ~**s** asthma

Asthmatiker [ast'ma:tikɐ] **der;** ~**s,** ~**, Asthmatikerin die;** ~**,** ~**nen** asthmatic

asthmatisch 1. *Adj.* asthmatic. **2.** *adv.* asthmatically; ~ **bedingte Beschwerden** complaints linked to asthma

astig *Adj.* knotty

Ast·loch das knot-hole

astral [as'tra:l] *Adj.* astral

Astral·leib der astral body

ast·rein 1. *Adj. (ugs.) (in Ordnung)* on the level *(coll.)*; *(echt)* genuine; *(salopp: prima, toll)* fantastic *(coll.)*; great *(coll.)*. **2.** *adv. (salopp: prima)* fantastically *(coll.)*

Astrologe [astro'lo:gə] **der;** ~**n,** ~**n** astrologer; *(fig.)* forecaster; pundit; **DDR-/Kreml-**~ *(fig.)* GDR-watcher/Kremlinwatcher *or* Kremlinologist

Astrologie die; ~: astrology *no art.*

Astrologin die; ~**,** ~**nen** *s.* **Astrologe**

astrologisch 1. *Adj.* astrological. **2.** *adv.* astrologically; **sich** ~ **beraten lassen** consult an astrologer

Astronaut [astro'naut] **der;** ~**en,** ~**en** astronaut

Astronautik [astro'nautɪk] **die;** ~: astronautics *sing., no art.*

Astronautin die; ~**,** ~**nen** astronaut; *s. auch* **-in**

astronautisch 1. *Adj.* astronautical. **2.** *adv.* astronautically; ~ **interessiert** interested in astronautics; **jmdn.** ~ **ausbilden** train sb. in astronautics

Astronom [astro'no:m] **der;** ~**en,** ~**en** astronomer

Astronomie die; ~: astronomy *no art.*

Astronomin die; ~**,** ~**nen** astronomer

astronomisch *Adj.* astronomical

astro-, Astro- [astro-]: ~**physik die** astrophysics *sing., no art.*; ~**physikalisch 1.** *Adj.* astrophysical; **2.** *adv.* astrophysically; ~**physiker der** astrophysicist

Ast·werk das; ~**[e]s** branches *pl.*

ASU *Abk.* **Abgassonderuntersuchung**

Äsung die; ~**,** ~**en** *(Jägerspr.)* grazing

Asyl [a'zy:l] **das;** ~**s,** ~**e a)** [political] asylum; **jmdm.** ~ **gewähren** grant sb. asylum; **b)** *(Obdachlosen~)* hostel [for the homeless]

Asylant [azy'lant **der;** ~**en,** ~**en, Asylantin die;** ~**,** ~**nen** person granted [political] asylum; *(Asylbewerber)* person seeking [political] asylum

Asyl-: ~**bewerber der** person seeking [political] asylum; ~**recht das** *(Rechtsw.)* **a)** right of [political] asylum; **b)** *(eines Staates)* right to grant [political] asylum; ~**werber der;** ~**s,** ~ *(österr.) s.* ~**bewerber**

Asymmetrie die asymmetry

asymmetrisch 1. *Adj.* asymmetrical. **2.** *adv.* asymmetrically

asynchron 1. *Adj.* asynchronous; **Bild und Ton sind** ~: sound and picture are out of synchronization. **2.** *adv.* asynchronously

Aszendent [astsɛn'dɛnt] **der;** ~**en,** ~**en** *(Astron., Astrol., Genealogie)* ascendant

A. T. *Abk.* **Altes Testament** OT

ata ['ata] *in* ~ **[~] gehen** *(Kinderspr.)* go walkies *(child lang., coll.)*

Atavismus [ata'vɪsmʊs] **der;** ~**, Atavismen** *(Biol., Psych.)* atavism

atavistisch *(Biol., Psych.)* **1.** *Adj.* atavistic. **2.** *adv.* atavistically

Atelier [atə'li̯e:] **das;** ~**s,** ~**s** studio

Atelier-: ~**aufnahme die** *(Film, Fot.)* studio shot; ~**fest das** studio party; ~**wohnung die** studio flat *(Brit.)* *or (Amer.)* apartment

Atem ['a:təm] **der;** ~**s** breath; **sein** ~ **wurde schneller** his breathing became faster; **einen kurzen** ~ **haben** be short of breath; *(fig.)* not have much staying-power; **einen langen/den längeren** ~ **haben** *(fig.)* have great/the greater staying power; **jmdn. in** ~ **halten** *(in Spannung halten)* keep sb. in suspense; *(pausenlos beschäftigen)* keep sb. busy *or* at it; **den** ~ **anhalten** hold one's breath; **jmdm. den** ~ **verschlagen** take sb.'s breath away; ~ **holen** *od. (geh.)* **schöpfen** *(auch fig.)* get one's breath back; **außer** ~ **sein/geraten** *od.* **kommen** be/get out of breath; **[wieder] zu** ~ **kommen** get one's breath back; **nach** ~ **ringen** *(geh.)* gasp for air; *s. auch* **ausgehen 1 b**

atem-, Atem-: ~**beklemmung die** shortness of breath; ~**beraubend 1.** *Adj.* breath-taking; **2.** *adv.* breath-takingly; ~**beschwerden** *Pl.* trouble *sing.* with one's breathing; ~**holen das** breathing; **der Taucher kam zum** ~**holen an die Oberfläche** the diver came up to the surface for air; ~**los 1.** *Adj.* breathless; **2.** *adv.* breathlessly; ~**losigkeit die;** ~: breathlessness; ~**luft die;** *o. Pl.* the air one breathes; ~**maske die** *(Med.)* breathing-mask; ~**not die;** *o. Pl.* difficulty in breathing; ~**pause die** breathing space; ~**technik die** breathing technique; ~**übung die** breathing exercise; ~**wege** *Pl.* respiratory tract *sing. or* passages; ~**zug der** breath; **bis zum letzten** ~**zug** *(geh.)* to the last breath; **in einem** *od.* **im selben** ~**zug** in the same breath

Atheismus [ate'ɪsmʊs] **der;** ~: atheism *no art.*

Atheist der; ~**en,** ~**en, Atheistin die;** ~**,** ~**nen** atheist

atheistisch 1. *Adj.* atheistic. **2.** *adv.*

atheistically; **er ist ~ erzogen worden** he had an atheistic upbringing

Athen [a'te:n] **(das)**; ~s Athens

Athener 1. *indekl. Adj.; nicht präd.* Athens *attrib.*; of Athens *postpos.* **2. der;** ~s, ~: Athenian; *s. auch* **Kölner**

athenisch *Adj.* Athenian

Äther ['ɛ:tɐ] **der;** ~s, ~ *(Chemie, Physik, geh.)* ether

ätherisch [ɛ'te:rɪʃ] *Adj. (Chemie, dichter.)* ethereal

Äther-: ~narkose die *(Med.)* ether anaesthesia; **~wellen** *Pl. (veralt.)* waves in the ether

Äthiopien [ɛ'tio:pi̯ən] **(das)**; ~s Ethiopia

Äthiopier der; ~s, ~, **Äthiopierin die;** ~, ~nen Ethiopian; *s. auch* **-in**

Athlet [at'le:t] **der;** ~en, ~en **a)** *(Sportler)* athlete; **b)** *(ugs.: kräftiger Mann)* muscleman

Athletik [at'le:tɪk] **die;** ~: athletics *sing., no art.*

Athletin die; ~, ~nen athlete; *s. auch* **-in**

athletisch *Adj.* athletic

Äthyl·alkohol der *(Chemie)* ethyl alcohol; ethanol

Äthylen [ɛty'le:n] **das;** ~s *(Chemie)* ethylene

Atlant [at'lant] **der;** ~en, ~en *(Archit.)* telamon; atlas

Atlanten *s.* [1]**Atlas, Atlant**

Atlantik [at'lantɪk] **der;** -s Atlantic

atlantisch *(Geogr.) Adj.* Atlantic; **der Atlantische Ozean** the Atlantic Ocean

[1]**Atlas** ['atlas] **der;** ~ *od.* ~ses, **Atlanten** *od.* ~se atlas

[2]**Atlas der;** ~ *od.* ~ses, ~se *(Textilw.)* atlas

atmen ['a:tmən] **1.** *itr. V.* breathe; *(Physiol., Bot.)* respire. **2.** *tr. V. (geh., auch fig.: erfüllt sein von)* breathe

Atmosphäre [atmo'sfɛ:rə] **die;** ~, ~n *(auch fig.)* atmosphere

atmosphärisch 1. *Adj.* atmospheric; *s. auch* **Störung b. 2.** *adv.* atmospherically

Atmung die; ~: breathing; *(Physiol., Bot.)* respiration

Atmungs-: ~apparat der *(Med.)* respirator; **~organ das** respiratory organ

Ätna ['ɛ:tna] **der;** ~[s] Mount Etna

Atoll [a'tɔl] **das;** ~s, ~e atoll

Atom [a'to:m] **das;** ~s, ~e atom

atomar [ato'ma:ɐ̯] **1.** *Adj.* atomic; *(Atomwaffen betreffend)* nuclear; nuclear, atomic ⟨*age, weapons*⟩. **2.** *adv.* **~ angetrieben** nuclear-powered; atomic-powered; **~ aufrüsten** build up nuclear arms

Atom-, atom-: ~bombe die nuclear bomb; atom bomb; **~bomben·sicher** *Adj.* nuclear-bomb-proof; **~bombenversuch der** nuclear [weapons] test; **~bunker der** fall-out shelter; **~energie die;** *o. Pl.* nuclear *or* atomic energy *no indef. art.*; **~explosion die** nuclear *or* atomic explosion; **~gewicht das** atomic weight

atomisieren *tr. V.* **a)** *(vernichten)* **etw. ~:** smash sth. to atoms; **b)** *(zerstäuben)* atomize ⟨*liquid*⟩; **c)** *(abwertend: zerstückelnd behandeln)* atomize

Atomismus der; ~ *(Philos.)* atomism *no art.*

atom-, Atom-: ~kern der atomic nucleus; **~klub der** *(Politik ugs.)* nuclear club; **~kraft die;** *o. Pl.* nuclear *or* atomic power *no indef. art.*; **~kraft·werk das** nuclear *or* atomic power-station; **~krieg der** nuclear war; **~macht die** nuclear power; **~meiler der** atomic pile; **~modell das** *(Physik)* model of the/an atom; **~müll der** nuclear *or* atomic waste; **~physik die** nuclear *or* atomic physics *sing., no art.*; **~physiker der** nuclear *or* atomic physicist; **~pilz der** mushroom cloud; **~rakete die** nuclear *or* atomic missile; **~reaktor der** nuclear reactor; **~spreng·kopf der** nuclear warhead; **~stopp der** nuclear freeze; **~streit·macht die** nuclear force; **~strom der** *(ugs.)* electricity generated by nuclear power; **~test·stopp·abkommen das** *(Politik)* nuclear test ban treaty; **~tod der;** *o. Pl.* death in a nuclear war/accident; **„Kampf dem ~tod!"** 'ban the bomb'; **~-U-Boot das** nuclear[-powered] submarine; **~uhr die** atomic clock; **~untersee·boot das** *s.* ~-U-Boot; **~waffe die** nuclear *or* atomic weapon; **~waffen·frei** *Adj.* nuclear-free; **~waffen-sperr·vertrag der** *(Politik)* Nuclear Nonproliferation Treaty; **~zeichen das** *(Chemie)* [chemical] symbol; **~zeit·alter das;** *o. Pl.* nuclear *or* atomic age; **~zerfall der** *(Physik)* radioactive decay; **~zertrümmerung die** *(Physik)* splitting of the atom

atonal *(Musik) Adj.* atonal

Atonalität die; ~ *(Musik)* atonality

atoxisch *Adj. (bes. Biol., Med.)* non-toxic

Atrium ['a:triʊm] **das;** ~s, **Atrien** atrium

Atrium·haus das *(Archit.)* house with an atrium

ätsch [ɛ:tʃ] *Interj. (Kinderspr.)* ha ha

Attaché [ata'ʃe:] **der;** ~s, ~s attaché

Attacke [a'takə] **die;** ~, ~n **a)** *(auch Med.)* attack **(auf** + *Akk.* on); **b)** *(Reiter~)* [cavalry] charge; **eine ~ [gegen jmdn./etw.] reiten** charge [sb./sth.]; *(fig.)* make an attack [on sb./sth.]

attackieren *tr. V.* **a)** attack; **b)** *(Milit.: zu Pferde)* charge

Attentat ['atnta:t] **das;** ~[e]s, ~e assassination attempt; *(erfolgreiches)* assassination; **ein ~ auf jmdn. verüben** make an attempt on sb.'s life/assassinate sb.; **ein ~ [auf jmdn.] vorhaben** *(fig. ugs. scherzh.)* want to ask a favour [of sb.]

Attentäter ['atnte:tɐ] **der;** ~s, ~, **Attentäterin die;** ~, ~nen would-be assassin; *(bei erfolgreichem Attentat)* assassin

Attest [a'tɛst] **das;** ~[e]s, ~e medical certificate; doctor's certificate

attestieren *tr. V.* certify; **jmdm. seine Unzurechnungsfähigkeit ~:** certify sb. as not responsible for his/her own actions

Attika ['atika] **(das)**; ~s Attica

attisch ['atɪʃ] *Adj.* Attic

Attitüde [ati'ty:də] **die;** ~, ~n *(geh.)* posture

Attraktion [atrak'tsi̯o:n] **die;** ~, ~en attraction

attraktiv [atrak'ti:f] **1.** *Adj.* attractive. **2.** *adv.* attractively

Attraktivität [atraktivi'tɛ:t] **die;** ~: attractiveness

Attrappe [a'trapə] **die;** ~, ~n dummy; **die ~ eines Fernsehgeräts/einer Flasche** a dummy television set/bottle

Attribut [atri'bu:t] **das;** ~[e]s, ~e attribute

attributiv [atribu'ti:f] *(Sprachw.)* **1.** *Adj.* attributive. **2.** *adv.* attributively

Attribut·satz der *(Sprachw.)* attributive clause

atü [a'ty:] *(veralt.) Abk.* **Atmosphärenüberdruck; 1 ~:** 2 atm.; **3 ~:** 4 atm.

atypisch *(geh.)* **1.** *Adj.* atypical. **2.** *adv.* atypically

atzen ['atsn] *tr. V. (Jägerspr.)* feed

ätzen ['ɛtsn] **1.** *tr. V.* **a)** etch; **b)** *(Med.)* cauterize ⟨*wound*⟩. **2.** *itr. V.* corrode

ätzend 1. *Adj.* **a)** corrosive; *(fig.)* caustic ⟨*wit, remark, criticism*⟩; pungent ⟨*smell*⟩; acrid ⟨*smoke*⟩; **b)** *(Jugendspr.) (gut)* great *(coll.)*; ace *(sl.)*; *(schlecht)* grotty *(Brit. sl.)*; grot *(Brit. sl.)*. **2.** *adv.* caustically ⟨*ironic, critical*⟩

Ätz·natron das *(Chemie)* caustic soda

Atzung die; ~, ~en *(Jägerspr.)* **a)** *(Fütterung)* feeding; **b)** *(Nahrung)* food; *(fig. scherzh.)* fodder

Ätzung die; ~, ~en **a)** etching; **b)** *(Med.)* cauterization

au [au̯] *Interj.* **a)** *(bei Schmerz)* ow; ouch; **b)** *(bei Überraschung, Begeisterung)* oh

Au die; ~, ~en *(südd., österr.)* *s.* **Aue a**

aua ['au̯a] *Interj. (ugs.; Kinderspr.)* ow; ouch

Aubergine [obɛr'ʒi:nə] **die;** ~, ~n aubergine *(Brit.)*; egg-plant

auch [au̯x] **1.** *Adv.* **a)** *(ebenso, ebenfalls)* as well; too; also; **Klaus war ~ dabei** Klaus was there as well *or* too; Klaus was also there; **Ich gehe jetzt. – Ich ~:** I'm going now – So am I; **Mir ist warm. – Mir ~:** I feel warm – So do I; **... – Ja, das ~: ...** – Yes, that too; **~ gut!** that's all right too; **das kann ich ~!** I can do that too; **was er verspricht, tut er ~:** what he promises to do, he does; **wenn er sagt, er kommt, dann kommt er ~:** if he says he's going to come, then he'll come; **nicht nur ..., sondern ~ ...:** not only ..., but also ...; **grüß deine Frau und ~ die Kinder** give my regards to your wife and the children too; **sehr gut, aber ~ teuer** very good but expensive too; **~ das noch!** that's all I/we *etc.* need!; **oder ~:** or; **oder ~ nicht** or not, as the case may be; **das weiß ich ~ nicht** I don't know either; **ich weiß ~ das nicht** I don't know that either; **ich habe ~ keine Lust/kein Geld** I don't feel like it either/don't have any money either; **das hat ~ nichts genützt** that did not help either; **wir waren unter anderem ~ in Florenz** we were in Florence, among other places; *s. auch* **sowohl; b)** *(sogar, selbst)* even; **~ wenn** even if; **wenn ~:** even if *or* though; **ohne ~ nur zu fragen/eine Sekunde zu zögern** without even asking/hesitating for a second; **c)** *(außerdem, im übrigen)* besides; **und ich sehe ~ gar nicht ein, warum ...:** nor do I see why ...; and besides, I don't see why ... **2.** *Partikel* **a)** *not translated* **etwas anderes habe ich ~ nicht erwartet** I never expected anything else; **du bist aber ~ ein Trottel** *(ugs.)* you're a real idiot[, you are] *(coll.)*; **so schlimm ist es ~ [wieder] nicht** it's not as bad as all that; **den Teufel ~:** damn it [all]!; **nun hör aber ~ zu!** now listen!; **wozu [denn] ~?** what's the point? why should I/you *etc.?*; **b)** *(zweifelnd)* **bist du dir ~ im klaren, was das bedeutet?** are you sure you unterstand what that means?; **bist du ~ glücklich?** are you truly happy?; **lügst du ~ nicht?** you're not lying, are you?; **c)** *(mit Interrogativpron.)* **wo .../wer .../wann .../was ... usw. ~:** wherever/whoever/whenever/whatever *etc.* ...; **wie dem ~ sei** however that may be; **d)** *(konzessiv)* **mag er ~ noch so klug sein** however clever he may be; no matter how clever he is; **so oft ich ~ anrief** however often I rang; no matter how often I rang; **so gern ich es ~ täte, ...:** much as I should like to [do it]; **so sehr er sich ~ bemühte** much as he tried; **wenn ~!** never mind

Audienz [au̯'di̯ɛnts] **die;** ~, ~en audience

Audimax [au̯di'maks] **das;** ~ *(Studentenspr.)* main lecture hall

audiovisuell [au̯di̯ovi'zu̯ɛl] **1.** *Adj.* audio-visual. **2.** *adv.* audio-visually

auditiv [au̯di'ti:f] **1.** *Adj.* auditory. **2.** *adv.* auditorily

Auditorium [au̯di'to:ri̯ʊm] **das;** ~s, **Auditorien a)** *(Hörsaal)* auditorium; **~ maximum** *(Hochschulw.)* main lecture hall; **b)** *(Zuhörerschaft)* audience

Aue ['au̯ə] **die;** ~, ~en **a)** *(dichter.)* mead *(poet.)*; meadow; **b)** *(Geogr.)* water meadow

Auen·wald der riverside forest

Auer- ['au̯ɐ-]: **~hahn der** [cock] capercaillie; **~henne die** [female *or* hen] capercaillie; **~huhn das** capercaillie; **~ochse der** aurochs

auf [au̯f] **1.** *Präp. mit Dat.* **a)** on; **~ See** at sea; **~ dem Baum** in the tree; **~ der Erde** on earth; **~ der Welt** in the world; **~ der Straße** in the street; **~ dem Platz** in the square; **~ meinem Konto** in my account; **~ den Hebriden/Skye** in the Hebrides/on Skye; **~ Meereshöhe** at sea level; **~ beiden Augen blind** blind in both eyes; **das Thermometer steht ~ 15°** the thermometer stands at *or* says *or* reads 15°; **b)** *(bei Räumen, Gebäuden, Institutionen)* at ⟨*post office, town, hall, police station*⟩; ~ **seinem Zimmer** *(ugs.)* in his room; **Geld** ~ **der Bank haben** have money in the bank; ~ **der Polizei** *(ugs.)* at the police station; ~ **der Schule/Uni** at school/university; **c)** *(bei Veranstaltungen o. ä.)* at ⟨*party, wedding*⟩; on ⟨*course, trip, walk, holiday, tour*⟩; **d) was hat es damit** ~ **sich?** what's it all about?; **damit hat es nichts/etwas** ~ **sich** there is nothing/something in it. **2.** *Präp. mit Akk.* **a)** on; on to; **sich** ~ **einen Stuhl setzen** sit down on a chair; **sich** ~ **das Bett legen** lie down on the bed; **er nahm den Rucksack** ~ **den Rücken** he lifted the rucksack up on to his back; ~ **einen Berg steigen** climb up a mountain; **sich** *(Dat.)* **einen Hut** ~ **den Kopf setzen** put a hat on [one's head]; ~ **den Mond fliegen** fly to the moon; ~ **die See hinausfahren** go out to sea; **jmdm.** ~ **den Fuß treten** step on sb.'s foot; ~ **die Straße gehen** go [out] into the street; ~ **den Grund des Meeres sinken** sink to the bottom of the sea; **jmdn.** ~ **den Rücken legen** lay sb. on his/her back; **jmdn.** ~ **den Rücken drehen** turn sb. on to his/her back; ~ **die Hebriden** to the Hebrides; ~ **die andere Seite der Schranke gehen** go over to the other side of the barrier; **etw.** ~ **ein Konto überweisen** transfer sth. to an account; **das Thermometer ist** ~ **0° gefallen** the thermometer has fallen to 0°; ~ **ihn!** *(ugs.)* get him!; **b)** *(bei Institutionen, Veranstaltungen)* to; ~ **die Schule/Uni gehen** go to school/university; ~ **einen Lehrgang gehen** go on a course; ~ **Reisen/Urlaub/Tournee gehen** go travelling/on holiday/on tour; **c)** *(bei Entfernungen)* ~ **10 km [Entfernung]** for [a distance of] 10 km; **wir näherten uns der Hütte [bis]** ~ **30 m** we approached to within 30 m of the hut; **d)** *(zeitlich)* for; ~ **Jahre [hinaus]** for years [to come]; **etw.** ~ **nächsten Mittwoch festlegen/verschieben** arrange sth. for/postpone sth. until next Wednesday; **die Nacht von Sonntag** ~ **Montag** Sunday night; **das fällt** ~ **einen Montag** it falls on a Monday; **wir verschieben es** ~ **den 3. Mai** we'll postpone it to the 3 May; **sich** ~ **morgen vertagen** adjourn until tomorrow; **komm doch mal** ~ **eine Tasse Tee herüber** come round for a cup of tea some time; **e)** *(zur Angabe der Art und Weise)* ~ **diese Art und Weise** in this way; ~ **die Tour erreichst du bei mir nichts** *(ugs.)* you won't get anywhere with me like that; **komm mir bloß nicht** ~ **die Sentimentale!** *(salopp)* don't try *or* come the old sentimental bit with me! *(sl.)*; **auf die Billige** *(salopp)* on the cheap; ~ **deutsch** in German; ~ **das sorgfältigste/herzlichste** *(geh.)* most carefully/warmly; ~ **a enden** end in a; **Wörter** ~ **a** words ending in a; **f)** *(auf Grund)* ~ **Wunsch** on request; ~ **vielfachen Wunsch/wiederholte Aufforderung [hin]** in response to numerous requests/repeated demands; ~ **meine Bitte** at my request; ~ **seine Initiative** on his initiative; ~ **Befehl** on command; ~ **meinen Vorschlag [hin]** at my suggestion; **erst** ~ **meinen Brief [hin]** only as a result of my letter; **g)** *(sonstige Verwendungen)* **ein Teelöffel** ~ **einen Liter Wasser** one teaspoon to one litre of water; **das Bier geht** ~ **mich** *(ugs.)* the beer's on 'me *(coll.)*; ~ **wen geht die Cola?** who's paying for the Coke?; **Welle** ~ **Welle brandete ans Ufer** wave upon wave broke on the shore; **einen Text** ~ **orthographische Fehler [hin] durchsehen** examine a text for orthographical errors; **jmdn.** ~ **Tb untersuchen** examine sb. for TB; **jmdn.** ~ **seine Eignung prüfen** test sb.'s suitability; ~ **die Sekunde/den Millimeter [genau]** [precise] to the second/millimetre; **ein Kabel** ~ **1,50 m kürzen/abschneiden** shorten a cable to 1.50 m; ~ **ein gutes Gelingen** to our/your success; ~ **deine Gesundheit** your health; ~ **bald/morgen!** *(bes. südd.)* see you soon/tomorrow; ~ **10 zählen** *(bes. südd.)* count [up] to 10; *s. auch* **einmal 1 a; machen 3 f. 3.** *Adv.* **a)** *(Aufforderung, sich zu erheben)* ~! up you get!; *(zu einem Hund)* up!; **Sprung** ~! **Marsch, marsch!** *(Milit.)* Up! At the double!; **b) sie waren längst** ~ **und davon** they had made off long before; **jetzt heißt's** ~ **und davon** it's time to be off; *s. auch* **aufsein, aufmachen, davonsein, davonmachen; c)** *(bes. südd.: los)* come on; ~ **geht's** off we go; let's go; **d)** *(Aufforderung, sich aufzumachen)* ~ **ins Schwimmbad!/nach Schifferstadt!** come on, off to the swimming-pool!/to Schifferstadt!; **e)** ~ **und ab** *od. (geh.)* **nieder** up and down; **das Auf und Ab** the up-and-down movement; **das Auf und Ab des Lebens** *(fig.)* the ups and downs of life; **f)** ~ **und ab** *(hin und her)* up and down; to and fro; **g)** *(Aufforderung, sich etw. aufzusetzen)* **Helm/Hut/Brille** ~! helmet/hat/glasses on!; **h)** *(Aufforderung, etw. zu öffnen)* **Fenster/Türen/Mund** ~! open the window/doors/your mouth!. **4.** ~ **daß** *Konj. (veralt.)* so that; ~ **daß er sich nicht erkälte[te]** lest he should catch [a] cold

auf|arbeiten *tr. V.* **a)** *(erledigen)* catch up with ⟨*correspondence etc.*⟩; **b)** *(studieren, analysieren)* review ⟨*literature, material*⟩; look back on and reappraise ⟨*one's past, childhood*⟩; **c)** *(restaurieren, überholen)* refurbish

Aufarbeitung die; ~, ~**en a)** *(Erledigung)* **die** ~**arbeitung der Post** catching up with the post *(Brit.) or* mail; **b)** *(das Studieren, Analysieren)* **die** ~ **der Literatur/Kindheit** reviewing the literature/looking back on and reappraising one's childhood; **c)** *(Restaurierung)* refurbishing

auf|atmen *itr. V.* **a)** *(fig.: erleichtert sein)* breathe a sigh of relief; **ein Aufatmen** a sigh of relief; **b)** *(tief atmen)* breathe deeply

auf|backen *regelm. (auch unr.) tr. V.* crisp up ⟨*bread, rolls, etc.*⟩

auf|bahren *tr. V.* lay out ⟨*body, corpse*⟩; **jmdn./einen Toten** ~: lay out sb.'s body; **aufgebahrt sein** ⟨*king, president, etc.*⟩ lie in state

Auf·bau der; ~**[e]s,** ~**ten a)** *o. Pl. (das Aufbauen)* construction; building; *(das Wiederaufbauen)* reconstruction; rebuilding; **b)** *o. Pl. (von Staat, Ökonomie, gesellschaftlicher Ordnung)* building; **den wirtschaftlichen** ~ **beschleunigen** speed up economic development; **c)** *o. Pl. (Biol.)* synthesis; **d)** *o. Pl. (Struktur)* structure; **e)** *Pl. (Schiffbau)* superstructure *sing.*; **f)** *(Bauw.)* superstructure; **einen zweistöckigen** ~ **genehmigen** approve the addition of two extra storeys; **g)** *(Kfz-W.)* body

Aufbau·arbeit die the construction work; *(bei Wiederaufbau)* reconstruction work

auf|bauen 1. *tr. V.* **a)** *auch itr. (errichten, aufstellen)* erect ⟨*hut, kiosk, podium*⟩; set up ⟨*equipment, train set*⟩; build ⟨*house, bridge*⟩; put up ⟨*tent*⟩; *(wiederaufbauen)* rebuild ⟨*house, bridge*⟩; **ein Haus neu** ~: rebuild a house; **b)** *(hinstellen, arrangieren)* lay *or* set out ⟨*food, presents, etc.*⟩; **c)** *(fig.: schaffen)* build ⟨*state, economy, social order, life, political party, etc.*⟩; build up ⟨*business, organization, army, spy network*⟩; **sich** *(Dat.)* **ein neues Leben** ~: build a new life [for oneself]; **d)** *(fig.: strukturieren)* structure; **e)** *(fig.: fördern)* **jmdn./etw. zu etw.** ~: build sb./sth. up into sth.; **jmdn. als etw.** ~: build sb. up as sth.; **f)** *(gründen)* **etw. auf etw.** *(Dat.)* ~: base sth. upon sth.; **g)** *(Biol.)* synthesize. **2.** *itr. V.* **auf etw.** *(Dat.)* ~: be based on sth. **3.** *refl. V.* **a)** *(ugs.: sich hinstellen)* plant oneself (**vor** + *Dat.* in front of); **b)** *(sich zusammensetzen)* be composed (**aus** of); **c)** *(sich auftürmen, sich bilden)* ⟨*clouds, pressure, tension, etc.*⟩ build up

aufbauend *Adj.* constructive ⟨*criticism, geological process*⟩; restorative ⟨*medicine*⟩; nutrient ⟨*substance*⟩

auf|bäumen ['aufbɔymən] *refl. V.* rear up; **sich gegen jmdn./etw.** ~ *(fig.)* rise up against sb./sth.

Aufbau·prinzip das structural principle

auf|bauschen 1. *tr. V.* **a)** *(aufblähen)* billow; billow, belly [out] ⟨*sail*⟩; **b)** *(fig.: hochspielen)* blow up *(coll.)*; exaggerate. **2.** *refl. V. (fig.: sich auswachsen)* **sich [zu etw.]** ~: blow up [into sth.] *(coll.)*

Aufbauten *s.* **Aufbau**

auf|begehren *itr. V. (geh.)* rebel

auf|behalten *unr. tr. V.* **etw.** ~: keep sth. on

auf|beißen *unr. tr. V.* **etw.** ~: bite sth. open; **sich** *(Dat.)* **die Lippe** ~: bite one's lip [and make it bleed]

auf|bekommen *unr. tr. V.* **a)** *(öffnen können)* **etw.** ~: get sth. open; **b)** *(aufessen können)* manage to eat; **c)** *(aufsetzen können)* **etw.** ~: get sth. on; **d)** *(aufgegeben bekommen)* be given

auf|bereiten *tr. V.* **a)** *(Hüttenw., Bergbau)* dress, prepare ⟨*ore, coal*⟩; **Erz magnetisch** ~: separate ore magnetically; **b)** *(Wasserwirtsch.)* purify; treat; **c)** *(Kerntechnik)* reprocess; **d)** *(Statistik)* process; **e)** *(geh.) (bearbeiten)* adapt; *(erschließen)* reconstruct; **etw. literarisch/dramatisch** ~: put sth. into literary/dramatic form

Auf·bereitung die *s.* **aufbereiten a-e:** dressing; preparation; purification; treatment; reprocessing; processing; adaptation; reconstruction

Aufbereitungs·anlage die *(Hüttenw.)* preparation plant; *(Wasserwirtsch.)* purification works *sing.*; treatment plant; *(Kerntechnik)* reprocessing plant

auf|bessern *tr. V.* improve; increase ⟨*pension, wages, etc.*⟩

Auf·besserung die improvement (*Gen.* in); *(bei Renten, Löhnen, Gehältern)* increase (*Gen.* in); **zur** ~ **seines Taschengeldes/seiner Sprachkenntnisse** to increase his pocket money/to improve his linguistic proficiency

auf|bewahren *tr. V.* keep; store, keep ⟨*medicines, food, provisions*⟩; *(fig.: bewahren, erhalten)* preserve ⟨*memory, name, writings*⟩; **die Fahrkarte/das Testament mußt du gut** ~: you must keep your ticket safe/keep the will in a safe place; **etw. kühl** ~: store sth. in a cool place

Auf·bewahrung die a) *s.* **aufbewahren:** keeping; storage; **jmdm. etw. zur** ~ **geben/anvertrauen** give sth. to sb. for safe keeping/entrust sb. with the care of sth.; **bei** ~ **im Kühlschrank** if kept in a refrigerator; **b)** *(Verkehrsw.)* left-luggage office *(Brit.)*; baggage check room *(Amer.)*

Aufbewahrungs-: ~**ort der: das ist kein geeigneter** ~**ort für Dokumente/Lebensmittel** that is not a suitable place to keep documents/keep *or* store food; ~**schein der** *(Verkehrsw.)* left-luggage ticket *(Brit.)*; baggage check *or* ticket *(Amer.)*

auf|biegen 1. *unr. tr. V.* **a) etw.** ~: bend sth. open; **b)** *(hochbiegen)* bend up[wards]. **2.** *unr. refl. V.* **a)** bend open; **b)** *(sich hochbiegen)* bend up[wards]

auf|bieten *unr. tr. V.* **a)** *(aufwenden)* exert ⟨*strength, energy, will-power, influence, authority*⟩; call on ⟨*skill, wit, powers of persuasion or eloquence*⟩; **b)** *(einsetzen)* call in ⟨*police, troops*⟩; **c)** *(Milit. veralt.: ausheben)* call up ⟨*troops*⟩; raise ⟨*army*⟩; **d)** *(zur Eheschließung)* **ein Brautpaar** ~: read *or* call the banns of a couple to be married; **e)** *(bei Versteigerung)* **etw. [mit 400 Mark]** ~: put sth. up for auction [at a starting price of 400 marks]

Aufbietung die; ~ **a) unter** ~ **aller Kräfte/seiner ganzen Überredungskunst** summoning up all one's strength/calling on all one's

persuasive skills; **b)** *(Milit. veralt.)* calling up; *(einer Armee)* raising
auf|binden *unr. tr. V.* **a)** *(öffnen, lösen)* untie; undo; **sich/jmdm. die Schuhe ~:** undo one's/sb.'s shoes; **b)** *(hochbinden)* tie *or* put up ‹*hair*›; tie ‹*plant*› up straight; **jmdm./sich die Haare ~:** tie *or* put up sb.'s/one's hair; **c)** *(auf den Rücken binden)* **jmdm./einem Tier eine Last ~:** tie a burden on to sb.'s/an animal's back; **d)** *(ugs.: weismachen)* **wer hat dir das aufgebunden?** who spun you that yarn?; **jmdm. ein Märchen/eine Fabel ~:** spin sb. a yarn; *s.* **auch Bär; e)** *(binden auf)* **etw. auf etw.** *(Akk.)* **~:** tie sth. on to sth.; **f)** *(Buchw.: binden)* bind
auf|blähen 1. *tr. V.* distend ‹*body, stomach*›; puff out ‹*cheeks, feathers*›; flare ‹*nostrils*›; billow, fill, belly [out] ‹*sail*›; billow ‹*washing, clothing*›; *(fig.: vergrößern)* over-inflate; **ein aufgeblähter Beamtenapparat** *(fig.)* an overblown bureaucracy. **2.** *refl. V.* **a)** ‹*sail*› billow *or* belly out; ‹*balloon, lungs, chest*› expand; ‹*stomach*› swell up, become swollen *or* distended; **b)** *(abwertend: sich aufspielen)* puff oneself up
Auf·blähung die *(fig.)* over-expansion
aufblasbar *Adj.* inflatable
auf|blasen 1. *unr. tr. V.* blow up; inflate; **die Backen ~:** puff out one's cheeks; **etw. zu etw. ~** *(fig.)* blow sth. up into sth. **2.** *unr. refl. V. (ugs. abwertend: sich aufspielen);* **sich ~ [wie ein Frosch]** puff oneself up **(mit** about); *s. auch* **aufgeblasen 2**
auf|bleiben *unr. itr. V.; mit sein* **a)** *(geöffnet bleiben)* stay open; **b)** *(nicht zu Bett gehen)* stay up
auf|blenden 1. *tr. V. (Kfz-W.)* **die Scheinwerfer ~:** switch one's headlights to full beam; **mit aufgeblendeten Scheinwerfern fahren** drive with headlights on full beam. **2.** *itr. V.* **a)** *(Kfz-W.)* switch to full beam; **b)** *(Fot., Film)* open up the lens; increase the [lens] aperture
auf|blicken *itr. V.* **a)** look up; *(kurz)* glance up; **von etw. ~:** look/glance up from sth.; **b)** *(verehrend)* **zu jmdm. ~:** look up to sb.
auf|blinken *itr. V.* **a)** ‹*light*› flash; ‹*metal*› glint; ‹*star*› blink; **b)** *(ugs.: kurz aufblenden)* flash one's headlights
auf|blitzen *itr. V.* flash; ‹*wave, white-caps*› sparkle
auf|blühen *itr. V.; mit sein* **a)** bloom; come into bloom; ‹*bud*› open; **eine halb/voll aufgeblühte Tulpe** a half-open tulip/a tulip in full bloom; **b)** *(fig.: aufleben)* blossom [out]; **c)** *(fig.: einen Aufschwung nehmen)* ‹*trade, business, town, industry*› flourish and expand; ‹*cultural life, science*› blossom and flourish
auf|bocken *tr. V.* **etw. ~:** jack sth. up
auf|bohren *tr. V.* **etw. ~:** drill a hole in sth.; drill ‹*tooth*›; bore out ‹*cylinder, engine*›
auf|branden *itr. V.; mit sein (geh.)* **die Wellen brandeten an den Felsen auf** the waves broke against the rock with a roar; **Beifall/Jubel brandete auf** *(fig.)* thunderous applause/cheering burst out
auf|braten *unr. tr. V.* **etw. ~:** fry sth. up [again]
auf|brauchen *tr. V.* use up
auf|brausen *itr. V.; mit sein* **a)** *(zornig werden)* flare up; **schnell/leicht ~:** be quick-tempered *or* hot-tempered; have a quick temper; **b)** *(zu brausen beginnen)* ‹*sea, surf, wave*› surge [up]; ‹*liquid*› seethe, boil up; ‹*wind*› rise to a roar; **Beifall/Jubel brauste auf** there was a sudden roar of applause/a thunderous cheer went up
aufbrausend *Adj.* quick-tempered; hot-tempered; **ein ~es Temperament haben** be quick-tempered *or* hot-tempered; have a quick temper
auf|brechen 1. *unr. tr. V.* **a)** *(öffnen)* break open ‹*lock, safe, box, crate, etc.*›; break into ‹*car*›; force [open] ‹*door*›; break up ‹*ground, surface*›; *(geh.: aufreißen)* tear open ‹*letter, telegram*›; *(fig.)* break down ‹*[social] structures*›; break ‹*system*›; **b)** *(Jägerspr.: ausnehmen)* gut. **2.** *unr. itr. V.; mit sein* **a)** *(sich öffnen)* ‹*bud*› open [up], burst [open]; ‹*ice [sheet], surface, ground*› break up; ‹*wound*› open; **alte Wunden brechen auf** *(fig.)* old wounds are opening [again]; **b)** *(sich auf den Weg machen)* set off, start out **(zu** on); **c)** *(geh.: spürbar werden)* become evident; emerge
auf|brennen *unr. tr. V.* **einem Tier ein Zeichen/ein Mal ~:** brand an animal; **jmdm. eins ~** *(salopp: auf jmdn. schießen)* let sb. have it
auf|bringen *unr. tr. V.* **a)** *(beschaffen)* find; raise, find ‹*money*›; *(fig.)* find, summon [up] ‹*strength, energy, courage*›; find ‹*patience*›; **b)** *(kreieren)* introduce, start ‹*fashion, custom*›; introduce ‹*slogan, theory*›; start, put about ‹*rumour*›; **c)** *(in Wut bringen)* **jmdn. ~:** make sb. angry; infuriate sb.; **d)** *(aufwiegeln)* **jmdn. gegen jmdn./etw. ~:** set sb. against sb./sth.; **e)** *(auftragen)* put on, apply ‹*paint, ointment, varnish, etc.*›; **f)** *(Seew.)* seize; *(in den Hafen bringen)* bring in; **g)** *(bes. südd.) s.* **aufbekommen a, b, c**
Auf·bruch der a) departure; *(fig. geh.)* awakening; **im ~ begriffen sein** be on the point of departure *or* of setting off; *(fig. geh.)* experience an awakening; **das Zeichen zum ~ geben** give the signal to set off *or* leave; **zum ~ rüsten** get ready to set off *or* leave; **b)** *(aufgebrochene Stelle)* crack
Aufbruchs·stimmung die; *o. Pl.* **es herrschte allgemeine ~:** everybody was getting ready to go; **bist du schon in ~?** are you all ready to go?
auf|brühen *tr. V.* brew [up]
auf|brüllen *itr. V.* let out *or* give a roar; ‹*animal*› bellow
auf|brummen *tr. V. (ugs.)* **jmdm. etw. ~:** slap sth. on sb. *(coll.)*; **einem Schüler viele Hausaufgaben ~:** lumber *(Brit.) or* burden a pupil with a lot of homework; **jmdm. die Kosten für etw. ~:** land sb. with the costs for sth.
auf|bügeln *tr. V.* iron; **etw. [auf etw.** *(Akk.)*] **~:** iron sth. on [to sth.]; **Flicken zum Aufbügeln** iron-on patches
auf|bürden *tr. V. (geh.)* **jmdm./einem Tier etw. ~:** load sth. on to sb./an animal; **jmdm./sich etw. ~** *(fig.)* burden sb./oneself with sth.; **jmdm. die Schuld ~:** put the blame on sb.
auf|bürsten *tr. V.* **etw. ~:** brush sth. up; give sth. a brush-up
auf|decken 1. *tr. V.* **a)** uncover; **das Bett ~:** pull back the covers; **sich im Schlaf ~:** throw off one's covers; **b)** *(Kartenspiele)* show; **die** *od.* **seine Karten ~** *(fig.)* lay one's cards on the table *(fig.)*; **c)** *(enthüllen)* expose ‹*corruption, error, weakness, misdeeds, crime, plot, abuse, etc.*›; *(erkennen und bewußtmachen)* reveal, uncover ‹*connections, motive, processes, cause, error, weakness, contradiction, etc.*›; **d)** *(für eine Mahlzeit)* **etw. ~:** put sth. on the table. **2.** *itr. V.* lay the table
Auf·deckung die *s.* **aufdecken 1c:** exposure; revelation; uncovering
auf|donnern *refl. V. (ugs. abwertend)* tart *(Brit.) or* doll oneself up *(coll.)*; get tarted *(Brit.) or* dolled up *(coll.)*
auf|drängen 1. *tr. V.* **jmdm. etw. ~:** force sth. on sb.; **jmdm. seine Ansichten ~:** force *or* impose one's views on sb. **2.** *refl. V.* **a) sich jmdm. ~:** force one's company *or* oneself on sb.; **ich will mich aber nicht ~:** I don't want to impose; **b)** *(fig.: in den Sinn kommen)* **mir drängte sich der Verdacht auf, daß ...:** I couldn't help suspecting that ...; **dieser Gedanke drängt sich [einem] förmlich auf** one simply can't help but think so; the thought is unavoidable
auf|drehen 1. *tr. V.* **a)** *(öffnen)* unscrew ‹*bottle-cap, nut*›; undo ‹*screw*›; turn on ‹*tap, gas, water*›; open ‹*valve, bottle, vice*›; **b)** *(ugs.: laut stellen)* turn up ‹*radio, record-player, etc.*›; **c)** *(ugs.: aufziehen)* wind up ‹*musical box, watch, toy, etc.*›; **d)** *(zu Locken drehen)* turn up, twist up ‹*moustache*›; **sich/jmdm. die Haare ~:** put one's/sb.'s hair in curlers. **2.** *itr. V. (ugs.)* **a)** *(das Tempo steigern)* **[voll] ~:** put one's foot [right] down *(coll.)*; step on the gas *(Amer.)*; *(fig.)* step the pace [right] up; **b)** *(in Schwung kommen)* get into the mood; get going
auf·dringlich 1. *Adj.* importunate, *(coll.)* pushy ‹*person*›; insistent ‹*music, advertisement, questioning*›; pestering *attrib.* ‹*journalist*›; pungent ‹*perfume, smell*›; loud, gaudy ‹*colour, wallpaper*›; **~e Vertraulichkeit** over-familiarity; **~e Freundlichkeit** over-friendliness; **sei nicht so ~!** don't pester so!; **~ riechen** have a pungent smell; be pungent. **2.** *adv.* ‹*behave*› importunately, *(coll.)* pushily; ‹*ask*› insistently
Aufdringlichkeit die; ~, ~en a) *o. Pl. s.* **aufdringlich:** insistent manner; insistence; importunity, pushiness *(coll.)*; pungency; **b)** *(Äußerung, Handlung)* piece of over-familiarity; **die ~en der Männer** the over-familiarity *sing.* of the men
auf|dröseln ['aufdrø:zl̩n] *tr. V. (ugs., auch fig.)* unravel; unpick ‹*piece of knitting*›
Auf·druck der; ~[e]s, ~e a) imprint; **b)** *(Philat.) s.* **²Überdruck**
auf|drucken *tr. V.* **etw. auf etw.** *(Akk.)* **~:** print sth. on sth.; **Briefumschläge mit aufgedruckter Adresse** envelopes with the address printed on them
auf|drücken *tr. V.* **a)** *(öffnen)* push open; **b)** *(aufplatzen lassen)* squeeze ‹*pimple, boil*›; **c)** *(aufstempeln, aufprägen)* **etw. auf etw.** *(Akk.)* **~:** stamp sth. on sth.; **jmdm. einen Kuß ~:** plant a kiss on sb.; **einer Sache** *(Dat.)* **sein Gepräge ~** *(fig.)* leave one's mark *or* stamp on sth.; *s. auch* **Stempel a; d)** *(auf etw. drücken)* **etw. auf etw.** *(Akk.)* **~:** press sth. on to sth.; **drück den Bleistift nicht so fest auf** don't press so hard with your pencil
auf·einander *Adv.* **a)** on top of one another *or* each other; **die Bücher sollen ~ liegen** the books should lie one on top of the other; **b) zwei Autos waren ~ aufgefahren** two cars had collided with each other *or* one another; **~ warten** wait for each other *or* one another; **~ zugehen** walk towards *or* approach one another *or* each other
aufeinander-: ~|beißen *unr. tr. V.* **die Zähne ~beißen** clench one's teeth; **~|drücken** *tr. V.* press together
Aufeinander·folge die; ~: sequence; **in rascher ~:** in rapid *or* quick succession
aufeinander-: ~|folgen *itr. V.; mit sein* follow each other *or* one another; **~folgend** successive; **an mehreren ~folgenden Tagen** several days running; on several successive days; **~|hängen 1.** *tr. V.* **die Mäntel ~hängen** hang the coats one on top of the other; **2.** *unr. itr. V.* **a)** hang one on top of the other; hang on top of each other *or* one another; **b)** *(fig. ugs.)* hang around together; **wenn es regnet, hängt man den ganzen Tag im Hotel ~:** when it rains, people hang around on top of each other all day in the hotel; **~|häufen** *tr. V.* pile ‹*books etc.*› on top of each other *or* one another; **~|hetzen** *tr. V.* set ‹*dogs etc.*› on each other *or* one another; **~|legen 1.** *tr. V.* lay ‹*planks etc.*› one on top of the other; **2.** *refl. V.* lie on top of each other *or* one another; **~|liegen** *unr. itr. V.* lie on top of each other *or* one another; **~|prallen** *itr. V.; mit sein* crash into each other *or* one another; collide; ‹*armies*› clash; *(fig.)* ‹*opinions*› clash; **~|pressen** *tr. V.* press together; **~|schichten** *tr. V.* stack up;

~|**schlagen 1.** *unr. tr. V.* strike *or* knock together; bang ⟨*cymbals*⟩ together; **2.** *unr. itr. V.; mit sein* strike *or* knock against each other *or* one another; ~|**setzen 1.** *tr. V.* put ⟨*stones etc.*⟩ one on top of the other; **2.** *refl. V.* sit on top of each other *or* one another; ~|**sitzen** *unr. itr. V.* sit on top of each other *or* one another; *(fig.: eng wohnen)* live on top of each other *or* one another; ~|**stapeln** *tr. V.* stack ⟨*planks etc.*⟩ one on top of the other; ~|**stoßen** *unr. itr. V.; mit sein* ⟨*buffers*⟩ bump together; ⟨*lines, streets*⟩ meet; *(fig.)* ⟨*people*⟩ bump *or* run into each other *or* one another; ⟨*cultures*⟩ meet; ⟨*opinions*⟩ clash; ~|**treffen** *unr. itr. V.; mit sein* ⟨*teams, enemies, opponents, streets*⟩ meet; ⟨*missiles*⟩ collide, hit each other *or* one another; ~|**türmen** *tr. V.* stack ⟨*crates etc.*⟩ [up] one on top of the other

Aufenthalt ['aufɛnthalt] **der; ~[e]s, ~e a)** stay; **der ~ im Depot ist verboten** personnel/the public *etc.* are not permitted to remain within in the depot; **~ nehmen** *(geh.)* reside; **b)** *(Fahrtunterbrechung)* stop; **der Zug hatte dort [10 Minuten] ~:** the train stopped there [for 10 minutes]; **ohne ~ durchfahren** travel through non-stop *or* without stopping; **c)** *(geh.: Ort)* residence

-aufenthalt der: Frankreich~/Italien~: stay in France/Italy

Aufenthalts-: ~bewilligung die *s.* **~erlaubnis; ~dauer die** length of stay; **bei einer ~dauer von weniger als sechs Monaten** for a stay of less than six months; **~erlaubnis die** residence permit; **~genehmigung die** *s.* **~erlaubnis; ~ort der** [place of] residence; **jmds. ~ort ermitteln** establish sb.'s whereabouts *pl.*; **~raum der** *(in einer Schule o. ä.)* common-room *(Brit.)*; *(in einer Jugendherberge)* day-room; *(in einem Betrieb o. ä.)* recreation-room; *(in einem Hotel o. ä.)* lounge

auf|erlegen, auf·erlegen *tr. V. (geh.)* **jmdm. etw. ~:** impose sth. on sb.; **du solltest dir etwas Zurückhaltung ~:** you should exercise some restraint; **die Kosten wurden dem Kläger auferlegt** costs were awarded against the plaintiff; **jmdm. eine schwere Prüfung ~:** subject sb. to *or* put sb. through a severe test

auf|erstehen *unr. itr. V.; mit sein* rise [again]; **von den Toten ~:** rise from the dead; **Christus ist auferstanden** Christ is risen

Auferstehung die; ~, ~en resurrection

auf·erwecken *tr. V.* **jmdn. ~:** bring sb. back to life; raise sb. from the dead; **jmdn. von den Toten ~:** raise sb. from the dead; **der Lärm hätte einen Toten ~ können** *(fig.)* the noise was enough to waken the dead

Auf·erweckung die: die ~ eines Toten raising someone from the dead

auf|essen *unr. tr. (auch itr.) V.* eat up

auf|fächern 1. *tr. V.* fan [out]; *(fig.)* set out. **2.** *refl. V.* fan out; **sich in Einzeldisziplinen ~:** develop into seperate disciplines

auf|fädeln *tr. V.* **etw. [auf etw.** *(Akk.)***] ~:** thread sth. on to sth.

auf|fahren 1. *unr. itr. V.; mit sein* **a)** *(aufprallen)* **auf ein anderes Fahrzeug ~:** drive *or* run into the back of another vehicle; **auf etw./jmdn. ~:** drive *or* run into sth./sb.; **das Schiff ist auf ein Riff aufgefahren** the ship has run aground on a reef; **b)** *(aufschließen)* **auf den Vordermann zu dicht ~:** drive too close to the car in front; tail-gate; **fahr doch nicht so dicht** *od.* **nah auf!** don't drive so close!; **zu dichtes Auffahren** driving too close to the vehicle in front; tail-gating; **c)** *(vorfahren)* drive up; **d)** *(in Stellung gehen)* move up [into position]; **e)** *(Bergmannsspr.)* go/come up; **aufgefahren kommen** come up; **f)** *(gen Himmel fahren)* ascend; **g)** *(aufschrecken)* start; **aus dem Schlaf ~:** awake with a start; **h)** *(aufbrausen)* flare up. **2.** *unr. tr. V.* **a)** *(in Stellung bringen)* bring *or* move up; **b)** *(ugs.: auftischen)* serve up

auf·fahrend *Adj.* quick-tempered; hot-tempered

Auf·fahrt die a) *(das Hinauffahren)* climb; drive up; **die ~ zum Gipfel** the drive up to the summit; **b)** *(zu Gebäuden)* drive; **c)** *(zur Autobahn)* slip-road *(Brit.)*; access road *(Amer.)*; **d)** *(schweiz.) (Himmelfahrt)* Ascension; *(Himmelfahrtstag)* Ascension [Day]

Auffahrts·fest das *(schweiz.)* feast of the Ascension

Auffahr·unfall der rear-end collision

auf|fallen *unr. itr. V.; mit sein* **a)** *(auffällig sein)* stand out; **diese Fettflecken/Druckfehler fallen kaum auf** these grease-marks/printing errors are hardly noticeable; **tu das so, daß es nicht auffällt** do it so that it doesn't attract attention *or* so that nobody notices; **er fällt durch seine abstehenden Ohren auf** the fact that his ears stick out makes him conspicuous; **seine Abwesenheit fiel nicht auf** his absence was not noticed; **um nicht aufzufallen** so as not to attract attention; **sie will nur ~:** she just wants to attract attention; **jmdm. fällt etw. auf** sb. notices sth.; sth. strikes sb.; **fällt dir an diesem Satz etwas auf?** does anything strike you about that sentence?; **er ist mir angenehm/unangenehm aufgefallen** he made a good/bad impression on me; **ist Ihnen nichts aufgefallen?** did you not notice anything?; did nothing strike you?; **so etwas fällt sofort/nie auf** that sort of thing will be noticed right away/will never be noticed; **es fiel allgemein auf, daß ...:** it was generally noticed that ...; **b)** *(auftreffen)* fall (**auf +** *Akk.* on [to]); strike (**auf +** *Akk.* sth.); **das ~de Licht** the light falling on [to] *or* striking the surface *etc.*; *(Optik)* the incident light

auffallend 1. *Adj. (auffällig)* conspicuous; *(eindrucksvoll, bemerkenswert)* striking ⟨*contrast, figure, appearance, beauty, similarity*⟩; **das Auffallendste an ihr** the most striking thing about her. **2.** *adv. (auffällig)* conspicuously; *(eindrucksvoll, bemerkenswert)* ⟨*contrast, differ*⟩ strikingly; **stimmt ~!** *(scherzh.)* you're so right!

auf·fällig 1. *Adj.* conspicuous; garish, loud ⟨*colour*⟩; **eine recht ~e Erscheinung sein** have a most striking appearance. **2.** *adv.* conspicuously; **sich ~ kleiden** dress showily; **~er hätte er es nicht machen können** he couldn't have made it more obvious [if he had tried]

Auf·fälligkeit die a) *o. Pl.* conspicuousness; *(Grellheit)* garishness; loudness; **b)** *(etw. Auffälliges)* distinctive feature

auf|falten 1. *tr. V.* fold open; unfold. **2.** *refl. V. (Geol.)* fold upward

auf|fangen *unr. tr. V.* **a)** *(fangen)* catch; *(fig.)* regain control of ⟨*aircraft*⟩; **b)** *(aufnehmen, sammeln)* collect; collect, catch ⟨*liquid*⟩; *(fig.)* receive ⟨*refugees*⟩; **c)** *(wahrnehmen)* catch ⟨*words, conversation*⟩; *(Funkw.: empfangen)* pick up; **d)** *(absorbieren)* absorb; **e)** *(Milit.: aufhalten)* hold ⟨*attack, advance*⟩; **f)** *(Handarb.)* pick up ⟨*stitch*⟩; **g)** *(ausgleichen)* offset ⟨*price increase etc.*⟩

Auffang·lager das reception camp

auf|fassen *tr. V.* **a)** *(ansehen als)* **etw. als etw. ~:** see *or* regard sth. as sth.; **etw. als Scherz/Kompliment/Beleidigung/Kritik ~:** take sth. as a joke/compliment/insult/criticism; **etw. persönlich/falsch ~:** take sth. personally/misunderstand sth.; **b)** *(begreifen)* grasp; comprehend

Auf·fassung die a) *(Meinung, Ansicht)* view; *(Begriff)* conception; **nach meiner ~:** in my view; **der ~ sein, daß ...:** take the view that ...; be of the opinion that ...; **eine andere ~ von etw. haben** take a different view of sth.; **b)** *o. Pl. s.* **Auffassungsgabe**

Auffassungs-: ~gabe die powers *pl.* of comprehension; **eine leichte/schnelle ~gabe haben** be quick on the uptake; **~sache die** in **~sache sein** depend on one's point of view; **~vermögen das;** *o. Pl. s.* **~gabe**

auf|fegen *tr. (auch itr.) V. (bes. nordd.)* sweep up

auffindbar *Adj.* findable; **der Schlüssel muß doch ~ sein!** we must be able to find the key somewhere!; **es ist nirgends/nicht ~:** it's nowhere to be found/it can't be *or* isn't to be found; **schwer/leicht ~ sein** be hard/easy to find

auf|finden *unr. tr. V.* find

auf|fischen *tr. V. (ugs.)* fish out *(coll.)*

auf|flackern *itr. V.; mit sein* flicker up; *(fig.)* ⟨*hope*⟩ flicker up; ⟨*revolt, unrest, passion, anger*⟩ flare up

auf|flammen *itr. V.; mit sein (auch fig.)* flare up; **in seinen Augen flammte Zorn auf** *(fig.)* his eyes flashed with anger

auf|fliegen *unr. itr. V.; mit sein* **a)** *(hochfliegen)* fly up; **b)** *(sich öffnen)* fly open; **c)** *(ugs.: scheitern)* ⟨*illegal organization, drug ring*⟩ be *or* get busted *(coll.)*; **den Parteitag/einen Schmugglerring ~ lassen** ruin *or (Brit. sl.)* scupper the party conference/bust a smuggling ring *(coll.)*

auf|fordern *tr. V.* **a)** *auch itr.* **jmdn. ~, etw. zu tun** call upon *or* ask sb. to do sth.; **jmdn. zur Teilnahme/Zahlung ~:** call upon *or* ask sb. to take part/ask sb. for payment; **ich fordere Sie zum letzten Mal auf, ...:** I am asking you for the last time ...; **jmdn. dringend ~, etw. zu tun** urgently request sb. to do sth.; **b)** *(einladen, ermuntern)* **jmdn. ~, etw. zu tun** invite *or* ask sb. to do sth.; **jmdn. zu einem Spaziergang/zum Mitspielen/Sitzen ~:** invite sb. for a walk/invite *or* ask sb. to join in/sit down; **jmdn. [zum Tanz] ~:** ask sb. to dance

auffordernd 1. *Adj.* **mit einer ~en Geste** with a gesture of invitation; **mit ~em Blick** with a look of encouragement. **2.** *adv.* encouragingly

Auf·forderung die a) request; *(nachdrücklicher)* demand; **nach dreimaliger/mehrmaliger ~:** after three/repeated requests; **b)** *(Einladung, Ermunterung)* invitation

Aufforderungs·satz der *(Sprachw.) clause/sentence expressing a wish, desire, or command*

auf|forsten 1. *tr. V.* afforest; *(wieder ~)* reforest; **einen Wald ~:** restock a forest. **2.** *itr. V.* establish woods; *(wieder ~)* reestablish the woods

Aufforstung die; ~, ~en afforestation; *(Wieder~)* reforestation; **die ~ der Wälder** restocking the forests

auf|fressen 1. *unr. tr. V.* **a)** eat up; *(fig.)* swallow up ⟨*small business*⟩; eat up ⟨*savings, money, etc.*⟩; **er wird dich [deswegen] nicht [gleich] ~** *(ugs.)* he won't *or* isn't going to bite your head off [for that]; **b)** *(fig. ugs.: krank machen)* **jmdn. ~:** eat sb. up; **c)** *(fig.: auflösen)* **etw. ~:** ⟨*acid etc.*⟩ eat sth. **2.** *unr. itr. V.* ⟨*animal*⟩ eat [all] its food up; *(salopp)* ⟨*person*⟩ eat [everything] up

auf|frischen 1. *tr. V.* **a)** *(wieder frisch machen)* freshen up; brighten up ⟨*colour, paintwork*⟩; renovate ⟨*polish, furniture*⟩; *(restaurieren)* restore ⟨*tapestry, fresco, etc.*⟩; *(fig.)* revive ⟨*old memories*⟩; renew ⟨*acquaintance, friendship*⟩; **seine Englischkenntnisse ~:** brush up one's [knowledge of] English; **b)** *(auffüllen)* stock up on ⟨*supplies*⟩. **2.** *itr. V.; auch mit sein* ⟨*wind*⟩ freshen

Auffrischung die; ~, ~en *s.* **auffrischen: a)** freshening up; brightening up; renovation; restoration; renewal; **zur ~ meiner Englischkenntnisse** to brush up my [knowledge of] English; **b) die ~ der Biervorräte** *usw.* stocking up on beer [supplies] *etc.*

aufführbar *Adj.* stageable ⟨*play, ballet, opera*⟩; performable ⟨*piece of music*⟩

auf|führen 1. *tr. V.* **a)** put on, stage ⟨*play,*

ballet, opera⟩; screen, put on ⟨*film*⟩; perform ⟨*piece of music*⟩; put on ⟨*concert*⟩; **führ doch nicht so ein Theater auf!** don't make such a fuss!; **b)** *(nennen)* cite, quote, adduce ⟨*example, reason, fact*⟩; cite ⟨*witness*⟩; **Waren/Preise in einem Verzeichnis ~:** list goods/prices. **2.** *refl. V.* behave; **er hat sich wieder einmal aufgeführt** he made another fuss

Auf·führung die a) performance; **zur ~ bringen** *(Papierdt.)* put on, stage ⟨*play, ballet, opera*⟩; screen, put on ⟨*film*⟩; perform ⟨*piece of music*⟩; put on ⟨*concert*⟩; **zur ~ gelangen** *od.* **kommen** *(Papierdt.)* ⟨*play, ballet, opera*⟩ be staged; ⟨*film*⟩ be screened; ⟨*piece of music, composer*⟩ be performed; ⟨*concert*⟩ be put on; **b)** *(Nennung) s.* **aufführen 1 b:** citation; quotation; listing

Aufführungs·recht das performing rights *pl.*

auf|füllen *tr. V.* **a)** *(vollfüllen, füllen)* fill up; fill in ⟨*hole, gap, crack*⟩; **b)** *(fig.: ergänzen)* replenish ⟨*stocks*⟩; bring ⟨*team, battalion, etc.*⟩ up to full strength; **c)** *(ugs.: nachfüllen)* **Wasser/Öl/Benzin ~:** top up *(Brit.) or (Amer.)* fill up with water/oil/fill up with petrol *(Brit.) or (Amer.)* gasoline. **2.** *refl. V. (Met.)* ⟨*low-pressure area*⟩ fill

auf|futtern *tr. (auch itr.) V. (fam.)* eat up

auf|füttern *tr. V.* rear ⟨*animal*⟩ **(mit** on)

Auf·gabe die a) *(zu Bewältigendes)* task; **sich** *(Dat.)* **zur ~ machen, etw. zu tun** make it one's task *or* job to do sth.; **sich** *(Dat.)* **etw. zur ~ machen** make sth. one's task *or* job; **b)** *(Pflicht)* task; responsibility; duty; **c)** *(fig.: Zweck, Funktion)* function; **d)** *(Schulw.) (Übung)* exercise; *(Prüfungs~)* question; **e)** *(Schulw.: Haus~)* piece of homework; **~n** homework *sing.*; **ich muß noch ~n machen** I still have homework to do; **f)** *(Rechen~, Mathematik~)* problem; **g)** *(Beendigung)* abandonment; **h)** *(Kapitulation)* retirement; *(im Schach)* resignation; **jmdn. zur ~ zwingen** force sb. to retire/resign; **i)** *(Verzicht)* giving up; *(eines Plans, einer Forderung)* giving up; abandonment; dropping; *(eines Berufs, Versuchs)* giving up; abandonment; **j)** *(einer Postsendung)* posting *(Brit.)*; mailing *(Amer.)*; *(eines Telegramms)* handing in; *(einer Bestellung, einer Annonce)* placing; **k)** *(von Gepäck)* depositing; *(am Flughafen)* checking in; **l)** *(bes. Volleyball)* service

auf|gabeln *tr. V. (salopp)* pick up; **wo hat die Firma bloß diesen Analphabeten aufgegabelt?** where on earth did the firm get hold of this illiterate?

Aufgaben-: ~bereich der, ~gebiet das area of responsibility; **~stellung die** nature of the task; **sich mit der neuen ~stellung vertraut machen** *(bei Ressortwechsel)* familiarize oneself with one's new duties *or* responsibilities; **~verteilung die a)** *(das Verteilen)* allocation of duties *or* responsibilities; **b)** *(das Verteiltsein)* distribution of responsibilities

Aufgabe-: ~ort der *(Postw.)* place of posting *(Brit.) or (Amer.)* mailing; **~stempel der** *(Postw.)* postmark [showing time and place of posting *(Brit.) or (Amer.)* mailing]

Auf·gang der a) *(Sonnen~, Mond~ usw.)* rising; **b)** *(Treppe)* stairs *pl.*; staircase; stairway; *(in einem Bahnhof, zu einer Galerie, einer Tribüne)* steps *pl.*; **c)** *(Weg)* **der ~ zur Burgruine** the path up to the ruined castle; **d)** *(Turnen)* mount **(auf +** *Akk.* on to)

auf|geben 1. *unr. tr. V.* **a)** *(beenden)* give up; **gib's auf!** *(ugs.)* you might as well give up!; why don't you give up!; **b)** *(sich trennen von)* give up ⟨*habit, job, flat, business, practice, etc.*⟩; give up, abandon, drop ⟨*plans, demand*⟩; give up, abandon ⟨*profession, attempt*⟩; give up, stop ⟨*smoking, drinking*⟩; **c)** *(verloren geben)* give up ⟨*patient*⟩; give up hope on *or* with ⟨*wayward son, daughter, etc.*⟩; give up, abandon ⟨*chessman*⟩; **sich selbst ~:** give oneself up for lost; **d)** *(nicht länger zu gewinnen versuchen)* give up ⟨*struggle*⟩; retire from ⟨*race, competition*⟩; **eine Partie ~:** concede a game; **e)** *(übergeben, übermitteln)* post *(Brit.)*, mail ⟨*letter, parcel*⟩; hand in, *(telefonisch)* phone in ⟨*telegram*⟩; place ⟨*advertisement, order*⟩; check ⟨*luggage*⟩ in; *(am Flughafen)* check ⟨*baggage*⟩ in; *(zur Aufbewahrung im Bahnhof)* deposit ⟨*luggage*⟩; **f)** *(Schulw.: als Hausaufgabe)* set *(Brit.)*; assign *(Amer.)*; **viel/nichts ~:** set *(Brit.) or (Amer.)* assign a lot of/no homework; **g)** *(zur Lösung vorlegen)* **jmdm. ein Rätsel/eine Frage ~:** set *(Brit.) or (Amer.)* assign sb. a puzzle/pose sb. a question; **h)** *(geh. veralt.: auftragen, auferlegen)* **jmdm. ~, etw. zu tun** charge sb. with doing sth.; **es war ihr aufgegeben, schweigend zu dulden** it was her lot to suffer in silence; **i)** *(landsch.: auf den Teller geben)* serve [up]; **jmdm. etw. ~:** serve sb. [up] sth. **2.** *unr. itr. V.* **a)** give up; *(im Sport)* retire; *(Schach)* resign; **b)** *s.* **aufschlagen 1 d; c)** *(landsch.: Essen auf den Teller geben)* dish up; **jmdm. ~:** serve sb.; **jmdm. zum zweiten Mal ~:** give sb. a second helping

auf·geblasen 1. *2. Part. v.* **aufblasen. 2.** *Adj.* puffed up

Aufgeblasenheit die; ~: self-importance

Auf·gebot das a) *(aufgebotene Menge)* contingent; *(Sport: Mannschaft)* contingent; squad; *(an Arbeitern)* squad; **ein gewaltiges ~ an Polizisten/Fahrzeugen/Material** a huge force of police/array of vehicles/materials; **b)** *(zur Heirat)* notice of an/the intended marriage; *(kirchlich)* banns *pl.*; **das ~ bestellen** give notice of an/the intended marriage; *(kirchlich)* put up the banns

auf·gedreht 1. *2. Part. v.* **aufdrehen. 2.** *Adj. (ugs.)* in high spirits *pred.*; **er war unheimlich ~:** he was in tremendously high spirits

auf·gedunsen *Adj.* bloated

auf|gehen *unr. itr. V.; mit sein* **a)** *(am Horizont erscheinen)* rise; **b)** *(sich öffnen [lassen])* ⟨*door, parachute, wound*⟩ open; ⟨*stage curtain*⟩ go up, rise; ⟨*knot, button, zip, bandage, shoelace, stitching*⟩ come undone; ⟨*boil, pimple, blister*⟩ burst; ⟨*flower, bud*⟩ open [up]; **das Weckglas ist wieder aufgegangen** the top has come off the preserving jar; **c)** *(keimen)* come up; **d)** *(aufgetrieben werden)* ⟨*dough, cake*⟩ rise; **e)** *(Math.)* ⟨*calculation*⟩ work out, come out; ⟨*equation*⟩ come out; **3 geht in 12 auf** 3 goes into 12; 12 is divisible by 3; **12 durch 3 geht glatt** *od.* **genau auf** 3 goes into 12 without a remainder; **7 durch 3 geht nicht auf** threes into seven won't go; **seine Rechnung ging nicht auf** *(fig.)* he had miscalculated; **die Patience geht auf** *(fig.)* the game of patience comes out; **f)** *(klarwerden)* **etw. geht jmdm. auf** sb. realizes sth.; **der Sinn dieses Satzes ist mir noch nicht ganz aufgegangen** I don't quite grasp the meaning of this sentence; **g)** *(einbezogen werden)* **in etw.** *(Dat.)* **~:** become absorbed into sth.; *s. auch* **Flamme; h)** *(Erfüllung finden)* **in etw.** *(Dat.)* **~:** be completely absorbed in sth.; **er geht ganz in seiner Familie auf** his whole life revolves around his family; **i)** *(Jagdw.: beginnen)* **die Jagd geht im August auf** the hunting season *or* open season starts in August

auf|geilen *tr. V. (salopp)* **jmdn. [mit/durch etw.] ~:** get sb. randy [with sth.]; **sich [an etw.** *(Dat.)***] ~:** get randy [with sth.]; *(fig.)* get worked up [about sth.]

aufgeklärt 1. *2. Part. v.* **aufklären. 2.** *Adj.* enlightened; *(sexualkundlich)* **~ sein/werden** know/be taught the facts of life; *s. auch* **Absolutismus**

Aufgeklärtheit die; ~: enlightened views *pl.*; **bei aller ~:** although he is/they are *etc.* so enlightened

aufgekratzt 1. *2. Part. v.* **aufkratzen. 2.** *Adj. (ugs.)* in high spirits *pred.*; **in ~er Stimmung** in high spirits

Auf·geld das *(landsch.) s.* **Aufschlag b**

auf·gelegt 1. *2. Part. v.* **auflegen. 2.** *Adj.* **a)** *(gelaunt)* **gut/schlecht/heiter** *usw.* **~ sein** be in a good/bad/cheerful *etc.* mood; **zu etw. ~ sein** be in the mood for sth.; **dazu ~ sein, etw. zu tun** be in the mood to do sth.; **b)** *nicht präd. (offensichtlich)* **ein ~er Schwindel** a blatant swindle

auf·gelöst 1. *2. Part. v.* **auflösen. 2.** *Adj.* distraught; **vor Schmerz/Trauer/Freude ~ sein** be beside oneself with pain/grief/joy; *s. auch* **Träne**

aufgeräumt 1. *2. Part. v.* **aufräumen. 2.** *Adj.* jovial

aufgeregt 1. *2. Part. v.* **aufregen. 2.** *Adj.* *(erregt)* excited; *(nervös, beunruhigt)* agitated. **3.** *adv. (erregt)* exitedly; *(nervös, beunruhigt)* agitatedly

Aufgeregtheit die; ~: excitement; agitation; *(Nervosität)* agitation

auf·geschlossen 1. *2. Part. v.* **aufschließen. 2.** *Adj.* open-minded **(gegenüber** as regards, about); *(interessiert, empfänglich)* receptive, open (+ *Dat.*, **für** to); *(mitteilsam)* communicative); *(zugänglich)* approachable; **einer Sache** *(Dat.)* **~ gegenüberstehen** be open-minded about sth.

Auf·geschlossenheit die *s.* **aufschließen 2:** open-mindedness; receptiveness; openness; communicativeness; approachableness

auf·geschmissen *Adj. (ugs.)* *in* **[ganz] [schön] ~ sein** be [right] up the creek *(sl.)*; be in a [real] fix

auf·geschossen *2. Part. v.* **aufschießen**

aufgesetzt 1. *2. Part. v.* **aufsetzen. 2.** *Adj.* put on

aufgestellt 1. *2. Part. v.* **aufstellen. 2.** *Adj. (schweiz.) s.* **aufgeschlossen**

aufgeweckt 1. *2. Part. v.* **aufwecken. 2.** *Adj.* bright; sharp

Aufgewecktheit die; ~: brightness; sharpness

auf|gießen *unr. tr. V.* **a)** *(aufbrühen)* make, brew [up] ⟨*tea*⟩; make ⟨*coffee*⟩; **b)** *(gießen auf, daraufgießen)* **etw. [auf etw.** *(Akk.)***] ~:** pour sth. on [to sth.]; **c)** *(übergießen)* **etw. mit Milch/Wasser** *usw.* **~:** pour milk/water *etc.* on [to] sth.

auf|gliedern *tr. V.* subdivide, break down, split up **(in +** *Akk.* into); structure ⟨*essay*⟩; *(nach Kategorien)* categorize; **aufgegliedert nach Berufen/Einkommen** broken down by occupation/income

Auf·gliederung die *s.* **aufgliedern:** subdivision; breakdown; structuring; categorization

auf|glimmen *unr. (auch regelm.) itr. V.; mit sein* [begin to] glimmer; *(fig.)* ⟨*hope, suspicion*⟩ flicker up

auf|glühen *itr. V.; mit sein* [begin to] glow; *(fig.)* ⟨*passion*⟩ begin to burn; **eine Hoffnung glühte in ihm auf** he felt a gleam of hope

auf|graben *unr. tr. V. (umgraben)* dig over; *(freilegen)* dig up

auf|greifen *unr. tr. V.* **a)** *(festnehmen)* pick up; **b)** *(sich befassen mit)* take *or* pick up ⟨*subject, suggestion*⟩; **c)** *(fortsetzen)* take up again; continue

auf Grund, aufgrund *s.* **Grund c**

Auf·guß der infusion; *(fig.)* rehash

Aufguß·beutel der; *(Teebeutel)* tea-bag; *(für Kräutertee)* herb sachet

auf|haben *(ugs.)* **1.** *unr. tr. V.* **a)** *(aufgesetzt haben)* have on; wear; **sie hat ihre Brille nicht aufgehabt** she didn't have her glasses on; she wasn't wearing her glasses; **b)** *(geöffnet haben)* have ⟨*zip*⟩ undone; have ⟨*door, window, jacket, blouse*⟩ open; **die Augen ~:** have one's eyes open; **seinen Laden/sein Büro ~:** have one's shop/office open; be open; **c)** *(aufbekommen haben)* have got

⟨*cupboard, case, safe, etc.*⟩ open; have got ⟨*knot, zip*⟩ undone; **d)** *(für die Schule)* **etw. ~:** have sth. as homework; **viel/wenig ~:** have a lot of/not have much homework; **haben wir etwas in** *od.* **für Englisch auf?** have we got any English homework?; **e)** *(aufgegessen haben)* have eaten up *or* finished. **2.** *unr. itr. V.* ⟨*shop, office*⟩ be open; **wir haben bis 17.30 auf** we are open until 5.30 p.m.

auf|hacken *tr. V. (mit einer Hacke)* break up; *(mit dem Schnabel)* peck *or* break open

auf|halsen ['aufhalzn̩] *tr. V. (ugs.)* **jmdm./sich etw. ~:** saddle sb./oneself with sth.; **sich** *(Dat.)* **etw. ~ lassen** get oneself saddled with sth.

auf|halten 1. *unr. tr. V.* **a)** *(anhalten)* halt; halt, check ⟨*inflation, advance, rise in unemployment*⟩; **jmdn. an der Grenze ~:** hold sb. up at the border; **b)** *(stören)* hold up; **c)** *(ugs.: geöffnet halten)* hold ⟨*sack, door, etc.*⟩ open; **die Augen [und Ohren] ~:** keep one's eyes [and ears] open; **die Hand ~** *(auch fig.)* hold out one's hand. **2.** *unr. refl. V.* **a)** *(sich befassen)* **sich mit jmdm./etw. ~:** spend [a long] time on sb./sth.; **sich zu lange mit jmdm./etw. ~:** spend too long on sb./sth.; **sich bei etw. ~:** linger over sth.; **b)** *(verweilen)* stay; **tagsüber hielt er sich im Museum auf** he spent the day in the museum; **sich im Winter in der Küche ~:** live in the kitchen in the winter; **der Gesuchte soll sich in Frankreich ~:** the wanted man is thought to be in France

auf|hängen 1. *tr. V.* **a)** *(auf etw. hängen)* hang up; hang ⟨*picture, curtains*⟩; **die Wäsche ~:** hang up the washing *or (Amer.)* wash; *(draußen)* hang out the washing; **den Hörer ~:** hang up; **b)** *(erhängen)* hang; **jmdn. an etw.** *(Dat.)* **~:** hang sb. from sth.; **c)** *(ugs.)* **jmdm. etw. ~** *(andrehen)* palm sth. off on sb.; *(glauben machen)* talk sb. into believing sth.; *(aufbürden)* saddle sb. with sth.; **d) etw. an einer Frage/einem bestimmten Fall** *usw.* **~:** use a question/a specific case *etc.* as a peg to hang sth. on. **2.** *refl. V. (sich erhängen)* hang oneself; **wo kann ich mich ~?** *(ugs. scherzh.)* where can I hang up my things?

Aufhänger der; ~s, ~ a) *(Schlaufe)* loop; **b)** *(fig.: aktuelles Ereignis)* peg; **ein guter ~ für etw.** a good peg to hang sth. on

Aufhängung die; ~ *(Technik)* suspension

auf|hauen *unr. (ugs. auch regelm.) tr. V.* **a)** *(öffnen)* knock a hole in ⟨*ice, wall*⟩; crack open ⟨*nut, coconut*⟩; **b)** *(ugs.: verletzen)* **sich** *(Dat.)* **das Knie/die Stirn usw. ~:** gash one's knee/forehead *etc.*

auf|häufen 1. *tr. V.* pile up; *(fig.)* amass ⟨*treasure, riches*⟩. **2.** *refl. V. (auch fig.)* pile up; accumulate

auf|heben *unr. tr. V.* **a)** *(hochheben)* pick up; pick *or* lift up ⟨*heavy object, burden*⟩; lift [off] ⟨*lid, cover*⟩; **b)** *(aufbewahren)* keep; preserve; **gut/schlecht aufgehoben sein** be/not be in good hands **(bei** with); **dein Geheimnis ist bei mir sicher aufgehoben** your secret is quite safe with me; **c)** *(abschaffen)* abolish; repeal ⟨*law*⟩; rescind, revoke ⟨*order, instruction*⟩; cancel ⟨*contract*⟩; lift ⟨*ban, prohibition*⟩; **das neue Gesetz hebt die alte Regelung auf** the new law supersedes the old regulation; *s. auch* **aufschieben a; d)** *(ausgleichen)* cancel out; neutralize, cancel ⟨*effect*⟩; **sich [gegenseitig] ~:** cancel each other out; **e)** *(beenden)* close ⟨*meeting*⟩; lift ⟨*blockade, siege, martial law*⟩; **die Tafel ~** *(geh.)* bring the meal to a close; **f)** *(erheben)* **die Hand/den Kopf ~:** raise one's hand/head

Aufheben das; ~s *in* **viel ~[s]/kein ~ von jmdm./etw. machen** make a great fuss/not make any fuss about sb./sth.; **ohne jedes/großes ~:** without any/a great deal of *or* much fuss

Auf·hebung die a) *(Abschaffung) s.* **aufheben c:** abolition; repeal; rescindment; revocation; cancellation; lifting; **b)** *(Beendigung) s.* **aufheben e:** closure; lifting

auf|heitern 1. *tr. V. (heiterer stimmen)* cheer up; brighten up ⟨*life*⟩. **2.** *refl. V.* **a)** *(froher werden)* ⟨*mood, face, expression*⟩ brighten; **b)** *(heller werden)* ⟨*weather*⟩ clear *or* brighten up; ⟨*sky*⟩ brighten. **3.** *itr. V.* **es heitert auf** it is clearing up; **zeitweilig ~d** [some] bright periods

Aufheiterung die; ~, ~en a) *(des Wetters)* bright period; **b)** *(Erheiterung)* cheering up; **zur allgemeinen ~:** to cheer everyone up

auf|heizen *(bes. Physik, Technik)* **1.** *tr. V.* heat [up]; *(fig.)* inflame ⟨*tensions, conflict*⟩; fuel ⟨*mistrust*⟩. **2.** *refl. V.* heat up

auf|helfen *unr. itr. V.* **a)** *(beim Aufstehen helfen)* **jmdm. ~:** help sb. up; *(fig.)* help sb. [to get] back on his/her feet again; **b)** *(aufbessern)* boost ⟨*self-confidence, income*⟩

auf|hellen 1. *tr. V.* **a)** *(heller machen)* brighten; lighten ⟨*hair, shadow, darkness*⟩; *(fig.)* brighten [up] ⟨*mood, life*⟩; **b)** *(klären)* shed *or* cast *or* throw light on. **2.** *refl. V.* **a)** *(hell werden)* ⟨*sky*⟩ brighten; ⟨*hair*⟩ turn *or* go lighter; ⟨*day, weather*⟩ brighten [up]; **sein Gesicht/seine Miene hellte sich auf** his face/expression brightened; **es hat sich aufgehellt** it's brightened up; **b)** *(durchschaubar werden)* ⟨*sense, meaning*⟩ become clear

Aufheller der; ~s, ~ a) *(Fot.)* fill-in photo flood; **b)** *(in Waschmitteln)* colour-intensifier; brightener; **c)** *(ugs.: Medikament)* pep pill *(coll.)*

auf|hetzen *tr. V.* incite; **jmdn. zur Meuterei/zu Gewalttaten ~:** incite sb. to mutiny/violence

Aufhetzung die; ~, ~en incitement

auf|heulen *itr. V.* **a)** *(heulen)* ⟨*siren*⟩ wail; ⟨*animal*⟩ howl; ⟨*engine, crowd*⟩ give a roar; **b)** *(ugs.: weinen)* howl

auf|holen 1. *tr. V.* make up ⟨*time, delay*⟩; make up, pull back ⟨*lead*⟩; catch up on ⟨*studies, neglected work*⟩; **ein paar Sekunden/Meter ~:** make up *or* pull back a few seconds/metres. **2.** *itr. V.* **a)** catch up; ⟨*train*⟩ make up time; ⟨*athlete, competitor*⟩ make up ground; *(Zeit ~)* make up time; **b)** *(Börsenw.)* ⟨*shares*⟩ rise

auf|horchen *itr. V.* prick up one's ears; **die Öffentlichkeit ~ lassen** *(fig.)* make the public [sit up and] take notice

auf|hören *itr. V.* stop; ⟨*friendship*⟩ end; *(ugs.: das Arbeitsverhältnis aufgeben)* finish; **das muß ~!** this has got to stop!; **da hört [sich] doch alles auf!** *(ugs.)* that really is the limit! *(coll.)*; **die Musik hörte auf** the music ended *or* came to an end; *(wurde abgebrochen)* the music stopped; **es hat aufgehört zu schneien** it's stopped snowing; **[damit] ~, etw. zu tun** stop doing sth.; **nicht [damit] ~, etw. zu tun** keep on doing sth.; **hört mit dem Lärm/Unsinn auf** stop that noise/nonsense; **ich habe mit dem Buch aufgehört und ein anderes angefangen** I've stopped reading that book and started another; **mit dem Fußboden kannst du jetzt aufhören, der ist sauber genug** you can leave the floor now, it's clean enough; **ich höre hier bald auf** I'm just about to finish; *(kündige bald)* I'm giving up this job soon; **ohne aufzuhören** without stopping; *s. auch* **Spaß b**

auf|jagen *tr. V.* start ⟨*game, animals*⟩ from cover; put up ⟨*birds*⟩; **jmdn. aus dem Schlaf ~** *(fig.)* rouse sb. [violently] from his/her sleep

auf|jauchzen *itr. V.;* **[vor Freude/Entzücken** *usw.***] ~:** shout for joy/with delight *etc.*

auf|jaulen *itr. V.* howl; give a howl

Auf·kauf der buying up; **durch Aufkäufe kleiner Firmen** by buying up smaller firms

auf|kaufen *tr. V.* buy up

Auf·käufer der buyer

auf|kehren *tr. (auch itr.) V. (bes. südd.)* sweep up

auf|keimen *itr. V.; mit sein* sprout; *(fig.)* ⟨*suspicion, doubt, fear, longing, reluctance*⟩ begin to grow; ⟨*hope, passion, love, sympathy*⟩ burgeon

aufklappbar *Adj.* ⟨*chair, table*⟩ which folds open; folding *attrib.* ⟨*chair, table*⟩; fold-back ⟨*car hood*⟩; opening *attrib.* ⟨*window*⟩; hinged ⟨*flap, lid*⟩; **eine zu einem Doppelbett ~e Couch** a settee which converts into a double bed

auf|klappen 1. *tr. V.* open, fold open ⟨*chair, table*⟩; open [up] ⟨*suitcase, trunk*⟩; fold back ⟨*car hood*⟩; open ⟨*window, door, book, knife*⟩. **2.** *itr. V.; mit sein* ⟨*shutters, door*⟩ open, swing open

auf|klaren *itr. V. (Met.)* ⟨*sky*⟩ clear; ⟨*weather*⟩ clear up; **örtlich ~d** clearing locally

auf|klären 1. *tr. V.* **a)** *(klären)* clear up ⟨*matter, mystery, question, misunderstanding, error, confusion*⟩; solve ⟨*crime, problem*⟩; elucidate, explain ⟨*event, incident, cause*⟩; resolve ⟨*contradiction, disagreement*⟩; **b)** *(unterrichten)* enlighten; *(informieren)* inform; **jmdn. über jmdn./etw. ~:** enlighten/inform sb. about sb./sth.; **jmdn. [darüber] ~, wie .../ was ...:** enlighten/inform sb. how .../what ...; **c)** *(sexualkundlich)* **ein Kind ~:** tell a child the facts of life; educate a child in sexual matters; **d)** *(Milit.)* reconnoitre. **2.** *refl. V.* **a)** *(sich klären)* ⟨*misunderstanding, mystery*⟩ be cleared up; **b)** *(sich aufhellen)* ⟨*weather*⟩ clear up; brighten [up]; ⟨*sky*⟩ clear, brighten

Aufklärer der; ~s, ~ a) *(hist.)* philosopher of the Enlightenment; **b)** *(Luftwaffe: Flugzeug)* reconnaissance plane *or* aircraft; **c)** *(Milit.: Soldat, Spion)* scout

aufklärerisch 1. *Adj.* ⟨*mission, intention*⟩ to instruct and inform, to combat ignorance. **2.** *adv.* **~ wirken** instruct and inform; combat ignorance

Auf·klärung die a) *s.* **aufklären 1 a:** clearing up; solution; elucidation; explanation; resolution; **ihm gelang die ~ des Verbrechens** he succeeded in solving the crime; **b)** *(Information)* information; **jmdm. einige ~en geben** give sb. some information *sing.*; **c)** *(Belehrung)* enlightenment; *(von offizieller Stelle)* informing; **um ~ darüber bitten, was vorgefallen ist** ask to be told what has happened; **d)** *o. Pl. (über Sexualität)* education in sexual matters; **die ~ der Kinder** telling the children the facts of life; **e)** *o. Pl. (hist.)* **die ~:** the Enlightenment; **f)** *(Milit.)* reconnaissance

Aufklärungs-: ~arbeit die educational work; **politische ~arbeit** political education; **~buch das** sex education book; **~film der** sex education film; **~flug der** *(Luftwaffe)* reconnaissance flight *or* mission; **~flug·zeug das** *(Luftwaffe)* reconnaissance plane *or* aircraft; **~kampagne die** information campaign; **~schrift die** information pamphlet; **~ziel das** *(Milit.)* reconnaissance objective

auf|klauben *tr. V. (landsch., auch fig.)* pick up

auf|kleben *tr. V.* stick on; *(mit Kleister)* paste on; *(mit Klebstoff, Leim)* stick *or* glue on

Auf·kleber der sticker; adhesive label

auf|klinken *tr. V.* open ⟨*door*⟩ by the handle

auf|klopfen *tr. V.* **a)** *(öffnen)* crack open; **b)** *(aufschütteln)* plump up ⟨*cushion etc.*⟩

auf|knacken *tr. V.* **a)** crack [open] ⟨*nut, cherry-stone, etc.*⟩; **b)** *(ugs.: aufbrechen)* break into ⟨*car, desk, drawer*⟩; break down ⟨*door*⟩; crack ⟨*safe*⟩

auf|knien 1. *itr. V.; auch mit sein (Turnen)* kneel **(auf +** *Akk. od. Dat.* on). **2.** *refl. V.* kneel **(auf +** *Akk./Dat.* on)

auf|knöpfen *tr. V.* **a)** unbutton; undo; **b) etw. auf etw.** *(Akk.)* **~:** button sth. on to sth.

auf|knoten *tr. V.* untie, undo ⟨*parcel, bundle, etc.*⟩; unknot ⟨*string, rope*⟩

auf|knüpfen *(ugs.)* **1.** *tr. V.* **a)** *(erhängen)* string up *(coll.)*, hang **(an** + *Dat.* from); **b)** *(aufknoten)* undo, untie ⟨*knot, parcel, bundle*⟩; unknot ⟨*string, rope*⟩. **2.** *refl. V.* hang oneself

auf|kochen 1. *tr. V.* **a)** *(zum Kochen bringen)* bring to the boil; **b)** *(noch einmal kochen)* reboil. **2.** *itr. V.* **a)** *mit sein (zu kochen beginnen)* come to the boil; **etw. ~ lassen** bring sth. to the boil; **b)** *(südd., österr.: üppig kochen)* prepare a magnificent spread

auf|kommen *unr. itr. V.; mit sein* **a)** *(entstehen)* ⟨*wind*⟩ spring up; ⟨*storm, gale*⟩ blow up; ⟨*fog*⟩ come down; ⟨*rumour*⟩ start; ⟨*suspicion, doubt, feeling*⟩ arise; ⟨*fashion, style, invention*⟩ come in; ⟨*boredom*⟩ set in; ⟨*mood, atmosphere*⟩ develop; **etw. ~ lassen** give rise to sth.; **b) ~ für** *(bezahlen)* bear, pay ⟨*costs*⟩; pay for ⟨*damage*⟩; pay, defray ⟨*expenses*⟩; be liable for ⟨*debts*⟩; stand ⟨*loss*⟩; **für jmdn. ~:** pay for sb.'s upkeep; **c) ~ für** *(Verantwortung tragen für)* be responsible for; **d) er läßt niemanden neben sich** *(Dat.)* **~:** he won't let anybody become a rival; he brooks no rivals *(literary)*; **e)** *(auftreffen)* land **(auf** + *Akk.* on); **f)** *(Sport: aufholen) (beim Wettlauf)* close the gap; *(Fußball, Boxen)* come back; **g)** *(sich behaupten)* **gegen jmdn./etw. ~:** prevail against sb./sth.; **h)** *(bes. südd.: entdeckt werden)* be discovered; **wenn das aufkommt, ...:** if it comes out, ...; **i)** *(Seemannsspr.: in Sicht kommen)* approach

Aufkommen das; ~s, ~ *(Wirtsch.)* revenue **(aus** from)

auf|kratzen *tr. V.* **a)** *(öffnen)* scratch open ⟨*wound, sore*⟩; **b)** *(verletzen)* scratch

auf|kreischen *itr. V.* ⟨*person*⟩ shriek, give a shriek; ⟨*brake, saw*⟩ screech

auf|krempeln *tr. V.* roll up ⟨*sleeves, trousers*⟩; **jmdm./sich die Ärmel ~:** roll up sb.'s/one's sleeves

auf|kreuzen *itr. V.* **a)** *mit sein (ugs.: erscheinen)* turn up; **b)** *auch mit sein (Seemannsspr.)* **gegen den Wind ~:** beat to windward

auf|kriegen *(ugs.) s.* **aufbekommen**

auf|künden *(geh., schweiz.),* **auf|kündigen** *tr. V.* terminate ⟨*lease, contract*⟩; cancel ⟨*subscription, membership*⟩; foreclose ⟨*mortgage*⟩; **seinen Dienst ~:** hand in one's notice; **jmdm. die Freundschaft/den Gehorsam ~** *(geh.)* break off one's friendship with sb./refuse sb. further obedience

Auf·kündigung die *s.* **aufkündigen:** termination; cancellation; foreclosure; breaking off

Aufl. *Abk.* **Auflage** ed.

auf|lachen *itr. V.* give a laugh; laugh; *(schallend)* burst out laughing

auf|laden 1. *unr. tr. (auch itr.) V.* **a)** load **(auf** + *Akk.* on [to]); **b)** *(ugs.: tragen lassen)* **jmdm. etw. ~:** load sb. with sth.; *(fig.)* saddle *or* load sb. with sth.; **c)** *(Physik: elektrisch laden)* charge [up] ⟨*battery*⟩; put ⟨*battery*⟩ on charge; *(nach Entladung auch)* recharge; **emotional aufgeladen** *(fig.)* emotionally charged; **d)** *(Kfz-W.)* supercharge ⟨*engine*⟩. **2.** *unr. refl. V. (Physik)* ⟨*battery*⟩ charge, become charged; *(nach Entladung)* recharge; become recharged; **sich elektrostatisch ~:** become electrostatically charged

Auf·ladung die a) *(Kfz-W.)* supercharging; **b)** *(Physik) (das Aufladen)* charging [up]; *(nach Entladung)* recharging

Auf·lage die a) *(Buchw.)* edition; *(gedruckte ~ einer Zeitung)* print run; *(verkaufte ~ einer Zeitung)* circulation; **dieses Buch/diese Zeitung hat hohe ~n erreicht** large numbers of copies of this book have been sold/this newspaper has reached high circulation figures; **sieben ~n erleben** go through seven editions; **b)** *(bes. Rechtsw.: Verpflichtung)* condition; **mit der ~, etw. zu tun** with the condition that *or* on condition that one does sth.; **[es] jmdm. zur ~ machen, daß ...:** impose on sb. the condition that ...; **c)** *(DDR Wirtsch.)* target; **d)** *(auf Sitzmöbeln)* cushion; **e)** *(Metallüberzug)* plating; **eine ~ aus Silber haben** be silver-plated; **f)** *(Stütze)* rest; support

Auflage·fläche die supporting surface

Auflagen·höhe die *(Buchw.)* number of copies printed; *(einer Zeitung)* circulation

auflagen·stark *Adj.* high-circulation ⟨*newspaper, magazine*⟩; **~ sein** have a high *or* large circulation

Auf·lager das *(Bauw.)* support; bearer; *(beweglich)* bearing

auflandig *(Seemannsspr.)* onshore

auf|lassen *unr. tr. V.* **a)** *(ugs.: offenlassen)* leave open; **b)** *(ugs.: aufbehalten)* keep on; **c)** *(ugs.: aufbleiben lassen)* let ⟨*child*⟩ stay up; **d)** *(aufsteigen lassen)* send up ⟨*balloon, rocket, satellite*⟩; release ⟨*carrier pigeon*⟩; **e)** *(bes. südd., österr.: schließen, Bergbau: stillegen)* close *or* shut down; **eine aufgelassene Grube** a closed-down pit

Auflassung die; ~, ~en *(bes. südd., österr.: Schließung; Bergbau: Stillegung)* closing *or* shutting down

auf|lauern *itr. V.* **jmdm. ~:** lie in wait for sb.; *(~ und angreifen)* waylay sb.

Auf·lauf der a) *(Menschen~)* crowd; **b)** *(Speise)* soufflé

auf|laufen *unr. itr. V.; mit sein* **a)** *(Seemannsspr.)* run aground **(auf** + *Akk. od. Dat.* on); **b)** *(Sport)* **zur Spitze/zu den Führenden ~:** move to the front/catch up with the leaders; **c)** *(aufprallen)* **auf jmdn./etw. ~:** run into sb./sth.; **jmdn. ~ lassen** *(Fußball)* body-check sb.; **d)** *(sich ansammeln)* accumulate; mount up

Auflauf·form die baking-dish; *(für Eierspeisen)* soufflé dish

auf|leben *itr. V.; mit sein* revive; *(fig.: wieder munter werden)* come to life; liven up; **etw. ~ lassen** revive sth.

auf|lecken *tr. V.* lap up

auf|legen 1. *tr. V.* **a)** *(auf etw. legen)* put on ⟨*record, coal, logs, table-cloth, adhesive plaster, saddle*⟩; **noch ein Gedeck ~:** set another place; **das Silber ~:** put out the silverware; **jmdm. das Fleisch ~:** serve sb. his/her meat; **jmdm. die Hand ~** ⟨*faith-healer*⟩ lay one's hands on sb.; **den Hörer ~:** put down the receiver; **b)** *(Buchw.)* publish; **ein Buch neu** *od.* **wieder ~:** bring out a new edition of a book; *(nachdrucken)* reprint a book; **c)** *(Finanzw.)* issue, float ⟨*shares*⟩; **d)** *(Seemannsspr.)* lay up ⟨*ship*⟩. **2.** *itr. V. (den Hörer ~)* hang up; ring off *(Brit.)*

auf|lehnen 1. *refl. V.* **sich gegen jmdn./etw. ~:** rebel *or* revolt against sb./sth. **2.** *tr. V. (landsch.: aufstützen)* **sich/die Arme auf etw.** *(Akk. od. Dat.)* **~:** lean on sth./lean *or* rest one's arms on sth.

Auflehnung die; ~, ~en rebellion; revolt

auf|leimen *tr. V.* glue on **(auf** + *Akk.* to)

auf|lesen *unr. tr. V.* **a)** *(aufsammeln)* pick up; gather [up]; *(fig. ugs.: sich holen)* pick up, catch ⟨*germ, disease, illness*⟩; **b)** *(ugs.: mitnehmen)* pick up; **jmdn. von der Straße ~:** pick sb. up off the street

auf|leuchten *itr. V.; auch mit sein* light up; *(für kurze Zeit)* flash; ⟨*brake-light*⟩ come on; ⟨*star*⟩ shine out; *(fig.)* ⟨*eyes, face*⟩ light up

auf|liegen 1. *unr. itr. V.* **a)** *(auf etw. liegen)* lie, rest **(auf** + *Dat.* on); **b)** *(Seemannsspr.)* be laid up. **2.** *unr. refl. V. (ugs.: sich wundliegen)* get bedsores

auf|listen *tr. V.* list

Auflistung die; ~, ~en a) *o. Pl. (das Auflisten)* listing; **b)** *(Liste)* list

auf|lockern 1. *tr. V.* **a)** *(locker machen)* break up, loosen ⟨*soil*⟩; loosen ⟨*stuffing, hair*⟩; **die Muskeln ~:** loosen up one's muscles; **aufgelockerte Bewölkung** broken cloud; **b)** *(abwechslungsreicher machen)* introduce some variety into ⟨*landscape, lesson, lecture*⟩; relieve, break up ⟨*pattern, façade*⟩; **c)** *(unbeschwerter machen)* make ⟨*mood, atmosphere, evening*⟩ more relaxed. **2.** *refl. V. (seine Muskeln lockern)* loosen up

Auf·lockerung die a) *(des Bodens)* breaking up; loosening; *(einer Füllung, des Haars)* loosening; *(der Muskeln)* loosening up; **b)** *(einer Fassade, eines Musters)* relieving; breaking up; **zur ~ des Unterrichts/Vortrags** to introduce some variety into the lesson/lecture; **c) zur ~ der Stimmung/Atmosphäre/des Abends** to make the mood/atmosphere/evening more relaxed

auf|lodern *itr. V.; mit sein (geh.)* ⟨*fire*⟩ blaze *or* flare up; ⟨*flames*⟩ leap up; *(fig.)* ⟨*jealousy, hatred, anger, passion*⟩ flare up; **wie eine Fackel ~:** go up like a torch

auflösbar *Adj.* soluble; soluble, solvable ⟨*equation, problem*⟩; dissoluble ⟨*marriage*⟩

Auf·lösbarkeit die; ~: *s.* **auflösbar:** solubility; solvability; dissolubility

auf|lösen 1. *tr. V.* **a)** dissolve; resolve ⟨*difficulty, contradiction*⟩; solve ⟨*puzzle, equation*⟩; break off ⟨*engagement*⟩; terminate, cancel ⟨*arrangement, contract, agreement*⟩; dissolve, disband ⟨*organization*⟩; remove ⟨*brackets*⟩; **etw. in seine Bestandteile ~:** resolve sth. into its constituent parts; *s. auch* **Haushalt; b)** *(geh.: aufbinden)* undo, untie ⟨*knot, shoelace, plait*⟩; let down ⟨*hair*⟩; *(fig.)* disentangle; **c)** *(Musik)* cancel ⟨*accidental*⟩; resolve ⟨*discord*⟩; **d)** *(Optik, Fot.)* resolve. **2.** *refl. V.* **a)** dissolve; ⟨*parliament*⟩ dissolve itself; ⟨*crowd, demonstration*⟩ break up; ⟨*fog, mist*⟩ disperse, lift; ⟨*cloud*⟩ break up; *(fig.)* ⟨*resistance, vision*⟩ dissolve; ⟨*empire, kingdom, social order*⟩ disintegrate; **sich in etw.** *(Akk.)***/in nichts ~** *(auch fig.)* dissolve into sth./into nothing; **b)** *(geh.: aufgehen)* ⟨*shoelace, hair, bow*⟩ come undone; **c)** *(sich aufklären)* ⟨*misunderstanding, difficulty, contradiction*⟩ be resolved; ⟨*puzzle, equation*⟩ be solved; *s. auch* **aufgelöst 2**

Auf·lösung die a) *s.* **auflösen 1 a–d:** dissolving; resolution; solution; breaking off; termination; cancellation; dissolution; disbandment; removal; undoing; untying; disentanglement; **b)** *s.* **auflösen 2 a:** dissolving; dispersing; lifting; breaking up; *(fig.)* dissolving; disintegration; **c)** *(Verstörtheit)* distraction

Auflösungs-: ~erscheinung die sign of disintegration; **~zeichen das** *(Musik)* natural

auflüpfisch [ˈaʊ̯flʏpfɪʃ] *Adj., adv. (schweiz.) s.* **aufmüpfig**

auf|machen 1. *tr. V.* **a)** *(öffnen)* open; undo ⟨*button, knot*⟩; open, undo ⟨*parcel, packet*⟩; **b)** *(ugs.: eröffnen)* open [up] ⟨*shop, theatre, business, etc.*⟩; **c)** *(gestalten)* get up; present; **das wurde von der Presse groß aufgemacht** the press gave it headline treatment. **2.** *itr. V.* **a)** *(geöffnet werden)* ⟨*shop, office, etc.*⟩ open; **b)** *(ugs.: die Tür öffnen)* open up; open the door; **jmdm. ~:** open the door to sb.; **mach auf!** open up!; **c)** *(ugs.: eröffnet werden)* ⟨*shop, business*⟩ open [up]. **3.** *refl. V. (aufbrechen)* set out; start [out]

Auf·macher der *(Zeitungsw.) (Schlagzeile)* lead headline; *(Bild)* main front-page photograph

Aufmachung die; ~, ~en a) *(Gestaltung)* presentation; *(Kleidung)* get-up; **ein Buch in ansprechender ~:** an attractively presented book; **b)** *(Zeitungsw.)* **die Zeitungen haben darüber in großer ~ berichtet** it was splashed across the pages of the newspapers; **c)** *s.* **Aufmacher**

auf|malen *tr. V.* paint on

Auf·marsch der a) *(Milit.: zum Kampf)* deployment; **b)** *(Parade)* march-past; parade; **c)** *(schweiz.: Zulauf)* attendance

Aufmarsch·gebiet das *(Milit.)* deployment area

auf|marschieren *itr. V.; mit sein* draw up; assemble; *(heranmarschieren)* march up; *(vorbeimarschieren)* march past; parade; ‹*demonstrators, delegations*› parade; **die Zeugen zur Vernehmung ~ lassen** *(salopp)* march the witnesses in for examination; **Truppen sind an der Grenze aufmarschiert** troops were deployed along the border

auf|meißeln *tr. V.* chisel open

auf|merken *itr. V.* **a)** *(aufhorchen)* [sit up and] take notice; **b)** *(geh.: aufpassen)* pay attention (**auf** + *Akk.* to)

aufmerksam 1. *Adj.* **a)** *(konzentriert)* attentive ‹*pupil, reader, observer*›; keen, sharp ‹*eyes*›; **~e Nachbarn hatten bemerkt, daß ...:** observant neighbours had noticed that ...; **jmdn. auf jmdn./etw. ~ machen** draw sb.'s attention to sb./sth.; bring sb./sth. to sb.'s notice; **jmdn. darauf ~ machen, daß ...:** draw sb.'s attention to *or* bring to sb.'s notice the fact that ...; **auf jmdn./etw. ~ werden** become aware of *or* notice sb./sth.; **~ werden** notice; **b)** *(höflich)* attentive; **danke, sehr ~:** thank you, that's very *or* most kind of you. **2.** *adv.* attentively

Aufmerksamkeit die; ~, ~en a) *o. Pl. (Konzentration)* attention; **jmds. ~** *(Dat.)* **entgehen** escape sb.'s attention; **b)** *(Höflichkeit)* attentiveness; **c)** *(Geschenk)* **eine [kleine] ~:** a small gift

auf|möbeln *tr. V. (ugs.)* **a)** *(verbessern)* do up; **seinen Ruf/seine Deutschkenntnisse ~:** polish up one's reputation/knowledge of German; **b)** *(beleben)* pep *or* buck up *(coll.)*; *(aufmuntern)* buck *(coll.) or* cheer up

auf|montieren *tr. V.* mount; fit [on]

auf|motzen *tr. V. (ugs.)* tart up *(Brit. coll.)*; doll up *(coll.)*; repackage ‹*edition, novel, record*›; *(schneller machen)* soup up *(coll.)* ‹*car, engine*›

auf|mucken, auf|mucksen *itr. V. (ugs.)* kick up *or* make a fuss; **gegen etw. ~:** balk at sth.

auf|muntern *tr. V.* **a)** *(aufheitern)* cheer up; **b)** *(beleben)* liven up; pep up *(coll.)*; **c)** *(ermutigen)* encourage; **jmdn. zum Weitermachen/Widerstand/Kampf** *usw.* **~:** encourage sb. to carry on/resist/ fight *etc.*

Aufmunterung die; ~, ~en a) *(Aufheiterung)* cheering up; **b)** *(Belebung)* livening up; pepping up *(coll.)*; **eine Tasse Kaffee zur ~:** a cup of coffee to liven *or (coll.)* pep me/you *etc.* up; **c)** *(Ermutigung)* encouragement

aufmüpfig ['aufmʏpfɪç] *(ugs.)* **1.** *Adj.* rebellious. **2.** *adv.* rebelliously

Aufmüpfigkeit die; ~: rebelliousness

auf|nähen *tr. V.* sew on; **etw. auf etw.** *(Akk.)* **~:** sew sth. on [to] sth.

Aufnahme die; ~, ~n a) *(Beginn) (von Verhandlungen, Gesprächen)* opening; starting; *(der Arbeit, einer Ermittlung, der Produktion)* start; *(von Beziehungen, Verbindungen)* establishment; *(von Studien, einer Tätigkeit)* taking up; **vor ~ der Arbeit** before starting work; **b)** *(Empfang)* reception; *(Beherbergung)* accommodation; **jmds. ~ in ein Krankenhaus** sb.'s admission to hospital; **jmdm. eine herzliche ~ bereiten** give sb. a warm reception; **sie fanden ~ bei einer Familie** they were taken in [and looked after] by a family; **c)** *(in einen Verein, eine Schule, Organisation)* admission (**in** + *Akk.* into); **d)** *(von Hypotheken, Geld, Anleihen)* raising; **e)** *(Aufzeichnung)* taking down; *(von Personalien, eines Diktats)* taking [down]; **die ~ des Protokolls der Sitzung** taking the minutes of the meeting; **f)** *(das Fotografieren)* photographing; *(eines Bildes)* taking; *(das Filmen)* shooting; filming; **bei der ~:** while taking the photograph/ while shooting *or* filming; **g)** *(Bild)* picture; shot; photo[graph]; **eine ~ machen** take a picture *or* shot *or* photo[graph]; **h)** *(das Aufnehmen auf Tonträger, das Aufgenommene)* recording; **i)** *(Anklang)* reception; response (*Gen.* to); **j)** *o. Pl. (Einverleibung, Absorption)* absorption; **k)** *(das Einschließen, Verzeichnen)* inclusion; **die ~ eines Wortes in den Wortschatz** the adoption of a word into the language; **l)** *(~raum)* reception *(Brit.)*; reception office *(Amer.)*; **in der ~ warten** wait in reception *(Brit.) or (Amer.)* the reception office

aufnahme-, Aufnahme-: ~antrag der application for membership; **~bedingung die a)** condition of admission; **~bedingungen** conditions *or* terms of admission; **b)** *Pl. (bei Tonaufnahme)* recording conditions; *(Fot., Film)* shooting conditions; **~fähig** *Adj.* **a)** *(konzentriert)* receptive (**für** to); **ich bin nicht mehr ~fähig** I can't take any more in; **b)** *(Wirtsch.)* receptive ‹*market*›; **~fähigkeit die;** *o. Pl.* **a)** *(Konzentration)* receptivity (**für** to); ability to take things in; **b)** *(Wirtsch.)* receptivity (**für** to); **~gebühr die** enrolment fee; **~land das** host country; **~leiter der** *(Film, Rundf., Ferns.)* production manager; **~prüfung die** entrance examination; **~studio das** *(Tonstudio)* recording studio; *(Filmstudio)* film studio; **~wagen der** recording van

aufnahms-, Aufnahms- *(österr.) s.* **aufnahme-, Aufnahme-**

auf|nehmen *unr. tr. V.* **a)** *(hochheben)* pick up; lift up; *(aufsammeln)* pick up; *(fig.)* **es mit jmdm./etw. ~/nicht ~ können** be a/no match for sb./sth.; **an Intelligenz kann es keiner mit ihm ~:** nobody can compare with him for intelligence; **b)** *(beginnen mit)* open, start ‹*negotiations, talks*›; establish ‹*relations, contacts*›; take up ‹*studies, activity, occupation*›; start ‹*production, investigation*›; *(fortsetzen)* take up ‹*idea, theme*›; **den Kampf gegen etw. ~** *(fig.)* take up the fight against sth.; **etw. wieder ~:** resume sth.; **um ein Wort des Kanzlers aufzunehmen** to borrow an expression used by the chancellor; **c)** *(empfangen)* receive; *(beherbergen)* take in; *(fig.: umhüllen)* ‹*night, darkness, mist*› envelop; **in ein** *od.* **einem Krankenhaus aufgenommen werden** be admitted to hospital; **d)** *(beitreten lassen)* admit (**in** + *Akk.* to); **jmdn. als Mitglied in einen Verein** *usw.* **~:** admit sb. as a member of a club *etc.*; admit sb. to membership of a club *etc.*; **jmdn. als Teilhaber in sein Geschäft ~:** bring sb. into one's business as a partner; **e)** *(einschließen, verzeichnen)* include; **f)** *(fassen)* take; hold; absorb ‹*immigrants, goods, workers*›; **g)** *(erfassen)* take in, absorb ‹*impressions, information, etc.*›; **etw. ganz in sich ~:** take sth. in *or* absorb sth. completely; **h)** *(absorbieren)* absorb; **wieder Nahrung ~** ‹*patient*› take food again; **i)** *(leihen)* raise ‹*mortgage, money, loan*›; **j)** *(reagieren auf)* receive; **etw. positiv/mit Begeisterung ~:** give sth. a positive/ an enthusiastic reception; **k)** *(aufschreiben)* take down; take [down] ‹*dictation, particulars*›; *(Kartographie)* survey and record ‹*area, district*›; **l)** *(fotografieren)* take ‹*picture*›; take a photograph of, photograph ‹*scene, subject*›; *(filmen)* film; **m)** *(auf Tonträger)* record; **n)** *(Handarbeit)* increase ‹*stitch*›; **o)** *(bes. Fußball)* take ‹*ball*›; ‹*goalkeeper*› take, gather ‹*ball*›; **p)** *(nordd.: aufwischen)* mop *or* wipe up; **q)** *(österr.: einstellen)* take on ‹*staff, workers*›

Aufnehmer der; ~s, ~ *(nordd.)* cloth

äufnen ['ɔyfnən] *tr. V. (schweiz.)* accumulate ‹*money, fortune*›

auf|nesteln *tr. V.* undo

auf|norden *tr. V. (ns.)* nordicize

auf|nötigen *tr. V.* **jmdm. etw. ~:** force sth. on sb.; **die Lage nötigt uns Zurückhaltung auf** the situation forces us to be cautious

auf|oktroyieren ['aufǀɔktroaji:rən] *tr. V.* **jmdm. etw. ~:** impose *or* force sth. on sb.

auf|opfern 1. *tr. V. (geh.: opfern)* sacrifice (*Dat.* to). **2.** *refl. V. (sich einsetzen)* devote oneself sacrificingly (**für** to)

aufopfernd 1. *Adj.* self-sacrificing ‹*person, love, work*›. **2.** *adv.* self-sacrificingly

Auf·opferung die a) *(das Opfern)* sacrifice; **b)** *(das Sicheinsetzen)* self-sacrifice

aufopferungs·voll *s.* **aufopfernd**

auf|packen *tr. V.* **etw. ~:** load sth. on; **jmdm./einem Tier etw. ~:** load sth. on to sb./an animal; **sich** *(Dat.)* **etw. ~:** load oneself with sth.; **jmdm./sich etw. ~** *(fig.)* burden sb./oneself with sth.

auf|päppeln *tr. V.* feed up; *(fig.)* pep up

auf|passen *itr. V.* **a)** look *or* watch out; *(konzentriert sein)* pay attention; **paß mal auf!** *(ugs.) (du wirst sehen)* you just watch!; *(hör mal zu!)* now listen; *(sei aufmerksam!)* pay attention!; **aufgepaßt!** *(ugs.)* look *or* watch out!; **kannst du denn nicht ~?** can't you be more careful?; **wir haben immer aufgepaßt, aber jetzt ist meine Frau doch schwanger** *(ugs.)* we've always been careful, but my wife's got pregnant all the same *(coll.)*; **b)** *(beaufsichtigen)* **auf jmdn./etw. ~:** keep an eye on sb./sth.

Aufpasser der; ~s, ~ a) *(abwertend)* spy; **b)** *(Wärter, Bewacher)* guard; *(aus Gründen des Anstands)* chaperon

Aufpasserin die; ~, ~nen a) *(abwertend)* spy; **b)** *(Wärterin)* guard; *(Anstandsdame)* protector; chaperon

auf|peitschen *tr. V.* **a)** *(bewegen)* whip up ‹*sea, waves*›; **b)** *(erregen)* inflame ‹*passions, emotions, senses*›; inflame, stir up ‹*populace, crowd*›

auf|peppen ['aufpɛpn̩] *tr. V. (salopp)* pep up *(coll.)*

auf|pflanzen 1. *tr. V.* **a)** *(aufstellen)* set up; **b)** fix ‹*bayonet*›. **2.** *refl. V.* **sich vor jmdm./etw. ~** *(ugs.)* plant oneself in front of sb./sth.

auf|pfropfen *tr. V. (auch fig.)* graft on (**auf** + *Akk.* to)

auf|picken *tr. V.* **a)** *(aufnehmen)* ‹*bird*› peck up; *(fig. ugs.)* pick up ‹*expression, idea, piece of information*›; **b)** *(öffnen)* peck open; **c)** *(österr.: aufkleben)* stick on (**auf** + *Akk.* to)

auf|platzen *itr. V.; mit sein* burst open; ‹*seam, cushion*› split open; ‹*wound*› open up

auf|plustern 1. *tr. V.* ruffle [up] ‹*feathers*›; puff up ‹*cheeks*›; *(fig. ugs.: aufbauschen)* blow up (**zu** into). **2.** *refl. V.* **a)** ‹*bird*› ruffle [up] its feathers; **b)** *(ugs. abwertend: sich wichtig tun)* puff oneself up

auf|polieren *tr. V. (auch fig.)* polish up

auf|polstern *tr. V.* reupholster

auf|prägen *tr. V.* emboss; stamp; **jmdm./einer Sache einen Stempel ~** *(fig.)* leave one's/its mark on sb./sth.

Auf·prall der; ~[e]s, ~e impact

auf|prallen *itr. V.; mit sein* **auf etw.** *(Akk., seltener Dat.)* **~:** strike *or* hit sth.; *(auf etw. auffahren)* collide with *or* run into sth.

Auf·preis der extra *or* additional charge; **gegen ~:** for an extra *or* additional charge

auf|probieren *tr. V.* try on ‹*hat, cap, spectacles*›

auf|pulvern *tr. (auch itr.) V. (ugs.)* pep up *(coll.)*; boost, lift ‹*morale*›; **Kaffee pulvert [einen] auf** coffee peps you up *(coll.)*

auf|pumpen 1. *tr. V.* pump up, inflate ‹*tyre*›; inflate ‹*air mattress, rubber boat*›; pump up *or* inflate the tyres of *or* on ‹*bicycle*›. **2.** *refl. V. (ugs.)* ‹*bird*› ruffle [up] its feathers

auf|putschen *tr. V. (abwertend)* **a)** *(stimulieren)* stimulate; arouse ‹*passions, urge*›;

~de Mittel stimulants; **jmdn./sich mit Kaffee ~:** give sb. coffee/drink coffee as a stimulant; **b)** *(aufhetzen)* incite; stir up (**gegen** against)
Aufputsch·mittel das stimulant
Auf·putz der get-up; **die Häuser standen in festlichem ~:** the houses were festively decorated
auf|putzen *tr. V.* **a)** decorate ‹*Christmas tree, building, etc.*›; **b)** *(fig. ugs.)* **mit bürgerlichen Ideen aufgeputzter Sozialismus** socialism dressed up in bourgeois ideas
auf|quellen *unr. itr. V.; mit sein* **a)** *(größer werden)* swell up; ‹*dough*› rise; **aufgequollene Augen/Wangen** swollen eyes/cheeks; **b)** *(geh.: emporsteigen, auch fig.)* well *or* rise up; ‹*smoke*› rise [up]
auf|raffen 1. *tr. V. (hochnehmen)* gather up. **2.** *refl. V.* **a)** *(sich erheben)* pull oneself up [on to one's feet]; struggle to one's feet; **b)** *(sich überwinden)* pull oneself together; **sich dazu ~, etw. zu tun** bring oneself to do sth.; **sich zu einer Arbeit/Entscheidung ~:** bring oneself to do a piece of work/come to a decision
auf|ragen *itr. V.* tower [up]; ‹*tower, mountain range*› rise up
auf|rappeln *refl. V. (ugs.)* **a)** *s.* **aufraffen 2a, b; b)** *(Schwäche überwinden)* recover
auf|rauchen *tr. V.* finish [smoking] ‹*cigarette, pipe, etc.*›; **die ganze Schachtel/alle Zigaretten ~:** get through *or* smoke the whole packet/all the cigarettes
auf|rauhen *tr. V.* roughen [up]; nap ‹*cloth*›
auf|räumen 1. *tr. V.* **a)** *(in Ordnung bringen)* tidy *or* clear up; *(fig.)* sort out; **b)** *(wegräumen)* clear *or* put away. **2.** *itr. V.* **a)** *(Ordnung machen)* tidy *or* clear up; *(fig.)* sort things out; **b)** *(beseitigen)* **mit jmdm./etw. ~:** eliminate sb./sth.
Aufräumungs·arbeiten *Pl.* clearance work *sing.*
auf|rechnen *tr. V.* **a)** *(berechnen)* charge for; **b)** *(verrechnen)* **etw. gegen etw. ~:** set sth. off against sth.
auf·recht 1. *Adj.* **a)** *(aufgerichtet)* upright ‹*position*›; upright, erect ‹*posture, bearing*›; **der ~e Gang ist für den Menschen charakteristisch** human beings characteristically walk upright; **etw. ~ hinstellen** place sth. upright *or* in an upright position; **b)** *(redlich)* upright. **2.** *adv. (aufgerichtet)* ‹*walk, sit, hold oneself*› straight, erect; **die Aussicht/Hoffnung hält ihn ~** *(fig.)* the prospect/hope keeps him going; **sich kaum noch ~ halten können** be hardly able to stand
aufrecht|erhalten *unr. tr. V.* maintain; maintain, keep up ‹*deception, fiction, contact, custom*›; keep to ‹*decision*›; **nur der Gedanke an ein kühles Bier erhielt ihn aufrecht** *(fig.)* it was only the thought of a cool beer that kept him going
Aufrecht·erhaltung die *s.* **aufrechterhalten:** maintenance; keeping up; **zur ~ des Kontakts** in order to maintain contact
auf|regen 1. *tr. V. (erregen)* excite; *(ärgerlich machen)* annoy; irritate; *(beunruhigen)* agitate; *(ugs.: entrüsten)* upset; **du regst mich auf** you're getting on my nerves. **2.** *refl. V.* get worked up (**über** + *Akk.* about)
Auf·regung die *(Erregung)* excitement *no pl.*; *(Beunruhigung)* agitation *no pl.*; **jmdn. in ~ versetzen** make sb. excited/agitated; **nur keine ~!** don't get excited!; **alles war in heller ~:** everything was in utter confusion; **der Vorfall hat das ganze Land in ~ versetzt** the whole country is in an uproar over the case
auf|reiben 1. *unr. tr. V.* **a)** *(zermürben)* wear down; **b)** *(vernichten)* wipe out; **c)** *(wund reiben)* **sich** *(Dat.)* **die Hände/Fersen** *usw.* **~:** rub one's hands/heels *etc.* sore; **das Seil hatte ihm die Hände aufgerieben** the rope had chafed his hands. **2.** *unr. refl. V.* wear oneself out
aufreibend 1. *Adj.* wearing; trying ‹*day, time*›; *(stärker)* gruelling. **2.** *adv.* tryingly, exasperatingly
auf|reihen 1. *tr. V.* **a)** thread ‹*beads, pearls*›; **b)** *(aufstellen)* line up; put in a row/rows. **2.** *refl. V. (sich aufstellen)* line up
auf|reißen 1. *unr. tr. V.* **a)** *(öffnen)* tear *or* rip open; tear open ‹*collar, shirt, etc.*›; wrench open ‹*drawer*›; fling open ‹*door, window*›; **die Augen/den Mund ~:** open one's eyes/mouth wide; **b)** *(beschädigen)* tear *or* rip open; rip, tear ‹*clothes*›; break up ‹*road, soil*›; **sich** *(Dat.)* **die Haut/den Ellbogen/Ärmel ~:** gash one's skin/elbow/rip *or* tear one's sleeve; **c)** *(bes. Fußballjargon)* open up ‹*defence*›; **d)** *(aufbrechen)* tear up ‹*road surface, pavement*›; **e)** *(Bautechnik)* make a drawing of; **f)** *(salopp: Kontakt finden mit)* pick up *(coll.)*; **g)** *(salopp: sich verschaffen)* get hold of; get, land oneself ‹*job*›. **2.** *itr. V.; mit sein (auseinanderreißen)* ‹*clothes*› tear, rip; ‹*seam*› split; ‹*wound*› open; ‹*clouds*› break up
auf|reizen *tr. V.* **a)** *(erregen)* excite ‹*senses, imagination*›; rouse ‹*passions*›; *(wütend machen)* provoke; **b)** *(aufwiegeln)* incite; **jmdn. zum Widerstand ~:** incite sb. to resist
auf·reizend 1. *Adj.* provocative. **2.** *adv.* provocatively
auf|ribbeln *tr. V. (ugs.)* unpick
Aufrichte die; ~, ~n *(schweiz.)* topping-out ceremony
auf|richten 1. *tr. V.* **a)** *(hochrichten)* **den Kopf/Oberkörper ~:** raise one's head/upper body; **jmdn. ~** *(auf die Beine stellen)* help sb. up; **jmdn. im Bett ~:** sit sb. up in bed; **sich ~:** stand up [straight]; *(aus gebückter Haltung)* straighten up; *(nach einem Sturz)* get to one's feet; **sich im Bett ~:** sit up in bed; **sich zur vollen Länge ~:** draw oneself up to one's full height; **b)** *(errichten)* erect; put up; *(fig.)* build up ‹*business, empire*›; **c)** *(trösten)* **jmdn. [wieder] ~:** give fresh heart to sb.; **d)** *(beleben)* restore ‹*pride, self-confidence*›; **jmds. Mut ~:** give sb. new courage. **2.** *refl. V. (Mut schöpfen)* take heart; **sich an jmdm./etw. [wieder] ~:** take heart from sb./sth.
auf·richtig 1. *Adj.* honest, sincere ‹*person, efforts*›; sincere ‹*regret, sympathy, affection*›; genuine ‹*pleasure, admiration*›; **~ zu jmdm.** *od.* **gegen jmdn. sein** be honest *or* straightforward with sb.; **wenn ich ~ sein soll** to be honest *or* frank. **2.** *adv.* sincerely; ‹*speak*› honestly, frankly
Auf·richtigkeit die sincerity; *(eines Menschen)* honesty; sincerity
Auf·riß der a) *(Bautechnik)* elevation; **etw. im ~ darstellen** draw sth. in elevation; **b)** *(Darstellung)* outline
Aufriß·zeichnung die *(Bautechnik)* elevation
auf|ritzen *tr. V.* **a)** *(öffnen)* slit [open]; **b)** *(verletzen)* scratch; **sich** *(Dat.)* **die Haut/den Arm ~:** scratch oneself/one's arm
auf|rollen *tr. V.* **a)** *(zusammenrollen)* roll up; coil *or* roll up ‹*hose, cable*›; *(auf eine Rolle)* roll up ‹*hose, cable*›; **sich** *(Dat.)* **die Haare ~** *(ugs.)* put one's hair up in rollers *or* curlers; **b)** *(auseinanderrollen)* unroll; unfurl ‹*flag*›; **c)** *(aufkrempeln)* roll up ‹*sleeve, trouser-leg*›; **d)** *(erörtern)* go into ‹*subject, question*›; **der Prozeß mußte noch einmal aufgerollt werden** the case had to be retried; **e)** *(Milit.)* **den Feind ~:** turn ‹*enemy, enemy position*›
auf|rücken *itr. V.; mit sein* **a)** *(aufschließen)* move up; **dicht aufgerückt stehen** stand close [up] together; **b)** *(befördert werden)* move up; be promoted; **zum Major ~:** be promoted to major; **in eine leitende Stellung ~:** rise to a managerial position
Auf·ruf der a) *(das Aufrufen)* call; **„Eintritt nur nach ~“** 'do not enter until called'; **b)** *(Appell)* appeal (**an** + *Akk.* to); **einen ~ an jmdn. richten** appeal to sb.; **c)** *(DV)* call; **d)** *(Bankw.)* calling-in
auf|rufen *unr. tr. V.* **a)** *auch itr. (auffordern)* **jmdn. ~, etw. zu tun** call upon sb. to do sth.; **jmdn. zum Widerstand/zu Spenden ~:** call on sb. to resist/for donations; **zum [Generallstreik ~:** call a [general] strike; **b)** *(namentlich)* call ‹*name*›; **jmdn. ~:** call sb.; call sb.'s name; **einen Schüler ~:** call upon a pupil to answer; **c)** *(Rechtsw.)* appeal for ‹*witnesses*› [to come forward]; **etwaige Erben ~:** call on possible heirs to make themselves known; **d)** *(DV)* call
Aufruhr der; ~s, ~e a) *(Widerstand)* revolt; rebellion; **in ~ sein** be in revolt; **b)** *o. Pl. (Erregung)* turmoil; **jmdn./etw. in ~ versetzen** plunge *or* throw sb./sth. into [a state of] turmoil
auf|rühren *tr. V.* **a)** stir up; **b)** *(geh.: hervorrufen)* stir up, rouse ‹*feelings*›; **c)** *(in Erinnerung rufen)* stir up ‹*memory*›; rake up ‹*scandal, story*›; **d)** *(geh.: erregen)* upset; disturb
Aufrührer der; ~s, ~, Aufrührerin die; ~, ~nen rabble-rouser
aufrührerisch 1. *Adj.* **a)** *(aufwiegelnd)* seditious; inflammatory; **b)** *nicht präd. (in Aufruhr befindlich)* rebellious. **2.** *adv. (aufwiegelnd)* seditiously
auf|runden *tr. V.* round off (**auf** + *Akk.* to)
auf|rüsten *tr., itr. V.* arm; **wieder ~:** rearm
Auf·rüstung die armament
auf|rütteln *tr. V.* **jmdn. [aus dem Schlaf] ~:** shake sb. out of his/her sleep; **jmds. Gewissen ~** *(fig.)* stir sb.'s conscience; **jmdn. aus seiner Apathie/Lethargie** *usw.* **~** *(fig.)* shake sb. out of his/her apathy/lethargy *etc.*
aufs *Präp. + Art.* **a) = auf das; b) ~ Klo gehen** *(ugs.)* go to the loo *(Brit. coll.)* or *(Amer. coll.)* john; **sich ~ Bitten verlegen** resort to appeals
auf|sagen *tr. V.* **a)** *(sagen)* recite; **b)** *(geh.: aufkündigen)* **[jmdm.] seinen Dienst ~:** give in one's notice [to sb.] *(Brit.)*; give [one's] notice [to sb.] *(Amer.)*; **jmdm. die Freundschaft ~:** break with sb.
auf|sammeln *tr. V.* **a)** *(aufheben)* pick *or* gather up; **b)** *(ugs.: aufgreifen)* pick up
aufsässig ['aufzɛsɪç] **1.** *Adj.* **a)** *(trotzig)* recalcitrant; **b)** *(veralt.: rebellisch)* rebellious. **2.** *adv.* **a)** *(trotzig)* recalcitrantly; **b)** *(veralt.: rebellisch)* rebelliously
Aufsässigkeit die; ~, ~en a) *o. Pl. (Trotz)* recalcitrance; *(Rebellion)* rebelliousness; **b)** *(Handlung)* piece of recalcitrance/rebelliousness
auf|satteln *tr. V.* saddle ‹*horse*›; hitch up ‹*trailer, sled*›
Auf·satz der a) *(Schul~, Abhandlung)* essay; *(in einer Zeitschrift)* article; **b)** *(Aufbau)* top *or* upper part; **c)** *(Orgelbau)* resonator; **d)** *(Tafel~)* epergne
Aufsatz-: ~heft das essay book; **~thema das** essay subject
auf|saugen *unr. (auch regelm.) tr. V.* soak up; *(fig.)* absorb; *(verschlucken)* absorb; swallow up
auf|schauen *(südd., österr., schweiz.) s.* **aufblicken**
auf|schaukeln *refl. V.* **a)** *(Techn.)* ‹*vehicle*› start rocking more and more violently; **b)** *(ugs.: sich steigern)* ‹*excitement etc.*› build up
auf|schäumen 1. *itr. V.; meist mit sein* ‹*champagne, beer, etc.*› foam up; ‹*sea*› foam. **2.** *tr. V. (Technik)* **etw. auf die Wand ~:** apply sth. to *or* spray sth. on to the wall as a foam
auf|scheinen *unr. itr. V.; mit sein (auch fig., auch österr. Amtsspr.)* appear
auf|scheuchen *tr. V.* **a)** *(aufjagen)* put up ‹*birds, animals*›; **b)** *(ugs.: in Unruhe versetzen)* startle; **jmdn. aus seiner Gleichgültigkeit/Lethargie** *usw.* **~:** shake *or* jolt sb. out of his/her apathy/lethargy
auf|scheuern 1. *tr. V. (verletzen)* chafe;

sich *(Dat.)* **die Haut/die Fersen ~:** chafe one's skin/heels. **2.** *refl. V. (verletzt werden)* become chafed *or* sore

auf|schichten *tr. V.* stack up; build [up] ‹*wall, mound, stack, pile*›; pile up ‹*straw*› [in layers]

auf|schieben *unr. tr. V.* **a)** *(verschieben)* postpone; put off; **aufgeschoben ist nicht aufgehoben** there'll be another opportunity; there is always another time; **b)** slide open ‹*door, window*›; slide *or* draw back ‹*bolt*›

auf|schießen 1. *unr. itr. V.; mit sein* **a)** *(nach oben schießen)* shoot up; ‹*flames*› shoot *or* leap up; **b)** *(schnell wachsen)* shoot up; **ein lang aufgeschossener Junge** a tall gangling *or* gangly youth. **2.** *unr. tr. V. (Seemannsspr.)* coil [up]

Auf·schlag der a) *(das Aufprallen)* impact; **b)** *(Preis~)* extra charge; surcharge; **c)** *(Ärmel~)* cuff; *(Hosen~)* turn-up; *(Revers)* lapel; **d)** *(Tennis usw.)* serve; service; **jetzt habe ich ~:** now it's my serve

auf|schlagen 1. *unr. itr. V.* **a)** *mit sein (aufprallen)* **auf etw.** *(Dat. od. Akk.)* **~:** hit *or* strike sth.; **mit der Stirn/dem Kopf ~:** hit one's forehead/head on sth.; **b)** *auch mit sein (teurer werden)* ‹*price, rent, costs*› go up; **c)** *(Tennis usw.)* serve; **Sie schlagen auf!** it's your serve *or* service; **d)** *(auflodern)* ‹*flames*› leap up; ‹*fire*› leap *or* blaze up. **2.** *unr. tr. V.* **a)** *(öffnen)* crack ‹*nut, egg*› [open]; knock a hole in ‹*ice*›; **sich** *(Dat.)* **das Knie/den Kopf ~:** fall and cut one's knee/head; **b)** *(aufblättern)* open ‹*book, newspaper*›; *(zurückschlagen)* turn back ‹*bedclothes, blanket*›; **schlagt S. 15 auf!** turn to page 15; **c) die Augen ~:** open one's eyes; **d)** *(hoch-, umschlagen)* turn up ‹*collar, sleeve, trouser-leg*›; **e)** *(aufbauen)* set up ‹*camp*›; pitch, put up ‹*tent*›; put up ‹*bed, hut, scaffolding*›; **f)** *(erhöhen)* put up, raise, increase ‹*prices*›; **5% auf etw.** *(Akk.)* **~:** put 5% on sth.; **g)** *(sich niederlassen)* **seinen Wohnsitz in der Hauptstadt/einem Bauernhaus ~:** take up residence in the capital/a farmhouse; **h)** *(Stricken)* cast on

Auf·schläger der *(Tennis usw.)* server

Aufschlag-: ~fehler der *(Tennis usw.)* [service] fault; **~zünder der** percussion fuse

auf|schlecken *tr. V.* lap up

auf|schließen 1. *unr. tr. V.* **a)** unlock; **jmdm. die Tür ~:** unlock the door for sb.; **b)** *(Bergbau)* develop; **c)** *(Chemie, Biol.)* break down; **d)** *(Amtsspr.: erschließen)* develop. **2.** *unr. itr. V.* **a) [jmdm.] ~:** unlock the door/gate *etc.* [for sb.]; **b)** *(aufrücken)* close up; *(Milit.)* close ranks; **die Autos fuhren dicht aufgeschlossen** the cars were bumper to bumper; **c)** *(Sport)* catch up **(zu** with)

auf|schlitzen *tr. V.* slit open; slash open ‹*stomach, dress*›

auf|schluchzen *tr. V.* give a sob; *(stoßweise schluchzen)* sob convulsively

Auf·schluß der a) *(Auskunft)* information *no pl.;* **über etw.** *(Akk.)* **~ geben** give *or* provide information about sth.; **jmdm. über etw.** *(Akk.)* **~ geben** inform sb. about sth.; **über etw.** *(Akk.)* **~ verlangen** demand an explanation of sth.; **b)** *(Bergbau)* development; **c)** *(Chemie, Biol.)* breaking up; **d)** *(im Gefängnis)* **um 7 Uhr ist ~:** the cells are unlocked at 7 o'clock

auf|schlüsseln *tr. V.* break down **(nach** according to)

Aufschlüsselung, Aufschlüßlung die; ~, **~en** breakdown

aufschluß·reich *Adj.* informative; *(enthüllend)* revealing

auf|schnallen *tr. V.* **a)** *(öffnen)* unbuckle; unstrap; unbuckle, unfasten ‹*belt*›; **b)** *(befestigen)* strap on; **sich** *(Dat.)* **den Rucksack ~:** strap one's rucksack on [to] one's back

auf|schnappen 1. *tr. V.* **a)** *(ugs.: hören)* pick up; **b)** *(auffangen)* snap up. **2.** *itr. V.; mit sein (sich öffnen)* snap *or* spring open

auf|schneiden 1. *unr. tr. V.* **a)** *(öffnen)* cut open; cut ‹*knot*›; lance ‹*abscess, boil*›; **sich** *(Dat.)* **den Finger ~:** cut one's finger [open]; **ein neues Buch ~:** cut the pages of a new book; **b)** *(zerteilen)* cut, slice ‹*bread, cake, cheese*›; carve, slice ‹*meat, poultry*›. **2.** *unr. itr. V. (ugs. abwertend: prahlen)* boast, brag **(mit** about)

Auf·schneider der *(ugs. abwertend)* boaster; braggart

Auf·schneiderei die *(ugs. abwertend)* boasting; bragging

auf|schnellen *itr. V.; mit sein* leap up

Auf·schnitt der; *o. Pl.* [assorted] cold meats *pl.*/cheeses *pl.*; **kalter ~:** cold cuts *pl.*

auf|schnüren *tr. V.* undo, untie ‹*knot, parcel, string*›; unlace, undo ‹*shoe, boot, corset*›

auf|schrauben *tr. V.* **a)** *(öffnen, lösen)* unscrew; unscrew the top of ‹*bottle, jar, etc.*›; **b)** *(auf etw. schrauben, mit Schrauben befestigen)* screw on **(auf** + *Akk.* to)

auf|schrecken 1. *tr. V.* *(erschrecken)* startle; make ‹*person*› jump; **jmdn. aus dem Schlaf ~:** startle sb. from his/her sleep. **2.** *itr. V.; im Präsens und Prät. auch unr.; mit sein* start [up]; **aus dem Schlaf ~:** awake with a start; start from one's sleep; **aus einem Traum/seinen Gedanken ~:** start from a dream/one's reflections

Auf·schrei der cry; *(stärker)* yell; *(schriller)* scream; **ein ~ der Empörung** *od.* **Entrüstung** *(fig.)* an outcry

auf|schreiben 1. *unr. tr. V.* **a)** write down; **[sich** *(Dat.)***] etw. ~:** make a note of sth.; **er wurde von einem Polizisten aufgeschrieben** the policeman took his name and particulars; **b)** *(ugs.: verordnen)* prescribe ‹*medicine*›. **2.** *unr. itr. V. (bes. südd., österr.: anschreiben)* give credit; **bei jmdm. ~ lassen** get credit from sb.

auf|schreien *unr. itr. V.* cry out; *(stärker)* yell out; *(schrill)* scream

Auf·schrift die a) *(Beschriftung)* inscription; *(Etikett)* label; **b)** *(Anschrift)* address

Auf·schub der delay; *(absichtliche Verschiebung)* postponement; **die Sache duldet keinen ~:** the matter brooks no delay; **jmdm. ~ gewähren** *(Zahlungs~)* allow *or* grant sb. a period of grace; **ein ~ der Hinrichtung** a reprieve

auf|schürfen *tr. V.* **sich** *(Dat.)* **das Knie/die Haut ~:** graze one's knee/oneself

auf|schütteln *tr. V.* shake *or* plump up ‹*pillow, cushion*›

auf|schütten *tr. V.* **a)** *(auf etw. schütten)* pour on ‹*liquid*›; **etw. auf etw.** *(Akk.)* **~:** pour sth. on *or* over sth.; **noch etwas Kohle [auf die Glut] ~:** put some more coal on [the fire]; **b)** *(aufhäufen)* pile up; pile *or* heap up ‹*sand, earth, straw*›; **c)** *(errichten)* build ‹*dam, embankment, pile*›; *(erhöhen)* raise ‹*road*›; *(verbreitern)* widen ‹*road*›; **d)** *(Geol.)* deposit

Aufschüttung die; ~, **~en a)** *(Erhöhung)* earth bank; **b)** *(Geol.)* deposit

auf|schwatzen, *(bes. südd.)* **auf|schwätzen** *tr. V.* **jmdm. etw. ~:** talk sb. into having sth.; **sich** *(Dat.)* **etw. ~ lassen** be talked into having sth.

auf|schwellen 1. *unr. itr. V.; mit sein* **a)** *(dick werden)* swell up; **aufgeschwollene Leiber/Wangen** swollen bodies/cheeks; **b)** *(laut werden)* swell. **2.** *tr. V. (auch fig.)* swell

auf|schwemmen *tr. V.* **jmdn./jmds. Gesicht ~:** make sb./sb.'s face bloated

auf|schwingen 1. *unr. refl. V.* **a)** *(emporfliegen)* ‹*bird*› soar up; **b)** *(sich aufraffen)* **sich ~, etw. zu tun** bring oneself to do sth.; **sich zum Arbeiten/zu einem Entschluß/Brief ~:** bring oneself to get down to work/bring oneself to make a decision/write a letter; **c) sich zum Sittenrichter/Diktator** *usw.* **~:** set oneself up as a judge of morals/as a dictator *etc.* **2.** *unr. itr. V. (Turnen)* swing [oneself] up

Auf·schwung der a) *(Auftrieb)* uplift; **das gab mir neuen ~:** that gave me a lift; **b)** *(gute Entwicklung)* upswing; upturn *(Gen.* in); **einen ~ erleben** experience an upswing *or* upturn; **c)** *(Turnen)* swing up

auf|sehen *unr. itr. V.* **a)** look up; **b)** *(bewundern)* **zu jmdm. ~:** look up to sb.

Aufsehen das; ~s stir; sensation; **[großes] ~ erregen** cause *or* create a [great] stir *or* sensation; **sich ohne großes ~ davonmachen** make off without causing a lot of fuss; **um jedes ~ zu vermeiden, reiste er inkognito** to avoid causing *or* creating a stir, he travelled incognito

aufsehen·erregend *Adj.* sensational

Auf·seher der *(im Gefängnis)* warder *(Brit.)*; [prison] guard *(Amer.)*; *(im Park)* park-keeper; *(im Museum, auf dem Parkplatz)* attendant; *(bei Prüfungen)* invigilator *(Brit.)*; proctor *(Amer.)*; *(auf einem Gut, Sklaven~)* overseer; *(im Warenhaus)* shopwalker *(Brit.)*; floorwalker *(Amer.)*

Aufseherin die; ~, **~nen** *(im Gefängnis)* warder *(Brit.)*; [prison] guard *(Amer.)*; *(im Museum)* attendant; *(bei Prüfungen)* invigilator *(Brit.)*; proctor *(Amer.)*; *(im Warenhaus)* shopwalker *(Brit.)*; floorwalker *(Amer.)*

auf|sein *unr. itr. V.; mit sein; nur im Inf. und Part. zusammengeschrieben (ugs.)* **a)** be open; **b)** *(nicht im Bett sein)* be up

auf|setzen 1. *tr. V.* **a)** put on ‹*hat, glasses, mask*›; **eine Miene/ein Lächeln ~** *(fig.)* put on an expression/a smile; **sich** *(Dat.)* **etw. ~:** put sth. on; **b)** *(aufs Feuer setzen)* put on; **Wasser [zum Kochen] ~:** put water on [to boil]; **c)** *(entwerfen)* draft; *(verfassen)* draw up ‹*minutes, contract, will*›; **d)** *(aufrecht hinsetzen)* **jmdn. ~:** sit sb. up; **sich ~:** sit up; **e)** *(auf eine Unterlage)* set down; lower ‹*record-player arm*›; **den Fuß ~:** put one's foot on the ground *or* down; **f)** *(aufschichten)* stack [up]; **g)** *(aufrecht hinstellen)* set up ‹*skittles*›; **h)** *(Seemannsspr.)* beach; **i)** *(Flugw.)* land ‹*aircraft*›; set ‹*aircraft*› down. **2.** *itr. V.* ‹*aircraft*› touch down, land; *s. auch* **aufgesetzt 2; Horn a; Dämpfer b**

Auf·setzer der *(Fußball, Handball)* bouncer; bouncing ball

auf|seufzen *itr. V.* **[laut/tief] ~:** heave a [loud/deep] sigh

Auf·sicht die a) *o. Pl.* *(Überwachung)* supervision; *(bei Prüfungen)* invigilation *(Brit.)*; proctoring *(Amer.)*; **[die] ~ haben** *od.* **führen** be in charge **(über** + *Akk.* of); *(bei Prüfungen)* invigilate *(Brit.)*; proctor *(Amer.)*; **ohne ~:** unsupervised; without supervision; **unter [jmds.] ~** *(Dat.)* under [sb.'s] supervision; **unter ärztlicher/polizeilicher ~:** under medical/police supervision; **während der Pause auf dem Schulhof ~ haben** ‹*teacher*› be on duty during break; **b)** *(Person)* person in charge; *(Lehrer)* teacher in charge *or* on duty; *(im Museum)* attendant

aufsicht·führend *Adj.; nicht präd.* in charge *postpos.*; supervising ‹*authority*›; ‹*teacher*› in charge *or* on duty

Aufsicht·führende der/die; *adj. Dekl.; s.* **Aufsicht b**

Aufsichts-: ~beamte der attendant; *(im Bahnhof)* supervisor; **~pflicht die** *(Rechtsw.)* legal responsibility *or* obligation to exercise proper supervision; **die elterliche ~pflicht** legal parental responsibility to keep children under proper supervision; **~rat der** *(Wirtsch.)* **a)** *(Gremium)* board of directors; supervisory board; **b)** *(Mitglied)* member of the board [of directors] *or* supervisory board

auf|sitzen *unr. itr. V.* **a)** *mit sein (auf ein Reittier)* mount; *(auf ein Fahrzeug)* get on;

auf ein Pferd ~: mount a horse; **aufgesessen!** *(Milit.)* mount!; **b)** *mit sein (Turnen)* come to a sitting position; **c)** *mit sein (hereinfallen)* **jmdm./einer Sache ~**: be taken in by sb./sth.; **d)** *(ugs.: aufrecht sitzen)* sit up; **e)** *(aufliegen)* **auf etw.** *(Dat.)* **~**: ⟨*machine part, beam, etc.*⟩ sit on sth.; **f)** *(Seemannsspr.)* be grounded *or* aground

Aufsitzer der; ~s, ~ *(österr.)* flop *(coll.)*

auf|spalten 1. *unr. (auch regelm.) tr. V.* split; *(fig.)* split [up]. **2.** *unr. refl. V.* split

Auf·spaltung die splitting; *(fig.)* splitting [up]

auf|spannen *tr. V.* **a)** *(öffnen)* open, put up ⟨*umbrella, parasol*⟩; stretch out ⟨*net, jumping-sheet*⟩; put up ⟨*tennis-net, badminton-net, etc.*⟩; **b)** *(spannen)* stretch, mount ⟨*canvas*⟩ **(auf +** *Akk.* **on)**

auf|sparen *tr. V. (auch fig.)* save [up]; keep

auf|speichern 1. *tr. V. (auch fig.)* store up; **seine aufgespeicherte Wut/Energie** *(fig.)* his pent-up rage/energy. **2.** *refl. V. (auch fig.)* build up

auf|sperren *tr. V.* **a)** *(ugs.: öffnen)* **[weit] ~**: open wide; **b)** *(bes. südd., österr.: aufschließen)* unlock

auf|spielen 1. *refl. V.* **a)** *(ugs. abwertend: angeben)* put on airs; **sich vor jmdm. ~**: show off in front of sb.; **b)** *(als etw. hinstellen)* **sich als Held/Märtyrer ~**: act the hero/martyr; **sich als Kenner/als jmds. Anwalt ~**: set oneself up as an expert/as sb.'s lawyer. **2.** *itr. V.* **a)** *(musizieren)* play; **zum Tanz ~**: play dance music; **b)** *(Sport)* **groß/eindrucksvoll ~**: give a fine/impressive display

auf|spießen *tr. V.* **a)** run ⟨*animal, person*⟩ through; skewer ⟨*piece of meat*⟩; *(mit der Gabel)* take ⟨*piece of meat*⟩ on one's fork; *(auf die Hörner nehmen)* gore; **jmdn. mit seinen Blicken ~** *(fig.)* look daggers at sb.; **b)** *(befestigen)* pin ⟨*butterfly, insect*⟩

auf|splittern 1. *itr. V.; mit sein* ⟨*wood*⟩ splinter. **2.** *tr. V. (in Teile auflösen)* split up ⟨*party, group, country, etc.*⟩. **3.** *refl. V.* ⟨*party, group, country, etc.*⟩ split up

Aufsplitterung die; ~, ~en *s.* **aufsplittern**: splintering; splitting up

auf|sprengen *tr. V.* force [open]; break open; *(mit Sprengstoff)* blow open

auf|springen *unr. itr. V.; mit sein* **a)** *(hochspringen)* jump *or* leap up; **b)** *(auf ein Fahrzeug)* jump on; **auf etw.** *(Akk.)* **~**: jump on [to] sth.; **c)** *(rissig werden)* crack; ⟨*skin, lips*⟩ crack, chap; **d)** *(sich öffnen)* ⟨*door, window*⟩ fly or burst open; ⟨*bud, seed-pod*⟩ burst open; **e)** *(auftreffen)* bounce

auf|spriten ['aufʃprıtn̩] *tr. V.* fortify ⟨*wine*⟩

auf|spritzen 1. *itr. V.; mit sein* **a)** *(hochspritzen)* ⟨*blood*⟩ spurt [up]; ⟨*mud, spray, waves, sea, surf*⟩ spray up; **b)** *(ugs.: aufspringen)* leap up; leap to one's feet. **2.** *tr. V.* spray on; **etw. auf etw.** *(Akk.)* **~**: spray sth. on [to] sth.

auf|sprudeln *itr. V.; mit sein* ⟨*spring, water*⟩ bubble up

auf|sprühen 1. *tr. V.* spray on; **etw. auf etw.** *(Akk.)* **~**: spray sth. on [to] sth. **2.** *itr. V.; mit sein* ⟨*flames*⟩ shoot up; ⟨*sparks, spray*⟩ fly up; ⟨*water*⟩ spray up

Auf·sprung der landing; *(eines Balls)* bounce

auf|spulen *tr. V.* wind ⟨*cotton, ribbon, fishing-line*⟩ on to a/the reel *or* spool

auf|spüren *tr. V. (auch fig.)* track down

auf|stacheln *tr. V.* **a)** *(aufhetzen)* incite; **jmdn. zur Revolte/zum Widerstand** *usw.* **~**: incite sb. to revolt/offer resistance *etc.*; **b)** *(anspornen)* spur on ⟨*person, team*⟩; fire ⟨*passion, jealousy, imagination, etc.*⟩

auf|stampfen *itr. V.* stamp; **mit dem Fuß ~**: stamp one's foot

Auf·stand der rebellion; revolt; **im ~**: in rebellion *or* revolt

auf·ständisch *Adj.* rebellious; rebel *attrib.*, insurgent ⟨*army unit*⟩

Aufständische der/die; *adj. Dekl.* rebel; insurgent

auf|stapeln *tr. V.* stack up

auf|stauen 1. *refl. V.* ⟨*water*⟩ pile up; *(fig.)* ⟨*anger, aggression, bitterness, etc.*⟩ build up; **aufgestaute Wut/Erbitterung** *usw. (fig.)* pent-up rage/bitterness *etc.* **2.** *tr. V.* dam [up]; **etw. in sich** *(Dat.)* **~** *(fig.)* bottle sth. up inside [one]

auf|stechen *unr. tr. V.* **a)** lance, prick ⟨*boil*⟩; prick ⟨*blister*⟩; lance ⟨*abscess*⟩; **jmdm./sich eine Blase ~**: prick sb.'s/one's blister; **b)** *(ugs.: aufdecken)* uncover; bring to light

auf|stecken 1. *tr. V.* **a)** put up ⟨*curtains*⟩; turn up ⟨*hem, dress, trousers*⟩; **sich** *(Dat.)* **das Haar/die Zöpfe ~**: pin *or* put one's hair/plaits up; **sie trug das Haar aufgesteckt** she wore her hair up; **Kerzen auf den Leuchter ~**: put candles on the candelabrum; **b)** *(ugs.: aufgeben)* **etw. ~**: give sth. up; pack sth. in *(sl.)*; **einen Plan ~**: give up a plan. **2.** *itr. V. (bes. Sport: aufgeben)* retire

auf|stehen *unr. itr. V.* **a)** *mit sein (vom Sitzplatz)* stand up; *(aus dem Liegen)* get up; get to one's feet; *(aus dem Bett)* **get up**; *(als Kranker)* get up; get out of bed; **aus seinem Sessel ~**: get up from one's chair; **vom Tisch ~**: rise from the table; **für jmdn. im Bus ~**: get up for sb. in the bus; **da mußt du früher** *od.* **eher ~!** *(ugs.)* you'll have to be a lot sharper than that!; *s. auch* **Huhn a**; **b)** *(offenstehen)* ⟨*door, window, etc.*⟩ be open; **c)** *mit sein (geh. veralt.: sich auflehnen)* rise in revolt; **gegen jmdn./etw. ~**: rise [up] against sb./sth.

auf|steigen *unr. itr. V.; mit sein* **a)** *(auf ein Fahrrad, einen Wagen usw.)* get *or* climb on; **auf etw.** *(Akk.)* **~**: get *or* climb on [to] sth.; **auf ein Pferd ~**: get on [to] *or* mount a horse; **b)** *(bergan steigen)* climb; **zum Gipfel ~**: climb [up] to the top *or* summit; **c)** *(hochsteigen)* ⟨*smoke, mist, sap, air, moon, sun*⟩ rise; ⟨*storm*⟩ gather; **eine ~de Linie** *(fig.)* an ascending line; **d)** *(beruflich, gesellschaftlich)* rise **(zu** to); **zum Direktor ~**: rise to the post of *or* to be manager; **zu Macht und Einfluß ~**: rise to power and influence; **e)** *(hochfliegen)* go up; ⟨*bird*⟩ soar up; **in** *od.* **mit einem Ballon ~**: go up in a balloon; **f)** **an die Oberfläche ~**: rise to the surface; **g)** *(geh.: entstehen)* **in jmdm. ~** ⟨*hatred, revulsion, fear, etc.*⟩ rise [up] in sb.; ⟨*memory, thought*⟩ come into sb.'s mind; ⟨*doubt*⟩ arise in sb.'s mind; ⟨*tears*⟩ well up inside sb.; **h)** *(Sport)* be promoted, go up **(in +** *Akk.* to); **i)** *(geh.: aufragen)* rise up; tower

Auf·steiger der a) ein [sozialer] ~: a social climber; **b)** *(Sport) (aufsteigende Mannschaft)* promotion team *or* side; *(aufgestiegene Mannschaft)* newly promoted side

auf|stellen 1. *tr. V.* **a)** *(hinstellen)* put up **(auf +** *Akk.* **on)**; set up ⟨*skittles*⟩; *(aufrecht hinstellen)* stand up; **b)** *(postieren)* post; station; **c)** *(auswählen)* select, pick ⟨*team, player*⟩; put together ⟨*team of experts*⟩; raise ⟨*army*⟩; **jmdn. für ein Spiel ~** *(Sport)* play sb. in a match; pick *or* select sb. for a match; **d)** *(nominieren)* nominate; put up; **jmdn. als Kandidaten ~**: nominate sb. *or* put sb. up as a candidate; **e)** *(errichten)* put up; put up, erect ⟨*scaffolding, monument*⟩; put in, install ⟨*machine*⟩; **f)** *(hochstellen)* erect ⟨*spines*⟩; turn up ⟨*collar*⟩; **die Ohren ~** ⟨*animal*⟩ prick up its ears; **g)** *(ausarbeiten)* work out ⟨*programme, budget, plan*⟩; draw up ⟨*contract, statute, balance sheet*⟩; make [out], draw up ⟨*list*⟩; set up ⟨*hypothesis*⟩; establish ⟨*norm*⟩; prepare ⟨*statistics*⟩; **eine Formel für etw. ~**: devise a formula for sth.; **h)** *(erzielen)* set up, establish ⟨*record*⟩; **i)** *(formulieren)* put forward ⟨*theory, conjecture, demand*⟩; **j)** *(bes. südd.: aufsetzen)* put on ⟨*soup, potatoes, etc.*⟩; **k)** *(nordd.) s.* **anstellen f. 2.** *refl. V.* **a)** *(postieren)* position *or* place oneself; take up position; *(in einer Reihe, zum Tanz)* line up; **sich im Kreis ~**: form a circle; **sich in Reih und Glied ~** *(Milit.)* fall in; **b)** ⟨*hairs, bristles*⟩ rise

Auf·stellung die a) *s.* **aufstellen 1 a**: putting up; setting up; standing up; **b)** *s.* **aufstellen e**: putting up; erection; installation; **c)** *(einer Mannschaft, eines Spielers)* selection; picking; *(einer Spezialeinheit)* putting together; *(eines Heeres)* raising; *(aufgestellte Mannschaft)* [team] line-up; **d)** *(Nominierung)* nomination; **e)** *(Milit.)* **~ nehmen** *od.* **beziehen** line up; **das Bataillon hatte vor dem Palast ~ genommen** *od.* **bezogen** the battalion was drawn up in front of the palace; **f)** *s.* **aufstellen g**: working out; drawing up; making out; setting up; establishment; preparation; **g)** *(das Erzielen)* setting up; establishment; **h)** *(das Formulieren)* putting forward; **i)** *(Liste)* list; *(Tabelle)* table

auf|stemmen *tr. V.* **a)** *(öffnen)* force ⟨*door*⟩ open [with a crowbar]; force *or* prise ⟨*box*⟩ open [with a crowbar]; **b)** *(aufstützen)* **seinen Fuß/Arm ~**: brace one's foot/arm **(auf +** *Akk.* **on)**

auf|stieben *unr. itr. V.; mit sein* fly up

Aufstieg der; ~[e]s, ~e a) *(das Hinaufsteigen)* climb; ascent; **b)** *(Aufwärtsentwicklung)* rise; **den ~ zum Geschäftsleiter/in den Vorstand schaffen** succeed in rising to the position of manager/rising to become a member of the board of directors; **ein wirtschaftlicher/sozialer ~**: economic/social advancement; **c)** *(Sport)* promotion **(in +** *Akk.* to); **d)** *(Weg)* way up; **ein gefährlicher ~ zum Gipfel** a dangerous route up *or* ascent to the summit

Aufstiegs-: **~chance die** prospect of promotion; **~spiel das** *(Sport)* promotion decider

auf|stöbern *tr. V.* **a)** *(aufjagen)* put up ⟨*birds, animals*⟩; **b)** *(entdecken)* track down; run to earth

auf|stocken *tr. (auch itr.) V.* **a) ein Gebäude ~**: add a storey to a building; **wir haben aufgestockt** we've added another storey; **b)** *(vermehren, erweitern)* increase ⟨*capital, budget, funds, pensions*⟩; build up ⟨*supplies*⟩; **die Gesellschaft stockt auf** the company is increasing its capital

auf|stöhnen *itr. V.* groan; **laut/erleichtert ~**: give *or* utter a loud groan/a sigh of relief

auf|stören *tr. V.* **a)** *(aufschrecken)* put up ⟨*bird, animal*⟩; disturb ⟨*wasps' nest, anthill*⟩; **b)** *(stören)* disturb

auf|stoßen 1. *unr. tr. V.* **a)** *(öffnen)* push open; *(mit einem Fußtritt)* kick open; **b)** *(heftig aufsetzen)* **etw. auf etw.** *(Akk.)* **~**: bang sth. down on sth.; **den Stock auf den Boden ~**: thump one's stick on the ground; **c)** *(verletzen)* **sich** *(Dat.)* **den Ellbogen** *usw.* **~**: graze one's elbow *etc.* **2.** *unr. itr. V.* **a)** *(rülpsen)* belch; burp *(coll.)*; ⟨*baby*⟩ bring up wind, *(coll.)* burp; **b)** *auch mit sein (Aufstoßen verursachen)* **[jmdm.] ~**: repeat [on sb.]; **das könnte Ihnen übel ~** *(fig.)* you might have to pay dearly for that *(fig.)*; you could live to regret that; **c)** *mit sein (ugs.: auffallen)* **jmdm. ~**: strike sb.

auf|streben *itr. V. (geh.)* tower [up]; **steil ~de Felswände** towering rock walls

aufstrebend *Adj.* rising ⟨*talent, bourgeoisie, industry*⟩; ⟨*nation, people*⟩ striving for progress; **ein ~er junger Mann** an ambitious and up-and-coming young man

auf|streichen *unr. tr. V.* spread ⟨*butter, jam, etc.*⟩ **(auf +** *Akk.* **on)**; put on, apply ⟨*ointment, paint*⟩ **(auf +** *Akk.* **to)**

auf|streuen *tr. V.* sprinkle on; **etw. auf etw.** *(Akk.)* **~**: sprinkle sth. on sth.; **den Tieren Stroh ~**: put down straw for the animals

Auf·strich der a) *(Brot~)* spread; **b)** *(Schriftw.)* upstroke; **c)** *(Musik)* up-bow

auf|stülpen *tr. V.* **a)** *(stülpen auf)* **etw. auf**

etw. *(Akk.)* ~: plonk sth. on sth.; **b)** *(hochschlagen)* turn *or* roll up ‹*sleeves, trousers*›; turn up ‹*collar*›; **die Lippen** ~ *(fig.)* purse one's lips; *(verführerisch)* pout

auf|stützen 1. *tr. V.* **a)** *(auf etw. stützen)* **die Ellbogen/Arme auf etw.** *(Akk. od. Dat.)* **~:** rest one's elbows/arms on sth.; **mit aufgestütztem Kopf** with one's head resting on one's hands; **b)** *(aufrichten)* **jmdn./sich [im Bett] ~:** prop sb./oneself up [in bed]. **2.** *refl. V.* support oneself

auf|suchen *tr. V.* **a)** *(hingehen zu)* call on, go and see ‹*friends, relatives*›; visit ‹*museum, grave, monument*›; **den Arzt ~:** go to the doctor; go and see the doctor; **die Toilette ~:** go to the toilet *or* lavatory; **b)** *(in einem Buch usw.)* look up

auf|summen, auf|summieren 1. *tr. V.* *(DV)* sum. **2.** *refl. V.* add *or* mount up

auf|takeln ['aufta:kl̩n] *refl. V.* *(ugs. abwertend)* tart *(Brit.)* *or* doll oneself up *(coll.)*; **aufgetakelt** tarted *(Brit.)* or dolled up *(coll.)*

Auf·takt der a) prelude; *(Beginn)* start; **den ~ zu etw. bilden** form the prelude to sth./be the start of sth.; **b)** *(Musik)* upbeat; anacrusis; **c)** *(Verslehre)* anacrusis

auf|tanken 1. *tr. V.* fill up; refuel ‹*aircraft*›; **2 000 Liter ~** ‹*aircraft*› take on 2,000 litres; **neue Kräfte ~** *(fig.)* recharge one's batteries *(fig.)*. **2.** *itr. V.* fill up; ‹*aircraft*› refuel

auf|tauchen *itr. V.; mit sein* **a)** *(aus dem Wasser)* surface; ‹*frogman, diver*› surface, come up; **b)** *(sichtbar werden)* appear; *(aus dem Dunkel, dem Nebel)* emerge; appear; **c)** *(erscheinen, gefunden werden)* turn up; *(fig.)* ‹*problem, question, difficulties*› crop up, arise

auf|tauen 1. *tr. V.* thaw ‹*ice, frozen food*›; thaw [out] ‹*earth, ground*›; defrost ‹*windscreen*›; ‹*sun*› thaw the ice on ‹*windscreen*›. **2.** *itr. V.; mit sein (auch fig.)* thaw; ‹*earth, ground*› thaw [out]; **der See ist wieder aufgetaut** the ice on the lake has melted

auf|teilen *tr. V.* **a)** *(verteilen)* share out (**unter** + *Akk. od. Dat.* among); **b)** *(aufgliedern)* divide [up] (**in** + *Akk.* into)

Auf·teilung die *s.* **aufteilen a, b:** sharing out (**unter** + *Akk. od. Dat.* among); dividing [up] (**in** + *Akk.* into)

auf|tischen 1. *tr. V.* **a)** *(servieren)* serve [up]; **jmdm. etw. ~:** serve sb. with sth.; **b)** *(ugs. abwertend: erzählen)* serve up ‹*excuses, lies, etc.*›; **jmdm. etw. ~:** serve sb. up with sth. **2.** *itr. V.* **jmdm. reichlich ~:** serve sb. up a substantial meal

Auftrag der; ~[e]s, Aufträge a) *(Anweisung)* instructions *pl.*; *(Aufgabe)* task; job; **in jmds. ~** *(Dat.)* on sb.'s instructions; **Luigi, ich habe einen ~ für dich** I've got a job for you, Luigi; **im ~ des/der ...** *(für jmdn.)* on behalf of the ...; *(auf jmds. Anweisung)* on the instructions of the ...; **jmdm. den ~ geben** *od.* **erteilen, etw. zu tun** instruct sb. to do sth.; give sb. the job of doing sth.; **einen ~ ausführen** carry out an instruction *or* order; **den ~ haben, etw. zu tun** have been instructed to do sth.; **b)** *(Bestellung)* order; *(bei Künstlern, Architekten usw.)* commission; **ein ~ über** *od.* **auf etw.** *(Akk.)* an order/a commission for sth.; **etw. in ~ geben** *(Kaufmannsspr.)* order/commission sth. (**bei** from); **c)** *(Mission)* task; mission; **d)** *(das Auftragen [von Farbe])* application

auf|tragen 1. *unr. tr. V.* **a) jmdm. ~, etw. zu tun** instruct sb. to do sth.; **jmdm. eine Besorgung/eine Botschaft ~:** instruct sb. to get sth./to deliver a message; **er hat mir aufgetragen, dich zu grüßen** he asked me to pass on his regards; **b)** *(aufstreichen)* apply, put on ‹*paint, make-up, ointment, etc.*›; **etw. auf etw.** *(Akk. od. Dat.)* **~:** apply sth. to sth.; put sth. on sth.; **c)** *(verschleißen)* wear out ‹*clothes*›; **d)** *(geh.: servieren)* serve [up]. **2.** *unr. itr. V.* **a)** ‹*clothes*› be too bulky; **b)** *(ugs.: übertreiben)* **dick** *od.* **stark ~:** lay it on thick *(sl.)*

Auftrag-: ~geber der client; customer; *(eines Künstlers, Architekten, Schriftstellers usw.)* client; **~nehmer der** contractor

auftrags-, Auftrags-: ~buch das *(Kaufmannsspr.)* order book; **~gemäß 1.** *Adj.; nicht präd.* in accordance with instructions *postpos.*; **2.** *adv.* as instructed; as ordered; as per instructions; **~lage die** *(Kaufmannsspr.)* situation as regards orders; **~rückgang der** *(Kaufmannsspr.)* falling-off of orders; **~werk das** commissioned work

auf|treffen *unr. itr. V.; mit sein* **auf etw.** *(Akk.)* **~:** strike *or* hit sth.; **mit der Stirn auf etw.** *(Akk.)* **~:** hit one's forehead on sth.

auf|treiben 1. *unr. tr. V.* **a)** *(aufwirbeln)* raise ‹*dust*›; blow up ‹*dry leaves, sand*›; **b)** *(aufblähen)* bloat; swell; make ‹*dough*› rise; **c)** *(ugs.: ausfindig machen)* get hold of; **ein Quartier ~:** find somewhere to stay; **d)** *(auf den Markt)* drive ‹*livestock*› to market; *(auf die Almen)* drive ‹*cattle, livestock*› up to [the] high pastures. **2.** *unr. itr. V.; mit sein* ‹*body, corpse, face*› become bloated *or* swollen; ‹*dough*› rise

auf|trennen *tr. V.* unpick; undo; unpick ‹*garment*›

auf|treten 1. *unr. itr. V.; mit sein* **a)** tread; **er kann mit dem verletzten Bein nicht ~:** he can't walk on *or* put his weight on his injured leg; **b)** *(sich benehmen)* behave; **forsch/schüchtern ~:** have a forceful/shy manner; **mit Entschlossenheit ~:** act with firmness; **c)** *(fungieren)* appear; **als Zeuge/Kläger ~:** appear as a witness/a plaintiff; **als Vermittler/Sachverständiger ~:** act as mediator/be called in as an expert; **gegen jmdn./etw. ~:** speak out against sb./sth.; **d)** *(als Künstler, Sänger usw.)* appear; **sie ist seit Jahren nicht mehr aufgetreten** she hasn't given any public performances for years; **zum ersten Mal ~:** make one's first appearance; **e)** *(die Bühne betreten)* enter; **f)** *(auftauchen)* ‹*problem, question, difficulty*› crop up, arise; ‹*difference of opinion*› arise; *(vorkommen)* occur; ‹*pest, symptom, danger*› appear. **2.** *unr. tr. V.* kick open ‹*door, gate*›

Auftreten das; ~s a) *(Benehmen)* manner; **b)** *(das Fungieren)* appearance; **c)** *(das Vorkommen)* occurrence; *(von Schädlingen, Gefahren)* appearance; **seit dem ~ von Aids** since the appearance of AIDS

Auf·trieb der a) *o. Pl. (Physik)* buoyancy; *(in der Luft)* lift; **b)** *o. Pl. (Elan, Aufschwung)* impetus; **das hat ihm ~/neuen ~ gegeben** that has given him a lift/given him new impetus; **neuen ~ erhalten** ‹*industry, economy*› receive a boost; **c)** *(von Vieh zum Markt)* **der ~ an** *od.* **von Ferkeln** *usw.* the number of piglets *etc.* [brought] for sale; **d)** *(auf Almen)* **der ~ des Viehs** the driving of cattle up to [the] high pastures

Auftriebs·kraft die *(Physik)* buoyancy; *(in der Luft)* lift

Auf·tritt der a) *(als Künstler, Sänger usw.)* appearance; **b)** *(Theater: das Auftreten)* entrance; *(Szene)* scene; **er hat erst im 3. Akt seinen ~:** he doesn't make his entrance until the third act; **c)** *(Streit)* row; **jmdm. einen ~ machen** go off the deep end at sb. *(coll.)*

auf|trumpfen *itr. V.* show one's superiority; show how good one is; **„Na siehst du", trumpfte sie auf** there you are, she crowed; **mit seinem Wissen/seinen Leistungen ~:** show off with one's knowledge/achievements

auf|tun 1. *unr. refl. V.* *(geh.: sich öffnen)* open; *(fig.)* ‹*abyss, plain, street, new world, new horizons*› open up; **sich jmdm. ~:** open up before sb. **2.** *unr. tr. V.* **a)** *(ugs.: entdecken)* find; **b)** *(ugs.: servieren)* **jmdm./sich etw. ~:** help sb./oneself to sth.; **c)** *(geh.: öffnen)* open ‹*door, window*›; **den Mund/die Augen ~:** open one's mouth/eyes; **d)** *(landsch.: aufsetzen)* put on ‹*hat, spectacles, etc.*›. **3.** *unr. itr. V.* **jmdm./sich ~:** help sb./oneself (**von** to)

auf|türmen 1. *tr. V.* pile up (**zu** into). **2.** *refl. V.* ‹*mountain range*› tower up; *(fig.)* ‹*work, problems, difficulties*› pile up

auf|wachen *itr. V.; mit sein (auch fig.)* wake up, awaken (**aus** from); **aus der Narkose/Ohnmacht ~:** come round from the anaesthetic/faint

auf|wachsen *unr. itr. V.; mit sein* grow up

auf|wallen *itr. V.; mit sein* boil up; **etw. ~ lassen** bring sth. to the boil; **in jmdm. ~** *(fig. geh.)* ‹*joy, tenderness, hatred, passion, etc.*› surge [up] within sb.

Auf·wallung die; ~, ~en *(geh.)* surge

Auf·wand der; ~[e]s a) expenditure (**an** + *Dat.* of); *(das Aufgewendete)* cost; expense; **mit einem ~ von 1,5 Mio. Mark** at a cost of 1.5 million marks; **ein unnützer ~ an Zeit** a waste of time; **der dazu nötige ~ an Zeit/Kraft** the time/energy needed; **b)** *(Luxus)* extravagance; **~ [mit etw.] treiben** be extravagant [with sth.]

Aufwands·entschädigung die expense allowance

auf|wärmen 1. *tr. V.* heat *or* warm up ‹*food*›; *(fig. ugs.: wieder erwähnen)* rake *or* drag up. **2.** *refl. V.* **a)** *(sich wärmen)* warm oneself up; **b)** *(Sport)* warm up

Aufwarte·frau die *(bes. md.)* cleaning woman; domestic help

auf|warten *itr. V.* **a)** *(geh.)* **jmdm. mit etw. ~** *(anbieten)* offer sb. sth.; *(vorsetzen)* serve sb. [with] sth.; **b)** *(zu bieten haben)* **mit etw. ~:** come up with sth.; **c)** *(veralt.: bedienen)* **jmdm. ~:** wait *or* attend on sb.; **bei Tisch ~:** wait *or* serve at table

aufwärts *Adv.* upwards; *(bergauf)* upwards; uphill; **den Fluß ~:** upstream; **~!** *(beim Fahrstuhl)* going up!; **vom Major [an] ~:** from major up

-aufwärts *Adv.* **[weiter] rhein~/mosel~:** further up the Rhine/Mosel; **rhein~/mosel~ segeln** sail up the Rhine/Mosel

aufwärts-, Aufwärts-: ~entwicklung die upward trend; **~|führen** *tr. V.* *(fig.)* lead towards prosperity; **~|gehen** *unr. itr. V.; mit sein (unpers.)* **mit seiner Gesundheit/dem Land/Geschäft geht es ~:** his health is improving/the country/firm is doing better; **mit ihm geht es ~** *(gesundheitlich)* he's getting better; *(finanziell, geschäftlich, beruflich, in der Schule)* he's doing better; **~haken der** *(Boxen)* uppercut; **~trend der** upward trend

Auf·wartung die *in* **jmdm. seine ~ machen** *(geh.)* make *or* pay a courtesy call on sb.; pay sb. a courtesy visit

Aufwasch der; ~[e]s *(bes. md.)* *s.* **¹Abwasch**

auf|waschen *unr. tr., itr. V.* *(bes. md.)* wash up; **das ist ein/geht in einem Aufwaschen** *(ugs.)* it can all be done in one go

auf|wecken *tr. V.* wake [up]; waken; *(fig.)* waken; *s. auch* **aufgeweckt**

auf|wehen 1. *tr. V.* **a)** *(hochwehen)* blow up; raise, blow up ‹*dust*›; **b)** *(aufhäufen)* pile up ‹*snow, leaves, etc.*›; **c)** *(öffnen)* blow open. **2.** *itr. V.; mit sein (emporwirbeln)* blow up

auf|weichen 1. *tr. V.* soften; *(fig.)* weaken ‹*system*›; **den Boden ~:** make the ground soft *or* sodden. **2.** *itr. V.; mit sein* become soft; soften up; *(fig.)* weaken

auf|weisen *unr. tr. V.* **a)** *(zeigen)* demonstrate; show; **b)** *(erkennen lassen)* show; exhibit; **der Ort hat viele Sehenswürdigkeiten aufzuweisen** the town has many sights to offer

auf|wenden *unr. (auch regelm.) tr. V.* use ‹*skill, influence*›; expend ‹*energy, resources*›; spend ‹*money, time*›; **viel Geld/**

seine ganze Freizeit für etw. ~: spend a great deal of money/all one's spare time on sth.

auf·wendig 1. *Adj.* lavish; *(kostspielig)* costly; expensive. **2.** *adv.* lavishly; *(kostspielig)* expensively

Auf·wendung die a) *s.* **aufwenden:** using; expenditure; spending; **unter ~ von etw.** by using/expending/spending sth.; **b)** *Pl. (Kosten)* expenditure *sing.*

auf|werfen 1. *unr. tr. V.* **a)** *(aufhäufen)* pile *or* heap up ⟨*earth, snow, etc.*⟩; build, raise ⟨*embankment, dam, etc.*⟩; **b)** *(öffnen)* fling open ⟨*door, window*⟩; **c)** *(ansprechen)* raise ⟨*problem, question*⟩; **d)** *(hochwerfen)* throw up; **den Kopf ~:** toss one's head; **e)** *(schürzen)* **die Lippen ~:** purse one's lips; **aufgeworfene Lippen** pursed lips. **2.** *unr. refl. V. (abwertend: sich aufspielen)* **sich zu etw. ~:** set oneself up as sth.; **sich zum Richter ~:** set oneself up as judge

auf|werten *tr. V.* **a)** *auch itr.* revalue; **b)** *(fig.)* enhance the status of; enhance ⟨*standing, reputation, status*⟩

Auf·wertung die revaluation; **dieses Amt hat durch ihn eine ~ erfahren** he has enhanced the status of this office

auf|wickeln *tr. V.* **a)** wind up; *(ohne Rolle, Spule)* roll *or* coil up; **b)** *(auf Lockenwickler)* **jmdm./sich die Haare ~:** put sb.'s/one's hair in curlers; **sich** *(Dat.)* **die Haare ~ lassen** have one's hair curled; **c)** *(öffnen)* unwrap, undo ⟨*parcel, bundle*⟩

Aufwiegelei die; ~, ~en *(abwertend)* incitement [to revolt]

auf|wiegeln ['aufvi:gl̩n] *tr. V. (abwertend)* incite; stir up (**gegen** against); **jmdn. zum Aufstand/Streik ~:** incite sb. to rebel/strike

Aufwiegelung die; ~, ~en *(abwertend)* incitement; **die ~ der Massen zum Widerstand** inciting the masses to resist

auf|wiegen *unr. tr. V.* make up for; **die Vorteile wiegen die Nachteile auf** the advantages offset the disadvantages; *s. auch* **Gold**

Aufwiegler der; ~s, ~, Aufwieglerin die; ~, ~nen *(abwertend)* agitator

aufwieglerisch *(abwertend)* **1.** *Adj.* seditious; inflammatory, seditious ⟨*speech, pamphlet*⟩. **2.** *adv.* seditiously

Aufwieglung *s.* **Aufwiegelung**

Auf·wind der *(Met.)* anabatic wind; *(Flugw.)* up-current; **wieder ~ bekommen** *(fig.)* get new impetus (**durch** from)

auf|wirbeln 1. *tr. V.* swirl up; swirl up, raise ⟨*dust*⟩; *s. auch* **Staub. 2.** *itr. V.; mit sein* swirl up

auf|wischen *tr. V.* **a)** *(entfernen)* wipe *or* mop up; **b)** *(säubern)* wipe ⟨*floor*⟩; *(mit Wasser)* wash; **die Küche/das Badezimmer ~:** wipe/wash the kitchen/bathroom floor

auf|wogen *itr. V.; mit sein (dichter.)* ⟨*sea*⟩ surge

auf|wühlen *tr. V.* churn up ⟨*water, sea, mud, soil*⟩; *(fig.)* stir ⟨*person, emotions, passions*⟩ deeply; *(auf schmerzhafte Weise)* upset ⟨*person*⟩ deeply; **ein ~des Erlebnis** *(fig.)* a deeply moving experience; **jmdn. bis ins Innerste ~:** move sb. to the depths of his/her soul

auf|zahlen *(südd., österr.)* **1.** *tr. V.* **20 Mark ~:** pay 20 marks on top; pay an extra 20 marks. **2.** *itr. V.* pay extra; make an additional payment

Auf·zahlung die *(südd., österr.)* additional payment

auf|zählen *tr. V.* enumerate; list; enumerate, give ⟨*dates, names, facts*⟩

Auf·zählung die a) *(das Aufzählen)* enumeration; listing; **b)** *(Liste)* list

auf|zäumen *tr. V.* bridle ⟨*horse*⟩; **etw. verkehrt ~** *(fig.)* go about sth. the wrong way; *s. auch* **Pferd a**

auf|zehren *(geh.)* **1.** *tr. V.* exhaust ⟨*food, supplies, savings*⟩; *(fig.)* consume, sap ⟨*energy, strength*⟩. **2.** *refl. V.* wear oneself out; ⟨*energy, supplies, money, etc.*⟩ give out

auf|zeichnen *tr. V.* **a)** *(notieren)* record; **b)** *(zeichnen)* draw

Auf·zeichnung die a) *(das Notieren)* recording; **b)** *(das Aufgezeichnete)* record; *(Film~, Magnetband~)* recording; **~en** *(Notizen)* notes; **c)** *(das Zeichnen)* drawing

auf|zeigen *tr. V. (nachweisen)* demonstrate; show; *(darlegen)* expound; *(hinweisen auf)* point out; highlight

auf|ziehen 1. *unr. tr. V.* **a)** *(öffnen)* pull open ⟨*drawer*⟩; open, draw [back] ⟨*curtains*⟩; undo ⟨*zip*⟩; undo, untie ⟨*bow*⟩; **b)** *(die Feder spannen von)* wind up ⟨*clock, watch, toy, etc.*⟩; **c)** *(spannen, aufkleben)* mount ⟨*photograph, print, etc.*⟩ (**auf** + *Akk.* on); stretch ⟨*canvas*⟩; **Saiten/neue Saiten auf ein Instrument ~:** string/restring an instrument; **neue Saiten ~:** put new strings on; *s. auch* **Saite; d)** *(großziehen)* bring up, raise ⟨*children*⟩; raise, rear ⟨*animals*⟩; raise ⟨*plants, vegetables*⟩; **e)** *(ugs.: gründen)* set up ⟨*company, department, business, political party, organization, system*⟩; **f)** *(ugs.: durchführen)* organize, stage ⟨*festival, event, campaign, rally*⟩; **wir haben das Ganze völlig falsch aufgezogen** we've gone about it completely the wrong way; **g)** *(ugs.: verspotten)* rib *(coll.)*, tease (**mit, wegen** about); **sie hat ihn damit aufgezogen, daß er so große Ohren hat** she ribbed him *(coll.) or* poked fun at him because of his big ears; **h)** *(nach oben ziehen)* pull *or* draw up; haul up ⟨*fishing nets, heavy load*⟩; hoist, run up ⟨*flag*⟩; hoist ⟨*sail*⟩; raise ⟨*barrier, curtain, sluice-gate, signal, drawbridge, etc.*⟩; **i)** *(auftrennen)* undo; unpick; unpick ⟨*garment*⟩; **j)** *(auf eine Spritze)* draw up ⟨*vaccine etc.*⟩; **k)** *(füllen)* fill ⟨*hypodermic syringe*⟩. **2.** *unr. itr. V.; mit sein* **a)** *(näher kommen)* ⟨*storm*⟩ gather, come up; ⟨*clouds*⟩ gather; ⟨*star, mist, haze*⟩ come up; **b)** *(sich aufstellen)* take up position; *(aufmarschieren)* march up

Auf·zucht die raising; rearing

Auf·zug der a) *(Lift)* lift *(Brit.)*; elevator *(Amer.)*; *(Lasten~, Bau~)* hoist; **b)** *(abwertend: Aufmachung)* get-up; **c)** *(Theater: Akt)* act; **d)** *(Aufmarsch)* parade; *(feierlicher Zug)* procession; **der ~ der Garde** the mounting of the guard

Aufzugs·schacht der lift *(Brit.) or (Amer.)* elevator shaft

auf|zwingen 1. *unr. tr. V.* **jmdm. etw. ~:** force sth. [up]on sb.; **jmdm. seinen Willen ~:** impose one's will [up]on sb. **2.** *unr. refl. V.* **sich jmdm. ~:** impose oneself *or* force one's company [up]on sb.; **der Gedanke zwingt sich [einem] ja förmlich auf** the idea positively forces itself upon you

Aug·apfel der eyeball; **er hütet das wie seinen ~:** it's his most treasured possession; **sie ist der ~ ihrer Großmutter** *(fig.)* she is the apple of her grandmother's eye

Auge ['augə] **das; ~s, ~n a)** eye; **gute/schlechte ~n haben** have good/poor eyesight; **er hat so gute ~n, daß ...:** his eyesight is so good that ...; **meine ~n sind schlechter geworden** my eyesight has deteriorated; **auf einem ~ blind sein** be blind in one eye; *(fig.)* have two different sets of standards; **ich konnte ihm nicht in die ~n sehen** *(fig.)* I could not look him in the eye; **etw. mit eigenen ~n gesehen haben** have seen sth. with one's own eyes; **die ~n schließen** *od.* **zumachen** close *or* shut one's eyes; **mit bloßem ~:** with the naked eye; **ihm fallen die ~n zu** his eyelids are drooping; **ganz kleine ~n haben** *(fig.)* be all sleepy; **~n links/rechts/geradeaus!** *(Milit.)* eyes left/right/front!; **mit verbundenen ~n** blindfold[ed]; **jmdn. aus großen ~n unschuldig ansehen** look at sb. all wide-eyed and innocent; **hast du keine ~n im Kopf?** haven't you got eyes in your head?; are you blind?; **etw. im ~ haben** have sth. in one's eye; *(fig.: haben wollen)* have one's eye on sth.; **das ~ des Gesetzes** *(fig.: Polizist)* the law *(coll.)*; **so weit das ~ reicht** as far as the eye can see; **die ~n sind größer als der Magen** *od.* **Bauch** *(fig. ugs.)* your *etc.* eyes are bigger than your *etc.* belly; **ihr/ihm** *usw.* **gingen die ~n auf** *(fig.)* the scales fell from her/his *etc.* eyes; **ihm/ihr** *usw.* **werden die ~n noch aufgehen** *(fig.)* he/she *etc.* is in for a rude awakening; **da wird er ~n machen** *(fig. ugs.)* his eyes will pop out of his head; **ihnen fielen fast die ~n aus dem Kopf** their eyes nearly popped out of their heads; **ein ~ voll Schlaf nehmen** *(fig. ugs.)* have forty winks *or* a short nap; **da blieb kein ~ trocken** *(fig. ugs.)* everyone laughed till they cried *or* till the tears ran down their faces; *(es blieb niemand verschont)* no one was safe; **ich traute meinen [eigenen] ~n nicht** *(ugs.)* I couldn't believe my eyes; **~n wie ein Luchs haben** have eyes like a lynx; **ich habe doch hinten keine ~n** *(ugs.)* I haven't got eyes in the back of my head; **nur ~n für jmdn. haben** *(fig.)* have eyes only for sb.; **ich kann doch meine ~n nicht überall haben!** I can't be looking everywhere at once; **sie hat ihre ~n überall** she doesn't miss a thing; **[große] ~n machen** *(fig. ugs.)* be wide-eyed; **jmdm. [schöne] ~n machen** *(fig. veralt.)* make eyes at sb.; **die ~n offen haben** *od.* **offenhalten [ob, ...]** *(fig.)* keep one's eyes open [and see whether ...]; **die ~n vor etw.** *(Dat.)* **verschließen** *(fig.)* shut *or* close one's eyes to sth.; **sich** *(Dat.)* **nach jmdm./etw. die ~n ausgucken** *od.* **aus dem Kopf sehen** *(fig. ugs.)* look out eagerly *or* expectantly for sb./sth.; **ein ~** *od.* **beide ~n zudrücken** *(fig.)* turn a blind eye; **ein ~ auf jmdn./etw. geworfen haben** *(fig.)* have taken a liking to sb./have one's eye on sth.; **ein ~ auf jmdn./etw. haben** *(achtgeben)* keep an eye on sb./sth.; *(Gefallen finden)* have taken a fancy to sb./have one's eye on sth.; **ein ~/ein sicheres ~ für etw. haben** have an eye/a sure eye for sth.; **kein ~ von jmdm. lassen** *(fig.)* not take one's eyes off sb.; **ich habe ja schließlich ~n im Kopf** *(ugs.)* I'm not blind, you know; **jmdm. die ~n öffnen** *(fig.)* open sb.'s eyes; **sich** *(Dat.)* **die ~n ausweinen** *od.* **aus dem Kopf weinen** *(fig.)* cry one's eyes out; **jmdn./etw. nicht aus den ~n lassen** not take one's eyes off sb./sth.; not let sb./sth. out of one's sight; **jmdn./etw. aus dem ~** *od.* **den ~n verlieren** lose sight of sb./sth.; *(fig.)* lose contact *or* touch with sb./lose touch with sth.; **ich kann vor Arbeit/Müdigkeit nicht mehr aus den ~n gucken** *(ugs.)* I've got so much work I don't know whether I'm coming or going/I'm so tired I can't see straight; **aus den ~n, aus dem Sinn!** *(Spr.)* out of sight, out of mind; **geh mir aus den ~n!** get out of my sight!; **ein solches Ereignis muß auch etwas fürs ~ sein** such an event must also have visual appeal; **das ist mehr fürs ~:** it's only [there] for decoration; **jmdm./einander ~ in ~ gegenüberstehen** face sb./one another; **Aug' in Aug'** *(veralt.)* face to face; **jmdn./etw. im ~ behalten** *(fig.)* keep an eye on sb./bear *or* keep sth. in mind; **in jmds. ~n** *(Dat.) (fig.)* to sb.'s mind; in sb.'s opinion; **jmdm. ins ~** *od.* **in die ~n fallen** *od.* **springen** *(fig.)* hit sb. in the eye; **etw. ins ~ fassen** *(fig.)* consider sth.; think about sth.; **ins ~ fassen, etw. zu tun** *(fig.)* have it in mind to do sth.; contemplate doing sth.; **einer Sache** *(Dat.)* **ins ~ sehen** *(fig.)* face sth.; **der Wahrheit/Gefahr ins ~ sehen** *(fig.)* face up to the truth/danger; **ins ~ gehen** *(fig. ugs.) (schlimm ausgehen)* end in disaster; *(erfolglos ausgehen)* end in failure; **mit einem lachenden und einem weinenden ~** *(fig.)* with mixed feelings; **mit offenen ~n schlafen** *(ugs.)* be day-dreaming; **mit offenen ~n durch die Welt gehen** *(fig.)* walk about with one's eyes open; **jmdn./etw. mit anderen** *od.* **neuen ~n betrachten** *od.* **ansehen** *(fig.)* see sb./sth. in a different *or* new light; **~ um ~, Zahn um Zahn** an eye for an eye, a tooth for a tooth; **unter vier ~n** *(fig.)* in private; **unter jmds. ~n** *(Dat.)* right in front of sb.; right under sb.'s nose; **komm mir nicht mehr unter die ~n!** never let me set eyes on you again!; **jmdm. jeden Wunsch von den ~n ablesen** *(fig.)* anticipate sb.'s every wish; **vor aller ~n** in front of everybody; **jmdm. etw. vor ~n führen** *od.* **halten** *od.* **stellen** *(fig.)* bring sth. home to sb.; **wenn man sich** *(Dat.)* **das mal vor ~n führt** *(fig.)* when you stop and think about it; **jmdn./etw. vor ~n haben** *(fig.)* see sb./sth. in one's mind's eye; *s. auch* **auskratzen 1 a; beleidigen; blau; [1]Null b; schließen 1 a; schwarz 1 a; schweben a; zutun; b)** *(auf Würfeln, Spielkarten, Dominosteinen)* pip; **drei ~n werfen** throw a three; **wie viele ~n hat er geworfen?** how many has he thrown?; **c)** *(Keim)* eye; bud; *(bei Kartoffeln)* eye; **d)** *s.* **Fettauge**

äugeln ['ɔyg!n] **1.** *itr. V. (hinsehen)* **nach jmdm./etw. ~:** cast secret glances at sb./sth. **2.** *tr. V. (Gartenbau)* bud

äugen ['ɔygn̩] *itr. V.* peer

Augen-: ~abstand der *(Med.)* interocular distance; **~arzt der** eye specialist; **~aufschlag der** [upward] glance; **mit unschuldigem ~aufschlag** with wide-eyed innocence; **~binde die** blindfold; *(Verband)* eye bandage

Augen·blick [*auch:* --'-] **der** moment; **alle ~e** *(ugs.)* all the time; *s. auch* **[1]Moment**

augenblicklich [*auch:* --'--] **1.** *Adj.; nicht präd.* **a)** *(unverzüglich)* immediate; **b)** *(gegenwärtig)* present; *(vorübergehend)* temporary; *(einen Augenblick dauernd)* momentary. **2.** *adv.* **a)** *(sofort)* immediately; at once; **b)** *(zur Zeit)* at the moment

augen·blicks *Adv.* immediately; at once

Augenblicks-: ~erfolg der short-lived success; **~sache die** matter of a moment

augen-, Augen-: ~braue die eyebrow; **~brauen·stift der** eyebrow pencil; **~deckel der** *(ugs.)* eyelid; **~fällig 1.** *Adj.* striking; *(offensichtlich)* obvious; **2.** *adv.* strikingly; *(offensichtlich)* obviously; **~farbe die** colour of one's eyes; **~fehler der** eye defect; **~fleck der** *(Biol.)* eye-spot; ocellus; **~glas das;** *Pl.* **~gläser** *(österr., sonst Amtsspr.) (Monokel)* monocle; *(Zwicker)* pince-nez; **~gläser** *(Brille)* spectacles; **~heil·kunde die** ophthalmology; **~höhe die** eye-level; **in/auf ~höhe** at/to eye-level; **~höhle die** eye socket; **~klappe die** eye-patch; **~klinik die** eye hospital; **~krankheit die** eye-disease; disease of the eye; **~lid das** eyelid; **~Make-up das** eye make-up; **~maß das;** *o. Pl.* **ein gutes/schlechtes ~maß haben** have a good eye/no eye for distances; **jegliches ~maß verlieren** *(fig.)* lose all sense of proportion; **~mensch der** *(ugs.)* visual type *or* person; **~merk das: sein ~merk auf jmdn./etw. richten** *od.* **lenken** give one's attention to sb./sth.; **~optiker der** ophthalmic optician; **~paar das** *(geh.)* pair of eyes; **~ränder** *Pl.* rims of one's/the eyes; **sie hatte gerötete ~ränder** the rims of her eyes were red; **~ringe** *Pl.* rings under the eyes; **~schatten** *Pl.* shadows under the eyes

Augen·schein der; *o. Pl. (geh.)* **a)** *(Eindruck)* appearance; **dem ~ nach** by all appearances; **dem ersten ~ nach** at first sight; **allem ~ zum Trotz** despite all appearances; **b)** *(Betrachtung)* inspection; **jmdn./etw. in ~ nehmen** have a close look at sb./sth.; give sb./sth. a close inspection

augen·scheinlich *(geh.)* **1.** *Adj. (scheinbar)* apparent; evident; *(sichtbar)* obvious; evident. **2.** *adv. (scheinbar)* apparently; evidently; *(sichtbar)* obviously; evidently

augen-, Augen-: ~schmaus der *(scherzh.)* feast for the eyes; **~spiegel der** *(Med.)* ophthalmoscope; **~spiegelung die** *(Med.)* ophthalmoscopy; **~stern der a)** *(dichter.: Pupille)* pupil; **b)** *(veralt.: Liebstes)* apple of one's eye; **~trost der** *(Bot.)* eyebright; **~weide die;** *o. Pl.* feast for the eyes; **~wimper die** eyelash; **~winkel der** corner of one's eye; **~wischerei die** eyewash; **~zahn der** eye-tooth; **~zeuge der** eyewitness; **~zeuge sein** be an eyewitness; **~zeugen·bericht der** eyewitness report; **~zwinkern das; ~s: mit einem ~zwinkern** with a wink; **durch ~zwinkern** by winking; **~zwinkernd 1.** *Adj.; nicht präd.* tacit ⟨*agreement*⟩; **2.** *adv.* with a wink

Augias·stall [au'gi:as-] **der;** *o. Pl. (geh.)* Augean stables; **den ~ ausmisten** *od.* **reinigen** create order out of chaos

-äugig [-ɔygɪç] *Adj.* -eyed; **ein~/blau~/groß~/hell~:** one-eyed/blue-eyed/big-eyed/bright-eyed

Augur ['aʊgʊr] **der; ~s** *od.* **~en** [-'gu:rən], **~en** *(geh., spött.)* pundit

Auguren·lächeln das *(geh.)* knowing smile

[1]August [aʊ'gʊst] **der; ~[e]s** *od.* **~, ~e** August; *s. auch* **April**

[2]August ['aʊgʊst] *in* **dummer ~:** clown

augusteisch [aʊgʊs'te:ɪʃ] *Adj. in* **~es Zeitalter** *(geh.)* Augustan age

Augustiner [aʊgʊs'ti:nɐ] **der; ~s, ~:** Augustinian monk

Augustinus [aʊgʊs'ti:nʊs] **(der)** St Augustine

Auktion [aʊk'tsio:n] **die; ~, ~en** auction

Auktionator [aʊktsio'na:tɔr] **der; ~s, ~en** [-na'to:rən] auctioneer

Aula ['aʊla] **die; ~, Aulen** *od.* **~s** *(einer Universität)* [great] hall; *(einer Schule)* [assembly] hall

Au-pair-Mädchen [o'pɛ:r-] **das** au pair [girl]

Aura ['aʊra] **die; ~, Auren** *(geh.)* aura

Aureole [aʊre'o:lə] **die; ~, ~n a)** *(Heiligenschein)* aureole; halo; **b)** *(Met.)* aureole

aus [aʊs] **1.** *Präp. mit Dat.* **a)** *(räumlich: aus dem Inneren von)* out of; **~ dem Bett steigen** get out of bed; **~ der Flasche trinken** drink out of the bottle *or* from the bottle; **b)** *(Herkunft, Quelle, Ausgangspunkt angebend, auch zeitlich)* from; **~ Spanien/Griechenland** *usw.* from Spain/Greece *etc.*; **er kommt** *od.* **stammt ~** *od.* **ist gebürtig ~ Hamburg** he comes from Hamburg; **~ der Ferne** from a distance; *(von weitem)* from far away; **jmdm. etw. ~ dem Urlaub mitbringen** bring sth. back from holiday *or (Amer.)* one's vacation for sb.; **~ guter Familie stammen** come from a good family; **~ dem Deutschen ins Englische** from German into English; **etw. ~ dem Zusammenhang reißen** take sth. out of [its] context; **c)** *(Veränderung eines Zustandes angebend)* **~ der Mode/Übung sein** be out of fashion/training; **~ dem Gleichgewicht** out of balance; **~ tiefem Schlaf erwachen** awake from a deep sleep; **d)** *(Grund, Ursache angebend)* out of; **etw. ~ Erfahrung wissen** know sth. from experience; **~ folgendem Grund** for the following reason; **~ Versehen** inadvertently; by mistake; **~ einer Laune heraus** on impulse; **~ Furcht vor** for fear of; **~ Spaß/Jux** *(ugs.)* for fun/a laugh; **ein Verbrechen ~ Leidenschaft** a crime of passion; **~ sich heraus** on one's own initiative; of one's own accord; **e)** *(hergestellt ~)* made of; **eine Bank ~ Holz/Stein** a bench made of wood/stone; a wooden/stone bench; **etw. ~ Fertigteilen bauen** build sth. out of prefabricated components; **eine Figur ~ Holz schnitzen** carve a figure in wood; **~ etw. bestehen** consist of sth.; **f)** *(Entwicklung angebend)* **~ ihm ist ein guter Arzt geworden** he made a good doctor; **~ der Sache wird nichts** nothing will come of it; **~ den Raupen entwickeln sich Schmetterlinge** caterpillars develop into butterflies; **einen Soldaten ~ jmdm. machen** make a soldier out of sb.; **etwas ~ sich machen** make something of oneself; **~ ihm ist nichts geworden** he never made anything of his life; **g)** *(österr.: in)* in; **eine Prüfung ~ Biologie** an examination in biology. **2.** *Adv.* **a)** *(ugs.: vorbei, Schluß)* **~ jetzt!** that's enough; **~, habe ich gesagt** that's enough, I said; **~ und vorbei** over and done with; *s. auch* **aussein, aushaben** *usw.*; **b)** *(als Aufforderung: ausschalten)* **„~"** *(an Lichtschaltern)* 'out'; *(an Geräten)* 'off'; **Licht/Radio ~!** lights *pl.* out!/turn the radio off; **c) vom Flugplatz/Fenster/obersten Stockwerk ~:** from the airport/window/top storey; **von hier/München ~:** from here/Munich; **von seinem Standpunkt ~:** from his point of view; **von mir ~** *(ugs.)* if you like *or* want; **von sich** *(Dat.)* **~:** of one's own accord; *s. auch* **[2]ein**

Aus das; ~ a) der Ball ging ins ~ *(Tennis)* the ball was out; *(Fußball)* the ball went out of play; **den Ball ins ~ schlagen** hit the ball out; **b)** *(Sport: das Ausscheiden)* exit; *(fig.)* end

aus|arbeiten 1. *tr. V.* **a)** *(erstellen)* work out, develop ⟨*guidelines, system, method*⟩; prepare, draw up ⟨*agenda, draft, regulations, contract*⟩; prepare ⟨*leaflet*⟩; **b)** *(vollenden)* work out the details of ⟨*plan, proposal, list, lecture, etc.*⟩; elaborate the details of ⟨*picture, drawing*⟩. **2.** *refl. V. (durch Sport, körperliche Anstrengung)* work out; have a work-out

Ausarbeitung die; ~, ~en a) *s.* **ausarbeiten 1 a:** working out; developing; preparation; drawing up; **b)** *s.* **ausarbeiten 1 b:** working out the details; elaboration of the details

aus|arten *itr. V.; mit sein* **a)** degenerate **(in + Akk., zu** into); **b)** *(sich schlecht benehmen)* become unruly

aus|atmen *itr., tr. V.* breathe out; exhale

aus|backen *regelm. (auch unr.) tr. V. (Kochk.)* **a)** *(in Fett)* fry; **b)** *(fertigbacken)* **etw. ~:** bake sth. until it is done

aus|baden *tr. V. (ugs.)* carry *or* take the can for *(Brit. sl.)*; take the rap for *(sl.)*

aus|baggern *tr. V.* **a)** excavate ⟨*hole, basement, ditch, etc.*⟩; **b)** *(säubern)* dredge ⟨*channel, river bed, etc.*⟩; **c)** *(herausholen)* dredge up ⟨*mud, detritus, etc.*⟩

aus|balancieren 1. *tr. V. (auch fig.)* balance. **2.** *refl. V.* balance; *(fig.)* balance out

aus|baldowern *tr. V. (ugs.)* spy out

Aus·ball der *(Ballspiele)* **auf ~ entscheiden** decide that the ball was out; **bei ~:** when the ball goes out of play

Aus·bau der; ~[e]s a) *(Erweiterung)* extension; *(einer Straße)* improvement; **ein ~ des Hauses** an extension to the house; **der ~ der Beziehungen zwischen zwei Staaten/Organisationen** the building of closer relations between two states/organizations; **b)** *(Ausgestaltung)* conversion **(zu** into); **c)** *(Entfernung)* removal **(aus** from)

aus|bauen *tr. V.* **a)** *(entfernen)* remove **(aus** from); **b)** *(erweitern)* extend; *(fig.)* build up, cultivate ⟨*friendship, relationship*⟩; expand ⟨*theory, knowledge, market*⟩; **eine Fachhochschule zu einer Universität ~:** expand *or* enlarge a college into a university; **eine Straße ~:** improve a road; **seinen Vorsprung weiter ~** *(fig.)* extend one's lead; **seine Position ~** *(fig.)* consolidate *or* strengthen one's position; **ein Gebäude zu einem** *od.* **als Theater ~:** convert a building into a theatre *or* for use as a theatre

ausbau·fähig *Adj.* ⟨*building etc.*⟩ suitable for extension; ⟨*market*⟩ that can be expanded; ⟨*position, job*⟩ with [good] prospects; **er hat ~e Englischkenntnisse** he has a good grounding in English

aus|bedingen *unr. refl. V.* **sich** *(Dat.)* **etw. ~:** *(etw. verlangen)* insist on sth.; *(etw. zur Bedingung machen)* make sth. a condition;

sich *(Dat.)* das Recht/die Freiheit ~, etw. zu tun reserve the right/freedom to do sth.
aus|beißen *unr. refl. V.* **sich** *(Dat.)* **einen Zahn** ~: break a tooth (**an** + *Dat.* on); **sich** *(Dat.)* **an einem Problem die Zähne** ~ *(fig.)* sweat over a problem
aus|bekommen *unr. tr. V. (ugs.)* get off
aus|bessern *tr. V.* **a)** *(reparieren)* repair; fix *(Amer.)*; mend ‹*clothes*›; touch up ‹*paintwork*›; **b)** *(beseitigen)* mend; **einen Schaden an etw.** *(Dat.)* ~: repair damage to sth.
Aus·besserung die repair
ausbesserungs-, Ausbesserungs-: **~arbeiten** *Pl.* repairs; repair work *sing.*; **~bedürftig** *Adj.* in need of repair *postpos.*; **~werk das** *(Eisenb.)* repair shed
aus|beulen 1. *tr. V.* **a)** remove a/the dent/the dents in; *(mit einem Hammer)* beat out; **b)** *(dehnen)* make baggy; **ausgebeulte Knie** baggy knees. **2.** *refl. V.* ‹*trousers*› go baggy; ‹*pocket*› bulge
Aus·beute die yield; *(einer Untersuchung)* results *pl.*; *(eines Einkaufsbummels)* spoils *pl.*; **unsere ganze ~ betrug drei Pilze** we ended up with only three mushrooms between us
aus|beuteln *tr. V. (bes. österr.)* shake out
aus|beuten *tr. V. (auch abwertend)* exploit
Ausbeuter der; ~s, ~, Ausbeuterin die; ~, ~nen *(abwertend)* exploiter
ausbeuterisch *(abwertend)* **1.** *Adj.* exploitative. **2.** *adv.* exploitatively
Ausbeuter·klasse die; ~ *(abwertend)* exploiting class
Ausbeutung die; ~, ~en exploitation
aus|bezahlen *tr. V.* **a)** *(auszahlen)* pay [out]; **er bekommt 2 000 DM ausbezahlt** his take-home pay is 2,000 marks; **b)** *(entlohnen)* pay; *(und entlassen)* pay off; **c)** *(abfinden)* buy out ‹*shareholder, joint heir, etc.*›
Aus·bezahlung die *s.* **ausbezahlen:** payment; paying; paying off; buying out
aus|bilden 1. *tr. V.* **a)** *(schulen, unterrichten)* train; **sich in etw.** *(Dat.)* **~ lassen** take a training in sth.; *(studieren)* study sth.; **sich als** *od.* **zu etw. ~ lassen** train to be sth.; *(studieren)* study to be sth.; **sich im Gesang/Zeichnen ~ lassen** take singing lessons/study drawing; **jmdn. an einem Instrument/einer Maschine ~:** teach sb. to play an instrument/train sb. on a machine *or* to use a machine; **b)** *(fördern)* cultivate, develop ‹*talent, skill, feeling, etc.*›; **c)** *(entwickeln)* develop; *(gestalten)* design; *(formen)* shape; form. **2.** *refl. V.* **a)** *(sich schulen)* **sich in etw.** *(Dat.)* ~: take a training in sth.; *(studieren)* study sth.; **b)** *(sich entwickeln)* develop
Ausbilder der; ~s, ~, Ausbilderin die; ~, ~nen instructor
Ausbildner der; ~s, ~ *(österr.)* instructor
Aus·bildung die a) *(Schulung)* training; **sich noch in der ~ befinden** still be training; *(an einer Lehranstalt)* still be at college; **b)** *(Entwicklung)* development
Ausbildungs-: ~bei·hilfe die [education] grant; *(für Berufsschüler, Lehrlinge)* training grant; **~beruf der** trade requiring an apprenticeship; **~förderung die** provision of [education] grants; *(für Berufsschüler, Lehrlinge)* provision of training grants; **~gang der** training syllabus; **~platz der** trainee post; *(für Lehrlinge)* apprenticeship; **~stätte die** place of training; **~vertrag der** articles of apprenticeship
aus|bitten *unr. refl. V.* **a)** *(geh.: erbitten)* **sich** *(Dat.)* **von jmdm. etw. ~:** request sth. from sb.; ask sb. for sth.; **b)** *(verlangen)* **sich** *(Dat.)* **etw. ~:** demand sth.; **ich bitte mir Ruhe/mehr Sorgfalt aus** I must insist on silence/that you take more care
aus|blasen *unr. tr. V.* **a)** *(löschen, ausatmen)* blow out; **b)** *(leer blasen)* blow ‹*egg*›
aus|blassen *itr. V.; mit sein (geh.)* fade
aus|bleiben *unr. itr. V.; mit sein* **a)** *(nicht eintreten)* ‹*effect, disaster, success, reward*› fail to materialize; ‹*symptom*› be absent, not appear; **es konnte nicht ~, daß ...:** it was inevitable that ...; **das Ausbleiben einer Nachricht** the abscence *or* lack of any news; **beim Ausbleiben der Regelblutung** if a period is missed; **b)** *(fernbleiben)* ‹*guests, visitors, customers*› stay away, fail to appear; ‹*order, commission, help, offer, support, rain*› fail to arrive; **wenn jahrelang der Regen ausbleibt** if the rains fail year after year; **sein Ausbleiben** his abscence; **c)** *(nicht heimkommen)* stay out; **d)** *(ugs.: ausgeschaltet bleiben)* stay off; **e)** *(stocken)* ‹*pulse, breathing*› stop
aus|bleichen 1. *unr. itr. V.; mit sein* fade; **ausgebleichte Gebeine/Haare** bleached bones/hair. **2.** *tr. V.* bleach; ‹*light, sun*› fade ‹*material, curtains, etc.*›
aus|blenden 1. *tr. V. (Rundf., Ferns., Film)* fade out; *(fig.: nicht berücksichtigen)* take no account of, leave out of account ‹*facts, information*›. **2.** *refl. V. (Rundf., Ferns.)* **sich [aus einer Übertragung] ~:** fade oneself out of a transmission
Aus·blendung die *(Film, Rundf., Ferns.)* fade-out; **nach unserer ~ aus der Übertragung** after we leave this transmission
Aus·blick der a) view (**auf** + *Akk.* of); **jmdm. den ~ versperren** block *or* obstruct sb.'s view; **ein Zimmer mit ~ aufs Meer/auf die Berge** a room overlooking the sea/with a view of the mountains; **b)** *(Vorausschau)* **jmdm. einen ~ auf etw.** *(Akk.)* **geben** give sb. a preview of sth.; **einen optimistischen ~ in die Zukunft gestatten** permit an optimistic view of the prospects for the future
aus|blicken *itr. V. (geh.)* **nach jmdm./etw. ~:** look out for sb./sth.
aus|bluten *itr. V.; mit sein* bleed to death; *(fig.)* bleed dry; **~ lassen** bleed ‹*animal*›
aus|bohren *tr. V.* **a)** *(bohren)* bore; *(mit Bohrgerät)* drill; *(erweitern)* drill out; **b)** *(entfernen)* bore out; *(mit Bohrgerät)* drill out
aus|bomben *tr. V.* bomb out; *s. auch* **Ausgebombte**
aus|booten *tr. V.* **a)** *(ugs.: verdrängen)* get rid of (**aus** from); **b)** *(Seew.: an Land bringen)* disembark ‹*passengers*› by boat
aus|borgen *tr. V. (ugs.)* **a)** *(sich ausleihen)* [**sich** *(Dat.)*] **etw. ~:** borrow sth. (**von, bei** from); **b)** *(überlassen)* **jmdm. etw. ~:** lend sb. sth.; lend sth. to sb.
aus|braten 1. *unr. itr. V.; mit sein* ‹*fat*› run out (**aus** of). **2.** *unr. tr. V. (auslassen)* fry the fat out of ‹*bacon*›
aus|brechen 1. *unr. itr. V.; mit sein* **a)** *(entkommen, auch Milit.)* break out (**aus** of); *(fig.)* break free (**aus** from); **b)** *(austreten)* **jmdm. bricht der [kalte] Schweiß aus** sb. breaks into a [cold] sweat; **c)** ‹*volcano*› erupt; **d)** *(beginnen)* break out; ‹*crisis*› break; ‹*misery, despair*› set in; *s. auch* **Wohlstand; e) in Gelächter/Weinen ~:** burst out laughing/crying; **in Beifall/Tränen ~:** burst into applause/tears; **in den Ruf ~ „...“** break into the cry, '...'; **in Schweiß ~:** break out into a sweat; **in Zorn/Wut ~:** explode with anger/rage; **f)** *(sich lösen)* ‹*hook, dowel, etc.*› come out; **ihm waren zwei Zähne ausgebrochen** he had broken two teeth; **g)** *(Richtung ändern)* ‹*car, horse*› swerve. **2.** *unr. tr. V.* **a)** take *or* knock down ‹*wall*›; **Steine aus einer Wand ~:** knock stones out of a wall; **sich** *(Dat.)* **einen Zahn ~:** break a tooth; **eine Tür/ein Fenster [in einer Mauer] ~:** put a doorway/window [in a wall]; **b)** *(erbrechen)* bring up; vomit [up]
Aus·brecher der *(ugs.)* escaped prisoner *or* convict; *(gewohnheitsmäßiger)* jail-breaker
aus|breiten 1. *tr. V.* **a)** *(entfalten)* spread [out] ‹*map, cloth, sheet, etc.*›; open out ‹*fan, newspaper*›; *(nebeneinanderlegen)* spread out; **ein Tuch über etw.** *(Akk. od. Dat.)* **~:** spread *or* put a cloth over sth.; **seine Wünsche/Pläne/Ansichten/sein Leben vor jmdm. ~** *(fig.)* unfold one's desires/plans/views/life story to sb.; **b)** *(ausstrecken)* **die Arme/Flügel ~:** spread one's arms/its wings; **die Arme nach jmdm. ~:** stretch out one's arms to sb. **2.** *refl. V.* **a)** *(sich verbreiten)* spread; **b)** *(ugs.: sich breitmachen)* spread oneself out; **c)** *(sich erstrecken)* extend; stretch [out]; **d)** *(abwertend: erörtern)* **sich über etw.** *(Akk.)* **~:** go on [at great length] about sth.
aus|brennen 1. *unr. itr. V.; mit sein* **a)** *(zu Ende brennen)* burn out; **ausgebrannte Kernbrennstäbe** *(fig.)* spent nuclear fuel rods; **b)** *(zerstört werden)* ‹*building, room*› be gutted, be burnt out; ‹*ship, aircraft, vehicle*› be burnt out; **ausgebrannt sein** be burnt out; **c)** *(ugs.: seine Habe verlieren)* be burnt out. **2.** *unr. tr. V.* **a)** *(reinigen)* cauterize ‹*wound*›; **b)** *(entfernen)* burn out; burn off ‹*weeds*›; *s. auch* **ausgebrannt 2**
aus|bringen *unr. tr. V.* **a)** *(sprechen)* propose; **einen Trinkspruch** *od.* **Toast auf jmdn./etw. ~:** propose a toast to sb./sth.; **b)** *(Seemannsspr.)* lower ‹*boat, anchor*›; lay, lower ‹*net*›; lay *or* run out ‹*mooring-line*›
Aus·bruch der a) *(Flucht)* escape; *(lit. or fig.)*, break-out *(also Mil.)* (**aus** from); **an ~ denken** think of escape; **b)** *(Beginn)* outbreak; **vor/nach ~ des Krieges** before/after the outbreak of war; **zum ~ kommen** break out; ‹*crisis, storm*› break; **c)** *(Gefühls~)* outburst; *(stärker)* explosion; *(von Wut, Zorn)* eruption; explosion; **zum ~ kommen** explode; erupt; **d)** *(eines Vulkans)* eruption
Ausbruchs·versuch der attempted break-out *or* escape; *(fig.)* attempt to break free; *(Milit.)* attempted break-out
aus|brüten *tr. V.* **a)** hatch out; *(im Brutkasten)* incubate; **b)** *(ugs.: sich ausdenken)* hatch [up] ‹*plot, scheme*›; **c) etwas/einen Infekt ~** *(ugs.: krank werden)* be going down with something/an infection
aus|buchen *tr. V. (Kaufmannsspr., Bankw.)* **etw. ~** *(streichen)* delete sth. from the accounts; *(abschreiben)* write sth. off; *s. auch* **ausgebucht 2**
aus|buchten *tr. V.* bulge; widen ‹*road*› *(to form a parking area, passing point, etc.)*
Ausbuchtung die; ~, ~en bulge
aus|buddeln *tr. V. (ugs., auch fig.)* dig up
aus|bügeln *tr. V.* **a)** *(ugs.: bereinigen)* iron out ‹*differences, problem, misunderstanding, defect*›; make good ‹*loss, mistake*›; **b)** iron ‹*shirt, dress, etc.*›; press ‹*seam, suit, trousers*›; iron out ‹*crease, fold*›
aus|buhen *tr. V. (ugs.)* boo
Aus·bund der *(oft iron.)* **ein ~ an** *od.* **von Tugend** a paragon *or* model of virtue; **ein ~ an** *od.* **von Bosheit/Frechheit** malice/impudence itself *or* personified
aus|bürgern *tr. V.* **jmdn. ~:** deprive sb. of citizenship
Ausbürgerung die; ~, ~en deprivation of citizenship
aus|bürsten *tr. V.* brush out ‹*dust, dirt*› (**aus** of); brush ‹*clothes, upholstery, etc.*›
aus|büxen ['ausbʏksn̩] *itr. V.; mit sein (ugs.)* skedaddle *(coll.)*; scarper *(Brit. sl.)*; **jmdm. ~:** run away from sb.; **vor jmdm./etw. ~:** run away from sb./sth.
Aus·dauer die staying power; stamina; *(Beharrlichkeit)* perseverance; *(Hartnäckigkeit)* persistence; **[beim Lernen, Lesen] ~/keine ~ haben** have/lack perseverance [when it comes to learning, reading]
aus·dauernd 1. *Adj.* **a)** ‹*runner, swimmer, etc.*› with stamina *or* staying power; *(beharrlich)* persevering; tenacious; *(hartnäckig)* persistent; unflagging ‹*diligence, enthusiasm, efforts*›; enduring ‹*love, sympathy*›; **b)** *(Bot.)* perennial. **2.** *adv.* perseveringly; tenaciously; *(hartnäckig)* persistently

Aus·dauer·training das stamina training

aus·dehnbar *Adj.* ⟨*company, market*⟩ capable of expansion; ⟨*norm, application, etc.*⟩ capable of extension *or* of being extended (**auf** + *Akk.* to); elastic ⟨*material*⟩

aus|dehnen 1. *tr. V.* **a)** *(räumlich)* stretch ⟨*clothes, piece of elastic*⟩; expand ⟨*rail*⟩; *(fig.)* extend ⟨*power, borders, trading links*⟩; expand, increase ⟨*capacity*⟩; **b)** *(einbeziehen)* **etw. auf etw.** *(Akk.)* **~:** extend sth. to sth.; **c)** *(zeitlich)* prolong; **ein ausgedehntes Frühstück** a leisurely breakfast; **ausgedehnte Ausflüge/Spaziergänge** extended trips/walks. **2.** *refl. V.* **a)** *(räumlich)* ⟨*metal, water, gas, etc.*⟩ expand; ⟨*fog, mist, fire, epidemic*⟩ spread; *(fig.)* ⟨*business, firm, trade*⟩ expand; **b)** *(zeitlich)* go on (**bis** until); **c)** *(sich erstrecken)* extend; **ein ausgedehnter Park** an extensive park; **sich bis zum Meer ~:** extend *or* stretch to the sea

Aus·dehnung die a) *(Zunahme an Volumen, Vergrößerung)* expansion; *(fig.: der Macht, von Beziehungen, Grenzen)* extension; **b)** *(zeitlich)* prolongation; *(von Öffnungszeiten)* extension; **c)** *(Ausmaß, Größe)* extent

ausdehnungs-, Ausdehnungs-: ~fähig *Adj. (bes. Physik)* expansible; capable of expansion *postpos.*; **~fähigkeit die** *(bes. Physik)* expansibility; **~koeffizient der** *(Physik)* coefficient of expansion

aus|denken 1. *unr. refl. V.* **sich** *(Dat.)* **etw. ~:** think of sth.; *(erfinden)* think sth. up; *(sich vorstellen)* imagine sth.; **sich** *(Dat.)* **etw. in allen Einzelheiten ~:** think sth. out in every detail; **da mußt du dir schon etwas anderes ~!** you'll have to come up with *or* think of something better than that! **2.** *unr. tr. V. (zu Ende denken)* **etw. ~:** think sth. out *or* through [completely]; **[das ist] nicht auszudenken** it's impossible to imagine; *(zu schrecklich)* it does not bear thinking about

aus|deuten *tr. V.* interpret; **etw. falsch ~:** misinterpret sth.; **etw. dahin ~, daß ...:** interpret sth. to mean that ...

aus|deutschen *tr. V. (österr.)* **jmdm. etw. ~:** explain sth. to sb. in words of one syllable

Aus·deutung die interpretation

aus|dienen *itr. V. (Milit. veralt.)* **ausgedient haben** have finished *or* completed one's military service; *(fig. ugs.)* have had it *(coll.)*; *s. auch* **ausgedient 2**

aus|diskutieren *tr. V.* **etw. ~:** discuss sth. fully *or* thoroughly

aus|dorren *s.* **ausdörren 2**

aus|dörren 1. *tr. V.* dry up; dry up, parch ⟨*land, soil*⟩; parch ⟨*throat, lips*⟩. **2.** *itr. V.; mit sein* dry up; ⟨*land, soil*⟩ dry up, become parched; ⟨*plant*⟩ wither

aus|drehen *tr. V.* **a)** *(ausschalten)* switch *or* turn off ⟨*radio, light, engine*⟩; turn off ⟨*gas*⟩; **b)** *(Technik)* drill [out] ⟨*hole*⟩

[1]**Aus·druck der; ~[e]s, Ausdrücke a)** *(Wort)* expression; *(Terminus)* term; **du sollst nicht solche Ausdrücke gebrauchen** you mustn't use language like that; **Sie haben sich im ~ vergriffen** your choice of words is most unfortunate; **dumm/ärgerlich** *usw.* **ist gar kein ~:** stupid/angry *etc.* isn't the word for it; **b)** *o. Pl. (Ausdrucksweise, Gesichts~)* expression; **etw. zum ~ bringen** express sth.; give expression to sth.; **einer Sache** *(Dat.)* **~ geben** *od.* **verleihen** *(geh.)* express sth.; **mit dem ~ der Entrüstung/des Dankes** with an expression of indignation/thanks; **in etw.** *(Dat.)* **zum ~ kommen** be expressed *or* find expression in sth.

[2]**Aus·druck der; ~[e]s, ~e** *(Nachrichtenw., DV)* print-out

aus|drucken 1. *tr. V.* **a)** *(Druckerspr.: fertig drucken)* finish printing ⟨*book etc.*⟩; **b)** *(Nachrichtenw., DV)* print out; **c)** *(angeben, aufführen)* **im Katalog [mit 400 DM] ausgedruckt** listed in the catalogue [at 400 marks]; **in Abänderung unseres ausgedruckten Programms** in a change to our advertised programme. **2.** *itr. V. (Druckerspr.)* **gut/schlecht ~:** print well/badly

aus|drücken 1. *tr. V.* **a)** *(auspressen)* squeeze ⟨*juice*⟩ out; squeeze [out] ⟨*lemon, orange, grape, etc.*⟩; squeeze out ⟨*sponge*⟩; squeeze ⟨*boil, pimple*⟩; **den Saft aus einer Zitrone ~:** squeeze *or* press the juice out of *or* from a lemon; **b)** *(auslöschen)* stub out ⟨*cigarette*⟩; pinch out ⟨*candle*⟩; **c)** *(formulieren, widerspiegeln)* express; **anders ausgedrückt** to put it another way; **... und das ist noch milde ausgedrückt** ..., and that's putting it mildly; **jmdm. seinen Dank ~:** express one's thanks to sb.; **etw. in** *od.* **mit Worten ~:** express sth. in *or* put sth. into words; **seine Miene drückte Zufriedenheit aus** his expression was one of contentment. **2.** *refl. V.* **a)** *(sich äußern)* express oneself; **um mich gelinde/höflich auszudrücken** to put it mildly/politely; **b)** *(offenbar werden)* be expressed

ausdrücklich [*od.* -'--] **1.** *Adj.; nicht präd.* express *attrib.* ⟨*command, wish, etc.*⟩; explicit ⟨*reservation*⟩; **gegen jmds. ~es Verbot** although sb. has/had expressly forbidden it. **2.** *adv.* expressly; ⟨*mention*⟩ explicitly; **etw. ~ betonen** give sth. particular emphasis

ausdrucks-, Ausdrucks-: ~fähigkeit die expressiveness; *(sprachliche Gewandtheit)* articulateness; **~kraft die;** *o. Pl.* expressive power; expressiveness; **~los 1.** *Adj.* **a)** expressionless; **b)** *(ohne Ausdruckskraft)* unexpressive ⟨*style, delivery, etc.*⟩; **2.** *adv.* **a)** expressionlessly; **b)** *(ohne Ausdruckskraft)* unexpressively; **~losigkeit die;** *o. Pl.* **a)** expressionlessness; **b)** *(Fehlen von Ausdruckskraft)* lack of expressiveness; **~mittel das** means of expression; **~schwach 1.** *Adj.* unexpressive; **~schwach sein** be lacking in expression; **2.** *adv.* unexpressively; **~stark 1.** *Adj.* expressive; forceful ⟨*language*⟩; bold ⟨*pattern, colour*⟩; **2.** *adv.* expressively; **~tanz der;** *o. Pl.* expressive dance; **~voll 1.** *Adj.* expressive; **2.** *adv.* expressively; **~weise die** way of expressing oneself

aus|dünnen *tr. V.* thin out

aus|dünsten 1. *tr. V. (ausströmen)* give off; ⟨*factory*⟩ emit ⟨*fumes etc.*⟩. **2.** *itr. V. (Feuchtigkeit abgeben)* transpire

Aus·dünstung die a) *(das Ausdünsten)* transpiration; **b)** *(Dampf)* vapour; *(Geruch)* odour

aus·einander *Adv.* **a)** *(voneinander getrennt)* apart; **etw. ~ schreiben** write sth. as separate words; **zwei Schüler ~ setzen** seat two pupils apart; **weit ~ stehen** be far apart; ⟨*teeth*⟩ be widely spaced; ⟨*eyes, legs*⟩ be wide apart; **sie sind [im Alter] ein Jahr ~:** they are a year apart in age; **~!** get away from each other!; break it up!; **~ sein** *(ugs.) (sich getrennt haben)* have separated; have split up; *(aufgelöst sein)* ⟨*engagement*⟩ have been broken off; be off; ⟨*marriage, relationship, friendship*⟩ have broken up; **b)** *(eines aus dem anderen)* **Behauptungen/Formeln** *usw.* **~ ableiten** deduce propositions/formulae *etc.* one from another

auseinander-, Auseinander-: ~|bekommen *unr. tr. V.* **etw./zwei Sachen ~bekommen [können]** be able to get sth./two things apart; **~|biegen** *unr. tr. V.* **Drähte/Zweige** *usw.* **~biegen** bend wires/twigs *etc.* apart; **~|brechen 1.** *unr. itr. V.; mit sein (auch fig.)* break up; **2.** *unr. tr. V.* **etw. ~brechen** break sth. up; **~|breiten** *tr. V.* **etw. ~breiten** spread sth. out; **~|bringen** *unr. tr. V. (ugs.)* **a)** *(voneinander lösen)* separate ⟨*objects, combatants*⟩; **b)** *(entzweien)* split up ⟨*family*⟩; **das hat die beiden auseinandergebracht** this led to the two of them parting company; **nichts kann sie ~bringen** nothing can part them; **~|dividieren** *tr. V.* split up; **zwei Verbündete ~zudividieren suchen** seek to drive a wedge between two allies; **~|entwickeln** *refl. V.* develop away from each other *or* one another; ⟨*friends, partners, etc.*⟩ grow apart [from each other *or* one another]; **~|fallen** *unr. itr. V.; mit sein* fall apart; **~|falten** *tr. V.* unfold; open ⟨*newspaper*⟩; **~|gehen** *unr. itr. V.; mit sein* **a)** *(sich trennen, sich teilen)* part; ⟨*crowd*⟩ disperse; **b)** *(nicht übereinstimmen)* ⟨*opinions, views*⟩ differ, diverge; **c)** *(sich verzweigen)* ⟨*streets, traffic lanes*⟩ diverge; **d)** *(ugs.: sich wieder lösen)* ⟨*relationship, marriage*⟩ break up; **e)** *(ugs.: dick werden)* get round and podgy; *s. auch* **Hefekloß; f)** *(ugs.: entzweigehen)* come apart; **~|halten** *unr. tr. V.* **zwei Dinge ~halten** distinguish between two things; **zwei Namen ~halten** keep two names apart; **zwei Sprachen/Menschen ~halten** tell two languages/people apart; **~|jagen** *tr. V.* scatter; **~|klaffen** *itr. V.* **a)** ⟨*hole, wound*⟩ gape; **b)** *(fig.: nicht übereinstimmen)* be poles apart; **~|klamüsern** [~klamy:zɐn] *tr. V. (nordd. ugs.)* **a)** *(mühsam ordnen)* unravel; sort out; **b)** *(erklären)* **[jmdm.] etw. ~klamüsern** make sense of sth. [for sb.]; **~|kriegen** *tr. V. (ugs.) s.* **~bekommen; ~|laufen** *unr. itr. V.; mit sein* **a)** *(in verschiedene Richtungen laufen)* run off in different directions; ⟨*crowd*⟩ scatter; **b)** *(in verschiedenen Richtungen verlaufen)* ⟨*paths, roads, etc.*⟩ diverge; **c)** *(verlaufen)* ⟨*ink, paint, etc.*⟩ run; **d)** *(zerlaufen)* ⟨*ice-cream, cheese*⟩ go runny; ⟨*dough*⟩ spread; **~|leben** *refl. V.* grow apart (**mit** from); **~|nehmen** *unr. tr. V.* **a)** *(zerlegen)* **etw. ~nehmen** take sth. apart; dismantle sth.; **b)** *(salopp: besiegen)* **jmdn. ~nehmen** take sb. apart *(coll.)*; **~|pflücken** *tr. V. s.* **zerpflücken; ~|reißen** *unr. tr. V.* **a)** tear up; **eine Familie ~reißen** *(fig.)* tear a family apart; **Freunde/Liebende ~reißen** *(fig.)* part *or* separate friends/lovers; **b)** *(zerfetzen)* **etw. ~reißen** tear *or* rip sth. apart; **~|rücken 1.** *tr. V.* **Sachen ~rücken** move things apart; **2.** *itr. V.; mit sein* move apart; **~|schrauben** *tr. V.* **etw. ~schrauben** unscrew sth. and take it apart; **~|setzen 1.** *tr. V.* **jmdm. etw. ~setzen** explain sth. to sb.; **2.** *refl. V.* **a)** *(sich befassen)* **er hat sich mit diesem Problem/Thema seit Jahren ~gesetzt** he's concerned himself with this problem/subject for years; **ein Mensch, der sich mit den Dingen [ernsthaft] ~setzt** a person who gives things serious thought; **b)** *(etw. Strittiges klären)* **sich mit jmdm. ~setzen** have it out with sb.; argue the/a matter out with sb.; **sich mit seinen Gläubigern ~setzen** battle with one's creditors; **~setzung die; ~, ~en a)** *(eingehende Beschäftigung)* examination (**mit** of); **b)** *(Diskussion)* debate, discussion (**über** + *Akk.* about, on); **c)** *(Streit)* argument; *(zwischen Arbeitgeber und Arbeitnehmer)* dispute; **es kam wegen etw. zu einer ~setzung** an argument/a dispute developed over sth.; **d)** *(Kampfhandlung)* clash; **es kam zu ~setzungen zwischen Polizisten und Demonstranten** there were clashes between police and demonstrators; **e)** *(Rechtsw.)* partition; **~|sprengen 1.** *tr. V.* **a)** *(sprengen)* **etw. ~sprengen** blow sth. up; **b)** *(zerbersten lassen)* **etw. ~sprengen** burst sth. [apart *or* open]; **2.** *itr. V.; mit sein* scatter; **~|stieben** *unr. (auch regelm.) itr. V.; mit sein* scatter; **~|streben** *itr. V.* **a)** *mit sein (sich voneinander wegbewegen)* disperse; ⟨*lines*⟩ diverge; **b)** *(sich trennen wollen)* begin to go their separate ways; **c)** *(divergieren)* ⟨*opinions, trends, forces, etc.*⟩ diverge; **~|treiben 1.** *unr. tr. V.* scatter ⟨*birds, animals*⟩; disperse ⟨*crowd, demonstrators, clouds*⟩; **der Wind trieb die beiden Boote ~:** the wind drove the two boats apart; **2.** *unr. itr. V.; mit sein* ⟨*boats, balloons*⟩ drift apart, *(in alle Richtungen)* drift off in all directions; **~|ziehen**

1. *unr. tr. V.* **a)** *(dehnen)* stretch; extend ⟨*reading-lamp arm, telescope*⟩; **b)** *(trennen)* pull apart; **den Ausziehtisch ~ziehen** pull out the table leaf; **c)** *(aufziehen)* draw *or* pull back ⟨*curtains*⟩; **2.** *unr. refl. V.* spread out; ⟨*column, competitors in race*⟩ string *or* spread out

aus|erkiesen *unr. tr. V. (geh., Präsensformen dicht. veralt.)* choose; **zu etw. auserkoren sein** be chosen for sth.

Aus·erkorene der/die; *adj. Dekl. (scherzh.)* intended *(coll.)*

aus·erlesen 1. *Adj. (geh.)* select ⟨*company, audience*⟩; choice ⟨*fruits, wines, etc.*⟩; exquisite ⟨*taste*⟩; **von ~er Eleganz** of exquisite elegance. **2.** *adv. (überaus)* exquisitely ⟨*beautiful, fine, charming*⟩

aus|ersehen *unr. tr. V. (geh.)* choose

aus|erwählen *tr. V. (geh.)* choose; **zu etw. auserwählt sein** be chosen for sth.; **das auserwählte Volk** *(jüd. Rel.)* the chosen people

Aus·erwählte der/die; *adj. Dekl.* **a)** *(geh.)* chosen one; **die ~n** the chosen; **b)** *(scherzh.) (Freund[in])* beloved *(joc.)*; *(Verlobte[r])* intended *(coll.)*

aus·fahrbar *Adj.* telescopic ⟨*aerial*⟩; retractable, pop-up ⟨*headlights*⟩

aus|fahren 1. *unr. tr. V.* **a) jmdn. ~** *(im Kinderwagen, Rollstuhl)* take sb. out for a walk; *(im Auto o. ä.)* take sb. out for a drive *or* ride; **b)** *(ausliefern)* deliver ⟨*newspapers, parcels, laundry*⟩; **c)** *(Technik: nach außen bringen)* extend ⟨*aerial, crane, landing-flaps, telescope, etc.*⟩; lower ⟨*undercarriage*⟩; raise ⟨*periscope*⟩; **d)** *(abnutzen)* damage; **ausgefahrene Straßen** rutted and damaged roads; *s. auch* **Gleis b; e)** *mit sein* **eine Kurve ~:** take a bend wide; **f)** *(maximal beschleunigen)* drive ⟨*car*⟩ flat out; run ⟨*engine*⟩ at full power; **g)** *(die Kapazität ausnutzen)* **etw. voll/zu 40 % ~:** operate *or* run sth. at full capacity/40 % of capacity; **h)** *(Seemannsspr.: ausbringen)* lay out, run out ⟨*warp, cable*⟩; run out ⟨*anchor*⟩; rig out, set ⟨*boom*⟩. **2.** *unr. itr. V.; mit sein* **a)** *(spazierenfahren)* go out for a drive; **b)** *(hinausfahren)* ⟨*boat, ship*⟩ put to sea; ⟨*train*⟩ leave, pull out; ⟨*car, lorry*⟩ leave; **aus dem Hafen ~:** leave harbour; **der Zug fuhr aus dem Bahnhof aus** the train pulled out of *or* left the station; **c)** *(Bergmannsspr.: aus dem Schacht fahren)* come up; **d)** *(Technik: hervorkommen)* extend; **e)** *(den Körper verlassen)* **[von jmdm.] ~** ⟨*evil spirit etc.*⟩ leave sb.

Aus·fahrt die a) *(Stelle zum Hinausfahren, Autobahn~)* exit (*Gen.* from); **die ~ Bremen-Ost** the Bremen-East exit; the exit for Bremen East; **b)** *(das Hinausfahren)* departure; *(Bergmannsspr.: aus dem Schacht)* ascent; **bei der ~ aus dem Bahnhof sahen wir ...:** as the train pulled out of *or* left the station, we saw ...; **bei der ~ aus dem Hafen tutete das Schiff** as it left [the] habour, the ship hooted; **der Zug hat keine ~:** the train has not been given the signal for departure; **c)** *(Spazierfahrt) (mit dem Auto)* drive; *(mit dem Fahrrad, Motorrad)* ride; **eine ~ machen** go for a drive/ride

Ausfahrt·signal das *(Eisenb.)* starting-signal

Ausfahrts-: ~schild das; *Pl.* **~schilder** exit sign; **~signal das** *(Eisenb.) s.* **Ausfahrtsignal; ~straße die** exit [road]

Aus·fall der a) *(das Nichtstattfinden)* cancellation; **ein hoher ~ an Unterrichtsstunden** a large number of cancelled lessons; **b)** *(Einbuße, Verlust)* loss; *(an Einnahmen, Lohn)* drop (*Gen.* in); **c)** *(Technik) (eines Motors)* failure; *(einer Maschine, eines Autos)* breakdown; *(fig.: eines Organs)* failure; loss of function; **d)** *o. Pl. (das Ausscheiden)* retirement; *(vor einem Rennen)* withdrawal; *(Abwesenheit)* absence; **nach [dem] ~ von vier Läufern** after four runners had retired *or* dropped out; **e)** *(das Herausfallen)* **zum ~ der Haare/Zähne führen** cause hair loss/cause teeth to fall out; **f)** *(Ergebnis)* outcome; result; **g)** *(beleidigende Äußerungen)* attack **(gegen** on); **h)** *(Fechten)* lunge; **im ~:** in the lunge position; **i)** *(Gewichtheben)* split; **in den ~ springen** split the legs; **j)** *(Turnen)* splits *pl.*; **k)** *(Milit.: Ausbruch)* rally; sortie

aus|fallen *unr. itr. V.; mit sein* **a)** *(herausfallen)* fall out; **mir fallen die Haare aus** my hair is falling out; **b)** *(nicht stattfinden)* be cancelled; **etw. ~ lassen** cancel sth.; **der Unterricht/die Schule fällt morgen aus** lessons are cancelled/there is no school tomorrow; **c)** *(ausscheiden)* drop out; *(während eines Rennens)* retire; drop out; *(fehlen)* be absent; **wenn der Pilot ausfällt, muß der Kopilot das Steuer übernehmen** if the pilot becomes unable to fly the plane, the co-pilot must take over the controls; **d)** *(nicht mehr funktionieren)* ⟨*engine, brakes, signal*⟩ fail; ⟨*machine, car*⟩ break down; **der Strom fiel aus** there was a power failure; **e)** *(ein bestimmtes Ergebnis zeigen)* turn out; **gut/schlecht** *usw.* **~:** turn out well/badly *etc.*; **wie ist die Prüfung ausgefallen?** *(für dich)* how did you do in the examination?; *(insgesamt)* what were the examination results like?; **die Niederlage fiel sehr deutlich aus** the defeat turned out to be *or* was most decisive; **f)** *(Milit.: einen Ausfall machen)* make a sortie; **g)** *(Chemie: sich abscheiden)* be precipitated; **h)** *(Sprachw.: wegfallen)* be dropped; *s. auch* **ausgefallen 2**

aus|fällen *tr. V. (Chemie)* precipitate

ausfallend *Adj.* **[gegen jmdn.] ~ sein/werden** be/become abusive [towards sb.]

aus·fällig *Adj. s.* **ausfallend**

Ausfalls·erscheinung die *(Med.)* deficiency symptom

Ausfall·straße die *(Verkehrsw.)* main road [leading] out of the/a town/city

Ausfall[s]·winkel der *(Physik)* angle of reflection

Ausfall·zeit die *(Versicherungsw.)* credited service period

aus|fasern *itr. V.; meist mit sein* fray

aus|fechten *unr. tr. V.* fight out

aus|fegen *tr. (auch itr.) V. (bes. nordd.)* sweep up ⟨*dirt*⟩; sweep out ⟨*room etc.*⟩; *s. auch* **eisern c**

aus|feilen *tr. V.* file down ⟨*key, cogwheel, etc.*⟩; file [out] ⟨*hole*⟩; *(fig.)* polish ⟨*speech, essay, poem, etc.*⟩

aus|fertigen *tr. V. (Amtsspr.)* **a)** *(ausstellen)* draw up ⟨*document, agreement, will, etc.*⟩; issue ⟨*passport, certificate*⟩; make out ⟨*bill, receipt*⟩; **b)** *(unterzeichnen)* sign

Aus·fertigung die *(Amtsspr.)* **a)** *s.* **ausfertigen a:** drawing up; issuing; making out; **b)** *(Exemplar)* copy; **in doppelter/dreifacher ~:** in duplicate/triplicate; **etw. in vier ~en einreichen** submit four copies of sth.

aus·findig *Adv.* **in jmdn./etw. ~ machen** find sb./sth.

aus|flicken *tr. V. (ugs.)* patch up

aus|fliegen 1. *unr. itr. V.; mit sein* **a)** *(hinausfliegen)* fly out; **die ganze Familie ist ausgeflogen** *(ugs. fig.)* the whole family has gone out [for a walk/drive *etc.*]; **b)** *(flügge werden)* leave the nest. **2.** *unr. tr. V.* **jmdn./etw. ~:** fly sb./sth. out; *(per Luftbrücke)* air-lift sb./sth.

aus|fließen *unr. itr. V.; mit sein (herausfließen)* flow *or* run out **(aus** of)

aus|flippen *itr. V.; mit sein (salopp)* **a)** freak out *(sl.)*; **ausgeflippt** *(im Drogenrausch)* freaked *or* spaced out *(sl.)*; **eine ausgeflippte Idee** a freaky idea *(sl.)*; **b)** *(überschnappen)* flip one's lid *or* one's top *(sl.)*

Aus·flucht die; ~, **Ausflüchte** [-flʏçtə] excuse; **Ausflüchte machen** make excuses

Aus·flug der a) outing; *(vom Reisebüro o. ä. organisiert)* excursion; *(Wanderung)* ramble; walk; *(fig.)* excursion; **einen ~ machen** go on an outing/excursion; go for a ramble *or* walk; **b)** *(das Ausschwärmen)* flight [from the nest/hive]; **c)** *(Imkerei: Flugloch)* [hive-]entrance

Ausflügler ['ausfly:klɐ] **der;** ~s, ~, **Ausflüglerin die;** ~, **~nen** tripper *(Brit.)*; day-tripper; excursionist *(Amer.)*

Ausflugs-: ~dampfer der pleasure steamer; *(allgemeiner)* excursion boat; **~lokal das** restaurant/café catering for [day-]trippers; **~ort der** resort for [day-]trippers; **~verkehr der** *(am Wochenende)* weekend holiday traffic; *(an Feiertagen)* holiday traffic; **~ziel das** destination for [day-]trippers; **unser ~ziel war ...:** the destination of our excursion *or* outing was ...

Aus·fluß der a) *o. Pl. (das Ausfließen)* outflow; *(von Gas)* escape; **b)** *(Med.: Absonderung)* discharge; **c)** *(geh.: Auswirkung)* product; **d)** *(Abfluß)* outlet; **e)** *(Technik: ausfließende Menge)* outflow

aus|folgen *tr. V. (österr.)* issue; release ⟨*body*⟩

aus|formen *tr. V.* **a)** *(formen)* shape **(zu** into); **b)** *(endgültig gestalten)* give final shape to ⟨*text, work of art*⟩

aus|formulieren *tr. V.* formulate ⟨*ideas, questions*⟩; flesh out ⟨*paper*⟩ [from notes]

Aus·formung die a) *o. Pl. (das Ausformen)* shaping; **b)** *(Gestalt)* form

aus|forschen *tr. V.* **a)** *(ausfragen)* question **(nach** about); **b)** *(herausfinden)* find out; *(erforschen)* investigate; *(zu Spionagezwecken)* gather information on; **c)** *(österr. Amtsspr.: ausfindig machen)* find

Aus·forschung die a) *(Befragung)* questioning; **b)** *(das Herausfinden)* finding out; *(das Erforschen)* investigation; **zur ~ von militärischen Betrieben** to gather information about military establishments; **c)** *(österr. Amtsspr.: Ermittlung)* finding

aus|fragen *tr. V.* **jmdn. ~:** question sb., ask sb. questions **(nach, über +** *Akk.* about); *(verhören)* interrogate sb. **(nach, über +** *Akk.* about); **so fragt man die Leute aus** that would be telling

aus|fransen 1. *itr. V.; mit sein* fray. **2.** *tr. V.* fringe

aus|fressen *unr. tr. V.* **etw. ausgefressen haben** *(ugs.)* have been up to sth. *(coll.)*

Aus·fuhr die; ~, **~en a)** *o. Pl. (das Exportieren)* export; **b)** *(Export)* exports *pl.*

ausführbar *Adj.* **a)** *(durchführbar)* practicable; workable ⟨*plan*⟩; **b)** *(für die Ausfuhr geeignet)* exportable

aus|führen *tr. V.* **a)** *(ausgehen mit)* **jmdn. ~:** take sb. out; **b)** *(spazierenführen)* take ⟨*person, animal*⟩ for a walk; take *or* lead ⟨*prisoners*⟩ out for their exercise; **c)** *(exportieren)* export; **d)** *(durchführen)* carry out ⟨*work, repairs, plan, threat*⟩; execute, carry out ⟨*command, order, commission*⟩; execute, perform ⟨*movement, dance-step*⟩; put ⟨*idea, suggestion*⟩ into practice; perform ⟨*operation*⟩; perform, carry out ⟨*experiment, analysis*⟩; **die ~de Gewalt** *(Politik)* the executive power; **e)** *(Fußball, Eishockey usw.)* take ⟨*penalty, free kick, corner*⟩; **f)** *(ausarbeiten)* **etw. ~:** work sth. out in detail *or* fully; **etw. näher ~:** work sth. out in more detail; **g)** *(erläutern, darlegen)* explain

Ausfuhr-: ~gut das; *meist Pl.* article for export; **~güter** goods for export; **~hafen der** port of exportation; **~land das;** *Pl.* **~länder** *(Wirtsch.)* **a)** *(Land, das ausführt)* exporting country; **b)** *(Land, in das ausgeführt wird)* export market

ausführlich [*auch:* -'--] **1.** *Adj.* detailed, full ⟨*account, description, report, discussion*⟩; thorough, detailed, full ⟨*investigation, debate*⟩; detailed ⟨*introduction, instruction, letter*⟩; **~ werden** go into detail. **2.** *adv.* in detail; ⟨*investigate*⟩ thoroughly, fully; **etw. ~er/sehr ~ beschreiben** describe sth. in more *or* greater/in great detail

Ausführlichkeit [*auch:* -'---] **die;** ~ *s.* **ausführlich 1:** fullness; thoroughness; exhaustiveness; **mit großer** ~: in great detail; *(umständlich)* at great length

Ausfuhr-: ~prämie die *(Wirtsch.)* export premium; **~sperre die** *(Wirtsch.) s.* **~verbot**

Aus·führung die a) *o. Pl. (das Durchführen) s.* **ausführen d:** carrying out; execution; performing; implementation; playing; giving; **zur ~ gelangen** *od.* **kommen** *(Papierdt.)* ‹*plan*› be carried out *or* put into effect; **b)** *(Fußball, Eishockey)* taking; **nach der ~ des Freistoßes** after the free kick has/had been taken; **c)** *(Art der Herstellung) (Version)* version; *(äußere ~)* finish; *(Modell)* model; *(Stil)* style; **in der gleichen ~:** of the same design; **d)** *(Darlegung)* explanation; *(Bemerkung)* remark; observation; **e)** *o. Pl. (Ausarbeitung)* **der Entwurf war fertig, jetzt ging es an die ~ des Romans/der Einzelheiten** the draft was ready, and the next task was to work the novel out in detail/to work out the details

Ausfuhr·verbot das *(Wirtsch.)* export embargo

aus|füllen *tr. V.* **a)** *(füllen)* fill in ‹*trench, excavation, gravel pit*›; *(zustopfen)* fill ‹*hole, joint*›; **b)** *(beanspruchen, einnehmen)* take up ‹*space*›; ‹*person*› fill ‹*chair, doorway, etc.*›; **ihr Leben ist ganz mit Arbeit ausgefüllt** her life is completely taken up by work; **c)** *(die erforderlichen Angaben eintragen in)* fill in ‹*form, crossword puzzle*›; write *or* make out ‹*prescription, cheque*›; **d)** *(verbringen)* fill ‹*pause*›; **seine freie Zeit mit etw. ~:** fill [up] one's free time with sth.; **er füllte die Wartezeit mit Lesen aus** he filled in the time [he had to wait] with reading; **e)** *(in Anspruch nehmen)* take up; **f)** *(bekleiden, versehen)* **seinen Posten gut/nicht ~:** do one's job well/not do one's job; **g)** *(innerlich befriedigen)* **jmdn. ~:** fulfil sb.; give sb. fulfilment; **ihr Beruf füllt sie ganz aus** she finds complete fulfilment in her work; **er lebt ein ausgefülltes Leben** he lives a full life

aus|füttern *tr. V.* line

Aus·gabe die a) *o. Pl. (das Austeilen)* distribution; giving out; *(von Essen)* serving; **die ~ des Essens erfolgt ab ...:** lunch/dinner *etc.* is [served] from ...; **b)** *o. Pl. (das Aushändigen)* issuing; *(von Meldungen, Nachrichten)* release; **nach ~ des Befehls** after the order was/had been issued; **c)** *(Geld~)* item of expenditure; expense; **~n** expenditure *sing.* **(für** on); **seine ~n überstiegen seine Einnahmen** his outgoings exceeded his income; **d)** *(Edition, Auflage)* edition; *(Nummer einer Zeitschrift; Finanzw., Postw.)* issue; **~ erster/letzter Hand** *first/last edition personally supervised by the author;* **die letzte ~ der Tagesschau** *(fig.)* the late news bulletin; **e)** *s.* **Ausgabestelle; f)** *(Ausführung, auch fig.)* version; **g)** *(DV)* output

Ausgabe·kurs der *(Finanzw.)* issue price

Ausgaben-: ~buch das petty-cash book; **~politik die;** *o. Pl.* expenditure policy

Ausgabe·stelle die *(Schalter)* issuing counter; *(Büro)* issuing office

Aus·gang der a) *o. Pl. (Erlaubnis zum Ausgehen)* time off; *(von Soldaten)* leave; **zwei Tage ~ haben** ‹*servant*› have two days off; ‹*soldier*› have a two-day pass; **bis sechs Uhr ~ haben** ‹*servant*› be free till six; ‹*soldier*› have a pass until six; **b)** *(Tür ins Freie)* exit *(Gen.* from); **c)** *(Endpunkt, Grenze)* **am ~ des Dorfes/der Allee/des Waldes** at the end of the village/avenue/on the edge of the forest; **d)** *(Anat.: Öffnung eines Organs)* outlet; **e)** *o. Pl. (Ende)* end; *(eines Romans, Films usw.)* ending; **f)** *o. Pl. (Ergebnis)* outcome; *(eines Wettbewerbs)* result; **ein Unfall mit tödlichem ~:** an accident with fatal consequences; a fatal accident; **g)** *o. Pl. (Ausgangspunkt)* starting-point; **seinen ~ von etw. nehmen** take sth. as one's starting-point; ‹*style, plan, suggestion*› originate with sth.; **h)** *o. Pl. (Bürow.: Postversand)* posting *(Brit.)*; mailing; **i)** *(Bürow.: abgehende Post)* outgoing mail; **j)** *(Spaziergang)* walk; **das war der erste ~ des Rekonvaleszenten** that was the convalescent's first time out

ausgangs 1. *Adv.* **~ von** on the outskirts of. **2.** *Präp. mit Gen.* **a)** *(räumlich)* coming out of; **b)** *(zeitlich)* at the end of; **ein Mann ~ der Fünfziger** a man in his late fifties

Ausgangs-: ~basis die starting-point; **~lage die** initial position *or* situation; **~position die** initial position; starting position; *(bei einem Rennen)* starting position; **~punkt der** starting-point; **~sperre die** *(bes. Milit.) (für Zivilisten)* curfew; *(für Soldaten)* confinement to barracks; **[eine] ~sperre verhängen** impose a curfew/confine the soldiers/regiment *etc.* to barracks; **~sperre haben** be confined to barracks; **~sprache die** *(Sprachw.)* source language; **~stellung die a)** *(Sport)* starting position; **b)** *(Milit.)* initial position; **~zeile die** *(Druckw.)* break-line

aus|geben 1. *unr. tr. V.* **a)** *(austeilen)* distribute; give out; serve ‹*food, drinks*›; **b)** *(aushändigen, erteilen; Finanzw., Postw.: herausgeben)* issue; *(fig.)* put about ‹*story, rumour*›; **c)** *(verbrauchen)* spend ‹*money*› **(für** on); **d)** *(ugs.: spendieren)* **einen ~:** treat everybody; *(eine Runde geben)* stand a round of drinks *(coll.)*; **ich gebe [dir] einen aus** I'll treat you; **e)** *(fälschlich bezeichnen)* **jmdn./etw. als** *od.* **für jmdn./etw. ~:** pretend sb./sth. is sb./sth.; **sich als jmd./etw.** *od.* **für jmdn./etw. ~:** pretend to be sb./sth.; **f)** *(DV)* output. **2.** *unr. refl. V.* **sich [völlig** *od.* **vollständig] ~:** push oneself right to the limit

ausgebeult *2. Part. v.* **ausbeulen**

ausgebombt *2. Part. v.* **ausbomben**

Ausgebombte der/die; *adj. Dekl.* person who has/had been bombed out; **die ~n** those who have/had been bombed out

aus·gebrannt 1. *2. Part. v.* **ausbrennen. 2.** *Adj. (fig.)* burnt out

ausgebucht 1. *2. Part. v.* **ausbuchen. 2.** *Adj. (ausverkauft, belegt, auch fig. ugs.)* booked up

ausgebufft ['ausgəbʊft] *Adj. (salopp) (clever)* canny; *(durchtrieben)* crafty

Aus·geburt die *(geh. abwertend)* **a)** *(übles Erzeugnis)* evil product; **eine ~ der Hölle** the spawn of hell; **b)** *(Inbegriff)* epitome

aus·gedient 1. *2. Part. v.* **ausdienen. 2.** *Adj. (ugs.: unbrauchbar)* worn out, *(Brit. sl.)* clapped out, *(Amer. sl.)* beat up ‹*vehicle, engine, etc.*›

ausgedörrt *2. Part. v.* **ausdörren**

aus·gefallen 1. *2. Part. v.* **ausfallen. 2.** *Adj.* unusual

Ausgeflippte der/die; *adj. Dekl. (salopp)* drop-out *(coll.)*

ausgefranst *2. Part. v.* **ausfransen**

ausgefuchst *Adj. (ugs.)* wily; crafty; **~e Spezialisten** experienced specialists

ausgeglichen 1. *2. Part. v.* **ausgleichen. 2.** *Adj.* **a)** *(harmonisch)* balanced, harmonious ‹*structure, façade, etc.*›; well-balanced ‹*person*›; **ein ~es Wesen haben** have an even *or* well-balanced temperament; **b)** *(stabil)* stable; equable ‹*climate*›; **c)** *(Sport)* even

Ausgeglichenheit die; ~ *(einer Struktur, Fassade usw.)* balance; harmony; **die ~ ihres Wesens/ihre ~:** the eveness of her temperament

aus·gegoren *Adj.* **[voll] ~:** fully fermented; *(fig.)* fully worked out ‹*plan, idea*›

Ausgeh·anzug der best suit; *(Milit.)* walking-out uniform *(Brit.)*

aus|gehen 1. *unr. itr. V.; mit sein* **a)** *(irgendwohin gehen)* go out; **er geht selten aus** he doesn't go out much; **b)** *(fast aufgebraucht sein; auch fig.)* run out; **jmdm. geht etw. aus** sb. is running out of sth.; **ihr ging die Geduld/der Gesprächsstoff aus** *(fig.)* she ran out of patience/conversation; **ihm geht der Atem** *od.* **die Luft** *od. (ugs.)* **die Puste aus** *(er gerät außer Atem)* he is getting short *or* out of breath; he is running out of puff *(Brit. coll.)*; *(er verliert seine Kraft, Energie)* he is running out of steam *(fig.)*; *(er ist finanziell am Ende)* he is going broke *(coll.)*; **c)** *(ausfallen)* fall out; **mir gehen die Haare aus** I'm losing my hair; my hair is falling out; **d)** *(aufhören zu brennen)* go out; **e)** *(enden)* end; **unentschieden ~:** end in a draw; **gut/schlecht ~:** turn out well/badly; ‹*story, film*› end happily/unhappily; *s. auch* **leer a; straffrei; f)** *(herrühren)* **von jmdm./etw. ~:** come from sb./sth.; **g) von etw. ~** *(etw. zugrunde legen)* take sth. as one's starting-point; **gehen wir davon aus, daß ...:** let us assume that ...; let us start from the assumption that ...; **du gehst von falschen Voraussetzungen aus** you're starting from false assumptions; **h) auf Abenteuer ~:** look for adventure; **auf Entdeckungen ~:** be bent on making discoveries; **auf Eroberungen ~** *(scherzh.)* set out *or* be aiming to make a few conquests; **i)** *(seinen Ausgang nehmen)* **vom Hauptplatz** *usw.* **~** ‹*road*› lead off from the main square *etc.*; *(strahlenförmig)* radiate from the main square *etc.*; **j)** *(ausgestrahlt werden)* radiate; **von jmdm./etw. geht Ruhe/Sicherheit aus** sb./sth. radiates calm/confidence; **k)** *(abgeschickt werden)* be sent off; **die ~de Post** the outgoing mail; **l)** *(blasser werden)* ‹*colour*› run; ‹*fabric*› fade. **2.** *unr. refl. V. (österr.: ausreichen)* be enough; ‹*equation, calculation*› come out; **es geht sich aus** there's enough; *(zeitlich)* there's enough time

ausgehend *Adj.; nicht präd.* **im ~en Mittelalter** towards the end of the Middle Ages; **das ~e 19. Jahrhundert** the end of *or* closing years of the 19th century

ausgehungert 1. *2. Part. v.* **aushungern. 2.** *Adj.* **a)** *(sehr hungrig)* starving; **nach etw. ~ sein** *(fig.)* be starved of sth.; **b)** *(abgezehrt)* emaciated

Ausgeh-: ~uniform die *(Milit.)* walking-out uniform *(Brit.)*; **~verbot das** curfew; *(Milit.)* confinement to barracks

ausgeklügelt *2. Part. v.* **ausklügeln**

ausgekocht 1. *2. Part. v.* **auskochen. 2.** *Adj. (ugs. abwertend: durchtrieben)* crafty

aus·gelassen 1. *2. Part. v.* **auslassen. 2.** *Adj.* exuberant ‹*mood, person*›; lively ‹*party, celebration*›; *(wild)* boisterous. **3.** *adv.* exuberantly; *(wild)* boisterously; **nebenan wurde ~ gefeiert** there was a lively party going on next door

Aus·gelassenheit die exuberance; *(Wildheit)* boisterousness

Ausgeliefertsein das; ~**s** helplessness

aus·gelitten *Adj.* **in er hat ~** *(geh.)* he has been released from his suffering

aus·gemacht 1. *2. Part. v.* **ausmachen. 2.** *Adj.* **a)** *(beschlossen)* agreed; **es ist [eine] ~e Sache, daß ...:** it is an accepted fact that ...; **b)** *nicht präd. (vollkommen)* complete; complete, utter ‹*nonsense*›; **eine ~e Dummheit** downright stupidity. **3.** *adv. (überaus)* extremely; *(ausgesprochen)* decidedly

aus·genommen 1. *2. Part. v.* **ausnehmen. 2.** *Konj. (außer)* except; apart from; **alle sind anwesend, ~ er** *od.* **er ~:** everyone is present apart from *or* except him; **er kommt bestimmt, ~ es regnet** he's sure to come, unless it rains

ausgepicht ['ausgəpɪçt] *Adj. (ugs.)* crafty; **ein ~er Bursche** a wily customer *(coll.)*

ausgeprägt 1. *2. Part. v.* **ausprägen. 2.** *Adj. (ausgesprochen, stark entwickelt)* distinctive ‹*personality, character*›; marked ‹*inclination, tendency, disinclination*›; pronounced ‹*feature, tendency*›; **einen ~en Sinn für etw. haben** have a highly developed sense of sth.

ausgepumpt 1. *2. Part. v.* **auspumpen.** 2. *Adj. (salopp: erschöpft)* knackered *(Brit. sl.)*; shattered *(Brit. coll.)*; tuckered out *(Amer. coll.)*

ausgerechnet 1. *2. Part. v.* **ausrechnen.** 2. *Adv. (ugs.:* **gerade)** ~ **heute/morgen** today/tomorrow of all days; ~ **hier** here of all places; ~ **Sie** you of all people; ~ **jetzt kommt er/muß er kommen** he would have to come [just] now [of all times]; ~ **ihm muß das passieren** it would have to happen to him of all people; ~ **das** that of all things

aus·geschlafen 1. *2. Part. v.* **ausschlafen.** 2. *Adj. (ugs.: gewitzt)* wide-awake

aus·geschlossen 1. *2. Part. v.* **ausschließen.** 2. *Adj.; nicht attr.* **das ist** ~: that is out of the question; **es ist nicht** ~, **daß ...:** one cannot rule out the possibility that ...; it is not impossible that ...; **jeder Irrtum ist** ~: there can be no possibility of a mistake

aus·geschnitten 1. *2. Part. v.* **ausschneiden.** 2. *Adj.* low-cut ‹*dress, blouse, etc.*›; **ein tief/weit ~es Kleid** a dress with a plunging neckline; a very low-cut dress

ausgesorgt *Adj. (ugs.)* **[finanziell] ~ haben** be comfortably off

ausgespielt 1. *2. Part. v.* **ausspielen.** 2. *Adj. in* ~ **haben** be finished; **bei mir hat er** ~ *(ugs.)* he's had it as far as I'm concerned *(coll.)*

aus·gesprochen 1. *2. Part. v.* **aussprechen.** 2. *Adj.* definite, marked ‹*preference, inclination, resemblance*›; pronounced ‹*dislike*›; marked ‹*contrast*›; **~es Pech/Glück haben** be decidedly unlucky/lucky; **ein ~es Talent für etw.** a definite talent for sth.; **ein ~er Gegner von etw. sein** be a strong opponent of sth. 3. *adv. (besonders)* decidedly; downright ‹*stupid, ridiculous, ugly*›

aus|gestalten *tr. V.* **a)** *(in bestimmter Weise gestalten)* arrange; *(formulieren)* formulate; **b)** *(ausbauen)* develop **(zu** into)

Aus·gestaltung die a) *o. Pl.; s.* **ausgestalten a, b:** arrangement; development; formulation; **b)** *(Form)* form

ausgestellt 1. *2. Part. v.* **ausstellen.** 2. *Adj.* flared ‹*skirts, trousers, etc.*›

aus·gestorben 1. *2. Part. v.* **aussterben.** 2. *Adj.* **[wie]** ~: deserted; **die Stadt ist wie** ~: this is like a ghost town

Ausgestoßene der/die; *adj. Dekl.* outcast

aus·gesucht 1. *2. Part. v.* **aussuchen.** 2. *Adj.* **a)** *(erlesen)* choice; exquisite ‹*jewellery, clothes, furniture*›; select ‹*company*›; **b)** *(besonders groß)* exceptional; extreme; **c)** *(wenig Auswahl bietend)* **diese Sachen sind ziemlich** ~: there aren't many good things left. 3. *adv.* exceptionally; extremely

aus·gewachsen 1. *2. Part. v.* **auswachsen.** 2. *Adj.* **a)** fully-grown; adult ‹*man, woman*›; **b)** *(fig. ugs.) (richtig)* real ‹*storm, gale*›; *(groß)* full-blown ‹*scandal*›; utter, complete ‹*nonsense, fool, idiot*›

aus·gewogen 1. *2. Part. v.* **auswiegen.** 2. *Adj. (ausgeglichen)* balanced; [well-]balanced ‹*personality*›. 3. *adv.* in a balanced way

Aus·gewogenheit die; ~: balance

ausgezeichnet [*od.* '--'--] 1. *2. Part. v.* **auszeichnen.** 2. *Adj.* excellent; outstanding ‹*expert*›. 3. *adv.* excellently; ~ **Tennis spielen können** be an excellent tennis player; **sie paßt ~ zu ihm** she suits him very well indeed

ausgiebig ['ausgi:bɪç] 1. *Adj.* **a)** substantial, large ‹*meal*›; good long ‹*walk, sleep, rest, drive*›; extensive ‹*study*›; abundant ‹*credit*›; **ein ~er Regen** continuous heavy rain; **~en Gebrauch von etw. machen** make full use of sth.; **b)** *(veralt.) s.* **ergiebig.** 2. *adv.* ‹*profit*› handsomely; ‹*read*› extensively; **von etw.** ~ **Gebrauch machen** make full use of sth.; ~ **frühstücken** eat a substantial breakfast; ~ **wandern** walk extensively; **etw.** ~ **betrachten** have a long close look at sth.; **sich ~ strecken** have a good stretch; ~ **gähnen** have a good yawn

aus|gießen *unr. tr. V.* **a)** *(aus einem Gefäß gießen)* pour out **(aus** of); **b)** *(leeren)* empty; **c)** *(geh.: über jmdn./etw. gießen)* pour **(über** + *Akk.* over); **seinen Spott/seine Verachtung/seinen Zorn über jmdn.** ~: pour scorn/contempt on sb./vent one's rage on sb.; **d)** *(Technik: ausfüllen)* fill **(mit** with)

Ausgießung die; ~ *in* **die ~ des Heiligen Geistes** *(christl. Rel.)* the effusion of the Holy Spirit

Ausgleich der; ~[e]s, ~e a) *(von Unregelmäßigkeiten)* evening out; *(von Spannungen)* easing; *(von Differenzen, Gegensätzen)* reconciliation; *(eines Konflikts)* settlement; *(Schadensersatz)* compensation; *(einer Rechnung, Schuld)* settlement; *(eines Kontos)* balancing; **einen ~ der verschiedenen Interessen anstreben** strive to reconcile differing interests; **um ~ bemüht sein** be at pains to promote compromise; **als** *od.* **zum ~ für etw.** to make up *or* compensate for sth.; **im Büro hat er wenig Bewegung, deshalb spielt er Tennis zum** ~: he doesn't get much exercise in the office, so, to compensate, he plays tennis; **eine auf ~ und Zusammenarbeit gerichtete Politik** policies aimed at conciliation and cooperation; **zum ~ Ihrer Rechnung/Ihres Kontos** in settlement of your invoice/to balance your account; **einen ~ in etw.** *(Dat.)* **finden** be made up *or* compensated for by sth.; **b)** *(Gleichgewicht)* balance; **c)** *o. Pl. (Sport)* equalizer; **den ~ erzielen, zum ~ kommen** equalize; score the equalizer

aus|gleichen 1. *unr. tr. V.* even out ‹*irregularities, differences in height*›; ease ‹*tensions*›; reconcile ‹*differences of opinions, contradictions*›; settle ‹*conflict*›; redress ‹*injustice*›; compensate for ‹*damage*›; equalize, balance ‹*forces, values*›; make up for, compensate for ‹*misfortune, lack*›; *(Kaufmannsspr.)* settle ‹*bill, debt*›; discharge ‹*obligation*›; make up ‹*loss*›; *(Bankw.)* balance ‹*account, budget*›; **etw. durch etw.** ~: compensate for sth. by sth.; make up for sth. with sth.; **~de Gerechtigkeit** poetic justice; *s. auch* **ausgeglichen 2.** 2. *unr. refl. V.* **a)** *(sich nivellieren)* balance out; *(sich ganz aufheben)* cancel each other out; **das gleicht sich wieder aus** one thing makes up for the other; **b)** *(Kaufmannsspr., Bankw.)* ‹*account, budget*› balance. 3. *unr. itr. V. (Sport)* equalize; **zum 3:3** ~: level the scores at three all

Ausgleichs-: ~amt das *authority which administers system of compensation paid to individuals for damage and losses during and immediately after the Second World War;* **~getriebe das** *(Technik)* differential gear; **~sport der** sport for fitness; **~tor das, ~treffer der** *(Ballspiele)* equalizer; **~zahlung die** compensation payment

aus|gleiten *unr. itr. V.; mit sein (geh.) s.* **ausrutschen**

aus|gliedern *tr. V.* hive off; *(fig.: ausklammern)* exclude

aus|glühen *tr. V.* **a)** *(Med.)* sterilize by heating; **b)** *(Technik)* anneal

aus|graben *unr. tr. V.* dig up; dig [out] ‹*trench, hole*›; dig out ‹*trapped person, avalanche victim, etc.*›; dig up, excavate ‹*archaeological object*›; excavate ‹*temple, settlement, etc.*›; dig, lift ‹*potatoes*›; *(aus dem Grab)* disinter, exhume ‹*body, corpse*›; *(fig. ugs.)* dig up; dig up, unearth ‹*old manuscripts, maps, etc.*›; **eine alte Geschichte wieder** ~ *(fig.)* dig *or* rake up an old story; *s. auch* **Kriegsbeil**

Aus·grabung die *(Archäol.)* **a)** *(das Ausgraben)* excavation; **b)** *(Fund)* find

Ausgrabungs-: ~arbeit die; *meist Pl.* excavation work *no pl.;* **~stätte die** excavation site

aus|greifen *unr. itr. V.* step out; **~d** extended ‹*gallop*›; striding ‹*movement*›; long ‹*stride*›; **weit ~d** widely spreading ‹*branches*›; *(fig.)* wide-ranging ‹*speech*›; large-scale ‹*plans, objectives*›

aus|grenzen *tr. V.* mark off **(aus** from); mark out ‹*area*›; *(ausklammern, isolieren)* exclude **(aus** from)

Ausgrenzung die; ~: marking off; *(einer Fläche)* marking out; *(Ausklammerung, Isolierung)* exclusion

aus|gründen *tr. V. (Wirtsch.)* hive off **(aus** from)

Ausguck der; ~[e]s, ~e a) *(ugs., auch Seemannsspr.)* look-out post; ~ **halten** keep a look-out **(nach** for); **b)** *(Seemannsspr.: Matrose)* look-out

aus|gucken *itr. V. (ugs.)* keep a look-out **(nach** for); *s. auch* **Auge a**

Aus·guß der a) *(Becken)* sink; **b)** *(Abfluß)* wastepipe; **c)** *(landsch.: Tülle)* spout

aus|haben *(ugs.)* 1. *unr. tr. V.* **a)** *(ausgelesen haben)* have finished; **b)** *(ausgezogen haben)* have taken off. 2. *unr. itr. V. (Schule, Unterricht beendet haben)* finish school

aus|hacken *tr. V.* **a)** hoe ‹*weeds*›; lift ‹*potatoes, turnips, etc.*› using a hoe; **b)** *(auspicken)* **jmdm. die Augen** ~: peck out sb.'s eyes; *s. auch* **Krähe; c)** *(österr.: zerlegen)* cut up

aus|haken 1. *tr. V.* unhook. 2. *refl. V.* come unhooked; ‹*zip-fastener*› come undone. 3. *itr. V. (unpers.)* **es hakte bei ihr aus** *(ugs.) (sie begriff es nicht)* she just didn't get it; *(ihre Geduld war zu Ende)* she lost her patience

aus|halten 1. *unr. tr. V.* **a)** *(ertragen)* stand, bear, endure ‹*pain, suffering, hunger, blow, noise, misery, heat, etc.*›; withstand ‹*attack, pressure, load, test, wear and tear*›; stand up to ‹*strain, operation*›; **er konnte es zu Hause nicht mehr** ~: he couldn't stand it at home any more; **er hält es nirgends lange aus** he never stays in one place for long; *(wechselt häufig die Stellung)* he never stays in one job for long; **den Vergleich mit jmdm./etw.** ~: stand comparison with sb./sth.; **es läßt sich** ~: it's bearable; I can put up with it; **hier läßt es sich** ~: I could get to like this place; **er konnte es im Bett nicht** ~: he couldn't stand being in bed; **es ist nicht/nicht mehr zum Aushalten** it is/has become unbearable *or* more than anyone can bear; **es ist nicht mehr zum Aushalten mit dir** you've become unbearable; **das Material muß viel** ~: the material has to take a lot of wear [and tear]; **b)** *(ugs. abwertend: jmds. Unterhalt bezahlen)* keep; **er läßt sich von seiner Freundin** ~: he gets his girl-friend to keep him; **c)** *(Musik: anhalten)* hold. 2. *unr. itr. V. (durchhalten)* hold out

aus|handeln *tr. V.* negotiate

aus|händigen *tr. V.* hand over; issue ‹*passport, document, etc.*›; **jmdm. etw.** ~: hand sth. over to sb./issue sb. with sth.

Aushändigung die; ~: handing over; *(eines Passes, Dokuments usw.)* issue

Aus·hang der notice; **einen ~ machen** put up a notice

Aushänge·bogen der *(Druckw.)* advance sheet

[1]**aus|hängen** *unr. itr. V.* ‹*notice, timetable, etc.*› have been put up; **am Schwarzen Brett** ~: be up on the notice-board *(Brit.) or (Amer.)* bulletin board

[2]**aus|hängen** 1. *tr. V.* **a)** *(öffentlich anschlagen)* put up ‹*notice, timetable, etc.*›; **b)** *(herausheben)* take ‹*door*› off its hinges; take ‹*window*› out; unhitch ‹*coupling*›. 2. *refl. V.* **a)** *(sich lösen)* ‹*chain*› come undone *or* unfastened; ‹*shutter, door, etc.*› come off its hinges; **b)** *(sich glätten)* ‹*crease*› drop out

Aus·hänger der *(Druckw.) s.* **Aushängebogen**

Aushänge·schild das; *Pl.* **~er** [advertising] sign; advertisement *(lit. or fig.)*

aus|harren *itr. V. (geh.)* hold out; **an jmds. Seite** *(Dat.)* **~:** remain at sb.'s side; **auf seinem Posten ~:** remain *or* wait at one's post

aus|härten *tr., itr. V. (Technik)* cure

aus|hauchen *tr. V. (geh.)* give off ‹*smell, fumes*›; exhale, give off ‹*perfume, scent*›; **seinen Geist** *od.* **sein Leben** *od.* **seine Seele ~** *(geh. verhüll.)* breathe one's last *(literary)*

aus|hauen *unr. tr. V.* **a)** *(hineinschlagen)* hew out; **b)** *(ausmeißeln)* carve ‹*statue, inscription, etc.*›; **c)** *(fällen)* thin out ‹*trees*›; **d)** *(roden)* clear ‹*forest, vineyard, etc.*›; **e)** *(auslichten)* prune ‹*trees, bushes, etc.*›

aushäusig ['aushɔyzɪç] *Adj.* out-of-house, *(Amer.)* independent ‹*worker, contractor*›; **[viel] ~ sein** be away from home [a great deal]

aus|heben *unr. tr. V.* **a)** *(ausschaufeln)* dig out ‹*earth, sand, etc.*›; dig ‹*channel, trench, grave*›; **b)** *s.* **²aushängen 1 b; c)** *(aus dem Nest nehmen)* steal ‹*eggs, birds*›; *(leeren)* rob ‹*nest*›; *(fig.: unschädlich machen)* break up ‹*gang, ring, etc.*›; raid ‹*club, casino, hiding-place, outpost*›; pick up, catch ‹*criminal, terrorist*›; **d)** *(österr.)* empty ‹*post-box*›; **e)** *(veralt.: einziehen)* levy, recruit ‹*troops, army*›; **f)** *(Ringen)* **jmdn. ~:** execute a pick-up on sb.

aus|hebern *tr. V. (Med.)* **jmdm. den Magen ~:** pump out sb.'s stomach

aus|hecken *tr. V. (ugs.)* hatch ‹*plan, intrigue*›; plan ‹*attack*›; **immer neue Streiche ~:** keep on thinking up new tricks

aus|heilen 1. *itr. V.; mit sein* ‹*injury, organ*› heal [up]; ‹*patient, illness*› be cured. **2.** *tr. V.* **bis er seine Verletzung ausgeheilt hatte** until his injury had healed

aus|helfen *unr. itr. V.* help out; **jmdm. [mit** *od.* **bei etw.] ~:** help sb. out [with sth.]

aus|heulen *(ugs.) refl. V.* **sich bei jmdm. ~:** cry one's heart out on sb.'s shoulder

Aus·hilfe die a) *o. Pl. (das Aushelfen)* help; **sie arbeitet in der Kantine zur ~:** she helps out in the canteen; **b)** *(Aushilfskraft)* temporary worker; *(in Läden, Gaststätten)* temporary helper *or* assistant; *(Sekretärin)* temporary secretary; temp *(coll.)*; **als ~ arbeiten** help out on a temporary basis

Aushilfs-, aushilfs-: ~arbeit die; *meist Pl.* temporary work *no pl.*; **~arbeiten** *Pl.* temporary work *sing.*; temporary jobs; **~kraft die** temporary worker; *(in Läden, Gaststätten)* temporary helper *or* assistant; *(Sekretärin)* temporary secretary; temp *(coll.)*; **~weise** *adv.* on a temporary basis

aus|höhlen *tr. V.* hollow out; erode ‹*rock, cliff, etc.*›; *(fig.: untergraben)* undermine; **ausgehöhlte Wangen** *(fig.)* hollow cheeks; **einen Begriff ~** *(fig.)* render a concept meaningless

Aushöhlung die; ~, ~en a) *o. Pl. s.* **aushöhlen:** hollowing out; erosion; undermining; **b)** *(ausgehöhlte Stelle)* hollow

aus|holen 1. *itr. V.* **a)** *(zu einer Bewegung ansetzen)* **[mit dem Arm] ~:** draw back one's arm; *(zum Schlag)* raise one's arm; **er holte zum Schlag aus** he raised his fist/sword *etc.* to strike; **er holte zum Wurf aus** he drew back his arm ready to throw; **zum Gegenschlag ~** *(fig.)* prepare to counter-attack; **zu einem Coup ~** *(fig.)* prepare a coup; **b)** *(ausgreifen)* step out; **[weit] ~de Schritte** long strides; **c)** *(weitschweifig sein)* range far afield; *(weit zurückgehen)* go back a long way. **2.** *tr. V. (landsch.: ausfragen)* **jmdn. über etw.** *(Akk.) od.* **nach etw. ~:** question *or* *(coll.)* quiz sb. about sth.

aus|holzen *tr. V.* **a)** *(lichten)* thin out; **b)** *(abholzen)* clear

aus|horchen *tr. V.* **jmdn. über etw.** *(Akk.) od.* **nach etw. ~:** sound sb. out about sth.

Aus·hub der *(Tiefbau)* **a)** *o. Pl.* excavation; **b)** *(ausgehobene Erde)* excavated material

aus|hungern *tr. V.* starve out ‹*city, fortress, garrison, etc.*›; *s. auch* **ausgehungert 2**

aus|husten 1. *tr. V.* cough up. **2.** *itr., auch refl. V. (zu Ende husten)* finish coughing

aus|ixen *tr. V. (ugs.)* x out

aus|jäten *tr. V.* weed ‹*garden, flower-bed*›; weed out ‹*dandelions etc.*›; **Unkraut ~:** weed

aus|kämmen *tr. V.* **a)** *(entfernen)* comb out ‹*dust, dirt*›; **jmdm./sich etw. aus dem Haar ~:** comb sth. out of sb.'s/one's hair; **b)** *(glätten, ordnen)* comb out ‹*hair*›

aus|kegeln *tr. V.* **a) einen Pokal** *usw.* **~:** bowl for a cup *etc.*; **b)** *(südd., österr.: ausrenken)* **sich/jmdm. den Arm ~:** put one's/sb.'s arm out [of joint]

aus|kehren *tr. (auch itr.) V. (bes. südd.) s.* **ausfegen**

aus|keimen *itr. V.; auch mit sein* germinate; ‹*potatoes*› sprout

aus|kennen *unr. refl. V. (in einer Stadt, an einem Ort usw.)* know one's way around *or* about; *(in einem Fach, einer Angelegenheit usw.)* know what's what; **sie kennt sich in dieser Stadt aus** she knows her way around the town; **man kennt sich bei ihm nicht aus** you don't know where you are with him; **sich [gut] mit/in etw.** *(Dat.)* **~:** know [a lot] about sth.; **sich mit den Klassikern/jmds. Jargon ~:** be familiar with the classics/sb.'s jargon; **sich bei den Frauen ~:** know a lot about women

aus|kernen *tr. V.* stone

aus|kippen *tr. V.* **a)** *(entfernen aus)* tip out; **b)** *(leeren)* empty

aus|klammern *tr. V.* **a)** *(Math.)* place outside the brackets; **b)** *(beiseite lassen)* leave aside; *(nicht zulassen)* exclude

aus|klamüsern *tr. V. (ugs.)* figure *or* work out

Aus·klang der a) *(geh.; Abschluß)* end; **zum ~ der Saison/des Festes** to end *or* close the season/festival; **b)** *(Musik: Ende)* final notes/chord/chorus *etc.*; **einen heiteren ~ haben** end brightly

ausklappbar ['ausklapba:ɐ̯] *Adj.* fold-out; **die Couch ist ~:** the couch folds out

aus|klarieren *tr. V. (Zollw., Seew.)* clear

aus|klauben *tr. V. (südd., österr., schweiz.)* pick out

aus|kleiden 1. *tr. V.* **a)** *(geh.: entkleiden)* undress; **b)** *(überziehen mit)* line. **2.** *refl. V. (geh.)* undress; disrobe *(formal)*

Aus·kleidung die lining; *(eines Schwimmbeckens, Gartenteichs)* liner

aus|klingen *unr. itr. V.* **a)** *mit sein (ausgehen)* end; **b)** *mit sein (verklingen)* ‹*song*› finish; ‹*music, final notes*› die away; **c)** ‹*bell*› cease *or* stop ringing

aus|klinken 1. *tr. (auch itr.) V.* release. **2.** *refl. V.* release itself/themselves; *(fig.)* opt out

aus|klopfen *tr. V.* **a)** *(entfernen) (mit einem Stock, Schläger)* beat out (**aus +** *Dat.* of); *(durch Anklopfen)* knock *or* tap out (**aus +** *Dat.* of); **b)** *(säubern)* beat ‹*carpet*›; knock *or* tap ‹*pipe*› out

Aus·klopfer der; ~s, ~: carpet-beater

aus|klügeln *tr. V.* think out; work out; **ein ausgeklügeltes System** a cleverly devised system

aus|kneifen *unr. itr. V.; mit sein (ugs.)* run away (**vor, aus** from)

aus|knipsen *tr. V. (ugs.)* switch *or* turn off

aus|knobeln *tr. V. (ugs.)* **a)** *(durch Knobeln entscheiden)* **sie knobelten aus, wer anfangen sollte** they threw dice to decide who would start; **die nächste Runde Bier ~:** throw dice to decide who will stand the next round of beer; **b)** *(austüfteln)* work out

ausknöpfbar ['ausknœpfba:ɐ̯] *Adj.* removable, detachable ‹*lining*›

aus|kochen *tr. V.* **a)** *(kochen, säubern)* boil; **b)** *(keimfrei machen)* sterilize ‹*instruments etc.*› [in boiling water]; **c)** *(salopp abwertend: sich ausdenken)* concoct; *s. auch* **ausgekocht 2**

aus|kommen *unr. itr. V.; mit sein* **a)** *(ausreichend haben, zurechtkommen)* **mit etw. ~:** manage on *or (coll.)* get by on sth.; **ohne jmdn./etw. ~:** manage without *or (coll.)* get by without sb./sth.; **der Motor kommt mit sechs Litern aus** the engine can run for a hundred kilometres on six litres; **b)** *(sich verstehen)* **mit jmdm. [gut] ~:** get along *or* on [well] with sb.; **mit ihm ist einfach nicht auszukommen** he's just impossible to get on with; **c)** *(südd., österr.: entkommen)* escape (**aus +** *Dat.* from); **d)** *(bes. schweiz.: bekannt werden)* get out

Auskommen das; ~s a) *(Lebensunterhalt)* livelihood; **sein ~ haben** make a living; **b) mit ihm/ihr ist kein ~:** he/she is quite impossible [to get on with]

auskömmlich ['auskœmlɪç] **1.** *Adj.* adequate; **ein ~es Gehalt haben** earn enough to live on. **2.** *adv.* adequately

aus|kosten *tr. V. (geh.)* **a)** *(genießen)* **etw. ~:** enjoy sth. to the full; **b)** *(erleiden)* suffer

aus|kotzen *(derb)* **1.** *tr. V.* puke up *(sl.)*. **2.** *refl. V.* puke *(sl.)*; **sich bei jmdm. ~** *(fig.)* have a bloody good moan to sb. *(Brit. sl.)*

aus|kramen *tr. V. (ugs.)* dig out; *(fig.)* dig up ‹*memories, knowledge, story*›

aus|kratzen 1. *tr. V.* **a)** *(entfernen)* scrape out ‹*dirt, remains, deposit, etc.*› (**aus** from); scratch ‹*words, writing, inscription*› out; *(reinigen)* scrape [out] ‹*bowl, pan, etc.*›; **jmdm. am liebsten die Augen ~ mögen** *(ugs.)* want to scratch sb.'s eyes out; **b)** *(Med.) s.* **ausschaben b. 2.** *itr. V.; mit sein (salopp)* do a bunk *(Brit. sl.)*; beat it *(sl.)*; **vor jmdm. ~:** beat it to avoid sb.

Auskratzung die; ~, ~en *(Med.) s.* **Ausschabung**

aus|kriechen *unr. itr. V.; mit sein* hatch [out]

aus|kriegen *tr. V. (ugs.) s.* **ausbekommen**

aus|kristallisieren 1. *tr. V.* crystallize out. **2.** *itr. V.; mit sein* crystallize out

aus|kugeln *tr. V.* **sich** *(Dat.)* **den Arm/die Schulter** *usw.* **~:** put one's arm/shoulder *etc.* out [of joint]; dislocate one's arm/shoulder *etc.*; **jmdm. den Arm/die Schulter ~:** dislocate sb.'s arm/shoulder *etc.*

aus|kühlen 1. *tr. V.* chill ‹*person, body*› through. **2.** *itr. V.; mit sein* cool down

Aus·kühlung die; *o. Pl.* loss of body heat; exposure

auskultieren [auskʊl'ti:rən] *tr. V. (Med.)* auscultate

aus|kundschaften *tr. V.* find out; trace ‹*arrival, relative*›; find ‹*opportunity*›; track down ‹*refuge, criminal, enemy, etc.*›; sound out ‹*mood, attitude*›; spy out ‹*place*›

Auskunft die; ~, Auskünfte a) *(Information)* piece of information; **Auskünfte** information *sing.*; **[jmdm. über etw.** *(Akk.)***] ~ geben** *od.* **erteilen** give [sb.] information [about sth.]; **sie gab auf alle Fragen ~:** she answered all the questions; **können Sie mir bitte ~ geben, wann ...?** *(geh.)* can you please tell me when ...?; **~/Auskünfte über jmdn./etw. einholen** *od.* **einziehen** obtain information about sb./sth.; *s. auch* **näher b; b)** *o. Pl. (Stelle)* information desk/counter/office/centre *etc.*; *(Fernspr.)* directory enquiries *no art. (Brit.)*; directory information *no art. (Amer.)*; **„~"** 'Information'; 'Enquiries' *(Brit.)*

Auskunftei die; ~, ~en private detective agency; *(Kredit~)* credit reference agency

Auskunfts-: ~beamte der *(Schalterbeamte)* enquiry office clerk *(Brit.)*; information office clerk *(Amer.)*; *(Bahnsteigbeamte)* inspector; **~büro das** information office; enquiry office *(Brit.)*; **~dienst der** *(Fernspr.)* directory enquiries *no art. (Brit.)*; directory information *no art. (Amer.)*; **~pflicht die;** *o. Pl. (Rechtsw.)* obligation to provide information; **~schalter der** information counter; **~stelle die** information office

aus|kuppeln *itr. V.* disengage the clutch; declutch
aus|kurieren *tr. V.* heal ‹*wound*› [completely]; **jmdn.** ~: cure sb. [completely]; **der Spieler, der seit Wochen eine Oberschenkelzerrung auskuriert** the player, who has been recovering from a thigh strain for weeks
aus|lachen *tr. V.* **jmdn.** ~: laugh at sb.; **laß dich nicht** ~: don't be ridiculous
[1]**aus|laden** *unr. tr. V.* unload (**aus** from)
[2]**aus|laden** *unr. tr. V.* **jmdn.** ~: cancel one's invitation to sb.
ausladend *Adj.* prominent ‹*forehead*›; jutting ‹*chin*›; broad ‹*shoulders*›; extensive ‹*roots*›; widely spreading ‹*branches*›; *(fig.)* sweeping ‹*gestures, movements*›
Aus·lage die a) *Pl. (Unkosten)* expenses; **unsere ~n für Strom/Heizung/Wasser** *usw.* our outlay *sing.* on electricity/heating/water *etc.*; **b)** *(ausgestellte Ware)* item *or* article on display; **~n** goods on display; **c)** *(Schaufenster)* shop-window; window display; *(Vitrine)* display cabinet; **d)** *(Boxen)* stance; **in der linken/rechten** ~ **boxen** use the orthodox stance/be a southpaw *(coll.)* *or* left-hander; **e)** *(Fechten)* on-guard position; **f)** *(Rudern)* recovery; **in die** ~ **gehen** recover
Aus·land das; *o. Pl.* foreign countries *pl.*; **im/ins** ~: abroad; **aus dem** ~: from abroad; **aus dem sozialistischen und dem kapitalistischen** ~: from other countries, both socialist and capitalist; **die Literatur/Intervention/Hilfe des ~s** foreign literature/intervention/aid; **die Meinung des ~s** opinion abroad; **das** ~ **hat zurückhaltend reagiert** foreign reaction *or* the reaction of other countries *pl.* was guarded
Ausländer der; ~s, ~: foreigner; alien *(Admin. lang., Law)*; ~ **sein** be a foreigner
ausländer·feindlich *Adj.* hostile to foreigners *postpos.*
Ausländerin die; ~, ~**nen** *s.* **Ausländer;** *s. auch* **-in**
ausländisch *Adj.; nicht präd.* foreign; exotic ‹*plant, animal*›
Auslands-: ~anleihe die *(Bankw.)* foreign loan; **~aufenthalt der** stay abroad; **~beziehungen** *Pl.* foreign relations; **~deutsche der/die** expatriate German; German national living abroad; **~gespräch das** *(Fernspr.)* international call; **~korrespondent der** foreign correspondent; **~reise die** trip abroad; **~schule die** *school run by one country on another's territory*; **~schutz·brief der** *(Versicherungsw.)* international travel cover documents *pl.*; **~tournee die** foreign tour; **~vertretung die a)** *(von Firmen usw.)* foreign agency; **b)** *(diplomatische Vertretung)* foreign mission
aus|langen *itr. V. (landsch.)* **a)** *(ausholen)* **[mit dem Arm]** ~: draw back one's arm; *(zum Schlag)* raise one's hand; **nach jmdm.** ~: raise one's a arm to hit sb.; **b)** *(ausreichen)* be enough
Auslaß der; Auslasses, Auslässe *(Technik)* outlet
aus|lassen 1. *unr. tr. V.* **a)** *(weglassen)* leave out; leave out, omit ‹*detail, passage, word, etc.*›; **b)** *(versäumen)* miss ‹*chance, opportunity, etc.*›; **c)** *(abreagieren)* vent (**an** + *Dat.* on); release ‹*tension*›; **seinen Ärger/Zorn/seine Wut an jmdm.** ~: vent one's anger on sb.; take one's anger out on sb.; **d)** *(ugs.: nicht tragen, nicht einschalten)* **etw.** ~: leave sth. off; **e)** *(zerlassen)* melt ‹*bacon fat*› down; melt ‹*butter*›; **f)** *(länger machen)* let down; *(weiter machen)* let out. **2.** *unr. refl. V. (abwertend: sich äußern)* talk, speak (**über** + *Akk.* about); *(schriftlich)* write (**über** + *Akk.* about); *(sich verbreiten)* hold forth (**über** + *Akk.* about); **sich im Detail/näher** ~: go into detail/more detail; *s. auch* **ausgelassen 2, 3**
Auslassung die; ~, ~**en a)** *(Weglassung)* omission; **b)** *meist Pl. (oft abwertend: Äußerung)* remark
Auslassungs-: ~punkte *Pl.* omission marks; ellipsis *sing.*; **~zeichen das** *(Sprachw.)* apostrophe
aus|lasten *tr. V.* **a)** *(volladen)* fully load; **b)** *(voll ausnutzen)* **etw.** ~: use sth. to full capacity; **seine/ihre** *usw.* **Kapazität** ~ ‹*mine, factory, etc.*› be working to full capacity; **ausgelastet sein** ‹*mine, factory, etc.*› be working to full capacity; **c)** *(voll beanspruchen)* fully occupy; *(befriedigen)* fulfil
aus|latschen *tr. V. (ugs.)* wear ‹*shoes etc.*› out of shape
Auslauf der a) *o. Pl.* **keinen/zuwenig** ~ **haben** have no/too little chance to run around outside; **der Hund braucht viel** ~: the dog needs plenty of exercise; **b)** *(Raum)* space to run around in; *(für Hühner, Enten usw.)* run; *(für Pferde)* paddock; **c)** *(Fechten)* runback; *(Ski)* outrun; run-out; **d)** *(Abfluß)* outlet
aus|laufen 1. *unr. itr. V.; mit sein* **a)** *(herausfließen)* run out (**aus** of); ‹*pus*› drain; **b)** *(leer laufen)* empty; ‹*eye*› drain; ‹*egg*› run out; *(undicht sein)* leak; **c)** *(in See stechen)* sail, set sail (**nach** for); **d)** *(erlöschen)* ‹*contract, agreement, etc.*› run out; **e)** *(nicht fortgesetzt werden)* ‹*model, line*› be dropped *or* discontinued; **etw.** ~ **lassen** drop *or* discontinue sth.; **f)** *(zum Stillstand kommen)* come *or* roll to a stop; **g)** *(auseinanderlaufen)* ‹*colour, ink, etc.*› run; **h)** *(Sport: abbremsen)* slow down; **i)** *(enden)* ‹*path, road, etc.*› end, *(allmählich)* peter out; **j)** *(übergehen)* run (**in** + *Akk.* into); **spitz ~de Türme** towers tapering to a point; **k)** *(einen bestimmten Ausgang nehmen)* end. **2.** *unr. refl. V.* **die Kinder konnten sich mal richtig** ~: the children could run about to their heart's content
Aus·läufer der a) *(Geogr.)* foothill *usu. in pl.*; **b)** *(Met.) (eines Hochs)* ridge; *(eines Tiefs)* trough; **c)** *(Bot.)* runner; **d)** *(schweiz.: Bote)* delivery man/boy
aus|laugen *tr. V.* leach ‹*soil*›; leach [out] ‹*salts etc.*› (**aus** from); *(fig.)* drain, exhaust, wear out ‹*person*›; exhaust ‹*economy*›
Aus·laut der *(Sprachw.)* final sound; auslaut; **im** ~: in final position
aus|lauten *itr. V. (Sprachw.)* **auf „d"** ~: have 'd' in final position; **ein ~der Konsonant** a final consonant
aus|läuten *tr. V.* **a) das alte Jahr** ~: ring out the old year; **b)** *(veralt.: bekanntmachen)* ring out; proclaim
aus|leben 1. *refl. V.* **a)** *(das Leben genießen)* live life to the full; **sich in seiner Arbeit** ~: find complete fulfilment in one's work; **b)** *(sich entfalten)* find *or* be given complete expression. **2.** *tr. V. (geh.: verwirklichen)* give full expression to; realize ‹*talent*›
aus|lecken *tr. (auch itr.) V.* lick out (**aus** of)
aus|leeren *tr. V.* empty [out]; empty ‹*ashtray, dustbin, etc.*›; *(austrinken)* drain
aus|legen *tr. V.* **a)** *(zur Ansicht, Einsicht hinlegen)* lay out; display ‹*goods, exhibits*›; **b)** *(bedecken mit)* **etw. mit Fliesen/Teppichboden** ~: tile/carpet sth.; **einen Schrank [mit Papier]** ~: line a cupboard [with paper]; **c)** *(leihen)* lend; **jmdm. etw.** *od.* **etw. für jmdn.** ~: lend sb. sth.; lend sth. to sb.; **ich habe das Porto für dich ausgelegt** I paid the postage for you; **d)** *(interpretieren)* interpret; **etw. falsch** ~: misinterpret sth.; **etw. als Furcht** ~: take sth. to be fear; **e)** *(für Tiere)* lay ‹*bait*›; put down ‹*poison*›; set ‹*trap, net*›; **f)** *(Technik: verlegen)* lay ‹*mine, cable, fuse, etc.*›; **g)** *(Landw.)* plant; **h)** *(Technik: auf eine bestimmte Leistung hin)* **etw. auf** *od.* **für etw.** ~: design sth. for sth.
Ausleger der; ~s, ~ **a)** *(eines Krans)* jib; boom; **b)** *(Bootsbau)* outrigger
Auslege·ware die carpeting
Auslegung die; ~, ~**en** interpretation
aus|leiern *(ugs.)* **1.** *itr. V.; mit sein* wear out; ‹*clothes*› go baggy; **ausgeleiert** worn out; baggy ‹*pullover, trousers, etc.*›. **2.** *refl. V.* wear out; ‹*pullover, trousers*› go baggy; ‹*elastic band, material*› lose its stretch. **3.** *tr. V.* wear out; make ‹*pullover, trousers, etc.*› go baggy; make ‹*rubber band*› lose its stretch
Ausleihe die; ~, ~**n a)** *o. Pl. (das Ausleihen)* lending; **b)** *(Stelle)* issue desk
aus|leihen *unr. tr. V.* **a)** *(leihen)* borrow; **[sich** *(Dat.)***] etw. von jmdm.** ~: borrow sth. from sb.; **b)** *(verleihen)* lend; **jmdm.** *od.* **an jmdn. etw.** ~: lend sb. sth.; lend sth. to sb.
aus|lernen *itr. V.* finish one's apprenticeship; **ein ausgelernter Schreiner** a trained carpenter; **man lernt nie aus** *(Spr.)* you learn something new every day
Aus·lese die a) *o. Pl. (Auswahl)* selection; **eine** ~ **treffen** make a selection; **b)** *(geh.: Elite)* elite; cream; **c)** *(Wein) fine wine made with selected bunches of fully ripe grapes*
[1]**aus|lesen** *unr. tr. V.* **a)** *(aussondern)* pick out (**aus** from); **b)** *(von Minderwertigem befreien)* sort ‹*peas, lentils, etc.*›
[2]**aus|lesen** *unr. tr. V. (ugs.)* **etw.** ~: finish [reading] sth.; **etw. in einem Zug** ~: read sth. [from beginning to end] at one sitting
Auslese·verfahren das selection process
aus|leuchten *tr. V.* illuminate; *(fig.)* throw light on; *(untersuchen)* probe; **die Bühne** ~: floodlight the stage
aus|lichten *tr. (auch itr.) V.* prune ‹*bush, tree, etc.*›; thin ‹*wood, area, etc.*›
aus|liefern *tr. V.* **a)** *(übergeben)* **jmdm. etw.** *od.* **etw. an jmdn.** ~: hand sth. over to sb.; **jmdn. an ein Land** ~: extradite sb. to a country; **jmdm./einer Sache ausgeliefert sein** *(fig.)* be at the mercy of sb./sth.; **b)** *auch itr. (Kaufmannsspr.: liefern)* deliver
Aus·lieferung die a) *(Übergabe)* handing over; *(an ein Land)* extradition; **jmds.** ~ **fordern** demand that sb. be handed over/extradited; **b)** *(Kaufmannsspr.: Lieferung)* delivery
Auslieferungs-: ~abkommen das *s.* **~vertrag; ~antrag der** application for extradition; **~lager das** *(Wirtsch.)* distribution centre; **~vertrag der** extradition treaty
aus|liegen *unr. itr. V.* **a)** *(zur Ansicht, Einsicht)* be displayed; ‹*newspapers, plans, etc.*› be laid out, be available; **b)** *(zum Fang)* ‹*trap*› be set
Aus·linie die *(Ballspiele)* touchline
aus|loben *tr. V.* **10 000 DM** ~: offer a reward of 10,000 marks; *(bei einem Wettbewerb)* offer a prize of 10,000 marks
aus|löffeln *tr. V.* **a)** *(aufessen)* **etw.** ~: spoon up [all of] sth.; **jetzt muß** *od.* **kann er die Suppe ~[, die er sich eingebrockt hat]** *(fig.)* he's made his [own] bed and now he must lie in it; **b)** *(leer essen)* spoon up everything out of ‹*plate, bowl, etc.*›
aus|löschen *tr. V.* **a)** *(löschen)* extinguish, put out ‹*fire, lamp*›; snuff, put out, extinguish ‹*candle*›; *(geh.)* extinguish ‹*light*›; **b)** *(beseitigen)* rub out, erase ‹*drawing, writing*›; ‹*wind, rain*› obliterate ‹*tracks, writing*›; *(fig.)* obliterate, wipe out ‹*memory*›; extinguish ‹*life*›; wipe out ‹*people, population*›
aus|losen *tr. V.* **etw.** ~: draw lots for sth.; **es wurde ausgelost, wer beginnt** lots were drawn to decide who would start; **den Gewinner** ~: draw lots to decide the winner
aus|lösen 1. *tr. V.* **a)** *(in Gang setzen)* trigger ‹*mechanism, device, etc.*›; set off, trigger ‹*alarm*›; release ‹*camera shutter*›; **b)** *(hervorrufen, herbeiführen)* provoke ‹*discussion, anger, laughter, reaction, outrage, heart attack, sympathy*›; cause ‹*sorrow, horror, surprise, disappointment, panic, war*›; excite, arouse ‹*interest, enthusiasm*›; evoke ‹*memories*›; draw ‹*applause*›; trigger [off] ‹*crisis, chain of events, rebellion, strike*›; **c)** *(veralt.:*

einlösen, freikaufen) redeem; **d)** *(südd., österr.: lösen aus, von)* remove, take out (**aus** from); shell ‹*peas, beans*›. **2.** *refl. V.* ‹*alarm*› go off

Auslöser der; ~s, ~ *(Fot.)* shutter release; *(fig., Psych., Verhaltensf.)* trigger

Aus·losung die draw

Aus·lösung die a) *(Betätigung) (eines Mechanismus)* triggering; *(eines Alarms)* setting off; triggering; **b)** *(Hervorrufung, Herbeiführung) s.* **auslösen b:** provocation; causing; exciting; arousal; evocation; drawing; triggering [off]; **c)** *(veralt.: Einlösung, Freikauf)* redemption

aus|loten *tr. V.* **a)** *(Seew.)* sound the depth of; sound, plumb ‹*depth*›; *(fig.)* sound out ‹*intentions*›; **ein Problem ~** *(fig.)* try to get to the bottom of a problem; **b)** *(Bauw.)* plumb ‹*wall*›

aus|lüften 1. *tr., itr. V.* air. **2.** *refl. V. (ugs. scherzh.)* get some fresh air

aus|lutschen *tr. V. (ugs.)* suck out ‹*juice*›; suck the juice from ‹*orange, lemon, etc.*›

aus|machen *tr. V.* **a)** *(ugs.: ausschalten, auslöschen)* put out ‹*light, fire, cigarette, candle*›; turn *or* switch off ‹*television, radio, hi-fi*›; turn off ‹*gas*›; **b)** *(vereinbaren)* agree; **einen Termin/ein Honorar ~:** agree [on] a deadline/fee; **etw. mit jmdm. ~:** agree sth. with sb.; **c)** *(auszeichnen, kennzeichnen)* make up; constitute; **was einen großen Künstler ausmacht** what goes to make a great artist; **die Farben machen den Reiz seiner Bilder aus** it is the colours which make his pictures attractive; **d)** *(ins Gewicht fallen)* make a difference; **wenig/nichts/viel ~:** make little/no/a great *or* big difference; **e)** *(stören)* **das macht mir nichts aus** I don't mind [that]; **macht es Ihnen etwas aus, wenn ...?** would you mind if ...?; **würde es Ihnen etwas ~, den Platz zu wechseln?** would you mind swapping places?; **f)** *(klären)* settle; **etw. mit sich allein/mit seinem Gewissen ~:** sort sth. out for oneself/with one's conscience; **g)** *(erkennen)* make out; **es läßt sich nicht mit Sicherheit ~, ob ...:** it cannot be determined with certainty whether ...; **h)** *(betragen)* come to; **der Zeitunterschied/die Entfernung macht ... aus** the time difference/distance is ...; *s. auch* **ausgemacht**

aus|malen 1. *tr. V.* **a)** *(mit Farbe ausfüllen)* colour in; **b)** *(mit Malereien ausschmücken)* **das Innere einer Kirche ~:** decorate the interior of a church with murals/frescoes *etc.*; **c)** *(schildern)* describe. **2.** *refl. V.* **sich** *(Dat.)* **etw. ~:** picture sth. to oneself; imagine sth.; **das hatte ich mir so schön ausgemalt** I had pictured it as being so beautiful

aus|manövrieren *tr. V.* outmanœuvre

aus|marschieren *itr. V.; mit sein* march out (**aus** of)

Aus·maß das a) *(Größe, Ausdehnung)* size; dimensions *pl.*; **die ~e des Rumpfs/Kraters** *usw.* the size *sing. or* dimensions of the fuselage/crater *etc.*; **gewaltige ~e haben** be of huge *or* vast dimensions; **b)** *(Umfang, Grad)* extent; **bis zu einem gewissen ~:** to a certain extent; **erschreckende ~e annehmen** assume horrifying dimensions; **eine Katastrophe unvorstellbaren ~es** a disaster on an unimaginable scale

aus|mergeln ['ausmɛrgl̩n] *tr. V.* emaciate; **ausgemergelt** gaunt, emaciated ‹*face, body*›

aus|merzen ['ausmɛrtsn̩] *tr. V.* **a)** *(ausrotten)* eradicate ‹*pests, insects, weeds, etc.*›; **b)** *(beseitigen)* eliminate ‹*errors, slips, etc.*›; eliminate, cut out ‹*offensive passages*›; **c)** *(aussondern)* cull ‹*animal*›

aus|messen *unr. tr. V.* measure up

aus|misten *tr. (auch itr.) V.* **a)** *(von Mist säubern)* muck out; **b)** *(ugs.: von Unbrauchbarem leeren, aussortieren)* clear out

aus|mustern *tr. V.* **a)** *(Milit.: als untauglich erklären)* **jmdn. ~:** reject sb. as unfit [for service]; **b)** *(als unbrauchbar ausscheiden)* take ‹*vehicle, machine*› out of service

Aus·nahme die; ~, ~n exception; **mit ~ von Peter/des Pfarrers** with the exception of Peter/of the priest; **ohne ~:** without exception; **mit** *od.* **bei jmdm. eine ~ machen** make an exception in sb.'s case; **~n bestätigen die Regel, keine Regel ohne ~:** the exception proves the rule

Ausnahme-: ~erscheinung die exceptional phenomenon; **~fall der** exceptional case; **im ~fall** in exceptional cases; **~situation die** exceptional situation; **~zustand der** state of emergency

ausnahms-: ~los 1. *Adj.; nicht präd.* unanimous ‹*approval, agreement*›; **2.** *adv.* without exception; **~weise** *Adv.* by way of *or* as an exception; **Dürfen wir mitkommen? – Ausnahmsweise ja** May we come too? – Yes, just this once; **er hat es mir ~weise erlaubt** he gave me permission by way of an exception; **kann ich heute ~weise früher weg?** can I go earlier today, just as a special exception?; **wenn ich ~weise keinen Schirm bei mir habe** when, just for once, I don't have my umbrella with me

aus|nehmen 1. *unr. tr. V.* **a)** gut ‹*fish, rabbit, chicken*›; **b)** *(ausschließen von)* exclude; *(gesondert behandeln)* make an exception of; **jeder irrt sich einmal, ich nehme mich nicht aus** everyone makes mistakes once in a while, and I'm no exception; *s. auch* **ausgenommen 2; c)** *(die Eier herausnehmen aus)* rob ‹*nest*›; **d)** *(ugs. abwertend: neppen)* **jmdn. ~:** fleece sb. **2.** *unr. refl. V. (geh.: wirken)* look; *(sich anhören)* sound

ausnehmend *(geh.)* **1.** *Adj.; nicht präd.* exceptional. **2.** *adv.* exceptionally

aus|nüchtern *tr., itr., refl. V.* sober up

Ausnüchterung die; ~, ~en sobering up; **jmdn. zur ~ auf die Wache bringen** take sb. to the [police] station to sober up

Ausnüchterungs·zelle die drying-out cell

aus|nutzen, *(bes. südd., österr.)* **aus|nützen** *tr. V.* **a)** *(nutzen)* **etw. [voll] ~:** take [full] advantage of sth.; make [full] use of sth.; **den Raum/seine Zeit für etw. ~:** use the space/one's time for sth.; **b)** *(Vorteil ziehen aus)* take advantage of; *(ausbeuten)* exploit

Aus·nutzung die, *(bes. südd., österr.)* **Ausnützung die; ~:** use; *(Ausbeutung)* exploitation; **unter voller ~ einer Sache** *(Gen.)* making full use of sth.

aus|packen 1. *tr., itr. V.* unpack (**aus** from); unwrap ‹*present*›; *(fig. ugs.: erzählen)* come out with. **2.** *itr. V. (ugs.)* **a)** *(Geheimnisse verraten)* talk *(coll.)*; squeal *(sl.)*; **b)** *(seine Meinung sagen)* sound off

aus|peitschen *tr. V.* whip; *(auf Grund eines Gerichtsurteils)* flog

Auspeitschung die; ~, ~en whipping; *(auf Grund eines Gerichtsurteils)* flogging

aus|pennen *(salopp)* **1.** *itr., refl. V.* have a decent *or* good kip *(Brit. sl.) or* sleep-in. **2.** *tr. V.* **seinen Rausch ~:** sleep it off

aus|pfeifen *unr. tr. V.* **jmdn./etw. ~:** give sb./sth. the bird

aus|pflanzen *tr. V.* plant out

Auspizium [aus'pi:tsiʊm] **das; ~s, Auspizien;** *meist Pl. (geh.)* auspice; **unter jmds. Auspizien** *(Dat.)* under sb.'s auspices

aus|plaudern *tr. V.* let out; blab

aus|plündern *tr. V.* **a)** *(ausrauben)* **jmdn./etw. ~:** rob sb./sth. [of everything]; **b)** *(völlig plündern, auch fig.)* plunder

aus|polstern *tr. V.* pad; pad ‹*jacket, coat, etc.*› [out]; **gut ausgepolstert sein** *(fig. scherzh.)* be well upholstered *(joc.)*

aus|posaunen *tr. V. (ugs. abwertend)* tell the whole world about *(fig.)*

aus|powern [-po:vɐn] *tr. V. (ugs. abwertend)* bleed ‹*organization, country, nation*› dry *or* white; exploit ‹*workers, masses*›; *(fig.)* impoverish ‹*soil, fields, market*›

aus|prägen 1. *refl. V.* **a)** *(offenbar werden)* show itself; ‹*contradiction*› manifest itself; **b)** *(sich herausbilden)* develop; ‹*peculiarity*› become more pronounced; *s. auch* **ausgeprägt 2. 2.** *tr. V. (prägen)* mint (**zu** into)

Aus·prägung die a) *(das Prägen)* minting; **b)** *(charakteristische Form)* form; **c)** *(das Sichherausbilden)* development [in a more pronounced form]; *(der Persönlichkeit)* moulding

aus|pressen *tr. V.* press *or* squeeze out ‹*juice*›; squeeze ‹*orange, lemon*›; *(mit einer Presse)* press the juice from ‹*grapes etc.*›; press out ‹*juice, oil*›; *(fig.: ausbeuten)* squeeze ‹*country, population, etc.*› [dry]; *(fig.: ausfragen)* grill; *(aus Neugier)* pump; *s. auch* **Zitrone**

aus|probieren *tr. V.* try out

Aus·puff der exhaust

Auspuff-: ~gase *Pl.* exhaust fumes *pl.*; **~rohr das** exhaust pipe; **~topf der** silencer *(Brit.)*; muffler *(Amer.)*

aus|pumpen *tr. V.* pump out; *s. auch* **ausgepumpt 2**

aus|punkten *tr. V. (Boxen)* outpoint; beat on points; *(fig.)* outdo

aus|pusten *tr. V. (ugs.)* blow out; blow ‹*egg*›

aus|putzen 1. *tr. V.* **a)** *(auslichten, beschneiden)* prune; **b)** *(bes. südd.: reinigen)* clean out; **c)** *(veralt.: schmücken)* deck out. **2.** *itr. V. (Fußball)* play as sweeper

Aus·putzer der; ~s, ~ *(Fußball)* sweeper

aus|quartieren *tr. V.* move out; billet out ‹*troops*›

aus|quatschen *(salopp)* **1.** *tr. V.* let out; blab; **alles ~:** spill the beans *(coll.)*. **2.** *refl. V.* **sich mit jmdm. ~:** have a really *or (Amer.)* real good chat with sb.; *(sich aussprechen)* have a heart-to-heart with sb. *(coll.)*

aus|quetschen *tr. V.* **a)** squeeze out; squeeze ‹*orange, lemon, etc.*›; **b)** *(ugs.: ausfragen)* grill; *(aus Neugier)* pump; *s. auch* **Zitrone**

aus|radieren *tr. V.* rub out; erase; *(fig.)* annihilate, wipe out ‹*village, city, etc.*›; liquidate ‹*person*›

aus|rangieren *tr. V. (ugs.)* throw out; discard; scrap ‹*vehicle, machine*›; **ausrangierte Fahrzeuge** scrap vehicles

aus|rasieren *tr. V.* shave ‹*neck, leg, etc.*›; shave off ‹*hair*›; **jmdm./sich die Haare im Nacken/den Nacken ~:** shave sb.'s/one's neck

[1]**aus|rasten** *itr. V.; mit sein (Technik)* disengage; **er rastete aus, es rastete bei ihm aus** *(fig. salopp)* something snapped in him

[2]**aus|rasten** *itr., refl. V. (südd., österr.)* have a decent *or* good rest

aus|rauben *tr. V.* rob

aus|räubern *tr. V.* raid; rob; *(scherzh.: plündern)* raid; **jmdn. ~:** rob sb. [of everything]; *(fig.)* clean sb. out

aus|räuchern *tr. V. (auch fig.)* smoke out; fumigate ‹*room*›

aus|raufen *tr. V.* pull *or* tear out; **ich könnte mir die Haare ~** *(fig.)* I could kick myself

aus|räumen 1. *tr. V.* **a)** *(herausnehmen)* clear out (**aus** of); clear *or* move out ‹*furniture*› (**aus** of); **b)** *(leer räumen)* clear out; **c)** *(beseitigen)* clear up; dispel ‹*prejudice, suspicion, misgivings*›; **d)** *(ugs.: ausrauben)* clear out *(coll.)*; **e)** *(Med.)* remove; *(mit der Kürette)* curette. **2.** *itr. V.* clear everything out

aus|rechnen 1. *tr. V.* **a)** *(lösen)* work out; **b)** *(errechnen)* work out; calculate. **2.** *refl. V.* **das kannst du dir leicht ~** *(ugs.)* you can easily work that out [for yourself]; **sich** *(Dat.)* **Vorteile/gute Chancen ~:** reckon that one has advantages/good prospects; *s. auch* **ausgerechnet 2**

Aus·rede die excuse

aus|reden 1. *itr. V. (zu Ende reden)* finish

[speaking]. **2.** *tr. V.* **jmdm. etw. ~:** talk sb. out of sth.; **sie versuchten, ihm das Mädchen auszureden** *(ugs.)* they tried to persuade him to give up the girl. **3.** *refl. V. (südd., österr.) s.* **aussprechen 2 c**

aus|regnen *itr., refl. V. (unpers.)* stop raining

aus|reiben *unr. tr. V.* **a)** *(entfernen aus)* rub out ‹*stain etc.*›; **b)** *(reinigen)* rub ‹*pot, pan, etc.*› clean; wipe out ‹*glasses*›; **sich** *(Dat.)* **die Augen ~:** rub one's eyes; **c)** *(österr.: scheuern)* scrub

aus|reichen *itr. V.* **a)** *(genügen)* be enough *or* sufficient **(zu** for); **die Zeit/der Platz reicht [nicht] aus** there's [not] enough *or* sufficient time/space; **b)** *(ugs.: auskommen)* get by *(coll.)*, manage **(mit** on)

ausreichend 1. *Adj.* sufficient; enough; *(als Note)* fair. **2.** *adv.* sufficiently; **etw. ~ begründen/erklären** give an adequate justification for/explanation of sth.

aus|reifen *itr. V.; mit sein* ‹*fruit, cereal, etc.*› ripen fully; ‹*cheese, wine, etc.*› mature fully; *(fig.)* mature [fully]

Aus·reise die: jmdm. die ~ verweigern refuse sb. permission to leave [the/a country]; **vor/bei der ~:** before/when leaving the country

Ausreise-: ~erlaubnis die, ~genehmigung die exit permit

aus|reisen *itr. V.; mit sein* leave [the country]; **aus einem Land/nach Österreich** *usw.* **~:** leave a country/go to Austria *etc.*

ausreise·willig *Adj.* wanting to leave the country *postpos.*

aus|reißen 1. *unr. tr. V.* tear out; pull out ‹*plants, weeds*›; **jmdm. die Haare ~:** tear sb.'s hair out; **einer Fliege** *(Dat.)* **die Beine/Flügel ~:** pull a fly's legs/wings off. **2.** *unr. itr. V.; mit sein* **a)** *(sich lösen)* ‹*sleeve*› come off *or* away; ‹*button, handle*› come off; *(einreißen)* ‹*buttonhole*› tear; ‹seam› split, pull apart; **b)** *(ugs.: weglaufen)* run away *(Dat.* from); **von zu Hause ~:** run away from home; **c)** *(Sport: Vorsprung gewinnen)* break away *(Dat.* from)

Aus·reißer der a) *(ugs.)* runaway; **b)** *(Statistik)* outlier; **c)** *(Sport: Läufer/Radfahrer)* runner/rider breaking away from the field; **d)** *(Schießsport)* stray bullet

Ausreißerin die; ~, ~nen *s.* **Ausreißer a, c**

aus|reiten 1. *unr. itr. V.; mit sein* **a)** *(wegreiten)* ride out **(aus** of); **b)** *(einen Ausritt machen)* go for a ride; go riding. **2.** *unr. tr. V. (Reitsport)* **a)** *(bewegen)* exercise; **b)** *(die Höchstleistung abfordern)* **ein Pferd ~:** ride a horse to its limit

aus|reizen *tr. V. (Kartenspiel)* **seine Karten ~:** bid the full value of one's cards

aus|renken *tr. V.* dislocate; **jmdm./sich den Arm ~:** dislocate sb.'s/one's arm; **sich [nach jmdm.] den Hals ~** *(ugs.)* crane one's neck [to look for sb.]

aus|richten 1. *tr. V.* **a)** *(übermitteln)* **jmdm. etw. ~:** tell sb. sth.; **ich werde es ~:** I'll pass the message on; **kann ich ihm etwas ~?** can I give him a message?; **richte ihr einen Gruß [von mir] aus** give her my regards; **jmdm. ~, daß ...:** tell sb. that ...; **b)** *(einheitlich anordnen)* line up; **etw./sich in einer Linie ~:** line sth. up/line up; **c)** *(Technik: in eine bestimmte Lage bringen)* align, line up **(auf +** *Akk.* with); **d)** *(fig.)* **etw. auf jmdn./etw. ~:** orientate sth. towards sb./sth.; **sein ganzes Denken und Handeln auf etw.** *(Akk.)* **~:** direct all one's thoughts and energies towards sth.; **etw. nach** *od.* **an jmdm./etw. ~:** gear sth. to sb./sth.; **seine Entscheidung an den Bedürfnissen der Menschen ~:** make one's decision to fit in with people's needs; **reformerisch/kommunistisch ausgerichtet sein** be oriented towards reform/be communist in one's/its orientations; **e)** *(erwirken)* accomplish; achieve; **bei jmdm. wenig/nichts ~ können** not be able to get very far/anywhere with sb.; **gegen jmdn./etw. etwas ~ können** be able to do something against sb./sth.; **gegen ihn wirst du nichts ~ können** you won't be able to do anything about him; **f)** *(veranstalten)* organize; **jmdm. die Hochzeit ~:** make the arrangements for sb.'s wedding; **g)** *(schweiz.: zahlen)* pay **(an +** *Akk.* to); make ‹*payment*›. **2.** *refl. V.* **a)** *(Milit.)* dress ranks; **sich nach seinem Vorder-/Hinter-/Nebenmann ~:** line [oneself] up with the person in front/behind/next to one; **b) sich an einem Vorbild ~:** follow an example

Aus·richtung die a) *(Technik: das Ausrichten)* alignment; **b)** *(Orientierung)* orientation **(auf +** *Akk.* towards); *(an Bedürfnissen, Interessen)* gearing **(an +** *Dat.*, **nach** to); **c)** *(Veranstaltung)* organization; **die ~ einer Hochzeit** making the arrangements for a wedding; **d)** *(schweiz.: Zahlung)* payment

aus|ringen *unr. tr. V. (bes. ostmitteld.) s.* **auswringen**

aus|rinnen *unr. itr. V.; mit sein (bes. südd., österr.)* **a)** *(herausfließen)* run out; **b)** *(leer werden)* empty

Aus·ritt der a) *(das Ausreiten)* riding out; **b)** *(Spazierritt)* ride [out]

aus|roden *tr. V.* root *or* grub up ‹*tree, bush*›; *clear* ‹*forest*›

aus|rollen 1. *tr. V.* roll out. **2.** *itr. V.; mit sein* roll to a stop

aus|rotten *tr. V.* eradicate ‹*weeds, vermin, etc.*›; *(fig.)* wipe out ‹*family, enemy, etc.*›; eradicate, stamp out ‹*superstition, idea, evil, etc.*›; eliminate ‹*error*›

aus|rücken 1. *itr. V.; mit sein* **a)** *(bes. Milit.: in den Einsatz gehen)* move out; ‹*fire brigade, police*› turn out; **b)** *(ugs.: weglaufen)* make off; **seinen Bewachern ~:** give one's guards the slip; **von zu Hause ~:** run away from home. **2.** *tr. V.* **a)** *(Druckw.)* **etw. [nach links/rechts] ~:** set sth. out to the left/right; **b)** *(Technik: auskuppeln)* disengage

Aus·ruf der cry

aus|rufen *unr. tr. V.* **a)** *(äußern)* call out; **„Schön!" rief er aus** 'Lovely', he exclaimed; **jmdn.** *od.* **jmds. Namen ~ lassen** have a call put out for sb.; *(im Hotel)* have sb. paged; **die Haltestellen ~:** call out [the names of] the stops; **b)** *(offiziell verkünden)* proclaim; declare ‹*state of emergency*›; call ‹*strike*›; **jmdn. zum König/als Präsidenten ~:** proclaim sb. king/president; **c)** *(zum Kauf anbieten)* **seine Waren ~:** cry one's wares

Ausrufe-: ~satz der *(Sprachw.)* exclamation; exclamatory clause; **~wort das;** *Pl.* **~wörter** *(Sprachw.)* interjection; **~zeichen das** exclamation mark

Ausrufung die; ~, ~en *s.* **ausrufen b:** proclamation; declaration; calling; **nach seiner ~ zum König/Präsidenten** after he had been proclaimed king/president

Ausrufungs·zeichen das *(österr., schweiz.)* exclamation mark

aus|ruhen 1. *refl., itr. V. (sich erholen)* have a rest; **[sich] ein wenig/richtig ~:** rest a little/have a proper *or* good rest; **ausgeruht sein** be rested; *s. auch* **Lorbeer c. 2.** *tr. V. (ruhen lassen)* rest

aus|rupfen *tr. V.* pluck out ‹*feathers, hair*›; pull up ‹*grass, weeds, flowers*›

aus|rüsten *tr. V.* **a)** equip; equip, fit out ‹*ship*›; **ein Auto mit Sicherheitsgurten ~:** fit safety belts to a car; fit a car with safety belts; **b)** *(Textilw.: veredeln)* finish

Aus·rüstung die a) *o. Pl. (das Ausrüsten)* equipping; *(von Schiffen)* equipping; fitting out; **die ~ des Autos mit Gurten** *usw.* the fitting of belts *etc.* to the car; **b)** *(Ausrüstungsgegenstände, technische Einrichtung)* equipment *no pl.*; **eine neue ~:** a new set of equipment; **technische ~en** technical equipment *sing.*; **c)** *(Textilw.)* finishing

Ausrüstungs·gegenstand der item of equipment

aus|rutschen *itr. V.; mit sein* slip; *(fig.)* put one's foot in it; **jmdm. rutscht das Beil/die Feder aus** sb.'s axe/pen slips

Ausrutscher der; ~s, ~ a) *(ugs., auch fig.)* slip; **b)** *(Sport: Niederlage)* surprise defeat

Aus·saat die a) sowing; **mit der ~ beginnen** begin sowing; **b)** *(Saatgut)* seed

aus|säen *tr. (auch itr.) V. (auch fig.)* sow

Aus·sage die a) *(Feststellung)* statement; stated view; **nach ~ von Experten** according to what the experts say; **b)** *(vor Gericht, bei der Polizei)* statement; **eine ~ machen** make a statement; give evidence; **die ~ verweigern** refuse to make a statement; *(vor Gericht)* refuse to give evidence; **~ steht gegen ~:** it's one person's word against another's; **c)** *(geistiger Gehalt)* message; **dem Gemälde fehlt jede ~:** the painting conveys nothing

Aussage·kraft die; *o. Pl.* meaningfulness; *(Ausdruckskraft)* expressiveness

aussage·kräftig *Adj.* meaningful; *(ausdruckskräftig)* expressive

aus|sagen 1. *tr. V.* **a)** *(zum Ausdruck bringen)* say; **damit wird ausgesagt, daß ...:** this expresses the idea that ...; **b)** *(eine bestimmte Aussagekraft haben)* ‹*picture, novel, etc.*› express; **c)** *(vor Gericht, vor der Polizei)* **~, daß ...:** state that ...; *(unter Eid)* testify that ... **2.** *itr. V.* make a statement; *(unter Eid)* testify

aus|sägen *tr. V.* saw out

Aussage-: ~satz der *(Sprachw.)* affirmative clause; **~verweigerung die** *(Rechtsw.)* refusal to give evidence

Aus·satz der; *o. Pl. (Med. veralt., fig.)* leprosy

aussätzig *Adj. (Med. veralt., fig.)* leprous

Aussätzige der/die; *adj. Dekl. (Med. veralt., fig.)* leper

aus|saufen *unr. tr. (auch itr.) V.* **a)** ‹*animal*› drink [up] ‹*water etc.*› **(aus** out of); empty ‹*trough etc.*›; **b)** *(derb)* **den ganzen Schnaps/eine halbe Flasche [Schnaps] ~:** drink all the schnapps/half a bottle [of schnapps]; **ein Glas Bier in einem Zuge ~:** down a glass of beer in one *(sl.)*

aus|saugen *regelm. (geh. auch unr.) tr. V.* **a)** suck out **(aus** of); *(leer saugen)* suck dry; **eine Wunde/Apfelsine ~:** suck the poison out of a wound/suck the juice from an orange; **b)** *(fig.: ausbeuten)* **jmdn./etw. ~:** bleed sb./sth. [white]; **jmdn. bis aufs Blut** *od.* **Mark ~:** bleed sb. white

aus|schaben *tr. V.* **a)** scrape out; **b)** *(Med.)* remove; *(mit der Kürette)* curette

Ausschabung die; ~, ~en *s.* **Kürettage**

aus|schachten *tr. V.* excavate; sink ‹*well, shaft*›

Ausschachtung die; ~, ~en a) *(das Ausschachten)* excavation; *(eines Brunnens, Schachtes)* sinking; **b)** *(Grube, Schacht usw.)* excavation

aus|schälen *tr. V. (auch Med.)* remove **(aus** from)

aus|schalten *tr. V.* **a)** *(abstellen)* switch *or* turn off; **b)** *(ausschließen)* eliminate; exclude ‹*emotion, influence*›; dismiss ‹*doubt, objection*›; shut out ‹*feeling, thought*›

Aus·schaltung die a) *(das Abstellen)* switching *or* turning off; **bei ~ des Geräts** when switching *or* turning off the apparatus; **b)** *(Eliminierung) s.* **ausschalten b:** elimination; exclusion; dismissal

Aus·schank der; ~[e]s, Ausschänke ['ausʃɛŋkə] **a)** *o. Pl.* serving; **„Heute kein ~"** 'closed today'; **„Kein ~ an Jugendliche unter 16 Jahren"** 'persons under sixteen will not be served with alcoholic drinks'; **b)** *(Schanktisch)* bar; counter; **c)** *(Gaststätte)* bar; pub *(Brit. coll.)*; bar *(Amer.)*

Aus·schau *in* **nach jmdm./etw. ~ halten** look out for *or* keep a look-out for sb./sth.

aus|schauen *itr. V.* **a)** *(Ausschau halten)*

nach jmdm./etw. ~ *(auch fig.)* look out for *or* keep a look-out for sb./sth.; **b)** *(südd., österr.) s.* **aussehen**
aus|schaufeln *tr. V.* dig out ⟨*earth, rubble, buried person*⟩; dig ⟨*trench, grave, hole, etc.*⟩
Ausscheid der; ~**[e]s**, ~**e** *(bes. DDR Sport)* qualifier
aus|scheiden 1. *unr. itr. V.; mit sein* **a)** *(eine Gemeinschaft verlassen)* **aus etw.** ~: leave sth.; **aus dem Amt** ~: leave office; **b)** *(Sport)* be eliminated; *(wegen Defekt, Verletzung)* retire; **c)** *(nicht in Betracht kommen)* **diese Möglichkeit/dieser Kandidat scheidet aus** this possibility/candidate has to be ruled out. **2.** *unr. tr. V.* **a)** *(absondern) (Physiol.)* excrete ⟨*waste*⟩; eliminate, expel ⟨*poison*⟩; exude ⟨*sweat*⟩; *(Chem.)* precipitate; **b)** *(aussondern)* eliminate; rule out ⟨*proposal, possibility*⟩
Aus·scheidung die a) *o. Pl. s.* **ausscheiden 2 a:** excretion; elimination; expulsion; exudation; precipitation; **b)** *Pl. (Physiol.)* excreta; **c)** *(Sport)* qualifier
Ausscheidungs-: ~**kampf der** *(Sport)* qualifier; ~**organ das** *(Physiol.)* excretory organ; ~**runde die** *(Sport)* qualifying round; ~**spiel das** *(Sport)* qualifying game *or* match
aus|schelten *unr. tr. V.* scold
aus|schenken 1. *tr. V.* **a)** *(servieren)* serve ⟨*alcohol, drink*⟩; **b)** *(eingießen)* pour out; *(verteilen)* serve. **2.** *itr. V.* serve drinks
aus|scheren *itr. V.; mit sein* **a)** *(eine Gruppe, Reihe usw. verlassen)* ⟨*car, driver*⟩ pull out; ⟨*ship*⟩ break out of [the] line; ⟨*aircraft*⟩ peel off, break formation; *(fig.) (aus einer Organisation)* pull out **(aus** of); **b)** *(aus der Spur geraten)* skid
aus|schicken *tr. V.* send out
aus|schießen *unr. tr. V.* **a) jmdm. ein Auge** ~: shoot sb.'s eye out; **b)** *(Druckw.)* impose; **c)** *(Schießsport)* hold ⟨*competition*⟩; shoot for ⟨*prize*⟩; **den besten Schützen** ~: hold a competition to find the best marksman; **die Sache** ~ *(salopp)* ⟨*cowboys etc.*⟩ shoot it out *(sl.)*
aus|schiffen *tr. V.* disembark ⟨*passengers*⟩; unload ⟨*cargo*⟩
aus|schildern *tr. V.* signpost
aus|schimpfen *tr. V.* **jmdn.** ~: give sb. a telling-off; tell sb. off
aus|schlachten *tr. V.* **a)** *(ugs.: brauchbare Teile ausbauen aus)* cannibalize ⟨*machine, vehicle*⟩; break ⟨*vehicle*⟩ for spares; **b)** *(ugs. abwertend: ausnutzen)* exploit; **etw. politisch** ~: make political capital out of sth.; **c)** eviscerate ⟨*animal*⟩
aus|schlafen 1. *unr. itr., refl. V.* have a good *or* proper sleep; **[hast du jetzt] ausgeschlafen?** have you had a long enough sleep?; **ich hatte** *od.* **war nicht ausgeschlafen** I hadn't had enough sleep. **2.** *unr. tr. V.* **seinen Rausch** ~: sleep off the effects of alcohol
Aus·schlag der a) *(Haut~)* rash; **[einen]** ~ **bekommen** break out *or* come out in a rash; **b)** *(Abweichung) (einer Magnetnadel, Waage)* deflection; *(eines Pendels)* swing; **den** ~ **geben** *(fig.)* turn *or* tip the scales *(fig.)*; **das gab den** ~ **für seine Entscheidung** that was the crucial factor in his decision; that decided him
aus|schlagen 1. *unr. tr. V.* **a)** *(herausschlagen)* knock out; **jmdm. einen Zahn** ~: knock one of sb.'s teeth out; **b)** *(ablehnen)* turn down; reject; refuse ⟨*inheritance*⟩; **c)** *(löschen)* beat out ⟨*fire*⟩; **d)** *(auskleiden)* line ⟨*room, walls*⟩; **e)** *(Handw.: breit schlagen)* beat out. **2.** *unr. itr. V.* **a)** *(stoßen)* ⟨*horse*⟩ kick; **b)** *auch mit sein (schwingen)* ⟨*needle, pointer*⟩ be deflected, swing; ⟨*divining-rod*⟩ dip; ⟨*scales*⟩ turn; ⟨*pendulum*⟩ swing; **c)** *auch mit sein (sprießen)* come out [in bud]; **d)** *(zu Ende schlagen)* **ausgeschlagen haben** ⟨*clock*⟩ have stopped striking; *(fig. geh.)* ⟨*heart*⟩ have stopped [beating]; **e)** *mit sein (sich entwickeln)* turn out; **zu jmds. Nachteil** ~: turn out to sb.'s disadvantage
ausschlag·gebend *Adj.* decisive; **das war** ~ **für seine Entscheidung** that was the crucial factor in his decision; that decided him
aus|schlecken *s.* **auslecken**
aus|schließen *unr. tr. V.* **a)** *(aus einer Gemeinschaft entfernen)* expel **(aus** from); **b)** *(nicht teilnehmen lassen)* exclude **(aus** from); **er schließt sich von allem aus** he won't join in anything; **c)** *(ausnehmen)* exclude; exclude, rule out ⟨*possibility*⟩; **die zwei Behauptungen schließen einander aus** the two statements are mutually exclusive; **d)** *(unmöglich machen)* **jedes Mißverständnis/jeden Irrtum** *usw.* ~: rule out all possibility of misunderstanding/error *etc.*; **es ist nicht auszuschließen, daß ...:** one cannot rule out the possibility that ...; **e)** *(aussperren)* lock out; **f)** *(Druckw.)* justify; *s. auch* **ausgeschlossen 2**
aus·schließlich [*od.* '-'--, -'--] **1.** *Adj.; nicht präd. (alleinig)* exclusive; exclusive, sole ⟨*concern, right*⟩. **2.** *Adv. (nur)* exclusively; **das ist** ~ **sein Verdienst** the credit is his alone. **3.** *Präp. mit Gen. (ohne, außer)* excluding; exclusive of; **der Preis versteht sich** ~ **Porto** the price does not include postage
Ausschließlichkeit [*od.* '-'---] **die**; ~: exclusiveness; **er widmet sich seinem Beruf mit einer** ~, **die ...:** he devotes himself to his job with a single-mindedness which ...
Aus·schlupf der way out; *(Möglichkeit zum Entkommen)* means of escape
aus|schlüpfen *itr. V.; mit sein* hatch [out]; ⟨*butterfly*⟩ emerge
aus|schlürfen *tr. V.* sip ⟨*drink*⟩ noisily; suck ⟨*oyster, egg*⟩; **sein Glas/seine Tasse** ~: empty one's glass/cup noisily
Aus·schluß der a) *(das Ausschließen)* exclusion **(von** from); *(aus einer Gemeinschaft)* expulsion **(aus** from); *(aus einem Wettbewerb)* disqualification **(aus** from); **unter** ~ **der Öffentlichkeit** with the public excluded; *(Rechtsw.)* in camera; **b)** *(Druckw.)* spaces *pl.*; spacing material
aus|schmücken *tr. V.* decorate; deck out; *(fig.)* embellish ⟨*story, incident, report, etc.*⟩
Ausschmückung die; ~, ~**en a)** *s.* **ausschmücken:** decoration; decking out; embellishment; **b)** *(etw. Ausschmückendes)* decoration; *(erfundene Einzelheit)* embellishment
aus|schnaufen *(österr., südd. ugs.) s.* **verschnaufen**
aus|schneiden *unr. tr. V.* **a)** *(herausschneiden)* cut out; **b)** prune ⟨*tree*⟩; **einen Apfel** ~: cut the rotten parts out of an apple; *s. auch* **ausgeschnitten 2**
Aus·schnitt der a) *(Zeitungs~)* cutting; clipping; **b)** *(Hals~)* neck; **ein tiefer** ~: a plunging neck-line; **er versuchte, ihr in den** ~ **zu gucken** he tried to look down the front of her dress; **c)** *(Teil, Auszug)* part; *(eines Textes)* excerpt; *(eines Films)* clip; excerpt; *(Bild~)* detail; **etw. in** ~**en lesen/kennenlernen** read/show/get to know parts of sth.; **d)** *(Kreis~)* sector; **e)** *(Loch)* [cut-out] opening
ausschnitt·weise 1. *Adj.; nicht präd.* **die** ~ **Lektüre ist unbefriedigend** reading extracts is unsatisfactory; **die** ~ **Wiedergabe einer Rede/Vorführung eines Films** the reporting of parts of a speech/showing clips from a film. **2.** *adv.* **etw.** ~ **zitieren/abdrucken** quote/print extracts from sth.; **einen Film** ~ **zeigen** show clips from a film
aus|schnitzen *tr. V.* **etw.** ~: carve sth. out
aus|schöpfen *tr. V.* **a)** *(herausschöpfen)* scoop out **(aus** from); *(mit dem Schöpflöffel)* ladle out **(aus** of); **Wasser aus einem Boot** ~: bale water out of a boat; **b)** *(leeren)* bale ⟨*boat*⟩ out; **c)** *(voll ausnutzen)* exhaust; **alle Lebensgenüsse voll** ~: enjoy to the full all the pleasures life has to offer
aus|schrauben *tr. V.* screw out **(aus** of)
aus|schreiben *unr. tr. V.* **a)** *(nicht abgekürzt schreiben)* **etw.** ~: write sth. out in full; **einen Betrag** ~: write an amount out in words; **b)** *(ausstellen)* write *or* make out ⟨*cheque, invoice, receipt*⟩; **c)** *(bekanntgeben)* announce, call ⟨*election, meeting*⟩; impose ⟨*tax*⟩; advertise ⟨*flat, job*⟩; put ⟨*supply order etc.*⟩ out to tender
Aus·schreibung die a) *s.* **ausschreiben c:** announcement; calling; imposition; advertisement; **die** ~ **von Lieferungen** the invitation of tenders for supplies; **b)** *(Text)* announcement; *(bei Wahlen)* election notice; *(Steuerw.)* schedule; *(Anzeige, Inserat)* advertisement; *(Angebotseinholung)* invitation to tender
aus|schreien 1. *unr. tr. V.: s.* **ausrufen c. 2.** *unr. refl. V.* **sich** *(Dat.)* **die Kehle** *od.* **die Lunge** ~: shout *or* yell one's head off
aus|schreiten *(geh.)* **1.** *unr. itr. V.; mit sein* step out. **2.** *unr. tr. V.* **eine Strecke** ~: pace out a distance
Ausschreitung die; ~, ~**en**; *meist Pl.* **a)** *(Gewalttätigkeit)* act of violence; **es kam zu** ~**en** violence broke out; **b)** *(veralt.: Ausschweifung)* excess
aus|schulen *tr. V.* **ausgeschult werden** leave school
Aus·schulung die: nach der ~: after leaving school
Aus·schuß der a) *(Kommission)* committee; **b)** *o. Pl. (Waren)* rejects *pl.*
Ausschuß-: ~**mitglied das** committee member; ~**quote die** reject rate; ~**sitzung die** committee meeting; ~**ware die** rejects *pl.*
aus|schütteln *tr. V.* shake ⟨*dust, tablecloth, etc.*⟩ out
aus|schütten *tr. V.* **a)** tip out ⟨*water, sand, coal, etc.*⟩; *(ausleeren)* empty ⟨*bucket, bowl, container*⟩; *(verschütten)* spill; **jmdm. seinen Kummer** ~ *(fig.)* recount one's woes *pl.* to sb.; **sich vor Lachen** ~ **[wollen]** *(ugs.)* split one's sides laughing; die laughing *(coll.)*; *s. auch* **Herz b**; **b)** *(auszahlen)* distribute ⟨*dividends, prizes, etc.*⟩
Ausschüttung die; ~, ~**en a)** distribution; **b)** *(Börsenw.)* dividend [paid]
aus|schwärmen *itr. V.; mit sein (auch fig.)* swarm out; ⟨*soldiers*⟩ deploy; *(fächerartig)* fan out
aus|schwefeln *tr. V.* **a)** *(desinfizieren)* sulphur; fumigate with sulphur; **b)** *(entfernen)* smoke out ⟨*insects, vermin*⟩ with sulphur
aus|schweifen *itr. V.; mit sein* **a)** ⟨*imagination*⟩ run riot; **b)** *(in seiner Lebensweise)* indulge in excess
ausschweifend 1. *Adj.* wild ⟨*imagination, emotion, hope, desire, orgy*⟩; extravagant ⟨*idea*⟩; exaggerated ⟨*account, portrayal*⟩; riotous, wild ⟨*enjoyment*⟩; dissolute, dissipated ⟨*life*⟩; dissolute ⟨*person*⟩. **2.** *adv.* ~ **leben** lead a dissolute life
Ausschweifung die; ~, ~**en** *(im Genießen)* dissolution; dissipation; **nächtliche** ~**en** nightly excesses; *(stärker)* nightly orgies
aus|schweigen *unr. refl. V.* remain silent
aus|schwemmen *tr. V.* **a)** wash out; wash *or* flush out ⟨*impurities, poisons*⟩; **b)** *(aushöhlen)* erode ⟨*rock*⟩; erode, wash away ⟨*beach, river bank*⟩
aus|schwenken 1. *tr. V.* **a)** *(nach außen schwenken)* swing out; **b)** *(reinigen)* rinse out. **2.** *itr. V.; mit sein* ⟨*lorry, tram*⟩ swing out; *(Milit.)* ⟨*rearguard etc.*⟩ wheel; **nach rechts/links** ~**!** left-wheel/right-wheel!
aus|schwitzen *tr. V.* **a)** *(ausscheiden)* sweat out; **eine Erkältung** ~ *(fig.)* sweat out a cold; **b)** *(aussondern)* ⟨*wall, stone, etc.*⟩ sweat ⟨*moisture etc.*⟩; ⟨*tree, plant*⟩ exude ⟨*sap etc.*⟩; **c)** *(Kochk.)* sweat ⟨*onion, flour*⟩
aus|segnen *tr. V. (christl. Kirchen)* give the last blessing to ⟨*dead person*⟩

aus|sehen *unr. itr. V.* look (**wie** like); **gut ~:** look good; *(gesund)* look well; *(schön)* be good-looking; **zum Fürchten ~:** look terrifying; **es sieht nach Regen aus** it looks like rain; **nach etwas/nichts ~** *(ugs.)* look something special/not look anything special; **wie sieht ein Okapi aus?** what does an okapi look like?; **wie sieht's aus, kannst du mitkommen?** *(ugs.)* how are you fixed, can you come with us? *(coll.)*; **na, wie sieht's aus, wie weit seid ihr?** *(ugs.)* how is it going, how far have you got *(Brit.)* or *(Amer.)* are you?; **wie sieht der denn aus?!** what does he look like!; just look at him!; **ich habe [vielleicht] ausgesehen!** I looked a real sight!; **es sieht danach** *od.* **so aus, als ob ...:** it looks as if ...; **Erfolgreicher junger Unternehmer! Der sieht [mir] gerade danach aus!** *(iron.)* A successful young executive! I bet!; **sehe ich so** *od.* **danach aus?** *(ugs.)* what do you take me for?; **so siehst du aus!** *(ugs.)* you've got another think coming *(coll.)*; that's what you think!; **es sieht [nicht] gut mit ihm/damit aus** things [don't] look good for him/on that front; *s. auch* **danach d**

Aussehen das; ~s appearance; **dem ~ nach** going *or* judging by appearances; **etw. nach dem ~ beurteilen** judge sth. by appearances

aus|sein *unr. itr. V.; mit sein; nur im Inf. und Part. zusammengeschrieben* **a)** *(zu Ende sein)* ⟨*play, film, war*⟩ be over, have ended; **wann ist die Vorstellung aus?** what time does the performance end?; **die Schule ist aus** school is out *or* has finished; **mit ihm ist es aus** he's had it *(coll.)*; he's finished; **es ist aus mit dem schönen Leben/der Faulenzerei** the good life is over/[there'll be] no more lazing around; **zwischen uns ist es aus** it's [all] over between us; **b)** *(nicht mehr brennen)* ⟨*fire, candle, etc.*⟩ be out; **c)** *(ausgeschaltet sein)* ⟨*radio, television, light, etc.*⟩ be off; **d)** *(erreichen wollen)* **auf etw.** *(Akk.)* **~:** be after *or* interested in sth.; **e)** *(Sport)* ⟨*ball*⟩ be out; **f)** *(ausgegangen sein)* ⟨*person*⟩ be out; **g)** *(bes. Kindersp.: ausgeschieden sein)* be out

außen ['ausn̩] *Adv.* **a)** outside; **die Vase ist ~ bemalt** the vase is painted on the outside; **~ an der Windschutzscheibe** on the outside of the windscreen; **nach ~ hin** on the outside; outwardly; **das Fenster geht nach ~ auf** the window opens outwards; **von dem Skandal darf nichts nach ~ dringen** *(fig.)* nothing must get out about the scandal; **er ist nur auf Wirkung nach ~ [hin] bedacht** *(fig.)* he is only concerned with [outward] effect; **von ~:** from the outside; **Hilfe von ~ nötig haben** *(fig.)* need outside help; **er läuft/spielt ~** *(Sport)* he's running in the outside lane/playing on the wing; **~ vor bleiben** *(ugs.)* be ignored; **jmdn./etw. ~ vor lassen** *(ugs.)* ignore sb./sth.; **~ vor lassen, daß ...** *(ugs.)* ignore the fact that ...; **b)** *(österr.: [hier] draußen)* outside; out here; **hier ~:** out here

Außen der; ~, ~ *(Sport)* wing; winger

Außen-: ~ansicht die exterior view; **~antenne die** outdoor aerial; **~arbeiten** *Pl.* outside work; **~aufnahme die** *(Film)* exterior [shot]; location shot; **~bahn die** *(Sport)* outside lane; **~bezirk der** outlying district

Außenborder [-bɔrdɐ] **der;** ~s, ~ *(ugs.: Motor, Boot)* outboard

Außenbord·motor der outboard motor

außenbords *Adv. (Seemannsspr.)* outboard; **das Schiff muß ~ gestrichen werden** the hull of the ship must be painted

aus|senden *unr. (auch regelm.) tr. V.* **a)** *(wegschicken)* send out; **b)** *(ausstrahlen)* send out, emit ⟨*rays, light, etc.*⟩; transmit ⟨*news, radio programme, etc.*⟩

außen-, Außen-: ~dienst der: im ~dienst sein *od.* **arbeiten, ~dienst machen** *od.* **haben** be working out of the office; ⟨*salesman*⟩ be on the road; **~durchmesser der** external diameter; **~fläche die** outer surface; *(der Hand)* back [of the hand]; **~geleitet** *Adj. (Soziol.)* other-directed; **~handel der;** *o. Pl.* foreign trade *no art.*; **~handels·bilanz die** balance of trade; **~haut die** [outer] skin; *(aus Metallplatten)* shell plating; **~kurve die** outside bend; **~läufer der** *(Ballspiele)* wing half; **~linie die** *(Ballspiele)* touch-line; **~minister der** Foreign Minister; Foreign Secretary *(Brit.)*; Secretary of State *(Amer.)*; **~ministerium das** Foreign Ministry; Foreign and Commonwealth Office *(Brit.)*; Foreign Office *(Brit. coll.)*; State Department *(Amer.)*; **~netz das** *(Ballspiele)* outside of the net; **~pfosten der** *(Ballspiele)* outside of the post; **~politik die** foreign politics *sing.*; *(bestimmte)* foreign policy/policies *pl.*; **~politiker der** politician concerned with foreign affairs; **~politisch 1.** *Adj.* foreign-policy *attrib.* ⟨*debate*⟩; ⟨*question*⟩ relating to foreign policy; ⟨*mistake*⟩ in foreign policy; ⟨*reporting*⟩ of foreign affairs; ⟨*experience*⟩ in foreign affairs; ⟨*speaker, expert*⟩ on foreign affairs; **auf ~politischem Gebiet** in foreign affairs; **2.** *adv.* as regards foreign policy; **~politisch gesehen** from the point of view of foreign policy; **~politisch unter Druck geraten** come under foreign pressure; **~posten der** outpost; **~rist der** *(bes. Fußball)* outside of the *or* one's foot; **~rolle die** flick-up; **~seite die** outside; *(eines Stoffes)* right side; *(fig.: eines Menschen)* exterior

Außenseiter der; ~s, ~, **Außenseiterin die;** ~, ~nen *(Sport, fig.)* outsider

Außen-: ~spiegel der exterior mirror; **~stände** *Pl.* outstanding debts *or* accounts

Außenstehende der/die; *adj. Dekl.* outsider

Außen-: ~stelle die branch; **~stürmer der** *(Ballspiele)* winger; outside forward; **~tasche die** outside pocket; **~temperatur die** outside temperature; *(im Freien herrschende Temperatur)* outdoor temperature; **bei 15° ~temperatur** when the temperature outdoors is 15°; **~wand die** external *or* outside wall; **~welt die** outside world; **~winkel der** exterior angle; **~wirtschaft die;** *o. Pl.* foreign trade and investment

außer ['ausɐ] **1.** *Präp. mit Dat.* **a)** *(abgesehen von)* apart from; aside from *(Amer.)*; *(ausgenommen auch)* except [for]; **alle ~ mir** all except [for] me; **b)** *(außerhalb von)* out of; **~ Atem** out of breath; **~ Haus[es]/Land[es] sein** be out of the house/country; **~ Landes gehen** leave the country; **~ Zweifel stehen** be beyond doubt; **~ sich sein** be beside oneself (**vor** with); **c)** *(zusätzlich zu)* in addition to. **2.** *Präp. mit Akk.* **etw. ~ jeden Zweifel stellen** make sth. very clear *or* clear beyond all doubt; **vor Wut/Dankbarkeit/Erleichterung ~ sich geraten** become beside oneself with rage/be overcome with gratitude/relief; *s. auch* **[3]Acht; Betrieb b; Dienst b; Frage c; Gefecht a; Kraft g; Kurs b; Zeit b; Zweifel. 3.** *Konj. (es sei denn)* except; **ich komme, ~ es regnet** I'll come unless it rains; **~ daß ...:** except that ...; **~ wenn ...:** except when ...; **niemand ~ ich selbst** nobody but me

äußer... ['ɔysɐ...] *Adj.; nicht präd.* **a)** *(sich außen befindend)* outer ⟨*layer, courtyard, ring road*⟩; outer, outside ⟨*wall, door*⟩; external ⟨*diameter*⟩; outside ⟨*pocket*⟩; outlying ⟨*district, area*⟩; external ⟨*injury*⟩; **die ~e Seite** the outside; **b)** *(von außen kommend)* external ⟨*cause, force, etc.*⟩; **c)** *(von außen wahrnehmbar)* outward ⟨*appearance, similarity, effect, etc.*⟩; external ⟨*form, circumstances*⟩; **d)** *(auswärtig)* foreign ; **Minister des Äußeren** *s.* **Außenminister**

außer-, Außer-: ~acht·lassen [--'---] **das, ~achtlassung** [--'---] **die; ~:** disregard; **unter ~achtlassen** *od.* **~achtlassung der Vorschriften** disregarding *or* ignoring the regulations; **~beruflich** *Adj.* ⟨*interests, pressures, etc.*⟩ outside one's job; **~dem** [*auch:* --'-] *Adv. (dazu)* as well; besides; *(überdies)* besides; anyway; **sie ist Ärztin, Politikerin und ~dem noch Mutter von drei Kindern** she is a doctor, a politician, and a mother of three children as well; **~dienstlich 1.** *Adj.* private; social, unofficial ⟨*event*⟩; unofficial ⟨*commitment, activity*⟩; **2.** *adv.* out of working hours; **mit jmdm. ~dienstlich verkehren** meet with sb. on a social basis

Äußere das; ~n [outward] appearance; **das ~ täuscht oft** appearances are often deceptive; **dem ~n nach zu urteilen** to judge by appearances; judging by appearances

außer-, Außer-: ~ehelich 1. *Adj.* extramarital ⟨*relationship*⟩; illegitimate ⟨*child, birth*⟩; **2.** *adv.* outside marriage; **ein ~ehelich geborenes Kind** a child born out of wedlock; **~europäisch** *Adj.* non-European; **Reisen ins ~europäische Ausland** journeys to countries outside Europe; **~fahrplan·mäßig** [--'----] **1.** *Adj.* unscheduled ⟨*train, bus*⟩; **2.** *adv.* **dieser Zug verkehrt ~fahrplanmäßig** this train is not a scheduled one; **~gerichtlich** *(Rechtsw.)* **1.** *Adj.* out of court *attrib.* ⟨*settlement, arrangement*⟩; ⟨*settlement, arrangement*⟩ arrived at *or* reached out of court; **2.** *adv.* **sich ~gerichtlich einigen** arrive at *or* reach a settlement out of court; **~gewöhnlich 1.** *Adj.* **a)** *(vom Üblichen abweichend)* unusual; **dies ist ein ganz ~gewöhnlicher Fall** this case is quite out of the ordinary; this is a most unusual case; **b)** *(das Gewohnte übertreffend)* exceptional; **2.** *adv.* **a)** *(unüblich)* unusually; **b)** *(sehr)* exceptionally; **~halb 1.** *Präp. mit Gen.* outside; **~halb der Legalität** *(fig.)* outside the law; **~halb der Sprechstunde/Dienstzeit** out of *or* outside consulting hours/working hours *or* office hours; **2.** *Adv.* out of town; **~halb von Bremen wohnen** live outside Bremen; **nach/von ~halb** out of/from out of town; **~irdisch 1.** *Adj.* **a)** *(nicht auf der Erde)* ⟨*phenomenon, object*⟩ in space; **b)** *(von einem anderen Planeten)* extraterrestrial; *(fig. dichter.)* heavenly ⟨*beauty etc.*⟩; **2.** *adv.* **a)** *(nicht auf der Erde)* ⟨*stationed etc.*⟩ in space; **b)** *(fig. dichter.: überirdisch)* **~irdisch anmutende Musik** heavenly-sounding music; **~kirchlich 1.** *Adj.* civil ⟨*wedding*⟩; non-ecclesiastical ⟨*organization*⟩; **2.** *adv.* **sie sind ~kirchlich getraut** they had a civil wedding; they had a registry-office wedding *(Brit.)*; **~kraft·setzung** [--'---] **die** repeal; *(des Kriegsrechts)* lifting

äußerlich 1. *Adj.* **a)** *(an der Außenseite)* external ⟨*use, injury*⟩; **zur ~en Anwendung** for external use; **b)** *(nach außen hin)* outward ⟨*appearance, calm, similarity, etc.*⟩; **c)** *(oberflächlich)* superficial; **einer Sache** *(Dat.)* **~ sein** *(geh.)* be extrinsic to sth. **2.** *adv.* **a)** *(an der Außenseite)* externally; **b)** *(nach außen hin)* outwardly; **~ gesehen** on the face of it

Äußerlichkeit die; ~, **~en a)** *(äußere Form)* formality; **b)** *(Unwesentliches)* minor point; **c)** *Pl. (Aussehen)* appearances; **d)** *Pl. (Philos., Rel.)* externals

äußern 1. *tr. V.* express, voice ⟨*opinion, view, criticism, reservations, disapproval, doubt*⟩; express ⟨*joy, happiness, wish*⟩; voice ⟨*suspicion*⟩. **2.** *refl. V.* **a)** *(Stellung nehmen)* **sich über etw.** *(Akk.)* **~:** give one's view on sth.; **ich möchte mich dazu jetzt nicht ~:** I don't want to comment on that at present; **sich abfällig/begeistert über etw.** *(Akk.)* **~:** make disparaging remarks about sth./speak enthusiastically about sth.; **sich dahin gehend ~, daß ...:** make a comment to the effect that ...; **b)** *(in Erscheinung treten)* ⟨*illness*⟩ manifest itself (**in** + *Dat.*, **durch** in); ⟨*emotion*⟩ show itself, be expressed (**in** + *Dat.* in, **durch** through)

außer-: ~ordentlich 1. *Adj.* **a)** *(ungewöhnlich)* extraordinary; **b)** *(zusätzlich)* extraordinary ⟨*meeting*⟩; special ⟨*court, conference*⟩; *s. auch* **Professor a; c)** *(das Gewohnte übertreffend)* exceptional; 2. *adv. (sehr)* exceptionally; ⟨*value*⟩ highly; extremely ⟨*pleased, relieved*⟩; **~ordentlich viel Mühe** an enormous *or* exceptional amount of trouble; **~orts** *Adv. (schweizer., österr.)* out of town; **~parlamentarisch** 1. *Adj.* extra-parliamentary ⟨*opposition, organization, etc.*⟩; 2. *adv.* outside parliament; **~plan·mäßig** *Adj.* **a)** unscheduled; unbudgeted ⟨*expenditure*⟩; *s. auch* **Professor a; b)** *s.* **~fahrplanmäßig; ~schulisch** 1. *Adj.* ⟨*topics, problems*⟩ unconnected with school; out-of-school *attrib.* ⟨*activities*⟩; ⟨*interests*⟩ outside school; 2. *adv.* outside school; **~sprachlich** *Adj.* extra-linguistic

äußerst *Adv.* extremely; extremely, exceedingly ⟨*important*⟩; **~ knapp gewinnen/entkommen** *usw.* only just win/escape *etc.*

äußerst... *Adj.; nicht präd.* **a)** extreme; **mit ~er Umsicht/Behutsamkeit/Mißbilligung** with extreme *or* the utmost circumspection/care/disapproval; **mit ~er Willenskraft** using all one's will-power; **aufs ~e erschrocken/angestrengt/verwirrt** frightened in the extreme/strained to the utmost/utterly confused; **von ~er Wichtigkeit sein** be of extreme *or* the utmost importance; **im ~en Norden/Süden der Stadt/des Landes** in the northernmost/southernmost part of the town/in the far north/south of the country; **b)** *(letztmöglich)* latest possible, last possible ⟨*date, deadline*⟩; *(höchst...)* highest ⟨*price*⟩; *(niedrigst...)* lowest ⟨*price*⟩; **das Äußerste wagen/versuchen** risk/try everything; **bis zum Äußersten gehen** go to the last extreme; **c)** *(schlimmst...)* worst; **im ~en Fall** if the worst comes/came to the worst; **auf das Äußerste gefaßt sein** be prepared for the worst; *s. auch* **äußer... a**

außer·stand [*auch:* '---], **außerstande** *Adv.* **~ sein, etw. zu tun** *(nicht befähigt)* be unable to do sth.; *(nicht in der Lage)* not be in a position to *or* not be able to do sth.; **jmdn. ~ setzen, etw. zu tun** make it impossible for sb. to do sth.

äußersten·falls *Adv.* **a)** at most; **~ bis 19⁰⁰** until 7 p.m. at the outside; **b)** *s.* **schlimmstenfalls**

außertourlich [-tu:ɐ̯lɪç] *(österr.)* 1. *Adj.* additional ⟨*bus, train*⟩; additional, special ⟨*concert*⟩. 2. *adv.* in addition; **~ befördert werden** be promoted ahead of turn

Äußerung die; ~, ~en a) *(Bemerkung)* comment; remark; **eine amtliche ~:** an official comment *or* statement; **b)** *(Ausdruck)* expression

aus|setzen 1. *tr. V.* **a)** *(verlassen)* abandon ⟨*baby, animal*⟩; *(auf einer einsamen Insel)* maroon; *(ansiedeln)* release ⟨*animal*⟩ [into the wild]; *(ins Freiland bringen)* plant out ⟨*plants, seedlings*⟩; **b)** *(auf See)* launch, lower ⟨*boat*⟩; get ⟨*passengers*⟩ into the boats; *(an Land bringen)* put ⟨*passengers*⟩ ashore; **c)** *(der Einwirkung von etw. überlassen)* expose (*Dat.* to); **jmdm. ausgesetzt sein** be at sb.'s mercy; **dem Spott/der Kritik/einer Gefahr** *usw.* **ausgesetzt sein** be exposed to ridicule/criticism/a danger *etc.*; **Belastungen/Mißdeutungen ausgesetzt werden** be subject to strains/misinterpretations; **d)** *in* **an jmdm./etw./allem etwas auszusetzen haben** find fault with sb./sth./everything; **was hast du an ihm/daran auszusetzen?** what don't you like about him/it?; **daran war nichts auszusetzen** there was nothing wrong with that; **ich habe nur eines daran auszusetzen** I've only one objection to make about it; **e)** *(zur Verfügung stellen)* offer ⟨*reward, prize, salary*⟩; bequeath, leave ⟨*inheritance*⟩; **eine große Summe für etw. ~:** provide a large sum for sth.; **jmdm.** *od.* **für jmdn. eine Rente ~:** provide sb. with a pension; settle an annuity on sb.; **f)** *(Kaufmannsspr.)* prepare ⟨*consignment*⟩ [for packing]; **g)** *(unterbrechen)* interrupt; **h)** *(Rechtsw.)* suspend ⟨*proceedings*⟩; defer ⟨*judgement, imprisonment*⟩; *s. auch* **Bewährung a.** 2. *itr. V.* **a)** *(aufhören)* stop; ⟨*engine, machine*⟩ cut out, stop; ⟨*heart*⟩ stop [beating]; **b)** *(eine Pause machen)* ⟨*player*⟩ miss a turn; **mit etw. ~:** stop sth.; **mit der Arbeit/dem Training [ein paar Wochen] ~:** stop work/training [for a few weeks]; **mit seinem Studium ~:** interrupt one's studies; **mit den Tabletten ~:** stop taking the tablets

Aus·setzer der *(Kaufmannsspr.) employee who prepares consignments etc. for packing*

Aussetzung die; ~, ~en a) *s.* **aussetzen 1a:** abandonment; marooning; release [into the wild]; planting out; **b)** *s.* **aussetzen 1b:** launching; lowering; **c)** *s.* **aussetzen 1e:** offering; bequesting; leaving; **d)** *s.* **aussetzen 1h:** suspension; deferment

Aus·sicht die a) *(Blick)* view (**auf** + *Akk.* of); **ein Zimmer mit ~ aufs Meer** a room overlooking the sea; **jmdm. die ~ nehmen/versperren** block *or* obstruct sb.'s view; **b)** *(Perspektive)* prospect (**auf** + *Akk.* of); **das sind ja vielleicht [heitere] ~en!** *(iron.)* that's a fine prospect! *(iron.)*; **~ auf etw.** *(Akk.)* **haben** have the prospect of sth.; **sie hat nicht die geringste ~ auf Erfolg** she hasn't the slightest chance *or* prospect of success; **er hat gute ~en, gewählt zu werden** he stands a good chance of being elected; **etw. in ~ haben** have the prospect of sth.; have sth. in prospect; **jmdn./etw. für etw. in ~ nehmen** consider sb./sth. for sth.; **in ~ stehen** be in prospect; **jmdm. etw. in ~ stellen** hold out the prospect of sth. to sb.; **weitere ~en** *(Met.)* further outlook *sing.*

aussichts·los 1. *Adj.* hopeless. 2. *adv.* hopelessly

Aussichtslosigkeit die; ~: hopelessness

aussichts-, Aussichts-: ~punkt der vantage point; **~reich** *Adj.* **a)** promising; **b)** *(österr.: mit schöner Aussicht)* **in ~reicher Wohnlage** offering attractive views *postpos.*; **~turm der** look-out *or* observation tower; **~voll** *Adj.* promising; **~wagen der** observation car

aus|sieben *tr. V.* sift out; screen ⟨*coal*⟩; filter out ⟨*frequencies*⟩; *(fig.)* select; pick out ⟨*candidates etc.*⟩; weed out ⟨*weak candidates etc.*⟩

aus|siedeln *tr. V.* move out and resettle; *(evakuieren)* evacuate

Aussiedelung die; ~, ~en *s.* **Aussiedlung**

Aus·siedler der *(Auswanderer)* emigrant; *(Evakuierter)* evacuee; *(Umsiedler)* resettled person

Aussiedler·hof der *farm, formerly part of a strip-farming system and with its buildings in the village, now resited away from the village on a single area of land*

Aus·siedlung die *(Evakuierung)* evacuation; *(Umsiedlung)* resettlement

aus|sinnen *unr. tr. V. (geh.)* think up; devise ⟨*plan*⟩

aus|sitzen *unr. tr. V.* **etw. ~:** sit sth. out

aus|söhnen 1. *refl. V.* **sich mit jmdm./***(fig.)* **etw. ~:** become reconciled with sb./to sth.; **sie haben sich ausgesöhnt** they have become reconciled; they have made it up. 2. *tr. (auch itr.) V.* reconcile; **jmdn. mit jmdm./***(fig.)* **etw. ~:** reconcile sb. with sb./to sth.

Aussöhnung die; ~, ~en reconciliation

aus|sondern *tr. V.* **a)** *(ausscheiden)* weed out; **ausgesonderte Ware** reject goods *pl.*; **b)** *(auswählen)* sort *or* pick out; select

Aussonderung die; ~, ~en a) weeding out; **b)** *(das Auswählen)* selection

aus|sortieren *tr. V.* sort out

aus|spähen 1. *itr. V. (ausschauen)* keep a look-out (**nach** for). 2. *tr. V. (auskundschaften)* spy out; spy on ⟨*organization*⟩

aus|spannen 1. *tr. V.* **a)** unharness, unhitch ⟨*horse, mule*⟩; unyoke ⟨*oxen*⟩; **b)** *(salopp: wegnehmen)* **jmdm. etw. ~:** get sb. to part with sth.; **jmdm. den Freund/die Freundin ~:** pinch sb.'s boy-friend/girl-friend *(sl.)*; **c)** *(lösen)* unhitch ⟨*cart, plough, etc.*⟩; take out ⟨*sheet of paper*⟩ (**aus** of); **d)** *(ausbreiten)* spread out ⟨*cloth, net*⟩; stretch ⟨*rope, cable, line*⟩; **die Flügel ~:** spread its/their wings. 2. *itr. V.* **a)** *(ausruhen)* take *or* have a break; **b)** *(Pferde ~)* unharness *or* unhitch the horses; *(Ochsen ~)* unyoke the oxen

Aus·spannung die relaxation

aus|sparen *tr. V.* leave ⟨*line etc.*⟩ blank; *(fig.)* leave out; omit; **eine ausgesparte Lücke** a gap left free

Aussparung die; ~, ~en a) *(das Aussparen)* leaving blank; **b)** *(Stelle)* gap; *(im Text)* blank space

aus|speien *(geh.)* 1. *unr. tr. V.* **a)** *(ausspucken)* spit out; **b)** *(erbrechen)* bring up; vomit [up]. 2. *unr. itr. V.* spit; **vor jmdm. ~:** spit at sb.'s feet

aus|sperren 1. *tr. V.* **a)** *(ausschließen)* lock out; shut ⟨*animal*⟩ out; **b)** *(im Streik)* lock out. 2. *itr. V.* organize a lock-out; lock the work-force out

Aus·sperrung die lock-out

aus|spielen 1. *tr. V.* **a)** *(Kartenspiel)* lead; **sein ganzes Wissen ~** *(fig.)* make use of all one's knowledge; bring all one's knowledge to bear; **einen/seinen letzten Trumpf ~** *(fig.)* play one's last trump card; **b)** *(manipulieren)* **jmdn./etw. gegen jmdn./etw. ~:** play sb./sth. off against sb./sth.; **c)** *(Sport: spielen um)* play for ⟨*cup, title, etc.*⟩; **d)** *(als Preis aussetzen)* put up as ⟨*prize money*⟩; **e)** *(Sport) (deklassieren)* outplay; *(umspielen)* beat; go round; **f)** *(Theater)* act out; *s. auch* **ausgespielt 2.** 2. *itr. V. (Kartenspiel)* lead; **wer spielt aus?** whose lead is it?

aus|spinnen *unr. tr. V.* elaborate ⟨*story, idea*⟩; develop, pursue ⟨*train of thought*⟩

aus|spionieren *tr. V.* **a)** *(entdecken, herausbekommen)* spy out; **die Zahlenkombination des Safes ~:** discover the combination of the safe by spying; **b)** *(ugs.: aushorchen)* pump

aus|spotten *tr. V. (bes. österr., schweiz.) s.* **verspotten**

Aus·sprache die a) *(von Wörtern)* pronunciation; *(Art des Artikulierens)* articulation; *(Akzent)* accent; *s. auch* **feucht; b)** *(Gespräch)* discussion; *(zwangloseres)* talk; **eine offene ~ herbeiführen** bring things out into the open

Aussprache-: ~angabe die, ~bezeichnung die phonetic transcription; **~angaben haben** show pronunciation; **~wörterbuch das** pronouncing dictionary; dictionary of pronunciation

aussprechbar *Adj.* pronounceable; **nicht ~:** unpronounceable; impossible to pronounce *postpos.*; unrepeatable ⟨*thought, idea, wish*⟩

aus|sprechen 1. *unr. tr. V.* **a)** pronounce; **b)** *(ausdrücken)* express; voice ⟨*suspicion, request*⟩; *(verkünden)* pronounce ⟨*judgement, sentence, etc.*⟩; grant ⟨*divorce*⟩; **~, daß ...:** state that ...; **der Regierung sein Vertrauen ~:** pass a vote of confidence in the government. 2. *unr. refl. V.* **a)** *(sich sprechen lassen)* be pronounced; **ihr Name spricht sich schwer aus** her name is difficult to pronounce; **b)** *(äußern)* speak; **sich lobend/mißbilligend über jmdn./etw. ~:** speak highly/disapprovingly of sb./sth.; **er hat sich nicht näher darüber ausgesprochen** he did not say anything further about it; **sich für jmdn./etw. ~:** declare *or* pronounce oneself in favour of sb./sth.; **sich gegen jmdn./etw. ~:** declare *or* pronounce oneself against sb./sth.; **c)** *(offen sprechen)* say what's on one's mind; **sich über etw.** *(Akk.)*

mit *od.* **bei jmdm. ~:** have a heart-to-heart talk with sb. about sth.; **na los, sprich dich aus!** *(ugs.)* come on, get it off your chest!; **d)** *(Strittiges klären)* have it out, talk things out (**mit** with); **wir haben uns über alles ausgesprochen** we had everything out. **3.** *unr. itr. V. (zu Ende sprechen)* finish [speaking]; *s. auch* **ausgesprochen 2, 3**

aus|spritzen *tr. V.* **a)** squirt out ⟨*liquid, contents*⟩; **sein Gift gegen jmdn. ~** *(fig.)* spit venom at sb.; **b)** *(reinigen)* flush out; rinse out ⟨*tooth*⟩; syringe ⟨*ear*⟩; **c)** *(löschen)* put out ⟨*fire*⟩ [with a hose/hoses]

Aus·spruch der remark; *(Sinnspruch)* saying

aus|spucken 1. *itr. V.* spit; **vor jmdm. ~:** spit at sb.'s feet. **2.** *tr. V.* **a)** spit out; *(fig. ugs.)* ⟨*machine, factory, computer*⟩ spew out; cough up *(sl.)* ⟨*money*⟩; regurgitate ⟨*facts, information, etc.*⟩; **nun los, spuck's aus, sei nicht so schüchtern!** *(ugs. fig.)* come on, spit it out and don't be so shy!; **b)** *(ugs.: erbrechen)* sick up *(Brit. coll.)*; throw up

aus|spülen *tr. V.* **a)** *(reinigen)* rinse out; *(Med.)* irrigate; wash out; **sich** *(Dat.)* **den Mund ~:** rinse one's mouth out; **b)** *(entfernen)* flush *or* wash out; ⟨*river, sea*⟩ wash away, erode ⟨*soil, rock*⟩

Aus·spülung die *s.* **ausspülen a, b:** rinsing out; irrigation; washing out; flushing *or* washing out; washing away; erosion

aus|staffieren ['aus∫ta,fi:rən] *tr. V.* kit *or* rig out; fit out, furnish ⟨*room etc.*⟩; *(verkleiden)* dress up; **sie hat ihre Tochter sonntäglich ausstaffiert** she dressed her daughter up in her Sunday best

Aus·staffierung die outfit; get-up *(coll.)*

Aus·stand der strike; **im ~ sein** be on strike; **in den ~ treten** go on strike

aus·ständig *Adj. (südd., österr.: ausstehend)* outstanding

aus|stanzen *tr. V.* punch out

aus|statten ['aus∫tatn̩] *tr. V.* provide (**mit** with); *(mit Kleidung)* provide; fit out; *(mit Gerät)* equip ⟨*office, kitchen, hospital, school, etc.*⟩; *(mit Möbeln, Teppichen, Gardinen usw.)* furnish ⟨*room, flat, office, etc.*⟩; **mit Rechten/Befugnissen ausgestattet sein** be vested with powers/authority *sing.*; have powers/authority *no pl.* vested in one; **mit Talent ausgestattet sein** be endowed with talent; **ein prächtig ausgestatteter Band** a splendidly produced volume

Ausstattung die; ~, ~en a) *(das Ausstatten) s.* **ausstatten:** provision; fitting out; equipping; furnishing; vesting; production; **b)** *(Ausrüstung)* equipment; *(Innen~ eines Autos)* trim; **c)** *(Einrichtung)* furnishings *pl.*; **d)** *(Aufmachung) (eines Films, Theaterstücks)* décor and costumes; *(Verpackung)* packaging; *(eines Buchs)* design and layout; *(typographisch)* design

Ausstattungs-: ~film der period film; **~stück das** spectacular [opera/play *etc.*]

aus|stechen *unr. tr. V.* **a) jmdm. die Augen ~:** put *or* gouge sb.'s eyes out; **b)** *(entfernen)* dig up ⟨*plants*⟩; cut ⟨*turf*⟩; **c)** *(herstellen)* dig [out] ⟨*trench, hole, etc.*⟩; *(Kochk.)* press *or* cut out ⟨*biscuits*⟩; **d)** *(übertreffen)* outdo; **jmdn. bei jmdm. ~:** oust sb. in sb.'s affections/esteem/favour; **jmdn. in etw.** *(Dat.)* **~:** outshine sb. *or* put sb. in the shade in sth.

aus|stehen 1. *unr. itr. V.* **noch ~** ⟨*debt*⟩ be outstanding; ⟨*decision*⟩ be still to be taken, have not yet been taken; ⟨*book*⟩ be still to appear; ⟨*solution*⟩ be still to be found; **ihre Entscheidung/Antwort steht noch aus** I am/we are *etc.* still awaiting their decision/reply; **eine offizielle Bestätigung steht noch aus** there has as yet been no official confirmation; **~de Forderungen** outstanding demands; **Geld ~ haben** *(ugs.)* have money owing [one]; **euer Besuch bei mir steht noch aus** you still owe me a visit. **2.** *unr. tr. V. (ertragen)* endure ⟨*pain, suffering*⟩; suffer ⟨*worry, anxiety*⟩; *(erdulden)* put up with; **ausgestanden sein** be all over; **ich kann ihn/das nicht ~:** I can't stand *or* bear him/it

aus|steigen *unr. itr. V.; mit sein;* **a)** *(aus einem Auto, Boot)* get out (**aus** of); *(aus einem Zug, Bus)* get off; alight *(formal)*; *(Fliegerspr.: abspringen)* bale out; **aus einem Zug/Bus ~:** get off a train/bus; alight from a train/bus *(formal)*; **alles ~!** all change!; **b)** *(ugs.: sich nicht mehr beteiligen)* **~ aus** opt out of; give up ⟨*show business, job*⟩; leave ⟨*project*⟩; **c)** *(Sport: aus einem Rennen o. ä.)* drop out (**aus** of); retire (**aus** from); **d)** *(ugs.: der Gesellschaft den Rücken kehren)* drop out

Aussteiger der; ~s, ~, Aussteigerin die; ~, ~nen *(ugs.)* drop-out *(coll.)*

aus|stellen *tr. V.* **a)** *auch itr. (im Schaufenster)* put on display; display; *(im Museum, auf einer Messe)* exhibit; **ausgestellt sein** ⟨*goods*⟩ be on display/be exhibited; ⟨*painting*⟩ be exhibited; **die Galerie wird Hans Meyer ~:** the gallery is going to put on a Hans Meyer exhibition; **bekannte Künstler/viele Betriebe stellen hier aus** famous artists/many firms exhibit here; **b)** *(ausfertigen)* make out, write [out] ⟨*cheque, prescription, receipt*⟩; make out ⟨*bill*⟩; issue ⟨*visa, passport, certificate*⟩; **einen Scheck auf jmdn. ~:** make out a cheque to sb.; **c)** *(ugs.: ausschalten)* turn *or* switch off ⟨*cooker, radio, heating, engine*⟩; **d)** *(nach außen stellen)* open out ⟨*window*⟩; roll out ⟨*blind*⟩; pull out ⟨*aerial*⟩; **e)** *(aufstellen)* put up ⟨*poster, sign*⟩; post ⟨*sentry*⟩; set ⟨*trap*⟩; *s. auch* **ausgestellt 2**

Aussteller der; ~s, ~, Ausstellerin die; ~, ~nen a) *(auf Messen)* exhibitor; **b)** *(eines Dokuments)* issuer; *(Behörde)* issuing authority; *(eines Schecks)* drawer

Aus·stellung die a) *(das Präsentieren)* exhibiting; **b)** *(das Ausfertigen) s.* **ausstellen b:** making out; writing [out]; issuing; **Datum und Ort der ~:** date and place of issue; **c)** *(Veranstaltung)* exhibition; **d)** *(das Aufstellen) s.* **ausstellen e:** putting up; posting; setting

Ausstellungs-: ~datum das date of issue; **~fläche die** exhibition area; **~gelände das** exhibition site; **~halle die** exhibition hall; **~katalog der** exhibition catalogue; **~ort der** place of issue; **~raum der a)** *o. Pl.* exhibition space; **b)** *(Zimmer)* exhibition room; **~stand der** exhibition stand; **~stück das** *(in Schaufenstern usw.)* display item; *(in Museen usw.)* exhibit; *(auf Messen)* **dieses Fahrzeug ist ein ~stück** this vehicle is for display purposes only; **dein Auto ist ja nicht gerade ein ~stück!** *(iron.)* your car isn't exactly much to look at!

Aussterbe·etat der *(ugs.)* **in auf dem ~ sein** *od.* **stehen, sich auf dem ~ befinden** be on its last legs

aus|sterben *unr. itr. V.; mit sein (auch fig.)* die out; ⟨*species*⟩ die out, become extinct; **ein ~des Handwerk** *(fig.)* a dying craft; **die Dummen sterben nicht** *od.* **nie aus** there's one born every minute

Aus·steuer die trousseau *(consisting mainly of household linen)*

aus|steuern *tr. V.* **a)** *(Elektronik)* modulate ⟨*signal, wave*⟩; *(bei der Aufnahme)* control the recording level of; control the power level of ⟨*amplifier*⟩; **b) ein Auto ~:** [use the steering-wheel to] bring a car under control; **c)** *(Versicherungsw.)* **jmdn. ~:** end sb.'s entitlement to benefits

Ausstieg der; ~[e]s, ~e a) *(Ausgang)* exit; *(Tür)* door[s]; *(~luke)* hatch; **b)** *o. Pl. (das Aussteigen)* climbing out (**aus** of); **„kein ~"** 'no exit'; **der ~ aus dem Bus/Zug** getting off the bus/train; alighting from the bus/train *(formal)*; **der ~ aus der Höhle** the way up out of the cave; **c)** *(fig.)* **ein ~ aus dem heiklen Thema** a way of getting off the awkward subject

aus|stopfen *tr. V.* stuff ⟨*cushion, animal, doll, etc.*⟩; fill ⟨*crack*⟩

Aus·stoß der; *o. Pl. (Wirtsch.)* output

aus|stoßen *unr. tr. V.* **a)** *(nach außen pressen)* expel; give off, emit ⟨*gas, fumes, smoke*⟩; fire ⟨*torpedo*⟩; **b)** give ⟨*cry, whistle, laugh, etc.*⟩; let out ⟨*cry, scream, yell*⟩; heave, give ⟨*sigh*⟩; utter ⟨*curse, threat, accusation, etc.*⟩; **c) jmdm. ein Auge ~:** put sb.'s eye out; **sich** *(Dat.)* **einen Zahn ~:** knock a tooth out; **d)** *(ausschließen) (aus einem Verein, einer Gesellschaft)* expel (**aus** from); *(aus der Armee)* drum out (**aus** of); **sich ausgestoßen fühlen** feel an outcast; *s. auch* **Ausgestoßene; e)** *(Wirtsch.)* turn out; produce

aus|strahlen 1. *tr. V.* **a)** *(verbreiten, auch fig.)* radiate; radiate, give off ⟨*heat*⟩; ⟨*lamp*⟩ give out ⟨*light*⟩; **b)** *(Rundf., Ferns.)* broadcast; transmit; **c)** *(ausleuchten)* floodlight. **2.** *itr. V.* **a)** *(ausgehen)* radiate; ⟨*heat*⟩ radiate, be given off; ⟨*light*⟩ be given out; *(fig.)* ⟨*pain*⟩ spread, extend; **b)** *(wirken)* **auf jmdn./etw. ~:** communicate itself to sb./influence sth.

Aus·strahlung die a) *(Wirkung)* radiation; *(eines Menschen)* charisma; **~ haben** ⟨*person*⟩ have charisma; **b)** *(Rundf., Ferns.)* transmission

aus|strecken 1. *tr. V.* extend, stretch out ⟨*arms, legs*⟩; stretch out ⟨*hand*⟩; put out ⟨*feelers*⟩; stick *or* put out ⟨*tongue*⟩; **mit ausgestreckten Armen** with arms extended; with outstretched arms. **2.** *refl. V.* stretch [oneself] out; **ausgestreckt am Boden liegen** lie stretched out on the floor

aus|streichen *unr. tr. V.* **a)** *(durchstreichen)* cross *or* strike out; delete; *(fig.)* obliterate; **jmds. Namen auf einer Liste ~:** cross sb.'s name off a list; **b)** *(verteilen)* spread; **c)** *(Kochk.)* grease ⟨*tin, pan, etc.*⟩; **d)** *(füllen)* fill, smooth over ⟨*cracks*⟩

aus|streuen *tr. V.* **a)** *(verstreuen)* scatter; distribute ⟨*gifts, leaflets, money*⟩; spread, put about ⟨*rumour, story, lies, etc.*⟩; **er ließ ~, daß ...:** he caused the rumour to be spread about that ...; **b)** *(bestreuen)* **etw. mit etw. ~:** sprinkle sth. with sth.

Aus·strich der *(Med., Biol.)* smear

aus|strömen 1. *tr. V.* radiate ⟨*warmth*⟩; give off ⟨*scent*⟩; *(fig.)* radiate ⟨*optimism, confidence, etc.*⟩. **2.** *itr. V.; mit sein* stream *or* pour out; ⟨*gas, steam*⟩ escape; **etw. strömt von jmdm./etw. aus** *(fig.)* sb./sth. radiates sth.

aus|suchen *tr. V.* choose; pick; **such dir was aus!** choose what you want; take your pick; **man kann es sich nicht immer ~:** there isn't always any choice in the matter; *s. auch* **ausgesucht 2, 3**

aus|sülzen *refl. V. (salopp) (lange reden)* go on [and on]; *(zu Ende reden)* finish spouting

aus|täfeln *tr. V.* panel

aus|tapezieren *tr. V.* paper

aus|tarieren *tr. V.* **a)** *(ins Gleichgewicht bringen)* balance ⟨*scales*⟩; **b)** *(österr.: Tara feststellen von)* determine the tare of

Aus·tausch der a) exchange; **im ~ für** *od.* **gegen** in exchange for; **b)** *(das Ersetzen)* replacement (**gegen** with); *(Sport)* substitution (**gegen** by)

austauschbar *Adj.* interchangeable; *(ersetzbar)* replaceable ⟨*parts etc.*⟩

aus|tauschen 1. *tr. V.* **a)** exchange (**gegen** for); **b)** *(ersetzen)* replace (**gegen** with); *(Sport)* substitute (**gegen** by). **2.** *refl. V. (über etw. sprechen)* exchange views/experiences [with each other]

Austausch-: ~motor der *(Kfz-W.)* replacement engine; **~schüler der** exchange pupil *or* student

aus|teilen *tr. V.* distribute (**unter** + *Dat.*

among, **an** + *Akk.* to); *(aushändigen)* hand *or* give out ‹*books, post, etc.*› (**an** + *Akk.* to); issue, give ‹*orders*›; deal [out] ‹*cards*›; give out ‹*marks, grades*›; administer ‹*sacrament*›; *(servieren)* serve ‹*food etc.*›; *(fig.)* give ‹*blessing*›; **Prügel ~** *(fig.)* hand out beatings

Aus·teilung die *s.* **austeilen:** distribution; handing *or* giving out; issuing; giving; dealing [out]; administering; serving

Auster ['austɐ] **die; ~, ~n** oyster

Austern-: ~bank die; *Pl.* **~bänke** oysterbed; oyster-bank; **~fischer der** oystercatcher; **~park der** oyster-farm; **~zucht die** oyster-farming

aus|tilgen *tr. V.* **a)** *(vernichten)* exterminate ‹*pests, race*›; eradicate ‹*weeds*›; wipe out, eradicate ‹*disease*›; **b)** *(streichen, auch fig.)* obliterate

aus|toben 1. *refl. V.* **a)** *(spielen)* romp about; have a good romp; **b)** *(sich amüsieren)* indulge oneself; **die Jugend will sich ~:** youth must have its fling. **2.** *tr. V. (abreagieren)* work off ‹*anger etc.*› (**an** + *Dat.* on)

aus|tollen *refl. V. (ugs.)* romp about; have a good romp

Austrag der; ~[e]s a) *(das Austragen)* settlement; resolution; **b)** *(Sport)* holding; **c)** *(österr.) s.* **Altenteil**

aus|tragen *unr. tr. V.* **a)** *(zustellen)* deliver ‹*newspapers, post*›; **b)** *(im Mutterleib)* carry ‹*child*› to full term; *(nicht abtreiben)* have ‹*child*›; **c)** *(ausfechten)* settle; *(bis zum Ende)* carry on ‹*quarrel, hostilities*›; settle, resolve ‹*conflict, differences*›; fight out ‹*battle*›; **etw. vor Gericht ~:** take sth. to court; **einen Streit mit jmdm. ~:** have it out with sb.; **d)** *(Sport)* hold ‹*race, competition, etc.*›; **e)** *(löschen)* delete, take out ‹*data, figures*›; *(aus einer Liste)* cross ‹*person, name*› off

Aus·träger der delivery boy/man; *(Zeitungsjunge)* newspaper boy

Aus·trägerin die delivery woman/girl; *(Zeitungsmädchen)* newspaper girl

Austragung die; ~, ~en a) carrying on; *(bis zum Ende) (eines Streits)* settlement; **b)** *(Sport)* holding

Austragungs-: ~modus der *(bes. Sport)* procedure; **~ort der** *(Sport)* venue

Australide [austra'li:də] **der/die;** *adj. Dekl.* Australoid

Australien [aus'tra:li̯ən] **(das); ~s** Australia; **~ und Ozeanien** Australasia

Australier der; ~s, ~, Australierin die; ~, ~nen Australian; **er/sie ist ~:** he/she is [an] Australian

australisch *Adj.* Australian

aus|träumen *itr. (auch tr.) V.* finish dreaming; **der Traum [vom Glück] ist ausgeträumt** the dream [of happiness] is over

aus|treiben 1. *unr. tr. V.* **a)** *(verbannen)* exorcize, cast out ‹*evil spirit, demon*›; **b)** *(abgewöhnen)* **jmdm. etw. ~:** cure sb. of sth.; **c)** *(geh.: vertreiben, auch fig.)* drive out (**aus** from); **d)** *(auf die Weide)* drive ‹*cattle, sheep*› out to pasture; **e)** *(hervorbringen)* put forth ‹*leaves, buds*›; produce ‹*blossom*›. **2.** *unr. itr. V.* **a)** *(ausschlagen)* sprout; **b)** *(hervorkommen)* ‹*shoot, bud*› appear

Austreibung die; ~, ~en expulsion (**aus** from); *(von Dämonen)* exorcism; casting out

aus|treten 1. *unr. tr. V.* **a)** tread out ‹*spark, cigarette-end*›; trample out ‹*fire*›; **b)** *(bahnen)* tread out ‹*path*›; **ausgetretene Pfade** *(fig.)* well-trodden paths; **c)** *(abnutzen)* wear down; **eine ausgetretene Steintreppe** a stone staircase with worn-down steps; **d)** *(weiten)* wear out ‹*old shoes*›; break in ‹*new shoes*›. **2.** *unr. itr. V.; mit sein* **a)** *(ugs.: zur Toilette gehen)* pay a call *(coll.)*; **der Schüler fragte, ob er ~ dürfe** the pupil asked to be excused; **b)** *(ausscheiden)* **aus etw. ~:** leave sth.; **aus einer Vereinigung ~:** resign from a society; **c)** *(Jägerspr.)* come out into the open; **aus der Deckung ~:** break cover; **d)** *(nach außen gelangen)* come out; *(entweichen)* escape; ‹*blood*› issue; ‹*pus*› be discharged

Austriazismus [austria'tsɪsmʊs] **der; ~, Austriazismen** Austrianism

aus|tricksen *tr. V. (ugs.)* trick

aus|trinken 1. *tr. V.* finish, drink up ‹*wine, beer, coffee, etc.*›; finish, drain ‹*glass, bottle, etc.*›. **2.** *itr. V.* drink up

Aus·tritt der a) *(das Ausscheiden)* leaving; *(aus einem Verband, einer Vereinigung)* resignation (**aus** from); **seinen ~ aus der Partei/Kirche erklären** announce that one is leaving the party/church; **die Partei hatte viele ~e zu verzeichnen** the party recorded a large drop in membership; **b)** *(das Hervorquellen)* outflow; *(das Entweichen)* escape; *(von Blut)* issue; *(von Eiter)* discharge

Austritts·erklärung die [notice of] resignation

aus|trocknen 1. *tr. V.* **a)** *(ausdörren)* dry out; dry up ‹*river bed, marsh*›; parch ‹*throat*›; **b)** *(trockenlegen)* drain ‹*marsh, swamp*›. **2.** *itr. V.; mit sein* dry out; ‹*river bed, pond, etc.*› dry up; ‹*skin, hair*› become dry; ‹*throat*› become parched

Austro·marxismus [austro-] **der** Austro-Marxism

aus|trompeten *tr. V. (ugs.) s.* **ausposaunen**

aus|trudeln 1. *itr. V. (ugs.)* **etw. ~ lassen** let sth. fizzle out. **2.** *tr. V. (ugs.) s.* **auswürfeln**

aus|tüfteln *tr. V. (ugs.) (ausarbeiten)* work out; *(ersinnen)* think up

aus|üben *tr. V.* **a)** *(nachgehen)* practise ‹*art, craft*›; follow ‹*profession*›; carry on ‹*trade*›; do ‹*job*›; **welche Tätigkeit üben Sie aus?** what is your occupation?; **b)** *(innehaben)* hold ‹*office*›; wield, exercise ‹*power*›; exercise ‹*control*›; *(wahrnehmen)* exercise ‹*right*›; *(wirksam werden lassen)* exert

Aus·übung die *o. Pl.; s.* **ausüben:** practising; following; carrying on; doing; holding; wielding; exercising

aus|ufern *itr. V.; mit sein* **a)** *(überhandnehmen)* get out of hand; **b)** *(selten: über die Ufer treten)* burst *or* break its banks

Aus·verkauf der [clearance] sale; *(wegen Geschäftsaufgabe)* closing-down *(Brit.) or (Amer.)* liquidation sale; *(fig.: Verrat)* sellout; **etw. im ~ kaufen** buy sth. at the sale[s]

aus|verkaufen *tr. V.* **a)** *(verkaufen)* sell out of; **Mineralwasser ist ausverkauft** there is no mineral water left [in stock]; **b)** *(räumen)* sell off, clear ‹*stock*›; clear ‹*warehouse, shop*›

ausverkauft *Adj.* sold out; **vor ~em Haus spielen** play to a full house; **~e Ränge** *(Sport)* packed stands

aus|wachsen 1. *unr. refl. V.* **a)** *(sich normalisieren)* right *or* correct itself; **b)** *(sich entwickeln)* grow (**zu** into). **2.** *unr. itr. V.; mit sein* **a)** *(ugs.: verzweifeln)* go round the bend *(coll.)*; **zum Auswachsen sein** be enough to drive you up the wall *(coll.)*; **b)** *(keimen)* sprout prematurely

Aus·wahl die a) *(das Auswählen)* choice; selection; **Sie haben die [freie] ~:** the choice is yours; you can choose whichever you like; **drei Sorten/Tee und Kaffee stehen zur Wahl** there are three kinds to choose from/one can choose between tea and coffee; **bei uns stehen Ihnen mehr als 600 Wagen zur ~:** we offer you a choice of over 600 cars; **eine ~ treffen** make a selection; **b)** *(Auslese)* selection; *(von Gedichten, Erzählungen)* anthology; selection; **c)** *(Sortiment)* range; **viel/wenig ~ haben** have a wide/limited selection (**an** + *Dat.*, **von** of); **hier hat man keine ~:** there is no choice here; **Backwaren in reicher ~:** a wide selection of bread, cakes, and pastries; **d)** *(Sport: Mannschaft)* [selected] team

Auswahl·band der; *Pl.* **-bände** anthology

aus|wählen *tr. V.* choose, select (**aus** from, **unter** + *Dat.* from among); **sich** *(Dat.)* **etw. ~:** choose *or* select sth. [for oneself]

Auswahl-: ~mannschaft die *(Sport)* [selected] team; **~möglichkeit die** choice; **~prinzip das** method of selection; **~spieler der** *(Sport)* [selected] player

aus|walzen *tr. V.* roll out ‹*metal*›; *(fig. ugs.)* drag out ‹*subject*›; **eine Geschichte zu einem Roman ~:** spin a story out into a novel

Aus·wanderer der emigrant

aus|wandern *itr. V.; mit sein* emigrate (**nach, in** + *Akk.* to); ‹*tribe*› migrate

Aus·wanderung die emigration

auswärtig ['ausvɛrtɪç] *Adj.; nicht präd.* **a)** *(woanders befindlich)* non-local; **eine ~e Filiale/Bank** a branch/bank in another area/town; **b)** *(von woanders stammend)* ‹*student, guest, etc.*› from out of town; **c)** *(das Ausland betreffend)* foreign; **der Minister des Auswärtigen** the Foreign Minister; the Foreign Secretary *(Brit.)*; the Secretary of State *(Amer.)*; **das Auswärtige Amt** the Foreign Ministry; the Foreign and Commonwealth Office *(Brit.)*; the Foreign Office *(Brit. coll.)*; the State Department *(Amer.)*; **der ~e Dienst** the foreign service

auswärts *Adv.* **a)** *(nach außen)* outwards; **b)** *(nicht zu Hause)* ‹*sleep, live*› away from home; **~ essen** eat out; **c)** *(nicht am Ort)* in another town; *(Sport)* away; **ich habe ~ zu tun** I have to do a few things out of town; **~ sprechen** *(ugs. scherzh.)* talk foreign *(coll.)*

Auswärts-: ~sieg der *(Sport)* away win; **~spiel das** *(Sport)* away match *or* game

aus|waschen *unr. tr. V.* **a)** wash out; *(ausspülen)* rinse out; **b)** *(Geol.)* erode

auswechselbar *Adj.* changeable; exchangeable; *(untereinander)* interchangeable; *(ersetzbar)* replaceable

aus|wechseln 1. *tr. V.* **a)** change (**gegen** + *Akk.* for); **b)** *(ersetzen)* replace (**gegen** with); *(Sport)* substitute ‹*player*›; **A gegen B ~:** replace A by B; **sie war wie ausgewechselt** she was a different person. **2.** *itr. V. (Sport)* bring on a substitute; make a substitution

Auswechsel·spieler der *(Sport)* substitute

Auswechselung, Auswechslung die; ~, ~en change; *(Ersatz)* replacement; *(Sport)* substitution; **die ~ von A gegen B** the replacement of A by B

Aus·weg der way out (**aus** of); **der letzte ~ für jmdn. sein** be a last resort for sb.

ausweg·los 1. *Adj.* hopeless. **2.** *adv.* hopelessly

Ausweglosigkeit die; ~: hopelessness

aus|weichen *unr. itr. V.; mit sein* **a)** *(Platz machen)* make way (*Dat.* for); *(wegen Gefahren, Hindernissen)* get out of the way (*Dat.* of); **[nach] rechts/nach der Seite ~:** move to the right/move aside to make way/get out of the way; **b)** *(entgehen wollen)* get out of the way (*Dat.* of); **einem Schlag/Angriff ~:** dodge a blow/evade an attack; **c)** *(meiden)* **dem Feind ~:** avoid [contact with] the enemy; **jmdm./einem Kampf/Hindernis ~** *(auch fig.)* avoid sb./a fight/an obstacle; **einer Frage/Entscheidung/einem Zwang/Verbot ~:** evade a question/decision/obligation/ban; **~de Antworten** evasive answers; **der Beantwortung weiterer Fragen ~:** avoid answering any more questions; **d)** *(zurückgreifen)* **auf etw.** *(Akk.)* **~:** switch [over] to sth.

Ausweich·manöver das evasive manœuvre; **~** *Pl.* evasive action *sing.*; **das sind doch nur ~** *(fig.)* these are just evasions

aus|weinen 1. *refl. V.* have a good cry; **sie hat sich bei mir darüber ausgeweint** *(ugs.)* she had a cry on my shoulder about it. **2.** *tr. V. (geh.)* **seinen Kummer/sein Elend ~:** find relief for one's sorrow/misery in tears; *s. auch* **Auge a. 3.** *itr. V.* finish crying

Ausweis ['auswais] **der;** ~es, ~e **a)** card; *(Personal~, Kennkarte)* identity card; *(Mitglieds~)* membership card; **b)** *(österr. veralt.: Zeugnis)* certificate; *(Schulzeugnis)* report; **c)** *in* **nach** ~ *(Papierdt.) s.* **ausweislich**
aus|weisen 1. *unr. tr. V.* **a)** *(aus dem Land)* expel (**aus** from); **b)** *(erkennen lassen)* **jmdn. als etw.** ~: show that sb. is/was sth.; **seine Papiere wiesen ihn als ... aus** his papers proved *or* established his identity as ...; **c)** *(angeben)* reveal; **d)** *(zeigen)* demonstrate ⟨*ability, skill, etc.*⟩. **2.** *unr. refl. V.* **a)** *(seinen Ausweis zeigen)* prove *or* establish one's identity [by showing one's papers]; **können Sie sich ~?** do you have any means of identification?; **b)** *(sich erweisen)* **sich als etw.** ~: prove oneself to be sth.
ausweislich *Präp. mit Gen. (Papierdt.)* according to
Ausweis·papiere *Pl.* identity papers
Aus·weisung die expulsion (**aus** from)
aus|weiten 1. *tr. V. (dehnen)* stretch; *(fig.: erweitern)* expand (**zu** into); extend ⟨*jurisdiction, study*⟩. **2.** *refl. V.* **a)** *(zu weit werden)* stretch; **b)** *(sich erweitern)* expand; **sich zur Krise** ~: develop *or* grow into a crisis
Ausweitung die; ~, ~en expansion; *(des Studiums, der Gerichtsbarkeit)* extension
aus·wendig *Adv.* **etw.** ~ **können/lernen** know/learn sth. [off] by heart; **etw.** ~ **spielen/aufsagen** play/recite sth. from memory; **das kenne ich ja schon** ~ *(ugs. abwertend fig.)* I know it backwards; *s. auch* **inwendig**
Auswendig·lernen das learning by heart
aus|werfen *unr. tr. V.* **a)** cast ⟨*net, anchor, rope, line, etc.*⟩; **b)** *(herausschleudern)* throw out ⟨*sparks*⟩; ⟨*volcano*⟩ eject, spew out ⟨*lava, ash, etc.*⟩; eject ⟨*cartridge-case*⟩; **c)** *(geh.: ausspucken)* cough up ⟨*blood, phlegm, etc.*⟩; **d)** *(ausschaufeln)* throw up ⟨*earth, sand, etc.*⟩; **e)** *(anlegen)* dig [out] ⟨*trench, pit, ditch, etc.*⟩; **f)** *(zur Ausgabe bestimmen)* allocate ⟨*sum*⟩; pay [out] ⟨*dividend, premium, etc.*⟩; **g)** *(produzieren)* produce; turn out; **h)** **jmdm. ein Auge** ~: put sb.'s eye out *(by throwing sth.)*
auswertbar *Adj.* **a) leicht/schwer** ~ **sein** be easy/difficult to analyse and evaluate; **maschinell** ~: machine-analysable; **b)** *(nutzbar)* utilizable
aus|werten *tr. V.* **a)** analyse and evaluate; **b)** *(nutzbar machen)* utilize
Aus·wertung die a) analysis and evaluation; *(das Nutzbarmachen)* utilization; **b)** *(Ergebnis)* analysis
aus|wetzen *tr. V.: s.* **Scharte a**
aus|wickeln *tr. V.* **a)** *(Verpackung entfernen)* unwrap (**aus** from); **b)** unwind ⟨*person*⟩ (**aus** from)
aus|wiegen *unr. tr. V.* **a)** *(das Gewicht feststellen)* weigh; **b)** *(portionsweise)* weigh out; *s. auch* **ausgewogen 2, 3**
aus|winden *unr. tr. V. (südd., schweiz.)* wring out
aus|wirken *refl. V.* have an effect (**auf** + *Akk.* on); **sich in etw.** *(Dat.)* ~: result in sth.; **sich günstig/negativ** *usw.* ~: have a favourable/an unfavourable *etc.* effect (**auf** + *Akk.* on); **sich zu jmds. Vorteil** ~: work to sb.'s advantage
Aus·wirkung die *(Wirkung)* effect (**auf** + *Akk.* on); *(Folge)* consequence (**auf** + *Akk.* for); *(Rückwirkung)* repercussion (**auf** + *Akk.* on)
aus|wischen 1. *tr. V.* **a)** *(entfernen)* wipe ⟨*dirt etc.*⟩ out (**aus** of); **b)** *(säubern)* wipe [clean]; **sich** *(Dat.)* **die Augen** ~: wipe one's eyes; **c)** *in* **jmdm. eins** ~ *(ugs.)* get one's own back on sb. *(coll.)*. **2.** *itr. V.; mit sein (ugs.)* get away, escape (*Dat.* from)
aus|wringen *unr. tr. V. (bes. nordd.)* wring out
Aus·wuchs der a) *(Wucherung)* growth; excrescence *(Med., Bot.)*; *(Mißbildung)* deformity; **b)** *(fig.)* unhealthy product; *(Folge)* harmful consequence; *(Übersteigerung, Mißstand)* excess; **c)** *o. Pl. (Landw.)* premature sprouting of the kernel
aus|wuchten *tr. V. (Technik)* **die Räder** ~: balance the wheels
Aus·wurf der a) *(Med.)* sputum; **~/blutigen ~ haben** be bringing up phlegm/coughing up blood; **b)** *o. Pl. (das Auswerfen)* ejection; **c)** *(Lava, Geröll usw.)* ejected material; ejecta *pl.*; **d)** *o. Pl. (abwertend: Abschaum)* scum
aus|würfeln *tr. V.* **eine Runde Bier** *usw.* ~: throw dice to decide who will pay for a round of beer *etc.*
aus|zacken *tr. V.* serrate; *(mit der Zickzackschere)* pink ⟨*fabric*⟩
aus|zahlen 1. *tr. V.* **a)** *(aushändigen)* pay out; **sich** *(Dat.)* **einen Scheck ~ lassen** cash a cheque; **ausgezahlt bekommt er 1650 Mark** his net pay is 1,650 marks; **b)** *(entlohnen)* pay off; buy out ⟨*business partner, shareholder, etc.*⟩. **2.** *refl. V. (sich lohnen)* pay off; *(einbringen)* pay; **Verbrechen zahlen sich nicht aus** crime doesn't pay
aus|zählen *tr. V.* **a)** *(zählen)* count [up] ⟨*votes etc.*⟩; **b)** *(Boxen)* count out; **c)** *auch itr. (aussondern)* choose by counting; *(bei Kinderspielen)* count out
Aus·zahlung die a) *(das Aushändigen)* paying out; **b)** *(das Entlohnen)* paying off; *(eines Geschäftspartners)* buying out
Aus·zählung die counting [up]; **mit der ~ wurde bereits begonnen** the count had already started
aus|zanken *tr. V. (bes. ostmd.)* **jmdn.** ~: give sb. a scolding *or* a telling off
aus|zehren *tr. V. (geh.)* exhaust ⟨*person, soil*⟩; ⟨*disease*⟩ debilitate ⟨*person*⟩; *(abzehren)* emaciate ⟨*person*⟩
Auszehrung die; ~: **a)** *(Kräfteverfall)* emaciation; **b)** *(veralt.: Schwindsucht)* consumption
aus|zeichnen 1. *tr. V.* **a)** *(mit einem Preisschild)* mark, price (**mit** at); **etw. mit einem Preisschild** ~: put a price-tag on sth.; **b)** *(ehren)* honour; **jmdn. mit einem Orden** ~: decorate sb. [with a medal]; **jmdn./etw. mit einem Preis/Titel** ~: award a prize/title to sb./sth.; **c)** *(Druckw.: hervorheben)* display; **wichtige Stellen sind durch Kursivschrift ausgezeichnet** important sections are displayed in italics; **d)** *(Druckw.: zum Satz fertigmachen)* mark up; **e)** *(bevorzugt behandeln)* single out for special favour; *(ehren)* single out for special honour; **jmdn. mit** *od.* **durch etw.** ~: *(bevorzugt behandeln)* favour sb. with sth.; *(ehren)* honour sb. with sth.; **f)** *(kennzeichnen)* distinguish (**gegenüber, vor** + *Dat.* from); **Klugheit und Fleiß zeichneten ihn aus** he was distinguished by his intelligence and industriousness. **2.** *refl. V. (sich hervortun) (durch eine Eigenschaft)* stand out (**durch** for); *(durch Leistung)* ⟨*person*⟩ distinguish oneself (**durch** by); **sich als Politiker/im Sport** ~: distinguish oneself as a politician/at sport; **der Stoff zeichnet sich durch seine Haltbarkeit aus** the outstanding feature of the material is its durability; *s. auch* **ausgezeichnet 2, 3**
Aus·zeichnung die a) *o. Pl. (von Waren)* marking; **b)** *(Schildchen)* [price-]ticket *or* tag; **c)** *(Ehrung)* honouring; *(mit Orden)* decoration; *(Gunstbeweis)* mark of favour; **die ~ mit dem „Oscar" war sein größter Erfolg** the award of the Oscar was his greatest success; **die ~ der Preisträger** the presentation of awards to the winners; **d)** *(Orden)* decoration; *(Preis)* award; prize; **e)** *o. Pl. (Druckw.: das Hervorheben)* displaying; **f)** *o. Pl. (Druckw.: das Satzfertigmachen)* marking up; **g)** *(Druckw.: Zeichen im Manuskript)* mark; **h)** *in* **mit** ~: with distinction
Aus·zeit die *(Basketball, Volleyball, Schach)* time-out
ausziehbar *Adj.* extendible; telescopic ⟨*aerial*⟩; extending *attrib.* ⟨*ladder*⟩; sliding-leaf *attrib.* ⟨*table*⟩
aus|ziehen 1. *unr. tr. V.* **a)** *(vergrößern)* pull out ⟨*couch*⟩; extend ⟨*table, tripod, etc.*⟩; **b)** *(ablegen)* take off, remove ⟨*clothes*⟩; **c)** *(entkleiden)* undress; **sich** ~: undress; get undressed; **sich ganz/nackt** ~: strip off *or* undress completely; **jmdn. mit den Augen** ~ *(ugs.)* undress sb. with one's eyes; **d)** *(auszupfen)* pull out ⟨*hair etc.*⟩; **e)** *(herausschreiben)* extract ⟨*words, passages, etc.*⟩; **f)** *(nachzeichnen)* draw in; **mit Tusche** ~: ink in; **ausgezogene und punktierte Linien** continuous and dotted lines. **2.** *unr. itr. V.; mit sein* **a)** *(aus einer Wohnung usw.)* move out (**aus** of); **b)** *(losgehen)* set off; **auf Abenteuer/zur Jagd** ~: set off *or* out in search of adventure/for the hunt
Auszieh·tisch der extending table; sliding-leaf table
aus|zischen *tr. V.* hiss ⟨*speaker, play, etc.*⟩
Auszubildende der/die; *adj. Dekl. (bes. Amtsspr.)* trainee; *(im Handwerk)* apprentice
Aus·zug der a) *(das Ausziehen)* move; **b)** *(Abschrift)* extract; *(Bankw.)* statement; **c)** *(Textstelle)* extract; excerpt; **d)** *(das Hinausgehen)* departure; *(feierlich)* procession (**aus** out of); *(als Protest)* walk out; **der ~ der Kinder Israel** *(bibl.)* the Exodus; **e)** *(Extrakt)* extract; **f)** *(schweiz.) first age-group of men liable for military service*
auszugs·weise *Adv.* in extracts *or* excerpts; **etw. ~ lesen** read extracts from sth.
aus|zupfen *tr. V.* pluck out; pull out ⟨*weeds*⟩
autark [au'tark] *Adj.* **a)** *(Wirtsch.)* self-sufficient; autarkic *as tech. term;* **b)** *(geh.: eigenständig, selbstgenügsam)* independent; self-sufficient
Autarkie [autar'ki:] **die;** ~, ~n **a)** *(Wirtsch.)* self-sufficiency; autarky *as tech. term;* **b)** *(geh.: Selbstgenügsamkeit)* self-sufficiency; independence
authentisch [au'tɛntɪʃ] **1.** *Adj. (echt)* authentic; *(zuverlässig)* reliable ⟨*report*⟩. **2.** *adv.* authentically; ⟨*prove*⟩ reliably
Authentizität [autɛntitsi'tɛ:t] **die;** ~ *(geh.)* authenticity
Autismus [au'tɪsmʊs] **der;** ~ *(Med.)* autism
autistisch *(Med.)* **1.** *Adj.* autistic. **2.** *adv.* autistically
Auto ['auto] **das;** ~s, ~s car; automobile *(Amer.)*; ~ **fahren** drive [a car]; *(mitfahren)* go in the car; **mit dem ~ fahren** go by car; **er hat wie ein Auto geguckt** *(ugs.)* his eyes popped out of his head
Auto·atlas der road atlas
Auto·bahn die motorway *(Brit.)*; expressway *(Amer.)*; *(mit Gebühren)* turnpike *(Amer.)*; *(in Germany, Austria, Switzerland also)* autobahn
Autobahn-: **~auf·fahrt die** motorway access road *(Brit.)*; expressway entrance [ramp] *(Amer.)*; **~aus·fahrt die** motorway *(Brit.) or (Amer.)* expressway exit; **~dreieck das** motorway *(Brit.) or (Amer.)* expressway junction *or* merging point; **~gebühr die** motorway *(Brit.) or (Amer.)* expressway toll; **~kreuz das** motorway *(Brit.) or (Amer.)* expressway interchange; **~rast·stätte die** motorway *(Brit.) or (Amer.)* expressway service area; **~vignette die** *s.* **Gebührenvignette**; **~zubringer der** motorway *(Brit.) or (Amer.)* expressway approach road *or* feeder [road]
auto-, Auto-: **~biographie** [-----'-] **die** autobiography; **~biographisch** [----'--] **1.** *Adj.* autobiographical; **2.** *adv.* autobiographically; **~bus der** bus; *(Reisebus)* coach; **~car der** *(schweiz.)* coach
Autodafé [autoda'fe:] **das;** ~s, ~s **a)** *(hist.: Ketzerverbrennung)* auto-da-fé; **b)** *(Bücherverbrennung)* book-burning
Auto·didakt [-di'dakt] **der;** ~en, ~en,

Autodidaktin die; ~, ~nen autodidact; ~ **sein** be an autodidact; be self-taught
auto·didaktisch 1. *Adj.* self-study *attrib.*, self-teaching *attrib.* ‹*aids, materials*›; **~es Studium** self-study; self-instruction. **2.** *adv.* **sich ~ weiterbilden** continue one's education by self-study
Autodrom das; ~s, ~e a) *s.* **Motodrom; b)** *(österr.: für Skooter)* dodgems *pl.*; bumper cars *pl.*
auto-, Auto-: ~elektrik die automotive electrics *pl.*; *(Anlage)* [car] electrical system; **~erotik die** auto-eroticism *no art.*; **~fähre die** car ferry; **~fahren das** driving; motoring; **~fahrer der** [car-]driver; **~fahrer·gruß der** *(ugs.) driver's tapping of the forehead in response to stupid action by other driver, cyclist, pedestrian, etc.*; **~fahrt die** drive; **~frei** *Adj.* ‹*day, time*› when no cars are/were allowed on the road; ‹*place*› where no cars are/were allowed; **X ist ~frei** no cars are allowed in X; **~fried·hof der** *(ugs.)* car dump; **~gen** [~'ge:n] **1.** *Adj.* **a)** *(Technik)* **~genes Schneiden/Schweißen** gas *or* oxy-acetylene cutting/welding; **b)** *(Psych.)* **~genes Training** autogenic training; autogenics; **2.** *adv. (Technik)* **~gen schweißen/schneiden** weld/cut using an oxy-acetylene flame; **~gramm** [--'-] **das; ~s, ~e** autograph; **~gramm·jäger** [--'--] **der** autograph-hunter; **~hypnose** [---'--] **die** *(Psych.)* autohypnosis; **~karte die** road map; **~kino das** drive-in cinema; **~knakker der** *(ugs.)* car-burglar; **~kolonne die** line of cars; **~krat** [auto'kra:t] **der; ~en, ~en** autocrat; **~kratie** [---'-] **die; ~, ~n** autocracy; **~kratisch** [--'--] **1.** *Adj.* autocratic; **2.** *adv.* autocratically; **~marder der** car-burglar; **~marke die** make of car
Automat [auto'ma:t] **der; ~en, ~en a)** *(Verkaufs~)* [slot-]machine; vending-machine; *(Spiel~)* slot-machine; fruit-machine; *(Musik~)* juke-box; **b)** *(in der Produktion, auch fig.: Mensch)* robot; automaton; **ich bin doch kein ~:** I'm not a machine; **c)** *(Math., DV)* automaton
Automaten-: ~knacker der *(ugs.)* thief who breaks into slot-machines; **~restaurant das** vending-machine restaurant; automat *(Amer.)*
Automatik die; ~, ~en *(Technik)* **a)** *(Vorrichtung)* automatic control mechanism; *(Getriebe~)* automatic transmission; **eine ~ haben** ‹*car*› have automatic transmission; ‹*camera*› have automatic exposure control; **b)** *(Vorgang)* automatic process
Automatik·gurt der *(Kfz-W.)* inertia-reel belt
Automation die; ~: automation
automatisch *(auch fig.)* **1.** *Adj.* automatic. **2.** *adv.* automatically
automatisieren *tr. V.* automate
Automatisierung die; ~, ~en automation
Automatismus der; ~, Automatismen a) *(Technik, fig.)* automatic mechanism; **b)** *(Med., Biol., Psych.)* automatism *no art.*
Auto-: ~mechaniker der motor mechanic; **~minute die: zehn ~minuten entfernt sein** be ten minutes [away] by car; be ten minutes' drive [away]; **~mobil** [---'-] **das; ~s, ~e** *(geh.)* motor car; automobile *(Amer.)*
Automobil-: ~aus·stellung die motor show *(Brit.)*; automobile show *(Amer.)*; **~bau der** car manufacture; **~industrie die** motor industry
auto-, Auto-: ~mobilist [----'-] **der; ~en, ~en** *(bes. schweiz.)* motorist; car-driver; **~mobil·klub** [---'--] **der** motoring organization; **~nom** [--'-] **1.** *Adj.* autonomous; autonomic ‹*nervous system*›; **2.** *adv.* autonomously; **~nomie** [---'-] **die; ~, ~n** autonomy; **~nummer die** [car] registration number; **~papiere** *Pl.* car documents; **~pilot der** *(Flugw.)* autopilot
Autopsie [autɔ'psi:] **die; ~, ~n** *(Med.)* autopsy; post-mortem [examination]
Autor ['autɔr] **der; ~s, ~en** [-'to:rən] author
Auto-: ~radio das car radio; **~reifen der** car tyre; **~reise·zug der** Motorail train *(Brit.)*; auto train *(Amer.)*
Autoren·kollektiv das authors' collective
Auto-: ~rennen das *(Sportart)* motor *(Brit.) or (Amer.)* auto racing; *(Veranstaltung)* motor *(Brit.) or (Amer.)* auto race; **~reparatur die** car repair; repair to the/a car
Autorin die; ~, ~nen authoress; author
Autorisation [autoriza'tsio:n] **die; ~, ~en** authorization
autorisieren *tr. V.* authorize
autoritär [autori'tɛ:ɐ̯] **1.** *Adj.* authoritarian. **2.** *adv.* in an authoritarian manner
Autorität [autori'tɛ:t] **die; ~, ~en** authority; **als ~ auf einem Gebiet gelten** be regarded as an authority in a field
autoritativ [autorita'ti:f] **1.** *Adj. (geh.)* authoritative. **2.** *adv.* authoritatively
autoritäts·gläubig *Adj.* trusting in authority *pred.*
Autoritäts·gläubigkeit die trust in authority
Autor·korrektur die *(Buchw.)* author's correction; *(Fahne)* author's proof; *(Korrekturlesen)* author's reading of the proofs
Autorschaft die; ~: authorship
auto-, Auto-: ~schalter der drive-in counter; **~schlange die** queue *or* line of cars; **~schlosser der** *s.* **~mechaniker; ~schlüssel der** car key; **~skooter der** dodgem; bumper car; **~stopp der** hitch-hiking; hitching *(coll.)*; **per** *od.* **mit ~stopp fahren, ~stopp machen** hitch-hike; hitch *(coll.)*; **~strich der** *(ugs.) area where prostitutes wait to be picked up by kerb-crawlers*; **~stunde die: zwei ~stunden entfernt sein** be two hours [away] by car; be two hours' drive [away]; **~suggestion** [----'-] **die** *(Psych.)* auto-suggestion; **~telefon das** car telephone; **~test der** car test; **~tür die** car door; **~typie** [---'-] **die; ~, ~n** *(Druckw.)* half-tone photoengraving; **~unfall der** car accident; **~verkehr der** [motor] traffic; **~verleih der, ~vermietung die** car hire *(Brit.) or* rental firm *or* service; **~werkstatt die** garage; car repair shop; **~zubehör das** car accessories *pl.*
autsch [autʃ] *Interj.* ouch; ow
Au·wald der *s.* **Auenwald**
auweh [au've:] *Interj.* oh dear; *(Ausruf des Schmerzes)* ouch
auwei[a] [au'vai(a)] *Interj. (ugs.)* oh dear
Avance [a'vã:sə] **die; ~, ~n** *in* **jmdm. ~n machen** make advances to sb.; *(geh.: einen Flirt beginnen)* make advances to sb.
avancieren [avã'si:rən] *itr. V.; mit sein (geh.)* **zu etw. ~:** be promoted to sth. *(also iron.)*; rise to sth.; **zum Bestseller ~** *(fig.)* become a best seller
Avantgarde [avã'gardə] **die; ~, ~n** avant-garde; *(Politik)* vanguard *(fig.)*
Avantgardismus der; ~: avant-gardism
Avantgardist der; ~en, ~en member of the avant-garde; avant-gardist
avantgardistisch 1. *Adj.* avant-garde. **2.** *adv.* ‹*paint etc.*› in an avant-garde style
AvD [a:fau'de:] **der;** ~ *Abk.*: **Automobilclub von Deutschland** Automobile Club of Germany
Ave-Maria ['a:vema'ri:a] **das; ~[s], ~[s]** *(kath. Kirche)* Ave Maria; Hail Mary
Avers [a'vɛrs] **der; ~es, ~e** *(Münzk.)* obverse
Aversion [avɛr'zio:n] **die; ~, ~en** aversion; **eine ~** *od.* **~en gegen jmdn./etw. haben** have an aversion to sb./sth.
Avis [a'vi:] **der** *od.* **das;** ~ *(Kaufmannsspr., Bankw.)* advice; *(schriftlich)* advice note
avisieren [avi'zi:rən] *tr. V. (bes. Wirtsch.)* send notification of; advise *or* notify of
Aviso [a'vi:zo] **das; ~s, ~s** *(österr.) s.* **Avis**
Avocado [avo'ka:do] **die; ~, ~s** avocado [pear]
Axel ['aksl] **der; ~s, ~** *(Eis-, Rollkunstlauf)* axel
axial [a'ksia:l] *Adj. (Technik)* axial
Axiom [a'ksio:m] **das; ~s, ~e** axiom
Axiomatik [aksio'ma:tɪk] **die; ~ a)** *(Lehre)* axiomatics *sing.*; *no art.*; study of axioms; **b)** *(Verfahren)* axiomatization
axiomatisch 1. *Adj.* axiomatic. **2.** *adv.* axiomatically
Axt [akst] **die; ~, Äxte** ['ɛkstə] axe; **die ~ im Haus erspart den Zimmermann** *(Spr.)* it saves trouble if you don't have to get someone in; **sich benehmen wie die ~ im Walde** behave like a boor
Axt·hieb der blow of the/an axe
Azalee [atsa'le:ə], **Azalie** [a'tsa:liə] **die; ~, ~n** azalea
Azetat *s.* **Acetat**
Azimut [atsi'mu:t] **das** *od.* **der; ~s** *(Astron.)* azimuth
Azoren [a'tso:rən] *Pl.* **die ~:** the Azores
Azteke [ats'te:kə] **der; ~n, ~n** Aztec
Azteken·reich das Aztec empire
Azubi ['a:tsubi] **der; ~s, ~s/die; ~, ~s** *(ugs.) s.* **Auszubildende**
Azur [a'tsu:ɐ̯] **der; ~s** *(dichter.)* **a)** *(Farbe)* azure; **b)** *(Himmel)* azure *(literary)*
azur·blau, azurn *Adj. (geh.)* azure[-blue]
azyklisch ['atsy:klɪʃ] *Adj.* **a)** *(unregelmäßig)* irregular; **b)** *(Bot., Chemie)* acyclic

B

b, B [be:] **das; ~, ~ a)** *(Buchstabe)* b/B; **b)** *(Musik)* [key of] B flat; *s. auch* **a, A**
B die; ~ *Abk.* **Bundesstraße** ≈ A *(Brit.)*
BA [be:'|a:] **die;** ~ *Abk.* **Bundesanstalt für Arbeit**
BAB [be:|a:'be:] **die;** ~ *Abk.* **Bundesautobahn** ≈ M *(Brit.)*
babbeln ['babl̩n] *(landsch. ugs.) itr., tr. V. (auch abwertend)* babble
Babel ['ba:bl̩] **1. (das); ~s** Babel; **der Turm zu ~:** the Tower of Babel. **2. das; ~s, ~ a)** *(Sünden~)* hotbed of vice; sink of iniquity; **b)** *(vielsprachiger Ort)* babel
Baby ['be:bi] **das; ~s, ~s** *od.* **Babies** baby
Baby-: ~artikel *Pl.* baby goods; **~ausstattung die** layette
Babylon ['ba:bylɔn] **1. (das); ~s** Babylon. **2. das; ~s, ~s** *s.* **Babel 2**
Babylonien [baby'lo:niən] **(das); ~s** Babylonia
Babylonier der; ~s, ~: Babylonian
babylonisch *Adj.* Babylonian; **ein ~es Sprachgewirr** a babel of languages; **der Babylonische Turm** the Tower of Babel
baby-, Baby-: ~sitten [-sɪtn̩] *itr. V.; nur im Inf. (ugs.)* babysit; **~sitter** [-sɪtɐ] **der; ~s, ~, ~sitterin die; ~, ~nen** baby-sitter; **~sitting** [-sɪtɪŋ] **das; ~s** baby-sitting; **~speck der** *(ugs.)* puppy fat *(Brit.)*; baby fat *(Amer.)*; **~strich der** *(ugs.)* child pros-

tution; ~**waage die** baby scales; ~**wäsche die** baby clothes
bacchantisch [ba'xantɪʃ] *(geh.)* **1.** *Adj.* Bacchanalian. **2.** *adv.* in a Bacchanalian manner *or* fashion
Bach [bax] **der; ~[e]s, Bäche** ['bɛçə] **a)** stream; brook; **den ~ runtergehen** *(ugs.)* get pushed into the background; **b)** *(Rinnsal)* stream [of water]; *s. auch* **Bächlein**
bach·ab *Adv.* downstream
Bache ['baxə] *(Jägerspr.)* **die; ~, ~n** wild sow
Bächelchen ['bɛçlçən] **das; ~s, ~:** rivulet
Bach·forelle die brown trout
Bächlein ['bɛçlain] **das; ~s, ~:** rivulet; **ein ~ machen** *(Kinderspr.)* do a wee-wee *(child lang.)*
Bach·stelze die *(Motacilla alba alba)* white wagtail; *(M.a. yarrellii)* pied wagtail
Back [bak] **die; ~, ~en** *(Seemannsspr.)* **a)** *(Decksaufbau)* forecastle; fo'c's'le; **b)** *(Schüssel)* wooden serving bowl *(in which sailors' food is served)*; **c)** *(Tisch)* mess-table; **d)** *(Tischgemeinschaft)* mess
Back·blech das baking-sheet
Back·bord das *(Seew., Luftf.)* port [sɪde]; **über ~:** over the port side
backbord[s] ['bakbɔrt(s)] *Adv.* *(Seew., Luftf.)* on the port side
Bäckchen ['bɛkçən] **das; ~s, ~:** [little] cheek
Backe ['bakə] **die; ~, ~n a)** *(Wange)* cheek; **au ~!** *(ugs.)* oh heck *(coll.)*; *s. auch* **voll 1 a; b)** *(ugs.: Gesäß~)* buttock; cheek *(sl.)*; *s. auch* **abreißen c; c)** *(Seitenteil) (eines Schraubstocks)* jaw; cheek; *(eines Gewehrs)* cheek-piece; *(Brems~) (eines Autos)* shoe; *(eines Fahrrads)* block
[1]**backen** ['bakn̩] **1.** *unr. itr. V.* **a)** bake; do the baking; **ich backe immer selbst** I do all my own baking; **b)** *(garen)* ⟨*cake etc.*⟩ bake; **der Kuchen muß noch 10 Minuten ~:** the cake has to stay in the oven for another 10 minutes; **c)** ⟨*oven*⟩ bake. **2.** *unr. tr. V.* **a)** bake ⟨*cakes, bread, etc.*⟩; **ich backe vieles selbst** I do a lot of my own baking; *(fig.)* **das frisch gebackene Ehepaar** *(ugs.)* the newly-weds *pl. (coll.)*; **eine frisch gebackene Ärztin** *(ugs.)* a newly-fledged doctor; **b)** *(bes. südd.: braten)* roast; *(in der Bratpfanne)* fry; **c)** *(trocknen)* dry ⟨*fruit, mushrooms, etc.*⟩; bake ⟨*brick*⟩
[2]**backen** *(bes. nordd.)* **1.** *itr. V.* ⟨*snow, earth*⟩ stick (**an** + *Dat.* to). **2.** *tr. V.* stick (**an** + *Akk.* on to)
Backen-: ~bart der side-whiskers *pl.*; sideboards *pl. (sl.)*; **~bremse die** *(Technik) (eines Autos)* shoe brake; *(eines Fahrrads)* block brake; **~knochen der** cheek-bone; **~streich der** *(veralt.)* slap in the face; **~tasche die** [cheek] pouch; **~zahn der** molar; **kleiner** *od.* **vorderer/großer** *od.* **hinterer ~zahn** premolar/back molar
Bäcker ['bɛkɐ] **der; ~s, ~ a)** baker; **~ lernen** learn the baker's trade; learn to be a baker; **er will ~ werden/ist ~:** he wants to be/is a baker; **b)** *(Geschäft)* baker's [shop]; **zum ~ gehen** go to the baker's; **beim ~:** at the baker's
Back·erbsen *Pl. (Kochk.) small crisp round noodles added to soup*
Bäckerei die; ~, ~en a) *(Bäckerladen)* baker's [shop]; *(Backstube)* bakery; **b)** *o. Pl. (das Backen)* baking; **c)** *(Handwerk)* bakery trade; **d)** *(südd., österr.) s.* **Backwerk**
Bäcker-: ~geselle der journeyman baker; **~hand·werk das** bakery trade
Bäckerin die; ~, ~nen baker
Bäcker-: ~innung die bakers' guild; **~junge der** *(Gehilfe)* baker's boy *or* lad; *(Lehrling)* baker's apprentice; **~laden der** baker's shop; **~lehre die** baker's apprenticeship; **~lehrling der** baker's apprentice; **~meister der** master baker
Bäckers·frau die baker's wife
back-, Back-: ~fertig *Adj.* oven-ready; **~fisch der a)** *(Kochk.)* fried fish *(in breadcrumbs)*; **b)** *(veralt.: Mädchen)* teenager; teenage girl; **~form die** baking-tin *(Brit.)*; baking-pan *(Amer.)*; *(für Kuchen)* cake-tin *(Brit.)*; cake-pan *(Amer.)*; *(aus Ton)* earthenware baking-mould
Background ['bɛkgraunt] **der; ~s, ~s** background
Backhähnchen das fried chicken *(in breadcrumbs)*
Back-: ~hendl das *(österr.)*, **~huhn das** fried chicken *(in breadcrumbs)*; **~mulde die** *s.* **~trog; ~obst das** dried fruit; **~ofen der** oven; *(beim Bäcker)* [baker's] oven; **~pfeife die** *(bes. nordd.)* slap in the face; **~pfeifen·gesicht das** *(salopp abwertend) s.* **Ohrfeigengesicht; ~pflaume die** prune; **~pulver das** baking-powder; **~rohr das** *(südd., österr.)*, **~röhre die** oven; **~stein der** brick; **~stein·bau der;** *Pl.* **-bauten** brick building; **~stein·gotik die** *(Kunstwiss.)* brick Gothic [architecture]; **~stube die** bakery; bakehouse; **~trog der** kneading trough; dough tray *or* trough; **~waren** *Pl.* bread, cakes, and pastries; **~werk das;** *o. Pl.* biscuits *or (Amer.)* cookies and pastries
Bad [ba:t] **das; ~[e]s, Bäder** ['bɛ:dɐ] **a)** *(Wasser)* bath; **[sich** *(Dat.)*] **ein ~ einlaufen lassen** run [oneself] a bath; **b)** *(das Baden)* bath; *(das Schwimmen)* swim; *(im Meer o. ä.)* bathe; **ein ~ nehmen** *(geh.)* have *or* take a bath; *(schwimmen)* go for a swim; *(im Meer o. ä.)* bathe; **nach dem ~** after bathing; **beim ~ im Meer/***(fig.)* **in der Sonne** when bathing in the sea/sun-bathing; **jmdm. Bäder verordnen** *(Med.)* prescribe a course of baths for sb.; **c)** *(Badezimmer)* bathroom; **ein Zimmer mit ~:** a room with [private] bath; **d)** *(Schwimm~)* [swimming-]pool; swimming-bath; **e)** *(Heil~)* spa; *(See~)* [seaside] resort; **f)** *(Technik, Chemie)* bath
Bade-: ~anstalt die swimming baths *pl.* *(Brit.)*; public pool *(Amer.)*; **~an·zug der** swimming *or* bathing costume; swimsuit; **~arzt der** spa doctor; **~gast der a)** *(im Schwimmbad)* bather; swimmer; **b)** *(im Kurort)* visitor to a/the spa; **~hose die** swimming *or* bathing trunks *pl*; **~kabine die** changing-cubicle *(Brit.)*; locker *(Amer.)*; **~kappe die** swimming *or* bathing cap; **~kur die** course of treatment at a spa; **~mantel der** dressing-gown; bathrobe; *(Strandkleidung)* beach robe; **~matte die** bath-mat; **~meister der** swimming-pool attendant; **~mütze die** swimming *or* bathing cap
baden 1. *itr. V.* **a)** *(in der Wanne)* have *or* take a bath; bath; **warm/kalt ~:** have *or* take a hot/cold bath; **b)** *(schwimmen)* bathe; swim; **~ gehen** go for a bathe *or* a swim; go bathing *or* swimming; **[bei** *od.* **mit etw.] ~ gehen** *(ugs.)* come a cropper *(coll.)* [over sth.]. **2.** *tr. V.* bath ⟨*child, patient, etc.*⟩; bathe ⟨*wound, face, eye, etc.*⟩; **in Schweiß gebadet** *(fig.)* bathed in sweat; **du bist wohl als Kind zu heiß gebadet worden!** *(ugs. scherzh.)* you must have been dropped on your head as a baby
Baden ['ba:dn̩] **(das); ~s** Baden
Badener ['ba:dənɐ], *(ugs.)* **Badenser** [ba'dɛnzɐ] **der; ~s, ~:** inhabitant of Baden; *(von Geburt)* native of Baden; *s. auch* **Kölner**
Bade-: ~ofen der bath-water heater; **~ort der a)** *(Seebad)* [seaside] resort; **b)** *(Kurort)* spa; **~platz der** bathing-place
Bader der; ~s, ~ *(hist.)* barber[-surgeon]
Bäder *s.* **Bad**
Bade-: ~sachen *Pl.* bathing *or* swimming things; **~saison die** bathing *or* swimming season; *(im Kurort)* spa season; **~salz das** bath salts *pl.*; **~schwamm der** [bath] sponge; **~strand der** bathing-beach; **~tuch das** bath towel; **~wanne die** bath[-tub]; **~wasser das** bath water; **~wetter das** bathing weather; weather warm enough *or* suitable for bathing *or* swimming; **~zeit die a)** *(bei Heilbehandlungen)* immersion time; **b)** *(in ~anstalten)* swimming time; **die ~zeit ist beendet** the pool is now closing; **c)** *s.***~saison; ~zeug das** *(ugs.)* bathing *or* swimming things *pl.*; **~zimmer das** bathroom; **~zu·satz der** *(~salz)* bath salts; *(Schaumbad)* bubble bath
badisch *Adj.* of Baden *postpos.*; ⟨*wine, produce, etc.*⟩ from Baden; **die ~e Mundart** the Baden dialect; **das Badische** *(Sprachw.)* the Baden dialect; *(Region)* Baden
Badminton ['bɛtmɪntən] **das; ~:** badminton
baff [baf] *in* **~ sein** *(ugs.)* be flabbergasted
BAföG ['ba:fœk] **das; ~** *Abk.* **Bundesausbildungsförderungsgesetz; [300 DM] ~ bekommen** get a [state] grant [of 300 marks]
Bagage [ba'ga:ʒə] **die; ~, ~n** *(abwertend) (Familie)* tribe *(derog.)*; *(Gesindel)* rabble; crowd *(coll.)*; **die ganze ~:** the whole lot of them
Bagatell-: ~betrag der trifling amount; **~delikt das** *(Rechtsw.)* petty *or* minor offence
Bagatelle [baga'tɛlə] **die; ~, ~n a)** *(Kleinigkeit)* trifle; bagatelle; **das ist keine ~:** it's no mere trifle; **b)** *(Musik)* bagatelle
bagatellisieren 1. *tr. V.* trivialize; minimize. **2.** *itr. V.* trivialize matters
Bagatell-: ~sache die petty *or* minor case; **~schaden der** minor damage *no indef. art.*; **~schäden** minor damage *sing.*
Bagger ['bagɐ] **der; ~s, ~:** excavator; digger; *(Schwimmbagger)* dredger
Bagger·führer der excavator driver; *(eines Schwimmbaggers)* dredger master
baggern 1. *itr. V.* **a)** excavate; *(mit dem Schwimmbagger)* dredge; **b)** *(Volleyball)* dig the ball. **2.** *tr. V.* **a)** excavate; *(mit dem Schwimmbagger)* dredge; **b)** *(Volleyball)* dig ⟨*ball*⟩
Bagger·see der flooded gravel-pit
Baguette [ba'gɛt] **die; ~, ~n** baguette
bah [ba:] *Interj.* ugh
bäh [bɛ:] *Interj.* **a)** *(bei Ekel)* ugh; *(schadenfroh)* hee-hee; tee-hee; **b)** *(von Schafen)* baa
Bahama·inseln [ba'ha:ma-], **Bahamas** *Pl.* **die ~:** the Bahamas
bähen ['bɛ:ən] *tr. V. (südd., österr., schweiz.)* toast ⟨*bread, roll, etc.*⟩
Bahn [ba:n] **die; ~, ~en a)** *(Weg)* path; way; *(von Wasser)* course; **sich** *(Dat.)* **~ brechen** ⟨*invention, idea*⟩ establish itself; **einer Sache ~ brechen** pave *or* prepare the way for sth.; **jmdn. aus der ~ werfen** *od.* **bringen** *od.* **schleudern** *(fig.)* knock sb. sideways *(fig.)*; **auf die schiefe ~ geraten** *(fig.)* go astray; *s. auch* **ebnen; tüchtig 1 a; b)** *(Strecke)* path; *(Umlaufbahn)* orbit; *(einer Rakete)* [flight-] path; *(eines Geschosses)* trajectory; **sich in neuen ~en bewegen** *(fig.)* break new *or* fresh ground *(fig.)*; **etw. [wieder] in die richtige ~ lenken** *(fig.)* get sth. [back] on the right track *(fig.)*; **c)** *(Sport)* track; *(für Pferderennen)* course *(Brit.)*; track *(Amer.)*; *(für einzelne Teilnehmer)* lane; *(Kegel~)* alley; *(Schlitten~, Bob~)* run; *(Bowling~)* lane; **~ frei!** make way!; get out of the way!; **d)** *(Fahr~)* lane; **e)** *(Eisen~)* train; *(~netz)* railways *pl.*; railroad *pl. (Amer.)*; **jmdn. zur ~ bringen/an der ~ abholen** take sb. to/pick sb. up from the station; **mit der** *od.* **per ~:** by train; **~ fahren** go by train; **f)** *(Straßen~)* tram; streetcar *(Amer.)*; **g)** *(Schienenweg)* railway [track]; **h)** *(Streifen) (Stoff~)* length; *(Tapeten~)* strip; length; *(eines Rocks)* panel
bahn-, Bahn-: ~amtlich *Adj. (Amtsspr.)* official railway; **~arbeiter der** railway *or* *(Amer.)* railroad worker; **~beamte der** railway *or (Amer.)* railroad official; **~bre-**

chend *Adj.* pioneering; ~brechend für etw. sein pave *or* prepare the way for sth.; Bahnbrechendes geleistet haben have done pioneering work; ~brecher der, ~brecherin die pioneer; ~bus der railway bus
Bähnchen ['bɛːnçən] das; ~s, ~: narrow-gauge railway; *(in Vergnügungsparks usw.)* miniature railway
Bahn·damm der railway *or (Amer.)* railroad embankment
bahnen *tr. V.* clear ⟨*way, path*⟩; ⟨*river etc.*⟩ carve out ⟨*channel, bed*⟩; jmdm./einer Sache einen Weg ~: clear the *or* a way for sb./sth.; *(fig.)* pave *or* prepare the way for sb./sth.; sich *(Dat.)* einen Weg durch etw. ~: force a *or* one's way through sth.
bahnen·weise *Adv.* in lengths; *(bei Tapeten)* in strips *or* lengths
bahn-, Bahn-: ~fahrt die train *or* rail journey; ~frei *(Kaufmannsspr.) Adj., adv.* free on rail; ~gleis das railway *or (Amer.)* railroad track *or* line
Bahn·hof der [railway *or (Amer.)* railroad] station; ~ Käfertal Käfertal station; sich im/am ~ treffen meet at the station; ich verstehe nur ~ *(ugs.)* it's [all] double Dutch to me; [ein] großer ~ *(ugs.)* the red-carpet treatment; jmdm. einen großen ~ bereiten *(ugs.)* roll *or* put out the red carpet for sb.
Bahnhofs-: ~buch·handlung die station bookshop; *(Bücherstand)* station bookstall; ~gast·stätte die station restaurant; ~halle die station concourse; ~hotel das station hotel; ~mission die ≈ Travellers' Aid *(charitable organization for helping rail travellers in need of care or assistance)*; ~platz der square in front of the station; ~restaurant das station restaurant; ~vor·platz der station forecourt; ~vorstand der, ~vorsteher der station-master; ~wirtschaft die station buffet
bahn-, Bahn-: ~körper der permanent way; ~lagernd 1. *Adj.* to be collected from the station *postpos.*; 2. *adv.* Waren ~lagernd schicken send goods to await collection at the station; ~linie die railway *or (Amer.)* railroad line; ~meisterei die; ~, ~en permanent way *(Brit.) or (Amer.)* railroad maintenance department; ~polizei die railway *or (Amer.)* railroad police; ~post die travelling *or* railway post office *(Brit.)*; ~reise die train *or* rail journey; *(Pauschalreise)* package holiday *(Brit.) or (Amer.)* vacation trip by train; ~reisende der/die [rail] passenger; ~schranke die level-crossing *(Brit.) or (Amer.)* grade crossing barrier/gate; ~station die [railway *or (Amer.)* railroad] halt *(Brit.) or (Amer.)* stop; ~steig [~ʃtaik] der; ~[e]s, ~e [station] platform; ~steig·karte die platform ticket; ~über·führung die a) underbridge; underline bridge; b) *(ugs.: Brücke über die Bahnlinie)* bridge over the/a railway *or (Amer.)* railroad; ~über·gang der level-crossing *(Brit.)*; grade *or* railroad crossing *(Amer.)*; ~unter·führung die a) overbridge; overline bridge; b) *(ugs.: Brücke für die Eisenbahn)* railway *or (Amer.)* railroad bridge; ~verbindung die rail *(Brit.) or* train connection; ~wärter der level-crossing keeper *(Brit.)*; *(Streckenwärter)* linesman *(Brit.)*; trackman *(Amer.)*; ~wärter·häuschen das level-crossing keeper's hut *(Brit.)*
Bahre ['baːrə] die; ~, ~n a) *(Kranken~)* stretcher; b) *(Toten~)* bier
Bahr·tuch das; *Pl.* Bahrtücher pall
Bai [bai] die; ~, ~en bay
bairisch ['bairɪʃ] *Adj.* Bavarian
Baiser [bɛ'zeː] das; ~s, ~s meringue
Baisse ['bɛːsə] die; ~, ~n *(Börsenw.)* fall; auf ~ spekulieren speculate for a fall; bear
Baisse·spekulant der, **Baissier** [bɛ'sieː] der; ~s, ~s *(Börsenw.)* bear
Bajonett [bajo'nɛt] das; ~[e]s, ~e bayonet
Bajonett-: ~fassung die *(Elektrot.)* bayonet socket; ~verschluß der bayonet connection
Bajuware [baju'vaːrə] der; ~n, ~n *(scherzh.)* Bavarian
bajuwarisch *Adj. (scherzh.)* Bavarian
Bake ['baːkə] die; ~, ~n a) *(vor Eisenbahnübergängen, an Autobahnen)* countdown marker; b) *(zur Absperrung)* [movable] barrier; c) *(für Schiffe, Flugzeuge)* beacon; d) *(Vermessungsw.)* ranging-pole; range-pole
Bakelit Ⓦᶻ [bakə'liːt] das; ~s bakelite (P)
Baken·tonne die *(Seew.)* marker buoy
Bakkarat ['bakara(t)] das; ~s baccarat
Bakken ['bakn̩] der; ~s, ~ *(Skispringen)* [jumping-]hill
Bakschisch ['bakʃɪʃ] das; ~[e]s, ~e baksheesh
Bakterie [bak'teːriə] die; ~, ~n bacterium; voller ~n full of germs
bakteriell [bakte'riɛl] *(Med., Biol.)* 1. *Adj.* bacterial. 2. *adv.* ~ verursacht caused by bacteria
Bakterien-: ~kultur die bacterial culture; ~träger der carrier
Bakteriologe [bakterio'loːgə] der; ~n, ~n, **Bakteriologin** die; ~, ~nen bacteriologist
Bakteriologie die; ~: bacteriology *no art.*
bakteriologisch 1. *Adj.* bacteriological. 2. *adv.* ⟨*investigate, detect*⟩ using bacteriological methods
bakterizid [bakteri'tsiːt] *(Med.)* 1. *Adj.* bactericidal. 2. *adv.* ~ wirken act as a bactericide; have a bactericidal effect
Bakterizid das; ~s, ~e bactericide
Balalaika [bala'laika] die; ~, ~s *od.* Balalaiken balalaika
Balance [ba'laŋsə] die; ~, ~n balance; die ~ halten/verlieren keep/lose one's balance; die ~ zwischen ... und ... halten *(fig.)* keep a balance between ... and ...
Balance·akt der *(auch fig.)* balancing act
balancieren [balaŋ'siːrən] 1. *itr. V.; mit sein (auch fig.)* balance; über etw. *(Akk.)* ~: pick one's way precariously across sth. 2. *tr. V.* balance
Balancier·stange die balancing pole
balbieren [bal'biːrən] *tr. V. s.* Löffel a
bald [balt] *Adv.* a) eher ['eːɐ̯], am ehesten [-'eːəstn̩] *(in kurzer Zeit)* soon; *(leicht, rasch)* quickly; easily; ~ danach *od.* darauf soon afterwards; so ~ als *od.* wie möglich as soon as possible; möglichst ~: as soon as possible; so etwas kommt so ~ nicht wieder vor something like that won't happen again in a long while *or (coll.)* in a hurry; bist du ~ still? will you just be quiet; wird's ~? how much longer are you going to be?; get a move on, will you; bis *od.* auf ~: see you soon; seit ~ zwei Jahren for nearly two years; b) *(ugs.: fast)* almost; nearly; das ist ~ nicht mehr schön that's getting beyond a joke *(Brit.)*; that's not funny any more *(Amer.)*; c) *(veralt.)* in ~ ..., ~ ...: now ..., now ...; ~ so, ~ so now this way, now that
Baldachin ['baldaxiːn] der; ~s, ~e baldachin; *(über dem Bett)* canopy
Bälde ['bɛldə] in in ~ *(Papierdt.)* in the near future
baldig *Adj.; nicht präd.* speedy; quick; auf ~es Wiedersehen *(geh.)* see you again soon
baldigst *Adv.* as soon as possible
bald·möglichst *(Papierdt.) adv.* as soon as possible
baldowern [bal'doːvɐn] *(ugs.)* 1. *tr. V.* check out. 2. *itr. V.* check everything out
Baldrian ['baldriaːn] der; ~s, ~e valerian
Baldrian·tropfen *Pl.* valerian drops
Balearen [bale'aːrən] *Pl.* die ~: the Balearic Islands
[1]**Balg** [balk] der; ~[e]s, Bälge ['bɛlgə] a) *(von Tieren)* pelt; skin; *(eines Vogels)* skin; einem Tier den ~ abziehen skin an animal; b) *(salopp) (Bauch)* belly; *(Leib)* body; *s. auch* rücken 2a; c) *(Bot. od. südd.) (Haut)* skin; *(Hülle, Schote)* pod; d) *(Blase~; bei einer Kamera)* bellows *pl.*
[2]**Balg** das; ~[e]s, Bälger ['bɛlgɐ] *od.* Bälge ['bɛlgə] *(ugs., oft abwertend)* kid *(sl.)*; brat *(derog.)*
balgen *refl. V. (ugs.)* scrap *(coll.)*; sich um etw. ~: scrap *(coll.)* over sth.; *(fig.)* fight over sth.
Balgen der; ~s, ~ *(Fot.)* bellows *pl.*
Balgerei die; ~, ~en *(ugs.)* scrap *(coll.)*
Balg·geschwulst die sebaceous cyst
Balkan ['balkaːn] der; ~s a) *(~halbinsel)* der ~: the Balkans; auf dem ~: in the Balkans; b) *(Gebirge)* Balkan Mountains
Balkan·halb·insel die Balkan Peninsula
balkanisieren *tr. V. (auch fig.)* Balkanize
Balkanisierung die; ~, ~en *(auch fig.)* Balkanization
Balkan·staat der Balkan State
Balken ['balkn̩] der; ~s, ~ a) *(Holz~)* beam; *(aus Stahl)* beam; girder; *(Stütz~)* prop; shore; lügen, daß sich die ~ biegen tell a [complete] pack of lies; *s. auch* Splitter, Wasser a; b) *(Her.)* fess; c) *(Schwebe~)* beam; d) *(Musik)* cross-stroke; e) *(Waage~)* beam; f) *(Leichtathletik) (beim Weitsprung)* take-off board; *(beim Kugelstoßen)* stop-board; toe-board; g) *(dicker Strich)* thick stroke; *(fette Linie)* thick line
Balken-: ~decke die ceiling with wooden beams; ~konstruktion die timber-frame structure; ~über·schrift die *(Zeitungsw.)* banner headline; ~waage die beam-balance
Balkon [bal'kɔŋ, bal'koːn] der; ~s, ~s [bal'kɔŋs] *od.* ~e [bal'koːnə] a) balcony; b) *(Theater)* [dress] circle; *(im Kino)* circle; ~ sitzen sit in the [dress] circle; c) *(ugs.: Busen)* big boobs *pl. (sl.)*; big bust
Balkonien [bal'koːniən] (das); ~s *(ugs. scherzh.)* nach ~ fahren stay at home and relax on one's own balcony
Balkon-: ~pflanze die balcony plant; ~tür die balcony door; ~zimmer das room with a balcony
Ball [bal] der; ~[e]s, Bälle ['bɛlə] a) ball; ~ spielen play ball; am ~ sein have the ball; *(fig. ugs.)* be in touch; be on the ball *(coll.)*; am ~ bleiben keep [possession of] the ball; *(fig.)* stick *(coll.) or* keep at it; hart am ~ bleiben *(fig. ugs.)* stay right with it *(coll.)*; jmdm./einander/sich [gegenseitig] die Bälle zuspielen *od.* zuwerfen *(fig.)* feed sb./each other lines; b) *(Sportjargon: Schuß, Wurf)* ball; *(aufs Tor)* shot; c) *(Fest)* ball; d) *(Punkt) (Tennis)* point; *(Baseball)* ball; e) *(fig.: Kugel)* ball; der glühende ~ der Sonne *(geh.)* the fiery orb of the sun
ballaballa [bala'bala] *Adj.; nicht attr. (salopp)* crackers *(sl.)*; daft
Ballade [ba'laːdə] die; ~, ~n ballad
balladenhaft, balladesk [bala'dɛsk] *Adj.* ballad-like
Ballast [ba'last] der; ~[e]s, ~e ballast; *(fig.: in Buch, Artikel usw.)* padding; ~ abwerfen *od.* über Bord werfen shed *or* jettison ballast; *(fig.)* rid oneself of unnecessary burdens; jmdn./etw. als ~ empfinden *(fig.)* find sb./sth. a burden *or* an encumbrance
Ballast·stoffe *Pl. (Med.)* roughage *sing.*
Bällchen ['bɛlçən] das; ~s, ~: [little] ball
ballen 1. *tr. V.* clench ⟨*fist*⟩; crumple ⟨*paper*⟩ into a ball; press ⟨*snow etc.*⟩ into a ball; *s. auch* Faust; geballt 2. 2. *refl. V.* ⟨*clouds*⟩ gather, build up; ⟨*crowd*⟩ gather; ⟨*traffic*⟩ build up; ⟨*fist*⟩ clench; *(fig.)* ⟨*problems, difficulties, etc.*⟩ accumulate, mount up
Ballen der; ~s, ~ a) *(Packen)* bale; ein ~ Stroh/Stoff a bale of straw/cloth; b) *(Hand~, Fuß~)* ball; *(bei Tieren)* pad; c) *(Med.)* bunion; d) *(Wurzel~)* [root-]ball
ballen·weise *Adv.* by the bale
Ballerei die; ~, ~en *(ugs.)* shoot-out
Ballerina [balə'riːna] die; ~, Ballerinen ballerina; ballet-dancer

Baller·mann der; *Pl.* **-männer** *(ugs.)* shooting-iron *(sl.)*; shooter *(coll.)*
ballern *(ugs.)* **1.** *itr. V.* **a)** *(schießen)* fire [away]; bang away; **b)** *(schlagen)* bang, hammer **(gegen** on). **2.** *tr. V.* **a)** *(werfen)* hurl; **b) jmdm. eine ~:** sock sb. one *(sl.)*; **c)** *(Sportjargon)* fire ‹*ball*›
Ballett [ba'lɛt] **das; ~[e]s, ~e** ballet; **beim ~ sein** *(ugs.)* be a dancer with the ballet; be a ballet-dancer
Ballett·abend der evening ballet programme *or* performance
Ballettänzer der, Ballettänzerin die ballet-dancer
Balletteuse [balɛ'tø:zə] **die; ~, ~n** dancer
Ballett-: ~meister der ballet-master; **~musik die** ballet music; **~ratte die** *(ugs. scherzh.)* ballet-pupil; **~röckchen das** tutu; **~schuh der** ballet shoe; **~schule die** ballet school; **~tänzer** *s.* **Ballettänzer; ~truppe die** ballet company; *(im Gegensatz zu den Solotänzern)* corps de ballet
Ball-: ~führung die *(Ballspiele)* ball control; **~haus das** real-tennis court; *(hist.)* tennis court
Ballistik die; ~: ballistics *sing., no art.*
Ballistiker der; ~s, ~: ballistics expert
ballistisch 1. *Adj.; nicht präd.* ballistic. **2.** *adv.* ballistically
Ball-: ~junge der ballboy; **~kleid das** ball dress *or* gown; **~königin die** belle of the ball; **~künstler der** *(Fußballjargon)* artist with the ball
Ballon [ba'lɔŋ] **der; ~s, ~s a)** balloon; **b)** *(salopp: Kopf)* nut *(sl.)*; **eins auf** *od.* **an den ~ kriegen** get hit on the nut *(sl.)*; **[so] einen ~ kriegen** *od.* **bekommen** go as red as a beetroot; **c)** *(Flasche)* demijohn; **d)** *(Chemie)* carboy
Ballon-: ~mütze die Mao cap; **~reifen der** balloon tyre
Ball-: ~saal der ballroom; **~spiel das** ball game; **~spielen das; ~s** playing ball *no art.*; **~spielen verboten** no ball games; **~technik die** ball control
Ballung ['balʊŋ] **die; ~, ~en** build-up; concentration; *(fig.: von Problemen, Schwierigkeiten)* accumulation
Ballungs-: ~gebiet das, ~raum der conurbation; **~zentrum das** centre of population; **ein ~zentrum der chemischen Industrie** a centre of the chemical industry
Ball·wechsel der *(Tennis, Tischtennis, Badminton)* rally
Balsam ['balza:m] **der; ~s, ~e** balsam; balm; *(fig.)* balm; **~ auf jmds. Wunden gießen** *(fig.)* pour balm on sb.'s wounds
balsamieren *s.* **einbalsamieren**
balsamisch 1. *Adj.* **a)** *(wohlriechend)* balmy; fragrant; *(lindernd)* soothing ‹*cream, ointment, etc.*›; **b)** *(Balsam enthaltend)* balsamic. **2.** *adv.* fragrantly ‹*scented*›; soothingly ‹*cooling*›
Balte ['baltə] **der; ~n, ~n, Baltin die; ~, ~nen** person *or* man/woman from the Baltic; Balt; **er ist ~:** he comes from the Baltic
Baltikum ['baltikʊm] **das; ~s** Baltic States *pl.*
baltisch *Adj.* Baltic
Balustrade [balʊs'tra:də] **die; ~, ~n** balustrade
Balz [balts] **die; ~, ~en a)** *(Liebesspiel)* courtship display; **b)** *(Zeit)* mating season
balzen *itr. V.* perform its/their courtship display
Balz·zeit die mating season
Bambi ['bambi] **das; ~s, ~s** *(Kinderspr.)* little deer
Bambule [bam'bu:lə] **die; ~, ~n** *(salopp)* shindy; **~ machen** go on the rampage
Bambus ['bambʊs] **der; ~** *od.* **~ses, ~se** bamboo
Bambus-: ~rohr das bamboo [cane]; **~sprossen** *Pl.* bamboo shoots; **~vorhang der** *(Politik)* bamboo curtain

Bammel ['baml̩] **der; ~s** *(ugs.)* **~ vor jmdm./etw. haben** be scared stiff of sb./sth. *(coll.)*
bammeln *(bes. nordd.) s.* **baumeln**
banal [ba'na:l] **1.** *Adj.* **a)** *(abwertend: platt)* banal; trite, banal ‹*speech, reply, response, excuse*›; **b)** *(gewöhnlich)* commonplace; ordinary. **2.** *adv.* **a)** *(abwertend: platt)* banally; tritely; **b)** *(gewöhnlich)* **~ gesagt** to put it plainly and simply
banalisieren *tr. V.* make ‹*idea*› seem trite; trivialize ‹*idea, feeling*›
Banalität die; ~, ~en a) *o. Pl. (das Banalsein) s.* **banal 1a, b:** banality; triteness; commonplaceness; ordinariness; **b)** *(Äußerung)* banality
Banane [ba'na:nə] **die; ~, ~n** banana
Bananen-: ~dampfer der banana boat; **~flanke die** *(Fußballjargon)* curving cross; **~republik die** *(abwertend)* banana republic; **~schale die** banana-skin; **~split, das; ~, ~s** banana split; **~stecker der** *(Elektrot.)* banana plug
Banause [ba'nauzə] **der; ~n, ~n** *(abwertend)* philistine
banausenhaft *(abwertend)* **1.** *Adj.* philistine. **2.** *adv.* in a philistine way
Banausentum das; ~s *(abwertend)* philistinism *no indef. art.*
banausisch *s.* **banausenhaft**
band [bant] *1. u. 3. Pers. Sg. Prät. v.* **binden**
[1]Band das; ~[e]s, Bänder ['bɛndɐ] **a)** *(Schmuck~; auch fig.)* ribbon; *(Haar~, Hut~)* band; *(Schürzen~)* string; *(zum Zusammenhalten, Kleben)* tape; *(für Sicherheitsgurte usw.)* webbing; **das Blaue ~:** the Blue Ribband *or* Ribbon; **das Bundesverdienstkreuz am ~e** the Federal Service Cross on a ribbon; **b)** *(Meß~)* tape-measure; measuring-tape; *(Farb~)* ribbon; *(Ziel~, Isolier~)* tape; **c)** *(Ton~)* [magnetic] tape; **etw. auf ~** *(Akk.)* **aufnehmen** tape[-record] sth.; **etw. auf ~** *(Akk.)* **sprechen/diktieren** record/dictate sth. on to tape; **d)** *(Förder~)* conveyor belt; *(Fließ~)* production line; **am ~ stehen** work on the production line; **vom ~ laufen** come off the production line; **etw. auf ~** *(Akk.)* **legen** put sth. into production; **am laufenden ~** *(ugs.)* nonstop; continuously; **e)** *(Anat.)* ligament; **f)** *(Säge~)* band; **g)** *(Beschlag)* hinge; **h)** *(Metall~ um Ballen usw.)* band; *(Faß~)* hoop; **i)** *(Nachrichtenw.)* [frequency] band
[2]Band der; ~[e]s, Bände ['bɛndə] volume; **etw. spricht Bände** *(ugs.)* sth. speaks volumes
[3]Band [bɛnt] **die; ~, ~s** band; *(Beat~, Rock~ usw.)* band; group
[4]Band das; ~[e]s, ~e a) *(dichter. veralt.: Fessel)* bond; fetter; shackle; **jmdn. in ~e schlagen** clap sb. in irons; **in ~en liegen** lie in chains; **b)** *(fig.: Unfreiheit)* **~e** shackles; **frei von allen ~en** free from all ties; **c)** *(fig.: Bindung)* **ein ~ der Liebe/Freundschaft** a bond of love/friendship; **die ~e des Bluts** the ties of blood; **verwandtschaftliche ~e** family ties; **zarte ~e knüpfen** *(geh., scherzh.)* start a romance
Bandage [ban'da:ʒə] **die; ~, ~n** bandage; **mit harten ~n kämpfen** *(fig.)* fight with the gloves off *(fig.)*
bandagieren [banda'ʒi:rən] *tr. V.* bandage
Band-: ~aufnahme die tape recording; **~breite die a)** *(Nachrichtenw.)* bandwidth; **b)** *(fig.: Bereich, Umfang)* range
[1]Bändchen ['bɛntçən] **das; ~s, ~:** little ribbon
[2]Bändchen das; ~s, ~ *(kleines Buch)* little volume
[1]Bande ['bandə] **die; ~, ~n a)** *(Verbrecher~)* gang; **b)** *(ugs.: Gruppe)* mob *(sl.)*; crew
[2]Bande die; ~, ~n a) *(Sport)* [perimeter] barrier; *(mit Reklame)* billboards *pl.*; *(Billard)* cushion; *(der Reitbahn)* rail; *(der Kegelbahn)* side; edge; *(im Zirkus)* ring fence; *(der Eisbahn)* boards *pl.*; **b)** *(Physik)* band

Band·eisen das strip iron
Bandel ['bandl̩] **das; ~s, ~** *(bayr., österr. ugs.)*, **Bändel** ['bɛndl̩] **der; ~s, ~** *(schweiz. ugs.) s.* **Bendel**
Banden-: ~bildung die formation of an armed gang; **~chef der** *(ugs.)*, **~führer der** gang leader; **~krieg der** gang war; **~spektrum das** *(Physik)* band spectrum; **~unwesen das** *s.* **~wesen; ~werbung die** *advertising on hoardings around the perimeter of a football pitch etc.*; **~wesen das** gangsterism; activities of the criminal gangs
Bänder *s.* **[1]Band**
Banderole [bandə'ro:lə] **die; ~, ~n a)** *(Steuer~)* revenue stamp *or* seal; **b)** *(Kunstwiss.)* banderole
Bänder-: ~riß der *(Med.)* torn ligament; **~zerrung die** *(Med.)* pulled ligament
Band-: ~förderer der *(Technik)* conveyor belt; **~geschwindigkeit die** tape speed
-bändig [-bɛndɪç] *adj. (Buchw.)* -volume; **viel~/acht~:** multi-volume/eight-volume ‹*encyclopaedia etc.*›; ‹*encyclopaedia etc.*› in many/eight volumes
bändigen ['bɛndɪgn̩] *tr. V.* tame ‹*animal*›; control ‹*person, anger, child, thoughts, voice*›; *(fig.)* control, master, overcome ‹*desire, urge, etc.*›; bring ‹*fire*› under control; keep ‹*floods, river, natural forces*› in check; overcome ‹*tiredness*›
Bändigung die; ~: *s.* **bändigen:** taming; controlling; mastering; overcoming; **die ~ von Naturgewalten** keeping natural forces in check
Bandit [ban'di:t] **der; ~en, ~en** bandit; brigand; *(fam. scherzh.)* rascal; *(fig. abwertend)* robber; **einarmiger ~** *(ugs.)* one-armed bandit *(sl.)*
Band·keramik die *(Archäol.)* **a)** Bandkeramik; band ceramics; **~en** Bandkeramik pieces; **b)** *o. Pl. (Epoche)* Danubian I stage
Bandleader ['bɛntli:dɐ] **der; ~s, ~:** bandleader
Band-: ~maß das tape-measure; measuring-tape; **~nudeln** *Pl.* tagliatelle *sing.*; **~säge die** band-saw; **~scheibe die** [intervertebral] disc; **~scheiben·schaden der** slipped disc; **~scheiben·vorfall der** *(Med.)* prolapsed intervertebral disc *(Med.)*; slipped disc; **~stahl der** strip steel; steel strip; **~wurm der** tapeworm; **~wurm·satz der** *(ugs.)* interminable sentence
bang [baŋ] *s.* **bange**
Bang·büx[e] die *(nordd. ugs.)* scaredy-cat *(coll.)*; chicken *(coll.)*
bange; banger, bangst... *od.* **bänger** [bɛŋɐ], **bängst...** [bɛŋst...] **1.** *Adj.* afraid; scared; *(besorgt)* anxious; worried; **mir ist/wurde ~ [zumute]** I am *or* feel/became scared *or* frightened; **das wirst du schon schaffen, da ist mir gar nicht ~:** you'll manage that all right, I'm sure of it; **jmdm.** *od.* **jmdn. ~ machen** scare *or* frighten sb.; **ihm wurde ~ und bänger** he became more and more afraid *or* scared; **mir ist ~ vor ihm/davor** I'm afraid *or* frightened *or* scared of him/it; **~ machen** *od.* **Bangemachen gilt nicht** *(ugs.)*; *(gekniffen wird nicht)* you can't chicken out now *(sl.)*; *(ich lasse mich nicht ängstigen)* you can't put the wind up *(sl.) or* scare me. **2.** *adv.* anxiously
Bange die; ~ *(bes. nordd.)* fear; **[nur] keine ~!** don't be afraid; *(sei nicht besorgt)* don't worry; **da habe ich keine ~:** I've no fears about that; **[große] ~ vor jmdm./etw. haben** be [very] scared *or* frightened of sb./sth.
bangen *itr. V.* be anxious *or* worried; **um jmdn./etw. ~:** be anxious *or* worried about sb./sth.; worry about sb./sth.; **ihm bangt [es] vor dir/der Operation** he's afraid *or* frightened of you/the operation
Bangigkeit die; ~ *(Furcht)* fear; *(Beklemmung)* apprehension; *(Besorgnis)* anxiety

Bangladesch [baŋgla'dɛʃ] **(das); ~s** Bangladesh
bänglich ['bɛŋlɪç] **1.** *Adj.* nervous; timid. **2.** *adv.* nervously; timidly
Bạngnis die; ~, ~se *(geh.) (Furcht)* fear; *(Besorgnis)* anxiety; *(Beklommenheit)* trepidation
Banjo ['banjo] **das; ~s, ~s** banjo
¹Bank [baŋk] **die; ~, Bänke** ['bɛŋkə] **a)** *(Sitz~, Parlaments~, Schul~; Sport: Ersatz~, Turngerät)* bench; *(mit Lehne)* bench seat; *(Kirchen~)* pew; *(Anklage~)* dock; **setz dich in deine ~!** *(Schul~)* sit at your desk; **etw. auf die lange ~ schieben** *(ugs.)* put sth. off; **vor leeren Bänken spielen** play to an empty house; **durch die ~** *(ugs.)* every single one; the whole lot of them; **b)** *(Werk~)* work-bench; *(Dreh~)* lathe; **c)** *(Sand~)* sandbank; **d)** *(Austern~)* bed; *(Korallen~)* [coral] reef; **e)** *(Nebel~, Wolken~)* bank; **f)** *(Geol.)* layer; bed; **g)** *(Ringen)* crouch [position]
²Bạnk die; ~, ~en a) bank; **Geld auf der ~ [liegen] haben** have money in the bank; **ein Konto bei einer ~ eröffnen** open an account with a bank; **bei einer ~ arbeiten** *od.* **sein** work in a bank; **Geld bei der ~ abheben** withdraw money from the bank; **b)** *(Glücksspiel)* bank; **die ~ sprengen** break the bank; **die ~ halten** be [the] banker; have the bank
Bạnk-: ~angestellte der/die; *adj. Dekl., (veralt.)* **~beamte der** bank employee
Bänkchen ['bɛŋkçən] **das; ~s, ~:** little *or* small bench; *(mit Lehne)* little *or* small seat
Bạnk-: ~direktor der director of a/the bank; **~ein·bruch der** bank raid
Bänkel- ['bɛŋkl-]: **~lied das** street ballad; **~sang der** performance of street ballads; **~sänger der** singer of street ballads
Bạnker der; ~s, ~ *(ugs.)* banker
bankerott [baŋkə'rɔt] *s.* **bankrott**
Bankert ['baŋkɐt] **der; ~s, ~e** *(veralt. abwertend)* bastard
¹Bankett [baŋ'kɛt] **das; ~[e]s, ~e** banquet
²Bankẹtt das; ~[e]s, ~e, Bankẹtte die; ~, ~n a) *(an Straßen)* shoulder; *(unbefestigt)* verge; **„~[e] nicht befahrbar"** 'soft verges'; **b)** *(an Häusern)* footing
Bạnk-: ~fach das a) *o. Pl. (Berufsgebiet)* banking *no art.;* banking profession; **b)** *(Schließfach)* safe-deposit box; **~filiale die** branch of a/the bank; **~gebäude das** bank; **~geheimnis das** *(Wirtsch.)* bankers' duty to maintain confidentiality; **~gut·haben das** bank balance; **~halter der** *(Glücksspiel)* banker; **~haus das** banking house
Bankier [baŋ'kie:] **der; ~s, ~s** banker
Bạnk-: ~kauf·mann der [qualified] bank/building society/stock market clerk; **~konto das** bank account; **~kredit der** bank loan; **~lehre die;** *o. Pl.* training as a bank clerk; **~leit·zahl die** bank sorting code; **~nachbar der** *(Schulw.)* **er war mein ~nachbar** he sat next to me [at school]; **~note die** banknote; bill *(Amer.)*; **~raub der** bank robbery; **~räuber der** bank robber
bankrott [baŋ'krɔt] *Adj.* **a)** bankrupt; **jmdn./etw. ~ machen** bankrupt sb./sth.; **~ gehen** go bankrupt; **b)** *(fig.) (moralisch)* bankrupt; *(politisch)* discredited
Bankrọtt der; ~[e]s, ~e a) bankruptcy; **seinen ~ anmelden** *od.* **ansagen** *od.* **erklären** declare oneself bankrupt; **~ machen** go bankrupt; **b)** *(fig.)* downfall; *(moralisch)* bankruptcy
Bankrọtt·erklärung die declaration of bankruptcy; *(fig.)* declaration of [one's own] failure
Bankrotteur [baŋkrɔ'tø:ɐ̯] **der; ~s, ~e** bankrupt
Bạnk-: ~überfall der bank raid; **~üblich** *Adj.* **das ist ~üblich** that is normal banking practice; **~übliche Zinssätze** normal bank interest rates; **~verbindung die** particulars of one's bank account; **~verkehr der** bank transactions *pl.;* **~vollmacht die** third-party mandate; *(given by firm)* signing powers *pl.;* **~wesen das;** *o. Pl.* banking system
Bann [ban] **der; ~[e]s a)** *(hist.)* excommunication; **den ~ über jmdn. aussprechen** *od.* **verhängen, jmdn. mit dem ~ belegen, jmdn. in den ~ tun** excommunicate sb.; **b)** *(geh.: Wirkung)* spell; **in jmds. ~/im ~e einer Sache stehen** be under sb.'s spell/under the spell of sth.; **jmdn. in seinen ~ schlagen** *od.* **ziehen** cast one's/its spell over sb.
Bạnn·bulle die *(hist.)* bull of excommunication
bạnnen *tr. V.* **a)** *(festhalten)* entrance; captivate; **[wie] gebannt** ‹*watch, listen, etc.*› spellbound; **ein Geschehen auf die Leinwand/auf Zelluloid ~** *(fig.)* capture an event on canvas/film; *s. auch* **Platte a; b)** *(vertreiben)* exorcize ‹*spirit*›; avert, ward off ‹*danger*›; banish ‹*worries, poverty*›; *(geh.)* banish ‹*disease*›; **c)** *(hist.: exkommunizieren)* excommunicate
Bạnner das; ~s, ~: banner; **das ~ der Freiheit/des Fortschritts hochhalten** *(fig.)* hold high the banner of freedom/progress
Bạnner·träger der *(auch fig.)* standard-bearer
Bạnn·fluch der *(hist.)* excommunication; anathema; **den ~ gegen jmdn. schleudern** excommunicate *or* anathematize sb.
bạnnig *Adv. (nordd. ugs.)* extremely; terribly *(coll.)*
Bạnn-: ~kreis der *(geh.)* influence; **in jmds. ~kreis/in den ~kreis einer Sache geraten** fall under sb.'s influence/the influence of sth.; **~meile die** *restricted area surrounding government buildings, where no public meetings or marches may be held;* **~spruch der** *(hist.)* excommunication; anathema
Bạntam- ['bantam-]: **~gewicht das** *(Schwerathletik)* **a)** *o. Pl.* bantamweight; *s. auch* **Fliegengewicht; b)** *(Sportler) s.* **~gewichtler; ~gewichtler** [~gə'vɪçtlɐ] **der; ~s, ~:** bantamweight; **~huhn das** bantam
Bantu ['bantu] **der; ~[s], ~[s]** Bantu
Bạntu-: ~frau die Bantu woman; **~sprache die** Bantu language
Baptismus [bap'tɪsmʊs] **der; ~:** Baptist faith
Baptịst der; ~en, ~en Baptist
Baptisterium [baptɪs'te:ri̯ʊm] **das; ~s, Baptisterien** *(christl. Rel., Kunstwiss.)* **a)** *(Gebäude)* baptistery; **b)** *(Taufbecken)* [baptismal] font; *(in einer Baptistenkapelle)* baptistery
Baptịstin die; ~, ~nen Baptist
baptịstisch *Adj.* Baptist
bar [ba:ɐ̯] **1.** *Adj.* **a)** *nicht präd.* cash; **~es Geld** cash; **in ~:** in cash; **etw. [in] ~ bezahlen** pay for sth. in cash; pay cash for sth.; **Verkauf/Reparaturen nur gegen ~:** cash sales only/repairs must be prepaid in cash; **gegen ~ verkauft/gekauft** sold/bought for cash; *s. auch* **Münze a; b)** *nicht präd. (pur)* pure; sheer; utter, pure, sheer ‹*nonsense*›; absolute ‹*reality*›; **c)** *(veralt.: nackt)* bare; **~en Hauptes** bareheaded; **einer Sache** *(Gen.)* **~ [sein]** *(geh.)* [be] devoid of *or* without sth. **2.** *adv.* in cash; **~ auf die Hand** *(ugs.) od. (salopp)* **Kralle** cash on the nail
¹Bar die; ~, ~s a) *(Nachtlokal)* night-club; bar; **b)** *(Theke)* bar
²Bar das; ~s, ~s; *bei Maßangaben ungebeugt (Physik, Met.)* bar
¹Bär [bɛ:ɐ̯] **der; ~en, ~en** bear; **ein richtiger ~** *(ugs.)* a hulking great brute of a man *(fig. coll.)*; **ich bin hungrig wie ein ~** *(ugs.)* I'm so hungry I could eat a horse *(coll.)*; **er ist stark/schläft wie ein ~** *(ugs.)* he is as strong as an ox/sleeps like a log; **der Große/Kleine ~** *(Astron.)* the Great/Little Bear; Ursa Major/Minor; **jmdm. einen ~en aufbinden** have sb. on *(coll.)*; pull sb.'s leg
²Bär der; ~s, ~en *(Technik)* ram
Baracke [ba'rakə] **die; ~, ~n** hut; **eine elende ~:** a miserable shack
Barạcken-: ~lager das hutted camp; **~siedlung die** shanty town
Barbar [bar'ba:ɐ̯] **der; ~en, ~en** *(auch hist.)* barbarian
Barbarei die; ~, ~en a) *(Roheit)* barbarity; **b)** *(Kulturlosigkeit)* barbarism *no indef. art.*
Barbarin die; ~, ~nen *(auch hist.)* barbarian
barbarisch 1. *Adj.* **a)** *(roh)* barbarous; savage; barbarous, brutal ‹*torture*›; **b)** *(unzivilisiert)* barbaric, uncivilized ‹*person*›; **c)** *(furchtbar)* dreadful *(coll.)*, terrible *(coll.)*‹*noise, cold, etc.*›; **d)** *(hist.)* barbarian. **2.** *adv.* **a)** *(roh)* barbarously; ‹*torture*› barbarously, brutally; **b)** *(unzivilisiert)* barbarically; in an uncivilized manner; **c)** *(sehr)* dreadfully *(coll.)*; terribly *(coll.)*
Barbarịsmus der; ~, Barbarịsmen *(Sprachw.)* barbarism
Barbe ['barbə] **die; ~, ~n** *(Zool.)* barbel
bärbeißig [-baisɪç] **1.** *Adj.* gruff. **2.** *adv.* gruffly
Bar-: ~bestand der *(Buchf.)* cash in hand; *(Finanzw.)* cash reserve; **~betrag der** cash sum; **ein ~betrag von 800 DM** a sum of 800 marks in cash
Barbier [bar'bi:ɐ̯] **der; ~s, ~e** *(veralt., noch scherzh.)* barber
barbieren *tr. V. (veralt.)* **jmdn. ~:** shave sb.; *(den Bart beschneiden)* trim sb.'s beard
Barbiturat [barbitu'ra:t] **das; ~s, ~e** *(Pharm.)* barbiturate
Barbitur·säure [barbi'tu:ɐ̯-] **die** *(Chemie)* barbituric acid
bar-: ~brüstig [-brʏstɪç] *Adj.;* bare-breasted; **~busig** [-bu:zɪç] *Adj.* topless ‹*pin-up, waitress, etc.*›
Barchent ['barçn̩t] **der; ~[e]s, ~e** barchent
Bar·dame die barmaid; *(verhüll.: Prostituierte)* hostess
Barde ['bardə] **der; ~n, ~n** bard
bären-, Bären-: ~dienst der *in* **jmdm. einen ~dienst erweisen** do sb. a disservice; **~dreck der** *(südd., österr.)* liquorice; **~fell das** bearskin; **~fell·mütze die** bearskin; **~führer der a)** *(veralt.)* bear-trainer; **b)** *(ugs. scherzh.: Fremdenführer)* guide; **für jmdn. den ~führer abgeben/spielen** show *or* shepherd sb. around; **~haut die** *in* **auf der ~haut liegen** *(ugs.)* lounge *or* laze about; **~hunger der** *(ugs.)* **einen ~hunger haben/kriegen** be famished *(coll.) or* starving *(coll.)*/get famished *(coll.) or* ravenous *(coll.)*; **~kräfte** *Pl. (ugs.)* the strength *sing.* of an ox; **~kräfte haben** be as strong as an ox; **~natur die** *(ugs.)* very tough constitution; **eine ~natur haben** be very tough; **~ruhe die** *(ugs.)* complete unflappability *(coll.)*; **eine ~ruhe haben** be completely unflappable *(coll.)*; **~stạrk** *Adj.* as strong as an ox *postpos.*
Barett [ba'rɛt] **das; ~[e]s, ~e** *(eines Geistlichen)* biretta; *(eines Richters, Professors)* cap; *(Baskenmütze)* beret
bar-, Bar-: ~fuß *indekl. Adj.* barefooted; **~fuß herumlaufen/gehen** run about/go barefoot; **~fuß·arzt der** barefoot doctor; **~füßer der; ~s, ~:** discalced *or* barefoot monk; **~füßerin die; ~, ~nen** discalced nun; **~füßig** [~fy:sɪç] *Adj. (geh.)* barefooted
barg [bark] *1. u. 3. Pers. Sg. Prät. v.* **bergen**
bar-, Bar-: ~geld das cash; **~geld·los 1.** *Adj.* cashless; **2.** *adv.* without using cash; **~geschäft das** *(Kaufmannsspr.)* cash transaction; **~häuptig** [~hɔyptɪç] *Adj. (geh.)* bareheaded; **~hocker der** bar stool
Bärin ['bɛ:rɪn] **die; ~, ~nen** she-bear
Bariton ['ba(:)ritɔn] **der; ~s, ~e a)** baritone [voice]; **b)** *o. Pl. (im Chor)* baritones *pl.;* **c)**

o. Pl. (Partie) baritone part; **d)** *(Sänger)* baritone
Bariton·schlüssel der *(Musik)* baritone clef
Barium ['ba:ri̯ʊm] **das; ~s** *(Chemie)* barium
Bark [bark] **die; ~, ~en** barque
Barkarole [barka'ro:lə] **die; ~, ~n** *(Musik)* barcarole
Barkasse [bar'kasə] **die; ~, ~n** launch
Bar·kauf der *(Kaufmannsspr.)* cash purchase; **3% Skonto bei ~ geben** give a 3% discount on cash purchases
Barke ['barkə] **die; ~, ~n** [small] rowing-boat
Bar·keeper ['ba:ɐ̯ki:pɐ] **der; ~s, ~:** barman; barkeeper *(Amer.)*
Bärlapp ['bɛ:ɐ̯lap] **der; ~s, ~e** *(Bot.)* lycopod
Bar-: ~mädchen das bar hostess; **~mann der;** *Pl.* **~männer** barman; barkeeper *(Amer.)*
barmen ['barmən] *itr. V. (nordd.)* lament *(literary)*
barmherzig [barm'hɛrtsɪç] *(geh.)* **1.** *Adj.* merciful; compassionate; *(mildtätig)* charitable; **selig sind die Barmherzigen** *(bibl.)* blessed are the merciful; **~er Gott/Himmel!** merciful God/Heaven!; **die Barmherzigen Brüder/Schwestern** the hospitallers/ the Sisters of Mercy; *s. auch* **Samariter. 2.** *adv.* mercifully; compassionately; *(mildtätig)* charitably
Barmherzigkeit die; ~ *(geh.)* mercy; compassion; *(Mildtätigkeit)* charity; **gegen jmdn. ~ üben** show compassion/charity towards sb.
Bar·mittel *Pl.* cash resources
Bar·mixer der barman; barkeeper *(Amer.)*
barock [ba'rɔk] **1.** *Adj.* **a)** baroque; **b)** *(schwülstig)* baroque, florid ⟨*style etc.*⟩; *(üppig)* voluptuous ⟨*figure*⟩. **2.** *adv.* **a)** ⟨*conceived, designed, etc.*⟩ in the baroque style; **b)** *(schwülstig)* floridly
Barock das *od.* **der; ~[s] a)** *(Stil)* baroque; **das Zeitalter des ~:** the baroque period *or* age; **b)** *(Zeit)* baroque period *or* age
Barock-: ~dichtung die baroque poetry; **~engel der** baroque angel; **~kirche die** baroque church; **~musik die** baroque music; **~zeit die** baroque period *or* age
Barometer [baro'me:tɐ] **das** barometer; **das ~ steht auf Sturm** the barometer is pointing to 'Storm'; *(fig.)* the atmosphere is very strained
Barometer·stand der barometer reading
baro·metrisch *Adj.* barometric
Baron [ba'ro:n] **der; ~s, ~e** baron; *(als Anrede)* **[Herr] ~:** ≈ my lord
Baroneß, Baronesse [baro'nɛs(ə)] **die; ~, Baronessen** baroness *(baron's daughter)*; *(als Anrede)* **[verehrte] ~:** ≈ my lady
Baronin die; ~, ~nen baroness *(baron's wife)*; *(als Anrede)* **[Frau] ~:** ≈ my lady
Barrakuda [bara'ku:da] **der; ~s, ~s** *(Zool.)* barracuda
Barras ['baras] **der; ~** *(Soldatenspr.)* army; **beim ~:** in the army; **zum ~ müssen** have to go into the army
Barrel ['bɛrəl] **das; ~s, ~s** barrel; **10 ~[s] Öl** ten barrels of oil
Barren ['barən] **der; ~s, ~ a)** *(Gold~, Silber~ usw.)* bar; **b)** *(Sport)* parallel bars *pl.*; **c)** *(südd., österr.: Trog)* trough
Barriere [ba'ri̯e:rə] **die; ~, ~n** *(auch fig.)* barrier
Barrikade [bari'ka:də] **die; ~, ~n** barricade; **auf die ~n gehen** *od.* **steigen** *(ugs.)* go on the warpath
Barrikaden·kampf der fight on the barricades; **Barrikadenkämpfe** fighting *sing.* on the barricades
barsch [barʃ] **1.** *Adj.* curt. **2.** *adv.* curtly; **jmdn. ~ anfahren** snap at sb.
Barsch der; ~[e]s, ~e *(Zool.)* perch
Barschaft die; ~, ~en [ready] cash; **seine ganze ~ bestand aus 20 Mark** all he had was 20 marks
Bar·scheck der open *or* uncrossed cheque
Barschheit die; ~: curtness
Barsoi [bar'zɔy] **der; ~s, ~s** borzoi
Bar·sortiment das *(Buchhandel)* book wholesaler's; book distribution centre
barst [barst] *1. u. 3. Pers. Sg. Prät. v.* **bersten**
Bart [ba:ɐ̯t] **der; ~[e]s, Bärte** ['bɛ:ɐ̯tə] **a)** *(Kinn~)* beard; *(Oberlippen~, Schnurr~)* moustache; **er bekommt jetzt einen ~:** his beard is starting to grow; **sich** *(Dat.)* **einen ~ wachsen** *od.* **stehen lassen** grow a beard; **einen acht Tage alten ~ haben** have a week's growth on one's chin; *(fig.)* **der ~ ist ab** *(ugs.)* that's quite enough; **wenn er das noch mal macht, dann ist der ~ aber ab** if he does it once more, that'll be it *(coll.)*; **der Witz hat [so] einen ~** *(ugs.)* that joke is as old as the hills; **beim ~e des Propheten** *(scherzh.)* cross my heart; **etw. in seinen ~ brummen** *od.* **murmeln** mumble sth.; **jmdm. um den ~ gehen** *(abwertend)* butter sb. up; **b)** *(von Ziegen, Vögeln, Getreide, Muscheln)* beard; *(von Katzen, Mäusen, Robben)* whiskers *pl.*; **c)** *(am Schlüssel)* bit
Bart·binde die moustache-trainer
Bärtchen ['bɛ:ɐ̯tçən] **das; ~s, ~:** [small] beard; *(Schnurr~)* [thin] moustache
Barteln ['bartl̩n] *Pl. (Zool.)* barbels
Barten·wal der *(Zool.)* whalebone whale
Bart-: ~faden der *(Zool.)* barbel; **~flaum der** down; **~flechte die a)** *(an Bäumen)* lichen of the family Usneaceae; *(Usnea)* old man's beard; **b)** *(beim Menschen)* sycosis; **~geier der** *(Zool.)* bearded vulture; **~haar das** beard; *(von Robben)* whiskers *pl.*
Bar·theke die bar
Barthel ['bartl̩] *in* **wissen, wo ~ [den] Most holt** *(ugs.)* know every trick in the book
bärtig ['bɛ:ɐ̯tɪç] *Adj.* bearded; **Bärtige** men with beards
bart-, Bart-: ~los *Adj.* beardless; **~nelke die** sweet william; **~stoppel die** piece of stubble; **~stoppeln** stubble *sing.*; **~tracht die** style of beard; **~träger der** man with a beard; **~wuchs der** growth of beard; **starken ~wuchs haben** have a strong growth of beard; **~wuchs bei Frauen** women's facial hair
Bar·vermögen das cash resources *pl.*
Baryt [ba'ry:t] **der; ~[e]s, ~e** *(Mineral.)* barytes
Bar-: ~zahlung die cash payment; **bei ~zahlung** for cash payment; if payment is made in cash; **~zahlungs·rabatt der** cash discount
Basalt [ba'zalt] **der; ~[e]s, ~e** basalt
Basal·temperatur [ba'za:l-] **die** *(Med.)* basal body temperature
Basar [ba'za:ɐ̯] **der; ~s, ~e a)** *(im Orient, Wohltätigkeits~)* bazaar; **b)** *(DDR) (Warenhaus)* department store; *(Ladenstraße)* shopping precinct *or (Amer.)* mall
¹Base ['ba:zə] **die; ~, ~n a)** *(veralt.: Cousine)* cousin; **b)** *(schweiz.: Tante)* aunt
²Base die; ~, ~n *(Chemie)* base
Baseball ['beɪsbɔ:l] **der; ~s** baseball
Basedow- ['ba:zədo-]: **~-Augen** *Pl.* bulging eyes; **~-Krankheit, Basedowsche Krankheit die** *(Med.)* exophthalmic goitre; Graves' disease
Basel ['ba:zl̩] **(das); ~s** Basle
Basen *s.* **Basis, Base**
basieren *itr. V.* **auf etw.** *(Dat.)* **~:** be based on sth.
Basilika [ba'zi:lika] **die; ~, Basiliken** *(Kunstwiss.)* basilica
Basilikum [ba'zi:likʊm] **das; ~s** basil
Basilisk [bazi'lɪsk] **der; ~en, ~en** *(Fabeltier, Leguan)* basilisk
Basilisken·blick der basilisk stare
Basis ['ba:zɪs] **die; ~, Basen a)** *(Grundlage)* basis; **auf einer festen ~ ruhen** have a firm basis; **etw. auf eine feste ~ stellen** put sth. on a firm foundation *(fig.)*; **b)** *(Math., Architekt., Fläche, Zahl, Milit.)* base; **c)** *(marx.)* base; **~ und Überbau** base and superstructure; **d)** *(Politik)* grass roots *pl.*; **an der ~ arbeiten** work at grass-roots level
Basis·arbeit die; *o. Pl. (Politik)* work at grass-roots level
basisch *(Chemie)* **1.** *Adj.* basic. **2.** *adv.* ⟨*react*⟩ as a base
Basis-: ~demokratie die *(Politik)* grass-roots democracy; **~gruppe die** *(Politik)* action group *(usually left-wing)*; **~lager das** base camp
Baske ['baskə] **der; ~n, ~n** Basque
Basken-: ~land das Basque region; **~mütze die** beret
Basket·ball ['ba(:)skətbal] **der** basketball
Baskin die; ~, ~nen Basque
baskisch *Adj.* Basque
Basler ['ba:zlɐ] **1.** *Adj.; nicht präd.* of Basle *postpos.* **2. der; ~s, ~:** native of Basle; *(Einwohner)* inhabitant of Basle; *s. auch* **Kölner**
Bas·relief ['ba-] **das** *(Kunstwiss.)* bas-relief
baß [bas] *Adv. in* **~ erstaunt sein** *(veralt.)* be quite taken aback
Baß der; Basses, Bässe ['bɛsə] *(Musik)* **a)** *(Stimmlage)* bass [voice]; **b)** *o. Pl. (im Chor)* basses *pl.*; bass section; **c)** *o. Pl. (Partie)* bass part; **d)** *(Sänger)* bass; **e)** *(Instrument)* double-bass; bass *(coll.)*; **f)** *(Lautsprecher)* bass speaker; woofer
Baß·bariton der bass-baritone
Basset ['bæsɪt] **der; ~s, ~s** basset[-hound]
Bassett·horn [ba'sɛt-] **das** basset-horn
Baß·geige die *(volkst.)* double-bass
Bassin [ba'sɛ̃:] **das; ~s, ~s** *(Schwimm~)* pool; *(im Garten)* pond
Bassist der; ~en, ~en *(Musik)* **a)** *(Sänger)* bass; **b)** *(Instrumentalist)* double-bass player; bassist; *(in einer Rockband)* bass guitarist
Baß-: ~klarinette die bass clarinet; **~lautsprecher der** bass loudspeaker; woofer; **~saite die** bass string; **~schlüssel der** *(Musik)* bass clef; **~stimme die** bass voice
Bast [bast] **der; ~[e]s, ~e a)** bast; *(Raffia~)* raffia; **b)** *(Jägerspr.)* velvet
basta ['basta] *Interj. (ugs.)* that's enough; **und damit ~!** and that's that
Bastard ['bastart] **der; ~s, ~e a)** *(veralt.: uneheliches Kind)* bastard; **b)** *(Biol.)* hybrid; **c)** *(salopp)* bastard
Bastard·schrift die *(Druckw.)* bastard type
Bastel-: ~arbeit die a) *(Gegenstand)* piece of handicraft work; **~arbeiten** handicraft work *sing.*; **b)** *o. Pl.* handicraft work; **~ecke die** *(in einer Zeitung, Zeitschrift)* handicraft corner *or* column
Bastelei die; ~, ~en; a) *(Gegenstand)* piece of handicraft work; **~en** handicraft work *sing.*; **b)** *(ugs.: das Basteln)* handicraft work
basteln ['bastl̩n] **1.** *tr. V.* make; make, build ⟨*model, device*⟩. **2.** *itr. V. (Bastelarbeiten herstellen)* make things [with one's hands]; do handicraft work; **an etw.** *(Dat.)* **~:** be working on sth.; *(etw. herstellen)* be making sth.; *(etw. laienhaft bearbeiten)* tinker with sth.; **sein Hobby ist Basteln** his hobby is making things [with his hands]; his hobby is handicraft work
Bast·faser die bast fibre
Bastille [bas'ti:jə] **die; ~:** Bastille
Bastion [bas'ti̯o:n] **die; ~, ~en** bastion
Bastler ['bastlɐ] **der; ~s, ~, Bastlerin die; ~, ~nen** handicraft enthusiast; **ein guter/leidenschaftlicher ~ sein** be good *or* clever with one's hands/love making [and repairing] things
Bastonade [basto'na:də] **die; ~, ~n** bastinado
Bast·rock der bast skirt; *(aus Raffia)* raffia skirt
bat [ba:t] *1. u. 3. Pers. Sg. Prät. v.* **bitten**

BAT [be:|a:'te:] *Abk.* **Bundesangestelltentarif**

Bataille [ba'taljə] **die;** ~, ~**n** *(veralt.)* battle

Bataillon [batal'jo:n] **das;** ~**s,** ~**e** *(Milit.)* battalion

Bataillons-: ~führer der, ~kommandeur der *(Milit.)* battalion commander

Bathy·sphäre [baty-] **die** *(Meereskunde)* abyssal zone

Batik ['ba:tɪk] **der;** ~**s,** ~**en** *od.* **die;** ~, ~**en** batik

batiken 1. *tr. V.* **etw.** ~: decorate sth. with batik work. **2.** *itr. V.* do batik work

Batist [ba'tɪst] **der;** ~**[e]s,** ~**e** batiste

batisten *Adj.; nicht präd.* batiste

Batterie [batə'ri:] **die;** ~, ~**n; a)** *(Milit., Elektrot., Technik)* battery; **b)** *(ugs.: große Anzahl)* battery; *(von Flaschen)* rows *pl.*

batterie-, Batterie-: ~betrieb der; *o. Pl.* battery operation; **auf ~betrieb laufen** run on batteries; **~betrieben** *Adj.* battery-operated; **~gerät das** battery[-operated] device; *(Radio)* battery-set

Batzen ['batsn̩] **der;** ~**s,** ~ **a)** *(ugs.: Klumpen)* lump; **b)** *(ugs.: Menge)* pile *(coll.)*; **ein [schöner** *od.* **ganzer]** ~ **Geld** a pile *(coll.)* [of money]; **c)** *(MA.: Münze)* batz

¹Bau [bau̯] **der;** ~**[e]s,** ~**ten a)** *o. Pl. (Errichtung)* building; construction; **im** ~ **sein, sich im** ~ **befinden** be under construction; **mit dem** ~ **[von etw.] beginnen** start construction [of sth.]; start building [sth.]; **b)** *(Gebäude)* building; **c)** *o. Pl. (~stelle)* building site; **auf dem** ~ **arbeiten** *(Bauarbeiter sein)* be in the building trade; **auf den** *od.* **zum** ~ **gehen** *(Bauarbeiter werden)* go into the building trade; **vom** ~ **sein** *(fig. ugs.)* be an expert; **d)** *o. Pl. (Struktur)* structure; **e)** *o. Pl. (Körper~)* build; **von schmalem** ~ **sein** be slenderly built; have a slender physique; **f)** *o. Pl. (Landw.: An~)* growing

²Bau [bau̯] **der;** ~**[e]s,** ~**e a)** *(Höhle) (Kaninchen~)* burrow; hole; *(Fuchs~)* earth; *(Wolfs~)* lair; *(Dachs~)* sett; earth; *(Biber~)* lodge; **b)** *o. Pl. (ugs.: Wohnung)* **nicht aus dem** ~ **gehen/kommen** not stick *or* put one's nose outside the door *(coll.)*; **c)** *o. Pl. (Soldatenspr.: Strafe)* glasshouse *(Mil. sl.)*; **er bekam sieben Tage** ~: he got seven days in the glasshouse; **d)** *o. Pl. (Bergmannsspr.: Stollen)* workings *pl.*

-bau der; ~**s** *(Landw.)* -growing

Bau-: ~ab·schnitt der phase *or* stage of building; **~amt das** department of planning and building inspection; **~arbeiten** *Pl.* building *or* construction work *sing.*; *(Straßenarbeiten)* road-works; **~arbeiter der** building *or* construction worker; **~art die** type of construction; **ein Haus in italienischer ~art** a house built in the Italian style; **~auf·sicht die** supervision of building *or* construction [work]; **~beginn der** start of building *or* construction; **~boom der** building boom; **~bude die** site hut; **~büro das** site office

Bauch [baux] **der;** ~**[e]s, Bäuche** ['bɔyçə] **a)** stomach; belly; abdomen *(Anat.)*; tummy *(coll.)*; *(fig.: von Schiffen, Flugzeugen)* belly; **mir tut der** ~ **weh** I have [a] stomach-ache *or (coll.)* tummy-ache; **sich** *(Dat.)* **den** ~ **vollschlagen** *(ugs.)* stuff oneself *(coll.)*; **jmdm. den** ~ **aufschneiden** *(salopp)* cut sb. open; **ein Kind im** ~ **haben** *(ugs.)* have a baby on the way; **er hat ihr einen dicken** ~ **gemacht** *(salopp)* he put her in the club *(sl.)*; **ein voller** ~ **studiert nicht gern** *(Spr.)* you can't work hard on a full stomach; **ich habe nichts im** ~ *(ugs.)* I haven't had anything to eat; **sich** *(Dat.)* **[vor Lachen] den** ~ **halten** *(ugs.)* split one's sides [with laughing]; *(fig.)* **auf den** ~ **fallen** *(ugs.)* come a cropper *(sl.)* **(mit** with); **vor jmdm. auf dem** ~ **liegen** *od.* **kriechen** *(ugs. abwertend)* crawl *or* grovel to sb.; **aus dem hohlen** ~ *(salopp)* off the top of one's head *(sl.)*; **b)** *(Wölbung)* paunch; corporation *(coll.)*; *(fig.: eines Kruges usw.)* belly; **c)** *(Kochk.) (beim Schwein)* belly; *(beim Kalb)* flank

Bauch-: ~an·satz der beginnings *pl.* of a paunch; **~atmung die;** *o. Pl.* abdominal respiration; **~binde die a)** woollen body-belt; **b)** *(ugs.: bei Zigarren, Büchern)* band; **~decke die** *(Med.)* abdominal wall; **~fell das** *(Anat.)* peritoneum; **~fleisch das** *(Kochk.) (vom Schwein)* belly pork; *(vom Rind)* flank; **~flosse die** *(Zool.)* ventral fin; **~gegend die;** *o. Pl.* stomach region; region of the stomach; **~grimmen das** *(veralt.)* stomach ache *or* pains *pl.*; **~höhle die** *(Anat.)* abdominal cavity; **~höhlenschwangerschaft die** *(Med.)* abdominal pregnancy

bauchig *Adj.* bulbous

Bauch-: ~klatscher [~klatʃɐ] **der;** ~**s,** ~ *(ugs.)* belly-flop *(coll.)*; **~kneifen das;** ~**s** stomach-ache *or* pains *pl.*; **~laden der** vendor's tray; **~lage die;** *o. Pl.* prone position; **in der ~lage schlafen** sleep on one's front; **~landung die** *(ugs.)* belly-landing

Bäuchlein ['bɔyçlai̯n] **das;** ~**s,** ~: stomach; tummy *(coll.)*

bäuchlings ['bɔyçlɪŋs] *Adv.* on one's stomach

bauch-, Bauch-: ~muskel der; *meist Pl.* stomach muscle; **~nabel der** *(ugs.)* belly-button *(coll.)*; tummy-button *(coll.)*; **~pinseln** *tr. V.: s.* **gebauchpinselt; ~reden** *itr. V.: nur Inf. gebr.* ventriloquize; **~redner der** ventriloquist; **~schmerz der;** *meist Pl.* stomach pain; **~schmerzen** stomach-ache *sing.*; stomach pains; **~schuß der** shot in the stomach; *(Verwundung)* stomach wound; **~speck der a)** *(Kochk.)* belly of pork; **b)** *(ugs.: Fettansatz)* spare tyre *(coll.)*; **~speichel·drüse die** pancreas; **~tanz der** belly-dance; **~tanzen** *itr. V.; nur Inf. gebr.* belly-dance; **~tänzerin die** belly-dancer

Bauchung die; ~, ~**en** bulge

Bauch-: ~weh das *(ugs.)* tummy-ache *(coll.)*; stomach-ache; **~welle die** *(Turnen)* hip-circle

Baude ['baudə] **die;** ~, ~**n** *(ostmd.)* mountain hut; *(Berggasthof)* mountain inn

Bau-: ~denkmal das architectural monument; **~element das** component

bauen 1. *tr. V.* **a)** build, construct ⟨*house, road, bridge, etc.*⟩; build ⟨*nest, lair*⟩; make ⟨*burrow*⟩; **sich** *(Dat.)* **ein Haus** ~: have a house built; **sich** *(Dat.)* **sein Haus selbst** ~: build one's own house; *s. auch* **Bett a; b)** *(entwickeln, herstellen)* build ⟨*model, vehicle, aircraft, organ*⟩; make ⟨*violin, piano*⟩; **sich** *(Dat.)* **einen Anzug** ~ **lassen** *(ugs. scherzh.)* have a suit made; **einen Satz** ~ *(Sprachw.)* construct a sentence; **c)** *(ugs.)* **das Abitur/seinen Doktor** ~: do one's Abitur/Ph.D.; **d)** *(ugs.: verursachen)* **einen Unfall** ~: have an accident; **e)** *(Landw.: an~)* grow; **f)** *(veralt.: bestellen)* cultivate. **2.** *itr. V.* **a)** build; **wir wollen** ~: we want to build a house; *(bauen lassen)* we want to have a house built; **zur Zeit wird nicht viel gebaut** there's not much building going on at the moment; **solide/großzügig** ~: build solidly/on a lavish scale; **modern** ~: build in a modern style; **hoch** ~: put up high-rise buildings; **an etw.** *(Dat.)* ~: do building work on sth.; **b)** *(vertrauen)* **auf jmdn./etw.** ~: rely on sb./sth.

¹Bauer ['bauɐ] **der;** ~**n,** ~**n a)** *(Landwirt)* farmer; *(als Vertreter einer ärmlichen Klasse)* peasant; *(ugs. abwertend)* peasant; **die dümmsten** ~**n haben die dicksten Kartoffeln** *(abwertend)* fortune favours fools *(prov.)*; **was der** ~ **nicht kennt, das frißt er nicht** *(abwertend)* some people won't eat anything they've never seen before; **b)** *(beim Schach)* pawn; **c)** *(in Kartenspielen)* jack; **d)** *(beim Kegeln)* corner; copper

²Bauer das *od.* **der;** ~**s,** ~: [bird-]cage

-bauer der; ~**s,** ~ *(Bauw.)* -constructor

Bäuerchen ['bɔyɐçən] **das;** ~**s,** ~ **a) [ein]** ~ **machen** *(Kinderspr.)* burp; **b)** *s.* **Bäuerlein**

Bäuerin ['bɔyərɪn] **die;** ~, ~**nen** *(Landwirtin)* [lady] farmer; *(Frau eines Landwirts)* farmer's wife; *(als Vertreterin einer ärmlichen Klasse)* peasant [woman]

Bäuerlein ['bɔyɐlai̯n] **das;** ~**s,** ~: [simple] peasant

bäuerlich ['bɔyɐlɪç] **1.** *Adj. (landwirtschaftlich)* farming *attrib.*; *(ländlich)* rural; **kleine** ~**e Betriebe** small farms. **2.** *adv.* rurally

Bauern-: ~auf·stand der peasants' revolt; **~brot das** *s.* **Landbrot; ~bub der** *(südd., österr., schweiz.) s.* **~junge; ~bursche der** *s.* **~junge; ~dorf das** farming village; **~fang der** *in* **auf ~fang ausgehen** *(ugs. abwertend)* set out to con people out of their money *(coll.)*; **~fänger der** *(ugs. abwertend)* con man *(coll.)*; **~fängerei die;** ~ *(ugs. abwertend)* con tricks *pl. (coll.)*; **das ist ~fängerei** it's a con *(coll.)*; **~frühstück das** *fried potatoes mixed with scrambled egg and bacon;* **~gut das** farm; **~haus das** farmhouse; **~hoch·zeit die** country wedding; **~hof der** farm; **~junge der** country lad; *(~sohn)* farmer's son; **~kalender der** farming calendar; **~krieg der** *(hist.)* peasants' revolt; **der Große ~krieg, die ~kriege** the Peasant[s'] War; **~legen das;** ~**s** driving out small farmers; **~lümmel der** *(abwertend)* loutish yokel; **~mädchen das** country girl; *(~tochter)* farmer's daughter; **~möbel** *Pl.* rustic-style furniture *sing.*; **~partei die a)** Agrarian Party; **b)** *(DDR)* Peasants' Party; **~regel die** country saying

Bauernschaft die; ~: farmers *pl.*; farming community; *(als ärmliche Klasse)* peasantry; peasants *pl.*

bauern-, Bauern-: ~schlau 1. *Adj.* cunning; sly; crafty; **2.** *adv.* cunningly; slyly; craftily; **~schläue die** peasant cunning *or* slyness *or* craftiness; **~sohn der** farmer's son; **~stand der** farming community; **~stube die** room furnished in rustic style; **~tochter die** farmer's daughter; **~tölpel der** *(abwertend)* yokel; country bumpkin

Bauerntum das; ~**s** *(Bauernstand)* farming community; *(bäuerliches Wesen)* character of the farming community

Bauers-: ~frau die farmer's wife; *(Landwirtin)* [lady] farmer; *(Frau vom Lande)* countrywoman; **~leute** *Pl.* **a)** *(veralt.)* country folk; **b)** *(Bauer und Bäuerin)* **die [beiden] ~leute** the farmer and his wife; **~mann der;** *Pl.* **~leute** *(veralt.)* countryman

bau-, Bau-: ~erwartungs·land das; *o. Pl.* land shortly to be made available for building; **~fach das** building trade; **~fällig** *Adj.* ramshackle; badly dilapidated; unsafe ⟨*roof, ceiling*⟩; **~fälligkeit die;** *o. Pl.* bad state of dilapidation; badly dilapidated state; **~firma die** building *or* construction firm; **~flucht die, ~flucht·linie die** building line; **~gelände das** *(~stelle)* building site; *(~land)* building land; **~genehmigung die** planning permission and building regulations clearance; **~genossenschaft die** *co-operative housing association which builds and maintains houses or flats for its members;* **~gerüst das** scaffolding; **~gewerbe das** building trade; **~grube die** excavation; **~handwerk das** building trade; **~handwerker der** skilled building worker; building craftsman; **~helfer der** builder's mate; **~herr der** client *(for whom a house etc. is being built)*; **„~herr: Stadt Mannheim"** 'under construction for the city of Mannheim'; **er ist ~herr** he is having a house built; **~holz das** building timber; **~hütte die a)** site hut; **b)** *(MA.)* stonemasons' lodge; **~ingenieur der** building engineer; **~jahr das** year of construction; *(bei Autos)* year of manufacture; **für Modelle dieses ~jahres** for models manufactured in that year; **das ~jahr des Hauses** the year in which the house was built; **welches ~jahr ist dein Wagen?** what year is your car?; **mein Auto ist ~jahr 75** my car is a 1975 model; **~kasten der** construction set *or* kit; *(mit Holzklötzen)* box of bricks; **~kasten·system das;** *o. Pl.* unit construction system; **~klotz der** building-brick; **~klötze[r] staunen** *(salopp)* be staggered *(coll.)* *or* flabbergasted; **~klötzchen das** building-brick; **~kolonne die** construction gang; **~kosten** *Pl.* building *or* construction costs; **~kosten·zuschuß der** *contribution to cost of building, rebuilding, or renovation paid by tenant to landlord;* **~kran der** construction crane; **~kunst die;** *o. Pl. (geh.)* architecture; **~land das;** *o. Pl.* building land; **~leiter der** clerk of the works; **~leitung die;** *o. Pl.* engineers supervising the building *or* construction work; *(~büro)* site office

baulich 1. *Adj.; nicht präd.* structural ‹*alteration, condition, defect, etc.*›; architectural ‹*character, value*›; **~e Anlagen** buildings. **2.** *adv.* **ein Gebäude ~ verbessern/verändern** carry out structural improvements/alterations to a building; **den Stadtkern ~ neugestalten** redevelop the town centre

Baulichkeit die; ~, ~en building

Bau-: ~los das section; **~löwe der** *(ugs. abwertend)* building speculator; **~lücke die** vacant lot

Baum [baum] **der;** ~[e]s, **Bäume** ['bɔymə] **a)** tree; **auf einen ~ klettern** climb up [into] a tree; **er ist stark wie ein ~:** he's as strong as an ox; *(fig.)* **es ist dafür gesorgt, daß die Bäume nicht in den Himmel wachsen** nobody has everything his own way all of the time; **alte Bäume soll man nicht verpflanzen** old people are happiest left in their familiar surroundings; **Bäume ausreißen können** *(ugs.)* be *or* feel ready to tackle anything; **der ~ der Erkenntnis** *(bibl.)* the Tree of Knowledge; **vom ~ der Erkenntnis essen** learn by experience; find out for oneself; **zwischen ~ und Borke sitzen** *od.* **stecken** be on the horns of a dilemma; *s. auch* **Wald; b)** *(ugs.: Weihnachtsbaum)* [Christmas] tree; **den ~ anzünden** light the candles on the tree; **c)** *(Seemannsspr.)* boom

Bau·markt der a) building *or* construction market; **b)** *(Kaufhaus)* DIY hypermarket

baum·arm *Adj.* very thinly wooded; **relativ ~:** relatively thinly wooded

Bau-: ~maschine die piece of construction plant *or* machinery; **~maschinen** construction plant *sing. or* machinery; **~maßnahme die** *(Amtsspr.)* building project; **~material das** building material; *(~materialien)* building materials *pl.*

Baum-: ~bestand der tree stock; **~blüte die a)** blossoming of the trees; **b)** *(Zeitraum)* **zur ~blüte/während der ~blüte** when/while the trees are in blossom

Bäumchen ['bɔymçən] **das;** ~s, ~: small tree; *(junger Baum)* sapling; young tree; **~, wechsle dich** *(Kinderspiel)* puss in the corner; *(ugs. scherzh.: Partnerwechsel)* partner-swapping

Bau·meister der a) *(hist.)* [architect and] master builder; **b)** *(Bautechniker, Bauhandwerker)* master builder; *(Bauunternehmer)* building contractor *(with professional qualifications)*

baumeln ['baum|n] *itr. V.* **a)** *(ugs.)* dangle (**an** + *Dat.* from); **die Beine ~ lassen** dangle one's legs; **b)** *(derb: gehängt werden)* swing *(sl.)*

bäumen ['bɔymən] *refl. V.: s.* **aufbäumen**

baum-, Baum-: ~farn der tree-fern; **~frevel der** unlawful and malicious damaging of trees; **~grenze die** tree-line; timber-line; **~gruppe die** clump of trees; **~krone die** treetop; crown [of the/a tree]; **~kuchen der** *tall cylindrical cake, hollow in the centre;* **~lang** *Adj. (ugs.)* tremendously tall *(coll.);* **~läufer der** *(Zool.)* tree-creeper; **~los** *Adj.* treeless; **~reich** *Adj.* wooded; **~riese der** *(geh.)* giant tree; **~rinde die** bark [of trees]; **~schere die** tree-pruner; **~schule die** tree nursery; **~stamm der** tree-trunk; **~stark** *Adj.* as strong as an ox *postpos.;* **~sterben das** dying-off of trees; **~strunk der** dead tree-stump; **~stumpf der** tree-stump; **~wachs das** grafting-wax

Baum·wolle die cotton

baum·wollen *Adj.; nicht präd.* cotton

Baumwoll-: ~ernte die cotton harvest; **~pflücker der** cotton-picker; **~plantage die** cotton plantation; **~spinnerei die a)** cotton-spinning; **b)** *(Betrieb)* cotton-mill

Baum·wurzel die tree-root

bau-, Bau-: ~ordnung die building regulations *pl.;* **~plan der** *(Entwurf, Zeichnung)* building plans *pl.; (für eine Maschine)* designs *pl.; (fig.)* structure; **~planung die** building design; **~platz der** site for building *or* construction; **~polizei die;** *o. Pl.* building inspectorate; **~polizeilich 1.** *Adj.; nicht präd.* building ‹*regulations*›; **eine ~polizeiliche Kontrolle** a visit from the building inspector/inspectors; **2.** *adv.* ‹*detected, approved, etc.*› by the building inspectorate; **~preis der** building costs *pl.;* **~rat der** chief architect; **~recht das** planning laws and building regulations *pl.;* **~reif** *Adj.* **ein ~reifes Grundstück** a cleared building plot; **~reihe die** series; *(bei Lokomotiven)* class

bäurisch ['bɔyrɪʃ] *(abwertend)* **1.** *Adj.* boorish; oafish. **2.** *adv.* boorishly; oafishly

Bau-: ~ruine die *(ugs.)* building abandoned only half-finished; **~satz der** kit

Bausch [bauʃ] **der;** ~[e]s, ~e *od.* **Bäusche** ['bɔyʃə] **a)** *(am Kleid, Ärmel)* puff; **einen ~ machen** *(ugs.)* ‹*dress*› bulge; **b) ein ~ Watte** a wad of cotton wool; **c) etw. in ~ und Bogen verwerfen/verdammen** reject/condemn sth. wholesale

Bau·schaffende [-ʃafn̩də] **der/die;** *adj. Dekl. (DDR)* building *or* construction worker

Bäuschchen ['bɔyʃçən] **das;** ~s, ~: [small] wad

bauschen 1. *tr. V.* billow, fill ‹*sail, curtains, etc.*›; **gebauschte Ärmel** puffed *or* puff sleeves. **2.** *refl. V.* ‹*dress, sleeve*› puff out; *(ungewollt)* bunch up; become bunched up; *(im Wind)* ‹*curtain, flag, etc.*› billow [out]

bauschig 1. *Adj.* puffed ‹*dress*›; baggy ‹*trousers*›. **2.** *adv.* **~ fallen** ‹*skirt*› be full

Bau-: ~schlosser der fitter [in the building trade]; **~schutt der** building-rubble; **~soldat der** *(DDR) conscript allowed to do non-military (esp. building) work*

bau·sparen *itr. V.; nur Inf. gebr.* save with a building society

Bau·sparer der building-society investor

Bauspar-: ~kasse die ≈ building society; **~vertrag der** savings contract with a building society *(to save a specified sum which earns interest and is later used to pay for the building of a house)*

Bau-: ~stahl der structural steel; **~stein der a)** building stone; **b)** *(Bestandteil)* element; component; *(Elektronik, DV)* module; **die ~steine der Materie** the constituents of matter; **c)** *(~klötzchen)* building-brick; **~stelle die** building site; *(beim Straßenbau)* road-works *pl.; (bei der Eisenbahn)* site of engineering works; **„Betreten der ~stelle verboten"** 'no entry *or* access for unauthorized persons'; **die Strecke war wegen einer ~stelle gesperrt** the road was closed because of road-works/the line was closed because of engineering works; **~stil der** architectural style; **im italienischen ~stil** in the Italian style; **~stoff der a)** building material; **b)** *(Biol.)* nutrient; **~stopp der** suspension of building work (**für** on); **~substanz die** *o. Pl.* fabric [of the building/buildings]; *(Bestand an Gebäuden)* building stock; **~summe die** building costs *pl.;* **~tätigkeit die;** *o. Pl.* building activity; **~teil das** component

Bauten *Pl.: s.* **Bau**

Bau-: ~tischler der [building] joiner; **~unternehmen das** building firm; **~unternehmer der** building contractor; builder; **~vorhaben das** building project; **~weise die a)** method of building *or* construction; **b)** *(~art)* type of construction; **in geschlossener/offener ~weise errichtet** built as terrace houses/detached houses; **~werk das** building; *(Brücke, Staudamm)* structure; **~wirtschaft die;** *o. Pl.* building *or* construction industry

Bauxit [bau'ksi:t] **der;** ~s, ~e bauxite

bauz [bauts] *Interj.* flop

Bau-: ~zaun der site fence; **~zeichnung die** construction drawing; **~zeit die** construction time

Bayer ['baiɐ] **der;** ~n, ~n, **Bayerin die;** ~, ~nen Bavarian

bay[e]risch 1. *Adj.* Bavarian; **der Bayerische Wald** the Bayerischer Wald; the Bavarian Forest. **2.** *adv.* **~ sprechen** speak Bavarian dialect; *(mit bayerischem Akzent)* speak with a Bavarian accent; **~ gekleidet** dressed in Bavarian costume; *s. auch* **deutsch, badisch**

Bayern ['baiɐn] **(das);** ~s Bavaria

Bazi ['ba:tsi] **der;** ~, ~ *(südd., österr. abwertend)* **a)** *(Faulpelz)* lazy good-for-nothing; **b)** *(Wichtigtuer)* big-head *(coll.)*

Bazille [ba'tsɪlə] **die;** ~, ~n *(ugs.) s.* **Bazillus**

Bazillen·träger der carrier

Bazillus [ba'tsɪlʊs] **der;** ~, **Bazillen a)** bacillus; **b)** *(fig.)* cancer; **der ~ der Korruption** the cancer of corruption

Bazooka [ba'zu:ka] **die;** ~, ~s bazooka

Bd. *Abk.* **Band** Vol.

Bde. *Abk.* **Bände** Vols.

BDM [be:de:'|ɛm] **der;** ~ *Abk.* **Bund Deutscher Mädel** *(ns.) National Socialist organization for girls*

B-Dur ['be:-] **das;** ~ *(Musik)* B flat major; *s. auch* **A-Dur**

BE *Abk.* **Broteinheit**

beabsichtigen [bə'|apzɪçtɪgn̩] *tr. V.* intend; **~, etw. zu tun** intend *or* mean to do sth.; **das war nicht beabsichtigt** it wasn't intentional *or* deliberate; **was hast du mit dieser Frage beabsichtigt?** what did you mean by your question?; **die beabsichtigte Wirkung** the intended *or* desired effect

beachten *tr. V.* **a)** observe, follow ‹*rule, regulations*›; follow ‹*instruction*›; heed, follow ‹*advice*›; obey ‹*traffic signs*›; observe ‹*formalities*›; **b)** *(berücksichtigen)* **etw. ~:** take account of sth.; *(Aufmerksamkeit schenken)* pay attention to *or* take notice of sth.; **es ist zu ~, daß ...:** please note that ...; **c)** *(beobachten)* notice; **jmdn. nicht ~:** ignore sb.

beachtens·wert *Adj.* remarkable; *(erwähnenswert)* noteworthy

beachtlich 1. *Adj.* **a)** *(erheblich)* considerable; marked, considerable ‹*improvement, increase, change, etc.*›; notable, considerable ‹*success*›; **er verdient jetzt ~e zehntausend Mark im Monat** he is now earning as much as ten thousand marks a month; **b)** *(anerkennenswert)* important ‹*job, post*›; **Beachtliches leisten** make one's mark; **c)** *(Amtsspr.: zu berücksichtigen)* **~ sein** have to be given due consideration. **2.** *adv.* considerably; ‹*improve, increase, change*› markedly, considerably

Beachtung die a) *(Einhaltung) s.* **beachten a:** observance; following; heeding; obeying; **bei ~ der Regeln** if one observes *or* follows the rules; **b)** *(Berücksichtigung)* consideration; **unter ~ aller Umstände** taking all the circumstances into account; **c)** *(Aufmerksamkeit)* attention; **~/keinerlei ~ finden** receive attention/be ignored completely; **jmdm./einer Sache ~/keine ~ schenken** pay attention/no attention to sb./sth.; take notice/no notice of sb./sth.

beackern *tr. V.* **a)** *(ugs.: bearbeiten)* go over ⟨*subject*⟩; plough through ⟨*literature, regulations*⟩; **b)** *(ugs.: überreden)* **jmdn. ~:** work on sb. *(coll.)*; **c)** *(bebauen)* cultivate

Beamte [bəˈlamtə] **der;** *adj. Dekl.* official; *(Staats~)* [permanent] civil servant; *(Kommunal~)* [established] local government officer *or* official; *(Polizei~)* [police] officer; *(Zoll~)* [customs] officer *or* official; **ein typischer ~r** a typical civil servant; **ein kleiner ~r** *(meist abwertend)* a minor *or (derog.)* petty official

Beamten-: ~apparat der bureaucracy; **~beleidigung die** insulting a public servant; **~bestechung die** bribery of a public servant/public servants; **~deutsch das** *(abwertend)* officialese *(derog.)*; **~laufbahn die** career in the civil service *or* as a civil servant; **die ~laufbahn einschlagen** join *or* enter the civil service; become a civil servant; **~recht das;** *o. Pl.* administrative law; **~seele die** *(abwertend)* petty official *or* bureaucrat; **~silo der** *(ugs. scherzh.)* huge impersonal office-block full of bureaucrats

Beamtentum das; ~s a) civil service mentality; **b)** *(Beamtenschaft)* civil servants *pl.*; civil service; *(in den Gemeinden)* local government officers *or* officials *pl.*

Beamten·verhältnis das: im ~ stehen be a [permanent] civil servant; **ins ~ übernommen werden** attain permanent status

beamtet *Adj.* **~ sein** have permanent civil-servant status; **ein ~er Lehrer** a teacher with permanent civil-servant status

Beamtete der/die; *adj. Dekl. (Amtsspr.) s.* **Beamte, Beamtin**

Beamtin die; ~, ~nen *s.* **Beamte;** *(Polizei~)* [woman] police officer

beängstigen *tr. V. (veralt.)* alarm

beängstigend 1. *Adj.* worrying ⟨*feeling*⟩; unsettling ⟨*sign*⟩; eerie ⟨*silence*⟩; alarming ⟨*speed*⟩; **ein ~es Gedränge** a frightening crush of people; **sein Zustand ist ~:** his condition is giving cause for anxiety. **2.** *adv.* alarmingly; **~ schnell** at an alarming speed

beanspruchen *tr. V.* **a)** claim; **etw. ~ können** be entitled to expect sth.; **b)** *(ausnutzen)* make use of ⟨*person, equipment*⟩; take advantage of ⟨*hospitality, offer of help, services*⟩; **jmds. Geduld übermäßig ~:** try *or* strain sb.'s patience; **c)** *(abverlangen)* demand ⟨*energy, attention, stamina*⟩; **das beansprucht ihn sehr/wenig** that demands a lot/doesn't demand much of him; **sein Beruf beansprucht ihn sehr/völlig** his job is very demanding/takes up all his time and energy; **d)** *(benötigen)* take up ⟨*time, space, etc.*⟩

Beanspruchung die; ~, ~en a) demands *pl.* (*Gen.* on); **b)** *(Inanspruchnahme)* **die ~ durch den Beruf** the demands of his/her job; **~en** *(Dat.)* **ausgesetzt werden** ⟨*material, machine*⟩ be subjected to stresses *or* strains

beanstanden, *(österr. auch)* **beanständen** *tr. V.* object to; take exception to; *(sich beklagen über)* complain about; **an der Arbeit ist nichts/allerlei zu ~:** there ist nothing/there are all sorts of things wrong with the work; **die Waren wurden beanstandet** there were complaints about the goods; **~, daß ...:** complain that ...

Beanstandung die; ~, ~en complaint; **Anlaß zu ~en geben** give cause for complaint *sing.*

beantragen *tr. V.* **a)** apply for; **~, versetzt zu werden** apply to be transferred; apply for a transfer; **etw. bei den Behörden ~:** apply to the authorities for sth.; **b)** *(fordern)* call for; demand; **c)** *(vorschlagen)* propose; **~, etw. zu tun** propose doing sth.; **Schluß der Debatte ~:** move the closure

beantworten *tr. V.* answer; reply to, answer ⟨*letter*⟩; respond to ⟨*insult*⟩; return ⟨*greeting*⟩; **jmdm. eine Frage ~:** answer a question for sb.; **bitte ~ Sie meine Frage mit Ja oder Nein** please answer yes or no to my question

Beantwortung die; ~, ~en a) die ~ einer Frage/eines Briefes an answer to a question/a reply *or* an answer to a letter; **in ~** *(Amtsspr.)* in reply (*Gen.* to); **zur ~ Ihrer Frage** in order to answer your question; **b)** *(Reaktion)* response; **die ~ seiner Beleidigung** the response to his insult

bearbeiten *tr. V.* **a)** deal with; work on, handle ⟨*case*⟩; **b)** *(adaptieren)* adapt (**für** for); **ein Buch völlig neu ~:** revise a book completely; **ein Stück für Klavier ~:** arrange a piece for the piano; **c)** *(behandeln)* treat (**mit** with); work ⟨*wood, metal, leather, etc.*⟩; **etw. mit Politur/einem Hammer/einer Feile** *usw.* **~:** polish/hammer/file *etc.* sth.; **etw. mit einer Drahtbürste ~:** work on sth. with a wire brush; **d)** cultivate ⟨*field, land*⟩; *(fig. ugs.)* hammer away on ⟨*piano, organ*⟩; **den Boden ~:** work the soil; **e)** *(ugs.: schlagen)* beat [repeatedly]; **jmdn. mit den Fäusten ~:** pummel sb.; **f)** *(untersuchen)* treat, examine ⟨*subject, aspect*⟩; **g)** *(ugs.: überreden)* work on; **jmdn. ~, daß er etw. macht** work on sb. to get him to do sth.

Bearbeiter der, Bearbeiterin die a) der zuständige Bearbeiter the person who is dealing/who dealt with the matter; **sie war nicht die Bearbeiterin des Antrags** she did not deal with the application; **b)** *(eines Romans, Schauspiels)* adapter; *(eines Textes)* reviser; *(Herausgeber)* editor; *(eines Musikstücks)* arranger

Bearbeitung die; ~, ~en a) die ~ eines Antrags/eines Falles *usw.* dealing with an application/working on *or* handling a case *etc.*; **die ~ der Post ist ...:** dealing with the mail is...; **b)** *(Fassung, Veränderung)* adaptation; *(eines Musikstücks)* arrangement; **die englische ~:** the English version; **c)** *(Behandlung)* treatment; *(von Holz, Metall, Leder usw.)* working; **die ~ des Metalls ist schwer** it is difficult to work the metal; **zur weiteren ~:** in order to be worked further/for further treatment; **d)** *(Untersuchung)* examination; *(eines Themas)* treatment

Bearbeitungs-: ~gebühr die administrative charge; *(Bankw.)* handling charge; **~methode die: ~methoden für Stahl** *usw.* methods of working steel *etc.*; **~zeit die: die ~zeit für etw.** the time required to deal with sth.

beargwöhnen *tr. V.* **jmdn./etw. ~:** be suspicious of sb./sth.; regard sb./sth. with suspicion; **beargwöhnt werden** be regarded with suspicion

Beat [bi:t] **der; ~[s] a)** beat; **b)** *(Musikrichtung)* beat [music]

Beat-: ~band die beat group; **~club der:** *s.* **~lokal; ~fan der** beat fan; **~lokal das** beat club

beatmen *tr. V. (Med.)* **jmdn. [künstlich] ~:** administer artificial respiration to sb.; *(während einer Operation)* ventilate sb.

Beatmung die; ~, ~en: [künstliche] ~: artificial respiration; *(während einer Operation)* ventilation

Beatmungs·gerät das respirator

Beat·musik die beat music

Beatnik [ˈbi:tnɪk] **der; ~s, ~s** beatnik

Beat·schuppen der *(ugs.)* beat club

Beau [bo:] **der; ~s, ~s** dandy

Beaufort·skala [ˈbo:fɐt-] **die;** *o. Pl. (Met.)* Beaufort scale

beaufsichtigen *tr. V.* supervise; mind, look after ⟨*child*⟩; **jmdn. bei der Arbeit ~:** supervise sb. while he/she is working

Beaufsichtigung die; ~, ~en supervision; **unter ~ stehen** be kept under supervision

beauftragen *tr. V.* **a) jmdn./einen Ausschuß** *usw.* **mit etw. ~:** entrust sb./a committee *etc.* with sth.; charge sb./a committee *etc.* with sth.; **jmdn./einen Ausschuß** *usw.* **~, etw. zu tun** give sb./a committee *etc.* the job *or* task of doing sth.; **jmdn. ~, die Urkunden zu unterschreiben** authorize sb. to sign the documents; **man hat mich beauftragt, Sie darüber zu informieren** I have been asked to tell you about this; **einen Künstler/Architekten ~, etw. zu tun** commission an artist/architect to do sth.; **b)** *(beordern)* **jmdn. ~, etw. zu tun** order sb. to do sth.

Beauftragte der/die; *adj. Dekl.* representative; **der ~ der DDR für Kirchenfragen** the GDR official responsible for church affairs

beaugapfeln *tr. V. (scherzh.)* **jmdn./etw. ~:** give sb./sth. the once-over *(coll.)*

beäugen *tr. V.* eye ⟨*person*⟩; inspect ⟨*thing*⟩

beaugenscheinigen [bəˈlaugn̩ʃainɪgn̩] *tr. V. (Amtsspr., scherzh.)* inspect

Beauté [boˈte:] **die; ~, ~s** *(geh.)* beauty

bebändert [bəˈbɛndɐt] *Adj.* decorated with ribbons; beribboned

bebauen *tr. V.* **a)** build on; develop; **ein Gelände mit Häusern ~:** build houses on a site; **mit etw. bebaut werden** have sth. built on it; **b)** cultivate ⟨*land*⟩; **einen Acker mit Kartoffeln ~:** grow potatoes in a field

Bebauung die; ~, ~en a) *(mit Gebäuden)* development; **b)** *(Gebäude)* buildings *pl.*; **das Gebiet hat eine völlig uneinheitliche ~:** the buildings in this area lack any unity of style; **c)** *(eines Ackers)* cultivation

Bebauungs·plan der development plan

Bébé [beˈbe:] **das; ~s, ~s** *(schweiz.)* baby

beben [ˈbe:bn̩] *itr. V.* **a)** shake; tremble; **b)** *(geh.: zittern)* tremble, shake (**vor** + *Dat.* with); ⟨*lips*⟩ tremble; ⟨*knees*⟩ shake

Beben das; ~s, ~ a) shaking; trembling; **b)** *(Erd~)* quake *(coll.)*; earthquake; **c)** *(geh.: Zittern)* shaking; trembling; **das ~ seiner Stimme** the tremble in his voice

bebildern *tr. V.* illustrate

Bebilderung die; ~, ~en illustrations *pl.*

bebrillt [bəˈbrɪlt] *Adj.* bespectacled

bebrüten *tr. V.* **a)** brood; incubate; **b)** *(Biol.)* incubate

Béchamel·soße [beʃaˈmɛl-] **die** *(Kochk.)* béchamel [sauce]

Becher [ˈbɛçɐ] **der; ~s, ~ a)** *(Glas~, Porzellan~)* glass; tumbler; *(Plastik~)* beaker; cup; *(Eis~) (aus Glas, Metall)* sundae dish; *(aus Pappe)* tub; *(Joghurt~)* carton; **ein ~ Eis** a tub of ice cream; **b)** *(bei Pflanzen)* cupule; cup

Becher·glas das *(Chemie)* beaker

bechern *tr., itr. V. (ugs. scherzh.)* **[einen] ~:** have a few *(coll.)*; **bis zum frühen Morgen ~:** booze into the small hours

Becher·werk das *(Technik)* bucket elevator

becircen [bəˈtsɪrtsn̩] *tr. V. (ugs.)* **a)** bewitch ⟨*man*⟩; **b)** *(überreden)* **jmdn. ~[, daß er etw. tut]** wrap sb. round one's little finger [and get him to do sth.]

Becken [ˈbɛkn̩] **das; ~s, ~ a)** *(Wasch~)* basin; *(Abwasch~)* sink; *(Toiletten~)* pan; bowl; **b)** *(Anat.)* pelvis; **c)** *Pl. (Musik)* cymbals; **d)** *(Schwimm~)* pool; *(Plansch~)* paddling-pool; *(eines Brunnens, einer Schleuse)* basin; *(Fisch~)* pond; **e)** *(Geol.)* basin

Becken-: ~bruch der *(Med.)* pelvic fracture; fractured pelvis; **~end·lage die** *(Med.)* breech position; **~knochen der** hip-bone; pelvic bone

Beckmesser [ˈbɛkmɛsɐ] **der; ~s, ~** *(abwertend)* caviller; carper

Beckmesserei die; ~, ~en *(abwertend)* cavilling; carping

beckmessern *itr. V. (abwertend)* cavil; carp

bedachen [bəˈdaxn̩] *tr. V.* put the roof on ‹*house*›; **bedacht** roofed; covered ‹*bridge*›

bedacht 1. *2. Part. v.* **bedenken; bedachen. 2.** *Adj.* **a)** carefully considered; *(umsichtig)* circumspect; **b) auf etw.** *(Akk.)* **~ sein** be intent on sth.; **auf seinen eigenen Vorteil ~ sein** have an eye to one's own advantage; **darauf ~/sehr ~ sein, etw. zu tun** be intent on doing sth./be [most] anxious to do sth.; **[ängstlich] darauf ~ sein, daß etw. nicht geschieht** be [extremely] anxious to prevent sth. from happening; **er ist stets auf korrekte Kleidung ~:** he makes a point of being correctly dressed. **3.** *adv.* in a carefully considered way; *(umsichtig)* circumspectly

Bedacht der *in* **ohne ~:** rashly; without thinking *or* forethought; **mit ~:** in a carefully considered way; *(umsichtig)* circumspectly; **voll ~:** very carefully; **auf etw.** *(Akk.)* **~ nehmen** *(geh.)* pay regard to sth.

Bedachte der/die; *adj. Dekl. (Rechtsw.)* beneficiary; *(eines Legats)* legatee

bedächtig [bəˈdɛçtɪç] **1.** *Adj.* **a)** deliberate; measured ‹*steps, stride, speech*›; **b)** *(besonnen)* thoughtful; well-considered ‹*words*›; *(vorsichtig)* careful. **2.** *adv.* **a)** deliberately; **~ reden** speak in measured tones; **b)** *(besonnen)* thoughtfully; *(vorsichtig)* carefully

Bedächtigkeit die; ~ a) deliberateness; **b)** *(Besonnenheit)* thoughtfulness; *(Vorsichtigkeit)* carefulness

bedachtsam *(geh.)* **1.** *Adj.* thoughtful; *(vorsichtig)* careful. **2.** *adv.* thoughtfully; *(vorsichtig)* carefully

Bedachung die; ~, ~en a) *o. Pl.* roofing; **b)** *(Dach)* roof

bedang [bəˈdaŋ] *1. u. 3. Pers. Sg. Prät. v.* **²bedingen**

bedanken 1. *refl. V.* say thank you; express one's thanks; **ich bedanke mich** thank you; *(ugs. iron.: nein danke!)* thank you ˈvery much; **sich bei jmdm. [für etw.] ~:** thank sb. *or* say thank you to sb. [for sth.]; **sich bei jmdm. ~, daß er/sie etw. getan hat** thank sb. for doing sth.; **dafür kannst du dich bei ihm ~** *(ugs. iron.)* you've got him to thank for that *(iron.)*. **2.** *tr. V. (geh.)* **etw. ~:** express one's thanks for sth.; **Seien Sie herzlich bedankt** please accept my/our warmest thanks

Bedarf [bəˈdarf] **der; ~[e]s a)** need (**an** + *Dat.* of); requirement (**an** + *Dat.* for); *(Bedarfsmenge)* needs *pl.*; requirements *pl.*; **Dinge des täglichen ~s** everyday necessities; **der persönliche ~:** one's personal needs *pl.*; **bei ~:** if and when the need arises; if required; **bei dringendem ~:** in cases of urgent need; **~ an etw.** *(Dat.)* **haben** *(Kaufmannsspr.)* require sth.; **je nach ~:** as required; **kein ~!** *(salopp)* I don't feel like it; **b)** *(Nachfrage)* demand (**an** + *Dat.* for); **dafür besteht kein ~:** there is no demand for it/them; **mein ~ an Überraschungen ist für heute gedeckt** *(fig.)* I've had enough surprises for ˈone day

-bedarf der; ~[e]s ... requirement

bedarfs-, Bedarfs-: ~ampel die *(Verkehrsw.)* pedestrian-controlled *or* -operated lights; **~deckung die** satisfaction of its/one's needs *or* requirements; **~fall der** *in* **im ~fall[e]** if required; if the need arises/arose; **~gerecht 1.** *Adj.* designed to meet requirements; tailor-made; **eine ~gerechte Versorgung der Bevölkerung** a supply system tailored to the needs of the people; **2.** *adv.* in line with demand; **~güter** *Pl.* consumer goods; **~halte·stelle die** request stop; **~weckung die; ~:** stimulation of demand

bedauerlich *Adj.* regrettable; unfortunate

bedauerlicher·weise *Adv.* regrettably; unfortunately

bedauern *tr., itr. V.* **a)** feel sorry for; **sie hat es gern, bedauert zu werden** she likes people to feel sorry for her; **sie läßt sich gerne ~:** she likes being pitied; **b)** *(schade finden)* regret; **ich bedaure sehr, daß ...:** I am very sorry that ...; **wir ~, Ihnen mitteilen zu müssen** we regret to [have to] inform you; **bedaure!** sorry!

Bedauern das; ~s a) sympathy; **jmdm. sein ~ ausdrücken** offer one's sympathy to sb.; **b)** *(Betrübnis)* regret; **zu meinem ~:** to my regret; **ich habe zu meinem ~ gehört, daß ...:** I was sorry to hear that ...; **zu unserem ~ müssen wir Ihnen mitteilen, daß ...:** we regret to [have to] inform you that ...; it is with regret that we must inform you that ...; **mit ~:** with regret; **mit ~ habe ich festgestellt, daß ...:** I have discovered to my regret that ...

bedauerns-: ~wert *(geh.)*, **~würdig** *Adj.* unfortunate ‹*person, coincidence*›; regrettable, unfortunate ‹*incident*›

bedecken 1. *tr. V.* **a)** cover (**mit** with); **mit etw. bedeckt sein** be covered with sth.; **von Schlamm/Schmutz bedeckt sein** be covered in mud/dirt; **b)** *(österr.: ausgleichen)* meet ‹*costs*›. **2.** *refl. V.* cover oneself up

bedeckt *Adj.* overcast ‹*sky*›; **bei ~em Himmel** when the sky is overcast; **sich ~ halten** *(fig.)* keep a low profile

Bedecktsamer [-za:mɐ] **der; ~s, ~** *(Bot.)* angiosperm

bedecktsamig [-za:mɪç] *Adj. (Bot.)* angiospermous

Bedeckung die; *o. Pl.* **a)** covering; **b)** *(Schutz)* guard; **zehn Mann ~:** a ten-man bodyguard *sing.*; **c)** *(das Bedeckende)* covering; **d)** *(österr.: Deckung)* meeting

bedenken 1. *unr. tr. V.* **a)** consider; think about; **wenn ich es recht bedenke/wenn man es recht bedenkt** when I/you stop and think about it; **~, daß ...:** consider *or* think that ...; **b)** *(beachten)* take into consideration; **du mußt ~, daß ...:** you should bear in mind that *or* take into consideration the fact that ...; **ich gebe [dir]/er gab [uns] zu ~, daß ...:** I would ask you/he asked us to bear in mind that *or* take into consideration the fact that ...; **c)** *(geh.: beschenken)* **jmdn. reich ~:** shower sb. with gifts; **jmdn. mit etw. ~:** present sb. with sth.; **jmdn. großzügig mit Lob ~:** lavish praise on sb. **2.** *refl. V.* reflect; think; **ohne sich lange zu ~:** without stopping to reflect

Bedenken das; ~s, ~ a) *o. Pl.* reflection; **nach kurzem/langem ~:** after a moment's/after much reflection *or* consideration; **ohne ~:** without hesitation; **b)** *(Zweifel)* doubt; reservation; **~ haben** *od.* **hegen** *od. (geh.)* **tragen** have doubts *or* reservations (**gegen** about); **aber jetzt kommen mir ~:** but now I'm having second thoughts

bedenken·los 1. *Adj.* unconsidered; *(ohne Zögern)* unhesitating; prompt ‹*intervention*›; *(skrupellos)* unscrupulous. **2.** *adv.* without a moment's hesitation; without stopping to think; *(ohne Zögern)* without hesitation; ‹*intervene*› promptly; *(skrupellos)* unscrupulously

Bedenkenlosigkeit die; ~: lack of consideration; *(mangelndes Zögern)* absence of any hesitation; *(Skrupellosigkeit)* unscrupulousness; lack of scruples

bedenkens·wert *Adj.* ‹*argument, suggestion*› worthy of consideration; **~ sein** be worth considering *or* worthy of consideration

bedenklich 1. *Adj.* **a)** dubious, questionable ‹*methods, transactions, etc.*›; **b)** *(bedrohlich)* alarming; disturbing; **~ sein/werden** be giving/be starting to give cause for concern; **c)** *(besorgt)* concerned; apprehensive; anxious; **ein ~es Gesicht machen** look concerned *etc.*; **das machte** *od.* **stimmte mich ~** *(ließ mich nachdenken)* that gave me food for thought; *(machte mich ängstlich)* that gave me cause for concern. **2.** *adv.* **a)** alarmingly; disturbingly; **b)** *(besorgt)* apprehensively; anxiously

Bedenklichkeit die; ~ a) dubiousness; questionableness; **b)** *(Bedrohlichkeit)* alarming *or* disturbing nature

Bedenk·zeit die; *o. Pl.* time for reflection; **um ~/einige Tage ~ bitten** ask for some time/a few days to think about it; **nach einer kurzen ~:** after a pause for thought; **ich gebe Ihnen vierundzwanzig Stunden ~:** I'll give you twenty-four hours to think about it

bedeppert [bəˈdɛpɐt] *(salopp) Adj. (ratlos)* confused and embarrassed; *(töricht, dümmlich)* gormless *(coll.)*; *(niedergeschlagen)* crestfallen

bedeuten *tr. V.* **a)** *(bezeichnen, heißen)* mean; **was bedeutet dieses Wort?** what does that word mean?; what is the meaning of that word?; **was soll das ~?** what does that mean?; **er weiß, was es bedeutet, krank zu sein** he knows what it means to be ill; **„Ph. D." bedeutet Doktor der Philosophie** 'Ph.D.' stands for Doctor of Philosophy; **was bedeutet diese Zeremonie?** what's ˈthe significance of this ceremony?; **b)** *(sein)* represent; **das bedeutet ein Wagnis** that is being really daring; **einen Eingriff in die Pressefreiheit ~:** amount to *or* represent an attack on press freedom; **c)** *(hindeuten auf)* mean; **das bedeutet nichts Gutes** that bodes ill; that's a bad sign; **schönes Wetter ~:** mean good weather; be a sign of good weather to come; **d)** *(wichtig sein)* mean; **Geld bedeutet ihm nichts** money means nothing to him; **das hat nichts zu ~:** that doesn't mean anything; **e)** *(geh.: anraten)* **jmdm. ~, etw. zu tun** intimate *or* indicate to sb. that he/she should do sth.; **f)** *(veralt.: belehren)* inform

bedeutend 1. *Adj.* **a)** *(wichtig)* significant, important ‹*step, event, role, measure, etc.*›; important ‹*city, port, artist, writer, etc.*›; **b)** *(groß)* considerable; substantial; considerable ‹*success*›; substantial ‹*pension*›. **2.** *adv.* considerably

bedeutsam 1. *Adj.* **a)** *s.* **bedeutend; b)** *(vielsagend)* meaningful; significant. **2.** *adv.* meaningfully; significantly

Bedeutung die; ~, ~en a) *o. Pl.* meaning; significance; **einer Sache** *(Dat.)* **zu große ~ beimessen** attach too much significance to sth.; **b)** *(Wort~)* meaning; **c)** *o. Pl. (Tragweite)* significance; importance; **[an] ~ gewinnen** become more significant; **nichts von ~:** nothing important *or* significant; nothing of [any] importance *or* significance; **d)** *(Berühmtheit)* importance; **ein Mann von ~:** an important figure

bedeutungs-, Bedeutungs-: ~erweiterung die *(Sprachw.)* extension of meaning; **~gehalt der** semantic content *(Ling.)*; meaning; **~lehre die** *(Sprachw.)* semantics; **~los** *Adj.* insignificant; unimportant; **~losigkeit die; ~:** insignificance; unimportance; **~schwer** *Adj. (geh.)* loaded with meaning; *(folgenschwer)* critical; momentous; **~unterschied der** *(Sprachw.)* difference in meaning; **~verengung die** *(Sprachw.)* restriction of meaning; **~voll 1.** *Adj.* **a)** significant; **b)** *(vielsagend)* meaningful; meaning ‹*look*›; **2.** *adv.* meaningfully; significantly; **~wandel der** *(Sprachw.)* change in *or* of meaning; semantic change *(Ling.)*; **~wörter·buch das** defining dictionary

bedienen 1. *tr. V.* **a)** wait on; ‹*waiter, waitress*› wait on, serve; ‹*sales assistant*› serve; *(salopp: sexuell)* satisfy; **jmdn. vorn und hinten ~** *(ugs.)* wait on sb. hand and foot; **werden Sie schon bedient?** are you being served?; **aufmerksam bedient werden** receive attentive service; **b)** *(handhaben)* operate ‹*machine*›; **c)** *in* **[mit etw.] gut/schlecht bedient sein** *(ugs.)* be well-served/

ill-served [by sth.]; **mit diesem Artikel sind Sie gut bedient** this article will give you good value for money; **bedient sein** *(salopp)* have had enough; have had all one can take; **d)** *(Kartenspiel)* play; **Kreuz/Trumpf ~:** play a club/trump; **eine Farbe ~:** follow suit; **e)** *(Fußball)* **jmdn. ~:** pass to sb.; **die Stürmer mit hervorragenden Pässen ~:** provide the forwards with excellent service; **f)** ⟨*means of transport*⟩ serve; operate on ⟨*route*⟩; maintain ⟨*network of routes*⟩. **2.** *itr. V.* **a)** *(im Restaurant, Geschäft)* serve; **wer bedient hier?** who is serving here?; **b)** *(Kartenspiel)* follow suit; **falsch ~:** revoke. **3.** *refl. V.* **a)** help oneself; **sich selbst ~** *(im Geschäft, Restaurant usw.)* serve oneself; **b)** *(geh.)* **sich einer Sache** *(Gen.)* **~:** make use of *or* use sth.

Bedienerin die; ~, ~nen *(österr.)* cleaning woman

bedienstet [bəˈdiːnstət] *Adj. in* ~ **sein** *(österr.)* be employed **(bei** by)

Bedienstete der/die; *adj. Dekl.* **a)** *(Amtsspr.)* employee; **b)** *(veralt.: Diener)* servant

Bediente [bəˈdiːntə] **der/die;** *adj. Dekl. (veralt.)* servant

Bedienung die; ~, ~en a) *o. Pl. (das Bedienen)* service; ~ **inbegriffen** service included; **b)** *o. Pl. (das Handhaben)* operation; **für die ~ dieser Maschine bekommt er ...:** for operating this machine he receives ...; **c)** *(Person) (in einem Lokal)* waiter/waitress; *(in einem Geschäft)* [sales] assistant; *(gesamtes Personal)* staff; **hallo, ~!** waiter/waitress!; **d)** *(österr.)* cleaning woman

Bedienungs-: ~an·leitung die operating instructions *pl.*; *(Heft)* instruction book; **~auf·schlag der, ~geld das:** *s.* **~zuschlag; ~fehler der** operator's error; **~mannschaft die** operating crew; *(am Geschütz)* gun crew; **~zu·schlag der** service charge

¹bedingen [bəˈdɪŋən] *tr. V.* **a)** cause; **b)** *(erfordern)* require; demand; *(voraussetzen)* presuppose; **c)** *(abhängig sein von)* **einander ~:** be interdependent *or* mutually dependent

²bedingen *unr. refl. V. (veralt.)* **sich** *(Dat.)* **etw. ~:** stipulate sth.; make sth. a condition

bedingt [bəˈdɪŋt] **1.** *Adj.* **a)** qualified ⟨*praise, acceptance, approval*⟩; **b)** *(von etw. abhängig)* conditional; **~er Reflex** *(Physiol.)* conditioned reflex; **psychologisch ~ sein** have psychological causes. **2.** *adv.* **~ richtig/gelten** partly/be partly true; **nur ~ tauglich** fit for certain duties only

-bedingt *Adj.* associated with *postpos.*; due to *postpos.*; **alters~:** associated with old age *postpos.*; **berufsbedingte Krankheiten** occupational illnesses; **witterungsbedingte Schäden** damage caused by the weather

Bedingtheit die; ~, ~en a) *(Abhängigkeit)* relative nature; *(Begrenztheit)* limited *or* restricted nature; **b)** *(Bestimmtheit)* **wechselseitige ~:** interdependence; mutual dependence

Bedingung die; ~, ~en condition; **etw. zur ~ machen** make sth. a condition; **zu annehmbaren ~en** on acceptable terms; **unter diesen ~en** on these conditions; **unter keiner ~:** under no circumstances; **unter der ~, daß ...:** on condition that ...; **~ ist, daß ...:** it is a condition that ...

bedingungs-, Bedingungs-: ~form die *(Sprachw.)* conditional; **~los 1.** *Adj.* unconditional ⟨*surrender, acceptance, etc.*⟩; absolute, unquestioning ⟨*obedience, loyalty, devotion*⟩; **2.** *adv.* ⟨*surrender, accept, etc.*⟩ unconditionally; ⟨*subordinate oneself*⟩ unquestioningly; **sich ~los für jmdn. einsetzen** give sb. one's unqualified support; **~satz der** *(Sprachw.)* conditional clause

bedrängen *tr. V.* **a)** besiege ⟨*town, fortress, person*⟩; put ⟨*opposing player*⟩ under pressure; **vom Feind bedrängt sein** be hard pressed by the enemy; **mit Fragen bedrängt werden** be assailed with questions; **b)** *(belästigen)* pester; **c)** *(belasten)* distress; **von Zweifeln bedrängt** beset with doubts; **in einer bedrängten/sehr bedrängten Lage sein** be hard-pressed/be in a difficult/desperate situation *or* in dire straits *pl.*

Bedrängnis die; ~, ~se *(geh.) (innere Not)* distress; *(wirtschaftliche Not)* [great] difficulties *pl.*; **in ~ geraten/sein** get into/be in great difficulties *pl.*; **in arger ~:** in dire straits *pl.*; **jmdn. in ~ bringen** cause sb. great difficulties/distress

bedripst [bəˈdrɪpst] *Adj. (nordd. ugs.) (ratlos)* confused and embarrassed; *(niedergeschlagen)* crestfallen

bedrohen *tr. V.* **a)** threaten; **b)** *(gefährden)* threaten; endanger; **den Frieden ~:** be a threat *or* danger to peace; **vom Feuer bedroht sein** be in danger of catching fire; **vom Aussterben bedroht sein** be threatened with extinction

bedrohlich 1. *Adj. (drohend)* threatening, menacing ⟨*gesture*⟩; *(unheilverkündend)* ominous; *(gefährlich)* dangerous. **2.** *adv. (drohend)* threateningly; menacingly; *(unheilverkündend)* ominously; *(gefährlich)* dangerously; **~ nahe kommen** come ominously/dangerously near

Bedrohlichkeit die; ~: dangerousness; *(einer Krankheit usw.)* dangerous nature

Bedrohung die threat *(Gen.* to); **in ständiger ~:** under a constant threat

bedrucken *tr. V.* print; **etw. mit einer Adresse ~:** print an address on sth.; **ein mit Blumen bedrucktes Kleid** a flower-print dress

bedrücken *tr. V.* **a)** depress; **es bedrückt mich, daß ...:** I feel depressed that ...; **bedrückt dich was?** is something weighing on your mind?; **b)** *(veralt.: unterdrücken)* oppress

bedrückend *Adj.* oppressive; depressing ⟨*sight, thought, news*⟩

bedruckt *Adj.* printed; print *attrib.* ⟨*dress etc.*⟩

bedrückt *Adj.* depressed; oppressed ⟨*people*⟩

Bedrückung die; ~, ~en depression; *(eines Volkes)* oppression

Beduine [beduˈiːnə] **der; ~n, ~n** Bed[o]uin

bedungen [bəˈdʊŋən] *2. Part. v.* **²bedingen**

bedürfen *unr. itr. V. (geh.)* **jmds./einer Sache ~:** require *or* need sb./sth.; **es bedarf einer Sache** there is need for sth.; **es bedarf nur eines Wortes von Ihnen** you need only say so; **es bedarf keines weiteren Wortes** no more need be said; **es bedarf einiger Mühe** *(geh.)* some effort is needed *or* required

Bedürfnis das; ~ses, ~se need **(nach** for); **dafür besteht kein ~:** there is no necessity for that; **das ~ haben, etw. zu tun** feel a need to do sth.; **ein ~ nach etw. haben** be in need of sth.; **es war mir ein ~, das zu tun** I felt the need to do it

bedürfnis-, Bedürfnis-: ~anstalt die *(Amtsspr.)* public convenience; **~befriedigung die** satisfaction of one's needs; *(polit. Ökonomie)* satisfaction of needs; **~los 1.** *Adj.* ⟨*person*⟩ with few [material] needs; modest, simple ⟨*life*⟩; **~los sein** have few [material] needs; **2.** *adv.* **~los leben** have a [very] modest life-style; **~losigkeit die; ~:** lack of [material] needs

bedürftig *Adj.* **a)** needy; **die Bedürftigen** the needy; those in need; **b)** *in* **jmds./einer Sache ~ sein** *(geh.)* be in need of sb./sth.

Bedürftigkeit die; ~: neediness; **die ~ einer Familie feststellen** means-test a family

beduseln *refl. V. (ugs.)* get merry *(coll.)*; **ich war beduselt** *(fig.)* my head was spinning

Beef·steak [ˈbiːfsteːk] **das** [beef]steak; **deutsches ~:** ≈ beefburger

beehren *(geh.)* **1.** *tr. V.* **a) jmdn. mit seinem Besuch/seiner Anwesenheit ~** *(auch iron.)* honour sb. with a visit/one's presence; **b)** *(gespreizt: besuchen)* **~ Sie uns bald wieder** *(im Geschäft/privat)* we hope to have the pleasure of your custom/company again. **2.** *refl. V.* **sich ~, etw. zu tun** have the honour to do sth.

beeiden [bəˈ|aidn̩] *tr. V.* **~, daß ...:** swear [on oath] that ...; **eine Aussage ~:** swear to the truth of a statement

beeidigen [bəˈ|aɪdɪgn̩] **a)** *(geh.) s.* **beeiden; b)** *(veralt.: vereidigen)* swear in; **ein beeidigter Zeuge** a sworn witness

beeilen *refl. V.* **a)** hurry [up] *(coll.)*; **beeil dich!** hurry [up]; **sich bei einer Arbeit ~:** hurry over a task; **du mußt dich aber mächtig beeilt haben** *(ugs.)* you must have really got a move on *(coll.)*; **b)** *(nicht zögern)* **sich ~, etw. zu tun** hasten to do sth.

Beeilung *Interj.* **[los], ~!** *(ugs.)*, **~ bitte!** *(ugs.)* get a move on! *(coll.)*; hurry up! *(coll.)*

beeindrucken *tr. V.* impress; **sich von etw. ~ lassen** be impressed by sth.; **~d** impressive

beeinflußbar *Adj.* **leicht/schwer ~ sein** ⟨*person*⟩ be easily influenced/hard *or* difficult to influence; **das ist nicht ~:** it cannot be influenced

beeinflussen [bəˈ|ainflʊsn̩] *tr. V.* influence; influence, affect ⟨*result, process, etc.*⟩; **jmdn./etw. positiv/nachhaltig ~:** have a positive/lasting influence on sb./sth.; **sich leicht ~ lassen** be easily influenced

Beeinflussung die; ~, ~en a) *(das Einflußnehmen)* influencing; **seine ~ durch die Schule** the influence of the school on him; **b)** *(Einfluß)* influence

beeinträchtigen [bəˈ|aintrɛçtɪgn̩] *tr. V.* restrict ⟨*sights, freedom*⟩; detract from, spoil ⟨*pleasure, enjoyment*⟩; spoil ⟨*appetite, good humour*⟩; detract from, diminish ⟨*value*⟩; diminish, impair ⟨*quality*⟩; impair ⟨*reactions, efficiency, vision, hearing*⟩; damage, harm ⟨*sales, reputation*⟩; reduce ⟨*production*⟩; **jmdn. in seiner Freiheit ~:** restrict sb.'s freedom; **sich beeinträchtigt fühlen** feel hampered

Beeinträchtigung die; ~, ~en: *s.* **beeinträchtigen:** restriction; detracting (+ *Gen.* from); spoiling; diminution; impairment; damage *(Gen.* to); harm *(Gen.* to); reduction; **eine ~ der Freiheit** a restriction on one's freedom

beelenden *tr. V. (schweiz.)* sadden

Beelzebub [ˈbeːltsə-] **(der)** Beelzebub; **den Teufel mit** *od.* **durch ~ austreiben** *(fig.)* replace one evil by *or* with another

beenden, beendigen *tr. V.* end; finish ⟨*piece of work, dissertation, etc.*⟩; end, conclude ⟨*negotiations, letter, lecture*⟩; complete, finish ⟨*studies*⟩; end, bring to an end ⟨*meeting, relationship, dispute, strike*⟩; **das Fest wurde mit einem Feuerwerk beendet** the celebration ended with a firework display; **damit ~ wir unser heutiges Programm** that brings to an end our programmes for today

Beendigung die; ~, Beendung die; ~ *(Ende)* end; *(Fertigstellung)* completion; **nach/vor ~ des Unterrichts** after/before school is/was over

beengen *tr. V.* hinder, restrict ⟨*movements*⟩; *(fig.)* restrict ⟨*freedom [of action]*⟩; **das Kleid/dieses Zimmer beengt mich** the dress hinders *or* restricts my movements/this room ist too cramped for me; **beengt wohnen** live in cramped surroundings *or* conditions; **sich beengt fühlen** feel cramped; *(fig.: durch Regeln usw.)* feel constricted; **diese kleinbürgerliche Atmosphäre beengte ihn** *(fig.)* he found this petit-bourgeois atmosphere stifling *or* restricting

Beengtheit die; ~ *(von Räumen)* crampedness; **ein Gefühl der ~:** a feeling of being cramped

beerben *tr. V.* **jmdn.** ~: inherit sb's estate
beerdigen [bə'|e:ɐ̯dɪgn̩] *tr. V.* bury; **jmdn. kirchlich** ~: give sb. a Christian burial
Beerdigung die; ~, ~**en** *(Bestattung)* burial; *(Trauerfeier)* funeral; **auf der falschen** ~ **sein** *(salopp, scherzh.)* have come to the wrong place
Beerdigungs·institut das [firm *sing.* of] undertakers *pl. or* funeral directors *pl.*
Beere ['be:rə] **die;** ~, ~**n** berry
Beeren-: ~**auslese die** *wine made from selected overripe grapes;* ~**obst das** soft fruit
Beet [be:t] **das;** ~**[e]s,** ~**e** *(Blumen~)* bed; *(Gemüse~)* plot
Beete *s.* **Bete**
befähigen [bə'fɛ:ɪgn̩] *tr. V.* **jmdn.** ~, **etw. zu tun** enable sb. to do sth.; ⟨*qualifications, training, etc.*⟩ qualify sb. to do sth.
befähigt 1. *2. Part. v.* **befähigen. 2.** *Adj.* **a)** *(qualifiziert)* qualified; **b)** *(begabt)* gifted
Befähigung die; ~ **a)** *(Qualifikation)* qualification; **die** ~ **zum Internisten/Hochschulstudium/Richteramt** the qualifications *pl.* for becoming an internist/studying at university/being a judge; **b)** *(Können)* ability; *(Talent)* talent; **seine** ~ **zum Schriftsteller** his talent as a writer *or* for writing
Befähigungs·nachweis der *(Amtsspr.)* proof of one's qualifications
befahl [bə'fa:l] *1. u. 3. Pers. Sg. Prät. v.* **befehlen**
befahrbar *Adj.* passable; navigable ⟨*canal, river*⟩; **nicht** ~: impassable/unnavigable
[1]**befahren** *unr. tr. V.* **a)** drive on, use ⟨*road*⟩; drive across, use ⟨*bridge, pass*⟩; use ⟨*railway line*⟩; **die Straße kann nur im Sommer** ~ **werden** this road is passable only in summer; **die Straße ist nur in einer Richtung zu** ~: traffic can only use the road in one direction; **„Seitenstreifen nicht** ~**!"** 'keep off verges'; **die Straße ist stark/wenig** ~: the road is heavily/little used; **eine stark** ~**e Straße** a busy road; **b)** sail ⟨*sea*⟩; navigate, sail up/down ⟨*river, canal*⟩; **eine stark** ~**e Wasserstraße** a busy waterway; **die Weltmeere** ~: sail the oceans; **c)** *(Bergmannsspr.)* **eine Grube** ~: go down a mine
[2]**befahren** *Adj.* **a)** *(Seemannsspr.)* seasoned; experienced; **b)** *(Jägerspr.)* inhabited ⟨*earth etc.*⟩
Befall der; ~**[e]s:** ~ *(Landw.)* attack (*Gen.* on; **durch, von** by)
befallen *unr. tr. V.* **a)** *(überkommen)* overcome; ⟨*misfortune*⟩ befall; **Fieber/eine Grippe befiel ihn** *(geh.)* he was stricken by fever/influenza; **von Panik/Angst/Heimweh** *usw.* ~ **werden** be seized *or* overcome with *or* by panic/fear/homesickness *etc.*; **von einer Ohnmacht/Schwäche/von Resignation** ~ **werden** faint/feel faint/be overcome with a feeling of resignation; **b)** ⟨*pests*⟩ attack
befangen 1. *Adj.* **a)** *(gehemmt)* self-conscious, awkward ⟨*person*⟩; **jmdn.** ~ **machen** make sb. self-conscious *or* awkward; **b)** *(bes. Rechtsw.: voreingenommen)* biased; **einen Richter als** ~ **ablehnen** challenge a judge on grounds of bias; **c) in einem Glauben/Irrtum** ~ **sein** *(geh.)* labour under a belief/misapprehension; **in Vorurteilen** ~ **sein** be prejudiced. **2.** *adv.* self-consciously; awkwardly
Befangenheit die; ~ **a)** self-consciousness; awkwardness; **b)** *(bes. Rechtsw.: Voreingenommenheit)* bias
Befangenheits·antrag der *(Rechtsw.)* challenge on grounds of bias
befassen 1. *refl. V.* **sich mit etw.** ~: occupy oneself with sth.; *(studieren)* study sth.; ⟨*article, book*⟩ deal with sth.; **sich nicht mit Kleinigkeiten** ~: not concern *or* bother oneself with trivial details; **mit diesem Thema haben wir uns lange genug befaßt** we've spent enough time on this subject; **sich mit jmdm./einem Fall/einer Angelegenheit** ~: deal with *or* attend to sb./a case/matter; **ich habe mich schon mit dieser Sache befaßt** I've already been into this matter; **sich viel mit jmdm.** ~: give sb. a great deal of attention; spend a great deal of time with sb.; **sich mit jedem Kind einzeln** ~: ⟨*teacher*⟩ give each child individual attention. **2.** *tr. V. (bes. Amtsspr.)* **jmdn. mit etw.** ~: get *or* instruct sb. to deal with sth.; **die mit diesem Fall befaßte Behörde** the authorities dealing *or* involved with this case
befehden [bə'fe:dn̩] *tr. V.* **a)** *(hist.)* feud with; **b)** *(geh.)* attack ⟨*plan, proposal, etc.*⟩; **sich/einander** ~: feud [with each other]; attack each other
Befehl [bə'fe:l] **der;** ~**[e]s,** ~**e a)** order; command; **jmdm. den** ~ **geben, etw. zu tun** order *or* command sb. to do sth.; **den** ~ **haben, etw. zu tun** be under orders *or* have been ordered to do sth.; **auf jmds.** ~ *(Akk.)* on sb.'s orders; **auf** ~ **handeln** act under orders; ~ **ist** ~: orders are orders; **zu** ~ **[Herr Leutnant/Oberst/General/Kapitän]!** yes, sir!; aye, aye, sir! *(Navy);* **dein Wunsch ist** *od.* **sei mir** ~ *(ugs. scherzh.)* your wish is my command; **b)** *(Befehlsgewalt)* command; **den** ~ **über jmdn./etw. haben** have command of *or* be in command of sb./sth.; **unter jmds.** ~ *(Dat.)* **stehen** be under sb.'s command; **den** ~ **übernehmen** take command; **c)** *(DV)* instruction; command
befehlen 1. *unr. tr., itr. V.* **a)** order; *(Milit.)* order; command; *(heißen)* tell; **jmdm. Stillschweigen** ~: order sb. to keep silent; **man befahl ihm zu warten** he was told to wait; **er befahl die Räumung des Dorfes** he ordered the village to be cleared; **er befiehlt gern** he likes to order people about; **von Ihnen lasse ich mir nichts** ~: I don't take orders from you; **[ganz] wie Sie** ~ *(veralt.)* [just] as you wish; ~ **gnädige Frau sonst noch etwas?** *(veralt.)* is there anything else, ma'am?; **b)** *(beordern)* order; *(zu sich)* summon; **jmdn. zum Rapport** ~: order/summon sb. to report; **c)** *(geh. veralt.)* commend; **seine Seele Gott/in Gottes Hände** ~ *(bibl.)* commend one's soul to God; **befiehl dem Herrn deine Wege!** *(bibl.)* commit thy ways unto the Lord. **2.** *unr. itr. V.* have command; be in command; **über eine Armee** ~: have command of *or* be in command of an army
befehligen *tr. V.* have command of; be in command of; **von ... befehligt werden** be commanded by ...; be under the command of ...
befehls-, Befehls-: ~**aus·gabe die** *(Milit.)* issuing of orders; briefing; ~**bereich der** [area of] command; ~**empfänger der** recipient of an order/orders; **bloße** ~**empfänger [der Zentrale] sein** just follow *or* take orders [from headquarters]; ~**form die** *(Sprachw.)* imperative [form]; ~**gemäß 1.** *Adj.* **die** ~**gemäße Durchführung des Plans** *usw.* carrying out the plan *etc.* in accordance with orders *or* as ordered; **2.** *adv.* in accordance with orders; as ordered; ~**gewalt die;** *o. Pl.* command (**über** + *Akk.* of); **jmds.** ~**gewalt** *(Dat.)* **unterstehen** be under sb.'s command; ~**haber** [~ha:bɐ] **der;** ~**s,** ~ *(Milit.)* commander; ~**notstand der** *(Rechtsw.)* **unter** ~**notstand handeln** be acting under orders; **in einem** ~**notstand sein/sich in einem** ~**notstand befinden** have to obey orders; ~**satz der** *(Sprachw.)* imperative sentence; ~**stab der** *(Eisenb.)* station-official's rod and signalling-disc; ≈ guard's flag; ~**ton der;** *o. Pl.* peremptory tone; ~**verweigerung die** refusal to obey an order/orders; ~**widrig 1.** *Adj.* contrary to orders *postpos.*; **2.** *adv.* contrary to orders
befeinden *tr. V.* be hostile to; **die Juden wurden dort befeindet** there was hostility to the Jews there
befestigen *tr. V.* **a)** fix (**mit** with); **etw. mit Stecknadeln/Bindfaden** ~: fasten sth. with pins/string; **etw. mit Schrauben/Leim** ~: fasten *or* fix sth. with screws/fix *or* stick sth. with glue; **etw. an der Wand** ~: fix sth. to the wall; **einen Anhänger an einem Koffer** ~: attach *or* fasten a label to a case; **ein Boot an einem Pfosten** ~: tie up *or* moor a boat to a post; **b)** *(haltbar machen)* stabilize ⟨*bank, embankment*⟩; make up ⟨*road, path, etc.*⟩; **c)** *(sichern)* fortify ⟨*town etc.*⟩; strengthen ⟨*border*⟩; **d)** *(festigen)* consolidate ⟨*reputation, authority*⟩; enhance ⟨*standing*⟩; strengthen ⟨*friendship, confidence*⟩
Befestigung die; ~, ~**en a)** *(Milit.)* fortification; **b)** *s.* **befestigen a:** fixing; fastening; attachment; tying up; mooring; **c)** *(Haltbarmachung) (eines Ufers)* stabilization; *(eines Weges)* making up; **d)** *(Stärkung) s.* **befestigen d:** consolidation; enhancement; strengthening
Befestigungs-: ~**an·lage die** fortifications *pl.*; ~**linie die** line of fortifications
befeuchten [bə'fɔyçtn̩] *tr. V.* moisten; damp ⟨*hair, cloth*⟩; **von Tränen/Tau befeuchtet** moist *or* wet with tears/dew
befeuern *tr. V.* **a)** *(beheizen)* fuel; **b)** *(beschießen)* shoot at; fire on; **c)** *(ugs.: bewerfen)* pelt (**mit** with); **d)** *(geh.: anfeuern)* inspire; **e)** *(Schiffahrt, Flugw.)* mark ⟨*coastline, runway, etc.*⟩ with lights *or* beacons
Befeuerung die lights *pl.*; beacons *pl.*
Beffchen ['bɛfçən] **das;** ~**s,** ~: [collar *sing.* with] bands *pl. (worn esp. by Protestant clergymen)*
befiehlst [bə'fi:lst], **befiehlt** [bə'fi:lt] *2., 3. Pers. Sg. Präsens v.* **befehlen**
befinden 1. *unr. refl. V.* be; **sich im Urlaub/auf Reisen** ~: be on holiday/be away on a trip; **unter ihnen befand sich jemand, der ...:** among them there was somebody who ...; **sich wohl** ~ *(geh.)* be well. **2.** *unr. tr. V. (geh.)* **a) etw. für gut/richtig** ~: find *or* consider sth. [to be] good/right; **jmdn. für tauglich** ~: declare sb. [to be] fit; **jmdn. für** *od.* **als schuldig** ~: find sb. guilty; **b)** *(äußern)* declare; assert. **3.** *unr. itr. V.* **über etw.** *(Akk.)* ~: decide [on] sth.; make a decision on sth.; **darüber habe ich nicht zu** ~: that's not for me to decide
Befinden das; ~**s a)** health; *(eines Patienten)* condition; **sich nach jmds.** ~ **erkundigen** enquire after *or* about sb.'s health; **wie ist Ihr** ~ **heute?** *(geh.)* how are you today?; **b)** *(geh.: Urteil)* judgement; **etw. nach eigenem** ~ **entscheiden** use one's own judgement in deciding sth.; **nach seinem/ihrem [eigenen]** ~: in his/her [own] judgement *or* estimation
befindlich *Adj.* **a)** *nicht präd. (liegend)* to be found *postpos.*; **das in der Kasse** ~**e Geld** the money in the till; **eine am Stadtrand** ~**e Siedlung** an estate [situated] on the edge of town; **b)** *(in einem Zustand)* **die im Bau** ~**en Häuser** the houses [which are/were] under construction
Befindlichkeit die; ~, ~**en** *(geh.)* state
befingern *tr. V. (salopp)* finger
beflaggen *tr. V.* **etw.** ~: decorate *or* [be]deck sth. with flags; **ein Schiff** ~: dress a ship
Beflaggung die; ~: decoration with flags; *(eines Schiffes)* dressing
beflecken *tr. V.* **a)** stain; **sich mit Blut** ~ *(verhüll. geh.)* stain one's hand with blood; **b)** *(fig.)* besmirch; stain; defile ⟨*sanctity*⟩
Befleckung die; ~ *(fig.)* besmirching; staining; *(eines Heiligtums)* defilement
befleißigen *refl. V. (geh.)* **sich eines klaren Stils/höflicheren Tons** *usw.* ~: make a great effort to cultivate a clear style/to adopt a more polite tone of voice *etc.*; **sich größter Zurückhaltung** ~: endeavour to exercise the greatest restraint
befliegen *unr. tr. V.* fly ⟨*route*⟩; **eine stark beflogene Route** a route with heavy [air] traffic

beflissen [bəˈflɪsn̩] *(geh.)* **1.** *Adj.* keen; eager; *(emsig)* assiduous; zealous; **~ sein/ängstlich ~ sein, etw. zu tun** be keen *or* eager/anxious to do sth. **2.** *adv.* keenly; eagerly; *(emsig)* assiduously; zealously

Beflissenheit die; ~: keenness; eagerness; *(Emsigkeit)* assiduousness; zeal

beflissentlich *Adj.; nicht präd.: s.* **geflissentlich**

beflügeln *tr. V. (geh.)* **a) jmdn. ~:** inspire sb.; ⟨*success, praise*⟩ spur sb. on, inspire sb.; **b)** *(schneller machen)* **jmds. Schritte/Gang ~:** ⟨*fear, joy*⟩ wing sb.'s steps; **jmdn. ~:** spur sb. on

befohlen [bəˈfoːlən] *2. Part. v.* **befehlen**

befolgen *tr. V.* follow, obey ⟨*instruction, grammatical rule*⟩; obey, comply with ⟨*law, regulation*⟩; follow, take ⟨*advice*⟩; follow ⟨*suggestion*⟩

Befolgung die; ~: *s.* **befolgen:** following; obedience (*Gen.* to); compliance (*Gen.* with); **die ~ des Gesetzes** obedience to *or* compliance with the law

Beförderer der carrier

befördern *tr. V.* **a)** carry; transport; convey; **etw. mit der Post/per Schiff/Luftfracht ~** *(schicken)* send sth. by post/sea/air; **jmdn. ins Freie** *od.* **an die Luft ~** *(ugs.)* chuck *(coll.) or* throw sb. out; *s. auch* **Jenseits; b)** *(aufrücken lassen)* promote; **zum Direktor befördert werden** be promoted to director

Beförderung die a) *o. Pl. (Waren~)* carriage; transport; conveyance; *(Personen~)* transport; conveyance; **Schäden, die bei der ~ entstehen** damage in transit; **die ~ per Luft/zu Lande** carriage *or* transport by air/road; **Züge zur ~ der Urlaubsreisenden** trains to carry the holiday passengers; **b)** *(das Aufrücken)* promotion **(zu** to)

Beförderungs-: ~bedingungen *Pl.* conditions of carriage; **~kosten** *Pl.* cost *sing.* of transport *or* transportation; transport *or* transportation costs; **~mittel das** means of transport; **~pflicht die** *obligation on bus companies, airlines, etc. to accept and convey passengers and goods*

befrachten *tr. V.* load **(mit** with); **mit Emotionen befrachtet** *(fig.)* ⟨*discussion etc.*⟩ charged with emotion; **mit Geschichte befrachtet** *(fig.)*⟨*castle, church, etc.*⟩ steeped in history

Befrachter der; ~s, ~: freighter

befrackt *Adj.* **ein ~er Herr** a gentleman wearing *or* in tails

befragen *tr. V.* **a)** *(ausfragen)* question **(über +** *Akk.* about); **einen Zeugen ~:** question *or* examine a witness; **auf Befragen** when questioned; **b)** *(fragen)* ask; consult; **jmdn. nach seiner Meinung ~:** ask sb. for his/her opinion; **ein Orakel/die Karten ~:** consult an oracle/the cards

Befragte der/die; *adj. Dekl.* man/woman/person questioned; **20% der ~n** 20% of those questioned

Befragung die; ~, ~en a) questioning; *(vor Gericht)* questioning; examination; **eine ~ aller Schüler vornehmen** question all the pupils; **b)** *(Konsultation)* consultation; **nach ~ des Arztes** after consulting the doctor; **c)** *(Umfrage)* opinion poll

befreien 1. *tr. V.* **a)** free ⟨*prisoner*⟩; set ⟨*animal*⟩ free; **jmdn. aus den Händen seiner Entführer ~:** rescue sb. from the hands of his/her abductors; **b)** *(frei machen)* liberate ⟨*country, people*⟩ **(von** from); **c)** *(freistellen)* exempt **(von** from); **jmdn. vom Turnunterricht/Wehrdienst/von einer Pflicht ~:** excuse sb. [from] physical education/exempt sb. from military service/release sb. from an obligation; **jmdn. von einer Aufgabe ~:** excuse sb. from *or* let sb. off a task; **d)** *(erlösen)* **jmdn. von Schmerzen ~:** free sb. of pain; **von seinen Leiden befreit werden** *(durch den Tod)* be released from one's sufferings; **jmdn. von Angst/einer Sorge ~:** remove sb.'s fear/free sb. of a worry; **ein ~des Lachen** a laugh which breaks/broke the tension; **e)** *(reinigen)* **die Straße von Schnee/Eis ~:** clear the road of snow/ice; **etw. von Läusen ~:** rid sth. of lice. **2.** *refl. V.* free oneself **(von** from); **sich von Vorurteilen/traditionellen Denkweisen ~:** rid oneself of prejudice *sing.*/break away from traditional ways of thinking

Befreier der, Befreierin die; ~, ~nen liberator

befreit 1. *Adj.* relieved; **sich ~ fühlen** feel relieved. **2.** *adv.* with relief; **~ aufatmen** heave a sigh of relief

Befreiung die; ~ a) freeing; **eine ~ des Kindes aus den Händen der Entführer ...:** rescuing the child from the hands of its abductors ...; **b)** *(das Freiwerden)* liberation; **die ~ der Frau** the emancipation of women; **c)** *(Erlösung)* **die ~ von Schmerzen** release from pain; **d)** *(Erleichterung)* relief; **e)** *(Freistellung)* exemption; **um ~ vom Sportunterricht/von einer Pflicht bitten** ask to be excused [from] sport/released from an obligation

Befreiungs-: ~armee die army of liberation; **~bewegung die** liberation movement; **~front die** liberation front; **~kampf der** liberation struggle; **~krieg der a)** war of liberation; **b)** *Pl. (hist.)* Wars of Liberation *(1813–1815);* **~versuch der** rescue bid *or* attempt; *(Ausbruchsversuch)* escape bid *or* attempt

befremden [bəˈfrɛmdn̩] **1.** *tr. V.* **jmdn. ~:** put sb. off; *(erstaunen)* take sb. aback; **es befremdete ihn, daß ...:** he was taken aback [to find] that ... **2.** *itr. V.* be disturbing

Befremden das; ~s surprise and displeasure

befremdlich *(geh.)* **1.** *Adj.* strange; odd. **2.** *adv.* strangely

Befremdung die; ~ *s.* **Befremden**

befreunden [bəˈfrɔyndn̩] *refl. V.* **a)** make *or* become friends **(mit** with); **sich miteinander ~:** make *or* become friends; **b)** *(gewöhnen)* **sich mit etw. ~:** get used to sth.

befreundet *Adj.* **[gut** *od.* **eng] ~ sein** be [good *or* close] friends **(mit** with); **ein uns** *(Dat.)* **~es Ehepaar/~er Schauspieler** a couple with whom we are friends/an actor who is a friend of ours; **~e Familien/Kinder** families which are friendly with each other/children who are friends; **das ~e Ausland** friendly [foreign] countries

befrieden *tr. V. (geh.)* bring peace to ⟨*country*⟩; **das Land ist jetzt befriedet** *(oft verhüll.)* the country is now at peace

befriedigen [bəˈfriːdɪɡn̩] *tr. (auch itr.) V.* **a)** satisfy; satisfy, meet ⟨*demand, need*⟩; satisfy, fulfil ⟨*wish*⟩; satisfy, gratify ⟨*lust*⟩; **seine Gläubiger ~:** satisfy one's creditors; **das Ergebnis befriedigte mich** the result satisfied me *or* was satisfactory to me; **seine Leistung befriedigte [nicht]** his performance was [un]satisfactory; **leicht/schwer zu ~ sein** be easy/hard to satisfy; be easily/not easily satisfied; **b)** *(ausfüllen)* ⟨*job, occupation, etc.*⟩ fulfil; **c)** *(sexuell)* satisfy; **sich [selbst] ~:** masturbate

befriedigend 1. *Adj.* **a)** satisfactory; satisfactory, adequate ⟨*reply, performance*⟩; **nicht ~ sein** be unsatisfactory/inadequate; **in Latein hat er „~" bekommen** ≈ he got a C in Latin; **b)** *(erfüllend)* ⟨*job, occupation, etc.*⟩ fulfilling. **2.** *adv.* satisfactorily; ⟨*answer*⟩ satisfactorily, adequately

befriedigt 1. *Adj.* satisfied. **2.** *adv.* with satisfaction

Befriedigung die; ~ a) *s.* **befriedigen a:** satisfaction; meeting; fulfilment; gratification; **sexuelle ~:** sexual satisfaction; **zur ~ deiner Neugier** to satisfy your curiosity; **b)** *(Genugtuung)* satisfaction; **~ darin finden, etw. zu tun** get satisfaction from doing sth.

Befriedung die; ~: ein Plan zur ~ des Landes a plan to bring peace to the country

befristen *tr. V.* **etw. ~:** limit the duration of sth. **(auf +** *Akk.* to)

befristet *Adj.* temporary ⟨*visa*⟩; fixed-term ⟨*ban, contract*⟩; **ein auf zwei Jahre ~er Vertrag** a two-year fixed-term contract; **~ sein** ⟨*visa, permit*⟩ be valid for a limited period [only]; **auf ein Jahr ~ sein** ⟨*visa, permit*⟩ be valid for one year; **ein auf zwei Jahre ~es Abkommen** an agreement running for *or* lasting two years

Befristung die; ~, ~en setting of a time limit/time limits; **mit einer ~ auf fünf Jahre gelten** have a time-limit of five years

befruchten *tr. V.* **a)** fertilize ⟨*egg*⟩; pollinate ⟨*flower*⟩; impregnate ⟨*female*⟩; *(fig. geh.)* make ⟨*fields, land*⟩ fertile; **ein Tier künstlich ~:** artificially inseminate an animal; **b)** *(geh.)* **jmdn./etw. ~, einen ~den Einfluß auf jmdn./etw. haben** have *or* be a stimulating *or* inspiring influence [up]on sb./sth.

Befruchtung die; ~, ~en a) *s.* **befruchten a:** fertilization; pollination; impregnation; **künstliche ~:** artificial insemination; **b)** *(geh.: Anregung)* stimulation; inspiration

befugen *tr. V.* authorize; **dazu befugt sein, etw. zu tun** be authorized to do sth.; **befugte/nicht befugte Personen** authorized/unauthorized persons

Befugnis die; ~, ~se authority; **seine ~se überschreiten** exceed one's authority *sing.;* **die ~ haben, etw. zu tun** have the authority to do sth.; be authorized to do sth.

befühlen *tr. V.* feel; *(streicheln)* run one's fingers over; fondle

befummeln *tr. V. (ugs.)* **a)** paw *(coll.);* **b)** *(sexuell berühren)* grope *(sl.);* feel up *(sl.);* **c)** *(regeln, erledigen)* fix; take care of

Befund der *(bes. Med.)* result[s *pl.*]; **ohne ~:** negative

befürchten *tr. V.* fear; **ich befürchte, daß ...:** I am afraid that ...; **das Schlimmste ~:** fear the worst; **das ist nicht zu ~:** there is no fear of that; **eine militärische Auseinandersetzung ~:** fear that there may be a military conflict

Befürchtung die; ~, ~en fear; **die ~ haben** *od. (geh.)* **hegen, daß ...:** be afraid that ...

befürworten [bəˈfyːɐ̯vɔrtn̩] *tr. V.* support; *(genehmigen)* approve

Befürworter der; ~s, ~, Befürworterin die; ~, ~nen supporter

Befürwortung die; ~, ~en support; *(Genehmigung)* approval

begaben *tr. V. (geh.)* endow

begabt [bəˈɡaːpt] *Adj.* talented; gifted; **vielseitig ~ sein** be many-talented; have many talents; **für etw. ~ sein** have a gift *or* talent for sth.

Begabte der/die; *adj. Dekl.* gifted *or* talented person/man/woman *etc.*

Begabten·förderung die assistance to gifted pupils/students

Begabung die; ~, ~en a) *(Talent)* talent; gift; **eine ~ [für etw.] haben** have a gift *or* talent [for sth.]; **die ~ haben, etw. zu tun** *(iron.)* have a talent for *or* the knack of doing sth. *(iron.);* **b)** *(begabter Mensch)* talented person/man/woman *etc.;* talent; **er war eine musikalische ~:** he had a talent for music

begaffen *tr. V. (ugs. abwertend)* gawp at *(coll.);* stare at

begann [bəˈɡan] *1. u. 3. Pers. Sg. Prät. v.* **beginnen**

begasen [bəˈɡaːzn̩] *tr. V. (Landw.)* gas

begatten [bəˈɡatn̩] **1.** *tr. V.* mate with; ⟨*man, husband*⟩ copulate with; ⟨*stallion, bull*⟩ cover. **2.** *refl. V.* mate; ⟨*persons*⟩ copulate

Begattung die mating; *(bei Menschen)* copulation

Begattungs·organe *Pl.* reproductive organs

begaunern *tr. V. (ugs. abwertend)* **jmdn. ~:** rip sb. off *(sl.)*; swindle sb.

begeben *unr. refl. V. (geh.)* **a)** proceed; make one's way; go; **sich nach Hause/ins Hotel ~:** proceed *or* make one's way *or* go home/into the hotel; **sich auf den Heimweg ~:** start for home; **sich zu Bett ~:** retire to bed; **sich in ärztliche Behandlung ~:** get medical treatment; go to a doctor for treatment; *s. auch* **Gefahr; b)** *(beginnen)* commence; **sich daran ~, etw. zu tun** commence doing sth.; **sich an die Arbeit ~:** commence work; **c)** *(unpers.: geschehen)* happen; occur; **es begab sich aber zu der Zeit, daß ...** *(bibl.)* and it came to pass in those days that ...; **d)** *(verzichten auf)* **sich einer Möglichkeit/eines Rechts** *usw.* **~:** forgo an opportunity/a right *etc.*

Begebenheit die; ~, ~en *(geh.)* event; occurrence

begegnen [bəˈgeːgnən] *itr. V.; mit sein* **a) jmdm. ~:** meet sb.; **sich** *(Dat.) od.* **einander ~:** meet [each other]; **ihre Blicke begegneten sich** *(Dat.) (geh.)* their eyes met; **b)** *(antreffen)* **einer Sache** *(Dat.)* **~:** encounter sth.; come across sth.; **solche Ausdrücke ~ einem** one encounters such expressions; **c)** *(geh.: widerfahren)* **etw. begegnet jmdm.** sth. happens to sb.; **d)** *(geh.: behandeln)* **jmdm. freundlich/höflich** *usw.* **~:** behave in a friendly/polite *etc.* way towards sb.; treat sb. in a friendly/polite *etc.* way; **einem Vorschlag kühl ~:** treat a suggestion with coolness; **e)** *(geh.: entgegentreten)* counter ‹*accusation, attack*›; combat ‹*illness, disease; misuse of drugs, alcohol, etc.*›; meet ‹*difficulty, danger*›; deal with ‹*emergency*›

Begegnung die; ~, ~en a) meeting; *(das Antreffen)* encounter; **eine Stätte internationaler ~en** an international meeting-place; **b)** *(Sport)* match; **die ~ Schweden gegen Italien** the match between Sweden and Italy

Begegnungs·stätte die *(Amtsspr.)* community centre

begehbar *Adj.* **der Weg ist nicht ~:** the path cannot be used *or* is impassable; **ein ~es Dach** a roof that is safe to walk on; **etw. besser ~ machen** make sth. easier to walk along

begehen *unr. tr. V.* **a)** commit ‹*crime, adultery, indiscretion, sin, suicide, faux-pas, etc.*›; make ‹*mistake*›; **eine [furchtbare] Dummheit/Taktlosigkeit ~:** do something [really] stupid/tactless; **einen Mord an jmdm. ~:** murder sb.; **ein oft begangener Fehler** a frequent *or* common mistake; *s. auch* **Verrat; b)** *(geh.: feiern)* celebrate; **ein Fest würdig ~:** celebrate an occasion fittingly; **c)** *(abgehen)* inspect [on foot]; **d)** *(gehen)* walk along ‹*path*›; walk across ‹*bridge*›; *(benutzen)* use

Begehr [bəˈgeːɐ̯] **der** *od.* **das; ~s** *(veralt.)* wish; desire; **was ist euer ~?** what is it that you require?

begehren *tr. V.* **a)** *(haben wollen)* desire; wish for; desire ‹*woman*›; **ein Mädchen zur Frau ~** *(veralt.)* ask for a girl's hand in marriage; **du sollst nicht ~ ...** *(bibl.)* thou shalt not covet ...; *s. auch* **Herz b; b)** *(veralt.: wollen)* desire; **c)** *(bitten um)* ask for

Begehren das; ~s *(geh.)* desire, wish **(nach** for); **jmdn. nach seinem ~ fragen** inquire *or* ask what sb. desires; **einem ~ entsprechen** grant sb.'s request

begehrens·wert *Adj.* desirable

begehrlich 1. *Adj. (gierig)* greedy; *(verlangend)* longing. **2.** *adv. (gierig)* greedily; *(verlangend)* longingly

Begehrlichkeit die; ~, ~en *(Gier)* greed; *(Verlangen)* desire

begehrt *Adj.* much sought-after; **~ bei den Damen sein** be much in demand with the ladies

Begehung die; ~, ~en a) *o. Pl. (Ausführung)* **die ~ eines Verbrechens/eines Fehlers** committing a crime/making a mistake; **b)** *(Feier)* celebration; **c)** *(das Abgehen)* inspection [on foot]

begeifern *tr. V. (abwertend: schmähen)* run down; vilify

begeistern 1. *tr. V.* **jmdn. [für etw.] ~:** fill *or* fire sb. with enthusiasm [for sth.]; **das Publikum ~:** fire the audience; **das kann mich nicht ~:** that leaves me cold. **2.** *refl. V.* get *or* be enthusiastic **(für** about); **sich an der schönen Landschaft/für die Oper ~:** be very fond of the beautiful scenery/be keen on opera

begeisternd *Adj.* rousing

begeistert 1. *Adj.* enthusiastic; **von jmdm./etw. ~ sein** be taken by *or* with sb./be enthusiastic about sth. **2.** *adv.* enthusiastically

Begeisterung die; ~: enthusiasm; **etw. aus ~ tun** do sth. out of enthusiasm; **in ~ geraten** become *or* get enthusiastic

begeisterungs-, Begeisterungs-: ~fähig *Adj.* ‹*children, people, etc.*› who are able to get enthusiastic *or* are capable of enthusiasm; **~fähig sein** be able to get enthusiastic; **er ist sehr ~fähig** his enthusiasm is easily aroused; **~fähigkeit die;** *o. Pl.* capacity for enthusiasm; **~sturm der** storm of enthusiastic applause

Begier die *(geh.)*, **Begierde** [bəˈgiːɐ̯də] **die; ~, ~n** desire **(nach** for); **fleischliche ~n** *(veralt.)* desires of the flesh; carnal desires

begierig 1. *Adj.* eager; *(gierig)* greedy; hungry; **ganz ~ auf jmds. Besuch** *(Akk.)* **sein** be eagerly looking forward to sb.'s visit; **~ sein, etw. zu tun** be [desperately] eager to do sth.; **mit ~en Blicken** with hungry *or* greedy glances. **2.** *adv.* eagerly; *(gierig)* greedily; hungrily

begießen *unr. tr. V.* **a)** water ‹*plants*›; baste ‹*meat*›; **jmdn./etw. mit Wasser ~:** pour water over sb./sth.; **b)** *(ugs.)* **etw. ~:** celebrate sth. with a drink; **das muß begossen werden** that calls for a drink; *s. auch* **Nase**

Beginn [bəˈgɪn] **der; ~[e]s** start; beginning; **[gleich] zu** *od.* **am ~:** [right] at the start *or* beginning; **mit ~ des Semesters** at the start of the semester

beginnen 1. *unr. itr. V.* start; begin; **mit einer Arbeit/dem Studium ~:** start *or* begin a piece of work/one's studies; **mit dem Bau ~:** start *or* begin building; **dort beginnt der Wald** the forest starts there. **2.** *unr. tr. V.* **a)** start; begin; start ‹*argument*›; **b)** *(unternehmen)* go *or* set about; **~, etw. zu tun** go *or* set about doing sth.; **was hättet ihr nur ohne mich begonnen?** what would you have done without me?; **nichts mit sich zu ~ wissen** not know what to do with oneself

Beginnen das; ~s *(geh.)* enterprise

beginnend *Adj.; nicht präd.* incipient; **mit der ~en Morgendämmerung** as dawn begins/began to break; **im ~en 19. Jahrhundert** at the beginning of the 19th century

beglaubigen [bəˈglaubɪgn̩] *tr. V.* **a)** certify; authenticate ‹*account, report, etc.*›; **eine beglaubigte Kopie** a certified copy; *s. auch* **notariell; b)** *(akkreditieren)* accredit **(***Dat.***, bei** to)

Beglaubigung die; ~, ~en a) certification; *(eines Berichts)* authentication; **zur ~:** for certification; to be certified; **b)** *(Akkreditierung)* accreditation

Beglaubigungs·schreiben das letter of accreditation

begleichen *unr. tr. V.* settle, pay ‹*bill, debt*›; pay ‹*sum*›; **mit jmdm. eine Rechnung zu ~ haben** *(fig.)* have a score to settle with sb.

Begleichung die; ~ *(einer Rechnung, einer Schuld)* settlement; payment; *(einer Summe)* payment; **ein Scheck zur ~ meiner Schulden** a cheque in payment of my debts

Begleit·brief der covering *or* accompanying letter

begleiten *tr. V.* **a)** accompany; escort ‹*ship*›; **jmdn. zur Tür ~:** show sb. to the door; **jmdn. nach Hause ~:** see sb. home; **b)** *(Musik)* accompany **(an, auf +** *Dat.* on); **c)** *(fig.)* accompany; **von Erfolg begleitet werden** be attended by success; **etw. mit einem Kommentar ~:** add a commentary to sth.

Begleiter der; ~s, ~, Begleiterin die; ~, ~nen a) companion; *(zum Schutz)* escort; *(Führer[in])* guide; **ihr ständiger ~/seine ständige Begleiterin** *(verhüll.)* his/her constant companion; **b)** *(Musik)* accompanist

Begleit-: ~erscheinung die concomitant; *(einer Krankheit)* accompanying symptom; **das Alter und seine unangenehmen ~erscheinungen** old age and its attendant ills; **~instrument das** accompanying instrument; **~musik die** background music; *(fig.)* accompaniment; **~papiere** *Pl.* accompanying documents; **~person die** escort; **Kinder haben nur mit einer ~person Zutritt** children must be accompanied by an adult; **~schein der** *(Zollw.)* [customs] bond note; **~schiff das** escort [vessel]; **~schreiben das** *s.* **~brief; ~text der** accompanying text; **~um·stand der** attendant circumstance

Begleitung die; ~, ~en a) *o. Pl.* **er bot uns seine ~ an** he offered to accompany us; **in ~ einer Frau/eines Erwachsenen** in the company of *or* accompanied by a woman/an adult; **er ist in ~ hier** he's here with someone; **b)** *(Musik)* accompaniment; **ohne ~ singen/spielen** sing/play unaccompanied *or* without accompaniment; **die ~ übernehmen** take over as accompanist; **c)** *(Person[en])* companion[s]; *(zum Schutz)* escort

beglotzen *tr. V. (ugs.)* gawp at *(coll.)*

beglücken *tr. V. (geh.)* **jmdn. ~:** make sb. happy; delight sb.; **jmdn. mit etw. ~** *(oft iron.)* favour sb. with sth.; **die Frauen/Männer ~:** gratify women/men; **ein ~des Erlebnis** a gladdening experience

Beglücker der; ~s, ~: bringer of happiness *(Gen.* to)

beglückt 1. *Adj.* happy; delighted. **2.** *adv.* happily; delightedly

Beglückung die; ~, ~en a) zur ~ der Menschheit beitragen contribute to the sum of human happiness; **die ~ des Volkes** bringing Utopia to the people; **b)** *(Glück)* happiness; delight

beglück·wünschen *tr. V.* congratulate **(zu** on); **sich zu etw. ~:** congratulate oneself on sth.

begnaden [bəˈgnaːdn̩] *tr. V. (geh.)* bless

begnadet *Adj. (geh.)* divinely gifted

begnadigen *tr. V.* pardon; reprieve; **einen zum Tode Verurteilten zu „lebenslänglich" ~:** commute the convicted prisoner's death sentence to life imprisonment

Begnadigung die; ~, ~en reprieving; *(Straferlaß)* pardon; reprieve

Begnadigungs-: ~gesuch das application for reprieve; **~recht das;** *o. Pl.* right to grant reprieve

begnügen [bəˈgnyːgn̩] *refl. V.* **sich mit etw. ~:** content oneself *or* make do with sth.; **sich damit ~, etw. zu tun** content oneself with doing sth.

Begonie [beˈgoːni̯ə] **die; ~, ~n** begonia

begonnen [bəˈgɔnən] *2. Part. v.* **beginnen**

begraben *unr. tr. V.* **a)** bury; **dort möchte ich nicht ~ sein** *(ugs.)* I wouldn't live there if you paid me *(coll.)*; **b)** *(fig.: aufgeben)* abandon ‹*hope, plan, etc.*›; **du kannst dich ~ lassen** *(ugs.)* you may as well give up; **du kannst dich mit diesem Plan ~ lassen** *(ugs.)* that plan won't get you anywhere

Begräbnis [bəˈgrɛːpnɪs] **das; ~ses, ~se** burial; *(~feier)* funeral

Begräbnis-: ~feier die funeral; **~kosten** *Pl.* funeral expenses; **~stätte die** *(geh.)* burial-place

begradigen [bəˈgraːdɪgn̩] *tr. V.* straighten

Begradigung die; ~, ~en straightening

begrast [bəˈgraːst] *Adj.* grass-covered

begreifbar *Adj.* comprehensible; understandable; **schwer ~ sein** be difficult to comprehend *or* understand

begreifen 1. *unr. tr. V.* **a)** understand; understand, grasp, comprehend ⟨*connection, problem, meaning, necessity of sth., concept*⟩; **er konnte nicht ~, was geschehen war** he could not grasp what had happened; **kaum zu ~ sein** be almost incomprehensible; **hast du mich begriffen?** you understand?; **b)** *(Verständnis zeigen für)* understand; **das begreife, wer will** it's beyond me; **c)** *(geh.: betrachten)* regard, see **(als** as); **d) etw. in sich ~** *(veralt.)* include sth.; **e)** *(ugs.: befühlen)* feel; *(betasten)* touch. **2.** *itr. V.* understand; **schnell** *od.* **leicht/langsam** *od.* **schwer ~:** be quick/slow on the uptake; be quick/slow to grasp things

begreiflich *Adj.* understandable; **das ist mir nicht ~:** I can't understand it; **jmdm. etw. ~ machen** make sb. understand sth.

begreiflicher·weise *Adv.* understandably; **~ hat er das abgelehnt** understandably enough, he refused

begrenzen *tr. V.* **a)** limit, restrict **(auf +** *Akk.* to); **b)** *(die Grenze bilden von)* mark the boundary of; **durch etw. begrenzt sein** be bounded by sth.

begrenzt *Adj.* limited; restricted

Begrenztheit die; ~: limitedness

Begrenzung die; ~, ~en a) *(Grenze)* boundary; *(Zaun)* boundary fence; **b)** *(das Begrenzen)* limiting; restriction; *(der Geschwindigkeit)* restriction

Begriff der a) concept; *(Terminus)* term; **in ~en denken** think abstractly; **b)** *(Auffassung)* idea; **einen/keinen ~ von etw. haben** have an idea/no idea of sth.; **keinen ~ davon haben, wie ...:** have no idea how ...; **sich** *(Dat.)* **keinen ~ von etw. machen können** not be able to imagine sth.; **nach menschlichen ~en** in human terms; **für meine ~e** in my estimation; **ein/kein ~ sein** be/not be well known; **jmdm. ein/kein ~ sein** mean something/nothing to sb.; **der ganzen Welt ein ~ sein** be known all over the world; **c) im ~ sein** *od.* **stehen, etw. zu tun** be about to do sth.; **d)** *(Begreifen)* **schwer** *od.* **langsam von ~ sein** *(ugs. abwertend)* be slow on the uptake

begriffen [bəˈgrɪfn̩] **1.** *2. Part. v.* **begreifen. 2.** *Adj. in* **im Aufbruch/Fallen ~ sein** be leaving/falling; **in der Entwicklung/im Bau ~ sein** be in [the] process of development/construction

begrifflich 1. *Adj.* conceptual. **2.** *adv.* conceptually; **~ denken** think abstractly

begriffs-, Begriffs-: ~bestimmung die definition [of the/a concept]; **~mäßig** *Adj., adv.: s.* **begrifflich; ~stutzig,** *(österr.:)* **~stützig** *(abwertend)* **1.** *Adj.* obtuse; slow-witted; gormless *(coll.)*; **2.** *adv.* obtusely; slow-wittedly; gormlessly *(coll.)*; **~stutzigkeit,** *(österr.:)* **~stützigkeit die; ~** *(abwertend)* obtuseness; slow-wittedness; gormlessness *(coll.)*; **~vermögen das;** *o. Pl.* comprehension; **über jmds. ~vermögen** *(Akk.)* **hinausgehen** be beyond sb.'s comprehension *or* grasp; **~verwirrung die** conceptual confusion

begründen 1. *tr. V.* **a)** substantiate ⟨*statement, charge, claim*⟩; give reasons for ⟨*decision, refusal, opinion*⟩; **womit** *od.* **wie begründet sie ihren Entschluß/ihr Verhalten?** what reasons does she give for her decision?/how does she account for her behaviour?; **etw. sachlich ~:** give objective reasons for sth.; **~, warum man etw. tut** give one's reason[s] for doing sth.; **er begründete seinen Meinungswechsel damit, daß ...:** he gave as the reason for his change of opinion the fact that ...; **ein Urteil ~:** give the grounds for a judgement; *s. auch* **begründet; b)** *(gründen)* found; establish ⟨*fame, reputation*⟩; start ⟨*family*⟩; **einen Hausstand ~:** set up house. **2.** *refl. V.* be based; **wie begründet sich das?** what is that based on?

Begründer der founder

begründet *Adj.* well-founded; reasonable ⟨*demand, objection, complaint*⟩; **sachlich ~:** objectively based; **nicht ~:** unfounded; **in etw.** *(Dat.)* **~ sein** be the result of sth.

Begründung die; ~, ~en a) reason[s]; **mit der ~, daß ...:** on the grounds that ...; **seine ~ war ...:** the reason/reasons he gave was/were ...; **für diese These fehlt eine ~:** there is no evidence to support this thesis; **etw. zur ~ einer Sache** *(Gen.)* **sagen** give sth. as the reason for sth.; **ohne jede ~:** without giving any reasons; **b)** *(Gründung)* founding; establishment; *(eines Hausstands)* setting up; *(einer Familie)* starting

begrünen *tr. V.* **etw. ~:** plant greenery in/on sth.; *(mit Rasen)* grass sth.; **etw. [mit Rasen/Bäumen/Sträuchern** *usw.***] ~:** plant sth. with grass/trees/shrubs *etc.*

begrüßen *tr. V.* **a)** greet; ⟨*host, hostess*⟩ greet, welcome; **ich freue mich, Sie in meinem Hause ~ zu dürfen** *(geh.)* it's a pleasure to welcome you into my home; **ich begrüße Sie** how do you do?; **es würde uns freuen, wenn wir Sie Freitag abend bei uns ~ dürften** *(geh.)* we should be delighted to have the pleasure of your company on Friday evening; **b)** *(gutheißen)* welcome ⟨*suggestion, proposal*⟩; **ich begrüße es, daß ...:** I am glad that ...; **es wäre zu ~, wenn ...:** it would be a welcome development if ...; **c)** *(schweiz.)* consult

begrüßens·wert *Adj.* welcome

Begrüßung die; ~, ~en greeting; *(von Gästen)* welcoming; *(Zeremonie)* welcome *(Gen.* for); **jmdm. zur ~ einen Strauß Blumen überreichen** welcome sb. with a bouquet of flowers; **sich** *od.* *(geh.)* **einander zur ~ die Hand schütteln** shake hands by way of greeting

Begrüßungs-: ~an·sprache die speech of welcome; welcoming speech; **~geld das** *(hist.) money paid to GDR citizens when visiting West Berlin or the FRG;* **~kuß der** welcoming kiss; **~rede die** *s.* **~ansprache; ~wort das;** *Pl.* **~worte** word of welcome

begucken *tr. V. (ugs.)* look at; have *or* take a look at; **laß dich mal ~:** let's have *or* take a look at you

begünstigen [bəˈgʏnstɪgn̩] *tr. V.* **a)** favour; encourage ⟨*exports, trade, growth*⟩; further ⟨*plan*⟩; **vom Rückenwind begünstigt** assisted *or* helped by a following wind; **vom Schicksal begünstigt werden** be blessed by fate; **b)** *(bevorzugen)* favour; show favour to; **c)** *(Rechtsw.)* **jmdn. ~:** be an accessory of sb. after the fact

Begünstigung die; ~, ~en a) *s.* **begünstigen a:** favouring; encouragement; furthering; **b)** *(Bevorzugung)* preferential treatment; **c)** *(Rechtsw.)* being an accessory after the fact

begutachten *tr. V.* **a)** examine and report on; **ein Gemälde/das Flugzeugwrack ~, um etw. festzustellen** examine a painting/the [aircraft] wreckage in order to establish sth.; **ein Gebäude ~:** carry out a survey of a building; **b)** *(ugs.)* look at; have *or* take a look at; **laß dich mal ~!** let's have *or* take a look at you

Begutachter der; ~s, ~: *s.* **Gutachter**

Begutachtung die; ~, ~en examination; *(von Gebäuden)* survey; **eine schriftliche ~:** a written report

begütert [bəˈgyːtɐt] *Adj.* **a)** wealthy; affluent; **b)** *(veralt.)* landed *attrib.* ⟨*gentry, nobility, etc.*⟩; **~ sein** own land

begütigen [bəˈgyːtɪgn̩] *tr. V.* placate; mollify; pacify; **~d auf jmdn. einreden** speak soothingly to sb.

Begütigung die; ~, ~en placating; mollifying; pacifying

behaart [bəˈhaːɐ̯t] *Adj.* hairy; **grau/schwarz/stark ~ sein** be covered with grey/black hair/covered with hair; **stark ~e Beine** very hairy legs

Behaarung die; ~, ~en covering of hair; *(Haar)* hair *no indef. art.*; **seine starke ~ auf dem Rücken** the thick hair on his back

behäbig [bəˈhɛːbɪç] **1.** *Adj.* **a)** stolid and portly; **b)** *(langsam und schwerfällig)* slow and ponderous; **c)** *(geruhsam und gemütlich)* placid and easy-going; **d)** *(ausladend)* large and solid ⟨*furniture, house*⟩. **2.** *adv.* slowly and ponderously

Behäbigkeit die; ~ a) portliness; stoutness; **b)** *(Langsamkeit)* slowness and ponderousness; **c)** *(ausladende Form)* size and solidity

behacken *tr. V.* **a)** hoe ⟨*plants*⟩; **b)** *(hacken an)* hack at

behaftet *Adj. (geh.)* **mit einem Makel/einer Krankheit ~ sein** be marked with a blemish/afflicted with a disease; **mit einem schlechten Ruf/einem Fehler/Laster ~ sein** have a bad name/a defect/be tainted with a vice; **mit Fehlern ~ sein** contain defects

behagen [bəˈhaːgn̩] *itr. V.* please; **das behagt mir/behagt mir nicht** that pleases/does not please me; I like/do not like that; **er behagt mir gar nicht** I don't like him at all

Behagen das; ~s *(Zufriedenheit)* contentment; *(Vergnügen)* pleasure; **mit [sichtlichem] ~:** with [obvious] contentment/pleasure; **etw. mit ~ essen** eat sth. with relish

behaglich 1. *Adj.* **a)** comfortable; comfortable, cosy ⟨*atmosphere, room, home, etc.*⟩; **es jmdm./sich ~ machen** make sb./oneself comfortable; **b)** *(genießerisch, zufrieden)* contented. **2.** *adv.* **a)** comfortably, cosily ⟨*warm, furnished*⟩; **b)** *(genießerisch, zufrieden)* contentedly

Behaglichkeit die; ~: *s.* **behaglich 1: a)** comfortableness; cosiness; **b)** contentment

behalten *unr. tr. V.* **a)** keep; keep on ⟨*workers, employees*⟩; keep, retain ⟨*value, expressive power, etc.*⟩; **den Hut auf dem Kopf ~:** keep one's hat on; **Nahrung bei sich ~:** keep food down; **jmdn. als Gast bei sich ~:** have sb. stay on as one's guest; **etw. für sich ~:** keep sth. to oneself; **die Nerven/die Ruhe ~:** keep one's nerve/keep calm; **ob wir das gute Wetter ~?** will the good weather hold?; **b)** *(zurück~)* be left with; **einen Herzschaden** *usw.* **~:** be left with a weak heart *etc.*; **sie behielt von dem Unfall ein steifes Knie** the accident left her with a stiff knee; **c)** *(sich merken)* remember ⟨*number, date*⟩; **ich habe die Adresse nicht ~:** I've forgotten the address; **er kann Geschichtszahlen schlecht ~:** he has no memory for historical dates; **jmdn. in freundlicher Erinnerung ~:** have fond memories of sb.; *s. auch* **Recht d**

Behälter [bəˈhɛltɐ] **der; ~s, ~ a)** container; *(für Abfälle)* receptacle; **b)** *(Container)* container

Behälter-: ~schiff das container ship; **~verkehr der** container traffic

Behältnis das; ~ses, ~se *(geh.)* container

behämmern *tr. V.* hammer

behämmert *Adj. (salopp) s.* **bekloppt**

behandeln *tr. V.* **a)** *(umgehen mit)* treat ⟨*person*⟩; handle ⟨*matter, machine, device*⟩; **jmdn. freundlich/herablassend/schlecht ~:** treat sb. in a friendly way/condescendingly/badly; **eine Maschine sachgemäß ~:** handle *or* use a machine correctly; **sie weiß, wie man Kinder/den Chef ~ muß** she knows how to handle children/the manager; **b)** *(bearbeiten)* treat **(mit** with); **c)** *(darstellen, analysieren)* deal with, treat ⟨*subject, question; theme*⟩; **d)** *(ärztlich)* treat ⟨*patient, illness, symptom*⟩ **(mit** with; **auf +** *Akk.,* **wegen** for); **jmdn. ambulant/stationär ~:** give sb. treatment as an out-patient/in-patient; **der ~de Arzt** the doctor treating the patient

Behandlung die; ~, ~en a) treatment; **eine solche ~ lasse ich mir nicht gefallen** I won't stand for being treated like that; **bessere ~ verdienen** deserve better treatment *or* to be treated better; **bei einem/diesem Arzt in ~ sein** be under medical treatment/this doctor; **b)** *(Besprechung)* discussion; *(Analyse)* treatment

behandlungs-, Behandlungs-: ~bedürftig *Adj.* **~bedürftig sein** require treatment; **~kosten** *Pl.* cost *sing.* of treatment; **~methode die** method of treatment; **~pflicht die** *obligation on a doctor to respond to a call for medical assistance;* **~raum der** treatment room; **~stuhl der** chair for the patient; *(beim Zahnarzt)* [dentist's] chair; **~weise die** *s.* **~methode**

behandschuht *Adj.* gloved

Behang der; ~[e]s, Behänge a) *(Wand~)* hanging; **b)** *(am Baum)* decoration; *(Ertrag)* crop; **c)** *(Jägerspr.) (Ohr)* lop-ear; *(Ohren)* lop-ears *pl.*

behangen *Adj.* **ein mit Äpfeln ~er Baum** a tree laden with apples; **mit Schmuck ~:** festooned with jewellery

behängen *tr. V.* **a) etw. mit etw. ~:** hang *or* decorate sth. with sth.; **b)** *(ugs. abwertend)* **jmdn./sich mit etw. ~:** festoon sb./oneself with sth.

beharken *tr. V.* **a)** *(Soldatenspr.)* rake with gunfire; **b)** *(salopp)* pitch into *(coll.)*; set about *(coll.)*

beharren *itr. V.* **a) auf etw.** *(Dat.)* **~** *(etw. nicht aufgeben)* persist in sth.; *(auf etw. bestehen)* insist on sth.; **darauf ~, etw. zu tun** insist on doing sth.; **b)** *(beharrlich behaupten)* insist; **c)** *(geh: bleiben) (an einem Ort)* remain; *(in einem Zustand)* persist

Beharren das; ~s insistence

beharrlich 1. *Adj.* dogged; persistent. **2.** *adv.* doggedly; persistently; **~ bei seiner Meinung bleiben** stick doggedly to one's opinion

Beharrlichkeit die; ~: doggedness; persistence

Beharrung die; ~: persistence

Beharrungs·vermögen das *(Physik)* inertia

behauchen *tr. V.* **a)** breathe on; **b)** *(Phon.)* aspirate; **behauchte Konsonanten** aspirates

behauen *unr. tr. V.* hew; **roh ~e Steine** rough-hewn stone blocks

behaupten [bə'hauptn̩] **1.** *tr. V.* **a)** maintain; assert; **~, jmd. zu sein/etw. zu wissen** claim to be sb./know sth.; **das kann man nicht ~:** you cannot say that; **man behauptet** *od.* **es wird behauptet, daß ...:** it is said *or* claimed that ...; *s. auch* **steif 2 c; b)** *(verteidigen)* maintain ⟨*position*⟩; retain ⟨*record*⟩; *s. auch* **Feld f. 2.** *refl. V.* **a)** assert oneself; *(nicht untergehen)* hold one's ground; *(dableiben)* survive; **die Kirche/der Dollar konnte sich ~:** the church/the dollar was able to maintain its position; **b)** *(Sport)* win through

Behauptung die; ~, ~en a) claim; assertion; **b)** *(Verteidigung)* **für die ~ seiner Stellung kämpfen** fight to maintain one's position; **c)** *(Durchsetzung)* assertion

behausen *tr. V. (geh.)* house; accommodate; accommodate, put up ⟨*guest*⟩

Behausung die; ~, ~en a) *(geh.: das Behausen)* housing; accommodation; **b)** *(oft abwertend: Wohnung)* dwelling

Behaviorismus [bihevi̯ə'rɪsmʊs] **der; ~** *(Verhaltensf.)* behaviourism *no art.*

behavioristisch *(Biol., Psych.)* **1.** *Adj.* behaviourist. **2.** *adv.* behaviouristically

beheben *unr. tr. V.* **a)** remove ⟨*doubt, danger, difficulty*⟩; repair ⟨*damage*⟩; remedy ⟨*abuse, defect*⟩; clear ⟨*disturbance*⟩; **b)** *(österr.: abheben)* withdraw ⟨*money*⟩

Behebung die; ~, ~en a) *o. Pl.*: *s.* **beheben a:** removal; repair; remedying; clearing; **b)** *(österr.: Abhebung)* withdrawal

beheimaten *tr. V.* provide a home for ⟨*person*⟩; **Tiere/Pflanzen in einer Gegend ~:** introduce animals/plants into an area

beheimatet *Adj.* **a)** *(heimisch)* **an einem Ort/in einem Land ~ sein** ⟨*plant, animal, tribe, race*⟩ be native *or* indigenous to a place/country; ⟨*person*⟩ come from a place/country; **wo ist er ~?** where does he come from?; **b)** *(ansässig)* resident (**in** + *Dat.* in)

beheizbar *Adj.* heatable; **eine ~e Heckscheibe** a heated rear window

beheizen *tr. V.* heat

Beheizung die; ~: heating

Behelf [bə'hɛlf] **der; ~[e]s, ~e** *(Notlösung)* stopgap; makeshift; *(Ersatz)* substitute

behelfen *unr. refl. V.* **a) sich mit etw. ~:** make do *or* manage with sth.; **b)** *(zurechtkommen)* get by; manage; **sich allein ~:** get by *or* manage on one's own

behelfs-, Behelfs-: ~aus·fahrt die *(Verkehrsw.)* temporary exit *(from a motorway)*; **~heim das** makeshift *or* temporary home; **~mäßig 1.** *Adj.* makeshift; temporary; **2.** *adv.* in a makeshift way *or* fashion; **~unterkunft die** temporary dwelling; **~weise** *Adv.* *(vorübergehend)* temporarily; *(ersatzweise)* as a substitute

behelligen [bə'hɛlɪgn̩] *tr. V.* *(lästig werden für)* bother; *(zudringlich werden gegenüber)* pester

Behelligung die; ~, ~en: ich verbitte mir solche ~en stop bothering *or* pestering me

behelmt [bə'hɛlmt] *Adj.* helmeted

behend [bə'hɛnt], **behende 1.** *Adj.* *(geschickt)* deft; adroit; *(flink)* nimble; agile. **2.** *adv.*; *s. Adj.*: deftly; adroitly; nimbly; agilely

Behendigkeit die; ~: *s.* **behende 1:** deftness; adroitness; nimbleness; agilety

beherbergen *tr. V.* **a)** accommodate, put up ⟨*guest*⟩; **b)** *(Raum bieten für)* accommodate; **c)** *(enthalten)* contain

Beherbergung die; ~: accommodation

Beherbergungs·gewerbe das hotel trade

beherrschen 1. *tr. V.* **a)** rule; **den Markt ~:** dominate *or* control the market; **von Haßgefühlen/Leidenschaften beherrscht sein** *(geh.)* be ruled by feelings of hatred/by passions; **b)** *(meistern)* control ⟨*vehicle, animal*⟩; be in control of ⟨*situation*⟩; **c)** *(bestimmen, dominieren)* dominate ⟨*townscape, landscape, discussions, relationship*⟩; **d)** *(zügeln)* control ⟨*feelings*⟩; control, curb ⟨*impatience*⟩; **seine Zunge ~** *(geh.)* curb one's tongue; **e)** *(gut können)* have mastered ⟨*instrument, trade*⟩; have a good command of ⟨*language*⟩; **es kostet viele Jahre ständiger Übung, ein Instrument zu ~:** it takes many years of constant practice to master an instrument; **Englisch fast so gut wie Deutsch ~:** speak English almost as well as German. **2.** *refl. V.* control oneself; **ich kann mich ~** *(iron.)* I can resist the temptation *(iron.)*; **kannst du dich so wenig ~, daß ...?** have you got so little self-control that ...?

Beherrscher der; ~s, ~: ruler

beherrscht 1. *Adj.* self-controlled. **2.** with self-control; **völlig ~:** with complete self-control

Beherrschtheit die; ~: self-control

Beherrschung die; ~ a) control; *(Verwaltung)* rule; *(eines Markts)* domination; control; **b)** *(das Meistern)* control; **c)** *(Beherrschtheit)* self-control; **seine** *od.* **die ~ verlieren** lose one's self-control; **d)** *(das Können)* mastery

beherzigen [bə'hɛrtsɪgn̩] *tr. V.* **etw. ~:** take sth. to heart; heed sth.

beherzigens·wert *Adj.* worth taking to heart *or* heeding *postpos.*

Beherzigung die; ~: heeding; **dies zur ~!** I want you to heed *or* take good heed of this

beherzt 1. *Adj.* spirited; **einige Beherzte** a few brave souls. **2.** *adv.* spiritedly

Beherztheit die; ~: spirit

behexen *tr. V.* bewitch

behilflich [bə'hɪlflɪç] *Adj.* **jmdm. [beim Aufräumen** *usw.*] **~ sein** help sb. [clear up *or* with the clearing-up *etc.*]; **kann ich [Ihnen] ~ sein?** can I help [you]?

behindern *tr. V.* **a)** hinder; hamper, impede ⟨*movement*⟩; hold up ⟨*traffic*⟩; impede ⟨*view*⟩; **jmdn. in etw.** *(Dat.)* **~:** hinder sb. in sth.; **ein behindertes Kind** a handicapped child; **b)** *(Sport, Verkehrsw.)* obstruct

Behinderte der/die; *adj. Dekl.* handicapped person; **die ~n** the handicapped; **WC für ~:** toilet for disabled persons

Behinderung die; ~, ~en a) um ~en bei der Zollabfertigung zu vermeiden to avoid hold-ups at customs; **zur ~ des Flugverkehrs beitragen** help to cause delays to air traffic; **~ der Sicht** obstruction to the view; **b)** *(Sport, Verkehrsw.)* obstruction; **Falschparken mit ~:** parking illegally and causing an obstruction; **c)** *(Hindernis)* hindrance; **d)** *(Gebrechen)* handicap

behobeln *tr. V.* plane

behorchen *tr. V.* **a)** *(ugs.)* listen to; **b)** *(belauschen)* eavesdrop on

Behörde [bə'hø:ɐ̯də] **die; ~, ~n a)** authority; *(Amt, Abteilung)* department; **die ~n** the authorities; **b)** *(Gebäude)* government offices *pl.*/[local] council offices *pl.*

Behörden-: ~apparat der administrative apparatus; *(abwertend: Bürokratie)* bureaucracy; **~deutsch das** *(abwertend)* officialese

behördlich 1. *Adj.*; *nicht präd.* official; **~e Genehmigung** permission from the authorities; official permission; **auf ~e Anordnung** by order of the authorities. **2.** *adv.* officially; **das ist ~ genehmigt worden** it has been approved by the authorities

behördlicher·seits *Adv.* *(durch die Behörde)* by the authorities; *(seitens der Behörde)* on the part of the authorities

behost [bə'ho:st] *Adj.* *(ugs.)* in trousers *postpos.*

Behuf der; ~[e]s, ~e *in* **zu diesem ~[e]** *(veralt.)* to this end

behufs *Präp. mit Gen.* *(veralt.)* with a view to

behuft [bə'hu:ft] *Adj.* hooved

behum[p]sen [bə'hʊmpsn̩, bə'hʊmzn̩] *tr. V.* *(ugs., bes. ostmd.)* diddle *(sl.)*

behüten *tr. V.* *(bewahren, beschützen)* protect (**vor** + *Dat.* from); *(sorgen für)* take care of; *(bewachen)* guard; **ein Geheimnis ~:** keep a secret; **jmdn. vor einer Gefahr ~:** keep *or* safeguard sb. from a danger; **[Gott] behüte!** God *or* Heaven forbid!

Behüter der; ~s, ~ *(geh.)* protector

behütet *Adj.* sheltered ⟨*upbringing, life*⟩

behutsam [bə'hu:tza:m] **1.** *Adj.* careful; cautious; cautious, discreet ⟨*question*⟩; *(zartfühlend)* gentle. **2.** *adv.* carefully; cautiously; *(zartfühlend)* gently

Behutsamkeit die; ~: care; caution; *(Zartgefühl)* gentleness

bei [bai̯] *Präp. mit Dat.* **a)** *(nahe)* near; *(dicht an, neben)* by; **die Schlacht ~ Leipzig** the battle of Leipzig; **irgendwo ~ Stuttgart** somewhere near Stuttgart; **nahe ~m Bahnhof** near the station; **~m Gepäck/Auto** *usw.* **bleiben** stay with the luggage/car; **wer steht da ~ ihm?** who is standing there with him?; **sich ~ jmdm. entschuldigen/beklagen/erkundigen** apologize/complain to sb./ask sb.; **wir haben Physik ~ Herrn Meyer** we do physics with Mr Meyer; **der Wert liegt ~ 10 000 Mark** the value is around *or* about ten thousand marks; **~m Fenster herausschauen** *(österr.)* look out of the window; **b)** *(unter)* among; **war heute ein Brief für mich ~ der Post?** was there a letter for me in the post today?; **c)** *(an)* by; **jmdn. ~ der Hand nehmen** take sb. by the hand; **jmdn. ~ der Schulter packen** seize sb. by the shoulder; *s.*

auch **beim b; d)** *(im Wohnbereich) (längerfristig)* with; *(kurzfristig)* at; **~ uns tut man das nicht** we don't do that; **~ mir [zu Hause]** at my house; **~ uns um die Ecke/gegenüber** round the corner from us/opposite us; **~ seinen Eltern leben** live with one's parents; **wir sind ~ ihr eingeladen** we have been invited to her house; **wir treffen uns ~ uns/Peter** we'll meet at our/Peter's place; **morgen schlafe ich ~ meinen Großeltern** I'm sleeping at my grandparents' tomorrow; **~ uns in Österreich** in Austria [where I/we come from/live]; **[hier/damals] ~ uns in Österreich** here in Austria/in Austria in those days; **wir haben ~ [den] Clarks gefeiert** we went to a party at the Clarks'; *(im Geschäft)* **beim Bäcker/Fleischer** *usw.* at the baker's/butcher's *etc.*; **~ uns in der Firma** in our company; **~ Schmidt** *(auf Briefen)* c/o Schmidt; **e)** *(im geistigen Bereich)* with; **~ jmdm. Verständnis finden** get sympathy and understanding from sb.; **die Verantwortung liegt ~ Ihnen** responsibility lies with you; **f)** *(im Arbeitsbereich)* **~ einer Firma sein** be with a company; **~ jmdm./einem Verlag arbeiten** work for sb./a publishing house; **~ der Bundeswehr/Luftwaffe sein** be in the forces/air force; *s. auch* **bei a; g)** *(im Bereich eines Vorgangs)* at; **~ einer Hochzeit/einem Empfang** *usw.* **sein** be at a wedding/reception *etc.*; **~ der Organisation von etw./~ einer Aufführung mitwirken** be involved in the organization of sth./appear in a production; **h)** *(im Werk von)* **~ Goethe** in Goethe; **~ Schiller heißt es ...:** Schiller says *or* writes that ...; **i)** *(im Falle von)* in the case of; **wie ~ den Römern** as with the Romans; **hoffentlich geht es nicht wie ~ mir** I hope the same thing doesn't happen as happened in my case; **j)** *(im eigenen Bereich)* with; **etw. ~ sich haben** have sth. with *or* on one; **~ sich [selbst] anfangen** start with oneself; **nicht [ganz] ~ sich sein** be not quite with it; **~ mir ist es zehn Uhr** I make it ten o'clock; **k)** *(Zeitpunkt)* at ‹*beginning, end*›; **~ seiner Ankunft/seinem Eintritt** on his arrival/entry; **~ diesen Worten errötete er** at this he blushed; **l)** *(Zeitspanne)* **~ Tag/Nacht** by day/night; **~ Sonnenaufgang/-untergang** at sunrise/sunset; **~ unserer Begegnung** at our meeting; **~ einem Unfall** in an accident; **~ einer Schlägerei** in a brawl; **~ Tisch sein** be at table; **~ der Arbeit** at work; *s. auch* **beim b; m)** *(gleichzeitig mit)* with; **~ zunehmendem Alter** with advancing age; **n)** *(modal)* **~ Tag und Nacht** day and night; **~ Tageslicht** by daylight; **~ Nebel** in fog; **~ Kälte** when it's cold; **~ einem Glas Wein** over a glass of wine; **~ offenem Fenster schlafen** sleep with the window open; **o)** *(betreffs)* with; **das gilt auch ~ ...:** this applies to ... also; **~ so etwas ist er geschickt** he is skilled at things like that; **p)** *(im Falle von)* **„~ Feuer Scheibe einschlagen"** 'in case of fire, break glass'; **„~ Regen Schleudergefahr"** 'slippery when wet'; **~ hohem Fieber** when sb. has a high temperature; **q)** *(auf Grund von)* with; **~ dieser Hitze** in this heat; **~ diesem Sturm/Lärm** with this storm blowing/noise going on; **~ deinen guten Augen/ihrem Talent** with your good eyesight/her talent; **er erblaßte ~ der Nachricht** he turned pale at the news; **r)** *(trotz)* **~ all seinem Engagement/seinen Bemühungen** in spite of *or* despite *or* for all his commitment/efforts; **~ allem Verständnis, aber ich kann das nicht** much as I sympathize, I cannot do that; **s)** *(in Beteuerungsformeln)* by; **~ Gott!** by God!; **~ meiner Ehre!** *(veralt.)* upon my honour!

bei|behalten *unr. tr. V.* keep, retain ‹*distinction, wording, penalty, measure, practice, laws*›; keep up ‹*custom, habit*›; continue, maintain ‹*way of life*›; keep to ‹*course, method*›; preserve, maintain ‹*attitude*›

Beibehaltung die; ~: *s.* **beibehalten:** keeping; retention; keeping up; continuance; maintenance; preservation

bei|biegen *unr. tr. V. (ugs.)* **jmdm. etw. ~:** get sb. to understand sth.

Bei·blatt das insert

Bei·boot das ship's boat

bei|bringen *unr. tr. V.* **a) jmdm. etw. ~:** teach sb. sth.; **jmdm. Gehorsam ~:** teach sb. obedience; **ich werde dir ~, mich zu betrügen!** *(ugs.)* I'll teach you to cheat me! *(coll.)*; **b)** *(ugs.: mitteilen)* **jmdm. ~, daß ...:** break it to sb. that ...; **c)** *(zufügen)* **jmdm./sich etw. ~:** inflict sth. on sb./oneself; **d)** *(beschaffen)* produce ‹*witness, evidence*›; provide, supply ‹*reference, proof*›; produce, furnish ‹*money*›

Beichte ['baiçtə] **die; ~, ~n** confession *no def. art.*; **zur ~ gehen** go to confession; **jmdm. die ~ abnehmen** hear sb.'s confession

beichten 1. *itr. V.* go to confession; **~ gehen** go to confession. **2.** *tr. V. (fig.)* confess

Beicht-: ~formel die form of confession; **~geheimnis das** seal of confession; **~gespräch das** *(kath. Rel.)* talk with the priest before confession; **~stuhl der** confessional; **~vater der** father confessor

beid-: ~armig 1. *Adj.* two-handed; *(mit beiden Armen gleich geschickt)* ambidextrous; **2.** *adv.* with both hands; **~beinig 1.** *Adj.* two-legged; **2.** *adv.* with both feet

beide ['baidə] *Indefinitpron. u. Zahlw.* **a)** *mit Art. od. Pron.* **die/seine ~n Brüder** the/his two brothers; *(mit Nachdruck)* both the/his brothers; **die ~n ersten Strophen** the first two verses; **kennst du die ~n?** do you know those two?; **alle ~:** both of us/you/them; **sie sind alle ~ sehr schön** they're both very nice; both of them are very nice; **sie sind ~ nicht hübsch** neither of them is pretty; **ihr/euch ~:** you two; **Ihr/euch ~ nicht** neither of you; **wir/uns ~:** the two of us/both of us; **b)** *o. Art.* both; **er hat ~ Eltern verloren** he has lost both [his] parents; **mit ~n Händen** with both hands; **~ Male** both times; **ich habe ~ gekannt** I knew both of them; **~ haben hier gearbeitet** both [of them] worked here; **einer/eins von ~n** one of the two; **keiner/keins von ~n** neither [of them]; **c)** *Neutr. Sg.* both *pl.*; **~s ist möglich** either is possible; **ich glaube ~s/~s nicht** I believe both things/neither thing; **das ist ~s nicht richtig** neither of those is correct; **er hat sich in ~m geirrt** he was wrong on both counts; **er hatte von ~m wenig Ahnung** he had little idea of either

beide·mal *Adv.* both times

beiderlei ['baidɐ'lai] *Gattungssz., indekl.* **~ Geschlechts** of both sexes; **von ~ Art** of both kinds; **das Abendmahl in** *od.* **unter ~ Gestalt** *(ev. Rel.)* communion in both kinds

beider·seitig 1. *Adj.* mutual ‹*decision, agreement*›; **~e Freude** joy on both sides; **zur ~en Überraschung** to the surprise of both of us/them; **in ~em Einverständnis** by mutual agreement. **2.** *adv.* by both sides; **eine ~ interessierende Frage** a question of interest to both sides. **3.** *Adv.* on both sides

beider·seits 1. *Präp. mit Gen.* on both sides of. **2.** *Adv.* on both sides

beid-: ~füßig *Adj., adv.* with both feet; **~händig 1.** *Adj.* **a)** *(mit beiden Händen gleich geschickt)* ambidextrous; **b)** *(mit beiden Händen)* two-handed; **2.** *adv.* with two hands; **eine ~händig geschlagene Rückhand** a two-handed backhand

bei|drehen *itr. V. (Seemannsspr.)* heave to

beid·seitig 1. *Adj.* mutual. **2.** *adv.* **a)** *(auf beiden Seiten)* ‹*be printed etc.*› on both sides; **~ gelähmt sein** be paralysed down both sides; **b)** *(gegenseitig)* *s.* **beiderseitig 2**

beidseits *(bes. schweiz.)* *s.* **beiderseits**

bei·einander *Adv.* together; **~ Trost suchen** seek comfort from each other

beieinander-, Beieinander-: ~|haben *unr. tr. V.* **etw. ~haben** have got sth. together; **du hast/er hat** *usw.* **nicht alle** *od.* **sie nicht richtig ~** *(ugs.)* he's/you're *etc.* not all there *(coll.)*; **~|halten** *unr. tr. V.* keep together; **~|liegen** *unr. itr. V.* lie together; **~|sein** *unr. itr. V.; mit sein (nur im Inf. und Part. zusammengeschrieben) (ordentlich sein)* be neat and tidy; **gut/schlecht ~sein** *(ugs.)* be in good/bad shape; **nicht ganz ~sein** *(ugs.)* be not quite all there *(coll.)*; **~sein das** get-together; **~|sitzen** *unr. itr. V.* sit together; **~|stehen** *unr. itr. V.* stand together

Bei·fahrer der, Bei·fahrerin die a) *(im Kfz)* [front-seat] passenger; *(auf dem Motorrad)* pillion passenger; *(im Beiwagen)* sidecar passenger; **b)** *(berufsmäßig)* co-driver; *(auf einem LKW)* driver's mate

Beifahrer·sitz der *(im Kfz)* passenger seat; *(eines Motorrads)* pillion

Bei·fall der; *o. Pl.* **a)** applause; *(Zurufe)* cheers *pl.*; cheering; *(Händeklatschen)* applause; clapping; **stürmischer** *od.* **tosender ~:** a storm of applause; **~ klatschen/spenden** applaud; **b)** *(Zustimmung)* approval; **~ finden** meet with approval

beifall·heischend *Adj. (geh.)* *s.* **Beifall:** looking for applause/approval; **jmdn. ~ ansehen** look at sb. in the hope of getting applause/approval

bei·fällig 1. *Adj.* approving; favourable ‹*judgement*›; **~es Gemurmel** murmurs *pl.* of approval. **2.** *adv.* approvingly; **~ nicken** nod approvingly *or* in approval; **~ aufgenommen werden** be received favourably *or* with approval

Beifall·klatschen das clapping; applause

Beifalls-: ~äußerung die expression of approval; **~bekundung die, ~bezeigung die; ~, ~en** demonstration of approval; **~kundgebung die** ovation; **~kundgebungen** ovation *sing.*; **~ruf der** shout of approval; cheer; **~sturm der** storm of applause

bei|fügen *tr. V.* **a)** *(dazulegen)* **einer Bewerbung etw. ~:** enclose sth. with an application; **einem Paket eine Zollerklärung ~:** attach a customs declaration to a parcel; **einem Blumenstrauß eine Grußkarte ~:** put a greetings card in with a bouquet; **b)** *(hinzufügen)* add; **dem Teig Zucker/Mehl ~:** add sugar/flour to the mixture

Bei·fügung die a) *(Sprachw.)* attribute; **b)** *o. Pl. (Amtsspr.: das Beifügen)* **unter ~ eines Lebenslaufs/Schecks** enclosing a curriculum vitae/cheque

Bei·fuß der; *o. Pl. (Bot.)* artemisia; *(Artemisia vulgaris)* mugwort

Bei·gabe die a) *o. Pl. (das Beigeben)* **unter ~** *(Dat.)* **von etw.** adding sth.; **b)** *(Hinzugefügtes)* addition; *(Beilage)* side-dish

beige [be:ʃ] *Adj.* beige; **ein ~** *od. (ugs.)* **~s Kleid** a ~ dress

Beige das; ~, ~ *od. (ugs.)* **~s** beige

bei|geben 1. *unr. tr. V.* **a)** *(hinzufügen)* add (*Dat.* to); **b)** *(mitgeben)* assign (*Dat.* to). **2.** *unr. itr. V.* **in klein ~** *(ugs.)* give in

beige·farben *Adj.* beige[-coloured]

bei|gehen *unr. itr. V.; mit sein (nordd.)* *s.* **darangehen**

Beigeordnete der/die; *adj. Dekl.* ≈ town council official

Bei·geschmack der; *o. Pl.* **einen bitteren** *usw.* **~ haben** have a slightly bitter *etc.* taste [to it]; taste slightly bitter *etc.*; **dieses Wort hat einen negativen ~** *(fig.)* this word has slightly negative overtones *pl.*; **einen ~ von Petroleum haben** have a slight taste of paraffin *(Brit.)* or *(Amer.)* kerosene; taste slightly of petrol

bei|gesellen *(geh.)* **1.** *tr. V.* **jmdm. jmdn. ~:** put sb. with sb. **2.** *refl. V.* **sich jmdm. ~:** attach oneself to sb.

Bei·heft das *(zum Lehrbuch)* supplement; *(einer Zeitschrift)* supplementary number

bei|heften *tr. V.* einer Sache *(Dat.)* etw. ~: attach sth. to sth.

Bei·hilfe die a) *(materielle Hilfe)* aid; assistance; *(Geldunterstützung)* [financial] aid *or* assistance; *(Zuschuß für Kleidung, Heizung, Miete, Kinderreiche, Studenten usw.)* allowance; *(Subvention)* subsidy; b) *o. Pl. (Rechtsw.: Mithilfe)* aiding and abetting; jmdn. wegen ~ zum Mord anklagen charge sb. with aiding and abetting a murder *or* with acting as accessory to a murder

Bei·klang der *(geh.)* [accompanying] sound; *(fig.)* overtone[s *pl.*]; underlying note

Bei·koch der assistant chef

bei|kommen *unr. itr. V.; mit sein* a) *(gewachsen sein)* jmdm. ~: get the better of sb.; b) *(bewältigen)* den Schwierigkeiten/der Unruhe/jmds. Sturheit ~: overcome the difficulties/deal with the unrest/cope with sb.'s obstinacy; c) *(ugs.: herbeikommen)* come; d) *(ugs. heranreichen)* reach; e) *unpers. (geh.)* es kommt jmdm. bei, etw. zu tun sb. has the idea of doing sth.

Bei·kost die diet supplement; vitaminreiche/nahrhafte ~ bekommen have a vitamin-rich/nutritious supplementary diet

Beil [bail] das; ~[e]s, ~e a) axe; *(kleiner)* hatchet; *(Fleischer~)* cleaver; b) *(Fall~)* guillotine

bei|laden *unr. tr. V.* a) *(zuladen)* add; b) *(Rechtsw.)* summon ‹*third party interested in the outcome of a case*›

Bei·ladung die additional load

Bei·lage die a) *(Zeitungs~)* supplement; b) *(zu Speisen)* side-dish; *(Gemüse~)* vegetables *pl.*; *(Salat~)* side-salad; ein Fleischgericht mit diversen ~n a meat dish with a selection of trimmings; c) *(das Beilegen)* enclosure; unter ~ von ...: enclosing ...; gegen ~ von Rückporto if return postage is enclosed; d) *(österr.: Anlage)* enclosure (zu with)

Bei·lager das a) *(geh. veralt.: Beischlaf)* sexual intercourse; b) *(hist.: Akt der Eheschließung)* consummation of the marriage

bei·läufig 1. *Adj.* a) *(nebensächlich)* casual; casual, passing ‹*remark, mention*›; b) *(österr.: ungefähr)* approximate; rough. 2. *adv.* a) *(nebenbei)* casually; etw. ~ erwähnen *od.* bemerken mention sth. casually *or* in passing; ~ bemerkt, ...: incidentally, ...; etw. ~ erfahren learn sth. by chance; jmdn. ~ ausfragen get information unobtrusively from sb.; b) *(österr.: ungefähr)* approximately; roughly

Beiläufigkeit die; ~, ~en a) *o. Pl. (Nonchalance)* casualness; b) *(Nebensächlichkeit)* triviality; ~en trivia

bei|legen *tr. V.* a) *(dazulegen)* enclose; *(einem Buch, einer Zeitschrift)* insert (*Dat.* in); einem Brief *usw.* etw. ~: enclose sth. with a letter *etc.*; b) *(schlichten)* settle ‹*dispute, controversy, etc.*›; c) *(beimessen)* attach; einer Sache *(Dat.)* Gewicht/Bedeutung *usw.* ~: attach weight/importance *etc.* to sth.; d) *(geben, verleihen)* jmdm. einen Titel/Namen ~: bestow *or* confer a title/bestow a name on sb.; sich *(Dat.)* einen Titel/Namen ~: assume *or* adopt a title/name

Beilegung die; ~, ~en settlement

beileibe [bai'laibə] *Adv.* ~ nicht certainly not; er ist ~ kein Genie he is by no means a genius

Bei·leid das sympathy; [mein] herzliches *od.* aufrichtiges ~! please accept my sincere condolences; jmdm. sein [aufrichtiges] ~ [zu etw.] aussprechen offer one's [sincere] condolences *pl.* to sb. [on sth.]

Beileids-: **~besuch** der visit of condolence; visit to offer one's condolences; **~bezeigung** die; ~, ~en, **~bezeugung** die expression of sympathy; **~karte** die condolence *or* sympathy card

Beil·hieb der blow with an/the axe

bei|liegen *unr. itr. V.* a) *(beigefügt sein)* einem Brief ~: be enclosed with a letter; dem Buch liegt ein Prospekt bei the book contains a catalogue as an insert; b) *(geh. veralt.: Geschlechtsverkehr haben mit)* jmdm. ~: lie with sb. *(arch.)*; c) *(Seemannsspr.)* lie to

bei·liegend *(Amtsspr.) Adj.* enclosed; ~ senden wir ...: please find enclosed ...

beim [baim] *Präp.* + *Art.* a) = bei dem; b) jmdn. ~ Ärmel zupfen tug at sb.'s sleeve; ~ Film sein be in films; c) *(zeitlich)* er will ~ Arbeiten nicht gestört werden he doesn't want to be disturbed when *or* while [he's] working; ~ Essen spricht man nicht you shouldn't talk while [you're] eating; den Hund darf man ~ Fressen nicht stören you mustn't disturb the dog while it's eating; ~ Verlassen des Gebäudes when *or* on leaving the building; ~ Fasching at carnival time; ~ Lesen/Essen/Duschen sein be reading/be having breakfast/dinner *etc.*/be taking a shower

bei|mengen *tr. V.* add (*Dat.* to)

Beimengung die; ~, ~en a) *o. Pl. (das Beimengen)* addition; b) *(Zusatz)* admixture

bei|messen *unr. tr. V.* attach; jmdm./einer Sache Bedeutung/Wert *usw.* ~: attach importance/value *etc.* to sb./sth.

bei|mischen *tr. V. (geh.)* add (*Dat.* to); meiner Bewunderung war Grauen beigemischt *(fig.)* my admiration was tinged with horror

Bei·mischung die a) *o. Pl. (das Beimischen)* addition; b) *(Zusatz)* admixture

Bein [bain] das; ~[e]s, ~e a) leg; jmdm. ~e machen *(ugs.)* make sb. get a move on *(coll.)*; du hast jüngere ~e *(ugs.)* your legs are younger than mine; ein langes ~ machen *(Fußballjargon)* make a sliding tackle; ein ~ stehen lassen *(Fußballjargon)* put *or (coll.)* stick one's foot out; sich *(Dat.)* die ~e nach etw. ablaufen *(fig.)* chase round everywhere for sth.; er hat sich *(Dat.)* kein ~ ausgerissen *(ugs.)* he didn't over-exert himself; jmdm. ein ~ stellen *(zum Stolpern bringen)* trip sb.; *(fig.: hereinlegen)* put *or* throw a spanner *or (Amer.)* a monkey-wrench in sb.'s works; jmdm. [einen] Knüppel *od.* Prügel zwischen die ~e werfen *(fig.)* put *or* throw a spanner *or (Amer.)* a monkey-wrench in sb.'s works; das hat ~e gekriegt *(fig. ugs.)* it seems to have [grown legs and] walked *(coll.)*; die ~e in die Hand *od.* unter die Arme nehmen *(fig. ugs.) (sich beeilen)* step on it *(coll.)*; *(weglaufen)* take to one's heels; die ~e unter jmds. Tisch strecken *(fig. ugs.)* live at sb.'s expense; sich *(Dat.)* die ~e in den Bauch stehen *(fig. ugs.)* cool one's heels; alles, was ~e hat *(fig. ugs.)* everyone who possibly can; wieder auf den ~en sein be back on one's feet again; [wieder] auf die ~e kommen *(ugs.)* get back on one's/its feet [again]; jmdn./etw. [wieder] auf die ~e bringen *(ugs.)* put sb./sth. back on his/her/its feet again; eine Firma/Expedition/ein Programm auf die ~e stellen *(ugs.)* start a business/mount an expedition/put together a programme; jmdm. auf die ~e helfen help sb. to his/her feet; *(fig. ugs.)* help to get *or* put sb. back on his/her feet again; ich kann mich nicht mehr/kaum noch auf den ~en halten I can't/can hardly stand up; auf eigenen ~en stehen *(fig.)* stand on one's own two feet; support oneself; auf schwachen ~en stehen *(fig.)* ‹*argument*› rest on shaky foundations; ‹*firm*› be in a precarious position; das geht in die ~e *(Alkohol)* it makes you unsteady on your feet; *(Musik)* it makes you want to get up and dance; mit beiden ~en im Leben *od.* [fest] auf der Erde stehen have both feet [firmly] on the ground; mit dem linken ~ zuerst aufgestanden sein *(ugs.)* have got out of bed on the wrong side; mit einem ~ im Gefängnis/Grab[e] stehen *(fig.)* stand a good chance of ending up in prison/have one foot in the grave; von einem ~ aufs andere treten *(ugs.)* shift from one foot to the other; auf einem ~ kann man nicht stehen *(scherzh.)* one drink isn't enough to wet one's whistle; *s. auch* Klotz a; Kopf e; vertreten 2; b) *(Hosen~, Teil eines Möbelstükkes, Stativ)* leg; c) *(nordd.: Fuß)* foot; d) *(südd., österr., schweiz.: Knochen)* bone; jmdm. in die ~e fahren go right through sb.; *s. auch* ²Mark a

bei·nah[e] ['baina:(ə)] *Adv.* almost; nearly; wir wären ~ zu spät gekommen we were nearly too late; ich möchte ~ sagen, daß ...: I would almost say that ...

Beinahe·zusammenstoß der *(Flugw.)* airmiss

Bei·name der epithet

bein-, Bein-: **~amputation** die leg amputation; **~amputiert** *Adj.* ‹*person*› with a *or* one leg/both [his/her] legs amputated; sie ist ~: she has had a leg/both [her] legs amputated; **~arbeit** die *(beim Boxen, Ringen, Tanzen)* footwork; *(beim Schwimmen)* leg action; **~bruch** der broken leg; das ist [doch] kein ~bruch! *(ugs.)* it's not the end of the world *(coll.)*

beinern ['bainən] *Adj.* a) *(knöchern)* bone *attrib.*; made of bone *postpos.*; b) *(aus Elfenbein)* ivory *attrib.*; made of ivory *postpos.*

Bein-: **~fleisch** das *(österr.)* beef cooked and served on the bone; **~freiheit** die legroom

beinhalten [bə'|ınhaltn̩] *tr. V. (Papierdt.)* involve

bein·hart *(österr., südd.)* 1. *Adj.* rock-hard; tough ‹*movie*›; ‹*person*› as hard as nails. 2. *adv.* ~ gefroren frozen hard; ~ spielen *(Sportjargon)* be hard and physical

Bein·haus das *(hist.)* charnel-house

-beinig *Adj.* -legged; drei~/lang~: three-legged/long-legged; ein zwölf~es Insekt an insect with twelve legs

Bein-: **~kleid** das; *meist Pl. (veralt.)* trousers *pl.*; **~leiden** das *(Med.)* leg condition

Beinling ['bainlıŋ] der; ~s, ~e *(veralt.)* leg

Bein-: **~prothese** die artificial leg; **~schere** die *(Ringen)* leg scissors *sing.*; **~schiene** die a) *(Sport)* [long] shin pad; *(Cricket, Hockey)* pad; b) *(Teil der Rüstung)* greave *usu. in pl.*; **~stumpf** der stump [of the leg]

bei|ordnen *tr. V.* a) jmdm. jmdn. ~: assign sb. to assist sb.; b) *(Rechtsw.)* als Pflichtverteidiger beigeordnet werden be called in as duty solicitor *(Brit.) or (Amer.)* court-appointed lawyer; c) *(Sprachw.) s.* nebenordnen

Bei·ordnung die a) *(Sprachw.)* co-ordination; b) *(Rechtsw.)* assignment

Bei·pack der extra item [ordered]

bei|packen *tr. V.* einer Warensendung etw. ~: pack sth. in with a consignment of goods

Beipack·zettel der instruction leaflet

bei|pflichten ['baipflıçtn̩] *itr. V.* jmdm. [in einer Sache] ~: agree with sb. [on sth.]; einem Vorschlag *usw.* ~: agree with a proposal *etc.*; Sie werden mir darin ~, daß ...: you will agree with me that ...

Bei·programm das supporting programme

Bei·rat der a) *(Gremium)* advisory committee *or* board; b) *(veralt.: Berater)* adviser

beirren *tr. V.* sich durch nichts/von niemandem ~ lassen not be put off *or* deterred by anything/anybody; not let anything/anybody put one off *or* deter one; nichts konnte ihn in seinen Ansichten ~: nothing could shake him in his views

Beirut [bai'ru:t] (das); ~s Beirut

beisammen [bai'zamən] *Adv.* together

beisammen-, Beisammen-: **~|haben** *unr. tr. V.* a) *(gesammelt haben)* have got together; **b) er hat nicht alle ~** *(ugs.)* he's not all there *(coll.)*; he's a bit soft in the head *(coll.)*; **~|halten** *unr. tr. V.* keep together; hold on to ‹*money*›; **~|sein** *unr. itr. V.; mit sein; nur im Inf. und 2. Part. zusammengeschr. (ugs.)* **[gut] ~sein** be in good health *or* shape; **~sein das** get-together; **~|sitzen** *unr. itr. V.* sit together

Bei·satz der *(Sprachw.)* appositive

Bei·schlaf der *(geh., Rechtsw.)* sexual intercourse

bei|schließen *unr. tr. V. (österr.)* **einem Brief** *usw.* **etw. ~:** enclose sth. with a letter *etc.*

Bei·schluß der *(österr.: Anlage)* enclosure

Bei·segel das *(Segeln)* additional sail

Bei·sein das *in* **im ~ von jmdm., in jmds. ~:** in the presence of sb. *or* in sb.'s presence; **ohne ~ von jmdm., ohne jmds. ~:** in the absence of sb. *or* in sb.'s absence

bei·seite *Adv.* **a)** *(auf die Seite)* aside; **jmdn. ~ ziehen/schieben** draw/push sb. to one side *or* aside; **etw. ~ bringen** get sth. hidden away; hide sth. away; **etw. ~ lassen** *(fig.)* leave sth. aside; **etw. ~ legen** *(sparen)* put sth. by *or* aside; *(Angefangenes weglegen)* put *or* lay sth. aside; **jmdn./die Leiche ~ schaffen** *(ugs.)* get rid of sb./the body; **die Beute/das Geld ~ schaffen** *(ugs.)* stash *(sl.)* *or* hide the loot/money away; **jmdn./etw. ~ schieben** *(fig.)* push sb./sth. aside; **b)** *(auf der Seite)* on *or* to one side; **~ stehen** *(fig.)* take second place

Beis[e]l ['baizl] **das; ~s, ~** *od.* **~n** *(österr.)* pub *(Brit. coll.)*; bar *(Amer.)*

bei|setzen *tr. V.* **a)** *(geh.: beerdigen)* bury; inter; lay to rest; inter ‹*ashes*›; **b)** *(Seemannsspr.)* set, hoist ‹*sail*›

Bei·setzung die; ~, ~en *(geh.)* funeral; burial

Beisetzungs·feierlichkeiten *Pl.* funeral [ceremony] *sing.*

Bei·sitz der assessorship; **den ~ haben** act as assessor

Bei·sitzer der; ~s, ~, Bei·sitzerin die; ~, ~nen assessor; *(bei Ausschüssen)* committee member

Bei·spiel das a) example **(für** of**)**; **zum ~:** for example *or* instance; **wie zum ~:** as for example; such as; **ohne ~ sein** be without parallel *or* unparalleled; *(unerhört sein)* be outrageous; **b)** *(Vorbild)* example; **ein warnendes ~:** a warning; **jmdm. ein ~ geben** set an example to sb.; **sich** *(Dat.)* **an jmdm./etw. ein ~ nehmen** follow sb.'s example/take sth. as one's example; **mit gutem ~ vorangehen** set a good example

beispiel·gebend *Adj.* exemplary; **~ für jmdn. sein** be an example to sb.

beispielhaft 1. *Adj.* exemplary. **2.** *adv.* in an exemplary fashion

beispiel-, Beispiel-: ~halber *Adv.: s.* **beispielshalber; ~los 1.** *Adj.* unparalleled; *(unerhört)* outrageous; **2.** *adv.* incomparably ‹*well, badly, etc.*›; **~ erfolgreich/grausam** with unparalleled success/cruelty; **~satz der** *(Sprachw.)* example sentence; illustrative sentence

beispiels-: ~halber *Adv.* for example *or* instance; **etw. ~halber anführen** offer *or* give sth. by way of example; **~weise** *Adv.* for example *or* instance

bei|springen *unr. itr. V.; mit sein* **jmdm. [in der Not] ~:** leap *or* rush to sb.'s aid *or* assistance [in an emergency]; **jmdm. mit Geld ~:** help sb. out with money

beißen ['baisn̩] **1.** *unr. tr., itr. V.* **a)** bite; **in etw.** *(Akk.)* **~:** bite into sth.; **auf etw.** *(Akk.)* **~:** bite on sth.; **an den Nägeln ~:** bite one's nails; **sich** *(Dat.)* **die Lippen wund ~:** bite one's lips till they bleed; **ich habe mich** *od.* **mir auf die Zunge/in die Lippe gebissen** I've bitten my tongue/lip; **der Hund hat mir** *od.* **mich ins Bein gebissen** the dog bit me in the leg; **nach jmdm./etw. ~:** snap at sb./sth.; **der Hund biß [wild] um sich** the dog snapped [wildly] in all directions; **b)** *(bissig sein; auch fig.)* bite; **c)** *(ätzen)* sting; **in die** *od.* **in den Augen ~:** sting one's eyes; make one's eyes sting; **auf der Zunge ~:** burn the tongue; **d)** *(Angelsport: an~)* bite; **e)** *(kauen)* **nicht mehr [richtig] ~ können** no longer be able to chew things [properly]; **nichts/nicht viel zu ~ haben** *(fig.)* have nothing/not have much to eat; **sich in den Arsch** *(derb) od.* **Hintern** *(salopp)* **~** *(fig.)* kick oneself. **2.** *unr. refl. V. (ugs.)* ‹*colours, clothes*› clash

beißend *Adj.; nicht präd.* biting ‹*cold*›; acrid ‹*smoke, fumes*›; sharp ‹*frost*›; biting, cutting ‹*wind*›; pungent, sharp ‹*smell, taste*›; *(fig.)* biting ‹*ridicule*›; cutting ‹*irony*›

Beißerchen das; ~s, ~ *(fam.)* toothy-peg *(child lang.)*

Beißerei die; ~, ~en fight

Beiß-: ~ring der teething-ring; **~zange die** *s.* **Kneifzange**

Bei·stand der a) *o. Pl. (geh.: Hilfe)* aid; assistance; help; **jmdm. ~ leisten** give sb. aid *or* assistance; come to sb.'s aid *or* assistance; **b)** *(Rechtsw.: Rechtshelfer) lay person acting in support of a defendant*

Beistands-: ~abkommen das *(Politik)* treaty of mutual assistance; **~pakt der** *(Politik)* mutual assistance pact; **~vertrag der** *(Politik)* treaty of mutual assistance

bei|stehen *unr. itr. V.* **jmdm. ~:** aid *or* assist *or* help sb.; *(zur Seite stehen)* stand by sb.

bei|stellen *itr. V. (österr.: bereitstellen)* make available; provide

Beistell-: ~möbel *Pl.* occasional furniture *sing.*; **~tisch der, ~tischchen das** occasional table; *(im Restaurant)* side-table

Bei·steuer die; *o. Pl. (südd.)* contribution

bei|steuern *tr. V.* contribute; make ‹*contribution*›

bei|stimmen *itr. V.: s.* **zustimmen**

Bei·strich der *(veralt.)* comma

Beitel ['baitl] **der; ~s, ~:** chisel

Beitrag ['baitra:k] **der; ~[e]s, Beiträge** ['baitrɛ:gə] **a)** *(Zahlung, Mitwirkung)* contribution; *(Versicherungs~)* premium; *(Mitglieds~)* subscription; **einen ~ zu etw. leisten** make a contribution to sth.; **b)** *(Aufsatz, Kommentar)* article **(zu** on**)**; *(in einer Zeitschrift, einem Sammelband)* article, contribution **(zu** on**)**

bei|tragen *unr. tr., itr. V.* contribute **(zu** to**)**; **das Seine/viel zu etw. ~:** contribute one's share/a great deal to sth.

beitrags-, Beitrags-: ~frei *Adj.* non-contributory; ‹*person*› not liable to pay contributions; **~gruppe, ~klasse die** *(Sozialw.)* contribution class *(Brit.)*; insurance group *(Amer.)*; **~marke die** stamp; **~pflicht die** *(Sozialw.)* liability to pay contributions; **~pflichtig** *Adj. (Sozialw.)* ‹*employee*› liable to pay contributions; ‹*earnings*› on which contributions are payable; **~satz der** contribution rate; **~zahlung die** contribution

bei|treiben *unr. tr. V. (Rechtsw.)* enforce payment of

Beitreibung die; ~, ~en *(Rechtsw.)* enforcement of payment

bei|treten *unr. itr. V.; mit sein* **a)** *(Mitglied werden bei)* join; **einem Verein** *usw.* **~:** join a club *etc.*; **b)** *(sich anschließen an)* **einem Abkommen/Pakt ~:** accede to an agreement/a pact; **c)** *(Rechtsw.)* **einem Verfahren/einer Verhandlung ~:** attend proceedings *pl.*/a hearing

Bei·tritt der a) *(Eintritt)* joining; **seinen ~ erklären** affirm one's wish to become a member; **b)** *(Rechtsw.)* **jmds. ~ anordnen** *od.* **verfügen** order sb. to attend [the proceedings]

Beitritts·erklärung die declaration *(affirming one's wish to become a member)*

Bei·wagen der a) *(Seitenwagen)* side-car; **b)** *(veralt.: Anhänger) (einer U-Bahn)* car; *(einer Straßenbahn)* trailer

Beiwagen-: ~fahrer der side-car passenger; **~maschine die** motor-cycle combination *(Brit.)*; side-car motor cycle *(Amer.)*

Bei·werk das; *o. Pl.* accessories *pl.*; **in Opern ist die Handlung oft nur ~:** in opera the plot is often of only secondary importance

bei|willigen *itr. V. (schweiz.) s.* **zustimmen**

bei|wohnen *itr. V.* **a)** *(geh.: anwesend sein)* **einer Sache** *(Dat.)* **~:** be present at *or* attend sth.; **b)** *(veralt. verhüll.)* **jmdm. ~:** lie with sb. *(arch.)*

Bei·wort das; ~[e]s, Beiwörter a) *s.* **Adjektiv; b)** *(Epitheton)* epithet

Beiz [baits] **die; ~, ~en** *(schweiz.) s.* ^{3}**Beize**

^{1}**Beize** ['baitsə] **die; ~, ~n a)** *(Holzbearb.)* [wood-]stain; **b)** *(Gerberei)* bate; **c)** *(Textilbearb.)* mordant; **d)** *(Metallbearb.)* pickle; **e)** *(Landw.)* disinfectant; seed-dressing; **f)** *(Tabakind.)* sauce; **g)** *(Kochk.)* marinade; **h)** *(das Beizen) s.* **beizen:** staining; bating; mordanting; pickling; disinfecting; sauce casing; marinading

^{2}**Beize die; ~, ~n** *(Jagdw.)* hawking

^{3}**Beize die; ~, ~n** *(schweiz.)* pub *(Brit. coll.)*; bar *(Amer.)*

beizeiten [bai'tsaitn̩] *Adv.* in good time

^{1}**beizen** ['baitsn̩] *tr. V. (mit Beize behandeln)* **a)** *(Holzbearb.)* stain; **b)** *(Gerberei)* bate; **c)** *(Textilbearb.)* mordant; **d)** *(Landw.)* disinfect, dress ‹*seed*›; **e)** *(Metallbearb., Tabakind.)* pickle; **f)** *(Kochk.)* marinade

^{2}**beizen** *tr., itr. V. (Jägerspr.)* hawk

Beizer der; ~s, ~: stainer

bei|ziehen *unr. tr. V. (südd., österr., schweiz.)* call in ‹*lawyer, psychologist, expert, etc.*›; bring in, enlist ‹*helpers*›; consult, make use of ‹*reference book etc.*›

Bei·ziehung die *(südd., österr., schweiz.)* calling in

Beiz-: ~jagd die *s.* ^{2}**Beize; ~vogel der** falcon; hawk

bejahen [bə'ja:ən] **1.** *tr. V.* **a)** *(mit Ja beantworten)* **etw. ~:** give an affirmative answer to sth.; answer sth. in the affirmative; **b)** *(gutheißen, befürworten)* approve of; **das Leben ~:** have a positive *or* an affirmative attitude to life. **2.** *itr. V.* answer in the affirmative; give an affirmative answer; **sie bejahte lebhaft** she replied with an animated 'yes'

bejahend 1. *Adj.* affirmative; affirmative, positive ‹*attitude*›. **2.** *adv.* ‹*answer*› in the affirmative; ‹*nod*› affirmatively

bejahrt [bə'ja:ɐt] *Adj. (geh.)* advanced in years

Bejahrtheit die; ~: advanced age

Bejahung die; ~, ~en a) affirmative answer *or* reply; **ein Zeichen/eine Geste der ~:** an affirmative sign/gesture; **b)** *(das Gutheißen)* approval

bejammern *tr. V.* lament; **die Toten ~:** lament for the dead; **dazu neigen, sich selbst zu ~:** tend towards self-pity

bejammerns·wert *Adj.* pitiable ‹*person*›; wretched ‹*situation*›; lamentable, pitiable ‹*condition, state*›; pitiful ‹*sight*›

bejubeln *tr. V.* cheer; acclaim; **jmdn. als Helden** *usw.* **~:** acclaim sb. as a hero *etc.*

bekacken *(vulg.)* **1.** *tr. V.* shit *(vulg.)* in ‹*nappy etc.*›; **bekackte Windeln** shitty nappies *(Brit.) or (Amer.)* diapers *(vulg.)*. **2.** *refl. V.* shit oneself *(vulg.)*

bekakeln *tr. V. (ugs.)* talk over; discuss

bekämpfen *tr. V.* **a)** fight against; **sich [gegenseitig] ~:** fight [one another *or* each other]; **b)** *(einzudämmen versuchen)* combat, fight ‹*disease, epidemic, pest*›; combat ‹*unemployment, crime, alcoholism*›; curb ‹*curiosity, prejudice*›

Bekämpfung die; ~ a) fight (+ *Gen.* against); **zur ~ des Feindes aufrufen** call for battle against the enemy; **b)** *s.* **bekämpfen**

b: combating; fighting; curbing; **zur ~ einer Krankheit beitragen** contribute to combating *or* fighting a disease; **unsere Aufgabe ist die ~ der Kriminalität/Arbeitslosigkeit** our task is to combat crime/unemployment

bekannt [bəˈkant] **1.** *2. Part. v.* **bekennen. 2.** *Adj.* **a)** *(von vielen gewußt)* well-known; **es wurde ~, daß ...:** it became known that ...; **für etw. ~ sein** be well known for sth.; **es ist nichts davon ~:** nothing is known concerning it; **wegen etw. ~ sein** be well-known on account of sth.; **b)** *(berühmt)* well-known; famous; **~er sein** be better known; **international ~ sein** be internationally known *or* famous; **c)** *(vertraut, bewußt)* **die Aufgaben sind ihm ~:** he knows what his duties are; **sie ist mir ~:** I know her; **davon ist mir nichts ~:** I know nothing about that; **mit jmdm. ~ sein/werden** know *or* be acquainted with sb./get to know *or* become acquainted with sb.; **mit etw. ~ sein/werden** be/become familiar *or* acquainted with sth.; **jmdn./sich mit jmdm. ~ machen** introduce sb./oneself to sb.; **Darf ich ~ machen? Meine Eltern** may I introduce my parents?; **jmdn./sich mit etw. ~ machen** acquaint sb./oneself with sth.; **jmdm. ~ vorkommen** seem familiar to sb.; **der Witz kommt mir ~ vor** I think I've heard that joke somewhere before

Bekạnnte der/die *adj. Dekl.* **a)** acquaintance; **b)** *(verhüll.: Freund/Freundin)* boyfriend/girl[-friend]

Bekạnnten·kreis der circle of acquaintances; **jmds. engerer** *od.* **näherer ~:** sb.'s circle of close acquaintances

bekạnnter·maßen *Adv. (Papierdt.) s.* **bekanntlich**

Bekạnnt·gabe die; ~: announcement

bekạnnt|geben *unr. tr. V.* announce

Bekạnntheit die; ~ a) *(Kenntnis)* acquaintance, familiarity (*Gen.* with); **b)** *(Berühmtheit)* fame

Bekạnntheits·grad der; ~es: einen großen ~ haben be very well known

bekạnntlich *Adv.* as is well known; **etw. ist ~ der Fall** it is known that sth. is the case; sth. is known to be the case; **der Walfisch ist ~ ein Säugetier** it is well known that the whale is a mammal; **~ sind Steuererhöhungen sehr unbeliebt** we all know that tax increases are highly unpopular

bekạnnt|machen *tr. V.* announce; *(der Öffentlichkeit)* make public; *(veröffentlichen)* publish

Bekạnnt·machung die; ~, ~en a) *o. Pl. (das ~machen)* announcement; *(das Veröffentlichen)* publication; **b)** *(Mitteilung)* announcement; notice

Bekạnntschaft die; ~; ~en a) *o. Pl. (Bekanntsein)* acquaintance; **bei näherer ~:** on closer acquaintance; **jmds. ~ machen** make sb.'s acquaintance; **du wirst bald mit der Polizei ~ machen** *(ugs.)* you're going to get into trouble with the police soon; **dein Hosenboden wird gleich mit meiner Hand ~ machen** *(ugs.)* you'll feel my hand across your backside any minute; **b)** *(Mensch, den man kennt)* acquaintance; *(Bekanntenkreis)* circle of acquaintances

bekạnnt|werden *unr. itr. V.; mit sein; nur im Inf. und 2. Part. zusammengeschr.* become known; become public knowledge

beka̲ufen *refl. V.* make a bad buy

beke̲hren 1. *tr. V.* convert (**zu** to); **jmdn. zum Anhänger des Buddhismus/Nacktbadens/Monetarismus ~:** convert sb. to Buddhism/nude bathing/monetarism; **vom Alkohol bekehrt sein** have turned one's back on alcohol. **2.** *refl. V.* become converted (**zu** to)

Beke̲hrer der; ~s, ~, Beke̲hrerin die; ~, ~nen converter; *(Missionar)* missionary

Beke̲hrte der/die; *adj. Dekl.* convert

Beke̲hrung die; ~, ~en *(auch fig.)* conversion (**zu** to)

bekẹnnen 1. *unr. tr. V.* **a)** *(eingestehen)* admit ‹*mistake, defeat*›; confess ‹*sin*›; admit, confess ‹*guilt, truth*›; **b)** *(Rel.)* profess; **die Bekennende Kirche** *(hist.)* the Confessional Church. **2.** *refl. V.* **sich zu Buddha/Mohammed ~:** profess *or* declare one's faith in Buddha/Muhammad; **nur wenige seiner früheren Freunde bekannten sich zu ihm** only a few of his former friends stood by him; **sich zu seiner Vergangenheit ~:** acknowledge one's past; **sich zu seiner Schuld ~:** admit *or* confess one's guilt; **sich zum Sozialismus ~:** declare one's belief in socialism; **sich schuldig/nicht schuldig ~:** admit *or* confess/not admit *or* not confess one's guilt; *(vor Gericht)* plead guilty/not guilty; **sich zu einem Bombenanschlag ~:** claim responsibility for a bomb attack; **sich als jmd[n]. ~:** admit *or* confess that one is sb.; admit *or* confess to being sb.

Bekẹnner der confessor

Bekẹnner-: ~brief, der letter (*Gen.* from) claiming responsibility; **~geist der, ~mut der;** *o. Pl.* courage of one's convictions

Bekẹnntnis das; ~ses, ~se a) *(Eingeständnis)* confession; **ein ~ ablegen** make a confession; **b)** *(Eintreten)* **ein ~ für die Sache des Friedens/zum Frieden** a declaration of belief in the cause of peace/a declaration for peace; **ein ~ zum Christentum/zur Demokratie ablegen** profess one's faith in Christianity/declare one's belief in democracy; **c)** *(Konfession)* denomination; **d)** *(formulierter Inhalt)* confession; **das Augsburger ~:** the Confession of Augsburg

bekẹnntnis-, Bekẹnntnis-: ~freiheit die; *o. Pl.* religious freedom; freedom of worship; **~kirche die;** *o. Pl.* Confessional Church; **~los** *Adj.* not belonging to any denomination *postpos., not pred.*; **~los sein** not belong to any denomination; **~schule die** denominational school

beki̲eken *tr. V. (nordd. ugs.)* look at; have a look at

bekifft [bəˈkɪft] *Adj. (ugs.)* stoned *(sl.)*

bekla̲gen 1. *tr. V. (geh.)* **a)** *(betrauern)* mourn; **Menschenleben waren nicht zu ~:** there were no fatalities; there was no loss of life; **b)** *(bedauern)* lament; **sein/jmds. Los ~:** lament *or* bewail one's fate/deplore sb.'s fate; **wir haben einen großen Umsatzrückgang zu ~:** we have to note with regret a large drop in sales. **2.** *refl. V.* complain; **sich über jmdn./etw. ~:** complain about sb./sth.; **ich kann mich nicht ~:** I can't complain; **du kannst dich nicht ~:** you've got nothing to complain about *or* no reason to complain

bekla̲gens-: ~wert, ~würdig *(geh.)* **1.** *Adj.* pitiful ‹*sight, impression*›; pitiable ‹*person*›; lamentable, pitiable, deplorable ‹*condition, state*›; wretched ‹*situation*›; **2.** *adv.* lamentably; deplorably

beklagt [bəˈklaːkt] *Adj.; nicht präd.* **die ~e Partei** the defendant; *(bei Ehescheidungen)* the respondent; **die ~en Personen** the defendants

Bekla̲gte der/die; *adj. Dekl.* defendant; *(bei Ehescheidungen)* respondent

beklạtschen *tr. V.* **a)** clap; applaud; **b)** *(ugs.: klatschen über)* gossip about

bekla̲uen *tr. V. (salopp)* rob; do *(sl.)*

bekle̲ben *tr. V.* **eine Wand** *usw.* **mit etw. ~:** stick sth. all over a wall *etc.*; **mit etw. beklebt sein** have sth. stuck all over it

beklẹckern *(ugs.)* **1.** *tr. V.* **seinen Schlips** *usw.* **mit Soße** *usw.* **~:** drop *or* spill sauce *etc.* down one's tie *etc.*; **mit Senf bekleckerte Teller** plates smeared with mustard. **2.** *refl. V.* **ich habe mich bekleckert** I've dropped *or* spilled sth. down myself; **sich mit Soße** *usw.* **~:** drop *or* spill sauce *etc.* down oneself; *s. auch* **Ruhm**

beklẹcksen *tr. V.* spatter; **etw. mit Tinte** *usw.* **~:** spatter ink *etc.* on sth.

bekle̲iden *tr. V.* **a)** clothe; **mit etw. bekleidet sein** be dressed in *or* be wearing sth.; **b)** *(geh.: innehaben)* occupy, hold ‹*office, position*›; **c)** *(geh. veralt.: versehen)* **jmdn. mit etw. ~:** bestow sth. on sb.

Bekle̲idung die clothing; clothes *pl.*; garments *pl.*; *(Aufmachung)* dress; attire

Bekle̲idungs-: ~gewerbe das, ~handwerk das clothing trade; **~industrie die** clothing industry; **~stück das** *s.* **Kleidungsstück; ~vorschriften** *Pl.* dress regulations; regulations governing dress

bekle̲istern *tr. V. (ugs.)* **a)** *(mit Kleister bestreichen)* apply paste to; **b)** *(bekleben)* **etw. mit Aufklebern** *usw.* **~:** plaster stickers *etc.* all over sth.

beklẹmmen *tr. V.* oppress; **jmdm. das Herz** *od.* **jmds. Herz ~** *(geh.)* weigh upon sb.'s heart

beklẹmmend 1. *Adj.* oppressive. **2.** *adv.* oppressively

Beklẹmmung die; ~, ~en oppressive feeling; *(Angst)* [feeling of] unease; *(stärker)* [feeling of] apprehension; **ich bekomme** *od.* **kriege ~en** I feel as if I'm being stifled

beklommen [bəˈklɔmən] **1.** *Adj.* uneasy; shaky ‹*voice*›; *(stärker)* apprehensive. **2.** *adv.* uneasily; *(stärker)* apprehensively

Beklọmmenheit die; ~: uneasiness; *(stärker)* apprehensiveness

beklö̲nen *tr. V. (nordd. ugs.)* talk over

beklọpfen *tr. V.* tap

bekloppt [bəˈklɔpt] *Adj. (salopp)* barmy *(Brit. sl.)*; loony *(sl.)*; **dieser ~e Fahrer** this nut-case of a driver *(Brit. sl.)*; this nutty driver *(sl.)*; **ein Bekloppter** a nut-case *(Brit. sl.)*; a nut *(sl.)*

beknạckt *Adj. (salopp)* lousy *(sl.)*; **ein ~er Typ** a berk *(Brit. sl.)*; a jerk *(sl.)*; **so was Beknacktes** what a load of rubbish! *(coll.)*

bekni̲en *tr. V. (ugs.)* beg

bekọchen *tr. V. (ugs.)* cook for

bekö̲dern *tr. V. (Angeln)* bait ‹*hook*›

bekọmmen 1. *unr. tr. V.* **a)** *(erhalten)* get; get, receive ‹*money, letter, reply, news, orders*›; **ich habe seit Monaten keinen Brief mehr von ihm ~:** I haven't had a letter from him for months; **Anschluß/eine Verbindung [zu einem Ort] ~:** get through [to a place]; **fünf Tage Urlaub ~:** get five days' holiday *(Brit.) or (Amer.)* vacation; **drei Monate Gefängnis ~:** get *or* receive three months in prison; **eine Flasche** *usw.* **an den Kopf ~:** get hit on the head with a bottle *etc.*; **was ~ Sie?** *(im Geschäft)* can I help you?; *(im Lokal, Restaurant)* what would you like?; *(wieviel Geld?)* how much is that?; *(bei mehreren Sachen)* how much does that come to?; **wir ~ Regen/besseres Wetter** we're going to get some rain/some better weather; there's rain/better weather on the way; **sie bekommt ein Kind** she's expecting a baby; **wann bekommt sie ihr Kind?** when is the baby due?; **b)** *(finden, erlangen)* get; obtain; catch ‹*train, bus, flight*›; **eine Vorstellung/einen Eindruck von etw. ~:** get some *or* an idea/impression of sth.; **seinen Willen ~:** get one's way; **c)** *(ein bestimmtes Ziel erreichen)* get; **etw. durch die Tür/in den Kofferraum ~:** get sth. through the door/into the boot *(Brit.) or (Amer.)* trunk; **etw. zu Papier ~:** get sth. down on paper; **jmdn. nicht aus dem Bett ~:** be unable to get sb. out of bed *or* up; **jmdn. zum Reden ~:** get sb. to talk; **jmdn. dazu ~, die Wahrheit zu sagen** get sb. to tell the truth; **etw. sauber/wohnlich ~:** get sth. clean/make sth. homely *or* comfortable; **d)** *(entwickeln, erleiden)* get ‹*goose-pimples, measles, spots, diarrhoea, practice, experience, etc.*›; **Hunger/Durst ~:** get hungry/thirsty; **einen roten Kopf/eine Glatze ~:** go red/bald; **Mut/Angst ~:** take heart/become frightened; **Gestalt/Form ~:** take shape; **er bekommt einen Bart** he's growing a beard; **sie bekommt eine Brust** her breasts are developing; **Zähne ~:**

‹*baby*› teethe; **er bekommt seine Weisheitszähne** his wisdom teeth are coming through; **e)** (+ *Inf.*) **etw. zu essen/trinken ~:** have sth. to eat/drink; **wo bekomme ich etwas zu essen/trinken?** where can I get something to eat/drink?; **etw./jmdn. zu fassen ~:** get hold of sth./lay one's hands on sb.; *s. auch* **hören, spüren; f)** + *2. Part.* get; **etw. geschenkt ~:** get [given] sth. *or* be given sth. as a present; **etw. direkt vom Verlag geschickt ~:** get sth. direct from the publisher; **seine Arbeit von anderen gemacht ~:** get one's work done by other people; **g)** *in* **es nicht über sich** *(Akk.)* **~, etw. zu tun** be unable to bring oneself to do sth. **2.** *unr. itr. V.; mit sein* **jmdm. gut ~:** do sb. good; be good for sb.; **jmdm. [gut] ~:** ‹*food, medicine*› agree with sb.; **jmdm. schlecht** *od.* **nicht ~:** not be good for sb.; not do sb. any good; ‹*food, medicine*› not agree with sb.; **wohl bekomm's!** your [very good] health!

bekömmlich [bəˈkœmlɪç] *Adj.* easily digestible; **leicht/schwer ~ sein** be easily digestible/difficult to digest

Bekömmlichkeit die; ~: easy digestibility

beköstigen [bəˈkœstɪgn̩] *tr. V.* cater for; **er wird von seiner Tante beköstigt** he gets his meals provided by his aunt

Beköstigung die; ~: a) catering *no indef. art.*; **b)** *(Kost)* food *no indef. art.*

bekotzen *tr. V. (derb)* puke over *(coarse)*

bekräftigen *tr. V.* reinforce ‹*statement*›; reaffirm ‹*promise*›; confirm, strengthen ‹*suspicion, conviction*›; **eine Vereinbarung durch Handschlag ~:** seal an agreement with a handshake

Bekräftigung die confirmation

bekränzen [bəˈkrɛntsn̩] *tr. V.* **jmdn./etw. ~:** crown sb. with a wreath/garland sth.

bekreuzen 1. *tr. V. (kath. Kirche)* make the sign of the cross over. **2.** *refl. V. s.* **bekreuzigen**

bekreuzigen *refl. V. (kath. Kirche)* cross oneself

bekriegen *tr. V.* wage war on; *(fig.)* fight; **bekriegt werden** be attacked; **sich ~:** be at war; *(fig.)* fight [each other *or* one another]

bekritteln *tr. V. (abwertend)* find fault with *(in a petty way)*

bekritzeln *tr. V.* scribble on; **die Wände waren von oben bis unten bekritzelt** the walls were covered with graffiti; **die Buchränder mit Anmerkungen ~:** scribble comments in the margins of the book

bekrönen *tr. V. (auch fig., Archit.)* crown

bekucken *(nordd.) s.* **begucken**

bekümmern *tr. V.* **jmdn. ~:** cause sb. worry; **das braucht dich nicht zu ~:** you needn't worry about that

Bekümmernis die *(geh.)* worry; trouble; *(stärker)* distress

bekümmert [bəˈkʏmɐt] **1.** *Adj.* worried; troubled; *(stärker)* distressed. **2.** *adv.* **~ schweigen** maintain a worried silence

bekunden [bəˈkʊndn̩] **1.** *tr. V.* **a)** *(geh.: zeigen)* express; **b)** *(Rechtsw.: bezeugen)* make ‹*statement*›; **er bekundete, daß ...:** he testified that ... **2.** *refl. V. (geh.: sich zeigen)* manifest itself

Bekunden das *in* **nach seinem/ihrem** *usw.* **eigenen ~:** according to his/her *etc.* own statement[s]

Bekundung die; ~, ~en expression; *(Aussage)* statement

belabern *tr. V. (salopp abwertend)* keep on [and on] at

belächeln *tr. V.* smile [pityingly/tolerantly *etc.*] at; **belächelt werden** meet with a pitying smile

belachen *tr. V.* laugh at

[1]**beladen** *unr. tr. V.* **a)** *(mit einer Ladung versehen)* load ‹*ship*›; load [up] ‹*car, wagon*›; **Be- und Entladen gestattet/verboten** loading and unloading permitted/no loading or unloading; **b)** *(zu tragen geben)* load up ‹*horse, donkey*›; **c)** *(reich bedecken)* load ‹*table*›

[2]**beladen** *Adj.* loaded, laden (**mit** with); **mit etw. ~ sein** be laden with sth.; **sie war schwer mit Paketen ~:** she was loaded *or* laden down with parcels; **mit Sorgen/Schuld ~ sein** *(fig.)* ‹*person*› be burdened with cares/guilt; **mit einem Fluch ~ sein** be under a curse

Belag [bəˈlaːk] **der; ~[e]s, Beläge** [bəˈlɛːgə] **a)** *(Schicht)* coating; film; *(Zungen~)* fur *no indef. art.*; coating; *(Zahn~)* film; **Sie haben einen ~ auf der Zunge** your tongue is coated; **b)** *(Fußboden~)* covering; *(Straßen~)* surface; *(Brems~)* lining; **c)** *(von Kuchen, Pizza, halben Brötchen)* topping; *(von Sandwiches)* filling

Belagerer [bəˈlaːgərɐ] **der; ~s, ~:** besieger

belagern *tr. V.* **a)** *(Milit.)* besiege; lay siege to; **b)** *(fig.: bedrängen)* besiege

Belagerung die; ~, ~en a) *(Milit.)* siege; **b)** *o. Pl. (fig.: Bedrängung)* besieging

Belagerungs-: ~maschine die siege-machine; **~zu·stand der;** *o. Pl.* state of siege; *(Ausnahmezustand)* state of emergency; **den ~zustand ausrufen** declare a state of siege/emergency; **über die Stadt wurde der ~zustand verhängt** the town was declared under siege/a state of emergency was declared in the town

Belang [bəˈlaŋ] **der; ~[e]s, ~e a)** *o. Pl. (Bedeutung)* **[für etw.] von/ohne ~ sein** be of importance/of no importance [for sth.]; **für jmdn. von/ohne ~ sein** be important/not be important to sb.; **b)** *Pl. (Interessen)* interests; **jmds. ~e wahrnehmen/vertreten** look after/represent sb.'s interests

belangen *tr. V.* **a)** *(Rechtsw.)* sue; *(strafrechtlich)* prosecute; **jmdn. wegen etw. ~:** sue/prosecute sb. for sth.; **b)** *(veralt. unpers.: betreffen)* **was mich/ihn** *usw.* **belangt, so ...:** as far as I am/he *etc.* is concerned, ...

belang-, Belang-: ~los *Adj. (trivial)* trivial; *(unerheblich)* of no importance (**für** for); **~losigkeit die; ~, ~en a)** *o. Pl. (Trivialität)* triviality; *(Unerheblichkeit)* unimportance; **b)** *(triviale Äußerung)* triviality; **~voll** *Adj. (geh.)* important (**für** for)

belassen *unr. tr. V.* **a)** *(unverändert lassen)* leave; **jmdn. in seinem Amt ~:** keep sb. in his/her post; **~ wir es dabei** let's leave it at that; **b)** *(überlassen)* **jmdm. etw. ~:** let sb. keep sth.

belastbar *Adj.* **a)** *(mit Last, Gewicht)* tough, resilient ‹*material*›; ‹*material*› able to withstand stress *pred.*; **[nur] mit 3,5 t ~ sein** be able to take a load of [only] 3.5 t; **b)** *(beanspruchbar)* tough, resilient ‹*person*›; **seelisch/körperlich ~ sein** be emotionally/physically tough *or* resilient; be able to stand emotional/physical stress; **ein ~er Mitarbeiter** an employee who can work under pressure; **die Umwelt ist nicht weiter ~:** the pressures on the environment have become intolerable

Belastbarkeit die; ~, ~n a) *(von Material)* ability to withstand stress; *(von Konstruktionen)* load-bearing capacity; **b)** *(von Menschen)* toughness; resilience; *(von Mitarbeitern)* ability to work under pressure

belasten *tr. V.* **a)** *(beschweren)* load ‹*vehicle etc.*›; put weight on ‹*ski*›; **der Fahrstuhl darf nur mit vier Personen belastet werden** the lift *(Brit.) or (Amer.)* elevator must not carry more than four persons; **b)** *(beeinträchtigen)* pollute ‹*atmosphere*›; put pressure on ‹*environment*›; **c)** *(in Anspruch nehmen)* burden (**mit** with); **d)** *(zu schaffen machen)* **jmdn. ~:** ‹*responsibility, guilt*› weigh upon sb.; ‹*thought*› weigh upon sb.'s mind; **Fett belastet den Magen** fat puts a strain on the stomach; **es belastet ihn seelisch schwer, daß ihn seine Frau verlassen hat** the fact that his wife has left him is causing him great emotional strain and distress; **e)** *(Rechtsw.: schuldig erscheinen lassen)* incriminate; **~des Material** incriminating evidence; **f)** *(Geldw.)* **jmds. Konto mit 100 DM ~:** debit sb.'s account with 100 DM; **jmdn. mit zusätzlichen Steuern ~:** increase the tax burden on sb.; **den Staatshaushalt ~:** place a burden on the national budget; **das Haus ist mit einer Hypothek belastet** the house is encumbered with a mortgage

belästigen [bəˈlɛstɪgn̩] *tr. V.* bother; *(sehr aufdringlich)* pester; *(sexuell)* molest; **sich von etw. belästigt fühlen** regard sth. as a nuisance

Belästigung die; ~, ~en: am schlimmsten empfanden wir die ~ durch die Reporter/Insekten we found the worst thing was being pestered by reporters/bothered by insects; **etw. als ~ empfinden** regard sth. as a nuisance

Belastung [bəˈlastʊŋ] **die; ~, ~en a) die ~ der Atmosphäre/Umwelt durch Schadstoffe** the pollution of the atmosphere by harmful substances/the pressure on the environment caused by harmful substances; **b)** *(Inanspruchnahme)* strain; **für jmdn. eine ~ sein** put a strain on sb.; **c)** *(Bürde, Sorge)* burden; **das stellte eine schwere seelische ~ für sie dar** it was causing her great strain and distress; **d)** *(Rechtsw.: Beschuldigung)* incrimination; **e)** *(Geldw.)* charge; *(steuerlich)* burden; **außergewöhnliche ~en** extraordinary expenses *(partly deductible as a charge on one's income)*; **eine weitere ~ meines Kontos kann ich mir nicht erlauben** I can't afford to draw any more money from my account; **f)** *(Beschwerung)* loading; **die maximale ~ der Brückenpfeiler** the safe maximum load for the bridge piers

belastungs-, Belastungs-: ~-EKG das *(Med.)* electrocardiogram after effort; **~fähig** *Adj. s.* **belastbar; ~grenze die** limit; *(der Atmosphäre, des Wasserhaushalts)* maximum tolerable level of pollution; **~material das** *(Rechtsw.)* incriminating evidence; **~probe die** *(bei Menschen)* endurance test; *(bei Materialien)* stress test; *(bei Konstruktionen)* load test; **~spitze die** *(Elektrot.)* peak load; **~zeuge der** *(Rechtsw.)* witness for the prosecution

belatschern [bəˈlaːtʃɐn] *tr. V. (berlin. salopp)* **a) jmdn. ~, daß er etw. macht** talk sb. into doing sth.; **er hat mich belatschert** he talked me into it; **b)** *(ansprechen)* accost

belauben *refl. V.* come into leaf; **belaubte Pappeln** poplars in leaf

Belaubung die; ~ a) coming into leaf; **b)** *(Laubwerk)* foliage; leaves *pl.*

belauern *tr. V.* **jmdn. ~:** *(versteckt beobachten)* watch sb. from hiding; *(mit lauerndem Blick beobachten)* eye *or* watch sb. carefully; keep a watchful eye on sb.

belaufen *unr. refl. V.* **sich auf ...**(*Akk.*) **~:** amount *or* come to ...; ‹*rent, price*› come to ..., be ...

belauschen *tr. V.* **a)** eavesdrop on; **b)** *(geh.: beobachten)* observe

Belcanto [belˈkanto] **der; ~s** *(Musik)* bel canto

beleben 1. *tr. V.* **a)** *(in Schwung bringen)* enliven; liven up *(coll.)*; *(wieder~)* put new life into; stimulate ‹*demand*›; **b)** *(lebendig gestalten)* enliven; brighten up; **c)** *(lebendig machen)* give life to; **d)** *(bevölkern)* inhabit; populate. **2.** *refl. V.* **a)** *(lebhafter werden)* ‹*eyes*› light up; ‹*face*› brighten [up]; ‹*market, economic activity*› revive, pick up; **b)** *(lebendig, bevölkert werden)* come to life; **sich neu belebt fühlen** feel revived

belebend 1. *Adj.* stimulating; invigorating. **2.** *adv.* **~ wirken** have a stimulating *or* invigorating effect

belebt *Adj.* **a)** *(lebhaft, bevölkert)* busy ‹*street, crossing, town, etc.*›; **b)** *(lebendig, auch fig.)* living; **die ~e Natur** the living world of nature

Belebtheit die; ~: bustle; bustling activity

Belebung die; ~, ~en revival; **eine ~ der Wirtschaft** a revival in the economy; **eine ~ des Absatzes** a stimulation of demand; **ein Getränk** *usw.* **zur ~**: a drink *etc.* to revive oneself

belecken *tr. V.* lick; **von Kultur/Geschichte nicht/wenig beleckt sein** *(fig. ugs.)* have no/not much trace of culture/knowledge of history

Beleg [bə'le:k] **der;** ~[e]s, ~e **a)** *(Beweisstück)* piece of [supporting] documentary evidence; *(Quittung)* receipt; ~e [supporting] documentary proof *sing. or* evidence *sing. no indef. art.*/receipts; **b)** *(Beispiel)* instance, example **(für** of); *(Quellennachweis)* reference; **als ~ für etw.** as evidence for sth.; **ein ~ für ein Wort** an example of the use of a word; **c)** *(Archäol.: Fundstück)* find

Beleg·arzt der doctor on duty *(who shares responsibility for hospital in-patients)*

belegbar *Adj.* verifiable

belegen 1. *tr. V.* **a)** *(Milit.: beschießen)* bombard; *(mit Bomben)* attack; **b)** *(mit Belag versehen)* cover ‹*floor*› **(mit** with); fill ‹*flan base, sandwich*›; top ‹*open sandwich*›; **eine Scheibe Brot mit Schinken/Käse ~**: put some ham/cheese on a slice of bread; **c)** *(reservieren)* reserve, book ‹*seat, table, room*›; *(nutzen)* occupy ‹*seat, room, etc.*›; *(Hochschulw.)* enrol for, register for ‹*seminar, lecture-course*›; **d)** *(Sport)* **den ersten/letzten Platz ~**: come first *or* take first place/come last; **e)** *(nachweisen)* prove; give a reference for ‹*quotation*›; *(fig.)* substantiate ‹*demand*›; **etw. mit** *od.* **durch Quittungen ~**: support sth. with receipts; **f)** *(versehen)* **jmdn./etw. mit etw. ~**: impose sth. on sb./sth.; **jmdn. mit einem Spitznamen ~**: give sb. a nickname; **g) eine Schule mit Flüchtlingen ~**: accommodate refugees in a school. **2.** *itr. V. (Hochschulw.)* enrol *or* register [for seminars/lectures] for the coming semester

Beleg-: ~exemplar das voucher copy; *(für Autoren)* author's copy; **~frist die** *(Hochschulw.)* enrolment period; **~leser der** *(DV)* document-reader; **~material das** documentary evidence

Belegschaft die; ~, ~en staff; employees *pl.*

Belegschafts-: ~aktie die employees' share; **~mitglied das** employee; **~versammlung die** meeting of the staff

Beleg-: ~stelle die reference; **~stück das** *s.* **~exemplar**

belegt 1. *2. Part. v.* **belegen. 2.** *Adj.* **a) ein ~es Brot** *(offen)* an open *or (Amer.)* open-face sandwich; *(zugeklappt)* a sandwich; **ein ~es Brötchen** *(offen)* a roll with topping; an open-face roll *(Amer.)*; *(zugeklappt)* a filled roll; a sandwich roll *(Amer.)*; **b)** *(mit Belag bedeckt)* coated, furred ‹*tongue, tonsils*›; **c)** *(heiser)* husky ‹*voice*›; **eine ~e Stimme haben** be hoarse; **d)** *(nicht mehr frei)* ‹*room, flat*› occupied; ‹*hotel, hospital*› full

Belegung die; ~, ~en *(Reservierung)* reservation; booking; *(Nutzung)* occupying

belehnen *tr. V.* **a)** *(hist.)* **jmdn. mit Land/einem Amt ~**: enfeoff sb. with land/in an office; **b)** *(schweiz.) s.* **beleihen**

belehrbar *Adj.* teachable

belehren *tr. V.* **a)** *(lehren)* teach; instruct; *(aufklären)* enlighten; *(informieren)* inform; advise; **jmdn. über etw.** *(Akk.)* ~: inform sb. about sth.; **jmdn. über seine Rechte ~/die Bedeutung des Eides ~** *(Rechtsw.)* inform *or* advise sb. of his/her rights/caution *or* warn sb. about the meaning of the oath; **b)** *(von einer irrigen Meinung abbringen)* **sich ~ lassen** [be willing to] listen *or* take advice *or* be told; **ich bin belehrt** I've learnt something; **sich eines anderen ~ lassen müssen** learn otherwise; *s. auch* **besser**

belehrend *Adj.* didactic

Belehrung die; ~, ~en **a)** *(das Belehrtwerden)* instruction; **b)** *(Zurechtweisung)* lecture; **c)** *(Rechtsw.)* caution; warning

beleibt [bə'laipt] *Adj. (geh.)* stout; portly; corpulent

Beleibtheit die; ~: *(geh.)* stoutness; portliness; corpulence

beleidigen [bə'laidɪgn̩] *tr. V.* insult; offend; **jmds. Ehre ~**: offend sb.'s honour; **~d** offensive; **~de Äußerungen** *(Rechtsw.)* *(schriftlich)* libellous statements; *(mündlich)* slanderous statements; **das beleidigt mein Ohr/mein Auge** *(fig.)* it offends my ear/eye

beleidigt *Adj.* insulted; offended; *(gekränkt)* offended; **ein ~es Gesicht machen** put on a hurt expression; **er ist schnell ~**: he easily takes offence; **jmdn. ~ ansehen** give sb. an offended look

Beleidigung die; ~, ~en insult; *(Rechtsw.)* *(schriftlich)* libel; *(mündlich)* slander; **etw. als ~ empfinden** regard sth. as an insult; **eine ~ für das Auge/Ohr** *(fig.)* an offence to the eye/ear

Beleidigungs-: ~klage die *(Rechtsw.)* *(wegen schriftlicher Beleidigung)* action for libel; libel action; *(wegen mündlicher Beleidigung)* action for slander; slander action; **eine ~klage gegen jmdn. erheben** sue sb. for libel/slander; bring an action for libel/slander against sb.; **~prozeß der** *(Rechtsw.)* *(wegen schriftlicher Beleidigung)* libel suit; *(wegen mündlicher Beleidigung)* slander suit

beleihen *unr. tr. V.* **a)** *(als Pfand nehmen)* grant a loan on the security of; grant a mortgage on ‹*home, property*›; raise money on ‹*insurance, policy*›; **etw. ~ lassen** raise a loan/mortgage on sth.; **ihr Schmuck wurde mit 15 000 DM beliehen** she raised a loan of 15,000 DM on her jewellery; **b)** *(hist.) s.* **belehnen a**

Beleihung die; ~, ~en: **die ~ von etw.** raising a loan on sth.

belemmern [bə'lɛmɐn] *tr. V. (nordd. ugs.)* bother; *(sehr aufdringlich)* pester

belemmert *Adj. (ugs.)* **a)** *(niedergedrückt)* miserable; **er stand [wie] ~ da** he stood there miserably; **b)** *(scheußlich)* awful *(coll.)*; terrible *(coll.)*; dreadful *(coll.)*

belesen *Adj.* well-read

Belesenheit die; ~: **[große] ~**: [very] wide reading

Beletage [bɛle'ta:ʒə] **die;** ~, ~n *(veralt.)* first floor *(Brit.)*; second floor *(Amer.)*

beleuchten *tr. V.* **a)** illuminate; light up; light ‹*stairs, room, street, etc.*›; **festlich beleuchtet** festively lit; **b)** *(fig.: untersuchen)* examine ‹*topic, problem*›

Beleuchter der; ~s, ~ *(Theater, Film)* lighting technician

Beleuchter·brücke die *(Theater, Film)* lighting bridge

Beleuchterin die; ~, ~nen *(Theater, Film)* lighting technician

Beleuchtung die; ~, ~en **a)** *(Licht)* light; **die ~ in der Stadt fiel aus** all the lights *pl.* of the town went out; **b)** *(das Beleuchten)* lighting; *(Anstrahlung)* illumination; **c)** *(fig.: Untersuchung)* examination

Beleuchtungs-: ~an·lage die lighting installation; **~effekt der** lighting effect; **~technik die** lighting engineering

beleumdet [bə'lɔymdət], **beleumundet** [bə'lɔymʊndət] *Adj.* **übel/gut ~ sein** have a bad/good reputation

belfern ['bɛlfɐn] **1.** *itr. V. (ugs.)* bark; *(fig.)* ‹*cannon*› boom; ‹*rifle*› crack. **2.** *tr. V.* bark; bark [out] ‹*order*›

Belgien ['bɛlgi̯ən] **(das);** ~s Belgium

Belgier ['bɛlgi̯ɐ] **der;** ~s, ~, **Belgierin die;** ~, ~nen Belgian; *s. auch* **-in**

belgisch *Adj.* Belgian; *s. auch* **deutsch; ²Deutsche**

Belgrad ['bɛlgra:t] **(das);** ~s Belgrade

belichten 1. *tr. V.* **a)** *(Fot.)* expose; **eine Aufnahme richtig/falsch ~**: give a shot the right/wrong exposure; **b)** *(fachspr.: beleuchten)* light. **2.** *itr. V. (Fot.)* **richtig/falsch/kurz ~**: use the right/wrong exposure/a short exposure time

Belichtung die a) *(Fot.)* exposure; **b)** *(fachspr.: Licht)* light

Belichtungs-: ~automatik die *(Fot.)* automatic exposure control; **~dauer die** *(Fot.) s.* **~zeit; ~messer der** *(Fot.)* exposure meter; **~tabelle die** *(Fot.)* exposure table; **~zeit die** *(Fot.)* exposure time

belieben *(geh.) itr. V. (unpers.)* **[ganz] wie es dir beliebt** [just] as you like; **was beliebt?** *(veralt.)* what can I do for you?; **wie beliebt?** *(veralt.)* I beg your pardon?; **~, etw. zu tun** like doing sth.; **Sie ~ zu scherzen** *(iron.)* you are joking, of course; **ihr könnt tun, was euch** *(Dat.)* **beliebt** you can do what you like

Belieben das; ~s: **es steht in deinem ~/es bleibt Ihrem ~ überlassen** it is up to you; **nach ~**: just as you/they *etc.* like

beliebig 1. *Adj.* any; **du kannst ein ~es Beispiel/einen ~en Tag wählen** you can choose any example/day you like; **fünf ~e Personen** any five people; **in ~er Reihenfolge** in any order; **eine ~e Reihe von Beispielen** an arbitrary series of examples; **die Reihenfolge/Farbe ist ~**: any order/colour will do. **2.** *adv.* as you like/he likes *etc.*; **~ lange/viele** as long/many as you like/he likes *etc.*; **wähle eine ~ große Zahl** choose any number[, as high as] you like; **wir konnten ~ lange wegbleiben** we could stay out [for] as long as we liked; **diese beiden Begriffe sind nicht ~ austauschbar** these two terms are not interchangeable at will

beliebt *Adj.* popular; favourite *attrib.*; **sich [bei jmdm.] ~ machen** make oneself popular [with sb.]

Beliebtheit die; ~: popularity; **sich großer ~** *(Gen.)* **erfreuen** *(geh.)* enjoy great popularity

beliefern *tr. V.* supply; **jmdn. mit etw. ~**: supply sb. with sth.

Belieferung die supply; **die ~ von jmdm. mit etw.** supplying sb. with sth.

Belladonna [bɛla'dɔna] **die;** ~, **Belladonnen** *(Bot., Pharm.)* belladonna

bellen ['bɛlən] **1.** *itr. V.* **a)** ‹*dog, fox*› bark; ‹*hound*› bay; *(fig.)* ‹*cannon*› boom; **b)** *(laut husten)* have a hacking cough; **ein ~der Husten** a hacking cough. **2.** *tr. V. (abwertend)* bark out ‹*orders*›

Belletristik [bɛle'trɪstɪk] **die;** ~: belles-lettres *pl.*

belletristisch 1. *Adj.* belletristic ‹*literature*›; **ein ~er Verlag** a publishing house specializing in belletristic literature. **2.** *adv.* **er hat seine Darstellung ~ aufgelockert** he made his account lighter and more entertaining

belobigen [bə'lo:bɪgn̩] *tr. V.* commend

Belobigung die; ~, ~en commendation; **jmdm. eine ~ aussprechen** commend sb.

Belobigungs·schreiben das letter of commendation

belohnen *tr. V.* **a)** *(beschenken)* reward; **jmdn. mit/für etw. ~**: reward sb. with/for sth.; **b)** *(vergelten)* repay, reward ‹*patience, loyalty, trust*›

Belohnung die; ~, ~en **a)** *(Lohn)* reward; **eine ~ für etw. aussetzen** offer a reward for sth.; **b)** *o. Pl. (das Belohnen)* rewarding

Belt [bɛlt] **der;** ~s *(Geogr.)* **der Kleine/Große ~**: The Little/Great Belt

belüften *tr. V.* ventilate; *(auslüften)* air; **das Zimmer wurde nur durch eine kleine Luke in der Decke belüftet** the only means of ventilation in the room was a small skylight

Belüftung die ventilation

Belüftungs·anlage die ventilation system

¹Beluga [be'lu:ga] **die;** ~, ~s *(Zool.)* beluga [sturgeon]; *(Wal)* white whale

²Beluga der; ~s beluga caviare

belügen *unr. tr. V.* **jmdn. ~:** lie to *or* tell lies to sb.; **sich selbst ~:** deceive oneself; *s. auch* **Strich**

belustigen 1. *tr. V.* **jmdn. ~:** amuse sb.; *(zum Lachen bringen)* make sb. laugh. **2.** *refl. V.* **a)** *(geh.)* **sich über jmdn./etw. ~:** make fun of *or* laugh at sb./sth.; **b)** *(veralt.: sich vergnügen)* amuse oneself

belustigt 1. *Adj.* amused. **2.** *adv.* in amusement

Belustigung die; ~, ~en a) *(Fest, Vergnügen)* entertainment; **b)** *o. Pl. (Belustigtsein, Belustigtwerden)* amusement; **der allgemeinen ~ dienen** serve to amuse everybody

bemächtigen [bəˈmɛçtɪgn̩] *refl. V. (geh.)* **a)** *(in seine Gewalt bringen)* **sich einer Sache/eines Menschen ~:** seize sth./a person; **sich der Regierungsgewalt/des Thrones ~:** seize power/the throne; **b)** *(überkommen)* **Angst bemächtigte sich seiner** he was seized by fear; **Unruhe/Unsicherheit bemächtigte sich seiner** a feeling of unease/uncertainty came over him; **Entsetzen bemächtigte sich eines jeden** everyone was horrified

bemäkeln *tr. V. (ugs.)* find fault with

bemalen 1. *tr. V.* **a)** *(bunt streichen)* paint; *(verzieren)* decorate ‹*porcelain etc.*›; **mit etw. bemalt sein** be painted/decorated with sth.; **b)** *(ugs.: stark schminken)* paint. **2.** *refl. V. (ugs.)* paint one's face; put on one's war-paint *(coll.)*; **warum hast du dich so bemalt?** why have you put so much war-paint on? *(coll.)*

Bemalung die; ~, ~en a) *o. Pl. (Bemalen)* painting; *(Verzierung)* decorating; **b)** *(Farbschicht)* painting

bemängeln [bəˈmɛŋl̩n] *tr. V.* find fault with; **Bremsen/Reifen ~:** find the brakes/tyres to be faulty; **etw. an jmdm./etw. ~:** criticize sth. about sb./sth.

Bemäng[e]lung die; ~, ~en criticism; **die häufige ~ von Fabrikationsfehlern** the frequent complaints about *or* of manufacturing defects

bemannen *tr. V.* man

Bemannung die; ~, ~en a) *(das Bemannen)* manning; **b)** *(Mannschaft)* crew

bemänteln [bəˈmɛntl̩n] *tr. V.* cover up

Bemänt[e]lung die; ~, ~en covering up

Bembel [ˈbɛmbl̩] **der; ~s, ~** *(hess.: Krug)* mug; *(zum Servieren)* jug; pitcher

bemeistern *(geh. veralt.)* **1.** *tr. V.* master; control ‹*rage, excitement, etc.*›. **2.** *refl. V.* control oneself

bemerkbar *Adj.* noticeable; perceptible; **sich ~ machen** *(auf sich aufmerksam machen)* attract attention [to oneself]; *(eine Wirkung ausüben, sich zeigen)* ‹*disadvantage*› become apparent; ‹*tiredness*› make itself felt; **mach dich ~, wenn du etwas brauchst** if you need anything, let me know

bemerken *tr. V.* **a)** *(wahrnehmen)* notice; **ich wurde nicht bemerkt** I was unobserved; **sie bemerkte zu spät, daß ...:** she realized too late that ...; **b)** *(äußern)* remark; **nebenbei bemerkt** by the way; incidentally

Bemerken das; ~s *(Amtsspr.) in* **mit dem ~ ...:** with the comment ...

bemerkenswert 1. *Adj. (beachtlich, bedeutend)* remarkable; notable; *(Aufmerksamkeit verdienend, auffallend)* remarkable. **2.** *adv.* remarkably

Bemerkung die; ~, ~en a) *(Äußerung)* remark; comment; **b)** *(Notiz)* note; *(Anmerkung)* comment

bemessen 1. *unr. tr. V.* **etw. nach etw. ~:** measure sth. according to sth.; **die Zeit ist kurz/sehr knapp ~:** time is short *or* limited/very limited; **das Trinkgeld war reichlich ~:** the tips were generous. **2.** *unr. refl. V. (Amtsspr.)* **sich ~ nach** be measured on the basis of; **die Vergütung bemißt sich nach ...:** payment is calculated on the basis of ...

Bemessung die calculation; **die ~ der Strafe richtet sich nach der Schwere des Deliktes** the penalty is fixed in accordance with the seriousness of the offence

Bemessungs·grundlage die *(Amtsspr.)* basis for assessment

bemitleiden *tr. V.* pity; feel sorry for; **er ist zu ~:** he is to be pitied; **sich selbst ~:** feel sorry for oneself

bemitleidens·wert *Adj.* pitiable

Bemitleidung die; ~: pity *no indef. art.* (+ *Gen.* for)

bemittelt *Adj. (veralt.)* well-to-do; well off

Bemme [ˈbɛmə] **die; ~, ~n** *(ostmd.)* open *or (Amer.)* open-face sandwich; *(mit Butter bestrichen)* slice of bread and butter; *(zusammengeklappt)* sandwich

bemogeln *tr. V. (ugs.)* cheat; diddle *(Brit. sl.)*; con *(sl.)*

bemoost *Adj.* mossy; covered in moss *postpos.*; **ein ~es Haupt** *(ugs., bes. Studentenspr.)* a perpetual student

bemühen 1. *refl. V.* **a)** *(sich anstrengen)* try; make an effort; **sich sehr ~:** try hard; make a great effort; **sich ~, etw. zu tun** try *or* endeavour to do sth.; **bemüht sein, etw. zu tun** endeavour to do sth.; **bitte, ~ Sie sich nicht [weiter]!** please do not trouble yourself [any further]; **b)** *(sich kümmern)* **sich um jmdn./etw. ~:** seek to help sb./endeavour *or* strive to achieve sth.; **um das Wohl der Hotelgäste bemüht sein** make every effort to ensure the comfort and enjoyment of the hotel patrons; **c)** *(zu erlangen suchen)* **sich um etw. ~:** try *or* endeavour to obtain sth.; **sich um eine Stelle/Wohnung ~:** try to get a job/a flat *(Brit.) or (Amer.)* apartment; **sich um eine Dame ~:** pay every attention to a lady; **sich um einen Regisseur/Trainer/Wissenschaftler ~:** try *or* endeavour to obtain the services of a director/manager/scientist; **d)** *(geh.: sich begeben)* proceed *(formal)*; **er hat sich sogar in meine Wohnung bemüht** he even took the trouble to go/come to my flat. **2.** *tr. V. (geh.)* **a)** *(in Anspruch nehmen)* trouble; call in, call upon the services of ‹*lawyer, architect, etc.*›; *(als Beweis heranziehen)* bring in a quotation/quotations from ‹*author, philosopher, etc.*›; **b)** *(bitten, zu kommen)* trouble sb. to come; **jmdn. ins oberste Stockwerk ~:** trouble sb. to come/go up to the top floor

Bemühen das; ~s *(geh.)* effort; endeavour; **unser ~ um eine Sanierung dieses Stadtteils** our efforts *pl. or* endeavours *pl.* to redevelop this part of the town; **trotz jahrelangen ~s** despite years of effort

bemühend *Adj. (schweiz.)* [painfully] embarrassing; *(unerfreulich)* unpleasant

bemüht 1. *2. Part. v.* **bemühen. 2.** *Adj.* forced; forced, constrained ‹*cheerfulness*›; constrained ‹*person*›

Bemühung die; ~, ~en a) *(Anstrengung)* effort; endeavour; **alle ~en waren vergeblich** all efforts were in vain; **trotz aller ~en, allen ~en zum Trotz** in spite of *or* despite all our/his *etc.* efforts; **vielen Dank für Ihre ~en** thank you very much for your efforts *or* trouble; **niemand wollte ihn in seinen ~en unterstützen** no one wanted to support him in his endeavours; **b)** *Pl. (Dienstleistung)* services

bemüßigen *refl. V. (geh.)* **sich einer Sache** *(Gen.)* **~:** make use of sth.

bemüßigt [bəˈmyːsɪçt] *(geh. iron.) in* **sich ~ sehen** *od.* **fühlen** *od.* **finden, etw. zu tun** feel obliged to do sth.; feel it incumbent on oneself to do sth.

bemuttern *tr. V.* mother

Bemutterung die; ~, ~en mothering

benachbart *Adj.* neighbouring *attrib.*; **~e Fachgebiete** related fields of study; **ihre Häuser sind ~:** their houses are next door to each other

benachrichtigen [bəˈnaːxrɪçtɪgn̩] *tr. V.* inform; notify; **jmdn. von etw. ~:** inform *or* notify sb. of *or* about sth.

Benachrichtigung die; ~, ~en notification; **ich bitte um sofortige ~:** I wish to be informed *or* notified immediately; **warum habt ihr uns denn keine ~ geschickt?** why didn't you contact us *or* let us know?

benachteiligen *tr. V.* put at a disadvantage; ‹*disability*› handicap; *(diskriminieren)* discriminate against; **sich benachteiligt fühlen** feel at a disadvantage/feel discriminated against; **er fühlte sich von seinen Lehrern benachteiligt** he felt unfairly treated by his teachers; **ein wirtschaftlich benachteiligtes Gebiet** an economically deprived area; **die sozial benachteiligten Schichten** the underprivileged classes

Benachteiligte der/die; *adj. Dekl.* disadvantaged person; **die ~n** the disadvantaged; those at a disadvantage; **die sozial ~n** the underprivileged; the socially deprived

Benachteiligung die; ~, ~en *(Vorgang)* discrimination (*Gen.* against); *(Zustand)* disadvantage (*Gen.* to); **der Firma wurde eine ~ der Frauen vorgeworfen** the firm was accused of discriminating against women

benagen *tr. V.* gnaw *or* nibble [at] ‹*bread, cheese, etc.*›; gnaw [at] ‹*tree, bark, etc.*›

benähen *tr. V.* **einen Rock** *usw.* **mit etw. ~:** sew sth. on to a skirt *etc.*

benässen *tr. V. (geh.)* wet

Bendel [ˈbɛndl̩] **der** *od.* **das; ~s, ~** *(landsch.)* ribbon; *(Schuh~)* shoe-lace; **jmdn. am ~ haben** *(ugs.)* have got sb. on a string

benebeln *tr. V.* befuddle; **mit benebeltem Kopf aufwachen** wake up with a muzzy head

Benediktiner [benedɪkˈtiːnɐ] **der; ~s, ~ a)** *(Mönch)* Benedictine [monk]; **b)** *(Kräuterlikör)* benedictine

Benediktinerin die; ~, ~nen Benedictine [nun]

Benediktiner·orden der Benedictine order; order of St. Benedict

Benefiz [beneˈfiːts] **das; ~es, ~e a)** *(veralt.: Vorstellung)* benefit performance; **b)** *(Wohltätigkeitsveranstaltung)* charity performance/match, *etc.*

Benefiz·spiel das charity game *or* match

benehmen 1. *unr. refl. V.* behave (**wie** like); *(in bezug auf Umgangsformen)* behave [oneself]; **sich schlecht ~:** behave badly; misbehave; **sie kann sich einfach nicht ~:** she simply does not know how to behave; **wenn du dich nicht ~ kannst, ...:** if you can't behave yourself, ... **2.** *unr. tr. V. (geh.: wegnehmen)* **es benahm mir den Atem** it took my breath away

Benehmen das; ~s a) behaviour; **kein ~ haben** have no manners *pl.*; **b)** *(Amtsspr.) in* **sich mit jmdm. ins ~ setzen** make contact with sb.

beneiden *tr. V.* envy; be envious of; **jmdn. um etw. ~:** envy sb. sth.; **du bist [nicht] zu ~:** I [don't] envy you

beneidens·wert 1. *Adj.* enviable. **2.** *adv.* enviably

Benelux [ˈbeːnelʊks] *Abk.* Benelux

Benelux·staaten *Pl.* Benelux countries

benennen *unr. tr. V.* **a)** *(mit einem Namen versehen)* name; **etw./jmdn. nach jmdm. ~:** name sth./name *or* call sb. after *or (Amer.)* for sb.; **b)** *(namhaft machen)* call ‹*witness*›; **jmdn. als Kandidaten ~:** nominate sb. as a candidate; **jmdn. als** *od.* **zum Zeugen ~:** call sb. as a witness

Benennung die a) *o. Pl. (Namengebung)* naming; **b)** *(das Namhaftmachen)* **durch ~ zweier weiterer Zeugen** by calling two more witnesses; **c)** *(Name)* name; *(Bezeichnung)* designation

benetzen *tr. V. (geh.)* moisten; ‹*dew*› cover; **mit Tau/von Schweiß benetzt** covered *or* wet with dew/damp with perspiration

Bengale [bɛŋˈgaːlə] **der; ~n, ~n, Bengalin die; ~, ~nen** Bengali; Bengalese

Bengalen (das); ~s Bengal

Bengali [bɛŋ'ga:li] **das;** ~[s] Bengali

bengalisch *Adj.* Bengalese; Bengali, Bengalese ⟨*people, language*⟩; **~e Beleuchtung, ~es Feuer** Bengal light *or* fire

Bengel ['bɛŋl̩] **der;** ~s, ~ *od. (nordd.)* ~s **a)** *(abwertend: junger Bursche)* young rascal; **b)** *(fam.: kleiner Junge)* little lad *or* boy; **ein süßer** ~: a dear little lad *or* boy; **c)** *(veralt.: Knüppel)* stick

Benimm [bə'nɪm] **der;** ~s *(ugs.)* manners *pl.*; **jmdm.** ~ **beibringen** teach sb. some manners

Benjamin ['bɛnjami:n] **der;** ~s, ~e *(scherzh.)* youngest boy; **er ist der** ~ **der Familie** he's the baby of the family

benommen [be'nɔmən] **1.** *2. Part. v.* **benehmen. 2.** *Adj.* bemused; dazed; *(durch Fieber, Medikamente, Alkohol)* muzzy **(von** from)

Benommenheit die; ~: bemused *or* dazed state; *(durch Fieber, Medikamente, Alkohol)* muzziness

benoten *tr. V.* mark *(Brit.)*; grade *(Amer.)*; **einen Test mit „gut"** ~: mark a test 'good' *(Brit.)*; assign a grade of 'good' to a test *(Amer.)*

benötigen *tr. V.* need; require; **das benötigte Geld** the necessary money

Benotung die; ~, ~en **a)** *o. Pl. (das Benoten)* marking *(Brit.)*; grading *(Amer.)*; **sich um eine gerechte** ~ **bemühen** try *or* endeavour to mark *(Brit.) or (Amer.)* grade fairly; **b)** *(Note)* mark *(Brit.)*; grade *(Amer.)*

benutzbar *Adj.* usable; **„Aufzug vorübergehend nicht ~"** 'lift temporarily out of service'; **schwer** ~: difficult to use

benutzen, *(bes. südd.)* **benützen** *tr. V.* use **(für** for); take, use ⟨*car, lift*⟩; take ⟨*train, taxi*⟩; use, consult ⟨*reference book*⟩; **das benutzte Geschirr** the dirty dishes; **etw. als Vorwand/Alibi** ~: use sth. as an excuse/alibi; **wir benutzten den freien Tag zu einem Ausflug** we made use of *or* took advantage of the free day to go on an excursion

Benutzer, *(bes. südd.)* **Benützer der;** ~s, ~: user; *(eines entliehenen Buchs)* borrower

benutzer·freundlich *Adj.* user-friendly

Benutzer·kreis der users *pl.*; *(von Büchereien)* borrowers *pl.*; **ein großer** ~: a large number of users/borrowers

Benutzung, *(bes. südd.)* **Benützung die;** ~: use; **jmdm. etw. zur** ~ **überlassen** give sb. the use of sth.; allow sb. to use sth.; **in** ~ *(Dat.)* **sein** be in use; **etw. in** ~ *(Akk.)* **nehmen** bring sth. into use; **etw. zur** ~ **freigeben** open sth.; **unter** ~ **einer Sache** *(Gen.)* making use of sth.

Benutzungs-: **~gebühr die** charge; *(in Büchereien)* borrowing charge; **die ~gebühr für etw.** the charge for using/borrowing sth.; **~ordnung die: die ~ordnung der Badeanstalt/Bibliothek** *usw.* the rules and conditions *pl.* for the use of the pool/library *etc.*

Benzin [bɛn'tsi:n] **das;** ~s petrol *(Brit.)*; gasoline *(Amer.)*; gas *(Amer. coll.)*; *(Wasch~)* benzine; *(Feuerzeug~)* petrol *(Brit.)*; gasoline *(Amer.)*; *lighter fuel*

Benzin-: **~dunst der** petrol *(Brit.) or (Amer.)* gasoline fumes *pl.*; **~einspritzung die;** ~ *(Kfz-W.)* fuel injection

Benziner der; ~s, ~ *(ugs.)* car that runs on petrol *(Brit.) or (Amer.)* gasoline; car with a petrol *(Brit.) or (Amer.)* gasoline engine; petrol-driven *(Brit.) or (Amer.)* gasoline-powered car

Benzin-: **~feuerzeug das** petrol *(Brit.) or (Amer.)* gasoline lighter; **~gut·schein der** petrol (Brit.) or (Amer.) gasoline coupon; **~hahn der** *(Kfz-W.)* fuel *or* petrol *(Brit.) or (Amer.)* gasoline tap; *s. auch* **Ölhahn; ~kanister der** petrol *(Brit.) or (Amer.)* gasoline can; **~leitung die** fuel pipe; **~motor der** petrol *(Brit.) or (Amer.)* gasoline engine; **~preis der** price of petrol *(Brit.) or (Amer.)* gasoline; **~pumpe die** petrol *(Brit.) or (Amer.)* gasoline pump; **~tank der** petrol *(Brit.) or (Amer.)* gasoline tank; **~uhr die** *(Kfz-W.)* fuel gauge; **~verbrauch der** fuel consumption

Benzoe ['bɛntsoe] **die;** ~ *(Chemie)* [gum] benzoin

Benzoe·säure die; *o. Pl. (Chemie)* benzoic acid

Benzol [bɛn'tso:l] **das;** ~s, ~e *(Chemie)* benzene

beobachtbar *Adj.* observable

beobachten [bə'|o:baxtn̩] *tr. V.* **a)** observe; watch; *(als Zeuge)* see; **er hat beobachtet, wie sie das Radio stahl** he watched her steal the radio; **jmdn.** ~ **lassen** put sb. under surveillance; have sb. watched; **b)** *(bemerken)* notice; observe; **etw. an jmdm.** ~: notice sth. about sb.; **eine Veränderung an jmdm.** ~: notice a change in sb.; **c)** *(geh.: beachten)* observe

Beobachter der; ~s, ~: observer

Beobachtung die; ~, ~en **a)** *(das Beobachten, die Feststellung)* observation; **~en anstellen** keep a watch; **zur** ~: for observation; **unter** ~ **stehen** be kept under surveillance; **b)** *(geh.: Beachtung)* observation

Beobachtungs-: **~ballon der** observation ballon; **~gabe die;** *o. Pl.* powers *pl.* of observation; **~posten der** observation post; **auf ~posten stehen** be on look-out duty; **~station die a)** *(im Krankenhaus)* observation ward; **b)** *s.* **Wetterstation**

beölen *refl. V. (Jugendspr.)* kill *or (coarse)* piss oneself laughing

beordern *tr. V.* order; **jmdn. nach Hause/ins Ausland** ~: order *or* summon sb. home/order sb. [to go] abroad

bepacken *tr. V.* load; **etw./jmdn./sich mit etw.** ~: load sth. up with/load sb./oneself with sth.

bepflanzen *tr. V.* plant **(mit** with)

Bepflanzung die a) *(das Bepflanzen)* planting **(mit** with); **b)** *(Pflanzen)* plants *pl.* (*Gen.* in)

bepflastern *tr. V.* **a)** *(ugs.)* put a plaster on ⟨*wound etc.*⟩; **b)** *(mit Pflasterung versehen)* pave; *(fig.: mit Orden, Aufklebern usw.)* plaster; **c)** *(Soldatenspr.: bombardieren)* plaster *(sl.)*; bombard

bepinkeln *(ugs.)* **1.** *tr. V.* pee on *(coll.)*. **2.** *refl. V.* wet oneself

bepinseln *tr. V.* **a)** *(ugs.: einpinseln)* paint ⟨*gums*⟩; brush ⟨*dough, cake-mixture*⟩; **b)** *(ugs. abwertend: anstreichen)* paint; **etw. mit Farbe** ~: paint sth.

bepissen *tr. V. (derb)* piss on *(coarse)*

Beplankung [bə'plaŋkʊŋ] **die;** ~, ~en *(Boots~)* planking; *(Flugzeug~)* skin

bepudern *tr. V.* powder

bequasseln *tr. V. (salopp) s.* **bequatschen a**

bequatschen *tr. V. (salopp)* **a)** *(bereden)* **etw. [ausführlich]** ~: have a [long] jaw about sth. *(coll.)*; **b)** *(überreden)* persuade; **jmdn.** ~, **daß er mitkommt** talk sb. into coming along

bequem [bə'kve:m] **1.** *Adj.* **a)** *(angenehm)* comfortable; **es sich** *(Dat.)* ~ **machen** make oneself comfortable; **machen Sie es sich** ~: make yourself at home; **b)** *(mühelos)* easy; **ein ~es Leben führen** have an easy *or* comfortable life; **c)** *(abwertend: träge)* lazy; idle. **2.** *adv.* **a)** *(angenehm)* comfortably; **liegen/sitzen Sie** ~ **so?** are you comfortable like that?; **b)** *(leicht)* easily; comfortably

bequemen *refl. V. (geh.)* **a)** *(abwertend)* **sich dazu** ~, **etw. zu tun** *(sich herablassen)* condescend *or* deign to do sth.; *(sich endlich entschließen)* bring oneself to do sth; **b)** *(veralt.: sich fügen)* become adapted (*Dat.* to)

bequemlich *Adj. (veralt.) s.* **bequem**

Bequemlichkeit die; ~, ~en **a)** *(Annehmlichkeit, Komfort)* comfort; **b)** *o. Pl. (Trägheit)* laziness; idleness; **aus [reiner]** ~: out of [sheer] laziness *or* idleness

berappen [bə'rapn̩] *tr., itr. V. (ugs.)* cough up *(sl.)*, shell out *(sl.)*, fork over *(sl.)* ⟨*money*⟩

beraten 1. *unr. tr. V.* **a)** advise; **jmdn. gut/schlecht** ~: give sb. good/bad advice; **sich** ~ **lassen** take *or* get advice **(von** from); **du bist gut** ~, **wenn du ...:** you'd be well advised to ...; **b)** *(besprechen)* discuss ⟨*plan, matter*⟩. **2.** *unr. itr. V.* **über etw.** *(Akk.)* ~: discuss sth.; **sie berieten lange** they were a long time in discussion. **3.** *unr. refl. V.* **sich mit jmdm.** ~, **ob ...:** discuss with sb. whether ...; **sich mit seinem Anwalt** ~: consult one's lawyer

beratend *Adj.* advisory, consultative ⟨*function, role, etc.*⟩

Berater der; ~s, ~, **Beraterin die;** ~, ~nen adviser

Berater-: **~stab der** team of advisers; **~vertrag der** consultancy contract

beratschlagen [bə'ra:tʃla:gn̩] **1.** *tr. V.* discuss. **2.** *itr. V.* **über etw.** *(Akk.)* ~: discuss sth.

Beratschlagung die; ~, ~en discussion

Beratung die; ~, ~en **a)** advice *no indef. art.*; *(durch Arzt, Rechtsanwalt)* consultation; **ohne juristische** ~: without [taking] legal advice; **b)** *(Besprechung)* discussion; **Gegenstand der** ~ **war ...:** the subject under discussion was ...; **sich zur** ~ **zurückziehen** withdraw for discussions *pl.*; **c)** *s.* **Beratungsstelle**

Beratungs-: **~kosten** *Pl.* consultation fees; **~stelle die** advice centre *(Brit.)*; counseling center *(Amer.)*; **~zimmer das** conference room

berauben *tr. V. (auch fig.)* rob; **jmdn. einer Sache** *(Gen.)* ~ *(geh.)* rob sb. of sth.; **jmdn. seiner Freiheit/Hoffnungen** ~ *(fig.)* deprive sb. of his/her freedom/hopes

Beraubung die; ~, ~en robbing *no indef. art.*

berauschen *(geh.)* **1.** *tr. V. (auch fig.)* intoxicate; ⟨*alcohol*⟩ intoxicate, inebriate; ⟨*drug*⟩ make euphoric; ⟨*speed*⟩ exhilarate; **der Erfolg/die Macht berauschte ihn** he was intoxicated *or* drunk with success/drunk with power. **2.** *refl. V.* become intoxicated; **sich an etw.** *(Dat.)* ~: become intoxicated with sth.; **sich an seinen eigenen Worten** ~: become carried away by one's own words

berauschend 1. *Adj.* intoxicating; ~ **auf jmdn. wirken** have an intoxicating effect on sb.; heady, intoxicating ⟨*perfume, scent*⟩; **das ist nicht** ~ *(ugs.)* it's nothing very special *or (coll.)* nothing to write home about. **2.** *adv.* ~ **schön** enchantingly beautiful; **der Abend war** ~ **schön** *(iron.)* the evening was just great *(iron.)*

Berber ['bɛrbɐ] **der;** ~s, ~ **a)** Berber; **b)** *(Teppich)* Berber carpet/rug; **c)** *(Pferderasse)* Barbary horse; **d)** *(Nichtseßhafter)* tramp

Berberitze [bɛrbə'rɪtsə] **die;** ~, ~n *(Bot.)* common barberry

Berber·teppich der Berber carpet/rug

berechenbar [bə'rɛçn̩ba:ɐ̯] *Adj.* calculable; predictable ⟨*behaviour*⟩

Berechenbarkeit die; ~: calculability; *(des Verhaltens)* predictability

berechnen *tr. V.* **a)** *(ermitteln)* calculate ⟨*quantity, cost, price, risk, etc.*⟩; predict ⟨*behaviour, consequences*⟩; *(fig.)* calculate ⟨*effect*⟩; **b)** *(anrechnen)* charge; **jmdm. etw. mit 10 Mark** ~: charge sb. 10 marks for sth.; **jmdm. etw. nicht** ~: not charge sb. for sth.; **für etw. nichts** ~: not charge for sth.; make no charge for sth.; **jmdm. zuviel** ~: overcharge sb.; charge sb. too much; **c)** *(kalkulieren)* calculate; *(vorsehen)* intend ; **der Architekt berechnete die Bauzeit auf sieben Monate** the architect estimated that the construction time would be seven months; **für sechs Personen berechnet sein** ⟨*recipe, buffet*⟩ be for six people

berechnend *Adj.* calculating

Berechnung die a) *(das Berechnen)* calculation; **nach meiner ~, meiner ~ nach** according to my calculations *pl.*; **b)** *o. Pl. (abwertend: Eigennutz)* [calculating] self-interest; **etw. aus ~ tun** do sth. from motives of self-interest; **c)** *o. Pl. (Überlegung)* deliberation; calculation; **mit kühler ~ vorgehen** act with cool deliberation

berechtigen [bəˈrɛçtɪgn̩] **1.** *tr. V.* entitle; **jmdn. ~, etw. zu tun** entitle sb. *or* give sb. the right to do sth.; **das berechtigt ihn zu dieser Kritik** it entitles him *or* gives him the right to criticize [in this way]. **2.** *itr. V.* **die Karte berechtigt zum Eintritt** the ticket entitles the bearer to admission; **sein Talent berechtigt zu den schönsten Hoffnungen** his talent gives grounds for very great hopes indeed; **das berechtigt zu der Annahme, daß ...:** it justifies the assumption that ...

berechtigt *Adj.* justified, legitimate ⟨*demand, criticism, objection, doubt, complaint, hope*⟩; just ⟨*accusation*⟩; **jmd. ist ~, etw. zu tun** sb. is authorized to do sth.

berechtigterweise *Adv. (Papierdt.)* legitimately; with justification

Berechtigung die; ~, ~en a) *(Befugnis)* entitlement; *(Recht)* right; **mit welcher ~ kritisiert er mich?** what right has he to criticize me?; **b)** *(Rechtmäßigkeit)* legitimacy; **seine/ihre ~ haben** be justified *or* legitimate

Berechtigungs·schein der authorization; *(zum Zutritt, Einlaß usw.)* pass

bereden 1. *tr. V.* **a)** *(besprechen)* talk over; discuss; **b)** *(überreden)* **jmdn. ~, etw. zu tun** talk sb. into doing sth.; **sich ~ lassen, etw. zu tun** let oneself be talked into doing sth. **2.** *refl. V.* **sich [mit jmdm.] über etw.** *(Akk.)* **~:** talk sth. over *or* discuss sth. [with sb.]

beredsam [bəˈreːtzaːm] **1.** *Adj. (beredt)* eloquent; *(iron.: redefreudig)* **~ sein** have the gift of the gab *(coll.)*. **2.** *adv. (beredt)* eloquently; *(iron.: redefreudig)* **~ für etw. werben** use one's gift of the gab to promote sth. *(coll.)*

Beredsamkeit die; ~ *s.* **beredsam:** eloquence; gift of the gab *(coll.)*

beredt [bəˈreːt] **1.** *Adj. (auch fig.)* eloquent; **~es Zeugnis von etw. ablegen** bear eloquent witness to sth.; **es herrschte ein ~es Schweigen** there was a meaningful silence. **2.** *adv.* eloquently

beregnen *tr. V.* water ⟨*field*⟩ using an overhead sprinkling system; water ⟨*lawn*⟩ using a sprinkler

Beregnung die; ~ *s.* **beregnen:** watering using an overhead sprinkling system/a sprinkler

Beregnungs·anlage die overhead sprinkling system

Bereich der; ~[e]s, ~e a) *(Gebiet)* area; **im ~/außerhalb des ~s der Stadt** within/outside the town; **im nördlichen ~:** in northern areas *pl.*; **b)** *(Sphäre)* sphere; area; *(Fachgebiet)* field; area; **in jmds. ~** *(Akk.)* **fallen** be [within] sb.'s province; **im ~ des Möglichen liegen** be within the bounds *pl.* of possibility; **aus dem ~ der Kunst/Politik** from the sphere of art/politics; **c)** *(Wirkungsfeld)* **im privaten/staatlichen ~:** in the private/public sector; **sich im ~ eines Tiefs befinden** be under the influence of a low-pressure area

bereichern [bəˈraiçɐn] **1.** *refl. V.* get rich; **sich an jmdm./etw. ~:** make a great deal of money at sb.'s expense/out of sth. **2.** *tr. V.* enrich; enlarge, increase ⟨*collection, knowledge*⟩; **diese Erfahrung hat mich bereichert** I gained a lot from the experience

Bereicherung die; ~, ~en a) *(das Sichbereichern)* money-making; **b)** *(Nutzen)* valuable acquisition; **eine wertvolle ~ der koreanischen Literatur** a valuable addition to Korean literature

[1]**bereifen** *tr. V.* put tyres on ⟨*car*⟩; put a tyre on ⟨*wheel*⟩; **neu ~:** put a new tyre/new tyres on; **gut bereift sein** ⟨*car*⟩ have good tyres

[2]**bereifen 1.** *tr. V.* cover with hoar-frost *or* rime. **2.** *itr. V.* become covered with hoar-frost *or* rime

Bereifung die; ~, ~en [set *sing.* of] tyres *pl.*

bereinigen 1. *tr. V.* **a)** *(klären)* clear up ⟨*misunderstanding*⟩; settle, resolve ⟨*dispute*⟩; **mit jmdm. etw. zu ~ haben** have sth. to sort out with sb.; **b)** *(verbessern)* correct ⟨*text*⟩; adjust, correct ⟨*statistics*⟩ **(um** for). **2.** *refl. V.* resolve itself; sort itself out

Bereinigung die *(eines Mißverständnisses)* clearing up; *(eines Streites)* settlement; resolution; *(eines Textes)* correction; *(einer Statistik)* adjustment; correction

bereisen *tr. V.* travel around *or* about; travel through ⟨*towns*⟩; *(beruflich)* ⟨*representative etc.*⟩ cover ⟨*area*⟩; **fremde Länder ~:** travel in foreign countries; **ganz Afrika ~:** travel throughout Africa

bereit [bəˈrait] *Adj.* **a)** *(fertig, gerüstet)* **in ~ sein** be ready; **sich ~ halten** be ready; **der Arzt mußte sich auf Abruf ~ halten** the doctor was on call; **etw. ~ haben** have sth. ready; **b)** *(gewillt)* **in ~ sein, etw. zu tun** be willing *or* ready *or* prepared to do sth.; **sich ~ zeigen/finden, etw. zu tun** show oneself/be willing *or* ready *or* prepared to do sth.; **sich ~ erklären, etw. zu tun** declare oneself willing *or* ready to do sth.

bereiten 1. *tr. V.* **a)** *(zu~)* prepare; make ⟨*tea, coffee*⟩; run ⟨*bath*⟩; **jmdm.** *od.* **für jmdn. etw. ~:** prepare/make/run sth. for sb.; **b)** *(zufügen)* cause ⟨*trouble, sorrow, frustration, difficulty, etc.*⟩; **jmdm. Freude/einen begeisterten Empfang ~:** give sb. great pleasure/an enthusiastic reception; **einer Sache** *(Dat.)* **ein Ende ~:** put an end to sth. **2.** *refl. V. (geh.: sich vorbereiten)* prepare oneself; **sich zum Sterben ~:** prepare to die

bereit-: ~|halten *unr. tr. V.* have ready; *(für Notfälle)* keep ready; **~|legen** *tr. V.* lay out ready; **jmdm.** *od.* **für jmdn. etw. ~legen** lay sth. out ready for sb.; **~|liegen** *unr. itr. V.* be ready; ⟨*surgical instruments, tools, papers*⟩ be laid out ready; **~|machen** *tr. V.* get ready; make up ⟨*bed*⟩

bereits *Adv.* already; **sie sind ~ gestern angekommen** they [in fact] arrived yesterday; **~ seit fünf Jahren** for [as long as] five years; **~ vor drei Stunden** three 'hours ago; **~ damals** even then *or* at that time; **~ im 17. Jh.** as early as the 17th century; **~ am nächsten Tag** by the very next day; **~ in zwei Wochen** in only two weeks' time

Bereitschaft die; ~; ~en a) *o. Pl.* willingness; readiness; preparedness; **etw. in ~ haben** have sth. ready; **b)** *o. Pl. (ugs.: ~dienst)* **~ haben** ⟨*doctor, nurse*⟩ be on call; ⟨*policeman, fireman*⟩ be on stand-by duty; ⟨*chemist's*⟩ be on rota duty *(for dispensing outside normal hours)*; **c)** *(Einheit)* unit

Bereitschafts-: ~arzt der doctor on call; **~dienst der: ~dienst haben** ⟨*doctor, nurse*⟩ be on call; ⟨*policeman, fireman*⟩ be on stand-by duty; ⟨*chemist's*⟩ be on rota duty *(for dispensing outside normal hours)*; **~polizei die** police; *(bei Demonstrationen usw.)* riot police

bereit-: ~|stehen *unr. itr. V.* be ready; ⟨*car, train, aircraft*⟩ be waiting; ⟨*troops*⟩ be standing by; **für uns steht ein Auto ~:** a car is/will be waiting for us; **etw. ~stehen haben** have sth. ready; **~|stellen** *tr. V.* place ready; get ready ⟨*food, drinks*⟩; provide, make available ⟨*money, funds*⟩; **die Getränke sind nebenan ~gestellt** the drinks are ready next door

Bereitung die; ~: *(Papierdt.)* preparation; *(von Tee, Kaffee)* making

bereit·willig 1. *Adj.*; *nicht präd.* willing. **2.** *adv.* readily

Bereitwilligkeit die; ~: willingness

berennen *unr. tr. V.* storm, attack ⟨*castle, fortress*⟩; *(Sport)* storm, *(Amer.)* rush ⟨*goal*⟩

berenten *tr. V. (Amtsspr.)* **jmdn. ~:** retire sb. on a pension; **sich ~ lassen** retire on a pension

bereuen 1. *tr. V.* regret; **seine Sünden ~:** repent [of] one's sins; **ich bereue, daß ...:** I'm sorry *or* I regret that ...; **nichts zu ~ haben** have no regrets. **2.** *itr. V.* be sorry; *(Rel.)* repent

Berg [bɛrk] **der; ~[e]s, ~e a)** hill; *(im Hochgebirge)* mountain; **über ~ und Tal** up hill and down dale; **~ Heil!** *greeting between mountaineers;* **wenn der ~ nicht zum Propheten kommt, muß der Prophet zum ~e kommen** *(Spr.)* if the mountain won't come to Muhammad, then Muhammad must go to the mountain *(prov.)*; **jmdm. goldene ~e versprechen** *(fig.)* promise sb. the moon; **mit etw. hinter dem** *od.* **hinterm ~ halten** *(fig.)* keep sth. to oneself; keep quiet about sth.; **mit seiner Meinung nicht hinter dem** *od.* **hinterm ~ halten** *(fig.)* not keep one's views *pl.* to oneself; not hesitate to speak one's mind; **~e versetzen [können]** *(fig.)* [be able to] move mountains *(fig.)*; **über den ~ sein** *(ugs.)* be out of the wood *(Brit.)* or *(Amer.)* woods; ⟨*patient*⟩ be on the mend, have turned the corner; **[längst] über alle ~e sein** *(ugs.)* be miles away; **b)** *Pl. (Gebirge)* mountains; **in die ~e fahren** go up into the mountains; **c)** *(Haufen)* enormous *or* huge pile; *(von Akten, Abfall auch)* mountain

berg-, Berg-: ~ab [-ˈ-] *Adv.* downhill; **einen steilen Weg ~ab fahren** go down a steep path; **mit dem Patienten/der Firma geht es ~ab** *(fig. ugs)* the patient's getting worse/the firm's going downhill; **~abwärts** [-ˈ--] *Adv.* downhill; **~ahorn der** sycamore [maple]; **~akademie die** school of mining

Bergamotte [bɛrgaˈmɔtə] **die; ~, ~n a)** *(Pomeranze)* bergamot [orange]; **b)** *(Birne)* bergamot [pear]

berg-, Berg-: ~amt das [local] mining authority; **~an** [-ˈ-] *s.* **~auf; ~arbeiter der** miner; mineworker; **~auf** [-ˈ-] *Adv.* uphill; **es geht ~auf mit der Firma** *(fig. ugs.)* things are looking up for the firm; **mit dem Patienten geht's ~auf** the patient's on the mend; **~aufwärts** [-ˈ--] *Adv.* uphill; **~bahn die** mountain railway; *(Seilbahn)* mountain cableway; **~bau der;** *o. Pl.* mining; **~bauer der** mountain farmer; **~dorf das** mountain village

berge·hoch *s.* **berghoch**

Berge·lohn der salvage payment

bergen *unr. tr. V.* **a)** *(retten)* rescue, save ⟨*person*⟩; salvage ⟨*ship*⟩; salvage, recover ⟨*cargo, belongings*⟩; *(einbringen)* gather *or* get in ⟨*harvest*⟩; **jmdn. tot/lebend ~:** recover sb.'s body/rescue sb. alive; **sich geborgen fühlen** feel safe; **die Segel ~** *(Seemannsspr.)* take in *or* furl the sails; **b)** *(geh.: enthalten)* hold; **Gefahren/Vorteile in sich** *(Dat.)* **~** *(fig.)* hold dangers/have advantages; **c)** *(geh.: ver~)* hide; *(vor Regen)* shelter; *(vor Sonne)* protect; **den Kopf in den Händen ~:** bury one's head in one's hands

berg-, Berg-: ~fach das mining *no art.*; **~fahrt die a)** *(Schiffahrt)* passage upstream; **b)** *(Hochgebirgstour)* mountaineering expedition; **auf ~fahrt gehen** go mountaineering; **~fest das** *(ugs.)* party to celebrate reaching the half-way stage; **~fex** [~fɛks] **der; ~es, ~e** *(ugs.)* enthusiastic climber; mountaineering freak *(coll.)*; **~fried** [-friːt] **der; ~[e]s, ~e** keep; **~führer der** mountain guide; **~geist der;** *Pl.* **~geister** *legendary sorcerer, kobold, gnome, or giant living inside a mountain;* **~gipfel der** mountain peak *or* top; summit; **~grat der** mountain ridge; **~hoch 1.** *Adj.* as high as a mountain/as mountains; mountainous ⟨*waves, seas*⟩; **2.** *adv.* **~hoch aufsteigende Wellen** mountainous waves *or* seas; **~hütte die** mountain hut

bergig *Adj.* hilly; *(mit hohen Bergen)* mountainous

Berg-: ~ingenieur der [qualified] mining engineer; **~kessel der** corrie; cirque; **~kette die** range *or* chain of mountains; mountain range *or* chain; **~krankheit die** mountain sickness; **~kristall der** rock crystal; **~kuppe die** [rounded] peak *or* mountain-top; **~land das** hilly country *no indef. art.; (mit hohen Bergen)* mountainous country *no indef. art.;* **das spanische ~land** the hill country of Spain; **das Schottische ~land** the Highlands of Scotland
Bergler ['bɛrklɐ] **der; ~s, ~:** mountain-dweller
Berg·mann der; *Pl.* **Bergleute** miner; mineworker
berg·männisch [-mɛnɪʃ] **1.** *Adj.* miner's *attrib.* **2.** *adv.* by miners
Bergmanns-: ~gruß der miner's greeting; **~sprache die** mining terminology
berg-, Berg-: ~massiv das massif; **~not die: in ~not sein/geraten** ⟨*climber*⟩ be/get into difficulties while climbing [in the mountains]; **jmdn. aus ~not retten** rescue sb. who has got into difficulties while climbing [in the mountains]; **~predigt die;** *o. Pl.* Sermon on the Mount; **~recht das;** *o. Pl.* laws relating to mining; **~rennen das** *(Motorsport)* hill-climbing; **ein ~rennen** a hill-climb; **~rettungs·dienst der** *s.* **~wacht; ~riese der** giant of a mountain; **~rücken der** mountain ridge; **~rutsch der** landslide; landslip; **~sattel der** saddle; col; **~schuh der** mountaineering boot; **~see der** mountain lake; **~spitze die** [mountain] peak; mountain top; **~sport der** mountaineering; mountain-climbing; **~station die** top station; **~steigen** *unr. itr. V.; mit haben od. sein; nur im Inf. und Part.* go mountaineering *or* mountain-climbing; **~steigen das; ~s** mountaineering *no art.;* mountain-climbing *no art.;* **~steiger der, ~steigerin die; ~, ~nen** mountaineer; mountain-climber; **~steigerisch 1.** *Adj.; nicht präd.* mountaineering; **2.** *adv.* **~steigerisch [gesehen]** from a mountaineering point of view; **~stock der a)** *(Spazierstock)* alpenstock; **b)** *s.* **Gebirgsstock; ~straße die a)** mountain road; **b)** *(Geogr.)* **die ~straße** the Bergstraße *(hilly wine-growing and orchard district between Darmstadt and Heidelberg);* **~sturz der** rock fall; **~tour die** trip up into the mountains; *(zu Fuß)* mountain climb; *(Wanderung)* hike in the mountains; **~-und-Tal-Bahn die** roller-coaster; switch back *(Brit.);* big dipper *(Brit.);* **~-und-Tal-Fahrt die** journey full of steep climbs and descents; **das war die reinste ~-und-Tal-Fahrt** it was just like going up and down on a roller-coaster *or (Brit.)* switchback
Bergung die; ~, ~en a) *(Erste Hilfe)* rescue; saving; **b)** *(von Schiffen, Gut)* salvaging; salvage; **c)** *(der Ernte)* gathering in
Bergungs-: ~arbeiten *Pl.* rescue work *sing.;* **~kommando das** rescue team; **~schiff das** salvage vessel; **~versuch der** rescue attempt; *(Versuch, ein Schiff zu bergen)* salvage attempt
Berg-: ~volk das mountain people; **~vor·sprung der** spur; *(Absatz)* ledge; **~wacht die;** *o. Pl.* mountain rescue service; **~wand die** mountain face; **~wanderung die** hike in the mountains; **~welt die** *(geh.)* mountain landscape
Berg·werk das mine; **im ~ arbeiten** work down the mine
Bergwerks·gesellschaft die mining company
Berg-: ~wesen das; *o. Pl.* mining *no art.;* **~wiese die** mountain pasture
Beriberi [beri'be:ri] **die; ~** *(Med.)* beriberi
Bericht [bə'rɪçt] **der; ~[e]s, ~e** report; **einen ~ von etw.** *od.* **über etw.** *(Akk.)* **geben** give a report on sth.; **[jmdm.] [von etw.] ~ erstatten** report *or* give a report [to sb.] [on sth.]
berichten *tr., itr. V.* report; **jmdm. etw. ~:** report sth. to sb.; **über etw.** *(Akk.) od.* **von etw. ~:** report on sth.; **es wird berichtet, daß ...:** it is reported that ...; **es wird soeben berichtet, daß ...:** reports are coming in that ...; **mir ist berichtet worden, daß ...:** I have heard a report/reports that ...; **wie uns berichtet wurde** according to reports reaching us
Bericht-: ~erstatter [-ɛɐ̯ʃtatɐ] **der; ~s, ~:** reporter; *(Referent)* rapporteur; **unser ~erstatter aus Paris** our Paris correspondent; **~erstattung die** reporting *no indef. art.;* **zur ~erstattung zurückgerufen werden** ⟨*ambassador etc.*⟩ be recalled to make a report; **die ~erstattung durch Presse und Rundfunk über diese Ereignisse** press and radio coverage of these events; **~haus das** *(schweiz.)* information centre
berichtigen *tr. V.* correct
Berichtigung die; ~, ~en correction; *(berichtigte Fassung)* corrected version; **der Lehrer gab uns die Arbeiten zur ~ zurück** the teacher gave the work back to us for the corrections to be done
Berichts-: ~heft das *(Schulw.) (apprentice's/trainee's)* record book; **~jahr das** *(bes. Wirtsch.)* year [covered by the report]
beriechen *unr. tr. V.* **a)** *(riechen an)* smell; sniff [at]; **b)** *(ugs.: vorsichtig Kontakt aufnehmen mit)* **sich [gegenseitig] ~:** size each other *or* one another up
berieseln *tr. V.* **a)** *(besprühen)* water ⟨*field*⟩ using an overhead sprinkling system; water ⟨*lawn*⟩ using a sprinkler; **b)** *(ugs. abwertend)* **mit Werbung/Musik berieselt werden** be subjected to a constant [unobtrusive] stream of advertisements/to constant background music
Berieselung die a) *s.* **berieseln:** watering using an overhead sprinkling system/a sprinkler; **b)** *(ugs. abwertend)* **die ständige ~ mit Musik** subjection to constant background music
Berieselungs·anlage die sprinkler system
beringen *tr. V.* put a ring on; ring ⟨*bird*⟩
Bering·straße ['be:rɪŋ-] **die** *(Geogr.)* Bering Strait
beringt *Adj.* beringed ⟨*finger, hand*⟩; ⟨*hand*⟩ covered with rings
beritten a) *(reitend)* mounted; on horseback *postpos.;* **b)** *(mit Pferden ausgerüstet)* mounted; **gut ~ sein** have good mounts *or* horses
Berittene der/die; *adj. Dekl.* rider; horseman/horsewoman
Berlin [bɛr'li:n] **(das); ~s** Berlin
[1]Berliner 1. *Adj.; nicht präd.* Berlin; **~ Weiße [mit Schuß]** *light, very fizzy beer flavoured with a dash of raspberry juice or woodruff.* **2. der; ~s, ~:** Berliner; *s. auch* **Kölner**
[2]Berliner der; ~s, ~: *(~ Pfannkuchen)* [jam *(Brit.) or (Amer.)* jelly] doughnut
Berlinerin die; ~, ~nen Berliner; *s. auch* **-in**
berlinerisch *Adj. (ugs.) s.* **berlinisch**
berlinern *itr. V. (ugs.)* speak [in] Berlin dialect
berlinisch *Adj.* Berlin *attrib.;* **im Berlinischen** *(Sprachw.)* in Berlin dialect; **„Schrippe" ist ~:** 'Schrippe' is Berlin dialect
Bermuda·inseln [bɛr'mu:da-] *Pl.* Bermuda *sing., no art.;* Bermudas
Bermudas *Pl.* **a)** Bermudas; Bermuda *sing., no art.;* **b)** *s.* **Bermudashorts**
Bermuda·shorts *Pl.* Bermuda shorts
Bern [bɛrn] **(das); ~s** Bern[e]
Berner 1. *Adj.; nicht präd.* Bernese; **eine ~ Zeitung** a Bern[e] newspaper; **die ~ Konvention:** the Berne Convention; **das ~ Oberland** the Bernese Oberland. **2. der; ~s, ~:** Bernese
Bernhardiner [bɛrnhar'di:nɐ] **der; ~s, ~:** St. Bernard [dog]
Bern·stein ['bɛrn-] **der;** *o. Pl.* amber
bernstein·farben *Adj.* amber[-coloured]
Berserker [bɛr'zɛrkɐ] **der; ~s, ~ a)** *(hist.)* berserker; berserk; **b) wie ein ~ arbeiten** work like mad; **wie ein ~ auf jmdn. einschlagen** go berserk and attack sb.
bersten ['bɛrstn̩] *unr. itr. V.; mit sein (geh.)* ⟨*ice*⟩ break *or* crack up; ⟨*glass*⟩ shatter [into pieces]; ⟨*wall*⟩ crack up; **[bis] zum Bersten voll** *od.* **gefüllt sein** be full to bursting-point; **vor Neugier/Ungeduld/Freude/Zorn ~** *(fig.)* be bursting with curiosity/impatience/joy/rage
berüchtigt [bə'rʏçtɪçt] *Adj.* notorious (**wegen** for); *(verrufen)* disreputable; **als Raufbold ~ sein** be a notorious ruffian
berücken *tr. V. (geh.)* captivate; charm; enchant; **ein ~der Anblick** an enchanting *or* a bewitching sight
berücksichtigen [bə'rʏkzɪçtɪgn̩] *tr. V.* **a)** *(einbeziehen)* take into account *or* consideration; **jmds. Alter ~:** make allowances for sb.'s age; **b)** *(beachten)* consider ⟨*applicant, application, suggestion*⟩
Berücksichtigung die; ~ a) *(das Einbeziehen)* **bei ~ aller Umstände** taking all the circumstances into account; **in** *od.* **unter ~ der Vor- und Nachteile** taking account of all the advantages and disadvantages; **b)** *(Beachtung)* consideration; **eine ~ Ihres Auftrags ist nicht möglich** we cannot consider your application
Beruf der; ~[e]s, ~e a) occupation; *(akademischer, wissenschaftlicher, medizinischer ~)* profession; *(handwerklicher ~)* trade; *(Stellung)* job; *(Laufbahn)* career; **was sind Sie von ~?** what do you do for a living?; what is your occupation?; **er ist von ~ Bäcker/Lehrer** *od.* **Bäcker/Lehrer von ~:** he's a baker by trade/a teacher by profession; **20 Jahre im ~ stehen** have been in the profession/trade for 20 years; **von ~s wegen** because of one's job; **den ~ verfehlt haben** *(scherzh.)* have missed one's vocation; *s. auch* **ergreifen, frei; b)** *(geh. veralt.) s.* **Berufung b**
[1]berufen 1. *unr. tr. V.* **a)** *(einsetzen)* appoint; **jmdn. auf einen Lehrstuhl/in ein Amt ~:** appoint sb. to a chair/an office; **b)** *(ugs.: beschreien)* **berufe es nicht!** don't speak too soon!; **ich will es nicht ~, aber bisher hat die Sache immer geklappt** I don't want to tempt fate *or* providence, but until now it's worked every time; **c)** *(veralt.: zusammenrufen)* call, summon ⟨*person*⟩ **(zu** to); call a meeting of ⟨*council, cabinet, etc.*⟩. **2.** *unr. refl. V.* **sich auf etw.** *(Akk.)* **~:** refer to sth.; quote *or* cite sth.; **sich auf jmdn. als Zeugen ~:** appeal to sb. as a witness; **wenn Sie sich vorstellen, können Sie sich auf mich ~:** when you introduce yourself, you can mention my name
[2]berufen *Adj.* **a)** competent; **aus ~em Munde** from somebody *or* one competent *or* qualified to speak; **b)** *(prädestiniert)* **sich dazu ~ fühlen, etw. zu tun** feel called to do sth.; feel one has a mission to do sth.; **sich zu großen Taten ~ fühlen** feel called to great things; **zum Dichter/zu Höherem ~ sein** have a vocation as a poet/be destined for greater things
beruflich 1. *Adj.; nicht präd.* occupational, vocational ⟨*training etc.*⟩; *(bei akademischen Berufen)* professional ⟨*training etc.*⟩; **seine ~e Tätigkeit** his occupation; **er hat ~e Probleme** he has problems at work *or* in his job; **aus ~en Gründen** because of one's job; *(bei akademischen Berufen)* for professional reasons. **2.** *adv.* **meine Reise war ~ bedingt** my trip was business-related; **~ erfolgreich sein** be successful in one's career; **~ viel unterwegs sein** be away a lot on business; **sich ~ weiterbilden** undertake further job training; **~ verhindert sein** be detained by one's work
berufs-, Berufs-: ~armee die *s.* **~heer;**

~aus·bildung die occupational *or* vocational training; *(als Lehrer, Wissenschaftler, Arzt)* professional training; **eine [solide] ~ausbildung [als etw.] bekommen** receive [a thorough] training [as sth.]; **~aussichten** *Pl.* job prospects *(in a particular profession etc.)*; **~beamte der** ≈ established civil servant; *s. auch* **Beamte**; **~beamtentum das** civil service with life-long job security; **~bedingt** *Adj.* occupational ‹*disease*›; ‹*expenses, difficulties*› connected with one's job; **~berater der** vocational adviser; **~beratung die** vocational guidance; **~bezeichnung die** job title; **~bezogen** *Adj.* vocationally orientated; **~bild das** outline of a/the profession/trade as a career; **~bildend** *Adj.* **~bildende Schule** vocational training school; **~boxer der** professional boxer; **~erfahren** *Adj.* [professionally] experienced; with considerable [professional] experience *postpos., not pred.*; **~erfahrung die;** *o. Pl.* [professional] experience; **~ethos das** *(geh.)* professional code of ethics; **~fach·schule die** vocational college *(providing full-time vocational training)*; **~fahrer der** [professional] driver; **~feuerwehr die** [professional] fire service; **~fremd** *Adj.* ‹*task, work, job*› unconnected with the profession/trade for which one has been trained; **„Berufsfremde werden eingearbeitet"** '[on-the-job] training will be given where necessary'; **~geheimnis das** professional secret; *(Schweigepflicht)* professional secrecy; **~genossenschaft die** *professional/trade association having liability for industrial safety and insurance*; **~gruppe die** occupational group; **~heer das** regular *or* professional army; **~kleidung die** [prescribed] work[ing] clothes *pl.*; **~krankheit die** occupational disease; **~leben das** working life; **im ~leben stehen** be working; **ins ~leben treten** start one's working life; start in one's first job; **~mäßig 1.** *Adj.; nicht präd.* professional; **2.** *adv.* professionally; **~offizier der** regular officer; **~politiker der** professional politician; **~richter der** full-time salaried judge; **~risiko das** occupational risk; **~schule die** vocational school; **~schüler der** student at a vocational school; **~soldat der** regular *or* professional soldier; **~sportler der** professional sportsman; **~stand der** profession; *(Gewerbe)* trade; **~ständisch** *Adj.* professional; **~tätig** *Adj.* working *attrib.*; **es gibt mehr ~tätige Männer als Frauen** more men than women have a job *or* are in paid employment; **[halbtags] ~tätig sein** work [part-time]; **~tätige der/die;** *adj. Dekl.* working person; **~tätige** *Pl.* working people; **~unfähigkeit die** incapacity *(to follow one's profession/trade)*; **~verband der** professional/trade association; **~verbot das** *debarment from practising a particular profession or trade; (für den öffentlichen Dienst) official debarment, on political grounds, from all civil service professions*; **~verbrecher der** professional criminal; **~verkehr der** rush-hour traffic; **~wahl die;** *o. Pl.* choice of career; **~wechsel der** change of career; **~wunsch der** preferred choice of career; **~zweig der** branch of the profession/trade

Berufung die; ~, ~en **a)** *(für ein Amt)* offer of an appointment (**auf, in, an** + *Akk.* to); **seit seiner ~ nach ...:** since he took up the appointment in ...; **b)** *(innerer Auftrag)* vocation; **die ~ zum Künstler in sich** *(Dat.)* **verspüren** feel one has a vocation as an artist; **c)** *(das Sichberufen)* **unter ~** *(Dat.)* **auf jmdn./etw.** referring *or* with reference to sb./sth.; **d)** *(Rechtsw.: Einspruch)* appeal; **~ einlegen** lodge an appeal; appeal; **in die ~ gehen** appeal; **e)** *(veralt.: Einberufung)* summoning

Berufungs-: ~frist die *(Rechtsw.)* period within which an appeal must be lodged; period allowed for an appeal; **~instanz die** *(Rechtsw.)* court of appeal; **~verfahren das** *(Rechtsw.)* appeal proceedings *pl.*

beruhen *itr. V.* **auf etw.** *(Dat.)* **~:** be based on sth.; **etw. auf sich** *(Dat.)* **~ lassen** let sth. rest; *s. auch* **Gegenseitigkeit**

beruhigen [bəˈruːɪgn̩] **1.** *tr. V.* calm [down]; quieten, pacify ‹*child, baby*›; *(trösten)* soothe; *(die Befürchtung nehmen)* reassure; salve, soothe ‹*conscience*›; **die Nerven/den Magen ~:** calm one's nerves/settle the stomach; **beruhigt schlafen/nach Hause gehen können** be able to sleep/go home with one's mind set at ease. **2.** *refl. V.* ‹*person*› calm down; ‹*wind*› drop, die down; ‹*sea*› become calm; ‹*storm*› abate, die down; ‹*struggle, traffic*› lessen; ‹*rush of people*› subside; ‹*prices, stock exchange, stomach*› settle down; **die Lage beruhigt sich** the situation is becoming more stable; **meine Nerven haben sich beruhigt** my nerves have steadied

Beruhigung die; ~ **a)** *s.* **beruhigen 1:** calming [down]; quietening; pacifying; soothing; salving; reassurance; **jmdm. etw. zur ~ geben** give sb. sth. to calm him/her [down]; **b)** *(das Ruhigwerden)*; **eine ~ des Wetters ist vorauszusehen** the weather can be expected to become more settled; **zu Ihrer ~ kann ich sagen, ...:** you'll be reassured to know that ...; **jmdm. ein Gefühl der ~ geben** reassure sb.; **eine ~ der politischen Lage ist nicht zu erwarten** we should not expect that the political situation will become more stable

Beruhigungs-: ~mittel das sedative; tranquillizer; **~pille die** sedative [pill]; tranquillizer; *(fig.)* sop; **~spritze die** sedative injection; **~zelle die** cooling-off cell; holding cell; **~zigarette die** calming cigarette; cigarette to calm one's nerves

berühmt [bəˈryːmt] *Adj.* famous; **durch diesen Roman wurde er ~:** the novel made him famous; **wegen** *od.* **für etw. ~ sein** be famous for sth.; **das ist nicht gerade ~** *(ugs. iron.)* it's nothing to write home about *(coll.)* or no big deal *(coll.)*

berühmt-berüchtigt *Adj.* notorious

Berühmtheit die; ~, ~en **a)** *o. Pl. (Ruhm)* fame; **~ erlangen/gewinnen** become famous/win fame; **zu trauriger ~ gelangen** become notorious; **b)** *(Mensch)* celebrity

berühren *tr. V.* **a)** *(anrühren)* touch; **sich** *od. (geh.)* **einander ~:** touch; **„Bitte Waren nicht ~!"** 'please do not touch the merchandise'; **b)** *(kurz erwähnen)* touch on ‹*topic, issue, question*›; **c)** *(beeindrucken)* affect; **das berührte ihn seltsam/schmerzlich** he was strangely affected/painfully moved by it; **wir fühlten uns davon unangenehm/peinlich berührt** it made an unpleasant impression on us/made us feel embarrassed; **das berührt mich [überhaupt] nicht** it's a matter of [complete] indifference to me

Berührung die; ~, ~en **a)** *(das Berühren)* touch; **mit etw. in ~** *(Akk.)* **kommen** come into contact with sth.; **jede ~ mit jmdm. vermeiden** avoid all physical contact with sb.; **bei der geringsten ~:** at the slightest touch; **b)** *(Kontakt)* contact; **mit jmdm./etw. in ~** *(Akk.)* **kommen** come into contact with sb./sth.; **jmdn. in ~** *(Akk.)* **mit jmdm./etw. bringen** bring sb. into contact with sb./sth.; **c)** *o. Pl. (Erwähnung)* mention

berührungs-, Berührungs-: ~angst die *(Psych.)* fear of contact; haptephobia *(Psych.)*; **~los** *(Physik, Technik)* **1.** *Adj.* contactless; non-contact; **2.** *adv.* without direct contact; **~punkt der a)** *(Math.)* point of contact *or* tangency; **b)** *(Gemeinsamkeit)* point of contact; **politische ~punkte mit jmdm. besitzen** have the same views as sb. on a number of political issues

Beryll [beˈrʏl] **der;** ~s, ~e *(Mineral.)* beryl

Beryllium [beˈrʏli̯ʊm] **das;** ~s *(Chemie)* beryllium

besabbern *tr. V. (salopp)* slobber [on *or* over]

besäen *tr. V.* sow

besagen *tr. V.* say; *(bedeuten)* mean; **das besagt noch gar nichts/sehr viel** that doesn't mean anything/means a great deal

besagt *Adj.; nicht präd. (Amtsspr.)* aforementioned

besamen [bəˈzaːmən] *tr. V.* fertilize; *(künstlich)* inseminate

besammeln *refl. V. (schweiz.) s.* **versammeln**

Besammlung die; ~, ~en *(schweiz.) s.* **Versammlung**

Besamung die; ~, ~en fertilization; *(künstlich)* insemination

Besan [beˈzaːn] **der;** ~s, ~e **a)** *(Segel)* mizen[-sail]; **b)** *(~mast)* mizen-mast

besänftigen [bəˈzɛnftɪgn̩] **1.** *tr. V.* calm [down]; pacify; calm, soothe ‹*temper*›. **2.** *refl. V.* calm down; ‹*sea*› become calm

Besänftigung die; ~: calming [down]; pacifying; *(von jmds. Zorn)* calming; soothing

Besan·mast der mizen-mast

besät [bəˈzɛːt] *Adj.* sown (**mit** with); *(fig.)* covered (**mit, von** with); **mit Blütenblättern/Sternen ~:** strewn with petals/studded with stars

Besatz der a) *(Mode: Borte)* trimming *no indef. art.*; **b)** *(Jagdw., Landw., Fischereiw.)* stock

Besatzer [bəˈzatsɐ] **der;** ~s, ~: member of the occupying forces; **die ~:** the occupying forces

Besatzung die a) *(Mannschaft)* crew; **b)** *(Milit.: Verteidigungstruppe)* garrison; **c)** *(Milit.: Okkupationstruppen)* occupying troops *pl. or* forces *pl.*

Besatzungs-: ~armee die occupying army; army of occupation; **~kind das** *child of a [coloured] member of the occupying forces and a local woman*; **~macht die** occupying power; **~truppen** *Pl.* occupying troops *or* forces; **~zone die** occupied zone

besaufen *unr. refl. V. (salopp)* get boozed up *(Brit. sl.) or* canned *(Brit. sl.) or* bombed *(Amer. sl.)*; *s. auch* **sinnlos 2 c**

Besäufnis [bəˈzɔʏfnɪs] **die;** ~, ~se *od.* **das;** ~ses, ~se *(salopp)* booze-up *(Brit. sl.)*: blast *(Amer. sl.)*

besäuseln *refl. V. (ugs.)* get merry *(Brit. coll.) or* tipsy; **besäuselt** merry *(coll.)*; tipsy

beschädigen *tr. V.* damage

Beschädigte der/die; *adj. Dekl. (veralt.)* disabled person

Beschädigung die a) *o. Pl. (das Beschädigen)* damaging; **b)** *(Schaden)* damage; **zahlreiche/mehrere ~en** a lot of/quite a lot of damage *sing.*

beschaffbar *Adj.* obtainable; **schwer/leicht ~:** difficult/easy to obtain

¹beschaffen *tr. V.* obtain; get; get ‹*job*›; **ein Quartier ~:** find accommodation; **jmdm. etw. ~:** obtain/get sb. sth. *or* sth. for sb.; **sich** *(Dat.)* **Geld/die Genehmigung ~:** get [hold of] money/get *or* obtain the permit/licence

²beschaffen *Adj.* **so ~ sein, daß ...:** ‹*goods, materials*› be made in such a way that ...; ‹*substance*› be such that ...

Beschaffenheit die; ~: composition; *(von Menschen)* make-up; **rauhe/glatte ~:** roughness/smoothness

Beschaffung die *s.* **beschaffen**: obtaining; getting; finding

Beschaffungs-: ~amt das; *o. Pl. (Milit.)* ≈ Procurement Executive *(Brit.) or (Amer.)* Office; **~kosten** *Pl.* procurement cost *sing.*; cost *sing.* of acquisition; **~kriminalität die** crime in the pursuit of drug acquisition

beschäftigen [bəˈʃɛftɪgn̩] **1.** *refl. V.* **sich mit etw. ~:** occupy *or* busy oneself with sth.;

sich viel mit Musik/den Kindern ~: devote a great deal of one's time to music/the children; **sich mit den Schriften Hegels ~:** be engaged in a study of the writings of Hegel; **sich mit einem Fall ~:** deal with a case; **mit etw. beschäftigt sein** be [busy] working on sth.; **sehr beschäftigt sein** be very busy. **2.** *tr. V.* **a)** *(geistig in Anspruch nehmen)* **jmdn. ~:** be on sb.'s mind; preoccupy sb.; **was beschäftigt dich so?** what's on your mind?; **Märchen ~ die Phantasie der Kinder** fairy stories engage children's imaginations; **b)** *(angestellt haben)* employ ‹*workers, staff*›; **bei einer Firma beschäftigt sein** work for a firm; **c)** *(zu tun geben)* occupy; **jmdn. mit etw. ~:** give sb. sth. to occupy him/her; **du mußt die Kinder ~:** you must keep the children occupied

Beschäftigte der/die; *adj. Dekl.* employee; **die Fabrik/das Kaufhaus hat 500 ~:** the factory has a workforce/the department store has a staff of 500

Beschäftigung die; ~, ~en a) *(Tätigkeit)* activity; occupation; **bei dieser ~ solltest du ihn nicht stören** you shouldn't disturb him while he's occupied with that; **einer ~ nachgehen** pursue an activity; **b)** *(berufliche Tätigkeit)* job; **seiner ~ nachgehen** go about one's business; **er geht wieder seiner ~ nach** he's now back at work; **ohne ~ sein** not be working; *(unfreiwillig)* be unemployed; **c)** *(mit einer Frage, einem Problem)* consideration **(mit** of**)**; *(Untersuchung, Studium)* study **(mit** of**)**; **d)** *o. Pl. (das Angestelltwerden)* employment; **e)** *o. Pl. (das Beschäftigtsein)* **die ~ in diesem Betrieb/im Staatsdienst** working for this firm/in the Civil Service

beschäftigungs-, Beschäftigungs-: ~grad der *(Wirtsch.)* level of employment; **~los** *Adj.* **a)** *(untätig)* **~ sein** have nothing to do; **b)** *(ohne Arbeit)* **~ sein** not be working; *(unfreiwillig)* be unemployed; **~therapie die** *(Med.)* occupational therapy

beschälen *tr. V.* cover, serve ‹*mare*›

Beschäler der; ~s, ~: breeding stallion; stud-horse

beschallen *tr. V.* **a)** fill with sound; **b)** *(Med.)* treat with ultrasonic waves *or* ultrasound

beschämen *tr. V.* shame; **jmdn. durch seine Großmütigkeit ~:** make sb. ashamed by one's generosity

beschämend 1. *Adj.* **a)** *(schändlich)* shameful; **b)** *(demütigend)* humiliating; **für jmdn. ~ sein** be humiliating for sb.; bring humiliation upon sb. **2.** *adv.* shamefully

beschämt *Adj.* ashamed; abashed; **ein ~es Gesicht** a shamefaced expression; **sich ~ fühlen** be ashamed *or* abashed

Beschämung die; ~: shame; **zu meiner ~ muß ich gestehen, daß ...:** to my shame I must confess that ...

beschatten *tr. V.* **a)** *(geh.)* shade; *(fig.)* overshadow, cast a cloud over ‹*event*›; cloud ‹*face*›; **b)** *(heimlich überwachen)* shadow; **jmdn. ~ lassen** have sb. shadowed; **c)** *(Fußball, Hockey)* mark closely

Beschatter der; ~s, ~: shadow

Beschattung die; ~ *(eines Verdächtigen)* shadowing

Beschau die inspection

beschauen *tr. V. (bes. md.) s.* **betrachten**

Beschauer der; ~s, ~: viewer

beschaulich [bəˈʃaulɪç] **1.** *Adj.* **a)** *(behaglich)* peaceful, tranquil ‹*life, manner, etc.*›; meditative, contemplative ‹*person, character*›; **b)** *(kath. Rel.)* **~e Orden** contemplative orders. **2.** *adv.* peacefully; tranquilly

Beschaulichkeit die; ~: peacefulness; tranquillity

Bescheid [bəˈʃait] **der; ~[e]s, ~e a)** *(Auskunft)* information; *(Antwort)* answer; reply; **jmdm. ~ geben** *od.* **sagen[, ob ...]** let sb. know or tell sb. [whether ...]; **sage bitte im Restaurant ~, daß ...:** please let the restaurant know *or* let them know in the restaurant that ...; **jmdm. ~ sagen** *(ugs.: sich beschweren)* give sb. a piece of one's mind *(coll.)*; **[über etw.** *(Akk.)***] ~ wissen** know [about sth.]; **in einer Stadt/mit Autos ~ wissen** know one's way around a town/know about cars; **jmdm. ~ stoßen** *(ugs.)* give sb. a dressing-down *(coll.)*; **Entschuldigung, wissen Sie hier ~?** excuse me, do you know your way around here?; **b)** *(Entscheidung)* decision; **ein abschlägiger/günstiger ~:** a refusal/a positive reply

[1]**bescheiden 1.** *unr. tr. V.* **a)** *(Amtsspr.: Mitteilung machen an)* **jmdn./etw. abschlägig ~:** turn sb./sth. down; refuse sb./sth.; **jmdn. ~[, daß ...]** inform *or* notify sb. [that ...]; **b)** *(geh.: zuteil werden lassen)* **jmdm. etw. ~:** grant sb. sth.; **es war ihm nicht beschieden, den Erfolg seines Romans zu erleben** it was not granted to him to live to see the success of his novel. **2.** *unr. refl. V. (geh.)* be content; **man muß sich ~ können** one has to be able to make do with less *or* moderate one's needs

[2]**bescheiden 1.** *Adj.* **a)** *(unaufdringlich)* modest; modest, unassuming ‹*person, behaviour*›; **b)** *(einfach)* modest; simple ‹*meal*›; **darf ich die ~e Frage stellen, wie ...?** *(auch iron.)* may I venture to ask how ...?; **aus ~en Anfängen** from modest *or* humble beginnings; **in ~en Verhältnissen aufwachsen** grow up in humble circumstances; **c)** *(dürftig)* modest ‹*salary, results, pension, etc.*›; **d)** *(ugs. verhüll.: sehr schlecht)* lousy *(sl.)*; bloody awful *(Brit. coll.)*. **2.** *adv.* modestly; **darf ich mal ganz ~ anfragen, wie ...?** *(auch iron.)* may I venture to ask how ...?

Bescheidenheit die; ~: modesty; **keine falsche ~!** don't be shy!; **~ ist eine Zier, doch weiter kommt man ohne ihr** *(scherzh.)* modesty is a virtue, but it doesn't get you very far; **aus falscher ~:** out of false modesty

Bescheidung die; *o. Pl. (geh.)* moderation in one's needs

bescheinen *unr. tr. V.* shine [up]on; **vom Mond/von der Sonne beschienen** moonlit/sunlit

bescheinigen [bəˈʃainɪgn̩] *tr. V.* **etw. ~:** confirm sth. in writing; **den Tod [auf dem Totenschein] ~:** sign the death certificate; **jmdm. den Empfang des Geldes ~:** acknowledge receipt of the money; *(durch Quittung)* give sb. a receipt for the money; **sich** *(Dat.)* **~ lassen, daß man arbeitsunfähig ist/die Rechnung bezahlt hat** get oneself certified as unfit for work/get a receipt for the bill; **du wirst deinen Fehler noch bereuen, das kann ich dir ~** *(fig.)* you'll regret your mistake, I can guarantee you that

Bescheinigung die; ~, ~en a) *(Schriftstück)* written confirmation *no indef. art.*; *(Schein)* certificate; *(Quittung)* receipt; **eine ~ des Arztes** a doctor's certificate; a certificate from the doctor; a medical certificate; **b)** *o. Pl. (das Bescheinigen)* confirmation in writing

bescheißen *unr. tr. V. (derb)* **jmdn. ~:** rip sb. off *(sl.)*; screw sb. *(coarse)*; **jmdn. um etw. ~:** do sb. out of sth. *(sl.)*

beschenken *tr. V.* **jmdn. ~:** give sb. a present/presents; **jmdn. reich ~:** shower sb. with presents; **jmdn. mit etw. ~:** give sb. sth. as a present; **sich [gegenseitig] ~:** give each other presents

bescheren 1. *tr. V.* **a)** *(schenken)* **jmdn. [mit etw.] ~:** give sb. [sth. as] a Christmas present/Christmas presents; **jmdm. etw. ~:** give sb. sth. for Christmas; **b)** *(zuteil werden lassen)* **ihnen waren keine Kinder beschert** they were not blessed with children; **ich bin gespannt, was uns dieser Tag ~ wird** I wonder what today will bring; **ihm waren noch viele Jahre des Glücks beschert** he was granted many more happy years. **2.** *itr. V.* **nach dem Abendessen wird beschert** the presents are given out after supper

Bescherung die; ~, ~en a) *(zu Weihnachten)* giving out of the Christmas presents; **die Kinder konnten die ~ kaum erwarten** the children could hardly wait for the presents to be given out; **b)** *(ugs. iron.: unangenehme Überraschung)* **das ist ja eine schöne ~:** this is a pretty kettle of fish; **jetzt haben wir die ~:** that's done it, I told you so; **nun guck dir die ~ an** just look at this mess

bescheuert *Adj. (salopp)* **a)** *(verrückt)* barmy *(Brit. sl.)*; nuts *(sl.)*; **b)** *(unangenehm)* stupid ‹*task, party, etc.*›; **jmdn./etw. ~ finden** find sb./sth. a real pain [in the neck] *(coll.)*

beschichten *tr. V. (Technik)* coat; **mit Kunststoff beschichtet** plastic-coated

Beschichtung die; ~, ~en *(Technik)* coating

beschicken *tr. V.* **a)** supply ‹*market, shop*›; send representatives to ‹*meeting, congress, etc.*›; send exhibits to ‹*art exhibition*›; **b)** *(Technik: füllen)* charge ‹*furnace*›

beschickert [bəˈʃɪkɐt] *Adj. (ugs.: angetrunken)* tipsy; merry *(Brit. coll.)*

Beschickung die; ~, ~en *(Technik: eines Hochofens) (das Beschicken)* charging; *(Füllung)* charge

beschießen *unr. tr. V.* **a)** fire *or* shoot at; *(mit Artillerie)* bombard; **b)** *(Kernphysik)* bombard

Beschießung die; ~, ~en *s.* **beschießen: a) die ~ der feindlichen Flugzeuge** firing *or* shooting at the enemy aircraft; **hält diese ~ weiter an, ...:** if this firing *or* shooting/bombardment continues ...; **b) die ~ mit Neutronen/Alphateilchen** bombardment with neutrons/alpha particles

beschildern *tr. V.* label ‹*jar etc.*›; put up direction-signs along ‹*road, path*›

Beschilderung die a) labelling; **die ~ der Straße/des Wanderwegs** putting up direction-signs along the road/footpath; **b)** *(Schilder)* direction signs

beschimpfen *tr. V.* abuse; swear at; **ich lasse mich von Ihnen nicht ~!** I won't stand for being sworn at *or* abused by you

Beschimpfung die; ~, ~en a) *(das Beschimpfen)* abuse *no indef. art.*; **die öffentliche ~ des Staatsoberhaupts** publicly insulting the head of state; **b)** *(Äußerung)* insult; **~en** abuse *sing.*; insults

beschirmen *tr. V. (geh.)* **a)** *(beschützen)* protect **(vor** + *Dat.* from**)**; **b)** *(vor Licht)* shade

beschirmt *Adj. (scherzh.)* **~ sein** have an *or* one's umbrella [with one]

Beschiß der; Beschisses *(derb)* rip-off *(sl.)*; **das ist doch alles ~!** it's a rip-off *(sl.)* *or* swindle

beschissen [bəˈʃɪsn̩] *(derb)* **1.** *Adj.* lousy *(sl.)*; shitty *(vulg.)*. **2.** *adv.* ‹*behave*› in a bloody awful manner *(Brit. coll.)*, shittily *(vulg.)*; **ihm geht es ~:** he's having a lousy *or* *(Brit.)* bloody awful time of it *(sl.)*

beschlafen *unr. tr. V. (ugs.)* **a)** *(den Beischlaf ausüben mit)* lay *(sl.)*; sleep with; **b)** *(überdenken)* sleep on

Beschlag der a) *(an Truhen)* metal fitting; *(an Fenstern, Türen, Möbelstücken, Sätteln)* metal mount; *(Scharnier)* hinge; *(Schließe)* clasp; **b)** *in* **jmdn./etw. mit ~ belegen** *od.* **in ~ nehmen, jmdn./etw. in ~ halten** monopolize sb./sth.; **c)** *(Hufeisen)* horseshoe

[1]**beschlagen 1.** *unr. tr. V.* shoe ‹*horse*›; **ein Faß mit Reifen ~:** hoop a barrel; **Schuhsohlen mit Nägeln ~:** stud the soles of shoes with [hob]nails. **2.** *unr. itr. V.*; *mit sein* ‹*window*› mist up *(Brit.)*, fog up *(Amer.)*; *(durch Dampf)* steam up; **~e Scheiben** misted-up/fogged-up/steamed-up windows. **3.** *unr. refl. V.* mist up *(Brit.)*; fog up *(Amer.)*; *(durch Dampf)* steam up

²**beschlagen** *Adj.* knowledgeable; **in etw.** *(Dat.)* **[gut] ~ sein** be knowledgeable about sth.; **auf einem Gebiet ~ sein** be knowledgeable about *or* well-versed in a subject

Beschlagenheit die; **~:** thorough *or* sound knowledge (**auf** + *Dat.* of)

Beschlag·nahme [-na:mə] **die; ~, ~n** seizure; confiscation

beschlagnahmen *tr. V.* **a)** *(konfiszieren)* seize; confiscate; **b)** *(scherzh.: in Anspruch nehmen)* **jmdn. ~:** monopolize sb.

Beschlagnahmung die; ~, ~en *s.* **Beschlagnahme**

beschleichen *unr. tr. V.* **a)** *(heranschleichen an)* creep up on *or* to; steal up to; ⟨*hunter*⟩ stalk ⟨*game, prey*⟩; **b)** *(geh.: überkommen)* creep over

beschleunigen [bəˈʃlɔynɪgn̩] **1.** *tr. V.* speed up; increase ⟨*speed*⟩; quicken ⟨*pace, step[s], pulse*⟩; accelerate ⟨*atomic particle*⟩; speed up, expedite ⟨*work, delivery*⟩; hasten ⟨*departure, collapse*⟩; accelerate, speed up, expedite ⟨*process*⟩; **etw. beschleunigt erledigen** deal with sth. as a matter of priority. **2.** *refl. V.* ⟨*speed, heart-rate*⟩ increase; ⟨*pulse*⟩ quicken. **3.** *itr. V.* ⟨*car*⟩ accelerate; ⟨*engine*⟩ speed up

Beschleuniger der; ~s, ~ *(Kernphysik)* accelerator

Beschleunigung die; ~, ~en a) *s.* **beschleunigen 1:** speeding up; increasing; quickening; acceleration; expedition; hastening; **eine ~ der Arbeit erreichen** speed up the work; **eine weitere ~ des Tempos** a further increase in speed; **b)** *(ugs.: ~svermögen)* acceleration; **eine gute ~ haben** have good acceleration; **c)** *(Physik)* acceleration

Beschleunigungs-: ~anlage die *s.* **Beschleuniger; ~vermögen das;** *o. Pl. (Technik) (eines Kfz)* acceleration; *(eines Motors)* throttle response; **~wert der** *(Technik)* acceleration figure

beschließen 1. *unr. tr. V.* **a)** *(entscheiden)* **~, etw. zu tun** decide *or* resolve to do sth.; **das ist beschlossene Sache** it's settled; **b)** *(einen Mehrheitsbeschluß fassen über)* pass ⟨*law*⟩; **~, etw. zu tun** resolve to do sth.; **c)** *(beenden)* end; end, conclude ⟨*lecture*⟩; end, close ⟨*letter*⟩; **seine Tage ~** *(geh.)* end one's days. **2.** *unr. itr. V.* **über etw.** *(Akk.)* **~:** decide concerning sth.

beschlossen [bəˈʃlɔsn̩] **1.** *2. Part. v.* **beschließen. 2.** *in* **in etw.** *(Dat.)* **~ sein** *od.* **liegen** *(geh.)* be summed up in sth.

Beschluß der a) *(Entscheidung)* decision; *(gemeinsam festgelegt)* resolution; **einen ~ fassen** come to a decision/pass a resolution; **laut ~ des Gerichtes/der Direktion** in accordance with the decision of the court/management; **b)** *o. Pl. (veralt.: Ende)* end; **zum ~:** to end *or* conclude

beschluß-, Beschluß-: ~fähig *Adj.* quorate; **~fähig sein** have a quorum; be quorate; **~fähigkeit die;** *o. Pl.* presence of a quorum; **die ~fähigkeit herstellen** make a quorum; **~fassung die** *(Amtsspr.)* **einen Entwurf zur ~fassung vorlegen** submit a draft resolution; **~organ das** decision-making body; **~unfähig** *Adj.* inquorate; **~unfähig sein** not have a quorum; be inquorate

beschmeißen *unr. tr. V. (salopp)* **jmdn./sich [gegenseitig] mit etw. ~:** pelt sb./each other with sth.; **jmdn./etw. mit Schmutz** *od.* **Dreck ~** *(fig.)* fling mud at sb./sth.

beschmieren *tr. V.* **a) etw./sich ~:** get sth./oneself in a mess; **sich** *(Dat.)* **die Kleidung/Hände mit etw. ~:** smear *or* get sth. [smeared] all over one's clothes/hands; **b)** *(abwertend) (bemalen)* daub paint all over; *(bekritzeln)* scrawl *or* scribble all over; **c)** *(bestreichen)* **sein Brot mit etw. ~:** spread sth. on one's bread; **das Brot mit Butter ~:** butter the bread; **etw. mit Fett/Salbe ~:** grease sth./smear ointment on sth.; **d)** *(abwertend: vollschreiben)* cover ⟨*paper*⟩

beschmunzeln *tr. V.* smile at

beschmutzen *tr. V.* **etw. ~:** make sth. dirty; **ganz beschmutzt sein** be covered in dirt; **jmds. Namen/Gedenken ~** *(fig.)* besmirch sb.'s name/memory; **sich ~** *(verhüll.)* dirty oneself

beschneiden *unr. tr. V.* **a)** *(stutzen)* cut, trim, clip ⟨*hedge*⟩; prune, cut back ⟨*bush*⟩; cut back ⟨*tree*⟩; trim ⟨*book block*⟩; **einem Vogel die Flügel ~:** clip a bird's wings; **b)** *(Med., Rel.)* circumcise; **ein Beschnittener** a circumcised boy/man; **c)** *(einschränken)* cut ⟨*salary, income, wages*⟩; restrict ⟨*rights*⟩; **jmdn. in seinen Rechten ~:** restrict sb.'s rights

Beschneidung die; ~, ~en a) *(das Stutzen) s.* **beschneiden a:** trimming; cutting; clipping; pruning; cutting back; **b)** *(Einschränkung) s.* **beschneiden c:** cutting; restriction; **die ~ seines Einkommens in Kauf nehmen** accept a cut in [one's] income; **c)** *(Med., Rel.)* circumcision

beschneit *Adj.* snow-covered

beschnüffeln *tr. V.* **a)** *(beriechen)* sniff at; **b)** *(ugs.: prüfen)* **jmdn./sich ~:** size sb./each other up; **c)** *(ugs. abwertend: bespitzeln)* spy on

beschnuppern *tr. V.: s.* **beschnüffeln a, b**

beschönigen [bəˈʃø:nɪgn̩] *tr. V.* gloss over

Beschönigung die; ~, ~en glossing over; **das wäre eine ~:** that would be to gloss over the true situation

beschränken [bəˈʃrɛŋkn̩] **1.** *tr. V.* restrict; limit; **etw. auf etw.** *(Akk.)* **~:** restrict *or* limit sth. to sth.; **jmdn. in seinen Rechten ~:** restrict sb.'s rights; **die Mittel sind beschränkt** my/our *etc.* resources are limited; **beschränkte Verhältnisse** straitened circumstances. **2.** *refl. V.* tighten one's belt *(fig.)*; **sich auf etw.** *(Akk.)* **~:** restrict *or* confine oneself to sth.

beschrankt *Adj.* ⟨*level crossing*⟩ with barriers; **~ sein** have barriers

beschränkt 1. *Adj.* **a)** *(abwertend: dumm)* dull-witted; **b)** *(engstirnig)* ⟨*person*⟩ of restricted *or* limited outlook; narrow-minded ⟨*person*⟩; narrow[-minded] ⟨*views, outlook*⟩; **~ sein** have a restricted *or* limited outlook; be narrow-minded; **einen ~en Horizont haben** have limited horizons *pl.* **2.** *adv.* narrow-mindedly; in a narrow-minded way

Beschränktheit die; ~: a) *(Dummheit)* lack of intelligence; **in ihrer ~:** with her limited intelligence; **b)** *(das Begrenztsein)* limitedness; restrictedness

Beschränkung die; ~, ~en a) *o. Pl. (das Beschränken)* limitation; restriction; **b)** *(das, was beschränkt)* restriction; **jmdm./einer Sache ~en auferlegen** impose restrictions on sb./sth.

beschreiben *unr. tr. V.* **a)** write on; *(vollschreiben)* write ⟨*page, side, etc.*⟩; **eng beschriebene Seiten** closely written pages; **b)** *(darstellen)* describe; **ich kann dir [gar] nicht ~, wie ..., es ist [gar] nicht zu ~, wie ...:** I [simply] can't tell you how ...; **ihre Leiden waren nicht zu ~:** her sufferings were indescribable *or* beyond description; **wer beschreibt seine Freude, als ...:** who could describe his joy when ...; **c)** *(durch Kreisbewegung herstellen)* describe ⟨*circle, orbit, curve, etc.*⟩

Beschreibung die; ~, ~en a) description; **jeder ~ spotten** defy *or* be beyond description; **b)** *(Gebrauchsanweisung)* instructions *pl.*

beschreien *unr. tr. V.: s.* ¹**berufen 1 b**

beschreiten *unr. tr. V. (geh.)* walk along ⟨*path etc.*⟩; **neue Wege ~** *(fig.)* tread new paths; ⟨*medicine, technology, etc.*⟩ pursue new methods; **den Rechtsweg ~:** have recourse to litigation

Beschrieb der *(schweiz.)* description

beschriften [bəˈʃrɪftn̩] *tr. V.* label; address ⟨*envelope, letter*⟩; inscribe ⟨*stone*⟩; letter ⟨*sign*⟩

Beschriftung die; ~, ~en a) *o. Pl.* labelling; *(eines Briefes)* addressing; *(eines Steines)* inscribing; *(eines Schildes)* lettering; **b)** *(Aufschrift)* label; *(eines Briefes)* address; *(eines Steines)* inscription; *(eines Schildes)* lettering

beschuhen [bəˈʃu:ən] *tr. V. (Technik)* shoe; tip [with metal]

beschuht *Adj.* shod; **ein weiß ~er Fuß** a foot [shod] in a white shoe

beschuldigen [bəˈʃʊldɪgn̩] *tr. V.* accuse (+ *Gen.* of); **jmdn. des Mordes/des Mordes an seiner Frau ~:** accuse sb. of murder/of the murder of his wife; **jmdn. ~, etw. getan zu haben/etw. zu sein** accuse sb. of doing/being sth.

Beschuldigte der/die; *adj. Dekl.* accused

Beschuldigung die; ~, ~en accusation; **~en gegen jmdn. erheben** make accusations against sb.

beschummeln *tr. V. (ugs.),* **beschupsen** *tr. V. (salopp)* cheat; diddle *(Brit. coll.)*; burn *(Amer. sl.)*; **jmdn. um etw. ~:** diddle *(Brit. sl.) or (coll.)* do sb. out of sth.

Beschuß der a) fire; *(aus Kanonen)* shelling; *(mit Pfeilen)* shooting; **unter ~ nehmen** fire at/shell/shoot at; *(fig.: kritisieren)* attack; **[heftig** *od.* **stark] unter ~ geraten/stehen** *od.* **liegen** *(auch fig.)* come/be under [heavy] fire; **b)** *(Physik)* **~ mit Neutronen** *usw.* bombardment with neutrons *etc.*

beschützen *tr. V.* protect (**vor** + *Dat.* from); **~d den Arm um jmdn. legen** put a protective arm around sb.; **~de Werkstätte** sheltered workshop

Beschützer der; ~s, ~, Beschützerin die; ~, ~nen protector (**vor** from)

beschwatzen, *(bes. südd.)* **beschwätzen** *tr. V. (ugs.)* **a) jmdn. ~:** talk sb. round; **jmdn. zu etw. ~:** talk sb. into sth.; **jmdn. ~, etw. zu tun** talk sb. into doing sth.; **b)** *(bereden)* chat about *or* over

Beschwerde [bəˈʃve:ɐ̯də] **die; ~, ~n a)** complaint (**gegen, über** + *Akk.* about); **~ führen** *(Amtsspr.) od.* **einlegen** *(Rechtsw.)* lodge a complaint; *(gegen einen Entscheid)* lodge an appeal; **b)** *Pl. (Schmerz)* pain *sing.*; *(Leiden)* trouble *sing.*; **er fragte mich nach meinen ~n** he asked me what the trouble was; **jmdm. [ziemliche/große] ~n machen** give sb. [quite a lot of/considerable] pain; **~n [mit der Verdauung** *usw.* **] haben** have trouble [with one's digestion *etc.*]; **die ~n des Alters** the aches and pains *or* infirmities of old age

beschwerde-, Beschwerde-: ~ausschuß der *(DDR)* appeal tribunal *(against actions of official bodies)*; **~buch das** complaints book; **~frei 1.** *Adj.* trouble-free; *(ohne Schmerzen)* free from pain *postpos.*; **2.** *adv.* without pain; **relativ ~frei leben** live a life relatively free from pain; **~frist die** *(Rechtsw.)* time-limit for lodging an appeal; **~führer der** complainant; *(gegen einen Entscheid)* appellant; **~weg der;** *o. Pl.* **auf dem ~weg** by appealing; by means of an appeal

beschweren [bəˈʃve:rən] **1.** *refl. V.* complain (**über** + *Akk.*, **wegen** *about*); **sich bei jmdm. ~:** complain to sb. **2.** *tr. V.* weight; *(etw. Schweres auflegen)* weight down; *(fig.: belasten)* burden ⟨*person, memory*⟩

beschwerlich 1. *Adj.* arduous; *(ermüdend)* exhausting; **jmdm. ~ fallen** *(veralt., geh.)* ⟨*person, children*⟩ be a burden to sb.; **jmdm. fällt etw. ~** *(veralt. geh.)* sb. finds sth. troublesome. **2.** *adv.* laboriously; with an effort

Beschwerlichkeit die; ~, ~en a) *o. Pl.* arduousness; **b)** *Pl. (Anstrengungen)* tribulations

Beschwernis die; ~, ~se *(geh.)* tribulation
Beschwerung die; ~, ~en a) *o. Pl.* weighting; **zur ~:** in order to weigh it [down]; **b)** *(Gegenstand)* weight; **etw. als ~ benutzen** use sth. as ballast
beschwichtigen [bəˈʃvɪçtɪgn̩] *tr. V.* pacify; calm ‹*excitement*›; placate, mollify ‹*anger etc.*›; **sein Gewissen ~:** ease one's conscience; **er versucht [uns] zu ~, wenn wir in Streit geraten** he tries to conciliate *or* placate us when we quarrel; **~de Worte** soothing words
Beschwichtigung die; ~, ~en pacification; *(des Zorns, Hasses)* mollification
Beschwichtigungs·politik die policy of appeasement
beschwindeln *tr. V. (ugs.)* **jmdn. ~:** tell sb. a fib/fibs; *(betrügen)* hoodwink sb.
beschwingt [bəˈʃvɪŋt] **1.** *Adj.* elated, lively ‹*mood*›; lively, lilting ‹*tune, melody*›; **~ sein/sich ~ fühlen** ‹*person*› be/feel elated; **~en Schrittes/Fußes** *(geh.)* with a spring in one's step. **2.** *adv.* **~ gehen** walk with a spring in one's step; **~ tanzen** dance with great élan
Beschwingtheit die; ~: elation; *(einer Melodie)* liveliness; *(des Ganges)* springiness
beschwipst [bəˈʃvɪpst] *Adj.* tipsy
beschwören *unr. tr. V.* **a) ~, daß ...:** swear that ...; **etw. ~:** swear to sth.; **eine Aussage ~:** swear a statement on *or* under oath; **b)** charm ‹*snake*›; **c)** *(erscheinen lassen)* invoke, conjure up ‹*spirit*›; *(fig.)* evoke, conjure up ‹*pictures, memories, etc.*›; **ein Unheil ~:** make a disaster happen *(by thinking/talking about it)*; **die Vergangenheit ~:** revive memories of the past; **d)** *(bitten)* beg; implore; **in ~dem Ton** in a beseeching *or* imploring tone; **mit ~dem Blick** with an imploring glance; **sie sah ihn ~d an** she looked at him imploringly; **e)** *(veralt.: bannen)* exorcize ‹*evil spirit*›
Beschwörung die; ~, ~en a) *(Zauberspruch)* spell; incantation; **b)** *(Bitte)* entreaty; **c)** *(das Erscheinenlassen)* invoking; conjuring up
Beschwörungs·formel die incantation
beseelen [bəˈzeːlən] *tr. V.* animate; **ein fester Glaube beseelte ihn** a steadfast faith was his inspiration
besehen *unr. tr. V.* have a look at; **sich** *(Dat.)* **etw. [genau] ~:** have a [close] look at sth.; inspect sth. [closely]; **er besah sich im Spiegel** he looked at himself in the mirror
beseitigen [bəˈzaitɪgn̩] *tr. V.* **a)** *(entfernen)* remove; get rid of; eliminate ‹*error, difficulty*›; dispose of ‹*rubbish*›; clear ‹*snow*›; eradicate ‹*injustice, abuse*›; **b)** *(verhüll.: ermorden)* dispose of; eliminate
Beseitigung die; ~ a) removal; *(eines Fehlers, einer Schwierigkeit)* elimination; *(des Müll s)* disposal; *(eines Mißstands)* eradication; **b)** *(verhüll.: Ermordung)* elimination
beseligen [bəˈzeːlɪgn̩] *tr. V.* fill with delight *or* joy; **ein ~des Gefühl/ein ~der Gedanke** a delightful *or* blissful feeling/thought
Besen [ˈbeːzn̩] **der; ~s, ~ a)** broom; *(Reisig~)* besom; *(Hand~)* brush; **~ und Schaufel** dustpan and brush; **die Hexe auf ihrem ~:** the witch on her broomstick; **ich fress' einen ~, wenn das stimmt** *(salopp)* I'll eat my hat if that's right *(coll.)*; **neue ~ kehren gut** *(Spr.)* a new broom sweeps clean *(prov.)*; **mit eisernem ~ [aus]kehren** *(fig.)* apply drastic remedies; **b)** *(salopp abwertend: Frau)* battleaxe *(coll.)*
besen-, Besen-: ~binder der broommaker; *(von Reisig~)* besom-maker; **~ginster der** *(Bot.)* broom; **~kammer die** broom-cupboard; broom-closet *(Amer.)*; **~macher der** broom-maker; **~rein** *Adj.* swept clean *postpos.*; **~schrank der** *s.* **~kammer; ~stiel der** broom-handle; *(eines Reisigbesens)* broomstick; **er läuft herum, als habe er einen ~stiel verschluckt** *(ugs.)* he runs around as stiff as a ramrod
besessen [bəˈzɛsn̩] **1.** *2. Part. v.* **besitzen. 2.** *Adj.* **a)** possessed; **vom Teufel ~ sein** be possessed by *or (dated)* of the Devil; **wie ~:** like one possessed; **b)** *(heftig ergriffen)* obsessive ‹*gambler*›; fanatical ‹*racing driver, footballer, etc.*›; **von einer Idee** *usw.* **~ sein** be obsessed with an idea *etc.*
Besessene der/die; *adj. Dekl.* **ein ~r/eine ~:** one possessed; **zum/zur ~n werden** become like one possessed; become fanatical
Besessenheit die; ~ a) *(durch einen Dämon, Teufel)* possession; **b)** *(Ergriffenheit)* obsessiveness; **mit wahrer ~:** in a truly obsessive manner; **zur ~ werden** become obsessive *or* an obsession
besetzen *tr. V.* **a)** *(mit Pelz, Spitzen)* edge; trim; **mit Perlen/Edelsteinen besetzt** set with pearls/precious stones; **b)** *(belegen; auch Milit.: erobern)* occupy; *(füllen)* fill (**mit** with); *(Jagdw., Fischereiw.)* stock ‹*shoot, pond, etc.*›; *(reservieren)* keep, reserve ‹*seat, table, etc.*›; **der Bus kann mit 50 Personen besetzt werden** the bus can carry 50 people; **c)** *(vergeben)* fill ‹*post, position, role, etc.*›; cast ‹*role, play, etc.*›; **einen Ausschuß ~:** fill [the places on] a committee; **die frei werdenden Stellungen werden nicht mehr neu besetzt** no new appointments are being made to positions which become vacant
besetzt *Adj.* occupied; ‹*table, seat*› taken *pred.*; ‹*washing-machine, drier, etc.*› in use *pred.*; *(gefüllt)* full; filled to capacity; **es** *od.* **die Leitung/die Nummer ist ~:** the line/number is engaged *or (Amer.)* busy; **er ist im Moment ~:** he is occupied *or* busy at the moment; **die amerikanisch ~e Zone** the American zone of occupation
Besetzt·zeichen das *(Fernspr.)* engaged tone *(Brit.)*; busy signal *(Amer.)*
Besetzung die; ~, ~en a) *(einer Stellung)* filling; *(einer Rolle)* casting; *(eines Ausschusses)* composition; *(Jagdw., Fischereiw.)* stocking *no indef. art.*; **b)** *(Mitwirkende) (Film, Theater usw.)* cast; *(einer Popgruppe)* line-up; **das Stück in hervorragender ~ sehen** see the play with an outstanding cast; **in der besten/der neuen ~ antreten** *(Sport)* ‹*team*› field its best side/new line-up; **die erste/zweite ~** *(Theater)* the first/second cast; **c)** *(Eroberung)* occupation; **die ~ des Brückenkopfes** the taking of the bridgehead
besichtigen [bəˈzɪçtɪgn̩] *tr. V.* see ‹*sights*›; see the sights of ‹*town*›; look round ‹*building*›; view ‹*house, flat*›; *(prüfend)* inspect ‹*troops, joc.: baby, girl-friend*›
Besichtigung die; ~, ~en viewing; *(Führung)* tour; *(Prüfung von Truppen)* inspection; **etw. zur ~ freigeben** open sth. to visitors *or* to the public; **die ~ der Kirche ist zwischen 10 und 16 Uhr möglich** the church is open to visitors between 10 a.m. and 4 p.m.
Besichtigungs-: ~reise die sightseeing trip; **~zeit die** opening time
besiedeln *tr. V.* **a)** settle (**mit** with); **neu ~:** resettle; **ein dicht/dünn besiedeltes Land** a densely/thinly populated country; **b)** *(heimisch sein in)* ‹*animal, plant*› inhabit, be found in
Besiedlung die settlement
Besiedlungs·dichte die population density
besiegeln *tr. V.* set the seal on; **sein Schicksal ist besiegelt** his fate is sealed
Besieg[e]lung die; ~, ~en sealing; **die ~ von etw. sein** seal sth.; **zur ~ des Geschäftes/unserer Freundschaft** to seal the transaction/our friendship
besiegen *tr. V.* **a)** defeat; **sich besiegt geben** admit defeat; **b)** *(überwinden)* overcome ‹*doubts, difficulties, curiosity, etc.*›
Besiegte der/die; *adj. Dekl.* loser
besingen *unr. tr. V.* **a)** *(geh.)* celebrate in verse; *(durch ein Lied)* celebrate in song; **b) eine Platte ~:** make a record [of songs]
besinnen 1. *unr. refl. V.* **a)** think it *or* things over; **sich anders/eines Besseren ~:** change one's mind/think better of it; **b)** *(sich erinnern)* **sich [auf jmdn./etw.] ~:** remember *or* recall [sb./sth.]; **sich darauf ~, wann ...:** recall when ...; **wenn ich mich recht besinne** if I remember correctly; **c)** *(sich bewußt werden)* **sich auf die Bedeutung von etw. ~:** become aware of the significance of sth. **2.** *unr. tr. V.* reflect on
besinnlich *Adj.* contemplative; thoughtful ‹*person*›; reflective ‹*story*›; **in einer ~en Stunde** in a quiet moment; when one has time to think; **ein ~er Abend** an evening of reflection
Besinnlichkeit die; ~: contemplation; **Stunden der ~:** moments of reflection
Besinnung die; ~ a) consciousness; **die ~ verlieren** *(das Bewußtsein verlieren)* lose consciousness; *(ohnmächtig werden)* faint; **ohne** *od.* **nicht bei ~:** unconscious; **[wieder] zur ~ kommen** come to; regain consciousness; **b)** *(Nachdenken)* reflection; **zur ~ kommen** stop and think things over; **ehe ich recht zur ~ kommen konnte** before I had time to think; **jmdn. zur ~ bringen** bring sb. to his/her senses
Besinnungs·aufsatz der reflective essay
besinnungs·los 1. *Adj.* **a)** *(bewußtlos)* unconscious; **b)** *(fig.)* mindless, blind ‹*rage, hatred*›; **~ vor Angst** out of one's mind with fear. **2.** *adv.* mindlessly; **~ auf jmdn. einschlagen** hit out at sb. in a blind *or* uncontrollable rage
Besinnungslosigkeit die; ~: unconsciousness *no art.*; **er betrank sich bis zur ~:** he drank himself into oblivion
Besitz der a) property; **nur wenig ~ haben** have only a few possessions *pl.*; **jmdm. den rechtmäßigen ~ [einer Sache** *(Gen.)* **] streitig machen** dispute sb.'s legal title to his/her property [in sth.]; **b)** *(das Besitzen)* possession; **sich in jmds. ~** *(Dat.)* **befinden, in jmds. ~** *(Dat.)* **sein** be in sb.'s possession; **es befindet sich seit mehreren Generationen im ~ unserer Familie** it has been in our family for several generations; **sich in privatem ~ befinden** be privately owned; be in private ownership *or* hands; **in amerikanischem ~:** in American ownership; **in jmds. ~** *(Akk.)* **übergehen** *od.* **kommen** pass *or* come into sb.'s possession; **in den ~ eines Hauses** *usw.* **kommen** become the owner of a house *etc.*; *(durch eigene Bemühungen)* gain possession of a house *etc.*; **im ~ einer Sache** *(Gen.)* **/von etw. sein, etw. in ~ haben** be in possession of sth.; possess sth.; **im vollen ~ seiner geistigen Kräfte sein** be in full possession of one's faculties; **etw. in [seinen] ~ nehmen, von etw. ~ ergreifen** take possession of sth.; **von jmdm. ~ ergreifen** *(geh.)* take hold of sb.; **c)** *(Land~)* estate
besitz-, Besitz-: ~anspruch der claim to ownership; **einen ~anspruch auf etw.** *(Akk.)* **anmelden** file a claim to ownership of sth.; **~anzeigend** *Adj. (Sprachw.)* possessive; **~bürgertum das** property-owning bourgeoisie
besitzen *unr. tr. V.* **a)** own; have ‹*quality, talent, etc.*›; *(nachdrücklicher)* possess; **seit wann besitzt er ein Auto?** since when does he own a car?; how long has he had a car?; **alles, was er besaß** all he possessed; **keinen Pfennig ~** *(ugs.)* not have a penny to one's name; **er besaß die Frechheit/Unverschämtheit, zu ...:** he had the cheek *or* nerve/impertinence to ...; **die ~de Klasse** the propertied class; **das Recht ~, zu ...:** have the right to ...; **b)** *(geh. verhüll.)* **eine Frau ~:** possess a woman
Besitzer der; ~s, ~ a) owner; *(eines Be-*

triebs usw.) proprietor *(formal);* **den ~ wechseln** change hands *pl.;* **b)** *(österr.)* property-owner

besitz·ergreifend *Adj.* ‹*troops etc.*› taking possession

Besitz·ergreifung die seizure

Besitzerin die; ~, ~nen *s.* **Besitzer**

Besitzer-: ~stolz der pride of ownership; **voller ~stolz** very much the proud owner; **~wechsel der** change of ownership

besitz-, Besitz-: ~gier die cupidity; acquisitiveness; **~los** *Adj.* destitute; **die ~lose Klasse** the propertyless class; **~nahme die** appropriation; *(mit Gewalt)* seizure; **~stand der** standard of living; **den ~stand wahren** maintain living standards

Besitztum das; ~s, Besitztümer [-ty:mɐ] **a)** possession; **b)** *(Gut)* estate

Besitzung die; ~, ~en *(geh.)* estate

Besitz·verhältnisse *Pl.* matters relating to ownership; *(marxistische Theorie)* conditions of ownership

besoffen [bəˈzɔfn̩] **1.** *2. Part. v.* **besaufen. 2.** *Adj. (salopp)* boozed [up] *(sl.);* plastered *(sl.);* pissed *pred. (sl.);* **völlig ~:** completely stoned *(sl.);* blind drunk

Besoffene der/die; *adj. Dekl. (salopp)* drunk

besohlen *tr. V.* sole; **neu ~:** resole

Besohlung die; ~ a) soling; **eine neue ~ der Schuhe** resoling the shoes; **b)** *(Sohle)* sole

besolden *tr. V.* pay ‹*soldier*›; pay ‹*civil servant*› his/her salary; **eine gut besoldete Stelle** a well-paid job

Besoldung [bəˈzɔldʊŋ] **die; ~, ~en** pay; *(Gehalt)* salary

Besoldungs-: ~gruppe die salary bracket; **~ordnung die** [tables of] pay scales *pl. (for civil servants)*

besonder... [bəˈzɔndɐ...] *Adj.; nicht präd.* special; *(mehr als gewohnt)* particular ‹*pleasure, enthusiasm, effort, etc.*›; *(hervorragend)* exceptional ‹*quality, beauty, etc.*›; **im ~en** in particular; **im allgemeinen und im ~en** in general and in particular; **ein ~es Ereignis** an unusual *or* a special event; **keine ~en Vorkommnisse wurden gemeldet** no incidents of any particular note were reported; **~e Merkmale** *(im Paß usw.)* distinguishing marks; **~en Wert auf etw.** *(Akk.)* **legen** lay particular emphasis on sth.; **keine ~e Leistung** no great achievement; **einen ~en Geschmack haben** ‹*person*› have exceptional taste; ‹*dish*› have an unusual taste; **es ist mir eine [ganz] ~e Freude/Ehre** it is a particular pleasure/honour for me

Besondere das; *adj. Dekl.* **a) etwas [ganz] ~s** something [really] special; **nichts ~s** nothing special; *(nichts Interessantes)* nothing of note *or* worth mentioning; **das ist doch nichts ~s** there's nothing special *or* unusual about that; **das ~ daran** the special thing about it; **b)** *(Einzelerscheinung)* **vom ~n zum Allgemeinen kommen** proceed from the particular to the general

Besonderheit die; ~, ~en special *or* distinctive feature; *(Eigenart)* peculiarity; **dieser Fall stellt eine ~ dar** this is a special case

besonders *Adv.* **a)** particularly; **~ du solltest das wissen** you of all people should know that; **~ bei schönem Wetter** especially in fine weather; **das hat ihn ~ gefreut** that gave him particular pleasure; **das braucht man wohl nicht ~ zu erwähnen** presumably one does not have to mention this specifically; **nicht ~ viel Geld haben** not be particularly well off; **b) nicht ~ sein** be nothing special; be nothing to write home about; **ich fand den Film nicht ~:** I didn't think the film was anything special *or* was up to much; **es geht ihm nicht ~:** he doesn't feel too well; **c)** *(getrennt)* separately

besonnen [bəˈzɔnən] **1.** *2. Part. v.* **besinnen. 2.** *Adj.* prudent; *(umsichtig)* circumspect; **ruhig und ~:** calm and collected; **~es Urteil** considered judgement. **3.** *adv.* prudently; *(umsichtig)* circumspectly

Besonnenheit die; ~: *s.* **besonnen 2:** prudence; circumspection

besonnt [bəˈzɔnt] *Adj.* sunlit

besorgen *tr. V.* **a)** get; *(kaufen)* buy; **jmdm. etw. ~:** get/buy sb. sth. *or* sth. for sb.; **ich will mir das Buch ~:** I want to get the book [for myself]; **b)** *(ugs. verhüll.: stehlen)* **sich** *(Dat.)* **etw. ~:** help oneself to sth.; **c)** *(erledigen)* take care of; deal with; prepare ‹*edition*›; **einen Brief ~:** post a letter; **er besorgte die Auswahl der Gedichte** he was responsible for the selection of poems; **was du heute kannst ~, das verschiebe nicht auf morgen** *(Spr.)* never put off to tomorrow what you can do today *(prov.);* **d)** *(betreuen)* look after ‹*children, flowers, etc.*›; **jmdm. den Haushalt/die Wäsche ~:** keep house/do the washing for sb.; **e) es jmdm. ~:** *(ugs.: heimzahlen)* get back at sb. *(coll.);* get one's own back on sb. *(Brit. coll.); (derb: geschlechtlich befriedigen)* give it to sb. *(sl.)*

Besorgnis die; ~, ~se concern; **echte ~ [um jmdn./über etw.** *(Akk.)***] empfinden** be genuinely concerned [about sb./sth.]; **jmds. ~ erregen** cause sb. concern; **jmds. ~se zerstreuen** put an end to sb.'s worries

besorgnis·erregend *Adj.* serious; **~ sein** give cause for concern

besorgt 1. *Adj.* worried **(über +** *Akk.,* **um** about); concerned *usu. pred.* **(über +** *Akk.,* **um** about); **er macht einen sehr ~en Eindruck** he appears to be very concerned; **sie war rührend um das Wohl ihrer Gäste ~:** she showed a touching concern for the well-being of her guests; **er war ~, es könnte etwas passieren** he was concerned lest something should happen *or* worried that something might happen. **2.** *adv.* with concern; *(ängstlich)* anxiously; **sich sehr ~ äußern** express one's great concern

Besorgtheit die; ~: concern

Besorgung die; ~, ~en a) purchase; **[einige] ~en machen** do some shopping; **kleinere ~en machen** do odd bits of shopping; **b)** *o. Pl. (das Beschaffen)* getting; *(das Kaufen)* buying; **c)** *o. Pl. (das Betreuen)* **die ~ des Haushalts** *usw.* looking after the household *etc.*

bespannen *tr. V.* **a)** cover ‹*wall, chair, car, etc.*›; string ‹*racket, instrument*›; **b)** *(mit Zugtieren)* **einen Wagen mit einem Pferd ~:** harness a horse to a cart; **mit zwei Schimmeln bespannt** harnessed to *or* pulled by two white horses

Bespannung die; ~, ~en covering; *(eines Schlägers, eines Instruments)* stringing

bespeien *unr. tr. V. (geh.)* spit at

bespiegeln *tr. V.* **a) sein eigenes Ich** *od.* **sich selbst ~:** contemplate one's own ego; **b)** *(darstellen)* mirror; portray

bespielbar *Adj.* **a) das Band ist nicht mehr ~:** one can no longer record on this tape; **b)** *(Sport)* playable ‹*ground, tennis-court*›

bespielen *tr. V.* **a)** make a recording on ‹*tape, cassette*›; **ein Band mit Liedern ~:** record songs on a tape; **die Kassette ist schon bespielt** the cassette already has a recording on it; **b)** *(Theaterw.)* **eine Bühne ~:** play a theatre

bespitzeln *tr. V.* spy on

Bespitz[e]lung die; ~, ~en spying

bespötteln *tr. V.* mock; make fun of

besprechen 1. *unr. tr. V.* **a)** discuss; talk over; *(rezensieren)* review; **gut/schlecht besprochen werden** get a good/bad review; *(mehrfach)* get good/bad reviews; **b)** *(aufnehmen)* **eine Kassette ~:** make a [voice] recording on a cassette; *(statt eines Briefes)* record a message on a cassette; **eine Platte mit Gedichten ~:** make a record of poems; **c)** *(beschwören)* **etw. ~:** utter a magic incantation *or* spell over sth. **2.** *unr. refl. V.* confer **(über +** *Akk.* about); **sich [ausführlich] über etw.** *(Akk.)* **~:** discuss sth. [in detail]; **sich mit jmdm. ~:** have a talk with sb.; confer with sb. *(formal)*

Besprechung die; ~, ~en a) discussion; *(Konferenz)* meeting; **in einer ~ sein, [gerade] eine ~ haben** be in a meeting; **b)** *(Rezension)* review *(Gen.,* **von** of); **c)** *(das Beschwören)* incantation

Besprechungs·exemplar das *(Buchw.)* review copy

besprengen *tr. V.* sprinkle

besprenkeln *tr. V.* spatter

bespringen *unr. tr. V.* ‹*stallion, bull, etc.*› cover, mount ‹*mare, cow, etc.*›

bespritzen *tr. V.* **a)** splash; *(mit einem Wasserstrahl)* spray; **b)** *(beschmutzen)* bespatter

besprühen *tr. V.* spray

bespucken *tr. V.* **jmdn. [mit etw.] ~:** spit [sth.] at sb.

Bessemer·birne [ˈbɛsəmɐ-] **die** *(Metallbearb.)* Bessemer converter

besser [ˈbɛsɐ] **1.** *s.* **gut; wohl 1 f. 2.** *Adj.* **a)** better; **~ dran sein** be better off; **[auch] schon [mal] ~e Zeiten gesehen haben** *(ugs.)* have seen better days; **es wäre ~, du hieltest deinen Mund** it would be better if you kept your mouth shut; **~ werden** get better; ‹*work etc.*› improve; **um so ~:** so much the better; all the better; **es wurde noch ~** *(iron.)* there was more *or* better to come *(iron.);* that wasn't the best of it *(iron.);* **das wäre ja noch ~!** *(iron.)* that really is the limit!; **ich habe Besseres zu tun** I've got better things to do; **~ ist ~:** better safe than sorry; just to be on the safe side; **jmdn. eines Besseren belehren** *(geh.)* put sb. right; **schließlich hat er sich doch eines Besseren belehren lassen** in the end he accepted that he was wrong; *s. auch* **besinnen; b)** *(sozial höher gestellt)* superior; upper-class; **~e** *od.* **die ~en Kreise** more elevated circles; **es verkehren hier die ~en Leute** you get a better *or* superior class of people here; **eine ~e Gegend/Adresse** a smart[er] *or* [more] respectable area/address; **c)** *(abwertend)* glorified; **wir arbeiten in einer ~en Baracke** we work in a glorified hut. **3.** *adv.* **a) [immer] alles ~ wissen** always know better; **es ~ haben** be better off; *(es leichter haben)* have an easier time of it; **es kommt noch ~** *(iron.)* it gets even better *(iron.);* **~ gesagt** to be [more] precise; **sie war nicht ganz offen, oder ~ gesagt, sie hat uns belogen** she was not quite frank, or to put it bluntly, she lied to us; **b)** *(lieber)* **das läßt du ~ sein** *od. (ugs.)* **bleiben** you'd better not do that; **er ließe es ~ bleiben, sich einzumischen** he would be better advised not to interfere; **er täte ~ daran, zu ...:** he would do better to ...; **geh ~ zum Arzt** you'd better go to the doctor

besser|gehen *unr. itr. V.; mit sein* **jmdm. geht es besser** sb. feels better; **kurze Zeit später ging es ihr schon wieder besser** a short time later, she had already recovered

Bessergestellte [-gəʃtɛltə] *Pl.; adj. Dekl.* **die ~n** the better off; the well-to-do

bessern 1. *refl. V.* improve; ‹*person*› mend one's ways. **2.** *tr. V.* improve; reform ‹*criminal*›

besser|stellen *tr. V.* **jmdn. [finanziell] ~:** improve sb.'s [financial] position

Besserung die; ~: a) *(Genesung)* recovery; **[ich wünsche dir] gute ~:** [I hope you] get well soon; **sich auf dem Wege der ~ befinden** be on the road to recovery *or* on the mend; **b)** *(Verbesserung)* improvement (+ *Gen.* in); *(eines Kriminellen)* reform; **~ geloben** promise to mend one's ways

Besserungs·anstalt die *(ugs. veralt.)* reform school; reformatory *(esp. Amer.)*

besser-, Besser-: ~wissen das *s.* **~wisserei; ~wisser der; ~s, ~** *(abwertend)* know-all; smart aleck; **~wisserei** [----ˈ-] **die; ~** *(abwertend)* superior attitude; **~wisserisch** *Adj. (abwertend)* superior;

know-all; **sei nicht so ~wisserisch!** don't always pretend you know better

bẹst... ['bɛst...] **1.** *s.* **gut. 2.** *Adj.* **a)** *attr.* best; **aus ~em Hause sein** *od.* **stammen** come from one of the very best families; **bei ~er Gesundheit/Laune sein** be in the best of health/spirits *pl.*; **im ~en Falle** at best; **er wird im ~en Falle mit einer Geldstrafe davonkommen** the best he can hope for is to get off with a fine; **in den ~en Jahren, im ~en Alter** in one's prime; **~e** *od.* **die ~en Grüße an ...** *(Akk.)* best wishes to ...; **mit den ~en Grüßen** *od.* **Wünschen** with best wishes; *(als Briefschluß)* ≈ yours sincerely; **~en Dank** many thanks *pl.*; *s. auch* **Dank, Familie, Weg, Wille; b) es ist** *od.* **wäre das ~e, wenn ...:** it would be best if ...; **es wäre das ~e, zu ...:** it would be best to ...; **er hielt es für das ~e, sofort abzureisen** he thought it best to leave immediately; **am ~en** best; **am ~en fährst du mit dem Zug** it would be best for you to go by train; **du bleibst am ~en zu Hause** you had best stay at home; **alles aufs ~e regeln** *od.* **richten** arrange everything in the best way possible; **es steht nicht zum ~en mit etw.** things are not going too well for sth.; **mit seiner Gesundheit steht es nicht zum ~en** his health is none too good; **der/die/das nächste ~e ...:** the first ... one comes across; **sie hat den ersten ~en Mann geheiratet, der ihr über den Weg lief** she married the first man who happened to cross her path; **eine Geschichte/einen Witz zum ~en geben** entertain [those present] with a story/a joke; **jmdn. zum ~en halten** *od.* **haben** pull sb.'s leg; **c)** *subst.* best; **der Beste in unserer Gruppe** the best person in our group; **der/die Beste der Klasse** the best [pupil/student] in the class; **das Beste vom Besten** the very best; **das Beste ist gerade gut genug** only the best is good enough; **sein Bestes tun** do one's best; **das Beste aus etw./daraus machen** make the best of sth./of it; **aufs** *od.* **auf das Beste hoffen** hope for the best; **ich will nur dein Bestes** I am doing this for your own good; **zu deinem Besten** for your benefit; in your best interests *pl.*

bestallen [bəˈʃtalən] *tr. V. (Amtsspr.)* appoint **(zu, als** as)

Bestạllung die *(Amtsspr.)* appointment **(zu, als** as)

Bestạllungs·urkunde die *(Amtsspr.)* certificate of appointment

Bestạnd der a) *o. Pl.* continued existence; survival; **keinen ~ haben, nicht von ~ sein** not last; not last long; **b)** *(Vorrat)* stock **(an** + *Dat.* of); *s. auch* **eisern 1 d; c)** *(Forstw.)* **~ von Eichen und Buchen** [mixed] stand of oaks and beeches; **Bestände durchforsten** thin out standing timber; **d)** *(österr.: Dauer des Bestehens)* **nach 15jährigem ~:** after 15 years of existence; after existing for 15 years; **e)** *(südd., österr.: Pacht)* **etw. in ~ haben/geben** lease sth./lease sth. [out]

bestanden [bəˈʃtandn̩] **1.** *2. Part. v.* **bestehen. 2.** *Adj.* **a) von** *od.* **mit etw. ~ sein** have sth. growing on it; **mit Blumen ~e Wiesen** flower-covered meadows; meadows full of flowers; **mit Tannen ~e Hügel** fir-covered hills; **b) nach ~er Prüfung** after passing one's examination; **c)** *(schweiz.: alt)* elderly

bestạ̈ndig 1. *Adj.* **a)** *nicht präd. (dauernd)* constant; **b)** *(gleichbleibend)* constant; steadfast ⟨*person*⟩; *(zuverlässig)* reliable; settled ⟨*weather*⟩; *(Chemie)* stable ⟨*compound*⟩; **seine Leistungen sind ~:** his work is consistent; **c)** *(widerstandsfähig)* resistant **(gegen, gegenüber** to). **2.** *adv.* **a)** constantly; **sie klagt ~:** she is constantly *or* for ever complaining; **b)** *(gleichbleibend)* consistently

-beständig *adj.* **hitze~/wetter~/säure~:** heat-/weather-/acid-resistant

Bestạ̈ndigkeit die; ~ a) constancy; steadfastness; *(bei der Arbeit)* consistency; *(Zuverlässigkeit)* reliability; **b)** *(Widerstandsfähigkeit)* resistance **(gegen, gegenüber** to)

Bestạnds·aufnahme die stock-taking; **[eine] ~ machen** do a stock-taking; take inventory *(Amer.)*; *(fig.)* take stock

Bestạnd·teil der component; **ein notwendiger ~ unserer Nahrung** an essential part *or* element of our diet; **sich in seine ~e auflösen** fall apart; fall to pieces; **etw. in seine [sämtlichen] ~e zerlegen** dismantle sth. [completely]

Bẹst·arbeiter der *(DDR)* best worker *(worker receiving an award as being the most efficient in his department, factory, etc.)*

bestạ̈rken 1. *tr. V.* confirm; **jmdn. in seinem Plan** *od.* **Vorsatz** *od.* **darin ~, etw. zu tun** strengthen sb.'s resolve *or* confirm sb. in his/her resolve to do sth. **2.** *refl. V.* grow

Bestạ̈rkung die confirmation

bestätigen [bəˈʃtɛːtɪgn̩] **1.** *tr. V.* confirm; endorse ⟨*document*⟩; acknowledge ⟨*receipt*⟩; **ein Urteil ~** *(Rechtsw.)* uphold a judgement; **jmdn. [in seinem Amt] als Schulleiter** *usw.* **~:** confirm sb.'s appointment as headmaster *(Brit.) or (Amer.)* principal *etc.*; **hiermit wird bestätigt, daß ...** *(in Urkunden)* this is to confirm *or* certify that ...; **jmdm. [schriftlich] ~, daß er ...:** give sb. [written] confirmation that he ...; certify that sb. ...; **sich in seiner Meinung/in seinen Vorurteilen bestätigt fühlen** have one's opinion/prejudices reinforced; **einen Brief/eine Bestellung ~** *(Kaufmannsspr.)* acknowledge [receipt of] a letter/an order. **2.** *refl. V.* be confirmed; ⟨*rumour*⟩ prove to be true; **damit hat sich meine Vermutung bestätigt** this confirmed my supposition

Bestạ̈tigung die; ~, ~en confirmation; *(des Empfangs)* acknowledgement; *(schriftlich)* letter of confirmation; **zur ~ seiner Aussage erbrachte er Beweise** he produced evidence to support *or* back up his statement; **die ~ [in seinem Amt] als ...:** the confirmation of his appointment as ...

bestatten [bəˈʃtatn̩] *tr. V. (geh.)* inter *(formal)*; bury; **bestattet werden** be laid to rest

Bestạtter der; ~s, ~: undertaker; mortician *(Amer.)*; *(bei Firmennamen)* funeral director

Bestạttung die; ~, ~en *(geh.)* interment *(formal)*; burial; *(Feierlichkeit)* funeral; „Meier und Schulze, ~en" 'Meier und Schulze, Funeral Directors *or (Amer.)* Morticians'

Bestạttungs-: ~institut das, ~unternehmen das [firm of] undertakers *pl. or* funeral directors *pl.*; funeral parlor *(Amer.)*

bestäuben [bəˈʃtɔybn̩] *tr. V.* **a)** dust; **b)** *(Biol.)* pollinate

Bestäubung die; ~, ~en *(Biol.)* pollination

bestaunen *tr. V.* marvel at; *(bewundernd anstarren)* gaze in wonder at; *(bewundernd anerkennen)* be lost in admiration for

bẹst·bezahlt *Adj.*; *nicht präd.* best-paid

bẹste *s.* **best...**

Bẹste das; ~n *s.* **best... c**

bestẹchen 1. *unr. tr. V.* **a)** bribe; **b)** *(für sich einnehmen)* win over, captivate ⟨*audience etc.*⟩. **2.** *unr. itr. V.* win people over

bestẹchend *Adj.* attractive; captivating, winning ⟨*smile, charm*⟩; persuasive ⟨*argument, logic*⟩; tempting ⟨*offer*⟩; **von ~er Logik** irresistibly logical; **in ~er Form** *(Sport)* in irresistible form

bestẹchlich *Adj.* corruptible; open to bribery *postpos.*

Bestẹchlichkeit die; ~: corruptibility

Bestẹchung die; ~, ~en bribery *no indef. art.*; **eine ~:** a case of bribery; **der ~ eines Beamten/der ~ schuldig sein** be guilty of bribing of an official/of bribery; **aktive ~** *(Rechtsw.)* giving bribes; **passive ~** *(Rechtsw.)* accepting bribes

Bestẹchungs-: ~geld das bribe; **~skandal der** bribery scandal; **~summe die** bribe; **~versuch der** attempted bribery

Besteck [bəˈʃtɛk] **das; ~[e]s, ~e a)** cutlery setting; **noch ein ~ auflegen** lay another place; **~e putzen** polish cutlery; **b)** *o. Pl. (ugs.: Gesamtheit der Bestecke)* cutlery; **c)** *(Med.)* [set *sing.* of] instruments *pl.*; **d)** *(Seemannsspr.)* fix; *(aus Kurs und Geschwindigkeit bestimmt)* dead reckoning [position]

bestẹcken *tr. V.* **A mit B ~:** stick B in/on A; **der Adventskranz war mit Tannenzapfen besteckt** the Advent wreath had fir-cones stuck in it

Bestẹck-: ~kasten der cutlery-box; *(größer)* canteen; **~schublade die** cutlery-drawer

bestehen 1. *unr. itr. V.* **a)** exist; **die Schule besteht noch nicht sehr lange** the school has not been in existence *or* has not been going for very long; **es besteht [die] Aussicht/Gefahr, daß ...:** there is a prospect/danger that ...; **darüber bestand noch immer keine Klarheit** it was still unclear; **es besteht noch** *od.* **noch besteht die Hoffnung, daß ...:** there is still hope that ...; **b)** *(fortdauern)* survive; last; *(standhalten)* hold one's own; **gegen diese Konkurrenz werden wir kaum ~ können** we shall hardly be able to survive *or* keep going in the face of this competition; **seine Arbeit kann vor jeder Kritik ~:** his work can stand up to any criticism; **in einer Gefahr** *usw.* **~:** prove oneself in a dangerous situation *etc.*; **c)** *(zusammengesetzt sein)* **aus etw. ~:** consist of sth.; *(aus einem Material)* be made of sth.; **in etw.** *(Dat.)* **~:** consist of *or* in sth.; **ihre Aufgabe besteht in der Aufstellung der Liste** her task is to draw up the list; **der Unterschied besteht darin, daß ...:** the difference is that ...; **eine Möglichkeit besteht darin, zu beweisen ...:** one possibility would be to prove ...; **d)** *(beharren)* **auf etw.** *(Dat.)* **~:** insist on sth.; **er bestand darauf, den Chef zu sprechen** he insisted on seeing the boss; **ich bestehe darauf, daß man mich darüber informiert** I insist that I be *or* on being informed about it; **e)** *(die Prüfung ~)* pass [the examination]. **2.** *unr. tr. V.* **a)** pass ⟨*test, examination*⟩; **b)** *(ertragen)* withstand ⟨*blows of fate*⟩; face up to ⟨*difficulties*⟩

Bestẹhen das; ~s a) existence; **die Firma feiert ihr 10jähriges ~:** the firm is celebrating its tenth anniversary; **seit ~ der Bundesrepublik** since the Federal Republic came into existence; since the founding of the Federal Republic; **b)** *(einer Prüfung)* passing; **mit ~ der Prüfung** on passing the examination; **c)** *(Beharren)* insistence **(auf** + *Dat.* on)

bestẹhen|bleiben *unr. itr. V.*; *mit sein* remain; ⟨*doubt*⟩ persist; ⟨*regulation*⟩ remain in force

bestẹhend *Adj.* existing; current ⟨*conditions*⟩; **das seit 5 Jahren ~e Gesetz** the law which has been in existence for five years

bestẹhen|lassen *unr. tr. V.* retain; allow ⟨*objection etc.*⟩ to stand

bestẹhlen *unr. tr. V.* **jmdn. [um etw.] ~:** rob sb. [of sth.]

besteigen *unr. tr. V.* **a)** climb; mount ⟨*horse, bicycle*⟩; climb into ⟨*pulpit*⟩; ascend ⟨*throne*⟩; **b)** *(betreten)* board ⟨*ship, aircraft*⟩; get on ⟨*bus, train*⟩; **c)** *s.* **bespringen**

Besteigung die ascent

Bestẹll-: ~block der *(Kaufmannsspr.)* order-pad; **~buch das** *(Buchhandel)* order-book

bestẹllen 1. *tr. V.* **a)** order **(bei** from); **sich** *(Dat.)* **etw. ~:** order sth. [for oneself]; **würden Sie mir bitte ein Taxi ~?** would you order me a taxi?; **b)** *(reservieren lassen)* reserve ⟨*table, tickets*⟩; **c)** *(kommen lassen)* **jmdn. [für 10 Uhr] zu sich ~:** ask sb. to go/come to see one [at 10 o'clock]; **jmdn. in ein Café ~:** ask sb. to meet one in a café; **beim**

od. **zum Arzt bestellt sein** have an appointment with the doctor; **dastehen wie bestellt und nicht abgeholt** *(ugs. scherzh.)* stand there like a little boy/girl lost; **d)** *(ausrichten)* **jmdm. etw. ~:** pass on sth. to sb.; tell sb. sth.; **bestell deinem Mann schöne Grüße von mir** give your husband my regards; **würden Sie Ihrer Kollegin etwas von mir ~?** would you give your colleague a message from me?; **er läßt dir ~, daß ...:** he left a message [for you] that ...; **nichts/nicht viel zu ~ haben** have no say/little *or* not much say; **e)** *(ernennen)* appoint **(zu, als** as); **f)** *(bearbeiten)* cultivate, till ‹*field*›; keep, look after ‹*garden*›; **g) es ist um jmdn./etw.** *od.* **mit jmdm./etw. schlecht bestellt** sb./sth. is in a bad way; **mit seiner Gesundheit ist es schlecht bestellt** he is in poor health. **2.** *itr. V.* order

Bestẹller der; ~s, ~: customer *(who has ordered sth.)*

Bestẹlliste die check-list *(of goods for ordering)*

Bestẹll-: ~nummer die order number; **~schein der** order form

Bestẹllung die a) order **(über, auf + *Akk.*** for); *(das Bestellen)* ordering *no indef. art.*; **bei ~ von/bei ~en über mehr als 1 000 Stück** if more than 1,000 are ordered/for orders of more than 1,000; **auf ~:** to order; *(im Lokal)* **eine ~ aufgeben** give one's order; **jmds. ~/die ~en aufnehmen** take sb.'s/the orders; **b)** *(Reservierung)* reservation; **c)** *(Nachricht)* **eine ~ übermitteln** *od.* **ausrichten** pass on a message; **d)** *(das Ernennen)* appointment; *(Wahl)* selection; **e)** *(das Bearbeiten)* cultivation; tilling; **~ des Gartens** gardening; work on the garden

Bestẹll·zettel der order-form

bẹsten·falls *Adv.* at best

Bẹsten·liste die *(Sport)* list of top athletes/sportsmen

bẹstens *Adv.* **a)** excellently; extremely well; **sich ~ verstehen** get on splendidly; **sich ~ unterhalten** have a splendid time; **b)** *(vielmals)* **jmdn. ~ grüßen** give sb. one's best wishes; **wir danken Ihnen/bedanken uns ~:** we thank you very much

besteuern *tr. V.* tax; **besteuert sein** be subject to tax; **höher besteuert werden** be more heavily taxed; **etw. höher ~:** increase the tax on sth.

Besteuerung die taxation; **bei einer ~ des Einkommens von 45 %** where income is taxed at [a rate of] 45 %

bẹst-, Bẹst-: ~form die; *o. Pl. (Sport)* best form; **in ~form** in top form; **~gehaßt** *Adj.; nicht präd. (ugs. iron.)* most heartily disliked; **~gekleidet** *Adj.; nicht präd.* best-dressed

bestialisch [bɛs'ti̯a:lɪʃ] **1.** *Adj.* **a)** *(abwertend)* bestial; **b)** *nicht präd. (ugs.: schrecklich)* ghastly *(coll.)*; awful *(coll.)*. **2.** *adv.* **a)** *(abwertend)* in a bestial manner; **~ schreien** scream like a wild beast; **b)** *(ugs.: schrecklich)* awfully *(coll.)*; unbearably; **~ kalt** beastly cold

Bestialität [bɛsti̯ali'tɛ:t] **die; ~, ~en a)** *o. Pl.* bestiality; **ein Verbrechen von solcher ~:** a crime of such a bestial nature *or* of such brutality; **b)** *(Tat)* brutality; atrocity

Bestiarium [bɛs'ti̯a:ri̯ʊm] **das; ~s, Bestiarien** bestiary

bestịcken *tr. V.* embroider; **ein mit Perlen besticktes Kleid** a dress sewn with pearls

Bestie ['bɛsti̯ə] **die; ~, ~n** *(auch fig. abwertend)* beast

bestịmmbar *Adj.* ascertainable; *(identifizierbar)* identifiable; **nicht [genau] ~ sein** be impossible to ascertain/identify [precisely]

bestịmmen 1. *tr. V.* **a)** *(festsetzen)* decide on; fix ‹*price, time, etc.*›; **das Gesetz bestimmt, daß ...:** the law provides that ...; **nichts zu ~ haben** have no say; **jmdn. zum** *od.* **als Nachfolger ~:** decide on sb. as one's successor; *(nennen)* name sb. as one's successor; **b)** *(vorsehen)* destine; intend; set aside ‹*money*›; **das ist für dich bestimmt** that is meant for you; **er ist zu Höherem bestimmt** he is destined for higher things; **füreinander bestimmt sein** be meant for each other; **c)** *(ermitteln, definieren)* identify ‹*part of speech, find, plant, etc.*›; determine ‹*age, position*›; define ‹*meaning*›; **d)** *(prägen)* determine the character of; give ‹*landscape, townscape*› its character; **unser Leben ~:** play a dominant *or* decisive role in our lives; **e)** *(veranlassen)* **jmdn. zum Nachgeben/Bleiben ~:** induce sb. to give in /stay; **sich von jmdm. zu etw. ~ lassen** allow sb. to talk one into sth. **2.** *itr. V.* **a)** make the decisions; **hier bestimme ich** I'm in charge *or* the boss here; my word goes around here; **b)** *(verfügen)* **über jmdn. ~:** tell sb. what to do; **[frei] über etw.** *(Akk.)* **~:** do as one wishes with sth.

bestịmmend 1. *Adj.* decisive; determining. **2.** *adv.* decisively

bestịmmt 1. *Adj.* **a)** *nicht präd. (speziell)* particular; *(gewiß)* certain; *(genau)* definite; **soll es ein ~es Buch sein?** have you a particular book in mind?; **es sind immer ganz ~e Leute, die so was tun** it is always a particular type of person who does something like that; **ich habe schon eine ~e Vorstellung davon, wie ...:** I already have a clear *or* definite idea of how ...; **ich kann noch nichts Bestimmtes sagen** I can say nothing definite *or* I cannot say anything definite yet; **ich habe nichts Bestimmtes vor** I am not doing anything in particular; **b)** *(festgelegt)* fixed; given ‹*quantity*›; **c)** *(Sprachw.)* definite ‹*article etc.*›; **d)** *(entschieden)* firm; **in sehr ~em Ton** very firmly; in a very firm voice; **~es Auftreten** resolute manner. **2.** *adv.* **a)** *(deutlich)* clearly; *(genau)* precisely; **b)** *(entschieden)* firmly; **sich ~ gegen etw. aussprechen** express one's firm opposition to sth. **3.** *Adv.* for certain; **du weißt es doch [ganz] ~ noch** I'm sure you must remember it; **ganz ~, ich komme** I'll definitely come; yes, certainly, I'll come; **Vergiß sie nicht wieder. – Nein, ~ nicht** Don't forget them again – Don't worry, I won't; **sie wird das ~ schaffen** she is certain *or* bound to manage it; **er hat es ~ vergessen** he is bound to have forgotten; **ich habe das ~ liegengelassen** I must have left it behind; **das ist ~ nicht richtig** that can't be right

Bestịmmtheit die; ~ a) firmness; *(im Auftreten)* decisiveness; **etw. mit aller ~ sagen/ablehnen** say sth. very firmly/reject sth. categorically; **b)** *(Gewißheit)* **mit ~:** for certain

Bestịmmung die a) *o. Pl. (das Festsetzen)* fixing; **b)** *(Vorschrift)* regulation; **gesetzliche ~en** legal requirements; **c)** *o. Pl. (Zweck)* purpose; **eine Brücke** *usw.* **ihrer ~ übergeben** [officially] open a bridge *etc.*; **d)** *(das Ermitteln)* identification; *(eines Begriffs)* definition; *(des Alters, der Position)* determination; *(der Bedeutung)* definition; **~ der Satzteile** distinguishing the parts of a sentence; parsing; **e)** *(Sprachw.)* modifier; **adverbiale ~:** adverbial qualification; **f)** *o. Pl. (Schicksal)* **das ist ~:** that is destiny *or* fate; **göttliche ~:** Divine Providence; **es war höhere ~, daß wir uns begegneten** it was ordained [by fate] that we should meet; **g)** *(veralt.: Bestimmungsort)* destination

bestịmmungs-, Bestịmmungs-: ~bahnhof der *(Eisenb.)* destination; **~gemäß** *Adv.* in accordance with the regulations *or* requirements [of the law]; **~hafen der** [port of] destination; **~ort der;** *Pl.* **~orte** destination; **~wort das;** *Pl.* **~wörter** *(Sprachw.)* qualifying element *(of a compound)*; modifier

bẹst-, Bẹst-: ~leistung die best performance; *(absolute ~leistung)* record; **persönliche ~leistung** personal best; **~mann der;** *Pl.* **~männer** *(Seew.)* mate *(of a coaster)*; **~marke die** *(Sport)* record; **~möglich 1.** *Adj.* best possible; **das Bestmögliche tun/getan haben** do the best one can/have done the best one could; **2.** *adv.* as well as possible *or* as one possibly can

Best.-Nr. *Abk.* **Bestellnummer** order no.

bestochen [bə'ʃtɔxn̩] *2. Part. v.* **bestechen**

bestrafen *tr. V.* punish **(für, wegen** for); **es wird mit Gefängnis bestraft** it is punishable by imprisonment

Bestrafung die; ~, ~en punishment; *(Rechtsw.)* penalty; *(Geldstrafe)* fine

bestrahlen *tr. V.* **a)** *(beleuchten)* illuminate; floodlight ‹*building*›; *(scheinen auf)* ‹*sun etc.*› shine on; *(erhellen)* light up; **b)** *(Med.)* treat ‹*tumour, part of body*› using radiotherapy; *(mit Höhensonne)* use sunray *or* sun-lamp treatment on ‹*part of body*›

Bestrahlung die; ~, ~en a) *(Med.)* radiation [treatment] *no indef. art.*; *(bes. mit Röntgenstrahlen)* radiotherapy *no art.*; *(mit Höhensonne)* sun-ray *or* sun-lamp treatment; **b)** *(das Beleuchten)* illumination; *(eines Gebäudes)* floodlighting; *(der Bühne)* lighting; **eine intensive ~ durch die Sonne** concentrated exposure to the sun's rays

Bestrahlungs·lampe die radiation lamp; *(Höhensonne)* sun[-ray] lamp

Bestreben das endeavour[s *pl.*]; **in seinem** *od.* **im ~, keine Schwächen zu zeigen** in his efforts *or* endeavours to show no weakness

bestrebt *Adj.* **~/sehr ~ sein, etw. zu tun** endeavour/take great pains *or* go to great trouble to do sth.

Bestrebung die; ~, ~en effort; *(Versuch)* attempt

bestreichen *unr. tr. V.* **A mit B ~:** spread B on A; **sein Brot mit Butter ~:** spread butter on one's bread; butter one's bread; **den Braten/das Hähnchen mit Öl** *usw.* **~:** baste the roast/chicken with oil *etc.*; **die Plätzchen mit Eigelb ~:** brush *or* coat the biscuits *(Brit.)* *or (Amer.)* cookies with egg yolk

bestreiken *tr. V.* take strike action against; **diese Firma wird bestreikt** there is a strike [on] at this firm

bestreitbar *Adj.* disputable; questionable, dubious ‹*argument*›; **es ist nicht ~[, daß ...]:** it is indisputable *or* cannot be denied [that ...]

bestreiten *unr. tr. V.* **a)** dispute; contest; *(leugnen)* deny; **er bestreitet, daß ...:** he denies that ...; **es läßt sich nicht/wohl kaum ~, daß ...:** it cannot/can hardly be denied that ...; there is no disputing/it can hardly be disputed that ...; **jmdm. ein Recht auf etw.** *(Akk.)* **~:** dispute *or* challenge sb.'s right to sth.; **b)** *(finanzieren)* finance ‹*studies*›; pay for ‹*studies, sb.'s keep, etc.*›; meet ‹*costs, expenses*›; **c)** *(gestalten)* carry ‹*programme, conversation, etc.*›; **d)** *(Sport)* take part in ‹*game*›

Bestreitung die; ~ a) financing; **b) eine ~ seiner Aussage liegt mir fern** I have no intention of disputing *or* challenging his statement

bestreuen *tr. V.* **etw. mit Zucker ~:** sprinkle sth. with sugar; **einen Weg mit Sand/Salz ~:** scatter sand on a path/salt a path

bestricken *tr. V.* **a)** ensnare; captivate; **b)** *(für andere stricken)* knit things for

bestrumpft [bə'ʃtrʊmpft] *Adj.* stockinged; **lila ~:** in mauve stockings

Bestseller ['bɛstzɛlɐ] **der; ~s, ~:** best seller

Bẹstseller-: ~autor der best-selling author; **~liste die** best-seller list

bestücken *tr. V.* fit; equip; *(mit Waffen)* arm; *(mit Waren)* stock [up]

Bestückung die; ~, ~en equipment; *(mit Waffen)* armament; *(mit Waren)* stocking; **eine ordnungsgemäße ~ des Lagers garantieren** ensure that the correct stock level is maintained at the warehouse

bestuhlen [bə'ʃtu:lən] *tr. V.* provide with seats

Bestuhlung die; ~, ~en a) fitting of [the] seats (*Gen.* in); **b)** *(Stühle)* seating

bestürmen *tr. V.* **a)** storm; *(Fußball)* besiege ⟨*goal*⟩; **b)** *(bedrängen)* besiege **(mit** with)

Bestürmung die storming; *(Angriff)* assault

bestürzen *tr. V.* dismay; *(erschüttern)* shake; *(erschrecken)* alarm; **es hat ihn sehr bestürzt zu hören, daß ...:** he was deeply dismayed to hear that ...

bestürzend *Adj.* disturbing; *(erschreckend)* alarming

bestürzt 1. *Adj.* dismayed **(über** + *Akk.* about); *(erschrocken)* alarmed **(über** + *Akk.* about); **sie machte ein [sehr] ~es Gesicht** her face fell [a mile *(coll.)*]; she looked [deeply] dismayed. **2.** *adv.* with dismay *or* consternation; **jmdn. [ganz** *od.* **sehr] ~ ansehen** look at sb. in *or* with [great] consternation

Bestürzung die; ~: dismay; consternation, **mit ~ feststellen, daß ...:** find to one's consternation that ...

bestußt [bə'ʃtʊst] *Adj. (salopp)* barmy *(Brit. sl.)*; loopy *(sl.)*

Best-: ~wert der; *meist Pl.* optimum result; *(Bestleistung)* maximum performance figure; *(beim Wettbewerb)* maximum mark; **~zeit die** *(Sport)* best time; **[persönliche] ~zeit** personal best [time]; **~zeit laufen/schwimmen** run/swim a best time/one's personal best *or* one's best time

Besuch [bə'zu:x] **der; ~[e]s, ~e a)** visit; **ein ~ bei jmdm.** a visit to sb.; *(kurz)* a call on sb.; **~ eines Museums** *usw.* visit to a museum *etc.*; **bei seinem letzten ~:** on his last visit; **wir erwarten den ~ alter Freunde** we are expecting a visit from some old friends; **~ von jmdm. bekommen** receive a visit from sb.; **auf** *od.* **zu ~ kommen** come for a visit; *(auf länger)* come to stay; **er ist bei uns auf ~:** he is staying with us; **jmdm. einen ~ abstatten** pay sb. a visit; **b)** *(das Besuchen)* visiting; *(Teilnahme)* attendance; **der ~ der Schule/Vorlesungen/Gottesdienste** attendance at school/lectures/services; **die Konzerte erfreuen sich eines regen ~s** the concerts are well attended; **c)** *(Gast)* visitor; *(Gäste)* visitors *pl.*; **~ bekommen/erwarten** have/expect visitors/a visitor; **ich bekomme gleich ~:** I've got visitors/a visitor coming any minute

-besuch der: Deutschland~/England~/USA-Besuch visit to Germany/England/the USA; **Messe~:** visit to the/a fair

besuchen *tr. V.* **a)** visit ⟨*person*⟩; *(weniger formell)* go to see ⟨*person*⟩; **gestern hat mich ein alter Bekannter besucht** yesterday an old friend came to see me *or* called on me; **b)** visit ⟨*place*⟩; go to ⟨*exhibition, theatre, museum, etc.*⟩; *(zur Besichtigung)* go to see ⟨*church, exhibition, etc.*⟩; **die Schule/Universität ~:** go to *or (formal)* attend school/university; **hast du diese Ausstellung schon besucht?** have you been to [see] this exhibition yet?; **er hat sämtliche Lokale der Umgebung besucht** he patronized all the pubs *(Brit. coll.) or (Amer.)* bars in the neighbourhood; *s. auch* **besucht**

Besucher der visitor; **~ eines Museums** *usw.* visitor to a museum *etc.*; **die ~ des Theaters** the theatre audience; the theatregoers; **er ist ständiger ~ der Oper/von Konzerten** he is a regular opera-goer/concertgoer; **alle ~ des Kurses/der Vorstellung/des Vortrags** all those attending the course/performance/lecture

-besucher der: Berlin~: visitor to Berlin; **Messe~:** visitor to the/a fair

Besucherin die; ~, ~nen *s.* **Besucher**

Besucher-: ~strom der stream of visitors; **~zahl die** number of visitors

Besuchs-: ~erlaubnis die visiting permit; **~ritze die** *(ugs. scherzh.)* join between the [twin] beds; **~tag der** visiting day; **~zeit die** visiting time *or* hours *pl.*; **es ist keine ~zeit** it is not visiting time

besucht *Adj.* **gut/schlecht ~:** well/poorly attended ⟨*lecture, performance, etc.*⟩; much/little frequented ⟨*restaurant etc.*⟩

besudeln *tr. V. (geh. abwertend)* besmirch; **jmds. Andenken/Namen ~** *(fig.)* cast a slur on sb.'s memory/name

Beta ['be:ta] **das; ~[s], ~s** beta

Beta·blocker [-blɔkɐ] **der; ~s, ~** *(Med.)* betablocker

betagt [bə'ta:kt] *Adj. (geh.)* elderly; *(scherzh.)* ancient ⟨*car etc.*⟩; **noch als ~er Mann** even in his old age

Betagtheit die; ~ *(geh.)* old age

betanken *tr. V.* refuel

betasten *tr. V.* feel [with one's fingers]

Beta-: ~strahlen *Pl. (Physik)* beta rays; **~teilchen das** *(Physik)* beta particle

betätigen 1. *refl. V.* busy *or* occupy oneself; **sich politisch/literarisch/körperlich ~:** engage in political/literary/physical activity; **sich als etw. ~:** act as sth.; **wenn du dich ~ willst, kannst du mir beim Spülen helfen** if you want to do something [useful], you can help me with the washing-up. **2.** *tr. V.* operate ⟨*lever, switch, flush, etc.*⟩; press ⟨*button*⟩; apply ⟨*brake*⟩

Betätigung die; ~, ~en a) activity; **ich werde schon eine ~ für dich finden** I'll find you something to do; **b)** *o. Pl. (das Bedienen)* operation; *(einer Bremse)* application; *(eines Knopfes)* pressing

Betätigungs-: ~drang der [compulsive] urge to be up and doing [something]; **~feld das** sphere of activity

betatschen *tr. V. (salopp abwertend)* finger; *(sexuell)* paw *(coll.)*

betäuben [bə'tɔybn̩] *tr. V.* **a)** *(Med.)* anaesthetize; make numb, deaden ⟨*nerve*⟩; **einen Patienten örtlich ~:** give a patient a local anaesthetic; **b)** *(unterdrücken)* ease, deaden ⟨*pain*⟩; quell, still ⟨*unease, fear*⟩; **seinen Kummer mit Alkohol ~** *(fig.)* drown one's sorrows [in drink]; **c)** *(benommen machen)* daze; *(mit einem Schlag)* stun; **ein ~der Duft** a heady *or* intoxicating scent; **ein ~der Lärm** a deafening noise

Betäubung die; ~, ~en a) *(Med.)* anaesthetization; *(Narkose)* anaesthesia; **eine örtliche ~ vornehmen** administer a local anaesthetic; **zur ~ der Schmerzen** to deaden the pain; **b)** *(Benommenheit)* daze

Betäubungs·mittel das narcotic; *(Med.)* anaesthetic

Betäubungsmittel·gesetz das narcotics law *(regulating the use of cocaine, morphine, cannabis, etc.)*

betaut [bə'taut] *Adj. (geh.)* covered in dew *postpos.*; bedewed *(literary)*

Bet·bruder ['be:t-] **der** *(abwertend)* overpions type *(coll.)*

Bete ['be:tə] **die; ~, ~n** *in* **rote ~:** beetroot *(Brit.)*; [red] beet *(Amer.)*

beteilen *tr. V. (österr.)* provide **(mit** with)

beteiligen 1. *refl. V.* **sich an etw.** *(Dat.)* **~:** participate *or* take part in sth.; **er hat sich kaum an der Diskussion beteiligt** he took hardly any part in the discussion; **sich an einem Geschäft ~:** take a share in *or* come in on a deal; **sich an etw. mit einer Million ~:** contribute a million to sth. **2.** *tr. V.* **jmdn. [mit 10%] an etw.** *(Dat.)* **~:** give sb. a [10%] share of sth.

beteiligt *Adj.* **a)** involved **(an** + *Dat.* in); **b)** *(finanziell)* **an einem Unternehmen/am Gewinn ~ sein** have a share in a business/in the profit; **er ist mit 20000 DM ~:** he has a 20,000 mark share

Beteiligte der/die; *adj. Dekl.* person involved **(an** + *Dat.* in); *(an einem Spiel, einer Sitzung usw.)* participant **(an** + *Dat.* in); **die [meisten] an dem Unfall/der Affäre ~n** [most of] those involved in the accident/affair

Beteiligung die; ~, ~en a) *(Teilnahme)* participation **(an** + *Dat.* in); *(Zahl der Beteiligten)* number of participants **(an** + *Dat.* in); *(an einem Verbrechen)* involvement **(an** + *Dat.* in); **unter ~ von** with the participation of; **b)** *(Anteil)* share **(an** + *Dat.* in); **eine ~ am Gewinn/Umsatz** a share in the profits/turnover

Betel ['be:tl̩] **der; ~s** betel

Betel·nuß die betel-nut

beten ['be:tn̩] **1.** *itr. V.* pray **(für, um** for); **zu Gott ~, daß etw. geschehen möge** pray to God that sth. should happen; **es wird gebetet** prayers are said. **2.** *tr. V.* say ⟨*prayer*⟩

Beter der; ~s, ~, Beterin die; ~, ~nen prayer (= *one who prays*)

beteuern [bə'tɔyɐn] *tr. V.* affirm; assert, protest ⟨*one's innocence*⟩; **jmdm. seine Liebe ~:** avow one's love to sb.; **sie beteuerte, daß sie mit dieser Sache nichts zu tun habe** she protested that she had nothing to do with this business

Beteuerung die; ~, ~en *s.* **beteuern:** affirmation; assertion; protestation

Bet·haus das synagogue

betiteln [bə'ti:tl̩n] *tr. V.* **a)** *(ugs. abwertend)* **jmdn. [mit] X/mit einem Schimpfnamen ~:** call sb. X/a rude name; **b)** *(mit Titel anreden)* **jmdn. [mit] Doktor/Professor ~:** address sb. as *or* call sb. 'Doctor'/'Professor'; **c)** *(mit Titel versehen)* give ⟨*book etc.*⟩ a title

Beton [be'tɔŋ, *bes. österr.:* be'to:n] **der; ~s, ~s** [-ɔŋs] *od.* **~e** [-o:nə] concrete

Beton-: ~bau der; *Pl.* **~bauten a)** concrete building; **b)** *o. Pl. (Bauweise)* concrete construction *no art.*; **~bunker der a)** concrete bunker; *(Luftschutzbunker)* concrete shelter; **b)** *(abwertend: ~bau)* concrete box

betonen [bə'to:nən] *tr. V.* **a)** stress ⟨*word, syllable*⟩; accent ⟨*syllable, beat*⟩; **ein Wort falsch ~:** put the wrong stress on a word; **b)** *(hervorheben)* emphasize; **ich möchte ~, daß ...:** I should like to emphasize *or* stress that ...; **warum betont er seine Herkunft so?** why does he lay such stress on his origins?; **die Taille ~:** accentuate the waist

betonieren [beto'ni:rən] *tr. V.* **a)** concrete; surface ⟨*road etc.*⟩ with concrete; lay a concrete floor in ⟨*cellar etc.*⟩; **frisch betonierte Fläche** recently laid concrete; **b)** *(festlegen)* harden ⟨*attitude*⟩; reinforce ⟨*prejudice*⟩

Betonierung die; ~, ~en a) concreting; **b)** *(Betondecke)* concrete surface

Beton-: ~klotz der a) concrete block; **b)** *(abwertend: massiver ~bau)* concrete monolith; **~kopf der** *(abwertend)* hardliner; **~mischer der, ~misch·maschine die** concrete-mixer

betont [bə'to:nt] **1.** *Adj.* **a)** stressed; accented; **b)** *(bewußt)* pointed, studied; deliberate, studied ⟨*simplicity, elegance*⟩. **2.** *adv.* pointedly; deliberately; **sich ~ sportlich kleiden** wear clothes with a strong *or* pronounced sporting character; **sich ~ zurückhaltend verhalten** behave with studied reserve

Beton·träger der concrete beam

Betonung die; ~, ~en a) stressing; accenting; **b)** *(Akzent)* stress; accent *(esp. Mus.)*; *(Intonation)* intonation; **c)** *(das Hervorheben)* emphasis (*Gen.* on); *(von Formen, Farben)* accentuation; **ein Lernprogramm mit ~ des Musisch-Kreativen** a syllabus with the emphasis on artistic creativity

Betonungs·zeichen das stress-mark

Beton·wüste die *(ugs. abwertend)* concrete desert

betören [bə'tø:rən] *tr. V. (geh.)* **a)** captivate; bewitch; **b)** *(verblenden)* beguile, entice ⟨*purchaser, consumer*⟩

Betörung die; ~, ~en *(geh.)* captivation; bewitching

betr. *Abk.* **betreffs, betrifft** re

Betr. *Abk.* **Betreff** re

Betracht [bəˈtraxt] *in* **jmdn./etw. in ~ ziehen** consider sb./sth.; **jmdn./etw. außer ~ lassen** discount *or* disregard sb./sth.; **eine Frage außer ~ lassen** pass over a question; *(zeitweilig)* leave a question on one side; **er/sie kommt/kommt nicht in ~:** he/she can/cannot be considered; **das kommt nicht in ~:** that is not worth considering; that is out of the question; **außer ~ bleiben** be passed over; *(zeitweilig)* be left on one side

betrachten *tr. V.* **a)** look at; *(bei einer Tätigkeit)* watch; observe; *(fig.: studieren)* observe, study ⟨*history, development, etc.*⟩; **sich** *(Dat.)* **etw. [genau] ~:** take a [close] look at sth.; watch *or* observe sth. [closely]; **sich im Spiegel ~:** look at oneself in the mirror; *(längere Zeit)* contemplate oneself in the mirror; **jmdn. von oben bis unten ~:** look sb. up and down; **genau/bei Licht betrachtet** *(fig.)* upon closer consideration/seen in the light of day; **b)** *(für etw. halten)* **jmdn./etw. als ... ~:** regard sb./sth. as ...; **sich als jmds. Freund ~:** regard oneself as *or* consider oneself sb.'s friend; **c)** *(beurteilen)* consider; view; **objektiv betrachtet** viewed objectively; from an objective point of view; **so betrachtet** seen in this light *or* from this point of view

Betrachter der; ~s, ~: observer

beträchtlich [bəˈtrɛçtlɪç] **1.** *Adj.* considerable; **um ein ~es** to a considerable degree. **2.** *adv.* considerably

Betrachtung die; ~, ~en a) *o. Pl.* contemplation; *(Untersuchung)* examination; **bei genauer[er] ~:** upon close[r] examination; *(fig.)* upon close[r] consideration; **bei nachträglicher ~:** [viewed] in retrospect; **b)** *(Überlegung)* observation; **~en über etw.** *(Akk.)* **anstellen** make observations *or* comments about sth.

Betrachtungs·weise die way of looking at things; *(Standpunkt)* point of view

Betrag [beˈtraːk] **der; ~[e]s, Beträge** [bəˈtrɛːgə] sum; amount; **ein Scheck über einen ~ von 1000 DM** a cheque for 1,000 marks; **~ dankend erhalten** *(auf Quittungen)* received *or* paid with thanks

betragen 1. *unr. itr. V.* be; *(bei Geldsummen)* come to; amount to; **die Zeitdifferenz beträgt 3 Stunden** the time difference is three hours. **2.** *unr. refl. V.* behave **(gegenüber, gegen** towards)

Betragen das; ~s behaviour; *(in der Schule)* conduct; **in ~ eine gute Note bekommen** get a good mark for conduct

Betragens·note die mark for conduct

betrauen *tr. V.* **jmdn. mit etw. ~:** entrust sb. with sth.; **jmdn. damit ~, etw. zu tun** entrust sb. with the task of doing sth.

betrauern *tr. V.* mourn ⟨*death, loss*⟩; **jmdn. ~:** mourn for sb.

beträufeln *tr. V.* sprinkle **(mit** with drops of)

Betrauung die; ~: entrusting

Betreff [bəˈtrɛf] **der; ~[e]s, ~e** *(Amtsspr., Kaufmannsspr.)* subject; matter; *(~zeile)* heading; reference line; **den ~ angeben** state the subject [of the letter]; *(im Brief)* **~: Ihr Schreiben vom 26. d. M.** re: your letter of the 26th inst.

betreffen *unr. tr. V.* **a)** concern; ⟨*new rule, change, etc.*⟩ affect; **was mich betrifft, ...:** as far as I'm concerned ...; **was mich betrifft, bin ich** *od.* **ich bin einverstanden** for my part I am in agreement; **was das betrifft, ...:** as regards that; as far as that goes; **b)** *(geh.: widerfahren)* befall; **c)** *(geh. veralt.: bestürzt machen)* hurt; **es hat mich schmerzhaft betroffen zu hören, daß ...:** it saddened me to hear that ...; **d)** *(geh. veralt.: ertappen)* apprehend

betreffend *Adj.* concerning; **der ~e Sachbearbeiter** the person concerned with *or* dealing with this matter; **in dem ~en Fall** in the case concerned *or* in question

Betreffende der/die; *adj. Dekl.* person concerned; **die ~n** the people concerned

betreffs *Präp. mit Gen. (Amtsspr., Kaufmannsspr.)* concerning

betreiben *unr. tr. V.* **a)** tackle ⟨*task*⟩; proceed with, *(energisch)* press ahead with ⟨*task, case, etc.*⟩; pursue ⟨*policy, studies*⟩; carry on ⟨*trade*⟩; **auf jmds./sein Betreiben** *(Akk.)* **[hin]** at the instigation of sb./at his instigation; **das Tischlerhandwerk ~:** ply the carpenter's trade; **b)** *(führen)* run ⟨*business, shop*⟩; **Radsport ~:** go in for cycling as a sport; **c)** *(antreiben)* drive **(mit** by); **etw. elektrisch ~:** drive sth. by electricity *or* electrically; **ein atomar/mit Dampf betriebenes Schiff** a nuclear-powered/steam-powered ship; **d)** *(schweiz.: Rechtsw.)* sue *(for payment of a debt)*

Betreibung die; ~, ~en: die ~ eines Geschäfts/einer Anlage running a business/driving a plant

betreßt [bəˈtrɛst] *Adj.* braided

[1]**betreten** *unr. tr. V. (hineintreten in)* enter; *(treten auf)* walk *or* step on to; *(begehen)* walk on ⟨*carpet, grass, etc.*⟩; **er hat das Haus nicht mehr** *od.* **nie wieder ~:** he never set foot in the house again; **„Betreten verboten"** 'Keep off'; *(kein Eintritt)* 'Keep out'; **„Betreten der Baustelle verboten"** 'Building site. No entry *or* Keep out'; **den Rasen nicht ~:** keep off the grass; *s. auch* **Neuland**

[2]**betreten 1.** *Adj.* embarrassed; **ein ~es Gesicht machen** look embarrassed. **2.** *adv.* with embarrassment; **man schwieg ~:** there was an embarrassed silence

Betretenheit die; ~: embarrassment

betreuen [bəˈtrɔyən] *tr. V.* look after; care for ⟨*invalid*⟩; supervise ⟨*youth group*⟩; see to the needs of ⟨*tourists, sportsmen*⟩; look after, be in charge of ⟨*department etc.*⟩

Betreuer der; ~s, ~ *(für Alte, Kranke, Behinderte)* social worker; *(für Kinder)* minder; *(für Entlassene aus Krankenhaus/Gefängnis)* after-care worker; *(für Sportler, Künstler)* manager; *(für Touristen)* courier; travel guide; *(einer Delegation)* secretary

Betreuerin die; ~, ~nen a) *(Kinder~)* child-minder; *(ganztägig)* nanny *(Brit.)*; nursemaid *(Amer.)*; *(Krankenpflegerin)* nurse; **b)** *s.* **Betreuer**

Betreuung die; ~ a) care *no indef. art.*; **die ~ der Gäste** taking care of the guests; **jmdn. zur ~ des Großvaters einstellen** take on sb. to look after *or* care for grandfather; **zwei Reiseleiter waren zu unserer ~ vorhanden** there were two couriers *or* travel guides to see to our needs; **b)** *(Person)* minder; *(Krankenpfleger)* nurse

Betrieb der; ~[e]s, ~e a) business; *(Firma)* firm; **ein staatlicher ~:** a state-owned *or* nationalized concern; **ein landwirtschaftlicher ~:** an agricultural holding; **im ~ sein/bleiben/essen** be/stay/eat at work; *s. auch* **volkseigen; b)** *o. Pl. (das In-Funktion-Sein)* operation; *(Arbeitsprozeß)* working process; operations *pl., no art.*; **in ~ sein** be running; be in operation; **außer ~ sein** be out of order; **in/außer ~ setzen** start up/stop ⟨*machine etc.*⟩; *(ein-/ausschalten)* switch on/off; **in ~ nehmen** put into operation; put ⟨*bus, train*⟩ into service; **ein Kraftwerk wird in ~ genommen** a power-plant is commissioned; **den ~ einstellen** close down *or* cease operations; *(in einer Fabrik)* stop work; *(einer Buslinie o. ä.)* withdraw the service; **den [ganzen] ~ aufhalten** *(ugs.)* hold everybody up; **c)** *o. Pl. (ugs.: Treiben)* bustle; commotion; *(Verkehr)* traffic; **es herrscht großer ~, es ist viel ~:** it's very busy; **bei dem ~ kann man nicht arbeiten** one cannot work with all that [commotion] going on

betrieblich *Adj.; nicht präd.* firm's; company; *(inner~)* internal; within the company *postpos.*; **aus ~en Gründen** for reasons to do with the state of the company

betriebsam 1. *Adj.* busy; *(ständig ~)* constantly on the go *postpos.*; **~e Naturen** hyperactive types; eager beavers *(coll.)*; *(Frauen)* busy bees *(coll.)*. **2.** *adv.* busily

Betriebsamkeit die; ~: [bustling] activity; **eine hektische ~ an den Tag legen** become frantically busy

betriebs-, Betriebs-: ~angehörige der/die employee; *Pl.* company staff; **~an·leitung die, ~an·weisung die** operating instructions *pl.*; *(Heft)* instruction manual; **~arzt der** company doctor; **~aus·flug der** staff outing; **~begehung die** *(DDR)* factory *etc.* inspection tour; **~bereit** *Adj.* ready to be put into operation *postpos.*; **~bereit sein** be operational; **~besichtigung die** visit to a firm; *(Fabrikbesichtigung)* factory visit; *(eines landwirtschaftlichen Betriebs)* farm visit; **~blind** *Adj.* inured to the shortcomings of working methods *postpos.*; professionally blinkered; **~blind werden** get into a rut *or* become blinkered in one's work; **~blindheit die** blinkered attitude to one's work; **~eigen** *Adj.* company-owned; *(DDR)* for employees *postpos.*; company ⟨*flat, sports ground*⟩; **~erlaubnis die** operating permit; **~ferien** *Pl.* firm's annual close-down *sing.*; **das Geschäft hat ~ferien** the shop is closed for its annual holidays; **„Wegen ~ferien geschlossen"** 'closed for annual holidays'; **~ferien·lager das** *(DDR)* holiday camp for employees' children and apprentices; **~fertig** *Adj.*: *s.* **~bereit; ~fest das** firm's party; **~fremd** *Adj.* who are not company employees *postpos., not pred.*; outside; **„Zutritt Betriebsfremden nicht gestattet"** 'Staff Only'; **~frieden der** harmonious relationship between employer and employed *(which all parties are obliged to uphold)*; industrial peace; **~führer der** *s.* **~leiter; ~führung die** *s.* **~leitung; ~geheimnis das** company secret; trade secret *(also fig.)*; **das ~geheimnis verletzen** infringe the confidentiality of company matters; **~gewerkschafts·leitung die** *(DDR)* trade union committee *(of an enterprise)*; **~gruppe die** trade union membership *(within one company)*; **~intern 1.** *Adj.* internal; internal company *attrib.*; **2.** *adv.* internally; within the company; **~kampfgruppe die** *(DDR veralt.)* [reservist] workers' militia *(within an enterprise)*; **~kapital das a)** working capital; **b)** *(Anfangskapital)* initial capital; **~kinder·garten der** play school for employees' children; **~klima das** working atmosphere; **~kosten** *Pl.* running costs; *(einer Firma)* operating costs; **~kranken·kasse die** company sickness insurance scheme; **~leiter der** manager; *(einer Fabrik)* works manager; **~leitung die** management [of the firm]; **~nudel die** *(ugs.)* **a)** live wire in the office; *(Komiker)* office comedian; **b)** *(übergeschäftige Person)* eager beaver *(coll.)*; *(Frau)* busy bee *(coll.)*; **~obmann der** workers' representative *(in a small firm)*; **~prüfung die** audit of a/the firm's accounts *(by the taxation authorities)*; **~rat der;** *Pl.*: **~räte a)** works committee; **b)** *(Person)* member of a/the works committee; **~rats·mitglied das** member of a/the works committee; **~rats·vorsitzende der/die** chairman of a/the works committee; **~rente die** company pension; **~ruhe die: ~ruhe haben** ⟨*business, factory*⟩ be closed; **~schließung die** closure [of a/the firm]; **~schluß der** *(im Geschäft)* end of business hours; *(in der Fabrik)* end of working hours; **kurz vor ~schluß** shortly before it was time to go home *or (coll.)* knocking-off time; **nach ~schluß geht er gleich nach**

Hause after work he goes straight home; **~sicher** *Adj.* [operationally] safe; **~sicher sein** be safe to operate *or* run; **~sicherheit die** [operational] safety; *(in der Fabrik)* safety at work; **~stillegung die** closure [of a/the firm]; *(eines Werks)* works closure; **~störung die** malfunction; **~treue die** loyalty to a/the company; **10jährige ~treue** 10 years' service with a/the company; **~unfall der a)** *(veralt.)* industrial accident; **b)** *(ugs.: Ungeschicklichkeit)* slip-up; little mishap; **~vereinbarung die** *agreement between 'Betriebsrat' and management;* **~verfassung die** code of industrial relations *(covering worker participation and representation);* **~verfassungs·gesetz das** industrial realtions law *(for the private sector);* **~versammlung die** meeting of the work-force; **~wirt der** graduate in business management; **~wirtschaft die;** *o. Pl.* business management; **~wirtschaftlich 1.** *Adj.* business management *attrib.;* **2.** *adv.* from the business management standpoint; **~wirtschafts·lehre die;** *o. Pl.* [theory of] business management; *(Fach)* management studies *sing., no art.;* **~wissenschaft die;** *o. Pl.: s.* **~wirtschaftslehre; ~zeitung die** company newspaper

betrinken *unr. refl. V.* get drunk; **sich fürchterlich/sinnlos ~:** get terribly/blind drunk

betroffen [bəˈtrɔfn̩] **1.** *2. Part. v.* **betreffen. 2.** *Adj.* upset; *(bestürzt)* dismayed; **zutiefst** *od.* **im Innersten ~:** extremely upset; *(gekränkt)* deeply hurt. **3.** *adv.* in dismay *or* consternation; **~ schweigen** be too upset/ dismayed to say anything

Betroffene der/die; *adj. Dekl.* person affected; **die von ... ~n** those affected by ...

Betroffenheit die; ~: dismay; consternation

betrog [bəˈtroːk] *1. u. 3. Pers. Sg. Prät. v.* **betrügen**

betrogen *2. Part. v.* **betrügen**

betrüben 1. *tr. V.* sadden; **seine Eltern durch sein Verhalten ~:** cause one's parents distress through one's behaviour. **2.** *refl. V. (geh. veralt.)* **sich über etw.** *(Akk.)* **~:** become dejected *or* depressed about sth.

betrüblich *Adj.* gloomy; *(deprimierend)* depressing; **ich muß Ihnen die ~e Mitteilung machen, daß ...:** unfortunately I have to inform you that ...

betrüblicher·weise *Adv.* unfortunately; *(traurigerweise)* sadly

Betrübnis [bəˈtryːpnɪs] **die;** ~, **~se** *(geh.)* sadness

betrübt [bəˈtryːpt] **1.** *Adj. (traurig)* sad **(über +** *Akk.* about); *(deprimiert)* dismayed, depressed **(über +** *Akk.* about); gloomy ⟨*face etc.*⟩; **~ aussehen** look gloomy; *s. auch* **Tod. 2.** sadly; *(schwermütig)* gloomily

betrug [bəˈtruːk] *1. u. 3. Pers. Sg. Prät. v.* **betragen**

Betrug der; ~[e]s; *Pl. schweiz.:* **Betrüge** deception; *(Mogelei)* cheating *no indef. art.; (Delikt)* fraud; **das ist [glatter] ~:** that's [plain] fraud/cheating; **mehrfacher** *od. (Rechtsw.)* **fortgesetzter ~:** repeated fraud; **ein frommer ~:** a well-meaning deception; *(Selbsttäuschung)* [a case of] self-deception

betrügen 1. *unr. tr. V.* **a)** deceive; be unfaithful to ⟨*husband, wife*⟩; *(Rechtsw.)* defraud ⟨*firm, customer, etc.*⟩; *(beim Spielen)* cheat; **sich [in etw.** *(Dat.)***] betrogen sehen** be deceived [in sth.]; *(in seinem Vertrauen)* be betrayed [in sth.]; *(enttäuscht)* be let down [in sth.]; **er sah sich in all seinen Hoffnungen betrogen** all his hopes were dashed; he was disappointed in all his hopes; **sich selbst ~:** deceive oneself; **b)** *(um etw. bringen)* **jmdn. um 100 DM ~:** cheat *or (coll.)* do sb. out of 100 marks; *(arglistig)* swindle sb. out of 100 marks; **um sein Recht betrogen werden** be cheated of one's rights. **2.** *unr. itr. V.* cheat; *(bei Geschäften)* swindle people

Betrüger der; ~s, ~: swindler; *(Hochstapler)* con man *(coll.); (beim Spielen)* cheat; *(der Ehefrau)* deceiver

Betrügerei die; ~, **~en** deception; *(beim Spielen usw.)* cheating; *(bei Geschäften)* swindling; **eine kleine ~:** a bit of a swindle *or* of swindling; a bit of cheating; **deine ~en** your swindling *sing.*/cheating *sing.*

Betrügerin die; ~, **~nen** swindler; *(beim Spielen)* cheat; *(des Ehemanns)* deceiver

betrügerisch *Adj.* deceitful; *(Rechtsw.)* fraudulent; **in ~er Absicht** with intent to deceive

betrunken [bəˈtrʊŋkn̩] **1.** *2. Part. v.* **betrinken. 2.** *Adj.* drunken *attrib.;* drunk *pred.;* **ein total ~er Fahrer** a completely drunk and incapable driver. **3.** *adv.* drunkenly

Betrunkene der/die; *adj. Dekl.* drunk; **eine ~:** a drunken woman

Bet-: ~saal der meeting-hall; [primitive] chapel; **~schwester die** *(abwertend)* over-pious type *(coll.);* **~stuhl der** prayer-stool

Bett [bɛt] **das;** ~[e]s, **~en a)** bed; **das ~ machen** make the bed; **die ~en bauen** *(ugs. scherzh.)* make the beds; **jmdm. das Frühstück ans ~ bringen** bring sb. breakfast in bed; **sie ging an sein ~/saß an seinem ~:** she went to/sat at his bedside; **jmdn. aus dem ~ holen** *(ugs.)* get sb. out of bed; **er kommt nur schwer aus dem ~:** he doesn't like getting up; **im ~:** in bed; **[mit Fieber] im ~ liegen** be in bed [with a temperature]; **ins** *od.* **zu ~ gehen, sich ins** *od.* **zu ~ legen** go to bed; **ins ~ fallen** *(ugs.)* fall into bed; **die Kinder ins ~ bringen** put the children to bed; **das ~ hüten [müssen]** *(fig.)* [have to] stay in bed; **er hütet seit einer Woche das ~** *(fig.)* he has been in bed for a week; **das ~ mit jmdm. teilen** *(fig. geh.)* share bed and board with sb.; live together with sb.; **mit jmdm. ins ~ gehen** *od.* **steigen** *(fig. ugs.)* go to bed with sb.; **sich ins gemachte ~ legen** *(fig.)* have everything handed to one on a plate *(fig.); s. auch* **fesseln, klingeln; b)** *(Feder~)* duvet; **c)** *(Fluß~)* bed; **der Fluß hat sich ein neues ~ gesucht** the river has formed a new bed; **d)** *(Technik)* bed

Bet·tag der *s.* **Buß- und Bettag**

Bett-: ~an·zug der *(schweiz.),* **~bezug der** duvet cover; **~couch die** bed-settee; studio couch; **~decke die a)** blanket; *(gesteppt)* quilt; **b)** *(Tagesdecke)* bedspread

Bettel [ˈbɛtl̩] **der;** ~s **a)** *(ugs.)* junk *(coll.);* **b)** *(veralt.: Betteln)* begging *no art.*

bettel-, Bettel-: ~arm *Adj.* destitute; penniless; **~brief der** begging letter

Bettelei die; ~, **~en** begging *no art.*

Bettel-: ~mann der; *Pl.:* **~leute** *(veralt.)* beggar; **~mönch der** mendicant friar

betteln [ˈbɛtl̩n] *itr. V.* beg **(um** for); **~ gehen** go begging; **„Betteln verboten!"** 'No begging'; **bei jmdm. um etw. ~:** beg sb. for sth.; **darum ~, aufbleiben zu dürfen** beg to be allowed to stay up

Bettel-: ~orden der mendicant order; **~stab der** *in* **jmdn. an den ~stab bringen** reduce sb. to penury; **~weib das** *(veralt.)* beggar woman

betten *(geh.)* **1.** *tr. V.* **a)** lay; **jmdn. flach ~:** lay sb. [down] flat; **jmdn. weich ~:** make a soft bed for sb. to lie on; **weich gebettet sein** *(fig.)* have an easy time of it; be feather-bedded; **b)** *(einbetten)* **etw. in etw.** *(Akk.)* **~:** embed sth. in sth. **2.** *refl. V. (fig.)* **wie man sich bettet, so liegt man** as you make your bed, so you must lie on it; **sich weich ~:** feather one's nest

Betten-: ~berg der surplus of beds; **~burg die a)** *(Hotel)* giant hotel; **b)** *(Urlaubsort)* over-developed resort; **~machen das** making the beds *no art.; (allgemein)* making beds *no art.;* **das tägliche ~machen** the daily making of beds; **~mangel der** shortage of beds

bett-, Bett-: ~feder die a) bedspring; **b)** *Pl. (Füllung)* [pillow/bed-]feathers; **~flasche die** hot-water bottle; **~genosse der, ~genossin die** bedfellow; **~geschichte die** *(abwertend)* **a)** *(Verhältnis)* purely physical relationship; **seine ~geschichten schildern** describe one's bedroom experiences; **b)** *(Klatschgeschichte)* bedroom saga; **~geschichten der Filmstars** gossip about film stars' love-lives; **~gestell das** bedstead; **~häschen das, ~hase der** *(ugs. scherzh.)* sex kitten; **~himmel der** bed canopy; **~hupferl** [~hʊpfɐl] **das;** ~s, ~: bedtime treat; **~jäckchen das, ~jacke die** bed-jacket; **~kante die** edge of the bed; **~kasten der** bedding box *(under a bed);* **~lade die** *(südd., österr.) s.* **~gestell; ~lägerig** [~lɛːgərɪç] *Adj.* bedridden; **~laken das** sheet; **~lektüre die** bedtime reading *no indef. art.*

Bettler [ˈbɛtlɐ] **der;** ~s, ~: beggar

Bettlerin die; ~, **~nen** beggar [woman]

bett-, Bett-: ~nässen das; ~s bed-wetting *no art.;* **~nässer der** bed wetter; **~pfanne die** bedpan; **~reif** *Adj. (ugs.)* ready for bed *pred.;* **~ruhe die** bed-rest; **zwei Wochen [absolute] ~ruhe** two weeks of [complete] bed-rest; **~schwere die;** *o. Pl.* *in* **die nötige** *od.* **notwendige ~schwere haben** *(ugs.)* be ready for one's bed; **~statt die; ~statt, ~stätten** [~ʃtɛtn̩] *(südd., österr.),* **~stelle die** *s.* **~gestell; ~szene die** *(Film)* bedroom scene; **~tuch** *s.* **Bettuch; ~über·zug der** duvet cover

Bettuch das sheet

Bett·umrandung die bedside carpeting *(on three sides of the bed)*

Bettung die; ~, **~en** *(Eisenb., Straßenbau)* road-bed

Bett-: ~vorlage die, ~vorleger der bedside rug; **~wäsche die** bed-linen; **~zeug das;** *o. Pl. (ugs.)* bedclothes *pl.*

betucht [bəˈtuːxt] *Adj. (ugs.)* **[gut] ~:** well-heeled *(coll.);* well-off

betulich [bəˈtuːlɪç] **1.** *Adj.* **a)** fussy; *(besorgt)* worried; agitated; **b)** *(gemächlich)* leisurely; unhurried. **2.** *adv.* **a)** fussily; **b)** *(gemächlich)* in a calm unhurried way

Betulichkeit die; ~ **a)** fussiness; *(Besorgtheit)* agitation; **b)** *(Gemächlichkeit)* calm unhurried manner

betun *unr. refl. V. (ugs.)* fuss around

betupfen *tr. V.* dab

betuppen [bəˈtʊpn̩] *(nordwestd. ugs.) tr. V.* diddle *(Brit. coll.);* do *(coll.)*

betütern [bəˈtyːtɐn] *(nordd. ugs.)* **1.** *tr. V.* mollycoddle. **2.** *refl. V.* get merry *or* tipsy

betütert *Adj. (nordd. ugs.)* **a)** *(beschwipst)* merry; tipsy; **b)** *(verwirrt)* not quite with it *pred. (coll.)*

beugbar *Adj. (Sprachw.)* declinable ⟨*noun, adjective*⟩; conjugable ⟨*verb*⟩

Beuge [ˈbɔygə] **die;** ~, **~n a)** *(Turnen)* bend; **eine ~ machen** bend over; *(Knie~)* **in die ~ gehen** do a knees-bend; **b)** *(Biegung)* bend; **c)** *(Arm~/Bein~)* crook of one's arm *or* elbow/knee

Beuge·haft die *(Rechtsw.)* coercive detention

Beugel [ˈbɔygl̩] **das;** ~s, ~ *(österr.)* filled croissant

Beuge·muskel der *(Anat.)* flexor

beugen 1. *tr. V.* **a)** bend; bow ⟨*head*⟩; **den Rumpf ~:** bend from the waist; **gebeugt gehen** walk with a stoop; **vom Alter/vom Kummer gebeugt** *(geh.)* bent *or* bowed with age *postpos.*/bowed down with grief *postpos.;* **b)** *(geh.: brechen)* **jmdn. ~:** break sb.'s resistance; **jmds. Starrsinn/Stolz ~:** break sb.'s stubborn/proud nature; **c)** *(Sprachw.: flektieren)* inflect ⟨*word*⟩; decline ⟨*noun, adjective*⟩; conjugate ⟨*verb*⟩; **stark/schwach gebeugt werden** be strong/weak; have strong/weak endings; ein stark/schwach gebeugtes Adjektiv an adjective with strong/weak endings; d) (Rechtsw.) bend ⟨law⟩; das Recht ~: pervert the course of justice; e) (Physik) diffract ⟨light ray etc.⟩. 2. refl. V. a) bend over; (sich bücken) stoop; sich nach vorn/hinten ~: bend forwards/bend over backwards; sich aus dem Fenster ~: lean out of the window; sich über den Tisch/das Geländer usw. ~: lean over the table/the banisters etc.; er beugte sich über ihre Hand he bowed his head over her hand; b) (sich fügen) give way; give in; sich dem Druck ~: yield or give way to pressure; sich der Mehrheit ~: bow to the will of the majority

Beugung die; ~, ~en a) (das Biegen) bending; (Biegung) bend; b) (Sprachw.) inflexion; (eines Substantivs) declension; (eines Verbs) conjugation; ein Adjektiv mit starker/schwacher ~: an adjective with strong/weak endings or inflexion; c) (Rechtsw.: des Gesetzes) bending; ~ des Rechts perversion of justice; d) (Physik) diffraction

Beugungs·endung die s. Flexionsendung

Beule ['bɔylə] die; ~, ~n a) bump; swelling; (Furunkel) boil; b) (Vertiefung) dent (an + Dat. in); (Vorwölbung) bump; bulge

beulen itr. V. bulge; ⟨trousers⟩ be baggy

Beulen·pest die bubonic plague

beunruhigen [bə'|ʊnru:ɪgn̩] 1. tr. V. worry; es beunruhigte ihn sehr it made him very worried; über etw. (Akk.) beunruhigt sein be worried about sth.; bist du nicht beunruhigt darüber, daß ...? aren't you worried that ...? 2. refl. V. worry (um, wegen about)

Beunruhigung die; ~, ~en worry; concern; eine deutliche ~: an obvious sense of concern

beurkunden [bə'|u:ɐ̯kʊndn̩] tr. V. record; (belegen) document, provide a record of

beurlauben [bə'|u:ɐ̯laubn̩] 1. tr. V. a) jmdn. [für zwei Tage] ~: give sb. [two days'] leave of absence; sich ~ lassen obtain leave of absence; beurlaubt sein be on leave [of absence]; Professor X ist in diesem Semester beurlaubt Professor X is on sabbatical leave this term; b) (suspendieren) suspend. 2. refl. V. (veralt.) take one's leave

Beurlaubung die; ~, ~en a) leave of absence no indef. art.; eine [einjährige] ~ beantragen apply for [one year's] leave of absence; ⟨professor⟩ apply for a [one-year] sabbatical; b) (Suspendierung) suspension

beurteilen tr. V. judge; assess; etw. falsch ~: misjudge sth.; assess sth. wrongly; sie ~ die Lage als kritisch they judge the situation to be critical or see the situation as critical; er kann doch nicht ~, was wirklich passiert ist he cannot possibly tell or is in no position to say what really happened

Beurteilung die; ~, ~en a) judgement; (einer Lage usw.) assessment; bei nüchterner ~ der Ereignisse muß man ...: if one views the events dispassionately, one has to ...; b) (Gutachten) assessment; (für eine Bewerbung) reference

Beurteilungs·maßstab der criterion of judgement/assessment

Beuschel ['bɔyʃl] das; ~s, ~ a) (österr., bayr.) dish made of finely chopped lights usu. with heart and other offal; b) (österr. salopp: Lunge) lung; c) (österr. salopp: Eingeweide) guts pl. (coll.)

¹Beute ['bɔytə] die; ~, ~n a) (Gestohlenes) haul; loot no indef. art.; (Kriegs~) booty; spoils pl.; eine ~ in Millionenhöhe machen make a haul worth millions; fette ~ machen get rich pickings pl.; b) (von Raubtieren) prey; (eines Jägers) bag; [seine] ~ schlagen catch one's prey; leichte ~: easy prey; c) (geh.: Opfer) prey (+ Gen. to); eine ~ der Flammen werden be consumed by the flames

²Beute die; ~, ~n (Imkerspr.) hive

beute·gierig Adj. a) rapacious; on the prowl postpos.; ravening ⟨wolf⟩; b) (auf Raub aus) greedy for loot postpos.

Beutel ['bɔytl̩] der; ~s, ~ a) bag; (kleiner, für Tabak usw.) pouch; b) (ugs.: Geld~) purse; jmds. ~ ist leer sb. is broke (coll.); tief in den ~ greifen müssen have to dig deep into one's pocket; etw. reißt ein großes Loch in jmds. ~: sth. makes a big hole in sb.'s pocket; c) (Zool.) pouch

beuteln 1. tr. V. a) (südd., österr.: schütteln) shake; b) (fig.: hart bedrängen) batter; das Leben hat ihn gebeutelt life has given him some hard knocks; c) (übervorteilen) jmdn. ~: take sb. for a ride (sl.). 2. itr. V. bulge; ⟨trousers⟩ be baggy

Beutel-: ~ratte die opossum; ~schneider der (veralt.) a) cutpurse (arch.); (Gauner) crook; b) (geh.: Nepper) shark; racketeer; ~tier das marsupial

Beute·zug der thieving spree; raid

Beutler ['bɔytlɐ] der; ~s, ~ (Zool.) marsupial

bevölkern [bə'fœlkɐn] 1. tr. V. populate; inhabit; (besiedeln) settle; (fig.) fill; invade; ein stark/dünn od. wenig bevölkertes Land a densely/thinly or sparsely populated country; von Touristen bevölkert (fig.) full of tourists. 2. refl. V. become populated; ⟨bar, restaurant, etc.⟩ fill up

Bevölkerung die; ~, ~en a) population; (Volk) people; b) o. Pl. (Besiedlung) settling

Bevölkerungs-: ~abnahme die decline in population; ~dichte die population density; ~explosion die population explosion; ~gruppe die section of the population; ~schicht die section or stratum of society; ~schwund der s. ~abnahme; ~statistik die demography no art.; ~zahl die population; ~zunahme die, ~zuwachs der increase in population

bevollmächtigen [bə'fɔlmɛçtɪgn̩] tr. V. jmdn. [dazu] ~, etw. zu tun authorize sb. to do sth.; (in Rechtshandlungen) give sb. power of attorney to do sth.

Bevollmächtigte der/die; adj. Dekl. authorized representative

Bevollmächtigung die; ~, ~en authorization; (Rechtsw.) power of attorney

bevor [bə'fo:ɐ̯] Konj. before; noch ~ ich antworten konnte before I could [even] reply; ~ du nicht unterschreibst/unterschrieben hast until you sign/have signed

bevor·munden tr. V. jmdn. ~: impose one's will on sb.; sie wollen sich nicht länger ~ lassen they do not want to be dictated to any longer

Bevormundung die; ~, ~en imposing one's will (+ Gen. on); wie kann sie sich diese ~ durch ihre Eltern gefallen lassen? how can she put up with her parents telling her what to do?

bevor·raten tr. V. (Amtsspr.) lay in stocks of ⟨goods, materials⟩; gut bevorratet werden/sein be kept/be well stocked or supplied

bevor|stehen unr. itr. V. be near; be about to happen; [unmittelbar] ~: be imminent; jmdm. steht etw. bevor sth. is in store for sb.; mir steht etwas Schlimmes bevor there's something unpleasant in store for me; die schwerste Prüfung steht ihm noch bevor he has still to face his severest test; his severest test is still to come

bevorstehend Adj. forthcoming; coming ⟨winter⟩; [unmittelbar] ~: imminent; die [dir/uns] ~en Probleme the problems facing you/us

bevorzugen [bə'fo:ɐ̯tsu:gn̩] tr. V. a) prefer (vor + Dat. to); b) (begünstigen) favour; give preference or preferential treatment to (vor + Dat. over)

bevorzugt 1. Adj. favoured; (privilegiert) privileged; preferential ⟨treatment⟩. 2. adv. jmdn. ~ behandeln give sb. preferential treatment; jmdn. ~ abfertigen/bedienen give sb. priority or precedence/serve sb. first; etw. ~ erledigen/bearbeiten give sth. priority

Bevorzugung die; ~, ~en preferential treatment; preference (Gen., von for)

bewachen tr. V. guard; (Ballspiele) mark; die Gefangenen werden streng bewacht a close watch is kept on the prisoners; the prisoners are closely guarded; ihr Mann bewacht sie wie ein Schießhund her husband watches over her like a guard dog; bewachter Parkplatz car park with an attendant

Bewacher der; ~s, ~: guard; (Ballspiele) marker

bewachsen unr. tr. V. grow over; cover; eine mit Efeu ~e Laube a summerhouse overgrown with ivy; an ivy-covered summerhouse; ein dicht ~es Tal/Blumenbeet a valley full of dense vegetation/a border packed with flowers

Bewachung die; ~, ~en a) guarding; (Ballspiele) marking; zur ~ des Geländes to guard the site; unter scharfer ~: closely guarded; jmdn. unter ~ stellen put sb. under guard; sich der ~ entziehen (Ballspiele) escape one's marker/markers; b) (Wachmannschaft) guard

bewaffnen [bə'vafnən] 1. tr. V. arm; ein Heer [neu] ~: supply an army with [new] weapons. 2. refl. V. (auch fig.) arm oneself (mit with)

bewaffnet Adj. armed; bis an die Zähne ~: armed to the teeth; ~er Raubüberfall/Widerstand armed robbery/resistance; mit Fotoapparaten ~ (fig.) armed with cameras

Bewaffnete der/die; adj. Dekl. armed man/woman/person; ~: people bearing arms; armed men/women

Bewaffnung die; ~, ~en a) arming; b) (Waffen) weapons pl.

bewahren tr. V. a) jmdn. vor etw. (Dat.) ~: protect or preserve sb. from sth.; vor einer Enttäuschung bewahrt bleiben be saved or spared a disappointment; [Gott od. i] bewahre! good Lord, no!; (Gott behüte) God forbid!; b) (erhalten) seine Fassung od. Haltung ~: keep or retain one's composure; Stillschweigen/Treue ~: remain silent/faithful; sich (Dat.) etw. ~: retain or preserve sth.; c) (geh.: auf~) keep; etw. im Gedächtnis ~ (fig.) preserve the memory of sth.; etw. im Herzen ~ (fig.) treasure sth. in one's heart

bewähren 1. refl. V. prove oneself/itself; prove one's/its worth; sich als [guter] Freund ~: prove to be a [good] friend; sich im Leben ~: prove oneself in life; make something of one's life; das Gerät hat sich doch noch bewährt this apparatus has turned out to be useful after all; sich gut/schlecht ~: prove/not prove to be worth while or a success; sich am besten ~: prove to be best; unsere Freundschaft hat sich über all die Jahre bewährt our friendship has stood the test of time over all these years. 2. tr. V. (veralt.) prove

bewahrheiten [bə'va:ɐ̯haitn̩] refl. V. prove to be true; an ihm bewahrheitet sich der Spruch, daß ...: he demonstrates the truth of the saying that ...

bewährt Adj. proven ⟨method, design, etc.⟩; well-tried, tried and tested ⟨recipe, cure⟩; reliable ⟨worker⟩

Bewahrung die; ~ a) protection no indef. art. (vor + Dat. from); b) (geh.: Auf~) keeping; c) (Beibehaltung) zur ~ seines Andenkens to preserve his memory

Bewährung die; ~, ~en a) (Rechtsw.) probation; 3 Monate Gefängnis mit ~: three months suspended sentence [with probation]; eine Strafe zur ~ aussetzen [conditionally] suspend a sentence on probation; b) (das Sichbewähren) proving; (das Testen) testing

Bewährungs-: ~auf·lage die (Rechtsw.)

obligation imposed as a condition of sentence being suspended; **~frist die** *(Rechtsw.)* period of probation; **~helfer der** probation officer; **~hilfe die** *(Rechtsw.)* probation supervision; *(Dienst)* probation service; **~probe die** [crucial] test; trial [of one's/its worth]; **jmdn./jmds. Nerven auf eine [harte] ~probe stellen** subject sb. to a [severe] test/be a severe test of sb.'s nerves; **~zeit die** *(Rechtsw.)* probation period

bewaldet [bəˈvaldət] *Adj.* wooded

Bewaldung die; ~, ~en a) tree cover; *(Wälder)* woodlands *pl.;* **eine spärliche ~:** a few trees *pl.;* **b)** *(Aufforstung)* afforestation *no indef. art.*

bewältigen [bəˈvɛltɪgn̩] *tr. V.* deal with; cope with; overcome ⟨*difficulty, problem*⟩; cover ⟨*distance*⟩; *(innerlich verarbeiten)* get over ⟨*experience*⟩; **die Vergangenheit ~:** come to terms with the past

Bewältigung die; ~, ~en *s.* **bewältigen:** coping with; overcoming; covering; getting over, coming to terms with; **zur ~ der Arbeit** *usw.* to deal *or* cope with the work *etc.*

bewandert [bəˈvandɐt] *Adj.* well-versed; knowledgeable; **auf einem Gebiet/in etw.** *(Dat.)* **~ sein** be well-versed *or* well up in a subject/in sth.

Bewandtnis [bəˈvantnɪs] **die; ~, ~se: mit etw. hat es [s]eine eigene/besondere ~:** there's a particular explanation for sth. *or* a [special] story behind sth.; **mit jmdm. hat es seine eigene/besondere ~:** there's a special story about sb.; sb. is a special case; **damit hat es folgende ~:** the story behind *or* reason for it is this

bewässern *tr. V.* irrigate; *(begießen)* water

Bewässerung die; ~, ~en irrigation; *(das Begießen)* watering

Bewässerungs-: ~an·lage die irrigation system; *(für Grünflächen usw.)* watering system; **~graben der** irrigation ditch; **~kanal der** irrigation channel; **~system das** irrigation system

bewegbar *Adj.* movable

[1]bewegen [bəˈveːgn̩] **1.** *tr. V.* **a)** move; **den Koffer von der Stelle ~:** move *or* shift the suitcase [from the spot]; **die Pferde/den Hund ~:** exercise the horses/the dog; **Erde ~:** shift *or* remove earth; **b)** *(ergreifen)* move; **eine ~de Rede** a moving speech; **niemand wußte, was ihn so bewegte** nobody knew what was affecting him so deeply; **c)** *(innerlich beschäftigen)* preoccupy; **das bewegt mich schon lange** I have been preoccupied with this *or* this has exercised my mind for a long time. **2.** *refl. V.* **a)** move; **die Blätter bewegten sich sanft** the leaves stirred gently; **der Hund bewegte sich nicht** the dog did not stir *or* was quite still; **b)** *(ugs.: sich Bewegung verschaffen)* **ich muß mich ein bißchen ~:** I must get some exercise; **du solltest/mußt dich mehr ~:** you ought to/must take more exercise; **c)** *(fig.)* **seine Ausführungen ~ sich in der gleichen Richtung** his comments have the same drift *or* are on the same lines; **d)** *(schwanken)* vary; fluctuate; **der Preis bewegt sich zwischen 10 DM und 20 DM** the price varies *or* fluctuates between 10 and 20 marks; **e)** *(sich verhalten)* behave; **sich mit großer Sicherheit ~:** bear oneself with great confidence

[2]bewegen *unr. tr. V.* **jmdn. dazu ~, etw. zu tun** ⟨*thing*⟩ make sb. do sth., induce sb. to do sth.; *(überreden)* ⟨*person*⟩ prevail upon *or* persuade sb. to do sth.; **jmdn. zu etw. ~:** talk sb. into sth.; **jmdn. zum Einlenken ~:** persuade sb. to give way

Beweg·grund der motive

beweglich 1. *Adj.* **a)** movable; mobile ⟨*troops etc.*⟩; moving ⟨*target*⟩; **die ~en Teile einer Maschine** the moving parts of a machine; **seine ~e Habe** one's goods and chattels *pl.;* one's personal effects *pl.;* **~e Feste** movable feasts; **etw. ist leicht/schwer ~:** sth. is easy/difficult to move; **b)** *(rege)* agile, active ⟨*mind*⟩; *(wendig)* flexible ⟨*policy*⟩; **geistig ~ sein** be nimble-minded; have an agile mind; **c)** *(veralt.: rührend)* moving. **2.** *adv.* *(veralt.)* movingly

Beweglichkeit die; ~ a) mobility; **b)** *(Wendigkeit)* agility; **taktische ~:** tactical flexibility

bewegt [bəˈveːkt] **1.** *2. Part. v.* **[1]bewegen. 2.** *Adj.* **a)** eventful; *(unruhig)* turbulent; **ein ~es Leben** an eventful/turbulent life; **sie hat eine ~e Vergangenheit** she has a colourful past; **b)** *(gerührt)* moved *pred.;* emotional ⟨*words, voice*⟩; **mit tief ~en Worten/~er Stimme** in words/a voice heavy with emotion; **c)** *(unruhig)* **leicht/stark ~:** ⟨*sea*⟩ slightly choppy/very rough

Bewegung die; ~, ~ a) movement; *(bes. Technik, Physik)* motion; *(von Erdmassen)* moving; **in ~ sein** ⟨*person*⟩ be on the move; ⟨*thing*⟩ be in motion; **sie ist immer in ~:** she is never still; **jmdn. in ~ bringen/halten** get sb. moving *or* going/keep sb. on the go; **eine Maschine** *usw.* **in ~ setzen** start [up] a machine *etc.;* **sich in ~ setzen** ⟨*train etc.*⟩ start to move; ⟨*procession*⟩ move off; ⟨*person*⟩ get moving; *s. auch* **Hebel; b)** *(körperliche ~)* exercise; **c)** *(Ergriffenheit)* emotion; **große ~ auslösen** arouse strong emotions *pl. or* feelings *pl.;* **d)** *(Bestreben, Gruppe)* movement

bewegungs-, Bewegungs-: ~ab·lauf der sequence of movements; **~drang der** urge to be on the move; **~energie die;** *o. Pl. (Physik)* kinetic energy; **~freiheit die;** *o. Pl.* freedom of movement; **~krieg der** mobile warfare; **~los 1.** *Adj.* motionless; **vor Schreck ~los** paralysed with fright; **2.** *adv.* without moving; **~los liegen/sitzen/stehen** lie/sit/stand motionless; **~losigkeit die; ~:** motionlessness; immobility; **~studie die** time and motion study; **~therapie die** physical *or* exercise therapy; **~unfähig** *Adj.* unable to move *postpos.;* *(gelähmt)* paralysed; ⟨*vehicle*⟩ immobilized

bewehren *tr. V. (veralt.)* arm ⟨*person*⟩; fortify ⟨*castle*⟩

beweih·räuchern [bəˈvairɔyçən] *tr. V.* surround with incense; *(fig. abwertend)* idolize; **sich selbst ~:** sing one's own praises; blow one's own trumpet

Beweih·räucherung die *(fig. abwertend)* idolization; adulation

beweinen *tr. V.* lament; *(weinend)* weep over; **jmdn./jmds. Tod ~:** mourn sb./sb.'s passing

Beweinung die; ~: die ~ Christi the mourning of Christ

Beweis [bəˈvais] **der; ~es, ~e** proof (*Gen.,* **für** of); *(Zeugnis)* evidence; **belastende ~e** incriminating evidence; **einen ~/~e für etw. haben** have proof/evidence of sth.; **haben Sie einen ~ dafür, daß ...?** have you any proof/evidence that ...?; **als** *od.* **zum ~ seiner Aussage/Theorie** to substantiate *or* in support of his statement/theory; **bis zum ~ des Gegenteils** until there is proof/evidence to the contrary; **den ~ für etw. antreten** *od.* **erbringen** produce proof [in support] of sth.; **aus Mangel an ~en** owing to lack of evidence; **etw. unter ~ stellen** *(Amtsspr.)* provide proof of sth.; **sie lassen sich kaum unter ~ stellen** they are hardly susceptible of proof; **jmdm. einen ~ seines Vertrauens/seiner Hochachtung geben** give sb. a token of one's trust/esteem; **zahlreiche ~e der Anteilnahme** numerous expressions of sympathy

Beweis-: ~antrag der *(Rechtsw.)* application to produce evidence; **~aufnahme die** *(Rechtsw.)* hearing of [the] evidence

beweisbar *Adj.* provable; susceptible of proof *postpos.;* **das ist nicht ~:** it cannot be proved

beweisen 1. *unr. tr. V.* **a)** prove; **jmdm. seine Beteiligung an etw.** *(Dat.)* **~:** prove sb.'s participation in sth.; **dem Angeklagten konnte die Tat nicht bewiesen werden** it could not be proved that the accused committed the deed; **was [noch] zu ~ wäre** which has yet to be proved; **was zu ~ war** which was the point at issue *or* which needed clarifying; **b)** *(zeigen)* show; **damit beweist er seine mangelnde Einsicht** that shows his lack of understanding. **2.** *unr. refl. V.* prove oneself *or* one's worth (**vor** + *Dat.* to)

beweis-, Beweis-: ~erhebung die *s.* **~aufnahme; ~führung die a)** *(Rechtsw.)* presentation of the evidence *or* case; **b)** *(Argumentation)* reasoning; argumentation; **~gegen·stand der** *(Rechtsw.)* issue; **~kraft die;** *o. Pl.* value as evidence; *(einer Argumentation)* cogency; **~kräftig** *Adj.* of value as evidence *postpos.;* *(Rechtsw.)* of probative value *postpos.;* cogent ⟨*reasoning*⟩; conclusive ⟨*test result*⟩; **~last die;** *o. Pl. (Rechtsw.)* **a)** *(~pflicht)* burden of proof; **b)** *(Nachteil) disadvantage due to one's inability to prove a fact material to one's case;* **~material das** evidence; *(~stück)* piece of evidence; **~mittel das** *(Rechtsw.)* form of evidence; **~not die;** *o. Pl.* want of proof; lack of evidence; **sich in ~not befinden** lack evidence; be short of evidence; **~pflichtig** *Adj. (Rechtsw.)* **für etw. ~pflichtig sein** be obliged to furnish proof of sth.; **~stück das** piece of evidence; **~stücke [für etw.]** evidence *sing.* [of sth.]

bewenden *unr. V. in* **es bei** *od.* **mit etw. ~ lassen** [have to] content oneself with sth.

Bewenden das; ~s: damit hat es sein ~: that is the end of the matter; **damit, daß sie entlassen wird, wird es keineswegs sein ~ haben** even if she is dismissed, the matter won't end there

bewerben *unr. refl. V.* apply (**um** for); **sich bei einer Firma** *usw.* **~:** apply to a company *etc.* [for a job]; **sich als Buchhalter** *usw.* **~:** apply for a job as a bookkeeper *etc.;* **die Firma bewarb sich um den Auftrag** the firm competed for the contract

Bewerber der, Bewerberin die a) applicant; *(Sport: Titel~)* contender; **b)** *(veralt.: Freier)* suitor; *s. auch* **-in**

Bewerbung die application (**um** for)

Bewerbungs-: ~bogen der application form; **~schreiben das** letter of application; **~unterlagen** *Pl.* documents in support of an/the application

bewerfen *unr. tr. V.* **a) jmdn./etw. mit etw. ~:** throw sth. at sb./sth.; **jmdn. mit [faulen] Eiern ~:** pelt sb. with [rotten] eggs; **jmds. Namen mit Schmutz ~** *(fig.)* sling mud at sb. *(fig.);* drag sb.'s good name through the mud; **b)** *(Bauw.)* render ⟨*wall*⟩; **mit Lehm beworfen** covered *or* faced with clay

bewerkstelligen [bəˈvɛrkʃtɛlɪgn̩] *tr. V.* pull off, manage ⟨*deal, sale, etc.*⟩; **es ~, etw. zu tun** contrive *or* manage to do sth.

Bewerkstelligung die managing

bewertbar *Adj.* assessable

bewerten *tr. V.* assess; rate; *(dem Geldwert nach)* value (**mit** at); *(beurteilen)* judge ⟨*person*⟩; *(Schulw., Sport)* mark; grade *(Amer.);* **etw. als Heldentat ~:** rate sth. as a heroic deed; **etw. zu hoch/niedrig ~:** overrate/underrate sth.; *(dem Geldwert nach)* overvalue/undervalue sth.; **Arbeiten schlecht ~** *(Schulw.)* give work low marks *or (Amer.)* grades; **einen Aufsatz mit [der Note] „gut" ~:** mark *or (Amer.)* grade an essay 'good'; **eine Kür mit Noten zwischen 5,6 und 5,9 ~** *(Eiskunstlauf, Turnen)* give a programme marks between 5.6 and 5.9

Bewertung die a) *(das Bewerten)* assessment; *(des Geldwerts)* valuation; *(eines Menschen)* judgement; *(das Benoten einer Schularbeit)* marking; grading *(Amer.);* **b)** *(Äußerung)* assessment; *(Note)* mark; grade *(Amer.)*

Bewertungs·maß·stab der criterion of assessment
bewies [bə'vi:s] *1. u. 3. Pers. Sg. Prät. v.* **beweisen**
bewiesen [bə'vi:zn̩] *1. u. 3. Pers. Pl. Prät. u. 2. Part. v.* **beweisen**
bewiesenermaßen *Adv.* demonstrably; as can be proved
bewilligen [bə'vɪlɪgn̩] *tr. V.* grant; award ⟨*salary, grant*⟩; *(im Parlament usw.)* approve ⟨*sum, tax increase, etc.*⟩; **jmdm. eine Stundung/zwei Mitarbeiter** *usw.* **~:** allow sb. deferment/two assistants *etc.*
Bewilligung die; ~, ~en granting; *(Zustimmung)* approval; *(eines Gehalts, Stipendiums)* award
bewimpert [bə'vɪmpɐt] *Adj.* lashed; *(Zool.)* ciliate
bewirken *tr. V.* bring about; cause; **~, daß etw. geschieht** cause sth. to happen; **damit/dadurch hast du nur bewirkt, daß ...:** all you have achieved by this *or* the only effect of this is that ...; **nichts/das Gegenteil bei jmdm. ~:** have *or* produce no effect/the opposite effect on sb.; **durch gutes Zureden bewirkt man bei ihm nichts** you don't get anywhere with him by talking to him nicely
bewirten [bə'vɪrtn̩] *tr. V.* feed; **jmdn. mit etw. ~:** serve sth. to sb.; serve sb. sth.
bewirtschaften *tr. V.* **a)** run, manage ⟨*estate, farm, restaurant, business, etc.*⟩; **b)** *(bestellen)* farm ⟨*fields, land*⟩; cultivate ⟨*field*⟩; **c)** *(staatlich lenken)* ration; **den Wohnraum ~:** make living accommodation subject to government control; **Devisen ~:** operate currency controls
Bewirtschaftung die; ~, ~en a) running; management; **b)** *(Bestellung)* farming; cultivation; **c)** *(staatliche Lenkung)* government control
Bewirtung die; ~, ~en provision of food and drink; *(Gastfreundschaft)* hospitality; **die ~ der Gäste** catering for the guests
bewitzeln *tr. V.* joke about; poke fun at
bewog [bə'vo:k] *1. u. 3. Pers. Sg. Prät. v.* **²bewegen**
bewogen *2. Part. v.* **²bewegen**
bewohnbar *Adj.* habitable
Bewohnbarkeit die; ~: suitability *or* fitness for habitation
bewohnen *tr. V.* inhabit, live in ⟨*house, area*⟩; live in ⟨*room, flat*⟩; live on ⟨*4th storey etc.*⟩; ⟨*animal, plant*⟩ be found in
Bewohner der; ~s, ~, Bewohnerin die; ~, ~nen *(eines Hauses, einer Wohnung)* occupant; *(einer Stadt, eines Gebietes)* inhabitant; **ein ~ der Steppe** *(Mensch)* a steppe-dweller; *(Tier, Pflanze)* a native of the steppes; **ein ~ des Waldes** a forest-dweller; *(Tier)* a woodland creature
Bewohnerschaft die; ~, ~en inhabitants *pl.*; *(eines Wohnblocks)* occupants *pl.*
bewohnt *Adj.* occupied ⟨*house etc.*⟩; inhabited ⟨*area*⟩; **ist das Haus noch ~?** is the house still lived in *or* occupied?
bewölken [bə'vœlkn̩] *refl. V.* cloud over; become overcast; **seine Stirn bewölkte sich** *(fig.)* his face darkened
bewölkt *Adj.* cloudy; overcast; **dicht** *od.* **stark ~:** heavily overcast; **der Himmel ist nur leicht ~:** there is only a light cloud cover
Bewölkung die; ~, ~en a) *o. Pl.* clouding over; **b)** *(Wolkendecke)* cloud [cover]; **wechselnde ~:** variable amounts *pl.* of cloud
Bewölkungs-: ~auf·lockerung die breaking up of the cloud cover; **~zunahme die** increase in the cloud cover
Bewuchs der plant cover; vegetation *no indef. art.*
Bewunderer der; ~s, ~, Bewunderin die; ~, ~nen admirer
bewundern *tr. V.* admire **(wegen, für** for); **ich kann sie nur ~:** I really admire her
bewunderns-: ~wert, ~würdig 1. *Adj.* admirable; worthy of admiration *postpos.*; **2.** *adv.* admirably; in an admirable fashion
Bewunderung die; ~, ~en admiration
bewunderungs·würdig *s.* **bewundernswert**
Bewurf der *(Bauw.)* rendering
bewußt [bə'vʊst] **1.** *Adj.* **a)** *(im Bewußtsein vorhanden)* conscious ⟨*reaction, behaviour, etc.*⟩; *(absichtlich)* deliberate ⟨*lie, deception, attack, etc.*⟩; **~e Ablehnung** conscious *or* deliberate rejection; **ein ~er Sozialist** a convinced socialist; **etw. ist/wird jmdm. ~:** sb. is/becomes aware of sth.; sb. realizes sth.; **mir war nicht recht ~, was ich tat** I was not really conscious of what I was doing; **b)** *(klar erkennend)* **ein ~er Mensch** a thinking person; **sich** *(Dat.)* **einer Sache** *(Gen.)* **~ sein/werden** be/become aware *or* conscious of something; **c)** *nicht präd. (bekannt)* particular; *(fraglich)* in question *postpos.* **2.** *adv.* **a)** *(absichtlich)* deliberately; **b)** *(klar erkennend)* consciously; **~er leben** live with greater awareness
Bewußtheit die; ~: deliberateness
bewußt·los *Adj.* unconscious; **~ zusammenbrechen** collapse unconscious; **der/die Bewußtlose** the unconscious man/woman
Bewußtlosigkeit die; ~: unconsciousness; **aus der ~ erwachen** regain consciousness; **bis zur ~** *(ugs.)* ad nauseam
bewußt|machen *tr. V.* **jmdm. etw. ~:** make sb. realize sth.; **sich** *(Dat.)* **etw. ~:** realize sth.
Bewußt·sein das a) *(deutliches Wissen)* awareness; **im ~ seiner Kraft** [secure] in the knowledge *or* awareness of one's strength; **im ~, seine Pflicht getan zu haben** conscious of having done one's duty; **sich** *(Dat.)* **etw. ins ~ rufen** remember *or* recall sth.; **jmdm. etw. ins ~ bringen** remind sb. of sth.; **gewisse Themen in das allgemeine ~ bringen** make the general public aware of certain issues; bring certain issues to the notice of the general public; **etw. mit ~ erleben** be fully aware of sth. [one is experiencing]; **jmdm. zu[m] ~ kommen** become clear to sb.; **jetzt erst kam ihr zu ~, daß ...:** only now did she realize that ...; **b)** *(Psych., Politik, Philos. usw.)* consciousness; **ein historisches ~:** a consciousness *or* awareness of history; **c)** *(geistige Klarheit)* consciousness; **das ~ verlieren** lose consciousness; **wieder zu ~ kommen, das ~ wiedererlangen** regain consciousness; **bei vollem ~ sein** be fully conscious; **bei vollem ~ operiert werden** be operated on while fully conscious
bewußtseins-, Bewußtseins-: ~bildung die; *o. Pl.* creation of [greater] awareness; **eine politische ~bildung** the creation of political consciousness *or* awareness; **~erweiternd 1.** *Adj.* mind-expanding; psychedelic; **2.** *adv.* **~erweiternd wirken** have a mind-expanding effect; **~erweiterung die** expansion of consciousness; **~spaltung die** *(Med., Psych.)* split consciousness; schizophrenia; **~störung die** disturbance of consciousness; **~trübung die** clouding *or* dimming of consciousness; **~verändernd 1.** *Adj.* mind-bending ⟨*drug*⟩; **dieses Erlebnis war ~verändernd** this experience changed sb.'s outlook; **2.** *adv.* **auf jmdn. ~verändernd wirken** change sb.'s awareness; **~veränderung die** change of awareness *or* outlook
Bewußtwerdung die; ~: development of awareness
bez. *Abk.* **bezahlt** pd.
bezahlbar *Adj.* affordable; *(wirtschaftlich vernünftig)* economic; **diese Miete ist für ihn kaum ~:** he can hardly afford this rent
bezahlen 1. *tr. V.* pay ⟨*person, bill, taxes, rent, amount*⟩; pay for ⟨*goods etc.*⟩; **etw. [in] bar ~:** pay [in] cash for sth.; **etw. mit [einem] Scheck ~:** pay for sth. by cheque; **jmdm. etw. ~:** pay for sth. for sb.; **bekommst du das Essen bezahlt?** do you get your meals paid for?; **[jmdm.] für etw. 10 DM ~:** pay [sb.] 10 marks for sth.; **bezahlter Urlaub** paid leave; holiday[s] with pay; **er mußte seinen Leichtsinn teuer ~** *(fig.)* he had to pay dearly for his carelessness; **das macht sich bezahlt** it pays off; **als ob er's bezahlt bekäme** *od.* **kriegte** *(ugs.)* for all he's worth *(coll.)*; like a mad thing. **2.** *itr. V.* pay; **Herr Ober, ich möchte ~** *od.* **bitte ~:** waiter, the bill *or* *(Amer.)* check please; **heute bezahle ich** it's on me today *(coll.)*
Bezahlung die payment; *(Lohn, Gehalt)* pay; **die ~ der Waren** the payment for the goods; **gegen ~ arbeiten** work for payment *or* money
bezähmen 1. *tr. V.* **a)** contain, control ⟨*wrath, curiosity, impatience*⟩; restrain ⟨*desire*⟩; **b)** *(veralt.: zähmen)* tame. **2.** *refl. V.* restrain oneself
bezaubern 1. *tr. V.* enchant; **von etw. bezaubert** enchanted with *or* by sth. **2.** *itr. V.* enchant; be enchanting
bezaubernd 1. *Adj.* enchanting; **es war ~ von euch, das Fest zu geben** it was wonderfully kind of you to give the party. **2.** *adv.* enchantingly
bezecht [bə'tsɛçt] *Adj.* drunken *attrib.*; drunk *pred.*
bezeichnen *tr. V.* **a) jmdn./sich/etw. als etw. ~:** call sb./oneself/sth. sth.; describe sb./oneself/sth. as sth.; **das muß man schon als anmaßend ~:** that can only be described as arrogant; **wie bezeichnet man das?** what is it called?; **mit dem Wort bezeichnet man eine Art Jacke** this word is used to denote *or* describe a kind of jacket; **jmdn. als Halunken** *od.* **mit dem Wort Halunke ~:** describe sb. as a scoundrel; call sb. a scoundrel; **jmdn. als Feigling ~:** call sb. a coward; **etw. als Verrat ~:** call sth. treachery; **so kann man das auch ~:** that's one way of describing it; **b)** *(Name sein für)* denote; **c)** *(markieren)* mark; *(durch Zeichen angeben)* indicate
bezeichnend *Adj.* characteristic, typical *(für* of); *(bedeutsam)* significant; **das ist ~ für ihn** that is typical *or* characteristic of him
bezeichnender·weise *Adv.* characteristically; typically; *(als Zeichen dafür)* significantly
Bezeichnung die a) *o. Pl.* marking; *(Angabe durch Zeichen)* indication; **b)** *(Name)* name; **mir fällt die richtige ~ dafür nicht ein** I can't think of the right word for it/them
bezeigen *(geh.)* **1.** *tr. V.* show; give proof of ⟨*courage*⟩; **jmdm. Ehrfurcht** *od.* **Respekt ~:** show sb. respect. **2.** *refl. V.* **sich dankbar/erkenntlich ~:** show one's gratitude/appreciation
bezeugen *tr. V.* **a)** testify to; **er/sie bezeugte, daß ...:** he/she testified that ...; **der Ort ist schon im 8. Jh. [dokumentarisch] bezeugt** [the existence of] this place is documented as early as the 8th century; **b)** *(bezeigen)* show; **jmdm. sein Wohlwollen ~:** give sb. proof of one's goodwill
Bezeugung die a) attestation; *(das Bezeugen)* testifying (*Gen.* to); **b)** *(das Bezeigen)* showing; demonstration
bezichtigen [bə'tsɪçtɪgn̩] *tr. V.* accuse; **jmdn. des Verrats ~:** accuse sb. of treachery; **jmdn. ~, etw. getan zu haben** *od.* **er/sie habe etw. getan** accuse sb. of having done sth.
Bezichtigung die; ~, ~en accusation
beziehbar *Adj.* **a)** ready for occupation *postpos.*; **b)** *(anwendbar)* applicable **(auf +** *Akk.* to)
beziehen 1. *unr. tr. V.* **a)** cover, put a cover/covers on ⟨*seat, cushion, umbrella, etc.*⟩; **die Betten frisch ~:** put clean sheets on the beds; **einen Schirm neu ~:** re-cover an umbrella; **das Sofa ist mit Leder bezogen** the

sofa is upholstered in leather; **b)** *(einziehen in)* move into ⟨*house, office*⟩; **c)** *(Milit.)* take up ⟨*position, post*⟩; **einen klaren Standpunkt ~** *(fig.)* adopt a clear position; take a definite stand; *s. auch* **Stellung; d)** *(regelmäßig erhalten)* receive, obtain [one's supply of] ⟨*goods*⟩; take ⟨*newspaper*⟩; draw, receive ⟨*pension, salary*⟩; **Prügel ~** *(ugs.)* get a hiding *(coll.)*; **e)** *(in Beziehung setzen)* apply **(auf +** *Akk.* to); **etw. auf sich ~:** take sth. personally; **seine Kritik auf etw.** *(Akk.)* **~:** direct one's criticism at sth. **2.** *unr. refl. V.* **a) es/der Himmel bezieht sich** it/the sky is clouding over *or* becoming overcast; **b) sich auf jmdn./etw. ~** *(sich berufen auf)* ⟨*person, letter, etc.*⟩ refer to sb./sth.; *(betreffen)* ⟨*question, statement, etc.*⟩ relate to sb./sth.; **wir ~ uns auf Ihr Schreiben vom 28. 8./unser Telefongespräch** with reference to your letter of 28 August/our telephone conversation; **diese Kritik bezieht sich nicht auf dich** this criticism is not aimed at you

Bezieher der; ~s, ~, Bezieherin die; ~, ~nen *(einer Zeitung)* reader; subscriber *(Gen.,* **von** to); *(einer Rente, eines Gehalts)* recipient; *s. auch* **-in**

Beziehung die a) *(Verbindung)* relations *pl.* **(zu** with); **gute ~en** *od.* **eine gute ~ zu jmdm./einer Firma haben** have good relations with sb./a firm; be on good terms with sb./a firm; **intime ~en zu jmdm. haben** have intimate relations with sb.; **diplomatische ~en aufnehmen/unterhalten/abbrechen** establish/maintain/break off diplomatic relations; **b)** *Pl. (Verbindungen, die Vorteile verschaffen)* connections **(zu** with); **etw. durch ~en bekommen** get sth. through connections; **seine ~en spielen lassen** pull some strings; **c)** *(Verhältnis)* relationship **(zwischen** between, **zu** with); *(Verständnis)* affinity **(zu** for); **zu jmdm. keine ~ haben** be unable to relate to sb.; **er hat keine ~ zur Kunst** he has a blind spot where the arts are concerned; the arts are a closed book to him; **d)** *(Zusammenhang)* connection **(zu** with); **zwischen A und B besteht keine/eine ~:** there is no/a connection between A and B; **A zu B in ~ setzen** relate A to B; see A in relation to B; **A und B in ~ zueinander setzen** relate A and B to each other; connect *or* link A and B; **das steht in keiner ~ dazu** that is not connected with *or* related to it; **in dieser/jeder ~:** in this/every respect; **in mancher ~:** in many respects; **mit ~ auf etw.** *(Akk.)* with reference to sth.

beziehungs-, Beziehungs-: ~kiste die *(ugs.)* relationship; **~los 1.** *Adj.* unconnected; unrelated; **2.** *adv.* without any connection; **~reich** *Adj.* evocative; rich in associations *postpos.*; *(vielseitig)* many-faceted; **~weise** *Konj.* **a)** *(oder vielmehr)* that is; or to be precise; **b)** *(und im anderen Fall)* and ... respectively; *(oder)* or; **die beiden Münzen waren aus Kupfer ~ aus Nickel** the two coins were made of copper and of nickel respectively; **sie sind in Schwarz ~ in Weiß lieferbar** they are available in black or in white

beziffern [bəˈtsɪfɐn] **1.** *tr. V.* **a)** *(numerieren)* number; **bezifferter Baß** *(Musik)* figured bass; **b)** *(angeben)* estimate **(auf +** *Akk.* at); **den Schaden auf 3 000 DM ~:** estimate the damage at 3,000 marks. **2.** *refl. V.* **sich auf 10 Millionen** *(Akk.)* **DM ~:** come *or* amount to 10 million marks

Bezifferung die; ~, ~en a) numbering; **b)** *(Zahlen)* numbers *pl.*

Bezirk [bəˈtsɪrk] **der; ~[e]s, ~e a)** district; **Vertreter für den ~ Südhessen** representative for the South Hessen area; **b)** *(Verwaltungs~)* [administrative] district; *(DDR)* [administrative] area; *(in West-Berlin)* borough; **c)** *(DDR: Behörde)* local *or* area authority; **auf dem ~:** at the local *or* area authority offices *pl.*

bezirklich *Adj.* district *attrib.*; *(DDR)* area *attrib.*

Bezirks-: ~amt das district *or (DDR)* area authority; **~bürger·meister der** Borough Mayor *(in West Berlin)*; **~gericht das** district *or (DDR)* area court; **~haupt·mann der;** *Pl.* **~hauptleute** *(österr.)* chief officer of an administrative district; **~haupt·mannschaft die** *(österr.)* district authority; **auf der ~hauptmannschaft** at the district authority offices; **~klasse die** *(Sport)* district *or (DDR)* area league; **~leiter der a)** *(DDR)* head of the area administration; **b)** *(Kaufmannsspr.)* area manager; **~regierung die** *(BRD)* district authority; **~stadt die** *(DDR)* chief town of the area; area capital; **~tag der** *(DDR)* area assembly; **~verordneten·versammlung die** borough assembly *(in West Berlin)*

bezirzen [bəˈtsɪrtsn̩] *s.* **becircen**

bezog [bəˈtsoːk] *1. u. 3. Pers. Sg. Prät. v.* **beziehen**

bezogen 1. *2. Part. v.* **beziehen. 2.** *Adj.* **~ auf jmdn./etw.** [seen] in relation to sb./sth.

-bezogen *Adj.* -related

Bezogene der/die; *adj. Dekl.* drawee *(of cheque)*

bezug [bəˈtsuːk] **in ~ auf jmdn./etw.** concerning *or* regarding sb./sth.

Bezug der a) *(für Kissen usw.)* cover; *(für Polstermöbel)* loose cover; slip-cover *(Amer.)*; *(für Betten)* duvet cover; *(für Kopfkissen)* pillowcase; **b)** *o. Pl. (Erwerb)* obtaining; *(Kauf)* purchase; **~ einer Zeitung** taking a newspaper; **bei ~ von mehr als 100 Stück** if more than 100 are ordered; **c)** *Pl. (österr. auch Sg.) (Gehalt)* salary *sing.*; **die Bezüge der Beamten** the salaries of the civil servants; **d)** *(Verbindung)* connection, link **(zu** with); **der Film vermeidet jeden ~ zur Gegenwart** this film avoids all allusion to the present; **mit** *od.* **unter ~ auf etw.** *(Akk.) (Amtsspr., Kaufmannsspr.)* with reference to sth.; **auf etw.** *(Akk.)* **~ nehmen** *(Amtsspr., Kaufmannspr.)* refer to sth.; **~ nehmend auf unser Telex** with reference to our telex

Bezüger [bəˈtsyːgɐ] **der; ~s, ~** *(schweiz.)* **a)** *s.* **Bezieher; b)** *(von Steuern)* collector

bezüglich [bəˈtsyːklɪç] **1.** *Präp. mit Gen.* concerning; regarding. **2.** *Adj.* **auf etw.** *(Akk.)* **~:** relating to sth.; **die darauf ~en Paragraphen** the relevant paragraphs; **~es Fürwort** *(Sprachw.)* relative pronoun

Bezugnahme [bəˈtsuːknaːmə] **die; ~, ~n** *(Amtsspr.)* reference; **unter ~ auf etw.** *(Akk.)* with reference to sth.

bezugs-, Bezugs-: ~aktie die *(Wirtsch.)* new share; **~berechtigt** *Adj.* entitled to receive goods/payment *postpos.*; **~berechtigt sind folgende** the following are entitled to benefit; **~fertig** *Adj.* ready to move into *pred.*; **eine ~fertige Wohnung** a flat *(Brit.) or (Amer.)* apartment that is ready to move into; **~person die** *(Psych., Soziol.)* **jedes Kind braucht eine ~person** every child needs someone it can relate to and take as an example; **~preis der** [subscription] price; **~punkt der** point of reference; **~quelle die** source of supply; *(Firma)* supplier; **~recht das** *(Wirtsch.)* preemptive *or* subscription right; **~satz der** *(Sprachw.)* relative clause; **~schein der** [ration] coupon; **auf ~schein** on coupons *pl.*; **~system das a)** *(Koordinatensystem)* reference frame; **b)** *(System des Denkens usw.)* terms *pl.* of reference

bezuschussen [bəˈtsuːʃʊsn̩] *tr. V. (Amtsspr.)* subsidize

Bezuschussung die; ~, ~en a) subsidization; **b)** *(Betrag)* subsidy

bezwecken [bəˈtsvɛkn̩] *tr. V.* aim to achieve; aim at; **was willst du damit ~?** what do you expect to achieve by [doing] that?; **was soll das ~?** what is the point of that?; what is that supposed to achieve?

bezweifeln *tr. V.* doubt; question; **sie bezweifelt, daß** *od.* **ob ...:** she doubts whether ...; **ich bezweifle nicht, daß ...:** I do not doubt that ...; **das ist nicht zu ~:** there is no doubt about that; **das möchte ich doch ~:** I have my doubts about that

bezwingbar *Adj.* **a)** *(zu besiegen)* conquerable; *(fig.)* controllable; **er/sie/es ist ~:** he/she/it can be beaten *or* overcome; **b)** *(zu bewältigen)* manageable; negotiable ⟨*course, slope*⟩

bezwingen 1. *unr. tr. V.* conquer ⟨*enemy, mountain, pain, etc.*⟩; defeat ⟨*opponent*⟩; take, capture ⟨*fortress*⟩; master ⟨*pain, hunger*⟩; **seinen Zorn/seine Neugier ~:** keep one's anger/curiosity under control; **er konnte diese Piste/diesen Paß nicht ~:** he was unable to negotiate this course/pass. **2.** *unr. refl. V.* control *or* restrain oneself

bezwingend *Adj.* compelling; irresistible ⟨*smile*⟩

Bezwinger der, Bezwingerin die; ~, ~nen conqueror

Bezwingung die; ~, ~en a) defeat; *(Sieg)* victory **(+** *Gen.* over); *(fig.)* control; **b)** *(Bewältigung)* conquest

BfA [beːɛfˈaː] **die; ~** *Abk.*: **a) Bundesanstalt für Arbeit; b) Bundesversicherungsanstalt für Angestellte**

BGB [beːgeːˈbeː] *Abk.*: **Bürgerliches Gesetzbuch**

BGH [beːgeːˈhaː] **der; ~** *Abk.*: **Bundesgerichtshof**

BGS [beːgeːˈɛs] **der; ~** *Abk.*: **Bundesgrenzschutz**

BH [beːˈhaː] **der; ~[s], ~[s]** *Abk.*: **Büstenhalter** bra

bi [biː] *Adj.; nicht attr. (salopp)* bi *(sl.)*

Biathlon [ˈbiːatlɔn] **das; ~s, ~s** *(Sport)* biathlon

bibbern [ˈbɪbɐn] *itr. V. (ugs.) (vor Kälte)* shiver **(vor** with); *(vor Angst)* shake, tremble **(vor** with); **um jmdn./etw. ~:** fear *or* tremble for sb./sth.

Bibel [ˈbiːbl̩] **die; ~, ~n** *(auch fig.)* Bible

bibel-, Bibel-: ~fest *Adj.* well versed in the Bible *postpos.*; who knows his/her *etc.* Bible *postpos., not pred.*; **du bist ziemlich ~fest** you know your Bible pretty well; **~forscher der** *(veralt.)* Jehovah's Witness; **~spruch der** biblical saying; **~stunde die** *Bible reading with discussion and prayer;* **~vers der** verse from the Bible; **~wort das;** *Pl.* **~worte** biblical saying

[1]Biber [ˈbiːbɐ] **der; ~s, ~:** beaver; **Mantel aus ~:** beaver coat

[2]Biber der *od.* **das; ~s** *(Stoff)* flannelette

Biber-: ~geil das; ~[e]s castor; **~pelz der** beaver [fur]; *(einzelner Pelz)* beaver pelt; **ein Mantel** *usw.* **aus ~pelz** a beaver coat *etc.*; **~schwanz a)** beaver's tail; **b)** *(Ziegel)* plain *or* plane tile *(with curved lower edge)*

Bibliograph [biblioˈgraːf] **der; ~en, ~en** bibliographer

Bibliographie die; ~, ~n bibliography

bibliographieren *tr. V.* **a) Bücher/Titel ~:** list books/titles in a bibliography; **b)** *(Daten feststellen)* establish the bibliographical details of ⟨*book, essay*⟩; identify ⟨*book*⟩; identify the source of ⟨*essay etc.*⟩

Bibliographin die; ~, ~nen *s.* **Bibliograph**

bibliographisch 1. *Adj.* bibliographical. **2.** *adv.* bibliographically; as a bibliography

Bibliomane [biblioˈmaːnə] **der; ~n, ~n** bibliomaniac

Bibliomanie die; ~: bibliomania

bibliophil [biblioˈfiːl] *Adj.* **a)** bibliophilic ⟨*interests etc.*⟩; bibliophile ⟨*collector*⟩; **b)** *(wertvoll)* for the bibliophile *postpos.*; **~e Ausgabe** collector's edition

Bibliophile der/die; *adj. Dekl.* bibliophile; book-lover

Bibliophilie die; ~: bibliophily *(formal)*; love of books

Bibliothek [biblioˈteːk] **die; ~, ~en** library;

bei *od.* an einer ~ angestellt sein have a job in a library
Bibliothekar [bibliote'ka:ɐ] **der; ~s, ~e, Bibliothekarin die; ~, ~nen** librarian
Bibliotheks-: ~benutzer der library-user; **„die ~benutzer werden gebeten, ...":** 'readers are requested ...'; **~katalog der** library catalogue; **~wesen das;** *o. Pl.* library system
biblisch ['bi:blɪʃ] *Adj.* biblical; **ein ~es Alter** a grand old age
Bick·beere ['bɪk-] **die** *(nordd.) s.* **Heidelbeere**
Bidet [bi'de:] **das; ~s, ~s** bidet
bieder ['bi:dɐ] **1.** *Adj.* **a)** unsophisticated; *(langweilig)* stolid; *(treuherzig)* trusting; **b)** *(veralt.: rechtschaffen)* upright. **2.** *adv.* in an unsophisticated manner; **etw. brav und ~ ausführen** carry sth. out faithfully and unquestioningly
Biederkeit die; ~ a) *(Rechtschaffenheit)* [bourgeois] probity; [stolid] uprightness; **b)** *(Rückständigkeit)* conventional attitudes *pl.*; *(Einfältigkeit)* lack of sophistication
Bieder·mann der; *Pl.* **Biedermänner a)** *(veralt.)* man of integrity *or* probity; **b)** *(Spießer)* petty bourgeois
biedermännisch ['bi:dɐmɛnɪʃ] *Adj.* **a)** *(veralt.)* stolidly upright; **b)** *(spießig)* stuffily correct; petty bourgeois
Biedermeier das; ~s Biedermeier [period/style]
Biedermeier-: ~stil der; *o. Pl.* Biedermeier style; **~sträußchen das** *small bouquet wrapped in white lace-paper;* **~zeit die;** *o. Pl.* Biedermeier period
Bieder·sinn der; *o. Pl. (geh.)* [stolid] uprightness; moral rectitude
biegbar *Adj.* flexible; pliable ‹*material*›; **leicht ~:** easily bent
Biege ['bi:gə] **die; ~, ~n** bend; **eine ~ drehen** *(salopp)* stretch one's legs; **eine ~ fahren/fliegen** *(salopp)* go for a spin [in the car/aircraft]
biegen ['bi:gn̩] **1.** *unr. tr. V.* **a)** bend; incline ‹*head*›; **das Recht ~** *(fig. veralt.)* bend the law; **mit gebogenem Rücken sitzen** sit with one's back hunched; **b)** *(österr., Sprachw.) s.* **beugen 1 c. 2.** *unr. refl. V.* bend; *(nachgeben)* give; sag; **der Tisch bog sich unter der Last der Speisen** the table sagged *or* groaned under the weight of the food; **sich vor Lachen ~** *(ugs.)* double up with laughter; **ihre Augenbrauen ~/ihre Nase biegt sich nach oben** her eyebrows curve upward/her nose is turned up. **3.** *unr. itr. V.; mit sein* **a)** turn; **um die Ecke ~:** turn the corner; ‹*car*› take the corner; **b) auf Biegen oder** *od.* **und Brechen** *(ugs.)* at all costs; by hook or by crook; **es geht auf Biegen oder** *od.* **und Brechen** *(ugs.)* it has come to the crunch *or (Amer.)* showdown
biegsam *Adj.* flexible; pliable ‹*material*›; supple ‹*joints, person*›; **ein ~er Charakter** *(fig.)* a malleable personality
Biegsamkeit die; ~ *s.* **biegsam:** flexibility; pliability; suppleness; *(fig.)* malleability
Biegung die; ~, ~en a) bend; **eine [enge] ~ nach rechts machen** bend [sharply] to the right; **b)** *(österr. Sprachw.) s.* **Beugung b**
Biene ['bi:nə] **die; ~, ~n a)** bee; **b)** *(ugs. veralt.: Mädchen)* bird *(Brit. sl.)*; dame *(Amer. sl.)*; **eine flotte ~:** a smashing bird *(Brit. sl.)*; a luscious piece *(sl.)*
Bienen-: ~fleiß der unflagging industry; **mit wahrem ~fleiß ging er daran** he set about it industriously; **~haus das** apiary; **~honig der** bees' honey; **~kasten der** beehive; *(as tech. term)* frame hive; **~königin die** queen bee; **~korb der** straw hive; **~schwarm der** swarm of bees; **~sprache die** language of bees; **~staat der** bee-colony; **~stich der a)** bee-sting; **b)** *(Kuchen) cake with a topping of sugar and almonds (and sometimes a cream filling);* **~stock der** beehive; **~wachs das** beeswax; **~zucht die** beekeeping; **~züchter der** beekeeper
Biennale [biɛ'na:lə] **die; ~, ~n** biennial
Bier [bi:ɐ] **das; ~[e]s,** *(Sorten:)* **~e** beer; **ein kleines/großes ~:** a small/large [glass of] beer; **zwei ~:** two beers; two glasses of beer; **10 verschiedene ~e** ten different beers *or* types of beer; **das ist [nicht] mein ~** *(ugs.)* that is [not] my affair *or* business; **etw. wie sauer** *od.* **saures ~ anpreisen** praise sth. to the skies in an effort to get rid of it/them
Bier-: ~bar die beer-bar; **~bauch der** *(ugs. spött.)* beer belly; **~brauer der** [beer-]brewer; **~brauerei die a)** *o. Pl.* **die ~brauerei** the brewing of beer; brewing beer; **b)** *(Betrieb)* brewery
Bierchen das; ~s, ~ *(ugs.)* **a)** *(gute Sorte)* **so ein ~:** such a beer; a beer like that; **das ist ein ~!** that's quite some beer! *(Brit.)*; great beer! *(Amer.)*; **b)** *(Glas Bier)* little [glass of] beer
bier-, Bier-: ~deckel der beer-mat; **~dose die** beer can; **~durst der: [schrecklichen] ~durst haben** be [badly] in need of a beer; **~ernst** *(ugs.)* **1.** *Adj.* deadly serious; solemn; **2.** *adv.* solemnly; **so ~ernst** with such deadly seriousness; **~ernst der** deadly seriousness; **~faß das** beer-barrel; **~filz der** beer-mat; **~flasche die** beer-bottle; *(voll)* bottle of beer; **~garten der** beer garden; **~glas das** beer-glass; **~kasten der** beer-crate; **~keller der** beer cellar; **~kneipe die** ≈ pub *(Brit. coll.)*; beerhouse *(Amer.)*; **~krug der** beer-mug; *(aus Glas, Zinn)* tankard; **~kutscher der** *(ugs.)* brewery delivery driver; **~laune die** *(ugs.)* **in einer ~laune, aus einer ~laune heraus** in an exuberant mood; **~leiche die** *(ugs. scherzh.)* drunk lying dead to the world; **~lokal das** pub *(Brit. coll.)*; beerhouse *(Amer.)*; **~ruhe die** *(ugs.)* unruffled calm; unflappability *(coll.)*; **~schinken der** *slicing sausage containing pieces of ham;* **~schwemme die** beer hall; **~seidel das** beer-mug; *(aus Glas, Zinn)* tankard; **~selig** *(scherzh.)* **1.** *Adj.* beery ‹*mood*›; **~selig, wie er war** in his beerily happy state; **2.** *adv.* in a beerily happy state; ‹*laugh*› in beery merriment; **~stube die** ≈ small pub *(Brit. coll.)*; beer bar *(Amer.)*; **~suppe die** *soup containing beer, sugar, and eggs or rye bread;* **~tisch der: am ~tisch** over a glass of beer; in the pub *(Brit. coll.) or (Amer.)* bar; **~trinker der, ~trinkerin die** beer-drinker; **~verlag der, ~vertrieb der** beer wholesaler's; **~wärmer der** beer-warmer; **~wurst die** *smoked slicing sausage containing beef, pork, bacon, and spices;* **~zeitung die** joke newspaper *(made up for a closed group);* **~zelt das** beer tent; **~zipfel der** *tag worn by member of a student corporation, bearing its colours*
Biese ['bi:zə] **die; ~, ~n a)** *(bes. Milit.)* trouser-stripe; *(Paspel)* piping; **b)** *(Fältchen)* tuck
Biest [bi:st] **das; ~[e]s, ~er** *(ugs. abwertend)* **a)** *(Tier, Gegenstand)* wretched thing; *(Bestie)* creature; **ein riesiges ~ von einem Elefanten** a huge elephant; **b)** *(Mensch)* beast *(derog.)*; wretch; **das freche ~:** the cheeky devil *(coll.)*
Biesterei die; ~, ~en *(ugs. abwertend) (Gemeinheit)* beastly trick *(coll.)*; *(etw. Ärgerliches)* blasted nuisance *(coll.)*
biestig *(ugs. abwertend)* **1.** *Adj.* **a)** beastly *(coll.)* (zu to); **ganz schön ~ werden** turn really nasty; **b)** *(unangenehm)* filthy, beastly *(coll.)*‹*weather*›; frightful *(coll.)*‹*cold*›. **2.** *adv.* **a)** *(gemein)* nastily; in a beastly way *(coll.)*; **b)** *(sehr)* horribly *(coll.)*
Biet [bi:t] **das; ~[e]s, ~e** *(schweiz.)* area
bieten ['bi:tn̩] **1.** *unr. tr. V.* **a)** offer; put on ‹*programme etc.*›; provide ‹*shelter, guarantee, etc.*›; *(bei Auktionen, Kartenspielen)* bid **(für, auf +** *Akk.* for); **jmdm. Geld/eine Chance ~:** offer sb. money/a chance; **wir ~ beim Pokern bis zu 5 DM** we play poker for stakes of up to five marks; **was** *od.* **wieviel bietest du mir dafür?** what will you give me for it?; **jmdm. den Arm ~** *(geh.)* offer sb. one's arm; **jmdm. die Hand zur Versöhnung ~** *(fig. geh.)* hold out the olive-branch to sb.; **für Jugendliche wird nichts geboten** there is nothing for young people to do; **eine hervorragende Leistung ~:** put up an outstanding performance; **das bietet keine Schwierigkeiten** that presents no difficulties; **das Stadion bietet Platz für 40 000 Personen** the stadium has room for *or* can hold 40,000 people; **b) ein schreckliches/gespenstisches** *usw.* **Bild ~:** present a terrible/eerie *etc.* picture; be a terrible/eerie *etc.* sight; **einen prächtigen Anblick ~:** look splendid; be a splendid sight; **c)** *(zumuten)* **das lasse ich mir nicht ~:** I won't put up with *or* stand for that. **2.** *unr. refl. V.* **sich jmdm. ~:** present itself to sb.; **es bietet sich ...:** there is ...; **hier bietet sich dir eine Chance** this is an opportunity for you; this offers you an opportunity; **ihnen bot sich ein Bild des Grauens** a horrific sight confronted them. **3.** *unr. itr. V.* bid **(auf +** *Akk.* for); **jeder kann auf einer Auktion ~:** anyone can make a bid at an auction
Bieter der; ~s, ~, Bieterin die; ~, ~nen bidder
Bifokal·brille [bifo'ka:l-] **die** bifocal spectacles *pl.*; bifocals *pl.*
Bigamie [biga'mi:] **die; ~, ~n** bigamy *no def. art.*
Bigamist der; ~en, ~en bigamist
Big Band ['bɪg 'bænd] **die; ~ ~, ~ ~s** big band
Big Business ['bɪg 'bɪznɪs] **das; ~ ~:** big business *no art.*; **zum ~ ~ gehören** belong to the world of big business
bigott [bi'gɔt] *(abwertend)* **1.** *Adj.* **a)** religiose; over-devout; **b)** *(scheinheilig)* sanctimonious; holier-than-thou; *(heuchlerisch)* hypocritical; **~e Heuchler** sanctimonious hypocrites. **2.** *adv.* sanctimoniously; *(heuchlerisch)* hypocritically
Bigotterie [bigɔtə'ri:] **die; ~** *(abwertend)* religious bigotry; religiosity; *(Scheinheiligkeit)* sanctimoniousness
Bijou [bi'ʒu:] **das; ~s, ~s** *(veralt., schweiz.)* piece of jewellery; **~s** jewellery *sing.*
Bijouterie [biʒutə'ri:] **die; ~, ~n** *(veralt., schweiz.)* jeweller's shop
Bikini [bi'ki:ni] **der; ~s, ~s** bikini; **im ~:** in a bikini/in bikinis
bi·konkav *Adj. (Optik)* biconcave
bi·konvex *Adj. (Optik)* biconvex
bi·labial *Adj. (Phon.)* bilabial
Bilanz [bi'lants] **die; ~, ~en a)** *(Kaufmannsspr., Wirtsch.)* balance sheet; **die ~ des Jahres** the year's results *pl.*; **eine ~ aufstellen** make up the accounts *pl.*; draw up a balance sheet; **b)** *(Ergebnis)* outcome; *(Endeffekt)* net result; **erfreuliche ~:** happy outcome; **~ ziehen** take stock; sum things up; **[die] ~ aus etw. ziehen** draw conclusions *pl.* about sth.; *(rückblickend)* take stock of sth.
Bilanz-: ~analyse die *(Wirtsch., Kaufmannsspr.)* balance sheet analysis; **~buchhalter der** *(Wirtsch., Kaufmannsspr.)* [stewardship] accountant
bilanzieren *(Wirtsch., Kaufmannsspr.)* **1.** *itr. V.* balance; **mit ... DM ~:** show a balance of ... marks. **2.** *tr. V.* balance ‹*account*›; show ‹*turnover*› in the balance sheet; *(fig.)* sum up
Bilanz-: ~prüfer der *(Wirtsch., Kaufmannsspr.)* auditor; **~summe die** *(Wirtsch., Kaufmannsspr.)* balance-sheet total
bi·lateral *(Politik)* **1.** *Adj.* bilateral. **2.** *adv.* bilaterally

Bild [bɪlt] **das; ~[e]s, ~er a)** picture; *(in einem Buch usw.)* illustration; *(Spielkarte)* picture *or* court card; **ein ~ [von jmdm./etw.] machen** take a picture [of sb./sth.]; **wieviele ~er hast du noch auf dem Film?** how many photos *or* exposures have you left on the film?; **ein ~ von einem Mann/einer Frau sein** be a fine specimen of a man/woman; be a fine-looking man/woman; **ein lebendes ~:** a tableau vivant; **b)** *(Aussehen)* appearance; *(Anblick)* sight; **das ~ der Stadt** the appearance of the town; the townscape; **ein ~ des Jammers sein** *od.* **bieten** be a pathetic sight; **ein ~ für [die] Götter [sein]** *(scherzh.)* [be] a sight for sore eyes; **c)** *(Metapher)* image; metaphor; **im ~ bleiben** extend *or* continue the metaphor; **d)** *(Abbild)* image; *(Spiegel~)* reflection; **er ist [ganz] das ~ seines Vaters** he is the [very] image of his father; **e)** *(Vorstellung)* image; **ein falsches/merkwürdiges ~ von etw. haben** have a wrong impression/curious idea of sth.; **sich** *(Dat.)* **ein ~ von jmdm./etw. machen** form an impression of sb./sth.; **jmdn. [über etw.** *(Akk.)*] **ins ~ setzen** put sb. in the picture [about sth.]; **[über etw.** *(Akk.)*] **im ~e sein** be in the picture [about sth.]; **ich bin im ~e** *(als Reaktion: ich verstehe)* I'm with you; **f)** *(Theater)* scene

Bild-: ~archiv das picture library; **~aus·fall der** loss of picture *or* vision; **~aus·schnitt der** section of a/the picture; *(bes. Kunst)* detail; **~autor der** photographer *(who takes the photographs for a book)*; **~band der** copiously illustrated book

bildbar *Adj.* formable **(aus** from); malleable ‹*personality, mind*›; **schwer ~e Laute** sounds which are difficult to form

Bild-: ~bei·lage die pictorial *or* illustrated supplement; **~bericht der** photo-reportage; **~beschreibung die** picture description; **~dokument das** pictorial document; *(Film)* pictorial record

bilden 1. *tr. V.* **a)** form **(aus** from); *(modellieren)* mould **(aus** from); **den Charakter ~:** form *or* mould sb.'s personality; **eine Gasse ~:** make a path *or* passage; **sich** *(Dat.)* **ein Urteil [über jmdn./etw.] ~:** form an opinion [of sb./sth.]; **b)** *(ansammeln)* build up ‹*fund, capital*›; **c)** *(darstellen)* be, represent ‹*exception etc.*›; constitute ‹*rule etc.*›; **den Höhepunkt des Abends bildete sein Auftritt** his appearance was the high spot of the evening; **d)** *(erziehen)* educate; **Reisen bildet den Geist** travel broadens the mind. **2.** *refl. V.* **a)** *(entstehen)* form; **eine starke Opposition bildete sich** a strong opposition developed *or* came into being; **b)** *(lernen)* educate oneself. **3.** *itr. V.* **Lesen bildet** reading educates *or* cultivates the mind; **Reisen bildet** travel broadens the mind

bildend *Adj.* **a) die ~e Kunst, die ~en Künste** the plastic arts *pl.* *(including painting and architecture)*; **b)** *(belehrend)* educational

Bilder·bogen der pictorial broadsheet

Bilder·buch das picture-book *(for children)*; **aussehen wie im** *od.* **aus dem ~:** look a picture

Bilderbuch-: perfect ‹*landing, weather*›; picture-book ‹*weather, village*›; story-book ‹*marriage, career*›; archetypal ‹*Catholic, proletarian, capitalist*›

Bilder-: ~geschichte die picture story; *(Comic)* strip cartoon; **~kult der** idolatry; **~rahmen der** picture-frame; **~rätsel das** picture puzzle; *(Rebus)* rebus; **~schrift die** pictographic [system of] writing; *(Hieroglyphen)* hieroglyphics *pl.*; **~sturm der** *(hist.)* iconoclasm; **~stürmer der** *(hist.; auch fig.)* iconoclast

bild-, Bild-: ~fläche die: auf der ~fläche erscheinen *(ugs.)* appear on the scene; *(auftauchen)* turn up; **von der ~fläche verschwinden** *(ugs.)* *(rasch weggehen)* make oneself scarce *(coll.)*; *(aus der Öffentlichkeit verschwinden)* disappear from the scene; **~folge die a)** *o. Pl.* *(im Film)* sequence of shots; **b)** [picture] sequence; **~frequenz die** *(Film, Ferns.)* picture frequency; **~geschichte die** *s.* **Bildergeschichte; ~haft 1.** *Adj.* graphic; pictorial, illustrative ‹*language, sense, etc.*›; vivid ‹*imagination, clarity, etc.*›; **2.** *adv.* graphically; *(lebhaft)* vividly; **~haftigkeit die; ~:** vividness; graphic quality; *(der Sprache)* pictorial *or* illustrative quality; **~hauer der** sculptor; **~hauerei** [---'-] **die** sculpture *no def. art.*; **~hauerin die; ~, ~nen** sculptress; **~hauerisch** [~haʊ̯ərɪʃ] *Adj.; nicht präd.* sculptural; **~hauer·kunst die** *s.* **Bildhauerei; ~hübsch** *Adj.* really lovely; stunningly beautiful ‹*girl*›

bildlich 1. *Adj.* pictorial; *(übertragen)* figurative; **~er Ausdruck, ~e Wendung** figure of speech; image. **2.** *adv.* **a)** pictorially; **sich etw. ~ vorstellen** picture sth. to oneself; **b)** figuratively; **~ gesprochen** metaphorically speaking

Bild-: ~material das pictures *pl.* **(über +** *Akk.* of); *(Fotos/Film)* photographic/film material **(über +** *Akk.* of); **~mischer der, ~mischerin die** *(Ferns.)* vision-mixer

bildnerisch 1. *Adj.* artistic; creative ‹*abilities*›. **2.** *adv.* artistically

Bildnis ['bɪltnɪs] **das; ~ses, ~se** portrait; *(Plastik)* sculpture

Bild-: ~platte die video disc; **~plattenspieler der** video disc player; **~qualität die** picture quality; **~reportage die** photo-reportage; **~reporter der** photo-journalist; **~röhre die** *(Ferns.)* picture tube

bildsam *Adj.* *(geh.)* malleable; impressionable

Bild·schärfe die *(Fot., Ferns.)* definition

Bild·schirm der *(Ferns., Informationst.)* screen; **am ~ arbeiten** work at *or* with a VDU; **einen Text am ~ korrigieren** correct a text on screen

bildschirm-, Bildschirm-: ~arbeit die VDU work *no art., no pl.*; **~gerät das** VDU; visual display unit; **~gerecht** *Adj.* in screen format *postpos.*; **~text der** viewdata; **~zeitung die** teletext

bild-, Bild-: ~schnitzer der wood-carver; wood-sculptor; **~schön** *Adj.* really lovely; stunningly beautiful ‹*girl, woman*›; **~seite die a)** *(einer Münze)* obverse; *(beim Werfen)* **die ~seite ist oben** it's heads; **b)** *(bei Büchern, Zeitungen)* picture page; **zwei ~seiten** two pages of pictures; **~serie die** series *or* sequence of pictures; **~stelle die** picture and film library; **~stock der** wayside shrine; **~störung die** interference *no def. art.* on vision; **~synchron** *Adj.* *(Film, Ferns.)* synchronized [with the picture]; **~telefon das** video telephone; **~teppich der** tapestry

Bildung die; ~, ~en a) *(Erziehung)* education; *(Kultur)* culture; **eine umfassende ~:** a broad educational and cultural background; **das gehört zur allgemeinen ~:** that is something every educated person should know; **[keine] ~ haben** be [un]educated; *([un]kultiviert sein)* be [un]cultivated *or* [un]cultured; **b)** *(das Formen, Schaffung)* formation; **die ~ einer Untersuchungskommission** setting up a committee of investigation; **c)** *(Form, Gestalt)* form; shape; **die seltsamen ~en der Wolken/Eiskristalle** the strange formations of the clouds/ice crystals

bildungs-, Bildungs-: ~anstalt die *(Amtsspr.)* educational establishment; **~arbeit die;** *o. Pl.* educational work *no art.*; **~beflissen** *Adj.* keen on education *postpos.*; *(sich bilden wollend)* keen on self-improvement *postpos.*; **~bürger der** [traditionally educated] middle-class intellectual; **~chancen** *Pl.* educational opportunities; **~dünkel der** intellectual arrogance *or* snobbery; **~einrichtung die** *s.* **~anstalt; ~erlebnis das** formative experience; **~fähig** *Adj.* fast-learning; receptive to teaching *postpos.*; **~feindlich** *Adj.* hostile to education *postpos.*; anti-education; **~gang der** educational career; **~grad der** level of education; **~gut das** material for one's general education; *(Kulturgut)* cultural heritage; **~hunger der** thirst for education; **~hungrig** *Adj.* eager to be educated *postpos.*; **~ideal das** educational ideal; **~lücke die** gap in one's education; **das ist eine ~lücke!** that's culpable ignorance!; **~monopol das** monopoly of education; **~not·stand der** state of emergency in education; **~politik die** educational policy; **~politisch** *Adj.* educational-policy *attrib.* ‹*measure, strategy*›; ‹*discussion*› concerning educational policy; **~reform die** educational reform; **~reise die** educational tour; **~roman der** *(Literaturw.)* novel of character development; Bildungsroman; **~stätte die** *(geh.)* educational establishment; *(Universität)* seat of learning; **~urlaub der** educational leave; **~weg der** educational course; **der zweite ~weg** the second chance to study; the alternative way of studying *(in adult classes)*; **auf dem zweiten ~weg** using the second chance to study *(in adult classes)*; **~wesen das;** *o. Pl.* education system; **das ~wesen** education

Bild-: ~unter·schrift die caption; **~wand die** [projection] screen; **~werfer der** epidiascope; **~werk das** *(geh.)* sculpture; **~wörter·buch das** pictorial dictionary; *(für Kinder)* picture dictionary; **~zuschrift die** reply enclosing a photograph

Bilge ['bɪlgə] **die; ~, ~n** *(Seemannsspr.)* bilge

bilingual [bilɪŋ'gu̯a:l] **1.** *Adj.* bilingual. **2.** *adv.* bilingually

Billard ['bɪljart, *österr.:* bi'ja:ɐ̯] **das; ~s, ~e,** *österr.:* **~s** billiards

Billard-: ~kugel die billiard-ball; **~stock der** billiard-cue; **~tisch der** billiard-table

Billet *(schweiz.)*, **Billett** [bɪl'jɛt] **das; ~[e]s, ~e** *od.* **~s a)** *(schweiz., sonst veralt.)* [entrance] ticket; **b)** *(schweiz., sonst veralt.)* [train/tram/bus-]ticket; **c)** *(österr., sonst veralt.)* note; **d)** *(österr.: Glückwunschkarte)* greetings card *(Brit.)*; greeting card *(Amer.)*

Billiarde [bɪ'li̯ardə] **die; ~, ~n** thousand million million; quadrillion *(Amer.)*

billig ['bɪlɪç] **1.** *Adj.* **a)** cheap; **ein ~er Preis** *(ugs.)* a low price; **b)** *(abwertend: primitiv)* shabby, cheap ‹*trick*›; feeble ‹*excuse*›; **ist dir das nicht zu ~?** isn't that beneath you?; **ein ~er Trost** cold comfort; **c)** *(veralt.: angemessen)* reasonable; proper. **2.** *adv.* **a)** cheaply; **~ einkaufen** shop cheaply; **~ abzugeben** *(in Anzeigen)* for sale cheap; **~ davonkommen** *(fig. ugs.)* get off lightly; **b)** *(veralt.: angemessen)* **nicht mehr als ~:** no more than is reasonable *or* proper; **jeder ~ denkende Mensch** any fair-minded person; *s. auch* **recht**

Billig·angebot das special *or* cut-price offer

billigen *tr. V.* approve; **~, daß jmd. etw. tut** approve of sb.'s doing sth.; **ich kann nicht ~, daß du dich daran beteiligst** I cannot approve of *or* condone your taking part; **etw. stillschweigend ~:** give sth. one's tacit approval

billigermaßen, billigerweise *Adv.* rightly; justifiably

Billig-: ~flagge die flag of convenience; **~flug der** cheap flight

Billigkeit die; ~ a) cheapness; low cost; **b)** *(Rechtsw. od. geh.)* fairness; equitableness

Billig-: ~laden der cut-price shop; **~lohn der** low wages *pl.*; **~lohn·land das** low-

wage country; ~**preis der** low price; *(verbilligter Preis)* cut price
Billigung die; ~: approval; **jmds. ~ finden** meet with *or* receive sb.'s approval
Billig·ware die cheap goods *pl.*
Billion [bɪ'li̯o:n] **die;** ~, ~**en** million million; trillion *(Amer.)*
Bilsen·kraut ['bɪlzn̩-] **das;** *o. Pl.* henbane
Bilux·lampe ['bi:lʊks-] **die** twin-filament bulb
bim [bɪm] *Interj.* ding; ~, **bam** ding dong
Bimbam *in* **[ach du] heiliger ~!** *(ugs.)* [oh] my sainted aunt! *(sl.)*; glory be! *(sl.)*
Bi·metall das *(Technik)* bimetallic strip; **aus ~:** bimetallic
Bimmel ['bɪml̩] **die;** ~, ~**n** *(ugs.)* [ting-a-ling] bell
Bimmel·bahn die *(ugs. scherzh.)* narrow-gauge railway *(with a warning bell)*
Bimmelei die; ~ *(ugs. abwertend)* constant ringing; *(lautmalend)* ting-a-ling-a-ling
bimmeln *itr. V. (ugs.)* ring
Bimse ['bɪmzə] *Pl. (ugs.)* ~ **kriegen** get a walloping *(sl.) or* thrashing
bimsen *tr. V. (ugs.)* **a)** *(drillen)* drill; **b)** *(einexerzieren)* practise; **c)** *(Schülerspr.: pauken)* mug up *(sl.)*
Bims·stein ['bɪms-] **der a)** pumice-stone; **b)** *o. Pl. (Gestein)* pumice; **c)** *(Baustein)* pumice block
bin [bɪn] *1. Pers. Sg. Präsens v.* ¹**sein**
binar [bi'na:ɐ̯], **binär** [bi'nɛ:ɐ̯], **binarisch** [bi'na:rɪʃ] *Adj. (fachspr.)* binary
binaural [binau̯'ra:l] *Adj. (Med., Technik)* binaural
Binde ['bɪndə] **die;** ~, ~**n a)** *(Verband)* bandage; *(Augen~)* blindfold; **b)** *(Arm~)* armband; **c)** *(ugs.: Damen~)* [sanitary] towel *(Brit.) or (Amer.)* napkin; **d)** *(veralt.: Krawatte)* tie; **sich** *(Dat.)* **einen hinter die ~ gießen** *od.* **kippen** *(ugs.)* have a drink or two
Binde-: ~**gewebe das** *(Anat.)* connective tissue; ~**glied das** [connecting] link; ~**haut die** *(Anat.)* conjunctiva; ~**haut·entzündung die** *(Med.)* conjunctivitis *no art.*; ~**mittel das** binder
binden 1. *unr. tr. V.* **a)** *(bündeln)* tie; **etw. zu etw. ~:** tie sth. into sth.; **b)** *(herstellen)* make up ‹*wreath, bouquet*›; make ‹*broom*›; **c)** *(fesseln)* bind; **jmdn. an Händen und Füßen ~:** bind sb. hand and foot; *s. auch* **gebunden, Hand; d)** *(verpflichten)* bind; **ich bin zu jung, um mich schon zu ~:** I am too young to be tied down; **nicht mehr gebunden sein** be free of any ties; **e)** *(befestigen, auch fig.)* tie **(an** + *Dat.* to); **nicht an einen Ort gebunden sein** *(fig.)* not be tied to one place; **jmdn. an sich** *(Akk.)* ~ *(fig.)* make sb. dependent on one; **f)** *(knüpfen)* tie ‹*knot, bow, etc.*›; knot ‹*tie*›; **g)** *(festhalten)* bind ‹*soil, mixture, etc.*›; thicken ‹*sauce*›; **der Regen bindet den Staub** the rain lays the dust; **h)** *(Buchw.)* bind; **i)** *(Musik)* slur; **j)** *(Verslehre)* **Wörter durch Reime ~:** link words in rhyme; **in gebundener Rede/Sprache** in verse. **2.** *unr. itr. V. (fest machen)* bind
bindend *Adj.* binding **(für** on); definite ‹*answer*›
Binder der; ~**s,** ~ **a)** *(Krawatte)* tie; **b)** *(Bindemittel)* binder; **c)** *(Landw.)* [reaper-]binder; **d)** *(Bauw.: Stein)* header; **e)** *(Bauw.: Dachbalken)* [roof] truss
Binderei die; ~, ~**en a)** *(Blumen~)* wreath and bouquet department; **b)** *(Buch~)* bindery
Binde-: ~**strich der** hyphen; ~**wort das** *(Sprachw.)* conjunction
Bind·faden der string; **ein [Stück] ~:** a piece of string; **es regnet Bindfäden** *(ugs.)* it's raining cats and dogs *(coll.)*
Bindung die; ~, ~**en a)** *(Beziehung)* relationship **(an** + *Akk.* to); **seine politische ~ an die Sozialdemokraten** his political commitment to *or* ties with the Social Democrats; **b)** *(Verbundenheit)* attachment **(an** + *Akk.* to); **c)** *(Ski~)* binding; **d)** *(Chemie)* bond; **e)** *(Weberei)* weave
Bingo ['bɪŋgo] **das;** ~**[s]** bingo
binnen ['bɪnən] *Präp. mit Dat. od. (geh.) Gen.* within; ~ **Jahresfrist** within a year; ~ **kurzem** soon
binnen-, Binnen-: ~**bords** *Adv. (Seemannsspr.)* inboard; ~**deich der** inner dike; ~**deutsch 1.** *Adj.* ‹*dialect*› spoken in Germany; ‹*word, expression, etc.*› used in Germany; **2.** *adv.* in Germany; ~**fischerei die** freshwater fishing; ~**gewässer das** inland water; ~**hafen der** inland port; ~**handel der** domestic *or* home trade; ~**land das** *o. Pl.* interior; **im ~land** inland; ~**ländisch** *Adj.; nicht präd.* inland; ~**markt der** *(Wirtsch.)* domestic *or* home market; **europäischer ~markt** internal European market; ~**meer das** inland sea; ~**reim der** *(Literaturw.)* internal rhyme; ~**schiffahrt die** inland navigation; ~**schiffer der** member of an inland ship's crew; *(auf Schlepp-, Schubkahn)* bargee *(Brit.)*; bargeman *(Amer.)*; ~**see der** lake; ~**staat der** land locked country *or* state; ~**zoll der** internal duty *or* tariff
binokular [binoku'la:ɐ̯] *Adj.* binocular
Binom [bi'no:m] **das;** ~**s,** ~**e** *(Math.)* binomial
binomisch *Adj. (Math.)* binomial
Binse ['bɪnzə] **die;** ~, ~**n** *(Bot.)* rush; **in die ~n gehen** *(ugs.) (mißlingen)* fall through; *(verlorengehen, entzweigehen)* go for a burton *(Brit. sl.)*; come to grief *(Amer.)*; ‹*money*› go down the drain *(coll.)*; ‹*vehicle, machine*› pack up *(sl.)*; **die Prüfung ist in die ~n gegangen** the exam was a disaster
Binsen·weisheit die truism
Bio ['bi:o] *o. Art. (Schülerspr.)* biol *(school sl.)*; biology
bio-, Bio: ~**aktiv 1.** *Adj.* biological ‹*washing powder*›; **2.** *adv.* biologically; ~**chemie die** biochemistry; ~**chemisch** *Adj.* biochemical; ~**dynamisch 1.** *Adj.* organic; **2.** *adv.* organically; ~**gas** ['---] **das** *(Ökologie)* biogas; ~**genese die** biogenesis; ~**genetisch** *Adj.* biogenetic; ~**graph der;** ~**en,** ~**en** biographer; ~**graphie die;** ~, ~**n a)** *(Beschreibung)* biography; **b)** *(Lebenslauf)* life [history]; ~**graphin die;** ~, ~**nen** biographer; ~**graphisch** *Adj.* biographical; ~**laden** ['----] **der** *(ugs.)* health-food shop; ~**loge der;** ~**n,** ~**n** biologist; ~**logie die;** ~: biology *no art.*; ~**login die;** ~, ~**nen** biologist; *s. auch* **-in;** ~**logisch 1.** *Adj.* **a)** biological; **ein ~logisches Standardwerk** a standard work of biology; **b)** *(natürlich)* natural ‹*medicine, cosmetic, etc.*›; **2.** *adv.* **a)** biologically; **b)** *(natürlich)* naturally; ~**masse** *die* biomass
Bionik [bi'o:nɪk] **die;** ~: bionics *sing., no art.*
Bio·physik die biophysics *sing., no art.*
bio·physikalisch *Adj.* biophysical
Biopsie [bio'psi:] **die;** ~, ~**n** *(Med.)* biopsy
Bio-: ~**rhythmus der** biorhythm; ~**sphäre** [--'--] **die** biosphere
Biotop [bio'to:p] **der** *od.* **das;** ~**s,** ~**e** *(Biol.)* biotope
Bio·wissenschaften *Pl.* life sciences
bi·polar *Adj. (bes. Math., Physik)* bipolar
bi·quadratisch *Adj. (Math.)* biquadratic
Bircher·mü[e]sli ['bɪrçɐmy:(ə)sli] **das** muesli *(made with fresh fruit)*
Birke ['bɪrkə] **die;** ~, ~**n a)** *(Baum)* birch[-tree]; **b)** *o. Pl. (Holz)* birch[wood]
Birken-: ~**holz das;** *o. Pl.* birch[wood]; ~**wald der** birch-wood; *(größer)* birch forest; ~**wasser das;** *Pl.* ~**wässer** hair lotion made from birch sap
Birk-: ~**hahn der** blackcock; ~**huhn das** black grouse
Birma ['bɪrma] **(das);** ~**s** Burma
Birmane [bɪr'ma:nə] **der;** ~**n,** ~**n, Birmanin die;** ~, ~**nen** Burmese; *s. auch* **-in**
Birn·baum der a) pear-tree; **b)** *(o. Pl.: Holz)* pear-wood
Birne ['bɪrnə] **die;** ~, ~**n a)** pear; **b)** *(Glüh~)* [light-]bulb; **c)** *(salopp: Kopf)* nut *(sl.)*; **eine weiche ~ haben** *(salopp)* be soft in the head
Birnen·geist der pear brandy
bis [bɪs] **1.** *Präp. mit Akk.* **a)** *(zeitlich)* until; till; *(die ganze Zeit über und bis zu einem bestimmten Zeitpunkt)* up to; up until; up till; *(nicht später als)* by; **ich muß bis fünf Uhr warten** I have to wait until *or* till five o'clock; ~ **[einschließlich] Freitag** by Friday; **von Dienstag ~ Donnerstag** from Tuesday to Thursday; Tuesday through Thursday *(Amer.)*; **von sechs ~ sieben [Uhr]** from six until *or* till seven [o'clock]; ~ **Ende März ist er zurück/verreist** he'll be back by/away until the end of March; ~ **dann** *od.* **dahin will ich Ergebnisse sehen/muß ich mich noch gedulden** I want to see results by then/I must be patient until then; ~ **wann dauert das Konzert?** till *or* until when does the concert go on?; how long does the concert last?; ~ **jetzt ist nichts geschehen** up to now *or* so far nothing has happened; ~ **dann/gleich/später/morgen/nachher!** see you then/in a while/later/tomorrow/later!; ~ **spätestens Montag** *od.* **Montag spätestens** by Monday at the latest; **er ist [nur] ~ 17 Uhr hier** he is [only] here until *or* till 5 o'clock; **er ist [spätestens] ~ 17 Uhr hier** he will be here by 5 o'clock [at the latest]; *s. auch* **dato; b)** *(räumlich)* to; **dieser Zug fährt nur ~ Offenburg** this train only goes to *or* as far as Offenburg; ~ **wohin fährt der Bus?** how far does the bus go?; **nur ~ Seite 100** only up to *or* as far as page 100; ~ **5 000 Mark** up to 5,000 marks; **von Anfang ~ Ende** from beginning to end; ~ **dahin sind es 2 km** it's 2 km to there; **c)** *in* ~ **auf** *(einschließlich)* down to; *(mit Ausnahme von)* except for; ~ **auf weiteres** for the time being; **d)** *in* ~ **zu** up to; **Städte ~ zu 50 000 Einwohnern** towns of up to 50,000 inhabitants. **2.** *Adv.* ~ **zu 6 Personen** up to six people; **Kinder ~ 6 Jahre** children up to the age of six *or* up to six years of age; **die Feier dauerte ~ gegen 10 Uhr** the party went on until *or* till about 10 o'clock; ~ **gegen 10 Uhr ist es fertig** it will be ready by about 10 o'clock; ~ **nach Köln** to Cologne; ~ **an die Decke** up to the ceiling; ~ **ins kleinste** *od.* **letzte** down to the smallest *or* last detail. **3.** *Konj.* **a)** *(nebenordnend)* to; **vier ~ fünf** four to five; **heiter ~ wolkig** fair or cloudy; **b)** *(bevor nicht)* until; till; ~ **daß der Tod euch scheidet** *(geh.)* until *or* till death do you part; **c)** *(österr.: sobald)* when; **gleich ~ er aufgewacht ist** as soon as he's woken up
Bisam ['bi:zam] **der;** ~**s,** ~**e** *od.* ~**s a)** *s.* **Moschus; b)** *(Pelz)* musquash
Bisam·ratte die musk-rat
Bischof ['bɪʃɔf] **der;** ~**s, Bischöfe** ['bɪʃœfə] bishop
bischöflich *Adj.* episcopal
Bischofs-: ~**amt das** episcopate; office of bishop; ~**hut der** bishop's hat; ~**konferenz die** conference of bishops; ~**mütze die** [bishop's] mitre; ~**sitz der** seat of a/the bishopric; ~**stab der** [bishop's] crosier *or* crook; ~**stadt die** *s.* ~**sitz**
Bise ['bi:zə] **die;** ~, ~**n** *(schweiz.) north[-east] wind to the north of the Alps;* bise
Bi·sexualität die bisexuality
bi·sexuell 1. *Adj.* bisexual. **2.** *adv.* bisexually
bis·her *Adv.* up to now; *(aber jetzt nicht mehr)* until now; till now; ~ **war alles in Ordnung** everything has been all right up to now/everything was all right until *or* till now; **er hat sich ~ nicht gemeldet** he hasn't been in touch up to now *or* as yet; **das wußte ich ~ nicht** I didn't know that till now *or* before; **ein ~ unbekanntes Buch** a hitherto *or* previously unknown book

bisherig *Adj.; nicht präd.* *(vorherig)* previous; *(momentan)* present; sie ziehen um, ihre ~e Wohnung wird zu klein they are moving – their present flat is getting too small; sie sind umgezogen, ihre ~e Wohnung wurde zu klein they have moved – their previous flat became too small

Biskaya [bɪs'ka:ja] die; ~: die ~/der Golf von ~: the Bay of Biscay

Biskuit [bɪs'kvi:t] das *od.* der; ~[e]s, ~s *od.* ~e a) sponge biscuit; b) *(~teig)* sponge

Biskuit-: ~rolle die Swiss roll; ~teig der sponge mixture

bis·lang *Adv.: s.* bisher

Bismarck·hering ['bɪsmark-] der Bismarck herring

Bison ['bi:zɔn] der; ~s, ~s bison

Biß [bɪs] der; Bisses, Bisse; a) bite; b) *(ugs.: Engagement)* punch

bißchen *indekl. Indefinitpron.* a) *(in der Funktion eines Adjektivs)* ein ~ Geld/Brot/Milch/Wasser a bit of *or* a little money/bread/a drop of *or* a little milk/water; ich würde ihm kein ~ Geld mehr leihen I wouldn't lend him any more money at all; das ~ Geld/Farbe that [little] bit of money/[little] drop of paint; ein/kein ~ Angst haben be a bit/not a bit frightened; b) *(in der Funktion eines Adverbs)* ein/kein ~: a bit *or* a little/not a *or* one bit; ich werde mich ein ~ aufs Ohr legen I'm going to lie down for a bit; er hat mir kein ~ geholfen he didn't help me one [little] bit; ein klein ~: a little bit; ein ~ zuviel/mehr a bit too much/a bit more; ein ~ sehr teuer sein be getting rather expensive; c) *(in der Funktion eines Substantivs)* ein ~: a bit; a little; *(bei Flüssigkeiten)* a drop; a little; von dem ~ werde ich nicht satt that little bit/drop won't fill me up; das/kein ~: the little [bit]/not a *or* one bit; *s. auch* lieb 1d

bissel ['bɪsl̩] *(südd., österr. ugs.) s.* bißchen

Bissen der; ~s, ~: mouthful; laß mich mal einen kleinen ~ davon probieren let me try a small piece *or* a little bit; sie brachte keinen ~ herunter she couldn't eat a thing; ich muß erst mal einen ~ essen I must have a bite to eat first; ein fetter ~ *(fig.)* a really good deal; jmdm. die ~ in den Mund zählen *(fig.)* watch how much sb. eats; ihm blieb der ~ im Hals[e] stecken *(ugs.)* the food stuck in his throat; sich *(Dat.)* jeden *od.* den letzten ~ vom Munde absparen scrimp [and save]

bisserl ['bɪsɐl] *s.* bissel

bissig 1. *Adj.* a) ~ sein ⟨*dog*⟩ bite; ein ~er Hund a dog that bites; „Vorsicht, ~er Hund" 'beware of the dog'; b) cutting, caustic ⟨*remark, tone, etc.*⟩; du brauchst doch nicht gleich so ~ zu werden there's no need to bite my/his *etc.* head off; c) *(Sportjargon)* ein ~er Spieler a sharp, attacking player. 2. *adv.* *(boshaft)* ⟨*say*⟩ cuttingly, caustically; ⟨*grin*⟩ maliciously

Bissigkeit die; ~, ~en a) *o. Pl.* *(von Hunden)*; Kettenhunde neigen zur ~: dogs that are chained up tend to bite; b) *o. Pl.* *(Schärfe)* die ~ seiner Antwort zeigte nur, wie wütend er war his cutting *or* caustic answer just showed how angry he was; c) *(Bemerkung)* cutting *or* caustic remark

Biß·wunde die bite

bist [bɪst] *2. Pers. Sg. Präsens v.* sein

biste *(ugs.)* = bist du; *s. auch* haste

Bistro ['bɪstro] das; ~s, ~s bistro

Bistum ['bɪstu:m] das; ~s, Bistümer ['bɪsty:mɐ] bishopric; diocese; das ~ Limburg the diocese of Limburg

bis·weilen *Adv. (geh.)* from time to time; now and then

Bit [bɪt] das; ~[s], ~[s] *(DV)* bit

Bitt·brief der letter of request; *(Bittgesuch)* petition

bitte ['bɪtə] *Höflichkeitsformel* a) *(bittend)* please; können Sie mir ~ sagen ...? could you please tell me ...?; ~ nicht! no, please don't!; *(ich möchte nicht)* I'd rather not; ~ nach Ihnen after you; ~, ~ machen *(Kinderspr.)* clap hands [to mean 'please']; b) *(auffordernd)* please; der Nächste ~! next please!; ja, ~? *(am Telefon)* hello?; yes?; nehmen Sie ~ Platz please sit down; ~[, treten Sie ein]! *(geh.)* come in!; ~ hier, hier ~! over here, please!; ~ [schön]? *(im Laden)* can I help you?; *(im Lokal)* what would you like?; Hast du mal ein Tempotuch für mich? – Bitte [schön *od.* sehr]! Could you let me have a tissue? – There you are; ~, gern/selbstverständlich certainly/of course; Entschuldigung! – Bitte! I'm sorry – That's all right; ~, nur zu [go on,] help yourself; c) *(bejahend)* please; aber ~! yes, do; ~ ja!, ja ~! yes please!; d) *(Dank erwidernd)* ~ [schön *od.* sehr] not at all; you're welcome; e) *(nachfragend)* [wie] ~? sorry?; *(iron.)* what?; f) *(mißbilligend)* all right; aber ~, macht, was ihr wollt just [go ahead and] do what you want; na ~! there you are!

Bitte die; ~, ~n request; *(inständig)* plea; eine große ~ [an jmdn.]/nur die eine ~ haben have a [great] favour to ask [of sb.]/have [just] one request *or* just one thing to ask; auf seine ~ hin at his request; jmdm. keine ~ abschlagen *od.* ausschlagen können not be able to refuse sb. anything

bitten 1. *unr. itr. V.* a) um etw. ~: ask for *or* request sth.; *(inständig)* beg for sth.; der Blinde bat um eine milde Gabe the blind man begged for alms; ich bitte einen Moment um Geduld/Ihre Aufmerksamkeit I must ask you to be patient for a moment/may I ask for your attention for a moment; darf ich [um den nächsten Tanz] ~? may I have the pleasure [of the next dance]?; [ich] bitte gehorsamst, gehen zu dürfen *(veralt., scherzh.)* [I] respectfully beg permission to leave; es half ihm kein Bitten pleading was *or* pleas were of no avail; ~ und betteln beg and plead; b) *(einladen)* ask; ich lasse ~: [please] ask him/her/them to come in; der Herr Konsul läßt ~: the consul will see you now; darf ich zu Tisch ~? may I ask you to come and sit down at the table?; c) *(geh.: Fürsprache einlegen)* plead; bei jmdm. für jmdn. ~: plead with sb. on sb.'s behalf. 2. *unr. tr. V.* a) *(sich höflich wenden an)* jmdn. um etw. ~: ask sb. for sth.; darf ich Sie um Feuer/ein Glas Wasser ~? could I ask you for a light/a glass of water, please?; darf ich die Herrschaften um Geduld/Ruhe ~? could I ask you to be patient/silent?; es wird gebeten, die Tiere nicht zu füttern please do not feed the animals; allmächtiger Gott, wir ~ Dich, erhöre uns! almighty God, we beseech Thee to hear us; ich bitte dich um alles in der Welt I beg [of] you; [aber] ich bitte dich/Sie! [please] don't mention it; so, jetzt geht ihr ins Bett, aber ein bißchen plötzlich, wenn ich ~ darf into bed with you, at once if you please; darum möchte ich doch sehr gebeten haben! *(ugs.)* I should hope so *(coll.)*; ich muß doch [sehr] ~! really!; er ließ sich nicht lange *od.* erst ~: he didn't have to be asked twice; er läßt sich gern ~: he likes to be asked; jmdn. zu sich ~: ask sb. to come and see one; b) *(einladen)* ask, invite; jmdn. zum Tee [zu sich] ~: ask *or* invite sb. to tea; jmdn. ins Haus/Zimmer ~: ask *or* invite sb. [to come] in; jmdn. zum Tanz ~: ask sb. to dance; er wurde für neun Uhr zur Direktion gebeten he was asked to be at the manager's office at 9 o'clock; jmdn. zu Tisch ~: ask sb. to come and sit down at the table

bitter 1. *Adj.* a) bitter; plain ⟨*chocolate*⟩; b) *(schmerzlich)* bitter ⟨*experience, irony, contempt, disappointment, etc.*⟩; painful, hard ⟨*loss*⟩; painful, bitter, hard ⟨*truth*⟩; hard ⟨*time, fate, etc.*⟩; eine ~e Lehre a hard lesson; bis zum ~en Ende to the bitter end; das ist mein ~ster Ernst I am deadly serious; eine solche Erfahrung ist ~: an experience like that is a bitter one; c) *(verbittert)* bitter; ein ~es Gefühl a feeling of bitterness; er hatte einen ~en Zug um den Mund he had a look of bitterness on his face; jmdn. ~ machen embitter sb.; make sb. bitter; d) *(groß, schwer)* bitter ⟨*cold, tears, grief, remorse, regret*⟩; dire ⟨*need*⟩; desperate ⟨*poverty*⟩; grievous ⟨*injustice, harm*⟩; es herrschte [eine] ~e Kälte it was bitterly cold; e) *(verbittert)* bitter ⟨*enemy*⟩. 2. *adv.* a) *(verbittert)* bitterly; b) *(sehr stark)* desperately; ⟨*regret*⟩ bitterly; etw. ~ nötig haben be in dire need of sth.; das wird sich ~ rächen you'll/he'll *etc.* pay dearly for that

bitter-: ~arm *Adj.; präd. getrennt geschr.* wretchedly poor; ~böse 1. *Adj.* furious; 2. *adv.* furiously; ~ernst 1. *Adj.* deadly serious; damit ist es mir ~ernst! I am deadly serious; 2. *adv.* ich meine das ~ernst I mean it deadly seriously; ~kalt *Adj.; präd. getrennt geschr.* bitterly cold

Bitterkeit die; ~ a) *(auch fig.)* bitterness; b) *(Verbitterung)* bitterness

bitterlich 1. *Adj.* slightly bitter ⟨*taste*⟩; etwas ~: slightly bitter. 2. *adv.* *(heftig)* ⟨*cry, complain, etc.*⟩ bitterly

Bitter-: ~mandel die bitter almond; ~mandel·öl das bitter almond oil; oil of bitter almonds

Bitternis die; ~, ~se *(geh.)* a) *(Geschmack)* bitterness; b) *(Gefühl)* bitterness; *(Leiden)* suffering

Bitter·salz das Epsom salts *pl.*

bitter·süß *Adj. (auch fig.)* bitter-sweet

Bitte·schön das; ~s: mit einem höflichen ~ überreichte er das Geschenk he said politely 'this is for you' as he presented the gift

Bitt-: ~gang der a) *(zu jmdm.)* ein ~gang [nach einem Ort] going [to a place] with a request; einen ~gang zu jmdm. machen go to sb. with a request; b) *(kath. Rel.:* ~*prozession)* Rogation procession; ~gebet das *(Rel.)* prayer of supplication; ~gesuch das petition; ~gottes·dienst der *(Rel.)* Rogation service; ~prozession die *(kath. Rel.)* Rogation procession

bitt·schön *(ugs. Höflichkeitsformel)* ~, der Herr there we are, sir; Vielen Dank. – Bittschön, gern geschehen Thank you very much – My pleasure; *s. auch* bitte b

Bitt-: ~schreiben das petition; ~schrift die petition; ~steller [~ʃtɛlɐ] der; ~s, ~, ~stellerin die; ~, ~nen petitioner

Bitumen [bi'tu:mən] das; ~s, ~ *(auch:)* Bitumina [-mina] *(Chemie)* bitumen

bitzeln ['bɪtsl̩n] *itr. V. (südd., westd.)* tingle; ⟨*fabric, itching-powder, etc.*⟩ prickle

bivalent [bivə'lɛnt] *Adj. (Chemie, Sprachw.)* bivalent

Biwak ['bi:vak] das; ~s, ~s *(bes. Milit., Bergsteigen)* bivouac

biwakieren *itr. V. (bes. Milit., Bergsteigen)* bivouac

bizarr [bi'tsar] 1. *Adj.* bizarre; fantastic, grotesque ⟨*coral reef, tree, formation, etc.*⟩. 2. *adv.* bizarrely

Bizarrerie [bitsarə'ri:] die; ~, ~n bizarreness; *(Handlung)* bizarre action

Bizeps ['bi:tsɛps] der; ~[es], ~e biceps

BKA [be:ka:'|a:] das; ~[s] *Abk.:* Bundeskriminalamt

B-Klarinette ['be:-] die B-flat clarinet

Blabla [bla'bla:] das; ~[s] *(ugs.)* blah[-blah] *(coll.)*

Blach·feld ['blax-] das *(dichter. veralt.)* plain; champaign *(literary)*

Black-box-Methode ['blɛkbɔks-] die *(Kybernetik)* black-box method

Blackout ['blɛkaut] das *od.* der; ~[s], ~s black-out

blaffen ['blafn̩], **bläffen** ['blɛfn̩] *itr. V.* a) bark; give a short bark; *(kläffen)* yap; b) *(schimpfen)* snap

Bläh·bauch der *(ugs.)* bloated belly; einen ~ kriegen/haben get/be bloated

blähen ['blɛ:ən] **1.** *tr. V.* **a)** swell, distend ⟨*stomach*⟩; billow, fill, belly [out] ⟨*sail*⟩; billow ⟨*sheet, curtain, clothing*⟩; **b)** *(aufblasen)* flare ⟨*nostrils*⟩; **mit vor Stolz geblähter Brust schritt er ...:** his chest swollen with pride, he strode ... **2.** *refl. V.* **a)** *(rund werden)* ⟨*sail*⟩ billow *or* belly out; ⟨*nostrils*⟩ dilate; **b)** *(angeben)* puff oneself up. **3.** *itr. V. (Blähungen verursachen)* cause flatulence *or* wind; **~de Speisen** flatulent foods; **das bläht fürchterlich** it causes terrible flatulence

Blähung die; ~, ~en flatulence *no art., no pl.;* wind *no art., no pl.;* **~en** flatulence *sing.;* wind *sing.;* **eine ~ abgehen lassen** break wind

blaken ['bla:kn̩] *itr. V. (nordd.)* smoke

bläken ['blɛ:kn̩] *itr. V. (ugs. abwertend)* ⟨*child*⟩ yell; bawl; ⟨*animal*⟩ bellow

blakig *Adj. (nordd.)* smoky *pred.*

blamabel [bla'ma:bl̩] **1.** *Adj.* shameful, disgraceful ⟨*behaviour etc.*⟩; embarrassing ⟨*situation*⟩. **2.** *adv.* shamefully; disgracefully

Blamage [bla'ma:ʒə] **die;** ~, ~n disgrace

blamieren [bla'mi:rən] **1.** *tr. V. (bloßstellen)* disgrace; *(in Verlegenheit bringen)* embarrass. **2.** *refl. V. (sich bloßstellen)* disgrace oneself; *(sich lächerlich machen)* make a fool of oneself

blanchieren [blã'ʃi:rən] *tr. V. (Kochk.)* blanch

blank [blaŋk] *Adj.* **a)** *(glänzend)* shiny; **etw. ~ reiben/polieren** rub/polish sth. till it shines; **die Gläser werden nicht ~:** the glasses won't polish to a shine; **b)** *(ugs.: abgewetzt)* shiny; **c)** *(unbekleidet)* bare; naked; **mit ~en Beinen kannst du nicht gehen** you can't go without any tights/stockings/socks on; **d)** *(ugs.: mittellos)* **~ sein** be broke *(coll.);* **e)** *(bloß)* bare ⟨*wood, plaster, earth, etc.*⟩; **er ist mit dem ~en Messer auf mich losgegangen** he came at me with his knife drawn; **f)** *(rein)* pure; sheer; utter ⟨*mockery*⟩; **g)** *(dichter.: hell)* bright; **der ~e Hans** *(dichter. nordd.)* the stormy North Sea; **h)** *(österr.: ohne Mantel)* coatless; without a coat

Blankett [blaŋ'kɛt] **das;** ~s, ~e **a)** *(Wirtsch.)* blank [form]; *(mit Blankounterschrift)* signed blank [form]; **b)** *(Technik)* blank

blanko ['blaŋko] *Adv.* **a)** *(bei Schriftstücken)* blank; **ich schreibe dir mal ~ einen Scheck aus** I'll write you a blank cheque; **b)** *(bei Papier)* plain

Blanko-: ~scheck der *(Wirtsch., fig.)* blank cheque; **~unter·schrift die** blank signature; **~vollmacht die** *(Wirtsch., fig.)* carte blanche

blank·poliert *Adj.; präd. getrennt geschr.* brightly polished

Blank·vers der blank verse

Bläschen ['blɛ:sçən] **das;** ~s, ~ **a)** [small] bubble; **b)** *(in der Haut)* [small] blister

Bläschen·aus·schlag der *(Med.)* herpes simplex

Blase ['bla:zə] **die;** ~, ~n **a)** bubble; *(im Farbenanstrich)* blister; **~n werfen** *od.* **ziehen** ⟨*paint*⟩ blister; ⟨*wallpaper*⟩ bubble; **es regnet ~n** it's pelting [down]; **b)** *(in der Haut)* blister; **sich** *(Dat.)* **~n laufen** get blisters [from walking/running]; **c)** *(Harn~)* bladder; **eine erkältete ~ haben/sich** *(Dat.)* **die ~ erkälten** have/get a chill in the bladder; **eine schwache ~ haben** *(ugs.)* have a weak bladder; **d)** *(salopp abwertend: Leute)* mob *(sl.)*

Blase·balg der bellows *pl.;* pair of bellows

blasen 1. *unr. itr. V.* **a)** blow; **b)** *(ein Blasinstrument spielen)* play; **auf dem Kamm ~:** play the comb; **c) zum Angriff/Rückzug/Aufbruch ~:** sound the charge/retreat/departure; **d)** *(wehen)* ⟨*wind*⟩ blow; **e)** *(bes. südd., österr.: kühlen)* **in die Suppe/auf eine Brandwunde ~:** blow on one's soup/a burn. **2.** *unr. tr. V.* **a)** blow; **b)** *(spielen)* play ⟨*musical instrument, tune, melody, etc.*⟩; **c)** *(wehen)* ⟨*wind*⟩ blow; **d)** *(formen)* blow ⟨*bottle, glass, etc.*⟩; **e)** *(derb)* suck off *(sl.);* **jmdm. einen ~:** suck sb. off *(sl.);* give sb. a blow job *(sl.).* **3.** *unr. unpers. V.* **es bläst** it's windy *or* blowy

Blasen-: ~bildung die blistering; **sonst kommt es zur ~bildung** or blisters will form; **~katarrh der** *(Med.)* cystitis *no indef. art.;* **~leiden das** bladder complaint; **ein ~leiden haben** have bladder trouble *or* a bladder complaint; **~stein der** *(Med.)* bladderstone; vesical calculus *(Med.);* **~tee der** *herbal tea taken for bladder complaints*

Bläser ['blɛ:zɐ] **der;** ~s, ~ **a)** *(Musik)* wind player; **die ~:** the wind section *sing.;* **b)** *(Bergmannsspr.)* blower

Bläser·ensemble das wind ensemble

Bläserin die; ~, ~nen *(Musik)* wind player

Bläser·quartett das wind quartet

blasiert [bla'zi:ɐt] *(abwertend)* **1.** *Adj.* blasé. **2.** *adv.* in a blasé way

Blasiertheit die; ~: blasé attitude

blasig *Adj.* blistered ⟨*paint, skin*⟩; bubbly ⟨*liquid*⟩; [light and] frothy ⟨*dough*⟩

Blas-: ~instrument das wind instrument; **~kapelle die** brass band; **~musik die** brass-band music; *(~kapelle)* brass band; **~orchester das** brass band

Blasphemie [blasfe'mi:] **die;** ~, ~n blasphemy

blasphemisch 1. *Adj.* blasphemous. **2.** *adv.* blasphemously

Blas·rohr das a) *(Waffe)* blowpipe; **b)** *(Technik)* blast pipe

blaß [blas] **1.** *Adj.* **a)** pale ⟨*face, skin, colour, complexion*⟩; pale, wan ⟨*light, glow*⟩; faint ⟨*writing*⟩; *(fig.)* colourless ⟨*account, portrayal, etc.*⟩; **~ werden** turn *or* go pale; *(vor Angst, Schreck)* pale; turn *or* go pale; **Rot macht dich ~:** red makes you look pale [in the face]; **~ wie eine Wand/wie der Tod** white as a sheet/deathly pale; **~ vor Neid sein/werden** *(fig.)* be/turn *or* go green with envy; **b)** *(schwach)* faint, dim ⟨*recollection, suspicion*⟩; faint ⟨*hope, similarity*⟩; only slight ⟨*effect*⟩; **c) der ~e Neid** sheer *or* pure envy. **2.** *adv. (matt)* palely

blaß·blau *Adj.* pale blue

Blässe ['blɛsə] **die;** ~ *(der Haut)* paleness; pallor; *(der Farbe)* paleness; *(des Lichts)* paleness; wanness

Bläß·huhn ['blɛs-] **das** coot

bläßlich 1. *Adj.* **a)** rather pale; palish; **b)** *(unscheinbar, nichtssagend)* colourless ⟨*person, account, portrayal, etc.*⟩. **2.** *adv. (nichtssagend)* colourlessly

blaß·rosa *indekl. Adj.* pale pink

Blatt [blat] **das;** ~[e]s, **Blätter** ['blɛtɐ] **a)** *(von Pflanzen)* leaf; **kein ~ vor den Mund nehmen** not mince one's words; **b)** *(Papier)* sheet; **ein ~ Papier** a sheet of paper; **fliegende Blätter** loose leaves *or* sheets; **[noch] ein unbeschriebenes ~ sein** *(ugs.) (unerfahren sein)* be inexperienced; *(unbekannt sein)* be an unknown quantity; **c)** *(Buchseite usw.)* page; leaf; **etw. vom ~ spielen** sight-read sth.; **auf einem anderen ~ stehen** *(fig.)* be [quite] another *or* a different matter; **d)** *(Zeitung)* paper; **e)** *(Spielkarten)* hand; **das ~ hat sich gewendet** *(ugs.)* things have changed; **f)** *(am Werkzeug, Ruder)* blade; **g)** *(Graphik)* print; **h)** *(Jägerspr.)* shoulder

Blatt·ader die leaf vein

Blättchen ['blɛtçən] **das;** ~s, ~ **a)** *(von Pflanzen)* [small] leaf; **b)** *(Papier)* [small] sheet; **c)** *(abwertend: Zeitung)* rag *(derog.)*

Blätter·dach das leafy canopy

blätterig *s.* **blattrig**

blätterig *s.* **blättrig**

-blätterig *s.* **-blättrig**

Blattern *Pl.* smallpox *sing.*

blättern ['blɛtɐn] **1.** *itr. V.* **a) in einem Buch ~:** leaf through a book; **b)** *mit sein (zerfallen)* flake; **c)** *mit sein (sich ablösen)* ⟨*paint, plaster, etc.*⟩ flake off. **2.** *tr. V.* put down [one by one]; **er blätterte mir 50 Mark auf den Tisch** he counted me out fifty marks in notes on the table

Blatter·narbe die pock-mark

blatternarbig *Adj.* pock-marked

Blätter-: ~pilz der agaric; **~schmuck der** *(geh.)* foliage; **~teig der** puff pastry; **~teig·gebäck das** puff pastries *pl.;* **~wald der** *(scherzh.)* press; **es rauscht im ~:** there are murmurings *or* rumblings in the press; **~werk das;** *o. Pl.* foliage

blatt, Blatt-: ~feder die *(Technik)* leaf spring; **~gewächs das** *(Bot.)* foliage plant; **~gold das;** *o. Pl.* gold leaf; **~grün das** *o. Pl.* chlorophyll; **~knospe die** leaf-bud; **~laus die** aphid; greenfly; **~los** *Adj.* leafless; **~metall das** foil; **~pflanze die** foliage plant

blattrig *Adj.* pock-marked

blättrig *Adj.* **a)** *(von Pflanzen)* leafy; **b)** *(abblätternd)* flaky

-blättrig *adj.* -leaved

blatt-, Blatt-: ~säge die wide-bladed [hand]saw; **~salat der** green salad; **~silber das** silver leaf; **~wanze die** lygus bug; **~weise** *Adv.* **a)** *(bei Pflanzen)* leaf by leaf; **b)** *(bei Papier)* sheet by sheet; **~werk das;** *o. Pl. (geh.)* foliage

blau [blau] *Adj.* blue; **ein ~es Auge [haben/** *(ugs.)* **kriegen]** [have/get] a black eye; **mit einem ~en Auge davonkommen** *(fig. ugs.)* get off fairly lightly; **jmdm. ein ~es Auge hauen** *od.* **schlagen** give sb. a black eye; **etw. nicht nur wegen jds. schöner ~er Augen tun** not do sth. just out of the goodness of one's heart; **ein ~er Fleck** a bruise; **die ~en Jungs** *(ugs.: die Marine)* the boys in blue; **der ~e Planet** Earth; **die ~e Stunde** *(dichter.)* the twilight hour; **die ~e Blume [der Romantik]** the Blue Flower [of the Romantics]; **ein ~er Brief** *(ugs.) (Kündigung)* one's cards *pl.; (Schulw.) letter informing parents that their child is in danger of having to repeat a year;* **Forelle ~** *(Kochk.)* blue trout; **einen ~en Montag einlegen** *od.* **machen** *(ugs.)* skip work on Monday; **sein ~es Wunder erleben** *(ugs.)* get a nasty surprise; **jmdm. ~en Dunst vormachen** *(ugs.)* pull the wool over sb.'s eyes; **~ sein** *(fig. ugs.)* be tight *(coll.) or* canned *(sl.);* **~ sein wie ein Veilchen** *od.* **wie eine [Strand]haubitze** *od.* **wie [zehn]tausend Mann** *(salopp)* be [completely] canned *(sl.)*

Blau das; ~s, ~ *od. (ugs.:)* ~s blue

blau-, Blau-: ~alge die blue-green alga; **~äugig** *Adj.* **a)** blue-eyed; **b)** *(naiv)* naive; **~äugigkeit** [~ɔygɪçkait] **die;** ~ *(fig.)* naïvety; **~bart der** Bluebeard; **~beere die** bilberry; whortleberry; **~blütig** *Adj. (meist iron.)* blue-blooded

[1]**Blaue** ['blauə] **das;** ~n blue; **das ~ vom Himmel [herunter]lügen** *(ugs.)* lie like anything; tell a pack of lies; **jmdm. das ~ vom Himmel [herunter] versprechen** *(ugs.)* promise sb. the earth *or* the moon; **wir wollen einfach ins ~ fahren** we'll just set off and see where we end up; *s. auch* **Fahrt c**

[2]**Blaue der;** ~n, ~n *(ugs.)* **a)** *(Hundertmarkschein)* hundred-mark note; **acht ~ kosten** cost eight hundred marks; **b)** *(veralt.: Polizist)* cop *(sl.);* copper *(sl.)*

Bläue ['blɔyə] **die;** ~ *(geh.)* blue; blueness; *(des Himmels)* blue

bläuen *tr. V.* **a)** *(färben)* dye ⟨*material, clothes, etc.*⟩ blue; turn ⟨*litmus-paper*⟩ blue; **b)** *(aufhellen)* blue

blau-, Blau-: ~färbung die blue colour; blueness; **~felchen das** Blaufelchen; whitefish; **~filter der** *od.* **das** *(Fot.)* blue filter; **~fuchs der a)** *(Tier)* Arctic fox; blue fox; **b)** *(Fell)* blue fox [fur]; **~grau** *Adj.* blue-grey; bluish grey; **~grün** *Adj.* blue-green; bluish green; **~hemd das** *(DDR)* **a)** *(Hemd)* blue shirt [of the Free German Youth]; **b)** *(ugs.: Mitglied)* member of the Free German Youth; **~holz das** logwood;

~kabis der *(schweiz.)*, ~kohl der *(bes. nordd.)*, ~kraut das *(südd., österr.) s.* Rotkohl

bläulich *Adj.* bluish

Blau·licht das flashing blue light; ein Krankenwagen raste mit ~ vorbei an ambulance raced past with [its] blue light flashing

blau-, Blau-: ~|machen *(ugs.)* **1.** *itr. V.* skip work; **2.** *tr. V.* den Freitag ~machen skip work on Friday; ~mann der; *Pl.* ~männer *(ugs.)* boiler suit; ~meise die blue tit; ~papier das [blue] carbon paper; ~pause die blueprint; ~rot *Adj.* purple; ~säure die; *o. Pl. (Chemie)* prussic acid; hydrocyanic acid; ~schimmel der blue mould; ~schwarz *Adj.* blue-black; ~stichig [~ʃtɪçɪç] *Adj. (Fot.)* with a blue cast *postpos., not pred.*; ~stichig sein have a blue cast; ~stift der blue pencil; ~strumpf der *(abwertend)* bluestocking; ~tanne die blue spruce; Colorado spruce; ~wal der blue whale

Blazer ['ble:zɐ] der; ~s, ~: blazer

Blech [blɛç] das; ~[e]s, ~e **a)** *o. Pl. (Metall)* sheet metal; **b)** *(Platte)* metal sheet; *(Grob~)* metal plate; **c)** *(Back~)* [baking] tray; **d)** *o. Pl. (ugs.: Unsinn)* rubbish; nonsense; tripe *(sl.)*; **e)** *o. Pl. (ugs. abwertend: Orden)* medals *pl.*; gongs *pl. (sl.)*; **f)** *(Musik: ~bläser)* brass

Blech-: ~bläser der brass-player; die ~bläser *(im Orchester)* the brass [section] *sing.*; ~blas·instrument das brass instrument; ~büchse die, ~dose die tin; ~eimer der metal bucket

blechen *tr., itr. V. (ugs.)* cough up *(sl.)*; fork out *(sl.)*

blechern ['blɛçɐn] *Adj.* **1. a)** *nicht präd. (aus Blech)* metal; **b)** *(metallisch klingend)* tinny ⟨*sound, voice*⟩. **2.** *adv. (metallisch)* tinnily

Blech-: ~instrument das brass instrument; ~kiste die *(ugs. abwertend)* crate *(sl.)*; ~lawine die *(ugs. scherzh.)* solid line of cars; ~musik die *(abwertend)* brass-band music; ~napf der metal bowl

Blechner der; ~s, ~ *(südd.) s.* Klempner

Blech-: ~schaden der *(Kfz-W.)* damage *no indef. art.* to the bodywork; ~schere die metal-shears *pl.*; ~schmied der *(nordwestd.) s.* Klempner; ~trommel die tin drum

blecken ['blɛkn̩] *tr. V.* die Zähne ~: bare one's/its teeth

[1]Blei [blai] das; ~[e]s, ~e **a)** lead; ~ gießen *pour lead into cold water to tell one's fortune for the coming year*; jmdm. wie ~ in den Gliedern *od.* Knochen liegen ⟨*tiredness, exhaustion, shock, etc.*⟩ make sb.'s limbs feel like lead; jmdm. wie ~ im Magen liegen *(schwer verdaulich sein)* weigh heavily on sb.'s stomach; *(jmdn. bedrücken)* prey on sb.'s mind; **b)** *(Lot)* plumb[-bob]; **c)** *(veralt.) (Gewehrkugeln)* lead

[2]Blei der *od.* das; ~[e]s, ~e *(~stift)* pencil

Bleibe die; ~, ~n place to stay; keine ~ haben have nowhere to stay

bleiben ['blaibn̩] *unr. itr. V.; mit sein* **a)** *(an einem Ort)* stay; remain; ~ Sie bitte am Apparat hold the line please; wo bleibt er so lange? where has he got to?; wo bleibst du denn so lange? where have you been *or* what's been keeping you all this time?; wo bleibt der Kaffee? where has the coffee got to?; what has happened to the coffee?; wo sind die Blumen geblieben? what's happened to the flowers?; wo ~ nur die Jahre? how the years have flown!; zum Abendessen ~: stay for supper; auf dem Weg ~: keep to *or* stay on the path; da ~ wir ganz unter *(Dat.) od.* für uns there will just be us; jmdm. in Erinnerung *od.* im Gedächtnis ~: stay in sb.'s mind *or* memory; von etw. ~ *(ugs.)* stay *or* keep away from sth.; das bleibt unter uns *(Dat.)* that's [just] between ourselves; zusehen, wo man bleibt *(ugs.)* have to fend for oneself; ich kann sehen, wo ich bleibe I'm left to shift for myself; jmdn. zum Bleiben auffordern ask sb. to stay; hier ist meines Bleibens nicht länger *(veralt., scherzh.)* I shall not stay here any longer; bleibe im Lande, und nähre dich redlich there's a good living to be had in your own country; *s. auch* Rahmen b; Sache b; **b)** *(Zustand, Eigenschaft beibehalten)* stay; remain; der Kuchen bleibt mehrere Tage frisch the cake will keep for several days; bleib ruhig! keep calm!; das Geschäft bleibt heute geschlossen the shop is closed today; der Brief blieb unbeantwortet the letter went *or* remained unanswered; unbestraft/unbeachtet ~: go unpunished/go unnoticed *or* escape notice; dieser Tag wird uns *(Dat.)* immer unvergessen ~: we shall always remember this day; sitzen ~: stay *or* remain sitting down *or* seated; ~ Sie doch bitte sitzen please don't get up; ich bleibe lieber stehen I would rather stand; Freunde ~: remain friends; go on being friends; **c)** *(übrigbleiben)* be left; remain; uns *(Dat.)* bleibt noch Zeit we still have time; bis zur Abreise bleibt uns weniger als eine Stunde there is less than an hour before we leave; es blieb ihm keine Hoffnung mehr he had no hope left; was bleibt mir dann noch? what shall I have left?; *s. auch* Wahl; **d)** *(für die Zukunft)*; es bleibt abzuwarten, ob ...: it remains to be seen whether ...; es bleibt zu hoffen, daß ...: we can only hope that ...; bei dem Wein ~ wir we'll stick to *or* with *or* keep to this wine; **e)** *(nicht ändern)* bei etw. ~: keep *or* stick to sth.; ich bleibe dabei, daß ...: I still say that ...; dabei bleibt es! that's that; that's the end of it; **f)** *(verhüll.: sterben)* im Feld/im Krieg/auf See ~: die *or* fall in action/die in the war/at sea

bleibend *Adj.* lasting; permanent ⟨*damage*⟩

bleiben|lassen *unr. tr. V.* **a)** *(nicht tun)* etw. ~: give sth. a miss; forget sth.; das wirst du mal schön ~: you can forget about that; **b)** *(aufhören)* das Rauchen ~: give up *or* stop smoking

bleich [blaiç] *Adj.* **a)** pale; ~ vor Angst/Wut sein be white with fear/rage; ~ wie eine Wand/wie der Tod white as a sheet/deathly pale; ~ werden turn *or* go pale; *(vor Angst, Schreck)* pale; turn *or* go pale; **b)** *(geh.: fahl)* pale ⟨*light, gleam*⟩

Bleiche die; ~, ~n **a)** *(veralt.: für Wäsche)* bleaching field; bleaching-ground; **b)** *o. Pl. (geh.: Blässe)* paleness; *(des Gesichts, der Haut)* pallor; paleness

[1]bleichen *tr. V.* bleach

[2]bleichen *regelm. (veralt. auch unr.) itr. V.* become bleached; bleach; in der Sonne ~: be bleached by the sun

bleich, Bleich-: ~gesicht das *Pl.* ~gesichter **a)** pale face; *(ugs.: blasser Mensch)* pale-faced *or* pasty-faced type *(coll.)*; **b)** *(scherzh.: Weißer)* pale-face; ~gesichtig *Adj. (ugs.)* pale-faced; pasty-faced; ~mittel das bleach; bleaching agent; ~sucht die *o. Pl. (veralt.)* chlorosis; greensickness; ~süchtig *Adj. (veralt.)* chlorotic; greensick

bleiern ['blaiɐn] **1.** *Adj.* **a)** *nicht präd. (aus Blei)* lead; er schwimmt wie eine ~e Ente *(ugs. scherzh.)* he can't swim for toffee *(Brit. sl.) or* swim a stroke; **b)** *(geh.: bleifarben)* leaden ⟨*sky, grey*⟩; **c)** *(schwer)* heavy ⟨*sleep, tiredness, etc.*⟩; leaden ⟨*heaviness*⟩; seine Füße waren ~: his feet were like lead. **2.** *adv. (fig.: schwer)* heavily; es lag ihr ~ in den Gliedern her limbs felt like lead *or* as heavy as lead

blei-, Blei-: ~erz das lead ore; ~farben, ~farbig *Adj.* lead-coloured; lead-grey; leaden ⟨*sky*⟩; ~frei **1.** *Adj.* unleaded ⟨*fuel*⟩; **2.** *adv.* ~ fahren/tanken drive on/use unleaded fuel; ~fuß der *in* mit ~fuß fahren *(ugs. scherzh.)* drive with one's foot down to the floor; ~gehalt der lead content; ~gewicht das *(auch fig.)* lead weight; ~gießen das *pouring lead into cold water to tell one's fortune for the coming year*; ~glanz der *(Mineral.)* galena; ~glas das lead glass; ~haltig *Adj.* ⟨*petrol, paint, etc.*⟩ containing lead; plumbiferous, lead-bearing ⟨*ore*⟩; ~haltig sein ⟨*petrol, paint, etc.*⟩ contain lead; die Luft hier ist ziemlich ~haltig *(salopp scherzh.)* there's plenty of lead flying around; ~hütte die lead works *sing.*; ~kristall das lead crystal; ~kugel die **a)** *(Geschoß)* lead bullet; **b)** *(Kugel)* lead ball; ~oxyd das *(Chemie)* lead oxide; ~satz der; *o. Pl. (Druckw.)* hot-metal composition; ~schürze die lead apron; ~schwer **1.** *Adj.* heavy as lead *postpos.*; **2.** *adv.* heavily; like a heavy *or* lead weight; ~soldat der lead soldier

Blei·stift der pencil; mit ~: in pencil

Bleistift-: ~absatz der stiletto heel; ~mine die [pencil] lead; ~spitzer der pencil-sharpener; ~zeichnung die pencil drawing

Blei·vergiftung die lead-poisoning

Blende die; ~, ~n **a)** *(Lichtschutz)* shade; *(am Fenster)* blind; *(im Auto)* [sun-]visor; **b)** *(Optik, Film, Fot.: Vorrichtung)* diaphragm; die ~ öffnen/schließen open up the aperture/stop down; **c)** *(Film, Fot.: Blendenzahl)* aperture setting; f-number; mit *od.* bei ~ 8 at [an aperture setting of] f/8; ~ 11 einstellen set the aperture to *or* at f/11; **d)** *(Film: Einstellung)* fade; einen Film mit einer ~ anfangen/enden lassen start a film with a fade-in/end a film with a fade-out; **e)** *(Stoffstreifen)* trimming; **f)** *(Archit.)* blind window/arch/niche *etc.*; **g)** *(Chemie)* blende

blenden **1.** *tr. V.* **a)** *(auch beeindrucken, täuschen)* dazzle; **b)** *(blind machen)* blind; **c)** *(Kürschnerei)* blend. **2.** *itr. V.* **a)** ⟨*light*⟩ be dazzling; **b)** *(täuschen)* dazzle people

Blenden·automatik die *(Fot.)* automatic aperture control

blendend **1.** *Adj.* splendid; brilliant ⟨*musician, dancer, speech, achievement, etc.*⟩; es geht mir ~: I feel wonderfully well *or* wonderful. **2.** *adv.* wir haben uns ~ amüsiert we had a wonderful *or* marvellous time

Blender der; ~s, ~ *(ugs.)* fraud; phoney *(sl.)*

blend·frei *Adj.* **a)** *(nicht blendend)* non-dazzle; **b)** *(nicht spiegelnd)* non-dazzle; non-reflective

Blend·laterne die dark lantern

Blendung die; ~, ~en **a)** dazzling; **b)** *(Täuschung)* deception; **c)** *(Strafe)* blinding; **d)** *(Kürschnerei)* blending

Blend·werk das *(geh. abwertend)* deception; ein ~ des Teufels a trap set by the devil

Blesse ['blɛsə] die; ~, ~n **a)** *(Fleck)* blaze; **b)** *(Tier)* horse/cow *etc.* with a/the blaze

Bleß·huhn das *s.* Bläßhuhn

blessiert [blɛsi:ɐ̯t] *Adj. (geh., scherzh.) (verletzt)* injured; *(verwundet)* wounded

Blessur [blɛ'su:ɐ̯] die; ~, ~en *(veralt., scherzh.) (Verletzung)* injury; *(Wunde)* wound

bleu [blø:] *indekl. Adj., nicht attr.* light *or* pale blue

Bleu das; ~s, ~ *od. (ugs.)* ~s light *or* pale blue

blich [blɪç] *1. u. 3. Pers. Sg. Prät. v.* [2]bleichen

Blick [blɪk] der; ~[e]s, ~e **a)** *(das Anschauen)* look; *(flüchtig)* glance; jmdm. einen ~/sich ~e zuwerfen give sb. a look/exchange glances; einen kurzen ~ auf etw. *(Akk.)* werfen take a quick look at *or* glance [briefly] at sth.; einen ~ riskieren *(ugs.)* venture a glance; jmds. ~ *(Dat.)* ausweichen avoid sb.'s glance *or* eye; jmds. ~ *(Akk.)* erwidern return sb.'s look *or* gaze; ein ~ in die Vergangenheit/Zukunft a look back [into the past]/a look into the future; auf den ersten ~: at first glance; auf den zweiten ~: look ing at it again *or* a second time; **etw. mit einem ~ sehen** see sth. at a glance; **keinen ~ für jmdn./etw. haben** take no notice of sb./sth.; **jmdn./etw. im ~ haben** be looking at sb./sth.; **wenn ~e töten könnten!** if looks could kill; **einen ~ hinter die Kulissen werfen** *od.* **tun** take a look behind the scenes; **den ~ heben** *(geh.)* raise one's eyes; look up; **den ~ senken** *(geh.)* lower one's eyes; look down; **mein ~ fiel auf den Brief** my eye fell on the letter; the letter caught my eye; **er wendete keinen ~ von der attraktiven Frau** his eyes never left the attractive woman; **jmdn. mit seinen ~en verschlingen** devour sb. with one's eyes; **jmdn. mit ~en durchbohren** look piercingly at sb.; *s. auch* **Liebe a; würdigen b; b)** *o. Pl. (Ausdruck)* look in one's eyes; **mit mißtrauischem ~:** with a suspicious look in one's eye; **mit zärtlichem ~:** with a tender look in one's eyes; *s. auch* **böse; c)** *(Aussicht)* view; **ein Zimmer mit ~ aufs Meer** a room with a sea view; **jmdn./etw. aus dem ~ verlieren** lose sight of sb./sth.; **etw. im ~ haben** be able to see sth.; **d)** *o. Pl. (Urteil[skraft])* eye; **einen sicheren/geschulten ~ für etw. haben** have a sure/trained eye for sth.; **keinen ~ für etw. haben** have no eye for sth.; **seinen ~ für etw. schärfen** sharpen one's awareness of sth.

blịcken 1. *itr. V.* look; *(flüchtig)* glance; **jmdm. gerade in die Augen ~:** look sb. straight in the eye; **zur Seite ~:** look away; **auf das vergangene Jahr ~** *(fig.)* look back on the past year; **das läßt tief ~** *(ugs.)* that's very revealing. **2.** *tr. V.:* **sich ~ lassen** put in an appearance; **laß dich mal wieder ~:** come again some time; **er hat sich lange nicht mehr ~ lassen** he hasn't been seen for a long time; **sie wagt es nicht, sich ~ zu lassen** she dare not show her face; **er läßt sich ja nie ~:** he's never around *(coll.)*

Blịck-: ~fang der eye-catcher; **als ~fang dienen** serve to catch the eye; **~feld das** field of vision *or* view; **er hat ein recht enges ~feld** *(fig.)* he has really narrow horizons *pl.;* **jmdn./etw. ins ~feld der Öffentlichkeit rücken** make sb./sth. the focus of public attention; **~kontakt der** eye-contact; **~punkt der** view; field of vision; **im ~punkt der Öffentlichkeit stehen** *(fig.)* be in the public eye; **jmdn. in den ~punkt rücken** *(fig.)* single sb. out; **in den ~punkt treten** *(fig.)* become the focus of attention; enter the limelight; **~richtung die a)** line of sight *or* vision; **in ~richtung [nach] rechts** to the *or* on your right; looking to your right; **b)** *(fig.)* perspective; **~winkel der a)** angle of vision; **b)** *(fig.)* point of view; viewpoint; perspective

blieb [bli:p] *1. u. 3. Pers. Sg. Prät. v.* **bleiben**

blies [bli:s] *1. u. 3. Pers. Sg. Prät. v.* **blasen**

blind [blɪnt] **1.** *Adj.* **a)** blind; **~ werden** go blind; **auf einem Auge ~ sein** be blind in one eye; **auf dem Auge ist sie ~** *(fig. ugs.)* she refuses to see that; **~ für etw. sein** be blind to sth.; **~ vor Tränen** *(geh.)* blinded by tears; *s. auch* **Huhn; b)** *(maßlos)* blind ‹*rage, hatred, fear, etc.*›; indiscriminate ‹*violence*›; **c)** *(kritiklos)* blind ‹*obedience, enthusiasm, belief, etc.* ›; **~er Eifer schadet nur** *(Spr.)* haste makes waste *(prov.);* **d)** *(trübe)* clouded ‹*glass*›; dull, tarnished ‹*metal*›; **e)** *(verdeckt)* concealed; invisible ‹*seam*›; **ein ~er Passagier** a stowaway; **f) ~er Alarm** a false alarm; **g)** *(undurchschaubar)* **der ~e Zufall** pure *or* sheer chance; **das ~e Walten des Schicksals** *(geh.)* the unfathomable workings *pl.* of fate; **h)** *(vorgetäuscht)* false ‹*pocket, buttonhole, etc.*›; blind ‹*window, arch, etc.*›. **2.** *adv.* **a)** *(ohne hinzusehen)* without looking; *(wahllos)* blindly; wildly; **b)** *(unkritisch)* ‹*trust*› implicitly; ‹*obey*› blindly; **c)** *(verdeckt)* **der Mantel wird ~ geknöpft** the coat has concealed buttons

Blịnd·band der; *Pl.* **~bände** *(Buchw.)* dummy

Blịnd·darm der a) *(Anat.: Teil des Dickdarms)* caecum; **b)** *(volkst.: Wurmfortsatz)* appendix

Blịnd·darm-: ~entzündung die *(volkst.)* appendicitis; **~operation die** *(volkst.)* appendix operation; **~reizung die** *(volkst.)* grumbling appendix

Blịnde der/die; *adj. Dekl.* blind person; blind man/woman; **die ~n** the blind; **das sieht doch ein ~r [mit dem Krückstock]** *(ugs.)* anyone *or* any fool can see that; *s. auch* **einäugig**

Blịnde·kuh *o. Art.* blind man's buff

Blịnden-: ~anstalt die *s.* **~heim; ~führer der** blind person's guide; **~heim das** home for the blind; **~hund der** guide-dog; **~schrift die** Braille; **~stock der** white stick

blịnd-, Blịnd-: ~fenster das *(Bauw.)* blind window; **~|fliegen** *unr. itr. V.; mit sein* fly blind; **~flug der** blind flight; *(das Blindfliegen)* blind flying; **im ~flug** ‹*land, take off, etc.*› blind; **~gänger der a)** *(Geschoß)* unexploded shell; dud *(sl.);* **b)** *(salopp: Versager)* dead loss *(coll.)*

Blịndheit die; ~ *(auch fig.)* blindness; **[wie] mit ~ geschlagen sein** be [as if struck] blind

Blịnd·landung die *(Flugw.)* blind landing

blindlings ['blɪntlɪŋs] *Adv.* blindly; ‹*trust*› implicitly

blịnd-, Blịnd-: ~material das *(Druckw.)* spacing material; **~schleiche** [~ʃlaiçə] **die; ~, ~n** slowworm; blindworm; **~|schreiben** *unr. tr., itr. V.* touch-type; **~spiel das** *(Schach)* blindfold game; **~wütig 1.** *Adj.* raging ‹*anger, hatred, fury, etc.*›; wild ‹*rage*›; **~wütige Schläge** furious blows; **2.** *adv.* in a blind rage *or* fury; **~wütigkeit die; ~:** blind rage *or* fury

blinken ['blɪŋkn̩] **1.** *itr. V.* **a)** *(Verkehrsw.)* indicate; **b)** *(Signal geben)* **mit Lampen ~:** flash lamps; **c)** *(leuchten)* ‹*light, glass, crystal*› flash; ‹*star*› twinkle; ‹*metal, fish*› gleam; ‹*water, wine*› sparkle; **das ganze Haus blinkte vor Sauberkeit** the whole house was sparkling clean. **2.** *tr. V. (Signal geben)* flash; **SOS ~:** flash an SOS [signal]

Blinker der; ~s, ~ a) *(am Auto)* indicator [light]; winker; **b)** *(Angeln)* spoon[-bait]

Blịnk-: ~feuer das *(Seew.)* flashing light; **~gerät das** *(Milit.)* signalling apparatus; signal lamp; **~leuchte die** *(Kfz-W.)* indicator [light]; winker; **~licht das** *(Verkehrsw.)* flashing light; **~licht·anlage die** *(Verkehrsw.)* flashing lights *pl.;* **~signal das, ~zeichen das** flashlight signal

blinzeln ['blɪnts̩ln] *itr. V.* blink; *(mit einem Auge, um ein Zeichen zu geben)* wink

Blitz [blɪts] **der; ~es, ~e a)** *(bei Gewitter)* lightning *no indef. art.;* **ein ~:** a flash of lightning; **der ~ hat eingeschlagen** lightning has struck; **war das ein ~?** was that [a flash of] lightning?; **seine Augen schossen ~e** *(fig.)* his eyes flashed; **potz ~!** *(veralt.)* upon my soul!; good heavens!; **[schnell] wie der ~:** like lightning; as fast as lightning; **wie ein geölter ~** *(ugs.)* like greased lightning; **wie ein ~ aus heiterem Himmel** like a bolt from the blue; **wie ein ~ einschlagen** be a bombshell; **wie vom ~ getroffen** thunderstruck; **b)** *(~licht)* flash

blịtz-, Blịtz-: ~ab·leiter der lightning-conductor; **~aktion die** lightning operation; **~angriff der** *(Milit.)* lightning attack; **~artig 1.** *Adj.; nicht präd.* lightning; **2.** *adv.* like lightning; ‹*disappear*› in a flash; **~blạnk** *Adj. (ugs.)* **~blank [geputzt]** sparkling clean; brightly polished ‹*shoes*›

blịtzeblạnk *s.* **blitzblank**

blịtzen 1. *itr. V.* **a)** *unpers. (bei Gewitter)* **es blitzte** *(einmal)* there was a flash of lightning; *(mehrmals)* there was lightning; there were flashes of lightning; **bei dir blitzt es** *(ugs. scherzh.)* your slip is showing; Charlie's dead *(Brit. coll.);* it's snowing down south *(Brit. coll.);* **b)** *(glänzen)* ‹*light, glass, crystal*› flash; ‹*metal*› gleam; **sie hatte weiße, ~de Zähne** she had sparkling white teeth; **das Haus blitzte vor Sauberkeit** the house was sparkling clean; **Zorn blitzte aus ihren Augen** *(fig.)* her eyes flashed with anger; **c)** *(nackt laufen)* streak *(coll.);* **d)** *(ugs.: mit Blitzlicht)* use [a] flash; **er fing wie wild an zu ~:** he started to flash away like mad *(coll.).* **2.** *tr. V. (ugs.: mit Blitzlicht)* take a flash photo of

Blịtzer der; ~s, ~, Blịtzerin die; ~, ~nen *(ugs.)* streaker *(coll.)*

Blịtzes·schnelle die *in* **in** *od.* **mit ~:** at lightning speed; ‹*disappear*› in a flash

blịtz-, Blịtz-: ~gerät das *(Fot.)* flash [unit]; flash-gun; **~gescheit** *Adj.* very bright; **~gespräch das** priority call *(with tenfold call charge);* **~krieg der** *(Milit.)* blitzkrieg; **~licht das;** *Pl.* **~lichter** flash[light]; **mit ~licht** by flash[light]; **~licht·aufnahme die** flash[light] photograph; **~licht·foto das** flash photo[graph]; **~reise die** flying visit; **~sauber** *Adj.* **~sauber [geputzt]** sparkling clean; **~schlag der** flash of lightning; **von einem ~schlag getroffen werden** be struck *or* hit by lightning; **~schnẹll 1.** *Adj.* lightning *attrib.;* **~schnell sein** be like lightning; **2.** *adv.* like lightning; ‹*disappear*› in a flash; **das alles geschah so ~schnell, daß ...:** it all happened so quickly that ...; **~sieg der** *(Milit.)* lightning victory; **~start der** lightning start; **~telegramm das** priority telegram *(with tenfold charge);* **~um·frage die** lightning poll; **~würfel der** *(Fot.)* flash-cube

Blizzard ['blɪzɐt] **der; ~s, ~s** blizzard

blochen ['blɔxn̩] *tr., itr. V. (bes. schweiz.)* polish

Blocher der; ~s, ~ *(schweiz.)* floor-polisher

Block [blɔk] **der; ~[e]s, Blöcke** ['blœkə] *od.* **~s a)** *Pl.* **Blöcke** *(Brocken)* block; *(Fels~)* boulder; **b)** *(Wohn~)* block; **c)** *Pl.* **Blöcke** *(Gruppierung von politischen Kräften, Staaten)* bloc; **d)** *(Schreib~)* pad; **e)** *(Basketball)* screen; *(Volleyball)* block; **f)** *Pl.* **~s** *(Eisenb.)* block; **g)** *(Philat.)* block; **h)** *(ns.: Organisationseinheit)* block [of houses]

Blockade [blɔ'ka:də] **die; ~, ~n a)** *(Absperrung)* blockade; **eine ~ brechen** run a blockade; **b)** *(Druckw.)* [space marked by] turned letter[s] *(indicating missing or illegible material)*

Blockade·brecher der blockade-runner

Blọck-: ~bildung die formation *or* creation of a bloc/blocs; **~buchstabe der** block capital *or* letter

blọcken 1. *tr. V.* **a)** *(südd.: bohnern)* polish; **b)** *(bes. Boxen: abfangen; Ballspiele: sperren)* block. **2.** *itr. V.* **a)** *(südd.: bohnern)* polish; **b)** *(bes. Boxen: abfangen; Ballspiele: sperren)* block; **c)** *(Jägerspr.)* perch

blọck-, Blọck-: ~flöte die recorder; **~frei** *Adj.* non-aligned ‹*country, state*›; **~freie der;** *adj. Dekl.* non-aligned country *or* state; **~haus das, ~hütte die** log cabin

blockieren 1. *tr. V.* **a)** *(sperren)* blockade ‹*country, port*›; block ‹*access road, border crossing-point, etc.*›; **b)** *(verstopfen)* block; jam ‹*telephone line*›; **c)** *(unterbrechen)* block ‹*supply*›; stop, halt ‹*traffic*›; **d)** *(anhalten)* lock ‹*wheel, machine, etc.*›; **e)** *(unterbinden)* block ‹*negotiations, proposal, etc.*›; **f)** *(Druckw.)* mark with turned letter[s] *etc. (to indicate missing or illegible material).* **2.** *itr. V. (stehen bleiben)* ‹*wheels*› lock; ‹*gears*› jam

Blockierung die; ~, ~en *s.* **blockieren:** blockade; blocking; locking; jamming; stopping; halting

Blọck-: ~partei die *(bes. DDR)* bloc party; **~politik die** *(bes. DDR)* bloc policy; **~schokolade die** cooking chocolate; **~schrift die** block capitals *pl. or* letters *pl.;* **~staaten** *Pl.* aligned countries *or* states;

die ~staaten des Westens und des Ostens the countries of the Western and Eastern blocs; **~stunde die** *(Schulw.)* double period; **~unterricht der** theme-work teaching *no art.*; teaching using the theme method *or* approach *no art.*; **~wart der** *(ns.)* block warden

blöd[e] ['blø:t, 'blø:də] **1.** *Adj.* **a)** *(schwachsinnig)* mentally deficient; imbecilic; **b)** *(unsinnig, ugs.: dumm)* stupid; idiotic *(coll.)*; **c)** *(ugs.: unangenehm)* stupid; **das Blöde ist nur, daß ...:** the stupid thing is that ... **2.** *adv.* **a)** *(schwachsinnig)* imbecilically; **b)** *(unsinnig, ugs.: dumm)* stupidly; idiotically *(coll.)*; **er hat vielleicht ~ geguckt** a really stupid look came across his face; **frag doch nicht so ~:** don't ask such stupid *or (coll.)* idiotic questions; **c)** *(ärgerlich)* stupidly

Blödel ['blø:dl] **der; ~s, ~** *s.* **Blödian**

Blödelei die; ~, ~en a) *o. Pl.* messing *or* fooling about *no indef. art.*; **b)** *(Äußerung)* silly joke

blödeln *itr. V.* **a)** mess *or* fool about; **b)** *(sich äußern)* make silly jokes

blöder·weise *Adv. (ugs.)* stupidly

Blöd·hammel der *(salopp abwertend)* stupid fool *or (coll.)* idiot *or (Brit. sl.)* twit *or (Amer. sl.)* jerk

Blödheit die; ~, ~en a) *o. Pl. (Dummsein)* stupidity; **b)** *(dumme Äußerung)* stupid remark; *(dumme Tat)* stupidity; **c)** *o. Pl. (Schwachsinnigkeit)* mental deficiency; imbecility

Blödian ['blø:dia:n] **der; ~s, ~e** *(ugs. abwertend)* idiot *(coll.)*; fool

Blödler der; ~s, ~ *(ugs.)* silly joker

Blödling der; ~s, ~e *s.* **Blödian**

blöd-, Blöd-: ~mann der; *Pl.* **~männer** *(salopp)* stupid idiot *(coll.)* or fool; **~sinn der;** *o. Pl. (ugs. abwertend)* nonsense; **jetzt habe ich ~sinn gemacht** now I've [gone and] messed it up; **mach doch keinen ~sinn!** don't be stupid; **was machst du denn da für einen ~sinn?** what are you messing about at?; **hör jetzt auf mit dem ~sinn** stop that nonsense; stop fooling *or* messing around; **höherer ~sinn** *(iron.)* high-flown nonsense; **~sinnig 1.** *Adj.* **a)** *(ugs.: unsinnig)* stupid; idiotic *(coll.)*; **b)** *(schwachsinnig)* mentally deficient; imbecilic; **2.** *adv. (ugs.)* stupidly; idiotically *(coll.)*; **frag doch nicht so ~sinnig** don't ask such stupid *or (coll.)* idiotic questions; **~sinnigkeit die; ~** *(ugs.)* stupidity; idiocy *(coll.)*

blöken ['blø:kn̩] *itr. V.* ‹*sheep*› bleat; ‹*cattle*› low

blond [blɔnt] *Adj.* fair-haired, blond ‹*man, race*›; blonde, fair-haired ‹*woman*›; blond/blonde, fair ‹*hair*›; **ein ~es Gift** *(ugs. scherzh.)* a blonde bombshell

Blond das; ~s blond; *(von Frauenhaar)* blonde; **ihr ~ ist aus der Tube** her blonde hair comes from a bottle

[1]Blonde der/die; *adj. Dekl. (blonder Mann)* fair-haired *or* blond man; *(blonde Frau)* blonde

[2]Blonde das *od.* **die;** *adj. Dekl. (ugs.: Bier)* light beer; ≈ lager

blond-: ~gefärbt *Adj.*; *präd. getrennt geschr.* dyed blond/blonde; **~gelockt** *Adj.*; *präd. getrennt geschr.* fair curly *attrib.* ‹*hair*›; ‹*girl, child, etc.*› with fair curly hair

blondieren *tr. V.* bleach; *(mit Färbemittel)* dye blond/blonde; **sich ~ lassen** have one's hair bleached/dyed blond/blonde

Blondierung die; ~, ~en a) *o. Pl.*; *s.* **blondieren:** bleaching; dyeing blond/blonde; **b)** *(blonde Farbe)* blond colour

Blondine [blɔn'di:nə] **die; ~, ~n** blonde

Blond·kopf der a) *(Kopf)* blond/blonde hair; fair hair; **b)** *(Kind)* blond/blonde child; fair-haired child

bloß [blo:s] **1.** *Adj.* **a)** *(nackt)* bare; naked; **du kannst nicht mit ~en Beinen gehen** you can't go without tights/stockings/socks; **mit ~em Oberkörper** stripped to the waist; **den Pullover kann man nicht auf der ~en Haut tragen** you can't wear this pullover next to the skin *or* with nothing on underneath; **mit ~em Kopf** bare-headed; **mit ~en Füßen** barefoot; **mit ~en Händen** with one's bare hands; **auf der ~en Erde** on the ground; **b)** *(nichts als)* mere ‹*words, promises, triviality, suspicion, etc.*›; **der ~e Gedanke daran** the mere *or* very thought of it; **er kam mit dem ~en Schrecken davon** he escaped with no more than a fright; **nach dem ~en Augenschein beurteilen** judge simply by appearances; **ein ~er Zufall** mere *or* pure chance; **~es Gerede** mere gossip. **2.** *Adv. (ugs.: nur)* only; **ich habe ~ noch zehn Mark** I only have ten marks left; **das ist alles ~ deine Schuld** it's all your fault; **ich habe das Buch, ~ weiß ich nicht mehr, wo ich es hingelegt habe** I've got the book, but *or* only I don't know where I've put it. **3.** *in* **nicht ~ ..., sondern auch ...:** not only ..., but also ...; **er sagt das nicht ~, er glaubt es auch** he doesn't just say it, he believes it as well. **4.** *Partikel (verstärkend)* **was hast du dir ~ dabei gedacht?** what on earth *or* whatever were you thinking of?; **sieh ~ zu, daß ...:** just make sure that ...; **wie konnte das ~ geschehen?** how on earth did it happen?

Blöße ['blø:sə] **die; ~, ~n a)** *(geh.: Nacktheit)* nakedness; **b) sich** *(Dat.)* **eine/keine ~ geben** show a/not show any weakness; **er wollte sich** *(Dat.)* **nicht die ~ geben, das einzugestehen** he didn't want to show a weakness by admitting it; **jmdm. eine ~ bieten** reveal a weakness to sb.; **c)** *(Gerberei)* skin prepared for tanning; **d)** *(im Wald)* clearing; **e)** *(Fechten)* target; **eine ~ freigeben** *od.* **öffnen** present a target

bloß-, Bloß-: ~|legen *tr. V.* uncover; expose; *(fig.) (herausfinden)* uncover; reveal; *(enthüllen)* expose; reveal ‹*error, defect, etc.*›; **~|liegen** *unr. itr. V.*; *mit sein* be uncovered *or* exposed; **~|stellen** *tr. V.* show up; unmask, expose ‹*swindler, criminal, etc.*›; **sich ~stellen** show oneself up; **~stellung die** *s.* **~stellen:** showing up; unmasking; exposure; **~|strampeln** *refl. V.* kick the *or* one's covers off

Blouson [blu'zõ:] **das** *od.* **der; ~[s], ~s** blouson; bomber jacket

blubbern ['blʊbɐn] *itr. V. (ugs.)* **a)** *(Blasen bilden)* bubble; **b)** *(undeutlich reden)* mutter; mumble

Blücher ['blʏçɐ] *in* **er/sie geht ran wie ~** *(ugs.)* he/she really goes hard at it

Bluejeans, Blue jeans ['blu:dʒi:ns] *Pl. od.* **die; ~, ~:** [blue] jeans *pl.*; denims *pl.*; **er trug eine ~:** he wore [a pair of] jeans *or* denims

Blues [blu:s] **der; ~, ~** *(Musik, Tanz)* blues *pl.*

Bluff [blʊf] **der; ~s, ~s** bluff

bluffen *tr., itr. V.* bluff

blühen ['bly:ən] *itr. V.* **a)** ‹*plant*› flower, bloom, be in flower *or* bloom; ‹*flower*› bloom, be in bloom, be out; ‹*tree*› be in blossom; **~de Gärten/Wiesen** gardens/meadows full of flowers; **es blüht** there are flowers in bloom; **diese Rosensorte blüht rot** this type of rose has red flowers; **Azaleen zum Blühen bringen** get azaleas to flower; **b)** *(florieren)* flourish; thrive; **c)** *(ugs.: bevorstehen)* **jmdm. ~:** be in store for sb.; **das gleiche blüht mir nächste Woche** I've got the same thing coming [to me] next week; **da blüht dir ja was Nettes** *(iron.)* that'll be nice for you *(iron.)*; **das kann dir auch noch ~:** the same may *or* could happen to you; **sonst blüht dir was!** otherwise you'll catch it!

blühend *Adj.* **a)** *(frisch, gesund)* glowing ‹*colour, complexion, etc.*›; radiant ‹*health*›; **ein ~es Geschäft** a flourishing trade; **er sieht ~ aus** he looks marvellous *or* the picture of health; **aussehen wie das ~e Leben** look the very picture of health; **sie starb im ~en Alter von 20 Jahren** she died at 20, in the full bloom of youth; **b)** *(übertrieben)* vivid, lively ‹*imagination*›; absolute, utter ‹*nonsense*›

Blühet die; ~ *(schweiz.)* blossom

Blümchen ['bly:mçən] **das; ~s, ~:** [little] flower

Blümchen·kaffee der *(ugs. scherzh.)* **a)** weak coffee; **b)** *(Kaffee-Ersatz)* coffee substitute

Blume ['blu:mə] **die; ~, ~n a)** *(auch fig. dichter.)* flower; **vielen Dank für die ~n** *(iron.)* thank you very much *(iron.)*; thanks for nothing; **etw. durch die ~ sagen** say sth. in a roundabout way; **jmdm. etw. durch die ~ sagen** *od.* **zu verstehen geben** tell sb. sth. in a roundabout way; **b)** *(des Weines)* bouquet; **c)** *(des Biers)* head; **d)** *(Jägerspr.: des Hasen, Kaninchens)* tail; scut

blumen-, Blumen-: ~beet das flower-bed; **~bukett das** *(geh.)* bouquet [of flowers]; **~draht der** florist's wire; **~erde die** potting compost; **~fenster das** window full of flowers; *(spezielles Fenster)* flower window; **~flor der** *(geh.)* abundance of flowers; **~frau die** flower-woman; **~fülle die** *o. Pl.* abundance of flowers; **~garten der** flower-garden; **~geschäft das** florist's; flower-shop; **~geschmückt** *Adj.* flower-bedecked; adorned with flowers *postpos.*; **~gruß der** bouquet of flowers; **~händler der** florist; **~kasten der** flower-box; *(vor einem Fenster)* window box; **~kind das** flower child; **~kohl der** cauliflower; **~korb der** *(für Blumen)* flower-basket; *(mit Blumen)* basket of flowers; **~kranz der** floral wreath; garland of flowers; **~laden der** *s.* **~geschäft; ~mädchen das** flower-girl; **~markt der** flower-market; **~muster das** floral pattern; **~pracht die** magnificent display of flowers; **~rabatte die** flower-border; herbaceous border; **~reich 1.** *Adj.* **a)** *(voller Blumen)* full of flowers *postpos.*; flowery; **b)** flowery ‹*language, style, etc.*›; **2.** *adv.* ‹*speak*› in a flowery way; ‹*write*› in a flowery style; **~schale die** *(Schale für Blumen)* plant-bowl; *(Schale mit Blumen)* bowl of plants; **~schmuck der** floral decoration; **~stand der** flower-stall; **~stock der** [flowering] pot plant; **~strauß der** bunch of flowers; *(Bukett)* bouquet of flowers; **~teppich der** carpet of flowers; **~topf der a)** *(Topf für Pflanzen)* flowerpot; **b)** *(ugs.: Topfpflanze)* [flowering] pot plant; **damit kannst du keinen ~topf gewinnen** *(ugs.)* that won't get you anywhere; **~uhr die** floral clock; **~vase die** *(Vase für Blumen)* [flower] vase; *(Vase mit Blumen)* vase of flowers; **~zwiebel die** bulb

blümerant [blymə'rant] *Adj.* queasy; **mir ist ~:** I feel queasy

blumig 1. *Adj.* flowery ‹*language, style, perfume, wine, etc.*›. **2.** *adv.* ‹*speak*› in a flowery way; ‹*write*› in a flowery style

Blunze ['blʊntsə] **die; ~, ~n, Blunzen die; ~, ~** *(bayr., österr.)* **a)** black pudding; **b)** *(ugs. abwertend: Frau)* fat cow *(sl. derog.)*

Bluse ['blu:zə] **die; ~, ~n** blouse; **ganz schön etwas in** *od.* **unter der ~ haben** *(salopp)* be well stacked *(sl. joc.)* or well endowed *(joc.)*; **jmdm. an die ~ gehen** *(salopp)* try to grope sb.'s boobs *pl. (sl.)*

Blüse ['bly:zə] **die; ~, ~n** *(Seemannsspr.)* light

blusig 1. *Adj.* bloused. **2.** *adv.* **~ geschnitten/fallend** bloused

Blust [blu:st] **der** *od.* **das** *(veralt., schweiz.)* blossom

Blut [blu:t] **das; ~[e]s** blood; **deine Stirn ist ja voller ~:** your forehead is covered in blood; **~ abgenommen bekommen** have a blood sample taken; **gleich ins ~ gehen** pass straight into the bloodstream; **jmdm. steigt das ~ in den Kopf** the blood rushes to sb.'s head; **es wurde viel ~ vergossen** there was a great deal of bloodshed; **er kann kein ~ sehen** he can't stand the sight of blood; **er lag in seinem ~:** he lay in a pool of blood; **~ und Boden** *(ns.)* blood and soil; **wenn sie so was sieht, kocht ihr das ~ in den Adern** *(fig.)* when she sees something like that, it makes her blood boil; **den Zuschauern gefror** *od.* **stockte** *od.* **gerann das ~ in den Adern** *(fig.)* the spectators' blood ran cold; **heißes/feuriges ~ haben** *(fig.)* be hot-blooded; **französisches/russisches ~ in den Adern haben** *(fig.)* have French/Russian blood in one *or* in one's veins *(fig.)*; **~ ist dicker als Wasser** *(fig.)* blood is thicker than water *(fig.)*; **ein junges Blut** *(fig. dichter.)* a young thing *(fig.)*; **an jmds. Händen klebt ~** *(fig. geh.)* there is blood on sb.'s hands *(fig.)*; **blaues ~ in den Adern haben** *(fig.)* have blue blood in one's veins *(fig.)*; **kaltes ~ bewahren** *(fig.)* remain cold and unmoved; **böses ~ machen** *od.* **schaffen** *(fig.)* cause *or* create bad blood; **~ und Wasser schwitzen** *(fig. ugs.)* sweat blood *(fig. coll.)*; **~ geleckt haben** *(fig. ugs.)* have got a taste for it; **[nur/immer] ruhig ~!** *(ugs.)* keep your hair on! *(Brit. sl.)*; keep your cool! *(coll.)*; **jmdn. bis aufs ~ quälen** *od.* **peinigen** *(fig.)* torment sb. mercilessly; **jmdm. im ~ liegen** *(fig.)* be in sb.'s blood *(fig.)*; **ins ~ gehen** get into one's blood; really get one going; **etw. mit seinem ~ besiegeln** *(dichter.)* lay down one's life for sth.; **nach [jmds.] ~ lechzen** *od.* **dürsten** *(geh.)* thirst for [sb.'s] blood *(fig.)*

blut-, Blut-: ~ader die *(Anat.)* vein; **~alkohol der** blood alcohol level; **~andrang der** *(Med.)* congestion; hyperaemia *(Med.)*; **~apfelsine die** *s.* **~orange**; **~arm** *Adj. (Med.)* anaemic; **~armut die** *(Med.)* anaemia; **~auffrischung die** *(fig.)* **die Firma braucht eine ~auffrischung** the company needs some new blood; **~aus·strich der** *(Med.)* blood smear; **~aus·tausch der** *(Med.)* exchange transfusion; **~bad das** blood-bath; **~bahn die** bloodstream; **~bank die**; *Pl.* **~banken** *(Med.)* blood bank; **~befleckt** *Adj.* bloodstained; **seine Hände sind ~befleckt** *(fig.)* he has blood on his hands *(fig.)*; **~beschmiert** *Adj.* smeared with blood *postpos.*; **~bild das** *(Med.)* blood picture; **~bildend** *Adj. (Med.)* haematinic; **~bildung die** *(Med.)* blood-formation; **~blase die** blood blister; **~buche die** copper beech; **~druck der**; *o. Pl.* blood pressure; **~druck·messung die** blood-pressure test; **~drucksenkend** *Adj. (Med.)* anti-hypertensive; **~dürstig** *Adj. (geh.)* bloodthirsty

Blüte ['bly:tə] **die; ~, ~n a)** flower; bloom; *(eines Baums)* blossom; **die ~ der Jugend** *(dichter.)* the flower of the young men; **~n treiben** flower; bloom; ⟨*tree*⟩ blossom; **seltsame** *od.* **wunderliche ~n treiben** *(fig.)* produce strange effects; ⟨*custom, fashion*⟩ take strange forms; **seine Phantasie trieb üppige/die seltsamsten ~n** *(fig.)* his imagination produced extravagant/the strangest fancies; **b)** *(das Blühen)* flowering; blooming; *(Baum~)* blossoming; **die ~ der Tulpen/Obstbäume hat schon begonnen** the tulips have started to flower *or* bloom/the fruit-trees have started to blossom; **in [voller] ~ stehen** be in [full] flower *or* bloom/blossom; **in der ~ seiner Jahre** *(fig. geh.)* in his prime; in the prime of his life; **c)** *(geh.: Entwicklungsstand)* **seine/ihre ~ erreichen** ⟨*culture*⟩ reach its full flowering; **die Renaissance war für die Kunst eine Zeit der ~:** art flourished during the Renaissance; **d)** *(ugs.: falsche Banknote)* dud note *(sl.)*; **e)** *(ugs. abwertend: unfähiger Mensch)* duffer

Blut·egel der leech

bluten *itr. V.* **a)** *(Blut verlieren)* bleed **(aus** from); **mir blutet das Herz** *(iron.)* it makes my heart bleed *(iron.)*; **~den Herzens, mit ~dem Herzen** with a heavy heart; **wie ein Schwein ~** *(derb)* bleed like a stuck pig; **b)** *(ugs.: viel bezahlen)* **[ganz schön] ~:** cough up *(sl.) or* fork out *(sl.)* a[n awful] lot of money **(für** for)

Blüten-: ~blatt das petal; **~flor der** *(dichter.)* abundance of flowers; **~honig der** blossom honey; **~hülle die** *(Bot.)* perianth; **~kelch der** *(Bot.)* calyx; **~knospe die** flower-bud; **~lese die** *(veralt.)* florilegium *(arch.)*; **~meer das** *(geh.)* sea of flowers; **~pflanze die** *(Bot.)* flowering plant; **~stand der** *(Bot.)* inflorescence; **~staub der** *(Bot.)* pollen

Blut·entnahme die taking of a blood sample; **zur ~entnahme zum Arzt gehen** go to the doctor to have a blood sample taken

blüten·weiß *Adj.* sparkling white

Blüten·zweig der flowering branch; *(kleiner)* flowering twig

Bluter ['blu:tɐ] **der; ~s, ~** *(Med.)* haemophiliac

Blut·erguß der haematoma; *(blauer Fleck)* bruise

Bluter·krankheit die haemophilia *no art.*

Blüte·zeit die a) die ~ der Geranien ist von Mai bis Oktober geraniums flower *or* are in flower from May to October; **während der ~ der Obstbäume** when the fruit-trees are/were in blossom; **b)** *(fig.)* heyday; **seine ~ erleben** ⟨*culture, empire*⟩ be in its heyday; **das frühe 17. Jahrhundert war eine ~ des Dramas** drama flourished in the early 17th century

blut-, Blut-: ~farb·stoff der *(Physiol.)* haemoglobin; **~fleck[en] der** blood-stain; **~flüssigkeit die** *s.* **~plasma**; **~gefäß das** *(Anat.)* blood-vessel; **~geld das** *(veralt.)* blood money; **~gerinnsel das** blood-clot; **~gerinnung die** *(Physiol.)* clotting of the blood; **~gerüst das** *(geh.)* scaffold; **~getränkt** *Adj.* blood-soaked; **~gier die** *(auch fig.)* blood-lust; **~gierig** *Adj. (auch fig.)* bloodthirsty; **~gruppe die** *(Med.)* blood group; blood type; **jmds. ~gruppe bestimmen** *od.* **feststellen** blood-type sb.; type sb.'s blood; **er hatte ~gruppe 0** he was blood group 0; **~gruppen·bestimmung die** *(Med.)* blood-typing; **~gruppen·untersuchung die** *(Med.)* blood test; **~hoch·druck der** *(Med.)* high blood pressure; **~hund der** bloodhound; *(fig.)* bloodthirsty murderer

blutig 1. *Adj.* **a)** bloody; **jmdn. ~ schlagen** beat sb. to a pulp; **~ geschlagen werden** be left battered and bleeding; **b)** *nicht präd. (fig. ugs.: total, völlig)* absolute, complete ⟨*beginner, layman, etc.*⟩; **das ist mein ~er Ernst!** I am deadly serious. **2.** *adv.* bloodily; **sich ~ rächen** take bloody revenge

blut-, Blut-: ~jung *Adj.* very young; **~konserve die** *(Med.)* container of stored blood; **~konserven** stored blood; **~körperchen das** *(Anat.)* blood corpuscle; **rote/weiße ~körperchen** red/white corpuscles; **~krebs der** *(Med.)* leukaemia; **~kreis·lauf der** *(Physiol.)* blood circulation; **~kuchen der** *(Med.)* blood clot; clot of blood; **~lache die** pool of blood; **~leer** *Adj.* bloodless; **ihr Gesicht wurde ganz ~leer** the blood drained from her face; **~leere die** restricted blood supply; ischaemia *(Med.)*; **~mangel der a)** lack of blood; **b)** *(Anämie)* anaemia; **~orange die** blood orange; **~pfropf der** *(Physiol.)* blood clot; clot of blood; **~plasma das** *(Physiol.)* blood plasma; **~plättchen das** *(Physiol.)* blood platelet; **~probe die** *(Med.)* **a)** *(~entnahme, ~untersuchung)* blood test; **b)** *(kleine ~menge)* blood sample; **~rache die** blood revenge; blood vengeance; **~rausch der** *(geh.)* murderous frenzy; **~reinigend** blood-cleansing; **~reinigung die** purification of the blood; **~reinigungs·tee der** blood-cleansing tea; **~rot** *Adj.* blood-red; **~rünstig** [-rʏnstɪç] **1.** *Adj.* bloodthirsty; **2.** *adv.* bloodthirstily; **~sauger der a)** *(Insekt, abwertend: Ausbeuter)* bloodsucker; **b)** *(Vampir)* vampire

Bluts-: ~bande *Pl.* blood ties; **~brüderschaft die** blood brotherhood; **~brüderschaft schließen** become blood brothers

blut-, Blut-: ~schande die incest; **~schänder der, ~schänderin die** incestuous person; **~schänderisch** *Adj.* incestuous; **~schuld die** *(geh.)* blood-guilt; **~schwamm der** *(Med.)* strawberry mark; **~senkung die** *(Med.)* erythrocyte sedimentation test; **zur ~senkung gehen** *(ugs.)* go to have a sedimentation test; **~serum das** *(Physiol.)* blood serum; **~spende die** *(das Spenden)* giving *no indef. art.* of blood; donation of blood; *(~menge)* blood-donation; **~spender der** blood-donor; **~spende·zentrale die** blood-donor centre; **~spucken das** spitting of blood; haemoptysis *(Med.)*; **~spur die a)** trail of blood; **b)** *Pl. (auf Kleidung o. ä.)* traces of blood; **~stillend** *Adj.* styptic; **~stillende Mittel** styptics; **~strom der** bloodstream

Bluts·tropfen der drop of blood

Blut·sturz der a) *(ugs.: aus Mund und Nase)* **er erlitt einen ~sturz** he was bleeding from [his] nose and mouth; **b)** *(Med.)* haemorrhage

bluts-, Bluts-: ~verwandt *Adj.* related by blood *postpos.*; **sie ist nicht ~verwandt mit ihm** she is not related to him by blood; **sie sind nicht ~verwandt** they are not blood relations; **~verwandte der/die** blood relation; **~verwandtschaft die** blood relationship

blut-, Blut-: ~tat die *(geh.)* bloody deed; **~transfusion die** blood-transfusion; **~triefend** *Adj.*; *nicht präd.* dripping with blood *pred.*; **~überströmt** *Adj.* streaming with blood *pred.*; covered in blood *pred.*; **~übertragung die** blood-transfusion

Blut-und-Boden-Dichtung die; ~ *(abwertend)* blood-and-soil literature

Blutung die; ~, ~en a) bleeding *no indef. art., no pl.*; haemorrhage; **innere/äußere ~en** internal/external bleeding *sing.*; **eine ~ im Gehirn** a brain haemorrhage; **b)** *(Regel~)* period

blut-, Blut-: ~unterlaufen *Adj.* suffused with blood *postpos.*; bloodshot ⟨*eyes*⟩; **~untersuchung die** *(Med.)* blood test; **~vergießen das; ~s** bloodshed; **~vergiftung die** blood-poisoning *no indef. art., no pl.*; **~verlust der** loss of blood; **~verschmiert** *Adj.* blood-stained, smeared with blood *pred.*; **~wäsche die** *(Med.)* purification of the blood; **~wurst die** black pudding; **~zirkulation die** blood circulation; **~zoll der** *(geh.)* toll of lives; **~zucker der** *(Physiol.)* blood sugar; **~zucker·spiegel der** *(Physiol.)* blood-sugar level; **~zufuhr die** blood supply

b-Moll ['be:mɔl] **das; ~:** B flat minor; *s. auch* **a-Moll**

BND [be:lɛn'de:] **der; ~** *Abk.* **Bundesnachrichtendienst**

Bö [bø:] **die; ~, ~en** gust [of wind]; *(mit Niederschlag)* squall; **in ~en orkanartig** gusting to hurricane force

Boa ['bo:a] **die; ~, ~s** *(Schlange, Feder~)* boa

Bob [bɔp] **der; ~, ~s** bob[-sleigh]

Bob-: ~bahn die bob[-sleigh] run; **~fahrer der** bobber; **~mannschaft die** bob [-sleigh] team; **~rennen das** bob[-sleigh] racing; *(einzelne Veranstaltung)* bob [-sleigh] race; **~sport der** bob-sleighing; **~tail** [~teɪl] **der** [Old English] sheep-dog

Boccia ['bɔtʃa] **das;** ~[s] *od.* **die;** ~: boccie; boccia

[1]Bock [bɔk] **der;** ~[e]s, **Böcke** ['bœkə] **a)** *(Reh~, Kaninchen~)* buck; *(Ziegen~)* billy-goat; he-goat; *(Schafs~)* ram; **ein steifer ~** *od.* **steif wie ein ~ sein** *(ugs.)* be as stiff as a board; **stur wie ein ~ sein** *(ugs.)* be as stubborn as a mule; **stinken wie ein ~** *(salopp)* stink to high heaven *(coll.)*; **jmdn. stößt der ~** *(ugs.)* sb. is being contrary *(coll.)*; **etw. aus ~ tun** *(ugs.)* do sth. just for the fun of it; **einen ~ schießen** *(fig. ugs.)* boob *(Brit. sl.)*; make a boo-boo *(Amer. coll.)*; *(einen Fauxpas begehen)* drop a clanger *(sl.)*; **den ~ zum Gärtner machen** *(ugs.)* be asking for trouble; **die Böcke von den Schafen trennen** *(fig.)* separate the sheep from the goats; **einen/keinen ~ auf etw.** *(Akk.)* **haben** *(ugs.)* fancy/not fancy sth.; **einen/keinen ~ haben, etw. zu tun** *(ugs.)* fancy/not fancy doing sth.; **b)** *(ugs.: Schimpfwort)* **der geile alte ~:** the randy old goat; **sturer ~!** you stubborn git *(sl. derog.)*; **c)** *(Gestell)* trestle; **d)** *(Turnen)* buck; **e)** *(Kutsch~)* box

[2]Bock das; ~s *(Bier)* bock [beer]

bock-, Bock-: ~beinig *(ugs.)* **1.** *Adj.* contrary *(coll.)*; stubborn and awkward; **2.** *adv.* contrarily *(coll.)*; **~bier das** bock [beer]

bocken *itr. V.* **a)** *(nicht weitergehen)* refuse to go on; *(vor einer Hürde)* refuse; *(sich aufbäumen)* buck; rear; **die alte Karre bockt mal wieder** *(salopp)* the old heap is playing up again *(coll.)*; **b)** *(fam.: trotzig sein)* be stubborn and awkward; play up *(coll.)*; **c)** *(Landw.: brünstig sein)* be on heat; **d)** *(derb: koitieren)* have it away *or* off *(sl.)*; have a screw *(vulg.)*

bockig 1. *Adj.* stubborn and awkward; contrary *(coll.)*. **2.** *adv.* stubbornly [and awkwardly]; contrarily *(coll.)*

Bock-: ~kitz das *(Jägerspr.)* young buck; **~mist der** *(salopp)* bilge *no indef. art. (sl.)*; bullshit *no indef. art. (coarse)*; **einen ziemlichen ~mist verzapfen** come out with a load of bilge; **einen schönen ~mist machen** make a real cock-up *(Brit. sl.) or* a holy mess

Bocks-: ~bart der a) *(bei der Ziege)* [goat's] beard; *(beim Mann)* goatee [beard]; **b)** *(Bot.)* goat's-beard; **~beutel der a)** *(Flasche)* bocksbeutel; *wide, bulbous bottle for fine Franconian wines;* **b)** *(Wein) o. Pl.* bocksbeutel wine; *Franconian wine sold in a bocksbeutel*

Bock·schein der *(salopp) (prostitute's)* certificate of health

Bocks-: ~fuß der goat's foot; **~horn das sich [nicht] [von jmdm.] ins ~horn jagen lassen** *(ugs.) (sich [nicht] einschüchtern lassen)* [not] let oneself be browbeaten [by sb.]; *(sich [nicht] erschrecken und verwirren lassen)* [not] let oneself get worked up into a state [by sb.]

Bock-: ~springen das *(Turnen)* vaulting [over the buck]; *(ohne Gerät)* leapfrog; **~sprung der a)** *(Turnen) (Disziplin)* vaulting [over the buck]; *(einzelner Sprung)* vault [over the buck]; **b)** *(ungelenker Sprung)* [ungainly] jump *or* leap; **~sprünge machen** jump *or* leap about; **vor Freude ~sprünge machen** jump for joy; **~wurst die** bockwurst

Boden ['bo:dn̩] **der;** ~s, **Böden** ['bø:dn̩] **a)** *(Erde)* ground; soil; **er wäre am liebsten im ~ versunken** he wished the ground would open and swallow him up; **den ~ für jmdn./etw. [vor]bereiten** prepare the ground for sb./sth.; **[bei jmdm.] auf fruchtbaren ~ fallen** ⟨*advice, warning*⟩ have some effect [on sb.]; **etw. [nicht] aus dem ~ stampfen können** [not] be able to conjure sth. up [out of thin air]; **wie aus dem ~ gestampft** *od.* **gewachsen** as if by magic; **b)** *(Fuß~)* floor; **bei ihr kann man vom ~ essen** her floors are so clean that you could eat off them; **zu ~ fallen/sich zu ~ fallen lassen** fall/drop to the ground; **der Boxer ging zu ~:** the boxer went down; **die Augen zu ~ schlagen** look down; **jmdn. zu ~ schlagen** *od. (geh.)* **strecken** knock sb. down; floor sb.; *(fig.)* **sich auf unsicherem ~ bewegen** be on shaky ground *(fig.)*; **sich auf schwankenden ~ begeben** get into a risky area *(fig.)*; **jmdm. wird der ~ unter den Füßen zu heiß** *od.* **brennt der ~ unter den Füßen** *(ugs.)* things are getting too hot for sb. *(fig.)*; **festen ~ unter den Füßen haben** be back on terra firma; *(Tatsachen behaupten)* be on firm ground; *(wirtschaftlich gesichert sein)* be firmly on one's feet; **jmdm. den ~ unter den Füßen wegziehen** cut the ground from under sb.'s feet; **einem Gerücht/einer Theorie den ~ entziehen** scotch a rumour/explode a theory; **sie hatte das Gefühl, den ~ unter den Füßen zu verlieren** she felt the ground fall from beneath her feet; **er scheint völlig den ~ unter den Füßen verloren zu haben** the bottom seems to have dropped out of his world; **am ~ liegen** be bankrupt; **am ~ zerstört [sein]** *(ugs.)* [be] shattered *(coll.)*; **jmdn zu ~ drücken** ⟨*cares, worries*⟩ get on top of sb.; **c)** *o. Pl. (Grundlage)* **bleiben wir doch auf dem ~ der Tatsachen** let's stick to the facts; **hart auf den ~ der Wirklichkeit zurückgeholt werden** be brought back down to earth with a bump *(fig.)*; **auf dem ~ der Verfassung/des Gesetzes stehen** ⟨*person*⟩ be within the constitution/law; **d)** *o. Pl. (Terrain)* **heiliger ~:** holy ground; **feindlicher ~:** enemy territory; **auf französischem ~:** on French soil; **~ gutmachen** *od.* **wettmachen** *(ugs.)* make up ground; **[an] ~ gewinnen/verlieren** gain/lose ground; **e)** *(unterste Fläche)* bottom; *(Hosen~)* seat; *(Torten~)* base; **auf dem ~ des Meeres** at the bottom of the sea; on the sea-bed; *s. auch* **doppelt; f)** *(Dach~, Heu~)* loft; *(Wäsche~)* drying-room; **auf dem ~:** in the loft/drying-room

boden-, Boden-: ~abwehr die *(Milit.)* ground defence; **~bearbeitung die** cultivation of the land; tillage; **~belag der** *(Teppich, Linoleum)* floor-covering; *(Fliesen, Parkett)* flooring; **~beschaffenheit die a)** *(der Erde)* condition of the soil; **b)** *(des Fußbodens)* condition of the ground; conditions *pl.* underfoot; **~biologie die** soil biology; **~-Boden-Rakete die** *(Milit.)* surface-to-surface missile; **~erosion die** soil erosion; **~ertrag der** crop yield; **~feuchtigkeit die** soil moisture; **~fräse die** *(Landw.)* rotary cultivator; **~freiheit die** *(Technik)* ground clearance; **~frost der** ground frost; **~gefecht das** *(Milit.)* ground battle; **~haftung die** *(Kfz-W.)* road-holding *no indef. art.*; **~heizung die** underfloor heating; **~kammer die** attic; **~kampf der a)** *(Judo, Ringen)* groundwork; **b)** *(Milit.)* ground battle; **~kunde die** soil science; **~lang** *Adj.* full-length ⟨*skirt, dress, etc.*⟩; **~los** *Adj.* **a)** *(tief)* bottomless; **ins Bodenlose fallen** fall into a bottomless abyss; **b)** *(ugs.: unerhört)* incredible, unbelievable ⟨*foolishness, meanness, etc.*⟩; **~-Luft-Rakete die** *(Milit.)* surface-to-air missile; **~nähe die** *(Flugw.)* **in ~nähe** at a low level; **~nebel der** ground mist; *(dichter)* ground fog; **~nutzung die** agricultural land use; **~personal das** *(Flugw.)* ground staff; **~raum der** loft; **~recht das** *(Rechtsw.)* land law; **~reform die** land reform; **~rente die** ground rent; **~satz der** sediment; *(von Kaffee)* grounds *pl.*; *(fig.) (Rest)* residue; *(Grundbestandteil)* basic component *or* ingredient; **~schätze** *Pl.* mineral resources

Boden·see der; *o. Pl.* Lake Constance

boden-, Boden-: ~sicht die *(Flugw.)* ground visibility; **~spekulation die** land speculation; **~ständig** *Adj.* indigenous, native ⟨*culture, population, etc.*⟩; local ⟨*custom, craft, cuisine, tradition*⟩; ⟨*novel*⟩ rooted in the soil; **~ständigkeit die;** ~: **die ~ständigkeit des echten Kölners geht so weit, daß ...:** the roots of the genuine native of Cologne go so deep that ...; **die Schwarzwaldbauern verlieren ihre ~ständigkeit** the farmers of the Black Forest are losing the close links with their native soil; **~station die** *(Raumf.)* ground station; **~streitkräfte** *Pl.*: *s.* **~truppen; ~treppe die** attic stairs *pl.*; **~truppen** *Pl.* ground forces *or* troops; **~turnen das** floor exercises *pl.*; **~vase die** large vase *(standing on the floor)*; **~verhältnisse** *Pl.* ground conditions; **~welle die a)** *(Unebenheit)* bump; **b)** *(Funkw.)* ground wave; **~wichse die** *(schweiz.)* floor-polish

bodigen ['bo:dɪgn̩] *tr. V. (schweiz.: besiegen)* beat; defeat

Bodmerei [bo:dmə'rai] **die;** ~, ~en *(Seew.)* bottomry

Bodybuilder ['bɔdibɪldɐ] **der;** ~s, ~: bodybuilder

Bodybuilding [bɔdibɪldɪŋ] **das;** ~s bodybuilding *no art.*; **~ betreiben** do bodybuilding exercises

Bodycheck ['bɔditʃɛk] **der;** ~s, ~s *(Eishockey)* body-check

Böe ['bø:ə] **die;** ~, ~n *s.* **Bö**

Bofist ['bo:fɪst] **der;** ~[e]s, ~e puff-ball

bog [bo:k] *1. u. 3. Pers. Sg. Prät. v.* **biegen**

Bogen ['bo:gn̩] **der;** ~s, ~, *(südd., österr.:)* **Bögen** ['bø:gn̩] **a)** *(gebogene Linie)* curve; *(Math.)* arc; *(Skifahren)* turn; *(Schlittschuhlaufen)* curve; **einen ~ schlagen** move in a curve; **der Weg macht/beschreibt einen ~:** the path bends/the path describes a curve; **immer, wenn ich sie auf der Straße sehe, mache ich einen großen ~** *(fig. ugs.)* whenever I see her in the street I make a detour [round her]; **einen großen ~ um jmdn./etw. machen** *(fig. ugs.)* give sb./sth. a wide berth; **das Wasser spritzte in hohem ~ heraus** the water spurted out in a great arc; **in hohem ~ hinausfliegen** *(fig. ugs.)* be chucked out *(sl.)*; **große ~ spucken** *(ugs.)* talk big; *s. auch* **heraushaben; b)** *(Archit.)* arch; **c)** *(Waffe)* bow; **den ~ überspannen** *(fig.)* go too far; **d)** *(Musik: Geigen~ usw.)* bow; **e)** *(Papier~)* sheet; **ein ~ Schreibpapier/Packpapier** a sheet of writing-paper/wrapping-paper; **ein A4-~:** a sheet of A4 paper; **f)** *(Musik: Zeichen)* slur; *(bei gleicher Notenhöhe)* tie

bogen-, Bogen-: ~brücke die arch bridge; **~fenster das** arched window; **~förmig** *Adj.* arched; **~führung die** *(Musik)* bowing *no indef. art.*; **~gang der a)** *(Arkaden)* arcade; **b)** *(Anat.)* semicircular canal; **~lampe die** *(Elektrot.)* arc lamp; **~pfeiler der** pillar *or* column of the/an arch; **~säge die** coping saw; **~schießen das** *(Sport)* archery *no art.*; **~schütze der** *(Sport)* archer

Boheme [bo'e:m] **die;** ~: bohemian world *or* society

Bohemien [boe'mi̯ɛ̃:] **der;** ~s, ~s bohemian

Bohle ['bo:lə] **die;** ~, ~n [thick] plank

Bohlen·belag der planking *no indef. art.*

böhmakeln ['bø:makl̩n] *itr. V. (österr. ugs. abwertend)* speak with a dreadful Czech accent

Böhme ['bø:mə] **der;** ~n, ~n Bohemian

Böhmen ['bø:mən] *(das)*; ~s Bohemia

Böhmer·wald der Bohemian Forest

Böhmin die; ~, ~nen Bohemian; *s. auch* **-in**

böhmisch *Adj.* Bohemian

Böhnchen ['bø:nçən] **das;** ~s, ~: [small] bean

Bohne ['bo:nə] **die;** ~, ~n bean; **grüne ~n** green beans; French beans *(Brit.)*; **dicke/weiße ~n** broad/haricot beans; **gebackene ~n** casserole *sing.* of beans with pork; **blaue ~n** *(Soldatenspr. veralt., noch scherzh.)* bullets; **nicht die ~** *(ugs.)* not one little bit

Bohnen-: **~ein·topf der** bean stew; **~kaffee der a)** *(Bohnen)* real coffee; **gemahlener ~kaffee** ground coffee; **b)** *(Getränk)* real coffee; **~kraut das** savory; **~salat der** bean salad; **~stange die** *(auch ugs.: Mensch)* beanpole; **~stroh das: dumm wie ~stroh** *(ugs.)* as thick as two short planks *(coll.)*; **~suppe die** bean soup
Bohner der; ~s, ~ *s.* **Bohnerbesen**
Bohner-: **~besen der** floor-polisher; floor-polishing brush; **~maschine die** floor-polisher; floor-polishing machine
bohnern *tr., itr. V.* polish; **hier ist frisch gebohnert** this floor has/these stairs have *etc.* been freshly polished; **„Vorsicht, frisch gebohnert!"** 'freshly polished floor/stairs *etc.*'
Bohner·wachs das floor-polish
bohren ['bo:rən] **1.** *tr. V.* **a)** bore; *(mit Bohrer, Bohrmaschine)* drill, bore ‹*hole*›; sink ‹*well, shaft*›; bore, drive ‹*tunnel*›; sink ‹*pole, post etc.*› **(in + *Akk.*** into); **b)** *(bearbeiten)* drill ‹*wood, concrete, etc.*›; **c)** *(drücken in)* poke **(in + *Akk.*** in[to]). **2.** *itr. V.* **a)** *(eine Bohrung vornehmen)* drill; **in einem Zahn ~:** drill a tooth; **in der Nase ~:** pick one's nose; **nach Öl/Wasser** *usw.* **~:** drill for oil/water *etc.*; **b)** *(fig.: nagen)* gnaw; **Zweifel bohrten in ihm** he had nagging doubts; **c)** *(ugs.: drängen, fragen)* keep on; **jetzt hört auf zu ~:** now, don't keep on; **ich habe so lange gebohrt, bis ...:** I kept on and on until ... **3.** *refl. V. (eindringen)* bore its way; **das Flugzeug hatte sich tief in die Erde gebohrt** the aircraft had buried itself deep in the ground
bohrend *Adj.* **a)** gnawing ‹*pain, hunger, remorse*›; **b)** *(hartnäckig)* piercing ‹*look etc.*›; probing ‹*question*›
Bohrer der; ~s, ~ a) *(Gerät)* drill; *(zum Vorbohren)* gimlet; **b)** *(Arbeiter)* driller
Bohr-: **~insel die** drilling rig; *(für Öl)* drilling rig; oil rig; **~loch das** borehole; *(in Metall, Holz)* drill-hole; *(einer Ölquelle)* well; **~maschine die** drill; **~meißel der** bit; **~probe die** core [sample]; **~turm der** derrick
Bohrung die; ~, ~en a) *s.* **bohren 1 a:** drilling; boring; sinking; driving; **b)** *(Bohrloch)* borehole; *(in Holz, Metall)* drill-hole; **c)** *(lichte Weite)* **die ~ des Zylinders** the bore of the cylinder
böig *Adj.* gusty; *(mit Niederschlag)* squally; **~ auffrischend** freshening in gusts/squalls
Boiler ['bɔylɐ] **der; ~s, ~:** boiler; *(im Haushalt)* water-heater
Boje ['bo:jə] **die; ~, ~n** buoy
Bolero [bo'le:ro] **der; ~s, ~s a)** *(Tanz, Jacke)* bolero; **b)** *(Hut)* bolero hat
Bolid [bo'li:t] **der; ~s** *od.* **~en, ~e** *od.* **~en** *(Astron.)* bolide
Bolivianer [boli'vi̯a:nɐ] **der; ~s, ~, Bolivianerin die; ~, ~nen** Bolivian; *s. auch* **-in**
bolivianisch *Adj.* Bolivian
Bolivien [bo'li:vi̯ən] **(das); ~s** Bolivia
bölken ['bœlkn̩] *itr. V. (nordd., westd.)* ‹*cow*› moo; ‹*sheep*› bleat; ‹*person*› bawl, shout
¹Bolle ['bɔlə] **die; ~, ~n** *(berlin.)* **a)** *(Zwiebel)* onion; **b)** *(Loch in der Socke)* hole
²Bolle *o. Art.; in* **sich wie ~ [auf dem Milchwagen] amüsieren** *(berlin.)* have a marvellous *or (coll.)* great time
Böller ['bœlɐ] **der; ~s, ~ a)** *(Geschütz)* [small] cannon *(used on ceremonial occasions)*; **b)** *(Feuerwerkskörper)* banger
bollern ['bɔlɐn] *itr. V.; mit sein (bes. nordd.)* thud; **die Kinder bollerten die Treppe hinunter** the children clattered down the stairs
böllern *itr. V.* **es wurde 21mal geböllert** there was a 21-gun salute
Böller·schuß der gun salute; **der Admiral wurde mit fünf Böllerschüssen begrüßt** the admiral was greeted with a five-gun salute
Boller·wagen der *(nordd.)* handcart
Bollette [bɔ'lɛtə] **die; ~, ~n** *(österr. Amtsspr.)* customs declaration
Boll·werk das a) *(Befestigung)* bulwark; *(fig.)* bulwark; bastion; stronghold; **b)** *(Kai)* quay
Bolschewik [bɔlʃe'vɪk] **der; ~en, ~i,** *(abwertend:)* **~en a)** *(hist.)* Bolshevik; **b)** *(abwertend: Kommunist)* Bolshevik; Commie *(sl.)*
bolschewisieren [bɔlʃevi'zi:rən] *tr. V.* Bolshevize
Bolschewismus [bɔlʃe'vɪsmʊs] **der; ~:** Bolshevism *no art.*
Bolschewist der; ~en, ~en Bolshevist
bolschewistisch 1. *Adj.* **a)** Bolshevik; Bolshevist; **b)** *(abwertend)* Bolshevik; bolshy *(sl).* **2.** *adv.* **a) ~ geführt** Bolshevik-led; led by the Bolsheviks; **b)** *(abwertend)* **~ unterwandert sein** be Bolshevik-infiltrated; be infiltrated by the Bolsheviks
bolzen ['bɔltsn̩] *(ugs.)* **1.** *itr. V. (Fußball spielen)* kick the ball about. **2.** *tr. V. (treten)* slam, *(coll.)* belt ‹*ball*›; kick ‹*stone*›
Bolzen der; ~s, ~ a) *(Stift)* pin; bolt; *(mit Gewinde)* bolt; **b)** *(Geschoß)* bolt
bolzen·gerade 1. *Adj.* perfectly *or* absolutely straight ‹*back*›. **2.** *adv.* ‹*sit, stand*› bolt upright
Bolzen·schneider der bolt-cutters *pl.*
Bolzerei die; ~, ~en *(ugs.)* [aimless] kick-about
Bolz·platz der [children's] football area; **hier war in meiner Jugend der ~:** this is where we used to have kick-abouts *(Brit.)* when I was young
bömakeln *s.* **böhmakeln**
Bombardement [bɔmbardə'mã:] **das; ~s, ~s a)** *(Milit. veralt.: Artilleriebeschuß)* bombardment; **b)** *(Milit.: Bombenabwurf)* bombing; **c)** *(ugs.: Überhäufung)* **ein ~ mit Briefen/von Fragen** a flood of letters/deluge of questions
bombardieren [bɔmbar'di:rən] *tr. V.* **a)** *(Milit. veralt.: beschießen)* bombard; **b)** *(Milit.: Bomben abwerfen auf)* bomb; **c)** *(ugs.: bewerfen, überhäufen)* bombard
Bombardierung die; ~, ~en a) *(Milit. veralt.: Beschuß)* bombardment; **b)** *(Milit.: Bombenabwurf)* bombing; **c)** *(ugs.: das Bewerfen)* bombardment; **d)** *(ugs.: Überhäufung)* **die ~ mit Fragen/Bitten** the rush of questions/requests
Bombast [bɔm'bast] **der; ~[e]s** *(abwertend)* bombast *no indef. art.*
bombastisch *(abwertend)* **1.** *Adj.* bombastic ‹*speech, language, style, etc.*›; ostentatious ‹*architecture, production*›. **2.** *adv.* ‹*speak, write*› bombastically; ostentatiously ‹*dressed*›
Bombe ['bɔmbə] **die; ~, ~n a)** *(Sprengkörper)* bomb; **die Nachricht schlug ein wie eine ~:** the news came as a bombshell; **die ~ ist geplatzt** *(fig. ugs.)* the balloon has gone up *(fig.)*; **b)** *o. Pl. (ugs.: Atom~)* **die ~:** the bomb *(coll.)*; **c)** *(Sportjargon: Schuß)* thunderbolt; tremendous shot *(coll.)*; **d)** *(Geol.)* bomb; **e)** *(ugs.: Hut)* bowler [hat]
bomben 1. *tr. V. (ugs.: bombardieren)* bomb. **2.** *itr. V. (Sportjargon: schießen)* slam; blast *(coll.)*
bomben-, Bomben-: **~angriff der** bomb attack; bombing raid; **einen ~angriff fliegen** fly a bombing raid; **~an·schlag der** bomb attack; **~attentat das** bomb attack; **~drohung die** bomb threat; **~erfolg der** *(ugs.)* smash hit *(sl.)*; **~fest** *Adj.* **a)** *(unzerstörbar)* bomb-proof; **b)** ['-'-] *(ugs.: unveränderbar)* dead certain; **~fest stehen** be dead certain; be a dead cert *(Brit. sl.)*; **mein Entschluß steht ~fest** my mind is completely made up; **~flug·zeug das** bomber; **~form die** *(ugs.)* top form; **~gehalt das** *(ugs.)* tremendous salary *(coll.)*; **er kriegt doch sicher ein ~gehalt** he must earn a fortune *or (sl.)* bomb; **~geschäft das** *(ugs.)* **ein ~geschäft machen** do a roaring trade; **ein/kein ~geschäft sein** be/not be a gold mine *(fig.)*; **~geschwader das** bomber wing; bomber group *(Amer.)*; **~krater der** bomb crater; **~nacht die** night of bombing; **~rolle die** *(ugs.)* tremendous *or* terrific part *(coll.)*; **~schaden der** bomb damage *no indef. art.*; **~schuß der** *(Sportjargon)* thunderbolt; tremendous shot *(coll.)*; **~sicher 1.** *Adj.* **a)** *(unzerstörbar)* bomb-proof; **b)** ['-'-] *(ugs.: gewiß)* dead certain; **das ist eine ~sichere Sache** that's dead certain; that's a dead cert *(Brit. sl.)* or a sure thing *(Amer.)*; **ein ~sicherer Tip** a dead cert [tip] *(Brit. sl.)*; a sure thing *(Amer.)*; **2.** *adv. (ugs.: gewiß)* as sure as eggs are eggs *(coll.)*; **~splitter der** bomb fragment *or* splinter; **~stimmung die** *(ugs.)* tremendous *or* fantastic atmosphere *(coll.)*; **~teppich der: das Gebiet wurde mit einem ~teppich belegt** the area was carpet-bombed; **~terror der** terrorist bombing; **~trichter der** bomb crater
Bomber der; ~s, ~ a) *(ugs.: Flugzeug)* bomber; **b)** *(Sportjargon)* **der ~ der Nation** the player with the fiercest shot in the country
Bomber·verband der bomber wing; bomber group *(Amer.)*
bombig *(ugs.)* **1.** *Adj.* super *(coll.)*; smashing *(coll.)*; terrific *(coll.)*; fantastic *(coll.)*. **2.** *adv.* **sich ~ schlagen** make a terrific *or* fantastic showing *(coll.)*
Bommel ['bɔml̩] **die; ~, ~n** *od.* **der; ~s, ~** *(bes. nordd.)* bobble; pompom
Bon [bɔŋ] **der; ~s, ~s a)** voucher; coupon; **b)** *(Kassenzettel)* receipt; sales slip
Bonbon [bɔŋ'bɔŋ] **der** *od. (österr. nur)* **das; ~s, ~s a)** sweet; candy *(Amer.)*; *(fig.)* treat; **b)** *(ugs. scherzh.; bes. ns.: Parteiabzeichen)* [party] badge
bonbon·farben, bonbon·farbig *Adj. (abwertend)* candy-coloured
Bonbonniere [bɔŋbɔ'ni̯e:rə] **die; ~, ~n a)** *(Behälter)* sweet-jar *(Brit.)*; candy jar *(Amer.)*; **b)** *(Schachtel)* box of chocolates
bonbon-, Bonbon-: **~papier das** sweet-wrapper; sweet-paper; **~rosa** *indekl. Adj.* candy pink; bright pink
bongen ['bɔŋən] *(ugs.)* **1.** *tr. V.* ring up; **gebongt sein** *(ugs.)* be fine; **ist gebongt!** *(ugs.)* fine! **2.** *itr. V.* **ich habe falsch gebongt** I've rung up the wrong amount
Bongo ['bɔŋgo] **das; ~[s], ~s** *od.* **die; ~, ~s** bongo [drum]
Bonhomie [bɔno'mi:] **die; ~, ~n** *(geh.)* bonhomie
Bonifatius [boni'fa:tsi̯ʊs], **Bonifaz** [boni'fa:ts] **(der)** Boniface
Bonität [boni'tɛ:t] **die; ~** *(Kaufmannsspr.)* creditworthiness; [good] credit rating *(Amer.)*
Bonmot [bõ'mo:] **das; ~s, ~s** bon mot
Bonn (das); ~s Bonn
Bonner 1. *indekl. Adj.; nicht präd.* Bonn; **die ~ Regierung** the FRG Government. **2. der; ~s, ~:** inhabitant of Bonn; *(von Geburt)* native of Bonn; **die ~** *(Politik ugs.)* the Government; *s. auch* **Kölner**
Bonsai der; ~s, ~s bonsai [tree]
Bonus ['bo:nʊs] **der; ~** *od.* **Bonusses, ~** *od.* **Bonusse,** *(auch:)* **Boni** ['bo:ni] **a)** *(Kaufmannsspr.) (Rabatt)* discount; *(Dividende)* extra dividend; *(Versicherungsw.)* bonus; **b)** *(Schadenfreiheitsrabatt)* [no-claims] bonus; **c)** *(Punktvorteil)* bonus points *pl.*
Bon·vivant [bõvi'vã:] **der; ~s, ~s** *(geh.)* bon vivant
Bonze ['bɔntsə] **der; ~n, ~n a)** *(abwertend: Funktionär)* bigwig *(coll.)*; big noise *(sl.)*; big wheel *(Amer. sl.)*; **b)** *(Mönch)* bonze
Boogie-Woogie ['bʊgi'vʊgi] **der; ~[s], ~s** boogie-woogie
Boom [bu:m] **der; ~s, ~s** boom
Boot [bo:t] **das; ~[e]s, ~e** boat; **wir sitzen alle in einem** *od.* **im selben ~** *(fig. ugs.)* we're all in the same boat

Boots-: ~bau der *o. Pl.* boat-building *no art.;* **~fahrt die** boat trip; **~haken der** boat-hook; **~haus das** boathouse; **~länge die** [boat's] length; **~mann der** *Pl.* **~leute a)** *(Handelsmarine)* ≈ boatswain, bosun; **b)** *(Bundesmarine)* ≈ petty officer; **~steg der** landing-stage; **~verleih der a)** *(das Verleihen)* boat-hire; hiring of boats; **b)** *(Unternehmen)* boat-hire [business]

Bor [bo:ɐ̯] **das; ~s** *(Chemie)* boron

Borax ['bo:raks] **der; ~[es]** *(Chemie)* borax

[1]**Bord** [bɔrt] **das; ~[e]s, ~e a)** *(Wandbrett)* shelf; **b)** *(veralt., noch schweiz.: Abhang)* bank

[2]**Bord der; ~[e]s, ~e** *(eines Schiffes)* side; **an ~:** on board; **an ~ eines Schiffes/der „Baltic"** on board *or* aboard a ship/the 'Baltic'; **alle Mann an ~!** all aboard!; **über ~:** overboard; **über ~ gehen** go overboard; **Mann über ~!** man overboard!; **etw. über ~ werfen** *(auch fig.)* throw sth. overboard; **von ~ gehen** leave the ship; ‹*passengers at destination*› disembark, leave the ship; *(aus dem Flugzeug)* leave the aircraft

Bord-: ~buch das log[-book]; **~case** [-keıs] **das** *od.* **der; ~, ~** *od.* **~s** flight case; **~computer der** on-board computer

bordeaux *indekl. Adj. s.* **bordeauxrot**

Bordeaux [bɔr'do:] **der; ~, ~** [bɔr'do:s] *s.* **Bordeauxwein**

bordeaux·rot *Adj.* bordeaux-red; claret

Bordeaux·wein der Bordeaux [wine]; **roter ~:** claret

bord·eigen *Adj.* ships/plane's [own] *attrib.*

Bordell [bɔr'dɛl] **das; ~s, ~e** brothel; **in ein ~ gehen** visit a brothel

Bordell-: ~besucher der patron of a/the brothel; **~gegend die** red-light district

Bord-: ~flugzeug das ship's aircraft; **~funk der** [ship's/aircraft] radio; **~funker der** radio operator; **~kamera die** on-board camera; **~personal das** *(Flugw.)* cabin crew; **~rechner der** *s.* **~computer; ~stein der** kerb; **~stein·kante die** [edge of the] kerb

Bordüre [bɔr'dy:rə] **die; ~, ~n** edging

Bord-: ~waffen *Pl.* armament *sing.;* **~wand die** [ship's] side/side [of the/an aircraft]

Boreas ['bo:reas] **der; ~:** north wind

Borg [bɔrk] *in* **auf ~** *(veralt.)* on credit; on tick *(Brit. coll.);* on the cuff *(Amer. coll.)*

borgen ['bɔrgn̩] *tr., itr. V.* **a)** *(geben)* lend; **jmdm. etw. ~:** lend sb. sth.; lend sth. to sb.; **b)** *(erhalten)* borrow; **[sich** *(Dat.)***] etw. von jmdm. ~:** borrow sth. from sb.

Borgis ['bɔrgıs] **die; ~** *(Druckw.)* 9-point type; bourgeois *(Hist.)*

Borke ['bɔrkə] **die; ~, ~n a)** *(Rinde)* bark; **b)** *(ugs.: auf Wunden)* scab

Borken-: ~flechte die *([Tier]med.)* ringworm; **~käfer der** bark beetle; **~krepp der** bark crêpe; crépon; **~schokolade die** *thin-sheet chocolate made into rough-surfaced rolls;* chocolate bark

borkig *Adj.* **a)** *(rissig)* cracked ‹*earth*›; chapped, cracked ‹*skin*›; **b)** *(ugs.)* ‹*knee, arm, etc.*› covered in scabs

Born [bɔrn] **der; ~[e]s, ~e** *(dichter.)* spring; fount *(poet./rhet.)*

borniert [bɔr'ni:ɐ̯t] *(abwertend)* **1.** *Adj.* narrow-minded; bigoted. **2.** *adv.* in a narrow-minded *or* bigoted way

Borniertheit die; ~, ~en a) *o. Pl. (Eigenschaft)* narrow-mindedness; bigotry; **b)** *(Äußerung, Handlung)* piece of narrow-mindedness *or* bigotry

Borretsch ['bɔrɛtʃ] **der; ~[e]s** borage

Bor-: ~salbe die boric acid ointment; **~säure die** *(Chemie)* boric acid *(Chem.);* boracic acid

Börse ['bœrzə] **die; ~, ~n a)** *(Aktien~)* stock market; **an der ~:** on the stock market; **b)** *(Gebäude)* stock exchange; **c)** *(geh. veralt.: Geld~)* purse; **d)** *(Boxen)* purse

Börsen-: ~beginn der opening of the [stock] market; **bei ~beginn** when the [stock] market opens/opened; **~bericht der** stock-market report; **~fähig, ~gängig** *Adj. (Wirtsch.)* ‹*commodity, security, etc.*› negotiable on the stock market; **~geschäft das** stock-market transaction; **~krach der** stock-market crash; collapse of the [stock] market; **~kurs der** [stock-]market price; **~makler der** stockbroker; **~notierung die** [stock-exchange] quotation; **~schluß der** close of the [stock] market; **bei ~schluß** when the [stock] market closes/closed; **~spekulation die** speculation on the stock market; **~sturz der** *s.* **~krach; ~tendenz die** [stock-]market trend; **~tip der** market tip

Börsianer der; ~s, ~ *(ugs.)* **a)** *(Makler)* stockbroker; **b)** *(Spekulant)* stock-market speculator

Borste ['bɔrstə] **die; ~, ~n a)** bristle; **b)** *Pl. (ugs.: beim Menschen)* hair *sing.;* **seine ~n aufstellen** *(fig.)* bristle

Borsten·vieh das *(ugs.) (Schwein)* pig; *(Schweine)* pigs *pl.*

borstig 1. *Adj.* **a)** *(struppig)* bristly; **b)** *(grob)* crusty ‹*person, manner, etc.*›. **2.** *adv. (grob)* crustily

Borte ['bɔrtə] **die; ~, ~n** braiding *no indef. art.;* trimming *no indef. art.;* edging *no indef. art.*

Bor·wasser das boric acid [eye-]lotion

bös [bø:s] *s.* **böse 1 c, d, 2**

bös·artig 1. *Adj.* **a)** *(heimtückisch)* malicious ‹*person, remark, etc.*›; vicious ‹*animal*›; **b)** *(Med.)* malignant; **2.** *adv. (heimtückisch)* maliciously

Bös·artigkeit die a) maliciousness; *(von Tieren)* viciousness; **b)** *(Med.)* malignancy

Böschung ['bœʃʊŋ] **die; ~, ~en** *(an der Straße)* bank; embankment; *(am Bahndamm)* embankment; *(am Fluß)* bank

Böschungs·winkel der gradient

böse ['bø:zə] **1.** *Adj.* **a)** *(verwerflich)* wicked; evil; **eine ~ Zunge haben** have a wicked *or* malicious tongue; **Schneewittchen hatte eine ~ Stiefmutter** Snow White had a wicked stepmother; **etw. aus ~r Absicht/~m Willen tun** do sth. with evil intent; **Böses mit Gutem vergelten** repay evil with good; **jmdm. Böses tun** *(geh.)* do sb. harm; **ich will dir doch nichts Böses** I don't mean you any harm; *(bei Rat, Bemerkung)* I don't mean it nastily; **b)** *nicht präd. (übel)* bad ‹*times, illness, dream, etc.*›; nasty ‹*experience, affair, situation, trick, surprise, etc.*›; **ein ~s Ende nehmen** end in disaster; **eine ~ Geschichte** a bad *or* nasty business; **nichts Böses ahnen** be unsuspecting; **nichts Böses ahnend** unsuspectingly; not suspecting anything is/was wrong; **den ~n Blick haben** have the evil eye; **die ~ Sieben** *(fig.)* the unlucky seven; **c)** *(ugs.) (wütend)* mad *(coll.); (verärgert)* cross *(coll.);* **~ mit jmdm.** *od.* **auf jmdn. werden** get mad at/cross with sb. *(coll.);* **~ auf jmdn.** *od.* **mit jmdm. sein** be mad at/cross with sb. *(coll.);* **~ über etw.** *(Akk.)* **sein** be mad at/cross about sth. *(coll.);* **im ~n auseinandergehen** part on bad terms; *s. auch* **Blut; d)** *(fam.: ungezogen)* naughty; **e)** *nicht präd. (ugs.: entzündet)* bad, sore ‹*knee, finger, etc.*›; **f)** *nicht präd. (ugs.: arg)* terrible *(coll.)* ‹*pain, fall, shock, disappointment, storm, etc.*›. **2.** *adv.* **a)** *(übel)* ‹*end*› badly; **mit ihm wird es noch ~ enden** he'll come to a bad end; **das wird ~ enden** it is bound to end in disaster; **es war doch nicht ~ gemeint** I didn't mean it nastily; **b)** *(ugs.) (wütend)* angrily; *(verärgert)* crossly *(coll.);* **c)** *(ugs.: arg)* terribly *(coll.);* ‹*hurt*› badly; **er hat sich ~ geirrt** he was badly wrong; **er ist ~ gefallen** he had a nasty fall *(coll.)*

[1]**Böse der/die;** *adj. Dekl.* evil *or* wicked person; **er spielt den ~n** he plays the villain *or* *(coll.)* baddy; **die ~n kommen in die Hölle** the wicked go to hell

[2]**Böse der;** *adj. Dekl., o. Pl. (veralt.: Teufel)* the Evil One; the Devil

Böse·wicht der *Pl.* **~wichter a)** *(ugs. scherzh.: Schlingel)* rascal; **b)** *(veralt., noch fig.: Schuft)* villain; **jedesmal bin ich der ~** *(fig.)* I'm always the villain of the piece

boshaft ['bo:shaft] **1.** *Adj.* malicious. **2.** *adv.* maliciously

Boshaftigkeit die; ~, ~en a) *o. Pl.* maliciousness; **b)** *(Bemerkung)* malicious remark; *(Handlung)* piece of maliciousness

Bosheit die; ~, ~en a) *o. Pl. (Art)* malice; **mit konstanter ~:** out of sheer spite; **b)** *(Bemerkung)* malicious remark; *(Handlung)* piece of maliciousness

Boskop ['bɔskɔp], **Boskoop** ['bɔsko:p] **der; ~s, ~:** russet

Bosporus ['bɔsporʊs] **der; ~:** Bosporus

Boß [bɔs] **der; Bosses, Bosse** *(ugs.)* boss *(coll.)*

Bossa Nova ['bɔsa'no:va] **der; ~~, ~~s** bossa nova

bosseln ['bɔsl̩n] *tr., itr. V. (ugs.)* **etw./an etw.** *(Dat.)* **~:** beaver away *(Brit.) or* slave away making sth.; **er braucht immer was zu ~:** he always needs to be working on *or* making something

bös-, Bös-: ~willig 1. *Adj.* malicious; wilful ‹*desertion*›; **2.** *adv.* maliciously; wilfully ‹*desert*›; **~willigkeit die; ~:** malice; maliciousness

bot [bo:t] *1. u. 3. Pers. Sg. Prät. v.* **bieten**

Botanik [bo'ta:nık] **die; ~ a)** botany *no art.;* **b)** *(ugs.: Natur)* nature

Botaniker der; ~s, ~, Botanikerin die; ~, ~nen botanist; *s. auch* **-in**

botanisch 1. *Adj.* botanical. **2.** *adv.* botanically

botanisieren *itr. V.* botanize

Botanisier·trommel die *(veralt.)* [botanist's] vasculum

Bötchen ['bø:tçən] **das; ~s, ~** little boat

Bote ['bo:tə] **der; ~n, ~n a)** *(Überbringer)* messenger; *(fig.)* herald; harbinger; **b)** *(Laufbursche)* errand-boy; messenger[-boy]

Boten-: ~dienst der job as a messenger/errand-boy; **sie verdient sich ein Taschengeld durch ~dienste** she earns pocket money as a messenger *or* by carrying messages/running errands; **~gang der** errand; **~gänge erledigen** run errands; **~lohn der** [messenger's/errand-boy's] payment *or* tip

Botin die; ~, ~nen *s.* **Bote a, b:** messenger; errand-girl

bot·mäßig *(geh. veralt.)* **1.** *Adj. (gehorsam)* obedient; *(untertänig)* submissive. **2.** *adv. (gehorsam)* obediently; *(untertänig)* submissively

Botmäßigkeit die; ~ *(geh. veralt.)* **a)** *(Herrschaft)* dominion; sway; **b)** *(Gehorsam)* obedience; *(Untertänigkeit)* submissiveness

Botschaft die; ~, ~en a) *(geh.: Nachricht)* message; **die freudige ~:** the good *or* happy news; **die Frohe ~** *(christl. Rel.)* the Gospel; **b)** *(Verlautbarung)* message; **c)** *(diplomatische Vertretung, auch Gebäude)* embassy

-botschaft die: Friedens-/Kriegs-/Sieges~: news of peace/war/victory

Botschafter der; ~s, ~, Botschafterin die; ~, ~nen ambassador

Botschafts-: ~rat der counsellor; **~sekretär der** [embassy] secretary

Böttcher ['bœtçɐ] **der; ~s, ~:** cooper

Böttcherei die; ~, ~en a) *o. Pl. (Handwerk)* cooper's trade; cooperage *no art.;* **b)** *(Werkstatt)* cooper's workshop; cooperage

Bottich ['bɔtıç] **der; ~s, ~e** tub

Bottnische Meer·busen ['bɔtnıʃə -] **der** Gulf of Bothnia

[1]**Bouclé** [bu'kle:] **das; ~s, ~s** bouclé [yarn]

[2]**Bouclé der; ~s, ~s a)** *(Stoff)* bouclé; **b)** *(Teppich)* bouclé carpet

Boudoir [bu'do̯a:ɐ̯] **das; ~s, ~s** *(veralt.)* boudoir

Bouillabaisse [buja'bɛ:s] **die; ~, ~s** [-'bɛ:s] *(Kochk.)* bouillabaisse

Bouillon [bul'jɔŋ] **die; ~, ~s a)** *(Brühe)* bouillon; consommé; **b)** *(Med.)* bouillon; broth

Bouillon·würfel der bouillon cube

Boule [bu:l] **das; ~[s], ~s** *od.* **die; ~, ~s** boule[s *pl.*]

Boulette *s.* **Bulette**

Boulevard [bulə'va:ɐ̯] **der; ~s, ~s** boulevard

Boulevard-: ~blatt das *s.* **~zeitung; ~presse die** *(abwertend)* popular press; **~stück das** *(Theater)* boulevard drama; **~theater das** light theatre; **~zeitung die** *(abwertend)* popular rag *(derog.)*; tabloid

Bouquet [bu'ke:] **das; ~s, ~s** *s.* **Bukett**

Bourbone [bʊr'bo:nə] **der; ~n, ~n** *(hist.)* Bourbon

bourgeois [bʊr'ʒo̯a] *Adj. (abwertend, auch Soziol.)* bourgeois

Bourgeois der; ~, ~ *(abwertend, auch Soziol.)* bourgeois

Bourgeoisie [bʊrʒo̯a'zi:] **die; ~, ~n** *(abwertend, auch Soziol.)* bourgeoisie

Boutique [bu'ti:k] **die; ~, ~s** *od.* **~n** boutique

Bovist *s.* **Bofist**

Bowden·zug ['baudn̩-] **der** *(Technik)* Bowden cable

Bowle ['bo:lə] **die; ~, ~n a)** punch *(made of wine, champagne, sugar, and fruit or spices)*; **b)** *(Gefäß)* punch-bowl

bowlen ['boʊlən] *itr. V. (Sport) (auf der Bahn)* bowl; *(auf dem Rasen)* play bowls

Bowlen·glas das; *Pl.* **~gläser** punch-glass

Bowler ['boʊlɐ] **der; ~s, ~:** bowler [hat]

Bowling ['boʊlɪŋ] **das; ~s, ~s** *(auf der Bahn)* [ten-pin] bowling; *(auf dem Rasen)* bowls; **~ spielen gehen** go [ten-pin] bowling/go to play bowls

Bowling·bahn die [ten-pin] bowling-alley

Box [bɔks] **die; ~, ~en a)** *(Lautsprecher)* speaker; **b)** *(Pferde-)* [loose] box; **c)** *(für Autos)* [partitioned off] [parking-]space; **d)** *(Kamera)* box camera; **e)** *(Behälter)* box; **f)** *(Montageplatz)* pit; **an den ~en** in the pits

Boxcalf *s.* **Boxkalf**

boxen 1. *itr. V.* box; **gegen jmdn. ~:** fight sb.; box [against] sb.; **um die Weltmeisterschaft** *usw.* **~:** fight for the world championship *etc.*; **jmdm. in den Magen ~:** punch sb. in the stomach. **2.** *tr. V.* **a)** *(schlagen)* punch; **b)** *(Sportjargon: kämpfen gegen)* fight. **3.** *refl. V.* **a)** *(ugs.: Weg bahnen)* fight one's way; **b)** *(ugs.: sich prügeln)* have a punch-up *(coll.) or* fight; **hört auf, euch zu ~:** stop fighting

Boxer der; ~s, ~ a) *(Sportler, Hund)* boxer; **b)** *(ugs.: Schlag)* punch

Boxer·aufstand der; *o. Pl. (hist.)* Boxer Rebellion

boxerisch *Adj.; nicht präd.* boxing ‹*skill, know-how, etc.*›

Boxer-: ~motor der *(Technik)* horizontally opposed engine; **~nase die** boxer's nose

Box·hand·schuh der boxing-glove

Box·kalf [-kalf] **das; ~s, ~s** boxcalf

Box-: ~kampf der a) *(Kampf)* boxing match; *(im Streit)* fist-fight; **er hat 200 ~kämpfe ausgetragen** he's had 200 fights *or* bouts; **b)** *o. Pl. (Disziplin)* boxing *no art.*; **~ring der** boxing ring; **~sport der;** *o. Pl.* boxing *no art.*; **~staffel die** boxing team

Boy [bɔy] **der; ~s, ~s a)** *(Diener)* servant; *(im Hotel)* page-boy; **b)** *(Jugendspr.) (junger Mann)* boy; *(Freund)* boy-friend

Boykott [bɔy'kɔt] **der; ~[e]s, ~s** boycott; **einem Land den ~ erklären** declare a boycott of a country

Boykott·hetze die *(DDR Amtspr., Rechtsw.)* anti-state agitation

boykottieren *tr. V.* boycott

Boykott·maßnahme die boycott [action]; **sich zu weiteren ~n gegen ein Land entschließen** decide to tighten the boycott of a country

Bozen ['bo:tsn̩] **(das); ~s** Bolzano

BR [be:|'ɛr] **der; ~** *Abk.:* **Bayrischer Rundfunk** Bavarian Radio

brabbeln ['brabl̩n] *tr., itr. V. (ugs.)* mutter; mumble; ‹*baby*› babble

Brabbel·wasser das *(ugs. scherzh.)* **a)** schnapps; **b) ~ getrunken haben** *(ugs. scherzh.)* have verbal diarrhoea *(sl.)*

[1]**brach** [bra:x] *1. u. 3. Pers. Sg. Prät. v.* **brechen**

[2]**brach** *Adj. (veralt.)* fallow; *(auf Dauer)* uncultivated; waste

Brache die; ~, ~n a) *(Feld)* [piece of] fallow land; *(auf Dauer)* [piece of] uncultivated *or* waste land; **b)** *(Zeit)* fallow period

brachial [bra'xi̯a:l] *Adj.* **a)** violent; **~e Gewalt** brute force; **b)** *(Med.)* brachial

Brachial·gewalt die; *o. Pl.* brute force

Brachiosaurus [braxi̯o'zaurʊs] **der; ~, Brachiosaurier** [...zauri̯ɐ] brachiosaurus

Brach·land das fallow [land]; *(auf Dauer)* uncultivated *or* waste land

brach|liegen *unr. itr. V. (auch fig.)* lie fallow; *(auf Dauer)* lie waste

brachte ['braxtə] *1. u. 3. Pers. Sg. Prät. v.* **bringen**

Brach·vogel der curlew

brackig *Adj. (niederd.)* brackish

Brack·wasser das brackish water

Brahmane [bra'ma:nə] **der; ~n, ~n, Brahmanin die; ~, ~en** Brahmin

brahmanisch *Adj.* Brahminical

Brainstorming ['breɪnstɔ:mɪŋ] **das; ~s** brainstorming; **ein ~:** a brainstorming session

bramarbasieren [bramarba'zi:rən] *itr. V. (geh. abwertend)* brag, boast **(von** about)

Bram·segel ['bra:m-] **das** topgallant sail

Branche ['brã:ʃə] **die; ~, ~n a)** [branch of] industry; **alle ~n der Bekleidungsindustrie** all branches of the clothing industry; **er kennt sich in der ~ am besten aus** he has the most knowledge of the industry; **b)** *(Fachgebiet)* field; **die ~ wechseln** move into a different field

branche[n]-, Branche[n]-: ~fremd *Adj.* new to the industry *postpos.*; ‹*person*› who knows nothing of the industry *postpos., not pred.*; **~kenntnisse** *Pl.* knowledge *sing.* of the industry; **~kundig** *Adj.* experienced in the industry *postpos.*; with knowledge of the industry *postpos., not pred.*; **~üblich** *Adj.* usual in the industry *postpos.*; **im Baugewerbe ~üblich** usual in the building industry

Branchen·verzeichnis das classified directory; *(Telefonbuch)* yellow pages *pl.*

Brand [brant] **der; ~[e]s, Brände** ['brɛndə] **a)** fire; **b)** *(Brennen)* **beim ~ der Scheune** when the barn caught fire; **in ~ geraten** catch fire; **etw. in ~ setzen** *od.* **stecken** set fire to sth.; set sth. on fire; **c)** *(ugs.: Durst)* raging thirst; **einen fürchterlichen ~ haben** have a terrible thirst; **d)** *o. Pl. (Med.)* **[trockener/feuchter] ~:** [dry/moist] gangrene; **e)** *o. Pl. (Bot.)* blight

brand-, Brand-: ~aktuell *Adj.* very latest ‹*news*›; up-to-the-minute ‹*report*›; red-hot ‹*news item, issue*›; highly topical ‹*book*›; **~an·schlag der** arson attack **(auf + Akk.** on); **~bekämpfung die** fire-fighting *no art.*; **~binde die** dressing [for burns]; **~blase die** [burn] blister; **~bombe die** fire-bomb; incendiary bomb; **~direktor der** chief fire officer; fire chief *(Amer.)*; **~eilig** *Adj. (ugs.)* extremely urgent

branden *itr. V. (geh.)* break; **~der Beifall** *(fig.)* thunderous applause

Branden·burg (das); ~s Brandenburg

Brandenburger *indekl. Adj.; nicht präd.* **das ~ Tor** the Brandenburg Gate

brand-, Brand-: ~fackel die firebrand; flaming torch; **~fleck der** burn mark; **~gefahr die** danger of fire; **bei ~gefahr** when there is danger of fire; **~gefährlich** *Adj.* perilous; highly dangerous; **~geruch der** smell of burning; **~herd der** source of the fire

brandig *Adj.* **a)** ‹*smell*› of burning; burnt ‹*taste*›; **es riecht ~:** there is a smell of burning; **b)** *(Med.)* gangrenous; **c)** *(Bot.)* suffering from blight *postpos.*

brand-, Brand-: ~kasse die fire insurance company; **katastrophe die** disastrous fire; **~leger** [~le:gɐ] **der; ~s, ~** *(österr.) s.* **~stifter; ~legung die; ~, ~en** *(österr.) s.* **~stiftung; ~mal das** *(geh.)* burn mark; *(fig.: Stigma)* stigma; **~marken** *tr. V.* brand ‹*person*›; denounce ‹*thing*›; **jmdn. [als Verräter] ~marken** brand sb. [as a traitor]; **~mauer die** fire wall; **~meister der** chief fire officer; fire chief *(Amer.)*; **~neu** *Adj. (ugs.)* brand-new; **~opfer das a)** *(Rel.)* burnt offering; **b)** *(Opfer eines Brandes)* fire victim; victim of the/a fire; **~rede die** fiery tirade; **~salbe die** ointment for burns; **~satz der** incendiary mixture; **~schaden der** fire damage *no pl., no indef. art.*; **die ~schäden in den Wäldern** the damage to forests caused by fire; **~schatzen** *tr. V. (hist.)* pillage and threaten to burn; **~schatzung die; ~, ~en** *(hist.)* pillaging and threat of burning; **~schutz der;** *o. Pl.* fire safety *no art.*; **~sohle die** insole; **~stelle die a)** scene of the fire; **b)** *(verbrannte Stelle)* burn; *(größer)* burnt patch; **~stifter der** arsonist; **~stiftung die** arson; **eine ~stiftung** a case of arson; **~teig der** *(Kochk.)* choux pastry

Brandung die; ~, ~en surf; breakers *pl.*; **die ~ donnerte gegen die Felsen** the breakers crashed against the rocks; **bei starker ~:** when the surf is high

Brandungs-: ~boot das surf-boat; **~welle die** breaker

Brand-: ~versicherung die fire insurance; *(Gesellschaft)* fire-insurance company; **~wache die a)** fire-watcher; *(Mannschaft)* fire-watchers *pl.*; **b)** *(Dienst)* fire-watch; **~wunde die** burn; *(Verbrühung)* scald; **~zeichen das** brand

brannte ['brantə] *1. u. 3. Pers. Sg. Prät. v.* **brennen**

Brannt·wein der spirits *pl.*; **Wodka ist ein ~:** vodka is a type of spirit

Branntwein-: ~brenner der distiller; **~monopol das** monopoly of spirits; liquor monopoly *(Amer.)*; **~steuer die** tax on spirits; liquor tax *(Amer.)*

[1]**Brasil** [bra'zi:l] **der; ~s, ~e** *od.* **~s** Brazil[ian] tobacco

[2]**Brasil die; ~, ~[s]** Brazil cigar

Brasil·holz das Brazil-wood

Brasilianer [brazi'li̯a:nɐ] **der; ~s, ~, Brasilianerin die; ~, ~nen** Brazilian; *s. auch* **-in**

brasilianisch *Adj.* Brazilian

Brasilien [bra'zi:li̯ən] **(das); ~s** Brazil

Brasil-: ~tabak der Brazil[ian] tobacco; **~zigarre die** Brazil cigar

Brasse ['brasə] **die; ~, ~n** *(Seemannsspr.)* brace

brät [brɛ:t] *3. Pers. Sg. Präsens v.* **braten**

Brät das; ~s *lean minced pork used esp. as filling for sausages*

Brat·apfel der baked apple

braten ['bra:tn̩] **1.** *unr. tr. V. (auf dem Herd)* fry; *(im Backofen) (mit Fett, im eigenen Saft)* roast; *(ohne Fett)* bake; **etw. braun ~:** fry sth. until it is brown; **etw. am Spieß ~:** roast sth. on a spit. **2.** *unr. itr. V. (auf dem Herd)* fry; *(im Backofen) (mit Fett, im eigenen Saft)* roast; *(ohne Fett)* bake; **in der Sonne ~** *(fig.)* roast in the sun

Braten der; ~s, ~ joint; *(gebratene Portion)* roast [meat] *no indef. art.*; **sonntags gab es bei uns immer ~:** we always had a roast *or* a joint on Sundays; **kalter ~:** cold meat; **den fetten ~ konnte er sich nicht entgehen lassen** *(fig. ugs.)* he couldn't miss the chance of making such a big killing *(coll.)*; **den ~ riechen** *(fig. ugs.)* smell a rat

Braten-: ~fett das [meat] fat; [meat] juices *pl.*; **~rock der** *(veralt. scherzh.)* frock-coat; **~saft der** meat juice[s *pl.*]; **~soße die** gravy; **~wender der** slice; turner

Brat-: ~fett das [cooking] fat; **~fisch der** fried fish; **~hähnchen das,** *(südd., österr.)* **~hendl das a)** roast chicken; *(gegrillt)* broiled chicken; **b)** *(Hähnchen zum Braten)* roasting chicken; *(zum Grillen)* broiling chicken; **~hering der** fried herring; **~huhn das, ~hühnchen das** *s.* **~hähnchen; ~kartoffeln** *Pl.* fried potatoes; home fries *(Amer.)*; *s. auch* **daher b; ~kartoffel·verhältnis das** *(ugs. veralt.)* **er hat ein ~kartoffelverhältnis mit ihr** he treats her as his meal-ticket; **~ofen der** oven; **~pfanne die** frying-pan; **~röhre die** *s.* **~ofen; ~rost der** grill

Bratsche ['bra:tʃə] **die; ~, ~n** *(Musik)* viola

Bratschen·schlüssel der *(Musik) s.* **Altschlüssel**

Bratschist der; ~en, ~en, Bratschistin die; ~, ~nen violist; viola-player

Brat-: ~spieß der a) spit; **b)** *(Gericht)* kebab; **~wurst die a)** [fried/grilled] sausage; **b)** *(Wurst zum Braten)* sausage [for frying/grilling]

Brauch [braux] **der; ~[e]s, Bräuche** ['brɔyçə] custom; **so ist es ~, so will es der ~:** that's the custom; **das ist bei ihnen so ~:** that's their custom; **nach altem ~:** in accordance with an old custom

brauchbar 1. *Adj.* useful; *(benutzbar)* usable; wearable ‹*clothes*›; *(ordentlich)* decent ‹*worker, pupil*›; **er ist ganz ~:** he is a decent worker/pupil *etc.* **2.** *adv.* **er schreibt/arbeitet ganz ~:** he's a useful writer/he does useful work

Brauchbarkeit die; ~ usefulness; *(Benutzbarkeit)* usability

brauchen 1. *tr. V.* **a)** *(benötigen)* need; **alles, was man zum Leben braucht** everything one needs in order to live reasonably; **ich kann dich jetzt nicht ~** *(fam.)* I don't want you around just now; **deine guten Ratschläge kann ich nicht ~:** I can well do without your advice; **b)** *(aufwenden müssen)* **mit dem Fahrrad/Auto braucht er nur zehn Minuten** it only takes him ten minutes on his bicycle/by car; **er hat für die Arbeit Jahre gebraucht** the work took him years; **wie lange brauchst du dafür?** how long will it take you?; *(im allgemeinen)* how long does it take you?; **c)** *(benutzen, verwenden, verbrauchen)* use; **ich könnte es gut ~:** I could do with it. **2.** *itr. V. (geh. veralt.: bedürfen)* **es braucht keines weiteren Beweises** no further proof is needed *or* necessary. **3.** *mit Inf. mit „zu", verneintes od. eingeschränktes Modalverb* need; **du brauchst nicht zu helfen** there is no need [for you] to help; you don't need to help; **du brauchst doch nicht gleich zu weinen** there's no need to start crying; **das hättest du nicht zu tun ~:** there was no need to do it; you needn't have done that; **das hätte nicht zu sein ~:** that needn't have happened; **es braucht nicht sofort zu sein** it doesn't need *or* have to be done immediately; **du brauchst es [mir] nur zu sagen** you only have to tell me; **du brauchst es nur zu sagen** you only have to say so

Brauchtum das; ~s, Brauchtümer [-ty:mɐ] custom; **zum ~ dieser Region gehört ...:** one of the customs in this area is ...

Braue ['brauə] **die; ~, ~n** [eye]brow

brauen 1. *tr. V.* **a)** brew; **b)** *(ugs.: aufbrühen, zubereiten)* brew [up] ‹*tea, coffee*›; concoct ‹*potion etc.*›; mix ‹*cocktail*›. **2.** *itr. V.* **a)** *(Bier ~)* brew [beer]; **b)** *(dichter.: wallen)* ‹*mist, fog*› gather

Brauer der; ~s, ~: brewer

Brauerei die; ~, ~en a) *o. Pl.* brewing; **b)** *(Betrieb)* brewery

Brau-: ~haus das brewery; **~meister der** master brewer

braun [braun] *Adj.* **a)** brown; **~werden** *(sonnengebräunt)* get brown; get a tan; **sich von der Sonne ~ brennen lassen** sit/lie in the sun and get a tan; **b)** *(abwertend: nationalsozialistisch)* Nazi; **er war ~:** he was a Nazi

Braun das; ~s, ~, *(ugs.)* **~s** brown

braun·äugig *Adj.* brown-eyed; **~ sein** have brown eyes

Braun·bär der brown bear

Braune der; *adj. Dekl.* **a)** bay [horse]; **b)** *(österr.: Kaffee)* [cup of] white coffee *(Brit.)*; [cup of] coffee with milk/cream

Bräune ['brɔynə] **die; ~:** [sun-]tan

bräunen 1. *tr. V.* **a)** tan; **die Sonne hat sein Gesicht stark gebräunt** the sun has tanned his face a deep brown; **b)** *(Kochk.)* brown. **2.** *itr. V.* **a) die südliche Sonne bräunt stark** the Southern sun gives you a good tan; **b)** *(Kochk.)* ‹*meat*› brown; ‹*cake*› go golden brown; ‹*butter*› go brown

braun-, Braun-: ~gebrannt *Adj.* [sun-]tanned; **~hemd das** *(ns.)* **a)** brown shirt; **b)** *(Träger des ~hemds)* Brown-shirt; **~kohl der** *s.* **Grünkohl; ~kohle die** brown coal; lignite

bräunlich *Adj.* brownish

Braunschweig ['braunʃvaik] **(das); -s** Braunschweig; Brunswick *(Hist.)*

braunschweigisch *Adj.* Braunschweig *attrib.*; *s. auch* **hannoversch**

Bräunung die; ~, ~en browning; *(durch die Sonne)* [sun-]tan

Bräunungs·studio das solarium

Braus [braus] *s.* **Saus**

Brause ['brauzə] **die; ~, ~n a)** fizzy drink; *(~pulver)* sherbet; **b)** *(veralt.: Dusche)* shower; **sich unter die ~ stellen** take *or* have a shower; **c)** *(Sprühteil) (einer Gießkanne)* rose; *(einer Dusche)* shower head

Brause-: ~bad das *(veralt.)* **a)** shower[-bath]; **b)** *(Duschbad)* shower; **ein ~bad nehmen** take *or* have a shower; **~kopf der** *(veralt.)* hothead; **~limonade die** fizzy lemonade

brausen 1. *itr. V.* **a)** ‹*wind, water, etc.*› roar; *(fig.)* ‹*organ, applause, etc.*› thunder; **hier braust der Verkehr bei Tag und Nacht** there is a constant roar of traffic here day and night; **b)** *(duschen)* [take *or* have a] shower; **c)** *(sich schnell bewegen)* race. **2.** *tr. V.* put ‹*children etc.*› under the shower. **3.** *refl. V.* [take *or* have a] shower

Brausen das; ~s roar; **das ~ in meinen Ohren** the ringing *or* buzzing in my ears

Brause-: ~pulver das sherbet; **~tablette die** effervescent tablet

Braut [braut] **die; ~, Bräute** ['brɔytə] **a)** bride; **b)** *(Verlobte)* fiancée; bride-to-be; **c)** *(ugs.: Freundin)* girl[-friend]

-braut die *(ugs.)* **Fußball~:** football player's/fan's girl-friend/wife; **Rocker~:** rocker's girl; *(Mitglied der Bande)* girl rocker

Braut-: ~bett das *(hist.)* bridal bed; **~eltern** *Pl.* bride's parents

Bräutigam ['brɔytɪgam] **der; ~s, ~e a)** [bride]groom; **b)** *(veralt.: Verlobter)* fiancé; husband-to-be

Braut-: ~jungfer die bridesmaid; **~kleid das** wedding dress; **~kranz der** bridal wreath; **~leute** *Pl.*: *s.* **~paar; ~mutter die** bride's mother; **~nacht die** wedding night; **~paar das** bridal couple; bride and groom; **~schau die;** *o. Pl.* **in auf ~schau gehen, ~schau halten** *(ugs. scherzh.)* go *or* be looking for a wife; **~schleier der** bridal veil; **~vater der** bride's father

brav [bra:f] **1.** *Adj.* **a)** *(artig)* good; **sei [schön] ~:** be good; **sei ein ~es Kind** be a good boy/girl; **b)** *(redlich)* honest; upright; **er soll ein ~es Mädchen heiraten** he should marry a good honest girl; **c)** *(hausbacken)* plain and conservative ‹*clothes*›; **d)** *(veralt.: tapfer)* brave. **2.** *adv.* **a) nun iß schön ~ deine Suppe** be a good boy/girl and eat up your soup; eat up your soup like a good boy/girl; **die Kinder spielten ~ in ihrem Zimmer** the children were being good and playing quietly in their room; **b)** *(redlich)* honestly; **c)** *(bieder)* **[recht] ~ spielen/schreiben** play/write quite nicely; **d)** *(veralt.: tapfer)* bravely

bravo ['bra:vo] *Interj.* bravo

Bravo das; ~s, ~s cheer; **das laute ~ der Zuschauer** the loud cheers *or* cheering of the audience; **ein ~ für ...:** three cheers for ...

Bravo·ruf der cheer

Bravour [bra'vu:ɐ̯] **die; ~ a)** stylishness; **mit ~:** with style and élan; **b)** *(Tapferkeit)* daring and bravery

Bravour·leistung die brilliant performance

bravourös [bravu'rø:s] **1.** *Adj.* **a)** *(rasant)* **mit ~em Tempo** at magnificent speed; **b)** *(meisterhaft)* brilliant. **2.** *adv.* **a)** *(rasant)* with great dash; **b)** *(meisterhaft)* brilliantly

Bravour·stück das piece of bravura; brilliant performance

BRD [be:|ɛr'de:] **die; ~** *(nicht amtlich) Abk.* **Bundesrepublik Deutschland** FRG

Break [breɪk] **das; ~s, ~s** *(Sport, Musik)* break

Breakdance [breɪkdæns] **der; ~[s]** breakdancing

brechbar *Adj.* **a)** breakable; **nicht ~:** unbreakable; **b)** *(ablenkbar)* refrangible

Brech-: ~bohne die French bean *(Brit.)*; green bean; **~durch·fall der** diarrhoea and vomiting *no indef. art.*; **~eisen das** *s.* **~stange**

brechen ['brɛçn] **1.** *unr. tr. V.* **a)** break; cut ‹*marble, slate, etc.*›; **Blumen ~** *(dichter.)* pluck flowers; **sich** *(Dat.)* **den Arm/das Genick ~:** break one's arm/neck; **nichts zu ~ und zu beißen haben** *(geh.)* not have anything at all to eat; **b)** *(ablenken)* break ‹*water etc.*›; refract ‹*light*›; **c)** *(bezwingen)* overcome ‹*resistance*›; break ‹*will, silence, record, blockade, etc.*›; **d)** *(nicht einhalten)* break ‹*agreement, contract, promise, the law, etc.*›; **e)** *(ugs.: erbrechen)* bring up. **2.** *unr. itr. V.* **a)** *mit sein* break; ‹*leather*› crack; **mir bricht das Herz** *(fig.)* it breaks my heart; **brechend voll sein** be full to bursting; **b)** *(Beziehungen aufgeben)* break; **er brach mit der Familientradition** he broke [away from] the family tradition; **mit einer Gewohnheit ~:** break a habit; **c)** *mit sein (hervorkommen)* break **(durch** through); **d)** *(ugs.: sich erbrechen)* throw up. **3.** *unr. refl. V.* ‹*waves etc.*› break **(an** + *Dat.* on); ‹*rays etc.*› be refracted

Brecher der; ~s, ~ a) *(Welle)* breaker; **b)** *(Maschine)* crusher

Brech-: ~mittel das emetic; **der Mann ist ein echtes ~mittel** *(fig. ugs. abwertend)* that man makes me sick *(coll.) or (coarse)* want to puke; **~reiz der** nausea; **~stange die** crowbar; **mit der ~stange vorgehen** *(fig.)* go about it with a sledgehammer; **ein Sieg mit der ~stange** *(Sport)* a victory by sheer force

brecht[i]sch ['brɛçt(ɪ)ʃ] *Adj.* Brechtian

Brechung die; ~, ~en a) *(Physik)* refraction; **b)** *(Sprachw.)* breaking

Brechungs·winkel der *(Physik)* angle of refraction

Bredouille [bre'dʊljə] **die; ~, ~n** *(ugs.)* **in der ~ sein** *od.* **sitzen** be in real trouble; **in die ~ kommen** get into real trouble

Bregen ['bre:gn̩] **der; ~s, ~** *(nordd.)* brains *pl.*

Brei [brai] **der; ~[e]s, ~e** *(Hafer~)* porridge *(Brit.)*, oatmeal *(Amer.) no indef. art.*; *(Reis~)* rice pudding; *(Grieß~)* semolina *no indef. art.*; **etw. zu einem ~ verrühren**

make sth. into a mash *or* purée; **um den [heißen] ~ herumreden** *(ugs.)* beat about the bush
breiig *Adj.* mushy; **eine ~e Masse** a thick paste
breit [brait] **1.** *Adj.* **a)** wide ⟨*street, river, bridge, window, margin, etc.*⟩; broad, wide ⟨*hips, face, shoulders, forehead, etc.*⟩; **etw. ~er machen** widen sth.; **einen ~en Buckel** *od.* **Rücken haben** *(fig. ugs.)* have broad shoulders *(fig.)*; **die Beine ~ machen** *(auch fig.)* open one's legs; **die Schuhe ~ treten** stretch one's shoes out of shape; **ein ~es Lachen** a guffaw; **eine ~e Aussprache** a broad accent; **b)** *(bei Maßangaben)* wide; **ein 5 cm ~er Saum** a hem 5 cm wide; **einen Finger ~ sein** be the width of a finger *or* a finger's breadth; **c)** *(groß)* **die ~e Masse** the general public; most people *pl.*; **die ~e Öffentlichkeit** the general public; **~e Bevölkerungsschichten** large sections of the population; **ein ~es Interesse finden** arouse a great deal of interest; **d)** *(ugs.: im Rausch)* high *(coll.)*; stoned *(sl.)*. **2.** *adv.* **a) ~ gebaut** sturdily *or* well built; **~ lachen** guffaw; **etw. ~ darstellen** *(fig.)* describe sth. in great detail; **b) der Stoff liegt doppelt ~**: the material is double width
breit·beinig 1. *Adj.*; *nicht präd.* rolling ⟨*gait*⟩. **2.** *adv.* with one's legs apart; **er stand ~ vor uns** he stood squarely in front of us
Breite die; ~, ~n a) width; breadth; *(bei Maßangaben)* width; **etw. der ~ nach durchsägen** saw through sth. widthways *or* widthwise; **etw. in epischer ~ schildern** *(fig.)* describe sth. in great detail *or* down to the last detail; **in die ~ gehen** *(ugs.)* put on weight; **b)** *(Geogr.)* latitude; **auf/unter 50° nördlicher ~**: at/below latitude 50° north; **c)** *Pl.* *(Gebiet)* **in diesen ~n** in these latitudes
breiten *(geh.)* *tr.*, *refl. V.* spread
Breiten-: ~grad der degree of latitude; **New York und Mailand liegen auf demselben ~**: New York and Milan have the same latitude; **der 30. ~grad** the 30th parallel; **~kreis der** [line of] latitude; parallel; **~sport der** popular sport; **~wirkung die** widespread effect
breit-, Breit-: ~flächig *Adj.* wide; **~flächig gebaut** built over a wide area *postpos.*; **~gefächert** *Adj.*; *nicht präd.* wide ⟨*range, choice*⟩; **~krempig** *Adj.* broad-brimmed; **~|machen** *refl. V.* *(ugs.)* **a)** take up room; **mach dich nicht so ~**: don't take up so much room; **b)** *(sich ausbreiten)* be spreading; **c)** *(sich niederlassen)* make oneself at home; **~randig** *Adj.* broad-brimmed; **~|schlagen** *unr. tr. V.* *(ugs.)* **sich zu etw. ~schlagen lassen** let oneself be talked into sth.; **er ließ sich ~schlagen** he let himself be persuaded; **~schult[e]rig** *Adj.* broad-shouldered; **~schwanz der** caracul; broadtail; **~seite die a)** *(eines Tisches, Gebäudes, Zimmers usw.)* long side; *(eines Schiffes)* side; **b)** *([Abfeuern der] Geschütze)* broadside; **~spur die** *(Eisenb.)* broad gauge; **~spurig** *Adj.* broad-gauge ⟨*railway etc.*⟩; ⟨*car etc.*⟩ with a wide track; **~|treten** *unr. tr. V.* *(ugs. abwertend)* go on about; **das Thema ist breitgetreten** this subject has been flogged to death; **~wand die** *(Kino)* wide *or* big screen; **~wand·film der** wide-screen *or* big-screen film
Bremer 1. *indekl. Adj.*; *nicht präd.* Bremen; **der ~ Hafen** the Port of Bremen. **2. der; ~s, ~**: native/inhabitant of Bremen; *s. auch* **Kölner**
bremisch *Adj.* Bremen *attrib.*
Brems-: ~backe die *(Kfz-W.)* brake-shoe; **~belag der** *(Kfz-W.)* brake lining
[1]**Bremse** ['brɛmzə] **die; ~, ~n** brake; **auf die ~ treten** put on the brakes
[2]**Bremse die; ~, ~n** *(Insekt)* horse-fly
bremsen 1. *itr. V.* brake; **der Dynamo bremst ganz erheblich** the dynamo has quite a considerable braking effect. **2.** *tr. V.* **a)** brake; *(um zu halten)* stop; **b)** *(fig.)* slow down ⟨*rate, development, production, etc.*⟩; restrict ⟨*imports etc.*⟩; **jmdn. ~** *(ugs.)* stop sb.; **er ist nicht [mehr] zu ~** *(ugs.)* there's no stopping him. **3.** *refl. V.* *(ugs.)* stop oneself; hold oneself back
Bremser der; ~s, ~ *(Eisenb., Bobsport)* brakeman
Brems-: ~flüssigkeit die *(Kfz-W.)* brake fluid; **~hebel der** brake arm; **~klotz der a)** *(am Fahrrad)* brake-block; *(am Wagen)* brake-pad; **b)** *(Klotz, der vor das Rad geschoben wird)* [wheel] chock; **c)** *(fig.)* obstacle to progress; **~kraft·verstärker der** *(Kfz-W.)* brake servo; **~leitung die** *(Kfz-W.)* brake-pipe; **~leuchte die, ~licht das**; *Pl.* **~lichter** brake-light; **~pedal das** brake-pedal; **~probe die** brake test; **~scheibe die** *(Kfz-W.)* brake-disc; **~spur die** skid-mark; **~trommel die** *(Kfz-W.)* brake-drum
Bremsung die; ~, ~en braking
Brems-: ~weg der braking distance; **~zylinder der** *(Kfz-W.)* brake-cylinder
brenn-, Brenn-: ~bar *Adj.* [in]flammable; combustible; **leicht ~bar** highly [in]flammable *or* combustible; **~dauer die**; *o. Pl.* **a)** *(einer Glühlampe)* life; **b)** *(im Brennofen)* firing time; **~eisen das a)** *s.* **~schere**; **b)** *(für Brandzeichen)* branding-iron
brennen ['brɛnən] **1.** *unr. itr. V.* **a)** ⟨*wood etc.*⟩ burn; ⟨*house etc.*⟩ burn, be on fire; **schnell/leicht ~**: catch fire quickly/easily; **es brennt!** fire!; **in der Hotelbar hat es gebrannt** there was a fire in the hotel bar; **wo brennt's denn?** *(fig. ugs.)* what's the panic?; **b)** *(glühen)* be alight; **c)** *(leuchten)* be on; **in ihrem Zimmer brennt Licht** there is a light on in her room; **das Licht ~ lassen** leave the light on; **die Birne/Kerze brennt ganz schwach** the bulb is glowing very dimly/the candle is burning very low; **d)** *(scheinen)* **die Sonne brannte so stark** the sun was so strong; **die Sonne brannte** the sun was burning down; **e)** *(schmerzen)* ⟨*wound etc.*⟩ burn, sting; ⟨*feet etc.*⟩ hurt, be sore; **mir ~ die Augen** my eyes are stinging *or* smarting; **Pfeffer brennt auf der Zunge** pepper burns the tongue; **f)** *(trachten)* **darauf ~, etw. zu tun** be dying *or* longing to do sth.; **auf Rache ~**: be bent on *or* dying for revenge; **g)** *(ungeduldig sein)* **vor Neugier ~**: be dying to know; **er brannte vor Ehrgeiz** he was burning with ambition. **2.** *unr. tr. V.* **a)** burn ⟨*hole, pattern, etc.*⟩; **einem Tier ein Zeichen ins Fell ~**: brand an animal; **gebranntes Kind scheut das Feuer** *(Spr.)* once bitten, twice shy *(prov.)*; **b)** *(mit Hitze behandeln)* fire ⟨*porcelain etc.*⟩; distil ⟨*spirits*⟩; **gebrannter Kalk** quicklime; **c)** *(rösten)* roast ⟨*coffee-beans, almonds, etc.*⟩; brown ⟨*flour, sugar, etc.*⟩
brennend 1. *Adj.* *(auch fig.)* burning; urgent ⟨*topic, subject*⟩; lighted ⟨*cigarette*⟩; raging ⟨*thirst*⟩; violent ⟨*homesickness*⟩. **2.** *adv.* **ich würde ~ gern mal ein Wochenende dort verbringen** I should absolutely love to spend a weekend there; **ich wüßte ~ gern, ob ...**: I'm dying to know whether ...; **es scheint dich ja ~ zu interessieren, was besprochen wurde** you seem to be dying to know what was discussed
Brenner der; ~s, ~: burner
Brennerei die; ~, ~en a) *o. Pl.* distilling; **b)** *(Betrieb)* distillery
Brennessel ['brɛnnɛsl] **die; ~, ~n** stinging nettle
Brenn-: ~glas das burning-glass; **~holz das**; *o. Pl.* firewood; **~material das** fuel; **wir benutzen alte Zeitungen als ~material** we use old newspapers to burn on the fire; **~nessel die** *s.* **Brennessel**; **~ofen der** kiln; **~punkt der** *(auch Mathematik, Optik)* focus; **im ~punkt des Interesses stehen** be the focus of attention *or* interest; **in den ~punkt der Diskussion rücken** become the focal point of discussion; **~schere die** curling-tongs *pl.* *(Brit.)*; curling iron *(Amer.)*; **~spiegel der** *(Optik)* burning-mirror; **~spiritus der** methylated spirits; **~stab der** *(Kerntechnik)* fuel rod; **~stoff der** fuel; **~weite die** *(Optik)* focal length
brenzlig ['brɛntslɪç] *Adj.* **a)** ⟨*smell, taste, etc.*⟩ of burning *not pred.*; **~ riechen/schmecken** smell of burning/taste burnt; **b)** *(ugs.: bedenklich)* dicey *(sl.)*; **mir wird die Sache zu ~**: things are getting too hot for me
Bresche ['brɛʃə] **die; ~, ~n** gap; breach; **[für jmdn.] in die ~ springen** stand in [for sb.]; **für jmdn./etw. eine ~ schlagen** give one's backing to sb./sth.
Bretagne [bre'tanjə] **die; ~**: Brittany
Bretone [bre'to:nə] **der; ~n, ~n, Bretonin die; ~, ~nen** Breton
Brett [brɛt] **das; ~[e]s, ~er a)** board; *(lang und dick)* plank; *(Diele)* floorboard; **hier ist die Welt [wie] mit ~ern vernagelt** *(ugs.)* this place is like the end of the earth; **das Schwarze ~**: the notice-board; **ein ~ vor dem Kopf haben** *(fig. ugs.)* be thick; **ich habe heute einfach ein ~ vor dem Kopf** *(fig. ugs.)* I just can't think straight today; **das ~ bohren, wo es am dünnsten ist** *(fig. ugs.)* take the easy way out; **b)** *(für Spiele)* board; **c)** *Pl.* *(Skisport)* skis; **d)** *Pl.* *(Bühne)* stage *sing.*; boards; **auf den ~ern stehen** be on [the] stage *or* on the boards; **die ~er, die die Welt bedeuten** *(geh.)* the stage *sing.*; the boards; **e)** *Pl.* *(Boxen)* floor *sing.*; canvas *sing.*; **er schickte seinen Gegner auf die ~er** he put his opponent on the canvas; he floored his opponent
Brettchen das; ~s, ~ a) *wooden board used for breakfast*; **b)** *(zum Schneiden)* board
Brettel ['brɛtl] **das; ~s, ~[n]** *(südd., österr.)* **a)** board; **b)** *Pl.* *(Skisport)* skis
Bretter-: ~boden der wooden floor; **~bude die** [wooden] hut, shack; **~verschlag der** [wooden] shed; **~wand die** wooden wall *or* partition; **~zaun der** wooden fence
Brett·spiel das board game
Brevier [bre'vi:ɐ̯] **das; ~s, ~e a)** *(kath. Rel.)* breviary; **b)** *(Leitfaden)* guide **(für** to)
Brezel ['bre:tsl̩] **die; ~, ~n, Brezen** ['bre:tsn̩] **der; ~s, ~** *od.* **die; ~, ~** *(österr.)* pretzel
Bridge [brɪtʃ] **das; ~**: bridge
Brief [bri:f] **der; ~[e]s, ~e a)** letter; **blauer ~** *(ugs.)* warning letter; **offener ~** *(fig.)* open letter; **jmdm. ~ und Siegel [auf etw. (Akk.)] geben** *(fig.)* promise sb. faithfully *or* give sb. one's word [on sth.]; **b)** *(Rauschgiftpäckchen)* deck
Brief-: ~beschwerer der; ~s, ~: paper-weight; **~block der**; *Pl.* **~blocks** writing-pad; letter-pad; **~bogen der** sheet of writing-paper *or* notepaper; **~bögen mit Kopf** letter-headed writing-paper *sing.* *or* notepaper *sing.*; **~bombe die** letter-bomb
Briefchen das; ~s, ~ a) ein ~ Nähnadeln/Streichhölzer a packet of needles/book of matches; **b)** *(kurzer Brief)* note
Brief-: ~druck·sache die *(Postw.)* printed paper *(sent as a letter)*; **eine ~drucksache** a piece of printed matter; **die Gebühren für ~drucksachen** the rates for printed matter *sing.*; **~freund der, ~freundin die** pen-friend; pen-pal *(coll.)*; **~geheimnis das** privacy of the post; secrecy of correspondence; **~karte die** correspondence card; **~kasten der a)** post-box; pillar-box *(Brit.)*; **b)** *(privat)* letter-box; **lebender/toter ~kasten** *(Geheimdienstjargon)* [live] letter-box/letter-box; **c)** *(in der Zeitung)* agony column *(coll.)*
Briefkasten-: ~firma die accommodation address; **~tante die** *(ugs. scherzh.)* agony aunt *(coll.)*

Brief-: ~kopf der a) letter-heading; **b)** *(aufgedruckt)* letter-head; **~kuvert das** *(veralt.)* *s.* **~umschlag**
brieflich 1. *Adj.; nicht präd.* written. **2.** *adv.* by letter
Brief·marke die [postage] stamp
Briefmarken-: ~album das stamp-album; **~sammler der** stamp-collector; philatelist; **~sammlung die** stamp-collection; **wollen Sie sich meine ~sammlung ansehen?** *(fig. verhüll.)* come up and see my etchings *(joc.)*
Brief-: ~öffner der letter-opener; **~papier das** writing-paper; notepaper; **~partner der, ~partnerin die** pen-friend; **~porto das** [letter] rate; **~post die** letter post; **~roman der** epistolary novel; **~schreiber der** [letter-]writer; **~sendung die** item sent by letter post; **~tasche die** wallet; **~taube die** carrier pigeon; **~träger der** postman; letter-carrier *(Amer.)*; **~trägerin die** postwoman; female letter-carrier *(Amer.)*; **~um·schlag der** envelope; **~waage die** letter-scales *pl.*; **~wahl die** postal vote; **~wechsel der a)** correspondence; **einen ~wechsel führen** have a *or* be in correspondence; **mit jmdm. in ~wechsel stehen** be in correspondence *or* correspond with sb.; **b)** *(gesammelte Briefe)* correspondence
Brie·käse ['bri:-] **der** Brie
Bries [bri:s] **das; ~es, ~e** thymus [gland] *(esp. of calf)*; *(Kochk.)* sweetbreads *pl.*
briet [bri:t] *1. u. 3. Pers. Sg. Prät. v.* **braten**
Brigade [bri'ga:də] **die; ~, ~n a)** *(Milit.)* brigade; **b)** *(DDR)* work team; [work] brigade
Brigade-: ~führer der *s.* **Brigadier; ~general der** *(Milit.)* brigadier
Brigadier a) [briga'die:] **der; ~s, ~s** *(Milit.)* brigadier; **b)** [briga'die: *od.* briga'di:ɐ] **der; ~s, ~s** *od.* **~e** *(DDR)* [work] team leader; brigade leader
Brigadierin die; ~, ~nen *(DDR)* [work] team leader; brigade leader; *s. auch* **-in**
Brigg [brɪk] **die; ~, ~s** *(Seew.)* brig
Brikett [bri'kɛt] **das; ~s, ~s** briquette
brillant [brɪl'jant] **1.** *Adj.* brilliant. **2.** *adv.* brilliantly
[1]**Brillant** [brɪl'jant] **der; ~en, ~en** brilliant
[2]**Brillant die; ~** *(Druckw.)* 3-point type
Brillantine [brɪljan'ti:nə] **die; ~, ~n** *(veralt.)* brilliantine
Brillant-: ~kollier das *(brilliant-cut)* diamond necklace; **~ring der** *(brilliant-cut)* diamond ring; **~schliff der** brilliant cut; **~schmuck der;** *o. Pl. (brilliant-cut)* diamond jewellery
Brillanz [brɪl'jants] **die; ~ a)** brilliance; **b)** *(Akustik)* clarity; sound quality
Brille ['brɪlə] **die; ~, ~n a)** glasses *pl.*; spectacles *pl.*; specs *(coll.) pl.*; **eine ~:** a pair of glasses *or* spectacles; **eine ~ tragen** wear glasses *or* spectacles; **etw. durch eine gefärbte ~ sehen** *(fig.)* look at sth. subjectively *or* from one's own point of view; **etw. durch eine rosa[rote] ~ sehen** *od.* **betrachten** *(fig.)* see sth. through rose-coloured *or* rose-tinted spectacles; **b)** *(ugs.: Klosett~)* [lavatory *or* toilet] seat
Brillen-: ~etui das, ~futteral das glasses-case; spectacle-case; **~gestell das** spectacle-frame; [glasses-]frame; **~glas das** [spectacle-]lens; **~schlange die a)** *(Zool.)* spectacled cobra; **b)** *(ugs. scherzh.)* **in der Schule wurde ich oft ~schlange genannt** I was often called 'four-eyes' at school; **~träger der** person who wears glasses; person with glasses
brillieren [brɪl'ji:rən] *itr. V. (geh.)* be brilliant
Brimborium [brɪm'bo:riʊm] **das; ~s** *(ugs. abwertend)* hoo-ha *(coll.)*
bringen ['brɪŋən] *unr. tr. V.* **a)** *(her~)* bring; *(hin~)* take; **sie brachte mir/ich brachte ihr ein Geschenk** she brought me/I took her a present; **Unglück/Unheil [über jmdn.] ~:** bring misfortune/disaster [upon sb.]; **jmdm. Glück/Unglück ~:** bring sb. [good] luck/bad luck; **jmdm. eine Nachricht ~:** bring sb. news; **der letzte Winter brachte uns viel Schnee** *(fig.)* we had a lot of snow last winter; **b)** *(begleiten)* take; **jmdn. nach Hause/zum Bahnhof ~:** take sb. home/to the station; **das Auto in die Garage ~:** put the car in the garage; **die Kinder ins Bett** *od.* **zu Bett ~:** put the children to bed; **c) es zu etwas/nichts ~:** get somewhere/get nowhere *or* not get anywhere; **er hat es zu nichts weiter gebracht als zum Redaktionsassistenten** he didn't get further than assistant editor; **es bis zum Direktor ~:** make it to director; **es zu hohem Ansehen ~:** acquire standing *or* a high reputation; **es weit ~:** get on *or* do very well; **es im Leben weit ~:** go far in life; **d) jmdn. ins Gefängnis ~** ⟨*crime, misdeed*⟩ land sb. in prison *or* gaol; **eine Sache vor Gericht ~:** take a matter to court; **das Gespräch auf etw./ein anderes Thema ~:** bring the conversation round to sth./change the topic of conversation; **jmdn. wieder auf den rechten Weg ~** *(fig.)* get sb. back on the straight and narrow; **jmdn. zum Lachen/zur Verzweiflung ~:** make sb. laugh/drive sb. to despair; **jmdn. dazu ~, etw. zu tun** get sb. to do sth.; **du hast mich auf eine gute Idee gebracht** you have given me a good idea; **etw. hinter sich ~** *(ugs.)* get sth. over and done with; **es nicht über sich** *(Akk.)* **~ [können], etw. zu tun** not be able to bring oneself to do sth.; **etw. an sich** *(Akk.)* **~** *(ugs.)* collar sth. *(sl.)*; **e)** *(mit Präp.* **um)** **jmdn. um seinen Besitz ~:** do sb. out of his property; **jmdn. um den Schlaf/Verstand ~:** rob sb. of his/her sleep/drive sb. mad; **f)** *(veröffentlichen)* publish; **die Zeitschrift bringt jetzt eine Artikelserie über ...:** the magazine is running a series of articles about ...; **was bringt denn die Zeitung heute darüber?** what does it say about it in today's paper?; **alle Zeitungen brachten Berichte über das Massaker** all the papers carried reports of the massacre; **g)** *(senden)* broadcast; **um 23.00 Uhr ~ wir die letzten Nachrichten** the late-night news will be at 11 o'clock; **das Fernsehen bringt eine Sondersendung** there is a special programme on television; **einen Film im Fernsehen ~:** show a film on television; **das Fernsehen hat nichts darüber gebracht** there was nothing about it on television; **h)** *(darbringen)* **das/ein Opfer ~:** make the/a sacrifice; **eine Nummer/ein Ständchen ~:** perform a number/a serenade; **i)** *(erbringen)* **einen großen Gewinn/hohe Zinsen ~:** make a large profit/earn high interest; **das Gemälde brachte 50 000 DM** the painting fetched 50,000 marks; **das bringt nichts** *(ugs.)* it's pointless; **j) das bringt es mit sich, daß ...:** that means that ...; **seine Krankheit bringt es mit sich, daß ...:** it's because of *or* to do with his illness that ...; **k)** *(verursachen)* cause ⟨*trouble, confusion*⟩; **es kann dir doch nur Vorteile ~:** it can only be to your advantage; **l)** *(salopp: schaffen, erreichen)* **das bringst du doch nicht** you'll never do it; **der Wagen/diese Kneipe bringt's doch nicht** the car/this pub is no good; **der Wagen bringt 210 km/h** the car can *or* will do 210 km/h; **m)** *(hinein~, heraus~, bewegen)* get **(in** + *Akk.* into, **aus** out of); **der Schrank ist viel zu groß, als daß ich ihn allein von der Stelle ~ könnte** the cupboard is far too big for me to shift on my own; **den Wagen zum Laufen ~:** get the car to go; **ich bringe den Schlüssel nicht ins Schloß** *(bes. südd.)* I can't get the key into the lock
Bring·schuld die *(Rechtsw.) debt to be paid at the creditor's domicile*
brisant [bri'zant] *Adj.* explosive; **ein recht ~es Unternehmen** a highly risky undertaking; **~e Sprengstoffe** highly explosive materials
Brisanz [bri'zants] **die; ~, ~en a)** *o. Pl.* explosiveness; explosive nature; **ein Thema von hoher politischer ~:** a highly explosive political subject; **b)** *(Waffenkunde)* explosive force
Brise ['bri:zə] **die; ~, ~n** breeze
Britannien [bri'taniən] **(das); ~s** Britain; *(hist.)* Britannia
Brite ['brɪtə] **der; ~n, ~n** Briton; **die ~n** the British; **er ist [kein] ~:** he is [not] British; **der ~ gewann eine Medaille** the British athlete/scholar *etc.* won a medal
Britin die; ~, ~nen Briton; British girl/woman; **die ~nen** the British [girls/women]; **sie ist [keine] ~:** she is [not] British; *s. auch* **-in**
britisch *Adj.* British; **die Britischen Inseln** the British Isles
Bröckchen ['brœkçən] **das; ~s, ~:** bit; small piece
bröckchen·weise *Adv. s.* **brockenweise**
bröckelig *Adj.* crumbly
bröckeln ['brœkl̩n] *tr., itr. V.* **a)** crumble; **b)** *mit sein* **von der Decke/Wand ~:** crumble away from the ceiling/wall
Brocken ['brɔkn̩] **der; ~s, ~ a)** *(von Brot)* hunk, chunk; *(von Fleisch)* chunk; *(von Lehm, Kohle, Erde)* lump; **b)** *(fig.)* **ein paar ~ Englisch** a smattering of English; **ein paar ~ eines Gesprächs auffangen** catch a few snatches of a conversation; **jmdm. einen fetten ~ wegschnappen** *(ugs.)* snap up a real opportunity from under sb.'s nose; **das war ein harter ~** *(ugs.)* that was a tough *or* a hard nut to crack; **c)** *(ugs.: dicke Person)* lump; **ist das ein ~!** what a big fat lump he/she is!
brocken·weise *Adv. (auch fig.)* bit by bit
bröcklig *s.* **bröckelig**
brodeln ['bro:dl̩n] *itr. V.* bubble; **es brodelt in der Masse/Bevölkerung** *(fig.)* there is seething unrest among the masses/in the population
Brodem ['bro:dəm] *(geh.)* vapour *(literary)*
Broiler ['brɔylɐ] **der; ~s, ~** *(DDR) s.* **Brathähnchen**
Brokat [bro'ka:t] **der; ~[e]s, ~e** brocade
Brokat·kleid das brocade dress
Brokkoli ['brɔkoli] *Pl.* broccoli *sing.*
Brom [bro:m] **das; ~s** *(Chemie)* bromine
Brom·beere ['brɔm-] **die a)** bramble; blackberry-bush; **b)** *(Frucht)* blackberry; **~n pflücken gehen** go blackberrying
Brombeer-: ~konfitüre die, ~marmelade die blackberry jam; **~strauch der** bramble; blackberry-bush
Bronchial-: ~asthma das *(Med.)* bronchial asthma; **~katarrh der** *(Med.) s.* **Bronchitis; ~tee der** bronchial tea
Bronchie ['brɔnçiə] **die; ~, ~n** *(Med.)* bronchial tube; bronchus
Bronchitis ['brɔnçi:tɪs] **die; ~, Bronchitiden** *(Med.)* bronchitis
Bronze ['brõ:sə] **die; ~:** bronze; **diese Leistung reichte gerade noch für ~** *(Sportjargon)* this performance was just enough to get a bronze; *s. auch* **Gold**
Bronze·medaille die bronze medal
bronzen ['brõ:sn̩] *Adj.* bronze ⟨*object*⟩; bronzed ⟨*skin*⟩; **~ schimmern** glint like bronze
Bronze·zeit die Bronze Age
Brosame ['bro:za:mə] **die; ~, ~n** *(geh. veralt., auch fig.)* crumb
Brosche ['brɔʃə] **die; ~, ~n** brooch
broschiert [brɔ'ʃi:rt] *Adj.* paperback; **eine ~e Ausgabe** a paperback *or* soft-cover edition; **~e Heftchen** booklets
Broschüre [brɔ'ʃy:rə] **die; ~, ~n** booklet; pamphlet; *(Reiseprospekt)* brochure
Brösel ['brø:zl] **der; ~s, ~,** *(österr.)* **das; ~s, ~:** breadcrumb
bröselig *Adj.* crumbly

bröseln 1. *itr. V.* crumble. 2. *tr. V.* crumble

Brot [bro:t] **das; ~[e]s, ~e a)** bread *no pl., no indef. art.; (Laib ~)* loaf [of bread]; **wes ~ ich ess', des Lied ich sing'** *(Spr.)* he/she is not going to bite the hand that feeds him/her; **Bier ist flüssiges ~** *(scherzh.)* beer is full of nourishment; **der Mensch lebt nicht vom ~ allein** *(Spr.)* man shall not live by bread alone *(bibl.)*; **~ und Arbeit finden** find a paid job; **b)** *(Scheibe Brot)* slice [of bread]; **c)** *s.* **Butterbrot; d)** *(Lebensunterhalt)* daily bread *(fig.)*; **das ist ein hartes ~:** it's a hard way to earn a *or* your living

Brot-: ~aufstrich der spread; **~belag der** topping; *(im zusammengeklappten Brot)* filling; **~beruf der** occupation that enables one to make a living; **~beutel der** satchel

Brötchen ['brø:tçən] **das; ~s, ~:** roll; **kleinere ~ backen [müssen]** *(fig. ugs.)* [have to] lower one's sights; **seine/die ~ verdienen** *(ugs.)* earn one's/the daily bread

Brötchen·geber der; ~s, ~ *(scherzh.)* employer

brot-, Brot-: ~einheit die carbohydrate unit; **~erwerb der** way to earn a living; **~fabrik die** bakery *(producing bread on a large scale)*; **~frucht·baum der** breadfruit tree; **~kanten der** [bread] crust; **~kasten der** bread-bin; **~korb der** bread-basket; **jmdm. den ~korb höher hängen** *(ugs.)* put sb. on short rations; *(fig.)* put the squeeze on sb. *(sl.)*; **~krume die, ~krümel der** breadcrumb; **~kruste die** [bread] crust; **~laib der** loaf [of bread]; **~los** *Adj.* unemployed; **jmdn. ~los machen** put sb. out of work; **das ist eine ~lose Kunst** there's no money in that; **~maschine die** bread-slicer; **~messer das** bread-knife; **~neid der** jealousy of sb.'s position/salary; **~rinde die** [bread] crust; **~scheibe die** slice of bread; **~schneide·maschine die** *s.* **~maschine; ~studium das;** *o. Pl.* **für einen großen Teil der Studenten heute ist die Medizin ein reines ~studium** a lot of today's students choose medicine because it will get them a well-paid job; **~teig der** bread dough; **~zeit die** *(südd.)* **a)** *(Pause)* [tea-/coffee-/lunch-]break; **b)** *o. Pl. (Vesper)* snack; *(Vesperbrot)* sandwiches *pl.*

brr [br̩] *Interj.* **a)** *(bei Kälte)* brr; *(vor Ekel)* ugh; **b)** *(Zuruf an Zugtier)* whoa

BRT *Abk.* **Bruttoregistertonne** grt

¹Bruch [brʊx] **der; ~[e]s, Brüche** ['brʏçə] **a)** *(das Brechen)* break; **der ~ des Deiches/Dammes** the breaching *(Brit.) or (Amer.)* breaking of the dike/dam; **das hätte ~ geben können** *(ugs.)* there could have been a crash; **~ machen** *(ugs.)* break things; *(Fliegerspr.)* crash; **in die Brüche gehen** *(zerbrechen)* break; get broken; *(enden)* break up; **zu ~ gehen** break; get broken; **etw. zu ~ fahren** smash sth. up; **b)** *(~stelle)* break; **die Brüche im Deich** the breaches *(Brit.) or (Amer.)* breaks in the dike; **c)** *(Med.: Knochen~)* fracture; break; **d)** *(Med.: Eingeweide~)* hernia; rupture; **sich** *(Dat.)* **einen ~ heben** rupture oneself *or* give oneself a hernia [by lifting sth.]; **e)** *(fig.) (eines Versprechens)* breaking; *(eines Abkommens, Gesetzes, einer Verfassung)* break; violation; *(mit der Vergangenheit, Tradition, Partei)* break **(mit** with); *(einer Freundschaft)* break; *(einer Ehe)* break-up; **ein ~ des Waffenstillstandes** a violation of the cease-fire; **der ~ mit dem Elternhaus** the break with home; **es kam zum ~ zwischen ihnen** they broke up; **f)** *(Math.)* fraction; **g)** *(Kaufmannsspr.: beschädigte Ware)* **diese Schokolade ist ~:** this chocolate is broken; **h)** *(Falte)* crease; **nach dem ~ falten** fold along the crease/creases; **i)** *(salopp: Einbruch)* break-in; **einen ~ machen** do a break-in

²Bruch der *od.* **das; ~[e]s, Brüche** *(Sumpfland)* marsh

bruch-, Bruch-: ~band das; *Pl.* **~bänder** *(Med.)* truss; **~bude die** *(ugs. abwertend)* hovel; dump *(coll.)*; **~fest** *Adj.* unbreakable

brüchig ['brʏçɪç] *Adj.* **a)** brittle, crumbly ⟨*rock, brickwork*⟩; **das Leder mit Creme einreiben, damit es nicht ~ wird** rub cream into the leather to keep it from cracking; **der Stoff ist ziemlich ~:** the material is splitting quite a bit; **b)** *(fig.)* crumbling ⟨*relationship, marriage, etc.*⟩; **c)** *(rauh)* rough; cracked

Brüchigkeit die; ~ a) brittleness; crumbliness; **b) die ~ ihrer Beziehung/Ehe ist für alle offenbar** it is obvious to everyone that their relationship/marriage is breaking up; **c)** *(Rauheit)* roughness

bruch-, Bruch-: ~|landen *itr. V.; mit sein; nur im Inf. u. 2. Part.* crash-land; make a crash-landing; **~landung die** crash-landing; **~los** *Adj.* without a break *postpos.*; **~operation die** hernia operation; **~pilot der** *(ugs.)* crash-happy pilot; **~rechnen** *itr. V.; nur im Inf.* do fractions; **~rechnen das** fractions *pl.*; **jmdm. [das] ~rechnen beibringen** teach sb. how to do fractions; **beim ~rechnen ...:** when doing fractions ...; **~rechnung die** fractions *pl.*; **~schaden der** breakage; **~schokolade die** broken chocolate; **~sicher** *Adj.* unbreakable; **~stein der** undressed stone; **~stelle die** break; *(von Knochen auch)* fracture; **die ~stelle mit Klebstoff bestreichen** apply adhesive to the broken area; **~strich der** fraction line; **~stück das** fragment; *(großes Stück)* piece; *(fig.)* snatch; **~stückhaft 1.** *Adj.* fragmentary; **2.** *adv.* in a fragmentary way; **~teil der** fraction; **im ~teil einer Sekunde** in a fraction of a second; in a split second; **er kam um den ~teil einer Sekunde zu spät** he came a split second too late; **~zahl die** fraction

Brücke ['brʏkə] **die; ~, ~n a)** *(auch: Schiffs~, Zahnmed., Bodenturnen, Ringen)* bridge; **die** *od.* **alle ~n hinter sich** *(Dat.)* **abbrechen** *(fig.)*; burn one's bridges *(fig.)*; **jmdm. eine [goldene] ~** *od.* **[goldene] ~n bauen** *(fig.)* make things easier for sb.; **b)** *(Landungs~)* gangway; gangplank; **c)** *(Teppich)* rug; **d)** *(Anat.)* pons [Varolii]

Brücken-: ~bau der; *Pl.* **~bauten a)** *o. Pl.* building *or* construction of a/the bridge; *(allgemein)* bridge-building; bridge construction; **b)** *(Brücke)* bridge [structure]; **~bogen der** arch [of a/the bridge]; **~geländer das** parapet; railing; **~heilige der/die** sculptured saint [on a/the bridge]; **~kopf der** *(Milit., auch fig.)* bridgehead; **~pfeiler der** pier [of a/the bridge]; **~waage die** weighbridge; **~zoll der** [bridge] toll; **~zoll bezahlen** pay a [bridge] toll

Bruder ['bru:dɐ] **der; ~s, Brüder** ['bry:dɐ] **a)** *(auch: Mitmensch, Mönch)* brother; **die Brüder Müller** the Müller brothers; the brothers Müller; **~ Peter** Brother Peter; **und willst du nicht mein ~ sein, so schlag' ich dir den Schädel ein** if you're not my friend, then I'll treat you as an enemy; **der große ~** *(fig.)* Big Brother; **der große/kleine ~** *(fig. scherzh.)* the larger/smaller edition; **unter Brüdern** *(fig. ugs. scherzh.)* between *or* amongst friends; **b)** *(ugs. abwertend: Mann)* guy *(sl.)*; **ein ziemlich windiger ~:** a bit of a dodgy *(Brit.) or* shady character *(coll.)*; **~ Lustig** *od.* **Leichtfuß** *(veralt. scherzh.)* light-hearted fellow; *s. auch* **warm 1c**

Bruder·bund der *(geh., bes. DDR)* comradeship; fraternal links *pl.*

Brüderchen ['bry:dɐçən] **das; ~s, ~:** little brother; **ein kleines ~:** a little brother

Bruder-: ~herz das; *o. Pl. (veralt., noch scherzh.)* dear brother; **hör mal, ~herz** listen, brother dear; **~krieg der** fratricidal war; **~kuß der** brotherly kiss; **~land das** *(geh., bes. DDR)* fraternal country

brüderlich 1. *Adj.* brotherly; *(im politischen Bereich)* fraternal. **2.** *adv.* in a brotherly way; *(im politischen Bereich)* fraternally; **etw. ~ [mit jmdm.] teilen** share sth. [with sb.] in a fair and generous way

Brüderlichkeit die; ~: brotherliness; *(im politischen Bereich)* fraternity

Bruder-: ~liebe die brotherly love; **~mord der** fratricide; **~mörder der, ~mörderin die** fratricide

Bruder·partei die *(bes. DDR)* fraternal party

Bruderschaft die; ~, Brüderschaft die; ~, ~en a) *o. Pl.* **[mit jmdm.] ~ trinken** drink to close friendship [with sb.] *(agreeing to use the familiar 'du' form)*; **b)** *(Rel.)* brotherhood

Bruder-: ~volk das a) *(bes. DDR)* sister people; **b)** *(veralt. geh.)* kindred people; **~zwist der** feud between brothers; *(im politischen Bereich)* fraternal feud

Brühe ['bry:ə] **die; ~, ~n a)** stock; *(als Suppe)* clear soup; broth; **b)** *(ugs. abwertend: Getränk)* muck; **eine abscheuliche ~** *(fig.)* a revolting concoction; **c)** *(abwertend: verschmutztes Wasser)* dirty *or* filthy water; **d)** *(Kochk.: Kochwasser)* water; **e)** *(ugs.: Schweiß)* sweat

brühen *tr. V.* **a)** blanch; **b)** *(auf~)* brew, make ⟨*tea*⟩; make ⟨*coffee, soup*⟩

brüh-, Brüh-: ~warm *(ugs.)* **1.** *Adj.* hot ⟨*news*⟩; very latest ⟨*gossip etc.*⟩; **2.** *adv.* **etw. ~warm weitererzählen** pass sth. on *or* spread sth. around straight away; **~würfel der** stock cube; **~wurst die** sausage *(which is heated in boiling water)*

Brüll·affe der *(Zool.)* howler [monkey]; howling monkey

brüllen ['brʏlən] **1.** *itr. V.* **a)** ⟨*bull, cow, etc.*⟩ bellow; ⟨*lion, tiger, etc.*⟩ roar; ⟨*elephant*⟩ trumpet; **b)** *(ugs.: schreien)* roar; shout; **vor Schmerzen/Lachen ~:** roar with pain/laughter; **brüll nicht so!** there's no need to shout like that; **nach jmdm. ~:** shout to *or* for sb.; **~des Gelächter** roars *pl.* of laughter; **das ist [ja] zum Brüllen** *(ugs.)* it's a [real] scream; what a scream; **c)** *(ugs.: weinen)* howl; bawl; **er brüllte wie am Spieß** he bawled his head off. **2.** *tr. V.* yell; shout

Brumm-: ~bär der *(ugs.)* grouch *(coll.)*; **~baß der a)** *(ugs.)* deep *or* bass voice; **b)** *s.* **Kontrabaß**

brummeln ['brʊml̩n] *tr., itr. V. (ugs.)* mumble; mutter

brummen ['brʊmən] *tr., itr. V.* **a)** ⟨*insect*⟩ buzz; ⟨*bear*⟩ growl; ⟨*engine etc.*⟩ drone; **mir brummt der Schädel** *od.* **Kopf** *(ugs.)* my head is buzzing; **b)** *(sich ~d bewegen)* ⟨*fly etc.*⟩ buzz; ⟨*lorry etc.*⟩ thunder; ⟨*moped*⟩ buzz; **c)** *(unmelodisch singen)* drone; **d)** *(mürrisch sprechen)* mumble; mutter; **e)** *(ugs. veralt.: in Haft sein)* do time; **zwei Jahre ~:** do two years; **f)** *(ugs.: nachsitzen)* stay behind

Brummer der; ~s, ~ *(ugs.)* **a)** *(Fliege)* bluebottle; **b)** *(Lkw)* heavy lorry *(Brit.) or* truck

Brummi der; ~s, ~s *(ugs.)* lorry *(Brit.)*; truck

brummig *(ugs.)* **1.** *Adj.* grumpy. **2.** *adv.* grumpily

Brumm-: ~kreisel der humming top; **~schädel der** *(ugs.)* thick head; **~ton der** humming noise

brünett [bry'nɛt] *Adj.* dark-haired ⟨*person*⟩; dark ⟨*hair*⟩; **sie ist ~:** she's [a] brunette

Brünette die; ~, ~n brunette

Brunft [brʊnft] **die; ~, Brünfte** ['brʏnftə] *(Jägerspr.) s.* **Brunst**

brunften *itr. V. (Jägerspr.) s.* **brunsten**

Brunft·hirsch der *(Jägerspr.)* rutting stag

brunftig *Adj. (Jägerspr.)* rutting ⟨*male animal*⟩; ⟨*female animal*⟩ in *or* on heat

Brunft-: ~schrei der *(Jägerspr.)* bell; **~zeit** *(Jägerspr.) s.* **Brunstzeit**

Brunnen ['brʊnən] **der; ~s, ~ a)** well; *(fig. geh.)* fountain *(literary)*; **den ~ [erst] zu-**

decken, wenn das Kind hineingefallen ist lock the stable door after the horse has bolted *(fig.)*; **b)** *(Spring~)* fountain; **c)** *(Wasser einer Heilquelle)* spring water; ~ **trinken** take the waters *pl.*

Brunnen-: **~becken das** basin [of a/the fountain]; **~figur die** figure on a/the fountain; **~haus das** pump-room; **~kresse die** watercress; **~kur die** [spa] cure; **eine ~kur machen** take a cure/a course of treatment at a spa; **~putzer der** *in* **schaffen wie ein ~putzer** *(ugs., bes. südwestd.)* slave away; work like a horse; **~vergifter der; ~s, ~:** water-poisoner; *(fig. abwertend)* trouble-maker; **~vergiftung die** water-poisoning; *(fig. abwertend)* trouble-making

Brünnlein ['brʏnlain] **das; ~s, ~ a)** [little] well; **b)** *(Springbrunnen)* [little] fountain

Brunst [brʊnst] **die; ~, Brünste** ['brʏnstə] *(von männlichen Tieren)* rut; *(von weiblichen Tieren)* heat; **Männchen/Weibchen in der ~:** rutting males/females in *or* on heat

brunsten *itr. V.* ⟨*male animal*⟩ rut; ⟨*female animal*⟩ be in *or* on heat

brünstig ['brʏnstɪç] **1.** *Adj.* rutting ⟨*male animal*⟩; ⟨*female animal*⟩ in *or* on heat. **2.** *adv.* ~ **röhren** bell

Brunst-: **~schrei der** bell; **~zeit die** *(bei männlichen Tieren)* rut; rutting season; *(bei weiblichen Tieren)* [season of] heat

brunzen ['brʊntsn̩] *itr. V. (landsch. derb)* [have a] piss *(coarse)*; take a leak *(sl.)*

brüsk [brʏsk] **1.** *Adj.* brusque; abrupt. **2.** *adv.* brusquely; abruptly

brüskieren *tr. V.* offend; *(stärker)* insult; *(schneiden)* snub

Brüskierung die; ~, ~en *s.* **brüskieren:** piece of offensive behaviour; insult; snub

Brüssel ['brʏsl̩] **(das); ~s** Brussels

Brüsseler 1. *indekl. Adj.; nicht präd.* Brussels; ~ **Spitzen** Brussels lace *sing.* **2. der; ~s, ~:** inhabitant of Brussels; *(von Geburt)* native of Brussels; *s. auch* **Kölner**

Brust [brʊst] **die; ~, Brüste** ['brʏstə] **a)** *o. Pl.* chest; *(fig. geh.)* breast; heart; ~ **an ~:** face to face; **sich in die ~ werfen** puff oneself up; **mit geschwellter ~:** proudly; as proud as a peacock; **er sang aus voller ~:** he sang lustily; **einen zur ~ nehmen** *(ugs.)* have a drink or two; **schwach auf der ~ sein** *(ugs.: anfällig sein)* have a weak chest; *(ugs.: wenig Geld haben)* be short [of money]; **b)** *(der Frau)* breast; **einem Kind die ~ geben** breast-feed a baby; **c)** *o. Pl. (Hähnchen~)* breast; *(Rinder~)* brisket; **d)** *o. Pl. (Sport)* breast-stroke

Brust-: **~bein das** breastbone; **~beutel der** purse *(worn around the neck)*; **~drüse die** *(Anat.)* mammary gland

brüsten ['brʏstn̩] *refl. V. (abwertend)* **sich mit etw. ~:** boast *or* brag about sth.

brust-, Brust-: **~fell·entzündung die** *(Med.)* pleurisy; **~flosse die** *(Zool.) (bei Fischen)* pectoral fin; *(beim Wal)* flipper; **~haar das** hair on the chest; chest hair; **~harnisch der** *(hist.)* breastplate; **~hoch** *Adj.* chest-high; **~höhe die;** *o. Pl.* **in ~höhe** at chest height; **~höhle die** *(Anat.)* thoracic cavity; **~kasten** *(ugs.)* chest; **~kind das** *(ugs.)* breast-fed baby; **~korb der** *(Anat.)* thorax *(Anat.)*; **~krebs der** breast cancer; cancer of the breast; **~schutz der** *(Fechten)* plastron; **~schwimmen** *itr. unr. V.; nur im Inf.* do [the] breast-stroke; **~schwimmen das** breast-stroke; **~stimme die** *(Musik)* chest-voice; **~stück das** *(Kochk.)* breast; *(vom Rind)* brisket; **~tasche die** breast pocket; *(Innentasche)* inside breast pocket; *(an der Latzhose)* front pocket; **~tee der** pectoral tea; **~ton der** *(Musik)* chest tone; **im ~ton der Überzeugung** *(fig.)* with utter conviction; **~tuch das** neckerchief *(worn with traditional costume)*; **~umfang der** chest measurement; *(bei Frauen)* bust measurement

Brüstung die; ~, ~en a) parapet; *(Balkon~)* balustrade; *(Logen~)* ledge; **b)** *(Fenster~)* breast

Brust-: **~warze die** nipple; **~wickel der** *(Med.)* chest compress; **~wirbel der** *(Anat.)* thoracic vertebra

Brut [bru:t] **die; ~, ~en a)** *(das Brüten)* brooding; **b)** *(Jungtiere, auch fig. scherzh.: Kinder)* brood; **c)** *o. Pl. (abwertend: Gesindel)* mob

brutal [bru'ta:l] **1.** *Adj.* brutal; violent ⟨*attack, programme, etc.*⟩; brute ⟨*force, strength*⟩. **2.** *adv.* brutally

brutalisieren *tr. V.* brutalize

Brutalisierung die; ~: brutalization

Brutalität [brutali'tɛ:t] **die; ~, ~en a)** *o. Pl.* brutality; **b)** *(Handlung)* act of brutality *or* violence

Brut·apparat der incubator

brüten ['bry:tn̩] **1.** *itr. V.* **a)** brood; **b)** *(geh.: lasten)* hang heavily; **~de Hitze** stifling heat; **c)** *(grübeln)* ponder **(über +** *Dat.* over); **über einem Plan ~:** work on a plan; **in dumpfes Brüten versinken** *od.* **verfallen** fall to brooding. **2.** *tr. V. (Kernphysik)* breed

brütend heiß *Adj.; nicht präd. (ugs.)* boiling *or* stifling hot

Brüter der; ~s, ~ *(Kernphysik)* breeder; **schneller ~:** fast breeder

Brut-: **~henne die** sitting hen; **~hitze die** *(ugs.)* stifling *or* sweltering heat; **~kasten der** incubator; **in ihrem Haus ist eine Hitze wie in einem ~kasten** it's like an oven in her house; **~pflege die** *(Zool.)* care of the brood; **~reaktor der** *(Kernphysik)* breeder reactor; **~stätte die** breeding-ground; *(fig.)* breeding-ground **(***Gen.***, für** for); hotbed **(***Gen.***, für** for)

brutto ['brʊto] *Adv.* gross; ~ **4 000 DM, 4 000 DM ~:** 4,000 marks gross; ~ **800 kg** 800 kilos gross

Brutto-: **~einkommen das** gross income; **~ertrag der** gross return; **~gehalt das** gross salary; **~gewicht das** gross weight; **~inlands·produkt das** *(Wirtsch.)* gross domestic product; **~preis der** full price; **~raum·zahl die** gross register tonnage; **~register·tonne die** *(Seew.)* gross register[ed]ton; **~sozial·produkt das** *(Wirtsch.)* gross national product

brutzeln ['brʊtsl̩n] **1.** *itr. V.* sizzle; **die Kartoffeln müssen noch 10 Minuten ~:** the potatoes have to fry [gently] for another ten minutes. **2.** *tr. V. (ugs.)* fry [up]; **sich** *(Dat.)* **etw. ~:** fry oneself sth.

Bruyère·holz [bry'jɛ:r-] **das** brierwood

Btx [be:te:'ɪks] *Abk.* **Bildschirmtext**

Bub [bu:p] **der; ~en, ~en** *(südd., österr., schweiz.)* boy; lad

Bübchen ['by:pçən] **das; ~s, ~** *(südd., österr., schweiz.)* [little] boy; [little] lad

Bube ['bu:bə] **der; ~n, ~n a)** *(Kartenspiele)* jack; knave; **b)** *(veralt. abwertend)* rogue; knave; **der böse ~:** the bad boy

Buben-: **~streich der a)** childish prank; **b)** *(veralt.: Übeltat)* knavish trick; **~stück das** *(veralt.)* knavish trick

Bubi ['bu:bi] **der; ~s, ~s a)** [little] boy *or* lad *or* fellow; **b)** *(salopp abwertend: Schnösel)* young lad

Bubi-: **~kopf der** bobbed hair[cut]; bob; **sie hat sich** *(Dat.)* **einen ~kopf schneiden lassen** she had her hair bobbed; **~kragen der** *(veralt.)* Peter Pan collar

bübisch ['by:bɪʃ] **1.** *Adj.* **a)** mischievous; **b)** *(veralt. abwertend: schurkisch)* villainous. **2.** *adv.; see* **Adj.:** mischievously; villainously

Buch [bu:x] **das; ~[e]s, Bücher** ['by:çɐ] **a)** book; **über seinen Büchern sitzen** pore over one's books; **das Goldene ~ der Stadt** the visitors' book of the town; **sie ist ein aufgeschlagenes** *od.* **offenes ~ für mich** I can read her like an open book; **das ~ der Bücher** the Book of Books; **wie ein ~ reden** *(ugs.)* talk nineteen to the dozen; **ein Detektiv/ein Faulpelz, wie er im ~e steht** a classic [example of a] detective/a complete lazy-bones; **ein ~ mit sieben Siegeln** a closed book; a complete mystery; **sich [mit etw.] ins ~ der Geschichte eintragen** *(geh.)* go down in the annals *pl.* of history [for sth.]; **ein schlaues ~** *(ugs.)* a reference book/textbook; **die fünf Bücher Mose** the Pentateuch; **das erste/zweite/dritte/vierte/fünfte ~ Mose** Genesis/Exodus/Leviticus/Numbers/Deuteronomy; **b)** *(Dreh~)* script; **c)** *(Geschäfts~)* book; **er führt selbst die Bücher** he keeps his own books *or* accounts; **über etw.** *(Akk.)* **~ führen/genau ~ führen** keep a record of sth./keep an exact record of sth.; **zu ~[e] schlagen** *(den Etat beeinflussen)* be reflected in the budget; *(ins Gewicht fallen)* have a big influence; **es schlägt mit ca. 200 DM zu ~[e]** it makes a difference of about 200 marks; **d)** *(Wettliste)* book; **~ machen** make a book

Buch-: **~besprechung die** book-review; **~binder der** bookbinder; **~binderei die a)** *o. Pl.* bookbinding; **b)** *(Betrieb)* bindery; **~block der;** *Pl.* **~blocks** book block; **~deckel der** [book] cover *(front or back)*; **~druck der;** *o. Pl.* letterpress printing; **im ~druck** in letterpress; **~drucker der** printer; **~druckerei die a)** *o. Pl.* letterpress printing; **b)** *(Betrieb)* printing works; **~drucker·kunst die;** *o. Pl.* art of printing

Buche die; ~, ~n a) beech[-tree]; **b)** *o. Pl. (Holz)* beech[wood]

Buch-: **~ecker die** beech-nut; **~einband der** binding; [book] cover

¹buchen *tr. V.* **a)** enter; **etw. auf ein Konto ~:** enter sth. into an account; **etw. als Erfolg ~** *(fig.)* count sth. as a success; **einen Sieg für sich ~** *(fig.)* chalk up a victory; **b)** *(vorbestellen)* book ⟨*holiday, trip, flight*⟩; book, reserve ⟨*seat, berth, room*⟩

²buchen *Adj.; nicht präd.* beech; of beech[wood] *postpos.*

Buchen-: **~hain der** beech-grove; **~holz das** beechwood; **~wald der** beech-wood

Bücher-: **~bord das a)** *s.* **~brett; b)** *s.* **~regal; ~brett das** bookshelf

Bücherei die; ~, ~en library

Bücher-: **~freund der** book-lover; **~gestell das** bookshelves *pl.*; **~kiste die** book-crate; *(Kiste mit Büchern)* crate of books; **~narr der** book-fiend; **sie ist ein wahrer ~narr** she's really mad on books; **~regal das** bookshelves *pl.*; **~schrank der** bookcase; **~sendung die: etw. als ~sendung aufgeben/schicken** send sth. at printed paper rate; **das ist eine ~sendung** this can be/has been sent at printed paper rate; **~stube die** bookshop; **~stütze die** book-end; **~verbot das** *(kath. Kirche)* ban on books; **~verbrennung die** burning of books; **~wand die a)** bookshelf unit; **b)** *(Wand mit ~regal)* wall of bookshelves; **~weisheit die** *(abwertend)* book-learning; **~wurm der** *(scherzh.)* bookworm

Buch-: **~fink der** chaffinch; **~form die** *in* **in ~form** in book form; **~führung die** bookkeeping; **einfache/doppelte ~führung** single/double-entry bookkeeping; **~gemeinschaft die** book club; **~halter der, ~halterin die** bookkeeper

buchhalterisch 1. *Adj.* bookkeeping *attrib.* **2.** *adv.* **~ gesehen** from a bookkeeping point of view

Buch-: **~haltung die a)** accountancy; **b)** *(Abteilung)* accounts department; **~handel der;** *o. Pl.* book trade; **im ~handel erhältlich** available from bookshops; **~händler der, ~händlerin die** bookseller; **~handlung die** bookshop; **„~handlung Franz Maier"** 'Franz Maier's Bookshop'; **~hülle die** [book-]cover; **~illustration die** book illustration; **~klub der** book club; **~kritik die** book-review; **~laden der** *s.* **~handlung**

Büchlein das; ~s, ~: little book
Buch-: ~macher der bookmaker; bookie *(coll.)*; **~malerei die;** *o. Pl.* illumination; **~messe die** book fair; **~prüfer der** auditor; **~rücken der** spine
Buchs·baum ['bʊks-] **der** box[-tree]
Buchse ['bʊksə] **die; ~, ~n a)** *(Elektrot.)* socket; **b)** *(Technik)* bush; liner
Büchse ['bʏksə] **die; ~, ~n a)** tin; **die ~ der Pandora** Pandora's box; **b)** *(ugs.: Sammel~)* [collecting-]box; **c)** *(Gewehr)* rifle; *(Schrot~)* shotgun; **jmdm. vor die ~ kommen** come into sb.'s sights *pl.*
Büchsen-: ~fleisch das tinned *(Brit.) or (Amer.)* canned meat; **~gemüse das** tinned *(Brit.) or (Amer.)* canned vegetables *pl.*; **~macher der** gunsmith; **~milch die** tinned *(Brit.) or (Amer.)* canned milk; **~öffner der** tin-opener *(Brit.)*; can opener *(Amer.)*
Buchstabe ['bu:xʃta:bə] **der; ~ns, ~n** letter; *(Druckw.)* character; **ein großer/kleiner ~:** a capital [letter]/small letter; **nach dem ~n des Gesetzes** *(fig.)* according to the letter of the law; **sich auf seine vier ~n setzen** *(ugs. scherzh.)* sit [oneself] down
buchstaben-, Buchstaben-: ~getreu 1. *Adj.* literal; **2.** *adv.* to the letter; **~rätsel das** word-puzzle; **~rechnung die;** *o. Pl.* simple algebra; **~schloß das** letter-lock; **~schrift die** alphabetic script; **~wort das;** *Pl.* **~wörter** acronym
buchstabieren *tr. V.* **a)** spell; **b)** *(mühsam lesen)* spell out
buchstäblich ['bu:xʃtɛ:plɪç] **1.** *Adv.* literally. **2.** *Adj.* literal
Buch·stütze die *s.* **Bücherstütze**
Bucht [bʊxt] **die; ~, ~en a)** bay; **b)** *(für Schweine)* sty; *(für Pferde)* stall
Buchtel ['bʊxtl̩] **die; ~, ~n** *(österr.)* yeast pastry with jam or poppy-seed filling
Buch·titel der title
Buchung die; ~, ~en a) entry; **b)** *s.* [1]**buchen b:** booking; reservation
Buchungs·maschine die accounting machine
Buch-: ~weizen der buckwheat; **~wesen das;** *o. Pl.* book trade; *(Studienfach)* the book trade; **~wissen das** *(abwertend)* book-learning; **das ist nur ~wissen** that is only knowledge gained from books; **~zeichen das** bookmark[er]
Bücke ['bʏkə] **die; ~, ~n** *(Turnen)* stoop vault
Buckel ['bʊkl̩] **der; ~s, ~ a)** *(ugs.: Rücken)* back; **den ~ voll kriegen** get a good hiding *(coll.)*; **einen ~ machen** ⟨*cat*⟩ arch its back; ⟨*person*⟩ hunch one's shoulders; **rutsch mir den ~ runter!** *(salopp)* get lost! *(sl.)*; **der kann** *od.* **soll mir mal den ~ runterrutschen** *(salopp)* he can get lost *or* take a running jump *(sl.)*; **den ~ voll Schulden haben** be up to one's neck *or* ears in debt; **den ~ hinhalten** *(fig.)* take the blame; carry the can *(sl.)*; **einen krummen ~ machen, den ~ krumm machen** *(fig.)* bow and scrape; kowtow; **genug/viel auf dem ~ haben** *(fig.)* have enough/a lot on one's plate *(fig.)*; **schon 40 Jahre** *od.* **Jährchen auf dem ~ haben** be 40 already; **wenn du so viele Jahre auf dem ~ hast wie ich** when you are as old as I am; *s. auch* **breit 1 a; b)** *(Rückenverkrümmung)* hunchback; hump; **c)** *(ugs.: Hügel)* hillock; **d)** *(ugs.: gewölbte Stelle)* bump
buckelig *s.* **bucklig**
buckeln *itr. V. (ugs.)* **a)** *(abwertend)* bow and scrape; kowtow; **vor jmdm. ~:** kowtow to sb.; **nach oben ~ und nach unten treten** bow to superiors and kick underlings; **b)** ⟨*cat*⟩ arch its back
Buckel·rind das zebu
bücken ['bʏkn̩] *refl. V.* bend down; **sich nach etw. ~:** bend down to pick sth. up
bucklig *Adj.* **a)** hunchbacked; humpbacked; **b)** *(ugs.: uneben)* bumpy

Bucklige der/die; *adj. Dekl.* hunchback; humpback
[1]**Bückling** ['bʏklɪŋ] **der; ~s, ~e** *(ugs. scherzh.: Verbeugung)* bow
[2]**Bückling der; ~s, ~e** *(Hering)* smoked herring; bloater
Büdchen ['by:tçən] **das; ~s, ~:** little hut
Buddel ['bʊdl̩] **die; ~, ~n** *(nordd.)* bottle
Buddelei ['bʊdə'lai̯] **die; ~, ~en** *(ugs. abwertend)* digging *no pl.*; **eine ~** a piece fo digging
Buddel·kasten der sand-pit
buddeln *(ugs.)* **1.** *itr. V.* dig; **die Kinder ~ im Garten/im Sand** the children are digging about in the garden/sand. **2.** *tr. V.* **a)** dig ⟨*hole, tunnel*⟩; **b)** *(ausgraben)* dig up; **etw. aus der Erde ~:** dig sth. up out of the ground
Buddha ['bʊda] **der; ~s, ~s** Buddha
Buddhismus der; ~: Buddhism *no art.*
Buddhist der; ~en, ~en, Buddhistin die; ~, ~nen Buddhist
buddhistisch 1. *Adj.* Buddhist *attrib.* **2.** *adv.* **~ beeinflußt** influenced by Buddhism
Bude ['bu:də] **die; ~, ~n a)** kiosk; *(Markt~)* stall; *(Jahrmarkts~)* booth; **b)** *(Bau~)* hut; **c)** *(ugs.: Haus)* dump *(coll.)*; **d)** *(ugs.: Zimmer)* room; digs *pl. (Brit. coll.)*; **Leben in die ~ bringen** liven the place up; **mir fällt die ~ auf den Kopf** I'm feeling *or* getting claustrophobic; **[jmdm.] die ~ auf den Kopf stellen** turn the *or* sb.'s place upside down; **jmdm. die ~ einrennen** pester *or* badger sb.; **jmdm. auf die ~ rücken** *(mit einem Anliegen)* go/come round to sb.'s place; *(als Besuch)* drop in on sb.; **e)** *(ugs. abwertend: Laden, Lokal)* outfit *(coll.)*
Budel ['bu:dl̩] **die; ~, ~n** *(bayr., österr.)* counter
Buden-: ~besitzer der stall-holder; stall-keeper; **~zauber der** *(ugs. veralt.)* **~zauber machen** have a rave-up *(sl.)*
Budget [bʏ'dʒe:] **das; ~s, ~s** budget
budgetär [bʏdʒe'tɛ:ɐ̯] *Adj.* budgetary
Budget-: ~beratung die budget discussion; **~entwurf der** draft budget
Budike [bu'di:kə] **die; ~, ~n** *(berl.)* **a)** little shop; **b)** *(Lokal)* pub *(Brit. coll.)*; bar
Budiker der; ~s, ~ *(berl.)* landlord
Budo ['bu:do] **das; ~s** budo
Büfett [by'fɛt] **das; ~[e]s, ~s** *od.* **~e a)** sideboard; **b)** *(Schanktisch)* bar; **c)** *(Verkaufstisch)* counter; **d) kaltes ~:** cold buffet; **e)** *(schweiz.: Bahnhofsrestaurant)* station restaurant
Büfett·fräulein das barmaid *(Brit.)*
Büfettier [byfɛ'ti̯e:] **der; ~s, ~s** barman
Büffel ['bʏfl̩] **der; ~s, ~:** buffalo
Büffelei die *(ugs.)* swotting *no pl. (Brit. sl.)*
Büffel-: ~herde die herd of buffalo; **~leder das** buffalo-hide
büffeln *(ugs.)* **1.** *itr. V.* swot *(Brit. sl.)*; cram. **2.** *tr. V.* swot up *(Brit. sl.)*; cram
Buffet, *(österr. auch:)* **Büffet** [by'fɛt] **das; ~s, ~s** *s.* **Büfett**
Buffo ['bʊfo] **der; ~s, ~s** *od.* **Buffi** buffo
Bug [bu:k] **der; ~[e]s, ~e** *u.* **Büge** ['by:gə] **a)** *Pl.:* **Buge** *(Schiffs~)* bow; *(Flugzeug~)* nose; **jmdm. eine vor den ~ knallen** *(salopp) (einen Schlag versetzen)* sock *(sl.) or* give sb. one; *(einschüchtern)* sock *(sl.) or* give it to sb.; *s. auch* **Schuß a; b)** *(Schulterstück)* shoulder; **c)** *Pl.:* **Büge** *(Technik)* brace; strut
Bügel ['by:gl̩] **der; ~s, ~ a)** hanger; **über einen/einem ~:** on a hanger; **b)** *(Steig~)* stirrup; **c)** *(Brillen~)* ear-piece; **d)** *(an einer Tasche, Geldbörse)* frame; **e)** *(Griff einer Handtasche)* handle; **f)** *(Stromabnehmer)* bow; pantograph; **g)** *(Säge~)* frame; **h)** *(Gewehr~)* trigger-guard
bügel-, Bügel-: ~automat der *s.* **~maschine; ~brett das** ironing-board; **~eisen das** iron; **~falte die** [trouser] crease; **~frei** *Adj.* non-iron; **~maschine die** ironing-machine

bügeln *tr., itr. V.* iron ⟨*clothes*⟩; *s. auch* **gebügelt**
Bügel·säge die hack-saw
Buggy ['bagi] **der; ~s, ~s** buggy
Bügler der; ~s, ~, Büglerin die; ~, ~nen ironer
Bug-: ~rad das *(Flugw.)* nose-wheel; **~see die** *(Seemannsspr.) s.* **~welle**
Bugsier·dampfer der *(Seemannsspr.)* tug [boat]
bugsieren [bʊ'ksi:rən] *tr. V.* **a)** *(ugs.)* shift; manœuvre; steer ⟨*person*⟩; **b)** *(Seemannsspr.)* tow
Bug-: ~spriet das *od.* **der** *(Seemannsspr.)* bowsprit; **~welle die** *(Seemannsspr.)* bow wave
buh [bu:] *Interj.* boo; **~ rufen** boo
Buh das; ~s, ~s *(ugs.)* boo; **die ~s** the boos *or* booing *sing.*
Buhei [bu'hai̯] **das; ~s** *(bes. westd.)* fuss
buhen *itr. V. (ugs.)* boo
Bühl [by:l] **der; ~[e]s, ~e** *(südd., schweiz., österr.)* hill
[1]**Buhle** ['bu:lə] **der; ~n, ~n** *(dichter. veralt.)* paramour
[2]**Buhle die; ~, ~n** *(dichter. veralt.)* paramour; mistress
buhlen ['bu:lən] *itr. V.* **a)** *(abwertend)* **um jmds. Gunst ~:** court sb.'s favour; **um jmds. Anerkennung ~:** strive for recognition by sb.; **um jmdn. ~** *(veralt.)* court *or* woo sb.; **b)** *(veralt.: eine Liebschaft haben)* **mit jmdm. ~:** have a liaison with sb.
Buhler der; ~s, ~ a) *s.* [1]**Buhle; b)** *(geh. abwertend: Werber)* wooer
buhlerisch *(veralt. abwertend)* **1.** *Adj.* **a)** amorous; **b)** *(werbend)* ingratiating. **2.** *adv.* **a)** amorously; **b)** *(werbend)* ingratiatingly
Buh·mann der; *Pl.* **Buhmänner** *(ugs.)* **a)** whipping-boy; scapegoat; **b)** *(Schreckgestalt)* bogyman
Buhne ['bu:nə] **die; ~, ~n** groyne
Bühne ['by:nə] **die; ~, ~n a)** stage; **es gab mehrmals Beifall auf offener ~:** there were several rounds of applause during the play; **ein Stück auf die ~ bringen** put on *or* stage a play; **seit Monaten steht er jeden Abend als Faust auf der ~:** he has been playing Faust [on the stage] every evening for months; **auf der politischen ~** *(fig.)* on the political scene; **über die ~ bringen** *(ugs.)* finish ⟨*process*⟩; get ⟨*event*⟩ over; **über die ~ gehen** *(ugs.)* go off; **von der ~ des Lebens abtreten** *(geh. verhüll.)* depart this life; **von der ~ abtreten** disappear from *or* leave the scene; **b)** *(Theater)* theatre; **die Städtischen ~n Köln** the Cologne municipal theatres; **das Stück ging über alle ~n** the play was put on *or* staged in all the theatres; **an** *od.* **bei der ~ sein** be on the stage *or* in the theatre; **zur ~ gehen** go on the stage *or* into the theatre; **c)** *(landsch.: Dachboden)* attic; loft; **d)** *(landsch.: Heuboden)* [hay] loft; **e)** *(Hebe~)* lift; ramp
bühnen-, Bühnen-: ~anweisung die stage direction; **~arbeiter der** stage-hand; **~aus·sprache die** standard *or* received pronunciation; **~ausstattung die** stage set; **~autor der** playwright; **~bearbeitung die** stage adaptation; **~beleuchtung die** stage lighting; **~bild das** [stage] set; **~bildner der; ~s, ~, ~bildnerin die; ~, ~nen** stage *or* set designer; **~dekoration die** [stage] setting; stage decoration; **~dichtung die** drama; theatre; **~effekt der** stage effect; **~eingang der** stage door; **~erfahrung die** stage experience; **~erfolg der a)** stage success; **das Stück hatte einen großen ~erfolg** the play was a big success; **b)** *(Theaterstück)* stage hit; **ein großer ~erfolg am Broadway** a big Broadway hit; **~fassung die** *s.* **~bearbeitung; ~gerecht** *Adj.* ⟨*form*⟩ suitable for the stage; stage ⟨*adaptation*⟩; **etw. ~gerecht bearbeiten** adapt sth. for the stage; **~himmel der** cyc-

lorama; **~kunst die** *s.* **Schauspielkunst; ~maler der** scene-painter; **~manuskript das** script; **~musik die** incidental music; **~raum der** stage [and backstage]; **~reif** *Adj.* ‹*play etc.*› ready for the stage; ‹*imitation etc.*› worthy of the stage; dramatic ‹*entrance etc.*›; **~schaffende der/die;** *adj. Dekl.* dramatic artist; **~stück das** stage play; **~technik die;** *o. Pl.* stage equipment *or* machinery; **~werk das** work for the stage; *(im engeren Sinne: dramatisches Werk)* dramatic work; **~wirksam** *Adj.* effective on the stage *pred.*; **~wirkung die** dramatic effectiveness

Buh·ruf der boo

buk [bu:k] *1. u. 3. Pers. Sg. Prät. v.* **backen**

Bukarest ['bu:karɛst] **(das); ~s** Bucharest

Bukett [bu'kɛt] **das; ~s, ~s** *od.* **~e a)** *(geh.)* bouquet; **ein ~ Rosen** a bouquet of roses; **b)** *(bei Wein)* bouquet

Bukolik [bu'ko:lɪk] **die; ~** *(Literaturw.)* bucolic *or* pastoral poetry

bukolisch *Adj.* **a)** *(Literaturw.)* bucolic; pastoral; **b** *(geh.: idyllisch)* idyllic

Bulette [bu'lɛtə] **die; ~, ~n** *(bes. berl.)* rissole; **ran an die ~n!** *(ugs.)* go to it! *(coll.)*

Bulgare [bʊl'ga:rə] **der; ~n, ~n** Bulgarian

Bulgarien [bʊl'ga:ri̯ən] **(das); ~s** Bulgaria

Bulgarin die; ~, ~nen Bulgarian; *s. auch* **-in**

bulgarisch *Adj.* Bulgarian; *s. auch* **deutsch, Deutsch**

Bulk·ladung ['bʌlk-] **die** *(Seemannsspr.)* bulk cargo

Bull- [bʊl-]: **~auge das** circular porthole; **~dogge die** bulldog

Bulldozer ['bʊldo:zɐ] **der; ~s, ~:** bulldozer

[1]**Bulle** ['bʊlə] **der; ~n, ~n a)** bull; **b)** *(ugs. abwertend: Mann)* great ox; big bull; **d)** *(salopp abwertend: Polizist)* cop *(sl.)*; **die ~n kommen!** here come the fuzz *(sl.)* *or* the cops *(sl.)*!

[2]**Bulle die; ~, ~n a)** *(päpstlicher Erlaß)* bull; *s. auch* **golden; b)** *(Urkundensiegel)* bulla

bullen-, Bullen-: ~beißer der a) *s.* **Bulldogge; b)** *(ugs. abwertend: Mensch)* aggressive fellow; **~hitze die** *(ugs.)* sweltering *or* boiling heat; **~kalb das** bull-calf; **~stark** *Adj. (ugs.)* as strong as an ox *pred.*

bullern ['bʊlɐn] *itr. V. (ugs.)* ‹*water*› bubble [away]; ‹*fire etc.*› roar [away]

Bulletin [byl'tɛ̃:] **das; ~s, ~s** bulletin

bullig 1. *Adj.* **a)** beefy, stocky ‹*person, appearance, etc.*›; chunky, hefty ‹*car*›; **b)** *(drückend)* sweltering, boiling ‹*heat*›; **2.** *adv.* swelteringly; **~ heiß** boiling hot

Bull·terrier der bull-terrier

Bully ['bʊli] **das; ~s, ~s** *(Sport)* bully; **das ~ ausführen** take a bully

bum [bʊm] *Interj.* bang

Bumerang ['bʊməraŋ] **der; ~s, ~e** *od.* **~s** boomerang; **es erwies sich als ~** *(fig.)* it boomeranged [on him/her/them]

Bumerang·effekt der boomerang effect

Bummel ['bʊml̩] **der; ~s, ~ a)** stroll **(durch** around); **einen ~ [durch den Park] machen** go for *or* take a stroll [in the park]; **b)** *(durch Lokale)* pub-crawl *(coll.)*

Bummelant [bʊmə'lant] **der; ~en, ~en** *(ugs. abwertend)* **a)** slowcoach *(Brit.)*; slowpoke *(Amer.)*; dawdler; **b)** *(Faulenzer)* idler; loafer

Bummelei die; ~, ~en *(ugs. abwertend)* **a)** dawdling; **b)** *(Faulenzerei)* idling *or* loafing about

bummelig *(ugs. abwertend)* **1.** *Adj.* **a)** slow; **b)** *(nachlässig)* slovenly; slipshod. **2.** *adv.* **a)** slowly; **b)** *(nachlässig)* in a slovenly *or* slipshod way

Bummel·liese die *(ugs. abwertend)* slowcoach; dawdler

bummeln *itr. V.* **a)** *mit sein (ugs.)* stroll **(durch** around); **[im Park] ~ gehen** go for *or* take a stroll [in the park]; **b)** *mit sein (ugs.: durch Lokale)* go round the pubs *(Brit. coll.)*; go on a pub-crawl *(Brit. coll.)*; **c)** *(ugs. abwertend: trödeln)* dawdle; **bei den Schulaufgaben ~:** dawdle over one's homework; **d)** *(ugs. abwertend: faulenzen)* laze about; do nothing

Bummel-: ~streik der go-slow; *(bei Beamten usw.)* work to rule; **in einen ~streik treten** go on a go-slow; **~zug der** *(ugs.)* slow *or* stopping train

bummern ['bʊmɐn] *itr. V. (landsch.)* bang; **gegen die Tür ~:** bang on the door

Bummler der; -s, ~ *(ugs.)* **a)** *(Spaziergänger)* stroller; **b)** *s.* **Bummelant**

bummlig *s.* **bummelig**

bums [bʊms] *Interj.* bang!; **es machte laut ~:** there was a loud bang *or* thud

Bums der; ~es, ~e a) *(ugs.)* bang; *(dumpfer)* thud; thump; **b)** *(salopp abwertend: Lokal)* dive *(coll.)*; **c)** *(salopp abwertend: Tanzvergnügen)* hop *(coll.)*; **d)** *(Fußballjargon)* **einen unerhörten ~ haben** have a tremendous shot

bumsen 1. *itr. V. (ugs.)* **a)** *unpers.* **es bumste ganz furchtbar** there was a terrible bang/thud *or* thump; **es bumste an der Tür** there was a bang/thump on the door; **an dieser Kreuzung bumst es mindestens einmal am Tag** *(fig.)* there's at least one smash *or* crash a day at this junction; **hör auf, oder es bumst [gleich]!** *(fig.)* stop it, or you'll catch it [in a minute]! *(coll.)*; **b)** *(schlagen)* bang; *(dumpfer)* thump; **gegen die Tür ~:** bang/thump on the door; **c)** *mit sein (stoßen)* bang; bash; **er ist mit dem Kopf gegen die Wand gebumst** he banged *or* bashed his head on the wall; **d)** *(salopp: koitieren)* have it off *(sl.)*; screw *(vulg.)*. **2.** *tr. V.* **a)** *(Fußballjargon)* thump; **b)** *(salopp: koitieren mit)* have it off with *(sl.)*; screw *(vulg.)*; **gebumst werden** get laid *(sl.)*; be screwed *(vulg.)*

bums-, Bums-: ~lokal das *(ugs. abwertend)* dive *(coll.)*; **~musik die** *(ugs. abwertend)* oompah music *(coll.)*; **~voll** *Adj. (salopp)* full to bursting *pred.*

[1]**Bund** [bʊnt] **der; ~[e]s, Bünde** ['bʏndə] **a)** *(Verband, Vereinigung)* association; society; *(Bündnis, Pakt)* alliance; **der Dritte im ~e** *(fig.)* the third in the trio; **der Alte ~/der Neue ~** *(Rel.)* the Old/New Testament; **den ~ der Ehe eingehen, den ~ fürs Leben schließen** *(geh.)* enter into the bond of marriage; **mit jmdm. im ~e sein** *od.* **stehen** be in league with sb.; **b)** *(föderativer Staat)* federation; **der ~ und die Länder** the Federation *or* Federal Government and the Länder *or* States; *(in Austria)* the Federation *or* Federal Government and the provinces; **c)** *(ugs.: Bundeswehr)* forces *pl*; **beim ~:** in the forces *pl.*; **zum ~ gehen** do one's military service; **er hat sich freiwillig zum ~ gemeldet** he joined up voluntarily; **d)** *(an Röcken od. Hosen)* waistband; **e)** *(an Instrumenten)* fret

[2]**Bund das; ~[e]s, ~e** bunch; **ein ~ Petersilie/Mohrrüben/Spargel** a bunch of parsley/carrots/asparagus

Bündchen ['bʏntçən] **das; ~s, ~** *(am Hals)* [neck-]band; *(am Ärmel)* [sleeve-]band; *(an der Taille)* [waist]band; *(am Knöchel)* [ankle-]band

Bündel ['bʏndl̩] **das; ~s, ~ a)** bundle; **ein ~ von Fragen** *(fig.)* a set *or* cluster of questions; **ein hilfloses/schreiendes ~** *(ugs.)* a helpless/howling little bundle; **jeder hat sein ~ zu tragen** *(fig.)* everybody has his cross to bear; **sein ~ packen** *od.* **schnüren** pack one's bags *pl.*; **b)** *(Zusammengebundenes)* bundle; sheaf; **c)** *(Geom.)* sheaf

bündeln *tr. V.* bundle up ‹*newspapers, old clothes, rags, etc.*›; tie ‹*banknotes etc.*› into bundles/a bundle; tie ‹*flowers, radishes, carrots, etc.*› into bunches/a bunch; sheave ‹*straw, hay, etc.*›

bündel·weise *Adv.* by the bundle; in bundles; *(bei Blumen, Möhren, Radieschen usw.)* by the bunch; in bunches

bundes-, Bundes-: ~amt das federal department **(für** of); *(schweiz.)* federal office **(für** of); **~angestellten·tarif* der;** *o. Pl.* [civil servants'] statutory salary scale; **~anleihe die** government bond; **~anstalt die** federal institute **(für** of); **~anwalt der a)*** Federal Prosecutor; **b)** *(*; beim Bundesverwaltungsgericht)* prosecutor in the Supreme Administrative Court ; **c)** *(schweiz.)* public prosecutor; **~anwaltschaft* die a)** Federal Supreme Court prosecutors *pl.*; **b)** *(beim ~verwaltungsgericht)* Supreme Administrative Court prosecutors *pl.*; **~anzeiger* der** federal gazette; **~arbeitsgericht* das** Federal Labour Court; **~ausbildungs·förderungsgesetz* das** Federal Education and Training Assistance Act; **~autobahn die** *(*, österr.)* federal motorway; **~bahn die** Federal Railway; **~bank die** federal bank; **die Deutsche ~bank*** the German Federal Bank; **~beamte der** federal civil servant; **~behörde die** federal authority; **~bruder der** fellow member [of a/the students' association]; **~bürger* der** West German citizen; **~deutsch*** *Adj.* West German; **der ~deutsche Alltag** everyday life in West Germany; **~deutsche* der/die;** *adj. Dekl.* West German; **~ebene die: auf ~ebene** at federal *or* national level; **~eigen** *Adj.* federal-owned; nationalized; **~gebiet* das** federal territory; **das ~gebiet** West Germany; **~genosse der** ally; **~gericht das** Federal Court; **~gerichts·hof* der;** *o. Pl.* Federal Supreme Court; **~gesetzblatt das** Federal Law Gazette; **~grenzschutz* der** Federal Border Police; **~haupt·stadt die** federal capital; **~haus das;** *o. Pl.* Federal Parliament; *(Gebäude)* federal parliament [building]; **~haushalt der** *(*, österr.)* federal *or* national budget; **~heer das** *(österr., schweiz.)* [federal] armed forces *pl.*; **~kabinett* das** Federal Cabinet; **~kanzlei die** *(*, schweiz.)* Federal Chancellery; **~kanzler der a)** *(*, österr.)* Federal Chancellor; **b)** *(schweiz.)* Chancellor of the Confederation; **~kanzler·amt das** *(*, österr.)* Federal Chancellery; **~kriminal·amt* das** Federal Criminal Investigation Agency; **~lade die** *(jüd. Rel.)* Ark of the Covenant; **~land das** [federal] state; *(österr.)* province; **~liga die** national *or* federal division; **~ligist** [~ligɪst] **der; ~en, ~en** team in the national *or* federal division; **~marine* die** Federal Navy; West German Navy; **~minister der** *(*, österr.)* Federal Minister; **~ministerium das** *(*, österr.)* Federal Ministry; **~mittel** *Pl.* federal funds; **~nachrichten·dienst* der** Federal Intelligence Agency; **~post die** Federal Post Office; **die Deutsche ~post*** the West German [Federal] Post Office; **~präsident der a)** *(*, österr.)* [Federal] President; **b)** *(schweiz.)* President of the Confederation; **~rat der a)** (*) [Federal] Upper House of Parliament; Bundesrat; **b)** *(österr., schweiz.)* Federal Council; **~rechnungs·hof* der** Federal Audit Office; **~recht das** federal law; **~regierung die** Federal Government; **~republik die** federal republic; **die ~republik Deutschland** The Federal Republic of Germany; **~republikanisch*** *Adj.; nicht präd.* West German; **~richter der** federal judge; **~sieger der** national winner; **~staat der** federal state; **~straße die** *(*, österr.)* federal highway; ≈ A road *(Brit.)*

Bundes·tag* der [Federal] Lower House of Parliament; Bundestag

Bundestags-: ~abgeordnete* der/die member of parliament; member of the Bundestag; **~fraktion* die** parliamentary group; group in the Bundestag; **~präsi-**

* *(Bundesrepublik Deutschland)*

dent* **der** President of the Bundestag; **~wahl*** **die** parliamentary *or* general election

bundes-, Bundes-: **~trainer der** national team manager; national coach; **~treue die** federal allegiance; **~verband der** federal association; **~verband der Deutschen Industrie*** Federation of German Industries; **~verdienst·kreuz*** **das** Order of Merit of the Federal Republic; **~verfassung die** federal constitution; **~verfassungs·gericht*** **das** Federal Constitutional Court; **~versammlung die** *(*, schweiz.)* Federal Assembly; **~versicherungs·anstalt*** **die** federal insurance institution; **die ~versicherungsanstalt für Angestellte** the Federal Insurance Institution [for salaried employees]; **~verwaltungs·gericht*** **das** Supreme Administrative Court; **~wehr*** **die**; *o. Pl.* [Federal] Armed Forces *pl.*; **~weit 1.** *Adj.; nicht präd.* nation-wide; national; **2.** *adv.* nation-wide; nationally; **~zwang*** **der** federal obligation

Bund-: **~falten** *Pl.* pleats; **~falten·hose die** pleat[ed]-front trousers *pl.*; **~hose die** knee-breeches

bündig ['bʏndɪç] **1.** *Adj.* **a)** concise; succinct; **b)** *(schlüssig)* conclusive; *s. auch* **kurz 1b**; **c)** *(Bauw.)* flush; level. **2.** *adv.* **a)** concisely; succinctly; *s. auch* **kurz 2b**; **b)** *(schlüssig)* conclusively; **c)** *(Bauw.)* flush

Bündigkeit die; ~ a) conciseness; succinctness; **b)** *(Schlüssigkeit)* conclusiveness

Bündnis ['bʏntnɪs] **das; ~ses, ~se** alliance

bündnis-, Bündnis-: **~frei** *Adj.* non-aligned; **~partner der** ally; **~politik die a)** alliance policy; **b)** *(um Bündnisse zu schließen)* policy of alliance; **~system das** system of alliance; **das atlantische ~system** the Atlantic alliances *pl.*; **~treue die** loyalty to the alliance

Bund·weite die waist; *(Maß)* waist measurement

Bungalow ['bʊŋgalo] **der; ~s, ~s** bungalow

Bunker ['bʊŋkɐ] **der; ~s, ~ a)** *(auch Behälter)* bunker; *(für Getreide)* silo; *(für Raketen)* silo; bunker; **b)** *(Luftschutz~)* air-raid shelter; **c)** *(salopp: Gefängnis)* clink *(sl.)*

bunkern 1. *tr. V.* **a)** bunker ⟨*coal*⟩; store ⟨*grain etc.*⟩; **b)** *(salopp: verstecken)* stash away *(sl.)*. **2.** *itr. V. (Seemannsspr.)* refuel

Bunsen·brenner ['bʊnzn̩-] **der** Bunsen burner

bunt [bʊnt] **1.** *Adj.* **a)** *(farbig)* coloured; *(vielfarbig)* colourful; **~e Farben/Kleidung** bright colours/brightly coloured *or* colourful clothes; **~e Luftballons** different coloured balloons; **zu ~e Kleidung** garish clothing; **b)** *(fig.)* colourful ⟨*sight*⟩; varied ⟨*programme etc.*⟩; **ein ~er Abend** a social [evening]; **ein ~er Teller [mit Äpfeln, Nüssen und Süßigkeiten]** a plate of assorted fruit, nuts, and sweets *(Brit.) or (Amer.)* candy; **Männer und Frauen bilden eine ~e Reihe** men and women alternate; **Buntes** *(DDR ugs.)* West German currency; *s. auch* **Hund a**; **c)** *(ungeordnet)* confused ⟨*muddle etc.*⟩; **ein ~es Treiben** a real hustle and bustle; **jetzt wird es mir zu ~** *(ugs.)* that's *or* it's too much. **2.** *adv.* **a)** colourfully; **die Vorhänge waren ~ geblümt** the curtains had a colourful floral pattern; **etw. ~ bemalen/streichen** paint sth. a bright colour/in bright colours; **~ gekleidet sein** be colourfully dressed; have colourful clothes; **b)** *(fig.)* **ein ~ gemischtes Programm** a varied programme; **ein ~ gemischtes Publikum** a very mixed audience/*(im Restaurant)* clientele; **c)** *(ungeordnet)* **~ durcheinander liegen** be in a complete muddle; **es zu ~ treiben** *(ugs.)* go too far; overdo it

bunt-, Bunt-: **~bemalt** *Adj.; präd. getrennt geschrieben* brightly *or* colourfully painted; **~druck der; ~es, ~e a)** *o. Pl. (Verfahren)* colour printing; **b)** *(Gedrucktes)* colour print; **~film der** *s.* **Farbfilm**; **~geblümt** *Adj.; präd. getrennt geschrieben* with a colourful floral pattern *or* design *postpos., not pred.*; **~gefärbt** *Adj.; präd. getrennt geschrieben* multicoloured; **~gefiedert** *Adj.; präd. getrennt geschrieben* with colourful *or* brightly coloured feathers *postpos., not pred.*; **~metall das** non-ferrous metal; **~papier das** coloured paper; **~sand·stein der a)** red sandstone; **b)** *o. Pl. (Geol.)* Bunter; **~scheckig** *Adj.* spotted; **~schillernd** *Adj.* iridescent; **~specht der** spotted woodpecker; **~stift der** coloured pencil/crayon; **~wäsche die** coloureds *pl.*

Bürde ['bʏrdə] **die; ~, ~n** *(geh.)* weight; load; *(fig.)* burden; **jmdm. zur ~ werden** *(fig.)* become a burden to sb.

bürden *tr. V. (geh. veralt.)* **die Verantwortung für etw. auf jmds. Schultern** *(Akk.)* **~:** burden sb. with the responsibility for sth.

Bure ['bu:rə] **der; ~n, ~n** Boer

Buren·krieg der Boer War

Bürette [bʏ'rɛtə] **die; ~, ~n** *(Chemie)* burette

Burg die; ~, ~en a) castle; **b)** *(Strand~)* wall of sand; **c)** *(Sand~)* [sand-]castle; **d)** *(Jägerspr.)* lodge

Burg-: **~anlage die** castle buildings *pl.*; castle complex; **~berg der** castle hill; *(aufgeschüttet)* castle mound; **~bewohner der** inhabitant of a/the castle; **die ~bewohner** those living in the castle

Bürge ['bʏrgə] **der; ~n, ~n a)** guarantor; **einen ~n stellen** offer surety *or* a guarantor; **er muß zwei ~n stellen** he has to give the names of two guarantors; **b)** *(fig.)* guarantee

bürgen *itr. V.* **a) für jmdn./etw. ~:** vouch for *or* act as guarantor for sb./vouch for or guarantee sth.; **wer bürgt mir dafür, daß ich das Geld zurückbekomme?** who can guarantee *or* what guarantee do I have that I'll get the money back?; **b)** *(fig.)* guarantee; **der Name bürgt für Qualität** the name is a guarantee of quality

Bürger der; ~s, ~ a) *(Staats~)* citizen; **akademischer ~** *(veralt.)* [university] student; *s. auch* **Uniform**; **b)** *(einer Gemeinde)* citizen; resident; **die Bremer ~:** the citizens *or* people of Bremen; **die ~ von Calais** the burghers of Calais; **c)** *(Bourgeois)* bourgeois

Bürger-: **~aktion die** public campaign; **~beauftragte der/die** ombudsman; **~begehren das** public petition; **~beteiligung die** public participation *or* involvement; **~entscheid der** local referendum; **~forum das** open forum; public debate; **~haus das** [bourgeois] town house

Bürgerin die; ~, ~nen a) *(Staats~)* citizen; **b)** *(einer Gemeinde)* citizen; resident; **c)** *(zur Bourgeoisie gehörend)* bourgeois[e]

Bürger-: **~initiative die** citizens' action group; **~krieg der** civil war; **der Spanische ~krieg** the Spanish Civil War

bürgerlich 1. *Adj.* **a)** *nicht präd. (staats~)* civil ⟨*rights, marriage, etc.*⟩; civic ⟨*duties*⟩; **das Bürgerliche Gesetzbuch** the [German] Civil Code; **sein ~er Name** his real name; **b)** *(dem Bürgertum zugehörig)* middle-class; **die ~e Küche** good plain cooking; good home cooking; **das ~e Trauerspiel** domestic tragedy; **c)** *(Polit.)* non-socialist; *(nicht marxistisch)* non-Marxist; **d)** *(abwertend: spießerhaft)* bourgeois. **2.** *adv.* **a)** ⟨*think, etc.*⟩ in a middle-class way; **~ leben** live a middle-class life; **gut ~ essen** have a good plain meal; *(gewohnheitsmäßig)* eat good plain food; **b)** *(abwertend: spießerhaft)* in a bourgeois way; **dieses ~ engstirnige Denken** this bourgeois, narrow-minded way of thinking

Bürgerliche der/die; *adj. Dekl.* **a)** *(Nichtadlige)* commoner; **b)** *(Polit.)* non-socialist

Bürgerlichkeit die; ~: middle-class *or* bourgeois way of life; **eine erdrückende Atmosphäre der ~:** a stifling middle-class *or* bourgeois atmosphere

bürger-, Bürger-: **~meister der** mayor; **~meister·amt das a)** *(Gemeindeverwaltung)* local authority; **b)** *(Amt des ~meisters)* office of mayor; **c)** *(Gebäude)* local council offices *pl.*; **~meisterin die** mayor; **~mut der** *s.* **Zivilcourage**; **~nah** *Adj.* which/who reflects the general public's interests *postpos., not pred.*; **~nahe Politik** politics for the people; **~nähe die: ~nähe in der Politik** politics for the people; **~nähe bewahren** keep a close relationship with the people; **~pflicht die** civic duty; duty as a citizen; *s. auch* **Ruhe f**; **~recht das** one of the civil rights; **~rechte** civil rights; **~rechtler der; ~s, ~, ~rechtlerin die; ~, ~nen** civil-rights campaigner; **~rechts·bewegung die** civil-rights movement; **~rechts·kämpfer der** *s.* **~rechtler**

Bürgerschaft die; ~, ~en a) citizens *pl.*; **die ganze ~:** all the citizens; **b)** *(in Hamburg u. Bremen)* city parliament

Bürger·schreck der bogey of the middle classes

Bürgers-: **~frau die** *(veralt.)* **a)** middle-class woman; **b)** *(zur Bourgeoisie gehörend)* bourgeoise; **~mann der;** *Pl.:* **~leute** *(veralt.)* **a)** middle-class man; **b)** *(zur Bourgeoisie gehörend)* bourgeois

Bürger-: **~sohn der a)** son of a middle-class family; **b)** *(zur Bourgeoisie gehörend)* son of a bourgeois family; **~stand der** *o. Pl. (veralt.)* **a)** middle class; **b)** *(Großbürgertum)* bourgeoisie; **~steig der** pavement *(Brit.)*; sidewalk *(Amer.)*

Bürgertum das; ~s a) middle class; **b)** *(wohlhabender Bürgerstand)* bourgeoisie

Bürger·wehr die vigilante group

Burg-: **~fräulein das** *(hist.)* daughter of the lord of the/a castle; **~fried der; ~[e]s, ~e** *s.* **Bergfried**; **~friede der a)** truce; **b)** *(hist.: Schutz)* castle precincts *pl.*; **~graben der** [castle] moat; **~graf der** *(hist.)* burgrave; **~gräfin die** *(hist.)* chatelaine; **~herr der** *(hist.)* lord of the/a castle; **~herrin die** *(hist.)* lady of the/a castle

Bürgin ['bʏrgɪn] **die; ~, ~nen** *s.* **Bürge**

Burg·ruine die castle ruins *pl.*; ruined castle

Bürgschaft die; ~, ~en a) *(Rechtsw.)* guarantee; security; **die ~ für jmdn./etw. übernehmen** agree to act as sb.'s guarantor/to guarantee sth.; **b)** *(Garantie)* guarantee; **~ für etw. leisten** vouch for *or* guarantee sth.; **c)** *(Betrag)* penalty

Bürgschafts-: **~erklärung die** guarantee; **~nehmer der** creditor

Burgund [bʊr'gʊnt] **(das); ~s** Burgundy

Burgunder der; ~s, ~ a) *(Einwohner, auch hist.)* Burgundian; **b)** *(Wein)* burgundy

Burgunder·wein der burgundy

Burg-: **~verlies das** [castle] dungeon; **~vogt der** *s.* **~graf**

Burin die; ~, ~nen Boer; *s. auch* **-in**

Burkina Faso [bʊr'ki:na 'fa:zo] **(das)** Burkina

Burkiner der; ~s, ~, Burkinerin die; ~, ~nen Burkinan; *s. auch* **-in**

burkinisch *Adj.* Burkinan

burlesk [bʊr'lɛsk] *Adj.* burlesque

Burleske die; ~, ~n *(Theater, Musik)* burlesque

Burma ['bʊrma] *s.* **Birma**

Burnus ['bʊrnʊs] **der; ~ses, ~se** burnous

Büro [bʏ'ro] **das; ~s, ~s** office

Büro-: **~angestellte der/die** office-worker; **~arbeit die** office work *no pl.*; **alle ~arbeiten** all types of office work; **~artikel der** item of office equipment; **~artikel**

* *(Bundesrepublik Deutschland)*

Pl. office supplies *or* equipment; **~bedarf der** office supplies *pl.*; **~gehilfe der** office-boy; **~gehilfin die** office-girl; **~haus das** office-block; **~hengst der** *(ugs. abwertend)* office-clerk; pen-pusher *(coll.)*; **~kaufmann der** [qualified] office executive; **~klammer die** paper-clip; **~kraft die** clerical worker

Bürokrat [byro'kra:t] **der; ~en, ~en** *(abwertend)* bureaucrat

Bürokratie [byrokra'ti:] **die; ~, ~n** bureaucracy

Bürokratin die; ~, ~nen bureaucrat

bürokratisch 1. *Adj.* bureaucratic. **2.** *adv.* bureaucratically

bürokratisieren *tr. V.* bureaucratize

Bürokratismus der; ~ *(abwertend)* bureaucracy

Büro-: ~maschine die office machine; **~material das** *s.* **~bedarf; ~mensch der** *(ugs.)* office-clerk; **~schluß der** [office] closing-time; **bei uns ist um 17 h ~schluß** our office closes at 5 o'clock; **nach ~schluß** after the office closes/the offices close; after office hours; **~tätigkeit die;** *o. Pl.* **eine ~tätigkeit** office work; an office job; **Mädchen für leichte ~tätigkeit gesucht** girl required to carry out basic clerical duties; **~vorsteher der** *(veralt.)* office manager *or* supervisor; **~zeit die** office hours *pl.*; **während der ~zeit** during office hours

Bursch [bʊrʃ] **der; ~en, ~en a)** *member of a student fraternity;* **b)** *s.* **Bursche**

Bürschchen ['bʏrʃçən] **das; ~, ~:** little fellow; little chap; **ein freches ~:** a cheeky little devil; **sei vorsichtig, mein ~:** be careful, sonny *or* laddie

Bursche ['bʊrʃə] **der; ~n, ~n a)** boy; lad; **b)** *(junger Mann)* young man; **die jungen ~n aus dem Dorf** the village youths; **er hält sich für einen ganz tollen ~n** *(ugs.)* he thinks he's really something; **er ist ein toller ~** *(ugs.)* he's a reckless devil; **c)** *(abwertend: Kerl)* guy *(sl.)*; character; **ein übler ~:** a nasty piece of work *(coll.)*; **d)** *(ugs.: Prachtexemplar)* specimen; **der Hecht, den er gefangen hat, ist ein prächtiger ~:** the pike he caught is a real whopper *(sl.)*; **e)** *(Milit. hist.)* batman; orderly; **f)** *s.* **Bursch a**

Burschenschaft die; ~, ~en students' duelling society

Burschenschafter der; ~s, ~: member of a/the students' duelling society

burschikos [bʊrʃi'ko:s] **1.** *Adj.* **a)** sporty ⟨*clothes, look*⟩; [tom]boyish ⟨*behaviour, girl, haircut*⟩; **b)** *(ungezwungen)* casual ⟨*comment, behaviour, etc.*⟩. **2.** *adv.* **a)** [tom]boyishly; **sich ~ benehmen** behave like a [tom]boy; **b)** *(ungezwungen)* in a colloquial way

Burschikosität [bʊrʃikozi'tɛ:t] **die; ~, ~en** *s.* **burschikos 1:** sportiness; [tom]boyishness; casualness

Burse ['bʊrzə] **die; ~, ~n** *(hist.)* hostel *(for students and journeymen)*

Bürste ['bʏrstə] **die; ~, ~n a)** brush; **b)** *(Haarschnitt)* crew cut; **c)** *(Elektrot.)* brush

bürsten *tr. V.* **a)** brush; **b)** *(vulg.: koitieren)* screw *(vulg.)*

Bürsten-: ~abzug der *(Druckw.)* brush proof; **~binder der a)** *(veralt.) s.* **~macher; b) trinken** *(ugs.)* **od. saufen** *(salopp)* **wie ein ~binder** drink like a fish; **~macher der** broom- and brushmaker; **~schnitt der** crew cut

Bürzel ['bʏrtsl̩] **der; ~s, ~ a)** *(Zool.)* rump; **b)** *(Jägerspr.)* tail

Bus [bʊs] **der; ~ses, ~se** bus; *(Privat- und Reisebus auch)* coach

Bus·bahn·hof der bus station; *(für Reisebusse auch)* coach station

Busch [bʊʃ] **der; ~[e]s, Büsche** ['bʏʃə] **a)** bush; *(fig.)* **auf den ~ klopfen** *(ugs.)* sound things out; **bei jmdm. auf den ~ klopfen** *(ugs.)* sound sb. out; **mit etw. hinterm ~ halten** *(ugs.)* keep sth. to oneself; **es ist etw. im ~** *(ugs.)* something's up; **sich [seitwärts] in die Büsche schlagen** *(ugs.)* slip away; **b)** *(Geogr.)* bush; **c)** *(ugs.: Urwald)* jungle; **aus dem ~ kommen** have come from the backwoods *pl.*; **d)** *(Strauß)* bunch; **e)** *(Büschel)* tuft; **ein ~ Haare/Federn** a tuft of hair/feathers

Busch·bohne die dwarf bean

Büschel ['bʏʃl̩] **das; ~s, ~** *(von Haaren, Federn, Gras usw.)* tuft; *(von Heu, Stroh)* handful; **ein ~ Federn** a tuft of feathers

büschel·weise *Adv. s.* **Büschel:** in tufts/in handfuls; **~ Unkraut** whole clumps of weeds

Buschen der; ~s, ~ *(südd., österr. ugs.)* **ein ~ [Blumen/Zweige]** a bunch [of flowers]/bundle [of twigs]; **einen ~ über die Tür hängen** hang a bundle of twigs above the door

Buschen·schenke die *(österr.) s.* **Straußwirtschaft**

buschig *Adj.* bushy; **~e Rosen** rose-bushes

Busch·klepper der *(veralt.)* highwayman *(Hist.)*

Busch-: ~mann der Bushman; **~messer das** machete; **~werk das;** *o. Pl.* bushes *pl.*; **~wind·röschen das** wood anemone

Busen ['bu:zn̩] **der; ~s, ~ a)** bust; **sie hat wenig ~** *(ugs.)* she has very little bosom; **in dem Film wurde viel ~ gezeigt** *(ugs.)* in this film there was plenty of bosom on display; **eine Schlange od. Natter an seinem ~ nähren** *(veralt.)* nourish a viper in one's bosom *(literary)*; **b)** *(dichter. veralt.: Brust)* bosom; breast; **am ~ der Natur** *(fig. scherzh.)* in the bosom of nature; **c)** *(dichter. veralt.: Inneres)* bosom; heart; **d)** *(dichter. veralt.: Mieder)* bodice; bosom

busen-, Busen-: ~frei *Adj.* topless; **~freund der, ~freundin die** *(oft iron.)* bosom friend; **~star der** *(ugs.)* sex symbol

Bus-: ~fahrer der bus-driver; *(von Reisebussen auch)* coach-driver; **~halte·stelle die** bus-stop; *(von Reisebussen auch)* coach-stop; **~linie die** bus-route; **mein Haus liegt an der ~linie 7** my house is on the number 7 bus-route

Bussard ['bʊsart] **der; ~s, ~e** *(Zool.)* buzzard

Buße ['bu:sə] **die; ~, ~n a)** *(Rel.)* penance *no art.*; **~ tun** *(veralt.)* do penance; **b)** *o. Pl.* *(Reue)* repentance; **c)** *(Rechtsw.)* damages *pl.*; **d)** *(schweiz. Rechtsspr.: Geldstrafe)* fine

Bussel ['bʊsl̩] **das; ~s, ~[n]** *s.* **Busserl**

busseln *s.* **busserln**

büßen ['by:sn̩] **1.** *tr. V.* **a)** *(Rel.: sühnen)* atone for; expiate; **b)** *(bestraft werden für)* atone for; **das sollst du mir ~:** you'll pay for that; **c)** *(fig.: bezahlen)* pay for. **2.** *itr. V.* **a)** *(Rel.)* **für etw. ~:** atone for *or* expiate sth.; **b)** *(bestraft werden)* suffer; **c)** *(fig.: bezahlen)* pay

Büßer der; ~s, ~ *(Rel.)* penitent

Büßer-: ~gewand das, ~hemd das penitential robe; **sich im ~hemd zeigen, im ~hemd erscheinen** *(fig.)* show repentance

Büßerin die; ~, ~nen *(Rel.)* penitent

Busserl ['bʊsɐl] **das; ~s, ~[n]** *(südd., österr. ugs.)* kiss

busserln *tr., itr. V.* *(südd., österr. ugs.)* kiss

buß-, Buß-: ~feier die *(kath. Rel.) s.* **~gottesdienst; ~fertig** *(Rel.)* **1.** *Adj.* penitent; *(fig.)* repentant; **2.** *adv.* penitently; **~fertigkeit die** *o. Pl.* *(Rel.)* penitence; *(fig.)* repentance; **~gang der** *(geh.)* **einen ~gang antreten od. machen** go to beg for forgiveness; **~gebet das** *(Rel.)* prayer of repentance *or* penitence; **~geld das** *(Rechtsw.)* fine; **~geld·bescheid der** official demand for payment of a fine; **einen ~geldbescheid bekommen** be fined **(von** by); **~gesang der** *(Rel.)* hymn of repentance; **~gottes·dienst der** *(kath. Rel.)* service of confession and general absolution

Bussi ['bʊsi] **das; ~s, ~s** *(ugs.)* kiss

Bussole [bʊ'so:lə] **die; ~, ~n** compass; *(Elektrot.)* galvanometer

Buß-: ~prediger der repentance-preacher; **~predigt die** sermon calling to repentance; **~sakrament das** *(Rel.)* sacrament of penance; **~tag der a)** *(kath. Rel.)* day of repentance; **b)** *s.* **~- und Bettag; ~- und Bettag der** *(ev. Kirche)* Wednesday eleven days before Advent *(as day of penance)*

Büsten·halter der bra; brassière *(formal)*

Bus-: ~verbindung die a) *(Linie)* bus service; **b)** *(Anschluß)* bus connection; *(für Reisebusse auch)* coach connection; **~verkehr der** bus service; *(von Fernreisebussen auch)* coach service

Butan [bu'ta:n] **das; ~s, ~e** *(Chemie)* butane

Butan·gas das butane gas

Butt [bʊt] **der; ~[e]s, ~e** flounder; butt

Bütt [bʏt] **die; ~, ~en** speaker's platform; [carnival] soap-box; **in der ~ stehen** stand on the platform *or* soap-box; **in die ~ steigen** take the platform; get up on the soap-box

Butte die; ~, ~n a) *(südd., österr., schweiz.) s.* **Bütte; b)** *(Winzerspr.)* dosser; pannier

Bütte die; ~, ~n a) tub; **b)** *(Papierherstellung)* vat

Büttel ['bʏtl̩] **der; ~s, ~ a)** *(abwertend)* lackey; **b)** *(veralt.: Häscher)* bailiff; **c)** *(geh. abwertend: Polizist)* minion of the law

Bütten das; ~s *s.* **~papier**

Bütten-: ~papier das handmade paper *(with deckle-edge)*; **~rand der** deckle-edge; **~rede die** carnival speech; **~redner der** carnival speaker

Butter ['bʊtɐ] **die; ~:** butter; **gute ~** *(veralt.)* butter; **[es ist] alles in ~** *(ugs.)* everything's fine; **sie läßt sich** *(Dat.)* **nicht die ~ vom Brot nehmen** *(ugs.)* she doesn't let anyone put one over on her; **jmdm. die ~ aufs od. auf dem Brot nicht gönnen** *(ugs.)* begrudge sb. everything

Butter-: ~bemme die *(ostmd.) s.* **~brot; ~berg der;** *o. Pl.* *(ugs.)* butter mountain; **~blume die** *(Löwenzahn)* dandelion; *(Sumpfdotterblume)* marsh marigold; *(Hahnenfuß)* buttercup; **~brot das** piece *or* slice of bread and butter; *(zugeklappt)* sandwich; **ein ~brot mit Schinken** a slice of bread and butter with ham on it/a ham sandwich; **für ein ~brot** *(ugs.)* for next to nothing; ⟨*buy, sell*⟩ for a song; **mußt du mir ständig aufs ~brot streichen od. schmieren, daß ...?** *(ugs.)* do you have to keep rubbing it in that ...?; **~brot·papier das** greaseproof paper; **~creme die** butter-cream; **~creme·torte die** butter-cream cake; **~dose die** butter-dish; **~fahrt die** *(ugs.)* sea trip to buy duty-free goods; **~faß das** [butter-]churn; **~fett das** butter-fat; **~flöckchen das** flake of butter

Butterfly ['bʌtəflai] **der; ~s a)** *(Schwimmen)* butterfly [stroke]; **b)** *(Eiskunstlauf)* split jump

butter·gelb *Adj.* butter yellow

butterig *Adj.* buttery

Butter-: ~käse der rich creamy cheese; **~keks der** butter biscuit; **~krem die** *(ugs. auch:)* **der** *s.* **~creme; ~messer das** butter-knife; **~milch die** buttermilk

buttern 1. *itr. V.* make butter. **2.** *tr. V.* **a)** butter; grease ⟨*baking tray*⟩ with butter; **b)** *(ugs.: aufwenden)* put **(in** + *Akk.* into)

butter-, Butter-: ~pilz der boletus lutens; **~säure die** *(Chemie)* butyric acid; **~schmalz das** clarified butter; **~stulle die** *(nordd., bes. berlin.) s.* **~brot; ~teig der** short pastry [made with butter]; **~weich 1.** *Adj.* **a)** beautifully soft; **eine ~weiche Landung** *(fig.)* a [really] soft landing; **b)** *(ohne Festigkeit)* vague ⟨*agreement, promise*⟩; **wenn man ihm schmeichelt, wird er ~weich** if you flatter him, he's like putty in your hands; **c)** *(Sportjargon)* gentle ⟨*shot, pass*⟩;

2. *adv.* **a)** gently; **die Maschine landete ~weich** the machine landed gently; **b)** *(Sportjargon)* gently

Buttje ['bʊtjə], **Buttjer** ['bʊtjɐ] **der;** ~s, ~s *(nordd.)* kid *(coll.)*

Büttner ['bʏtnɐ] **der;** ~s, ~ *s.* **Böttcher**

Button [bʌtn] **der;** ~s, ~s badge

buttrig *s.* **butterig**

Butze·mann der; *Pl.* **~männer** *(fam.)* bogyman

bützen ['bʏtsn̩] *tr., itr. V. (rhein.)* kiss

Butzen·scheibe die bull's-eye pane

Büx [bʏks] **die;** ~, ~en, **Buxe** ['bʊksə] **die;** ~, ~n *(nordd.)* trousers *pl.;* pants *pl. (Amer.);* **zwei Büxen** *od.* **Buxen** two pairs of trousers *or (Amer.)* pants

Buxtehude [bʊkstə'hu:də] *in* **in/aus/nach ~** *(fig. ugs.)* at/from/to the back of beyond

BV die; ~ *Abk. (schweiz.)* **Bundesversammlung**

BVG das; ~s *Abk.* **a) Bundesverwaltungsgericht; b) Bundesverfassungsgericht; c) Betriebsverfassungsgesetz**

b.w. *Abk.* **bitte wenden** p.t.o.

Bypass ['baipɑs] **der;** ~es, **Bypässe** *(Med.)* bypass

Byte [bait] **das;** ~[s], ~[s] *(DV)* byte

Byzantiner [bʏtsan'ti:nɐ] **der;** ~s, ~ Byzantine

byzantinisch *Adj.* Byzantine; **das Byzantinische Reich** the Byzantine Empire

Byzantinismus der; ~ *(geh. abwertend)* obsequiousness; sycophancy

Byzantinistik die; ~: Byzantine studies *pl., no art.*

Byzanz [bʏ'tsants] **(das); Byzanz'** Byzantium

bzgl. *Abk.* **bezüglich**

bzw. *Abk.* **beziehungsweise**

C

c, C [tse:] **das;** ~, ~: **a)** *(Buchstabe)* c/C; **b)** *(Musik)* [key of] C; *s. auch* **a, A**

C *Abk.* **Celsius** C

ca. *Abk.* **cirka** c.

Cabaret [kaba're:] *s.* **Kabarett**

Cabrio *s.* **Kabrio**

Cabriolet [kabrio'le:] *s.* **Kabriolett**

cachieren *s.* **kaschieren**

Café [ka'fe:] **das;** ~s, ~s café; **ins ~ gehen** go to a/the café

Cafeteria [kafetə'ri:a] **die;** ~, ~s cafeteria

cal *Abk.* **[Gramm]kalorie** cal.

Calcium *s.* **Kalzium**

Callgirl ['kɔ:lgə:l] **das;** ~s, ~s call-girl

Callgirl·ring der call-girl ring

Calvados [kalva'do:s] **der;** ~, ~ calvados

calvinistisch *s.* **kalvinistisch**

Calypso [ka'lɪpso] **der;** ~[s], ~s calypso

Camembert ['kamәmbe:ɐ] **der;** ~s, ~s Camembert

Camion [ka'mjõ] **der;** ~s, ~s *(schweiz.)* lorry *(Brit.);* truck *(Amer.)*

Camouflage [kamu'fla:ʒə] **die;** ~, ~n *(bes. Milit.; veralt.)* camouflage

camouflieren *tr. V. (veralt.)* camouflage

Camp [kɛmp] **das;** ~s, ~s camp

campen ['kɛmpn̩] *itr. V.* camp

Camper der; ~s, ~, **Camperin die;** ~, ~nen camper

Camping ['kɛmpɪŋ] **das;** ~s camping; **zum ~ [nach X] fahren** go camping [in X]

Camping-: ~aus·rüstung die camping equipment; **~beutel der** duffle-bag; **~bus der** motor caravan; camper; **~führer der** camping guide[book]; **~platz der** campsite; campground *(Amer.);* **~stuhl der** [folding] camp-chair; **~tisch der** [folding] camp-table

Campus ['kampʊs] **der;** ~ *(Hochschulw.)* campus

Canaille *s.* **Kanaille**

Canasta [ka'nasta] **das;** ~s canasta

Cancan [kã'kã:] **der;** ~s, ~s cancan

Candela [kan'de:la] **die;** ~, ~ *(Physik)* candela

Cannabis ['kanabɪs] **der;** ~: cannabis

Cannelloni [kanɛ'lo:ni] *Pl.* cannelloni

Cañon ['kanjɔn] **der;** ~s, ~s canyon

Canossa *s.* **Kanossa**

Canto ['kanto] **der;** ~s, ~s *(Literaturw.)* canto

Cantus ['kantʊs] **der;** ~, ~ *(Musik)* cantus; principal *or* melody voice

Cape [ke:p] **das;** ~s, ~s cape

Cappuccino [kapʊ'tʃi:no] **der;** ~[s], ~[s] cappuccino

Capriccio [ka'prɪtʃo] **das;** ~s, ~s *(Musik)* capriccio

Car [ka:ɐ] **der;** ~s, ~s *(schweiz.)* coach

Caravan ['ka(:)ravan] **der;** ~s, ~s **a)** *(Kombi)* estate car; station wagon *(Amer.);* **b)** *(Wohnwagen)* caravan; trailer *(Amer.)*

Carbid *s.* **Karbid**

Caritas ['ka:ritas] **die;** ~ Caritas *(Catholic welfare organization);* **ich bin doch nicht von der ~!** *(ugs.)* I'm not a charitable institution!

Carnet [de passages] [kar'nɛ (də pa'sa:ʒə)] **das;** ~ [~], ~s [~] [kar'nɛ (~)] *(Verkehrsw.)* carnet

cartesianisch [karte'zi̯a:nɪʃ] *Adj.* Cartesian

Cartoon [kar'tu:n] **der** *od.* **das;** ~[s], ~s cartoon

Casanova [kaza'no:va] **der;** ~[s], ~s Casanova

Cäsar ['tsɛ:zar] **(der)** Caesar

Cäsaren- [tsɛ'za:rən-]: **~herrschaft die** dictatorship; **~wahn·sinn der** [dictatorial] megalomania

Cäsarismus [tsɛza'rɪsmʊs] **der;** ~ Caesarism; absolutism

Cäsaropapismus [tsɛzaropa'pɪsmʊs] **der;** ~: Caesaropapism *no art.*

Cashew·nuß ['kɛʃu-] **die** cashew-nut

Cash-flow [kæʃ'floʊ] **der;** ~s *(Wirtsch.)* [gross] cash flow

Casino *s.* **Kasino**

Cassata [ka'sa:ta] **die** *od.* **das;** ~, ~s cassata

Cassette *s.* **Kassette**

Catch-as-catch-can ['kætʃəz'kætʃ'kæn] **das;** ~: catch-as-catch-can; all-in wrestling

catchen ['kɛtʃn] *itr. V.* do all-in wrestling; **das Catchen** all-in wrestling

Catcher ['kɛtʃɐ] **der;** ~s, ~: all-in wrestler

Cayenne·pfeffer [ka'jɛn-] **der** cayenne [pepper]

CB-Funk [tse:'be:-] **der;** ~s *(Nachrichtent.)* CB radio

cbm *Abk. (veralt.)* **Kubikmeter** m^3

ccm *Abk. (veralt.)* **Kubikzentimeter** c.c.

CD-Platte [tse:'de:-] **die** compact disc

CD-Spieler [tse:'de:-] **der** compact-disc player

CDU [tse:de:'|u:] **die;** ~ *Abk.* **Christlich-Demokratische Union [Deutschlands]** [German] Christian Democratic Party

C-Dur ['tse:-] **das;** ~: C major; *s. auch* **A-Dur**

C-Dur-Dreiklang der C major triad

Cedille [se'di:j(ə)] **die;** ~, ~n *(Sprachw.)* cedilla

Cellist [tʃɛ'lɪst] **der;** ~en, ~en, **Cellistin die;** ~, ~nen cellist; *s. auch* **-in**

Cello ['tʃɛlo] **das;** ~s, ~s *od.* **Celli** cello

Cello·konzert das cello concerto

Cellophan Ⓦ **das;** ~s, **Cellophane** Ⓦ [tsɛlo'fa:n(ə)] **die;** ~ Cellophane **(P)**

Celsius ['tsɛlzi̯ʊs] *o. Art.* centigrade; Celsius *(Phys.)*

Celsius·skala die Celsius *or* centigrade scale

Cembalo ['tʃɛmbalo] **das;** ~s, ~s *od.* **Cembali** harpsichord

Cent [tsɛnt] **der;** ~[s], ~[s] cent

Center ['sɛntɐ] **das;** ~s, ~ **a)** *(Großmarkt)* centre; **b)** *(Einkaufszentrum)* shopping centre *or (Amer.)* mall

Centime [sã'ti:m] **der;** ~[s], ~s centime

Cercle ['sɛrkl] **der;** ~s, ~s **a) ~ halten** *(veralt.)* hold court; **b)** *(österr.: im Theater)* front stalls *pl.*

Cervelat ['sɛrvəla] **der;** ~s, ~s *(schweiz.)* cervelat [sausage]

ces, Ces [tsɛs] **das;** ~ *(Musik)* C flat

Ces-Dur das; ~[s] C flat major; *s. auch* **A-Dur**

Ćevapčići [tʃe'vaptʃɪtʃi] *Pl.: Serbian spiced and grilled mince fingers*

Ceylon ['tsailɔn] **(das);** ~s *(hist.)* Ceylon *(Hist.)*

Ceylonese der; ~n, ~n, **Ceylonesin die;** ~, ~nen *(hist.)* Ceylonese

cf. *Abk.* **conferatur** cf.

C-Flöte ['tse:-] **die** soprano recorder

Cha-Cha-Cha ['tʃa 'tʃa 'tʃa] **der;** ~[s], ~s cha-cha-cha

Chaise ['ʃɛ:zə] **die;** ~, ~n **a)** *(veralt.: Kutsche)* [closed] chaise; **b)** *(ugs. abwertend: Auto)* jalopy; banger *(Brit. sl.)*

Chaise-longue [ʃɛzə'lõ:k] **die;** ~, ~n *od.* ~s chaise longue

Chalet [ʃa'le:] **das;** ~s, ~s **a)** Alpine [cowherd's] hut; **b)** *(Landhaus)* [Swiss] chalet

Chamäleon [ka'mɛ:leɔn] **das;** ~s, ~s *(auch fig.)* chameleon

Chamois [ʃa'mo̯a] **das;** ~ **a)** *(Farbe)* chamois; parchment [colour]; **b)** *s.* **~leder**

Chamois·leder das chamois[-leather]

Champagner [ʃam'panjɐ] **der;** ~s, ~ champagne *(from Champagne)*

champagner·farben *Adj.* champagne-coloured

Champignon ['ʃampɪnjɔn] **der;** ~s, ~s mushroom

Champion ['tʃɛmpi̯ən] **der;** ~s, ~s *(Sport)* champion; *(Mannschaft)* champions *pl.*

Chance ['ʃã:sə] **die;** ~, ~n **a)** *(Gelegenheit)* chance; **eine ~/keine ~/mehr ~n haben, etw. zu tun** have a chance/no chance/more chance of doing sth.; **die ~n [zu gewinnen] stehen eins zu hundert** the chances [of winning] are one in a hundred; *(bes. beim Wetten)* the odds [against winning] are 100:1 *or* a hundred to one; **ich gebe dir eine letzte ~:** I'll give you one last chance; **eine/keine ~ sehen, zu ...:** see a/no chance *or* hope of ...; **sie rechnen sich** *(Dat.)* **eine ~ aus, 2 Punkte zu machen** they reckon they have a chance of scoring 2 points; **~n/eine ~ vergeben** *(Sport)* give away chances/a chance; **b)** *Pl. (Aussichten)* prospects; **seine ~n stehen gut/schlecht** his prospects are good/poor; **[bei jmdm] ~n haben** stand a chance [with sb.]

Chancen·gleichheit die; *o. Pl. (Päd., Soziol.)* equality of opportunity *no art.*

changieren [ʃã'ʒi:rən] *itr. V.* shimmer *(in different colours);* iridesce; **~d** iridescent; **~de Seide** shot silk

Chanson [ʃã'sõ:] **das;** ~s, ~s chanson; cabaret-style song

Chansonette, Chansonnette [ʃãsɔ'nɛtə] **die;** ~, ~n chanteuse; *(im Kabarett)* cabaret singer

Chansonnier [ʃãsɔ'ni̯e:] **der; ~s, ~s** singer/composer of chansons; chansonnier
Chaos ['ka:ɔs] **das;** ~ chaos *no art.*; **in der Wohnung herrschte ein einziges ~:** the flat *(Brit.)* or *(Amer.)* apartment was in total chaos
Chaot [ka'o:t] **der; ~en, ~en a)** *(Politik)* anarchist *(trying to undermine society)*; *(bei Demonstrationen)* violent demonstrator; **b)** *(salopp: unordentlicher Mensch)* **ein [furchtbarer] ~ sein** be [terribly] disorganized
chaotisch 1. *Adj.* chaotic. **2.** *adv.* chaotically; **es geht ~ zu** there is chaos
Chapeau claque [ʃapo'klak] **der; ~ ~, ~x ~s** [ʃapo'klak] opera-hat
Charade *s.* **Scharade**
Charakter [ka'raktɐ] **der; ~s, ~e** [...'te:rə] **a)** character; personality; **etw. prägt** *od.* **formt den ~:** sth. moulds one's character *or* is character-forming; **die seinen ~ prägenden** *od.* **formenden Jahre** his formative years; **Geld verdirbt den ~:** money spoils people; **sie hat einen schwierigen/ist ein schwieriger ~:** she has/is a complex personality; **gegensätzliche ~e haben/sein** have entirely different personalities/be quite different in personality *or* character; **er ist ein mieser ~** *(ugs.)* he's a lousy so-and-so *(sl.)*; **b)** *o. Pl.* *(~stärke)* [strength of] character; **keinen ~ haben** lack [strength of] character; be spineless; **c)** *o. Pl.* *(Eigenart)* character; **die Mitteilung hat vertraulichen ~:** the communication is of a confidential nature
charakter-, Charakter-: ~an·lage die; *meist Pl.* trait; **gute/schlechte ~anlagen haben** have good/bad qualities *or* a good/bad disposition; **~bild das** profile; **~bildend** *Adj.* character-forming; **~bildung die;** *o. Pl.* formation of character; **jmds. ~bildung** the formation of sb.'s character; **~darsteller der** actor of complex parts; **~darstellerin die** actress of complex parts; **~eigenschaft die** characteristic; trait; **~fehler der** fault [of character]; **~fest** *Adj.* steadfast; **~festigkeit die** firmness *or* strength of character
charakterisieren *tr. V.* characterize
Charakterisierung die; ~, ~en characterization; *(Schilderung)* portrayal
Charakteristik die; ~, ~en characterization
Charakteristikum das; ~s, Charakteristika *(geh.)* characteristic (+ *Gen. od.* **für** of)
charakteristisch 1. *Adj.* characteristic, typical **(für** of). **2.** *adv.* characteristically; in a typical manner
charakteristischerweise *Adv.* characteristically [for him/her]
Charakter·kopf der striking head; **ein ~ sein** have a magnificent *or* striking head
charakterlich 1. *Adj.* character *attrib.* ⟨*defect, development, training*⟩; personal ⟨*qualities*⟩; **~e Veränderungen** personality changes. **2.** *adv.* in [respect of] character; **jmdn. ~ formen** mould sb.'s character; *(schulen)* give sb. character-training
charakter·los 1. *Adj.* unprincipled; characterless, colourless ⟨*style, playing, townscape*⟩; *(niederträchtig)* despicable; *(labil)* spineless. **2.** *adv.* in an unprincipled fashion; *(ohne Ausdruck)* colourlessly; drearily; *(niederträchtig)* despicably; *(labil)* spinelessly
Charakterlosigkeit die; ~, ~en a) *o. Pl.* lack of principle; *(Niederträchtigkeit)* despicableness; *(Labilität)* weakness of character; spinelessness; **b)** *(Handlung)* unprincipled/despicable action; *(Äußerung)* unprincipled/despicable remark
Charakterologie [karakterolo'gi:] **die; ~:** characterology *no art.*
charakter-, Charakter-: ~rolle die *(Theater)* complex part *or* character; **~schwach** *Adj.* of weak character *postpos.*; spineless; **~schwäche die** weakness of character; spinelessness *no pl.*; **~schwein das** *(ugs. abwertend)* unprincipled bastard *(coll.)*; **~stärke die;** *o. Pl.* strength of character; *(Entschlossenheit)* strength of mind; **~studie die** character study; **~voll** *Adj.* **a)** *(~fest)* steadfast; showing strength of character *postpos., not pred.*; **b)** *(ausdrucksvoll)* distinctive; ⟨*house etc.*⟩ of character; strongly characterized, individual ⟨*features*⟩; **~zug der** characteristic
Charge ['ʃarʒə] **die; ~, ~n a)** *(bes. Milit.: Dienstgrad, Person)* rank; **die unteren ~n** the lower ranks *(Mil.)*/orders; **die oberen ~n** the upper ranks *(Mil.)*/echelons; **b)** *(Theater: Nebenrolle)* small character part
Charisma ['ça:rısma] **das; ~s, Charismen** charisma
charismatisch [çarıs'ma:tıʃ] *Adj.* charismatic
Charleston ['tʃarlstn̩] **der; ~, ~s** Charleston
charmant [ʃar'mant] **1.** *Adj.* charming; **sich von seiner ~esten Seite zeigen** show one's most attractive side. **2.** *adv.* charmingly; with much charm
Charme [ʃarm] **der; ~s** charm; **seinen ganzen ~ spielen lassen** *od.* **aufbieten** turn on all one's charm
Charmeur [ʃar'mø:ɐ̯] **der; ~s, ~s** *od.* **~e** charmer
Charmeuse [ʃar'mø:z] **die; ~** *(Textilw.)* charmeuse
Charta ['karta] **die; ~, ~s** *(Politik)* charter
Charter ['tʃartɐ] **der; ~s, ~s** charter agreement
Charter-: ~flug der charter flight; **~maschine die** chartered aircraft
chartern *tr. V.* charter ⟨*aircraft, boat*⟩; hire [the services of] ⟨*guide, firm*⟩
Charts [tʃarts] *Pl.* charts
chassidisch [xa'si:dıʃ] *Adj.* *(jüd. Rel.)* Hasidic
Chassidismus der; ~ *(jüd. Rel.)* Hasidism *no art.*
Chassis [ʃa'si:] **das; ~** [ʃa'si:(s)], **~** [ʃa'si:s] *(Kfz-W., Elektrot.)* chassis
Chateaubriand [ʃatobri'ã:] **das; ~[s], ~s** *(Kochk.)* Chateaubriand [steak]
Chauffeur [ʃɔ'fø:ɐ̯] **der; ~s, ~e** driver; *(privat angestellt)* chauffeur
chauffieren *(veralt.)* *tr., itr. V.* drive
Chaussee [ʃo'se:] **die; ~, ~n** *(veralt.)* *(surfaced)* [high] road; highway *(Amer.)*
Chauvi ['ʃo:vi] **der; ~s, ~s** *(ugs. abwertend)* male chauvinist *(coll. derog.)*
Chauvinismus [ʃovi'nısmʊs] **der; ~:** chauvinism; **männlicher ~:** male chauvinism
Chauvinist der; ~en, ~en *(abwertend)* chauvinist; *(männlicher ~)* male chauvinist
Chauvinistin die; ~, ~nen chauvinist
chauvinistisch *(abwertend)* **1.** *Adj.* chauvinistic; *(männlich-~)* male chauvinist. **2.** *adv.* chauvinistically; *(männlich-~)* in a male chauvinist way
Check *(schweiz.)* *s.* **Scheck**
checken ['tʃɛkn̩] *tr. V.* **a)** *(bes. Technik: kontrollieren)* check; examine; **sich [vom Arzt] ~ lassen** *(ugs.)* have a check-up [from the doctor]; **b)** *(salopp: begreifen)* twig *(coll.)*; *(bemerken)* spot; **ich habe das noch nicht gecheckt** I haven't got it yet; **c)** *(Eishockey: stoppen)* check ⟨*player*⟩
Check·liste die check-list; *(Passagierliste)* passenger list
Chef [ʃɛf] **der; ~s, ~s a)** *(Leiter)* *(einer Firma, Abteilung, Regierung)* head; *(der Polizei, des Generalstabs)* chief; *(einer Partei, Bande)* leader; *(Vorgesetzter)* superior; boss *(coll.)*; **wer ist denn hier der ~?** who's in charge here?; **b)** *(salopp: Anrede)* **hallo, ~:** hey, chief *or* squire *(Brit. coll.)*; hey mister *(Amer. coll.)*
Chef- *in Zus.* chief
Chef-: ~arzt der *head of one or more specialist departments in a hospital*; *(Direktor)* superintendent *(of small hospital)*; **~dramaturg der** *(Theater)* [chief] literary adviser; **~etage die** management floor; **Unruhe in den ~etagen auslösen** cause a flutter in the boardrooms; **~ideologe der** leading ideologist
Chefin die; ~, ~nen a) *(Leiterin)* *(einer Firma, Abteilung, Regierung)* head; *(einer Partei, Bande)* leader; *(Vorgesetzte)* superior; boss *(coll.)*; **b)** *(ugs.: Frau des Chefs)* boss's wife *(coll.)*; **c)** *(salopp: Anrede)* missis *(sl.)*; ma'am *(Amer.)*
Chef-: ~koch der chef; head cook; **~redakteur der** chief editor; *(Verlagsw. auch)* managing editor; **~sekretärin die** director's secretary; **~visite die** senior consultant's round *(in the wards)*
Chemie [çe'mi:] **die; ~ a)** *(Wissenschaft)* chemistry *no art.*; **b)** *(ugs.: Chemikalien)* chemicals *pl.*; **der Pudding ist reine ~:** the pudding is nothing but chemicals *or* is purely synthetic
Chemie-: ~arbeiter der chemical worker; **~betrieb der** chemical firm; **~faser die** synthetic *or* man-made fibre; **~ingenieur der** chemical engineer; **~laborant der, ~laborantin die** chemical laboratory assistant; **~werker der** *(ugs.)* chemical worker
Chemikalie [çemi'ka:li̯ə] **die; ~, ~n** chemical
Chemiker ['çe:mikɐ] **der; ~s, ~, Chemikerin die; ~, ~nen** *(graduate)* chemist; *s. auch* **-in**
Cheminée ['ʃmıne] **das; ~s, ~s** *(schweiz.)* open fireplace
chemisch 1. *Adj.* chemical; **~er Versuch** chemistry experiment; **eine/die ~e Reinigung** a/the dry cleaner's; *(Vorgang)* dry cleaning; **die ~e Keule** Chemical Mace **(P).** **2.** *adv.* chemically; **~ bleichen** bleach with chemicals
chemisieren *tr. V.* *(DDR)* chemicalize; make increased use of chemicals in ⟨*agriculture*⟩
chemo-, Chemo-: ~techniker der industrial chemist; *(Chemieingenieur)* chemical engineer; **~therapeutisch** *Adj.* *(Med.)* chemotherapeutic; **~therapie die** *(Med.)* chemotherapy; **mit einer ~therapie beginnen** start a course of chemotherapy
Chenille [ʃə'nıljə] **die; ~, ~n** chenille
Cherry Brandy ['tʃɛri 'brɛndi] **der; ~ ~s, ~ ~s** cherry brandy
Cherub ['çe:rʊp] **der; ~s, Cherubim** ['çe:rubi:m] *od.* **Cherubinen** [çe:ru'bi:nən] *(Rel.)* cherub
cherubinisch *Adj.* cherubic
Chester·käse ['tʃɛstɐ-] **der** *(usu. processed)* Cheddar cheese
chevaleresk [ʃəvalə'rɛsk] *(geh.)* **1.** *Adj.* chivalrous; gentlemanly. **2.** *adv.* chivalrously
Chevreau·leder [ʃə'vro:-] **das** kid
Chianti ['ki̯anti] **der; ~[s]** Chianti
Chiasmus ['çi̯asmʊs] **der; ~** *(Rhet.)* chiasmus *no art.*
chic *usw. s.* **schick** *usw.*
Chicorée ['ʃikore] **der; ~s** *od.* **die; ~:** chicory
Chiffon ['ʃıfõ] **der; ~s, ~s** chiffon
Chiffre ['ʃıfrə] **die; ~, ~n a)** *(Zeichen)* symbol; **b)** *(Geheimzeichen)* cipher; **~n** cipher *sing.*; **in ~n** *(Dat.)* **schreiben** write in code; **c)** *(in Annoncen)* box number; **Zuschriften unter ~ ...:** reply quoting box no. ...; **d)** *(Rhet.)* cipher
Chiffre·schrift die code
chiffrieren *tr. V.* [en]code; **chiffriert** coded; in [a secret] code *postpos.*
Chignon [ʃın'jõ:] **der; ~s, ~s** chignon
Chihuahua [tʃi'u̯au̯a] **der; ~s, ~s** chihuahua
Chile ['tʃi:le, 'çi:lə] **(das); ~s** Chile

Chilene [tʃi'le:nə, çi'le:nə] **der; ~n, ~n, Chilenin die; ~, ~nen** Chilean; *s. auch* **-in**
chilenisch *Adj.* Chilean
Chile·salpeter der Chile salpeter *or* nitre
Chili ['tʃi:li] **der; ~s, ~es a)** *Pl. (Schoten)* chillies; **b)** *o. Pl. (Gewürz)* chilli [powder]; **c)** *s.* **Chilisoße**
Chiliasmus [çi'liasmʊs] **der;** ~ *(christl. Rel.)* chiliasm *no art.*
Chili·soße die chilli sauce
Chimäre [çi:mɛ:rə] **die; ~, ~n a)** *s.* **Schimäre; b)** *(Biol.)* chimera
China ['çi:na] **(das); ~s** China
China-: ~kracher der Chinese cracker; **~kohl der** Chinese cabbage; *(im Handel)* Chinese leaves *pl.*; **~papier das** rice paper
¹Chinchilla [tʃɪn'tʃɪla] **das; ~s, ~s a)** *(Pelz)* chinchilla; **b)** *(Kaninchen)* chinchilla [rabbit]
²Chinchilla die; ~, ~s *(Zool.)* chinchilla
Chinese [çi'ne:zə] **der; ~n, ~n** Chinese; **zum ~n essen gehen** *(ugs.)* eat Chinese *(coll.)*
Chinesin die; ~, ~nen Chinese; *s. auch* **-in**
chinesisch 1. *Adj.* Chinese; **~er Tee** China tea; **die Chinesische Mauer** the Great Wall of China. **2.** *adv.* in the Chinese manner *or* style; **~ essen** have a Chinese meal; eat Chinese *(coll.)*
-chinesisch das; ~[s] ... jargon
Chinin [çi'ni:n] **das; ~s** quinine
chinin·haltig *Adj.* containing quinine *postpos., not pred.*; **~ sein** contain quinine
Chintz [tʃɪnts] **der; ~** chintz
Chip [tʃɪp] **der; ~s, ~s a)** *(Spielmarke)* chip; **b)** *(Kartoffel~)* [potato] crisp *(Brit.) or (Amer.)* chip; **c)** *(Elektronik)* [micro]chip
Chippendale ['tʃɪpəndeɪl] **das; ~[s]** Chippendale
Chiromant [çiro'mant] **der; ~en, ~en** palmist
Chiromantie die; ~ chiromancy *no art.*; palmistry *no art.*
Chiropraktik die; ~ *(Med.)* chiropractic *no art.*
Chiropraktiker der; ~s, ~ *(Med.)* chiropractor
Chirurg [çi'rʊrk] **der; ~en, ~en** surgeon
Chirurgie [çirʊr'gi] **die; ~, ~n a)** *o. Pl. (Disziplin)* surgery *no art.*; **b)** *(Abteilung)* surgical department; *(Station)* surgical ward; **auf der ~ liegen** be in the surgical ward
Chirurgin die; ~, ~nen surgeon; *s. auch* **-in**
chirurgisch 1. *Adj., nicht präd.* surgical. **2.** *adv. (operativ)* surgically; by surgery
Chitin [çi'ti:n] **das; ~s** chitin
Chitin·panzer der *(Zool.)* chitinous exoskeleton
Chlor [klo:ɐ̯] **das; ~s** chlorine
Chloral [klo'ra:l] **das; ~s** *(Chemie)* chloral
Chlorat [klo'ra:t] **das; ~s, ~e** *(Chemie)* chlorate
chloren *tr. V.* chlorinate
chlor·haltig *Adj.* containing chlorine *postpos., not pred.*; **~/stark ~ sein** contain chlorine/have a high chlorine content
Chlorid [klo'ri:t] **das; ~s, ~e** *(Chemie)* chloride
chlorieren *tr. V. (Chemie)* chlorinate
chlorig *Adj.* **~e Säure** *(Chemie)* chlorous acid
Chloroform [kloro'fɔrm] **das; ~s** chloroform
chloroformieren *tr. V.* chloroform
Chlorophyll [kloro'fʏl] **das; ~s** *(Bot.)* chlorophyll
Chlor-: ~säure die *(Chemie)* chloric acid; **~wasser das a)** *(ugs.: gechlortes Wasser)* chlorinated water; **b)** *(Chemie)* chlorine water; **~wasser·stoff der** *(Chemie)* hydrogen chloride
Choke [tʃoʊk] **der; ~s, ~s, Choker** [tʃoʊkɐ] **der; ~s, ~** *(Kfz-W.)* [manual] choke
Cholera ['ko:lera] **die; ~** *(Med.)* cholera
Choleriker [ko'le:rikɐ] **der; ~s, ~ a)** choleric type *or (Psych.)* subject; **ein klassischer ~**: a textbook example of the choleric temperament; **b)** *(ugs.: jähzorniger Mensch)* irascible person; **ein ~ sein** have a short fuse
cholerisch 1. *Adj.* irascible; choleric ‹*temperament*›. **2.** *adv.* irascibly
Cholesterin [çolɛste'ri:n] **das; ~s** *(Med.)* cholesterol
Cholesterin·spiegel der *(Physiol.)* cholesterol level
¹Chor [ko:ɐ̯] **der; ~[e]s, Chöre** ['kø:rə] **a)** choir; *(in Oper, Sinfonie)* chorus; **im ~ rufen/brüllen** shout/roar in chorus; **b)** *(Komposition; im Theater)* chorus
²Chor der *od. (selten:)* **das; ~[e]s, ~e** *od.* **Chöre a)** *(Altarraum)* choir; **b)** *(Empore)* choir loft; *(mit der Orgel)* organ loft
Choral [ko'ra:l] **der; ~s, Choräle** [ko'rɛ:lə] **a)** *(Kirchenlied)* chorale; **b)** *(Gregorianischer ~)* [Gregorian] chant
Choral-: ~bearbeitung die *(Musik)* arrangement of a chorale; **~vor·spiel das** *(Musik)* chorale prelude
Choreograph [koreo'gra:f] **der; ~en, ~en** choreographer
Choreographie die; ~, ~n choreography
choreographieren *tr., itr. V.* choreograph
Choreographin die; ~, ~nen choreographer; *s. auch* **-in**
choreographisch *Adj.* choreographic
Chor-: ~frau die *(kath. Rel.)* canoness; **~führer der** *(Theater)* leader of the chorus; **~gebet das** *(kath. Rel.)* canonical hour *(as part of divine office)*; **~gestühl das** choir-stalls *pl.*; **~herr der** *(kath. Rel.)* canon [regular]
Chorist der; ~en, ~en *s.* **Chorsänger**
Choristin die; ~, ~nen *s.* **Chorsängerin**
Chor-: ~knabe der choirboy; chorister; **~konzert das** choral concert; **~leiter der** chorus-master; *(des Kirchenchors)* choirmaster; **~musik die** choral music; **~rock der** surplice; **~sänger der, ~sängerin die** member of the chorus
Chorus ['ko:rʊs] **der; ~, ~se** *(Jazz)* theme
Chose ['ʃo:zə] **die; ~, ~n** *(ugs.)* **a)** *(Angelegenheit)* business *(derog.)*; **b)** *(Gegenstände)* stuff; **die ganze ~**: the whole lot *(coll.) or (sl.)* shoot *or (sl.)* caboodle
Chow-Chow [tʃau 'tʃau] **der; ~s, ~s** chow
¹Christ [krɪst] **der; ~en, ~en** Christian
²Christ (der) *(Christus)* Christ
christ-, Christ-: ~baum der a) *(bes. südd.)* Christmas tree; **nicht alle auf dem ~baum haben** *(ugs.)* be dotty *(Brit. coll.)*; be not quite all there *(Brit. coll.)*; be missing some marbles *(sl.)*; **b)** *(milit. Jargon: Leuchtsignale)* target marker [flare]; **~baum-** *s.* **Weihnachtsbaum-**; **~demokrat der** *(Politik)* Christian Democrat; **~demokratisch** *(Politik)* **1.** *Adj.* Christian-Democrat; **2.** *adv.* in a Christian-Democrat manner *or* spirit; **~demokratisch regiert** governed by Christian Democrats
Christen-: ~gemeinde die Christian community; **~glaube[n] der** Christian faith
Christenheit die; ~ Christendom *no art.*; **die ganze ~**: the whole Christian community; all Christians *pl.*
Christen·lehre die; *o. Pl.* **a)** *(christl. Kirchen)* [Church] teaching of Christian doctrine; **b)** *(DDR Schulw.)* Christian religious instruction
Christentum das; ~s Christianity *no art.*; *(Glaube)* Christian faith; **sich zum ~ bekennen** profess the Christian faith; declare oneself a Christian
Christen·verfolgung die persecution of Christians
Christ·fest das *(veralt., noch südd., österr.) s.* **Weihnachtsfest**
christianisieren [krɪstiani'zi:rən] **1.** *tr. V.* Christianize; convert to Christianity. **2.** *itr. V.* make conversions to Christianity
Christianisierung die; ~ Christianization
Christin die; ~, ~nen Christian; *s. auch* **-in**
christ-, Christ-: ~katholisch *Adj. (schweiz.) s.* **altkatholisch; ~kind das;** *o. Pl.* **a)** *(Jesus)* infant Jesus; Christ-child; **b)** *(weihnachtliche Gestalt)* Christ-child *(as bringer of Christmas gifts)*; **er glaubt noch ans ~kind** *(fig. iron.)* he still believes in Father Christmas; **c)** *(bes. südd., österr.: Geschenk)* Christmas present; **~kindchen das** *s.* **~kind a, b; ~kindl das** *(südd., österr.) s.* **~kind a, b, c; ~königs·fest das** *(kath. Rel.)* feast of Christ the King
christlich 1. *Adj.* Christian; **die ~e Seefahrt** *(scherzh.)* seafaring; **wir stehen um halb neun auf – eine halbwegs ~e Zeit** *(ugs. scherzh.)* we get up at half-past eight – a more or less civilized time. **2.** *adv.* in a [truly] Christian spirit; **~ leben** live a Christian life; **Kinder ~ erziehen** give children a Christian upbringing; **~ geprägt** imbued with Christian principles
Christlichkeit die; ~: Christian spirit
Christ-: ~messe die *(kath. Rel.)* Christmas Mass; **~mette die** *(kath. Rel.)* Christmas Mass; *(ev. Rel.)* midnight service [on Christmas Eve]; **~nacht die** Christmas night
Christoph ['krɪstɔf] **(der)** Christopher
Christophorus [krɪs'to:forʊs] **(der): der heilige ~**: St Christopher
Christ-: ~rose die Christmas rose; **~stollen der** [German] Christmas loaf *(with candied fruit, almonds, etc.)*
Christus ['krɪstʊs] **(der); ~** *od.* **Christi** Christ; **1000 vor/nach Christi Geburt** 1000 BC/AD 1000
Christus-: ~dorn der *(Bot.)* crown of thorns; **~kopf der** *(Kunst)* head of Christ; **~monogramm das** Christogram; chi-rho
Christ·vesper die *(kath. u. ev. Rel.)* Christmas Eve vespers *(with music)*
Chrom [kro:m] **das; ~s** chromium
Chromatik [kro'ma:tɪk] **die; ~ a)** *(Musik)* chromaticism; **b)** *(Physik)* chromatics *pl.*
chromatisch *Adj.* chromatic
chrom-, Chrom-: ~blitzend *Adj.* gleaming with chrome *postpos.*; **~dioxyd·kassette die** chrome[-dioxide] cassette; **~gelb das** chrome yellow; **~leder das** chrome leather; **~nickel·stahl der** chrome-nickel steel
Chromosom [kromo'zo:m] **das; ~s, ~en** *(Biol.)* chromosome
Chromosomen·satz der *(Biol.)* chromosome set
Chromosphäre [kromo'sfɛ:rə] **die** *(Astron.)* chromosphere
Chrom·stahl der chrome steel
Chronik ['kro:nɪk] **die; ~, ~en** chronicle
chronisch 1. *Adj. (Med., auch ugs.)* chronic; **an ~em Geldmangel leiden** *(ugs.)* suffer from a chronic shortage of money. **2.** *adv. (Med., auch ugs.)* chronically
Chronist [kro'nɪst] **der; ~en, ~en** chronicler
Chronistik die; ~: historiography *no art.*
Chronologie die; ~: chronology; **die ~ der Ereignisse** *od.* **des Geschehens** the sequence of events; **[nach] unserer/jüdischer ~**: according to our/the Jewish calendar
chronologisch 1. *Adj.* chronological; **~er Fehler** mistake regarding the date. **2.** *adv.* chronologically; in chronological order
Chronometer [krono'me:tɐ] **das; ~s, ~**: chronometer
chronometrisch 1. *Adj.* chronometric. **2.** *adv.* chronometrically
Chrysantheme [krʏzan'te:mə] **die; ~, ~n** chrysanthemum
Chuzpe ['xʊtspə] **die; ~** *(salopp abwertend)* chutzpah; **die ~ haben, etw. zu tun** have the nerve to do sth. *(coll.)*
CIA ['si:aɪ'eɪ] **der** *od.* **die; ~**: CIA
Cicero die *od. (schweiz.)* **der; ~, ~** *(Druckw.)* pica; 12-point type

Cidre [si:dʀ] **der; ~s** [Normandy/Brittany] cider
Cimbal *s.* **Zimbal**
Cineast [sine'ast] **der; ~en, ~en a)** *(Filmschaffender)* film-maker; **b)** *(Kenner)* film expert; *(Filmfan)* film fan
circa *s.* **zirka**
Circe ['tsɪrtsə] **die; ~, ~n** Circe; enchantress
Circulus vitiosus ['tsɪrkulʊs vi'tsio:zʊs] **der; ~ ~, Circuli vitiosi** *(geh.)* vicious circle
Circus *s.* **Zirkus**
cis, Cis [tsɪs] **das; ~, ~** *(Musik)* C sharp
Cis-Dur das; ~[s] *(Musik)* C sharp major; *s. auch* **A-Dur**
cis-Moll das; ~[s] *(Musik)* C sharp minor; *s. auch* **a-Moll**
Citoyen [sitoa'jɛ̃:] **der; ~s, ~s** *(politically aware)* citizen
City ['sɪti] **die; ~, ~s** city centre
Clair-obscur [klɛrɔps'ky:ʀ] **das; ~[s]** *(Kunst)* chiaroscuro
Clan [kla:n] **der; ~s, ~e** *od.* **~s a)** *(salopp: Interessengemeinschaft)* clique; **b)** *(in Schottland; auch salopp: Familie)* clan
Claque ['klakə] **die; ~** claque; hired applauders *pl.*
Claqueur [kla'kø:ʀ] **der; ~s, ~e** claqueur; hired applauder
Clavicembalo [klavi'tʃɛmbalo] **das; ~s, ~s** *(Musik)* harpsichord
clean [kli:n] *indekl. Adj.; nicht attr. (ugs.)* clean *(coll.)*; **~ werden** come off drugs
Clearing ['kli:rɪŋ] **das; ~s, ~s** *(Wirtsch.)* clearing
clever ['klɛvɐ] **1.** *Adj. (raffiniert)* shrewd; *(intelligent, geschickt)* clever; smart. **2.** *adv.*: *s. Adj.*: shrewdly; cleverly; smartly
Cleverneß ['klɛvɐnɛs] **die; ~** *s.* **clever 1:** shrewdness; cleverness; smartness *(Amer.)*
Cliché *s.* **Klischee**
Clinch [klɪntʃ] **der; ~[e]s a)** *(Boxen)* clinch; **in den ~ gehen** go into a clinch; **b)** *(ugs.: Auseinandersetzung)* conflict; **mit jmdm. im ~ liegen** be locked in dispute with sb.; **[mit jmdm.] in den ~ gehen** start quarrelling *or* wrangling [with sb.]
clinchen *itr. V. (Boxen)* go into a clinch
Clip *s.* **Ohrklipp**
Clipper Ⓦⓩ ['klɪpɐ] **der; ~s, ~** *(veralt.)* [long-haul] airliner *(on overseas routes)*
Clique ['klɪkə] **die; ~, ~n a)** *(abwertend: Interessengemeinschaft)* clique; **b)** *(Freundeskreis)* set; lot *(coll.)*; *(größere Gruppe)* crowd *(coll.)*; *(Jugendliche)* gang *(coll.)*; **er gehört mit zur unserer ~:** he's one of our crowd *(coll.) or* lot *(coll.)*
Cliquen-: ~[un]wesen das; *o. Pl.*, **~wirtschaft die** *(ugs. abwertend)* clique system
Clivia ['kli:via] **die; ~, Clivien** *(Bot.)* clivia
Clochard [klɔ'ʃa:r] **der; ~[s], ~s** down-and-out; tramp
Clog [klɔk] **der; ~s, ~s** clog
Clou [klu:] **der; ~s, ~s** *(ugs.)* main point; *(Glanzpunkt)* highlight; **der besondere ~:** the really special thing [about it]; **das ist doch gerade der ~:** but that's the great thing about it
Clown [klaun] **der; ~s, ~s** clown; **sich zum ~ machen** make oneself look a fool *or* look ridiculous; **jmdn. zum ~ machen** make a clown of sb.; treat sb. as a clown
Clownerie [klaunə'ri:] **die; ~, ~n: ~[n]** clowning *no pl.*
Club *s.* **Klub**
Cluster ['klastɐ] **der; ~s, ~[s]** *(Kernphysik, Musik, Sprachw.)* cluster
cm *Abk.*: **Zentimeter** cm.
c-Moll [tse:-] **das; ~** C minor; *s. auch* **a-Moll**
Co. *Abk.*: **Compagnie** Co.
Coach [koutʃ] **der; ~[s], ~s** *(Sport)* coach; *(bes. Fußball: Trainer)* manager
coachen ['koutʃn] *tr., itr. V. (Sport)* coach; *(Trainer sein)* manage

Coca ['ko:ka] **das; ~[s], ~s** *od.* **die; ~, ~s** *(ugs.)* Coke **(P)**
Cockerspaniel ['kɔkɐ-] **der; ~s, ~s** cocker spaniel
Cockpit ['kɔkpɪt] **das; ~s, ~s** cockpit; *(bei großen Linienflugzeugen)* flight deck
Cocktail ['kɔkteɪl] **der; ~s, ~s a)** *(Getränk; auch Salat usw.)* cocktail; **b)** *(Party)* cocktail party; *(DDR: Empfang)* reception
Cocktail-: ~empfang der [cocktail] reception; **~kleid das** cocktail dress; **~party die** cocktail party; **~schürze die** hostess apron
Code *s.* **Kode**
Codein *s.* **Kodein**
Codex *s.* **Kodex**
Cœur [kø:ʀ] **das; ~[s], ~[s]** *(Kartenspiel)* hearts *pl.*; *(einzelne Karte)* heart; *s. auch* **²Pik**
cognac ['kɔnjak] *indekl. Adj.; nicht attr.* cognac[-coloured]
Cognac Ⓦⓩ **der; ~s, ~s** Cognac
cognac·farben *Adj.* cognac[-coloured]
Coiffeur [koa'fø:ʀ] **der; ~s, ~e, Coiffeuse** [koa'fø:zə] **die; ~, ~n** *(schweiz., sonst geh.: Friseur/Friseuse)* hairdresser; *(Schöpfer/Schöpferin von Haarmoden)* hair-stylist
Coiffure [koa'fy:ʀ] **die; ~, ~n a)** *o. Pl. (geh.: Frisierkunst)* hairdressing; *(Schöpfung von Haarmoden)* hair-styling; **b)** *(schweiz.: Frisiersalon)* hairdresser's [salon]
Cola ['ko:la] **das; ~[s], ~s** *od.* **die; ~, ~s** *(ugs.)* Coke **(P)**
Collage [kɔ'la:ʒə] **die; ~, ~n** collage; *(als Form/Technik)* **die ~:** collage
Collie ['kɔli] **der; ~s, ~s** collie
Colloquium *s.* **Kolloquium**
Colonia·kübel [ko'lo:nia-] **der** *(österr.)* dustbin; garbage *or* trash can *(Amer.)*
Color- ['ko'lɔ:ɐ-] *(Fot.)* **~film/~dia/~negativ** colour film/slide/negative
Colt Ⓦⓩ [kɔlt] **der; ~s, ~s** Colt **(P)** [revolver]
Combo ['kɔmbo] **die; ~, ~s** small (jazz *or* dance) band; combo *(sl.)*
Comeback [kam'bɛk] **das; ~[s], ~s** come-back; **ein ~ feiern** stage a come-back
COMECON, Comecon ['kɔmekɔn] **der** *od.* **das; ~:** Comecon
Comic ['kɔmɪk] **der; ~s, ~s a)** comic strip; *(Heft)* comic; **b)** *(Film)* cartoon film
Comic-: ~heft das comic; **~held der** comic-strip hero
Comic strip ['kɔmɪk 'strɪp] **der; ~ ~[s], ~ ~s** comic strip
Composer [kɔm'po:zɐ] **der; ~s, ~** *(Druckw.)* composer
Computer [kɔm'pju:tɐ] **der; ~s, ~:** computer; **über ~** *(Akk.)* **gehen** *od.* **laufen** be computerized; be done by computer; **auf ~** *(Akk.)* **umstellen** computerize
computer-, Computer-: ~an·lage computer system; **~blitz der** *(Fot.)* computerized [electronic] flash; **~diagnostik die** *(Med.)* computer[-aided] diagnosis; **~gerecht 1.** *Adj.* computer-compatible; **2.** *adv.* in computer-compatible form; **~gesteuert** *Adj.* computer-controlled; **~gestützt** *Adj.* computer-assisted
computerisieren *tr. V.* computerize ‹*data, system*›; *(aufbereiten)* make ‹*data*› computer-compatible
Computer-: ~kunst die; *o. Pl.* computerized art; **~satz der;** *o. Pl. (Druckw.)* computer setting
Comte [kõ:t] **der; ~, ~s** *(French)* count
Comtesse [kõ'tɛs] **die; ~, ~n** *s.* **Komteß**
Concept-art ['kɔnsɛptla:ɐt] **die; ~** *(Kunstwiss.)* concept[ual] art
Concerto grosso [kɔn'tʃɛrto 'grɔso] **das; ~ ~, Concerti grossi** *(Musik)* concerto grosso
Concierge [kõ'sɪɛrʃ] **der/die; ~, ~s** concierge
Conditio sine qua non [kɔn'di:tsio 'zi:nə 'kva: 'no:n] **die; ~ ~ ~ ~** *(Philos.)* sine qua non

Conférencier [kõferã'sie:] **der; ~s, ~s** compère *(Brit.)*; master of ceremonies
Confiserie *s.* **Konfiserie**
Confiteor [kɔn'fi:teɔr] **das; ~** *(kath. Rel.)* Confiteor; general confession
Connaisseur [kɔnɛ'sø:ʀ] **der; ~s, ~s** *(geh.)* connoisseur
Consommé [kõsɔ'me:] **die; ~, ~s** *od.* **das; ~s, ~s** *(Kochk.)* consommé
Container [kɔn'te:nɐ] **der; ~s, ~:** container; *(für Müll)* [refuse] skip; *(für Altglas)* bottle-bank
Container-: ~bahn·hof der container station; **~hafen der** container port *or* terminal; **~schiff das** container ship; **~verkehr der;** *o. Pl.* container traffic *no art.*
Contenance [kõtə'nã:s(ə)] **die; ~** *(geh.)* composure; **die ~ [be]wahren/verlieren** keep/lose one's composure *or* countenance
Contergan Ⓦⓩ [kɔntɛr'ga:n] **das; ~s** thalidomide
Contergan·kind das thalidomide child
cool [ku:l] *(ugs.)* **1.** *Adj.* **a)** *(gelassen)* cool; **~ bleiben** keep one's cool *(sl.)*; **b)** *(gut)* fabulous *(coll.)*; **c)** *(reell)* reliable; *(anständig)* decent; reasonable. **2.** *adv.* **a)** *(gelassen)* coolly; **b)** *(gut)* fabulously *(coll.)*; **c)** *(anständig)* decently; reasonably
Cool Jazz ['ku:l 'dʒæz] **der; ~ ~:** cool jazz
Copilot *s.* **Kopilot**
Copyright ['kɔpirait] **das; ~s, ~s** copyright
coram publico ['ko:ram] *(geh.)* in public
Cord [kɔrt] **der; ~[e]s, ~e** *od.* **~s** cord; *(~samt)* corduroy
Cord-: ~an·zug der cord/corduroy suit; **~hose die** [pair *sing.* of] corduroy trousers *pl. or* cords *pl.*; **~jeans** *Pl.* corduroy jeans; cords
Cordon bleu [kɔrdõ'blø] **das; ~ ~, ~s ~s** [kɔrdõ'blø] *(Kochk.)* veal escalope cordon bleu
Cord-: ~rock der corduroy skirt; **~samt der** corduroy
Core [kɔ:] **das; ~[s], ~s** *(Kernphysik)* core
Corned beef ['kɔ:nd 'bi:f] **das; ~ ~:** corned beef
Corner ['kɔ:nə] **der; ~s, ~** *(österr. Fußball)* corner [kick]
Corn-flakes ['kɔ:nfleɪks] *Pl.* cornflakes
Cornichon [kɔrni'ʃõ:] **das; ~s, ~s** [fine-quality] gherkin
Corona *s.* **Korona**
Corps *s.* **Korps**
Corpus *s.* **Korpus**
Corpus delicti ['kɔrpʊs de'lɪkti] **das; ~ ~, Corpora** ['kɔrpora] **delicti a)** *(Rechtsspr.)* weapon [used]; **b)** *(meist scherzh.: Beweisstück)* piece of incriminating evidence
Corso *s.* **Korso**
Cortison *s.* **Kortison**
Costa Rica ['kɔsta 'ri:ka] **(das); ~s** Costa Rica
Costaricaner der; ~s, ~ Costa Rican
costaricanisch *Adj.* Costa Rican
CO-Test [tse'lo:-] **der** *(Kfz-W.)* exhaust emission test *(for carbon monoxide content)*
Couch [kautʃ] **die,** *(schweiz. auch:)* **der; ~, ~es** sofa; **auf die ~ müssen** *(fig.)* need to see a psychiatrist
Couch-: ~garnitur die three-piece suite; **~tisch der** coffee-table
Couleur [ku'lø:ʀ] **die; ~, ~s a)** *o. Pl. (Richtung)* shade [of opinion]; persuasion; **Politiker jeglicher ~:** politicians of every shade of opinion *or* of every hue; **b)** *(Studentenspr.: Band u. Mütze)* fraternity colours *pl.*; **~ tragen** wear one's fraternity's colours
Coulomb [ku'lõ:] **das; ~s, ~** *(Physik)* coulomb
Countdown ['kaunt'daun] **der** *od.* **das; ~[s], ~s** *(Raumf., auch fig.)* countdown
Country-music ['kʌntrɪmju:zɪk] **die; ~:** country music
Coup [ku:] **der; ~s, ~s** coup; **einen ~ landen** *(ugs.)* pull off a coup

Coupé [ku'pe:] **das; ~s, ~s a)** coupé; **b)** *(österr., sonst veralt.: Abteil)* compartment
Couplet [ku'ple:] **das; ~s, ~s** satirical song *(with refrain)*
Coupon [ku'põ:] **der; ~s, ~s a)** *(Gutschein)* coupon; voucher; *(im Café)* ticket; *(zum Abreißen)* counterfoil; **auf** *od.* **für** *od.* **gegen diesen ~ bekommen Sie ...:** for this voucher you will receive ...; **b)** *(Finanzw.)* [interest] coupon; **c)** *(Stoff)* piece; length
Cour [ku:ɐ̯] *in* **einer Frau/Dame die ~ machen** *od.* **schneiden** *(veralt.)* pay court to a woman/lady
Courage [ku'ra:ʒə] **die; ~** *(ugs.)* courage; **im letzten Moment verließ sie die ~:** at the last moment she lost her nerve; *s. auch* **Angst**
couragiert [kura'ʒi:ɐ̯t] **1.** *Adj. (mutig)* courageous; *(beherzt)* spirited. **2.** *adv. s.* **1:** courageously; spiritedly
Courtage [kʊr'ta:ʒə] **die; ~, ~n** brokerage; broker's commission
Courtoisie [kʊrtoa'zi:] **die; ~, ~n** *(veralt.)* courtesy
Cousin [ku'zɛ̃:] **der; ~s, ~s** *(male)* cousin; *s. auch* **Grad a**
Cousine [ku'zi:nə] **die; ~, ~n** *(female)* cousin
Couturier [kutʏ'rie:] **der; ~, ~s** couturier
Couvert [ku've:ɐ̯] **das; ~s, ~s a)** *s.* **Kuvert; b)** *(für Bettdecken)* [quilt] cover
Cover ['kavɐ] **das; ~s, ~s a)** *(von Illustrierten)* cover; **b)** *(von Schallplatten)* sleeve
Cover·girl das cover girl
Cowboy ['kaubɔy] **der; ~s, ~s** cowboy
Cowboy-: ~hut der cowboy hat; stetson; **~stiefel der** cowboy boot
Cox Orange ['kɔks|orã:ʒə] **der; ~ ~, ~ ~** Cox's orange pippin
Crack [krɛk] **der; ~s, ~s** ace; crack player; *(Athlet)* crack athlete; **ein ~ im Schwimmen/Radfahren** a crack swimmer/cyclist
Cracker ['krɛkɐ] **der; ~s, ~[s]** cracker
Credo *s.* **Kredo**
creme [kre:m] *indekl. Adj.; nicht attr.* cream
Creme [kre:m] **die; ~, ~s,** *(schweiz.:)* **~n a)** *(Kosmetik, Kochk.)* cream; **b)** *o. Pl. (oft iron.: Oberschicht)* cream; top people; **die ~ der Gesellschaft** the cream of society
creme·farben *Adj.* cream[-coloured]
cremen *tr. V. s.* **eincremen**
Creme-: ~schnitte die cream slice; **~törtchen das** cream tart[let]; **~torte die** cream cake *or* gateau
cremig 1. *Adj.* creamy; **etw. ~ schlagen** beat sth. into a cream. **2.** *adv.* like cream
¹Crêpe [krɛp] **die; ~, ~s** *(Kochk.)* crêpe
²Crêpe der; ~, ~s *s.* **Krepp**
Crescendo [krɛ'ʃɛndo] **das; ~s, ~s** *(Musik)* crescendo
Crew [kru:] **die; ~, ~s a)** *(eines Schiffs/Flugzeugs)* crew; **b)** *(Gruppe)* team; **c)** *(Marine: Kadetten)* group of cadets *(in the same year);* class
Croissant [kroa'sã:] **das; ~[s], ~s** croissant
Cromargan Ⓦⓩ [kromar'ga:n] **das; ~s** stainless [chrome-nickel] steel
Croquette *s.* **Krokette**
Cross-country [krɔs'kantri] **das; ~[s], ~s** *(Sport)* cross-country [race]
Croupier [kru'pie:] **der; ~s, ~s** croupier
Crux [krʊks] **die; ~ a)** *(Schwierigkeit)* trouble (+ *Gen.,* **bei** with); **b)** *(Sorgen)* **man hat seine ~ mit ihnen** they are a real trial; *(sie sind eine Last)* they are a real burden
Csárdás ['tʃardas] **der; ~, ~:** csardas
C-Schlüssel ['tse:-] **der** *(Musik)* C clef
ČSFR [tʃe:|ɛs|ɛf'|ɛr] **die; ~** *Abk.:* **Tschechoslowakei**
ČSSR [tʃe:|ɛs|ɛs'|ɛr] *(hist.) s.* **ČSFR**
CSU [tse:|ɛs'|u:] **die; ~** *Abk.:* **Christlich-Soziale Union** CSU
c.t. [tse:'te:] *Abk.:* **cum tempore; Beginn: 20 Uhr ~:** 8.15 start
cum grano salis [kʊm 'gra:no 'za:lɪs] *(geh.)* taken with a pinch of salt
cum laude [kʊm 'laudə] *(Hochschulw.)* with distinction; *third of four grades of successful doctoral examination*
cum tempore [kʊm 'tɛmpore] *(Hochschulw.)* 15 minutes after the time indicated; observing
Cunnilingus [kʊni'lɪŋgʊs] **der; ~, Cunnilingi** *(Sexualk.)* cunnilingus
Cup [kap] **der; ~s, ~s** cup
Cup·finale das *(Fußball)* Cup Final; *(andere Sportarten)* final of the Cup
Cupido [ku'pi:do] **(der); ~s** *(Myth.)* Cupid
Curettage *s.* **Kürettage**
Curie [kʏ'ri:] **das; ~, ~** *(Physik)* curie
Curling ['kə:lɪŋ] **das; ~s** *(Sport)* curling
curricular [kʊriku'la:ɐ̯] *Adj.; nicht präd. (Päd.)* curricular
Curriculum [kʊ'ri:kulʊm] **das; ~s, Curricula** *(Päd.)* curriculum; *(genauer festgelegt)* syllabus
Curriculum·forschung die curricular research
Curry ['kœri] **das; ~s, ~s a)** *(auch:* **der)** curry-powder; **b)** *(Gericht)* curry
Curry-: ~sauce, ~soße die curry sauce; **~wurst die** *sliced fried sausage sprinkled with curry powder and served with ketchup*
Cut [kœt, kat] **der; ~s, ~s a)** *(Sakko)* morning coat; **b)** *(Boxen)* cut *(esp. above the eye)*
Cutaway ['kœtəve] **der; ~s, ~s** *s.* **Cut a**
cutten ['katn̩] *tr., itr. V. (Film, Rundf., Ferns.)* cut; edit
Cutter ['katɐ] **der; ~s, ~, Cutterin die; ~, ~nen** *(Film, Ferns., Rundf.)* editor
cuttern *s.* **cutten**
CVJM [tse:faujɔt'|ɛm] **der; ~** *Abk.:* **a) Christlicher Verein Junger Männer** YMCA; **b) Christlicher Verein Junger Menschen;** *combined form of YMCA and YWCA*
CVP [tse:fau'pe:] **die; ~** *(schweiz.) Abk.:* **Christlich-demokratische Volkspartei** Christian-Democratic People's Party
c_w-Wert der *(Technik)* c_d [value]
Cyan [tsy̆a:n] **das; ~s** *(Chem.)* cyanogen
Cyanid [tsy̆a'ni:t] **das; ~s, ~e** *(Chemie)* cyanide
Cymbal *s.* **Zimbal**

D

d, D [de:] **das; ~, ~ a)** *(Buchstabe)* d/D; **b)** *(Musik)* [key of] D; *s. auch* **a, A**
D *Abk.* **Damen**
da [da:] **1.** *Adv.* **a)** *(dort)* there; **da draußen/drinnen/drüben/unten** out/in/over/down there; **da hinten/vorn[e]** [there] at the back/front; **da hinab/hinauf/hinüber** down/up/over that way; **geh da herum** go round that way; **he, Sie da!** hey, you there!; **der Kerl da** that fellow [over there]; **ich möchte von dem da** I'd like some of that one; **halt, wer da?** *(Milit.)* halt, who goes there?; **hallo, wer ist denn da?** *(am Telefon)* hello, who's that [speaking]?; **gleich sind wir da** we're almost there; we'll be there in a minute; **ach, da ist meine Brille!** so 'that's where my glasses are!; oh, 'there are my glasses!; **da bist du ja!** there you are [at last]!; **da, ein Reh!** look, [there's] a deer!; **da, wo die Straße nach X abzweigt** where the road to X turns off; at the turning for X; **da und da** at such-and-such a place; **da und dort** here and there; *(manchmal)* now and again *or* then; **b)** *(hier)* here; **da bin ich** here I am; **da hast du das Buch** here's the book; **da, nimm schon!** here [you are], take it!; *s. auch* **dasein, dahaben; c)** *(zeitlich)* then; *(in dem Augenblick)* at that moment; **ich hatte mich gerade ins Bett gelegt, da klingelte das Telefon** I had just got into bed when the telephone rang; **von da an** from then on; **in meiner Jugend, da war alles besser** back in my young days, everything was better [then]; **d)** *(deshalb)* **der Zug war schon weg, da habe ich den Bus genommen** the train had already gone, so I took the bus; **e)** *(ugs.: in diesem Fall)* **da kann man nichts machen** there's nothing one can do about it *or* that; **was gibt's denn da zu lachen?** what's there to laugh about [there]?; what's funny about that?; **da kann ich [ja] nur lachen!** that's plain ridiculous!; that just makes me laugh!; **was tut man da?** what does one do in a case like this?; **f)** *(altertümelnd: nach Relativpronomen; wird nicht übersetzt)* **..., der da sagt ...,** who says; **g)** *(hervorhebend; wird meist nicht übersetzt)* **ich habe da einen Kollegen, der ...:** I have a colleague who ...; **da fällt mir noch was ein** [oh yes] another thought strikes me; **h)** *(Note: in North German colloquial usage pronominal adverbs are often divided so that* **da** *appears on its own with the remainder of the adverb at the end of the clause: see footnotes under* **dabei, dafür, dagegen, daher, damit, danach, davon, davor, dazu, dazwischen***).* **2.** *Konj.* **a)** *(weil)* as; since; **da ich ein Feigling bin, wagte ich es nicht** being a coward *or* since I'm a coward I didn't dare to; **da es [gerade] regnet** as *or* seeing that it's raining; **b)** *(geh.: als)* when; **jetzt, da es feststand, daß ...:** now that it was definite that ...
da-: 1. *Bei den aus* **da-** *od.* **dar-** *und einer Präposition gebildeten Adverbien* **(dabei, dafür, damit, daran** *usw.) wird* **da[r]-** *im allgemeinen durch* it *oder, wenn es sich auf einen Plural bezieht, durch* them *übersetzt; z. B.* **es gibt nur eine Tür, jeder muß dadurch** there is only one door and everyone has to pass through it; **die Tulpen sind schön; wieviel verlangen Sie dafür?** the tulips are nice; how much are you asking for them? *Wenn jedoch der Bestandteil* **da[r]-** *besonders betont ist, dann ist* that *bzw.* those *die angemessenere Übersetzung:* **also darauf willst du hinaus!** so that's what you're getting at! **Haben die Spritzen nicht geholfen? – Nein, dadurch ist ihm nur noch schlechter geworden** Didn't the injections help? – No, those only made him worse. *Wenn auf das Adverb ein* **daß** *mit Nebensatz folgt, bietet sich häufig die Formulierung* the fact that *an:* **dadurch gekennzeichnet, daß ...** characterized by the fact that ... *Wenn Haupt- u. Nebensatz dasselbe Subjekt haben oder wenn ein Infinitivsatz angeschlossen ist, kommt man durch die Verbindung von Präposition und Verbalsubstantiv zu einer eleganten Übersetzung:* **wir sind dafür, daß wir weitermachen** *od.* **weiterzumachen** we are in favour of continuing. *Das ist manchmal sogar bei verschiedenen Subjekten möglich, wenn man ein Possessivpronomen* (his, our *usw.*) *hinzusetzt:* **er ist dafür, daß wir weitermachen** he is in favour of our continuing. **2.** *Die Einträge für diese Adverbien berücksichtigen nur einen Teil der möglichen Kontextbeispiele mit Verben oder Substantiven. Es empfiehlt sich deshalb, auch unter den jeweiligen Verben oder Substantiven nachzuschlagen; so kann man z. B. die Übersetzung für* **danach fragen** (ask about it/them) *über* **nach etw.**

fragen *unter dem Stichwort* **fragen** *erschließen*
d. Ä. *Abk.:* **der Ältere**
da|behalten *unr. tr. V.* keep [there]; *(hier behalten)* keep here; **sie hat die Kinder gleich ~:** she simply kept the children at her place; **kann ich das Buch ~?** can I keep the book [here]?
da·bei *Adv.* **a)** *(bei etw.)* with it/them; *(bei jmdm.)* with him/her/them; *(beigeschlossen)* enclosed; **eine Tankstelle mit einer Werkstatt ~:** a filling station with its own workshop [attached]; **nahe ~** *(in der Nähe)* near it; close by; **wir wollen es ~ lassen** *(fig.)* we'll leave it at that; **b)** *(währenddessen)* at the same time; *(bei diesem Anlaß)* then; on that occasion; **er aß weiter und redete ~:** he went on eating and talked as he did so; **die ~ entstehenden Kosten** the expense involved; **er ist ~ gesehen worden, wie er das Geld nahm** he was seen [in the act of] taking the money; **eine unangenehme Reparatur – man muß ~ unterm Auto liegen** an unpleasant job – you have to lie under the car to do it; **ich hoffe, Sie haben alle ~ etwas gelernt** I hope you have all learned something from it *or* in the process; **eine Massenkarambolage – ~ gab es zwei Tote** a big pile-up – two people were killed [in it]; **~ kam es zu erbitterten Kämpfen** this gave rise to bitter fighting; **c)** *(außerdem)* **~ [auch]** what is more; **es war eiskalt und [auch] naß ~:** it was freezing cold and damp into the bargain; **er ist sehr beschäftigt, aber ~ immer freundlich** he is very busy but even so always friendly; **d)** *(hinsichtlich des Erwähnten)* about it/them; **was hast du dir denn ~ gedacht?** what were you thinking of?; what came over you?; **er hat sich nichts ~ gedacht** he saw no harm in it; **ich fühle mich ganz und gar nicht wohl ~:** I am not at all happy about it; **da ist doch nichts ~!** there's really no harm in it!; *(es ist nicht schwierig)* there's nothing to it!; *s. auch* **bleiben e; da-; e)** *(obwohl)* but; **er suchte nach dem Brief, ~ hatte er ihn in der Hand** he was looking for the letter and all the time he had it in his hand; *NB In senses* **a, b,** *and* **d** *the word can occur in two parts in North German coll. usage, e.g.* **da ist eine Karte bei** there is a card with it
dabei-: ~|bleiben *unr. itr. V.; mit sein (dort)* stay there; be there; *(bei einer Tätigkeit)* stick to it; *(bei einer Firma, der Armee)* stay on; **~|haben** *unr. tr. V.* have with one; **ich habe kein Geld ~:** I haven't got any money with me *or* on me; **sie wollte die Kinder nicht ~haben** *(ugs.)* she didn't want to have the children there *or* around; **~|sein** *unr. itr. V.; mit sein (Zusschr. nur im Inf. u. 2. Part.)* **a)** *(anwesend sein)* be there; be present (**bei** at); *(teilnehmen)* take part (**bei** in); **bei der Sitzung ~sein** be at *or* attend the meeting; **~sein ist alles!** it's taking part that counts; **Wer kommt mit? – Ich bin ~!** Who's coming? – Count me in!; **ein wenig Angst ist immer ~:** there is always an element of fear; **b)** *(gerade tun)* **[gerade] ~sein, etw. zu tun** be just doing sth.; **Spülst du das Geschirr? – Ich bin schon ~:** Will you wash up? – I'm already in the middle of it; **~|sitzen** *unr. itr. V.* sit there; **~|stehen** *unr. itr. V.* stand by; stand there
da|bleiben *unr. itr. V.; mit sein* stay there; *(hier bleiben)* stay here; **[noch] ~:** stay on
da capo [da'ka:po] **a)** *(Musik)* da capo; **b)** *(Beifallsruf)* **~!** encore!
d'accord [da'ko:ɐ̯] *(bes. österr.)* **mit jmdm. ~ gehen** *od.* **sein** agree with sb.
Dach [dax] **das; ~[e]s, Dächer** ['dɛçɐ] **a)** roof; **[ganz oben] unterm ~** *od. (ugs. scherzh.)* **unterm ~ juchhe** [right up] in the attic; **ein/kein ~ über dem Kopf haben** *(ugs.)* have a/no roof over one's head; **[mit jmdm.] unter einem ~ leben** live under the same roof [with *or* as sb.]; **etw. unter ~ und Fach bringen** get sth. [safely] under cover; bring in sth.; *(fig.: erfolgreich beenden)* get sth. all wrapped up; **unter ~ und Fach sein** be under cover; ⟨*harvest*⟩ be safely [gathered] in; *(fig.: erfolgreich beendet)* wrapped up; ⟨*contract etc.*⟩ be signed and sealed; **das ~ der Welt** *(fig.)* the roof of the world; **b)** *(fig. ugs.)* **jmdm. aufs ~ steigen** give sb. a piece of one's mind; ⟨*superior officer etc.*⟩ haul sb. over the coals; **jmdm. eins aufs ~ geben** bash sb. over the head; *(tadeln)* give sb. a dressing down; tear a strip off sb. *(sl.)*; **eins aufs ~ bekommen** *od.* **kriegen** get a bash on the head; *(eine Rüge erhalten)* get it in the neck *(coll.)*
dach-, Dach-: ~antenne die roof-aerial; roof antenna *(Amer.)*; **~balken der** roof-beam; **~boden der** loft; **auf dem ~boden** in the loft; **~decker** [~dɛkɐ] **der; ~s, ~:** roofer; *(für Reetdächer)* thatcher; **das kannst du halten wie ein ~decker** *(ugs.)* it's all the same to me; **~decker·arbeiten** *Pl.* roofing work *sing.*; *(mit Reet)* thatching work *sing.*; **~fenster das** skylight; *(Dachgaube)* dormer window; **~first der** [roof-] ridge; **~förmig** *Adj.* roof-shaped; **~förmiger Vorsprung** rooflike projection; **~garten der a)** roof-garden; **b)** *s.* **~terrasse; ~gaube die** *(bes. Bauw.)* dormer window; **~gebälk das** roof-timbers *pl.*; **~gepäck·träger der** *(Kfz-W.)* roof-rack; **~geschoß das** attic [storey]; **~gesellschaft die** *(Wirtsch.)* holding company; **~gesims das** eaves *pl.*; **~gestühl das** *s.* **~stuhl; ~giebel der** gable; **~gleiche** [~glaiçə] **die; ~, ~n** *(österr.) s.* **Richtfest; ~hase der** *(scherzh.)* cat; moggie *(sl.)*; **~kammer die** attic [room]; *(ärmlich)* garret; **~konstruktion die a)** roof-structure; *(Entwurf)* roof-design; **b)** *(das Konstruieren)* construction of the roof; **~lawine die** *mass of snow sliding from a roof*
Dächlein ['dɛçlain] **das; ~s, ~:** little roof
Dach-: ~luke die skylight; **~organisation die** umbrella organization; **~pappe die** roofing-felt; **~pfanne die** pantile; **~platte die** flat tile; *(Schindel)* shingle; *(aus Schiefer)* slate; **~reiter der** ridge turret; **~rinne die** gutter
Dachs [daks] **der; ~es, ~e a)** *(Tier)* badger; **b)** *(ugs.: unerfahrener Bursche)* greenhorn; **er ist noch ein ganz junger ~:** he's still wet behind the ears; **c)** *(ugs.: Kind)* **vorlauter** *od.* **frecher kleiner ~:** little rascal; young whipper- snapper
Dachs-: ~bär der *(Jägerspr.)* [male] badger; **~bau der;** *Pl.* **~e** badger's earth *or* set
Dach: ~schaden der a) *o. Pl. (ugs.)* **einen ~schaden haben** be not quite right in the head; be slightly screwy *(sl.)*; **b)** *(Schaden am Dach)* roof-damage; **~schiefer der** roofing-slate; **~schindel die** [roof-] shingle; **~schräge die** roof angle; pitch of the roof
Dachs·hund der *(fachspr.) s.* **Dackel a**
Dächsin ['dɛksɪn] **die; ~, ~nen** [female] badger; badger sow
Dach-: ~sparren der rafter; **~stroh das** straw thatch; **~stübchen das** *(veralt.)* little attic room; *(ärmlich)* garret; **~stube die** *(veralt.) s.* **~kammer; ~stuhl der** roof-truss
dachte ['daxtə] *1. u. 3. Pers. Sg. Prät. v.* **denken**
Dach-: ~terrasse die roof-terrace; **~traufe die** eaves *pl.*; **~verband der** *s.* **~organisation; ~wohnung die** attic flat *(Brit.) or (Amer.)* apartment; **~ziegel der** roof-tile; **~ziegel·verband der** *(Med.)* [rib-]strapping; **~zimmer das** attic room
Dackel ['dakl] **der; ~s, ~ a)** *(Hund)* dachshund; **b)** *(Schimpfwort)* clot *(sl.)*
Dackel·beine *Pl. (ugs. scherzh.)* [stumpy] bow legs
Dada ['dada] **der; ~[s] a)** Dada; **b)** *(Gruppe)* Dada[ist group]
Dada-Bewegung die Dadaist movement; Dadaism
Dadaismus der; ~: Dadaism *no art.*
Dadaist der; ~en, ~en, Dadaistin die; ~, ~nen Dadaist
dadaistisch *Adj.* Dadaist
da·dran *(ugs.) s.* **daran**
da·drauf *(ugs.) s.* **darauf**
da·draus *(ugs.) s.* **daraus**
da·drin *(ugs.) s.* **darin**
da·drinnen *(ugs.) s.* **darinnen**
da·drüber *(ugs.) s.* **darüber**
da·drum *(ugs.) s.* **darum**
da·drunter *(ugs.) s.* **darunter**
da·durch *Adv.* **a)** *(durch diese Öffnung hindurch)* through it/them; *(geh.: wodurch)* through which; **soll ich dadurch gehen oder dadurch?** should I go through this one or that one *or* through here or through there?; **b)** *(durch diesen Umstand)* as a result; *(durch dieses Mittel)* in this way; by this [means]; **ich nehme den D-Zug, ~ bin ich zwanzig Minuten eher da** I'll take the express, that way I'll get there twenty minutes earlier; **er hat sich ~ selbst geschadet** by doing this he has damaged his own interests; **c) ~, daß er es [nicht] tat, konnte er ...:** as a result of [not] doing it *or* by [not] doing it he was able to ...; **~, daß er älter ist, hat er einige Vorteile** he has several advantages by virtue of being older *or* because he is older; *s. auch* **da-**
da·für *Adv.* **a)** *(für diese Sache, diesen Zweck)* for it/them; **~ gebe ich gern etwas [Geld]** I'll gladly give some money for that; **~ haben wir Sie schließlich eingestellt!** after all, that's what we took you on for!; **Magenschmerzen? Pfefferminztee ist sehr gut ~** *(ugs.)* Stomach ache? Peppermint tea is very good for that; **~, daß ...:** considering that ...; *(damit)* so that ...; **~ sorgen [, daß ...]** see to it [that ...]; **der Grund ~, daß ...** the reason why ...; **b)** *(zugunsten dieser Sache)* for it; **~ sein** be in favour [of it]; **ich bin ganz ~:** I'm all for it; **er ist nicht ~, daß sie allein fährt** he's against her going alone; **das ist ein/kein Beweis ~, daß ...:** this is proof/no proof that ... *or* proves/does not prove that ...; **ein Beispiel ~ ist ...:** an example of this is ...; **alles spricht ~, daß ...:** all the evidence *or* everything suggests that ...; **c)** *(als Gegenleistung)* in return [for it]; *(beim Tausch)* in exchange; *(statt dessen)* instead; **heute hat er keine Zeit, ~ will er morgen kommen** he has no time today, so he wants to come tomorrow instead; **in Mathematik ist er zwar eine Niete, aber ~ kann er sehr gut zeichnen** he is useless at maths, but then *or* on the other hand he can draw very well; **d)** *(als etw. [geltend])* **der Stein ist kein Rubin, aber man könnte ihn ~ halten** the stone is not a ruby, but one might think it was *or* take it for one; **er ist schon 60, aber ~ hält ihn niemand** he is 60 but nobody would think so; **sie ist ihre Mutter, nicht ihre Schwester, aber sie könnte ~ gelten** she is her mother, not her sister, though she could pass for it; *s. auch* **da-;** NB *In senses* **a, b,** *and* **d** *the word can occur in two parts in North German coll. usage, e.g.* **da kriege ich nichts für** I'm getting nothing for it
dafür-: ~|halten *unr. itr. V. (geh.)* consider; be of the opinion; **nach meinem Dafürhalten** in my opinion; **~|können** *unr. tr. V.* **in etwas/nichts ~können** be/not be responsible; **~ kann er nichts** *od. (nordd. ugs.)* **da kann er nichts für [, daß ...]:** it's not his fault [that ...]; he can't help it [that ...]; **die können sehr wohl etwas ~, daß es so ist** they are very much responsible for things being the way they are; **~|stehen** *unr. itr. V.* **a)** *(veralt.: bürgen)* **~stehen, daß ...:** guarantee that ...; **~stehen, wie sich die Kinder beneh-**

men be responsible for the way the children behave; **b)** *(österr.: sich lohnen)* **das** *od.* **es steht [nicht] ~**: it is [not] worth it

DAG [de:/a:'ge:] **die;** ~ *Abk. (Bundesrepublik Deutschland):* **Deutsche Angestellten-Gewerkschaft** German Employees' Union

dagegen *Adv.* **a)** *(gegen das Genannte)* against it/them; **der Wagen raste auf den Pfeiler zu und prallte ~**: the car careered towards the pillar and crashed into it; **er stieß aus Versehen ~**: he knocked into it by mistake; **ich protestiere energisch ~, daß Sie mich verleumden** I must protest strongly against this slander; **etwas ~ haben** have sth. against it; object [to it]; **ich habe nichts ~**: I've no objection; I don't mind; **haben Sie etwas** *od. (ugs.)* **was ~, wenn ...?** do you mind if ...?; **was hat er ~, daß wir Freunde sind?** why does he object to our being friends?; **~ sein** be opposed to it *or* against it; **die Mehrheit war ~, das Angebot anzunehmen** the majority was against *or* opposed to accepting the offer; **wir kennen kein Mittel ~**: we know of no cure for it; **~ kann man nichts machen** there is nothing one can do about it; **b)** *konjunktional (im Vergleich dazu)* by *or* in comparison; compared with that; *(jedoch)* on the other hand; **sein Sohn ist dunkelhaarig, seine Tochter ~ blond** his son has dark hair, but his daughter on the other hand is blonde; **c)** *(als Gegenwert)* in exchange; **er hat ein anderes Gerät ~ eingetauscht** he got another machine in exchange [for it]; *s. auch* **da-;** NB *In senses* **a, c** *the word can occur in two parts in North German coll. usage, e.g.* **da kann niemand gegen sein** nobody can have any objection [to that]

dagegen-: ~|halten *unr. tr. V.* **a)** *(entgegnen)* counter; *(einwenden)* object; **er hielt ~, daß ...**: his rejoinder *or* answer was that ...; **b)** *(ugs.: vergleichen)* hold it/them against; compare it/them with; **halte das Original ~**: compare it with the original; **~|setzen** *tr. V.* put forward [in opposition]; **„Das stimmt doch gar nicht", setzte er ~**: 'That's quite untrue,' he objected; **nichts ~zusetzen haben** offer no counter-argument; *(nichts einwenden)* make no objection; *(es nicht leugnen)* not deny it; **~|sprechen** *unr. itr. V.* be against it/them; **zahlreiche Gründe sprechen/nichts spricht ~, daß du ein paar Tage freinimmst** there are numerous reasons/there is no reason why you should not take a couple of days off; **was spricht ~?** what is the objection?; **~|stellen** *refl. V.* oppose it; **~|stemmen** *refl. V.* oppose it vigorously; fight it

da|haben *unr. tr. V. (Zusschr. nur im Inf. u. 2. Part.) (ugs.)* have [here]; *(im Hause)* have in the house; **mal sehen, ob ich noch eins da habe** I'll see whether I've got one left

da·heim *Adv. (bes. südd., österr., schweiz.)* **a)** *(zu Hause)* at home; *(nach Präp.)* home; **ich bin für niemanden ~**: I'm not at home to anybody; **~ anrufen** phone *or* ring home; **wie geht es ~?** how are things at home?; **sind Sie hier ~?** do you live here?; **bei mir ~**: at my place; **~ ist ~!** there's no place like home! *(prov.);* east, west, home's best *(prov.);* **b)** *(in der Heimat)* [back] home; **bei uns ~**: back home where I/we come from; **nach ~ schreiben** write home; **wo bist du ~?** where do you come from?

Daheim das; ~s *(bes. südd., österr., schweiz.)* home

Daheim·gebliebene der/die; *adj. Dekl.* one who stayed at home; **die ~gebliebenen** those who stayed at home; those back home

da·her *Adv.* **a)** *(von dort)* from there; **~ habe ich meine neuen Stiefel** that's where I got my new boots from; **von ~ droht keine Gefahr** there is no danger from 'that quarter; **~ weht also der Wind!** *(ugs.)* so 'that's the way the wind blows! *(fig.);* **b)** *(durch diesen Umstand)* hence; **~ kommt seine gute Laune** that's why he's in a good mood; that's the reason for his good mood; **das/die Krankheit kommt ~, daß ...**: the reason for this/the illness is that ...; **~ der Name Bratkartoffel!** *(scherzh.)* that explains it; so that's why!; **~ wußte er das** *od.* **hat er das** that's how he knew; that's where he got it from; **c)** *konjunktional (deshalb)* therefore; so; **d)** *(bes. südd.: hierhin)* here; NB *In senses* **a, b,** *and* **d** *the word can occur in two parts in coll. usage, e.g.* **da hast du die Klamotten her** that's where you got those clothes from

daher-, Daher-: ~|bringen *unr. tr. V. (südd., österr.)* **a)** *(mitbringen)* bring [with one]; *(nach Hause)* bring home; **b)** *(abwertend: sagen)* come out with *(coll.);* **~|fliegen** *unr. itr. V.; mit sein* **a)** *(umherfliegen)* fly around; **b)** *(heranfliegen)* fly up; **~geflogen kommen** come flying along; *(auf jmdn. zu)* come flying up; **~gelaufen** *Adj.; nicht präd. (abwertend)* that nobody's heard of *postpos.;* **jeder ~gelaufene Kerl** any guy who comes along; any Tom, Dick, or Harry; **~gelaufene der/die;** *adj. Dekl. (abwertend)* nonentity; **jeder ~gelaufene** absolutely anybody [who comes along]; **~|kommen** *unr. itr. V.* come along; *(gemütlich)* stroll along; *(auf jmdn. zu)* come/stroll up; *(auftreten)* turn up; **wie kann man nur in so einem Aufzug ~kommen?** how can one go around dressed like that?; **~reden** *(abwertend)* **1.** *itr. V.* **a)** talk off the cuff; **b)** *(viel reden)* blather on; **[so] dumm ~reden** talk [such] rubbish; **2.** *tr. V.* **a)** say off the cuff; **b)** *(wortreich sagen)* prattle; **was er so ~redet** his blathering on; the things he comes out with

da·hier *Adv. (österr., schweiz., sonst veralt.)* here

da|hin a) *(nach dort)* there; **~ und dorthin** this way and that; **b)** *(fig.)* **~ mußte es kommen** it had to come to that; **~ hat ihn seine Wettleidenschaft gebracht** that's where his betting mania has got him; **du wirst es ~ bringen, daß ...**: you'll carry things *or* matters so far that ...; **c) bis ~**: to there; *(zeitlich)* until then; **bis ~ sind es 75 km** it's 75 km from here; **bis ~ sind es noch zehn Minuten** there are another ten minutes to go until then; **es steht mir bis ~** *(ugs.)* I am sick and tired of it *or* fed up to the back teeth with it *(coll.);* **d)** [-'-] *(verloren, vorbei)* **~ sein** be *or* have gone; **mein neuer Mantel ist ~**: my new coat is ruined *or (coll.)* has had it; **e)** *(in diesem Sinne)* **~ [gehend], daß ...**: to the effect that ...; **man kann dieses Schreiben auch ~ [gehend] auslegen/verstehen, daß ...**: one can also interpret/take this letter as meaning that ...

da·hinab *Adv.* down there; down that way

da·hinauf *Adv.* up there; up that way

da·hinaus *Adv.* out there; *(in die Richtung)* out that way

dahin-: ~|bewegen *refl. V.* move on one's way; **~|dämmern** *itr. V.; mit sein* be semiconscious; **~|eilen** *itr. V.; mit sein (geh.)* hurry along *or* on one's way; ⟨*time*⟩ fly [past]

da·hinein *Adv.* in there; *(hier hinein)* in here

dahin-: ~|fahren *unr. itr. V.; mit sein* **a)** *(dichter.: wegfahren)* depart; **b)** *(dichter.: vorbeifahren)* go *or* pass on one's/its way; **c)** *(veralt.: sterben)* pass away; depart this life *(literary);* **~|fliegen** *unr. itr. V.; mit sein (dichter.)* **a)** *(wegfliegen)* fly on its way; ⟨*person*⟩ fly away; **b)** *(vergehen)* fly past; **~|fließen** *unr. itr. V.; mit sein (geh.)* flow along *or* on its way

da·hingegen *Adv.* on the other hand

dahin-: ~|gehen *unr. itr. V.; mit sein* **a)** *(geh.: vergehen)* pass; ⟨*years*⟩ go by; **b)** *(geh.: vorbeigehen)* go *or* pass on one's way; **c)** *(verhüll.: sterben)* pass away; **~gestellt** *in* **es ist** *od.* **bleibt ~gestellt** it remains to be seen; **ob etwas Vernünftiges dabei herauskommt, sei ~gestellt** we must wait and see whether this produces any useful result; **etw. ~gestellt sein lassen** leave sth. open [for the moment]; **~|jagen** *itr. V.; mit sein (geh.)* tear *or* race along; **~|kümmern** *itr. V.; mit sein (geh.)* fade away; *(im Gefängnis usw.)* languish; **~|leben** *itr. V.* live one's life; **~|plätschern** *itr. V.; mit sein* **das Gespräch plätscherte an der Oberfläche dahin** the conversation was very superficial *or* remained at the level of small talk; **~|raffen** *tr. V. (geh. verhüll.)* carry off; **~|sagen** *tr. V.* say without thinking; **das war nur so ~gesagt** that was just a casual *or* off-the-cuff remark; **~|scheiden** *unr. itr. V.; mit sein (geh. verhüll.)* pass away; depart this life *(literary);* **~|schwinden** *unr. itr. V.; mit sein (geh.)* **a)** *(abnehmen)* dwindle; ⟨*courage, interest, hope*⟩ fade; **b)** *(vergehen)* pass; **~|siechen** *itr. V.; mit sein (geh.)* waste away; **~|stehen** *unr. itr. V.* **[es] steht [noch] ~**: [it] remains to be seen

da·hinten *Adv.* over there

da·hinter *Adv.* behind it/them; *(folgend)* after it/them; **ein Haus mit einem Garten ~**: a house with a garden behind *or* at the back; **was sich wohl ~ verbirgt?** *(fig.)* what can be behind it?; *s. auch* **da-**

dahinter·her *Adj.; nur präd. (ugs.)* **~ sein** make a big effort; put oneself out; **nie macht ihr eure Aufgaben von euch aus, ich muß immer ~ sein** you never do your homework without being reminded, I've always got to keep on at you

dahinter-: ~|klemmen *refl. V.,* **~|knien** *refl. V. (ugs.)* buckle down to it; pull one's finger out *(sl.);* **~|kommen** *unr. itr. V.; mit sein (ugs.)* find out; **~|machen** *refl. V. (ugs.)* get down to it; **mach dich ~!** get on with it!; **~|setzen** *refl. V. (ugs.) s.* **~klemmen; ~|stecken** *itr. V. (ugs.)* **a)** *(als Grund, Urheber)* be behind it/them; **b)** *(Sinn haben)* **es steckt nichts/nicht viel ~**: there is nothing/not much to it/them; **~|stehen** *unr. itr. V.* **a)** *(dafür eintreten)* be behind it/them; [fully] support it/them; *(bei eigenen Erklärungen, Entscheidungen)* stand by it/them; **b)** *(zugrunde liegen)* be behind it/them; be at the root of it/them

da|hinüber *Adv.* over/across there

da|hinunter *Adv.* down there; *(in diese Richtung)* down that way

dahin-: ~|vegetieren *itr. V.* **[elend] ~vegetieren** drag out a miserable existence; **~|ziehen 1.** *unr. itr. V.; mit sein* go *or* move on one's/its way; ⟨*clouds*⟩ drift by; **2.** *unr. refl. V.* ⟨*path*⟩ pass along

Dahlie ['da:li̯ə] **die; ~, ~n** dahlia

Dakapo [da'ka:po] **das; ~s, ~s** *(Musik)* encore

daktylisch [dak'tʏ:lɪʃ] *Adj. (Verslehre)* dactylic

Daktylo- ['daktʏlo]: **~graphin** [~'gra:fɪn] **die; ~, ~nen** *(schweiz.)* typist; **~skopie** [~sko'pi:] **die; ~, ~n** dactyloscopy *no art.;* fingerprint identification *no art.*

Daktylus ['daktʏlʊs] **der; ~, Daktylen** *(Verslehre)* dactyl

da-: ~|lassen *unr. tr. V. (ugs.)* leave [here]; *(dort lassen)* leave there; **[jmdm.] keine Nachricht ~lassen** leave [sb.] no message; **~|liegen** *unr. itr. V.* lie there; ⟨*building etc.*⟩ stand there

Dalk [dalk] **der; ~[e]s, ~e** *(südd., österr. ugs.)* [clumsy] clot *(Brit. sl.);* jerk *(sl.)*

Dalken *Pl. (österr.)* [yeast-dough] fritters

dalkert ['dalkɐt] *(südd., österr. ugs.)* **1.** *Adj.* daft; **~e Kuh** silly woman *(derog.).* **2.** *adv.* stupidly

Dalle ['dalə] **die; ~, ~n** *(bes. südd.)* dent

Dalles ['daləs] **der; ~** *(ugs.)* **im ~ sein** be broke *(coll.)*

dalli ['dali] *Adv. (ugs.)* **aber [ein bißchen] ~!** and make it snappy *(coll.)*; **[~] ~!** get a move on!; *(beim Laufen)* come on, at the double!

Dalmatien [dal'ma:tsiən] **(das); ~s** Dalmatia

Dalmatiner [dalma'ti:nɐ] **der; ~s, ~** Dalmatian

dalmatinisch *Adj.* Dalmatian

damalig ['da:ma:lıç] *Adj.; nicht präd.* at that *or* the time *postpos.*; **der ~e Bundeskanzler** the then Federal Chancellor; the Federal Chancellor at that *or* the time; **das ~e Leben** life in those days; **die ~e Regierung** the government of the day; **unter den ~en Umständen** in the circumstances obtaining at the time; **im ~en Gallien** in what was then Gaul

damals ['da:ma:ls] *Adv.* then; at that time; **~, als ...:** at the time *or* in the days when ...; **von ~:** of that time *or* those days; *(aus dieser Zeit)* from that time *or* those days; **seit ~:** since then; **wie es ~war** what it was like in those days

Damast [da'mast] **der; ~[e]s, ~e** damask

damasten *Adj. (geh.)* damask

Damaszener·klinge [damas'tse:nɐ-] **die** Damascus blade

damaszieren [damas'tsi:rən] *tr. V.* damascene ⟨*blade, sword*⟩

Dämchen ['dɛ:mçən] **das; ~s, ~ a)** little lady; **b)** *(Kind)* [proper] little lady; little madam; **c)** *(abwertend: Prostituierte)* lady of the night

Dame ['da:mə] **die; ~, ~n a)** *(Frau)* lady; **sehr verehrte** *od.* **meine ~n und Herren!** ladies and gentlemen; **was wünschen Sie, meine ~?** may I help you, madam?; **ein Abend mit ~n** a ladies' night; **die Abfahrt/die 200 Meter der ~n** *(Sport)* the women's downhill/200 metres; **bei den ~n siegte die deutsche Staffel** *(Sport)* the German team won in the women's event; **die ~ des Hauses** the lady of the house; **meine Alte ~** *(veralt. scherzh.)* my mater *(dated sl.)*; **ganz ~ sein** be the complete lady; *s. auch* **Welt f; b)** *(Schach, Kartenspiele)* queen; **c)** *o. Pl. (Spiel)* draughts *(Brit.)*; checkers *(Amer.)*; **d)** *(Doppelstein)* king

Dame·brett das draught-board *(Brit.)*; checkerboard *(Amer.)*

Dämel ['dɛ:ml̩] **der; ~s, ~** *(salopp)* fool; **du ~!** you clot! *(Brit. sl.)*; you jerk! *(sl.)*

Damen-: ~bart der [unwanted] facial hair; **~begleitung die: in/ohne ~begleitung** in the company of a lady/unaccompanied; with/without a female companion; **~bekanntschaft die** lady friend; **eine ~bekanntschaft machen** *(ugs.)* meet *or* get to know someone of the opposite sex; **~besuch der** lady visitor/visitors; **~besuch ist ab 20^{00} untersagt** no female visitors after 8 p.m.; **~binde die** sanitary towel *(Brit.) or (Amer.)* napkin; **~doppel das** *(Sport)* women's doubles *pl.*; **~einzel das** *(Sport)* women's singles *pl.*; **~fahr·rad das** lady's bicycle; **~friseur der** ladies' hairdresser; **~fußball der;** *o. Pl.* women's football; **~garnitur die** set of women's underwear; **~gesellschaft die a)** ladies' party; **b)** *o. Pl. (Begleitung von Damen)* female company; **in ~gesellschaft** in the company of a lady/of ladies

damenhaft 1. *Adj.* ladylike; **~e Kleidung** clothes fit for a lady. **2.** *adv.* like a lady; in a ladylike manner

Damen-: ~kapelle die women's band; **~konfektion die** ladies' wear; **~kränzchen das** *(veralt.)* ladies' circle; **~mannschaft die** women's team; **~rad das** lady's bicycle; **~salon der** ladies' hairdressing salon *(Brit.)*; beauty salon *(Amer.)*; **~sattel der** side-saddle; **im ~sattel reiten** ride side-saddle; **~schuh der** lady's shoe; **~schuhe** ladies' shoes; **~sitz der** *(Reiten)* **im ~sitz reiten** ride side-saddle; **~stift das** *(veralt.)* home for elderly gentlewomen *(esp. members of the aristocracy)*; **~toilette die a)** *(WC)* ladies' toilet; ladies' rest-room *(Amer.)*; **b)** *(Kleidung)* ladies' [formal] wear; **~unter·wäsche die** ladies' underwear; **~wahl die;** *o. Pl.* ladies' choice; **jetzt ist ~wahl** now it's the ladies' turn to choose their partners; **~welt die;** *o. Pl. (scherzh.)* **die ~welt** the ladies *pl.*; the fair sex

Dame-: ~spiel das a) das ~spiel draughts *(Brit.)*; checkers *(Amer.)*; **b)** *(Partie)* game of draught *or (Amer.)* checkers; **~stein der** draughtsman *(Brit.)*; checker *(Amer.)*

Dam·hirsch ['dam-] **der** fallow deer; *(männliches Tier)* fallow buck

damisch ['da:mıʃ] *(südd., österr. ugs.)* **1.** *Adj.* **a)** *(dumm)* stupid; **b)** *nicht attr. (schwindlig)* dizzy. **2.** *adv. (dumm)* stupidly

da·mit 1. *Adv.* **a)** *(mit dieser Sache)* with it/them; **was will er ~ [machen]?** what's he going to do with it/them?; **meint er mich ~?** does he mean me?; **ich bin gleich ~ fertig** I'll be finished in a moment; **du hast recht ~ gehabt** you were right there *or* about that; **er hatte nicht ~ gerechnet** he had not expected that *or* reckoned with that; **~ habe ich nichts zu tun** I have nothing to do with it/them; **er kommt immer wieder ~ an** he's for ever harping on it; **was ist denn ~?** what's the matter with it/them?; what about it/them?; **wie wäre es ~?** how about it?; **~ hat es noch Zeit** there's no hurry about that/those; **Schluß** *od.* **genug ~!** that's enough [of that]; **hör auf ~!** stop it!; **her ~!** let's have it/them!; hand it/them over!; **b)** *(gleichzeitig)* with that; thereupon; **c)** *(daher)* thus; as a result; **er hatte kein Alibi, und gehörte ~ zu den Verdächtigen** he had no alibi and was therefore one of the suspects; *s. auch* **da-**; *NB In sense* **a** *the word can occur in two parts in North German coll. usage, e.g.* **da habe ich nicht mit gerechnet** I didn't expect that. **2.** *Konj.* so that; **er kam früher, ~ sie mehr Zeit hatten** *od. (geh.)* **hätten** he came earlier so that they would have more time

Dämlack ['dɛ:mlak] **der; ~s, ~e** *od.* **~s** *(salopp)* clot *(Brit. sl.)*; twerp *(sl.)*; jerk *(sl.)*

dämlich ['dɛ:mlıç] *(ugs. abwertend)* **1.** *Adj.* stupid. **2.** *adv.* stupidly; **~ fragen** ask stupid questions

Dämlichkeit die; ~, ~en *(ugs. abwertend)* **a)** *o. Pl. (Art)* stupidity; **b)** *(Handlung)* piece of stupidity

Damm [dam] **der; ~[e]s, Dämme** ['dɛmə] **a)** *(Schutzwall)* embankment; levee *(Amer.)*; *(Deich)* dike; *(Stau~)* dam; *(durch Wasser, Watt, Sumpf)* causeway; *(fig.)* bulwark **(gegen** against); **einen ~ gegen etw. errichten** *(fig.)* form a barrier *or* defence against sth.; **b)** *(Straßen~, Bahn~)* embankment; **c)** *(nord[ost]d.: Straße)* road[way]; **d)** *(fig.)* **wieder/nicht auf dem ~ sein** *(ugs.)* be fit *or* in good shape again/not be fit *or* in good shape; **jmdn. wieder auf den ~ bringen** *(ugs.)* put sb. back on his/her feet; **e)** *(Anat.)* perineum

Dämm- insulating

Damm·bruch der *s.* **Damm:** breach in a dam/dike; collapse of an embankment/a causeway

dämmen ['dɛmən] *tr. V.* **a)** *(geh.: aufhalten)* hold back; dam ⟨*river, stream*⟩; stem ⟨*flood*⟩; **b)** *(Technik: nicht durchlassen)* retain, keep in ⟨*heat*⟩; *(ausschließen)* keep out ⟨*noise, heat*⟩

Dämmer der; ~s *(dichter.)* twilight; *(Halbdunkel)* half-light; **der ~ des Halbschlafs** *(fig.)* stupefied half-sleep

dämmerig *s.* **dämmrig**

Dämmer·licht das; *o. Pl.* twilight; *(trübes Licht)* dim light

dämmern ['dɛmɐn] *itr. V.* **a) es dämmert** *(morgens)* it is getting light; *(abends)* it is getting dark; *(mit Zeitangabe)* it gets light/dark; **der Morgen dämmert** the day is dawning *or* breaking; **der Abend dämmert** dusk is falling; **b)** *(ugs.: klarwerden)* **jmdm. ~:** dawn upon sb.; **mir dämmert da etwas** the penny is beginning to drop; *(ich habe einen Verdacht)* I am beginning to smell a rat; **jetzt dämmert's [bei] mir** now I'm beginning to understand; **c)** *(im Halbschlaf)* doze; **vor sich hin ~:** doze; *(nicht klar bei Bewußtsein)* be semi-conscious

Dämmer-: ~schlaf der a) *(Halbschlaf)* half-sleep; doze; **b)** *(Med.)* twilight sleep; **~schoppen der** [early] evening drink; **~stündchen das** early evening get-together; **~stunde die** *(geh.)* twilight hour; **in der ~stunde** at twilight *or* dusk

Dämmerung die; ~, ~en a) *(Abend~)* twilight; dusk; **in der [abendlichen] ~:** in the twilight *or* gloaming; **bei** *od.* **mit/vor Einbruch der ~:** at/before dusk *or* nightfall; **die Stunden der ~:** the twilight hours; **b)** *(Morgen~)* dawn; daybreak; **die ~ bricht an** dawn *or* day is breaking; **bei** *od.* **mit/vor Anbruch der ~:** at/before dawn *or* daybreak; **c)** *o. Pl. (Halbdunkel)* semi-darkness; half-light; **der Raum lag in tiefer ~:** the room was in deep shadow *or* gloom

Dämmer·zustand der a) *(Halbschlaf)* half-sleep; doze; **b)** *(Bewußtseinstrübung)* semi-conscious state; coma

dämmrig *Adj.* **a) es ist** *od.* **wird schon ~** *(morgens)* it is beginning to get light; day is breaking; *(abends)* it is beginning to get dark; night is falling; **draußen ist es noch ~:** it is still quite dark outside; **b)** *(halbdunkel)* gloomy; dim ⟨*light*⟩

Damm-: ~riß der *(Med.)* perineal tear; **~schnitt der** *(Med.)* episiotomy

Dämmung die; ~, ~en *(Technik)* insulation

Damm·weg der embankment/dike path; *(Verbindung durch Wasser, Watt, Sumpf)* causeway

Damokles·schwert ['da:moklɛs-] **das; ~[e]s** *(geh.)* sword of Damocles

Dämon ['dɛ:mɔn] **der; ~s, ~en** [dɛ'mo:nən] **a)** *(böser Geist)* demon; **gute und böse ~en** good and evil spirits; **b)** *(geh.: im Menschen)* daemon; daemonic inner force

dämonenhaft *Adj.* demoniac

Dämonie [dɛmo'ni:] **die; ~, ~n** *(geh.)* daemonic power; *(eines Künstlers)* daemonic genius; **eine** *od.* **die ~ des Schicksals** a cruel stroke of fate

dämonisch 1. *Adj.* daemonic; *(teuflisch)* diabolical. **2.** *adv.* daemonically; **~ grinsen** grin like a demon

dämonisieren *tr. V.* demonize; portray as a demon/demons

Dämonisierung die; ~, ~en demonization; portrayal as a demon/demons

Dämonismus der; ~ demonism *no art.*

Dampf [dampf] **der; ~[e]s, Dämpfe** ['dɛmpfə] **a)** steam *no pl., no indef. art.*; *(Rauch)* smoke *no pl., no indef. art.*; *(Physik)* [water] vapour *as tech. term, no pl., no indef. art.*; **wallende Dämpfe** clouds of steam; **giftige Dämpfe einatmen** breathe in toxic vapour *or* fumes; **etw. mit ~ behandeln** steam sth.; **mit ~ betrieben [werden] [be]** steam-powered *or* steam-driven; **unter ~** *(Dat.)* **stehen** *od.* **sein** have steam up; **~ aufmachen** *(veralt.: stärker feuern)* get up [more] steam; *(ugs.: energischer spielen)* put on an effort; **da ist/aus etw. ist der ~ raus** *(ugs.)* it/sth. has lost its momentum; **~ ablassen** *(auch ugs.: Ärger abreagieren)* let off steam; **jmdm. ~ [unterm Hintern] machen** *(ugs.)* make sb. get on with it; put pressure on sb.; **~ drauf haben** *(ugs.)* be really shifting *(sl.) or* moving; *(vital sein)* be full of beans; **~ dahinter/hinter etw.** *(Akk.)* **machen** *od.* **setzen** *(ugs.) (sich beeilen)* get a move on/get a move on with sth.; *(andere zur Eile treiben)* get things *pl.*/sth. moving; **dieser**

Boxer hat ~ in den Fäusten this boxer packs quite a punch; **b)** *(ugs.: Angst)* **vor jmdm./etw. [mächtigen** *od.* **unheimlichen] ~ haben** be [absolutely] terrified of sb./in a [blue] funk about sth. *(sl.)*; **c)** *(bayr.: Alkoholrausch)* **einen ~ haben** be drunk

Dampf-: ~antrieb der steam drive; *(Eisenb.)* steam traction; **mit ~antrieb** steam-driven; **~bad das** steam *or* Turkish bath; *(Raum)* steam *or* Turkish baths *pl.*; **~boot das** steamboat; **~bügel·eisen das** steam iron; **~druck der;** *Pl.* **~drücke** steam pressure

dampfen *itr. V.* **a)** *(Dampf abgeben)* steam (**vor** + *Dat.* with, due to); **b)** *mit sein (fahren)* steam; **c)** *mit sein (ugs.: mit Zug, Schiff reisen)* chug; *(wegfahren)* chug off

dämpfen ['dɛmpfn̩] *tr. V.* **a)** *(mit Dampf garen)* steam ⟨*fish, vegetables, potatoes*⟩; **b)** *(glätten)* press with a damp cloth; *(mit Dampfbügeleisen)* steam-iron; **c)** *(mildern)* muffle, deaden ⟨*sound*⟩; attenuate ⟨*high notes*⟩; dim, turn down ⟨*lights*⟩; **die** *od.* **seine Stimme ~:** lower one's voice; **den Ton einer Trompete ~:** mute a trumpet; *s. auch* **gedämpft; d)** *(abschwächen)* cushion, absorb ⟨*blow, impact, shock*⟩; damp ⟨*vibrations*⟩; *(fig.)* temper, diminish ⟨*joy*⟩; dampen ⟨*enthusiasm*⟩; assuage ⟨*sb.'s wrath*⟩; calm ⟨*anger, excitement*⟩; *(Wirtsch.)* curb ⟨*price rises*⟩; slow down ⟨*inflation*⟩

Dampfer der; ~s, ~ steamer; **mit dem ~ fahren** go by steamer; **auf dem falschen ~ sein** *od.* **sitzen** *(fig. ugs.)* be barking up the wrong tree; have got it wrong

Dämpfer der; ~s, ~ a) *(beim Klavier)* damper; *(bei Streich- u. Blasinstrumenten)* mute; **b)** *(fig.)* **einen ~ bekommen** *(ugs.)* have one's enthusiasm dampened; *(gerügt werden)* be taken down a peg or two; **jmdm. einen ~ aufsetzen** dampen sb.'s enthusiasm; **c)** *(Technik)* damper; *(Stoß~)* shock absorber

Dampfer·linie die steamer service; *(Gesellschaft)* steamship line

dampf-, Dampf-: ~förmig *Adj.* vaporous; vapour *attrib.* ⟨*state*⟩; **~hammer der** steam-hammer; **~heizung die** steam heating

dampfig *Adj.* steamy; *(dunstig)* misty

Dampf-: ~kessel der boiler; **~kochtopf der** pressure-cooker; **~kraft die;** *o. Pl.* steam power; **~kraft·werk das** steam[-driven] power station; **~lok[omotive] die** steam locomotive *or* engine; **~maschine die** steam engine; **~nudel die** *(südd., Kochk.)* steamed yeast dumpling; **aufgehen wie eine ~nudel** *(ugs.)* fill out like a balloon; **~pfeife die** steam whistle; *(mit Druckluft betrieben)* compressed-air whistle; **~schiff das** steamer; *(bes. hist.)* steamship; **~schiffahrt die** steam navigation; **~turbine die** steam turbine

Dämpfung die; ~, ~en a) *(der Stimme)* lowering; *(von hohen Tönen)* attenuation; *(von Licht)* dimming; **~ des Schalls/der Töne** deadening of sound/sounds; **b)** *(Stoß~)* cushioning; absorption; *(von Schwingungen)* damping; *(fig.) (von Freude, Leidenschaft)* tempering; diminishing; *(von Begeisterung)* dampening; *(von Wut, Aufregung)* calming; *(Wirtsch.: des Preisauftriebs)* curbing; *(der Konjunktur)* slowing down

Dampf·walze die a) steamroller; **b)** *(ugs. scherzh.: Frau)* mountain of flesh

Dam·wild das; *o. Pl.* fallow deer *pl.*

da·nach *Adv.* **a)** *(zeitlich)* after it/that; then; **noch tagelang ~:** for days after[wards]; **eine Stunde ~:** an hour later; **ich dusche gern kalt, ~ fühlt man sich gleich viel frischer** I like cold shower, you feel really refreshed afterwards; **b)** *(räumlich: dahinter)* after it/them; **voran gingen die Eltern, ~ kamen die Kinder** the parents went in front, the children following after *or* behind; **Kommt Mainz vor oder nach Wiesbaden? - Danach** Is Mainz before or after Wiesbaden? - After; **c)** *(ein Ziel angebend)* towards it/them; **er sprang/griff ~:** he jumped/made a grab for it/them; **~ laßt uns alle streben** let us all strive for that; **d)** *(entsprechend)* in accordance with it/them; **ein Brief ist gekommen; ~ ist sie schon unterwegs** a letter has arrived, according to which she is already on her way; **~ zu urteilen** to judge by that; **ihr kennt die Regeln, nun richtet euch ~!** you know the rules, so stick to *or* abide by them; **~ steht mir nicht der Sinn,** *(ugs.)* **mir ist nicht ~:** I'm not in the mood; I don't feel like it; **es sieht ~ aus/~ aus, als ob ...:** it looks like it/looks as though ...; **~ siehst du [gerade] aus!** *(ugs. iron.)* tell that to the Marines!; **es ist billig, aber es ist auch ~** *(ugs.)* it's cheap and looks it; **es ist nur ein kleiner Schnellimbiß, und das Essen ist auch ~:** it's only a small snack bar and the food's what you might expect; *s. auch* **da-;** NB *In sense* **d** *the word can occur in two parts in North German coll. usage, e.g.* **es ist billig, da ist es aber auch nach** it's cheap and looks it

Danaer·geschenk ['da:naɐ-] **das** *(geh.)* Greek gift

Dancing ['da:nsɪŋ] **das; ~s, ~s** *(bes. österr.)* **a)** *(Lokal)* dance hall; **b)** *(Veranstaltung)* dance

Dandy ['dɛndi] **der; ~s, ~s** dandy

dandyhaft 1. *Adj.* dandyish; foppish ⟨*manner*⟩. **2.** *adv.* like a dandy/dandies

Dandytum das; ~s a) *(Art)* dandyish nature; **b)** *(Schicht)* **das ~:** the dandies *pl.* *(as a group)*

Däne ['dɛ:nə] **der; ~n, ~n** Dane; **er ist ~:** he is Danish *or* a Dane

da·neben *Adv.* **a)** *(an der/die Seite davon)* next to *or* beside him/her/it/them *etc.*; **b)** *(im Vergleich dazu)* in comparison; **c)** *(außerdem)* in addition [to that]; besides [that]; **man muß ~ auch berücksichtigen, wie schwer es ist** one must consider at the same time *or* as well how difficult it is

daneben-: ~|benehmen *unr. refl. V. (ugs.)* blot one's copybook *(coll.)*; spoil one's record; *(sich aufführen)* make an exhibition of oneself; **~|fallen** *unr. itr. V.; mit sein* miss; **~|gehen** *unr. itr. V.; mit sein* **a)** *(das Ziel verfehlen)* miss [the target]; **b)** *(ugs.: fehlschlagen)* misfire; be a flop *(sl.)*; **das geht sowieso ~:** it won't be any good; **~|geraten** *unr. itr. V.; mit sein (ugs.)* **[jmdm.] ~geraten** go wrong [on sb.]; **~|greifen** *unr. itr. V.* **a)** *(vorbeigreifen)* miss [one's aim] *(when reaching for sth.)*; **beim Klavierspielen ~greifen** play a wrong note/some wrong notes on the piano; **b)** *(ugs.)* **im Ausdruck ~greifen** *(aus Unkenntnis)* say the wrong thing; *(aus Taktlosigkeit)* put one's foot in it; **mit seiner Prognose ~greifen** be wide of the mark with one's prognosis; **~|halten** *unr. tr. V. (ugs.: vergleichen)* **wenn man X ~hält** when compared with X; **~|hauen** *unr. tr. V.;* **a)** *(nicht treffen)* miss; **b)** *(ugs.: sich irren)* be wide of the mark; **mit der Antwort hat er ziemlich ~gehauen** his answer was well wide of the mark *or (coll.)* way out; **~|liegen** *unr. itr. V. (ugs.)* be wide of the mark; **mit dieser Meinung liegst du aber sehr ~:** your estimation is quite wrong *or (coll.)* way out; **~|schießen** *unr. itr. V.* **a)** *(Ziel verfehlen)* miss [the target]; **mit Absicht ~:** shoot to miss; **b)** *s.* **~hauen b; ~|sein** *unr. itr. V.; Zusschr. nur im Inf. u. 2. Part. (ugs.) (verwirrt sein)* be in a complete daze; *(sich unwohl fühlen)* not be oneself; be under the weather *(coll.)*; **~|tippen** *itr. V. (ugs.)* guess wrong; **~getippt!** wrong!; **~|treffen** *unr. itr. V.* miss [the target]; **danebengetroffen!** missed!

Dänemark ['dɛ:nəmark] **(das); ~s** Denmark

dang [daŋ] *1. u. 3. Pers. Sg. Prät. v.* **dingen**

da·nieden *Adv. (dichter. veralt.)* here below [on earth]

danieder|liegen *unr. itr. V. (geh.)* **a)** *(krank sein)* be laid low; **schwer [krank]/sterbend ~:** lie seriously ill/dying; **b)** *(Wirtsch.)* ⟨*trade, economy*⟩ be depressed

Dänin die; ~, ~nen Dane; Danish woman/girl; *s. auch* **-in**

dänisch ['dɛ:nɪʃ] *Adj.* Danish; *s. auch* **deutsch, Deutsch**

dank [daŋk] *Präp. mit Dat. u. Gen. im Sg. u. meist mit Gen. im Pl.* thanks to; **~ einem Zufall** *od.* **eines Zufalls** by chance; owing to a coincidence

Dank der; ~[e]s a) thanks *pl.*; **jmdm. seinen ~ abstatten** offer one's thanks to sb.; **jmdm. seinen [herzlichen/allerherzlichsten] ~ aussprechen** express one's/sincere/most sincere/thanks *or* gratitude to sb.; **jmdm. ~ sagen** thank sb.; offer one's thanks to sb.; **jmdm. [großen] ~ schulden** *od.* **schuldig sein** *(geh.)*, **jmdm. zu [großem] ~ verpflichtet sein** owe sb. a [great] debt of gratitude; **kein Wort des ~es sagen** not say *or* offer a word of thanks; **als** *od.* **zum ~ dafür, daß ich seinen Hund in Pflege genommen hatte** as a way of saying 'thank you' to me for looking after his dog; **zum ~ dafür hat sie mir noch ins Gesicht gespuckt** *(iron.)* all the thanks I got was that she spat in my face; **und das ist nun der ~ dafür** *(iron.)* so that's all the thanks I get!; **zum ~ für seine Verdienste** in grateful recognition of his services; **mit vielem** *od.* **bestem ~ zurück** thanks for the loan; *(bes. geschrieben)* returned with thanks!; **etw. mit ~ annehmen** accept sth. with thanks; **von [tiefem] ~ erfüllt sein** *(geh.)* be filled with a [deep] sense of gratitude; **damit wird er [bei mir] wenig/keinen ~ ernten** he won't get much/any thanks [from me] for that; **b)** *(in Dankesformeln)* **haben Sie ~!** please accept my thanks; **vielen/besten/herzlichen ~!** thank you very much; many thanks; **vielen ~, daß du mir beim Umzug geholfen hast** thank you very much for helping me with the move; **[nein,] vielen ~!** *(iron.)* no, thank you!; **tausend ~!** *(ugs.)* very many thanks [indeed]; *s. auch* **heiß**

Dank·adresse die [official] letter of thanks

dankbar 1. *Adj.* **a)** *(voller Dank)* grateful; *(anerkennend)* appreciative ⟨*child, audience, etc.*⟩; **in ~er Anerkennung** *(+ Gen.)*/**Erinnerung an** *(+ Akk.)* in grateful recognition/memory of; **[jmdm.] für etw. ~ sein** be grateful [to sb.] for sth.; **sich ~ zeigen** show one's gratitude *or* appreciation; **sie sind für jede Abwechslung ~:** they are thankful for any diversion; **für eine baldige Antwort wären wir ~:** we should be grateful for an early reply; **ich wäre Ihnen sehr ~, wenn Sie ... könnten** I should be very grateful if you could ...; **b)** *(lohnend)* rewarding ⟨*job, part, task, etc.*⟩; **c)** *(ugs.: haltbar)* hard-wearing ⟨*material, clothes*⟩; *(unempfindlich)* easy-care ⟨*garment, plant, etc.*⟩. **2.** *adv.* gratefully; **etw. ~ annehmen** *od.* **entgegennehmen** accept sth. gratefully *or* with thanks; **jmdn. ~ anblicken** give sb. a look of gratitude

Dankbarkeit die; ~: gratitude; **etw. aus ~ tun** do sth. out of gratitude; **in/mit [aufrichtiger/tiefer] ~:** in/with [sincere/deep] gratitude

Dank·brief der letter of thanks; thank-you letter

danke ['daŋkə] *Höflichkeitsformel* thank you; *(ablehnend)* no, thank you; **Darf ich Ihnen noch Tee nachgießen? – Ja ~[, gern]** May I pour you some more tea? – Yes, please[, I'd like some]; **Gefällt es Ihnen hier bei uns? – Ja ~, sehr sogar** Do you like it here? – Yes, thank you, very much; **nein ~, ~ nein** no, thank you; **Soll ich Ihnen helfen? – Danke, es geht schon** Shall I help you? – No thank you *or* No thanks, it's all right; ~ **schön/sehr/vielmals** thank you very much; ~ **schön sagen** say 'thank you'; **Wie geht's? – Mir geht's** ~ *(ugs.)* How are you? – I'm OK [thanks] *(coll.)*; **sonst geht's dir [wohl]** ~**!** *(ugs.)* what do you think you're doing?; have you taken leave of your senses?

danken 1. *itr. V. (Dank aussprechen)* thank; **jmdm. für etw. [vielmals]** ~: thank sb. [very much] for sth.; **ich danke Ihnen vielmals** thank you very much; **er dankte kurz und verließ das Zimmer** he said a quick 'thank you' and left the room; **danke der [gütigen] Nachfrage!** *(meist scherzh. od. iron.)* thanks for asking; kind of you to ask; **Betrag ~d erhalten** [payment] received with thanks; **~d ablehnen** decline with thanks; **dafür danke ich bestens** *(iron.)* thanks a lot *(coll.)*; **na, ich danke!** *(ugs.)* no, 'thank you!; **ich danke für Obst und Südfrüchte** *(ugs.)* no, thanks; *s. auch* **Knie. 2.** *tr. V.* **a) [aber bitte,] nichts zu** ~: don't mention it; not at all; **es wird einem noch nicht einmal gedankt** you don't even get any thanks [for it]; **sie hat ihm seine Hilfe schlecht gedankt** she gave him a poor reward for his help; **er dankte ihnen ihre Güte mit Ungehorsam** *(iron.)* the only reward they got [from him] for their kindness was disobedience; **b)** *(geh.: verdanken)* **jmdm. etw.** ~: owe sb. sth.; owe sth. to sb.; **nur diesem Umstand ist es zu** ~, **daß ...**: it was only thanks to this that ...

dankens·wert *Adj.* commendable ⟨*effort etc.*⟩; **es ist ~, daß er uns hilft** it is kind *or* very good of him to help [us]

dankenswerter·weise *Adv.* kindly; generously; ~ **haben sich viele freiwillig gemeldet** commendably many have volunteered

Danke·schön das; ~**s** thank-you; **ein [herzliches]** ~ **sagen** express one's [sincere] thanks; **nicht einmal ein** ~ **bekommen** not get so much as a thank-you

Dankes·wort das word of thanks

Dank-: ~gebet das prayer of thanksgiving; **~gottes·dienst der** thanksgiving service; **~sagung die;** ~, **~en** *(Text)* expression of thanks; *(Karte)* note of thanks; *(Brief)* letter of thanks; **~schreiben das** letter of thanks

dann [dan] *Adv.* **a)** then; **was machen wir ~?** what shall we do then *or* after that?; **was ~?** what happens then?; **noch drei Tage, ~ ist Ostern** another three days and it will be Easter; **was soll ~ werden?** what will happen then?; **bis ~**: see you then; ~ **und** ~: at such and such a time; *(an dem und dem Tag)* on such and such a date; **von ~ bis ~**: from such and such a date/time to such and such a date/time; ~ **und wann** now and then; **b)** *(räumlich: dahinter)* **zuerst kam die Kapelle, ~ folgten die Pfadfinder** first came the band, then *or* followed by the Scouts; **an die Gärten schließt sich ~ Ödland an** then at the end of the gardens there is a piece of wasteland; **c)** *(rangmäßig danach)* **er ist der Klassenbeste, ~ kommt sein Bruder** he is top of the class, followed by his brother *or* then comes his brother; **d)** *(unter diesen Umständen)* ~ **will ich nicht weiter stören** then *or* in that case I won't disturb you any further; **na ~!** well, that's different!; **[na,]** ~ **eben nicht!** in that case, forget it!; ~ **bis morgen** see you tomorrow, then; **wenn er selbst nicht hinfahren kann, wer ~?** if he can't go there himself, who can?; **nur ~, wenn ...**: only if ...; **lehnt er ab, ~ werden wir klagen** if he refuses, [then] we shall complain; **e)** *(außerdem)* ~ **noch ...**: then ... as well; **und ~ kommt noch die Mehrwertsteuer hinzu** and then there's VAT *(Brit.) or (Amer.)* tax to add on top of that; **zuletzt fiel ~ noch der Strom aus** finally to top it all there was a power failure; **f)** *(demnach)* ~ **hast du also die ganze Zeit mit zugehört** so you've been listening the whole time; **g)** *(schließlich)* **es hat ~ doch noch geklappt** it was all right in the end

dannen ['danən] *Adv.* **in von** ~ *(veralt.)* from thence *(arch./literary)*; **von ~ eilen/gehen** hasten away/depart

dantesk [dan'tɛsk] *Adj. (geh.)* Dantesque

dantisch ['dantɪʃ] *Adj.* Dantean

Danzig ['dantsɪç] **(das);** ~**s** Gdansk; *(vor 1945)* Danzig

daran [da'ran] *Adv.* **a)** *(an dieser/diese Stelle, an diesem/diesen Gegenstand)* on it/them; **es klebt etwas ~**: something is sticking to it/them; **es hängt etwas ~**: something is hanging from it/them; **er klammert sich** ~ *(auch fig.)* he clings to it; ~ **riechen** take a sniff at it/them; ~ **vorbei** past it/them; **kommen wir noch einmal ~ vorbei?** shall we be passing it/them again?; **dicht ~**: close to it/them; **nahe ~ sein, etw. zu tun** be on the point of doing sth.; **b)** *(hinsichtlich dieser Sache)* about it/them; **denken Sie ~**: think about it/them; **das Beste/Schlimmste ~**: the best/worst part of *or* about it/them; ~ **ist nichts zu machen** there's nothing one can do about it; ~ **wird sich nichts ändern** nothing will alter this fact; **kein Wort ~ ist wahr** not a word of it is true; **er arbeitet schon lange ~**: he has been working on it/them for a long time; **wir haben keinen Bedarf mehr ~**: we no longer have any need of it/them; **mir liegt viel ~**: it means a lot to me; **mir liegt ~, zu erfahren, wie er zu der Sache steht** I'd really like *or* I'd be interested to know his view of this matter; **Sie werden viel Freude ~ haben** you will get a lot of pleasure from it; **c)** *(auf Grund dieser Sache)* **ich wäre beinahe ~ erstickt** I almost choked on it; it almost made me choke; **er ist ~ gestorben** he died of it; **d)** *(an diesen Vorgang)* ~ **anschließend** *od.* **im Anschluß ~ fand eine Diskussion statt** after that there was a discussion; *s. auch* **da-; dran**

daran- (*s. auch* **dran-)**: **~|geben** *unr. tr. V. (geh.)* sacrifice; **~|gehen** *unr. itr. V.; mit sein* set about it; **~gehen, etw. zu tun** set about doing sth.; **~|machen** *refl. V. (ugs.)* set about it; *(ernstlich)* get down to it; **sich ~machen, etw. zu tun** get down to/set about doing sth.; **~|setzen 1.** *tr. V.* devote ⟨*energy etc.*⟩ to it; summon up ⟨*ambition*⟩ for it; *(aufs Spiel setzen)* risk ⟨*one's life, one's honour*⟩ for it; **er hat alles** *od.* **alle seine Kräfte ~gesetzt, um dieses Ziel zu erreichen** he spared no effort to achieve *or* devoted all his energy to achieving this aim; **2.** *refl. V. (ugs.: in Angriff nehmen)* get down to it; **sich ~setzen, etw. zu tun** get down to doing sth.; **~|wenden** *unr. od. regelm. tr. V. (geh.)* devote ⟨*time, effort*⟩ to it

darauf [da'rauf] *Adv.* **a)** *(auf dieser/diese Stelle)* on it/them; *(oben ~)* on top of it/them; **er ißt gern Frikadellen mit Senf ~**: he likes eating rissoles with mustard on top; **er goß Wasser ~**: he poured water on [to] it/them; **b)** *(auf ein Ziel hin)* **er hat ~ geschossen** he shot at it/them ; ~ **müßt ihr zugehen** that's what you must head towards *or* make for; **ich muß ~ dringen** I must insist on it; **er ist ganz versessen ~**: he is mad [keen] on it *(sl.)*; **also darauf willst du hinaus** so 'that's what you're getting at; ~ **wollen wir anstoßen!** let's drink to that!; **c)** *(auf diese Angelegenheit)* about it; **wir kamen nur kurz ~ zu sprechen** we only talked about it briefly *or* touched on it; **wie kommt du nur ~?** what makes you think that?; **wie kommst du ~, so etwas anzunehmen?** how do you come to assume such a thing?; **d)** *(danach)* after that; **erst ein Blitz, unmittelbar ~ ein Donnerschlag** first there was lightning, immediately followed by a clap of thunder; **ein Jahr ~ / kurz ~ starb er** he died a year later/shortly afterwards; **zuerst kamen die Kinder, ~ folgten die Festwagen** first came the children, then followed *or* followed by the floats; **e)** *(infolgedessen, daraufhin)* because of that; as a result; **f) der Gutschein ist verfallen, ~ bekommen Sie nichts mehr** the voucher is out of date, you won't get anything on *or* for that; ~ **fußen alle unsere Überlegungen** all our deliberations are based on it *or* this; *s. auch* **da-; drauf; tags**

darauf- (*s. auch* **drauf-)**: **~folgend** *Adj.; nicht präd.* following; **dieser und der ~folgende Wagen** this car and the one behind *or* following it; **am ~folgenden Tag** the following day; next day; **~hin** [--'-] *Adv.* **a)** *(infolgedessen)* as a result [of this/that]; consequently; *(zeitlich)* thereupon; **b)** *(unter diesem Gesichtspunkt)* with a view to this/that; **etw. ~hin prüfen, ob es geeignet ist** examine sth. to see whether it is suitable

daraus [da'raus] *Adv.* **a)** *(aus diesem Raum, Behälter o. ä. heraus)* from it/them; out of it/them; **er holte eine Flasche und goß ~ ein** he fetched a bottle and poured out drinks from it; **sie öffnete den Koffer und holte ein Kleid ~ hervor** she opened the suitcase and took out a dress *or* took a dress out of it; **b)** *(aus dieser Angelegenheit, Sache)* from it/them; out of it/them; **wir alle wissen das und sollten ~ lernen** we all know that and should learn from it; **sie hat ihm nie einen Vorwurf ~ gemacht** she never reproached him for it *or* made an issue out of it; **mach dir nichts ~** don't worry about it; **dieser Stoff ist hübsch, ~ nähe ich mir ein Kleid** this material is pretty, I'm going to make myself a dress out of it; **Kartoffeln sind nicht nur zum Essen da, viele machen Schnaps ~**: potatoes are not only for eating – a lot of people make schnapps from them; ~ **ist eine große Firma geworden** it has become *or* turned into a large business; **was ist ~ geworden?** what has become of it?; ~ **wird nichts** nothing will come of it; **c)** *(aus dieser Quelle, Unterlage)* from it/them; ~ **geht eindeutig hervor, daß ...**: from this it is clear that ...

darben ['darbn̩] *itr. V. (geh.)* **a)** *(in Not leben)* live in want; *(sich sehr einschränken)* go short; pinch and scrape; **die ~den Massen** the indigent *or* destitute masses; **wir haben sehr gedarbt** we suffered great want; **b)** *(Hunger leiden)* go hungry

dar|bieten *(geh.)* **1.** *unr. tr. V.* **a)** *(anbieten)* offer; serve ⟨*drinks, food*⟩; **die dargebotene Hand ausschlagen** *(fig.)* reject the proffered hand [of friendship] *(fig.)*; **b)** *(aufführen, vortragen)* perform; **es wurden Gedichte und Lieder dargeboten** a recital of poems and songs was presented. **2.** *unr. refl. V.* **sich jmds. Blicken ~**: expose oneself to sb.'s gaze; **eine herrliche Aussicht bot sich uns dar** a marvellous view met our eyes

Darbietung die; ~, **~en** *(geh.)* **a)** presentation; **b)** *(Aufführung)* performance; *(beim Varieté usw.)* act

dar|bringen *unr. tr. V.* offer; **jmdm. ein Ständchen ~**: serenade sb.

darein [da'rain] *Adv. (geh.)* in it/them; *s. auch* **da-**

darein-: ~|finden *unr. refl. V. (geh.)* come to terms with it; *(sich daran gewöhnen)* become accustomed to it; **~|fügen** *refl. V. (geh.)* resign oneself to it; **~|reden** *itr. V.* **jmdm. ~**: meddle *or* interfere in sb.'s affairs/decisions *etc.*; *(unterbrechen)* interrupt sb.; **niemand hat ihm ~zureden** nobody has any right to [try to] tell him what to do; **~|setzen** *tr. V.* devote to it; **alles** *od.* **seine ganze Energie ~setzen, etw. zu tun** concentrate all one's efforts on doing sth.; **er setzt seinen ganzen Ehrgeiz ~, als erster fertig zu sein** he has made it his great ambition to finish first

darf [darf] *1. u. 3. Pers. Sg. Präsens v.* **dürfen**

darfst [darfst] *2. Pers. Sg. Präsens v.* **dürfen**

darin [da'rɪn] *Adv.* **a)** *(in dieser Sache o. ä.)* in it/them; *(drinnen)* inside [it/them]; **die ~ enthaltenen Briefe** the letters contained in it/them *or (formal)* therein; **b)** *(in dieser Hinsicht)* in that respect; **~ stimme ich völlig mit Ihnen überein** I entirely agree with you there; *s. auch* **da-**
darinnen [da'rɪnən] *Adv. (geh.)* in it/them; therein *(formal)*
dar|legen *tr. V.* explain; set forth ⟨*reasons, facts*⟩; expound ⟨*theory*⟩; **jmdm. etw. ~:** explain sth. to sb.; **etw. schriftlich ~:** set sth. out in writing
Darlegung die; ~, ~en explanation
Darlehen ['da:ɐ̯le:ən] **das; ~s, ~:** loan; **ein ~ aufnehmen** get *or* raise a loan; **jmdm. ein ~ gewähren** give *or* grant sb. a loan
Darlehens-: ~kasse die credit bank; **~nehmer der** *(Bankw.)* borrower; **~summe die** amount of the loan; **eine ~summe von ...:** a loan amounting to ...; **~vertrag der** loan agreement
Darm [darm] **der; ~|e|s, Därme** ['dɛrmə] **a)** intestines *pl.*; bowels *pl.*; **[jmdm.] auf den ~ schlagen** give sb. diarrhoea; **den ~ entleeren** evacuate *or* empty one's bowels; **Erkrankungen des ~es** intestinal diseases; **b)** *(als Saiten)* gut; **c)** *(als Wursthaut)* skin
Darm-: ~aus·gang der *(Anat.)* anus; **~blutung die** *(Med.)* intestinal haemorrhage; **~bruch der** *(Med.)* enterocele; **~entleerung die** evacuation of the bowels; **~grippe die** gastric influenza; **~katarrh der** *(Med.)* enteritis; **~krebs der;** *o. Pl.* cancer of the intestine *or* bowels; **~saite die** gut string; **~spülung die** *(Med.)* enema; **~tätigkeit die;** *o. Pl. (Med.)* functioning of the bowels; **~trägheit die** *(Med.)* constipation; **~trakt der** *(Anat.)* intestinal tract; **~verschlingung die** *(Med.)* volvulus; **~verschluß der** *(Med.)* intestinal obstruction
darnach *(veralt.) s.* **danach**
darneben *(veralt.) s.* **daneben**
darnieder- *s.* **danieder-**
darob [da'rɔp] *Adv. (veralt.)* **a)** *(darüber)* about it/them; **er wunderte sich ~, daß ...:** he was surprised that ...; **b)** *(deswegen)* because of it; *s. auch* **da-**
Darre ['darə] **die; ~, ~n a)** *(Vorrichtung)* [drying] kiln; **b)** *(das Darren)* drying
dar|reichen *tr. V. (geh.)* **a)** *(anbieten)* proffer; **b)** *(überreichen)* **jmdm. ein Geschenk** *usw.* **~:** present sb. with a gift *etc.*
darren *tr. V.* dry
Darr-: ~gewicht das [kiln-]dry weight *(of wood)*; **~malz das** [kiln-]dried malt
darstellbar *Adj.* **a)** *(abbildbar)* depictable; portrayable; **ist das graphisch ~?** can that be represented graphically?; **graphisch ~e Entwicklungen** developments which can be shown on a graph *or* diagram; **b)** *(spielbar)* playable ⟨*part*⟩; **c)** *(Chemie)* **ein leicht ~er Stoff** a material which can easily be produced
dar|stellen 1. *tr. V.* **a)** *(abbilden)* depict; portray; **etw. graphisch ~:** present sth. graphically; *(als Graph)* show sth. on a graph; **wen/was stellt dieses Bild dar?** whom does this picture portray/what does this picture represent?; **die ~de Geometrie** descriptive geometry; **die ~de Kunst** the performing arts *pl.*; **ein ~der Künstler** a performer; **b)** *(verkörpern)* play; act; **den Othello ~:** play *or* act [the part of] Othello; **etwas/mehr/nichts ~:** make [a bit of] an impression/more of an impression/not make any sort of an impression; ⟨*gift etc.*⟩ look good/look better/not look anything special; **c)** *(schildern)* describe ⟨*person, incident, etc.*⟩; present ⟨*matter, argument*⟩; **falsch/verzerrt ~:** misrepresent/distort ⟨*facts*⟩; **es wurde dann so dargestellt, als sei das unser Wunsch gewesen** it was then put in such a way as to suggest that we had wanted it; **so schlimm, wie du ihn darstellst, ist er auch nicht** he is not as bad as you make him out to be; **d)** *(sein, bedeuten)* represent; constitute; **das zweite Kind stellt eine große Belastung für sie dar** the second child means a heavy load for her; **e)** *(Chemie)* produce. **2.** *refl. V.* **a)** *(sich erweisen, sich zeigen)* prove [to be]; turn out to be; **sich jmdm. als ... ~:** appear to sb. as ...; **nach dem Bericht stellt sich die Sache ungefähr so dar** according to the report the situation appears to be roughly this; **b)** *(sich selbst schildern)* portray oneself **(als + *Akk.*** as); **sie lieben es, sich als Wohltäter darzustellen** they like to present themselves in the role of benefactors
Darsteller der; ~s, ~ actor; **der ~ des Hamlet** the actor playing Hamlet; **berühmt als ~ des Hamlet** famous for his portrayal of Hamlet *or* as an interpreter of Hamlet
Darstellerin die; ~, ~nen actress; *s. auch* **Darsteller**
darstellerisch 1. *Adj.; nicht präd.* acting *attrib.*; **das Darstellerische** the interpretative aspect; **eine einmalige ~e Leistung** a marvellow piece of acting; **ihre ~en Fähigkeiten** her abilities as an actress. **2.** *adv.* from an acting point of view
Darstellung die a) representation; *(Schilderung)* portrayal ; *(Bild)* picture; **graphische/schematische ~:** diagram; *(Graph)* graph; **b)** *(Beschreibung, Bericht)* description; account; **bei seiner ~ der geschichtlichen Tatsachen** in his account *or* rendering of the historical facts; **c)** *(einer Theaterrolle)* interpretation; performance; *(einer Szene usw.)* performance; **seine ~ des Mephisto** his portrayal *or* interpretation of Mephisto; **etw. zur ~ bringen** portray sth.; *(aufführen)* perform sth.; **d)** *(Chemie)* production
Darstellungs-: ~form die form of representation; **~mittel das** representational technique; *(eines Schauspielers)* acting technique
dar|tun *unr. tr. V. (geh.) (darlegen)* state ⟨*fact, one's reasons*⟩; *(erklären)* explain; *(demonstrieren)* demonstrate; **er hat zur Genüge dargetan, wie ...:** he gave a sufficient account of how ...
darüber *Adv.* **a)** *(über dem Genannten)* over *or* above it/them; **wir wohnen im zweiten Stock und er ~:** we live on the second floor and he lives above us; **b)** *(über das Genannte [hinweg])* over it/them; **~ führen zu wenige Brücken** too few bridges go across it/them; **~ hinaus** in additon [to that]; *(noch obendrein)* what is more; **~ hinaussein** *(zu alt/erfahren genug für etw. sein)* be beyond that stage [now]; *(etw. überwunden haben)* have got over it; **c)** *(über dieser/diese Angelegenheit)* about it/them; **~ kann kein Zweifel bestehen** there can be no doubt about it; **ich habe fast den ganzen Tag ~ gesessen** I spent almost the whole day over *or* on it; **~ wollen wir hinwegsehen** we will overlook it; **d)** *(über diese Grenze, dieses Maß hinaus)* above [that]; over [that]; **Kinder im Alter von 5 Jahren und ~:** children of 5 and over; **der Preis beträgt 50 Mark oder etwas ~:** the price is 50 marks or a bit more; **Ist es schon 12 Uhr? – Aber ja, es ist schon 10 Minuten ~:** Is it twelve o'clock yet? – Oh yes, it's already ten past; **man braucht 4 Wochen, manchmal auch etwas ~:** it takes four weeks, sometimes rather longer *or* more; **e)** *(währenddessen)* in the process; **es war ~ Abend geworden** meanwhile it had become evening; **f)** *(währenddessen und deshalb)* because of it/them; as a result; **der Film war so spannend, daß er ~ seine Sorgen vergaß** the film was so exciting that it made him forget his worries; *s. auch* **da-**
darüber-: ~|fahren *unr. itr. V.; mit sein* run over it/them; **sie fuhr rasch mit der Hand/mit einem Tuch ~:** she quickly ran her hand over it/wiped it with a cloth; **~|liegen** *unr. itr. V.* be higher; **sie liegen mit ihrem Angebot weit ~:** their offer is much higher; **~|machen** *refl. V. (ugs.)* get down to it/them; *(essen)* get stuck into it *(sl.)*; *(trinken)* get to work on it; **~|stehen** *unr. itr. V.* be above such things; **~|steigen** *unr. itr. V.; mit sein* climb over it/them
darum [da'rʊm] *Adv.* **a)** *(um diese Stelle herum)* [a]round it/them; **ein Häuschen mit einem Garten ~ [herum]** a little house surrounded by a garden; **b)** *(hinsichtlich dieser Angelegenheit)* **ich werde mich ~ bemühen** I will try to deal with it; *(versuchen, es zu bekommen)* I'll try to get it; **sie wird nicht ~ herumkommen, es zu tun** she won't get out of *or* avoid doing it; **~ ist es mir nicht zu tun, ~ geht es mir nicht** that's not the point as far as I'm concerned; that's not what I'm after; **es geht mir ~, eine Einigung zu erzielen** my concern *or* aim is to reach an agreement; **c)** ['--] *(deswegen)* because of that; for that reason; **ach, ~ ist er so schlecht gelaunt!** so that's why he's in such a bad mood!; **er ist zwar klein, aber ~ nicht schwach** he is small but that doesn't mean that he's weak; **Warum weinst du? – Darum!** Why are you crying? – Because!; *s. auch* **da-**
darum-: ~|binden *unr. tr. V.* tie [a]round it/them; **~|kommen** *unr. itr. V.; mit sein* lose it/them; **~kommen, etw. zu tun** miss the opportunity of doing sth.; miss out on [doing] sth. *(coll.)*; **~|legen** *tr. V.* put around it/them
darunter [da'rʊntɐ] *Adv.* **a)** *(unter dem Genannten/das Genannte)* under *or* beneath it/them; **wir wohnen im 2. Stock und er ~:** we live on the second floor and he lives under us *or* on the floor below; **sie hatte nichts ~ an** she was wearing nothing underneath; **b)** *(unter dieser Grenze, diesem Maß)* less; **10° oder etwas ~:** 10° or a bit less; **~ kann ich die Vase nicht verkaufen** I can't sell the vase for less; **Bewerber im Alter von 40 Jahren und ~:** applicants aged 40 and under; **~ tut er es nicht** *(ugs.)* he's not satisfied with anything less; **c)** *(unter dieser Sache)* **was verstehen Sie ~?** what do you understand by that?; **was hat man ~ zu verstehen?** what is one to make of it/that?; what is it/that supposed to mean?; **sie hat sehr ~ gelitten** she suffered a great deal from *or* because of it/that; **d)** *(unter dieser/diese Menge, dazwischen)* amongst them; **in vielen Ländern, ~ der Schweiz** in many countries, including Switzerland; *s. auch* **da-**
darunter-: ~|bleiben *unr. itr. V.; mit sein* remain lower; *(niedriger sein)* be lower; **viele forderten 20 %, wir blieben aber ~:** many demanded 20 %, but we kept below this; **~|fallen** *unr. itr. V.; mit sein* be included; be amongst them; *(in diese Kategorie)* come under it; **~|gehen** *unr. itr. V.; mit sein* **a)** *(ugs.) (unter diese Sache passen)* fit *or* go underneath; **b)** *(diese Grenze unterschreiten)* go below that; **~|liegen** *unr. itr. V.* be lower; *(weniger bekommen)* get less; **die Parallelklasse liegt mit ihren Leistungen ~:** the parallel class's performance is not as good; **~|mischen 1.** *tr. V.* mix in; mix with it; **2.** *refl. V.* mingle with it/them; **~|schreiben** *unr. tr. V.* write underneath *or* at the bottom; *(als Unterschrift)* sign underneath *or* at the bottom; *(mit der Schreibmaschine)* type underneath *or* at the bottom; **~|setzen** *tr. V.* put ⟨*signature, name*⟩ to it
Darwinismus [darvi'nɪsmʊs] **der; ~:** Darwinism *no art.*
darwinistisch 1. *Adj.* Darwinian; Darwinist. **2.** *adv.* in Darwinian terms

das [das] **1.** *best. Art.* the; **das Leben im Dschungel** life in the jungle; **das Weihnachtsfest** Christmas; **das Frankreich/London des 19. Jahrhunderts** nineteenth-century France/London; **das Laufen/Sprechen fällt ihm schwer** walking/talking is difficult for him; **das Gute/Schöne** what is good/beautiful. **2.** *Demonstrativpron.* **a)** *attr.* **dạs Kind/Buch/Auto war es** it was 'that child/book/car; **b)** *selbständig* **dạs [da]** that one; **dạs [hier]** this one [here]; **das mit dem blonden Haar/roten Umschlag** the one with the fair hair/red cover; **das Schwein, das!** the dirty pig!; **mein Auto, das ist kaputt** *(ugs.)* oh, my car – it's conked out *(coll.)*. **3.** *Relativpron. (Mensch)* who; that; *(Sache, Tier)* which; that; **das Mädchen, das da drüben entlanggeht** the girl walking along over there; **ich sah ein Mädchen/Hündchen, das aus dem Fenster schaute** I saw a girl/little dog looking out of the window

dạ|sein *unr. itr. V.; mit sein; Zusschr. nur im Inf. u. Part.* **a)** be there; *(hier sein)* be here; *(übrig sein)* be left; **ist Herr X da?** is Mr X about *or* available?; **er ist schon da** he has already arrived; **der neue Katalog ist da** the new catalogue is in; **ist ein Brief für mich da?** is there a letter for me?; **es ist niemand da** there is nobody there/here; **es muß noch Brot ~:** there must be some bread left; **du mußt essen, was da ist** you must eat what there is; **der Schlüssel ist wieder da** the key is back again; *(ist gefunden worden)* the key has turned up [again]; **ich bin gleich wieder da** I'll be right *or* straight back; **ich melde mich, wenn ich wieder da bin** I'll get in touch when I get back; **es/sie sind nur dazu da, zu ...:** it only exists/they only exist to ...; its/their only purpose is to ...; **dafür** *od.* **dazu ist es ja da!** that's what it's [there] for!; **b)** *(sich ereignen)* occur; ‹*moment*› have arrived; ‹*situation*› have arisen; **ein solcher Fall ist noch nie dagewesen** such a case has never occurred before *or* is unprecedented; **er überbot alles bisher Dagewesene** he surpassed all previous achievements; **c)** *(existieren, leben)* be left; be still alive; **da warst du noch gar nicht da** *(ugs.)* you weren't around then; that was before your time; **sie war nur noch für ihn da** he had her to himself; **d)** *(ugs.: klar bei Bewußtsein sein)* **ganz** *od.* **voll ~:** be completely with it *(coll.)*; **ich bin noch nicht ganz da** I'm not quite with it yet *(coll.)*; I haven't quite come round yet; **er ist [geistig] wieder voll da** he is in full possession of his faculties again

Da·sein das; *o. Pl.* **a)** *(Vorhandensein)* existence; **etw. ins ~ rufen** create sth.; *(gründen)* found sth.; **b)** *(menschliche Existenz)* life; **sich/jmdm. das ~ erleichtern** make life easier for oneself/sb.; **ein trauriges ~ führen** lead a miserable existence; *s. auch* **fristen, Kampf; c)** *(Zugegensein)* presence

Daseins-: ~berechtigung die right to exist; **das findet darin** *od.* **dadurch seine ~berechtigung** this justifies its existence; **~form die** form *or* mode of existence; **~freude die** *s.* **Lebensfreude; ~kampf der** struggle for existence

da·sẹlbst *Adv. (geh. veralt.)* there

dạ|sitzen *unr. itr. V.* **a)** sit there; **b)** *(ugs.: ohne etw. auskommen müssen)* be left [there]; **ich saß ohne Geld da** I was stuck there without any money; **jetzt sitzen wir da!** now we're stuck!

dạsjenige *s.* **derjenige**

daß [das] *Konj.* **a)** that; **entschuldigen Sie bitte, ~ ich mich verspätet habe** please forgive me for being late; please forgive my being late; **ich weiß, ~ du recht hast** I know [that] you are right; **ich verstehe nicht, ~ sie ihn geheiratet hat** I don't understand why she married him; **es ist schon 3 Jahre her, ~ wir zum letzten Mal im Theater waren** it is three years since *or* it was three years ago when we last went to the theatre; **b)** *(nach Pronominaladverbien o. ä.)* [the fact] that; *(bei gleichen Subjekten)* **er leidet darunter, ~ er kleiner ist** he suffers from the fact that he is smaller *or* from being smaller; **Wissen erwirbt man dadurch, ~ man viel liest** one acquires knowledge by reading a great deal; *(bei verschiedenen Subjekten)* **das liegt daran, ~ du nicht aufgepaßt hast** that is due to the fact that you did not pay attention; that comes from your not paying attention; **ich bin dagegen, ~ er geht** I am against his going; **c)** *(mit Konsekutivsatz)* that; **[so] ~:** so that; in such a way that; **ich bin so müde, ~ ich kaum gehen kann** I am so tired [that] I can hardly walk; **er lachte so [sehr], ~ ihm die Tränen in die Augen traten** he laughed so much that he almost cried; **d)** *(mit Finalsatz)* so that; **hilf ihm doch, ~ er endlich fertig wird** do help him so that he'll finally be ready/finished; **e)** *(mit Wunschsatz)* if only; **~ er doch käme!** if only he would come!; **~ ihn doch der Teufel hole!** to hell with him!; **~ mir das nicht noch einmal passiert!** see that it doesn't happen again!; **o ~ ich dich bald wiedersehe!** *(poet.)* oh that I may see you again soon!; **f)** *(bedauernder Ausruf)* **~ er so jung sterben mußte!** how terrible *or* it's so sad that he had to die so young!; **~ mir das passieren mußte!** why did it have to [go and] happen to me!; *s. auch* **als, [an]statt, auf, außer, nur, ohne, kaum**

dassẹlbe *s.* **derselbe**

dassẹlbige *s.* **derselbige**

Dassel·fliege die bot-fly

dạ|stehen *unr. itr. V.* **a)** *([untätig] stehen)* [just] stand there; **wie stehst du denn da!** what a way to stand!; **krumm ~:** slouch; **~ wie die Kuh** *od.* **der Ochs vorm neuen Tor** *od.* **Scheunentor** *od.* **vorm Berg** *(salopp)* be completely baffled; **b)** *(in einer bestimmten Lage sein)* find oneself; **gut/schlecht/[ganz] anders ~:** be in a good/bad/[quite] different position; **[ganz] allein ~:** be [all] alone in the world; **nun, wie stehe ich jetzt da?** *(ugs.)* just look at me now!; *(bei einer bestimmten Leistung)* how about that?; *(verzweifelt)* now I'm sunk! *(coll.)*; **wie stehen wir denn jetzt vor den Nachbarn da?** what will the neighbours think of us now?; **mit leeren Händen/als Lügner** *usw.* **~:** be left empty-handed/looking like a liar *etc.*

Datei [da'tai] **die; ~, ~en** data file

Daten ['da:tn̩] *Pl. (Angaben)* data; *(persönliche ~)* particulars; **die technischen ~ eines Typs** the technical specification *sing.* of a model; *s. auch* **Datum a, c**

Daten-: ~bank die; *Pl.* **~banken** data bank; **~bestand der** data base; **~erfassung die;** *o. Pl.* data collection *or* capture; **~schutz der** data protection; **~schutzbeauftragte der/die** data protection officer; **~technik die** data systems [engineering]; **~träger der** data carrier; **~typist der; ~en, ~en, ~typistin die; ~, ~en** data processing keyboarder; **~verarbeitung die** data processing *no def. art.*; **~verarbeitungs·anlage die** data processor; *(größeres System)* data processing system

datieren [da'ti:rən] **1.** *tr. V.* date; **vom 1. Mai datiert** dated 1 May; **archäologische Funde [ins 3. Jh.] ~:** date archaeological finds [to the third century AD]. **2.** *itr. V. (stammen)* date **(aus** from); **der Brief datierte vom 4. Mai** the letter was dated 4 May

Dativ ['da:ti:f] **der; ~s, ~e** *(Sprachw.)* dative [case]; *(Wort im ~)* dative [form]; **im/mit dem ~ stehen** be in/take the dative [case]

Dạtiv·objekt das *(Sprachw.)* indirect object

dato ['da:to] *in* **bis ~** *(Kaufmannsspr., sonst ugs.)* to date

Dạto·wechsel der *(Bankw.)* time-bill

Datscha ['datʃa] **die; ~, ~s** *od.* **Datschen, Datsche** ['datʃə] **die; ~, ~n** *(DDR)* dacha

Dattel ['datl̩] **die; ~, ~n** date

Dạttel-: ~palme die date-palm; **~traube die** *popular name for various large, elongated black grapes*

Datterich ['datərɪç] *s.* **Tatterich**

Datum ['da:tʊm] **das; ~s, Daten** ['da:tn̩] **a)** *(Zeitangabe, Zeitpunkt)* date; **das heutige ~:** the date today; today's date; **was für ein/welches ~ haben wir heute?** what is the date today?; **der Brief trägt das ~ vom 6. Mai** the letter is dated 6 May; **unter dem heutigen/gestrigen ~ übersandten wir Ihnen ...:** in today's/yesterday's mail we sent you ...; **ein Schriftstück mit dem ~ versehen** date a document; **eine Entdeckung neueren ~s** a recent discovery; **b)** *(Faktum)* fact

Datums-: ~grenze die date-line; **~stempel der** date-stamp

Daube ['daubə] **die; ~, ~n a)** *(am Faß)* stave; **b)** *(beim Eisschießen)* tee

Dauer ['dauɐ] **die; ~, ~n a)** *(Zeitraum)* length; duration; **die ~ eines Vertrags** the term of a contract; **die ~ des Besuchs** the length of the visit; **von kurzer** *od.* **nicht von [langer] ~ sein** not last long; be short-lived; **für die ~ eines Jahres** *od.* **von einem Jahr** for a period of one year; **während der ~ unseres Aufenthalts** for the duration of our stay; *(die ganze Zeit)* throughout our whole stay; **b)** *(Fortbestehen)* **von ~ sein** last [long]; **ihr Glück hatte keine ~** *od.* **war nicht von ~:** her happiness was short-lived *or* did not last [long]; **auf die ~:** in the long run; **der Lärm ist auf die ~ nicht zu ertragen** the noise is not tolerable for any length of time; **auf die ~ möchte ich hier nicht wohnen** I wouldn't want to live here permanently *or* indefinitely; **auf ~:** permanently; for good; **er hat die Stelle jetzt auf ~:** his job is now permanent; he now has tenure *(Amer. Sch./Univ.)*

dauer-, Dauer-: ~arbeitslose der/die long-term unemployed person; **~auftrag der** *(Finanzw.)* standing order; **per** *od.* **durch ~auftrag** by standing order; **~ausweis der** long-term pass; **~belastung die** continual *or* constant strain; *(Technik)* permanent load; **~beschäftigung die** permanent job *or (formal)* position; **~brenner der a)** *(Ofen)* slow-burning stove; **b)** *(ugs.: Theaterstück usw.)* long-running success; *(Schlager)* evergreen; **~einrichtung die** permanent institution; **~erfolg der** long-running success; **~erscheinung die** permanent feature **(bei, in** of); **~frost der** long period of frost; **es herrschte ~frost** there was a long period of frost; **~gast der a)** *(im Hotel usw.)* long-stay guest *or* resident; *(scherzh.: Besucher)* long-term visitor *(who outstays his/her welcome)*; **b)** *(im Lokal)* regular; **~geschwindigkeit die** cruising speed; **~haft 1.** *Adj.* **a)** *(von langer Dauer)* [long-]lasting, enduring ‹*peace, friendship, etc.*›; **b)** *(haltbar)* durable; hard-wearing; **2.** *adv.* lastingly; with long-lasting effect; **~karte die** season ticket; **~lauf der** jogging *no art.*; **ein ~lauf** a jog; **einen ~lauf machen** go for a jog; go jogging; **im ~lauf** at a jog; **~lösung die** permanent solution; **~lutscher der** large lollipop; all-day sucker *(Amer.)*; **~mieter der** long-term tenant

[1]**dauern** *itr. V.* last; ‹*job etc.*› take; **der Film dauert zwei Stunden** the film lasts [for] *or* goes on for two hours; **bei ihm dauert alles furchtbar lange** everything takes him a terribly long time; **einen Moment, es dauert nicht lange** just a minute, it won't take long; **etw. dauert seine Zeit** sth. takes time; **ein Weilchen wird es schon noch ~:** it will be *or* take a little while longer; **es dauert mir zu lange** it takes too long for me; **das dauert** *(ugs.)* that will take [some] time; **diese Freundschaft wird ~** *(geh.)* this friendship will last *or* endure

²dauern *tr. V. (geh.)* **die Waisen dauerten ihn** he felt sorry for the orphans; **es dauert mich, daß ...:** I regret *or* I am sorry that ...
dauernd 1. *Adj.; nicht präd.* constant, perpetual ⟨*noise, interruptions, etc.*⟩; permanent ⟨*institution*⟩; **~er Wohnsitz** permanent residence. **2.** *adv.* constantly; *(immer)* always; the whole time; **er kommt ~ zu spät** he is for ever *or* keeps on arriving late
Dauer-: ~obst das fruit which keeps well; **~parker der; ~s, ~:** resident with a parking permit; *(im Parkhaus)* holder of a reserved parking-space; **~redner der** *(abwertend)* voluble speaker; **~regelung die** permanent arrangement; **~regen der** continuous rain; **~schach das** perpetual check; **~schaden der** *(Med.)* **ein ~schaden/~schäden** permanent damage *no indef. art.*; *(Verletzung)* permanent injury; **~stellung die** permanent position; **~strom der** *(Elektrot.)* constant current; **~test der** long-term test; **~ton der** continuous tone; **~welle die** perm; permanent wave; **sie will sich** *(Dat.)* **~wellen legen lassen** *od.* *(ugs.)* **machen lassen** she wants to have her hair permed; **~wurst die** smoked sausage *(with good keeping properties, esp. salami)*; **~zustand der** permanent state [of affairs]; **zum ~zustand werden** become permanent *or* a permanent state
Däumchen ['dɔymçən] **das; ~s, ~:** little thumb; **~ drehen** *(ugs.)* twiddle one's thumbs
Daumen ['daumən] **der; ~s, ~:** thumb; **am ~ lutschen** suck one's thumb; *(fig. ugs.)* [sit there and] starve; **jmdm.** *od.* **für jmdn. den** *od.* **die ~ drücken** *od.* **halten** keep one's fingers crossed for sb.; **auf etw.** *(Dat.)* **den ~ haben, auf etw.** *(Akk.)* **den ~ halten** *(ugs.)* keep a careful eye *or* check on sth.; **jmdm. den ~ aufs Auge drücken** *(ugs.)* put the screws *pl.* on sb.; **[etw.] über den ~ peilen** *(ugs.)* make a guesstimate [of sth.] *(coll.)*; **über den ~ gepeilt** at a rough estimate
daumen-, Daumen-: ~ab·druck der thumb-print; **~breit** *Adj.* as wide as your thumb *postpos.*; ≈ an inch across *postpos.*; **~lutscher der** *(oft abwertend)* thumb-sucker; **~nagel der** thumb-nail; **~register das** thumb-index; **~schrauben** *Pl.* *(hist.)* thumbscrews; **jmdm. die ~schrauben anlegen** *(fig.)* put the screws on sb.
Däumling ['dɔymlɪŋ] **der; ~s, ~e a)** *o. Pl.* *(Märchengestalt)* Tom Thumb; **b)** *(Schutzkappe)* thumb-stall
Daune ['daunə] **die; ~, ~n** down [feather]; **~n** down *sing.*; **man geht weich wie auf ~n** it's like walking on thistledown
daunen-, Daunen-: ~bett das down-filled quilt; **~kissen das** down[-filled] cushion; *(für das Bett)* down[-filled] pillow; **~weich** *Adj.* downy soft; as soft as down *postpos.*
Daus [daus] *(veralt.) in* **ei der ~!, was der ~!** what the deuce *or* dickens! *(coll.)*
David ['da:fɪt] **(der)** David
David[s]·stern der star of David
davon [da'fɔn] *Adv.* **a)** *(von dieser Stelle entfernt)* from it/them; *(von dort)* from there; *(mit Entfernungsangabe)* away [from it/them]; **nur einige Meter ~ [entfernt] ist eine Mauer** there is a wall only a few metres away [from it]; **wir sind noch weit ~ entfernt** *(fig.)* we are still a long way from that; we still have a long way to go; **b)** *(von dieser Stelle weg)* from it/them; **sie konnte die Augen nicht ~ abwenden** she could not take her eyes off it *or* away from it; **dies ist die Hauptstraße, und ~ zweigen einige Nebenstraßen ab** this is the main road and a few side-roads branch off it; **c)** *(hinsichtlich dieser Sache, darüber)* about it/them; **er redet nur davon** he talks only of this; he talks of *or* about nothing else; **d)** *(durch diese Angelegenheit verursacht, dadurch)* by it/them; thereby; **~ betroffen sein** be affected by it/them; **~ wirst du krank** it will make you ill; **~ kriegt man Durchfall** you get diarrhoea from [eating] that/those; that gives/those give you diarrhoea; **das kommt ~!** *(ugs.)* [there you are,] that's what happens; *(es geschieht dir usw. recht)* it serves you/him/her/them right; **das kommt ~, daß du nicht genug schläfst** that's the result of [your] not getting enough sleep; **das hast du nun ~!** that's what comes of it!; **~ hast du doch nichts** you won't *or* don't get anything out of it; there's nothing in it for you; **e)** *(als Teil eines Ganzen; dessen, deren)* of it/them; **das Gegenteil ~ ist wahr** the opposite [of this] is true; **ich hätte gern ein halbes Pfund ~:** I would like half a pound of that/those; **geben Sie mir vier ~:** give me four of them; **hast du schon ~ gegessen/genommen?** have you had/taken some of that/those?; **f)** *(aus diesem Material, auf dieser Grundlage)* from *or* out of it/them; **hier ist Wolle, du kannst dir einen Schal ~ stricken** here is some wool, you can knit yourself a scarf with it; **~ kann man nicht leben** you can't live on that; *s. auch* **da-;** *NB The word can occur in two parts in North German coll. usage, e.g.* **da weiß ich nichts von** I don't know anything about it
davon-: ~|bleiben *unr. itr. V.; mit sein* keep away; **du sollst ~bleiben!** don't touch it/them!; leave it/them alone!; **~|fahren** *unr. itr. V.; mit sein* leave; *(mit dem Auto)* drive away *or* off; *(mit dem Fahrrad, Motorrad)* ride away *or* off; **dem ~fahrenden Zug nachschauen** look after the departing train; *(aus dem Bahnhof)* watch the train as it pulls out; **jmdm. ~fahren** leave sb. behind; **ich muß mich beeilen, sonst fährt mir der Bus ~:** I must hurry or the bus will leave without me *or* I'll miss the bus; **er fährt allen ~** *(ist schneller als alle)* he leaves the rest standing; **~|fliegen** *unr. itr. V.; mit sein* fly away *or* off; **~|gehen** *unr. itr. V.; mit sein* walk away *or* off; **~|kommen** *unr. itr. V.; mit sein* get away; escape; **mit dem Leben ~kommen** escape with one's life; **mit dem Schrecken/einer Geldstrafe ~kommen** get off with a fright/a fine; **~|lassen** *unr. tr. V. in* **die Finger ~lassen** *s.* **Finger a; ~|laufen** *unr. itr. V.; mit sein* **a)** *(weglaufen)* run away; **er ist mir ~gelaufen** he's made off; **es ist zum Davonlaufen** *(ugs.)* it really turns you off *(coll.)*; it makes you want to run a mile; **b)** *(ugs.: überraschend verlassen)* **jmdm. ~laufen** walk out on sb.; **dieser Partei laufen die Wähler ~:** the voters are deserting this party; **c)** *(unkontrollierbar steigen)* spiral; **die Kosten des Projekts sind uns ~gelaufen** the costs of the project have got out of control; **die Preise laufen den Einkommen ~:** prices are outstripping incomes; **~|machen** *refl. V.* make off **(mit** with); **~|schleichen** *unr. itr. V mit sein; auch refl. V.* slink off *or* away; **~|sein** *unr. itr. V.; mit sein; Zusschr. nur im Inf. u. im 2. Part. (ugs.)* **seine Frau ist mit einem andern ~:** his wife has run off with another man; **~|stehlen** *unr. refl. V. (geh.)* steal away; **~|tragen** *unr. tr. V.* **a)** *(wegtragen)* carry away; take away ⟨*rubbish*⟩; **b)** *(geh.: erringen)* win, gain ⟨*a victory, fame*⟩; **den Sieg ~tragen** win; be victorious; *(Sport)* be the winner/winners; **c)** *(geh.: sich zuziehen)* receive, suffer ⟨*injuries*⟩; **~|ziehen** *unr. itr. V.; mit sein* **a)** *(Sport)* pull away; **b)** *(weggehen)* go on one's way
davor [da'fo:ɐ̯] *Adv.* **a)** *(vor dieser/diese Stelle)* in front of it/them; **ein Haus mit einem Garten ~:** a house with a garden at the front *or* in front; **Kommt Mainz vor oder nach Wiesbaden? – Davor** Is Mainz before or after Wiesbaden? – Before; **b)** *(zeitlich)* before [it/them]; **~ macht er einen Dauerlauf von 30 Minuten** he goes jogging for 30 minutes beforehand *or* first; **c)** *(in Verbindung mit bestimmten Verben und Substantiven)* **wir haben ihn ~ gewarnt** we warned him of *or* about it/them; **er hat Angst ~, erwischt zu werden** he is afraid of being caught; **wir sind ~ geschützt** we are protected from it/them; *s. auch* **da-;** *NB In some uses under* **a** *and* **c** *the word occurs in North German colloquial usage in two parts, e.g.* **da habe ich keine Angst vor** I'm not afraid of it/them
davor-: ~|legen 1. *tr. V.* put in front of it/them; **2.** *refl. V.* lie down in front of it/them; **~|liegen** *unr. itr. V.* lie in front of it/them; **die ~liegende Matte** the mat [lying] in front of it; *(vor der Längsseite)* the mat [lying] beside it; **~|schieben 1.** *unr. tr. V.* push in front if it/them; **2.** *unr. refl. V.* move in front of it/them; *(bedecken)* cover it/them; **~|stehen** *unr. itr. V.* **a)** *(vor dieser Sache)* stand in front of it/them; *(vor einem Haus usw.)* stand outside; **b)** *(vor diesem Ereignis usw.)* **kurz ~stehen** be close to it; *(vor einer Tat)* be about to do it; **~|stellen 1.** *tr. V.* put in front of it/them; **2.** *refl. V.* plant oneself in front of it/them
dazu [da'tsu:] *Adv.* **a)** *(zusätzlich zu dieser Sache)* with it/them; *(gleichzeitig)* at the same time; *(außerdem)* what is more; **~ reicht man am besten Salat** it's/they're best served with lettuce/salad; **er ist dumm und ~ auch noch frech** he is stupid and insolent into the bargain; **b)** *(darüber)* about *or* on it/them; **was meinen Sie ~?** what do you think about it?; what is your opinion on this?; **c)** *(zu diesem Zweck)* for it; *(es zu tun)* to do it; **d)** *(zu diesem Ergebnis)* to it; **ich kann nichts ~ tun** I can't do anything to help; **er ist zu alt ~:** he is too old for it; **~ reicht das Geld nicht** we haven't enough money for that; **~ sind sie ja da!** that's what they are there for!; **~ kann ich dir nur raten** I would strongly advise you to do it; **im Widerspruch** *od.* **Gegensatz ~:** contrary to this/that; **~ war sie nicht in der Lage** she was not in a position to do it *or* do so; **er hatte ~ keine Lust** he didn't want to *or* didn't feel like it; **ich komme nie ~/nie ~, es zu tun** I never get round to it/to doing it; **wie komme ich ~?** *(ugs.)* it would never occur to me; why on earth should I?; *s. auch* **da-;** *NB In senses b and d the word occurs in North German colloquial usage in two parts, e.g.* **da habe ich keine Lust zu** I don't feel like it
dazu-: ~|geben *unr. tr. V.* **a)** *(beisteuern)* give towards it; **b)** *(zusätzlich geben)* add; give as well; **c)** *(Kochk.)* add; *s. auch* **Senf; ~|gehören** *tr. V.* **a)** *(zu dieser Sache, Kategorie gehören)* belong to it/them; *(als Zusatz)* go with it/them; **der Wein gehört ~:** *(ist nicht wegzudenken)* the wine belongs with it; you have to have wine, it's all part of it; *(ist im Preis inbegriffen)* the wine is included [in the price]; **das gehört [mit] ~:** it's all part of it; *(es ist Sitte)* it's the done thing *(coll.)*; **alles, was ~gehört** everything that goes with it/them; **b)** *(erforderlich sein)* **sie hat alles, was ~gehört, um Karriere zu machen** she has what it takes to make a successful career; **es gehört Mut/schon einiges ~:** it takes courage/quite something; **~gehörig** *Adj.; nicht präd.* **a)** appropriate; which goes/go with it/them *postpos.*; *(farblich usw. passend)* matching; **ein Schloß und die ~gehörigen Schlüssel** a lock and the keys that fit it; **b)** *(erforderlich)* necessary; **~|gesellen** *refl. V.* join in; *(als Zuschauer)* gather round; **~|kommen** *unr. itr. V.; mit sein* **a)** *(hinkommen)* arrive [on the scene]; turn up; **b)** *(außerdem kommen)* **es kommen noch einige Gäste ~:** there are still some guests to come; **kommt noch etwas ~?** *(fig.)* is there anything else [you would like]?; **~ kommt, daß ...** *(fig.)* what's more, ...; on top

of that, ...; *s. auch* **kommen m**; **~|lernen** *tr., itr. V.* **[etwas] ~ lernen** learn [something new]; **man kann immer noch [etwas] ~lernen** there's always something [new] to learn
da·zu·mal *Adv. (veralt., noch scherzh. altertümelnd)* in those days; *s. auch* **Anno**
dazu-: ~|rechnen *tr. V.* add on; **wenn man noch ~rechnet ...** *(fig.)* when you also consider ...; **~|setzen** *refl. V.* sit down next to him/her/you/them; **darf ich mich ~setzen?** may I join you *or* sit here?; **~|tun** *unr. tr. V. (ugs.)* add; **das Seine ~tun** do one's bit; *(mit Geld)* chip in *(coll.)*; **ohne jmds. Dazutun** without sb.'s help; *(ohne jmds. Beteiligung)* without involving sb.; **~|verdienen** *tr., itr. V.* earn ⟨*sth.*⟩ extra; *(als Nebenbeschäftigung)* earn ⟨*sth.*⟩ on the side; **seine Frau verdient noch [etwas] ~:** his wife earns something as well
dazwischen [da'tsvɪʃn̩] *Adv.* **a)** in between; between them; *(darunter)* among them; **b)** *(unterwegs)* on the way; *(währenddessen)* during this
dazwischen-: ~|fahren *unr. itr. V.; mit sein* **a)** *(eingreifen)* step in [and sort things out]; **b)** *(unterbrechen)* break in; **~|funken** *itr. V. (ugs.)* put a spanner in the works; *(sich einmischen)* put one's oar in; **jmdm. ~funken** put a spoke in sb.'s wheel; mess it up for sb.; **~|kommen** *unr. itr. V.; mit sein* **a)** *(zwischen diese Dinge kommen)* **mit dem Hemd/Finger ~kommen** get one's shirt/finger caught [in it]; **b)** *(als Störung auftreten)* **[jmdm.] ~kommen** complicate matters [for sb.]; *(es verhindern)* prevent it; **mir ist etwas ~gekommen** I had problems; *(immer noch)* I've got problems; **wenn nur nichts ~kommt** as long as there are no hitches *or* complications; **c)** *(dazwischen an der Reihe sein)* **[noch] ~kommen** come in between; **~|liegen** *unr. itr. V.;* lie in between; **Jahre lagen ~:** years had passed; **da liegen doch schon Tage ~:** that was days ago; **die ~liegende Zeit/Strecke** the intervening period/distance; **die ~liegenden Ereignisse** the events which have/had occurred in the mean while; **~|reden** *itr. V.* **a)** *(unterbrechen)* interrupt; **b)** *(umzustimmen versuchen)* **jmdm. ~reden** try to make sb. change his/her mind; **~|rufen 1.** *unr. itr. V.* interrupt [by shouting]; **2.** *unr. tr. V.* interrupt [loudly] with; interject; **~|schalten** *tr. V.* **a)** *(Elektrot.)* insert; **b)** *(fig.)* interpose; *(vorteilhaft)* use as an intermediary; **~|stehen** *unr. itr. V.* **a)** *(Einigung verhindern)* be obstructive; stand in the way; **b)** *(zwischen diesen Gegensätzen stehen)* be [somewhere] in the middle; **c)** *(zwischen den Erwähnten stehen)* stand amongst them; **~|treten** *unr. itr. V.; mit sein* **a)** *(eingreifen)* intervene; **sein Dazwischentreten** his intervention; **b)** *(Uneinigkeit verursachen)* come between them
DB *Abk.* **Deutsche Bundesbahn** German Federal Railways
DBP *Abk.* **Deutsche Bundespost** German Federal Post Office
DDR [de:de:'ʔɛr] **die; ~** *Abk.* **Deutsche Demokratische Republik** GDR; East Germany *(in popular use)*
DDR-Bürger der GDR citizen; East German *(in popular use)*
D-Dur ['de:du:ɐ̯] **das; ~[s]** D major; *s. auch* **C-Dur**
Deal [di:l] **der** *od.* **das; ~s, ~s** *(salopp)* deal
dealen ['di:lən] *itr. V. (ugs.)* push drugs; **mit LSD ~:** push LSD
Dealer der; ~s, ~, Dealerin die; ~, ~nen *(ugs.)* pusher
Debakel [de'ba:kl̩] **das; ~s, ~:** debacle; fiasco; *(schwere Niederlage)* rout
Debatte [de'batə] **die; ~, ~n** debate **(über + Akk.** on); *(Streit)* argument **(über + Akk.** about); **etw. in die ~ werfen** introduce *or* bring sth. into the debate; **[nicht] zur ~ stehen** [not] be under discussion; *(auf der Tagesordnung)* [not] be on the agenda; **etw. zur ~ stellen** put sth. up for discussion
debattieren *tr., itr. V.* debate; *(weniger formell)* discuss; **[mit jmdm.] über etw. ~:** discuss sth. [with sb.]
Debattier·klub der debating society
Debet ['de:bɛt] **das; ~s, ~s** *(Finanzw.)* debit [side]
debil [de'bi:l] *Adj.* **a)** *(Med.)* mentally subnormal; **b)** *(abwertend)* feeble-minded
Debilität [debili'tɛ:t] **die; ~ a)** *(Med.)* mental subnormality; **b)** *(abwertend)* feeble-mindedness
Debitor ['de:bitɔr] **der; ~s, ~en** [debi'to:rən] *(Finanzw.)* debtor
Debüt [de'by:] **das; ~s, ~s** debut; **sein ~ [als Autor** *usw.***] geben** make one's debut [as an author *etc.*]
Debütant [deby'tant] **der; ~en, ~en** newcomer [making his debut]; *(in einer Mannschaft, Truppe, usw.)* new face
Debütantin die; ~, ~nen a) *s.* **Debütant; b)** *(in der Gesellschaft)* debutante
Debütantinnen·ball der debutantes' ball
debütieren [deby'ti:rən] *itr. V.* make one's debut
Dechant [dɛ'çant] **der; ~en, ~en** *(kath. Kirche)* dean
dechiffrieren *tr. V.* decipher ⟨*code, message*⟩; decode ⟨*message, (fig.) conventions*⟩
Deck [dɛk] **das; ~[e]s, ~s a)** *(eines Schiffes)* deck; **alle Mann an ~!** all hands on deck!; **auf ~ sein** be on deck; **unter ~ gehen** go below [decks]; **auf dem obersten/im mittleren/unteren ~:** on the top/middle/lower deck; **b)** *(Park~)* storey; level; **auf ~ 6 fahren** drive up to level 6; **c)** *(im Autobus)* deck
Deck-: ~adresse die accommodation *or (Amer.)* cover address; **~an·strich der** top coat; **~auf·bauten** *Pl.* superstructure *sing.*; **~bett das** *s.* **Oberbett; ~blatt das a)** *(Bot.)* bract; **b)** *(von Zigarre)* wrapper; **c)** *(Titelblatt)* title-page
Deckchen das; ~s, ~ a) small tablecloth; **b)** *(Zier~, Häkel~)* [small] crocheted mat *or* cover
Decke ['dɛkə] **die; ~, ~n a)** *(Tisch~)* tablecloth; **eine neue ~ auflegen** put a clean cloth on [the table]; **b)** *(Woll~, Pferde~, auch fig.)* blanket; *(Reise~)* rug; *(Deckbett, Stepp~)* quilt; *(Tages~)* bedspread; **sich** *(Dat.)* **die ~ über den Kopf ziehen** pull the covers *pl.* over one's head; **unter die ~ kriechen** slip under the covers; **sich nach der ~ strecken [müssen]** *(ugs.)* [have to] cut one's coat according to one's cloth; **mit jmdm. unter einer ~ stecken** *(ugs.)* be hand in glove with sb.; be in cahoots with sb. *(sl.)*; **c)** *(Zimmer~)* ceiling; **mir fällt die ~ auf den Kopf** *(ugs.) (ich bekomme Platzangst)* I feel claustrophobic *or* shut in; *(ich langweile mich)* I get sick of [the sight of] these four walls; **an die ~ gehen** *(ugs.)* hit the roof *(coll.)*; **[vor Freude] [bis] an die ~ springen** jump for joy; **d)** *(Radmantel)* [outer] cover; **e)** *(Fahrbahn~)* surface; **f)** *(Buchw.: Bucheinband)* cover; **g)** *(Jägerspr.: Haut, Fell)* skin
Deckel ['dɛkl̩] **der; ~s, ~ a)** lid; *(auf Flaschen, Gläsern usw.)* top; *(Schacht~, Uhr~, Buch~ usw.)* cover; **b)** *(Bier~)* beer-mat; **c)** *(salopp: Kopfbedeckung)* headgear *no pl.*; **jmdm. eins auf den ~ geben** *(ugs.)* haul sb. over the coals; take sb. to task
Deckel·krug der tankard *(with a lid)*
deckeln *tr. V. (ugs.)* take to task; tell off
decken 1. *tr. V.* **a)** *(breiten, legen)* spread; **b)** *(mit einem Dach o. ä. versehen)* roof ⟨*house*⟩; cover ⟨*roof*⟩; **ein Dach/Haus mit Ziegeln/Stroh ~:** tile/thatch a roof/house; **c) den Tisch ~:** lay *or* set the table; **es ist [für fünf Personen] gedeckt** the table is set [for five]; **d)** *(schützen)* cover; *(bes. Fußball: abschirmen)* mark ⟨*player*⟩; *(vor Gericht usw.)* cover up for ⟨*accomplice, crime, etc.*⟩; **e)** *(befriedigen)* satisfy, meet ⟨*need, demand*⟩; **mein Bedarf ist gedeckt** *(ugs.)* I've had enough; **f)** *(Finanzw., Versicherungsw.)* cover; **g)** *(genau beschreiben)* describe accurately; cover; **h)** *(begatten)* cover; ⟨*stallion*⟩ serve ⟨*mare*⟩. **2.** *itr. V.* **a)** *(Fußball)* mark; *(Boxen)* keep up one's guard; **besser ~:** improve one's marking/guard; **b)** *(den Tisch ~)* lay *or* set the table; **c)** ⟨*colour*⟩ cover. **3.** *refl. V.* **a)** *(Geom.)* be congruent; **b)** *(gleich sein)* coincide; tally; **ihre Aussage deckt sich nicht mit seiner** her statement does not agree with his
Decken-: ~balken der ceiling beam; **~beleuchtung die** ceiling light; **~gemälde das** ceiling painting; **~malerei die** ceiling painting; **~träger der** [iron] ceiling joist
Deck-: ~farbe die paint *(which covers well)*; body-colour; *(für Gouachen)* gouache colour; **~feder die** cover; tectrix *(Ornith.)*; **~flügel der** elytron; **~haar das a)** *(bei Tieren)* guard hair; **b)** *(bei Menschen)* top hair; **~hengst der** stud-horse; breeding stallion; **~mantel der, ~mäntelchen das;** *o. Pl. (abwertend)* cover; **unter dem ~mantel der Entwicklungshilfe** *usw.* using development aid *etc.* as a blind *or* cover; under the guise of development aid *etc.*; **~name der** alias; assumed name; *(eines Spions, milit. Programms)* code name; *(einer Organisation)* cover name; **~plane die** waterproof cover; *(bes. geteert)* tarpaulin; **~platte die** cover; **~station die** stud
Deckung die; ~, ~en a) *o. Pl. (das Schützen)* covering *(esp. Mil.)*; *(Feuerschutz)* covering fire; *(Boxen, Fechten)* guard; *(bes. Fußball)* marking; *(Schach)* protection; **b)** *(Schutz; auch fig.)* cover *(esp. Mil.)*; *(Schach)* defence; *(Boxen)* guard; *(bes. Fußball: die deckenden Spieler)* defence; **~ nehmen, in ~ gehen** take cover; **~ suchen/in ~ bleiben** look for/stay under cover; **[volle] ~!** take cover!; **c)** *(Finanzw.: das Begleichen) o. Pl.* meeting; **zur ~ seiner Schulden** to meet his debts; **d)** *(Finanzw.: Sicherheit)* cover[ing]; **der Scheck ist ohne ~:** the cheque is not covered; **als ~ für seine Schulden** as security for his debts; **e)** *(Befriedigung)* satisfaction; **f)** *(Übereinstimmung)* **Pläne** *usw.* **zur ~ bringen** make plans *etc.* agree; bring plans *etc.* into line; **g)** *(von Tieren: Begatten)* covering; *(einer Stute)* service
deckungs-, Deckungs-: ~auf·lage die *(Verlagsw.)* break-even quantity; **~fehler der** *(bes. Fußball)* marking error; **~gleich** *Adj. (Geom.)* congruent; **unsere Meinungen sind ~gleich** *(fig.)* our opinions coincide *or* are the same
Deck-: ~weiß das opaque white; **~wort das** code word
decodieren *s.* **dekodieren**
Decrescendo [dekre'ʃɛndo] **das; ~s, ~s** *od.* **Decrescendi** *(Musik)* decrescendo
Dedikation [dedika'tsio:n] **die; ~, ~en** dedication
Dedikations·exemplar das presentation copy *(containing dedication)*
dedizieren [dedi'tsi:rən] *tr. V.* dedicate; **jmdm. ein Exemplar ~:** inscribe a copy to sb.
Deduktion [dedʊk'tsio:n] **die; ~, ~en** *(Philos., Kybernetik)* deduction
deduktiv [dedʊk'ti:f] *(Philos.)* **1.** *Adj.* deductive. **2.** *adv.* deductively; **~ folgern** conclude by deduction
deduzieren [dedu'tsi:rən] *tr. V. (bes. Philos.)* deduce
Deern [de:ɐ̯n] **die; ~, ~s** *(nordd.)* lass
Deez *s.* **Dez**
DEFA ['de:fa] **die; ~** *(DDR) Abk.* **Deutsche Film-Aktiengesellschaft** *(nationalized East German film company)*

de facto [de: 'fakto] *Adv.* de facto *(esp. Polit., Law)*; in reality
De-facto-Anerkennung die de facto recognition
Defaitismus *usw. (schweiz.) s.* **Defätismus** *usw.*
Defäkation [defɛka'tsi̯o:n] **die; ~, ~en** *(Med.)* defecation
Defätismus [defɛ'tɪsmʊs] **der; ~** *(oft abwertend)* defeatism
Defätist der; ~en, ~en *(abwertend)* defeatist
defätistisch *(oft abwertend)* **1.** *Adj.* defeatist. **2.** *adv.* in a defeatist manner
defekt [de'fɛkt] *Adj.* **a)** defective; faulty; **~ sein** have a defect; be faulty; *(nicht funktionieren)* not be working; **b)** *(fig.)* deficient ⟨*mind, understanding*⟩
Defekt der; ~[e]s, ~e a) defect, fault **(an** + *Dat.* in); **b)** *(Psych., Med.)* defect **(an** + *Dat.* in); **Heilung mit bleibendem ~:** cure leaving a permanent handicap
defektiv [defɛk'ti:f] *Adj. (Sprachw.)* defective
Defektivum [defɛk'ti:vʊm] **das; ~s, Defektiva** *(Sprachw.)* defective
defensiv [defɛn'zi:f] **1.** *Adj.* **a)** *(verteidigend; auch Sport)* defensive; **b)** *(sicherheitsbewußt)* safety-conscious. **2.** *adv.* **a)** *(verteidigend; auch Sport)* defensively; **b)** *(sicherheitsbewußt)* in a safety-conscious manner
Defensive die; ~, ~n a) defensive; **in der ~:** on the defensive; **jmdn. in die ~ drängen** force sb. on [to] the defensive; **in die ~ geraten** go on [to] the defensive; **b)** *(Sport)* **die ~:** defensive play; **aus der ~ heraus** from defensive positions *pl.*
Defensiv-: ~krieg der defensive war; **~spiel das** *(Sport)* defensive play
Defilee [defi'le:] **das; ~s, ~s,** *(auch:)* **~n** parade; march past
defilieren [defi'li:rən] *itr. V.; mit haben od. sein* **vor jmdm./etw. ~:** parade before *or* march past sb./sth.
definierbar *Adj.* definable; *(identifizierbar)* identifiable; **nicht [näher] ~:** indefinable; *(nicht zu identifizieren)* unidentifiable
definieren [defi'ni:rən] **1.** *tr. V.* define; *(identifizieren)* identify. **2.** *refl. V. (sich als etw. verstehen)* describe oneself **(durch** in terms of)
Definition [defini'tsi̯o:n] **die; ~, ~en** definition
definitiv [defini'ti:f] **1.** *Adj.* definitive; final ⟨*answer, decision*⟩; *(sicher)* definite. **2.** *adv.* finally; *(sicher)* definitely
definitorisch [defini'to:rɪʃ] **1.** *Adj.* ⟨*problem*⟩ of definition; ⟨*skill*⟩ at defining. **2.** *adv.* with regard to definition
defizient [defi'tsi̯ɛnt] *Adj.* deficient
Defizit ['de:fitsɪt] **das; ~s, ~e a)** *(Fehlbetrag)* deficit; **b)** *(Mangel)* deficiency; **~ an etw.** *(Dat.)* lack of sth.
defizitär [defitsi'tɛ:ɐ̯] **1.** *Adj.* **a)** *(Defizit aufweisend)* ⟨*trade etc.*⟩ which shows/showed a deficit *not pred.*; ⟨*firm etc.*⟩ which runs/ran at a loss *not pred.*; **b)** *(Defizit verursachend)* which leads/led to a deficit *postpos., not pred.* **2.** *adv.* **~[er] arbeiten** *od.* **wirtschaften** show a [bigger] deficit; run at a [bigger] loss
Deflation [defla'tsi̯o:n] **die; ~, ~en** *(Wirtsch.)* deflation
deflationär [deflatsi̯o'nɛ:ɐ̯], **deflationistisch** *Adj. (Wirtsch.)* deflationary
Deflations·politik die *(Wirtsch.)* deflationary policy
Deflektor [de'flɛktɔr] **der; ~s, ~en** [-'to:rən] *(Technik)* deflector
Defloration [deflora'tsi̯o:n] **die; ~, ~en** *(Med.)* defloration
deflorieren [deflo'ri:rən] *tr. V.* deflower
Deformation die a) *(Physik)* deformation; **b)** *(Med.)* deformation; *(Mißbildung)* deformity
deformieren *tr. V.* **a)** *(verformen)* distort; put out of shape; **deformiert** out of shape *pred.*; distorted; **b)** *(entstellen)* deform *(also fig.)*; *(verunstalten)* disfigure ⟨*face etc.*⟩; *(verstümmeln)* mutilate
Deformierung die a) *o. Pl. (Verformung)* deformation; distortion; **b)** *(Entstellung)* deformation; *(Verunstaltung)* disfigurement; *(Verstümmelung)* mutilation; *(Mißbildung)* deformity
Deformität [defɔrmi'tɛ:t] **die; ~, ~en** *(Med.)* deformity
Defraudant [defrau̯'dant] **der; ~en, ~en** *(veralt.)* defrauder; swindler; *(bei Unterschlagung)* embezzler
Defroster [de'frɔstɐ] **der; ~s, ~ a)** *(Gerät)* defroster; **b)** *(Spray)* de-icer
deftig ['dɛftɪç] *(ugs.)* **1.** *Adj.* **a)** [good] solid *attrib.*, good and solid *pred.* ⟨*meal etc.*⟩; [nice] big, [nice] fat ⟨*sausage etc.*⟩; *(tüchtig)* [really] big ⟨*surprise*⟩; sound ⟨*hiding*⟩; *(hoch)* tremendous, *(coll.)* terrific ⟨*price, bill, etc.*⟩; **b)** *(derb)* crude, coarse ⟨*joke, speech, etc.*⟩. **2.** *adv.* good and proper *(coll.)*
¹Degen der; ~s, ~ *(hist.)* [doughty] warrior
²Degen ['de:gn̩] **der; ~s, ~ a)** *(Waffe)* [light] sword *(esp. for duelling)*; *(Rapier)* rapier; **b)** *(Sportgerät)* épée
Degeneration [degenera'tsi̯o:n] **die; ~, ~en** degeneration **(zu** into)
Degenerations·erscheinung die sign of degeneration
degenerativ [degenera'ti:f] **1.** *Adj.* degenerative. **2.** *adv.* **es ist ~ verändert** it has degenerated
degenerieren [degene'ri:rən] *itr. V.; mit sein* degenerate **(zu** into)
degeneriert *Adj.* degenerate; *(überzüchtet)* overbred
Degen-: ~fechten das épée [fencing] *no art.*; **~klinge die** sword-blade; **~korb der** [sword-]guard; **~scheide die** scabbard
degoutant [degu'tant] *(geh.)* **1.** *Adj.* disgusting. **2.** *adv.* in a disgusting manner
degoutieren [degu'ti:rən] *tr. V. (geh.)* disgust
degradieren [degra'di:rən] *tr. V.* **a)** *(im Rang o. ä.)* demote; **vom Feldwebel zum einfachen Schützen degradiert werden** be demoted from [the rank of] sergeant to [a] mere private; **b)** *(herabwürdigen)* **jmdn./etw. zu etw. ~:** reduce sb./sth. to [the level of] sth.
Degradierung die; ~, ~en a) *(im Rang)* demotion; **b)** *(Herabwürdigung)* degradation; reduction **(zu** to the level of)
Degression [degrɛ'si̯o:n] **die; ~, ~en a)** *(Wirtsch.)* progressive reduction [of unit cost]; **b)** *(Steuerw.)* degression
degressiv [degrɛ'si:f] *Adj. (Wirtsch., Steuerw.)* degressive
degustieren [degʊs'ti:rən] *tr. V. (bes. schweiz.)* taste; sample
dehnbar *Adj.* **a)** *(elastisch)* ⟨*material etc.*⟩ that stretches *not pred.*; elastic ⟨*waistband etc.*⟩; stretch ⟨*fabric*⟩; **etw. ist ~:** sth. can be stretched; **b)** *(fig.: vage)* elastic; **das ist ein ~er Begriff** it's a loose concept; that can mean what you want it to mean
Dehnbarkeit die; ~ *(auch fig.)* elasticity
dehnen ['de:nən] **1.** *tr. V.* **a)** stretch; **b)** *(lang aussprechen)* lengthen, draw out ⟨*vowel, word*⟩; **etw. gedehnt sagen/aussprechen** say/pronounce sth. slowly; *(lässig)* drawl sth. **2.** *refl. V.* **a)** stretch; **er dehnte sich wohlig** he stretched [himself] luxuriantly; **b)** *(lange dauern)* **sich endlos ~:** go on for ever *(coll.)*; go on and on; **die Minuten ~ sich zu Stunden** the minutes seem like hours
Dehnung die; ~, ~en a) *o. Pl. (das Dehnen)* stretching; *(eines Vokals)* lengthening; **b)** *(Dehnbarkeit)* elasticity
Dehnungs-: ~fuge die *(Bauw.)* expansion joint; **~-h das; ~, ~** *(Phon.)* 'h' lengthening the preceding vowel; **~zeichen das** *(Phon.)* length-mark
dehydrieren *tr. V. (Chemie)* dehydrogenate
Deibel ['dai̯bl̩] *s.* **Deiwel**
Deich [dai̯ç] **der; ~[e]s, ~e** dike; **mit etw. über den ~ gehen** *(nordd.)* make off with sth.
Deich-: ~bau der; *o. Pl.* building of a/the dike; *(allgemein)* dike-building; **~bruch der** breach *(Brit.) or (Amer.)* break in the dike; *(Brechen des Deiches)* breaching *(Brit.) or (Amer.)* breaking of the dike; **~genossenschaft die** *s.* **~verband; ~graf der** *(veralt.) s.* **~vorsteher; ~krone die** top of the dike
Deichsel ['dai̯ksl̩] **die; ~, ~n** shaft; *(in der Mitte)* pole; *(aus zwei Stangen)* shafts *pl.*
Deichsel·kreuz das a) *(Griff)* shaft-handle; **b)** *(Symbol)* Y[-shaped] cross
deichseln *tr. V. (ugs.)* fix; *(durch eine List)* wangle *(sl.)*
Deich-: ~verband der association of owners of diked land; **~vorland das** *land above mean high-water mark on the seaward side of a dike;* **~vorsteher der** chairman of a 'Deichverband'
deifizieren [deifi'tsi:rən] *tr. V. (geh.)* deify
¹dein, *(in Briefen)* **Dein** [dai̯n] *Possessivpron.* your; *(Rel., auch altertümelnd)* thy; **viele Grüße von Deinem Emil/Deiner Karin/Deinen Müllers** with best wishes, yours Emil/Karin/the Müllers; **~ Wille geschehe** *(Rel.: im Vaterunser)* Thy will be done; **heute abend kannst du ~en Humphrey Bogart im Fernsehen sehen** you can watch your beloved Humphrey Bogart *or* that Humphrey Bogart of yours on television tonight; **das Buch dort, ist das ~[e]s?** that book over there, is it yours?; **sind das ihre Schuhe oder ~e?** are those her shoes or yours?; **das war nicht mein Wunsch, sondern ~er** *od. (geh.)* **der ~e** it was not my wish but yours; **ewig/stets der Deine** *(geh.)* yours ever; **du und die Deinen** *(geh.)* you and yours *or* your family; **der/die Deine** *(geh.)* your husband/wife; **das Deine** *(geh.)* your possessions *pl. or* property; **du mußt das Deine tun** *(was du kannst)* you must do what you can; *(deinen Teil)* you must do your bit *or* share; *s. auch* **¹mein**
²dein *(geh. veralt.),* **deiner** *Gen. des Personalpronomens* **du** *(geh.)* of you; **ich gedenke ~ auf ewig** I will always remember you; **man lachte ~:** they laughed at you
deiner·seits ['dai̯nɐ'zai̯ts] *Adv. (von deiner Seite)* on your part; *(auf deiner Seite)* for your part
deines·gleichen *indekl. Pron.* people *pl.* like you; *(abwertend)* the likes *pl.* of you; your sort *or* kind; **unter ~:** amongst your own sort *or* kind; **für dich und ~** *(abwertend)* for your sort; for the likes of you
deines·teils *Adv.* for your part
deinet·halben *(veralt.) s.* **deinetwegen a**
deinet·wegen *Adv.* **a)** because of you; on your account; *(für dich)* on your behalf; *(dir zuliebe)* for your sake; **ich habe mir ~ große Sorgen gemacht** I have been very worried about you *or* on your account; **b)** *(du hast nichts dagegen)* **du hast gesagt, ~ könnten wir gehen** you said we could go as far as you were concerned
deinet·willen *Adv. in* **um ~:** for your sake
deinige ['dai̯nɪgə] *Possessivpron. (geh. veralt.)* **der/die/das ~:** yours; **die Deinigen** your family *sing.*; **das Deinige** what is yours; your property; **du mußt das Deinige tun** *(was du kannst)* you must do what you can; *(deinen Teil)* you must do your bit *or* share
Deismus [de'ɪsmʊs] **der; ~:** deism *no art.*
deistisch *Adj.* deistic
Deiwel ['dai̯vl̩] *(nordd.),* **Deixel** ['dai̯ksl̩] *(südd.)* **der; ~s** devil; *s. auch* **Teufel**
de jure [de: 'ju:rə] *Adv.* de jure; legally
De-jure-Anerkennung die de jure recognition

Deka ['dɛka] **das;** ~**[s],** ~ *(österr.)* decagram
Dekade [de'ka:də] **die;** ~, ~**n a)** *(zehn Tage)* ten days *pl.*; **b)** *(zehn Jahre)* decade
dekadent [deka'dɛnt] *Adj.* decadent
Dekadenz [deka'dɛnts] **die;** ~: decadence
dekadisch *Adj.* ~**es Zahlensystem** decimal system; ~**er Logarithmus** *(Math.)* common logarithm
Deka-: ~**eder das** *(Geom.)* decahedron; ~**gramm das** decagram; ~**liter der** decalitre
Dekalog [deka'lo:k] **der;** ~**[e]s** *(Rel.)* decalogue
Dekan [de'ka:n] **der;** ~**s,** ~**e a)** *(Universität)* dean; **b)** *(kath. Kirche)* dean; **c)** *(ev. Kirche)* superintendent
Dekanat [deka'na:t] **das;** ~**s,** ~**e a)** *(Universität)* dean's office; **b)** *(kath. Kirche)* deanery; **c)** *(Amt eines Dekans)* office of dean
dekartellisieren [dekartɛli'zi:rən] *tr. V.* *(Wirtsch.)* decartelize
dekatieren [deka'ti:rən] *tr. V.* *(Textilw.)* decatise
Deklamation [deklama'tsio:n] **die;** ~, ~**en a)** *(Vortrag)* recitation; **b)** *(abwertend: hohles Gerede)* [empty] rhetoric *no pl.*
deklamatorisch [deklama'to:rɪʃ] **1.** *Adj.* **a)** *(ausdrucksvoll)* declamatory; **b)** *(abwertend: hohl)* rhetorical. **2.** *adv.* **a)** *(ausdrucksvoll)* expressively; **b)** *(abwertend: hohl klingend)* rhetorically; in expansive terms
deklamieren [dekla'mi:rən] *tr., itr. V.* recite
Deklaration [deklara'tsio:n] **die;** ~, ~**en** *(Politik, Zoll-, Steuer-, Postwesen)* declaration
deklarieren [dekla'ri:rən] *tr. V.* declare; **etw. als etw.** ~: declare sth. to be sth.; **zur atomwaffenfreien Zone deklariert werden** be declared a nuclear-free zone
deklassieren *tr. V.* **a)** *(Soziol.)* disadvantage; **b)** *(herabsetzen)* reduce; downgrade; **c)** *(Sport)* outclass; *(beim Rennen)* leave standing
Deklassierung die; ~, ~**en a)** *(Soziol.)* disadvantaging; reduction in circumstances; **b)** *o. Pl. (Herabsetzung)* downgrading; **c)** *o. Pl. (Sport)* outclassing
deklinabel [dekli'na:bl̩] *Adj. (Sprachw.)* declinable
Deklination [deklina'tsio:n] **die;** ~, ~**en a)** *(Sprachw.)* declension; **die starke/schwache** ~: the strong/weak declension; **b)** *(Astron., Physik)* declination
deklinierbar *Adj. (Sprachw.)* declinable
deklinieren [dekli'ni:rən] *tr. V. (Sprachw.)* decline; **ein Wort schwach/stark** ~: decline a word as weak/strong
dekodieren *tr. V. (fachspr.)* decode
Dekolleté [dekɔl'te:] **das;** ~**s,** ~**s** low[-cut] neckline; décolletage; **Kleid mit tiefem** ~: very low-cut dress; dress with a plunging neckline
dekolletieren [dekɔl'ti:rən] *tr. V.* make *or* cut with a low neckline
dekolletiert *Adj.* **a)** *(ausgeschnitten)* décolleté; low-cut ‹*back, neckline*›; **b)** *(Dekolleté tragend)* ~**e Damen** ladies in low-cut dresses; **[tief]** ~ **sein** *od.* **gehen** wear a [very] low-cut dress/[very] low-cut dresses
Dekolonisation die decolonization
dekolonisieren *tr. V.* decolonize
Dekompression die decompression
Dekompressions·kammer die decompression chamber
Dekontamination die decontamination
Dekonzentration die *(der Verwaltung)* decentralization; *(der Industrie usw.)* deconcentration
Dekor [de'ko:ɐ̯] **das;** ~**s,** ~**s** *od.* ~**e a)** *(Verzierung)* decoration; *(Muster)* pattern; **ein Zimmer im** ~ **der dreißiger Jahre** a room in the 1930s style; **b)** *(Theater, Film)* décor; setting
Dekorateur [dekora'tø:ɐ̯] **der;** ~**s,** ~**e, Dekorateurin die;** ~, ~**nen** *(Schaufenster~)* window-dresser; *(von Innenräumen)* interior decorator *or* designer; *(Dekorationsmaler)* scene-painter
Dekoration [dekora'tsio:n] **die;** ~, ~**en a)** *o. Pl. (das Dekorieren)* decoration; *(von Schaufenstern)* window-dressing; **zur** ~: for decoration; **b)** *(Schmuck, Ausstattung)* decorations *pl.*; *(Schaufenster~)* window display; *(Theater, Film)* set; scenery *no pl.*; **bloße** ~ **sein** be purely for decoration purposes; **c)** *(Orden[verleihung])* decoration
Dekorations-: ~**maler der** interior decorator; *(Theater)* [stage] decorator; scene-painter; ~**stoff der** furnishing fabric; ~**stück das** part of the décor; *(Theater)* piece of scenery
dekorativ [dekora'ti:f] **1.** *Adj.* decorative. **2.** *adv.* decoratively
dekorieren [deko'ri:rən] *tr. V.* **a)** *(ausschmücken)* decorate ‹*room etc.*›; dress ‹*shop-window*›; **b)** *(mit Orden auszeichnen)* decorate **(mit** with)
Dekorierung die; ~, ~**en** *s.* **Dekoration a, c**
Dekorum [de'ko:rʊm] **das;** ~**s** *(veralt.)* decorum *no art.*; **das** ~ **verletzen/wahren** offend against/observe the proprieties *pl.*
Dekostoff ['de:ko-] **der** furnishing fabric
Dekrescendo *s.* **Decrescendo**
Dekret [de'kre:t] **das;** ~**[e]s,** ~**e** decree
dekretieren *tr. V.* decree
dekuvrieren [deku'vri:rən] **1.** *tr. V.* *(entlarven)* expose. **2.** *refl. V.* *(schlechte Züge zeigen)* reveal oneself; **sich als etw.** ~: reveal oneself to be sth.
Deleatur [dele'a:tʊr] **das;** ~**s,** ~, **Deleatur·zeichen das** *(Druckw.)* deletion mark
Delegation [delega'tsio:n] **die;** ~, ~**en** delegation **(an** + *Akk.* to; **bei** at)
Delegations·chef der head of a/the delegation
delegieren [dele'gi:rən] *tr. V.* **a)** *(abordnen)* send as a delegate/as delegates **(zu** to); **jmdn. ins Komitee** ~: select sb. as one's representative on the committee; **b)** *(übertragen)* delegate ‹*task etc.*› **(an** + *Akk.* to)
Delegierte der/die; *adj. Dekl.* delegate; *(Sport)* representative **(bei** at)
Delegierten-: ~**konferenz die** delegates' *or* delegate conference; ~**versammlung die** delegates' *or* delegate assembly
delektieren [delɛk'ti:rən] **1.** *tr. V.* **jmdn. mit etw.** ~: entertain *or* regale sb. with sth. **2.** *refl. V.* **sich an etw.** *(Dat.)* ~: regale oneself with sth.; *(fig.)* take delight in sth.
delikat [deli'ka:t] **1.** *Adj.* **a)** *(wohlschmeckend)* delicious; *(fein)* subtle, delicate ‹*bouquet, aroma*›; ~ **riechen** have a delicate bouquet/aroma; **b)** *(Diskretion erfordernd, heikel)* delicate; *(geh.: empfindlich)* **in so persönlichen Dingen ist sie sehr** ~: she is very sensitive about such personal matters; **c)** *(geh.: behutsam)* discreet; *(taktvoll)* tactful; ~**e Andeutung** subtle *or* discreet reference. **2.** *adv.* **a)** *(lecker)* deliciously; **b)** *(geh.: behutsam)* delicately; **etw.** ~ **behandeln** handle sth. tactfully *or* discreetly
Delikatesse [delika'tɛsə] **die;** ~, ~**n a)** *(Leckerbissen)* delicacy; *(fig.)* treat; **als besondere** ~: as a special delicacy/treat; **b)** *o. Pl. (geh.: Feingefühl)* delicacy; *(Takt)* tact; discretion; **eine Angelegenheit mit** ~ **behandeln** handle a matter discreetly
Delikatessen·geschäft, Delikateß·geschäft das delicatessen
Delikateß·gurke die [fine-quality] gherkin
Delikt [de'lɪkt] **das;** ~**[e]s,** ~**e** offence
delinquent [delɪŋ'kvɛnt] *Adj. (bes. Rechtw.)* delinquent; criminal ‹*conduct*›
Delinquent der; ~**en,** ~**en** offender
Delinquenz die; ~ *(bes. Rechtsw.)* delinquency
delirieren [deli'ri:rən] *itr. V.* be delirious
Delirium [de'li:riʊm] **das;** ~**s, Delirien** delirium; **im** ~ **liegen/sein** lie/be in a delirium; **im** ~ **reden** speak in one's delirium
Delirium tremens [~ 'tre:mɛns] **das;** ~ ~ *(Med.)* delirium tremens; **im** ~ **sterben** die in a state of delirium [tremens]
deliziös [deli'tsiø:s] *(geh.)* **1.** *Adj.* delicious; delectable; ~ **schmecken** taste delicious. **2.** *adv.* deliciously
Delle ['dɛlə] **die;** ~, ~**n a)** *(ugs.)* dent; **eine** ~ **in die Stoßstange fahren** drive into something and dent one's bumper; **b)** *(Geogr.)* hollow
delogieren *tr. V. (bes. österr.)* evict
[1]**Delphin** [dɛl'fi:n] **der;** ~**s,** ~**e** dolphin
[2]**Delphin das;** ~**s** *(Schwimmen)* butterfly [stroke]
Delphinarium [dɛlfi'na:riʊm] **das;** ~**s, Delphinarien** dolphinarium
Delphin·schwimmen das butterfly
delphisch ['dɛlfɪʃ] **1.** *Adj.* Delphic ‹*oracle*›; enigmatic ‹*remark etc.*›. **2.** *adv.* enigmatically
[1]**Delta** ['dɛlta] **das;** ~**[s],** ~**[s]** *(Buchstabe)* delta
[2]**Delta das;** ~**s,** ~**s** *od.* **Delten** *(Fluß~)* delta
delta-, Delta-: ~**förmig** *Adj.* delta-shaped; triangular; deltaic ‹*estuary*›; ~**mündung die** delta [estuary]; ~**strahlen** *Pl. (Kernphysik)* delta rays
De-Luxe-Ausstattung [də'lyks-] **die: eine** ~ **haben** be fitted with de luxe equipment; ‹*car etc.*› be a de luxe model; ‹*room*› have de luxe fittings
dem [de:m] **1.** *best. Art., Dat. Sg. v.* [1]**der 1** *u.* **das 1: ich gab dem Mann/dem Kind das Buch** I gave the man/the child the book; I gave the book to the man/to the child; **hast du dem Peter das Geld gegeben?** *(ugs.)* have you given Peter the money?; **ich half dem Mann/dem Kind** I helped the man/the child; **er hat sich dem Okkultismus zugewandt** he turned to occultism; **aus dem Libanon/Baltikum kommen** come from Lebanon/the Baltic area; **dem Theater/Kino seinen Ruhm verdanken** owe one's fame to the stage/films. **2.** *Demonstrativpron., Dat. Sg. v.* [1]**der 2** *u.* **das 2: a)** *attr.* **gib es dem Mann/Kind** give it to 'that man/child; **mit dem Messer kann man fast alles schneiden** you can cut almost anything with 'that knife; **b)** *selbständig* **gib es nicht dem, sondern dem da!** don't give it to him, give it to that man/child *etc.*; **Zwiebeln schneide ich nicht mit dem [hier], sondern mit dem da** I chop onions with 'that knife, not with this one. **3.** *Relativpron., Dat. Sg. v.* [1]**der 3** *u.* **das 3** *(Mensch)* **der Mann/das Kind, dem ich das Geld gab** the man/the child to whom I gave the money *or (coll.)* [that] I gave the money to; **der Mann, dem ich geholfen habe** the man whom *or* that I helped; *(Sache)* **das Messer, mit dem ich Zwiebeln schneide** the knife with which I chop onions *or (coll.)* that I chop onions with
Demagoge [dema'go:gə] **der;** ~**n,** ~**n** *(abwertend)* demagogue
Demagogie [demago'gi:] **die;** ~, ~**n** *(abwertend)* demagogy
demagogisch *(abwertend)* **1.** *Adj.* demagogic. **2.** *adv.* by demagogic means; *(zu* ~*en Zwecken)* for demagogic purposes; ~ **reden** talk like a demagogue
Demarche [de'marʃ(ə)] **die;** ~, ~**n** *(Dipl.)* diplomatic move
Demarkation [demarka'tsio:n] **die;** ~, ~**en** demarcation; *(Staatsgrenze)* frontier
Demarkations·linie die demarcation line
demarkieren *tr. V.* demarcate
demaskieren 1. *refl. V.* **a)** *(Maske ablegen)* unmask; take one's mask off; **b)** *(sich offenbaren)* reveal oneself [as what one is]; appear in one's true colours; **sich als etw.** ~: reveal *or* show oneself to be sth. **2.** *tr. V.*

(entlarven) unmask; expose; **jmdn. als etw. ~:** reveal sb. as sth.
Dementi [de'mɛnti] **das; ~s, ~s** denial
dementieren 1. *tr. V.* deny. **2.** *itr. V.* deny it
Dementierung die; ~, ~en denial
dem·entsprechend 1. *Adj.* appropriate; **das Wetter war schlecht und die Stimmung ~:** the weather was bad and the general mood was correspondingly bad *or* bad too; **Er hat eine Villa in Cannes und eine Luxusjacht. Sein Einkommen ist auch ~:** He has a villa in Cannes and a luxury yacht. And he has an income to match *or* to go with it. **2.** *adv.* accordingly; *(vor Adjektiven)* correspondingly; **~ wird er bezahlt** he is paid accordingly
dem-: ~gegenüber *Adv.* in contrast; *(jedoch)* on the other hand; **~gemäß 1.** *adv.* **a)** *(infolgedessen)* consequently; **b)** *(entsprechend)* accordingly; **2.** *Adj.* in accordance with it/them *postpos.*; *(angemessen)* appropriate; **ein Zimmer mit Vollpension kostet nur 18 Mark – das Essen ist ~:** a room with full board only costs 18 marks – the food is what you'd expect [at that price]
Demimonde [dəmi'mõ:d] **die; ~** *(abwertend)* demi-monde
Demission die; ~, ~en *(Politik)* resignation; **jmdn. zur ~ zwingen** force sb. to resign; **um seine ~ bitten** ask to be relieved of one's duties
demissionieren *itr. V.* **a)** *(Politik: zurücktreten)* resign; **b)** *(schweiz.: kündigen)* hand in one's notice **(auf + Akk.** for)
dem-: ~jenigen *s.* derjenige; **~nach** *Adv.* therefore; *(laut dessen)* according to that; **~nächst** *Adv.* in the near future; shortly; **~nächst in diesem Theater** coming soon [to this theatre]; *(ugs. scherzh.)* some time soon
Demo ['dɛmo] **die; ~, ~s** *(ugs.)* demo; **auf der ~:** at the demo
demobilisieren *tr. V.* **a)** demobilize ⟨*army, industry*⟩; **b)** *(veralt.: entlassen)* discharge ⟨*soldier*⟩
Demobilisierung die; ~, ~en demobilization
Demodulation die; ~, ~en *(Nachrichtent.)* demodulation
Demo·graphie die demography *no art.*
demo·graphisch 1. *Adj.* demographic. **2.** *adv.* demographically
Demokrat [demo'kra:t] **der; ~en, ~en a)** democrat; **b)** *(Parteimitglied)* Democrat
Demokratie [demokra'ti:] **die; ~, ~n a)** *o. Pl. (Prinzip)* democracy *no art.*; **zur ~ zurückkehren** return to democracy *or* democratic government; **b)** *(Staat)* democracy
Demokratie·verständnis das understanding *or* conception of democracy
demokratisch 1. *Adj.* **a)** democratic ⟨*principle, process, etc.*⟩; **b)** *(zur Demokratischen Partei gehörend)* Democratic. **2.** *adv.* democratically; **es wurde ~ gewählt** democratic elections were held; **bei uns geht es ~ zu** we run things on democratic lines; **~ eingestellt sein** have democratic attitudes
demokratisieren *tr. V.* **a)** democratize; make democratic; **b)** *(allgemein zugänglich machen)* make generally available; make ⟨*art*⟩ generally accessible; bring ⟨*art, fashion*⟩ to the people
Demokratisierung die; ~ a) *(eines Staates, einer Institution)* democratization; **b)** *(das Zugänglichmachen)*; **die ~ der Mode/des Reisens** making fashion/travel generally available *or* accessible
demolieren [demo'li:rən] *tr. V.* **a)** *(zerstören)* wreck; smash up ⟨*furniture*⟩; **b)** *(österr.: abreißen)* demolish
Demolierung die; ~, ~en a) *(Zerstörung)* wrecking; *(von Möbeln)* smashing up; **b)** *(österr.: Abriß)* demolition
Demonstrant [demɔn'strant] **der; ~en, ~en** demonstrator
Demonstrantin die; ~, ~nen demonstrator; *s. auch* **~in**
Demonstration [demɔnstra'tsio:n] **die; ~, ~en a)** *(Protestkundgebung)* demonstration **(für** in support of, **gegen** against); **b)** *(Bekundung, Veranschaulichung)* demonstration; **zur ~ seines guten Willens** as a demonstration of *or* to demonstrate his good will
Demonstrations-: ~marsch der demonstration; *(gegen etw.)* protest march; **~objekt das** exhibit *(used to demonstrate a point)*; **~recht das** right to demonstrate; **~verbot das** ban on demonstrations; **~zug der** column *or* procession of demonstrators
demonstrativ [demɔnstra'ti:f] **1.** *Adj.* **a)** *(betont)* demonstrative; pointed; **ein ~es Nein** an emphatic no; **b)** *(Sprachw.)* demonstrative; **c)** *(anschaulich)* graphic ⟨*example etc.*⟩. **2.** *adv.* pointedly; *(aus Protest)* in protest; **ich sah ~ weg** I intentionally looked the other way; **sie blieben ~ sitzen** they remained seated in protest *or* to make their point
Demonstrativ·pronomen das *(Sprachwissenschaft)* demonstrative pronoun
demonstrieren [demɔn'stri:rən] **1.** *itr. V.* demonstrate **(für** in support of, **gegen** against). **2.** *tr. V.* demonstrate; **jmdm. etw. ~:** demonstrate sth. to sb.
Demontage [demɔn'ta:ʒə] **die; ~, ~n** *(auch fig.)* dismantling; *(eines Schiffes)* breaking-up; **soziale ~** *(Politik)* dismantling of the welfare state
demontieren *tr. V.* **a)** *(abbrechen)* dismantle; *(zerlegen)* break up ⟨*ship, aircraft*⟩; **b)** *(abmontieren)* take off; **c)** *(fig.)* eradicate ⟨*prejudices*⟩; damage ⟨*reputation*⟩
Demontierung die; ~, ~en *s.* **Demontage**
Demoralisation [demoraliza'tsio:n] **die; ~, ~en** *s.* **Demoralisierung**
demoralisieren *tr. V.* **a)** *(Moral untergraben)* corrupt; **b)** *(entmutigen)* demoralize
Demoralisierung die; ~, ~en demoralization; *(Sittenverfall)* moral decline
Demoskop [demo'sko:p] **der; ~en, ~en** opinion pollster
Demoskopie [demosko'pi:] **die; ~, ~n a)** *o. Pl. (Meinungsforschung)* [public] opinion research *no art.*; **b)** *(Umfrage)* opinion poll
Demoskopin die; ~, ~nen opinion pollster
demoskopisch 1. *Adj.*; *nicht präd.* opinion research ⟨*institute, methods, data, etc.*⟩; ⟨*data etc.*⟩ from opinion polls *or* opinion research; **das ~e Ergebnis** the result of the opinion poll; **~e Umfrage** [public] opinion poll. **2.** *adv.* through opinion polls *or* research; **etw. ~ untersuchen** conduct an opinion poll on sth.
dem·selben *s.* derselbe
Demut ['de:mu:t] **die; ~:** humility; **in** *od.* **mit ~:** with humility
demütig ['de:my:tıç] **1.** *Adj.* humble; *(respektvoll)* respectful. **2.** *adv.* humbly; *(respektvoll)* respectfully
demütigen 1. *tr. V.* humiliate; humble ⟨*sb.'s pride*⟩. **2.** *refl. V.* humble oneself; **sich vor jmdm. ~:** humble oneself before sb.
Demütigung die; ~, ~en humiliation
Demuts·gebärde die *(Verhaltensf.)* attitude of submission
dem·zufolge *Adv.* consequently; therefore
[1]**den** [de:n] **1.** *best. Art., Akk. Sg. v.* [1]**der 1: ich sah den Mann/den Hund/den Stein** I saw the man/the dog/the stone; **wir haben den „Faust" gelesen** we read 'Faust'; **hast du den Peter gesehen?** *(ugs.)* have you seen Peter?; **in den Libanon reisen** travel to Lebanon; **den Sozialismus/Kapitalismus ablehnen** reject socialism/capitalism. **2.** *Demonstrativpron., Akk. Sg. v.* [1]**der 2: a)** *attr.* **ich meine den Mann/den Hund/den Stein, nicht den anderen** I mean 'that man/'that dog/'that stone, not the other; **b)** *selbständig* **ich meine den [da]** I mean 'that one. **3.** *Relativpron., Akk. Sg. v.* [1]**der 3: der Mann/Hund/Stein, den ich gesehen habe** the man/dog/stone that I saw
[2]**den 1.** *best. Art., Dat. Pl. v.* [1]**der 1,** [1]**die 1, das 1: ich gab es den Männern/Frauen/Kindern** I gave it to the men/women/children; **ich habe mich mit den Berichten/Theorien/Büchern befaßt** I dealt with the reports/theories/books; **er war bei den Müllers zu Besuch** *(ugs.)* he visited the Müllers. **2.** *Demonstrativpron., Dat. Pl. v.* [1]**der 2 a,** [1]**die 2 a, das 2 a: ich gab es den Männern/den Frauen/den Kindern** I gave it to 'those men/'those women/'those children
Denaturalisation die; ~, ~en denaturalization
denaturalisieren *tr. V.* denaturalize
denaturieren [denatu'ri:rən] **1.** *tr. V.* **a)** *(geh.: verändern)* warp the personality of; *(entmenschen)* dehumanize; **b)** *(bes. Chemie)* denature ⟨*alcohol, foodstuffs, protein, fissile material, etc.*⟩. **2.** *itr. V.*; *mit sein (geh.)* **zu etw. ~:** degenerate into sth.
Dendrit [dɛn'dri:t] **der; ~en, ~en** *(Geol., Anat.)* dendrite
denen ['de:nən] **1.** *Demonstrativpron., Dat. Pl. v.* [1]**der 2 b,** [1]**die 2 b, das 2 b: gib es ~, nicht den anderen** give it to 'them, not to the others; **~ gehört das Buch** the book belongs to 'them; **~, die uns geholfen haben, helfen wir auch** we help those who have helped us. **2.** *Relativpron., Dat. Pl. v.* [1]**der 3,** [1]**die 3, das 3: die Menschen, ~ wir Geld gegeben haben** the people to whom we gave money; **die Tiere, ~ er geholfen hat** the animals that he helped; **die Bücher, mit ~ sie aufgewachsen ist** the books she grew up with
dengeln ['dɛŋl̩n] *tr. V. (Landw.)* sharpen *(by hammering out irregularities)*
Den Haag [de:n 'ha:k] **(das); ~ ~s** The Hague
denjenigen *s.* derjenige
Denk-: ~an·satz der intellectual approach; **~an·stoß der** something to think about; **jmdm. einen ~anstoß geben** give sb. food for thought; **~art die** way of thinking; **~auf·gabe die** brain-teaser
denkbar 1. *Adj.* conceivable; **in einem Zustand, wie er schlimmer nicht ~ ist** in the worst state imaginable. **2.** *adv. (sehr, äußerst)* extremely; **die Lösung ist ~ leicht** the solution could not be easier *or* is as easy as could be; **die ~ beste Methode** the best method imaginable
denken ['dɛŋkn̩] **1.** *unr. itr. V.* think **(an** *od.* *[südd., österr.]* **auf +** *Akk.* of, **über +** *Akk.* about); **kleinlich/liberal/edel ~:** be petty-minded / liberal-minded / noble-minded; **spießig/reaktionär ~:** have a bourgeois/reactionary mind *or* bourgeois/reactionary views; **wie denkst du darüber?** what do you think about it?; what's your opinion of it?; **ich weiß nicht, wie ich darüber ~ soll** I don't know what to think *or* make of it; **erst ~, dann handeln** think before you act; **der Mensch denkt, [und] Gott lenkt** *(Spr.)* man proposes, God disposes; **Denken ist Glückssache** you/he/she *etc.* thought wrong; **~de Menschen** thinking people; **so darfst du nicht ~:** you mustn't think that; **schlecht von jmdm. ~:** think badly of sb.; **jmdm. zu ~ geben** make sb. think; *(stutzig machen)* make sb. suspicious; **denk mal, Eva hat sich verlobt!** just think, Eva has got engaged!; **denk mal an!** *(spött.)* just imagine!; imagine that!; **denk daran, daß .../zu ...:** don't forget that .../to ...; **ich darf gar nicht an die Kosten ~:** I daren't think of the cost; the cost doesn't bear thinking about; **der wird noch an mich ~:** I'll give him something to remember; **das geschieht schon, solange ich ~ kann** this has been going on as long as I can remember; **ich muß an meine Familie ~:** I have to think

of *or* consider my family; **an was für einen Schuh haben Sie denn gedacht?** what sort of shoe did you have in mind?; **ich komme nach Hause, denke an nichts Böses** I came home, quite unsuspecting; **ich denke nicht daran!** no way!; not on your life!; **ich denke nicht daran, das zu tun** I've no intention *or* I wouldn't dream of doing that. **2.** *unr. tr. V.* think; **was sollen bloß die Nachbarn ~?** what will the neighbours think?; **einen Gedanken zu Ende ~:** think an idea through; **er dachte den gleichen Gedanken** the same thought occurred to him; **ich habe nichts Böses dabei gedacht** I didn't mean any harm [by it]; **das denke ich auch** I think so too; **ich denke schon** I think so; **was od. wieviel haben Sie denn gedacht?** how much did you have in mind?; **wer hätte das gedacht?** who would have thought it?; **[typischer Fall von] denkste!** *(ugs.)* how wrong can one be!; *(da irrst du dich)* that's what 'you think!; **da weiß man nicht, was man ~ soll** one doesn't know what to think; **das hätte ich nie von dir gedacht** I would never have thought it of you; **eine gedachte Linie** an imaginary line; **ein gedachter Punkt** an imaginary point. **3.** *unr. refl. V.* **a)** *(sich vorstellen)* think; imagine; **ich habe mir gedacht, daß wir ein paar Tage in Urlaub fahren** I was thinking *or* thought that we could go on holiday for a few days; **du kannst dir ~, daß ...:** you can imagine that ...; as you can imagine, ...; **das kann ich mir ~/nicht ~:** I can well believe/cannot believe that; **das habe ich mir so gedacht** I imagined it like this; this is what I had in mind; **das hast du dir so gedacht!** that's what you thought; **das hättest du dir doch ~ können, daß ...:** you should have realized that ...; **das habe ich mir [gleich] gedacht** that's [just] what I thought; *(bei Verdacht)* I thought *or* suspected as much; **das hätte ich mir ~ können!** I might have known it!; **ich denke mir mein[en] Teil** I can put two and two together *or* work things out for myself; **b) sich** *(Dat.)* **etw. bei etw. ~** *(beabsichtigen)* mean sth. by sth.; **ich habe mir nichts [Böses] dabei gedacht** I didn't mean any harm [by it]; **er denkt sich nichts dabei** he doesn't think anything of it; *s. auch* **gedacht**

Denken das; ~s thinking; *(Denkweise)* thought; **logisches/abstraktes ~:** logical/abstract thought

Denker der; ~s, ~: thinker

denkerisch 1. *Adj.* intellectual. 2. *adv.* intellectually

Denker·stirn die *(oft scherzh.)* intellectual's high brow

denk-, Denk-: ~fähig *Adj.* capable of thinking *postpos.*; intellectually able; **~fähigkeit die;** *o. Pl.* ability to think; intellectual capacity; **~faul** *Adj.* mentally lazy; **sei nicht so ~faul** use your brains; **~fehler der** flaw in one's reasoning; **das war ein ~fehler** that was poor thinking

Denk·mal das; ~s, Denkmäler *od. (geh.)* **Denkmale a)** *(Monument)* monument; memorial; **jmdm. ein ~ errichten** *od.* **setzen** erect *or* put up a memorial to sb.; **mit der Klinik hat er sich ein ~ gesetzt** *(fig.)* by building the clinic he has ensured that his name will live on; **b)** *(Zeugnis)* monument

Denkmal[s]-: ~pflege die preservation of historic monuments; **~schutz der** protection of historic monuments; **unter ~schutz stehen/stellen** be/put under a preservation order

Denk-: ~modell das hypothesis; **~pause die** pause for thought; **eine ~pause machen** *od.* **einlegen** pause for thought; *(bei Verhandlungen usw.)* have a break [to think things over]; **~schrift die** memorandum; **~sport·auf·gabe die** brain-teaser; **~spruch der** maxim; motto; **~übung die** intellectual exercise

Denkungs·art die way of thinking

denk-, Denk- ~vermögen das: [kreatives] ~vermögen ability to think [creatively]; **~weise die** way of thinking; [mental] attitude; **eine solch niedrige ~weise** such low-mindedness; **~würdig** *Adj.* memorable; **~würdigkeit die a)** *o. Pl.* memorable nature; **der ~würdigkeit eines Ereignisses bewußt** aware how memorable an event is; **b)** *Pl. (Ereignisse)* memorable events; **~zettel der** warning; lesson; **jmdm. einen ~zettel verpassen** teach sb. a lesson

denn [dɛn] **1.** *Konj.* **a)** *(kausal)* for; because; **b)** *(geh.: als)* than; **schöner/besser/größer ~ je [zuvor]** more beautiful/better/greater than ever; **c)** *(konzessiv)* **es sei ~, ...:** unless ...; **ich spreche nicht mehr mit ihm, er müßte sich ~ geändert haben** *(veralt.)* I'm not speaking to him again unless he changes his ways; *s. auch* **geschweige. 2.** *Partikel* **a)** *(in Fragesätzen: oft nicht übersetzt)* **Die Kirschen sind wahnsinnig teuer! – Wieviel kosten sie ~?** The cherries are frightfully expensive! – How much are they then?; **was ist ~ da los?** what 'is going on there?; **ist er ~ krank gewesen?** has he been ill, then?; **wie geht es dir ~?** tell me, how are you?; **wer will ~ aufgeben?** who is talking of giving up?; **ist das ~ so wichtig?** is that really so important?; **was muß ich ~ machen?** what am I to do, then?; **wie hieß sie ~ noch?** now what was her name?; **wie heißt du ~?** tell me your name; **wieso ~?** why is that?; *(stärker)* what ever for?; **warum ~ nicht?** why ever not?; **was soll das ~?** what's all this about?; *(wozu ist das gut?)* what's this in aid of?; **was ~ [sonst]?** well, what [else] then?; **wohin [fahrt ihr] ~?** where [are you going] then?; **b)** *(in Aussagesätzen verstärkend, oft folgernd)* **so wollen wir ~ zur Abstimmung kommen** let's get on with the voting now; **das ist ~ doch die Höhe!** that really is the limit!; **er starb ~ auch bald** and so he soon died. **3.** *Adv. (nordd.: dann)* then **na, ~ man los!** right then, let's get going!

dennoch ['dɛnɔx] *Adv.* nevertheless; even so; **ein höfliches und ~ eisiges Lächeln** a polite yet frosty smile

Denotat [deno'ta:t] **das; ~s, ~e** *(Sprachw.)* denotation

Denotation [denota'tsio:n] **die; ~, ~en** *(Logik, Sprachw.)* denotation

denselben *s.* **derselbe**

dental [dɛn'ta:l] **1.** *Adj. (Anat., Med., Sprachw.)* dental; **~e Laute** dentals. **2.** *adv. (Sprachw.)* dentally

Dental der; ~s, ~e *(Sprachw.)* dental

Dentist [dɛn'tɪst] **der; ~en, ~en, Dentistin die; ~, ~nen** *(veralt.)* dentist

Denunziant [denʊn'tsiant] **der; ~en, ~en** *(abwertend)* informer; grass *(sl.)*

Denunziation [denʊntsia'tsio:n] **die; ~, ~en** *(abwertend)* denunciation *(by an informer)*

denunziatorisch [denʊntsia'to:rɪʃ] *Adj. (abwertend)* **a)** *(denunzierend)* **ein ~es Klima** a climate which favours informing; **~e Äußerungen seines eigenen Vaters** statements informing against him made by his own father; **b)** *(öffentlich verurteilend)* denunciatory; condemnatory

denunzieren [denʊn'tsi:rən] *tr. V. (abwertend)* **a)** *(anzeigen)* denounce; *(bei der Polizei)* inform against; grass on *(sl.)* **(bei** to); **b)** *(als negativ hinstellen)* denounce

Deo ['de:o] **das; ~s, ~s, Deodorant** [deodo'rant] **das; ~s, ~s** *(auch:)* **~e** deodorant

deodorierend [de|odo'ri:rənt] *Adj.* deodorant

Deo·spray das deodorant spray

Departement [departə'mã:, *schweiz.:* departə'mɛnt] **das; ~s, ~s** *od. (schweiz.:)* **~e** department

Dependance [depã'dã:s] **die; ~, ~n a)** *(Hotelw.)* annexe; **b)** *(Zweigstelle)* branch

Dependenz [depɛn'dɛnts] **die; ~, ~en a)** *(Philos.)* dependence **(von** on); **b)** *(Sprachw.)* dependency

Dependenz·grammatik die *(Sprachw.)* dependency grammar

Depesche [de'pɛʃə] **die; ~, ~n** *(veralt.)* telegram **(an** + *Akk.* to)

depeschieren *(veralt.)* **1.** *tr. V.* send a telegram giving ⟨*time of arrival etc.*⟩; **~, daß ...:** wire that ... *(coll.)*. **2.** *itr. V.* send a telegram **(an** + *Akk.* to)

deplaciert, deplaziert [depla'tsi:ɐt] *Adj.* out of place *pred.*; misplaced ⟨*remark etc.*⟩

Depolarisation die *(Physik)* depolarization

Deponie [depo'ni:] **die; ~, ~n** tip *(Brit.)*; dump; **geordnete ~:** controlled tip *(Brit.)*, sanitary landfill *(Amer.) (subsequently covered and planted with trees etc.)*

deponieren *tr. V.* **a)** *(im Safe o. ä.)* deposit **(bei** with); **b)** *(an einem bestimmten Platz)* put

Deponierung die; ~: depositing

Deportation [depɔrta'tsio:n] **die; ~, ~en** transportation **(in** + *Akk.*, **nach** to); *(ins Ausland)* deportation **(in** + *Akk.*, **nach** to)

deportieren [depɔr'ti:rən] *tr. V.* transport **(in** + *Akk.*, **nach** to); *(ins Ausland)* deport **(in** + *Akk.*, **nach** to)

Deportierte der/die; *adj. Dekl.* transportee; *(ins Ausland)* deportee

Depositar [depozi'ta:ɐ], **Depositär** [depozi'tɛ:ɐ] **der; ~s, ~e** *(Finanzw.)* depositary

Depositen [depo'zi:tn̩] *Pl. (Finanzw.)* deposits

Depot [de'po:] **das; ~s, ~s a)** *(Aufbewahrungsort)* depot; *(Lagerhaus)* warehouse; *(für Möbel usw.)* depository; *(im Freien, für Munition o. ä.)* dump; *(für Straßenbahnen, Omnibusse)* depot; garage; *(in einer Bank)* strong-room; safe deposit; **b)** *(hinterlegte Wertgegenstände)* deposits *pl.*; **c)** *(Med.)* deposit

Depot-: ~fett das *(Biol., Med.)* adipose; **~fund der** *(Archäol.)* cache [find]; **~geschäft das** *(Finanzw.)* safe-deposit business; **~präparat das** *(Med.)* depot preparation

Depp [dɛp] **der; ~en** *(auch:)* **~s, ~en** *(auch:)* **~e** *(bes. südd., österr., schweiz. abwertend)* **a)** *(Dummkopf)* twit *(sl.)*; nitwit *(coll.)*; **und ich ~ bin darauf reingefallen** and like a fool I fell for it; **b)** *(Schwachsinniger)* cretin

deppert ['dɛpɐt] *(südd., österr. abwertend)* **1.** *Adj.* stupid; *(begriffsstutzig)* thick. **2.** *adv.* **stell dich doch nicht so ~ an** don't act so stupid

Depression [deprɛ'sio:n] **die; ~, ~en** *(Wirtsch., Psych., Met.)* depression; **an ~en leiden** suffer from [fits *pl.* of] depression *sing.*

depressiv [deprɛ'si:f] **1.** *Adj.* **a)** depressive; **b)** *(Wirtsch.)* depressive ⟨*effect*⟩; depressed ⟨*phase*⟩. **2.** *adv.* **a) ~ veranlagt sein** have a tendency towards depression; **b)** *(Wirtsch.)* **den Markt ~ beeinflussen** have a depressive influence on *or* depress the market

Depressivität [deprɛsivi'tɛ:t] **die; ~** *(Psych.)* depression

deprimieren [depri:mi:rən] *tr. V.* depress

deprimierend *Adj.* depressing

deprimiert **1.** *Adj.* depressed. **2.** *adv.* dejectedly

Deputat [depu'ta:t] **das, ~[e]s, ~e a)** *(Schulw.)* teaching load; **mit einem halben ~ unterrichten** have half the normal teaching load; **b)** *(Sachleistung)* payment in kind; **ein ~ Kohlen/Milch** *usw.* **erhalten** receive free coal/milk *etc.*

Deputation [deputa'tsio:n] **die; ~, ~en** deputation; *(bei Konferenzen)* delegation

deputieren [depu'ti:rən] *tr. V.* depute; delegate; **jmdn. zu einer Konferenz ~:** depute *or* delegate sb. to attend a conference

Deputierte der/die; *adj. Dekl. (Mitglied einer Deputation)* delegate; *(Abgeordnete[r])* deputy

[1]der [de:ɐ̯] **1.** *best. Art. Nom.* the; **der Kleine** the little boy; **der Tod** death; **der Montag/April/Winter** Monday/April/winter; **der „Faust"***/(ugs.)* **der Dieter** 'Faust'/Dieter; **der Kapitalismus/Sozialismus/Buddhismus/Islam** capitalism/socialism/Buddhism/Islam; **der 1. FC Köln** Cologne FC; **er ist der Fußballer/Komponist** he's 'the footballer/composer; **der Washingtonplatz** Washington Square; **der Bodensee/Mount Everest** Lake Constance/Mount Everest; **der Iran/Sudan** Iran/the Sudan; **der Mensch/Mann ist ...:** man is .../men are ... **2.** *Demonstrativpron.* **a)** *attr.* **der Mann war es** it was 'that man; **b)** *selbständig* he; **der war es** it was 'him; **der und arbeiten!** *(ugs.)* [what,] him work! *(coll.);* **der mit der Glatze** *(ugs.)* him with the bald head *(coll.);* **der [da]** *(Mann/Junge)* that man/boy; *(Gegenstand, Tier)* that one; **der [hier]** *(Mann/Junge)* this man/boy; *(Gegenstand, Tier)* this one; **der Idiot, der!** *(salopp)* what an idiot!. **3.** *Relativpron. (Mensch)* who; that; *(Sache, Tier)* which; that; **der Mann, der da drüben entlanggeht** the man walking along over there; **ich sah einen Mann/Hund, der aus dem Fenster schaute** I saw a man/dog looking out of the window. **4.** *Relativ- u. Demonstrativpron.* the one who; **der das getan hat** the man *etc.* who did it

[2]der 1. *best. Art.* **a)** *Gen. Sg. v.* **[1]die 1: der Hut der Frau** the woman's hat; **der Henkel der Tasse** the handle of the cup; **das Wiehern der Stute** the neighing of the mare; the mare's neighing; **die Freuden der Liebe** the joys of love; **der Untergang der „Titanic"** the sinking of the Titanic; **am Ende der Hauptstraße** at the end of the High Street; **der Einfluß der NATO/UNO** the influence of NATO/the UN; **b)** *Dat. Sg. v.* **[1]die 1: sein schwarzes Haar hat er von der Mutter** he got his black hair from his mother; **der Henkel an der Tasse** the handle of the cup; **sein Buch ist der Callas gewidmet** his book is dedicated to Callas; **in der Türkei** in Turkey; **seit der Aufklärung** since the Enlightenment; **c)** *Gen. Pl. v.* **[1]der 1, [1]die 1, [1]das 1: das Haus der Freunde** our/their *etc.* friends' house; **das Zimmer der Schwestern** our/their *etc.* sisters' room; **das Bellen der Hunde** the barking of the dogs. **2.** *Demonstrativpron.* **a)** *Gen. Sg. v.* **[1]die 2: es ist das Kind der Frau, die gestern hier war** he's/she's the child of the woman who was here yesterday; **b)** *Dat. Sg. v.* **[1]die 2** *attr.* **der Frau [da/hier] gehört es** it belongs to that woman there/this woman here; *selbständig* **gib es der da!** *(ugs.)* give it to 'her; **alles nur wegen der** *(ugs.)* all because of her; **c)** *Gen. Pl. v.* **[1]die 2: die Ansichten der Leute lehne ich ab** I reject the views of those people. **3.** *Relativpron.; Dat. Sg. v.* **[1]die 3** *(Mensch)* **die Frau, der ich es gegeben habe** the woman to whom I gave it; the woman I gave it to; *(Tier, Sache)* **die Katze, der er einen Tritt gab** the cat [that] he kicked; **die Lawine, unter der er begraben wurde** the avalanche under which he was buried

derangiert [derã'ʒi:ɐ̯t] *Adj.* dishevelled

der·art *Adv.* **jmdn. ~ schlecht/unfreundlich behandeln, daß ...;** treat sb. so badly/in such an unfriendly way that ...; **~ gute Vorbereitungen** such good preparations; **eine ~ schöne Frau** such a beautiful woman; **es hat lange nicht mehr ~ geregnet** it hasn't rained as hard as that for a long time; **sie hat ~ geschrien, daß ...:** she screamed so much that ...

der·artig 1. *Adj.; nicht präd.* such; **ein ~er Wutausbruch** such a fit of fury; **~es things** *pl.* like that; **etwas Derartiges** a thing like that; such a thing. **2.** *adv. s.* **derart**

derb [dɛrp] **1.** *Adj.* **a)** strong, tough ⟨*material*⟩; stout, strong, sturdy ⟨*shoes*⟩; **b)** *(kräftig)* solid, substantial ⟨*food*⟩; **c)** *(kraftvoll, deftig)* earthy ⟨*scenes, humour*⟩; **d)** *(unverblümt)* crude, coarse ⟨*expression, language*⟩; **e)** *(unfreundlich)* gruff. **2.** *adv.* **a)** strongly ⟨*made, woven, etc.*⟩; **b)** *(heftig)* roughly; **c)** *(kraftvoll, deftig)* earthily; **um es einmal ~ zu sagen** to put it crudely; **d)** *(unverblümt)* crudely; coarsely; **e)** *(unfreundlich)* gruffly

Derbheit die; ~, ~en a) *o. Pl. s.* **derb c, d:** earthiness; crudity; coarseness; **b)** *(Äußerung)* crudity

derb·knochig *Adj.* big-boned

Derby ['dɛrbi] **das; ~s, ~s a)** *(Pferdesport)* Derby; **b)** *(Fußball)* derby; **das ~ der beiden Lokalrivalen** the local derby

der·einst *Adv.* **a)** *(geh.)* one *or* some day; **b)** *(veralt.)* once; at one time; **der·einstig** *Adj.; nicht präd. (geh.)* future

deren ['de:rən] **1.** *Relativpron.* **a)** *Gen. Sg. v.* **[1]die 3** *attr. (Menschen)* whose; *(Sachen, Tiere)* of which; **die Katastrophe, ~ Folgen furchtbar waren** the disaster, the consequences of which were frightful; *selbständig* **die Großmutter, ~ wir uns gerne erinnern** our grandmother, of whom we have fond memories; **eine Anrede, ~ er sich gern bediente** a form of address which *or* that he liked to use; **b)** *Gen., Pl. v.* **[1]der 3, [1]die 3, das 3** *attr. (Menschen)* whose; *(Sachen, Tiere)* **Maßnahmen, ~ Folgen wir noch nicht absehen können** measures, the consequences of which we cannot yet foresee. **2.** *Demonstrativpron.* **a)** *Gen. Sg. v.* **[1]die 2** *attr.* **meine Tante, ihre Freundin und ~ Hund** my aunt, her friend and 'her dog; **die Universität und ~ Abteilungen** the university and its departments; *selbständig* **Tante Frieda? Deren erinnere ich mich nicht mehr** Aunt Frieda? I don't remember 'her; **b)** *Gen. Pl. v.* **[1]der 2, [1]die 2, das 2** *attr.* **meine Verwandten und ~ Kinder** my relatives and their children; **die Schulen und ~ Lehrpersonal** the schools and their teaching staff; *selbständig* **Bücher/Kinder? Deren hat er genug** *(geh.)* Books/Children? He's got enough of those

derent-: ~halben *Adv. (veralt.),* **~wegen** *Adv.* **1.** *relativ* on whose account; on account of whom; because of whom; *(von Sachen)* on account of which; because of which; **die Frau, ~wegen er seine Familie verlassen hat** the woman on whose account *or* for whom he left his family; **die Tasche, ~wegen du das ganze Haus abgesucht hast** the purse for which you searched the entire house; **2.** *demonstrativ* because of them; **~willen** *Adv.* **1.** *relativ* **um ~willen** for whose sake; for the sake of whom; *(von Sachen)* for the sake of which; **die Erbstücke, um ~willen sich die Kinder zerstritten** the heirlooms over which the children fell out; **die Parkplätze, um ~willen es so heiße Diskussionen gab** the car parks about which there were such impassioned debates; **2.** *demonstrativ* **um ~willen** for her/their sake

derer ['de:rɐ] *Demonstrativpron.; Gen. Pl. v.* **[1]der 2, [1]die 2, das 2;** *vorausweisend* **das Schicksal ~, die verschollen sind** the fate of those who are missing; **die Zahl ~, die das glauben, nimmt ab** the number of people who believe that is declining; **das Schloß ~ von Fleckenstein** *(geh.)* the castle of the family Fleckenstein

deret-: *s.* **derent-**

der·gestalt *Adv. (geh.)* **~, daß ...:** in such a way that ...; **Widrigkeiten, die uns ~ belasten[, daß ...]** adversities which weigh so heavily upon us [that ...]; **~ ausgerüstet/vorbereitet** thus equipped/prepared

der·gleichen *indekl. Demonstrativpron.* **a)** *attr.* such; like that *postpos., not pred.;* **b)** *alleinstehend* that sort of thing; such things *pl.;* things *pl.* like that; **nichts ~:** nothing of the sort; **es gibt ~ mehr** there's more of that sort of thing; **und ~ [mehr]** and suchlike; **nichts ~ tun** do nothing of the sort

Derivat [deri'va:t] **das; ~[e]s, ~e** *(Chemie, Sprachw., Biol.)* derivative

Derivativ [deriva'ti:f] **das; ~s, ~e** *(Sprachw.)* derivative

der·jenige [-je:nɪgə], **die·jenige, das·jenige** *Demonstrativpron.* **a)** *mit Relativsatz* **derjenige, der ...:** *(Mensch)* the one who ...; *(Sache)* the one which ...; **die Kinder derjenigen, die ...:** the children of those who ...; **er ist immer derjenige, welcher** *(ugs.)* it's always him *(coll.);* **ach, du bist diejenige, welche** *(ugs.)* oh, so you're the one; **b)** *mit nachfolgendem Gen.* that; **diejenigen** those; **seine Frau ist charmanter als diejenige seines Bruders** *(geh.)* his wife is more charming than his brother's

derlei ['de:ɐ̯lai] *indekl. Demonstrativpron.* **a)** *attr.* such; like that *postpos., not pred.;* **b)** *selbständig* that sort of thing; such things *pl.;* things *pl.* like that

der·maßen *Adv.* **~ schön** *usw.,* **daß ...:** so beautiful *etc.* that ...; **ein ~ intelligenter Mensch** such an intelligent person; **er hat mich ~ belogen, daß ...:** he has lied to me so much that ...

Dermatologe [dɛrmato'lo:gə] **der; ~n, ~n** dermatologist

Dermatologie [dɛrmatolo'gi:] **die; ~:** dermatology *no art.*

Dermatologin die; ~, ~nen dermatologist

Dermato·plastik die *(Med.)* dermatoplasty *(Med.);* plastic surgery

Dero ['de:ro] *indekl. Pron. (veralt.)* Your

ders. *Abk.* **derselbe**

derselbe [de:ɐ̯'zɛlbə], **dieselbe, dasselbe,** *Pl.* **dieselben** *Demonstrativpron.* **a)** *attr.* the same; **derselbe Mann/dieselbe Frau/dasselbe Dorf** the same man/woman/village; **b)** *selbständig* the same one; **er sagt immer dasselbe** he always says the same thing; **sie ist immer noch [ganz] dieselbe** she is still [exactly] the same; **es sind immer dieselben, die ...:** it's always the same people *or* ones who ...; **noch einmal dasselbe, bitte** *(ugs.)* [the] same again please; **c)** *selbständig (Amtsspr. veralt.)* the same; **derselben/desselben** of same; **... des Angeklagten. Derselbe hatte ...:** ... of the defendant. He had ...

derselbige [de:ɐ̯'zɛlbɪgə], **dieselbige, dasselbige,** *Pl.* **dieselbigen** *(veralt.) s.* **derselbe**

der·weil[en] 1. *Adv.* meanwhile; in the meantime. **2.** *Konj.* while

Derwisch ['dɛrvɪʃ] **der; ~[e]s, ~e** dervish

der·zeit *Adv.* **a)** *(zur Zeit)* at present; at the moment; **b)** *(veralt.: damals)* at that time; then

der·zeitig *Adj.; nicht präd.* **a)** *(jetzig)* present; current; **b)** *(veralt.: damalig)* at that time *postpos.*

[1]des [dɛs] **1.** *best. Art.; Gen. Sg. v.* **[1]der 1, das 1: die Mütze des Jungen** the boy's cap; **das Wiehern des Pferdes** the neighing of the horse; the horse's neighing; **das Klingeln des Telefons** the ringing of the telephone; **er hat das schwarze Haar des Vaters** he has his father's black hair; **nördlich des Schillerplatzes** to the north of Schiller Square. **2.** *Demonstrativpron.; Gen. Sg. v.* **[1]der 2, das 2: er ist der Sohn des Mannes, der gestern hier war** he's the son of the man who was here yesterday

[2]des *(veralt.)* **a)** *s.* **dessen; b)** *s.* **wes**

[3]des, Des das; ~, ~ *(Musik)* D flat

Desaster [de'zastɐ] **das; ~s, ~:** disaster

desavouieren [dɛs|avu'i:rən] *tr. V. (geh.)* **a)** *(bloßstellen)* expose; **b)** *(nicht anerkennen)* repudiate

Desavouierung die; ~, ~en *s.* **desavouieren:** exposure; repudiation

Des-Dur [*auch* '–'–] **das** D flat major; *s. auch* **C-Dur**

desensibilisieren *tr. V. (Fot., Med., fig.)* desensitize
Deserteur [dezɛr'tø:ɐ̯] **der; ~s, ~e** *(Milit.)* deserter
desertieren *itr. V.; mit sein (Milit., fig.)* desert
Desertion [dezɛr'tsi̯o:n] **die; ~, ~en** *(Milit.)* desertion
des·gleichen *Adv.* likewise; **er ist Antialkoholiker, ~ seine Frau** he is a teetotaller, as is *or* and so is his wife; **es fehlt an Papier, ~ an Schreibmaschinen** there's a shortage of paper and also [of] typewriters
des·halb *Adv.* for that reason; because of that; **~ bin ich zu dir gekommen** that is why I came to you; **aber ~ ist sie nicht dumm** but that doesn't mean she is stupid; **~ also!** so that's why *or* the reason!; **er war krank, [und] ~ konnte er nicht kommen** he was ill, [and] so he couldn't come; **..., aber ~ könnt ihr gerne noch bleiben** ..., but you're still welcome so stay
Desiderat [dezidɛ'ra:t] **das; ~[e]s, ~e, Desideratum** [dezide'ra:tʊm] **das; ~s, Desiderata a)** *(Buchw.)* suggestion; **dieses Buch ist schon seit langem ein ~ in unserer Bibliothek** it was suggested a long time ago that our library should acquire this book; **b)** *(geh.: Erwünschtes)* desideratum
Design [di'zain] **das; ~s, ~s** design
Designat [dezɪ'gna:t] **das; ~[e]s, ~e** *(Sprachw., Logik)* designatum
Designation [dezɪgna'tsi̯o:n] **die; ~, ~en** designation
Designer [di'zainɐ] **der; ~s, ~, Designerin die; ~, ~nen** designer
designieren [dezɪ'gni:rən] *tr. V. (geh.)* designate (**zu** as)
desillusionieren [dɛsɪluzi̯o'ni:rən] *tr. V.* disillusion
Desillusionierung die; ~, ~en disillusionment
Des·infektion [dɛs|-] **die** disinfection; **zur ~**: to disinfect it/them
Desinfektions·mittel das disinfectant
des·infizieren *tr. V.* disinfect
Des·infizierung die disinfection
Des·information die disinformation *no indef. art.*; **~en** disinformation *sing.*
Des·integration die *(Soziol., Psych.)* disintegration
Des·interesse das lack of interest (**an** + *Dat.* in)
des·interessiert 1. *Adj.* uninterested. **2.** *adv.* uninterestedly
Deskription [deskrɪp'tsi̯o:n] **die; ~, ~en** *(geh.)* description
deskriptiv [deskrɪp'ti:f] **1.** *Adj.* descriptive. **2.** *adv.* descriptively
Desodorant [dɛs|odo'rant] *s.* **Deodorant**
desolat [dezo'la:t] *Adj. (geh.)* wretched
Des·organisation die *(geh.)* **a)** disintegration; **b)** *(fehlende Planung)* disorganization *no indef. art.*; lack of organization
des·orientieren *tr. V.* disorientate
Des·orientiertheit, Des·orientierung die; ~: confusion
Des·oxidation *(fachspr.)*, **Des·oxydation die** deoxidation
Desoxyribo[se]nuklein·säure [dɛs|ɔksyri'bo(:zə)nukle'i:n-] **die** *(Biochemie)* deoxyribonucleic acid
despektierlich [despɛk'ti:ɐ̯lɪç] *(geh.)* **1.** *Adj. (abfällig, geringschätzig)* disparaging; *(respektlos)* disrespectful. **2.** *adv.; s.* **1**: disparagingly; disrespectfully
Desperado [dɛspe'ra:do] **der; ~s, ~s** desperado
desperat [dɛspe'ra:t] *Adj. (geh.)* desperate; **eine ~e Stimmung** a mood of desperation
Despot [dɛs'po:t] **der; ~en, ~en** despot; *(fig. abwertend)* tyrant
Despotie [dɛspo'ti:] **die, ~, ~n** despotism
despotisch 1. *Adj.* despotic. **2.** *adv.* despotically
Despotismus der; ~: despotism
des·selben *s.* **derselbe**
dessen ['dɛsn̩] **1.** *Relativpron.; Gen. Sg. v.* **¹der 3, das 3** *attr. (Mensch)* whose; **der Onkel, ~ Besuch wir erwarten** the uncle from whom we are expecting a visit; *(Sache, Tier)* **der Garten, ~ Fläche 2 000 m² beträgt** the garden, the area of which is 2,000 m²; *selbständig* **der Großvater, ~ wir uns gern erinnern** our grandfather, of whom we have fond memories; **ein Sprichwort, ~ er sich gern bedient** a proverb which *or* that he likes to use. **2.** *Demonstrativpron.; Gen. Sg. v.* **¹der 2, das 2** *attr.* **mein Onkel, sein Sohn und ~ Hund** my uncle, his son, and 'his dog; **das Waldsterben und ~ Folgen** the death of the forests and its consequences; *selbständig* **Onkel August? Dessen erinnere ich mich noch sehr gut** Uncle August? I remember 'him well
dessent-: ~halben *(veralt.)*, **~wegen** *Adv.* **1.** *relativ* on whose account; on account of whom; because of whom; *(von Sachen)* on account of which; because of which, **das Verbrechen, ~wegen er verurteilt wurde** the crime of which he was convicted; **2.** *demonstrativ* because of him; *(von Sachen)* because of this; **~willen** *Adv.* **1.** *relativ* **um ~willen** for whose sake; for the sake of whom; *(von Sachen)* for the sake of which; **das Treffen, um ~willen wir dorthin reisten** the meeting for which we travelled there; **2.** *demonstrativ* **um ~willen** for his sake
dessen·ungeachtet *Adv.* nevertheless; notwithstanding [this]
Dessert [dɛ'sɛ:ɐ̯] **das; ~s, ~s** dessert
Dessert-: ~teller der dessert plate; **~wein der** dessert wine
Dessin [dɛ'sɛ̃:] **das; ~s, ~s a)** design; pattern; **b)** *(Entwurf)* design; **c)** *(Billard)* path [of the ball]
Dessous [dɛ'su:] **das; ~** [dɛ'su:(s)], **~** [dɛ'su:s] *(geh.) (ladies')* underwear *no indef. art.*
destabilisieren *tr. V. (Politik)* destabilize
Destabilisierung die; ~, ~en *(Politik)* destabilization
Destillat [dɛstɪ'la:t] **das; ~[e]s, ~e** distillate
Destillateur [dɛstɪla'tø:ɐ̯] **der; ~s, ~e** distiller
Destillation [dɛstɪla'tsi̯o:n] **die; ~, ~en a)** *(Chemie)* distillation; **b)** *(von Weinbrand)* distilling; *(Anlage)* distillery
Destillator [dɛstɪ'la:tɔr] **der; ~s, ~en** [-la'to:rən] still
Destille [dɛs'tɪlə] **die; ~, ~n a)** bar; **b)** *(Branntweinbrennerei)* distillery
destillieren *tr. V.* **a)** *(Chemie)* distil; **destilliertes Wasser** distilled water; **b)** *(fig.)* condense (**zu** into); **aus einer Dokumentation eine Reportage ~**: condense records into a report
Destillier·kolben der distillation flask
desto *Konj., nur vor Komp.* **je eher, ~ besser** the sooner the better; **~ ängstlicher** the more anxious/anxiously; **ich schätzte ihn ~ mehr** I appreciated him all the more; **~ schlimmer für ihn** so much the worse for him; **~ besser für uns** all the better for us
Destruktion [destrʊk'tsi̯o:n] **die; ~, ~en** destruction
Destruktions·trieb der *(Psych.)* destructive urge
destruktiv [destrʊk'ti:f] **1.** *Adj.* destructive. **2.** *adv.* destructively; **~ auf etw.** *(Akk.)* **wirken** have a destructive effect on sth.
Destruktivität [destrʃktivi'tɛ:t] **die; ~**: destructiveness
des·wegen *Adv. s.* **deshalb**
Deszendent [destsɛn'dɛnt] **der; ~en, ~en** *(Genealogie, Astrol.)* descendant
Deszendenz·theorie die theory of evolution
Detail [de'tai] **das; ~s, ~s** detail; **ins ~ gehen** go into detail; **in allen ~s** in the fullest detail; **bis ins [kleinste] ~**: down to the smallest detail
detail-, Detail-: ~frage die question of detail; **~getreu 1.** *Adj.* accurate in every detail *postpos.*; **2.** *adv.* accurately in every detail; **~kenntnisse** *Pl.* detailed knowledge *sing.*
detaillieren [deta'ji:rən] *tr. V.* explain ⟨*plan, suggestion, etc.*⟩ in detail; **etw. genauer ~**: explain sth. in more *or* greater detail
detailliert 1. *Adj.* detailed. **2.** *adv.* in detail; **sehr ~**: in great detail
Detail·schilderung die detailed account; *(Beschreibung)* detailed description
Detektei [detɛk'tai] **die; ~, ~en** [private] detective agency
Detektiv [detɛk'ti:f] **der; ~s, ~e** [private] detective; **die ~e von Scotland Yard** the detectives from Scotland Yard
Detektiv-: ~büro das *s.* **Detektei**; **~geschichte die** detective story
Detektivin die; ~, ~nen [private] detective
detektivisch 1. *Adj.* **mit ~em Scharfsinn** with the keen perception of a detective; **in ~er Kleinarbeit** by detailed detective work. **2.** *adv.* like a detective
Detektiv·roman der detective novel
Detektor [de'tɛktɔr] **der; ~s, ~en** [-'to:rən] *(Technik, Funkw.)* detector
Detergens [de'tɛrgɛns] **das; ~, Detergenzien** *(Chemie)* detergent
Determinante [detɛrmi'nantə] **die; ~, ~n** *(Math., Biol.)* determinant
Determination [detɛrmina'tsi̯o:n] **die; ~, ~en** *(Philos., Biol., Psych.)* determination
determinieren *tr. V.* determine
Determiniertheit die; ~ *(Philos.)* determined nature; **die gesellschaftliche ~ der Sprache** the socially determined nature of language
Determinismus der; ~ *(Philos.)* determinism *no art.*
deterministisch 1. *Adj.* deterministic. **2.** *adv.* deterministically
Detonation [detona'tsi̯o:n] **die; ~, ~en** detonation; explosion; **eine Bombe zur ~ bringen** detonate a bomb
detonieren [deto'ni:rən] *itr. V.; mit sein* detonate; explode
Deubel ['dɔybl̩] **der; ~s, ~** *(nordd.) s.* **Teufel**
deucht ['dɔyçt] *3. Pers. Sg. Präsens v.* **dünken**
deuchte *3. Pers. Sg. Prät. v.* **dünken**
Deut [dɔyt] **keinen ~**: not one bit; **du bist keinen ~ besser als er** you're not one bit *or* whit better than he is
deutbar *Adj.* interpretable
Deutelei die; ~, ~en *(abwertend)* speculation
deuteln ['dɔytl̩n] *itr. V.* quibble (**an** + *Dat.* about); **daran gibt es nichts zu ~**: there are no ifs and buts about it
deuten ['dɔytn̩] **1.** *itr. V.* **a)** point; **[mit dem Finger] auf jmdn./etw. ~**: point [one's finger] at sb./sth.; **b)** *(hinweisen)* **auf etw.** *(Akk.)* **~**: point to *or* indicate sth.; **sein Verhalten deutet darauf hin, daß ...**: his behaviour indicates that .... **2.** *tr. V.* interpret; **die Zukunft ~**: read the future; **etw. falsch ~**: misinterpret sth.
Deuter der; ~s, ~ a) interpreter; **b)** *(österr.: Tip)* hint; clue
deutlich 1. *Adj.* **a)** clear; **daraus wird ~, daß/wie ...**: this makes it clear that/how ...; **b)** *(eindeutig)* clear; plain; clear, distinct ⟨*recollection, feeling*⟩; clear ⟨*victory*⟩; **das ist ~**: that is [quite] plain *or* clear; **das war ~ [genug]** that was clear *or* plain enough; **~ werden** make oneself plain *or* clear; **muß ich noch ~er werden?** do I have to speak more plainly?. **2.** *adv.* **a)** clearly; **~ sichtbar/erkennbar/hörbar sein** be clearly *or* plainly visible/recognizable/audible; **b)** *(eindeutig)* clearly; plainly; **[klar und] ~ sagen, daß ...**:

make it [perfectly *or* quite] clear that ...; **jmdm. etw. ~ zu verstehen geben** make sth. clear *or* plain to sb.

Deutlichkeit die; ~, ~en a) *o. Pl.* clarity; **b)** *o. Pl. (Eindeutigkeit)* clearness; plainness; *(von Erinnerungen)* clearness; distinctness; **in** *od.* **mit aller ~ sagen, daß ...:** make it perfectly clear *or* plain that ...; **seine Antwort ließ an ~ nichts zu wünschen übrig** his answer could not have been clearer; **c)** *Pl. (Grobheiten)* rude remarks

deutlichkeits·halber *Adv.* for the sake of clarity

deutsch [dɔytʃ] **1.** *Adj.* **a)** German; **die ~e Schrift** German script; **~er Schäferhund** Alsatian; German shepherd [dog]; **mit typisch ~er Gründlichkeit** with typical Teutonic *or* German thoroughness; **Deutsche Mark** Deutschmark; German mark; **der Deutsche Orden** the Teutonic Order; **Deutsche Bundesbahn** German Federal Railway; **Deutsche Bundespost** German Federal Post Office; **Deutsche Demokratische Republik** German Democratic Republic; **Deutscher Fußball-Bund** German Football Association; **Deutscher Gewerkschaftsbund** German Trade Union Federation; **das Deutsche Reich** the German Reich *or* Empire; **Deutsche Presse-Agentur** German Press Agency; **Deutsches Rotes Kreuz** German Red Cross; **b)** *(die Sprache betreffend)* German; **etw. auf ~ sagen** say sth. in German; **auf** *od.* **in ~ geschrieben sein** be written in German; **was heißt das Wort auf ~?** what is the word in German?; what is the German for that word?; **auf [gut] ~** *(ugs.)* in plain English; **die ~e Schweiz** German-speaking Switzerland. **2.** *adv.*; **~ sprechen/schreiben** speak/write German; **~ geschrieben sein** be written in German; **~ fühlen** feel German; **etw. ~ aussprechen** pronounce sth. in a German way; **mit jmdm. ~ reden** *od.* **sprechen** *(fig. ugs.)* be blunt with *or* speak bluntly to sb.; **dieses Gebiet war damals ~ besetzt/verwaltet** this area was under German occupation/administration at that time

Deutsch das; ~[s] a) German; **gutes/fließend ~ sprechen** speak good/fluent German; **ein perfektes ~:** faultless *or* perfect German; **kein ~ [mehr] verstehen** *(ugs.)* not understand plain English; **b)** *o. Art. (Unterrichtsfach)* German *no art.*; **er ist gut in ~:** he's good at German; **wen habt ihr in ~?** who do you have for German?

Deutsch·amerikaner der German-American

deutsch-amerikanisch *Adj.; nicht präd.* German-American

Deutsch·arbeit die *(Schulw.)* German test

deutsch-deutsch *Adj.; nicht präd.* intra-German

[1]**Deutsche** ['dɔytʃə] **der/die;** *adj. Dekl.* German; **~[r] sein** be German; **er ist kein ~r** he's not German; **als ~r** as a German; **er hat eine ~ geheiratet** he married a German girl/woman

[2]**Deutsche das; ~ a)** *mit best. Art.* German; **das ~ ist ...:** German is ...; **aus dem ~n/ins ~ übersetzen** translate from/into German; **b)** *(deutsche Eigenart)* **alles ~:** all things *pl. or* everything German; **das typische ~ daran** what is/was typically German about it

Deutschen·feind der anti-German; Germanophobe

deutsch-englisch *Adj.* Anglo-German ⟨*relations, co-operation, etc.*⟩; German-English ⟨*dictionary, anthology, etc.*⟩

Deutschen·haß der hatred of the Germans; Germanophobia *no indef. art.*

deutsch-, Deutsch-: ~feindlich *Adj.* anti-German; Germanophobe; **~feindlichkeit die** Germanophobia *no indef. art.*; anti-German feeling; **~-französisch** *Adj.* Franco-German ⟨*relations, border, etc.*⟩; German-French ⟨*dictionary, anthology, etc.*⟩; **der Deutsch-Französische Krieg** the Franco-Prussian War; **~freundlich** *Adj.* pro-German; Germanophile; **~herren** *Pl. (hist.)* Teutonic Knights; **~herren·orden der** *(hist.)* Teutonic Order of Knights; **~kanadier der** German-Canadian

Deutschland (das); ~s Germany; **die beiden ~:** the two Germanies

Deutschland-: ~fahrt die trip through Germany; **~frage die** *(Politik)* German question; **~lied das** the song 'Deutschland, Deutschland über alles'; **~politik die** *(innerdeutsche Politik)* intra-German policy; *(gegenüber ~)* policy towards Germany; **~politisch 1.** *Adj.* ⟨*speaker*⟩ for intra-German affairs; ⟨*committee*⟩ on intra-German affairs; **2.** *adv.* ⟨*interested*⟩ in intra-German affairs; **~politisch gesehen** from the point of view of intra-German affairs; **~reise die** trip to Germany; *(Rundreise)* tour of Germany

deutsch-, Deutsch-: ~lehrer der German teacher; **~schweiz die** *(schweiz.)* German-speaking Switzerland; **~schweizer der** German-Swiss; **~schweizerisch** *Adj.* German-Swiss; **~sowjetisch** *Adj., nicht präd.* German-Soviet; **~sprachig** *Adj.* **a)** German-speaking; **Deutschsprachige** *Pl.* German speakers; **b)** *(in deutscher Sprache)* German-language *attrib.* ⟨*newspaper, edition, broadcast*⟩; ⟨*teaching*⟩ in German; German ⟨*literature*⟩; **~sprachlich** *Adj.* German[-language *attrib.*]; **~sprechend** *Adj.; nicht präd.* German-speaking; **~stämmig** *Adj.* of German origin *postpos.*; **Deutschstämmige** *Pl.* ethnic Germans; **~stunde die** German lesson

Deutschtum das; ~s a) *(deutsche Wesensart)* Germanness; **b)** *(Volkszugehörigkeit)* German nationality; **c)** *(die Deutschen)* Germans *pl.*

Deutschtümelei [-ty:mə'lai] **die; ~, ~en** *(abwertend)* jingoistic emphasis on things German

Deutsch·unterricht der German teaching; *(Unterrichtsstunde)* German lesson; **~ erteilen** *or* **geben** teach German; *s. auch* **Englischunterricht; Unterricht**

Deutung die; ~, ~en interpretation

Deutungs·versuch der attempt at interpretation; **ein ~ dieser Parabel** an attempt to interpret this parable

Devalvation [devalva'tsio:n] **die; ~, ~en** *(Finanzw.)* devaluation

Devise [de'vi:zə] **die; ~, ~n** motto; **sich** *(Dat.)* **etw. zur ~ machen** make sth. one's motto

Devisen *Pl.* foreign exchange *sing.*; *(Sorten)* foreign currency *sing. or* exchange *sing.*

Devisen-: ~abkommen das *(Politik)* foreign exchange agreement; **~bewirtschaftung die** foreign exchange control; **~börse die** foreign exchange market; **~bringer der** foreign exchange earner; **~geschäft das** foreign exchange business *or* dealings *pl.*; *(einzelne Transaktion)* foreign exchange transaction; **~kurs der** exchange rate; rate of exchange; **~markt der** foreign exchange market; **~schmuggel der** [foreign] currency smuggling; **~sperre die** exchange embargo; **~vergehen das** currency offence; breach of exchange control regulations

devot [de'vo:t] *(geh.)* **1.** *Adj.* **a)** *(abwertend)* obsequious; **b)** *(veralt.: demütig)* humble. **2.** *adv.* **a)** *(abwertend)* obsequiously; **b)** *(veralt.: demütig)* humbly

Devotionalien [devotsio'na:liən] *Pl. (Rel.)* devotional objects

Dextrose [dɛks'tro:zə] **die; ~:** dextrose

Dez [de:ts] **der; ~es, ~e** *(salopp)* nut *(sl.)*; bonce *(sl.)*

Dez. *Abk.* **Dezember** Dec.

Dezember [de'tsɛmbɐ] **der; ~s, ~:** December; *s. auch* **April**

Dezennium [de'tsɛnium] **das; ~s, Dezennien** *(geh.)* decennium; decade

dezent [de'tsɛnt] **1.** *Adj.* quiet ⟨*colour, pattern, suit*⟩; subdued ⟨*lighting, music*⟩; discreet ⟨*smile, behaviour*⟩; gentle ⟨*irony*⟩. **2.** *adv.* discreetly; ⟨*dress*⟩ unostentatiously

dezentral 1. *Adj.* **a)** non-central ⟨*location*⟩; **b)** *(von verschiedenen Stellen ausgehend)* decentralized. **2.** *adv.* **a)** outside the centre; **b)** *s.* **1 b:** decentrally

Dezentralisation die; ~, ~en decentralization

dezentralisieren *tr. V.* decentralize

Dezentralisierung die; ~, ~en decentralization

Dezenz [de'tsɛnts] **die; ~ a)** discreetness; **b)** *(Eleganz)* unostentatious elegance

Dezernat [detsɛr'na:t] **das; ~[e]s, ~e** department

Dezernent [detsɛr'nɛnt] **der; ~en, ~en** head of department

dezi-, Dezi- ['de:tsi-]: deci

Dezibel [detsi'bɛl] **das; ~s, ~:** decibel

dezidiert [detsi'di:ɐt] *(geh.)* **1.** *Adj.* firm ⟨*demand, view*⟩; **mit einigen ~en Fragen** with some determined questioning. **2.** *adv.* ⟨*support, demand*⟩ firmly; ⟨*question*⟩ determinedly

Dezi-: ~gramm das decigram; **~liter der** *od.* **das** decilitre

dezimal [detsi'ma:l] *Adj.* decimal

Dezimal-: ~bruch der decimal [fraction]; **~klassifikation die;** *o. Pl.* decimal *or* Dewey classification; **~rechnung die** decimal arithmetic *no art.*; **~stelle die** decimal place; **~system das** decimal system; **~waage die** decimal balance; **~zahl die** decimal [number]

Dezime [de'tsi:mə] **die; ~, ~n** *(Musik)* tenth

Dezi·meter der *od.* **das** decimetre

dezimieren [detsi'mi:rən] **1.** *tr. V.* decimate. **2.** *refl. V.* be drastically reduced

Dezimierung die; ~, ~en a) decimation; **b)** *(starker Rückgang)* drastic reduction (*Gen.* in)

DFB [de:|ɛf'be:] **der; ~** *Abk.* **Deutscher Fußball-Bund**

DGB [de:ge:'be:] **der; ~** *Abk.* **Deutscher Gewerkschaftsbund** West German Trade Union Federation

dgl. *Abk.* **dergleichen, desgleichen**

d. Gr. *Abk.* **der/die Große**

d. h. *Abk.* **das heißt** i. e.

Di. *Abk.* **Dienstag** Tue[s].

Dia ['di:a] **das; ~s, ~s** slide; transparency

Diabetes [dia'be:tɛs] **der; ~:** diabetes

Diabetiker [dia'be:tikɐ] **der; ~s, ~, Diabetikerin, die; ~, ~nen** diabetic

diabetisch *Adj.* diabetic

Dia·betrachter der [slide-]viewer

Diabolik [dia'bo:lɪk] **die; ~** *(geh.)* diabolic malevolence

diabolisch *(geh.)* **1.** *Adj.* diabolic; diabolically malevolent. **2.** *adv.* with diabolic malevolence

diachron [dia'kro:n] **1.** *Adj.* diachronic. **2.** *adv.* diachronically

Diachronie [diakro'ni:] **die; ~** *(Sprachw.)* diachrony *no art.*

diachronisch *Adj. s.* **diachron**

Diadem [dia'de:m] **das; ~s, ~e** diadem

Diadochen [dia'dɔxn̩] *Pl. (geh.)* rivals for the succession

Diadochen·kämpfe *Pl. (geh.)* power struggle *sing.*

Diagnose [dia'gno:zə] **die; ~, ~n** diagnosis; **eine ~ stellen** make a diagnosis

Diagnose·zentrum das diagnostic clinic

Diagnostik [dia'gnɔstɪk] **die; ~** *(Med., Psych.)* diagnostics *sing., no art.*

Diagnostiker der; ~s, ~, Diagnostikerin die; ~, ~nen *(Med., Psych.)* diagnostician

diagnọstisch 1. *Adj.* diagnostic. **2.** *adv.* diagnostically
diagnostizieren [diagnɔsti'tsi:rən] **1.** *tr. V.* diagnose. **2.** *itr. V.* **auf etw.** *(Akk.)* **~:** diagnose sth.
diagonal [diago'na:l] **1.** *Adj.* diagonal. **2.** *adv.* diagonally; **etw. ~ lesen** *(ugs.)* skim through sth.
Diagonạle die; ~, ~n diagonal
Diagrạmm das graph; *(von Gegenständen)* diagram
Diakon [dia'ko:n] **der; ~s** *od.* **~en, ~e[n]** *(christl. Kirche)* deacon
Diakonie [diako'ni:] **die; ~** *(ev. Kirche)* welfare and social work
diakọnisch *Adj.; nicht präd. (ev. Kirche)* welfare and social ⟨*work, facilities, etc.*⟩
Diakonisse [diako'nɪsə] **die; ~, ~n** *(ev. Kirche)* deaconess
dia·krịtisch *Adj.* **in ~es Zeichen** *(Sprachw.)* diacritical mark *or* sign; diacritic
Dialekt [dia'lɛkt] **der; ~[e]s, ~e** dialect; **~ sprechen** speak in dialect
dialektal [dialɛk'ta:l] *Adj.* dialectal
dialẹkt-, Dialẹkt-: ~ausdruck der; *Pl.* **~ausdrücke** dialect expression; **~forschung die** dialect research; **~frei 1.** *Adj.* **~freies Deutsch sprechen** speak German without a trace of [any] dialect; **2.** *adv.* **~frei sprechen** speak without a trace of [any] dialect
Dialektik [dia'lɛktɪk] **die; ~ a)** *(Philos.)* dialectics *pl.; (Diamat)* dialectic; **b)** *(Gegensätzlichkeit)* conflicting nature
Dialẹktiker der; ~s, ~, Dialẹktikerin die; ~, ~nen *(Philos.)* dialectician
dialẹktisch 1. *Adj.* **a)** *(Philos.)* dialectical; **b)** *s.* **dialektal. 2.** *adv.* dialectically
Dialog [dia'lo:k] **der; ~[e]s, ~e** dialogue
dialọgisch *Adj.* dialogic; ⟨*story*⟩ in dialogue form
Dialyse [dia'ly:zə] **die; ~, ~n** *(Physik, Chemie, Med.)* dialysis
Dialyse·zentrum das dialysis centre
[1]Diamant [dia'mant] **der; ~en, ~en** diamond
[2]Diamạnt die; ~ *(Druckw.)* diamond *(4½ points Pica)*; brilliant *(4 points Pica)*
diamạnten *Adj.; nicht präd.* diamond
Diamạnt[en]-: ~schleifer der diamond cutter; **~schmuck der** diamond jewellery; diamonds *pl.*; **~staub der** diamond dust
Diamat, DIAMAT [dia'ma(:)t] **der; ~** *Abk.* **dialektischer Materialismus**
diametral [diame'tra:l] **1.** *Adj.* **a)** *(Geom.)* diametral; **b)** *(fig. geh.)*; diametrical ⟨*opposition*⟩; diametrically opposed ⟨*views*⟩; **im ~en Gegensatz zu etw. stehen** be diametrically opposed to sth. **2.** *adv. (geh.)* diametrically; **~ entgegengesetzt sein** be diametrically opposed
Dịa-: ~positiv das slide; transparency; **~projektor der** slide projector; **~rahmen der** slide mount
Diärese [diɛ're:zə] **die; ~, ~n** *(Sprachw., Metrik, Rhet., Philos.)* diaeresis
Diarrhö, Diarrhöe [dia'rø:] **die; ~, Diarrhọ̈en** *(Med.)* diarrhoea
Diaspora [di'aspora] **die; ~:** Diaspora
Diastole [di'astole] **die; ~, ~n** [dia'sto:lən] *(Med.)* diastole
diät [di'ɛ:t] *adv.* **~ kochen** cook according to a/one's diet; **~ essen** be on a diet; **[strikt] ~ leben** keep to a [strict] diet
Diạ̈t die; ~, ~en diet; **eine ~ einhalten** keep to a diet; **nach einer ~ leben** live on a diet; **jmdn. auf ~ setzen** put sb. on a diet
Diạ̈t-: ~assistent der, ~assistentin die dietician; **~bier das** diabetic beer
Diạ̈ten *Pl.* [parliamentary] allowance *sing.*
Diätetik [diɛ'te:tɪk] **die; ~, ~en** dietetics *sing., no art.*
diätẹtisch *Adj.* dietetic; dietary; **eine ~e Lebensweise** living on a diet
Diạ̈t·fahrplan der *(ugs.)* diet
Diätịst der; ~en, ~en, Diätịstin die; ~, ~nen dietician
Diạ̈t-: ~koch der, ~köchin die dietary cook; **~kost die** dietary food; **~küche die a)** dietary kitchen; **b)** *o. Pl. (Schonkost)* dietary food; **~kur die** diet cure
Diatonik [dia'to:nɪk] **die; ~** *(Musik)* diatonicism; diatonic system
diatọnisch *Adj. (Musik)* diatonic
Diạ̈t·plan der dietary plan; diet plan; diet
dich [dɪç] **1.** *Akk. des Personalpron.* **du** you. **2.** *Akk. des Reflexivpron. der 2. Pers. Sg.* yourself; **wäschst du dich?** are you washing [yourself]?; **entschuldige dich!** apologize!
Dichotomie [dɪçoto'mi:] **die; ~, ~n** *(Bot., Philos., Sprachw.)* dichotomy
dicht [dɪçt] **1.** *Adj.* **a)** thick ⟨*hair, fur, plumage, moss*⟩; thick, dense ⟨*foliage, fog, cloud*⟩; dense ⟨*forest, thicket, hedge, crowd*⟩; heavy, dense ⟨*traffic*⟩; densely ranked, close-ranked ⟨*rows of houses*⟩; heavy ⟨*snowstorm*⟩; *(fig.)* dense ⟨*prose, dialogue, etc.*⟩; full, packed ⟨*programme*⟩; **in ~er Folge** in rapid *or* quick succession; **b)** *(undurchlässig) (für Luft)* airtight; *(für Wasser)* watertight ⟨*shoes*⟩; *(für Licht)* heavy ⟨*curtains, shutters*⟩; **~ machen** seal ⟨*crack*⟩; make airtight/watertight; seal the crack[s]/leak[s] in ⟨*roof, window, etc.*⟩; waterproof ⟨*material, umbrella, etc.*⟩; **nicht ganz ~ sein** *(salopp)* have a screw loose *(coll.)*; **c)** *(ugs.: geschlossen)* shut; closed. **2.** *adv.* **a)** densely ⟨*populated*⟩; thickly, densely ⟨*wooded*⟩; tightly ⟨*packed*⟩; heavily ⟨*built up*⟩; **~ verschneit** thick with snow; **~ besetzt** full; packed; **~ behaart** [very] hairy; **~ an ~** *od.* **~ gedrängt stehen/sitzen** stand/sit close together; **das Dorf war ~ verschneit** the village was covered in a thick blanket of snow *or* was deep in snow; **b)** *(undurchlässig)* tightly; **c)** *mit Präp. (nahe)* **~ neben** right next to; **sich ~ bei jmdn. halten** keep close to sb.; **~ daran** hard by; **~ nebeneinander** close together; **~ vor/hinter ihm** right *or* just in front of/behind him; **die Polizei ist ihm ~ auf den Fersen** the police are hard *or* close on his heels; **d)** *(zeitlich: unmittelbar)* **ich war ~ daran, es zu tun** I was just about to do it; **~ bevorstehen** be imminent; **das Fest steht ~ bevor** the party is almost upon us/them *etc.*
dịcht-: ~auf *Adv.* close behind; **~bebaut** *Adj. (präd. getrennt geschrieben)* heavily built-up; **~behaart** *Adj. (präd. getrennt geschrieben)* [very] hairy; **~belaubt** *Adj. (präd. getrennt geschrieben)* densely foliated; **~besetzt** *Adj. (präd. getrennt geschrieben)* full; packed; **~besiedelt** *Adj. (präd. getrennt geschrieben)* densely populated; **~bevölkert** *Adj. (präd. getrennt geschrieben)* densely populated; **~bewachsen** *Adj. (präd. getrennt geschrieben)* covered with dense vegetation *postpos.*
Dichte ['dɪçtə] **die; ~ a)** *(Physik, fig.)* density; **b)** *(Undurchdringlichkeit)* **ein Nebel von solcher ~:** such [a] dense *or* thick fog
[1]dichten ['dɪçtn̩] **1.** *itr. V.* **[gut] ~:** make a good seal. **2.** *tr. V.* make airtight/watertight; seal ⟨*joint etc.*⟩; seal the crack[s]/leak[s] in ⟨*window, roof, etc.*⟩
[2]dịchten 1. *itr. V.* **a)** write poetry; **b) sein ganzes Dichten und Trachten** all his thoughts and endeavours. **2.** *tr. V. (verfassen)* write; compose
Dịchter der; ~s, ~: poet; *(Schriftsteller)* writer; author
Dịchter·fürst der *(veralt.)* prince among poets; *(Schriftsteller)* prince among writers
Dịchterin die; ~, ~nen poet[ess]; *(Schriftstellerin)* writer; author[ess]
dịchterisch 1. *Adj.* poetic; *(schriftstellerisch)* literary. **2.** *adv.*; *s.* **1:** poetically; literarily
Dịchter-: ~komponist der poet/writer and composer; **~kreis der** circle of poets; *(von Schriftstellern)* circle of writers; **~lesung die** reading *(by a poet or writer from his own works)*
Dịchterling der; ~s, ~e *(abwertend)* poetaster *(derog.)*; rhymester *(derog.)*
Dịchter-: ~schule die school of poets; *(von Schriftstellern)* school of writers; **~sprache die** poetic language
dịcht-: ~gedrängt *Adj. (präd getrennt geschrieben)* tightly *or* closely packed; **~|halten** *unr. itr. V. (ugs.)* keep one's mouth shut *(coll.)*
Dịcht·kunst die a) art of poetry; **b)** *(Fähigkeit, Talent)* poetic talent; **c)** *(Poesie)* poetry *no art.*
dịcht|machen *(ugs.)* **1.** *tr. V.* shut; close; *(endgültig)* shut *or* close down; **die Polizei hat ihm die Bar dichtgemacht** the police shut *or* closed down his bar. **2.** *itr. V.* **a)** shut; close; *(endgültig)* shut *or* close down; **b)** *(Sportjargon)* **hinten ~:** close the game down at the back
[1]Dịchtung die; ~, ~en a) *o. Pl.* sealing; **zur ~ der Fugen** to seal the joints; **b)** *(Vorrichtung)* seal; *(am Hahn usw.)* washer; *(am Vergaser, Zylinder usw.)* gasket
[2]Dịchtung die; ~, ~en a) literary work; work of literature; *(in Versform)* poetic work; poem; *(fig. ugs.)* fiction; **~ und Wahrheit** fact and fiction; truth and fantasy; **Goethes „~ und Wahrheit"** Goethe's 'Poetry and Truth'; **b)** *o. Pl. (Dichtkunst)* literature; *(in Versform)* poetry
Dịchtungs-: ~masse die sealing compound; sealant; **~mittel das** integral waterproofing agent *or* waterproofer; **~ring der, ~scheibe die** sealing ring; *(am Hahn)* washer
dick [dɪk] **1.** *Adj.* **a)** thick; thick, chunky ⟨*pullover*⟩; stout ⟨*tree*⟩; fat ⟨*person, arms, legs, behind, etc.*⟩; big ⟨*bust*⟩; **~ und rund** *od.* **fett sein** *(ugs.)* be round and fat; **~ werden** get fat; **das Kleid macht ~:** the dress makes you look fat; **Kuchen macht ~:** cakes are fattening *or* make you fat; **ein ~es Auto fahren** *(fig. ugs.)* drive a great big car *(coll.)*; **ein Mädchen ~ machen** *(salopp)* put a girl in the club *(sl.)*; **b)** *(mit Maßangaben)* thick; **5 cm ~ sein** be 5 cm thick; **5 cm ~e Bretter** planks 5 cm thick; 5 cm thick planks; **c)** *(stark)* thick ⟨*carpet, wall, layer*⟩; **mit jmdm. durch ~ und dünn gehen** stay *or* stick with sb. through thick and thin; **es nicht so ~ haben** *(ugs.)* not be very well off; **d)** *(ugs.: angeschwollen)* swollen ⟨*cheek, ankle, tonsils, etc.*⟩; **e)** *(dicht, ~flüssig)* thick ⟨*hair, fog, soup, sauce, etc.*⟩; **im ~sten Verkehr** *(fig. ugs.)* in the heaviest traffic; **mitten in der ~sten Arbeit** *(fig. ugs.)* just when we're/they're *etc.* right up to our/their *etc.* necks in work *(coll.)*; **f)** *(ugs.: außergewöhnlich groß)* big ⟨*mistake, order*⟩; hefty, *(coll.)* fat ⟨*fee, premium, salary*⟩; **einen ~en Tadel verdienen** deserve heavy criticism; **jmdm. ein ~es Lob aussprechen** give sb. a great deal of prise *or* high praise; **das ~e Ende kommt noch** *(ugs.)* the worst is yet to come; **g)** *(ugs.: eng)* close ⟨*friends, friendship, etc.*⟩. **2.** *adv.* **a) etw. ~ unterstreichen** underline sth. heavily; **sich ~ anziehen** wrap up warm[ly]; **b)** *(mit Maßangabe)* **etw. 5 cm ~ schneiden/auftragen** *usw.* cut/apply sth. 5 cm. thick; **c)** *(stark)* thickly; **~ geschminkt/bemalt** heavily made up; **~ auftragen** *(ugs. abwertend)* lay it on thick *(sl.)*; **d) ~ geschwollen** *(ugs.)* badly swollen; **e) ~ befreundet sein** *(ugs.)* be close friends
dịck-, Dịck-: ~bauch der *(scherzh.)* fatty; *(mit Spitzbauch)* pot-belly: **~bauchig** *Adj.* large-bellied, big-bellied ⟨*vase, pot, etc.*⟩; **~bäuchig** *Adj.* corpulent; portly; *(mit Spitzbauch)* pot-bellied ⟨*person*⟩; **~darm der** *(Anat.)* large intestine
dịcke *Adv. (ugs.)* easily; **wir haben noch ~**

Zeit we've got plenty of time; **von etw. ~ genug haben** have had quite enough of sth.; **jmdn./etw. ~ haben** *(salopp)* have had a bellyful of sb./sth.

[1]**Dịcke die; ~:** thickness; *(von Menschen, Körperteilen)* fatness

[2]**Dịcke der/die;** *adj. Dekl.* **a)** *(ugs.)* fatty *(coll.)*; fat man/woman; **die ~n** *(im allgemeinen)* fatties *(coll.)*; fat people; **b)** *(Kosename)* podge *(coll.)*

dịcken 1. *tr. V.* thicken. **2.** *itr. V.; auch mit sein* thicken

Dịckerchen das; ~s, ~ *(ugs. scherzh.)* podge *(coll.)*

dịcke|tun *unr. refl. V. (ugs. abwertend)* show off; *(durch Reden)* boast; brag; **sich mit etw. ~:** boast *or* brag about sth.; **sich mit seiner Kraft ~:** show off one's strength

dịck-, Dịck-: ~fellig *(ugs. abwertend)* **1.** *Adj.* thick-skinned; **~fellig sein** have a thick skin; be thick-skinned; **2.** *adv.* in a thick-skinned way; **~felligkeit die; ~** *(ugs. abwertend)* insensitivity; **~flüssig** *Adj.* thick; viscous *(as tech. term)*; **~flüssigkeit die;** *o. Pl.* thickness; viscosity *(as tech. term)*; **~häuter der; ~s, ~:** pachyderm; *(fig.)* thick-skinned person

Dickicht ['dɪkɪçt] **das; ~[e]s, ~e** thicket; *(im Wald)* dense undergrowth *no indef. art.*; *(fig.)* jungle

dịck-, Dịck-: ~kopf der *(ugs.)* mule *(coll.)*; **du bist ein ~kopf** you're as stubborn as a mule; **einen ~kopf haben** be stubborn *or* pigheaded; **~köpfig** *(ugs.)* **1.** *Adj.* stubborn; pigheaded; **2.** *adv.* stubbornly; pigheadedly; **~leibig** *Adj. (geh.)* corpulent; fat; *(fig.)* thick, fat ‹*document, book*›; **~leibigkeit die; ~** *(geh.)* corpulence; fatness

dịcklich *Adj.* **a)** plumpish; chubby; **b)** *(dickflüssig)* thick

dịck-, Dịck-: ~macher der *(ugs.)* fattening food; **~milch die** sour milk; **~schädel der** *s.* **~kopf; ~schalig** *Adj.* thick-skinned ‹*orange, tomato, etc.*›; **~|tun** *unr. refl. V. s.* **dicketun; ~wạndig** *Adj.* thick-walled, thick-sided ‹*vessel, container*›; **~wanst der** *(salopp abwertend)* fatso *(sl.)*

Didaktik [di'daktɪk] **die; ~, ~en a)** *o. Pl.* didactics *sing., no art.*; theory of teaching and methodology; **b)** *(Unterrichtsmethode)* teaching method

Didạktiker der; ~s, ~, Didạktikerin die; ~, ~nen a) educationalist; **b)** *(jmd. mit didaktischen Fähigkeiten)* teacher

didạktisch 1. *Adj.* didactic. **2.** *adv.* didactically

[1]**die 1.** *best. Art. Nom.* the; **die Kleine** the little girl; **die Liebe/Freundschaft** love/friendship; **die „Iphigenie"/**(*ugs.*) **Helga** 'Iphigenia'/Helga; **die Demokratie/Diktatur/Monarchie** democracy/dictatorship/monarchy; **die Bardot** *(ugs.)* Bardot; **die [Frankfurter] Eintracht** *(ugs.)* Eintracht Frankfurt; **sie ist die Sängerin/Schauspielerin** she's 'the singer/actress; **die Marktstraße** Market Street; **die Schweiz/Türkei** Switzerland/Turkey; **die Frau/Menschheit** women *pl.*/mankind; **die „Concorde"/„Klaus Störtebeker"** 'Concorde'/the 'Klaus Störtebeker'; **die Kunst/Oper** art/opera. **2.** *Demonstrativpron.* **a)** *attr.* **die Frau war es** it was 'that woman; **b)** *selbständig* she; **die war es** it was 'her; **die und arbeiten!** *(ugs.)* [what,] her work!; **die mit dem Hund/den lila Haaren** *(ugs.)* her with the dog/purple hair; **die [da]** *(Frau, Mädchen)* that woman/girl; *(Gegenstand, Tier)* that one; **die blöde Kuh, die!** *(fig. salopp)* what a silly cow! *(sl.)*. **3.** *Relativpron. Nom. (Mensch)* who; that; *(Sache, Tier)* which; that; **die Frau, die da drüben entlanggeht** the woman walking along over there; **ich sah eine Frau/Katze, die aus dem Fenster schaute** I saw a women/cat looking out of the window. **4.** *Relativ- u. Demonstrativpron.* the one who; **die das getan hat** the woman *etc.* who did it

[2]**die 1.** *best. Art.* **a)** *Akk. Sg. v.* [1]**die 1: ich sah die Frau/Ratte** I saw the women/rat; **wir sahen die „Zauberflöte"** we saw the 'Magic Flute'; **hast du die Ute gesehen?** *(ugs.)* have you seen Ute?; **er hat die Callas geheiratet** *(ugs.)* he married Callas; **ich fuhr durch die Marktstraße** I drove through Market Street; **b)** *Nom. u. Akk. Pl. v.* [1]**der 1,** [1]**die 1, das 1: [er fragte] die Männer/Frauen/Kinder** [he asked] the men/women/children. **2.** *Demonstrativpron. Nom. u. Akk. Pl. v.* [1]**der 1,** [1]**die 1, das 1:** *attr.* **ich meine die Männer/Frauen/Kinder, die gestern hier waren** I mean those men/women/children who were here yesterday; *selbständig* **ich meine die [da]** I mean 'them. **3.** *Relativpron.* **a)** *Akk. Sg. v.* [1]**die 3:** *(bei Menschen)* **die Frau, die ich gesehen habe** the woman who *or* that I saw; *(bei Sachen, Tieren)* **die Straße, die ich entlangging** the street [that *or* which] I walked along; **die Maus, die die Katze fing** the mouse which *or* that the cat caught; **b)** *Nom. u. Akk. Pl. v.* [1]**der 3,** [1]**die 3, das 3:** *(bei Menschen)* **die Männer/Frauen/Kinder, die ich gesehen habe/die dort gehen** the men/women/children I saw/walking along over there; *(bei Sachen, Tieren)* **die Nägel/Birnen/Bücher, die da liegen/die jemand da hingelegt hat** the nails/pears/books lying there/which somebody put there

Dieb [di:p] **der; ~[e]s, ~e** thief; **haltet den ~!** stop thief!

Dieberei die; ~, ~en a) *o. Pl. (das Stehlen)* thieving; **b)** *(Diebstahl)* theft

Diebes-: ~bande die *(abwertend)* gang of thieves; **~beute die** stolen goods *pl. or* property; **~gut das** stolen goods *pl. or* property; **~nest das** thieves' hide-out; **~tour die auf ~tour gehen/sein** go/have gone [out] thieving *or* stealing; **auf ~touren sein** have been [out] thieving *or* stealing on a number of occasions

Diebin die; ~, ~nen [woman] thief; *s. auch* **-in**

diebisch 1. *Adj.* **a)** *nicht präd.* thieving; **b)** *(verstohlen)* mischievous. **2.** *adv.* mischievously; **sich ~ über etw.** *(Akk.)* **freuen** take a mischievous pleasure in sth.

Diebstahl ['di:p-ʃta:l] **der; ~[e]s, Diebstähle** ['di:p-ʃtɛ:lə] theft; **einfacher ~:** theft; **schwerer ~:** burglary and theft; **räuberischer ~:** *robbery accompanied by use of violence to keep possession of the stolen property;* **[ein] geistiger ~:** plagiarism *no indef. art*

Diebstahl·versicherung die insurance against theft

die·jenige, diejenigen *s.* **derjenige**

Diele ['di:lə] **die; ~, ~n a)** hall[way]; **b)** *(Fußbodenbrett)* floor-board

dielẹktrisch [die'lɛktrɪʃ] *Adj. (Physik, Elektrot.)* dielectric

dielen *tr. V.* lay floor-boards in ‹*room*›; board ‹*floor*›

Dielen·brett das floor-board

dienen ['di:nən] *itr. V.* **a)** be in service; **jmdm. ~:** serve sb.; **als Magd ~:** serve as a maid; **der Gerechtigkeit ~** *(geh.)* serve the cause of justice; **bei Hof ~:** wait *or* serve at court; *s. auch* **Herr; b)** *(veralt.: Militärdienst tun)* do military service; **beim Heer ~:** serve in the army; **acht Jahre ~:** do eight years' military service; *s. auch* **gedient 2; c)** *(nützlich sein)* serve; **das dient einer guten Sache** it is in a good cause; **diese Maßnahmen ~ der Sicherheit am Arbeitsplatz** these measures help towards safety at work; **d)** *(helfen)* help (**in +** *Dat.* in); **womit kann ich ~?** what can I do for you?; can I help you?; **mit 20 DM wäre mir schon gedient** 20 marks would do; **damit ist mir wenig gedient** it's not much help *or* use to me; **damit kann ich leider nicht ~:** I'm afraid I can't help you there; **e)** *(verwendet werden)* serve; **als Museum ~:** serve *or* be used as a museum; **als Ersatz/Vorwand ~:** serve as a substitute/pretext; **das soll dir als Warnung ~:** let that serve as *or* be a warning to you; **zur Unterstützung einer Theorie ~:** serve to support a theory

Diener der; ~s, ~ servant; **einen ~ machen** *(ugs.)*; bow; make a bow; *s. auch* **stumm**

Dienerin ['di:nərɪn] **die; ~, ~nen** maid; servant

dienern *itr. V. (abwertend)* bow; *(fig.)* bow and scrape

Dienerschaft die; ~: servants *pl.*; domestic staff

dienlich *Adj.* helpful; useful; **jmdm./einer Sache ~ sein** be helpful *or* of help to sb./sth.; **kann ich Ihnen mit etwas ~ sein?** *(geh.)* can I be of any assistance to you?

Dienst [di:nst] **der; ~[e]s, ~e a)** *o. Pl. (Tätigkeit)* work; *(von Soldaten, Polizeibeamten, Krankenhauspersonal usw.)* duty; **seinen ~ antreten** start work/go on duty; **zum ~ gehen** go to work/go on duty; **~ haben** be at work/on duty; ‹*doctor*› be on call; ‹*chemist*› be open; **außerhalb des ~es** outside work/when off duty; **im ~ sein** be at work/on duty; **nicht im ~ sein** not be at work/be off duty; **der Unteroffizier vom ~:** *(Milit.)* the duty NCO; **der Chef vom ~** *(Zeitungsw.)* the duty editor; **~ ist ~, und Schnaps ist Schnaps** *(ugs.)* you shouldn't mix business and pleasure; **b)** *(Arbeitsverhältnis)* post; **den** *od.* **seinen ~ quittieren** resign one's post; *(Milit.)* leave the service; ‹*officer*› resign one's commission; **jmdn. aus dem ~/seinen ~en entlassen** dismiss sb.; **jmdn. in ~ nehmen** *(veralt.)* employ *or* engage sb.; **in jmds. ~[en] sein** *od.* **stehen** *(veralt.)* be in sb.'s employ; **Major** *usw.* **außer ~ [sein]** [be a] retired major *etc.*; **im ~ einer guten Sache** *(Gen.)* **stehen** be in a good cause; **sich in den ~ einer guten Sache** *(Gen.)* **stellen** devote oneself to a good cause; **etw. in ~ stellen** put sth. into service *or* commission; **c)** *o. Pl. (Tätigkeitsbereich)* service; **der höhere ~ der Beamtenlaufbahn** the senior civil service; *s. auch* **öffentlich; d)** *(Hilfe)* **seine ~e [anbieten]** [offer] one's services; **jmdm. einen ~ tun** help sb.; **~ am Kunden** *(ugs.)* customer service; **seinen ~ tun** ‹*machine, appliance*› serve its purpose; **jmdm. gute ~e tun** serve sb. well; give sb. good service; **jmdm. mit etw. einen schlechten ~ erweisen** do sb. a disservice *or* a bad turn with sth.; **zu jmds. ~en** *od.* **jmdm. zu ~en sein** *od.* **stehen** *(geh.)* be at sb.'s disposal *or* service; **jmdm. den ~ versagen** fail sb.; **e)** *(Hilfs~)* service; *(Nachrichten~, Spionage~)* [intelligence] service; **f)** *(Kunstwiss.)* respond

-dienst der service; **Schicht~** shift work

Dienst-: ~abteil das *(Eisenb.)* guard's compartment; **~adel der** *(hist.) nobility whose titles derive from being in the king's service*

Diens·tag [di:ns-] **der** Tuesday; **am ~:** on Tuesday; *(jeden ~)* on Tuesday; **~, der 1. Juni** Tuesday the first of June; Tuesday, 1 June; **am ~, dem 1. Juni** *od.* **den 1. Juni** on Tuesday 1 June *or* June 1st; **er kommt ~:** he is coming on Tuesday; **die letzten ~e** the last few Tuesdays; **eines ~s** one Tuesday; **den ganzen ~ über** all day Tuesday; the whole of Tuesday; **~ morgen/nachmittag/abend** Tuesday morning/afternoon/evening; **~ morgens/abends** on Tuesday mornings/evenings; **~ mittags** Tuesday lunchtimes; **ab nächsten** *od.* **nächstem ~:** from next Tuesday [onwards]; **die Nacht von ~ auf** *od.* **zum Mittwoch** Tuesday night; **~ in einer Woche** *od.* **in acht Tagen** Tuesday week; a week on Tuesday; **~ vor einer Woche** a week last Tuesday

Dienstag·abend der Tuesday evening

dienstägig ['di:nstɛ:gɪç] *Adj.; nicht präd.* **die/unsere ~e Sendung** *usw.* Tuesday's programme *etc.*; the/our programme *etc.* on Tuesday

dienstäglich 1. *Adj.; nicht präd.* [regular] Tuesday. **2.** *adv.* on Tuesday

Dienstag-: ~mittag der Tuesday lunchtime; **~morgen der** Tuesday morning; **~nachmittag der** Tuesday afternoon

diens·tags *Adv.* on Tuesday[s]; **~ abends/morgens** on Tuesday evening[s]/morning[s]; on a Tuesday evening/morning

Dienstag·vormittag der Tuesday morning

dienst-, Dienst-: ~alter das length of service; **er hat ein ~alter von 6 Jahren** he has 6 years of service; **~älteste der/die** longest-serving person; **~an·tritt der** commencement of one's duties; **~an·weisung die** instruction; **laut ~anweisung** according to instructions *pl.*; **~auf·fassung die** conception of duty; **~auf·sicht die**; *o. Pl.* supervision; **die ~aufsicht liegt bei ...:** ... has supervisory responsibility; **~aufsichts·beschwerde die** complaint to the supervising authority *(about a public servant or government department)*; **~ausweis der** [official] identity card; **~bar** *Adj.* **sich jmdm. ~bar erzeigen** *(veralt.)* show one's willingness to serve sb.; **ein ~barer Geist** *(ugs. scherzh.)* a ministering angel; **sich** *(Dat.)* **jmdn./etw. ~bar machen** get good service from sb./utilize sth.; **einer Sache** *(Dat.)* **jmdn./etw. ~bar machen** make sb./sth. serve sth.; **sich** *(Dat.)* **die Kräfte der Natur/die Atomenergie ~bar machen** harness the power of nature/atomic energy; **~barkeit die; ~, ~en a)** *o. Pl. (geh.)* **jmdn. in seine ~barkeit bringen** bring sb. under one's power; **in jmds. ~barkeit geraten** come under sb.'s power; **b)** *o. Pl. (hist.)* bondage; servitude; **c)** *(jur.)* easement; **~beflissen 1.** *Adj.* zealous; eager; **2.** *adv.* zealously; eagerly; **~beflissenheit die** zeal; eagerness; **~beginn der** start of work; **vor/nach/bei ~beginn** before/after/at the start of work; **~bereich der** area of responsibility; **~bereit** *Adj.* ‹*chemist*› open *pred.*; ‹*doctor*› on call *or* duty; ‹*dentist*› on duty; **die nächste ~bereite Apotheke** the nearest chemist that is/was open; **~bereitschaft die ~bereitschaft haben** ‹*chemist*› be open; ‹*doctor*› be on call *or* duty; ‹*dentist*› be on duty; **~bezüge** *Pl.* salary *sing.*; **~bote der** servant; **~boten·eingang der** tradesmen's entrance; **~bezeichnung die** title; **~eid der** official oath; **~eifer der** zeal; eagerness; **~eifrig 1.** *Adj.* zealous; eager; **2.** *adv.* zealously; eagerly; **~enthebung die** suspension from duty; **~fähig** *Adj.* fit for work *postpos.*; *(Milit.)* fit for service *postpos.*; **~fahrt die** *s.* **~reise**; **~frei** *Adj.* free ‹*time*›; **an ~freien Tagen** on days off; **~frei haben/bekommen** have/get time off; **am Montag ~frei haben** have Monday off; **Heiligabend ist ~frei** Christmas Eve is a holiday; **~gebrauch der** *in* **nur für den ~gebrauch bestimmt** for official use only; **~geheimnis das a)** professional secret; *(im Staatsdienst)* official secret; **b)** *o. Pl.* professional secrecy; *(im Staatsdienst)* official secrecy; **unter das ~geheimnis fallen** be a professional/official secret; **~geschäfte** *Pl.* business *sing.*; **in ~geschäften** on business; *(von Beamten)* on official business; **~gespräch das a)** business meeting; *(von Beamten)* official meeting; **b)** *(Telefongespräch)* business call; *(von Beamten)* official call; **~grad der** *(Milit.)* rank; **~gradabzeichen das** *(Milit.)* insignia [of rank]; **~habend** *Adj.; nicht präd.* duty ‹*officer*›; ‹*official, doctor*› on duty; **~habende der/die**; *adj. Dekl. (Offizier)* duty officer; *(Beamter/Arzt)* official/doctor on duty; **~herr der** employer; **~hund der** dog used for police/security work; **ein Polizist mit seinem ~hund** a policeman with his dog; **~jahr das** year of service; **~jubiläum das** anniversary; **anläßlich seines 25jährigen ~jubiläums** to mark his completion of 25 years' service; **~kleidung die** uniform; **~kleidung tragen** wear a uniform; **~leistung die** *(auch Wirtsch.)* service

Dienstleistungs-: ~abend der late opening evening; **~betrieb der** *(Wirtsch.)* business in the service sector; **~gewerbe das** *(Wirtsch.)* service industries *pl.*; **~sektor der** *(Wirtsch.)* service sector

dienstlich 1. *Adj.* **a)** business ‹*call*›; *(im Staatsdienst)* official ‹*letter, call, etc.*›; **b)** *(offiziell)* official; **~ werden** *(ugs.)* get businesslike and formal. **2.** *adv.* on business; *(im Staatsdienst)* on official business

dienst-, Dienst-: ~mädchen das *(veralt.)* maid; **~magd die** *(veralt.)* maid; **~mann der**; *Pl.*: **~männer** *od.* **~leute** *(veralt.)* porter; **~marke die** [police] identification badge; ≈ warrant card *(Brit.) or (Amer.)* ID card; **~mütze die** regulation cap; **~nehmer der, ~nehmerin die** *(österr.) s.* **Arbeitnehmer**; **~ordnung die** official regulations *pl.*; **~personal das** servants *pl.*; *(in einem Hotel)* domestic staff; **~pflicht die a)** *o. Pl.* compulsory service; **b)** *(bei Beamten)* duty; **~pflichtig** *Adj.* liable for compulsory service *postpos.*; **~pistole die** service pistol; **~plan der** duty roster; **~rang der** *(Milit.)* rank; **~recht das** ≈ civil service law; **~rechtlich 1.** *Adj.* ≈ under civil service law *postpos.*; **2.** *adv.* ≈ under civil service law; ≈ ‹*regulated*› by civil service law; **~reise die** business trip; **auf ~reise sein** be on a business trip *or* away on business; **~sache die a)** official matter; **b)** *(Schreiben)* official letter; **c)** *(Postw.)* item of official mail; *(Brief)* official letter; **~schluß der**; *o. Pl.* end of work; **um 17 Uhr ist ~schluß** work finishes at 5 o'clock; **nach ~schluß** after work; **~schluß haben** finish work/have finished work; **~schreiben das** official letter; **~stelle die** office; *(Abteilung)* department; **~stellen·leiter der** office head; *(einer Abteilung)* department head; **~stempel der** official stamp; **~stunden** *Pl.* **a)** working hours; **während der ~stunden** during working hours; **b)** *(Öffnungszeiten)* **~stunden haben** be open; **~tauglich** *Adj. (Milit.)* fit for service *postpos.*; **~tuend** *Adj.; nicht präd. s.* **~habend**; **~tuende der/die**; *adj. Dekl. s.* **~habende**; **~unfähig** *Adj.* unfit for work *postpos.*; *(Milit.)* unfit for service *postpos.*; **~untauglich** *Adj. (Milit.)* unfit for service *postpos.*; **~vergehen das** offence against [official] regulations; **~verhältnis das** *contractual relationship between employee and employer in the public service*; **ein ~verhältnis eingehen** become a public employee; **~verpflichten** *tr. V. (nur im Inf. u. 2. Part.)* conscript; **~vertrag der** contract of employment; **~vorschrift die** regulations *pl.*; *(Milit.)* service regulations; **~wagen der** official car; *(Geschäftswagen)* company car; **~weg der** proper *or* official channels *pl.*; **den ~weg gehen** *od.* **einhalten** go through the proper *or* official channels; **auf dem ~weg** through the proper *or* official channels; **~wohnung die** *(von Firmen)* company flat *(Brit.) or (Amer.)* apartment; *(von staatlichen Stellen)* government flat *(Brit.) or (Amer.)* apartment; *(vom Militär)* army/navy/air force flat *(Brit.) or (Amer.)* apartment; **~zeit die a)** period of service; **eine ~zeit von 40 Jahren** 40 years' service; **b)** *(tägliche Arbeitszeit)* working hours *pl.*; **außerhalb der ~zeit** outside working hours; **~zeugnis das** testimonial; **~zimmer das** office

dies [di:s] *s.* **dieser**

dies·bezüglich 1. *Adj.; nicht präd.* relating to *or* regarding this *postpos., not pred.* **2.** *adv.* regarding this; on this matter

diese ['di:zə] *s.* **dieser**

Diesel ['di:zl̩] **der; ~[s], ~** diesel

die·selbe *s.* **derselbe**

die·selbige *s.* **derselbige**

Diesel-: ~kraft·stoff der diesel fuel; **~lokomotive die** diesel locomotive; **~motor der** diesel engine; **~öl das** diesel oil

dieser ['di:zɐ], **diese, dieses, dies** *Demonstrativpron.* **a)** *attr.* this; *Pl.* these; **dieses Buch/diese Bücher [da]** that book/those books [there]; **diesen Sommer/diese Weihnachten** this summer/this Christmas; **[zu] Anfang dieses Jahres/dieser Woche** at the beginning of this year/this week; **in dieser Nacht wird es noch schneien/begann es zu schneien** it will snow tonight/it started to snow that night; **er hat dieser Tage Geburtstag** it's his birthday within the next few days; **ich habe ihn dieser Tage noch gesehen** I saw him the other day; **diese Inge ist doch ein Goldschatz/Idiot** that Inge is a treasure/an idiot, isn't she?; **wer ist denn diese Inge?** who is this Inge?; **diese Russen** these *or* those Russians; **b)** *selbständig* **diese[r] [hier/da]** this one [here]/that one [there]; **diese** *Pl.* **[hier/da]** these [here]/those [there]; **dies alles** all this; **diese ..., jene ...** *(geh.)* the latter ..., the former ...; **dies und das,** *(geh.)* **dieses und jenes** this and that; **dieser und jener** *(geh.) (einige)* some [people] *pl.*; *(ein paar)* a few [people] *pl.*; **dieser oder jener** *(geh.) (der eine oder andere)* someone or other; *(mancher)* some people *pl.*

dieser·art *(geh.)* **1.** *indekl. Demonstrativpron.* of this/that kind *postpos.*. **2.** *Adv.* in this/that way

dieses *s.* **dieser**

diesig *Adj.* hazy

dies-: ~jährig *Adj.; nicht präd.* this year's; **unser ~jähriges Treffen** our meeting this year; **~mal** *Adv.* this time; **~seitig** *Adj.; nicht präd.* **a) das ~seitige Rheinufer** this side of the Rhine; **die ~seitigen Grenzdörfer** the villages on this side of the border; **b)** *(geh.)* worldly; secular ‹*world*›; **~seits 1.** *Präp. mit Gen.* on this side of; **2.** *Adv.* **~seits von** on this side of

Diesseits das; ~: im ~: in this world; **das ~:** this world

Dietrich ['di:trɪç] **der; ~s, ~e** picklock; *(Nachschlüssel)* skeleton key

die·weil *(veralt.)* **1.** *Konj.* **a)** *(zeitl.)* while; **b)** *(kausal)* because. **2.** *adv.* in the mean time *or* the mean while

diffamatorisch [dɪfama'to:rɪʃ] *Adj. (geh.)* defamatory

diffamieren [dɪfa'mi:rən] *tr. V.* defame; **~de Äußerungen** defamatory utterances

Diffamierung die; ~, ~en defamation; *(Bemerkung)* defamatory statement; **eine ~ des Gegners** defamation of one's opponent's character

Differential [dɪfərɛn'tsia:l] **das; ~s, ~e a)** *(Math.)* differential; **b)** *(Technik)* differential [gear]

Differential-: ~getriebe das *(Technik)* differential [gear]; **~gleichung die** *(Math.)* differential equation; **~rechnung die** *(Math.)* differential calculus

Differenz [dɪfə'rɛnts] **die; ~, ~en a)** *(auch Math.)* difference; **b)** *(Meinungsverschiedenheit)* difference [of opinion]

Differenz·betrag der difference

differenzier·bar *Adj.* **a)** distinguishable; **b)** *(Math.)* differentiable

differenzieren 1. *tr. V.* **a)** be discriminating in ‹*judgement, opinion*›; *(unterscheiden)* differentiate; **b)** *(Math.)* differentiate; **c)** *(DDR Landw.)* grade. **2.** *itr. V.* differentiate; make a distinction/distinctions **(zwischen** between); *(bei einem Urteil, einer Behauptung)* be discriminating; **genau ~:** make a precise distinction/precise distinctions. **3.** *refl. V.* ‹*methods*› become more subtly differentiated; ‹*life, language*› become more complex; ⟨*taste*⟩ become more sophisticated

differenziert 1. *Adj.* subtly differentiated ⟨*methods, colours*⟩; complex ⟨*life, language, person, emotional life*⟩; sophisticated ⟨*taste*⟩; diverse ⟨*range*⟩; **ein sehr ~er Bericht** a precise and subtle analysis. **2.** *adv.* **~ urteilen** be discriminating in one's judgement; **etw. ~ darlegen** give a precise and subtle analysis of sth.

Differenziertheit die; ~ *s.* **differenziert 1:** differentiation; complexity; sophistication; diversity

Differenzierung die; ~, **~en** *(von Methoden)* greater differentiation; *(des Lebens, der Sprache)* greater complexity; *(des Geschmacks)* greater sophistication

Differenz·menge die *(Math.)* **die ~ A\B** the complement of the set B relative to A

differieren [dɪfəˈriːrən] *itr. V. (geh.)* differ **(um** by)

diffizil [dɪfiˈtsiːl] *Adj. (geh.)* difficult; *(kompliziert)* complex; *(peinlich genau)* meticulous

diffus [dɪˈfuːs] **1.** *Adj.* **a)** *(Physik, Chemie)* diffuse; **b)** *(geh.)* vague; vague and confused ⟨*idea, statement, etc.*⟩. **2.** *adv.* in a vague and confused way

Diffusion [dɪfuˈzioːn] **die;** ~, **~en** *(Physik, Chemie)* diffusion

Digestivum [digɛsˈtiːvʊm] **das;** **~s, Digestiva a)** digestive; digestant; **b)** *(Chemie)* digestive

digital [digiˈtaːl] *(DV)* **1.** *Adj.* digital. **2.** *adv.* digitally

Digital·anzeige die digital display

digitalisieren *tr. V. (DV)* digitalize

Digital-: ~rechner der *(DV)* digital computer; *(Taschenrechner)* digital calculator; **~uhr die** digital clock; *(Armbanduhr)* digital watch

Dikta *s.* **Diktum**

Diktaphon [dɪktaˈfoːn] **das; ~s, ~e** Dictaphone **(P)**

Diktat [dɪkˈtaːt] **das; ~[e]s, ~e a)** dictation; **nach ~ schreiben** take dictation; **etw. nach ~ schreiben** write/type sth. from dictation; **b)** *(das Diktierte)* dictation; **ein ~ aufnehmen** take dictation; **c)** *(Schulw.)* dictation; **d)** *(geh.: Befehl)* dictate; *(Politik)* diktat; **das ~ der Mode** the dictates *pl.* of fashion

Diktator [dɪkˈtaːtɔr] **der; ~s, ~en** [-ˈtoːrən] *(auch fig.)* dictator

diktatorisch 1. *Adj. (auch fig.)* dictatorial. **2.** *adv. (auch fig.)* dictatorially

Diktatur [dɪktaˈtuːɐ̯] **die;** ~, **~en** *(auch fig.)* dictatorship

diktieren [dɪkˈtieren] *tr. V.* dictate

Diktier·gerät das dictating machine

Diktion [dɪkˈtsioːn] **die;** ~, **~en** *(geh.)* style and diction

Diktionär [dɪktsioˈnɛːɐ̯] **das** *od.* **der; ~s, ~e** *(veralt.)* dictionary

Diktum [ˈdɪktʊm] **das; ~s, Dikta** *(geh.)* **a)** dictum; **b)** *(veralt.: Entscheid)* dictum; pronouncement

dilatorisch [dilaˈtoːrɪʃ] *(geh.)* **1.** *Adj.* dilatory. **2.** *adv.* dilatorily; in a dilatory manner

Dilemma [diˈlɛma] **das; ~s, ~s** *od.* **Dilemmata** dilemma

Dilettant [dilɛˈtant] **der; ~en, ~en, Dilettantin die;** ~, **~nen** *(auch abwertend)* dilettante

dilettantisch *(abwertend)* **1.** *Adj.* dilettante; amateurish. **2.** *adv.* amateurishly

Dilettantismus der; ~ *(meist abwertend)* dilettantism; amateurism

dilettieren [dilɛˈtiːrən] *itr. V. (geh.)* dabble

Dill [dɪl] **der; ~[e]s, ~e,** *österr. auch:* **Dille die;** ~, **~n** *(Gattung)* Anethum; **Echter Dill** dill

Diluvium [diˈluːvi̯ʊm] **das; ~s** *(Geol. veralt.)* **das ~:** the Pleistocene

Dimension [dimɛnˈzioːn] **die;** ~, **~en** *(Physik, fig.)* dimension

-dimensional [dimɛnzioˈnaːl] *Adj.* -dimensional; **mehr~/drei~** multi-/three-dimensional

dimensionieren *tr. V. (Technik)* dimension

Diminuendo [dimiˈnuɛndo] **das; ~s, ~s** *od.* **Diminuendi** *(Musik)* diminuendo

diminutiv [diminuˈtiːf] *Adj.; nicht präd. (Sprachw.)* diminutive

Diminutiv das; ~s, ~e *(Sprachw.)* diminutive

Dimmer [ˈdɪmɐ] **der; ~s,** ~ *(Elektrot.)* dimmer

DIN [diːn] *Abk.* **Deutsche Industrie-Norm[en]** *German Industrial Standard[s];* DIN; **DIN-Format** DIN size; **DIN-A4-Format** A4

dinarisch [diˈnaːrɪʃ] *Adj.* Dinaric

Diner [diˈneː] **das; ~s, ~s a)** *(geh.)* [formal] dinner; **b)** *(Abendessen)* dinner

[1]Ding [dɪŋ] **das; ~[e]s, ~e a)** *(Gegenstand, Objekt)* thing; **das ~ an sich** *(Philos.)* the thing-in-itself; **die Welt der ~e** *(Philos.)* the world of material objects; **jedes ~ hat zwei Seiten** there are two sides to everything; *s. auch* **Namen; b)** *Pl. (Ereignisse)* things; **nach Lage der ~e** the way things are; **wie die ~ stehen** as things stand; **über den ~en stehen** be above such things; *s. auch* **harren; c)** *Pl. (Angelegenheiten)* matters; **persönliche/private ~e** personal/private matters; **in ~en des Geschmacks** in matters of taste; **wie ich die ~e sehe** as I see things *or* matters; **reden wir von anderen ~en** let's talk about something else; **gut ~ will Weile haben** it takes time to do a thing well; **die Letzten ~e** the last things; **ein ~ der Unmöglichkeit sein** be quite impossible; **das geht nicht mit rechten ~en zu** there's something funny about it; **vor allen ~en** above all; **d) guter ~e sein** *(geh.)* be in good spirits; **e)** *(Hist.) s.* **Thing**

[2]Ding das; [e]s, ~er a) *(ugs.: Gegenstand, Sache)* thing; **das ist ja ein ~!** that's really something; **ein ~ drehen** ⟨*criminal*⟩ pull a job *(sl.)*; **jmdm. ein ~ verpassen** *(salopp)* clout sb. one *(coll.)*; **mach keine ~er!** stop having me on *(Brit. coll.)*; stop putting me on *(Amer. coll.)*; **b)** *(ugs.: Mädchen)* thing; creature; **c)** *(salopp: Penis)* thing *(coll.)*; tool *(sl.)*

dingen *unr. tr. V.* **a)** *(geh.)* hire; **ein gedungener Schreiberling** a mercenary hack; **ein gedungener Mörder** a hired killer; **b)** *(veralt.: anstellen)* hire; take on

ding·fest *in* **jmdn. ~ machen** arrest *or* apprehend sb.

Dinghi, Dingi [ˈdɪŋgi] **das; ~s, ~s** dinghy

dinglich *Adj.* **a)** real; **die ~e Welt** the material world; the world of objects; **b)** *(Rechtsspr.)* real ⟨*right, security, etc.*⟩

[1]Dings [dɪŋs] **der/die;** ~ *(ugs.: Mensch)* thingamy *(coll.)*; thingumajig *(coll.)*; what's-his-name/-her-name

[2]Dings das; ~ *(ugs.)* **a)** *(Gegenstand)* thingamy *(coll.)*; thingumajig *(coll.)* what-d'you-call-it; **b)** *o. Art. (Ort)* what's-its-name; what's-it-called

Dings·bums [-bʊms] **der/die/das** *s.* **[1]Dings, [2]Dings**

Ding·wort das naming word

dinieren [diˈniːrən] *itr. V. (geh.)* dine

Dinkel [ˈdɪŋkl̩] **der; ~s,** ~ *(Landw.)* spelt

Dinner [ˈdɪnɐ] **das; ~s, ~[s]** dinner

Dinosaurier [dinoˈzaurie̯] dinosaur

Diode [diˈoːdə] **die;** ~, **~n** *(Elektrot.)* diode

Diolen Ⓦz [dioˈleːn] **das; ~s** *(Textilind.)* Terylene **(P)**

dionysisch [dioˈnyːzɪʃ] **1.** *Adj.* Dionysiac; Dionysian. **2.** *adv.* Dionysiacally

Diopter [diˈɔptɐ] **das; ~s,** ~ *(am Gewehr)* [optical] sight; *(an einer Kamera)* [direct-vision] frame finder

Dioptrie [diɔpˈtriː] **die;** ~, **~n** *(Optik)* dioptre

Dioskuren [diɔsˈkuːrən] *Pl. (geh.)* heavenly twins; inseparable friends

Dioxid [ˈdiː|ɔksiːt] *(fachspr.),* **Dioxyd** [ˈdiː|ɔksyːt] **das; ~s, ~e** *(Chemie)* dioxide

Dioxin [ˈdiː|ɔksiːn] **das; ~s** *(Chemie)* dioxin

Diözesan der; ~en, ~en member of the/a diocese

Diözese [diøˈtseːzə] **die;** ~, **~n** diocese

Diphtherie [dɪfteˈriː] **die;** ~, **~n** *(Med.)* diphtheria

diphtherisch *Adj. (Med.)* diphtherial

Diphthong [dɪfˈtɔŋ] **der; ~s, ~e** *(Sprachw.)* diphthong

diphthongieren [dɪftɔŋˈgiːrən] *tr. V. (Sprachw.)* diphthongize

Diphthongierung die; ~, **~en** *(Sprachw.)* diphthongization

diphthongisch *(Sprachw.)* **1.** *Adj.* diphthongal. **2.** *adv.* **etw. ~ aussprechen** pronounce sth. as a diphthong

Dipl.-Ing. *Abk.* **Diplomingenieur** *academically qualified engineer*

Dipl.-Kfm. *Abk.* **Diplomkaufmann** *holder of a diploma in commerce*

Dipl.-Landw. *Abk.* **Diplomlandwirt** *holder of a diploma in agriculture*

diploid [diploˈiːt] *Adj. (Biol.)* diploid

Diplom [diˈploːm] **das; ~s, ~e a)** ≈ [first] degree *(in a scientific or technical subject); (für einen Handwerksberuf)* diploma; **sein ~ machen** do one's *or* a degree/diploma; **b)** *(Urkunde)* ≈ degree certificate *(in a scientific or technical subject); (für einen Handwerksberuf)* diploma

Diplom-: qualified

Diplom·arbeit die ≈ degree dissertation *(for a first degree in a scientific or technical subject); (für einen Handwerksberuf)* dissertation [submitted for a/the diploma]

Diplomat [diploˈmaːt] **der; ~en, ~en** *(auch fig.)* diplomat

Diplomaten-: ~gepäck das diplomatic bags *pl. or* baggage; **~koffer der** attaché case; executive case; **~viertel das** embassy district

Diplomatie [diplomaˈtiː] **die;** ~ **a)** diplomacy; **b)** *(die Diplomaten)* diplomatic corps

Diplomatin die; ~, **~nen** *(auch fig.)* diplomat

diplomatisch *(auch fig.)* **1.** *Adj.* diplomatic. **2.** *adv.* diplomatically

diplomieren *tr. V. (Hochschulw.)* **jmdn. ~:** award sb. a degree/diploma

diplomiert *Adj.* qualified

Diplom·prüfung die ≈ degree examination *(in a scientific or technical subject); (für einen Handwerksberuf)* diploma examination

Dipol [ˈdiːpoːl] **der; ~s, ~e** *(Physik, Antenne)* dipole

Dipol·antenne die dipole antenna

dippen [ˈdɪpn̩] *tr. V. (Seemannsspr.)* dip ⟨*flag*⟩

dir [diːɐ̯] **1.** *Dat. des Personalpron.* **du** to you; *(nach Präpositionen)* you; **ich gab es ~:** I gave it to you; **ich gab ~ das Buch** I gave you the book; **Freunde von ~:** friends of yours; **gehen wir zu ~:** let's go to your place; *s. auch* **mir 1 a, b. 2.** *Dat. des Reflexivpron. der 2. Pers. Sg.* yourself; **hast du ~ seine Vorschläge genau überlegt?** have you given careful thought to his suggestions?; **hast du ~ gedacht, daß ...:** did you think that ...; **du willst ~ ein neues Kleid kaufen** you want to buy yourself a new dress; **nimm ~ noch von dem Braten** help yourself to some more roast

direkt [diˈrɛkt] **1.** *Adj.* direct. **2.** *adv.* **a)** *(geradewegs)* straight; directly; **b)** *(sofort)* directly; straight; **etw. ~ übertragen** broadcast sth. live; **c)** *(nahe)* directly; **~ am Marktplatz** right by the market square; **d)** *(unmittelbar)* direct; **sich ~ mit jmdm. verbinden lassen** get a direct line to sb.; **e)** *(unverblümt)* directly; **f)** *(ugs.: geradezu)* really; really, positively ⟨*dangerous, witty*⟩

Direkt·flug der direct flight

Direktheit die; ~: directness

Direktion [dirɛk'tsi̯o:n] **die; ~, ~en a)** *o. Pl.* management; *(von gemeinnützigen, staatlichen Einrichtungen)* administration; **b)** *(die Geschäftsleiter)* management; **c)** *(Büroräume)* managers' offices *pl.*

Direktions-: ~assistent der management trainee; **~sekretärin die** manager's secretary

Direktive [dirɛk'ti:və] **die; ~, ~n** *(geh.)* directive

Direkt·mandat das *(Politik)* **[über] ~:** [by] direct mandate

Direktor [di'rɛktɔr] **der; ~s, ~en** [...'to:rən] **a)** *(Schulw.)* headmaster; *(von Hochschulinstituten)* director; *(von Fachschulen usw.)* principal; **b)** *(einer gemeinnützigen Einrichtung)* director; *(einer Strafanstalt)* governor; **c)** *(Wirtsch.)* director; manager; *(einer bestimmten Abteilung)* manager

Direktorat [dirɛkto'ra:t] **das; ~[e]s, ~e a)** *(Amt, Amtszeit) (einer Schule)* headship; *(gemeinnütziger Einrichtungen)* directorship; **b)** *(Dienstzimmer)* headmaster's/headmistress's office

Direktoren·sessel der *(ugs.)* directorship; managership

direktorial [dirɛkto'ri̯a:l] *Adj.* directorial

Direktorin [dirɛk'to:rɪn] **die; ~, ~nen a)** *(Schulw.)* headmistress; *(von Hochschulinstituten)* director; *(von Fachschulen usw.)* principal; **b)** *s.* **Direktor b, c;** *s. auch* **-in**

Direktorium [dirɛk'to:ri̯ʊm] **das; ~s, Direktorien** board of directors

Direktrice [dirɛk'tri:sə] **die; ~, ~n** head designer; *(in einem Einzelhandelsgeschäft)* manageress

Direkt-: ~sendung die *s.* **~übertragung; ~student der** *(DDR)* campus student; **~studium das** *(DDR)* campus course; **~übertragung die** live transmission *or* broadcast; **~verbindung die a)** *(Eisenb.)* direct connection; through train; *(Flugw.)* direct flight; **b)** *(Fernspr.)* direct [telephone] connection; **~wahl die a) in** *od.* **durch ~wahl** by direct election; **b)** *o. Pl.* direct dialling

Direx ['di:rɛks] **der; ~, ~e,/die; ~, ~en** *(Schülerspr.)* head

Dirigent [diri'gɛnt] **der; ~en, ~en** conductor

Dirigenten-: ~pult das conductor's rostrum; **~stab der, ~stock der** [conductor's] baton

dirigieren [diri'gi:rən] *tr. V.* **a)** *auch itr.* conduct; **b)** *(führen)* steer ‹*person*›; **jmdn. an einen Ort ~:** send sb. to a place; **c)** run ‹*business, company*›; **d)** *(lenken)* steer ‹*vehicle*›; *(fahren)* drive

Dirigismus [diri'gɪsmʊs] **der; ~** *(Wirtsch.)* dirigisme

dirigistisch *(Wirtsch.)* **1.** *Adj.* dirigiste. **2.** *adv.* in a dirigiste manner

Dirn [dɪrn] **die; ~, ~en a)** *(bayr., österr.)* maid; **b)** *(nordd.)* girl; lass *(esp. Scot.)*

Dirndl ['dɪrndl̩] **das; ~s, ~:** dirndl

Dirndl·kleid das dirndl

Dirne ['dɪrnə] **die; ~, ~n a)** prostitute; **b)** *(veralt.: Mädchen)* girl; lass *(esp. Scot.)*

Dirnen·viertel das red-light district

Dis [dɪs] **das; ~, ~** *(Musik)* D sharp

Disagio [dɪs'|a:dʒo] **das; ~s** *(Finanzw.)* disagio

Discjockey ['dɪskdʒɔke] **der** *s.* **Diskjockey**

Disco ['dɪsko:] **die; ~, ~s** disco

Discount-: [dɪs'kaunt] discount; **~geschäft/~preis** discount shop/price

Dis-Dur [*auch* '-'–] **das; ~** *(Musik)* D sharp major; *s. auch* **A-Dur**

Disengagement [dɪsɪn'geɪdʒmənt] **das; ~s** *(Politik)* disengagement

Disharmonie [*auch:* '----] **die a)** *(Musik)* disharmony; discord; dissonance; **b)** *(von Farben)* clash; **c)** *(geh.: Uneinigkeit)* disagreement; disharmony *no indef. art.*; **solche ~n** such disharmony *sing. or* disagreements

disharmonieren *itr. V.* **a)** *(Musik)* be discordant *or* dissonant; **b)** ‹*colours*› clash; **c)** *(geh.: uneinig sein)* disagree

disharmonisch *Adj.* **a)** *(Musik)* disharmonious; discordant; dissonant; **b)** *(nicht zusammenstimmend)* clashing ‹*colours*›; **c)** *(geh.: uneinig)* disharmonious

Disjunktion [dɪsjʊnk'tsi̯o:n] **die; ~, ~en** *(Logik)* disjunction

disjunktiv [dɪsjʊŋk'ti:f] *Adj. (Sprachw.)* disjunctive

Diskant [dɪs'kant] **der; ~s, ~e a) in einen schneidenden ~ umschlagen** ‹*voice*› become gratingly shrill; **b)** *(einer Singstimme, beim Klavier)* treble; **c)** *(beim Cantus firmus)* descant

Diskette [dɪs'kɛtə] **die; ~, ~n** *(DV)* floppy disc

Disketten·lauf·werk *das (DV)* [floppy-] disc drive

Disk·jockey ['dɪskdʒɔke] **der** disc jockey

Disko *s.* **Disco**

Diskont [dɪs'kɔnt] **der; ~s, ~e** *(Finanzw.)* **a)** discount; **b)** discount rate

Diskonten *Pl. (Finanzw.)* inland *or* domestic bills of exchange

Diskont·erhöhung die *(Finanzw.)* raising of the discount rate

diskontieren *tr. V. (Finanzw.)* discount

Diskontinuität die; ~, ~en a) discontinuity; **b)** *(Politik) principle that bills not passed before the end of a legislative period must be reintroduced in the next parliament*

Diskont·satz der *(Finanzw.)* discount rate

Diskothek [dɪsko'te:k] **die; ~, ~en a)** *(Tanzlokal)* discothèque; **b)** *(Schallplatten)* record collection; **c)** *(Raum für Schallplatten)* record library

diskreditieren [dɪskredi'ti:rən] *tr. V.* discredit

Diskrepanz [dɪskre'pants] **die; ~, ~en** discrepancy **(zwischen** between**)**

diskret [dɪs'kre:t] **1.** *Adj.* **a)** *(vertraulich)* confidential ‹*discussion, report*›; *(unauffällig)* discreet ‹*action*›; **b)** *(taktvoll)* tactful ‹*behaviour, reserve*›; **sie ist sehr ~:** she is very discreet; **c)** *(dezent)* quiet ‹*colour, elegance*›; subtle ‹*perfume*›; **d)** *(Technik, Physik, Math.)* discrete. **2.** *adv.* **a)** *(vertraulich)* confidentially; **etw. ~ behandeln** treat sth. in confidence; **b)** *(taktvoll)* tactfully; **sich ~ zurückziehen** retire discreetly; **c)** *(dezent)* discreetly; **~ gemustert sein** have a subdued pattern

Diskretion [dɪskre'tsi̯o:n] **die; ~ a)** *(Verschwiegenheit, Takt)* discretion; **in einer Angelegenheit äußerste/strengste ~ wahren** treat a matter in the strictest confidence; **~ [ist] Ehrensache** you can rely on my discretion; **b)** *(Unaufdringlichkeit)* discreetness

diskriminieren [dɪskrimi'ni:rən] *tr. V.* **a)** *(herabwürdigen)* disparage; **b)** *(benachteiligen)* discriminate against

Diskriminierung die; ~, ~en a) discrimination **(von** against**)**; **b)** *(Handlung)* act of discrimination; *(Äußerung)* discriminatory remark

Diskurs [dɪs'kʊrs] **der; ~es, ~e a)** *(Abhandlung)* discourse; **b)** *(geh.: Unterhaltung)* discourse *no indef. art. (literary)*; conversation; **einen ~ [mit jmdm.] haben/führen** have *or* hold a conversation [with sb.]; **c)** *(Wortwechsel)* exchange [of words]; altercation; **d)** *(Sprachw.)* discourse

diskursiv [dɪskʊr'zi:f] *(Philos.)* **1.** *Adj.* discursive. **2.** *adv.* discursively

Diskus ['dɪskʊs] **der; ~** *od.* **~ses, Disken** *od.* **~se** *(Leichtathletik)* discus

Diskussion [dɪskʊ'si̯o:n] **die; ~, ~en** discussion; *(Gesprächsrunde, Tagesgespräch)* discussion; debate; **etw. zur ~ stellen** put sth. up for discussion; **[nicht] zur ~ stehen** [not] be under discussion

Diskussions-: ~abend der discussion [evening]; **~beitrag der** contribution to a/the discussion; **~grund·lage die** basis of a/the discussion; **als ~grundlage dienen** serve as a basis for [a/the] discussion; **~leiter der** chairman [of the discussion]; **~teilnehmer der** participant [in a/the discussion]

Diskus-: ~werfen das *(Leichtathletik)* [throwing the] discus; **das ~werfen ist ...:** [throwing] the discus is ...; **die Meisterschaften im ~werfen** the discus championships; **~werfer der, werferin die** discus thrower; **~wurf der** *(Leichtathletik)* **a)** *o. Pl. (Disziplin)* throwing the discus; **beim ~wurf** in the discus; **b)** *(einzelner Wurf)* [discus] throw

diskutabel [dɪsku'ta:bl̩] *Adj.*, **diskutierbar** *Adj.* **[äußerst] ~:** [very well] worth considering *or* discussing *postpos.*

diskutieren [dɪsku'ti:rən] **1.** *itr. V.* **a) über etw.** *(Akk.)* **~:** discuss sth.; **darüber wird viel zu viel diskutiert** there's much too much discussion about that; **darüber läßt sich ~:** that's debatable; **wir haben stundenlang diskutiert** our discussion went on for hours. **2.** *tr. V.* discuss

dis-Moll ['dɪs-] **das;** *(Musik)* D sharp minor; *s. auch* **a-Moll**

disparat *Adj.* disparate

Dispatcher [dɪs'pɛtʃɐ] **der; ~s, ~** *(DDR Technik)* controller

Dispens [dɪs'pɛns] **der; ~es, ~e** *(österr. u. kath. Kirche nur:)* **die; ~, ~en** *(bes. kath. Kirche)* dispensation **(von** from**)**

dispensieren *tr. V. (auch fig.)* dispense *(form., Eccl.)*, excuse **(von** from**)**

Dispensierung die; ~, ~en a) *(Befreiung)* dispensation *(form., Eccl.)*, exemption **(von** from**)**; **b)** *(Pharm.)* dispensing; **Wartezeit bei ~en** waiting period for dispensed *or* made-up prescriptions

Dispersion [dɪspɛr'zi̯o:n] **die; ~, ~en** *(Physik, Chemie)* dispersion

Dispersions·farbe die emulsion paint

Disponent [dɪspo'nɛnt] **der; ~en, ~en a)** *(Wirtsch.)* junior departmental manager; **b)** *(am Theater)* manager

Disponentin die; ~, ~nen a) *(Wirtsch.)* junior departmental manager; **b)** *(am Theater)* manageress

disponibel [dɪspo'ni:bl̩] *Adj.* *(verfügbar)* available; *(vielseitig einsetzbar)* versatile

disponieren 1. *itr. V.* **a)** *(verfügen)* **über jmdn./etw. ~** *(zur Verfügung haben)* have sb./sth. at one's disposal; **nach Belieben über jmdn./etw. ~:** do just as one wishes *or* likes with sb./sth.; **b)** *(vorausplanen)* plan ahead

disponiert *Adj.* **a) gut/schlecht ~ sein** be in good form *or* on form/be in bad form *or* off form; **b)** *(Med.)* **für** *od.* **zu etw. ~ sein** be disposed to sth.

Disposition [dɪspozi'tsi̯o:n] **die; ~, ~en a)** *(Verfügungsgewalt)* right of disposal; **jmdm. zur** *od.* **zu jmds. ~ stehen** be at sb.'s disposal; **jmdm. etw. zur ~ stellen** place sth. at sb.'s disposal; **jmdn. zur ~ stellen** *(Amtsspr.)* suspend sb.; **b)** *(Planung)* arrangement; **~en treffen** make arrangements; **c)** *(Gliederung)* plan; **d)** *(Med.: Anlage)* disposition **(zu, für** to**)**

Dispositions·kredit der *(Finanzw.)* overdraft facility

Disput [dɪs'pu:t] **der; ~[e]s, ~e** *(geh.)* dispute, argument **(über +** *Akk.* about**)**

disputabel [dɪspu'ta:bl̩] *Adj.* *(geh.)* disputable

Disputation [dɪsputa'tsi̯o:n] **die; ~, ~en** *(Hochschulw., geh.: Streit)* disputation

disputieren *itr. V. (geh.)* discuss; *(streiten)* dispute; **über etw.** *(Akk.)* **~:** discuss/dispute sth.

Disqualifikation die *(auch Sport)* disqualification

disqualifizieren *tr. V. (auch Sport)* disqualify

Disqualifizierung die; ~, ~en *(auch Sport)* disqualification

Diss. *Abk.* **Dissertation** diss.

Dissens [dɪ'sɛns] **der;** ~es, ~e *(geh.)* dissent *no indef. art.;* disagreement **(über + Akk.** over)

Dissertation [dɪsɛrta'tsi̯o:n] **die;** ~, ~en [doctoral] dissertation *or* thesis

Dissident [dɪsi'dɛnt] **der;** ~en, ~en, **Dissidentin, die;** ~, ~nen dissident; *(Rel.)* nonbeliever

Dissimilation [dɪsimila'tsi̯o:n] **die;** ~, ~en *(Sprachw., Biol.)* dissimilation

dissimilieren *tr. V. (Sprachw., Biol.)* dissimilate

dissonant [dɪso'nant] *Adj. (Musik)* dissonant

Dissonanz [dɪso'nants] **die;** ~, ~en *(Musik)* dissonance

Distanz [dɪs'tants] **die;** ~, ~en **a)** *(Abstand)* distance; **in einiger** ~: some distance away; ~ **zu etw. gewinnen** *(fig.)* distance oneself from sth.; **b)** *o. Pl. (Rangunterschied, Zurückhaltung)* ~ **wahren** *od.* **halten** keep one's distance; **die soziale** ~: the social gap; **auf** ~ **bleiben** *od.* **gehen** keep one's distance; **c)** *(Leichtathletik, Rennsport)* distance; **gegen Ende der** ~: towards the end of the race; **d)** *(Boxen: Abstand, Rundenzahl)* distance; **jmdn. auf** ~ **halten** keep sb. at long range

distanzieren 1. *refl. V.* **sich von jmdm./etw.** ~: dissociate oneself from sb./sth. **2.** *tr. V. (Sport: überrunden)* outdistance, outpace **(um** by); *(schlagen)* beat **(um** by)

distanziert 1. *Adj.* distant; reserved; reserved ⟨*politeness*⟩. **2.** *adv.* in a distant *or* reserved manner; with reserve

Distel ['dɪstl̩] **die;** ~, ~n thistle

Distel·fink der goldfinch

Distichon ['dɪstɪçɔn] **das;** ~s, **Distichen** *(Verslehre)* distich

distinguiert [dɪstɪŋ'gi:ɐ̯t] *(geh.)* **1.** *Adj.* distinguished. **2.** *adv.* in a distinguished manner

Distribution [dɪstribu'tsi̯o:n] **die;** ~, ~en *(auch Wirtsch., Math., Sprachw.)* distribution

distributiv [dɪstribu'ti:f] *Adj. (Sprachw., Math.)* distributive

Distrikt [dɪs'trɪkt] **der;** ~[e]s, ~e district; area; *(Bezirk)* district

Disziplin [dɪstsi'pli:n] **die;** ~, ~en **a)** *o. Pl. (Ordnung)* discipline; ~ **halten** keep discipline; *(sich diszipliniert verhalten)* behave in a disciplined way; **b)** *o. Pl. (Selbstbeherrschung)* [self-]discipline; **c)** *(Wissenschaftszweig, Sport)* discipline

disziplinär [dɪstsipli'nɛ:ɐ̯] *(bes. österr.)* **1.** *Adj.* disciplinary. **2.** *adv.* **gegen jmdn.** ~ **vorgehen** take disciplinary action against sb.

disziplinarisch 1. *Adj.* **a)** disciplinary; **b)** *(streng)* severe. **2.** *adv.* **a) gegen jmdn.** ~ **vorgehen** take disciplinary action against sb.; **jmdm.** ~ **unterstellt sein** be answerable to sb. in matters of discipline; **b)** *(streng)* **jmdn.** ~ **bestrafen** punish sb. severely

Disziplinar-: ~**maßnahme die;** *meist Pl.* disciplinary measure; ~**strafe die a)** *(Sport)* disciplinary penalty; **mit einer** ~**strafe rechnen müssen** have to expect disciplinary action; **eine hohe** ~**strafe** a heavy fine; **er erhielt eine** ~**strafe von 100 DM** he was fined 100 marks; **b)** *(Eishockey)* misconduct penalty; **c)** *(veralt.)* disciplinary measure; ~**verfahren das** disciplinary proceedings *pl.*

disziplinieren 1. *tr. V.* discipline. **2.** *refl. V.* discipline oneself

diszipliniert 1. *Adj.* **a)** *(geordnet)* well-disciplined; **b)** *(beherrscht)* disciplined. **2.** *adv.* **a)** *(geordnet)* in a well-disciplined way; **b)** *(beherrscht)* in a disciplined way

Disziplinierung die; ~, ~en disciplining *no indef. art.*

disziplin-, Disziplin-: ~**los 1.** *Adj.* undisciplined; **2.** *adv.* in an undisciplined way; ~**losigkeit die;** ~: lack of discipline; ~**schwierigkeiten** *Pl.* discipline problems; problems in maintaining discipline

dithyrambisch *Adj. (Literaturw.)* dithyrambic

Dithyrambus [dity'rambʊs] **der;** ~, **Dithyramben a)** *(Literaturw.)* dithyramb

dito ['di:to] *Adv. (Kaufmannsspr., auch ugs.)* ditto

Diuretikum [diu're:tikʊm] **das;** ~s, **Diuretika** *(Med.)* diuretic

diuretisch *(Med.) Adj.* diuretic

Diva ['di:va] **die;** ~, ~s *u.* **Diven a)** *(Künstlerin)* prima donna; diva; *(Film~)* great [film] star; **b)** *(eingebildeter Mensch)* prima donna

divergent [divɛr'gɛnt] **1.** *Adj. (auch fig., Math.)* divergent. **2.** *adv. (auch fig., Math.)* divergently; ~ **verlaufen** diverge

Divergenz [divɛr'gɛnts] **die;** ~, ~en *(auch Math.)* divergence; *(Meinungsverschiedenheit)* divergence of opinion

divergieren *itr. V. (auch Math.)* diverge

divers... [di'vɛrs...] *Adj.; nicht präd.* various; *(von derselben Sorte)* several; **die** ~**esten ...:** the most diverse ...

Diversifikation [divɛrzifika'tsi̯o:n] **die;** ~, ~en *(Wirtsch.)* diversification

diversifizieren [divɛrzifi'tsi:rən] *tr., itr. V. (Wirtsch.)* diversify

Diversion [divɛr'zi̯o:n] **die;** ~, ~en *(bes. DDR)* subversion

Divertimento [divɛrti'mɛnto] **das;** ~s, ~s *u.* **Divertimenti** *(Musik)* divertimento

Divertissement [divɛrtɪsə'mã:] **das;** ~s, ~s *(Musik)* divertissement

Dividend [divi'dɛnt] **der;** ~en, ~en *(Math.)* dividend

Dividende [divi'dɛndə] **die;** ~, ~n *(Börsenw., Wirtsch.)* dividend

Dividenden·ausschüttung die *(Börsenw., Wirtsch.)* payment of the dividend/of dividends

dividieren [divi'di:rən] *tr. V. (Math.)* divide

Divis [di'vi:s] **das;** ~es, ~e *(Druckw.)* hyphen

Division [divi'zi̯o:n] **die;** ~, ~en *(Math., Milit.)* division

Divisions·kommandeur der *(Milit.)* divisional commander

Divisor [di'vi:zɔr] **der;** ~s, ~en [-vi'zo:rən] *(Math.)* divisor

Diwan ['di:va:n] **der;** ~s, ~e *(veralt.: Sofa, Literaturw.: Gedichte)* divan

Dixieland ['dɪksɪlænd] **der;** ~[s] Dixieland

d. J. *Abk.* **a) dieses Jahres; b) der/die Jüngere**

DJH [de:jɔt'ha:] **der;** ~ *Abk.* **Deutscher Jugendherbergsverband** German Youth Hostel Association

DKP [de:ka:'pe:] **die;** ~ *Abk.* **Deutsche Kommunistische Partei** Communist Party of Germany

DLRG [de:|ɛl|ɛr'ge:] **die;** ~ *Abk.* **Deutsche Lebens-Rettungs-Gesellschaft** German Life Saving Society

dm *Abk.* **Dezimeter** dm

DM *Abk.* **Deutsche Mark** DM

d. M. *Abk.* **dieses Monats** inst.; **am 13. d. M.** on the thirteenth inst.

d-Moll ['de:mɔl] **das;** ~ *(Musik)* D minor; *s. auch* **a-Moll**

DNS [de:|ɛn'|ɛs] **die;** ~ *Abk. (Chemie)* **Desoxyribonukleinsäure** DNA

do. *Abk.* **dito** do.

Do. *Abk.* **Donnerstag** Thur[s].

Dobermann ['do:bɐman] **der;** ~s, **Dobermänner** Dobermann [pinscher]

doch [dɔx] **1.** *Konj.* but. **2.** *Adv.* **a)** *(jedoch)* but; **b)** *(dennoch)* all the same; still; *(trotzdem)* nevertheless; all the same; *(wider Erwarten)* after all; **aber ich habe ihn** ~ **erkannt** but I recognized him all the same; but I still recognized him; **und** ~: and yet; **aber die Ausstellung war** ~ **ganz interessant** but the exhibition was actually quite interesting; **c)** *(geh.: weil)* **wußte er** ~, **daß ...:** because he knew that ...; **d)** *(als Antwort)* **Das kannst du nicht! – Doch!** You can't do that! – [Oh] yes I can!; **Das stimmt nicht! – Doch!** That's not right! – [Oh] yes it is!; **Hast du keinen Hunger? – Doch!** Aren't you hungry? – Yes [I am]!; **doch schon, aber ...:** yes, I do/he does *etc.,* but ...; **e)** *(Angezweifeltes richtigstellend: tatsächlich)* **er war also** ~ **der Mörder!** so he 'was the murderer!; **sie hat es also** ~ **gesagt** so she 'did say it; **f)** *(etw. für unnütz erklärend)* in any case; **du kannst mir** ~ **nicht helfen** there's nothing you can do to help me. **3.** *Partikel* **a)** *(auffordernd, Ungeduld, Empörung ausdrückend) oft nicht übersetzt* **das hättest du** ~ **wissen müssen** you [really] should have known that; **du hast** ~ **selbst gesagt, daß ...** *(rechtfertigend)* you did say yourself that ...; **gib mir** ~ **bitte mal die Zeitung** pass me the paper, please; **Kinder, seid** ~ **nicht so laut!** don't make so much noise, children!; **reg dich** ~ **nicht so auf!** don't get so worked up!; **paß** ~ **auf!** [oh,] do be careful!; **das ist** ~ **nicht zu glauben** that's just incredible; **b)** *(Zweifel ausdrückend)* **du hast** ~ **meinen Brief erhalten?** you did get my letter, didn't you?; **es wird ihm** ~ **nichts passiert sein?** you don't think something has happened to him[, do you]?; **c)** *(Bestätigung erwartend)* **Sie kommen** ~ **morgen?** you will be coming tomorrow, won't you?; **d)** *(Überraschung ausdrückend)* **das ist** ~ **Karl!** there's Karl! **e)** *(an Bekanntes erinnernd)* **er ist** ~ **nicht mehr der jüngste** he's not as young as he used to be[, you know]; **ich bin** ~ **deine Schwester** I 'am your sister[, you know]; **g)** *(nach Vergessenem fragend)* **wie war** ~ **sein Name?** now what was his name?; **h)** *(verstärkt Bejahung/Verneinung ausdrückend)* **gewiß/sicher** ~: [why] certainly; of course; **ja** ~: [yes,] all right *or (coll.)* OK; **nein** ~: [no,] of course not; **nicht** ~**!** *(abwehrend)* [no,] don't!; **sollen sie** ~**!** let them, then!; well, let them!; **i)** *(Wunsch verstärkend)* **wäre es** ~ **...:** if only it were ...

Docht [dɔxt] **der;** ~[e]s, ~e wick

Docht·schere die snuffers *pl.*

Dock [dɔk] **das;** ~s, ~s dock

Dock·arbeiter der dock-worker; docker

Docke die; ~, ~n **a)** *(Garnbündel)* skein; **b)** *(Getreidebündel)* shock; stook; **c)** *(südd.: Puppe)* doll

[1]**docken** *tr. V.* shock, stook ⟨*corn*⟩; wind ⟨*thread*⟩ into a skein/skeins

[2]**docken 1.** *itr. V. (Seew., Raumf.)* dock. **2.** *tr. V. (Seew.)* dock ⟨*ship*⟩; put ⟨*ship*⟩ in dock

Docker der; ~s, ~: docker

Dock·hafen der dock

Dodekaeder [dodeka'|e:dɐ] **das;** ~s, ~ *(Geom.)* dodecahedron

Dodekaphonie [dodekafo'ni:] **die;** ~ *(Musik)* twelve-tone technique

Doge ['do:ʒə] **der;** ~n, ~n doge

Dogge ['dɔgə] **die;** ~, ~n **a) deutsche** ~: Great Dane; **b) englische** ~: mastiff

Dogma ['dɔgma] **das;** ~s, **Dogmen** *(bes. kath. Kirche, auch fig.)* dogma

Dogmatik [dɔ'gma:tɪk] **die;** ~, ~en **a)** *(Theol.)* dogmatics *sing., no art.;* **b)** *(fig. abwertend)* dogmatism

Dogmatiker der; ~s, ~, **Dogmatikerin die;** ~, ~nen *(Theol., auch fig.)* dogmatist

dogmatisch *(Theol., auch fig.)* **1.** *Adj.* dogmatic. **2.** *adv.* dogmatically

dogmatisieren *tr. V. (Theol., auch fig.)* dogmatize

Dogmatismus der; ~ *(oft abwertend)* dogmatism

Dogmen·geschichte die; *o. Pl. (Theol.)* history of dogma

Dohle ['do:lə] **die;** ~, ~n jackdaw

Dohne ['do:nə] **die;** ~, ~n springe

Döhnkes ['dø:nkəs] *Pl. (nordd.)* stories; yarns
Doktor ['dɔktɔr] **der; ~s, ~en** [-'to:rən] **a)** *o. Pl. (Titel)* doctorate; doctor's degree; **den/seinen ~ machen** do a/one's doctorate; **den ~ haben** have a doctorate *or* doctor's degree; **zum ~ promoviert werden** be awarded one's doctorate *or* doctor's degree; **b)** *(Träger)* doctor; **er ist ~ der Philosophie** he is a doctor of philosophy; **guten Tag, Frau ~!** hello, Doctor; *(Frau eines ~s)* hello, Mrs X; **Herr ~ Krause** Doctor Krause; **c)** *(ugs.: Arzt)* doctor; **der Onkel ~** *(Kinderspr.)* the nice doctor; **~ spielen** play doctors and nurses
Doktorand [dɔkto'rant] **der; ~en, ~en** student taking his/her doctorate; **er ist ~ bei Professor Meier** he is studying for his doctorate under Professor Meier
Doktoranden·kolloquium das research students' colloquium
Doktorandin die; ~, ~nen *s.* **Doktorand**
Doktor·arbeit die doctoral thesis *or* dissertation (**über** + *Akk.* on)
Doktorat [dɔkto'ra:t] **das; ~[e]s, ~e a)** *(veralt.: Doktorwürde)* doctorate; **b)** *(österr.) s.* **Doktorprüfung**
Doktor-: ~diplom das Ph. D. certificate; doctoral diploma *(Amer.)*; **~examen das** *s.* **~prüfung**; **~grad der** doctorate; doctor's degree; **den ~grad erwerben** gain *or* get one's doctorate *or* doctor's degree; **~hut der a)** *(Hut)* doctor's cap; **b)** *(ugs.) s.* **~grad**
Doktorin die; ~, ~nen doctor; *s. auch* **-in**
Doktor-: ~ingenieur der doctor of engineering science; **~prüfung die** examination for a/one's doctorate; **~titel der** title of doctor; **den ~titel führen** *(sich ~ nennen)* call oneself doctor; *(den ~grad haben)* have a doctorate *or* doctor's degree; **~vater der** *(ugs.)* [thesis] supervisor; **~würde die** doctorate; doctor's degree
Doktrin [dɔk'tri:n] **die; ~, ~en** doctrine
doktrinär [dɔktri'nɛ:ɐ̯] **1.** *Adj.* doctrinal; *(abwertend: starr, einseitig)* doctrinaire. **2.** *adv.* doctrinally; *(abwertend: starr, einseitig)* in a doctrinaire way
Doktrinär der; ~, ~e a) *(Verfechter einer Doktrin)* advocate of a/the doctrine; **b)** *(abwertend)* doctrinaire
Dokument [doku'mɛnt] **das; ~[e]s, ~e a)** *(Urkunde)* document; **b)** *(Zeugnis)* document; record; **c)** *(DDR: Parteibuch)* party membership book
Dokumentalist [dɔkumɛnta'lɪst] **der; ~en, ~en** *(DDR)*, **Dokumentar** [dɔkumɛn'ta:r] **der; ~s, ~e** documentalist
Dokumentar-: ~bericht der documentary report; **~film der** documentary [film]
dokumentarisch 1. *Adj.* documentary. **2.** *adv.* **etw. ~ belegen** provide documentary evidence of *or* for sth.; **etw. ~ festhalten** make a documentary record of sth.
Dokumentar-: ~literatur die documentary literature; **~theater das** documentary drama
Dokumentation [dɔkumɛnta'tsi̯o:n] **die; ~, ~en a)** *o. Pl. (das Dokumentieren)* documentation; **b)** *(Material)* documentary account; *(Bericht)* documentary report; **c)** *o. Pl. (das Beweisen)* demonstration; **d)** *(Beweis, Ausdruck)* evidence
dokumentieren 1. *tr. V.* **a)** *(bekunden)* demonstrate ⟨*readiness, cast of mind, sympathy, interest*⟩; express, register ⟨*protest*⟩; **b)** *(belegen)* document; **c)** *(darstellen)* record ⟨*behaviour, event*⟩. **2.** *refl. V. (offenbar werden)* **sich in** *od.* **an etw.** *(Dat.)* **~:** be demonstrated by sth.
Dolby ⓦⓩ ['dɔlbi] **das; ~s** Dolby system **(P)**
Dolce vita ['dɔltʃə 'vi:ta] **das** *od.* **die; ~ ~:** dolce vita; **~ ~ machen** *(ugs.)* live a life of luxury and pleasure
Dolch [dɔlç] **der; ~[e]s, ~e** dagger
Dolch-: ~stich der stab [with a dagger]; **~stoß der a)** *(Stoß)* dagger-thrust; **b)** *(fig.: Hinterhalt)* stab in the back; **~stoß·legende die** myth of the stab in the back
Dolde ['dɔldə] **die; ~, ~n** *(Bot.)* umbel
Dolden-: ~blütler der *(Bot.)* **a)** *(aus der Ordnung ~blütler) plant of the order Umbelliflorae;* **b)** *s.* **~gewächs; ~gewächs das** *(Bot.)* umbellifer
Dole ['do:lə] **die; ~, ~n** *(südd.)* drain
doll [dɔl] *(bes. nordd., salopp)* **1.** *Adj.* **a)** *(ungewöhnlich)* incredible; amazing; **b)** *(verrückt)* batty *(sl.)*; *s. auch* **oll**; **c)** *(großartig)* fantastic *(coll.)*; great *(coll.)*; *(iron.)* great *(coll.)*; **d)** *(schlimm)* dreadful *(coll.)*. **2.** *adv.* **a)** *(verrückt)* like a madman; **b)** *(großartig)* fantastically [well] *(coll.)*; **c)** *(sehr)* ⟨*hurt*⟩ dreadfully *(coll.)*, like mad; ⟨*shake, rain*⟩ good and hard *(coll.)*; **es regnet immer ~er** it's chucking it down harder than ever *(coll.)*; **sich ~ freuen** be terribly pleased *(coll.)*
Dollar ['dɔla:ɐ̯] **der; ~[s], ~s** dollar; **zwei ~:** two dollars
Dollar-: ~kurs der dollar rate; **~zeichen das** dollar sign
Dolle die; ~, ~n rowlock
Doll·punkt der *(ugs.)* bone of contention
Dolly ['dɔli] **der; ~[s], ~s** *(Film)* dolly
Dolmetsch ['dɔlmɛtʃ] **der; ~[e]s, ~e a)** *(bes. österr.: Dolmetscher)* interpreter; **b)** *(geh.: Fürsprecher, Verkünder)* spokesman (*Gen.* for)
dolmetschen 1. *itr. V. (übersetzen)* act as interpreter (**bei** at); *(als Dolmetscher arbeiten)* work as *or* be an interpreter. **2.** *tr. V.* act as interpreter at ⟨*discussion etc.*⟩
Dolmetscher der; ~s, ~ interpreter; **sich über einen** *od.* **mit Hilfe eines ~ unterhalten** talk through an interpreter
Dolmetscherin die; ~, ~nen *s.* **Dolmetscher**; *s. auch* **-in**
Dolmetscher-: ~institut das, ~schule die institute *or* school of interpreting
Dolomit [dolo'mi:t] **der; ~s, ~e** *(Geol.)* dolomite
Dolomiten *Pl.* **die ~:** the Dolomites
Dom [do:m] **der; ~[e]s, ~e a)** cathedral; *(fig.)* dome; **der Kölner ~, der ~ zu Köln** Cologne Cathedral; **b)** *(Geol.)* dome
Domäne [do'mɛ:nə] **die; ~, ~n a)** *(Spezialgebiet)* domain; **b)** *(Staatsgut)* demesne
Domestik [domɛs'ti:k] **der; ~en, ~en** *(veralt. abwertend)* domestic
Domestikation [domɛstika'tsi̯o:n] **die; ~, ~en** domestication
Domestike der; ~n, ~n *s.* **Domestik**
Domestikin die; ~, ~nen *(verhüll.)* sub girl *(coll.)*
domestizieren [domɛsti'tsi:rən] *tr. V.* domesticate; *(fig.)* tame; subdue
Dom-: ~freiheit die *(hist.) area of a city, usually around the cathedral, under the jurisdiction of the Church;* **~herr der** *(kath. Rel.)* canon
[1]**Domina** ['do:mina] **die; ~, Dominä** abbess; mother superior
[2]**Domina die; ~, ~s** *(verhüll.)* mistress; dominatrix
dominant [domi'nant] **1.** *Adj. (auch Biol.)* dominant. **2.** *adv.* dominantly
Dominant·akkord der *(Musik)* dominant chord
Dominante die; ~, ~n a) *(Hauptmerkmal)* dominant feature; **b)** *(Musik) (Quint)* dominant; *(Dreiklang) s.* **Dominantakkord**
Dominant·sept·akkord der *(Musik)* dominant seventh chord
Dominanz [domi'nants] **die; ~, ~en** *(auch Biol.)* dominance
dominieren [domi'ni:rən] **1.** *itr. V.* dominate; ⟨*aspect*⟩ predominate, dominate; **~d** dominant. **2.** *tr. V.* dominate
Dominikaner [domini'ka:nɐ] **der; ~s, ~, Dominikanerin die; ~, ~nen a)** *(Mönch/Nonne)* Dominican; **b)** *(Einwohner/Einwohnerin der Dominikanischen Republik)* Dominican
Dominikaner·orden der *o. Pl.* Dominican order
dominikanisch *Adj.* Dominican; **die Dominikanische Republik** the Dominican Republic
[1]**Domino** ['do:mino] **der; ~s, ~s** *(Mantel, Person)* domino
[2]**Domino das; ~s, ~s** *(Spiel)* dominoes *sing.*
[3]**Domino der; ~s, ~s** *(österr.: ~stein)* domino
Domino-: ~spiel das a) dominoes *sing.*; **b)** *(~steine)* [set *sing.* of] dominoes *pl.*; **c)** *(~partie)* game of dominoes; **~stein der a)** *(Spielstein)* domino; **b)** *(Gebäck) small chocolate-covered cake with layers of marzipan, jam, and gingerbread*
Domizil [domi'tsi:l] **das; ~s, ~e a)** *(geh.)* domicile; residence; **bei jmdm./in einer Stadt** *usw.* **~ nehmen** take up residence with sb./in a town *etc.*; **b)** *(Finanzw.)* place of payment
domizilieren *tr. V. (Finanzw.)* domicile
Dom-: ~kapitel das *(kath. Kirche)* cathedral chapter; **~kapitular der** *(kath. Kirche)* canon; **~pfaff der; ~en** *od.* **~s, ~en** *(Zool.)* bullfinch; **~prediger der** *(ev. Kirche)* cathedral preacher; **~probst der** *(kath. Kirche)* dean; provost
Dompteur [dɔmp'tø:ɐ̯] **der; ~s, ~e, Dompteuse** [dɔmp'tø:zə] **die; ~, ~n** tamer
Donau ['do:nau̯] **die; ~:** Danube
Donau-: ~monarchie die; ~ *(hist.)* Austro-Hungarian Empire; **~schwaben** *Pl. German settlers on the middle Danube*
Dönkes ['dœnkəs] *Pl. (nordd.) s.* **Döhnkes**
Donner ['dɔnɐ] **der; ~s, ~** *(auch fig.)* thunder; **der erste ~:** the first clap *or* peal of thunder; **wie vom ~ gerührt dastehen** *od.* **sein** be thunderstruck; **~ und Blitz** *od.* **Doria!** *(veralt.)* by Jove! *(dated coll.)*
Donner-: ~balken der *(salopp)* bog *(Brit. sl.)*; latrine; *(Sitzstange)* latrine seat; **~getöse das;** *o. Pl.* thunderous din; **~gott der;** *o. Pl.* god of thunder; **~keil der a)** *o. Art. (ugs.: Ausruf des Erstaunens)* my word; **b)** *(Werkzeug, Belemnit)* thunderstone; **~littchen** [-'lɪtçən], **~lüttchen** [-'lʏtçən] *o. Art. (nordd.: Ausruf des Erstaunens)* my word; wow
donnern 1. *itr. V.* **a)** *(unpers.)* thunder; **es hat gedonnert und geblitzt** there was thunder and lightning; **b)** *(fig.)* ⟨*gun*⟩ thunder, boom [out]; ⟨*engine*⟩ roar; ⟨*hooves*⟩ thunder; **~der Applaus** thunderous applause; **c)** *mit sein (sich laut fortbewegen)* ⟨*train, avalanche, etc.*⟩ thunder; **d)** *(ugs.: schlagen)* thump, hammer (**an** + *Akk.*, **gegen** on); **e)** *mit sein (ugs.: prallen)* **gegen etw. ~:** smash into sth.; **der Ball donnerte an die Latte** the ball slammed against the bar; **f)** *(ugs.: schimpfen)* **gegen etw. ~:** rage against sth. **2.** *tr. V.* **a)** *(ugs.: schleudern)* sling *(coll.)*; hurl; **b)** *(ugs.: schlagen)* slam; **jmdm. eine** *od.* **ein paar ~:** thump sb.; give sb. a good thumping; **c)** *(ugs.: schimpfen)* thunder
Donner·schlag der clap *or* peal of thunder; **die Nachricht traf uns wie ein ~:** the news completely stunned us
Donners·tag der Thursday; *s. auch* **Dienstag**
donnerstags *Adv.* on Thursday[s]; *s. auch* **dienstags**
Donner-: ~stimme die thundering voice; **~wetter das a)** *(ugs.: Krach)* row; **das wird ein [schönes] ~wetter geben** *od.* **setzen** that will cause a hell of a row *(coll.)*; **ein ~wetter über sich ergehen lassen müssen** be given what for *(sl.)*; **b)** ['--'--] *o. Art. (ugs.: Ausruf der Verärgerung)* **zum ~wetter [noch einmal]!** damn it!; **warum, zum ~wetter, ...?** why, for Heaven's sake, ...?; **c)** ['--'--] *o. Art.*

(ugs.: Ausruf der Bewunderung) my word; wow

Don Quichotte [dɔnki'ʃɔt] **(der)** Don Quixote

Donquichotterie [dɔnkiʃɔtə'ri:] **die; ~, ~n** quixotism; quixotry

doof [do:f] *(ugs. abwertend)* **1.** *Adj.* **a)** *(einfältig)* stupid; dumb *(coll.)*; dopey *(sl.)*; **~ bleibt ~[, da helfen keine Pillen]** once a fool, always a fool; **b)** *(langweilig)* boring; **c)** *nicht präd. (ärgerlich)* stupid. **2.** *adv. (beschränkt)* stupidly; **da hat er vielleicht ~ geguckt** he didn't half make *(Brit.)* or really made a stupid face

Doofheit die; ~, ~en *(ugs. abwertend)* **a)** *o. Pl.* stupidity; dumbness *(coll.)*; **b)** *(Äußerung)* stupid *or (coll.)* dumb remark

Doofi ['do:fi] **der; ~[s], ~s** *(ugs.)* dope *(coll.)*; dummy; [stupid] twit *(sl.)*; **steh nicht da wie Klein ~ mit Plüschohren!** stop looking so stupid!

Doofkopp [-kɔp] **der; ~s, Doofköppe** [-kœpə], **Doofmann der; ~[e]s, Doofmänner** *(ugs. abwertend)* dope *(coll.)*; dummy; [stupid] twit *(sl.)*

dopen ['dɔpn̩] *tr. V.* dope ⟨*horse etc.*⟩; **jmdn. ~:** give sb. drugs; **gedopt sein** ⟨*athlete*⟩ have taken drugs; **sich ~:** take drugs

Doping ['dɔpɪŋ] **das; ~s, ~s a)** *(bei Sportlern)* taking drugs; *(das Verabreichen von Drogen)* administering drugs; **b)** *(von Pferden usw.)* doping

Doppel ['dɔpl̩] **das, ~s, ~ a)** *(Kopie)* duplicate; copy; **b)** *(Sport)* doubles *sing. or pl.*; **im gemischten/das gemischte ~ gewinnen** win the mixed doubles; **ein ~:** a game of doubles; *(im Turnier)* a doubles match

doppel-, Doppel-: ~adler der double eagle; **~agent der** double agent; **~album das** double album *or* LP; **~-b das** *(Musik)* double flat; **~band der** double[-sized] volume; **~belastung die** double burden *or* load; **~belichtung die** *(Fot.)* double exposure; **~beschluß der** *(Politik)* twin-track decision; **~besteuerung die** double taxation; **~bett das** double bed; **~bock das** extra-strong bock beer; **~bödig** [~bø:dɪç] **1.** *Adj.* ambiguous; **2.** *adv.* ambiguously; **~bödigkeit die; ~, ~en** ambiguity; **~bogen der** double sheet; **~bruch der** *(Math.)* compound *or* complex fraction; **~decker der; ~s, ~ a)** *(Flugzeug)* biplane; **b)** *(Omnibus)* double-decker [bus]; **~deutig** [~dɔytɪç] **1.** *Adj.* **a)** ambiguous; **b)** *(anzüglich)* suggestive; **eine ~deutige Bemerkung** a double entendre; **2.** *adv.* **a)** ambiguously; **b)** *(anzüglich)* suggestively; **~deutigkeit die; ~, ~en a)** ambiguity; **b)** *(Anzüglichkeit)* suggestiveness; *(anzügliche Äußerung)* double entendre; **~fenster das** double-glazed window; **~fenster haben** have double glazing; **~flinte die** double-barrelled shotgun; **~gänger der; ~s, ~, ~gängerin die; ~, ~nen** double; **~gleisig 1.** *Adj.* **a)** *(mit zwei Gleisen)* double-tracked; **b)** *(zwielichtig)* dubious; **2.** *adv.* **a)** *(mit zwei Gleisen)* **diese Strecke ist ~gleisig ausgebaut** this section is double-tracked *or* has two tracks; **~gleisig fahren** *(fig.)* adopt a two-pronged strategy; **b)** *(zwielichtig)* dubiously; **~griff der** *(Musik)* double-stop; **~haus das** pair of semi-detached houses; **~haus·hälfte die** semi[-detached house]; **~heft das** double issue; **~hoch·zeit die** double wedding; **~kinn das** double chin; **~knoten der** double knot; **~konsonant der** *(Sprachw.)* double consonant; **~konzert das** double concerto; **~kopf der;** *o. Pl. (Kartenspiel)* Doppelkopf; **~lauf der** double barrel; **~laut der** *(Sprachw.)* **a)** *(Diphthong)* diphthong; **b)** *(~konsonant)* double consonant; **c)** *(~vokal)* double vowel; **~leben das** double life; **~moral die** double standards *pl.*; **~mord der** double murder

doppeln *tr. V.* **a)** *(südd., österr.)* resole; **b)** *(DV)* reproduce

doppel-, Doppel-: ~naht die French seam; **~name der** double-barrelled name *(Brit.)*; hyphenated name; **~paß der** *(Fußball)* one-two; **~punkt der** colon; **~reihig** *Adj. s.* **zweireihig; ~rolle die** dual role; **~schicht die** double shift; **eine ~schicht fahren** work a double shift; **~schlag der a)** *(Musik)* turn; **b)** *(Tennis, Tischtennis, Badminton)* double hit; **~seite die** *(Zeitungsw.)* double page; **~seitig 1.** *Adj.* **a)** *(Zeitungsw.)* two-page *attrib.*; double-page *attrib.*; **b)** *(Med.)* double ⟨*pleurisy, pneumonia*⟩; bilateral ⟨*paralysis*⟩; **2.** *adv.* **a)** *(Zeitungsw.)* **~seitig gedruckt** printed across two pages *or* a double page; **b)** *(Med.)* **~seitig gelähmt** paralysed on both sides; **~sieg der** first and second place; **einen ~sieg feiern** celebrate taking first and second place; **~sinnig 1.** *Adj.* ambiguous; **2.** *adv.* ambiguously; **~spiel das a)** *(Sport)* doubles *sing.* or *pl.*; **b)** *(abwertend: Unehrlichkeit)* double game; **~steck·dose die** *(Elektrot.)* double socket; **~stecker der** *(Elektrot.)* two-way plug *or* adapter; **~stöckig** *Adj.* two-storey ⟨*house*⟩; double-decker *attrib.* ⟨*bus*⟩; *(fig.)* double ⟨*whisky etc.*⟩; **ein ~stöckiges Bett** a bunk-bed; **~stunde die** double period

doppelt 1. *Adj.* **a)** *(zweifach)* double; dual ⟨*nationality*⟩; **die ~e Länge/Breite/Menge** double *or* twice the length/breadth/quantity; **~e Buchführung** *(Kaufmannsspr.)* double-entry bookkeeping; **ein ~er Klarer** *(ugs.)* a double schnapps; **ein ~er Boden** a false bottom; **b)** *(besonders groß, stark)* redoubled ⟨*enthusiasm, attention*⟩; **mit ~er Kraft arbeiten** work with twice as much energy; **2.** *adv.* **a)** *(zweimal)* **~ konzentriert** double concentrated; **der Stoff liegt ~:** the material is double-width; **~ genäht hält besser** *(Spr.)* it's better to be on the safe side; better safe than sorry; **das ist ~ gemoppelt** *(ugs.)* that's just saying the same thing twice over; **~ so groß/alt wie ...:** twice as large/old as ...; **~ soviel** twice as much; **das/diese Platte habe ich ~:** I have two of them/two copies of this record; **etw. ~ nehmen** double sth. up; **~ sehen** see double; **etw. ~ und dreifach bereuen/prüfen** regret sth. deeply/test and retest sth.; **b)** *(ganz besonders, noch mehr)* **~ einsam** twice as lonely; **sich ~ anstrengen** try twice as hard; **es ~ bereuen, daß ...:** be even more sorry that ...

¹Doppelte das; *adj. Dekl.* **das ~ bezahlen** pay twice as much; pay double; **um/auf das ~ steigen** triple/double; **etw. um das ~ erhöhen** triple sth.; **um das ~ größer** three times as large; **das ~ leisten** do double the work *or* twice as much work

²Doppelte der; *adj. Dekl. (ugs.)* double

doppelt·kohlen·sauer *Adj. (Chemie)* **...saures Natron** sodium bicarbonate; bicarbonate of soda; **...saurer Kalk** calcium bicarbonate

Doppelt·sehen das; ~s *(Med.)* double vision; diplopia *(Med.)*

Doppel·tür die double door

Doppelung die; ~, ~en doubling

doppel-, Doppel-: ~verdiener der a) *Pl. (Eheleute)* married couple who are both earning; **b)** *(mit zwei Einkommen)* person with an income from two jobs; **~verdiener sein** have an income from two jobs; **~vokal der** *(Sprachw.)* double vowel; **~zentner der** 100 kilograms; quintal; **~zimmer das** double room; **~züngig** [-tsʏnɪç] *(abwertend)* **1.** *Adj.* two-faced; **2.** *adv.* **~züngig reden** be two-faced; **~züngigkeit die; ~** *(abwertend) s.* **~züngig:** double-facedness; two-facedness

Doppler·effekt der; ~[e]s *(Physik)* Doppler effect

Dorado [do'ra:do] *s.* **Eldorado**

Dorf [dɔrf] **das; ~[e]s, Dörfer** ['dœrfɐ] *(auch ugs.: die Einwohner)* village; **auf dem ~:** in the country; **vom ~ kommen** *od.* **stammen** come from the country; **aufs ~ ziehen** move to the country; **über die Dörfer** from village to village; **über die Dörfer fahren** drive on country roads; **das olympische ~:** the Olympic village; **das sind mir/für mich böhmische Dörfer** *(ugs.)* it's all Greek to me; **auf/über die Dörfer gehen** *(Skat)* lead the side suits; **aus** *od.* **in jedem ~ einen Hund haben** *(Skat)* have a more or less even distribution; *s. auch* **potemkinsch**

Dorf-: ~akademie die *(DDR)* village adult education centre; **~älteste der** village elder; **~anger der** village green; **~bewohner der** villager

Dörfchen ['dœrfçən] **das; ~s, ~:** small village; hamlet

Dorf·depp der *(bes. südd., österr.)* village idiot

dörfisch 1. *Adj.* rustic. **2.** *adv.* rustically

Dorf-: ~jugend die young people *pl.* of the village; village youth; **~krug der** *(nordd.)* village inn *or (Brit. coll.)* pub

Dörfler ['dœrflɐ] **der; ~s, ~, Dörflerin die; ~, ~nen** villager

dörflich *Adj.* village *attrib.* ⟨*life, traditions, etc.*⟩; *(ländlich)* rural ⟨*character*⟩

Dorf-: ~polizist der village policeman; **~schenke die** village inn *or (Brit. coll.)* pub; **~schönheit die** village beauty; **~schulze der** *(veralt.)* mayor of the/a village; **~trottel der** village idiot

dorisch ['do:rɪʃ] *Adj.* **a)** *(Archit.)* Doric; **b)** *(Musik)* Dorian ⟨*mode*⟩

¹Dorn [dɔrn] **der; ~[e]s, ~en** *(ugs. auch:)* **Dörner** ['dœrnɐ] **a)** *(an Rosen o. ä.)* thorn; **jmdm. ein ~ im Auge sein** annoy sb. intensely; **sein Weg war voller ~en** *(fig. geh.)* his life was no bed of roses; **b)** *(Bot.)* thorn; spine; **c)** *(dichter.: ~busch)* thorn-bush

²Dorn der; ~[e]s, ~e a) *(Metallstift)* spike; *(an der Gürtelschnalle)* tongue; **b)** *(Technik) (zum Weiten von Löchern o. ä.)* punch; *(zum Biegen von Blechen o. ä.)* mandrel

Dorn·busch der thorn-bush; **der brennende ~** *(bibl.)* the burning bush

dornen-, Dornen-: ~gestrüpp das tangle of thorn-bushes; **~krone die** crown of thorns; **~reich** *Adj. (fig. geh.)* hard ⟨*life, fate*⟩; thorny ⟨*path*⟩; **~strauch der** thorn-bush; **~voll** *Adj. (fig. geh.) s.* **~reich**

Dorn·fort·satz der *(Anat.)* spinous process

dornig *Adj.* **a)** *(mit Dornen)* thorny; **b)** *(geh.: schwierig)* hard ⟨*life, fate*⟩; thorny ⟨*path, subject, question*⟩

Dorn-: ~röschen (das) the Sleeping Beauty; **~röschen·schlaf der** *(iron.)* long sleep

dorren ['dɔrən] *itr. V.; mit sein (geh.)* dry up

dörren ['dœrən] **1.** *tr. V. (trocken machen)* dry. **2.** *itr. V.; mit sein* dry

Dörr-: ~fleisch das *(südd.)* lean bacon; **~obst das** dried fruit; **~pflaume die** prune

dorsal [dɔr'za:l] *Adj.* **a)** *(Med.)* dorsal ⟨*artery, nerve*⟩; spinal ⟨*curvature*⟩; **b)** *(Phon.)* dorsal

Dorsch [dɔrʃ] **der; ~[e]s, ~e** cod; *(junger Kabeljau)* codling

dort [dɔrt] *Adv.* there; *s. auch* **da 1 a**

dort-: ~|behalten *unr. tr. V.* **jmdn./etw. ~behalten** keep sb./sth. there; **~|bleiben** *unr. itr. V.; mit sein* stay there; **~her** *Adv.* **[von] ~her** from there; **~hin** *Adv.* there; **bis ~hin** as far as there; **ich ging ~hin, wo der Wagen wartete** I went to where the car was waiting; **~hinab** *Adv.* down there; down that way; **~hinauf** *Adv.* up there; up that way; **bis ~hinauf** up to there; **~hinaus** *Adv.* out there; *(in diese Richtung)* out that way; **frech bis ~hinaus** *(ugs.)* [as] cheeky as anything; **das ärgert mich bis ~hinaus** *(ugs.)*

that really gets me *or* my goat *(sl.)*; **~hinein** *Adv.* in there; **~hinunter** *Adv.* down there
dortig *Adj.; nicht präd.* there *postpos.*
dort·zu·lande *Adv. (geh.)* in that country; there
Döschen ['dø:sçən] **das; ~s, ~** *s.* **Dose a:** small tin/box
Dose ['do:zə] **die; ~, ~n a)** *(Blech~)* tin; *(Pillen~)* box; *(Zucker~)* bowl; **b)** *(Konserven~)* can; tin *(Brit.)*; *(Bier~)* can; **Bier aus der ~:** canned beer; beer in cans; **c)** *(Steck~)* socket
dösen ['dø:zn̩] *itr. V. (ugs.)* doze; **vor sich hin ~:** doze
dosen-, Dosen-: ~bier das canned beer; **~fertig** *Adj.* ready in the can *or (Brit.)* tin *postpos.*; **~fleisch das** canned *or (Brit.)* tinned meat; **~milch die** canned *or (Brit.)* tinned milk; **~öffner der** can opener; tin-opener *(Brit.)*
dosierbar *Adj.* **etw. ist genau** *od.* **exakt ~:** sth. can be measured out in precise *or* exact doses
dosieren *tr. V.* **etw. ~:** measure out the required dose of sth.; *(zuführen)* administer the required dose of sth.; **ein Medikament genau/niedriger ~:** measure out/administer an exact/a smaller dose of a medicine; **sorgfältig dosierte Mengen** carefully measured doses; **seine Zuneigung sehr dosiert verteilen** *(fig.)* dispense one's affection in very small doses
Dosierung die; ~, ~en a) *o. Pl.* measuring out; *(das Zuführen)* administering; *(fig.)* dispensing; **b)** *s.* **Dosis**
dösig ['dø:zɪç] *(ugs.)* **1.** *Adj.* **a)** *(schläfrig)* drowsy; dozy; **b)** *(benommen)* dopey *(sl.)*; **ich habe einen ganz ~en Kopf** my head is all muzzy; **c)** *(unaufmerksam)* dozy *(coll.)*. **2.** *adv.* **a)** *(schläfrig)* drowsily; **b)** *(benommen)* dopily *(sl.)*; **c)** *(unaufmerksam)* dozily *(coll.)*
Dosimeter [dozi'me:tɐ] **das; ~s, ~** *(Physik)* dosimeter
Dosis ['do:zɪs] **die; ~, Dosen** *(auch fig.)* dose; **die tägliche ~:** the daily dosage
Döskopp ['dø:skɔp] **der; ~s, Dösköppe** ['dø:skœpə] *(salopp)* dozy twit *(Brit. sl.)*; dim-wit
Dossier [dɔ'si̯e:] **das,** *(veraltet:)* **der; ~s, ~s** dossier
Dotation [dota'tsi̯o:n] **die; ~, ~en** endowment
dotieren [do'ti:rən] *tr. V.* **a) eine Position gut/mit 5000 DM ~:** offer a good salary/a salary of 5,000 marks with a position; **b)** *(Physik)* dope
dotiert 1. *2. Part. v.* **dotieren. 2.** *Adj.* **eine gut/mit 5000 DM im Monat ~e Stellung** a well-paid position/a position with a monthly salary of 5,000 marks; **das Rennen ist gut ~:** good prize-money is being put up for the race
Dotierung die; ~, ~en a) *o. Pl. (das Dotieren)* **die ~ des Wettbewerbs/Rennens** putting up the prize-money for the competition/race; **b)** *(Entgelt)* remuneration; salary; *(Preis, Gewinn)* prize
Dotter ['dɔtɐ] **der** *od.* **das; ~s, ~ a)** *(Eigelb)* yolk; **b)** *(Zool.: Nährsubstanz)* vitellus; yolk
dotter-, Dotter-: ~blume die marsh marigold; **~gelb** *Adj.* bright yellow; **~sack der** *(Zool.)* yolk-sac
doubeln ['du:bl̩n] **1.** *tr. V.* stand in for ⟨*actor*⟩; use a stand-in for ⟨*scene*⟩; **sich ~ lassen** use *or* have a stand-in. **2.** *itr. V.* **für jmdn. ~:** stand in for sb.
Double ['du:bl̩] **das; ~s, ~s a)** *(Ersatzdarsteller[in])* stand-in; **b)** *(Doppelgänger, Sport: doppelter Gewinn)* double; **c)** *(Musik: Variation)* double
Doublé [du'ble:] **das; ~s, ~s a)** *(Schmuck)* rolled gold; **b)** *(Fechten)* double hit
doublieren *s.* **dublieren**
Douglasie [du'gla:zi̯ə] **die; ~, ~n, Douglas·fichte** ['du:glas-], **Douglas·tanne die** Douglas fir *or* spruce
down [daʊn] *Adj.; nicht attr. (salopp)* down
Doyen [do̯a'jɛ̃:] **der; ~s, ~s** doyen
Doyenne [do̯a'jɛn] **die; ~, ~n** doyenne
Dozent [do'tsɛnt] **der; ~en, ~en, Dozentin die; ~, ~nen** lecturer **(für** in); s. auch **-in**
Dozentur [dotsɛn'tu:ɐ̯] **die; ~, ~en** lectureship **(für** in)
dozieren [do'tsi:rən] **1.** *itr. V.* **a)** *(lehren)* lecture **(über +** *Akk.* on, **an +** *Dat.* at); **b)** *(belehrend reden)* lecture. **2.** *tr. V.* **„...", dozierte sie** '...,' she said in a lecturing tone
dpa [de:pe:'|a:] **die;** ~ *Abk.* **Deutsche Presse-Agentur** West German Press Agency
Dr. *Abk.*: **Doktor** Dr; *s. auch* **Dr. phil.**
Drache ['draxə] **der; ~n, ~n** *(Myth.)* dragon
Drachen der; ~s, ~ a) *(Papier~)* kite; **einen ~ steigen lassen** fly a kite; **b)** *(salopp: zänkische Frau)* dragon; **c)** *(Fluggerät)* hang-glider; **d)** *(Segelboot)* dragon
Drachen-: ~blut das *(Myth.; Chemie)* dragon's blood; **~fliegen das; ~s** *(Sport)* hang-gliding; **~saat die** *(geh.)* seeds *pl.* of discord
Dragée, Dragee [dra'ʒe:] **das; ~s, ~s** dragée
Dragoner [dra'go:nɐ] **der; ~s, ~ a)** *(salopp: resolute Frau)* battleaxe *(coll.)*; **b)** *(hist.: Soldat)* dragoon
Draht [dra:t] **der; ~[e]s, Drähte** ['drɛ:tə] **a)** *(dünnes Metall)* wire; **b)** *(Leitung)* wire; cable; *(Telefonleitung)* line; wire; **c)** *(Telefonverbindung)* line; **per** *od.* **über ~:** by wire *or* cable; **hast du einen ~ zur Polizei?** *(fig.)* have you got a direct line to the police?; **heißer ~:** hot line; **auf ~ sein** *(ugs.)* be on the ball *(coll.)*; **jmdn. auf ~ bringen** *(ugs.)* make sb. get a move on
Draht-: ~aus·löser der *(Fot.)* cable release; **~bürste die** wire brush
Drähtchen ['drɛ:tçən] **das; ~s, ~:** little wire
drahten *tr. V. (veralt.)* wire *(coll.)*; *(ins Ausland)* cable; **an jmdn./nach Paris ~, daß ...:** wire/cable sb./Paris to say that ...
Draht-: ~esel der *(ugs. scherzh.)* bike *(coll.)*; **~funk der** wired radio; **~geflecht das** wire mesh; **~gitter das** wire netting *no indef. art.*; **~glas das** wire glass
drahtig *Adj.* wiry ⟨*person, hair*⟩
draht-, Draht-: ~los *(Nachrichtenw.)* **1.** *Adj.* wireless; **2.** *adv.* **etw. ~los telegrafieren/übermitteln** radio sth.; **~schere die** wire-cutters *pl.*; **~seil das** [steel] cable; **~seil·bahn die** cable railway; **~seil·künstler der** tightrope walker; **~verhau der** *od.* **das** *(Barriere)* wire entanglement; *(Käfig)* wire enclosure; **~zange die** cutting pliers *pl.*; **~zaun der** wire fence; **~zieher** [-tsi:ɐ] **der a)** *(Beruf)* wire-drawer; **b)** *(Hintermann)* wire puller; **~zieherei die; ~, ~en** wire works
Drainage [drɛ'na:ʒə] **die; ~, ~n** *(Med., Landw., Kfz-W.)* drainage
drainieren [drɛ'ni:rən] *tr. V. (Med., Landw.)* drain
Draisine [drai̯'zi:nə] **die; ~, ~n a)** *(Laufrad)* dandy-horse; **b)** *(Schienenfahrzeug)* trolley
drakonisch [dra'ko:nɪʃ] **1.** *Adj.* Draconian. **2.** *adv.* in a Draconian way
drall [dral] *Adj.* strapping ⟨*girl*⟩; full, rounded ⟨*cheeks, face, bottom*⟩
Drall der; ~[e]s, ~e a) *(bei Feuerwaffen)* rifling; **b)** *(eines Geschosses, Balls)* spin; **er hat einen ~ nach rechts** *(fig.)* he leans to the right *or* has right-wing tendencies; **c)** *(Physik) (Verdrehung)* torsion; *(Rotation)* rotation; *(Drehimpuls)* angular momentum
Dralon Ⓦ ['dra:lɔn] **das; ~[s]** Dralon (P)
Drama ['dra:ma] **das; ~s, Dramen** drama; **ein einziges/furchtbares ~** *(fig.)* an absolute/a terrible disaster; **das ~ um die Entführung** *(fig.)* the drama of *or* surrounding the hijack
Dramatik [dra'ma:tɪk] **die; ~:** drama
Dramatiker der; ~s, ~: dramatist
dramatisch 1. *Adj.* dramatic. **2.** *adv.* dramatically; **der Autor hat den Stoff ~ bearbeitet** the author adapted the material as a drama *or* for the stage
dramatisieren *tr. V.* dramatize
Dramaturg [drama'tʊrk] **der; ~en, ~en** *(Theater)* literary and artistic director *(who also plans the programme of performances and advises on choice of costumes, scenery, etc.)*; *(Rundf., Ferns.)* script editor
Dramaturgie [dramatʊr'gi:] **die; ~, ~n a)** *(Dramenlehre)* dramaturgy; **b)** *(Gestaltung)* dramatization; **c)** *(Abteilung) (Theater)* literary and artistic director's department; *(Rundf., Ferns.)* script department
Dramaturgin die; ~, ~nen *s.* **Dramaturg**
dramaturgisch 1. *Adj.* dramaturgical; *(gestalterisch)* dramaturgical; dramatic; **die ~e Abteilung** *(Theater)* the literary and artistic director's department; *(Rundfunk, Fernsehen)* the script department. **2.** *adv.* **~ wirkungsvoll in Szene gesetzt** staged effectively; **~ gerechtfertigt** justified on dramaturgical grounds
dran [dran] *Adv. (ugs.)* **a)** *(an einer/eine Sache)* **das Schild bleibt ~:** the sign stays up; **gib noch etwas Mehl ~:** add some more flour; **halt deine Hand mal hier ~:** put your hand on this; **häng das Schild ~!** put the sign up!; **ich komme/kann nicht ~:** I can't reach; **mach doch ein Schild ~:** put a sign up; **b) arm ~ sein** be in a bad way; **gut/schlecht ~ sein** be well off/badly off; *(sich gut/schlecht fühlen)* be well/not very well; **früh/spät ~ sein** be early/late; **an dem Gerücht ist was ~:** there is something in the rumour; **an ihm ist doch nichts ~:** he's got nothing going for him *(coll.)*; *(er ist sehr mager)* there's nothing of him; **ich bin ~** *od. (scherzh.)* **am ~sten** *(ich bin an der Reihe)* it's my turn; I'm next; *(ich werde zur Verantwortung gezogen)* I'll be for the high jump *or (sl.)* for it *(Brit.)*; I'll be under the gun *(Amer.)*; **nicht wissen wie** *od.* **wo man ~ ist** not know where one stands; **nicht wissen wie** *od.* **wo man mit jmdm. ~ ist** not know where one is with sb.; *s. auch:* **daran; dranbleiben; drangeben; dranhängen** *usw.*; **glauben**
Dränage [drɛ'na:ʒə] **die; ~, ~n** *(auch Med.)* drainage
dran|bleiben *unr. itr. V.; mit sein (ugs.) (am Telefon)* hold *or (coll.)* hang on; *(an der Arbeit)* stick at it *(coll.)*; **am Gegner/an der Arbeit ~:** stick to one's opponent *(coll.)*/stick at one's work *(coll.)*; *s. auch* **dran a**
drang [draŋ] *1. u. 3. Pers. Sg. Prät. v.* **dringen**
Drang der; ~[e]s, Dränge ['drɛŋə] **a)** *(Antrieb)* urge; **ein ~ nach Bewegung/Freiheit** an urge to move/be free; **b)** *o. Pl. (Bedrängnis)* pressure
dränge ['drɛŋə] *1. u. 3. Pers. Sg. Konjunktiv II v.* **dringen**
dran-: ~|geben *unr. tr. V.* give up ⟨*time*⟩; give, sacrifice ⟨*one's life*⟩; *s. auch* **dran a; ~|gehen** *unr. itr. V.; mit sein (ugs.)* **a)** *(berühren)* touch; **b)** *(in Angriff nehmen)* **~gehen, etw. zu tun** get down to doing sth.
Drängelei die; ~, ~en *(abwertend)* **a)** pushing [and shoving]; **hören Sie doch mit Ihrer ~ auf** stop pushing [and shoving]; **b)** *(mit Wünschen, Bitten)* pestering
drängeln ['drɛŋl̩n] *(ugs.)* **1.** *itr. V.* **a)** *(schieben)* push [and shove]; **b)** *(auf jmdn. einreden)* go on *(coll.)*; **zum Aufbruch ~:** go on about it being time to leave *(coll.)*. **2.** *tr. V.* **a)** *(schieben)* push; shove; **b)** *(einreden auf)* pester; go on at *(coll.)*. **3.** *refl. V.* **sich nach vorn/durch die Menge** *usw.* **~:** push one's way to the front/through the crowd *etc.*; **sich danach ~, etw. zu tun** *(fig.)* fall over oneself to do sth. *(coll.)*
drängen ['drɛŋən] **1.** *itr. V.* **a)** *(schieben)*

push; **die Menge drängte zum Ausgang** the crowd pressed towards the exit; **b)** *(fordern)* demand; **auf etw.** *(Akk.)* **~:** press for sth.; **zum Aufbruch ~:** insist that it is/was time to leave; **zur Eile ~:** hurry us/them *etc.* up; **darauf ~, daß ...:** insist that ...; **c) die Zeit drängt** time is pressing; **~de Fragen/Probleme** pressing *or* urgent questions/problems; **d)** *(Sport)* press *or* push forward. **2.** *tr. V.* **a)** *(schieben)* push; **b)** *(antreiben)* press; urge; **jmdn. zur Bezahlung ~:** press sb. to pay; **es drängt mich, Ihnen zu sagen, daß ...:** I feel I have to *or* must tell you that ... **3.** *refl. V.* ‹*visitors, spectators, etc.*› crowd, throng; ‹*crowd*› throng; **sich nach vorn/durch die Menge ~:** push one's way to the front/through the crowd; **sich in den Vordergrund ~** *(fig.)* make oneself the centre of attention

Dränger der; ~s, ~ *s.* **Stürmer b**

Drängerei die; ~, ~en *(abwertend)* pushing [and shoving]

Drangsal ['draŋza:l] **die; ~, ~e** *(geh.)* *(Not)* hardship; *(Qual)* suffering

drangsalieren *tr. V.* *(abwertend)* *(quälen)* torment; *(plagen)* plague

dran-: ~|halten *unr. refl. V.* *(ugs.)* get a move on *(coll.)*; *s. auch* **dran a; ¹~|hängen** *(ugs.)* **1.** *tr. V.* **a)** *(aufwenden)* **viel Zeit/Geld ~hängen** put a lot of time/money into it; **b)** *(anschließen)* **ein paar Tage an seinen Urlaub ~:** add a few days on to one's holiday *(Brit.)* *or* *(Amer.)* vacation; **2.** *refl. V.* *(verfolgen)* stay *or* *(coll.)* stick close behind; *s. auch* **dran a; ²~|hängen** *unr. itr. V.* **da hängt noch viel Arbeit dran** it still needs a lot of work

dränieren [drɛ'ni:rən] *tr. V.* *(auch Med.)* drain

dran-: ~|kommen *unr. itr. V.*; *mit sein* *(ugs.)* have one's turn; *(beim Spielen)* have one's turn *or* go; **ich kam als erste/erster ~:** it was my turn first; *(beim Arzt, Zahnarzt usw.)* I was the first one; **wer kommt jetzt ~?** who's next?; **jeder von uns kommt mal ~** *(verhüll.)* we've all got to go some time; **ich bin heute in Latein ~gekommen** *(aufgerufen worden)* I got picked on to answer in Latin today *(coll.)*; *s. auch* **dran a; ~|kriegen** *tr. V.* *(ugs.)* **jmdn. ~kriegen** get sb.; *(zum Arbeiten bringen)* get sb. at it *(coll.)*; **~|machen** *refl. V.* *(ugs.)* **sich ~machen, etw. zu tun** get down to doing sth.; **wenn sich die Kinder ~machen, ist der Kuchen gleich weg** once the children get started on it the cake won't last long; *s. auch* **dran a; ~|nehmen** *unr. tr. V.* *(ugs.)* *(beim Friseur usw.)* see to; *(beim Arzt)* see; **jmdn. ~nehmen** *(in der Schule)* pick on sb. [to answer]; **~|setzen** *(ugs.)* **1.** *tr. V.* *(einsetzen)* **seine ganze Kraft ~setzen, etw. zu erreichen** put all one's energy into achieving sth.; **alles ~setzen** put everything into it; make every effort; **2.** *refl. V.* *(beginnen)* get down to it

dransten ['dranstn̩] *s.* **dran b**

dran|wollen *unr. itr. V.* *(ugs.)* want [to have] a turn; *(beim Spielen)* want [to have] a turn *or* go

Draperie [drapə'ri:] **die; ~, ~n** *(veralt.)* drapery

drapieren [dra'pi:rən] *tr. V.* drape

Dräsine *s.* **Draisine**

Drastik ['drastɪk] **die; ~** *(eines Witzes, Schwanks)* crude explicitness; *(eines Berichts usw.)* graphicness

drastisch 1. *Adj.* **a)** crudely explicit ‹*joke, story, etc.*›; graphic ‹*report, account*›; **b)** *(empfindlich spürbar)* drastic ‹*measure, means*›. **2.** *adv.* **a)** *(grob)* with crude explicitness; *(deutlich)* graphically; **b)** *(einschneidend)* drastically; ‹*punish*› severely

drauf [drauf] *Adv.* *(ugs.)* on it; **da wäre ich nie ~ gekommen** I would never have thought of that; **da lege ich keinen Wert ~:** it's not important to me; **da zeigt sich, wer was ~ hat** that'll show who can and who can't; **da kannst du mal zeigen, was du ~ hast** here's your chance to show what you can do; **die Rolle/die dollsten Sprüche/90 Sachen ~ haben** have *or* know the part off pat *(Brit.)* *or* *(Amer.)* have the part down pat/have the most amazing patter/be doing 90; **~ und dran sein, etw. zu tun** be just about to do *or* be on the verge of doing sth.; **halt mal den Finger hier ~:** put your finger on here; **ich kriege den Deckel nicht ~:** I can't get the lid on; **der Deckel geht nicht ~:** the lid won't go on; **mach einen neuen Deckel ~:** put a new lid on [it]; *s. auch* **darauf a–e; draufgehen; draufhalten** *usw.*; **scheißen**

drauf-, Drauf-: ~|bekommen *unr. tr. V.* *(ugs.)* *in* **eins ~bekommen** *(gescholten werden)* get it in the neck *(coll.)*; *(geschlagen werden)* get a smack; **~gänger der** daredevil; *(veralt.: Frauenheld)* lady-killer; **~gängerisch** *Adj.* daring; audacious; **~gängertum das; ~s** daredevilry; **~|geben** *unr. tr. V.* *(ugs.)* **a)** *(dazugeben)* **etw./was ~geben** add sth./add a bit on; **b)** *in* **jmdm. eins ~geben** *(schlagen)* give sb. a smack; *(zurechtweisen)* put sb. in his/her place; **c)** *(österr.: als Zugabe)* **etw. ~geben** play/sing/dance *etc.* sth. as an encore; **~|gehen** *unr. itr. V.*; *mit sein* *(ugs.)* **a)** *(umkommen)* kick the bucket *(sl.)*; **b)** *(verbraucht werden)* go; **für etw. ~gehen** ‹*money*› go on sth.; **für diese Sitzungen geht immer viel Zeit drauf** these meetings always take up a lot of time; **c)** *(entzweigehen)* get busted *(coll.)* *or* broken; **~|halten** *unr. itr. V.* *(ugs.)* shoot; **~halten und abdrücken** aim and fire; **~|hauen** *unr. itr. V.* *(ugs.)* **mein Arm tut noch weh, da darfst du nicht ~hauen** my arm still hurts, you're not to bash it; **einen ~hauen** have a booze-up *(Brit. coll.)*; go on a binge *(sl.)*; **~|kommen** *unr. itr. V.*; *mit sein* *(ugs.)* **jmdm. ~kommen** get on to sb.; **jmdm. ~kommen, daß er etw. tut** catch sb. doing sth.; *s. auch* **drauf; ~kriegen** *tr. V.* *(ugs.)* **eins ~kriegen** *(zu einem Kind: geschlagen werden)* get smacked; *(besiegt werden)* get a thrashing; **~|legen** *(ugs.)* **1.** *tr. V.* **150 DM/noch etwas ~legen** fork out *(sl.)* an extra 150 marks/a bit more; **2.** *itr. V.* lay out *(sl.)*; **ich lege dabei noch ~:** it's costing me money; *s. auch* **drauf**

drauf·los *Adv.* **nichts wie ~!** go on!

drauflos-: ~|arbeiten *itr. V.* work away; *(anfangen zu arbeiten)* get straight down to work; **~|gehen** *unr. itr. V.*; *mit sein* *(ugs.)* get going; **~|reden** *itr. V.* talk away; *(anfangen zu reden)* start talking away; **~|schimpfen** *itr. V.* *(ugs.)* curse away; *(anfangen zu schimpfen)* start cursing away; **~|wirtschaften** *itr. V.* *(ugs. abwertend)* splash out money right, left, and centre *(Brit. coll.)*; throw one's money around

drauf-: ~|machen *tr. V.* **einen ~machen** *(ugs.)* paint the town red; **~|stehen** *unr. itr. V.* *(ugs.)* be on it; **~|zahlen** *(ugs.)* **1.** *tr. V.* **noch etwas/1250 DM ~zahlen** fork out *(sl.)* *or* pay a bit more/an extra 1,250 marks; **2.** *itr. V.* *(Unkosten haben)* **ich zahle dabei noch ~:** it's costing me money; **diejenige sein, die immer nur ~zahlt** *(fig.)* be the one who makes all the sacrifices

draus [draus] *Adv.* *(ugs.)* *s.* **daraus**

draußen ['drausn̩] *Adv.* **a)** *(außerhalb)* outside; **hier/da ~:** out here/there; **~ vor der Tür** at the door; **nach/von ~:** outside/from outside; **„Hunde müssen ~ bleiben"** 'no dogs[, please]'; **bleib ~:** stay outside; **~ auf dem Land** *(fig.)* out in the country; **b)** *(irgendwo)* out there; **da/hier ~:** out there/here; **weit/weiter ~:** far/further out; **~ in der Welt** *(fig.)* in the world outside

drechseln ['drɛksl̩n] *tr. V.* turn; *(fig. iron.)* compose ‹*statement*›; turn ‹*phrase, verse*›

Drechsler der; ~s, ~: turner

Drechsler-: ~arbeit die piece of turned work; **~arbeiten** [pieces *pl.* of] turned work *sing.*; **~bank die** lathe

Drechslerei die; ~, ~en turner's workshop; turnery

Drechslerin die; ~, ~nen *s.* **Drechsler**

Dreck [drɛk] **der; ~[e]s a)** *(ugs.)* dirt; *(sehr viel/ekelerregend)* filth; *(Schlamm)* mud; *(Kot)* mess; muck; **in den ~ fallen** fall in the dirt/mud/muck; **deine Hände sind schwarz vor ~:** your hands are filthy [dirty]; **vor ~ starren** be covered in dirt; be filthy [dirty]; **~ machen** make a mess; **~ am Stecken haben** have a skeleton in the cupboard *(Brit.)* *or* *(Amer.)* closet; **aus dem [gröbsten] ~ [heraus] sein** *(ugs.)* be over the worst; **jmdn. aus dem ~ ziehen** *(ugs.)* take sb. out of the gutter; **etw. in den ~ ziehen** *od.* **treten** drag sth. through the mud *or* mire; **im ~ stecken/sitzen** *(ugs.)* be in a [real] mess *or* in the mire; **mit ~ und Speck** *(ugs.)* unwashed; **jmdn./etw. mit ~ bewerfen** throw *or* *(coll.)* sling mud at sb./sth.; **b)** *(salopp abwertend: Angelegenheit)* **bei/wegen jedem ~ regt er sich auf** he gets worked up about every piddling little thing *(coll.)*; **mach deinen ~ allein** do it yourself; **kümmere dich um deinen eigenen ~:** mind your own damn business; **ein ~** *od.* **der letzte ~ sein** *(salopp abwertend)* be the lowest of the low; **das geht dich einen ~ an** *(salopp)* none of your damned business *(sl.)*; **er kümmert sich einen ~ darum** *(salopp)* he doesn't give a damn about it; **er hat uns einen ~ zu befehlen** *(salopp)* he's got no damn right to order us around; **jmdn. wie [den letzten] ~ behandeln** *(ugs.)* treat sb. like dirt; **c)** *(salopp abwertend: Zeug)* rubbish *no indef. art.*; junk *no indef. art.*; *(Nahrungsmittel)* junk *no indef. art.*

Dreck-: ~arbeit die *(salopp)* **a)** *(schmutzige Arbeit)* dirty *or* messy work *no indef. art., no pl.*; dirty *or* messy job; **b)** *(minderwertige Arbeit)* dirty *or* menial work *no indef. art., no pl.*; dirty *or* menial job; **~ding das** *(salopp)* **a)** *(schmutziges Ding)* dirty *or* filthy thing; **b)** *(minderwertiges Ding)* damn thing *(coll.)*; **~eimer der** *(südd. ugs.)* rubbish bin; **~fink der** *(salopp)* filthy pig *(coll.)*; *(Kind, das etw. schmutzig macht)* mucky pup *(Brit. coll.)*; **~fleck der** *(ugs.)* stain; dirty mark

dreckig 1. *Adj.* **a)** *(ugs.: schmutzig, ungepflegt, auch fig.)* dirty; *(sehr/ekelerregend schmutzig, auch fig.)* filthy; **mach dich nicht ~:** don't get yourself dirty; **b)** *(salopp abwertend: unverschämt)* cheeky; **c)** *nicht präd.* *(salopp abwertend: gemein)* dirty, filthy ‹*swine etc.*›; foul ‹*crime*›. **2.** *adv.* **a) es geht ihm ~** *(ugs.)* he's in a bad way; **b)** *(salopp abwertend: unverschämt)* cheekily; **~ grinsen** have a cheeky grin on one's face

Dreck-: ~loch *(salopp abwertend)* *(Zimmer)* dump *(coll.)*; *(Wohnung)* dump *(coll.)*; hole *(coll.)*; **~nest das** *(salopp abwertend)* hole *(coll.)*; dump *(coll.)*; **~sack der** *(derb)* bastard *(coll.)*; **der ~sack von Torhüter** that dirty bastard of a goalkeeper; **~sau die** *(derb)* dirty *or* filthy swine; **~schaufel die** *(ugs.)* dustpan; **~schleuder die** *(derb abwertend)* **a)** *(Mundwerk)* foul mouth; **halt deine ~schleuder!** keep your filthy trap shut *(sl.)*; **b)** *(Mensch)* foul-mouth; **~schwein das** *(derb)* dirty *or* filthy swine

Drecks·kerl der *(derb)* dirty *or* filthy swine

Dreck-: ~spatz der a) *(fam.: Kind)* grubby little so-and-so *(coll.)*; *(Kind, das etw. schmutzig macht)* mucky pup *(Brit. coll.)*; **b)** *(ugs.: Ärger erregender Mensch)* filthy so-and-so *(coll.)*; **~wetter das** *(ugs. abwertend)* lousy *(sl.)* *or* filthy weather; **~zeug das** *(ugs. abwertend)* rubbish *no indef. art.*; junk *no indef. art.*; *(Nahrungsmittel)* junk *no indef. art.*

Dreh [dre:] **der; ~s, ~s** *(ugs.)* **a)** *(Einfall, Kunstgriff)* **den ~ heraushaben[, wie man es**

macht] have [got] the knack [of doing it]; **auf/hinter den richtigen ~ kommen** get the knack *or* the hang of it *(coll.)*; **b)** *in* **um den ~:** about that

Dreh-: ~achse die axis [of rotation]; **~arbeiten** *Pl. (Film)* shooting *sing.* **(zu** of); **die ~arbeiten fanden in ... statt** the film was shot in ...; **~bank die** lathe

drehbar 1. *Adj.* revolving *attrib.* ⟨*stand, stage*⟩; swivel *attrib.* ⟨*chair*⟩; **~ sein** revolve/swivel. **2.** *adv.* **~ gelagert** pivoted

Dreh-: ~bewegung die rotary motion; rotation; **sie machte eine rasche ~bewegung** she turned *or* spun round quickly; **~bleistift der** propelling pencil *(Brit.)*; mechanical pencil *(Amer.)*; **~brücke die** swing bridge; **~buch das** screenplay; [film] script; **~buch·autor der** script-writer; *(als Berufsbez.)* screen-writer; script-writer; **~bühne die** revolving stage

drehen 1. *tr. V.* **a)** turn; **du kannst es ~ und wenden, wie du willst** *(fig.)* whichever way you look at it; **b)** *(ugs.: einstellen)* **das Radio laut/leise ~:** turn the radio up/down; **die Flamme klein/die Heizung auf klein ~:** turn the heat/heating down; **c)** *(formen)* twist ⟨*rope, thread*⟩; roll ⟨*cigarette*⟩; make ⟨*pill*⟩ by rolling; **sich** *(Dat.)* **eine [Zigarette] ~:** roll a cigarette; **d)** *(Film)* shoot ⟨*scene*⟩; film ⟨*report*⟩; make, shoot ⟨*film*⟩; ⟨*star*⟩ make ⟨*film*⟩; **e)** *(ugs. abwertend: beeinflussen)* **es so ~, daß ...:** work it so that ... *(sl.)*; **daran ist nichts zu ~ und zu deuteln** there are no two ways about it; **f)** *(ugs. abwertend: anstellen)* **etwas ~:** get up to sth.; *s. auch* **[2]Ding a, krumm, Mangel, Nase, Runde, Strick, Wolf. 2.** *itr. V.* **a)** *(Richtung ändern)* ⟨*car*⟩ turn; ⟨*wind*⟩ change, shift; **b) an etw.** *(Dat.)* **~:** turn sth.; *(spielend, aus Langeweile)* twiddle sth.; **am Radio ~:** turn/twiddle a knob/knobs on the radio; **da muß einer dran gedreht haben** *(salopp)* somebody must have fiddled about *or* messed around with it; **c)** *(Film)* shoot [a/the film]; film. **3.** *refl. V.* **a)** turn; ⟨*wind*⟩ change, shift; *(um eine Achse)* turn; rotate; revolve; *(um einen Mittelpunkt)* revolve **(um** around); *(sehr schnell)* spin; **sie drehten sich im Tanz** they spun around; **mir dreht sich alles** *(ugs.)* everything's going round and round; **sich auf den Bauch ~:** turn over on to one's stomach; **b)** *(ugs.: zum Gegenstand haben)* **sich um etw. ~:** be about sth.; **es dreht sich darum, daß ...:** it's about the fact that ...; **alles dreht sich um ihn** everything revolves around him; *(er steht im Mittelpunkt des Interesses)* he is the centre of attention; **c)** *(österr. ugs.: aufbrechen)* push off *(sl.)*

Dreher der; ~s, ~ a) *(Beruf)* lathe-operator; **b)** *(Tanz) Austrian folk dance, similar to the Ländler*

Dreherin die; ~, ~nen *s.* **Dreher a**

Dreh-: ~feld das *(Elektrot.)* rotating field; **~impuls der** *(Physik)* angular momentum; **~kolben·motor der** rotary engine; **~kran der** revolving *or* slewing crane; **~kreuz das** turnstile; **~maschine die** lathe; **~moment das** *(Physik)* torque; **~orgel die** barrel-organ; **~ort der** *(Film)* location; **~pause die** *(Film)* break in shooting; **~punkt der** pivot; *(eines Sturms)* centre; **der ~- und Angelpunkt einer Sache** *(fig.)* the key element in sth.; **~restaurant das** revolving restaurant; **~schalter der** rotary switch; **~scheibe die** *(Eisenb.)* turntable; *(fig.)* hub; **~strom der** *(Elektrot.)* three-phase current; **~stuhl der** swivel chair; **~tag der** *(Film)* day of shooting; **~tür die** revolving door

Drehung die; ~, ~en a) turn; *(um eine Achse)* turn; rotation; revolution; *(um einen Mittelpunkt)* revolution; *(sehr schnell)* spin; *(beim Motor)* revolution; **eine halbe/ganze ~:** a half/complete turn; **eine ~ um 180° [machen]** [do] a 180° turn; *(fig.)* [do] a complete about-face; **b)** *(das Drehen)* turning; *(sehr schnell)* spinning

Dreh-: ~wurm der a) *in* **einen** *od.* **den ~wurm kriegen/haben** *(salopp)* get/feel giddy; **b)** *(Finne)* coenurus; **~zahl die** revolutions *or (coll.)* revs *(esp. per minute)*; **bei einer bestimmten ~zahl** at a particular number of revolutions *or (coll.)* revs per minute; **~zahl·bereich der: im unteren/oberen ~zahlbereich** at lower/higher revs *(coll.)*; **~zahl·messer der** revolution counter; rev counter *(coll.)*; tachometer

drei *Kardinalz.* three; **er ißt/arbeitet für ~:** he eats enough for three/does the work of three people; **aller guten Dinge sind ~!** all good things come in threes; *(nach zwei mißglückten Versuchen)* third time lucky!; **nicht bis ~ zählen können** *(ugs.)* be as thick as two [short] planks *(Brit. coll.)*; be dead from the neck up *(coll.)*; *s. auch* **[1]acht; heilig a**

Drei die; ~, ~en three; **eine ~ schreiben/bekommen** *(Schulw.)* get a C; *s. auch* **[1]Acht a, b, d, e; Zwei b**

drei-, Drei-: ~achser der *(ugs.)* three-axled vehicle; **~achtel takt der** *(Musik)* three-eight time; **~ad[e]rig** *Adj. (Elektrot.)* three-core; **~akter der** three-act play; **~bändig** *Adj.* three-volume; **~bein das** *(ugs.)* three-legged stool; **~beinig** *Adj.* three-legged; **~bett·zimmer das** room with three beds; **~blättrig** *Adj. (Bot.)* three-leaved; trifoliate *(Bot.)*

3-D-Brille [draiˈdeː-] **die** 3-D glasses *pl.*

3-D-Effekt der 3-D effect

drei-, Drei-: ~dimensional 1. *Adj.* three-dimensional; **2.** *adv.* three-dimensionally; in three dimensions; **einen Film ~dimensional sehen** watch a film in 3-D; **~eck das; ~s, ~e a)** *(Geom.)* triangle; **das Goldene ~eck** the Golden Triangle; **b)** *(bes. Fußball)* top corner; **~eckig** *Adj.* triangular; three-cornered; **~ecks·verhältnis das** eternal triangle; **~ein·halb** *Bruchz.* three and a half; **~einig** *Adj. in* **der ~einige Gott** *(christl. Rel.)* the triune God[head]; **~einigkeit die** *(christl. Rel.)* trinity; **die Heilige ~einigkeit** the [Holy] Trinity

Dreier der; ~s, ~ a) *(ugs.) s.* **Drei; b)** *(ugs.: im Lotto)* three winning numbers; **c)** *(hist.: Münze)* three-pfennig piece; **d)** *(Golf)* threesome; **e)** *(ugs.: Sprungbrett)* three-metre board; *s. auch* **Achter c, d**

Dreier-: ~kombination die *(Ski)* Alpine combined event; **~reihe die** row of three; **~takt der** *(Musik)* triple time

dreierlei *Gattungsz.; indekl.* **a)** *attr.* three kinds *or* sorts of; three different ⟨*sorts, kinds, sizes, possibilities*⟩; **b)** *subst.* three [different] things

drei-, Drei-: ~fach *Vervielfältigungsz.* triple; **die ~fache Menge** three times *or* triple the amount; three times as much; **ein ~fach[es] Hoch!** three cheers!; **ein ~fach verschnürtes Paket** a parcel tied three times; **~fach verstärkt** triple reinforced; *s. auch* **achtfach; ~fache das;** *adj. Dekl.* **das ~fache essen/kosten** eat/cost three times as much; **das ~fache von 3 ist 9** three times three is nine; **auf ein ~faches** *od.* **auf das ~fache steigen** treble; triple; *s. auch* **Achtfache; ~faltigkeit** [-ˈ---] **die; ~** *(christl. Rel.)* Trinity; **~farben·druck** [-ˈ---] **der a)** *o. Pl. (Verfahren)* three-colour process; **im ~farbendruck [gedruckt]** printed by the three-colour process; **b)** *(einzelner Druck)* three-colour print; **~felder·wirtschaft** [-ˈ----] **die;** *o. Pl.* three-field *or* three-course system; **~fuß der a)** *(für Kessel usw.)* trivet; tripod; **b)** *(Schemel)* three-legged stool; **c)** *(zum Besohlen)* three-way last; **~gang·schaltung die** three-speed gearbox *or* gears *pl. or (Amer.)* gear-shift; **~gespann das** team of three horses; *(fig.: von Direktoren o. ä.)* triumvirate; **eine Kutsche mit ~gespann** a three-horse carriage; **das unzertrennliche ~gespann** *(fig.)* the inseparable trio *or* threesome; **~gestrichen** *Adj. (Musik)* **das ~gestrichene C** the C two octaves above middle C; **~gestrichene Oktave** three-line octave; **~groschen·heft** [-ˈ---] **das** *(abwertend)* cheap novelette; dime novel *(Amer.)*

Dreiheit die; ~: trinity

drei-, Drei-: ~hundert *Kardinalz.* three hundred; **~jährig** *Adj. (3 Jahre alt)* three-year-old *attrib.*; *(3 Jahre dauernd)* three-year *attrib.*; *s. auch* **achtjährig; ~jährlich 1.** *Adj.* three-yearly; triennial; **2.** *adv.* every three years; triennially; *s. auch* **achtjährlich; ~kampf der** *(Sport)* triathlon; **~kantig** *Adj.* three-sided; triangular; **~kantstahl der** *(Technik)* triangular section steel [rod]; **~käse·hoch** [-ˈ---] **der; ~s, ~s** *(ugs. scherzh.)* [little] nipper *(Brit. sl.)*; little kid *(sl.)*; **~klang der** triad; **~klassen·wahlrecht** [-ˈ----] **das** *(hist.)* three-class franchise; **~könige** [-ˈ---] *Pl.; o. Art.* Epiphany *sing.*; **an** *od.* **zu/nach ~könige** at/after Epiphany; **~köpfig** *Adj.* ⟨*family, crew*⟩ of three; three-headed ⟨*monster*⟩; **~länder·eck** [-ˈ---] **das; ~s, ~e** *region where three countries meet*; **~mal** *Adv.* three times; *s. auch* **achtmal; ~malig** *Adj.; nicht präd.* **eine ~malige Warnung/Wiederholung** three warnings/repeats; *s. auch* **achtmalig; ~meilen·zone** [-ˈ----] **die** three-mile zone; **~meter·brett** [-ˈ---] **das** three-metre board

drein *(ugs.) s.* **darein**

drein-: ~|blicken *itr. V.* **mürrisch** *usw.* **~blicken** look morose *etc.*; **~|finden** *unr. refl. V. (ugs.)* get used to things; **~|reden** *itr. V. (ugs.)* **jmdm. ~reden** *(sich einmischen)* interfere in sb.'s affairs; *(jmdm. Vorschriften machen)* tell sb. what to do; **~|schauen** *itr. V. s.* **~blicken; ~|schlagen** *unr. itr. V. (ugs.)* lay into him/her/them *etc. (coll.)*

drei-, Drei-: ~phasen·strom [-ˈ---] **der** *(Elektrot.)* three-phase current; **~polig** *Adj. (Elektrot.)* three-core ⟨*cable*⟩; three-pin ⟨*adapter*⟩; **~punkt·gurt der** lap and diagonal belt; **~rad das a)** *(Kinderfahrrad)* tricycle; **b)** *(Kleintransporter)* three-wheeled van; **~räd[e]rig** *Adj.* three-wheeled; **~satz der, ~satz·rechnung die;** *o. Pl.* rule of three; **~schiffig** *Adj. (Archit.)* with a nave and two aisles *postpos.*; **~seitig** *Adj.* three-sided ⟨*figure*⟩; three-page ⟨*letter, leaflet, etc.*⟩; **~sekunden·regel** [-ˈ----] **die** *(Sport)* three-second rule; **~silbig** *Adj.* trisyllabic; three-syllable *attrib.*; **~spaltig** *(Druckw.)* **1.** *Adj.* three-column; *s. auch* **achtspaltig; 2.** *adv.* ⟨*printed, set*⟩ in three columns; **~spänner der; ~s, ~:** three-horse carriage; **~spitz der** *(hist.)* tricorn; three-cornered hat; **~sprachig 1.** *Adj.* trilingual; **2.** *adv.* **a) ~sprachig erzogen werden** be brought up speaking three languages; **b)** ⟨*written*⟩ in three languages; *s. auch* **zweisprachig; ~sprung der** triple jump

dreißig [ˈdraisɪç] *Kardinalz.* thirty; *s. auch* **achtzig**

Dreißig die; ~: thirty

dreißiger *indekl. Adj.; nicht präd.* **ein ~ Jahrgang** a '3'30 vintage; **die ~ Jahre** the thirties

[1]Dreißiger der; ~s, ~ *(30jähriger)* thirty-year-old; *s. auch* **[1]Achtziger b, c**

[2]Dreißiger die; ~, ~ *(ugs.)* **a)** *(Briefmarke)* thirty-pfennig/schilling *etc.* stamp; **b)** *(Zigarre)* thirty-pfennig cigar

[3]Dreißiger *Pl.* thirties; **eine Frau in den ~n** a woman in her thirties

dreißig-, Dreißig-: ~jährig *Adj. (30 Jahre alt)* thirty-year-old *attrib.*; *(30 Jahre dauernd)* thirty-year *attrib.*; **der Dreißigjährige Krieg** the Thirty Years' War; *s. auch* **achtjährig; ~jährige der/die;** *adj. Dekl.* thirty-year-old; **~pfennig·marke** [-ˈ----] **die** thirty-pfennig stamp

dreißigst... ['draisıçst...] *Ordinalz.* thirtieth; *s. auch* **acht...; achtzigst...**

Dreißigstel das; ~s, ~: thirtieth

dreist [draist] **1.** *Adj.* brazen; barefaced ⟨*lie*⟩. **2.** *adv.* brazenly

drei·stellig *Adj.* three-figure *attrib.* ⟨*number, sum*⟩; *s. auch* **achtstellig**

Dreistigkeit die; ~, ~en a) *o. Pl. (Art)* brazenness; **er besaß die ~, zu ...:** he had the audacity *or* cheek to ...; **b)** *(Handlung)* brazen act; *(Bemerkung)* brazen remark

drei-, Drei-: ~stimmig 1. *Adj.* ⟨*song*⟩ for three voices; three-voice ⟨*choir*⟩; three-part ⟨*singing*⟩; **2.** *adv.* ⟨*sing*⟩ in three voices; ⟨*play*⟩ in three parts; **~stöckig 1.** *Adj.* three-storey *attrib.; s. auch* **achtstöckig; 2.** *adv.* ⟨*build*⟩ three storeys high; **~stufen·rakete** [-'-----] **die** three-stage rocket; **~stündig** *Adj.* three-hour *attrib.; s. auch* **achtstündig; ~stündlich 1.** *Adj.* three-hourly; **2.** *adv.* every three hours; **~tägig** *Adj. (3 Tage alt)* three-day-old *attrib.; (3 Tage dauernd)* three-day *attrib.; s. auch* **achttägig; ~täglich 1.** *Adj.* **in ~täglichem Wechsel** on a three-day rota; **2.** *adv.* every three days; **~tausend** *Kardinalz.* three thousand; **~tausender der** mountain more than three thousand metres high; **~teilig** *Adj.* three-part *attrib.* ⟨*documentary, novel, etc.*⟩; three-piece *attrib.* ⟨*suit*⟩; **~teilig sein** be in three parts/consist of three pieces; **~viertel** *Bruchz.* three-quarters; **~viertel Liter/eine ~viertel Stunde** three-quarters of a litre/of an hour; **die Flasche ist ~viertel leer** the bottle is three-quarters empty; *s. auch* **¹acht; Viertel a; ~viertel·lang** [-'---] *Adj.* three-quarter-length; **~viertel·liter·flasche** [---'----] **die** three-quarter-litre bottle; **~viertel·mehrheit** [-'----] **die** three-quarters majority; **~viertel·stunde** [---'--] **die** three-quarters of an hour; **~viertel·takt** [-'---] **der** three-four time; **im ~vierteltakt** in three-four time; **~wege·katalysator der** *(Kfz-W.)* three-way catalytic converter; **~wertig** *Adj.* **a)** *(Chemie)* trivalent; **b)** *(Sprachw.)* three-place *attrib.;* **~wöchentlich 1.** *Adj.* three-weekly; **2.** *adv.* every three weeks; *s. auch* **achtwöchentlich; ~wöchig** *Adj. (3 Wochen alt)* three-week-old *attrib.; (3 Wochen dauernd)* three-week *attrib.;* **~zack der; ~s, ~e** trident; **~zackig** *Adj.* three-pointed; **~zehn** *Kardinalz.* thirteen; **jetzt schlägt's aber ~!** *(ugs.)* that's going too far; *s. auch* **achtzehn; ~zehntel das** thirteenth; **~zeilig** *Adj.* three-line *attrib.;* **~zeilig sein** have three lines; **~zimmer·wohnung die** three-room flat *(Brit.) or (Amer.)* apartment

Dresche ['drɛʃə] **die; ~** *(salopp)* walloping *(sl.);* thrashing; **~ kriegen** get a walloping *(sl.) or* thrashing

dreschen 1. *unr. tr. V.* **a)** thresh; **b)** *(salopp: prügeln)* wallop *(sl.);* thrash; **c)** *(salopp: schießen)* wallop *(sl.)* ⟨*ball*⟩; **den Ball ins Netz ~:** slam the ball into the net *(coll.); s. auch* **Skat. 2.** *unr. itr. V.* **a)** thresh; **b)** *(salopp: schlagen)* thump; bang; **mit der Faust auf den Tisch ~:** bang one's fist on the table; pound *or* bang the table with one's fist

Drescher der; ~s, ~: thresher

Dresch-: ~flegel der flail; **~maschine die** threshing-machine

Dresden ['dre:sdn̩] **(das); ~s** Dresden

Dresd[e]ner ['dre:sd(ə)nɐ] **1.** *Adj.; nicht präd.* Dresden. **2. der; ~s, ~:** native of Dresden; *(Einwohner)* inhabitant of Dresden; *s. auch* **Kölner**

Dreß [drɛs] **der; ~** *od.* **Dresses, Dresse;** *(österr. auch* **die; ~, Dressen) a)** *(Sportkleidung)* kit *(Brit.); (Fußball, Hockey usw.)* kit *(Brit.);* strip *(Brit. coll.);* **b)** *(ugs.: Kleidung)* outfit

Dresseur [drɛ'sø:ɐ̯] **der; ~s, ~e** [animal-]trainer

dressierbar *Adj.* trainable; **nicht/gut ~:** untrainable/easy to train

dressieren *tr. V.* **a)** train ⟨*animal*⟩; **darauf dressiert sein, etw. zu tun** be trained to do sth.; **der Hund ist auf den Mann dressiert** the dog is trained to attack people; **b)** *(Kochk.)* dress ⟨*poultry, fish, game*⟩; decorate ⟨*cake etc.*⟩; pipe ⟨*icing, marzipan, etc.*⟩

Dressing ['drɛsıŋ] **das; ~s, ~s** dressing

Dressman ['drɛsmən] **der; ~s, Dressmen** male model

Dressur [drɛ'su:ɐ̯] **die; ~, ~en a)** training; *(fig. abwertend)* conditioning; **b)** *(Kunststück)* trick; **c)** *(Dressurreiten)* dressage

Dressur-: ~pferd das dressage horse; **~prüfung die** *(Reiten)* dressage [test]; **~reiten das** dressage

dribbeln ['drıbl̩n] *itr. V. (Ballspiele)* dribble [the ball]

Dribbling ['drıblıŋ] **das; ~s, ~s** *(Ballspiele)* piece of dribbling; **seine Stärken sind Kopfball und ~:** his strengths are heading and dribbling

Drift [drıft] *s.* **Trift a**

driften *itr. V.; mit sein (auch fig.)* drift

¹Drill [drıl] **der; ~[e]s** drilling; *(Milit.)* drill

²Drill der; ~s, ~e *s.* **Drillich**

Drill·bohrer der drill

drillen *tr. V.* **a)** *(auch Milit.)* drill; **auf etw.** *(Akk.)* **gedrillt sein** be well-drilled in sth.; **jmdn. auf Angriff ~:** train sb. to attack; **b)** *(Landw.)* drill; **c)** *(bohren)* drill ⟨*hole*⟩

Drillich ['drılıç] **der; ~s, ~e** drill

Drillich·zeug das [heavy cotton twill] overalls *pl.*

Drilling ['drılıŋ] **der; ~s, ~e a)** *(Geschwister)* triplet; **b)** *(Gewehr)* triple-barrelled shotgun

Drill·maschine die *(Landw.)* drill

drin [drın] *Adv.* **a)** *(ugs.: darin)* in it; **da könnte für mich was ~ sein** something might come out of it [for me]; **das/mehr als 2000 DM ist nicht ~:** that/any more than 2,000 marks is not on *(Brit. coll.) or (Amer. coll.)* is no go; **es ist noch alles ~** *(bei einem Fußballspiel usw.)* there's still everything to play for; **nach drei Tagen ist man wieder ~** *(wieder eingearbeitet)* after three days you're back in the swing of things; *s. auch* **darin; b)** *(ugs.: drinnen)* inside; **hier/da ~:** in here/there; *s. auch* **drinnen**

dringen ['drıŋən] *unr. itr. V.* **a)** *mit sein (gelangen)* ⟨*water, smell, etc.*⟩ penetrate, come through; ⟨*news*⟩ get through; **in etw.** *(Akk.)* **~:** get into *or* penetrate sth.; **durch etw. ~:** come through *or* penetrate sth.; ⟨*person*⟩ push one's way through sth.; **die Nachricht ist nicht bis zu mir gedrungen** the news did not get through to me; **in** *od.* **an die Öffentlichkeit ~:** get out; become public knowledge; **b)** *mit sein (geh.: einwirken)* **in jmdn. ~:** press *or* urge sb.; **mit Fragen/Ermahnungen in jmdn. ~:** ply sb. with questions/press warnings on sb.; **sich gedrungen fühlen, etw. zu tun** *(veralt.)* feel obliged *or* compelled to do sth.; **c)** *(fordern)* **auf etw.** *(Akk.)* **~:** insist upon sth.

dringend 1. *Adj.* **a)** *(eilig)* urgent; **b)** *(eindringlich, stark)* urgent ⟨*appeal*⟩; strong ⟨*suspicion, advice*⟩; compelling ⟨*need*⟩. **2.** *adv.* **a)** *(sofort)* urgently; **b)** *(zwingend)* ⟨*recommend, advise, suspect*⟩ strongly; **jmdn. ~ bitten, etw. zu tun** insist that sb. does sth.; **~ erforderlich sein** be imperative *or* essential

dringlich ['drıŋlıç] **1.** *Adj.* urgent. **2.** *adv.* urgently; **jmdn. ~ bitten, etw. zu tun** plead hard with sb. to do sth.

Dringlichkeit die; ~: urgency

Dringlichkeits·antrag der *(Parl.)* emergency motion

Drink [drıŋk] **der; ~[s], ~s** drink

drinnen ['drınən] *Adv.* inside; *(im Haus)* indoors; inside; **von ~:** from inside/indoors; **nach ~ gehen** go in[side]/indoors; **~ im Haus** indoors; **hier/da ~:** in here/there

drin-: ~|sitzen *unr. itr. V. (ugs.)* be right in it *(coll.);* **~|stecken** *itr. V. (ugs.)* **a)** *(beschäftigt sein)* **[bis über beide Ohren] in etw.** *(Dat.)* **~stecken** be up to one's ears in sth. *(coll.);* **b)** *(vorhanden sein)* **ich bin überzeugt, daß viel in ihm ~steckt** I am convinced he has a lot in him; **da steckt nichts für dich ~:** there's nothing in it for you; **da steckt viel Arbeit ~:** there's a lot of work in that; **c)** *(voraussehen können)* **da steckt man nicht ~:** there's no [way of] telling; **~|stehen** *unr. itr. V.; südd. auch mit sein* **in etw.** *(Dat.)* **~stehen** be in sth.

dritt [drıt] *in* **wir waren zu ~:** there were three of us; **eine Ehe zu ~:** a ménage à trois; *s. auch* **²acht**

dritt... *Ordinalz.* third; **wer ist der Dritte im Bunde?** who is the third person?; **in Gegenwart Dritter** in the presence of other people; **ein Drittes wäre noch zu erwägen** there is a third point that ought to be considered; **wenn zwei sich streiten, freut sich der Dritte** *(Spr.)* when two people argue, somebody else benefits; **der lachende Dritte** the one to benefit *(from a dispute between two others); s. auch* **acht...**

dritt·best... *Adj.* third-best

Dritteil das; ~s, ~e *(veralt.),* **Drittel das,** *(schweiz. meist* **der); ~s, ~:** third

dritteln *tr. V.* split *or* divide ⟨*cost, profit*⟩ three ways; divide ⟨*number*⟩ by three

drittens *Adv.* thirdly

dritt-, Dritt-: ~größt... *Adj.* third-largest; **~höchst...** *Adj.* third-highest; **~klassig** *Adj. (meist abwertend)* third-class ⟨*hotel, railway carriage*⟩; third-rate ⟨*actor, novel, artist*⟩; **~kläßler der; ~s ~:** third-former; **~letzt...** *Adj.* antepenultimate; **~schuldner der** *(Rechtsw.)* garnishee

Drive [draif] **der; ~s, ~s** *(auch Jazz, Golf, Tennis)* drive

Dr. jur. *Abk.* **doctor juris** LL D; *s. auch* **Dr. phil.**

DRK [de:|ɛr'ka:] **das; ~** *Abk.* **Deutsches Rotes Kreuz** German Red Cross

Dr. med. *Abk.* **doctor medicinae** MD; *s. auch* **Dr. phil.**

Dr. med. dent. *Abk.* **doctor medicinae dentoriae** DMD; *s. auch* **Dr. phil.**

drob [drɔp] *s.* **darob**

droben ['dro:bn̩] *Adv. (südd., österr., sonst geh.)* up there; **da/hier ~:** up there/here

Droge ['dro:gə] **die; ~, ~n** drug; **unter ~n stehen** be on drugs

dröge ['drø:gə] *(nordd.)* **1.** *Adj. (auch fig.)* dry. **2.** *adv.* drily

drogen-, Drogen-: ~abhängig *Adj.* addicted to drugs *postpos.;* **~abhängig sein/werden** be/become a drug addict; **~abhängige der/die;** *adj. Dekl.* drug addict; **~abhängigkeit die** drug addiction; **~handel der** drug trafficking; **~süchtig** *Adj. s.* **~abhängig; ~szene die** drug scene; **~tote der/die** drug-related death

Drogerie [drogə'ri:] **die; ~, ~n** chemist's [shop] *(Brit.);* drugstore *(Amer.)*

Drogist der; ~en, ~en, Drogistin die; ~, ~nen chemist *(Brit.);* druggist *(Amer.)*

Droh·brief der threatening letter

drohen ['dro:ən] *itr. V.* threaten; **er drohte ihm mit erhobenem Zeigefinger** he raised a warning finger to him; **jmdm. mit etw. ~:** threaten sb. with sth.; **die Regierung hat mit dem Abbruch der diplomatischen Beziehungen gedroht** the government threatened to break off diplomatic relations; **den Angeklagten droht die Todesstrafe** the accused are threatened with the death penalty; **ein Gewitter drohte** a storm was threatening

drohend 1. *Adj.* impending ⟨*danger, strike, disaster*⟩; threatening ⟨*gesture, clouds*⟩. **2.** *adv.* threateningly

Droh·gebärde die threatening gesture

Drohn [dro:n] **der; ~en, ~en, Drohne die; ~, ~n** drone

dröhnen ['drø:nən] *itr. V.* **a)** ‹*voice, music*› boom; ‹*machine*› roar; ‹*room etc.*› resound (**von** with); **~er Applaus** thunderous applause; **er brach in ~des Gelächter aus** he roared with laughter; **mir dröhnt der Schädel** *(ugs.)* my head's ringing; **b)** *(Drogenjargon: Rausch verursachen)* **das dröhnt** it gives you a high *(sl.)*
Dröhnung die; ~, ~en *(Drogenjargon)* **a)** *(Dosis)* fix *(sl.)*; **b)** *(Rausch)* high *(sl.)*
Drohung die; ~, ~en threat; **eine ~ wahr machen** carry out a threat
drollig ['drɔlɪç] **1.** *Adj.* **a)** *(spaßig)* funny; comical; *(niedlich)* sweet; cute *(Amer.)*; **b)** *(seltsam)* odd; peculiar; **werde nicht ~:** don't get funny. **2.** *adv.* **a)** *(spaßig)* comically; *(niedlich)* sweetly; cutely *(Amer.)*; **b)** *(seltsam)* oddly; peculiarly
Dromedar ['dro:meda:ɐ̯] **das; ~s, ~e** dromedary
Drops [drɔps] **der** *od.* **das; ~, ~:** fruit *or (Brit.)* acid drop; **saurer** *od.* **saures ~:** acid drop *(Brit.)*; sour ball *(Amer.)*
drosch [drɔʃ] *1. u. 3. Pers. Sg. Prät. v.* **dreschen**
Droschke ['drɔʃkə] **die; ~, ~n a)** hackney carriage; **b)** *(veralt.: Taxi)* [taxi-]cab
Droschken-: ~kutscher der hackney coachman; **~platz der** *(Amtsspr.)* taxi-rank
[1]**Drossel** ['drɔsl̩] **die; ~, ~n** thrush
[2]**Drossel die; ~, ~n** *(Technik) s.* **~spule, ~ventil**
Drossel·klappe die *(Technik)* throttle *or* butterfly valve
drosseln *tr. V.* **a)** turn down ‹*heating, air-conditioning*›; throttle back ‹*engine*›; reduce *or* restrict the flow of ‹*steam, air*›; check ‹*flow*›; **b)** *(herabsetzen)* reduce; cut back *or* down; reduce ‹*speed*›
Drossel·spule die *(Elektrot.)* choking coil
Drosselung die; ~, ~en *s.* **drosseln:** turning down; throttling back; reduction *or* restriction of the flow; checking; reduction; cutback
Drossel·ventil das *(Technik)* throttle valve
Dr. phil. *Abk.* **doctor philosophiae** Dr; **~ ~ Hans Schulz** Dr Hans Schulz; Hans Schulz, Ph. D.; **sie ist ~ ~, nicht Dr. med.** she is a Ph. D. *or* a Doctor of Philosophy, not a Doctor of Medicine
Dr. rer. nat. *Abk.* **doctor rerum naturalium** Doctor of Natural Science
Dr. rer. pol. *Abk.* **doctor rerum politicarum** Doctor of Political Science
Dr. theol. *Abk.* **doctor theologiae** DD
drüben ['dry:bn̩] *Adv.* **a) dort** *od.* **da ~:** over there; **~ auf der anderen Seite** over on the other side; **b)** *(in der DDR)* in the East; *(in der Bundesrepublik, in West-Berlin)* in the West; **von ~ kommen** come from across the border/sea *etc.*
drüber ['dry:bɐ] *(ugs.) s.* **darüber**
drüber- *(ugs.) s.* **darüber-**
[1]**Druck** [drʊk] **der; ~[e]s, Drücke** ['drʏkə] **a)** *(Physik)* pressure; **einen ~ im Kopf/Magen haben** *(fig.)* have a feeling of pressure in one's head/stomach; **b)** *o. Pl. (das Drücken)* **ein ~ auf den Knopf** a touch of *or* on the button; **c)** *o. Pl. (Zwang)* pressure; **auf jmdn. ~ ausüben** put pressure on sb.; **unter ~ stehen/handeln** be/act under pressure; **jmdn. unter ~ setzen** put pressure on sb.; **~ dahinter machen** *(ugs.)* put some pressure on; **in** *od.* **im ~ sein** *(ugs.)* be under pressure of time; **d)** *Pl.* **~s** *(Drogenjargon: Injektion)* fix *(sl.)*; **sich** *(Dat.)* **einen ~ setzen** give oneself a fix *(sl.)*
[2]**Druck der; ~[e]s, ~e a)** *o. Pl. (das Drucken)* printing; *(Art des Drucks)* print; **in ~ gehen** go to press; **etw. in ~ geben** send sth. to press; **~ und Verlag Meier & Sohn** printed and published by Meier and son; **im ~ erscheinen** appear in print; **im ~ sein** be being printed; **b)** *(Bild, Graphik usw.)* print; **c)** *Pl.* **~s** *(Textilw.)* print; **d)** *(~schrift)* printed work; **frühe persische ~e** early printed works from Persia
Druck-: ~ab·fall der *(Physik)* drop *or* fall in pressure; **~an·zug der** pressure suit; **~anstieg der** *(Physik)* rise *or* increase in pressure; **~ausgleich der** *(Physik, Med.) (Vorgang)* equalization of pressure; *(Zustand)* balance of pressure; **~blei·stift der** propelling pencil; **~bogen der** printed sheet; **~buchstabe der** block letter *or* capital
Drückeberger ['drʏkəbɛrgɐ] **der; ~s, ~** *(ugs. abwertend)* shirker
Drückebergerei die; ~ *(ugs. abwertend)* shirking
druck·empfindlich *Adj.* pressure-sensitive ‹*material*›; easily bruised ‹*fruit*›; ‹*area of the body*› sensitive to pressure
drucken *tr., itr. V.* print
drücken ['drʏkn̩] **1.** *tr. V.* **a)** *(pressen)* press; press, push ‹*button*›; **jmdm. die Hand ~:** squeeze sb.'s hand; **jmdn. zur Seite/an die Wand ~:** push sb. aside/against the wall; **jmdn. ans Herz** *od.* **an sich** *(Akk.)* **~:** clasp sb. to one's breast; **jmdm. etw. in die Hand ~:** press sth. into sb.'s hand; **b)** *(heraus~)* squeeze ‹*juice, pus*› **(aus** out of); **c)** *(liebkosen)* **jmdn. ~:** hug [and squeeze] sb.; **d)** *(Druck verursachen, quetschen)* ‹*shoe, corset, bandage, etc.*› pinch; **e)** *(geh.: be~)* ‹*conscience*› weigh heavily [up]on sb.; **jmds. Stimmung ~:** depress sb.'s spirits; **f)** *(herabsetzen)* push *or* force down ‹*price, rate*›; depress ‹*sales*›; bring down ‹*standard*›; **den Rekord ~:** beat *or* break the record; **den Rekord um zwei Sekunden ~:** take two seconds off the record; **g)** *(Kartenspiel)* discard; **h)** *(Gewichtheben)* press; **i)** *(Drogenjargon: injizieren)* **sich** *(Dat.)* **einen Schuß ~:** give oneself a fix *(sl.)*. **2.** *itr. V.* **a)** press; **auf den Knopf ~:** press *or* push the button; **„bitte ~":** 'push'; **die Hitze drückt** *od.* **ist drückend** *(fig.)* the heat is oppressive; **das drückte auf die Stimmung/unsere gute Laune** *(fig.)* it spoilt the atmosphere/dampened our spirits; *s. auch* **Tränendrüse; b)** *(Druck verursachen)* ‹*shoe, corset, bandage*› pinch; **der Rucksack drückt** the rucksack is pressing *or* digging into me; **c)** *(herabsetzen)* **auf etw.** *(Akk.)* **~:** push *or* force sth. down; **d)** *(Drogenjargon)* fix *(sl.)*. **3.** *refl. V.* **a) sich in die Ecke ~:** squeeze [oneself] into the corner; **die Kinder drückten sich ängstlich in die Ecke** the children huddled frightened in the corner; **sich aus dem Saal ~:** slip out of the hall; **b)** *(ugs.)* shirk; **sich vor etw.** *(Dat.)* **~:** get out of *or* dodge sth.; **sich vor einer Pflicht/Verantwortung/Aussprache ~:** shirk a duty/responsibility/avoid a frank discussion; **sich vor der Arbeit/ums Bezahlen ~:** get out of *or* avoid doing any work/paying
drückend *Adj.* **a)** burdensome ‹*responsibility*›; grinding ‹*poverty*›; heavy ‹*debt, taxes*›; serious ‹*worries*›; **b)** *(schwül)* oppressive
Drucker der; ~s, ~: printer
Drücker der; ~s, ~ a) *(Tür~)* handle; *(eines Schnappschlosses)* latch; *(Abzug am Gewehr)* trigger; **auf den letzten ~** *(ugs.)* at the very last minute; **b)** *(Knopf)* [push-]button; *(Klingelknopf)* [bell] push; **am ~ sitzen** *od.* **sein** *(fig. ugs.)* be in charge; **c)** *(ugs.: Werber)* hawker of magazine subscriptions; **d)** *(ugs.: Unterton, Nuance)* touch
Druckerei die; ~, ~en printing-works; *(Firma)* printing-house; printer's
Druckerei·arbeiter der print worker
Drucker·farbe die *s.* **Druckfarbe**
Druck·erlaubnis die permission to print; **die ~ verweigern** refuse to allow the book/article *etc.* to be printed
Drucker-: ~presse die *s.* **Druckmaschine; ~schwärze die** printer's *or* printing ink; **~sprache die** printers' terminology; **~zeichen das** printer's mark
druck-, Druck-: ~erzeugnis das piece of printed matter; **~erzeugnisse** printed matter *sing.*; **~fahne die** galley proof; **~farbe die** printer's *or* printing ink; **~fehler der** misprint; printer's error; **~fehler·teufel der** *(scherzh.)* misprint gremlin; **~fertig** *Adj.* ready for press *pred.*; **~fest** *Adj.* pressure-resistant; **~form die** [type-]forme; **~frisch** *Adj.* hot off the press *postpos.*; **~graphik die** *(Kunstwiss.)* graphic reproduction; **~kabine die** pressurized cabin; **~knopf der a)** press-stud *(Brit.)*; snap-fastener; **b)** *(an Geräten)* push-button; **~kosten** *Pl.* printing costs
Drucklegung die; ~, ~en printing; **die ~** *od.* **mit der ~ beginnen** go to press
druck-, Druck-: ~luft die *(Physik)* compressed air; **~luft·bremse die** air brake; **~maschine die** printing-press; **~messer der** *(Physik)* pressure gauge; **~mittel das** means of bringing pressure to bear **(gegenüber** on); **~papier das** printing paper; **~platte die** [printing] plate; **~posten der** *(ugs.)* cushy job *(coll.)*; **~pumpe die** *(Technik)* pressure pump; **~punkt der a)** *(bei Waffen)* first trigger pressure; **b)** *(bei Flugzeugen)* centre of pressure; **~reif 1.** *Adj.* ready for publication; *(~fertig)* ready for press; *(fig.)* polished, perfectly formulated ‹*phrase, reply*›; **2.** *adv.* ‹*speak*› in a polished manner; **~sache die a)** *(Postw.)* printed matter; **b)** *(Druckw.)* printed stationery; **~schrift die a)** block letters *pl.*; **b)** *(Schriftart)* type[-face]; **c)** *(Schriftwerk)* pamphlet
drucksen ['drʊksn̩] *itr. V. (ugs.)* hum and haw *(coll.)*
druck-, Druck-: ~stelle die mark *(where pressure has been applied)*; *(an Obst)* bruise; **die ~stelle von der Zahnklammer** the tender spot where the brace has/had been pressing; **~stock der** block; **~taste die** push-button; **~technisch 1.** *Adj.* printing *attrib.* ‹*process*›; **ein ~technisches Problem** a problem from the point of view of printing. **2.** *adv.* from the point of view of printing; **~type die** type; **~verband der** pressure bandage; **~verfahren das** printing process; **~vorlage die** printer's copy; **~wasser·reaktor der** pressurized-water reactor; **~welle die** *(Physik)* shock wave; **~werk das** publication; printed work; **~wesen das;** *o. Pl.* printing; **~zylinder der** *(Fotoreproduktion)* printing cylinder; *(Offsetdruck)* impression cylinder
Drude ['dru:də] **die; ~, ~n** *(Myth.) nocturnal female spirit that causes nightmares*
Druden·fuß der pentagram
druff [drʊf] *(ugs. landsch.) s.* **drauf**
Druide [dru'i:də] **der; ~n, ~n** *(hist.)* druid
drum [drʊm] *Adv. (ugs.)* **a)** *s.* **darum; b)** [a]round; **um etw. ~ herum** [all] [a]round sth.; **ein Haus mit einem Garten ~:** a house with a garden [a]round it; **~ rumreden** beat about *or (Amer.)* around the bush; **eben ~:** that's precisely why; **sei's ~:** never mind; [that's] too bad; **alles, was ~ und dran ist** *od.* **hängt** all the things that go with it; *(bei einer Sachlage)* all the circumstances; **alles** *od.* **das [ganze] Drum und Dran** *(bei einer Mahlzeit)* all the trimmings; *(bei einer Feierlichkeit)* all the palaver that goes with it *(coll.)*
drum-: *(ugs.) s.* **darum-**
Drum·herum das; ~s everything that goes/went with it
Drummer ['dramɐ] **der; ~s, ~** *(Musik)* drummer
Drums [drams] *Pl. (Musik)* drums; **an den ~:** on [the] drums
drunten ['drʊntn̩] *Adv. (südd., österr.)* down there
drunter ['drʊntɐ] *Adv. (ugs.)* underneath; **es** *od.* **alles geht ~ und drüber** everything is topsy-turvy; things are completely chaotic; **das Drunter und Drüber** the confusion

drunter- *(ugs.) s.* **darunter-**

Drusch [drʊʃ] **der; ~[e]s, ~e a)** threshing; **b)** *(Ertrag)* threshed corn; grain

¹Druse ['dru:zə] **der; ~n, ~n** Druze

²Druse die; ~, ~n a) *(Geol.)* geode; druse; **b)** *(Pferdekrankheit)* strangles *sing.*

Drüse ['dry:zə] **die; ~, ~n** gland

Drüsen-: ~funktion die glandular function; **~schwellung die** glandular swelling

drusisch *Adj.* Druse

DSB [de:|ɛs'be:] **der; ~** *Abk.* **Deutscher Sportbund**

Dschingis-Khan ['dʒɪŋɡɪs'ka:n] **(der)** Genghis Khan

Dschungel ['dʒʊŋl] **der; ~s, ~** *(auch fig.)* jungle; *(von Konflikten, Leidenschaften)* tangle

Dschungel-: ~fieber das jungle yellow fever; **~krieg der** jungle war; *(Kriegsführung)* jungle warfare

Dschunke ['dʒʊŋkə] **die; ~, ~n** junk

DSF [de:|ɛs'ɛf] **die; ~:** *Abk. (DDR)* **Gesellschaft für Deutsch-Sowjetische Freundschaft**

DSG [de:|ɛs'ge:] **die; ~** *Abk.* **Deutsche Schlafwagen- und Speisewagen-Gesellschaft**

dt. *Abk.* **deutsch** G.

Dtzd. *Abk.* **Dutzend** doz.

du [du:] *Personalpron.; 2. Pers. Sg. Nom.* you; thou *(arch.)*; *(in Briefen)* **Du** you; **du zueinander sagen** use the familiar form in addressing one another; say 'du' to each other; **[mit jmdm.] per du sein** be on familiar terms *or* use the familiar form of address [with sb.]; **mit jmdm. auf du und du stehen** be on familiar terms with sb.; **du Glücklicher/Idiot!** you lucky thing/you idiot!; **unser Vater, der du bist im Himmel** *(bibl.)* our Father which art in heaven; **du, ich kann nicht länger warten** [listen,] I can't wait any longer; **du bist es** it's 'you; **mach du das doch** 'you do it; *s. auch (Gen.)* **deiner,** *(Dat.)* **dir,** *(Akk.)* **dich**

Du das; ~[s], ~[s] 'du' *no art.*: the familiar form 'du'; **jmdm. das ~ anbieten** suggest to sb. that he/she use [the familiar form] 'du' *or* the familiar form of address

dual [du'a:l] *Adj.* dual

Dual der; ~s, ~e, Dualis [du'a:lɪs] **der; ~, Duale** *(Sprachw.)* dual

Dualismus der; ~ *(Philos., geh.)* dualism

dualistisch *Adj. (Philos., geh.)* dualistic

Dualität [duali'tɛ:t] **die; ~:** duality

Dual·system das *(Math.)* binary system

Dübel ['dy:bl] **der; ~s, ~:** plug; *(Holz~)* dowel

dübeln *tr. V.* **etw. ~:** fix sth. using a plug/plugs

dubios [du'bio:s], **dubiös** [du'biø:s] *Adj. (geh.)* dubious; **ich finde es ~, daß ...:** I find it suspicious that ...

Dublee [du'ble:] **das; ~s, ~s** rolled gold [plate]

Dublette [du'blɛtə] **die; ~, ~n a)** duplicate; **b)** *(bei Edelsteinen)* doublet; **c)** *(Boxen)* one-two

dublieren [du'bli:rən] *tr. V.* **a)** plate with gold; **b)** *(Spinnerei)* double; ply; **c)** *(Kunstwiss.)* reline

ducken ['dʊkn̩] **1.** *refl. V.* duck; *(fig. abwertend)* humble oneself **(vor** + *Dat.* before); *(vor Angst)* cower; **sich vor jmds. Fäusten ~:** duck to avoid sb.'s fists. **2.** *tr. V.* **a)** duck ‹*head [and shoulders]*›; **b)** *(abwertend) (einschüchtern)* intimidate; *(demütigen)* humiliate. **3.** *itr. V.* humble oneself **(vor** + *Dat.* before)

Duckmäuser ['dʊkmɔyzɐ] **der; ~s, ~** *(abwertend)* moral coward

duckmäuserisch *(abwertend)* **1.** *Adj.* ‹*behaviour etc.*› showing moral cowardice. **2.** *adv.* ‹*behave*› in a way that shows moral cowardice

Duckmäusertum das; ~s *(abwertend)* moral cowardice

Dudelei die; ~, ~en *(ugs. abwertend) (auf einem Blasinstrument)* tootling; *(aus dem Radio, Fernsehen usw.)* drone; droning

Dudel·kasten der *(salopp abwertend) (Radio)* radio; *(Plattenspieler)* record-player

dudeln ['du:dl̩n] **1.** *tr. V. (auf Blasinstrument)* tootle; *(singen)* sing tunelessly. **2.** *itr. V.* ‹*radio, television, etc.*› drone on; ‹*barrel organ*› grind away

Dudel·sack der bagpipes *pl.*

Dudelsack·pfeifer der; ~s, ~: piper; bagpipe-player

Duell [du'ɛl] **das; ~s, ~e a)** duel; **jmdn. zum ~ [heraus]fordern** challenge sb. to a duel; **ein ~ auf Pistolen** a duel with pistols; **b)** *(Sport)* contest (*Gen.* between); **c)** *(Wortgefecht)* duel of words

Duellant [duɛ'lant] **der; ~en, ~en** duellist

duellieren *refl. V.* fight a duel **(um** over)

Duett [du'ɛt] **das; ~[e]s, ~e a)** *(Musik)* duet; **im ~ singen** sing a duet; **etw. im ~ singen** sing sth. as a duet; **im ~ schreien/heulen** *(fig. ugs.)* scream/weep in unison; **b)** *(Duo, Paar)* duo; pair

Dufflecoat ['dʌfəlkoʊt] **der; ~s, ~s** duffle-coat

Duft [dʊft] **der; ~[e]s, Düfte** ['dʏftə] **a)** pleasant smell; scent; *(Zool.)* scent; *(von Parfüm, Blumen)* scent; fragrance; *(von Kaffee, frischem Brot, Tabak)* aroma; *(iron.)* beautiful smell *(iron.)*; **den ~ der großen, weiten Welt schnuppern** *(fig.)* get a taste of the big, wide world; **b)** *(schweiz.: Rauhreif)* hoar-frost

-duft der: Flieder~/Veilchen~/Jasmin~ *usw.* scent of lilac/violets/jasmine *etc.*

Düftchen ['dʏftçən] **das; ~s, ~:** pleasant aroma *or* smell; *(iron.)* beautiful whiff *or* smell

Duft·drüse die *(Zool.)* scent gland

dufte ['dʊftə] *(ugs.)* **1.** *Adj.* great *(coll.)*. **2.** *adv.* ‹*dressed, behave*› smashingly *(coll.)*; ‹*taste*› great *(coll.)*

duften ['dʊftn̩] *itr. V.* smell **(nach** of); **nicht ~:** not smell; have no smell; **die Rosen ~ gut** the roses smell lovely *or* have a lovely scent; **es duftet nach Kaffee** it smells of coffee; there's a smell of coffee

duftend *Adj.* sweet-smelling; fragrant; **angenehm/stark ~:** pleasant-/strong-smelling

duftig *Adj.* **a)** gossamer-fine ‹*dress, material*›; soft and fine ‹*hair*›; **b)** *(dichter.)* hazy

Duft-: ~marke die *(Zool.)* scent mark; **~note die** fragrance; **~stoff der a)** *(Biol.)* scent; **b)** *(bei Kosmetika)* aromatic substance *or* essence; **~wasser das;** *Pl.* **~wässer a)** *(scherzh.: Parfüm)* perfume; scent; **b)** *(Eau de Toilette)* toilet water; **~wolke die** cloud of perfume

duhn [du:n] *s.* **dun**

Dukaten [du'ka:tn̩] **der; ~s, ~** *(hist.)* ducat

Dukaten-: ~esel der *(ugs. scherzh.)* **ein ~esel sein** be made of money; **~gold das** fine gold; **~scheißer der** *(salopp) s.* **~esel**

Duktus ['dʊktʊs] **der; ~** *(geh.)* characteristic style; *(eines Gemäldes)* characteristic lines *pl. or* style; *(einer Handschrift)* characteristic shape *or* appearance

dulden ['dʊldn̩] **1.** *tr. V.* **a)** tolerate; put up with; **keinen Widerspruch ~:** tolerate *or (literary)* brook no contradiction; **die Arbeit duldet keinen Aufschub** the work will admit no delay; **b)** *(Aufenthalt gestatten)* **jmdn. ~:** tolerate *or* put up with sb.'s presence; **er war nur geduldet** his presence was only tolerated; he was here/there only on sufferance; **c)** *(geh.: er~)* endure. **2.** *itr. V. (geh.)* suffer

Dulder der; ~s, ~, Dulderin die; ~, ~nen patient sufferer

Dulder·miene die *(iron.)* martyred expression; **mit ~:** with a martyred expression

duldsam ['dʊltza:m] **1.** *Adj.* tolerant **(gegen** towards); *(geduldig)* patient. **2.** *adv.* tolerantly; *(geduldig)* patiently

Duldsamkeit die; ~: tolerance; *(Geduld)* patience

Duldung die; ~: toleration; **stillschweigende ~:** tacit permission; connivance

Dumdum [dʊm'dʊm] **das; ~[s], ~[s], Dumdum·geschoß das** dumdum [bullet]

dumm [dʊm], **dümmer** ['dʏmɐ], **dümmst...** ['dʏmst...] **1.** *Adj.* **a)** *(nicht intelligent)* stupid; stupid, thick, dense ‹*person*›; **jmdn. wie einen ~en Jungen behandeln** treat sb. like a stupid child; **[nicht] so ~ sein, wie man aussieht** [not] be as stupid as one looks; **sich ~ stellen** act stupid; **~ geboren, nichts dazugelernt** *(salopp)* stupid idiot! *(coll.)*; **sich nicht für ~ verkaufen lassen** *(ugs.)* not be taken in; **du willst mich wohl für ~ verkaufen!** you're trying to have me on *(Brit. coll.) or (Amer.coll.)* put me on; **sich ~ und dämlich** *od.* **dusselig reden/verdienen/essen** *(ugs.)* talk till one is blue in the face/earn a fortune/eat oneself silly; **b)** *(unvernünftig)* foolish; stupid; daft; **so etwas Dummes!** how stupid!; **c)** *(ugs.: töricht, albern)* idiotic; silly; stupid; **eine ~e Gans** a silly goose; **das ist mir [einfach] zu ~** *(ugs.)* I've had enough of it; **d)** *(ugs.: unangenehm)* nasty ‹*feeling, suspicion*›; annoying ‹*habit*›; awful *(coll.)* ‹*experience, business, coincidence*›; **so etwas Dummes!** how annoying!; **mir ist etwas Dummes passiert** something awful happened to me *(coll.)*; **e)** *(ugs.: benommen)* **mir ist ganz ~ im Kopf** my head is swimming. **2.** *adv.* **a)** *(ugs.: töricht)* foolishly; stupidly; **frag nicht so ~:** don't ask such silly *or* stupid questions; **b)** *(ugs.: unangenehm)* ‹*end*› badly *or* unpleasantly; **jmdm. ~ kommen** be cheeky *or* insolent to sb.

Dummchen ['dʊmçən] **das; ~s, ~** *s.* **Dummerchen**

dumm·dreist 1. *Adj.* brashly impertinent. **2.** *adv.* in a brashly impertinent manner

Dumme der/die; *adj. Dekl.* fool; **einen ~n finden, der etw. macht** find somebody stupid enough to do sth.; **die ~n werden nicht alle** there's one born every minute; **der ~ sein** *(ugs.)* be the loser

Dumme·jungen·streich der *(ugs.)* silly prank

Dummen·fang der; *o. Pl. (abwertend)* duping of unsuspecting people; **auf ~ gehen/aussein** go looking/be out looking for unsuspecting people to dupe

Dummerchen ['dʊmɐçən] **das; ~s, ~** *(fam.)* nitwit *(coll.)*; ninny; silly little boy/girl

dummer·weise *Adv.* **a)** *(leider)* unfortunately; *(ärgerlicherweise)* annoyingly; irritatingly; **b)** *(törichterweise)* foolishly; like a fool; stupidly

Dummheit die; ~, ~en a) *o. Pl.* stupidity; **wenn ~ weh täte, müßte er den ganzen Tag schreien** *(salopp)* he's as thick as two short planks *(Brit. coll.) or (Amer.)* as dumb as an ox; **b)** *(unkluge Handlung)* stupid *or* foolish thing; **es war eine große ~, deine Warnung nicht ernst zu nehmen** it was extremely stupid not to heed your warning; **[mach] keine ~en!** don't do anything stupid *or* foolish; **lauter** *od.* **nur ~en im Kopf haben** have a head full of silly ideas

Dumm·kopf der *(ugs.)* nitwit *(coll.)*; [silly] fool *or* idiot; blockhead

dümmlich ['dʏmlɪç] **1.** *Adj.* simple-minded. **2.** *adv.* ‹*grin, smile*› [rather] foolishly *or* stupidly

Dümmling ['dʏmlɪŋ] **der; ~s, ~e** *(ugs.)* dimwit *(coll.)*

Dumms·dorf (das) *(scherzh.)* **ich bin doch nicht aus ~!** I wasn't born yesterday!; **du bist wohl aus ~!** you must be stupid!

dümpeln ['dʏmpl̩n] *itr. V. (Seemannsspr.)* roll [gently]

dumpf [dʊmpf] **1.** *Adj.* **a)** dull ‹*thud, rumble of thunder*›; muffled ‹*sound, thump*›; **b)** *(muffig)* musty; **c)** *(stumpfsinnig)* dull; dull and expressionless ⟨*look*⟩; numb ⟨*indifference*⟩; stifling ⟨*small-town atmosphere*⟩; **d)** *(undeutlich)* dull ⟨*pain, anger*⟩; dim ⟨*memory, recollection*⟩; vague, hazy ⟨*conception, idea*⟩; **e)** *(veralt.: benommen)* dazed; stupefied ⟨*half-sleep*⟩. **2.** *adv.* **a)** ⟨*echo*⟩ hollowly; ~ **auf etw.** *(Akk.)* **aufschlagen** land with a dull thud on sth.; **b)** *(stumpfsinnig)* apathetically; numbly; ~ **vor sich hin blicken** gaze dully *or* apathetically into space; **c)** *(undeutlich)* vaguely ⟨*remember*⟩

Dumpfheit die; ~ **a)** *(Stumpfsinn)* torpor; apathy; **b)** *(Benommenheit)* numbness

dumpfig *Adj.* *(muffig)* musty; *(moderig)* fusty; mouldy; *(stickig)* stuffy ⟨*atmosphere*⟩

Dumping ['dampɪŋ] **das;** ~**s** *(Wirtsch.)* dumping

Dumping·preis der dumping price

dun [du:n] *Adj.; nicht attr. (nordd. salopp)* plastered *(sl.)*; well oiled *(sl.)*

Düne ['dy:nə] **die;** ~, ~**n** [sand-]dune

Dung [dʊŋ] **der;** ~**[e]s** dung; manure

Dünge·mittel das fertilizer

düngen ['dʏŋən] **1.** *tr. V.* fertilize ⟨*soil, lawn, etc.*⟩; spread fertilizer on ⟨*field*⟩; scatter fertilizer around ⟨*plants*⟩. **2.** *itr. V.* ⟨*person*⟩ put on fertilizer; **gut** ~ ⟨*substance*⟩ be a good fertilizer

Dünger der; ~**s**, ~: fertilizer

Dung·haufen der dunghill; dung *or* manure heap

Düngung die; ~, ~**en a)** use of fertilizers; **die** ~ **mit Chemikalien** the use of chemical fertilizers; **b)** *(Dünger)* fertilizer

dunkel ['dʊŋkl] **1.** *Adj.* **a)** dark; **es wird** ~: it's getting dark; **es wird um 22 h** ~: it gets dark about 10 o'clock; **im Dunkeln** in the dark; **im** ~**n bleiben** *(fig.)* ⟨*person*⟩ remain unidentified; ⟨*sb.'s identity etc.*⟩ remain a mystery; ⟨*future events*⟩ remain uncertain; **im** ~**n tappen** *(fig.)* grope around *or* about in the dark; **b)** *(unerfreulich)* dark ⟨*chapter in one's life*⟩; black ⟨*day*⟩; darker ⟨*side of life*⟩; **c)** *(fast schwarz)* dark; **dunkles Brot** brown bread; **dunkles Bier** dark beer *(darker than bitter)*; **eine dunkle Brille** dark glasses *pl.*; **d)** *(tief)* deep ⟨*voice, note*⟩; **e)** *(unbestimmt)* vague; dim, faint, vague ⟨*recollection*⟩; dark ⟨*hint, foreboding, suspicion*⟩; **in dunkler Vorzeit** in the dim and distant past; **jmdn. [über etw.** *(Akk.)***] im** ~**n lassen** *(fig.)* leave sb. in the dark [about sth.]; **f)** *(abwertend: zweifelhaft)* dubious; shady; **dunkle Geschäfte machen** be involved in shady transactions *or* deals. **2.** *adv.* **a)** *(tief)* ⟨*speak*⟩ in a deep voice; **b)** *(unbestimmt)* vaguely; ⟨*remember*⟩ vaguely, dimly

Dunkel das; ~**s a)** *(geh.)* darkness; **im** ~ **der Nacht** *(geh.)* in the darkness of the night; **b)** *(Rätselhaftigkeit)* obscurity, mystery **(um** surrounding); **in** ~ **gehüllt sein** be shrouded in mystery

Dünkel ['dʏŋkl] **der;** ~**s** *(geh. abwertend)* *(Überheblichkeit)* arrogance; haughtiness; *(Einbildung)* conceit[edness]; **einen ungeheuren** ~ **haben** be immensely arrogant *or* conceited

dunkel-: ~**äugig** *Adj.* dark-eyed; ~**blau** *Adj.* dark blue; ~**blond** *Adj.* light brown ⟨*hair*⟩; ⟨*person*⟩ with light brown hair; ~**blond sein** have light brown hair; ~**braun** *Adj.* dark brown; ~**grau** *Adj.* dark grey; ~**grün** *Adj.* dark green; ~**haarig** *Adj.* dark-haired

Dunkel·haft die confinement in a darkened cell

dünkelhaft 1. *Adj.* *(überheblich)* arrogant; haughty; *(eingebildet)* conceited. **2.** *adv.* *(hochmütig)* arrogantly; haughtily; *(eingebildet)* conceitedly

dunkel·häutig *Adj.* dark-skinned

Dunkelheit die; ~ **a)** darkness; **bei** ~: during the hours of darkness; **bei Einbruch der** ~: at nightfall; *s. auch* **Einbruch; b)** *(geh.: dunkle Tönung)* darkness

Dunkel-: ~**kammer die** dark-room; ~**mann der;** *Pl.* ~**männer** *(abwertend)* **a)** shady character; **b)** *(veralt.: Obskurant)* obscurantist

dunkeln 1. *itr. V.* **a)** *(unpers.)* **es dunkelt** *(geh.)* it is growing dark; **b)** *mit sein* grow *or* go darker; darken; **c)** *(dichter.)* ⟨*evening, night*⟩ fall. **2.** *tr. V.* make darker; darken

dunkel-, Dunkel-: ~**rot** *Adj.* dark red; *(tiefrot)* deep red; ~**werden das;** ~**s** nightfall; **vor dem** ~**werden** before nightfall; ~**ziffer die** number of unrecorded cases

dünken ['dʏŋkn̩] *(geh. veralt.)* **1.** *unr. tr. V.* **mich dünkt, er hat recht** methinks he is right *(arch.)*. **2.** *refl. V.* **er dünkt sich etwas Besseres/ein Held [zu sein]** he regards himself as superior/a hero; he thinks that he is superior/a hero

Dünkirchen ['dy:nkɪrçn̩] **(das);** ~**s** Dunkirk

dünn [dʏn] **1.** *Adj.* **a)** thin ⟨*slice, layer, etc.*⟩; slim ⟨*book*⟩; **b)** *(mager)* thin ⟨*person*⟩; **sich** ~ **machen** *(scherzh.)* squash *or* *(Amer.)* scrunch up [a bit]; **c)** *(leicht)* thin, light ⟨*clothing, fabric*⟩; fine ⟨*stocking*⟩; *(fig.)* thin, rarefied ⟨*air*⟩; fine ⟨*mist, rain*⟩; **d)** *(spärlich)* thin ⟨*hair*⟩; sparse ⟨*tree, cover, vegetation*⟩; **e)** *(wenig gehaltvoll)* thin ⟨*soup*⟩; weak, watery ⟨*coffee, tea*⟩; watery ⟨*beer*⟩; **f)** *(~flüssig)* thin ⟨*paint, lubricating oil*⟩; runny ⟨*batter*⟩; **g)** *(schwach)* thin ⟨*voice*⟩; weak, faint ⟨*smile*⟩; faint ⟨*scent*⟩. **2.** *adv.* **a)** ~ **geschnittene Wurst/~ geschnittener Käse** thinly sliced sausage/cheese; **etw.** ~ **auftragen** apply sth. thinly; **b)** *(leicht)* lightly ⟨*dressed*⟩; **c)** *(spärlich)* ~ **besiedelt sein** be thinly *or* sparsely populated *or* inhabited; *s. auch* **säen; d)** *(schwach)* ⟨*smile*⟩ weakly, faintly

dünn-, Dünn-: ~**besiedelt,** ~**bevölkert** *Adj. (präd. getrennt geschrieben)* thinly *or* sparsely populated *or* inhabited; ~**bier das** *(veralt.)* small beer; ~**brett·bohrer der** *(salopp abwertend)* **er ist ein** ~**brettbohrer** he likes to take the easy way out; ~**darm der** *(Anat.)* small intestine; ~**druck der** *Pl.* ~**drucke** thin-paper *or* India paper edition; ~**druck·aus·gabe die** thin-paper *or* India paper edition; ~**druck·papier das** India paper

[1]Dünne die; ~ *(Technik)* thinness

[2]Dünne der/die; *adj. Dekl. (ugs.)* thin man/woman; **die** ~**n** thin people

dünne|machen *s.* **dünnmachen**

dunnemals ['dʊnəma:ls] *s.* **Anno**

dünn-, Dünn-: ~**flüssig** *Adj.* thin; runny ⟨*batter etc.*⟩; ~**gesät** *Adj. (präd. getrennt geschrieben) (ugs.)* rare; ~**häutig** *Adj.* *(auch fig.)* thin-skinned; ~**|machen** *refl. V.* *(ugs.)* make oneself scarce *(coll.)*; ~**pfiff der;** *o. Pl. (salopp)*, ~**schiß der** *(derb)* the runs *pl. (coll.)*; the shits *pl. (vulg.)*; ~**wandig** *Adj.* thin-walled

Dunst [dʊnst] **der;** ~**[e]s, Dünste** ['dʏnstə] **a)** *o. Pl.* haze; *(Nebel)* mist; **b)** *(Geruch)* smell; *(Ausdünstung)* fumes *pl.*; *(stickige, dumpfe Luft)* fug *(coll.)*; **jmdm. blauen** ~ **vormachen** *(ugs.)* pull the wool over sb.'s eyes; **keinen [blassen]** ~ **von etw. haben** *(ugs.)* have not the foggiest *or* faintest idea about sth.

Dunst·abzugs·haube die extractor hood

dunsten *itr. V. (geh.)* **a)** smell, give off a smell **(nach** of); **b)** *(dampfen)* steam

dünsten ['dʏnstn̩] *tr. V.* steam ⟨*fish, vegetables*⟩; braise ⟨*meat*⟩; stew ⟨*fruit*⟩

Dunst·glocke die pall of haze

dunstig *Adj.* **a)** hazy; *(neblig)* misty; **b)** *(verräuchert)* smoky; *(stickig)* stuffy

Dunst·kreis der *(fig.)* orbit

Dunst·obst *(österr.)*, **Dünst·obst das** stewed fruit

Dunst-: ~**schicht die** layer of haze; *(Nebelschicht)* layer of mist; ~**schleier der** veil of haze; *(Nebelschleier)* veil of mist; ~**wolke die** cloud of smog; *(stickige, dumpfe Luft)* fug *(coll.)*

Dünung die; ~, ~**en** swell

Duo ['du:o] **das;** ~**s**, ~**s** *(Musik)* **a)** *(Stück)* duet; **b)** *(Ausführende)* ⟨*piano etc.*⟩ duet; *(fig. scherzh.)* duo; pair

Duodez- [duo'de:ts]: ~**band der** duodecimo *or* twelvemo edition; ~**fürst der** *(abwertend)* princeling; petty *or* minor prince; ~**fürstentum das** *(abwertend)* petty *or* minor princedom; ~**staat der** *(abwertend)* minor state

Duo·dezimal·system das duodecimal system

düpieren [dy'pi:rən] *tr. V. (geh.)* dupe

Duplikat [dupli'ka:t] **das;** ~**[e]s**, ~**e** duplicate

Duplikation [duplika'tsi̯o:n] **die;** ~, ~**en** *(geh., Genetik)* duplication

Duplizität [duplitsi'tɛ:t] **die;** ~, ~**en** *(geh.)* duplication

Dur [du:ɐ̯] **das;** ~ *(Musik)* major [key]; **in** ~ **enden** finish in a major key

Dur·akkord der *(Musik)* major chord

durativ ['du:rati:f] *Adj. (Sprachw.)* durative

durch [dʊrç] **1.** *Präp. mit Akk.* **a)** *(räumlich)* through; ~ **die Straßen/die Stadt bummeln** stroll through the streets/the town; ~ **ganz Europa reisen** travel all over *or* throughout Europe; ~ **einen Fluß waten** wade across a river; *s. auch* **Kopf; b)** *(modal)* by; **etw.** ~ **Boten/die Post schicken** send sth. by courier/post *(Brit.)* *or* mail; **etw.** ~ **Lautsprecher/das Fernsehen bekanntgeben** announce sth. over the loudspeakers/on television; **sie ist** ~ **das Fernsehen bekannt geworden** she became famous through television; **etw.** ~ **jmdn. bekommen** get *or* obtain sth. through sb.; **zehn [geteilt]** ~ **zwei** ten divided by two; **c)** *(österr.: zeitlich)* ~ **Wochen/Jahre** for weeks/years; ~ **sein ganzes Leben** throughout *or* all his life. **2.** *Adv.* **a)** *(hin~)* **das ganze Jahr** ~: throughout the whole year; all year; **die ganze Zeit** ~: the whole time; all the time; **b)** *(ugs.: vorbei)* **es war 3 Uhr** ~: it was past *or* gone 3 o'clock; **c)** ~ **und** ~ **naß/überzeugt** wet through [and through]/completely *or* totally convinced; **jmdm.** ~ **und** ~ **gehen** go right through sb.; **er ist ein Lügner** ~ **und** ~: he's an out and out liar; *s. auch* **durchsein**

durch|ackern *(ugs.)* **1.** *tr. V.* plough through. **2.** *refl. V.* **sich durch etw.** ~: plough [one's way] through sth.

durch|arbeiten 1. *tr. V.* **a) die Nacht/Pause** *usw.* ~: work through the night/break *etc.*; **b)** *(lesen und auswerten)* work *or* go through ⟨*book, article*⟩; **c)** *(ausarbeiten)* work out ⟨*speech, essay*⟩; **d)** *(durchkneten)* work *or* knead thoroughly ⟨*dough*⟩; massage *or* knead thoroughly ⟨*muscles*⟩. **2.** *itr. V.* work through. **3.** *refl. V. (auch fig.)* work one's way through

durch|atmen *itr. V.* take a deep breath/deep breaths; breathe deeply

durch·aus *Adv.* **a)** ~ **mitkommen wollen** [absolutely] insist on coming too; **das ist** ~ **nötig/ zu empfehlen** it is absolutely necessary/definitely to be recommended; **Muß das sein?** ~ **Ja,** ~: Is that necessary? – Yes, absolutely; **wenn du** ~ **willst** if you really insist; **b)** *(völlig)* perfectly, quite ⟨*correct, possible, understandable*⟩; **das ist** ~ **richtig** that is entirely right; **ich bin** ~ **Ihrer Meinung** I am entirely of your opinion; **man kann** ~ **vermuten, daß ...**: one can quite reasonably suppose *or* assume that ...; **ein** ~ **annehmbarer Vorschlag/gelungener Abend** an eminently acceptable suggestion/thoroughly successful evening; **c)** *(verneint)* **das hat** ~ **nichts damit zu tun** that's got nothing at all *or* whatsoever to do with it; ~ **nicht ins Wasser/darüber sprechen wollen** absolutely refuse to go into the water/talk about it; **es ist** ~ **nicht so einfach wie ...**: it is by no means as easy as ...; **das ist** ~ **kein Scherz** it is certainly no joke; **für so etwas habe ich** ~

kein Verständnis I have absolutely no time for that sort of thing
durch|backen **1.** *itr. V.* bake through. **2.** *tr. V.* **etw. richtig ~:** bake sth. right the way through
[1]**durch|beißen** **1.** *unr. tr. V.* bite through. **2.** *unr. refl. V.* *(ugs.)* [manage to] struggle through
[2]**durch·beißen** *unr. tr. V.* bite through; **jmdm. die Kehle ~:** tear *or* rip sb.'s throat open
durch|bekommen *unr. tr. V.* **etw. ~:** get sth. through; *(zerlegen)* get *or* cut through sth.
durch|betteln *refl. V.* **sich überall ~:** beg one's way through life
durch|biegen **1.** *unr. tr. V.* **etw. ~:** bend sth. as far as possible; **seinen Rücken/sein Kreuz ~:** straighten one's back. **2.** *unr. refl. V.* sag
durch|blasen **1.** *unr. tr. V.* **a)** *(durch Hindurchblasen reinigen)* **etw. ~:** clear sth. by blowing through it; **b)** *(treiben)* **etw. durch etw. ~:** blow sth. through sth.; **c)** *(durchdringen)* ‹*wind*› blow right through ‹*person*›. **2.** *unr. itr. V.* **~ durch** ‹*wind*› blow through ‹*cracks, thin coat, etc.*›
[1]**durch|blättern,** [2]**durch·blättern** *tr. V.* leaf through ‹*book, file, etc.*›
durch|bleuen *tr. V.* *(ugs.)* **jmdn. ~:** give sb. a good hiding *(coll.) or* thrashing
Durch·blick der a) *(ugs.)* **den [absoluten] ~ haben** know [exactly] what's going on; **den ~ verlieren** no longer know what's going on; lose track of what's going on; **b)** *(Ausblick)* view **(auf +** *Akk.* of)
durch|blicken *itr. V.* **a)** look through; **durch etw. ~:** look through sth.; **b)** *(ugs.)* **ich blicke da nicht durch** I can't make head or tail of it; **blickst du bei dieser Aufgabe durch?** can you make head or tail of this exercise?; **c) ~ lassen, daß .../wie ...:** hint that .../at how ...; **etw. ~ lassen** hint at sth.
[1]**durch|bluten** *itr. V.* **a) die Wunde blutete durch** blood from the wound soaked through [the bandage/dressing *etc.*]; **b)** *mit sein* ‹*bandage etc.*› become soaked with blood
[2]**durch·bluten** *tr. V.* **a)** supply ‹*body, limb, etc.*› with blood; **seine Beine sind schlecht durchblutet** the circulation in his legs is poor; **b)** *(mit Blut tränken)* **etw. ~:** soak sth. with blood
Durch·blutung die; *o. Pl.* flow *or* supply of blood (+ *Gen.* to); [blood-]circulation
durchblutungs·fördernd *Adj.* ‹*substance*› which stimulates the [blood-]circulation; **~ fördernd sein** stimulate the [blood-]circulation
Durchblutungs·störung die disturbance of the blood supply
[1]**durch|bohren** **1.** *tr. V.* drill *or* bore through ‹*wall, plank*›; drill, bore ‹*hole*›. **2.** *itr. V.* **durch etw. ~:** drill *or* bore through sth. **3.** *refl. V.* **sich durch etw. ~** ‹*woodworm etc.*› bore its way through sth.; ‹*spear, iron paling*› go right through sth.
[2]**durch·bohren** *tr. V.* pierce; **jmdn. mit ~den Blicken ansehen** *(fig.)* look piercingly *or* penetratingly at sb.
durch|boxen *(ugs.)* **1.** *refl. V.* fight one's way through; *(fig.)* battle through. **2.** *tr. V.* force *or* push through ‹*law, measure, bill, etc.*›; **einen Kandidaten ~:** bring pressure to bear to get a candidate appointed
durch|braten *unr. tr. V.* **etw. ~:** cook *or* roast sth. till it is well done; **ich möchte mein Steak durchgebraten** I'd like my steak well done
[1]**durch|brechen** **1.** *unr. tr. V.* **a)** *(zerbrechen)* **etw. ~:** break sth. in two; **b)** *(eine Öffnung brechen)* **eine Tür/ein Fenster ~:** make a door/window. **2.** *unr. itr. V.; mit sein* **a)** break in two; **der Blinddarm/das Magengeschwür ist durchgebrochen** *(Med.)* the appendix has burst/the gastric ulcer has perforated; **b)** *(hervorkommen)* ‹*sun*› break through; ‹*new tooth*› come through; ‹*bud*› appear; *(fig.)* ‹*rage, hatred*› erupt; **c)** *(einbrechen)* fall through ‹*ice, floor, etc.*›; **durch etw. ~:** fall through sth.; **d)** *(Milit.: sich einen Weg bahnen)* break through
[2]**durch·brechen** *unr. tr. V.* break through ‹*sound barrier*›; break *or* burst through ‹*crowd barrier*›; ‹*car*› crash through ‹*railings etc.*›; *(fig.)* break ‹*law, convention*›
durch|brennen *unr. itr. V.; mit sein* **a)** ‹*heating coil, light bulb*› burn out; ‹*fuse*› blow; **da ist ihm die Sicherung durchgebrannt** *(fig. salopp)* he blew a fuse *(sl.) or* his top *(coll.)*; **b)** *(ugs.: weglaufen)* *(von zu Hause)* run away; *(mit der Kasse)* run off; abscond; *(mit dem Geliebten/der Geliebten)* run off; **c)** *(glühen)* ‹*coals, logs*› glow
durch|bringen *unr. tr. V.* **a)** *s.* **durchbekommen; b)** *(durch eine Kontrolle, über eine Grenze)* **etw. ~:** get sth. through; **c)** *(bei Wahlen)* **jmdn. ~:** get sb. elected; **d)** *(durchsetzen)* get ‹*bill*› through; get ‹*motion*› passed; get ‹*proposal*› accepted; **e)** *(versorgen)* **seine Familie/sich ~:** support one's family/oneself; **f)** *(verschwenden)* get through
durch·brochen **1.** *2. Part. v.* [2]**durchbrechen. 2.** *Adj.* open-work *attrib.* ‹*stockings, shoes, etc.*›
Durch·bruch der a) *(Milit., Geol., fig.)* breakthrough; **einer Idee** *(Dat.)* **zum ~ verhelfen** get an idea generally accepted; **b)** *(Öffnung)* opening; *(durch Gewalteinwirkung)* breach
durch|buchstabieren *tr. V.* spell out
[1]**durch|bummeln** *(ugs.) itr. V.* **a) bis zum Morgen ~:** live it up till morning *(coll.)*; **b)** *mit sein* **~ durch** wander through ‹*park, exhibition, etc.*›
[2]**durch·bummeln** *tr. V.* **die Nacht ~:** be on the spree all night *(coll.)*; **eine durchbummelte Nacht** a night on the spree *(coll.)*
durch|bürsten *tr. V.* brush ‹*hair*› thoroughly
durch|checken *tr. V.* check ‹*list, documents*› thoroughly; check ‹*car*› over thoroughly
durch·dacht **1.** *2. Part. v.* **durchdenken. 2.** *Adj.* **ein wenig/gut ~er Plan** a badly/well thought-out plan; **nicht [genügend] ~ sein** not be sufficiently well thought-out
durch·denken *unr. tr. V.* think over *or* through
durch|diskutieren *tr. V.* discuss thoroughly
durch|drängen *refl. V.* **sich [durch etw.] ~:** push *or* force one's way through [sth.]
durch|drehen **1.** *tr. V.* put ‹*meat etc.*› through the mincer *or (Amer.)* grinder; chop ‹*nuts etc.*› in the blender. **2.** *itr. V.* **a)** *auch mit sein (ugs.)* crack up *(coll.)*; go to pieces; **b)** ‹*wheels*› spin
[1]**durch|dringen** *unr. itr. V.; mit sein* **a)** ‹*rain, sun*› come through; **durch etw. ~:** penetrate sth.; come through sth.; **bis zu jmdm. ~** *(fig.)* ‹*rumour, story*› get through to sb.; **b)** *(sich durchsetzen)* **mit einem Vorschlag bei der Geschäftsleitung ~:** succeed in getting the management to accept one's suggestion; **der Redner drang mit seiner Stimme nicht durch** the speaker couldn't make himself heard
[2]**durch·dringen** *unr. tr. V.* **a)** penetrate; **kaum zu ~ sein** be almost impenetrable; **b)** *(erfüllen)* **jmdn. ~** ‹*idea*› take hold of sb. [completely]; **von der Wahrheit einer Behauptung durchdrungen sein** be totally convinced of the truth of a statement; **seine Schriften sind von diesen Ideen durchdrungen** his writings are imbued with these ideas
durch·dringend **1.** *Adj.* **a)** *(intensiv)* piercing, penetrating ‹*voice, look, scream, sound*›; **mit ~em Blick** with a piercing *or* penetrating look; **b)** *(penetrant)* pungent, penetrating ‹*smell*›. **2.** *adv.* **a) jmdn. ~ ansehen** look at a person piercingly *or* penetratingly; give sb. a piercing *or* penetrating look; **b)** *(penetrant)* **~ riechen/stinken** have a pungent *or* penetrating smell/stench
Durchdringung die; ~ a) penetration; *(Verschmelzung)* fusion; **b)** *(Erfassung)* comprehension
durch|drücken *tr. V.* **a) Püree** *usw.* **[durch ein Sieb/Tuch] ~:** press *or* pass purée *etc.* through a sieve/cloth; **b)** *(strecken)* straighten ‹*limb, back*›; **die Knie ~:** straighten one's legs; **c)** *(ugs.: durchsetzen)* manage to get ‹*extra holiday etc.*›; **seinen Antrag ~:** manage to force one's application through; **ein Gesetz im Parlament ~:** force a bill through Parliament
durch|dürfen *unr. itr. V.* *(ugs.)* be allowed through; **darf ich mal [hier] durch?** can I get through here?
durch·einander *Adv.* **~ sein** ‹*papers, desk, etc.*› be in a mess *or* a muddle; *(verwirrt sein)* be confused *or* in a state of confusion; *(aufgeregt sein)* be flustered *or (coll.)* in a state; **alles ~ essen/trinken** eat/drink everything indiscriminately
Durcheinander das; ~s a) muddle; mess; **in wirrem ~** *(fig.)* in wild confusion; **b)** *(Wirrwarr)* confusion
durcheinander-: ~|bringen *unr. tr. V.* **a)** *(in Unordnung bringen)* get ‹*room, flat*› into a mess; get ‹*papers, file*› into a muddle; muddle up ‹*papers, file*›; **b)** *(verwirren)* confuse; **c)** *(verwechseln)* confuse ‹*names etc.*›; get ‹*names etc.*› mixed up *or* muddled; **~|gehen** *unr. itr. V.; mit sein (ugs.)* **im Betrieb/Hause geht alles ~:** everything's in a real muddle at work/the whole house is in a muddle; **mir geht alles ~** *(fig.)* I'm getting everything muddled up; **~|geraten** *unr. itr. V.; mit sein* ‹*collection, letters*› get in a muddle; **~|kommen** *unr. itr. V.; mit sein* ‹*pictures, papers, etc.*› get into a muddle; ‹*person*› get into a muddle, get confused; **~|laufen** *unr. itr. V.; mit sein* run [around] in all directions; **~|reden** *itr. V.* all talk at once *or* at the same time; **~|rennen** *itr. V.; mit sein s.* **~laufen; ~|werfen** *unr. tr. V.* **a)** turn ‹*desk, cupboard, etc.*› upside down; muddle *or* jumble up ‹*papers*›; **b)** *(verwechseln)* mix *or* muddle up; get mixed *or* muddled up
durch|essen *unr. refl. V.* **a) sich bei jmdm. ~:** live on sb.'s hospitality; **b)** *(scherzh.)* **sich durch etw. ~:** eat one's way through sth.
durch|exerzieren *tr. V.* *(ugs.)* go through, practise ‹*rules, multiplication tables*›; rehearse ‹*situation*›
[1]**durch|fahren** *unr. itr. V.; mit sein* **a) [durch etw.] ~:** drive through [sth.]; **b)** *(nicht anhalten)* go straight through; *(mit dem Auto)* drive straight through; *(fahren, ohne umsteigen zu müssen)* travel direct; go straight through; **durch eine Stadt ~:** go/drive straight through a town; go/drive through a town without stopping; **der Zug fährt [in H.] durch** the train doesn't stop [at H.]; **der Zug fährt bis München durch** the train is non-stop to Munich; **die [ganze] Nacht ~:** travel/drive [right] through the night
[2]**durch·fahren** *unr. tr. V.* **a)** travel through; ‹*train*› pass through; *(mit dem Auto)* drive through; **b)** *(zurücklegen)* cover ‹*distance*›; complete ‹*course, lap*›; **c)** *(durchzucken)* **plötzlich durchfuhr ihn ein Schreck** he was seized with sudden fright; **auf einmal durchfuhr mich [der Gedanke], daß ...:** suddenly the thought *or* it flashed through my mind that ...
Durch·fahrt die a) *o. Pl.* *(das Durchfahren)* **„~ verboten"** 'no entry except for access'; **die ~ durch den Kanal** the passage through the canal; **bei der ~ durch den Tunnel** when

passing through the tunnel; **b)** *o. Pl. (Durchreise)* **auf der ~ sein** be passing through; be on the way through; **c)** *o. Pl. (Weiterfahrt)* **die ~ freigeben** allow vehicles through; **freie ~ haben** have right of way; **d)** *(Weg)* thoroughfare; **„bitte [die] ~ freihalten"** 'please do not obstruct'

Dụrchfahrts·straße die main road through

Dụrch·fall der a) diarrhoea *no art.;* **b)** *(ugs.: Versagen)* failure; **in der Prüfung einen ~ erleben** fail the exam *(coll.)*

dụrch|fallen *unr. itr. V.; mit sein* **a)** fall through; **durch etw. ~:** fall through sth.; **b)** *(ugs.: nicht bestehen)* fail; flunk *(Amer. coll.);* **bei etw./in etw.** *(Dat.)***/durch etw.** *(Akk.)* **~:** fail *or* flunk sth.; **c)** *(ugs.: erfolglos sein)* ⟨*play, performance*⟩ flop *(sl.);* be a flop *(sl.) or* failure; **bei der Kritik ~:** be a flop with *(sl.) or* fail to please the critics; **d)** *(ugs.: verlieren)* lose; not get in; be defeated; **bei der Wahl ~:** lose the election; be defeated in the election

dụrch|faulen *itr. V.; mit sein* rot through

dụrch|fechten 1. *unr. tr. V.* **seine Ansprüche/Forderungen ~:** fight successfully to establish one's claims/get one's demands accepted. **2.** *refl. V.* **sich [im Leben] ~:** battle one's way through [life]

dụrch|fegen *tr. V.* sweep [out] ⟨*room*⟩ thoroughly

¹dụrch|feiern *itr. V.* **[die ganze Nacht] ~:** celebrate all night

²durch·fei̱ern *tr. V.* **die [ganze] Nacht ~:** spend all night celebrating; celebrate all night; **nach durchfeierter Nacht** after celebrating all night

dụrch|feilen *tr. V.* **a)** file through; **b)** *(bearbeiten)* polish ⟨*essay, speech, etc.*⟩

dụrch|finden *unr. refl. V.* find one's way through; **sich durch etw. ~:** find one's way through sth.; **sich durch das U-Bahn-System/in der Stadt ~:** find one's way around the underground *(Brit.) or (Amer.)* subway system/the town; **ich finde mich in diesem Kuddelmuddel nicht mehr durch** I can't make head or tail of this muddle

¹dụrch|fliegen *unr. itr. V.; mit sein* **a) [durch etw.] ~:** fly through [sth.]; **unter der Brücke ~:** fly under the bridge; **b)** *(nicht zwischenlanden)* fly non-stop; **c)** *(ugs.: nicht bestehen)* **[in einem Examen/bei einer Prüfung] ~:** fail [an exam *(coll.)*]

²durch·fli̱egen *unr. tr. V.* **a)** fly through; fly over ⟨*country*⟩; fly along ⟨*air corridor*⟩; **b)** *(zurücklegen)* fly, cover ⟨*distance*⟩; **c)** *(lesen)* glance through ⟨*newspaper, post*⟩; skim through ⟨*novel*⟩

¹dụrch|fließen *unr. itr. V.; mit sein* **[durch etw.] ~:** flow through [sth.]

²durch·fli̱eßen *unr. tr. V.* flow through

Dụrch·flug der flight through; **der ~ durch den Luftkorridor/das Gebiet** the flight along the air corridor/over the area; **Passagiere auf dem ~** transit passengers; **auf dem ~ [nach Kanada] sein** be in transit [to Canada]

Dụrch·fluß der a) *o. Pl. (das Durchfließen)* flow; **b)** *(Öffnung in einem Damm)* [discharge] opening; outlet; *(zwischen Becken)* connection channel

durch·flu̱ten *tr. V. (geh.)* ⟨*river*⟩ flow through ⟨*country*⟩; ⟨*warmth, pleasant feeling*⟩ flood through ⟨*person*⟩; **Licht durchflutete den Raum** light flooded the room; the room was flooded with light

dụrch|formen *tr. V.* **etw. ~:** get sth. into its final shape; **etw. bis ins einzelne ~:** work sth. out down to the last detail

dụrch|formulieren *tr. V.* finalize the [exact] wording of ⟨*essay, thesis*⟩; **eine Rede ~:** prepare the wording of a speech in detail

durch·fọrschen *tr. V.* **a)** search ⟨*pocket, room, area, etc.*⟩ thoroughly; **b)** *(untersuchen)* make a thorough investigation *or* examination of ⟨*sources, literature on a subject*⟩; carry out research into ⟨*subject*⟩

¹dụrch|forsten, ²durch·fọrsten *tr. V.* **a)** *(Forstw.)* thin; **b)** *(durchsehen)* sift through ⟨*archives, regulations, etc.*⟩

dụrch|fragen *refl. V.* **sich [nach dem Bahnhof/zum Museum] ~:** find one's way [to the station/museum] by asking

¹dụrch|fressen 1. *unr. tr. V.* **a) ein Loch durch etw. ~:** eat a hole through *or* in sth.; **b)** *(zerstören, zersetzen)* eat through; ⟨*moths*⟩ eat holes in ⟨*pullover etc.*⟩. **2.** *unr. refl. V.* **a)** ⟨*maggot, woodworm*⟩ eat [its way] through; ⟨*rust*⟩ eat through; **b)** *(ugs. abwertend)* **sich bei jmdm. ~:** live on sb.'s hospitality; **c)** *(durcharbeiten)* plough through ⟨*book, statistics, etc.*⟩

²durch·frẹssen *Adj.* **von Motten ~ sein** be moth-eaten *or* full of moth-holes; **ein von Säure ~er Kittel** a coat full of acid holes

dụrch|frieren *unr. itr. V.; mit sein* **a)** get frozen stiff; get *or* become chilled to the marrow *or* bone; **durchgefroren sein** be frozen stiff *or* chilled to the bone; **b)** *(gefrieren)* ⟨*water, lake*⟩ freeze solid

durchfro̱ren *Adj.* frozen ⟨*face, hands*⟩; **~ sein** ⟨*person*⟩ be frozen stiff

dụrch|fühlen *tr. V.* **etw. durch etw. ~:** feel sth. through sth.; **jmds. Bitterkeit ~** *(fig.)* sense sb.'s bitterness

dụrchführbar *Adj.* practicable; feasible; workable; **ein leicht/schwer ~er Plan** a plan that is easy/difficult to carry out

Dụrchführbarkeit die; ~: practicability; feasibility; workability

dụrch|führen 1. *tr. V.* **a)** *(verwirklichen)* carry out ⟨*intention*⟩; put into effect, implement ⟨*decision, programme*⟩; carry out, put into effect, implement ⟨*plan*⟩; put into practice ⟨*idea*⟩; **b)** *(ausführen)* carry out ⟨*work, installation, investigation*⟩; perform, carry out ⟨*operation*⟩; take ⟨*measurement*⟩; **c)** *(veranstalten)* make ⟨*charity collection*⟩; hold ⟨*meeting, election, examination*⟩; carry out ⟨*census*⟩; **d)** *(zu Ende führen)* complete, finish ⟨*task*⟩; carry through ⟨*method, system*⟩; maintain, keep up ⟨*role*⟩. **2.** *itr. V.* **durch etw./unter etw.** *(Dat.)* **~** ⟨*track, road*⟩ go *or* run *or* pass through/under sth.

Dụrchfuhr-: ~handel der *(Wirtsch.)* transit trade; **~land das** *(Wirtsch.)* country of transit

Dụrch·führung die a) *(Verwirklichung) (einer Absicht)* carrying out; *(eines Plans, Programms)* carrying out, implementation; **zur ~ kommen** *od.* **gelangen** *(Papierdt.)* ⟨*decision, regulation*⟩ be implemented; **zur ~ bringen** *(Papierdt.)* enforce ⟨*regulation, law*⟩; **b)** *(Ausführung) (einer Arbeit)* carrying out; *(einer Operation)* performing; *(einer Messung)* taking; **c)** *(Einhaltung) (einer Idee)* carrying through; *(von Richtlinien)* putting into practice; **d)** *(Veranstaltung) (eines Kongresses usw.)* holding; *(eines Wettbewerbs)* staging

Dụrchführungs·verordnung die implementing order

dụrch|füttern *tr. V. (ugs.)* feed; support; **sich von jmdm. ~ lassen** live off sb.

Dụrch·gabe die *(von Nachrichten, Meldungen)* announcement; *(von Gewinnzahlen)* reading; **bei der ~ des Telegramms** when telephoning the telegram through

Dụrch·gang der a) „kein ~", „~ verboten" 'no thoroughfare'; **b)** *(Weg)* passage[way]; **c)** *(Phase)* stage; *(einer Versuchsreihe)* run; *(Sport, bei Wahlen, Wettbewerb)* round; **d)** *(Astron.)* transit

durch·gängig 1. *Adj.* general; *(universell)* universal; constant ⟨*feature*⟩; general ⟨*principle*⟩; continual, constant ⟨*use*⟩. **2.** *adv.* generally, universally ⟨*accepted*⟩; **~ mit Maschine geschrieben sein** be typed throughout

Dụrchgangs-: ~bahn·hof der through station; **~lager das** transit camp; **~straße die** *(fig.)* transitional stage; **~straße die** through road; thoroughfare; **~verkehr der a)** through traffic; **b)** *(Transitverkehr)* transit traffic

dụrch|geben *unr. tr. V.* announce ⟨*news*⟩; give ⟨*results, weather report, winning numbers*⟩; **eine Meldung im Radio/Fernsehen ~:** make an announcement on the radio/on television; **etw. in den Nachrichten ~:** announce sth. on the news; **telefonisch** *od.* **per Telefon ~:** telephone ⟨*telegram*⟩ through; give ⟨*traffic information*⟩ over the telephone; pass on ⟨*report, results*⟩ by telephone

dụrch|gehen 1. *unr. itr. V.; mit sein* **a) [durch etw.] ~:** go *or* walk through [sth.]; **„bitte weiter ~!"** 'pass *or* move right down, please'; **b)** *(hindurchdringen)* **[durch etw.] ~:** ⟨*rain, water*⟩ come through [sth.]; ⟨*wind*⟩ go through [sth.]; **c)** *(direkt zum Ziel führen)* ⟨*train, bus, flight*⟩ go [right] through (**bis** to); go direct; **d)** *(andauern)* ⟨*meeting, party, etc.*⟩ go on (**bis zu** until); **e)** *(verlaufen)* ⟨*path etc.*⟩ go *or* run through (**bis zu** to); ⟨*stripe*⟩ go *or* run right through; **f)** *(angenommen werden)* ⟨*application, claim*⟩ be accepted; ⟨*law*⟩ be passed; ⟨*motion*⟩ be carried; ⟨*bill*⟩ be passed, get through; **g)** *(hingenommen werden)* ⟨*discrepancy*⟩ be tolerated; ⟨*mistake, discourtesy*⟩ be allowed to *or* let pass, be overlooked; **[jmdm.] etw. ~ lassen** let sb. get away with sth.; **h)** *(davonstürmen)* ⟨*horse*⟩ bolt; **i)** *(ugs.: davonlaufen)* **mit etw./jmdm. ~:** run off with sth./sb.; **sie ist ihrem Mann durchgegangen** she ran off and left her husband; **j)** *(außer Kontrolle geraten)* **die Nerven gehen mit ihm durch** he loses his temper; **ihr Temperament/ihre Begeisterung geht mit ihr durch** her temperament/enthusiasm gets the better of her; **k)** *(ugs.: durchgebracht werden können)* **[durch etw.] ~:** go through [sth.]; **hinter etw.** *(Dat.)* **~:** go through behind sth.; **l)** *(ohne Unterbrechung zu Fuß gehen)* walk without a break; **m)** *(gehalten werden für)* **für neu/30 Jahre** *usw.* **~:** be taken to be *or* pass for new/thirty *etc.*. **2.** *unr. tr. V.; mit sein* go through ⟨*newspaper, text*⟩; **etw. Punkt für Punkt/Wort für Wort ~:** go through sth. point by point/word by word

durch·gehend 1. *Adj.* **a)** continuous ⟨*line, pattern, etc.*⟩; constantly recurring ⟨*motif*⟩; **b)** *(direkt)* through *attrib.* ⟨*train, carriage*⟩; direct ⟨*flight, connection*⟩. **2.** *adv.* **a) ~ geöffnet haben/bleiben** be/stay open all day; *(Tag und Nacht)* be/stay open 24 hours a day; **b)** *(in einer Linie)* **~ geknöpft werden/gefüttert sein** button all the way down/be lined throughout *or* fully lined

durch·gei̱stigt *Adj.* spiritual ⟨*person, appearance*⟩

durch·geschwitzt 1. *2. Part. v.* **durchschwitzen. 2.** *Adj.* ⟨*person*⟩ soaked *or* bathed in sweat; ⟨*clothes*⟩ soaked with sweat; sweat-soaked *attrib.* ⟨*clothes*⟩

dụrch|gestalten *tr. V.* work ⟨*theme, motif*⟩ out in detail; portray ⟨*experience*⟩ in detail

dụrch|gießen *unr. tr. V.;* **etw. [durch etw.] ~:** pour sth. through [sth.]; **etw. durch ein Tuch ~:** strain sth. through a cloth

dụrch|gliedern *tr. V.* structure

¹dụrch|glühen 1. *itr. V.; mit sein* **a)** *(entzweigehen)* ⟨*heating coil, light bulb*⟩ burn out; ⟨*fuse*⟩ blow; **b)** *(vollständig glühen)* ⟨*coals, log*⟩ glow right through. **2.** *tr. V.* **etw. ~:** heat sth. until it glows right through

²durch·glü̱hen *tr. V. (dichter.)* **von etw. durchglüht sein** be aglow with sth.

dụrch|graben 1. *unr. tr. V.* **einen Tunnel/Gang** *usw.* **[durch etw.] ~:** dig a tunnel/passage through [sth.]. **2.** *unr. refl. V.* **sich [durch etw.] ~** ⟨*miner*⟩ dig his way through [sth.]; ⟨*mole*⟩ tunnel its way through [sth.]

dụrch|greifen *unr. itr. V.* **a) [hart] ~:** take drastic measures *or* steps; **rücksichtslos/strenger ~:** take ruthless/more drastic measures *or* steps; **gegen die Demonstranten hart ~:** take drastic action against the demonstrators; **b) ~ durch** reach through

dụrch|gucken *itr. V. (ugs.)* **[durch etw.] ~:** peep *or* look through [sth.]; **durch jmds. Fernglas~:** have a look through sb.'s binoculars

dụrch|haben *unr. tr. V. (ugs.)* **a)** have finished with ⟨*book, newspaper*⟩; have got through ⟨*song, discussion point*⟩; **b)** *(zerteilt haben)* have got through; **c)** *(hindurchbewegt haben)* **etw. [durch etw.] ~:** have got sth. through [sth.]

dụrch|hacken *tr. V.* hack *or* chop through; *(mit einem Schlag)* chop through

Dụrchhalte·appell der *(bei einem Kampf)* appeal to hold out; *(bei einer schwierigen Aufgabe)* appeal to see it through

dụrch|halten 1. *unr. itr. V. (bei einem Kampf)* hold out; *(bei einer schwierigen Aufgabe)* see it through; *(beim Rennen)* stay the course. **2.** *unr. tr. V.* stand ⟨*strain, difficult working conditions*⟩; stand, keep up ⟨*pace*⟩; **eine Diät ~:** keep to a diet

Dụrchhalte-: ~parole die *(abwertend)* exhortation to hold out; **~vermögen das** staying-power; stamina; [power of] endurance

dụrch|hängen *unr. itr. V.* **a)** sag; **b)** *(ugs.)* be washed out *or* drained

dụrch|hauen 1. *regelm. (auch unr.) tr. V.* **a) etw. ~:** chop *or* split sth. in half; **b)** *(bahnen)* **sich** *(Dat.)* **einen Weg durch etw. ~:** hack one's *or* a way through sth. **2.** *tr. V. (ugs.)* **a)** *(verprügeln)* **jmdn. ~:** give sb. a good hiding *(coll.) or (sl.)* walloping; **b)** *(zerstören)* blow ⟨*fuse*⟩; wreck ⟨*power line*⟩. **3.** *unr. refl. V.* **sich [durch etw.] ~:** hack one's way through [sth.]

dụrch|hecheln *tr. V. (ugs. abwertend)* gossip about ⟨*person, behaviour*⟩

dụrch|heizen 1. *tr. V.* **a)** heat ⟨*house, offices, etc.*⟩ through; **b)** *(ohne Pause heizen)* heat ⟨*house, offices, etc.*⟩ continuously *or* day and night. **2.** *itr. V.* have *or* keep the heating on

dụrch|helfen *unr. itr. V.* **jmdm. [durch etw.] ~:** help a person through [sth.]; **ich werde mir schon ~:** I'll manage *or* get by

dụrch|hören *tr. V.* **a) etw. [durch etw.] ~:** hear sth. [through sth.]; **b)** *(heraushören)* sense, detect ⟨*bitterness, envy, etc.*⟩

dụrch|hungern *refl. V.* get by *or* struggle along on very little to eat

durch·ịrren *tr. V.* wander *or* roam [aimlessly] through

dụrch|ixen *tr. V. (ugs.)* x out ⟨*typing error*⟩

¹dụrch|kämmen *tr. V.* **a)** comb ⟨*hair*⟩ through; **b)** *(durchsuchen)* comb ⟨*area etc.*⟩

²durch·kạ̈mmen *tr. V.* comb ⟨*area etc.*⟩

dụrch|kämpfen 1. *tr. V.* **a)** fight ⟨*case*⟩ [right] to the end; fight one's way through ⟨*adversity*⟩; **b)** *(durchsetzen)* force through. **2.** *refl. V.* **a) sich [durch etw.] ~:** fight *or* battle one's way through [sth.]; **b)** *(durchstehen)* battle *or* struggle through; **c)** *(sich überwinden)* **sich dazu ~, etw. zu tun** bring oneself to do sth.

dụrch|kauen *tr. V.* **a) etw. [gut] ~:** chew sth. thoroughly *or* well; **b)** *(ugs.: besprechen)* go over and over

dụrch|klettern *itr. V.; mit sein* **[durch etw.] ~:** climb *or* clamber through [sth.]

dụrch|kneten *tr. V.* **a)** knead ⟨*dough etc.*⟩ thoroughly; **b)** *(ugs.: massieren)* knead ⟨*muscles etc.*⟩ thoroughly; **jmdn. ~:** give sb. a good hard massage

dụrch|knöpfen *tr. V.* button ⟨*dress, coat*⟩ all the way down; **das Kleid wird hinten durchgeknöpft** the dress buttons all the way up the back; **ein durchgeknöpftes Kleid** a button-through dress

dụrch|kochen *tr. V.* boil ⟨*stock, jam*⟩ thoroughly

dụrch|kommen *unr. itr. V.; mit sein* **a)** come through; *(mit Mühe hindurchgelangen)* get through; **durch etw. ~:** come/get through sth.; **es gab kein Durchkommen** there was no way through; **b)** *(ugs.: beim Telefonieren)* get through; **c)** *(durchgehen, -fahren usw.)* **durch etw. ~:** come *or* pass through sth.; **um fünf Uhr kommt der Zug [hier] durch** the train comes through [here] at five o'clock; **wenn du hier durchkommst, ...:** when you're passing through ...; **d)** *(sich zeigen)* ⟨*sun*⟩ come out; ⟨*character trait, upbringing*⟩ come through, become apparent; **manchmal kommt sein Dialekt durch** *(fig.)* sometimes his dialect becomes noticeable; **bei ihm kommt der Lehrer durch** *(fig.)* the teacher in him comes through; **e)** *(erfolgreich sein)* **mit dieser Einstellung wird er [im Leben] nicht ~:** he won't get anywhere *or* far [in life] with an attitude like that; **mit Freundlichkeit und Verbindlichkeit kann man überall besser ~:** you'll get a lot further by being friendly and obliging; **damit kommst du bei mir nicht durch** you won't get anywhere with me like that; **mit so einer Entschuldigung kommt man bei ihm nicht durch** you won't get away with an excuse like that with him; **f)** *(ugs.: überleben)* pull through; **g)** *(ugs.: durchdringen)* **[durch etw.] ~** ⟨*water, sand, etc.*⟩ come through [sth.]; **h)** *(durchgesagt werden)* be announced; **die Nachricht kam im Fernsehen/Radio durch** the news was announced on television/the radio; **i)** *(bestehen)* get through; pass; **in einer Prüfung ~:** get through *or* pass an examination; **j)** *(auskommen)* manage; get by; **mit seiner Rente ~:** get by *or* manage on one's pension

dụrch|komponieren *tr. V.* **a)** work ⟨*story, play*⟩ out in detail; **b)** *(Musik)* compose ⟨*song*⟩ with an individual setting for each verse; set ⟨*poem*⟩ to music with an individual setting for each stanza; **die Ballade ist durchkomponiert** the ballad is through-composed *or* durchkomponiert

dụrch|können *unr. itr. V. (ugs.)* **a)** *(durchgehen, -kommen dürfen)* **[durch etw.] ~:** be able to go/come through [sth.]; **Sie können hier nicht durch** you can't go/come through here; **kann ich mal durch, bitte?** can I get by, please?; excuse me, please; **b)** *(durchkommen)* **[durch etw.] ~:** be able to get through [sth.]

dụrch|konstruieren *tr. V.* **etw. ~:** design and construct sth. with great attention to detail

¹dụrch|kreuzen *tr. V.* cross through *or* out ⟨*mistake, irrelevant information*⟩

²durch·kre̲uzen *tr. V.* **a)** *(vereiteln)* thwart, frustrate ⟨*plan, intention, ambition, policy*⟩; **b)** *(geh.: durchfahren)* cross ⟨*continent, sea, etc.*⟩

dụrch|kriechen *unr. itr. V.; mit sein* **[durch etw.] ~:** crawl through [sth.]; **unter etw.** *(Dat.)* **~:** crawl [through] under sth.

dụrch|kriegen *tr. V. (ugs.) s.* **durchbekommen**

dụrch|laden 1. *unr. tr. V.* cock ⟨*pistol etc.*⟩ and rotate the cylinder. **2.** *unr. itr. V.* cock the trigger and rotate the cylinder

Durchlaß ['dʊrçlas] **der; Dụrchlasses, Durchlässe** ['dʊrçlɛsə] **a)** *(geh.)* permission to pass; *(Einlaß)* admittance; **sich** *(Dat.)* **~ verschaffen** obtain permission to pass/gain admittance; **b)** *(Öffnung)* gap; opening; *(für Wasser)* duct; conduit

dụrch|lassen *unr. tr. V.* **a) jmdn. [durch etw.] ~:** let *or* allow sb. through [sth.]; **den Ball ~** *(Sport)* ⟨*goalkeeper*⟩ let a goal in; **b)** *(durchlässig sein)* let ⟨*light, water, etc.*⟩ through; *(eindringen lassen)* let ⟨*light, water, etc.*⟩ in; **c)** *(ugs.: dulden)* **jmdn. etw. ~:** let sb. get away with sth.

durchlässig ['dʊrçlɛsɪç] *Adj.* **a)** permeable; *(porös)* porous; *(undicht)* leaky; ⟨*raincoat, shoe*⟩ that lets in water; **b)** *(offen)* open ⟨*system, border*⟩; **die Grenzen müssen durchlässiger werden** the borders must be opened up further; **im Verteidigungsministerium gab es eine ~e Stelle** *(fig.)* there had been a leak/leaks at the defence ministry

-durchlässig *Adj.* **gas-/luft-/wasser~** *usw.* **sein** be permeable to gas/air/water *etc.*

Dụrchlässigkeit die; ~ a) permeability; *(Porosität)* porosity; *(Undichte)* leakiness; **b)** *(Offenheit)* free interchange (+ *Gen.*, **zwischen** between)

Durchlaucht ['dʊrçla̲uxt] **die; ~, ~en Ihre/Seine ~:** Her/His [Serene] Highness; **[Euer] ~:** Your [Serene] Highness

Dụrch·lauf der a) *(Sport, DV)* run; **b)** *(von Wasser)* flow; **während des ~s des Wassers** while the water is flowing through; **c)** *(Ferns.)* preview *(of programme to gain approval for broadcast)*; *(Rundf.)* scrutiny

¹dụrch|laufen 1. *unr. itr. V.; mit sein* **a) [durch etw.] ~:** run through [sth.]; **b)** *(durchrinnen)* **[durch etw.] ~:** trickle through [sth.]; **der Kaffee ist durchgelaufen** the coffee is filtered; **c)** *(passieren)* ⟨*runners*⟩ run *or* pass through; **d)** *(ohne Pause laufen)* run without stopping; **e)** *(fortlaufen)* ⟨*balcony, frieze*⟩ run all the way along. **2.** *unr. tr. V.* go through ⟨*socks, soles of shoes*⟩

²durch·la̲ufen *unr. tr. V.* **a)** go *or* pass through ⟨*phase, stage*⟩; **b)** *(geh.: hindurchgehen durch)* ⟨*shudder, feeling, etc.*⟩ run through; **c)** *(zurücklegen)* run, cover ⟨*distance*⟩

dụrchlaufend 1. *Adj.* continuous. **2.** *adv.* ⟨*numbered, marked*⟩ in sequence

Dụrchlauf-: ~erhitzer der; ~s, ~: geyser; instantaneous water-heater; **~zeit die** processing time; *(DV)* run duration

dụrch|lavieren *refl. V. (ugs. abwertend)* get along by dint of some smart manœuvring

durch·le̲ben *tr. V.* live through; experience; experience ⟨*moments of bliss, terror, fright*⟩; **etw. wieder ~:** relive sth.

dụrch|legen *tr. V. (ugs.)* **die Straße/Leitung wird hier durchgelegt** the road/pipe will be laid through here

durch·le̲iden *unr. tr. V. (geh.)* endure; suffer

dụrch|leiten *tr. V.* **den Verkehr durch die Stadt ~:** direct the traffic through the town; **den Strom [durch das Gebiet] ~:** run electricity cables through [the area]

dụrch|lesen *unr. tr. V.* **etw. [ganz] ~:** read sth. [all the way] through; **wenn du das Buch durchgelesen hast** when you've finished reading the book; **sich** *(Dat.)* **etw. ~:** read sth. through; **etw. auf Fehler hin ~:** read sth. for errors

durch·le̲uchten *tr. V.* **a)** x-ray ⟨*patient, part of body*⟩; **sich ~ lassen** have an x-ray; **jmdm. den Magen ~:** x-ray sb.'s stomach; **b)** *(fig.: analysieren)* investigate ⟨*case, matter, problem, etc.*⟩ thoroughly *or* in depth; **jmds. Vergangenheit ~:** probe into *or* investigate sb.'s past; **jmdn. ~:** vet sb.

Durchle̲uchtung die; ~, ~en a) *(das Röntgen)* x-ray examination; **jmdn. zur ~ ins Krankenhaus schicken** send sb. to hospital for an x-ray; **b)** *(fig.: Analyse)* [thorough] investigation; *(von Bewerbern usw.)* vetting

dụrch|liegen 1. *unr. tr. V.* wear out ⟨*mattress, bed*⟩ [so that it sags in the middle]; **eine durchgelegene Matratze** a worn-out mattress. **2.** *refl. V.* ⟨*patient*⟩ develop *or* get bedsores

durch·lọ̈chern *tr. V.* **a)** make holes in; wear holes in ⟨*socks, shoes*⟩; ⟨*rust*⟩ eat holes in; **jmdn./etw. mit Schüssen ~:** riddle sb./sth. with bullets; **völlig durchlöchert sein** be full of holes; **b)** *(fig.: schwächen)* undermine ⟨*system*⟩ completely; render ⟨*principle*⟩ meaningless

durch|lotsen *tr. V. (ugs.)* **ein Schiff [durch etw.] ~:** pilot a ship through [sth.]; **jmdn. [durch die Stadt] ~:** guide sb. through [the town]

[1]**durch|lüften 1.** *tr. V.* air ‹*room, flat, etc.*› thoroughly. **2.** *itr. V.* air the place

[2]**durch·lüften** *tr. V. (fachspr.)* aerate ‹*soil*›; ventilate ‹*grain, woodpile*›

durch|machen *(ugs.)* **1.** *tr. V.* **a)** undergo ‹*change*›; complete ‹*training course*›; go through ‹*stage, phase*›; serve ‹*apprenticeship*›; **b)** *(erleiden)* go through; **sie hat schlimme Zeiten/viel durchgemacht** she's been through some bad times/a lot; **eine schwere Krankheit ~:** suffer *or* have a serious illness; **c)** *(durcharbeiten)* work through ‹*lunch-break, weekend, etc.*›. **2.** *itr. V. (durcharbeiten)* work [right] through; *(durchfeiern)* celebrate all night/day *etc.*; keep going all night/day *etc.*

durch|manövrieren *tr. V.* **etw. [durch etw.] ~:** manœuvre sth. through [sth.]; **jmdn. sicher durch alle Schwierigkeiten ~** *(fig.)* bring *or* lead sb. safely through all the difficulties

Durch·marsch der a) der ~ zur Grenze the march through to the frontier; **auf dem ~ sein** be marching through; **b)** *o. Pl. (salopp: Durchfall)* **~ haben/bekommen** have/get the runs *(coll.)*; **c)** *(Skat)* **einen ~ machen** *take all the tricks when ramsch is called*

durch|marschieren *itr. V.; mit sein* **[durch etw.] ~:** march through [sth.]

durch|mengen *tr. V.* **[gut] ~:** mix ‹*ingredients etc.*› thoroughly

durch·messen *unr. tr. V. (geh.)* cross ‹*room*›; traverse ‹*time and space*›; **das Zimmer mit großen Schritten ~:** stride across the room; cross the room with long strides

Durchmesser der; ~s, ~: diameter; **das mißt 3 m im ~:** it measures 3 m in diameter

[1]**durch|mischen** *tr. V.* **[gut/gründlich] ~:** mix ‹*ingredients etc.*› thoroughly

[2]**durch·mischen** *tr. V.* **etw. mit etw. ~:** mix sth. with sth.

durch|mogeln *refl. V. (ugs. abwertend)* cheat one's way through; *(sich hineinmogeln)* wangle one's way in *(sl.)*; **sich bei einer Prüfung** *usw.* **~:** get through an examination *etc.* by cheating

durch|müssen *unr. itr. V. (ugs.)* **[durch etw.] ~:** have to go through [sth.]; **da werden wir ~** *(fig.)* we'll have to see it *or* the thing through

durch·mustern *tr. V. (geh.)* examine closely; scrutinize

durch|nagen *tr. V.* gnaw through

Durchnahme ['dʊrçna:mə] **die; ~: bei ~ des Stoffes** while we/they *etc.* are/were going through the material

durch·nässen *tr. V.* soak; drench; **[völlig] durchnäßt sein** be soaking wet *or* wet through; **mit durchnäßten Kleidern** with soaking-wet clothes

durch|nehmen *unr. tr. V.* deal with, do ‹*subject, topic*›; go through ‹*material*›

durch|numerieren *tr. V.* number ‹*pages, seats, etc.*› consecutively from beginning to end

durch|organisieren *tr. V.* organize sth. well; **etw. perfekt ~:** organize sth. down to the last detail

durch|pauken *tr. V. (ugs.)* **a)** force through ‹*law, regulation, etc.*›; **b)** *(lernen)* swot up *(Brit.)*; bone up on *(Amer.)*

durch|pausen *tr. V.* trace

durch|peitschen *tr. V.* **a) jmdn. ~:** give sb. a flogging; flog sb.; **b)** *(ugs. abwertend)* railroad ‹*law, application, etc.*› through

durch|pennen *itr. V. (salopp)* sleep through; **ich habe bis 11 Uhr durchgepennt** I kipped till 11 o'clock *(sl.)*

durch·pflügen *tr. V.* plough through

durch|planen *tr. V.* **etw. ~:** plan sth. well

durch|plumpsen *itr. V.; mit sein (ugs.)* **a) [durch etw.] ~** ‹*person*› fall through [sth.]; ‹*small object*› drop *or* fall through [sth.]; **b)** *(bei einer Prüfung)* fail; flunk *(Amer. coll.)*; **bei/in etw.** *(Dat.)* **~:** fail *or* flunk sth.

durch|pressen *tr. V.* mash ‹*potatoes*›; purée ‹*fruit*› *(by pressing through a sieve)*; crush ‹*garlic*› *(in a press)*; **Kartoffeln/Obst durch ein Sieb ~:** press *or* pass potatoes/fruit through a sieve

durch|proben *tr. V.* **etw. ~:** run through *or* rehearse sth. from beginning to end

durch|probieren *tr. V.* taste *or* try ‹*wines, cakes, etc.*› one after another; try on ‹*dresses, suits, etc.*› one after another

durch|prügeln *tr. V. (ugs.)* give sb. a real beating *or (sl.)* walloping; give ‹*naughty child*› a good hiding *or (sl.)* walloping

durch·pulsen *tr. V. (geh.)* ‹*blood*› pulse through; **buntes Leben durchpulste die Straßen** *(fig.)* the streets pulsated with life

durch|pusten *tr. V. (ugs.)* **etw. ~:** clear sth. by blowing through it

durch·queren *tr. V.* cross; travel across ‹*country*›; ‹*train*› pass *or* go through ‹*country*›

durch|quetschen *refl. V. (ugs.)* **sich [durch etw.] ~:** squeeze one's way through [sth.]

durch|rasen *itr. V.; mit sein* **[durch etw.] ~:** tear through [sth.]

durch|rasseln *itr. V.; mit sein (salopp),* **durch|rauschen** *itr. V.; mit sein (ugs.) s.* **durchfallen b**

durch|rechnen *tr. V.* calculate ‹*costs etc.*› [down to the last penny]; check ‹*bill*› thoroughly

durch|regnen *itr. V. (unpers.)* **in der Küche** *usw.* **regnet es durch** the rain is coming through in the kitchen *etc.*; **es regnet durchs Dach durch** the rain is coming [in] through the roof; **die ganze Nacht ~:** rain all [through the] night; *s. auch* **durchgeregnet**

Durchreiche die; ~, ~n [serving-]hatch

durch|reichen *tr. V.* **etw. [durch etw.] ~:** pass *or* hand sth. through [sth.]

Durch·reise die journey through; **auf der ~ sein** be on the way through *or* passing through

[1]**durch|reisen** *itr. V.; mit sein* travel *or* pass through

[2]**durch·reisen** *tr. V.* travel through *or* across ‹*area, continent*›

Durch·reisende der/die person travelling through; **~ auf dem Weiterflug nach Rom** passengers travelling through *or* on to Rome

Durchreise·visum das transit visa

durch|reißen 1. *unr. tr. V.* **etw. ~:** tear sth. in two *or* in half. **2.** *unr. itr. V.; mit sein* ‹*fabric, garment*› rip, tear; ‹*thread, rope*› snap *or* break [in two]

durch|reiten *unr. itr. V.; mit sein* **[durch etw.] ~:** ride through [sth.]; **die ganze Nacht ~:** ride all night without stopping

durch|rennen *unr. itr. V.; mit sein* **[durch etw.] ~:** run through [sth.]

[1]**durch|rieseln** *itr. V.; mit sein* **[durch etw.] ~:** trickle through [sth.]

[2]**durch·rieseln** *tr. V.* ‹*feeling of horror or pleasure*› run through; **es durchrieselte sie kalt/heiß** a cold shiver ran through her/she felt a hot flush come over her

durch|ringen *unr. refl. V.* **sie hat sich endlich [zu einem Entschluß] durchgerungen** finally she managed to come to a decision; **wann wirst du dich dazu ~, es zu tun?** when are you going to bring yourself to do it?

durch|rinnen *unr. itr. V.; mit sein* **[durch etw.] ~:** run through [sth.]; **das Geld rinnt ihm zwischen den Fingern durch** *(fig.)* money burns a hole in his pocket

durch|rosten *itr. V.; mit sein* rust through

durch|rufen *unr. itr. V. (ugs.)* **[bei jmdm.] ~:** ring [sb.] up *(Brit.)*

durch|rühren *tr. V.* **etw. [gut] ~:** stir sth. [well]

durch|rutschen *itr. V.; mit sein* **a) [durch etw.] ~** ‹*object*› slip through [sth.]; ‹*person*› slide through [sth.]; **b)** *(ugs.: durchkommen)* manage to get through without doing any work

durch|rütteln *tr. V.* **jmdn. ~:** shake sb. about badly

durchs [dʊrçs] *Präp. + Art.* = **durch das**

durch|sacken *itr. V.; mit sein* ‹*aeroplane*› drop suddenly; *(bei zu geringer Geschwindigkeit)* stall

Durch·sage die announcement; *(an eine bestimmte Person)* message; **eine ~ machen** make an announcement

durch|sagen *tr. V. s.* **durchgeben**

[1]**durch|sägen,** [2]**durch·sägen** *tr. V.* saw through

durch|saufen *unr. itr. V. (derb)* **die ganze Nacht ~:** booze all night *(sl.)*

durch|sausen *itr. V.; mit sein (ugs.)* **a) [durch etw.] ~:** shoot through [sth.]; **b)** *(ugs.: durchfallen)* **[durch eine Prüfung] ~:** fail *or (Amer. coll.)* flunk [an examination]

durch|schalten 1. *tr. V. (Technik)* connect ‹*telephone line*› through; put ‹*telephone call*› through; switch ‹*signal, current, etc.*› through. **2.** *itr. V. (beim Autofahren)* ‹*car driver*› change up [quickly]

durchschaubar *Adj.* transparent; **leicht/schwer ~ sein** be easy/difficult to see through; *(verständlich)* be easy/difficult to understand; **leicht ~** ‹*lie, plan, intention*› that is easy to see through *or* is easily seen through; **ein leicht/schwer ~er Mensch** a person who is easy/difficult to see through; **etw. ~ machen** make sth. easy to understand

[1]**durch|schauen** *itr. V. s.* **durchsehen**

[2]**durch·schauen** *tr. V.* **a)** see through ‹*lie, plan, intention, person, etc.*›; see ‹*situation*› clearly; **du bist durchschaut** I've/we've seen through you; I/we know what you're up to; **~, worum es wirklich geht** see what it's really all about; **b)** *(verstehen)* understand

[1]**durch|scheinen** *unr. itr. V.* **[durch etw.] ~** ‹*sun, light*› shine through [sth.]; ‹*colour, pattern*› show through [sth.]

[2]**durch·scheinen** *unr. tr. V. (geh.)* ‹*sun*› fill ‹*room*› with light; **von Sonnenlicht durchschienen** filled with sunlight

durchscheinend *Adj. (lichtdurchlässig)* translucent; *(durchsichtig)* transparent; diaphanous ‹*fabric*›; translucent ‹*skin etc.*›

durch|scheuern 1. *tr. V.* wear through; **ein durchgescheuertes Kabel** a worn cable. **2.** *refl. V.* wear through

durch|schieben *unr. tr. V.* **etw. [durch etw.] ~:** push sth. through [sth.]; **einen Brief unter der Tür ~:** push a letter under the door

[1]**durch|schießen** *unr. tr. V.* **durch etw. ~:** shoot through sth.; **den Ball zwischen den Bäumen ~:** shoot the ball [through] between the trees

[2]**durch·schießen** *unr. tr. V.* **a) etw. ~:** shoot sth. through; **b)** *(Buchbinderei)* interleave; **c)** *(Druckw.)* space out; **d)** *(Textilind.)* interweave (**mit** with)

durch|schimmern *itr. V.* **a) [durch etw.] ~** ‹*light*› shimmer through [sth.]; ‹*colour*› gleam through [sth.]; **b)** *(fig.)* ‹*qualities, emotions*› show through

durch|schlafen *unr. itr. V.* sleep [right] through; **die ganze Nacht ~:** sleep all night [without waking]

Durch·schlag der a) *(Kopie)* carbon [copy]; **b)** *(Küchengerät)* colander; strainer; **c)** *(Kfz-W.)* puncture; **d)** *(Werkzeug)* punch; **e)** *(Elektrot.)* disruptive discharge

[1]**durch|schlagen 1.** *unr. tr. V.* **a) etw. ~:** chop *or* split sth. in two; **b)** *(schlagen)* **ein Loch/einen Nagel [durch etw.] ~:** knock a hole through [sth.]/knock *or* drive a nail through [sth.]. **2.** *unr. itr. V.* **a)** *mit sein* **[durch etw.] ~** ‹*dampness, water*› come through [sth.]; **das schlägt auf die Preise durch** *(fig.)* it has an effect on prices; **bei**

ihm schlägt die Mutter durch *(fig.)* he takes after his mother; **der Aristokrat in ihm schlägt durch** the aristocrat in him comes out; **b)** *mit sein ‹fuse›* blow; **c)** *(abführen)* have a strong laxative effect; **bei jmdm. ~:** go straight through sb. **3.** *refl. V.* **a)** struggle along; **b)** *(ein Ziel erreichen) (mit Gewalt)* fight one's way through; *(mit List)* make one's way through

[2]durch·schlagen *unr. tr. V.* smash

durchschlagend *Adj.* resounding *‹success›*; decisive *‹effect, measures›*; conclusive *‹evidence›*

Durchschlag·papier das copy paper

Durchschlags·kraft die a) *(Ballistik)* penetrating power; **b)** *(fig.: Wirkung)* power; force

durch|schlängeln *refl. V.* **sich [durch etw.] ~** *(auch fig.)* thread one's way through [sth.]

durch|schleichen *unr. refl. V.* **sich [durch etw.] ~:** slip *or* creep through [sth.]

durch|schleppen *tr. V. (ugs.)* carry *‹loss-making concern, non-productive worker›*; keep *‹needy relation etc.›*

durch|schleusen *tr. V.* **a)** *(ugs.)* **jmdn./etw. [durch etw.] ~:** guide sb./sth. through [sth.]; *(durchschmuggeln)* get sb./sth. through [sth.]; **b)** *(Schiffahrt)* **ein Schiff ~:** pass a ship through a lock

Durchschlupf ['dʊrçʃlʊpf] **der; ~[e]s, ~e** gap; *(Loch)* hole

durch|schlüpfen *itr. V.; mit sein* **[durch etw.] ~:** slip through [sth.]

durch|schmecken 1. *tr. V.* be able to taste **(bei** in). **2.** *itr. V.* come through [too strongly]

durch|schmoren *itr. V.; mit sein (ugs.) ‹cable›* burn through; *‹element›* burn out

durch|schmuggeln *tr. V.* **etw. [durch etw.] ~:** smuggle sth. through [sth.]

[1]durch|schneiden *unr. tr. V.* cut through *‹thread, cable›*; cut *‹ribbon, sheet of paper›* in two; cut *‹throat, umbilical cord›*; **etw. in der Mitte ~:** cut sth. in half

[2]durch·schneiden *unr. tr. V.* **a)** *s.* **[1]durchschneiden; b)** *(geh.) ‹road, river, valley›* cut through; *‹bow of boat›* slice through *‹waves›*; **das Land ist von Kanälen durchschnitten** the country is criss-crossed by canals

Durch·schnitt der; *o. Pl.* **a)** average; **im ~:** on average; **im ~ 110 km/h fahren** average 110 k.p.h.; do 110 k.p.h. on average; **b)** *(Mittelmaß)* **über/unter dem ~ liegen, guter/unterer ~ sein** be above/below average; **vom ~ abweichen** deviate from the norm; **c)** *(ugs.: Mehrheit)* majority; **der ~ ist ...:** the majority [of people] *or* people in general are ...; **d)** *(Math.)* mean; **e)** *(fachspr.)* [cross-]section

durchschnittlich 1. *Adj.* **a)** *nicht präd.* average *‹growth, performance, output›*; **b)** *(ugs.: mehrheitlich)* ordinary *‹life, person, etc.›*; **c)** *(mittelmäßig)* modest *‹intelligence, talent, performance, achievements›*; ordinary *‹appearance›*. **2.** *adv. ‹produce, spend, earn, etc.›* on [an] average; **~ groß sein** be of average height; **~ begabt sein** be moderately talented

Durchschnitts-: ~alter das average age; **~bürger der** average citizen; **~ehe die** ordinary marriage; *(Statistik)* average marriage; **~einkommen das** average income; **~geschwindigkeit die** average speed; **~gesicht das** ordinary face; **~leser der** average reader; **~lohn der** average wage; **~mensch der** average person; *(Alltagsmensch)* ordinary person; **für uns ~menschen** for ordinary people like ourselves; **~note die** *(Schulw.)* average grade; **~temperatur die** average temperature; **~wert der** average *or* mean value; **~zensur die** *s.* **~note**

[1]durch|schnüffeln, [2]durch·schnüffeln *tr. V. (abwertend)* poke *or* nose around in

Durchschreibe·block der duplicate pad

durch|schreiben *unr. tr. V.* make a carbon copy of

durch·schreiten *unr. tr. V. (geh.)* stride across *‹room›*; stride through *‹door, hall›*

Durch·schrift die carbon [copy]

Durch·schuß der a) bullet *or* gunshot wound *(where the bullet has passed right through)*; **b)** *(Schuß) shot in which the bullet passes through and emerges on the other side*; **c)** *(Druckw.) (Zwischenraum)* space; *(Blindmaterial)* lead; **d)** *(Textilw.)* weft; woof

durch|schütteln *tr. V.* **jmdn. ~:** give sb. a good shaking; **wir wurden im Bus tüchtig durchgeschüttelt** we were shaken about all over the place in the bus

durch·schweifen *tr. V. (dichter.)* roam *or* wander through; *(fig.) ‹gaze›* rove *or* wander

[1]durch|schwimmen *unr. itr. V.; mit sein* **[durch etw.] ~:** swim through [sth.]; **unter etw.** *(Dat.)* **~:** swim through under sth.

[2]durch·schwimmen *unr. tr. V.* swim *‹the Channel, course, etc.›*

durch|schwindeln *refl. V.* get along by cheating and lying

durch|schwitzen, durch·schwitzen *tr. V.* **ich habe mein Hemd** *usw.* **durchgeschwitzt** *od.* **durchschwitzt** my shirt *etc.* is soaked in sweat; *s. auch* **durchgeschwitzt**

durch|segeln *itr. V.; mit sein* **a) [durch etw.] ~:** sail through [sth.]; **zwischen den Felsen ~:** sail [through] between the rocks; **b)** *(Schülerspr.: durchfallen)* **[durch etw.] ~:** fail *or (Amer. coll.)* flunk sth.; **bei/in etw.** *(Dat.)* **~:** fail *or* flunk sth.

durch|sehen 1. *unr. itr. V.* **a) [durch etw.] ~:** look through [sth.]; **durch dieses Glas kann man nicht ~:** you can't see through this type of glass; **b)** *s.* **durchblicken b. 2.** *unr. tr. V.* **a)** look *or* check through *or* over *‹essay, homework, etc.›*; **etw. auf Fehler ~:** look *or* check through sth. for mistakes; **b)** *(lesen)* look through *‹newspaper, magazine›*

durch|seihen *tr. V. (Kochk.)* strain; pass *‹sauce, gravy›* through a sieve

durch|sein *unr. itr. V., mit sein; nur im Inf. u. Part. zusammengeschrieben (ugs.)* **a) [durch etw.] ~:** be through *or* have got through [sth.]; **durch den Fluß ~:** be across *or* have got across the river; **ist die Post/der Briefträger schon durch?** has the mail arrived/has the postman *(Brit.) or (Amer.)* mailman been?; **b)** *(vorbeigefahren sein) ‹train, cyclist›* have gone through; *(abgefahren sein) ‹train, bus, etc.›* have gone; **c)** *(fertig sein)* have finished; **durch etw. ~:** have got through sth.; **mit etw. ~:** have got through sth.; **d)** *(durchgescheuert sein)* have worn through; **e)** *(reif sein) ‹cheese›* be ripe; **f)** *(durchgebraten sein) ‹meat›* be well done; **g)** *(angenommen sein) ‹law, regulation›* have gone through; *‹35-hour week etc.›* have been adopted; **h)** *(gerettet sein) ‹sick or injured person›* be out of danger; **i) bei jmdm. unten ~:** be in sb.'s bad books; **j)** *(bestanden haben)* have got through

durchsetzbar *Adj.* enforceable *‹demand, claim›*; **diese Rentenerhöhung/Reform ist nicht ~:** it will be impossible to get this pension increase approved/to carry this reform through

[1]durch|setzen 1. *tr. V.* carry *or* put through *‹programme, reform›*; carry through *‹intention, plan›*; accomplish, achieve *‹objective›*; enforce *‹demand, claim›*; get *‹resolution›* accepted; **~, daß etw. geschieht** succeed in getting sth. done; **seinen Willen ~:** have one's [own] way. **2.** *refl. V.* assert oneself; *‹idea›* find *or* gain acceptance, become generally accepted *or* established; *‹fashion›* catch on *(coll.)*, find *or* gain acceptance; **sich gegen jmdn. ~:** assert oneself against sb.; **sich den Schülern gegenüber ~** *‹teacher›* assert one's authority over the pupils

[2]durch·setzen *tr. V.* **eine Gruppe mit Spitzeln/ein Land mit Spionen ~:** infiltrate informers into a group/spies into a country; **mit Nadelbäumen durchsetzt sein** be interspersed with conifers

Durchsetzung die; ~ *s.* **[1]durchsetzen:** carrying through; putting through; accomplishment; achievement; enforcement; **zur ~ unserer Forderungen** to enforce our demands

Durchsetzungs-: ~kraft die, ~vermögen das ability to assert oneself

Durch·sicht die look *or* check through; **nach [einer] ~ der Unterlagen** after looking *or* checking through the documents; **jmdm. etw. zur ~ geben** give sb. sth. to look *or* check through

durchsichtig *Adj.* **a)** transparent; see-through, transparent *‹night-dress, blouse›*; clear *‹air, water›*; **b)** *(durchschaubar)* transparent; **etw. ~ machen** make sth. comprehensible

durch|sickern *itr. V.; mit sein* **a)** seep through; **b)** *(bekannt werden) ‹news›* leak out; **es ist durchgesickert, daß ...:** news has leaked out that ...

[1]durch|sieben *tr. V.* sift, sieve *‹flour etc.›*; strain *‹tea etc.›*; *(fig.)* sift [through] *‹applicants etc.›*

[2]durch·sieben *tr. V. ‹bullets›* riddle; **von Kugeln durchsiebt** riddled with bullets

durch|sitzen 1. *unr. tr. V.* wear out *‹chair, seat›*; **seine Hose ~:** wear through *or* out the seat of one's trousers. **2.** *unr. refl. V. ‹chair, seat›* wear out, become worn out

durchsoffen *Adj. (derb)* **eine ~e Nacht** a night on the booze *(sl.)*

durch|sollen *itr. V. (ugs.)* **[durch etw.] ~:** *‹cupboard, cable›* be supposed to go through [sth.]; **soll der Schrank hier durch?** is the cupboard to go through here?

durchsonnt [dʊrç'zɔnt] *Adj. (dichter.)* sun-drenched; sunny; sunny, sun-filled *‹room, clearing›*

durch|spielen *tr. V.* **a)** act *‹scene›* through; play *‹piece of music›* through; **b)** *(fig.: durchgehen)* go through *‹alternatives, options›*; play *‹part, role›* to the end; *‹footballer›* play right through; **all die ganze Nacht ~** *‹card players etc.›* play all night [long]

durch|sprechen *unr. tr. V.* talk *‹matter etc.›* over; discuss *‹matter etc.›* thoroughly

durch|springen *unr. itr. V.; mit sein* **[durch etw.] ~:** jump *or* leap through [sth.]

durch|spülen *tr. V.* **etw. [gut/gründlich] ~:** rinse sth. thoroughly

durch|starten *itr. V.; mit sein* **a)** *(Flugw.)* begin climbing again *(instead of landing)*; **b)** *(Kfz-W.)* accelerate away again

[1]durch|stechen *unr. itr. V.* **mit einer Nadel** *usw.* **[durch etw.] ~:** stick a needle *etc.* through [sth.]

[2]durch·stechen *unr. tr. V.* pierce; cut through *‹isthmus›*; **sich** *(Dat.)* **die Ohrläppchen ~ lassen** have one's ears pierced

durch|stecken *tr. V.* **etw. [durch etw.] ~:** put *or (coll.)* stick sth. through [sth.]

durch|stehen *unr. tr. V.* **a)** stand *‹pace, boring job, living with sb.›*; come through *‹adventure, difficult situation›*; pass *‹test›*; get over *‹illness›*; **b)** *(Ski)* complete *‹jump, run›* without falling

Durchsteh·vermögen das staying power; stamina; [power of] endurance

durch|steigen *unr. itr. V.; mit sein* **a) [durch etw.] ~:** climb through [sth.]; **b)** *(salopp: verstehen)* get it *(coll.)*; **da steige ich nicht durch** I don't get it *(coll.)*

durch|stellen *tr. V.* put *‹call›* through **(in** *+ Akk.*, **auf** *+ Akk.* to)

durch|stemmen *tr. V.* chisel through, chisel a hole in *‹wall›*

Durch·stich der a) *o. Pl. (Vorgang)* cutting

through; **der ~ der Landenge** *usw.* cutting through the isthmus *etc.*; **b)** *(Verbindung)* cut; cutting

Durchstieg ['dʊrçʃti:k] **der; ~[e]s, ~e: einen ~ in den Zaun schneiden** cut a hole in the fence [through which one can/could climb]

[1]dụrch|stöbern *tr. V. (ugs.)* search all through ⟨*house*⟩; rummage through ⟨*cupboard, case, etc.*⟩; scour ⟨*wood, area*⟩

[2]durch·stọ̈bern *tr. V. (ugs.)* **a)** *s.* **durch|stöbern; b)** *(durchsuchen)* rummage around ⟨*shop*⟩ **(nach** in search of); rummage through ⟨*archives*⟩ **(nach** in search of)

Dụrch·stoß der *(Milit.)* breakthrough

[1]dụrch|stoßen *unr. itr. V.* **a) durch etw. ~:** knock a hole through sth.; break through sth.; **b)** *mit sein (Milit.)* break through **(bis zu** to)

[2]durch·stọßen *unr. tr. V.* break through; go through ⟨*cloud layer*⟩; rupture ⟨*hymen*⟩; smash ⟨*pane of glass*⟩; **die feindlichen Linien ~** *(Milit.)* break through the enemy lines

[1]dụrch|streichen *unr. tr. V.* **a)** cross through *or* out; delete; *(in Formularen)* delete; **b)** *(passieren)* **Gemüse/die Sauce [durch ein Sieb] ~:** pass vegetables through a sieve/strain the sauce [through a sieve]

[2]durch·streichen *unr. tr. V. (geh.)* roam ⟨*area*⟩; rove, roam ⟨*foreign parts*⟩

durch·streifen *tr. V.* **a)** *(geh.)* roam, wander through ⟨*fields, countryside*⟩; **b)** *(kontrollieren)* patrol

[1]dụrch|strömen *itr. V.; mit sein* **[durch etw.] ~:** flow through [sth.]; *(fig.)* ⟨*people, crowd*⟩ stream *or* pour through [sth.]

[2]durch·strömen *tr. V.* flow through

dụrch|strukturieren *tr. V.* **etw. ~:** structure sth. well; **ein gut durchstrukturierter Artikel** a well-structured article

[1]dụrch|suchen *tr. V.* search through

[2]durch·sụchen *tr. V.* search ⟨*house, car*⟩ **(nach** for); frisk, search ⟨*person*⟩ **(nach** for); search, scour ⟨*area*⟩ **(nach** for)

Durchsụchung die; ~, ~en search; **zur ~ einer Wohnung** in order to search a flat

Durchsụchungs·befehl der search warrant

[1]dụrch|tanzen 1. *itr. V.* **die ganze Nacht ~:** dance all night; dance the night away; **bis zum Morgen ~:** dance until morning. **2.** *tr. V.* wear out ⟨*shoes*⟩ [by] dancing

[2]durch·tạnzen *tr. V.* **die Nacht ~:** spend the night dancing; dance all night; **nach einer durchtanzten Nacht** after a night of *or* spent dancing

dụrch|testen *tr. V.* **a) jedes einzelne Gerät ~:** test each device individually; **b)** *(gründlich testen)* **etw. ~:** test sth. thoroughly

durch·toben *tr. V. (geh.)* rage through

dụrch|trainieren *tr. V.* get ⟨*athlete, team, body*⟩ into condition; **ein gut durchtrainierter Körper** a body in peak condition

durch·trạ̈nken *tr. V. (geh.)* soak *or* saturate [completely]; soak, steep ⟨*fruit*⟩

dụrch|treiben *unr. tr. V.* **a) Menschen/Tiere [durch etw.] ~:** drive people/animals through [sth.]; **b)** *(durchschlagen)* **einen Nagel** *usw.* **[durch etw.] ~:** drive a nail *etc.* through [sth.]

[1]dụrch|trennen, [2]durch·trẹnnen *tr. V.* cut [through] ⟨*wire, rope*⟩; sever ⟨*nerve, umbilical cord*⟩

dụrch|treten 1. *unr. tr. V.* press ⟨*clutch-, brake-pedal*⟩ right down; depress ⟨*clutch-, brake-pedal*⟩ completely. **2.** *unr. itr. V.* **a)** *mit sein* **[durch etw.] ~** ⟨*liquid, gas*⟩ come through [sth.]; **b)** *mit sein (ugs.: weitergehen)* ⟨*passenger*⟩ move along down *(in bus, train)*

durchtrieben *(abwertend)* **1.** *Adj.* crafty; sly. **2.** *adv.* craftily; slyly

Durchtriebenheit die; ~: craftiness; slyness

dụrch|trinken *unr. itr. V.* **die ganze Nacht ~:** drink all night; **bis zum Morgen ~:** drink right through till morning

dụrch|tropfen *itr. V.; mit sein* **[durch etw.] ~** ⟨*water*⟩ drip through [sth.]

[1]dụrch|wachen *itr. V.* stay awake; **die ganze Nacht ~:** stay awake all night

[2]durch·wạchen *tr. V.* **die Nacht/mehrere Nächte ~:** stay awake all night/[for] several nights running; **die Nacht am Bett des Kranken ~:** keep watch through the night at the patient's bedside

[1]dụrch|wachsen *unr. itr. V.; mit sein* **[durch etw.] ~** ⟨*plant*⟩ grow through sth.

[2]durch·wạchsen 1. *Adj.* **a) mit Unkraut ~ sein** ⟨*lawn*⟩ have weeds growing in it; **~er Speck** streaky bacon; **b)** *nicht attr. (ugs. scherzh.)* so-so. **2.** *adv.* **ihr geht es ~:** she has her ups and downs

dụrch|wagen *refl. V. (ugs.)* **sich [durch etw.] ~:** dare to go through sth.; venture through sth.

Dụrchwahl die; *o. Pl.* **a)** direct dialling; **b) mein Apparat ist mit/hat keine ~:** I have/don't have an outside line; **c)** *s.* **Durchwahlnummer**

dụrch|wählen *itr. V.* **a)** dial direct; **direkt nach Nairobi ~:** dial Nairobi direct; **in ein Land ~:** dial a country direct; **b)** *(bei Nebenstellenanlagen)* dial straight through

Dụrchwahl·nummer die the number of the/one's direct line

dụrch|walken *tr. V.* **a)** *(durchkneten)* **jmdn. ~** ⟨*masseur*⟩ give sb. a good, hard massage; **die Wäsche ~:** use a vigorous kneading action to get the washing clean; **b)** *(ugs.: verprügeln)* **jmdn. ~:** give sb. a good belting; *(als Strafe)* give sb. a good hiding

[1]dụrch|wandern *itr. V.; mit sein* walk *or* hike without a break; **den ganzen Tag ~:** walk *or* hike all day

[2]durch·wạndern *tr. V.* walk *or* hike through

[1]dụrch|wärmen, [2]durch·wạ̈rmen *tr. V.* **jmdn. ~:** warm sb. up

dụrch|waschen *unr. tr. V. (ugs.)* **etw. ~:** wash sth. through

[1]dụrch|waten *itr. V.; mit sein* **[durch etw.] ~:** wade through [sth.]

[2]durch·waten *tr. V.* wade across

durch·weben *regelm. (dichter. auch unr.) tr. V.* interweave **(mit** with)

durchweg ['dʊrçvɛk], *(österr. ugs.)* **durchwegs** ['dʊrçvɛ:ks] *Adv.* without exception; **er umgibt sich ~ mit Leuten, die ...:** he surrounds himself exclusively with people who ...; **die Vegetation ist ~ öde** the vegetation is uniformly dreary

[1]dụrch|wehen *itr. V.* **durch etw. ~** ⟨*wind*⟩ blow through sth.

[2]durch·wehen *tr. V. (geh.)* ⟨*breeze*⟩ waft through; *(fig.)* pervade

[1]dụrch|weichen *itr. V.; mit sein* ⟨*cardboard, paper*⟩ become *or* go [soft and] soggy

[2]durch·weichen *tr. V.* make ⟨*earth, path, etc.*⟩ sodden; **völlig durchweicht sein** *(fig.)* be drenched; be sopping wet

dụrch|werfen *unr. tr. V.* **etw. [durch etw.] ~:** throw sth. through [sth.]

dụrch|wetzen wear out ⟨*clothes*⟩; wear through ⟨*sleeves*⟩; **eine durchgewetzte Hose** a worn-out pair of trousers

dụrch|winden *unr. refl. V.* **sich [durch etw.] ~** ⟨*river*⟩ wind its way through [sth.]; ⟨*person*⟩ thread one's way through [sth.]

durch·wịrken *tr. V. s.* **durchweben**

dụrch|witschen *itr. V. (ugs.)* **[durch etw.] ~:** slip through [sth.]; **jmdm. ~** ⟨*word*⟩ escape sb.

dụrch|wollen *unr. itr. V. (ugs.)* **a) [durch etw.] ~** *(durchgehen wollen)* want to go through [sth.]; *(durchkommen wollen)* want to come through [sth.]; **unter etw.** *(Dat.)* **~:** want to go through under sth.; **b)** *(ein Hindernis durchqueren)* **[durch etw.] ~:** want to get through [sth.]

[1]dụrch|wühlen 1. *tr. V.* rummage through, ransack ⟨*drawers, cupboard, case*⟩ **(nach** in search of, looking for); turn ⟨*room, house*⟩ upside down **(nach** in search of, looking for). **2.** *refl. V. (ugs.)* **sich durch das Blumenbeet/die Erde ~** ⟨*mole*⟩ dig up the flower-bed/burrow through the earth; **sich durch einen Aktenstoß ~** *(fig.)* plough through a pile of documents

[2]durch·wühlen *tr. V.* **a)** *s.* **[1]durchwühlen 1; b)** *(aufwühlen)* churn up

dụrch|wurschteln, dụrch|wursteln *refl. V. (salopp)* muddle through

dụrch|zählen *tr. V.* count; count up ⟨*money, people*⟩

[1]dụrch|zechen *itr. V.* **bis zum Morgen ~:** drink until morning

[2]durch·zẹchen *tr. V.* **die Nacht ~:** spend all night drinking; **eine durchzechte Nacht** a night of drinking

dụrch|zeichnen *tr. V. s.* **durchpausen**

[1]dụrch|ziehen 1. *unr. tr. V.* **a) jmdn./etw. [durch etw.] ~:** pull sb./sth. through [sth.]; **ein Gummiband [durch etw.] ~:** draw an elastic through [sth.]; **b)** *(ugs.: durchführen)* get through ⟨*syllabus, programme*⟩; **wir müssen die Sache ~:** we must see the matter through; **c)** *(bis zum Anschlag ziehen)* pull ⟨*oar, saw-blade*⟩ right through; **d)** *(salopp: rauchen)* smoke; **einen [Joint] ~:** smoke a joint *(sl.)*; **e)** *(erstellen)* dig ⟨*ditch*⟩ through; **eine Mauer [durch den Saal] ~:** build a wall across [the room]. **2.** *unr. itr. V.; mit sein* **a) [durch ein Gebiet** *usw.*] **~:** pass through [an area *etc.*]; ⟨*soldiers*⟩ march through [an area *etc.*]; **b)** *(Kochk.)* ⟨*fruit, meat, etc.*⟩ soak; **gut durchgezogen sein** be well soaked

[2]durch·ziehen *unr. tr. V.* **a)** pass through ⟨*land, area*⟩; **b)** *(durchsetzen)* ⟨*river, road, ravine*⟩ run through, traverse ⟨*landscape*⟩; **von blauen Adern durchzogener Marmor** marble veined with blue; **c)** *(enthalten sein in)* ⟨*theme, motif, etc.*⟩ run through ⟨*book etc.*⟩; **d)** *(durchdringen)* ⟨*pain*⟩ shoot through ⟨*person*⟩; ⟨*smell, scent*⟩ suddenly fill ⟨*room*⟩; *(fig.)* ⟨*feeling, awareness*⟩ come over ⟨*person*⟩

durch·zụcken *tr. V.* ⟨*lightning, beam of light*⟩ flash across; **jmdn. ~** *(fig.)* ⟨*thought*⟩ flash through *or* cross sb.'s mind

Dụrch·zug der a) *o. Pl.* draught; **~ machen** create a draught; **auf ~ schalten** *(ugs.)*, **die Ohren auf ~ stellen** *(ugs.)* let it go in one ear and out the other; **b)** *(das Durchziehen)* passage through; *(von Truppen)* march through; **nach dem ~ des Schlechtwettergebietes** *(Met.)* once the area of bad weather has moved through

Dụrchzügler [-tsy:klɐ] **der; ~s, ~** *(Zool.)* bird of passage

Dụrchzugs·recht das *(Völkerr.)* right to march troops through

dụrch|zwängen 1. *tr. V.* **etw. [durch etw.] ~:** force *or* squeeze [sth.] through [sth.]. **2.** *refl. V.* **sich [durch etw.] ~:** force *or* squeeze one's way through [sth.]

Dur·drei·klang der *(Musik)* major triad

dürfen ['dʏrfn̩] **1.** *unr. Modalverb; 2. Part.* **~ a)** *(Erlaubnis haben zu)* **etw. tun ~:** be allowed *or* permitted to do sth.; **darf ich [das tun]?** may I [do that]?; **hier darf man nicht rauchen** smoking is prohibited here; **b)** *(in Höflichkeitsformeln)* **darf ich rauchen?** may I smoke?; **darf ich Sie bitten, das zu tun?** could I ask you to do that?; **darf** *od.* **dürfte ich mal Ihre Papiere sehen?** may I see your papers?; **darf ich um diesen Tanz bitten?** may I have [the pleasure of] this dance?; **was darf es sein?** can I help you?; **was möchten Sie trinken, was darf es sein?** what can I get you to drink?; **darf ich bitten?** *(um einen Tanz)* may I have the pleasure?; *(einzutreten)* won't you come in?; **Ruhe, wenn ich bitten darf!** will you please be quiet!; **c)** *(verneint)* **das darf man nicht tun** *(ist einem nicht erlaubt)* that is not allowed *or* permitted; *(sollte man nicht)* one shouldn't do that; **er hat es nicht tun ~:** he was not allowed *or* permitted to do it; **nein, das darfst du nicht** no, you may not; **ich darf morgen nicht verschlafen** I mustn't oversleep tomorrow; **du darfst nicht lügen!/jetzt nicht aufgeben!** *(solltest nicht)* you shouldn't tell lies!/give up now!; *(mußt nicht)* you mustn't tell lies!/give up now!; **ihm darf nichts geschehen** nothing must happen to him; **das darf nicht wahr sein** *(ugs.)* that's incredible; **das hätte nicht kommen ~!** *(ugs.)* he/you *etc.* shouldn't have said that; **d)** *(Grund haben zu)* **ich darf Ihnen mitteilen, daß ...:** I am able to inform you that ...; **darf ich annehmen, daß ...?** can I assume that ...?; **sie darf sich nicht beklagen** she can't complain; she has no reason to complain; **da darf sie sich nicht wundern** that shouldn't surprise her; **das darfst du mir glauben** you can take my word for it; **e)** *Konjunktiv II + Inf.* **das dürfte der Grund sein** that is probably the reason; *(ich nehme an, daß das der Grund ist)* that must be the reason; **es dürfte einfach sein, das zu tun** it should be *or* ought to be easy to do it; **das dürfte reichen** that should be enough. **2.** *unr. tr., itr. V.* **er hat es nicht gedurft** he was not allowed *or* permitted to; **darf ich ins Theater?** may I go to the theatre?; **darfst du das?** are you allowed to?; **Darf ich? – Ja, Sie ~:** May I? – Yes, you may

durfte ['dʊrftə], *1. u. 3. Pers. Sg. Prät. v.* **dürfen**

dürfte ['dʏrftə] *1. u. 3. Pers. Sg. Konjunktiv II v.* **dürfen**

dürftig ['dʏrftɪç] **1.** *Adj.* **a)** *(ärmlich)* poor; scanty, meagre ⟨*meal*⟩; scanty, poor ⟨*clothing*⟩; **b)** *(abwertend: unzulänglich)* poor ⟨*substitute, performance, light*⟩; feeble, poor ⟨*explanation*⟩; lame, feeble ⟨*excuse*⟩; scanty ⟨*knowledge, evidence, results*⟩; sparse ⟨*growth of hair*⟩; paltry, meagre ⟨*income*⟩; **c)** *(kümmerlich, unansehnlich)* puny ⟨*tree, person*⟩. **2.** *adv.* **a)** ⟨*live*⟩ poorly; scantily ⟨*dressed*⟩; **b)** *(abwertend: unzulänglich)* skimpily, scantily ⟨*furnished*⟩; poorly ⟨*attended*⟩; ⟨*report, formulate*⟩ sketchily; thinly ⟨*concealed*⟩

Dürftigkeit die; ~ *s.* **dürftig: a)** *(Ärmlichkeit)* poorness; scantiness; meagreness; **b)** *(abwertend: Unzulänglichkeit)* poorness; feebleness; lameness; scantiness; sparseness; paltriness; meagreness

dürr [dʏr] *Adj.* **a)** withered ⟨*branch*⟩; dry, dried up, withered ⟨*grass, leaves*⟩; arid, barren ⟨*ground, earth*⟩; **b)** *(mager)* skinny, scraggy, scrawny ⟨*legs, arms, body, person*⟩; **c)** *(unergiebig)* lean ⟨*years*⟩; bare ⟨*words, description*⟩

Dürre die; ~, ~n a) *(Trockenheit)* drought; **b)** *o. Pl. (Dürrheit)* aridity; barrenness; *(fig.: der Sprache)* dryness

Dürre-: ~jahr das year of drought; **~katastrophe die** catastrophic drought; **~periode die** period of drought

Durst [dʊrst] **der; ~[e]s** thirst; **~ haben** be thirsty; **~ bekommen** get *or* become thirsty; **seinen ~ löschen** *od.* **stillen** quench *or* slake one's thirst; **ich habe ~ auf ein Bier** *od.* **nach einem Bier** I could just drink a beer; **~ nach Ruhm/Wissen** *(fig. geh.)* a thirst for fame/knowledge; **ein Glas** *od.* **einen/etliche über den ~ trinken** *(ugs. scherzh.)* have one/a few too many; **Fisch macht ~:** fish makes one thirsty

dursten *(geh.) itr. V.* **a)** thirst; **~ müssen** have to go thirsty; **b)** *s.* **dürsten**

dürsten ['dʏrstn̩] *(dichter.)* **1.** *tr. V. (unpers.)* **mich dürstet** *od.* **es dürstet mich** I am thirsty; **ihn dürstete nach Rache** *(fig.)* he thirsted *or* was thirsty for revenge. **2.** *itr. V.* **nach Rache/Gerechtigkeit** *usw.* **~:** thirst for revenge/justice *etc.*

durstig *Adj.* thirsty; **das macht ~:** it makes you thirsty; it gives you a thirst

durst-, Durst-: ~löschend, ~stillend *Adj.* thirst-quenching; **~strecke die** lean period *or* time; **~streik der** refusal of fluids *(as a means of protest)*; **in einen ~streik treten** refuse fluids

Dur-: ~ton·art die *(Musik)* major key; **~ton·leiter die** *(Musik)* major scale

Dusch·bad das shower[-bath]

Dusche ['dʊʃə] **die; ~, ~n** shower; **unter die ~ gehen** take *or* have a shower; **unter der ~ sein** be in the shower; **eine heiße/kalte ~ nehmen** take *or* have a hot/cold shower; **eine kalte ~ [für jmdn.] sein, wie eine kalte ~ [auf jmdn.] wirken** *(ugs.)* be like a cold douche *or* a douche of cold water [on sb.]

duschen 1. *itr., refl. V.* take *or* have a shower; **[sich] warm/kalt ~:** take *or* have a warm/cold shower. **2.** *tr. V.* **jmdn. ~:** give sb. a shower

Düse ['dy:zə] **die; ~, ~n** *(Technik)* nozzle; *(eines Vergasers)* jet

Dusel ['du:zl̩] **der; ~s a)** *(ugs.)* luck; **~ haben** be jammy *(Brit. coll.) or* lucky; **sie hat [einen] ~ gehabt** her luck was in *(coll.)*; she was jammy *(Brit. coll.) or* lucky; **so ein ~:** that was lucky; **b)** *(nordd.: Schwindelgefühl)* daze; **einen ~ haben** feel dizzy; **c)** *(nordd.: Rausch)* fuddle; **im ~ sein** be in a fuddle

duselig *Adj. (ugs.) (angetrunken)* fuddled; tipsy; muzzy; *(benommen)* muzzy; *(schlaftrunken)* drowsy

duseln *itr. V. (ugs.)* doze

düsen *itr. V.; mit sein (ugs.)* dash

Düsen-: ~an·trieb der jet propulsion; **mit ~antrieb** jet-propelled; **~bomber der** jet bomber; **~clipper der** jet airliner; **~flugzeug das** jet aeroplane *or* aircraft *or* plane; **~jäger der** jet fighter; **~maschine die** jet [aeroplane *or* aircraft *or* plane]; **~motor der** jet engine; **~trieb·werk das** jet power plant; jet engine

Dussel ['dʊsl̩] **der; ~s, ~** *(ugs.)* dope *(coll.)*; idiot; clot *(Brit. sl.)*

Dusselei die; ~ *(ugs.)* stupidity

dusselig, dußlig *(ugs.)* **1.** *Adj.* **a)** gormless *(Brit. coll.)*; stupid; idiotic; **b)** *(nordd.: benommen)* dopey *(sl.)*; muzzy. **2.** *adv.* gormlessly *(Brit. coll.)*; stupidly

duster ['du:stɐ] *Adj. (nordd.)* dark

düster ['dy:stɐ] **1.** *Adj.* **a)** dark; gloomy; dim ⟨*light*⟩; dark ⟨*background*⟩; **b)** *(bedrückend)* gloomy, dismal ⟨*day, weather, surroundings*⟩; sombre ⟨*colour, music*⟩; gloomy, sombre ⟨*atmosphere, picture*⟩; **c)** *(unheilvoll)* gloomy ⟨*forecast, conception, etc.*⟩; dark ⟨*foreboding*⟩; **d)** *(schwermütig)* gloomy ⟨*expression, look, person*⟩; gloomy, depressing ⟨*atmosphere*⟩; gloomy, dark ⟨*thoughts*⟩; **e)** *(obskur)* shady ⟨*business, affair*⟩; **f)** *(unklar)* hazy ⟨*idea*⟩; dim, hazy ⟨*conception*⟩. **2.** *adv. (schwermütig)* gloomily

Düsterheit, Düsterkeit die; ~, Düsternis die; ~ *(geh.)* **a)** *s.* **düster a:** darkness; gloom; dimness; **b)** *s.* **düster b:** gloominess; dismalness; sombreness; **c)** *s.* **düster d:** gloominess; depressingness; darkness

Dutt [dʊt] **der; ~[e]s, ~e** *od.* **~s** bun

Dutte die; ~, ~n *(österr. ugs.)* teat

Duty-free-Shop ['dju:tɪ'fri:ʃɔp] **der; ~[s], ~s** duty-free shop

Dutzend ['dʊtsn̩t] **das; ~s, ~e a) Pl.: ~:** dozen; **ein [ganzes]/halbes ~:** a dozen/half a dozen; **zwei ~:** two dozen; **ein ~ Eier** a dozen eggs; **das ~ Schnecken kostet** *od.* **kosten 16 Mark** snails cost 16 marks a dozen; **davon gehen 12 auf ein ~** *(ugs.)* there is nothing special about it; **b) ~e** *(eine Menge)* dozens; **sie kamen in** *od.* **zu ~en** they came in [their] dozens *(coll.)*

dutzend-, Dutzend-: ~fach 1. *Adj.; nicht präd.* dozens of *attrib.*; **2.** *adv.* a dozen times; dozens of times; **~gesicht das** *(abwertend)* nondescript face; **~mal** *Adv.* a dozen times; dozens of times; **~mensch der** *(abwertend)* nondescript *or* run-of-the-mill person; **~typ der** *(abwertend)* nondescript *or* run-of-the-mill type; **~ware die** *(abwertend)* cheap mass-produced item; **~ware sein** be a cheap mass-produced item; **~weise** *Adv.* ⟨*arrive, leave*⟩ in [their] dozens *(coll.)*; **Artikel ~weise kaufen/verkaufen** buy/sell articles by the dozen

Duz·bruder der *(veralt.) s.* **Duzfreund**

duzen ['du:tsn̩] *tr. V.* call 'du' *(the familiar form of address)*; **sich ~:** call each other 'du'; **sich mit jmdm. ~:** call sb. 'du'

Duz-: ~freund der good friend *(whom one addresses with 'du')*; **~fuß der** *in* **mit jmdm. auf [dem] ~fuß stehen** *(ugs. veralt.)* use [the familiar form] 'du' *or* the familiar form of address with sb.

DVP [de:vau̯'pe:] **die; ~** *Abk. (DDR)* **Deutsche Volkspolizei**

dwars [dvars] *Adv. (Seemannsspr.)* abeam

Dynamik [dy'na:mɪk] **die; ~ a)** *(Physik)* dynamics *sing., no art.*; **b)** *(Triebkraft)* dynamism; **c)** *(Musik)* dynamics; **d)** *(Versicherungsw.)* **eine Lebensversicherung mit ~:** ≈ index-linked life insurance *(linked to changes in the national product)*

dynamisch [dy'na:mɪʃ] **1.** *Adj.* **a)** *(auch fig.)* dynamic; **~e Renten** ≈ index-linked pensions *(linked to changes in the national product)*; **eine ~e Lebensversicherung** ≈ index-linked life insurance *(linked to changes in the national product)*; **b)** *(Physik)* dynamic; **~e Gesetze** laws of dynamics; **d)** *(Musik)* dynamic. **2.** *adv.* dynamically

dynamisieren *tr. V.* **a) etw. ~:** make sth. dynamic; give sth. dynamism; **b)** *(anpassen)* adjust ⟨*pension*⟩

Dynamisierung die; ~, ~en a) eine ~ der Agrarpolitik making the agricultural policy more dynamic; **die ~ einer Bewegung auslösen** give a movement dynamism; **b)** *(Anpassung)* adjustment *(of pension)*

Dynamismus der; ~: dynamism

Dynamit [dyna'mi:t] **das; ~s** dynamite; **~ in den Fäusten/Beinen haben** *(fig.)* pack a powerful punch/have a powerful shot

Dynamo [dy'na:mo] **der; ~s, ~s** dynamo

Dynast [dy'nast] **der; ~en, ~en** *(hist.)* dynast

Dynastie die; ~, ~n dynasty

dynastisch *Adj.; nicht präd.* dynastic

Dys·funktion [dʏs-] **die** *(Med., Psych., Soziol.)* dysfunction

Dystonie [dʏsto'ni:] **die; ~, ~n** *(Med.)* dystonia; **vegetative ~:** neurodystonia

D-Zug ['de:-] **der** fast *or* express train; **ein alter Mann/eine alte Frau ist doch kein ~!** *(salopp)* I'm too old to hurry

D-Zug-: ~-Tempo das *(ugs.)* **im ~-Tempo:** in double-quick time; **~-Zuschlag der** fast train supplement

E

e, E [e:] **das; ~, ~ a)** *(Buchstabe)* e/E; **b)** *(Musik)* [key of] E; *s. auch* **a, A**

E *Abk.* Europastraße
Eau de Cologne ['o: də ko'lɔnjə] **das** *od.* **die; ~ ~ ~, Eaux de Cologne** ['o:--] eau-de-Cologne
Ebbe ['ɛbə] **die; ~, ~n a)** *(Bewegung)* ebb tide; **nach Eintritt der ~:** once the tide starts/had started to go out; **~ und Flut** ebb and flow; **b)** *(Zustand)* low tide; **es ist ~:** the tide is out; **bei ~:** at low tide; when the tide is/was out; **es herrschte ~ in seinem Geldbeutel** *od.* **in seiner Kasse** *(fig. ugs.)* he was short of cash *(coll.)*
Ebbe-und-Flut-Kraftwerk das tidal power-station
ebd. *Akk.* **ebenda, ebendort** ibid
eben ['e:bn̩] **1.** *Adj.* **a)** *(flach)* flat; **b)** *(glatt)* level ⟨*ground, path, stretch*⟩; **c)** *nicht präd. (veralt.: gleichmäßig)* even, smooth ⟨*gait*⟩. **2.** *adv.* **a)** *(gerade jetzt)* just; **hast du ~ etwas gesagt?** did you just say something?; **b)** *(kurz)* [for] a moment; **kann ich Sie ~ sprechen?** can I speak to you [for] a moment *or* minute?; **c)** *(gerade noch)* just [about]; **etw. ~ noch schaffen** only just manage sth.; **d)** *(genau)* precisely; **aus ~ diesem Grunde** for this very reason; for precisely this reason; **aus ~ diesem Grunde brauchen wir das Geld** that is exactly *or* precisely why we need the money; **ja, ~:** yes, exactly *or* precisely; **ja, ~ das meine ich auch** yes, that's just *or* exactly what I think. **3.** *Partikel* **a) nicht ~:** not exactly; **b)** *(nun einmal)* simply; **das ist ~ so** that's just the way it is; **so gut ich ~ kann** as well as I can in the circumstances
eben-, Eben-: ~bild das image; **ganz jmds. ~bild sein** be the spitting image of sb.; **~bürtig** [~bʏrtɪç] *Adj.* equal; **jmdm. ein ~bürtiger Gegner sein** be sb.'s equal; be a match for sb.; **jmdm. ~bürtig sein** be equal to sb.; be sb.'s equal; **die beiden waren sich ~bürtig** they were [both] equal; **~da** *Adv.* ibid *abbr.*; ibidem; **~der, ~die, ~das** *Demonstrativpron.* **~das meine ich** that's exactly what I mean; **~die, von der wir sprachen** the very one we were talking about; **~der war krank** he was the very one who was ill; **~derselbe, ~dieselbe, ~dasselbe** *Demonstrativpron.* the very same ⟨*person, thing*⟩; **~dieselbe meine ich** she's just the one I mean; **~dasselbe wollte ich auch kaufen** I wanted to buy the very same thing; **~deshalb, ~deswegen** *Adv.* that is/was precisely [the reason] why; **~dieser, ~diese, ~dieses** *Demonstrativpron.* **~dieses Thema wurde behandelt** this very topic was discussed; **~diese Regeln gelten in allen Abteilungen** these same rules apply in all departments; **~dieser wurde genannt** he was the very one who was mentioned
Ebene die, ~, ~n a) *(flaches Land)* plain; **in der ~:** on the plain; **b)** *(Geom., Physik)* plane; **zwei sich schneidende ~n** two intersecting planes; **c)** *(Stufe)* level; **auf einer rein wissenschaftlichen ~:** on a purely scientific plane *or* level; **auf höchster ~:** at the highest level; *s. auch* **schief**
eben-: ~erdig 1. *Adj.* ground-level; *(in Gebäuden)* ground-floor; one-storey ⟨*house*⟩; **~erdig sein** be on ground level/on the ground floor *or (Amer.)* first floor; **2.** *adv.* at ground level; *(in Gebäuden)* on the ground floor *or (Amer.)* first floor; **~falls** *Adv.* likewise; as well; **der Botschafter war ~falls eingeladen** the ambassador was likewise invited; the ambassador was invited as well; **danke, ~falls** thank you, [and] [the] same to you
Eben·holz das ebony
ebenholz·farben *Adj.* ebony
eben-, Eben-: ~maß, das; *o. Pl. (der Gesichtszüge)* regularity; *(des Körperbaus)* symmetry; even proportions *pl.*; *(von Versen)* regularity; harmony; **~mäßig 1.** *Adj.* regular ⟨*features*⟩; well-proportioned ⟨*figure*⟩; regular, harmonious ⟨*verse*⟩; **von ~mäßigem Wuchs** of even proportions; **2.** *adv.* **~mäßig geformt** *od.* **gestaltet** regularly shaped; **~mäßigkeit die; ~** *s.* **Ebenmaß**
eben·so *Adv.* **a)** *mit Adjektiven* just as; **~ groß/schön/gut wie ... sein** be just as big/beautiful/good as ...; **ein ~ frecher wie dummer Kerl** a fellow who is/was as impudent as he is/was stupid; **er ist/arbeitet ~ fleißig wie geschickt** he is as diligent as he is skilful/works as diligently as he does skilfully; **b)** *mit Verben* in exactly the same way; *(in demselben Maße)* just as much; **ich glaube, er wird es ~ machen wie wir** I think he'll do exactly the same as we [do]; **bei Tag ~ wie bei Nacht** in the daytime as well as by night; **er ist dagegen, und ich denke ~:** he's against it, and so am I; **mir geht es ~:** its just the same for me
ebenso-: ~gern *Adv.* **~gern mag ich Erdbeeren [wie ...]** I like strawberries just as much [as ...]; **~gern würde ich an den Strand gehen** I would just as soon go to the beach; **~gut** *Adv.* just as well; **~gut hätte er zu Hause bleiben können** he might just as well have stayed at home; **ich kann ~gut ein Taxi nehmen** I can just as easily take a taxi; **~häufig** *Adv. s.* **~oft; ~lange** *Adv.* for the same length of time; **~oft** *Adv.* just as often; just as frequently
eben·solch... *Demonstrativpron.* the same; **ich habe ebensolche Angst/Kopfschmerzen wie du** I am just as afraid as you are/I have a headache too
ebenso-: ~sehr *Adv.* **a)** *mit Adjektiven* just as; **b)** *mit Verben* just as much; **~viel** *Indefinitpron., Adv.* just as much; **~weit** *Adv.* as far; **~wenig** *Indefinitpron., Adv.* just as little; **man kann dieses ~wenig wie jenes tun** one cannot do this, any more than that; **er aß kein Gemüse, ~wenig mochte er Obst** he didn't eat vegetables and he didn't like fruit either; he didn't eat vegetables, nor did he like fruit
Eber ['e:bɐ] **der; ~s, ~:** boar; **wie ein angestochener ~** *(salopp)* like a [raving] maniac
Eber·esche die rowan; mountain ash
ebnen *tr. V.* level ⟨*ground*⟩; **jmdm. den Weg** *od.* **die Bahn ~** *(fig.)* smooth the way for sb.; **das Geld seines Vaters ebnete ihm alle Wege** *(fig.)* his father's money opened [up] all doors for him
echauffieren [eʃɔ'fi:rən] *tr. V. (geh.)* **a)** make hot; **sich ~:** get hot; **b)** *(aufregen)* excite; **sich ~:** get excited
echauffiert *Adj. (geh.)* **a)** hot; **b)** *(aufgeregt)* excited
Echo ['ɛço] **das; ~s, ~s** echo; **das ~ auf die Ankündigung/den Vorschlag** *(fig.)* the response to the announcement/the suggestion; **das ~ in der Presse** *(fig.)* the press reaction; the reaction in the press; **ein breites ~ finden** meet with a wide response
Echo·effekt der echo effect
echoen ['ɛçoən] **1.** *itr. V. (unpers.)* **es echot** there is an echo. **2.** *tr. V. (gedankenlos wiederholen)* echo
Echo-: ~lot das a) *(Seew.)* echo-sounder; sonic depth finder; **b)** *(Flugw.)* sonic altimeter; **~lotung die** *(Seew.)* echo-sounding
Echse ['ɛksə] **die; ~, ~n** *(Zool.)* **a)** saurian; **b)** *(Eid~)* lizard
echt [ɛçt] **1.** *Adj.* **a)** *(nicht nachgemacht)* genuine ⟨*gold, fur, coin, Scotch whisky, Persian carpet*⟩; authentic, genuine ⟨*signature, document*⟩; **ist das ~?** is that real gold/fur *etc.?*; **ein ~er Picasso** a genuine Picasso; **b)** *(wahr)* true, real ⟨*love, friendship*⟩; real, genuine ⟨*concern, sorrow, emergency, need*⟩; **sind seine Gefühle ~?** is he sincere?; **sie hat noch ~e Gefühle** her emotions are still natural ones; **c)** *nicht präd. (typisch)* real, typical ⟨*Bavarian, American, etc.*⟩; **d)** *(Math.)* proper ⟨*fraction*⟩; **e)** *(Textilw., Chemie)* fast ⟨*dye*⟩; **f)** *meist attr. (reinrassig)* thoroughbred ⟨*horse*⟩; pedigree ⟨*dog, cattle*⟩. **2.** *adv.* **a)** *(ugs. verstärkend)* really; **ich habe mich ~ gefreut** I was really pleased; **das ist ~ wahr/blöd** that's absolutely true/stupid; **das war eine Frechheit, aber ~:** it was a piece of downright cheek; **b)** *(typisch)* typically; **das ist ~ amerikanisch/Frau/Klaus** that's typically American/just like a woman/Klaus all over; **c)** *(unverfälscht)* **das Armband ist ~ golden** the bracelet is real gold
echt-, Echt-: ~gold das real *or* genuine gold; **~golden** *Adj.* real *or* genuine gold; **~haar·perücke die** [real] hair wig
Echtheit die; ~ a) genuineness; *(einer Unterschrift, eines Dokuments)* authenticity; genuineness; **b)** *(Textilw., Chemie)* fastness
Echt·silber das real silver; genuine silver
echt·silbern *Adj.* real silver; genuine silver
Eck [ɛk] **das; ~s, ~e a)** *(südd., österr.: Ecke)* corner; **über(s) ~:** diagonally; **b)** *(Sport: Torecke)* **das lange/kurze ~:** the far/near corner [of the goal]
Eckart ['ɛkart] **der** *in* **der getreue ~** *(fig.)* a faithful supporter
Eck-: ~ball der *(Sport)* corner[-kick/-hit/-throw]; **einen ~ball treten** take a corner; **einen ~ball verwandeln** score from a corner; **~bank die** corner seat; **~daten** *Pl.* basic information *sing.*
Ecke ['ɛkə] **die; ~, ~n a)** corner; **am liebsten hätte ich mich in eine ~ verkrochen** I felt like creeping off into a corner; **an der ~:** on *or* at the corner; **Nietzschestr., ~ Goethestr.** on the corner of Nietzschestrasse and Goethestrasse; Nietzschestrasse at Goethestrasse *(Amer.)*; **um die ~:** round the corner; **um die ~ biegen** turn the corner; go/come round the corner; **jmdn. in die ~ drängen** *(fig.)* get sb. in a corner *(fig.)*; **es brennt an allen ~n [und Enden** *od.* **Kanten]** *(fig.)* there's a terrible commotion everywhere *(coll.)*; **das Auto klapperte an allen ~n [und Enden** *od.* **Kanten]** every nut and bolt in the car rattled; **jmdn. um die ~ bringen** *(salopp)* bump sb. off *(sl.)*; **mit jmdm. um** *od.* **über sieben ~n verwandt sein** *(ugs.)* be distantly related to sb.; *s. auch* **fehlen f; b)** *(Ballspiele)* corner; **eine ~ treten** take a corner; **den Ball zur ~ schlagen** put the ball over for a corner; **in die lange/kurze ~:** in[to] the far/near corner; **eine lange/kurze ~ treten** take a long/short corner; **c)** *(Boxen)* corner; **d)** *(ugs.: Gegend)* corner; **ihr wohnt in einer schönen ~:** you live in a lovely spot; **e)** *(ugs., bes. nordd.: Strecke)* **ich komme noch eine ~ mit** I'll come a little way/a bit further with you; **bis dahin ist es noch eine ganze ~:** it's still quite some way there; **er ist eine ganze ~ besser als du** *(fig.)* he is a whole lot better than you are; **f)** *(keilförmiges Stück)* wedge; **eine ~ Käse** a wedge of cheese
Ecken·steher der *(ugs.)* street loafer
Ecker ['ɛkɐ] **die; ~, ~n a)** *(Buch~)* beechnut; **b)** *(selten: Eichel)* acorn
Eck-: ~fahne die *(Sport)* corner flag; **~fenster das** corner window; **~grundstück das** corner site; **~haus das** corner house; house on the/a corner; *(einer Häuserreihe)* end house
eckig 1. *Adj.* **a)** square; angular ⟨*features*⟩; **b)** *(ruckartig)* jerky ⟨*movement, walk, gait*⟩. **2.** *adv.* **sich ~ bewegen** move jerkily
Eck-: ~kneipe die *small friendly pub on a street-corner;* **~laden der** corner shop; **~lohn der** *(Wirtsch.)* basic *or* minimum wage; **~pfeiler der** corner pillar; *(fig.)* corner-stone; **~platz der** end seat; **~schrank der** corner cupboard; **~sitz der** *s.* **~platz; ~sofa das** corner sofa; **~stein der a)** corner-stone; head stone; *(fig.)* corner-stone; **b)** *(Kartenspiel) s.* **Karo; ~stoß der** *(Fußball)* corner-kick; **~tisch der** corner table; **~turm der** angle tower; **~wert der**

(Wirtsch.) standard [of value]; **~zahn der** canine tooth; **~zimmer das** corner room; **~zins der** *(Finanzw.) official minimum interest rate on savings*
Eclair [e'klɛ:ɐ̯] **das; ~s, ~s** éclair
Economy·klasse [ɪ'kɔnəmɪ-] **die** economy class; tourist class; **in der ~ fliegen** fly economy [class]
Ecuador [ekua'do:ɐ̯] **(das); ~s** Ecuador
Ecuadorianer [ekuado'ria:nɐ] **der; ~s, ~:** Ecuadorean
Edamer Käse ['e:damɐ -] **der** Edam cheese
Edda ['ɛda] **die; ~:** [Elder] Edda; **die jüngere ~:** the Younger Edda
edel ['e:dl̩] **1.** *Adj.* **a)** *nicht präd. (reinrassig)* thoroughbred ⟨*horse*⟩; species ⟨*rose*⟩; **b)** *(großmütig)* noble[-minded], high-minded ⟨*person*⟩; noble ⟨*thought, gesture, feelings, deed*⟩; honourable ⟨*motive*⟩; **seine edle Gesinnung** his nobility of mind *or* noble-mindedness; **c)** *(geh.: wohlgeformt)* finely-shaped; **von edlem Wuchs** of noble stature; **d)** *(geh.: vortrefflich)* fine ⟨*wine*⟩; high-grade ⟨*wood, timber*⟩; **die edlen Teile** *(scherzh.)* the vital parts [of the body]; **e)** *nicht präd. (veralt.: adlig)* noble; **aus edlem Geschlecht** of noble stock. **2.** *adv.* **~ handeln** act nobly; **~ geformt** finely-fashioned
Edel-: ~fäule die *(Winzerspr.)* noble rot; **~fräulein das** *(hist.)* [unmarried] noblewoman; **~gas das** *(Chemie)* noble *or* inert *or* rare gas; **~hirsch der** *s.* **Rothirsch; ~holz das** high-grade wood; high-grade timber
Edeling ['e:dəlɪŋ] **der; ~s, ~e** *(hist.) s.* **Edelmann**
edel-, Edel-: ~kastanie die sweet chestnut; Spanish chestnut; **~kitsch der** grandly pretentious kitsch; **~mann der;** *Pl.* **~leute** *od.* **~männer** *(hist.)* nobleman; noble; **~metall das a)** precious metal; **b)** *(Chem.)* noble metal; **~mut der** *(geh.)* nobility of mind; noble-mindedness; magnanimity; **~mütig** *Adj. (geh.)* noble-minded; magnanimous; **~nutte die** *(salopp)* high-class tart *(sl.)*; **~pilz·käse der** blue[-veined] cheese; **~reis das** scion; **~rost der** patina; **~schnulze die** *(abwertend)* example of pretentious schmaltz; **der Film/Roman war eine ~schnulze** the film/novel was pretentious schmaltz; **~stahl der** *(rostfreier Stahl)* stainless steel; *(Sonderstahl)* special steel
Edel·stein der precious stone; gem[stone]; **mit ~en besetzt** set with precious stones; **ein synthetischer ~:** a synthetic stone; an artificial stone
Edelstein·schleifer der gem-cutter
Edel-: ~tanne die silver fir; **~weiß das; ~[es], ~e** edelweiss; **~wild das** *s.* **Rotwild; ~zwicker der** Edelzwicker *(fine Alsatian wine)*
Eden ['e:dn̩] **a)** *in* **der Garten ~** *(bibl.)* the Garden of Eden; **b) das; ~[s]** *(Paradies)* earthly paradise
edieren [e'di:rən] *tr. V.* edit
Edikt [e'dɪkt] **das; ~[e]s, ~e** *(hist.)* edict
Edition [edi'tsio:n] **die; ~, ~en** *(das Herausgeben)* editing; *(Ausgabe)* edition
E-Dur ['e:du:ɐ̯] **das; ~** *(Musik)* E major; *s. auch* **A-Dur**
EDV *Abk.* **elektronische Datenverarbeitung** EDP
EEG [e:e:'ge:] **das; ~[s], ~[s]** *Abk.* **Elektroenzephalogramm** EEG; *s. auch* **EKG**
Efeu ['e:fɔy] **der; ~s** ivy
efeu·bewachsen *Adj.* ivy-covered; ivy-clad
Efeu·ranke die ivy-twine; ivy-bind
Effeff [ɛf'|ɛf] *in* **etw. aus dem ~ beherrschen** *od.* **verstehen** know sth. inside out; **etw. aus dem ~ machen/können** do/be able to do sth. just like that *(coll.)*
Effekt [ɛ'fɛkt] **der; ~[e]s, ~e** effect; **im ~:** in the end; **im ~ läuft beides auf das gleiche hinaus** in effect the two *or* both come to the same thing
Effekten [ɛ'fɛktn̩] *Pl. (Finanzw.)* securities
Effekten-: ~bank die investment bank *(also acting as an issuing house)*; **~börse die** stock exchange; **~geschäft das** dealing in securities; **~makler der** stockbroker
Effekt·hascherei [-haʃə'rai] **die; ~, ~en** *(abwertend)* straining for effect; showiness; **ohne jede ~:** without any showiness; **billige ~:** cheap straining for effect
effektiv [ɛfɛk'ti:f] **1.** *Adj.* **a)** *(wirksam)* effective; **ein ~er Schutz** an effective form of protection; **b)** *nicht präd. (tatsächlich)* effective ⟨*profit, price, benefit*⟩. **2.** *adv.* **a)** effectively; **b)** *(ugs.: ganz bestimmt)* really; **ich weiß ~ nichts** I really haven't a clue *(coll.)*; **da ist ~ nichts zu machen** there's really nothing that can be done about it
Effektivität [ɛfɛktivi'tɛ:t] **die; ~:** effectiveness
Effektiv·lohn der real wage[s]
effekt·voll 1. *Adj.* effective ⟨*speech, poem, contrast, pattern*⟩; dramatic ⟨*pause, gesture, entrance*⟩. **2.** *adv.* effectively
Effet [ɛ'fe:] **der; ~s, ~s** spin; *(Billard)* side; **den Ball mit ~ schlagen** put spin/side on the ball
effizient [ɛfi'tsiɛnt] **1.** *Adj. (geh.)* efficient. **2.** *adv.* efficiently
Effizienz [ɛfi'tsiɛnts] **die; ~, ~en** *(geh.)* efficiency; *(Wirksamkeit)* effectiveness
EFTA ['ɛfta] **die; ~** *Abk.* **Europäische Freihandelsassoziation** Efta; European Free Trade Association
EG [e:'ge:] **die; ~:** *Abk.* **a) Europäische Gemeinschaft[en]; die ~-Länder** the countries of the European Communities; **b) Erdgeschoß**
egal [e'ga:l] **1.** *Adj.* **a)** *nicht attr. (ugs.: einerlei)* **es ist jmdm. ~:** it makes no difference to sb.; it's all the same to sb.; *(es kümmert ihn nicht)* sb. couldn't care less; it's all the same to sb.; **das ist ~:** that doesn't make any difference; **das kann dir doch ~ sein** that's none of your business; that's no concern of yours; **[ganz] ~, wie/wer/warum/wo/ob ...:** no matter how/who/why/where/whether ...; **b)** *(ugs.: gleich[artig])* identical; **~ sein** be the same *or* identical; **sie hat nicht zwei ~e Stühle** *(ugs.)* she hasn't got two chairs the same. **2.** *adv.* **a) Bretter ~ schneiden** cut planks to the same size; **b)** *(bes. ostm.: fortwährend)* constantly
egalisieren *tr. V.* **a)** *(Sport)* equal ⟨*record*⟩; **den Vorsprung des Gegners ~:** wipe out the opponent's lead; **den Punktvorsprung ~:** level the scores; **b)** *(Textilw.)* level ⟨*colour*⟩; **c)** *(Technik, Handw.)* smooth; dress ⟨*leather*⟩
egalitär [egali'tɛ:ɐ̯] *Adj.* egalitarian. **2.** *adv.* in an egalitarian way
Egalität die; ~: equality
Egel ['e:gl̩] **der; ~s, ~:** leech
Egge ['ɛgə] **die; ~, ~n** *(Landw.)* harrow
eggen *tr. V. (Landw.)* harrow
Ego ['e:go] **das; ~, ~s** *(Psych.)* ego
Egoismus [ego'ɪsmʊs] **der; ~, Egoismen a)** *o. Pl. (Selbstsucht)* egoism; **gesunder ~:** healthy self-esteem; **b)** *Pl. (egoistische Eigenschaften)* egoistic traits; **wo persönliche Egoismen aufeinanderstoßen** where individual egos clash
Egoist [ego'ɪst] **der; ~en, ~en, Egoistin die; ~, ~nen** egoist
egoistisch 1. *Adj.* egoistic[al]. **2.** *adv.* egoistically
Ego·trip ['e:go-] **der** *(ugs.)* ego trip
Egozentrik [ego'tsɛntrɪk] **die; ~:** egocentric attitude
Egozentriker der; ~s, ~, Egozentrikerin, die; ~, ~nen egocentric
egozentrisch 1. *Adj.* egocentric. **2.** *adv.* egocentrically; **~ denken** be egocentric in the way one thinks
[1]**eh** [e:] *Interj. (ugs.)* **a)** hey; **b)** *(was?)* **das hast du nicht erwartet, ~?** you didn't expect that, did you [,eh]?
[2]**eh** *Adv.* **a)** *(bes. südd., österr.: sowieso)* anyway; in any case; **es ist ~ alles zu spät** it's too late anyway *or* in any case; **b) seit ~ und je** for as long as anyone can remember; for donkey's years *(coll.)*; **wie ~ und je** just as before; **es sieht aus wie ~ und je** it looks the same as ever *or* the same as it always has done
ehe ['e:ə] *Konj.* before; **~ ihr nicht still seid, kann ich euch das Märchen nicht vorlesen** I can't read you the fairy story until you're quiet; **~ ich das tue, gehe ich lieber ins Gefängnis** I would rather go to prison than do it
Ehe ['e:ə] **die; ~, ~n** marriage; **eine glückliche ~ führen** be happily married; lead a happy married life; **die ~ brechen** commit adultery *(geh. veralt.)*; **jmdm. die ~ versprechen** promise to marry sb.; **mit jmdm. eine ~ eingehen** marry sb.; **ihre ~ wurde vor dem Standesamt/in der Kirche geschlossen** they were married in a registry office/in church; **Geld/Kinder in die ~ mitbringen** bring money/children into the marriage; **in erster ~ war sie mit einem Arzt verheiratet** her first husband was a doctor; **aus erster ~:** from his/her first marriage; **in wilder ~ leben** *(veralt.)* live in sin *(dated)*; **eine ~ zur linken Hand** *(hist.)* a morganatic *or* left-handed marriage; *s. auch* [1]**Hafen f; Stand; wild 1 b**
ehe-, Ehe-: ~ähnlich *Adj.* **ein ~ähnliches Verhältnis** a common-law marriage; **in einem ~ähnlichen Verhältnis leben** live [together] as man and wife; cohabit; **~anbahnung die** *s.* **~vermittlung; ~berater der, ~beraterin die** marriage guidance counsellor; **~beratung die a)** marriage guidance *(Brit.)*; marriage counselling; **b)** *s.* **~beratungsstelle; ~beratungs·stelle die** marriage guidance *or (Amer.)* counseling centre *(Brit.)*; **~bett das** marriage-bed; *(Doppelbett)* double bed; **~brechen** *unr. itr. V.; nur im Inf. u. 1. Part. gebr. (geh. veralt.)* commit adultery; **du sollst nicht ~brechen** *(bibl.)* thou shalt not commit adultery; **~brecher der; ~s, ~:** adulterer; **~brecherin die; ~, ~nen** adulteress; **~brecherisch** *Adj.* adulterous; **~bruch der** adultery
ehe·dem *Adv. (geh.)* formerly; in former times; **wie ~:** as in former times; **von ~:** of former times
ehe-, Ehe-: ~feindlich *Adj.* **a)** *(der ~ abgeneigt)* misogamic ⟨*attitude, tendencies*⟩; **b)** *(die ~ erschwerend)* **ein ~feindlicher Beruf** an occupation which is difficult to combine with marriage; **~frau die** *(im Verhältnis zum ~mann)* wife; *(im Verhältnis zu anderen)* married woman; **~freuden** *Pl. (scherzh.)* joys of married life; **~gatte der** *(geh.)* husband; spouse; **beide ~gatten** both husband and wife; **~gattin die** *(geh.)* wife; spouse; **~gelübde das** *(geh.)* marriage vows *pl.*; **~gemeinschaft die** marriage partnership; **~glück das** wedded *or* married bliss; **~hälfte die** *(scherzh.)* better half *(joc.)*; **~hindernis das** *(Rechtsw.)* impediment to marriage; **~joch das;** *o. Pl. (scherzh.)* yoke of marriage *or* matrimony; **sich ins ~joch begeben** get hitched *(sl.)*; **~kandidat der** *(scherzh.)* marriage candidate; **~krach der** *(ugs.)* row; quarrel; **er hat immer ~krach zu Hause** he is always having rows at home with his wife; **sie hatten ihren ersten ~krach** they had the first row of their married life; **~krise die** marital crisis; **~leben das** maried life; **~leute** *Pl.* married couple; **die beiden ~leute** the husband and wife
ehelich 1. *Adj.* **a)** *nicht präd. (die Ehe betreffend)* marital; matrimonial; conjugal ⟨*rights, duties*⟩; **~e Gemeinschaft** marriage

partnership; ~**es Zusammenleben** married life; **b)** *(aus einer Ehe stammend)* legitimate ⟨*child*⟩; **ein Kind für ~ erklären** declare a child legitimate; legitimate a child. **2.** *adv.* **sich ~ verbinden** *(geh.)* enter into [holy] wedlock

ehelichen *tr. V. (veralt., scherzh.)* wed

ehe·los *Adj.* celibate

Ehelosigkeit die; ~: celibacy

ehemalig ['e:əmalıç] *Adj.* former; **ein ~er Offizier** a former *or* one-time officer; **meine ~e Wohnung** my old flat *(Brit.) or (Amer.)* apartment; **seine ~e Frau** his ex-wife; **seine Ehemalige/ihr Ehemaliger** *(ugs.)* his/her ex *(coll.)*

ehemals ['e:əmals] *Adv. (geh., veralt.)* formerly; in former times

ehe-, Ehe-: ~mann der; *Pl.* **~männer** husband; **als ~mann** as a married man; **~müde** *Adj.* tired of married life *postpos.*; **~mündig** *Adj. (Rechtsspr.)* of marriageable age *postpos.*; **~mündig sein** be of marriageable age *or* of an age to marry; **~mündigkeit die** *(Rechtsspr.)* being of marriageable age; **vor Eintritt der ~mündigkeit** before attaining marriageable age; **~paar das** married couple; **ein älteres ~paar** an elderly [married] couple; **~partner der** marriage partner

eher ['e:ɐ] *Adv.* **a)** *(früher)* earlier; sooner; **ich war ~ da als er** I was there earlier *or* sooner than he was; **je ~, desto lieber** *od.* **besser** the sooner the better; **b)** *(lieber)* rather; sooner; **~ will ich sterben als mit ihr zusammenwohnen** I'd rather *or* sooner die than live with her; **alles ~ als das** anything but that; **c)** *(wahrscheinlicher)* more likely; *(leichter)* more easily; **das ist schon ~ möglich** that's more likely; **er ist schon ~ mein Typ** he's more my type; **um so ~, als ...** [all] the more so as *or* because ...; **d)** *(mehr)* **er ist ~ faul als dumm** he is lazy rather than stupid; he's more lazy than stupid *(coll.)*; **~ wie ein Beamter als wie ein Künstler aussehen** look more like a civil servant than an artist; **seine Wohnung ist ~ klein** his flat *(Brit.) or (Amer.)* apartment is rather on the small side; **es geht ihm ~ besser** he's rather better; **alles ~ sein als ...:** be anything but ...

Ehe-: ~recht das; *o. Pl. (Rechtsw.)* marriage law; laws governing marriage; **~ring der** wedding-ring

ehern ['e:ɐn] *Adj.; nicht präd. (dichter.)* bronze; *(eisern)* iron; *(fig.: unbeugsam)* iron ⟨*will, law*⟩; **mit ~er Stirn** brazenly

Ehe-: ~sakrament das; *o. Pl. (kath. Rel.)* sacrament of marriage; **~scheidung die** divorce; **~schließung die** wedding *or* marriage ceremony; **standesamtliche ~schließung** registry office wedding

ehest... ['e:əst] **1.** *Adj.; nicht präd.* **zum ~en Termin** at the earliest possible date; **bei ~er Gelegenheit** at the earliest opportunity. **2.** *adv.* **a)** *(noch am liebsten)* best of all; **am ~en wäre er nach Peru gefahren** best of all he'd have liked to go to Peru; **b)** *(noch am wahrscheinlichsten)* most likely; **am ~en möglich sein** be most likely *or* the most likely possibility; **mit diesem Werkzeug wirst du es noch am ~en schaffen** you'll manage it easiest with this tool; **am ~en könnte man ihn/es mit ... vergleichen** he/it could be most nearly compared to ...

Ehe·stand der; *o. Pl.* marriage *no art.*; matrimony *no art.*; **in den ~ treten** *(geh.)* enter into matrimony

Ehestands·darlehen das *low-interest government-backed loan available to young married couples*

ehestens ['e:əstn̩s] *Adv.* **a)** *(frühestens)* at the earliest; **~ [am] Dienstag** [on] Tuesday at the earliest; **~ in drei Wochen** in three weeks at the earliest; **b)** *(österr.: baldmöglichst)* as soon as possible

ehe-, Ehe-: ~stifter der matchmaker; **~streit der** marital *or* matrimonial dispute; **~vermittlung die a)** arrangement of introductions between people wishing to marry; **~vermittlung durch Computer** matching prospective marriage partners by computer; **b)** *(Institut)* marriage bureau; **~vermittlungs·institut das** marriage bureau; **~versprechen das** promise of marriage; **~vertrag der** *(Rechtsw.)* marriage contract; **~weib das** *(veralt., scherzh.)* spouse *(arch., joc.)*; **~widrig** *(Rechtsspr.)* **1.** *Adj.* extramarital ⟨*relations*⟩; **~widriges Verhalten** behaviour constituting a matrimonial offence; **2.** *adv.* **sich ~widrig verhalten** commit a matrimonial offence; **~zwist der** *s.* **~streit**

Ehr-: ~ab·schneider der calumniator; vilifier; **~auf·fassung die** conception of honour

ehrbar 1. *Adj. (geh.)* respectable, worthy ⟨*person, occupation*⟩; honourable ⟨*intentions*⟩; **~e Leute** respectable *or* worthy people. **2.** *adv.* respectably

Ehrbarkeit die; ~: respectability; worthiness

Ehr·begriff der conception of honour

Ehre ['e:rə] **die; ~, ~n a)** *(Ansehen)* honour; **seine ~ verlieren/bewahren** lose/preserve one's self-respect; **jmdm./einer Sache [alle] ~ machen** do sb./sth. [great] credit; **in ~n alt werden** *(geh.)* grow old without dishonour; **jmds. Andenken** *(Akk.)* **in ~n halten** honour sb.'s memory; **etw. um der ~ willen tun** do sth. for the honour of it; **zu ihrer ~ sei gesagt, ...:** in fairness to her *or* to do her justice it should be said ...; **[ich] hab'** *od.* **habe die ~** *(österr., südd.)* pleased to meet you; **auf ~ und Gewissen** in all truthfulness *or* honesty; **er fragte mich auf ~ und Gewissen, ob ich ...:** he asked me whether in all truthfulness *or* honesty I ...; **auf ~!, bei meiner ~!** upon my [word of] honour!; **dein Eifer in [allen] ~n, aber ...:** your enthusiasm is not in doubt *or* in question, but ...; **deine Meinung in [allen] ~n, aber ich halte das nicht für richtig** with [all] due respect to your opinion, I still think that it is wrong; **~ verloren, alles verloren** *(Spr.)* take away my good name and take away my life *(prov.)*; **b)** *(Zeichen der Wertschätzung)* **jmdm./einer Sache ~ antun** pay tribute to sb./sth.; **jmdm./einer Sache zuviel ~ antun** overvalue sb./sth.; **die ~ haben, etw. zu tun** *(geh.)* have the honour of doing sth.; **wir geben uns die ~, die Vermählung unserer Tochter bekanntzugeben** *(geh.)* we have much pleasure in announcing *or* are very pleased to announce the marriage of our daughter; **wir geben uns die ~, Sie zu einem Gartenfest einzuladen** *(geh.)* we request the pleasure of your company at a garden-party; we have the honour of inviting you to a garden-party; **sich** *(Dat.)* **etw. zur ~ anrechnen** give oneself credit for sth.; regard sth. as being to one's credit; **jmdm. zur ~ gereichen** *(geh.)* bring honour to sb.; **etw. zur ~ Gottes tun** do sth. to the glory of God; **~, wem ~ gebührt** [give] credit where credit is due; **jmdm. die letzte ~ erweisen** pay one's last respects to sb.; **mit ihr kannst du ~/keine ~ einlegen** she's a/no credit to you; **damit kannst du [keine] ~ einlegen** that does you [no] credit; **mit diesen Manieren legst du keine ~ ein** you won't get very far with manners like that; **der Wahrheit** *(Dat.)* **die ~ geben** tell the truth; **um der Wahrheit die ~ zu geben** to tell the truth; to be [perfectly] honest; **mit ~n** with honour; **mit ~n überhäuft** loaded with honours; **er wurde in ~n entlassen** he went into an honourable retirement; **zu ~n des Staatsbesuchs/des Königs** in honour of the state visit/of the king; **wieder zu ~n kommen** come back into favour; **c)** *o. Pl. (Ehrgefühl)* sense of honour; *(Selbstachtung)* self-esteem; pride; **jmdm. gegen die ~ gehen** offend sb.'s sense of honour; **ein Mann von ~** *(geh.)* a man of honour; **er hat keine ~ im Leib[e]** he doesn't have an ounce of integrity in him; **jmdn. bei seiner ~ packen** *od.* **fassen** appeal to sb.'s sense of honour; **d)** *(veralt.: Jungfräulichkeit)* honour; **e)** *(Golf)* honour

ehren *tr. V.* **a)** *(Ehre erweisen)* honour; **ihre Einladung ehrt uns sehr** we are greatly honoured by her invitation; **für seine Verdienste wurde er mit einem Orden geehrt** he was awarded a medal in recognition of his services; **man ehrte den ausländischen Gast mit einem Empfang** a reception was held in honour of the foreign guest; **sehr geehrter Herr Müller!/sehr geehrte Frau Müller!** Dear Herr Müller/Dear Frau Müller; **b)** *(Ehre machen)* **deine Hilfsbereitschaft ehrt dich** your willingness to help does you credit; **sein Vertrauen ehrt mich** I'm honoured by his confidence in me; **c)** *(veralt.: achten)* respect; **du sollst Vater und Mutter ~** *(bibl.)* honour thy father and thy mother

ehren-, Ehren-: ~ab·zeichen das medal; **~amt das** honorary position *or* post; **~amtlich 1.** *Adj.* honorary ⟨*position, membership*⟩; voluntary ⟨*help, worker*⟩; **2.** *adv.* in an honorary capacity; *(freiwillig)* on a voluntary basis; **~bezeigung die** salute

Ehren·bürger der, Ehren·bürgerin die honorary citizen; **ein Ehrenbürger/eine Ehrenbürgerin der Stadt** a freeman of the town/city; **jmdn. zum ~bürger der Stadt ernennen** give sb. the freedom of the town/city

Ehren·bürger-: ~recht das, ~würde die: jmdm. das ~recht *od.* **die ~würde verleihen** admit sb. as a freeman

Ehren-: ~dame die lady-in-waiting; **~dienst der** *(geh.)* **seinen ~dienst leisten** have the privilege of serving; **~doktor der a)** honorary doctor; **b)** *(Titel)* honorary doctorate; **~doktor·würde die** honorary doctorate; **~erklärung die: eine ~erklärung [für jmdn.]** a statement that aspersions cast on sb. are without foundation; **~formation die** *(Milit.)* guard of honour; **~fried·hof der** war cemetery; **~garde die** guard of honour; **~gast der** guest of honour; **~geleit das** official escort; **~gericht das** disciplinary tribunal *or* court; *(Standesgericht)* professional tribunal

ehrenhaft 1. *Adj.* honourable ⟨*intentions, person*⟩; **ein ~er Mann** an honourable man; a man of honour. **2.** *adv.* ⟨*act*⟩ honourably

Ehrenhaftigkeit die; ~: sense of honour; **die ~ seiner Absichten** the honourableness of his intentions

ehren-, Ehren-: ~halber *Adv.* **jmdm. den Doktortitel ~halber verleihen** confer an honorary doctorate on sb.; **Doktor ~halber** honorary doctor; **~handel der;** *Pl.* **~händel** *(veralt.)* affair of honour; **~karte die** complimentary ticket; **~kodex der** code of honour; **~kompanie die** guard of honour; **~kränkung die** *(Rechtsspr.)* affront; insult; **~legion die** Legion of Honour; **~loge die** VIP box; box reserved for VIPs; **~mal das** monument; **~mann der;** *Pl.* **~männer** man of honour; **~mit·glied das** honorary member; **~nadel die** badge of honour *(in the form of a lapel-pin)*; **~name der: den ~namen ... erhalten/tragen** be honoured by being given/by bearing the name ...; **~pflicht die** bounden duty; **es ist meine ~pflicht, diese Aufgabe zu erfüllen** I'm honour bound to perform this task; **~platz der** place of honour; **die ~plätze** the seats of honour; **~präsident der** honorary president; **~preis der** special prize; special award; **~rechte** *Pl.* **die bürgerlichen ~rechte** civil rights *or* liberties; *s. auch* **Aberkennung**; **~rettung die: zu jmds. ~rettung etw. sagen** say sth. to clear sb.'s name; **zu ihrer ~rettung muß ich sagen, daß ...:** it must be said in her defence that ...; **~rührig** *Adj.* defamatory ⟨*allegations*⟩; insulting ⟨*behaviour*⟩; **etw. ist ~rührig** sth. is an insult to sb.'s honour; **~runde die** lap of honour; **eine ~runde laufen/fahren** *usw.* do a lap of honour; **eine ~runde drehen** *(Schülerspr.)* repeat *or (Brit.)* stay down a year [at school]; **~sache die a)** *(~pflicht)* **das ist ~sache** that is a point of honour; **Verschwiegenheit ist ~sache** I/we feel honour bound to stay silent; **~sache!** you can count on me!; **b)** *(Angelegenheit der Ehre)* **es handelt sich um eine ~sache** my/our *etc.* reputation *or* good name is at stake; **~salut der** salute; **man begrüßte ihn mit einem ~salut** a salute was fired to welcome him; **~schuld die** debt of honour; **~senator der** honorary member of the/a university senate; **~spalier das** guard of honour; **~tag der** *(geh.)* special day; **~titel der a)** *(für besondere Dienste)* [honorary] title; **b)** *(ehrende Anrede, Bezeichnung)* title; **~tor das, ~treffer der** *(Sport)* consolation goal; **~tribüne die** VIP stand; **~urkunde die** certificate; **~voll 1.** *Adj.* honourable ⟨*peace, death, compromise, occupation*⟩; creditable, gallant ⟨*attempt, conduct*⟩; **2.** *adv.* ⟨*act*⟩ honourably; **~vorsitzende der/die** honorary chairman; **~wache die a)** *(Wachtposten)* guard of honour; **b)** *(Dienst)* **Soldaten zur ~wache abkommandieren** detail soldiers to form a guard of honour; **~wache halten** keep vigil; **~wert** *Adj. (geh.)* worthy, honourable ⟨*person, occupation*⟩; **die Ehrenwerte Gesellschaft** the Mafia; **~wort das;** *pl.* **~worte: ~wort [!/?]** word of honour [!/?]; **sein ~wort brechen** break one's word; **auf [mein] ~wort** [I] promise; **großes ~wort!** *(scherzh.)* scout's honour! *(joc.)*; **Urlaub auf ~wort** *(Milit.)* parole; **~wörtlich 1.** *Adj.; nicht präd.* solemn ⟨*agreement, promise*⟩; ⟨*agreement, promise*⟩ on one's honour; **2.** *adv.* **es war ~wörtlich ausgemacht, daß ...:** he/they *etc.* had promised faithfully *or* made a solemn promise that ...; **~zeichen das** decoration

ehrerbietig ['e:ɐ̯lɛɐ̯bi:tɪç] **1.** *Adj. (geh.)* respectful; **sein ~es Gehabe** his deferential manner. **2.** *adv.* ⟨*greet*⟩ respectfully

Ehrerbietung die; ~ *(geh.)* respect

Ehr·furcht die reverence (**vor** + *Dat.* for); **[große] ~ vor jmdm./etw. haben** have [a great] respect for sb./sth.; **~ vor dem Leben** reverence for life; **jmdm. ~ einflößen** fill sb. with awe; **er hat vor nichts ~:** he has no respect for anything; nothing is sacred to him

ehrfurcht·gebietend 1. *Adj.* awe-inspiring ⟨*personality, cathedral*⟩; awesome ⟨*silence*⟩; authoritative ⟨*voice*⟩. **2.** *adv.* **~ auftreten** have an imposing presence

ehrfürchtig 1. *Adj.* reverent. **2.** *adv.* reverently

ehrfurchts-: ~los 1. *Adj.* irreverent; **2.** *adv.* irreverently; **~voll** *(geh.)* **1.** *Adj.* reverent; **mit ~voller Miene** with a reverential expression; **2.** *adv.* reverently

ehr-, Ehr-: ~gefühl das; *o. Pl.* sense of honour; *(Selbstachtung)* self-esteem; pride; **falsches ~gefühl** a misplaced sense of honour; **~geiz der** ambition; **sie hatte den ~geiz, Pilotin zu werden** her ambition was *or* it was her ambition to become a pilot; **seinen ~geiz dareinsetzen, etw. zu tun** make it one's ambition to do sth.; **~geizig 1.** *Adj.* ambitious; **wenig ~geizig sein** be lacking in ambition; **2.** *adv.* ambitiously; **~geizling** [~gaitslɪŋ] **der;** **~s, ~e** *(ugs. abwertend)* pushy individual *(coll.)*; pusher

ehrlich 1. *Adj.* **a)** honest ⟨*person, face, answer, deal*⟩; genuine ⟨*concern, desire, admiration*⟩; upright ⟨*character*⟩; honourable ⟨*intentions*⟩; *(wahrheitsgetreu)* truthful ⟨*answer, statement*⟩; **wenn ich ~ bin** if you want my honest opinion; **der ~e Finder gab die Brieftasche beim Fundbüro ab** the person who found the wallet handed it in *(Brit.) or (Amer.)* turned it in at the lost-property office; **dem ~en Finder winkt eine Belohnung von 10% der Gesamtsumme** a reward of 10% is offered [for the return of the money]; **~ währt am längsten** *(Spr.)* honesty is the best policy *(prov.)*; **b)** *(veralt.: anständig)* **seinen Namen wieder ~ machen** restore one's good name; **ein ~es Handwerk** an honest trade. **2.** *adv.* honestly; **etw. ~ teilen** share sth.; **~ spielen** play fairly; **es ~ mit jmdm. meinen** play straight with sb.; **~ gesagt** quite honestly; to be honest

ehrlicherweise *Adv.* **a)** in all honesty; **etw. ~ zugeben** own up and admit sth.; **b)** *(selten: ehrlich)* honestly

Ehrlichkeit die; ~ *s.* **ehrlich 1a:** honesty; genuineness; uprightness; honourableness; truthfulness

ehr-, Ehr-: ~los 1. *Adj.* dishonourable; **2.** *adv.* dishonourably; **~los aus dem Leben scheiden** depart this life in dishonour; **~losigkeit die;** ~: dishonourableness; **~pusselig, ~pußlig** *Adj. (ugs.)* ⟨*person*⟩ who is pompously concerned about his/her reputation

ehrsam *Adj. (geh. veralt.)* respectable, worthy ⟨*people, occupation*⟩

Ehrsamkeit die; ~: respectability

ehr-, Ehr-: ~sucht die; *o. Pl. (veralt.)* inordinate ambition; **~süchtig** *Adj. (veralt.)* inordinately ambitious; over-ambitious

Ehrung die; **~, ~en a)** *(das Ehren)* **die ~ der Preisträger** the prize-giving *(Brit.) or (Amer.)* awards ceremony; **bei der ~ der Sieger** when the winners were awarded their medals/trophies; **für jmdn. die höchste ~ sein** be the supreme accolade for sb.; **b)** *(Ehrenerweisung)* honour

ehr-, Ehr-: ~verlust der; *o. Pl. (Rechtsw.)* loss of civil rights; *(hist.)* attainder; **~würden (der);** **~[s]** *(kath. Kirche, veralt.)* **Euer ~würden** Reverend Father; **~würden Bruder Martin/Schwester Notburga** brother Martin/sister Notburga; **~würdig** *Adj.* **a)** *(ehrfurchtgebietend)* venerable ⟨*person*⟩; **ein ~würdiges Alter haben** ⟨*person*⟩ have reached a grand old age; ⟨*building*⟩ be of great age; **b)** *(kath. Kirche)* **~würdiger Vater/~würdige Mutter** Reverend Father/Mother

ei [ai] *Interj.* **a)** hey; *(abschätzig)* oho; *s. auch* **Daus; b)** *(Kinderspr.)* **ei [ei] machen** stroke sb. [affectionately]; **mach mal ei!** stroke me!

Ei [ai] **das;** **~[e]s, ~er a)** egg; *(Physiol., Zool.)* ovum; **aus dem ~ schlüpfen** hatch [out]; **verlorene** *od.* **pochierte ~er** poached eggs; **russische ~er** egg mayonnaise; Russian eggs; **sie geht wie auf [rohen] ~ern** *(fig.)* she is walking very carefully; **das ist ein [dickes] ~!** *(ugs.)* that's terrible; **ach, du dickes ~!** *(ugs.)* dash it! *(Brit. coll.)*; darn it! *(Amer. coll.)*; **das ~ des Kolumbus** *(fig.)* an inspired discovery; **wie aus dem ~ gepellt sein** *(fig.)* be dressed to the nines; **sich gleichen wie ein ~ dem anderen** be as like as two peas in a pod; **das ~ will klüger sein als die Henne** *(fig.)* stop trying to teach your grandmother to suck eggs; **ein ~ legen** lay an egg; *(ugs.: einen Plan ausbrüten)* hatch [out] a plan; *(derb: seine große Notdurft verrichten)* have *(Brit.) or (Amer.)* take a shit *(coarse)*; *s. auch* **Apfel; bewerfen; Pfanne; roh; ungelegt; b)** *(derb: Hode) meist Pl.* **~er** balls *(coarse)*; nuts *(Amer. coarse)*; **c)** *(salopp)* **zwölf ~er** twelve marks; *(zwölf Pfund)* twelve quid *(coll.)*; *(zwölf Dollar)* twelve bucks *(coll.)*; **d)** *(Sportjargon: Ball)* ball

eia ['aia] *s.* **ei b**

eiapopeia [aiapo'paia] *Interj. (Kinderspr.)* hushaby[e]; **~ machen** lull the baby to sleep

Eibe ['aibə] **die;** **~, ~n** yew[-tree]

Eibisch ['aibɪʃ] **der;** **~[e]s, ~e** *(Bot.)* marsh mallow

Eich-: ~amt das local weights and measures office *(Brit.)*; local bureau of standards *(Amer.)*; **~baum der** oak-tree; **~behörde die** ≈ Weights and Measures Inspectorate *(Brit.)*; ≈ National Bureau of Standards *(Amer.)*

Eiche ['aiçə] **die;** **~, ~n** oak[-tree]; *(Holz)* oak[-wood]

Eichel ['aiçl̩] **die;** **~, ~n a)** *(Frucht)* acorn; **b)** *(Anat.)* glans; **c)** *Pl.; o. Art. (Spielkartenfarbe)* acorns *pl.*; *s. auch* ²**Pik**

Eichel·häher der jay

¹**eichen** *tr. V.* calibrate ⟨*measuring instrument, thermometer*⟩; standardize ⟨*weights, measures, containers, products*⟩; adjust ⟨*weighing-scales*⟩; **darauf bin ich geeicht** *(ugs.)* that's in my line *(coll.)*

²**eichen** *Adj.; nicht präd.* oak[en] ⟨*furniture*⟩

Eichen-: ~baum der oak-tree; **~blatt das** oak-leaf; **~holz das** oak[-wood]; **ein Schreibtisch aus ~holz** an oak writing-desk; **~laub das a)** oak leaves *pl.*; **b)** *(Auszeichnung)* garland of oak [leaves]; **~sarg der** oak[en] coffin *or (Amer.)* casket; **~wald der** oak-wood; *(größer)* oak forest

Eich·gewicht das standard weight

Eich·hörnchen das, Eich·kätzchen das *(landsch.)*, **Eich·katze die** *(landsch.)* squirrel

Eich-: ~maß das standard measure; **~stempel der** verification stamp; **~strich der** [engraved] line showing the correct measure; **ein Glas bis zum ~strich füllen** fill a glass up to the line

Eid [ait] **der;** **~[e]s, ~e** oath; **einen ~ leisten** *od.* **ablegen** swear *or* take an oath; **einen ~ auf die Bibel schwören** swear an oath on the [Holy] Bible; **einen ~ auf die Verfassung schwören** solemnly swear to preserve, protect, and defend the constitution; **unter ~ [stehen]** [be] under *or* on oath; **etw. auf seinen ~ nehmen** swear to sth.; **ich nehme es auf meinen ~, daß ...:** I swear that ...; **der ~ des Hippokrates** the Hippocratic oath; **an ~es Statt erklären, daß ...** *(Rechtsspr.)* attest in an statutory declaration that ...

Eidam ['aidam] **der;** **~s, ~e** *(veralt.)* son-in-law

Eid·bruch der breach of one's oath; *(Rechtsw.)* perjury *no indef. art.*; **einen ~bruch begehen** break one's oath

eid·brüchig *Adj.* treacherous ⟨*allies*⟩; **~brüchig werden** break one's oath; *(Rechtsw.)* perjure oneself

Eidechse ['aidɛksə] **die;** **~, ~n** lizard

Eider- ['aidɐ-]: **~daune die** eider-down; **~ente die** eider [duck]

eides-, Eides-: ~belehrung die *(Rechtsw.) caution to those about to take the oath;* **~formel die** *(jur.)* wording of the oath; **die ~formel nachsprechen** repeat the [words of the] oath; **~stattlich 1.** *Adj. (Rechtsw.)* **eine ~stattliche Erklärung** a statutory declaration; **2.** *adv.* **~stattlich erklären** *od.* **versichern, daß ...:** attest in a statutory declaration that ...

Eidetik [ai'de:tɪk] **die;** ~ *(Psych.)* eidetic ability

eidetisch *Adj. (Psych.)* eidetic

eid-, Eid-: ~genosse der Swiss; *(Verbündeter)* confederate; **~genossenschaft die;** *o. Pl.* **die Schweizerische ~genossenschaft** the Swiss Confederation; **~genössisch** *Adj.* Swiss

eidlich 1. *Adj.* made under oath *postpos.* **2.** *adv.* on oath

Ei·dotter der *od.* **das** egg yolk

eier-, Eier-: ~becher der egg-cup; **~brikett das** ovoid; **~farbe die** *paint for decorating eggs as Easter gifts;* **~frucht die** egg-plant; aubergine; **~hand·granate die** Mills bomb *or* grenade; **~kohle die** egg-coal; **~kopf der a)** *(salopp)* egg-shaped head; **b)** *(ugs.: Intellektueller)* egghead *(coll.)*; **~kuchen der** pancake; *(Omelett)* omelette; **~laufen das** egg-and-spoon race; **~legend** *Adj. (Biol.)* oviparous; egg-laying; **~likör der** egg-liqueur; **~löffel der** egg-spoon

eiern *itr. V.* **a)** *(ugs.: ungleichmäßig rotieren)* wobble; **b)** *mit sein (salopp: sich wackelnd fortbewegen)* roll

eier-, Eier-: ~nudel die; *meist Pl.* egg noodle; **~pfann·kuchen der** *s.* **~kuchen; ~pflaume die** egg-plum; **~punsch der** egg-flip; egg-nog; **~salat der** egg salad; **~schale die** eggshell; **er hat noch die ~schalen hinter den Ohren** *(fig.)* he's still wet behind the ears *(fig.)*; **~schalen·farben** *Adj.* off-white

Eier-: ~schwamm der *(bes. österr.)* chanterelle; **~speise die a)** egg dish; **b)** *(österr.)* scrambled egg; **~stich der;** *o. Pl. (Kochk.)* cooked-egg garnish; royale; **~stock der** *(Physiol., Zool.)* ovary; **~stock·entzündung die** *(Med.)* ovaritis; **~tanz der** *(ugs.) (um eine heikle Angelegenheit)* intricate manœuvring *no indef. art.*; *(zwischen unangenehmen Alternativen)* treading carefully *no art.*; **einen [richtigen] ~tanz aufführen** *od.* **vollführen** engage in [really] intricate manœuvring/tread [very] carefully; **~uhr die** egg-timer; **~wärmer der** egg-cosy

Eifer ['aifɐ] **der; ~s** enthusiasm; *(Eifrigkeit)* eagerness; *(Emsigkeit)* zeal; **etw. voller ~ tun** do sth. with great enthusiasm; **in ~ geraten** become excited *or* heated; **etw. im ~ [des Gefechts] vergessen** forget sth. in the excitement; *s. auch* **blind 1 c**

Eiferer der; ~s, ~ *(geh.)* zealot

eifern *itr. V.* **a)** *(abwertend)* **für etw. ~:** agitate for sth.; **gegen etw. ~:** rail *or* agitate against sth.; **b)** *(geh.: heftig streben)* strive; **nach Macht ~:** strive for power

Eifer·sucht die jealousy **(auf +** *Akk.* of); **etw. aus ~ tun** do sth. out of jealousy

Eifersüchtelei [-zʏçtə'lai] **die; ~, ~en;** *meist Pl.* petty jealousy

eifer·süchtig 1. *Adj.* jealous **(auf +** *Akk.* of). **2.** *adv.* jealously

Eifersuchts-: ~szene die display of jealousy; **sie machte ihm eine ~szene** in a fit of jealousy she made a scene; **~tragödie die** tragedy due to jealousy; **es handelte sich um eine ~tragödie** the tragedy was the result of jealousy

Eiffel·turm ['aifl-] **der** Eiffel Tower

ei·förmig *Adj.* egg-shaped

eifrig 1. *Adj.* eager; constant ‹*reader*›; enthusiastic ‹*supporter, collector*›; *(fleißig)* assiduous; **die ganz Eifrigen** the really keen ones; **~ bei einer Sache sein** show keen interest in doing sth. **2.** *adv.* eagerly; **~ dabei sein, etw. zu tun** be busy doing sth.; **sich ~ um etw. bemühen** set about sth. eagerly; **sich ~ bemühen, etw. zu tun** set about doing sth. eagerly; **~ bemüht sein, etw. zu tun** be eager to do sth.

Ei·gelb das; ~[e]s, ~e egg yolk; **drei ~:** the yolks of three eggs; three [egg] yolks

eigen ['aign̩] *Adj.* **a)** *nicht präd. (jmdm. selbst gehörend)* own; *(selbständig)* separate; **mein ~er Bruder** my own brother; **eine ~e Wohnung haben** have one's own flat *(Brit.)* *or (Amer.)* apartment; **ein Zimmer mit ~em Eingang** a room with a separate entrance; **etw. mit ~en Augen sehen** see sth. with one's [very] own eyes; **seine ~e Meinung** his own opinion; **auf ~en Füßen** *od.* **Beinen stehen** stand on one's own two feet; **sich** *(Dat.)* **etw. zu ~ machen** adopt sth.; **etw. sein ~ nennen** *(geh., iron.)* call sth. one's own; **meinem Lehrer zu ~** *(geh.)* [dedicated] to my teacher; **b)** *(kennzeichnend)* characteristic; **mit einer ihr ~en Gebärde** with a gesture characteristic of her; with a characteristic gesture; **mit allem ihr ~en Charme** with all her characteristic charm; **c)** *(landsch.: gewissenhaft)* particular; **mit etw. ~ sein** be particular about sth.; **d)** *(veralt.: seltsam)* peculiar; strange; odd; **mir ist so ~ zumute** I feel so strange; I have the strangest feeling

-eigen *Adj.* **a)** *(im Besitz von)* belonging to the ‹*school, company, community*›; **b)** *(zugehörig)* intrinsic to the ‹*body, language*›; inherent in the ‹*system, period*›

eigen-, Eigen-: ~art die *(Wesensart)* particular nature; *(Zug)* peculiarity; **eine ~art dieser Stadt** one of the characteristic features of this city; **ihre merkwürdigen ~arten** her strange peculiarities; **~artig** *Adj.* peculiar; strange; odd; **~artigerweise** *Adv.* strangely [enough]; oddly [enough]; **~artigkeit die a)** *o. Pl.* peculiarity; strangeness; oddness; **b)** *(~artige Verhaltensweise)* peculiarity; eccentricity; oddity; **~bedarf der** own requirements *pl.*; *(eines Landes)* domestic requirements *pl.*; **~bericht der: „~bericht"** 'report from our own correspondent'; **nur die Lokalberichte sind ~berichte** only the local news reports are by staff reporters; **~besitz der** *(Rechtsspr.)* personal property; **~brötelei** [~brø:tə'lai] **die; ~, ~en** taking an [unduly] independent line; **~brötler** [~brø:tlɐ] **der; ~s, ~:** loner; lone wolf; **~brötlerisch 1.** *Adj.* solitary; **2.** *adv.* **sich ~brötlerisch verhalten** behave like a loner *or* a lone wolf; **~dynamik die** inherent dynamism; **eine ~dynamik entwickeln** develop a momentum of its own; **~finanzierung die** self-financing *no art.*; **etw. in ~finanzierung tun** finance sth. oneself; **~funktion die** *(Math., Phys.)* eigenfunction; **~gesetzlich 1.** *Adj.* **die ~gesetzliche Entwicklung der Wirtschaft** the development of the economy according to its own laws; **2.** *adv.* according to its/their own laws; **~gesetzlichkeit die** inherent laws *pl.*; **~gewicht das a)** own weight; **b)** *(Wirtsch.: Nettogewicht)* net weight; **~goal das** *(österr.) s.* **~tor; ~händig 1.** *Adj.* personal ‹*signature*›; personally inscribed ‹*dedication*›; holographic ‹*will, document*›; **2.** *adv.* **etw. ~händig unterschreiben/übergeben** sign/present sth. personally; **„~händig abzugeben"** 'to be delivered to the addressee in person'; **~heim das** house of one's own; **der Trend zum ~heim** the trend towards owning a house of one's own

Eigenheit die; ~, ~en peculiarity

eigen-, Eigen-: ~initiative die initiative of one's own; **auf ~initiative** on one's own initiative; **~interesse das** personal interest; **~kapital das** *(Wirtsch.)* equity capital; **~leben das;** *o. Pl.* life of one's own; **ein ~leben haben** *od.* **führen** live one's own life; **sein ~leben bewahren** continue to live a life of one's own; **~liebe die** amour propre; **~lob das** self-praise; **~lob stinkt!** *(ugs.)* self-praise is no recommendation; **~mächtig 1.** *Adj.* unauthorized ‹*decision*›; *(selbstherrlich)* high-handed; **2.** *adv.* **~mächtig handeln** act on one's own authority; *(selbstherrlich)* act high-handedly; **er ist ~mächtig mit meinem Auto gefahren** he took my car without permission; **etw. ~mächtig tun** do sth. without asking; **~mächtiger·weise** *Adv. s.* **~mächtig 2; ~mächtigkeit die; ~, ~en a)** *o. Pl.* high-handedness; **b)** *(~mächtige Handlung)* unauthorized action; **~mittel** *Pl.* own resources; **aus ~mitteln** out of *or* from one's own resources; **~name der** proper name; *(Ling.)* proper noun; **~nutz der; ~es** self-interest; **~nützig** [~nʏtsɪç] **1.** *Adj.* self-interested, self-seeking ‹*person*›; selfish ‹*motive*›; **2.** *adv.* selfishly; **~produktion die: aus ~produktion** home-made; home-grown ‹*fruit, vegetables, etc.*›; **das ist eine ~produktion** I/they *etc.* made it myself/themselves *etc;* **~regie die: etw. in ~regie tun** undertake sth. oneself

eigens *Adv.* specially; **~ für diesen Zweck** specifically for this purpose; **~ aus diesen Gründen** just *or* solely for these reasons

Eigenschaft die; ~, ~en *(von Menschen, Tieren, Pflanzen)* quality; characteristic; *(von Sachen, Stoffen)* property; **in seiner ~ als Mann/Vorsitzender** as a man/in his capacity as chairman

Eigenschafts·wort das adjective

eigen-, Eigen-: ~sinn der; *o. Pl.* obstinacy; stubbornness; **~sinnig 1.** *Adj.* obstinate; stubborn; **2.** *adv.* obstinately; stubbornly; **~sinnigkeit die; ~:** obstinacy; stubbornness; **~sinnigkeiten** obstinate *or* stubborn behaviour *sing.*; **~staatlich** *Adj.* **a)** *(souverän)* sovereign; **b)** *(den ~en Staat betreffend)* national; **~staatlichkeit die; ~:** sovereignty; *(von Bundesstaaten)* statehood; **~ständig 1.** *Adj.* independent; **2.** *adv.* independently; **~ständigkeit die; ~:** independence; **~sucht die; ~:** selfishness; **~süchtig 1.** *Adj.* selfish; **2.** *adv.* selfishly

eigentlich ['aign̩tlɪç] **1.** *Adj.; nicht präd.* *(wirklich)* actual; real; *(wahr)* true; *(ursprünglich)* original; **die ~e Bedeutung eines Wortes** the original meaning of a word; **das Eigentliche** the essential thing. **2.** *Partikel* **a)** *(tatsächlich, genaugenommen)* actually; really; **~ nicht** not really; **b)** *(Verstärkung)* **wann erscheint ~ der letzte Band?/warum kommst du ~ nicht mehr zu uns?** tell me, when will the last volume come out/why have you stopped coming to see us?; **~ müßte ich ja jetzt gehen, aber ...:** really, I ought to go now, but ...; **es ist ~ schade, daß ...:** actually, it's a pity that ...; **sind sie ~ verheiratet?** are they in fact married?; **wohnen Sie ~ in Köln oder in Bonn?** is it in Cologne or Bonn that you live?; **wußten Sie ~ schon, daß ...?** were you actually aware that ...?; **warst du ~ schon [ein]mal da?** have you in fact ever been there?; **ist daraus ~ was geworden?** *(ugs.)* did it ever come to anything?; **was soll das ~?** what's it all about?; **wer sind Sie ~?** who do you think you are?; **wissen Sie ~, wer ich bin?** do you know who 'I am?; **rauchen Sie ~ viel?** do you actually smoke a lot?; **was muß ~ noch alles passieren, bevor ...?** what else has got to happen before ...?; **was denkst du dir ~?** what do you think you're doing?; **was willst du ~?** what exactly do you want?

Eigentlichkeit die; ~ *(geh.)* authenticity

Eigen·tor das *(Ballspiele, fig.)* own goal; **ein ~ schießen** score an own goal; **zum ~ für jmdn. werden** *(fig.)* backfire on sb.

Eigentum das; ~s a) property; *(einschließlich Geld usw.)* assets *pl.*; **geistiges ~:** [one's own] intellectual creation; **sie haben sein geistiges ~ verwendet** they used his idea/ideas; **sich an fremdem ~ vergreifen** steal; **b)** *(Recht des Eigentümers)* ownership **(an +** *Dat.* of); **c)** *(veralt.: Grundbesitz)* property

Eigentümer ['aign̩ty:mɐ] **der; ~s, ~:** owner; *(Hotel~, Geschäfts~)* proprietor; owner

Eigentümerin die owner; *(Hotel~, Geschäfts~)* proprietress; proprietor; owner

eigentümlich ['aign̩ty:mlɪç] **1.** *Adj.* **a)** *(typisch)* peculiar; characteristic; **eine ihm ~e Geste** a gesture peculiar to him *or* characteristic of him; **b)** *(eigenartig)* peculiar; strange; odd. **2.** *adv.* peculiarly; strangely; oddly

eigentümlicherweise *Adv.* strangely enough; oddly enough

Eigentümlichkeit die; ~, ~en a) *o. Pl. (Eigenartigkeit)* peculiarity; strangeness; **b)** *(typischer Zug)* peculiarity

Eigentums-: ~bildung die acquisition of assets; **~delikt das** offence against property; **~recht das** right of ownership; **~rechte geltend machen** claim one's proprietary rights; **~streuung die** distribution of assets; **~vorbehalt der** *(Rechtsw.)* reservation of proprietary rights; **~wohnung**

die owner-occupied flat *(Brit.)*; condominium *or* co-op apartment *(Amer.)*; **eine ~wohnung kaufen** buy a flat *(Brit.) or (Amer.)* an apartment

eigen-, Eigen-: ~verantwortlich 1. *Adj.* responsible; **eine ~verantwortliche Tätigkeit** a job with responsibility; a responsible job; **2.** *adv.* **~verantwortlich handeln** act on one's own authority; **etw. ~verantwortlich bestimmen/entscheiden** decide sth. on one's own responsibility; **~wärme die** *(Biol.)* body temperature; **~wert der** intrinsic value; *(Math., Phys.)* eigenvalue; **~willig** *Adj.* **a)** self-willed ⟨*person*⟩; individual ⟨*style, idea*⟩; **b)** *(~sinnig)* obstinate; stubborn; **~willigkeit die; ~, ~en a)** *o. Pl. (von Menschen)* individualism; independence of mind; *(einer Behauptung, eines Kunstwerks, eines Stils usw.)* originality; unconventionality; **b)** *(Handlung)* display of self-will

eignen 1. *refl. V.* be suitable; **sich als** *od.* **zum Lehrer ~:** be suitable as a teacher; **er würde sich gut als** *od.* **zum Handwerker ~:** he would make a good craftsman; **das Buch eignet sich gut als Geschenk** this book makes a good present; **für solche Arbeiten eignet er sich besonders** he is particularly well suited for that kind of work; *s. auch* **geeignet. 2.** *itr. V. (geh., veralt.: eigen sein)* **jmdm. eignet etw.** sb. possesses sth.

eigne, eigner *s.* **eigen**

Eigner der; ~s, ~: owner

Eignung die; ~: suitability; aptitude; **seine ~ für diesen Beruf/als Lehrer** his suitability for this profession/as a teacher; **seine ~ zum Fliegen** his aptitude for flying

Eignungs-: ~prüfung die, ~test der aptitude test

Ei·klar, das; ~s, ~ *(österr.) s.* **Eiweiß a**

Ei·land das; ~[e]s, ~e *(veralt., dichter.)* isle *(poet.)*

Eil- [ail-]: **~bote der** special messenger; **etw. durch einen ~boten zustellen lassen** send sth. by special delivery *or* express; **„durch** *od.* **per ~boten"** *(veralt.)* 'express'; **~brief der** express letter

Eile ['ailə] **die; ~:** hurry; **ich habe [große] ~:** I'm in a [great] hurry; **ich habe keine ~:** I'm not in a *or* any hurry; **die Sache hat ~:** it's urgent *or* a matter of urgency; **die Sache hat keine ~:** there's no hurry; it's not urgent; **[immer] in ~ sein** [always] be in a hurry; **in der ~:** in her/our *etc.* hurry; **in aller ~:** in great haste; **jmdn. zur ~ antreiben** hurry sb. up

Ei·leiter der *(Anat.)* Fallopian tube

Eileiter-: *(Med.)* **~entzündung die** salpingitis; **~schwangerschaft die** tubal pregnancy

eilen 1. *itr. V.* **a)** *mit sein* hurry; hasten; *(besonders schnell)* rush; **nach Hause ~:** hurry/rush home; **jmdm. zu Hilfe ~:** rush to sb.'s aid; **eile mit Weile** *(Spr.)* more haste, less speed *(prov.)*; **b)** *(dringend sein)* ⟨*matter*⟩ be urgent; **„eilt!"** 'urgent'; **„eilt sehr!"** 'immediate'; **es eilt mir damit** it's urgent; I'm in a hurry; **es eilt ihm mit dem Umzug** he is in a hurry to move. **2.** *refl. V.* hurry; make haste

eilends *Adv. (unverzüglich)* immediately; without delay; *(geh.: geschwind)* hastily

eil-, Eil-: ~fertig *(geh.)* **1.** *Adj.* **a)** *(vorschnell)* rash; **b)** *(dienstbeflissen)* zealous; **2.** *adv.: s. Adj.* rashly; zealously; **~fertigkeit die;** *o. Pl.: s.* **~fertig:** rashness; zeal; **~fracht die** express freight; express goods *pl.*; **etw. per** *od.* **als ~fracht senden** send sth. express freight; **~gut das** fast freight; express goods *pl.*; **etw. als ~gut schicken** send sth. by fast freight

eilig 1. *Adj.* **a)** *(schnell)* hurried; **mit ~en Schritten** hurriedly; **es ~ haben** be in a hurry; **es weniger ~ haben** be in less of a hurry; **b)** *(dringend)* urgent ⟨*news*⟩; **~ sein** be urgent; **es [sehr] ~ mit etw. haben** be in a [great] hurry about sth.; **etw. Eiliges** sth. urgent; an urgent matter; **nichts Eiligeres zu tun haben, als ...** *(iron)* have nothing better to do than...; **er hatte nichts Eiligeres zu tun, als allen davon zu erzählen** he couldn't wait to tell everybody about it. **2.** *adv.* hurriedly; **~ laufen** run hurriedly; hurry

Eil-: ~marsch der *(Milit.)* forced march; **~paket das** express parcel; **~schritt der: im ~schritt laufen** walk with short, quick steps; **~sendung die** express consignment; *(Brief)* express letter; *(Paket)* express parcel; **~tempo das** *(ugs.)* **im ~tempo** in a rush; **im ~tempo ging es zum Bahnhof** we/they *etc.* rushed to the station; **~verfahren das** *(jur.)* summary proceedings *pl.*; **etw. im ~verfahren erledigen** *(fig. ugs.)* do sth. in a rush; **~zug der** semi-fast train; stopping train *(Brit.)*; **~zustellung die** *(Postw.)* express delivery

Eimer ['aimɐ] **der; ~s, ~ a)** bucket; *(Milch~)* pail; *(Abfall~)* bin; **ein ~ [voll] Wasser** a bucket of water; **es gießt wie aus ~n** *(ugs.)* it's raining cats and dogs *(coll.)*; it's coming down in buckets *(coll.)*; **im ~ sein** *(salopp)* be up the spout *(sl.)*; **mein Wagen ist im ~** *(salopp)* my car is a total wreck; **unsere Stimmung war im ~** *(salopp)* the atmosphere was totally ruined; **seine Gesundheit ist im ~** *(salopp)* he's a physical wreck; **b)** *(ugs. abwertend: altes Schiff)* tub

Eimer·bagger der bucket dredger

eimer·weise *Adv.* by the bucketful; in bucketfuls

¹ein [ain] **1.** *Kardinalz. (betont)* one; **~ Dollar/~e Mark/~ Jahr** one dollar/mark/year; **in ~em Tag** in one day; in a single day; **~ einziger Tag/Mensch** one single day/person; **ich will dir noch ~[e]s sagen** there's one more thing I'd like to tell you; **~[e]s gefällt mir daran/an ihr nicht** there's one thing I don't like about it/her; **das ~e Gute daran ist ...:** the only good thing about it is ...; **das ~e, das ich brauche** the one thing I need; **~er von beiden** one of the two; one or the other; **~er für alle, alle für ~en** one for all and all for one; **~ für allemal** once and for all; **~ und derselbe** one and the same; **er war ihr ~ und alles** he was everything to her; **das Buch bietet alles in ~em** the book has everything in one volume; **in ~em fort** *(geh.)* continuously; all the time. **2.** *unbest. Art. (unbetont)* a/an; **~ Kleid/Apfel/Mensch/Hotel** a dress/an apple/a human being/a[n] hotel; **~ Held/~ ehrlicher Mensch** a hero/an honest man/woman; **~ bißchen** *od.* **wenig** a little [bit]; **~ anderer** somebody else; **~ jeder** *(geh.)* each and every one; **~e Kälte ist das hier!** it's freezing here!; **~e Frechheit ist das!** what absolute cheek!; **was für ~ Wein!** what superb wine!; **was für ~e Unordnung!** what a mess!; **was für ~ Kleid hast du gekauft?** what sort of dress did you buy?; **das konnte nur ~ Beethoven schaffen** only a Beethoven could do that; **er besaß ~en Klee und ~en Picasso** he owned a Klee and a Picasso. **3.** *Indefinitpron. (betont)* **a)** *(irgendeiner)* one; **b)** *(man)* one; *(jemand)* someone; somebody; **wie soll das ~er wissen?** how is one supposed to know that?; **das mach mal ~em verständlich** try explaining that to anybody; **~e/~er/~[e]s der besten** one of the best [people/things]; **~s war offen und ~s zu** one was open and one shut; **kaum ~er** hardly anybody; **~er von uns/euch** one of us/you; **~er namens Mayer** *(meist abwertend)* a certain Mayer; **ist ~er bereit, mir zu helfen?** is anyone willing to help me?; **~er nach dem anderen** one after the other; one by one; **der ~e kommt, der andere geht** one comes, the other goes; **die ~en ..., die anderen ...:** some ..., the others ...; **er trinkt ganz gerne ~en** *(ugs.)* he likes [to have] a drink; **sieh [mal] ~er an!** *(ugs.)* [now just] look at that!; **du bist [mir] ~e/~er!** *(iron.)* you are a [right] one *(coll.)*; **das ist ~e/~er!** *(ugs.)* she's/he's quite a one *(coll.)*; **er ist belesen wie selten ~er** he's uncommonly well read; **c)** *(der-/die-/dasselbe)* **~er Meinung sein** be of the same opinion; **es kommt alles auf ~[e]s heraus** it all comes to the same thing [in the end]

²ein *(elliptisch)* **~ – aus** *(an Schaltern)* on – off; **~ und aus gehen** go in and out; **bei jmdm. ~ und aus gehen** be a regular visitor at sb.'s house; **ich wußte nicht ~ noch aus** I didn't know where to turn *or* what to do

ein·achsig *Adj.* single-axle

ein·adrig *Adj. (Elektrot.)* single-core

Einakter ['ain|aktɐ] **der; ~s, ~:** one-act play

einander [ai'nandɐ] *reziprokes Pron. (geh.)* each other; one another; **sie grüßten ~:** they greeted each other *or* one another; **liebet ~** *(bes. bibl.)* love one another; **~ widersprechende Behauptungen** mutually contradictory statements

ein|arbeiten *tr. V.* **a)** *(ausbilden)* train ⟨*employee*⟩; **er arbeitet sich gerade ein** he is training at present; **sich in etw.** *(Akk.)* **~:** become familiar *or* familiarize oneself with sth.; **b)** *(einfügen)* incorporate ⟨*quotation etc.*⟩ **(in +** *Akk.* into); **sie arbeitete einige Verzierungen in die Decke ein** she worked some patterns into the cover

Einarbeitung die; ~, ~en training; **die ~ in das neue Sachgebiet fiel ihm schwer** he found it difficult to familiarize himself with the new subject

Einarbeitungs·zeit die training period

ein·armig 1. *Adj.* one-armed; **ein Einarmiger** a one-armed man. **2.** *adv.* **~ Gewichte stemmen** lift weights with one hand

ein|äschern ['ain|ɛʃɐn] *tr. V.* **a)** *(niederbrennen)* **ein Gebäude ~:** burn a building to the ground *or* down; reduce a building to ashes; **eine Stadt ~:** reduce a town to ashes; **b)** cremate ⟨*corpse*⟩; **ich werde mich ~ lassen** I am going to be cremated

Einäscherung die; ~, ~en a) *(das Niederbrennen)* **die ~ des Gebäudes** the burning down of the building; **die ~ der Stadt** the destruction of the town by fire; **b)** *(Leichenverbrennung)* cremation

Einäscherungs·halle die crematorium

ein|atmen *tr., itr. V.* breathe in

einatomig ['ain|ato:mɪç] *Adj. (Chemie, Physik)* monatomic

ein·äugig *Adj.* one-eyed; single-lens ⟨*camera*⟩; **unter Blinden ist der Einäugige König** *(Spr.)* in the kingdom of the blind the one-eyed man is king *(prov.)*

Ein·bahn·straße die one-way street; **eine ~, aus der es kein Zurück mehr gab** *(fig.)* a path from which there could be no turning back *(fig.)*; **das Verhältnis darf keine ~ sein** there must be give and take on both sides

ein|balsamieren *tr. V.* embalm ⟨*corpse*⟩; **du kannst dich ~ lassen** *(fig. ugs.)* you might as well give up

Ein·band der; *Pl.* **-bände** binding; [book-] cover

Einband-: ~deckel der *(Buchw.)* board; **~entwurf der** cover design

ein·bändig *Adj.* one-volume

ein·basisch *Adj. (Chemie)* monobasic

Ein·bau der; ~s, ~ten a) *o. Pl. (das Einbauen)* fitting; *(eines Motors)* installation; **b)** *o. Pl. (Einfügung)* incorporation; insertion; **c)** *Pl. (Eingebautes)* fitted shelves/cupboards

ein|bauen *tr. V.* **a)** build in, fit ⟨*cupboard, kitchen*⟩; **b)** *(Technik)* install ⟨*engine, motor*⟩; **c)** *(einfügen)* insert, incorporate ⟨*chapter*⟩

Einbau·küche die fitted kitchen

Ein·baum der dug-out

Einbau-: ~möbel *Pl.* built-in furniture *sing.*; *(Schränke)* built-in cupboards; *(Regale)* fitted shelves; **~schrank der** built-in cupboard; *(für Kleidung)* built-in wardrobe

ein|begreifen *unr. tr. V. (geh.)* include; MWSt einbegriffen including VAT

ein|behalten *unr. tr. V.* a) *(zurückbehalten)* withhold; b) *(Amtsspr.: festsetzen)* detain

ein·beinig *Adj.* one-legged

ein|bekennen *unr. tr. V. (geh., bes. österr.)* s. eingestehen

Ein·bekenntnis das *(geh., bes. österr.)* s. Eingeständnis

ein|berechnen *tr. V.* s. einkalkulieren

ein|berufen *unr. tr. V.* a) summon; call; eine Versammlung/Sitzung ~: call *or* convene a meeting; den Bundestag ~: summon the Bundestag; eine Versammlung nach Berlin/eine Sitzung für den 30. Mai ~: call a meeting in Berlin/for 30 May; b) *(zur Wehrpflicht)* call up; conscript; draft *(Amer.)*; ~ werden be called up *or* conscripted; be drafted *(Amer.)*

Ein·berufene der/die; *adj. Dekl.* conscript; draftee *(Amer.)*

Ein·berufung die a) *(das Einberufen)* calling; die ~ des Parlaments the summoning of Parliament; b) *(zur Wehrpflicht)* call-up; conscription; draft *(Amer.)*

Einberufungs-: **~befehl** der, **~bescheid** der call-up papers *pl.*; draft card *(Amer.)*

ein|beschreiben *unr. tr. V. (Geom.)* inscribe ‹circle›; einem Dreieck einen Kreis ~: inscribe a circle in a triangle

ein|bestellen *tr. V. (Amtsspr.)* summon

ein|betonieren *tr. V.* concrete in; etw. in etw. *(Akk.)* ~: concrete sth. into sth.

ein|betten *tr. V.* a) embed (in + *Akk.* in); das Haus liegt eingebettet in ein Tal the house nestles in a valley; b) *(Sprachw.)* eingebettete Sätze embedded sentences

Einbett-: **~kabine** die single-berth cabin; **~zimmer** das single room

ein|beulen 1. *tr. V.* etw. ~: dent sth.; make a dent in sth.; ein eingebeulter Kotflügel a dented mudguard. 2. *refl. V.* become dented

ein|beziehen *unr. tr. V.* include; etw. in etw. *(Akk.)* ~: include sth. in sth.; jmdn. in eine Diskussion ~: involve sb. *or* get sb. involved in a discussion

Ein·beziehung die, **Ein·bezug** der *(schweiz.) o. Pl.* inclusion; unter ~ aller Faktoren taking all factors into account

ein|biegen 1. *unr. itr. V.; mit sein* turn; in eine Straße ~: turn into a street; [nach] links/rechts ~: turn left/right. 2. *unr. tr. V.* bend. 3. *unr. refl. V.* bend inwards

ein|bilden *refl. V.* a) sich *(Dat.)* etw. ~: imagine sth.; sich *(Dat.)* ~, daß ...: imagine that ...; ich bilde mir ein, daß ich ihn in der Stadt gesehen habe *(ugs.)* I think I saw him in town; eine eingebildete Krankheit an imaginary illness; was bildest du dir eigentlich ein? *(ugs.)* what do you think you are doing?; b) *(ugs.: übermäßig stolz sein)* er bildet sich *(Dat.)* ganz schön viel ein he thinks no end of himself *(coll.)*; he fancies himself no end *(coll.)*; sich *(Dat.)* ziemlich viel auf etw. ~: be terribly conceited about sth. *(coll.)*; darauf brauchst du dir nichts einzubilden there's no need to be stuck-up about it

Ein·bildung die; ~, ~en a) *o. Pl. (Phantasie)* imagination; b) *(falsche Vorstellung)* fantasy; das ist alles nur ~: it's all in the mind; c) *o. Pl. (Hochmut)* conceitedness; ~ ist auch eine Bildung *(ugs.)* you're letting your imagination run away with you

Einbildungs-: **~kraft** die, **~vermögen** das [powers *pl.* of] imagination; imaginative powers *pl.*

ein|bimsen *tr. V. (ugs.)* jmdm. etw. ~: drum sth. into sb.

ein|binden *unr. tr. V.* a) bind ‹book›; etw. neu ~: rebind sth.; b) *(einfügen)* er war in bestimmte Konventionen/Wertvorstellungen eingebunden *(fig.)* he was bound by certain conventions/subject to certain values; in die Verantwortung eingebunden constrained by responsibility; c) *(integrieren)* das Dorf muß in das Verkehrsnetz eingebunden werden the village must be linked into the transport system; den einzelnen in ein Kollektiv ~: make the individual part of a group; in ein System eingebunden bleiben remain part of a system; d) *(einhüllen)* wrap; bandage ‹limb›

Ein·bindung die a) *(Integration)* integration; die ~ der Bundesrepublik in die EG the fact that the Federal Republic forms part of the European Community; b) *(Bindung, Festgelegtsein)* gegen die zu starke ~ durch den Vertrag setzte er sich zur Wehr he fought against being bound *or* tied too closely by the contract

ein·blätt[e]rig *Adj. (Bot.)* monophyllous

ein|blenden *(Rundf., Ferns., Film)* 1. *tr. V.* insert; eine Nachricht in eine Sendung ~: interrupt a programme with a news flash; Geräusche/Musik/Szenen nachträglich ~: dub in sounds/music/scenes. 2. *refl. V.* sich in ein Fußballspiel ~: go over to a football match; sich in eine Direktübertragung ~: link up with a live transmission

Ein·blendung die *(Rundf., Ferns., Film)* insertion; *(Rückblende)* flashback (in + *Akk.* to)

ein|bleuen *tr. V.* jmdm. etw. ~: drum *or* hammer sth. into sb.

Ein·blick der a) *(Sicht)* den ~ in den Garten verhindern obstruct the view of the garden; ~ in etw. *(Akk.)* haben be able to see into sth.; b) *(Durchsicht)* ~ in etw. nehmen take a look at *or* examine sth.; jmdm. ~ in etw. *(Akk.)* gewähren allow *or* permit sb. to look at *or* examine sth.; keinen ~ in etw. *(Akk.)* haben not be permitted to look at *or* examine sth.; c) *(Kenntnis)* insight; [einen] ~ in etw. haben/gewinnen have/gain an insight into sth.

ein|bohnern *tr. V.* wax ‹floor, stairs›

ein|bohren 1. *tr. V.* drill; bore. 2. *refl. V.* sich in etw. *(Akk.)* ~: bore into sth.

ein|brechen 1. *unr. itr. V.* a) *mit haben od. sein* break in; in eine Bank/ein Geschäft ~: break into a bank/shop; bei jmdm. ~: burgle sb.; bei uns wurde eingebrochen we were burgled; we had a break-in; b) *mit sein (einstürzen)* ‹roof, ceiling› fall in, cave in; c) *mit sein (durchbrechen)* fall through; beim Eislaufen ~: fall *or* go through the ice while skating; d) *mit sein (eindringen)* in ein Land ~: invade a country; in die Verteidigungslinie ~: break through the line of defences; e) *mit sein (geh.: beginnen)* ‹night, darkness› fall; ‹winter› set in; f) *mit sein (salopp: scheitern)* [ganz schön] ~: come [badly] unstuck *(coll.)*; come a [fearful] cropper *(coll.)*; g) *mit sein (hineinstürzen)* burst in; in etw. *(Akk.)* ~: burst into sth. 2. *unr. tr. V.* break down ‹door, wall›; demolish ‹chimney›

Einbrecher der; ~s, ~: burglar

Einbrecher·bande die gang of burglars

Einbrecherin die; ~, ~nen burglar

Einbrenne ['ainbrɛnə] die; ~, ~n *(Kochk.: bes. südd., österr.)* roux

ein|brennen 1. *unr. tr. V.* ein Zeichen in Holz/auf eine Platte ~: burn a design into wood/bake a design on to a plate; einem Tier das Brandzeichen ~: brand an animal. 2. *unr. refl. V. (geh.)* das Erlebnis hatte sich tief in sein *od.* seinem Gedächtnis eingebrannt the experience had engraved itself on his memory

ein|bringen 1. *unr. tr. V.* a) *(hineinschaffen)* bring *or* gather in ‹harvest›; ein Schiff in den Hafen ~: bring a ship into port; das Werkstück in die Maschine ~: put the workpiece into the machine; b) *(verschaffen)* jmdm. viel Geld ~: bring sb. [in] a lot of money; Gewinn/Zinsen ~: yield a profit/bring in interest; jmdm. Ruhm/Ehre ~: bring sb. fame/honour; das hat nichts als Ärger eingebracht that's caused nothing but trouble; das bringt nichts ein it isn't worth it; c) *(Parl.: vorlegen)* introduce ‹bill›; einen Antrag im Parlament ~: introduce a bill into parliament; bring a bill before parliament; d) *(in eine Gemeinschaft, Gesellschaft usw.)* invest ‹capital, money›; etw. in eine Ehe ~: bring sth. into a marriage; etw. [in eine Situation] ~: contribute sth. [to a situation]; e) *(festsetzen)* catch, capture ‹escaped prisoners›; f) *(Druckw.)* take in ‹lines›. 2. *unr. refl. V.* sich in eine Beziehung ~: make one's own contribution to a relationship

Einbringung die; ~ a) *(Festsetzung)* capture; b) *(Parl.: von Gesetzen)* introduction

ein|brocken *tr. V. (ugs.)* sich/jmdm. etw. [Schönes] ~, sich/jmdm. eine schöne Suppe ~: land oneself/sb. in the soup *or* in it *(coll.)*; das hast du dir selbst eingebrockt you've only yourself to thank for that *(coll.)*

Ein·bruch der a) burglary; break-in; ein ~ in eine Bank a break-in at a bank; einen ~ verüben commit a burglary; b) *(das Einstürzen)* collapse; ein ~ der Börsenkurse *(fig.)* a slump in stock-market prices; c) *(Vorstoß)* breakthrough; der ~ des Feindes in ein Land the enemy invasion of a country; der ~ einer Kälte-/Hitzewelle *(fig.)* the onset of a cold wave *or* spell/a heat wave; d) *(Beginn)* vor ~ der Dunkelheit before it gets dark; der ~ des Winters the onset of winter; bei ~ der Nacht at nightfall; when night closes/closed in; bei ~ des Winters when winter sets/set in; e) *(salopp: das Scheitern)* einen ~ erleiden take a drubbing *or* hiding *(coll.)*; f) *(Geol.)* area of subsidence

einbruch[s]-, Einbruch[s]-: **~diebstahl** der burglary; breaking and entering; **~gefahr** die: „~gefahr" 'danger – thin ice'; **~sicher** *Adj.* burglar-proof

ein|buchten *tr. V. (salopp)* jmdn. ~: lock sb. up *(coll.)*; put sb. away *(coll.)*; s. auch eingebuchtet

Einbuchtung die; ~, ~en a) eine ~ der Straße a bend in the road; eine ~ der Küste a bay; an inlet; b) *(Delle)* dent; die ~ der Autotür the dent in the car door

ein|buddeln *tr. V. (ugs.)* bury; sich ~: dig oneself in

einbürgern 1. *tr. V.* naturalize ‹person, plant, animal›; introduce ‹custom, practice›. 2. *refl. V.* ‹custom, practice› become established; ‹person, plant, animal› become naturalized; sich in einer Sprache ~: become established as part of a language; das hat sich hier so eingebürgert it has become the practice here

Einbürgerung die; ~, ~en naturalization

Ein·buße die loss; schwere ~n erleiden suffer heavy losses; eine ~ an etw. *(Dat.)* a loss of sth.; das bedeutet eine [finanzielle] ~ für mich I shall be worse off financially

ein|büßen 1. *tr. V.* lose; *(durch eigene Schuld)* forfeit; sein Geld/seine Freiheit/sein Leben ~: lose/forfeit one's money/one's freedom/one's life. 2. *itr. V.* sie büßte an Ansehen ein her reputation suffered

ein|checken *tr., itr. V. (Flugw.)* check in

ein|cremen *tr. V.* put cream on ‹hands, back›; sich ~: put cream on; jmdm./sich die Hände/den Rücken ~: put cream on sb.'s/one's hands/back

ein|dämmen *tr. V.* a) dam ‹river›; embank, dike ‹land›; b) *(aufhalten)* check; stem

ein|dämmern *itr. V.; mit sein* doze off

Eindämmung die; ~, ~en s. eindämmen: damming; diking; checking, stemming; eine ~ des Drogenhandels scheint unmöglich it seems impossible to stem the flow of drugs

ein|dampfen *tr. V. (Chemie)* evaporate

ein|decken 1. *refl. V.* stock up; sich [für den Winter] mit etw. ~: stock up with sth. [for the winter]. **2.** *tr. V. (ugs.: überhäufen)* **jmdn. mit Arbeit/Fragen ~:** swamp sb. with work/questions; **mit etw. eingedeckt sein** be swamped with sth.

Eindecker der; ~s, ~ *(Flugw.)* monoplane

ein|deichen *tr. V.* dike ⟨*land*⟩; dike, embank ⟨*river*⟩

ein|dellen *tr. V. (ugs.)* dent [in]

eindeutig ['aindɔytɪç] **1.** *Adj.* **a)** *(klar)* clear; clear, definite ⟨*proof*⟩; **b)** *(nur eine Deutung zulassend)* unambiguous ⟨*concept*⟩. **2.** *adv. s. Adj.* clearly; unambiguously

Eindeutigkeit die; ~, ~en **a)** *o. Pl. s.* **eindeutig:** clarity; unambiguity; **b)** *meist Pl. (scherzh.: unanständiger Witz)* crudity

ein|deutschen *tr. V.* Germanize

Eindeutschung die; ~, ~en **a)** *o. Pl.* Germanization; **b)** *(eingedeutschtes Wort)* Germanized word

ein|dicken *tr., itr. V.* thicken

ein·dimensional *Adj.* one-dimensional; unidimensional; *(fig.)* one-dimensional ⟨*personality*⟩

ein|docken *tr. V. (Schiffbau)* dock

ein|dosen *tr. V.* can; tin *(Brit.)*

ein|dösen *itr. V. (ugs.) mit sein* doze off

ein|drängen 1. *itr. V.; mit sein* **auf jmdn. ~:** crowd around sb.; **Eindrücke/Erinnerungen drängten auf ihn ein** *(fig.)* impressions/memories crowded in [up]on him. **2.** *refl. V.* push one's way in; force one's way in

ein|drecken ['aindrɛkn̩] *tr. V. (ugs.)* **etw./sich ~:** get sth./oneself filthy; *(mit Schlamm usw.)* get sth./oneself covered in *or* with muck *(coll.)*

ein|drehen *tr. V.* **a)** *(hineindrehen)* screw in ⟨*light bulb*⟩ **(in +** *Akk.* into); **b) sich** *(Dat.)* **die Haare ~:** put one's hair in curlers *or* rollers; **sich** *(Dat.)* **die Haare ~ lassen** have one's hair curled

ein|dreschen *unr. itr. V. (ugs.)* **auf jmdn. ~:** lay into sb. *(coll.)*

ein|dringen *unr. itr. V.; mit sein* **a) in etw.** *(Akk.)* **~:** penetrate into sth.; ⟨*vermin*⟩ get into sth.; ⟨*bullet*⟩ pierce sth.; *(allmählich)* ⟨*water, sand, etc.*⟩ seep into sth.; **er drang in sie ein** he penetrated her *(sexually)*; **die ~de Kaltluft** the cold air that blows in; **b)** *(einbrechen)* **in ein Gebäude ~:** force an entry *or* one's way into a building; **Feinde sind in das Land eingedrungen** *(geh.)* enemies invaded the country; **in eine Gesellschaft ~** *(fig.)* be an uninvited guest; **c)** *(bedrängen)* set upon, attack ⟨*person*⟩; **mit Fragen auf jmdn. ~:** besiege *or* ply sb. with questions; **auf jmdn. ~[, etw. zu tun]** *(fig.)* press *or* urge sb. [to do sth.]

ein·dringlich 1. *Adj.* urgent ⟨*warning, entreaty*⟩; impressive ⟨*voice*⟩; forceful, powerful ⟨*speech, words*⟩. **2.** *adv.* ⟨*urge*⟩ strongly; ⟨*talk*⟩ insistently; **jmdn. auf das ~ste warnen** warn sb. most urgently

Ein·dringlichkeit die; ~ *s.* **eindringlich:** urgency; impressiveness; forcefulness

Eindringling ['aindrɪŋlɪŋ] **der;** ~s, ~e intruder

Ein·druck der; ~[e]s, **Eindrücke a)** *(Vorstellung, Wirkung)* impression; **einen ~ haben/gewinnen** have/get *or* gain an impression; **jmdn. nach dem ersten ~ beurteilen** judge sb. by first impressions; **einen guten ~ machen** make a good impression; **~ auf jmdn. machen** make an impression on sb.; **Eindrücke gewinnen** receive impressions; **er macht den ~ eines sehr gewissenhaften Menschen** he gives the impression of being a very conscientious person; **er konnte sich des ~s nicht erwehren, daß ...** *(geh.)* he had the strong impression that ...; he could not help thinking *or* feeling that ...; **sie stand noch unter dem ~ dieses schrecklichen Erlebnisses** she was still haunted by this terrible experience; **er stand noch ganz unter dem ~ seiner Indienreise** he was still under the spell of his journey to India; **er tat es nur, um [bei ihr] ~ zu schinden** *(ugs.)* he only did it to impress [her]; **b)** *(Spur)* impression

ein|drücken *tr. V.* **a)** *(verbiegen, zerbrechen)* smash in ⟨*mudguard, bumper*⟩; stave in ⟨*side of ship*⟩; smash ⟨*pier, column, support*⟩; break ⟨*window*⟩; crush ⟨*ribs*⟩; flatten ⟨*nose*⟩; **der Wind drückte alle Fenster ein** the wind blew all the windows in; **b)** *(hineindrücken)* **etw. [in etw.** *(Akk.)***] ~:** press *or* push sth. in[to sth.]

eindrucks-: ~los 1. *Adj.* unimpressive; **2.** *adv.* unimpressively; **~voll 1.** *Adj.* impressive; **2.** *adv.* impressively

ein|dübeln *tr. V.* **etw. in die Wand ~:** fix sth. into the wall with a plug/dowel

eine *s.* ¹**ein**

ein|ebnen *tr. V.* level; **der Unterschied ist eingeebnet worden** *(fig.)* the difference has been eliminated

Einebnung die; ~, ~en levelling; *(fig.)* elimination; **bei der ~ des Grundstücks** during the levelling of the site

Ein·ehe die monogamy *no art.*

eineiig ['ain|aiɪç] *Adj.* identical ⟨*twins*⟩

ein·eindeutig *Adj.* one-to-one ⟨*correspondence, relationship*⟩; **eine ~e Abbildung** a representation having a one-to-one correspondence with its original

ein·ein·halb *Bruchz.* one and a half; **~ Stunden/Jahre** an hour/a year and a half; one and a half hours/years

ein·ein·halb·fach *Vervielfältigungsz.* one and a half times; **die ~e Anzahl/Menge** one and a half times the number/amount

einen *tr. V. (geh.)* unite

ein|engen *tr. V.* **a) jmdn. ~:** restrict sb.'s movement[s]; **sich eingeengt fühlen** feel hemmed in *or* shut in; **b)** *(fig.: einschränken)* restrict; restrict, narrow down ⟨*concept*⟩; **jmdn. in seiner Freiheit ~:** restrict *or* curb sb.'s freedom

einer *s.* ¹**ein**

Einer der; ~s, ~ **a)** *(Math.)* unit; **b)** *(Sport)* single sculler; **im ~:** in the single sculls

einerlei ['ainɐlai] **1.** *Adj.; nicht attr. (unwichtig)* **~, ob/wo/wer** *usw.* no matter whether/where/who *etc.*; **es ist ~:** it makes no difference; **es ist ihm ~:** it is all the same *or* all one to him; *(es kümmert ihn nicht)* he does not care at all. **2.** *Gattungsz.; indekl.; nicht präd.* **von ~ Sorte** of one *or* of the same kind; **mit ~ Maß gemessen werden** be assessed according to one *or* the same standard

Einerlei das; ~s monotony; **das tägliche ~:** the monotony of everyday life; the daily grind *(coll.)*

einerseits ['ainɐ'zaits] *Adv.* on the one hand; **~ ..., andererseits ...:** on the one hand ..., on the other hand ...

Einer·stelle die *(Math.)* units place

eines *s.* ¹**ein**

eines·teils *Adv.* on the one hand; **~ ..., ander[e]nteils ...:** on the one hand ..., on the other hand ...

ein|exerzieren *tr. V.* drill, train ⟨*soldier, pupil, etc.*⟩; **jmdm. etw. ~:** drill *or* train sb. in sth.

ein·fach 1. *Adj.* **a)** *(nicht mehrfach)* single ⟨*knot, ticket, journey*⟩; **zweimal ~ [nach] Köln** two singles to Cologne; **b)** *(nicht schwierig)* simple, easy ⟨*task*⟩; **das ist ~:** that is simple *or* easy; **sich** *(Dat.)* **etw. [zu] ~ machen** make sth. [too] easy for oneself; **warum ~, wenn es auch kompliziert geht!** *(scherzh.)* the other way would be too simple, I suppose!; **c)** *(einleuchtend)* simple ⟨*explanation, reason*⟩; **aus dem ~en Grund, weil ...:** for the simple reason that ...; **d)** *(bescheiden)* simple ⟨*person, manner, life, dress, etc.*⟩; plain, simple ⟨*food*⟩; **er war nur ein ~er Mann** he was just an ordinary man; *s. auch* **Verhältnis. 2.** *adv.* **a)** *(bescheiden, einleuchtend)* simply; **sich betont ~ kleiden** dress very simply; **b)** *(nicht mehrfach)* **etw. ~ falten** fold sth. once. **3.** *Partikel (verstärkend)* simply; just; **das ist ~ unmöglich** that is simply *or* just impossible; **ich begreife es ~ nicht** I simply *or* just cannot understand it; **es ist ~ nicht zu begreifen, daß ...:** it's simply incomprehensible that ...

Einfachheit die; ~ **a)** *(einfache Gestaltung)* simplicity; **von verblüffender ~ sein** be of astonishing simplicity; **der ~ halber** for the sake of simplicity; for simplicity's sake; **b)** *(Bescheidenheit)* simplicity; *(der Nahrung)* plainness; simplicity

ein|fädeln 1. *tr. V.* **a)** thread ⟨*needle, tape*⟩ **(in +** *Akk.* into); thread up ⟨*sewing-machine*⟩; **einen [neuen] Faden ~:** [re]thread the needle; **b)** *(ugs.: geschickt einleiten)* engineer ⟨*scheme, plot*⟩; **das hat sie fein/schlau eingefädelt** she worked that nicely/craftily *(coll.)*. **2.** *refl. V. (Verkehrsw.)* filter in; **sich in den fließenden Verkehr ~:** filter into the flow of traffic. **3.** *itr. V. (Skisport)* become entangled in the gate

ein|fahren 1. *unr. itr. V.; mit sein* come in; ⟨*train*⟩ come *or* pull in; **in den Bahnhof ~:** come *or* pull into the station; **der Zug nach Hamburg ist soeben auf Gleis 5 eingefahren** the Hamburg train has just arrived at platform 5. **2.** *unr. tr. V.* **a)** bring in ⟨*harvest*⟩; **b)** *(beschädigen)* knock down ⟨*wall*⟩; smash in ⟨*mudguard*⟩; **c)** *(Kfz-W.)* run in ⟨*car*⟩; **d)** *(Technik)* retract ⟨*undercarriage, antenna*⟩; **e)** *(Wirtsch.)* make ⟨*profit, loss*⟩; set up ⟨*record*⟩. **3.** *unr. refl. V.* **a) sich mit einem Fahrzeug ~:** get used to a vehicle; **b)** *(sich einspielen)* **der neue Produktionsprozeß hat sich eingefahren** the new production process is now running smoothly; *s. auch* **eingefahren**

Einfahr·signal das *(Eisenb.)* home signal

Ein·fahrt die a) *o. Pl. (das Hineinfahren)* entry; **Vorsicht bei der ~ des Zuges!** stand clear [of the edge of the platform], the train is approaching; **b)** *(Zufahrt)* entrance; *(Autobahn~)* slip road; **„keine ~"** 'no entry'; **der Zug hat noch keine ~/hat ~ auf Gleis 5** the train is not yet able to pull in/is now approaching platform 5

Ein·fall der a) *(Idee)* idea; **ein sonderbarer ~:** a strange notion *or* idea; **auf den ~ kommen, etw. zu tun** have *or* get the idea of doing sth.; **sie hat Einfälle wie ein altes Haus** *(scherzh.)* she gets some strange ideas; **b)** *o. Pl. (Licht~)* incidence *(Optics)*; **c)** *(in ein Land usw.)* invasion **(in +** *Akk.* of); **d)** *(geh.: plötzliches Einsetzen) (des Winters)* onset; **bei ~ der Nacht** at nightfall

ein|fallen *unr. itr. V.; mit sein* **a) jmdm. fällt etw. ein** sb. thinks of sth.; sth. occurs to sb.; **fällt dir etwas ein, was wir tun könnten?** can you think of anything we can do?; **ihm fallen immer wieder neue Ausreden ein** he can always think of *or (coll.)* come up with new excuses; **was fällt dir denn ein!** what do you think you're doing?; how dare you?; **laß dir das ja nicht ~!** don't you dare!; **sich** *(Dat.)* **etw. ~ lassen [müssen]** [have to] think of sth.; **das fällt mir nicht im Schlaf** *od.* **im Traum[e] ein** I wouldn't dream of it *or* such a thing; **b)** *(in Erinnerung kommen)* **ihr Name fällt mir nicht ein** I cannot think of her name; **plötzlich fiel ihm seine Frau ein** suddenly he thought of his wife; **es wird dir schon [wieder] ~:** it will come [back] to you; **plötzlich fiel ihr ein, daß ...** *(merkte sie)* suddenly she realized that ...; *(erinnerte sie sich daran)* suddenly she remembered that ...; **c)** *(von Licht)* come in; **d)** *(gewaltsam eindringen)* **in ein Land ~:** invade a country; **e)** *(einstimmen, mitreden usw.)* join in; **in den Gesang ~:** join in the singing; **in ein Gespräch ~:** break into a conversation; **„Ja, natürlich", fiel er ein** 'Yes, of course,' he put in; **f)** *(geh.: plötzlich beginnen)* ⟨*winter*⟩ set in; ⟨*night*⟩ fall; ⟨*storm*⟩ break

einfalls-, Einfalls-: ~los 1. *Adj.* unimaginative; lacking in ideas; **2.** *adv.* unimaginatively; without imagination; **~losigkeit die;** ~: unimaginativeness; lack of ideas; **~reich 1.** *Adj.* imaginative; full of ideas; **2.** *adv.* imaginatively; with imagination; **~reichtum der;** *o. Pl.* imaginativeness; wealth of ideas; **~tor das** gateway

Einfall·straße die *(Verkehrsw.)* access road

Einfall[s]·winkel der *(Physik)* angle of incidence

Einfalt ['ainfalt] **die;** ~ **a)** *(Beschränktheit)* simpleness; simple-mindedness; **b)** *(geh.: Reinheit)* simplicity; innocence; **~ des Herzens** simplicity of heart

einfältig ['ainfɛltɪç] *Adj.* **a)** *(arglos)* simple; naïve; artless; naïve ⟨*remarks*⟩; **sei nicht so ~!** don't be so naïve!; **b)** *(beschränkt)* simple; simple-minded

Einfältigkeit die; ~ **a)** *(Arglosigkeit)* simplicity; naïvety; artlessness; **b)** *(Beschränktheit)* simpleness; simple-mindedness

Einfalts·pinsel der *(ugs. abwertend)* nincompoop

Ein·familien·haus das house *(as opposed to block of flats etc.)*

ein|fangen 1. *unr. tr. V.* **a)** catch, capture ⟨*fugitive, animal*⟩; **b)** *(geh.: wiedergeben)* capture ⟨*atmosphere, aura, etc.*⟩. **2.** *unr. refl. V. (ugs.: bekommen)* **sich** *(Dat.)* **eine Erkältung** *usw.* **~:** catch *or* get a cold *etc.*; **sich** *(Dat.)* **eine Tracht Prügel ~:** get a beating

ein|färben *tr. V.* **a)** dye ⟨*material, hair*⟩; **eine kommunistisch eingefärbte Zeitung** *(fig.)* a newspaper with a communist slant; **b)** *(Druckw.)* ink

ein·farbig, *(österr.)* **ein·färbig 1.** *Adj.* ⟨*material, dress*⟩ of one colour; plain ⟨*material, dress*⟩. **2.** *adv.* **das Sofa ~ beziehen** cover the sofa in material of one colour; **die Wände ~ streichen** paint the walls all one colour

ein|fassen *tr. V.* border, hem, edge ⟨*material, dress, tablecloth*⟩; frame ⟨*picture*⟩; set ⟨*gem*⟩; edge ⟨*lawn, flower-bed, grave*⟩; curb ⟨*source, spring*⟩

Ein·fassung die *s.* **einfassen:** border; hem; edging; frame; setting; *(von Brunnen, Quellen)* enclosure

ein|fetten *tr. V.* grease; dubbin ⟨*leather*⟩; **sich** *(Dat.)* **die Haut/Hände ~:** rub cream into one's skin/hands

ein|finden *unr. refl. V.* *(eintreffen)* arrive; *(sich treffen)* meet; *(zusammenkommen)* gather; *(sich melden)* be present; *(fig.)* ⟨*opportunity etc.*⟩ occur; **sich bei jmdm. ~:** report to sb.

ein|flechten *unr. tr. V.* **sich** *(Dat.)* **Bänder ins Haar ~:** plait *or* braid ribbons into one's hair; **ein Muster in einen Korb ~:** weave a pattern into a basket; **in eine Rede ein paar Scherze ~:** work a couple of jokes into a speech; **Episoden in einen Roman ~:** weave episodes into a novel; **wenn ich das kurz ~ darf** if I could turn to this for a moment

ein|flicken *tr. V.* *(ugs.)* stitch on; *(fig.)* shove in *(coll.)*

ein|fliegen 1. *unr. tr. V.* **a)** fly in ⟨*supplies, troops*⟩; **b)** flight-test, test-fly ⟨*aircraft*⟩; **c)** *(Wirtsch.)* make ⟨*profit, loss*⟩. **2.** *unr. itr. V.; mit sein* **a)** fly in; **eingeflogen kommen** come over by air; **in ein Gebiet ~:** fly into *or* enter a territory; **b)** *(in einen geschlossenen Raum)* ⟨*bees, doves, etc.*⟩ fly in; **in etw.** *(Akk.)* **~:** fly into sth.

ein|fließen *unr. itr. V.; mit sein* flow in; **von Norden fließt Kaltluft nach Westeuropa ein** *(fig.)* a cold northerly airstream is moving into Western Europe; **etw. in ein Gespräch ~ lassen** *(fig.)* slip sth. into a conversation; **~de Kalt-/Warmluft** *(Met.)* an inflow of cold/warm air

ein|flößen *tr. V.* **a) jmdm. Tee/Medizin ~:** pour tea/medicine into sb.'s mouth; **jmdm. mit Gewalt Alkohol ~:** force alcohol *or* drink down sb.['s throat]; **b)** *(fig.)* **jmdm. Angst ~:** put fear into sb.; arouse fear in sb.; **jmdm. Vertrauen ~:** inspire sb. with confidence; **jmdm. Ehrfurcht/Mut ~:** fill sb. with awe/courage; inspire awe/courage in sb.

Ein·flug der: ~ einer feindlichen Maschine an incursion by an enemy aircraft; **beim ~ in feindliches Hoheitsgebiet** while flying into enemy territory

Einflug-: ~loch das *(Zool.)* entrance [hole]; **~schneise die** *(Flugw.)* approach path

Ein·fluß der a) influence; **~ auf jmdn./etw. haben/ausüben** have/exert an influence on sb./sth.; **das entzieht sich meinem ~:** I have no influence over that; that is beyond my control; **unter jmds. ~** *(Dat.)* **stehen** be under sb.'s influence; **unter dem ~ von Alkohol** under the influence of alcohol; **~ auf etw.** *(Akk.)* **nehmen** influence sth.; **[einen] großen ~ besitzen** have a great deal of influence *or* sway; **b)** *(Met.)* inflow; **c)** *(fig.: von Kapital usw.)* influx

einfluß-, Einfluß-: ~bereich der, ~gebiet das sphere of influence; **~los** *Adj.* uninfluential; lacking in influence *postpos.*; **~nahme die;** ~: exertion of influence **(auf** + *Akk.* on); *(Versuch)* **~nahme auf jmdn.** attempt to influence sb.; **~reich** *Adj.* influential; **~sphäre die** sphere of influence

ein|flüstern 1. *tr. V. (oft abwertend)* **wer hat dir denn diesen Unsinn eingeflüstert?** who has put this nonsense into your head?; **laß dir nicht solche albernen Gerüchte ~:** don't be taken in by such silly gossip. **2.** *itr. V.* *(flüsternd sprechen)* whisper

Einflüsterung die; ~, **~en** *(geh. abwertend)* blandishment

ein|fordern *tr. V.* demand ⟨*payment*⟩; demand payment of ⟨*money, outstanding debts*⟩; **ein Gutachten ~:** ask for a report

ein·förmig 1. *Adj.* monotonous. **2.** *adv.* monotonously

Ein·förmigkeit die; ~, **~en** monotony

ein|fressen *unr. refl. V.* **sich in etw.** *(Akk.)* **~:** eat into sth.

ein|frieden, ein|friedigen *tr. V. (geh.)* enclose ⟨*plot of land*⟩

Einfriedung, Einfriedigung die; ~, **~en** means of enclosure; *(Zaun)* fence; *(Hecke)* hedge; *(Mauer)* wall

ein|frieren 1. *unr. itr. V.; mit sein* **a)** ⟨*water*⟩ freeze, turn to ice; ⟨*pond*⟩ freeze over; ⟨*pipes*⟩ freeze up; ⟨*ship*⟩ be frozen in; **ihr Lächeln war eingefroren** *(fig.)* her smile had frozen *(fig.)*; **b)** *(fig.)* ⟨*wages, credit*⟩ be frozen; ⟨*negotiations*⟩ break down. **2.** *unr. tr. V.* **a)** deep-freeze ⟨*food*⟩; **b)** *(beenden)* freeze ⟨*credit, project, plan*⟩; break off, suspend ⟨*negotiations*⟩; suspend ⟨*inquiry*⟩

ein|frosten *tr. V. s.* **einfrieren 2 a**

ein|fuchsen *tr. V.* *(ugs.)* **jmdn. auf etw.** *(Akk.)* **~:** drill sb. in sth.; **ein eingefuchster Spezialist/Trainer** an experienced specialist/trainer; **auf etw.** *(Akk.)* **eingefuchst sein** be well practised in sth.

ein|fügen 1. *tr. V.* fit in; **etw. in etw.** *(Akk.)* **~:** fit sth. into sth.; **etw. in einen Text ~:** insert sth. into a text; **ich möchte noch einfügen, daß ...** *(fig.)* I would like to add that .... **2.** *refl. V.* adapt; **sich in etw.** *(Akk.)* **~:** adapt oneself to sth.; **sich überall gut ~:** fit in well anywhere

Ein·fügung die insertion

ein|fühlen *refl. V.* **sich in jmdn. ~:** empathize with sb.; **ich kann mich gut in deine Lage ~:** I know exactly how you feel; I can well understand how you feel; **er kann sich gut in eine Rolle/in einen anderen ~:** he is good at getting into a part/putting himself in another person's place; **sich in die Atmosphäre des alten Moskau ~:** get the feel of the atmosphere in old Moscow

einfühlsam *Adj.* understanding; sensitive ⟨*interpretation, performance*⟩

Einfühlsamkeit die; ~: sensitivity

Ein·fühlung die; ~: empathy **(in** + *Akk.* with)

Einfühlungs·vermögen das ability to empathize; **mit ausgesprochenem ~ spielen/übersetzen** play/translate with great sensitivity for the work

Ein·fuhr die; ~, **~en a)** *o. Pl. (das Einführen)* import; importing; **b)** *(das Eingeführte)* import

ein|führen 1. *tr. V.* **a)** *(importieren)* import ⟨*goods, technology*⟩; **b)** *(als Neuerung)* introduce ⟨*fashion, method, technology*⟩; **c)** *(ein-, unterweisen)* introduce; initiate; **jmdn. in etw.** *(Akk.)* **~:** introduce sb. to sth.; initiate sb. into sth.; **jmdn. in sein Amt ~:** install sb. in office; **der neue Kollege wurde eingeführt** our *etc.* new colleague was introduced to *or* initiated into his new job; **d)** *(hineinschieben)* introduce, insert ⟨*catheter etc.*⟩ **(in** + *Akk.* into); **e)** *(vorstellen)* introduce; **jmdn. bei seinen Eltern ~:** introduce sb. to one's parents; **eine junge Dame in die Gesellschaft ~:** bring a young lady out; **jmdn. bei Hofe ~:** present sb. at court. **2.** *refl. V.* **a)** *(sich vorstellen)* introduce oneself; **du hast dich nicht sehr gut eingeführt** you didn't make a very good first impression; **b)** *(Kaufmannsspr.)* ⟨*shop, company*⟩ become established

Einfuhr-: ~erlaubnis, ~genehmigung die import licence; **~hafen der** port of entry; **~kontingent das** import quota; **~land das** importing country; importer; **~lizenz die** import licence; **~sperre die, ~stopp der** embargo *or* ban on imports

Ein·führung die a) introduction; **eine ~ in die Naturwissenschaften** an introduction to the natural sciences; **ihre ~ in die Gesellschaft/bei Hof** her introduction to society/her presentation at court; **die ~ in sein Amt** his installation in office; **b)** *(Einarbeitung)* introduction; initiation; induction; **c)** *(das Hineinschieben)* introduction; insertion

Einführungs-: ~kurs[us] der *(Schulw.)* introductory course; **~preis der** *(Kaufmannsspr.)* introductory price

Einfuhr-: ~verbot das *s.* **~sperre; ~zoll der** import duty

ein|füllen *tr. V.* **etw. in etw.** *(Akk.)* **~:** pour *or* put sth. into sth.; **Wasser in eine Flasche ~:** fill a bottle with water

Einfüll·stutzen der *(an Tanks)* filler pipe; *(an Haushaltsgeräten)* filling spout

ein|füttern *tr. V. (DV)* feed in; **einem Computer Daten ~:** feed data into a computer

Ein·gabe die a) *(Gesuch)* petition; *(Beschwerde)* complaint; **b)** *o. Pl. (das Verabreichen)* administration; **die ~ der Tabletten sollte alle zwei Stunden erfolgen** the tablets are to be taken every two hours; **c)** *(DV)* input

Eingabe·gerät das *(DV)* input device

Ein·gang der a) *(Tür, Pforte, Portal usw.)* entrance; **der ~ eines Hauses/eines Parks** the entrance of *or* to a house/a park; **„kein ~"** 'no entry'; **in etw.** *(Akk.)* **~ finden** *(fig.)* become established in sth.; **b)** *o. Pl. (von Post, Geld)* receipt; **c)** *meist Pl. (eingetroffene Post)* incoming mail

ein·gängig 1. *Adj.* catchy ⟨*song, melody*⟩; **ihr war das [nicht] ~** *(geh.)* it was [in]comprehensible to her. **2.** *adv.* **etw. ~ erklären** explain sth. simply and clearly

eingangs 1. *Adv.* at the beginning; at the start. **2.** *Präp.* + *Gen.* **~ der Kurve/Fußgängerzone** where the bend/pedestrian precinct begins *or* starts; **~ des Jahres** at the beginning *or* start of the year

Eingangs-: ~buch das *(Buchf.)* 'goods inward' book; **~datum das** *(Bürow.)* date of receipt; **~formel die** preamble; **~halle die** entrance hall; *(eines Hotels, Theaters)*

foyer; ~**pforte die** gateway; ~**stempel der** *(Bürow.)* date-stamp; ~**tür die** *(von Kaufhaus, Hotel usw.)* [entrance] door; *(von Wohnung, Haus usw.)* front door

ein|geben *unr. tr. V.* **a)** *(verabreichen)* give; **jmdm. Medizin ~:** give *or* administer medicine to sb.; **b)** *(DV)* feed in; **etw. in den Computer ~:** feed sth. into the computer; **c)** *(geh.: zu denken veranlassen)* **jmdm. eine Idee ~:** inspire sb. with an idea; **jmdm. den Wunsch ~, etw. zu tun** prompt sb. to do sth.

ein·gebildet 1. *2. Part. v.* **einbilden. 2.** *Adj.* **a)** *(imaginär)* imaginary ⟨*illness*⟩; **ein ~er Kranker** a malade imaginaire; **~e Schwangerschaft** false pregnancy; **b)** *(arrogant)* conceited; **auf etw.** *(Akk.)* **~ sein** be conceited about sth.; *s. auch* **Affe**

ein·geboren *Adj.* **a)** *nicht präd.* native ⟨*population etc.*⟩; **b)** *(geh.: angeboren)* inborn; innate; **c)** *(Rel.)* **Gottes ~er Sohn** the only begotten Son of God

Eingeborene der/die; *adj. Dekl. (veralt.)* native

eingebuchtet 1. *2. Part. v.* **einbuchten. 2.** *Adj.* indented ⟨*coastline*⟩

Eingebung die; ~, ~en inspiration; **es muß eine glückliche ~ gewesen sein** the idea was an inspiration; **einer ~ folgend** acting on a sudden impulse

eingedenk ['aingədɛŋk] *Adj.; nicht attr.* **einer Sache** *(Gen.)* **~ sein/bleiben** *(geh.)* be mindful of sth.; **~ dieser Sache ...:** bearing this in mind ...; **~ der Tatsache, daß ...:** bearing in mind that ...

ein·gefahren 1. *2. Part. v.* **einfahren. 2.** *Adj.* long-established; deep-rooted ⟨*prejudice*⟩; **sich auf** *od.* **in ~en Bahnen** *od.* **Gleisen bewegen** go on in the same old way

ein·gefallen 1. *2. Part. v.* **einfallen. 2.** *Adj.* gaunt ⟨*face*⟩; sunken, hollow ⟨*cheeks*⟩

eingefleischt ['aingəflaiʃt] *Adj., nicht präd.* confirmed ⟨*bachelor*⟩; inveterate ⟨*smoker*⟩; deep-rooted, ingrained ⟨*habit, prejudice*⟩

ein|gehen 1. *unr. itr. V.; mit sein* **a)** *(eintreffen)* arrive; be received; **der Brief ist nicht bei uns eingegangen** we have not received the letter; **b)** *(aufgenommen werden)* **in die Geschichte ~:** go down in history; **in die Weltliteratur ~:** find one's/its place in world literature; **in die ewige Ruhe ~** *(dichter.)* pass away; **in das Reich Gottes ~:** enter the kingdom of Heaven; **c)** *(schrumpfen)* shrink; **d)** *(Bezug nehmen)* **auf eine Frage/ein Problem ~/nicht ~:** go into *or* deal with/ignore a question/problem; **e)** *(entgegenkommen, sich widmen)* **auf jmdn. ~:** be responsive to sb.; **auf jmdn. nicht ~:** ignore sb.'s wishes; **f) auf ein Angebot ~/nicht ~:** accept/reject an offer; **g)** *(sterben)* ⟨*animal, plant*⟩ die; **ihm war die Kuh eingegangen** the cow had died on him *(coll.)*; **die Blumen gehen eine nach der anderen ein** the flowers are dying off; **h)** *(bankrott gehen)* ⟨*shop*⟩ close down; ⟨*newspaper, business*⟩ close down, fold [up]; **i)** *(einleuchten)* **ihm geht alles leicht ein** he's quick on the uptake *(coll.)*; he cottons on to things quickly *(coll.)*; **es will ihr nicht ~, daß ...:** she can't grasp the fact that ... **2.** *unr. tr. V.* enter into ⟨*contract, matrimony*⟩; take ⟨*risk*⟩; accept ⟨*obligation*⟩; **darauf gehe ich jede Wette ein** *(ugs.)* I'll bet you anything on that *(coll.)*

eingehend 1. *Adj.* detailed ⟨*discussion, explanation, report*⟩; **~e Verhandlungen** negotiations on every detail. **2.** *adv.* in detail; **~er** in more detail

ein·gekeilt 1. *2. Part. v.* **einkeilen. 2.** *Adj. (von beiden Seiten)* wedged in (**in, zwischen** + *Dat.* between); *(von allen Seiten)* hemmed in (**in** among); **mein Auto war ~:** my car was boxed in

Ein·gekochte das; ~n *s.* **Eingemachte a**

Ein·gemachte das; ~n a) preserved fruit/vegetables; **b)** *(fig.: Substanz)* **ans ~ gehen** *(ugs.)* draw on one's reserves; **jetzt geht's ans ~** *(ugs.)* now comes the crunch

ein|gemeinden *tr. V.* incorporate ⟨*village*⟩ (**in** + *Akk.*, **nach** into)

Eingemeindung die; ~, ~en incorporation

ein·genommen 1. *2. Part. v.* **einnehmen. 2. a)** *(eingebildet)* **von sich ~ sein** be conceited; **von etw. ~ sein** be conceited about sth.; **b)** *(begeistert)* **von jmdm./etw. ~ sein** be taken with sb./sth.; *(dauerhaft)* like sb. very much/be very fond of sth.

ein·geschlechtig *Adj. (Bot.)* unisexual

ein·geschnappt 1. *2. Part. v.* **einschnappen. 2.** *Adj. (ugs.: beleidigt)* huffy

ein·geschossig *Adj.* single-storey; one-storey; *s. auch* **achtstöckig; einstöckig**

ein·geschränkt 1. *2. Part. v.* **einschränken. 2.** *Adj.* **~es Haltverbot** prohibition of stopping except for certain purposes; **in ~en Verhältnissen leben** live in reduced circumstances. **3.** *adv.* **~ leben** live in reduced circumstances

ein·geschrieben 1. *2. Part. v.* **einschreiben. 2.** *Adj.* registered ⟨*letter, member*⟩; enrolled ⟨*student*⟩

ein·geschworen 1. *2. Part. v.* **einschwören. 2.** *Adj.* dedicated (**auf** + *Akk.* to); **ein ~er Freund/Gegner** a sworn friend/enemy; **die beiden waren darauf ~:** the two had agreed on it

ein·gesessen 1. *2. Part. v.* **einsitzen. 2.** *Adj.* established

Ein·gesessene der/die; *adj. Dekl.* established resident

ein·gespannt 1. *2. Part. v.* **einspannen. 2.** *Adj.* **stark ~:** very busy

ein·gespielt 1. *2. Part. v.* **einspielen. 2.** *Adj.* in practice; **aufeinander ~:** playing well together

ein·gesprengt 1. *2. Part. v.* **einsprengen. 2.** *Adj.* **mit ~en Kiefern/Heideflächen/Fremdwörtern** with a sprinkling of conifers/a few areas of heathland/occasional foreign words

eingestandenermaßen *Adv.* admittedly

Ein·geständnis das confession; admission

ein|gestehen *unr. tr. V.* admit, confess ⟨*guilt*⟩; admit, confess to ⟨*mistake, theft*⟩; **[sich] ~, daß ...:** admit [to oneself] that ...

ein·gestellt 1. *2. Part. v.* **einstellen. 2.** *Adj.* **fortschrittlich/modern ~:** progressively minded/not at all old-fashioned in one's views; **ich weiß nicht, wie er [politisch] ~ ist** I don't know what his [political] views are

ein·gestrichen 1. *2. Part. v.* **einstreichen. 2.** *Adj.; nicht präd. (Musik)* **das ~e A** the A above middle C; **das ~e C** middle C

Eingeweide ['aingəvaidə] **das; ~s, ~;** *meist Pl.* entrails *pl.*; innards *pl.*; **der Hunger wühlte in seinen Eingeweiden** *(geh.)* raging hunger gnawed his insides

Eingeweide·bruch der *(Med.)* hernia

Ein·geweihte der/die; *adj. Dekl.* initiate

ein|gewöhnen 1. *refl. V.* get used *or* accustomed to one's new surroundings; accustom oneself to one's new surroundings; **er hat sich hier gut eingewöhnt** he's settled down here very well; **sich an seinem neuen Arbeitsplatz/in eine neue Tätigkeit ~:** settle in at one's new place of work/get used to a new job. **2.** *tr. V.* **jmdn. in etw.** *(Akk.)* **~:** get sb. used *or* accustomed to sth.

Ein·gewöhnung die; *o. Pl. (am Arbeitsplatz usw.)* settling in *no art.*; **die ~ in seiner neuen Umgebung/an seinem neuen Arbeitsplatz fiel ihm schwer** he found it difficult to get used to his new surroundings/job

ein·gewurzelt 1. *2. Part. v.* **einwurzeln. 2.** *Adj.* ingrained; **ein tief ~es Mißtrauen** a deeply rooted *or* deep-seated mistrust

ein|gießen *unr. tr. (auch itr.) V.* pour in; **etw. in etw.** *(Akk.)* **~:** pour sth. into sth.; **den Kaffee/die Limonade ~:** pour [out] the coffee/lemonade

ein|gipsen *tr. V.* **a)** *(Handw.)* **einen Nagel/Haken ~:** fix a nail/hook in with plaster; **b)** *(Med.)* **ein Bein/einen Arm ~:** put *or* set a leg/arm in plaster

Ein·glas das *(veralt.)* monocle

eingleisig ['ainglaiziç] **1.** *Adj.* single-track ⟨*railway line*⟩. **2.** *adv.* **eine ~ befahrene Strecke** a single-track line; **~ denken/ausgerichtet sein** *(fig.)* be narrow in one's outlook; be narrow-minded

Eingleisigkeit die ~: *(fig.)* narrowness

ein|gliedern 1. *tr. V.* integrate (**in** + *Akk.* into); incorporate ⟨*village, company*⟩ (**in** + *Akk.* into); *(einordnen)* include (**in** + *Akk.* in). **2.** *refl. V.* **sich in etw.** *(Akk.)* **~:** fit into sth.

Ein·gliederung die *s.* **eingliedern:** integration; incorporation; inclusion

ein|graben *unr. tr. V.* **a)** bury ⟨*box, treasure*⟩ (**in** + *Akk.* in); sink ⟨*pile, pipe*⟩ (**in** + *Akk.* into); **sich in etw.** *(Akk.)* **~:** ⟨*claws*⟩ dig into sth.; **der Krebs grub sich in den Sand ein** the crab buried itself in the sand; **b)** *(einpflanzen)* plant ⟨*tree, bush*⟩ (**in** + *Akk.* in); **c)** *(eindrücken)* make, leave ⟨*imprint, hole*⟩ (**in** + *Akk.* in); **d)** *(geh.: einmeißeln)* engrave ⟨*inscription, epitaph, etc.*⟩ (**in** + *Akk.* on); **der Fluß hatte sich tief ins Tal eingegraben** *(fig.)* the river had carved a deep channel in the valley

ein|gravieren *tr. V.* engrave (**in** + *Akk.* on)

ein|greifen *unr. itr. V.* **a)** *(Einfluß nehmen)* intervene (**in** + *Akk.* in); **entschieden ~:** take decisive action; **das Eingreifen** intervention; **b)** *(Technik)* **in etw.** *(Akk.)* **~:** mesh with sth.

eingreifend *Adj.* drastic, radical ⟨*change*⟩; far-reaching ⟨*consequences*⟩

Eingreif·truppe die *(Milit.)* strike force

ein|grenzen *tr. V.* **a)** enclose; **von** *od.* **mit etw. eingegrenzt werden** be enclosed by sth.; **b)** *(fig.: beschränken)* limit, restrict ⟨*topic, discussion, etc.*⟩ (**auf** + *Akk.* to); restrict, circumscribe ⟨*freedom, rights, etc.*⟩

Ein·griff der a) intervention (**in** + *Akk.* in); **ein staatlicher ~ in die Wirtschaft** state intervention in the economy; **ein ~ in jmds. Intimsphäre** *(Akk.)* an intrusion upon sb.'s privacy; **ein ~ in jmds. Rechte** an infringement of sb.'s rights; **b)** *(Med.)* operation; **c)** *(Schlitz)* fly

ein|gruppieren *tr. V.* **jmdn. in eine Gehaltsstufe ~:** place sb. on a step on the salary scale

Ein·gruppierung die grading

ein|hacken *itr. V.* **auf jmdn./aufeinander/etw. ~:** peck at sb./each other/sth.; **auf jmdn. ~** *(fig. ugs.)* pick on sb.

ein|haken 1. *tr. V.* **a)** *(mit Haken befestigen)* fasten; **b) jmdn. ~:** take sb.'s arm; link arms with sb.; **die Demonstranten hakten sich ein** the demonstrators linked arms; **sie gingen eingehakt** they walked arm in arm. **2.** *refl. V.* **sich bei jmdm. ~:** link arms with sb.; take sb.'s arm. **3.** *itr. V. (ugs.)* butt in; **bei einem Punkt ~:** [butt in and] take up a point

ein·halb·mal *Wiederholungsz., Adv.* half; **~ so viel/groß/teuer** half as much/big/expensive

Ein·halt der *in* **jmdm./einer Sache ~ gebieten** *od.* **tun** *(geh.)* stop *or* halt sb./sth.

ein|halten 1. *unr. tr. V.* keep ⟨*appointment*⟩; meet ⟨*deadline, commitments*⟩; keep to ⟨*diet, speed-limit, agreement*⟩; observe ⟨*regulation*⟩; **die Gesetze ~:** obey the laws; **den Kurs ~:** stay on course. **2.** *unr. itr. V. (geh.)* stop; *(vorübergehend)* pause; stop; **mit/in etw.** *(Dat.)* **~:** stop doing sth.

Ein·haltung die; *o. Pl. (einer Verabredung)* keeping; *(einer Vorschrift)* observance; **die ~ der Diät/Geschwindigkeitsbegrenzung/Vereinbarung** keeping to the diet/speed-limit/agreement; **die ~ eines Termins** meeting a deadline; **die ~ des Kurses** staying on course

ein|hämmern 1. *itr. V.* **auf etw.** *(Akk.)* **~:** hammer on sth.; **auf jmdn. ~** *(fig.)* pummel *or* pound sb. **2.** *tr. V.* **jmdm. etw. ~:** hammer *or* drum sth. into sb. *or* sb.'s head

ein|handeln 1. *tr. V.* **etw. für/gegen etw. ~:** barter sth. for sth. **2.** *refl. V.* **a)** *(ugs.: hinnehmen müssen)* **sich** *(Dat.)* **etw. ~:** let oneself in for sth. *(coll.)*; **b)** *(ugs.: sich zuziehen)* catch, get ⟨*disease*⟩

einhändig ['ainhɛndɪç] **1.** *Adj.* one-handed. **2.** *adv.* with [only] one hand

ein|händigen *tr. V.* **jmdm. etw. ~:** hand sth. over to sb.

Ein·hand·segler der single-handed yachtsman; *(Boot)* single-hander; single-handed dinghy/yacht

ein|hängen 1. *tr. V.* hang ⟨*door*⟩; fit ⟨*window*⟩; put down ⟨*receiver*⟩. **2.** *itr. V. (Fernspr.: auflegen)* hang up. **3.** *refl. V.* **sich bei jmdm. ~:** take sb.'s arm; link arms with sb.; **sie gingen eingehängt** they walked arm in arm

ein|hauchen *tr. V (dichter.)* **jmdm./einer Sache etw. ~:** breathe sth. into sb./sth.

ein|hauen 1. *unr. tr. V.* **a)** *(zertrümmern)* smash [in] ⟨*window*⟩; break down ⟨*door*⟩; **jmdm. den Schädel ~** *(ugs.)* bash sb.'s head in *(coll.)*; **b)** *(hineinschlagen)* drive in, knock in ⟨*nail*⟩; **c)** *(einmeißeln)* carve. **2.** *unr. itr. V.* **a)** *(einschlagen)* **auf jmdn. ~:** lay into sb.; **b)** *(ugs.: essen)* stuff oneself *(coll.)*

ein|heben *unr. tr. V.* **a)** hang, fit ⟨*door*⟩; fit ⟨*window*⟩; put *or* lift ⟨*wagon, train*⟩ back on the rails; **b)** *(südd., österr.)* levy ⟨*tax, fine*⟩; charge ⟨*sum, fee*⟩

Einhebung die; ~, ~en *(südd., österr.) s.* **einheben b:** levying; charging

ein|heften *tr. V.* file

ein|heilen *itr. V. (Med.)* ⟨*graft*⟩ take

ein·heimisch *Adj.* native, indigenous ⟨*population, plant*⟩; native ⟨*culture, traditions*⟩; home *attrib.* ⟨*team*⟩

Einheimische der/die; *adj. Dekl.* local

ein|heimsen ['ainhaimzn̩] *tr. V. (ugs.)* collect ⟨*medals, good marks*⟩; rake in *(coll.)* ⟨*money, profits*⟩

Ein·heirat die marriage **(in +** *Akk.* into); **durch ~ in die Familie** by marrying into the family

ein|heiraten *itr. V.* **in eine Familie ~:** marry into a family

Einheit die; ~, ~en a) unity; **b)** *(Maß~, Milit.)* unit

einheitlich 1. *Adj.* **a)** *(in sich geschlossen)* unified; integrated; **der Film hatte keine ~e Handlung** there was no unity of action in the film; **b)** *(unterschiedslos)* uniform ⟨*dress*⟩; standardized ⟨*education*⟩; standard ⟨*procedure, practice*⟩. **2.** *adv.* **~ gekleidet sein** be dressed the same; **die Prüfungsbestimmungen ~ regeln** standardize the examination regulations; **~ gestaltet sein** be designed along the same lines; **alle waren ~ ausgebildet** they had all had the same training

Einheitlichkeit die; ~ *(der Kleidung)* uniformity; *(der Ausbildung, des Verfahrens)* standard nature

Einheits-: ~essen das institutional food; **~format das** standard size; **~front die** united front; **~gewerkschaft die** general trade union; **~kleidung die** uniform; **~kurz·schrift die** unified shorthand [system]; **~liste die** *(Politik)* unified list [of candidates]; single list [of candidates]; **~partei die** united party; **Sozialistische Einheitspartei Deutschlands** *(DDR)* Socialist Unity Party of Germany; **~preis der** standard *or* fixed price; **~staat der** centralized state; **~tarif der** standard tariff; **~wert der** *(Steuerw.)* rateable value

ein|heizen 1. *tr. V.* put on ⟨*stove, boiler*⟩; heat ⟨*room*⟩. **2.** *itr. V.* **a)** *(ugs.: zur Eile antreiben)* **jmdm. ~:** chivvy sb. along *(coll.)*; **b)** *(ugs.: bedrängen)* **jmdm. ~:** give sb. a kick up the backside *(coll.)*

einhellig ['ainhɛlɪç] **1.** *Adj.* unanimous. **2.** *adv.* unanimously

Einhelligkeit die; ~: unanimity

ein·her|gehen *unr. itr. V.; mit sein* **a)** *(geh.: gemächlich gehen)* walk about *or* around; **b)** *(fig.: begleitet sein)* **mit etw. ~:** be accompanied by sth.

einhöck[e]rig *Adj.* one-humped

ein|holen 1. *tr. V.* **a)** *(erreichen)* **jmdn./ein Fahrzeug ~:** catch up with sb./a vehicle; **b)** make up ⟨*arrears, time*⟩; pull back ⟨*lead*⟩; **c)** *(einziehen)* haul in, pull in ⟨*nets*⟩; lower ⟨*flag*⟩; **d)** *(ugs.: einkaufen)* buy, get ⟨*groceries*⟩; **e)** *(erbitten)* ask for, seek ⟨*reference, advice*⟩; make ⟨*enquiries*⟩. **2.** *itr. V. (ugs.)* **~ gehen** go shopping

Einhol-: ~netz das *(ugs.)* string bag; **~tasche die** *(ugs.)* shopping bag

Ein·horn das unicorn

Einhufer ['ainhu:fɐ] **der; ~s, ~** *(Zool.)* soliped; solidungulate

ein|hüllen *tr. V.* **sich/jmdn. in etw.** *(Akk.)* **~:** wrap oneself/sb. up in sth.; **der Schnee/Nebel hatte die Gipfel eingehüllt** snow blanketed the peaks/the peaks were shrouded in mist

ein·hundert *Kardinalz.* a *or* one hundred; *s. auch* **hundert; Hundert**

einig ['ainɪç] *Adj.* **a)** *(einmütig)* **sich** *(Dat.)* **~ sein** be agreed *or* in agreement; **sich** *(Dat.)* **~ werden** reach agreement; **mit jmdm. über etw.** *(Akk.)* **~ sein** be in agreement *or* agree with sb. about *or* on sth.; **mit jmdm. über etw.** *(Akk.)* **~ werden** reach agreement *or* agree with sb. about *or* on sth.; **b)** *(geeint)* united ⟨*nation*⟩

einig... ['aɪnɪg...] *Indefinitpron. u. unbest. Zahlwort* **a)** *Sg. (etwas)* some ⟨*effort, hope, courage*⟩; **bei ~em guten Willen** with a measure of good will; **in ~er Entfernung** some distance away; **b)** *Pl. (mehrere)* some; **~e wenige** a few; **~e hundert** several hundred; **~e dreißig** thirty or so; **c)** *Sg. u. Pl. (beträchtlich)* **~er Ärger** quite a bit *or* quite a lot of trouble; **ich könnte dir über ihn ~es erzählen** I could tell you a thing *or* two about him; **dazu gehört schon ~es** it takes something to do that

ein|igeln ['ain|i:gl̩n] *refl. V.* **a)** *(sich einrollen)* curl up into a ball; **b)** *(sich zurückziehen)* hide oneself away; **c)** *(Milit.)* take up a position of all-round defence

einige·mal *Adv.* a few times; on a few occasions

einigen 1. *tr. V.* unite. **2.** *refl. V.* come to an agreement; reach an agreement; **sich auf jmdn./etw. ~:** agree on sb./sth.; **sich mit jmdm. [über etw.]** *(Akk.)* **~:** come to *or* reach an agreement with sb. [about sth.]

einigermaßen *Adv.* rather; somewhat; **~ zufrieden** fairly *or* reasonably satisfied; **Wie geht's dir? – ~:** How are you? – Not too bad; **das Essen war ~** *(ugs.)* the meal was OK *(coll.)* *or* all right

einig|gehen *unr. itr. V.; mit sein* agree; be agreed; **in einer Sache ~:** agree *or* be agreed about *or* on a matter

Einigkeit die; ~ a) *(Einheit, Eintracht)* unity; **b)** *(Übereinstimmung)* agreement

Einigung die; ~, ~en a) *(Übereinkunft)* agreement; **[über etw.** *(Akk.)***] eine ~ erzielen** come to *or* reach [an] agreement [on sth.]; **b)** *(Vereinigung)* unification

Einigungs-: ~versuch der attempt to reach [an] agreement; **~vertrag der** *(Politik)* unification treaty

ein|impfen *tr. V.* **a)** *(ugs.)* **jmdm. etw. [immer wieder] ~:** drum sth. into sb. [over and over again]; **b)** *(Med.: einspritzen)* **jmdm./einem Tier etw. ~:** inject sb./an animal with sth.

ein|jagen *tr. V.* **jmdm. Angst/einen Schrecken ~:** give sb. a fright

ein·jährig *Adj.* **a)** *(ein Jahr alt)* one-year-old *attrib.*; one year old *pred.*; *(ein Jahr dauernd)* **eine ~e Strafe** a one-year sentence; **eine ~e Abwesenheit** an absence of a *or* one year; a year's absence; **eine ~e Frist** a period of a *or* one year; **b)** *(Bot.)* annual

[1]Einjährige das; *adj. Dekl. (Schulw. veralt.)* *school-leaving examination taken after six years at secondary school*

[2]Einjährige der/die; *adj. Dekl.* one-year-old

ein|kalkulieren *tr. V.* **a)** *(einplanen)* take into account; **b)** *(mitberechnen)* take into account; include

Ein·kammer·system das *(Politik)* unicameral system

ein|kapseln 1. *tr. V.* encapsulate. **2.** *refl. V.* encapsulate oneself; *(fig.)* withdraw into one's shell

Einkaräter ['ainkarɛ:tɐ] **der; ~s, ~:** one-carat gem

einkarätig ['ainkarɛ:tɪç] *Adj.* one-carat

ein|kassieren *tr. V.* **a)** *(einnehmen)* collect; **b)** *(ugs.: entwenden)* pinch *(sl.)*; nick *(Brit. sl.)*; **c)** *(salopp: festnehmen)* pinch *(sl.)*; nab

Ein·kauf der a) *(Besorgung)* buying; **[einige] Einkäufe machen** *od.* **erledigen** do some shopping; **b)** *(eingekaufte Ware)* purchase; **ein guter/schlechter ~:** a good/bad buy; **c)** *(für ein Unternehmen)* buying; purchasing; **einen ~ tätigen** make a purchase; **d)** *o. Pl. (Kaufmannsspr.)* buying *or* purchasing department; **die Abteilung ~:** the buying *or* purchasing department; **e)** *(Sport) (von Spielern)* purchase; *(eingekaufter Spieler)* new signing; **der Verein tätigte einige Einkäufe** the club bought some players; **f)** *(einer Teilhaberschaft)* **der ~ in eine Firma** buying oneself into a firm

ein|kaufen 1. *itr. V.* **a)** *(Einkäufe machen)* shop; **~ gehen** go shopping; do the *or* some shopping; **beim Bäcker/im Supermarkt ~:** shop at the baker's/the supermarket; **da hast du aber teuer eingekauft** you paid high prices there; **b)** *(Kaufmannsspr.)* do the buying *or* purchasing. **2.** *tr. V.* **a)** buy; purchase; buy in ⟨*stores, provisions*⟩; **etw. billig/günstig ~:** buy sth. cheaply/at a favourable price; **b)** *(Sport)* buy ⟨*player*⟩. **3.** *refl. V.* **sich in ein Seniorenheim ~:** buy a place in an old people's home; **sich in eine Firma ~:** buy oneself into a firm

Ein·käufer der, Ein·käuferin die *(Berufsbez.)* buyer; purchaser

Einkaufs-: ~abteilung die *s.* **Einkauf d; ~bummel der** [leisurely] shopping expedition; **einen ~bummel machen** go on a shopping expedition; **~genossenschaft die** purchasing co-operative; **~korb der** shopping basket; *(im Geschäft)* [wire-]basket; **~netz das** string bag; **~passage die** shopping arcade *or* *(Amer.)* mall; **~preis der** *(Kaufmannsspr.)* wholesale price; **~quelle die: eine gute ~quelle für etw. sein** a good place to buy sth.; **~tasche die** shopping bag; **~wagen der** [shopping] trolley *(Brit.)* *or* *(Amer.)* cart; **~zentrum das** shopping centre; *(Großmarkt)* hypermarket; **~zettel der** shopping-list

Einkehr ['ainke:ɐ̯] **die; ~ a)** *(geh. veralt.)* stop; **~ halten** stop; make a stop; **b)** *(geh.: Sammlung)* **~ halten** take stock of oneself and one's attitudes; **eine Stunde der ~:** time for reflection and taking stock

ein|kehren *itr. V.; mit sein* **a)** stop; **in einem Wirtshaus ~:** stop at an inn; **b)** *(geh.: sich einstellen)* come

ein|keilen *tr. V.* **mein Auto ist eingekeilt** my car is boxed in; **die Fans keilten die Spieler ein** the fans mobbed the players; *s. auch* **eingekeilt**

ein·keim·blättrig *Adj. (Bot.)* monocotyledonous

ein|kellern *tr. V.* store in the/a cellar

ein|kerben *tr. V.* cut *or* carve a notch/notches in; notch; **Zeichen in etw.** *(Akk.)* **~:** carve signs on sth.

Einkerbung die; ~, ~en *(Kerbe)* notch

ein|kerkern *tr. V. (geh.)* incarcerate

Einkerkerung die; ~, ~en incarceration

ein|kesseln *tr. V. (bes. Milit.)* surround; encircle

Einkesselung die; ~, ~en *(bes. Milit.)* encirclement

ein|kitten *tr. V.* fix in with putty

einklagbar *Adj.* legally recoverable ⟨*debts*⟩; **nicht alle Rechte sind ~:** not all rights can be obtained through legal action

ein|klagen *tr. V.* sue for ⟨*damages, compensation, etc.*⟩; **etw. ~:** take legal action in order to gain *or* obtain sth.; **Schulden ~:** sue for the recovery of debts

ein|klammern *tr. V.* **etw. ~:** put sth. in brackets; bracket sth.

Ein·klang der **a)** *(Übereinstimmung)* harmony; **im ~ mit jmdm. sein** be in accord *or* agreement with sb.; **im** *od.* **in ~ mit etw. stehen** accord with sth.; **zwei Dinge in ~ [miteinander] bringen** harmonize two things; **die Hausarbeit mit einem Beruf in ~ bringen** combine housework and a career; **b)** *(Musik)* unison

ein|klappen *tr. V.* fold up; shut, close ⟨*knife*⟩

ein|klarieren *tr. V. (Zollw., Seew.)* clear

Ein·klassen·schule die one-room school

ein·klassig *Adj. (Schulw.)* one-room ⟨*school*⟩; **der ~e Unterricht** the teaching of children of different age-groups in one class

ein|kleben *tr. V.* stick in; **Fotos ins Album ~:** stick photos into the album

ein|kleiden *tr. V.* **a) sich/jmdn. ~:** clothe oneself/sb.; **sich/jmdn. neu ~:** fit oneself/sb. out with a new set of clothes; **sich/jmdn. völlig neu ~:** buy oneself/sb. a complete new wardrobe; **b)** *(mit einer Uniform versehen)* kit out ⟨*soldier*⟩; clothe ⟨*priest, nun*⟩; **c)** *(fig.: umschreiben)* couch; **Ermahnungen in Fabeln ~:** couch warnings in the form of fables

ein|klemmen *tr. V.* **a)** *(quetschen)* catch; **jmdm./sich die Hand [in etw. (Dat.)] ~:** catch *or* trap sb.'s/one's hand [in sth.]; *s. auch* **Schwanz a; b)** *(fest einfügen)* clamp

ein|klinken 1. *tr. V.* latch ⟨*door*⟩; engage ⟨*latch*⟩. **2.** *itr. V.; mit sein* ⟨*door*⟩ click to *or* shut

ein|klopfen *tr. V.* knock in ⟨*nail*⟩; pat in ⟨*cream*⟩

ein|kneifen *unr. tr. V. s.* **Schwanz a**

ein|knicken 1. *tr. V.* bend; crease over ⟨*paper*⟩; *(brechen)* snap; **mit eingeknickten Knien** with knees bent. **2.** *itr. V.; mit sein* bend; *(brechen)* snap; **sie knickte beim Gehen ein** she went over on her ankle while walking along

ein|knöpfen *tr. V.* **etw. in etw.** *(Akk.)* **~:** button sth. into sth.

ein|kochen 1. *tr. V.* preserve ⟨*fruit, vegetables*⟩. **2.** *itr. V.* thicken; **eine eingekochte Soße** a thickened sauce

ein|kommen *unr. itr. V.; mit sein* **a)** *(geh.: nachsuchen)* **[bei jmdm.] um etw. ~** *(geh.)* apply [to sb.] for sth.; **b)** *(veralt.: eingehen)* ⟨*money*⟩ come in; **c)** *(Sport, Seemannsspr.)* come in; **als erster/letzter ~:** come in first/last

Einkommen das; ~s, ~: income; **~ aus Grundbesitz/unselbständiger Arbeit** income from property/from employment

einkommens-, Einkommens-: ~grenze die income limit; **~los** *Adj.* without an income *postpos.*; **~los sein** have no income; be without an income; **~schwach** *Adj.* low-income *attrib.*; **~stark** *Adj.* high-income *attrib.*

Einkommen·steuer die income tax

Einkommensteuer·erklärung die income tax return

einkommensteuerpflichtig [-pflıçtıç] *Adj.* liable for income tax *postpos.*

ein|köpfen *tr., itr. V. (Fußball)* head in; **er köpfte zum 1:0 ein** he headed in to make it *or* the score 1-0

ein|kreisen *tr. V.* **a)** *(durch einen Kreis markieren)* **etw. ~:** put a circle round sth.; **b)** *(umzingeln)* surround ⟨*person*⟩; surround, encircle ⟨*house, town, troops*⟩; **c)** *(fig.: eingrenzen)* circumscribe ⟨*problem*⟩

Einkreisung die; ~, ~en encirclement

ein|kriegen *(ugs.)* **1.** *tr. V. s.* **einholen 1a. 2.** *refl. V.* control oneself; **sie konnte sich vor Lachen nicht ~:** she couldn't stop laughing

Einkünfte ['ainkʏnftə] *Pl.* income *sing.* **(aus** from); **feste ~:** a regular income

ein|kuppeln *itr. V. (Kfz-W.)* engage the clutch

[1]**ein|laden** *unr. tr. V.* load **(in +** *Akk.* into) ⟨*goods*⟩

[2]**ein|laden** *unr. tr. V.* invite; **jmdn. zum Essen ~:** invite sb. for a meal; *(im Restaurant)* invite sb. out for a meal; **jmdn. in sein Landhaus/auf sein Boot ~:** invite sb. to one's country house/on to one's boat; **ich lade euch alle ein** this is on me; **sich einladen** *(scherzh.)* invite oneself; **jmdn. auf ein Bier/einen Kaffee ~:** invite sb. for a beer/a coffee; **jmdn. zu sich nach Hause ~:** invite sb. over

einladend 1. *Adj.* inviting ⟨*impression, atmosphere*⟩; tempting, appetizing ⟨*meal*⟩; **~e Worte** words of invitation. **2.** *adv.* invitingly

Ein·ladung die invitation; **einer ~** *(Dat.)* **folgen** accept an invitation

Einladungs-: ~karte die invitation [card]; **~schreiben** das [written] invitation

Ein·lage die **a)** *(in einem Brief)* enclosure; **b)** *(Kochk.) vegetables, meat balls, dumplings, etc. added to a clear soup;* **eine Brühe mit ~:** a clear soup with meat balls/dumpling *etc.*; **c)** *(Schuh~)* arch-support; **d)** *(Einschiebsel)* **eine witzige ~:** a witty *or* humorous aside; **eine musikalische ~:** a musical interlude; **e)** *(eingelegte Verzierung)* inlay; **f)** *(Zahnmed.)* temporary filling; **g)** *(Finanzw.) (Guthaben)* deposit; *(Beteiligung)* investment; **die ~n bei den Banken** bank deposits; **h)** *(Schneiderei)* padding; *(Versteifung)* interfacing

ein|lagern 1. *tr. V.* store; lay in ⟨*stores*⟩. **2.** *refl. V.* **sich [in etw. (Akk.)] ~:** be deposited [in sth.]

Ein·lagerung die **a)** *(Aufbewahren)* storage; **b)** *(das Abgelagerte)* deposit

ein|langen *itr. V.; mit sein (österr.)* arrive

Einlaß ['ainlas] der; **Einlasses, Einlässe** ['ainlɛsə] **a)** *o. Pl.* admission, admittance **(in +** *Akk.* to); **sich** *(Dat.)* **~ verschaffen** gain admission *or* admittance; **~ fordern** demand entry *or* admission; **jmdm. ~ gewähren** grant sb. admission *or* admittance; **b)** *(veralt.: Eingang)* entrance

ein|lassen 1. *unr. tr. V.* **a)** *(hereinlassen)* admit; let in; **b)** *(einfüllen)* run ⟨*water*⟩; **c)** *(einpassen)* **etw. in etw.** *(Akk.)* **~:** set sth. into sth. **2.** *unr. refl. V.* **a)** *(meist abwertend)* **sich mit jmdm. ~:** get mixed up *or* involved with sb.; **sie läßt sich mit vielen Männern ein** she goes with lots of different men *(coll.)*; **b) sich auf etw.** *(Akk.)* **~:** get involved in sth.; **sich auf einen Streit ~:** be drawn into *or* get involved in an argument; **auf dein Vorhaben lasse ich mich nicht ein** I don't want anything to do with your plan; **c)** *(Rechtsw.)* testify; **sich dahin gehend ~, daß ...:** testify that ...; make a statement to the effect that ...

Einlaß·karte die admission ticket

Einlassung die; ~, ~en *(Rechtsw.)* testimony; statement; **nach eigenen ~en** according to his/her *etc.* own testimony

Ein·lauf der **a)** *(Med.)* enema; **jmdm. einen ~ machen** give sb. an enema; **b)** *o. Pl. (Sport: Passieren der Ziellinie)* finish; **beim ~:** at the finish; **c)** *o. Pl. (Sport: Beginn einer Rennphase)* **beim ~ in die Gerade/das Stadion** entering the straight/the stadium; **d)** *(Sport: Reihenfolge)* placings *pl.*; **es gab folgenden ~:** the placings were as follows

ein|laufen 1. *unr. itr. V.; mit sein* **a)** *(Sport)* **ins Stadion ~:** run into *or* enter the stadium; **in die letzte Runde ~:** start the last lap; **b)** *(ankommen)* **der Zug/das Schiff läuft ein** the train/ship is coming in; **das Schiff läuft in den Hafen ein** the ship is coming into *or* entering port; **c)** *(kleiner werden)* ⟨*clothes*⟩ shrink; **d)** *(hineinfließen)* run in; **e)** *(eingehen)* ⟨*news, information*⟩ come in. **2.** *unr. tr. V.* **a)** wear in ⟨*shoes*⟩; **b) jmdm. das Haus** *od.* **die Tür** *od.* **die Bude ~** *(ugs.)* pester sb. all the time. **3.** *unr. refl. V. (Sport)* warm up

Einlauf·wette die *(Pferdesport)* place-bet

ein|läuten *tr. V.* ring in ⟨*Sunday, New Year*⟩; **die letzte Runde ~** *(Sport)* ring the bell to signal *or* for the start of the last lap; *(Boxen)* ring the bell for the [start of the] last round

ein|leben *refl. V.* settle down; **sich an einem Ort ~:** settle down in a place; **sich in einem Haus ~:** settle in in a house; **sich gut ~:** settle down well

Einlege·arbeit die *(Kunsthandwerk)* inlaid work; *(Gegenstand)* piece of inlaid work

ein|legen *tr. V.* **a) etw. in etw.** *(Akk.)* **~:** put sth. in sth.; **einen Film in eine Kamera ~:** put *or* load a film into a camera; **den ersten Gang ~:** engage first gear; **einen schnelleren Gang** *od.* **ein schnelleres Tempo einlegen** *(fig.)* get a move on *(coll.)*; **b)** *(Kochk.)* pickle; **eingelegte Zwiebeln/Heringe** pickled onions/herrings; **c)** *(Kunsthandwerk)* **in die Truhe waren Blumenmuster eingelegt** the chest had been inlaid with flower patterns; **d)** *(Friseurhandwerk)* set ⟨*hair*⟩; **sich/jmdm. die Haare ~:** set one's/sb.'s hair; **e)** *(einschieben)* put in, insert ⟨*film extracts etc.*⟩; put on ⟨*trains, buses*⟩; **eine Pause ~:** take a break; **f)** *(geltend machen)* lodge ⟨*protest*⟩; **sein Veto gegen etw. ~:** use one's veto against sth.; veto sth.; **ein gutes Wort für jmdn. ~:** put in a good word for sb.; *s. auch* **Ehre b**

Einleger der; ~s, ~ *(Bankw.)* depositor

Einlege·sohle die insole

ein|leiten *tr. V.* **a)** *(beginnen)* institute, start ⟨*search*⟩; introduce, take ⟨*measures, steps*⟩; open ⟨*negotiations, investigation, inquest*⟩; induce ⟨*birth*⟩; launch, open ⟨*campaign*⟩; **b)** *(eröffnen)* introduce ⟨*chapter*⟩; **der Roman leitete eine neue Epoche ein** the novel ushered in a new epoch; **einige ~de Worte sprechen** say a few words of introduction; make a few introductory remarks; **c)** *(hineinleiten)* lead ⟨*water*⟩ **(in +** *Akk.* into); discharge ⟨*effluent*⟩

Ein·leitung die **a)** *(einleitender Teil)* introduction; **die ~ eines Aufsatzes/Buches** the introduction to an essay/book; **b)** *(einer Suche)* institution; *(von Maßnahmen)* introduction; *(einer Untersuchung, von Verhandlungen)* opening; *(einer Geburt)* induction; ⟨*einer Kampagne*⟩ launching; opening; **c)** *(Eröffnung)* **als** *od.* **zur ~ des Empfanges** to open *or* start the reception; **ein Feuerwerk bildete die ~:** the opening event was a firework display; **d) die ~ giftiger Abwässer in etw.** *(Akk.)* the discharge of poisonous effluents into sth.

ein|lenken 1. *itr. V.* **a)** *(nachgeben)* give way; make concessions; **sein Einlenken führte zu einem Kompromiß** by giving way *or* making concessions he enabled a compromise to be reached; **b)** *mit sein (einbiegen)* **in eine Straße ~:** turn into a street. **2.** *tr. V.* steer ⟨*boat, rocket, etc.*⟩

ein|lesen 1. *unr. refl. V.* **sich in ein Buch ~:** get into a book. **2.** *unr. tr. V. (DV)* feed in; input; **etw. in den Speicher ~:** read sth. into the memory

ein|leuchten *tr. V.* **jmdm.** ~: be clear to sb.; **es leuchtet ihr nicht ein, daß sie es allein machen soll** she doesn't see why she should do it by herself; **das will mir nicht** ~: I don't see that

ein·leuchtend 1. *Adj.* plausible. 2. *adv.* plausibly

ein|liefern *tr. V.* **einen Brief bei der Post** ~: take a letter to the post office; **jmdn. ins Krankenhaus/Gefängnis** ~: take sb. to hospital/jail; **wir mußten unsere Großmutter ins Krankenhaus** ~ **[lassen]** we had to have our grandmother admitted to hospital

Ein·lieferung die admission (in + *Akk.* to); **die** ~ **eines Verurteilten [ins Gefängnis]** taking a convicted prisoner to jail; **er wehrte sich gegen seine** ~ **ins Krankenhaus** he fought against being admitted to hospital

Einlieferungs·schein der a) receipt; b) *(Postw.)* certificate of posting

ein·liegend *(Papierdt.) Adj.* enclosed; ~ **übersenden wir Ihnen ...**: please find enclosed ...

Einlieger·wohnung die ≈ granny flat

ein|lochen 1. *tr. V. (salopp)* **jmdn.** ~: put sb. away *(coll.)*; put sb. behind bars *(coll.)*. 2. *tr., itr. V. (Golf)* hole; *(Billard)* pot ⟨*ball*⟩

einlösbar *Adj.* redeemable; **das Versprechen ist nicht** ~: the promise can't be kept

ein|lösen *tr. V.* a) cash ⟨*cheque*⟩; cash [in] ⟨*token, voucher, bill of exchange*⟩; redeem ⟨*pledge, pawned article*⟩; **man wollte [mir] den Scheck nicht** ~: they wouldn't cash the cheque [for me]; b) *(geh.: erfüllen)* redeem ⟨*pledge*⟩; **sein Wort** ~: keep one's word

Ein·lösung die *(von Schecks)* cashing; *(von Pfändern, Versprechen)* redemption

ein|lullen *tr. V. (ugs.)* **jmdn.** ~: lull sb. to sleep; *(fig.)* lull sb.'s suspicions

ein|machen *tr. V.* preserve ⟨*fruit, vegetables*⟩; *(in Gläser)* bottle

Einmach·glas das preserving jar

einmal 1. *Adv.* a) *(ein Mal)* once; **noch** ~ **so groß [wie]** twice as big [as]; **etw. noch** ~ **tun** do sth. again; ~ **mehr** once more *or* again; ~ **sagt er dies, ein andermal das** first he says one thing, then another; ~ **ist keinmal** *(Spr.)* just once won't matter; it won't matter just this once; **auf** ~: all at once; suddenly; *(zugleich)* at once; b) ['-'-] *(später)* some day; one day; *(früher)* once; **es war** ~ **ein König, der ...**: once upon a time there was a king who ... 2. *Partikel* a) **daran ist nun** ~ **nichts mehr zu ändern** there's nothing more that can be done about it; **nicht** ~: not even; **wieder** ~: yet again; **wir wollen die Sache erst** ~ **in Ruhe besprechen** let's discuss the matter quietly first; b) **alle** ~ **zuhören!** listen everybody!; **hör** ~ **auf zu reden!** stop talking, will you!

Einmal·eins das; ~: [multiplication] tables *pl.*; **das kleine/große** ~: tables from 1 to 10/11 to 20; **das** ~ **der Kochkunst/Politik** *(fig.)* the fundamentals *pl.* of cookery/politics

Einmal·hand·tuch das disposable towel

einmalig 1. *Adj.* a) unique ⟨*opportunity, chance*⟩; one-off, single ⟨*payment, purchase*⟩; b) *(hervorragend)* superb ⟨*film, book, play, etc.*⟩; *(ugs.)* fantastic *(coll.)* ⟨*girl, woman*⟩. 2. *adv. (ugs.)* really fantastic *or* superb *(coll.)*; **das Fest war** ~ **schön** the party was really superb *or* really fantastic *(coll.)*

Einmaligkeit die; ~: uniqueness

Ein·mann-: ~**betrieb der** a) *(Firma)* one-man business; b) *(Arbeitsweise)* one-man operation; ~**bus der** one-man bus; ~**wagen der** one-man bus/tram *(Brit.) or (Amer.)* trolley

Ein·mark·stück das one-mark piece

Ein·marsch der a) entry; **der** ~ **ins Stadion** the march into the stadium; b) *(Besetzung)* invasion (in + *Akk.* of)

ein|marschieren *itr. V.; mit sein* a) march in; **ins Stadion** ~: march into the stadium; b) *(gewaltsam besetzen)* **in ein Land** ~: march into *or* invade a country

ein|massieren *tr. V.* massage *or* rub in

Einmaster ['ainmastɐ] **der**; ~s, ~ *(Seemannsspr.)* single-master

ein|mauern *tr. V.* a) immure ⟨*prisoner, traitor*⟩; wall in ⟨*relic, treasure*⟩; b) *(ins Mauerwerk einfügen)* **etw. in die Wand** *usw.* ~: set sth. into the wall *etc.*

ein|meißeln *tr. V.* **etw. in etw.** *(Akk.)* ~: carve sth. into *or* on sth. [with a chisel]

Ein·meter·brett das one-metre board

ein|mieten *refl. V.* **sich in einer Villa** ~: rent a villa; **sich in einer Pension** ~: rent a room in a boarding-house

ein|mischen 1. *refl. V.* interfere (in + *Akk.* in); **wenn ich mich kurz** ~ **darf** if I may butt in for a moment. 2. *tr. V.* mix in

Ein·mischung die interference (in + *Akk.* in); **verzeihen Sie meine** ~: excuse my butting in

einmonatig *Adj.; nicht präd.* a) *(einen Monat alt)* one-month-old *attrib.*; b) *(einen Monat dauernd)* one-month *attrib.*; *s. auch* **achtmonatig**

ein·monatlich 1. *Adj.* monthly; *s. auch* **achtmonatlich** 1. 2. *adv.* monthly; once a month

ein·motorig *Adj.* single-engined

ein|motten *tr. V.* **etw.** ~: put sth. into mothballs; *(fig.)* mothball

ein|mumme[l]n *tr. V. (ugs.)* wrap up; **sich [warm]** ~: wrap up *or* wrap oneself up [warmly]

ein|münden *itr. V.; auch mit sein* a) flow in; enter; **in einen Fluß** ~: flow into *or* enter a river; b) *(enden)* **in etw.** *(Akk.)* ~: lead into sth.

Ein·mündung die a) **die** ~ **der Mosel in den Rhein** the confluence of the Rhine and the Moselle; **die** ~ **des Kanals in den Fluß** the point where the canal flows into the river; b) *(von Straßen)* **die** ~ **der Straße in die Hauptstraße/den Platz** the junction of the street and the main road/the point where the road comes out into the square

einmütig ['ainmy:tɪç] 1. *Adj.* unanimous. 2. *adv.* unanimously

Einmütigkeit die; ~: unanimity (über + *Akk.* on)

ein|nachten *itr. V. (unpers.) (schweiz.)* get dark

ein|nähen *tr. V.* a) *(festnähen)* sew in; **etw. in etw.** *(Akk.)* ~: sew sth. into sth.; b) *(enger nähen)* take in

Einnahme die; ~, ~**en** a) *meist Pl.* income; *(Staats~)* revenue; *(Kassen~)* takings *pl.*; b) *o. Pl. (von Arzneimitteln)* taking; **wir empfehlen die** ~ **einer leichten Mahlzeit** it is advisable to take a light meal; **die** ~ **der Tabletten muß regelmäßig erfolgen** the tablets must be taken regularly; c) *o. Pl. (einer Stadt, Burg)* capture; taking; **die** ~ **Berlins** the capture *or* taking of Berlin

Einnahme·quelle die source of income; *(des Staates)* source of revenue

ein|nässen *tr., itr. V.* wet ⟨*bed*⟩; **er näßt noch ein** he's still wetting the bed

ein|nebeln 1. *tr. V.* shroud; blanket. 2. *refl. V.* a) *(Milit.)* put up a smokescreen; b) *(unpers.)* **es hat sich eingenebelt** a mist has come down

ein|nehmen *unr. tr. V.* a) *(kassieren)* take; *(verdienen)* earn; **er hat nicht viel an Trinkgeld eingenommen** he didn't make much by way of tips; b) *(zu sich nehmen)* take ⟨*medicine, tablets*⟩; **eine Mahlzeit** ~ *(geh.)* take a meal; partake of a meal *(literary)*; c) *(besetzen)* capture, take ⟨*town, fortress*⟩; d) **seinen Platz** ~: take one's place; *(sich setzen)* take one's seat *or* place; **eine Haltung/einen Standpunkt** ~ *(fig.)* take up *or* adopt an attitude/a position; **eine wichtige Stellung in der Kunst/Literatur** ~ *(fig.)* occupy an important place in the artistic/literary world; e) *(ausfüllen)* take up ⟨*amount of room*⟩; f) *(beeinflussen)* **jmdn. für sich** ~: win sb. over; **jmdn. gegen sich** ~: turn sb. against one; **gegen jmdn. eingenommen sein** be prejudiced against sb.; **von sich eingenommen sein** think a lot of oneself *(coll.)*; be very taken with oneself

einnehmend *Adj.* winning ⟨*manner*⟩; **ein** ~**es Wesen haben** *(scherzh.)* take everything one can get

ein|nicken *itr. V.; mit sein (ugs.)* nod off *(coll.)*

ein|nisten *refl. V.* a) *(meist abwertend: sich niederlassen)* **sich bei jmdm.** ~: park oneself on sb. *(coll.)*; b) *(ein Nest bauen)* build a nest/their nests; nest; c) *(Med.)* **das befruchtete Ei nistet sich im Uterus ein** the fertilized ovum is implanted in the uterus

Ein·öde die barren *or* featureless waste; *(Einsamkeit)* isolation; **die weißen** ~**n Alaskas** the white wastes of Alaska

Einöd·hof der *(südd., österr.)* isolated farm

ein|ölen *tr. V.* a) *(mit Öl einreiben)* **sich/jmdn.** ~: put *or* rub oil on oneself/sb.; b) *(ölen)* oil

ein|ordnen 1. *tr. V.* a) *(einfügen)* arrange; put in order; **etw. in Aktenordner** ~: sort sth. into files; file sth.; **Briefe in Fächer** ~: sort letters and place them in their correct pigeon-holes; b) *(klassifizieren)* classify; categorize, classify ⟨*writer, thinker, artist*⟩. 2. *refl. V.* a) *(Verkehrsw.)* get into the correct lane; **sich nach rechts/links** ~: get into the right-hand/left-hand lane; „~" 'get in lane'; b) *(sich einfügen)* **sich [in die Gemeinschaft]** ~: fit in[to the community]

Ein·ordnung die; *o. Pl. (in Karteien usw.)* arranging; *(Klassifizierung)* classification

ein|packen 1. *tr. V.* a) pack (in + *Akk.* in); *(einwickeln)* wrap [up]; b) *(ugs.: warm anziehen)* wrap up; **jmdn./sich warm/gut** ~: wrap sb./oneself up warmly. 2. *itr. V. (ugs.)* **er kann** ~: he's had it *(coll.)*; **pack ein!** *(hör auf!)* pack it in! *(coll.)*; give it a rest! *(coll.)*; *(verschwinde!)* get lost! *(coll.)*

ein|parken *tr., itr. V.* park

Ein·parteien-: one-party

ein|passen 1. *tr. V.* fit; install; **etw. in etw.** *(Akk.)* ~: fit sth. into sth. 2. *refl. V.* fit in

ein|pauken *tr. V.* **etw.** ~: mug up *(Brit.) or (Amer.)* bone up on sth. *(coll.)*; **jmdm. etw.** ~: drum *or* hammer sth. into sb.

Einpeitscher ['ainpaitʃɐ] **der**; ~s, ~ a) *(Agitator)* rabble-rouser; b) *(Parl.)* whip

ein|pendeln *refl. V.* settle down; cease to fluctuate

ein|pennen *itr. V.; mit sein (salopp)* drop *or* doze off

Ein·personen-: ~**haushalt der** single-person household; ~**stück das** *(Theater)* monodrama

Ein·pfennig·stück das one-pfennig piece

ein|pferchen *tr. V.* a) *(zusammendrängen)* **eingepfercht stehen/sein** stand/be crammed *or* crushed together; b) pen in ⟨*animals*⟩

ein|pflanzen *tr. V.* a) plant ⟨*flowers, shrubs, etc.*⟩; **jmdm. einen Sinn für Gerechtigkeit** ~ *(fig.)* implant in sb. a sense of justice; b) *(Med.)* implant; **jmdm. ein Organ** ~: implant an organ in[to] sb.

ein|pfropfen *tr. V.* graft (in + *Akk.* on)

Ein·phasen-Wechselstrom der *(Physik, Elektrot.)* single-phase current

einphasig *Adj. (Physik, Elektrot.)* single-phase

ein|pinseln *tr. V.* brush; paint ⟨*wound*⟩

ein|planen *tr. V.* **etw.** ~: include sth. in one's plans; **diese Verzögerung war nicht eingeplant** we/they *etc.* didn't plan on this delay

ein|pökeln *tr. V. (Kochk.)* salt

ein·polig *Adj. (Physik, Elektrot.)* single-pole

ein|prägen 1. *tr. V.* a) stamp (in + *Akk.* into, on); b) *(fig.)* **sich** *(Dat.)* **etw.** ~: memorize sth.; commit sth. to memory; **jmdm. ~, pünktlich zu sein** impress on sb. the importance of being punctual. **2.** *refl. V.* **das prägte sich ihm [für immer] ein** it made an [indelible] impression on him; **Werbetexte prägen sich einem leicht ein** advertising slogans are catchy

einprägsam 1. *Adj.* easily remembered; catchy, easily remembered ⟨*tune, melody, slogan*⟩. **2.** *adv.* **er hat das sehr ~ dargelegt** he expounded it in a way that made it easy to remember

ein|prasseln *itr. V.; mit sein* **auf jmdn./etw. ~:** rain down on sb./sth.; **die Fragen der Zuhörer prasselten auf ihn ein** the audience showered him with questions

ein|pressen *tr. V.* press in; **etw. in etw.** *(Akk.)* **~:** press sth. into sth.

ein|programmieren *tr. V. (DV)* input ⟨*data, figures, etc.*⟩; programme in ⟨*function, property*⟩

ein·prozentig *Adj.* one per cent *attrib.*; of one per cent *postpos.*

ein|prügeln 1. *itr. V.* **auf jmdn./ein Tier ~:** beat sb./an animal. **2.** *tr. V.* **jmdm. etw. ~** *(fig.)* drub *or* beat sth. into sb.

ein|pudern *tr. V.* powder; **sich** *(Dat.)* **das Gesicht ~:** powder one's face

ein|quartieren 1. *tr. V.* quarter, billet ⟨*troops*⟩; **die Opfer wurden vorläufig in Hotels einquartiert** the victims were given temporary accommodation in hotels; **sie quartierten ihre Freunde bei ihren Eltern ein** they put their friends up with their parents. **2.** *refl. V.* **sich bei jmdm. ~** *(Milit.)* be quartered with *or* billeted on sb.; **sich auf einem Bauernhof/bei seinen Eltern ~:** stay on a farm/with one's parents

Einquartierung die; ~, ~en a) *(Milit.)* quartering; billeting; **b) [sechs Mann] ~ haben** have [six] soldiers billeted on one

ein|quetschen *tr. V. s.* **einklemmen**

Ein·rad das unicycle

einräd[e]rig *Adj.* one-wheeled

ein|rahmen *tr. V.* frame; **sich** *(Dat.)* **etw. ~ lassen** have sth. framed; **er saß da, von zwei Damen eingerahmt** *(fig.)* he sat flanked by two ladies; **den Brief solltest du dir ~ lassen** *(iron.)* you ought to *or* should get that letter framed

ein|rammen *tr. V.* **a)** ram in; **etw. in den Boden ~:** ram sth. into the ground; **b)** *(zertrümmern)* smash up ⟨*car*⟩; break *or* batter down ⟨*door*⟩

ein|rasten *itr. V.; mit sein (Technik)* engage

ein|räuchern *tr. V.* envelope in smoke; **ein Zimmer ~:** fill a room with smoke; **die Gardinen ~:** get *or* make the curtains smoky; **jmdn. mit Tränengas ~:** use tear gas against sb.

ein|räumen *tr. V.* **a)** *(einordnen)* put away; **etw. in etw.** *(Akk.)* **~:** put sth. away in sth.; **Bücher wieder [ins Regal] ~:** put books back [on the shelf]; **b)** *(füllen)* **er mußte seinen Schrank ~:** he had to put his things away in his cupboard; **das Zimmer wieder ~:** put everything *or* all the furniture back into the room; **c)** *(zugestehen)* admit; concede; **jmdm. etw. ~:** admit sth. to sb.; **jmdm. einen Platz ~:** reserve sb. a seat; **jmdm. ein Recht/einen Kredit ~:** give *or* grant sb. a right/loan; **jmdm. das Recht ~, etw. zu tun** give *or* grant sb. the right to do sth.; **d)** *(Sprachw.)* **~de Konjunktion** concessive conjunction

ein|rechnen *tr. V.* include, take account of ⟨*costs etc.*⟩; **nicht eingerechnet die Trinkgelder** not including the tips

ein|reden 1. *tr. V.* **jmdm. etw. ~:** talk sb. into believing sth.; **er redete ihr ein, es zu kaufen** he persuaded her to buy it; he talked her into buying it; **sich** *(Dat.)* **~, daß ...:** persuade oneself that...; **das redest du dir bloß ein** you're just imagining it. **2.** *itr. V.* **auf jmdn. ~:** talk insistently to sb.; **laut/beruhigend auf jmdn. ~:** keep talking to sb. loudly/soothingly

ein|regnen 1. *refl. V. (unpers.)* **es hat sich eingeregnet** it's begun to rain steadily. **2.** *itr. V.; mit sein* get soaked [to the skin]

ein|regulieren *tr. V. (Technik)* set ⟨*temperature*⟩ **(auf + *Akk.*** at); **ein falsch einreguliertes Hörgerät** a wrongly adjusted hearing-aid

ein|reiben *unr. tr. V.* **Salbe [in die Haut] ~:** rub ointment in[to one's skin]; **jmdm. den Rücken ~:** rub lotion/ointment *etc.* into sb.'s back; **sich** *(Dat.)* **den Nacken/das Gesicht mit etw. ~:** rub sth. into one's neck/face

ein|reichen *tr. V.* **a)** submit ⟨*application*⟩; hand in, submit ⟨*piece of work, dissertation, thesis*⟩; lodge, make ⟨*complaint*⟩; tender ⟨*resignation*⟩; **b)** *(jur.)* file ⟨*suit, petition for divorce*⟩

ein|reihen 1. *refl. V.* **sich in etw.** *(Akk.)* **~:** join sth. **2.** *tr. V.* **jmdn. in eine Kategorie/Gruppe ~:** place sb. in a category/group; **sich in eine Gruppe** *usw.* **~:** become part of a group *etc.*

Einreiher der; ~s, ~: single-breasted suit/jacket

einreihig ['ainraiıç] **1.** *Adj.* single-breasted ⟨*suit*⟩. **2.** *adv.* in a single row *or* line; **ein ~ geknöpfter Mantel** a single-breasted overcoat

Ein·reise die entry; **bei der ~ nach Frankreich/in die ČSSR** on entry into France/Czechoslovakia; **jmdm. die ~ verweigern** refuse sb. entry

Einreise·erlaubnis die entry permit

ein|reisen *itr. V.; mit sein* enter; **nach Schweden ~:** enter Sweden

Einreise-: ~verbot das: jmdm. ~verbot erteilen refuse sb. entry; **~visum das** entry visa

ein|reißen 1. *unr. tr. V.* **a)** *(abreißen)* pull *or* tear down ⟨*building*⟩; **b)** *(einen Riß machen in)* tear; rip; **c) sich** *(Dat.)* **einen Dorn ~:** prick oneself on a thorn; **sich** *(Dat.)* **einen Splitter ~:** get a splinter in one's hand/foot *etc..* **2.** *unr. itr. V.; mit sein* **a)** *(einen Riß bekommen)* tear; rip; **b)** *(ugs.: sich verbreiten)* become a habit; **etw. ~ lassen** allow sth. to *or* let sth. become a habit; **eine Gewohnheit ~ lassen** allow a habit to catch on *(coll.) or* spread

Einreiß·haken der ceiling hook

ein|reiten 1. *unr. itr. V.; mit sein* ride in; **in etw.** *(Akk.)* **~:** ride into sth.. **2.** *unr. refl. V.* warm up; **sich mit einem Pferd ~:** get used to riding a horse

ein|renken *tr. V.* **a)** *(Med.)* set; reduce *(Med.)*; **jmdm. den Fuß/Arm [wieder] ~:** [re]set sb.'s foot/arm; **b)** *(ugs.: bereinigen)* **etw. ~:** sort *or* straighten sth. out; **das renkt sich ein** that will sort *or* straighten itself out

ein|rennen 1. *unr. tr. V. (aufbrechen)* break down ⟨*door*⟩; **jmdm. [wegen etw.] das Haus** *od.* **die Bude ~** *(ugs.)* pester sb. all the time [for sth.]; *s. auch* **offen. 2.** *unr. refl. V. (ugs.: sich verletzen)* **sich** *(Dat.)* **den Kopf an etw.** *(Dat.)* **~:** bash *or* bang one's head on *or* against sth.

ein|richten 1. *refl. V.* **a) sich gemütlich/schön ~:** furnish one's home comfortably/beautifully; **sich an einem Ort häuslich ~:** make oneself at home in a place; **b)** *(auskommen)* **sich [mit seinem Gehalt] ~:** get by *or* make ends meet [on one's salary]; **c)** *(sich vorbereiten)* **sich auf jmdn./etw. ~:** prepare for sb./sth.; **darauf war sie nicht eingerichtet** she was not prepared for that. **2.** *tr. V.* **a)** furnish ⟨*flat, house*⟩; fit out ⟨*shop, restaurant, hobbies room*⟩; equip ⟨*laboratory*⟩; **b)** *(ermöglichen)* arrange; **das läßt sich ~:** that can be arranged; **es so ~, daß ...:** arrange things so that ...; **c)** *(eröffnen)* open ⟨*branch, shop*⟩; set up ⟨*advisory centre*⟩; start, set up ⟨*business*⟩; **sich** *(Dat.)* **ein Geschäft/eine Modeboutique ~:** start a business/open a fashion boutique; **d)** *(Med.)* set; reduce *(Med.)*; **e)** *(umformen)* arrange ⟨*piece of music*⟩; adapt ⟨*play, novel, etc.*⟩; **f)** *(Math.)* **eine gemischte Zahl ~:** reduce a mixed number

Ein·richter der fitter

Ein·richtung die a) *o. Pl. (das Einrichten) (einer Wohnung)* furnishing; *(eines Musikstücks)* arrangement; *(eines Theaterstücks)* adaptation; *(Med.)* setting; reducing *(Med.)*; **b)** *(Mobiliar)* furnishings *pl.*; **c)** *(Geräte)* **~en** *(Geschäfts~)* fittings; *(Labor~)* equipment *sing.*; **sanitäre ~en** sanitary facilities; sanitation *sing.*; **d)** *(Institution, Gewohnheit)* institution; **öffentliche/staatliche ~en** public/state institutions

Einrichtungs-: ~gegen·stand der piece of furniture; **~haus das** [large] furniture store

ein|ritzen *tr. V.* carve; **seinen Namen in einen Stamm ~:** carve one's name on a tree trunk

ein|rollen 1. *tr. V.* roll up ⟨*carpet etc.*⟩; **sich/jmdm. die Haare ~:** put one's/sb.'s hair in curlers *or* rollers; **sich ~:** ⟨*hedgehog, cat*⟩ curl up. **2.** *itr. V.; mit sein* **a)** roll in; **der Zug rollt ein** the train is coming in

ein|rosten *itr. V.; mit sein* go rusty; rust up; **er ist/seine Knochen sind eingerostet** *(fig.)* his joints have stiffened up

ein|rücken 1. *itr. V.; mit sein* **a)** *(Milit.: einmarschieren)* move in; **in ein Land ~:** march into a country; **wieder in die Kaserne ~:** return to barracks; **b)** *(Milit. veralt.: eingezogen werden)* report for duty. **2.** *tr. V.* **a)** *(Schriftw.)* indent ⟨*line, heading, etc.*⟩; **b)** *(Zeitungsw.)* insert ⟨*advertisement, article*⟩

ein|rühren *tr. V.* stir in; **etw. in etw.** *(Akk.)* **~:** stir sth. into sth.

ein|rüsten *tr. V. (Bauw.)* put up *or* erect scaffolding around ⟨*building*⟩

eins [ains] **1.** *Kardinalz.* one; **es ist ~:** it is one o'clock; **Punkt ~:** on the stroke of one; at one o'clock precisely; **halb ~:** half past twelve; **Viertel nach/vor ~:** [a] quarter past/to one; **gegen/vor ~:** around/before one; **~ zu null** one-nil; **~ zu ~:** one all; **~ zu null für dich!** *(ugs.)* that's one up to you!; **die Nummer ~ sein** *(fig.)* be number one; **„~, zwei, drei!"** 'ready, steady, go'; **... und ~, zwei, drei, weg war er** and in a jiffy *(coll.) or* in no time he was gone; **~ a,** *(Kaufmannsspr. meist)* **I a** top-quality; **seine Arbeit ~ a erledigen** *(ugs.)* do a first-class job; *s. auch* **[1]acht. 2.** *Adj.; nicht attr.* **mir ist alles ~:** it's all the same *or* all one to me; **den Schrei hören und zu Hilfe eilen war für sie ~:** the moment she heard the cry, she was hurrying to help; **mit jmdm. über etw.** *(Akk.)* **~ sein/werden** be in/reach agreement with sb. about *or* on sth.; **sich mit jmdm. ~ wissen/fühlen** be/feel at one with sb. **3.** *Indefinitpron. s.* **[1]ein 3 b, c**

Eins die; ~, ~en a) one; **wie eine ~ stehen** *(ugs.)* stand as straight as a ramrod; **sie kocht/spielt Klavier wie eine ~** *(ugs.)* she's a fantastic cook/piano-player *(coll.)*; *s. auch* **[1]Acht a, e, g; b)** *(Schulnote)* one; A; *s. auch* **Zwei b**

Ein·saat die sowing

[1]ein|sacken *tr. V.* **a)** *(in Säcke füllen)* **etw. ~:** put sth. into sacks; **b)** *(ugs.: einstecken)* grab; pocket ⟨*money*⟩

[2]ein|sacken *itr. V.; mit sein* sink in; ⟨*building, pavement*⟩ subside

ein|sagen *itr. V. (südd., österr.)* **er sagte ihr ein** he whispered the answer to her

ein|sägen *tr. V.* **etw. ~:** saw into sth.

ein|salben *tr. V.* **den Arm ~:** rub ointment on *or* into one's arm; **sich/jmdn. ~:** rub ointment on [oneself]/rub ointment on sb.

ein|salzen *tr. V.* salt ⟨*fish, meat*⟩

einsam *Adj.* **a)** *(verlassen)* lonely ⟨*person, decision*⟩; **~ leben** live a lonely *or* solitary life; **sich ~ fühlen** feel lonely; **b)** *(einzeln)* solitary ⟨*rock, tree, wanderer*⟩; **~e Spitzenklasse sein** *(ugs.)* be in a class of its/his/her own; **c)** *(abgelegen)* isolated; **~ liegen** be situated miles from anywhere; **d)** *(menschenleer)* empty; deserted; **~ und verlassen [da]liegen** lie [there] lonely and deserted

Einsamkeit die; ~, ~en a) *(Verlassenheit)* loneliness; **b)** *(Alleinsein)* solitude; **c)** *(Abgeschiedenheit)* isolation

ein|sammeln *tr. V.* **a)** *(auflesen)* pick up; gather up; **die Kinder/Betrunkene ~** *(ugs.)* pick up *or* collect the children/pick up drunks; **b)** *(sich aushändigen lassen)* collect in; collect ⟨*tickets*⟩

ein|sargen *tr. V.* **einen Toten ~:** put the body of a dead person into a coffin; **laß dich doch ~!** *(salopp)* [go and] get stuffed *(Brit sl.)*; go to hell *(sl.)*

Ein·satz der a) *(eingesetztes Teil) (in Tischdecke, Kopfkissen usw.)* inset; *(in Kochtopf, Nähkasten usw.)* compartment; **b)** *(eingesetzter Betrag)* stake; **den ~ erhöhen** raise the stakes *pl.*; **c)** *o. Pl. (das Einsetzen) (von Maschinen, Gewehren, Wasserwerfern, Schlagstöcken)* use; *(von Truppen)* deployment; **unter ~ seines Lebens** at the risk of his life; **zum ~ kommen** *od.* **gelangen** *(Papierdt.)* ⟨*machine*⟩ come into operation; ⟨*police, troops*⟩ be brought into action, be used; ⟨*reserve player*⟩ be brought on *or* used; **jmdn./etw. zum ~ bringen** use sb./sth.; **d)** *(Engagement)* commitment; dedication; **~ zeigen** show commitment *or* dedication; **der ~ hat sich gelohnt** the effort was worthwhile; **e)** *(Milit.)* **im ~ sein/fallen** be in action *or* on active service/die in action; **einen ~ fliegen** *(Luftwaffe)* fly a mission; **f)** *(Musik)* **der ~ der Instrumente** the entry of the instruments; **der ~ der Violinen kam zu spät** the violins came in too late

einsatz-, Einsatz-: ~befehl der a) *(Befehl zum Einsatz)* order to go into action; **b)** *(Verantwortung)* **den ~befehl haben** have operational command; **~bereit** *Adj.* **a)** *(bereit, sich einzusetzen)* ⟨*worker*⟩ ready to work; ⟨*athlete*⟩ fit to compete; **b)** *(bereit, eingesetzt zu werden)* ready for use; **c)** *(Milit.)* combat-ready *attrib.*; ready for action *postpos.*; **~bereitschaft die** *s.* **einsatzbereit:** readiness to work; fitness to compete; readiness for use; combat-readiness; readiness for action; **~fähig** *Adj.* **a)** *(fähig, sich einzusetzen)* ⟨*athlete*⟩ fit to compete; **b)** *(verfügbar)* fit ⟨*player*⟩; ⟨*washing machine etc.*⟩ in working order; **~freudig** *Adj.* enthusiastic; **~gruppe die, ~kommando das** task force; **~leiter der a)** *(des Einsatzkommandos)* head of operations; **b)** *(des Einsatzes)* leader of the task force; **~plan der** plan of action; **~wagen der** *(der Polizei)* police car; *(der Feuerwehr)* fire-engine; *(Notarztwagen)* ambulance; *(der Straßenbahn)* relief; **~zentrale die** operations centre

ein|sauen *tr. V. (derb)* **sich/etw. ~:** get oneself/sth. covered in muck *(coll.)*

ein|saugen *unr. (auch regelm.) tr. V.* suck in ⟨*air, liquid*⟩; breathe [in] ⟨*fresh air*⟩; **die Bienen saugen den Nektar ein** the bees suck the nectar

ein|säumen *tr. V.* **a)** *(Schneiderei)* hem; **b)** *(einfassen)* edge ⟨*flower-bed, vegetable-patch*⟩; surround ⟨*property*⟩

ein|schalten 1. *tr. V.* **a)** switch *or* turn on ⟨*radio, TV, electricity, etc.*⟩; **einen anderen Sender ~:** switch *or* tune to another station; **b)** *(fig.: beteiligen)* call in ⟨*press, police, expert, etc.*⟩; **jmdn. in die Verhandlungen ~:** bring sb. into the negotiations; **c)** *(einfügen)* take ⟨*break*⟩. **2.** *refl. V.* **a)** switch [itself] on; come on; **b)** *(eingreifen)* intervene (**in +** *Akk.* in)

Einschalt·quote die *(Rundf.)* listening figures *pl.*; *(Ferns.)* viewing figures *pl.*

Ein·schaltung die a) *(Einschalten)* switching *or* turning on; **b)** *(Beteiligung)* calling in; **c)** *(Sprachw.)* parenthesis

ein|schärfen *tr. V.* **jmdm. etw. ~:** impress sth. [up]on sb.; **jmdm. ~, etw. zu tun** impress upon sb. that he/she must do sth.

ein|scharren *tr. V. (vergraben)* bury; *(lieblos begraben)* **jmdn. ~:** bury sb. hurriedly

ein|schätzen *tr. V.* **a)** judge ⟨*person*⟩; assess ⟨*situation, income, damages*⟩; *(schätzen)* estimate; **jmdn./eine Situation falsch ~:** misjudge sb./a situation; **jmdn./eine Leistung hoch/niedrig ~:** think highly/not think highly of sb./an achievement; **wie ich die Lage einschätze** as I see the situation; **b)** *(Steuerw.)* assess

Ein·schätzung die a) *s.* **einschätzen:** judging; assessment; estimation; **nach seiner/meiner ~:** in my estimation *or* judgement; **b)** *(Steuerw.)* assessment

ein|schäumen *tr. V.* **a)** *(mit Schaum bedecken)* lather; **sich/jmdm. die Haare ~:** lather one's/sb.'s hair; **b)** *(mit Schaumstoff umhüllen)* **etw. ~:** wrap sth. in foam [material]

ein|schenken *tr., itr. V.* **a)** *(eingießen)* pour [out]; **jmdm. etw. ~:** pour out sth. for sb.; **b)** *(füllen)* fill [up] ⟨*glass, cup*⟩; **er schenkte immer wieder ein** he kept on filling up my glass/cup/our/their *etc.* glasses/cups

ein|scheren *itr. V.; mit sein (Verkehrsw.)* **in** *od.* **auf eine Fahrspur ~:** get *or* move into a lane; **nach links/rechts ~:** get *or* move into the left-hand/right-hand lane; **in eine Lücke ~:** move into a space; **er scherte vor mir ein** he cut in in front of me

ein|schicken *tr. V.* send in; **etw. zur Reparatur ~:** send sth. [in] to be repaired

ein|schieben *unr. tr. V.* **a)** *(hineinschieben)* push in; **den Ball zum 1:0 ~** *(Fußballjargon)* put the ball away to make it *or* the score 1-0; **b)** *(einfügen)* put in; insert; put on ⟨*trains, buses*⟩; fit in ⟨*client, patient*⟩; **etw. in etw.** *(Akk.)* **~:** put *or* insert sth. into sth.

Ein·schienen·bahn die monorail

ein|schießen 1. *unr. tr. V.* **a)** *(zerstören)* demolish ⟨*wall, building*⟩ by gunfire; **das Fenster [mit einem Ball] ~** *(fig.)* smash the window [with a ball]; **b)** *(treffsicher machen)* try out, test ⟨*gun etc.*⟩; **c)** *(hineinschießen)* insert ⟨*dowel, plug*⟩; **d)** *(Sport)* kick in ⟨*ball*⟩; **den Ball zum 1:1 ~:** shoot a goal to make it *or* the score 1-1; **e)** *(einzahlen)* inject ⟨*capital, cash, etc.*⟩ (**in +** *Akk.* into); **f)** *(Druckw.)* interleave; insert; **g)** *(Weberei)* **den Faden ~:** shoot the weft; pick. **2.** *unr. refl. V.* **a)** *(treffsicher werden)* **sich [auf etw. Akk.)] ~:** find *or* get the range [of sth.]; **b)** *(Sport)* find *or* get the range; **c)** *(angreifen)* **sich [immer mehr] auf jmdn./etw. ~:** make sb./sth. the target of [increasingly frequent] attacks

ein|schiffen 1. *tr. V.* embark ⟨*passengers*⟩; load ⟨*cargo*⟩. **2.** *refl. V.* embark (**nach** for)

Einschiffung die; ~, ~en *s.* **einschiffen:** embarkation; loading

Einschiffungs·hafen der port of embarkation

ein|schlafen *unr. itr. V.; mit sein* **a)** fall asleep; go to sleep; **über der Zeitung ~:** fall asleep over the paper; **beim Fernsehen ~:** fall asleep while watching television *or* in front of the television; **ich kann nicht ~:** I can't get to sleep; **b)** *(verhüll.: sterben)* pass away *(euphem.)*; **c)** *(gefühllos werden)* go to sleep; **mein Bein ist eingeschlafen, mir ist das Bein eingeschlafen** my leg has gone to sleep; **d)** *(aufhören)* peter out

ein|schläfern *tr. V.* **a)** *(in Schlaf versetzen)* **jmdn. ~:** send sb. to sleep; **b)** *(betäuben)* **jmdn. ~:** put sb. to sleep; **c)** *(schmerzlos töten)* **ein Tier ~:** put an animal to sleep; **d)** *(beruhigen)* soothe, salve ⟨*conscience*⟩; dull ⟨*critical faculties*⟩

einschläfernd 1. *Adj.* soporific. **2.** *adv.* **~ wirken** have a soporific effect

Einschläferung die; ~, ~en a) *(Betäubung)* anaesthesia *no art.*; **b)** *(Tötung)* **der Tierarzt empfahl die ~:** the vet recommended putting the animal to sleep; **c)** *o. Pl. (Beruhigung) s.* **einschläfern d:** soothing; salving; dulling

Ein·schlag der a) *(Einschlagen)* **wir sahen den ~ des Blitzes/der Bomben** we saw the lightning strike/the bombs land; **b)** *(Stelle)* **wir sahen die Einschläge der Kugeln/der Bomben** we saw the bullet-holes/where the bombs had fallen *or* landed; **c)** *(Anteil)* element; **eine Familie mit südländischem ~:** a family with southern blood in it; **mit nihilistischem ~:** with an element of nihilism; **d)** *(Kfz-W.) (des Lenkrads)* turning; *(der Räder)* lock; **e)** *(Forstw.)* felling

ein|schlagen 1. *unr. tr. V.* **a)** *(hineinschlagen)* knock in; hammer in; **etw. in etw.** *(Akk.)* **~:** knock *or* hammer sth. into sth.; **b)** *(zertrümmern)* smash [in]; **c)** *(einwickeln)* wrap up ⟨*present*⟩; cover ⟨*book*⟩; **ein Kind in eine warme Decke ~:** wrap a child up in a warm blanket; **d)** *(wählen)* take ⟨*route, direction*⟩; take up ⟨*career*⟩; adopt ⟨*policy*⟩; **einen Kurs ~:** follow a course; *(fig.)* follow *or* pursue a course; **einen anderen Kurs ~** *(auch fig.)* change *or* alter course; **e)** *(Kfz-W.)* turn ⟨*[steering-]wheel*⟩; **f)** *(Schneiderei: umlegen)* take in; take up ⟨*trousers*⟩; **g)** *(Forstw.)* fell ⟨*trees*⟩. **2.** *unr. itr. V.* **a)** *(auftreffen)* ⟨*bomb*⟩ land; ⟨*lightning*⟩ strike; **bei uns hat es eingeschlagen** our house was struck by lightning; **b)** *(einprügeln)* **auf jmdn./etw. ~:** rain blows on *or* beat sb./sth.; **c)** *(durch Händedruck)* shake [hands] on it; *(fig.)* accept; **schlag ein!** shake on it!; **d)** *(Kfz-W.)* **nach links/rechts ~:** steer to the left/right; **e)** *(sich erfolgreich entwickeln)* come along *or* on well; come on well; **f)** *(Erfolg haben)* be a success

einschlägig ['ainʃlɛ:gɪç] **1.** *Adj.; nicht präd.* specialist ⟨*journal, shop*⟩; relevant ⟨*literature, passage*⟩. **2.** *adv.* **er ist ~ vorbestraft** he has previous convictions for a similar offence/similar offences; **der ~ vorbestrafte Angeklagte** the accused, who has/had previous convictions for a similar offence/similar offences

ein|schleichen *unr. refl. V.* steal *or* sneak *or* creep in; *(fig.)* creep in; **sich in etw.** *(Akk.)* **~:** steal *or* sneak *or* creep into sth.; **der Verdacht schleicht sich ein, daß ...:** one has a sneaking suspicion that ...

ein|schleifen 1. *unr. tr. V.* **a)** *(eingraben)* cut in; **etw. in etw.** *(Akk.)* **~:** cut sth. into sth.; **b)** *(Technik: einpassen)* grind in. **2.** *unr. refl. V. (bes. Psych.)* become established

ein|schleppen *tr. V.* tow in ⟨*ship, yacht, etc.*⟩; bring in, introduce ⟨*disease, pest*⟩; **Typhus in ein Land ~:** bring *or* introduce typhus into a country

ein|schleusen *tr. V.* smuggle in; **Agenten in ein Land/eine Terroristengruppe ~:** infiltrate agents into a country/a terrorist group

ein|schließen *unr. tr. V.* **a) etw. in etw.** *(Dat.)* **~:** lock sth. up [in sth.]; **jmdn./sich ~:** lock sb./oneself in; **jmdn. in ein[em] Zimmer ~:** lock sb. [up] in a room; **sich in ein[em] Zimmer ~:** lock oneself in a room; **b)** *(umgeben)* ⟨*wall*⟩ surround, enclose; ⟨*people*⟩ surround, encircle; **c)** *(einbegreifen)* **etw. in etw.** *(Akk.)* **~:** include sth. in sth.

einschließlich 1. *Präp. mit Gen. (stark dekl. Substantiv im Sg. ohne Artikel od. Attribut bleibt ungebeugt)* including; inclusive of; **~ der Unkosten** including expenses; **die Kosten ~ Porto** costs including *or* inclusive of postage; **sie verlor ihre Handtasche ~ aller Papiere** she lost her handbag and all the papers which were in it. **2.** *adv.* **bis ~ 30. Juni** up to and including 30 June; **bis Montag ~:** up to and including Monday

ein|schlummern *itr. V.; mit sein* **a)** *(geh.: einschlafen)* fall asleep; **b)** *(verhüll.: sterben)* pass away *(euphem.)*
Ein·schluß der a) *(Einbeziehung)* inclusion; **alle Staaten unter** *od.* **mit ~ dieses Landes** all states, including this country; **b)** *(Geol.)* inclusion
ein|schmeicheln *refl. V.* **sich bei jmdm. ~:** ingratiate oneself with sb.
einschmeichelnd *Adj.* beguiling ‹*music, voice*›; ingratiating ‹*manner*›
ein·schmeißen *unr. tr. V. (salopp)* smash [in] ‹*window*›
ein|schmelzen *unr. tr. V.* melt down
ein|schmieren *tr. V. (ugs.)* **a)** *(einfetten) (mit Creme)* cream ‹*face, hands, etc.*›; *(mit Fett)* grease; *(mit Öl)* oil; **die Kinder schmierten meine Schuhe mit Zahncreme ein** the children smeared toothpaste on my shoes *or* smeared my shoes with toothpaste; **b)** *(schmutzig machen)* **sich/etw. ~:** make *or* get oneself/sth. mucky *(coll.) or* dirty; **sich mit Eis ~:** get oneself covered in ice-cream
ein|schmuggeln *tr. V.* **a)** *(unerlaubt einführen)* smuggle in; **etw. in ein Land** *(Akk.)* **~:** smuggle sth. into a country; **b)** *(ugs.: unerlaubt Zutritt verschaffen)* **sich in etw.** *(Akk.)* **~:** sneak into sth.; **jmdn. in etw.** *(Akk.)* **~:** smuggle *or* sneak sb. into sth.
ein|schnappen *itr. V.; mit sein* **a)** ‹*door, lock*› click to; **b)** *(ugs.: schmollen)* go into a huff; *s. auch* **eingeschnappt 2**
ein|schneiden 1. *unr. tr. V.* **a)** *(hineinschneiden)* make a cut in; cut; ‹*rope*› cut into ‹*wrists*›; **das Papier an den Ecken ~:** make a cut at each of the corners of the paper; **b)** *(einritzen)* carve; **ein tief eingeschnittenes Tal** a deeply carved valley. **2.** *unr. itr. V.* **das Kleid schneidet an den Schultern ein** the dress cuts into my shoulders
einschneidend *Adj.* drastic, radical ‹*measure, change*›; drastic, far-reaching ‹*effect*›
ein|schneien *itr. V.; mit sein* ‹*person, car*› get snowed in; become snowbound; ‹*village, farm*› get snowed in, be cut off by snow; ‹*mountain pass*› be closed by snow; **eingeschneit sein** be snowed in
Ein·schnitt der a) *(Schnitt)* cut; incision *(Med.)*; **einen ~ machen** make a cut *or (Med.)* incision; **b)** *(eingeschnittene Stelle)* cut; *(Med.)* incision; *(im Gebirge)* cleft; **c)** *(Zäsur)* break; **d)** *(einschneidendes Ereignis)* [decisive] turning-point; decisive event
ein|schnüren *tr. V.* **a) sich/jmdm. die Taille ~:** lace one's/sb.'s waist; **sich ~:** lace oneself up [in one's corset]; **b)** *(einengen)* cut in; **es schnürt mich ein** it cuts into me
ein|schränken 1. *tr. V.* **a)** *(verringern)* reduce, curb ‹*expenditure, consumption, power*›; **das Trinken/Rauchen/Essen ~:** cut down on the amount one drinks/smokes/eats; **b)** *(einengen)* limit; restrict; **jmdn. in seinen Rechten/seiner Bewegungsfreiheit ~:** limit *or* restrict sb.'s rights/freedom of movement; **c)** *(relativieren)* qualify, modify ‹*remark*›. **2.** *refl. V.* economize; cut back on spending; **sich finanziell ~ müssen** have to cut back on one's spending; **sich im Rauchen/Trinken sehr ~:** cut down drastically on the amount one smokes/drinks; *s. auch* **eingeschränkt**
Einschränkung die; ~, ~en a) restriction; limitation; **jmdm. ~en auferlegen** impose restrictions on sb.; **sich** *(Dat.)* **erhebliche finanzielle ~en auferlegen müssen** have to make considerable economies; **b)** *(Vorbehalt)* reservation; **nur mit ~[en]** only with reservations *pl.*; **ohne ~[en]** without reservation; **mit der ~, daß ...:** with the [one] reservation that ...
ein|schrauben *tr. V.* screw in
Einschreibe-: ~brief der registered letter; **~gebühr die a)** *(Postw., Hochschulw.)* registration fee; **b)** *(in Vereinen usw.)* membership fee
ein|schreiben *unr. tr. V.* **a)** *(hineinschreiben)* write up; **b)** *(Postw.)* register ‹*letter*›; **einen Brief ~ lassen** register a letter; send a letter by registered mail; *s. auch* **eingeschrieben 2**; **c)** *(eintragen)* **sich/jmdn. [in eine Liste] ~:** write sb.'s/one's name down [on a list]; enter sb.'s/one's name [on a list]; **sich an einer Universität ~:** register at a university; **sich für einen Abendkurs ~:** enrol for an evening class; *s. auch* **eingeschrieben**; **d)** *(DV)* input
Ein·schreiben das *(Postw.)* registered letter; **per ~:** by registered mail
Ein·schreibung die *(Hochschulw.)* registration; *(für einen Abendkurs)* enrolment
ein|schreien *unr. itr. V.* **auf jmdn. ~:** shout at sb.
ein|schreiten *unr. itr. V.* intervene; **gegen jmdn./etw. ~:** take action against sb./sth.; **das Einschreiten der Polizei** intervention by the police
ein|schrumpfen *itr. V.; mit sein* shrivel up; *(fig.)* dwindle
Ein·schub der *(Schrift- u. Druckw.)* insertion
ein|schüchtern *tr. V.* intimidate; **sich ~ lassen** let oneself be intimidated; **wir lassen uns nicht ~:** we won't be intimidated
Einschüchterungs·versuch der attempt at intimidation
ein|schulen *tr. V.* **eingeschult werden** start school; **Sie müssen Ihr Kind mit 6 Jahren ~ lassen** you must ensure that your child starts school when he or she reaches the age of 6
Ein·schulung die: die Anforderungen für die ~ erfüllen meet the requirements for starting school; **wir müssen die ~ verlegen** we must postpone the date on which he/she starts school
Einschulungs·alter das age at which children start school
Ein·schuß der a) bullet wound; wound at point of entry; **b)** *(Raumf.)* **nach dem ~ in die Mondumlaufbahn** after the rocket has/had been put into orbit around the moon *or* into moon orbit; **c)** *(Weberei)* weft; woof; **d)** *(Sport)* **zum ~ kommen** shoot a goal
Einschuß-: ~loch das bullet-hole; **~stelle die** wound at point of entry; bullet wound
ein|schütten *tr. V.* pour in; **etw. in etw.** *(Akk.)* **~:** pour sth. into sth.; **den Schweinen das Futter ~:** pour the pigs their feed
ein|schweben *itr. V.; mit sein* glide in
ein|schweißen *tr. V.* **a)** weld in; **etw. in etw.** *(Akk.)* **~:** weld sth. into sth.; **b)** *(in Klarsichtfolien)* **etw. ~:** seal sth. in transparent film
ein|schwenken *itr. V.; mit sein* **a)** turn in; **in die Toreinfahrt ~:** turn into the gateway; **nach links ~:** wheel left; **b)** *(fig.)* fall into line; **er schwenkte auf einen neuen politischen Kurs ein** he changed course politically
ein|schwören *unr. tr. V.* **a)** *(durch Treueschwur binden)* **jmdn. ~:** swear sb. in; **b)** *(verpflichten)* **jmdn. auf etw.** *(Akk.)* **~:** swear sb. to sth.; *s.* **eingeschworen**
ein|segnen *tr. V.* **a)** *(ev. Religion landsch.: konfirmieren)* confirm; **b)** *(kath. Religion: weihen)* consecrate
Ein·segnung die *s.* **einsegnen:** confirmation; consecration
ein|sehen *unr. tr. V.* **a)** *(überblicken)* see into ‹*building, garden, etc.*›; **b)** *(prüfend lesen)* look at, see ‹*files*›; **c)** *(erkennen)* see; realize; **d)** *(begreifen)* understand, see
Einsehen das; ~s: ein ~ haben have *or* show [some] understanding; **kein ~ haben** have *or* show no understanding
ein|seifen *tr. V.* **a) jmdn./sich/etw. ~:** lather sb./oneself/sth.; **jmdn. mit Schnee ~** *(ugs.)* rub snow in sb's face; **b)** *(ugs.: betrügen)* **jmdn. ~:** con sb. *(coll.)*; put one over on sb. *(coll.)*
ein·seitig 1. *Adj.* **a)** on one side *postpos.*; unrequited ‹*love*›; one-sided ‹*friendship*›; **er hat eine ~e Lähmung** he's paralysed down one side; **b)** *(tendenziös)* one-sided, biased ‹*view, statement, etc.*›; one-sided ‹*person*›; **c)** *(nicht abwechslungsreich)* unbalanced ‹*diet*›; one-sided ‹*education*›; **ein sehr ~er Mensch** a person with narrow interests. **2.** *adv.* **a) etw. ~ bedrucken** print sth. on one side; **b)** *(tendenziös)* one-sidedly; **c)** *(nicht abwechslungsreich)* **sich ~ ernähren** have an unbalanced diet; **sehr ~ ausgebildet sein** have had a very one-sided education
Einseitigkeit die; ~, ~en *(Voreingenommenheit)* one-sidedness; bias
ein|senden *unr. (auch regelm.) tr. V.* send [in]; **etw. einem Verlag** *od.* **an einen Verlag ~:** send sth. to a publisher
Ein·sender der sender; *(bei einem Preisausschreiben)* entrant; **die ~ von Fotos werden gebeten ...:** we [would] ask all those who send in photographs ...
Einsende·schluß der closing date
Ein·sendung die letter/card/contribution/article *etc.*; *(bei einem Preisausschreiben)* entry
ein|senken *tr. V.* sink ‹*pile etc.*›; **etw. in etw.** *(Akk.)* **~:** sink sth. into sth.
Einser der; ~s, ~ *(ugs.)* **a)** *(Schulnote)* one; A; *s. auch* **Zweier a**; **b)** *(Buslinie)* number one [bus]
ein|setzen 1. *tr. V.* **a)** *(hineinsetzen)* put in; put in, fit ‹*window*›; insert, put in ‹*tooth, piece of fabric, value, word*›; **etw. in etw.** *(Akk.)* **~:** put/fit/insert sth. into sth.; **Karpfen in einen Teich ~:** stock a pond with carp; **b)** *(Verkehrsw.)* put on ‹*special train etc.*›; **c)** *(ernennen, in eine Position setzen)* appoint; **jmdn. zum** *od.* **als Erben ~:** appoint *or* name sb. one's heir; **jmdn. in ein Amt ~:** appoint sb. to an office; **der Monarch glaubte sich von Gott eingesetzt** the monarch believed he held his office by divine right; **d)** *(in Aktion treten lassen)* use ‹*weapon, machine*›; bring into action, use ‹*troops, police*›; bring on, use ‹*reserve player*›; **seine ganze Kraft ~:** use all one's strength; **e)** *(aufs Spiel setzen)* stake ‹*money*›; **f)** *(riskieren)* risk; put at risk; **sein Leben/seinen Ruf ~:** risk one's life/reputation; put one's life/reputation at risk. **2.** *itr. V.* start; begin; ‹*storm*› break; **mit etw. ~:** start *or* begin sth.; **dann setzte Regen ein** then it started *or* began to rain; **wenn [die] Ebbe/Flut einsetzt** when the tide begins to ebb/flow. **3.** *refl. V.* **a)** *(sich engagieren)* **ich werde mich dafür ~, daß Sie mehr Geld bekommen** I shall do what I can to see that you get more money; **sich für die Annahme des Gesetzes/die Rettung der Flüchtlinge ~:** do what one can to see that the law is passed/the refugees are saved; **sich selbstlos für die Armen ~:** lend aid unselfishly to the poor; **der Schüler/Minister setzt sich nicht genug ein** the pupil is lacking application/the minister is lacking in commitment; **b)** *(Fürsprache einlegen)* **sich für jmdn. ~:** support sb.'s cause
Einsetzung die, ~, ~en appointment **(in +** *Akk.* to)
Ein·sicht die a) *(das Einsehen)* view **(in +** *Akk.* into); **b)** *o. Pl. (Einblick)* **~ in die Akten nehmen** take *or* have a look at the files; **jmdm. ~ in etw.** *(Akk.)* **gewähren** allow sb. to look at *or* see sth.; **c)** *(Erkenntnis)* insight; **zu der ~ kommen, daß ...:** come to realize that ...; come to the realization that ...; **d)** *o. Pl. (Vernunft)* sense; reason; *(Verständnis)* understanding; **~ mit jmdm. haben** show [some] understanding for sb.; **zur ~ kommen** come to one's senses

einsichtig 1. *Adj.* **a)** *(verständnisvoll)* understanding; **jeder Einsichtige muß zugeben, daß ...:** anyone with any understanding of the situation must concede that ...; **b)** *(verständlich)* comprehensible, understandable, clear; **ihm war nicht ~, warum ...:** it was not clear to him why ...; he was not clear why ... **2.** *adv.* **sehr ~ vorgehen** show a great deal of understanding
Einsichtnahme die; ~, ~n *(Papierdt.)* **nach ~ in die Akten** after studying the files; **die Baupläne liegen zur ~ aus** the building plans are available for inspection
einsichts-: ~los *Adj.* **a)** *(verständnislos)* lacking in understanding *postpos.*; **b)** *(reuelos)* without remorse *postpos.*; **~voll** *Adj.* understanding
ein|sickern *itr. V.; mit sein* seep in; *(fig.)* trickle in
Einsiedelei [ainzi:də'lai] **die; ~, ~en** hermitage; *(fig.)* [country] retreat
Ein·siedler der hermit; *(fig.)* recluse
einsiedlerisch *Adj.* hermit-like; solitary
Einsiedler-: ~klause die hermitage; **~krebs der** hermit-crab
ein·silbig 1. *Adj.* **a)** monosyllabic ⟨*word*⟩; **b)** *(fig.)* taciturn ⟨*person*⟩; monosyllabic ⟨*answer*⟩. **2.** *adv. (fig.)* ⟨*answer*⟩ in monosyllables
Einsilbigkeit die; ~ *(fig.)* taciturnity
ein|singen *unr. refl. V.* get oneself into voice; ⟨*choir*⟩ get itself into voice
ein|sinken *unr. itr. V.* **a)** sink in; **in etw.** *(Dat.)* **~:** sink into sth.; **b)** *(zusammenfallen)* ⟨*roof*⟩ sag; **eingesunkene Wangen** sunken cheeks
ein|sitzen *unr. itr. V. (Rechtsw.)* serve a prison sentence; **er sitzt für drei Jahre ein** he is serving three years *or* a three-year sentence
Einsitzer der; ~s, ~: single-seater
einsitzig *Adj.* single-seater *attrib.*
ein|sortieren *tr. V.* sort ⟨*books, papers, etc.*⟩ and put them away; **Briefmarken/Fotos in ein Album ~:** put stamps/photos into an album; **Karteikarten ~:** file cards; **Briefe in Fächer ~:** sort letters into pigeonholes
ein·spaltig *(Druckw.)* **1.** *Adj.* single-column *attrib.* **2.** *adv.* ⟨*print, set*⟩ in one column
ein|spannen *tr. V.* **a)** harness ⟨*horse*⟩; **b)** *(in etw. spannen)*; **den Bogen [in die Schreibmaschine] ~:** put the sheet of paper in[to the typewriter]; **Stoff in einen Stickrahmen ~:** fix cloth into an embroidery frame; **das Werkstück [in den Schraubstock] ~:** clamp the work [in the vice]; **c)** *(ugs.: heranziehen)* rope in *(coll.)*; **er wollte uns für seine Zwecke ~:** he wanted to use us for his own ends; *s. auch* **eingespannt 2**
Einspänner ['ainʃpɛnɐ] **der; ~s, ~ a)** one-horse carriage; **b)** *(österr. Gastr.)* black coffee with whipped cream *(served in a glass)*
einspännig 1. *Adj.* one-horse *attrib.* ⟨*carriage*⟩. **2.** *adv.* **~ fahren** drive a one-horse carriage
ein|sparen *tr. V.* save, cut down on ⟨*costs, expenditure*⟩; save ⟨*time*⟩; save, economize on ⟨*energy, electricity, gas, materials*⟩; **Stellen/Arbeitsplätze ~:** cut down on the number of posts/cut down on staff
Einsparung die; ~, ~en saving **(an** + *Dat.* in); **~en an Kosten/Energie/Material** savings *or* economies in costs/energy/materials; **durch ~ an** *od.* **von Material** by economizing on *or* saving materials
Einsparungs·maßnahme die economy measure
ein|speicheln *tr. V.* insalivate
ein|speichern *tr. V. (DV)* feed in; input; **einem Computer etw. ~:** feed sth. into a computer
ein|speisen *tr. V. (Technik, DV)* feed in; **etw. in etw.** *(Akk.)* **~:** feed sth. into sth.
ein|sperren *tr. V.* **jmdn. ~:** lock sb. up
ein|spielen 1. *refl. V.* **a)** ⟨*musician, athlete, team, etc.*⟩ warm up; *(zum Saisonbeginn)* ⟨*athlete, team*⟩ get into practice; **sich aufeinander ~** *(fig.)* get used to each other's ways *or* one another; *s. auch* **eingespielt 1; b)** *(funktionieren)* get going [properly]. **2.** *tr. V.* **a)** *(einbringen)* make; bring in; **der Film hat seine Unkosten eingespielt** the film has covered its costs; **b)** play *or* break in ⟨*musical instrument*⟩; **c)** *(aufnehmen)* record
Einspiel·ergebnis das *(Film, Theater)* box-office takings *pl.*
ein|spinnen *unr. refl. V. (Zool.)* ⟨*insect*⟩ spin a cocoon around itself
einsprachig ['ainʃpra:xɪç] **1.** *Adj.* monolingual. **2.** *adv.* **~ aufwachsen** grow up speaking only one language; *s. auch* **zweisprachig**
ein|sprechen *unr. itr. V. s.* **einreden 2**
ein|sprengen *tr. V.* **etw. ~:** sprinkle sth. with water; damp sth.; *s. auch* **eingesprengt**
Einsprengsel ['ainʃprɛŋzl̩] **das; ~s, ~:** embedded particles *pl.*; **mit einigen philosophischen** *usw.* **~n** *(fig.)* with a sprinkling of philosophy *etc.*
ein|springen 1. *unr. itr. V.; mit sein* **a)** *(als Stellvertreter)* stand in; *(fig.: aushelfen)* step in and help out; **für jmdn. ~:** stand in for sb./step in and help sb. out; **b)** *(Turnen)* **in den Handstand ~:** perform a dive to handstand. **2.** *unr. refl. V. (Ski)* do practice jumps
Einspritz|düse die injection nozzle
ein|spritzen *tr. V. (auch Kfz-W.)* inject; **jmdm. etw. ~:** inject sb. with sth.
Einspritz-: ~motor der fuel-injection engine; **~pumpe die** injection pump
Ein·spruch der a) *(Einwand)* objection **(gegen** to); **~ gegen etw. erheben** raise an objection to sth.; **b)** *(Rechtsw.)* objection; *(gegen Urteil, Entscheidung)* appeal; **[gegen etw.] ~ einlegen** raise an objection [to sth.]; *(gegen Urteil, Entscheidung)* lodge an appeal [against sth.]
ein|sprühen *tr. V.* **die Windschutzscheibe mit einem Entfroster ~:** spray de-icer on [to] the windscreen *(Brit.) or (Amer.)* windshield; **sich** *(Dat.)* **das Haar ~:** put hairspray on one's hair
einspurig ['ainʃpu:rɪç] **1.** *Adj.* single-track ⟨*road*⟩. **2.** *adv.* **die Autobahn ist nur ~ befahrbar** only one lane of the motorway is open
Eins·sein das *(geh.)* oneness
einst [ainst] *Adv. (geh.)* **a)** *(früher)* once; **b)** *(der~)* some *or* one day; **~ wird kommen der Tag, da ...** *(dichter., veralt.)* the day will come when ...
ein|stampfen *tr. V.* pulp ⟨*books*⟩
Ein·stand der a) *(zum Dienstantritt)* **seinen ~ geben** celebrate starting a new job; **b)** *o. Pl. (Sport: erstes Spiel)* début; **seinen ~ geben** make one's début; play one's first match; **c)** *o. Pl. (Tennis)* deuce
ein|stanzen *tr. V. (Technik)* stamp in; **etw. auf etw.** *(Akk.)***/in etw.** *(Akk.)* **~:** stamp sth. into *or* on sth.
ein|stauben *itr. V.; mit sein* get dusty; get covered in dust; **eingestaubt sein** be dusty; be covered in dust
ein|stäuben *tr. V. (mit Mehl)* dust
ein|stechen 1. *unr. itr. V.* **a)** *(mit einer Stichwaffe)* **auf jmdn. ~:** stab sb.; **b)** *(Kartenspiel)* trump; play a trump. **2.** *unr. tr. V.* pierce, make ⟨*hole*⟩; **eine Nadel in etw.** *(Akk.)* **~:** stick *or* push a needle into sth.; **den Teig mit einer Gabel ~:** prick the dough with a fork
ein|stecken *tr. V.* **a)** *(in etw. stecken)* put in; **etw. in etw.** *(Akk.)* **~:** put sth. into sth.; **das Bügeleisen ~:** plug in the iron; **er steckte die Pistole/das Messer wieder ein** he put the pistol back in the holster/the knife back in the sheath; **b)** *(mitnehmen)* **[sich** *(Dat.)***] etw. ~:** take sth. with one; put sth. in one's pocket/case *etc.*; **c)** mail ⟨*letter*⟩; **d)** *(abwertend: für sich behalten)* pocket ⟨*money, profits*⟩; **e)** *(hinnehmen)* take ⟨*criticism, defeat, etc.*⟩; take, swallow ⟨*insult*⟩; **f)** *(ugs.: übertreffen)* outclass ⟨*competitors, opponents*⟩
Einsteck-: ~kamm der comb; **~tuch das** dress handkerchief
ein|stehen *unr. itr. V.* **a)** *(garantieren)* **für jmdn. ~:** vouch for sb.; **dafür ~, daß ...:** vouch [for the fact] that ...; **b)** *(verantwortlich gemacht werden)* **für etw. ~:** take responsibility for *or* assume liability for sth.; **für jmdn. ~:** take responsibility for *or* assume liability for sb.'s debts/misdeeds *etc.*; *(jmdm. treu bleiben)* stand by sb.
Einsteige·diebstahl der *(Rechtsw.)* *burglary involving entering, but not breaking into, a property*
ein|steigen *unr. itr. V.; mit sein* **a)** *(in ein Fahrzeug)* get in; **in ein Auto ~:** get into a car; **in den Bus ~:** get on the bus; **vorn/hinten ~** *(ins Auto)* get into the front/back; *(in den Bus)* get on at the front/back; **b)** *(eindringen)* **durch ein Fenster/über den Balkon ~:** climb in *or* get in through a window/over the balcony; **c)** *(ugs.: sich engagieren)* **in ein Geschäft/die Politik ~:** go into a business/into politics; **in die Frauenbewegung ~:** get involved in the women's movement; **[mit zwei Millionen] in ein Unternehmen ~:** take a [two million pound *etc.*] stake in a company; **d)** *(Bergsteigen)* **in eine Felswand ~:** tackle a rock-face; **e)** *(Sport)* tackle; **hart ~:** go in hard
einstellbar *Adj.* adjustable; **das ist genau ~:** it can be adjusted *or* set exactly
ein|stellen 1. *tr. V.* **a)** *(einordnen)* put away ⟨*books etc.*⟩; **b)** *(unterstellen)* put in ⟨*car, bicycle*⟩; **das Auto [in die Garage] ~:** put the car in [the garage]; **c)** *(auch itr.) (beschäftigen)* take on, employ ⟨*workers*⟩; **„VW stellt wieder ein"** 'VW is taking on new workers again'; **„wir stellen ein: Schweißer"** 'we have vacancies for welders'; **d)** *(regulieren)* adjust; set; focus ⟨*camera, telescope, binoculars*⟩; adjust ⟨*headlights*⟩; **die Kamera auf die richtige Entfernung ~:** set the camera to the correct distance; **das Radio laut/leiser ~:** put the radio on loud/turn the radio down; **ein Radio auf einen Sender ~:** tune a radio to a station; tune in to a station; **ein Programm [an der Waschmaschine] ~:** select a programme [on the washing-machine]; **e)** *(beenden)* stop; call off ⟨*search, strike*⟩; **das Feuer ~:** cease fire; **die Zeitung hat ihr Erscheinen eingestellt** the newspaper has ceased publication; **ein Gerichtsverfahren ~:** abandon court proceedings; **die Arbeit ~** ⟨*factory*⟩ close; ⟨*workers*⟩ stop work; **f)** *(Sport)* equal ⟨*record*⟩; **g)** *(Sport: vorbereiten)* **eine Mannschaft defensiv/offensiv ~:** train a team to play defensive/attacking football. **2.** *refl. V.* **a)** *(ankommen, auch fig.)* arrive; **b)** *(eintreten)* ⟨*pain, worry*⟩ begin; ⟨*success*⟩ come; ⟨*symptoms, consequences*⟩ appear; **starkes Erbrechen stellte sich ein** he/she began to vomit violently; **c)** *(einrichten)* **sich auf etw.** *(Akk.)* **~:** prepare oneself *or* get ready for sth.; **sich schnell auf neue Situationen ~:** adjust quickly to new situations; **sie war nicht auf Gäste eingestellt** she was not prepared for guests; **sich auf jmdn. ~:** adapt to sb.
Einstell·hebel der adjusting lever
ein·stellig *Adj.* single-figure *attrib.* ⟨*number*⟩
Einstell·platz der parking space; *(auf eigenem Grundstück)* carport
Ein·stellung die a) *(von Arbeitskräften)* employment; taking on; **b)** *(Regulierung)* adjustment; setting; *(eines Fernglases, einer Kamera)* focusing; *(von Scheinwerfern)* adjustment; **c)** *(Beendigung)* stopping; *(einer Suchaktion, eines Streiks)* calling off; **die ~**

der Produktion veranlassen order that production be stopped; **er drohte mit der ~ der Zahlungen** he threatened to stop the payments; **d)** *(Sport)* **die ~ eines Rekordes** the equalling of a record; **e)** *(Ansicht)* attitude; **ihre politische/religiöse ~:** her political/religious views *pl.*; **f)** *(Film)* take

Einstellungs-: ~bedingung die; *meist Pl.* requirement [for appointment]; **~gespräch das** interview; **~sperre die, ~stopp der** freeze on recruitment; **~termin der** starting date

einstens ['ainstn̩s] *(geh., veralt.) s.* **einst**

Ein·stich der a) insertion; **b)** *(~stelle)* puncture; prick

ein|sticken *tr. V.* embroider (**in** + *Akk.* on)

Ein·stieg der; ~[e]s, ~e a) *(Eingang)* entrance; *(Tür)* door/doors; **b)** *o. Pl. (das Einsteigen)* entry; **„kein ~"** 'exit only'; **c)** *(Bergsteigen)* **der ~ in die Nordwand** the start of the assault on the north face; **beim ~ in den Kamin** at the start of the climb up the chimney; **ein guter ~:** a good point to start the climb; **d)** *(fig.)* **der ~ in diese Problematik ist schwierig** these are difficult problems to approach

Einstieg·luke die hatch

Einstiegs·droge die come-on drug

einstig *Adj.; nicht präd.* former

ein|stimmen 1. *itr. V.* join in; *(veralt.: zustimmen)* agree; **in den Gesang ~:** join in the singing; **in das [allgemeine] Lachen ~** *(fig.)* join in the [general] laughter. **2.** *tr. V.* **jmdn. auf etw.** *(Akk.)* **~:** get sb. in the [right] mood for sth.

einstimmig 1. *Adj.* **a)** *(Musik)* **ein ~es Lied** a song for one voice; **b)** *(einmütig)* unanimous ⟨*decision, vote*⟩. **2.** *adv.* **a)** *(Musik)* **~ singen** sing in unison; **b)** *(einmütig)* unanimously

Einstimmigkeit die; ~: unanimity; **~ erzielen** achieve unanimity; reach unanimous agreement

Ein·stimmung die: zur *od.* **als ~ auf etw.** to get in the [right] mood for sth.

ein|stippen *tr. V. (bes. nordd.)* dip; dunk

einst·mals *Adv. (geh., veralt.)* formerly; in former times

ein·stöckig 1. *Adj.* single-storey *attrib.*; one-storey *attrib.*; **hier sind die meisten Häuser ~:** most of the houses here have one storey. **2.** *adv.* **hier darf nur ~ gebaut werden** single-storey *or* one-storey buildings only may be built here

ein|stöpseln *tr. V.* **a)** plug in ⟨*telephone, electrical device*⟩; **b)** put in, push in ⟨*cork etc.*⟩

ein|stoßen *unr. tr. V.* **a)** *(gewaltsam öffnen)* break down ⟨*door, wall*⟩; smash [in] ⟨*window*⟩; smash ⟨*mirror*⟩; **b)** *(durch Anstoßen verletzen)* break ⟨*nose, ribs*⟩; **sich** *(Dat.)* **den Kopf ~:** bang one's head

ein|strahlen 1. *itr. V.* **a)** *(hineinscheinen)* shine in; **das ~de Licht** the light shining in; **b) auf etw.** *(Akk.)* **~** ⟨*sun*⟩ irradiate sth. **2.** *tr. V. (Physik, Technik)* direct ⟨*beam etc.*⟩

Ein·strahlung die irradiation; *(Sonnen~)* insolation

ein|streichen *unr. tr. V.* **a) Brot mit Butter** *usw.* **~:** spread butter *etc.* on bread; **b)** *(ugs.: für sich behalten)* pocket ⟨*money, winnings, etc.*⟩; *(ugs. abwertend)* rake in *(coll.)* ⟨*money, profits, etc.*⟩; **c)** *(Theater)* cut ⟨*script, play*⟩

ein·streifig *(Verkehrsw.)* **1.** *Adj.* single-lane. **2.** *adv.* in a single-lane

ein|streuen *tr. V.* **a) etw. mit Sand ~:** strew *or* scatter sand on sth.; **b)** *(einfügen)* **er streute witzige Bemerkungen in seinen Vortrag ein** he sprinkled his lecture with witty remarks

ein|strömen *itr. V.* ⟨*water*⟩ pour *or* flood *or* stream in; ⟨*air, light*⟩ stream in; *(fig.)* ⟨*crowd, supporters*⟩ stream *or* pour in

ein·strophig *Adj.* one-verse *attrib.* ⟨*poem, song*⟩; ⟨*poem, song*⟩ consisting of one verse; **das Gedicht ist ~:** the poem consists of *or* has one verse *or* stanza

ein|studieren *tr. V.* rehearse

ein·studiert *Adj. (abwertend)* studied

Einstudierung die; ~, ~en a) *o. Pl.* rehearsal; **b)** *(Inszenierung)* production

ein|stufen *tr. V.* classify; categorize; **jmdn. in eine Kategorie/eine höhere Steuerklasse ~:** put sb. in a category/a higher income-tax bracket

ein·stufig *Adj.* single-stage ⟨*rocket*⟩

Einstufung ['ainʃtu:fʊŋ] **die, ~, ~en** classification; categorization

ein|stülpen *tr. V.* push in

ein·stündig *Adj.* one-hour *attrib.* ⟨*wait, delay*⟩; **nach ~em Warten** after a wait of one hour; after an hour's wait; *s. auch* **achtstündig**

ein|stürmen *itr. V.* **mit Fragen/Bitten auf jmdn. ~:** besiege sb. with questions/requests

Ein·sturz der collapse

ein|stürzen *itr. V.; mit sein* **a)** collapse; **eine Welt stürzte für sie ein** *(fig.)* her whole world collapsed *or* fell apart; **b)** *(fig.)* **auf jmdn. ~** ⟨*worries, problems*⟩ crowd in [up]on sb.

Einsturz·gefahr die; *o. Pl.* danger of collapse; **„Achtung, ~!"** 'danger – building unsafe'

einst·weilen *Adv.* **a)** *(vorläufig)* for the time being; temporarily; **b)** *(inzwischen)* in the mean time; meanwhile

einstweilig *Adj.; nicht präd. (Amtsspr.)* temporary; **eine ~e Verfügung/Anordnung** *(Rechtsw.)* a temporary injunction/order; **in den ~en Ruhestand versetzt werden** be suspended from duty

ein|suggerieren *itr. V.* **jmdm. etw. ~:** instil sth. into sb. by suggestion

Eins·werden das *(geh.)* becoming one *no art.*; **das ~ der Liebenden** the union of the lovers

ein·tägig *Adj.* one-day *attrib.*; **ein ~er Ausflug** a day tour; *s. auch* **achttägig**

Eintags·fliege die *(Zool.)* mayfly; *(fig. ugs.)* seven-day wonder; *(kein Dauerzustand)* passing phase

ein|tanzen *refl. V.* warm up

Ein·tänzer der *(veralt.)* gigolo

ein|tasten *tr. V. (Technik)* key in

ein|tauchen 1. *tr. V.* immerse; **den Pinsel in die Farbe ~:** dip the brush in the paint; **den Zwieback in den Tee ~:** dunk *or* dip the rusk in the tea. **2.** *itr. V.; mit sein* dive in; ⟨*submarine*⟩ dive

Ein·tausch der exchange; **im ~ gegen etw.** in exchange for sth.

ein|tauschen *tr. V.* exchange (**gegen** for)

ein·tausend *Kardinalz.* a *or* one thousand; *s. auch* **¹acht**

ein|teilen *tr. V.* **a)** divide up; classify ⟨*plants, species*⟩; **den Kuchen in zwölf Stücke ~:** divide *or* cut the cake [up] into twelve pieces; **b)** *(disponieren, verplanen)* organize; plan [out]; **sein Geld [besser] ~:** plan *or* organize one's finances [better]; **sich** *(Dat.)* **seine Arbeit ~:** organize *or* plan [out] one's work; **sich seine Vorräte ~:** plan out how to make one's provisions last; **c)** *(delegieren, abkommandieren)* **jmdn. für etw.** *od.* **zu etw. ~:** assign sb. to sth.

Einteiler der; ~s, ~ *(Mode)* one-piece bathing-suit

einteilig ['aintailɪç] *Adj.* one-piece ⟨*dress, bathing-suit*⟩

Ein·teilung die a) *(Gliederung)* division; dividing up; *(Biol.)* classification; **b)** *(planvolles Disponieren)* organization; planning; **bei besserer ~ seines Gehalts würde er ...:** if he planned out better how to spend his salary, he would...; **c)** *(Delegierung, Abkommandierung)* assignment

Eintel ['aintl̩] **das** *(schweiz. meist* **der***)*; **~s, ~:** whole

ein|tippen *tr. V. (in die Kasse)* register; *(in einen Rechner)* key in

eintönig ['aintø:nɪç] **1.** *Adj.* monotonous ⟨*landscape, work, life*⟩. **2.** *adv.* monotonously; ⟨*read*⟩ in a monotone

Eintönigkeit die; ~: monotony

Ein·topf der, Eintopf·gericht das *(Kochk.)* stew

Ein·tracht die; *o. Pl.* harmony; concord; **in ~ leben** live in harmony

ein·trächtig 1. *Adj.* harmonious. **2.** *adv.* harmoniously; **~ zusammenleben** live together in harmony

Eintrag ['aintra:k] **der; ~[e]s, Einträge** ['aintrɛ:gə] **a)** *o. Pl. (das Eintragen)* entering; **b)** *(Aktennotiz)* entry; **ein ~ ins Register** an entry in the register

ein|tragen *unr. tr. V.* **a)** *(einschreiben)* enter; copy out ⟨*essay*⟩; **einen Aufsatz in sein Heft ~:** copy an essay into one's exercise-book; *(einzeichnen)* mark in; enter; **seinen Namen** *od.* **sich [in eine Liste] ~:** enter one's name [on a list]; **b)** *(Amtsspr.)* register; **sich ~ lassen** register; **etw. auf seinen Namen ~ lassen** have sth. registered in one's name; **ein eingetragenes Warenzeichen** a registered trade mark; *s. auch* **Verein**; **c)** *(einbringen)* bring in ⟨*money*⟩; bring ⟨*criticism*⟩; win ⟨*goodwill*⟩; **das Geschäft trägt [einen] Gewinn ein** the business makes a profit; **das hat ihm nur Undank eingetragen** that only brought him ingratitude

einträglich ['aintrɛ:klɪç] *Adj.* profitable, lucrative ⟨*business, sideline*⟩; lucrative ⟨*work, job*⟩

Eintragung die; ~, ~en a) *(das Eintragen)* entering; **die ~ der Zinsen vornehmen lassen** have the interest entered [in one's account book]; **eine ~ ins Grundbuch bezahlen** pay to have a property *etc.* entered in the land register; **b)** *(Eingetragenes)* entry

ein|träufeln *tr. V.* **sich/jmdm. Augentropfen ~:** put drops in one's/sb.'s eyes; **jmdm. ein Medikament ~:** administer *or* give a medicine to sb. in drops

ein|treffen *unr. itr. V.; mit sein* **a)** *(ankommen)* arrive; **b)** *(verwirklicht werden)* ⟨*prophecy*⟩ come true

Ein·treffen das; *o. Pl.* arrival; **ich glaube nicht an das ~ dieser Prophezeiung** I don't believe that this prophecy will come true

ein|treiben *unr. tr. V.* **a)** *(kassieren)* collect ⟨*taxes, debts*⟩; *(durch Gerichtsverfahren)* recover ⟨*debts, money*⟩; **das Geld ~ lassen** take action to obtain the money; **b)** *(hineintreiben)* drive in ⟨*nail, stake*⟩

Eintreibung die; ~, ~en *(von Steuern, Schulden)* collection; *(durch Gerichtsverfahren)* recovery

ein|treten 1. *unr. itr. V.* **a)** *mit sein (einen Raum betreten)* enter; **in ein Zimmer ~:** enter a room; **bitte, treten Sie ein!** please come in; **die Eintretenden** those entering; **b)** *mit sein (Mitglied werden)* **in einen Verein/einen Orden ~:** join a club/enter a religious order; **c)** *mit sein (Raumfahrt)* **in die Erdumlaufbahn/Erdatmosphäre ~:** enter Earth orbit/the Earth's atmosphere; **d)** *mit sein* **in eine neue/schwierige Phase ~:** be entering a new/difficult phase; **in Verhandlungen ~:** enter into negotiations; **in die Beweisaufnahme ~** *(Rechtsw.)* proceed to hearing the evidence; **e)** *mit sein (sich ereignen)* occur; ⟨*silence*⟩ descend; ⟨*thaw*⟩ set in; ⟨*darkness, night*⟩ set in, fall; **bald trat eine Besserung ein** there was soon an improvement; **bei Eintreten der Dunkelheit** at nightfall; when darkness sets/set in; **das Unerwartete war eingetreten** the unexpected had occurred *or* happened; **f)** *mit sein (sich einsetzen)* **für jmdn./etw. ~:** stand up for sb./sth.; *(vor Gericht)* speak in sb.'s defence; **g) auf jmdn./etw. ~:** kick sb./sth. **2.** *unr. tr. V.* kick in

⟨*door, window, etc.*⟩. **3.** *unr. refl. V.* **sich** *(Dat.)* **etw. ~:** get sth. in one's foot
ein|trichtern *tr. V. (salopp)* **jmdm. etw. ~:** drum sth. into sb.; **jmdm. ~, daß ...:** drum into sb. that ...
Ein·tritt der a) entry; entrance; **sich** *(Dat.)* **[in etw.** *(Akk.)***] ~ verschaffen** gain entry [to sth.]; **beim ~ in die Adoleszenz** *(fig.)* when entering adolescence; **vor dem ~ in die Verhandlungen** *(fig.)* before entering into negotiations; **b)** *(Beitritt)* **der ~ in einen Verein/einen Orden** joining a club/entering a religious order; **c)** *(von Raketen)* entry; **beim ~ [in die Erdatmosphäre]** on entry [into the Earth's atmosphere]; **d)** *(Zugang, Eintrittsgeld)* admission; **[der] ~ [ist] frei** admission [is] free; **jmdm. den ~ [in etw.** *(Akk.)***] verwehren** refuse sb. admission [to sth.]; **e)** *(Beginn) (des Winters)* onset; **vor/nach ~ der Dunkelheit** before/after nightfall *or* dusk; **f)** *(eines Ereignisses)* occurrence; *(der Menstruation, Wehen)* onset; **bei ~ des Todes** when death occurs
Eintritts-: ~geld das admission charge *or* fee; entrance charge *or* fee; **~karte die** admission *or* entrance ticket; **~preis der** admission *or* entrance charge
ein|trocknen *itr. V.; mit sein* **a)** ⟨*paint, blood*⟩ dry; ⟨*water, toothpaste*⟩ dry up; **b)** *(verdorren)* ⟨*leather*⟩ dry out; ⟨*berry, fruit*⟩ shrivel
ein|trüben *refl. V. (Met.)* cloud over; become overcast; **es trübt sich ein** it's clouding over
Ein·trübung die cloudy spell
ein|trudeln *itr. V.; mit sein (ugs.)* drift in *(coll.)*
ein|tunken *tr. V. (landsch.)* **etw. in etw.** *(Akk.)* **~:** dip *or* dunk sth. in sth.
ein|tüten *tr. V.* bag
ein|üben *tr. V.* **a)** *(sich aneignen)* practise; **jede einzelne seiner Gesten wirkt sorgfältig eingeübt** all of his gestures seem carefully rehearsed; **b)** *(proben, trainieren)* **mit jmdm. etw. ~:** practise sth. with sb.
Ein·übung die a) *(Aneignung)* acquisition; **b)** *(Proben, Trainieren)* practising
Ein·uhr-: one o'clock ⟨*news, train*⟩
ein·und·ein·halb *s.* **anderthalb**
Einung die; ~, ~en *(dichter.) s.* **Einigung b**
ein|verleiben [-fɛɐ̯laibn̩] **1.** *tr. V.* annex ⟨*land, country*⟩. **2.** *refl. V. (sich zu eigen machen)* assimilate, absorb ⟨*knowledge, experience*⟩; *(scherzh.: zu sich nehmen)* put away *(coll.)*
Einvernahme die; ~, ~n *(Rechtsw., bes. österr. u. schweiz.)* examination
ein|vernehmen *unr. tr. V. (Rechtsw., bes. österr. u. schweiz.)* examine
Ein·vernehmen das; ~s harmony; *(Übereinstimmung)* agreement; **in freundschaftlichem/gutem ~ [mit jmdm.]** on friendly/good terms [with sb.]; *s. auch* **setzen 1c**
ein·vernehmlich *(Amtsspr.)* **1.** *Adv.* conjointly. **2.** *adj.* conjoint
einverstanden *Adj.; nicht attr.* **mit jmdm. ~ sein** *(einer Meinung)* be in agreement with sb.; agree with sb.; **mit jmdm./etw. ~ sein** *(zufrieden)* approve of sb./sth.; **sich [mit etw.] ~ erklären** agree [to sth.]; express one's agreement [to sth.]; **~!** *(ugs.)* okay! *(coll.)*; agreed!
ein·verständlich *(geh.)* **1.** *Adj.* mutually agreed; ⟨*divorce*⟩ by mutual consent. **2.** *adv.* by mutual consent
Ein·verständnis das a) *(Billigung)* consent **(zu** to); approval **(zu** of); **im ~ mit jmdm. handeln** act with sb.'s consent; **Ihr ~ vorausgesetzt** with your approval; if you are agreed; **b)** *(Übereinstimmung)* agreement; **zwischen ihnen herrscht ~:** there is agreement between them
Ein·waage die *(Kaufmannsspr.)* contents *pl.*
¹ein|wachsen *unr. itr. V.; mit sein* grow into the flesh; **eingewachsen** ingrown ⟨*toenail*⟩
²ein|wachsen *tr. V.* wax
Einwand der; ~[e]s, Einwände ['ainvɛndə] objection **(gegen** to)
Ein·wanderer der immigrant
ein|wandern *itr. V.; mit sein* immigrate **(in** + *Akk.* into)
Ein·wanderung die immigration; **eine Zunahme der ~en** an increase in the number of immigrants
Einwanderungs-: ~behörde die immigration authorities *pl.*; **~land das** immigration country; **~quote die** immigration quota; **~welle die** wave of immigrants
einwand·frei 1. *Adj.* **a)** *(ohne Fehler)* flawless; perfect; impeccable ⟨*behaviour*⟩; **das Fleisch ist noch ~:** the meat is still perfectly fresh; **b)** *(eindeutig)* indisputable, definite ⟨*proof*⟩; watertight ⟨*alibi*⟩. **2.** *adv.* **a)** perfectly; flawlessly; ⟨*behave*⟩ impeccably; **b)** beyond question *or* doubt; **es ist ~ erwiesen, daß ...:** it has been proved beyond question *or* doubt that ...
einwärts ['ainvɛrts] *Adv.* inwards
einwärts·gebogen *Adj.* concave
ein|weben *tr. V.* weave *or* work in; **etw. in etw.** *(Akk.)* **~:** weave *or* work sth. into sth.
ein|wechseln *tr. V.* **a)** *(wechseln, umtauschen)* change ⟨*money*⟩; **b)** *(Sport)* substitute ⟨*player*⟩
ein|wecken *tr. V.* preserve; preserve, bottle ⟨*fruit, vegetables*⟩
Einweck-: ~glas das preserving-jar; **~gummi der, ~ring der** rubber seal *(for preserving jar)*; **~topf der** preserving-pan
Ein·weg-: ~flasche die non-returnable bottle; **~packung die** disposable pack; **~spiegel der** one-way mirror; **~spritze die** disposable [hypodermic] syringe
ein|weichen *tr. V.* soak
ein|weihen *tr. V.* **a)** open [officially] ⟨*bridge, road*⟩; dedicate ⟨*monument*⟩; consecrate ⟨*church*⟩; **b)** *(ugs. scherzh.: zum erstenmal benutzen)* christen *(coll.)*; **c)** *(vertraut machen)* **jmdn. in etw.** *(Akk.)* **~:** let sb. in on sth.; **jmdn. in die Kunst des Strickens/in das Schachspiel ~:** initiate sb. into the art of knitting/the mysteries of chess
Einweihung die; ~, ~en [official] opening
ein|weisen *unr. tr. V.* **a) jmdn. in ein Krankenhaus ~:** have sb. admitted to hospital; **die Flüchtlinge wurden in eine Wohnung/ein Lager eingewiesen** the refugees were assigned a flat *(Brit.) or (Amer.)* apartment/sent to a camp; **b)** *(in eine Tätigkeit)* **jmdn. [in eine/die Arbeit] ~:** introduce sb. to a/the job; show sb. what a/the job involves; **c)** *(in ein Amt)* install; **jmdn. in sein Amt ~:** install sb.; **d)** *(Verkehrsw.)* direct
Ein·weisung die a) *(Unterbringung)* **~ in ein Krankenhaus** admission to a hospital; **sich gegen die ~ in ein Lager wehren** fight against being sent to a camp; **b)** introduction; **er wurde mit der ~ der neuen Mitarbeiter betraut** he was given the task of introducing the new members of staff to their jobs; **c)** *(Amtseinführung)* installation
ein|wenden *unr. (auch regelm.) tr. V.* **dagegen läßt sich manches/vieles ~:** there are a number of things/is a lot to be said against that; **dagegen ist nichts einzuwenden** there can be no objection to that; **„...", wandte er ein** '...,' he objected; **gegen etw. nichts einzuwenden haben** have no objection to sth.; have nothing against sth.
Ein·wendung die objection **[gegen** to]
ein|werfen 1. *unr. tr. V.* **a)** mail ⟨*letter, mail*⟩; put in, insert ⟨*coin*⟩; **b)** *(zertrümmern)* smash, break ⟨*window*⟩; **c)** *(Ballspiele)* throw in ⟨*ball*⟩; **d)** *(bemerken, sagen)* throw in ⟨*remark*⟩; **„...", warf sie ein** '...,' she interjected. **2.** *unr. itr. V. (Ballspiele) (vom Rand)* take the throw-in; *(ins Tor)* score
ein·wertig *Adj.* **a)** *(Chemie)* monovalent ⟨*atom*⟩; **b)** *(Sprachw.)* one-place ⟨*verb*⟩
ein|wickeln *tr. V.* **a)** wrap [up] ⟨*article, present*⟩; **jmdn./sich in etw.** *(Akk.)* **~:** wrap sb./oneself [up] in sth.; **b)** *(ugs.)* **jmdn. ~** *(überreden)* get round sb.; *(überlisten)* take sb. in
Einwickel·papier das wrapping paper
¹ein|wiegen *tr. V.* **jmdn. ~:** lull sb. to sleep; *(in der Wiege)* **ein Kind ~:** rock a child to sleep
²ein|wiegen *unr. tr. V. (Kaufmannsspr.)* weigh out
ein|willigen *itr. V.* agree, consent **(in** + *Akk.* to); **in ein Angebot ~:** accept an offer
Einwilligung die; ~, ~en agreement; consent; **seine ~ zu etw. geben** give one's consent to sth.; **ihre ~ in das Angebot** her acceptance of the offer
ein|winken *tr. V. (Verkehrsw.)* guide in ⟨*aircraft*⟩; guide *or* direct in ⟨*car*⟩; **ein Auto in eine Parklücke ~:** guide *or* direct a car into a parking space
ein|wirken 1. *itr. V.* **a)** *(beeinflussen)* **auf jmdn. ~:** influence sb.; exert *or* have an influence on sb.; **beruhigend auf jmdn. ~:** exert a soothing *or* calming influence on sb.; **b)** *(eine Wirkung ausüben)* have an effect **(auf** + *Akk.* on); **man lasse die Creme ~:** let the cream work in. **2.** *tr. V. (Handarb., Textilw.)* work in; **etw. in etw.** *(Akk.)* **~:** work sth. into sth.
Ein·wirkung die *(Einfluß)* influence; *(Wirkung)* effect; **unter ~ von Drogen stehen** be under the influence of drugs
ein·wöchig *Adj.* one-week *attrib.*; week-old ⟨*baby*⟩; week-long ⟨*conference*⟩
Einwohner der; ~s, ~, Einwohnerin die; ~, ~nen inhabitant; **die Stadt hat 3 Millionen ~:** the town has 3 million inhabitants *or* a population of 3 million
Einwohner·meldeamt das *local government office for registration of residents*
Einwohnerschaft die; ~: population; inhabitants *pl.*
Einwohner·zahl die population
Ein·wurf der a) *(Einwerfen)* insertion; *(von Briefen)* mailing; **b)** *(Ballspiele)* throw-in; **ein falscher ~:** a foul throw; **c)** *(Öffnung) (eines Briefkastens)* slit; *(einer Tür)* letterbox; **d)** *(Zwischenbemerkung)* interjection; *(kritisch)* objection; **einen kritischen ~ machen** raise an objection
ein|wurzeln *itr. (auch refl.) V.* root; *(fig.)* take root
Ein·zahl die; *o. Pl. (Sprachw.)* singular
ein|zahlen *tr. V.* pay in; deposit; **Geld auf sein Konto ~:** pay *or* deposit money into one's account; **die Miete ~:** pay in the rent
Ein·zahlung die payment; deposit; *(Überweisung)* payment
Einzahlungs-: ~beleg der counterfoil; **~schalter der** paying-in counter *(Brit.)*; deposit counter *(Amer.)*; **~schein der** pay[ing]-in slip *(Brit.)*; deposit slip
ein|zäunen *tr. V.* fence in; enclose; **ein Grundstück [mit etw.] ~:** fence a property in [with sth.]
Einzäunung die; ~, ~en a) *(das Einzäunen)* fencing-in; enclosure; **b)** *(Zaun)* fence; enclosure
ein|zeichnen *tr. V.* draw *or* mark in; **etw. in eine Karte ~:** draw *or* mark sth. in on a map
ein·zeilig *Adj.* **a)** one-line *attrib.*; *s. auch* **achtzeilig; b) eine ~e Küche** a fitted kitchen arranged along one wall
Einzel ['aintsl̩] **das; ~s, ~** *(Sport)* singles *pl.*; **der Sieger im ~:** the winner in the singles; **~ spielen** to play a singles match
Einzel-: ~aktion die independent action; **~an·fertigung die** custom-made article; *(Fahrzeug)* custom-built model; **~ausgabe die** separate edition; **~band der** individual *or* single volume; **~bett das** single bed; **~buchstabe der** *(Druckw.)* single

[piece of] type; single sort; **~darstellung die** *(eines Themas)* individual treatment; *(Abhandlung)* monograph; **~disziplin die** *(bes. Leichtathletik)* single event; **~erscheinung die** isolated occurrence; **~fahrer der** *(Motorsport)* solo rider; **~fahr·schein der** single; **~fall der a)** particular case; **im ~fall** in particular cases; **b)** *(Ausnahme)* isolated case; exception; **~feuer das** *(Milit.)* independent fire; **~frage die** individual question

Einzelgänger [-gɛŋɐ] **der; ~s, ~ a)** solitary person; loner; **b)** *(Tier)* lone animal

Einzelgängerin die; ~, ~nen solitary person; loner

Einzelgängertum das; ~s solitariness

Einzel-: ~gehöft das solitary farm; **~gewerkschaft die** member union; **~grab das** separate *or* individual grave; **~haft die** solitary confinement

Einzel·handel der retail trade; **das kostet im ~ 200 DM** it retails at 200 marks; **etw. im ~ kaufen** buy sth. retail

Einzelhandels-: ~geschäft das retail shop; retail store *(Amer.)*; **~kaufmann der** retail salesman; **~preis der** retail price

Einzel-: ~händler der retailer; retail trader; **~haus das** detached house

Einzelheit die; ~, ~en a) detail; **b)** *(einzelner Umstand)* particular; **bis in alle ~en** down to the last detail; **in ~en gehen** go into detail

Einzel-: ~interesse das individual interest; **~kind das** only child

Einzeller ['aintsɛlɐ] **der; ~s, ~** *(Biol.)* unicellular organism

einzellig ['aintsɛlɪç] *Adj. (Biol.)* unicellular; single-cell *attrib.*

einzeln *Adj.* **a)** *(für sich allein)* individual; **die ~en Bände eines Werkes** the individual *or* separate volumes of a work; **jede ~e Insel** each individual island; **ein ~er Schuh/Handschuh** an odd shoe/glove; **jede ~e ist ein Kunstwerk** each individual one is a work of art; **schon ein ~es von diesen Gläsern** just one of these glasses on its own; **„bitte ~ eintreten"** 'please enter one [person] at a time'; **alle Teile ~ verpacken** pack each piece individually; **~ reisen** travel alone *or* on one's own; **wir sind alle ~ gekommen** we all came separately; **sich um jeden ~en Gast kümmern** look after each guest individually; **b)** *(alleinstehend)* solitary ‹*building, tree*›; **eine ~e Dame/ein ~er Herr** a single lady/gentleman; **c)** *(wenige)* a few; *(einige)* some; **~e Regenschauer** scattered *or* isolated showers; **d)** *substantivisch (~er Mensch)* **der/jeder ~e** the/each individual; **als ~er** as an individual; **jeder ~e der Betroffenen wurde angehört** every [single] one of those concerned was given a hearing; **ein ~er** one individual; **für einen ~en geeignet** suitable for one person; **e)** *substantivisch* **~es** *(manches)* some things *pl.*; **das Einzelne** the particular; **vom Einzelnen zum Allgemeinen** from the particular to the general; **etw. im ~en besprechen** discuss sth. in detail; **ins ~e gehen** go into detail[s *pl.*]; **bis ins ~e** right down to the last detail

einzeln·stehend *Adj.* solitary

Einzel-: ~person die one person; individual; **als ~person** as an individual; **~preis der** individual price; **~rad·aufhängung die** *(Kfz-W.)* independent suspension; **~richter der** judge sitting singly; **~schicksal das** individual fate *or* destiny; **~staat der** individual state; **~stück das** individual piece *or* item; **~stunde die** private lesson; **~teil das** individual *or* separate part; **etw. in [seine] ~teile zerlegen** take sth. to pieces; **~therapie die** *(Med.)* individual therapy; **~unterricht der** individual tuition; **~wertung die** *(Sport)* individual placings *pl.*; **~wesen das** individual [being]; **der Mensch als ~wesen** man as an individual; **~wettbewerb der** *(Sport)* individual event; **~zelle die a)** *(für ~haft)* single cell; **b)** *(Biol.)* single cell; **~zimmer das** single room

ein|zementieren *tr. V.* cement in

einziehbar *Adj.* **a)** *(Technik)* retractable; **b)** *(Finanzw.)* recoverable

Einzieh·decke die duvet *(Brit.)*; continental quilt *(Brit.)*; stuffed quilt *(Amer.)*

ein|ziehen 1. *unr. tr. V.* **a)** put in ‹*duvet*›; thread in ‹*tape, elastic*›; **b)** *(einbauen)* put in ‹*wall, ceiling*›; **c)** *(einholen)* haul in, pull in ‹*net*›; retract, draw in ‹*feelers, claws*›; **den Kopf ~:** duck; **der Hund zog den Schwanz ein** the dog put its tail between its legs; *s. auch* **Schwanz a; d)** *(einatmen)* breathe in ‹*scent, fresh air*›; inhale ‹*smoke*›; **e)** *(einberufen)* call up, conscript ‹*recruits*›; **f)** *(beitreiben)* collect; **er läßt die Miete vom Konto ~:** he pays his rent by direct debit; **g)** *(beschlagnahmen)* confiscate; seize; **h)** *(aus dem Verkehr ziehen)* withdraw, call in ‹*coins, banknotes*›; **i)** *(Amtsspr.: einholen)* **Informationen/Erkundigungen ~:** gather information/make enquiries; **j)** *(Druckw.)* indent ‹*paragraph*›. **2.** *unr. itr. V.; mit sein* **a)** *(eindringen)* ‹*liquid*› soak in; **b)** *(einkehren)* enter; **der Frühling zieht ein** *(geh.)* spring comes *or* arrives; **dann zog bei uns wieder Ruhe ein** then we had peace and quiet again; **ins Parlament ~:** enter parliament; **c)** *(in eine Wohnung)* move in

Ein·ziehung die a) *(Einberufung)* call-up; conscription; drafting *(Amer.)*; **b)** *(Beitreibung)* collection; **c)** *(von Eigentum)* confiscation, seizure; *(von Münzen, Banknoten usw.)* withdrawal

einzig ['aintsɪç] **1.** *Adj.; o. Komp.; Sup. (ugs.:)* **~ste a)** *(alleinig)* only; single; *(intensivierend nach „ein" od. „kein")* single; **der ~e Sohn** the only son; **unser Einziger/unsere Einzige** our only son/daughter; **nur ein ~er** only one; **nicht ein ~es Stück** not one single piece; **es blieb nur ein ~er Ausweg** there was only one way out; **ihre ~e Freude war ihre Tochter** her daughter was her one and only joy; **das ~e, was er sah, war ...:** the only thing he saw was ...; **b)** *nicht präd. (völlig)* complete; absolute; one long ‹*torment*›; **c)** *(geh.: unvergleichlich)* unique; unparalleled; **~ in ihrer/seiner Art** unique in her/his/its [own] way. **2.** *adv.* **a)** *(intensivierend bei Adj.)* singularly; extraordinarily; **ein ~ schöner Tag** an extraordinarily beautiful day; **b)** *(ausschließlich)* only; **das ~ Wahre** the only thing; **das ~ Vernünftige/Richtige** the only sensible/right thing [to do]; **~ und allein** nobody/nothing but; solely; **~ ihm wollte sie sich anvertrauen** he was the only one she would confide in

einzig·artig 1. *Adj.* unique. **2.** *adv.* uniquely; **~ schön** extraordinarily beautiful

Einzigartigkeit die, Einzigkeit die uniqueness

Ein·zimmer-: ~apartment das, ~appartement das, ~wohnung die one-room flat *or (Amer.)* apartment

ein|zuckern *tr. V.* sprinkle with sugar

Ein·zug der a) entry (**in** + *Akk.* into); **der ~ des Winters** *(geh.)* the advent of winter; **[seinen] ~ halten** make one's entrance; **mit strahlendem Sonnenschein hielt der Frühling [seinen] ~:** glorious sunshine marked the beginning of spring; **der ~ ins Parlament** entry into parliament; **b)** *(in eine Wohnung)* move; **c)** *(Druckw.)* indentation

Einzugs-: ~bereich der, ~gebiet das catchment area

ein|zwängen *tr. V.* squeeze *or* hem in; ‹*corset*› constrict

Ein·zylinder·motor der single-cylinder engine

Eis [ais] **das; ~es a)** ice; **eine Flasche auf ~ legen** put a bottle on ice; **ein Whisky mit ~:** a whisky with ice *or* on the rocks; **etw. auf ~ legen** *(fig. ugs.)* put sth. on ice; shelve sth.; **jmdn. auf ~ legen** *(fig. salopp)* put sb. out of harm's way; **b)** *(Speise~)* ice-cream; **ein ~ am Stiel** an ice-lolly *(Brit.) or (Amer.)* ice pop

Eis-: ~bahn die ice-rink; **~bär der** polar bear; **~behälter der** ice bucket; **~becher der a)** *(~portion)* ice-cream sundae; **b)** *(Gefäß)* [ice-cream] sundae dish; **~bein das a)** *(Kochk.)* knuckle of pork; **b) ich habe ~beine** *(ugs. scherzh.)* my feet are like ice; **~berg der** iceberg; **die Spitze eines ~bergs** the tip of an iceberg; **~beutel der** ice-bag; ice-pack; **~blume die** frost flower; **~bombe die** *(Gastr.)* bombe glacée; **~brecher der** ice-breaker; **~café das** ice-cream parlour

Ei·schnee der stiffly beaten egg-white

Eis-: ~creme die ice-cream; **~diele die** ice-cream parlour

Eisen ['aizn̩] **das; ~s, ~: a)** *o. Pl.* iron; **aus ~ sein** be made of iron; **man muß das ~ schmieden, solange es heiß ist** *(Spr.)* strike while the iron is hot *(prov.)*; **b)** *(Werkzeug, Golf~)* iron; *(Jägerspr.)* trap; **jmdn. in ~ legen** *(veralt.)* put sb. in irons; *(fig.)* **ein heißes ~ anfassen** *od.* **anpacken** grasp the nettle; **das ist ein heißes ~:** that is a hot potato; **noch ein/mehrere ~ im Feuer haben** have another iron/several irons in the fire; **jmdn./etw. zum alten ~ werfen** *(ugs.)* throw sb./sth. on [to] the scrap-heap; **zum alten ~ gehören** belong on the scrap heap; **jmdn. zum alten ~ zählen** write sb. off [as too old]

Eisen·bahn die a) railway; railroad *(Amer.)*; **mit der ~ fahren** go *or* travel by train *or* rail; **es ist [die] [aller]höchste ~** *(ugs.)* it's high time; its' getting late; **b)** *(Bahnstrecke)* railway line; railroad track *(Amer.)*; **c)** *(Verwaltung)* railway[s]; railroad *(Amer.)*; **d)** *(Spielbahn)* train *or* railway set

Eisenbahn-: ~abteil das railway *or (Amer.)* railroad compartment; **~bau der** railway *or (Amer.)* railroad construction

Eisenbahner der; ~s, ~: railwayman; railroader *(Amer.)*

Eisenbahner-: ~gewerkschaft die railwaymen's union; **~streik der** railway *or (Amer.)* railroad strike

Eisenbahn-: ~fähre die train ferry; **~gesellschaft die** railway *or (Amer.)* railroad company; **~knotenpunkt der** railway *or (Amer.)* railroad junction; **~netz das** railway *or (Amer.)* railroad network; **~schaffner der** railway guard; railroad conductor *(Amer.)*; **~tunnel der** railway *or (Amer.)* railroad tunnel; **~unglück das** train crash; **~wagen der** railway carriage; railroad car *(Amer.)*; *(Güterwagen)* railway wagon; railroad car *(Amer.)*; **~waggon der** *(veralt.) s.* **~wagen**

eisen-, Eisen-: ~berg·werk das iron mine; **~beschlag der** piece of ironwork; **~beschläge** ironwork *sing.*; **~erz das** iron ore; **~farbe die** ferric oxide paint; **~feil·späne** *Pl.* iron filings; **~fresser der** *(ugs. abwertend)* big mouth *(coll.)*; **~gerüst das** iron scaffolding *no indef. art.*; **~gießerei die** *(Verfahren)* iron-smelting; *(Betrieb)* iron-foundry; **~guß der;** *o. Pl. (das Gießen)* iron-casting; *(Guß~)* cast iron; **~haltig** *Adj.* iron-bearing ‹*stone*›; ‹*food*› containing iron; **~hammer der a)** steam hammer; **b)** *(bild. Kunst)* trimming hammer; **~hart** *Adj.* as hard as iron *or* as a rock; *(fig.)* ‹*person*› as hard as nails; iron ‹*will*›; **~hut der a)** *(Bot.)* monks-hood; wolfs-bane; **b)** *(Hist.)* iron hat

Eisen·hütte die ironworks *sing. or pl.*; iron foundry

Eisenhütten-: ~industrie die iron industry; **~werk das** *s.* **Eisenhütte**

eisen-, Eisen-: ~industrie die iron industry; **~kern der** *(Elektrot.)* ferrite core; **~kette die** iron chain; **~kitt der** iron cement; ~**kraut das** *(Bot.)* vervain; ~**kur die** course of iron treatment; ~**legierung die** iron alloy; ~**mangel der** *(Med.)* iron deficiency; ~**nagel der** iron nail; ~**oxid** *(fachspr.)*, ~**oxyd das** iron oxide; ~**präparat das** iron preparation; ~**ring der** iron ring; ~**säge die** hack-saw; ~**schaffend** *Adj. in* ~**schaffende Industrie** iron-and-steel-producing industry; ~**schwamm der** *(Metall.)* sponge iron; ~**span der;** *meist Pl.* iron filing; ~**spat der** *(Mineral.)* siderite; ~**stange die** iron bar; ~**staub der** iron filings *pl.;* ~**sulfat das** ferrous sulphate; ~**teil das** iron part; ~**träger der** iron girder; ~**verarbeitend** *Adj.; nicht präd.* iron-processing ‹*industry, firm, etc.*›; ~**verhüttung die** iron smelting; ~**vitriol das** *(Chemie)* green vitriol; copperas; ferrous sulphate; ~**waren** *Pl.* ironmongery *sing.;* ~**waren·händler der** ironmonger; ~**zeit die** Iron Age

eisern ['aizɐn] **1.** *Adj.* **a)** *nicht präd. (aus Eisen)* iron; ~**e Lunge** *(Med.)* iron lung; **der ~e Vorhang** *(Theater)* the safety curtain; **der Eiserne Vorhang** *(Pol.)* the Iron Curtain; **das Eiserne Kreuz** the Iron Cross; **die Eiserne Jungfrau** the Iron Maiden; **b)** *(unerschütterlich)* iron ‹*discipline*›; unflagging ‹*energy*›; **mit ~em Willen** with a will of iron; **Eiserne Hochzeit** 65th wedding anniversary; **c)** *(unerbittlich)* iron; unyielding; iron ‹*discipline*›; **mit ~em Besen [aus]kehren** *od.* **[aus]fegen** make a ruthlessly clean sweep; **der Eiserne Kanzler** the Iron Chancellor; **d)** *(bleibend)* ~**er Bestand** emergency stock; **eine ~e Reserve** emergency reserves *pl.;* **die ~e Ration** the iron rations *pl.; (fig.)* one's last reserves *pl. or* standby. **2.** *adv.* **a)** *(unerschütterlich)* resolutely; ~ **bei etw. bleiben** stick tenaciously to sth.; ~ **schweigen** remain resolutely silent; **sich ~ an etw.** *(Akk.)* **halten** keep resolutely to sth.; ~ **sparen/trainieren** save/train with iron determination; **b)** *(unerbittlich)* ~ **Widerstand leisten** put up steadfast resistance; ~ **durchgreifen** take drastic measures *or* action; ~ **auf Disziplin bedacht sein** insist on iron discipline

Eises·kälte die icy cold

eis-, Eis-: ~**fach das** freezing compartment; ~**fischerei die** ice fishing; ~**fläche die** sheet *or* surface of ice; ~**frei** *Adj.* ice-free; free of ice *postpos.;* ~**gang der** drift ice; ~**gekühlt** *Adj.* iced ‹*drink*›; ~**glatt** *Adj.* **a)** icy ‹*road*›; **b)** ['-'-] *(ugs.)* ‹*floor, steps*› as slippery as ice; ~**glätte die** black ice; ~**grau** *Adj.* steely grey; **eine ~graue Alte** a hoary old woman; ~**heilige** *in die* ~**heiligen** *[feast days of] Three Saints (12, 13, 14 May);* ~**hockey das** ice hockey

eisig 1. *Adj.* **a)** *(kalt wie Eis)* icy ‹*wind, cold*›; icy [cold] ‹*water*›; **es ist ~:** it's icy cold; it's freezing; **b)** *(kalt ablehnend)* frosty, icy ‹*atmosphere*›; frosty ‹*smile*›. **2.** *adv.* **a)** ~ **kalt sein** be icy cold; **b)** *(ablehnend)* ‹*smile*› frostily; ~ **schweigen** maintain an icy silence; **jmdn. ~ empfangen** give sb. a frosty *or* icy reception

eisig·kalt *Adj. präd. getrennt geschrieben* ice-cold ‹*water*›; freezing cold ‹*weather*›

eis-, Eis-: ~**kaffee der** iced coffee; ~**kalt 1.** *Adj.* **a)** ice-cold ‹*drink*›; freezing cold ‹*weather*›; **sich ~kalt anfühlen** feel freezing cold; **b)** *(völlig gefühllos)* icy; ice-cold ‹*technocrat, businessman*›; **ein ~kalter Blick** a cold look. **2.** *adv.* **a) es lief mir ~kalt über den Rücken** a cold shiver went down my spine; **b) etw. ~kalt tun** *(kaltblütig)* do sth. in cold blood; *(lässig)* do sth. without turning a hair; **jmdn. ~kalt ansehen/abweisen** give sb. an icy *or* frosty look/coldly reject sb.'s request; **er ging ~kalt hin und sagte ...:** he went over there, cool as you like, and said ...; ~**kanal der** *(Sportjargon)* toboggan run; ~**karte die** *(Gastron.)* ice-cream menu; ~**kraut das** *(Bot.)* ice plant; ~**kristall das** ice crystal; ~**kübel der** ice bucket

Eis·kunst-: ~**lauf der** figure skating; ~**laufen das** figure skating; ~**läufer der** figure skater

eis-, Eis-: ~**lauf der** ice-skating; ~|**laufen** *unr. itr. V.; mit sein* ice-skate; ~**laufen das** ice-skating; ~**läufer der** ice-skater; ~**mann der;** *Pl.* ~**männer** *(ugs.)* ice-cream man; ~**maschine die** ice-cream maker; freezer *(Amer.);* ~**meer das: das Nördliche/Südliche ~meer** the Arctic/Antarctic Ocean; ~**pickel der** *(Bergsteigen)* ice-pick

Ei·sprung der *(Physiol.)* ovulation

eis-, Eis-: ~**regen der** sleet; ~**revue die** ice show; ~**schicht die** layer of ice; ~**schießen das** *(Sport) s.* ~**stockschießen;** ~**schnellauf der,** ~**schnellaufen das** speed skating; ~**schnelläufer der** *(Sport)* speed skater; ~**scholle die** ice-floe; ~**schrank der** refrigerator; ~**spalte die** crevasse; ~**sport der** ice sports *pl.;* ~**stadion das** ice rink; ~**stock der** *(Sport)* ice-stick; ~**stock·schießen das** *(Sport)* ice-stick shooting; Bavarian curling; ~**tanz der** *(Sport)* ice-dancing; ~**vogel der a)** kingfisher; **b)** *(Falter)* white admiral; ~**waffel die** [ice-cream] wafer; ~**wasser das;** *o. Pl.* **a)** *(~kaltes Wasser)* ice-cold water; **b)** *(Wasser mit ~stücken)* iced water; **c)** *(Schmelzwasser)* melt-water; ~**wein der** *wine made from grapes frozen on the vine;* ~**würfel der** ice cube; ~**zapfen der** icicle; ~**zeit die** ice age; ~**zeitlich** *Adj.* ice-age *attrib.*, of the ice age *postpos.*

eitel ['aitl] *Adj.* **a)** *(abwertend)* vain; ~ **wie ein Pfau [sein]** [be] as proud as a peacock; **b)** *(veralt.: nichtig)* vain ‹*hope*›; futile, vain ‹*endeavour*›; empty, idle ‹*talk*›; **c)** *indekl., nicht präd. (veralt.: rein)* pure; ~ **Freude** pure joy

Eitelkeit die; ~, ~**en** vanity

Eiter ['aitɐ] **der;** ~**s** pus

Eiter-: ~**beule die** boil; abscess; ~**herd der** pus focus; suppurative focus; ~**pickel der** spot; pimple

eitern *itr. V.* suppurate

eitrig *Adj.* suppurating; festering

Ei·weiß das a) *(des Hühnereis)* egg-white; albumen; ~ **und Dotter trennen** separate the egg-white and the yolk; **drei ~:** the whites of three eggs; **b)** *(Chemie, Biol.)* protein

eiweiß-, Eiweiß-: ~**arm** *Adj.* low-protein *attrib.;* low in protein *postpos.;* ~**bedarf der** protein requirement; ~**haltig** *Adj.* ‹*food*› containing protein; ~**mangel der** protein deficiency; ~**reich** *Adj.* high-protein *attrib.;* rich in protein *postpos.*

Ejakulation [ejakula'tsio:n] **die;** ~, ~**en** *(Physiol.)* ejaculation

EK [e:'ka:] **das;** ~**[s]** ~**[s]** Iron Cross

EKD [e:ka:'de:] **die;** ~ *Abk.* **Evangelische Kirche in Deutschland**

ekel ['e:kl] *Adj.; nicht präd. (veralt.)* **a)** nauseating; disgusting; vile; **b)** *(verwerflich)* nasty; odious

¹Ekel der; ~**s a)** *(Abscheu)* disgust; loathing; revulsion; **[einen]** ~ **vor etw.** *(Dat.)* **haben** have a loathing *or* revulsion for sth.; **[ein]** ~ **packte/erfüllte ihn** he was seized by/filled with disgust *etc.;* **ein ~ stieg in ihr hoch** she was overcome by a feeling of disgust *etc.;* **b)** *(Überdruß)* loathing; **einen ~ vor etw.** *(Dat.)* **entwickeln** come to loathe sth.

²Ekel das; ~**s,** ~ *(ugs. abwertend)* horror; **er ist ein [altes]** ~: he is a perfect horror *or* quite obnoxious

ekel·erregend *Adj.* disgusting; nauseating; revolting; ~**e Krankheiten** diseases which could cause offence

ekelhaft 1. *Adj.* disgusting, revolting, nauseating ‹*sight*›; nasty, *(coll.)* horrible ‹*weather, person*›; ~ **riechen/schmecken** smell/taste disgusting *or* revolting. **2.** *adv.* **a)** in a disgusting *or* revolting *or* nauseating way; **b)** *(ugs.: sehr)* terribly *(coll.)*, dreadfully *(coll.)* ‹*cold, hot*›

ekeln ['e:k|n] **1.** *refl. V.* be *or* feel disgusted *or* sickened; **sie ekelt sich vor Schlangen/Spinnen** *usw.* she finds snakes/spiders *etc.* repulsive; **sich vor jmdm./etw. ~:** find sb./sth. disgusting *or* revolting. **2.** *tr., itr. V. (unpers.)* **es ekelt mich** *od.* **mir ekelt davor** I find it disgusting *or* revolting. **3.** *tr. V.* **a) Hunde ~ ihn** he finds dogs repulsive; **b)** *(vertreiben)* **jmdn. aus dem Haus ~:** hound sb. out of the house

EKG [e:ka:'ge:] **das;** ~**[s],** ~**[s]** *Abk.* **Elektrokardiogramm** ECG; **ein ~ machen lassen** have an ECG

Eklat [e'kla(:)] **der;** ~**s,** ~**s** *(geh.) (Aufsehen, Skandal)* sensation; stir; *(Konfrontation)* row; altercation; **es kam zum ~:** it came to a row *or* [major] confrontation

eklatant [ekla'tant] *(geh.)* **1.** *Adj.* **a)** *(offensichtlich)* striking ‹*difference*›; flagrant, scandalous ‹*offence*›; **b)** *(sensationell)* sensational; spectacular. **2.** *adv.* flagrantly; ~ **gegen etw. verstoßen** be in flagrant breach of sth.

Eklektiker [e'klɛktikɐ] **der;** ~**s,** ~, **Eklektikerin die;** ~, ~**nen** eclectic

eklektisch 1. *Adj.* eclectic. **2.** *adv.* eclectically

Eklektizismus [eklɛkti'tsɪsmʊs] **der;** ~: eclecticism

eklig ['e:klɪç] **1.** *Adj.* **a)** disgusting, revolting, nauseating ‹*sight*›; nasty *(coll.)*, horrible ‹*weather, person*›; ~ **riechen/schmecken** smell/taste disgusting *or* revolting; **b)** *(ugs.: gemein)* mean; nasty; **sich ~ benehmen** be mean *or* nasty. **2.** *adv.* **a)** in a disgusting *or* revolting *or* nauseating way; **b)** *(ugs.: sehr)* terribly *(coll.)*, dreadfully *(coll.)* ‹*hot, cold*›

Eklipse [e'klɪpsə] **die;** ~, ~**n** *(Astron.)* eclipse

Ekliptik [e'klɪptɪk] **die;** ~, ~**en** *(Astron.)* ecliptic

Ekstase [ɛk'sta:zə] **die;** ~, ~**n** ecstasy; **in ~ geraten** go into ecstasies; become ecstatic; **jmdn. in ~ versetzen** send sb. into ecstasies; make sb. ecstatic

ekstatisch [ɛk'sta:tɪʃ] **1.** *Adj.* ecstatic. **2.** *adv.* ecstatically

Ektoderm ['ɛktodɛrm] **das;** ~**s,** ~**e** *(Zool.)* ectoderm

Ekto·plasma [ɛkto-] **das** *(Biol.; Parapsychologie)* ectoplasm

Ekzem das; ~**s,** ~**e** *(Med.)* eczema

ekzematös [ɛktsema'tø:s] *Adj. (Med.)* eczematous

Elaborat [elabo'ra:t] **das;** ~**[e]s,** ~**e** *(geh. abwertend)* pathetic concoction

elaboriert *Adj. (geh.)* elaborate ‹*style*›; elaborated; **ein ~er Code** *(Sprachw.)* an elaborated code

Elan [e'la:n] **der;** ~**s** zest; vigour

elan·voll 1. *Adj.* zestful; vigorous. **2.** *adv.* zestfully; vigorously

Elaste [e'lastə] *Pl. (Chemie)* elastomers

Elastik [e'lastɪk] **das;** ~**s,** ~**s** *od.* **die;** ~, ~**en** elasticated material; stretch fabric

elastisch 1. *Adj.* **a)** *(dehnbar)* elasticated ‹*material*›; springy, resilient ‹*surface*›; **b)** *(geschmeidig)* supple, lithe ‹*person, body*›; **c)** *(flexibel)* flexible ‹*tactics, rules*›. **2.** *adv.* **a)** *(geschmeidig)* supply; lithely; **sein ~ federnder Gang** his supple *or* lithe walk; **b)** *(flexibel)* flexibly

Elastizität [elastitsi'tɛ:t] **die;** ~: **a)** *(Dehnbarkeit)* elasticity; *(Federkraft)* springiness; **b)** *(Geschmeidigkeit)* suppleness; **c)** *(Flexibilität)* flexibility

Elativ ['e:lati:f] **der;** ~**s,** ~**e** *(Sprachw.)* absolute superlative; elative

Elb-Florenz ['ɛlp-] **das** Dresden

Elb·kähne *Pl. (nordd. scherzh.)* clodhoppers *(coll.)*

Elch [ɛlç] **der;** ~**[e]s,** ~**e** elk; *(in Nordamerika)* moose

Elch-: ~**bulle der** bull elk; ~**kuh die** cow elk
Eldorado [ɛldo'ra:do] **das;** ~**s,** ~**s** eldorado; **ein** ~ **der** *od.* **für Taucher** *(fig.)* a divers' paradise
Elefant [ele'fant] **der;** ~**en,** ~**en** elephant; **wie ein** ~ **im Porzellanladen** *(ugs.)* like a bull in a china shop; *s. auch* **Mücke**
Elefanten-: ~**baby das** baby elephant; *s. auch* ~**küken;** ~**bulle der** bull elephant; ~**haut die** elephant skin; **eine** ~**haut haben** *(fig. ugs.)* be thick-skinned; ~**herde die** elephant herd; ~**hochzeit die** *(Wirtsch. scherzh.)* giant merger; ~**kuh die** cow elephant; ~**küken das: er ist ein richtiges** ~**küken** *(ugs. scherzh.)* he looks just like a baby elephant; ~**rennen das** *(ugs. scherzh.)* race between two juggernauts
Elefantiasis [elefan'ti:azɪs] **die;** ~ *(Med.)* elephantiasis
elegant [ele'gant] **1.** *Adj.* **a)** *(geschmackvoll)* elegant, stylish ‹*dress, appearance*›; elegant ‹*society*›; **die** ~**e Welt** elegant society; **b)** *(harmonisch)* elegant, graceful ‹*movement*›; neat ‹*solution*›; **c)** *(kultiviert)* elegant, civilized ‹*taste*›; elegant ‹*style*›; civilized ‹*manner*›. **2.** *adv.* elegantly, stylishly ‹*dressed*›; **sich** ~ **aus der Affäre ziehen** get oneself gracefully out of it
Eleganz [ele'gants] **die;** ~ elegance; stylishness; **zeitlose/sportliche/lässige** ~: timeless/sporty/casual elegance
Elegie [ele'gi:] **die;** ~, ~**n** elegy
elegisch [e'le:gɪʃ] **1.** *Adj.* **a)** *(Dichtk.)* elegiac; **b)** *(fig.: wehmütig)* elegiac; mournful; plaintive. **2.** *adv.* ~ **gestimmt sein** feel in a mournful mood
elektrifizieren [elɛktrifi'tsi:rən] *tr. V.* electrify
Elektrifizierung die; ~, ~**en** electrification
Elektrik [e'lɛktrɪk] **die;** ~, ~**en** electrics *pl.*
Elektriker der; ~**s,** ~: electrician
elektrisch 1. *Adj.* electric ‹*current, light, heating, shock*›; electrical ‹*resistance, wiring, system*›; **der** ~**e Stuhl** the electric chair. **2.** *adv.* ~ **kochen** cook with electricity; ~ **geladen sein** be electrically charged; be charged with electricity; **sich** ~ **rasieren** use an electric shaver
Elektrische die; ~**n,** ~**n** *(veralt.)* tram *(Brit.)*; streetcar *(Amer.)*
elektrisieren 1. *tr. V.* **a)** *(Med.)* treat using electricity; **b)** *(fig.: entflammen)* electrify. **2.** *refl. V.* give oneself *or* get an electric shock
Elektrizität [elɛktritsi'tɛ:t] **die;** ~ *(Physik)* electricity; *(elektrische Energie)* electricity; [electric] power
Elektrizitäts-: ~**erzeugung die** generation of electricity; ~**gesellschaft die** electricity company; ~**versorgung die** [electric] power supply; ~**werk das** power station; ~**zähler der** electricity meter
elektro-, Elektro-: ~**antrieb der** electric drive; ~**artikel der** electrical appliance; ~**auto das** electric car; ~**chemie die** electrochemistry *no art.*; ~**chemisch 1.** *Adj.* electrochemical; **2.** *adv.* electrochemically; ~**chirurgie die** electrosurgery *no art.*
Elektrode [elɛk'tro:də] **die;** ~, ~**n** electrode
elektro-, Elektro-: ~**dynamik die** *(Physik)* electrodynamics *sing., no art.*; ~**dynamisch** *(Physik)* **1.** *Adj.* electrodynamic; **2.** *adv.* electrodynamically; ~**enzephalogramm das** *(Med.)* electroencephalogram; ~**fahrzeug das** electric vehicle; ~**gerät das** electrical appliance; ~**geschäft das** electrical shop *or (Amer.)* store; ~**handwerk das** electrical trade; ~**herd der** electric cooker; ~**industrie die** electrical goods industry; ~**ingenieur der** electrical engineer; ~**installateur der** electrical fitter; electrician; ~**kardiogramm das** *(Med.)* electrocardiogram; ~**karren der** electric trolley; ~**konzern der** electrical company
Elektrolyse [elɛktro'ly:zə] **die;** ~, ~**n** *(Chemie, Physik)* electrolysis
elektrolysieren *tr. V.* *(Chemie)* electrolyse
Elektrolyt [elɛktro'ly:t] **der;** ~**en** *od.* ~**s,** ~**en** *od.* ~**e** electrolyte
elektrolytisch *Adj.* electrolytic
elektro-, Elektro-: ~**magnet der** electromagnet; ~**magnetisch 1.** *Adj.* electromagnetic; **2.** *adv.* electromagnetically; ~**magnetismus der** electromagnetism *no art.*; ~**mechanik die** electrical engineering *no art.*; ~**mechanisch 1.** *Adj.* electromechanical; **2.** *adv.* electromechanically; ~**meter der** electrometer; ~**mobil das** electric car; ~**monteur der** *s.* ~**installateur;** ~**motor der** electric motor
Elektron [e'lɛktrɔn] **das;** ~**s,** ~**en** [-'tro:nən] *(Kernphysik)* electron
Elektronen-: ~**blitz der** electronic flash; ~**blitz·gerät das** *(Fot.)* electronic flash; ~**[ge]hirn das** *(ugs.)* electronic brain *(coll.)*; ~**hülle die** electron shell; ~**mikroskop das** electron microscope; ~**optik die** electron optics *sing., no art.*; ~**rechner der** electronic computer; ~**röhre die** electron tube *or* valve; ~**strahl der** *(Physik)* electron beam; ~**theorie die** electron theory; ~**volt das** electron volt
Elektronik [elɛk'tro:nɪk] **die;** ~ **a)** *o. Pl.* electronics *sing., no art.*; **b)** *(Bestandteile)* electronic parts *pl.*; electronics *pl.*
Elektroniker der; ~**s,** ~: electronics engineer
elektronisch 1. *Adj.* electronic. **2.** *adv.* electronically
Elektro-: ~**ofen der** *(Technik)* electric furnace; ~**rasierer der** electric shaver *or* razor; ~**rasur die** shaving *no art.* with an electric shaver *or* razor; ~**schock der** *(Med.)* electric shock; ~**schweißer der** arc welder
Elektroskop [elɛktro'sko:p] **das;** ~**s,** ~**e** electroscope
elektro-, Elektro-: ~**smog der** *(Jargon)* electronic smog; ~**statisch 1.** *Adj.* electrostatic; **2.** *adv.* electrostatically; ~**technik die** electrical engineering *no art.*; ~**techniker der a)** electronics engineer; **b)** *(Elektriker)* electrician; ~**technisch 1.** *Adj.* electrotechnical; ~**technische Industrie** electrical *or* electrotechnical industry; **2.** *adv.* electrotechnically; ~**therapie die** *(Med.)* electrotherapy; ~**wagen der** electric vehicle
Element [ele'mɛnt] **das;** ~**[e]s,** ~**e a)** element; **die vier** ~**e** the four elements; **die entfesselten** ~**e** *(geh.)* the raging elements; **er war/fühlte sich in seinem** ~: he was/felt in his element; **zwielichtige/kriminelle** ~**e** shady/criminal elements; **die** ~**e der Mathematik/Grammatik** *usw.* the elements *or* rudiments of mathematics/grammar *etc.*; **b)** *(Bauteil)* element; *(einer Schrankwand)* unit; **c)** *(Elektrot.)* cell; battery
elementar [elemɛn'ta:ɐ̯] **1.** *Adj.* **a)** *(grundlegend)* fundamental ‹*requirement, right, condition, insight, significance*›; **b)** *(einfach)* elementary, rudimentary ‹*knowledge*›; **ihm fehlen die** ~**sten Kenntnisse** he lacks the most elementary *or* rudimentary knowledge; **c)** *(naturhaft)* elemental ‹*force, forces*›. **2.** *adv.* with elemental force
Elementar-: ~**begriff der** elementary *or* basic concept; ~**gewalt die** elemental force; ~**kenntnisse** *Pl.* elementary *or* rudimentary knowledge *sing.*; ~**mathematik die** elementary mathematics *sing., no art.*; ~**stufe die** *(Schulw.)* pre-school level; ~**teilchen das** *(Physik)* elementary particle; ~**unterricht a)** *(Einführungsunterricht)* elementary instruction; **b)** *(Unterricht in der* ~*stufe)* pre-school teaching
Elen ['e:lɛn] **das** *od.* **der;** ~**s,** ~: *s.* **Elch**
elend ['e:lɛnt] **1.** *Adj.* **a)** wretched, miserable ‹*existence, life conditions, environment*›; **eines** ~**en Todes sterben** die a miserable death; **b)** *(krank)* **sich** ~ **fühlen** feel wretched *or (coll.)* awful; **mir ist/wird** ~: I feel/I am beginning to feel awful *or* terrible *(coll.)*; **c)** *(gemein)* despicable ‹*person, coward, allegation*›; **d)** *nicht präd. (ugs.: besonders groß)* dreadful *(coll.)* ‹*hunger, pain*›. **2.** *adv.* **a)** *(jämmerlich)* wretchedly; miserably; ~ **zugrunde gehen** come to a miserable *or* wretched end; **b)** *(ugs.: intensivierend)* dreadfully *(coll.)*
Elend das; ~**s a)** *(Leid)* misery; wretchedness; **das ganze Leben ist ein** ~: life is just a complete misery; **es ist ein** ~ **mit ihm** *(ugs.)* he's enough to drive you to despair; **das heulende** ~ **kriegen** *(ugs.)* start blubbering hysterically; **..., da kann man das heulende** ~ **kriegen** it's enough to make you weep; **wie das leibhaftige** ~ **aussehen** *(ugs.)* look like death warmed up *(coll.)*; **ein langes** ~ *(ugs. scherzh.)* a beanpole; *s. auch* **Häufchen; b)** *(Armut)* misery; destitution; **jmdn. ins** ~ **stürzen** plunge sb. into misery
elendig, elendiglich *Adv.* *(geh.)* miserably; wretchedly; ~ **zugrunde gehen** perish miserably; come to a wretched *or* miserable end
Elends-: ~**gestalt die** [poor] wretch; wretched figure; ~**quartier das** slum [dwelling]; ~**viertel das** slum area
Eleve [e'le:və] **der;** ~**n,** ~**n a)** *(Theater, Ballett)* student; **b)** *(Land- und Forstwirtsch.)* trainee; **c)** *(veralt. geh.: Schüler, Jünger)* acolyte; disciple
elf [ɛlf] *Kardinalz.* eleven; *s. auch* [1]**acht**
[1]**Elf die;** ~, ~**en a)** eleven; *s. auch* [1]**Acht a, e, g; b)** *(Sport)* team; side
[2]**Elf der;** ~**en,** ~**en** elf
Elfe ['ɛlfə] **die;** ~, ~**n** fairy
Elfen·bein das ivory; **schwarzes** ~ *(fig.)* black ivory
Elfenbein·arbeit die ivory piece
elfen·beinern *Adj.* ivory
elfenbein-, Elfenbein-: ~**farben** *Adj.* ivory-coloured; ~**küste die** Ivory Coast; ~**schnitzerei die a)** *o. Pl.* ivory-carving; **b)** *(Gegenstand)* ivory carving; ~**turm der** *(fig.)* ivory tower
elfenhaft *Adj.* elfish; elfin
Elfen-: ~**königin die** elfin queen; fairy queen; ~**reigen der** fairy dance
Elfer der; ~**s,** ~ **a)** *(Fußballjargon)* penalty; **b)** *(landsch.: Zahl Elf)* eleven; **c)** *(Buslinie)* number eleven
Elfer-: ~**rat der** *carnival committee consisting of eleven members;* ~**wette die** *(Sport) football pools [entry] requiring eleven selections;* **er hat sieben Richtige in der** ~**wette** he's got seven out of eleven on the pools
elf-: ~**fach** *Vervielfältigungsz.* elevenfold; **die** ~**fache Menge** eleven times the amount; *s. auch* **achtfach;** ~**mal** *Wiederholungsz.* eleven times; *s. auch* **achtmal**
Elf·meter der *(Fußball)* penalty; **einen** ~ **schießen** take a penalty
Elfmeter-: ~**punkt der** *(Fußball)* penalty spot; ~**schießen das** *(Fußball)* **durch** ~**schießen** by *or* on penalties; **es gab ein** ~**schießen** it was decided on penalties; ~**schütze der** *(Fußball)* penalty taker; ~**tor das** *(Fußball)* penalty
elft *in* **wir waren zu** ~: there were eleven of us; *s. auch* [2]**acht**
elft... *Ordinalz.* eleventh; *s. auch* **acht...**
elf·tausend *Kardinalz.* eleven thousand
Elftel ['ɛlftl̩] **das;** ~**s,** ~: eleventh
elftens *Adv.* eleventh
elidieren [eli'di:rən] *tr. V.* **a)** *(geh.: streichen)* delete; **b)** *(Sprachwiss.)* elide
Elimination [elimina'tsio:n] **die;** ~, ~**en** elimination
eliminieren [elimi'ni:rən] *tr. V.* eliminate
Eliminierung die; ~, ~**en** elimination
Elisabeth [e'li:zabɛt] **(die)** Elizabeth
elisabethanisch *Adj.* Elizabethan

Elision [eli'zi̯o:n] **die; ~, ~en** elision

elitär [eli'tɛ:ɐ̯] **1.** *Adj.* **a)** élitist; **ein ~es Bewußtsein** an élite-awareness; **b)** *(zu einer Elite gehörend)* élite *attrib.* **2.** *adv.* **er denkt/verhält sich ~:** he thinks/behaves in an élitist fashion

Elite [e'li:tə] **die; ~, ~n** élite; **die ~ der Sportler** the sporting élite

Elite-: ~denken das élitist thinking; élitism; **~truppe die** *(Milit.)* élite *or* crack force

Elixier [elɪ'ksi:ɐ̯] **das; ~s, ~e** elixir

Ell·bogen der; ~s, ~: elbow; **er/sie hat keine ~** *(fig. ugs.)* he/she isn't pushy enough *(coll.)*

Ellbogen-: ~freiheit die elbow-room; **~gesellschaft die** *(abwertend)* society where the weakest go to the wall; **~mensch der** *(abwertend)* pushy individual *(ugs.)*

Elle ['ɛlə] **die; ~, ~n a)** *(Anat.)* ulna; **b)** *(frühere Längeneinheit)* cubit; **c)** *(veralt.: Maßstock)* ≈ *yardstick;* **alles mit einer ~ messen** *(fig.)* measure everything by the same yardstick

Ellen·bogen *s.* **Ellbogen**

ellen·lang *Adj. (ugs.)* ⟨*list*⟩ as long as your arm; interminable ⟨*lecture, sermon*⟩*;* terribly long *(coll.)* ⟨*letter*⟩

Ellipse [ɛ'lɪpsə] **die; ~, ~n** ellipse; *(Sprachw., Rhet.)* ellipsis

Ellipsen·bahn die elliptical orbit

ellipsen·förmig 1. *Adj.* elliptical. **2.** *adv.* elliptically

elliptisch [ɛ'lɪptɪʃ] **1.** *Adj.* elliptical. **2.** *adv.* elliptically

Elms·feuer ['ɛlms-] **das** *(Met.)* St. Elmo's fire

Eloge [e'lo:ʒə] **die; ~, ~n** *(geh.)* eulogy

E-Lok die *(veralt.)* electric locomotive *or* engine

eloquent [elo'kvɛnt] *(geh.)* **1.** *Adj.* eloquent. **2.** *adv.* eloquently

Eloquenz die; ~ *(geh.)* eloquence

Elritze ['ɛlrɪtsə] **die; ~, ~n** *(Zool.)* minnow

Elsaß ['ɛlzas] **das; ~** *od.* **Elsasses** Alsace; **im/aus dem ~:** in/from Alsace

Elsässer ['ɛlzɛsɐ] **1.** *indekl. Adj.; nicht präd.* Alsatian. **2. der; ~s, ~:** Alsatian

Elsässerin die; ~, ~nen Alsatian; *s. auch* **-in**

elsässisch *Adj.* Alsatian

Elsaß-Lothringen (das) *(hist.)* Alsace-Lorraine

Elster ['ɛlstɐ] **die; ~, ~n** *(Zool.)* magpie; **wie eine ~ stehlen** be light-fingered; **eine diebische ~** *(fig.)* a pilferer

Elter ['ɛltɐ] **das** *od.* **der; ~s, ~n** *(Biol.)* parent

elterlich *Adj.; nicht präd.* parental

Eltern *Pl.* parents; **nicht von schlechten ~ sein** *(fig. ugs.)* be quite something

eltern-, Eltern-: ~abend der *(Schulw.)* parents' evening; **~aktiv das** *(DDR: Schulw.)* parents' committee; **~bei·rat der** *(Schulw.)* parents' association; **~haus das** parental home; **aus einem armen/katholischen ~haus kommen** come from a poor/Catholic home; **~liebe die** parental love; **~los 1.** *Adj.* parentless; orphaned; **ein ~loses Kind** a child without parents; an orphan; **2.** *adv.* **~los aufwachsen** grow up an orphan *or* without parents

Elternschaft die; ~ a) *(Schulw.)* parents' association; **b)** *(Elternsein)* parenthood; **geplante ~:** planned parenthood

Eltern-: ~sprech·tag der parents' day; **~teil der** parent; **~versammlung die** parents' meeting

elysäisch [ely'zɛ:ɪʃ], **elysisch** [e'ly:zɪʃ] *Adj., adv. (dichter.)* Elysian

Elysium [e'ly:zi̯ʊm] **das; ~s, Elysien** [e'ly:zi̯ən] *(dichter.)* Elysium

EM *Abk.* **Europameisterschaft[en]**

Email [e'mai̯] **das; ~s, ~s, Emaille** [e'maljə] **die; ~, ~n** enamel

Email[le]-: ~arbeit die *(Kunst)* **a)** enamel; **b)** *(~malerei)* enamel painting; **~geschirr das** enamelware; **~waren** *Pl.* enamelware *sing.*

emaillieren *tr. V.* enamel

Emanation [emana'tsi̯o:n] **die; ~, ~en** *(Philos.)* emanation

Emanze [e'mantsə] **die; ~, ~n** *(ugs., auch abwertend)* women's libber *(coll.)*

Emanzipation [emantsipa'tsi̯o:n] **die; ~, ~en** emancipation; **die ~ der Frau** the emancipation *or* liberation of women

Emanzipations·bewegung die liberation movement

emanzipatorisch [emantsipa'to:rɪʃ] *Adj. (geh.)* emancipatory ⟨*education*⟩

emanzipieren [emantsi'pi:rən] **1.** *refl. V.* **sich [von jmdm./etw.] ~:** emancipate oneself [from sb./sth.]. **2.** *tr. V.* emancipate

emanzipiert *Adj.* emancipated; emancipated, liberated ⟨*woman*⟩

Embargo [ɛm'bargo] **das; ~s, ~s** embargo

Emblem [ɛm'ble:m] **das; ~s, ~e** *od.* **~ata** emblem

Embolie [ɛmbo'li:] **die; ~, ~n** *(Med.)* embolism

Embonpoint [ãbõ'po̯ɛ̃:] **der** *od.* **das; ~s** *(geh. scherzh.)* embonpoint

Embryo ['ɛmbryo] **der; ~s, ~nen** [-y'o:nən] *od.* **~s** embryo

Embryoblast der; ~en, ~en *(Biol.)* cyst

embryonal *Adj.; nicht präd. (Med., Biol., fig.)* embryonic

Emendation [emɛnda'tsi̯o:n] **die; ~** *(Literaturw.)* emendation

emeritieren [emeri'ti:rən] *tr. V.* confer emeritus status on; **ein emeritierter Professor** an emeritus professor; a professor emeritus

Emeritierung die; ~, ~en: seit seiner ~: since he has been an emeritus professor

Emeritus [e'me:ritʊs] **der; ~, Emeriti** *(geh.)* emeritus professor

Emigrant [emi'grant] **der; ~en, ~en** emigrant; *(Flüchtling)* emigré

Emigranten·presse die emigré press

Emigrantin die; ~, ~nen *s.* **Emigrant**

Emigration [emigra'tsi̯o:n] **die; ~, ~en a)** *(das Emigrieren)* emigration; **die innere ~:** inner emigration *(particularly during the Nazi period in Germany);* **b)** *o. Pl. (die Fremde)* exile; **in der ~ leben** live in exile; **c)** *o. Pl. (die Emigranten)* emigrés *pl.*

emigrieren [emi'gri:rən] *itr. V.; mit sein* emigrate

eminent [emi'nɛnt] **1.** *(geh.) Adj.* eminent; **von ~er Bedeutung sein** be of the utmost significance. **2.** *adv.* eminently; **das ist ~ wichtig** that is of the utmost importance

Eminenz [emi'nɛnts] **die; ~, ~en** *(kath. Kirche)* eminence; **Eure/Seine ~:** Your/His Eminence; **eine graue ~:** an éminence grise; a grey eminence

Emir ['e:mɪr] **der; ~s, ~e** emir

Emirat das; ~[e]s, ~e emirate

Emissär [emɪ'sɛ:ɐ̯] **der; ~s, ~e** emissary

Emission [emɪ'si̯o:n] **a)** *(Physik, Ökologie)* emission; **b)** *(Ausgabe [von Briefmarken, Wertpapieren])* issue

Emissions·schutz·gesetz das anti-pollution law

Emitter [e'mɪtɐ] **der; ~s, ~** *(Technik)* emitter

emittieren *tr. V.* **a)** *(Finanzw.)* issue; **b)** *(in die Luft abblasen)* emit

Emmchen ['ɛmçən] *Pl. (ugs. veralt.)* marks

Emmentaler ['ɛmənta:lɐ] **der; ~s, ~:** Emmenthal [cheese]

e-Moll das E minor; *s. auch* **a-Moll**

Emotion [emo'tsi̯o:n] **die; ~, ~en** emotion

emotional 1. *Adj.* emotional ⟨*person, reaction, etc.*⟩*;* emotive ⟨*topic, question*⟩. **2.** *adv.* emotionally

emotionalisieren *tr. V. (geh.)* arouse emotions in, emotionalize ⟨*person*⟩*;* emotionalize ⟨*issue*⟩

Emotionalität die; ~: emotionalism; emotionality

emotionell *Adj. s.* **emotional**

emotions·geladen *Adj.* emotionally charged

E-Motor der electric motor

Empathie [ɛmpa'ti:] **die; ~** *(Psych.)* empathy

empfahl [ɛm'pfa:l] *1. u. 3. Pers. Sg. Prät. v.* **empfehlen**

empfand [ɛm'pfant] *1. u. 3. Pers. Sg. Prät. v.* **empfinden**

Empfang [ɛm'pfaŋ] **der; ~[e]s, Empfänge a)** *(Entgegennahme)* receipt; **bei ~:** on receipt; **etw. in ~ nehmen** accept sth.; **mit einer Strafpredigt in ~ genommen werden** *(iron.)* be welcomed *or* greeted with a dressing-down; **zahlbar bei ~:** payable on receipt; **b)** *(Funkw., Rundf., Ferns.)* reception; **auf ~ gehen/bleiben** *(Funkw.)* switch over to 'receive'/stay on 'receive'; **c)** *o. Pl. (geh.: Begrüßung)* reception; **d)** *(festliche Veranstaltung)* reception; **e)** *(Rezeption)* reception [desk]

empfangen 1. *unr. tr. V.* **a)** *(geh.)* receive; **einen Gast bei sich ~:** receive a guest at home; **die Sakramente ~** *(Rel.)* receive the sacraments; **b)** *(Funkw., Rundf., Ferns.)* receive; **c)** *(begrüßen)* receive, greet ⟨*person*⟩*;* **jmdn. mit Blumen ~:** greet sb. with flowers; **d)** *(geh.: angeregt werden zu)* conceive ⟨*idea*⟩*;* **eine Anregung [von jmdm.] ~:** receive a stimulus from sb.; **e)** *(geh.)* **ein Kind ~:** conceive a child. **2.** *unr. itr. V. (geh.: schwanger werden)* conceive

Empfänger [ɛm'pfɛŋɐ] **der; ~s, ~ a)** recipient; *(eines Briefs)* addressee; **~ unbekannt/verzogen/unbekannt verzogen** not known at this address/gone away/gone away, address unknown; **b)** *(Empfangsgerät)* receiver

-empfänger der *(Renten~ usw.)* recipient of ...

Empfängerin die; ~, ~nen *s.* **Empfänger a**

empfänglich *Adj.* **a)** *(leicht zugänglich)* receptive **(für** to); **b)** *(beeinflußbar)* susceptible; **für jmds. Charme/Schönheit ~ sein** be susceptible to sb.'s charm/beauty

Empfänglichkeit die; ~ a) *(Zugänglichkeit)* receptivity, receptiveness **(für** to); **b)** *(Beeinflußbarkeit)* susceptibility **(für** to)

Empfängnis die; ~: conception

empfängnis·verhütend *Adj.* **ein ~es Mittel** a contraceptive; **~ wirken** act as a contraceptive

Empfängnis·verhütung die contraception

Empfängnisverhütungs·mittel das contraceptive

Empfängnis·zeit *(Rechtsw.)* time of conception

empfangs-, Empfangs-: ~antenne die *(Rundf., Ferns.)* [receiving] aerial *(Brit.) or (Amer.)* antenna; **~berechtigt** *Adj.* authorized to receive payment/goods *postpos.;* **eine ~berechtigte Person** an authorized recipient; **~bereich der** *(Rundf., Ferns.)* reception area; **~bestätigung die** receipt; **~chef der** head receptionist; **~dame die** receptionist; **~gerät das** *(Funkw., Rundf., Ferns.)* receiver; **~halle die** reception lobby; **~saal der** reception hall; **~station die** *(Funkw., Rundf., Ferns.)* receiving station; *(Raumfahrt)* tracking station; **~zimmer das** reception room

empfehlen [ɛm'pfe:lən] **1.** *unr. tr. V.* **a) jmdm. etw./jmdn. ~:** recommend sth./sb. to sb.; **der empfohlene Richtpreis** *(Wirtsch.)* the recommended price; **~ Sie mich Ihrer Gattin** *(geh.)* convey my respects to your wife; **dieser Arzt/dies ist sehr zu ~:** this doctor/this is to be highly recommended; **b)** *(veralt.: anvertrauen)* commend **(***Dat.* to). **2.** *unr. refl. V.* **a)** *(geh.: sich verabschieden und gehen)* take one's leave; **darf ich**

mich ~? may I take my leave?; **b)** *(unpers.)* **es empfiehlt sich, ... zu ...:** it's advisable to...; **c)** *(geh.: sich als geeignet erweisen)* **sich [durch/wegen etw.] ~:** commend oneself/itself [because of sth.]

empfehlens·wert *Adj.* **a)** to be recommended *postpos.;* recommendable; **b)** *(ratsam)* advisable

Empfehlung die; ~, ~en a) recommendation; **sie kam auf ~:** she came on somebody's recommendation; **b)** *(Empfehlungsschreiben)* letter of recommendation; testimonial; **c)** *(höflicher Gruß)* **„eine ~ an Ihre Frau Mutter"** '[kind] regards to your mother'; **„mit freundlicher ~"** 'with kindest regards'

Empfehlungs·schreiben das letter of recommendation; testimonial

empfiehl [ɛm'pfi:l] *Imperativ Sg. v.* **empfehlen**

empfiehlst *2. Pers. Sg. Präsens v.* **empfehlen**

empfiehlt *3. Pers. Sg. Präsens v.* **empfehlen**

empfinden [ɛm'pfɪndn̩] *unr. tr. V.* **a)** *(wahrnehmen)* feel ⟨*pain, pleasure, bitterness, etc.*⟩; **etwas/nichts für jmdn. ~:** feel something/nothing for sb.; **b)** *(auffassen)* **etw. als Beleidigung ~:** feel sth. to be an insult; **jmdn. als Eindringling ~:** feel sb. to be an impostor; **das empfinde ich nicht so** I feel differently about it

Empfịnden das; ~s feeling; **für mein** *od.* **nach meinem ~:** to my mind

empfịndlich 1. *Adj.* **a)** *(sensibel, feinfühlig, auch fig.)* sensitive; fast ⟨*film*⟩; **eine ~e Stelle** a tender spot; **b)** *(leicht beleidigt)* sensitive, touchy ⟨*person*⟩; **c)** *(anfällig)* **zart und ~:** delicate; **~ gegen Viruserkrankungen** prone to virus infections; **d)** *(spürbar)* severe ⟨*punishment, shortage*⟩; harsh ⟨*punishment, measure*⟩; sharp ⟨*increase*⟩. **2.** *adv.* **a) ~ auf etw.** *(Akk.)* **reagieren** *(sensibel)* be susceptible to sth.; *(beleidigt)* react oversensitively to sth.; **b)** *(spürbar)* ⟨*punish*⟩ severely, harshly; ⟨*increase*⟩ sharply; **c)** *(intensivierend)* ⟨*hurt*⟩ badly; bitterly ⟨*cold*⟩; **der Streik machte sich für die Verbraucher sofort ~ bemerkbar** the strike had an immediate effect on the consumers

Empfịndlichkeit die; ~, ~en *s.* **empfindlich:** sensitivity; touchiness; severity; harshness; *(eines Films)* speed; **ihre ~ gegen Infektionen** her proneness *or* susceptibility to infections

empfịndsam 1. *Adj.* sensitive ⟨*nature*⟩; *(gefühlvoll)* sentimental. **2.** *adv.* sensitively; *(gefühlvoll)* sentimentally

Empfịndsamkeit die; ~: sensitivity; *(Literaturw.)* sentimentality

Empfịndung die; ~, ~en a) *(sinnliche Wahrnehmung)* sensation; sensory perception; **b)** *(Gefühl)* feeling; emotion

empfịndungs-, Empfịndungs-: ~los *Adj.* **a)** *(körperlich)* numb; without sensation *pred.;* **b)** *(seelisch)* insensitive; unfeeling; **~losigkeit die; ~ a)** *(körperlich)* numbness; lack of sensation; **b)** *(Gefühlskälte)* insensitivity; lack of feeling; **~nerv der** sensory nerve; **~vermögen das a)** *(physisch)* sensory perception; **b)** *(seelisch)* sensitivity

empfing [ɛm'pfɪŋ] *1. u. 3. Pers. Sg. Prät. v.* **empfangen**

empfohlen [ɛm'pfo:lən] **1.** *2. Part. v.* **empfehlen. 2.** *Adj.* recommended

empfunden [ɛm'pfʊndn̩] *2. Part. v.* **empfinden**

Emphase [ɛm'fa:zə] **die; ~, ~n** *(geh.)* emphasis

emphatisch [ɛm'fa:tɪʃ] **1.** *Adj. (geh.)* emphatic. **2.** *adv.* emphatically

[1]**Empire** [ã'pi:ɐ̯] **das; ~[s]** Empire

[2]**Empire** ['ɛmpaɪə] **das; ~[s]** *(Hist.)* Empire

Empire·stil [ã'pi:ɐ̯-] **der** Empire style

Empirie [ɛmpi'ri:] **die; ~ a)** *(Methode)* empirical method; **b)** *(Erfahrungswissen)* empirical knowledge

Empiriker der; ~s, ~: empiricist

empirisch 1. *Adj.* empirical. **2.** *adv.* empirically

Empirịsmus der; ~: empiricism

empor [ɛm'po:ɐ̯] *Adv. (geh.)* upwards; up

empor-: ~|arbeiten *refl. V. (geh.)* work one's way up; **~|blicken** *itr. V. (geh.)* look upwards *or (literary)* heavenwards; **zum Himmel ~blicken** raise one's eyes heavenwards *(literary)*

Empore die; ~, ~n gallery

empören [ɛm'pø:rən] **1.** *tr. V.* fill with indignation; incense; outrage. **2.** *refl. V.* **a)** *(zornig werden)* **sich über jmdn./etw. ~:** become indignant *or* incensed *or* outraged about sb./sth.; **b)** *(geh.: sich auflehnen)* **sich gegen jmdn./etw. ~:** rebel *or* rise against sb./sth.

empörend 1. *Adj.* outrageous. **2.** *adv.* outrageously

Empörer der; ~s, ~ *(geh.)* rebel

empörerisch *Adj. (geh.)* rebellious

empor-: ~|heben *unr. tr. V. (geh.)* raise; **~|kommen** *unr. itr. V.; mit sein (geh.)* **a)** *(nach oben kommen)* come up; **b)** *(fig.: aufsteigen)* rise

Emporkömmling [-kœmlɪŋ] **der; ~s, ~e** *(abwertend)* upstart; parvenu

empor-: ~|ragen *itr. V. (geh.)* rise [up]; **über etw.** *(Akk.)* **~ragen** tower above sth.; **~|recken 1.** *tr. V. (geh.)* raise; **2.** *refl. V.* rise; **~|schauen** *itr. V. (geh.)* raise one's eyes; **~|schwingen** *unr. refl. V. (geh.)* **sich ~schwingen** swing oneself aloft; **sich zu großen Taten ~schwingen** *(fig.)* rise to great deeds; **~|steigen** *unr. itr. V.; mit sein (geh.)* **a)** climb up; **an etw.** *(Dat.)* **~steigen** climb [up] sth.; **einen Berg/die Treppe ~steigen** climb a mountain/the stairs; **b)** ⟨*balloon, kite*⟩ rise aloft; **~|streben** *itr. V.; mit sein (geh.)* soar upwards; **ein ~strebender Künstler** an aspiring artist

empört 1. *Adj.* outraged ⟨*letter, look*⟩; **über jmdn./etw. ~ sein** be outraged at sth./about sb. **2.** *adv.* **jmdn./etw. ~ zurückweisen** reject sb./sth. indignantly *or* angrily

Empörung die; ~, ~en a) *o. Pl.* outrage; **b)** *(geh.: Aufstand)* rebellion; uprising

empor|züngeln *itr. V.; mit sein (geh.)* ⟨*flames*⟩ leap up

emsig ['ɛmzɪç] **1.** *Adj. (fleißig)* industrious, busy ⟨*person*⟩; *(geschäftig)* bustling ⟨*activity*⟩; *(übereifrig)* sedulous; **ein ~es Treiben** bustling activity; a hustle and bustle; **~ wie die Ameisen** *od.* **Bienen sein** be busy as bees. **2.** *adv. (fleißig)* industriously; busily; *(übereifrig)* sedulously

Ẹmsigkeit die; ~ *(Fleiß)* industriousness; business; *(Übereifer)* sedulousness

Emu ['e:mu] **der; ~s, ~s** *(Zool.)* emu

Emulgator [emʊl'ga:tɔr] **der; ~s, ~en** [-ga'to:rən] *(Chemie)* emulsifying agent; emulsifier

Emulsion [emʊl'zio:n] **die; ~, ~en** *(Chemie, Fot., Kosmetik)* emulsion

E-Musik die; ~: serious music

en bloc [ã'blɔk] *Adv.* en bloc

ẹnd-, Ẹnd-: ~abnehmer der *(Wirtsch.)* ultimate buyer; **~ab·rechnung die** final account; **~bahn·hof der** terminus; **~betont** *Adj. (Sprachw.)* ⟨*word*⟩ with final stress; **das Wort „Berlin" ist ~betont** the word 'Berlin' is stressed on the final syllable; **~betonung die** *(Sprachw.)* final stress; **~betrag der** final amount

Ẹndchen das; ~s, ~: little bit; small piece

Ẹnd·darm der *(Anat.) (Dickdarm)* large intestine; colon; *(Afterdarm)* rectum

Ẹnd·dreißiger der man in his late thirties

Ẹnde ['ɛndə] **das; ~s, ~n a)** end; **am ~ der Straße/Stadt** at the end of the road/town; **am ~ der Welt** *(scherzh.)* at the back of beyond; **etw. am richtigen/falschen ~ anfassen** *(fig.)* go about sth. the right/wrong way; **am/bis/gegen ~ des Monats/der Woche/des Jahres/des Jahrhunderts** at/by/towards the end of the month/week/year/century; **~ April** at the end of April; **bis ~ der Woche** by the end of the week; **am ~ des Buchs/Films** at the end of the book/film; **das ~ des Films hat mir nicht gefallen** I didn't like the ending of the film; **~ zwanzig** *od.* **der Zwanziger/fünfzig** *od.* **der Fünfziger sein** be in one's late twenties/fifties; **wenn die beiden sich zanken, finden sie kein ~:** once those two start quarrelling they never stop; **zu ~ sein** ⟨*patience, hostility, war*⟩ be at an end; **die Schule/das Kino/das Spiel ist zu ~:** school is over/the film/game has finished; **zu ~ gehen** ⟨*period of time*⟩ come to an end; ⟨*supplies, savings*⟩ run out; ⟨*contract*⟩ expire; **etw. zu ~ führen** *od.* **bringen** finish sth.; **ein Buch zu ~ lesen** read a book to the end; **alles hat ein ~** *od.* **muß ein ~ haben** everything has to [come to an] end sometime; **~ gut, alles gut** all's well that ends well *(prov.)*; **ein/kein ~ nehmen** come to an end/never come to an end; **einer Sache/seinem Leben ein ~ machen** *od.* **setzen** *(geh.)* put an end to sth./take one's life; **am ~ sein** *(ugs.)* be at the end of one's tether; **ich bin mit meiner Geduld am ~:** my patience is at an end; **mit etw. am ~ sein** be at *or* have reached the end of sth.; **mit ihm geht es zu ~** *(verhüll.)* he is nearing his end; **das ~ vom Lied** *(ugs.)* the end of the story; **am ~** *(schließlich)* when all is said and done; **am ~ wird er der Täter sein** *(nordd.)* he's probably the culprit; **das ~ der Wurst** the end [piece] of the sausage; **b)** *(ugs.: kleines Stück)* bit; piece; **ein ~ Schnur** a bit *or* piece of string; **c)** *(ugs.: Strecke)* **ein ganzes ~:** a pretty long way; **d)** *(Jägerspr.)* point; **e)** *(Seemannsspr.)* rope

Ẹnd·effekt der: im ~: in the end; in the final analysis

endemisch [ɛn'de:mɪʃ] **1.** *Adj. (Biol., Med.)* endemic. **2.** *adv.* endemically

endeln ['ɛndl̩n] *tr. V. (bayr., österr.)* turn in [and oversew] ⟨*hem, seam*⟩

ẹnden *itr. V.* **a)** end; ⟨*programme*⟩ end, finish; **der Zug endet in Berlin/hier** this train terminates in Berlin/here; **gut ~:** end well; **das wird nicht gut ~:** it's bound to end in disaster; **nicht ~ wollender Beifall** unending applause; **b)** *(sterben) mit sein* **in der Gosse/im Gefängnis ~:** end up in the gutter/in prison; *(dort sterben)* die in the gutter/end one's days in prison

Ẹnd·ergebnis das final result

en détail [ãde'taj] *Adv.* **a)** *(im einzelnen)* in detail; **b)** *(Kaufmannsspr. veralt.)* retail

ẹnd-, Ẹnd-: ~fünfziger der man in his late fifties; **~geschwindigkeit die** *s.* **Höchstgeschwindigkeit; ~gültig 1.** *Adj.* final ⟨*consent, answer, decision*⟩; conclusive ⟨*evidence*⟩; **etwas/nichts Endgültiges sagen/hören** say/hear something/nothing definite; **2.** *adv.* **das ist ~gültig vorbei** that's all over and done with; **sich ~gültig trennen** separate for good; **das ist jetzt ~gültig entschieden** it's been decided once and for all; **~gültigkeit die** finality; *(von Beweisen)* conclusiveness; **~halte·stelle die** terminus

endigen ['ɛndɪgn̩] *itr. V. (veralt.) s.* **enden**

Endivie [ɛn'di:viə] **die; ~, ~n** endive

Ẹnd-: ~kampf der *(Sport)* final; *(Milit.)* final battle; **~lagerung die** permanent disposal *(of nuclear waste)*; **~lauf der** *(Sport)* final; **~lauf·teilnehmer der** finalist

ẹndlich 1. *Adv.* **a)** *(nach langer Zeit)* at last; **na ~ [kommst du]!** [so you've arrived] at [long] last; **bist du ~ soweit?** are you ready at last?; **siehst du ~ ein, daß du unrecht hattest?** do you see now that you were wrong?; **halt ~ den Mund!** why don't you shut up?; **laß mich ~ in Ruhe mit deinem Geschwätz!**

stop your babbling and leave me in peace; **b)** *(schließlich)* in the end; eventually; **wir kamen ~ doch zu einer Einigung** we did reach an agreement in the end *or* eventually. **2.** *Adj.* finite ⟨*size, number*⟩

Ẹndlichkeit die; ~: finiteness

ẹnd·los 1. *Adj.* **a)** *(ohne Ende)* infinite; *(ringförmig)* endless, continuous ⟨*belt, chain*⟩; **b)** *(nicht enden wollend)* endless ⟨*road, desert, expanse, etc.*⟩; endless, infinite ⟨*patience*⟩; interminable ⟨*speech*⟩. **2.** *adv.* **~ lange dauern** be interminably long; go on and on; **~ lange reden** talk interminably; **~ warten** wait for ages

Ẹndlos·formular das: ein ~: continuous stationery; form paper *(Amer.)*

Ẹndlosigkeit die; ~: infinity; endlessness

Ẹnd-: ~lösung die a) *(selten: endgültige Lösung)* final solution; **b)** *(ns. verhüll.)* Final Solution *(to the Jewish question)*; **~moräne die** terminal moraine

Endogamie [ɛndoga'mi:] **die; ~** *(Völkerk.)* endogamy *no art.*

endogen [ɛndo'ge:n] *Adj. (Med., Psych., Bot.)* endogenous

Endoskop [ɛndo'sko:p] **das; ~s, ~e** *(Med.)* endoscope

endotherm [ɛndo'tɛrm] *Adj. (Physik, Chemie)* endothermic

Ẹnd-: ~phase die final stages *pl.*; **~produkt das** final *or* end product; **~punkt der** end; *(einer Reise)* last stop; **~reim der** end rhyme; **~resultat das** final result; **~runde die** *(Sport)* final; **~runden·teilnehmer der** *(Sport)* finalist; **~sechziger der** man in his late sixties; **~siebziger der** man in his late seventies; **~sieg der** *(bes. ns.)* final *or* ultimate victory; **~silbe die** [word-]final syllable; **~spiel das a)** *(Sport)* final; **b)** *(Schach)* end-game; **~spurt der** *(bes. Leichtathletik)* final spurt; **einen guten ~spurt haben** have a good finish; be good in the final spurt; **~stadium das** final stage; *(Med.)* terminal stage; **Krebs im ~stadium** terminal cancer; **~stand der** *(Sport)* final result; **~station die** terminus; **~station Krankenhaus** *(fig.)* finishing up in hospital; **~stück das** end; *(eines Brotes)* crust; **~summe die** [sum] total

Ẹndung die; ~, ~en *(Sprachw.)* ending

ẹndungs·los *Adj. (Sprachw.)* without an ending *postpos., not pred.*; uninflected

ẹnd-, Ẹnd-: ~verbraucher der *(Wirtsch.)* consumer; **~verbraucher·preis der** retail price; **~vierziger der** man in his late forties; **~zeit die** *(Rel.)* last days [of the world]; **~zeitlich** *Adj. (Rel.)* apocalyptic; **~ziel das** *(einer Reise)* final destination; *(Zweck)* ultimate aim *or* goal; **~ziffer die** final number; **das Los mit der ~ziffer 4** the coupon with a number ending in 4; **~zustand der** final state; **~zwanziger der** man in his late twenties; **~zweck der** ultimate purpose *or* object

Energie [enɛr'gi:] **die; ~, ~n a)** *(Physik)* energy; **b)** *o. Pl. (Tatkraft)* energy; vigour

energi̲e-, Energi̲e-: ~arm *Adj.* ⟨*country*⟩ lacking in energy resources; **~bedarf der** energy requirement; **~bewußt** *Adj.* energy-conscious; **~bündel das** *(ugs.)* bundle of energy; **~form die** form of energy; **~geladen** *Adj.* energetic, dynamic ⟨*person*⟩; **~gewinnung die** energy production; **~haushalt der** *(Physiol.)* energy balance; *(Wirtsch.)* control of the use of energy; **~intensiv** *Adj.* energy-intensive; **~krise die** energy crisis; **~los** *Adj.* lacking [in] energy *postpos.*; sluggish; **~politik die** energy policy; **~politisch 1.** *Adj.* **~politische Maßnahmen/Programme** energy measures/programmes; **2.** *adv.* in terms of energy policy; **~quelle die** energy source; source of energy; **neuzeitliche ~quellen** modern sources of energy; **~reich** *Adj.* energy-rich; **~reichtum der** energy wealth; **~satz der** *(Physik)* principle of the conservation of energy; **~sparer der** energy-saver; **~spender der** energy-giving substance; **~träger der** energy source; **~verbrauch der** energy consumption; **~verschwendung die a)** wasting of energy; **b)** *(Verschwendung von Tatkraft)* waste of energy; **~versorgung die** energy supply; **der ~versorgung** *(Dat.)* **dienen** serve to supply energy; **~wirtschaft die** energy sector; **~zufuhr die** supply of energy

energisch [e'nɛrgɪʃ] **1.** *Adj.* **a)** *(tatkräftig)* energetic, vigorous ⟨*person*⟩; firm ⟨*action*⟩; **~ werden** put one's foot down; **b)** *(von starkem Willen zeugend)* determined; forceful; **ein ~es Kinn** a strong chin; **c)** *(entschlossen)* forceful, firm ⟨*voice, words*⟩. **2.** *adv.* **a)** *(tatkräftig)* **~ durchgreifen** take drastic action; **etw. ~ verteidigen** defend sth. vigorously; **b)** *(entschlossen)* ⟨*reject, say*⟩ forcefully, firmly; ⟨*stress*⟩ emphatically; ⟨*deny*⟩ strenuously

enervieren [enɛr'vi:rən] *tr. V. (geh.)* enervate

Enfant terrible [ãfãtɛ'ribl] **das; ~ ~, ~s ~s** *(geh.)* enfant terrible

eng [ɛŋ] **1.** *Adj.* **a)** *(schmal)* narrow ⟨*valley, road, bed*⟩; **einen ~en Horizont** *od.* **Gesichtskreis haben** *(fig.)* have a narrow *or* limited outlook; **b)** *(dicht)* close ⟨*writing*⟩; **c)** *(fest anliegend)* close-fitting, tight; **ein ~es Kleid** a close-fitting dress; **der Anzug/Rock ist zu ~:** the suit/skirt is too tight; **d)** *(beschränkt)* narrow, restricted ⟨*interpretation, concept*⟩; cramped, constricted ⟨*room, space*⟩; **e)** *im Komp. u. Sup. (begrenzt)* **in die ~ere Wahl kommen** be short-listed *(Brit.)*; **in der ~eren Wahl sein** be on the short list *(Brit.)*; **im ~eren Sinne** in the stricter sense; **f)** *(nahe)* close ⟨*friend*⟩; **im ~sten Freundeskreis** among close friends; **die Hochzeit fand im ~sten Kreis der Familie statt** the wedding was attended by close relatives [only]; **die ~ere Verwandtschaft/Heimat** one's immediate relatives/home [area]. **2.** *adv.* **a)** *(dicht)* **~ schreiben** write closely together; **~ [zusammen] sitzen/stehen** sit/stand close together; **b)** *(fest anliegend)* **~ anliegen/sitzen** fit closely; **c)** *(beschränkt)* **etw. zu ~ auslegen** interpret sth. too narrowly; **das siehst du zu ~** *(ugs.)* there's more to it than that; **d)** *(nahe)* closely; **mit jmdm. ~ befreundet sein** be a close friend of sb.

Engadin ['ɛŋgadi:n] **das; ~s** Engadine

Engagement [ãgaʒə'mã:] **das; ~s, ~s a)** *o. Pl. (Einsatz)* involvement; **sein ~ für etw.** his commitment to sth.; **sein ~ gegen etw.** his committed stand against sth.; **b)** *(eines Künstlers)* engagement

engagi̲eren [ãga'ʒi:rən] **1.** *refl. V.* commit oneself, become committed **(für** to); **sich politisch ~:** become politically involved; **sich in einer Organisation ~:** be active in an organization; **sich in einem Land/Geschäft ~** *(verhüllend)* become involved in a country/business. **2.** *tr. V. (unter Vertrag nehmen)* engage ⟨*artist, actor, etc.*⟩

engagi̲ert *Adj.* **a)** *(entschieden für etw. eintretend)* committed ⟨*literature, film, director*⟩; **politisch/sozial ~ sein** be politically/socially committed *or* involved; **b)** *(angestellt)* engaged ⟨*artist, actor, etc.*⟩

Engagi̲ertheit die; ~: commitment; involvement

ẹng-: ~anliegend *Adj. (präd. getrennt geschrieben)* tight-fitting; close-fitting; **~bedruckt** *Adj. (präd. getrennt geschrieben)* closely-printed ⟨*page*⟩; **~befreundet** *Adj. (präd. getrennt geschrieben)* **die beiden ~befreundeten Professoren/Ehepaare** the two professors/[married] couples, who are/were close friends; **~begrenzt** *Adj. (präd. getrennt geschrieben)* limited; restricted; **~beschrieben** *Adj. (präd. getrennt geschrieben)* closely-written

Enge ['ɛŋə] **die; ~, ~n a)** *o. Pl.* confinement; restriction; **b)** *(veralt.: Engpaß) (Meeres~)* strait; *(Kanal~)* narrows *pl.*; **jmdn. in die ~ treiben** *(fig.)* drive sb. into a corner

Engel ['ɛŋl̩] **der; ~s, ~:** angel; **ich habe die ~ [im Himmel] singen** *od.* **pfeifen hören** *(ugs.)* it hurt like hell; **sie ist mein guter/ein rettender/ein wahrer ~:** she is my good/a guardian/a real angel; **er ist [auch] nicht gerade ein ~:** he's not exactly an angel

Ẹngelchen das; ~s, ~, Ẹngelein das; ~s, ~: little angel

ẹngel-, Ẹngel-: ~haft *Adj.* angelic; **~macher der, ~macherin die; ~, ~nen** backstreet abortionist; **~schar die** heavenly host; host of angels

Ẹngels-: ~geduld die patience of a saint; **~gesicht das** angelic face

ẹngel[s]·gleich *Adj.* angelic

Ẹngels·haar das angel's hair

Ẹngel[s]·kopf der cherub

Ẹngels-: ~miene die innocent look; **~musik die** heavenly music; **~zungen** *Pl. in* **mit ~zungen auf jmdn. einreden** use all one's powers of persuasion on sb.

Engerling ['ɛŋɐlɪŋ] **der; ~s, ~e** grub

ẹng·herzig 1. *Adj.* petty. **2.** *adv.* in a petty way

Ẹng·herzigkeit die; ~: pettiness

Ẹngland (das); ~s a) England; **b)** *(ugs.: Großbritannien)* Britain

Engländer ['ɛŋlɛndɐ] **der; ~s, ~ a)** Englishman/English boy; **er ist ~:** he is English *or* an Englishman; **die ~:** the English; **b)** *(ugs.: Brite)* British person/man; Britisher *(Amer.)*; **die ~:** the British; **c)** *(Schraubenschlüssel)* monkey wrench

Ẹngländerin die; ~, ~nen a) Englishwoman/English girl; **sie ist ~:** she is English *or* an Englishwoman; **b)** *(ugs.: Britin)* British person/woman; **die ~nen sind ...:** British women are ...

ẹngland·freundlich *Adj.* anglophile

[1]**ẹnglisch 1.** *Adj.* English; **~-deutsch** Anglo-German; English-German ⟨*dictionary*⟩; ⟨*book*⟩ in English and German; **die ~e Sprache/Literatur** the English language/English literature; **die ~e Krankheit** *(veralt.)* rickets; **Englisch Horn** *(fachspr.) s.* **Englischhorn; Englische Bulldogge** bulldog. **2.** *adv.* **~ sprechen** speak English; **~ [gebraten]** rare; underdone; **ein ~ abgefaßter Artikel** an article in English; *s. auch* **deutsch,** [2]**Deutsche**

[2]**ẹnglisch** *Adj.* **der Englische Gruß** the Angelic Salutation; the Ave Maria; the Hail Mary; **die Englischen Fräulein** *Institute of the Blessed Virgin Mary*; the 'English Ladies'; the 'English Virgins'

Ẹnglisch das; ~[s] English; **ein gutes/fehlerfreies ~ sprechen** speak good/perfect English; **das moderne ~/~ Chaucers** present day/Chaucerian English; *s. auch* **Deutsch**

ẹnglisch-, Ẹnglisch-: ~họrn das *(Musik)* cor anglais; **~lehrer der** 'English teacher; **~sprachig** *Adj.* **a)** *(in ~er Sprache)* English-language ⟨*book, magazine*⟩; **die ~sprachige Literatur** English literature; **b)** *(~sprechend)* English-speaking ⟨*population, country*⟩; **~unterricht der** English teaching; *(Unterrichtsstunde)* English lesson; **er gibt ~unterricht** he teaches English; **sie arbeitet im ~unterricht gut mit** she always pays attention in English lessons; **das habe ich im ~unterricht gelernt** I learnt that in English

English-Waltz ['ɪŋglɪʃ 'wɔ(:)l(t)s] **der; ~, ~:** slow waltz

ẹng·maschig 1. *Adj.* **a)** close-meshed ⟨*fabric*⟩; **b)** *(Sport)* tight. **2.** *adv.* **a) ~ stricken/gestrickt sein** knit/be knitted tightly; **b)** *(Sport)* **~ spielen** play tightly

Ẹng·paß der a) [narrow] pass; defile; **b)** *(fig.: in der Versorgung usw.)* bottle-neck

en gros [ã'gro] *(Kaufmannsspr.)* wholesale

ẹng-, Ẹng-: ~stirnig 1. *Adj. (abwertend)* narrow-minded ⟨*person*⟩; **2.** *adv.* **~stirnig denken/handeln** be narrow-minded in the way one thinks/acts; **~stirnigkeit die; ~:** narrow-mindedness; **~verwandt** *Adj. (präd. getrennt geschrieben)* closely related; **~zeilig** *Adv.* with the lines closely spaced

Enjambement [ãʒãbə'mã:] **das; ~s, ~s** *(Verslehre)* enjambment

¹Enkel ['ɛŋkl̩] **der; ~s, ~** *(nordd.)* ankle

²Ẹnkel der; ~s, ~ a) grandson; **b)** *(Nachfahr)* grandchild; **selbst unsere ~ werden sich daran erinnern** even our grandchildren and great-grandchildren will remember it

Ẹnkelin die; ~, ~nen granddaughter

Ẹnkel-: ~kind das grandchild; **~sohn der** grandson; **~tochter die** granddaughter

Enklave [ɛn'kla:və] **die; ~, ~n** enclave

enkodieren [ɛnko'di:rən] *tr. V.* encode

en masse [ã'mas] *(ugs.)* en masse

en miniature [ãminja'ty:r] in miniature; **der Eiffelturm ~ ~:** the Eiffel Tower in miniature; a miniature Eiffel Tower

enorm [e'nɔrm] **1.** *Adj.* enormous ⟨*sum, costs*⟩; tremendous *(coll.)* ⟨*effort*⟩; immense ⟨*strain*⟩; vast ⟨*knowledge, sum*⟩. **2.** *adv.* tremendously *(coll.)* ⟨*expensive, practical*⟩; **~ verdienen** earn an enormous amount *or* vast sums [of money]; **~ viel/viele** a tremendous *(coll.) or* an enormous amount/a tremendous *(coll.) or* an enormous number; **sich ~ freuen** *(ugs.)* be tremendously *(coll.)* pleased

en passant [ãpa'sã] **a)** *(beiläufig)* en passant; in passing; **b)** *(Schach)* en passant

Enquete [ã'kɛ:t(ə)] **die; ~, ~n a)** survey; **b)** *(österr.: Arbeitstagung)* meeting for discussion

Ensemble [ã'sã:bl̩] **das a)** *(Gruppe)* ensemble; **das ~ eines Theaters** the company of a theatre; **b)** *(Auftritt)* ensemble; **c)** *(Kleidungsstück)* outfit; ensemble; **d)** *(geh.: Gesamtheit)* ensemble

Ensẹmble-: ~mitglied das member of the ensemble/company; **~musik die** light music

entarten *itr. V.; mit sein* degenerate; **entartet** degenerate; **zu** *od.* **in** *(Akk.)* **etw. ~:** degenerate into sth.

Entartung die; ~, ~en degeneration

Entartungs·erscheinung die sign of degeneration; **das führte zu ~en** this led to degeneracy

entasten, entästen *tr. V. (Forstw.)* disbranch

entäußern *refl. V. (geh.)* **a) sich einer Sache** *(Gen.)* **~** *(entsagen)* renounce sth.; *(weggeben)* relinquish *or* give up sth.; **b)** *(Philos.)* be realized

Entäußerung die a) *(geh.: Verzicht)* renunciation; **b)** *(Weggabe)* giving up; **c)** *(Philos.)* realization

entbehren [ɛnt'be:rən] **1.** *tr. V.* **a)** *(geh.: vermissen)* miss ⟨*person*⟩; **b)** *(verzichten)* do without; spare; **etw./jmdn. nicht ~ können** not be able to spare sth./sb.; not be able to do without sth./sb.; **viel[es] ~ müssen** have to go without [a lot of things]. **2.** *itr. V. (geh.: ermangeln)* **einer Sache** *(Gen.)* **~:** lack *or* be without sth.

entbehrlich *Adj.* dispensable; unnecessary ⟨*action*⟩

Entbehrlichkeit die; ~: superfluousness; dispensability

Entbehrung die; ~, ~en privation; **große ~en auf sich** *(Akk.)* **nehmen** make great sacrifices

entbehrungs-: ~reich, ~voll *Adj.* ⟨*life, years*⟩ of privation

entbeinen *tr. V.* bone

entbieten *unr. tr. V. (geh.)* **a)** offer ⟨*best wishes, greetings*⟩; **jmdm. seine Grüße ~:** present one's compliments to sb.; **b)** *(veralt.: kommen lassen)* summon

entbinden 1. *unr. tr. V.* **a)** *(befreien)* **jmdn. von einem Versprechen ~:** release sb. from a promise; **seines Amtes** *od.* **von seinem Amt entbunden werden** be relieved of [one's] office; **b)** *(Geburtshilfe leisten)* **jmdn. ~:** deliver sb.; deliver sb.'s baby; **von einem Jungen/Mädchen entbunden werden** give birth to a boy/girl. **2.** *unr. itr. V. (gebären)* give birth; **zu Hause ~:** have one's baby at home

Entbindung die a) *(das Gebären)* **eine schwere/schmerzfreie ~:** a difficult/painless delivery *or* birth; **zur ~ in die Klinik müssen** have to go to hospital for the delivery *or* to have the baby; **bei der ~ anwesend sein** be present at the birth; **b)** *(Befreiung)* release; **um die ~ von seinem Amt bitten** ask to be relieved of one's duties

Entbindungs-: ~saal der delivery room; **~station die** maternity ward

entblättern 1. *refl. V.* **a)** ⟨*trees, shrubs*⟩ shed its/their leaves; **b)** *(scherzh.: sich ausziehen)* strip; take one's clothes off. **2.** *tr. V.* strip ⟨*trees*⟩ [of leaves]

entblöden *refl. V.* **sich nicht ~, etw. zu tun** *(geh. abwertend)* have the effrontery to do sth.

entblößen 1. *refl. V.* take one's clothes off; ⟨*exhibitionist*⟩ expose oneself; *(sein wahres Gesicht zeigen)* show oneself as one really is/was. **2.** *tr. V.* **a) den Arm ~:** uncover one's arm; **entblößt** bare; **mit entblößtem Kopf** without a hat; **sein Schwert ~** *(dichter.)* unsheathe one's sword; **b)** *(fig.)* reveal ⟨*feelings, thoughts*⟩

entbrennen *unr. itr. V.; mit sein (geh.)* **a)** *(beginnen)* ⟨*battle*⟩ break out; ⟨*quarrel*⟩ flare up; **b)** *(ergriffen werden)* **in Liebe entbrannt sein** be passionately in love; **in Zorn entbrannt sein** be inflamed with anger

Entchen ['ɛntçən] **das; ~s, ~:** duckling

entdecken 1. *tr. V.* **a)** *(finden)* discover; **eine Insel/ein chemisches Element ~:** discover an island/a chemical element; **b)** *(ausfindig machen)* **jmdn. ~:** find *or* spot sb.; **wir konnten ihn in dem Gewühl nicht ~:** we couldn't find him in the crowd; **etw. ~:** find *or* discover sth.; **c)** *(überraschend bemerken)* discover ⟨*theft*⟩; come across ⟨*acquaintance*⟩; **d)** *(veralt.: offenbaren)* **jmdm. etw. ~:** reveal *or (arch.)* discover sth. to sb. **2.** *refl. V. (veralt.: anvertrauen)* **sich jmdm. ~:** confide in sb.

Entdecker der; ~s, ~: discoverer; *(Forschungsreisender)* explorer

Entdecker·freude die joy of discovery

Entdeckerin die; ~, ~nen *s.* **Entdecker**

Entdeckung die; ~, ~en discovery

Entdeckungs·reise die voyage of discovery; *(zu Lande)* expedition; **auf ~/~n gehen** *(fig. scherzh.)* go exploring

Ente ['ɛntə] **die; ~, ~n a)** *(Vogel, Fleisch)* duck; **eine lahme ~** *(ugs.)* a slow-coach *(coll.)*; **sein Wagen ist eine richtige lahme ~** *(ugs.)* his car totally lacks oomph *(sl.) or* has no pick-up *(Amer. sl.)*; **b)** *(ugs.: Falschmeldung)* canard; spoof *(coll.)*; **c) kalte ~:** [cold] punch; **d)** *(ugs.: Auto)* Citroën 2CV car; **e)** *(ugs.: Uringefäß)* [bed-]bottle

entehren *tr. V.* dishonour; **~d** degrading

Entehrung die dishonouring

enteignen *tr. V.* expropriate

Enteignung die expropriation

enteilen *itr. V.; mit sein (geh.)* hasten away; *(fig.)* ⟨*hours, years, etc.*⟩ fly by

enteisen *tr. V.* de-ice

enteisenen *tr. V.* remove the iron from; **stark/schwach enteisent** with very low/slightly reduced iron content

Entelechie [ɛntelɛ'çi:] **die; ~, ~n** *(Philos.)* entelechy

Ẹnten-: ~braten der roast duck; **~ei das** duck's egg; **~feder die** duck's feather; **~flott das** *(nordd.) s.* **~grütze; ~gericht das** duck dish; **~grütze die** duckweed; **~jagd die** duck shooting; **eine ~jagd** a duck shoot; **~junge das** duckling; **~klein das; ~s** *(Kochk.)* duck's giblets *pl;* **~küken das** duckling; **~schnabel der a)** duck's bill; **b)** *(Schuh)* duck-bill

Entente [ã'tã:t(ə)] **die; ~, ~n** *(Politik)* entente

Ẹnten-: ~teich der duck pond; **~wal der** bottle-nosed whale

Ẹnter·beil das boarding pike

enterben *tr. V.* disinherit

Ẹnter·brücke die boarding bridge

Enterbung die; ~, ~en disinheritance

Ẹnter·haken der grapnel; grappling iron

Enterich ['ɛntərıç] **der; ~s, ~e** drake

entern ['ɛntɐn] **1.** *tr., itr. V.* board ⟨*ship*⟩. **2.** *itr. V.; mit sein* **in die Masten ~** *(Seemannsspr.)* climb the rigging. **3.** *tr. V. (ugs.: erklettern)* climb ⟨*fence, wall, etc.*⟩; climb on to ⟨*lorry, etc.*⟩

Ẹnter·säbel der *(hist.)* cutlass

Entertainer ['ɛntɐteınɐ] **der; ~s, ~:** entertainer

entfachen *tr. V. (geh.)* **a)** kindle, light ⟨*fire*⟩; **einen Brand ~:** start a fire; **b)** *(fig.: hervorrufen)* provoke, start ⟨*quarrel, argument*⟩; arouse ⟨*passion, enthusiasm*⟩

entfahren *unr. itr. V.; mit sein* **ihm entfuhr ein Fluch/ein Seufzer** he swore inadvertently/he let out a sigh

entfallen *unr. itr. V.; mit sein* **a)** *(aus dem Gedächtnis)* **der Name/das Wort ist mir ~:** the name/word escapes me *or* has slipped my mind; **das ist mir ~:** I have forgotten; **b)** *(zugeteilt werden)* **auf jmdn./etw. ~:** be allotted to sb./sth.; **auf jeden Erben entfielen 10 000 Mark** each heir received 10,000 marks; **auf jeden Miteigentümer ~ 50 000 Mark** *(müssen bezahlt werden)* each of the joint owners has to pay 50,000 marks; **c)** *(wegfallen)* lapse; **für Kinder ~ diese Gebühren** these charges do not apply *or* are not applicable to children; **aus Zeitmangel ~:** be omitted for lack of time; **d)** *(geh.)* **jmds. Händen ~:** slip *or* fall from sb.'s hands

entfalten 1. *tr. V.* **a)** *(auseinanderfalten)* open [up]; unfold, spread out ⟨*map etc.*⟩; ⟨*plant*⟩ open ⟨*leaves*⟩; **b)** *(zeigen)* show, display ⟨*ability, talent*⟩; **c)** *(darlegen)* expound ⟨*ideas, thoughts*⟩; present ⟨*plan*⟩; **d)** *(entwickeln)* begin to show *or* display ⟨*interest, enthusiasm, etc.*⟩. **2.** *refl. V.* **a)** *(sich entwickeln)* ⟨*personality, talent*⟩ develop; **sich frei ~:** develop one's own personality to the full; **b)** *(sich öffnen)* ⟨*flower, parachute*⟩ open [up]

Entfaltung die; ~, ~en a) *(Entwicklung)* development; **die ~ der Persönlichkeit** the development of one's personality; **zur ~ kommen** *od.* **gelangen** develop; **b)** *(Darstellung)* display; *(eines Plans)* exposition; presentation

entfärben 1. *tr. V.* take the colour out of ⟨*material, clothing*⟩. **2.** *refl. V.* ⟨*material, clothing, etc.*⟩ fade

Entfärber der colour *or* dye remover

entfernen 1. *tr. V.* **a)** remove ⟨*stain, wart, etc.*⟩; take out ⟨*tonsils etc.*⟩; **jmdn. von** *od.* **aus der Schule ~:** expel sb. [from school]; **jmdn. aus seinem Amt ~:** dismiss sb. from his office; **b)** *(geh.: fortbringen)* remove. **2.** *refl. V.* go away; **sich vom Weg ~:** go off *or* leave the path; **sich unerlaubt von der Truppe ~:** go absent without leave; **sich aus der Stadt/dem Büro ~:** leave [the] town/the office; **langsam entfernten sich die Schritte** the footsteps slowly receded

entfernt 1. *Adj.* **a)** *(fern)* remote; **das ist** *od.* **liegt weit ~ von der Stadt** it is a long way from the town *or* out of town; **er ist weit davon ~, das zu tun** *(fig.)* he does not have the slightest intention of doing that; **10 km/zwei Stunden [von einem Punkt] ~:** 10 km/two hours away [from a place]; **b)** *nicht präd. (weitläufig)* slight ⟨*acquaintance*⟩; distant ⟨*relation*⟩; **c)** *(schwach)* slight, vague ⟨*resemblance*⟩. **2.** *adv.* **a)** *(fern)* remotely; **das stört mich nicht im ~esten** that does not bother me in the slightest *or* in the least; **er dachte nicht ~** *od.* **im ~esten daran, das zu tun** he did not have the slightest intention of doing that; **b)** *(weitläufig)* slightly ⟨*acquainted*⟩; distantly ⟨*related*⟩; **mit jmdm. ~ verwandt sein** be distantly related to sb.; **c)** *(schwach)* slightly, vaguely; **sich ~ an etw.** *(Akk.)* **erinnern** remember sth. vaguely; have a vague recollection of sth.

Entfernung die; ~, ~en a) *(Abstand)* distance; *(beim Schießen)* range; **in einer ~ von 100 m** at a distance/range of 100 m.; 100 m. away; **auf eine ~ von 100 m** from a distance of 100 m.; **aus der ~:** from a distance; **b)** *(das Beseitigen)* removal; **c)** *(das Weggehen)* **unerlaubte ~ von der Truppe** absence without leave

Entfernungs·messer der *(Gerät)* rangefinder

entfesseln *tr. V.* unleash ⟨*war, riot, etc.*⟩; raise ⟨*laughter etc.*⟩; **die entfesselten Elemente** *od.* **Naturgewalten** the raging elements; **entfesselte Leidenschaften** *(geh.)* unbridled passions

Entfesselungs·künstler der escapologist

entfetten *tr. V.* skim ⟨*milk*⟩; scour ⟨*wool*⟩; dry ⟨*skin*⟩

Entfettungs·kur die diet to remove one's excess fat

entflammbar *Adj.* **a)** inflammable; **b)** *(begeisterungsfähig)* easily roused

entflammen 1. *tr. V.* arouse ⟨*enthusiasm etc*⟩; **jmdn. für etw. ~:** arouse sb.'s enthusiasm for sth. **2.** *itr. V.; mit sein* **a)** ⟨*hatred etc.*⟩ flare up; ⟨*battle, strike*⟩ break out; **er ist [in Liebe] für sie entflammt** he became enraptured with her; *(Zustand)* he is passionately in love with her

entflechten *unr. (auch regelm.) tr. V.* **a)** *(entwirren)* disentangle; **b)** *(Wirtsch.)* break up ⟨*cartel etc.*⟩

Entflechtung die; ~, ~en *(Wirtsch.)* breaking-up; break-up

entfleuchen *itr. V.; mit sein (altertümelnd scherzh.)* get *or* run away

entfliegen *unr. itr. V.; mit sein* fly away; **gestern ist uns** *(Dat.)* **unser Kanarienvogel entflogen** yesterday our canary got away; **„Wellensittich entflogen"** 'budgerigar lost'

entfliehen *unr. itr. V.; mit sein* **a)** escape; **jmdm. ~:** escape from sb.; **dem Alltag ~** *(geh.)* escape from the daily routine; **b)** *(geh.: entschwinden)* ⟨*time*⟩ fly by

entfremden 1. *tr. V.* **a)** *(fremd machen)* **jmdn. einer Sache** *(Dat.)* **~:** alienate *or* estrange sb. from sth.; **etw. seinem Zweck ~:** use sth. for a different purpose; **b)** *(Philos., Soziol.)* **entfremdet** alienated ⟨*person, work, etc.*⟩. **2.** *refl. V.* **sich jmdm./einer Sache ~:** become estranged from sb./unfamiliar with sth.

Entfremdung die; ~, ~en a) alienation; estrangement; **die ~ von jmdm./etw.** alienation *or* estrangement from sb./sth.; **die ~ zwischen Regierung und Volk** the government's alienation from the people; **b)** *(Philos., Soziol.)* alienation

entfrosten *tr. V.* defrost ⟨*refrigerator etc.*⟩; defrost, de-ice ⟨*windscreen etc.*⟩

Entfroster der; ~s, ~: defroster; de-icer

entführen *tr. V.* **a)** kidnap, abduct ⟨*child etc.*⟩; hijack ⟨*plane, lorry, etc.*⟩; **b)** *(scherzh.: mitnehmen)* steal; make off with

Entführer der *s.* **entführen a:** kidnapper; abducter; hijacker

Entführung die *s.* **entführen a:** kidnap; kidnapping; abduction; hijack; hijacking; **„Die ~ aus dem Serail"** 'Il Seraglio'

entgegen 1. *Adv.* **a)** *(auf ... zu)* towards; **der Sonne ~!** on towards the sun!; **b)** *(zuwider)* **alles, was ihnen ~ war** everything they did not like. **2.** *Präp. mit Dat.* **~ meinem Wunsch** against my wishes; **~ dem Befehl** contrary to orders

entgegen-, Entgegen-: ~|arbeiten *itr. V.* **jmdm./einer Sache** *(Dat.)* **~arbeiten** work against sb./sth.; **~|blicken** *itr. V. (geh.)* **a) jmdm. freudig/böse ~blicken** happily/angrily watch sb. coming; **b)** *(fig.: ~sehen)* **der Zukunft froh/mit Bangen ~blicken** look towards the future with joy/fear; **~|branden** *itr. V.; mit sein (geh.)* **dem Künstler brandete Beifall ~:** the artist received *or* was greeted with a great wave of applause; **~|bringen** *unr. tr. V. (fig.)* **jmdm. Liebe/Verständnis ~bringen** show sb. love/understanding; **~|eilen** *itr. V.; mit sein* **a) jmdm. ~eilen** hurry to meet sb.; **b)** *(fig.: ~gehen)* **einer Sache** *(Dat.)* **~eilen** rush towards sth.; **~|fahren** *unr. itr. V.; mit sein* **jmdm. ~fahren** come/go to meet sb.; **~|fiebern** *itr. V.* **einem Ereignis ~fiebern** look forward to an event with nervous anticipation; **~|gehen** *unr. itr. V.; mit sein* **a) jmdm. [ein Stück] ~gehen** go [a little way] to meet sb.; **b)** *(fig.)* **einer Katastrophe/schweren Zeiten ~gehen** be heading for *or* towards a catastrophe/hard times; **der Vollendung/dem Ende ~gehen** be approaching completion/its end; **~gesetzt 1.** *Adj.* **a)** *(umgekehrt)* opposite ⟨*end, direction*⟩; **sie gingen in ~gesetzter Richtung davon** they went off in opposite directions; **b)** *(gegensätzlich)* opposing; **~gesetzter Meinung sein** hold opposing views; **das Entgegengesetzte tun** do the opposite; **2.** *adv.* **genau ~gesetzt handeln/denken** do/think exactly the opposite; **~|halten** *unr. tr. V.* **a) jmdm. etw. ~halten** offer sth. to sb.; **b)** *(fig.: einwenden)* **einem Argument ein anderes ~halten** counter an argument with another; **~halten, daß ...:** counter that ...; **~|kommen** *unr. itr. V.; mit sein* **a)** *(zukommen auf)* **jmdm. ~kommen** come to meet sb.; **der ~kommende Verkehr** oncoming traffic; **b)** *(Zugeständnisse machen)* **jmdm. ~kommen** be accommodating towards sb.; **dem Verhandlungspartner ~kommen** make concessions to one's opposite number in the negotiations; **sie/das kam unseren Wünschen ~:** she complied with our wishes/it was what we wanted; **c)** *(entsprechen)* **einer Sache** *(Dat.)* **~kommen** comply with *or* fit in with sth.; **~kommen das a)** *(Konzilianz)* cooperation; **wenn er etwas mehr ~kommen gezeigt hätte** if he had shown a little more willingness to co-operate; **b)** *(Zugeständnis)* concession; **zu keinem ~kommen bereit sein** be unwilling to make any concessions; **~kommend** *Adj.* obliging; **~kommenderweise** *Adv.* obligingly; **~|laufen** *unr. itr. V.; mit sein* **a) jmdm. ~laufen** run to meet sb.; **b)** *(sich widersprechen)* **einander ~laufen** conflict with each other; **~nahme die** *(Amtsdt.)* receipt; **bei ~nahme** on receipt; **~|nehmen** *unr. itr. V.* receive; **ein Paket ~nehmen** accept a parcel; **~|schlagen** *unr. itr. V.* **a)** *mit sein* **eine Rauchwolke/ein übler Geruch schlug mir ~:** I encountered a cloud of smoke/a foul smell; **ihm schlug eine Welle der Entrüstung ~:** he was met by a wave of indignation; **b)** *(geh.)* **die Herzen schlugen ihm ~:** their/our *etc.* hearts went out to him; **~|sehen** *unr. itr. V.* **a) einer Sache** *(Dat.)* **~sehen** look forward to sth.; **einem Ereignis freudig ~sehen** look forward eagerly to an event; **b)** *(~blicken)* **den eintreffenden Gästen ~sehen** watch the guests arriving; **~|setzen** *tr. V.* **a) einer Sache** *(Dat.)* **etw. ~setzen** oppose sth. with sth.; **einer Sache** *(Dat.)* **Widerstand ~setzen** resist sth.; **b)** *(gegenüberstellen)* **einer Behauptung/einem Argument etw. ~setzen** counter a claim/an argument with sth.; **~|stehen** *unr. itr. V.* **a)** *(hinderlich sein)* **einer Sache** *(Dat.)* **~stehen** stand in the way of sth.; **dem steht nichts ~:** there's no reason why not; **b)** *(im Gegensatz stehen zu)* **einer Sache** *(Dat.)* **~stehen** conflict with sth.; **~|stellen** *tr. V.: s.* **~setzen b; ~|strecken** *tr. V.* **jmdm. etw. ~strecken** hold sth. out towards sb.; **~|treten** *unr. itr. V.; mit sein* **a)** *(in den Weg treten)* go/come up to; **einem Angreifer ~treten** go into action against an attacker; **Schwierigkeiten** *(Dat.)* **~treten** stand up to difficulties; **einem Angriff ~treten** answer an attack; **b)** *(sich wehren gegen)* **Vorwürfen/Anschuldigungen ~treten** answer reproaches/accusations; **~|wirken** *itr. V.* **einer Sache** *(Dat.)* **~wirken** [actively] oppose sth.; **die Regierung sollte diesem Mißbrauch ~wirken** the Government should do something to halt this abuse

entgegnen [ɛnt'ge:gnən] *tr. V.* retort; reply; **einer Sache** *(Dat.)* **etw. ~:** say sth. in reply to sth.; **jmdm. ~, daß ...:** reply that ...

Entgegnung die; ~, ~en retort; reply; **als ~ darauf** in reply

entgehen *unr. itr. V.; mit sein* **a)** *(entkommen)* escape; **einer Gefahr/Strafe** *(Dat.)* **~:** escape *or* avoid danger/punishment; **b)** *(versäumt, ausgelassen werden)* miss; **das darf man sich** *(Dat.)* **nicht ~ lassen** that is not to be missed; **c)** *(nicht bemerkt werden)* **jmdm. entgeht etw.** sb. misses sth.; sb. fails to see sth.; **ihm ist nicht entgangen, daß ...:** it has not escaped his notice that ...

entgeistert [ɛnt'gaistɐt] *Adj.* dumbfounded; **jmdn. ~ anstarren** stare at sb. in amazement *or* astonishment

Entgelt [ɛnt'gɛlt] **das; ~[e]s, ~e** payment; fee; **gegen** *od.* **für ein geringes ~:** for a small fee; **ohne ~:** free of charge

entgelten *unr. tr. V. (geh.)* pay for *(also fig.)*; **jmdm. eine Arbeit ~:** pay sb. a job; **jmdn. etw. ~ lassen** make sb. pay for sth.

entgeltlich *(Papierdt.)* **1.** *Adj.* payable. **2.** *adv.* on payment of a fee

entgiften *tr. V.* decontaminate ⟨*substance etc.*⟩; detoxicate ⟨*body etc.*⟩

Entgiftung die; ~, ~en decontamination; detoxication

entgleisen *itr. V.; mit sein* **a)** be derailed; **der Zug ist entgleist** the train was derailed; **das Entgleisen** the derailment; **b)** *(in Gesellschaft)* make *or* commit a/some faux pas

Entgleisung die; ~, ~en *s.* **entgleisen: a)** derailment; **b)** faux pas

entgleiten *unr. itr. V.; mit sein (geh.)* **a)** slip; **jmds. Händen ~:** slip from sb.'s hands; **b)** *(fig.)* **jmdm. entgleitet etw.** sb. loses his/her grip on sth.

entgräten *tr. V.* fillet; bone; **entgräteter Fisch** filleted fish

enthaaren *tr. V.* remove hair from; depilate *(formal)*

Enthaarungs·mittel das hair remover; depilatory

[1]enthalten 1. *unr. tr. V.* contain. **2.** *unr. refl. V.* **sich einer Sache** *(Gen.)* **~:** abstain from sth.; **sich der Stimme ~:** abstain; **sich jeder Meinung/Äußerung ~:** refrain from giving any opinion/making any comment

[2]enthalten *Adj.* **in etw.** *(Dat.)* **~ sein** be contained in sth.; **die im Wasser ~en Stoffe** the substances contained in water; **wie oft ist 4 in 12 ~?** how many times does 4 go into 12?; **das ist im Preis ~:** that is included in the price

enthaltsam 1. *Adj.* abstemious; *(sexuell)* abstinent. **2.** *adv.* **in bezug auf etw.** *(Akk.)* **~ sein** be moderate regarding sth.; **~ leben** live in abstinence

Enthaltsamkeit die; ~: abstinence

Enthaltung die abstention; **mit 20 Stimmen bei 3 ~en gewählt werden** be elected by 20 votes with 3 abstentions

enthärten *tr. V.* soften ⟨*water*⟩

Enthärtungs·mittel das [water] softener

enthaupten *tr. V. (geh.)* behead

Enthauptung die; ~, ~en *(geh.)* beheading
enthäuten *tr. V.* skin
entheben *unr. tr. V. (geh.)* relieve; **jmdn. seines Amtes ~**: relieve sb. of his/her office; **aller Sorgen enthoben sein** be relieved of all one's cares; **einer Verpflichtung enthoben werden** be released from an obligation
entheiligen *tr. V.* desecrate, profane ⟨*sabbath*⟩
enthemmen *tr., itr. V.* **jmdn. ~**: make sb. lose his/her inhibitions; free sb. from his/her inhibitions; **Alkohol enthemmt** alcohol takes away one's inhibitions
enthemmend 1. *Adj.* disinhibitory ⟨*effect, etc.*⟩. **2.** *adv.* ~ **wirken** take away sb.'s inhibitions
enthemmt 1. *s.* **enthemmen. 2.** *Adj.* uninhibited
Enthemmtheit die; ~, **Enthemmung die** loss of inhibition[s]; disinhibition *(Psych.)*
enthüllen 1. *tr. V.* **a)** unveil ⟨*monument etc.*⟩; reveal ⟨*face, etc.*⟩; **b)** *(offenbaren)* reveal ⟨*truth, secret*⟩; disclose ⟨*secret*⟩; *(Zeitungsw.)* expose ⟨*scandal*⟩. **2.** *refl. V. (sich offenbaren)* **sich [jmdm.] ~**: be revealed [to sb.]; **sich als etw. ~**: be revealed as *or* turn out to be sth.
Enthüllung die; ~, ~en *s.* **enthüllen: a)** *(das Enthüllen)* unveiling; revelation; disclosure; exposé; **b)** *(das Enthüllte)* revelation; disclosure
enthülsen *tr. V.* shell; pod
Enthusiasmus [ɛntuˈzi̯asmʊs] **der**; ~: enthusiasm
Enthusiast der; ~en, ~en, **Enthusiastin die**; ~, ~nen enthusiast
enthusiastisch 1. *Adj.* enthusiastic. **2.** *adv.* enthusiastically
Entität [ɛntiˈtɛːt] **die**; ~, ~en *(Philos.)* entity
entjungfern *tr. V.* deflower
Entjungferung die; ~, ~en defloration
entkalken *tr. V.* decalcify
entkeimen *tr. V.* **a)** *(keimfrei machen)* sterilize ⟨*water etc.*⟩; **b)** *(Triebe entfernen von)* remove the shoots from ⟨*potatoes etc.*⟩
entkernen *tr. V.* **a)** core ⟨*apple etc.*⟩; stone, remove stone from ⟨*plum etc.*⟩; remove pips from ⟨*grape etc.*⟩; **b)** *(Städtebau)* reduce the density of ⟨*town*⟩
entkleiden *tr. V. (geh.)* **a) jmdn./sich ~**: undress sb./undress; **die entkleidete Leiche einer Unbekannten** the unclothed body of an unknown woman; **b)** *(berauben)* strip; **jmdn. einer Sache** *(Gen.)* **~**: strip sb. of sth.
Entkleidung die undressing
entknoten 1. *tr. V.* untie, undo ⟨*string etc.*⟩; unravel ⟨*wool etc.*⟩. **2.** *refl. V. (fig.)* ⟨*plot etc.*⟩ unravel itself
entkoffeiniert [ɛntkɔfeiˈniːɐ̯t] *Adj.* decaffeinated
Entkolon[ial]isierung die decolonization
entkommen *unr. itr. V.; mit sein* escape; **jmdm./einer Sache ~**: escape *or* get away from sb./sth.; **es gibt kein Entkommen** there is no escape
entkorken *tr. V.* uncork ⟨*bottle*⟩
entkräften [ɛntˈkrɛftn̩] *tr. V.* **a)** weaken; **völlig ~**: exhaust; **von etw. [völlig] entkräftet sein** be [utterly] exhausted by sth.; **b)** *(widerlegen)* refute, invalidate ⟨*argument etc.*⟩; remove ⟨*suspicion etc.*⟩
Entkräftung die; ~, ~en **a)** debility; **völlige ~**: exhaustion; **an** *od.* **vor ~** *(Dat.)* **sterben** die of exhaustion; **b)** *(Widerlegung)* refutation; invalidation
entkrampfen 1. *tr. V.* **a)** relax ⟨*body etc.*⟩; loosen, relax ⟨*muscles etc.*⟩; **b)** *(fig.)* ease ⟨*situation, tension*⟩; **2.** *refl. V.* **a)** relax; **b)** *(fig.)* ⟨*atmosphere etc.*⟩ become relaxed
Entkrampfung die; ~, ~en *s.* **entkrampfen**: relaxation; loosening; easing
entkriminalisieren *tr. V.* legalize; make legal
entladen 1. *unr. tr. V.* unload ⟨*vehicle, ship, luggage, gun*⟩; discharge ⟨*battery*⟩; *s. auch* [1]**beladen a. 2.** *unr. refl. V.* **a)** ⟨*storm*⟩ break; **b)** *(fig.: hervorbrechen)* ⟨*anger etc.*⟩ erupt; ⟨*aggression etc.*⟩ be released; **sich in etw.** *(Dat.)* **~**: release itself in sth.; **c)** *(Elektrot.)* ⟨*battery*⟩ run down; **d)** ⟨*gun*⟩ go off
Entladung die *s.* **entladen 1, 2b**: unloading; discharge; eruption; release; **etw. zur ~ bringen** *(fig.)* cause sth. to erupt
entlang 1. *Präp. mit Akk. u. Dat.* along; **den Weg ~, ~ dem Weg** along the path. **2.** *Adv.* along; **hier/dort ~, bitte!** this/that way please!
entlang-: **~|fahren** *unr. itr. V.; mit sein* **a)** drive along; **die Straße/den** *od.* **am Fluß ~fahren** drive *or* go down the street/along the river; **b)** *(streichen)* go along; **er fuhr mit dem Finger die** *od.* **an der Tischkante ~**: he ran his finger along the edge of the table; **~|führen 1.** *tr. V.* lead along; **jmdn. die Straße ~führen** lead sb. along *or* down the street; **2.** *itr. V. (verlaufen)* run *or* go along; **die Straße führt am** *od.* **den Fluß ~**: the road runs *or* goes along the river; **~|gehen** *unr. itr. V.; mit sein* ⟨*person*⟩ go *or* walk along; **bitte gehen Sie hier ~**: [go] this way please; **~|kommen** *unr. itr. V.; mit sein* come along; **~|laufen** *unr. itr. V.; mit sein* **a)** go *or* walk/run along; **b)** *(verlaufen)* go *or* run along
entlarven *tr. V.* expose; **jmdn. als Schwindler ~**: expose sb. as *or* show sb. to be a swindler
Entlarvung die; ~, ~en exposure
Entlaß- *(südd.) s.* **Entlassungs-**
entlassen *unr. tr. V.* **a)** *(aus dem Gefängnis)* release; *(aus dem Krankenhaus, der Armee)* discharge; **jmd. wird aus der Schule ~**: sb. leaves school; **jmdn. aus der** *od.* **seiner Staatsbürgerschaft ~**: release sb. from citizenship; **b)** *(aus einem Arbeitsverhältnis)* dismiss; *(wegen Arbeitsmangels)* make redundant *(Brit.)*; lay off; **bei einer Firma ~ werden** be dismissed from/be made redundant *(Brit.) or* laid off by a company; **c)** *(geh.: gehen lassen)* release
Entlassung die; ~, ~en **a)** *(aus dem Gefängnis)* release; *(aus dem Krankenhaus, der Armee)* discharge; *(aus der Schule)* leaving; **~ aus der Staatsbürgerschaft** release from citizenship; **b)** *(aus einem Arbeitsverhältnis)* dismissal; *(wegen Arbeitsmangels)* redundancy *(Brit.)*; laying off; **c)** *(Entlassungsschreiben)* notice of dismissal; *(wegen Arbeitsmangels)* redundancy notice *(Brit.)*; pink slip *(Amer.)*
Entlassungs-: **~feier die** *(Schulw.)* school-leaving *or (Amer.)* graduation ceremony; **~gesuch das** resignation; **~papiere** *Pl. (eines Soldaten)* discharge papers; *(eines Häftlings)* release papers; **~schreiben das** *(Arbeitsw.)* notice of dismissal; *(wegen Arbeitsmangels)* redundancy notice *(Brit.)*; pink slip *(Amer.)*
entlasten *tr. V.* **a)** *(Rechtsspr.)* exonerate ⟨*defendant*⟩; **b)** *(Beanspruchung mindern)* **jmdn. ~**: relieve *or* take the load off sb.; **den Verkehr ~**: ease the traffic; **den Kreislauf ~**: relieve the strain on the circulation; **c)** *(erleichtern)* **sein Gewissen ~**: ease *or* relieve one's conscience; **d)** *(Finanzw.)* **sein Konto ~**: pay off the amount owed on one's account; **e)** *(Kaufmannssspr.)* approve the actions of ⟨*chairman, board, etc.*⟩
Entlastung die; ~, ~en **a)** *(Rechtsw.)* exoneration; defence; **zu jmds. ~**: in sb.'s defence; **b)** *(Minderung der Belastung)* relief; **die ~ eines Menschen/des Körpers/der Straßen** relief of the burden on a person/the body/the roads; **c)** *(Person od. Sache)* **eine große ~ für seinen Vater** a great help to his father; **eine ungeheure ~ für den Ortsverkehr** an enormous relief for local traffic; **d)** *(Erleichterung)* easing; relief; **wir senden Ihnen Ihre Unterlagen zu unserer ~ zurück** we are returning your documents for safe keeping; **e)** *(Finanzw.)* **die ~ eines Kontos** paying off the amount owed on an account; **f)** *(Kaufmannsspr.)* approval of the actions of ⟨*chairman, board, etc.*⟩
Entlastungs-: **~material das** *(Rechtsw.)* evidence for the defence; **~zeuge der** *(Rechtsw.)* witness for the defence; defence witness; **~zug der** *(Eisenb.)* relief train
entlauben 1. *tr. V.* strip ⟨*branch*⟩; defoliate ⟨*forest, area*⟩. **2.** *refl. V.* ⟨*tree*⟩ shed its leaves; **entlaubte Äste** bare branches
Entlaubung die; ~, ~en defoliation
Entlaubungs·mittel das defoliant
entlaufen *unr. itr. V.; mit sein* run away; **jmdm. ~**: run away from sb.; **ein ~er Sträfling/Sklave** an escaped convict/a runaway slave; **„Hund ~"** 'dog missing *or* lost'
entlausen *tr. V.* delouse
Entlausung die; ~, ~en delousing
entledigen *refl. V. (geh.)* **a) sich jmds./einer Sache** *(Gen.)* **~**: dispose of *or* rid oneself of sb./sth.; **b) sich eines Kleidungsstücks ~**: remove an item of clothing; **c)** *(erledigen)* **sich einer Aufgabe/einer Schuld/seiner Pflichten ~**: carry out a task/discharge a debt/one's duty
entleeren 1. *tr. V.* **a)** empty ⟨*ashtray etc.*⟩; evacuate ⟨*bowels, bladder*⟩. **2.** *refl. V.* **a)** *(leer werden)* empty; become empty; **b)** *(fig.: seinen Sinn verlieren)* ⟨*concept, tradition*⟩ lose its meaning
Entleerung die a) *(das Leermachen)* emptying; **b)** *(fig.: von Werten, Begriffen)* erosion; **c)** *(Med.)* evacuation
entlegen *Adj.* **a)** *(entfernt)* remote, out-of-the-way ⟨*place*⟩; **b)** *(abwegig)* remote, little-known ⟨*word, expression*⟩; out-of-the-way, odd ⟨*theory etc.*⟩
entlehnen *tr. V.* borrow (*Dat.*, **aus** from)
Entlehnung die; ~, ~en borrowing; **das Wort ist eine ~ aus dem Lateinischen** the word is borrowed *or* a borrowing from the Latin
entleiben *refl. V. (geh. veralt.)* take one's own life
entleihen *unr. tr. V.* borrow; **entliehene Bücher** borrowed books
Entleiher der; ~s, ~: borrower
Entlein [ˈɛntlai̯n] **das**; ~s, ~: duckling; **ein häßliches ~** *(ugs. scherzh.)* an ugly duckling
entloben *refl. V.* break off one's *or* the engagement
Entlobung die; ~, ~en breaking off [of] one's *or* the engagement
entlocken *tr. V. (geh.)* **jmdm. etw. ~**: elicit sth. from sb.; **jmdm. Begeisterung ~**: arouse enthusiasm in sb.; **jmdm. ein Geheimnis ~**: worm a secret out of sb.; **jmdm. ein Lächeln ~**: draw a smile from sb.
entlohnen, *(bes. schweiz.)* **entlöhnen** *tr. V.* pay; **jmdn. [für etw.] ~**: pay sb. [for sth.]
Entlohnung die; ~, ~en payment; *(Lohn)* pay
entlüften *tr. V.* **a)** ventilate; **b)** *(Technik)* bleed ⟨*brakes, radiator, etc.*⟩
Entlüfter der; ~s, ~ **a)** ventilator; **b)** *(Technik)* bleeder
Entlüftung die ventilation; *(Anlage)* ventilation [system]
Entlüftungs-: **~an·lage die** ventilation system; **~ventil das** air-release valve
entmachten *tr. V.* deprive of power
Entmachtung die; ~, ~en deprivation of power
entmannen *tr. V.* castrate; *(fig.)* emasculate
Entmannung die; ~, ~en castration; *(fig.)* emasculation
entmaterialisieren *tr. V. (bes. Philos.)* dematerialize
entmenschen, entmenschlichen *tr. V.* **a)** dehumanize; **b)** *(verrohen)* brutalize
entmenscht *Adj.* brutalized
entmieten *tr. V. (Amtsspr.)* drive out the tenants of

entmilitarisieren *tr. V.* demilitarize; **eine entmilitarisierte Zone** a demilitarized zone
Entmilitarisierung die demilitarization
entminen *tr. V.* clear of mines
entmisten *tr. V.* muck out
entmotten *tr. V. (Technik)* de-mothball
entmündigen *tr. V. (Rechtsw.)* incapacitate; *(fig.)* deprive of the right of decision
Entmündigung die; ~, ~en *(jur.)* incapacitation; *(fig.)* deprivation of the right of decision
entmutigen *tr. V.* discourage; dishearten; **laß dich nicht ~:** don't be discouraged
Entmutigung die; ~, ~en discouragement
Entmythologisierung die demythologization
Entnahme die; ~, ~n *(von Wasser)* drawing; *(von Geld, Blutprobe)* taking; *(von Blut)* extraction; *(von Organen)* removal
entnazifizieren [ɛntnatsifi'tsi:rən] *tr. V.* denazify
Entnazifizierung die; ~, ~en denazification
entnehmen *unr. tr. V.* **a)** *(herausnehmen aus)* **etw. [einer Sache** *(Dat.)***] ~:** take sth. [from sth.]; **der Kasse Geld ~:** take money out of the till; **jmdm. Blut/eine Blutprobe ~:** take a blood sample from sb.; **Organe ~:** remove organs; **b)** *(ersehen aus)* gather; **einer Sache** *(Dat.)* **etw. ~ können** be able to gather sth. from sth.; **wie wir Ihrem Schreiben ~, ...:** we gather from your letter that ...
entnerven *tr. V.* **jmdn. ~:** be nerve-racking for sb.
entnervend *Adj.* nerve-racking
entölen *tr. V.* remove fat from ‹*cocoa*›; **stark/schwach entölt** with very low/slightly reduced fat content *postpos., not pred.*
Entomologie [ɛntomolo'gi:] **die; ~:** entomology *no art.*
entpflichten *tr. V.* release
entprivatisieren *tr. V.* nationalize; take out of the private sector
entpuppen *refl. V.* **sich als etw./jmd. ~:** turn out to be sth./sb.
entquellen *unr. itr. V.; mit sein (geh.)* **einer Sache** *(Dat.)* **~:** pour from sth.; **Tränen entquollen ihren Augen** tears streamed from her eyes
entrahmen *tr. V.* skim ‹*milk*›
entraten *unr. itr. V. (geh.)* **jmds./einer Sache ~:** dispense with sb./sth.; **einer Sache** *(Gen.)* **~ müssen** have to do without sth.
enträtseln 1. *tr. V.* decipher ‹*code etc.*›; understand, fathom ‹*behaviour etc.*›. **2.** *refl. V.* ‹*mystery, secret, etc.*› be solved
entrechten *tr. V.* **jmdn. ~:** deprive sb. of his/her rights
Entrechtete der/die; *adj. Dekl.* person deprived of his/her rights
Entrecote [ãtrə'ko:t] **das; ~[s], ~s** *(Kochk.)* entrecôte
Entree [ã'tre:] **das; ~s, ~s a)** *(Kochk.)* entrée; **b)** *(Eingang)* [entrance] hall; **c)** *(Erscheinen)* entrance; **d)** *(bes. österr.: Eintrittsgeld)* entrance *or* admission fee
entreißen *unr. tr. V.* **a)** *(wegnehmen)* **jmdm. etw. ~:** snatch sth. from sb.; **b)** *(retten vor)* **jmdn. dem Tod ~:** save sb. from imminent death; **c)** *(geh.: befreien von)* **jmdn./etw. dem Vergessen ~:** rescue sb./sth. from oblivion
entrichten *tr. V. (Amtsspr.)* pay ‹*fee*›; **jede Familie mußte dem Krieg ihren Tribut ~** *(fig.)* the war took its toll of every family
entriegeln *tr. V.* unbolt
entrinden *tr. V.* strip the bark off; decorticate
entringen *(geh.)* **1.** *unr. tr. V. (wegnehmen)* **jmdm. etw. ~:** wrest sth. from sb. **2.** *unr. refl. V.* **sich [einer Sache** *(Dat.)***] ~:** escape [from sth.]; **ein Seufzer entrang sich ihrer Brust** she heaved a sigh
entrinnen *unr. itr. V.; mit sein (geh.)* **a)** *(entgehen)* **einer Sache** *(Dat.)* **~:** escape sth.; **b)** *(dichter.)* ‹*time*› fly by
entrollen 1. *tr. V. (geh.)* unroll. **2.** *refl. V. (fig.)* unfold
Entropie [ɛntro'pi:] **die; ~, ~n** *(fachspr.)* entropy
entrosten *tr. V.* derust
entrücken *tr. V. (geh.)* **jmdn. ~:** carry sb. [far] away *(fig.)* (*Dat.* from); **entrückt** carried away; transported; *(gedankenverloren)* lost in reverie; **jmdm./einer Sache entrückt sein** be far away from sb./sth.; **in eine bessere Welt entrückt** transported to a better world
Entrücktheit die; ~, ~en *(geh.)* reverie; **in völliger ~:** completely lost in reverie
entrümpeln [ɛnt'rʏmpl̩n] *tr. V.* clear out
Entrümpelung die; ~, ~en clear-out; clearing out
entrußen *tr. V.* clear of soot
entrüsten 1. *refl. V.* **sich [über etw.** *(Akk.)***] ~:** be indignant [at *or* about sth.]. **2.** *tr. V. (empören)* **jmdn. ~:** make sb. indignant; **über etw.** *(Akk.)* **entrüstet/aufs höchste entrüstet sein** be indignant/outraged at sth.; **etw. entrüstet tun** do sth. indignantly
Entrüstung die indignation **(über +** *Akk.* at, about)
entsaften *tr. V.* extract the juice from
Entsafter der; ~s, ~: juice-extractor
entsagen *itr. V. (geh.)* **einem Genuß ~:** renounce *or* forgo a pleasure; **der Welt ~:** renounce the world; **sie mußte lernen zu ~:** she had to learn self-denial
Entsagung die; ~, ~en *(geh.)* renunciation; **viele ~en auf sich** *(Akk.)* **nehmen** renounce many things
entsagungs·voll *Adj.* **a)** full of self-denial *postpos.*; **b)** *(Entsagungen verlangend)* full of privation *postpos.*
entsalzen *tr. V.* desalinate
Entsalzung die; ~, ~en desalination
Entsalzungs·anlage die desalination plant; *(bei Erdölgewinnung)* brine separator
Entsatz der; *o. Pl. (Milit.)* **a)** relief; **b)** *(~truppe)* relief troops *pl.*
entsäuern *tr. V.* deacidify; disacidify
entschädigen *tr. V.* compensate **(für** for); **jmdn. für etw. ~** *(fig.)* make up for sth.
Entschädigung die compensation *no indef. art.*
entschädigungs-, Entschädigungs-: ~los *Adj., adv.* without compensation; **~summe die** compensation *no indef. art.*
entschärfen *tr. V.* **a)** defuse, deactivate ‹*bomb etc.*›; control ‹*avalanche*›; blunt ‹*edge etc.*›; make ‹*hill, slope*› less steep; alleviate ‹*disaster, crisis*›; **b)** *(fig.)* defuse ‹*situation*›; tone down ‹*discussion, criticism*›
Entschärfung die; ~, ~en a) *(von Bomben usw.)* defusing; deactivation; **b)** *(fig.)* defusing; toning down
Entscheid [ɛnt'ʃait] **der; ~[e]s, ~e** decision
entscheiden 1. *unr. refl. V.* **a)** decide; **sich für/gegen jmdn./etw. ~:** decide on *or* in favour of/against sb./sth.; **sich nicht ~ können** be unable to make up one's mind; **b)** *(unpers.)* **morgen entscheidet es sich, ob ...:** I/we/you will know tomorrow wether ... **2.** *unr. itr. V.* **über etw.** *(Akk.)* **~:** decide on *or* settle sth. **3.** *unr. tr. V.* **a)** *(bestimmen)* decide on ‹*dispute*›; **der Richter entschied, daß ...:** the judge decided *or* ruled that ...; **b)** *(den Ausschlag geben für)* decide ‹*outcome, result*›
entscheidend 1. *Adj.* crucial ‹*problem, question, significance*›; decisive ‹*action*›; **die ~e Stimme** the deciding vote; **etwas/nichts Entscheidendes** something/nothing crucial *or* decisive. **2.** *adv.* **jmdn./etw. ~ beeinflussen** have a crucial *or* decisive influence on sb./sth.; **sich/etw. ~ verändern** change/change sth. decisively
Entscheidung die decision; *(Gerichts~)* ruling; *(Schwurgerichts~)* verdict; **etw. steht vor der ~:** sth. is just about to be decided; **einer ~** *(Dat.)* **ausweichen** avoid making a decision; **jmdn. vor die ~ stellen, etw. zu tun** leave the decision to sb. to do sth.
entscheidungs-, Entscheidungs-: ~befugnis die decision-making powers *pl.*; **~frage die** *(Sprachw.)* yes-no *or* polar question; **~gewalt die** power of decision; **~hilfe die** help *or* assistance in reaching a decision; **~kampf der** decisive struggle; *(Milit.)* decisive battle; **~schlacht die** decisive battle; **~spiel das** *(Sport)* deciding match; *(bei gleichem Rang)* play-off; **~träger der** decision-maker
entschieden 1. *2. Part. v.* **entscheiden. 2.** *Adj.* **a)** *(entschlossen)* determined; resolute; **b)** *(eindeutig)* definite. **3.** *adv.* resolutely; **etw. ~** *od.* **auf das ~ste ablehnen** reject sth. emphatically *or* categorically; **jmdn. sehr ~ antworten** give sb. a very definite answer; **das geht ~ zu weit** that is going much too far
Entschiedenheit die; ~: decisiveness; **etw. mit ~ behaupten/verneinen** state/deny sth. categorically; **etw. mit ~ fordern** demand sth. emphatically
entschlacken *tr. V.* cleanse
Entschlackung die; ~, ~en cleansing
entschlafen *unr. itr. V.; mit sein* **a)** *(verhüll.: sterben)* pass away; fall asleep *(euphem.)*; **sanft ~:** pass away peacefully; **b)** *(geh.: einschlafen)* fall asleep
entschleiern *tr. V. (geh.)* **a)** *(fig.)* reveal; uncover; **ein Geheimnis ~:** reveal a secret; **b)** unveil ‹*face*›
entschließen *unr. refl. V.* decide; make up one's mind; **sich ~, etw. zu tun** decide *or* resolve to do sth.; **sich dazu ~:** decide to do it; **sich zu einer Reise/zur Heirat ~:** decide to make a journey/to marry; **ich kann mich zu nichts ~:** I can't make up my mind; **sich anders ~:** change one's mind
Entschließung die resolution
entschlossen 1. *2. Part. v.* **entschließen. 2.** *Adj.* determined, resolute ‹*person*›; determined ‹*look etc.*›; **fest ~ [sein], etw. zu tun** [be] absolutely determined to do sth. **3.** *adv.* **~ handeln/durchgreifen** act resolutely *or* with determination/take determined action; **kurz ~:** on the spur of the moment; *(als Reaktion)* immediately
Entschlossenheit die; ~: determination; resolution; **in wilder ~:** fiercely determined; with fierce determination
entschlummern *itr. V.; mit sein* **a)** *(dichter.: einschlafen)* fall asleep; **b)** *s.* **entschlafen a**
entschlüpfen *itr. V.; mit sein* **a)** escape; slip away; **b)** ‹*remarks, words*› slip out
Entschluß der decision; **seinen ~ ändern** change one's mind; **aus eigenem ~:** on one's own initiative; of one's own volition
entschlüsseln *tr. V.* decipher; decode
Entschlüsselung die; ~, ~en deciphering; decoding
entschluß-, Entschluß-: ~freudig *Adj.* decisive; **~kraft die** decisiveness; **~los 1.** *Adj.* indecisive; **2.** *adv.* indecisively
entschuldbar *Adj.* excusable; pardonable
entschulden *tr. V.* free of debts; **einen Betrieb ~:** write off a business's debts
entschuldigen 1. *refl. V.* apologize; **sich bei jmdm. wegen** *od.* **für etw. ~:** apologize to sb. for sth.; **sich in aller Form ~:** apologize formally; make a formal apology. **2.** *tr. (auch itr.) V.* excuse ‹*person*›; **die Mutter entschuldigte ihren Sohn in der Schule** the mother had her son excused from school; **sich ~ lassen** ask to be excused; **sein Verhalten ist durch nichts zu ~:** his behaviour is inexcusable; **~ Sie [bitte]!** *(bei Fragen, Bitten)* excuse me; *(bedauernd)* excuse me; I'm sorry; **Sie müssen ~, daß ...:** I'm sorry, but ...
entschuldigend 1. *Adj.* apologetic; **~e Worte** words of apology. **2.** *adv.* apologetically

Entschuldigung die; ~, ~en a) *(Rechtfertigung)* excuse; **etw. zu seiner ~ sagen/anführen** say sth. in one's defence; **b)** *(schriftliche Mitteilung)* [excuse] note; letter of excuse; **c)** *(Höflichkeitsformel)* **~!** *(bei Fragen, Bitten)* excuse me; *(bedauernd)* excuse me; [I'm] sorry; **jmdn. für** *od.* **wegen etw. um ~ bitten** apologize to sb. for sth.; **d)** *(entschuldigende Äußerung)* apology

Entschuldigungs-: ~grund der excuse; **~schreiben das** letter of apology

entschweben *itr. V.; mit sein (geh., häufig iron.)* waft away

entschwefeln *tr. V. (Chemie)* desulphurize

entschwinden *unr. itr. V.; mit sein (geh.)* **a)** disappear; vanish; **jmds. Blicken ~:** disappear *or* vanish from sb.'s view *or* sight; **b)** *(vergehen)* ⟨*time*⟩ fly by

entseelt [ɛnt'ze:lt] *Adj. (geh.)* lifeless, dead *(also fig.)*

entsenden *unr. (auch regelm.) tr. V.* dispatch

Entsendung die; *o. Pl. (geh.)* dispatch

entsetzen 1. *refl. V.* be horrified; **sich vor** *od.* **bei dem Anblick von etw. ~:** be horrified at the sight of sth. **2.** *tr. V.* **a)** *(erschrecken)* horrify; **über etw.** *(Akk.)* **entsetzt sein** be horrified by sth.; **entsetzt starren** stare in horror; **b)** *(Milit.)* relieve

Entsetzen das; ~s horror; **vor ~ stumm** speechless with horror; **mit ~ bemerken** notice to one's horror; **ihn befiel lähmendes ~:** he was paralysed with horror

Entsetzens·schrei der cry of horror

entsetzlich 1. *Adj.* **a)** horrible, dreadful ⟨*accident, crime, etc.*⟩; **b)** *nicht präd. (ugs.: stark)* terrible ⟨*thirst, hunger*⟩; **einen ~en Durst haben** have a terrible thirst; be terribly thirsty. **2.** *adv.* terribly *(coll.)*; awfully; **es ist ~ kalt/warm/dunkel** it is terribly *(coll.) or* awfully cold/warm/dark

Entsetzlichkeit die; ~, ~en horribleness; dreadfulness

entseuchen *tr. V.* decontaminate

entsichern *tr. V.* **eine Pistole ~:** release the safety catch of a pistol; **das Gewehr war entsichert/nicht entsichert** the rifle had the safety catch off/on

entsinnen *unr. refl. V.* **sich jmds./einer Sache ~:** remember sb./sth.; **sich an jmdn./etw. ~:** remember sb./sth.

entsorgen *tr. V. (Amtsspr., Wirtsch.)* dispose of ⟨*waste etc.*⟩; **eine Stadt/ein Kernkraftwerk ~:** dispose of a town's/a nuclear power station's waste

Entsorgung die; ~, ~en *(Amtsspr., Wirtsch.)* waste disposal

entspannen 1. *tr. V.* **a)** *(lockern)* relax ⟨*body etc.*⟩; relax, loosen ⟨*muscles*⟩; **b)** *(von Spannung befreien)* relax the tension of ⟨*spring*⟩; reduce the surface tension of ⟨*water*⟩. **2.** *refl. V.* **a)** ⟨*person*⟩ relax; **b)** *(fig.)* ⟨*situation, tension*⟩ ease

Entspannung die; *o. Pl.* **a)** relaxation; **b)** *(politisch)* easing of tension; détente

Entspannungs-: ~politik die policy of détente; **~übung die** relaxation exercise

entspiegeln *tr. V.* bloom; **entspiegeltes Glas** coated glass

entspinnen *unr. refl. V.* develop; arise

entsprechen *unr. itr. V.* **a)** *(übereinstimmen mit)* **einer Sache** *(Dat.)* **~:** correspond to sth.; **der Wahrheit/den Tatsachen ~:** be in accordance with the truth/the facts; **den Erwartungen ~:** live up to one's expectations; **sich** *(Dat.) od. (geh.)* **einander ~:** correspond; **b)** *(nachkommen)* **einem Wunsch/einer Bitte ~:** comply with a wish/request; **den Anforderungen ~:** meet the requirements; **dem Anlaß ~:** be appropriate for the occasion; **dem Zweck ~:** suit the purpose

entsprechend 1. *Adj.* **a)** corresponding; *(angemessen)* appropriate ⟨*payment, reply, etc.*⟩; **b)** *nicht attr. (dem~)* in accordance *postpos.*; **das Wetter war schlecht und die Stimmung ~:** the weather was bad and the mood was the same; **c)** *nicht präd. (zuständig)* relevant ⟨*department etc.*⟩; ⟨*person*⟩ concerned. **2.** *adv.* **a)** *(angemessen)* appropriately; **b)** *(dem~)* accordingly. **3.** *Präp. mit Dativ:* **~ einer Sache** in accordance with sth.; **der Anweisung ~ handeln** act in accordance with *or* according to instructions; **es geht ihm den Umständen ~:** he is as well as can be expected [in the circumstances]

Entsprechung die; ~, ~en a) *(Übereinstimmung)* correspondence; **b)** *(Analogie)* parallel; **in einer Sache seine ~ haben** *od.* **finden** have its counterpart in sth.; **für dieses Wort gibt es keine deutsche ~:** there is no German equivalent for this word

entsprießen *unr. itr. V.; mit sein (geh.)* **einer Sache** *(Dat.)* **~:** spring from sth.; *(fig.: hervorgehen aus)* come from sth.

entspringen *unr. itr. V.; mit sein* **a)** ⟨*river*⟩ rise, have its source; **b)** *(entstehen aus)* **einer Sache** *(Dat.)* **~:** spring from sth.; **c)** *(entweichen aus)* escape; **ein entsprungener Häftling** an escaped prisoner; **dem Irrenhaus entsprungen sein** *(scherzh.)* be crazy

entstaatlichen *tr. V.* denationalize

Entstalinisierung [ɛntʃtalini'zi:rʊŋ] **die; ~:** destalinization

entstammen *itr. V.; mit sein* come from; *(herrühren von)* derive from; **einer Sache** *(Dat.)* **~:** come/derive from sth.

entstauben *tr. V.* dust; remove the dust from; *(fig.)* bring up to date

entstehen *unr. itr. V.; mit sein* **a)** originate; ⟨*quarrel, friendship, etc.*⟩ arise; ⟨*work of art*⟩ be created; ⟨*building, town, etc.*⟩ be built; ⟨*industry*⟩ emerge; ⟨*novel etc.*⟩ be written; **im Entstehen [begriffen] sein** be being created/built/written/be emerging; **b)** *(gebildet werden)* be formed (**aus** from, **durch** by); **c)** *(sich ergeben)* occur; *(als Folge)* result; **jmdm. ~ Kosten** sb. incurs costs; **hoffentlich ist nicht der Eindruck entstanden, daß ...:** I/we hope I/we have not given the impression that ...

Entstehung die; ~: origin; **die ~ des Lebens/der Arten** the origin of life/species; **die ~ dieser Stadt/Industrie** the building of this town/the emergence of this industry

Entstehungs-: ~geschichte die history of the origin[s]; **~ort der** place of origin; **~ursache die** [original] cause; **~zeit die** time of origin; *(Datum)* date of origin

entsteigen *unr. V.; mit sein (geh.)* **einer Kutsche** *(Dat.) usw.* **~** alight from a coach etc.

entsteinen *tr. V.* stone

entstellen *tr. V.* **a)** disfigure ⟨*person*⟩; distort ⟨*face*⟩; **b)** *(verfälschen)* distort ⟨*text, facts*⟩

Entstellung die a) *(Entstelltsein)* disfigurement; **b)** *(Verfälschung)* distortion

entstielen *tr. V.* remove the stalks from

entstören *tr. V. (Elektrot.)* suppress ⟨*engine, distributor, electrical appliance*⟩

Entstörungs·stelle die fault repair service

entströmen *tr. V.; mit sein (geh.)* pour out; ⟨*gas*⟩ escape; *(fig.)* ⟨*crowd*⟩ pour *or* stream out

enttabuisieren *tr. V. (geh.)* free from taboos

enttarnen *tr. V.* uncover; *(fig.)* discover; **etw. als etw. ~:** reveal sth. as sth.

Enttarnung die uncovering

enttäuschen 1. *tr. V.* disappoint; **unsere Hoffnungen wurden enttäuscht** our hopes were dashed; **jmdn. angenehm ~:** come as a pleasant surprise to sb. **2.** *itr. V.* **etw./jmd. enttäuscht** sth./sb. is disappointing *or* a disappointment

enttäuscht *Adj.* disappointed; dashed ⟨*hopes*⟩; **von jmdm. ~ sein** be disappointed in sb.; **von** *od.* **über etw. ~ sein** be disappointed by *or* at sth.

Enttäuschung die disappointment **(für** to); **jmdm. eine ~ bereiten** be a disappointment to sb.

entthronen *tr. V.* **a)** *(geh.)* dethrone ⟨*monarch*⟩; **b)** *(fig.: verdrängen)* take the title away from ⟨*champion etc.*⟩; remove ⟨*magnate*⟩ from power

Entthronung die; ~, ~en *(auch fig.)* dethronement

entvölkern [ɛnt'fœlkɐn] **1.** *tr. V.* depopulate. **2.** *refl. V.* become depopulated *or* deserted

Entvölkerung die; ~, ~en depopulation

ent·wachsen *unr. itr. V.; mit sein* **einer Sache** *(Dat.)* **~:** grow out of *or* outgrow sth.; *s. auch* **Kinderschuh**

entwaffnen *tr. V. (auch fig.)* disarm

entwaffnend 1. *Adj.* disarming. **2.** *adv.* disarmingly

Entwaffnung die; ~: disarming; *(der Bevölkerung, eines Landes)* disarmament

entwalden *tr. V.* deforest

entwarnen *itr. V.* sound *or* give the all-clear

Entwarnung die [sounding of the] all-clear

entwässern 1. *tr. V.* **a)** drain ⟨*meadow, area*⟩; **b)** *(Med.)* dehydrate. **2.** *itr. V. (abfließen)* flow

Entwässerung die; ~, ~en a) drainage; **b)** *(Kanalisation)* drainage [system]

Entwässerungs-: ~an·lage die drainage system; **~graben der** drainage ditch; **~netz das** drainage network

entweder *Konj.* **~ ... oder** either ... or

Entweder-Oder das; ~, ~: es gibt kein ~: there is no alternative *or* are no alternatives; **es gibt nur ein ~:** a choise has to be made

entweichen *unr. itr. V.; mit sein* **a)** *(ausströmen)* escape; **ihrem Gesicht entwich alles Blut** *(geh.)* the blood drained from her face; **b)** *(geh.: entfliehen)* escape

entweihen *tr. V.* desecrate; profane

Entweihung die; ~: desecration; profanation

entwenden *tr. V. (geh.)* purloin (*Dat.* **from)**

entwerfen *unr. tr. V.* **a)** design ⟨*furniture, dress*⟩; *(fig.)* draw ⟨*picture*⟩; **b)** *(ausarbeiten)* draft ⟨*novel etc.*⟩; draw up ⟨*plans etc.*⟩

entwerten *tr. V.* **a)** cancel ⟨*ticket, postage stamp*⟩; **b)** *(Finanzw.)* devalue ⟨*currency*⟩

Entwerter der; ~s, ~: ticket-cancelling machine

Entwertung die *s.* **entwerten:** cancellation; cancelling; devaluation

entwesen *tr. V. (Amtsspr.)* disinfest

Entwesung die; ~, ~en *(Amtsspr.)* disinfestation

entwickeln 1. *refl. V.* develop (**aus** from, **zu** into); **sie ist körperlich voll entwickelt** she is [physically] fully developed. **2.** *tr. V.* give off, produce ⟨*vapour, smell*⟩; show, display ⟨*ability, characteristic*⟩; develop ⟨*weapons, equipment, process, photograph, film*⟩; elaborate ⟨*theory, ideas*⟩

Entwickler der; ~s, ~ *(Fot.)* developer

Entwickler·bad das *(Fot.)* developing bath

Entwicklung die; ~, ~en a) development; *(von Dämpfen usw.)* production; **in der ~ sein** ⟨*young person*⟩ be adolescent *or* in one's adolescence; **in seiner [körperlichen] ~ zurückbleiben** be physically underdeveloped; **eine bestimmte ~ nehmen** show certain developments; **eine positive ~ zeichnet sich ab** positive developments *pl.* can be seen; **die ~ geht dahin, daß ...:** the trend is that ...; **etw. befindet sich in der ~:** sth. is [still] in the development stage; **b)** *(Darlegung)* elaboration; **c)** *(Fot.)* development; developing

entwicklungs-, Entwicklungs-: ~abschnitt der stage of development; **~alter**

das adolescence; **~dienst der** development aid service; **~fähig** *Adj.* capable of development; **~geschichte die** history of the development; **die ~geschichte der Menschheit/der Meerestiere** the evolution of man/of marine animals; **~geschichtlich 1.** *Adj.* historical; *(stammesgeschichtlich)* evolutionary. **2.** *adv.* **~geschichtlich bedeutsam** important historically/as regards evolution; **sich ~geschichtlich verändert haben** have evolved; **~helfer der** development aid worker; **~hilfe die** [development] aid; **~jahre** *Pl.* adolescence *sing.*; **in die ~jahre kommen** reach adolescence; **~kosten** *Pl.* development costs; **~land das;** *Pl.* **~länder** developing country; **~ministerium das** ministry of development aid; **~phase die** stage of development; **~politik die** development aid policy; **~roman der** *(Literaturw.)* novel showing the development of an individual's character; **~stand der** level of development; **~störung die** developmental disturbance; **~stufe die** stage of development; **~zeit die a)** *s.* **~alter; b)** *(~zeitraum)* period of development

entwinden *(geh.)* **1.** *unr. tr. V.* **jmdm. etw. ~:** wrest sth. from sb.. **2.** *unr. refl. V.* **sich jmdm./einer Sache ~:** wrest *or* free oneself from sb./sth.

entwirrbar *Adj.* **das Garnknäuel war kaum ~:** the ball of thread could scarcely be unravelled; **die vielen Handlungsstränge waren kaum ~:** the strands of the plot could scarcely be untangled

entwirren 1. *tr. V.* **a)** unravel, disentangle ‹*wool etc.*›; **b)** *(fig.)* unravel, sort out ‹*situation etc.*›. **2.** *refl. V.* sort itself out

entwischen *itr. V.; mit sein (ugs.)* get away; **aus dem Gefängnis ~:** get out of jail; **jmdm. ~:** give sb. the slip *(coll.)*

entwöhnen [ɛnt'vø:nən] *tr. V.* **a)** wean ‹*baby*›; **b)** *(geh.)* **jmdn. einer Sache** *(Dat.)* **~:** break sb. of the habit of [doing] sth.; **jmdn. [von einer Sucht] ~:** cure sb. [of an addiction]

entwürdigen *tr. V.* degrade

entwürdigend 1. *Adj.* degrading. **2.** *adv.* ‹*treat sb.*› in a degrading manner; degradingly ‹*low*›

Entwürdigung die degradation

Entwurf der a) design; **b)** *(Konzept)* draft; **der ~ zu einem Roman** the outline *or* draft of a novel

entwurmen *tr. V.* worm

entwurzeln *tr. V.* uproot ‹*tree etc., person*›; **ein entwurzelter Mensch** a rootless person

Entwurzelung die; ~, ~en uprooting

entzaubern *tr. V. (geh.)* **a)** free ‹*person*› from the spell; break the spell on ‹*person*›; **b) entzaubert werden** *(die Poesie, den Zauber verlieren)* lose its magic

entzerren *tr. V.* **a)** *(Technik)* correct; rectify; **b)** *(Fot.)* rectify

Entzerrer der; ~s, ~ a) *(Technik)* equalizer; **b)** *(Fot.)* rectifier;

entziehen 1. *unr. tr. V.* **a)** take away; **etw. jmdm./einer Sache ~:** take sth. away from sb./sth.; **jmdm. den Führerschein ~:** take sb.'s driving licence away; **jmdm. das Wort ~:** ask sb. to stop [speaking]; **b)** *(nicht zugestehen)* withdraw; **jmdm. das Vertrauen ~:** withdraw one's confidence in sb.; **c)** *(entfernen von, aus)* **etw. einer Sache** *(Dat.)* **~:** remove sth. from sth.; **d)** *(herausziehen aus)* **etw. einer Sache** *(Dat.)* **~:** extract sth. from sth.; **e)** *(ugs.: entwöhnen)* get ‹*addict*› off drugs; dry ‹*alcoholic*› out *(coll.)*. **2.** *unr. refl. V.* **sich jmds. Armen/Umklammerung ~:** free oneself from sb.'s arms/embrace; **ihrem Reiz konnte ich mich nicht ~:** I could not resist her/their charms; **sich der Gesellschaft** *(Dat.)* **~** *(geh.)* withdraw from society; **sich seinen Pflichten** *(Dat.)* **~:** shirk *or* evade one's duty; **sich einer Untersuchung** *(Dat.)* **~** *(geh.)* elude an investigation; **das entzieht sich meiner Kontrolle/Kenntnis** that is beyond my control/knowledge

Entziehung die a) withdrawal; loss; **b)** *(Entziehungskur)* withdrawal treatment *no indef. art.*; **eine ~ machen** take withdrawal treatment

Entziehungs-: ~anstalt die treatment centre; clinic; **~kur die** course of withdrawal treatment; withdrawal programme

entzifferbar *Adj.* decipherable

entziffern *tr. V.* **a)** decipher ‹*writing*›; **b)** *(entschlüsseln)* decipher, decode ‹*message*›

Entzifferung die; ~, ~en *s.* **entziffern:** deciphering; decoding

entzücken 1. *tr. V.* delight; **etw. entzückt jmdn.** sth. delights sb. *or* fills sb. with delight. **2.** *refl. V. (geh.)* **sich an etw.** *(Dat.)* **~:** be enraptured by sth.

Entzücken das; ~s *(geh.)* delight, joy **(an** + *Dat.* in)

entzückend 1. *Adj.* delightful; **das ist ja ~!** *(iron.)* [that's] charming! **2.** *adv.* delightfully

entzückt *Adj.* delighted; **von/über etw.** *(Akk.)* **~ sein** be delighted by/at sth.

Entzückung die; ~, ~en *(geh.)* joy; rapture

Entzug der; ~[e]s a) withdrawal; *(das Herausziehen)* extraction; **b)** *s.* **Entziehung b**

Entzugs·erscheinung die withdrawal symptom

entzündbar *Adj.* **a)** *(brennbar)* [in]flammable; **b)** *(fig.: erregbar)* easily roused

entzünden 1. *tr. V.* **a)** *(geh.: anzünden)* light ‹*fire*›; strike, light ‹*match*›; **b)** *(geh.: erregen)* kindle, arouse ‹*passion*›; arouse ‹*hatred*›. **2.** *refl. V.* **a)** catch fire; ignite; **b)** *(anschwellen)* become inflamed; **entzündete Augen haben** have inflamed eyes; **c)** *(geh.: entstehen)* **sich an etw.** *(Dat.)* **~:** ‹*quarrel*› be sparked off by sth.; ‹*temper*› flare at sth.

entzündlich *Adj.* **a)** [in]flammable ‹*substance*›; **b)** *(Med.)* inflammatory

Entzündlichkeit die; ~: [in]flammability

Entzündung die; ~, ~en inflammation

entzündungs·hemmend *Adj.* anti-inflammatory; antiphlogistic *(Med.)*

Entzündungs·herd der focus of inflammation

entzwei *Adj.; nicht attr. (geh.)* in pieces

entzwei|brechen *(geh.)* **1.** *unr. tr. V.* break into pieces. **2.** *unr. itr. V.; mit sein* break into pieces

entzweien 1. *refl. V.* **sich [mit jmdm.] ~:** fall out [with sb.]. **2.** *tr. V.* cause ‹*persons*› to fall out

entzwei- *(geh.)*: **~|gehen** *unr. itr. V.; mit sein (zerbrechen)* break; *(nicht mehr funktionieren)* cease to function; **~|machen** *tr. V.* break; **~|schlagen** *unr. tr. V.* smash to pieces

Entzweiung die; ~, ~en: eine ~ herbeiführen cause the two friends/countries *etc.* to fall out

en vogue [ã'vo:k] *(geh.)* **~ ~ sein** be fashionable *or* in vogue

Enzephalogramm [ɛntsefalo'gram] **das; ~s, ~e** *(Med.)* encephalogram

Enzian ['ɛntsia:n] **der; ~s, ~e a)** *(Bot.)* gentian; **b)** *(Schnaps)* enzian liqueur

enzian·blau *Adj.* gentian-blue

Enzyklika [ɛn'tsy:klika] **die; ~, Enzykliken** encyclical

Enzyklopädie [ɛntsyklopɛ'di:] **die; ~, ~n** encyclopaedia

enzyklopädisch 1. *Adj.* encyclopaedic. **2.** *adv.* encyclopaedically

Enzyklopädist der; ~en, ~en encyclopaedist

Enzym [ɛn'tsy:m] **das; ~s, ~e** *(Chemie)* enzyme

eo ipso ['e:o 'ɪpso] *(geh.)* ipso facto

Eolithikum [eo'li:tikʊm] **das; ~s** eolithic period

Epaulett [epo'lɛt] **das; ~s, ~s, Epaulette die; ~, ~n** epaulette

Epen *s.* **Epos**

ephemer [efe'me:ɐ̯] *Adj. (geh.)* ephemeral

Epidemie [epide'mi:] **die; ~, ~n** *(auch fig.)* epidemic

epidemisch 1. *Adj.* epidemic. **2.** *adv.* as/like an epidemic

Epidermis [epi'dɛrmɪs] **die; ~, Epidermen** *(Biol.)* epidermis

Epidiaskop [epidia'sko:p] **das; ~s, ~e** epidiascope

epigonal [epigo'na:l] *Adj. (geh.) s.* **epigonenhaft**

Epigone [epi'go:nə] **der; ~n, ~n** *(geh.)* imitator

epigonenhaft *Adj. (geh.)* imitative; unoriginal

Epigonentum das; ~s *(geh.)* imitativeness; unoriginality

Epigramm [epi'gram] **das; ~s, ~e** *(Literaturw.)* epigram

Epigrammatik die; ~ *(Literaturw.)* epigrammatism

epigrammatisch *Adj.* epigrammatic

Epik ['e:pɪk] **die; ~** *(Literaturw.)* epic poetry

Epiker der; ~s, ~: epic poet

Epikureer [epiku're:ɐ] **der; ~s, ~ a)** *(Philos.)* Epicurean; **b)** *(geh.)* epicurean

epikureisch *Adj.* **a)** *(Philos.)* Epicurean; **b)** *(geh.)* epicurean

Epilepsie [epilɛ'psi:] **die; ~, ~n** *(Med.)* epilepsy *no art.*

Epileptiker [epi'lɛptikɐ] **der; ~s, ~, Epileptikerin die; ~, ~nen** epileptic

epileptisch *Adj.* epileptic

Epilog [epi'lo:k] **der; ~s, ~e** epilogue

Epiphanias [epi'fa:nias] **das; ~:** Epiphany *no art.*

Epiphanie [epifa'ni:] **die; ~** *(Rel.)* epiphany

episch ['e:pɪʃ] **1.** *Adj.* epic. **2.** *adv.* in epic terms

Episkop [epi'sko:p] **das; ~s, ~e** episcope

Episkopal·kirche die a) episcopal church; **b)** *(ev. Kirche)* protestant church

Episkopat [epɪsko'pa:t] **das** *od.* **der; ~[e]s, ~e** *(Theol.)* **a)** *o. Pl. (Amt)* episcopate; **b)** *(Gesamtheit der Bischöfe)* episcopate; episcopacy

Episode [epi'zo:də] **die; ~, ~n** episode

episodenhaft, episodisch 1. *Adj.* episodic. **2.** *adv.* episodically

Epistel [e'pɪstl] **die; ~, ~n a)** *(bibl.)* epistle; **b)** *(kath. Kirche)* epistle; lesson; **jmdm. die ~ lesen** *(fig. veralt.)* read sb. a lesson

Epitaph [epi'ta:f] **das; ~s, ~e** *(geh.)* **a)** epitaph; **b)** *(Gedenktafel)* memorial plaque

Epithel [epi'te:l] **das; ~s, ~e** *(Biol.)* epithelium

Epitheton [e'pi:tetɔn] **das; ~s, Epitheta** *(Sprachw.)* epithet

Epizentrum das *(Geol.)* epicentre

epochal [epɔ'xa:l] *Adj.* epochal; epoch-making; epoch-making ‹*invention*›; *(fig. iron.)* world-shattering; monumental

Epoche [e'pɔxə] **die; ~, ~n** epoch; **~ machen** be epoch-making

epoche·machend *Adj.* epoch-making

Epos ['e:pɔs] **das; ~, Epen** epic [poem]; epos

Eprouvette [epru'vɛt] **die; ~, ~n** *(österr.)* test-tube

Equipage [ekvi'pa:ʒə] **die; ~, ~n** *(veralt.)* equipage

Equipe [e'kɪp] **die; ~, ~n** team

er [e:ɐ̯] *Personalpron. 3. Pers. Sg. Nom. Mask.* he; *(betont)* him; *(bei Dingen/Tieren)* it; *(bei männlichen Tieren)* he/him; it; **„Er"** *(auf Handtüchern, an Türen)* 'His'; **er war es, nicht sie** it was him, not her; **ich weiß mehr als er** I know more than he does; I know more than him *(coll.)*; **„Er, 42, Witwer ..."** 'widower, 42 ...'; **bring Er den Wein!** *(veralt.)* fetch the wine!; *s. auch* **ihm; ihn; seiner**

Er der; ~, ~s *(ugs.)* he; **ist es ein Er oder eine Sie?** is it a he or a she?

erachten *tr. V. (geh.)* consider; **etw. als** *od.* **für seine Pflicht ~:** consider sth. [to be] one's duty; **etw. als** *od.* **für notwendig ~:** consider *or* think sth. necessary
Erachten das *in* **meinem ~ nach, meines ~s** in my opinion
erahnen *tr. V.* imagine; guess
erarbeiten *tr. V.* **a)** *(erwerben)* work for; **[sich** *(Dat.)***] ein Vermögen ~:** make [oneself] a fortune; **b)** *(zu eigen machen)* work on; study; **[sich** *(Dat.)***] einen Text ~:** understand a text by working on it; **c)** *(erstellen)* work out ⟨*plan, programme, etc.*⟩
Erb- ['ɛrp-]: **~adel der** hereditary nobility; *(Titel)* hereditary title; **~an·lage die** *(Biol.)* hereditary disposition; **~an·spruch der** claim to an/the inheritance; **~an·teil der** share of an/the inheritance
erbarmen [ɛɐ̯'barmən] **1.** *refl. V. (geh.)* **sich jmds./einer Sache ~:** take pity on sb./sth.; **Herr, erbarme dich unser!** Lord, have mercy upon us. **2.** *tr. V.* **jmdn. ~:** arouse sb.'s pity; move sb. to pity
Erbarmen das; ~s pity; **mit jmdm. ~ haben** take pity on *or* feel pity for sb.; **er kennt kein ~:** he knows no pity *or* mercy; **zum ~:** pitifully; pathetically; **zum ~ sein** be pitiful *or* pathetic
erbarmens·wert *Adj.* pitiful
erbärmlich [ɛɐ̯'bɛrmlɪç] **1.** *Adj.* **a)** *(elend)* wretched; **b)** *(unzulänglich)* pathetic; **c)** *(abwertend: gemein)* mean; wretched; **d)** *nicht präd. (sehr groß)* terrible ⟨*hunger, thirst, fear, etc.*⟩. **2.** *adv. (intensivierend)* terribly ⟨*cold, hot, thirsty, hungry, etc.*⟩
Erbärmlichkeit die; ~: a) *(Elend)* wretchedness; **b)** *(abwertend: Gemeinheit)* meanness; wretchedness
erbarmungs-, Erbarmungs-: ~los 1. *Adj.* merciless; **2.** *adv.* mercilessly; **~losigkeit die; ~:** mercilessness; **~würdig** *Adj.* pitiful
erbauen 1. *tr. V.* **a)** build; **b)** *(geh.: erheben)* uplift; edify; **wir waren von seinen Plänen wenig erbaut** we were not exactly delighted about his plans. **2.** *refl. V. (geh.: sich erfreuen)* **sich an etw.** *(Dat.)* **~:** be uplifted *or* edified by sth.
Erbauer der; ~s, ~: architect
erbaulich *Adj.* edifying
Erbauung die; ~ *(Freude)* edification
Erbauungs·literatur die devotional literature
erb-, Erb-: ~bauer der a) *farmer owning property by hereditary right;* **b)** *(in ~pacht) farmer with hereditary right of tenure;* **~begräbnis das a)** *right to be buried in the family grave;* **b)** *s.* **Familiengrab; ~berechtigt** *Adj.* entitled to inherit; entitled to an/the inheritance; **die Erbberechtigten** the heirs; **~biologisch** *Adj.* genetic; **ein ~biologisches Gutachten** the opinion of an expert in genetics
[1]**Erbe** ['ɛrbə] **das; ~s a)** *(Vermögen)* inheritance; **das väterliche/mütterliche ~:** patrimony/maternal inheritance; **sein ~ antreten** come into one's inheritance; **b)** *(Vermächtnis)* heritage; legacy
[2]**Erbe der; ~n ~n** heir; **der rechtmäßige/mutmaßliche ~:** the rightful heir/heir presumptive; **jmdn. zum** *od.* **als ~n einsetzen** appoint sb. as one's heir; **am Ende war alles nur für die lachenden ~n** *(ugs.)* in the end it was all just for others to inherit; **die ~n** *(fig.)* future generations
Erbe·aneignung, Erbe·rezeption die *(DDR)* acquainting oneself with the nation's cultural heritage
erbeben *itr. V.; mit sein (geh.)* **a)** shake; tremble; **b)** *(fig.: erregt werden)* shake; quiver
erb-, Erb-: ~eigen *Adj.* inherited; **~eigenschaft die** *(Biol.)* hereditary characteristic; **~einsetzung die** *(Rechtsw.)* appointment of an/one's heir

erben *tr. (auch itr.) V.* inherit; **bei mir ist nichts zu ~** *(ugs.)* you won't get anything out of me
Erben·gemeinschaft die [community of] joint heirs
erbetteln *tr. V.* get by begging; **um eine Mahlzeit zu ~:** to beg for a meal
erbeuten [ɛɐ̯'bɔytn̩] *tr. V.* carry off, get away with ⟨*valuables, prey, etc.*⟩; capture ⟨*enemy plane, tank, etc.*⟩
erb-, Erb-: ~fähig *Adj. (Rechtsspr.)* heritable; **~faktor der** hereditary factor; **~fall der** *(Rechtsw.)* inheritance; **~fehler der** hereditary defect; **~feind der a)** traditional enemy; **b)** *(verhüll.: Teufel)* arch fiend
Erb·folge die a) succession; **die gesetzliche ~:** intestate succession; **b)** *(Thronfolge)* succession
Erbfolge-: ~krieg der war of succession; **~recht das** law of succession
Erb-: ~forschung die genetics *sing., no art.;* **~gut das** *(Biol.)* genotype; genetic make-up; **~hof der** ancestral estate; *(fig. Pol.)* perquisite
erbieten *unr. refl. V. (geh.)* **sich ~, etw. zu tun** offer to do sth.
Erbin die; ~, ~nen heiress
erbitten 1. *unr. tr. V. (geh.)* request; **„baldige Antwort erbeten"** 'early reply appreciated'. **2.** *unr. refl. V. (veralt.)* **sich ~ lassen, etw. zu tun** be prevailed upon to do sth.
erbittern *tr. V.* enrage; incense
erbittert 1. *Adj.* bitter ⟨*resistance, struggle*⟩. **2.** *adv.* **~ kämpfen** wage a bitter struggle
Erbitterung die; ~: bitterness
Erb·krankheit die hereditary disease
erblassen [ɛɐ̯'blasn̩] *itr. V.; mit sein (geh.)* go *or* turn pale; blanch *(literary); s. auch* **Neid**
Erblasser ['ɛrplasɐ] **der; ~s, ~** *(Rechtsw.)* testator
Erblasserin die; ~, ~nen *(Rechtsw.)* testatrix
Erb-: ~lehen das *(hist.)* hereditary fief; **~lehre die** *(Biol.)* genetics *sing.*
erbleichen *itr. V.; mit sein (geh.)* go *or* turn pale; blanch *(literary)*
erblich 1. *Adj.* hereditary ⟨*title, disease*⟩. **2.** *adv.* **er ist ~ belastet** he suffers from a hereditary condition; *(scherzh.)* it runs in his family
Erblichkeit die; ~ *(auch Biol.)* heritability
erblicken *tr. V. (geh.)* **a)** catch sight of; see; **b)** *(fig.)* see; **sie erblickte in mir eine Konkurrentin** she saw me as a rival; she saw a rival in me
erblinden *itr. V.; mit sein* **a)** go blind; lose one's sight; **b)** *(matt werden)* go *or* become dull
Erblindung die; ~: loss of sight
erblonden *itr. V.; mit sein (scherzh.)* go blonde
erblühen *itr. V.; mit sein (geh.)* **a)** bloom; blossom; **b)** *(sich entfalten)* blossom
Erb-: ~masse die a) *(Biol.)* genotype; genetic make-up; **b)** *(Rechtsspr.)* estate; **~monarchie die** hereditary monarchy; **~onkel der** *(ugs. scherzh.)* rich uncle
erbosen [ɛɐ̯'bo:zn̩] *(geh.)* **1.** *tr. V.* infuriate. **2.** *refl. V.* **sich über etw.** *(Akk.)* **~:** become furious about sth.
erbost *Adj.* angry, furious (**über** + *Akk.* at)
erbötig [ɛɐ̯'bø:tɪç] *Adj. (veralt.)* **sich ~ machen, etw. zu tun** offer to do sth.
Erb-: ~pacht die a) *(Rechtsw.)* hereditary lease; **b)** *(hist.)* fee simple; **~prinz der** heir to the throne
erbrechen 1. *unr. tr. V.* **a)** bring up ⟨*food*⟩; **b)** *(geh.: aufbrechen)* break open ⟨*safe etc.*⟩; **c)** *(veralt.: öffnen)* open ⟨*letter, seal*⟩. **2.** *unr. itr., refl. V. (geh.: sich übergeben)* **[sich] ~:** vomit; be sick
Erbrechen das; ~s vomiting; **bis zum ~** *(ugs.)* ad nauseam
Erb·recht das *(Rechtsw.)* **a)** *o. Pl.* law of inheritance; **b)** *(Anspruch)* right of inheritance
erbringen *unr. tr. V.* **a)** produce ⟨*proof, evidence*⟩; **b)** *(liefern)* produce ⟨*result etc.*⟩; yield ⟨*amount*⟩; result in ⟨*savings etc.*⟩; **die vorgesehene Leistung ~:** do the required work; **c)** *(aufbringen)* raise ⟨*funds etc.*⟩; put up ⟨*money etc.*⟩
Erbrochene [ɛɐ̯'brɔxənə] **das;** *adj. Dekl.* vomit
Erb·schaden der *(Genetik)* hereditary defect
Erbschaft die; ~, ~en inheritance; **eine ~ machen** come into an inheritance; **die ~ des Kolonialismus** *(fig.)* the legacy of colonialism
Erbschafts·anspruch der claim to an/the inheritance
Erbschaft[s]·steuer die estate *or* death duties *pl.*
Erb-: ~schein der certificate of inheritance; **~schleicher der; ~s, ~** *(abwertend)* legacy-hunter; **~schleicherei die; ~, ~en** *(abwertend)* legacy-hunting; **~schuld die** *(Rechtsw.)* inherited debt
Erbse ['ɛrpsə] **die; ~, ~n** pea; **grüne/getrocknete** *od.* **gelbe ~n** green/dried peas
erbsen·groß *Adj.* pea-size; the size of a pea *postpos.*
Erbs[en]·püree das pease pudding
Erbsen·suppe die a) pea soup; **b)** *(ugs.: Nebel)* pea souper
Erb-: ~stück das heirloom; **~sünde die** original sin; **~tante die** *(ugs. scherzh.)* rich aunt; **~teil das a)** share of an/the inheritance; **b)** *(fig.: Anlage)* inherited trait; **~träger der** *(Biol.)* gene; **~vertrag der** testamentary contract; **~verzicht der** renunciation of the/an inheritance
Erd-: ~achse die earth's axis; **~altertum das** *(Geol.)* Palaeozoic [era]; **~anziehung die** earth's gravitational pull; **~apfel der** *(bes. österr.) s.* **Kartoffel; ~arbeiten** *Pl. (Bauw.)* earth-moving *sing.;* **~arbeiter der** *(Bauw.)* labourer; navvy *(Brit.);* **~atmosphäre die** earth's atmosphere; **~bahn die** earth's orbit; **~ball der** *(geh.)* globe; earth; **~beben das** earthquake
erdbeben-, Erdbeben-: ~gebiet das earthquake area; **~herd der** seismic focus; hypocentre; **~messer der; ~s, ~:** seismograph; **~sicher** *Adj.* earthquake-proof ⟨*building, construction*⟩; ⟨*region etc.*⟩ free from earthquakes; **~warte die** seismological station; **~welle die** seismic wave
Erdbeer·bowle die strawberry punch
Erd·beere die strawberry
erdbeer·farben *Adj.* strawberry-coloured
Erd-: ~beschleunigung die acceleration of gravity; **~bestattung die** burial; interment; **~bevölkerung die** earth's population; **~bewegung die a)** *(in der Erdkruste)* tremor; **b)** *(Bauw.)* excavation; earthwork; **~bewohner der** inhabitant of the earth; *(Science Fiction)* earthling; **~boden der** ground; earth; **etw. dem ~boden gleichmachen** raze sth. to the ground; **sie ist wie vom ~boden verschluckt** it's as if the earth *or* ground had swallowed her up; **er wäre am liebsten in den ~boden versunken** he wished the earth *or* ground could have swallowed him up; **vom ~boden verschwinden** disappear from *or* off the face of the earth; **~bohrer der** *(Technik)* drill
Erde ['e:ɐ̯də] **die; ~, ~n a)** *(Erdreich)* soil; earth; **ein Klumpen ~:** a lump of earth; **etw. in die ~ rammen** ram sth. into the ground; **zu ~ werden** *(geh. verhüll.)* turn to dust; **b)** *o. Pl. (fester Boden)* ground; **etw. auf die ~ legen/stellen** put sth. down [on the ground]; **zu ebener ~:** on the ground floor *or (Amer.)* the first floor; **auf der ~ bleiben** *(fig.)* keep one's feet on the ground *(fig.);* **mit beiden Beinen** *od.* **Füßen fest auf der ~ stehen** *(fig.)* have one's feet firmly on the ground *(fig.);*

unter der ~ liegen *(geh. verhüll.)* be in one's grave; **jmdn. unter die ~ bringen** *(ugs.)* bury sb.; *(fig.: töten)* be the death of sb. *(coll.)*; **c)** *o. Pl. (Gebiet)* **ein ruhiges/idyllisches Fleckchen ~:** a peaceful/idyllic spot; **in heimatlicher/fremder ~ begraben werden** be buried in one's native soil/in foreign soil; *s. auch* **Taktik; d)** *o. Pl. (Welt)* earth; world; **auf ~n** *(bibl.)*, **auf der ~:** on earth; **die fernsten Winkel der ~:** the farthest corners of the globe; **auf der ganzen ~:** throughout the world; **e)** *o. Pl. (Planet)* Earth; **der Mars, der Jupiter und die ~:** Mars, Jupiter, and [the] Earth; **f)** *(Elektrot.)* earth

ẹrden *tr. V. (Elektrot.)* earth

Ẹrden-: ~bürger der earth-dweller; **ein neuer/kleiner ~bürger** *(scherzh.)* a new arrival; **~da·sein das** *(geh.)* earthly existence; **~jammer der** *(dichter.)* earthly misery; misery of the world

erdẹnkbar *Adj. s.* erdenklich

erdẹnken *unr. tr. V.* think *or* make up; **eine erdachte Geschichte** a made-up story

Ẹrden·kind das *(geh.)* child of the earth *(literary)*; mortal

erdẹnklich *Adj.* conceivable; imaginable; **alle** *od.* **jede ~e Mühe** every conceivable *or* the greatest possible trouble

Ẹrden-: ~kloß der *(veralt.: Mensch)* lump of clay; **~leben das** *(geh.)* earthly existence; **~wurm der** *(dichter. veralt.)* earthly being; mortal

ẹrd-, Ẹrd-: ~fern *Adj.* **a)** *(Astron.)* remote, distant ⟨*planet*⟩; distant ⟨*orbit*⟩; **b)** *(dichter.)* spiritual ⟨*world etc.*⟩; **~ferne die a)** *(Astron.)* apogee; **b)** *(dichter.)* remoteness [from the world]; **~gas das** natural gas; **~gebunden** *Adj. (geh.)* close to nature *postpos.*; **~geist der** earth spirit; **~geruch der** earthy smell; **~geschichte die;** *o. Pl.* history of the earth; **~geschichtlich 1.** *Adj.* relating to the earth's history *postpos., not pred.*; **2.** *adv.* in relation to the earth's history; **~geschoß das** ground floor; first floor *(Amer.)*; **im ~geschoß** on the ground floor; **~gravitation die** [earth's] gravitation; **~haufen der** mound of earth; **~hörnchen das; ~s, ~** *(Zool.)* chipmunk; ground-squirrel

erdịchten *tr. V.* manufacture; **das ist alles erdichtet** it's all a pure fabrication

ẹrdig *Adj.* **a)** earthy ⟨*mass, smell, taste*⟩; **b)** *(geh.: mit Erde beschmutzt)* muddy

ẹrd-, Ẹrd-: ~innere das interior of the earth; **~kabel das** underground cable; **~karte die** map of the earth; **~kern der** earth's core; **~klumpen der** lump of earth; clod [of earth]; **~kreis der** *(dichter.)* world; **~kröte die** toad; **~kruste die** earth's crust; **~kugel die a)** *(Planet)* terrestrial globe; earth; **b)** *(Globus)* globe; **~kunde die** geography; **~kundlich 1.** *Adj.* geographical; **2.** *adv.* geographically; **~leitung die** *(Elektrot.)* earth [connection]

Erdling ['e:ɐ̯dlɪŋ] **der; ~s, ~e** *(Science-fiction)* earthling

ẹrd-, Ẹrd-: ~loch das hole in the ground; *(Milit.)* foxhole; **~magnetismus der** terrestrial magnetism; **~massen** *Pl.* masses of earth; **~metall das** *(Chemie)* group III metal; **~mittel·alter das** *(Geol.)* Mesozoic [era]; **~mittel·punkt der** centre of the earth; **~nah** *Adj.* **a)** *(Astron.)* close to the earth *postpos.*; **b)** *(geh.)* down to earth; **~nuß die** peanut; ground-nut; **~nuß·butter die** peanut butter; **~nuß·öl das** ground-nut oil; **~ober·fläche die** earth's surface; **~öl das** oil; petroleum *(as tech. term)*

erdọlchen *tr. V. (geh.)* stab to death

ẹrdöl-, Ẹrdöl-: ~exportierend *Adj.* oil-exporting ⟨*country*⟩; **~feld das** oilfield; **~fọ̈rder·land das** oil-producing country; **~gewinnung die** oil production; **~leitung die** oil pipeline; **~produkt das** oil product; **~produzent der** oil-producing country; **~produzierend** *Adj.* oil-producing; **~raffinerie die** oil refinery

Ẹrd-: ~pol der terrestrial pole; **~reich das** soil

erdrẹisten *refl. V.* **sich ~, etw. zu tun** have the audacity to do sth.

erdrọ̈hnen *itr. V.; mit sein* **a)** *(ertönen)* roar; **b)** *(beben)* shake

erdrọsseln *tr. V.* strangle

Erdrọsselung die; ~, ~en strangling

Ẹrd·rotation die rotation of the earth

erdrụ̈cken *tr. V.* **a)** crush; **b)** *(fig.: belasten)* overwhelm; **die ständigen Geldsorgen erdrückten ihn** he was oppressed by the continual worries about money; **c)** *(fig.: nicht gelten lassen)* overshadow; **die Schrankwand erdrückt den kleinen Raum** these wall units are too overpowering in the small room

erdrụ̈ckend 1. *Adj.* overwhelming ⟨*evidence, superiority*⟩; oppressive ⟨*heat, silence*⟩. **2.** *adv.* overwhelmingly

Ẹrd-: ~rutsch der landslide; landslip; **ein politischer ~rutsch** a political landslide; **~rutsch·sieg der** *(Politik)* landslide victory; **~satellit der** earth satellite; **~schatten der** shadow of the earth; **~schicht die a)** layer of earth; **b)** *(Geol.)* stratum; **~schluß der** *(Elektrot.)* accidental earth contact; **~scholle die** lump of earth; clod [of earth]; **~spalte die** fissure [in the ground]; **~stoß der** earth tremor; **~teil der** continent; **~trabant der** *(geh.)* earth satellite

erdụlden *tr. V.* endure ⟨*sorrow, misfortune*⟩; tolerate ⟨*insults*⟩; *(über sich ergehen lassen)* undergo

Ẹrd-: ~um·drehung die rotation of the earth; **eine ~umdrehung** one revolution of the earth; **~um·fang der** circumference of the earth; **~umkreisung die** orbit of the earth; **~ụm·lauf·bahn die** orbit [of the earth]; **in die ~umlaufbahn eintreten** enter into orbit; **~um·rundung die** *(eines Schiffs)* circumnavigation of the earth; *(eines Raumschiffs)* orbit of the earth; **~umseg[e]lung die** circumnavigation of the earth

Ẹrdung die; ~, ~en *(Elektrot.)* **a)** *(das Erden)* earthing; **b)** *(Leitung)* earth [connection]

ẹrd-, Ẹrd-: ~verbunden, ~verhaftet, ~verwachsen *Adj. (geh.)* close to nature *postpos.*; **~wall der** wall of earth; *(Milit., Straßenbau)* earthwork; **~wärts** *Adv. (geh.)* earthward[s]; **~zeit·alter das** geological era

erẹifern *refl. V.* **sich über etw.** *(Akk.)* **~:** get excited about sth.; **sich schnell/unnötig ~:** quickly get worked up/get worked up about nothing

Erẹiferung die; ~: excitement

erẹignen *refl. V.* happen; ⟨*accident, mishap*⟩ occur

Ereignis [ɛɐ̯'|aignɪs] **das; ~ses, ~se** event; occurrence; **ein aufregendes/historisches ~:** an exciting/historical event; **das fröhliche ~ Eurer Hochzeit** the happy occasion of your marriage; **die ~se überstürzten sich** everything seemed to happen at once; **ein freudiges ~:** a happy event; **große ~se werfen ihren Schatten voraus** coming events cast their shadows before

erẹignis-: los 1. *Adj.* uneventful; **2.** *adv.* uneventfully; **~reich 1.** *Adj.* eventful; **2.** *adv.* eventfully

erẹilen *tr. V. (geh.)* **der Tod ereilte ihn** he died suddenly; **das gleiche Schicksal ereilte ihn** he met the same fate

Erektion [erɛk'tsio:n] **die; ~, ~en** erection

Eremit [ere'mi:t] **der; ~en, ~en** hermit

Eremitage [eremi'ta:ʒə] **die; ~, ~n** hermitage

Eremịten·leben das hermit's life

erẹrben *tr. V. (veralt.)* inherit ⟨*money, characteristics*⟩

erẹrbt *Adj.* inherited ⟨*fortune, ability*⟩; inherited, hereditary ⟨*characteristic etc.*⟩

erfạhrbar *Adj.* **~ sein** be able to be experienced; **einem Kind etw. ~ machen** bring sth. within a child's experience

¹erfạhren *unr. tr. V.* **a)** find out; learn; *(hören)* hear; **etw. Wichtiges/Neues/Einzelheiten ~:** find out something important/new/some details; **etw. von jmdm. ~:** find sth. out from sb.; **etw. über jmdn./etw. ~:** find out *or* hear sth. about sb./sth.; **etw. von etw. ~:** find out *or* learn/hear sth. about sth.; **etw. durch jmdn./etw. ~:** learn of sth. from sb./sth.; **b)** *(geh.: erleben)* experience; **viel Leid/Kummer ~:** suffer much sorrow/anxiety; *s. auch* **Leib a; c)** *(mitmachen)* undergo ⟨*change, experience, development, etc.*⟩; suffer ⟨*set-back*⟩

²erfạhren *Adj.* experienced

Erfạhrung die; ~, ~en experience; **über reiche/langjährige ~en verfügen** have extensive/years of experience; **eine Frau mit ~:** a woman of experience; **~en sammeln** gain experience *sing.*; **~en austauschen** share one's experiences; **bittere ~en sammeln müssen** have bitter experiences; **die ~ machen, daß ...:** learn by experience that ...; **durch ~ lernen** learn through experience; **aus ~ sprechen** speak from experience; **wir haben schlechte ~en mit ihm/damit gemacht** our experience of him/it has not been very good; **etw. in ~ bringen** discover sth.

erfạhrungs-, Erfạhrungs-: ~austausch der exchange of experiences; **~bericht der** report; **~gemäß** *Adv.* in our/my experience; **~gemäß ist es so, daß ...:** experience shows that ...; **~mäßig 1.** *Adj.* empirical; **2.** *adv.* empirically; **~tat·sache die** empirical fact; **~wert der** figure drawn from past experience; **~wissenschaft die** empirical science

erfạßbar *Adj.* ascertainable

erfạssen *tr. V.* **a)** *(mitreißen)* catch; **b)** *(begreifen)* grasp ⟨*situation, implications, etc.*⟩; **etw. intuitiv ~:** have an intuitive grasp of sth.; **du hast es erfaßt!** *(meist iron.)* you've got it!; **c)** *(registrieren)* register; record; **einen repräsentativen Bevölkerungsdurchschnitt ~:** record information on *or* from a representative cross-section of the population; **d)** *(einbeziehen)* cover; **e)** *(packen)* seize; **Angst/Freude erfaßte ihn** he was seized by fear/overcome with joy

Erfạssung die registration; **eine ~ der gesamten Bevölkerung/des Wohnraums** a survey of the whole population/living space

erfịnden *unr. tr. V.* **a)** invent; **b)** *(ausdenken)* make up ⟨*story, words*⟩; make up, invent ⟨*excuse*⟩; **sie hat die Arbeit [auch] nicht erfunden** *(iron.)* she is a lazy so-and-so *(coll.)*; **das ist alles erfunden** it is pure fabrication; *s. auch* **Pulver b**

Erfịnder der; ~s, ~, Erfịnderin die; ~, ~nen a) inventor; **b)** *(Urheber)* creator; **das ist nicht im Sinne des ~s** *(ugs.)* that's not what it was meant for

Erfịnder·geist der; *o. Pl.* inventive genius

erfịnderisch *Adj.* inventive; *(schlau)* resourceful

Erfịnder·schutz der *protection of inventors*; ≈ patent law

erfịndlich *Adj.* **nicht ~ sein** be unclear; **mir ist nicht ~, warum ...:** I do not see why ...

Erfịndung die; ~, ~en a) invention; **die ~en der Raumfahrttechnik** inventions in the field of space technology; **eine ~ machen** invent something; **er hat viele ~en gemacht** he has many inventions to his credit; **b)** *(Ausgedachtes)* invention; fabrication

erfịndungs-, Erfịndungs-: ~gabe die inventiveness; **~reich 1.** *Adj.* imaginative; **2.** *adv.* imaginatively; **~reichtum der** capacity for invention

erflehen *tr. V. (geh.)* beg; **jmds. Hilfe/Hilfe von jmdm.** ~: beg sb.'s help/beg help from sb.; **Vergebung** ~: beg for forgiveness

Erfolg [ɛɐ̯'fɔlk] **der;** ~**[e]s,** ~**e** success; **viel/keinen** ~ **haben** be very successful/be unsuccessful; **etw. mit/ohne** ~ **tun** do something successfully/without success; **ohne** ~ **bleiben** remain unsuccessful; **der** ~ **blieb aus** success was not forthcoming; **einen** ~ **erzielen** *od.* **erringen** achieve success; **von** ~ **begleitet/gekrönt sein** be accompanied by/crowned with success; **der** ~ **war, daß ...** *(ugs.)* the upshot was that ...

erfolgen *itr. V.; mit sein* take place; occur; **nach erfolgtem Umbau** when reconstruction has/had been completed; **auf seine Beschwerden erfolgte keine Reaktion** there was no reaction to his complaints; **es erfolgte keine weitere Stellungnahme** no further statement was forthcoming

erfolg-, Erfolg-: ~**gekrönt** *Adj. (geh.)* crowned with success; ~**los** 1. *Adj.* unsuccessful; 2. *adv.* unsuccessfully; ~**losigkeit die;** ~: lack of success; ~**reich** 1. *Adj.* successful; 2. *adv.* successfully

Erfolgs-: ~**aus·sicht die;** *meist Pl.* prospect of success; ~**autor der** successful author; ~**beteiligung die** profit-sharing; ~**chance die** chance of success; ~**denken das: das rücksichtslose** ~**denken** the thoughtless worship of success; ~**erlebnis das** feeling of achievement; **dieses** ~**erlebnis tat ihm gut** this experience of success did him good; ~**film der** successful film; ~**honorar das** contingent fee; ~**kurve die** path of success; *(eines Produkts)* sales graph; ~**meldung die** report of success; ~**mensch der** successful individual; ~**prämie die** *(eines Vertreters)* commission; *(eines Arbeiters)* bonus; ~**quote die** success rate; *(bei Prüfungen)* pass rate; ~**rezept das** recipe for success; ~**roman der** successful novel; ~**stück das** *(Theater)* successful play; ~**zahl die,** ~**ziffer die;** *meist Pl.* high success figure; *(Wirtsch.)* profit figure; ~**zwang der** pressure to succeed

erfolg·versprechend *Adj.* promising

erforderlich *Adj.* required; necessary

erforderlichenfalls *Adv. (Amtsspr.)* should it be necessary

erfordern *tr. V.* require; demand; **wenn es die Umstände** ~: if circumstances require

Erfordernis das; ~**ses,** ~**se** requirement

erforschen *tr. V.* discover ⟨*facts, causes, etc.*⟩; explore ⟨*country*⟩; find out ⟨*truth*⟩; **sein Gewissen** ~: search one's conscience

Erforscher der researcher; *(Forschungsreisender)* explorer

Erforschung die research (+ *Gen.* into); *(der Erde, des Weltalls usw.)* exploration

erfragen *tr. V.* ascertain; **Einzelheiten zu** ~ **bei ...**: further details can be obtained from ...

erfrechen *refl. V. (veralt., scherzh.)* **sich** ~, **etw. zu tun** have the audacity to do sth.

erfreuen 1. *tr. V.* please; **wir möchten Sie mit einem kleinen Geschenk** ~: we should like to give you a small present; **diese gute Nachricht hat uns sehr erfreut** we were very pleased to hear the good news; **sehr erfreut!** pleased to meet you. 2. *refl. V.* **a) sich an etw.** *(Dat.)* ~: take pleasure in sth.; **b)** *(geh.: genießen)* **sich einer Sache** *(Gen.)* ~: enjoy sth.; **sich bester Gesundheit** ~: enjoy the best of health

erfreulich *Adj.* pleasant; **eine** ~**e Mitteilung** a piece of good news; **es ist sehr** ~ **zu hören, daß es Ihnen besser geht** its very good to hear that you're better; **etwas/wenig/nichts Erfreuliches** something/hardly anything/nothing pleasant

erfreulicherweise *Adv.* happily

erfrieren 1. *unr. itr. V.; mit sein* **a)** ⟨*person, animal*⟩ freeze to death; ⟨*plant, harvest, etc.*⟩ be damaged by frost; suffer frost-damage; **er ist ganz erfroren** *(ugs.)* he's absolutely frozen; **b)** *(fig.: erstarren)* freeze; ⟨*feelings*⟩ cool. 2. *unr. refl. V.* **sich** *(Dat.)* **die Finger/Ohren** ~: get frostbite in one's fingers/ears

Erfrierung die; ~, ~**en** frostbite *no pl.*; ~**en an den Händen/Füßen** frostbitten hands/feet

Erfrierungs·tod der death from exposure

erfrischen 1. *tr. (auch itr.) V.* **a)** *(beleben)* refresh; **ein Abendspaziergang erfrischt sehr** an evening walk is very refreshing; **b)** *(anregen)* stimulate. 2. *refl. V.* freshen oneself up

erfrischend *(auch fig.)* 1. *Adj.* refreshing. 2. *adv.* refreshingly

Erfrischung die; ~, ~**en** *(auch fig.)* refreshment

Erfrischungs-: ~**getränk das** soft drink; **eisgekühlter Tee ist ein herrliches** ~**getränk** iced tea is a wonderfully refreshing drink; ~**raum der** refreshment room; ~**stand der** refreshment stand; ~**trunk der** *(geh.)* refreshing drink; ~**tuch das;** *Pl.* ~**tücher** tissue wipe; towelette

erfühlen *tr. V. (geh.)* sense

erfüllbar *Adj.* ~**e Wünsche/Bedingungen** wishes which can be granted/conditions which can be met; **Ihre Wünsche/Bedingungen sind nicht** ~: your wishes cannot be granted/your conditions cannot be met

erfüllen 1. *tr. V.* **a)** grant ⟨*wish, request*⟩; fulfil ⟨*contract*⟩; carry out ⟨*duty*⟩; meet ⟨*condition*⟩; **seinen Zweck** ~: serve its purpose; **der Tatbestand des Totschlags ist erfüllt** this constitutes a case of manslaughter; **b)** *(füllen)* fill; **die Luft war von süßem Duft erfüllt** a sweet perfume filled the air; **ein erfülltes Leben** *(geh.)* a full life; **c)** *(stark beschäftigen)* overcome; **eine Sehnsucht erfüllte sein Herz** a longing came over him; **jmdn. mit etw.** ~ *(geh.)* fill sb. with sth.; **d)** *(Math.)* satisfy. 2. *refl. V.* ⟨*wish*⟩ come true

Erfüllung die: die ~ **von Pflichten** the performance of duties; **sie glaubte nicht mehr an die** ~ **ihrer Wünsche** she no longer believed that her wishes would be granted; **in** ~ **gehen** come true; **in etw.** *(Dat.)* ~ **finden** find fulfilment in sth.

Erfüllungs-: ~**gehilfe der** *(Rechtsw.)* agent of vicarious liability; ~**ort der;** *Pl.* ~**e** *(Rechtsw.)* place of performance; ~**politik die** *(bes. ns.) policy of unconditional fulfilment of the reparations and disarmament clauses of the Treaty of Versailles;* ~**tag der** *(Rechtsw.)* day for settlement *(of debts)*

erfunden 1. *2. Part. v.* **erfinden.** 2. *Adj.* **eine** ~**e Geschichte** a fictional story; **das Abenteuer ist doch nur** ~: the adventure is just made up; **frei** ~: completely fictitious

Erg [ɛrk] **das;** ~**s,** ~ *(Physik)* erg

ergänzen [ɛɐ̯'gɛntsn̩] 1. *tr. V.* **a)** *(vervollständigen)* complete; *(erweitern)* add to; replenish ⟨*supply*⟩; amplify ⟨*remark, statement, etc.*⟩; amend ⟨*statute*⟩; **etw. wieder** ~: make sth. up; **er ergänzte seine Sammlung durch** *od.* **um einige wertvolle Stücke** he added some valuable pieces to his collection; **b)** *(hinzufügen)* ~**[d hinzufügen]** add ⟨*remark*⟩; **c)** *(hinzukommen zu)* **eine Jacke ergänzte das Sommerkleid** a jacket complemented the summer dress; **der neue Mitarbeiter ergänzt das Team hervorragend** the new employee makes up the team admirably; **d) sie** ~ **einander** *od.* **sich** they complement each other. 2. *refl. V.* **sich durch etw.** ~: be augmented by sth.

Ergänzung die; ~, ~**en a)** *(Vervollständigung)* completion; *(Erweiterung)* enlargement; **die** ~ **der Arbeitsgruppen** making up the working groups; **zur** ~ **des Gesagten/einer Sammlung** to amplify what has been said/in order to enlarge a collection; **die** ~ **eines Gesetzes** the amendment of a statute; **die** ~ **der Vorräte** the replenishment of supplies; **b)** *(Zusatz)* addition; *(zu einem Gesetz)* amendment; **c)** *(zusätzliche Bemerkung)* further remark; **d)** *(Sprachw.: Objekt)* object

Ergänzungs-: ~**ab·gabe die** *(Steuerw.)* surtax; ~**band der;** *Pl.* ~**bände** supplementary volume; supplement; ~**binde·strich der** *(Sprachw.)* hyphen; ~**frage die a)** *(Sprachw.)* wh-question; **b)** *(Zusatzfrage)* supplementary question

ergattern *tr. V. (ugs.)* manage to grab

ergaunern *tr. V.* get by underhand means; **wo hast du [dir] das Fahrrad ergaunert?** *(ugs.)* where did you pinch *or* swipe that bike? *(coll.)*

[1]**ergeben** 1. *unr. refl. V.* **a)** *(sich fügen)* **sich in etw.** *(Akk.)* ~: submit to sth.; **sich in sein Schicksal** ~: resign oneself *or* become resigned to one's fate; **b)** *(kapitulieren)* surrender **(jmdm.** to sb.); **sich [der Polizei** *(Dat.)*] ~: give oneself up [to the police]; **c)** *(folgen, entstehen)* ⟨*opportunity, difficulty, problem*⟩ arise **(aus** from); **bald ergab sich ein angeregtes Gespräch** soon a lively discussion was taking place; **es ergab sich so** it just turned out that way; **d)** *(sich hingeben)* **sich jmdm.** ~: give oneself to someone; **sich einer Sache** *(Dat.)* ~: abandon oneself to sth.; **sich dem Alkohol/***(ugs.)* **Suff** ~: take to alcohol/drink *or* the bottle. 2. *unr. tr. V.* result in; **die Ernte ergab rund 400 Zentner Kartoffeln** the harvest produced about 400 hundredweight of potatoes; **eins und eins ergibt zwei** one and one makes two

[2]**ergeben** 1. *Adj.* **a)** *(zugeneigt)* devoted; **b)** *(resignierend)* **mit** ~**er Miene** with an expression of resignation; **c)** *(geh.: devot)* obsequious; ~**sten Dank** *(veralt.)* humblest thanks; **Ihr sehr** ~**er ...** *(geh.)* yours most obediently, ...; **Ihr** ~**ster** *od.* **sehr** ~**er Diener** *(veralt.)* your most obedient servant *(arch.)*. 2. *adv.* **a)** devotedly; **b)** with resignation; **c)** *(geh.)* obsequiously; **jmdm.** ~**st danken** *(veralt.)* thank sb. most humbly

Ergebenheit die; ~ **a)** *(Treue)* devotion; **b)** *(Sichfügen)* resignation

Ergebenheits·adresse die declaration of loyalty; *(an Monarchen)* loyal address

Ergebnis das; ~**ses,** ~**se** result; **zu einem** ~ **kommen** reach a conclusion; **zu einem** ~ **führen** produce a result; **ohne** ~ **bleiben** lead to nothing

ergebnis·los 1. *Adj.* fruitless ⟨*discussion*⟩; **die Verhandlungen blieben/verliefen** ~**/wurden** ~ **abgebrochen** negotiations remained inconclusive/proceeded unprofitably/were broken off without a conclusion having been reached. 2. *adv.* fruitlessly

ergebnis·reich *Adj.* fruitful

Ergebung die; ~: resignation

ergebungs·voll 1. *Adj.* humble. 2. *adv.* humbly

ergehen 1. *unr. refl. V.* **a)** *(äußern)* **sich in etw.** *(Dat.)* ~: indulge in sth.; **sich in endlosen Reden** ~: get carried away in endless speeches; **b)** *(geh.: lustwandeln)* take a turn. 2. *unr. itr. V.; mit sein* **a)** *(geh.: erlassen werden)* ⟨*law*⟩ be enacted; **an ihn erging der Ruf einer bekannten Universität** he was offered a chair at a well-known university; **die Einladungen ergingen an alle Mitglieder** the invitations went to all members; **b)** *unpers. (widerfahren)* **jmdm. ergeht es gut/schlecht** things go well/badly for someone; **c) etw. über sich** *(Akk.)* ~ **lassen** let sth. wash over one

ergiebig [ɛɐ̯'gi:bɪç] *Adj.* rich ⟨*deposits, resources*⟩; productive ⟨*mine*⟩; fertile ⟨*fisheries, topic*⟩; **der neue Kaffee ist nicht so** ~**/ist** ~**er** the new coffee does not go as far/goes further

Ergiebigkeit die; ~: *s.* **ergiebig:** richness; productivity; fertility; **wegen der** ~ **des Kaffees/Tees** because the coffee/tea goes a long way

ergießen *unr. refl. V.* pour; **die Abwässer ~ sich in den Fluß** the effluent pours out into the river; **eine Menschenmasse ergoß sich in das Stadion** a mass of people poured into the stadium

erglänzen *itr. V.; mit sein (geh.)* ⟨*sun, light*⟩ appear; ⟨*sea, diamonds*⟩ begin to sparkle

erglühen *itr. V.; mit sein (geh.)* **a)** glow; **in Liebe [zu jmdm.] erglüht sein** be passionately in love [with sb.]; **b)** *(rot werden)* redden

ergo ['ɛrgo] *Adv.* ergo

Ergo·meter das; ~s, ~ *(Med.)* ergometer

Ergonomie [ɛrgono'mi:] **die,** ~, **Ergonomik** [ɛrgo'no:mɪk] **die;** ~: ergonomics *sing., no art.*

ergötzen *(geh.)* **1.** *tr. V.* enthrall; captivate. **2.** *refl. V.* **sich an etw.** *(Dat.)* ~: be delighted by sth.

Ergötzen das; ~s *(geh.)* delight

ergötzlich *(geh.)* **1.** *Adj.* delightful. **2.** *adv.* delightfully

ergrauen *itr. V.; mit sein* go *or* turn grey; **in Ehren ergraut sein** *(fig.)* have grown old with honour; **ein im Dienst ergrauter Beamter** *(fig.)* an official of long standing

ergreifen *unr. tr. V.* **a)** *(greifen)* grab; **jmds. Hand** ~: grasp sb.'s hand; **b)** *(festnehmen)* catch ⟨*thief etc.*⟩; **c)** *(fig.: erfassen)* seize; **von blindem Zorn ergriffen** *(geh.)* in the grip of blind anger; **d)** *(fig.: aufnehmen)* **einen Beruf** ~: take up a career; **die Initiative/eine Gelegenheit** ~: take the initiative/an opportunity; **e)** *(fig.: bewegen)* move

ergreifend 1. *Adj.* moving; **das ist ja** ~ *(iron.)* how moving. **2.** *adv.* movingly

Ergreifung die; ~ **a)** *(des Schuldigen)* capture; **b)** *(der Macht)* seizure

ergriffen *Adj.* moved

Ergriffenheit die; ~: **vor** ~ **schweigen** be too moved to speak; **vor** ~ **weinen** be moved to tears; **voller** ~: deeply moved

ergrimmen *(geh.)* **1.** *itr. V.; mit sein* be angry; **über etw.** *(Akk.)* **ergrimmt sein** be angry about something. **2.** *tr. V.* infuriate

ergründbar *Adj. s.* **ergründen:** ascertainable; discoverable; graspable; fathomable

ergründen *tr. V.* ascertain; discover ⟨*cause*⟩; grasp ⟨*concept*⟩; fathom ⟨*mystery*⟩

Ergründung die *s.* **ergründen:** ascertainment; discovery; grasping; fathoming

Erguß der a) *(Med.) (Blut~)* bruise; contusion; *(Samen~)* ejaculation; **b)** *(geh. abwertend)* outburst; **ein poetischer** ~: a poetic outpouring; **c)** *(Geol.)* eruption

erhaben *Adj.* **a)** *(weihevoll)* solemn ⟨*moment*⟩; awe-inspiring ⟨*sight*⟩; sublime ⟨*beauty*⟩; **b)** *(überlegen)* **über etw.** *(Akk.)* ~ **sein** be above sth.; **über jeden Zweifel** ~: beyond all criticism; **c)** *(hervortretend)* uneven ⟨*surface*⟩; embossed ⟨*pattern*⟩

Erhabenheit die; ~: grandeur; **eine Landschaft von solcher** ~: a landscape of such awe-inspiring grandeur; **die** ~ **des Augenblicks** the solemn grandeur of the moment

Erhalt der; ~[e]s *(Amtsdt.)* **a)** receipt; **den** ~ **eines Briefes bestätigen** acknowledge receipt of a letter; **bei** ~ **zahlen** pay on receipt; **b)** *s.* **Erhaltung**

erhalten 1. *unr. tr. V.* **a)** *(empfangen, bekommen)* receive ⟨*letter, news, gift*⟩; be given ⟨*order*⟩; get ⟨*good mark, impression*⟩; **eine hohe Geldstrafe** ~: be fined heavily; **er erhielt 3 Jahre Gefängnis** he was sentenced to 3 years in prison; **b)** *(bewahren)* preserve ⟨*town, building*⟩; conserve ⟨*energy*⟩; **diese Kleider sind noch gut** ~: these clothes are still in good condition; **jmdn. am Leben** ~: keep sb. alive; **er ist noch gut** ~ *(scherzh.)* he is well preserved; **c)** *(unterhalten)* support; **d)** *(als Endprodukt gewinnen)* obtain ⟨*sugar, oil, etc.*⟩. **2.** *unr. refl. V. (überdauern)* survive

Erhalter der *(Bewahrer)* preserver; *(der Familie)* bread-winner

erhältlich [ɛɐ̯'hɛltlɪç] *Adj.* obtainable

Erhaltung die; ~ *(des Friedens)* maintenance; *(der Arten, von Kunstschätzen)* preservation; *(der Energie)* conservation

Erhaltungs·satz der *(Physik)* principle of conservation

erhängen *tr. V.* **jmdn./sich** ~: hang sb./oneself; **Tod durch Erhängen** death by hanging

erhärten *tr. V.* **a)** strengthen ⟨*suspicion, assumption*⟩; substantiate ⟨*claim*⟩; **b)** *s.* **härten 1**

Erhärtung die; ~, ~**en a)** *(Bekräftigung)* substantiation; **b)** *s.* **Härtung**

erhaschen *tr. V. (geh., auch fig.)* catch

erheben 1. *unr. tr. V.* **a)** *(emporheben)* raise ⟨*one's arm/hand*⟩; **das Glas** ~: raise one's glass; **erhobenen Hauptes** with head held high; **die Stimme** ~: raise one's voice; **b)** *(verlangen)* levy ⟨*tax*⟩; charge ⟨*fee*⟩; **c)** *(befördern)* **jmdn. in den Adelsstand** ~: elevate sb. to the nobility; **d)** *(sammeln)* gather, collect ⟨*data, material*⟩; **e)** *(vorbringen)* **Anklage** ~: bring *or* prefer charges; **Protest** ~: make a protest; *s. auch* **Einspruch a; f)** *auch itr. (geh.: erbauen)* ⟨*art*⟩ edify; ⟨*music*⟩ uplift; **g)** *(bes. südd., österr.: feststellen)* ascertain ⟨*cause etc.*⟩. **2.** *unr. refl. V.* **a)** *(aufstehen)* rise; **sich von seinem Platz** ~: rise from one's seat; **b)** *(rebellieren)* rise up **(gegen** against); **c)** *(aufsteigen)* ⟨*bird, balloon*⟩ rise; **d)** *(hinauswachsen)* **sich über etw.** *(Akk.)* ~: rise above sth.; **e)** *(emporragen)* ⟨*tower, mountain*⟩ rise; **f)** *(geh.: sich besser dünken)* **sich über jmdn.** ~: feel superior to sb.; **g)** *(geh.: beginnen)* ⟨*cry*⟩ ring out; ⟨*storm*⟩ rise

erhebend *Adj.* uplifting

erheblich [ɛɐ̯'he:plɪç] **1.** *Adj.* considerable. **2.** *adv.* considerably

Erhebung die; ~, ~**en a)** *(Anhöhe)* elevation; **b)** *(Aufstand)* uprising; **c)** *(Umfrage)* survey; **d)** *(Einziehen) (von Steuern)* levying; *(von Gebühren)* charging; **e)** *(Beförderung)* elevation; **seine** ~ **in den Adelsstand** his elevation to the nobility; **f)** *(seelische Erbauung)* uplift

Erhebungs·zeitraum der *(Statistik)* period during which information is/was collected

erheischen *tr. V. (geh.)* demand; command ⟨*admiration*⟩

erheitern 1. *tr. V.* **jmdn.** ~: cheer sb. up. **2.** *refl. V. (geh.)* be amused; **seine Züge erheiterten sich** his face brightened up

Erheiterung die; ~, ~**en** amusement

erhellen 1. *tr. V.* **a)** *(beleuchten)* light up, illuminate ⟨*room, sky*⟩; **b)** *(erklären)* shed light on, illuminate ⟨*reason, relationship*⟩. **2.** *refl. V. (geh.: sich aufheitern)* ⟨*eyes, face*⟩ brighten. **3.** *itr. V. (veralt.: hervorgehen)* **daraus erhellt, daß ...:** it follows *or* is evident from this that ...

Erhellung die; ~ *(Erklärung)* illumination

erhitzen 1. *tr. V.* **a)** *(heiß machen)* heat ⟨*liquid*⟩; **jmdn.** ~: make sb. hot; **b)** *(fig.: erregen)* **die Gemüter** ~: make feelings run high. **2.** *refl. V.* **a)** heat up; ⟨*person*⟩ become hot; **b)** *(fig.: sich erregen)* ⟨*feelings*⟩ become heated

erhitzt *Adj.* heated

Erhitzung die; ~, ~**en** heating; *(Hitze)* heat

erhoffen *tr. V.* **sich** *(Dat.)* **viel/wenig von etw.** ~: expect a lot/little from sth.; **die erhoffte Änderung/Lohnerhöhung** the change/pay rise we/they had expected

erhöhen 1. *tr. V.* **a) eine Mauer [um einen Meter]** ~: make a wall [one metre] higher; **b)** *(steigern)* increase, raise ⟨*prices, productivity, etc.*⟩; **erhöhte/leicht erhöhte Temperatur haben** have a [high]/slight temperature; **erhöhter Blutdruck** somewhat high blood pressure; **erhöhte Gefahr** increased danger; **erhöhte Vorsicht** extra care; **c)** *(Musik)* raise ⟨*note*⟩. **2.** *refl. V.* ⟨*rent, prices*⟩ rise

Erhöhung die; ~, ~**en a)** *(Höhermachen)* raising; **die** ~ **der Schornsteine/Deiche** increasing the height of the chimneys/dikes; **b) eine** ~ **der Preise/Steuern** an increase in prices/taxes; **eine Erhöhung des Blutdrucks** a rise in blood pressure; **die** ~ **einer Dosis** the increasing of a dose; **c)** *(Musik)* raising [of a note]; **d)** *(Anhöhe)* hill

Erhöhungs-: ~winkel der *(Waffent.)* angle of elevation; **~zeichen das** *(Musik)* sharp [sign]

erholen *refl. V.* **a)** *(sich ausruhen)* **sich [gut]** ~: have a [good] rest; *(entspannen)* relax [thoroughly]; **die Kurse haben/die Wirtschaft hat sich erholt** *(fig.)* the rates of exchange have/the economy has recovered; **b)** *(genesen)* **sich von etw.** ~: recover from something

erholsam *Adj.* restful ⟨*weekend, holiday*⟩; **wandern ist sehr** ~: walking is very refreshing

Erholung die; ~ **a)** ~ **brauchen** *od.* **nötig haben** need a rest; **nach der langen Krankheit hat er** ~ **nötig** he needs to recuperate after his long illness; **zur** ~ **fahren** go on holiday to rest/relax; *(nach einer Krankheit)* go on holiday to convalesce; **eine** ~ **sein** be relaxing; **b)** *(fig.)* refreshing change

erholungs-, Erholungs-: ~aufenthalt der holiday; **~bedürftig** *Adj.* in need of a rest *postpos.*; **~bedürftig sein** need a rest; **~gebiet das** holiday area; **~heim das** holiday home; **~ort der;** *Pl.* ~e resort; **~pause die** break; **~reif** *Adj. (ugs.) s.* **~bedürftig; ~reise die** holiday trip; **~suchend** *Adj.* seeking relaxation *postpos.*; **~suchende der/die;** *adj. Dekl.* holidaymaker; **~urlaub der** holiday for convalescence; **~wert der** recreational value; **~zentrum das** leisure centre

erhören *tr. V. (geh.)* hear ⟨*plea, prayer*⟩; **einen Liebhaber** ~ *(veralt.)* yield to a lover

erigieren [eri'gi:rən] *itr. V.; mit sein* become erect; **erigiert** erect

Erika ['e:rika] **die;** ~, ~s *od.* **Eriken** [-kən] *(Bot.)* erica

erinnerlich *Adj.; nicht attr.* **wie** ~: as will be recalled; **soviel mir** ~ **ist** as I recall; **das ist mir nicht mehr** ~: I cannot remember that any more

erinnern [ɛɐ̯'lɪnɐn] **1.** *refl. V.* **sich an jmdn./etw. [gut/genau]** ~: remember sb./sth. [well/clearly]; **sich [daran]** ~, **daß ...:** remember *or* recall that ...; **wenn ich mich recht erinnere** if I remember rightly; **sich jmds./einer Sache** ~ *(geh.)* remember *or* recall sb./sth. **2.** *tr. V.* **a)** *(ins Bewußtsein rufen)* **jmdn. an etw./jmdn.** ~: remind sb. of sth./sb.; **jmdn. daran** ~, **etw. zu tun** remind sb. to do sth.; **b)** *(ugs., bes. nordd.)* **jmdn./etw.** ~: remember sb./sth. **3.** *itr. V.* **a) jmd./etw. erinnert an jmdn./etw.** sb./sth. reminds one of sb./sth.; **b)** *(zu bedenken geben)* **an etw.** *(Akk.)* ~: remind sb. of sth.; **ich möchte daran** ~, **daß ...:** let us not forget *or* overlook that ...

Erinnerung die; ~, ~**en a)** memory **(an** + *Akk.* of); **etw. [noch gut] in** ~ **haben** [still] remember sth. [well]; **etw. aus der** ~ **aufschreiben/sagen** write/say sth. from memory; **wenn mich die** ~ **nicht täuscht** if my memory does not deceive me; **sich** *(Dat.)* **etw. in die** ~ **zurückrufen** call something to mind again; **nach meiner** ~, **meiner** ~ **nach** as far as I remember; **seinen** ~**en nachhängen** lose oneself in one's memories; **jmdn./etw. in guter** ~ **behalten** have pleasant memories of sb./sth.; **zur** ~ **an jmdn./etw.** in memory of sb./sth.; **zur** ~ **an die Gefallenen wurde ein Denkmal errichtet** a monument was erected to the memory of those who had fallen; **b)** *(Erinnerungsstück)* remembrance; souvenir; **c)** *Pl. (Autobiographie)* memoirs; **d)** *(Zahlungsaufforderung)* reminder

Erinnerungs-: ~bild das memory; **~foto das** souvenir snapshot; **~lücke die** gap in one's memory; **da habe ich eine ~lücke** my mind is a blank about that; ~**medaille die** commemorative coin; ~**schreiben das** reminder; ~**stück das** keepsake; *(von einer Reise)* souvenir; ~**vermögen das** memory; ~**wert der** sentimental value

Erinnye [e'rɪnyə] **die; ~, ~n** *(Myth.)* Fury; Erinys

erjagen *tr. V.* **a)** *(erbeuten)* catch; **b)** *(gewinnen)* win ⟨*fame*⟩; make ⟨*money, fortune*⟩

erkalten *tr. V.; mit sein* cool; ⟨*limbs*⟩ grow cold; *(fig.)* ⟨*passion, feeling*⟩ cool

erkälten *refl. V.* catch cold; **sich** *(Dat.)* **den Magen ~**: get a chill on one's stomach; *s. auch* **Blase c**

Erkältung die; ~, ~en cold; **sich** *(Dat.)* **eine ~ zuziehen** *od. (ugs.)* **holen** catch a cold

Erkältungs·krankheit die cold

erkämpfen *tr. V.* win; **den Sieg ~**: gain a victory; **sich** *(Dat.)* **etw. ~ müssen** have to fight for sth.

erkaufen *tr. V.* **a)** *(durch Opfer)* win; **etw. teuer ~**: win something at great cost; **b)** *(durch Geld)* buy; **sich** *(Dat.)* **etw. ~**: buy oneself sth.

erkennbar 1. *Adj.* recognizable; *(sichtbar)* visible; *(schwach sichtbar)* discernible. **2.** *adv.* recognizably; *(sichtbar)* visibly

erkennen 1. *unr. tr. V.* **a)** *(deutlich sehen)* make out; **die Fingerabdrücke waren deutlich zu ~**: the fingerprints were clearly visible; **b)** *(identifizieren)* recognize (**an** + *Dat.* by); **der Täter wurde nicht erkannt** the culprit was not identified; **sich zu ~ geben** reveal one's identity; **sich als etw. zu erkennen geben** reveal oneself to be sth.; **c)** *(einschätzen)* recognize; perceive; acknowledge ⟨*error, mistake*⟩; **„erkenne dich selbst!"** 'know thyself!'; **d)** *(geh. veralt: begatten)* know *(arch.)*. **2.** *unr. itr. V.* **a)** *(Rechtsspr.)* **auf Freispruch ~**: grant an acquittal; **das Gericht erkannte auf 6 Jahre Gefängnis** the court passed a sentence of six years' imprisonment; **b)** *(Sport)* **auf Elfmeter/Freistoß ~**: award a penalty/free kick

erkenntlich *Adj.* **a) sich [für etw.] ~ zeigen** show one's appreciation for sth.; **b)** *s.* **erkennbar**

Erkenntlichkeit die; ~, ~en a) *o. Pl. (Dankbarkeit)* gratitude; **b)** *(Geschenk)* token of gratitude

Erkenntnis die; ~, ~se a) *(Einsicht)* discovery; **wissenschaftliche/wichtige/gesicherte ~se** scientific findings/important discoveries/firm insights; **zu der ~ kommen, daß ...**: come to the realization that ...; **b)** *o. Pl. (das Erkennen)* cognition; **der Baum der ~** *(bibl.)* the tree of knowledge

erkenntnis-, Erkenntnis-: ~drang der thirst for knowledge; **~kritik die** *(Philos.)* critique of knowledge; **~prozeß der** cognitive process; **~theoretisch** *(Philos.)* **1.** *Adj.* epistemological; **2.** *adv.* epistemologically; **~theorie die** *(Philos.)* theory of knowledge; epistemology *no art.*; **~vermögen das** powers *pl.* of cognition

erkennungs-, Erkennungs-: ~dienst der police records department; **~dienstlich 1.** *Adj.* **~dienstliche Behandlung** fingerprinting and photographing; **2.** *adv.* **Personen ~dienstlich erfassen** investigate persons through the police records department; **jmdn. ~dienstlich behandeln** take sb.'s fingerprints and photograph; **~marke die** identification disc; **~melodie die** *(einer Sendung)* theme music; *(eines Senders)* signature tune; **~zeichen das** sign [to recognize sb. by]

Erker ['ɛrkɐ] **der; ~s, ~**: bay window

Erker-: ~fenster das bay window; **~zimmer das** room with a bay window

erkiesen *unr. tr. V. (veralt. geh.)* choose

erklärbar *Adj.* explicable; **etw. ist ~**: sth. can be explained; **aus ~en Gründen** for reasons which can easily be explained

erklären 1. *tr. V.* **a)** explain; **jmdm. etw. ~**: explain sth. to sb.; **etw. an einem Beispiel ~**: explain sth. with an example; **b)** *(begründen)* explain (**durch** by); **c)** *(mitteilen)* state; declare; announce ⟨*one's resignation*⟩; **jmdm. den Krieg ~**: declare war on sb.; **d)** *(bezeichnen)* **jmdn. für tot ~**: pronounce someone dead; **etw. für ungültig/verbindlich ~**: declare something to be invalid/binding; **die Ehe wurde für ungültig erklärt** the marriage was declared void; **jmdn. zu etw. ~**: name sb. as sth. **2.** *refl. V.* **a) sich einverstanden/bereit ~**: declare oneself [to be] in agreement/willing; **sich zu einer Sache ~**: make a statement on sth.; **sich für jmdn./etw. ~** *(geh.)* declare one's support for sb./sth.; **sich gegen jmdn./etw. ~**: declare one's opposition to sb./sth.; **sich jmdm. ~** *(geh. veralt.)* declare one's love to someone; **b)** *(seine Begründung finden)* be explained; **das erklärt sich einfach/von selbst** that is easily explained/self-evident

erklärend 1. *Adj.* explanatory; **mit einigen ~en Worten** with a few words of explanation. **2.** *adv.* by way of explanation

erklärlich *Adj.* understandable; **es ist mir einfach nicht ~, wie ...**: I just can't understand how ...

erklärlicherweise *Adv.* understandably

erklärt *Adj.; nicht präd.* declared ⟨*opponent, intention*⟩; **er war der ~e Mittelpunkt** he was regarded by all as the centre of attraction

erklärtermaßen *Adv.* on one's own admission

Erklärung die; ~, ~en a) *(Darlegung)* explanation; **b)** *(Mitteilung)* statement; **eine ~ abgeben** make a statement

Erklärungs·versuch der attempt at an explanation

erklecklich [ɛɐ̯'klɛklɪç] *Adj.* considerable ⟨*sum, profit*⟩

erklettern *tr. V.* climb to the top of ⟨*rock, wall, mountain*⟩; climb to ⟨*summit*⟩

erklimmen *unr. tr. V. (geh.)* climb ⟨*wall, tree*⟩; **die oberste Stufe der Erfolgsleiter ~** *(fig.)* reach the top of the ladder to success

erklingen *unr. itr. V.; mit sein* ring out; **Musik ~ hören** hear the sound of music; **es erklang die Nationalhymne** the national anthem was played

erkoren [ɛɐ̯'ko:rən] *2. Part. v.* **erkiesen**

erkranken *itr. V.; mit sein* become ill (**an** + *Dat.* with); **er ist an einer Lungenentzündung erkrankt** he's got an inflammation of the lungs; **schwer erkrankt sein** be seriously ill; **ein erkrankter Kollege** a sick colleague

Erkrankung die; ~, ~en *(eines Menschen, Tieres)* illness; *(eines Körperteils)* disease

Erkrankungs·fall der: im ~: in event of illness; **die Versicherung schließt Erkrankungsfälle nicht ein** the insurance does not cover illness

erkühnen *refl. V. (geh.)* **sich ~, etw. zu tun** dare to do sth.

erkunden *tr. V.* reconnoitre ⟨*terrain*⟩; **die Situation ~**: find out what the situation is

erkundigen *refl. V.* **sich nach jmdm./etw. ~**: ask after sb./enquire about sth.; **sich ~, ob/wann ...**: enquire whether/when ...; *s. auch* **Befinden**

Erkundigung die; ~, ~en enquiry; **~en einholen** *od.* **einziehen** make enquiries

Erkundung die; ~, ~en *(meist Milit.)* reconnaissance; **auf ~ gehen** go out on reconnaissance

Erkundungs-: ~fahrt die exploratory trip; **eine ~fahrt machen** go exploring; **eine ~fahrt durch die Umgebung machen** explore the area; **~flug der** reconnaissance flight; **~trupp der** reconnaissance party

erkünstelt [ɛɐ̯'kʏnst|t] *Adj. (abwertend) s.* **gekünstelt 1**

Erlag·schein [ɛɐ̯'la:k-] **der** *(österr.) s.* **Zahlkarte**

erlahmen *itr. V.; mit sein* **a)** tire; become tired; ⟨*strength*⟩ flag; **b)** *(nachlassen)* ⟨*enthusiasm etc.*⟩ wane

erlangen *tr. V.* gain; obtain ⟨*credit, visa*⟩; reach ⟨*age*⟩

Erlangung die; ~: attainment; *(eines Kredits, Visums)* obtaining; *(von Stimmen)* gaining; **zur ~ der Doktorwürde** for the degree of doctor

Erlaß [ɛɐ̯'las] **der; Erlasses, Erlasse a)** *(Anordnung)* decree; **der ~ eines Ministers** a decree by a minister; a ministerial decree; **b)** *(Straf~, Schulden~ usw.)* remission; **c)** *o. Pl. (Verfügung) (eines Gesetzes, einer Bestimmung)* enactment; *(eines Dekrets)* issue; *(eines Verbots)* imposition

erlassen *unr. tr. V.* **a)** *(verkünden)* enact ⟨*law*⟩; declare ⟨*amnesty*⟩; issue ⟨*warrant*⟩; **b)** *(verzichten auf)* remit ⟨*sentence*⟩; **~ Sie es mir, das zu schildern** *(geh.)* excuse me from having to describe it

erlauben 1. *tr. V.* **a)** allow; **jmdm. ~, etw. zu tun** allow sb. to do sth.; **~ Sie mir, das Fenster zu öffnen?** *(geh.)* would you mind if I opened the window?; **es ist nicht erlaubt, den Rasen zu betreten** it is forbidden to walk on the grass; **[na], ~ Sie mal!** *(ugs.)* do you mind! *(coll.)*; **was ~ Sie sich!** how dare you!; **erlaubt ist, was gefällt** do what you feel like doing; **was nicht verboten ist, das ist erlaubt** if something's not forbidden then it's allowed; **b)** *(ermöglichen)* permit; **meine Gesundheit erlaubt es mir nicht** my health does not permit me to do it; **meine Zeit erlaubt es mir nicht** time does not allow. **2.** *refl. V.* **a)** *(sich die Freiheit nehmen)* **sich** *(Dat.)* **etw. ~**: permit oneself sth.; **du hast dir in letzter Zeit ziemlich viele Freiheiten erlaubt** you have been taking a lot of liberties recently; **sie erlaubt sich** *(Dat.)* **in letzter Zeit grobe Nachlässigkeiten** she's allowed herself to become extremely negligent recently; **über seine berufliche Leistung kann ich mir kein Urteil ~**: I do not feel free to comment on his professional competence; **sich** *(Dat.)* **alles ~**: do just as one pleases; **sich** *(Dat.)* **einen Scherz [mit jmdm.] ~**: play a trick [on someone]; **b)** *(sich leisten)* **sich** *(Dat.)* **etw. ~**: treat oneself to sth.; **das/solche teuren Geschenke kannst du dir nicht ~**: you cannot afford it/such expensive presents

Erlaubnis die; ~, ~se permission; *(Schriftstück)* permit; **jmdn. um ~ bitten, etw. zu tun** ask sb.'s permission *or* sb. for permission to do sth.; **jmdm. die ~ erteilen/verweigern, etw. zu tun** give/refuse sb. permission to do sth.

Erlaubnis·schein der permit

erlaucht [ɛɐ̯'lauxt] *Adj. (geh.)* illustrious

Erlaucht die; ~, ~en *(veralt.)* **Ihre/Seine ~**: Her Ladyship/His Lordship; **Euer ~**: Your Ladyship/Lordship

erläutern *tr. V.* explain; comment on ⟨*picture etc.*⟩; annotate ⟨*text*⟩; **näher ~**: clarify; **~de Anmerkungen** explanatory notes

Erläuterung die explanation; *(zu einem Bild usw.)* commentary; *(zu einem Text)* [explanatory] note

Erle ['ɛrlə] **die; ~, ~n** alder

erleben *tr. V.* experience; **etwas Schönes/Schreckliches ~**: have a pleasant/terrible experience; **das habe ich noch nie erlebt!** I've never heard of such a thing!; **er hat viel erlebt** he has seen a lot of life; **große Abenteuer ~**: have great adventures; **er wollte erst etwas ~**: he wanted to live it up a bit first; **so ängstlich hatte er sie noch nie erlebt** he had never seen her so afraid before; **etw. bewußt/intensiv ~**: be fully aware of sth./experience sth. to the full; **sie wünschte sich nur, die Hochzeit ihrer Tochter noch zu ~**: her only remaining wish was to be at her daughter's wedding; **er wird das nächste Jahr nicht mehr ~**: he won't see next year;

dieser Film erlebte einen völligen Reinfall this film was a complete flop *(coll.)*; **du kannst was ~!** *(ugs.)* you won't know what's hit you!; **sich als etw. ~:** feel oneself to be sth.; *s. auch* **erlebt**

Erleben das experience; **etw. aus eigenem ~ kennen** know something from one's own experience

Erlebens·fall der *(Versicherungsw.)* **im ~:** in the event of survival; **eine Versicherung auf den ~:** endowment assurance

Erlebnis das; ~ses, ~se experience; **das war ein ~:** what an experience!

Erlebnis-: ~auf·satz der *(Schulw.)* essay based on personal experience; **~fähigkeit die;** *o. Pl. (Psych.)* capacity for experience; **~hunger der** thirst for experience

erlebt *Adj.* **~e Rede** inner monologue; **~e Geschichte** a first-hand account

erledigen 1. *tr. V.* **a)** *(ausführen)* **einen Auftrag ~:** deal with a task; **ich muß noch einige Dinge erledigen** I must see to a few things; **so, damit wäre die Angelegenheit endlich erledigt** so now the matter is finally settled; **sie hat alles pünktlich erledigt** she got everything done on time; **schon erledigt!** that's already done; **b)** *(erschöpfen)* finish *(coll.)* ⟨*person*⟩; **der Umzug hat ihn völlig erledigt** the move finished him off completely *(coll.)*; *(ugs.: töten)* knock off *(sl.)*; *(fig.: zerstören)* destroy. **2.** *refl. V.* ⟨*matter, problem*⟩ resolve itself; **damit hat sich die Sache erledigt** that's that; **vieles erledigt sich von selbst** a lot of things sort them'selves out

erledigt *Adj.* closed ⟨*case*⟩; *(ugs.)* worn out ⟨*person*⟩

Erledigung die; ~, ~en a) *o. Pl. (Durchführung)* carrying out; *(Beendigung)* completion; *(einer Angelegenheit)* settling; **um baldige ~ wird gebeten** please give this matter your prompt attention; **b)** *(Besorgung)* **er hat noch einige ~en zu machen** he's got one or two more things to see to

erlegen *tr. V.* **a)** shoot ⟨*animal*⟩; **b)** *(österr.: entrichten)* pay ⟨*fee, charge*⟩

erleichtern 1. *tr. V.* **a)** *(einfacher machen)* make easier; **jmdm./sich die Arbeit ~:** make sb.'s/one's work easier; **b)** *(befreien)* relieve; **das hat ihn [sehr] erleichtert** that came as a [great] relief to him; **erleichtert aufatmen** breathe a sigh of relief; **c)** *(Gewicht verringern, fig.)* lighten; **sein Herz/sein Gewissen ~:** open one's heart/unburden one's conscience; **jmdn. um etw. ~** *(ugs. scherzh.)* relieve sb. of sth. **2.** *refl. V. (verhüll.: seine Notdurft verrichten)* relieve oneself

Erleichterung die; ~, ~en a) *o. Pl. (Vereinfachung)* **zur ~ der Arbeit** to make the work easier; **b)** *o. Pl. (Befreiung)* relief; **mit ~:** with relief; **voller ~:** with great relief; **~ empfinden** feel relieved; **c)** *(Verbesserung, Milderung)* alleviation; **es gab weitere ~en im Reiseverkehr** there was a further easing of travel restrictions

erleiden *unr. tr. V.* suffer

erlernbar *Adj.* learnable; **es ist leicht ~:** it can be easily learnt *or* is easy to learn; **eine ~e Fähigkeit** a faculty which can be acquired

erlernen *tr. V.* learn

[1]**erlesen** *unr. tr. V. (geh. veralt.)* choose

[2]**erlesen** *Adj.* superior ⟨*wine*⟩; choice ⟨*dish*⟩; **ein ~er Geschmack** a discriminating taste

Erlesenheit die; ~: exquisiteness

erleuchten *tr. V.* **a)** light; **Blitze erleuchteten den Himmel** the sky was lit up by flashes of lightning; **hell erleuchtete Fenster** brightly lit windows; **b)** *(geh.: mit Klarheit erfüllen)* inspire

Erleuchtung die; ~, ~en inspiration; **ihm kam eine ~:** he had a flash of inspiration

erliegen *unr. itr. V.; mit sein* **a)** succumb (*Dat.* to); **einem Irrtum ~:** be misled; **im Kampf ~** *(veralt.)* be vanquished in battle; **zum Erliegen kommen** come to a standstill; **etw. zum Erliegen bringen** bring sth. to a standstill; **b)** *(zum Opfer fallen)* **einer Krankheit** *(Dat.)* **~:** die from an illness

Erl·könig ['ɛrl-] **der a) „Der ~"** 'The erl-king'; **b)** *(Kfz-Jargon)* test model

erlogen *Adj.* made up; untruthful ⟨*story*⟩

Erlös [ɛɐ̯'lø:s] **der; ~es, ~e** proceeds *pl.*; **vom ~ seiner Bilder leben** live on the income from the sale of one's paintings

erlöschen *unr. itr. V.; mit sein* **a)** ⟨*fire*⟩ go out; **ein erloschener Vulkan** an extinct volcano; **die Lichter waren schon erloschen** the lights were already out; **b)** *(nachlassen)* ⟨*hope, feelings*⟩ wane; **c)** *(aussterben)* ⟨*family, clan*⟩ die out; **d)** *(zu bestehen aufhören)* ⟨*claim, obligation*⟩ cease; ⟨*firm, membership*⟩ cease to exist

erlösen *tr. V.* save, rescue (**von** from); **jmdn. von seinen Schmerzen ~:** release sb. from pain; **von einer Sorge erlöst sein** be relieved of a worry; **von einer Krankheit erlöst werden** *(verhüll.)* be released from an illness; **jmdn. ~** *(ugs. scherzh.)* take over from sb.; **und erlöse uns von dem Übel** *od.* **Bösen** *(bibl.)* and deliver us from evil

erlösend *Adj.* **das ~e Wort sprechen** say the magic word; **~ wirken** come as a relief

Erlöser der; ~s, ~ a) saviour; **b)** *(christl. Rel.)* redeemer

Erlösung die release (**von** from); *(christl. Rel.)* redemption; **es war eine ~ zu wissen, daß ...:** it was a relief to know that ...

ermächtigen *tr. V.* authorize; **[dazu] ermächtigt sein, etw. zu tun** be authorized to do sth.

Ermächtigung die; ~, ~en authorization

Ermächtigungs·gesetz das *(Politik, bes. ns.)* Enabling Act

ermahnen *tr. V.* admonish; tell *(coll.)*; *(warnen)* warn

Ermahnung die admonition; *(Warnung)* warning

ermangeln *itr. V. (geh.)* **einer Sache** *(Gen.)* **~:** lack sth.

Ermang[e]lung die; ~ *in* **in ~** (+ *Gen.*) *(geh.)* in the absence of; **in ~ eines Besseren** for lack of anything better

ermannen *refl. V. (geh.)* **sich ~, etw. zu tun** pluck up courage to do sth.

ermäßigen 1. *tr. V.* reduce. **2.** *refl. V.* be reduced

Ermäßigung die reduction

ermatten *(geh.)* **1.** *itr. V.; mit sein* ⟨*person*⟩ become exhausted; *(fig.)* ⟨*enthusiasm*⟩ wane. **2.** *tr. V. (matt machen)* exhaust, tire ⟨*person*⟩

ermattet *Adj.* exhausted

Ermattung die; ~: weariness; fatigue

ermessen *unr. tr. V.* estimate, gauge ⟨*consequences, implications*⟩; **daran können Sie ~, wie/ob ...:** that will give you some idea of how/whether ...; **die Bedeutung von etw. ~:** appreciate the significance of sth.

Ermessen das; ~s estimation; **nach eigenem ~:** in one's own estimation; **in jmds. ~** *(Dat.)* **liegen** be at sb.'s discretion; **nach menschlichem ~:** as far as anyone can judge; **etw. in jmds.** *(Akk.)* **~ stellen** leave sth. to sb.'s discretion

Ermessens-: ~entscheidung die discretionary decision; **~frage die** matter of discretion; **~mißbrauch der** abuse of one's powers of discretion; **~spiel·raum der** powers *pl.* of discretion; discretionary powers *pl.*

ermitteln 1. *tr. V.* **a)** *(herausfinden)* ascertain, determine ⟨*facts*⟩; discover ⟨*culprit, hideout, address*⟩; establish, determine ⟨*identity, origin*⟩; decide ⟨*winner*⟩; **b)** *(errechnen)* calculate ⟨*quota, rates, data*⟩. **2.** *itr. V. (Rechtsw.)* investigate; **gegen jmdn. ~:** investigate sb.; **in einer Sache ~:** investigate sth.

Ermittlung die; ~, ~en a) *(das Ermitteln) s.* **ermitteln a:** ascertainment; determination; discovery; establishment; **die ~ eines Gewinners** deciding a winner; **b)** *(Untersuchung) meist Pl.* investigation

Ermittlungs-: ~arbeit die investigatory work; **~aus·schuß der** committee of inquiry; **~beamte der** investigating officer; **~richter der** examining magistrate; **~verfahren das** *(Rechtsw.)* preliminary inquiry

ermöglichen *tr. V.* enable; **jmdm. etw. ~:** make sth. possible for sb.; **um einen besseren Gedankenaustausch zu ~:** to facilitate a better exchange of ideas

ermorden *tr. V.* murder; *(aus politischen Gründen)* assassinate

Ermordung die; ~, ~en murder; *(aus politischen Gründen)* assassination

ermüden 1. *itr. V.; mit sein* **a)** *(müde werden)* tire; become tired; **b)** *(Technik)* ⟨*metal*⟩ fatigue. **2.** *tr. V. (müde machen)* tire; make tired

ermüdend *Adj.* tiring

Ermüdung die; ~, ~en a) tiredness; **vor ~:** from tiredness; **b)** *(Technik)* metal fatigue

Ermüdungs-: ~erscheinung die sign of fatigue; **~zustand der** state of fatigue

ermuntern *tr. V.* **a) jmdn. [dazu] ~, etw. zu tun** encourage sb. to do sth.; **jmdn. zum Reden/zu einem Verbrechen ~:** encourage sb. to talk/to commit a crime; **b)** *(veralt.: wach machen)* liven up ⟨*person*⟩

ermunternd 1. *Adj.* encouraging. **2.** *adv.* encouragingly

Ermunterung die; ~, ~en a) *(Aufheiterung)* enlivenment; **zur ~ der Anwesenden** to the amusement of those present; **b)** *(Ermutigung)* encouragement; **c)** *(ermunternde Worte)* words *pl.* of encouragement

ermutigen *tr. V.* **a)** encourage; **b)** *s.* **ermuntern a**

ermutigend 1. *Adj.* encouraging. **2.** *adv.* encouragingly

Ermutigung die; ~, ~en a) encouragement; **zur ~:** to encourage; **b)** *(ermutigende Worte)* words *pl.* of encouragement

ernähren 1. *tr. V.* **a)** feed ⟨*young, child*⟩; **mit der Flasche ernährt werden** be bottle-fed; **b)** *(unterhalten)* keep ⟨*family, wife*⟩; **das ernährt seinen Mann** it provides a good living. **2.** *refl. V.* feed oneself; **sich von etw. ~:** live on sth.; ⟨*animal*⟩ feed on sth.; **sich vegetarisch ~:** live on a vegetarian diet

Ernährer der; ~s, ~, Ernährerin die; ~, ~nen breadwinner; provider

Ernährung die; ~: a) *(das Ernähren)* feeding; **b)** *(Nahrung)* diet; **gesunde/ungesunde ~:** a healthy/an unhealthy diet; **c)** *(Versorgung)* feeding; **zur ~ der Familie beitragen** contribute to feeding the family

Ernährungs-: ~lage die state of nutrition; **~lehre die** *(Med.)* dietetics *sing., no art.*; **~ministerium das** Ministry of Food; **~störung die** *(Med.)* nutritional disorder; **~weise die** diet; **~wissenschaft die** dietetics *sing., no art.*

ernennen *unr. tr. V.* **a) jmdn. zu etw. ~:** make sb. sth.; **b)** *(bestimmen)* appoint ⟨*deputy, ambassador*⟩

Ernennung die appointment (**zu** as)

Ernennungs·urkunde die certificate of appointment

Erneu[e]rer der; ~s, ~, Erneuerin die; ~, ~nen reviver

erneuern 1. *tr. V.* **a)** *(auswechseln)* replace; **b)** *(wiederherstellen)* renovate ⟨*roof, building*⟩; *(fig.)* thoroughly reform ⟨*system*⟩; **c)** *(beleben)* resume ⟨*relations*⟩; **d)** *(verlängern lassen)* extend, renew ⟨*permit, licence, contract*⟩. **2.** *refl. V.* ⟨*nature, growth*⟩ renew itself

Erneuerung die a) *(Auswechslung)* replacement; **b)** *(Wiederherstellung)* renovation; *(fig.)* thorough reform; **demokratische/religiöse ~:** democratic/religious revival; **c)** *(von Beziehungen)* resumption; **d)** *(Verlänge-*

rung eines Vertrages usw.) renewal; extension
erneuerungs·bedürftig *Adj.* in need of replacement *postpos.*
Erneuerungs·schein **der** *(Börsenw.)* talon
erneut 1. *Adj.; nicht präd.* renewed. **2.** *adv.* once again
erniedrigen *tr. V.* **a)** *(demütigen)* humiliate; **sich [selbst] ~:** lower oneself; **wer sich selbst erniedrigt, wird erhöht werden** *(bibl.)* he that shall humble himself shall be exalted; **b)** *(heruntersetzen)* lower, reduce ⟨*price, pressure*⟩; **c)** *(Musik)* lower ⟨*note*⟩
erniedrigend *Adj.* humiliating
Erniedrigung die; ~, ~en a) *(Demütigung)* humiliation; **b)** *(Senkung)* lowering; reduction (+ *Gen.* in); **c)** *(Musik)* lowering
Erniedrigungs·zeichen das *(Musik)* flat sign
ernst [ɛrnst] **1.** *Adj.* **a)** serious ⟨*face, expression, music, doubts*⟩; **~ bleiben** remain serious; keep a straight face *(coll.)*; **b)** *(aufrichtig)* genuine ⟨*intention, offer*⟩; **c)** *(gefahrvoll)* serious ⟨*injury*⟩; grave ⟨*situation*⟩; **etwas Ernstes** something serious. **2.** *adv.* seriously; **jmdn./etw. ~nehmen** take sb./sth. seriously; **es ~ mit etw. meinen** be serious about sth.
[1]**Ernst der; ~[e]s a)** *(ernster Wille)* seriousness; **das ist mein [voller] ~:** I mean that [quite] seriously; **es ist mir [bitterer] ~ damit** I'm [deadly] serious about it; **etw. im ~ sagen** say something in all seriousness; **etw. im ~ meinen** mean sth. seriously; **allen ~es** in all seriousness; **etw. mit ~ betreiben** apply oneself seriously to sth.; **[mit etw.] ~ machen** be serious [about sth.]; **er will jetzt ~ machen und morgen nach Peru fliegen** now he wants to turn words into action and fly to Peru tomorrow; **b)** *(Wirklichkeit)* **daraus wurde [blutiger/bitterer] ~:** it became [deadly] serious; **der ~ des Lebens** the serious side of life; **dann beginnt der ~ des Lebens** then life begins in earnest; **c)** *(Gefährlichkeit)* **der ~ der Lage** the seriousness of the situation; **d)** *(gemessene Haltung)* gravity
[2]**Ernst (der); ~s** Ernest
Ernst·fall der: eine Übung für den ~: a practice for the real thing; **im ~:** when the real thing happens
ernst·gemeint *Adj.* *(präd. getrennt geschrieben)* serious ⟨*offer, reply*⟩; sincere ⟨*wish*⟩
ernsthaft 1. *Adj.* serious; **etwas/nichts Ernsthaftes** something/nothing serious. **2.** *adv.* seriously; **jmdn. ~ an etw.** *(Akk.)* **erinnern** give sb. a stern reminder about sth.
Ernsthaftigkeit die; ~: seriousness
ernstlich 1. *Adj.* **a)** *(nachdrücklich)* serious ⟨*doubt, attempt, intention*⟩; **b)** *(aufrichtig)* genuine ⟨*wish*⟩; **c)** *(gefährlich)* serious ⟨*threat, danger, risk*⟩. **2.** *adv.* **a)** *(nachdrücklich)* seriously; **er hat ~ gefordert, daß ...:** he has demanded in all seriousness that ...; **b)** *(aufrichtig)* genuinely ⟨*sorry, repentant*⟩; **jmdm. ~ böse sein** be seriously annoyed with sb.; **c)** *(gefährlich)* seriously ⟨*ill, threatened*⟩; **~ gefährdet sein** be in serious danger
Ernte ['ɛrntə] **die; ~, ~n a)** *(das Ernten)* harvest; **bei der ~ sein** be bringing in the harvest; **während der ~:** at harvest time; **reiche/furchtbare ~ halten** *(fig. geh.)* take a heavy/terrible toll; **b)** *(Ertrag)* crop; **die ~ einbringen** bring in the harvest; **die ~ an Getreide/Kartoffeln/Tabak** the grain/potato/tobacco crop; **ihm ist die ganze ~ verhagelt** *(fig.)* he's had a bad blow
-ernte die; ~, ~n ... harvest; *(Ertrag)* ... crop
Ernte-: ~arbeit die harvest work; **~arbeiter der** harvester; **~aus·fall der** crop failure; **~dank·fest das** harvest festival; **~ein·satz der** assistance with the harvest; **jmdn. zum ~einsatz aufrufen** call upon sb. to help with the harvest; **~ertrag der** yield; **~maschine die** harvester; **~monat der** month of the harvest
ernten *tr. V.* harvest ⟨*cereal, fruit*⟩; *(fig.)* get ⟨*mockery, ingratitude*⟩; win ⟨*fame, praise*⟩
Ernte-: ~wagen der harvest wagon; **~wetter das: gutes/schlechtes ~wetter haben** have good/bad weather for the harvest; **~zeit die** harvest time; **in der ~zeit** at harvest time
ernüchtern *tr. V.* **a)** *(nüchtern machen)* sober up; **b)** *(fig.)* **jmdn. [völlig] ~:** bring sb. down to earth [with a bang]; **~d** sobering
Ernüchterung die; ~, ~en *(fig.)* disillusionment
Eroberer [ɛɐ̯'|o:bərɐ] **der; ~s, ~, Eroberin die; ~, ~nen** conqueror
erobern *tr. V.* **a)** conquer ⟨*country*⟩; take ⟨*town, fortress*⟩; **b)** *(fig.)* conquer ⟨*woman, market*⟩; seize ⟨*power*⟩; **[sich** *(Dat.)***] die Herzen ~:** win hearts; **eine Stadt/ein Land ~** *(scherzh.)* take a town/country by storm; *s. auch* **Sturm b**
Eroberung die; ~, ~en *(auch fig. scherzh.)* conquest; *(einer Stadt, Festung)* taking; **die ~ der Macht** the seizing of power; **~en machen** make conquests; *s. auch* **ausgehen h**
Eroberungs-: ~drang der; *o. Pl.* thirst for conquest; **~feld·zug der** campaign of conquest; **~krieg der** war of conquest
eröffnen 1. *tr. V.* **a)** open ⟨*shop, gallery, account*⟩; start ⟨*business, practice*⟩; **b)** *(beginnen)* open ⟨*meeting, conference*⟩; **das Feuer ~:** open fire; **eine Veranstaltung mit Musik ~:** begin an event with music; **c)** *(mitteilen)* **jmdm. etw. ~:** reveal sth. to sb.; **d) ein Testament ~:** read a will; **e)** *(Rechtsw., Wirtsch.)* **den Konkurs ~:** institute bankruptcy proceedings; **das Verfahren ~:** begin proceedings; **f) jmdm. neue Möglichkeiten ~:** open up new possibilities to sb.; **g)** *(Börsenw.)* ⟨*stock exchange*⟩ open. **2.** *refl. V.* *(sich bieten)* **sich jmdm. ~** ⟨*opportunity, possibility*⟩ present itself
Eröffnung die a) opening; *(einer Sitzung)* start; *(einer Schachpartie)* opening [move]; **b)** *(Mitteilung)* revelation; **ich muß dir eine ~ machen** I have something to tell you; **c)** *(Testaments~)* reading; **d)** *(Wirtsch.)* **die ~ des Konkurses** the institution of bankruptcy proceedings
Eröffnungs-: ~an·sprache die opening speech; **~beschluß der** *(Rechtsw.)* decision to begin court proceedings; **~bilanz die** *(Wirtsch.)* opening balance; **~feier die** opening ceremony; **~kurs der** *(Börsenw.)* opening price; **~spiel das** *(Sport)* opening game; **~tag der** *(einer Ausstellung, eines Kongresses usw.)* first day; *(eines Geschäftes usw.)* first day of opening; **~variante die** *(Schach)* opening variation; **~wehen** *Pl.* *(Med.)* dilation pains
erogen [ero'ge:n] *Adj.* erogenous ⟨*zone*⟩
erörtern [ɛɐ̯'|œrtɐn] *tr. V.* discuss
Erörterung die; ~, ~en discussion
Eros ['e:rɔs] **der; ~: a)** *(Gott)* Eros; **b)** *(sinnliche Liebe)* erotic love
Eros-Center das [licensed] brothel; eros centre
Erosion [ero'zio:n] **die; ~, ~en** erosion
Erosions·schutz der protection against erosion
Erotik [e'ro:tɪk] **die; ~:** eroticism
Erotika [e'ro:tika] *s.* **Erotikon**
Erotiker der; ~s, ~ a) eroticist; **b)** *(Autor)* erotic writer
Erotikon [e'ro:tikɔn] **das; ~s, Erotika a)** erotic work; **Erotika** erotica; **b)** *Pl.* *(Mittel)* aphrodisiacs
erotisch 1. *Adj.* erotic. **2.** *adv.* erotically
erotisieren *tr. V.* arouse sexual desire in; **~d wirken** have an erotic effect
Erotomane [eroto'ma:nə] **der; ~n, ~n** erotomaniac
Erotomanie die; ~: erotomania
Erotomanin die; ~, ~nen erotomaniac
Erpel ['ɛrpl̩] **der; ~s, ~:** drake
erpicht [ɛɐ̯'pɪçt] *Adj.* *in* **auf etw.** *(Akk.)* **~ sein** be keen on sth.
erpressen *tr. V.* **a)** *(nötigen)* blackmail; **jmdn. mit etw. ~:** blackmail sb. with sth.; **b)** *(erlangen)* extort ⟨*money, confession*⟩ **(von** from)
Erpresser der; ~s, ~: blackmailer
Erpresser·brief der blackmail letter
Erpresserin die; ~, ~nen blackmailer
erpresserisch 1. *Adj.* blackmailing *attrib.*; **diese Maßnahme ist ~:** this action amounts to blackmail; **in ~er Absicht** for the purpose of blackmail. **2.** *adv.* **~ vorgehen** use blackmail
Erpresser·methoden *Pl.* blackmail *sing.*
Erpressung die blackmail *no indef. art.*; *(von Geld, Geständnis)* extortion; *s. auch* **räuberisch 1 a**
Erpressungs·versuch der blackmail attempt
erproben *tr. V.* test ⟨*medicine*⟩ **(an +** *Akk.* on); **jmds. Zuverlässigkeit ~:** put sb.'s reliability to the test; **ein erprobter Soldat** an experienced soldier; **das ist seit langem erprobt** it is tried and tested
Erprobung die; ~, ~en testing
Erprobungs·flug der test *or* proving flight
erquicken [ɛɐ̯'kvɪkn̩] *tr. V.* *(geh.)* refresh; **das Herz ~:** gladden one's heart; **ich will euch ~** *(bibl.)* and I will give you rest
erquickend *Adj.* *(geh.)* refreshing
erquicklich *(geh.)* **1.** *Adj.* pleasant. **2.** *adv.* pleasantly
Erquickung die; ~, ~en *(geh.)* refreshment; **der Schlaf brachte ihm keine ~:** the sleep did not refresh him
Errata *s.* **Erratum**
erraten *unr. tr. V.* guess; **du hast es ~!** *(iron.)* you've guessed it!
erratisch [ɛ'ra:tɪʃ] *Adj.* *(Geol.)* erratic
Erratum [ɛ'ra:tʊm] **das; ~s, Errata** *(Druck- u. Schriftw.)* erratum
errechenbar *Adj.* calculable; **leicht/genau ~ sein** be easily/accurately calculated
errechnen 1. *tr. (auch itr.) V.* **a)** *(ausrechnen)* calculate ⟨*sum*⟩; **wie er errechnete** according to his calculations; **b)** *(erwarten)* count on ⟨*chance, advantage*⟩. **2.** *refl. V.* *(Papierdt.)* **sich aus etw. ~:** be calculated from sth.
erregbar *Adj.* excitable
Erregbarkeit die; ~: excitability
erregen 1. *tr. V.* **a)** annoy; **b)** *(sexuell)* arouse; **c)** *(verursachen)* arouse; **Aufsehen/Ärgernis ~:** cause a stir/annoyance; *s. auch* **öffentlich. 2.** *refl. V.* **sich über etw.** *(Akk.)* **~:** get excited about sth.
erregend *Adj.* exciting; *(sexuell)* arousing
Erreger der; ~s, ~ *(Med.)* pathogen
erregt 1. *Adj.* excited; *(sexuell)* aroused; **die ~en Gemüter** the hot tempers. **2.** *adv.* excitedly
Erregung die a) excitement; *(sexuell)* arousal; **in starke ~ geraten** become extremely excited; **vor ~:** with excitement; **b)** *(Verursachung)* **~ öffentlichen Ärgernisses** *(Rechtsspr.)* causing a public nuisance; **~ von Mißfallen** incurring displeasure
Erregungs·zustand der state of excitement; *(sexuell)* [state of] arousal
erreichbar *Adj.* **a)** within reach *postpos.*; **in ~er Höhe** at a reachable height; **b) der Ort ist mit dem Auto/Zug ~:** the place can be reached by car/train; **leicht ~ sein** be easy to reach; be easily reachable; **c) er ist [telefonisch] ~:** he can be contacted [by telephone]
erreichen *tr. V.* **a)** reach; **den Zug ~:** catch the train; **etw. ist zu Fuß/mit dem Bus/schnell zu ~:** sth. can be reached on foot/by bus/quickly; **b)** *(in Verbindung treten mit, ansprechen)* reach ⟨*viewers*⟩; **er ist telefo-**

nisch/um 10 Uhr/zu Hause zu ~: he can be contacted by telephone/at 10 o'clock/at home; c) *(durchsetzen)* achieve ⟨*goal, aim*⟩; **bei jmdm. etwas/nichts ~**: get somewhere/not get anywhere with sb.

Erreichung die; ~: reaching *no art.*; **bei** *od.* **mit ~ der Altersgrenze/Volljährigkeit** on reaching the age limit/one's majority

erretten *tr. V. (geh.)* save

Erretter der *(geh.)* saviour

errichten *tr. V.* **a)** build ⟨*house, bridge, etc.*⟩; **b)** *(aufstellen)* erect, put up ⟨*rostrum, barrier, etc.*⟩; **c)** *(einrichten)* found ⟨*company*⟩; set up ⟨*fund*⟩

erringen *unr. tr. V.* gain ⟨*victory*⟩; reach ⟨*first etc. place*⟩; win ⟨*majority*⟩; gain, win ⟨*sb.'s trust*⟩

erröten *itr. V.; mit sein* blush (**vor** with); **jmdn. zum Erröten bringen** make sb. blush

Errungenschaft [ɛɐ̯'rʊŋənʃaft] **die; ~, ~en** achievement; **meine neueste ~** *(ugs. scherzh.)* my latest acquisition

Ersatz der; ~es a) replacement; **als ~ für jmdn.** in place of sb.; **b)** *(Entschädigung)* compensation; **c)** *(Milit.)* reserve

ersatz-, Ersatz-: ~an·spruch der claim for damages; **~ansprüche stellen** claim damages; **~ball der** *(Sport)* new ball; **~bank die** *(Sport)* substitutes' bench; **~befriedigung die** *(Psych.)* vicarious satisfaction; **~dienst der** *community service as an alternative to military service*; **~dienst·leistende der;** *adj. Dekl.: person carrying out alternative service;* **~heer das** reserve army; **~kasse die** private health insurance company; **~los 1.** *Adj.* without replacement *postpos.*; **2.** *adv.* **etw. ~los streichen** cancel sth.; **ein Gesetz ~los streichen** strike a law from the statute books; **~mann der;** *Pl.* **~männer, ~leute** replacement; *(Sport)* substitute; **~mine die** refill; **~mittel das** substitute; **~pflichtig** *Adj.* liable to pay compensation *postpos.*; **~rad das** spare wheel; **~reifen der** spare tyre; **~religion die** substitute religion; **~spieler der** *(Sport)* substitute [player]

Ersatz·teil das *(bes. Technik)* spare part; spare *(Brit.)*

Ersatzteil-: ~lager das [spares] store; **~medizin die** spare-part surgery

Ersatz-: ~truppe die *(Milit.)* reserve troops *pl.*; **~weise** *Adv.* as an alternative

ersaufen *unr. itr. V.; mit sein* **a)** *(salopp)* drown; **b)** *(überflutet werden)* flood

ersäufen [ɛɐ̯'zɔyfn̩] *tr. V.* drown; **seinen Kummer im Alkohol ~** *(fig.)* drown one's sorrows [in drink]

erschaffen *unr. tr. V.* create; **wie Gott ihn ~ hat** *(scherzh. verhüll.)* in his birthday suit

Erschaffer der; ~s, ~ *(Rel.)* Creator

Erschaffung die creation

erschallen *unr. od. regelm. itr. V.; mit sein* ⟨*song, call*⟩ ring out; ⟨*music*⟩ sound

erschaudern *itr. V.; mit sein (geh.)* shudder (**bei** at)

erschauern *itr. V.; mit sein (geh.)* tremble (**vor** + *Dat.* with)

erscheinen *unr. itr. V.; mit sein* **a)** *(sichtbar werden, sich zeigen, auftreten)* appear; **jmdm. ~**: appear to sb.; **in der Schule/am Arbeitsplatz ~**: put in an appearance at school/at work; **vor Gericht ~**: appear in court; **um frühzeitiges/rechtzeitiges/zahlreiches Erscheinen wird gebeten** an early/a punctual arrival/a full turn-out is requested; **b)** *(herausgegeben werden)* ⟨*newspaper, periodical*⟩ appear; ⟨*book*⟩ be published; **c)** *(sich darstellen)* **jmdm. ratsam/unverständlich ~**: seem advisable/incomprehensible to sb.; *s. auch* **Licht a**

Erscheinung die; ~, ~en a) *(Vorgang)* phenomenon; *(Alters~, Krankheits~ usw.)* symptom; **in ~ treten** become evident; **das Fest der ~ des Herrn** *(christl. Rel.)* [the Feast of] the Epiphany; **b)** *(äußere Gestalt)* appearance; **eine stattliche/elegante ~ sein** be an imposing/elegant figure; **c)** *(Vision)* apparition; **eine ~/~en haben** see a vision/visions

Erscheinungs-: ~bild das appearance; **vom ~bild her** judging by appearance; **~fest das** Epiphany *no art.*; **~form die** manifestation; **~jahr das** year of publication; **~ort der** place of publication; **~tag der** day of publication; publication day; **~weise die a)** *s.* **~form; b) die ~weise einer Zeitung** the frequency of publication of a newspaper; **wöchentliche/monatliche ~weise** weekly/monthly publication; **„~weise: vierteljährlich"** 'published quarterly'; **~welt die** world perceived through the senses

erschießen *unr. tr. V.* shoot dead; **Tod durch Erschießen** death by firing squad; **erschossen sein** *(fig. ugs.)* be completely whacked *(Brit. coll.)*; **dann kann ich mich ~** *(ugs.)* I might as well end it all *(coll.)*; *s. auch* **Flucht a, standrechtlich 2**

Erschießung die; ~, ~en shooting; **eine sofortige/standrechtliche ~**: a summary execution [by firing squad]; **zur ~ abgeführt werden** be led away to be shot

Erschießungs·kommando das firing squad

erschlaffen *itr. V.; mit sein* **a)** *(kraftlos werden)* ⟨*muscle, limb*⟩ become limp; *(fig.)* ⟨*resistance, will*⟩ weaken; **seine Spannkraft war erschlafft** he had lost his vigour; **b)** *(welk werden)* ⟨*skin*⟩ grow slack

Erschlaffung die; ~ a) *(das Müdewerden)* weakening; **b)** *(das Welkwerden)* **bei ~ der Haut** when the skin grows slack

[1]**erschlagen** *unr. tr. V.* strike dead; kill; *(ugs.: erschöpfen)* wear out; **vom Blitz ~ werden** be struck dead by lightning; **jmdn. mit Argumenten ~** *(fig.)* defeat sb. with arguments

[2]**erschlagen** *Adj. (ugs.)* **a)** *(erschöpft)* worn out; **b)** *(verblüfft)* **wie ~ sein** be flabbergasted *(coll.)* *or* thunderstruck

erschleichen *unr. refl. V. (abwertend)* **sich** *(Dat.)* **etw. ~**: get sth. by devious means; **sich** *(Dat.)* **jmds. Gunst/Vertrauen ~**: worm oneself into sb.'s favour/confidence

erschließbar *Adj.* ascertainable ⟨*facts*⟩; **~e Rohstoffquellen** sources of raw materials which can be tapped; **~e Absatzmärkte** markets which can be opened up

erschließen 1. *unr. tr. V.* **a)** *(zugänglich machen)* develop ⟨*area, building land*⟩; open up ⟨*market*⟩; **jmdm. etw. ~** *(fig.)* make sth. accessible to sb.; **er hat mir ganz neue Welten erschlossen** he opened up a whole new world to me; **b)** *(nutzbar machen)* tap ⟨*resources, energy sources*⟩; **c)** *(ermitteln)* deduce ⟨*meaning, wording*⟩. **2.** *unr. refl. V.* **a)** *(verständlich werden)* **sich jmdm. ~**: become accessible to sb.; **b)** *(geh.: sich offenbaren)* **sich jmdm. ~**: confide in sb.

Erschließung die a) *(von Bauland)* development; *(von Märkten)* opening up; **b)** *(von Rohstoffen)* tapping; **c) zur ~ des Textes** in order to grasp the meaning of the text

Erschließungs·kosten *Pl. (Bauw.)* development costs *pl.*

erschöpfen 1. *tr. V. (auch fig.)* exhaust; **seine Kräfte ~**: drain one's strength. **2.** *refl. V.* **a)** *(sich beschränken)* **darin ~ sich ihre Kenntnisse** her knowledge does not go beyond that; **b)** *(zu Ende gehen)* ⟨*supplies, stores*⟩ run out; **seine Ideen haben sich erschöpft** he has run out of ideas

erschöpfend 1. *Adj.* exhaustive. **2.** *adv.* exhaustively

erschöpft *Adj.* exhausted

Erschöpfung die exhaustion; **bis zur ~**: to the point of exhaustion; **vor ~ einschlafen/umfallen** fall asleep from exhaustion/drop with exhaustion

Erschöpfungs-: ~tod der death from exhaustion; **den ~tod sterben** die from exhaustion; **~zu·stand der** state of exhaustion; **Müdigkeit und ~zustände** tiredness and exhaustion

[1]**erschrecken** *unr. itr. V.; mit sein* be startled; **vor etw.** *(Dat.)* *od.* **über etw.** *(Akk.)* **~**: be startled by sth.; **erschrick nicht!** don't be startled; **er war zutiefst/zu Tode erschrocken** he was frightened out of his wits/frightened to death

[2]**erschrecken** *tr. V.* frighten; scare; **du hast mich aber erschreckt!** you really gave me a scare

[3]**erschrecken** *unr. od. regelm. refl. V.* get a fright; **erschrick dich nicht!** don't be frightened

erschreckend *Adj.* **1.** alarming. **2.** *adv.* alarmingly

erschrocken 1. *2. Part. v.* [1]**erschrecken. 2.** *Adj.* frightened; **sie wandte sich ~ ab** she turned away in fright

erschüttern *tr. V. (auch fig.)* shake; **die Nachricht hat uns erschüttert** we were shaken by the news; **über etw.** *(Akk.)* **erschüttert sein** be shaken by sth.; **das kann mich nicht ~** *(ugs.)* that doesn't worry me

erschütternd *Adj.* deeply distressing ⟨*account, picture, news*⟩; deeply shocking ⟨*conditions*⟩

Erschütterung die; ~, ~en a) *(Bewegung)* *(durch Lkws usw.)* vibration; *(der Erde)* tremor; **wirtschaftliche ~en** *(fig.)* economic upheavals; **b)** *(Ergriffenheit)* shock; *(Trauer)* distress; **c) das trug zur ~ meines Glaubens/Vertrauens bei** that helped to shake my faith/confidence

erschütterungs-: ~fest *Adj.* shockproof; **~frei 1.** *Adj.* vibrationless; free from *or* without vibration *postpos.*; **ein ~freier Transport von etw.** transporting sth. without jolting; **2.** *adv.* without vibration

erschweren 1. *tr. V.* **etw. ~**: make sth. more difficult; **etw. durch etw. ~**: impede *or* hinder sth. by sth. **2.** *refl. V.* **sich [durch etw.] ~**: be hindered [by sth.]

erschwerend 1. *Adj.* complicating ⟨*factor*⟩; **~e Umstände** *(Rechtsw.)* aggravating circumstances. **2.** *adv.* **es kommt ~ hinzu, daß er ...**: to make matters worse he ...; **das kommt ~ hinzu** that is an added problem

Erschwernis die; ~, ~se difficulty

Erschwernis·zulage die *bonus for particularly hard work or shift work*

Erschwerung die; ~, ~en: eine ~ für etw. an impediment to sth.; **das ist eine ~ seiner Tätigkeit** that makes his job more difficult

erschwindeln *refl. V.* get by swindling; **sich** *(Dat.)* **etw. von jmdm. ~**: swindle sb. out of sth.

erschwinglich *Adj.* reasonable ⟨*price*⟩; **für jmdn. nicht ~ sein** not be within sb.'s reach; **dort sind die Mieten noch ~**: the rents there are still affordable

ersehen *unr. tr. V.* see; **aus etw. zu ~ sein** be evident from sth.

ersehnen *tr. V. (geh.)* long for

ersetzbar *Adj.* replaceable

ersetzen *tr. V.* **a)** replace; **etw./jmdn. durch etw./jmdn. ~**: replace sth./sb. by sth./sb.; **Talent durch Fleiß ~**: substitute hard work for talent; **ihn wird niemand ~ können** nobody will be able to take his place; **b)** *(erstatten)* **jmdm. einen Schaden ~**: compensate sb. for damages; **die Fahrtkosten ~**: reimburse travel expenses

Ersetzung die; ~, ~en *(von Kosten usw.)* reimbursement; **die ~ von Schäden** compensation for damage

ersichtlich *Adj.* apparent; **ohne ~en Grund** for no apparent reason; **etw. ist klar/nicht ~**: sth. is quite obvious/not clear; **hieraus ist ~, daß ...**: it is apparent from this that ...; **die Lieferbedingungen sind aus dem Kaufvertrag ~**: the conditions of delivery are contained in the contract of sale

ersinnen *unr. tr. V. (geh.)* devise

ersitzen 1. *unr. refl. V. (abwertend)* **als Beamter ersitzt man sich eine ansehnliche Pension** as a civil servant you get a considerable pension just by staying in your job long enough. **2.** *unr. tr. V. (Rechtsspr.)* obtain by prescription

erspähen *tr. V. (geh.)* espy *(literary)*; catch sight of; **einen Vorteil ~** *(fig.)* see an advantage

ersparen *tr. V.* **a)** *(erwerben)* save ‹*money*›; **sein/ihr erspartes Geld** *od.* **Erspartes** his/her savings; **b)** *(fernhalten von)* save, spare ‹*trouble, bother*›; save ‹*work*›; **er konnte ihr diese peinlichen Fragen nicht ~:** he could not spare her these awkward questions; **es bleibt einem nichts erspart** *(ugs.)* at least I/you *etc.* could have been spared that

Ersparnis die; ~, ~se a) *(österr. auch* **das; ~ses, ~se)** *(ersparte Summe)* savings *pl.*; **b)** *(Einsparung)* saving

Ersparnis·kasse die *(schweiz.)* savings bank

ersprießlich *Adj. (geh.)* profitable, fruitful ‹*contacts, collaboration*›; **das ist nicht sehr ~:** that is not very pleasant

erst [e:ɐ̯st] **1.** *Adv.* **a)** *(zu~)* first; **~ einmal** first [of all]; **wenn er ~ einmal in Wut gerät** once he becomes angry; **~ noch** first; **eine solche Frau muß ~ noch geboren werden** such a woman has not yet been born; **b)** *(nicht eher als)* **eben ~:** only just; **er will ~ in vierzehn Tagen/einer Stunde zurückkommen** he won't be back for a fortnight *(Brit.) or* for two weeks/for an hour; **~ nächste Woche/um 12 Uhr** not until next week/12 o'clock; **er war ~ zufrieden, als ...:** he was not satisfied until ...; **~ im 19. Jh. ...:** it was not until the nineteenth century that ...; **c)** *(nicht mehr als)* only; **~ eine Stunde/halb soviel** only an hour/half as much; **sie ist mit ihrer Arbeit ~ am Anfang** she is only just beginning her work. **2.** *Partikel* **so was lese ich gar nicht ~:** I dont even start reading that sort of stuff; **jetzt tue ich es ~ recht!** that makes me even more determined to do it; **er ist schon ziemlich arrogant, aber ~ seine Frau** he is quite arrogant but his wife is even worse

erst... *Ordinalz.* **a)** first; **der ~e Stock** the first *or (Amer.)* second floor; **etw. das ~e Mal tun** do sth. for the first time; **am Ersten [des Monats]** on the first [of the month]; **am nächsten Ersten** on the first [day] of next month; **als erstes** first of all; **der/die ~e** the first person; **als ~er/~e etw. tun** be the first to do sth.; **Karl der Erste** Charles the First; **fürs ~e** for the moment; **der/die/das ~e beste** the first suitable; **sie kaufte das ~e beste Kleid, das sie sah** she bought the first dress she saw; *s. auch* **zum h**; **b)** *(best...)* **das ~e Hotel** the best hotel; **der/die Erste [der Klasse]** the top boy/girl [of the class]; **sie kam als ~e ins Ziel** she was the first to reach the finish; **die Erste** *(Sportjargon: erste Mannschaft)* the first team

erstarken *itr. V.; mit sein (geh.)* regain one's strength; *(fig.)* grow stronger

Erstarkung die; ~ *(geh.)* strengthening

erstarren *itr. V.; mit sein* **a)** *(starr werden)* ‹*jelly, plaster*› set; **ihm erstarrte das Blut in den Adern** *(fig.)* the blood ran cold in his veins; **b)** *(steif werden)* ‹*limbs, fingers*› grow stiff; **c) vor Schreck/Entsetzen ~:** be paralysed by fear/with horror; **d)** *(geh.: leblos werden)* ossify

Erstarrung die; ~ a) *(Starrheit)* numbness; **b)** *(von Lava)* solidification; *(von Eisen)* hardening; **c)** *(von Gliedern)* stiffening; **d)** *(fig.: Absterben)* ossification

erstatten *tr. V.* **a)** reimburse ‹*expenses*›; **b) Anzeige gegen jmdn. ~:** report sb. [to the police]; **jmdm. Bericht über etw.** *(Akk.)* **~:** report on sth. to sb.; **[über etw.** *(Akk.)***] Meldung ~:** report [sth.]

Erstattung die; ~, ~en a) *(von Kosten)* reimbursement; **b) die ~ einer Anzeige** the reporting of sth. [to the police]; **er sah von der ~ einer Anzeige ab** he refrained from reporting it/us *etc.* to the police; **die ~ einer Meldung** the making of a report

Erst-: ~auf·führung die première; **~auflage die** first impression

erstaunen *tr. V.* astonish; amaze; **es erstaunte ihn nicht sonderlich** he wasn't particularly surprised

Erstaunen das; ~s astonishment; amazement; **jmdn. in ~ versetzen** astonish *or* amaze sb.

erstaunlich 1. *Adj.* astonishing, amazing ‹*achievement, number, amount*›; **das ~e ist, daß ...:** the astonishing *or* amazing thing is that ...; **das Erstaunliche an diesem Vorfall** the astonishing *or* amazing thing about this incident. **2.** *adv.* astonishingly; amazingly

erstaunlicher·weise *Adv.* astonishingly *or* amazingly [enough]

erstaunt *Adj.* astonished; amazed

erst-, Erst-: ~aus·gabe die first edition; **~aus·rüstung die** *(Kfz-W.)* original fittings *pl.*; **~ausstattung die** original furnishings *pl.*; **~best...** *Adj.* **der ~beste Wagen, der ihr angeboten wurde** the first car she was offered; **die ~beste Frau, die ihm über den Weg lief** the first woman he met; **bei ~bester Gelegenheit** at the first opportunity; **~beste der/die/das** *s.* **Nächstbeste**; **~besteigung die** first ascent; **Hillary gelang die ~besteigung des Mount Everest** Hillary made the first successful ascent of Mount Everest; **~druck der** *s.* **~ausgabe**

erstechen *unr. tr. V.* stab [to death]

erstehen 1. *unr. tr. V. (geh.: kaufen)* purchase. **2.** *unr. itr. V.; mit sein (geh.)* **a)** *(entstehen)* ‹*difficulties, problems*› arise; **b)** *(auferstehen)* rise; **„Christ ist erstanden"** 'Christ is risen'

Erste-Hilfe-Ausrüstung die first-aid kit

Erste-Hilfe-Leistung die administering of first aid; **zur ~ verpflichtet sein** be obliged to give first aid

ersteigen *unr. tr. V.* climb

ersteigern *tr. V.* buy [at an auction]

Ersteigung die ascent

erstellen *tr. V. (Papierdt.)* **a)** *(bauen)* build; **b)** *(anfertigen)* make ‹*assessment*›; draw up ‹*plan, report, list*›

Erstellung die a) *(Bau)* construction; building; **b)** *(Anfertigung) s.* **erstellen b:** making; drawing up

erste·mal *Adv.* **das ~:** for the first time

ersten·mal *Adv.* **zum ~:** for the first time; **beim ~:** the first time

erstens ['e:ɐ̯stn̩s] *Adv.* firstly; in the first place

erster... ['e:ɐ̯stɐ...] *Adj.* the former

Erste[r]-Klasse-Abteil das first-class compartment

ersterben *unr. itr. V.; mit sein (geh.)* ‹*flame*› die down; ‹*singing, murmuring*› die away; ‹*smile*› fade

erst-, Erst-: ~geboren *Adj.; nicht präd.* first-born; **der/die Erstgeborene** the first-born child; **~gebot das** first *or* opening bid; **~geburt die a)** first-born child; **b)** *o. Pl.* **[das Recht der] ~geburt** *(Rechtsw.)* [right of] primogeniture; **~geburts·recht das** right of primogeniture; **~genannt** *Adj.; nicht präd.* mentioned first *postpos.*; **der Erstgenannte** the one mentioned first

ersticken 1. *itr. V.; mit sein* suffocate; *(sich verschlucken)* choke; **an einem Knochen ~:** choke on a bone; **vor Lachen ~** *(ugs.)* choke with laughter; **zum Ersticken sein** ‹*heat*› be stifling; **in Arbeit ~** *(ugs.)* be swamped with work; **in Geld ~** *(ugs.)* be rolling in money. **2.** *tr. V.* **a)** *(töten)* suffocate; **die Tränen erstickten ihre Stimme** *(fig.)* she was choked by tears; **der Widerstand wurde erstickt** *(fig.)* resistance was suppressed; **etw. sofort** *od.* **im Keim ~** *(fig.)* nip sth. in the bud; **b)** *(löschen)* smother ‹*flames*›

Erstickung die; ~ a) *(Sterben)* suffocation; asphyxiation; **b)** *(Löschen)* smothering; **zur ~ der Flammen** to smother the flames

Erstickungs-: ~gefahr die danger of suffocation; **~tod der** death from suffocation; **den ~tod sterben** die from suffocation

erst-, Erst-: ~instanz die *(Rechtsw.)* court of first instance; **~klassig 1.** *Adj.* first-class; **~klassige Bedingungen** excellent conditions; **2.** *adv.* superbly; **da kann man ~klassig essen** you can get a first-class meal there; **da wird man ~klassig bedient** the service there is first-class; **~kläßler der; ~s, ~** *(südd., schweiz.) pupil in first class of primary school;* first-year pupil; **~kommunion die** *(kath. Rel.)* first communion

Erstling der; ~s, ~e first work

Erstlings-: ~ausstattung die first layette; **~film der** first film; **~roman der** first novel; **~werk das** first work

erstmalig 1. *Adj.* first. **2.** *adv.* for the first time

erstmals *Adv.* for the first time

Erst·plazierte der/die *(Sport) person gaining one of the first [three] places*

erstrahlen *itr. V.; mit sein* shine; **der ganze Park erstrahlte im Lichterglanz** the whole park was aglow with light

erstrangig *Adj.* **a)** *(vordringlich)* of top priority *postpos.*; **von ~er Bedeutung** of the utmost importance; **b)** *s.* **erstklassig 1**

erstreben *tr. V.* strive for

erstrebens·wert *Adj.* ‹*ideals etc.*› worth striving for; desirable ‹*situation*›

erstrecken *refl. V.* **a)** *(sich ausdehnen)* stretch; **sich bis an etw.** *(Akk.)* **~:** extend as far as sth.; **sich über ein Gebiet ~:** extend over *or* cover an area; **b)** *(dauern)* **sich über 10 Jahre ~:** carry on for 10 years; **c)** *(betreffen)* **sich auf jmdn./etw. ~:** affect sb./sth.; ‹*laws, regulations*› apply to sb./sth.

erstreiten *unr. tr. V. (geh.)* gain; **sich** *(Dat.)* **etw. ~ müssen** have to fight to get sth.; **sich ein Recht ~ müssen** have to fight for a right

Erst-: ~schlag der first strike; **~schlag·waffe die** first-strike weapon; **~sendung die** first broadcast; **~stimme die** first vote

Ersttags-: ~brief der *(Philat.)* first-day cover; **~stempel der** *(Philat.)* first-day stamp

Erst·täter der *(Rechtsw.)* first offender

erstunken [ɛɐ̯'ʃtʊŋkn̩] *in* **~ und erlogen sein** *(salopp)* be a pack of lies

erstürmen *tr. V.* take ‹*fortress, town*› by storm; **den Gipfel ~** *(geh.)* conquer the summit

Erstürmung die; ~, ~en storming

Erst-: ~wagen der main car; **~wähler der** first-time voter

ersuchen *tr. V. (geh.)* ask; **jmdn. um etw. ~:** request sth. of sb.; **jmdn. ~, etw. zu tun** request sb. to do sth.

Ersuchen das; ~s, ~: request **(an +** *Akk.* to); **auf ~ von .../des ...:** at the request of ...

ertappen *tr. V.* catch ‹*thief, burglar*›; **jmdn. dabei ~, wie er etw. tut** catch sb. in the act of doing sth.; **jmdn. beim Mogeln ~:** catch sb. cheating; **sich bei etw. ~:** catch oneself doing sth.; *s. auch* **frisch 1 a**

ertasten *tr. V.* **etw. ~:** make out sth. by touch; **sich** *(Dat.)* **seinen Weg ~:** feel one's way

erteilen *tr. V.* give ‹*advice, information*›; give, grant ‹*permission*›; **Unterricht ~:** teach; **Klavier-/Deutschunterricht ~:** give piano/German lessons; *s. auch* **Auftrag a; Lektion; Wort b**

Erteilung die giving; **die ~ der Arbeitsgenehmigung** granting of a work permit

ertönen *itr. V.; mit sein* **a)** *(laut werden)* sound; **er ließ seine tiefe Stimme ~:** his deep voice rang out; **b)** *(geh.)* **von etw. ~:** resound with sth.

Ertrag [ɛɐ̯'tra:k] **der;** ~[e]s, **Erträge** [ɛɐ̯'trɛ:gə] **a)** *(landwirtschaftliche Produkte)* yield; **b)** *(Gewinn)* return
ertragen *unr. tr. V.* bear ⟨*pain, shame, uncertainty*⟩; **etw. mit Geduld/Fassung ~:** bear sth. patiently/take sth. calmly; **es ist nicht mehr zu ~:** I can't stand it any longer; **Frauen können mehr Schmerz ~ als Männer** women can stand *or* tolerate more pain than men; **er mußte große Schmerzen ~:** he had to endure great pain
ertrag·fähig *Adj.* **a)** *(gewinnbringend)* profitable ⟨*investment etc.*⟩; **b)** *(fruchtbar)* fertile ⟨*soil*⟩
Ertrag·fähigkeit die; *o. Pl.: s.* **ertragfähig:** profitability; fertility
erträglich [ɛɐ̯'trɛ:klɪç] **1.** *Adj.* **a)** bearable ⟨*pain*⟩; tolerable ⟨*conditions, climate*⟩; **die Grenze des Erträglichen erreichen** be as much as one can endure; **b)** *(ugs.: annehmbar)* tolerable. **2.** *adv. (ugs.: annehmbar)* tolerably
ertrag-: ~los *Adj.* unprofitable ⟨*business*⟩; unproductive ⟨*land, soil*⟩; **~reich** *Adj.* lucrative ⟨*business*⟩; productive ⟨*land, soil*⟩
ertrags-, Ertrags-: ~arm *Adj.* unprofitable ⟨*year*⟩; poor ⟨*soil*⟩; **~ein·buße die** decrease in profits; **~lage die** profit situation; profits; **~minderung die** decrease in profits
Ertrag[s]-: ~steigerung die increase in profits; **~steuer die** *(Wirtsch.)* tax on profits
ertränken *tr. V.* drown; **seinen Kummer/seine Sorgen im Alkohol ~** *(fig.)* drown one's sorrows [in drink]
erträumen *refl. V.* dream of; **sie ist die Frau, die er sich** *(Dat.)* **erträumt hat** she's the woman of his dreams; **erträumte Welten** imaginary worlds
ertrinken *unr. itr. V.; mit sein* be drowned; drown; *(fig.)* be inundated; **in einer Flut von Anfragen ~** *(fig.)* be inundated with inquiries
Ertrinkende der/die; *adj. Dekl.* drowning person
ertrotzen *tr. V.* **sich** *(Dat.)* **etw. ~:** obtain sth. by sheer defiance
Ertrunkene der/die; *adj. Dekl.* drowned person
ertüchtigen 1. *tr. V.* toughen up ⟨*body*⟩. **2.** *refl. V.* **sich körperlich ~:** get/keep oneself fit
Ertüchtigung die; ~, ~**en** fitness; **jmdn. zur körperlichen ~ anhalten** encourage sb. to keep [himself/herself] physically fit
erübrigen 1. *tr. V.* spare ⟨*money, time*⟩; **etw. Geld/Zeit ~ können** have some money/time to spare. **2.** *refl. V.* be unnecessary; **es erübrigt sich, noch länger darüber zu sprechen** there's no point in talking about it any longer
eruieren [eru'i:rən] *tr. V.* find out; **jmdn. ~** *(österr.)* trace sb.
Eruierung die; ~, ~**en** investigation; **die ~ des Täters** *(österr.)* the tracing of the culprit
Eruption [erʊp'tsio:n] **die;** ~, ~**en** *(Geol., Med.)* eruption
Eruptiv·gestein [erʊp'ti:f-] **das** *(Geol.)* eruptive rock
erwachen *itr. V.; mit sein (geh.)* awake; wake up; *(fig.)* awake; **aus tiefem Schlaf ~:** awake from a deep sleep; **aus der Narkose ~:** come round; **aus seinen Tagträumen ~:** snap out of one's day-dreams; **ein neuer Tag erwacht** *(geh.)* a new day dawns
Erwachen das; ~**s** *(auch fig.)* awakening; **es wird ein böses ~ [für ihn] geben** *(fig.)* it'll be a rude awakening [for him]
[1]**erwachsen** *unr. itr. V.; mit sein* **a)** grow **(aus** out of); ⟨*rumour*⟩ spread; **b)** *(sich ergeben)* ⟨*difficulties, tasks*⟩ arise
[2]**erwachsen 1.** *Adj.* grown-up *attrib.*; **~ sein** be grown up; **~ werden** reach adulthood. **2.** *adv.* ⟨*behave*⟩ in an adult way
Erwachsene der/die; *adj. Dekl.* adult; grown-up
Erwachsenen-: ~alter das adulthood; **~bildung die;** *o. Pl.* adult education *no art.*
Erwachsen·sein das being an adult/adults *no art.*
erwägen *unr. tr. V.* consider
erwägens·wert *Adj.* worth considering *postpos.*; worthy of consideration *postpos.*
Erwägung die; ~, ~**en** consideration; **etw. in ~ ziehen** consider sth.; take sth. into consideration
erwählen *tr. V. (geh.)* choose
Erwählte der/die; *adj. Dekl. (Freund[in])* sweetheart; *(Bevorrechtigte)* **er gehört zu den wenigen ~n** he belongs to the select few
erwähnen *tr. V.* mention; **etw. mit keinem Wort ~:** make no mention of sth.; **jmdn. lobend ~:** speak in praise of sb.; **es muß lobend erwähnt werden, daß ...:** it must be said in his/her *etc.* praise that ...; **bereits erwähnt** aforementioned *attrib.*; **oben erwähnt** above mentioned *attrib.*
erwähnens·wert *Adj.* worth mentioning *postpos.*
Erwähnung die; ~, ~**en** mention; **das verdient [keine] ~:** that is [not] worth mentioning
erwandern *tr., refl. V.* **er hat [sich** *(Dat.)*] **ganz Frankreich erwandert** he's walked all round France
erwärmen 1. *tr. V.* **a)** *(warm machen)* heat; **das erwärmte uns** *(Dat.)* **das Herz** *(fig.)* that warmed our hearts; **b)** *(fig.: gewinnen)* **jmdn. für etw. ~:** win sb. over to sth. **2.** *refl. V. (warm werden)* ⟨*air, water*⟩ warm up; **sich für jmdn./etw. ~** *(fig.)* warm to sb./sth.; **für diese Idee kann ich mich nicht ~:** I cannot work up any enthusiasm for this idea
Erwärmung die; ~: **eine ~ der Luft/des Wassers** an increase in air/water temperature; **bei ~ der Flüssigkeit** when the liquid is heated
erwarten *tr. V.* **a)** expect ⟨*guests, phone call, post*⟩; **etw. ungeduldig/sehnlich ~:** wait impatiently/eagerly for sth; **jmdn. am Bahnhof ~:** wait for sb. at the station; **wir ~ ihn um 7 Uhr** we are expecting him at 7 o'clock; **ein Kind ~:** be expecting a baby; be expecting *(coll.)*; **ich kann meinen Urlaub kaum ~:** I can hardly wait for my holiday; **b)** *(rechnen mit)* **etw. von jmdm. ~:** expect sth. of sb.; **von jmdm. ~, daß er etw. tut** expect sb. to do sth.; **es ist** *od. (geh.)* **steht zu ~, daß ...:** it is to be expected that ...; **wider Erwarten** contrary to expectation; **[sich** *(Dat.)*] **von etw. viel/wenig/nichts ~:** expect a lot/little/nothing from sth.
Erwartung die; ~, ~**en** expectation; **~en in etw.** *(Akk.)* **setzen** have expectations of sth.; **die in ihn gesetzten ~en erfüllten sich nicht** the hopes placed in him were not fulfilled; **in freudiger ~:** in joyful anticipation; **die ~en [nicht] erfüllen** [not] come up to one's expectations
erwartungs-, Erwartungs-: ~gemäß *Adv.* as expected; **~horizont der** level of expectations; **~voll 1.** *Adj.* expectant; **2.** *adv.* expectantly
erwecken *tr. V.* **a)** *(auf~)* wake; **jmdn. vom Tode ~:** bring sb. back to life; **b)** *(erregen)* arouse ⟨*longing, mistrust, pity*⟩; **den Eindruck ~, als ...:** give the impression that ...
Erweckung die; ~, ~**en a)** *(Auf~)* resurrection; **b)** *(Erregung)* arousal; **c)** *(Mystik)* religious awakening; **d)** *(ev. Theol.)* religious revival
Erweckungs·bewegung die revivalist movement
erwehren *refl. V. (geh.)* **sich jmds./einer Sache ~:** fend *or* ward sb./sth. off; **sie konnte sich des Gefühls/des Eindrucks nicht ~, daß ...:** she could not help feeling/thinking that ...
erweichen 1. *tr. V.* soften; **jmdn./jmds. Herz ~** *(fig.)* soften sb.'s heart; **sich ~ lassen** *(fig.)* yield. **2.** *itr. V.; mit sein (aufweichen)* become soft
Erweichung die; ~, ~**en** softening
erweisen 1. *unr. tr. V.* **a)** prove; **es ist erwiesen, daß ...:** it has been proved that ...; **b)** *(bezeigen)* **jmdm. Achtung ~:** show respect to sb.; **jmdm. einen Gefallen ~:** do sb. a favour; **~ Sie mir die Ehre** *(geh.)* do me the honour. **2.** *unr. refl. V.* **sich als etw. ~:** prove to be sth.; **seine Behauptungen haben sich als falsch erwiesen** his assertions have proved false
erweislich *Adv. (geh.)* demonstrably
erweitern 1. *tr. V.* widen ⟨*river, road*⟩; expand ⟨*library, business*⟩; enlarge ⟨*collection*⟩; dilate ⟨*pupil, blood vessel*⟩; extend ⟨*power*⟩; **seinen Horizont/seine Kenntnisse ~:** broaden one's horizons/knowledge; **einen Bruch ~** *(Math.)* reduce a fraction to higher terms; **eine erweiterte Neuauflage** a new, expanded edition; **erweiterte Oberschule** *(DDR) (Stufe)* ≈ sixth form; *(Schule)* ≈ sixth-form college. **2.** *refl. V.* ⟨*road, river*⟩ widen; ⟨*pupil, blood vessel*⟩ dilate; **sich zu etw. ~:** widen into sth.
Erweiterung die; ~, ~**en** *s.* **erweitern:** widening; expansion; enlargement; dilation; extension; **die ~ eines Bruchs** the reduction of a fraction; **zur ~ seiner Fremdsprachkenntnisse ...:** to increase his knowledge of foreign languages ...
Erweiterungs·bau der; *Pl.* **~ten** extension
Erwerb [ɛɐ̯'vɛrp] **der;** ~[e]s **a) der ~ des Lebensunterhaltes** earning a living; **b)** *(Arbeit)* occupation; **ohne ~ sein** be unemployed; **c)** *(Aneignung)* acquisition; **d)** *(Kauf)* purchase; **e)** *(das Erworbene)* earnings *pl.*
erwerben *unr. tr. V.* **a)** *(verdienen)* earn; *(fig.)* win ⟨*fame*⟩; **sich** *(Dat.)* **großen Ruhm ~:** win great fame; **jmds. Vertrauen ~:** win *or* earn sb.'s trust; **b)** *(sich aneignen)* gain ⟨*experience, influence*⟩; acquire, gain ⟨*knowledge*⟩; **c)** acquire ⟨*property, works of art, etc.*⟩; **etw. käuflich ~** *(Papierdt.)* purchase sth.; **d)** *(Biol., Psych.)* acquire
erwerbs-, Erwerbs-: ~fähig *Adj.* capable of gainful employment *postpos.*; able to work *postpos.*; **~fähigkeit die;** *o. Pl.* ability to work; **~leben das** working life; **im ~leben stehen** be working; **~los** *Adj.: s.* **arbeitslos; ~lose der/die;** *adj. Dekl.: s.* **Arbeitslose; ~minderung die: eine ~minderung** a reduction in one's/sb.'s capacity for work; **~mittel das** means of livelihood; **~quelle die** source of income; **~sinn der;** *o. Pl.* business sense; **~tätig** *Adj.* gainfully employed; **~tätige der/die;** *adj. Dekl.* person in work; **die ~tätigen** those in work; **~unfähig** *Adj.* incapable of gainful employment *postpos.*; unable to work *postpos.*; **~unfähigkeit die** inability to work; **~zweig der** source of employment
Erwerbung die a) *(Aneignung)* acquisition; **b)** *(Erworbenes)* acquisition; *(Gekauftes)* purchase
erwidern [ɛɐ̯'vi:dɐn] *tr. V.* **a)** reply; **etw. auf etw.** *(Akk.)* **~:** say sth. in reply to sth.; **auf diese Beleidigung wußte sie nichts zu ~:** she could not think of a reply to this insult; **b)** *(reagieren auf)* return ⟨*greeting, visit*⟩; reciprocate ⟨*sb.'s feelings*⟩
Erwiderung die; ~, ~**en a)** *(Antwort)* reply **(auf +** *Akk.* to); **b)** *s.* **erwidern b:** return; reciprocation
erwiesen 1. *2. Part. v.* **erweisen. 2.** *Adj.* proved; **eine ~e Tatsache** a proven fact; **das ist doch längst ~:** that has long since been proved
erwiesener·maßen *Adv.* as has been proved; **er hat ~ die Unwahrheit gesagt** it has been proved that he didn't tell the truth

erwirken *tr. V.* obtain ‹*permit, release*›
Erwirkung die; *o. Pl.* obtainment
erwirtschaften *tr. V.* **etw. ~:** obtain sth. by careful management
erwischen *tr. V.* *(ugs.)* **a)** *(fassen, ertappen, erreichen)* catch ‹*culprit, train, bus*›; **jmdn. beim Abschreiben ~:** catch sb. copying; **b)** *(greifen)* grab; **jmdn. am Ärmel ~:** grab sb. by the sleeve; **c)** *(bekommen)* manage to catch *or* get; **d)** *(unpers.)* **es hat ihn erwischt** *(ugs.) (er ist tot)* he has bought it *(sl.)*; *(er ist krank)* he has got it; *(er ist verletzt)* he's been hurt; *(scherzh.: er ist verliebt)* he's got it bad *(coll.)*
erwünscht [ɛɐ̯'vʏnʃt] *Adj.* wanted; **das ~e Resultat** the desired result; **deine Anwesenheit ist dringend ~:** your presence is urgently required
erwürgen *tr. V.* strangle
Erz [ɛrts *od.* e:ɐ̯ts] **das; ~es, ~e** ore
Erz-: ~abbau der mining of ore; **~ader die** vein of ore
erzählen *tr. (auch itr.) V.* tell ‹*joke, story*›; **jmdm. etw. ~:** tell sb. sth.; **erzähl keine Märchen!** *(ugs.)* don't tell stories!; **dem werde ich was ~!** *(ugs.) (zurechtweisend)* I'll have something to say to him!; *(ablehnend)* I'll tell him where to get off! *(coll.)*; **einen Traum/ein Erlebnis ~:** recount a dream/an experience; **jmdm. von etw. ~:** tell sb. about sth.; **von etw. ~:** talk about sth.; **etw. von jmdm.** *od.* **über jmdn. ~:** tell sth. about sb.; **das kannst du einem anderen** *od. (ugs.)* **deiner Großmutter ~!** tell that to the [horse] marines *(Brit. coll.)*; pull the other leg *or* one *(coll.)*; **du kannst mir viel ~** *(ugs.)* you can say what you like
erzählens·wert *Adj.* ‹*things, stories*› worth telling
Erzähler der a) story-teller; **der ~ eines Romans** the narrator of a novel; **b)** *(Autor)* writer [of stories]; narrative writer; **„Deutsche ~"** 'Stories by German Authors'; 'German Narrative Writers'
erzählerisch *Adj.* narrative *attrib.*
Erzähl-: ~gut das narrative [writing]; **~kunst die** narrative art; **~technik die** narrative technique; **~weise die a)** narrative style; **b)** *(Literaturw.)* narrative form; **~zeit die;** *o. Pl. (Literaturw.)* narrative time
Erzählung die; ~, ~en a) narration; *(Bericht)* account; **b)** *(Literaturw.)* story; *(märchenhafte Geschichte)* tale
Erz-: ~bergbau der ore-mining *no art.*; **~bergwerk das** ore mine; **~bischof der** archbishop; **~bischöflich** *Adj.* archiepiscopal; **~bistum das, ~diözese die** archbishopric; archdiocese; **~dumm** *Adj. (ugs.)* incredibly stupid
erzen *Adj.; nicht präd. (geh.)* bronze
Erz·engel der archangel
erzeugen *tr. V.* **a)** produce; generate ‹*electricity*›; **b)** *(österr.: anfertigen)* manufacture; produce
Erzeuger der; ~s, ~ a) *(Vater)* father; **er ist zwar mein ~, aber ich betrachte ihn nicht als Vater** I may be his child, but I do not regard him as a father; **b)** *(Produzent)* producer; **vom ~ zum Verbraucher** from producer to consumer; **c)** *(österr.: Hersteller)* manufacturer
Erzeuger-: ~land das country of origin; **~preis der** manufacturer's price
Erzeugnis das *(auch fig.)* product; **landwirtschaftliche ~se** agricultural products *or* produce
Erzeugung die a) *(das Bewirken)* creation; **b)** *(das Produzieren) (von Lebensmitteln usw.)* production; *(von Industriewaren)* manufacture; *(Strom~)* generation; **c)** *(österr.: Herstellung)* manufacture
erz-, Erz-: ~feind der arch enemy; **~gang der** lode of ore; **~gauner der** *(ugs.)* arch villain; **~gehalt der** ore content; **~grube die** ore mine; **~haltig** *Adj.* ore-bearing; **~herzog der** archduke; **~herzogin die** archduchess; **~hütte die** ore-smelting works *sing.*
erziehbar *Adj.* educable; **der Junge ist sehr schwer ~:** the boy is a very difficult child
erziehen *unr. tr. V.* **a)** *(bilden u. fördern)* bring up; *(in der Schule)* educate; **ein Kind streng/sehr frei ~:** give a child a strict/very liberal upbringing/education; **b)** *(anleiten)* **jmdn. zum Verbrecher ~:** bring sb. up to criminal ways; **ein Kind zu Sauberkeit und Ordnung ~:** bring a child up to be clean and tidy; **jmdn./sich dazu ~, etw. zu tun** train sb./oneself to do sth.; *s. auch* **erzogen 2**
Erzieher der; ~s, ~, Erzieherin die; ~, ~nen educator; *(Pädagoge)* educationalist; *(Lehrer)* teacher
erzieherisch *s.* **pädagogisch 1a, 2a**
erziehlich *Adj. (bes. österr.)* educational
Erziehung die; *o. Pl.* **a)** *(das Erziehen)* upbringing; *(Schul~)* education; **eine gute ~ genießen** enjoy a good education; **b)** *(Manieren)* upbringing; breeding; **seine gute ~ vergessen** forget oneself
erziehungs-, Erziehungs-: ~anstalt die *(veralt.)* approved school; Borstal *(Brit.)*; **~berater der** *(Berufsbez.)* child guidance counsellor; **~beratung die a)** *(Beraten)* child guidance; **b)** *(Beratungsstelle)* child guidance clinic; **~berechtigt** *Adj.* having parental authority *postpos., not pred.*; **sein Großvater wurde ~berechtigt** his grandfather became his [legal] guardian; **~berechtigte der/die;** *adj. Dekl.* parent or [legal] guardian; **~frage die** question of upbringing; **~heim das** community home; **~maßnahme die** measure used in bringing up a child; **~methode die** educational method; teaching method; **~modell das** educational model; approach to education; **~roman der** *(Literaturw.)* novel describing the development of an individual's character; **~wesen das** educational system; education; **~wissenschaft die** education; **~wissenschaften studieren** study education *sing.*; **~wissenschaftler der** educationalist
erzielen *tr. V.* reach ‹*agreement, compromise, speed*›; achieve ‹*result, effect*›; make ‹*profit*›; obtain ‹*price*›; score ‹*goal*›
erzittern *itr. V.; mit sein* **a)** [begin to] shake *or* tremble; **etw. ~ lassen** shake sth.; **b)** *(geh.)* quiver; tremble
erz-, Erz-: ~konservativ *Adj.* ultraconservative; **~lager·stätte die** ore deposit; **~lügner der** inveterate liar; **~lump der** *(abwertend)* [low-down] scoundrel
erzogen 1. *2. Part. v.* **erziehen. 2.** *Adj.* **gut/schlecht ~ sein** have been brought up/not have been brought up properly
erz-, Erz-: ~reaktionär *Adj.* ultrareactionary; **~reaktionär der** ultrareactionary; **~schurke der** *(abwertend) s.* **Erzlump**
erzürnen *(geh.)* **1.** *tr. V.* anger; *(stärker)* incense; **erzürne ihn nicht** don't make him angry. **2.** *refl. V.* **sich über jmdn./etw. ~:** become *or* grow angry with sb./about sth.
Erz-: ~vater der *(Rel.)* patriarch; **~verhüttung die** ore smelting; **~vorkommen das** ore deposit
erzwingen *unr. tr. V.* force; **sich** *(Dat.)* **den Zutritt ~:** force an entry; **etw. von jmdm. ~:** force sth. out of sb.
erzwungenermaßen *Adv.* under duress
¹es [ɛs] *Personalpron.; 3. Pers. Sg. Nom. u. Akk. Neutr.* **a)** *(s. auch Gen.* **seiner;** *Dat.* **ihm)** *(bei Dingen)* it; *(bei weiblichen Personen)* she/her; *(bei männlichen Personen)* he/him; **b)** *bezieht sich auf ein Nomen mit beliebigem Genus* **Wer ist der Mann? – Es muß der Bruder des Gastgebers sein** Who is that man? – He/It must be the host's brother; **es waren Studenten** they were students; **keiner will es gewesen sein** no one will admit to it; **ich bin es** it's me; it is I *(formal)*; **er/sie ist es** it's him/her; it is he/she *(formal)*; **wir sind es** it's us; it is we *(formal)*; **ich bin/wir sind es, der/die ...:** I am the one/we are the ones who ...; *(förmlicher)* it is I/it is we who ...; **c)** *bezieht sich auf ein Adj.* **wir sind traurig, ihr seid es auch** we are sad, and you are too *or* so are you; **d)** *bezieht sich auf ein Prädikat* it; **er hat gelogen, will es aber nicht zugeben** he lied, but won't admit it; **er hatte es nicht anders erwartet** he hadn't expected anything else; **Wird man ihn dafür bestrafen? – Ich befürchte es** Will he be punished for it? – I fear so; **e)** *kündigt Subjekt od. Subjekt- und Objektsatz an* **es war einmal ein König** once upon a time there was a king; there was once a king; **es gibt keinen anderen Weg** there is no other way; **es war Karl, der ...:** it was Karl who ...; **es ist schön, daß ...:** it is nice that ...; **es wundert mich, daß ...:** I'm surprised that ...; **es sei denn, [daß] ...:** unless ...; **f)** *bezieht sich auf einen Sachverhalt* **es ist genug!** that's enough; **wir schaffen es** we'll manage it; **g)** *bei unpersönlicher Witterungsangabe* **es regnet/schneit/donnert** it rains/snows/thunders; *(jetzt)* it is raining/snowing/thundering; **es blitzt** there is lightning; **es stürmt** it is blowing a gale; **h)** *bei unpersönlicher Darstellung* **es hat geklopft** there was a knock; **es klingelte** there was a ring; **es klingelt** someone is ringing; **es knistert** there is something rustling; **in diesem Haus spukt es** this house is haunted; **es friert mich** I am cold; **i)** *bei Zustands- u. Artsätzen* **es ist 9 Uhr/spät/Nacht** it is 9 o'clock/late/night-time; **es wird schöner** the weather is improving; **es wird kälter** it's getting colder; **es wird Frühling** spring is on the way; **es geht ihm gut/schlecht** he is well/unwell; **j)** *bei passivischer Konstruktion* **es wird gelacht** there is laughter; **es wird um 6 Uhr angefangen** we/they *etc.* start at 6 o'clock; **es wurde uns befohlen, das Gebäude zu verlassen** we were ordered to leave the building; **k)** *bei reflexiver Konstruktion* **es läßt sich aushalten** it is bearable; **es lebt sich gut hier** it's a good life here; **l)** *als formales Objekt* **er hat es gut** he has it good; it's all right for him; **er meinte es gut** he meant well; **sie hat es mit dem Herzen** *(ugs.)* she has got heart trouble *or* something wrong with her heart; **er hat es mit seiner Sekretärin** *(salopp)* he's making it with his secretary *(sl.)*; *s. auch* **haben 1n**
²es, ¹Es das; ~, ~ *(Musik)* E flat
²Es das; ~, ~ *(Psych.)* id
³Es der; ~, ~ *(österr., ugs.)* schilling
E-Saite die E-string
Eschatologie [ɛsçatolo'gi:] **die; ~, ~n** [-ən] *(Theol.)* eschatology *no art.*
eschatologisch *Adj.* eschatological
Esche ['ɛʃə] **die; ~, ~n** *(Bot.)* ash
Es-Dur das E flat major; *s. auch* **A-Dur**
Esel ['e:zl̩] **der; ~s, ~ a)** donkey; ass; **bepackt** *od.* **beladen wie ein ~ sein** be loaded down like a pack-horse; **den hat der ~ im Galopp verloren** *(salopp)* he just appeared from nowhere *(coll.)*; **wenn es dem ~ zu wohl wird, geht er aufs Eis** *(Spr.)* you'll/he'll *etc.* come unstuck one of these days; **b)** *(ugs.: Dummkopf)* ass *(coll.)*; idiot *(coll.)*; **so ein alter ~:** what a stupid ass *or* idiot *(coll.)*; **du ~:** you ass!; *s. auch* **ich**
Eselei die; ~, ~en *(ugs.)* stupidity; **das war aber eine ~!** *(Handlung)* that was a stupid *or* silly thing to do; *(Bemerkung)* that was a stupid *or* silly thing to say
Eselein das; ~s, ~: little donkey
Esel-: ~füllen das ass-foal; **~hengst der** he-donkey; jackass
Eselin die; ~, ~nen she-donkey; jenny-ass
Esels-: ~brücke die *(ugs.)* mnemonic; **~milch die** ass's milk; **~ohr das** *(ugs.)* **a)** **~ohren haben** *(fig.)* have donkey's ears; **b)**

(umgeknickte Stelle) dog-ear; **ein Buch voller ~ohren** a dog-eared book; **~stute die** she-donkey; jenny[-ass]
Ẹsel·treiber der donkey-driver
Eskalation [ɛskala'tsio:n] **die; ~, ~en** escalation
eskalieren *tr., itr. V.* escalate
eskamotieren [ɛskamo'ti:rən] *tr. V.* conjure away; **Fakten ~:** explain facts away by sleight of hand
Eskapade [ɛska'pa:də] **die; ~, ~n** escapade; *(Seitensprung)* amorous adventure
Eskapismus [ɛska'pɪsmʊs] **der; ~** *(Psych.)* escapism *no art.*
eskapistisch *Adj.* escapist
Eskimo ['ɛskimo] **der; ~[s], ~[s]** Eskimo
eskimoisch *Adj.* Eskimo
Eskorte [ɛs'kɔrtə] **die; ~, ~n** escort; *(fig.)* entourage; **eine ~ der Polizei** a police escort
eskortieren *tr. V.* escort
ẹs-Moll das; ~: E flat minor; *s. auch* **a-Moll**
esoterisch [ezo'te:rɪʃ] **1.** *Adj.* esoteric. **2.** *adv.* esoterically
Espe ['ɛspə] **die; ~, ~n** aspen
Ẹspen·laub das *in* **wie ~ zittern** shake like a leaf
Esperanto [ɛspe'ranto] **das; ~[s]** Esperanto
Esplanade [ɛspla'na:də] **die; ~, ~n** esplanade
[1]Espresso [ɛs'prɛso] **der; ~[s], ~s** *od.* **Espręssi a)** *o. Pl.: dark blend of roasted coffee;* **b)** *(Getränk)* espresso [coffee]
[2]Espręsso das; ~[s], ~[s] *(Lokal)* espresso [bar]
Espręsso·maschine die espresso [machine]
Esprit [ɛs'pri:] **der; ~s** esprit
Essai ['ɛse, ɛ'se:] *s.* **Essay**
Ẹß·apfel der eating apple; eater *(Brit.)*
Essay ['ɛse] **der** *od.* **das; ~s, ~s** essay
Essayist der; ~en, ~en, Essayistin die; ~, ~nen essayist
essayistisch *Adj.* essayistic; **seine ~e Begabung** his talent as an essayist
ẹßbar *Adj.* edible; **ist etwas Eßbares im Haus?** *(ugs.)* is there anything to eat in the house?; **nicht ~ sein** be inedible
Ẹß·besteck das knife, fork, and spoon; **unser ~:** our cutlery; **zwei ~e** two sets of knife, fork, and spoon
Esse ['ɛsə] **die; ~, ~n a)** *(bes. ostmd.)* chimney; **b)** *(Herd)* hearth; forge
Ẹß·ecke die dining area
essen ['ɛsn̩] *unr. tr., itr. V.* eat; eat, drink ⟨*soup*⟩; **mittags ißt er meist im Restaurant** he usually lunches *or* has lunch at a restaurant; **etw. gern ~:** like sth.; **möchten Sie ein Stück Kuchen ~?** would you like a piece of cake?; **was gibt es zu ~?** what's for lunch/dinner/supper?; **von etw. ~:** eat some of sth.; **jmdm. etwas zu ~ machen** get sb. something to eat; **sich satt ~:** eat one's fill; **den Teller leer ~:** clear one's plate; **er ißt mich noch arm!** he'll eat me out of house and home!; **gut ~:** have a good meal; *(immer)* eat well; **warm/kalt ~:** have a hot/cold meal; **das Kind ißt schlecht** the child doesn't eat very much *or* has a poor appetite; **Kranke müssen gut ~:** you must eat properly when you're ill; **~ gehen** got out for a meal; **er ißt bei seiner Tante** he has his meals with his aunt; **es wird nichts so heiß gegessen, wie es gekocht wird** *(Spr.)* nothing is ever as bad as it seems; **selber ~ macht fett** *(ugs.)* I'm all right, Jack *(coll.)*; *s. auch* **Abend a; [1]Mittag a; [2]Mittag**
Ẹssen das; ~s, ~ a) *o. Pl.* **beim ~ sein** be having lunch/dinner/supper; **laßt euch nicht beim ~ stören** don't let me/us disturb your meal; **zum ~ gehen** go to lunch; **jmdn. zum ~ einladen** invite sb. for a meal; **b)** *(Mahlzeit)* meal; *(Fest~)* banquet; **zehn ~:** ten meals; **ein ~ [für jmdn.] geben** give a banquet [in sb.'s honour]; **c)** *(Speise)* food; **[das] ~ machen/kochen** get/cook the meal; **das ~ warm stellen** keep the lunch/dinner/supper hot; **das ~ wird kalt** lunch/dinner/supper is getting cold; the food is getting cold; **~ fassen!** *(Soldatenspr.)* come and get it!; **~ auf Rädern** meals on wheels; **d)** *(Verpflegung) o. Pl.* food; **~ und Trinken** food and drink
Ẹssen·fassen das *(Soldatenspr.)* **zum ~!** come and get it!; **beim ~:** at mess-time
Ẹssen[s]-: ~ausgabe die a) *(das Ausgeben)* serving of meals; **die ~ausgabe ist zwischen 12 und 14 Uhr** meals are *or* lunch is served between 12 [o'clock] and 2 o'clock; **b)** *(Stelle)* serving-hatch; **~marke die** meal-ticket; **~zeit die** mealtime; **während der ~zeit** during *or* at mealtimes
essentiell [ɛsɛn'tsi̯ɛl] **1.** *Adj. (geh., auch Chemie, Biol.)* essential. **2.** *adv. (geh.)* essentially
Essenz [ɛ'sɛnts] **die; ~, ~en** essence
Ẹsser der; ~s, ~: er ist ein guter/schlechter ~: he has a healthy/poor appetite; **ein zusätzlicher ~, den es zu ernähren gilt** an extra mouth to feed
Ẹß·geschirr das a) pots and pans; **b)** *(Milit.)* mess-kit
Ẹß·gewohnheiten *Pl.* eating habits
Essig ['ɛsɪç] **der; ~s, ~e** vinegar; **~ und Öl** oil and vinegar; **es ist mit etw. ~** *(ugs.)* sth. has fallen through completely *(coll.)*
ẹssig-, Ẹssig-: ~baum der staghorn sumac; **~essenz die** vinegar essence; **~flasche die** vinegar bottle; **~gurke die** pickled gherkin; **~sauce die** vinaigrette; French dressing; **~sauer** *Adj.* acetic; **~saure Tonerde** basic aluminium acetate; **~säure die** *(Chemie)* acetic acid; **~soße die:** *s.* **~sauce; ~-und-Öl-Ständer der** cruet-stand; **~wasser das** water with a little vinegar added
ẹß-, Ẹß-: ~kastanie die sweet chestnut; **~kohle die** dry steam coal; **~kultur die** gastronomy; **~löffel der** *(Suppenlöffel)* soup-spoon; *(für Nach-, Vorspeise)* dessert-spoon; **~löffel·weise** *Adv. (abmessend)* in dessert-spoonfuls; *(steigernd)* by the spoonful; **~lokal das** restaurant; **~lust die;** *o. Pl.* desire for something to eat; **~napf der** bowl; **~paket das** food parcel; **~platz der** dining area; **~stäbchen das** chopstick; **~teller der** dinner plate; **~tisch der** dining-table; **~waren** *Pl.* food *sing.*; **~zimmer das** dining-room; *(Möbel)* dining-room suite
Establishment [ɪs'tɛblɪʃmənt] **das; ~s, ~s** Establishment
Este ['e:stə] **der; ~n, ~n** Estonian
Ester ['ɛstɐ] **der; ~s, ~** *(Chemie)* ester
Estin die; ~, ~nen Estonian
Ẹst·land (das); ~s Estonia
Ẹstländer der; ~s, ~: *s.* **Este**
ẹstländisch, ẹstnisch *Adj.* Estonian; *s. auch* **deutsch; Deutsch**
Estrade [ɛs'tra:də] **die; ~, ~n a)** *(veralt.)* estrade; dais; platform; **b)** *(DDR)* open-air show
Estragon ['ɛstragɔn] **der; ~s** tarragon
Estrich ['ɛstrɪç] **der; ~s, ~e a)** composition *or* jointless floor; **b)** *(schweiz.)* attic; loft
Eszett [ɛs'tsɛt] **das; ~, ~:** [the letter] ß
Eta ['e:ta] **das; ~[s], ~s** eta
etablieren [eta'bli:rən] **1.** *tr. V. (gründen)* establish; set up. **2.** *refl. V.* **a)** *(sich niederlassen)* ⟨*shop*⟩ open up; ⟨*chain store*⟩ open up *or* set up branches; **sich als Juwelier ~:** set up as a jeweller; open up a jeweller's shop; **b)** *(sich einrichten)* settle in; **c)** *(gesellschaftlich)* become established
etabliert *Adj.* established; **er ist jetzt so entsetzlich ~** *(abwertend)* he is now so terribly conservative; **die Etablierten** the Establishment
Etablissement [etablɪs(ə)'mã:] **das; ~s, ~s** establishment
Etage [e'ta:ʒə] **die; ~, ~n** floor; storey; **in** *od.* **auf der dritten ~ wohnen** live on the third *or (Amer.)* fourth floor
Etagen-: ~bett das bunk-bed; **~haus das** block of flats *(Brit.) or (Amer.)* apartments; **~heizung die** *central heating serving one floor of a building;* **~kellner der** waiter [serving one floor of a hotel]; **~wohnung die** *flat (Brit.) or (Amer.) apartment occupying an entire floor*
Etagere [eta'ʒe:rə] **die; ~, ~n** *(veralt.)* étagère; whatnot
Etappe [e'tapə] **die; ~, ~n a)** *(Teilstrecke)* stage; leg; *(Rennsport)* stage; **b)** *(Stadium)* stage; **c)** *(Milit.)* back area; base; **jmdn. in die ~ versetzen** move sb. back behind the lines
etappen-, Etappen-: ~hase der, ~hengst der *(Soldatenspr. salopp)* base wallah *(Mil. sl.)*; **~sieg der** *(Rennsport)* stage-win; **der heutige ~sieg ging an ...:** the winner of today's stage was ...; **~weise** *Adv.* by *or* in stages; **~wertung die** *(Rennsport)* daily points classification; **~ziel das** *(Sport)* finish of the stage
Etat [e'ta:] **der; ~s, ~s** budget
etat-, Etat-: ~ausgleich der balancing of the budget; **~defizit das** budgetary deficit; **~kürzung die** cut in the budget; **die ~kürzungen im Bildungswesen** the cuts in the education budget; the education cuts; **~mäßig 1.** *Adj.* **a)** *(im Etat)* budgetary ⟨*expenditure*⟩; **b)** *(eingeplant)* budgeted ⟨*post, position*⟩; **der ~mäßige Mittelstürmer** *(Fußballjargon)* the regular centre-forward; **2.** *adv.* in the budget; **~stärke die** *(Milit.)* planned strength
etc. *Abk.* **et cetera** etc.
et cetera [ɛt'tse:tera] et cetera; **~ ~ pp.** ['-'---pe'pe:] *(ugs., scherzh.)* and so on and so forth *(coll.)*
etepetete [e:təpe'te:tə] *Adj. (ugs.)* fussy; finicky; pernickety *(coll.)*
Eternit Ⓦᶻ [etɛr'ni:t] **das** *od.* **der; ~s** asbestos cement
ETH *Abk.* **Eidgenössische Technische Hochschule** Swiss Federal Institute of Technology
Ethik ['e:tɪk] **die; ~, ~en a)** *(Sittenlehre)* ethics *sing.*; **b)** *o. Pl. (sittliche Normen)* ethics *pl.*; **c)** *(Werk über Ethik)* ethical work
Ethiker der; ~s, ~ a) *(Philos.)* moral philosopher; **b)** *(Moralist)* moralist
ethisch 1. *Adj.* ethical. **2.** *adv.* ethically
Ethnie [ɛt'ni:] **die; ~, ~n** *(Völkerk.)* ethnos
ethnisch ['ɛtnɪʃ] **1.** *Adj.* ethnic. **2.** *adv.* ethnically
Ethnograph [ɛtno'gra:f] **der; ~en, ~en** ethnographer
Ethnographie die; ~, ~n ethnography *no art.*
Ethnographin die; ~, ~nen ethnographer
Ethnologe [ɛtno'lo:gə] **der; ~n, ~n** ethnologist
Ethnologie die; ~, ~n ethnology *no art.*
Ethnologin die; ~, ~nen ethnologist
ethnologisch 1. *Adj.* ethnological. **2.** *adv.* ethnologically
Ethologie [etolo'gi:] **die; ~, ~n** ethology *no art.*
Ethos ['e:tɔs] **das; ~:** ethos; **das berufliche ~ der Ärzteschaft** doctors' professional ethics *pl.*
Etikett [eti'kɛt] **das; ~[e]s, ~en** *od.* **~e** *od.* **~s** label; **jmdn./etw. mit einem ~ versehen** *(fig.)* pin a label on sb./sth.
[1]Etikętte die; ~, ~n *(schweiz., österr.) s.* **Etikett**
[2]Etikętte die; ~, ~n etiquette; **die ~ wahren** observe the proprieties; **gegen die ~ verstoßen** commit a breach of etiquette
Etikęttenschwindel der *(abwertend)* playing with names
etikettieren [etikɛ'ti:rən] *tr. V.* label
etlich... ['ɛtlɪç...] *Indefinitpron. u. unbest.*

Zahlwort **a)** *(ugs., verstärkend) Sg.* quite a lot of; *Pl.* quite a few; a number of; **vor ~en Wochen** several *or* some weeks ago; **b)** *Sg. (veralt.: wenig)* a little; **~es bemerken** make a few remarks *or* comments; **~es sagen** say a few things; **c)** *Pl. (veralt.: einige)* a few; some; **~e der Gefangenen** a few *or* some of the prisoners

etliche·mal *Adv. (veralt.)* several times; a number of times

Etrusker [e'trʊskɐ] **der; ~s, ~:** Etruscan

etruskisch *Adj.* Etruscan; *s. auch* **deutsch**

Etsch die; ~: Adige

Etüde [e'ty:də] **die; ~, ~n** *(Musik)* étude

Etui [ɛt'vi:] **das; ~s, ~s** case

etwa ['ɛtva] **1.** *Adv.* **a)** *(ungefähr)* about; approximately; **~ 50 m/2 Wochen** about 50 m/2 weeks; **~ so groß wie ...:** about as large as ...; **wie lange wird die Fahrt ~ dauern?** roughly how long will the journey take?; **~ so** roughly like this; **das läßt sich ~ so erklären:** you could perhaps explain it like this; **in ~:** to some *or* a certain extent *or* degree; **können Sie mir in ~ sagen, wann ...?** can you give me any idea when ...?; **b)** *(beispielsweise)* for example; for instance; **vergleicht man ~ ...:** for example, if one compares ...; **wie ~ ...:** as, for example ...; **c)** *(schweiz.: bisweilen)* from time to time; now and then. **2.** *Part. (womöglich)* **hast du das ~ vergessen?** you haven't forgotten that, have you?; **störe ich ~?** am I disturbing you at all?; **falls sie ~ doch mitgeht, ...:** if she does happen to go ...; **du glaubst doch nicht ~, daß ...?** surely you don't think that ...?; **sie darf nicht ~ glauben, daß ...:** she mustn't think that ...

etwaig... ['ɛtva(:)ɪg...] *(Papierdt.) Adj.* possible ⟨*delays*⟩; **~e Mängel/Beschwerden** any faults/complaints [which might arise]; **bei ~en Beschwerden** in the event of any complaints

etwas ['ɛtvas] *Indefinitpron.* **a)** something; *(fragend, verneinend)* anything; **~ sagen/hören/sehen** say/hear/see something; **hast du ~ gesagt?** did you say something?; **irgend ~:** something; **erzähl ihm einfach irgend ~:** just tell him anything!; **es muß ~ geschehen** something has to *or* must be done; **wenn sie es wagt, dir ~ zu tun** if she dares to do anything to you; **~ gegen jmdn. haben** have something against sb.; **sie haben ~ miteinander** *(ugs.)* there is something going on between them; **~ für sich haben** *(ugs.)* have sth. in it; **dein Argument hat ~ für sich** *(ugs.)* there's something in your argument; **so ~:** a thing like that; **[so] ~ wie ...:** something like ...; **so ~ habe ich noch nie gesehen** I've never seen anything like it; **nein, so ~:** would you believe it!; **b)** *attr.* something; *(fragend, verneinend)* anything; **~ Schönes/Neues/Unangenehmes** something beautiful/new/unpleasant; **so ~ Schönes habe ich noch nie gesehen** I've never seen anything so beautiful before; **~ anderes** something else; *(fragend, verneinend)* anything else; **das ist ~ anderes** *(ugs.)* that's different; **c)** *(Bedeutsames)* **aus ihm wird ~:** he'll make something of himself *or* his life; **es zu ~ bringen** get somewhere; **~ gelten** count for something; **das will ~ heißen** that really is something; **d)** *(ein Teil)* some; *(fragend, verneinend)* any; **~ von dem Geld** some of the money; **kann ich auch ~ davon haben?** can I have some of it too?; **er weiß ~ von dieser Sache** he knows something about this matter; **sie hat ~ von einer Künstlerin an sich** *(Dat.)* she has *or* there is something of the artist about her; **e)** *(ein wenig)* a little; **noch ~ Milch** a little more *or* some more milk; **kannst du mir ~ Geld leihen?** can you lend me some money?; **~ lauter/besser** a little louder/better; **[noch] ~ spielen/lesen** play/read for a little while [longer]; **~ Englisch** a little *or* some English

Etwas das; ~, ~: something; **ein hilfloses ~:** a helpless little thing; **das gewisse ~:** that certain something

etwelch... ['ɛtvɛlç...] *Indefinitpron. (schweiz., österr.)* some

Etymologe [etymo'lo:gə] **der; ~n, ~n** etymologist

Etymologie die; ~, ~n etymology

Etymologin die; ~, ~nen etymologist

etymologisch *(Sprachw.)* **1.** *Adj.* etymological. **2.** *adv.* etymologically

etymologisieren *tr. V. (Sprachw.)* etymologize

Et-Zeichen ['ɛt-] **das** ampersand

Etzel ['ɛtsl̩] **(der)** Attila the Hun

euch, *(in Briefen)* **Euch** [ɔyç] **1.** *Dat. u. Akk. Pl. des Personalpron.* **ihr, Ihr** you; ye *(Bibl./arch.)*; **ich gebe ~ das** I'll give you it; I'll give it to you. **2.** *Dat. u. Akk. Pl. des Reflexivpron. der 2. Pers. Pl.* yourselves

Eucharistie [ɔyçarɪs'ti:] **die; ~, ~n** *(kath. Rel.)* Eucharist

eucharistisch *Adj. (kath. Rel.)* Eucharistic

[1]**euer,** *(in Briefen)* **Euer** ['ɔyɐ] *Possessivpron.* your; **Grüße von Eu[e]rer Helga/Eu[e]rem Hans** Best wishes, Yours, Helga/Hans; **Eu[e]re** *od.* **Euer Exzellenz** Your Excellency; **ist das/sind das eure?** is that/are they yours?; **es ist der Eu[e]re** *(geh.)* it is yours; **die Eu[e]ren** *od.* **Euern** *(geh.)* your family; **nehmt Euch das Eu[e]re** *(geh.)* take what is yours; **ihr müßt das Eu[e]re dazu tun** you must do your share; **ich verbleibe auf immer die Eu[e]re ...** *(veralt.)* I remain, yours for ever, ...; *s. auch* [1]**dein**

[2]**euer,** *(in Briefen)* **Euer** *Gen. des Personalpron.* **ihr** *(geh.)* **wir werden ~ gedenken** we will remember you

euerseits *s.* **eurerseits**

euersgleichen *s.* **euresgleichen**

euert-: ~halben *s.* **eurethalben; ~wegen** *s.* **euretwegen; ~willen** *s.* **euretwillen**

Eugenik [ɔy'ge:nɪk] **die; ~** *(Med.)* eugenics *sing.*

eugenisch *Adj. (Med.)* eugenic

Eukalyptus [ɔyka'lʏptʊs] **der; ~, Eukalypten** *od.* **~:** eucalyptus

Eukalyptus·bonbon das eucalyptus cough-sweet *(Brit.)*; cough-drop

Euklid [ɔy'kli:t] **(der)** Euclid

euklidisch *Adj. (Math.)* Euclidean

Eule ['ɔylə] **die; ~, ~n a)** owl; **~n nach Athen tragen** carry coals to Newcastle; send owls to Athens; **b)** *(salopp abwertend: Frau)* old boot *(sl.)*

eulen-, Eulen-: ~haft *Adj.* owlish; owllike; **~spiegel der** joker; *s. auch* **Till; ~spiegelei die; ~, ~en** caper; **~vogel der** *(Zool.)* owl

Eumel ['ɔyml̩] **der; ~s, ~** *(Jugendspr.)* twerp *(sl. derog.)*

Eunuch [ɔy'nu:x] **der; ~en, ~en, Eunuche der; ~n, ~n** eunuch

Eunuchen·stimme die *(ugs.)* squeaky, high-pitched voice

Euphemismus [ɔyfe'mɪsmʊs] **der; ~, Euphemismen** *(geh., Sprachw.)* euphemism

euphemistisch *(geh., Sprachw.)* **1.** *Adj.* euphemistic. **2.** *adv.* euphemistically

euphonisch [ɔy'fo:nɪʃ] *Adj. (Sprachw., Musik)* euphonic

Euphorie [ɔyfo'ri:] **die; ~, ~n** *(bes. Med., Psych.)* euphoria; **in [eine] ~ verfallen** go into a state of euphoria

euphorisch *(bes. Med., Psych.)* **1.** *Adj.* euphoric. **2.** *adv.* euphorically

Euphrat ['ɔyfrat] **der; ~[s]** Euphrates

Eurasien [ɔy'ra:zi̯ən] **(das); ~s** Eurasia

Eurasier der; ~s, ~, Eurasierin die; ~, ~nen Eurasian

eurasisch *Adj.* Eurasian

Euratom [ɔyra'to:m] **die; ~:** Euratom

eure, Eure ['ɔyrə] *s.* [1]**euer**

eurer·seits *Adv. (von eurer Seite)* on your part; *(auf eurer Seite)* for your part

eures·gleichen *indekl. Pron.* people *pl.* like you; *(abwertend)* the likes *pl.* of you; your sort *or* kind; *s. auch* **deinesgleichen**

euret-: ~halben [-halbn̩] *(veralt.)*, **~wegen** *Adv. (wegen euch)* because of you; on your account; *(für euch)* on your behalf; *(euch zuliebe)* for your sake; **ich mache mir ~wegen keine Sorgen** I don't worry about you; **~willen** *Adv.* **um ~willen** for your sake

Eurhythmie [ɔyrʏt'mi:] **die; ~ a)** *(bes. Tanz, Gymnastik)* eurhythmics *sing., no art.*; **b)** *(Med.)* eurhythmia

eurige ['ɔyrɪgə] *Possessivpron. (geh., veralt.)* **der/die/das ~:** yours; **das Eurige** *(Angelegenheit)* your affairs; *(Besitz)* what is yours

Eurocheque ['ɔyroʃɛk] **der; ~s, ~s** Eurocheque

Eurocheque·karte die Eurocheque card

Euro~: ~dollar der *(Wirtsch.)* Eurodollar; **~kommunismus der** Eurocommunism; **~krat** [~'kra:t] **der; ~en, ~en, ~kratin die; ~, ~nen** Eurocrat

Europa [ɔy'ro:pa] **(das); ~s** Europe

Europa·cup der *(Sport)* European cup

Europäer [ɔyro'pɛ:ɐ] **der; ~s, ~, Europäerin die; ~, ~nen** European

Europa·flagge die flag of the Council of Europe

europäisch [ɔyro'pɛ:ɪʃ] *Adj.* European; **die Europäische Gemeinschaft/Europäischen Gemeinschaften** the European Community/European Communities; **Europäische Wirtschaftsgemeinschaft** European Economic Community

europäisieren *tr. V.* Europeanize

Europäisierung die; ~, ~en Europeanization

europa-, Europa-: ~meister der *(Sport)* European champion; **~meisterschaft die** *(Sport)* **a)** *(Wettbewerb)* European Championship; **b)** *(Sieg)* championship of Europe, European title; **~minister der** minister for Europe; **~müde** *Adj.* disillusioned with the Common Market *postpos.*; **~parlament das;** *o. Pl.* European Parliament *or* Assembly; **~pokal der** *(Sport) s.* **Europacup; ~politik die** policy towards the EEC; **~rat der;** *o. Pl.* Council of Europe; **~rekord der** *(Sport)* European record; **~straße die** European long-distance road; **~wahlen** *Pl.* European elections

Euro·scheck der *s.* **Eurocheque**

Euro·vision die Eurovision

Eurythmie *s.* **Eurhythmie a**

Eustachische Röhre [ɔys'taxɪʃə -] **die; ~n ~, ~n ~n** *(Med., Zool.)* Eustachian tube

Euter ['ɔytɐ] **das** *od.* **der; ~s, ~:** udder

Euthanasie [ɔytana'zi:] **die; ~:** euthanasia *no art.*

e. V., E. V. *Abk.* **eingetragener Verein**

ev. *Abk.* **evangelisch** ev.

[1]**Eva** ['e:fa *od.* 'e:va] **(die)** Eve; *s. auch* [1]**Adam**

[2]**Eva die; ~, ~s** *(ugs. scherzh.: Frau)* **sie ist eine richtige ~:** she's a real little Eve

evakuieren [evaku'i:rən] *tr. V.* evacuate

Evakuierte der/die; *adj. Dekl.* evacuee

Evakuierung die; ~, ~en evacuation

Evaluation [evalua'tsi̯o:n] **die; ~, ~en a)** *(geh.)* valuation; **b)** *(Päd.)* evaluation

Evangelien·buch das Gospel

evangelikal [evangeli'ka:l] *Adj. (christl. Kirche)* evangelical

evangelisch [evaŋ'ge:lɪʃ] *Adj.* **a)** Protestant; **die ~e Kirche** the Protestant Church; **b)** *(des Evangeliums)* evangelical

evangelisch-lutherisch *Adj.* Lutheran

evangelisch-reformiert *Adj.* Reformed

evangelisieren *tr. V.* evangelize

Evangelist der; ~en, ~en evangelist

Evangelium [evaŋ'ge:li̯ʊm] **das; ~s, Evangelien a)** *o. Pl. (auch fig.)* gospel; **alles, was ihr Mann sagte, war [ein] ~ für sie** she took everything her husband said as gospel; **b)**

(christl. Rel.) Gospel; **das ~ des Johannes** St. John's Gospel
Evas- ['e:fas- *od.* 'e:vas-]: **~kostüm das** *in* **im ~kostüm** *(ugs. scherzh.)* in her birthday suit/their birthday suits *(coll. joc.)*; in the altogether *(coll. joc.)*; **~tochter die** *(scherzh.)* **eine echte ~tochter** a real little Eve
Eventual- [evɛn'tu̯a:l-]: **~fall der** eventuality; contingency; **für den ~fall** should the eventuality arise; **~haushalt der** *(Politik)* contingency reserve
Eventualität [evɛntu̯ali'tɛ:t] **die; ~, ~n** eventuality; contingency
eventuell [evɛn'tu̯ɛl] **1.** *Adj.; nicht präd.* possible ‹*objections, difficulties, applicants*›; ‹*objections, difficulties*› which might occur; **bei ~en Schäden** in the event *or* case of damage. **2.** *adv.* possibly; perhaps; **wir werden ~ morgen kommen** we may [possibly] come tomorrow; **können wir ~ bei euch übernachten?** can we stay the night at your house, if necessary?
Evergreen ['ɛvəgri:n] **der; ~s, ~s** old favourite
evident [evi'dɛnt] *Adj. (geh.)* **a)** *(einleuchtend)* convincing ‹*argument, proof*›; evident, self-evident ‹*truth*›; **b)** *(offenkundig)* evident, obvious ‹*disadvantage*›
Evidenz [evi'dɛnts] **die; ~, ~en** *(geh.) (einer Behauptung, eines Beweises)* convincingness; *(eines Satzes, einer Wahrheit)* self-evidence
Evolution [evolu'tsio:n] **die; ~, ~en** evolution
evolutionär [evolutsio'nɛ:ɐ] **1.** *Adj.* evolutionary. **2.** *adv.* by evolution
Evolutions·theorie die theory of evolution
evozieren [evo'tsi:rən] *tr. V. (geh.)* evoke
evtl. *Abk.* **eventuell**
EW *Abk.* **Elektrizitätswerk**
Ewer ['e:vɐ] **der; ~s, ~** *(nordd.)* ketch-rigged sailing barge
E-Werk das *s.* **Elektrizitätswerk**
EWG [e:ve:'ge:] **die; ~:** EEC
ewig ['e:vıç] **1.** *Adj.* eternal, everlasting ‹*life, peace*›; eternal, undying ‹*love*›; *(abwertend)* never-ending; **die Ewige Stadt** the Eternal City; **der Ewige Jude** the Wandering Jew; **ein ~er Student** *(scherzh.)* an eternal student; **das ~e Einerlei** the unending *or* never-ending monotony; **seit ~en Zeiten** for ages *(coll.)*; for donkey's years *(coll.)*; **das Ewige Licht** *(kath. Rel.)* the Sanctuary Lamp. **2.** *adv.* eternally; for ever; **~ warten** wait for ever; **~ dauern** take ages; **~ halten** last for ever *or* indefinitely; **auf ~:** for ever; **sein Name wird ~ leben** his name will live forever; **~ und drei Tage** *(ugs.)* for ever and a day; **~ kommt er mit denselben Problemen an** *(ugs.)* he is for ever coming along with the same problems; *s. auch* **immer a**
Ewig·gestrige der/die; *adj. Dekl. (abwertend)* **ein ~r sein** be an old reactionary
Ewigkeit die; ~, ~en a) eternity; **in ~:** for ever and ever; **in die ~ eingehen** *(geh. verhüll.)* find eternal rest; **b)** *(ugs.)* **es dauert eine [ganze] ~:** it takes [absolutely] ages *(coll.)*; **es ist eine [kleine] ~ her** it was ages ago *(coll.)*; **es muß ~en hersein, daß ...:** it must be ages since ... *(coll.)*; **seit ~en** for ages *(coll.)*; **in alle ~:** for ever
Ewigkeits-: ~sonntag, der *s.* **Totensonntag; ~wert der** *(geh.)* **es besitzt ~:** it will last for ever
ewiglich *Adv. (dichter. veralt.)* for ever; till the end of time
Ewig·weibliche das; ~n *(geh.)* **das ~:** the essential Feminine
ex [ɛks] *Adv. (ugs.)* **a) etw. ex trinken** drink sth. down in one *(coll.)*; knock sth. back in one *(sl.)*; **ex!** down in one! *(sl.)*; **b)** *(salopp: tot)* **der ist ex** he's snuffed it *(sl.)*
Ex- *(vor Personenbez.: vormalig)* ex-
exakt [ɛ'ksakt] **1.** *Adj.* exact; precise; **eine ~e Beschreibung** a precise description. **2.** *adv.* ‹*work etc.*› accurately; **~ [um] 12 Uhr** at 12 o'clock precisely; **~!** exactly!; precisely!
Exaktheit die; ~: precision; exactness
exaltieren [ɛksal'ti:rən] *refl. V.* get over-excited *or* worked up
exaltiert 1. *Adj. (hysterisch)* over-excited; *(überspannt)* exaggerated ‹*behaviour, gestures*›; *(überschwenglich)* effusive. **2.** *adv. (hysterisch)* over-excitedly; *(überschwenglich)* effusively
Exaltiertheit die; ~, ~en: *s.* **exaltiert:** over-excitedness; exaggeratedness; effusiveness
Examen [ɛ'ksa:mən] **das; ~s, ~** *od.* **Examina** [ɛ'ksa:mina] examination; exam *(coll.)*; **ein ~ machen** *od.* **ablegen** sit *or* take an examination; **~ haben** *(ugs.)* have examinations; **im ~ sein** *od.* **stehen** be in the middle of one's examinations; **im ~ durchfallen** fail the examination
Examens-: ~angst die examination nerves *pl.*; **~arbeit die** *written work presented for an examination;* **~kandidat der** examination candidate
examinieren *tr. V.* **a)** examine; **eine examinierte Krankenschwester** a qualified nurse; **b)** *(ausfragen)* question; **c)** *(veralt. geh.: prüfend untersuchen)* scrutinize ‹*appearance*›; investigate ‹*affair, matter*›
ex cathedra [ɛks'ka(:)tedra] *(kath. Rel.)* ex cathedra
Exegese [ɛkse'ge:zə] **die; ~, ~n** *(Theol.)* exegesis
Exeget [ɛkse'ge:t] **der; ~en, ~en** *(Theol.)* exegete
exekutieren [ɛkseku'ti:rən] *tr. V.* **a)** execute; **b)** *(österr.) s.* **pfänden**
Exekution [ɛkseku'tsio:n] **die; ~, ~en a)** execution; **b)** *(österr.) s.* **Pfändung**
Exekutions·kommando das firing squad
exekutiv [ɛkseku'ti:f] *Adj. (bes. Politik, Rechtsw.)* executive
Exekutiv·ausschuß der executive committee
Exekutive [ɛkseku'ti:və] **die; ~, ~n** *(Rechtsw., Politik)* executive
Exekutiv-: ~gewalt die *(Politik)* executive power; **~organ das** *(Politik)* executive body
Exekutor [ɛkse'ku:tɔr] **der; ~s, ~en** *(österr.)* bailiff
Exempel [ɛ'ksɛmpl̩] **das; ~s, ~:** example; **ein ~ [an jmdm.] statuieren** make an example [of sb.]; **zum ~** *(veralt.)* for example; *s. auch* **Probe a**
Exemplar [ɛksɛm'pla:ɐ] **das; ~s, ~e** specimen; *(Buch, Zeitung, Zeitschrift)* copy
exemplarisch [ɛksɛm'pla:rıʃ] **1.** *Adj.* exemplary; **eine ~e Strafe** an exemplary punishment; a deterrent sentence; **~ für etw. sein** be typical of sth. **2.** *adv.* by means of an example/examples; **jmdn. ~ bestrafen** punish sb. as an example to others
exemplifizieren [ɛksɛmplifi'tsi:rən] *tr. V. (geh.)* exemplify; **etw. an einem Beispiel ~:** illustrate sth. by an example
Exequien [ɛ'kse:kviən] *Pl. (kath. Kirche)* exequies
exerzieren [ɛksɛr'tsi:rən] **1.** *itr. V. (Milit.: Übungen machen)* drill. **2.** *tr. V.* **a)** *(Milit.: ausbilden)* drill ‹*soldiers*›; **b)** *(ugs.: üben)* practise; **c)** *(ausführen)* employ ‹*technique, method*›; follow ‹*procedure*›
Exerzier-: ~munition die *(Milit.)* dummy ammunition; **~platz der** *(Milit.)* parade ground; **~reglement das** *(Milit.)* drill regulations *pl.*
Exerzitien [ɛksɛr'tsi:tsiən] *Pl. (kath. Rel.)* religious *or* spiritual exercises
Exhaustor [ɛks'haustɔr] **der; ~s, ~en** *(Technik)* extractor fan
exhibitionieren [ɛkshibitsio'ni:rən] *itr., refl. V. (Psych.)* expose oneself
Exhibitionismus der; ~ *(Psych., fig.)* exhibitionism
Exhibitionist der; ~en, ~en, Exhibitionistin die; ~, ~nen *(Psych., fig.)* exhibitionist
exhibitionistisch *(Psych.)* **1.** *Adj.* exhibitionist. **2.** *adv.* **er ist ~ veranlagt** he has exhibitionist tendencies
exhumieren [ɛkshu'mi:rən] *tr. V.* exhume
Exhumierung die; ~, ~en exhumation
Exil [ɛ'ksi:l] **das; ~s, ~e** exile; **ins ~ gehen** go into exile
Exilant [ɛksi'lant] **der; ~en, ~en** exile
Exil·heimat die home in exile
exiliert [ɛksi'li:ɐt] *Adj.* exiled
Exilierte der/die; *adj. Dekl.* exile
Exil-: ~literatur die literature written in exile; **~regierung die** government in exile
existent [ɛksıs'tɛnt] *Adj.* existing; existent; **jmdn./etw. als nicht ~ betrachten** treat sb./sth. as if he/she/it did not exist
Existentialismus [ɛksıstɛntsia'lısmʊs] **der; ~** *(Philos.)* existentialism *no art.*
Existentialist der; ~en, ~en, Existentialistin die; ~, ~nen existentialist
existentialistisch 1. *Adj.* existentialist. **2.** *adv.* **~ beeinflußt** influenced by existentialism
existentiell [ɛksıstɛn'tsiɛl] *Adj. (Philos.)* existential; **in etw.** *(Dat.)* **eine ~e Bedrohung sehen** see in sth. a threat to one's existence
Existenz [ɛksıs'tɛnts] **die; ~, ~en a)** *(Dasein)* existence; **die nackte ~ retten** to escape with one's life; **b)** *(Lebensgrundlage)* livelihood; **sich** *(Dat.)* **eine ~ aufbauen** build a life for oneself; **jmdm. eine gesicherte ~ bieten** offer sb. a secure livelihood *or* living; **c)** *(Mensch)* **zweifelhafte ~en** dubious characters; **eine verkrachte ~** *(ugs.)* a dead-beat
existenz-, Existenz-: ~angst die angst; existential fear; **~bedingungen** *Pl.* living conditions; conditions of life; **~berechtigung die** right to exist; **diese Institution hat keine ~berechtigung mehr** there is no longer any justification for the existence of this institution; **~fähig** *Adj.* able to exist *or* to survive *postpos.*; **~frage die** matter of life and death; **~grund·lage die** basis of one's livelihood; **~kampf der** struggle for existence; **~minimum das** subsistence level; **am Rande des ~minimums leben** live at subsistence level; **die Löhne der Teepflücker liegen unter dem ~minimum** the tea-pickers earn less than a living wage; **~philosophie die** existential philosophy *no art.*
existieren [ɛksıs'ti:rən] *itr. V.* exist
Exitus ['ɛksitʊs] **der; ~** *(Med.)* death; **„~", konstatierte der Arzt** 'she's/he's dead,' confirmed the doctor
exkl. *Abk.* **exklusiv[e]** excl.
Exklave [ɛks'kla:və] **die; ~, ~n** exclave
exklusiv [ɛksklu'zi:f] **1.** *Adj.* exclusive. **2.** *adv.* exclusively; **[über etw.** *(Akk.)***] ~ berichten** run an exclusive report [on sth.]
Exklusiv·bericht der exclusive [report]
exklusive [ɛksklu'zi:və] *Präp.* + *Gen. (Kaufmannsspr.)* exclusive of; excluding
Exklusiv·interview das exclusive interview
Exklusivität [ɛkskluzivi'tɛ:t] **die; ~:** exclusiveness; exclusivity
Exklusiv·vertrag der exclusive contract
Ex·kommunikation die *(kath. Kirche)* excommunication
ex·kommunizieren *tr. V. (kath. Kirche)* excommunicate
Ex·könig der ex-king
Exkrement [ɛkskre'mɛnt] **das; ~[e]s, ~e;** *meist Pl. (bes. Med., Zool.)* excrement; **menschliche ~e** human excrement *sing.*
Exkret [ɛks'kre:t] **das; ~[e]s, ~e** *(Med., Zool.)* excretion; **~e** excreta; excretions
Exkulpation [ɛkskʊlpa'tsio:n] **die; ~, ~en** *(Rechtsw.)* exculpation
exkulpieren [ɛkskʊl'pi:rən] *tr. V. (Rechtsw.)* exculpate

Exkurs [ɛksˈkʊrs] **der;** ~**es,** ~**e** digression; *(in einem Buch)* excursus
Exkursion [ɛkskʊrˈzi̯o:n] **die;** ~, ~**en** study trip *or* tour
Exlibris [ɛksˈli:bri:s] **das;** ~, ~ *(Buchw., Graphik)* ex-libris; book-plate
Exmatrikulation [ɛksmatrikulaˈtsi̯o:n] **die;** ~, ~**en** *(Hochschulw.) removal of a student's name from the register on leaving a university*
exmatrikulieren [ɛksmatrikuˈli:rən] *tr. V. (Hochschulw.)* **jmdn./sich** ~: remove sb.'s name/have one's name removed from the university register
Ex·meister der *(Sport)* ex-champion
exmittieren [ɛksmɪˈti:rən] *tr. V. (Rechtsw.)* evict
Exmittierung die; ~, ~**en** *(Rechtsw.)* eviction
Exodus [ˈɛksodʊs] **der;** ~, ~**se** *(geh.)* exodus
exogen [ɛksoˈge:n] *Adj. (Med., Psych., Bot.)* exogenous
exorbitant [ɛksɔrbiˈtant] **1.** *Adj. (geh.)* exorbitant ‹*price*›. **2.** *adv.* exorbitantly
Exorzismus [ɛksɔrˈtsɪsmʊs] **der;** ~, **Exorzismen** *(Rel.)* exorcism
Exorzist der *(Rel.)* exorcist
Exot [ɛˈkso:t] **der;** ~**en,** ~**en a)** *(Mensch)* strange foreigner; **b)** *(Tier, Pflanze)* exotic
Exotin die; ~, ~**nen** *s.* **Exot a**
exotisch 1. *Adj.* exotic. **2.** *adv.* exotically
Expander [ɛksˈpandɐ] **der;** ~**s,** ~ *(Sport)* chest-expander
expandieren [ɛkspanˈdi:rən] *tr., itr. V.* expand
Expansion [ɛkspanˈzi̯o:n] **die;** ~, ~**en** expansion
expansionistisch *Adj. (Politik)* expansionist
expansions-, Expansions-: ~**freudig** *Adj.* **a)** *(Politik)* expansionist; **b)** *(Wirtsch.)* ~**freudige Unternehmen** businesses which are eager to expand; ~**kraft die** *(Physik, Technik)* expansive force; ~**krieg der** expansionist war; ~**politik die a)** expansionism; expansionist policy; **b)** *(Wirtsch.)* policy of expansion
expansiv [ɛkspanˈzi:f] **1.** *Adj.* **a)** *(Politik)* expansionist; **b)** *(Wirtsch.)* expansionary. **2.** *adv.* in an expansionary manner
expatriieren [ɛkspatriˈi:rən] *tr. V. (Politik, Rechtsw.)* expatriate
Expedient [ɛkspeˈdi̯ɛnt] **der;** ~**en,** ~**en a)** dispatch clerk; **b)** *(im Reisebüro)* travel agency clerk
expedieren [ɛkspeˈdi:rən] *tr. V.* dispatch; send; **jmdn. an einen anderen Ort** ~ *(ugs.)* pack sb. off somewhere else *(coll.)*
Expedition [ɛkspediˈtsi̯o:n] **die;** ~, ~**en a)** expedition; **b)** *(Versandabteilung)* dispatch department
Expeditions-: ~**korps das** *(Milit.)* expeditionary force; ~**leiter der** leader of the/an expedition
Experiment [ɛksperiˈmɛnt] **das;** ~**[e]s,** ~**e** experiment; **mach keine** ~**e!** *(ugs.) (sei vorsichtig)* don't take any unnecessary risks!; *(bleib bei dem, was du kennst)* why experiment unnecessarily?; **ein filmisches** ~: an experimental film
Experimental- [ɛksperimɛnˈta:l-]: ~**film der** experimental film; *(o. Pl.: Filmschaffen)* experimental cinema; ~**physik die** experimental physics
experimentell [ɛksperimɛnˈtɛl] **1.** *Adj.; nicht präd.* experimental. **2.** *adv.* experimentally; **etw.** ~ **beweisen/bestätigen** prove/confirm sth. experimentally *or* by experiment
experimentieren *itr. V.* experiment; **mit etw.** ~: experiment on *or* with sth.
experimentier-, Experimentier-: ~**freudig** *Adj.* keen to experiment; ~**stadium das** experimental stage; ~**theater das** experimental theatre

Experte [ɛksˈpɛrtə] **der;** ~**n,** ~**n, Expertin die;** ~, ~**nen** expert **(für in)**
Expertise [ɛkspɛrˈti:zə] **die;** ~, ~**n** expert's report; **eine** ~ **[über etw.] einholen** obtain an expert opinion [on sth.]
explizieren [ɛkspliˈtsi:rən] *tr. V. (geh.)* explicate
explizit [ɛkspliˈtsi:t] **1.** *Adj.* explicit. **2.** *adv.* ‹*describe, define*› explicitly
explizite [ɛksˈpli:tsitɛ] *Adv. (geh.)* explicitly
explodieren [ɛksploˈdi:rən] *itr. V.; mit sein (auch fig.)* explode; ‹*costs*› rocket
Explosion [ɛksploˈzi̯o:n] **die;** ~, ~**en** explosion; **etw. zur** ~ **bringen** detonate sth.; **eine** ~ **der Rohstoffpreise** *(fig.)* an explosion in the price of raw materials
explosions-, Explosions-: ~**artig 1.** *Adj.* explosive, astronomical ‹*growth, increase*›; **2.** *adv.* ‹*rise*› astronomically; ~**gefahr die;** *o. Pl.* danger of explosion; „~**gefahr!**" '[Danger,] Explosives!'; ~**herd der a)** centre of the explosion; **b)** *(Unruheherd)* trouble-spot; ~**krater der** crater; *(Bombenkrater)* bomb crater; ~**motor der** internal combustion engine; ~**welle die** shock wave
explosiv [ɛksploˈzi:f] **1.** *Adj.* **a)** *(auch fig.)* explosive; **b)** *(Sprachw.)* explosive; plosive; ~**e Laute** plosives. **2.** *adv.* explosively; ~ **reagieren** *(fig.)* react violently
Explosiv-: ~**geschoß das** explosive device; ~**laut der** *(Sprachw.)* explosive; plosive; ~**stoff der** *s.* **Sprengstoff**
Explosivität [ɛksplozivi'tɛ:t] **die** explosiveness
Exponat [ɛkspoˈna:t] **das;** ~**[e]s,** ~**e** exhibit
Exponent [ɛkspoˈnɛnt] **der;** ~**en,** ~**en** *(Math.)* exponent; *(fig.)* leading exponent
Exponential- [ɛksponɛnˈtsi̯a:l-] *(Math.)* exponential ‹*function, equation, curve*›
exponieren [ɛkspoˈni:rən] *tr. V. (geh.) (der Aufmerksamkeit aussetzen)* **jmdn./sich** ~: draw attention to sb./oneself; *(der Gefahr aussetzen)* lay sb./oneself open to attack
exponiert *Adj.* exposed
Export [ɛksˈpɔrt] **der;** ~**[e]s,** ~**e a)** *o. Pl. (das Exportieren)* export; exporting; **der** ~ **nach Afrika** exports to Africa; **b)** *(das Exportierte)* export; **c)** *Pl.* ~ *(*~*bier)* export
Export-: ~**ab·teilung die** export department; ~**artikel der** export; ~**bier das** export beer
Exporteur [ɛkspɔrˈtø:ɐ̯] **der;** ~**s,** ~**e** *(Wirtsch.)* exporter
Export-: ~**firma die** exporter; ~**geschäft das a)** export business; **b)** *(geschäftlicher Abschluß)* export deal; ~**handel der** export trade; ~**händler der** exporter
exportieren *tr., itr. V.* export
Export-: ~**kaufmann der** export salesman; ~**quote die** *ratio of the value of exports to that of the national product*
Exposé [ɛkspoˈze:] **das;** ~**s,** ~**s a)** exposé; report; **b)** *(eines Drehbuchs, Romans usw.)* outline
Exposition [ɛkspoziˈtsi̯o:n] **die;** ~, ~**en** exposition
expreß [ɛksˈprɛs] *Adv.* **a)** *(schnell)* express; **b)** *(veralt.: absichtlich)* on purpose; deliberately
Expreß der; Expresses *(bes. österr.)* express [train]
Expreß-: ~**brief der** *(veralt.)* express letter; ~**gut das** express freight; express goods *pl.*; **etw. als** ~**gut schicken** send sth. by express goods
Expressionismus [ɛksprɛsi̯oˈnɪsmʊs] **der** expressionism *no art.*
Expressionist der; ~**en,** ~**en, Expressionistin die;** ~, ~**nen** expressionist
expressionistisch 1. *Adj.* expressionist. **2.** *adv.* expressionistically; ‹*influenced*› by expressionism
expressis verbis [ɛksˈprɛsi:s -] *(geh.)* explicitly

expressiv [ɛksprɛˈsi:f] *Adj.* expressive; creative ‹*dance*›
Expreß-: ~**reinigung die** express [dry] cleaning service; ~**zug der** *(bes. schweiz.)* express [train]
Expropriation [ɛkspropri̯aˈtsi̯o:n] **die;** ~, ~**en** *(geh., Soziol.)* expropriation
exquisit [ɛkskviˈzi:t] **1.** *Adj.* exquisite. **2.** *adv.* exquisitely
Exquisit·geschäft das *(DDR)* shop selling foreign and luxury goods *(for GDR currency)*
ex tempore [ɛks ˈtɛmpore] *Adv. (Theater)* extempore
Extempore das; ~**s,** ~**s** *(Theater)* improvisation; extemporization
extemporieren *itr. V. (Theater)* improvise; extemporize
extensiv [ɛkstɛnˈzi:f] **1.** *Adj. (auch Landw.)* extensive. **2.** *adv.* **a)** *(auch Landw.)* extensively; **b)** *(Rechtsw.)* **ein Gesetz** ~ **auslegen** give an extensive interpretation to a law
Exterieur [ɛksteˈri̯ø:ɐ̯] **das;** ~**s,** ~**s** *u.* ~**e** *(geh.) (von Menschen)* appearance; *(von Gebäuden)* exterior
extern [ɛksˈtɛrn] *(Schulw.)* **1.** *Adj.* external; **ein** ~**er Schüler** a day boy/girl. **2.** *adv.* **eine Prüfung** ~ **ablegen** take an examination as an external candidate
Externe der/die; *adj. Dekl. (Schulw.)* day boy/girl; *(Prüfling)* external candidate
exterritorial [ɛkstɛritoˈri̯a:l] *Adj. (Völkerr.)* extraterritorial
Exterritorialität [ɛkstɛritori̯aliˈtɛ:t] **die** *(Völkerr.)* extraterritoriality
extra [ˈɛkstra] **1.** *Adv.* **a)** *(gesondert)* ‹*pay*› separately; **Getränke werden** ~ **berechnet** drinks are extra; *(ugs. auch attr.)* **ein** ~ **Bett** a spare bed; **b)** *(zusätzlich, besonders)* extra; ~ **fein gemahlener Kaffee** extra-fine ground coffee; **dafür brauche ich aber noch 10 DM** ~: but I need another 10 marks for that; **etwas** ~ **Schönes** something particularly nice; **c)** *(eigens)* especially; **etw.** ~ **für jmdn. tun** do sth. especially *or* just for sb.; ~ **deinetwegen** just because of you; **d)** *(ugs.: absichtlich)* **etw.** ~ **tun** do sth. on purpose. **2.** *Adj.; nicht attr. (bayr., österr.)* fussy; hard to please
Extra das; ~**s,** ~**s;** *meist Pl.* extra
extra-, Extra-: ~**aus·gabe die a)** *(Zeitung)* special edition; extra; **b)** *(Geldausgabe)* extra *or* additional expense; ~**blatt das** special edition; extra; ~**fahrt die** *(bes. schweiz.)* special excursion; ~**fein** *Adj. (ugs.)* really good; superb; ~**galaktisch** *Adj. (Astron.)* extragalactic
extrahieren [ɛkstraˈhi:rən] *tr. V. (Med., Chem.)* extract
Extrakt [ɛksˈtrakt] **der;** ~**[e]s,** ~**e a)** *fachspr. auch* **das** extract; **b)** *(Zusammenfassung)* summary; synopsis
Extraktion [ɛkstrakˈtsi̯o:n] **die;** ~, ~**en** *(Med., Chem.)* extraction
extra-, Extra-: ~**ordinarius der** *(Hochschulw.)* extraordinary professor; ~**polation** [~polaˈtsi̯o:n] *(Math.)* extrapolation; ~**polieren** *tr., itr. V. (Math.)* extrapolate; ~**post die** *(hist.)* postchaise; **mit** ~**post** *(veralt.)* by express post; ~**ration die** extra ration; ~**terrestrisch** [~tɛrɛstrɪʃ] *Adj. (Astron.)* extraterrestrial; ~**tour die** *(ugs. abwertend)* **sich** *(Dat.)* **ständig irgendwelche** ~**touren leisten** keep doing things off one's own bat *(Brit.) or* on one's own initiative
extravagant [-vaˈgant] **1.** *Adj.* flamboyant; flamboyantly furnished ‹*flat*›. **2.** *adv.* flamboyantly
Extravaganz [-vaˈgants] **die;** ~, ~**en a)** *o. Pl.* flamboyance; **b)** *(Sache)* ~**en** flamboyance *sing.*
extravertiert [-vɛrˈti:ɐ̯t] *Adj. (Psych.)* extrovert[ed]
Extravertiertheit die; ~ *(Psych.)* extroversion

Ẹxtra·wurst die a) *(fig. ugs.)* **eine ~ bekommen** get special treatment *or* special favours; **sie will immer eine ~ [gebraten] haben** she always expects to get special treatment; **b)** *(österr.) s.* **Lyoner**
extrem [ɛks'tre:m] **1.** *Adj.* extreme. **2.** *adv.* extremely; **das Unternehmen hat sich ~ vergrößert** the business has expanded enormously; **~ reagieren** react in an extreme manner
Extre̲m das; ~s, ~e extreme; **von einem ~ ins andere fallen** go from one extreme to another
Extre̲m·fall der extreme case
Extremịsmus der; ~, Extremịsmen extremism; **alle Extremismen** all forms of extremism
Extremịst der; ~en, ~en, Extremịstin die; ~, ~nen extremist
extremịstisch *Adj.* extremist
Extremität [ɛkstremi'tɛ:t] **die; ~, ~en a)** extremity; **b)** *(das Extremsein)* extremeness
Extre̲m-: ~punkt der *(Math.)* extremum; **~situation die** extreme situation; extremity; **~wert der** *(Math.)* extremum
extrovertiert [ɛkstrovɛr'ti:ɐ̯t] *s.* **extravertiert**
exzellent [ɛkstsɛ'lɛnt] *(geh.)* **1.** *Adj.* excellent. **2.** *adv.* excellently
Exzellenz [ɛkstsɛ'lɛnts] **die; ~, ~en** Excellency; **Eure/Seine ~:** Your/His Excellency
Exzenter [ɛks'tsɛntɐ] **der; ~s, ~** *(Technik)* tappet
Exzẹnter·welle die *(Technik)* camshaft; tappet shaft
Exzentriker [ɛks'tsɛntrikɐ] **der; ~s, ~:** eccentric
exzẹntrisch 1. *Adj.* eccentric. **2.** *adv.* eccentrically
Exzentrizität [ɛkstsɛntritsi'tɛ:t] **die; ~, ~en** eccentricity
exzeptionell [ɛkstsɛptsio'nɛl] *Adj. (geh.)* unusual; exceptional ‹*case, cirumstances*›; *(hervorragend)* exceptional
exzerpieren [ɛkstsɛr'pi:rən] *tr. V. (geh.)* extract ‹*reference*›; excerpt ‹*book*›
Exzerpt [ɛks'tsɛrpt] **das; ~[e]s, ~e** excerpt
Exzeß [ɛks'tsɛs] **der; Exzẹsses, Exzẹsse** excess; **etw. bis zum ~ trei̲ben** carry sth. to excess
exzessiv [ɛkstsɛ'si:f] **1.** *Adj.* excessive. **2.** *adv.* excessively
Eyeliner ['ailainɐ] **der; ~s, ~:** eye-liner
E̲-Zug der semi-fast train; stopping train *(Brit.)*

F

f, F [ɛf] **das; ~, ~ a)** *(Buchstabe)* f/F; **nach Schema F** according to a set pattern *or* routine; **b)** *(Musik)* [key of] F; *s. auch* **a/A**
f. *Abk.* **folgend** f.
F *Abk.* **Fahrenheit** F
Fa. *Abk.* **Firma**
Fabel ['fa:bl̩] **die; ~, ~n a)** *(Literaturw.)* *(Gattung)* fable; *(Kern einer Handlung)* plot; **b)** *(Erfundenes)* story; tale; fable; **[jmdm.] eine ~ auftischen** spin [sb.] a yarn; **ins Reich der ~ gehören** belong in the realm of fantasy
Fa̲bel-: ~buch das book of fables; **~dichter der** writer of fables
fa̲belhaft 1. *Adj.* **a)** *(ugs.: großartig)* fantastic *(coll.)*; **das ist ja ~:** that's [just] fantastic; **b)** *nicht präd. (unglaublich)* fabulous ‹*riches*›. **2.** *adv. (ugs.)* fantastically *(coll.)*; fabulously *(coll.)*
Fa̲bel-: ~tier das mythological *or* fabulous creature; **~welt die** fairy-tale world; fabulous world
Fabrik [fa'bri:k] **die; ~, ~en** factory; *(Papier~, Baumwollspinnerei)* mill; **eine chemische ~:** a chemical works; **in die ~ gehen** *(ugs.)* work in a factory
Fabri̲k·anlage die factory; *(Maschinen)* factory plant
Fabrikant [fabri'kant] **der; ~en, ~en** manufacturer
Fabri̲k·arbeiter der factory-worker
Fabrikat [fabri'ka:t] **das; ~[e]s, ~e** product; *(Marke)* make
Fabrikation [fabrika'tsio:n] **die; ~:** production; **die ~ einstellen** stop production
Fabrikatio̲ns-: ~fehler der manufacturing fault; factory fault; **~prozeß der, ~verfahren das** manufacturing process
fabri̲k-, Fabri̲k-: ~besitzer der factory-owner; **~direktor der** works *or* production manager; **~gebäude das** factory building; **~gelände das** factory site; **~neu** *Adj.* brand-new
fabri̲ks-, Fabri̲ks- *(bes. österr.) s.* **fabrik-, Fabrik-**
Fabri̲k-: ~schiff das factory ship; **~schorn·stein der** factory chimney; **~tor das** factory gate
fabrizieren [fabri'tsi:rən] *tr. V.* **a)** *(ugs. abwertend)* knock together *(coll.)*; **Unsinn ~:** make a mess of things; **b)** *(veralt.: herstellen)* manufacture; produce
fabulieren [fabu'li:rən] *itr. V.* invent stories; spin yarns
Fabuli̲er·lust die delight in making up stories
Facette [fa'sɛtə] **die; ~, ~n** facet
Facẹtten-: ~auge das compound eye; **~schliff der** faceting; **ein Schmuckstein mit ~schliff** a faceted gem
Fach [fax] **das; ~[e]s, Fächer** ['fɛçɐ] **a)** compartment; *(für Post)* pigeon-hole; **ein ~ für Wäsche** a shelf for linen; *s. auch* **Dach a; b)** *(Studienrichtung, Unterrichts~)* subject; *(Wissensgebiet)* field; *(Berufszweig)* trade; **ein Meister seines ~es** a master of his trade; **das schlägt [nicht] in mein ~:** that is [not] my province; **vom ~ sein** be an expert; **ein Mann vom ~:** an expert
fạch-, Fạch-: ~arbeiter der skilled worker; craftsman; **~arzt der** specialist **(für in)**; **~ausdruck der, ~begriff, der** technical *or* specialist term; **~bereich der** *(Hochschulw.)* faculty; school; *(in der Schule)* department; **~bezogen** *Adj.* specialized ‹*training*›; **~blatt das** specialist journal; **~buch das** *(Abhandlung)* specialist book; *(Nachschlagewerk)* reference book; *(Lehrbuch)* textbook
fächeln ['fɛçl̩n] **1.** *tr. V.* fan. **2.** *itr. V.* ‹*breeze*› blow gently
Fächer ['fɛçɐ] **der; ~s, ~:** fan; *(fig.)* range
fạ̈cher-, Fạ̈cher-: ~artig 1. *Adj.* fan-like; **2.** *adv.* like a fan; **~besen der** *(Gartenbau)* wire-tooth rake; **~gewölbe das** fan vault
fạ̈chern 1. *refl. V.* fan out. **2.** *tr. V. (fig.)* diversify; **das Angebot ist breit gefächert** there is a wide range to choose from
Fạ̈cher·palme die fan palm
Fạ̈cherung die; ~, ~en *(fig.)* diversity
fạch-, Fạch-: ~fremd *Adj.* **~fremde Methoden** methods alien to the subject; **~fremde Ausdrücke/Vorstellungen** layman's terms/ideas; **~gebiet das** field; **~gelehrte der/die** specialist **(für in)**; **~gerecht 1.** *Adj.* correct; **2.** *adv.* correctly; **~geschäft das** specialist shop; **ein ~geschäft für Sportartikel/Eisenwaren** *usw.* a specialist sports shop/ironmonger's; **~gespräch das** technical discussion; **~gruppe die** section; **~handel der** specialist shops *pl.*; **~hoch·schule die** college *(offering courses in a special subject)*; **~hochschule für Musik** academy of music; **~idiot der** *(abwertend) person who has no interests outside his/her subject*; **~jargon der** *(abwertend)* technical jargon; **~kenntnis die** specialized *or* specialist knowledge; **~kraft die** skilled worker; **~kreise** *Pl.* **in ~kreisen** in specialist circles; **~kundig 1.** *Adj.* knowledgeable; **2.** *adv.* **jmdn. ~kundig beraten** give sb. informed *or* expert advice; **~lehrer der** subject teacher
fạchlich 1. *Adj.* specialist ‹*knowledge, work*›; technical ‹*problem, explanation, experience*›; **~e Ausbildung/Qualifikation** training/qualification in the subject. **2.** *adv.* **etw. ~ beurteilen** give a professional opinion on sth.; **~ qualifiziert** qualified in the subject
fạch-, Fạch-: ~literatur die specialist literature; *(bes. naturwissenschaftlich auch)* technical literature; **in der medizinischen ~literatur** in the specialist medical literature; **~mann der** expert; **~männisch 1.** *Adj.* expert; **2.** *adv.* **jmdn. ~männisch beraten** give sb. expert advice; **~ober·schule die** *college specializing in particular subjects*; **~presse die** specialist/technical publications *pl.*; *s. auch* **~literatur; ~richtung die** *s.* **Fach b**
Fạchschaft die; ~, ~en a) *(einer Berufsgruppe)* professional association; **b)** *(von Studenten)* student body of the/a faculty
fạch-, Fạch-: ~schule die technical college; **~simpelei** [~zɪmpə'lai] **die; ~, ~en** *(ugs. abwertend)* shop-talk; **~simpeleien** shop-talk *sing.*; **~simpeln** [~zɪmpl̩n] *itr. V. (ugs. abwertend)* talk shop; **~sprache die** technical terminology *or* language; **~sprachlich** *Adj.* technical; **~tagung die** [specialist] conference; **~terminus der** specialist/technical term; *s. auch* **~literatur; ~text der** specialist text; **~übergreifend 1.** *Adj.* inter-disciplinary ‹*teaching*›; **2.** *adv.* ‹*think, argue*› along interdisciplinary lines; ‹*teach*› using interdisciplinary methods; **~verband der** trade association; **~welt die;** *o. Pl.* experts *pl.*; **in der ~welt** among experts
Fạch·werk das a) *o. Pl. (Bauweise)* half-timbered construction; **b)** *(Balkengerippe)* half-timbering
Fạchwerk·haus das half-timbered house
Fạch-: ~wissenschaftler der specialist; **~wort das;** *Pl.* **~wörter** technical *or* specialist term; **~wörter·buch das** specialist/technical dictionary; *s. auch* **~literatur; ~zeit·schrift die** specialist/technical journal; *s. auch* **~literatur**
Fackel ['fakl̩] **die; ~, ~n** torch; **die ~ des Krieges** *(fig.)* the flames of war; **die ~ der Revolution/der Hoffnung** *(fig.)* the flame of revolution/hope; **von ~n erleuchtet sein** be torchlit *or* lit by torches; **wie lebende ~n** like human torches
fạckeln *itr. V. (ugs.)* shilly-shally *(coll.)*; dither; **nicht lange gefackelt!** no shilly-shallying! *(coll.)*; don't dither about!
Fạckel-: ~schein der torchlight; **im ~schein** by torchlight; **~träger der** torch-bearer; **~zug der** torchlight procession
fad [fa:t] *(bes. südd., österr.) s.* **fade**
Fädchen ['fɛ:tçən] **das; ~s, ~:** short, thin thread
fade ['fa:də] *Adj.* **a)** *(schal)* insipid; **ein ~r Beigeschmack** *(fig.)* a flat after-taste; **b)** *(bes. südd., österr.: langweilig)* dull; **c)** *(südd., österr.: zimperlich)* **sei nicht ~!** don't be such a sissy!

fädeln ['fɛ:dl̩n] *tr. V.* thread; **etw. auf eine Schnur ~**: thread sth. on to a string

[1]**Faden** ['fa:dn̩] **der; ~s, Fäden** ['fɛ:dn̩] **a)** *(Garn)* thread; **ein ~**: a piece of thread; **sich wie ein roter ~ durch etw. ziehen** run like a thread through sth.; **der rote ~** *(fig.)* the central theme; **den ~ verlieren** *(fig.)* lose the thread; **er hat** *od.* **hält alle Fäden in der Hand** *(fig.)* he holds the reins; **er hält alle Fäden fest in der Hand** *(fig.)* he keeps a tight rein on everything; **an einem dünnen** *od.* **seidenen ~ hängen** *(fig.)* hang by a single thread; **seine Fäden spinnen** *(fig.)* spin a web of intrigue; **keinen trockenen ~ mehr am Leibe haben** *(ugs.)* be wet through *or* soaked to the skin; *s. auch* **Strich h; b)** *(fig.)* **ein schmaler ~ Blut** a thin trickle of blood; **graue Fäden im Haar haben** have a grey hair here and there; **Fäden ziehen** ⟨*cheese etc.*⟩ be soft and stringy; **c)** *(Med.)* suture; **die Fäden ziehen** remove the stitches

[2]**Faden der; ~s, ~** *(Seemannsspr.)* fathom

faden-, Faden-: ~kreuz das cross-hairs *pl.*; **~lauf der** grain [of the cloth]; **~molekül das** linear molecule; **~nudeln** *Pl. (Kochk.)* vermicelli *sing.*; **~scheinig** [-ʃainɪç] *Adj.* **a)** *(fig. abwertend: nicht glaubhaft)* threadbare ⟨*morality*⟩; flimsy ⟨*argument, reason, excuse*⟩; **b)** *(abgewetzt)* threadbare ⟨*clothes*⟩; **~spiel das** cat's cradle; **~stärke die** thickness *(of wool)*; **~wurm der** *(Zool.)* threadworm

Fadheit die; ~, ~en *s.* **fade a, b**: insipidness; dullness

Fagott [fa'gɔt] **das; ~[e]s, ~e** bassoon

Fagottist der; ~en, ~en, Fagottistin die; ~, ~nen bassoonist

Fähe ['fɛ:ə] **die; ~, ~n** *(Jägerspr.) (Fuchs~)* vixen; bitch; *(Dachs~)* sow; bitch

fähig ['fɛ:ɪç] *Adj.* **a)** *(begabt)* able; capable; **ich halte ihn für einen ~en Kopf** I think he has an able mind; **b)** *(bereit, in der Lage)* **zu etw. ~ sein** be capable of sth.; **er ist zu allem ~**: he is capable of anything; **~ sein, etw. zu tun** be capable of doing sth.

Fähigkeit die; ~, ~en a) *meist Pl. (Tüchtigkeit)* ability; capability; **menschliche ~en** human faculties; **geistige ~en** intellectual faculties *or* abilities; **praktische ~en** practical skills; **jmds. ~en wecken** awaken sb.'s talents; **seine ~en für etw. einsetzen** use one's abilities for sth.; **b)** *o. Pl. (Imstandesein)* ability **(zu** to)

Fähigkeits·nachweis der certificate of proficiency

fahl [fa:l] *Adj.* pale; pallid; wan ⟨*light, smile*⟩; **~ schien der Mond ins Zimmer** the moon shone wanly into the room

fahl-: ~blau *Adj.* pale-blue; **~blond** *Adj.* ash-blond; **~gelb** pale-yellow

Fahlheit die; ~: paleness; pallor

Fähnchen ['fɛ:nçən] **das; ~s, ~ a)** little flag; **~ schwenken** wave flags; **b)** *(ugs. abwertend: Kleid)* **ein billiges ~**: a cheap frock *(Brit.) or* dress

fahnden ['fa:ndn̩] *itr. V.* search **(nach** for)

Fahndung die; ~, ~en search

Fahndungs-: ~aktion die search operation; **~apparat der: der gesamte ~apparat der Polizei ist eingesetzt worden** the police have committed all their available resources to the search; **~blatt das, ~liste die** wanted list

Fahne ['fa:nə] **die; ~, ~n a)** flag; **b)** *(fig.)* **etw. auf seine ~n schreiben** espouse the cause of sth.; **seine ~ nach dem Wind[e] hängen** trim one's sails to the wind; **mit fliegenden ~n zu jmdm./etw. übergehen** *od. (abwertend)* **überlaufen** openly and suddenly turn one's coat; **zu den ~n eilen** *(veralt.)* join the colours; **jmdn. zu den ~n rufen** *(veralt.)* call sb. to the colours; **c)** *o. Pl. (ugs.: Alkoholgeruch)* smell of alcohol on sb.'s breath; **eine ~ haben** reek of alcohol; **d)** *(Druckw.)* galley

fahnen-, Fahnen-: ~eid der oath of allegiance; **~flucht die** desertion; **~flucht begehen** desert; **~flüchtig** *Adj.* **~flüchtig werden/sein** desert/be a deserter; **~geschmückt** *Adj.* decorated with flags *postpos.*; **~korrektur** *(Druckw.) (Fahne)* galley-proof; *(Korrekturlesen)* **die ~korrektur muß bald erfolgen** the galley-proofs will have to be read soon; **~mast der, ~stange die** flagpole; **das Ende der ~stange ist erreicht** *(fig.)* that's as far as we/they *etc.* can go; **~träger der** standard-bearer; **~weihe die** consecration of the flag

Fähnlein ['fɛ:nlain] **das; ~s, ~** *(hist.)* small troop

Fähnrich ['fɛ:nrɪç] **der; ~s, ~e** *(Milit.)* ~, *(Marine)* **~ zur See** ensign

Fahr·ausweis der a) *(Amtsspr.: Fahrschein)* ticket; **b)** *(schweiz.: Führerschein)* driving licence

Fahr·bahn die carriageway; **die linke/rechte ~**: the left-hand/right-hand side of the road; **beim Überqueren der ~**: when crossing the road *or (formeller)* carriageway

Fahrbahn-: ~belag der road surface; **~breite die** road width; **~markierung die** road-marking

fahrbar *Adj.* ⟨*table, bed*⟩ on castors; mobile ⟨*crane, kitchen, etc.*⟩; **ein ~er Untersatz** *(ugs.)* wheels *pl. (joc.)*

fahr·bereit *Adj.* ⟨*car etc.*⟩ in running order; **wir sind ~**: we're ready to go

Fahr·bereitschaft die motor pool

Fähr·betrieb der ferry service; *(von mehreren Fähren)* ferry services *pl.*

Fahr-: ~damm der *(bes. berlin.) s.* **~bahn; ~bücherei die** mobile library; **~dienst·leiter der** *(Eisenb.)* train controller; **~draht der** overhead contact wire

Fähre ['fɛ:rə] **die; ~, ~n** ferry

Fahr·eigenschaft die *(Kfz-W.)* handling characteristic; **~en** handling

fahren ['fa:rən] **1.** *unr. itr. V.; mit sein* **a)** *(als Fahrzeuglenker)* drive; *(mit dem Fahrrad, Motorrad usw.)* ride; *(mit dem Kinderroller)* scooter; *(auf Skiern)* ski; *(mit Rollschuhen)* [roller-]skate; *(mit Schlittschuhen)* [ice-]skate; *(mit dem Rodelschlitten)* toboggan; **mit dem Auto ~**: drive; *(her~ auch)* come by car; *(hin~ auch)* go by car; **mit dem Fahrrad/Motorrad ~**: cycle/motor cycle; come/go by bicycle/motor cycle; **mit 80 km/h ~**: drive/ride at 80 k.p.h.; **links/rechts ~**: drive on the left/right; *(abbiegen)* bear *or* turn left/right; **langsam ~**: drive/ride slowly; **langsamer ~**: slow down; **gegen etw. ~**: go into sth.; **wie fährt man am schnellsten zum Bahnhof?** what is the quickest route to the station [by car/motor cycle *etc.*]?; **b)** *(mit dem Auto usw. als Mitfahrer; mit dem Bus, der Straßenbahn, U-Bahn, dem Taxi, Zug, Schiff, Luftschiff, Schlitten usw., ugs. mit dem Flugzeug)* go; *(mit dem Aufzug/der Rolltreppe/der Seilbahn/dem Skilift)* take the lift *(Brit.) or (Amer.)* elevator/escalator/cable-car/ski-lift; *(mit der Achterbahn, dem Karussell usw.)* ride **(auf** + *Dat.* on); *(per Anhalter)* hitch-hike; **mit dem Auto/Bus/Zug** *usw.* **~**: go by car/bus/train *etc.*; **erster/zweiter Klasse/zum halben Preis ~**: travel *or* go first/second class/at half-price; **ich fahre nicht gern [im] Auto/Bus** I don't like travelling in cars/buses; **fährst du mit mir?** are you coming with me?; **sollen wir ~ oder zu Fuß gehen?** shall we go by car/bus *etc.* or walk?; **mit Chauffeur ~**: be driven round by a chauffeur; **ich will noch mal ~!** *(auf der Achterbahn usw.)* I want to have another ride!; **c)** *(reisen)* go; **in Urlaub ~**: go on holiday; **ins Wochenende ge~ sein** *(vom Arbeitsplatz aus gesehen)* have left for the weekend; *(von zu Hause)* have gone away for the weekend; *s. auch* **Himmel b; Hölle a; d)** *(los~)* go; leave; **e)** ⟨*motor vehicle, train, lift, cable-car*⟩ go; ⟨*ship*⟩ sail; **mein Auto fährt nicht** my car won't go; **der Wagen fährt sehr ruhig** the car is very quiet *or* runs very quietly; **der Aufzug fährt heute nicht** the lift *(Brit.) or (Amer.)* elevator is out of service today; **f)** *(verkehren)* run; **der Bus fährt alle fünf Minuten/bis Goetheplatz** the bus runs *or* goes every five minutes/goes to Goetheplatz; **hier fährt dreimal täglich eine Fähre** there are three ferries a day from here; **von München nach Passau fährt ein D-Zug** there's a fast train from Munich to Passau; **g)** *(mit bestimmtem Treibstoff)* **mit Diesel/Benzin ~**: run on diesel/petrol *(Brit.) or (Amer.)* gasoline; **mit Dampf/Atomkraft ~**: be steam-powered/atomic-powered; **h)** *(schnelle Bewegungen ausführen)* **in die Kleider ~**: leap into one's clothes; **in die Höhe ~**: jump up [with a start]; **der Blitz ist in einen Baum ge~**: the lightning struck a tree; **jmdm. an die Kehle ~**: leap at sb.'s throat; **sich** *(Dat.)* **mit der Hand durch das Haar ~**: run one's fingers through one's hair; **was ist denn in dich ge~?** *(fig.)* what's got into you?; **der Schreck fuhr ihm in die Glieder** *(fig.)* the shock went right through him; **ein Gedanke fuhr ihm durch den Kopf** *(fig.)* an idea flashed through his mind; **jmdm. über den Mund ~** *(fig.)* shut sb. up; **aus der Haut ~** *(ugs.)* blow one's top *(coll.)*; **i)** *(Erfahrungen machen)* **gut/schlecht mit jmdm./einer Sache ~**: get on well/badly with sb./sth.; **er ist schlecht damit ge~, den Arbeitsplatz zu wechseln** his change of job turned out badly for him. **2.** *unr. tr. V.* **a)** *(fortbewegen)* drive ⟨*car, lorry, train, etc.*⟩; ride ⟨*bicycle, motor cycle*⟩; **ein Boot ~**: sail a boat; **Auto/Motorrad/Roller ~**: drive [a car]/ride a motor cycle/scooter; **Kahn** *od.* **Boot/Kanu ~**: go boating/canoeing; **Ski ~**: ski; **Schlitten ~**: toboggan; **Rollschuh ~**: [roller-]skate; **Schlittschuh ~**: [ice-]skate; **Aufzug/Rolltreppe ~**: ride up and down in the lift *(Brit.) or (Amer.)* elevator/on the escalator; **Sessellift ~**: ride in a/the chair-lift; **U-Bahn ~**: ride on the underground *(Brit.) or (Amer.)* subway; **b)** *mit sein ([als Strecke] zurücklegen)* drive; *(mit dem Motorrad, Fahrrad)* ride; take ⟨*curve*⟩; **einen Umweg/eine Umleitung ~**: make a detour/follow a diversion; **der Zug fährt jetzt eine andere Strecke** the train takes a different route now; **er fährt seine 26. Runde** he is on his twenty-sixth lap; **c)** *(befördern)* drive, take ⟨*person*⟩; take ⟨*thing*⟩; ⟨*vehicle*⟩ take; ⟨*ship, lorry, etc.*⟩ carry ⟨*goods*⟩; *(zum Sprecher)* drive, bring ⟨*person*⟩; bring ⟨*thing*⟩; ⟨*vehicle*⟩ bring; **jmdn. über den Fluß ~**: ferry sb. across the river; **d)** *mit sein (mit einer bestimmten Geschwindigkeit)* **50/80 km/h ~**: do 50/80 k.p.h.; **hier muß man 50 km/h ~**: you've got to keep to 50 k.p.h. here; **e)** *meist mit sein (als Teilnehmer mitfahren bei)* **ein Rennen ~**: take part in a race; **f)** *meist mit sein (erzielen)* **einen Rekord ~**: set a record; **1:23:45/eine gute Zeit ~**: do *or* clock 1.23.45/a good time; **g)** *mit sein (leisten)* **der Wagen fährt 210 km/h** the car will do 210 k.p.h.; **h)** *(in einen schlechten Zustand bringen)* **ein Auto schrottreif** *od.* **zu Schrott ~**: write off a car; *(durch lange Beanspruchung)* run *or* drive a car into the ground; **eine Beule in den Kotflügel ~**: dent the wing; **jmdm. eine Schramme in den Kotflügel ~**: scratch sb.'s wing; **i)** *(als Treibstoff benutzen)* use ⟨*diesel, regular*⟩; **j)** *(auf Roll-, Schlittschuhen ausführen)* skate; **k)** *(Technik: bedienen)* operate; **einen Hochofen ~**: control a blast-furnace; **l)** *(Rundf.: senden)* broadcast ⟨*programme*⟩; **m)** *(arbeiten)* **eine Sonderschicht ~**: do *or* work an extra shift. **3.** *unr. refl. V.* **a) sich gut ~** ⟨*car*⟩ handle well, be easy to drive; **wie fährt sich so ein Rennboot?** how does a power-boat like that handle?; **b)** *mit sein (unpers.)* **in dem Wagen**

fährt es sich bequem the car gives a comfortable ride; **auf dieser Straße/mit dem Zug fährt es sich angenehm** this road is pleasant to drive on/it's pleasant travelling by train

fahrend *Adj.* itinerant; **~er Sänger** wandering minstrel; **~es Volk** travelling people *pl.*

Fahrenheit *s.* **Grad c**

fahren|lassen *unr. tr. V.* **a)** *(loslassen)* let go; **b)** *(aufgeben)* abandon ⟨*hope*⟩

Fahrens·mann der; *Pl.* **Fahrensmänner** *od.* **Fahrensleute** *(Seemannsspr.)* sailor

Fahrer der; ~s, ~: driver; **„Nicht mit dem ~ sprechen!"** 'Passengers must not talk to the driver'

Fahrerei die; ~, ~en *(Fahrweise)* driving; *(dauerndes Fahren)* driving/riding around

Fahrer-: ~flucht die: wegen ~flucht for failing to stop after [being involved in] an accident; **~flucht begehen** fail to stop after [being involved in] an accident; **~haus das** [driver's] cab

Fahrerin die; ~, ~nen driver; *s. auch* **-in**

fahrerisch 1. *Adj.; nicht präd.* **~es Können** driving skill; skill as a driver. **2.** *adv.* **jmdm. ~ überlegen sein** be a better driver than sb.

Fahrer·kabine die [driver's] cab

Fahr-: ~erlaubnis die *(Amtsspr.)* driving licence; **jmdm. die ~ entziehen** disqualify sb. from driving; **~gast der** passenger; **~geld das** fare; **~geld·erstattung die** reimbursement of travelling expenses; **~gelegenheit die** means of transport; **~gemeinschaft die** car pool; **~geschwindigkeit die** speed; **~gestell das a)** *(Kfz-W.)* chassis; **b)** *(bei Kränen, Eisenbahnwagen, Maschinen)* bogie *(Brit.)*; *(Lafette)* gun-carriage; *(beim Flugzeug)* undercarriage; **c)** *(scherzh.: Beine)* legs *pl.*

Fähr·hafen der ferry terminal

fahrig ['fa:rɪç] *Adj.* nervous, agitated ⟨*movements*⟩; nervous and fidgety ⟨*student, pupil*⟩

Fahrigkeit die; ~: nervousness and fidgetiness

Fahr·karte die ticket; **eine ~ schießen** *(ugs.)* miss completely

Fahrkarten-: ~ausgabe die ticket office; **~automat der** ticket machine; **~kontrolleur der** *(im Bus)* inspector; *(im Zug)* ticket inspector; **~schalter der** ticket window; **~verkäufer der** ticket-office clerk

fahr-, Fahr-: ~kilometer der *(im Bus)* kilometre [travelled]; *(eines Autos)* kilometre [covered]; **~komfort der** [passenger] comfort; **~kunst die** driving skills *pl.*; **~lässig 1.** *Adj.* negligent ⟨*behaviour*⟩; **~e Tötung/Körperverletzung** *(Rechtsw.)* causing death/injury through *or* by [culpable] negligence; **2.** *adv.* negligently; **er hat den Tod des Fußgängers ~lässig verschuldet** he was responsible for *or* guilty of causing the death of the pedestrian through *or* by culpable negligence; **~lässigkeit die** negligence; **~lehrer der** driving instructor; **~leistung die** performance

Fähr·mann der ferryman

Fahrnis die; ~, ~se *(Rechtsw.)* chattels *pl.*; movables *pl.*

Fährnis die; ~, ~se *(veralt.)* peril

Fahr·personal das crew

Fahr·plan der a) timetable; schedule *(Amer.)*; **den ~ einhalten** run to schedule *or* on time; **b)** *(ugs.: Vorhaben)* plans *pl.*; **den ~ durcheinanderbringen** upset the entire schedule *or* all the arrangements

fahrplan·mäßig 1. *Adj.* scheduled ⟨*departure, arrival*⟩; **der verspätete Schnellzug nach Köln, ~e Abfahrt 16.³⁰ ...:** the delayed fast train to Cologne, due to depart at 16.30, ... **2.** *adv.* ⟨*depart, arrive*⟩ according to schedule, on time

Fahr·praxis die driving experience

Fahr·preis der fare

Fahrpreis-: ~anzeiger der taximeter; **~erhöhung die** fare increase; increase in fares; **~ermäßigung die** reduction in fares; **eine ~ermäßigung erhalten** be given concessionary fares

Fahr·prüfung die driving test

Fahr·rad das bicycle; cycle; **mit dem ~ fahren** cycle; ride a bicycle

Fahrrad-: ~fahrer der cyclist; **~händler der** bicycle dealer; **etw. beim ~händler kaufen** buy sth. from a/the bicycle shop; **~handlung die** bicycle shop; **~kette die** bicycle chain; **~lampe die** bicycle lamp; **~pumpe die** bicycle pump; **~schlüssel der a)** *(für das Schloß)* bicycle-lock key; **b)** *(Schraubenschlüssel)* bicycle spanner; **~ständer der** bicycle rack *or* stand; **~weg der** cycle path

Fahr·rinne die shipping channel; fairway

Fahr·schein der ticket

Fahrschein-: ~automat der ticket machine; **~entwerter der** ticket cancelling machine; **~heft das** book of tickets

Fähr·schiff das ferry

Fahr-: ~schule die a) *(Unternehmen)* driving school; **b)** *(ugs.: Unterricht)* driving lessons *pl*; **~schüler der a)** learner driver; **b)** *pupil who must use transport to get to school;* **~sicherheit die** safe driving *no art.*; **die ~sicherheit erhöhen** make driving safer; **~spur die** traffic-lane; **die ~spur wechseln/beibehalten** change lanes/stay in one's lane

fährst [fɛ:ɐst] *2. Pers. Sg. Präsens v.* **fahren**

Fahr-: ~stil der style of driving; *(mit dem Rad)* style of riding; *(auf Skiern)* style of skiing; **~streifen der** *s.* **~spur**

Fahr·stuhl der lift *(Brit.)*; elevator *(Amer.)*; *(für Lasten)* hoist; **mit dem ~ fahren** take the lift/elevator

Fahrstuhl-: ~führer der lift attendant *(Brit.)*; elevator operator *(Amer.)*; **~schacht der** lift shaft *(Brit.)*; elevator shaft *(Amer.)*

Fahr·stunde die driving lesson

Fahrt [fa:ɐt] **die; ~, ~en a)** *o. Pl. (das Fahren)* journey; **„während der ~ nicht hinauslehnen!"** 'do not lean out of the window while the train is in motion'; **freie ~ haben** have a clear run; *(fig.)* have been given the green light; **b)** *(Reise)* journey; *(Schiffsreise)* voyage; **auf der ~:** on the journey; **c)** *(kurze Reise, Ausflug)* trip; *(Wanderung)* hike; **eine ~ [nach/zu X] machen** go on *or* take a trip [to X]; **eine ~ ins Blaue machen** *(mit dem Auto)* go for a drive; *(Veranstaltung)* go on a mystery tour; **auf ~ gehen** *(veralt.)* go hiking; **d)** *o. Pl. (Geschwindigkeit)* **in voller ~:** at full speed; **die ~ verlangsamen** slow down; decelerate; **die ~ beschleunigen** speed up; accelerate; **die ~ aufnehmen** gather speed; pick up speed; **kleine ~ machen** *(Seemannsspr.)* sail slowly; **in ~ kommen** *od.* **geraten** *(ugs.)* get going; *(böse werden)* get worked up; **jmdn. in ~ bringen** *(ugs.)* get sb. going; *(böse machen)* get sb. worked up; **e)** *(Seemannspr.)* **Kapitän auf großer ~:** foreign trade master; **das Patent für kleine ~:** master's certificate for coastal trade *or* home trade

-fahrt die; ~, ~en: Frankreich~/Ostasien~: trip to France/East Asia

fährt [fɛ:ɐt] *3. Pers. Sg. Präsens v.* **fahren**

fahr·tauglich *Adj.* fit to drive *postpos.*

Fahr·tauglichkeit die fitness to drive

fahrt-, Fahrt-: ~ausweis der *s.* **Fahrausweis; ~bereit** *s.* **fahrbereit; ~dauer die** travelling-time

Fährte ['fɛ:ɐtə] **die** tracks *pl.*; trail; **die ~ aufnehmen** pick up the trail *or* scent; **Hunde auf die ~ setzen** put hounds on the track; **jmds. ~ verfolgen** track sb.; **die richtige ~ finden** *(fig.)* get on the right track; **die falsche ~ verfolgen** *(fig.)* be on the wrong track; **jmdn. auf eine falsche ~ locken** *(fig.)* put sb. on the wrong track

Fahrten-: ~buch das a) *(Kontrollbuch)* logbook; **b)** *(Tagebuch)* [rambler's] diary; **~messer das** sheath-knife; **~schreiber der** tachograph; **~schwimmer der** advanced swimmer; **den ~schwimmer machen** *(ugs.)* take the advanced swimmer's test

Fahrt·kosten *Pl. (für öffentliche Verkehrsmittel)* fare/fares; *(für Autoreisen)* travel costs; **die ~ erstatten** pay travelling expenses

Fahr·treppe die escalator

Fahrt·richtung die direction; **in ~ Innenstadt** in the direction of the town centre; **die Autobahn ist in ~ Norden gesperrt** the northbound carriageway of the motorway is closed; **in ~ parken** park in the direction of the traffic; **die ~ ändern** change direction; **gegen die ~ sitzen** *(im Zug)* sit with one's back to the engine; *(im Bus)* facing backwards; **in ~ sitzen** *(im Zug)* sit facing the engine; *(im Bus)* facing forwards

Fahrtrichtungs·anzeiger der *(Kfz-W.)* **a)** *(Blinklicht)* [direction] indicator; **b)** *(Hinweistafel)* destination board

Fahrt·schreiber der *s.* **Fahrtenschreiber**

fahr·tüchtig *Adj.* ⟨*driver*⟩ fit to drive; ⟨*vehicle*⟩ roadworthy

Fahr·tüchtigkeit die *(des Fahrers)* fitness to drive; *(des Fahrzeugs)* roadworthiness

Fahrt-: ~unterbrechung die break [in the journey]; stop; **eine ~unterbrechung ist [nicht] möglich** passengers may [not] break their journey; **~wind der** airflow; **~ziel das** destination

fahr·untüchtig *Adj.* ⟨*driver*⟩ unfit to drive; ⟨*vehicle*⟩ unroadworthy

Fähr·verbindung die ferry link

Fahr-: ~verbot das disqualification from driving; driving ban; **jmdm. [ein] ~verbot erteilen** ban *or* disqualify sb. from driving; **~verhalten das a)** *(des Fahrers)* behaviour as a driver; **b)** *(des Fahrzeuges)* performance

Fähr·verkehr der ferry traffic

Fahr-: ~wasser das shipping channel; fairway; **in ein gefährliches ~wasser geraten** *(fig.)* get on to dangerous ground; **in ein politisches ~wasser geraten** *(fig.)* stumble into a political minefield; **in jmds. ~wasser schwimmen** *od.* **segeln** *(fig.)* follow [along] in sb.'s wake; **~weise die** way of driving; **seine ~weise** the way he drives; **~werk das a)** *(Flugw.)* undercarriage; **b)** *(Kfz-W.)* *s.* **~gestell; ~wind der a)** *(Segelfliegen)* wind; **b)** *s.* **Fahrtwind; ~zeit die** travelling time; **eine ~zeit von wenigen Minuten/Stunden** a few minutes'/hours' travelling time; **nach einer ~zeit von zwei Stunden** after travelling for two hours

Fahr·zeug das vehicle; *(Luft~)* aircraft; *(Wasser~)* vessel

Fahrzeug-: ~bau der motor manufacturing industry; **~brief der** *s.* **Kraftfahrzeugbrief; ~führer der** driver of a/the motor vehicle; **~halter der** registered keeper [of a/the vehicle]; **~kolonne die** convoy of vehicles; **~papiere** *Pl.* vehicle documents *pl.*; **~verkehr der** traffic

Faible ['fɛ:bl̩] **das; ~s, ~s** liking; *(Schwäche)* weakness; **ein ~ für etw. haben** have a weakness for sth.

fair [fɛ:ɐ] **1.** *Adj.* fair (**gegen** to). **2.** *adv.* fairly; **~ spielen** play fairly *or (coll.)* fair

Fairneß ['fɛ:ɐnɛs] **die; ~:** fairness

Fairneß·pokal der *(Sport) cup for the most sporting competitor*

Fair play ['fɛə'pleɪ] **das; ~ ~:** fair play

Fait accompli [fɛtakõ'pli] **das; ~ ~, ~s ~s** *(geh.)* fait accompli

Fäkalien [fɛ'ka:li̯ən] *Pl.* faeces *pl.*

Fakir ['fa:ki:ɐ, *österr.:* fa'ki:ɐ] **der; ~s, ~e** fakir

Faksimile [fak'zi:mile] **das; ~s, ~s** facsimile

Faksimile-: ~aus·gabe die facsimile edition; **~druck der** printed facsimile

Fakt [fakt] **das** *od.* **der; ~[e]s, ~en** *od.* **~s** fact

Fakten *s.* **Faktum**
Fakten-: ~material das facts *pl.*; **~wissen das** factual knowledge
Faktion [fak'tsio:n] **die; ~, ~en** *(veralt., schweiz.)* faction
faktisch 1. *Adj.; nicht präd.* real; actual; **der ~e Nachteil/Nutzen** the practical disadvantage/usefulness. **2.** *adv.* **a) das bedeutet ~...:** it means in effect...; **es ist ~ möglich/unmöglich** it is in actual fact possible/impossible; **b)** *(bes. österr. ugs.: praktisch, eigentlich)* more or less; virtually
Faktor ['faktɔr] **der; ~s, ~en** [-'to:rən] **a)** *(auch Math.)* factor; **der auslösende ~:** the immediate cause; **ein konstanter ~** *(Math.)* a constant; **b)** *(Berufsbez.) (in einer Setzerei)* composing-room foreman *or* supervisor; *(in einer Druckerei)* [printing-room] foreman *or* supervisor
Faktorei die; ~, ~en *(hist.)* foreign trading post; factory *(Hist.)*
Faktotum [fak'to:tʊm] **das; ~s, ~s** *od.* **Faktoten** *(scherzh.)* factotum
Faktum ['faktʊm] **das; ~s, Fakten** fact
Faktur [fak'tu:ɐ̯] **die; ~, ~en** *(Kaufmannsspr. veralt.)* invoice
fakturieren *itr. V.* do invoicing
Fakturier·maschine die invoicing machine
Fakturist der; ~en, ~en, Fakturistin die; ~, ~nen invoice clerk
Fakultas [fa'kʊltas] **die; ~, Fakultäten** [fakʊl'tɛ:tn̩] *(Schulw.)* qualification to teach; **die ~ für etw. haben** be qualified to teach sth.
Fakultät [fakʊl'tɛ:t] **die; ~, ~en** *(Hochschulw.)* **a)** *(Abteilung)* faculty; **die philosophische/medizinische/juristische ~:** the faculty of arts/medicine/law; **die ~ wechseln** change faculty; **b)** *(Lehrer und Studenten)* staff and students *(of a faculty)*; **c)** *(Räumlichkeiten)* faculty building; **d)** *(Math.)* factorial; **5 ~:** factorial 5
fakultativ [fakʊlta'ti:f] **1.** *Adj.* optional ⟨*subject, participation*⟩. **2.** *adv.* optionally
Falange [fa'laŋge] **die; ~:** Falange
Falangist der; ~en, ~en Falangist
falb [falp] *Adj. (geh.)* dun-coloured
Falbe ['falbə] **der; ~n, ~n** dun [horse]
Falbel ['falbl̩] **die; ~, ~n** *(Textilw.)* furbelow, flounce
Falke ['falkə] **der; ~n, ~n** *(auch Politik fig.)* hawk
Falken·beize die falconry
Falkenier [falkə'ni:ɐ̯] **der; ~s, ~e:** *s.* **Falkner**
Falkländer ['falklɛndɐ] **der, ~s, ~, Falkländerin die; ~, ~nen** Falklander
Falkland·inseln *Pl.* Falkland Islands; Falklands
Falkner der; ~s, ~: falconer
Falknerei die; ~, ~en a) *o. Pl. (Falkenbeize)* falconry; **b)** *(Anlage)* hawk-house
[1]**Fall** [fal] **der; ~[e]s, Fälle** ['fɛlə] **a)** *(Sturz)* fall; **zu ~ kommen** have a fall; **durch** *od.* **über etw.** *(Akk.)* **zu ~ kommen** *(fig.)* come to grief because of sth.; **jmdn. zu ~ bringen** *(fig.)* bring about sb.'s downfall; **der ~ einer Stadt** *(fig.)* the fall of a town; *s. auch* **Hochmut; b)** *(das Fallen)* descent; **der freie ~:** free fall; **c)** *(Ereignis, Vorkommnis)* case; *(zu erwartender Umstand)* eventuality; **für den äußersten** *od.* **schlimmsten ~, im schlimmsten ~:** if the worst comes to the worst; **im besten ~:** at best; **es ist [nicht] der ~:** it is [not] the case; **gesetzt den ~:** assuming; supposing; **für den ~, daß es morgen schön ist** in case it's fine tomorrow; **im ~e einer Veränderung** in the event of a change; **auf jeden ~:** in any case; **auf alle Fälle** in any case; **auf keinen ~:** on no account; **das ist doch ein ganz klarer ~:** it's perfectly clear; **jmds. ~ sein** *(fig. ugs.)* be sb.'s cup of tea; **klarer ~** *(ugs.)* it goes without saying; **in jedem ~:** in any case; **der ~ ist [für mich] erledigt** [as far as I'm concerned] that's the end of it; **d)** *(Rechtsw., Med., Grammatik)* case; **der 1./2./3./4. ~** *(Grammatik)* the nominative/genitive/dative/accusative case
[2]**Fall das; ~[e]s, ~en** *(Seemannsspr.)* halyard
Fall-: ~beil das guillotine; **~beschleunigung die** *(Physik)* gravitational acceleration
Falle ['falə] **die; ~, ~n a)** *(auch fig.)* trap; **in die ~ gehen** walk into the trap; **jmdm. eine ~ stellen** *(fig.)* set a trap for sb.; **jmdn. in eine ~ locken** *(fig.)* lure sb. into a trap; **jmdm. in die ~ gehen** *(fig.)* fall into sb.'s trap; **in der ~ sitzen** *(fig.)* be in a spot; **b)** *(salopp: Bett)* **in die ~ gehen** turn in *(coll.)*; **sich in die ~ hauen** hit the sack *or* hay *(sl.)*; **c)** *(Riegel am Türschloß)* catch; latch
fallen *unr. itr. V.; mit sein* **a)** fall; **etw. ~ lassen** drop sth.; **immer [wieder] auf die Füße ~** *(fig. ugs.)* always land on one's feet; **sich ins Gras/Bett/Heu ~ lassen** fall on to the grass/into bed/into the hay; *s. auch* **Decke c; Gewicht; Groschen b; Rahmen b; Schoß a; Schuppe a; stehen; Stein b; Stuhl a; Tür; Wasser a; Wolke; Würfel b; b)** *(hin~, stürzen)* fall [over]; **auf die Knie/in den Schmutz ~:** fall to one's knees/in the dirt; **über einen Stein ~:** trip over a stone; **im Fallen hat er den Schirmständer umgerissen** he pulled the umbrella stand over as he fell; *s. auch* **gefallen 2; Kopf a; Mund; Nase a; c)** *(sinken)* ⟨*prices*⟩ fall; ⟨*temperature, water level*⟩ fall, drop; ⟨*fever*⟩ subside; **im Preis ~:** go down *or* fall in price; *s. auch* **Arm a; Hals a; Knie a; Rücken a; Schloß a; Zügel a; d)** *(an einen bestimmten Ort gelangen, dringen)* ⟨*light, shadow, glance, choice, suspicion*⟩ fall; **die Wahl fiel auf ihn** the choice fell on him; **e)** *(abgegeben, erzielt werden)* ⟨*shot*⟩ be fired; *(Sport)* ⟨*goal*⟩ be scored; **f)** *(nach unten hängen)* ⟨*hair*⟩ fall; **die Haare ~ ihr ins Gesicht/auf die Schulter** her hair falls over her face/to her shoulders; **g)** *(im Kampf sterben)* die; fall *(literary)*; **im Krieg ~:** die in the war; **er ist bei Verdun ge~:** he died *or* fell at Verdun; **h)** *(aufgehoben, beseitigt werden)* ⟨*ban*⟩ be lifted; ⟨*tax*⟩ be abolished; ⟨*obstacle*⟩ be removed; ⟨*limitation*⟩ be overcome; *s. auch* **Opfer b; Tisch; i)** *(zu einer bestimmten Zeit stattfinden)* **in eine Zeit ~:** occur at a time; **mein Geburtstag fällt auf einen Samstag** my birthday falls on a Saturday; **in diese Zeit fällt der Höhepunkt der romantischen Dichtung** that time saw the heyday of Romantic poetry; **j)** *(zu einem Bereich gehören)* **in/unter eine Kategorie ~:** fall into *or* within a category; **unter ein Gesetz/eine Bestimmung ~:** come under a law/a regulation; **k)** *(zu~, zuteil werden)* **eine Erbschaft/ein Gebiet fällt an jmdn.** an inheritance/a piece of territory falls to sb.; **er ist seinen Feinden in die Hände ge~:** he has fallen into the hands of his enemies; **l)** *(geäußert werden)* ⟨*decision*⟩ be taken *or* made; **scharfe Worte/Bemerkungen fielen** harsh words were spoken/harsh remarks were made; **m)** *(ver~)* **in Trümmer ~:** collapse in ruins; **in Schwermut ~:** be overcome by melancholy; **in einen Dialekt ~:** lapse into a dialect; **in Trab ~:** break into a trot; *s. auch* **Last c; Rolle f; Ungnade; n)** *(erobert werden)* ⟨*town, stronghold*⟩ fall; **o)** *(geh.: ab~)* slope; fall
fällen ['fɛlən] *tr. V.* **a)** fell ⟨*tree, timber*⟩; **b)** *(verkünden)* **ein Urteil ~** ⟨*judge*⟩ pass sentence; ⟨*jury*⟩ return a verdict; **einen Schiedsspruch ~:** make a ruling; **c)** *(Milit.: zum Angriff senken)* lower ⟨*bayonet*⟩; **d)** *(Chemie)* precipitate
fallen|lassen *unr. tr. V.; 2. Part.* ~ *od. (seltener)* **fallengelassen a)** *(aufgeben)* abandon ⟨*plan, aim, project*⟩; **b)** *(sich lossagen von)* drop ⟨*friend, colleague*⟩; **c)** *(äußern)* let fall ⟨*remark*⟩; drop ⟨*hint*⟩
Fallen·steller der; ~s, ~: trapper
Fall-: ~geschwindigkeit die *(Physik)* velocity of fall; **~gesetz das** *(Physik)* law of gravity; **~gitter das** portcullis; **~grube die** pitfall; **~höhe die a)** *(Physik)* height of fall; **b)** *(Literaturw.)* extent of a/the dramatic hero's fall
fallieren *itr. V. (Finanzw.)* go bankrupt
fällig ['fɛlɪç] *Adj.* **a)** due; **eine ~e Reform** an overdue reform; **der Kerl ist ~** *(ugs.)* he's in for it *(sl.)*; **b)** *(zu bezahlen)* ⟨*sum of money*⟩ payable, due; **ein ~er Wechsel/~e Zinsen** a bill to mature/interest payable
Fälligkeit die; ~, ~en *(Wirtsch.)*, **Fälligkeits·termin der** settlement date; date of payment
Fall·obst das windfalls *pl.*
Fallout [fɔ:l'|aʊt] **der; ~s, ~s** *(Kernphysik)* fall-out
Fall-: ~reep das *(Seemannsspr.)* jack-ladder; **~rückzieher der** *(Fußball)* bicycle kick
falls [fals] *(Konj.)* **a)** *(wenn)* if; **~ es regnet/schneit** if it rains/snows; **b)** *(für den Fall, daß)* in case; **~ es regnen sollte** in case it should rain
Fall·schirm der parachute; **mit dem ~ abspringen** *(im Notfall)* parachute out; *(als Sport)* make a [parachute] jump; **mit dem ~ über Belgien abspringen** parachute out over Belgium; *(als Soldat, Spion)* parachute into Belgium
Fallschirm-: ~jäger der *(Luftwaffe)* paratrooper; **~springen das** parachuting *no art.*; **~springer der** parachutist
Fall-: ~strick der trap; snare; **jmdm. ~stricke legen** *(fig.)* set traps for sb.; **~studie die** case-study; **~sucht die;** *o. Pl. (veralt.)* falling sickness *(arch.)*; **~tür die** trapdoor
Fällungs·mittel das *(Chemie)* precipitant
fall-, Fall-: ~weise *Adv. (österr.) s.* **gelegentlich 2a; ~wind der** katabatic wind; **~wurf der** *(Handball)* falling throw
falsch [falʃ] **1.** *Adj.* **a)** *(unecht, imitiert)* false ⟨*teeth, plait*⟩; imitation ⟨*jewellery*⟩; **Falsche Akazie** *(Bot.)* false acacia; **~er Hase** *(Kochk.)* meat loaf; **b)** *(gefälscht)* counterfeit, forged ⟨*banknote*⟩; false, forged ⟨*passport*⟩; assumed ⟨*name*⟩; **c)** *(irrig, fehlerhaft)* wrong ⟨*impression, track, pronunciation*⟩; wrong, incorrect ⟨*answer*⟩; **auf der ~en Fährte sein** be on the wrong track; **logisch ~ sein** be logically false; **an den Falschen geraten** come to the wrong man; **alle Aufgaben ~ [gelöst] haben** have got all one's exercises wrong; **etw. in die ~e Kehle** *od.* **den ~en Hals bekommen** *(fig. ugs.)* take sth. the wrong way; *s. auch* **Licht a, Pferd a; d)** *(unangebracht)* false ⟨*shame, modesty*⟩; **e)** *(irreführend)* false ⟨*statement, promise*⟩; **unter Vorspiegelung ~er Tatsachen** under false pretences; **f)** *(abwertend: hinterhältig)* false ⟨*friend*⟩; **ein ~er Hund** *(salopp)* a two-faced so-and-so *(sl.)*; **eine ~e Schlange** *(fig.)* a snake in the grass; **ein ~es Spiel [mit jmdm.] treiben** play false with sb.; *s. auch* **Fuffziger; g)** *(bes. nordd.: erzürnt)* angry. **2.** *adv.* **a)** *(fehlerhaft)* wrongly; incorrectly; **~ singen** sing wrongly; **~ gehen/fahren** go the wrong way; **etw. ~ verstehen** misunderstand sth.; **die Uhr geht ~:** the clock is wrong; **~ informiert** *od.* **unterrichtet sein** be misinformed; **~ herum** *(verkehrt)* back to front; the wrong way round; *(auf dem Kopf)* upside down; *(links)* inside-out; *s. auch* **herum a, verbinden 1h; b)** *(irreführend)* **~ schwören** lie on oath
Falsch der; ~s *(geh., veralt.)* **in an jmdm. ist kein ~:** sb. is guileless; **ohne ~ sein** be completely guileless
Falsch-: ~aus·sage die *(Rechtsspr.)* **[eidliche] ~aussage** false testimony *or* evidence; **uneidliche ~aussage** false statement [not on oath]; **~eid der** *(Rechtsspr.)* unintentional false statement under oath

fälschen ['fɛlʃn̩] *tr. V.* forge, fake ⟨*signature, document, passport*⟩; forge ⟨*painting*⟩; forge, counterfeit ⟨*coin, banknote*⟩; falsify ⟨*history*⟩
Fälscher der; ~s, ~, **Fälscherin die;** ~, ~nen forger; counterfeiter
Falsch-: ~**fahrer der** *s.* **Geisterfahrer;** ~**geld das** counterfeit money
Falschheit die; ~ **a)** *(Hinterhältigkeit)* duplicity; deceitfulness; **b)** *(Unechtheit)* falseness; *(Fehlerhaftigkeit)* wrongness
fälschlich 1. *Adj.* ; *nicht präd.* false ⟨*claim, accusation*⟩; *(irrtümlich)* mistaken, false ⟨*assumption, suspicion*⟩. **2.** *adv.* falsely, wrongly ⟨*claim, accuse*⟩; mistakenly, falsely ⟨*assume, suspect*⟩
fälschlicher·weise *Adv.* by mistake; mistakenly
falsch-, Falsch-: ~|**liegen** *unr. itr. V. (ugs.)* be mistaken; ~**meldung die** false report; ~**münzer** ['~mʏntsɐ] **der** forger; counterfeiter; ~**münzerei** [~mʏntsə'rai] **die;** ~, ~en forgery; counterfeiting; ~|**spielen** *itr. V.* cheat; ~**spieler der** cheat; *(erwerbsmäßig)* card-sharp[er]
Fälschung die; ~, ~en **a)** fake; counterfeit; **b)** *(das Fälschen)* forging; counterfeiting
Falsett [fal'zɛt] **das;** ~[e]s, ~e *(Musik)* falsetto [voice]
Falsifikat [falzifi'ka:t] **das;** ~[e]s, ~e forgery; fake
Falsifikation [falzifika'tsio:n] **die;** ~, ~en falsification
falsifizieren [falzifi'tsi:rən] *tr. V.* falsify
faltbar *Adj.* collapsible ⟨*box, boat*⟩
Falt-: ~**blatt das** leaflet; *(in Zeitungen, Zeitschriften, Büchern)* insert; ~**boot das** collapsible boat
Fältchen ['fɛltçən] **das;** ~s, ~: wrinkle
Falte ['faltə] **die;** ~, ~n **a)** crease; ~**n schlagen** crease; **b)** *(im Stoff)* fold; *(mit scharfer Kante)* pleat; **c)** *(Haut~)* wrinkle; line; **die Stirn in ~n legen** *od.* **ziehen** *(nachdenklich)* knit one's brow; *(verärgert)* frown; **d)** *(Geol.)* fold
fälteln ['fɛltl̩n] *tr. V.* pleat
falten 1. *tr. V.* fold; **die Hände ~:** fold one's hands. **2.** *refl. V. (auch Geol.)* fold; ⟨*skin*⟩ wrinkle, become wrinkled
falten-, Falten-: ~**bildung die** *(auch Geol.)* folding; *(der Haut)* wrinkling; ~**frei** *Adj.* creaseless ⟨*fit*⟩; ~**gebirge das** [range of] fold mountains; ~**los** *Adj.* uncreased ⟨*garment*⟩; unwrinkled ⟨*skin*⟩; ~**reich** *Adj.* heavily pleated ⟨*robe*⟩; heavily lined ⟨*face*⟩; ~**rock der** pleated skirt; ~**wurf der** arrangement of the folds
Falter der; ~s, ~ *(Nacht~)* moth; *(Tag~)* butterfly
faltig a) *Adj.* ⟨*clothes*⟩ gathered [in folds]; wrinkled ⟨*skin, hands*⟩; **b)** *(zerknittert)* creased
-fältig [-fɛltɪç] *Adj., adv.* -fold; **hundert~/tausend~:** hundredfold/thousandfold
Falt-: ~**karte die** folding map; ~**karton der** collapsible cardboard box; ~**tür die** folding door
Faltung die; ~, ~en *(Geol.)* fold
Falz [falts] **der;** ~es, ~e **a)** *(Buchbinderei) (scharfe Faltlinie)* fold; *(Übergang zwischen Buchdeckel und -rücken)* groove; *(angehefteter Leinenstreifen)* guard; stub; **b)** *(bei Briefmarken)* hinge; **c)** *(Bauw., Holzverarb.)* rebate; rabbet; **d)** *(Technik)* lock seam; double seam
falzen *tr. V. (Buchbinderei)* fold; *(Technik)* seam
Falz·maschine die a) *(Buchbinderei)* folding machine; **b)** *(Technik)* seaming machine
Fama ['fa:ma] **die;** ~ *(geh.)* rumour; **es geht die ~, daß ...:** there is a rumour that ...
familial [fami'lia:l] *Adj. (Soziol.)* familial
familiär [fami'liɛ:ɐ̯] **1.** *Adj.* **a)** family ⟨*problems, worries*⟩; **aus ~en Gründen** for family reasons; **b)** *(zwanglos)* familiar; informal; informal ⟨*tone, relationship*⟩. **2.** *adv. (zwanglos)* **sich ~ ausdrücken** to talk in a familiar way
Familiarität [familiari'tɛ:t] **die;** ~, ~en familiarity
Familie [fa'mi:liə] **die;** ~, ~n **a)** family; ~ **Meyer** the Meyer family; ~ **haben** have a family; **eine ~ gründen** *(heiraten)* marry; *(Kinder bekommen)* start a family; **das bleibt in der ~:** it will stay in the family; it will go no further; **das kommt in den besten ~n vor** it happens in the best families; **das liegt in der ~:** it runs in the family; **b)** *(Biol.)* family
familien-, Familien-: ~**album das** family album; ~**angehörige der/die;** *adj. Dekl.* member of the family; ~**angelegenheit die** family affair *or* matter; **in dringenden ~angelegenheiten** on urgent family business; ~**anschluß der** personal contact [with a/the family]; ~**anzeigen** *Pl.* births, deaths, and marriages; ~**besitz der** family property; **im ~besitz** in the family's possession; **dieses Stück ist aus altem ~besitz** this piece is a family heirloom; ~**betrieb der** family business *or* firm; ~**bibel die** family bible; ~**bild das** *(Foto)* family photograph; *(Gemälde)* family picture; ~**chronik die** family history; ~**ehre die** family honour; ~**feier die** family party; ~**feindlich** *Adj.* ⟨*policy etc.*⟩ hostile to the family; ~**flasche die** family-sized bottle; ~**forschung die** genealogy; ~**für·sorge die** family welfare service; ~**gerecht** *Adj.* ⟨*accommodation etc.*⟩ suiting the needs of families; ~**grab das** family grave; ~**gruft die** family vault; ~**krach der** *(ugs.)* family row; **bei uns gibt es oft ~krach** we often have family rows; ~**kreis der** family circle; **im engsten ~kreis** in the immediate family; ~**leben das;** *o. Pl.* family life; ~**minister der** *minister responsible for family matters;* ~**mit·glied das** member of the family; ~**name der** surname; family name; ~**ober·haupt das** head of the family; ~**paß der** family passport; ~**planung die;** *o. Pl.* family planning *no art.*; ~**politik die;** *o. Pl.* policy/policies relating to the family; ~**recht das** family law; ~**roman der** family saga; ~**schmuck der** family jewels *pl.*; family jewellery; ~**sinn der** sense of commitment to the family; ~**stand der** marital status; ~**stück das** family heirloom; ~**treffen das** family meeting; ~**vater der:** ~**vater sein** be the father of a family; **ein guter ~vater** a good husband and father; ~**verhältnisse** *Pl.* family circumstances; family background; **aus geordneten ~verhältnissen kommen** have a stable family background; ~**vor·stand der** *(Amtsspr.)* head of the family; ~**wappen das** family coat of arms; ~**zu·sammen·führung die** re-uniting of families; ~**zuwachs der** addition[s] to the family; ~**zuwachs bekommen/erwarten** have/expect an addition to the family
famos [fa'mo:s] *(veralt.)* **1.** *Adj.* splendid. **2.** *adv.* splendidly
famulieren [famu'li:rən] *itr. V. (Med.)* do one's clinical training
Famulus ['fa:mulʊs] **der;** ~, ~se *od.* **Famuli** ['fa:muli] **a)** *(Med.) medical student doing his/her clinical training;* intern *(Amer.)*; **b)** *(veralt., scherzh.: Assistent)* famulus
Fan [fɛn] **der;** ~s, ~s fan
Fanal [fa'na:l] **das;** ~s, ~e *(geh.)* torch; **ein ~ für etw. setzen** light a torch for sth.
Fanatiker [fa'na:tikɐ] **der;** ~s, ~, **Fanatikerin die;** ~, ~nen fanatic; *(religiös)* fanatic; zealot
-fanatiker der: Frischluft~/Fußball~: fresh air/football fanatic
fanatisch 1. *Adj.* fanatical. **2.** *adv.* fanatically
fanatisieren *tr. V.* rouse to fanaticism; **der fanatisierte Mob** the fanatically excited mob
Fanatismus der; ~: fanaticism
fand [fant] *1. u. 3. Pers. Sg. Prät. v.* **finden**
Fandango [fan'daŋgo] **der;** ~s, ~s fandango
Fanfare [fan'fa:rə] **die;** ~, ~n **a)** herald's trumpet; **die ~ blasen** play the ceremonial trumpet; **b)** *(Signal)* fanfare; flourish; ~**n erklingen** fanfares are sounded; **c)** *(Musikstück)* fanfare; **d)** *(am Auto)* musical [air] horn
Fanfaren-: ~**klang der** sound of the fanfare; ~**zug der** parade of trumpeters
Fang [faŋ] **der;** ~[e]s, **Fänge** ['fɛŋə] **a)** *o. Pl. (Tier~)* trapping; *(von Fischen)* catching; **zum ~ auslaufen** put to sea [to fish]; **b)** *o. Pl. (Beute)* bag; *(von Fischen)* catch; haul; **einen guten ~ machen** *od.* **tun** *(fig.)* make a good catch; **c)** *(Jägerspr.: Fuß eines Raubvogels) Pl.* talons *pl.*; claws *pl.*; **was er einmal in den Fängen hat, rückt er nicht wieder heraus** *(fig. ugs.)* once something gets into his clutches, he doesn't let go; **d)** *Pl. (Jägerspr.: Fangzähne)* fangs *pl.*
Fang-: ~**arm der** *(Zool.)* tentacle; ~**ball der** catch; ~**eisen das** *(Jagdw.)* trap
fangen 1. *unr. tr. V.* **a)** *(ergreifen, fassen)* catch, trap ⟨*bird, animal*⟩; catch ⟨*fish*⟩; **die Katze fängt eine Maus** the cat catches a mouse; **eine ~** *(südd., österr. ugs.)* get a clip round the ear *(coll.)*; **b)** *(gefangennehmen)* catch, capture ⟨*fugitive etc.*⟩; **gefangene Soldaten** captured soldiers; **in Frankreich/Rußland gefangen sein** be a prisoner of war in France/Russia; **von etw. [ganz] gefangen sein** *(fig.)* be [quite] enthralled by sth.; **sich gefangen geben** give oneself up; surrender; **c)** *auch itr. (auffangen)* catch ⟨*ball*⟩; **er kann gut/nicht ~:** he's good/not good at catching. **2.** *unr. refl. V.* **a)** *(in eine Falle geraten, nicht mehr frei kommen)* get *or* be caught; **der Wind fängt sich in etw.** sth. catches the wind; *s. auch* **Schlinge b; b)** *(wieder in die normale Lage kommen)* **sich [gerade] noch ~:** [just] manage to steady oneself; **sich wieder ~** *(fig.)* recover
Fangen das; ~s: ~ **spielen** play tag *or* catch
Fänger ['fɛŋɐ] **der;** ~s, ~: catcher; *(von Großwild)* hunter
fang-, Fang-: ~**flotte die** fishing leet; ~**frage die** catch question; trick question; ~**frisch** *Adj.* fresh; freshly caught ⟨*fish*⟩; ~**gebiet das** fishing ground; ~**leine die a)** *(Seemannsspr.) (eines Schiffs)* hawser; *(eines Bootes)* mooring rope; **b)** *(Fallschirmspringen)* shroud line; ~**netz das a)** *(Fischereiw.)* [fishing] net; **b)** *(Flugw.)* arrester gear; **c)** *(Artistik)* safety net
Fango·packung ['faŋgo-] **die** *(Med.)* fango pack
Fang-: ~**prämie die** bounty; ~**riemen der** [binding] strap; ~**schaltung die** *(Fernspr.)* tracing device; interception circuit; ~**schuß der** *(Jagdw.)* coup de grâce; ~**zeit die** season
Fan- [fɛn-]: ~**klub der** fan club; ~**post die** fan mail
Fantasie [fanta'zi:] **die;** ~, ~n *(Musik)* fantasia
Faraday·käfig ['færədɪ-] **der** *(Physik)* Faraday cage
Farb-: ~**ab·stimmung die** colour balance; colour harmony; ~**band das** [typewriter] ribbon; ~**beutel der** paint bomb; ~**bild das a)** *(Aufnahme)* colour photo; **b)** *(Illustration)* colour picture; ~**dia das** colour slide; colour transparency; ~**druck der** colour print *or* reproduction
Farbe ['farbə] **die;** ~, ~n **a)** colour; ~ **bekommen/verlieren** get some colour/lose one's colour; **an ~ gewinnen/verlieren** *(fig.)* become more/less colourful; **die ~ wechseln** ⟨*person*⟩ blanch; **b)** *(Farbstoff) (für Texti-*

lien) dye; *(für Holz, Metall, Stein usw.)* paint; **~n mischen/auftragen** mix/apply paint; **die ~n laufen ineinander/verblassen** the colours are running together/are fading; **etw. in den schwärzesten/glühendsten ~n malen** *od.* **schildern** *(fig.)* paint the gloomiest possible picture/a rosy picture of sth.; **c)** *o. Pl. (Buntheit)* colour; **der Film ist in ~:** the film is in colour; **d)** *meist Pl. (Symbol eines Landes, einer Vereinigung)* **~n** colours; **die ~n seines Landes vertreten** represent one's country; **die ~ wechseln** *(fig.)* change sides; **e)** *(Spielkarten)* suit; **eine ~ bedienen** follow suit; **~ bekennen** *(fig. ugs.)* come clean *(coll.)*

farb-, Farb-: ~echt *Adj.* colour-fast; **~effekt der** colour effect; **~empfindlich** *Adj.* **a)** colour-sensitive ‹*film*›; **b)** *(nicht ~echt)* non-colour-fast

Färbe·mittel das dye

färben ['fɛrbn̩] **1.** *tr. V.* **a)** dye ‹*wool, material, hair*›; **etw. grün/schwarz/beige ~:** dye sth. green/black/beige; **sich** *(Dat.)* **das Haar blond ~ lassen** have one's hair dyed blond; **b)** *meist im 2. Part. (verändert darstellen)* **eine politisch gefärbte Rede** a speech with a political slant; **ein gefärbter Bericht** a biased report. **2.** *refl. V.* change colour; **sich schwarz/rot** *usw.* **~:** turn black/red *etc.* **3.** *itr. V. (ugs.: ab~)* **der Stoff/die Bluse färbt** the material/the blouse runs

-farben *Adj., adv.* **erd~/erdbeer~/creme~/haut~:** earth-/strawberry-/cream-/skin-coloured; **creme~ angestrichen** painted cream

farben-, Farben-: ~blind *Adj.* colour-blind; **~freudig** *Adj.*, **~froh** *Adj.* colourful; **~industrie die** paint industry; **~lehre die** theory of colour; **~pracht die** colourful splendour; **~prächtig** *Adj.* vibrant with colour *postpos.*; **~sinn der;** *o. Pl.* colour-sense; sense of colour; **~spiel das** play of colours; **~test der** *(Psych.)* colour test; **~tragend** *Adj.* ‹*student fraternity*› using traditional colours

Färber der; ~s, ~: dyer

Färberei die; ~, ~en a) *(Betrieb)* dye-works *sing.*; **b)** *o. Pl. (Verfahren)* dyeing

Färberin die; ~, ~nen dyer

Farb-: ~fernsehen das colour television; **~fernseher der** *(ugs.)* colour telly *(coll.)* *or* television; **~fernseh·gerät das** colour television [set]; **~film der** colour film; **~filter, der,** *fachspr. meist:* **das** colour filter; **~fleck der** paint spot; **~foto das** colour photo; **~fotografie die a)** *o. Pl. (Verfahren)* colour photography; **b)** *(Foto)* colour photograph; **~gebung, ~gestaltung die** colouring; choice of colours

farbig 1. *Adj.* **a)** coloured; **b)** *(bunt, fig.: anschaulich, lebhaft)* colourful ‹*dress, picture, description, tale*›; **~e [Kirchen]fenster** stained-glass [church-]windows. **2.** *adv.* colourfully

-farbig *Adj., adv. s.* **-farben**

Farbige der/die; *adj. Dekl.* coloured man/woman; coloured; **die ~n in Amerika/Südafrika** the coloured people in America/the Coloureds in South Africa

Farbigkeit die; ~ *(auch fig.)* colourfulness

Farb-: ~karte die colour chart *or* guide; **~klecks der** paint spot *or* splash; *(nicht aufgesogen)* blob of paint; paint spot; **~kombination die** colour combination; **~komposition die** colour composition

farblich 1. *Adj.* in colour *postpos.*; as regards colour *postpos.* **2.** *adv.* **etw. ~ aufeinander abstimmen** match sth. in colour

farb-, Farb-: ~los *Adj. (auch fig.)* colourless; clear ‹*varnish*›; neutral ‹*shoe polish*›; **~losigkeit die;** ~ *(auch fig.)* colourlessness; **~negativ das** *(Fot.)* colour negative; **~schicht die** layer of paint; *(beim Auftragen)* coat of paint; **~skala die** colour range; **~stift der a)** *(Buntstift)* coloured pencil; **b)** *(Filzstift)* coloured felt-tip *or* pen; **~stoff der a)** *(Med., Biol.)* pigment; **b)** *(für Textilien)* dye; **c)** *(für Lebensmittel)* colouring; **~ton der** shade; **~tupfen, ~tupfer der** spot of colour

Färbung die; ~, ~en a) *(Farbgebung)* colouring; colour; **b)** *(das Färben)* dyeing; **c)** *(fig.: Tendenz)* slant

Farb-: ~walze die *(Druckw.)* ink[ing] roller; **~wechsel der a)** *(wechselndes Auftreten von Farben)* variation in colour; **b)** *(Zool.)* ability to change skin-colour

Farce ['farsə] **die; ~, ~n a)** *(auch fig.)* farce; **b)** *(Kochk.)* stuffing; *(mit Fleisch)* forcemeat

farcieren *tr. V. (Kochk.)* fill; stuff

Farm [farm] **die; ~, ~en** farm

Farmer der; ~s, ~: farmer

Farn [farn] **der; ~[e]s, ~e** fern

Farn-: ~kraut das fern; **~wedel der** fern frond

Färse ['fɛrzə] **die; ~, ~n** heifer

Fasan [fa'za:n] **der; ~[e]s, ~e[n]** pheasant

Fasanerie [fazanə'ri:] **die; ~, ~n** pheasantry

faschieren *tr. V. (österr.)* mince

Faschierte das; *adj. Dekl. (österr.)* minced meat; mince

Faschine [fa'ʃi:nə] **die; ~, ~n** *(Straßenbau)* fascine; faggot

Fasching ['faʃɪŋ] **der; ~s, ~e** *od.* **~s** [pre-Lent] carnival; **im ~:** at carnival time

Faschings-: ~ball der carnival ball; **~kostüm das** fancy-dress costume [for carnival]; **~zug der** carnival procession

Faschismus [fa'ʃɪsmʊs] **der; ~:** fascism *no art.*; **Opfer des ~:** victim of fascism

Faschist der; ~en, ~en, Faschistin die; ~, ~nen fascist

faschistisch *Adj.* fascist

faschistoid [faʃɪsto'i:d] *Adj.* fascistic

Fase ['fa:zə] **die; ~, ~n** *(Technik)* bevel [edge]; chamfer [edge]

Faselei die; ~, ~en *(ugs. abwertend)* drivel; twaddle

faseln ['fa:zl̩n] *itr. V. (ugs. abwertend)* drivel; blather

fasen ['fa:zn̩] *tr. V. (Technik)* bevel; chamfer

Faser ['fa:zɐ] **die; ~, ~n** fibre; **mit jeder ~ seines Herzens an etw.** *(Dat.)* **hängen** *(fig. geh.)* love sth. with every fibre of one's being

Faser·glas das; *o. Pl. (Technik)* fibreglass

faserig *Adj.* fibrous ‹*paper*›; stringy ‹*meat*›

fasern *itr. V.* fray

faser-, Faser-: ~pflanze die fibre-plant; **~schonend** *Adj.* gentle [to fabrics]; **~stoff der** fibrous material

Fas·nacht ['fas-] **die;** *o. Pl. (bes. südd.) s.* **Fastnacht**

Faß [fas] **das; Fasses, Fässer** ['fɛsɐ] barrel; *(Öl~, Benzin~ usw.)* drum; *(kleines Bier~)* keg; *(kleines Sherry~, Portwein~ usw.)* cask; *(Butter~)* churn; **Bier vom ~:** draught beer; **Wein vom ~:** wine from the wood; **er ist [so] dick wie ein ~** *(ugs.)* he's as fat as a barrel; **er säuft wie ein ~** *(ugs.)* he drinks like a fish; **das schlägt dem ~ den Boden aus** *(ugs.)* that takes the biscuit *(Brit. coll.) or (coll.)* cake; **das bringt das ~ zum Überlaufen** that's the last straw; **ein ~ ohne Boden sein** be an endless drain on sb.'s resources; **ein ~ aufmachen** *(ugs.)* paint the town red

Fassade [fa'sa:də] **die; ~, ~n a)** façade; frontage; **b)** *(abwertend: äußere Erscheinung)* façade; front; **das ist nur [noch] ~:** it is just a façade *or* front; **sie hat eine hübsche ~:** she is pretty on the outside

Fassaden-: ~kletterer der; ~s, ~: cat-burglar; **~lift der** [workmen's/window-cleaners'] cradle; **~reiniger der** *workman who cleans the exteriors of buildings*

faßbar *Adj.* **a)** *(greifbar, konkret)* tangible, concrete ‹*results*›; **b)** *(verständlich)* comprehensible

Faß-: ~bier das draught beer; beer on draught; **~binder der; ~s, ~** *(bes. südd., österr.)* cooper

Fäßchen ['fɛsçən] **das; ~s, ~:** small barrel; [small] cask

fassen ['fasn̩] **1.** *tr. V.* **a)** *(greifen)* grasp; take hold of; **jmdn. am Arm ~:** take hold of sb.'s arm; **jmdn. bei der Hand ~:** take hold of sb.'s hand; take sb. by the hand; **etw. zu ~ bekommen** get a hold on sth.; **faß!** get *or* grab it/him!; *s. auch* **Ehre c; Fuß b; Kopf a; Nase a; Schopf a; Stier a; Wurzel a; b)** *(festnehmen)* catch ‹*thief, culprit*›; **c)** *(aufnehmen können)* ‹*hall, tank*› hold; **d)** *(begreifen)* **ich kann es nicht ~:** I cannot take it in; **das ist [doch] nicht zu fassen!** it's incredible; **e)** *(in verblaßter Bedeutung)* make, take ‹*decision*›; **Vertrauen** *od.* **Zutrauen zu jmdm. ~:** begin to feel confidence in *or* to trust sb.; **Mut ~:** take courage; **er konnte keinen klaren Gedanken ~:** he could not think clearly; *s. auch* **Auge a; Herz b; f)** *(in eine Fassung bringen)* set, mount ‹*jewel*›; curb ‹*spring, well*›; **g)** *(formulieren, gestalten)* **etw. in Worte/Verse ~:** put sth. into words/verse; **einen Begriff eng/weit ~:** define a concept narrowly/widely; **h)** *(geistig er~)* grasp; **i)** *(als Ladung aufnehmen)* take on ‹*load, goods*›; **j)** *(Soldatenspr.)* draw ‹*rations, supplies, ammunition*›. **2.** *itr. V.* **a)** *(greifen)* **nach etw. ~:** reach for sth.; **in etw.** *(Akk.)* **~:** put one's hand in sth.; **an etw.** *(Akk.)* **~:** touch sth.; **ins Leere ~:** grasp thin air; **b)** *(einrasten)* ‹*screw*› bite; ‹*cog*› mesh. **3.** *refl. V.* **a)** pull oneself together; recover [oneself]; **sich [schnell/allmählich] wieder ~:** recover [quickly/gradually]; **b)** **sich kurz ~:** be brief; *s. auch* **Geduld**

fässer·weise *Adv.* by the barrel

faßlich *Adj.* comprehensible; intelligible; **etw. in [leicht] ~er Form schreiben** write sth. in an easily comprehensible way

Fasson [fa'sõ:] **die; ~, ~s** style; shape; **keine ~ mehr haben** have become shapeless; **jeder muß nach seiner [eigenen]** *od.* **auf seine [eigene] ~ selig werden** everyone has to work out his own salvation

Fasson·schnitt der short back and sides

Fassung die; ~, ~en a) *(sprachliche, künstlerische Form)* version; **b)** *o. Pl. (Selbstbeherrschung, Haltung)* composure; self-control; **die ~ bewahren** keep one's composure; **die ~ verlieren** lose one's self-control; **jmdn. aus der ~ bringen** upset *or* ruffle sb.; **etw. mit ~ tragen** bear sth. calmly; **nach ~ ringen** struggle to retain one's composure; **c)** *(für Glühlampen)* holder; **d)** *(von Juwelen)* setting; *(Bilder~, Brillen~)* frame

fassungs-, Fassungs-: ~kraft die *s.* **Auffassungsgabe; ~los** *Adj.* stunned; **ich war einfach ~los** *(ugs.)* I was completely bewildered; **~los vor Schmerz sein** be beside oneself with grief; **jmdn. ~los anstarren** gaze at sb. in bewilderment; **~losigkeit die** the state of bewilderment; **~vermögen das;** *o. Pl.* capacity

fast [fast] *Adv.* almost; nearly; **~ nie** almost never; hardly ever; **~ nirgends** hardly anywhere; **~ nichts** almost nothing; hardly anything

fasten *itr. V.* fast; **das lange/kurze Fasten** the long/short fast

Fasten *Pl.* **a)** *(~zeit vor Ostern)* Lent *sing.*; **b)** *(Bußübungen)* Lenten works of penance

Fasten-: ~kur die drastic reducing diet; **eine ~kur machen** be/go on a drastic reducing diet; **~predigt die** *(kath. Rel.)* Lent[en] sermon; **~zeit die a)** *(Rel.)* time of fasting; **b)** *(kath. Rel.)* Lent

Fast·nacht die a) *(Faschingsdienstag)* Shrove Tuesday; **b)** *(Karneval)* carnival; Shrovetide; **während der ~:** at Shrovetide; at carnival time; **~ feiern** celebrate Shrovetide *or* the carnival

fast·nächtlich *Adj.; nicht präd.* Shrovetide; carnival

Fastnachts-: ~brauch der Shrovetide custom; **~dienstag der** Shrove Tuesday; **~kostüm das** [carnival] fancy dress; **~spiel das** *(Literaturw.)* Shrovetide play; **~treiben das** [carnival] hustle and bustle; **~zeit die** Shrovetide; **~zug der** carnival procession

Faszikel [fas'tsi:kl] **der; ~s, ~:** fascicle

Faszination [fastsina'tsio:n] **die; ~:** fascination; **eine ~ auf jmdn. ausüben** fascinate sb.

faszinieren [fastsi'ni:rən] *tr. V.* fascinate

fatal [fa'ta:l] *Adj.* **a)** *(peinlich, mißlich)* awkward; embarrassing; **~e Folgen haben** have unfortunate consequences; **sich als ~ erweisen** prove [to be] rather unfortunate; **b)** *(verhängnisvoll)* fatal

fataler·weise *Adv.* unfortunately

Fatalismus der; ~: fatalism

Fatalist der; ~en, ~en fatalist

fatalistisch 1. *Adj.* fatalistic. **2.** *adv.* fatalistically

Fata Morgana ['fa:ta mɔr'ga:na] **die; ~ ~, ~ Morganen** *od.* **~ ~s** fata morgana; mirage; *(fig.)* illusion

Fatum ['fa:tʊm] **das; ~s, Fata** *(geh.)* fate; destiny

Fatzke ['fatskə] **der; ~n** *od.* **~s, ~n** *od.* **~s** *(ugs. abwertend)* twit *(Brit. sl.)*; jerk *(sl.)*

fauchen ['fauxn̩] *itr. V.* **a)** ⟨*cat*⟩ hiss; ⟨*tiger*⟩ snarl; *(fig.)*⟨*engine*⟩ hiss; **b)** *(sich gereizt äußern)* snarl

faul [faul] **1.** *Adj.* **a)** *(verdorben)* rotten, bad ⟨*food*⟩; bad ⟨*tooth*⟩; rotten ⟨*wood*⟩; foul, stale ⟨*air*⟩; foul ⟨*water*⟩; **b)** *(träge)* lazy; idle; **zu ~ zu etw. sein/zu ~ sein, etw. zu tun** be too lazy *or* idle for sth./to do sth.; **er hat heute seinen ~en Tag** *(ugs.)* he's having a lazy day today; **er, nicht ~, übernahm die Leitung** he was not slow in taking over; **auf der ~en Haut liegen/sich auf die ~e Haut legen** take it easy; **c)** *(ugs.: nicht einwandfrei)* bad ⟨*joke*⟩; dud ⟨*cheque*⟩; false ⟨*peace*⟩; lame ⟨*excuse*⟩; shabby ⟨*compromise*⟩; shady ⟨*business, customer*⟩; **das ist doch [alles] ~er Zauber** it's [all] quite bogus; **etwas ist ~ im Staate Dänemark** something is rotten in the state of Denmark; **d)** *(säumig)* bad ⟨*debtor*⟩. **2.** *adv. (träge)* lazily; idly

Faul·baum der alder buckthorn; alder dogwood

Fäule ['fɔylə] **die; ~:** foulness

faulen *itr. V.; meist mit sein* ⟨*vegetables, fruit, straw, leaves, wood*⟩ rot; ⟨*water*⟩ go foul, stagnate; ⟨*meat*⟩ go off, putrefy; ⟨*fish*⟩ go off, go bad

faulenzen ['faulɛntsn̩] *itr. V.* laze about; loaf about *(derog.)*

Faulenzer der; ~s, ~: idler; lazy-bones *sing. (coll.)*

Faulenzerei die; ~, ~en *(abwertend)* idleness; laziness

Faulenzer·leben das life of idleness

Faul·gas das sludge *or* sewage gas

Faulheit die; ~: laziness; idleness; **vor ~ stinken** *(ugs.)* be bone-idle

faulig *Adj.* stagnating ⟨*water*⟩; putrefying ⟨*meat*⟩; ⟨*meat*⟩ which is going bad; rotting ⟨*vegetables, fruit*⟩; foul, putrid ⟨*smell*⟩; **~ schmecken/riechen** taste/smell bad *or* off

Fäulnis ['fɔylnɪs] **die; ~:** rottenness; *(fig.)* decadence; degeneracy; **in ~ übergehen** begin to rot

Fäulnis-: ~bakterie die putrefactive bacterium; **~erreger der** putrefactive agent; organism causing putrefaction

Faul-: ~pelz der *(fam.)* lazy-bones *sing. (coll.)*; **~schlamm der** sludge; **~tier das a)** *(Zool.)* sloth; **b)** *(ugs.: Faulenzer) s.* **~pelz**

Faun [faun] **der; ~[e]s, ~e** faun

Fauna ['fauna] **die; ~, Faunen** *(Zool.)* fauna

faunisch 1. *Adj. (geh.)* **a)** *(naturhaft)* faunlike; **b)** *(sinnesfroh)* lascivious. **2.** *adv.* lasciviously

Faust [faust] **die; ~, Fäuste** ['fɔystə] fist; **eine ~ machen, die Hand zur ~ ballen** clench one's fist; **die ~ ballen/öffnen** clench/unclench one's fist; **mit den Fäusten auf jmdn. losgehen** fly at sb. with one's fists; **jmdm. mit der ~ ins Gesicht schlagen** punch sb. in the face; **das paßt wie die ~ aufs Auge** *(ugs.) (paßt nicht)* that clashes horribly; *(paßt)* that matches perfectly; **er paßt zu ihr wie die ~ aufs Auge** *(ugs.)* they are like chalk and cheese *or* like night and day; **die ~ im Nacken spüren** *(fig.)* begin to feel the pressure; **die ~/Fäuste in der Tasche ballen** *(fig.)* be seething inwardly; **auf eigene ~:** on one's own initiative; off one's own bat *(coll.)*; **mit der ~ auf den Tisch schlagen** *od.* **hauen** *(fig.)* put one's foot down

Faust-: ~abwehr die *(Ballspiele)* save with the fists; **~ball der** faustball

Fäustchen ['fɔystçən] **das; ~s, ~:** fist; **sich** *(Dat.)* **ins ~ lachen** laugh up one's sleeve; *(aus finanziellen Gründen)* laugh all the way to the bank

faust·dick 1. *Adj.* as thick as a man's fist *postpos.*; **eine ~e Lüge** *(fig.)* a bare-faced lie. **2.** *adv.* **er hat es ~ hinter den Ohren** *(ugs.)* he's a crafty *or* sly one

Fäustel ['fɔystl] **der; ~s, ~:** club hammer; stonemason's hammer

fausten *tr. V.* fist, punch ⟨*ball*⟩

faust-, Faust-: ~groß *Adj.* as big as a fist *postpos.*; **~hand·schuh der** mitten; **~hieb der** punch

faustisch *Adj. (geh.)* Faustian

Faust-: ~kampf der *(geh.)* pugilism; boxing; *(Wettkampf)* boxing contest; **~kämpfer der** *(geh.)* pugilist; boxer; **~keil der** *(Archäol.)* hand-axe

Fäustling ['fɔystlɪŋ] **der; ~s, ~e** mitten

Faust-: ~pfand das security; *(fig.)* bargaining-counter; **ein ~pfand verlangen** demand security; **~recht das;** *o. Pl.* rule of force; **~regel die** rule of thumb; **~schlag der** punch; **jmdm. einen ~schlag versetzen** punch sb.

Fauteuil [fo'tø:j] **der; ~s, ~s** *(bes. österr., sonst veralt.)* armchair

Fauvismus [fo'vɪsmʊs] **der; ~** *(bild. Kunst)* fauvism *no art.*

Fauxpas [fo'pa] **der; ~, ~:** faux pas

favorisieren [favori'zi:rən] *tr. V.* **a)** *(geh.: bevorzugen)* favour; **b)** *(Sport)* **er ist klar favorisiert** he is the clear favourite

Favorit [favo'ri:t] **der; ~en, ~en** favourite

Favoriten·rolle die position as favourite

Favoritin die; ~, ~nen favourite

Fax [faks] **das; ~, ~[e]** fax

faxen *tr. V.* fax

Faxen *Pl. (ugs.)* **a)** *(dumme Späße)* fooling around; **nur ~ im Sinn** *od.* **Kopf haben** do nothing but fool around *or* play the fool; **laß die ~!** stop fooling around *or* playing the fool!; **b)** *(Grimassen)* **~ machen** *od.* **schneiden** make *or* pull faces

Fayence [fa'jã:s] **die; ~, ~n** faience

Fazialis [fa'tsia:lɪs] **der; ~** *(Anat.)* facial nerve

Fazit ['fa:tsɪt] **das; ~s, ~s** *od.* **~e** result; **das ~ [aus etw.] ziehen** sum [sth.] up

FCKW *Abk.* **Fluorchlorkohlenwasserstoff** CFC

FDGB [ɛfde:ge:'be:] **der; ~[s]** *Abk. (DDR)* **Freier Deutscher Gewerkschaftsbund**

FDJ [ɛfde:'jɔt] **die; ~** *Abk. (DDR)* **Freie Deutsche Jugend** Free German Youth

FDJler [ɛfde:'jɔtlɐ] **der; ~s, ~, FDJlerin die; ~, ~nen** *(DDR)* Free German Youth member

F.D.P. [ɛfde:'pe:] **die; ~** *Abk.* **Freie Demokratische Partei**

F-Dur ['ɛf-] **das; ~** *(Musik)* [key of] F major; *s. auch* **A-Dur**

Feature ['fi:tʃɐ] **das; ~s, ~s** *od.* **die; ~, ~s** *(Rundf., Ferns., Zeitungsw.)* feature

Feber ['fe:bɐ] **der; ~[s], ~** *(österr.)* February

Febr. *Abk.* **Februar** Feb.

Februar ['fe:brua:ɐ̯] **der; ~[s], ~e** February; *s. auch* **April**

Fecht-: ~bahn die [fencing] piste; **~boden der** *(Studentenspr.)* fencing room

fechten ['fɛçtn̩] *unr. itr., tr. V.* **a)** fence; **für etw. ~** *(fig. geh.)* fight for sth.; **b)** *(geh.: im Krieg kämpfen)* fight

Fechter der; ~s, ~: fencer

Fechter·flanke die *(Turnen)* flank vault

Fechterin die; ~, ~nen fencer; *s. auch* **-in**

Fecht-: ~hand·schuh der fencing glove; **~hieb der** cut; **~kampf der** rapier fight; *(Sport)* fencing bout; **~maske die** fencing mask; **~meister der** fencing master; **~sport der** fencing; **~stellung die** fencing stance; **~waffe die** fencing weapon

Fedajin [feda'ji:n] **der; ~[s], ~:** fedayin

Feder ['fe:dɐ] **die; ~, ~n a)** *(Vogel~)* feather; *(Gänse~)* quill; *(lange Hut~)* plume; **leicht wie eine ~ sein** be as light as a feather; **in die ~n kriechen** *(ugs.)* turn in *(coll.)*; **[noch] in den ~n liegen** *(ugs.)* [still] be in one's bed; **er ließ ~n** *od.* **mußte ~n lassen** *(ugs.)* he did not come out [of it] unscathed; **sich mit fremden ~n schmücken** strut in borrowed plumes; **b)** *(zum Schreiben)* nib; *(mit Halter)* pen; *(Gänse~)* quill[-pen]; **ein Mann der ~** *(geh.)* a man of letters; **eine spitze ~ führen** *(geh.)* wield a sharp pen; **aus berufener ~ stammen** *(geh.)* come from an authoritative source; **jmdm. etw. in die ~ diktieren** dictate sth. to sb.; **zur ~ greifen** *(geh.)* take up one's pen; **c)** *(Technik)* spring; **d)** *(Tischlerei)* tongue

Feder·antrieb der *(Technik)* clockwork

Feder·ball der a) *o. Pl. (Spiel)* badminton; **b)** *(Ball)* shuttlecock

Federball-: ~schläger der badminton racket; **~spiel das a)** *(Zubehör)* badminton rackets and shuttlecock; **b)** *o. Pl.* badminton

feder-, Feder-: ~bein das *(Technik) (am Auto)* suspension strut; *(am Motorrad)* telescopic arm; **~bett das** duvet *(Brit.)*; continental quilt *(Brit.)*; stuffed quilt *(Amer.)*; **~blume die** artificial flower [made of feathers]; **~boa die** feather boa; **~busch der a)** *(Hutzierde)* plume; **b)** *(eines Vogels)* crest; **~fuchser** [-fʊksɐ] **der; ~s, ~** *(abwertend)* pen-pusher; **~führend** *Adj.* in charge *postpos.*; **der ~führende Redakteur** the chief editor; **~führung die: unter der ~führung des Ministers** under the overall control of the minister; **die ~führung haben** have overall control; be in overall charge; **~gewicht** *(Schwerathletik)* **a)** *o. Pl. (Gewichtsklasse)* featherweight; *s. auch* **Fliegengewicht a; b)** *(Sportler)* featherweight; **~gewichtler der; ~s, ~:** featherweight; **~halter der** fountain-pen; **~kiel der** quill; **~kissen das** feather cushion; *(im Bett)* feather pillow; **~kleid das** *(geh.)* plumage; **~kraft die a)** tension [of a/the spring]; **b)** *(Elastizität)* springiness; **~leicht 1.** *Adj.* ⟨*person*⟩ as light as a feather; featherweight ⟨*object*⟩; **2.** *adv.* as lightly as a feather; **~lesen das: nicht viel ~lesen[s] mit jmdm./etw. machen** give sb./sth. short shrift; make short work of sb./sth.; **ohne viel ~lesen[s], ohne langes ~lesen** without much ado; **viel zu viel ~lesen[s] machen** make far too much fuss; **~mappe die** pen and pencil case; **~messer das** penknife

federn 1. *itr. V.* ⟨*springboard, floor, etc.*⟩ be springy; **in den Knien ~:** bend at the knees; **ein ~der Gang** a springy *or* bouncy walk; **mit ~den Schritten** with a spring in one's step. **2.** *tr. V.* **a)** *(mit einer Federung versehen)* spring; **das Auto ist gut/schlecht gefedert** the car has good/poor suspension; **das Bett ist gut gefedert** the bed is well-sprung; **b)** *s. auch* **teeren**

Feder-: ~ohr das ear-tuft; plumicorn; **~schaft der** shaft of a/the feather; **~schmuck der a)** *(Kopfschmuck)* feather head-dress; **b)** *(geh.: Gefieder)* plumage; **~spiel das** *(Jägerspr.)* lure; **~skizze die** pen-and-ink sketch; **~strich der** stroke of the pen; **du hast noch keinen ~strich getan** *(fig. ugs.)* you have not yet put pen to paper

Federung die; ~, ~en *(in Möbeln)* springs *pl.*; *(Kfz-W.)* suspension

Feder-: ~vieh das *(ugs.)* poultry; **~waage die** spring balance; **~weiße der;** *adj. Dekl.* new wine; **~werk das** spring mechanism; **~wild das** game birds *pl.*; **~wisch der** feather-duster; **~wolke die** wispy *or* fleecy cloud; **~zeichnung die** pen-and-ink drawing

Fee [fe:] **die; ~, ~n** fairy

Feedback ['fi:dbæk] **das; ~s, ~s** feedback

Feeling ['fi:lɪŋ] **das; ~s, ~s** feeling; *(Geschicklichkeit)* feel

feenhaft *Adj.* fairy-like

Feen-: ~königin die fairy queen; queen of the fairies; **~reich das** Fairyland; **ins ~reich** to Fairyland

Fege·feuer das purgatory

fegen ['fe:gn̩] **1.** *tr. V.* **a)** *(bes. nordd.: säubern)* sweep; **b)** *(schnell entfernen)* brush; **etwas vom Tisch ~:** brush sth. off the table; *(fig.)* brush sth. aside; **den Gegner vom Platz ~** *(Sportjargon)* wipe the floor with one's opponent/opponents; **c)** *(schnell treiben)* sweep; drive; **d)** *(bes. südd.: blank reiben)* scour ⟨*pots, pans*⟩; **e)** *auch itr. (Jägerspr.)* fray; **die Hirsche ~ [ihr Geweih]** the stags fray [their heads]. **2.** *itr. V.* **a)** sweep up; **b)** *mit sein (rasen, stürmen)* sweep; tear *(coll.)*

Feger der; ~s, ~ *(ugs.)* live-wire

Fehde ['fe:də] **die; ~, ~n** feud; **mit jmdm. in ~ liegen** be at feud with sb.; **literarische/politische ~n [mit jmdm.] austragen/ausfechten** *(fig. geh.)* carry on/fight out literary/political controversies [with sb.]

Fehde·hand·schuh der *(geh.)* **jmdm. den ~ hinwerfen** *od.* **vor die Füße werfen** throw down the gauntlet to sb.; **den ~ aufnehmen** *od.* **aufheben** take up the gauntlet

fehl [fe:l] *Adv.* **~ am Platz[e] sein** be out of place

Fehl *in* **ohne Fehl [und Tadel] sein** *(geh.)* be faultless *or* beyond reproach

Fehl·anzeige die a) *(ugs.: Ausdruck der Verneinung)* no chance *(coll.)*; **b)** *(Milit.)* nil return

fehlbar *Adj.* fallible

Fehlbarkeit die; ~: fallibility

Fehl-: ~bedienung die incorrect operation; **~besetzung die: so viele ~besetzungen** so many examples of miscasting; **[als Ophelia] eine ~besetzung sein** be miscast [in the role of Ophelia]; **~bestand der** shortage; deficiency; **~betrag der** *(bes. Kaufmannsspr.)* deficit; **~bildung die** *(Med.)* deformity; malformation; **~diagnose die** incorrect diagnosis; **~druck der;** *Pl.* **~drucke** *(Philat.)* misprint; **~ein·schätzung die** false assessment; *(einer Entwicklung)* misjudgement

fehlen *itr. V.* **a)** *(nicht vorhanden sein)* **ihm fehlt der Vater/das Geld** he has no father/no money; **ihr fehlt der Sinn dafür** she lacks a *or* has no feeling for it; **b)** *(ausbleiben)* be missing; be absent; **[un]entschuldigt ~:** be absent with[out] permission; **du darfst bei dieser Party nicht ~:** you mustn't miss this party; **diese Zutat darf bei dieser Soße nicht ~:** this ingredient is a must in this sauce; **c)** *(verschwunden sein)* be missing; be gone; **in der Kasse fehlt Geld** money is missing *or* has gone from the till; **d)** *(vermißt werden)* **er/das wird mir ~:** I shall miss him/that; **e)** *(erforderlich sein)* be needed; **zwei Punkte ~ nur noch** only two points are still needed; **ihm ~ noch zwei Punkte zum Sieg** he needs only two points to win; **es fehlte nicht viel, und ich wäre eingeschlafen** I all but fell asleep; **das fehlte mir gerade noch [zu meinem Glück], das hat mir gerade noch gefehlt** *(ugs.)* that's all I needed; **f)** *unpers. (mangeln)* **es fehlt an Lehrern** there is a lack of teachers; **es fehlt am Nötigsten** what is most needed is lacking; **bei ihnen fehlt es am Nötigsten** they lack what is most needed; **es an nichts ~ lassen** provide everything that is needed; **an mir soll es nicht ~:** I shall do my part; **es fehlt an allen Ecken und Enden** *od.* **Kanten [bei jmdm.]** sb. is short of everything; **g)** *(krank sein)* **was fehlt Ihnen?** what seems to be the matter?; **fehlt dir etwas?** is there something wrong?; are you all right?; **mir fehlt nichts** I'm all right; there is nothing wrong with me; **h) weit gefehlt!** *(geh.)* far from it!; **i)** *(geh.: sündigen)* do wrong; sin

Fehl-: ~entscheidung die wrong decision; **~entwicklung die** abortive development

Fehler der; ~s, ~ a) *(Unrichtigkeit, Irrtum)* mistake; error; *(Sport)* fault; **der Schiedsrichter entschied** *od.* **erkannte auf ~:** the referee called a fault; **b)** *(schlechte Eigenschaft)* fault; shortcoming; *(Gebrechen)* [physical] defect; **sein ~ ist, daß er ...:** it is a fault of his that ...; **c)** *(schadhafte Stelle)* flaw; blemish; **Textilien/Porzellan mit kleinen ~n** textiles/porcelain with small flaws *or* imperfections

fehler·frei 1. *Adj.* faultless, perfect ⟨*piece of work, dictation, etc.*⟩; correct ⟨*measurement*⟩; **ein ~es Deutsch sprechen/schreiben** speak/write faultless *or* perfect German; *(Reiten)* **ein ~er Durchgang** a clear round. **2.** *adv.* without any mistakes; *(Reiten)* without any faults; **ich spreche französisch, aber nicht ~:** I can speak French, but not perfectly

Fehler·grenze die margin of error; tolerance; **die ~ liegt bei 30 %** there's a 30 % margin of error

fehlerhaft *Adj.* faulty; defective; imperfect ⟨*pronunciation*⟩; incorrect ⟨*measurement*⟩; **eine ~e Stelle im Material** a defect in the material

fehler-, Fehler-: ~los 1. *Adj.* flawless; **2.** *adv.* flawlessly; without a mistake; **etw. ~los schreiben/aufsagen** write/recite sth. without a mistake; **~quelle die** source of error; **~quote die** *(Statistik, Schulw.)* error rate; **~rechnung die;** *o. Pl.* calculus of accidental error; **~suche die a)** *(bei der Reparatur)* **ein Gerät zur ~suche** a device for detecting faults; **b)** *(zur Kontrolle)* **bei der ~suche** when checking for faults; *(DV: im Programm)* when checking for errors; **~zahl die** number of mistakes *or* errors

fehl-, Fehl-: ~farbe die *(Kartenspiel) (Farbe, die einem Spieler fehlt)* void suit; *(Farbe, die nicht Trumpf ist)* plain suit; **mit einer ~farbe bedienen** follow with a non-trump card; **~geburt die** miscarriage; **~|gehen** *unr. itr. V.; mit sein (geh.)* **a)** *(sich irren)* go *or* be wrong; **in einer Annahme ~gehen** be wrong in an assumption; **b)** *(sich verlaufen)* lose one's way; **Sie können nicht ~gehen** you cannot go [far] wrong; **c)** *(nicht treffen)* ⟨*shot*⟩ miss [the mark]; **~griff der** mistake; wrong choice; **einen ~griff tun** make a mistake *or* the wrong choice; **~information die** piece of wrong information; **einer ~information aufsitzen** *(ugs.)* have been given wrong information; **auf einer ~information beruhen** be based on [a piece of] incorrect information; **~interpretation die** misinterpretation; **~investition die** *(bes. Wirtsch.)* **a)** bad investment; **b)** *(ugs.: Gegenstand)* **eine [glatte] ~investition sein** be a [total] waste of money; **~kalkulation die** miscalculation; **~kauf der** *(ugs.)* bad buy; **~konstruktion die: eine ~konstruktion sein** be badly designed; **~leistung die** *(Psych.)* slip; mistake; **eine Freudsche ~leistung** a Freudian slip; **~|leiten** *tr. V. (geh.)* misdirect; misdirect, misroute ⟨*transport, convoy*⟩; **~paß der** *(Ballspiele)* bad pass; **~planung die** [piece of] bad planning *no art.*; **~schlag der** failure; **~|schlagen** *unr. itr. V.; mit sein* fail; ⟨*hopes*⟩ come to nothing; **~schluß der** wrong conclusion; **~sichtig** [~zɪçtɪç] *Adj.* ⟨*person*⟩ with defective vision; **~sichtigkeit die** defective vision; **~start der a)** *(Leichtathletik)* false start; **b)** *(Flugw.)* faulty start; **c)** *(Raumf.)* abortive launch; **~tritt der a)** *(falscher Tritt)* false step; **b)** *(geh.: Verfehlung)* slip; indiscretion; *(veralt.: gesellschaftlich verpönte Liebesbeziehung)* indiscretion; **einen ~tritt begehen, sich eines ~tritts schuldig machen** commit an indiscretion; **~urteil das a)** *(Rechtsw.)* **ein ~urteil fällen** ⟨*jury*⟩ return a wrong verdict; ⟨*judge*⟩ pass a wrong judgement; **b)** *(falsche Beurteilung)* error of judgement; **ein ~urteil über etw.** *(Akk.)* **abgeben** make an incorrect assessment of sth.; **~verhalten das a)** *(fehlerhaftes Verhalten)* incorrect conduct; **~verhalten beim Überholen** incorrect action when overtaking; **b)** *(anormales Verhalten)* aberrant behaviour; **~versuch der** *(Gewichtheben, Hochsprung)* unsuccessful attempt; failure; *(Weitsprung)* foul jump; **~zündung die** *(Technik)* misfire

Fehn [fe:n] **das; ~[e]s, ~e** fen; marsh

Fehn·kultur die *(Landw.) method of cultivation which puts marshland to agricultural use*

feien ['faiən] *tr. V.; meist im 2. Part. (geh.)* protect **(gegen** against); **gegen Tropenkrankheiten gefeit sein** be immune to tropical diseases

Feier ['faiɐ] **die; ~, ~n a)** *(Veranstaltung)* party; *(aus festlichem Anlaß)* celebration; **zu** *od.* **anläßlich einer Begebenheit eine ~ veranstalten** celebrate an occasion with a party; **eine ~ in kleinem Rahmen/im Familienkreis** a small/family celebration/party; **keine ~ ohne Meier** *(scherzh.)* he/she *etc.* never misses a party; **b)** *(Zeremonie)* ceremony; **die ~ des heiligen Abendmahls** the celebration of Holy Communion; **zur ~ des Tages** *(oft scherzh.)* to mark the day; in honour of the occasion

Feier·abend der a) *(Zeit nach der Arbeit)* evening; **den ~ genießen** enjoy one's evening; **schönen ~!** have a nice evening; **b)** *(Arbeitsschluß)* finishing time; **nach ~:** after work; **~ machen** finish work; knock off; **für mich ist ~, dann ist** *od.* **mache ich ~** *(fig. ugs.)* I'm finished; I've had enough *(coll.)*

Feierabend-: ~beschäftigung die leisure pursuit; spare-time interest; **~heim das** *(DDR)* old people's home; **~lektüre die** leisure-time reading

Feierei die; ~, ~en *(ugs. abwertend)* **diese ständige ~:** these endless parties

feierlich 1. *Adj.* **a)** ceremonial; solemn; **eine ~e Handlung** a ceremonial act; **eine ~e Stille** a solemn silence; **das ist ja [schon] nicht mehr ~** *(ugs.)* it's got beyond a joke; **b)** *(emphatisch)* solemn ⟨*declaration*⟩. **2.** *adv.* **a)** solemnly; ceremoniously; **jmdm. ist ~ zumute** sb. is in a solemn mood *or* frame of mind; **~ verabschiedet werden** be given a ceremonious farewell; **b)** *(emphatisch)* solemnly ⟨*declare, swear, etc.*⟩

Feierlichkeit die; ~, ~en a) *o. Pl. (Würde, Ernst)* solemnity; **b)** *meist Pl. (feierliche Veranstaltung)* celebration; festivity

feiern 1. *tr. V.* **a)** *(festlich begehen)* celebrate ⟨*birthday, wedding, etc.*⟩; **man muß die Feste ~, wie sie fallen** you have to enjoy yourself while you can; **b)** *(ehren, umjubeln)* acclaim ⟨*artist, sportsman, etc.*⟩; **ein gefeierter Sportler/Dichter** a celebrated sportsman/poet; **Triumphe ~:** win the highest acclaim. **2.** *itr. V. (lustig beisammen sein)* celebrate; have a party

feier-, Feier-: ~schicht die *(Arbeitswelt)* cancelled shift; **eine ~schicht einlegen müssen** have one's shift cancelled; **~stunde die** ceremony; **jmdn. in/mit einer ~stunde ehren** hold a ceremony in sb.'s honour; **~tag der** holiday; **ein gesetzlicher/kirchlicher ~tag** a public holiday/religious festival; **an Sonn- und ~tagen** on Sundays and public holidays; **jmdm. schöne ~tage wünschen** wish sb. a good holiday; **für mich ist heute ein ~tag** *(fig.)* today is a very special *or* a red letter day for me; **~täglich** *Adj.* solemn ⟨*silence, mood*⟩; **~tags** *Adv.* **sonn- und ~tags** on Sundays and public holidays; **~tags·stimmung die** Sunday mood

feig, feige [faik, 'faigə] **1.** *Adj.* cowardly. **2.** *adv.* like a coward/like cowards; in a cowardly way

Feige die; ~, ~n fig

Feigen-: ~baum der fig tree; **~blatt das a)** *(Blatt)* fig-leaf; **b)** *(fig.: Verhüllung)* front; cover; **~kaktus der** Indian fig; prickly pear

Feigheit die; ~: cowardice; cowardliness; **~ vor dem Feind** *(Milit.)* cowardice in the face of the enemy

Feigling der; ~s, ~e coward

feil [fail] *Adj. (veralt.)* for sale *postpos.*; *(fig.)* venal; **eine ~e Dirne** *(veralt.)* a harlot; **für Geld ist nicht alles ~:** money can't buy everything

feil|bieten *unr. tr. V. (geh.)* offer ⟨*goods*⟩ for sale

Feile die; ~, ~n file; **etw. mit einer ~ bearbeiten** file sth.

feilen *tr., itr. V.* file; **etw. passend/rund ~:** file sth. to fit/into a round shape; **sich** *(Dat.)* **die Fingernägel ~:** file one's [finger-]nails

feil|halten *unr. tr. V. (veralt.)* offer ⟨*goods*⟩ for sale

feilschen ['failʃn̩] *itr. V.* haggle **(um** over); **nach langem/hartem Feilschen** after a long/hard bout of haggling

Feil-: ~span der filing; **~staub der** filings *pl.*

fein [fain] **1.** *Adj.* **a)** *(zart)* fine ⟨*material, line, mesh, etc.*⟩; **b)** *(aus kleinsten Teilchen bestehend)* fine ⟨*sand, powder*⟩; finely-ground ⟨*flour*⟩; finely-granulated ⟨*sugar*⟩; **etw. ~ mahlen** grind sth. fine; **c)** *(hochwertig)* high-quality ⟨*fruit, soap, etc.*⟩; fine ⟨*silver, gold, etc.*⟩; fancy ⟨*cakes, pastries, etc.*⟩; **nur das Feinste vom Feinen kaufen** buy only the best; **d)** *(ugs.: erfreulich)* great *(coll.)*; marvellous; **e)** *(~geschnitten)* finely shaped, delicate ⟨*hands, features, etc.*⟩; **f)** *(scharf, exakt)* keen, sensitive ⟨*hearing*⟩; keen ⟨*sense of smell*⟩; **eine ~e Nase für etw. haben** *(fig.)* have a good nose for sth.; **g)** *(listig, gerissen)* cunning ⟨*move, scheme*⟩; **h)** *(ugs.: anständig, nett)* great *(coll.)*, splendid ⟨*person*⟩; **eine ~e Verwandtschaft/Gesellschaft** *(iron.)* a fine *or* nice family/crowd; **i)** *(einfühlsam)* delicate ⟨*sense of humour*⟩; keen ⟨*sense, understanding*⟩; **ein ~es Gespür für etw. haben** have a good feeling for sth.; **j)** *(gediegen, vornehm)* refined ⟨*gentleman, lady*⟩; **du bist dir wohl zu ~ dafür!** *(ugs.)* I suppose you think it's beneath you; *s. auch* **Herr a. 2.** *adv.* **a)** *(gut, günstig)* **~ [he]raussein** *(ugs.)* be sitting pretty *(coll.)*; **Unterschiede ~ herausarbeiten** bring out subtle differences; **b)** *(listig, gerissen)* **~ ausgeklügelt** cleverly thought out; **c)** *(ugs.: bekräftigend)* **etw. ~ säuberlich aufschreiben** write sth. down nice and neatly; **~ brav sein** be a good boy/girl

Fein-: ~ab·stimmung die *(Technik)* fine tuning; **~arbeit die** detailed work; *(Technik)* precision work; **~bäckerei die** patisserie; **~bearbeitung die** *(Technik)* finishing; **~blech das** thin sheet metal

feind [faint] *Adj. (geh.)* in **jmdm./einer Sache ~ sein** be hostile towards sb./sth.

-feind der ...hater; **ein Hunde~/Fernseh~ sein** be anti dogs/television

Feind der; ~[e]s, ~e a) enemy; **er ist ein ~ des Alkohols** he is opposed to alcohol; **sich** *(Dat.)* **~e machen** make enemies; **sich** *(Dat.)* **jmdn. zum ~ machen** make an enemy of sb.; **liebet eure ~e** *(bibl.)* love thine enemy; **„~ hört mit"** 'careless talk costs lives'; **b)** *o. Pl. (feindliche Truppen)* enemy *constr. as pl.*; **[nichts wie] ran an den ~** *(fig. ugs.)* get/let's get going *or (sl.)* stuck in

Feind-: ~berührung die *(Milit.)* contact with the enemy; **~bild das** concept of the enemy

Feindes-: ~hand die *(veralt.)* **in ~hand geraten** *od.* **fallen** fall into the hands of the enemy; **von ~hand fallen** fall at the hands of the enemy; **~land das** *(veralt.)* enemy territory

Feind·flug der *(Luftwaffe)* operational flight [over enemy territory]

Feindin die; ~, ~nen *s.* **Feind a**

feindlich 1. *Adj.* **a)** hostile; **b)** *nicht präd. (Milit.)* enemy ⟨*attack, broadcast, activity*⟩. **2.** *adv.* in a hostile manner; with hostility

-feindlich *adj.* anti-⟨*Soviet, American, EEC, government, etc.*⟩; **familienfeindliche/kinderfeindliche Gesetze** laws which are hostile towards families/children

Feind·mächte *Pl.* enemy powers *pl.*

Feindschaft die; ~, ~en enmity; **zwischen ihnen herrscht bittere ~:** they are bitter enemies; **sich** *(Dat.)* **jmds. ~ zuziehen** make an enemy of sb.

feind·selig 1. *Adj.* hostile; **sich ~ gegen jmdn. zeigen** show hostility towards sb. **2.** *adv.* **sich ~ ansehen** look at each other in a hostile manner *or* with hostility

Feind·seligkeit die; ~, ~en hostility; **~en** *(Milit.)* hostilities

fein-, Fein-: ~einstellung die fine adjustment; **~frost der;** *o. Pl. (DDR)* deep-frozen foods *pl.*; **~fühlig 1.** *Adj.* sensitive; **2.** *adv.* sensitively; **~fühligkeit die; ~:** sensitivity; **~gebäck das** [fancy] cakes and pastries *pl.*; **~gefühl das** sensitivity; **~gehalt der** fineness; **~gemahlen** *Adj. (präd. getrennt geschrieben)* finely-ground; **~geschnitten** *Adj. (präd. getrennt geschrieben)* **a)** finely-chopped ⟨*herbs, vegetables, etc.*⟩; **b)** *(fig.: schön geformt)* delicate, finely shaped ⟨*face, hands, etc.*⟩; **~gewicht das** fineness; **~glied[e]rig** *Adj.* delicate; slender; **~gold das** fine gold; **~guß der** *(Metall)* precision casting

Feinheit die; ~, ~en a) *o. Pl. (zarte Beschaffenheit)* fineness; delicacy; **b)** *(Nuance, Andeutung)* subtlety; **die stilistischen ~en** the stylistic subtleties *or* nuances; **c)** *o. Pl. (Vornehmheit)* refinement

fein-, Fein-: ~körnig *Adj.* **a)** fine-grained, fine ⟨*sand, gravel, etc.*⟩; finely-granulated ⟨*sugar*⟩; **b)** *(Fot.)* fine-grain ⟨*film*⟩; **~kost die** delicatessen *pl.*; **~kost·geschäft das** delicatessen; **~|machen** *refl. V. (ugs.)* dress up; **~maschig** *Adj.* finely meshed, fine-mesh *attrib.* ⟨*net etc.*⟩; **~mechanik die** precision engineering *no art.*; **~mechaniker der** precision engineer; **~mechanisch** *Adj.; nicht präd.* precision ⟨*instrument*⟩; **~meß·gerät das** precision measuring-instrument; **~nervig** *Adj.* sensitive; **~säuberlich** *Adj. (österr.) s.* **säuberlich; ~|schleifen** *tr. V.* fine-grind; **~schmecker der; ~s, ~, ~schmeckerin die; ~, ~nen** gourmet; **~schmecker·lokal das** gourmet restaurant; **~schnitt der a)** *(Tabak)* fine cut; **b)** *(Film)* final editing; **~silber das** fine silver; **~sinnig 1.** *Adj.* sensitive and subtle; **2.** *adv.* in a sensitive and subtle manner; **~sinnigkeit die; ~:** sensitivity and subtlety

Feins·liebchen das *(dichter. veralt.)* sweetheart

Fein-: ~struktur die *(Physik, Med.)* fine structure; **~strumpf·hose die** sheer tights *pl. or* pantihose; **~unze die: eine ~unze Gold/Silber** an ounce of fine gold/silver; **~wäsche die** delicates *pl.*; **~wasch·mittel das** mild detergent

feist *Adj. (meist abwertend)* fat ⟨*face, fingers, etc.*⟩; **mit einem ~en Grinsen** *(fig.)* with a leer

feixen ['faiksn̩] *itr. V. (ugs.)* smirk

Felchen ['fɛlçn̩] **der; ~s, ~:** whitefish

Feld [fɛlt] **das; ~[e]s, ~er a)** *o. Pl. (geh.: unbebaute Bodenfläche)* country[side]; **freies ~:** open country[side]; **b)** *(bebaute Bodenfläche)* field; **auf dem ~ arbeiten** work in the field; **das ~ bestellen** till the field; **c)** *(Sport: Spiel~)* pitch; field [of play]; **d)** *(auf Formularen)* box; space; *(auf Brettspielen)* space; *(auf dem Schachbrett)* square; *(in Kassettendecken)* panel; **e)** *o. Pl. (Tätigkeitsbereich)* field; sphere; **das ~ der Wissenschaften** the field of science; **ein weites ~ [sein]** *(fig.)* [be] a wide sphere; **f)** *o. Pl. (veralt.: Schlacht~)* field [of battle]; **ins ~ rücken** *od.* **ziehen** *(veralt.)* go into battle; **gegen/für jmdn./etw. ins ~ ziehen** *(fig.)* crusade against/for sb./sth.; **das ~ behaupten** stand one's ground; **in der Politik behaupten nach wie vor Männer das ~:** politics is still dominated by men; **das ~ räumen** leave; get out; **jmdm. das ~ überlassen** hand over to sb.; leave sb. a clear field; **jmdn. aus dem ~[e] schlagen** eliminate sb.; get rid of sb.; **jmdm. das ~ streitig machen** compete with sb.; **etw. gegen jmdn./etw. ins ~ führen** bring up sth. against sb./sth.; **g)** *(Sport: geschlossene Gruppe)* field; **h)** *(Physik, Sprachw.)* field

feld-, Feld-: ~ahorn der field maple; **~arbeit die a)** work in the field; **b)** *(Wissensch.)* field-work; **~bahn die** narrow-gauge railway; light railway; **~bau der** agriculture; **~bett das** camp-bed; **~blume die** field flower; wild flower; **~ein[wärts]** [-'-(-)] *Adv.* across the field/fields; **~flasche die** *(Milit.)* canteen; water-bottle; **~forschung die** *(Wissensch.)* field-work; **~frucht die** arable crop; **~geistliche der** *(Milit. veralt.)* army chaplain; **~gottesdienst der** field-service; **~grau** *Adj.* field-grey; **~hand·ball der** field handball; fieldball; **~hase der** common hare; European hare

Feld·herr der *(veralt.)* commander

Feldherrn-: ~kunst die *(veralt.)* strategy; **~stab der** *(veralt.)* field marshal's baton

feld-, Feld-: ~hockey das *(Sport)* [field] hockey; **~huhn das** partridge; **~hüter der** *guard protecting crops from birds, thieves, etc.*; **~jäger der** *(Polizist)* military policeman; *(Polizei)* military police; **~küche die** *(bes. Milit.)* field kitchen; **~lager das** *(veralt.)* encampment; **~lazarett das** field hospital; **~linien** *Pl. (Physik)* field lines; **~marschall der** Field Marshal; **~marsch·mäßig 1.** *Adj.; nicht präd.* in full marching order *postpos.*; **2.** *adv.* **~marschmäßig angetreten/ausgerüstet sein** be lined up/be in full marching order; **~maus die** [European] common vole

Feld·post die forces' *(Brit.) or (Amer.)* military postal service

Feldpost-: ~brief der forces' *(Brit.) or (Amer.)* military letter; **~nummer die** forces' *(Brit.) or (Amer.)* military postal code

Feld-: ~prediger der *(veralt.)* army chaplain; **~rain der** balk; baulk; **~salat der** corn salad; lamb's lettuce

Feldscher ['fɛltʃeːɐ̯] **der; ~s, ~e** *(Milit.)* **a)** *(hist.: Wundarzt)* [unqualified] army doctor; **b)** *(DDR)* medical orderly

Feld-: ~schlacht die *(veralt.)* battle [in the field]; **~schütz der; ~en, ~en** field-guard; **~spat** [~ʃpaːt] **der; ~[e]s, ~späte** [~ʃpɛːtə] *od.* **~spate** feldspar; **~spieler der** player (excluding goalkeeper); ~**stärke** die (Physik) field strength; ~**stecher** der binoculars pl.; field glasses pl.; ~**stein** der stone; boulder; ~**studie** die (Wissensch.) field study; ~**theorie** die (Sprachw.) field theory; ~**überlegenheit** die (Sport) superiority; ~**versuch** der (Wissensch.) field experiment; ~**verweis** der (Sport) sending-off; **einen ~verweis gegen jmdn. aussprechen** send sb. off [the field]

Feld-Wald-und-Wiesen- (ugs.) run-of-the-mill; common-or-garden

Feld·webel [-ve:bl̩] der; ~s, ~ (Milit.) sergeant

Feld·weg der path; track

Feld·weibel [-vaibl̩] der; ~s, ~ (schweiz. Milit.) sergeant

Feld-: ~**zeichen** das (hist.) standard; flag; ~**zug** der (Milit., fig.) campaign

Felg·auf·schwung der (Turnen) upward circle forwards

Felge ['fɛlgə] die; ~, ~n a) (Radkranz) [wheel] rim; **die Reifen auf die ~n montieren** put the tyres on the wheels; b) (Turnen) circle

Felgen·bremse die (Technik) rim brake

Felg·um·schwung der (Turnen) circle

Fell [fɛl] das; ~[e]s, ~e a) (Haarkleid) fur; (Pferde~, Hunde~, Katzen~) coat; (Schaf~) fleece; skin; **ein weiches/glänzendes ~:** a soft/shiny coat; **einem Tier das ~ abziehen** skin an animal; **jmdm. das ~ über die Ohren ziehen** (fig. salopp) take sb. for a ride (sl.); b) o. Pl. (Material) fur; furskin; **ein Mantel aus [braunem] ~:** a [brown] fur coat; c) (abgezogene behaarte Haut) skin; hide; **ihm sind die** od. **alle ~e weg-** od. **davongeschwommen** (fig.) he has had all his hopes dashed; d) (salopp: Haut des Menschen) skin; (fig.) **ihm** od. **ihn juckt das ~** (ugs.) he is asking for a good hiding (coll.); **sich** (Dat.) **ein dickes ~ anschaffen** (ugs.) become thick-skinned; **ein dickes ~ haben** (ugs.) be thick-skinned or have a thick skin; **jmdm. das ~ versohlen** (ugs.) tan sb.'s hide; give sb. a good hiding (coll.); **das ~ versaufen** (ugs.) have a good drink to sb.'s memory

Fellache [fɛ'laxə] der; ~n, ~n, **Fellachin** die; ~, ~nen fellah

Fellatio [fɛ'la:tsio] die; ~: fellatio no art.

Fell·eisen das (veralt.) knapsack

Fell-: ~**handel** der skin trade; ~**jacke** die fur jacket; ~**mütze** die fur cap

Fels [fɛls] der; ~en, ~en a) o. Pl. (Gestein) rock; b) (geh.: Felsen) rock; **wie ein ~ in der Brandung stehen** stand as firm as a rock; s. auch ¹**wachsen a**

Fels-: ~**bild** das rock painting; ~**block** der; Pl. ~**blöcke** rock; boulder

Felsen ['fɛlzn̩] der; ~s, ~: rock; (an der Steilküste) cliff

felsen-, Felsen-: ~**bucht** die bay lined by cliffs; cliff-lined bay; ~**fest 1.** Adj. firm; unshakeable ⟨opinion, belief⟩; **2.** adv. ⟨believe, be convinced⟩ firmly; ~**grab** das rock tomb; ~**grotte** die grotto; cave; ~**höhle** die rock cave; ~**klippe** die rocky cliff; **an einer ~klippe zerschellen** be dashed to pieces on a rock; ~**küste** die rocky coast or coastline; ~**riff** das rocky reef; ~**tor** das (Geogr.) rock arch

Fels-: ~**geröll** das rocks pl.; boulders pl.; ~**haken** der (Bergsteigen) piton

felsig Adj. rocky

Fels-: ~**massiv** das [rock] massif; ~**nase** die ledge; ~**schlucht** die gorge; ravine; ~**spalte** die crevice [in the rock]; ~**vorsprung** der ledge; ~**wand** die rock face; **in der ~wand** on the rock face

fem. Abk. **feminin** fem.

Feme ['fe:mə] die; ~, ~n a) (hist.) vehmgericht; b) (Geheimgericht) kangaroo court

Feme-: ~**gericht** das s. **Feme**; ~**mord** der lynching

feminin [femi'ni:n] Adj. a) (geh.: weiblich) feminine ⟨characteristic, behaviour⟩; b) (abwertend: unmännlich) effeminate ⟨man, type⟩; c) (Sprachw.) feminine

Femininum ['fe:mini:nʊm] das; ~s, **Feminina** feminine noun

Feminismus der; ~, **Feminismen** a) o. Pl. (Frauenbewegung) feminism no art.; b) (Med., Zool.) feminism no art.

Feminist der; ~en, ~en, **Feministin** die; ~, ~nen feminist

feministisch Adj. feminist

Femme fatale [famfa'tal] die; ~ ~, ~s ~s (geh.) femme fatale

Fenchel ['fɛnçl̩] der; ~s fennel

Fenchel-: ~**knolle** die fennel; ~**öl** das fennel oil; ~**tee** der fennel tea

Fender ['fɛndɐ] der; ~s, ~ (Seew.) fender

Fenn [fɛn] das; ~[e]s, ~e (bes. nordd.) fen

Fennek ['fɛnɛk] der; ~s, ~s od. ~e fennec

Fenster ['fɛnstɐ] das; ~s, ~ (auch DV) window; **im ~ liegen** be leaning out of the window; **[sein] Geld zum ~ hinauswerfen** (fig.) throw [one's] money down the drain; **weg vom ~ sein** (ugs.) be right out of it

Fenster-: ~**bank** die window-sill; window-ledge; ~**bogen** der (Archit.) window arch; ~**brett** das s. ~**bank**; ~**brief[umschlag]** der window envelope; ~**brüstung** die window breast; ~**flügel** der [side of a/the] window; ~**front** die window frontage; ~**gips** der (Med.) fenstrated plaster; ~**gitter** das window grille or grating; ~**glas** das a) o. Pl. window glass; b) Pl. ~**gläser** (ungeschliffenes Glas) plain glass; **eine Brille aus ~glas** glasses with plain glass lenses; ~**griff** der window catch; ~**kitt** der window putty; ~**klappe** die shutter opening; ~**kreuz** das mullion and transom; ~**kurbel** die window handle; ~**laden** der [window] shutter; ~**leder** das wash-leather

fensterln ['fɛnstɐln] itr. V. (bes. südd., österr.) climb through one's sweetheart's window

fenster-, Fenster-: ~**los** Adj. windowless; ~**nische** die window recess; ~**öffnung** die window opening; ~**platz** der window-seat; seat by the window; ~**putzer** der window-cleaner; ~**rahmen** der window-frame; ~**ritze** die gap between window-pane and frame; ~**rose** die (Archit.) rose window; ~**scheibe** die window-pane; ~**sims** der od. das s. ~**bank**; ~**sturz** der a) **der Prager ~sturz** (Hist.) the Defenestration of Prague; b) (~abschluß) [window] lintel; ~**verband** der (Med.) fenestrated dressing

Ferial·tag [fe'ria:l-] der (österr.) s. **Ferientag**

Ferien ['fe:ri̯ən] Pl. a) (Arbeitspause) holiday (Brit.); vacation (Amer.); (Werks~) shut-down; holiday (Brit.); (Parlaments~) recess; (Hochschul~) vacation; **in den großen/während der großen ~:** in/during the summer holidays/vacation; **~ haben** have a or be on holiday/vacation; **das Parlament geht in die ~:** parliament goes into recess; b) (Urlaub) holiday[s pl.] (Brit.); vacation (Amer.); **in die ~ fahren** go on holiday/vacation

Ferien-: holiday... (Brit.); vacation... (Amer.); s. auch **Urlaubs-**

Ferien-: ~**arbeit** die vacation work; **eine ~arbeit** a vacation job; ~**aufenthalt** der holiday (Brit.); vacation (Amer.); ~**beginn** der start of the school holidays/vacation; ~**dorf** das holiday/vacation village; ~**erlebnis** das holiday/vacation experience; ~**gast** der holiday/vacation guest; ~**haus** das holiday/vacation house; ~**heim** das holiday/vacation home; ~**kind** das child on a state-subsidized holiday/vacation in the country or at the seaside; ~**kolonie** die [children's] holiday/vacation camp; ~**kurs** der vacation course; ~**lager** das holiday/vacation camp; ~**ordnung** die holiday/vacation dates pl.; ~**ort** der holiday/vacation resort; **ein idyllischer ~ort** an idyllic holiday/vacation spot or spot for a holiday/vacation; ~**paradies** das holiday[-maker's]/vacation[er's] paradise; ~**reise** die holiday/vacation trip; ~**sonder·zug** der special holiday/vacation train; holiday/vacation special; ~**tag** der day [of one's holiday (Brit.) or (Amer.) vacation]; ~**zeit** die holiday (Brit.); vacation (Amer.); **zu Beginn der ~zeit** at the beginning of the holidays/vacation; ~**zentrum** das holiday/vacation centre or resort

Ferkel ['fɛrkl̩] das; ~s, ~ a) (junges Schwein) piglet; b) (ugs. abwertend) pig; **du [altes] ~!** you [dirty] pig!

Ferkelei die; ~, ~en (ugs. abwertend) (Benehmen) filthy behaviour; (Bemerkung) dirty remark; **seine ~en** his filth sing. or smut sing.

ferkeln itr. V. a) (Ferkel werfen) farrow; b) (ugs. abwertend) be filthy

Fermate [fɛr'ma:tə] die; ~, ~n (Musik) pause

Ferment [fɛr'mɛnt] das; ~[e]s, ~e (veralt.) ferment (arch.); enzyme

Fermentation [fɛrmɛnta'tsio:n] die; ~, ~en fermentation

fermentieren tr. V. ferment

fern [fɛrn] **1.** Adj. a) (räumlich) distant, far-off, faraway ⟨country, region, etc.⟩; b) (zeitlich) distant ⟨past, future⟩; **eine Geschichte aus ~en Tagen** a story from far-off days; **in [nicht allzu] ~er Zukunft** in the [not too] distant future; **der Tag ist nicht mehr ~:** the day is not far off; **der Frieden ist ~er denn je** peace is farther away than ever. **2.** adv. **~ von der Heimat [sein/leben]** [be/live] far from home; **etw. von ~ betrachten** look at sth. from a distance; **von ~ betrachtet** (fig.) looked at from a distance; **so von ~ betrachtet würde ich ...:** looking at it from a distance, I should ...; **das sei ~ von mir, daß ich dich jemals verraten werde** (geh.) heaven forbid that I should ever betray you; s. auch **Osten c**; **nahe 2a. 3.** Präp. mit Dat. (geh.) far [away] from; a long way from; **~ der Heimat [leben]** [live] far from home or a long way from home

fern-, Fern-: ~**ab** [-'-] (geh.) **1.** Adv. far away; **~ab von aller Zivilisation** far [away] from all civilization; **2.** Präp. mit Dat. **~ab aller Zivilisation** far [away] from all civilization; ~**amt** das (veralt.) telephone exchange; ~**auslöser** der (Fot.) remote shutter release; ~**bahn** die main-line railway; ~**bahn·hof** der main-line station; ~**beben** das (Geol.) distant earthquake; ~**bedienung** die remote control; ~**bereich** der (bes. Fot.) distance; ~|**bleiben** unr. itr. V.; mit sein (geh.) stay away; **dem Unterricht ~bleiben** stay away from lessons; ~**blick** der view

ferne in von ~ (geh.) from far off or away

Ferne die; ~, ~n a) (räumlich) distance; **etw. in weiter ~ erblicken** see sth. in the far distance; **ein Gruß aus der ~:** greetings from afar or far away; **in die ~ ziehen** (geh.) travel to far-off parts [of the world]; b) (Zukunft) future; (Vergangenheit) past; **das liegt noch/schon in weiter ~:** that is still far off or a long time away/that was a long time ago

ferner Adv. a) in addition; furthermore; **er rangiert unter „~ liefen"** (fig.) he is an also-ran; b) (geh.: künftig) in [the] future; **auch ~ etw. tun** continue to do sth.

ferner... Adj. (Papierdt.) further

ferner·hin Adv. a) in [the] future; **wir werden ihn auch ~ unterstützen** we shall continue to support him. b) s. **ferner a**

fern-, Fern-: ~**fahrer** der long-distance lorry-driver (Brit.) or (Amer.) trucker; ~**fahrer·lokal** das transport café; ~**fahrt**

die long run *or* trip; **~flug der** long-distance *or* long-haul flight; **~gelenkt** *Adj.* remote-controlled; *(fig.: durch Geheimdienste usw.)* controlled; **eine ~gelenkte Rakete** a guided missile; **~geschoß das** *(Milit.)* long-range missile; **~gespräch das** long-distance call; trunk call; **ein ~gespräch mit jmdm./London führen** speak to *or* with sb./ London long-distance; **~gesteuert** *Adj. s.* **~gelenkt; ~glas das;** *Pl.* **~gläser** binoculars *pl.;* **etw. mit dem ~glas erkennen** make sth. out with binoculars; **~|gucken** *itr. V. (ugs.)* watch telly *(coll.) or* the box *(coll.);* **~|halten 1.** *unr. tr. V.* **jmdn./etw. von jmdm./etw. ~halten** keep sb./sth. away from sb./sth.; **2.** *unr. refl. V.* **sich von jmdm./ etw. ~halten** keep away from sb./sth.; **~heizung die** district heating system; **~her** *Adv. (geh.)* **[von] ~her** from afar; **~hin** *Adv. (geh.)* far off; **~kopierer der** fax machine; **~kurs[us] der** correspondence course; **~laster der** *(ugs.)* long-distance lorry *(Brit.) or (Amer.)* truck; **~last·fahrer der** long-distance lorry-driver *(Brit.) or (Amer.)* trucker; **~last·zug der** [long-distance] articulated lorry; **~lehr·gang der** correspondence course; **~leihe die a)** *(Dienststelle)* inter-library loans department; **b)** *(Leihverkehr)* inter-library loan system; **ein Buch über [die] ~leihe bestellen** order a book through inter-library loans; **~leitung die a)** *(Postw.)* long-distance line; **b)** *(Energiewirtsch.)* long-distance cable; **~|lenken** *tr. V.* operate by remote control; **~lenkung die** remote control; **~lenk·waffen** *Pl.* guided missiles; **~licht das** *(Kfz-W.)* full beam; **das ~licht anhaben** drive on full beam; **~|liegen** *unr. itr. V.* **das liegt mir ~:** that is the last thing I want to do; **es liegt mir ~, das zu tun** I shouldn't dream of doing that

Fern·melde-: ~amt das telephone exchange; **~gebühren** *Pl.* telephone charges; **~netz das** telecommunications network; **~satellit der** communications satellite; **~technik die;** *o. Pl.* telecommunications *sing., no art.;* **~truppe die** *(Milit.)* signal corps; **~turm der** telecommunications tower; **~verkehr der** telecommunication; **~wesen das** telecommunications *pl.*

fern-, Fern-: ~mündlich 1. *Adj.; nicht präd.* telephone ⟨*communication*⟩; **2.** *adv.* by telephone; **~ost** *o. Art.* Far East; **in/ nach ~ost** in/to the Far East; **~östlich** *Adj.; nicht präd.* Far Eastern; **eine ~östliche Schönheit** an oriental beauty; **~rohr das** telescope; **~ruf der** telephone number; **~ruf: 45678** telephone *or* tel.: 45678; **~schach das** correspondence chess; **~schaltung die** remote control system; **durch ~schaltung** by remote control; **~schreiben das** telex [message]; **~schreiber der** telex [machine]; teleprinter; **~schriftlich 1.** *Adj.; nicht präd.* telex ⟨*message*⟩; **2.** *adv.* by telex; **~schuß der** *(Ballspiele)* long-range shot

Fernseh-: ~ansager der, ~ansagerin die television announcer; **~anstalt die** television organization; **~antenne die** television aerial *(Brit.) or (Amer.)* antenna; **~apparat der** television [set]; **~aufzeichnung die** telerecording; **~diskussion die** [television] discussion programme; **~empfang der** television reception

fern|sehen *unr. itr. V.* watch television

Fern·sehen das; **~s** television; **im ~:** on television; **vom** *od.* **im ~ übertragen werden** be televised; be shown on television; **das ~ brachte eine Sendung über ...** *(Akk.)* they showed a programme about ... on television

Fern·seher der; **~s, ~** *(ugs.)* **a)** *(Gerät)* telly *(Brit. coll.);* TV; television; **b)** *(Zuschauer)* [television] viewer

Fernseh-: ~fassung die television version; **~film der** television film; **~gebühren** *Pl.* television licence fee; **~gerät das** television [set]; **~journalist der** television reporter; **~kamera die** television camera; **~lotterie die** television lottery; **~programm das a)** *(Sendungen)* television programmes *pl.;* **b)** *(Kanal)* television channel; **c)** *(Blatt, Programmheft)* television [programme] guide; **~publikum das** viewing public; **~reporter der** television reporter; **~satellit der** television satellite; **~schirm der** television screen; **~sender der** television transmitter; **~sendung die** television programme; **~serie die** television series; **~sessel der** television chair; **~spiel das** television play; **~spot der** television commercial; **~sprecher der** *s.* **~ansager; ~studio das** television studio; **~team das** television crew; **~techniker der** television engineer; **~truhe die** cabinet television; **~turm der** television tower; **~übertragung die** television broadcast; **~zuschauer der** television viewer

Fern·sicht die *(Aussicht)* view; *(gute Sicht)* visibility

fern·sichtig *Adj. s.* **weitsichtig**

Fern·sprech- *(bes. Amtsspr.) s.* **Telefon-**

Fernsprech-: ~amt das telephone [area] office; **~ansage·dienst der** telephone information service; **~an·schluß der** telephone; line; **noch keinen ~anschluß haben** not yet be connected to the telephone network; **~apparat der** telephone; **~auftrags·dienst der** telephone services *pl.;* **ich möchte mich vom ~auftragsdienst wecken lassen** I'd like to book an alarm call; **~auskunft die** directory enquiries *sing., no art.;* **eine Telefonnummer über die** *od.* **von der ~auskunft bekommen** get a [telephone] number from *or* through directory enquiries; **~automat der** coinbox telephone; pay phone; **~buch das** telephone book *or* directory

Fern·sprecher der telephone

Fernsprech-: ~gebühren *Pl.* telephone charges; **~nummer die** telephone number; **~säule die** roadside telephone; **~teilnehmer der** telephone subscriber; telephone customer *(Amer.);* **~verbindung die** telephone connection *or* link; **~verkehr der** telephone communication; **~zelle die** telephone-booth *or (Brit.)* -box; call-box *(Brit.)*

fern-, Fern-: ~|stehen *unr. itr. V. (geh.)* **jmdm. ~stehen** not be on close terms with sb.; **~|steuern** *tr. V. s.* **~lenken; ~steuerung die** *(Technik)* remote control; *(fig.: durch Geheimdienste usw.)* control; **~straße die** [principal] trunk road; major road; **~studium das a)** *(Studium ohne personale Medien)* correspondence course; ≈ Open University course *(Brit.);* **b)** *(DDR)* extramural studies *pl.;* **~trauung die** marriage by proxy; **~universität die** ≈ Open University *(Brit.);* **~unterricht der** correspondence courses *pl.;* **~verkehr der** long-distance traffic; **~verkehrs·mittel das** form of long-distance transport; **~verkehrs·straße die** *s.* **~straße; ~wahl die** *(Postw.)* [automatic] trunk dialling; long-distance dialling; **~wärme die** district heating; **~weh das** *(geh.)* wanderlust; **~ziel das a)** *(zeitlich)* long-term aim; **etw. als ~ziel anstreben** aim for sth. in the long term; **b)** *(räumlich)* distant destination; **~zug der** long-distance train

Ferrit [fɛ'ri:t] **der;** **~s, ~e** ferrite

Ferrit·antenne die ferrite-rod aerial *or (Amer.)* antenna

Ferro- [fɛro-] ferro-

Ferro·magnetismus der ferromagnetism

Ferse ['fɛrzə] **die;** **~, ~n** heel; **jmdm. in die ~n treten** kick sb. in the heel; *(fig.)* **sich an jmds. ~n** *(Akk.)***/sich jmdm. an die ~n heften** stick [hard] on sb.'s heels; **jmdm. [dicht] auf den ~n sitzen** *od.* **sein** *(ugs.)* be [hard *or* close] on sb.'s heels; **jmdm. auf den ~n bleiben** stick on sb.'s heels; stay on sb.'s tail; **ich habe die Polizei auf den ~n** *(ugs.)* the police are on my tail; **er hatte Löcher in den ~n** he had holes in the heels of his socks

Fersen-: ~bein das *(Anat.)* heel bone; calcaneum; **~geld** *in* **~geld geben** *(ugs. scherzh.)* take to one's heels

fertig ['fɛrtɪç] *Adj.* **a)** *(völlig hergestellt)* finished ⟨*manuscript, picture, etc.*⟩; **das Essen ist ~:** lunch/dinner *etc.* is ready; **und ~ ist der Lack** *od.* **die Laube** *(ugs.)* and there you are; and bob's your uncle *(Brit. coll.);* **b)** *nicht attr. (zu Ende)* finished; **[mit etw.] ~ sein/werden** have finished/finish [sth.]; **bist du ~?** have you finished?; **mit jmdm. ~ sein** *(ugs.)* be finished *or* through with sb.; **mit etw. ~ werden** *(fig.)* cope with sth.; **sie wird mit dem Jungen einfach nicht mehr ~** *(ugs.)* she cannot cope with the boy any more; **c)** *nicht attr. (bereit, verfügbar)* ready **(zu, für** for); **zum Abmarsch/Start ~ sein** be ready to march/ready for take-off; **auf die Plätze – ~ – los!** on your marks, get set, go! *(Sport); (bei Kindern auch:)* ready, steady, go!; **d)** *nicht attr. (ugs.: erschöpft)* shattered *(coll.);* **mit den Nerven ~ sein** be at the end of one's tether; **e)** *meist attr. (reif)* mature ⟨*person, artist, etc.*⟩

fertig-, Fertig-: ~bau der; *Pl.* **~ten a)** *(Gebäude)* prefabricated building; **b)** *o. Pl. (Herstellung)* prefabricated building; prefabrication; **~bau·weise die** prefabricated construction; prefabrication; **etw. in ~bauweise errichten** build sth. by the prefabricated method; **~|bekommen** *unr. tr. V.,* **~|bringen** *unr. tr. V.* **a)** *(imstande sein zu)* manage; **so etwas bringst auch nur du ~!** *(iron.)* only you could manage to do a thing like that!; **ich brächte es nicht ~, jmdn. zu erschießen** I couldn't bring myself to shoot anybody; **der bringt das ~!** *(iron.)* I wouldn't put it past him; **sie bringt es ~ und sagt ihr das** she is capable of saying that to her; **b)** *(zu Ende bringen)* finish

fertigen *tr. V.* make; **von Hand/maschinell gefertigte Waren** hand-made/machine-produced goods

Fertig-: ~erzeugnis das, ~fabrikat das finished product; **~gericht das** ready-to-serve meal; **ein ~gericht aus der Dose** a meal out of *or* from a tin *(Brit.) or (Amer.)* can; **~haus das** prefabricated house; prefab *(coll.)*

Fertigkeit die; **~, ~en** skill; **eine ~ in etw.** *(Dat.)* **haben** be skilled in *or* at sth.; **~ im Zeichnen/Nähen** skill in *or* at drawing/sewing

fertig-, Fertig-: ~|kriegen *tr. V. (ugs.) s.* **~bringen; ~|machen** *tr. V.* **a)** *(ugs.: beenden)* finish ⟨*task, job, etc.*⟩; **b)** *(ugs.: bereitmachen)* get ⟨*meals, beds*⟩ ready; **sich für etw. ~machen** get ready for sth.; **c)** *(erschöpfen)* **jmdn. ~machen** wear sb. out; *(durch Schikanen)* wear sb. down; **der Lärm macht mich [ganz] ~:** that noise is getting me down; **d)** *(deprimieren)* **jmdn. ~machen** get sb. down; **e)** *(salopp: zusammenschlagen, töten)* **jmdn. ~machen** do sb. in *(sl.);* **f)** *(ugs.: zurechtweisen)* **jmdn. ~machen** tear sb. off a strip *(sl.);* **~produkt das** finished product; **~|stellen** *tr. V.* complete; finish; **~stellung die** completion; **~teil das** prefabricated part

Fertigung die; **~:** production; manufacture

Fertigungs- production

Fertigungs-: ~kosten *Pl.* production *or* manufacturing costs; **~verfahren das** production *or* manufacturing process

Fertig·ware die finished product

Fertilität [fɛrtili'tɛ:t] **die;** **~** *(Biol., Med.)* fertility

¹Fes [fe:s] **der**; ~[es], ~[e] fez
fes, ²Fes [fɛs] **das**; ~, ~ *(Musik)* F flat
fesch [fɛʃ] *Adj.* **a)** *(bes. österr.: hübsch)* smart ‹*woman, suit, etc.*›; **b)** *(österr.: nett)* good; **sei ~ und komm mit!** be a sport and come too!
¹Fessel ['fɛsl] **die**; ~, ~n *meist Pl. (auch fig.)* fetter; shackle; *(Kette)* chain; **jmdm. ~n anlegen,** *(geh.)* **jmdn. in ~n legen** fetter sb./put sb. in chains
²Fẹssel die; ~, ~n *(Anat.)* **a)** *(bei Huftieren)* pastern; **b)** *(bei Menschen)* ankle
Fẹssel-: ~ballon der captive balloon; **~gelenk das** *(Zool.)* pastern-joint
fẹsseln *tr. V.* **a)** tie up; *(mit Ketten)* chain up; **jmdn. an etw.** *(Akk.)* **~:** tie/chain sb. to sth.; **jmdn. an Händen und Füßen ~:** tie sb. hand and foot; **jmdm. die Hände auf den Rücken ~:** tie sb.'s hands behind his/her back; **ans Bett/Haus/an den Rollstuhl gefesselt sein** *(fig.)* be confined to [one's] bed/tied to the house/confined to a wheelchair; **jmdn. an sich** *(Akk.)* **~** *(fig.)* bind sb. to oneself; **b)** *(faszinieren)* ‹*book*› grip; ‹*work, person*› fascinate; ‹*personality*› captivate; ‹*idea*› possess; **das Buch hat mich so gefesselt** I was so gripped by the book; **jmdn. durch etw. ~:** captivate sb. with sth.
Fẹsselung, Fẹßlung die; ~, ~en *(Schach)* block
fest [fɛst] **1.** *Adj.* **a)** *(nicht flüssig od. gasförmig)* solid; **~e Nahrung** solid food; **~e Gestalt** *od.* **Form[en] annehmen** take on a definite shape; **b)** *(straff)* firm, tight ‹*bandage*›; **c)** *(kräftig)* firm ‹*handshake*›; *(tief)* sound ‹*sleep*›; **d)** *(haltbar, solide)* sturdy ‹*shoes*›; tough, strong ‹*fabric*›; solid ‹*house, shell*›; **e)** *(energisch)* firm ‹*tread*›; steady ‹*voice*›; **eine ~e Hand brauchen** *(fig.)* need a firm hand; **f)** *(unbeirrbar)* **der ~en Überzeugung** *od.* **Meinung sein, daß ...:** be firmly convinced *or* of the firm opinion that ...; **g)** *(endgültig)* firm ‹*appointment, date*›; **eine ~e Zusage machen** make a firm *or* definite commitment; *s. auch* **Fuß b**; **h)** *nicht präd. (konstant)* fixed, permanent ‹*address*›; fixed ‹*income*›; **einen ~en Freund/eine ~e Freundin haben** have a steady boyfriend/girlfriend; **in ~en Händen sein** *(fig.)* be spoken for; **einen ~en Platz in etw.** *(Dat.)* **haben** *(fig.)* be firmly established in sth.; **i)** *(Milit. veralt.)* fortified ‹*position*›. **2.** *adv.* **a)** *(straff)* ‹*tie, grip*› tight[ly]; **b)** *(ugs. auch* **~e)** *(tüchtig)* ‹*work*› with a will; ‹*eat*› heartily; ‹*sleep*› soundly; **~ zuschlagen** plant a solid punch; **er schläft [gerade] ~:** he is fast asleep; **~ zulangen** tuck in; **~ feiern** have a real celebration; **immer ~[e] drauf** *od.* **druff!** *(salopp)* get stuck in! *(sl.)*; let him/them have it!; **c)** *(unbeirrbar)* ‹*believe, be convinced*› firmly; **sich auf jmdn./etw. ~ verlassen** rely one hundred per cent on sb./sth.; **d)** *(endgültig)* firmly; definitely; **etw. ~ vereinbaren** come to a firm *or* definite arrangement about sth.; **e)** *(auf Dauer)* permanently; **~ angestellt sein** be permanently employed *or* a permanent member of staff; **~ befreundet sein** be close friends; *(als Paar)* be going steady; **jmdn. ~ einstellen** give sb. a permanent job; employ sb. as a permanent member of staff
Fẹst das; ~[e]s, ~e **a)** *(Veranstaltung)* celebration; *(Party)* party; **man muß die ~e feiern, wie sie fallen** you don't get a chance for a celebration every day of the week; **es ist mir ein ~** *(scherzh.)* [it's] my pleasure; **b)** *(Feiertag)* festival; *(Kirchen~)* feast; festival; **bewegliches/unbewegliches ~:** movable/immovable feast; **frohes ~!** happy Christmas/Easter!
fẹst-, Fẹst-: ~akt der ceremony; **~angestellt** *Adj. (präd. getrennt geschrieben)* permanent; **~angestellte der/die**; *adj. Dekl.* permanent employee; **~ansprache die** address; **~|backen** *itr. V. (landsch.)* stick; **~|beißen** *unr. refl. V.* **sich in etw.** *(Dat.)* **~beißen** ‹*dog etc.*› sink its teeth firmly into sth.; **sich an einem Problem ~beißen** *(fig.)* get bogged down in a problem; **~beleuchtung die** festive lighting; **in ~beleuchtung erstrahlen** be ablaze with festive illuminations; **~besoldet** *Adj. (präd. getrennt geschrieben)* full-time [and] salaried; **~besoldete der/die**; *adj. Dekl.* full-time member of staff; **~|binden** *unr. tr. V.* tie [up]; **etw. an einem Baum/Pfosten ~binden** tie sth. to a tree/post; **~|bleiben** *unr. itr. V.; mit sein* stand firm; **~|drehen** *tr. V.* screw [up] tight
fẹste *Adv. (ugs.) s.* **fest 2 b**
Fẹste die; ~, ~n *(veralt.)* fortress; castle
fẹst-, Fẹst-: ~essen das banquet; **~|fahren** *unr. itr., refl. V. (itr. V. mit sein)* get stuck; *(fig.)* get bogged down; **der Wagen hat sich** *od.* **ist ~gefahren** the car got stuck; **~|fressen** *unr. refl. V.* **a)** *(sich verklemmen)* ‹*engine*› seize up; ‹*saw*› get stuck; **b)** *(fig.: sich einprägen)* **sich in jmdm. ~fressen** become fixed in sb.'s mind; **~|frieren** *unr. itr. V.; mit sein* freeze up; freeze solid; **~gabe die** *(geh.)* gift; **~gefügt** *Adj.* firmly established; **~gelage das** *s.* **Gelage**; **~geld das** *(Bankw.)* time deposit; **~gottes·dienst der** festival service; **~|haken 1.** *tr. V. (befestigen)* hook up; **etw. an etw.** *(Dat.)* **~haken** hook sth. to sth.; **2.** *refl. V.* get caught (**an** + *Dat.* on); **~halle die** festival hall; **~|halten 1.** *unr. tr. V.* **a)** *(halten, packen)* hold on to; **jmdn. am Arm ~halten** hold on to sb.'s arm; **etw. mit den Händen ~halten** hold sth. in one's hands; **b)** *(nicht weiterleiten)* withhold ‹*letter, parcel, etc.*›; **c)** *(verhaftet haben)* hold, detain ‹*suspect*›; **d)** *(aufzeichnen, fixieren)* record; capture; **etw. in Bild und Ton ~halten** record *or* capture sth. in sound and vision; **etw. mit der Kamera ~halten** capture sth. with the camera; **e)** *(konstatieren)* record; **~halten, daß ...:** record the fact that ...; **2.** *unr. refl. V. (sich anklammern)* **sich an jmdm./etw. ~halten** hold on to sb./sth.; **halt dich ~!** hold tight!; *(fig. ugs.)* brace yourself!; **3.** *unr. itr. V.* **an jmdm./etw. ~halten** stand by sb./sth.; **~|hängen** *unr. itr. V.* get caught; **[mit etw.] an/in etw.** *(Dat.)* **~hängen** get [sth.] caught on/in sth.
festigen ['fɛstɪgn̩] **1.** *tr. V.* strengthen ‹*friendship, alliance, marriage, etc.*›; consolidate ‹*position*›; **in sich** *(Dat.)* **gefestigt sein** be strong. **2.** *refl. V.* ‹*friendship, ties*› become stronger
Fẹstigkeit die; **~ a)** *(Entschlossenheit)* firmness; **b)** *(Standhaftigkeit)* steadfastness; resolution; **sein Ziel mit ~ verfolgen** pursue one's aim with [great] resolution; **c)** *(von Stoffen)* strength
Fẹstigkeits·lehre die; *o. Pl.* [theory of] strength of materials
Fẹstigung die; **~:** strengthening; *(einer Stellung)* consolidation
Festival ['fɛstivəl] **das**; ~s, ~s festival
Fẹstival·besucher der visitor to a/the festival
Festivität [fɛstivi'tɛ:t] **die**; ~, ~en *(veralt., scherzh.)* festivity; celebration
fẹst-, Fẹst-: ~|klammern 1. *tr. V.* **etw. [an etw.** *(Dat.)***] ~klammern** clip sth. on [to sth.]; **Wäsche an der Leine ~klammern** peg washing [up] on the line; **2.** *refl. V.* **sich an jmdm./etw. ~klammern** cling [on] to sb./sth.; **~|kleben 1.** *itr. V.; mit sein* stick (**an** + *Dat.* to); **2.** *tr. V.* stick; **etw. an etw.** *(Dat.)* **~kleben** stick sth. to sth.; **~kleid das** evening dress; **die Stadt legte ihr ~kleid an** *(fig. geh.)* the town took on a festive look; **~kleidung die** formal dress; **~|klemmen 1.** *itr. V.; mit sein* **~geklemmt sein** be stuck *or* jammed; **2.** *tr. V.* wedge; jam; **~|klopfen** *tr. V.* bang ‹*nail*› in *or* home; bang ‹*floor-board*› down; *(fig.)* finalize ‹*agreement*›; **~|knoten** *tr. V.* **etw. an etw.** *(Dat.)* **~knoten** tie sth. to sth.; **~komitee das** festival committee; **~komma das** *(DV)* fixed point; **~körper der** *(Physik)* solid; **~körper·physik die** solid-state physics *sing., no art.*; **~|krallen** *refl. V.* **sich in etw.** *(Dat.)* **~krallen** dig its claws into sth.; **sich an jmdm. ~krallen** cling to sb. with its claws; ‹*person*› cling [on] to sb.; **~land das**; *o. Pl.* **a)** *(Kontinent)* continent; *(im Gegensatz zu den Inseln)* mainland; **das europäische ~land** the continent of Europe/the European mainland; **b)** *(fester Boden)* land; **auf dem ~land** on dry land; **~ländisch** *Adj.; nicht präd.* **a)** *(kontinental)* continental ‹*climate, shelf, etc.*›; **b)** *(im Gegensatz zu den Inseln)* mainland *attrib.*; **~land[s]·sockel der** *(Geogr.)* continental shelf; **~|laufen 1.** *unr. itr., refl. V. (itr. V. mit sein)* ‹*ship*› run aground, get stuck; ‹*wheels*› jam, get jammed; *(fig.)* ‹*negotiations*› reach a deadlock; ‹*policy*› get bogged down; **das Schiff hat sich** *od.* **ist im Packeis ~gelaufen** the ship has got stuck in the pack-ice; **2.** *refl. V. (Sport)* **die Stürmer liefen sich immer wieder ~:** the forwards could not find a way through [the defence]; **~legbar** *Adj.* **das ist [nicht] eindeutig ~legbar** it can[not] definitely be established; **~|legen** *tr. V.* **a)** *(verbindlich regeln)* fix ‹*time, deadline, price*›; arrange ‹*programme*›; **etw. gesetzlich ~legen** prescribe sth. by law; **b)** *(verpflichten)* **sich [auf etw.** *(Akk.)***] ~legen [lassen]** commit oneself [to sth.]; **jmdn. [auf etw.** *(Akk.)***] ~legen** tie sb. down [to sth.]; **c)** *(Bankw.)* tie up ‹*money*›; **~legung die**; ~, ~en *s.* **~legen: a)** fixing; arrangement; **b)** commitment
fẹstlich 1. *Adj.* **a)** festive ‹*atmosphere*›; **b)** *(einem Fest gemäß)* formal ‹*dress*›. **2.** *adv.* **a)** festively; **b)** *(einem Fest gemäß)* formally; **etw. ~ begehen** celebrate sth.
Fẹstlichkeit die; ~, ~en **a)** *(Feier)* celebration; **b)** *(der Stimmung, Atmosphäre)* festiveness; *(Feierlichkeit, Würde)* solemnity
fẹst-, Fẹst-: ~|liegen *unr. itr. V.* **a)** *(nicht weiterkommen)* be stuck; **b)** *(~stehen)* have been fixed; ‹*programme*› have been arranged; **c)** *(Bankw.)* ‹*money*› be tied up; **~|machen 1.** *tr. V.* **a)** *(befestigen)* fix; *(fig.)* demonstrate ‹*characteristic, fault*›; **b)** *(fest vereinbaren)* arrange ‹*meeting etc.*›; **c)** *(Seemannsspr.)* moor ‹*boat*›; **2.** *itr. V. (Seemannsspr.) s.* **anlegen 2 a**; **~mahl das** *(geh.)* banquet; **~meter der** *od.* **das** cubic metre *(of solid timber)*; **~|nageln** *tr. V.* **a)** *(befestigen)* nail (**an** + *Dat.* to); **wie ~genagelt dastehen** *(ugs.)* stand there as though rooted to the spot; **b)** *(ugs.: festlegen)* **jmdn. [auf etw.** *(Akk.)***] ~nageln** tie sb. down [to sth.]; **sich auf etw.** *(Akk.)* **~nageln lassen** let oneself be tied [down] to sth.; **~nahme die**; ~, ~n arrest; **bei seiner ~nahme** when he was/is arrested; **~|nehmen** *unr. tr. V.* arrest; **jmdn. vorläufig ~nehmen** take sb. into custody
Feston [fɛs'tõ:] **das**; ~s, ~s festoon
fẹst-, Fẹst-: ~platte die *(DV)* fixed disc; **~platz der** fairground; **~preis der** *(Wirtsch.)* fixed price; **~programm das** festival programme; **~rede die** speech; **~redner der** speaker; **~|rennen** *unr. refl. V.* **a)** *(ugs.)* get tangled up; **b)** *(Sport) s.* **~laufen 2**; **~saal der** banqueting hall; *(Ballsaal)* ballroom; **~|saugen** *regelm. (auch unr.) refl. V.* attach itself (**an** + *Dat.* to); **~schmaus der** *(veralt.)* banquet; feast; **~schmuck der** festive decorations *pl.*; **im ~schmuck erstrahlen** be festively decorated; **~|schnallen** *tr. V.* tie (**an** + *Dat.* to); **der Pilot schnallte sich am Sitz ~:** the pilot strapped *or* fastened himself in; **~|schrauben** *tr. V.* screw [up] tight; **~|schreiben** *unr. tr. V.* establish; **~|schrift die** commemorative volume; *(für Gelehrten)* Festschrift; **~|setzen 1.** *tr. V.* **a)**

(~legen) fix ‹*time, deadline, price*›; lay down ‹*duties*›; **b)** *(in Haft nehmen)* detain; **2.** *refl. V.* **a)** ‹*dust*› collect, settle; ‹*idea*› take root; **diese Idee hat sich bei ihm ~gesetzt** this idea has become fixed in his mind; **b)** *(ugs.: sich niederlassen)* establish oneself; **~setzung die; ~, ~en** *s.* **~setzen 1: a)** fixing; laying down; **b)** *(selten)* detention; **~|sitzen** *unr. itr. V.* **a)** *(haften)* be stuck; **b)** *(nicht mehr weiterkommen)* be stuck; **~spiel das a)** *Pl.* festival; **die Bayreuther/ Edinburger ~spiele** the Bayreuth/Edinburgh Festival *sing.*; **b)** *(Bühnenstück)* festival production; **~spiel·haus das** festival theatre; **~|stecken 1.** *tr. V. (befestigen)* pin up; **2.** *regelm. (auch unr.) itr. V. (nicht weiterkommen)* be stuck; **~|stehen** *unr. itr. V.* **a)** *(~gelegt sein)* ‹*order, appointment, etc.*› have been fixed; **b)** *(unumstößlich sein)* ‹*decision*› be definite; ‹*fact*› be certain; **~ steht** *od.* **es steht ~, daß ...:** it is certain *or* definite that ...; **es steht ~, daß sie keine Chance haben** they certainly have no chance; **~stellbar** *Adj.* **a)** *(zu ermitteln)* ascertainable; **die Ursache ist nicht mehr ~stellbar** the cause can no longer be ascertained *or* established; **b)** *(wahrnehmbar)* detectable; diagnosable ‹*illness*›; **c)** *(arretierbar)* lockable; securable ‹*lock*›; **~|stellen** *tr. V.* **a)** *(ermitteln)* establish ‹*identity, age, facts*›; **das läßt sich [nicht] mit Sicherheit ~stellen** it can[not] be established with certainty *or* for certain; **b)** *(wahrnehmen)* detect; diagnose ‹*illness*›; **er stellte ~, daß er sich geirrt hatte** he realized that he was wrong; **sie mußte ~stellen, daß ...:** she realized that ...; **die Ärzte konnten nur noch den Tod ~stellen** all the doctors could do was [to] confirm that the patient/victim *etc.* was dead; **c)** *(aussprechen)* state ‹*fact*›; **ich muß ~stellen, daß ...:** I must *or* am bound to say that ...; **d)** *(arretieren)* secure, lock ‹*moving part*›; secure ‹*lock*›

Fẹststell-: ~hebel der locking lever; **~taste die** shift lock

Fẹst·stellung die a) *(Ermittlung)* establishment; **b)** *(Wahrnehmung)* realization; **die ~ machen, daß ...:** realize that ...; **c)** *(Erklärung)* statement; **die ~ treffen, daß ...:** observe that ...

Fẹst-: ~stimmung die festive atmosphere *or* mood; **~stoff·rakete die** solid-fuel rocket; **~tafel die** *(geh.)* banquet table

Fẹst·tag der a) holiday; *(Kirchenfest)* [religious] feast-day; *(Ehrentag)* special day; **b)** *(Festspieltag)* [day of a/the] festival; **die Berliner ~e** the Berlin Festival *sing.*

Fẹsttags·stimmung die festive atmosphere *or* mood

fẹst-: ~|treten *unr. tr. V.* tread down; **das tritt sich ~:** don't worry, it's good for the carpet *(iron.)*; **~umrissen** *Adj. (präd. getrennt geschrieben)* clear-cut; definite

Fẹstung die; ~, ~en a) *(Verteidigungsanlage)* fortress; **b)** *(hist.: Haft)* imprisonment [in a fortress]

Fẹstungs-: ~anlage die fortification; **~graben der** moat; **~haft die** *(hist.)* imprisonment [in a fortress]; **~mauer die** wall of a/the fortress

fẹst-, Fẹst-: ~veranstaltung die official function; **~verwurzelt** *Adj. (präd. getrennt geschrieben) (auch fig.)* deep-rooted; **~verzinslich** *Adj. (Bankw.)* fixed-interest *attrib.*; fixed-income *attrib.*; **~vortrag der** lecture; **~|wachsen** *unr. itr. V.; mit sein* **an** *od.* **auf etw.** *(Dat.)* **~wachsen** grow on [to] sth.; **~wiese die** festival site; **~zeit die** holiday *(Brit.)* or *(Amer.)* vacation [period]; **~zelt das** marquee; **~|ziehen** *unr. tr. V.* pull tight; **~zug der** procession

fetal [fe'ta:l] *Adj. (Med.)* foetal

Fete ['fe:tə] **die; ~, ~n** *(ugs.)* party; **eine ~ geben** *od.* **feiern** have *or* throw a party

Fetisch ['fe:tɪʃ] **der; ~s, ~e** *(Völkerk., fig.)* fetish

Fetischịsmus der; ~: fetishism *no art.*

Fetischịst der; ~en, ~en fetishist

fett [fɛt] **1.** *Adj.* **a)** *(~reich)* fatty ‹*food*›; **~er Speck** fat bacon; **das Fleisch war zu ~:** there was too much fat on the meat; **b)** *(sehr dick)* fat; **c)** *(ugs.: üppig, reich)* fat ‹*inheritance, wallet*›; **~e Jahre/Zeiten** rich years/good times; **~e Beute machen** make a rich haul; **d)** *(ertragreich)* rich ‹*soil*›; luxuriant ‹*vegetation*›; **e)** *(Druckw.)* bold; *(breiter, größer)* extra bold; **etw. ~ drucken** print sth. in bold/extra bold [type]. **2.** *adv.* **~ essen** eat fatty foods; **~ kochen** use a lot of fat [in cooking]; **~ lachen** guffaw

Fẹtt das; ~[e]s, ~e a) fat; **pflanzliche/tierische ~e** vegetable/animal fats; *(fig.)* **das ~ abschöpfen** *(ugs.)* cream off the best; **sein ~ [ab]bekommen** *od.* **[ab]kriegen** *(ugs.)* get one's come-uppance *(Amer.)*; **sein ~ [weg]haben** *(ugs.)* have been put in one's place *or* taught a lesson; **im ~ schwimmen** *(ugs.)* be rolling in it *(coll.)*; **b)** *o. Pl. (~gewebe)* fat; **~ ansetzen** ‹*animal*› fatten up; ‹*person*› put on weight; **die Gans hat viel ~:** the goose has a lot of fat on it; **~ schwimmt oben** *(Spr.)* fat people never drown!; *(fig.)* the rich never suffer

fẹtt-, Fẹtt-: ~ansatz der fat; **er neigt zu ~ansatz** he tends to get fat *or* to put on weight easily; **~arm 1.** *Adj.* low-fat ‹*food*›; low in fat *pred.*; **2.** *adv.* **~arm essen** eat low-fat foods; **~auge das** speck of fat; **~bauch der** *(ugs.)* paunch; fat stomach; **~bedarf der** fat requirement; **~creme die** enriched [skim] cream; **~depot das** *(Physiol.)* fat depot; **~druck der** bold type; **in ~druck** in bold [type]

fẹtten 1. *tr. V. (mit Fett einreiben)* grease. **2.** *itr. V. (Fett absondern)* be greasy

fẹtt-, Fẹtt-: ~film der greasy film; **~fleck[en] der** grease mark *or* spot; **~frei** *Adj.* non-fat; **~gebäck das, ~gebackene das;** *adj. Dekl.* cakes *pl.* fried in fat; **~gedruckt** *Adj. (präd. getrennt geschrieben)* bold; **~gehalt der** fat content; **~geschwulst die** fatty tumour; **~gewebe das** fatty tissue; **~haltig** *Adj.* fatty; **[sehr] ~haltig sein** contain [a lot of] fat; **~henne die** *(Bot.)* stonecrop; **Große ~henne** orpine; **~herz das** fatty heart; fat heart

fẹttig *Adj.* greasy; oily; greasy ‹*skin, saucepan, etc.*›

fẹtt-, Fẹtt-: ~kloß der *(ugs. abwertend)* fatty; fatso *(sl.)*; **~leber die** *(Med.)* fatty liver; **~leibig** *Adj.* obese; **~leibigkeit die; ~:** obesity; **~löslich** *Adj.* fat-soluble; **~näpfchen das** *in* **[bei jmdm.] ins ~näpfchen treten** *(scherzh.)* put one's foot in it [with sb.]; **~polster das** subcutaneous fat *no indef. art.*; fat pad; **~reich 1.** *Adj.* high-fat ‹*food*›; **2.** *adv.* **~reich essen** eat high-fat foods; **~sack der** *(salopp abwertend)* fatso *(sl.)*; **~säure die** *(Chemie)* fatty acid; **~schicht die** layer of fat; **~stift der a)** *(Schreibgerät)* grease pencil; lithographic pencil; **b)** *(Lippenstift)* lip salve; **~stoffwechsel der** fat metabolism; **~sucht die** *(Med.)* obesity; **~triefend** *Adj.* dripping with fat *postpos.*; **~wanst der** *(salopp abwertend)* fatso *(sl.)*; **~wulst der** *od.* **die** roll of fat

Fetus ['fe:tʊs] **der; ~** *od.* **~ses, ~se** *od.* **Fẹten** *(Med.)* foetus

fetzen ['fɛtsn̩] *tr. V. (ugs.)* tear; **die Musik/Platte fetzt unheimlich** *(Jugendspr.)* the music/record is really mind-blowing *(sl.)*

Fẹtzen der; ~s, ~ a) scrap; **die Tapete hängt in ~ von der Wand** the wallpaper is hanging [off the wall] in shreds; **das Kleid ist in ~:** the dress is in tatters; **etw. in ~ [zer]reißen** tear sth. to pieces *or* shreds; **in ~ gehen** *(ugs.)* fall apart *or* to pieces; **daß die ~ fliegen** *(ugs.)* like mad; **b)** *(abwertend: billiges Kleid)* **ein billiger ~:** cheap rags *pl.*

feucht [fɔyçt] *Adj.* damp ‹*cloth, wall, hair*›; tacky ‹*paint*›; humid ‹*climate*›; sweaty, clammy ‹*hands*›; moist ‹*lips*›; lubricated ‹*condom*›; **die ~e Schnauze des Hundes** the dog's wet nose; **Oberhemden müssen ~ gebügelt werden** shirts must be ironed damp; **Gardinen ~ aufhängen** hang curtains while [they are] still damp; **etw. ~ abwischen** wipe sth. with a damp cloth; **eine ~e Aussprache haben** *(scherzh.)* spit when one speaks; **ein ~er Abend** *(fig. ugs.)* a boozy evening *(coll.)*; **~e Augen bekommen** be close to tears; **das geht dich einen ~en Schmutz** *od.* **Kehricht an** *(ugs.)* that's none of your business

Feucht·biotop das *(Ökol.)* wetland

Feuchte die; ~: humidity

feucht-, Feucht-: ~fröhlich *Adj. (ugs. scherzh.)* merry ‹*company*›; boozy *(coll.)* ‹*evening*›; **~gebiet das** wet area; **~heiß** *Adj.* hot and humid

Feuchtigkeit die a) *(leichte Nässe)* moisture; **b)** *(das Feuchtsein)* dampness; **die ~ des Bodens/der Luft** the wetness of the soil/humidity of the air

Feuchtigkeits-: ~creme die *(Kosmetik)* moisturizing cream; moisturizer; **~gehalt der** moisture content; *(der Luft)* humidity; **~grad der** moisture level; *(der Luft)* humidity; **~messer der** hygrometer; **~schutz der** *(Bauw.)* damp protection; protection against damp

feucht-: ~kạlt *Adj.* cold and damp; **~wạrm** *Adj.* muggy; humid

feudal [fɔy'da:l] **1.** *Adj.* **a)** feudal ‹*system*›; **b)** *(aristokratisch)* aristocratic ‹*regiment etc.*›; **c)** *(ugs.: vornehm)* plush ‹*hotel etc.*›. **2.** *adv. (ugs.: vornehm)* **~ essen** have a slap-up meal *(coll.)*; **~ Urlaub machen** have a plush holiday

Feudal-: ~gesellschaft die feudal society; **~herr der** feudal lord; **~herrschaft die** feudalism

Feudalịsmus der; ~: feudalism *no art.*

feudalịstisch *Adj.* feudalistic

Feudal·staat der feudal state

Feuer ['fɔyɐ] **das; ~s, ~ a)** fire; **[ein Gegensatz] wie ~ und Wasser sein** be as different as chalk and cheese; **das Essen aufs ~ stellen/vom ~ nehmen** put the food on to cook/take the food off the heat; **jmdn. um ~ bitten** ask sb. for a light; **jmdm. ~ geben** give sb. a light; **das olympische ~:** the Olympic flame *or* torch; **mit dem ~ spielen** play with fire; **er ist ganz ehrlich, für ihn** *od.* **dafür lege ich die Hand ins ~:** he is totally honest, I'd swear to it; *s. auch* **brennen 2a; b)** *(Brand)* fire; blaze; **~!** fire!; **[für etw.] ~ und Flamme sein** be full of enthusiasm [for sth.]; **~ fangen** catch fire; *(fig.: sich verlieben)* be smitten; *(fig.: sich schnell begeistern)* be fired with enthusiasm; **für jmdn. durchs ~ gehen** go through hell and high water for sb.; **zwischen zwei ~ geraten** be caught between the devil and the deep blue sea; **jmdm. ~ unter dem Hintern machen** *(salopp)* put a squib under sb.; **c)** *o. Pl. (Milit.)* fire; **unter feindliches ~ geraten** come under enemy fire; **das ~ einstellen** cease fire; **jmdn./etw. unter ~ nehmen** fire on sb./sth.; **[gebt] ~!** fire!; **~ frei!** open fire!; **d)** *o. Pl. (Leuchten, Funkeln)* sparkle; blaze; **ihre Augen sprühten ~:** her eyes blazed [with fire]; **e)** *o. Pl. (innerer Schwung)* fire; passion; **das ~ der Jugend** the fire *or* passion of youth; **das Pferd/der Wein hat [viel] ~:** the horse has [a lot of] spirit/the wine is strong and full-bodied

feuer-, Feuer-: ~alarm der fire alarm; **~alarm geben** raise the [fire] alarm; **~anbeter der; ~s, ~** *(Rel.)* fire-worshipper; **~anzünder der; ~s, ~:** fire-lighter; **~befehl der** *(Milit.)* order to fire; **~bekämpfung die** fire-fighting; **~bereit** *Adj. (Milit.)* ready to fire *postpos.*; **~beständig** *Adj.* fire-resistant; **~bestattung die** cremation; **~bock der** fire-dog; andiron; **~bohne die** *(Bot.)* scarlet runner [bean]; **~büchse die a)** *(Technik)* firebox; **b)** *(veralt.: Gewehr)* musket; **~eifer der** enthusiasm; zest; **~einstellung die** cessation of fire; *(Waffenstillstand)* cease-fire; **~fest** *Adj.* heat-resistant ⟨*dish, plate*⟩; fire-proof ⟨*material*⟩; **~flüssig** *Adj.* molten ⟨*rock, lava*⟩; **~gefahr die** fire hazard *or* risk; **bei ~gefahr** when there is a risk of fire; **~gefährlich** *Adj.* [in]flammable; **~gefecht das** gun battle; **~haken der** poker; **~holz das;** *o. Pl.* firewood; **~kult der** fire cult

Fe̲uer·land (das); ~s Tierra del Fuego

Fe̲uerländer der; ~s, ~: Fuegian

Fe̲uer-: ~leiter die *(bei Häusern)* fire escape; *(beim ~wehrauto)* [fireman's] ladder; *(fahrbar)* turntable ladder; **~lösch·boot das** fireboat; **~löscher der;** ~s, ~: fire extinguisher; **~mal das** port-wine mark *or* stain; **~melder der** fire alarm

fe̲uern 1. *tr. V.* **a)** *(ugs.: entlassen)* fire *(coll.)*; sack *(coll.)*; **b)** *(ugs.: schleudern, werfen)* fling; **jmdm. eine ~** *(salopp)* belt sb. one; **c)** *(heizen)* fire ⟨*stove*⟩; **mit Holz ~:** have wood fires. **2.** *itr. V. (Milit.)* fire **(auf** + *Akk.* at)

fe̲uer-, Fe̲uer-: ~patsche die fire-beater; **~pause die** *(Milit.)* lull in the fighting; **~polizei die** *authorities responsible for fire precautions and fire-fighting;* **~probe die a)** *(Prüfung)* test; **die ~probe bestehen** pass the [acid] test; **b)** *(Gottesurteil)* ordeal by fire; **~qualle die** stinging jellyfish; **~rad das a)** *(~werkskörper)* Catherine wheel; **b)** *(Wagenrad)* fire wheel; **~rọt** *Adj.* fiery red; flaming red; **~rot werden** *(fig.)* turn crimson *or* scarlet; **~salamander der** fire salamander; **~säule die** column of fire

Fe̲uers·brunst die *(geh.)* great fire; conflagration

fe̲uer-, Fe̲uer-: ~schein der fiery glow; glow of the/a fire; **~schiff das** lightship; **~schlucker der** fire-eater; **~schutz der a)** *(Brandschutz)* fire prevention *or* protection; **b)** *(Milit.)* covering fire; **jmdm. ~schutz geben** cover sb.; **~sicher 1.** *Adj.* fire-proof; **2.** *adv.* **etw. ~sicher in einem Safe deponieren** deposit sth. in a fire-proof safe; **~sirene die** fire siren; **~speiend** *Adj.; nicht präd.* fire-breathing ⟨*dragon*⟩; ⟨*volcano*⟩ spewing fire; **~spritze die** fire hose; **~stätte die** hearth; **~stein der** flint; **~stelle die** [camp]fire; **~stellung die** *(Milit.)* firing position; **~stuhl der** *(ugs. scherzh.)* [motor]bike *(coll.)*; machine; **~taufe die** baptism of fire; **~teufel der** *(Pressejargon)* arsonist; **~tod der** *(geh.)* [death at] the stake; **den ~tod erleiden** be burnt at the stake; **~treppe die** fire escape; **~über·fall der** armed attack

Fe̲uerung die; ~, ~en **a)** *(Verbrennungsvorrichtung)* firing [system]; **b)** *o. Pl. (das Heizen)* heating; **c)** *o. Pl. (Brennstoff)* fuel

Fe̲uer-: ~versicherung die fire insurance; **~wache die** fire station; **~waffe die** firearm; **~wasser das;** *o. Pl. (ugs.)* firewater *(coll.)*

Fe̲uer·wehr die; ~, ~en fire service; **das ging ja wie die ~** *(ugs.)* that was quick; **der fährt ja wie die ~** *(ugs.)* he drives like a maniac

Fe̲uerwehr-: ~auto das fire engine; **~beil das** fireman's axe; **~mann der;** *Pl.* **~männer** *od.* **~leute** fireman; **~übung die** fire service drill; fire-fighting exercise

Fe̲uer-: ~werk das firework display; *(~werkskörper)* fireworks *pl.*; *(fig.)* barrage; **~werks·körper der** firework; **~zangen·bowle die** *burnt rum and red wine punch;* **~zeug das** lighter; **~zone die** *(Militär.)* firing zone

Feuilleton [fœjəˈtõ:] **das;** ~s, ~s **a)** *(Teil einer Zeitung)* arts section; **b)** *(literarischer Beitrag)* [literary] article

Feuilletonịsmus der; ~ *(oft abwertend)* literary journalese

Feuilletonịst der; ~en, ~en, **Feuilletonịstin die;** ~, ~nen arts writer *or* correspondent

feuilletonịstisch 1. *Adj.* *(unterhaltend)* literary journalistic ⟨*style*⟩; *(abwertend)* glib, facile ⟨*essay etc.*⟩. **2.** *adv.* in a literary journalistic style; *(abwertend)* glibly

Feuilletọn·teil der arts section

fe̲urig *Adj.* **a)** fiery ⟨*horse, spice, wine*⟩; passionate ⟨*speech*⟩; **b)** *(geh.: feuerrot)* flaming ⟨*sky, red, etc.*⟩; **c)** *(geh.: funkelnd)* blazing ⟨*precious stone*⟩

Fez [fe:ts] **der;** ~es *(ugs.)* lark *(coll.)*; **~ machen** lark about *(coll.)*; **hört mit dem ~ auf!** stop larking about *(coll.)*

ff [ɛfˈɛf] *Abk.* **sehr fein** superior-quality ⟨*sweets, cakes and pastries, etc.*⟩

ff. *Abk.* **folgende [Seiten]** ff.

Ffm. *Abk.* **Frankfurt am Main**

Fiaker [ˈfi̯akɐ] **der;** ~s, ~ *(österr.)* hackney carriage; cab

Fiale [ˈfi̯a:lə] **die;** ~, ~n *(Archit.)* pinnacle

Fiasko [ˈfi̯asko] **das;** ~s, ~s fiasco; **unser Urlaub war ein einziges ~:** our holiday was a total disaster *(coll.)*

Fibel [ˈfi:bl̩] **die;** ~, ~n **a)** *(Lesebuch)* reader; primer; **b)** *(Lehrbuch)* handbook; guide

Fiber [ˈfi:bɐ] **die;** ~, ~n fibre

Fibrille [fiˈbrɪlə] **die;** ~, ~n *(Med.)* fibril

Fibrin [fiˈbri:n] **das;** ~s *(Med.)* fibrin

Fibrom [fiˈbro:m] **das;** ~s, ~e *(Med.)* fibroma

Fiche [fi:ʃ] **der** *od.* **das;** ~s, ~s *(Informationst.)* [micro]fiche

ficht [fɪçt] *Imperativ Sg. u. 3. Pers. Sg. Präsens v.* **fechten**

Fịchte die; ~, ~n **a)** spruce; **b)** *(Rottanne)* Norway spruce

Fịchten-: ~brett das spruce board; **~holz das** spruce [wood]; **~nadel die** spruce needle; **~nadel·öl das** spruce oil; pine-needle oil; **~wald der** spruce forest

Fick [fɪk] **der;** ~s, ~s *(vulg.)* fuck *(coarse)*

fịcken *tr., itr. V. (vulg.)* fuck *(coarse)*; **mit jmdm. ~:** fuck sb.; **sie ließ sich von ihm ~:** she let him fuck her

Fickere̲i die; ~, ~en *(vulg.)* **a)** *o. Pl. (das Ficken)* fucking *(coarse)*; **b)** *(sexuelles Abenteuer)* fuck *(coarse)*

fick[e]rig [ˈfɪk(ə)rɪç] *Adj. (landsch.: nervös)* nervous

Fideikommiß [fideikɔˈmɪs] **das; Fideikommịsses, Fideikommịsse** *(Rechtsspr.)* entail; entailed estate

fidel [fiˈde:l] *Adj. (ugs.)* jolly, merry ⟨*company, person*⟩; **ein ~es Haus sein** be a *or* the cheerful type

Fidibus [ˈfi:dibʊs] **der;** ~ *od.* **~ses,** ~ *od.* **~se** *(scherzh.)* spill

Fidschianer [fɪˈdʒi̯a:nɐ] **der;** ~s, ~: Fijian

Fidschi·inseln [ˈfɪdʒi-] *Pl.* **die ~:** Fiji; the Fiji Islands

Fieber [ˈfi:bɐ] **das;** ~s **a)** [high] temperature; *(über 38 °C)* fever; **~ haben** have a [high] temperature/a fever; **hohes/ansteigendes ~ haben** have a high/rising temperature; **~ messen/bei jmdm. ~ messen** take one's/sb.'s temperature; **im ~:** in one's fever; **b)** *(geh.: Besessenheit)* fever; **vom ~ des Ehrgeizes gepackt sein** be consumed with ambition; **das ~ der Ungeduld hatte ihn ergriffen** he was in a fever of impatience; **im ~ der Erwartung** in a fever of anticipation; **im ~ des Wahlkampfs** in the heat of the election campaign

fi̲eber-, Fi̲eber-: ~anfall der attack *or* bout of fever; **~flecke[n]** *Pl.* fever spots; fever rash *sing.*; **~frei** *Adj.* ⟨*person*⟩ free from fever; **er ist wieder ~frei** his temperature is back to normal; **~glänzend** *Adj. (geh.)* feverish ⟨*eyes*⟩

fi̲eber·haft 1. *Adj.* **a)** feverish, febrile ⟨*infection, state, condition*⟩; **b)** *(angestrengt, hektisch)* feverish ⟨*activity*⟩; **eine ~e Tätigkeit entfalten** become feverishly active. **2.** *adv.* feverishly; **~ überlegen** think desperately hard

fi̲eberig *Adj. s.* **fiebrig**

Fi̲eber-: ~kurve die temperature chart; **~messer der** *s.* **~thermometer; ~mücke die** *(Zool.)* malaria mosquito

fi̲ebern *itr. V.* **a)** *(Fieber haben)* have *or* run a temperature; **b)** *(sehr aufgeregt sein)* **vor Aufregung/Erwartung** *(Dat.)* **~:** be in a fever of excitement/anticipation; **c)** *(heftig verlangen)* **nach etw. ~:** long desperately for sth.

fi̲eber-, Fi̲eber-: ~phantasie die; *meist Pl.* [feverish] delirium; **~senkend** *Adj.* antipyretic; **~senkende Mittel** antipyretics; **~thermometer das** [clinical] thermometer; **~wahn der** *(geh.)* [feverish] delirium; **im ~wahn** in his/her delirium

fi̲ebrig *Adj. (auch fig.)* feverish

Fiedel [ˈfi:dl̩] **die;** ~, ~n *(veralt., scherzh.)* fiddle

fi̲edeln *tr., itr. V. (scherzh., abwertend)* fiddle; **eine Melodie ~:** play a tune on the fiddle

Fiedler [ˈfi:dlɐ] **der;** ~s, ~ *(scherzh., abwertend)* fiddler

fiel [fi:l] *1. u. 3. Pers. Sg. Prät. v.* **fallen**

fiepen [ˈfi:pn̩] *itr. V.* **a)** ⟨*dog*⟩ whimper; ⟨*bird*⟩ cheep; **b)** *(Jägerspr.)* ⟨*deer*⟩ call

fies [fi:s] **1.** *Adj. (ugs.)* **a)** *(charakterlich)* nasty ⟨*person, character*⟩; **das finde ich ~:** I think that's mean; **b)** *(geschmacklich)* horrid *(coll.)*; awful *(coll.)*. **2.** *adv.* in a nasty way

Fiesling [ˈfi:slɪŋ] **der;** ~s, ~e *(salopp abwertend)* creep *(sl.)*

Fifa, FIFA [ˈfi:fa] **die;** ~: FIFA; International Football Federation

fifty-fifty [ˈfɪftɪˈfɪftɪ] *Adv. (ugs.)* **in ~ machen** go fifty-fifty; **die Sache wird am Ende wohl ~ ausgehen** things will no doubt work out even in the end

Figaro [ˈfigaro] **der;** ~s, ~s *(scherzh.)* hairdresser

Fight [fai̯t] **der;** ~s, ~s *(Sport)* fight

fighten [ˈfai̯tn̩] *itr. V. (Sport)* fight

Fighter [ˈfai̯tɐ] **der;** ~s, ~: fighter

Figur [fiˈgu:ɐ̯] **die;** ~, ~en **a)** *(Wuchs, Gestalt)* *(einer Frau)* figure; *(eines Mannes)* physique; **eine gute/schlechte ~ machen** cut a good/poor *or* sorry figure; **b)** *(Bildwerk)* figure; **c)** *(geometrisches Gebilde)* shape; **d)** *(Spielstein)* piece; **e)** *(Persönlichkeit)* figure; **f)** *(literarische Gestalt)* character; **die komische ~** *(Theater)* the comic character *or* figure; **eine komische ~:** a figure of fun; **g)** *(Tanzen, Eissport usw.)* figure; **~en laufen** skate figures; **h)** *meist Pl. (salopp: Mensch)* character *(coll.)*; **i)** *(Musik, Sprachw.)* figure

figural [figuˈra:l] *Adj.* figured

Figura̲l·musik die figurate *or* florid music

Figuration [figuraˈtsi̯o:n] **die;** ~, ~en *(Musik, Kunstwiss.)* figuration

figurativ [figuraˈti:f] *(Sprachw., Kunstw.)* **1.** *Adj.* figurative. **2.** *adv.* figuratively

figuri̲eren *itr. V. (geh.)* figure

Figurine [figuˈri:nə] **die;** ~, ~n **a)** *(Kunstwiss.)* figurine; **b)** *(bes. Theater)* costume design

figürlich [fiˈgy:ɐ̯lɪç] **1.** *Adj. (Kunstwiss.)* figured. **2.** *adv. (in bezug auf die Figur)* as far as her figure/his physique is concerned

Figu̲r·problem das; *meist Pl. (ugs.)* weight problem

Fiktion [fɪkˈtsi̯o:n] **die;** ~, ~en fiction

fiktional [fɪktsi̯oˈna:l] *Adj. (geh.)* fictional ⟨*significance*⟩; ⟨*work*⟩ of fiction

fiktiv [fɪkˈti:f] *Adj. (geh.)* fictitious

Filament [filaˈmɛnt] **das;** ~s, ~e *(Bot., Astron.)* filament

[1]**Filet** [fiˈle:] **das;** ~s, ~s *(Textilw.)* filet; netting

[2]**File̲t das;** ~s, ~s fillet; *(Rinder~, Schweine~)* fillet; filet

Filet·arbeit die *(Handarb.)* filet; netting
filetieren [file'ti:rən] *tr. V.* *(Kochk.)* fillet
Filet-: ~nadel die netting needle; **~steak das** fillet steak
Filial·betrieb der branch
Filiale [fi'lia:lə] **die; ~, ~n** branch
Filial·generation die *(Genetik)* filial generation
Filialist der; ~en, ~en *(Wirtsch.)* chain-store owner
Filial-: ~kirche die daughter church; subsidiary church; **~leiter der** branch manager
Filibuster [fili'bastɐ] **das; ~[s], ~** *(Parl.)* filibuster
filigran [fili'gra:n] *Adj.; nicht präd.* filigreed
Filigran das; ~s, ~e filigree
Filigran-: ~arbeit die [piece of] filigree work; **~schmuck der** filigree [jewellery]
Filipina [fili'pi:na] **die; ~, ~s** Filipina
Filipino der; ~s, ~s Filipino
Filius ['fi:li̯ʊs] **der; ~, ~se** *(scherzh.)* son
Film [fɪlm] **der; ~[e]s, ~e a)** *(Fot.)* film; **b)** *(Kino~)* film; movie *(Amer. coll.)*; **da ist bei ihm der ~ gerissen** *(fig. ugs.)* he's had a mental blackout; **der deutsche/brasilianische ~:** the German/Brazilian cinema; **c)** *o. Pl. (Filmbranche)* films *pl.*; **beim ~ sein** be in films; **d)** *(dünne Schicht)* film
Film-: ~amateur der amateur film-maker; **~archiv das** film library *or* archive; **~atelier das** film studio; **~aufnahme die** shot; **mit den ~aufnahmen beginnen** start filming *or* shooting; **~aus·rüstung die** filming equipment; **~bar die** [porno] film club; **~bericht der** film report; **~branche die** films *pl., no art.*; **~bühne die a)** *(Bildbühne)* film window; **b)** *s.* **Filmtheater**; **~cutter der, ~cutterin die** film editor; **~diva die** *(veralt.)* screen goddess
Filme·macher der film-maker
filmen 1. *tr. V.* **a)** film; **b)** *(ugs.: hereinlegen)* **jmdn. ~:** take sb. for a ride *(sl.)*. **2.** *itr. V.* film; make a film/films
Film-: ~festival das film festival; **~festspiele** *Pl.* film festival *sing.*; **~fritze der** *(salopp)* film guy *(sl.)*; **~geschäft das;** *o. Pl.* film business *or* industry; **~groteske die** film grotesquerie; **~held der** screen hero; **~industrie die** film industry
filmisch 1. *Adj.* cinematic ⟨*art etc.*⟩. **2.** *adv.* cinematically
Film-: ~kamera die film camera; *(Schmalfilmkamera)* cine-camera; **~kassette die** *(Fot.)* film cassette *or* cartridge; **~klub der** film club *or* society; **~komödie die** film comedy; comedy film; **~kopie die** [film] print; copy of a/the film; **~kritik die a)** *(Besprechung)* film review; **b)** *(~kritiker)* film critics *pl.*; **~kritiker der** film critic; **~kulisse die** film set; **das wäre eine ideale ~kulisse** that would be an ideal setting for a film; **~kunst die;** *o. Pl.* cinematic art; **~kunst·theater das** film theatre; **~lein·wand die** cinema screen; **~material das a)** *(Fot., Film: Aufnahmematerial)* film; **b)** *(Filme zu einem Thema)* film material; **~musik die** film music; *(eines einzelnen Films)* theme music
Filmographie [fɪlmogra'fi:] **die; ~, ~n** filmography *no art.*
Film-: ~palast der picture palace *(dated)*; *cinema*; **~preis der** film award; **~produzent der** film producer; **~projektor der** film projector; **~regisseur der** film director; **~riß der** *in* **einen ~riß haben** *(ugs.)* have a mental blackout; **~rolle die a)** *(schauspielerische Rolle)* film part *or* role; **jmdm. eine ~rolle anbieten** offer sb. a part in a film; **b)** *(Spule)* reel of film; **~schaffende der/die;** *adj. Dekl.* film-maker; **~schau·spieler der** film actor; **~schauspielerin die** film actress; **~spule die** film reel; **~stadt die a)** *(Studiokomplex)* film studios *pl.*; **b)** *(Zentrum)* centre of the film industry; **~star der** film star; **~studio das** film studio; **~technik die** film technology *no art.*; **~theater das** cinema; **~titel der** film title; **~verleih der** film distributor[s]; **~vor·führer der; ~s, ~:** film projectionist; **~vor·stellung die** film show; **~wirtschaft die;** *o. Pl.* film business *or* industry; **~zensur die** film censorship; *(Gremium)* film censors *pl.*; censor *(coll.)*
Filou [fi'lu:] **der** *(abwertend)* **a)** *(Spitzbube)* dog *(derog.)*; rogue; **b)** *(Verführer)* devil *(derog.)*
Filter ['fɪltɐ] **der,** *(fachspr. meist)* **das; ~s, ~:** filter; **Zigaretten ohne/mit ~:** plain/[filter-]tipped cigarettes
filter-, Filter-: ~fein *Adj.* finely-ground *attrib.*, filter-fine *attrib.* ⟨*coffee*⟩; **Kaffee ~fein mahlen** grind coffee fine[ly]; **~kaffee der** filter coffee; **~mund·stück das** filter-tip
filtern *tr. V.* filter
Filter-: ~papier das filter paper; **~presse die** *(Technik)* filter press; **~tüte die** filter; **~zigarette die** [filter-]tipped cigarette
Filtrat [fɪl'tra:t] **das; ~[e]s, ~e** *(Technik)* filtrate
Filtration [fɪltra'tsi̯o:n] **die; ~, ~en** *(Technik)* filtration
filtrieren *tr. V.* filter
Filz [fɪlts] **der; ~es, ~e a)** *(Material)* felt; **b)** *(filzartig Verschlungenes)* mass; mat; **c)** *(ugs. abwertend: geiziger Mensch)* miser; skinflint; **d)** *(Bierdeckel)* beer-mat; **e)** *(~hut)* felt hat; **f)** *(ugs. abwertend: Korruption)* corruption; graft *(coll.)*
filzen 1. *itr. V.* felt. **2.** *tr. V.* **a)** *(ugs.: durchsuchen)* search ⟨*room, car, etc.*⟩; frisk ⟨*person*⟩; **b)** *(salopp: berauben)* do over *(sl.)*; **c)** *(salopp: schlafen)* kip *(Brit. sl.)*
Filz·hut der felt hat
filzig *Adj.* **a)** *(verfilzt)* felted ⟨*wool*⟩; matted ⟨*hair*⟩; **b)** *(ugs.: geizig)* mean; tight-fisted
Filz-: ~latschen der *(ugs.)* slipper; **~laus die** *(Zool.)* crab louse
Filzokratie [fɪltsokra'ti:] **die; ~, ~n** *(abwertend)* corruption; graft *(coll.)*
Filz-: ~pantoffel der slipper; **~schreiber der** felt-tip pen; **~stiefel der** felt boot; **~stift der** felt-tip pen
Fimmel ['fɪml] **der; ~s, ~** *(ugs. abwertend)* **einen ~ für etw. haben** have a thing about sth. *(coll.)*; **du hast wohl einen ~!** there must be something the matter with you; you must be dotty *(Brit.)*; **das ist ein ~ von ihm** it's a strange habit of his; *(Idee)* it's a funny idea he has *(coll.)*
final [fi'na:l] *Adj.* *(Philos., Sprachw.)* final
Finale [fi'na:lə] **das; ~s, ~[s] a)** *(Sport: Endkampf)* final; **im ~ stehen** be in the final; **b)** *(spektakulärer Abschluß; Musik: Schlußsatz, -szene)* finale
Final·gegner der *(Sport)* opponent in the final
Finalist der; ~en, ~en *(Sport)* finalist
Finalität [finali'tɛ:t] **die, ~, ~en** *(bes. Philos.)* finality
Final·satz der *(Sprachw.)* final clause
Finanz [fi'nants] **die; ~ a)** *(Geldwesen)* finance *no art.*; **b)** *(~leute)* financial world
Finanz-: ~amt das a) *(Behörde)* ≈ Inland Revenue; **Ärger mit dem ~amt** trouble with the taxman; **b)** *(Gebäude)* tax office; **~aristokratie die** financial aristocracy; **~ausgleich der** *equalization of revenue and costs between government and local authorities*; **~beamte der** tax officer; **~buch·halter der** financial accountant; **~buch·haltung die** financial accountancy; **~dinge** *Pl.* financial matters
Finanzen *Pl.* **a)** *(ugs.: finanzielle Verhältnisse)* finances; **b)** *(Finanz- und Geldwesen)* finance *sing.*; **die Abteilung ~:** the finance department; **c)** *(Einkünfte des Staates)* [government] finances
Finanz-: ~genie das financial wizard; **~gericht das** *court dealing with tax disputes*; **~gruppe die** [financial] syndicate; **~hilfe die** financial aid; **~hoheit die** fiscal prerogative
finanziell [finan'tsi̯ɛl] **1.** *Adj.* financial. **2.** *adv.* financially; **jmdn. ~ unterstützen** give sb. financial support; **~ gesichert sein** be financially secure
Finanzier [finan'tsi̯e:] **der; ~s, ~s** financier
finanzieren *tr. V.* **a)** finance; *(fig.: bezahlen)* pay for; **frei/staatlich finanziert sein** be privately financed/financed by the state; **b)** *(Kaufmannsspr.: auf Kredit kaufen)* buy on credit; **etw. langfristig ~:** obtain long-term credit for sth.
Finanzierung die; ~, ~en a) financing; **b)** *(Gewährung eines Kredits)* credit *no indef. art.*; **eine langfristige ~:** long-term credit
Finanzierungs·plan der financial plan
finanz-, Finanz-: ~kapital das; *o. Pl.* financial capital; **~kontrolle die** *(Wirtsch.)* financial control; **~kraft die;** *o. Pl.* financial strength; **~kräftig** *Adj.* financially powerful; **~lage die** financial situation; **~minister der** minister of finance; ≈ Chancellor of the Exchequer *(Brit.)*; ≈ Secretary of the Treasury *(Amer.)*; **~ministerium das** Ministry of Finance; *(in GB u. USA)* ≈ Treasury; **~not die** financial difficulties *pl.*; **~planung die** financial planning; **~politik die** *(des Staates, eines Unternehmens)* financial policy; *(allgemeine)* politics of finance; **~politisch 1.** *Adj.* ⟨*questions etc.*⟩ relating to financial policy; **2.** *adv.* from the point of view of financial policy; **~reform die** financial reform; **~schwach** *Adj.* financially weak; **~spritze die** *(ugs.)* cash injection; **~stark** *Adj.* financially strong; **~verwaltung die** *regional department with responsibility for settling fiscal matters*; ≈ Board of Inland Revenue *(Brit.)*; ≈ Internal Revenue Service *(Amer.)*; **~wesen das;** *o. Pl.* **a)** system of public finances; **ein Ausdruck aus dem ~wesen** a financial expression; **b)** *s.* **~verwaltung**; **~wirtschaft die** public finances *pl.*; **~wissenschaft die** public finance
finassieren [fina'si:rən] *itr. V.* *(abwertend)* use trickery
Findel·kind ['fɪndḷ-] **das** foundling
finden ['fɪndn̩] **1.** *unr. tr. V.* **a)** *(entdecken)* find; **eine Spur von jmdm. ~:** get a lead on sb.; **keine Spur von jmdm. ~:** find no trace of sb.; **er/das ist nicht zu ~:** he/it is not to be found; **ich weiß nicht, was er an ihr findet** I don't know what he sees in her; **b)** *(erlangen, erwerben)* find ⟨*work, flat, wife, etc.*⟩; **Freunde ~:** make friends; **die Kraft/den Mut dazu ~, etw. zu tun** find the strength/the courage to do sth.; **c)** *(heraus~)* find ⟨*solution, mistake, pretext, excuse, answer*⟩; **einen Ausweg ~:** see a way out; **d)** *(einschätzen, beurteilen)* **etw. gut/richtig ~:** think sth. is good/right; **wie ~ Sie dieses Bild?** what do you think of this painting?; **nichts bei etw. ~:** not mind sth.; **ich finde nichts dabei** I don't mind; **wie finde ich denn das?** *(ugs.)* well, really!; **e)** *(erhalten)* **Hilfe [bei jmdm.] ~:** get help [from sb.]; *s. auch* **Anklang a; Beifall b; ²Gefallen; Gehör; Verwendung a; f)** *(vorfinden)* find; **er fand das Haus verlassen** he found the house deserted. **2.** *unr. refl. V.* **sich ~:** turn up; **es fand sich niemand/jemand, der das tun wollte** nobody wanted to do that/there was somebody who wanted to do that; **das/es wird sich alles ~** *(das wird sich aufklären)* it will all work out all right; **sich in sein Schicksal/seine Lage/seine neue Rolle ~** *(geh.)* come to terms with one's fate/situation/new role. **3.** *unr. itr. V.* **zu jmdm. ~:** find sb.; **nach einem Ort ~:** find the way to a place; **nach Hause ~:** find the way home; **zu sich selbst ~** *(fig.)* come to terms with oneself; **er gehört zu diesen Nachtmenschen,**

die nicht ins Bett ~ können he is one of these night-owls who just will not go to bed; **das Kind findet schon allein zur Schule** the child knows the way to school by himself/herself

Finder der; ~s, ~: finder; *s. auch* **ehrlich 1 a**

Finder·lohn der reward [for finding sth.]

Fin de siècle [fɛ̃d'sjɛkl] **das**; ~ ~ ~: fin de siècle; **die Kunst/Literatur des ~ ~ ~:** fin de siècle art/literature

findig *Adj.* resourceful; **ein ~er Kopf** a resourceful person; **er ist ~ im Aufspüren von Antiquitäten** he ist good at finding antiques

Findling ['fɪntlɪŋ] **der**; ~s, ~e **a)** *(Findelkind)* foundling; **b)** *(Geol.)* erratic block

Findlings·block der *(Geol.)* erratic block

Finesse [fi'nɛsə] **die**; ~, ~n **a)** *meist Pl. (Kunstgriff)* trick; **alle ~n von etw. beherrschen** know all the tricks of sth.; **b)** *meist Pl. (in der Ausstattung)* refinement; **mit allen ~n ausgestattet** equipped with every refinement; **c)** *(Schlauheit)* flair

fing [fɪŋ] *1. u. 3. Pers. Sg. Prät. v.* **fangen**

Finger ['fɪŋɐ] **der**; ~s, ~ **a)** finger; **mit dem ~ auf jmdn./etw. zeigen** *(auch fig.)* point one's finger at sb./sth.; **den ~ an die Lippen legen** put one's finger to one's lips; **einen Ring am ~ tragen** have a ring on one's finger; **den ~ am Abzug haben** have one's finger on the trigger; **mit den ~n schnippen** snap one's fingers; **sich** *(Dat.)* **die ~ wund schreiben** write one's fingers to the bone; **b)** *(fig.)* **das Geld zerrinnt ihm unter** *od.* **zwischen den ~n** money just runs through his fingers; **wenn man ihm den kleinen ~ reicht, nimmt er gleich die ganze Hand** if you give him an inch he takes a mile; **die ~ davonlassen/von etw. lassen** *(ugs.)* steer clear of it/of sth.; **sie macht keinen ~ krumm** *(ugs.)* she never lifts a finger; **lange ~ machen** *(ugs.)* get itchy fingers; **er rührte keinen ~:** he wouldn't lift a finger; **ich würde mir alle [zehn] ~ danach lecken** *(ugs.)* I'd give my eye-teeth for it; **die ~ in etw.** *(Dat.)***/im Spiel haben** *(ugs.)* have a hand in sth./have one's finger in the pie; **sich** *(Dat.)* **die ~ schmutzig machen** get one's hands dirty; **sich** *(Dat.)* **die ~ verbrennen** *(ugs.)* burn one's fingers *(fig.)*; **etw. an den ~n abzählen können** be able to count sth. on the fingers of one hand; **sich** *(Dat.)* **etw. an den [fünf** *od.* **zehn] ~n abzählen können** be able to see sth. straight away; **eine[n] an jedem ~ haben** *(ugs. scherz.)* have one for every day of the week; **jmdm. auf die ~ sehen** *od.* **gucken** *(ugs.)* keep a sharp eye on sb.; **jmdm. auf die ~ klopfen** *(ugs.)* rap sb. across the knuckles; **sich** *(Dat.)* **etw. aus den ~n saugen** *(ugs.)* make sth. up; **ihm** *od.* **ihn juckt es in den ~n [, etw. zu tun]** *(ugs.)* he is itching [to do sth.]; **dann juckt's mir in den ~n** *(ugs.)* then I get restless; **jmdm. in die ~ fallen** *od.* **geraten** *(ugs.)* fall into sb.'s hands; **etw. in die ~ bekommen** *od.* **kriegen** *(ugs.)* get hold of sth.; **wenn ich den in die ~ kriege!** *(ugs.)* wait till I get my hands on him *(coll.)*; **sich** *(Dat.)* **in den ~ geschnitten haben** *(ugs.)* have another think coming *(coll.)*; **etw. mit spitzen ~n anfassen** hold sth. at arm's length; **etw. mit dem kleinen ~ machen** *(ugs.)* do sth. with one's eyes shut; **jmdn. um den [kleinen] ~ wickeln** *(ugs.)* wrap sb. round one's little finger; **jmdm. unter die ~ kommen** *od.* **geraten** *(ugs.)* fall into sb.'s hands; **der elfte ~** *(salopp scherzh.)* one's third leg *(coll. joc.)*; **c)** *(Teil des Handschuhs)* finger

finger-, Finger-: ~abdruck der fingerprint; **jmdm. ~abdrücke abnehmen** take sb.'s fingerprints; **~beere die** *(Anat.)* finger pad; **~breit** *Adj.* as wide as a finger *postpos.*; half an inch wide *postpos.*; **~breit der**; ~, ~ *(Maßeinheit)* finger's width; *(fig.)* inch; **sie war nicht bereit, einen ~breit abzuweichen** *(fig.)* she was not prepared to budge an inch; **~dick** *Adj.* as thick as a finger *postpos.*; **Brot ~dick mit etw. bestreichen** spread bread thickly with sth.; **~druck der**; *o. Pl.* touch of a finger; **~fertig** *Adj.* nimble-fingered; **~fertigkeit die**; *o. Pl.* dexterity; **~gelenk das** finger joint; **~glied das** phalanx; **~hakeln** [~ha:kl̩n] **das**; ~s finger-wrestling; **~hand·schuh der** glove [with fingers]; **~hut der a)** thimble; **ein ~hut [voll]** *(fig.)* a thimbleful; **b)** *(Bot.)* foxglove; **~knochen der, ~knöchel der** knuckle; **~kuppe die** fingertip

fingern 1. *itr. V.* fiddle; **an etw.** *(Dat.)* **~:** fiddle with sth.; **nach etw. ~:** fumble [around] for sth. **2.** *tr. V.* **etw. aus der Tasche ~:** fish sth. out of one's pocket

Finger-: ~nagel der fingernail; **an den ~nägeln kauen** bite one's nails; **er gönnt ihr nicht das Schwarze unterm ~nagel** *(fig.)* he grudges her everything; **~rechnen das** counting on one's fingers *no art.*; **er beherrscht schon das ~rechnen** he can already count on his fingers; **~ring der** ring; **~satz der** *(Musik)* fingering; **~schale die** finger-bowl; **~schnippen das**; ~s snapping one's fingers; **sich mit ~schnippen melden** attract attention by snapping one's fingers

Finger·spitze die fingertip; **Künstler/musikalisch bis in die ~n sein** *(fig.)* be an artist/be musical to the tips of one's fingers; **das muß man in den ~n haben** *(fig.)* you have to have a feel for it

Fingerspitzen·gefühl das; *o. Pl.* feeling; **ein [besonderes] ~ für etw. haben** have a [special] feeling for sth.

Finger-: ~sprache die deaf-and-dumb language; *(alphabetische Zeichen)* deaf-and-dumb alphabet; **~übung die** *(Musik)* finger exercise; **~zeig** [~tsaik] **der**; ~s, ~e tip-off; **einen ~zeig erhalten** be given a hint; ⟨*police*⟩ be tipped off, get a tip-off; **für sie war es ein ~zeig des Schicksals** she took it as a sign

fingieren [fɪŋ'gi:rən] *tr. V.* fake ⟨*accident, break-in*⟩; **ein fingierter Name** a false name; **ein fingierter Briefwechsel** *(in der Literatur)* an imaginary correspondence

Finish ['fɪnɪʃ] **das**; ~s, ~s finish

finit [fi'ni:t] *Adj. (Sprachw.)* finite

Fink [fɪŋk] **der**; ~en, ~en finch

Finken-: ~schlag der; *o. Pl.* finch's song; **~vogel der** finch

Finn-Ding[h]i ['fɪndɪŋgi] **das**; ~s, ~s Finn dinghy

[1]**Finne** ['fɪnə] **der**; ~n, ~n Finn

[2]**Finne die**; ~, ~n **a)** *(Zool.)* fin; **b)** *(am Hammer)* peen

Finnen·dolch der [short, wide-bladed] dagger

Finnin die; ~, ~nen Finn

finnisch *Adj.* Finnish; **der Finnische Meerbusen** the Gulf of Finland; *s. auch* **deutsch, Deutsch, [2]Deutsche**

Finnland ['fɪnlant] **(das)**; ~s Finland

Finnlandisierung [fɪnlandi'zi:rʊŋ] **die**; ~ *(Pol.)* Finlandization

Finn·wal der *(Zool.)* fin whale; common rorqual

finster ['fɪnstɐ] **1.** *Adj.* **a)** dark; **im Finstern** in the dark; **b)** *(düster)* dark ⟨*house, forest, alleyway*⟩; dimly-lit ⟨*pub, district*⟩; **c)** *(dubios)* shady ⟨*plan, affair*⟩; **eine ~e Gestalt** a sinister figure; **d)** *(verdüstert, feindselig)* **eine ~e Miene [aufsetzen]** [assume] a black expression; **~e Gedanken gegen jmdn. hegen** have evil intentions against sb.; **e)** *(fig.)* **in diesen ~en Zeiten** in these dark times; **aus dem ~en Mittelalter** from the Dark Ages; **im ~n tappen** be groping in the dark. **2.** *adv.* **jmdn. ~ ansehen** give sb. a black look; **~ entschlossen sein, etw. zu tun** be grimly determined to do sth.

Finsternis die; ~, ~se **a)** darkness; *(auch bibl., fig.)* dark; **rabenschwarze ~:** pitch darkness; **in tiefer ~ liegen** be shrouded in darkness; **die Mächte/das Reich der ~:** the powers of darkness/the Kingdom of Darkness; **eine ägyptische ~:** stygian gloom; **b)** *(Astron.)* eclipse

Finte ['fɪntə] **die**; ~, ~n **a)** trick; **jmdn. durch eine ~ täuschen** deceive sb. by trickery; **alle ~n nützen Ihnen nichts** no trickery will help you; **b)** *(Fechten)* feint

finten·reich *Adj. (geh.)* skilful, tricky ⟨*opponent*⟩

finzelig, finzlig ['fɪnts(ə)lɪç] *Adj. (ugs.)* **~e Arbeit** fiddly work *(coll.)*; **~e Schrift** tiny writing

fipsig ['fɪpsɪç] *Adj. (ugs.)* undersized

Firlefanz ['fɪrləfants] **der**; ~es *(ugs. abwertend)* **a)** *(Tand, Flitter)* frippery; trumpery; **b)** *(Unsinn)* nonsense; **~ machen** fool around

firm [fɪrm] *Adj.* **in etw.** *(Dat.)* **~ sein** be well up in sth.; know sth. thoroughly

Firma ['fɪrma] **die**; ~, **Firmen a)** firm; company; **in einer ~ arbeiten** work for a firm *or* company; **die ~ ist erloschen** the company has been struck from the register; **„Fa. W. Bert & Söhne"** 'W. Bert & Sons'; **b)** *(ugs. abwertend: Sippschaft)* bunch *(sl.)*

Firmament [fɪrma'mɛnt] **das**; ~[e]s *(dichter.)* firmament

firmen *tr. V. (kath. Rel.)* confirm

firmen-, Firmen-: ~aufdruck der company letter heading; **~chef der** *s.* **~inhaber**; **~eigen** *Adj.* company *attrib.*; belonging to the company *postpos.*; **~eigen sein** belong to the company; **ein ~eigener LKW/eine ~eigene Kantine** a company lorry *(Brit.) or* truck/canteen; **~inhaber der** owner of the/a company; **~intern 1.** *Adj.* internal; internal company *attrib.*; **2.** *adv.* internally; within the company; **~name der** name of a/the company *or* firm; **~schild das** company's name plate; **~stempel der** company stamp; firm's stamp; **~wagen der** company car; **~zeichen das** trademark

firmieren *itr. V.* trade

Firmling ['fɪrmlɪŋ] **der**; ~s, ~e *(kath. Rel.)* confirmation candidate

Firm·pate der sponsor

Firmung die; ~, ~en confirmation; **jmdm. die ~ erteilen** confirm sb.

firn [fɪrn] *Adj.* mature ⟨*wine*⟩

Firn der; ~[e]s firn

Firn·feld das firn field

Firnis ['fɪrnɪs] **der**; ~ses, ~se varnish

Firn·schnee der firn snow

First [fɪrst] **der**; ~[e]s, ~e ridge

First-: ~höhe die height [to the ridge of the roof]; **eine ~höhe von 8,50 m aufweisen** be 8.50 m high; **~ziegel der** ridge tile

Fis [fɪs] **das**; ~, ~ *(Musik)* [key of] F sharp

Fisch [fɪʃ] **der**; ~[e]s, ~e **a)** fish; **[fünf] ~e fangen** catch [five] fish; **sie hatten viele ~e im Netz** they had a good catch; **fliegende ~e** flying fish; **gesund und munter wie ein ~ im Wasser** as fit as a fiddle; **stumm wie ein ~ sein** keep a stony silence; *(fig.)* **kleine ~e** *(ugs.)* small fry; **faule ~e** *(ugs.)* lame excuses; **die ~e füttern** *(ugs. scherzh.)* be seasick; **b)** *o. Pl. (Nahrungsmittel)* fish; **das ist weder ~ noch Fleisch** *(fig.)* that's neither fish nor fowl; **c)** *(Astrol.)* **die ~e** Pisces; the Fishes; **er ist [ein] ~:** he is a Piscean; **im Zeichen der ~e geboren sein** be born under [the sign of] Pisces; **d)** *(Druckerspr.) letter from the wrong fount*

fisch-, Fisch-: ~abfälle *Pl.* fish scraps; **~adler der** *(Zool.)* osprey; **~arm** *Adj.* poor as regards fish; **~auge das a)** fish eye; **er hat große, hervorquellende ~augen** *(fig.)* he's got big, protruding fish-like eyes; **b)** *(Fot.)* fisheye lens; **~becken das** fishpond; **~bein das**; *o. Pl.* whalebone; **~bestand der** fish population; **~besteck das** fish knife and fork; **~blase die a)** *(Schwimmblase)* fish-sound; **b)** *(Archit.)* vesica piscis; **~blut das** fish blood; **~blut**

in den Adern haben *(fig.)* be a cold fish; **~braterei die, ~brat·küche die** fried-fish shop; **~brötchen das** fish roll; **~bude die** *stall selling pickled and smoked fish;* **~bulette die** fishcake; **~dampfer der** steam trawler; **~ei das** fish egg

fischen 1. *tr. V.* **a)** fish for; **Forellen/Aale ~:** fish for trout/eels; **b)** *(ugs.)* **etw. aus etw. ~:** fish sth. out of sth. **2.** *itr. V.* fish; **~ gehen** go fishing; **nach etw. ~:** fish for sth.; **nach Komplimenten ~** *(fig.)* fish for compliments; *s. auch* **trüb 1 a**

Fischer der; ~s, ~ a) fisherman; **b)** *(ugs.: Angler)* angler

Fischer-: ~boot das fishing boat; **~dorf das** fishing village

Fischerei die; ~: fishing; **von der ~ leben** make a/one's living from fishing

Fischerei-: ~fahrzeug das fishing vessel; **~flotte die** fishing fleet; **~grenze die** fishing limit; **~hafen der** fish dock; *(Hafenort)* fishing port; **~recht das a)** fishing rights *pl.*, right of fishery *(Law)*; **b)** *o. Pl (Rechtsvorschriften)* fishing laws *pl.*; **~schiff das** fishing vessel; **~schutzboot das** fishery protection vessel; **~wesen das** fisheries *pl.*

Fischer-: ~hütte die, ~kate die fisherman's hut; **~netz das** fishing net; **~ring der** *(kath. Rel.)* Fisherman's Ring

Fisch-: ~fabrik die fish cannery; **~fabrik·schiff das** factory ship

Fisch·fang der; *o. Pl.* **vom ~ leben** make a/one's living by fishing; **auf ~ gehen** go fishing

Fischfang-: ~flotte die fishing fleet; **~gebiet das** fishing grounds *pl.;* fishery

fisch-, Fisch-: ~filet das fish fillet; **~frau die** fishwife; **~frikadelle die** fishcake; **~futter das** fish food; **~gabel die** fish fork; **~gang der** *(Gastr.)* fish course; **~gericht das** fish dish; **~geruch der** smell of fish; **~geschäft das** fishmonger's [shop] *(Brit.);* fish store *(Amer.);* **~gräte die** fish bone; **~grät[en]·muster das** *(Textilw.)* herringbone pattern; **ein Mantel/ein Anzug mit ~grätenmuster** a herringbone coat/suit; **~gräten·stich der** herringbone stitch; **~gründe** *Pl.* fishing grounds; **~guano der** fish guano; **~handel der** fish trade; **~händler der** fishmonger *(Brit.);* fish dealer *(Amer.); (Großhändler)* fish wholesaler; **~konserve die** canned fish; **~kutter der** fishing trawler; **~laden der** *s.* **~geschäft; ~laich der** *(Zool.)* fish spawn; **~lokal das** *s.* **~restaurant; ~markt der** fish market; **~mehl das** fish-meal; **~messer das** fish knife; **~milch die** *(Zool.)* milt; **~otter der** otter; **~paß der** fish ladder; **~reich** *Adj.* rich in fish *postpos.;* **~reiher der** *(Zool.)* common heron; **~restaurant das** fish restaurant; seafood restaurant; **~reuse die** fish trap; **~schuppe die** fish scale; **~schwanz der** fish's tail; **~schwarm der** shoal of fish; **~stäbchen das** *(Kochk.)* fish finger; **~sterben das** death of the fish; **~suppe die** fish soup; **~teich der** fish-pond; **~vergiftung die** fish poisoning; **~wanderung die** *(Zool.)* fish migration; **~weib das** *(meist abwertend)* fishwife; **~werker der** *(Berufsbez.)* fish-worker; **~wilderei die** illicit fishing; **~wirt der** *(Berufsbez.)* fish-farmer; **~wirtschaft die** fishing industry; **~zaun der** fish weir; fishgarth; **~zucht die** fish farming; **~zug der a)** *(ugs.: gewinnbringendes Unternehmen)* killing; **b)** *(Fischereiw.)* draught

Fis-Dur [auch: '-'-] **das; ~** *(Musik)* F sharp major; *s. auch* **A-Dur**

Fisimatenten [fizima'tɛntn̩] *Pl.* *(ugs.)* messing about *sing.;* **mach keine ~!** stop messing about; **es ist besser, Sie machen keine ~:** it will be better if you don't try anything silly

fiskalisch [fɪs'ka:lɪʃ] *Adj.* fiscal

Fiskus ['fɪskʊs] **der; ~, Fisken** *od.* **~se** Government *(as managing the State finances);* **das Erbe fällt dem ~ zu** the estate falls to the Crown *(Brit.)*/the Government *(Amer.)*

fis-Moll [auch: '-'-] **das; ~** *(Musik)* F sharp minor; *s. auch* **a-Moll**

fisselig ['fɪsəlɪç] *Adj. (bes. nordd.)* **a)** *(dünn, fein)* fine ⟨*wool, material*⟩; **b)** *(umständlich)* fiddly ⟨*work*⟩

fisseln ['fɪsl̩n] *itr. V. (unpers.) (bes. nordd.)* drizzle; **es fisselt** it is drizzling

Fissur [fɪ'su:ɐ̯] **die; ~, ~en** *(Med.)* fissure

Fistel ['fɪstl̩] **die; ~, ~n** *(Med.)* fistula

fisteln ['fɪstl̩n] *itr. V.* speak in a thin high-pitched voice

Fistel·stimme die a) *(hohe Stimme bei Männern)* thin high-pitched voice; **b)** *(Musik)* falsetto [voice]

fit [fɪt] *Adj.; nicht attr.* fit; **jmdn. ~ machen** get sb. fit; **sich ~ halten** keep fit; **das hält ~:** it keeps you fit

Fitness, Fitneß ['fɪtnɛs] **die; ~:** fitness

Fitness-, Fitneß-: ~raum der fitness room; **~training das** fitness training; **~zentrum das** fitness centre

Fittich ['fɪtɪç] **der; ~[e]s, ~e** *(dichter.)* wing; pinion; **jmdn. unter seine ~e nehmen** *(ugs. scherzh.)* take sb. under one's wing

Fitting ['fɪtɪŋ] **das; ~s, ~s** *(Technik)* fitting

Fitzel ['fɪts̮l] **der** *od.* **das; ~s, ~** *(bes. nordd.)* morsel

Fitzelchen das; ~s, ~ *(ugs.)* scrap; **nicht ein ~ war von seinem Reichtum übriggeblieben** he did not have a penny of his fortune left

fix [fɪks] **1.** *Adj.* **a)** *(ugs.: flink, wendig)* quick; **ein ~er Bursche** a bright lad; **b)** *(ugs.)* **~ und fertig** *(fertig vorbereitet)* quite finished; *(völlig erschöpft)* completely shattered *(coll.);* **c)** *(festgelegt)* fixed ⟨*cost, salary*⟩; **eine ~e Idee** an idée fixe. **2.** *adv. (ugs.)* quickly; **das geht ganz ~:** it won't take a jiffy *(coll.);* **mach ~!** hurry up!

Fixativ [fɪksa'ti:f] **das; ~s, ~e** fixative

Fixe ['fɪksə] **die; ~, ~n** *(Drogenjargon)* needle

fixen ['fɪksn̩] *itr. V.* **a)** *(Drogenjargon: spritzen)* fix *(sl.);* **b)** *(Börsenw.)* bear

Fixer der; ~s, ~ a) *(Drogenjargon)* fixer; **b)** *(Börsenw.)* bear

Fix·geschäft das *(Wirtsch.)* purchase for delivery at a fixed time

Fixier·bad das *(Fot.)* fixer

fixierbar *Adj.* definable

fixieren [fɪ'ksi:rən] *tr. V.* **a)** *(scharf ansehen)* fix one's gaze on; **jmdn./etw. scharf/kühl ~:** gaze sharply/coldly at sb./sth.; **b)** *(geh.: schriftlich niederlegen)* take down ⟨*interview, report, statement*⟩; **c)** *(geh.: verbindlich bestimmen)* fix ⟨*date*⟩; **der Zeitpunkt ist auf den 12. Mai fixiert worden** the date has been fixed as the twelfth of May; **d)** *(Fot.)* fix; **e)** *(Med.: festmachen)* set; **f)** *(Psych.)* **er ist stark auf seine Mutter fixiert** he has a strong mother-fixation; **sich auf** *(Akk.)***/an** *(Dat.)* **etw. ~:** devote oneself *or* give oneself up entirely to sth.

Fixier·salz das *(Fot.)* hypo

Fixierung die; ~, ~en a) *(starres Festlegen, -halten)* **die ~ auf eine Frage** concentration on a question; **die ~ auf seine Mutter** his mother-fixation; **b)** *(Festlegung)* determination

Fixigkeit die; ~ *(ugs.)* speed

Fix-: ~punkt der fixed point; **~stern der** *(Astron.)* fixed star

Fixum ['fɪksʊm] **das; ~s, Fixa** basic salary

Fix·zeit die core time

Fjord [fjɔrt] **der; ~[e]s, ~e** fiord

FKK [ɛf ka: 'ka:] *Abk.* **Freikörperkultur** nudism *no art.;* naturism *no art.*

FKK-: ~-Anhänger der nudist; naturist; **~-Strand der** nudist beach

Fla [fla:] **die; ~:** anti-aircraft defense; AA defence

flach [flax] *Adj.* **a)** *(eben)* flat ⟨*countryside, region, roof*⟩; **das ~e Land** the flat country; **sich ~ hinlegen** lay oneself [down] flat; **mit der ~en Hand** with the flat of one's hand; **b)** *(niedrig)* low ⟨*heels, building*⟩; flat ⟨*shoe*⟩; **c)** *(nicht tief)* shallow ⟨*water, river, etc., dish*⟩; **d)** *(abwertend: nichtssagend, unwesentlich)* shallow

flach-, Flach-: ~bau der; *Pl.* **~bauten** low building; **~bogen der** *(Archit.)* segmental arch; **~brüstig** *Adj.* flat-chested; **~dach das** flat roof; **~druck·verfahren das** planographic printing method

Fläche ['flɛçə] **die; ~, ~n a)** *(ebenes Gebiet)* area; **auf einer ~ von x m²** over an area of x square metres; **b)** *(Ober~, Außenseite)* surface; **c)** *(Math.)* area; *(einer dreidimensionalen Figur)* side; face; **d)** *(weite Land~, Wasser~)* expanse; **e)** *(von Kristallen)* facet

Flach·eisen das a) *(gewalztes Eisen)* flat bar; **b)** *(Werkzeug)* scorper

flächen-, Flächen-: ~ausdehnung die area; **~blitz der** sheet lightning; **~brand der** extensive blaze; **sich zu einem ~brand ausweiten** *(fig.)* spread like wildfire; **~gleich** *Adj.* of equal area *postpos.;* equal in area *postpos.;* **~haft 1.** *Adj.* extensive; **2.** *adv.* extensively; **~inhalt der** *(Math.)* area; **~maß das** *(Math.)* unit of square measure; **~nutzungs·plan der** land development plan; **~staat der** territorial state; **~wirkung die** surface effect

flach-, Flach-: ~|fallen *itr. V.; mit sein (ugs.)* ⟨*trip*⟩ fall through; ⟨*event*⟩ be cancelled; **das Kino fällt für dich heute ~:** you won't be going to the cinema today; **diese Subventionen sollen ~fallen** these subsidies will not be continued; **~feile die** flat file; **~glas das** sheet glass; **~hang der** slip-off slope

Flachheit die; ~, ~en a) *o. Pl. (abwertend)* shallowness; **b)** *(Bemerkung)* platitude

flächig 1. *Adj.* **a)** *(abgeflacht)* flat ⟨*features, shape*⟩; **b)** *(ausgedehnt)* extensive ⟨*area*⟩; **c)** *(Kunstw.)* two-dimensional ⟨*style, representation*⟩. **2.** *adv.* extensively

flach-, Flach-: ~kopf der *(abwertend)* numskull; **~küste die** *(Geogr.)* beach; **~land das;** *o. Pl.* lowland; **~länder der; ~s, ~:** lowlander; **~|legen 1.** *refl. V. (ugs.)* lie down; **2.** *tr. V. (zu Boden strecken)* floor ⟨*opponent*⟩; **~|liegen** *unr. itr. V. (ugs.)* be flat on one's back; **~mann der;** *Pl.* **~männer** *(ugs. scherzh.)* hip-flask; **~meißel der** flat chisel; **~moor das** *(Geog.)* low-moor bog; **~paß der** *(Fußball)* low pass; **einen ~paß [auf jmdn.] spielen** make a low pass [to sb.]; **~relief das** low relief; **~rennen das** *(Sport)* flat race

Flachs [flaks] **der; ~es a)** flax; **b)** *(ugs.: Ulk)* **das war doch nur ~:** I/he *etc.* was just having you on *(Brit. coll.) or (Amer. coll.)* putting you on; **ganz ohne ~:** no kidding *(coll.)*

flachs·blond *Adj.* flaxen ⟨*hair*⟩

Flach·schuß der *(Fußball)* low shot

flachsen ['flaksn̩] *itr. V.* **mit jmdm. ~** *(ugs.)* joke with sb.; **gerne ~:** like a joke

Flachserei die; ~, ~en *(ugs.)* joking; **das war doch nur ~:** it was just a joke

Flachs·kopf der flaxen-haired person; **beide Kinder waren ~köpfe** both of the children were flaxen-haired

Flach-: ~strecke die *(Leichtathletik)* flat race; **~zange die** flat tongs *pl.;* **~ziegel der** flat tile

flackern ['flakɐn] *itr. V.* flicker; **~des Kaminfeuer/Licht/~de Augen** flickering fire/light/eyes; **Erregung flackerte in seinem Blick** his eyes glinted with excitement

Flacker·schein der flickering light

Fladen ['fla:dn̩] **der; ~s, ~ a)** *flat, round unleavened cake made with oat or barley flour;* ≈ [large] oatcake *(Scot.);* **b)** *(Kuh~)* cowpat

Fladen·brot das unleavened bread

Flagellant [flagɛ'lant] **der;** ~**en,** ~**en** flagellant

Flagellantismus der; ~ *(Med., Psych.)* flagellantism *no art.*

Flagellation [flagɛla'tsio:n] **die,** ~ *(Med., Psych.)* flagellation

Flagellum [fla'gɛlʊm] **das;** ~**s, Flagellen** *(Biol.)* flagellum; *(Peitsche)* scourge

Flagge ['flagə] **die;** ~, ~**n** flag; **unter neutraler** ~ **fahren** sail under a neutral flag; **die** ~ **streichen** *(fig.)* strike the flag *(fig.)*; ~ **zeigen** *(fig.)* show one's colours; **unter falscher** ~ **segeln** *(fig.)* sail under false colours

flaggen 1. *itr. V.* put out the flags; **überall war geflaggt** the flags were flying everywhere. **2.** *tr. V.* **die Straßen sind geflaggt** the flags have been put out in the streets

Flaggen-: ~**alphabet das** international code of signals; ~**ehrung die** *s.* ~**parade;** ~**gala die** flag dressing; ~**gruß der** flag salute; ~**leine die** halyard; ~**mast der** flagstaff; ~**parade die** flag-raising/flag-lowering ceremony; ~**signal das** code flag signal; ~**tuch das;** *Pl.* ~**tuche** bunting

Flagg-: ~**leine die** halyard; ~**offizier der** flag officer; ~**schiff das** flagship

flagrant [fla'grant] *Adj.* flagrant

Flair [flɛ:ɐ̯] **das** *od.* **der;** ~**s a)** *(Fluidum, Aura)* air; **ein** ~ **von etw. haben** have an air of sth.; **b)** *(Talent)* flair; **ein** ~ **für etw. haben** have a flair for sth.

Flak [flak] **die;** ~, ~ *(Milit.)* anti-aircraft gun; AA gun

Flak-: ~**feuer das** anti-aircraft fire; flak; **wir wurden unter** ~**feuer genommen** we came under anti-aircraft fire *or* flak; ~**geschütz das** anti-aircraft gun; AA gun; ~**helfer der** anti-aircraft auxiliary; ~**soldat der** anti-aircraft soldier; ~**stellung die** anti-aircraft position; AA position

Flakon [fla'kõ:] **das** *od.* **der;** ~**s,** ~**s** bottle

flambieren [flam'bi:rən] *tr. V.* flambé; **flambiert** flambé; flambéed

Flamboyant [flãbo̯a'jã:] **der;** ~**s,** ~**s** *(Bot.)* flamboyant tree; royal poinciana tree

Flamboyant·stil der *(Archit.)* Flamboyant style

Flame ['fla:mə] **der;** ~**n,** ~**n** Fleming

Flamenco [fla'mɛŋko] **der;** ~**[s],** ~**s** flamenco

Flamin, Flämin ['flɛ:mɪn] **die;** ~, ~**nen** Fleming; *s. auch* **-in**

Flamingo [fla'mɪŋgo] **der;** ~**s,** ~**s** flamingo

flämisch ['flɛ:mɪʃ] *Adj.* Flemish

Flämmchen ['flɛmçən] **das;** ~**s,** ~**:** [small] flame

Flamme ['flamə] **die;** ~, ~**n a)** flame; **etw. auf kleiner/großer** ~ **kochen** cook sth. on a low/high flame *or* gas; **in [hellen]** ~**n stehen** be in flames; **in** ~**n aufgehen** go up in flames; **b)** *(Brennstelle)* burner; **ein Gasherd mit drei** ~**n** a gas stove with three burners; **c)** *(ugs. veralt.: Freundin)* flame

flammen ['flamən] *itr. V. (geh.)* blaze

Flammen·blume die *(Bot.)* phlox

flammend *Adj.* **a)** flaming; ~**es Haar** flaming red hair; **b)** *(fig.)* fiery ⟨*speech*⟩; ~**e Anklagen und Protestaktionen** fervent accusations and protests

Flammen-: ~**meer das** *(geh.)* sea of flame[s]; ~**tod der** *(geh.)* death by burning; **er konnte sie vor dem** ~**tod retten** he was able to save them from burning to death; **sie erlitt den** ~**tod** she was burnt to death; ~**werfer der** *(Milit.)* flame-thrower

Flammeri ['flaməri] **der;** ~**[s],** ~**s** *(Kochk.)* flummery

Flandern ['flandɐn] **(das);** ~**s** Flanders

Flanell [fla'nɛl] **der;** ~**s,** ~**e** flannel; **ein Anzug aus** ~**:** a flannel suit

Flanell-: ~**anzug der** flannel suit; ~**hose die** flannel trousers *pl.*

Flaneur [fla'nø:ɐ̯] **der;** ~**s,** ~**e** *(geh.)* flâneur

flanieren [fla'ni:rən] *itr. V.; mit Richtungsangabe mit sein* stroll

Flanke ['flaŋkə] **die;** ~, ~**n a)** *(Weiche)* flank; **b)** *(Ballspiele)* centre; **eine** ~ **geben** *od.* **schlagen** centre the ball; **eine** ~ **direkt aufnehmen** pick up a centre; **c)** *(Teil des Spielfeldes)* wing; **über die [rechte/linke]** ~ **spielen** play on the [right/left] wing; **d)** *(Turnen)* flank vault; **e)** *(Milit.)* flank; **f)** *(Fechten)* lower outside target

flanken *itr. V.* **a)** *(Ballspiele)* **[in die Mitte]** ~**:** centre the ball; **b)** *(Turnen)* flank vault; **über etw.** *(Akk.)* ~**:** flank vault over sth.

Flanken-: ~**ball der** *(Ballspiele)* centre; ~**deckung die** *(Milit.)* flank defence; ~**schutz der** *(Milit.)* flank protection

flankieren *tr. V.* flank; **von jmdm./etw. flankiert werden** be flanked by sb./sth.; ~**de Maßnahmen** *(fig.)* additional measures

Flansch [flanʃ] **der;** ~**[e]s,** ~**e** *(Technik)* flange

Flappe ['flapə] **die;** ~, ~**n** *(bes. nordd.; ugs.)* **eine** ~ **ziehen** sulk; **halt die** ~**!** shut up! *(coll.)*

Flaps [flaps] **der;** ~**es,** ~**e** *(ugs.)* lout

flapsig ['flapsɪç] *(ugs.)* **1.** *Adj.* rude. **2.** *adv.* rudely

Flasche ['flaʃə] **die;** ~, ~**n a)** bottle; **eine** ~ **Wein/Bier/Milch** a bottle of wine/beer/milk; **etw. auf** ~**n abfüllen** *od.* **ziehen** bottle sth.; **gibst du deinem Kind immer noch die** ~**?** are you still bottle-feeding your child?; **ich muß dem Kind noch die** ~ **geben** I must just feed the baby; **ein Tier mit der** ~ **großziehen** rear an animal by bottle; **zur** ~ **greifen** *(fig.)* take to the bottle; **b)** *(ugs. abwertend) (Feigling)* wet *(sl.)*; *(unfähiger Mensch)* **eine [richtige]** ~ **sein** be [completely] useless; **du** ~**!** you useless item! *(coll.)*

flaschen-, Flaschen-: ~**batterie die** *(ugs.)* hoard of bottles; ~**baum der** *(Bot.)* custard-apple tree; sweet-sop tree; ~**bier das** bottled beer; ~**bofist,** ~**bovist der** *(Bot.)* devil's tobacco pouch; ~**bürste die** bottle brush; ~**etikett das** label [on a/the bottle]; ~**gärung die** fermentation in the bottle; ~**gas das** bottled gas; ~**gestell das** bottle rack; ~**grün** *Adj.* bottle-green; ~**hals der** *(auch fig.)* bottleneck; ~**kind das** bottle-fed baby; **waren Sie ein Brustkind oder ein** ~**kind?** were you breast-fed or bottle-fed?; ~**korken der** cork; ~**kürbis der** *(Bot.)* bottle-gourd; ~**milch die a)** *(abgefüllte Milch)* bottled milk; **b)** *(Nahrung)* [liquid] baby food; baby milk; ~**öffner der** bottle-opener; ~**pfand das** deposit [on a/the bottle]; ~**post die** message in a/the bottle; ~**regal das** bottle-rack; ~**wein der** wine by the bottle; **offene und** ~**weine** wine by the bottle or by the glass; ~**weise** *Adv.* by the bottleful; ~**zug der** block and tackle

Flaschner ['flaʃnɐ] **der;** ~**s,** ~ *(südd., schweiz.)* plumber

Flatschen ['fla(:)tʃn̩] **der;** ~**s,** ~ *(ugs.)* *(Lehm~)* lump; *(Tapeten~)* strip

Flatter ['flatɐ] *in* **die** ~ **machen** *(salopp)* beat it *(coll.)*

Flatter-: ~**geist der** fickle person; ~**gras das** millet grass

flatterhaft *Adj.* fickle

Flatterhaftigkeit die; ~**:** fickleness

Flatter·mann der; *Pl.* ~**männer** *(salopp)* **a)** *o. Pl. (nervöse Unruhe)* jitters *pl. (coll.)*; **einen** ~ **haben** have the jitters; *(zitternde Hände)* be shaking all the time; **b)** *(scherzh.: Brathuhn)* roast chicken

flattern *itr. V.* **a)** *mit Richtungsangabe mit sein* flutter; **der Vogel flatterte in seinem Käfig** the bird fluttered its wings in its cage; **b)** *(zittern)* ⟨*hands*⟩ shake; ⟨*eyelids*⟩ flutter; **seine Nerven flatterten** *(fig.)* he got in a flap *(coll.)*; **c)** *mit sein (vom Wind weitergetragen werden)* flutter; **zu Boden** *od.* **auf den Boden** ~**:** flutter to the ground; **plötzlich flattert mir eine Postkarte auf den Tisch** *(fig.)* suddenly a postcard appears on the table; **d)** *(die Haftung verlieren)* ⟨*ski, wheel*⟩ lose its grip

Flatter-: ~**satz der** *(Druckw.)* unjustified setting; ~**tier das** *(Zool.)* flying mammal; ~**zunge die** *(Musik)* tonguing

flau [flau̯] **1.** *Adj.* **a)** *(schwach, matt)* slack ⟨*breeze*⟩; flat ⟨*atmosphere*⟩; **b)** *(leicht übel)* queasy ⟨*feeling*⟩; **mir ist** ~ **[vor Hunger]** I feel queasy [with hunger]. **2.** *adv. (Kaufmannsspr.)* **das Geschäft geht** ~**:** business is slack; **die Börse eröffnete** ~**:** the market got off to a slow start

Flaum [flau̯m] **der;** ~**[e]s a)** fuzz; **b)** *(~feder)* down

Flaum·bart der downy beard

Flaumer der; ~**s,** ~ *(schweiz.)* mop

Flaum-: ~**feder die** down feather; ~**haar das** down

flaumig *Adj.* **a)** downy ; **b)** *(österr.: schaumig, porös)* fluffy

Flausch [flau̯ʃ] **der;** ~**[e]s,** ~**e** brushed wool

flauschig *Adj.* fluffy

Flausch·jacke die brushed-wool jacket

Flause ['flau̯zə] **die;** ~, ~**n;** *meist Pl. (ugs.)* **a)** *(Unsinn)* **er hat nur** ~**n im Kopf** he can never think of anything sensible; **jmdm. die** ~**n austreiben** knock some sense into sb.; **laß doch die albernen** ~**n** stop messing about *(coll.)*; **b)** *(Ausflucht)* excuse; ~**n machen** make excuses

Flaute ['flau̯tə] **die;** ~, ~**n a)** *(Seemannsspr.)* calm; **b)** *(Kaufmannsspr.)* fall[-off] in trade; **in der** ~**:** in the doldrums; **es herrscht eine [allgemeine]** ~**:** trade is [generally] slack; **c)** *(Sport: Tiefpunkt)* **sie überwanden die** ~**:** they got over the bad patch [in the game]

Fläz [flɛ:ts] **der;** ~**es,** ~**e** *(ugs. abwertend)* lout

fläzen *refl. V. (ugs. abwertend)* **sich in den/im Sessel** ~**:** flop into/lounge in the armchair

Flebbe ['flɛbə] **die;** ~, ~**n** *(salopp)* identity card

Flechse ['flɛksə] **die;** ~, ~**n** sinew

Flecht·arbeit die piece of wickerwork; ~**en** wickerwork *sing.*

Flechte ['flɛçtə] **die;** ~, ~**n a)** *(Bot.)* lichen; **b)** *(Med.)* eczema; **c)** *(geh.: Zopf)* plait

flechten *unr. tr. V.* plait ⟨*hair*⟩; weave ⟨*basket, mat*⟩; **etw. zu einem Korb** ~**:** weave sth. into a basket; weave a basket out of sth.; **jmdn. aufs Rad** ~ *(hist.)* break sb. on the wheel

Flechter der; ~**s,** ~**, Flechterin die;** ~, ~**nen** basket-weaver

Flecht-: ~**werk das a)** *(Geflecht)* wickerwork; **b)** *(Archit.)* wattle and daub; ~**zaun der** wicker fence

Fleck [flɛk] **der;** ~**[e]s,** ~**e a)** *(verschmutzte Stelle)* stain; **voller** ~**e sein** be covered in stains; ~**e machen** leave stains; **das macht keine** ~**e** that does not leave stains *or* does not stain; **einen** ~ **auf der [weißen] Weste haben** *(fig. ugs.)* have blotted one's copybook; **b)** *(andersfarbige Stelle)* patch; **ein weißer** ~ **auf der Landkarte** a piece of uncharted territory; an uncharted region; *s. auch* **blau;** **c)** *(Stelle, Punkt)* spot; **er rührte sich nicht vom** ~**:** he didn't move an inch; **auf demselben** ~ **stehen** stand in the same place; **wir brachten den Stein nicht vom** ~**:** we couldn't budge the stone; **ich bin nicht vom** ~ **gekommen** *(fig.)* I didn't get anywhere; **am falschen** ~ **sparen** *(fig.)* save on the wrong things; **vom** ~ **weg** *(fig.)* on the spot; *s. auch* **Herz a**

Fleckchen das; ~**s,** ~**:** spot; **ein schönes** ~ **Erde** a lovely little spot

flecken *itr. V.* stain

Flecken der; ~**s,** ~ **a)** *s.* **Fleck a, b; b)** *(Ortschaft)* little place

flecken-, Flecken-: ~**entfernungsmittel das** stain *or* spot remover; ~**los 1.** *Adj.* **a)** spotless; **b)** *(einwandrei, tadellos)* without blemish *postpos.*; **2.** *adv.* spotlessly

Fleck·entferner der, Fleck·entfernungs·mittel das, Flecken·wasser das stain *or* spot remover
Fleckerl·teppich der *(bayr., österr.)* patchwork rug
Fleck·fieber das *(Med.)* typhus
fleckig ['flɛkɪç] *Adj.* **a)** *(verschmutzt)* stained; **ganz ~:** full of stains; **b)** *(gepunktet)* speckled ‹*apple*›; blotchy ‹*face, skin*›
fleddern ['flɛdɐn] *tr. V.* plunder, rob ‹*person*›; *(salopp)* ransack ‹*desk etc.*›
Fleder·maus ['fle:dɐ-] **die** bat
Fledermaus·ärmel der *(Textilw.)* batwing sleeve
Fleder·wisch der feather duster
Fleet [fle:t] **das; ~s, ~e** *(nordd.)* canal
Flegel ['fle:gl̩] **der; ~s, ~** *(abwertend)* lout
Flegel·alter das *s.* **Flegeljahre**
Flegelei die; ~, ~en *(abwertend)* loutish behaviour; **eine solche ~/solche ~en** such loutish behaviour
flegelhaft 1. *Adj. (abwertend)* loutish; boorish ‹*tone of voice*›. **2.** *adv.* loutishly
Flegel·jahre *Pl.* uncouth adolescence *sing.*; **in die ~ kommen/aus den ~n heraussein** reach/be past the awkward age *sing.*
flegeln *refl. V. (abwertend)* **sich auf ein Sofa/in einen Sessel ~:** flop on to a sofa/into an armchair
flehen ['fle:ən] *itr. V.* plead; **[bei jmdm.] um etw. ~:** plead [with sb.] for sth.; **mit ~der Stimme** with a pleading voice; **zu Gott/zum Himmel [um etw.] ~:** beg God/Heaven [for sth.]
flehentlich *Adv. (geh.)* pleadingly
Fleisch [flaiʃ] **das; ~[e]s a)** *(Muskelgewebe)* flesh; **das nackte ~:** one's bare flesh; **das rohe ~:** one's raw flesh; **viel ~ zeigen** *(ugs.)* show a lot of flesh; *(fig.)* **sein eigen[es] ~ und Blut** *(geh.)* his own flesh and blood; **jmdm. in ~ und Blut übergehen** become second nature to sb.; **sich** *(Dat.)* **ins eigene ~ schneiden** cut off one's nose to spite one's face; **vom ~ fallen** *(ugs.)* waste away; **b)** *(Nahrungsmittel)* meat; **c)** *(Frucht~)* flesh; **d)** **den Weg allen ~es gehen** *(geh.)* go the way of all flesh
fleisch-, Fleisch-: ~abfälle *Pl.* meat scraps; **~arm 1.** *Adj.* ‹*diet*› low in meat; **2.** *adv.* **ich esse sehr ~arm** I eat very little meat; **~beschau die** meat inspection; *(ugs. scherzh.)* cattle-market; **~beschauer der** meat inspector; **~brocken der** chunk of meat; **~brühe die** *(mit Einlage)* meat soup; *(klar)* bouillon; consommé; **~einlage die** added meat; **mit ~einlage** with meat added; **~einwaage die** meat content
Fleischer ['flaiʃɐ] **der; ~s, ~:** butcher; *s. auch* **Bäcker**
Fleischerei die; ~, ~en butcher's shop; **in der ~:** at the butcher's; *s. auch* **Bäckerei**
Fleischer-: ~geselle der butcher; **~haken der** meat hook; **~handwerk das** butchery trade; **~hund der** large fierce dog; **ein Gemüt wie ein ~hund haben** *(ugs.)* be a cold-blooded sort *(coll.)*; **~laden der** *s.* **Fleischerei**; **~meister der** master butcher; **~messer das** butcher's knife
Fleisches·lust die *(geh.)* carnal lust
fleisch-, Fleisch-: ~esser der meat-eater; **~extrakt der** meat extract; **~farben, ~farbig** *Adj.* flesh-coloured; **~fliege die** meat-fly; **~fondue das** *(Kochk.)* meat fondue; **~fressend** *Adj.; nicht präd. (Biol.)* carnivorous; **~fresser der; ~s, ~** *(Biol.)* carnivore; **~füllung die** *(Kochk.)* meat stuffing; *(in Pasteten)* meat filling; **~gang der** *(Gastr.)* meat course; **~gericht das** meat dish; **~geworden** *Adj.; nicht präd. (dichter.)* incarnate *(Theol.)*; ‹*innocence, virtue, etc.*› personified; **~haken der** meat hook; **~hauer der** *(österr.)* butcher
fleischig *Adj.* plump ‹*hands, face*›; fleshy ‹*leaf, fruit*›

Fleisch-: ~käse der meat loaf; **~kloß der a)** *(Kochk.)* meat ball; **b)** *s.* **~klumpen**; **~klößchen das** small meat ball; **~klumpen der** *(ugs.)* **a)** *(großes Stück ~)* chunk of meat; **b)** *(abwertend: Mensch)* mound of flesh; **~konserve die** tin of meat *(Brit.)*; can of meat *(Amer.)*; **~konserven** tinned meat *(Brit.)*; canned meat *(Amer.)*
fleischlich *Adj.* **a)** *nicht präd. (veralt.)* **~e Kost** *od.* **Nahrung** meat; **b)** *(geh. veralt.)* carnal; **allem Fleischlichen entsagen** renounce the flesh
fleisch-, Fleisch-: ~los 1. *Adj.* **a)** ‹*meal*› without meat; **b)** *(hager, mager)* bony ‹*hands, face*›; **2.** *adv.* ‹*cook*› without meat; **~maschine die** *(südd., österr.) s.* **~wolf**; **~messer das** carving knife; **~pastete die** *(Kochk.)* pâté; **~preis der** price of meat; **die ~preise** the meat prices; **~ration die** meat ration; **~salat der** *(Kochk.)* meat salad; **~seite die** *(Gerberei)* flesh side; **~stück das** piece of meat; **~topf der** meat pot; **sich nach den ~töpfen Ägyptens sehnen/zurücksehnen** long for/long to return to the good life; **~vergiftung die** food poisoning [from meat]; **~waren** *Pl.* meat products; **~- und Wurstwaren** meat and sausages; **~werdung die; ~** *(selten, dicht.)* incarnation; **~wolf der** mincer; **etw. durch den ~wolf drehen** put sth. through the mincer; mince sth.; **~wunde die** flesh-wound; **~wurst die** pork sausage
Fleiß [flais] **der; ~es a)** *(eifriges Streben)* hard work; *(Eigenschaft)* diligence; **mit großem ~:** diligently; **mit ihrem beharrlichen ~:** with her unceasing application; **viel ~ auf etw.** *(Akk.)* **verwenden** put a lot of effort into sth.; **durch ~ etw. erreichen** achieve sth. by hard work; **im ~ nachlassen** become slack; **ohne ~ kein Preis** *(Spr.)* success never comes easily; **b)** *(veralt., südd.: Absicht)* **mit ~:** on purpose
Fleiß·arbeit die task requiring great diligence; **eine reine ~** *(abwertend)* a [diligent but] routine piece of work
fleißig ['flaisɪç] **1.** *Adj.* **a)** *(arbeitsam)* hard-working; **~e Hände** willing hands; **sie sind ~ wie die Bienen** *od.* **Ameisen** they work like beavers; **b)** *nicht präd. (von Fleiß zeugend)* **eine ~e Arbeit** a diligent piece of work; **c)** *(regelmäßig, häufig)* **ein ~er Besucher** a frequent visitor (*Gen.* to); **d)** *(unermüdlich)* indefatigable ‹*collector*›; great ‹*walker*›. **2.** *adv.* **a)** ‹*work, study*› hard; **~ lernen** learn as much as one can; **b)** *(unermüdlich)* ‹*drink, spend*› steadily; ‹*collect*› regularly; **immer ~ hauen** keep on hitting; **c)** *(regelmäßig)* frequently; **geh nur ~ spazieren** do as much walking as you can
Fleiß·prüfung die *examination to assess application*
flektierbar *Adj. (Sprachw.)* inflectional
flektieren [flɛk'ti:rən] *(Sprachw.)* **1.** *tr. V.* inflect. **2.** *itr. V.* be inflected
flennen ['flɛnən] *itr. V. (ugs. abwertend)* blubber
fletschen ['flɛtʃn̩] *tr., itr. V.* **die Zähne** *od.* **mit den Zähnen ~:** bare one's teeth; **mit gefletschten Zähnen** with bared teeth
fleucht [flɔyçt] *s.* **kreucht**
Fleurop Ⓦ ['flɔyrɔp] **die** Interflora **(P)**
flexibel [flɛ'ksi:bl̩] **1.** *Adj.* flexible. **2.** *adv.* flexibly
Flexibilität [flɛksibili'tɛ:t] **die; ~:** flexibility
Flexion [flɛ'ksio:n] **die; ~, ~en a)** *(Sprachw.)* inflexion; *(von Adjektiven, Substantiven)* declension; *(von Verben)* conjugation; **b)** *(Med.)* flexion
flexions-, Flexions-: ~endung die *(Sprachw.)* inflectional suffix *or* ending; **~los** *Adj. (Sprachw.)* uninflected
Flexo·druck ['flɛkso-] **der** *(Druckw.)* flexographic printing
flicht *Imperativ Sg. u. 3. Pers. Sg. Präsens v.* **flechten**

Flick·arbeit die repair; **mit einer ~ beschäftigt sein** be repairing *or* mending something
flicken ['flɪkn̩] *tr. V.* mend ‹*trousers, dress*›; repair ‹*engine, cable*›; mend, repair ‹*wall, roof*›; **etw. notdürftig ~:** patch sth. up
Flicken der; ~s, ~: patch
Flicken-: ~decke die patchwork quilt; **~teppich der** patchwork rug
Flickflack ['flɪkflak] **der; ~s, ~s** *(Turnen)* flik-flak
Flick-: ~korb der sewing basket; **~schneider der** *(veralt.)* mending tailor; **~schuster der a)** *(veralt. abwertend)* mending shoemaker; cobbler; **b)** *(fig.: Nichtskönner)* bungler; **~schusterei die** *(fig. abwertend)* bungling; **~werk das;** *o. Pl. (abwertend)* botched-up job; **~wort das;** *Pl.* **~wörter** filler; **~zeug das** repair kit
Flieder ['fli:dɐ] **der; ~s, ~:** lilac
flieder-, Flieder-: ~duft der scent of lilac; **~farben, ~farbig** *Adj.* lilac; **~strauch der** lilac bush; **~tee der** elderberry tea
Fliege ['fli:gə] **die; ~, ~n a)** fly; **die Menschen starben wie die ~n** people were dying like flies; **er tut keiner ~ etwas zuleide/könnte keiner ~ etwas zuleide tun** he wouldn't/couldn't hurt a fly; *(fig.)* **ihn stört die ~ an der Wand** the least little thing annoys him; **zwei ~n mit einer Klappe schlagen** kill two birds with one stone; **die** *od.* **'ne ~ machen** *(salopp)* beat it *(sl.)*; **b)** *(Schleife)* bow-tie; **c)** *(Bärtchen)* shadow
fliegen 1. *unr. itr. V.* **a)** *mit sein* fly; **das ~de Personal** the air-crew; **im Wind ~:** be flying in the wind; **mit ~den Rockschößen** with flapping coat-tails; **die Funken flogen** sparks flew about; **in die Luft ~:** blow up; *s. auch* **Fahne b**; **b)** *mit sein (ugs.: geworfen werden)* **aus der Kurve ~:** skid off a/the bend; **vom Pferd/Fahrrad ~:** fall off a/the horse/bicycle; **c)** *mit sein (ugs.: entlassen werden)* be sacked *(coll.)*; get the sack *(coll.)*; **auf die Straße/aus einer Stellung ~:** get the sack *(coll.)*; *be thrown out*; **von der Schule ~:** be chucked out [of the school] *(coll.)*; **d)** *mit sein (ugs.: hinfallen, stürzen)* fall; **in einen Graben ~:** fall into a ditch; **über etw.** *(Akk.)* **~:** trip over sth.; **durch das Examen/eine Prüfung ~** *(fig.)* fail the exam/a test; **e)** *mit sein* **auf jmdn./etw. ~** *(ugs.)* go for sb./sth.; **er fliegt auf Blondinen** he makes a beeline for blondes; **f)** *meist mit sein (flattern, zittern)* ‹*pulse*› race; **sein Atem fliegt** he is gasping for breath; **er flog am ganzen Körper** he was trembling all over; **g)** *mit sein (eilen, rasen)* fly; race; **das Pferd flog wie ein Pfeil über die Bahn** the horse raced *or* flew over the track like a shot from a gun; **ihre Hand flog über das Papier** her hand flew over the paper; **in ~der Eile** *od.* **Hast** in a mad rush. **2.** *unr. tr. V.* **a)** *(steuern, fliegend befördern)* fly ‹*aircraft, passengers, goods*›; **b)** *auch mit sein (fliegend ausführen)* **einen Einsatz ~:** fly a mission; **einen Umweg ~:** make a detour; **eine Kurve ~:** describe a curve; **einen Looping ~:** loop the loop; **einen Angriff ~** *(Milit.)* make an attack. **3.** *refl. V.* **die Maschine fliegt sich gut/schlecht** the plane flies well/badly; **es fliegt sich gut/schlecht hier/heute** the flying is good/bad here/today
fliegend *Adj.; nicht präd.* flying; **ein ~er Händler** a pedlar; **~e Bauten** mobile buildings; **der Fliegende Holländer** the Flying Dutchman
Fliegen-: ~draht der fly screen; **~dreck der** fly droppings *pl.*; **~fänger der** fly-paper; **~fenster das** wire-mesh window; **~gewicht das** *(Schwerathletik)* **a)** *o. Pl.* flyweight; **die Meisterschaften im ~gewicht** the flyweight championships; **im ~gewicht starten** compete at flyweight; **b)** *s.* **~gewichtler**; **~gewichtler** [~gəvɪçtlɐ]

der; ~s, ~: flyweight; **~klatsche die** fly swat; **~kopf der** *(Druckw.) piece of type turned over to print as black oblong;* **~pilz der** fly agaric; **~schnäpper der** *(Zool.)* flycatcher; **~schrank der** meat-safe

Flieger der; ~s, ~ a) pilot; **er ist bei den ~n** *(Milit.)* he's in the air force; **b)** *(Radsport)* sprinter; **c)** *(Artistik)* trapeze artist; **d)** *(Zool.)* flyer

Flieger-: ~abwehr die *s.* **Flugabwehr; ~abzeichen das** *(Milit.)* flying badge; **~alarm der** air-raid warning; **~angriff der** air raid

Fliegerei die; ~: flying *no art.*

Flieger·horst der *(Milit.)* military airfield

Fliegerin die; ~, ~nen [woman] pilot

fliegerisch *Adj.; nicht präd.* aeronautical; **~e Eigenschaften** handling characteristics; handling *sing.*

Flieger-: ~jacke die flying jacket; **~krankheit die** altitude sickness; **~rennen das** *(Radsport)* sprint; **~schule die** flying school; **~sprache die** airmen's jargon; **~staffel die** *(Milit.)* [flying] squadron

Flieh·burg die refuge

fliehen ['fli:ən] **1.** *unr. itr. V.; mit sein (flüchten)* flee (**vor** + *Dat.* from); *(aus dem Gefängnis usw.)* escape (**aus** from); **ins Ausland/über die Grenze ~:** flee the country/escape over the border. **2.** *unr. tr. V. (geh.: meiden)* shun

fliehend *Adj.; nicht präd.* sloping ‹*forehead*›; receding ‹*chin*›

Flieh·kraft die *(Physik)* centrifugal force

Fliese ['fli:zə] **die; ~, ~n** tile; **etw. mit ~n auslegen** tile sth.

fliesen *tr. V.* tile

Fliesenleger [-le:gɐ] **der; ~s, ~:** tiler

Fließ-: ~arbeit die; *o. Pl.* assembly line production; **~band das** conveyor belt; **am ~band arbeiten** *od. (ugs.)* **stehen** work on the assembly line; **am ~band gefertigt werden** be produced on the assembly line; **~band·arbeit die** assembly-line work; **~band·arbeiter der** assembly-line worker; **~band·fertigung die** assembly-line production

fließen ['fli:sn̩] *unr. itr. V.; mit sein* **a)** flow; **ein Bach ist ein ~des Gewässer** a stream is a body of running water; **ein Zimmer mit ~dem [warmem und kaltem] Wasser** a room with [hot and cold] running water; **„Alles fließt", sagte Heraklit** 'All is flux', said Heraclitus; *(unpers.)* **es floß Blut** blood was shed; **b)** *(fig.)* **viele Devisen flossen ins Land** a great deal of foreign currency flowed into the country; **die Gaben flossen reichlich** donations were pouring in; **die Nachrichten aus diesem Gebiet flossen nur spärlich** news from this area came in very infrequently; **der Verkehr war ~d** the traffic kept moving; **die Grenzen [zwischen zwei Gebieten] sind ~d** the dividing-line [between two areas] is blurred; **~de Übergänge** fluid transitions; **die Verse flossen ihm aus der Feder** the verses flowed from his pen; **eine Sprache ~d sprechen** speak a language fluently

Fließ-: ~grenze die *(Technik)* yield point; **~heck das** *(Kfz-W.)* fastback; **~komma das** *(DV)* floating point; **~satz der** *(Druckw.)* undisplay; **~wasser das** *(Touristik)* running water

Flimmer-: ~epithel das *(Biol.)* ciliated epithelium; **~kasten der, ~kiste die** *(ugs.)* telly *(coll.)*; box *(coll.)*

flimmern ['flɪmɐn] *itr. V.; mit Richtungsangabe mit sein* ‹*water, air, surface*› shimmer; ‹*film*› flicker; **ihm flimmerte es vor den Augen** everything was swimming in front of his eyes; **über den Bildschirm ~** *(ugs.)* be served up on the box *(coll.)*

flink [flɪŋk] **1.** *Adj.* nimble ‹*fingers*›; sharp ‹*eyes*›; quick ‹*hands*›; **~ wie ein Wiesel** as quick as a flash; **er hat noch ~e Beine** *od.* **ist noch ~ auf den Beinen** *(ugs.)* he's still nippy on his pins *(coll.)*. **2.** *adv.* quickly; **mit etw. ~ bei der Hand sein** be very ready to do sth.; **aber ein bißchen ~!** *(ugs.)* and be quick about it!

Flinkheit die; ~ *s.* **flink 1:** nimbleness; sharpness; quickness

flink·züngig [-t͡syŋɪç] **1.** *Adj.* eloquent. **2.** *adv.* eloquently

Flinte ['flɪntə] **die; ~, ~n** shotgun; **alles, was ihm vor die ~ kommt** everything he gets in his sights; **der soll mir nur vor die ~ kommen!** *(fig. salopp)* if I can just get my hands on him; **die ~ ins Korn werfen** *(fig.)* throw in the towel

Flinten-: ~knall der gun-fire; **ein ~knall** a gunshot; **~kugel die** shotgun pellet; **~lauf der** shotgun barrel; **~weib das** *(abwertend)* soldier in skirts

Flip [flɪp] **der; ~s, ~s** flip

Flipflop·schaltung ['flɪpflɔp-] **die** *(Elektrot.)* flip-flop circuit

Flipper ['flɪpɐ] **der; ~s, ~, Flipper·automat der** pinball machine; **Flipper spielen** play pinball

flippern ['flɪpɐn] *itr. V. (ugs.)* play pinball

flirren ['flɪrən] *itr. V. (geh.)* ‹*heat, light, dust, etc.*› shimmer

Flirt [flɪrt] **der; ~s, ~s** flirtation; **einen ~ mit jmdm. anfangen/haben** start flirting with sb./flirt with sb.

flirten *itr. V.* flirt

Flittchen ['flɪtçən] **das; ~s, ~** *(ugs. abwertend)* floozie

Flitter ['flɪtɐ] **der; ~s, ~ a)** *o. Pl. (täuschender Glanz)* frippery; trumpery; **b)** *(Metallplättchen)* sequin

Flitter-: ~gold das Dutch metal; **~kram der** *(ugs. abwertend)* frippery; trumpery

flittern *itr. V. (ugs. scherzh.)* honeymoon

Flitter-: ~wochen *Pl.* honeymoon *sing.*; **in die ~wochen fahren** go on one's honeymoon; **~wöchner der** *(ugs. scherzh.)* honeymooner

Flitz[e]·bogen ['flɪt͡s(ə)-] **der** bow; *(fig.)* **gespannt sein wie ein ~:** be on tenterhooks; **ich bin gespannt wie ein ~, ob er kommen wird** I'm dying to see if he will come; **auf etw.** *(Akk.)* **gespannt sein wie ein ~:** be on tenterhooks waiting for sth.

flitzen ['flɪt͡sn̩] *itr. V.; mit sein (ugs.)* shoot; dart; **ich flitze mal gerade zum Fleischer** I'll just dash to the butcher's; **nach rechts und links ~:** dart to either side

Flitzer der; ~s, ~ *(ugs.)* sporty job *(coll.)*

floaten ['floʊtn̩] *tr., itr. V. (Wirtsch.)* float

Floating ['floʊtɪŋ] **das; ~s, ~s** *(Wirtsch.)* floating

F-Loch ['ɛf-] **das** *(Musik)* F-hole

flocht [flɔxt] *1. u. 3. Pers. Sg. Prät. v.* **flechten**

Flöckchen ['flœkçən] **das; ~s, ~** *(Schnee~)* flake; *(Staub~)* bit of fluff

Flocke ['flɔkə] **die; ~, ~n a) eine ~ Watte/Wolle** a bit of cottonwool/tuft of wool; **b)** *(Schnee~)* flake; **es schneit in dicken ~n** it's snowing large flakes; **c)** *(Schaum~)* blob; *(Staub~)* piece of fluff

Flocken-: ~blume die *(Bot.)* centaury; **~wirbel der** *(geh.)* whirl of snowflakes

flockig *Adj.* fluffy; **~er Schaum** blobs *pl.* of foam; **Butter ~ rühren** cream butter

Flock-: ~print der; ~[s] *(Textilw.)* flock printing; **~seide die** floss

flog [flo:k] *1. u. 3. Pers. Sg. Prät. v.* **fliegen**

floh [flo:] *1. u. 3. Pers. Sg. Prät. v.* **fliehen**

Floh [flo:] **der; ~[e]s, Flöhe** ['flø:ə] **a)** flea; *(fig.)* **lieber einen Sack [voll] Flöhe hüten, als ...:** even if you paid me a million pounds I wouldn't ...; **jmdm. einen ~ ins Ohr setzen** *(ugs.)* put an idea into sb.'s head; **die Flöhe husten** *od.* **niesen hören** *(ugs.)* know it all before it happens; **b)** *Pl. (salopp: Geld)* dough *sing. (sl.)*; bread *sing. (sl.)*

Floh·biß der flea-bite

flöhen ['flø:ən] *tr. V.* flea

Floh-: ~hüpfen das *(Kinderspiel)* tiddlywinks; **~kino das** *(ugs.)* flea-pit *(sl.)*; **~kraut das** *(Bot.)* fleabane; **~markt der** flea market; **~zirkus der** flea-circus

Flom[en] ['flo:m(ə)n] **der; ~s** *(nordd.)* leaf fat

Flop [flɔp] **der; ~s, ~s** *(ugs.)* flop *(coll.)*

¹Flor [flo:ɐ̯] **der; ~s, ~e** *(geh.)* **a)** *(Blütenpracht)* **im ~ stehen** be in full bloom; **einen zweiten ~ entfalten** have a second flush; **b)** *(Blumenfülle)* display

²Flor der; ~s, ~e, *selten:* **Flöre** ['flø:rə] **a)** *(zartes Gewebe)* gauze; **b)** *(Faserenden)* pile; **c)** *s.* **Trauerflor**

Flora ['flo:ra] **die; ~, Floren** flora

Flor·band das black band; mourning band

¹Florentiner [florɛn'ti:nɐ] **der; ~s, ~:** Florentine

²Florentiner der; ~s, ~ a) *(Hut)* picture hat; **b)** *(Gebäck)* florentine

Florentinerin die; ~, ~nen Florentine

florentinisch *Adj.* Florentine

Florenz [flo'rɛnt͡s] **(das); Florenz'** Florence

Florett [flo'rɛt] **das; ~[e]s, ~e a)** *(Stoßwaffe)* foil; **mit dem ~ fechten** fence with a foil; **b)** *o. Pl. (~fechten)* foils *sing.*; foil fencing *no art.*

Florett-: ~fechten das foil fencing *no art.*; **~fechter der** foil fencer

Flor·fliege die *(Zool.)* green lacewing

florieren [flo'ri:rən] *itr. V.* ‹*business*› flourish; **ein [gut] ~der Laden** a flourishing shop

Florist [flo'rɪst] **der; ~en, ~en, Floristin die; ~, ~nen a)** *(Blumenbinder)* [qualified] flower-arranger; **b)** *(Kenner einer Flora)* botanist; **c)** *(Blumenhändler)* florist

Flor·teppich der pile carpet

Floskel ['flɔskl̩] **die; ~, ~n** cliché; **der Brief enthält nichts außer abgedroschenen ~n** the letter is full of clichés *or* hackneyed phrases

floskelhaft 1. *Adj.* cliché-ridden; clichéd. **2.** *adv.* **sich ~ ausdrücken** talk in clichés

floß [flɔs] *1. u. 3. Pers. Sg. Prät. v.* **fließen**

Floß [flo:s] **das; ~es, Flöße** ['flø:sə] **a)** raft; **b)** *(an der Angel)* float

flöß·bar *Adj.* navigable by raft *postpos.*

Flosse ['flɔsə] **die; ~, ~n a)** *(Zool., Flugw.)* fin; **b)** *(zum Tauchen)* flipper; **c)** *(ugs. scherzh. od. abwertend: Hand)* paw

flößen ['flø:sn̩] *tr., itr. V.* float; **Baumstämme [auf dem Fluß] ~:** raft tree trunks [on the river]

Flossen·füß[l]er der *(Zool.)* pinniped

Flößer ['flø:sɐ] **der; ~s, ~:** raftsman

Flößerei [flø:sə'rai] **die; ~:** rafting

Floß-: ~fahrt die voyage by raft; **~gasse die** channel for rafts; **~holz das** rafted wood

Flotation [flota't͡si̯o:n] **die; ~, ~en** *(bes. Hüttenw.)* flotation

Flöte ['flø:tə] **die; ~, ~n a)** *(Musik)* flute; *(Block~)* recorder; **~ spielen** play the flute/recorder; **die ~ des Pan** the pipes of Pan; **b)** *(Skat)* **die [ganze] ~ herunterspielen** play a [straight] flush; **c)** *(hohes Glas)* flute

flöten ['flø:tn̩] **1.** *itr. V.* **a)** ‹*bird*› flute; **b)** *(ugs.: affektiert sprechen)* pipe; **in den sanftesten Tönen ~:** speak in wheedling tones. **2.** *tr. V.* whistle ‹*song, tune*›

flöten-, Flöten-: ~|gehen *unr. itr. V.; mit sein (ugs.)* **a)** *(verlorengehen)* ‹*money*› go down the drain; ‹*time*› be wasted; **seine Illusionen gingen ~:** his illusions went for a burton *(Brit. sl.)*; **b)** *(entzweigehen)* get smashed; **~kessel der** whistling kettle; **~konzert das a)** *(Musikstück)* flute concerto; **b)** *(Veranstaltung)* flute concert; **~musik die** flute music; **~register das** *(Musik)* flute stop; **~spiel das** flute-playing; **~spieler der** flute-player; **~ton der** sound of a flute; **jmdm. die ~töne beibringen** *(fig. ugs.)* teach sb. a thing or two *(coll.)*

Flötist [flø'tɪst] **der;** ~**en,** ~**en, Flötistin die;** ~, ~**nen** flautist
flott [flɔt] **1.** *Adj.* **a)** *(ugs.: schwungvoll)* lively ‹*music, dance, pace, style*›; snappy ‹*dialogue*›; **den** ~**en Otto haben** *(salopp)* have the runs *(coll.)*; **b)** *(ugs.: schick, modisch)* smart ‹*hat, suit, car*›; **c)** *(munter, hübsch)* stylish; smart; ~ **aussehen** look attractive; **d)** *(leichtlebig)* **ein** ~**es Leben führen** be fast-living; **e)** *nicht attr. (fahrbereit, wiederhergestellt)* seaworthy ‹*vessel*›; *(ugs.)* roadworthy ‹*vehicle*›; airworthy ‹*aircraft*›; **mein Auto ist wieder** ~**:** my car ist back on the road again. **2.** *adv.* ‹*work*› quickly; ‹*dance, write*› in a lively manner; ‹*be dressed*› smartly
flott|bekommen *unr. tr. V.: s.* **flottkriegen**
Flotte ['flɔtə] **die;** ~, ~**n** fleet
Flotten-: ~**abkommen das** naval treaty; ~**chef der** commander-in-chief of the/a fleet; ~**kommando das** fleet command; ~**parade die** naval parade; ~**stützpunkt der** naval base; ~**verband der** naval unit
Flottille [flɔ'tɪl(j)ə] **die;** ~, ~**n** flotilla
Flottillen·admiral der rear-admiral
flott-: ~**|kommen** *unr. itr. V.* get afloat; ~**|kriegen** *tr. V.* get ‹*boat*› afloat; get ‹*car*› going; ~**|machen** *tr. V.* refloat ‹*ship*›; get ‹*car*› back on the road; ~**weg** *Adv. (ugs.)* ~**weg arbeiten** keep at it
Flöz [flø:ts] **das;** ~**es,** ~**e** *(Bergbau)* seam
Fluch [flu:x] **der;** ~**[e]s, Flüche** ['fly:çə] **a)** *(Kraftwort)* curse; oath; **ein derber/lästerlicher** ~**:** a vulgar/blasphemous oath; **einen** ~ **ausstoßen/unterdrücken** utter/suppress an oath; **b)** *(Verwünschung)* curse; **einen** ~ **gegen jmdn. ausstoßen** utter a curse against sb.; **c)** *o. Pl. (Unheil, Verderben)* curse; **ein** ~ **liegt über/lastet auf jmdm.** there's a curse on sb.; **das ist der** ~ **der bösen Tat** that's the wages of sin
fluch·beladen *Adj. (geh.)* accursed
fluchen *itr. V.* **a)** *(Flüche ausstoßen)* curse; swear; **auf/über jmdn./etw.** ~**:** swear at *or* curse sb./sth.; **b)** *(verwünschen) (geh.)* curse; **jmdm./einer Sache** ~**:** curse sb./sth.
[1]**Flucht** [flʊxt] **die;** ~ **a)** *(Fliehen, Flüchten)* flight; **auf/während der** ~**:** while fleeing; *(von Gefangenen)* on the run; **jmdn. auf der** ~ **erschießen** shoot sb. while he/she is trying to escape; **auf** *od.* **während der** ~ **erschossen werden** be shot while trying to escape; **in wilder** ~ **davonjagen** run away in mad panic; **die** ~ **aus dem Gefängnis/aus einem Land** the escape from prison/from a country; **den Bankräubern/Gefangenen gelang die** ~**:** the bank robbers/prisoners succeeded in escaping; **die** ~ **ergreifen** ‹*prisoner*› make a dash for freedom; *(fig.)* make a dash for it; **jmdn. in die** ~ **schlagen** put sb. to flight; *s. auch* **Ägypten; b)** *(Ausweichen)* refuge; **ihr blieb nur noch die** ~ **in den Alkohol/das Rauschgift** the only thing left to her was to take refuge in alcohol/drugs; **die** ~ **in die Krankheit/Anonymität** taking refuge in illness/anonymity; **die** ~ **in die Krankheit antreten** take refuge in illness; **die** ~ **aus der Wirklichkeit/Verantwortung** escape from reality/responsibility; **die** ~ **nach vorn antreten** take the bull by the horns; **die** ~ **in die Öffentlichkeit antreten** make a public statement
[2]**Flucht die;** ~, ~**en a)** *(Bauw.: Häuser~, Arkaden~)* row; **die** ~ **der Fenster** the line of the windows; **b)** *(Zimmer~)* suite
flucht-, Flucht-: ~**artig 1.** *Adj.* hurried; hasty; **2.** *adv.* hurriedly; hastily; ~**auto das** getaway car; ~**burg die** refuge
flüchten ['flʏçtn] **1.** *itr. V.; mit sein* **vor jmdm./etw.** ~**:** flee from sb./sth.; **vor der Polizei** ~**:** run away from the police; *(mit Erfolg)* escape from the police; **zu jmdm.** ~**:** take refuge with sb.; **ins Ausland** ~**:** escape abroad; **unter ein schützendes Dach** ~**:** take shelter under a protective roof. **2.** *refl. V.* **sich in ein Bauernhaus** ~**:** take refuge in a farmhouse; **sich aufs Dach** ~**:** escape on to the roof
Flucht-: ~**fahrzeug das** getaway vehicle; ~**gefahr die** risk of an escape attempt; **es besteht** ~**gefahr/keine** ~**gefahr** there's a/no risk of an escape attempt; ~**helfer der** person who aids/aided an/the escape; ~**hilfe die** aiding an escape
flüchtig ['flʏçtɪç] **1.** *Adj.* **a)** *(flüchtend)* fugitive; **er ist noch** ~**:** he ist still at large; **ein** ~**er Dieb/Verbrecher** a wanted thief/criminal; **b)** *(oberflächlich)* cursory; superficial ‹*insight*›; **eine** ~**e Arbeit** a hurried piece of work; **c)** *(eilig, schnell)* quick; short ‹*visit, greeting*›; fleeting ‹*glance*›; **d)** *(vergänglich)* fleeting ‹*moment*›; quickly changing ‹*moods*›; sudden ‹*temper, whim*›; **e)** *(Chemie)* volatile. **2.** *adv.* **a)** *(oberflächlich)* cursorily; **b)** *(eilig)* hurriedly
Flüchtigkeit die; ~, ~**en a)** *(Oberflächlichkeit)* cursoriness; **b)** *s.* **Flüchtigkeitsfehler; c)** *(Vergänglichkeit)* fleetingness; **d)** *(Chemie)* volatility
Flüchtigkeits·fehler der slip; *(tadelnswert)* careless mistake
Flucht·kapital das *(Wirtsch.) capital which has been sent out of the country to evade tax*
Flüchtling ['flʏçtlɪŋ] **der;** ~**s,** ~**e** refugee
Flüchtlings-: ~**ausweis der** refugee's identity card; ~**elend das** hardship among refugees; ~**lager das** refugee camp; ~**treck der** long stream of refugees
Flucht-: ~**linie die** vanishing-line; ~**plan der** escape plan; ~**punkt der** *(Kunstwiss.)* vanishing-point; ~**reaktion die** *(Verhaltensf.)* escape reaction; ~**verdacht der: es besteht [kein]** ~**verdacht** he/she is [not] likely to try to escape; ~**versuch der** escape attempt; **einen** ~**versuch unternehmen** *od.* **machen** attempt to escape; ~**weg der** escape route; **sich** *(Dat.)* **den** ~**weg offenhalten** keep a way out open; **sich** *(Dat.)* **den** ~**weg freischießen** shoot one's way out
fluch·würdig *Adj. (geh.)* monstrous
Flug [flu:k] **der;** ~**[e]s, Flüge** ['fly:gə] **a)** *o. Pl.* flight; **im** ~**:** in flight; **die Urlaubstage/Stunden vergingen [wie] im** ~**e** the holiday/hours flew by; **b)** *(Flugreise)* flight; **c)** *(Skispringen)* jump; **einen** ~ **[sicher] stehen** land safely; **d)** *(Jägerspr.)* flock
flug-, Flug-: ~**abwehr die** *(Milit.)* anti-aircraft defence; ~**abwehr·rakete die** *(Milit.)* anti-aircraft missile; ~**angst die** fear of flying; ~**asche die** fly ash; ~**bahn die** trajectory; ~**ball der** *(Tennis)* volley; ~**begleiter der** steward; ~**begleiterin die** stewardess; ~**benzin das** aviation fuel; ~**bereit** *Adj.* ready for take-off *postpos.*; ~**betrieb der** air traffic; ~**bild das** *(Zool.)* flight silhouette; ~**blatt das** pamphlet; leaflet; ~**boot das** flying boat; ~**datenschreiber der** flight-recorder; ~**dauer die** flight time; ~**dienst der a)** *(Flugverkehr)* air service; **b)** *(Überwachungsdienst)* air traffic control; ~**dienst·leiter der** air traffic controller; ~**drache der** *(Zool.)* flying dragon; ~**echse die** *(Zool.)* pterosaurian; ~**eigenschaft die;** *meist Pl.* flying characteristic
Flügel ['fly:gl] **der;** ~**s,** ~ **a)** wing; **mit den** ~**n schlagen** flap its/their wings; **die** ~ **hängen lassen** *(fig. ugs.)* become disheartened; **jmdm. die** ~ **stutzen** *od.* **beschneiden** *(fig.)* clip sb.'s wings; **das verlieh ihm** ~ *(fig. geh.)* that gave *or* lent him wings *(literary)*; **b)** *(Altar~)* wing; *(Fenster~)* casement; *(Nasen~)* nostril; **der linke/rechte** ~ **der Lunge** the left/right lung; **c)** *(Klavier)* grand piano; **jmdn. auf dem** ~ **begleiten** accompany sb. on the piano; **d)** *(Milit., Ballspiele)* wing; **über die** ~ **spielen/angreifen** play/attack on the wings; **e)** *(Tragfläche, Partei~, Gebäude~)* wing; **f)** *(Schrauben~)* vane; *(Windmühlen~)* sail
flügel-, Flügel-: ~**altar der** winged altar; ~**decke die** *(Zool.)* elytron; wing-case; ~**fenster das** casement window; ~**horn das** *(Musik)* flugelhorn; ~**lahm** *Adj.* **a)** ‹*bird*› with an injured wing; **einen Vogel** ~**lahm schießen** wing a bird; **b)** *(fig.: mutlos, kraftlos)* lacking energy *postpos.*; limping ‹*organization*›; ~**mutter die** wing nut; ~**pumpe die** rotary pump; ~**rad das a)** impeller wheel; **b)** *(als Symbol)* winged wheel; ~**roß das** *(Myth.)* winged horse; ~**schlag der** beat of [its/their] wings; ~**schlagend** *Adj.; nicht präd.* beating its/their wings; ~**spann·weite die** *(Flugw., Zool.)* wing span; ~**stürmer der** *(Ballspiele)* wing forward; winger; ~**tür die** double door
flug-, Flug-: ~**entfernung die** distance by air; ~**erfahrung die** flying experience; ~**fähig** *Adj.* airworthy; ~**feld das** airfield; ~**gast der** [air] passenger
flügge ['flʏgə] *Adj.* fully-fledged; *(fig.: selbständig)* independent
Flug-: ~**geschwindigkeit die** *(eines Flugzeugs)* flying speed; *(eines Vogels)* speed of flight; ~**gesellschaft die** airline; ~**hafen der** airport; ~**hafen Frankfurt** Frankfurt airport; ~**hafen·restaurant das** airport restaurant; ~**hafer der** *(Bot.)* wild oat; ~**höhe die** altitude; **in einer** ~**höhe von ...:** at an altitude of ...; ~**hund der** *(Zool.)* flying fox; ~**ingenieur der** flight engineer; ~**kapitän der** captain; ~**kilometer der** [air] kilometre; ~**körper der** space vehicle; ~**lärm der** aircraft noise; ~**lehrer der** flying instructor; ~**leiter der** flight controller; ~**linie die a)** *(Strecke)* air route; **b)** *(Gesellschaft)* airline; ~**loch** *s.* **Einflugloch;** ~**lotse der** air traffic controller; ~**motor der** aircraft engine; ~**objekt das** flying object; **ein unbekanntes** ~**objekt** an unidentified flying object; ~**personal das** flight personnel; ~**plan der** flight schedule; ~**platz der** airfield; aerodrome; ~**preis der** air fare; ~**reise die** air journey; ~**route die** air route
flugs [flʊks] *Adv. (veralt.)* swiftly
flug-, Flug-: ~**sand der** wind-borne sand; ~**saurier der** *(Zool.)* pterosaurian; ~**schanze die** *(Skifliegen)* ski-jump *(used for ski-flying)*; ~**schein a)** pilot's licence; **b)** *(Flugticket)* air ticket; ~**schneise die** air corridor; ~**schreiber der** flight-recorder; ~**schrift die** pamphlet; ~**schüler der** trainee pilot; ~**sicherung die** air traffic control; ~**simulator der** flight simulator; ~**sport der** aerial sports; ~**steig der** pier; *(Ausgang)* ~**steig 5** gate 5; ~**stunde die** hour's flying time; **zwei** ~**stunden entfernt** two hours away by air; ~**tauglich** *Adj.* ‹*pilot*› fit to fly; ~**technik die a)** *(Technologie)* aeronautical engineering; **b)** *(fliegerisches Können)* flying technique; ~**technisch 1.** *Adj.; nicht präd.* aeronautical; **2.** *adv.* aeronautically; ~**ticket das** air ticket; ~**touristik die** tourism by air; ~**tüchtig** *Adj. s.* ~**fähig;** ~**unfähig** *Adj.* flightless ‹*bird*›; *(vorübergehend)* ‹*bird*› unable to fly; ‹*aircraft*› not airworthy; ~**verbindung die** air connection; ~**verkehr der** air traffic; **der** ~**verkehr nimmt ständig zu** the volume of air traffic is continually increasing; ~**wetter das** flying weather; ~**wetter·dienst der** meteorological service [for aviation]; ~**zeit die** flight time
Flug·zeug das; ~**[e]s,** ~**e** aeroplane *(Brit.)*; airplane *(Amer.)*; aircraft; **mit dem** ~ **reisen** travel by plane *or* air
Flugzeug-: ~**absturz der** plane crash; ~**bau der;** *o. Pl.* aircraft construction; ~**besatzung die** crew; ~**entführer der** [aircraft] hijacker; ~**entführung die** [aircraft] hijack[ing]; ~**halle die** hangar; ~**industrie die** aircraft industry; ~**katastrophe die** air disaster; ~**konstrukteur der** aircraft designer; ~**modell das** model

aeroplane; ~**mutterschiff das** seaplane carrier; ~**träger der** aircraft carrier; ~**typ der** model of aircraft; ~**unglück das** plane crash; ~**wrack das** wreckage of the/a plane **zwei ~wracks** the wreckage of two planes

Fluidum ['flu:idʊm] **das; ~s, Fluida** aura; atmosphere; **von ihr/davon geht ein gewisses ~ aus** she/it exudes a certain aura; **das ~ des Künstlers** the aura *or* atmosphere surrounding the artist

Fluktuation [flʊktu̯a'tsi̯o:n] **die; ~, ~en** *(bes. Wirtsch., Soziol.)* fluctuation (*Gen.* in)

fluktuieren [flʊktu'i:rən] *(bes. Wirtsch., Soziol.) itr. V.* fluctuate

Flunder ['flʊndɐ] **die; ~, ~n** flounder

Flunkerei [flʊŋkə'rai̯] **die; ~, ~en** *(ugs.)* **a)** *o. Pl. (Flunkern)* story-telling; **b)** *(Lügengeschichte)* tall story

flunkern ['flʊŋkɐn] *itr. V.* tell stories

Flunsch [flʊnʃ] **der; ~[e]s, ~e** *od.* **die; ~, ~en** *(ugs.)* pout; **eine[n] ~ ziehen** *od.* **machen** pout

[1]**Fluor** ['flu:ɔr] **das; ~s** *(Chemie)* fluorine

[2]**Fluor der; ~s** *(Med.)* vaginal discharge

Fluor·chlor·kohlen·wasserstoff der *(Chemie)* chlorofluorocarbon

Fluoreszenz [fluorɛs'tsɛnts] **die; ~:** fluorescence

fluoreszieren *itr. V.* fluoresce; be fluorescent; **das Wasser fluoresziert** the water is fluorescent; **eine fluoreszierende Flüssigkeit** a fluorescent liquid

Fluor·gehalt der *(Chemie)* fluorine content

Fluorid [fluo'ri:t] **das; ~[e]s, ~e** *(Chemie)* fluoride

Fluor·test der *(Paläont.)* fluorine test

[1]**Flur** [flu:ɐ̯] **der; ~[e]s, ~e** *(Korridor)* corridor; *(Diele)* [entrance] hall; **im/auf dem ~:** in the corridor/hall

[2]**Flur die; ~, ~en a)** *(landwirtschaftliche Nutzfläche)* farmland *no indef. art.*; **die ~ bereinigen** reallocate land; **die ~en** the fields; **b)** *(geh.: offenes Kulturland)* fields *pl.*; **allein auf weiter ~ sein** *od.* **stehen** *(fig.)* be all alone in the world; **er stand mit seiner Ansicht allein auf weiter ~:** he was a lone voice in the wilderness

Flur-: ~**begehung die** inspection of fields; ~**bereinigung die** reallocation of land; ~**fenster das** hall window/window in a/the corridor; ~**form die** layout of fields; ~**garderobe die** hall-stand; ~**hüter der** field guard; ~**name der** *name of a feature of the local landscape;* ~**schaden der** damage *no pl., no indef. art.* to farmland; ~**tür die** front door

Fluse ['flu:zə] **die; ~, ~n** *(bes. nordd.)* bit of fluff

flusen *itr. V.* shed fluff

Fluß [flʊs] **der; Flusses, Flüsse** ['flʏsɐ] **a)** river; **die Stadt liegt am ~:** the town stands on the river; **am ~ sitzen** sit by the river; **b)** *o. Pl. (fließende Bewegung)* flow; **der ~ des Verkehrs** the flow of traffic; **die Dinge sind noch im ~:** things are in a state of flux; **in ~ kommen** *od.* **geraten** get going; get under way; **etw. in ~ bringen** get sth. going

fluß-, Fluß-: ~**aal der** *(Zool.)* freshwater eel; ~**ab[wärts]** *Adv.* downstream; ~**arm der** river branch; river arm; ~**auf[wärts]** *Adv.* upstream; ~**barsch der** *(Zool.)* perch; ~**bett das** river bed

Flüßchen ['flʏsçən] **das; ~s, ~:** small river

Fluß-: ~**dampfer der** river steamer; ~**diagramm das** *(DV, Arbeitswiss.)* flow chart; ~**ebene die** flood plain; ~**fisch der** freshwater fish; ~**gott der** *(Myth.)* river god; ~**hafen der** river port

flüssig ['flʏsɪç] **1.** *Adj.* **a)** liquid ⟨*nourishment, fuel*⟩; molten ⟨*ore, glass*⟩; melted ⟨*butter*⟩; runny ⟨*honey*⟩; **sie konnte nur ~e Nahrung zu sich nehmen** she could only take liquids; **etw. ~ machen** melt sth.; **~es Brot** *(scherzh.)* beer; **b)** *(fließend, geläufig)* fluent; **~er Verkehr** free-flowing traffic; **c)** *(verfügbar, solvent)* **~es Kapital/Geld** ready capital/money; **~es Vermögen** liquid assets; **wieder ~ sein** *(ugs.)* have got some cash to play with again *(coll.)*; **nicht ~ sein** *(ugs.)* be skint *(Brit. coll.) or (coll.)* [flat]broke. **2.** *adv.* ⟨*write, speak*⟩ fluently; **der Verkehr lief ~:** the traffic was flowing freely; **~ ernährt werden müssen** be only able to take liquids

Flüssig·gas das liquid gas

Flüssigkeit die; ~, ~en a) liquid; *(auch Gas)* fluid; **b)** *(Geläufigkeit)* fluency

Flüssigkeits-: ~**aufnahme die** intake of fluids; ~**maß das** liquid measure

Flüssig·kristall·anzeige die *(Technik)* liquid crystal display

flüssig|machen *tr. V.* make available ⟨*money, funds*⟩

Flüssigseife die liquid soap

Fluß-: ~**krebs, der** *(Zool.)* crayfish; ~**landschaft die a)** *(Geogr.)* fluvial topography; **b)** *(Gemälde)* river landscape; ~**lauf der** course of a/the river; ~**mittel das** *(Technik)* flux; ~**mündung die** river mouth; *(mit Gezeiten)* estuary; ~**name der** river name; ~**niederung die** flood plain; ~**pferd das** hippopotamus; ~**regulierung die** river control; ~**schiffahrt die** river traffic; *(Navigation)* river navigation; ~**spat der** fluorite; fluorspar; ~**tal das** river valley; ~**ufer das** river bank; **das diesseitige/jenseitige ~ufer** the near/opposite bank [of the river]; ~**wasser das** river water

Flüster-: ~**gewölbe das** whispering gallery; ~**laut der** whisper; **~laute von sich geben** whisper

flüstern ['flʏstɐn] **1.** *itr. V.* whisper; **sich ~d unterhalten/verständigen** speak/communicate in whispers; **leises, beschwörendes Flüstern** quiet, pleading whispers. **2.** *tr. V.* whisper; **jmdm. etw. ins Ohr ~:** whisper sth. in sb.'s ear; **jmdm. [et]was ~** *(ugs.)* give sb. something to think about; **das kann ich dir ~** *(ugs.)* I can promise you that

Flüster-: ~**parole die** rumour; ~**propaganda die** underground propaganda; ~**ton der** whisper; **im ~ton sprechen** speak in whispers; ~**tüte die** *(ugs.)* megaphone; ~**witz der** underground joke

Flut [flu:t] **die; ~, ~en a)** *o. Pl.* tide; **die ~ steigt/ebbt ab** the tide is coming in/going out; **die steigende ~:** the incoming *or* rising tide; **mit der ~ aus-/einlaufen** sail with the tide/come in on the tide; **b)** *meist Pl. (geh.: Wassermasse)* flood; **aufgewühlte/schmutzige ~en** turbulent/dirty waters; **in den ~en umkommen** die in the floods; **eine ~ von Protesten** *(fig.)* a flood of protests

fluten 1. *itr. V.; mit sein (geh.)* flood; **in etw.** *(Akk.)* **~:** flood sth.; **Sonnenlicht flutete in den Raum** sunlight streamed into the room. **2.** *tr. V. (Seemannsspr.: unter Wasser setzen)* flood

Flut-: ~**höhe die** height of the tide; ~**katastrophe die** flood disaster; ~**licht das;** *o. Pl.* floodlight; ~**licht·anlage die** floodlight installation; floodlights *pl.*

flutschen ['flʊtʃn̩] *itr. V. (ugs., bes. nordd.)* **a)** *mit sein (gleiten)* slip; **jmdm. aus den Fingern/Händen ~:** slip out of sb.'s fingers/hands; **b)** *(glatt vonstatten gehen)* go smoothly; **es flutscht nur so** it's going extremely well

Flut-: ~**warnung die** flood warning; ~**welle die** tidal wave

fluvial [flu'vi̯a:l] *Adj. (Geol.)* fluvial

fm *Abk.* **Festmeter** solid m³

f-Moll ['ɛf-] F minor; *s. auch* **a-Moll**

focht [fɔxt] *1. u. 3. Pers. Sg. Prät. v.* **fechten**

Fock [fɔk] **die; ~, ~en** *(Seew.)* foresail; *(auf einer Jacht)* jib

Fock·mast der foremast

föderal [fødə'ra:l] *Adj. s.* **föderativ**

Föderalismus der; ~: federalism *no art.*

föderalistisch *Adj.* federalist

Föderation [fødəra'tsi̯o:n] **die; ~, ~en** federation

föderativ [fødəra'ti:f] **1.** *Adj.* federal. **2.** *adv.* federally

fohlen ['fo:lən] *itr. V.* foal

Fohlen das; ~s, ~: foal

Föhn [fø:n] **der; ~[e]s, ~e** föhn; **es war ~:** the föhn was blowing; **bei ~:** when the föhn is/was blowing

Föhn·krankheit die illness caused by föhn conditions

Föhre ['fø:rə] **die; ~, ~n** *(landsch.) s.* [2]**Kiefer**

Fokus ['fo:kʊs] **der; ~, ~se** *(Optik, Med.)* focus

fokussieren *tr., itr. V. (Optik)* focus

Folge ['fɔlgə] **die; ~, ~n a)** *(Auswirkung)* consequence; *(Ergebnis)* consequence; result; **das kann böse ~n nach sich ziehen** that could have dire consequences; **die ~n tragen müssen** have to take the consequences; **an den ~n eines Unfalls/eines Herzleidens sterben** die as a result of an accident/a heart condition; **etw. zur ~ haben** result in sth.; lead to sth.; **b)** *(Aufeinander~)* succession; *(zusammengehörend)* sequence; *(einer Sendung)* episode; *(eines Romans)* instalment; *(einer Zeitschrift)* issue; **in rascher ~:** in quick succession; **eine ~ von Bildern/ Tönen** a sequence of pictures/notes; **eine Fortsetzung in 10 ~n** a serialization in ten episodes; **c) einem Aufruf/einem Befehl/einer Einladung ~ leisten** *(Amtsspr.)* respond to an appeal/obey *or* follow an order/accept an invitation

Folge-: ~**ein·richtung die** community facility; ~**erscheinung die** consequence; ~**kosten** *Pl.* resulting costs; ~**kriminalität die** *crime arising from the need to acquire drugs etc.;* ~**lasten** *s.* ~**kosten**

folgen ['fɔlgn̩] *itr. V.* **a)** *mit sein* follow; **jmdm./einer Sache ~:** follow sb./sth.; **jmdm. im Amt/in der Regierung ~:** succeed sb. in office/in government; **auf etw.** *(Akk.)* **~:** follow sth.; come after sth.; **einer Rede/einem Vortrag ~ [können]** [be able to] follow a speech/a lecture; **kannst du mir ~?** *(oft scherzh.)* do you follow me?; **jmds. Beispiel** *(Dat.)* **~:** follow sb.'s example; **aus etw. ~:** follow from sth.; **daraus folgt, daß ...:** it follows from this that ...; **b)** *(gehorchen) auch mit sein* **jmds. Anordnungen/Befehlen ~:** follow *or* obey sb.'s orders; **seiner inneren Stimme/seinem Gefühl ~:** listen to one's inner voice/be ruled by one's feelings

folgend *Adj.* **der/die/das ~e** the next in order; **er sagte das ~e ...:** he said this ...; **~es** *od.* **das Folgende** the following [words *pl.*/passage *etc.*]; **aus ~em** *od.* **dem Folgenden geht hervor, daß ...:** it will be seen from what follows that ...; **alle ~en** all those who come/came after; **im ~en** *od.* **in ~em** in [the course of] the following discussion/passage *etc.*; **der/die Folgende** the one who follows/followed; **die Folgenden** those following

folgendermaßen *Adv.* as follows; *(so)* in the following way

folgen-: ~**los** *Adj.* without consequences *postpos.*; **das ist nicht ~los geblieben** that hasn't been without its consequences; ~**reich** *Adj.* ⟨*decision, event*⟩ fraught with consequences; *(bedeutsam)* momentous; ~**schwer** *Adj.* fateful ⟨*error, omission*⟩; ⟨*error, omission, accident*⟩ with serious consequences

folge·richtig 1. *Adj.* logical ⟨*decision, conclusion*⟩; consistent ⟨*behaviour, action*⟩. **2.** *adv.* ⟨*think, develop, conclude*⟩ logically; ⟨*act, behave*⟩ consistently

Folge·richtigkeit die *(einer Entscheidung, Schlußfolgerung)* logicality; *(eines Verhaltens, einer Handlung)* consistency

folgern ['fɔlgɐn] **1.** *tr. V.* **~, daß ...:** conclude that ...; **etw. aus etw.** ~: deduce *or* infer sth. from sth. **2.** *itr. V.* **richtig** ~: draw a/the correct conclusion; **voreilig** ~: jump to conclusions

Folgerung die; ~, ~en conclusion

Folge-: ~**satz der** *(Sprachw.)* consecutive clause; ~**schaden der a)** *meist Pl.* damaging after-effects; **b)** *(Versicherungsw.)* consequential damage

Folge·ton·horn das *s.* **Martinshorn**

folge·widrig 1. *Adj.* illogical ‹*conclusion*›; inconsistent ‹*behaviour*›. **2.** *adv.* ‹*conclude*› illogically; ‹*behave*› inconsistently

Folge·zeit die ensuing *or* following weeks/months/years *pl.*

folglich ['fɔlklɪç] *Adv.* consequently; as a result; *(ugs.: deshalb)* consequently; therefore

folgsam 1. *Adj.* obedient. **2.** *adv.* obediently

Folgsamkeit die; ~: obedience

Foliant [fo'li̯ant] **der;** ~**en,** ~**en** folio

Folie ['fo:li̯ə] **die;** ~, ~**n a)** *(Metall~)* foil; *(Plastik~)* film; **b)** *(Druckw.: Farbschicht)* [blocking] foil

Folio ['fo:li̯o] **das;** ~**s, Folien** *od.* ~**s** folio

Folio·band der; *Pl.* ~**bände** folio volume

Folklore [fɔlk'lo:rə] **die;** ~ **a)** *(Überlieferung)* folklore; **b)** *(Musik)* folk-music

Folklore·bluse die peasant blouse

Folkloristik die; ~: [study of] folklore

folkloristisch 1. *Adj.* folkloric. **2.** *adv.* in a folkloric way

Folk·song ['foʊk-] **der** folk-song

Follikel [fɔ'li:kl̩] **der;** ~**s,** ~ *(Med., Bot.)* follicle

Follikel·sprung der *(Med.)* ovulation

Folter ['fɔltɐ] **die;** ~, ~**n a)** torture; **bei jmdm. die** ~ **anwenden** use torture on sb.; **die** ~ **abschaffen** abolish the use of torture; **b)** *(~bank)* rack; **jmdn. auf die** ~ **legen** put sb. on the rack; **jmdn. auf die** ~ **spannen** *(fig.)* keep sb. in an agony of suspense; **c)** *(geh.: peinigende Qual)* torment

Folter·bank die; *Pl.* ~**bänke** rack

Folterer der; ~**s,** ~: torturer

Folter-: ~**kammer die,** ~**keller der** torture-chamber; ~**knecht der** torturer

foltern 1. *tr. V.* **a)** torture; **b)** *(fig. geh.)* torment. **2.** *itr. V.* use torture

Folter·qual die a) agony of torture; **b)** *(fig. geh.)* torment; ~**en erdulden** suffer torment; **jmdm. wahre** ~**en bereiten** be sheer torment to sb.

Folterung die; ~, ~**en** torture; **nach tagelangen** ~**en** after days of torture

Folter·werkzeug das instrument of torture

Fön Ⓦ [fø:n] **der;** ~**[e]s,** ~**e** hair-drier; **sich** *(Dat.)* **die Haare mit dem** ~ **trocknen** blow-dry one's hair

¹Fond [fõ:] **der;** ~**s,** ~**s** *(geh.)* rear compartment; back; **im** ~ **sitzen** sit in the back [seat]

²Fond der; ~**s,** ~**s** *(Kochk.)* juices *pl.*

Fondant [fõ'dã:] **der** *od.* **das;** ~**s,** ~**s** fondant

Fonds [fõ:] **der;** ~ [fõ:(s)], ~ [fõ:s] **a)** *(Vermögensreserve)* fund; **einen** ~ **bilden** set up a fund; **b)** *Pl. (Finanzw.)* government stocks; government bonds

Fondue [fõ'dy:] **die;** ~, ~**s** *od.* **das;** ~**s,** ~**s** *(Kochk.)* fondue

Fondue-: ~**gabel die** fondue fork; ~**gerät das** fondue set

fönen ['fø:nən] *tr. V.* blow-dry

Fono- *s.* **Phono-**

Fontäne [fɔn'tɛ:nə] **die;** ~, ~**n** jet; *(Springbrunnen)* fountain

Fontanelle [fɔnta'nɛlə] **die;** ~, ~**n** *(Anat.)* fontanelle

foppen ['fɔpn̩] *tr. V. (ugs.)* **jmdn.** ~: pull sb.'s leg *(coll.)*; put sb. on *(Amer. coll.)*; **jmdn. mit etw.** ~: make fun of sb. with sth.; **jmdn. mit einem Spitznamen** ~: make fun of sb. by calling him/her by his/her nickname

forcieren [fɔr'si:rən] *tr. V.* **a)** step up ‹*production*›; redouble, intensify ‹*efforts*›; speed up, push forward ‹*developments*›; **das Tempo/Rennen** ~ *(Sport)* force the pace; **er drängte auf eine forcierte Durchführung des Planes** he pressed for the plan to be forced through; **b)** *(Milit.)* force ‹*pass, stronghold, etc.*›

Forcierung die; ~, ~**en** *s.* **forcieren:** stepping up; redoubling; intensification; speeding up; pushing forward; forcing

Förde ['fø:ɐ̯də] **die;** ~, ~**n** long narrow inlet

Förder-: ~**anlage die** *(Technik)* conveyor; ~**band das** *(Technik)* conveyor belt

Förderer ['fœrdərɐ] **der;** ~**s,** ~ **a)** *(Gönner)* patron; **b)** *s.* **Förderanlage**

Förder-: ~**korb der** *(Bergbau)* cage; ~**leistung die** *(Bergbau, Technik)* output; production

förderlich *Adj.* beneficial; **für jmdn./etw.** ~ **sein** be beneficial *or* of benefit to sb./sth.; **guten Beziehungen** ~ **sein** be conducive to *or* promote good relations

Förder·maschine die *(Bergbau)* winding engine

fordern ['fɔrdɐn] *tr. V.* **a)** *(verlangen)* demand; **sein Recht** ~: demand one's rights; **Rechenschaft von jmdm.** ~: call sb. to account; **das Unglück hat 200 Menschenleben gefordert** the disaster claimed 200 lives; **b)** *(in Anspruch nehmen)* make demands on; **gefordert werden** have demands made on one; **von etw. gefordert werden** be stretched by sth.; **jmdn. zu stark** ~: make excessive *or* too many demands on sb.; **von einem Gegner gefordert werden** be stretched by an opponent; **c)** *(zum Zweikampf)* **jmdn. [zum Duell]** ~: challenge sb. [to a duel]; **jmdn. auf Pistolen/Säbel** ~ *(veralt.)* challenge sb. to a duel with pistols/sabres

fördern ['fœrdɐn] *tr. V.* **a)** promote ‹*trade, plan, project, good relations*›; patronize, support ‹*artist, art*›; further ‹*investigation*›; foster ‹*talent, tendency, new generation*›; improve ‹*appetite*›; aid ‹*digestion, sleep*›; ~**d auf etw.** *(Akk.)* **wirken** have a beneficial effect on sth.; **b)** *(Bergbau, Technik)* mine ‹*coal, ore*›; extract ‹*oil*›

Förder-: ~**schacht der** *(Bergbau)* winding shaft; ~**stufe die** *(Schulw.) phase of mixed-ability teaching intended to reveal the aptitudes and abilities of individual pupils;* ~**turm der** *(Bergbau)* head-frame; headgear

Forderung die; ~, ~**en a)** *(Anspruch)* demand; *(in bestimmter Höhe)* claim; **eine** ~ **erfüllen** meet a demand/a claim; **b)** *(Kaufmannsspr.)* claim **(an** + *Akk.* against); **eine** ~ **einklagen** sue for payment of a debt; **c)** *(zum Duell)* challenge; **eine** ~ **auf Pistolen/Säbel** *(veralt.)* a challenge to a duel with pistols/sabres

Förderung die; ~, ~**en a)** *o. Pl. s.* **fördern a:** promotion; patronage; support; furthering; fostering; improvement; aiding; **b)** *(Bergbau, Technik)* output; *(das Fördern)* mining; *(von Erdöl)* extraction; **die** ~ **steigt** output is increasing

-förderung die: Erdöl~/Erdgas~: extraction of petroleum/natural gas; **Silber~/Kali~:** mining of silver/potash

Förderungs·maßnahme die supportive measure

förderungs·würdig *Adj.* worthy *or* deserving of support *postpos.*

Förder·wagen der *(Bergbau)* mine car

Forelle [fo'rɛlə] **die;** ~, ~**n** trout; ~ **blau** *(Kochk.)* blue trout

Forellen-: ~**teich der** trout pond; ~**zucht die** trout-farming

forensisch [fo'rɛnzɪʃ] *Adj.* **a)** forensic; **b)** *(veralt.: rhetorisch)* oratorical

Forke ['fɔrkə] **die;** ~, ~**n** *(bes. nordd.)* fork

Form [fɔrm] **die;** ~, ~**en a)** *(Gestalt)* shape; **es hat die** ~ **einer Kugel/eines Rechtecks** it has the form of a sphere/rectangle; **[feste]** ~**[en] annehmen** take definite shape; **die Demonstration nahm häßliche** ~**en an** the demonstration began to look ugly; **in** ~ **von Tabletten/Briefmarken/Lebensmitteln/Subventionen** in the form of tablets/stamps/food/subsidies; **aus der** ~ **gehen** *(ugs. scherzh.)* lose one's figure; **b)** *(bes. Sport: Verfassung)* form; **in** ~ **sein** be on form; **in guter** ~ **sein** be in good form; **in schlechter** ~ **sein** be off form; **sich in** ~ **bringen** get on form; **zu großer** ~ **auflaufen** *(Jargon)* hit peak form; **c)** *(vorgeformtes Modell)* mould; *(Back~)* baking tin; **d)** *(Gestaltungsweise, Erscheinungs~, Darstellungs~)* form; **musikalische/künstlerische** ~: musical/artistic form; ~ **und Inhalt** form and content; **etw. in angemessene** ~ **kleiden** present sth. in an appropriate form; **e)** *(Umgangs~)* form; **ein Mensch ohne** ~**en** an ill-mannered person; **die** ~**[en] wahren** observe the proprieties; **etw. der** ~ **halber tun** do sth. for the sake of form *or* as a matter of form; **in aller** ~: formally

formal [fɔr'ma:l] **1.** *Adj.* formal; **ein** ~**er Fehler** a technical error; *(Rechtsw.)* procedural error. **2.** *adv.* formally; **eine** ~ **gute Lösung** a good solution from the point of view of form; ~ **im Recht sein** be technically in the right

Formaldehyd ['fɔrmlaldehy:t] **der;** ~**s** *(Biol., Med.)* formaldehyde

Formalie [fɔr'ma:li̯ə] **die;** ~, ~**n;** *meist Pl.* formality

Formalin Ⓦ [fɔrma'li:n] **das;** ~**s** formalin

formalisieren *tr. V.* formalize

Formalisierung die; ~, ~**en** formalization

Formalismus der; ~, **Formalismen** formalism

Formalist der; ~**en,** ~**en** formalist

formalistisch 1. *Adj.* formalistic. **2.** *adv.* formalistically

Formalität [fɔrmali'tɛ:t] **die;** ~, ~**en** formality

formaliter [fɔr'ma:litɐ] *Adv. (geh.)* formally

formal·juristisch, formal·rechtlich 1. *Adj.* technical; **ein rein** ~**er Standpunkt** a narrowly legalistic view. **2.** *adv.* technically

Form·anstieg der *(Sport)* improvement in form

Format [fɔr'ma:t] **das;** ~**[e]s,** ~**e a)** size; *(Buch~, Papier~, Bild~)* format; **b)** *o. Pl. (Persönlichkeit)* stature; **ihm fehlt das menschliche** ~: he lacks real personal stature; **eine Frau von** ~: a woman of stature; **c)** *o. Pl. (besonderes Niveau)* quality; **etw. hat/ist ohne** ~: sth. has/lacks class

Formation [fɔrma'tsi̯o:n] **die;** ~, ~**en a)** *(Herausbildung, Anordnung)* formation; *(einer Generation, Gesellschaft)* development; **b)** *(Gruppe)* group; **eine Hamburger** ~ *(Tanzsport)* a team from Hamburg; **c)** *(Milit.) (von Flugzeugen)* formation; *(von Soldaten)* unit; **d)** *(Geol., Bot.)* formation

Formations-: ~**flug der a)** *(Flug in Formation)* formation flying; **b)** *(Raumflug)* alignment of orbits; ~**tanz der** *(Tanzsport)* formation dancing

formbar *Adj.* malleable; soft ‹*bone*›; *(fig.)* malleable, pliable ‹*character, person*›

Formbarkeit die; ~: malleability; *(fig.)* malleability; pliability

form·beständig *Adj.* ~**beständig sein** keep its/their shape

Form·blatt das form

Formel ['fɔrml̩] **die;** ~, ~**n** formula; **die** ~ **des Eides** the wording of the oath; ~ **1/2** *(Motorsport)* Formula One/Two; ~**-1-Fahrer/-Wagen** Formula One driver/car

formelhaft 1. *Adj.* stereotyped ‹*style, mode of expression*›; **eine** ~**e Wendung** a stereotyped phrase. **2.** *adv.* **sich** ~ **ausdrücken** talk in stereotyped phrases

Formelhaftigkeit die; ~: stereotyped character

Formel·kram der *(ugs.)* **die Chemie mit ihrem ~:** chemistry and its awful formulae *pl.*
formell [fɔr'mɛl] **1.** *Adj.* formal. **2.** *adv.* formally; **die Einladung wurde rein ~ ausgesprochen** the invitation was made only as a matter of form; **er ist nur ~ im Recht** he's only technically in the right
Formel-: ~sammlung die formulary; **~sprache die: die ~sprache der Physik** the language of formulae as used in physics; **die mathematische ~sprache** the language of mathematical formulae; **~zeichen das** symbol
formen 1. *tr. V.* **a)** *(gestalten)* form; shape; **etw. in Ton/Gips ~:** shape *or* form sth. in clay/plaster; **schön geformte Möbel/Hände** finely shaped furniture/hands; **Laute/Silben ~:** form sounds/syllables; **b)** *(bilden, prägen)* mould, form ‹*character, personality*›; mould ‹*person*›; **jmdn. zu etw. ~:** mould sb. into sth. **2.** *refl. V.* take on a shape; *(fig.)* form; take shape
formen-, Formen-: ~lehre die a) *(Sprachw., Biol.)* morphology; **b)** *(Musik)* theory of [musical] form; **~reich** *Adj.* with its/their great variety of forms; **~reich sein** display a great variety of forms; **~reichtum der** great variety of forms; wealth of forms
Former der; ~s, ~ *(Berufsbez.)* moulder
Formerei die; ~, ~en moulding department
form-, Form-: ~fehler der a) *(in einem Verfahren, Dokument)* irregularity; **b)** *(Taktlosigkeit)* faux pas; breach of etiquette; **~frage die** formality; **~gebung die; ~, ~en** design; **~gerecht 1.** *Adj.* correct; proper; **2.** *adv.* correctly; properly; **~gestalter der** *s.* **Designer; ~gestaltung die** *s.* **Design**
formidabel [fɔrmi'da:bl] *Adj.* **a)** *(geh.: außergewöhnlich)* superb; **b)** *(veralt.: besorgniserregend)* formidable
formieren 1. *tr. V.* form ‹*team, party, organization*›; **der Feldherr formierte seine Truppen auf dem Hügel** the commander drew up his troops on the hill. **2.** *refl. V.* **a)** *(sich aufstellen)* form; **wir formierten uns zu einer Gruppe** we formed ourselves into a group; **sich neben der Tribüne ~:** assemble beside the rostrum; **b)** *(sich zusammenschließen)* be formed; **die formierte Gesellschaft** *(hist.)* the aligned society
Formierung die; ~, ~en formation; *(von Truppen)* drawing up
-förmig [-fœrmɪç] -shaped; *s. auch* **ei-, gabel-, kugelförmig** *usw.*
Form·krise die *(Sport)* bad patch; **in einer ~ sein** *od.* **stecken** be off form
förmlich ['fœrmlɪç] **1.** *Adj.* **a)** formal; **warum denn so ~?** why [be] so formal?; **b)** *nicht präd. (regelrecht)* positive; **ein ~er Schreck durchfuhr ihn** he got a real fright; **einen ~en Abscheu verspüren** feel positive revulsion. **2.** *adv.* **a)** *(steif, unpersönlich, offiziell)* formally; **b)** *(geradezu)* **sich ~ fürchten** be really afraid; **~ außer sich sein** be quite beside oneself; **jmdn. ~ zwingen, etw. zu tun** positively force sb. to do sth.
Förmlichkeit die; ~, ~en formality; **in aller ~ um etw. bitten** *(veraltend)* formally request sth.; **die juristischen ~en** the legal formalities; **bitte keine ~en!** please don't stand on ceremony!
form-, Form-: ~los 1. *Adj.* **a)** informal; **einen ~losen Antrag stellen** make an application without the official form[s]; apply informally; **b)** *(gestaltlos)* shapeless; **2.** *adv.* informally; **~losigkeit die; ~ a)** informality; **b)** *(Gestaltlosigkeit)* shapelessness; **~sache die** formality; **das ist [eine] reine ~sache** that is purely a formality; **~schön** *Adj.* elegant; **~tief das** *(Sport)* bad patch; **er steckt** *od.* **befindet sich in einem ~tief** he's badly off form
Formular [fɔrmu'la:ɐ̯] **das; ~s, ~e** form
formulieren [fɔrmu'li:rən] *tr. V.* formulate; **eine Frage noch einmal ~:** reformulate *or* rephrase a question
Formulierung die; ~, ~en a) *o. Pl. (das Formulieren)* formulation; *(eines Entwurfes, Gesetzes)* drafting; **b)** *(formulierter Text)* formulation; **politische/wissenschaftliche ~en** political/scientific phraseology *sing.*
Formung die; ~, ~en a) *(Gestaltung)* design; **die strenge ~ des Sonetts** strict sonnet form; **b)** *o. Pl. (Bildung, Erziehung)* moulding; *(des Charakters)* moulding; forming
form-, Form-: ~veränderung die change in shape; **~verstoß der** *s.* **~widrigkeit; ~vollendet 1.** *Adj.* perfectly executed ‹*pirouette, bow, etc.*›; ‹*poem*› perfect in form; **2.** *adv.* **etw. ~vollendet tun** do sth. faultlessly; **~vorschrift die** statutory form; **~widrig 1.** *Adj.* improper ‹*behaviour, expression*›; **2.** *adv.* improperly; **~widrigkeit die** impropriety
forsch [fɔrʃ] **1.** *Adj.* self-assertive; forceful; **einen ~en Eindruck machen** seem self-assertive *or* forceful; **mit ~en Schritten** with a brisk step; briskly. **2.** *adv.* self-assertively; forcefully
forschen *itr. V.* **a)** *(suchen)* **nach jmdm./etw. ~:** search *or* look for sb./sth.; **jmdn. ~d** *od.* **mit ~dem Blick betrachten** look at sb. searchingly; give sb. a searching look; **b)** *(als Wissenschaftler)* research; do research; **auf einem Gebiet ~:** research *or* do research in a field; **in [alten] Quellen ~:** research into [ancient] sources
Forscher der; ~s, ~ a) *(Wissenschaftler)* researcher; research scientist; **b)** *(Forschungsreisender)* explorer
Forscher-: ~drang der a) *(Wissensdurst)* thirst for new knowledge; **b)** *(Entdeckerfreude)* urge to explore; **~geist der** inquiring mind
Forscherin die; ~, ~nen *s.* **Forscher**
forscherisch 1. *Adj.* research *attrib.*; **~e Arbeit** research work. **2.** *adv.* **~ arbeiten** do research [work]
Forscher·team das research team
Forschheit die; ~: self-assertiveness; forcefulness
Forschung die; ~, ~en research; **~en [auf einem Gebiet] betreiben** do research [in a field]; **~ und Lehre** teaching and research
Forschungs-: ~anstalt die research establishment; **~arbeit die a)** piece of research; **b)** *o. Pl. s.* **Forschung; ~auftrag der** research assignment; **~bericht der** research report; **~ergebnis das** result of the research; **~gebiet das** field of research; **~gegen·stand der** research topic; **~institut das** research institute; **~labor[atorium] das** research laboratory; **~methode die** research method; **~programm das** research programme; **~rakete die** research rocket; **~reaktor der** research reactor; **~reise die** expedition; **~reisende der/die** explorer; **~satellit der** research satellite; **~schiff das** research vessel; **~stipendium das** research grant; **~tätigkeit die** research work; **~vorhaben das** research project; **~zentrum das** research centre; **~zweck der** purpose of the research; **für ~zwecke** for research purposes
Forst [fɔrst] **der; ~[e]s, ~e[n]** forest
Forst-: ~amt das forestry office; **~beamte der** forestry official
Förster ['fœrstɐ] **der; ~s, ~:** forest warden; forester; ranger *(Amer.)*
Försterei die; ~, ~en *s.* **Forsthaus**
forst-, Forst-: ~frevel der offence against the forest law; **~frevel begehen** break the forest law; **~haus das** forester's house; **~ingenieur der** senior forestry official *(with academic qualifications)*; **~nutzung die** [commercial] exploitation of forests; **~recht das** forest law; **~revier das** forest district; **~schaden der** damage *no pl., no indef. art.* to the forest; **~schädling der** forest pest; **~verwaltung die** forestry commission; **~wesen das;** *o. Pl.* forestry; **~wirtschaft die** forestry; **~wirtschaftlich 1.** *Adj.* commercial; **2.** *adv.* commercially
Forsythie [fɔr'zy:tsi̯ə] **die; ~, ~n a)** forsythia; **b)** *Pl. (Zweige)* sprigs of forsythia
fort [fɔrt] *Adv.* **a)** *(weg)* **sie ist schon ~:** she has already gone *or* left; **ihre Brille war ~:** her glasses had gone *or* had vanished; **~ mit dir!** be off with you!; away with you!; **~ mit ihr/damit!** take her/it away!; away with her/it!; **[schnell] ~!** run for it!; **b)** *(weiter)* **nur immer so ~:** just carry on as you are *or* like that; **und so ~:** and so on; and so forth; **in einem ~:** continuously
Fort [fo:ɐ̯] **das; ~s, ~s** fort
fort-, Fort- (*s. auch* **weg-, Weg-**): **~an** [-'-] *Adv.* from now/then on; **~bestand der;** *o. Pl.* continuation; *(eines Staates)* continued existence; **~|bestehen** *unr. itr. V.* remain; continue; ‹*nation*› remain in existence; *(beim alten bleiben)* remain the same; remain as before; **~|bewegen 1.** *tr. V.* move; shift; **2.** *refl. V.* move [along]; **~bewegung die;** *o. Pl.* locomotion; **~bewegungsmittel das** means of transport; **~|bilden** *tr. V.* **sich/jmdn. ~bilden** continue one's/sb.'s education; **die Lehrlinge wurden ~gebildet** the apprentices were given further training; **~bildung die;** *o. Pl.* further education; *(beruflich)* further training; **~bildungs·kurs der** further education course; *(beruflich)* training course; **~|bleiben** *unr. itr. V.; mit sein* fail to come; **du bist so lange ~geblieben!** you've been away so long!; **sein Fortbleiben beunruhigte mich** I was worried when he didn't turn up; **~|bringen** *unr. tr. V.: s.* **wegbringen; ~dauer die** continuation; **~|dauern** *itr. V.* continue; **~dauernder Widerstand** continuing/*(in der Vergangenheit)* continued resistance; **unter ~dauernden Beschuß geraten** come under continuous bombardment; **~|denken** *unr. itr. V.: s.* **wegdenken**
forte ['fɔrtə] *Adv. (Musik, Pharm.)* forte
Forte das; ~s, ~s *od.* **Forti** *(Mus.)* forte
fort-, Fort-: ~|eilen *itr. V.; mit sein (geh.)* hurry off *or* away; hasten away; **~|entwickeln 1.** *tr. V.* **etw. ~entwickeln** develop sth. further; **2.** *refl. V.* develop; **~|erben** *refl. V.* be passed on; be handed down; **sich auf jmdn. ~erben** pass to sb.; be handed down to sb.; **~|fahren 1.** *unr. itr. V.* **a)** *mit sein (abreisen)* leave; *(einen Ausflug machen)* go out; **b)** *auch mit sein (weitermachen)* **~fahren [,etw. zu tun]** continue *or* go on [doing sth.]; **in seiner Rede ~fahren** continue *or* go on with one's speech; **bitte, fahren Sie ~:** please continue; please go on; **2.** *unr. tr. V.* drive away; **jmdn. [mit dem Auto] ~fahren** drive *or* take sb. away [in a car]; **etw. [mit einem Auto] ~fahren** take sth. away [in a car]; **~fall der** ending; discontinuation; **~|fallen** *unr. itr. V.; mit sein* ‹*obstacle, misgiving*› be removed; ‹*words*› be omitted; ‹*conditions*› no longer apply; ‹*subsidy*› be discontinued; ‹*advantage*› be lost; **ein Kapitel ~fallen lassen** delete a chapter; **~|fliegen** *unr. itr. V.; mit sein: s.* **wegfliegen; ~|führen 1.** *tr. V.* **a)** lead away; **b)** *(fortsetzen)* continue, keep up ‹*tradition, business*›; continue, carry on ‹*another's work*›; **2.** *itr. V.* **von etw. ~führen** lead away from sth.; **~führung die** *s.* **~führen 1 b**; continuation; keeping up; carrying on; **sich zur ~führung von jmds. Geschäften bereit erklären** declare one's readiness to carry on sb.'s business; **~gang der;** *o. Pl.* **a)** departure **(aus** from); **b)** *(Weiterentwicklung)* progress; **seinen ~gang nehmen** progress; **~|geben** *unr. tr. V. s.* **weggeben; ~|gehen** *unr. itr. V.; mit sein* **a)** *(weggehen)* leave;

geh ~! go away!; geh nicht ~! don't go away!; don't leave!; b) *(andauern, verlaufen)* continue; go on; ~**geschritten** *Adj.* advanced; **in ~geschrittenem Alter** at an advanced age; **zu ~geschrittener Tageszeit** at a late hour; **die Krankheit befindet sich in einem ~geschrittenen Stadium** the disease has reached an advanced stage; ~**geschrittene der/die;** *adj. Dekl.* advanced student/ player; **ein Kurs[us] für ~geschrittene** a course for advanced students; an advanced course; ~**geschrittenen·kurs[us] der** advanced course; ~**gesetzt 1.** *Adj.; nicht präd.* continual; constant; **~gesetzter Betrug/~gesetzte Untreue** repeated fraud/ embezzlement; **2.** *adv.* continually; constantly; ~|**haben** *unr. tr. V.: s.* **weghaben a;** ~**hin** *Adv. (veralt.)* henceforth; henceforward

fortissimo [fɔr'tɪsimo] *Adv. (Musik)* fortissimo

Fortissimo das; ~s, ~s *od.* **Fortissimi** *(Musik)* fortissimo

fort-, Fort-: ~|**jagen** *tr. V.: s.* **wegjagen;** ~|**kommen** *unr. itr. V.; mit sein* **a)** *s.* **wegkommen a, b, d, f; b)** *(Erfolg haben)* get on; do well; **in der Schule/im Beruf ~kommen** get on at school/in one's job; ~**kommen das;** ~**s a)** *(das Vorwärtskommen, auch beruflich)* progress; **das wird für mein ~kommen nützlich sein** that will help me get ahead *or* get on; **b)** *(Lebensunterhalt)* living; **sein ~kommen finden** make a living; **das Gehalt reichte gerade für sein ~kommen** the money was just enough for him to get by on; ~|**können** *unr. itr. V.: s.* **wegkönnen;** ~|**lassen** *unr. tr. V.: s.* **weglassen;** ~|**laufen** *unr. itr. V.; mit sein* **a)** *s.* **weglaufen; b)** *(sich ~setzen)* continue; ~**laufend 1.** *Adj.* continuous; **die ~laufende Handlung der Fernsehserie** the ongoing plot of the television series; **~laufende Hefte** consecutive issues; **2.** *adv.* continuously; **~laufend numeriert** numbered consecutively; ~|**leben** *itr. V.: s.* **weiterleben;** ~|**legen** *tr. V.* put down *or* aside; ~|**loben** *tr. V.: s.* **wegloben;** ~|**machen** *(ugs.)* **1.** *refl. V.* get away; **2.** *itr. V.: s.* **weitermachen 1;** ~|**müssen** *unr. itr. V.: s.* **wegmüssen;** ~|**nehmen** *unr. tr. V.* take away; ~|**pflanzen** *refl. V.* **a)** *(sich vermehren)* reproduce [oneself/itself]; **b)** *(sich verbreiten)* ‹*idea, mood*› spread; ‹*sound, light*› travel, propagate; ~**pflanzung die a)** *(Vermehrung)* reproduction; **b)** *(Verbreitung)* transmission; *(von Schall, Licht)* propagation; *(von Ideen)* spread; ~**pflanzungs·fähig** *Adj.* capable of reproduction *postpos.;* ~**pflanzungs·trieb der** reproductive instinct; ~|**räumen** *tr. V.: s.* **wegräumen;** ~|**reisen** *itr. V.; mit sein: s.* **abreisen;** ~|**reißen** *unr. tr. V.* **a)** *(wegreißen)* tear away; **die Fluten rissen alles mit sich ~:** the floods swept everything away; **b)** *(begeistern)* **jmdn. ~reißen** carry *or* sweep sb. along; **jmdn. zu Beifallsstürmen ~reißen** rouse sb. to tumultuous applause; ~|**rennen** *unr. itr. V.; mit sein (ugs.)* run off *or* away; ~**satz der** *(Biol.)* process; ~|**schaffen** *tr. V.* take *or* carry away; ~|**scheren** *refl. V. (ugs.)* **scher dich ~!** clear off! *(coll.);* ~|**scheuchen** *tr. V.* shoo *or* chase away; ~|**schicken** *tr. V.: s.* **wegschicken;** ~|**schieben** *unr. tr. V.: s.* **wegschieben;** ~|**schleichen** *unr. itr., refl. V.: s.* **wegschleichen;** ~|**schleppen** *refl., tr. V.: s.* **wegschleppen;** ~|**schleudern** *tr. V.* fling away; ~|**schreiben** *unr. tr. V.* update; *(in die Zukunft)* project forward; ~**schreibung die** updating; *(in die Zukunft)* forward projection; ~|**schreiten** *unr. itr. V.; mit sein* ‹*process*› progress, continue; ‹*time*› move on; **die Zeit ist [weit] ~geschritten** it is getting on *or* late; **der Sommer ist [weit] ~geschritten** we are well into summer; **das Fortschreiten** progress; ~**schreitend** *Adj.* progressive; **mit ~schreitender Jahreszeit** as the year goes/went on; **mit ~schreitendem Alter** with advancing age; with the passing of the years; ~**schritt der** progress; **~schritte** progress *sing.;* **ein ~schritt** a step forward; **das ist schon ein ~schritt** that is some progress at least; **große ~schritte machen** make great progress; ~**schrittlich 1.** *Adj.* progressive; **2.** *adv.* progressively; ~**schrittlichkeit die;** ~**:** progressiveness; ~**schritts·feindlich** *Adj.* anti-progressive; ~**schritts·gläubig** *Adj.* **~schrittsgläubig/zu ~schrittsgläubig sein** put one's/too much faith in progress; **das ~schrittsgläubige 19. Jahrhundert** the nineteenth century with its implicit faith in progress; ~**schritts·gläubigkeit die** belief *or* faith in progress; ~|**schwemmen** *tr. V.* sweep away; ~|**sehnen** *refl. V.* long to go; ~|**setzen 1.** *tr. V.* continue; carry on; **den Weg zu Fuß/mit dem Auto ~setzen** continue by foot/car; **2.** *refl. V.* continue; ~**setzung die;** ~, ~**en a)** *(das ~setzen)* continuation; **[s]eine ~setzung finden** resume; **b)** *(anschließender Teil)* instalment; **in ~setzungen erscheinen** be published in instalments; **~setzung von S. 7** continued from p. 7; **~setzung folgt** to be continued; ~**setzungs·roman der** serial; serialized novel; ~|**spülen** *tr. V.: s.* **wegspülen;** ~|**stehlen** *unr. refl. V.* steal *or* sneak away; ~|**stoßen** *unr. tr. V.: s.* **wegstoßen;** ~|**stürzen** *itr. V.; mit sein* rush off *or* away; ~|**tragen** *unr. tr. V.: s.* **wegtragen;** ~|**treiben 1.** *unr. tr. V.* **a)** *(vertreiben, wegtreiben)* drive off *or* away; **er hat seinen Sohn ~getrieben** he made it impossible for his son to stay; **es trieb mich bald ~** I soon felt I had to leave; **b)** *(vorwärtstreiben)* sweep away; **2.** *itr. V.; mit sein* float away

Fortuna [fɔr'tu:na] **(die)** Fortune; ~ **lachte** *od.* **lächelte ihm** *(geh.)* Fortune smiled upon him

Fortune [fɔr'ty:n], *eingedeutscht:* **Fortüne** [fɔr'ty:nə] **die;** ~**:** luck; **keine/wenig ~ haben** have no/not much luck

fort-: ~|**währen** *itr. V. (geh.) s.* **~dauern;** ~|**während 1.** *Adj.; nicht präd.* continual; incessant; **2.** *adv.* continually; incessantly; ~|**werfen** *unr. tr. V.: s.* **wegwerfen;** ~|**wirken** *itr. V.* continue to have an effect; **das wirkt in uns ~:** the effect of it persists in us; **sein Vorbild wirkt in ihnen ~:** his example continues to exert an influence on them; **das Fortwirken antiker Motive** the continuing influence of ancient motifs; ~|**wollen** *unr. itr. V.* **a)** *s.* **wegwollen; b)** *(vorwärts wollen)* want to move; **seine Füße wollten nicht recht ~:** his feet did not seem to be able to carry him; ~|**zaubern** *tr. V.* **etw. ~zaubern** make sth. disappear; ~|**zerren** *tr. V.: s.* **wegzerren;** ~|**ziehen** *unr. tr., itr. V.: s.* **wegziehen**

Forum ['fo:rʊm] **das;** ~**s, Foren** *od.* **Fora a)** *(Personenkreis, Plattform, röm. Marktplatz)* forum; **b)** *Pl. nur* **Foren** *(Aussprache) (über Literatur)* symposium; *(über Politik)* forum discussion

fossil [fɔ'si:l] *Adj.* fossilized; fossil *attrib.*

Fossil das; ~**s,** ~**ien** fossil

[1]**Foto** ['fo:to] **das;** ~**s,** ~**s,** *(schweiz.:)* **die;** ~, ~**s** photo; **~s machen** *od. (ugs.:)* **schießen** take photos; **auf einem ~:** in a photo

[2]**Foto der;** ~**s,** ~**s** *(bes. südd. ugs.)* camera

Foto-: ~**album das** photo album; ~**apparat der** camera; ~**atelier das** photographic studio; ~**ecke die** [mounting] corner

fotogen [foto'ge:n] *Adj.* photogenic

Foto·geschäft das photographic shop

Foto·graf der; ~**en,** ~**en** photographer

Fotografie die; ~, ~**n a)** *o. Pl.* photography *no art.;* **b)** *(Lichtbild)* photograph

fotografieren 1. *tr. V.* photograph; take a photograph/photographs of; **sie läßt sich gern/ungern ~:** she likes/does not like being photographed *or* having her photograph taken; **Katzen lassen sich gut ~:** cats photograph well. **2.** *itr. V.* take photographs; **er fotografiert gut** *od.* **kann gut ~:** he is a good photographer; **[das] Fotografieren [ist] verboten!** photography prohibited

Fotografin die; ~, ~**nen** photographer

fotografisch 1. *Adj.* photographic. **2.** *adv.* photographically

foto-, Foto-: ~**kopie die** photocopy; ~**kopieren** *tr., itr. V.* photocopy; ~**kopierer der,** ~**kopier·gerät das** photocopier; photocopying machine

Foto-: ~**labor das** photographic laboratory; ~**modell das a)** photographic model; **b)** *(verhüll.: Prostituierte)* model; ~**montage die** photomontage; ~**papier das** photographic paper; ~**realismus der** *(bild. Kunst)* photo-realism *no art.;* ~**reporter der** press photographer; newspaper photographer; ~**safari die** photographic safari; ~**satz der** *(Druckw.) s.* **Lichtsatz;** ~**tasche die** camera bag; ~**wettbewerb der** photographic competition; ~**zeitschrift die** photographic magazine

Fötus *s.* **Fetus**

Fotze ['fɔtsə] **die;** ~, ~**n a)** *(vulg.: Vulva)* cunt *(coarse);* **b)** *(vulg.: Frau)* cunt *(coarse);* **c)** *(bayr. u. österr. ugs.: Mund)* gob *(sl.)*

foul [faul] *Adv. (Sport)* ~ **spielen** play dirty; be a dirty player; **er hat gerade ~ gespielt** he has just committed a foul

Foul das; ~**s,** ~**s** *(Sport)* foul **(an +** *Dat.* on)

Foul·elf·meter der *(Fußball)* penalty [for a foul]; **einen ~ verhängen** *od.* **geben** award *or* give a penalty

foulen ['faulən] *(Sport)* **1.** *tr. V.* foul. **2.** *itr. V.* commit a foul

Fox [fɔks] **der;** ~**[es],** ~**e a)** *s.* **Foxterrier; b)** *s.* **Foxtrott**

Fox·terrier der fox-terrier

Fox·trott [-trɔt] **der;** ~**s,** ~**e** *od.* ~**s** foxtrot; ~ **tanzen** foxtrot

Foyer [foa'je:] **das;** ~**s,** ~**s** foyer

FPÖ *Abk.* **Freiheitliche Partei Österreichs**

[1]**Fr.** *Abk.* **Franken** SFr.

[2]**Fr.** *Abk.* **Frau**

[3]**Fr.** *Abk.* **Freitag** Fri.

Fracht [fraxt] **die;** ~, ~**en a)** *(Schiffs~, Luft~)* cargo; freight; *(Bahn~, LKW~)* goods *pl.;* freight; **volle/halbe ~ führen** carry full/half freight; **b)** *(~kosten) (Schiffs~, Luft~)* freight; freightage; *(Bahn~, LKW~)* carriage

Fracht-: ~**brief der** consignment note; waybill; ~**dampfer der** *(veralt.)* steam freighter

Frachten·bahnhof der, Frachtenstation die *(österr.) s.* **Güterbahnhof**

Frachter der; ~**s,** ~**:** freighter

fracht-, Fracht-: ~**flugzeug das** cargo *or* freight plane; ~**frei 1.** *Adj.* carriage-free ‹*delivery*›; **2.** *adv.* ‹*deliver*› carriage free; ~**führer der** carrier; ~**geld das** *s.* **Fracht b;** ~**gut das** slow freight; slow goods *pl.;* **etw. als ~gut schicken** send sth. by slow goods; ~**kosten** *Pl.: s.* **Fracht b;** ~**raum der;** *o. Pl.* [cargo] hold; *(Platz)* [cargo] space; ~**schiff das** cargo ship

Frack [frak] **der;** ~**[e]s, Fräcke** ['frɛkə] tails *pl.;* evening dress; **einen ~ tragen** wear tails *or* evening dress; **im ~ erscheinen** turn up in tails *or* evening dress; **jmdm. saust der ~** *(fig. ugs. scherzh.)* sb. gets the wind up *(sl.)*

Frack-: ~**hemd das** dress shirt; ~**sausen das** *in* **~sausen haben** *(ugs.)* get the wind up *(sl.);* ~**schoß der;** *meist Pl.* coat-tail; ~**weste die** waistcoat *(worn with evening dress)*

Frage ['fra:gə] **die;** ~, ~**n a)** question; **jmdm.** *od.* **an jmdn. eine ~ stellen** put a question to sb.; **jmdm. eine ~ beantworten/auf jmds. ~** *(Akk.)* **antworten** reply to *or* answer sb.'s question; **eine ~ [zu etw.] haben** have a question [on sth.]; **sind noch ~n?** are there any questions?; **an jmdn. eine ~ richten** direct a question to sb.; **darf ich Ihnen eine ~ stellen?** may I put a question?; **eine ~ verneinen/bejahen** give a negative/positive answer to a question; **auf eine dumme ~ bekommt man eine dumme Antwort** ask a silly question [and you get a silly answer]; **b)** *(Problem)* question; *(Angelegenheit)* issue; **es erhebt sich/bleibt die ~, ob ...:** the question arises/remains whether ...; **eine soziale/politische ~:** a social/political issue; **die deutsche ~:** the German problem; **das ist [nur] eine ~ der Zeit** that is [only] a question *or* matter of time; **c)** *in* **das ist noch sehr die ~:** that is still very much the question; **das ist die große ~:** that is the big question; **das ist gar keine ~:** there's no doubt *or* question about it; **es ist** *od.* **steht außer ~, daß ...:** there is no doubt that ...; there is no question but that ...; **etw. in ~ stellen** call sth. into question; question sth.; **jmdn. in ~ stellen** cast doubt on sb.; **das stellt unsere Glaubwürdigkeit in ~:** it casts doubt on our credibility; **in ~ kommen** be possible; **für ein Stipendium kommen nur gute Schüler in ~:** only good pupils can be considered for a grant; **dieses Kleid kommt für mich nicht in ~:** I couldn't possibly wear this dress; **die für die Tat in ~ kommenden Personen** those suspected of the crime; **das kommt nicht in ~** *(ugs.)* that is out of the question; **ohne ~:** without question

Frage-: ~bogen der questionnaire; *(Formular)* form; **~bogen·aktion die** poll; **~für·wort das** *s.* **Interrogativpronomen**

fragen 1. *tr., itr. V.* **a)** ask; **er fragt immer so klug** he always asks *or* puts such astute questions; **neugierig/erstaunt ~:** ask inquisitively/in amazement; **gezielt ~:** ask *or* put well-aimed questions; **frag nicht so dumm!** *(ugs.)* don't ask such silly questions; **das fragst du noch?** *(ugs.)* need you ask?; **~ Sie lieber nicht** *(ugs.)* don't ask!; **da fragst du mich zuviel** that I don't know; I really can't say; **jmdn. ~d ansehen** look at sb. inquiringly; give sb. a questioning look; **~ kostet nichts** there is no harm in asking; **b)** *(sich erkundigen)* **nach etw. ~:** ask *or* inquire about sth.; **jmdn. nach/wegen etw. ~:** ask sb. about sth.; **nach dem Weg ~:** ask the way; **nach Einzelheiten ~:** ask for details; **nach jmds. Meinung ~:** ask [for] sb.'s opinion; **nach jmdm. ~** *(jmdn. suchen)* ask for sb.; *(über jmdn. Fragen stellen)* ask about sb.; *(nach jmds. Befinden ~)* ask after *or* about sb.; **wenn ich ~ darf** if you don't mind my asking; *(ungeduldig)* may I ask?; **c)** *(nachfragen)* ask for; **jmdn. um Rat/Erlaubnis ~:** ask sb. for advice/permission; **d)** *(verneint: sich nicht kümmern)* **nach jmdm./etw. nicht ~:** not care about sb./sth.; **ich frage den Teufel** *od.* **einen Dreck danach** *(salopp)* I couldn't care less [about it] *(coll.)*; I don't give a damn about it *(sl.)*. **2.** *refl. V.* **sich ~, ob ...:** wonder whether ...; **das frage ich mich auch** I was wondering that, too; *(unpers.)* **es fragt sich [nur], ob/wann ...:** the [only] question is whether/when ...

Fragen·komplex der set of problems

Fragerei die; ~, ~en *(abwertend)* questions *pl.*

Frage-: ~satz der interrogative sentence/clause; **ein direkter/indirekter ~satz** a direct/an indirect question; **~stellung die a)** *(Formulierung)* formulation of a/the question; **durch eine geschickte ~stellung** by skilled questioning; **b)** *(Problem)* problem; **~stunde die** *(Parl.)* question time; **~-und-Antwort-Spiel das** question-and-answer game; **~zeichen das** question mark; **ein ~zeichen setzen** put a question mark; **etw. mit einem [dicken/großen] ~zeichen versehen** *(fig.)* put a [big] question mark over sth. *(fig.)*; **dastehen/dasitzen wie ein ~zeichen** *(ugs.)* stand/sit like a hunchback

fragil [fra'gi:l] *Adj. (geh.)* fragile

fraglich ['fra:klɪç] *Adj.* **a)** *(unsicher)* doubtful; **b)** *nicht präd. (betreffend)* in question *postpos.*; relevant; **zur ~en Zeit** at the time in question; at the relevant time

fraglos *Adv.* without question; unquestionably

Fragment [fra'gmɛnt] **das; ~[e]s, ~e** fragment

fragmentarisch [fragmɛn'ta:rɪʃ] **1.** *Adj.* fragmentary. **2.** *adv.* **ein ~ überlieferter Text** a text preserved only as fragments/a fragment; **es ist nur ~ erhalten** it is preserved only in fragmentary form

frag·würdig *Adj.* **a)** questionable; **b)** *(zwielichtig)* dubious

Fragwürdigkeit die; ~, ~en a) questionableness; **b)** *(Zwielichtigkeit)* dubiousness

Fraktion [frak'tsio:n] **die; ~, ~en a)** *(Parl.)* parliamentary party; *(mit zwei Parteien)* parliamentary coalition; **b)** *(Sondergruppe)* faction; **c)** *(Chemie)* fraction

fraktionell [fraktsio'nɛl] *Adj.* within a/the party/group *postpos.*; internal ‹*conflict, agreement*›

fraktions-, Fraktions- *(Parl.)*: **~beschluß der** party/coalition decision; **~führer der** leader of the parliamentary party/coalition; **~kollege der** fellow parliamentary party/coalition member; **~los** *Adj.* independent; **~mit·glied das** member of a/the parliamentary party/coalition; **~sitzung die** meeting of the parliamentary party/coalition; **~stärke die a)** *minimum number of elected members necessary for a party to be allowed to form a parliamentary group;* **b)** *(Größe der Fraktion)* size of the parliamentary party; **~vorsitzende der/die** *s.* **~führer; ~zwang der** obligation to vote in accordance with party policy; **den ~zwang aufheben** allow a free vote

Fraktur [frak'tu:ɐ̯] **die; ~, ~en a)** *(Med.)* fracture; **b)** *(Schriftart)* Fraktur; **mit jmdm. ~ reden** *(ugs.)* talk straight with sb.

Franc [frã:] **der; ~, ~s** franc

Franchise ['fræntʃaɪz] **das; ~** *(Wirtsch.)* franchise

frank [fraŋk] *Adv.* **~ und frei** frankly and openly; openly and honestly

Franke der; ~n, ~n a) Franconian; **b)** *(hist.)* Frank

[1]**Franken (das); ~s** Franconia

[2]**Franken der; ~s, ~:** [Swiss] franc

[1]**Frankfurter** ['fraŋkfʊrtɐ] **die; ~, ~** *(Wurst)* frankfurter

[2]**Frankfurter 1.** *indekl. Adj.; nicht präd.* Frankfurt. **2. der; ~s, ~:** Frankfurter; *s. auch* **Kölner**

frankieren [fraŋ'ki:rən] *tr. V.* frank

Frankier·maschine die franking-machine

fränkisch ['frɛŋkɪʃ] *Adj.* **a)** Franconian; **b)** *(hist.)* Frankish; *s. auch* **deutsch, Deutsch, badisch**

franko ['fraŋko] *Adv. (Kaufmannsspr. veralt.)* carriage paid; *(mit der Post)* post-free

Franko·kanadier der French Canadian

frankophil [-'fi:l] *Adj.* Francophile

frankophon [-'fo:n] *Adj.* Francophone

Frank·reich (das); ~s France

Franktireur [frãti'rø:ɐ̯] **der; ~s, ~e** *od.* **~s** *(hist.)* franc tireur

Franse ['franzə] **die; ~, ~n** strand [of a/the fringe]; **die ~n der Decke/des Teppichs** the fringe of the rug/the carpet

fransen *itr. V.: s.* **ausfransen 1**

fransig 1. *Adj.* frayed ‹*shirt, trousers*›; straggly ‹*hair*›. **2.** *adv.* **das Haar hing ihr ~ ins Gesicht** her hair hung down over her face in untidy strands

[1]**Franz** [frants] **(der)** Francis

[2]**Franz das; ~** *(Schülerspr.)* French

Franz·branntwein der; *o. Pl. (veralt.)* alcoholic liniment

Franziskaner [frantsɪs'ka:nɐ] **der; ~s, ~:** Franciscan

Franziskaner-: ~kloster das Franciscan monastery; **~orden der** *(kath.)* Franciscan Order

Franzose [fran'tso:zə] **der; ~n, ~n a)** Frenchman; **er ist ~:** he is French *or* a Frenchman; **die ~n** the French; **b)** *(ugs.: Schraubenschlüssel)* screw wrench

Franzosen·krankheit die *(veralt.)* French disease *(dated)*; syphilis

Französin [fran'tsø:zɪn] **die; ~, ~nen** Frenchwoman

französisch 1. *Adj.* French; **ein ~es Bett** a double bed; **die Französische Schweiz** French-speaking Switzerland; **die Französische Revolution** the French Revolution; **die ~e Krankheit** *(veralt.) s.* **Franzosenkrankheit. 2.** *adv.* **es ~ machen** *(salopp)* have oral sex; **sich [auf] ~ empfehlen** *od.* **verabschieden** *(ugs.)* take French leave; *s. auch* **deutsch;** [2]**Deutsche**

Französisch das; ~[s] French; *s. auch* **Deutsch**

frappant [fra'pant] *Adj.* striking ‹*similarity*›; remarkable ‹*success, discovery*›

frappieren [fra'pi:rən] *tr. V. (geh.)* astonish; astound

frappierend *Adj.* astonishing; remarkable

Fräse ['frɛ:zə] **die; ~, ~n a)** *(für Holz)* moulding machine; *(für Metall)* milling machine; **b)** *s.* **Fräser a; c)** *(Boden~)* rotary cultivator

fräsen *tr. V.* **a)** shape ‹*wood*›; mill ‹*metal*›; form ‹*groove, thread*›; **b)** *(Landw.)* hoe [with a rotary cultivator]

Fräser der; ~s, ~ a) *(Werkzeug)* cutter; **b)** *(Metallbearb.)* milling-machine operator; *(Holzverarb.)* moulding-machine operator

Fräs·maschine die *s.* **Fräse a**

fraß [fra:s] *1. u. 3. Pers. Sg. Prät. v.* **fressen**

Fraß der; ~es a) *(Tiernahrung)* food; **einem Tier etw. als** *od.* **zum ~ vorwerfen** feed an animal with sth.; **jmdm. etw. zum ~ hin-** *od.* **vorwerfen** *(fig. abwertend)* let sb. have sth.; **b)** *(derb: schlechtes Essen)* muck; swill; **ein abscheulicher/widerlicher ~:** disgusting/repulsive muck; **c) vom ~ befallen sein** have been eaten away

Frater ['fra:tɐ] **der; ~s, Fratres** ['fra:tre:s] *(kath. Kirche)* lay brother

fraternisieren [fratɛrni'zi:rən] *itr. V. (geh.)* fraternize

Fraternisierung die; ~: fraternization

Fratz [frats] **der; ~es, ~e,** *(österr.:)* **~en, ~en a)** *(ugs.: niedliches Kind)* [little] rascal; **ein süßer ~:** a sweet little rascal; **b)** *(bes. südd., österr.: ungezogenes Kind)* brat

Fratze ['fratsə] **die; ~, ~n a)** *(häßliches Gesicht)* hideous face; hideous features *pl.*; **sein Gesicht war zu einer ~ deformiert** his face was hideously deformed; **b)** *(ugs.: Grimasse)* grimace; **jmdm. ~n schneiden** pull faces at sb.; **c)** *(abwertend: Gesicht)* mug *(sl.)*

fratzenhaft *Adj.* grotesque; hideous

frau [frau] *Indefinitpron. im Nom. (feministischer Sprachgebrauch) s.* [1]**man**

Frau die; ~, ~en a) woman; **zur ~ werden** *(verhüll.)* lose one's virginity; **typisch** *od.* **echt ~** *(ugs.)* typical of a woman; **die Gleichberechtigung der ~:** equal rights for women; **von ~ zu ~:** woman to woman; **b)** *(Ehe~)* wife; **wie Mann und ~ zusammenleben** live together as man *or* husband and wife; **jmdn. zur ~ nehmen** *(veralt.)* take sb. to wife *(arch.)*; **er hat eine Französin zur Frau** his wife is French; **willst du meine ~ werden?** will you be my wife?; **c)** *(Titel, Anrede)* **~ Schulze** Mrs Schulze; **~ Professor/Dr. Schulze** Professor/Dr. Schulze; **~ Ministerin/Direktorin/Studienrätin Schulze** Mrs/Miss/Ms Schulze; **~ Ministerin/Professor/Doktor** Minister/Professor/doctor; **~ Vorsitzende/Präsidentin** Madam Chairman/President; *(in Briefen)* **Sehr geehrte ~**

Schulze Dear Madam; *(bei persönlicher Bekanntschaft)* Dear Mrs/Miss/Ms Schulze; **[Sehr verehrte] gnädige ~:** [Dear] Madam; **gute ~** *(veralt.)* good lady; **Ihre ~ Gemahlin/Mutter** *(geh.)* your lady wife/lady mother *(dated)*; your wife/mother; **d)** *(Herrin)* lady; mistress; **die ~ des Hauses** the lady of the house; **Unsere Liebe ~** *(kath. Rel.)* Our Lady

Frauchen ['frauçən] **das; ~s, ~ a)** *(ugs.: Ehefrau)* wifie; **b)** *(Herrin eines Hundes)* mistress

frauen-, Frauen-: ~arbeit die a) *o. Pl. (Erwerbstätigkeit)* women's employment; **b)** *(für ~ geeignete Arbeit)* women's work; **c)** *(gesellschaftspolitisch)* work for the women's movement; **in der ~arbeit tätig sein** work in the women's movement; **~arzt der, ~ärztin die** gynaecologist; **~beruf der** women's occupation; **~bewegung die;** *o. Pl.* women's movement; **~emanzipation die** female emancipation; women's emancipation; **~fachschule die** women's technical college; **~farn der** *(Bot.)* lady fern; **~feind der** misogynist; **~feindlich** *Adj.* anti-women; **~frage die** issue of women's rights; **~funk der** women's [radio] programmes *pl.*; **~fuß·ball der** women's football; **~gefängnis das** women's prison; **~geschichten** *Pl. (ugs.)* affairs with women; **~gestalt die** female character; **~haar das a)** woman's hair; **b)** *(Bot.)* haircap moss; **~haar·farn der** *(Bot.)* maidenhair fern; **~hand die** *in* **von zarter ~hand** from the fair hand of a lady; **von zarter ~hand gepflegt** nursed by a woman's tender care; **~haus das a)** battered wives' refuge; **b)** *(veralt.)* brothel; **c)** *(Völkerk.)* unmarried girls' dormitory; **~heil·kunde die** gynaecology; **~held der** lady-killer; **~herz das** female heart; **sich auf ~herzen verstehen** know the way to a woman's heart; **~kenner der** connoisseur of women; **~kleider** *Pl.* women's clothes; **~klinik die** gynaecological hospital *or* clinic; **~kloster das** convent; nunnery; **~krankheit die, ~leiden das** gynaecological disorder; **Facharzt für ~krankheiten** gynaecologist; **~liebling der** favourite with the ladies; **~lohn der** women's pay *no indef. art.*; **~los** *Adj.* all-male; **~mörder der** killer of women; **~orden der** *(kath. Rel.)* women's order; **~recht das;** *meist Pl.* women's right; **~rechtlerin** [-rɛçtlərɪn] **die; ~, ~nen** feminist; Women's Libber *(coll.)*; **~sache die: das ist ~sache** that's a woman's job; **~schänder der** rapist; **~schuh der** *(Bot.)* lady's slipper; **~seite die** women's page

Frauens·person die *(veralt.)* female

Frauen-: ~sport der women's sport; **~station** *die* women's ward; **~stimme die a)** woman's voice; **b)** *(Parl.)* **die ~stimmen** the women's vote *sing.*; **~stimmrecht das** *s.* **~wahlrecht; ~tausch der** *(Völkerk.)* exchange of wives

Frauentum das; ~s *(geh.)* womanhood

Frauen-: ~turnen das ladies' *or* women's gymnastics *sing.*; **~über·schuß der** surplus of women; **~verband der** women's association; **~wahl·recht das** women's franchise; women's right to vote; **~zeitschrift die** women's magazine; **~zimmer das a)** *(abwertend)* female; **b)** *(veralt., landsch.)* woman

Fräulein ['frɔylain] **das; ~s, ~** *(ugs.* **~s) a)** *(junges ~)* young lady; *(ältliches ~)* spinster; **b)** *(Titel, Anrede)* **~ Mayer/Schulte** Miss Mayer/Schulte; **[sehr verehrtes] gnädiges ~ [X]** Dear Miss X; **c)** *(veralt.: Angestellte)* **~, wollen Sie ...:** Miss, would you ...; **das ~ hat uns schlecht bedient** the girl gave us bad service; **d)** *(Kellnerin)* **~, wir möchten zahlen** [Miss,] could we have the bill *(Brit.)* *or (Amer.)* check, pledase?; **das ~ kommt gleich** the waitress is just coming; **e) das ~ vom Amt** *(veralt.)* the operator

fraulich 1. *Adj.* feminine; *(reif)* womanly. **2.** *adv.* in a feminine/womanly way; **sich ~ kleiden** dress femininely/in a womanly way

Fraulichkeit die; ~: femininity; *(reifes Wesen)* womanliness

frech [frɛç] **1.** *Adj.* **a)** *(respektlos, unverschämt)* impertinent; impudent; cheeky; bare-faced ⟨*lie*⟩; **ein ~er Kerl** an impertinent chap; **~ werden/sein** become/be impertinent; **etw. mit ~er Stirn behaupten** *(fig.)* have the bare-faced cheek to say sth.; **~ wie Dreck** *od.* **Oskar sein** *(bes. berlin.)* be a cheeky devil *(coll.)*; **b)** *(keck, keß)* saucy. **2.** *adv. (respektlos, unverschämt)* impertinently; impudently; cheekily; **jmdn. ~ anlügen** tell sb. bare-faced lies; **jmdm. etw. ~ ins Gesicht sagen** say sth. quite unashamedly to sb.'s face; **jmdm. ~ ins Gesicht lachen** laugh in sb.'s face

Frech·dachs der *(ugs., meist scherzh.)* cheeky little thing

Frechheit die; ~, ~en a) *o. Pl. (Benehmen)* impertinence; impudence; cheek; **die ~ haben, etw. zu tun** have the impertinence *etc.* to do sth.; **das ist der Gipfel der ~!** that is the height of impertinence!; **b)** *(Äußerung)* impertinent *or* impudent *or* cheeky remark; **sich** *(Dat.)* **~en erlauben** be impertinent; **was erlauben Sie sich für ~en?** how dare you be so impertinent?

Frechling der; ~s, ~e *(geh.)* impudent rascal

Freesie ['fre:zi̯ə] **die; ~, ~n** freesia

Fregatte [fre'gatə] **die; ~, ~n a)** *(Marine)* frigate; **b)** *(abwertend: Frau)* **eine alte/aufgetakelte ~:** an old bag/overdressed old bag

Fregatten·kapitän der commander

frei [frai] **1.** *Adj.* **a)** *(unabhängig)* free ⟨*man, will, life, people, decision, etc.*⟩; **eine ~e Reichsstadt/Hansestadt** *(hist.)* a free imperial/Hanseatic city; **b)** *(nicht angestellt)* free-lance ⟨*writer, worker, etc.*⟩; **die ~en Berufe** the independent professions; **c)** *(ungezwungen)* free and easy; lax *(derog.)*; **ein ~es Benehmen haben** behave in a free and easy/lax way; **es herrschte ein ~er Ton** there was an informal atmosphere; **~e Liebe** free love; **d)** *(nicht mehr in Haft)* free; at liberty *pred.*; **e)** *(offen)* open; **ein ~es Gelände/~er Platz** open ground/an open square; **unter ~em Himmel** in the open [air]; outdoors; **auf ~er Strecke** *(Straße)* on the open road; *(Eisenbahn)* between stations; **ins Freie gehen** walk out into the open; **im Freien sitzen/übernachten** sit out of doors/spend the night in the open; **ständig im Freien übernachten** sleep rough; **f)** *(unbesetzt)* vacant; unoccupied; free; **ein ~er Stuhl/Platz** a vacant *or* free chair/seat; **Entschuldigung, ist hier noch ~?** excuse me, is this anyone's seat *etc.?*; **eine ~e Stelle** a vacancy; **ein Bett ist [noch] ~:** one bed is [still] free *or* not taken; **ist der Tisch ~?** is this table free?; **sind Sie ~?** are you free?; **den Weg/die Kreuzung ~ machen** clear the path/junction; **[jmdm.] Platz ~ lassen** leave [sb.] some space; **einige Seiten ~ lassen** leave some pages blank; **Ring ~!** *(Boxen)* seconds out!; **g)** *(kostenlos)* free ⟨*food, admission*⟩; **~e Verpflegung** free board; **der Eintritt ist ~:** admission is free [of charge]; **20 kg Gepäck ~ haben** have *or* be allowed a 20 kilogram baggage allowance; **Lieferung ~ Haus** carriage free; **~e Kost und Logis** *(veralt.)* free board and lodging; **h)** *(ungenau)* **eine ~e Übersetzung** a free *or* loose translation; **~ nach einer Vorlage** based [loosely] on a source; **i)** *(ohne Vorlage)* improvised; **in ~er Improvisation** in spontaneous improvisation; **j)** *(uneingeschränkt)* free; **~e Meinungsäußerung/Religionsausübung** free expression of opinion/practice of religion; **die ~e Arzt-/Berufswahl** the free choice of doctor/profession; **der Zug hat ~e Fahrt** the train can proceed; **der ~e Fall** *(Physik)* free fall; **k)** *(nicht beeinträchtigt)* free; **~ von Schuld/Schmerzen sein** be free of guilt/pain; **~ von Fehlern** without faults; **nicht ~ von Überheblichkeit** not without arrogance; **l)** *(verfügbar)* spare; free; **jede ~e Minute/Stunde** every spare *or* free minute/hour; **ich habe heute ~:** I've got today off; **er hat seinen ~en Sonnabend/Abend** this is his Saturday/evening off; **sich** *(Dat.)* **~ nehmen** *(ugs.)* take some time off; **er ist noch/nicht mehr ~:** he is still/no longer unattached; **m)** *(ohne Hilfsmittel)* **eine ~e Rede** an extempore speech; **aus ~er Hand zeichnen** draw free-hand; **n)** *(unbekleidet)* bare; **das Kleid läßt die Schultern ~:** the dress leaves the shoulders bare; **den Oberkörper ~ machen** strip to the waist; **o)** *(bes. Fußball)* unmarked; **der ~e Mann** the sweeper; **~ stehen** be [standing] unmarked; **p)** *(Chemie, Physik)* free; **~ werden** *(bei einer Reaktion)* be given off; **Elektronen werden ~:** electrons are released; **q)** *(in festen Wendungen)* **~e Hand haben** have a free hand; **jmdm. ~e Hand lassen** give sb. a free hand; **aus ~en Stücken** *(ugs.)* of one's own accord; voluntarily; **jmdn. auf ~en Fuß setzen** set sb. free; **auf ~em Fuß** *(von Verbrechern etc.)* at large; **~ ausgehen** get away scot-free; get away with it *(coll.)*; **ich bin so ~!** if I may ... **2.** *adv.* ⟨*act, speak, choose*⟩ freely; ⟨*translate*⟩ freely, loosely; **etw. ~ heraus sagen** say sth. freely; **~ herumlaufen** run around scot-free; **eine Rede ~ halten** make a speech without notes; **ein ~ praktizierender Arzt** a doctor in private practice; **die Personen sind/die Geschichte ist ~ erfunden** the characters are/the story is entirely fictional; **~ in der Luft schweben** hang in mid-air

frei-, Frei-: ~aktie die *(Börsenw.)* bonus share; **~bad das** open-air *or* outdoor swimming-pool; **~ballon der** free balloon; **~bank die** *place in slaughterhouse where lower-grade meat is sold*; **~|bekommen 1.** *unr. itr. V. (ugs.)* get time off; **ich habe nachmittags ~bekommen** I've got the afternoon off; **2.** *unr. tr. V.* **jmdn./etw. ~bekommen** get sb./sth. released; **~beruflich 1.** *Adj.* self-employed; free-lance ⟨*journalist, editor, architect, etc.*⟩; ⟨*doctor, lawyer*⟩ in private practice; **2.** *adv.* **~beruflich tätig sein/arbeiten** work free-lance/practise privately; **~betrag der** *(Steuerw.)* [tax] allowance; **~beuter** [-bɔytɐ] **der; ~s, ~ a)** *(hist.: Pirat)* freebooter; **b)** *(abwertend)* exploiter; **~beuterei die; ~ a)** *(hist.: Piraterie)* freebootery; **b)** *(abwertend)* exploitation; **~bier das** free beer; **~bleibend** *(Kaufmannsspr.)* **1.** *Adj.* **~bleibendes Angebot** provisional offer; **2.** *adv.* **die Preise verstehen sich ~bleibend** prices are subject to alteration; **~bord der** *(Schiffahrt)* freeboard; **~brief der a)** *in* **kein ~brief für etw. sein** be no excuse for sth.; **jmdm. einen ~brief für etw. geben** *od.* **ausstellen** give sb. a licence for sth.; **einen ~brief für etw. haben/einen ~brief haben, etw. zu tun** have authority for sth./to do sth.; *(fig.)* have a licence for sth./to do sth.; **etw. als ~brief für etw. ansehen/betrachten** regard sth. as a charter for sth.; **b)** *(hist.: Urkunde)* charter; **~demokrat der** Free Democrat; **~denker der** free thinker; **~denkertum das; ~s** free thought; free-thinking

Freie der/die; *adj. Dekl. (hist.)* freeman/freewoman

freien 1. *tr. V. (veralt.)* marry; wed; **jung gefreit hat nie gereut** *(Spr.)* marry young and you won't regret it. **2.** *itr. V.* **um ein Mädchen ~:** court *or* woo a girl

Freier der; ~s, ~ a) *(veralt.)* suitor; **b)** *(salopp: Kunde einer Dirne)* punter *(sl.)*

Freiers·füße *Pl. in* **auf ~n gehen** *(scherzh.)* be courting

frei-, Frei-: ~exemplar das *(Buch)* free copy; *(Zeitung)* free issue; **~fahr·schein der** free ticket; **~fahrt die** free trip; *(auf Karussell)* free turn *or* ride; **~fläche die** open space; **~flug der** free flight; **~frau die, ~fräulein das** baroness; **~gabe die a)** release; **die ~gabe der Wechselkurse** the lifting of controls on exchange rates; **b)** *(Übergabe)* opening [to the public]; **~|geben 1.** *unr. tr. V.* **a)** release ⟨*prisoner, footballer*⟩; decontrol ⟨*exchange rates*⟩; **jmdm. den Weg ~geben** let sb. through; **b)** open ⟨*motorway*⟩; pass ⟨*film*⟩; **etw. für den Verkehr/die Öffentlichkeit ~geben** open sth. to traffic/to the public; **der Film ist ab 18 freigegeben** the film has been passed 18; **2.** *unr. tr., itr. V.* **jmdm. ~geben** give sb. time off; **sich** *(Dat.)* **zwei Tage ~geben lassen** take two days off; **~gebig** [-ge:bɪç] *Adj.* generous; open-handed; **~gebig gegen jmdn. sein** *(veralt.)* be generous to sb.; **[nicht] sehr ~gebig mit etw. sein** be [not] very generous *or* open-handed with sth.; **~gebigkeit die** generosity; open-handedness; **~gehege das** outdoor *or* open-air enclosure; **~geist der** free thinker; **~geistig** *Adj.* free-thinking; **~gelände das** piece of open ground; *(Film)* studio lot; **~gelassene der/die;** *adj. Dekl. (hist.)* freedman/freedwoman *(Hist.)*; **~gepäck das** baggage allowance; **~grenze die** *(Steuerw.)* tax exemption limit; **~gut das** *(Zollw.)* duty-free goods *pl.*; **~|haben** *unr. tr., itr. V. (ugs.)* **ich habe [am** *od.* **den] Montag ~:** I've got Monday off; **~hafen der** free port; **~|halten** *unr. tr. V.* **a)** treat; **er hielt das ganze Lokal ~:** he stood drinks for everyone in the pub *(Brit.)* *or (Amer.)* bar; **b)** *(offenhalten)* keep ⟨*entrance, roadway*⟩ clear; **Einfahrt ~halten!** no parking in front of entrance; keep clear; **c)** *(reservieren)* **jmdm.** *od.* **für jmdn. einen Platz ~halten** keep a place for sb.; **sich ~halten** keep oneself free of engagements; **~hand·bücherei die** open-access library; **~handel der** free trade; **~handels·zone die** free-trade zone; **~händig** [-hɛndɪç] **1.** *Adj.* **a)** free-hand ⟨*drawing*⟩; offhand ⟨*shooting*⟩; **b)** *(Amtsspr.)* private ⟨*sale*⟩; **2.** *adv.* **a)** ⟨*cycle*⟩ without holding on; ⟨*draw*⟩ free-hand; ⟨*shoot*⟩ offhand; **b)** *(Amtsspr.)* ⟨*sell*⟩ privately; **~hand·zeichnen das** free-hand drawing

Freiheit die; ~, ~en a) freedom; **~, Gleichheit, Brüderlichkeit** Liberty, Equality, Fraternity; **die persönliche ~:** personal freedom *or* liberty; **die ~ der Presse** Press freedom; the freedom of the Press; **die akademische ~:** academic freedom; **jmdm. völlige ~ lassen** give sb. a completely free hand; **die ~ der Meere** *(Rechtsw.)* the freedom of the seas; **einem Gefangenen/Tier die ~ schenken** give a prisoner his/an animal its freedom; **jmdn. in ~ setzen** set sb. free; **b)** *(Vorrecht)* freedom; privilege; **[besondere] ~en genießen** enjoy [special] privileges; **sich** *(Dat.)* **gegen jmdn. ~en herausnehmen** take liberties with sb.; **die dichterische ~:** poetic licence; **sich** *(Dat.)* **die ~ nehmen, etw. zu tun** take the liberty of doing sth.

-freiheit die; ~: Gebühren~/Porto~: freedom from dues/postal charges; **Bewegungs~:** freedom of movement; **Entscheidungs~:** freedom of decision *or* choice

freiheitlich 1. *Adj.* liberal ⟨*philosophy, conscience*⟩; **~ und demokratisch** free and democratic. **2.** *adv.* liberally; **~ gesinnt sein** have liberal ideas

freiheits-, Freiheits-: ~beraubung die *(jur.)* wrongful detention; **~bewegung die** liberation movement; **~drang der;** *o. Pl.* desire for freedom; **~entzug der** imprisonment; **jmdn. zu zwei Jahren ~entzug verurteilen** sentence sb. to two years' imprisonment; **~kampf der** struggle for freedom; **~kämpfer der** freedom fighter; **~krieg der** war of liberation; **die ~kriege** *(hist.)* the War of Liberation; **~liebe die;** *o. Pl.* love of freedom *or* liberty; **~liebend** *Adj.* freedom-loving; **~rechte** *Pl.* civil rights; **~statue die** Statue of Liberty; **~strafe die** *(Rechtsw.)* term of imprisonment; prison sentence; **er wurde zu einer ~strafe von fünf Jahren/zu einer lebenslänglichen ~strafe verurteilt** he was sentenced to five years' imprisonment/given a life sentence

frei-, Frei-: ~heraus *Adv.* frankly; openly; **~heraus gesagt ...:** to put it frankly ...; **~herr der** baron; **~herrlich** *Adj.; nicht präd.* baronial

Freiin ['fraiɪn] **die; ~, ~nen** baroness

frei-, Frei-: ~|kämpfen *tr. V.* liberate; **sich ~kämpfen** fight one's way out; **~karte die** complimentary *or* free ticket; **~|kaufen** *tr. V.* ransom ⟨*hostage*⟩; buy the freedom of ⟨*slave*⟩; **sich von der Verantwortung/Schuld ~kaufen** *(fig.)* buy off one's responsibility/guilt; **~kirche die** Free Church; **~|kommen** *unr. itr. V.; mit sein* **aus dem Gefängnis ~kommen** be released from prison; leave prison; **aus jmds. Fängen ~kommen** escape from sb.'s clutches; **~körper·kultur die;** *o. Pl.* nudism *no art.*; naturism *no art.*; **~korps das** *(hist.)* volunteer corps; **~land·gemüse das** outdoor vegetables *pl.*; **~|lassen** *unr. tr. V.* set free; release; **~lassung die** release; **~lauf der** *(Technik)* neutral gear; *(beim Fahrrad)* free-wheel; **im ~lauf fahren** ⟨*driver*⟩ coast in neutral; ⟨*cyclist*⟩ free-wheel; **~|laufen** *unr. refl. V. (bes. Fuß- und Handball)* run into *or* find space; **~lebend** *Adj.* living in the wild *postpos.*; **~|legen** *tr. V.* uncover; **~leitung die** *(Technik)* overhead cable

freilich *Adv.* **a)** *(einschränkend)* **er arbeitet schnell, ~ nicht sehr gründlich** he works quickly, though admittedly he's not very thorough; **deine Theorie klingt zwar überzeugend, ~ ist eine wichtige Einschränkung zu machen** your theory sounds convincing, it's true, but there is one important reservation to be made; **ich werde morgen einmal bei dir vorbeischauen, lange bleiben kann ich ~ nicht** I'll call in on you tomorrow, though I shan't be able to stay long; **sie hat sehr viel Talent, ~ fehlt es ihr an Ausdauer** she has a great deal of talent, but she does lack staying power; **b)** *(einräumend)* **man muß ~ bedenken, daß ...:** one must of course bear in mind that ...; **~ scheinen die Tatsachen gegen meine Überlegungen zu sprechen ...:** admittedly the facts seem to contradict my ideas, but ...; **sie war sehr wütend auf ihren Mann, wozu sie ~ auch allen Grund hatte** she was furious with her husband, and of course she had every reason to be; **c)** *(bes. südd.: selbstverständlich)* of course; **ja ~:** [why] yes; of course

Frei·licht-: ~bühne die *s.* **~theater; ~museum das** open-air *or* outdoor museum; **~theater das** open-air *or* outdoor theatre

frei-, Frei-: ~los das a) free [lottery] ticket; **b)** *(Sport)* bye; **durch ~los die nächste Runde erreichen** get a bye into the next round; **~|machen 1.** *refl. V. (ugs.: frei nehmen)* **sich [für etw.] ~machen** take time off [for sth.]; **2.** *tr. V. (Postw.)* frank; **etw. mit 0,50 DM ~machen** put a 50-pfennig stamp on sth.; **~machung die; ~** *(Postw.)* franking; **~marke die** postage stamp; **~maurer der** Freemason; **~maurerei die;** *o. Pl.* Freemasonry; **~maurer·loge die** Freemasons' lodge; **~mut der** candidness; frankness; **mit ~mut sprechen** speak candidly *or* frankly; **~mütig 1.** *Adj.* candid; frank; **2.** *adv.* candidly; frankly; **~mütigkeit die; ~:** candidness; frankness; **~platz der a)** *([Hoch]schulw.)* scholarship; **b)** *(Sitzplatz)* free seat; **~|pressen** *tr. V.* **jmdn. ~pressen** obtain sb.'s release by threats; **~raum der** *(Psych., Soziol.)* space *no indef. art.* to be oneself; **unpolitische ~räume** areas where politics is not involved; **~religiös** *Adj.* non-denominational; **~saß, ~sasse der; ~sassen, ~sassen** *(hist.)* yeoman; tenant farmer; **~schaffend** *Adj.* free-lance; **Steuervergünstigungen für Freischaffende** tax concessions to self-employed persons; **~schar die** *(hist.)* corps of irregulars; **~schärler** [-ʃɛ:ɐ̯lɐ] **der; ~s, ~:** irregular [soldier]; **~|schaufeln** *tr. V.* clear ⟨*road*⟩ by shovelling; dig ⟨*person*⟩ free; **~|schießen** *unr. tr., refl. V.* **sich** *(Dat.)* **den Weg ~schießen** shoot one's way out; **jmdn. ~schießen** free sb. [in a gun battle]; **~|schwimmen** *unr. refl. V.* **sich ~schwimmen** pass the 15-minute swimming test; **inzwischen hat er sich ~geschwommen** *(fig.)* he has now got over his initial difficulties; **~|setzen** *tr. V.* **a)** *(Physik, Chemie, Med.)* release ⟨*energy*⟩; emit ⟨*rays, electrons, neutrons*⟩; release, give off ⟨*gas*⟩; **b)** *(Arbeitsw.)* release ⟨*staff*⟩; *(verhüll.)* make ⟨*staff*⟩ redundant; **~setzung die; ~, ~en a)** *(Physik, Chemie, Med.) (von Energie, Gas)* release; *(von Strahlung usw.)* emission; **b)** *(Arbeitsw.)* release ⟨*of staff*⟩; *(verhüll.)* redundancy; **~sinn der;** *o. Pl. (veralt.)* liberalism; **~sinnig** *Adj. (veralt.)* liberal; broadminded; **~spiel das** free turn; **~|spielen 1.** *tr. V. (Ballspiele)* **jmdn./sich ~spielen** create space for sb./oneself; **2.** *refl. V. (auf der Bühne)* settle into the performance; **~|sprechen** *unr. tr. V.* **a)** *(Rechtsw.)* acquit; **jmdn. von einer Anklage ~sprechen** acquit sb. of a charge; **b)** *(für unschuldig erklären)* exonerate **(von** from); **c)** *(Handw.)* release ⟨*apprentice*⟩; **~sprechung die; ~, ~en a)** *(Rechtsw.)* acquitting; **b)** *(Handw.)* release; **~spruch der** *(Rechtsw.)* acquittal; **~staat der** *(veralt.)* free state; **der ~staat Bayern** the Free State of Bavaria; **~statt, ~stätte die; ~, ~stätten** *(geh.)* sanctuary; **~|stehen** *unr. itr. V.* **a) es steht jmdm. ~, etw. zu tun** sb. is free to do sth.; **b)** ⟨*flat, house*⟩ be empty *or* vacant; ⟨*storeroom etc.*⟩ be empty; **~stelle die** *s.* **~platz a; ~|stellen** *tr. V.* **a) jmdm. etw. ~stellen** leave sth. up to sb.; let sb. decide sth.; **b)** *(befreien)* release ⟨*person*⟩; **jmdn. vom Wehrdienst ~stellen** exempt sb. from military service; **~stellung die** release; *(befristet)* leave; **~stempel der** *(Postw.)* postmark

Frei·stil der; *o. Pl. (Sport)* **a)** *s.* **~ringen; b)** *s.* **~schwimmen**

Freistil-: ~ringen das free-style wrestling; **~schwimmen das** free-style swimming

Frei-: ~stoß der *(Fußball)* free kick; **einen ~stoß schießen** *od.* **treten** take a free kick; **~stunde die** free hour; *(Schulstunde)* free period

Frei·tag der Friday; **ein schwarzer ~:** a black day; *s. auch* **Dienstag, Dienstag-**

freitags *Adv.* on Friday[s]; *s. auch* **dienstags**

frei-, Frei-: ~tod der *(verhüll.)* suicide *no art.*; **den ~tod wählen** choose to take one's own life; **~tragend** *Adj. (Bauw.)* suspended ⟨*floor*⟩; cantilever ⟨*bridge*⟩; **~treppe die** [flight of] steps; **~übung die;** *meist Pl. (Sport)* keep-fit exercise; **~übungen machen** do keep-fit exercises; **~umschlag der** stamped addressed envelope; s.a.e.; **~verkehr der** *(Bankw.)* unofficial market; kerb dealings *pl.*; **~wache die** *(Seemannsspr.)* watch below; **~weg** *Adv. (ugs.)* **wir können ~weg reden** we can talk freely *or* openly; **sag es ~weg** say it straight out; **~wild das** fair game; **zum ~wild werden** become fair game; **~willig 1.** *Adj.* voluntary ⟨*decision*⟩; optional ⟨*subject*⟩; **~willige Feuerwehr** volunteer fire brigade; **2.** *adv.* voluntarily; of one's own accord; **sich ~willig melden** volunteer; **~willig aus dem Leben scheiden** choose to end one's life; **~willige der/die;** *adj. Dekl.* volunteer; **~willige vor!** volunteers take one step forward!; **sich als ~williger zu etw. melden** volunteer for sth.; **~wurf der** free throw; **~zeichen das a)** *(volkst.)* dialling tone; **b)** *(Nachrichtenw.)* ringing tone; **~zeichnungs·klausel die** *(Rechtsw.)* exemption clause

Frei·zeit die; *o. Pl.* **a)** spare time; leisure time; *(Arbeitsw.)* time off in lieu; **in** *od.* **während der ~:** in/during one's spare time; **b)** *(Zusammenkunft)* [holiday/weekend] course; *(der Kirche)* retreat

Freizeit-: ~anzug der leisure suit; **~beschäftigung die** the hobby; leisure pursuit; **~gestaltung die** *(Soziol., Päd.)* leisure activity; **~hemd das** sports shirt; **~industrie die** leisure industry; **~kleidung die** casual clothes *pl.*; leisure wear *(Commerc.)*; **~wert der: eine Stadt mit hohem ~wert** a town with many leisure amenities

frei-, Frei-: ~zügig 1. *Adj.* **a)** *(großzügig)* generous, liberal ⟨*dosage, spending*⟩; liberal, flexible ⟨*interpretation of rule etc.*⟩; **~zügig im Geldausgeben** generous with one's money; **b)** *(gewagt, unmoralisch)* risqué, daring ⟨*remark, film, dress*⟩; permissive ⟨*attitude*⟩; **c)** *(frei in der Wahl des Wohnsitzes)* **~zügig sein** enjoy freedom of domicile; **ein ~zügiges Leben führen** live a nomadic life; be always on the move; **2.** *adv.* **Geld ~zügig ausgeben** be generous with one's money; **ein Gesetz ~zügig auslegen** interpret a law flexibly; **~zügigkeit die; ~ a)** *(Großzügigkeit)* liberalness; *(in Geldsachen)* generosity; *(von Interpretation)* flexibility; **b)** permissiveness; **c)** *(freie Wahl des Wohnsitzes)* freedom of domicile

fremd [frɛmt] *Adj.* **a)** *nicht präd.* foreign ⟨*country, government, customs, language*⟩; **b)** *nicht präd. (nicht eigen)* other people's; of others *postpos.*; **~es Eigentum** other people's property; the property of others; **sich in ~e Angelegenheiten mischen** interfere in other people's business; **etw. ohne ~e Hilfe schaffen** do sth. without anyone else's help; **unter ~em Namen** under an assumed name; **unter ~em Namen schreiben** write under a nom de plume *or* pseudonym; **~e Welten** other worlds; *s. auch* **Feder a; c)** *(unbekannt)* strange; **eine ~e Umgebung** strange *or* unknown surroundings *pl.*; **Rockmusik war ihr ~:** she knew nothing about rock music; **Hinterhältigkeit ist ihm ~:** underhandedness is foreign to his nature; **er fühlte sich sehr ~:** he felt very much a stranger; **sich** *(Dat.) od.* **einander ~ werden** become estranged; grow apart; **die Anziehungskraft des Fremden** the attraction of the unfamiliar; **d)** *(andersgeartet)* strange

fremd-, Fremd-: ~arbeiter der *(veralt., schweiz.)* foreign worker; **~artig** *Adj.* strange; *(exotisch)* exotic; **~artigkeit die** strangeness; *(Exotik)* exoticness; **~bestimmt** *Adj. (Politik, Wirtsch., Soziol.)* heteronomous; **~bestimmung die** *(Politik, Wirtsch., Soziol.)* heteronomy

¹Fremde ['frɛmdə] **der/die;** *adj. Dekl.* **a)** *(Unbekannte[r])* stranger; **b)** *(Ausländer)* foreigner; alien *(Admin. lang.)*; **c)** *(Besucher, Tourist)* visitor

²Fremde die; ~ *(geh.)* foreign parts *pl.*; abroad; **in die ~ ziehen** go off to foreign parts; go abroad

Fremd·einwirkung die *(Rechtsspr.)* **ohne ~:** without any other person *or* vehicle being involved; **der Unfall passierte ohne ~:** no other vehicle was involved in the accident; **liegt ~ vor?** was any other person involved?

fremdeln, *(schweiz.)* **fremden** *itr. V.* be afraid of strangers

fremden-, Fremden-: ~bett das hotel bed; **~buch das** hotel register; **~feindlich** *Adj.* hostile to strangers/foreigners *postpos.*; **~feindlichkeit die; ~:** xenophobia; **~führer der** tourist guide; **~heim das** guest-house; boarding-house; **~industrie die** tourist industry; tourist trade; **~legion die;** *o. Pl.* foreign legion; **~legionär der** legionnaire; **~paß der** alien's passport; **~polizei die;** *o. Pl. police department dealing with aliens;* **~verkehr der** tourism *no art.*; **~zimmer das a)** *(Hotelzimmer)* room; **~zimmer frei!** vacancies *(Brit.)*; vacancy *(Amer.)*; **b)** *(Gastzimmer)* guest room

fremd-, Fremd-: ~erregung die *(Technik)* separate excitation; **~finanzierung die** *(Finanzw.)* financing from outside sources; **~|gehen** *unr. itr. V.; mit sein (ugs.)* be unfaithful

Fremdheit die; ~: strangeness; *(Zurückhaltung)* reserve

fremd-, Fremd-: ~herrschaft die foreign domination *no art. or* rule *no art.*; **~kapital das** *(Wirtsch.)* outside capital; **~körper der a)** *(Med., Biol.)* foreign body; **b)** *(fig.)* **ein ~körper sein/ sich** *(Dat.)* **wie ein ~körper vorkommen** be/feel out of place; **~ländisch** [-lɛndɪʃ] *Adj.* foreign; *(exotisch)* exotic

Fremdling der; ~s, ~e *(veralt.)* stranger

Fremd·sprache die foreign language

Fremdsprachen-: ~korrespondentin die bilingual/multilingual secretary; **~unterricht der** teaching of foreign languages

fremd-, Fremd-: ~sprachig *Adj.* bilingual/multilingual ⟨*staff, secretary*⟩; foreign ⟨*literature*⟩; foreign-language ⟨*edition, teaching*⟩; **~sprachlich** *Adj.; nicht präd.* foreign-language ⟨*teaching*⟩; foreign ⟨*word*⟩; **~stoff der;** *meist Pl. (Med.)* foreign substance; **~verschulden das** involvement of another person; **ein ~verschulden an diesem Unfall ist unwahrscheinlich** it is unlikely that anyone else was involved in the accident; **~wort das;** *Pl.* **~wörter** foreign word; **Liebe ist für ihn ein ~wort** *(fig.)* he doesn't know the meaning of the word love; **~wörter·buch das** dictionary of foreign words

frenetisch [fre'neːtɪʃ] **1.** *Adj.* frenetic ⟨*applause*⟩. **2.** *adv.* ⟨*applaud*⟩ frenetically

frequentieren *tr. V.* frequent ⟨*pub, café*⟩; use ⟨*library*⟩; **eine stark frequentierte Straße** a heavily used road

Frequenz [fre'kvɛnts] **die; ~, ~en a)** *(Physik)* frequency; *(Med.: Puls~)* rate; **b)** *(Besucherzahl)* **die Schule hat eine geringe ~:** the school has low numbers; **die ~ der Touristen** *(bes. österr., schweiz.)* the number of tourists; **die ~ des Elternabends war gut** attendance at the parents' evening was good; **c)** *(Verkehrsdichte)* traffic density

Frequenz-: *(Technik)* **~bereich der** frequency range; **~modulation die** frequency modulation

Fresko ['frɛsko] **das; ~s, Fresken** *(Kunstwiss.)* fresco

Fresko·malerei die *(Kunstwiss.)* fresco; fresco-painting

Fressalien [frɛ'saːli̯ən] *Pl. (ugs. scherzh.)* grub *(sl.)*

Freß·beutel der a) *(ugs.: Brotbeutel)* lunch bag; **b)** *(für Pferde)* nosebag

Fresse ['frɛsə] **die; ~, ~n** *(derb)* **a)** *(Mund)* gob *(sl.)*; trap *(sl.)*; **eine große ~ haben** *(fig.)* have a big mouth *(coll.)*; **die ~ weit aufreißen** *(fig.)* shoot one's mouth off *(sl.)*; **[ach] du meine ~!** bloody hell! *(sl.)*; **die ~ halten** keep one's trap *or* gob shut *(sl.)*; **b)** *(Gesicht)* mug *(sl.)*; **jmdm. die ~ polieren** smash sb.'s face in *(sl.)*; **jmdm. eins vor** *od.* **auf die ~ geben** smash sb. in the face *(sl.)*

fressen 1. *unr. tr. V.* **a)** ⟨*animal*⟩ eat; *(sich ernähren von)* feed on; **einem Tier zu ~ geben** feed an animal; **sich satt ~:** eat its/her/his fill; **sich dick [und rund] ~:** get fat by overeating; **b)** *(ugs.: verschlingen)* swallow up ⟨*money, time, distance*⟩; drink ⟨*petrol*⟩; **c)** *(zerstören)* eat away; **d)** *(derb: von Menschen)* guzzle; *(fig.)* **er wird dich schon nicht ~** *(salopp)* he won't eat you *(coll.)*; **etw. gefressen haben** *(ugs.)* have understood sth.; **jmdn. gefressen haben** *(ugs.)* hate sb.'s guts *(coll.)*; **jmdn. zum Fressen gern haben** like sb. so much one could eat him/her. **2.** *unr. itr. V.* **a)** *(von Tieren)* feed; **friß, Vogel, oder stirb!** *(fig.)* you've got no option; **b)** *(zerstören)* **an etw.** *(Dat.)* **~:** ⟨*rust*⟩ eat away at sth.; ⟨*fire*⟩ begin to consume sth.; **Ärger und Sorgen fraßen an ihm** irritation and worry gnawed at him; **c)** *(derb: von Menschen)* stuff oneself *or* one's face *(sl.)*; **er frißt für drei** he eats enough for three. **3.** *unr. refl. V.* **sich durch/in etw.** *(Akk.)* **~:** eat one's way through/into sth.

Fressen das; ~s a) *(Futter) (für Hunde, Katzen usw.)* food; *(für Vieh)* feed; **b)** *(derb, oft abwertend: Essen)* grub *(sl.)*; **das ist ein gefundenes ~ für sie** *(fig.)* that's just what she needed; that's a real gift for her; **erst kommt das ~, dann kommt die Moral** you can't moralize on an empty stomach

Fresser der; ~s, ~ a) *(Tier)* **ein guter/langsamer ~:** a good/slow eater; **b)** *(derb: Mensch)* hungry mouth to feed

-fresser der; ~s, ~ *(ugs. abwertend)* **Kommunisten~:** Communist-hater

Fresserei die; ~, ~en *(derb abwertend)* guzzling; stuffing; **eine große ~:** a big blow-out *(sl.)*

freß-, Freß-: ~gier die *(abwertend) (bei Tieren)* voracity; *(bei Menschen)* greed; gluttony; **~gierig** *Adj.* voracious ⟨*animal*⟩; greedy, gluttonous ⟨*person*⟩; **~korb der** *(ugs.)* **a)** *(Verpflegungskorb)* picnic basket; **b)** *(Geschenkkorb)* hamper; **~lust die;** *o. Pl. (ugs.)* desire for food; **~napf der** feeding-bowl; **~paket das** *(ugs.)* food parcel; **~sack der** *(derb)* greedy pig *(sl.)*; **~sucht die;** *o. Pl.* [morbid] craving for food; **~trog der** [feeding-]trough; **~welle die** *(scherzh.)* wave of gluttony *or* over-eating; **~werk·zeuge** *Pl. (Zool.)* trophi

Frettchen ['frɛtçən] **das; ~s, ~** *(Zool.)* ferret

Freude ['frɔydə] **die; ~, ~n a)** joy; *(Vergnügen)* pleasure; *(Wonne)* delight; **~ an etw.** *(Dat.)* **haben** take pleasure in sth.; **~ am Leben haben** enjoy life; **die ~ an der Natur** enjoyment of nature; **das war eine große ~ für uns** that was a great pleasure for us; **eine wahre/reine ~:** a real pleasure *or* joy; **das war nicht gerade eine reine ~ für mich** it was not exactly fun for me; **jmdm. eine ~ machen** *od.* **bereiten** make sb. happy; **etw. aus lauter** *od.* **reiner ~ tun** do sth. out of sheer joy; *(aus Spaß)* do sth. just for the pleasure oft it; **vor ~ hüpfen/in die Hände klatschen** jump for joy/clap one's hands with joy; **zu unserer ~:** to our delight; **zu meiner ~ kann ich Ihnen mitteilen, daß ...:** I am pleased to be able to inform you that ...; **jmdm. die ~ verderben** spoil sb.'s enjoyment; **seine helle ~ an etw.** *(Dat.)* **haben** be delighted about sth.; **herrlich und in ~n leben** live happily; **geteilte ~ ist doppelte ~** *(Spr.)* a pleasure shared is a pleasure doubled; **Freud und Leid** *(geh.)* joy and sorrow; **mit ~n** with pleasure; **b)** *Pl. (Annehmlichkeit)* **die ~n des Alltags/der Liebe** the pleasures of everyday life/the joys of love

Freuden-: ~botschaft die glad news; **~fest das** celebration; **ein ~fest feiern** hold a celebration; **~feuer das** bonfire; **~gebrüll das, ~geheul das, ~geschrei das** cries *or* shouts of joy *pl.*; **~haus das** house of pleasure; **~mädchen das** *(verhüll.)* woman of easy virtue; **~rausch der** transport of joy; **~schrei der** cry *or* shout of joy; **einen ~schrei ausstoßen** shout for joy;

~spender der *(geh.)* source of pleasure; **~sprung der** joyful leap; **einen ~sprung machen** jump for joy; **~tag der** joyous *or* happy day; **~tanz der** *in* **einen [wilden** *od.* **wahren] ~tanz aufführen** *od.* **vollführen** dance for joy; **~taumel der** transport of delight *or* joy; **~träne die;** *meist Pl.* **~tränen weinen** *od.* **vergießen** cry *or* weep tears of happiness *or* joy

freude-: ~strahlend *Adj.* beaming with joy; radiant with joy; **mit ~strahlendem Gesicht** beaming with delight *or* joy; **~trunken** *Adj. (dichter.)* delirious with joy

Freudianer [frɔy'di̯a:nɐ] **der; ~s, ~:** Freudian

freudianisch *Adj.* Freudian

freudig 1. *Adj.* **a)** joyful, happy ⟨*face, feeling, greeting*⟩; joyous ⟨*heart*⟩; **in ~er Erwartung** in joyful anticipation; **b)** *(erfreulich)* delightful ⟨*surprise*⟩; **ein ~es Ereignis** *(verhüll.)* a happy event; **eine ~e Nachricht** good news; glad tidings *(literary)*. **2.** *adv.* **~ erregt** happy and excited; **von etw. ~ überrascht sein** be surprised and delighted about sth.; **etw. ~ tun** do sth. gladly *or* with pleasure; **etw. ~ erwarten** look forward to sth. with pleasure; **jmd./etw. ~ begrüßen** give sb./sth. a warm welcome; **~ arbeiten/seine Pflicht tun** work cheerfully/do one's duty willingly

-freudig *Adj.* **a)** *(Freude an etw. zeigend)* **lese~:** fond of reading; **b)** *(schnell bereit, etw. zu tun)* **experimentier~/kauf~:** keen *or* eager to experiment/buy; **beifalls~/entscheidungs~:** very ready to applaud/take decisions

Freudigkeit die; ~: joyfulness; *(Begeisterung)* enthusiasm

freud·los 1. *Adj.* joyless ⟨*days, existence*⟩; cheerless ⟨*surroundings*⟩. **2.** *adv.* joylessly; **~ arbeiten** work unenthusiastically

Freudsch [frɔytʃ] *Adj.* Freudian

freud·voll 1. *Adj.* joyful; joyous; happy. **2.** *adv.* joyfully; joyously; happily

freuen ['frɔyən] **1.** *refl. V.* be pleased *or* glad **(über +** *Akk.* about); *(froh sein)* be happy; **ich freue mich über das Geschenk** I am pleased with the present; **sich zu früh ~:** get carried away *or* rejoice too soon; **sich an jmdm./etw. ~** *(geh.)* take pleasure in sb./sth.; **sich auf etw.** *(Akk.)* **~:** look forward to sth.; **sich auf jmdn. ~:** look forward to seeing sb.; **sich mit jmdm. ~:** rejoice with sb.; **sich für jmdn. ~:** be pleased *or* glad for sb.; **ich freue mich, Ihnen mitteilen zu können, daß ...:** I am pleased to be able to inform you that ... **2.** *tr. V.* please; **es freut mich, daß ...:** I am pleased *or* glad that ...; **freut mich!** pleased to meet you; **es hat mich aufrichtig gefreut, Ihre Bekanntschaft zu machen** I'm delighted *or* very pleased to have met you; **das hat ihn sehr gefreut** he was very pleased about it

freund [frɔynt] *Adj.; nicht attr. (geh. veralt.)* **jmdm. ~ sein/bleiben** be/remain friends with sb.; **jedem Menschen ~ sein** be a friend to all men

Freund der; ~es, ~e a) friend; **unter ~en sein** be among friends; **jmdn. zu seinen ~en rechnen** regard *or* count sb. as a friend; **~e in der Not gehen hundert** *od.* **tausend auf ein Lot** *(Spr.)* friends are hard to find when you really need them; **~ und Feind** friend and foe; **dicke ~e sein** *(ugs.)* be bosom pals *or* buddies *(coll.)*; **du bist mir ja ein feiner ~!** *(iron.)* you're a fine friend; **b)** *(Verehrer, Geliebter)* boy-friend; *(älter)* gentleman-friend; **c)** *(Anhänger, Liebhaber)* lover; **ein ~ der Musik/Kunst/des Weines** a lover of music/art/wine; **ich bin kein ~ von großen Worten** *(fig.)* I am not one for fine words; **d)** *(Anrede)* **~[e]!** my friend[s]!; **hallo, alter ~!** hello, old friend

Freundchen das; ~s, ~ *(Anrede; [scherzh.] drohend)* my friend

Freundes-: ~hand die *(geh.)* hand of friendship; **~kreis der** circle of friends; **im engen ~kreis** among close friends; **~treue die** *(geh.)* loyalty as a friend

Freund-Feind-Denken das us-and-them attitude

Freundin die; ~, ~nen a) friend; **b)** *(Geliebte)* girl-friend; *(älter)* lady-friend

freundlich 1. *Adj.* **a)** *(liebenswürdig)* kind ⟨*face*⟩; kind, friendly ⟨*reception*⟩; friendly ⟨*smile*⟩; fond ⟨*farewell*⟩; **zu jmdm. ~ sein** be kind to sb.; **er war so ~, mir zu helfen** he was kind *or* good enough to help me; **würden Sie so ~ sein, mir den Weg zum Bahnhof zu zeigen?** would you be so kind *or* good as to show me the way to the station?; **bitte recht ~!** smile, please! ; **b)** *(angenehm)* pleasant ⟨*weather, surroundings*⟩; pleasant, congenial ⟨*atmosphere*⟩; pleasant, mild ⟨*climate*⟩; **eine ~e Stimmung/Tendenz an der Börse** *(Kaufmannsspr.)* a favourable mood/trend on the Stock Exchange; **c)** *(freundschaftlich)* friendly, amiable ⟨*person, manner*⟩; friendly ⟨*disposition, attitude, warning*⟩. **2.** *adv.* **a)** *(freundschaftlich)* **jmdn. ~ anhören/begrüßen** listen to/greet sb. amiably; **jmdm. ~ danken** thank sb. kindly; **jmdm. ~ gesinnt sein** be well-disposed towards sb.; **b)** *(angenehm)* **die Morgensonne schien ~ in das Zimmer** the morning sun cast its friendly light into the room

-freundlich *adj.* **a)** *(wohlgesinnt)* pro-; **regierungs~:** pro-government; **presse~:** friendly to the press *postpos.*; **b)** *(-gerecht)* **familien~/fußgänger~:** catering for the interests of families/pedestrians *postpos., not pred.*; **haut~:** kind to the skin *postpos.*; **benutzer~:** user-oriented

freundlicher·weise *Adv.* kindly; **sie hat mich ~ mit dem Auto mitgenommen** she was kind enough to take me in the car

Freundlichkeit die; ~, ~en a) *(Liebenswürdigkeit, Gefälligkeit)* kindness; **würden Sie die ~ haben, mit uns mitzukommen?** would you be so kind as to come with us?; **jmdm. ein paar ~en sagen** to make a few kind remarks to sb.; **jmdm. ~en erweisen** show kindness to sb.; be kind to sb.; **b)** *o. Pl. (angenehme Art)* pleasantness; friendliness; *(eines Zimmers, Hauses)* cheerfulness

freund·nachbarlich *Adj.* good-neighbourly

Freundschaft die; ~, ~en a) friendship; **die ~ zwischen uns/ihnen** the friendship between us/them; **mit jmdm. ~ schließen** make *or* become friends with sb.; **jmdm. etw. in aller ~ sagen** tell sb. sth. as a friend; **b)** *o. Pl. (DDR: Gruß der FDJ)* **~!** *greeting of the Free German Youth organization;* **c)** *(DDR: Pioniergruppe) school branch of the Pioneer organization*

freundschaftlich 1. *Adj.* friendly; amicable; **ein ~er Hinweis** a friendly piece of advice; **mit jmdm. auf ~em Fuße stehen** be on friendly *or* amicable terms with sb. **2.** *adv.* in a friendly way; amicably; **jmdm. ~ auf die Schulter klopfen** give sb. a friendly pat on the shoulder

Freundschafts-: ~bande *Pl. (geh.)* bonds of friendship; **~besuch der** *(bes. Politik)* goodwill visit; **~bezeigung die; ~, ~en** *(geh.)* gesture of friendship; **~dienst der** service rendered out of friendship; **jmdm. einen ~dienst erweisen** render sb. a service out of friendship; **~pakt der** *(Politik)* pact of friendship; **~preis der: etw. zu einem ~preis verkaufen** sell sth. at a specially reduced price; **~ring der** ring given as a token of friendship; **jmdm. einen ~ring schenken** give sb. a ring as a token of friendship; **~spiel das** *(Sport)* friendly match *or* game; friendly *(coll.)*; **~treffen das** *(bes. DDR)* friendly meeting; **~vertrag der** *(Politik)* treaty of friendship

Frevel ['fre:fl̩] **der; ~s, ~** *(geh., veralt.)* crime; outrage; **einen ~ an jmdm./etw. begehen** commit a crime against sb./sth.; **~ gegen Gott** sacrilege

frevelhaft *(geh.)* **1.** *Adj.* wicked ⟨*deed, rebellion, person*⟩; criminal ⟨*stupidity*⟩. **2.** *adv.* wickedly

freveln *itr. V. (geh.)* **an jmdm./gegen etw. ~:** commit a crime against sb./sth.; **gegen das Gesetz ~:** violate the law

Frevel·tat die *(geh.)* wicked deed; heinous crime

freventlich ['fre:fn̩tlɪç] *Adj. (veralt.) s.* **frevelhaft**

Frevler der; ~s, ~, Frevlerin die; ~, ~nen evil-doer; wicked person; *(gegen Gott)* sacrilegious person; *(Lästerer)* blasphemer

frevlerisch *Adj. s.* **frevelhaft**

friderizianisch [frideri'tsi̯a:nɪʃ] of Frederick the Great *postpos., not pred.*

Friede ['fri:də] **der; ~ns, ~n a)** *(älter, geh.) s.* **Frieden; b)** *(geh.)* **~ sei mit euch** peace be with you; **~ seiner Asche** *(Dat.)* God rest his soul; **~ auf Erden** peace on earth; **ruhe in ~n** Rest in Peace

Frieden der; ~s, ~ a) peace; **[mit dem Feind] ~ schließen** make peace [with the enemy]; **mit jmdm. ~ schließen** make one's peace with sb.; **mitten im ~:** in the middle of peace-time; **der eheliche/häusliche ~:** marital/domestic peace; **zwischen Gegnern ~ stiften** make peace between opponents; **um des lieben ~s willen** for the sake of peace and quiet; **er kann keinen ~ finden** he can find no peace; **der ~ der Natur** the peace *or* tranquillity of nature; **laß mich in ~!** *(ugs.)* leave me in peace!; leave me alone!; **seinen ~ mit jmdm. machen** make one's peace with sb.; **ich traue dem ~ nicht** *(ugs.)* it's too good to be true; **b)** *(Friedensschluß)* peace settlement; **den ~ diktieren** dictate the terms for peace *or* the terms of the peace settlement

friedens-, Friedens-: ~angebot das peace offer; **~apostel der** *(spött.)* peace-maker; **~appell der, ~auf·ruf der** appeal for peace; **einen ~appell** *od.* **~aufruf an die Völker richten** call upon the nations to make peace; **~bedingungen** *Pl.* peace terms; terms for peace; **~bemühungen** *Pl.* efforts to bring about peace; **~bewegung die** peace movement; **~bruch der** violation of the peace; **~demonstration die** peace demonstration; **~diktat das** dictated peace terms *pl.*; **das ~diktat der Siegermächte** the peace terms dictated by the victorious nations; **~engel der** angel of peace *(poet.)*; messenger of peace; **~fahrt die** *(DDR)* Peace Race; **~forschung die** peace studies *pl., no art.*; **~freund der** lover of peace; **~fürst der** *(bibl.)* Prince of Peace; **~garantie die** guarantee of peace; **~gefährdend** *Adj.* representing a threat to peace *postpos., not pred.*; **~gespräche** *Pl.* peace talks; **~glocken** *Pl.* **die ~glokken läuten** the bells are ringing to proclaim the peace; **~göttin die** goddess of peace; **~grenze die** *(DDR) frontier serving as guarantee of peace, esp. Oder-Neisse-Line;* **~kämpfer der** pacifist; **~konferenz die** peace conference; **~kundgebung die** peace rally; **~kuß der** *(kath. Rel.)* kiss of peace; pax; **~lager das** *(DDR) bloc of peace-loving nations;* **~liebe die** love of peace; **~nobel·preis der** Nobel Peace Prize; **~pfeife die** pipe of peace; **mit jmdm. die ~pfeife rauchen** *(fig.)* make one's peace with sb.; **laßt uns die ~pfeife rauchen!** *(fig.)* let us make peace; **~pflicht die** *(Arbeitswelt) obligation on employers and unions to avoid conflicts resulting in industrial action while a/the wages agreement is in force;* **~politik die** policy of peace; **~richter der** *lay magistrate dealing with minor offences;* ≈ Justice of the Peace; **~schluß der** peace settlement; **nach dem ~schluß** after the peace settlement had been reached; **~sehnsucht die** longing for peace; **~sicherung die** peace-keeping; **~stärke die** *(Milit.)* peace-time strength; **~stifter der** peacemaker; **~symbol das** symbol of peace; **~taube die** dove of peace; **~truppe die** peace-keeping force; **~verhandlungen** *Pl.* peace negotiations; peace talks; **~vertrag der** peace treaty; **~wille der** desire for peace; **~wirtschaft die** peace-time economy; **~zeiten** *Pl.* peace-time *sing.*

fried·fertig *Adj.* peaceable ‹*person, character*›; peaceful ‹*intentions*›; **selig sind die Friedfertigen** *(bibl.)* blessed are the peacemakers

Fried·fertigkeit die; ~: peaceableness

Fried·hof der cemetery; *(Kirchhof)* graveyard; churchyard

Friedhofs-: ~gärtner der cemetery gardener; **~kapelle die** cemetery chapel; **~ruhe die, ~stille die** stillness *or* quiet of the graveyard; *(fig.)* deathly stillness; deathly quiet; **~wärter der** cemetery attendant

friedlich ['fri:tlɪç] **1.** *Adj.* **a)** *(nicht kriegerisch)* peaceful; **auf ~em Wege** by peaceful means; **b)** *(ruhig, verträglich)* peaceable, peaceful ‹*character, person*›; peaceful, tranquil ‹*life, atmosphere, valley*›; **sei ~!** *(ugs.)* be quiet!. **2.** *adv.* ‹*live, sleep*› peacefully; **einen Streit ~ schlichten/beilegen** settle an argument peaceably *or* peacefully

Friedlichkeit die; ~: peaceableness; peacefulness; *(der Atmosphäre, eines Tals)* peacefulness; tranquillity

fried·liebend *Adj.* peace-loving

fried·los 1. *Adj.* **a)** *(geh.: ruhelos)* **er entsagte der ~en Welt** he renounced the unquiet world; **b)** *(hist.: geächtet)* outlawed ‹*person*›. **2.** *adv.* **a)** *(geh.: ruhelos)* **~ durchwanderte er die Welt** he wandered through the world, never finding peace; **b)** *(hist.: geächtet)* ‹*live*› as an outlaw

Friedrich ['fri:drɪç] **(der)** Frederick; **~ der Große** Frederick the Great

Friedrich Wilhelm der; ~ ~s, ~ ~s *(ugs. scherzh.: Unterschrift)* monicker *(coll. joc.)*

fried·voll *Adj. (geh.)* peaceful; tranquil

frieren ['fri:rən] *unr. itr. V.* **a)** *(Kälte empfinden)* be *or* feel cold; **erbärmlich/sehr ~:** be freezing/terribly cold; **er fror an den Händen/Beinen** he had [freezing] cold hands/legs; **b)** *mit sein (ge~)* freeze; **das Wasser/der Boden ist gefroren** the water/the ground is *or* has frozen; **steif gefroren sein** be frozen stiff; **blau gefroren sein** be blue with cold; **c)** *(unpers.: Kälte empfinden)* **mich/ihn/sie friert [es]** I am/he/she is cold; **d)** *(unpers.: ge~)* **es friert/hat gefroren** it is/was freezing; *s. auch* **Stein**

Fries [fri:s] **der; ~es, ~e** *(Archit., Textilw.)* frieze

Friese ['fri:zə] **der; ~n, ~n** [East] Frisian

friesisch *Adj.* [East] Frisian

frigid[e] [fri'gi:d(ə)] *Adj.* frigid

Frigidität [frigidi'tɛ:t] **die; ~:** frigidity

Frikadelle [frika'dɛlə] **die; ~, ~n** rissole

Frikandeau [frikan'do:] **das; ~s, ~s** *(Kochk.)* fricandeau

Frikassee [frika'se:] **das; ~s, ~s** *(Kochk.)* fricassee; **aus jmdm. ~ machen** *(salopp, scherzh.)* make mincemeat of sb. *(coll.)*

frikassieren *tr. V.* fricassee

Frikativ [frika'ti:f] **der; ~s, ~e** *(Sprachw.)* fricative

Friktion [frɪk'tsio:n] **die; ~, ~en** friction

frisch [frɪʃ] **1.** *Adj.* **a)** fresh; new-laid ‹*egg*›; fresh, clean ‹*linen*›; clean ‹*underwear*›; wet ‹*paint*›; **~e Luft schöpfen** *od. (ugs.)* **schnappen** get some fresh air; **mit ~en Kräften** with renewed strength; **~en Mut fassen** take heart again; **sich ~ machen** freshen oneself up; **jmdn. auf ~er Tat ertappen** catch sb. red-handed; **die Erinnerung daran ist noch ganz ~:** the memory of it is still quite fresh [in sb.'s mind]; **b)** *(munter)* fresh; **~ und munter sein** *(ugs.)* be bright and cheerful; **~, fromm, fröhlich, frei** fresh, pious, cheerful, free *(motto of 19th century physical education enthusiasts)*; **c)** *(kühl)* fresh ‹*wind, breeze*›; chilly ‹*night, air*›; **d)** *(leuchtend)* lively ‹*colours*›. **2.** *adv.* freshly; **~ gelegte Eier** new-laid eggs; **~ gebackenes Brot/gefallener Schnee** freshly baked bread/fallen snow; **Bier, ~ vom Faß** beer straight from the barrel; **~ gewaschen sein** ‹*person*› have just had a wash; ‹*garment*› have just been washed; **~ rasiert sein** have just had a shave; **er kommt ~ von der Universität** he has come straight from the university; **er kommt ~ vom Friseur** he has just been to the hairdresser's; **~ geputzte Schuhe/ausgehobene Gräber/gestrichene Bänke** newly cleaned shoes/dug graves/painted seats; **„Vorsicht, ~ gestrichen!"** 'wet paint'; **etw. ~ verputzen lassen** have sth. replastered; **die Betten ~ beziehen** put fresh *or* clean sheets on the beds; **~ gewagt ist halb gewonnen** *(Spr.)* nothing ventured, nothing gained *(prov.)*

frisch·auf *Adv. (veralt.)* let us be off

Frische die; ~ a) freshness; **b)** *(Lebhaftigkeit, frisches Aussehen)* **jugendliche ~:** youthful freshness; **geistige ~:** mental alertness; **körperliche ~:** physical fitness; vigour; **in voller körperlicher und geistiger ~:** hale and hearty in mind and body; **in erstaunlicher ~:** with amazing sprightliness; **in rosiger ~:** with a rosy freshness; **bis morgen in alter ~!** *(ugs.)* see you tomorrow!; **c)** *(Kühle, Reinheit)* freshness; **~ für den ganzen Tag** all-day freshness; **d)** *(von Farben)* liveliness

Frisch·ei das new-laid egg

frischen *tr. V. (Hüttenw.)* refine

frisch-, Frisch-: ~fisch der fresh fish; **~fleisch das** fresh meat; **~gebacken** *Adj.; nicht präd. (ugs.)* **ein ~gebackenes Ehepaar** a newly-wed couple; newly-weds *pl.*; **ein ~gebackener Doktor** a newly-qualified doctor; *s. auch* **frisch 2; ~gemüse das** fresh vegetables *pl.*; **~gewaschen** *Adj. (präd. getrennt geschrieben) s.* **frisch 2; ~gewicht das** weight when packed; **~halte·beutel der** airtight bag; **~halte·packung die** airtight pack; **~käse der** curd cheese

Frischling der; ~s, ~e a) *(Jägerspr.)* young boar; **b)** *(scherzh.)* new boy *or* girl

frisch-, Frisch-: ~luft die fresh air; **~luft·zufuhr die** fresh air supply; **~milch die** fresh milk; **~obst das** fresh fruit; **~wasser das** fresh water; **~weg** *Adv.* uninhibitedly; **~weg antworten** answer right away; **~zelle die** *(Med.)* living cell; **~zellen·therapie die** *(Med.)* Niehans's therapy

Friseur [fri'zø:ɐ̯] **der; ~s, ~e a)** hairdresser; *(Herren~)* hairdresser; barber; **b)** *(~salon) (für Frauen)* hairdresser's *(Brit.)*; beauty salon *(Amer.)*; *(für Herren)* hairdresser's; barber's; *s. auch* **Bäcker**

Friseur·salon der hairdressing *or* hairdresser's salon *(Brit.)*; *(für Frauen)* beauty salon *(Amer.)*; *(für Herren)* barber shop *(Amer.)*

Friseuse [fri'zø:zə] **die; ~, ~n** hairdresser

Frisier·creme die hair cream

frisieren [fri'zi:rən] *tr. V.* **a) jmdn./sich ~:** do sb.'s/one's hair; **sich ~ lassen** have one's hair done; **[sich** *(Dat.)***] die Haare ~:** do one's hair; **eine elegant frisierte Dame** an elegantly coiffured lady; **er war immer sorgfältig frisiert** he was always well-groomed; **b)** *(ugs.: verfälschen)* doctor ‹*reports, statistics*›; fiddle *(coll.)* ‹*accounts*›; **c)** *(Kfz-W.)* soup up *(coll.)* ‹*engine, vehicle*›

Frisier-: ~haube die *(hood-type)* hairdrier; **~kommode die** dressing-table; **~salon der** *s.* **Friseursalon; ~spiegel der** dressing-table mirror; **~stab der** curling-tongs *pl.*; **~um·hang der** cape

Frisör *s.* **Friseur**

Frisöse *s.* **Friseuse**

friß [frɪs] *Imperativ Sg. v.* **fressen**

frißt *2. u. 3. Pers. Sg. Präsens v.* **fressen**

Frist [frɪst] **die; ~, ~en a)** *(Zeitspanne)* time; period; **die ~ für die Anmeldung läuft ab** the time allowed for registration is running out; **[sich** *(Dat.)***] eine ~ von 3 Wochen setzen** set [oneself] a time limit of 3 weeks; **die ~ verlängern** extend the deadline; **in kürzester ~:** within a very short time; **b)** *(begrenzter Aufschub)* extension; **jmdm. drei Tage [als] ~ geben** give sb. three days' time; **eine letzte ~ von einem Monat** a final extension of one month; **c)** *(Zeitpunkt)* date; deadline; **[bis] zu dieser ~:** by that date

fristen *tr. V.* **ein kümmerliches Dasein** *od.* **Leben ~:** eke out a wretched existence; barely manage to survive

Fristen-: ~lösung die, ~regelung die abortion limit

frist-, Frist-: ~gemäß, ~gerecht *Adj., adv.* within the specified time *postpos.*; *(bei Anmeldung usw.)* before the closing date *postpos.*; **wir bitten Sie um eine ~gerechte Wahrnehmung der Liefertermine** it is requested that delivery dates should be met; **~los 1.** *Adj.* instant ‹*dismissal*›; **2.** *adv.* without notice; **jmdn.** *od.* **jmdm. ~los kündigen, jmdn. ~los entlassen** dismiss sb. without notice; **jmdm. ~los die Wohnung kündigen** ask sb. to quit without notice; **~verlängerung die** extension [of the/a time-limit]

Frisur [fri'zu:ɐ̯] **die; ~, ~en** hairstyle; hair-do *(coll.)*

Friteuse [fri'tø:zə] **die; ~, ~n** deep fryer

fritieren [fri'ti:rən] *tr. V.* deep-fry

Frittate [frɪ'ta:tə] **die; ~, ~n** *(bes. österr.)* pancake

Fritte ['frɪtə] **die; ~, ~n** *(ugs.)* chip

-fritze ['frɪtsə] **der; ~n, ~n** *(ugs., abwertend)* man

frivol [fri'vo:l] *Adj.* **a)** *(schamlos)* suggestive ‹*remark, picture, etc.*›; risqué ‹*joke*›; earthy ‹*man*›; flighty ‹*woman*›; **b)** *(leichtfertig)* frivolous; irresponsible

Frivolität [frivoli'tɛ:t] **die; ~, ~en a)** *o. Pl. s.* **frivol a:** suggestiveness; risqué nature; earthiness; flightiness; **b)** *(frivole Bemerkung)* risqué remark

Frivolitäten·arbeit die *(Handarb.)* tatting

Frl. *Abk.* **Fräulein**

froh [fro:] *Adj.* **a)** *(glücklich)* happy; cheerful ‹*person, mood*›; **jmdn. ~ machen** make sb. happy; cheer sb. up; **~e Ostern** happy Easter; **~e Weihnachten** happy *or* merry Christmas; **~es Fest** happy Christmas/Easter *etc.*; **~en Herzens** with a glad heart; **b)** *(ugs.: erleichtert)* pleased, glad **(über +** *Akk.* about); **du kannst ~ sein, daß ...:** you can be thankful *or* glad that ...; **da bin ich aber ~ [, daß ...]** I am glad [that ...]; **seines Lebens nicht mehr ~ werden** not enjoy life any more; **der soll seines Lebens nicht mehr ~ werden** we'll make his life a misery; **c)** *nicht präd. (erfreulich)* good ‹*news*›; happy ‹*event*›

froh-, Froh-: ~botschaft die; *o. Pl. (geh.)* glad tidings *pl.*; **~gelaunt** *Adj.* cheerful; **~gemut 1.** *Adj.* happy; **2.** *adv.* happily; in good spirits

fröhlich ['frø:lɪç] **1.** *Adj.* cheerful; happy; **~e Ostern** happy Easter; **~e Weihnachten** happy *or* merry Christmas; **eine ~e Gesellschaft** a happy crowd of people; **~es Treiben** merry-making; **~e Spiele** fun and games; **~e Tänze** dancing and merry-making. **2.** *adv. (unbekümmert)* blithely; cheerfully

Fröhlichkeit die; ~: cheerfulness; *(eines Festes, einer Feier)* gaiety

froh·lọcken *itr. V. (geh.)* **a)** *(Schadenfreude empfinden)* rejoice; gloat; **heimlich ~:** secretly rejoice; **b)** *(jubeln)* rejoice; exult; **frohlocket dem Herrn** sing joyfully unto the Lord

Froh-: ~natur die a) *o. Pl.* happy *or* cheerful nature; **b)** *(Mensch)* cheerful person; **~sinn der;** *o. Pl.* cheerfulness; gaiety

fromm [frɔm]; **frommer** *od.* **frömmer** ['frœmɐ], **frommst...** *od.* **frömmst... 1.** *Adj.* **a)** pious, devout ⟨*person*⟩; devout ⟨*Christian*⟩; **ein ~es Leben führen** lead a devout life; **~e Reden führen** talk piously; **b)** *(scheinheilig)* **ein ~er Augenaufschlag** a look of wide-eyed innocence; **~es Getue** pious affectation; **c)** *(wohlgemeint)* **eine ~e Lüge** a white lie; **einer ~en Täuschung unterliegen** deceive oneself; **ein ~er Wunsch** a pious hope; **d)** *(brav)* docile; **~ wie ein Lamm** meek as a lamb; **e)** *(veralt.: rechtschaffen)* worthy ⟨*person*⟩. **2.** *adv.* *(gläubig)* piously; *(brav)* docilely; **~ und rechtschaffen leben** *(veralt.)* live a worthy life

Frömmelei die; ~, ~en *(abwertend)* **a)** *o. Pl.* affected piety; **b)** *(Handlung)* sanctimonious act; **~en** sanctimonious behaviour *sing.*

frömmeln ['frœmḷn] *itr. V. (abwertend)* affect piety; **eine ~de Betschwester** an over-pious woman; **~des Geschwätz** sermonizing

frommen *itr. V. (unpers.) (veralt.)* **das frommt uns [nicht]** it will avail us [nothing]; *s. auch* **Nutz**

frömmer *s.* **fromm**

Frömmigkeit ['frœmɪçkait] **die; ~:** piety; devoutness

Frömmler ['frœmlɐ] **der; ~s, ~** *(abwertend)* [pious] hypocrite

frömmst ... *s.* **fromm**

Fron [fro:n] **die; ~, ~en a)** *(hist.)* corvée; **schwere ~ leisten** do hard forced labour; **b)** *(geh.: aufgezwungene Mühsal)* drudgery

Fron·arbeit die *s.* **Fron a**

Fronde ['frõ:də] **die; ~, ~n** *(geh.)* [political] faction

Fron·dienst der a) *s.* **Fron a; b)** *(schweiz.)* voluntary work

fronen *itr. V.* **a)** *(hist.)* do forced labour; **b)** *(geh.: unter Zwang arbeiten)* slave; toil

frönen ['frø:nən] *itr. V. (geh.)* **einer Neigung/einem Laster ~:** indulge an inclination/in a vice; **dem Alkohol ~:** indulge one's craving for alcohol; **einem Hobby ~:** devote oneself to a hobby

Fron·leichnam *o. Art.* [the feast of] Corpus Christi

Fronleichnams·prozession die Corpus Christi procession

Front [frɔnt] **die; ~, ~en a)** *(Gebäude~)* front; façade; **b)** *(Kampfgebiet)* front [line]; **an die ~ gehen** go to the front; **er war an der ~:** he fought at the front; **c)** *(Milit.: vorderste Linie)* front line; **auf breiter ~:** on a broad front; **in vorderster ~ kämpfen** fight at the very front; **die ~en haben sich verhärtet** *(fig.)* attitudes have hardened; **zwischen die ~en geraten** *(fig.)* be caught in the crossfire; **an zwei ~en kämpfen** *(fig.)* fight on two fronts; **klare ~en schaffen** clarify one's position; **d)** *(Milit.: einer Truppe)* **die ~ abnehmen/abschreiten** inspect the troops/guard of honour *etc.*; **gegen jmdn./etw. ~ machen** *(fig.)* make a stand against sb./sth.; **e)** *(Sport)* **in ~ [liegen]** [be] in front *or* in the lead; **in ~ gehen** go in front; **die Mannschaft lag mit 5:0 in ~:** the team was leading 5-0; **f)** *(Gruppe)* front; **die Nationale ~** *(DDR)* the National Front; **g)** *(Met.)* front

Front·abschnitt der *(Milit.)* sector of the front

frontal [frɔn'ta:l] **1.** *Adj.; nicht präd.* **a)** *(von vorn)* head-on ⟨*collision*⟩; **b)** *(nach vorn)* frontal ⟨*attack*⟩. **2.** *adv.* ⟨*collide*⟩ head-on; ⟨*attack*⟩ from the front

Frontal-: ~an·griff der frontal attack; **zum ~angriff übergehen** go over into a frontal attack; **~unterricht der** *(Päd.)* teacher-centred teaching; **~zusammen·stoß der** head-on collision

Front-: ~an·trieb der *(Kfz-W.)* front-wheel drive; **~begradigung die** *(Milit.)* straightening of the front; **~bericht der** *(Milit.)* report *or* dispatch from the front; **~dienst der** *(Milit.)* front-line service; service at the front; **~ein·satz der** *(Milit.)* front-line action; **~erfahrung die** *(Milit.)* experience of the front

Frontispiz [frɔnti'spi:ts] **das; ~es, ~e a)** *(Archit.)* pediment; frontispiece; **b)** *(Buchw.)* frontispiece

Front-: ~kämpfer der *(Milit.)* front-line soldier; **~linie die** *(Milit.)* front line; **~scheibe die** windscreen (Brit.); windshield *(Amer.)*; **~seite die** front page; **~soldat der** *(Milit.)* front-line soldier; **~stellung die a)** *(entschiedene Gegnerschaft)* hostile stance; **b)** *(Fechten)* guard position; **~urlaub der** *(Milit.)* leave from the front; **~wechsel der** *(fig.)* U-turn; volte-face

fror [fro:ɐ̯] *1. u. 3. Pers. Sg. Prät. v.* **frieren**

Frosch [frɔʃ] **der; ~[e]s, Frösche** ['frœʃə] **a)** frog; **einen ~ in der Kehle** *od.* **im Hals haben** have a frog in one's throat; **sei kein ~** *(ugs.)* don't be a spoilsport; **b)** *(Musik)* nut; **c)** *s.* **Knallfrosch**

Frosch-: ~auge das [frog's] eye; **[richtige] ~augen haben** *(fig.)* have [real] goggle-eyes; **~hüpfen das** leap-frog; **~klemme die** *(Technik)* stone tongs; nippers *pl.*; **~könig der** Frog Prince; **~laich der** frog-spawn; **~löffel der** *(Bot.)* water plantain; **~lurch der** *(Zool.)* anuran; salientian; **~mann der;** *Pl.* **~männer** frogman; **~perspektive die** worm's-eye view; **etw. aus der ~perspektive fotografieren** make a low-angle shot of sth.; **etw. aus der ~perspektive betrachten** *(fig.)* take a very narrow view of sth.; **~schenkel der** frog's leg; **~teich der** frog-pond; **~test der** *(Med.)* male frog test

Frost [frɔst] **der; ~[e]s, Fröste** ['frœstə] **a)** frost; **es herrscht** *od.* **ist [strenger] ~:** there is a [severe] frost; it is [very] frosty; **b)** *(Kälteempfindung)* fit of shivering

frost-, Frost-: ~anfällig *Adj.* sensitive *or* susceptible to frost *postpos.*; **~auf·bruch der** frost damage *no indef. art.*; **wegen der ~aufbrüche** because of the frost damage; **~beständig** *Adj.* frost-resistant; **~beule die** chilblain; **~boden der** frozen soil; *(ständig)* permafrost; **~ein·bruch der** sudden frost

frösteln ['frœstḷn] *itr. V.* **a)** feel chilly; **vor Kälte/Müdigkeit ~:** shiver with cold/tiredness; **mich überkommt** *od.* **durchläuft ein Frösteln** I feel a sudden chill; **b)** *(unpers.)* **es fröstelt ihn, ihn fröstelt** he feels chilly

frosten *tr. V. (fachspr.)* deep-freeze

Froster der; ~s, ~: freezing compartment

frost-, Frost-: ~frei *Adj.* **ein ~freier Winter** a winter without frost; **die Nacht war ~frei** there was no frost during the night; **~gefahr die;** *o. Pl.* danger of frost; **~grenze die** *(Met.)* 0 °C isotherm; *(Geol.)* frost line

frostig ['frɔstɪç] **1.** *Adj. (auch fig.)* frosty. **2.** *adv.* frostily; **sie lächelte ~:** she smiled frostily *or* icily; **jmdn. ~ empfangen** give sb. a frosty reception

Frostigkeit die; ~: frostiness

frost-, Frost-: ~klirrend *Adj.* crisp and frosty; **~salbe die** chilblain ointment; **~schaden der** frost damage; **durch die vielen ~schäden** due to extensive frost damage; **~schutz der** frost protection; protection from frost; **~schutz·mittel das a)** frost protection agent; **b)** *(Kfz-W.)* anti-freeze; **~sicher** *Adj.* frost-proof; **~warnung die** *(Met.)* frost warning; **~wetter das** freezing weather; frost

Frottee [frɔ'te:] **das** u. **der; ~s, ~s** terry towelling

Frottee-: ~handtuch das terry towel; **~kleid das** towelling dress

Frottier- [frɔ'ti:ɐ̯-] *s.* **Frottee-**

frottieren [frɔ'ti:rən] *tr. V.* rub; towel; **sich ~:** rub oneself down

Frotzelei die; ~, ~en *(ugs.)* **a)** *o. Pl.* teasing; **b)** *(Bemerkung)* teasing remark

frotzeln ['frɔtsḷn] **1.** *tr. V.* tease; **jmdn. wegen einer Sache ~:** tease sb. about sth.. **2.** *itr. V.* **über jmdn./etw. ~:** make fun of sb./sth.

Frucht [frʊxt] **die; ~, Früchte** ['frʏçtə] **a)** fruit; **Früchte tragen** *(auch fig.)* bear fruit; **Früchte ansetzen** start to fruit; **jmdm. wie eine reife ~ in den Schoß fallen** drop into sb.'s lap; **verbotene Früchte** *(fig.)* forbidden fruits; **die ~ ihres Leibes** *(fig. geh.)* the fruit of her womb; **b)** *(geh.: Ertrag)* fruit; **reiche Früchte tragen** bear rich fruit; **c)** *o. Pl.* *(landsch.: Getreide)* corn; crops *pl.*; **die ~ steht gut/schlecht [auf dem Halm]** the corn is coming on well/looks bad

frucht·bar *Adj.* fertile ⟨*soil, field, man, woman*⟩; prolific ⟨*breed*⟩; fruitful ⟨*work, idea*⟩; fruitful, rewarding ⟨*conversation*⟩; **eine Idee** *usw.* **für etw. ~ machen** allow sth. to benefit from an idea *etc.*

Fruchtbarkeit die; ~ *s.* **fruchtbar:** fertility; prolificness; fruitfulness

Fruchtbarkeits·kult der fertility cult

frucht-, Frucht-: ~becher der a) *(Eisbecher)* fruit sundae; **b)** *(Bot.)* cupule; **~blase die** *(Anat.)* amniotic sac; **~bonbon das** *od.* **der** fruit drop; **~bringend** *Adj.* fruitful; rewarding

Früchtchen ['frʏçtçən] **das; ~s, ~** *(ugs. abwertend: Tunichtgut)* good-for-nothing; **ein nettes/sauberes ~:** a right good-for-nothing

Frucht-: ~ein·waage die net weight [of fruit]; **~eis das** fruit ice-cream

fruchten *tr. V.* **nichts ~:** be no use; be of no avail; **[bei jmdm.] nicht[s] ~:** have no effect [on sb.]

Frucht-: ~fleisch das flesh; pulp; **~fliege die** fruit fly; **~folge die** *(Landw.)* rotation of crops

fruchtig *Adj.* fruity

frucht-, Frucht-: ~joghurt der *od.* **das** fruit yoghurt; **~kapsel die** *(Biol.)* capsule; **~knoten der** *(Bot.)* ovary; **~los** *Adj.* fruitless, vain ⟨*efforts*⟩; **alle Anstrengungen blieben ~los** all efforts proved in vain; **~losigkeit die; ~:** fruitlessness; **~presse die** fruit squeezer; **~saft der** fruit juice; **~salat der** fruit salad; **~säure die** fruit acid; **~stand der** *(Bot.)* multiple fruit; **~wasser das** *(Anat.)* amniotic fluid; waters *pl.* *(coll.)*; **~zucker der** fruit sugar; fructose

Fructose [frʊk'to:zə] **die; ~** *(Chemie)* fructose

frugal [fru'ga:l] **1.** *Adj.* frugal. **2.** *adv.* frugally

früh [fry:] **1.** *Adj.* **a)** early; **am ~en Morgen/Abend** early in the morning/evening; **von ~er Kindheit an** from early childhood; **b)** *(vorzeitig)* premature; **ein ~es Ende finden** come to an untimely end; **einen ~en Tod sterben** die an untimely *or* premature death. **2.** *adv.* early; **~ am Tage/morgens** early in the day/morning; **~ genug kommen** arrive in [good] time; **~er oder später** sooner or later; **heute/morgen/gestern ~:** this/tomorrow/yesterday morning; **um fünf Uhr ~:** at five o'clock in the morning; **von ~ bis spät** from morning till night; from dawn to dusk; *s. auch* **aufstehen; früher**

früh-, Früh-: ~auf *in* **von ~auf** from early childhood on[wards]; **~aufsteher der; ~s, ~:** early riser; early bird *(coll.)*; **~beet das** cold frame; *(geheizt)* [heated] frame; **~christlich** *Adj.* early Christian; **~diagnose die** *(Med.)* early diagnosis; **~dienst der** early duty; *(im Betrieb)* early shift; **~dienst haben** be on early duty/shift

Frühe die; ~: in der ~: *(geh.)* in the early morning; **in aller ~:** at the crack of dawn
Früh·ehe die early marriage
früher ['fry:ɐ] **1.** *Adj., nicht präd.* **a)** *(vergangen)* earlier; former; **in ~en Zeiten** in the past; in former times; **aus ~en Zeiten/Jahrhunderten** from the past/from past centuries; **eine ~e Auflage** an earlier edition; **b)** *(ehemalig)* former ‹*owner, occupant, friend*›. **2.** *adv.* formerly; **~ war er ganz anders** he used to be quite different at one time; **meine Bekannten von ~:** my former acquaintances; **ich kenne ihn [noch] von ~ [her]** I know him from some time ago; **diese Dinge waren ihm von ~ [her] vertraut** he had adready been familiar with such things; **an ~ denken** think back
Früh·erkennung die *(Med.)* early recognition *or* diagnosis
frühestens ['fry:əstn̩s] *Adv.* at the earliest; **~ in einer Woche/morgen** in a week/tomorrow at the earliest
frühest·möglich ['fry:əst'mø:klɪç] *Adj.; nicht präd.* earliest possible
früh-, Früh-: ~geburt die a) premature birth; **b)** *(Kind)* premature baby; **~gemüse das** early vegetables *pl.*; **~geschichte die;** *o. Pl.* ancient history; **die ~geschichte Europas** the early history of Europe; early European history; **~geschichtlich** *Adj.* **~geschichtliche Funde** finds dating back to early history; **aus ~geschichtlicher Zeit** dating back to early history; **~gottes·dienst der** early service; **~herbst der** early autumn; **~invalide der/die** premature invalid
Früh·jahr das spring; **im ~:** in spring
Frühjahrs-: ~kollektion die spring collection; **~messe die** *(Wirtsch.)* spring trade fair; **~müdigkeit die** springtime tiredness; **~putz der** spring-cleaning
früh-, Früh-: ~kapitalismus der early capitalism *no art.*; **~kapitalistisch** *Adj.* early capitalist; **~kartoffel die** early potato; **~kindlich** *Adj. (Psych.)* in early childhood *postpos.*; **~konzert das** [early] morning concert; **~kultur die a)** *(Geschichte)* early culture; **b)** *(Gartenbau)* forcing; **bei der ~kultur wachsen die Pflanzen schneller** when forced, plants grow more quickly
Frühling ['fry:lɪŋ] **der; ~s, ~e** spring; **im ~:** in [the] spring; **[im] ~ vergangenen/nächsten Jahres** last/next spring; in spring last/next year; **der ~ kommt** spring is coming; **vor dem nächsten ~:** before next spring; **im ~ 1979** in the spring of 1979; **im ~ des Lebens** *(geh.)* in the springtime of one's life; **seinen zweiten ~ erleben** *(fig. iron.)* relive one's youth
frühlings-, Frühlings-: ~anfang der first day of spring; **~gefühl das: ~gefühle haben/bekommen** *(ugs. scherzh.)* feel/get frisky *(coll.)*; **~haft** *Adj.* springlike; **~lied das** song about spring; **~punkt der** *(Astron.)* vernal equinox; **~rolle die** *(Kochk.)* spring roll; **~tag der** spring day; **~wetter das** spring weather; **~zeit die;** *o. Pl. (geh.)* spring [time]; springtide *(literary)*
früh-, Früh-: ~messe, ~mette die *(kath. Kirche)* early [morning] mass; **~morgens** [-'--] *Adv.* early in the morning; **~nebel der** early morning fog/mist; **~neu·hoch·deutsch das** Early New High German; **~reif** *Adj.* precocious ‹*child*›; early ‹*fruit, vegetables*›; **~rente die** early retirement pension; **~rentner der** *person who has retired early;* **~rentner werden/sein** retire/have retired early; **~schicht die** early shift; **~schicht haben** be on the early shift; **~schoppen der** morning drink; *(um Mittag)* lunchtime drink; **~sommer der** early summer; **~sport der** early-morning exercise; **~stadium das** early stage; **im ~stadium** at an early stage; **~start der** *(Sport)* false start
Früh·stück das; ~s, ~e a) breakfast; **das erste ~:** breakfast; **das zweite ~:** mid-morning snack; **b)** *(ugs.: Pause)* morning break; coffee break
frühstücken 1. *itr. V.* breakfast; have breakfast; **gut/ausgiebig ~:** have a good/hearty breakfast. **2.** *tr. V.* **Brot/Eier ~:** breakfast on bread/eggs; have bread/eggs for breakfast
Frühstücks-: ~brot das sandwiches *pl.* [for morning snack]; **~fernsehen das** breakfast television; **~fleisch das** luncheon meat; **~kartell das** *(Wirtsch. Jargon)* informal, illegal cartel; **~pause die** morning break; coffee break; **~speck der** bacon; bacon rashers *pl.*; **~teller der** tea plate
früh-, Früh-: ~verstorben *Adj. (präd. getrennt geschrieben)* **seine ~verstorbene Mutter** his mother, who died young; **~vollendet** *Adj. (präd. getrennt geschrieben) (geh.)* **der ~vollendete Dichter Keats** the poet Keats, whose life ended so soon; **ein Frühvollendeter** one whose genius was cut off by his/her untimely death; **~warn·system das** early warning system; **~werk das** early work; *(gesamtes)* early works *pl.*; **~zeit die** *(einer Kulturstufe)* early period; *(eines Künstlers)* early life; **~zeitig 1.** *Adj.* **a)** *(früh)* early; **b)** *(vorzeitig)* premature; untimely ‹*death*›; **der ~zeitige Winter** the early onset of winter; **2.** *adv.* **a)** *(früh)* early; *(im Leben, in der Entwicklung)* at an early stage; **das Verbrechen wurde ~zeitig aufgedeckt** the crime was uncovered at an early stage; **jmdn. ~zeitig benachrichtigen** let someone know in good time; **b)** *(vorzeitig)* prematurely; **~zug der** early [morning] train; **~zündung die** *(Technik)* pre-ignition
Fruktose *s.* **Fructose**
Frust [frʊst] **der; ~[e]s** *(ugs.)* frustration; **ihre Arbeit war der absolute ~:** her work was a real drag *(coll.)*; **der große ~ überkam ihn** he began to feel really browned off *(coll.)*
Frustration [frʊstra'tsio:n] **die; ~, ~en** *(Psych.)* frustration
frustrieren [frʊs'tri:rən] *tr. V.* frustrate
frustrierend *Adj.* frustrating
FS *Abk.* **Fernschreiben**
F-Schlüssel der *(Musik)* bass clef; F-clef
FU[B] ['ɛf'|u:('be:)] **die; ~** *Abk.* **Freie Universität [Berlin]**
Fuchs [fʊks] **der; ~es, Füchse** ['fʏksə] **a)** fox; **dort sagen sich ~ und Hase** *od.* **die Füchse gute Nacht** *(scherzh.)* it's in the middle of nowhere *or* at the back of beyond; **b)** *(ugs.: schlauer Mensch)* **ein schlauer ~:** a sly *or* cunning devil; **c)** *(Fell, Pelz)* fox[-fur]; **d)** *(Pferd)* chestnut; *(heller)* sorrel; **e)** *(ugs.: rothaariger Mensch)* carrot-top; **f)** *(Tagfalter)* tortoise-shell; **g)** *(Studentenspr.) first-year member of a student fraternity*
Fuchs·bau der; *Pl.* **~baue** fox-den
Füchschen ['fʏksçən] **das; ~s, ~:** little fox
fuchsen 1. *tr. V.* annoy; vex. **2.** *refl. V.* **sich [über etw.** *(Akk.)***] ~:** be annoyed [about sth.]
Fuchs-: ~falle die fox trap; **~fell das** fox-fur
Fuchsie ['fʊksiə] **die; ~, ~n** *(Bot.)* fuchsia
fuchsig *Adj.* **a)** *(ugs.: wütend)* mad *(coll.)*; furious; **b)** ginger ‹*hair*›
Füchsin ['fʏksɪn] **die; ~, ~nen** vixen
fuchs-, Fuchs-: ~jagd die fox-hunt; *(Schleppjagd)* drag-hunt; **~loch das** *s.* **Fuchsbau**; **~pelz der** fox-fur; **~rot** *Adj.* ginger; **~schwanz der a)** [fox's] brush; [fox] tail; **b)** *(Bot.)* amaranth; love-lies-bleeding; **c)** *(Werkzeug)* hand saw; **~teufels·wild** *Adj. (ugs.)* livid *(coll.)*; hopping mad *(coll.)*
Fuchtel ['fʊxtl̩] **die; ~, ~n a)** *o. Pl. (ugs.: strenge Zucht)* **jmdn. unter der/seiner ~ haben/halten** have/keep sb. under one's thumb; **b)** *(österr.: zänkische Frau)* shrew
fuchteln *itr. V. (ugs.)* **mit etw. ~:** wave sth. about; **mit etw. vor jmds. Gesicht/Nase ~:** wave sth. in sb.'s face
fuchtig ['fʊxtɪç] *Adj. (ugs.)* mad *(coll.)*; furious
Fuder ['fu:dɐ] **das; ~s, ~ a)** *(Wagenladung)* cart-load; **b)** *(ugs.: große Menge)* load *(coll.)*; **c)** *(fachspr.: Weinfaß)* tun
fuder·weise *Adv. (ugs.)* by the ton; **er ißt das ~:** he eats tons of it
fuffzehn ['fʊf-] *(ugs.) s.* **fünfzehn**
fuffzig ['fʊftsɪç] *(ugs.) s.* **fünfzig**
Fuffziger der; ~s, ~ *(ugs.)* fifty-pfennig piece; **ein falscher ~** *(salopp)* a real crook
Fug [fu:k] **der** *in* **mit ~ [und Recht]** rightly; justifiably
[1]Fuge ['fu:gə] **die; ~, ~n a)** joint; *(Zwischenraum)* gap; **der Stuhl/Tisch kracht in allen ~n** *(ugs.)* every joint in the chair/table creaks; **aus den ~n gehen** *od.* **geraten/sein** *(fig.)* be turned completely upside down *(fig.)*; **b)** *(Sprachw.)* juncture
[2]Fuge die; ~, ~n *(Musik)* fugue
fugen ['fu.gn̩] *tr. V.* **a)** *(verbinden)* join, joint ‹*timber*›; **b)** *(ausfüllen)* point ‹*brickwork*›; grout ‹*tiles*›
fügen ['fy:gn̩] **1.** *tr. V.* **a)** *(hinzu~)* place; set; **etw. zu etw. ~** *(fig.)* add sth. to sth.; **Wort an Wort ~:** string words together; **sie fügte Masche an Masche** she joined up the stitches one by one; **b)** *(geh.: zusammen~)* put together; **aus roten Ziegeln gefügt** built with red bricks; **lose gefügte Bretter** loosely jointed boards; **Bestandteile zu einem Ganzen ~** *(fig.)* join parts together to form a whole; **c)** *(geh.: bewirken)* ‹*fate*› ordain, decree; ‹*person*› arrange; **der Zufall hat es gefügt, daß ...:** fate decreed that ... **2.** *refl. V.* **a)** *(sich ein~)* **sich in etw.** *(Akk.)* **~:** fit into sth.; **im Garten fügte sich ein Beet an das andere** in the garden one flower-bed followed the next; **b)** *(gehorchen)* **sich ~:** fall into line; **sich jmdm./einer Sache** *(Dat.)* **~:** fall into line with sb./sth.; **er muß lernen, sich zu ~:** he must learn to toe the line; **sich in sein Schicksal ~:** submit to *or* accept one's fate; **c)** *(geh.: geschehen)* **es fügt sich gut, daß ...:** it is fortunate that ...; **die Umstände scheinen sich günstig zu ~:** circumstances seem to be favourable
fugenlos 1. *Adj.* smooth ‹*concrete wall*›; **eine ~e Trockenmauer** a dry stone wall with no gaps. **2.** *adv.* **die Tür schließt ~:** the door fits exactly
Fugen·zeichen das *(Sprachw.)* juncture marker
füglich *Adv. (veralt.)* with reason; justifiably
fügsam 1. *Adj.* obedient. **2.** *adv.* obediently
Fügsamkeit die; ~: obedience
Fügung die; ~, ~en a) eine ~ Gottes divine providence; **eine ~ des Schicksals** a stroke of fate; **in etw.** *(Dat.)* **eine glückliche ~ sehen** see providence at work in sth.; **b)** *(Sprachw.)* construction
fühlbar 1. *Adj.* **a)** noticeable ‹*lack, improvement, change, difference*›; **b)** *(wahrnehmbar)* perceptible ‹*touch, sound*›. **2.** *adv.* **a)** noticeably; **b)** *(wahrnehmbar)* perceptibly
fühlen ['fy:lən] **1.** *tr., itr. V.* feel ‹*pain, warmth, etc.*›; **jmdm. den Puls ~:** feel sb.'s pulse; **einen Drang/eine Kraft in sich** *(Dat.)* **~:** feel in oneself an urge/a strength; **jmdn. seine Verachtung ~ lassen** show sb. one's contempt; **[Mitleid] mit jmdm. ~:** feel [sympathy] for sb. **2.** *refl. V.* **sich krank/matt ~:** feel sick/weary; **sich bedroht/verfolgt ~:** feel threatened/persecuted; **sich zu jmdm. hingezogen/von jmdm. abgestoßen ~:** feel drawn to/repelled by sb.; **sich schuldig/betrogen ~:** feel guilty/betrayed; **sich zu etw. berufen ~:** feel called to be sth.; **sich zu etw. verpflichtet ~:** feel obliged *or* an obligation to do sth.; **sich als Künstler ~:** feel oneself

to be an artist; feel one is an artist; **der fühlt sich aber** *(ugs.)* he's really pleased with himself. **3.** *itr. V. (tastend prüfen)* **nach etw. ~:** feel for sth.

Fühler der; ~s, ~ a) *(Tentakel)* feeler; antenna; **seine/die ~ ausstrecken** put out feelers; **b)** *s.* **Meß~**

Fühl[er]·lehre die feeler gauge

fühl·los *Adj. (geh. veralt.)* unfeeling

Fühlung die; ~: contact; **mit jmdm. ~ bekommen/[auf]nehmen** get into contact with sb.; **mit einer Organisation/Regierung ~ haben** be in contact with an organization/a government

Fühlungnahme die; ~: initial contact; **die diplomatische ~ ist erfolgt** diplomatic contact has been established

fuhr [fu:ɐ̯] *1. u. 3. Pers. Sg. Prät. v.* **fahren**

Fuhrbetrieb der *s.* **Fuhrunternehmen**

Fuhre ['fu:rə] **die; ~, ~n a)** *(Wagenladung)* load; **eine ~ Sand/Kies** a load of sand/gravel; **b)** *(Transport) (Taxi)* fare; *(Laster)* trip; journey

führen ['fy:rən] **1.** *tr. V.* **a)** *(geleiten, bringen)* lead; **jmdn. an der Hand ~/zum Tisch ~:** lead sb. by the hand/to the table; **ein Tier an der Leine ~:** walk an animal on a lead; **jmdn. durch ein Haus/eine Stadt ~:** show sb. around a house/town; **jmdn. ins Theater/zu einem Ball ~:** take sb. to the theatre/ to a ball; **durch das Programm führt [Sie] Klaus Frank** Klaus Frank will present the programme; **jmdn. auf die richtige Spur ~:** put sb. on the right track; **eine Klasse zum Abitur ~:** take a class through to Abitur level; **ein Land ins Chaos ~:** plunge a country into chaos; **b)** *(verkaufen)* stock, sell ⟨*goods*⟩; **c)** *(durch~)* **Gespräche/Verhandlungen ~:** hold conversations/negotiations; **ein Orts-/Ferngespräch ~:** make a local/long-distance call; **ein unruhiges Leben ~:** lead a turbulent life; **eine glückliche Ehe ~:** be happily married; **einen Prozeß [gegen jmdn.] ~:** take legal action [against sb.]; **d)** *(verantwortlich leiten)* manage, run ⟨*company, business, pub, etc.*⟩; lead ⟨*party, country*⟩; command ⟨*regiment*⟩; chair ⟨*committee*⟩; **eine Reisegruppe ~:** be courier to a group of tourists; **e)** *(gelangen lassen)* take; **die Straße/Reise führte uns durch einen Wald** the road/journey took us through a forest; **was führt Sie zu mir?** what brings you to me?; **f)** *(Amtsspr.)* drive ⟨*train, motor, vehicle*⟩; navigate ⟨*ship*⟩; fly ⟨*aircraft*⟩; **g)** *(bewegen)* **die Hand an die Mütze/Stirn ~:** raise one's hand to one's cap/forehead; **h)** *(verlaufen lassen)* take; **die neue Autobahn um die Stadt ~:** take the new motorway round the city; **i)** *(als Kennzeichnung, Bezeichnung haben)* bear; **etw. in seinem Wappen ~:** have *or* bear sth. on one's coat of arms; **das Auto führt das Kennzeichen ...:** the car bears the registration number ...; **das Schiff führt die schwedische Flagge** the ship is flying the Swedish flag; **einen Titel/Künstlernamen ~:** have a title/use a stage name; **den Titel „Professor" ~:** use the title of professor; **j)** *(angelegt haben)* keep ⟨*diary, list, file*⟩; **k)** *(befördern)* carry; **die Leitung führt Gas** the pipe carries gas; **der Lkw führt Kohle** the truck *or (Brit.)* lorry is carrying coal; **der Zug führt einen Speisewagen** the train has a dining-car; **der Fluß führt Hochwasser** the river is in flood; **l)** *(registrieren)* **jmdn. in einer Liste/Kartei ~:** have sb. on a list/on file; **in einer Liste geführt werden** appear on a list; **wir ~ hier keinen Müller** there is no Müller here; **m)** *(tragen)* **etw. bei** *od.* **mit sich ~:** have sth. on one; **eine Waffe/einen Ausweis bei sich ~:** carry a weapon/a pass; **n)** *(handhaben)* wield ⟨*weapon*⟩. **2.** *itr. V.* **a)** lead; **die Straße führt nach .../durch ...:** the road leads *or* goes to .../goes through ...; **die Brücke führt über den Bach** the bridge goes over the stream; **das Rennen führt über zehn Runden** the race is over ten laps; **das führt zu weit** *(fig.)* that would be taking things too far; **b)** *(an der Spitze liegen)* lead; be ahead; **nach Punkten ~:** be ahead on points; **in der Tabelle ~:** be the league leaders; be at the top of the league; **mit 3 : 1 ~:** be leading 3–1; **c)** *(ein Ergebnis haben)* **zu etw. ~:** lead to sth.; **zum Ziel ~:** bring the desired result; **das führt zu nichts** *(ugs.)* that won't get you/us *etc.* anywhere *(coll.)*. **3.** *refl. V.* **sich gut/schlecht ~:** conduct oneself *or* behave well/badly; **er wurde frühzeitig aus dem Gefängnis entlassen, weil er sich gut geführt hatte** he got remission for good behaviour

führend *Adj.* leading ⟨*politician, figure, role*⟩; high-ranking ⟨*official*⟩; prominent ⟨*position*⟩; **auf einem Gebiet/in einer Sache ~ sein** be a leader in a field/in sth.

Führer der; ~s, ~ a) *(Leiter)* leader; **der ~** *(ns.)* the Führer; **b)** *(Fremden~)* guide; **c)** *(Handbuch)* guide[book] **(durch** to); **d)** *(Amtsspr., schweiz.: Fahrer)* driver

Führer-: ~befehl der *(ns.)* Führer's order; **~eigenschaft die;** *meist Pl.* quality of leadership; **~hauptquartier das** *(ns.)* Führer's headquarters *pl.;* Hitler's headquarters *pl.;* **~haus das** driver's cab

Führerin die; ~, ~nen *s.* **Führer a, b, d**

führer-, Führer-: ~kult der leader cult; **~los 1.** *Adj.* **a)** *(ohne Anführer)* leaderless; **b)** *(ohne Lenker)* driverless ⟨*car*⟩; pilotless ⟨*aircraft*⟩; unmanned ⟨*boat*⟩; **2.** *adv.* **a)** *(ohne Anführer)* without a leader; **b)** *(ohne Lenker) s.* **1b:** without a driver; without a pilot; unmanned; **~natur die a)** leader figure; **b)** *(Wesensart)* **er hat eine starke ~natur** he is clearly a born leader; **~persönlichkeit die** *s.* **~natur a; ~prinzip das** *(bes. ns.)* leadership principle

Führerschaft die; ~: leadership

Führer-: ~schein der driving licence *(Brit.);* driver's license *(Amer.);* **den ~schein machen** *(ugs.)* learn to drive; **jmdm. den ~schein entziehen** take away sb.'s licence; ban *or* disqualify sb. from driving; **~schein·entzug der** disqualification from driving; driving ban; **~sitz der** driving seat; driver's seat; **~stand der** driver's cab

Führ·hand die *(Boxen)* leading hand

Fuhr-: ~lohn der *(an die Spedition)* carriage charge; *(an den Fahrer)* carriage money; **~mann der;** *Pl.* **~leute a)** carter; *(einer Kutsche)* driver; **b)** *o. Pl. (Astron.)* **der ~mann** the Charioteer; **~park der** transport fleet

Führ·ring der *(Pferdesport)* paddock

Führung die; ~, ~en a) *o. Pl. s.* **führen 1d:** management; running; leadership; command; chairmanship; **die politische ~ übernehmen** take over political control *or* the political leadership; **b)** *(Fremden~)* guided tour; **an einer ~ teilnehmen** go on a guided tour; **c)** *o. Pl. (führende Position)* lead; **auf einem Gebiet/in etw.** *(Dat.)* **die ~ haben** be leading *or* the leader/leaders in a field/in sth.; **in ~ liegen/gehen** *(Sport)* be in/go into the lead; **d)** *o. Pl. (Erziehung)* guidance; **eine feste ~:** a firm hand; firm guidance; **e)** *o. Pl. (leitende Gruppe)* leaders *pl.; (einer Partei)* leadership; *(einer Firma)* directors *pl.; (eines Regiments)* commanders *pl.;* **f)** *o. Pl. (Betragen)* conduct; **wegen guter ~ vorzeitig entlassen werden** get remission for good behaviour; **g)** *o. Pl. (eines Registers, Protokolls usw.)* keeping; **h)** *o. Pl. (das Handhaben von Waffen)* wielding; **i)** *o. Pl. (Amtsspr.) (eines Kfz)* driving; *(eines Flugzeugs)* flying; **j)** *o. Pl. (eines Titels usw.)* use; **k)** *(Technik)* guide

Führungs-: ~an·spruch der claim to leadership; **einen ~anspruch erheben** lay claim to the leadership; **~auf·gabe die** *(im Betrieb)* management function; *(Politik)* leadership function; **~gremium das** executive committee; **~kraft die** manager; **~krise die** *(Politik)* leadership crisis; *(Wirtsch.)* boardroom crisis; **~rolle die** role as leader; **~schiene die** *(Technik)* guide rail; **~spitze die** *(Politik)* top leadership; *(im Betrieb)* top management; **~stab der** *(Milit.)* high command; *(im Betrieb)* top management; **~tor das, ~treffer der** *(Sport) goal which puts the/a team in the lead;* **das ~tor erzielen** score the goal which puts one's team in the lead; **~wechsel der** *(Politik)* change of leadership; *(Wirtsch.)* change of director/directors; **~zeugnis das** *document issued by police certifying that holder has no criminal record*

fuhr-, Fuhr-: ~unternehmen das haulage business; **~unternehmer der** haulage contractor; **~werk das** cart *(drawn by horse[s], ox[en], etc.); (veralt.: Wagen) (horse-drawn)* carriage; **~werken** *itr. V. (ugs.)* **mit etw. ~werken** wave sth. about; **sie ~werkte nervös mit ihrer Handtasche** she fumbled nervously with her handbag

Fülle ['fʏlə] **die; ~ a)** *(große Menge)* wealth; abundance; **eine ~ von Arbeit** an enormous amount of work; **in ~:** in plenty; in abundance; **b)** *(Intensität)* **die ganze ~ des Lebens** the fullness *or* richness of life; **die ~ seines Glücks** the extent of his happiness; **c)** *(Körper~)* corpulence; *(von Wein)* full-bodiedness; *(von Haar)* fullness; **zur ~ neigen** tend to corpulence; **sie ließ sich mit ihrer ganzen ~ auf das Sofa fallen** she let her whole weight drop on to the sofa

füllen 1. *tr. V.* **a)** *(vollmachen, an~)* fill; **eine Flasche/ein Glas [mit etw.] ~:** fill a bottle/a glass with sth.; **bis zum Rand gefüllt sein** be full to the brim; **der Saal ist bis auf den letzten Platz/halb gefüllt** the hall is completely/half full; *s. auch* **gefüllt 2; b)** *(fig.)* fill in ⟨*gap, time*⟩; **c)** *(mit einer Füllung versehen)* stuff ⟨*fowl, tomato, apple, mattress, toy*⟩; fill ⟨*tooth*⟩; *s. auch* **gefüllt 2; d)** *(schütten)* pour; **etw. in Flaschen ~:** bottle sth.; **etw. in Säcke ~:** put sth. into sacks; **e)** *(einnehmen)* fill ⟨*space etc.*⟩. **2.** *refl. V. (voll werden)* fill [up]; **sich mit etw. ~:** fill up with sth.

Füllen das; ~s, ~ *(geh.)* foal

Füller der; ~s, ~ a) *(ugs.)* [fountain-]pen; **b)** *(Zeitungsw.)* filler

Füll-: ~feder·halter der fountain-pen; **~gewicht das** net weight; **~horn das** horn of plenty; *(fig.)* cornucopia

füllig *Adj.* corpulent, portly ⟨*person*⟩; ample, portly ⟨*figure*⟩; full ⟨*face*⟩; ample ⟨*bosom*⟩

Füll-: ~masse die filler; **~material das** *(Druckw.)* furniture; spacing material

Füllsel ['fʏlzl̩] **das; ~s, ~ a)** *(Lückenfüller)* padding; **b)** *(in Lebensmitteln)* filling; *(in Geflügel)* stuffing

Füllung die; ~, ~en a) *(in Geflügel, Paprika)* stuffing; *(in Pasteten, Kuchen)* filling; *(in Schokolade, Pralinen)* centre; *(in Kissen, Matratzen)* stuffing; **b)** *(Zahnmed.)* filling; **c)** *(Teil der Tür)* panel; **d)** *o. Pl. (das Vollmachen)* filling

Füll·wort das; *Pl.* **-wörter** filler; *(Sprachw., Literaturw.)* expletive

fulminant [fʊlmi'nant] *Adj.* brilliant

Fummel [fʊml̩] **der; ~s, ~** *(salopp)* **a)** rags *pl.;* **b)** *(von Transvestiten)* drag [outfit]; **im ~:** in drag

Fummelei die; ~, ~en *(ugs.)* **a)** twiddling; **das ist eine furchtbare ~:** it's terribly fiddly; **b)** *(Petting)* petting; groping *(coll.);* **c)** *(Fußballjargon)* dribbling

fummeln 1. *itr. V.* **a)** *(ugs.: fingern)* fiddle; **an etw.** *(Dat.)* **~:** fiddle [around] with sth.; **nach etw. ~:** grope for *or* feel for sth.; **b)** *(ugs.: erotisch)* pet; **c)** *(Fußballjargon)* dribble. **2.** *tr. V.* **etw. in etw.** *(Akk.)***/aus etw. ~** *(ugs.)* get sth. in sth./out of sth.

Fund [fʊnt] **der**; ~[e]s, ~e *(auch Archäol.)* find; *(wissenschaftliche Entdeckung)* discovery

Fundament [fʊnda'mɛnt] **das**; ~[e]s, ~e **a)** *(Bauw.)* foundations *pl.*; **das ~ legen** *od.* **mauern** lay the foundations; **etw. bis auf die ~e abreißen** raze sth. to the ground; **etw. in seinen ~en erschüttern** *(fig.)* strike at the very foundations of sth.; **das ~ zu etw. legen** *(fig.)* lay the foundations for sth.; **an den ~en rütteln** *(fig.)* rock the very foundations; **b)** *(Basis)* base; basis; **ein solides ~ haben** have a solid base

fundamental [fʊndamɛn'ta:l] *Adj.* fundamental

Fundamentalismus der; ~: fundamentalism

Fundamentalist der; ~en, ~en, **Fundamentalistin die**; ~, ~nen fundamentalist; *s. auch* **-in**

Fundamental·satz der fundamental theorem

fundamentieren *tr. V. (Bauw.)* **ein Gebäude** ~: lay the foundations of a building; **schlecht fundamentiert sein** *(auch fig.)* have weak foundations

Fund-: ~**amt das** *(bes. österr.)*, ~**büro das** lost property office *(Brit.)*; lost and found office *(Amer.)*; ~**gegenstand der a)** *s.* ~**sache**; **b)** *(Archäol.)* find; ~**grube die** treasure-house

Fundi ['fʊndi] **der**; ~s, ~s/**die**; ~, ~s *(ugs.)* fundamentalist

fundieren [fʊn'di:rən] *tr. V.* **a)** *(geistig begründen, untermauern)* underpin; **ein wissenschaftlich fundierter Vortrag** a scientifically sound lecture; **b)** *(geh.: festigen)* sustain; **c)** *(finanziell sichern)* strengthen [financially]; **ein gut fundiertes Unternehmen** a [financially] sound business

fündig ['fʏndɪç] *Adj.* ~ **sein** yield something; ~ **werden** make a find; *(bei Bohrungen)* make a strike

Fund-: ~**ort der** place *or* site where sth. is/was found; ~**sache die** article found; ~**sachen** lost property *sing.*; ~**stätte die**, ~**stelle die** *s.* ~**ort**; ~**unterschlagung die** *(Rechtsw.)* larceny by finding

Fundus ['fʊndʊs] **der**; ~, ~ **a)** *(Requisition)* equipment store; **b)** *(Grundstock, -lage)* **einen [reichen] ~ von/an etw.** *(Dat.)* **haben** have a [rich] fund of sth.; **kein eigentlicher geistiger ~**: no real intellectual resources *pl.*

fünf [fʏnf] *Kardinalz.* five; ~**[e] gerade sein lassen** *(fig. ugs.)* let sth. pass; **man muß manchmal ~[e] gerade sein lassen** *(ugs.)* one has to turn a blind eye sometimes; **es ist ~ Minuten vor zwölf** it is five minutes to twelve; ~ **Minuten vor zwölf** *(fig.)* at the eleventh hour; at the last minute; *s. auch* **¹acht; Finger b; Sinn a**

Fünf die; ~, ~en five; **eine ~ schreiben/bekommen** *(Schulw.)* get an E; *s. auch* **¹Acht a, d, e, g; Zwei b**

fünf-, Fünf- *(s. auch* **acht-, Acht-**): ~**akter** [-|aktɐ] **der**; ~s, ~: five-act play; ~**eck das**; ~s, ~e pentagon; ~**eckig** *Adj.* pentagonal; five-cornered

Fünfer der; ~s, ~ *(ugs.)* **a)** *(Geldschein, Münze)* five; **b)** *(ugs.: Ziffer)* five; **c)** *(Lottogewinn)* five out of six; **d)** *(ugs.: Sprungturm)* five-metre board; *s. auch* **Achter c, d**

fünferlei *Gattungsz.; indekl.* **a)** *attr.* five kinds *or* sorts of; five different *attrib.* ‹*sorts, kinds, sizes, possibilities*›; **b)** *subst.* five [different] things

fünf-, Fünf-: ~**fach** *Vervielfältigungsz.* fivefold; quintuple; *s. auch* **achtfach**; ~**fache das**; *adj. Dekl.* five times as much; quintuple; *s. auch* **Achtfache**; ~**fältig** *Adj.* *(veralt.) s.* ~**fach**; ~**flach das**; ~s, ~e, ~**flächner der**; ~s, ~: pentahedron; ~**franken·stück das** five-franc piece; ~**füßig** *Adj. (Verslehre)* five-foot; ~**füßiger Jambus/Trochäus** iambic/trochaic pentameter; ~**gang·getriebe das** five-speed gearbox; ~**hebig** *Adj. (Verslehre) s.* ~**füßig**; ~**hundert** *Kardinalz.* five hundred; *s. auch* **hundert**; ~**hundert·jahr·feier die** quincentenary; ~**jahr[es]·plan der** five-year plan; ~**jährig** *Adj. (~ Jahre alt)* five-year-old; *(~ Jahre dauernd)* five-year; *s. auch* **achtjährig**; ~**jährlich 1.** *Adj.* five-yearly; quinquennial; **2.** *adv.* every five years; *s. auch* **achtjährlich**; ~**kampf der** *(Sport)* pentathlon; **der moderne ~kampf** the Modern Pentathlon; ~**kämpfer der**, ~**kämpferin die** *(Sport)* pentathlete; ~**köpfig** *Adj.* ‹*family, crew*› of five; five-headed ‹*monster*›;

Fünfling ['fʏnflɪŋ] **der**; ~s, ~e quintuplet; quin *(coll.)*

fünf-, Fünf-: ~**mal** *Adv.* five times; *s. auch* **achtmal**; ~**malig** *Adj.; nicht präd.* **eine ~malige Wiederholung** five repeats; *s. auch* **achtmalig**; ~**markstück das** five-mark piece; ~**meterplatt·form die** *(Wasserspringen)* five-metre platform; ~**meter·raum der** *(Fußball)* goal area; ~**pfennig·stück das** five-pfennig piece; ~**prozentig** *Adj.* five per cent; ~**prozent·klausel** *constitutional clause laying down that only parties with more than five per cent of the vote may be represented in parliament;* five per cent clause; ~**seitig** *Adj.* five-page ‹*letter, leaflet*›; *s. auch* **achtseitig**; ~**silber der**; ~s, ~: *s.* **Fünfsilbler**; ~**silbig** *Adj.* five-syllable; pentasyllabic; ~**silbler der**; ~s, ~ *(Verslehre)* five-syllable line; ~**stellig** *Adj.* five-figure ‹*number, sum*›; *s. auch* **achtstellig**; ~**stöckig** *Adj.* five-storey *attrib.*; *s. auch* **achtstöckig**; ~**strophig** [-ʃtro:fɪç] *Adj.* of five stanzas *or* verses *postpos., not pred.*

fünft [fʏnft] *in* **wir/sie waren zu ~**: there were five of us/them; *s. auch* **²acht**

fünft... *Ordinalz.* fifth; *s. auch* **acht...**

fünf-, Fünf-: ~**tage·woche die** five-day [working] week; ~**tägig** *Adj.* five-day; *s. auch* **achttägig**; ~**tausend** *Kardinalz.* five thousand; *s. auch* **tausend**

Fünfte der/die; *adj. Dekl.* fifth; **Kaiser Karl V.** *od.* **der ~**: the Emperor Charles V; *s. auch* **Achte**

fünfteilig *Adj.* five-part; *s. auch* **achtteilig**

fünftel ['fʏnftl] *Bruchz.* fifth; *s. auch* **achtel**

Fünftel das *(schweiz. meist* **der**); ~s, ~: fifth

fünftens ['fʏnftn̩s] *Adv.* fifthly; in the fifth place

fünf-, Fünf-: ~**tonner der**; ~s, ~: five-tonner; ~**uhr·tee der** [afternoon] tea; ~**viertel·takt** [-'---] **der** five-four time; ~**zehn** *Kardinalz.* fifteen; *s. auch* **achtzehn**; ~**zehn·jährig** *Adj. (15 Jahre alt)* fifteen-year-old *attrib.*; *(15 Jahre dauernd)* fifteen-year *attrib.*; *s. auch* **achtjährig**; ~**zehnt...** *Ordinalz.* fifteenth; *s. auch* **acht...**

fünfzig ['fʏnftsɪç] *Kardinalz.* fifty; *s. auch* **achtzig**

Fünfzig die; ~: fifty

fünfziger *indekl. Adj.; nicht präd.* **die ~ Jahre** the fifties; *s. auch* **achtziger**

¹Fünfziger der; ~s, ~ **a)** *(ugs.)* fifty-pfennig piece; **b)** *(50jähriger)* fifty-year-old; *s. auch* **¹Achtziger b, c**

²Fünfziger die; ~, ~ *(ugs.)* **a)** *(Briefmarke)* fifty-pfennig/shilling *etc.* stamp; **b)** *(Zigarre)* fifty-pfennig cigar

³Fünfziger *Pl.* fifties; *s. auch* **³Achtziger**

fünfzig-, Fünfzig-: ~**jährig** *Adj. (50 Jahre alt)* fifty-year-old *attrib.*; *(50 Jahre dauernd)* fifty-year *attrib.*; *s. auch* **achtjährig**; ~**pfennig·stück das** fifty-pfennig piece

fünfzigst... ['fʏnftsɪçst...] *Ordinalz.* fiftieth; *s. auch* **acht...; achtzigst...**

fungieren [fʊŋ'gi:rən] *itr. V.* **als etw.** ~ ‹*person*› act as sth.; ‹*word etc.*› function as sth.

Funk [fʊŋk] **der**; ~s **a)** *(drahtlose Übermittlung)* radio; **jmdn./etw. über ~** *(Akk.)* **anfordern** ask for sb./sth. by radio; **b)** *(Rund~)* radio; **beim ~ sein** *(ugs.) od.* **arbeiten** be *(coll.) or* work in radio

Funk-: ~**amateur der** radio ham; ~**anlage die** radio set; ~**ausstellung die** radio and television exhibition; ~**bake die** radio beacon; ~**bearbeitung die** radio adaptation; adaptation for radio; ~**bericht der** radio report; ~**bild das** radio photograph

Fünkchen ['fʏŋkçən] **das**; ~s, ~: *s.* **Funke b**

Funk·dienst der radio communication service

Funke ['fʊŋkə] **der**; ~ns, ~n **a)** *(glühendes Teilchen)* spark; ~**n sprühen** send out a shower of sparks; *(fig.)* ‹*eyes*› flash; **b)** *(fig.)* **der ~ der Begeisterung/Revolution** the spark of enthusiasm/revolution; **der auslösende ~ für meinen Entschluß war ...**: what finally triggered my decision was ...; **ein/kein ~** *od.* **Fünkchen [von] Verstand/Ehrgefühl/Mitleid** a/not a glimmer of understanding/shred of honour/scrap of sympathy; **arbeiten, daß die ~n stieben** *od.* **fliegen** *(fig.)* work like mad

funkeln ['fʊŋkl̩n] *itr. V.* ‹*light, star*› twinkle, sparkle; ‹*gold, diamonds*› glitter, sparkle; ‹*eyes*› blaze

funkel·nagel·neu *Adj. (ugs.)* brand new; spanking new *(coll.)*

funken ['fʊŋkn̩] **1.** *tr. V.* radio; ‹*transmitter*› broadcast; **SOS ~**: send out an SOS. **2.** *itr. V.; unpers. (fig. ugs.)* **es hat gefunkt** *(es hat Streit gegeben)* the sparks flew; *(die Sache geht in Ordnung)* it's worked out OK *(coll.)*; *(man hat sich verliebt)* something clicked between them/us *(coll.)*; **es hat bei ihm gefunkt** the penny's dropped [with him] *(coll.)*

funken-, Funken-: ~**bildung die** sparking *no art.*; ~**entladung die** spark discharge; ~**fänger der** *(Eisenb.)* spark-arrester; ~**flug der** flying sparks *pl.*; ~**mariechen das**; ~s, ~: red-coat girl *(in Rhenish carnival)*; ~**regen der** shower of sparks; ~**sprühend 1.** *Adj.* **ein ~sprühendes Feuer** a fire sending out showers of sparks; **2.** *adv.* **~sprühend raste die Lok vorbei** the engine thundered past, giving off showers of sparks

funk·entstören *tr. V.* fit with a suppressor/suppressors; suppress

Funk·entstörung die suppression of interference

Funker der; ~s, ~: radio operator

Funk-: ~**fern·steuerung die** radio control; ~**feuer das** *s.* ~**bake**; ~**gerät das** radio set; *(tragbar)* walkie-talkie; ~**haus das** broadcasting centre; ~**kolleg das** radio-based [adult education] course; ~**meldung die** radio message *or* report; ~**meß·technik die** radar; ~**navigation die** radio navigation; ~**ortung die** radio position-finding; ~**peiler der** [radio] direction-finder; ~**peilung die** [radio] direction-finding; ~**sprech·gerät das** radiophone; *(tragbar)* walkie-talkie; ~**sprech·verkehr der** radio telephony; ~**spruch der** radio signal; *(Nachricht)* radio message; ~**station die**, ~**stelle die** radio station; ~**stille die** radio silence; **bei ihm herrscht ~stille** *(fig.)* he's keeping quiet; ~**störung die** [radio] interference; *(mit Absicht)* jamming; ~**streife die** [police] radio patrol; ~**streifen·wagen der** radio patrol car; ~**taxi das** radio taxi; ~**technik die** radio technology; ~**telegramm das** radio telegram

Funktion [fʊnk'tsio:n] **die**; ~, ~en **a)** function; **b)** *o. Pl. (Tätigkeit, Arbeiten)* functioning, working; **außer/in ~ sein** be out of/in operation; **in ~** *(Akk.)* **treten** come into operation; **jmdn./etw. außer ~ setzen** put sb./sth. out of operation; **c)** *(Amt, Stellung)* function; **in seiner ~ als ...**: in his function as ...; **d)** *(Math., Sprachw.)* function

funktional [fʊŋktsi̯o'na:l] 1. Adj. functional. 2. adv. functionally

Funktionalismus der; ~: functionalism

Funktionär [fʊŋktsi̯o'nɛ:ɐ̯] **der**; ~s, ~e, **Funktionärin die**; ~, ~nen official; functionary

funktionell [fʊŋktsi̯o'nɛl] 1. Adj. functional. 2. adv. functionally

Funktionen·theorie die (Math.) theory of functions

funktionieren itr. V. work; function; **die gut ~de Organisation** the smooth organization

funktions-, Funktions-: **~fähig** Adj. able to function or work pred.; **~gerecht** 1. Adj. functional; 2. adv. functionally; **~los** Adj. ⟨person⟩ without a job to do; functionless ⟨equipment, object⟩; **~los werden** become unnecessary; **~sicher** 1. Adj. operatively sound; 2. adv. properly; **~störung die** (Med.) functional disorder; dysfunction; **~tüchtig** Adj. working ⟨equipment, part⟩; sound ⟨organ⟩; **~verb das** (Sprachw.) empty verb; **~wechsel der** change in function

Funk-: **~turm der** radio tower; **~verbindung die** radio contact; **~verkehr der** radio communication; **~wagen der** radio patrol car; **~weg der**: **auf dem ~weg** by radio

Funzel ['fʊnts̩l] **die**; ~, ~n (ugs., abwertend) useless lamp or light; **bei dieser ~**: in this gloomy light

für [fy:ɐ̯] 1. Präp. mit Akk. a) for; **~ etw. trainieren/kämpfen** train/fight for sth.; **~ jmdn. bestimmt sein** be meant for sb.; **das ist nichts ~ mich** that's not for me; **Lehrer/Professor/Minister ~ etw. sein** be a teacher/professor/minister of sth.; **zu jung/alt ~ etw. sein** be too young/old for sth.; **~ sich** by oneself; on one's own; **er ist am liebsten ganz ~ sich** he most prefers to be quite alone; **jetzt habe ich eine Küche ganz ~ mich** now I've a kitchen all to myself; **das ist gut ~ Husten** that's good for coughs; **sich ~ jmdn. freuen/schämen** be pleased/ashamed for sb.; **~ etw. verurteilt werden** be condemned for sth.; **etw. ~ 50 DM kaufen** buy sth. for 50 marks; **~ diese Jahreszeit ist es viel zu kalt** it's much too cold for this time of year; **~ 20 Minuten/drei Tage** for 20 minutes/three days; **~ morgen** for tomorrow; **~ immer** for ever; for good; **~ gewöhnlich** usually; **~ nichts und wieder nichts** for absolutely nothing; b) (zugunsten) for; **~ jmdn./etw. stimmen/sein** vote/be for or in favour of sb./sth.; **das hat etwas ~ sich** it has something to be said for it; **das Für und Wider** the pros and cons pl.; c) (als) **etw. ~ ungültig/zulässig erklären** declare sth. invalid/admissible; **jmdn. ~ tot erklären** declare sb. dead; d) (an Stelle) for; **~ jmdn. einspringen** take sb.'s place; **~ zwei arbeiten** do the work of two people; e) (als Stellvertreter) for; on behalf of; **~ jmdn. eine Erklärung abgeben** make an announcement on sb.'s behalf; f) (um) **Jahr ~ Jahr/Tag ~ Tag** year after year/day after day; **Punkt ~ Punkt/Schritt ~ Schritt** point by point/step by step; **Wort ~ Wort** word for word; s. auch **was 1.** 2. adv. (veralt.) **~ und ~**: for ever [and ever]; unto all generations (bibl.)

Furage [fu'ra:ʒə] **die**; ~ (Milit. veralt.) a) (Verpflegung) rations pl.; b) (Futter) forage

furagieren itr. V. (Milit. veralt.) forage

für·baß Adv. (veralt., noch scherzh.) onwards; **~ gehen/schreiten** proceed on one's way

Für·bitte die intercession; **[bei jmdm.] für jmdn. ~ einlegen** intercede [with sb.] for sb.

Furche ['fʊrçə] **die**; ~, ~n a) furrow; **[mit dem Pflug] ~n ziehen** plough furrows; **~n im Gesicht/auf der Stirn haben** have a furrowed face/brow; b) (Wagenspur) rut; c) (Rille) groove

furchen tr. V. (geh.) a) (Linien bilden) furrow; **die Stirn/die Brauen ~**: furrow one's brow; b) (Rillen ziehen) make ⟨ruts⟩; make ruts in ⟨ground, track⟩

Furcht [fʊrçt] **die**; ~: fear; **~ vor jmdm./etw. haben** fear sb./sth.; **~ vor Gespenstern haben** be afraid of ghosts; **von ~ erfaßt sein** (geh.) be seized by fear or dread; **jmdm. ~ einflößen** frighten sb.; **aus ~ vor jmdm./etw.** for fear of sb./sth.; **jmdn. in ~ und Schrecken versetzen** fill sb. with terror; terrify sb.

furchtbar 1. Adj. a) awful; frightful; dreadful; **~ aussehen** look awful or frightful; **es war mir ~, das tun zu müssen** it was awful [for me] to have to do it; b) (ugs.: unangenehm) awful (coll.); terrible (coll.); **ein ~er Angeber/Pedant** an awful or frightful show-off/pedant (coll.). 2. adv. (ugs.) awfully (coll.); terribly (coll.); **~ lachen [müssen]** laugh oneself silly (coll.); **das ist ~ einfach/teuer** it's awfully simple/expensive; **es dauerte ~ lange** it took an awfully long time; **jmdn. ~ beschimpfen/verprügeln** give sb. an awful talking-to/beating

furcht·einflößend Adj. frightening; fearsome; **es wirkte ~ auf uns** it frightened us

fürchten 1. refl. V. **sich [vor jmdm./etw.] ~**: be afraid or frightened [of sb./sth.]; **es ist/war zum Fürchten** it is/was quite frightening; **du siehst in diesem Anzug ja zum Fürchten aus** (scherzh.) you look quite frightful in that suit. 2. tr. V. fear; be afraid of; **jmdn./etw. ~**: fear or be afraid of sb./sth.; **jmdn./etw. wegen etw. ~**: fear sb./sth. because of sth.; **er war als strenger Prüfer gefürchtet** he was feared as a strict examiner; **ein gefürchteter Kritiker** a feared critic; **der gefürchtete Augenblick** the moment they/we etc. had been fearing; **Gott ~**: fear God; **ich fürchte, [daß] ...**: I'm afraid [that] ... 3. itr. V. **für od. um jmdn./etw. ~**: fear for sb./sth.

fürchterlich Adj. s. **furchtbar**

furcht·erregend Adj. frightening

furcht·los 1. Adj. fearless. 2. adv. fearlessly

Furcht·losigkeit die; ~: fearlessness

furchtsam ['fʊrçtza:m] 1. Adj. timid; fearful. 2. adv. timidly; fearfully

Furchtsamkeit die; ~, ~en timidity; fearfulness

Furchung die; ~, ~en (Biol.) cleavage; segmentation

fürder[hin] ['fʏrdɐ(hɪn)] Adv. (veralt.) in future

für·einander Adv. for one another; for each other

Furie ['fu:ri̯ə] **die**; ~, ~n Fury; **er rannte wie von ~n gehetzt davon** he ran off as if the devil were on his tail; **sie wurde zur ~** (fig.) she started acting like a woman possessed; **wie ~n gingen sie aufeinander los** they went for each other like wildcats

furios [fu'ri̯o:s] Adj. (geh. veralt.) rousing; stirring

für·lieb|nehmen unr. itr. V. (veralt.) s. **vorliebnehmen**

fürnehm ['fy:ɐ̯ne:m] Adj. (veralt., scherzh.) s. **vornehm**

Furnier [fʊr'ni:ɐ̯] **das**; ~s, ~e veneer

furnieren tr. V. veneer; **[mit] Eiche furniert sein** have an oak veneer

Furore [fu'ro:rə] in **~ machen** cause a sensation or stir

fürs [fy:ɐ̯s] Präp. + Art. a) = **für das**; b) **~ erste** for the time being

Für·sorge die; ~ a) (umsorgende Hilfe) care; b) (veralt.: Sozialhilfe) welfare; c) (veralt.: Sozialamt) social services pl.; d) (ugs.: Unterstützungsgeld) social security (Brit.); welfare (Amer.)

Fürsorge-: **~amt das** (veralt.) welfare office; **~arzt der** (veralt.) welfare service doctor; **~empfänger der** (ugs.) recipient of social security; **~empfänger sein** receive social security; **~erziehung die** upbringing in [local authority] care

für·sorgend 1. Adj. caring; thoughtful. 2. adv. caringly; thoughtfully

Fürsorge·pflicht die (jur.) employer's obligation to ensure the welfare of his/her employees

Fürsorger der; ~s, ~, **Fürsorgerin die**; ~, ~nen (veralt.) welfare worker

Fürsorge·unterstützung die (veralt.) social security (Brit.); welfare (Amer.)

für·sorglich 1. Adj. considerate; thoughtful. 2. adv. considerately; thoughtfully

Fürsorglichkeit die; ~: considerateness; thoughtfulness

Für·sprache die support; **bei jmdm. für jmdn. ~ einlegen** put in a good word for sb. with sb.

Fürsprech ['fy:ɐ̯ʃprɛç] **der**; ~s, ~e (veralt., geh.) s. **Fürsprecher**

Für·sprecher der, Für·sprecherin die a) advocate; **in jmdm. einen ~ haben** have an advocate in sb.; b) (schweiz.) s. **Rechtsanwalt**

Fürst [fʏrst] **der**; ~en, ~en prince; **der ~ der Hölle/Finsternis** (fig.) the Prince of Hell/Darkness; **gehe nie zu deinem ~, wenn du nicht gerufen wirst** (scherzh.) do not meet trouble half way

Fürst-: **~abt der** (hist.) prince-abbot; **~bischof der** (hist.) prince-bishop

Fürsten-: **~geschlecht das, ~haus das** royal house; **~hof der** prince's palace; **~krone die** prince's coronet; **~spiegel der** novel giving guidance for the conduct of princes; **~stand der**; o. Pl. rank of prince

Fürstentum das; ~s, **Fürstentümer** [-ty:mɐ] principality; **das ~ Liechtenstein/Monaco** the Principality of Liechtenstein/Monaco

Fürstin die; ~, ~nen princess

fürstlich 1. Adj. a) nicht präd. royal; b) (fig.: üppig) handsome; lavish. 2. adv. handsomely; lavishly; **~ speisen** enjoy a sumptuous meal

Fürstlichkeit die; ~, ~en royal personage

Furt [fʊrt] **die**; ~, ~en ford

Furunkel [fu'rʊŋk̩l] **der od. das**; ~s, ~: boil; furuncle

Furunkulose [furʊŋku'lo:zə] **die**; ~, ~n (Med.) furunculosis

für·wahr Adv. (geh. veralt.) of a truth (arch.); in truth (literary)

Für·witz der; ~es (veralt.) s. **Vorwitz**

Für·wort das; Pl. **-wörter** pronoun

Furz [fʊrts] **der**; ~es, **Fürze** ['fʏrtsə] (derb) fart (coarse); **einen ~ lassen** let off a fart; **jeder ~** (fig.) the slightest thing

furzen (derb) itr. V. fart (coarse)

Fusel ['fu:z̩l] **der**; ~s, ~ (ugs. abwertend) rotgut (coll. derog.)

Fusel-: **~geruch der** (ugs. abwertend) smell of cheap alcohol; **~öl das** fusel oil

Füsilier [fyzi'li:ɐ̯] **der**; ~s, ~e (schweiz., sonst veralt.) fusilier

füsilieren tr. V. (veralt.) execute by firing squad

Fusion [fu'zi̯o:n] **die**; ~, ~en a) amalgamation; (von Konzernen) merger; b) (Naturw.) fusion

fusionieren itr. V. merge

Fusions·reaktor der (Physik) fusion reactor

Fuß [fu:s] **der**; ~es, **Füße** ['fy:sə] a) foot; (südd., österr., schweiz.) leg; **sich (Dat.) den ~ verstauchen/brechen** sprain one's ankle/break a bone in one's foot; **mit bloßen Füßen** barefoot; with bare feet; **jmdm. auf den ~ treten** tread on sb.'s foot; **zu ~ gehen** go on foot; walk; **über seine eigenen Füße stolpern** trip over one's own feet; **gut/schlecht zu ~ sein** be a good/bad walker; **ich habe keinen ~ vor die Tür gesetzt** I did not set foot outside the door; **sich (Dat.) gegenseitig auf die Füße treten** tread on each other's toes; **jmdm. auf dem ~e folgen** follow at sb.'s heels; **bei ~! heel!; nimm die Füße weg!** *(ugs.)* move your feet!; **Gewehr bei ~ stehen** stand with ordered arms; **b)** *(fig.)* **stehenden ~es** *(veralt., geh.)* without delay; instanter *(arch.)*; **[festen] ~ fassen** find one's feet; **kalte Füße kriegen** *(ugs.)* get cold feet *(coll.)*; **sich** *(Dat.)* **die Füße nach etw. ablaufen** *od.* **wund laufen** chase round everywhere for sth.; **sich auf eigene Füße stellen** stand on one's own feet; **auf freiem ~ sein** be at large; **jmdn. auf freien ~ setzen** set sb. free; **auf großem ~ leben** live in great style; **mit jmdm. auf freundschaftlichem/gespanntem ~ stehen** *od.* **leben** be on friendly/less than friendly terms with sb.; **jmdm. auf die Füße treten** *(ugs.)* give sb. a good talking-to; **auf dem ~e folgen** follow swiftly; **jmdn. auf dem falschen ~ erwischen** *(Sportjargon)* wrong-foot sb.; **jmdn./etw. mit Füßen treten** trample on sb./sth.; **jmdm. etw. vor die Füße werfen** throw sth. in sb.'s face; **jmdm. zu Füßen liegen** *(geh.) (bewundern)* adore *or* worship sb.; *(anflehen)* go on one's bended knee to sb.; **jmdm. etw. zu Füßen legen** *(geh.)* lay sth. at sb.'s feet; *s. auch* **eigen a; Erde b; fallen a; Gefängnis a; Grab** *usw.*; **c)** *(tragender Teil) (einer Lampe)* base; *(eines Weinglases)* foot; *(eines Schranks, Sessels, Klaviers)* leg; **auf tönernen** *od.* **schwachen** *od.* **schwankenden Füßen stehen** *(fig.)* be unsoundly based; **d)** *o. Pl. (eines Berges)* foot; *(einer Säule)* base; **e)** *Pl.: ~ (Längenmaß)* foot; **zwei/drei ~:** two/three feet *or* foot; **f)** *(Teil des Strumpfes)* foot

fuß-, Fuß-: ~abdruck der footprint; **~abstreifer, ~abtreter der** shoe scraper; **~abwehr die** *(Ballspiele)* kick save; **~angel die** mantrap; *(fig.)* trap; **er hat sich in den ~angeln dieser Paragraphen verstrickt** he has got entangled in these legal clauses; **~bad das a)** foot-bath; **b)** *(ugs., scherzh.)* pool in the saucer

Fuß·ball der a) *o. Pl. (Ballspiel)* [Association] football; soccer *(coll.)*; **b)** *(Ball)* football; soccer ball *(coll.)*

Fuß·ballen der the ball of the/one's foot

Fußballer der; ~s, ~: footballer; soccer player *(coll.)*

fußballerisch *Adj.; nicht präd.* footballing

Fußball-: ~klub der *s.* **~verein; ~mannschaft die** football team; **~meisterschaft die** football championship; **~platz der** football ground; *(Spielfeld)* football pitch; **~schuh der** football boot; **~spiel das a)** football match; **b)** *o. Pl. (Sportart)* football *no art.*; **~spieler der** football player; **~tor das** [football] goal; **~toto das** *od.* **der** football pools *pl.*; **~verband der** football association; **~verein der** football club

Fuß-: ~bank die foot-stool; **~bekleidung die** footwear; **~bett das** foot-bed; **~boden der** floor

Fußboden-: ~belag der floor covering; **~heizung die** underfloor heating

fuß-, Fuß-: ~breit *Adj.* foot-wide; **~breit sein** be a foot wide; **~breit der; ~:** foot; **er wollte keinen ~breit nachgeben** *(fig.)* he would not budge an inch; **~bremse die** foot-brake; **~brett das** foot rest

Füßchen ['fy:sçən] **das; ~s, ~:** [little] foot

Fussel ['fʊsl] **die; ~, ~n** *od.* **der; ~s, ~[n]** fluff; **ein[e] ~:** a piece of fluff; some fluff

fusselig *Adj.* covered in fluff *postpos.*; *(ausgefranst)* frayed; **sich** *(Dat.)* **den Mund ~ reden** *(salopp)* talk till one is blue in the face *(coll.)*

fusseln *itr. V.* make fluff

fußen *itr. V.* **auf etw.** *(Dat.)* **~:** be based on sth.

Fuß·ende das foot

fuß-, Fuß-: ~fall der kowtow; **einen ~fall vor jmdm. machen** *(fig.)* kowtow to sb.; **~fällig 1.** *Adj.* humble; **2.** *adv.* **a) sie flehte den Fürsten ~fällig um Gnade an** she fell on her knees before the prince, begging him for mercy; **b)** *(fig.)* humbly; **~fehler der a)** *(bes. Hockey)* kick; **b)** *(Tennis)* foot fault; **~fesseln** *Pl.* shackles *(on the feet)*; **~frei** *Adj.* ankle-length ‹*dress, skirt, etc.*›

Fußgänger [-gɛŋɐ] **der; ~s, ~:** pedestrian

Fußgänger-: ~brücke die foot-bridge; **~tunnel der** pedestrian subway; **~über·gang der, ~über·weg der** pedestrian crossing; **~unter·führung die** pedestrian subway; **~verkehr der** pedestrian traffic; **~zone die** pedestrian precinct

fuß-, Fuß-: ~geher der *(österr.)* pedestrian; **~gelenk das** ankle; **~gymnastik die** foot exercises *pl.*; **~hebel der** foot pedal; **~hoch 1.** *Adj.* ankle-high ‹*grass etc.*›; ankle-deep ‹*water etc.*›; **2.** *adv.* ‹*rise, lie*› ankle-deep

-füßig [-fy:sɪç] *adj.* -footed ‹*animal*›; -legged ‹*chair, stool, insect*›; -foot ‹*line*›

fuß-, Fuß-: ~kalt *Adj.* **das Zimmer ist ~kalt** the room has a cold floor; **~kettchen das** anklet; **~knöchel der** ankle bone; **~krank** *Adj.* **~krank sein/werden** have/get bad feet; **~lage die** *(Med.)* footling presentation; **~lappen der** foot-cloth; **~leiden das** foot complaint; **~leiste die** skirting-board *(Brit.)*; baseboard *(Amer.)*

fußlig *s.* **fusselig**

Füßling ['fy:slɪŋ] **der; ~s, ~e** foot *(of sock, stocking)*

Fuß-: ~marsch der march; **ein ~marsch von zwei Stunden** *(fig.)* two hours' steady walk; **~matte die** doormat; **~nagel der** toe-nail; **~note die** footnote; **~pfad der** footpath; **~pflege die** foot treatment; *(beruflich)* chiropody; **zur ~pflege gehen** go to the chiropodist's; **~pfleger der** chiropodist; **~pilz der, ~pilz·erkrankung die** athlete's foot; **~puder der** foot powder; **~punkt der a)** *(Math.)* foot [of the perpendicular]; **b)** *(Astron.)* nadir; **~raste die** foot rest; **~ring der** leg ring; **~rücken der** instep; **~sack der** foot-muff; **~schalter der** foot switch; **~schaltung die** foot gear-change control; **~schemel der** foot-stool; **~schweiß der** foot perspiration; **~sohle die** sole [of the/one's foot]; **meine ~sohlen** the soles of my feet; **~soldat der** *(veralt.)* foot soldier; **~spitze die: auf den ~spitzen gehen/stehen** walk/stand on tiptoe; **~sprung der** *(ins Wasser)* feet-first jump; **einen ~sprung machen** jump feet first; **~spur die** footprint; *(Fährte)* line of footprints; tracks *pl.*; **~stapfen der; ~s, ~:** footprint; **in jmds. ~stapfen** *(Akk.)* **treten** *(fig.)* follow in sb.'s footsteps; **~steig der a)** *(veralt.)* footpath; **b)** *(Gehsteig)* pavement *(Brit.)*; sidewalk *(Amer.)*; **~stütze die** foot rest; **~tritt der a)** kick; **jmdm./einer Sache einen ~tritt geben** *od.* **versetzen** *(fig.)* give sb./sth. a kick; **einen ~tritt bekommen** *(fig.)* get a kick in the teeth *(coll.)*; **b)** *(Auftreten)* **jmdn. an seinem ~tritt erkennen** recognize sb. by his/her step; **~truppe die** *(Milit.)* infantry; **~volk das a)** *(hist.)* footmen *pl.*; **b)** *(abwertend: Untergeordnete)* lower ranks *pl.*; dogsbodies *pl.* *(coll.)*; **~wanderung die** ramble; **~waschung die** *(kath. Rel.)* pedilavium; foot-washing; **~weg der a)** *(Gehweg, Bürgersteig)* footpath; **b)** *(Gehen zu ~)* walk; **eine Stunde/zwei Stunden ~weg** one hour's/two hours' walk; **~zehe die** *(ugs.)* toe

Fut [fʊt] **die; ~, ~en** *(vulg.) s.* **Fotze a**

Futon ['fu:tɔn] **der; ~s, ~s** futon

futsch [fʊtʃ] *Adj.; nicht attr. (salopp)* **~ sein** have gone for a burton *(Brit. sl.)*

¹Futter ['fʊtɐ] **das; ~s** *(Tiernahrung)* feed; *(für Pferde, Kühe)* fodder; **dem Vieh ~ geben** feed the cattle; **gut im ~ sein** *od.* **stehen** *(ugs.)* be well-fed

²Futter das; ~s a) *(von Kleidungsstücken)* lining; **b)** *(Bauw.)* casing; **c)** *(Techn.)* chuck

Futterage [fʊtə'ra:ʒə] **die; ~** *(ugs.)* grub *(sl.)*

Futteral [fʊtə'ra:l] **das; ~s, ~e** case

Futter-: ~beutel der nose-bag; **~getreide das** fodder cereal; forage cereal; **~klee der** red clover; **~krippe die** manger; *(fig.)* **an der ~krippe sitzen** *(ugs.)* be in clover; **an die ~krippe kommen** *(ugs.)* get on the gravy train *(coll.)*; **~mittel das** animal food

futtern *(ugs.)* **1.** *tr. V.* eat. **2.** *itr. V.* feed; **futtert nur ordentlich!** tuck in; have a good feed

¹füttern ['fʏtɐn] *tr. V.* feed; **Vieh mit etw. ~:** feed cattle on sth.; **„bitte nicht ~!"** 'please do not feed the animals'; **etw. ~:** use sth. for feed; *(für Haustiere)* use sth. for food; **einen Computer mit etw. ~** *(fig.)* feed a computer with sth.; **jmdn. mit Bonbons/Schokolade ~:** stuff sb. with sweets/chocolate

²füttern *tr. V.* **a)** *(mit ²Futter ausstatten)* line; **mit Taft/Seide gefüttert** lined with taffeta/silk; **b)** *(ausmauern, auskleiden)* case

Futter-: ~napf der bowl; **~neid der a)** *(Verhaltensf.)* jealousy [as regards food]; **b)** *(fig. ugs.: Neid)* jealousy; envy; **~pflanze die** fodder plant; forage plant; **~rübe die** mangold; mangel-wurzel; **~silo der** *od.* **das** fodder silo; **~suche die** search for food; **auf ~suche/bei der ~suche** searching for food; **~trog der** feeding trough

¹Fütterung die; ~, ~en feeding

²Fütterung die; ~, ~en *(von Kleidungsstücken)* lining

Futter·verwerter der: ein guter/schlechter ~ sein fatten up well/badly; *(fig. salopp)* ‹*person*› get fat easily/never get fat

Futur [fu'tu:ɐ] **das; ~s, ~e** *(Sprachw.)* future [tense]; **das erste/zweite ~:** future/future perfect [tense]

Futurismus der; ~: Futurism *no art.*

futuristisch a) Futurist; **b)** *(die Futurologie betreffend)* futuristic

Futurologe [futuro'lo:gə] **der; ~n, ~n** futurologist

Futurologie die; ~: futurology

Futurum [fu'tu:rʊm] **das; ~s, Futura** *(veralt.) s.* **Futur**

F-Zug ['ɛf-] **der** [long-distance] express train

G

g, G [ge:] **das; ~, ~ a)** *(Buchstabe)* g/G; **b)** *(Musik)* [key of] G; *s. auch* **a, A**

g *Abk.* **a) Gramm** g; **b) Groschen**

gab [ga:p] *1. u. 3. Pers. Sg. Prät. v.* **geben**

Gabardine ['gabardi:n] **der; ~s** *od.* **die; ~:** gabardine

Gabe ['ga:bə] **die; ~, ~n a)** *(geh.: Geschenk)* gift; present; **eine ~ Gottes** a gift of God; **b)** *(Almosen, Spende)* alms *pl.*; *(an eine Sammlung)* donation; **eine milde/fromme ~:** alms *pl.*; **um eine ~ bitten** beg for alms; **c)** *(geh.: Begabung, Talent)* gift; **die ~ haben, etw. zu tun** have the gift *or (iron.)* knack of doing sth.; **d)** *o. Pl. (Med.: Verabreichung)* administration; **e)** *(Med.: Dosis)* dose

gäbe ['gɛ:bə] *1. u. 3. Pers. Sg. Konjunktiv II v.* **geben**; *s. auch* **gang**

Gabel ['ga:bl] **die;** ~, ~**n a)** *(Eßgerät)* fork; **b)** *(Heu~, Mist~)* pitchfork; **c)** *(Telefon~)* rest; cradle; **d)** *(Fahrrad~)* fork; **e)** *(Ast~)* fork; **f)** *(Jägerspr.)* fork; **g)** *(Deichsel)* shafts *pl.*

gabel-, Gabel-: ~bissen der a) piece of pickled herring; **b)** *s.* **Appetithappen; ~bock der** *(Zool.)* pronghorn [antelope]; **~deichsel die** shafts *pl.*; **~förmig 1.** *Adj.* forked; **2.** *adv.* **sich ~förmig teilen** fork; **~frühstück das** cold buffet; fork lunch

gabeln 1. *refl. V.* fork; *(fig.: sich teilen)* divide; **ein gegabelter Ast/Stock** a forked branch/stick. **2.** *tr. V.* fork ‹*hay, straw*›

Gabel-: ~schlüssel der flat spanner; **~stapler** [-ʃta:plɐ] **der;** ~**s,** ~: fork-lift truck

Gabelung die; ~, ~**en** fork

Gabel-: ~weihe die *(Zool.)* red kite; **~zinke die** prong

Gaben·tisch der gift table *(at Christmas and on birthdays)*; **ein reich gedeckter ~:** a table overflowing with gifts

Gabun [ga'bu:n], *(österr.)* **Gabon** [ga'bo:n] **(das);** ~**s** Gabon

gack, gack ['gak 'gak] *Interj.* cluck, cluck

gackern ['gakɐn] *itr. V.* **a)** cluck; **b)** *(ugs.: kichern, lachen)* cackle

Gaffel ['gafl] **die;** ~, ~**n** *(Seemannsspr.)* gaff

Gaffel-: ~schoner der *(Seemannsspr.)* fore-and-aft schooner; **~segel das** *(Seemannsspr.)* gaff-sail

gaffen ['gafn] *itr. V. (abwertend)* gape; gawp *(coll.)*

Gaffer der; ~**s,** ~: gaper; starer

Gag [gɛk] **der;** ~**s,** ~**s a)** *(Theater, Film)* gag; **b)** *(Besonderheit)* gimmick

Gagat [ga'ga:t] **der;** ~**[e]s,** ~**e** jet

Gage ['ga:ʒə] **die;** ~, ~**n** salary; *(für einzelnen Auftritt)* fee

gähnen ['gɛ:nən] *itr. V.* **a)** yawn; **im Saal herrschte ~de Leere** the hall was totally empty; **b)** *(geh.: sich auftun)* ‹*chasm, abyss*› yawn; ‹*hole*› gape; **ein ~der Abgrund** a yawning abyss

Gala ['ga:la, *auch* 'gala] **die;** ~ **a)** *(Festkleidung)* formal dress; gala dress; **sich in ~ werfen** *(ugs. scherzh.)* put on one's best bib and tucker *(coll.)*; **b)** *(~vorstellung)* gala

Gala-: ~abend der *s.* **~vorstellung; ~diner das** formal dinner; banquet; **~empfang der** gala reception; formal reception

galaktisch [ga'laktɪʃ] *Adj.* galactic; **~er Nebel** [galactic] nebula

Galaktose [galak'to:zə] **die;** ~, ~**n** *(Biol.)* galactose

Galan [ga'la:n] **der;** ~**s,** ~**e** *(ugs. abwertend)* lover boy *(coll. derog.)*

galant [ga'lant] **1.** *Adj.* **a)** *(veralt.)* gallant; **b)** *(amourös)* amorous ‹*adventure*›; **~e Dichtung** galant poetry *(of the late 17th century)*. **2.** *adv.* gallantly

Galanterie [galantə'ri:] **die;** ~, ~**n** *(veralt.)* gallantry

Galanterie·waren *Pl. (veralt.)* fashion accessories *pl.*

Gala-: ~uniform die full-dress uniform; **~vorstellung die** gala performance

Galaxie [gala'ksi:] **die;** ~, ~**n** *(Astron.)* galaxy

Galaxis [ga'laksɪs] **die;** ~ *(Astron.)* Galaxy

Gäle ['gɛ:lə] **der;** ~**n,** ~**n** Gael

Galeere [ga'le:rə] **die;** ~, ~**n** galley

Galeeren-: ~sklave der galley slave; **~sträfling der** galley slave

Galeone [gale'o:nə] **die;** ~, ~**n** *(hist.)* galleon

Galerie [galə'ri:] **die;** ~, ~**n a)** gallery; **b)** *(scherzh.: beträchtliche Anzahl)* **eine [ganze] ~ von etw.** a [whole] array of sth.; **c)** *(bes. österr., schweiz.: Tunnel)* tunnel; **d)** *(Teppich)* runner

Galerist [galə'rɪst] **der;** ~**en,** ~**en** gallery-owner

Galgen ['galgn̩] **der a)** gallows *sing.*; gibbet; **jmdn. zum [Tode am] ~ verurteilen** condemn sb. to [death on] the gallows; **jmdn. an den ~ bringen** *(ugs.)* bring sb. to the gallows; **am ~ enden** end up on the gallows; **b)** *(Mikrophon~)* boom

Galgen-: ~frist die reprieve; **~humor der** gallows humour; **~strick der, ~vogel der** *(ugs. abwertend)* rogue

Galicien [ga'li:tsi̯ən] **(das);** ~**s** Galicia *(in Spain)*

Galiläa [gali'lɛ:a] **(das);** ~**s** Galilee

Galiläer [gali'lɛ:ɐ] **(der);** ~**s,** ~: Galilean

Galilei [gali'le:i] **(der)** Galileo

Galions·figur [ga'li̯o:ns-] **die** figurehead

gälisch ['gɛ:lɪʃ] *Adj.* Gaelic

Galizien [ga'li:tsi̯ən] **(das);** ~**s** Galicia *(in E. Europe)*

Gall·apfel der oak-apple; gall

[1]**Galle** ['galə] **die;** ~, ~**n a)** *(Gallenblase)* gall[-bladder]; **b)** *(Sekret) (bei Tieren)* gall; *(bei Menschen)* bile; **bitter wie ~:** extremely bitter; **mir lief die ~ über** *od.* **kam die ~ hoch** *(fig.)* my blood boiled; **seine ~ verspritzen** *(fig.)* give bitter vent to one's feelings

[2]**Galle die;** ~, ~**n** *(Bot.)* gall

galle·bitter *Adj.* extremely bitter

Gallen-: ~blase die gall-bladder; **~gang der;** *meist Pl.* bile duct; **~kolik die** biliary colic; **~leiden das** gall-bladder complaint; **~stein der** gallstone; **~wege** *Pl.* biliary tract *sing.*; bile ducts

Gallert ['galɐt] **das;** ~**[e]s** jelly

gallert·artig *Adj.* jelly-like

Gallerte [ga'lɛrtə] **die;** ~, ~**n** *s.* **Gallert**

Gallien ['gali̯ən] **(das);** ~**s** Gaul

Gallier ['gali̯ɐ] **der;** ~**s,** ~: Gaul

gallig *Adj.* **a)** *(bitter)* **einen ~en Geschmack haben, ~ schmecken** taste of bile; **b)** *(verbittert)* caustic ‹*remark, humour, person*›

Gallions·figur die *s.* **Galionsfigur**

gallisch *Adj.* Gallic

Gallium ['gali̯ʊm] **das;** ~**s** *(Chemie)* gallium

Gallizismus [gali'tsɪsmʊs] **der;** ~, **Gallizismen** Gallicism

Gallone [ga'lo:nə] **die;** ~, ~**n** gallon

Gall·wespe die *(Zool.)* gall-wasp

Galopp [ga'lɔp] **der;** ~**s,** ~**s** *od.* ~**e a)** *(Gangart)* gallop; **im ~:** at a gallop; **in ~ fallen** break into a gallop; **in vollem** *od.* **gestrecktem ~:** at full gallop; **etw. im ~ machen** *(fig. ugs.)* race through sth.; **b)** *(Tanz)* galop

Galopp·bahn die *(Pferdesport)* race-track; racecourse

Galopper der; ~**s,** ~ *(Pferd)* racehorse; *(Reiter)* jockey

galoppieren *itr. V.; meist mit sein* gallop; **die ~de Schwindsucht/Inflation** galloping consumption/inflation

Galopp-: ~rennbahn die *s.* **Galoppbahn; ~rennen das** *(Pferdesport)* race

Galosche [ga'lɔʃə] **die;** ~, ~**n** galosh

galt [galt] *1. u. 3. Pers. Sg. Prät. v.* **gelten**

galvanisch [gal'va:nɪʃ] *Adj.* galvanic

Galvaniseur [galvani'zø:ɐ̯] **der;** ~**s,** ~**e** electroplater

galvanisieren *tr. V.* electroplate

Galvano [gal'va:no] **das;** ~**s,** ~**s** *(graph. Technik)* electro[type]

Galvano-: ~meter das *(Technik)* galvanometer; **~plastik die;** *o. Pl.* **a)** electroforming; **b)** *(Druckw.)* electrotyping; **~skop das;** ~**s,** ~**e** *(Technik)* galvanoscope

Gamasche [ga'maʃə] **die;** ~, ~**n** gaiter; *(bis zum Knöchel reichend)* spat

Gamaschen·hose die [pair of] leggings *pl.*

Gambe ['gambə] **die;** ~, ~**n** *(Musik)* viola da gamba

Gambia ['gambi̯a] **(das);** ~**s** the Gambia

Gambit [gam'bɪt] **das;** ~**s,** ~**s** *(Schach)* gambit

Gamelan ['ga:məlan], **Gamelang** ['ga:məlaŋ] **das;** ~**s,** ~**s** *(Musik)* gamelan

Gamet [ga'me:t] **der;** ~**en,** ~**en** *(Biol.)* gamete

Gamma ['gama] **das;** ~**[s],** ~**s** gamma

Gamma-: ~funktion die *(Math.)* gamma function; **~strahlen** *Pl. (Physik, Med.)* gamma rays

Gammel ['gaml] **der;** ~**s** *(ugs.)* junk *(coll.)*

Gammelei die; ~ *(ugs.)* drifting around; bumming around *(Amer. coll.)*

gammelig ['gam(ə)lɪç] *Adj. (ugs.)* **a)** *(ungenießbar)* bad; rotten; **der Fisch/das Fleisch/der Käse ist ~:** the fish/meat/cheese has gone off; **b)** *(unordentlich)* scruffy; **~ aussehen/herumlaufen** look scruffy/go round looking scruffy

Gammel-Look der scruffy *or* untidy look; **sie erschien im ~:** she appeared dressed as a drop-out *(coll.)*

gammeln ['gamln̩] *itr. V.* **a)** *(ugs.) (verderben)* go bad; go off; **b)** *(nichts tun)* loaf around; bum around *(Amer. coll.)*

Gammler ['gamlɐ] **der;** ~**s,** ~ *(ugs.)* drop-out *(coll.)*

gammlig *s.* **gammelig**

Gams [gams] **die;** ~, ~**en** *(Jägerspr., südd.) s.* **Gemse**

Gams·bart der *tuft of chamois hair used as a hat decoration*

gang [gaŋ] *in* **~ und gäbe sein** be quite usual; be the usual *or* accepted thing

[1]**Gang** [gaŋ] **der;** ~**[e]s, Gänge** ['gɛŋə] **a)** *(Gehweise)* walk; gait; **jmdn. am ~ erkennen** recognise sb. by the way he/she walks; **gemessenen ~es einherschreiten** *(geh.)* walk with a measured step; **b)** *(zu einem Ort)* **einen ~ in die Stadt machen** go to town; **sein erster ~ führte ihn in die Kneipe** the first place he went to was the pub; **jmdn. auf seinem letzten ~ begleiten** *(fig. geh.)* accompany sb. to his/her last *or* final resting-place; **einen schweren ~ tun** *od.* **gehen [müssen]** *(fig.)* [have to] do a difficult thing; **c)** *(Besorgung)* **ich habe noch einige Gänge zu machen** I still have some errands to do; **jmdm. einen ~ abnehmen** do an errand for sb.; **d)** *o. Pl. (Bewegung)* running; **die Maschine hatte einen ruhigen ~:** the machine ran quietly; **etw. in ~ bringen** *od.* **setzen** get sth. going; **etw. in ~ halten** keep sth. going; **in ~ sein** be going; **die Maschine ist in ~:** the machine is running; **in ~ kommen** get going; get off the ground; **e)** *o. Pl. (Verlauf)* course; **der ~ der Ereignisse/Verhandlungen** the course of events/negotiations; **seinen [gewohnten] ~ gehen** go on as usual; **im ~[e] sein** be in progress; **gegen ihn ist etwas im ~[e]** *(ugs.)* moves are being made against him; **f)** *(Technik)* gear; **den ersten ~ einlegen** engage first gear; **in den ersten ~ [zurück]schalten** change [down] into first gear; **einen ~ zulegen** *(fig. ugs.)* get a move on *(coll.)*; **einen ~ zurückschalten** *(fig. ugs.)* take things a bit easier; **g)** *(Flur) (in Zügen, Gebäuden usw.)* corridor; *(Verbindungs~)* passage[-way]; *(im Theater, Kino, Flugzeug)* aisle; **auf dem ~:** in the corridor/hall [way]; **h)** *(unterirdisch)* tunnel; passage[way]; *(im Bergwerk)* gallery; *(eines Tierbaus)* tunnel; *(von Insekten)* gallery; tunnel; **i)** *(Kochk.)* course; **j)** *(Fechten)* bout; **einen ~ ausfechten** *od.* **austragen** fight a bout; **k)** *(Geol.)* vein; seam; **l)** *(Technik) s.* **Gewindegang**

[2]**Gang** [gɛŋ] **die;** ~, ~**s** *(Bande)* gang

Gang·art die walk; way of walking; gait; *(eines Pferdes)* gait; **eine schnellere ~ anschlagen** step up the pace; *(Pferdesport)* increase to a faster pace *or* gait; **eine langsamere ~ einlegen** *(fig.)* take things more easily

gangbar *Adj.* passable; **nicht ~:** impassable; **jmdm. einen ~en Weg zeigen** *(fig.)* show sb. a feasible *or* practicable way

Gängel·band ['gɛŋəl-] **das** *in* **jmdn. am ~ führen** keep sb. in leading-reins; **am ~ gehen** be in leading reins

Gängelei die; ~, ~en *(ugs.)* spoon-feeding; **sie war seine ~ leid** she was tired of being treated like a child by him

gängeln ['gɛŋl̩n] *tr. V. (ugs.)* **jmdn. ~:** boss sb. around; tell sb. what to do

gang·genau *Adj.* accurate

Gang·genauigkeit die accuracy

gängig ['gɛŋɪç] *Adj.* **a)** *(üblich)* common; *(aktuell)* current; **b)** *(leicht verkäuflich)* popular; in demand *postpos.*; **c)** *(im Umlauf)* current; **d)** *(beweglich)* **[wieder] ~ machen** get ⟨*mechanism*⟩ working [again]; loosen [again] ⟨*lock, screw, etc.*⟩

Ganglien·zelle ['gaŋ(g)liən-] **die** *(Med.)* ganglion cell

Ganglion ['gaŋ(g)liɔn] **das**; ~s, **Ganglien** ['gaŋ(g)liən] *(Med.)* ganglion

Gangrän [gaŋ'grɛ:n] **die**; ~, ~en *od.* **das**; ~s, ~e *(Med.)* gangrene

Gang·schaltung die *(Technik)* gear system; *(Art)* gear-change; **hat dein Auto Automatik oder ~?** has your car got an automatic or manual gearbox?; **ein Fahrrad mit ~:** a bicycle with gears

Gangster ['gɛŋstɐ] **der**; ~s, ~ *(abwertend)* gangster

Gangster-: ~**bande die** gang [of criminals]; ~**boß der** *(ugs.)* gang boss; ~**braut die** gangster's moll *(coll.)*; ~**methoden** *Pl. (abwertend)* gangster tactics; ~**stück das** piece of villainy

Gangstertum das; ~s gangsterism

Gangway ['gæŋwei] **die**; ~, ~s gangway

Ganove [ga'no:və] **der**; ~n, ~n *(ugs. abwertend)* crook *(coll.)*

Gans [gans] **die**; ~, **Gänse** ['gɛnzə] **a)** goose; **b)** *(Braten)* [roast] goose; **c)** *(abwertend: weibliche Person)* **eine [dumme/alberne/blöde] ~:** a silly goose

Gänschen ['gɛnsçən] **das**; ~s, ~ **a)** *(junge Gans)* gosling; **b)** *(kleine Gans, naives Mädchen)* little goose

Gänse-: ~**blümchen das** daisy; ~**braten der** roast goose; ~**brust die** *(Kochk.)* breast of goose; ~**ei das** goose-egg; ~**feder die** goose-feather; goose-quill; ~**fett das** goose-fat; ~**füßchen das**; *meist Pl. (ugs.) s.* **Anführungszeichen**; ~**geier der** griffon vulture; ~**haut die** *(fig.)* goose-flesh; goose pimples *pl.*; **eine ~haut bekommen** *od.* **kriegen** get goose-flesh *or* goose-pimples; **ihm läuft eine ~haut über den Rücken** a cold shiver runs down his spine; ~**junge das** gosling; ~**kiel der** goose-quill; ~**klein das**; ~s *(Kochk.)* braised trimmings of goose; gänseklein; ~**leber die** goose-liver; ~**leber·pastete die** pâté de foie gras; ~**marsch** *in* **im ~marsch** in single *or* Indian file

Ganser ['ganzɐ] **der**; ~s, ~ *(südd., österr.)*, **Gänserich** ['gɛnzərıç] **der**; ~s, ~e gander

Gänse-: ~**schmalz das** goose dripping; ~**wein der**; *o. Pl. (ugs. scherzh.)* water; Adam's ale *or* wine *(coll. joc.)*

Ganter ['gantɐ] **der**; ~s, ~ *(nordd.) s.* **Gänserich**

ganz [gants] **1.** *Adj.* **a)** *nicht präd. (gesamt)* whole; entire; **den ~en Tag/das ~e Jahr** all day/year; **die ~e Welt/Stadt** the whole world/town; ~ **Europa/Afrika** the whole of Europe/Africa; **wir fuhren durch ~ Frankreich** we travelled all over France; **diese Arbeit fordert den ~en Mann** this work requires all one's efforts; ~**e Arbeit leisten** do a complete *or* proper job; **die ~e Geschichte** *od.* **Sache** *(ugs.)* the whole story *or* business; **b)** *nicht präd. (ugs.: alle)* **die ~en Kinder/Leute/Gläser** *usw.* all the children/people/glasses *etc.*; **die ~e Stadt/Straße** everybody in the town/street; **c)** *nicht präd. (vollständig)* whole; ~**e Zahlen** whole numbers; **eine ~e Note** *(Musik)* a semibreve *(Brit.)*; a whole note *(Amer.)*; **im ~en sechs Tage/drei Jahre** six days/three years in all *or* altogether; **im ~en ist seine Leistung gut** on the whole *or* all in all his performance is good; **der ~e Shakespeare** *(ugs.)* the whole of Shakespeare *(coll.)*; **d)** *nicht präd. (ugs.: ziemlich [viel])* **eine ~e Menge/ein ~er Haufen** quite a lot/quite a pile; ~**e Nächte/Tage** whole nights/days; **e)** *(ugs.: unversehrt)* intact; **etw. wieder ~ machen** mend sth.; **f)** *nicht präd. (ugs.: nur)* all of; ~**e 14 Jahre alt/10 Mark** all of fourteen [years old]/ten marks; **mit ~en drei Mann kann ich die Arbeit unmöglich schaffen** with only three men I can't possibly get the work done; **g)** *(richtig)* **ein ~er Mann** a real man; *s. auch* **groß 1k; Herz b. 2.** *adv.* **a)** *(vollkommen)* quite; **etw. ~ Blödes sagen** say sth. really stupid; **das ist mir ~ egal** it's all the same to me; I don't care; **etw. ~ vergessen** completely *or* quite forget sth.; **du bist ja ~ naß!** you're all wet!; **etwas ~ anderes** something quite different; **etw. ~ allein tun** *od.* **machen** do sth. entirely on one's own; **nicht ~:** not quite; ~ **deiner Meinung!** I quite agree [with you]; ~ **besonders** especially; **er hat sich ~ besonders viel Mühe gegeben** he took particular trouble; ~ **wie Sie wollen** just as you like; **sie ist ~ die Mutter/der Vater** she's the image of *or* just like her mother/father; **sie ist ~ Dame** she ist quite the lady; ~ **und gar** totally; utterly; **es ist ~ und gar nicht wahr** it is utterly *or* totally untrue; **etw. ~ oder gar nicht machen** do sth. properly or not at all; **ein Buch ~ lesen** read a book from cover to cover *or* all the way through; **b)** *(sehr, ziemlich)* quite; **es ist mir ~ recht** it's quite all right with me; ~ **gut/nett** quite good/nice; *s. auch* **Ohr**

Ganze das; *adj. Dekl.* **a)** *(Einheit)* whole; **das ~ im Auge behalten** keep looking at the whole; **etw. als ~s betrachten** see sth. as a whole; **b)** *(alles)* **das ~:** the whole thing; **das ~ gefällt mir gar nicht** I don't like anything about it; **aufs ~ gehen** *(ugs.)* go the whole hog *(coll.)*; **es geht ums ~:** everything's at stake

Gänze ['gɛntsə] *in* **in seiner/ihrer ~** *(geh.)* in its/their entirety; **zur ~** *(bes. österr.)* entirely; completely

Ganzheit die; ~, ~en entirety; *(Einheit)* unity; **etw. in seiner ~ erfassen** grasp sth. in its entirety

ganzheitlich *Adj. (Päd.)* integrated

Ganzheits-: ~**medizin die**; *o. Pl.* holistic medicine; ~**methode die** *(Päd.)* 'look and say' method; ~**psychologie die** 'Ganzheit' psychology; holism; ~**unterricht der** *(Päd.)* integrated teaching

ganz·jährig 1. *Adj.*; *nicht präd.* **die ~e Trockenperiode** the dry period lasting all year. **2.** *adv.* ~ **geöffnet** open throughout the year *or* all the year round

Ganz·leder das *(Buchw.)* **in ~ [gebunden]** bound in [full] leather

Ganzleder·band der; *Pl.* **-bände** *(Buchw.)* [full-]leather-bound volume

ganz·leinen *Adj.* **a)** *(Textilw.)* pure linen; **b)** *(Buchw.)* **ein ~er Einband** a cloth binding

Ganz·leinen·band der; *Pl.* **-bände** *(Buchw.)* cloth-bound book

gänzlich ['gɛntslıç] **1.** *Adv.* completely; entirely; ~ **unangebracht** quite inappropriate *or* out of place. **2.** *Adj.* complete; total

Ganz·massage die whole-body massage

ganz-, Ganz-: ~**sache die** *(Postw., Philat.)* entire; ~**seitig 1.** *Adj.* whole-page; **2.** *adv.* ~**seitig inserieren** *(einmal)* take a whole-page advertisement; *(auf Dauer)* use whole-page advertising; ~**tägig 1.** *Adj.*; *nicht präd.* all-day; **eine ~tägige Arbeit** a full-time job; **2.** *adv.* all day

ganz·tags *Adv.* ~ **arbeiten** work full-time

Ganztags-: ~**beschäftigung die**; *o. Pl.* full-time job; ~**schule die** all-day school; *(System)* all-day schooling *no art.*

Ganz·wort·methode die; *o. Pl. (Päd.)* 'look and say' method

[1]**gar** [ga:ɐ̯] *Adj.* **a)** cooked; done *pred.*; **etw. ist ~/erst halb ~:** sth. is cooked *or* done/only half-cooked *or* half-done; **etw. ~ kochen** cook sth. [until it is done]; **b)** *(Landw.)* ready for cultivation *postpos.*; **der Kompost ist ~:** the compost is ready for use

[2]**gar** *Partikel* **a)** *(überhaupt)* ~ **nicht [wahr]** not [true] at all; **sie konnte ~ nicht anders handeln** there was nothing else at all that she could do; ~ **nicht so übel** not bad at all; **das habe ich ~ nicht gewußt** I had no idea that that was so; ~ **nichts** nothing at all *or* whatsoever; **ich habe ~ keinen Hunger** I'm not at all *or* not in the least hungry; ~ **niemand** *od.* **keiner** nobody at all *or* whatsoever; ~ **keines** not a single one; ~ **kein Geld** no money at all; **b)** *(südd., österr., schweiz.: verstärkend)* ~ **zu** only too; **es waren ~ zu viele Leute da** there were just too many people there; **er wäre ~ zu gern gekommen** he would so much have liked to come; ~ **so** so very; **sei doch nicht ~ so stur!** don't be so [damned] stubborn; **c)** *(geh.: sogar)* even; **die Zeitungen setzten sich ~ für den Attentäter ein** the papers even came out in support of the assassin; **ich glaube ~, sie weint** I do believe she's crying; **d)** *(geh. veralt.: erst)* **er ist unangenehm genug, und ~ sein Bruder!** he's unpleasant enough, and as for his brother!; **e)** *(veralt.: sehr)* very; **du bist ~ früh gekommen** you have indeed come early; ~ **mancher** many a one *or* person; *s. auch* **ganz 2a**

Garage [ga'ra:ʒə] **die**; ~, ~n garage

Garagen-: ~**einfahrt die** garage entrance; ~**wagen der** garaged car

garagieren *tr. V. (österr., schweiz.)* park

Garant [ga'rant] **der**; ~en, ~en guarantor

Garantie [garan'ti:] **die**; ~, ~n **a)** *(Gewähr)* guarantee; **eine ~ für etw.** a guarantee of sth.; **für etw. keine ~ übernehmen** not guarantee sth.; **wir haben unter ~ nicht genug Geld** *(ugs.)* we're dead certain not to have enough money *(coll.)*; **b)** *(Kaufmannsspr.)* guarantee; warranty; **die ~ auf** *od.* **für das Auto ist abgelaufen** the guarantee on the car has run out; **eine ~ auf etw.** *(Akk.)* **geben** guarantee sth.; **für** *od.* **auf etw.** *(Akk.)* **ein Jahr ~ erhalten** get a one year guarantee on sth.; **c)** *(Sicherheit)* guarantee; surety

Garantie-: ~**anspruch der** right to claim under [the] guarantee; ~**frist die** guarantee period; ~**lohn der** guaranteed minimum wage

garantieren 1. *tr. V.* guarantee; **jmdm. etw. ~:** guarantee sb. sth. **2.** *itr. V.* **für etw. ~:** guarantee sth.; **ich kann für den Hund nicht ~:** I can't say for sure what the dog will do

garantiert *Adv. (ugs.)* **wir kommen ~ zu spät** we're dead certain to arrive late *(coll.)*

Garantie·schein der guarantee [certificate]

Garaus ['ga:ɐ̯laus] *in* **jmdm. den ~ machen** do sb. in *(coll.)*; **dem Ungeziefer/Unkraut den ~ machen** get rid of the vermin/weeds; **einem Gerücht den ~ machen** scotch a rumour

[1]**Garbe** ['garbə] **die**; ~, ~n **a)** *(Getreide~)* sheaf; **b)** *(Geschoß~)* burst of fire; **eine ~ abfeuern** fire a burst

[2]**Garbe die**; ~, ~n *s.* **Schafgarbe**

Gär·bottich der fermenter

Garçonnière die; ~, ~n *(österr.)* bed-sitter

Garde ['gardə] **die**; ~, ~n **a)** *(Leib~)* guard; **b)** *(Gruppe)* team; **von der alten ~ sein** *(ugs.)* be one of the old guard; **c)** *(Milit.: Elitetruppe)* the Guards *pl.*; **bei der ~:** in the Guards

Garde·maß das; *o. Pl.* **a)** *(hist.) minimum height for belonging to the Prussian Guards*; **b)** *(scherzh.)* ~ **haben** be as tall as a tree; **mit deinem ~ solltest du Basketballspieler werden** with your height you ought to be a basketball player

Gardenie [gar'de:niə] **die**; ~, ~n *(Bot.)* gardenia

Garde·regiment das Guards regiment
Garderobe [gardə'ro:bə] **die; ~, ~n a)** *o. Pl. (Oberbekleidung)* wardrobe; clothes *pl.;* **für diesen Anlaß fehlt ihm die passende ~:** he hasn't got suitable clothes for this occasion; **für ~ wird nicht gehaftet!** clothes are left at the owner's risk; **b)** *(Flur~)* coat-rack; **etw. an die ~ hängen** hang sth. up on the coat rack; **c)** *(Raum)* clothes cupboard *or (Amer.)* closet; **d)** *(im Theater o. ä.)* cloakroom; checkroom *(Amer.)*; **etw. an der ~ abgeben** hand sth. in at the cloakroom; **e)** *(Ankleideraum)* dressing-room
Garderoben-: ~frau die cloakroom *or (Amer.)* checkroom attendant; **~marke die** cloakroom *or (Amer.)* checkroom ticket; **~spiegel der** hall mirror; **~ständer der** coat-stand
Garderobier [gardəro'bi̯e:] **der; ~s, ~s** dresser
Garderobiere [gardəro'bi̯e:rə] **die; ~, ~n a)** dresser; **b)** *(veralt.) s.* **Garderobenfrau**
Gardine [gar'di:nə] **die; ~, ~n a)** net curtain; **b)** *(landsch., veralt.)* curtain; *s. auch* **schwedisch**
Gardinen-: ~leiste die curtain rail; **~predigt die** *(ugs.)* telling-off *(coll.)*; *(einer Ehefrau zu ihrem Mann)* curtain lecture; **jmdm. eine ~predigt halten** give sb. a [good] telling-off *(coll.)*/a curtain lecture; **~ring der** curtain ring; **~röllchen das** curtain runner; **~stange die** curtain rail; **~stoff der** curtain material
Gardist der; ~en, ~en guardsman
garen ['ga:rən] *tr., itr. V.* cook; **Fleisch/Gemüse ~ [lassen]** cook meat/vegetables
gären ['gɛ:rən] **1.** *regelm. (auch unr.) itr. V.* ferment; *(fig.)* seethe; **es gärt in ihm/der Masse** he/the crowd is seething [with anger]/afire [with hatred/passion]. **2.** *regelm. (auch unr.) tr. V.* ferment ‹*beer, tobacco*›
Gär·futter das *(Landw.)* silage *no pl.*
gar-, Gar-: ~gekocht *Adj.; nicht präd.* cooked; **~küche die** snack-bar
Gär·mittel das ferment; fermenting agent
Garn [garn] **das; ~[e]s, ~e a)** *(Faden)* thread; *(zum Weben, Stricken)* yarn; *(Näh~)* cotton; **b)** *(Seew.)* yarn; **c)** *(Seemannsspr.: Geschichte) in* **[s]ein ~ spinnen** spin a yarn; **d)** *(Jagdw., Fischereiw.: Netz)* net; **jmdm. ins ~ gehen** *(fig.)* fall *or* walk into sb.'s trap
Garnele [gar'ne:lə] **die; ~, ~n** shrimp
Gar·nichts der *od.* **das; ~, ~e** *(abwertend)* [absolute] nonentity
garnieren [gar'ni:rən] *tr. V.* **a)** *(schmücken)* decorate (*mit* with); **b)** *(Gastr.)* garnish
Garnierung die; ~, ~en a) garnish; **b)** *(Vorgang)* garnishing
Garnison [garni'zo:n] **die; ~, ~en** garrison
Garnison·stadt die garrison town
Garnitur [garni'tu:ɐ̯] **die; ~, ~en a)** *(zusammengehörige Stücke)* set; *(Wäsche)* set of [matching] underwear; *(Schreibtisch~)* desk-set; *(Möbel)* suite; **eine zwei-/dreiteilige ~:** a two-piece/three-piece suite; **b)** *(ugs.)* **die erste/zweite ~:** the first/second-rate people *pl.;* **zur ersten/zweiten ~ gehören, erste/zweite ~ sein** be first-/second-rate; **c)** *(Gastr.)* garnishing; garniture
Garn-: ~knäuel das *od.* **der** ball of thread; *(zum Weben)* ball of yarn; **~rolle die** reel; bobbin; *(von Nähgarn)* cotton reel; **~spule die** spool
Gär·prozeß der *s.* **Gärungsprozeß**
Garrotte [ga'rɔtə] **die; ~, ~n** garrotte
garstig ['garstɪç] *Adj.* **a)** *(boshaft)* nasty (**zu** to); bad ‹*behaviour*›; nasty, naughty, *(coll.)* horrid ‹*child*›; **b)** *(abscheulich)* horrible; nasty
Garstigkeit die; ~, ~en a) *o. Pl.* nastiness; *(eines Kindes)* naughtiness, *(coll.)* horridness; **b)** *(Handlung)* piece of nastiness; **~en** nastiness *sing.;* horridness *sing. (coll.)*; **c)** *(Äußerung)* nasty *or (coll.)* horrid remark

Gärtchen ['gɛrtçən] **das; ~s, ~:** little garden
Garten ['gartn̩] **der; ~s, Gärten** ['gɛrtn̩] garden; **ein [kleines] Stück ~:** a [small] bit of garden; **der ~ Eden** the Garden of Eden; **quer durch den ~** *(ugs.: verschiedene Sorten Gemüse)* all sorts of different vegetables; *(oft spöttisch: in bunter Vielfalt)* all sorts; a real mixture; *s. auch* **botanisch; zoologisch**
Garten-: ~anlage die garden; *(öffentlich)* park; gardens *pl.;* **~arbeit die** gardening; **~architekt der** landscape gardener; **~bank die;** *Pl.* **~bänke** garden seat
Garten·bau der; *o. Pl.* horticulture
Gartenbau-: ~betrieb der market garden; **~ingenieur der** horticulturist
Garten-: ~blume die garden flower; **~erde die** garden mould; **~fest das** garden party; **~freund der** amateur gardener; **~gerät das** garden tool; **~gestaltung die** landscaping; **~haus das a)** *(Haus im ~)* summer-house; garden house; **b)** *(Hinterhaus) dwelling situated at or forming the rear of a house and having its own garden;* **wir wohnen in der Goethestr. 10, im ~haus** we live at 10, Goethestrasse, at the back; **~hecke die** garden hedge; **~land das;** *o. Pl.* gardening land; **~laube die** summer-house; garden house; **~lokal das** beer garden; *(Restaurant)* open-air café; **~mauer die** garden wall; **~möbel das** piece of garden furniture; **~möbel** *Pl.* garden furniture *sing.;* **~party die** *s.* **~fest; ~schau die** horticultural show; **~schirm der** sunshade; **~schlauch der** garden hose; **~stadt die** garden city; **~stuhl der** garden chair; **~wirtschaft die** *s.* **~lokal; ~zaun der** garden fence; **~zwerg der a)** garden gnome; **b)** *(salopp abwertend)* little runt
Gärtner ['gɛrtnɐ] **der; ~s, ~:** gardener
Gärtnerei die; ~, ~en a) nursery; **b)** *o. Pl. (Gartenarbeit)* gardening
Gärtnerin die; ~, ~nen gardener
Gärtnerin·art die *in* **Schweinefleisch** *usw.* **nach ~** *(Gastr.)* pork *etc.* jardinière
gärtnerisch 1. *Adj.* **der ~e Pflanzenbau** the growing of garden plants; **~er Betrieb** nursery. **2.** *adv.* **sich gern ~ betätigen** enjoy gardening
Gärung die; ~, ~en a) fermentation; **etw. zur ~ ansetzen** start sth. fermenting; **b)** *(Erregung)* ferment; **in ~ sein** be in [a state of] ferment
Gärungs-: ~mittel das *s.* **Gärmittel; ~prozeß der** fermentation process
Gar·zeit die *(Kochk.)* cooking time
Gas [ga:s] **das; ~es, ~e a)** gas; **jmdn. mit ~ vergiften** gas sb.; **mit ~ heizen** have gas heating; **mit ~ kochen** cook with gas; use gas for cooking; **jmdm. das ~ abdrehen** *(fig. salopp)* force sb. out of business; **etw. aufs ~ stellen** put sth. on the cooker *or* the gas; **b)** *(Treibstoff)* petrol *(Brit.)*; gasoline *(Amer.)*; gas *(Amer. coll.)*; **ohne ~ den Berg hinunterfahren** drive down the mountain without using any petrol *etc.;* **~ wegnehmen** decelerate; take one's foot off the accelerator; **~ geben** accelerate; put one's foot down *(coll.)*; *(ugs. fig.: schneller gehen)* step on it *(coll.)*; **c)** *(ugs.: ~pedal)* accelerator; gas pedal *(Amer.)*; **aufs ~ treten** put one's foot down *(coll.)*; **vom ~ gehen** take one's foot off the accelerator
gas-, Gas-: ~ableser der [gas-]meter reader; gas man; **~anschluß der** gas connection; *(~hahn)* gas tap; **~anstalt die** *s.* **~werk; ~anzünder der** gas-lighter; **~austausch der** *(Biol., Med.)* gaseous exchange; **~automat der** coin-in-the-slot gas meter; **~bade·ofen der** gas water-heater; **~behälter der** gasholder; gasometer; **~beheizt** *Adj.* gas-heated; **ein ~beheizter Backofen** a gas oven; **~beleuchtung die** gas lighting; **~beton der** *(Bauw.)* cellular *or* aerated concrete; **~bombe die** gas bomb; **~brand der** *(Med.)* gas gangrene; **~brenner der** gas burner; **~dicht** *Adj.* gas-tight; **~druck der** gas pressure; **~entladung die** *(Physik)* gas discharge; **~entwicklung die** formation of gas; **~explosion die** gas explosion; **~fabrik die** gasworks *sing.;* **~feuerung die** gas-firing; **~feuerzeug das** gas lighter; **~flamme die** gas flame; **~flasche die** gas-cylinder; *(für einen Herd, Ofen)* gas bottle; gas container; **~förmig** *Adj.* gaseous; **~fuß der** *(ugs.)* **einen nervösen ~fuß haben** rev up impatiently at the lights *(coll.)*; **~gemisch das** mixture of gases; **~gerät das** gas appliance; **~geruch der** smell of gas; **~hahn der** gas tap; **den ~hahn aufdrehen** *(ugs. verhüll.)* end it all *(coll. euphem.)*; **jmdm. den ~hahn abdrehen** *(salopp)* force sb. out of business; **~hebel der** accelerator pedal; gas pedal *(Amer.)*; **~heizung die** gas heating; **~herd der** gas cooker; **~hülle die** atmosphere; **~kammer die** gas chamber; **~kessel der** gas holder; gasometer; **~kocher der** camping stove; **~koks der** gas coke; **~krieg der** gas war; *(Kriegführung)* gas warfare; **~lampe, ~laterne die** gas lamp; **~leitung die** gas pipe; *(Hauptrohr)* gas main; **~licht das** gaslight; **~-Luft-Gemisch das** *(Kfz-W.)* fuel-and-air mixture; **~mann der** *(ugs.)* gas man; **~maske die** gas mask; **~ofen der** gas heater
Gasolin [gazo'li:n] **das; ~s** gasoline
Gasometer [gazo'me:tɐ] **der** *(veralt.)* gasometer; gasholder
Gas-: ~pedal das accelerator [pedal]; gas pedal *(Amer.)*; **~pistole die** pistol that fires gas cartridges; **~rechnung die** gas bill; **~rohr das** gas pipe; *(Hauptrohr)* gas main; **~schlauch der** gas hose
Gasse ['gasə] **die; ~, ~n a)** lane; narrow street; *(österr.)* street; **auf der ~:** in the lane *or* narrow street; **die Salzburger Altstadt ist von kleinen, engen ~n durchzogen** the old part of Salzburg is a maze of little, narrow streets and alley-ways *or* passages; **[für jmdn.] eine ~ bilden** *(fig.)* make way *or* clear a path [for sb.]; **wir machten eine ~ für das Brautpaar** *(fig.)* we lined up to make a passage for the bride and groom; **jmdm./sich eine ~ durch die Menge bahnen** *(fig.)* clear a path for sb./force one's way through the crowd; **b)** *(Fußball)* opening; **eine ~ öffnen** make an opening; **c)** *(Rugby)* line-out; **d)** *(Kegeln)* **in die rechte/linke ~ zielen/werfen** *aim/throw at the right-hand/left-hand gap between the lines of skittles*
gassen-, Gassen-: ~hauer der *(ugs.)* popular song; **~junge der** *(abwertend)* street urchin; **~seitig** *Adj. (österr.)* ‹*room etc.*› facing the street; **~seitig sein** face the street; **~wohnung die** *(österr.)* flat facing the street; **~wort das;** *Pl.* **~wörter** coarse word; **er benutzt die ordinärsten ~wörter** he uses the most vulgar gutter language
Gassi ['gasi] *in* **~ gehen** *(ugs.)* go walkies *(Brit. coll.)*
[1]**Gast** [gast] **der; ~[e]s, Gäste** ['gɛstə] **a)** *(auch zahlender ~)* guest; **ungebetene Gäste** *(auch fig.)* uninvited guests; *(bei einer Party usw. auch)* gatecrashers; **das Glück war ein seltener ~ bei ihr** *(fig.)* she hadn't known much happiness; **bei jmdm. zu ~ sein** be sb.'s guest/guests; **jmdn. zu ~ haben** have sb. as one's guest/guests; **jmdn. zu ~ laden** *od.* **bitten** *(geh.)* request the pleasure of sb.'s company; **b)** *(Besucher eines Lokals)* patron; **c)** *(Besucher)* visitor; **ein ~ in einem Land** a visitor to a country; **als ~ im Studio war X** the studio guest was X; **d)** *(Künstler[in])* guest star
[2]**Gast der; ~[e]s, ~en** *od.* **Gäste** *(Seemannsspr.)* man; *(Boots~)* crewman; *(Signal~)* signalman
Gas·tanker der gas tanker
Gast-: ~arbeiter der immigrant *or* foreign

or guest worker; **~bett das** *(im Hotel)* bed; *(im Haus)* spare bed; **~dozent der** *(Hochschulw.)* visiting lecturer
Gäste-: ~buch das guest book; **~handtuch das** guest-towel; **~haus das** guest-house; **~zimmer das** *(privat)* guest room; spare room; *(im Hotel)* room
gast-, Gast-: ~frei *Adj.* hospitable; **~freiheit die;** *o. Pl.* hospitality; **~freund der** *(veralt.)* **a)** *(~geber)* host; **b)** *(Besucher)* guest; **~freundlich** *Adj.* hospitable; **~freundschaft die** hospitality; **~gebend** *Adj.; nicht präd.* host ⟨*city, nation, etc.*⟩; **die ~gebende Mannschaft** the home team *or* side; **~geber der a)** host; **b)** *meist Pl. (Sport)* **der/die ~geber** the home team *or* side; **~geberin die; ~, ~nen** hostess; **~geschenk das** gift [for one's host/hostess]; **~haus das, ~hof der** inn; **~hörer der** *student who with permission attends lectures and seminars at a university without working for a degree;* auditor *(Amer.)*
gastieren *itr. V.* appear as a guest; give a guest performance; **das Orchester gastiert in N.** the orchestra is giving a guest performance in N; **der ~de Tenor** the guest tenor
Gast-: ~konzert das guest concert; **~land das** host country
gastlich 1. *Adj.* hospitable; **~e Aufnahme finden** have a hospitable reception; be received hospitably. **2.** *adv.* hospitably
Gastlichkeit die; ~: hospitality
Gast-: ~mahl das *(geh.)* banquet; **Platons „~mahl"** Plato's 'Symposium'; **~mannschaft die** *(Sport)* visiting team
Gas·tod der death by gassing; **den ~ erleiden** be gassed
Gast-: ~professor der visiting professor; **~recht das** right to hospitality; **jmdm. ~recht gewähren/das ~recht verweigern** grant/refuse sb. hospitality; **~recht genießen** enjoy the privileges of a guest; **das ~recht mißbrauchen** abuse one's position as a guest; **~redner der** guest speaker
Gastritis [gas'tri:tɪs] **die; ~, Gastritiden** *(Med.)* gastritis
Gast·rolle die guest role *or* part; **in einer ~ auftreten** make a guest appearance; appear as a guest
gastro-, Gastro- [gastro:-]: **~nom** [~'no:m] **der; ~en, ~en** restaurateur; **~nomie** [~no'mi:] **die; ~ a)** *(Gaststättengewerbe)* restaurant trade; *(Versorgung, Service)* catering *no art.;* **b)** *(Kochk.)* gastronomy; **~nomisch** [~'no:mɪʃ] *Adj.* gastronomic; **~skopie** [~sko'pi:] **die** *(Med.)* gastroscopy
Gast·spiel das guest performance; **ein [kurzes] ~ geben** *(fig. scherzh.)* stay for a short time
Gastspiel·reise die tour; **eine ~ durch Japan** a tour of Japan; **auf ~:** on tour
Gast·stätte die public house; *(Speiselokal)* restaurant
Gaststätten·gewerbe das pub/restaurant trade
Gast·stube die bar; *(in einem Speiselokal)* restaurant
Gas·turbine die gas turbine
Gast-: ~vorlesung die guest lecture; **~vorstellung die** guest performance; **~wirt der** publican; landlord; *(eines Restaurants)* [restaurant] proprietor *or* owner; *(Pächter)* restaurant manager; **~wirtschaft die** *s.* **~stätte; ~zimmer das** *s.* **Gästezimmer**
Gas-: ~uhr die gas meter; **~verbrauch der** gas consumption; **~verflüssigung die** *(Technik, Physik)* liquefaction of gases; **~vergiftung die** gas-poisoning *no indef. art.;* **~versorgung die** gas supply; **~wasch·flasche die** *(Technik)* gas washer; *(Chemie)* gas-washing bottle; **~werk das** gasworks *sing.;* **~wolke die** cloud of gas; **~zähler der** gas meter

Gatt [gat] **das; ~[e]s, ~en** *od.* **~s** *(Seemannsspr.)* eyelet hole
GATT [gat] **das; ~:** GATT
Gatte ['gatə] **der; ~n, ~n a)** *(geh.: Ehemann)* husband; **b)** *Pl. (veralt.: Eheleute)* couple; husband and wife
Gatten-: ~liebe die *(geh.)* conjugal love; love of one's husband/wife; **~mord der** *(Rechtsw., sonst geh.)* murder of one's husband/wife
Gatter ['gatɐ] **das; ~s, ~ a)** *(Zaun)* fence; *(Lattenzaun)* fence; paling; **b)** *(Tor)* gate; **c)** *(Jägerspr.: Gehege)* [game] preserve; **d)** *(Pferdesport)* rails *pl.;* **e)** *(Textilw.)* creel; **f)** *(Elektronik)* gate
Gatter-: ~säge die *(Technik)* gang saw; **~tor das** gate
Gattin ['gatɪn] **die; ~, ~nen** *(geh.)* wife; **die besten Grüße an Ihre ~:** my regards to your lady wife
Gattung ['gatʊŋ] **die; ~, ~en a)** kind; sort; *(Kunst~)* genre; form; **Menschen/Dinge verschiedener ~:** all sorts of people/things of different kinds *or* sorts; **b)** *(Biol.)* genus; **c)** *(Milit.)* service
Gattungs-: ~begriff der generic concept; **~name der** generic name; **~zahl·wort das;** *Pl.* **...wörter** *(Sprachw.) numeral showing how many different kinds ('achterlei' etc.);* variative numeral
Gau [gau̯] **der; ~[e]s, ~e a)** *tribal district in Germanic times;* **b)** *(ns.: Organisationseinheit) administrative district during the Nazi period;* **c)** *(Gebiet)* region
Gäu [gɔy̯] **das; ~[e]s, ~e** *(österr., schweiz.) s.* **Gau a**
Gaube ['gau̯bə] **die; ~, ~n** dormer [window]
Gauchheil ['gau̯xhai̯l] **der; ~[e]s, ~e** *(Bot.)* anagallis; pimpernel
Gaucho ['gau̯tʃo] **der; ~[s], ~s** gaucho
Gaudi ['gau̯di] **das; ~s** *(bayr., österr.:* **die; ~)** *(ugs.)* bit of fun; **eine große ~ haben** have a lot of *or* great fun; **eine ~ sein** be a lot of *or* great fun
Gaudium ['gau̯diʊm] **das; ~s** amusement; entertainment; **zum allgemeinen ~:** to everyone's amusement; to the amusement of everyone *or* all
Gaukel·bild das *(veralt.)* phantasm; **ein ~ deiner Phantasie** a figment of your imagination
Gaukelei die; ~, ~en *(geh.)* **a)** *(Vorspiegelung)* trickery *no indef. art., no pl.;* **~en** trickery *sing.; tricks;* **b)** *(Possenspiel)* trick
gaukeln ['gau̯kl̩n] *itr. V.; mit sein (dichter.)* ⟨*glow-worm*⟩ flicker; ⟨*butterfly*⟩ flutter; **der ~de Flug der Fledermäuse** the dancing flight of the bats
Gaukel·spiel das *(geh.)* deception
Gaukler der; ~s, ~ a) *(veralt.: Taschenspieler)* itinerant entertainer; **b)** *(geh.: Betrüger)* charlatan; mountebank; trickster; **c)** *(Zool.)* bateleur [eagle]
Gauklerin die; ~, ~nen *s.* **Gaukler a, b**
Gaul [gau̯l] **der; ~[e]s, Gäule** ['gɔy̯lə] **a)** *(abwertend)* nag *(derog.);* hack *(derog.);* **b)** *(veralt.)* horse; **einem geschenkten ~ schaut man nicht ins Maul** *(Spr.)* never look a gift-horse in the mouth
Gau·leiter der *(ns.)* gauleiter
Gaullismus [go'lɪsmʊs] **der; ~:** Gaullism
Gaumen ['gau̯mən] **der; ~s, ~ a)** palate; roof of the mouth; **der weiche/harte ~:** the soft/hard palate; **b)** *(geh.: Geschmacksorgan)* palate; **das ist etw. für einen verwöhnten ~:** this is sth. for the real gourmet
Gaumen-: ~freude die; *meist Pl. (geh.),* **~kitzel der** *(geh.)* delicacy; **~laut der** guttural; **~mandel die** *(Anat.)* [palatine] tonsil; **~platte die** upper [dental] plate; **~segel das** *(Anat.)* soft palate; velum *(Anat.);* **~spalte die** *(Med.)* cleft palate; **~zäpfchen das** uvula
Gauner ['gau̯nɐ] **der; ~s, ~ a)** *(abwertend)* crook *(coll.);* rogue; **ein ausgemachter/kleiner ~:** an out-and-out crook *(coll.) or* rogue/a small-time crook *(coll.);* **b)** *(ugs.: schlauer Mensch)* cunning devil *(coll.);* sly customer *(coll.)*
Gauner·bande die gang *or* band of crooks *(coll.)*
Gaunerei die; ~, ~en swindle; *(das Gaunern)* swindling
Gauner·komödie die comedy thriller
gaunern 1. *itr. V.* swindle; cheat. **2.** *refl. V.* **sich durchs Leben ~:** cheat one's way through life
Gauner-: ~sprache die thieves' cant *or* Latin; **~streich der, ~stück das** swindle; piece of roguery
gautschen ['gau̯tʃn̩] *tr. V.* **a)** *(Papierherstellung)* couch; **b)** *(Druckw.)* **jmdn. ~:** give sb. a ducking *(initiation ceremony for those finishing an apprenticeship in the printing trade)*
Gautscher der; ~s, ~ *(Papierherstellung)* coucher
Gaza·streifen ['ga:za-] **der** Gaza Strip
Gaze ['ga:zə] **die; ~, ~n** gauze; *(Draht~)* gauze; [wire-]mesh
Gaze-: ~bausch der gauze swab; **~binde die** gauze bandage
Gazelle [ga'tsɛlə] **die; ~, ~n** gazelle
Gaze·schleier der gauze veil
Gazette [ga'tsɛtə] **die; ~, ~n** newspaper; rag *(coll. derog.)*
Gaze·tupfer der *s.* **Gazebausch**
Gdańsk [gdai̯sk] **(das); ~s** *(amtl. Form in der DDR) s.* **Danzig**
G-Dur ['ge:-] **das; ~** *(Musik)* G major; *s. auch* **A-Dur**
geachtet 1. *2. Part. v.* **achten. 2.** *Adj.* respected; **~ und respektiert** esteemed and respected; **bei jmdm. ~ sein** be respected *or* held in esteem by sb.
Geächtete der/die; *adj. Dekl.* outlaw
Geächze das; ~s groaning; groans *pl.*
Geäder [gə'|ɛ:dɐ] **das; ~s** venation; veins *pl.; (beim Menschen)* veins *pl.*
geadert, geädert *Adj.* veined
Geäfter [gə'|ɛftɐ] **das; ~s, ~** *(Jägerspr.)* dew-claws *pl.*
Gealbere das; ~s *(ugs. abwertend)* messing about *or* around *(coll.)*
geartet *Adj.* **es ist [ganz] anders ~, als ich mir vorgestellt hatte** it is [quite] different [in kind] from what I'd imagined; **wie [auch] immer die Situation ~ ist** whatever the situation may be; **kein wie auch immer ~er Reiz** no stimulus of any kind; **dieses besonders ~e Material** this special material; **sie ist so ~, daß ...:** her nature is such that ...; **gutmütig ~:** good-natured; **sie ist ganz anders ~:** she is quite different; she has quite a different nature
Geäst [gə'|ɛst] **das; ~[e]s** branches *pl.;* boughs *pl.*
geb. *Abk.* **a) geboren; b) geborene**
Gebäck [gə'bɛk] **das; ~[e]s, ~e** cakes and pastries *pl.; (Kekse)* biscuits *pl.; (Törtchen)* tarts *pl.*
gebacken *2. Part. v.* **backen**
Gebäck-: ~schale die cake dish; **~zange die** cake tongs *pl.*
Gebälk [gə'bɛlk] **das; ~[e]s, ~e a)** *(Balkenwerk)* beams *pl.; (Dach~)* rafters *pl.;* **es knistert** *od.* **kracht im ~** *(fig.)* there are signs that things are beginning to fall apart *(fig.);* **b)** *(antike Archit.)* entablature
Geballere das; ~s *(ugs. abwertend)* banging
geballt [gə'balt] **1.** *2. Part. v.* **ballen. 2.** *Adj.; nicht präd.* concentrated; **mit ~er Kraft einen neuen Angriff starten** concentrate one's forces in a new attack; **eine ~e Ladung** *(Milit.)* a concentrated charge; **jmdm. eine ~e Ladung Sand ins Gesicht werfen** *(fig. ugs.)* chuck a load of sand in sb.'s face *(coll.)*
gebar *1. u. 3. Pers. Sg. Prät. v.* **gebären**
Gebärde [gə'bɛ:ɐ̯də] **die; ~, ~n** gesture; **mit vielen ~n** with much gesticulation

gebärden *refl. V.* **sich seltsam/wie ein Rasender/wie toll ~:** behave *or* act oddly/like a madman/as if one were mad

Gebärden-: ~spiel das gestures *pl.*; gesticulation[s *pl.*]; **~sprache die** *(Zeichensprache)* sign language; *(Taubstummensprache)* deaf-and-dumb language

Gebaren das; ~s *(oft abwertend)* conduct; behaviour

gebären [gə'bɛ:rən] *unr. tr. V.* bear; give birth to; **jmdm. ein Kind ~** *(geh.)* bear sb. a child; **wo bist du geboren?** where were you born?; **einen Gedanken/eine Idee ~** *(fig.)* generate a thought/give birth to an idea; *s. auch* **geboren**

gebär·freudig *Adj.* prolific

Gebär·mutter die; ~, -mütter womb

Gebärmutter·krebs der *(Med.)* cancer of the womb

gebauchpinselt [gə'bauxpɪnzlt] *in* **sich ~ fühlen** *(ugs. scherzh.)* feel flattered

Gebäude [gə'bɔydə] **das; ~s, ~ a)** *(Bauwerk)* building; **b)** *(Gefüge)* structure; **kunstvolles ~:** edifice; **das ~ einer Theorie/ Wissenschaft** the structure of a theory/of a science; **ein ~ von Lügen** a tissue of lies

Gebäude-: ~komplex der complex of buildings; **~teil der** part of the building

gebaut 1. *2. Part. v.* **bauen. 2.** *Adj.* **gut ~ sein** have a good figure; **gut ~e Mannequins** models with good figures; **so wie du ~ bist ...** *(ugs.)* with a figure like yours ...; *(fig.)* you being what you are ... *(coll.)*

gebe·freudig *Adj.* generous; openhanded

Gebein das; ~[e]s, ~e a) *Pl. (geh.: Skelett)* bones *pl.*; *(sterbliche Reste)* [mortal] remains; **b) ihr fuhr der Schreck durchs ~** *(veralt.)* her whole body shook with fear

Gebell das; ~[e]s barking; *(der Jagdhunde)* baying; *(fig.: von Geschützen)* booming

geben ['ge:bn̩] **1.** *unr. tr. V.* **a)** give; *(reichen)* give; hand; pass; **jmdm. zu essen/trinken ~:** give sb. sth. to eat/drink; **jmdm. [zur Begrüßung] die Hand ~:** shake sb.'s hand [in greeting]; **~ Sie mir bitte Herrn N.** please put me through to Mr N.; **ich gäbe viel darum, wenn ich das machen könnte** I'd give a lot to be able to do that; **jmdm. etw. in die Hand ~:** give sb. sth.; **etw. [nicht] aus der Hand ~:** [not] let go of sth.; **ich gebe Ihnen die Vase für 130 Mark** I'll let you have the vase for 130 marks; **~ Sie mir bitte eine Schachtel Zigaretten/ein Bier** I'll have a packet of cigarettes/a beer, please; **können Sie mir zwei Plätze ~?** can you give me *or* let me have two seats?; **jmdm. seine ganze Liebe ~** *(fig.)* give sb. all one's love; **Geben ist seliger denn Nehmen** *(Spr.)* it is more blessed to give than to receive *(prov.)*; **b)** *(über~)* **jmdn. zu jmdm. in die Lehre ~:** apprentice sb. to sb.; **etw. in Druck** *(Akk.) od.* **zum Druck ~:** send sth. to press *or* to be printed; **jmdm. etw. als** *od.* **zum Pfand ~:** give sb. sth. as [a] security; **etw. [bei jmdm.] in Verwahrung ~:** hand sth. in [to sb.] for safe keeping; **etw. zur Reparatur ~:** take sth. [in] to be repaired; **etw. zur Post ~:** post sth.; *s. auch* **Pflege; c)** *(gewähren)* give; **jmdm. eine Genehmigung/ein Interview ~:** give sb. permission/an interview; **einen Elfmeter/eine Ecke ~** *(Sport)* award a penalty/ corner; **d)** *(bieten)* give; **es hat mir nichts ge~:** I didn't gain anything from *or* get anything out of it; **jmdm. ein gutes/schlechtes Beispiel ~:** set sb. a good/bad example; **e)** *(versetzen)* give; **jmdm. einen Klaps/Tritt ~:** give sb. a slap/kick; **es jmdm. ~** *(ugs.: jmdm. die Meinung sagen)* give sb. what for *(coll.)*; *(jmdn. verprügeln)* let sb. have it; **gib [es] ihm!** *(ugs.)* let him have it!; **f)** *(erteilen)* give; **Unterricht ~:** teach; **eine Lektion ~:** give a lesson; **Französisch ~:** teach French; **jmdm. Antwort ~:** give sb. an answer; **jmdm. Auskunft/Aufschluß ~:** give sb. information; **g)** *(hervorbringen)* give ⟨*milk, shade, light*⟩; **etw. gibt Flecken** *(ugs.)* sth. stains; **h)** *(veranstalten)* give, throw ⟨*party*⟩; give, lay on ⟨*banquet*⟩; give ⟨*dinner-party, ball*⟩; **ein Fest ~:** give *or* hold a party *or* celebration; **i)** *(aufführen)* give ⟨*concert, performance*⟩; **das Theater gibt nächste Woche den „Faust"** the theatre is putting on 'Faust' next week; **was wird heute ge~?** what's on today?; **die Schauspielerin gibt ihr Debüt** the actress is making her debut; **j)** *(er~)* **drei mal drei gibt neun** three threes are nine; three times three is *or* makes nine; **eins plus eins gibt zwei** one and one is *or* makes two; **das gibt [k]einen Sinn** that makes [no] sense; **ein Wort gab das andere** one word led to another; **k)** *(vermitteln)* give; **jmdm./einer Sache neue Impulse/Anregungen ~:** give sb./sth. a fresh impulse/ stimulus; **etw. ist jmdm. nicht ge~:** sb. just hasn't got sth.; **es ist ihm nicht ge~, eine gute Rede zu halten** he just hasn't got what it takes to be a good speaker; **l)** *(äußern)* **etw. von sich ~:** utter sth.; **Unsinn/dummes Zeug von sich ~** *(abwertend)* talk nonsense/rubbish; **keinen Laut/Ton von sich ~:** not make a sound; **m) viel/wenig auf etw.** *(Akk.)* **~:** set great/little store by sth.; **n)** *(hinzu~)* add; put in; **etw. an das Essen ~:** add sth. to *or* put sth. into the food; **o)** *(ugs.: erbrechen)* **alles wieder von sich ~:** bring *or (coll.)* sick everything up again; **p)** *(Ballspiele: ab~)* pass; **den Ball nach links ~:** pass the ball [to the] left; **q)** *(darstellen)* play ⟨*role*⟩. **2.** *unr. tr. V. (unpers.)* **a)** *(vorhanden sein)* **es gibt** there is/are; **es gibt einen/keinen Gott** God exists/does not exist; **das gibt es wohl häufiger** it happens all the time; **daß es so etwas heutzutage überhaupt noch gibt!** I'm surprised that such things still go on nowadays; **zu meiner Zeit gab es das nicht** it wasn't like that in my day; **gibt es noch etwas?** *(ugs.)* is there anything else?; **das gibt es ja gar nicht** I don't believe it; you're joking *(coll.)*; **Ein Hund mit fünf Beinen? Das gibt es ja gar nicht** A dog with five legs? There's no such thing!; **was gibt es Neues?** what's new? *(coll.)*; **bei mir gibt's nichts Neues** I haven't got any news; **Kommen Sie herein. Was gibt es?** Come in. What's the matter *or (coll.)* what's up?; **was gibt's denn da?** what's going on over there?; **was es nicht alles gibt!** *(ugs.)* what will they think of next?; **gibt es dich auch noch?** *(ugs.)* are you still around? *(coll.)*; **da gibt's nichts** *(ugs.)* there's no denying it *or* no doubt about it; **da gibt's nichts, da würde ich sofort protestieren** there's nothing else for it, I'd protest immediately in that case; **b)** *(angeboten werden)* **was gibt es zu essen/trinken?** what is there to eat/drink?; **was gibt es denn zum Mittagessen?** what's for lunch?; **heute gibt's Schweinefleisch** we're having pork today; **im Theater/Fernsehen gibt es heute abend ...:** ... is on at the theatre/on television this evening; **c)** *(einsetzen)* **morgen gibt es Schnee/Sturm** it'll snow tomorrow/ there'll be a storm tomorrow; **es gibt Schereien/Streit** there'll be trouble/a row; **gleich/sonst gibt's was** *(ugs.)* there'll be trouble in a minute/otherwise. **3.** *unr. itr. V.* **a)** *(Karten austeilen)* deal; **wer gibt?** whose deal is it?; **b)** *(Sport: aufschlagen)* serve. **4.** *unr. refl. V.* **a) sich [natürlich/steif] ~:** act *or* behave [naturally/stiffly]; **er gab sich nach außen hin gelassen** he gave the appearance of being relaxed; **deine Art, dich zu ~:** the way you behave; **b)** *(nachlassen)* **das Fieber wird sich ~:** his/her *etc.* temperature will drop; **sein Eifer wird sich bald ~:** his enthusiasm will soon wear off *or* cool; **das gibt sich/wird sich noch ~:** it will get better

gebenedeit [gəbene'dait] *Adj. (christl. Rel.)* blessed; **die ~e Jungfrau** the Blessed Virgin Mary

Geber der; ~s, ~ a) *(veralt.: Gebender)* giver; donor; **b)** *(Technik)* transducer

Geber·laune die; *o. Pl.* generous mood; **in ~:** in a generous mood

Gebet [gə'be:t] **das; ~[e]s, ~e** prayer; **ein ~ sprechen** say a prayer; **sein ~ verrichten** say one's prayers *pl.*; **das ~ des Herrn** *(geh.)* the Lord's Prayer; **jmdn. ins ~ nehmen** *(ugs.)* give sb. a dressing down; take sb. to task

Gebet·buch das prayer-book

gebeten *2. Part. v.* **bitten**

Gebets-: ~mühle die prayer wheel; **~teppich der** *(islam. Rel.)* prayer mat

gebeut [gə'bɔyt] *(veralt.) 3. Pers. Sg. Präsens v.* **gebieten**

gebiert [gə'bi:ɐ̯t] *3. Pers. Sg. Präsens v.* **gebären**

Gebiet [gə'bi:t] **das; ~[e]s, ~e a)** *(Landstrich)* region; area; **b)** *(Staats~)* territory; **c)** *(Bereich)* field; sphere; **auf dem ~ der Wirtschaft/Politik** in the field *or* sphere of economics/politics; **d)** *(Fach)* field; **auf einem ~ führend sein** be the leader in a field

gebieten *(geh.)* **1.** *unr. tr. V.* **a)** *(befehlen, fordern)* command; order; **jmdm. ~, etw. zu tun** command *or* order sb. to do sth.; **eine Respekt ~de Persönlichkeit** a figure who commands/commanded respect; **b)** *(erfordern)* demand; bid; *s. auch* **Einhalt. 2.** *unr. itr. V.* **a) über etw.** *(Akk.)* **~:** command sth.; have command over sth.; **über ein Land/ Volk ~:** hold sway over a country/people; **b)** *(verfügen)* **über Geld ~:** have money at one's disposal; **er gebietet über beträchtliche Körperkräfte** he is a man of considerable strength

Gebieter der; ~s, ~ *(veralt.)* master; **~ über 400 Sklaven** master of 400 slaves

Gebieterin die; ~, ~nen *(veralt.)* mistress

gebieterisch *(geh.)* **1.** *Adj.* imperious; *(herrisch)* domineering; overbearing; peremptory ⟨*tone*⟩. **2.** *adv.* imperiously; **die Lage erfordert ~, daß ...:** the situation makes it [absolutely] imperative that ...

gebiets-, Gebiets-: ~abtretung die cession *or* ceding of territory; **~anspruch der** territorial claim; **~körperschaft die** *(Rechtsw.)* regional authority; **~reform die** local government reorganization; **~weise** *Adv.* locally; in some areas

Gebilde [gə'bɪldə] **das; ~s, ~** *(Gegenstand)* object; *(Bauwerk)* construction; structure; *(Form)* shape; **ein kompliziertes geistiges ~** *(fig.)* a complicated intellectual construct; **diese Dinge sind ~ seiner Phantasie** *(fig.)* these things are products of his imagination

gebildet 1. *2. Part. v.* **bilden. 2.** *Adj.* educated; *(kultiviert)* cultured; **er ist sehr ~:** he is very well educated; **vielseitig ~:** broadly educated; **er ist vielseitig ~:** he has a broad education; **akademisch ~ sein** have had an academic training. **3.** *adv.* **sich ~ unterhalten** have a cultured conversation

Gebimmel das; ~s *(ugs.)* ringing; *(von kleinen Glocken)* tinkling

Gebinde das; ~s, ~ *(Blumenarrangement)* arrangement; *(Bund, Strauß)* bunch; *(von kleinen Blumen)* posy

Gebirge [gə'bɪrgə] **das; ~s, ~ a)** mountain range; range of mountains; **ein ~ von Schutt** *(fig.)* a mountain of rubble *(fig.)*; **b)** *(Gebirgsgegend)* mountains *pl.*; **c)** *(Bergbau)* rock

gebirgig *Adj.* mountainous

Gebirgs-: ~ausläufer der foothill; **~bach der** mountain stream; **~bahn die** mountain railway; **~bewohner der** mountain dweller; **~jäger der** *(Milit.)* **a)** *(Soldat)* mountain soldier; **b)** *Pl. (Waffengattung)* mountain troops *pl.*; **~kamm der** mountain ridge *or* crest; **~kette die** mountain chain *or* range; **~klima das** mountain climate; **~landschaft die** mountainous region; *(Ausblick)* mountain scenery; *(Ge-*

mälde) mountain landscape; **~massiv das** massif; **~paß der** mountain pass; **~stock der** massif; **~truppe die** *(Milit.) s.* **~jäger b; ~volk das** mountain people; *(Stamm)* mountain tribe; **~zug der** mountain range

Gebiß das; Gebisses, Gebisse a) *(Zähne)* set of teeth; teeth *pl.*; **sein ~ zeigen/entblößen** bare one's teeth; **b)** *(Zahnersatz)* denture; plate *(coll.)*; *(für die Zähne beider Kiefer)* dentures *pl.*; set of false teeth; false teeth *pl.*; **ein [künstliches] ~ anpassen** fit a denture/dentures *or* [a set of] false teeth; **c)** *(am Pferdezaum)* bit

gebissen [gə'bɪsn̩] *2. Part. v.* **beißen**

Gebläse [gə'blɛ:zə] **das; ~s, ~** *(Technik)* fan; *(Kfz-W.: am Vergaser)* supercharger

Gebläse·motor der *(Kfz-W.)* supercharged engine

geblasen *2. Part. v.* **blasen**

geblichen [gə'blɪçn̩] *2. Part. v.* **bleichen**

Geblödel das; ~s *(ugs.)* silly chatter; twaddle *(coll.)*

geblümt [gə'bly:mt] *Adj.* **a)** flowered; **b)** *(geziert)* flowery ‹*style etc.*›

Geblüt [gə'bly:t] **das; ~[e]s** *(geh.)* blood; **von königlichem ~ sein** be of royal blood; **eine Prinzessin von ~:** a princess of the blood

gebogen 1. *2. Part. v.* **biegen. 2.** *Adj.* bent; **eine aufwärts ~e Nase** an upturned nose

geboren [gə'bo:rən] **1.** *2. Part. v.* **gebären. 2.** *Adj.* **blind/taub ~ sein** be born blind/deaf; **Frau Anna Schmitz ~e Meyer** Mrs Anna Schmitz née Meyer; **sie ist eine ~e von Schiller** she is a von Schiller by birth; **der ~e Schauspieler** *usw.* **sein** be a born actor *etc.*; **zum Musiker** *usw.* **~ sein** be born to be a musician *etc.*; be a born musician *etc.*

geborgen 1. *2. Part. v.* **bergen. 2.** *Adj.* safe; secure; **sich bei jmdm. ~ fühlen** feel safe and secure with sb.; **sicher und ~ sein** be safe and secure

Geborgenheit die; ~: security

geborsten [gə'bɔrstn̩] *2. Part. v.* **bersten**

gebot *1. u. 3. Pers. Sg. Prät. v.* **gebieten**

Gebot das; ~[e]s, ~e a) *(Grundsatz)* precept; **das ~ der Fairneß/Höflichkeit verlangt es, daß ...:** fairness/politeness demands that ...; **das oberste/erste ~:** the highest precept; **die Zehn ~e** *(Rel.)* the Ten Commandments; **b)** *(Vorschrift)* regulation; **c)** *(geh.: Befehl)* command; *(Verordnung)* decree; **auf jmds. ~** *(Akk.)* **[hin]** at sb.'s command; **d)** *in* **jmdm. zu ~[e] stehen** *(geh.)* be at sb.'s command/disposal; **e)** *(Erfordernis)* **ein ~ der Vernunft/Klugheit** a dictate of reason/good sense; **es ist ein ~ der Vernunft/Klugheit, etw. zu tun** reason/good sense dictates that one does sth.; **es ist das ~ der Stunde, nicht länger zu zögern** *(geh.)* our present predicament demands that we hesitate no longer; **etw. ist das ~ der Stunde** *(geh.)* sth. is the order of the day; **f)** *(Kaufmannsspr.)* bid; **verkaufe X gegen ~:** offers [are] invited for X

geboten 1. *2. Part. v.* **bieten, gebieten. 2.** *Adj.* *(ratsam)* advisable; *(notwendig)* necessary; *(unbedingt ~)* imperative; **mit der ~en Sorgfalt** with [all] due care; **mit dem ~en Respekt** with all due respect

Gebots·schild das *(Verkehrsw.)* regulatory sign

Gebr. *Abk.* **Gebrüder** Bros.

gebracht [gə'braxt] *2. Part. v.* **bringen**

gebrandmarkt *2. Part. v.* **brandmarken**

gebrannt [gə'brant] *2. Part. v.* **brennen**

gebraten *2. Part. v.* **braten**

Gebräu [gə'brɔy] **das; ~[e]s, ~e** *(meist abwertend)* brew; concoction *(derog.)*

Gebrauch der a) *o. Pl. (Benutzung)* use; **für den persönlichen/täglichen ~:** for personal/daily use; **vor ~ gut schütteln!** shake well before use; **von etw. ~ machen** make use of sth.; **von seinem Recht ~ machen** avail oneself of *or* exercise one's rights *pl.*; **außer ~ kommen** fall into disuse; **etw. in ~ nehmen** start using sth.; **etw. in** *od.* **im ~ haben** be using sth.; **in** *od.* **im ~ sein** be in use; **b)** *meist Pl. (Brauch)* custom

gebrauchen *tr. V.* use; **das kann ich gut ~:** I can make good use of that; I can just do with that *(coll.)*; **er ist zu nichts zu ~** *(ugs.)* he is useless; **sie ist zu allem zu ~:** she is always a useful person to have around; **den Verstand/eine List ~:** use one's common sense/a subterfuge; **er könnte einen neuen Mantel ~** *(ugs.)* he could do with *or (coll.)* use a new coat; **ich kann jetzt keine Störung ~** *(ugs.)* I don't want to be disturbed just now

gebräuchlich [gə'brɔyçlɪç] *Adj.* **a)** *(üblich)* normal; usual; customary; **b)** *(häufig)* common

gebrauchs-, Gebrauchs-: ~an·leitung die, ~an·weisung die instructions *pl. or* directions *pl.* [for use]; **~artikel der** basic consumer item; **~artikel** *Pl.* basic consumer goods; **~fähig** *Adj.* usable; in working order *pred.*; **etw. ~fähig machen** make sth. usable; put sth. in working order; **~fertig** *Adj.* ready for use *pred.*; **~gegen·stand der** item of practical use; **~graphik die** commercial art; **~graphiker der** commercial artist; **~gut das;** *meist Pl.* consumer item; **~güter** consumer goods; **langlebige ~güter** consumer durables; **~muster das** *(Rechtsw.)* registered design; **~muster·schutz der** *(Rechtsw.)* protection of designs; **~wert der** utility value

gebraucht 1. *2. Part. v.* **brauchen, gebrauchen. 2.** *Adj.* second-hand ‹*bicycle, clothes, etc.*›; used, second-hand ‹*car*›; used ‹*handkerchief*›; **etw. ~ kaufen** buy sth. second-hand

Gebraucht-: ~wagen der used *or* second-hand car; **~wagen·händler der** used-car dealer; second-hand car dealer; **~ware die;** *meist Pl.* second-hand item; **~n** second-hand goods

Gebrause das; ~s *(des Meeres, der Wellen)* thundering; roar[ing]; booming; *(des Sturms, Windes)* roar[ing]; *(des Verkehrs)* roar

gebrechen *unr. itr. V. (unpers.) (geh.)* **jmdm. gebricht etw., jmdm. gebricht es an etw.** *(Dat.)* sb. is lacking in *or* lacks sth.

Gebrechen das; ~s, ~ *(geh.)* affliction

gebrechlich *Adj.* infirm; frail; **die Alten und Gebrechlichen** the aged and infirm

Gebrechlichkeit die; ~: infirmity; frailty

gebrochen [gə'brɔxn̩] **1.** *2. Part. v.* **brechen. 2.** *Adj.* **a)** *(fehlerhaft)* **~es Englisch/Deutsch** broken English/German; **b)** *(niedergedrückt)* broken; **er ist ein ~er Mensch** he is a broken man; **c)** *(gestört)* **ein ~es Verhältnis zu jmdm./etw. haben** have a disturbed relationship to sb./sth. **3.** *adv.* **~ Deutsch sprechen** speak broken German

Gebrodel das; ~s boiling; bubbling; *(fig.)* turmoil

Gebrüder *Pl.* **a)** *(Kaufmannsspr.)* **die ~ Meyer** Meyer Brothers; **b)** *(veralt.)* **die ~ Schulze** the brothers Schulze

Gebrüll das; ~[e]s a) roaring; *(von Rindern)* bellowing; **b)** *(ugs.) (lautes Schreien)* bellowing; yelling; *(einer Menschenmenge)* roaring; **auf sie mit ~!** *(scherzh.)* go for *or* get them!; **c)** *(ugs.: lautes Weinen)* bawling

Gebrumm das; ~[e]s *(von Bären)* growling; *(von Flugzeugen, Bienen)* droning; *(von Insekten)* buzz[ing]; **ein zustimmendes ~** *(fig.)* a growl of assent

Gebrumme das; ~s *(ugs. abwertend) (von Flugzeugen, Motorrädern, Bienen)* droning; *(von Insekten)* buzz[ing]

gebückt 1. *2. Part. v.* **bücken. 2.** *Adj.* **in ~er Haltung** bending forward; **~ gehen** walk with a stoop

gebügelt *2. Part. v.* **bügeln;** *s. auch* **geschniegelt**

Gebühr [gə'by:ɐ̯] **die; ~, ~en a)** charge; *(Maut)* toll; *(Anwalts~)* fee; *(Fernseh~)* licence fee; *(Vermittlungs~)* commission *no pl.*; fee; *(Post~)* postage *no pl.*; **~ bezahlt Empfänger** postage will be paid by addressee; **b) jmds. Leistungen nach ~ anerkennen** give due recognition to sb.'s achievements; **ich werde dich nach ~ belohnen** I shall reward you appropriately; **über ~** *(Akk.)* unduly; excessively

gebühren *(geh.)* **1.** *itr. V.* **jmdm. gebührt Achtung** *usw.* **[für etw.]** sb. deserves respect *etc.* [for sth.]; respect *etc.* is due to sb. [for sth.]. **2.** *refl. V.* **wie es sich gebührt** as is fitting *or* proper; **er bewahrte die Haltung, wie es sich für einen König gebührt** he kept his composure, as befitted a king

Gebühren·anzeiger der *(Fernspr.)* telephone meter

gebührend 1. *Adj.* fitting; proper; *(angemessen)* fitting; suitable; **in ~em Abstand** at a proper distance; **mit ~er Sorgfalt** with due care; **jmdm. die ~e Achtung erweisen** show sb. due *or* proper respect; show sb. the respect due to him/her. **2.** *adv.* fittingly; in a fitting manner

gebührender·maßen, gebührender·weise *Adv.* fittingly; in a fitting manner

gebühren-, Gebühren-: ~einheit die *(Fernspr.)* [tariff] unit; **~erhöhung die** *s.* **Gebühr a:** increase in charges/fees; *(Erhöhung der Fernseh~)* licence fee increase; **~erlaß der** *s.* **Gebühr a:** remission of charges/fees; *(der Fernseh~)* remission of the licence fee; **~ermäßigung die** *s.* **Gebühr a:** reduction of charges/fees; **~frei 1.** *Adj.* free of charge *pred.*; post-free ‹*letter, packet, etc.*›; **2.** *adv.* free of charge; **einen Brief ~frei schicken** send a letter post-free; **~marke die** revenue stamp; fiscal stamp; **~ordnung die** *s.* **Gebühr a:** scale of charges/fees; **~pflichtig 1.** *Adj.* **eine ~pflichtige Verwarnung** a fine and a caution; **2.** *adv.* **jmdn. ~pflichtig verwarnen** fine and caution sb.; **~vignette die** [Swiss] motorway fee sticker

gebührlich *Adj. (veralt.) s.* **gebührend**

gebunden 1. *2. Part. v.* **binden. 2.** *Adj.* **a)** *(verpflichtet)* bound; **an ein Versprechen/das Haus ~ sein** be bound by a promise/tied to one's home; **sich [an etw.** *(Akk.)***] ~ fühlen** feel bound by sth.; **b)** *(verlobt)* engaged; *(verheiratet)* married; **c)** *(festgesetzt)* fixed ‹*book prices*›

Gebundenheit die; ~: ein Gefühl der ~: a feeling of being tied [down]

Geburt [gə'bu:ɐ̯t] **die; ~, ~en** birth; **von ~ an** from birth; **vor/nach Christi ~:** before/after the birth of Christ; **von hoher ~ sein** *(geh.)* be of noble birth; **ein Deutscher/Engländer von ~:** a German/Englishman by birth; **das war eine schwere ~** *(fig. ugs.)* it wasn't easy; it took some doing *(coll.)*

geburten-, Geburten-: ~beschränkung die population control; **~kontrolle die;** *o. Pl.*, **~regelung die;** *o. Pl.* birth control; **~rückgang der** decrease in the birth rate; **~schwach** *Adj.* **ein ~schwacher Jahrgang** a year with a low birth rate; **~stark** *Adj.* **ein ~starker Jahrgang** a year with a high birth rate; **~überschuß der** excess of births over deaths; **~ziffer die** birth rate

gebürtig [gə'bʏrtɪç] *Adj.* **ein ~er Schwabe** a Swabian by birth; **aus Ungarn/Paris ~ sein** be Hungarian/Parisian by birth

Geburts-: ~anzeige die birth announcement; **~datum das** date of birth; **~fehler der** congenital defect; **~haus das: das ~haus Beethovens** the house where Beethoven was born; Beethoven's birthplace; **~helfer der** *(Arzt)* obstetrician; *(Laie)* assistant [at a/the birth]; **~helferin die** obstetrician; *(Hebamme)* midwife; **~hilfe die** *(Med.)* obstetrics *sing.*; *(von einer Heb-*

amme) midwifery; ~jahr das year of birth; 1848 ist das ~jahr der Demokratie in Deutschland (fig.) the year 1848 marks the birth of democracy in Germany; ~ort der place of birth; birthplace; ~schein der s. ~urkunde; ~stadt die native town/city; ~stunde die hour of birth; die ~stunde des Reiches schlug, als er den Thron bestieg (fig.) with his accession to the throne the empire was born

Geburts·tag der a) birthday; jmdm. zum ~ gratulieren wish sb. [a] happy birthday or many happy returns of the day; sich (Dat.) etw. zum ~ wünschen want sth. for one's birthday; er hat morgen ~: it's his birthday tomorrow; b) (Geburtsdatum) date of birth

Geburtstags-: ~feier die birthday party; ~geschenk das birthday present; ~kind das (scherzh.) birthday boy/girl; ~torte die birthday cake; ~überraschung die birthday surprise

Geburts-: ~trauma das (Med., Psych.) birth trauma; ~ur·kunde die birth certificate; ~wehen Pl. labour pains; (fig.) birth pangs; ~zange die obstetric forceps pl.

Gebüsch [gəˈbʏʃ] das; ~[e]s, ~e bushes pl.; clump of bushes; ein niedriges ~: a clump of low bushes; some low bushes pl.; sich im ~ verstecken hide in the bushes

Geck [gɛk] der; ~en, ~en (abwertend) dandy; fop

geckenhaft 1. Adj. dandyish; foppish. 2. adv. er kleidet sich ~: he dresses like a dandy

Gecko [ˈgɛko] der; ~s, ~s od. ~nen [-ˈ--] (Zool.) gecko

gedacht [gəˈdaxt] 1. 2. Part. v. denken, gedenken. 2. Adj. für jmdn./etw. ~ sein be meant or intended for sb./sth.; so war das nicht ~: that wasn't what I intended

Gedächtnis [gəˈdɛçtnɪs] das; ~ses, ~se a) memory; den Alten läßt sein ~ im Stich the old man's memory fails him; sich (Dat.) etw. ins ~ [zurück]rufen recall sth.; etw. aus dem ~ aufsagen recite sth. from memory; jmdm. etw. aus dem ~ sagen tell sb. sth. from memory; das ist meinem ~ entfallen it has slipped my mind; das ist mir noch frisch im ~: it is still fresh in my memory; du hast ein kurzes ~ (ugs.) you have a short memory; jmds. ~ (Dat.) nachhelfen jog sb.'s memory; ein ~ wie ein Sieb haben (ugs.) have a memory like a sieve (coll.); b) (Andenken) memory; remembrance; zum ~ an jmdn. in memory or remembrance of sb.

Gedächtnis-: ~feier die s. Gedenkfeier; ~gottes·dienst der service of remembrance; memorial service; ~hilfe die s. ~stütze; ~lücke die gap in one's memory; ~rede die s. Gedenkrede; ~schwäche die; o. Pl. weak or poor memory; (Med., Psych.) defective or weakened memory; ~schwund der loss of memory; amnesia; ~störung die (bes. Med., Psych.) defect of memory; memory defect; ~stütze die memory aid; mnemonic

gedämpft 1. 2. Part. v. dämpfen. 2. Adj. subdued ⟨mood⟩; subdued, soft ⟨light⟩; subdued, muted ⟨colour⟩; muffled ⟨sound⟩; mit ~er Stimme in a low or hushed voice; ~e Schwingungen (Physik) damped vibrations

Gedanke der; ~ns, ~n a) thought; ein guter/vernünftiger ~: a good/sensible idea; einen ~n aufgreifen take up an idea; einen ~n zu Ende denken follow a thought through; seinen ~n nachhängen abandon oneself to one's thoughts; jmdn. auf andere ~n bringen take sb.'s mind off things; in ~n verloren od. versunken [sein] [be] lost or deep in thought; er war ganz in ~n he was lost in thought; in ~n ganz woanders sein have one's mind on something completely different; be miles away (coll.); mit seinen ~n nicht bei der Sache sein have one's mind on something else; ich bin in ~n immer bei dir I'm always with you in my thoughts; sich mit einem ~n vertraut machen get used to an idea; ~n sind frei thoughts are free; jmds. ~n lesen read sb.'s thoughts or mind; ~n lesen können be able to read people's thoughts or to mind-read; sich (Dat.) [um jmdn./etw. od. wegen jmds./etw.] ~n machen be worried [about sb./sth.]; mach dir keine ~n (ugs.) don't worry; sich über etw. (Akk.) ~n machen (länger nachdenken) think about or ponder sth.; b) o. Pl. der ~ an etw. (Akk.) the thought of sth.; bei dem ~n, hingehen zu müssen at the thought of having to go; kein ~ [daran]! (ugs.) out of the question!; no way! (coll.); kein ~ daran, daß ich rechtzeitig fertig werde (ugs.) there's no chance that I'll be finished on time; c) Pl. (Meinung) ideas; seine eigenen ~n über etw. haben have one's own ideas about sth.; seine ~n [über etw. (Akk.)] austauschen exchange views [about sth.]; d) (Einfall) idea; das bringt mich auf einen ~n that gives me an idea; mir kommt ein ~: I've had an idea; mir kam der ~, wir könnten ...: it occurred to me that we could ...; auf dumme ~n kommen (ugs.) get silly ideas (coll.); sich mit dem ~n tragen, etw. zu tun entertain the idea of or consider doing sth.; mit dem ~n spielen[, etw. zu tun] be toying with the idea [of doing sth.]; e) (Idee) idea; der ~ des Friedens the idea of peace

gedanken-, Gedanken-: ~armut die paucity of ideas; unoriginality; ~austausch der exchange of ideas; ~blitz der (ugs. scherzh.) brainwave (coll.); ~flug der flight of intellect; ~freiheit die; o. Pl. freedom of thought; ~gang der train of thought; ~gebäude das edifice of ideas; ~gut das thought; christliches ~gut Christian thought; staatszersetzendes ~gut subversive ideas pl.; ~lesen das mind-reading; ~los 1. Adj. (unüberlegt) unconsidered; thoughtless; (oberflächlich) thoughtless; (zerstreut) absent-minded; 2. adv. (zerstreut) absent-mindedly; (unüberlegt) without thinking; thoughtlessly; ~losigkeit die (Zerstreutheit) absent-mindedness; (Unüberlegtheit) lack of thought; thoughtlessness; ~lyrik die (Literaturw.) philosophical poetry; ~reichtum der (eines Menschen) fertility of ideas; (eines Werkes) wealth of ideas; ~schritt der logical step; ~spiel das intellectual pastime or game; ~splitter der s. Aphorismus; ~sprung der mental leap; jump from one idea to another; ~strich der dash; ~übertragung die telepathy no indef. art.; thought-transference no indef. art.; ~verloren Adv. lost in thought; ~voll 1. Adj. pensive; thoughtful; 2. adv. pensively; thoughtfully; ~vorbehalt der (Rechtsw.) mental reservation; ~welt die intellectual world

gedanklich [gəˈdaŋklɪç] 1. Adj.; nicht präd. intellectual; ein ~er Fehler an error in reasoning; die ~e Klarheit in diesem Werk the clarity of thought in this work. 2. adv. intellectually

Gedärm [gəˈdɛrm] das; ~[e]s, ~e intestines pl.; bowels pl., (eines Tieres) entrails pl.

Gedeck das; ~[e]s, ~e a) place setting; cover; ein ~ auflegen lay or set a place; b) (Menü) set meal; c) (Getränk) drink [with a cover charge]

gedeckt 1. 2. Part. v. decken. 2. Adj. subdued; muted; s. auch Apfelkuchen

Gedeih in auf ~ und Verderb for good or ill; for better or [for] worse; jmdm. auf ~ und Verderb ausgeliefert sein be entirely at sb.'s mercy

gedeihen [gəˈdaiən] unr. itr. V.; mit sein a) thrive; (wirtschaftlich) flourish; prosper; gut/schlecht gediehen sein have/not have thrived; b) (fortschreiten) progress; noch nicht sehr weit gediehen sein have not yet progressed very far

gedeihlich 1. Adj. (geh.) thriving, flourishing, successful ⟨business⟩; successful ⟨development, co-operation⟩; beneficial ⟨effect etc.⟩. 2. adv. successfully

ge·denken unr. itr. V. a) (geh.: zurückdenken, sich erinnern) jmds./einer Sache od. (schweiz.) jmdm./einer Sache (Dat.) ~: remember sb./sth.; (erwähnen) recall sb./sth.; (in einer Feier) commemorate sb./sth.; b) (beabsichtigen) intend

Gedenken das; ~s (geh.) remembrance; memory; Worte des ~s words of remembrance; zum ~ an jmdn./etw. in memory or remembrance of sb./sth.

Gedenk-: ~feier die commemoration; commemorative ceremony; ~gottesdienst der s. Gedächtnisgottesdienst; ~marke die (Philat.) commemorative stamp; ~minute die minute's silence; eine ~minute einlegen observe a minute's silence; ~münze die commemorative coin; ~rede die commemorative speech; ~stätte die memorial; ~stein der memorial or commemorative stone; ~stunde die hour of commemoration; ~tafel die commemorative plaque; ~tag der day of remembrance; commemoration day

Gedicht das; ~[e]s, ~e poem; Goethes ~e Goethe's poetry sing. or poems; das Steak/Kleid ist ein ~ (fig. ugs.) the steak is just superb/the dress is just heavenly

Gedicht-: ~interpretation die interpretation of a poem; ~sammlung die collection of poems; (von mehreren Dichtern) anthology of poetry or verse; poetry anthology

gediegen [gəˈdiːgn̩] 1. Adj. a) (solide) solid, solidly-made ⟨furniture⟩; sound, solid ⟨piece of work⟩; well-made ⟨clothing⟩; ~e Kenntnisse/ein ~es Wissen sound knowledge; ein ~er Charakter a sterling character; b) (rein) pure ⟨gold, silver, etc.⟩; (in der Natur rein vorkommend) native ⟨metal⟩; c) (ugs.: komisch) hilarious; eine ~e Marke/Type sein be good fun (coll.); d) (wunderlich) odd; peculiar. 2. adv. ~ gebaut/verarbeitet solidly built/made

Gediegenheit die; ~: solidity; (von Kleidung) sound manufacture; (von Metall) purity

gedieh [gəˈdiː] 1. u. 3. Pers. Sg. Prät. v. gedeihen

gediehen 2. Part. v. gedeihen

gedient [gəˈdiːnt] 1. 2. Part. v. dienen. 2. Adj. ein ~er Soldat a former soldier

Gedinge das; ~s, ~ (Bergmannsspr.: Akkordlohn) piece-rate pay; (Vereinbarung) piece-work agreement; im ~ arbeiten work on a piece-work basis

Gedöns [gəˈdøːns] das; ~es (landsch.) fuss; ein ~ machen make a fuss

Gedränge das; ~s a) (das Drängeln) pushing and shoving; (Menschenmenge) crush; crowd; vor der Theaterkasse herrschte ein großes ~: there was a big crush in front of the box-office; b) in ins ~ kommen od. geraten get into difficulties; mit dem Termin/der Zeit ins ~ kommen od. geraten have problems meeting the deadline/get into difficulties through lack of time; d) (Rugby) scrum; scrummage

gedrängt 1. 2. Part. v. drängen. 2. Adj. compressed, condensed ⟨account⟩; terse, succinct ⟨style, description⟩; crowded ⟨timetable, agenda⟩. 3. adv. ~ schreiben write succinctly or tersely; etw. ~ behandeln treat sth. in a condensed form

gedroschen [gəˈdrɔʃn̩] 2. Part. v. dreschen

gedrückt 1. 2. Part. v. drücken. 2. Adj. dejected, depressed ⟨mood⟩

gedrungen [gəˈdrʊŋən] 1. 2. Part. v. dringen. 2. Adj. stocky; thick-set

Gedrungenheit die; ~: stockiness
Gedudel das; ~s *(ugs. abwertend)* tootling; *(im Radio)* noise
Geduld [gə'dʊlt] **die;** ~: patience; **meine ~ ist erschöpft/am Ende** my patience is exhausted/at an end; **die ~ verlieren** lose one's patience; **keine ~ [zu etw.] haben** have no patience [with sth.]; **mit jmdm. ~ haben** be patient with sb.; **haben Sie bitte noch ein wenig ~**: please bear with me/us *etc.* a little while longer; **ihm riß die ~**: his patience snapped *or* gave way; **mir reißt die ~**: my patience is wearing thin; I'm losing all patience; **sich in ~ fassen** exercise *or* have patience; **mit ~ und Spucke** *(fig. salopp)* with a little patience [and ingenuity]
gedulden *refl. V.* be patient; **~ Sie sich bitte ein paar Minuten** please be so good as to wait a few minutes
geduldig 1. *Adj.* patient; **ein ~er Patient** a good patient; **~ wie ein Lamm** meek as a lamb. **2.** *adv.* patiently
Gedulds-: ~faden der *in* **mir/ihm** *etc.* **reißt der ~faden** *(ugs.)* my/his *etc.* patience is wearing thin; **~probe die** trial of one's patience; **das ist eine harte ~probe für mich** that sorely tries my patience; **auf eine harte ~probe gestellt werden** have one's patience sorely tried; **~spiel das** puzzle; *(fig.)* Chinese puzzle
gedungen [gə'dʊŋən] *2. Part. v.* **dingen**
gedunsen [gə'dʊnzn̩] *Adj. s.* **aufgedunsen**
gedurft [gə'dʊrft] *2. Part. v.* **dürfen**
geeignet 1. *2. Part. v.* **eignen. 2.** *Adj.* suitable; *(richtig)* right; **er ist der ~e Mann für diese Aufgabe** he's the right man for this job; **im ~en Augenblick** at the right moment; **ich war für diese Arbeit nicht ~**: I wasn't suited to the work
Geest [ge:st] **die;** ~: *sandy heathland on N. German coast*
Gefahr die; ~, ~en **a)** *(gefährliche Lage)* danger; *(Bedrohung)* danger; threat; **die ~en meines Berufs** the hazards of my job; **die ~en des Dschungels** the perils of the jungle; **eine ~ für jmdn./etw.** a danger to sb./sth.; **in ~ kommen/geraten** get into danger; **jmdn./etw. in ~ bringen** put sb./sth. in danger; **sich in ~ begeben** put oneself in danger; expose oneself to danger; **in ~ sein** be in danger; ⟨*rights, plans*⟩ be in jeopardy *or* peril; **außer ~ sein** be out of danger; **bei ~**: in case of emergency; **sie liebt die ~**: she likes living dangerously; **b)** *(Risiko)* risk; **jmdn./sich einer ~ aussetzen** run *or* take a risk; **es besteht die Gefahr, daß ...**: there is a danger *or* risk that ...; **auf die ~ hin, daß das passiert** at the risk of that happening; **~ laufen, etw. zu tun** risk *or* run the risk of doing sth.; **auf eigene ~**: at one's own risk; **wer sich in ~ begibt, kommt darin um** if you keep on taking risks, you'll come to grief eventually
gefahr·bringend *Adj.* dangerous
gefährden [gə'fɛ:ɐ̯dn̩] *tr. V.* endanger; jeopardize ⟨*enterprise, success, position, etc.*⟩; *(aufs Spiel setzen)* put at risk; **sich ~**: put oneself in danger
gefährdet *Adj.* ⟨*people, adolescents, etc.*⟩ at risk *postpos.*
Gefährdung die; ~, ~en **a)** *o. Pl.* endangering; *(eines Unternehmens, einer Position usw.)* jeopardizing; **b)** *(Gefahr)* threat (+ *Gen.* to)
gefahren *2. Part. v.* **fahren**
Gefahren-: ~bereich der danger area *or* zone; **~herd der** source of danger; **~quelle die** source of danger; **~zone die** danger zone *or* area; **~zulage die** danger money *no indef. art.*
gefährlich [gə'fɛ:ɐ̯lɪç] **1.** *Adj.* dangerous; *(gewagt)* risky; **ein Mann im ~en Alter** *(fig.)* a man at a dangerous age; **[für jmdn./etw.] ~ sein** be dangerous [for sb./sth.]; **er könnte mir ~ werden** he could be a threat *or* a danger to me; *(fig.)* I could fall for him [in a big way]; **das ist [alles] nicht so ~**: it's not disastrous; **ein ~er Plan/~es Unternehmen** a risky plan/enterprise; **ein ~es Spiel treiben** play a dangerous game. **2.** *adv.* dangerously
Gefährlichkeit die; ~: dangerousness; *(Gewagtheit)* riskiness
gefahr·los 1. *Adj.* safe. **2.** *adv.* safely
Gefahr·losigkeit die; ~: safety; safeness
Gefährt das; ~[e]s, ~e *(geh.)* vehicle
Gefährte der; ~n, ~n, **Gefährtin die;** ~, ~en *(geh.)* companion; *(Ehemann/Ehefrau)* partner in life
gefahr·voll *Adj.* dangerous; perilous
Gefälle [gə'fɛlə] **das;** ~s, ~ **a)** *(Neigungsgrad)* slope; incline; *(eines Flusses)* drop; *(einer Straße)* gradient; **ein ~ von fünf Prozent** a gradient of one in twenty *or* of five per cent; **das Gelände hat ein leichtes ~**: the land slopes gently; **b)** *(Unterschied)* difference; **das geistige/soziale ~**: the difference in intellect/social class
[1]**gefallen** *unr. itr. V.* **a) das gefällt mir** I like it; **das gefällt ihm gut/gar nicht** he likes it very much *or (coll.)* a lot/doesn't like it at all; **es gefiel ihr, wie er sich bewegte** she liked the way he moved; **zu ~ wissen** know how to make oneself liked [by everyone]; **weißt du, was mir an dir/dem Bild so gut gefällt?** do you know what I like so much about you/the picture?; **mir gefällt es hier** I like it here; **er gefällt mir [ganz und gar] nicht** *(ugs.: sieht krank aus)* he looks in a bad way to me *(coll.)*; **die Sache gefällt mir nicht** *(ugs.)* I don't like [the look of] it *(coll.)*; **wenn es dem Herrn gefällt** *(geh.)* if it please God; if it is God's will; **b)** *(ugs.)* **in sich** *(Dat.)* **etw. ~ lassen** put up with sth.; **das lasse ich mir nicht länger ~**: I won't put up with it *or* stand for it any longer; **das lasse ich mir ~!** there's nothing I like better; that's just the job *(coll.)*; **c)** *(abwertend)* **sich** *(Dat.)* **in einer Rolle ~**: enjoy *or* like playing a role; fancy oneself in a role *(coll.)*; **er gefällt sich in der Rolle des Intellektuellen** he likes playing the intellectual; **er gefällt sich in Übertreibungen** he likes to exaggerate
[2]**gefallen 1.** *2. Part. v.* **fallen, gefallen. 2.** *Adj.* fallen ⟨*angel etc.*⟩; **ein ~es Mädchen** *(veralt.)* a fallen woman
[1]**Gefallen der;** ~s, ~: favour; **jmdm. einen ~ tun** *od.* **erweisen** do sb. a favour; **tu mir den** *od.* **einen ~, und ...!** *(ugs.)* do me a favour and ...; **jmdn. um einen ~ bitten** ask a favour of sb.
[2]**Gefallen das;** ~s pleasure; **etw. mit ~ betrachten** get pleasure from *or* enjoy looking at sth.; **~ an jmdm./aneinander finden** like sb./each other; **an etw.** *(Dat.)* **~ finden** get *or* derive pleasure from sth.; enjoy sth.; **jmdm. etw. zu ~ tun** do sth. to please sb.
Gefallene der; *adj. Dekl.* soldier killed in action; **die ~n** the fallen; those killed *or* those who fell in action
Gefallenen·denkmal das war memorial
Gefälle·strecke die incline
ge·fällig 1. *Adj.* **a)** *(hilfsbereit)* obliging; helpful; **jmdm. ~ sein** oblige *or* help sb.; **sich ~ zeigen/[als] ~ erweisen** show oneself willing to oblige *or* help; **b)** *(anziehend)* pleasing; agreeable; pleasant, agreeable ⟨*programme, behaviour*⟩; **c)** *nicht attr. (gewünscht)* **folgen Sie mir, wenn's ~ ist!** follow me, if you please; **noch ein Kaffee ~?** would you like *or* care for another coffee?. **2.** *adv.* pleasingly; agreeably
Gefälligkeit die; ~, ~en **a)** *(Hilfeleistung)* favour; **jmdm. eine [kleine] ~ erweisen** do sb. a [small] favour; **b)** *o. Pl. (Hilfsbereitschaft)* obligingness; helpfulness; **etw. aus reiner ~ tun** do sth. just to be obliging; **c)** *(ansprechende Art)* agreeableness; pleasantness
Gefälligkeits·akzept das, Gefälligkeits·wechsel der *(Bankw.)* accommodation bill
gefälligst [gə'fɛlɪçst] *Adv. (ugs.)* kindly; **laß das ~!** kindly stop that
Gefäll·strecke die *s.* **Gefällestrecke**
Gefall·sucht die; ~; *o. Pl. (veralt.)* vanity
gefall·süchtig *Adj. (veralt.)* vain
gefangen *2. Part. v.* **fangen**
Gefangene der/die; *adj. Dekl.* **a)** prisoner; captive; **~ machen** take prisoners; **b)** *(Häftling, Kriegs~)* prisoner
Gefangenen-: ~austausch der exchange of prisoners; **~befreiung die** *(Rechtsw.)* aiding and abetting the escape of a prisoner; **~haus das** *(österr.) s.* **Gefängnis; ~lager das** prisoner of war camp; prison camp
gefangen-, Gefangen-: ~|halten *unr. tr. V.* **a) jmdn./ein Tier ~halten** hold sb. prisoner *or* captive/keep an animal in captivity; **b)** *(geh.: begeistern)* **jmdn./jmds. Aufmerksamkeit ~halten** hold sb. enthralled/rivet sb.'s attention; **~nahme die;** ~: capture; **bei seiner ~nahme** when he was captured; **~|nehmen** *unr. tr. V.* **a) jmdn. ~nehmen** capture sb.; take sb. prisoner; **b)** *(begeistern)* captivate; enthral
Gefangenschaft die; ~, ~en captivity; **in ~ sein/geraten** be a prisoner/be taken prisoner; **in russischer ~ sein** be a prisoner of the Russians
gefangen|setzen *tr. V. (geh.)* imprison
Gefängnis [gə'fɛŋnɪs] **das;** ~ses, ~se **a)** *(Strafanstalt)* prison; gaol; **jmdn. ins ~ bringen/werfen** put/throw sb. in[to] prison; **im ~ sein** *od.* **sitzen** be in prison; **ins ~ kommen** be sent to prison; **mit einem Bein** *od.* **Fuß im ~ stehen** be only just on the right side of the law; **b)** *(Strafe)* imprisonment; **darauf steht ~**: that is punishable by imprisonment *or* a prison sentence; **ein Vergehen mit ~ bestrafen** punish an offence with imprisonment; **jmdn. zu zwei Jahren ~ verurteilen** sentence sb. to two years' imprisonment *or* two years in prison
Gefängnis-: ~arzt der prison doctor; **~direktor der** prison governor; **~geistliche der** prison chaplain; **~haft die** imprisonment; **~hof der** prison yard; **~kleidung die** prison uniform; **~mauer die** prison wall; **~strafe die** prison sentence; **eine ~strafe verbüßen** *od. (ugs.)* **absitzen** serve a prison sentence; **eine ~strafe von sechs Monaten** six months' imprisonment; six months in prison; **jmdn. zu einer ~strafe [von acht Monaten] verurteilen** send sb. to prison [for eight months]; **~wärter der** prison officer; [prison] warder; **~zelle die** prison cell
Gefasel das; ~s *(ugs. abwertend)* twaddle *(coll.)*; drivel *(derog.)*
Gefäß [gə'fɛ:s] **das;** ~es, ~e **a)** *(Behälter)* vessel; container; **b)** *(Med.)* vessel; **c)** *(Fechten)* coquille
gefäß-, Gefäß-: ~erweiternd *(Med.)* **1.** *Adj.* vaso-dilating; **2.** *adv.* **~erweiternd wirken** have a vaso-dilating effect; **~erweiterung die** *(Med.)* vascular dilation; **~leiden das** *(Med.)* vascular complaint
gefaßt [gə'fast] **1.** *2. Part. v.* **fassen. 2.** *Adj.* **a)** *(beherrscht)* calm; composed; **mit ~er Haltung** with composure; **mit ~er Stimme** in a calm voice; **b)** *in* **auf etw.** *(Akk.)* **[nicht] ~ sein** [not] be prepared for sth.; **sich auf etw.** *(Akk.)* **~ machen** prepare oneself for sth.; **der kann sich auf was ~ machen** *(ugs.)* he'll catch it *or* be for it *(coll.)*. **3.** *adv.* calmly; with composure
Gefaßtheit die calmness; composure
gefäß-, Gefäß-: ~verengend *(Med.)* **1.** *Adj.* vaso-constrictive; **2.** *adv.* **~verengend wirken** have a vaso-constrictive effect; **~verengung die** *(Med.)* vasoconstriction; vascular constriction; **~wand die** *(Med.)* vascular wall

Gefecht das; ~[e]s, ~e **a)** battle; engagement *(Milit.)*; **ein schweres/kurzes ~:** fierce fighting/a skirmish; **sich** *(Dat.)***/dem Feind ein ~ liefern** engage each other/the enemy in battle; **die Truppen ins ~ führen** lead the troops into battle; **ein hitziges ~** *(fig.)* a heated exchange; **jmdn./etw. außer ~ setzen** put sb./sth. out of action; **klar zum ~!** *(Marine)* clear for action!; **b)** *(Fechten)* bout; *s. auch* **Eifer**

gefechts-, Gefechts-: ~ausbildung die *(Milit.)* combat training; battle training; **~bereich der** *(Milit.)* battle zone; battle area; combat zone *(Amer.)*; **~bereit** *Adj.* *(Milit.)* ready for action *or* battle *postpos.*; combat-ready; **~bereitschaft die** *(Milit.)* readiness for action; readiness for battle; **sich in ~bereitschaft befinden** be ready for action *or* battle; **~einheit die** *(Milit.)* fighting unit; **~klar** *Adj. s.* **~bereit; ~kopf der** *(Milit.)* warhead; **~mäßig** *(Milit.)* **1.** *Adj.* ⟨*equipment*⟩ for active service; combat ⟨*firing practice, formation, etc.*⟩; **2.** *adv.* **~mäßig ausgerüstet** equipped for active service *or* for battle; **~pause die** lull in the fighting; **~stand der** *(Milit.)* battle headquarters *pl.*; command post; *(Luftw.)* operations room; **~stärke die** *(Milit.)* fighting strength; **~turm der** *(Milit.)* turret; **~übung die** *(Milit.)* combat exercise; field exercise

gefedert *2. Part. v.* **federn**

gefehlt 1. *2. Part. v.* **fehlen. 2.** *Adj.* **weit ~!** wide of the mark!

Gefeilsche das; ~s haggling

gefeit *2. Part. v.* **feien**

gefestigt 1. *2. Part. v.* **festigen. 2.** *Adj.* assured ⟨*beliefs*⟩; secure ⟨*person*⟩; established ⟨*tradition*⟩

Gefiedel das; ~s *(abwertend)* fiddling

Gefieder [gəˈfi:dɐ] **das;** ~s, ~: plumage; feathers *pl.*

gefiedert *Adj.* **a)** *(mit Federn)* feathered; **unsere ~en Freunde** our feathered friends; **b)** *(Bot.)* pinnate; **paarig/unpaarig ~:** abruptly pinnate/odd-pinnate

Gefilde [gəˈfɪldə] **das;** ~s, ~ *(geh.)* **anmutige/sonnige ~:** pleasant/sunny climes *(literary)*; **die ~ der Seligen** *(griech. Myth.)* the Elysian Fields; **wieder in heimatlichen ~n sein** *(scherzh.)* be back under one's native skies

gefingert 1. *2. Part. v.* **fingern. 2.** *Adj.* *(Bot.)* digitate[d]; palmate

gefinkelt [gəˈfɪŋkl̩t] *Adj.* *(österr.)* cunning; crafty; shrewd

geflammt 1. *2. Part. v.* **flammen. 2.** *Adj.* mottled, wavy-grained ⟨*wood*⟩; mottled ⟨*tile*⟩; watered, moiré ⟨*silk, fabric*⟩

Geflatter das; ~s fluttering

Geflecht das; ~[e]s, ~e **a)** *(Flechtwerk)* wickerwork *no art.*; **ein ~ aus Binsen** interlaced rushes *pl.*; **b)** *(fig.: dichtes Netz)* tangle; **ein wirres/dichtes ~ von Zweigen und Wurzeln** a tangled/dense network of twigs and roots

gefleckt 1. *2. Part. v.* **flecken. 2.** *Adj.* spotty, blotchy ⟨*skin, face*⟩; spotted ⟨*leopard skin*⟩

Geflenne das; ~s *(ugs. abwertend)* bawling; blubbering

Geflimmer das; ~s *(auf dem Bildschirm, auf der Filmleinwand)* flickering; *(von Sternen)* twinkling

geflissentlich [gəˈflɪsn̩tlɪç] **1.** *Adj.; nicht präd.* **a)** *(absichtlich)* deliberate; **b)** *(Amtsspr. veralt.: freundlich)* **zu Ihrer ~en Kenntnisnahme/Beachtung** for your information/for your esteemed consideration. **2.** *adv.* deliberately; **jmdm. ~ aus dem Wege gehen** studiously avoid sb.

geflochten [gəˈflɔxtn̩] *2. Part. v.* **flechten**

geflogen [gəˈflo:gn̩] *2. Part. v.* **fliegen**

geflohen [gəˈflo:ən] *2. Part. v.* **fliehen**

geflossen [gəˈflɔsn̩] *2. Part. v.* **fließen**

Gefluche das; ~s *(ugs. abwertend)* swearing; cursing

Geflügel das; ~s *(Federvieh, Fleisch)* poultry

Geflügel-: ~farm die poultry farm; **~haltung die** poultry-farming; **~händler der** poulterer; **~handlung die** poulterer's [shop]; **~salat der** chicken salad/turkey salad *etc.*; **~schere die** poultry shears *pl.*

geflügelt *Adj.* winged ⟨*insect, seed*⟩; **ein ~es Wort** *(fig.)* a standard *or* familiar quotation

Geflügel-: ~zucht die poultry-breeding; **~züchter der** poultry-breeder

Geflunker das; ~s *(ugs.)* fibbing *(coll.)*

Geflüster das; ~s whispering

gefochten [gəˈfɔxtn̩] *2. Part. v.* **fechten**

Gefolge das; ~s, ~ **a)** *(Begleitung)* entourage; retinue; **etw. im ~ haben** lead to sth.; bring sth. in its wake; **b)** *(Trauergeleit)* cortège

Gefolgschaft die; ~, **~en a)** *o. Pl.* *(Gehorsam)* **jmdm. ~ leisten** obey *or* follow sb.; give one's allegiance to sb.; **jmdm. die ~ aufsagen** *od.* **kündigen** refuse to obey sb. any longer; renounce one's allegiance to sb.; **jmdm. die ~ verweigern** refuse to obey *or* follow sb.; refuse to give sb. one's allegiance; **b)** *(hist.)* *band of young nobles bound to a peer leader by an oath of fealty;* ≈ followers *pl.*

Gefolgs·mann der; *Pl.* **-männer** *od.* **-leute** *member of a Gefolgschaft;* ≈ follower; *(fig.)* follower

Gefrage das; ~s *(abwertend)* questions *pl.*

gefragt 1. *2. Part. v.* **fragen. 2.** *Adj.* ⟨*artist, craftsman, product*⟩ in great demand; sought-after ⟨*artist, craftsman, product*⟩; **~ sein** *od.* **werden** be in great demand

gefräßig [gəˈfrɛ:sɪç] *Adj.* *(abwertend)* greedy; gluttonous; voracious ⟨*animal, insect*⟩

Gefräßigkeit die; ~ *(abwertend)* greediness; gluttony; *(von Tieren)* voracity

Gefreite [gəˈfraitə] **der;** *adj. Dekl.* *(Milit.)* lance-corporal *(Brit.)*; private first class *(Amer.)*; *(Marine)* able seaman; *(Luftw.)* aircraftman first class *(Brit.)*; airman third class *(Amer.)*

gefressen *2. Part. v.* **fressen**

Gefrier-: ~anlage die freezing plant; **~apparat der** freezing unit; freezer

gefrieren 1. *unr. itr. V.; mit sein (auch fig.)* freeze; *s. auch* **Blut. 2.** *unr. tr. V.* *(einfrieren)* freeze

gefrier-, Gefrier-: ~fach das freezing compartment; **~fleisch das** frozen meat; **~gemüse das** frozen vegetables *pl.*; **~getrocknet** *2. Part. v.* **~trocknen; ~gut das** frozen food; **~punkt der** freezing-point; **Temperaturen über/unter dem ~punkt** temperatures above/below freezing; **~raum der** freezer; deep-freeze room; **~schrank der** [upright] freezer; **~schutz·mittel das** *s.* **Frostschutzmittel; ~|trocknen** *tr. V.; meist im Inf. u. 2. Part.* freeze-dry; **~truhe die** [chest] freezer

gefroren [gəˈfro:rən] *2. Part. v.* **frieren, gefrieren**

Gefror[e]ne das; *adj. Dekl.* *(südd., österr.)* ice cream

Gefrotzel das; ~s *(ugs.)* ribbing *(coll.)*

Gefuchtel das; ~s gesticulating

Gefüge das; ~s, ~ **a)** *(Zusammengefügtes)* structure; construction; **ein ~ aus Balken/Steinen** a construction of beams/stones; **b)** *(Aufbau, Struktur)* structure; **das syntaktische ~:** the syntactical structure; **das wirtschaftliche/soziale ~:** the economic/social fabric

gefügig *Adj.* submissive; compliant; docile ⟨*animal*⟩; **ein ~es Werkzeug** *(fig.)* a willing tool; **sich** *(Dat.)* **jmdn. ~ machen/jmdn. seinen Wünschen ~ machen** make sb. submit to one's will/one's wishes

Gefügigkeit die; ~: submissiveness; compliance; *(von Tieren)* docility

Gefühl das; ~s, ~e **a)** *(Wahrnehmung)* sensation; feeling; **ein ~ für Wärme und Kälte haben** be able to feel *or* tell the difference between hot and cold; **kein ~ im Arm haben** have no feeling in one's arm; **ein ~ des Schmerzes/der Kälte** a sensation of pain/cold; **b)** *(Gemütsverfassung)* feeling; **ein ~ der Einsamkeit/der Scham** a sense *or* feeling of loneliness/shame; **ein beglückendes/beängstigendes ~ überkam/ergriff sie** she was filled with a feeling of happiness/gripped by a feeling of anxiety; **kein ~ haben** have no feelings; **mit gemischten ~en** with mixed feelings; **drei Mark sind das höchste der Gefühle** *(ugs.)* three marks is the most I'm prepared to pay; *(was man dafür verlangen kann)* it won't fetch more than three marks; **c)** *(Ahnung)* feeling; **ein/das ~ haben, als ob ...:** have a/the feeling that ...; **etw. im ~ haben** have a feeling *or* a premonition of sth.; **d)** *(Verständnis, Gespür)* sense; instinct; **ein ~ für Rhythmus/Gut und Böse** a sense of rhythm/right and wrong; **sich auf sein ~ verlassen** trust one's feelings *or* instinct; **etw. nach ~ tun** do sth. by instinct

gefühlig *Adj.* *(abwertend)* mushy, mawkish ⟨*play, film, etc.*⟩; mawkish ⟨*person*⟩

gefühl·los *Adj.* **a)** *(ohne Wahrnehmung)* numb; **~ gegen Schmerzen** insensitive to pain; **b)** *(herzlos, kalt)* unfeeling; callous

Gefühllosigkeit die; ~ **a)** numbness; lack of sensation; **b)** *(Mangel an Mitleid)* unfeelingness; callousness

gefühls-, Gefühls-: ~aktiv *Adj.* supersensitive, extra sensitive ⟨*condom*⟩; **~arm** *Adj.* lacking in feeling; **~armut die** lack of feeling; **~ausbruch der** outburst [of emotion]; **~betont 1.** *Adj.* emotional ⟨*speech, argument*⟩; **2.** *adv.* **~betont handeln** be guided by one's emotions; **~dinge** *Pl.* emotional matters *pl.*; **~duselei** [-du:zəˈlai] **die;** ~ *(ugs. abwertend)* mawkishness; mawkish sentimentality; **~kalt** *Adj.* **a)** cold; unfeeling; **b)** *(frigide)* frigid; **~kälte die a)** coldness; unfeelingness; **b)** *(Frigidität)* frigidity; **~leben das** emotional life; **~mäßig 1.** *Adj.* emotional ⟨*reaction*⟩; ⟨*action*⟩ based on emotion; **2.** *adv.* **es hat sich ~mäßig auf ihn stark ausgewirkt** it has affected him deeply; **rein ~mäßig würde ich sagen, daß ...:** my own, purely instinctive, feeling would be to say that ...; **~mensch der** emotionalist; person guided by his/her emotions; **~nerv der** sensory nerve; **~regung die** emotion; **~roheit die** callousness; **~sache die** matter of feel *or* instinct; **~tiefe die** *(geh.)* depth of feeling; **~überschwang der** flood of emotion; **in seinem ~überschwang** carried away by emotion; **~welt die** emotions *pl.*

gefühl·voll 1. *Adj.* **a)** *(empfindsam)* sensitive; **b)** *(ausdrucksvoll)* expressive. **2.** *adv.* sensitively; expressively; with feeling

gefüllt 1. *2. Part. v.* **füllen. 2. ~e Bonbons** sweets *(Brit.)* *or* *(Amer.)* candies with centres; **~e Tomaten/Paprikaschoten** stuffed tomatoes/peppers; **~er Flieder/~e Geranien** double lilac/geraniums; **eine [gut] ~e Brieftasche** a well-stuffed *or* bulging wallet

Gefummel das; ~s *(ugs. abwertend)* **a)** fiddling *(coll.)*; **laß doch das ~ an der Tischdecke!** stop fiddling with the table-cloth!; **b)** *(erotisch)* pawing *(coll.)*

gefunden [gəˈfʊndn̩] *2. Part. v.* **finden;** *s. auch* **Fressen b**

gefurcht 1. *2. Part. v.* **furchen. 2.** *Adj.* lined; wrinkled

gefürchtet 1. *2. Part. v.* **fürchten. 2.** *Adj.* dreaded; feared ⟨*despot, opponent*⟩

gefüttert *2. Part. v.* **füttern**

gegabelt 1. *2. Part. v.* **gabeln. 2.** *Adj.* forked ⟨*branch, stick, tail*⟩

Gegạcker das; ~s a) *(dauerndes Gackern)* cackling; **b)** *(ugs.: Kichern)* giggling

gegạngen *2. Part. v.* **gehen**

gegẹben 1. *2. Part. v.* **geben. 2.** *Adj.* **a)** *(vorhanden)* given; **etw. als ~ voraussetzen/hinnehmen** take sth. for granted; **aus ~em Anlaß** for certain reasons *(specified or not)*; **aus ~em Anlaß kann ich nicht umhin, auch einige Worte der Kritik zu äußern** [there are reasons why] I cannot refrain from offering some criticisms; **unter den ~en Umständen** in these circumstances; **eine ~e Größe/Zahl** *(Math.)* a given magnitude/number; **b)** *(passend)* right; proper; **das ist das gegebene** that's the best thing; **zu ~er Zeit** in due course; at the appropriate time

gegẹbenen·falls *Adv.* should the occasion arise; *(wenn nötig)* if necessary; *(auf einem Formular)* if applicable

Gegẹbenheit die; ~, ~en; *meist Pl.* condition; *(Tatsache)* fact; **die wirtschaftlichen und sozialen ~en** the economic and social conditions

gegen ['ge:gn̩] **1.** *Präp. mit Akk.* **a)** towards; *(an)* against; **das Dia ~ das Licht halten** hold the slide up to *or* against the light; **~ die Tür schlagen** bang on the door; **~ etw. stoßen** knock into *or* against sth.; **das ist [nicht] ~ Sie gerichtet** that is [not] aimed against you; **ein Mittel ~ Husten/Krebs** a cough medicine/a cure for cancer; **~ jmdn. spielen/gewinnen** play [against] sb./win against sb.; **etwas/nichts ~ jmdn. haben** have something/nothing against sb.; **~ die Abmachung** contrary to *or* against the agreement; **~ alle Vernunft/bessere Einsicht** against all reason/one's better judgement; **~ jmds. Willen/Befehl** against *or* contrary to sb.'s wishes/orders; **b)** *(ungefähr um)* **~ Abend/Morgen** towards evening/dawn; **~ 4^{00} nachts** around 4 a. m. *or* 4 o'clock in the morning; **c)** *(im Vergleich zu)* compared with; in comparison with; **~ gestern** compared with yesterday; **ich wette hundert ~ eins, daß er ...:** I'll bet you a hundred to one he ...; **d)** *(im Ausgleich für)* for; **etw. ~ bar verkaufen/tauschen** sell/exchange sth. for cash; **etw. ~ Quittung erhalten** receive sth. against a receipt; **e)** *(veralt.: gegenüber)* **~ jmdn. freundlich/höflich sein** be pleasant/polite to *or* towards sb.; **~ jmdn./sich streng sein** be strict with sb./oneself. **2.** *Adv. (ungefähr)* about; around

Gẹgen-: ~angebot das counter-offer; **~angriff der** counter-attack; **zum ~angriff ansetzen** mount *or* launch a counter-attack; **~antrag der** *(im Parlament)* counter-motion; **~anzeige die** *(Med.)* contra-indication; **~argument das** counter-argument; **~beispiel das** example to the contrary; counter-example; **~beschuldigung die** countercharge; counter-accusation; **~besuch der** return visit; **~bewegung die a)** counter-movement; **b)** *(Musik) (bei der Melodie)* inversion; *(bei Tonleitern usw.)* contrary motion; **~beweis der** evidence to the contrary, counter-evidence *no indef. art., no pl.*; **den ~beweis antreten** *od.* **führen** produce evidence to the contrary *or* counter-evidence; **~buchung die** *(Buchf.)* cross-entry

Gegend ['ge:gn̩t] **die; ~, ~en a)** *(Landschaft)* landscape; *(geographisches Gebiet)* region; **die ~ ist flach/gebirgig** the region is flat/mountainous; **durch die ~ latschen/kurven** *(salopp)* traipse around *(coll.)*/drive around; **in der ~ herumbrüllen** *(salopp)* bawl one's head off *(coll.)*; **b)** *(Umgebung)* area; neighbourhood; *(Stadtviertel)* district; neighbourhood; *(Einwohnerschaft)* neighbourhood; **in der ~ von/um Hamburg** in the Hamburg area; **in der ~ des Parks** in the neighbourhood of the park; **ein Einbrecher/eine Jugendbande macht die ~ unsicher** *(ugs.)* there is a burglar about in the neighbourhood/a gang of youths are making a nuisance of themselves in this area; **c) in der ~ des Magens/der Leber** in the region of the stomach/the liver; **d)** *(Richtung)* direction

Gẹgen-: ~darstellung die: eine ~darstellung [der Sache] an account [of the matter] from an opposing point of view; **~demonstration die** counter-demonstration; **~dienst der** service in return; *(Gefälligkeit)* favour in return; **~druck der** counter-pressure; *(fig.)* resistance

gegen·einạnder *Adv.* **a)** against each other *or* one another; *(im Austausch)* **man tauschte die Geiseln ~ aus** the hostages were exchanged; **es ist schwierig, diese beiden Begriffe/Epochen ~ abzugrenzen** it is difficult to distinguish these two concepts/to divide these two periods from each other; **die beiden haben etwas ~:** those two have got something against each other; **b)** *(zueinander)* to[wards] each other *or* one another

Gẹgen·einander das; ~s conflict

gegeneinạnder-: ~|halten *unr. tr. V.* **a)** *(nebeneinanderhalten)* **zwei Dinge ~halten** hold two things up together *or* side by side; **b)** *(vergleichen)* compare; put side by side; **~|prallen** *itr. V.; mit sein* collide; **~|schlagen 1.** *unr. tr. V.* beat against each other; knock ⟨*heads*⟩ against each other; strike ⟨*flints*⟩ against each other; **2.** *unr. itr. V.; mit sein* bang against each other; **~|stellen** *itr. V.* **a) Bretter/Fahrräder ~stellen** stand planks/bicycles [up] against one another; **b)** *(vergleichen)* compare; put side by side

gegen-, Gẹgen-: ~entwurf der alternative draft; **~erklärung die** counter-statement; rebuttal; **~fahrbahn die** opposite carriageway; **~forderung die a)** counter-condition; **b)** *(Forderung eines Schuldners)* counter-claim; **~frage die** question in return; counter-question; **auf eine Frage mit einer ~frage antworten** answer a question with another question; **~gabe die** *(geh.)* present *or* gift in return; **~gerade die** *(Leichtathletik)* back straight; **~gewalt die** counter-violence; **~gewicht das** counterweight; **ein ~gewicht zu** *od.* **gegen etw. bilden** *(fig.)* counterbalance sth.; **~gift das** antidote; **~grund der** *s.* **Grund c; ~|halten** *unr. tr., itr. V. (nordd. ugs.)* **[die Hand/den Finger] ~halten** hold one's hand/finger against it; **~kandidat der** opposing candidate; rival candidate; **~klage die** *(Rechtsw.)* counter-claim; countercharge; **~klage [gegen jmdn.] erheben** bring a counter-claim *or* counter-charge/countercharges *pl.* [against sb.]; **~kläger der** *(Rechtsw.)* counterclaimant; **~könig der** *(hist.)* rival claimant to the throne; **~kraft die** opposing force; counter-force; **~kultur die** counter-culture; alternative culture; **~kurs der** *(Flugw.)* reciprocal course; **auf ~kurs gehen** set a reciprocal course; *(fig.)* steer an opposite course; **~läufig 1.** *Adj.* opposed ⟨*pistons*⟩; contra-rotating ⟨*propellers*⟩; **eine ~läufige Entwicklung/Tendenz** *(fig.)* a reverse development/trend; **2.** *adv.* **sich ~läufig bewegen** ⟨*pistons*⟩ be opposed; ⟨*propellers*⟩ contra-rotate; **~leistung die** service in return; consideration; **als ~leistung für etw.** in return for sth.; **zu einer ~leistung bereit sein** be prepared to do sth. in return; **~|lenken** *itr. V.* turn the wheel to correct the line; **~|lesen** *unr. tr. V.* read as a check

Gẹgen·licht das; *o. Pl. (bes. Fot.)* backlighting

Gẹgenlicht·aufnahme die *(Fot.)* photograph taken/taking a picture against the light; contre-jour photograph

gẹgen-, Gẹgen-: ~liebe die *in* **[bei jmdm.] ~liebe finden** *od.* **auf ~liebe stoßen** find favour [with sb.]; **~maßnahme die** counter-measure; **~meinung die** opposing *or* dissenting view; **~mittel das** *(gegen Gift)* antidote; *(gegen Krankheit)* remedy; **ein ~mittel für ein Gift/gegen eine Krankheit** an antidote for *or* to a poison/a remedy for a disease; **~mutter die** *(Technik)* locking nut; lock-nut; **~offensive die** *(Milit.)* counter-offensive; **~papst der** *(hist.)* antipope; **~part der** *(geh.)* counterpart; *(Gegner)* opponent; **~partei die** opposing side; other side; *(Sport)* opposing side *or* team; **~plan der** *(DDR Wirtsch.)* counter-plan *(to supplement the national economic plan)*; **~pol der** *(auch fig.)* opposite pole; *(Math.)* antipole; **~probe die a)** *(einer Behauptung, These)* cross-check; **durch die ~probe** by cross-checking; **die ~probe machen** carry out a cross-check; *(bei einer Rechnung)* work the sum the other way round; **b)** *(bei Abstimmungen durch Handzeichen od. Aufstehen)* recount in which the opposite motion is put; **~propaganda die** counter-propaganda; **~rechnung die** contra account; check account; **[jmdm.] die ~rechnung aufmachen** make out a contra account for sb.; *(fig.)* reply with one's own set of figures; **~rede die a)** *(geh.: Erwiderung)* reply; rejoinder; **Rede und ~rede** dialogue; **ein amüsantes Spiel von Rede und ~rede** an amusing series of exchanges; **b)** *(Widerrede)* contradiction; *(Einspruch)* objection; **~reformation die** *(hist.)* Counter-Reformation; **~revolution die** counter-revolution; **~richtung die** opposite direction; **~ruder das** *(Flugw.)* **a)** *(zur Erleichterung des Steuerns)* servo tab; **b)** *(zur Einhaltung der Fluglage)* trim tab; **~satz der a)** *(Gegenteil)* opposite; **einen schroffen/diametralen ~satz zu etw./jmdm. bilden** contrast sharply with/be diametrically opposed to sth./sb.; **im ~satz zu** in contrast to *or* with; unlike; **~sätze ziehen sich an** opposites attract; **b)** *(Widerspruch)* conflict; **im krassen/scharfen ~satz zu etw. stehen** be in stark/sharp conflict with sth.; **c)** *Pl. (Meinungsverschiedenheiten)* **~sätze abbauen/überbrücken** reduce/reconcile differences; **~sätzlich 1.** *Adj.* conflicting ⟨*views, opinions, etc.*⟩; **~sätzliche Fronten** opposing alignments; **2.** *adv.* **etw. ~sätzlich beurteilen** judge sth. completely differently; **~schlag der** counterstroke; **zum ~schlag ausholen** prepare to counter-attack *or* strike back; **~seite die a)** *(einer Straße, eines Flusses usw.)* other side; far side; **b)** *s.* **~partei; ~seitig 1.** *Adj.* **a)** *(wechselseitig)* mutual ⟨*aid, consideration, love, consent, services*⟩; reciprocal ⟨*aid, obligation, services*⟩; **in ~seitiger Abhängigkeit stehen** be mutually dependent; be dependent on each other *or* one another; **b)** *(beide Seiten betreffend)* **eine ~seitige Abmachung** a bilateral arrangement; **in ~seitigem Einvernehmen** by mutual agreement; **2.** *adv.* **sich ~seitig helfen/überbieten** help/outdo each other *or* one another; **~seitigkeit die** reciprocity; **auf ~seitigkeit** *(Dat.)* **beruhen** be mutual; **~sinn der** *in* **im ~sinn** in the opposite direction; **~spieler der a)** *(Widersacher)* opponent; **b)** *(Sport)* opposite number; **c)** *(Theater)* antagonist; **~spionage die** counter-espionage; **~sprechanlage die** intercom [system]; *(Fernspr.)* duplex system; **~sprech·verkehr der** two-way communication

Gẹgen·stand der a) *(Ding, Körper)* object; **Gegenstände des täglichen Gebrauchs/Bedarfs** objects *or* articles of everyday use; **b)** *o. Pl. (Thema)* subject; topic; **etw. zum ~ haben** deal with sth.; be concerned with sth.; **c)** *(Objekt, Ziel)* **der ~ seiner Zuneigung/seines Hasses** the object of his affections/of his hatred; **zum ~ der Kritik werden** become the target *or* butt of criticism; **d)** *(österr.: Schulfach)* subject

gegenständlich ['ge:gn̩ʃtɛntlɪç] *Adj.* *(Kunst)* representational; *(Philos.)* objective

gegenstands·los *Adj.* **a)** *(hinfällig)* invalid; **das hat unsere Pläne ~los gemacht** that's made nonsense of our plans; **b)** *(grundlos, unbegründet)* unsubstantiated, unfounded ‹*accusation, complaint*›; baseless ‹*fear*›; unfounded ‹*jealousy*›; **c)** *(abstrakt)* non-representational; abstract

Gegenstands·wort das *(Sprachw.)* concrete noun

gegen-, Gegen-: ~|steuern *itr. V.* **a)** *s.* **~lenken; b)** *(fig.)* take countermeasures; **~stimme die a)** vote against; **ohne ~stimme** unanimously; **das Gesetz passierte mit 380 Jastimmen und 80 ~stimmen das Parlament** the law was passed by Parliament by 380 votes to 80; **b)** *(gegenteilige Meinung)* dissenting voice; **c)** *(Musik)* counterpart; **~stoß der a)** *s.* **~schlag; b)** *s.* **~angriff; ~strömung die** counter-current; **~stück das a)** *(Pendant)* companion piece; *(fig.)* counterpart; **b)** *s.* **~teil; ~teil das** opposite; **im ~teil** on the contrary; **ganz im ~teil:** far from it; quite the reverse; **die Stimmung schlug ins ~teil um** the mood changed completely; **~teilig** *Adj.* opposite; contrary; **~teiliger Meinung/Ansicht sein** hold the opposite opinion *or* view; be of the opposite opinion; **~teilige Aussagen** contradictory statements; **~tor das, ~treffer der** *(Sport)* goal for the other side; **ein ~tor** *od.* **einen ~treffer hinnehmen müssen** concede a goal

gegen·über 1. *Präp. mit Dat.* **a)** *(auf der entgegengesetzten Seite)* opposite; **~ dem Bahnhof/Rathaus, dem Bahnhof/Rathaus ~:** opposite the station/town hall; **b)** *(in bezug auf)* **~ jmdm.** *od.* **jmdm. ~ freundlich/streng sein** be kind to/strict with sb.; **~ einer Sache** *od.* **einer Sache ~ skeptisch sein** be sceptical about sth.; **~ uns** *od.* **uns ~ brauchst du wirklich keine Hemmungen zu haben** you really needn't have any inhibitions with us; **c)** *(im Vergleich zu)* compared with; in comparison with; **~ jmdm. im Vorteil sein** have an advantage over sb. **2.** *Adv.* opposite; **er wohnt schräg ~:** he lives diagonally opposite

Gegen·über das; ~s, ~ a) *(gegenübersitzende/-stehende Person)* person [sitting/standing] opposite; *(Gesprächspartner)* person one is talking to; **b)** *(Bewohner eines gegenüberliegenden Gebäudes)* person living opposite; **kein ~ haben** have no one living opposite

gegenüber-, Gegenüber-: ~|liegen *unr. itr. V.* **sich** *(Dat.)* *od.* **einander ~liegen** face each other *or* one another; **auf der ~liegenden Seite/am ~liegenden Ufer** on the opposite side/bank; **~|sehen** *unr. refl. V.* **sich jmdm./etw. ~sehen** find oneself facing sb./sth.; **sich einer Sache** *(Dat.)* **~sehen** *(fig.)* be faced with sth.; **~|sitzen** *unr. itr. V.* **jmdm./sich ~sitzen** sit opposite *or* facing sb./each other; **~|stehen** *unr. itr. V.* **a)** *(zugewandt stehen)* **jmdm./einer Sache ~stehen** stand facing sb./sth.; **jmdm. Auge in Auge ~stehen** confront sb. face to face; **Schwierigkeiten/Problemen ~stehen** *(fig.)* be faced *or* confronted with difficulties/problems; **b)** *(eingestellt sein)* **jmdm./einer Sache feindlich/wohlwollend ~stehen** be ill/well disposed towards sb./sth.; **jmdm./einer Sache mißtrauisch ~stehen** be mistrustful of sb./sth.; *s. auch* **ablehnend; c)** *(Sport)* **sich ~stehen** face each other *or* one another; meet; **d)** *(im Widerstreit stehen)* **sich ~stehen** stand directly opposed to each other *or* one another; **~|stellen** *tr. V.* **a)** *(konfrontieren)* confront; **jmdn. einem Zeugen ~stellen** to confront sb. with a witness; **b)** *(in Beziehung bringen)* compare; **~stellung die a)** *(Konfrontation)* confrontation; **b)** *(Vergleich)* comparison; **~|treten** *unr. itr. V.;* *mit sein* face; **Schwierigkeiten** *(Dat.)* **~treten** face [up to] difficulties

Gegen-: ~verkehr der oncoming traffic; **~vorschlag der** counter-proposal

Gegenwart [-vart] **die; ~ a)** present; *(heutige Zeit)* present [time *or* day]; **bis in die ~ fortwirken** continue [down] to the present day; **die Literatur/Musik der ~:** contemporary literature/music; **b)** *(Anwesenheit)* presence; **in ~ von anderen** in the presence of others; **c)** *(Grammatik)* present [tense]

gegenwärtig [-vɛrtɪç] **1.** *Adj.* **a)** *nicht präd.* present; *(heutig)* present[-day]; current; **b)** *(geh.: erinnerlich)* **ich habe die Begebenheit nicht ~:** I cannot recall the event; **sich** *(Dat.)* **etw. ~ halten** keep sth. in mind; **c)** *(veralt.: anwesend, zugegen)* present; **bei etw. ~ sein** be present at sth.; **in dieser mittelalterlichen Stadt ist die Geschichte überall ~** *(fig.)* history is all around one in this medieval town. **2.** *adv.* at present; at the moment; *(heute)* at present; currently

gegenwarts-, Gegenwarts-: ~bezogen *Adj.* relevant to the present day *or* to today *postpos.;* **~fern** *Adj.* remote from the present *postpos.;* **~fremd** *Adj.* out of touch with the present *or* with today; **~kunde die** *(Schulw.)* political and social studies *sing., no art.;* **~kunst die** contemporary art *no art.;* **~literatur die** contemporary literature *no art.;* **~nah[e] 1.** *Adj.* relevant to the present day *or* to today *postpos.;* *(aktuell)* topical; **2.** *adv.* **~nah denken** be up to date in one's thinking; **~nah unterrichten** teach in accordance with contemporary ideas; **~schaffen das** *(DDR)* contemporary creative work in the arts; **~sprache die** present-day language; **die deutsche ~sprache** modern German; **~stück das** contemporary play

gegen-, Gegen-: ~wehr die; *o. Pl.* resistance; **[keine] ~wehr leisten** put up [no] resistance; **~wert der** equivalent; **der volle ~wert für das gestohlene Auto** the full replacement value of the stolen car; **~wind der** head wind; **~winkel der** *(Math.)* opposite angle; **~wirkung die** reaction; **~|zeichnen** *tr. V.* countersign; **~zug der a)** *(Brettspiele, fig.)* countermove; *(Polit.)* reciprocal gesture; **im ~zug** *(fig.)* in return for; **b)** *(entgegenkommender Zug)* train in the opposite direction; **c)** *s.* **~angriff**

gegessen [gə'gɛsn̩] *2. Part. v.* **essen**

geglichen [gə'glɪçn̩] *2. Part. v.* **gleichen**

geglitten [gə'glɪtn̩] *2. Part. v.* **gleiten**

Geglitzer das; ~s *(von Edelsteinen)* glitter; sparkle; *(von Sternen)* twinkling

geglommen [gə'glɔmən] *2. Part. v.* **glimmen**

Geglucks[e] das; ~[e]s chuckling; *(lauter)* chortling; **laß doch mal dein ~:** stop [that] chuckling/chortling

Gegner ['ge:gnɐ] **der; ~s, ~ a)** adversary; opponent; *(Rivale)* rival; **ein ~ der Todesstrafe sein** oppose *or* be an opponent of; **b)** *(Sport)* opponent; *(Mannschaft)* opposing team; **der ~ war für uns viel zu stark** the opposition was far too strong for us; **c)** *(feindliches Heer)* enemy

Gegnerin die; ~, ~nen a) *s.* **Gegner a; b)** *(Sport)* opponent

gegnerisch *Adj.; nicht präd.* **a)** opposing; **b)** *(Sport)* opposing ‹*team, player, etc.*›; opponents' ‹*goal*›; **c)** *(Milit.)* enemy

Gegnerschaft die; ~ a) *(Einstellung)* hostility; antagonism; **b)** *(Gesamtheit der Gegner)* opposition

gegolten [gə'gɔltn̩] *2. Part. v.* **gelten**

gegoren [gə'go:rən] *2. Part. v.* **gären**

gegossen [gə'gɔsn̩] *2. Part. v.* **gießen**

gegriffen [gə'grɪfn̩] *2. Part. v.* **greifen**

Gegrinse das; ~s *(abwertend)* grinning

Gegröle das; ~s *(ugs. abwertend)* [raucous] bawling and shouting; *(Gesang)* raucous singing

Gegrunze das; ~s *(abwertend)* grunting

Gehabe das; ~s *(abwertend)* affected behaviour; **ihr wichtigtuerisches ~:** her pompous behaviour

gehaben *refl. V.* *(veralt., noch scherzh.)* *in* **gehab dich wohl!/gehabt euch wohl!/~ Sie sich wohl!** farewell!

Gehaben das; ~s *(geh. veralt.)* behaviour; demeanour

gehabt 1. *2. Part. v.* **haben. 2.** *Adj.; nicht präd.* *(ugs.: schon dagewesen)* same old *(coll.);* usual; **wie ~:** as before; **[es ist] alles wie ~:** everything's just the same *or* just as before

Gehackte [gə'haktə] **das;** *adj. Dekl.* mince[meat]; **~s vom Rind/Schwein** minced beef/pork

[1]**Gehalt der; ~[e]s, ~e a)** *(gedanklicher Inhalt)* meaning; **intellektueller/religiöser ~:** intellectual/religious content; **b)** *(Anteil)* content; **ein hoher ~ an Gold/Blei** a high gold/lead content

[2]**Gehalt das,** *österr. auch:* **der; ~[e]s, Gehälter** [gə'hɛltɐ] salary; **ein hohes/niedriges ~ beziehen** draw a large/small salary; **1000 DM ~, ein ~ von 1000 DM** a salary of 1,000 marks

gehalten 1. *2. Part. v.* **halten. 2.** *Adj.* **a)** *(geh.)* **~ sein, etw. zu tun** be obliged *or* required to do sth.; **b)** *(Mus.)* held; tenuto

gehalt·los *Adj.* unnutritious ‹*food*›; ‹*wine*› lacking in body; *(fig.)* vacuous; empty; lacking in substance *postpos., not pred.*

Gehaltlosigkeit die; ~ *(von Nahrungsmitteln)* lack of nutritional value; *(fig.)* vacuousness; emptiness; lack of substance

Gehalts-: ~ab·rechnung die salary statement; payslip; **~ab·zug der** deduction from salary; **~an·spruch der** salary claim; pay claim; **~auf·besserung die** increase in salary; **zur ~aufbesserung** in order to increase one's salary; **~aus·zahlung die** payment of salary/salaries; **~empfänger der** salary earner; **~erhöhung die** salary increase; rise [in salary]; *(regelmäßig)* increment; **~forderung die** salary claim; pay claim; **~gruppe die** salary group *or* bracket; *(innerhalb einer Firma)* grade; **~konto das** *account into which the/one's salary is paid;* **~kürzung die** salary cut; cut in salary; **~liste die** payroll; **auf jmds. ~liste** *(Dat.)* **stehen** *(fig.)* be on sb.'s payroll; be in sb.'s pocket; **~pfändung die** attachment of earnings; **~streifen der** payslip; **~stufe die** salary bracket; **~vorrückung die** *(österr.)* increment; **~vor·schuß der** advance [on one's salary]; **~zahlung die** payment of salary/salaries; **~zu·lage die** salary increase; *(regelmäßig)* increment; *(zusätzlich)* bonus

gehalt·voll *Adj.* nutritious, nourishing ‹*food*›; full-bodied ‹*wine*›; ‹*novel, speech*› rich in substance *postpos.*

Gehänge das; ~s, ~ a) *(Girlande)* festoon; *(Kranz)* garland; *(Ohrring)* ear-pendant; **b)** *(österr.: Bergabhang)* slope; **c)** *(Jagdw., sonst veralt.)* belt *(with scabbard for hunting-knife, sword, etc.);* **d)** *(vulg.: Hoden)* balls *(coarse)*

gehangen *2. Part. v.* [1]**hängen**

Gehängte [gə'hɛŋtə] **der/die;** *adj. Dekl.* hanged man/woman; **die ~n** the hanged

geharnischt [gə'harnɪʃt] **1.** *Adj.* **a)** *(scharf, energisch)* sharp, sharply-worded, strongly-worded ‹*letter, protest, reply*›; strongly-worded ‹*speech, article*›; **b)** *(hist.: gepanzert)* **ein ~er Ritter** a knight in armour. **2.** *adv.* sharply

gehässig [gə'hɛsɪç] *Adj.* *(abwertend)* spiteful; **~ von jmdm. reden/sprechen** be spiteful about sb.

Gehässigkeit die; ~, ~en a) *o. Pl.* *(Wesen)* spitefulness; **b)** *meist Pl.* *(Äußerung)* spiteful remark

gehauen *2. Part. v.* **hauen**

gehäuft **1.** *2. Part. v.* **häufen. 2.** *Adj.* **ein ~er Teelöffel/Eßlöffel** a heaped teaspoon/tablespoon. **3.** *adv.* in large numbers

Gehäuse [gəˈhɔyzə] **das; ~s, ~ a)** *(einer Maschine, Welle)* casing; housing; *(einer Kamera, Uhr)* case; casing; *(einer Lampe)* housing; *(Pistolen~, Gewehr~)* casing; **b)** *(Schnecken~ usw.)* shell; **c)** *(Kern~)* core; **d)** *(Sportjargon: Tor)* goal

geh·behindert *Adj.* able to walk only with difficulty *postpos.;* disabled; **sie ist stark ~behindert** she can walk only with great difficulty

Geh·behinderung die disability [which makes walking difficult]

Gehege das; ~s, ~ a) *(Jägerspr.: Revier)* preserve; **jmdm. ins ~ kommen** *(fig.)* poach on sb.'s preserve; **sich** *(Dat.)* **[gegenseitig] ins ~ kommen** *(fig.)* encroach on each other's territory; **b)** *(im Zoo)* enclosure

geheim 1. *Adj.* **a)** secret; **streng ~:** top *or* highly secret; **im ~en** in secret; secretly; **Geheimer Rat** *(hist.)* *(Gremium)* Privy Council; *(Mitglied)* privy councillor; **b)** *(mysteriös)* mysterious. **2.** *adv.* **~ abstimmen** vote by secret ballot

geheim-, Geheim-: ~abkommen das secret agreement; **~agent der** secret agent; **~befehl der** secret order; **~bund der** secret society; **~bündelei die; ~** *(veralt.)* membership of an illegal secret society; **~code der** *s.* **~kode; ~dienst der** secret service; **~diplomatie die** secret diplomacy; *(neben der offiziellen Diplomatie)* behind-the-scenes diplomacy; **~fach das** secret compartment; *(Schublade)* secret drawer; **~gang der** secret passage; **~|halten** *unr. tr. V.* keep secret; **Pläne/Entwürfe ~halten** keep plans/drawings secret

Geheim·haltung die; *o. Pl.* observance of secrecy; **zur ~ verpflichtet sein** be pledged to secrecy

Geheimhaltungs·pflicht die obligation to maintain secrecy

Geheim-: ~kode der secret code; **~lehre die** esoteric doctrine; **~material das** secret papers *pl. or* documents *pl.;* **militärisches ~material** secret military papers *or* documents

Geheimnis das; ~ses, ~se a) secret; **ein ~ lüften/enträtseln** unravel a secret; **vor jmdm. [keine] ~se haben** have [no] secrets from sb.; **jmdn. in die ~se einer Sache einweihen** initiate *or* let sb. into the secrets of sth.; **ein/kein ~ aus etw. machen** make a big/no secret of sth.; **das ist das ganze ~:** that's all there is to it; **ein offenes** *od.* **öffentliches ~:** an open secret; **b)** *(Unerforschtes)* mystery; secret; **die ~se der Natur/des Lebens** the mysteries *or* secrets of nature/life

geheimnis-, Geheimnis-: ~krämer der *(ugs.)* mystery-monger; **~krämerei die; ~** *s.* **~tuerei; ~träger der** person cleared for access to secret information; **~tuerei die; ~** *(ugs. abwertend)* secretiveness; mystery-mongering; **~tuerisch** *(ugs. abwertend)* **1.** *Adj.* secretive; **2.** *adv.* secretively; **~umwittert, ~umwoben** *Adj.* *(geh.)* shrouded in mystery *postpos.;* mysterious; **~verrat der** *(Rechtsspr.)* betrayal of secrets; **~voll 1.** *Adj.* mysterious; **auf ~volle Weise** in a mysterious way; mysteriously; **2.** *adv.* mysteriously; **~voll tun** be mysterious; act mysteriously

Geheim-: ~polizei die secret police; **~polizist der** member of the secret police

Geheim·rat der Privy Councillor *(purely honorary title)*

Geheimrats·ecken *Pl.* *(ugs. scherzh.)* receding hairline *sing.;* **er hat schon ~:** he's receding *or* going bald [at the temples] already

geheim-, Geheim-: ~rezept das secret recipe; **~sache die** classified information *no indef. art., no pl.;* **~schrift die** secret writing *no indef. art., no pl.;* cipher; **~sender der** secret transmitter; **~sitzung die** secret session; closed meeting; **~sprache die** secret language; **~tinte die** invisible ink; **~tip der** inside tip; **~|tun** *unr. itr. V.* *(ugs. abwertend)* be secretive; **mit etw. ~tun** be secretive about sth.; **~tür die** secret door; **~vertrag der** secret treaty *or* agreement; **~waffe die** *(Milit.)* secret weapon; **~wissenschaft die** occult science; **~zeichen das** secret sign

Geheiß das; ~es *(geh.)* behest *(literary);* command; **auf jmds. ~:** at sb.'s behest *or* command

gehemmt 1. *2. Part. v.* **hemmen. 2.** *Adj.* inhibited

gehen [ˈge:ən] **1.** *unr. itr. V.; mit sein* **a)** *(sich zu Fuß fortbewegen)* walk; go; **auf und ab ~:** walk up and down; **über die Straße ~:** cross the street; **wo er geht und steht** wherever he goes *or* is; no matter where he goes *or* is; **etw. geht durch die Presse** *(fig.)* sth. is in the papers; **b)** *(sich irgendwohin begeben)* go; **schwimmen/tanzen ~:** go swimming/dancing; **schlafen ~:** go to bed; **zu jmdm. ~:** go to see sb.; go and see sb. *(coll.);* **zum Arzt ~:** go to the doctor; **nach London/Mannheim ~:** move to London/Mannheim; **aufs Amt/auf den Markt ~:** go to the office/the market; **an die Arbeit ~** *(fig.)* get down to work; **er geht auf die 60** *(fig.)* he is approaching *or (coll.)* pushing 60; **in sich** *(Akk.)* **~:** take stock of oneself; **c)** *(regelmäßig besuchen)* attend; **in die** *od.* **zur Schule ~:** be at *or* attend school; **wieviel Jahre mußt du noch in die Schule ~?** how many more years have you got at school?; **d)** *(weg~)* go; leave; **ich muß jetzt/bald ~:** I must leave now/soon; **Sie können ~:** you may go; **gegangen werden** *(ugs. scherzh.)* be sacked *(coll.);* **der Minister/Offizier mußte ~:** the Minister/officer had to resign; **er ist von uns gegangen** *(verhüll.)* he has passed away *or* passed over *(euphem.);* **jmdn. lieber ~ als kommen sehen** be always glad to see the back of sb.; **geh mir mit deinen politischen Schlagworten** spare me the political slogans; **e)** *(ugs.: [ab]fahren)* leave; **der Zug geht um zehn Uhr** the train leaves at ten o'clock; **f)** *(in Funktion sein)* work; **etw. geht wieder/nicht mehr** sth. is working again/has stopped working; **meine Uhr geht falsch/richtig** my watch is wrong/right; **das Telefon/die Klingel geht ununterbrochen** the telephone/the bell never stops ringing; **g)** *(möglich sein)* **ja, das geht** yes, I/we can manage that; **das geht nicht** that can't be done; that's impossible; *(ist nicht zulässig)* that's not on *(Brit. coll.);* no way *(coll.);* **Donnerstag geht auch** Thursday's a possibility *or* all right too; **es geht einfach nicht, daß du so spät nach Hause kommst** it simply won't do for you to come home so late; **es geht leider nicht anders** unfortunately there's nothing else for it; **das wird schwer/schlecht ~:** that will be difficult; **auf diese Weise geht es nicht/sicher** it won't/is bound to work this way; **h)** *(ugs.: gerade noch angehen)* **es geht so** it could be worse; **das Essen ging ja noch, aber der Wein war ungenießbar** the food was passable, but the wine was undrinkable; **Wie war die Feier? – Es ging so** How was the party? – [It was] all right *or* [It] could have been worse; **Hast du gut geschlafen? – Es geht** Did you sleep well? – Not too bad *or* So-so; **der Anfang ging, aber der Schluß des Films war idiotisch** the film began fairly well, but the end was absolutely stupid; **i)** *(sich entwickeln)* **der Laden/das Geschäft geht gut/gar nicht** the shop/business is doing well/not doing well at all; **es geht alles nach Wunsch/Plan** everything is going according to plan; **alles geht drunter und drüber** *(ugs.)* everything's at sixes and sevens; **die Anfangszeile geht ...** *(fig.)* the first line goes *or* runs ...; **wie geht die Melodie?** *(fig.)* how does the tune go?; what's the tune?; **vor sich ~:** go on; happen; **j)** *(sich ausdehnen bis)* **das Wasser geht mir bis an die Knie** the water comes up to *or* reaches my knees; **ich gehe ihm bis zu den Schultern** I come up to his shoulders; **in die Hunderte/Tausende ~:** run into [the] hundreds/thousands; **das geht über mein Vermögen/meinen Horizont** *(fig.)* that is beyond me; **diese Nachricht würde über ihre Kräfte ~** *(fig.)* this news would be too much for her; **es geht [doch] nichts über ...** *(+ Akk.)* *(fig.)* there is nothing like *or* nothing to beat ...; nothing beats ...; **das geht zu weit** *(fig.)* that's going too far; **k)** *(unpers.)* **jmdm. geht es gut/schlecht** *(gesundheitlich)* sb. is well/not well; *(geschäftlich)* sb. is doing well/badly; **wie geht es dir/Ihnen?** how are you?; **mir geht es ähnlich** it's the same with me; same here *(coll.);* **wie geht's, wie steht's?** *(ugs.)* how are things?; **l)** *(unpers.)* *(sich um etw. handeln)* **es geht um mehr als ...:** there is more at stake than ...; **jmdm. geht es um etw.** sth. matters to sb.; **ihr geht es nur um Geld** she only thinks about money; **worum geht es hier?** what is this all about?; **bei dieser Sache geht es um viel Geld** this involves a great deal of money; **wenn es ums Geld geht, versteht er keinen Spaß** he takes money matters very seriously; **Ich hätte eine Frage. – Worum geht es denn?** I have a question. – What [is it] about?; *s. auch* **darum b; m)** *(tätig werden)* **in den Staatsdienst/in die Industrie/die Politik ~:** join the Civil Service/go into industry/politics; **zum Film/Theater ~:** go into films/on the stage; **ins Kloster ~:** enter a monastery/convent; **als Kellner/Prostituierte ~:** work as *or* be a waiter/prostitute; **n)** *(ugs.: sich kleiden)* **gut/schlecht gekleidet ~:** be well/badly dressed; **in kurz/lang ~:** wear a short/long dress/skirt; **als Zigeuner/Matrose ~:** go as a gypsy/a sailor; **o)** *(ugs.: sich zu schaffen machen an)* **du sollst nicht an meine Sachen ~:** you must not mess around with my things; *(benutzen)* you must not take my things; **die Kinder sind an den Kuchen/das Geld gegangen** the children have been at the cake/money *(coll.);* **p)** *(ein Liebespaar sein)* **mit jmdm. ~:** go out with sb.; **q)** *(absetzbar sein)* **[gut/schlecht] ~:** sell [well/slowly]; **r)** *(passen)* go; **in den Kofferraum geht nur ein Koffer** only one case will go into the boot; **s)** *(aufgeteilt werden)* **etw. geht in zwei/drei Teile** sth. is shared out *or* divided two/three ways; **t)** *(verlaufen)* go; **die Straße geht geradeaus/nach links** the road goes *or* runs straight ahead/turns to the left; **wohin geht diese Straße?** where does this road go *or* lead to?; **u)** *(gerichtet sein auf)* **nach der Hauptstraße ~:** face the main road; **die Fenster ~ alle nach Süden** all the windows face south; **gegen jmdn./etw. gehen** *(fig.)* be aimed *or* directed at sb./sth.; **das geht gegen meine Überzeugung** that goes against my convictions; **v)** *(als Maßstab nehmen)* **nach jmdm./etw. ~:** go by sb./sth.; **wenn es nach mir geht, fangen wir jetzt an** I'd be quite happy if we began now; **w)** *s.* **aufgehen d. 2.** *unr. tr. V.* *(zurücklegen)* **eine Strecke ~:** cover *or* do a distance; **er ist eine Strecke mit uns gegangen** he walked with us for some of the way; **einen Umweg ~:** make a detour; **10 km ~:** walk 10 km.; **einen Weg in 30 Minuten ~:** do a walk in 30 minutes; **seine eigenen Wege ~** *(fig.)* go one's own way; **lerne doch, deine eigenen Wege zu ~** *(fig.)* learn to stand on your own two feet. **3.** *unr. refl. V.* *(unpers.)* **in diesen Schuhen geht es sich sehr bequem** these shoes are very comfortable [to walk in]; **auf dem Weg ging es sich schlecht** the going on the track was difficult

Gehen das; ~s a) walking; **er hat Schmerzen**

beim ~: it hurts him to walk; **b)** *(Leichtathletik)* walking; **der Sieger im 50-km-~:** the winner of the 50 km walk

Gehenkte [gəˈhɛŋktə] **der/die;** *adj. Dekl.* hanged man/woman; **die ~n** the hanged

gehen|lassen 1. *unr. refl. V. (sich nicht beherrschen)* lose control of oneself; *(sich vernachlässigen)* let oneself go. **2.** *unr. tr. V. (ugs.: in Ruhe lassen)* leave alone

Geher [ˈgeːɐ] **der; ~s, ~ a)** *(Leichtathletik)* walker; **b)** *(Bergsteigen)* hill/mountain walker

geheuer [gəˈhɔyɐ] *Adj.* **a) in diesem Gebäude ist es nicht ~:** this building is eerie; this building feels as if it's haunted *(coll.)*; **in der Ruine soll es nicht ganz ~ sein** there is said to be something eerie about the ruins; **b) ihr war doch nicht [ganz] ~:** she felt [a little] uneasy; **c) diese Angelegenheit ist nicht ganz ~:** there's something odd *or* suspicious about this business

Geheul das; ~[e]s a) *(auch fig.)* howling; **b)** *(ugs. abwertend: Weinen)* bawling; wailing

Geheule das; ~s *s.* **Geheul b**

geh·fähig *Adj.* ⟨*patient*⟩ who is able to walk *postpos., not pred.*; walking ⟨*wounded*⟩; **~ sein** be able to walk

Geh·gips der *plaster which allows the patient to walk*

Gehilfe [gəˈhɪlfə] **der; ~n, ~n, Gehilfin die; ~, ~nen a)** qualified assistant; **b)** *(veralt.: Helfer/Helferin)* helper; assistant

Gehirn das; ~[e]s, ~e a) brain; **b)** *(ugs.: Verstand)* mind; **sein ~ anstrengen** *od.* **sich** *(Dat.)* **das ~ zermartern** rack one's brain[s]

Gehirn-: ~blutung die *(Med.)* cerebral haemorrhage; encephalorrhagia *(Med.)*; **~chirurgie die** brain surgery; **~erschütterung die** *(Med.)* concussion; **~erweichung die** *(Med.)* softening of the brain; encephalomalacia *(Med.)*; **~haut die** *s.* **Hirnhaut; ~haut·entzündung die** *s.* **Hirnhautentzündung; ~kasten der** *(salopp scherzh.)* [thick] skull; **~schlag der** *(Med.)* stroke; [cerebral] apoplexy *no art. (Med.)*; **~substanz die** brain matter; **graue/weiße ~substanz** grey/white matter; **~tätigkeit die;** *o. Pl.* brain activity; **~tumor der** *s.* **Hirntumor; ~wäsche die** brainwashing *no indef. art.*; **jmdn. einer ~wäsche unterziehen** brainwash sb.; **~zelle die** brain cell

gehoben [gəˈhoːbn̩] **1.** *2. Part. v.* **heben. 2.** *Adj.* **a)** higher ⟨*income*⟩; senior ⟨*position*⟩; **der ~e Dienst** the higher [levels of the] Civil Service; **die ~e Beamtenlaufbahn einschlagen** ≈ enter the Civil Service as an Administrative Trainee *(Brit.)*; **der ~e Mittelstand** the upper middle class; **b)** *(anspruchsvoll)* **Kleidung für den ~en Geschmack** clothes for those with discerning taste; **Artikel für den ~en Bedarf** luxury goods; **die ~e Unterhaltungsliteratur** up-market popular literature; **c)** *(gewählt)* elevated, refined ⟨*language, expression*⟩; **d)** *(feierlich)* festive ⟨*mood*⟩; **in ~er Stimmung sein** be in high spirits. **3.** *adv.* **sich ~ ausdrücken** use elevated *or* refined language

Gehöft [gəˈhœft, -ˈhøːft] **das; ~[e]s, ~e** farm[stead]

geholfen [gəˈhɔlfn̩] *2. Part. v.* **helfen**

Gehölz [gəˈhœlts] **das; ~es, ~e a)** *(Wäldchen)* copse; spinney *(Brit.)*; **b)** *Pl. (Holzgewächse)* woody plants

Gehör [gəˈhøːɐ̯] **das; ~[e]s** [sense of] hearing; **ein scharfes/gutes ~ haben** have acute/good hearing; **[etw.] nach dem ~ singen/spielen** sing/play [sth.] by ear; **das absolute ~ [haben]** *(Musik)* [have] absolute pitch; **~/kein ~ finden** meet with *or* get a/no response; **jmdm./einer Sache [kein] ~ schenken** [not] listen to sb./sth.; **sich** *(Dat.)* **~ verschaffen** make oneself heard; **um ~ bitten** ask for a hearing; **ein Lied/Gedicht/Musikstück zu ~ bringen** *(geh.)* sing a song/recite a poem/perform a piece of music

gehorchen [gəˈhɔrçn̩] *itr. V.* **a)** *(Gehorsam leisten)* **jmdm. ~:** obey sb.; **b)** *(sich leiten, lenken lassen)* **einer Sache** *(Dat.)* **~:** respond to sth.; **das Auto gehorchte dem Fahrer nicht mehr** the car wouldn't respond when the driver turned the wheel; **einer Laune/Stimmung** *(Dat.)* **~:** yield to a caprice/mood

gehören 1. *itr. V.* **a)** *(Eigentum sein)* **jmdm. ~:** belong to sb.; **das Haus gehört uns nicht** the house doesn't belong to us; we don't own the house; **der Jugend gehört die Zukunft** the future belongs to the young; **dir will ich ~** *(dichter.)* I want to be yours; **ihr Herz gehört einem anderen** *(geh.)* her heart belongs to another; **b)** *(Teil eines Ganzen sein)* **zu jmds. Freunden ~:** be one of sb.'s friends; **zu jmds. Aufgaben ~:** be part of sb.'s duties; **c)** *(passend sein)* **dein Roller gehört doch nicht in die Küche!** your scooter does not belong in the kitchen!; **das gehört nicht/durchaus hierher** that is not to the point/is very much to the point; **dieses Problem/Thema gehört nicht/durchaus hierher** this problem/topic is not relevant/certainly relevant here; **du gehörst ins Bett** you should be in bed; **d)** *(nötig sein)* **es hat viel Fleiß dazu gehört, dieses Projekt durchzuführen** it took *or* called for a lot of hard work to carry through this project; **dazu gehört sehr viel/einiges** that takes a lot/something; **dazu gehört nicht viel** that doesn't take much; **auf diese Weise sein Geld zu verdienen, dazu gehört nicht viel** earning one's living like this is nothing to be proud of; **e)** *(bes. südd.)* **er gehört geohrfeigt** he deserves *or (coll.)* needs a box round the ears; **du gehörst eingesperrt** *(ugs.)* you ought to be locked up. **2.** *refl. V. (sich schicken)* be fitting; **es gehört sich [nicht], ... zu ...:** it is [not] good manners to ...; **wie es sich gehört** comme il faut; **benimm dich, wie es sich gehört** behave properly

Gehör·gang der *(Anat.)* auditory canal

gehörig 1. *Adj.* **a)** *nicht präd. (gebührend)* proper; **jmdm. den ~en Respekt/die ~e Achtung erweisen** show sb. proper *or* due respect; **b)** *nicht präd. (ugs.: beträchtlich)* **ein ~er Schrecken/eine ~e Portion Mut/Ausdauer** a good fright/a good deal of courage/perseverance; **c)** *(zu~)* **zu etw. ~ sein** be part of sth.; belong to sth.; **jmdm. ~ sein** *(geh.)* belong to sb.; be owned by sb.; **[nicht] zur momentanen Fragestellung ~:** [not] relevant to the question [under discussion]. **2.** *adv.* **a)** *(gebührend)* properly; **b)** *(ugs.: beträchtlich)* **~ essen/trinken** eat/drink properly *or* heartily; **er hat ~ geschimpft** he didn't half grumble *(coll.)*; *s. auch* **¹Marsch b; Meinung**

Gehör·knöchelchen *Pl. (Anat.)* auditory ossicles

gehör·los *Adj.* deaf

Gehörn [gəˈhœrn] **das; ~[e]s, ~e a)** horns *pl.*; **b)** *(Jägerspr.)* antlers *pl.*

Gehör·nerv der auditory nerve

gehörnt *Adj.* **a)** *(mit einem Gehörn)* horned; *(mit einem Geweih)* antlered; **b)** *(scherzh. verhüll.: betrogen)* cuckolded; **ein ~er Ehemann** a cuckold

Gehör·organ das organ of hearing

gehorsam [gəˈhoːɐ̯zaːm] **1.** *Adj.* **a)** *(artig, brav)* obedient; **jmdm. ~ sein** *(geh.)* be obedient to sb.; **b)** *(veralt. als Höflichkeitsformel)* humble; *(als Briefschluß)* **Ihr ~ster Diener** your most obedient servant. **2.** *adv. (veralt. als Höflichkeitsformel)* humbly

Gehorsam der; ~s obedience; **~ gegenüber jmdm.** obedience to sb.; **jmdm. ~ leisten/den ~ verweigern** obey/refuse to obey sb.

Gehorsamkeit die obedience

Gehorsams-: ~pflicht die; *o. Pl. (Milit.)* duty to obey orders; **~verweigerung die;** *o. Pl. (Milit.)* insubordination; refusal to obey orders

Gehör·sinn der; *o. Pl.* [sense of] hearing

Geh·rock der frock-coat

Gehrung [ˈgeːrʊŋ] **die; ~, ~en** *(Handw., Technik)* mitre [joint]

Geh·steig der pavement *(Brit.)*; sidewalk *(Amer.)*

Geht·nicht·mehr das *in* **bis zum ~** *(salopp)* ad nauseam; **das habe ich bis zum ~ erklärt/gehört** I've explained it ad nauseam *or* till I'm blue in the face *(coll.)*/I've heard it so often I'm sick of it *(coll.)*

Gehupe das; ~s honking; hooting

Geh-: ~versuch der; *meist Pl. (eines Kindes)* attempt at walking; *(nach einem Unfall)* attempt at walking again; **~weg der** *s.* **~steig; ~werkzeuge** *Pl. (ugs. scherzh.)* legs

Geier [ˈgaiɐ] **der; ~s, ~:** vulture; **hol' dich/hol's der ~** *(ugs.)* to hell with you/it *(coll.)*; **weiß der ~** *(salopp)* God only knows *(sl.)*; Christ knows *(sl.)*

Geifer [ˈgaifɐ] **der; ~s a)** *(Speichel)* slaver; spittle; slobber; *(von Tieren)* slaver; slobber; *(schäumend)* foam; froth; **b)** *(geh. abwertend: Gehässigkeit)* venom; vituperation

Geiferer der; ~s, ~ *(geh. abwertend)* vituperator; venomous speaker/writer *etc.*

geifern *itr. V.* **a)** slaver; slobber; **b)** *(abwertend: gehässig reden)* **gegen jmdn./über etw.** *(Akk.)* **~:** discharge one's venom at sb./sth.

Geige [ˈgaigə] **die; ~, ~n** violin; fiddle *(coll./derog.)*; **~ spielen** play the violin; **die erste ~ spielen** *(ugs.)* play first fiddle; call the tune; **die zweite ~ spielen** *(ugs.)* play second fiddle

geigen 1. *itr. V.* **a)** *(ugs.: Geige spielen)* play the fiddle *(coll.) or* the violin; **b)** *(ugs.: von Insekten)* chirp; chirr. **2.** *tr. V.* **a)** *(ugs.: auf der Geige spielen)* **einen Walzer/ein Solo ~:** play a waltz/a solo on the fiddle *(coll.) or* violin; **jmdm. die Meinung ~:** give sb. a piece of one's mind; **b)** *(salopp: koitieren mit)* lay *(sl.)*; shag *(sl.)*; have it off with *(sl.)*

Geigen-: ~bau der violin-making; **~bauer der** violin-maker; **~bogen der** violin bow; **~hals der** neck of the/a violin; **~kasten der** violin case; **~musik die** violin music; **~saite die** violin string; **~spiel das** violin-playing; **~spieler der** violin-player

Geiger der; ~s, ~: violin-player; violinist

Geiger·zähler der *(Physik)* Geiger counter

geil [gail] **1.** *Adj.* **a)** *(oft abwertend: sexuell erregt)* randy; horny *(sl.)*; *(lüstern)* lecherous; **auf jmdn. ~ sein** lust for *or* after sb.; **~e alte Männer** old lechers; dirty old men; **b)** *(Landw.)* rank ⟨*vegetation, growth, plant*⟩; over-rich, over-manured ⟨*soil*⟩; **c)** *(Jugendspr.)* great *(coll.)*; fabulous *(coll.)*. **2.** *adv.* **a)** *(oft abwertend)* lecherously; **b)** *(Landw.)* **~ wuchern/emporschießen** grow rank; **c)** *(Jugendspr.)* fabulously *(coll.)*

Geilheit die; ~: *s.* **geil 1: a)** randiness; horniness *(sl.)*; lecherousness; **b)** *(Landw.)* rankness; over-richness

Geisel [ˈgaizl̩] **die; ~, ~n** hostage; **jmdn. als ~ behalten** *od.* **festhalten** hold sb. hostage; **jmdn. als** *od.* **zur ~ nehmen** take sb. hostage

Geisel-: ~drama das *(Pressejargon)* hostage drama; **~gangster der** *(Pressejargon) s.* **~nehmer; ~nahme die** the taking of hostages; **„Bankraub mit ~nahme zweier Kunden"** 'Bank raid. Two customers taken hostage'; **~nehmer der** terrorist/guerrilla *etc.* holding the hostages

Geisha [ˈgeːʃa] **die; ~, ~s** geisha

Geiß [gais] **die; ~, ~en a)** *(südd., österr., schweiz.: Ziege)* [nanny-]goat; **b)** *(Jägerspr.)* doe

Geiß-: ~bart der a) *o. Pl. (Bot.)* goat's-beard; **b)** *(österr.: Spitzbart)* goatee; **~blatt das;** *o. Pl. (Bot.)* honeysuckle; woodbine

Geißel [ˈgaisl̩] **die; ~, ~n a)** *(hist., auch fig.)* scourge; **b)** *(Biol.)* flagellum; **c)** *(bes. südd.: Peitsche)* whip

geißeln *tr. V.* **a)** *(anprangern, tadeln)* castigate; **b)** *(plagen)* plague; **c)** *(hist.: züchtigen)* scourge

Geißel·tierchen das *(Biol.)* flagellate

Geißelung die; ~, ~en a) *(Anprangern)* castigation; **b)** *(hist.: Züchtigung)* scourging

Geiß·fuß der a) *o. Pl. (Bot.)* Aegopodium; **gewöhnlicher ~:** ground elder; goutweed; **b)** *(Handw., Technik)* V-shaped gouge

Geißlein das; ~s, ~: little goat

Geißler ['gaislɐ] **der; ~s, ~:** *s.* **Flagellant**

Geist [gaist] **der; ~[e]s, ~er a)** *o. Pl. (Verstand)* mind; **jmds. ~ ist verwirrt/gestört** sb. is mentally deranged/disturbed; **jmdm. mit etw. auf den ~ gehen** *(salopp)* get on sb.'s nerves with sth.; **den** *od.* **seinen ~ aufgeben** *(geh./ugs. scherzh., auch fig.)* give up the ghost; **im ~[e]** in my/his *etc.* mind's eye; **im ~ werde ich dabei sein** I shall be there in spirit; **den** *od.* **seinen ~ aushauchen** *(geh. verhüll.)* breathe one's last; pass away; **der ~ ist willig, aber das Fleisch ist schwach** *(bibl.)* the spirit is willing, but the flesh is weak; **b)** *o. Pl. (Scharfsinn)* wit, **einen sprühenden ~ haben** have a sparkling wit; **Mangel an ~:** lack of intellect *or* intelligence; **c)** *o. Pl. (innere Einstellung)* spirit; **im ~ der Zeit** in the spirit of the age; **ein schlechter ~ in der Mannschaft** poor morale in the team; **... wes ~es Kind er/sie** *usw.* **ist** the kind of person he/she *etc.* is; **d)** *(denkender Mensch)* mind; intellect; **ein großer/kleiner ~:** a great mind/a person of limited intellect; **hier** *od.* **da scheiden sich die ~er** this is where opinions differ; **große ~er stört das nicht** *(ugs. scherzh.)* it doesn't worry me/her *etc.*; not to worry *(coll.)*; **e)** *(Mensch mit bestimmten Eigenschaften)* spirit; **ein dienstbarer ~** *(ugs. scherzh.)* a servant; **f)** *(überirdisches Wesen)* spirit; **der Heilige ~** *(christl. Rel.)* the Holy Ghost *or* Spirit; **der böse ~:** the evil spirit; **g)** *(Gespenst)* ghost; **~er gehen im Schloß um/spuken im Schloß** the castle is haunted; **von allen guten ~ern verlassen sein** have taken leave of one's senses; be out of one's mind

Geister-: ~bahn die ghost train; **~beschwörer der** exorcist; *(der die Geister heraufbeschwört)* necromancer; **~beschwörung die** exorcism; *(das Heraufbeschwören)* necromancy; **~erscheinung die** apparition; phantom; **~fahrer der** *person driving on the wrong side of the road or the wrong carriageway;* **~geschichte die** ghost story

geisterhaft 1. *Adj.* ghostly; spectral; eerie ⟨*atmosphere*⟩. **2.** *adv.* eerily

Geister·hand die *in* **wie von** *od.* **durch ~:** as if by an invisible hand

geistern ['gaistɐn] *itr. V.; mit sein* ⟨*ghost*⟩ wander; *(fig.)* wander like a ghost; **Irrlichter geisterten über das Moor** will o' the wisps drifted eerily across the moor; **diese Idee geisterte immer noch durch seinen Kopf** he still had this idea in his head

Geister-: ~seher der ghost-seer; *(Hellseher)* visionary; **~stadt die** ghost town; **~stunde die** witching hour

geistes-, Geistes-: ~abwesend 1. *Adj.* absent-minded; **2.** *adv.* absent-mindedly; **~abwesenheit die** absent-mindedness; **~anlage die** intellectual ability *or* gift; **~arbeiter der** brain-worker; **~armut die** poverty of mind; **~art die** cast of mind; **~blitz der** *(ugs.)* brainwave; flash of inspiration; **~gaben** *Pl.* intellectual gifts; **~gegenwart die** presence of mind; **~gegenwärtig 1.** *Adj.* quick-witted; **2.** *adv.* with great presence of mind; **~geschichte die** history of ideas; intellectual history; **~geschichtlich 1.** *Adj.* ⟨*work, method, etc.*⟩ relating to the history of ideas, relating to intellectual history; **eine ~geschichtliche Tradition** an intellectual tradition; a tradition of ideas; **2.** *adv.* **etw. ~geschichtlich einordnen** place sth. in the history of ideas; **~gestört** mentally disturbed; **~größe die a)** *o. Pl. (Kraft des Geistes)* greatness of mind; **b)** *(Mensch)* genius; intellectual giant; **~haltung die** attitude [of mind]; **~kraft die** mental ability; **~kräfte** *Pl.* mental powers; **~krank** *Adj.* mentally ill; [mentally] deranged; **~kranke der/die** mentally ill person; *(im Krankenhaus)* mental patient; **~krankheit die** mental illness; **~leben das** intellectual life; **~richtung die** school of thought; **~riese der** *(ugs.)* great genius; **~schaffende der/die;** *adj. Dekl. (bes. DDR)* intellectual; **~schärfe die** keenness of intellect; **~schwäche die;** *o. Pl.* feeble-mindedness; mental deficiency; **~störung die** mental disturbance *or* disorder; **~strömung die** current of thought; **~tätigkeit die** mental activity; **~verfassung die** state of mind; mental state; **~verwandt** *Adj.* spiritually akin; **wir sind ~verwandt** we are kindred spirits; **~verwirrung die** mental confusion; *(~gestörtheit)* [mental] derangement; **~welt die** *(geh.)* **a)** *(Welt des ~es)* world of the mind; **b)** *(Gesamtheit der geistig Interessierten)* intelligentsia; **~wissenschaften** *Pl.* arts; humanities; **~wissenschaftler der** arts scholar; scholar in the humanities; **~wissenschaftlich 1.** *Adj.* **~wissenschaftliche Fächer** arts subjects; **2.** *adv.* ⟨*interested, be distinguished*⟩ in arts subjects; **~zustand der;** *o. Pl.* mental condition; mental state; **jmdn. auf seinen ~zustand untersuchen lassen** have sb.'s mental condition examined; **du solltest dich mal auf deinen ~zustand untersuchen lassen** *(ugs.)* you need your head examined *(coll.)*

geistig 1. *Adj.; nicht präd.* **a)** intellectual; *(Psych.)* mental; **~e und körperliche Arbeit** physical work and brain-work; **er verlebte seine Rentnerjahre in ~er Frische** he remained mentally alert throughout the years of his retirement; **der ~e Vater/Urheber** the spiritual father/author; **in ~er Umnachtung** *(geh.)* in a state of mental derangement; **das ~e Erbe** the spiritual legacy; **~es Eigentum** intellectual property; **~er Diebstahl** plagiarism; **ein ~es Band** *(fig. geh.)* a spiritual bond; **~-kulturell** intellectual and cultural; **das ~-kulturelle Leben** *(bes. DDR)* the intellectual and cultural scene; **ein ~-kulturelles Zentrum** *(bes. DDR)* a centre of learning and the arts; **~-schöpferische Arbeit** *(bes. DDR)* intellectual and creative work; **b)** *(alkoholisch)* **~e Getränke** alcoholic drinks *or* beverages. **2.** *adv.* **~ träge/rege sein** be mentally lazy/active; **~ überlegen** intellectually superior; **~ zurückgeblieben** mentally retarded; **~ weggetreten sein** *(ugs.)* be miles away *(coll.)*

Geistigkeit die; ~: intellectuality

geistlich *Adj.; nicht präd.* sacred ⟨*song, music*⟩; religious ⟨*order*⟩; religious, devotional ⟨*book, writings*⟩; spiritual ⟨*matter, support*⟩; spiritual, religious ⟨*leader*⟩; ecclesiastical ⟨*office, dignitary*⟩; **der ~e Stand** the clergy; **in den ~en Stand eintreten** take holy orders

Geistliche der; *adj. Dekl.* clergyman; priest; *(einer Freikirche)* minister; *(Militär~, Gefängnis~)* chaplain

Geistlichkeit die; ~: clergy

geist-, Geist-: ~los *Adj.* *(dumm)* dim-witted; witless; *(ohne ernsten Gehalt)* trivial; shallow ⟨*conversation*⟩; **~losigkeit die; ~** *(Dummheit)* dim-wittedness; witlessness; *(Trivialität)* triviality; **~reich 1.** *Adj.* *(amüsant)* witty; *(elegant)* elegant; *(klug)* clever; *(unterhaltsam)* entertaining; **nicht gerade ~reich aussehen** *(ugs.)* look pretty stupid *(coll.)*; **2.** *adv.: s. Adj.:* wittily; elegantly; cleverly; entertainingly; **~sprühend** *Adj.* brilliantly witty; **~tötend** *Adj.* soul-destroying ⟨*work, job*⟩; stupefyingly boring ⟨*chatter, drivel*⟩; **~voll** *Adj.* brilliantly witty ⟨*joke, satire*⟩; brilliant ⟨*idea*⟩; intellectually stimulating ⟨*conversation, book*⟩

Geiz [gaits] **der; ~es** *(abwertend)* meanness; *(Knauserigkeit)* miserliness

geizen *itr. V.* **a)** *(übertrieben sparsam sein)* be mean; **mit etw. ~:** be mean *or* stingy with sth.; **mit Lob ~** *(fig.)* be sparing with one's praise; **sie geizt nicht mit ihren Reizen** *(fig. iron.)* she doesn't mind displaying her charms; **b)** *(veralt.: heftig verlangen)* **nach etw. ~:** crave [for] sth.; *(gierig)* be greedy for sth.

Geiz·hals der *(abwertend)* skinflint

geizig *Adj.* mean; *(knauserig)* miserly

Geiz·kragen der *(ugs. abwertend)* skinflint

Gejammer[e] das; ~s *(abwertend)* yammering *(coll.)*; belly-aching *(sl.)*

Gejauchze das; ~s rejoicing; jubilation; **ihr ~ hallte durch das ganze Haus** their joyful cheers echoed through the house

Gejaul[e] das; ~s *(abwertend)* howling

Gejohl[e] [gə'jo:l(ə)] **das; ~s** *(abwertend)* howling; **mit lautstarkem ~:** with loud howls *pl.*

gekannt [gə'kant] *2. Part. v.* **kennen**

Gekeif[e] [ge'kaif(ə)] **das; ~s** scolding; nagging

Gekicher das; ~s giggling

Gekläff[e] das; ~[e]s *(abwertend; auch fig.)* yapping

Geklapper das; ~s clatter[ing]

Geklatsch[e] das; ~s *(abwertend)* **a)** *(Beifallklatschen)* clapping; **b)** *(Tratsch)* gossiping

gekleidet 1. *2. Part. v.* **kleiden. 2.** *Adj.* dressed; **gut/schlecht ~ sein** be well/badly dressed

Geklimper das; ~s *(abwertend)* plunking

Geklingel das; ~s *(abwertend)* ringing

geklungen [gə'klʊŋən] *2. Part. v.* **klingen**

Geknall[e] das; ~s *(ugs. abwertend)* banging; *(von Schüssen, einer Peitsche)* cracking; *(von Korken)* popping

Geknatter das; ~s *(eines Autos, Motors, Motorrades)* clattering; *(eines Maschinengewehrs)* rattling; *(eines Segels)* flapping; *(eines Radios)* crackle

geknickt 1. *2. Part. v.* **knicken. 2.** *Adj.* *(ugs.)* dejected; downcast

gekniffen *2. Part. v.* **kneifen**

Geknister das; ~s rustling; rustle; *(von Holz, Feuer)* crackling; crackle

gekommen *2. Part. v.* **kommen**

gekonnt [gə'kɔnt] **1.** *2. Part. v.* **können. 2.** *Adj.* accomplished; *(hervorragend ausgeführt)* masterly. **3.** *adv.* in an accomplished manner; *(hervorragend)* in masterly fashion

gekoren [gə'ko:rən] *2. Part. v.* **küren, kiesen**

Gekrächz[e] das; ~s cawing; *(einer heiseren Stimme)* croaking; *(von Papageien)* squawking

Gekrakel das; ~s *(ugs. abwertend)* scrawl; scribble

Gekreisch[e] das; ~s *(von Vögeln)* screeching; *(von Menschen)* shrieking; squealing; *(von Rädern, Bremsen)* squealing

gekrischen [gə'krɪʃn̩] *2. Part. v.* **kreischen**

Gekritzel[e] das; ~s *(abwertend)* scribble; scrawl

gekrochen *2. Part. v.* **kriechen**

Gekröse [gə'krø:zə] **das; ~s, ~ a)** *(Kochk.)* *(vom Kalb)* tripe; *(vom Schwein)* chitterlings *pl.*; *(von Geflügel)* giblets *pl.*; **b)** *(Anat.)* mesentery

gekünstelt [gə'kʏnstl̩t] **1.** *Adj.* artificial; **ein ~es Lächeln** a forced smile; **ein ~es Benehmen** affected behaviour. **2.** *adv.* **er lächelte ~:** he gave a forced smile; **sie spricht immer so ~:** she always talks so affectedly

Gel [ge:l] **das; ~s, ~e** *(Chemie)* gel

Gelaber[e] das; ~s *(ugs. abwertend)* rabbiting *(coll.)* or babbling on

Gelächter [gəˈlɛçtɐ] **das; ~s, ~:** laughter; **ein lautes/schallendes ~:** loud/ringing laughter; **in ~ ausbrechen** burst out laughing; *s. auch* **homerisch**

gelackmeiert [gəˈlakmaiɐt] *Adj.; nicht attr. (salopp scherzh.)* had *(sl.)*; conned *(coll.)*; **ich bin/du bist** *usw.* **der Gelackmeierte** I'm/you're *etc.* the one who's been had *(sl.)*

geladen 1. *2. Part. v.* **laden. 2.** *in* **~ sein** be furious *or (coll.)* livid; **[auf jmdn./etw.] ~ sein** be furious *or (Brit. coll.)* livid [with sb./about sth.]

Gelage das; ~s, ~: feast; banquet; *(abwertend)* orgy of eating and drinking

Gelähmte der/die; *adj. Dekl.* paralytic

Gelände [gəˈlɛndə] **das; ~s, ~ a)** *(Landschaft)* ground; terrain; **das ~ steigt an/fällt ab** the ground rises/falls; **das ~ durchkämmen/erkunden** comb/reconnoitre the ground; **b)** *(Grundstück)* site; *(von Schule, Krankenhaus usw.)* grounds *pl.*; **das ~ absperren** cordon off the area; **c)** *(Milit.)* **~ gewinnen/verlieren** gain/lose ground

gelände-, Gelände-: ~darstellung die *(Geogr.)* relief mapping; **~fahrt die** cross-country drive; *(das Fahren)* cross-country driving; **~fahrzeug das** cross-country vehicle; **~gängig** *Adj.* cross-country *attrib.* ⟨*vehicle*⟩; ⟨*vehicle*⟩ suitable for cross-country driving; **~lauf der** *(Leichtathletik)* cross-country run; *(Wettbewerb)* cross-country race; *(das Laufen)* cross-country running

Geländer [gəˈlɛndɐ] **das; ~s, ~:** banisters *pl.*; handrail; *(am Balkon, an einer Brücke)* railing[s *pl.*]; *(aus Stein)* balustrades; parapet

Gelände-: ~reifen der cross-country tyre; **~ritt der a)** cross-country ride; **b)** *(Reitsport)* endurance competition; **~spiel das** scouting game; **~sport der** scrambling; **~übung die** *(Milit.)* field exercise; **~wagen der** *s.* **~fahrzeug**

gelang *3. Pers. Sg. Prät. v.* **gelingen**

gelänge *3. Pers. Sg. Konjunktiv II v.* **gelingen**

gelangen *itr. V.; mit sein* **a) an etw.** *(Akk.)***/zu etw. ~:** arrive at *or* reach sth.; **ans Ziel ~:** arrive at *or* reach one's destination; **an die Öffentlichkeit ~:** reach the public; leak out; **in jmds. Besitz ~:** come into sb.'s possession; **in den Besitz von etw. ~:** gain possession of sth.; **b)** *(fig.)* **zu Geld ~** *(durch Arbeit)* make money; *(durch Erbe)* come into money; **zu Ansehen ~:** gain esteem *or* standing; **zu Ehre ~:** attain honour; **zu Ruhm ~:** achieve fame; **an die Macht ~:** come to power; **zu der Erkenntnis ~, daß ...:** come to the realization that ...; realize that ...; **c)** *als Funktionsverb* **zur Aufführung ~:** be presented *or* performed; **zur Auszahlung/Verteilung ~:** be paid [out]/distributed

Gelaß [gəˈlas] **das; Gelasses, Gelasse** *(geh.)* [small, dark] room *or* chamber; *(Verlies)* dungeon

gelassen 1. *2. Part. v.* **lassen. 2.** *Adj.* calm; *(gefaßt)* composed; **~ bleiben** keep calm *or* cool. **3.** *adv.* calmly

Gelassenheit die; ~: calmness; *(Gefaßtheit)* composure

Gelaster das; ~s *(abwertend)* making malicious remarks

Gelatine [ʒelaˈtiːnə] **die; ~:** gelatine

Geläuf das; ~[e]s, ~e a) *(Jägerspr.)* tracks *pl.*; track; spoor; **b)** *(Sport)* track, course

gelaufen *2. Part. v.* **laufen**

geläufig 1. *Adj.* **a)** *(vertraut)* familiar, common ⟨*expression, concept*⟩; **etw. ist jmdm. ~:** sb. is familiar with sth.; **b)** *(fließend, perfekt)* fluent. **2.** *adv.* fluently; **~ Englisch sprechen** speak fluent English; speak English fluently; be fluent in English

Geläufigkeit die; ~ a) *(Bekanntheit)* familiarity; **b)** *(Perfektion)* fluency

gelaunt [gəˈlaunt] **gut/schlecht ~ sein** be in a good/bad mood; **wie ist sie ~?** what sort of mood is she in?; **zu etw. ~ sein** *(veralt.)* be in the mood for sth.

Geläut das; ~[e]s, ~e a) *(Glocken)* chime; **b)** *s.* **Geläute**

Geläute das; ~s ringing; *(harmonisch)* chiming

gelb [gɛlp] *Adj.* yellow; **die ~e Gefahr** *(abwertend)* the yellow peril; **die ~e Karte** *(Fußball)* the yellow card; **vor Neid ~ werden** turn green with envy; **der Gelbe Fluß/das Gelbe Meer** the Yellow River/Sea; **das Gelbe vom Ei** the egg-yolk; **das ist nicht das Gelbe vom Ei** *(fig. ugs.)* that's no great shakes *(sl.)*

Gelb das; ~s, ~ *od. (ugs.)* **~s** yellow; **bei ~ über die Ampel fahren** go through *or* crash the lights on amber; *s. auch* **Blau**

gelb·braun *Adj.* yellowish-brown

Gelbe [ˈgɛlbə] **der/die;** *adj. Dekl. (abwertend)* Oriental

gelb-, Gelb-: ~fieber das *(Med.)* yellow fever; **~filter der** *od. (fachspr. meist)* **das** *(Fot.)* yellow filter; **~grün** *Adj.* yellowish-green; **~körper der** *(Anat.)* corpus luteum; **~kreuz das;** *o. Pl.* mustard gas

gelblich *Adj.* yellowish; yellowed ⟨*paper*⟩; sallow ⟨*skin*⟩

gelb-, Gelb-: ~licht das; *o. Pl. (Verkehrsw.)* amber [light]; **~sucht die;** *o. Pl. (Med.)* jaundice; icterus *(Med.)*; **~süchtig** *Adj.* jaundiced; **~wurz[el] die** *(Bot.)* turmeric

Geld [gɛlt] **das; ~es, ~er a)** *o. Pl.* money; **großes ~:** large denominations *pl.*; **kleines/bares ~:** change/cash; **etw. bedeutet bares ~:** sth. is worth hard cash; **~ scheffeln** rake in the money; **etw. für teures ~ erwerben** pay a lot of money for sth.; **es ist für ~ nicht zu haben** money cannot buy it; **mit ~ nicht umgehen können** be hopeless about money; **das ist hinausgeworfenes ~:** that is a waste of money *or (coll.)* money down the drain; **ohne ~ dastehen** be left penniless; **ins ~ gehen** *(ugs.)* run away with the money *(coll.)*; **~ stinkt nicht** *(Spr.)* money has no smell; **~ regiert die Welt** *(Spr.)* money makes the world go round; **~ allein macht nicht glücklich [***(scherzh.)***, aber es hilft]** *(Spr.)* money isn't everything[, but it helps]; **~ und Gut** *(geh.)* all one's wealth and possessions; **hier liegt das ~ auf der Straße** *(fig.)* the streets here are paved with gold; **das große ~ machen** make a lot of money; **sein ~ unter die Leute bringen** spend one's money; **jmdm. das ~ aus der Tasche ziehen** get *or* wheedle money out of sb.; **~ wie Heu haben, im ~ schwimmen** be rolling in money *or* in it *(coll.)*; **nicht für ~ und gute Worte** *(ugs.)* not for love or money; **zu ~ kommen** get hold of [some] money; **etw. zu ~ machen** turn sth. into money *or* cash; **b)** *meist Pl. (größere Summe)* money; **öffentliche/staatliche ~er** public/state money *sing. or* funds; **c)** *(Börsenw.) s.* **Geldkurs**

geld-, Geld-: ~adel der financial aristocracy; **~angelegenheit die;** *meist Pl.* money *or* financial matter; **seine ~angelegenheiten regeln** settle one's affairs; **~anlage die** investment; **~automat der** cash dispenser; **~betrag der** sum *or* amount [of money]; **~beutel der** *(bes. südd.)* purse; **auf dem** *od.* **seinem ~beutel sitzen** *(ugs. abwertend)* be tight-fisted; **~bombe die** night-safe box; **~börse die** purse; **~briefträger der** *postman who delivers items containing money or on which money is payable;* **~buße die** fine; **~entwertung die** depreciation of the/a currency; **~erwerb der a) zum ~erwerb arbeiten** work [in order] to earn money; **seine Malerei dient nicht dem ~erwerb** he does not paint for the money; **b)** *(Tätigkeit)* **seinem ~erwerb nachgehen** earn one's living; **~forderung die** claim [for money]; **eine ~forderung an jmdn. haben** have a claim against sb.; **~frage die** question of money; **~geber der** financial backer; *(für Forschungen usw.)* sponsor; **~geschäft das** financial transaction; money transaction; **~geschenk das** gift of money; **~gier die** *(abwertend)* greed; avarice; **~gierig** *Adj. (abwertend)* greedy; avaricious; **~hahn der** *in* **[jmdm.] den ~hahn ab-** *od.* **zudrehen** *(ugs.)* cut off sb.'s supply of money; **~heirat die: das ist eine reine ~heirat** he just married her for her money/she just married him for his money; **~herrschaft die** plutocracy

geldig *Adj. (österr.)* rich; wealthy

Geld-: ~institut das financial institution; **~katze die** *(hist.) large leather purse worn on or as a belt;* **~klemme die** *(ugs.)* financial straits *pl. or* difficulties *pl.*; **~knappheit die** shortage of money; **~kurs der** *(Börsenw.)* bid price; **~leute** *s.* **~mann**

geldlich *Adj.; nicht präd.* financial

Geld-: ~mangel der; *o. Pl.* lack of money; **~mann der;** *Pl.* **~leute** financier; **~markt der** *(Wirtsch.)* money market; **~mittel** *Pl.* financial resources; funds; **~not die** financial straits *pl. or* difficulties *pl.*; **~politik die** monetary policy; **~prämie die** cash bonus; *(~preis)* cash prize; **~preis der** cash prize; *(bei einem Turnier)* prize money; **~quelle die** source of income; *(für den Staat)* source of revenue; **~sache die** *s.* **~angelegenheit; ~sack der a)** money-bag; **b)** *(veralt.) s.* **~beutel; c)** *(ugs. abwertend: geiziger Mensch)* money-bags *sing.*; **~schein der** banknote; bill *(Amer.)*; **~schöpfung die** *(Finanzw.)* creation of money; **~schrank der** safe; **~schrank·knacker der** *(ugs.)* safe-breaker; safe-cracker; **~schuld die** [money *or* financial] debt; **~schwemme die** *(ugs.)* glut of money; **~schwierigkeiten** *Pl.* financial difficulties *or* straits; **~sorgen** *Pl.* money troubles; financial worries; **~sorte die** (Bankw.) currency; **~spende die** donation; contribution; **~spritze die** *s.* **Finanzspritze; ~strafe die** fine; **jmdn. zu einer ~strafe verurteilen** fine sb.; **~stück das** coin; **~summe die** sum [of money]; **~tasche die** purse; **~umlauf der** circulation of money; **~umtausch der** *s.* **~wechsel; ~verlegenheit die** *(verhüll.)* financial embarrassment; **in ~verlegenheit sein** be financially embarrassed; **~verleiher der** money-lender; **~verlust der** financial loss; **~verschwendung die** waste of money; **das wäre reinste ~verschwendung** that would be a sheer waste of money; **~wasch·anlage die** *(ugs.)* money-laundering scheme; **~wechsel der** exchanging of money; **„~wechsel"** 'bureau de change'; 'change'; **~wert der a)** *(Wert eines Gegenstandes)* cash value; **b)** *(innerer ~wert)* value of money; *(äußerer ~wert)* value of the/a currency; **~wesen das;** *o. Pl.* finance *no art.*; **~zu·wendung die** allowance [of money]; *(~geschenk)* gift of money

geleckt 1. *2. Part. v.* **²lecken. 2.** *Adj. in* **wie ~ aussehen** *(ugs.)* look all spruced up

Gelee [ʒeˈleː] **der** *od.* **das; ~s, ~s** jelly; **Aale in ~:** jellied eels

Gelege das; ~s, ~ *(von Vögeln)* clutch of eggs; *(von Reptilien, Insekten)* batch of eggs

gelegen 1. *2. Part. v.* **liegen. 2.** *Adj.* **a)** *(passend)* convenient; **das kommt mir ~:** that comes just at the right time for me; **b)** *(liegend)* situated

Gelegenheit die; ~, ~en a) *(günstiger Augenblick)* opportunity; **jmdm. [die] ~ geben, etw. zu tun** give sb. the opportunity of doing *or* to do sth.; **die ~ nutzen** make the most of the opportunity; **bei nächster ~:** at the next opportunity; **bei ~:** some time; **~ macht Diebe** opportunity makes the thief *(prov.)*;

die ~ beim Schopf[e] fassen *od.* ergreifen grab *or* seize the opportunity with both hands; **b)** *(Anlaß)* occasion; **ein Anzug für alle ~en** a suit that can be worn on any occasion

Gelegenheits-: ~arbeit die casual work; **~arbeiter der** casual worker; **~dieb der** opportunist thief; **~dichtung die** occasional poetry; **~kauf der** bargain

gelegentlich 1. *Adj.; nicht präd.* occasional. **2.** *adv.* **a)** *(manchmal)* occasionally; **b)** *(bei Gelegenheit)* some time. **3.** *Präp. + Gen. (Amtsspr.)* on the occasion of

gelehrig [gə'le:rɪç] **1.** *Adj.* ⟨*child*⟩ who is quick to learn *or* quick at picking things up; ⟨*animal*⟩ that is quick to learn. **2.** *adv.* **sich ~ anstellen** be quick to learn

Gelehrigkeit die; ~: quickness to learn

gelehrsam *Adj.* **a)** *s.* **gelehrig; b)** *(veralt.: gelehrt)* learned; erudite

Gelehrsamkeit die; ~: learning; erudition

gelehrt 1. *2. Part. v.* **lehren. 2.** *Adj.* **a)** *(kenntnisreich)* learned; erudite; **b)** *(auf gründlichen Kenntnissen beruhend)* scholarly; **c)** *(abwertend: schwer verständlich)* highbrow. **3.** *adv.* **a)** learnedly; eruditely; **b)** *(abwertend: schwer verständlich)* in a highbrow way

Gelehrte der/die; *adj. Dekl.* scholar; **darüber streiten sich die ~n** *od.* **sind sich die ~n noch nicht einig** the experts disagree on that; *(fig.)* that's a moot point

Gelehrten-: ~dasein das scholarly life *or* existence; **~streit der** dispute among scholars

Geleise das; ~s, ~ *(österr., sonst geh.) s.* **Gleis**

Geleit das; ~[e]s, ~e a) *(geh.: das Begleiten)* **sie bot uns ihr ~ an** she offered to accompany *or* escort us; **freies** *od.* **sicheres ~** *(Rechtsw.)* safe-conduct; **jmdm. das ~ geben** *(geh.)* accompany *or* escort sb.; **jmdm. das letzte ~ geben** *(geh. verhüll.)* attend sb.'s funeral; **zum ~:** as a preface; **„zum ~"** 'preface'; **b)** *(Eskorte)* escort; *(Gefolge)* entourage; retinue

geleiten *tr. V. (geh.)* escort; *(begleiten)* accompany; escort; **jmdn. zur Tür ~:** see sb. to the door; show sb. out

Geleit-: ~schiff das *(Milit.)* escort vessel; **~schutz der** *(Milit.)* escort; **jmdm. ~schutz geben** provide an escort for sb.; **~wort das** *(geh.)* preface; **~zug der** *(Milit.)* convoy

Gelenk [gə'lɛŋk] **das; ~[e]s, ~e a)** joint; **es kracht** *od.* **knackt in den ~en** my/your *etc.* joints creak; **b)** *(Technik)* joint; *(Scharnier~)* hinge

Gelenk-: ~entzündung die *(Med.)* arthritis; **~fahrzeug das** articulated vehicle

gelenkig 1. *Adj.* agile ⟨*person*⟩; *(geschmeidig)* supple ⟨*limb*⟩. **2.** *adv.* **a)** agilely; **b)** *(Technik)* **~ gelagert** *(mittels Scharnier)* hinge-mounted; *(mittels Drehzapfen)* swivel-mounted

Gelenkigkeit die; ~: agility; *(von Gliedmaßen)* suppleness

Gelenk-: ~kapsel die *(Anat.)* joint capsule; articular capsule; **~kopf der** *(Anat.)* head of a/the bone; **~pfanne die** *(Anat.)* socket of a/the joint; **~rheumatismus der** *(Med.)* articular rheumatism; **~schmiere die** *(Anat.)* synovial fluid; **~welle die** *(Kfz-W.)* cardan shaft

gelernt 1. *2. Part. v.* **lernen. 2.** *Adj.; nicht präd.* qualified

gelesen *2. Part. v.* **lesen**

Gelichter das; ~s *(veralt. abwertend)* rabble; riff-raff

Geliebte [gə'li:ptə] **der/die;** *adj. Dekl.* **a)** lover/mistress; **b)** *(geh. veralt.)* beloved

geliefert 1. *2. Part. v.* **liefern. 2.** *Adj.* **in ~ sein** *(salopp)* be sunk *(coll.)*; have had it *(coll.)*

geliehen [gə'li:ən] *2. Part. v.* **leihen**

gelieren [ʒe'li:rən] *itr. V.* set

Gelier·zucker der preserving sugar

gelind[e] 1. *Adj.* **a)** *(schonend)* mild; **b)** *(geh. veralt.: mild, sanft)* mild ⟨*climate*⟩; light ⟨*punishment*⟩; slight ⟨*pain*⟩. **2.** *adv.* mildly; **~e gesagt** to put it mildly

gelingen [gə'lɪŋən] *unr. itr. V.; mit sein* succeed; **es gelang ihr, es zu tun** she succeeded in doing it; **es gelang ihr nicht, es zu tun** she did not succeed in doing it; she failed to do it; **möge dir dein Vorhaben gelingen** I hope you succeed with *or* accomplish your plan; **das wollte ihr nicht ~:** she couldn't seem to manage it; **eine gelungene Arbeit** a successful piece of work; *s. auch* **gelungen 2**

Gelingen das; ~s success; **auf ein gutes ~ hoffen** hope for success; **jmdm. gutes ~ wünschen** wish sb. every success; **gutes ~!** the best of luck!

gelitten [gə'lɪtn̩] *2. Part. v.* **leiden**

¹gell [gɛl] **1.** *Adj. (geh.)* piercing; shrill. **2.** *adv.* **~ aufschreien** let out *or* give a piercing scream *or* shriek

²gell[e] ['gɛl(ə)] *Interj. (südd.) s.* **gelt**

gellen ['gɛlən] *itr. V.* **a)** *(hell schallen)* ring out; **ein Schrei gellte durch die Nacht** a scream *or* shriek pierced the night; **jmdm. in den Ohren ~:** make sb.'s ears ring; **~des Gelächter** shrill peals of laughter; **~d aufschreien** let out *or* give a piercing scream *or* shriek; **b)** *(nachhallen)* ring; **uns gellten die Ohren** our ears rang; **von etw. ~:** ring with sth.

geloben *tr. V. (geh.)* vow; **Besserung/Armut ~:** promise solemnly to improve/take a vow of poverty; **jmdm. Treue ~:** vow to be faithful to sb.; **sich** *(Dat.)* **~, etw. zu tun** vow to oneself *or* make a solemn resolve to do sth.; **das Gelobte Land** the Promised Land

Gelöbnis [gə'lø:pnɪs] **das; ~ses, ~se** *(geh.)* vow; **ein ~ ablegen** *od.* **leisten** make *or* take a vow

gelogen *2. Part. v.* **lügen**

gelöst [gə'lø:st] **1.** *2. Part. v.* **lösen. 2.** *Adj.* relaxed

Gelöstheit die; ~: relaxed mood

Gelse ['gɛlzə] **die; ~, ~n** *(österr.)* mosquito, gnat

gelt [gɛlt] *Interj. (südd., österr. ugs.)* **~, du bist mir doch nicht böse?** you're not angry with me, are you?; **er kommt doch morgen zurück, ~?** he'll be coming back tomorrow, won't he *or (coll.)* right?

gelten ['gɛltn̩] **1.** *unr. itr. V.* **a)** *(gültig sein)* be valid; ⟨*banknote, coin*⟩ be legal tender; ⟨*law, regulation, agreement*⟩ be in force; ⟨*price*⟩ be effective; **etw. gilt für jmdn.** sth. applies to sb.; **das gilt auch für dich/Sie!** *(ugs.)* that includes you!; that goes for you too!; **das gilt nicht!** that doesn't count!; **~de Preise** current prices; **nach ~dem Recht** in accordance with the law as it [now] stands; **die ~de Meinung** the generally accepted opinion; **etw. [nicht] ~ lassen** [not] accept sth.; **b)** *(angesehen werden)* **als etw. ~:** be regarded as sth.; be considered [to be] sth.; **er galt als klug/Favorit** he was regarded as clever/the favourite; he was considered [to be] clever/the favourite; **c)** (+ *Dat.*) *(bestimmt sein für)* be directed at; **die Bemerkung gilt dir** the remark is aimed at you; **der Beifall galt auch dem Regisseur** the applause was also for the director. **2.** *unr. tr. V.* **a)** *(wert sein)* **sein Wort gilt viel/wenig** his word carries a lot of/little weight; **was gilt die Wette?** what do you bet?; **etw. gilt jmdm. mehr als ...:** sth. is worth *or* means more to sb. than ...; **b)** *unpers. (darauf ankommen, daß)* **es gilt, Zeit zu gewinnen/rasch zu handeln** it is essential to gain time/act swiftly; **es gilt einen Versuch** the only thing to do is to make an attempt; **c)** *unpers. (geh.: auf dem Spiel stehen)* **es gilt dein Leben** *od.* **deinen Kopf** your life is at stake

geltend in etw. ~ machen assert sth.; **einige Bedenken/einen Einwand ~ machen** express some doubts/raise an objection; **sich ~ machen** begin to show; begin to make itself/themselves felt; *s. auch* **gelten 1 a**

Geltendmachung die; ~ *(Amtsspr.)* assertion

Geltung die; ~ a) *(Gültigkeit)* validity; **~ haben** ⟨*banknote, coin*⟩ be legal tender; ⟨*law, regulation, agreement*⟩ be in force; ⟨*price*⟩ be effective; **für jmdn. ~ haben** apply to sb.; **b)** *(Wirkung)* recognition; **jmdm./sich/einer Sache ~ verschaffen** gain *or* win recognition for sb./oneself/sth.; **an ~ verlieren** ⟨*value, principle, etc.*⟩ lose its importance, become less important; **etw. zur ~ bringen** show something to its best advantage; **zur ~ kommen** show to [its best] advantage

Geltungs-: ~bedürfnis das need for recognition; **~bereich der** scope; **unter den ~bereich eines Gesetzes fallen** come within the scope of a law; **~bereich dieser Verordnung ist Hessen** the area in which the regulation is in force is Hesse; **~dauer die** period of validity; **die ~dauer des Vertrags/Gesetzes** the period during which the agreement/law is in force; **~drang der** *s.* **~bedürfnis; ~sucht die** [pathological] craving for recognition; **~trieb der** *(~bedürfnis)* need for recognition; *(~sucht)* craving for recognition

Gelump[e] [gə'lʊmp(ə)] **das; ~s** *(ugs. abwertend)* **a)** *(Plunder)* junk; rubbish; **b)** *(Gesindel)* riff-raff; rabble

gelungen [gə'lʊŋən] **1.** *2. Part. v.* **gelingen. 2.** *Adj.* **a)** *(ugs.: spaßig)* priceless; **das finde ich ~:** what a laugh!; **b)** *(ansprechend)* inspired

Gelüst das; ~[e]s, ~e, Gelüste das; ~s, ~ *(geh.)* longing; strong desire; *(zwingend, krankhaft)* craving; **ein ~ nach** *od.* **auf etw.** *(Akk.)* **haben** have a longing *or* a strong desire/a craving for sth.

gelüsten *tr. V. (unpers.)* **es gelüstet ihn nach ...:** he has a longing for ...; *(zwingend, krankhaft)* he has a craving for ...

gemach [gə'ma(:)x] *Adv. (veralt.)* **[nur/immer] ~!** not so fast!; take it easy!

Gemach [gə'ma(:)x] **das; ~[e]s, Gemächer** [gə'mɛ(:)çɐ] *(veralt. geh.)* apartment

gemächlich [gə'mɛ(:)çlɪç] **1.** *Adj.* leisurely; **ein ~es Leben führen** take life easily. **2.** *adv.* in a leisurely manner; **~ wandern** stroll

Gemächlichkeit die; ~: leisureliness; **etw. mit ~ machen** do sth. at a leisurely pace

gemacht 1. *2. Part. v.* **machen. 2. in ein ~er Mann sein** *(ugs.)* be a made man; **zu** *od.* **für etw. [nicht] ~ sein** *(ugs.)* [not] be made for sth.; **ich bin nicht dazu ~, einen solchen Posten auszufüllen** I'm not cut out for a job like this

Gemächt das; ~[e]s, Gemächte das; ~s *(scherzh., veralt.)* privy parts *pl. (arch.)*

Gemahl der; ~s, ~e *(geh.)* consort; husband; **bitte grüßen Sie Ihren Herrn ~:** please give my regards to your husband

Gemahlin die; ~, ~nen *(geh.)* consort; wife; **eine Empfehlung an die Frau ~:** my compliments to your wife

gemahnen *tr., itr. V. (geh.)* **jmdn. an etw.** *(Akk.)* **~:** remind sb. of sth.; **diese Gedenktafel soll an die Opfer beider Weltkriege ~:** this memorial plaque is to commemorate the dead of two World Wars

Gemälde [gə'mɛ:ldə] **das; ~s, ~:** painting

Gemälde-: ~ausstellung die exhibition of paintings; **~galerie die** picture gallery; **~sammlung die** collection of paintings

gemäß [gə'mɛ:s] **1.** *Präp. + Dat.* in accordance with; **~ Paragraph 15/Artikel 12** under section 15/article 12. **2.** *Adj.* **jmdm./einer Sache ~ sein** be appropriate for sb./to sth.; **eine deinen Leistungen ~e Arbeit** a job suited to your abilities

-gemäß *Adj.* in accordance with ⟨*tradition etc.*⟩; **berufs~:** in accordance with the standards of the profession; **art~:** appropriate [for the species *postpos.*]

gemäßigt 1. *2. Part. v.* **mäßigen. 2.** *Adj.* moderate; modest ⟨*life-style*⟩; more restrained ⟨*version*⟩; qualified ⟨*optimism*⟩; temperate ⟨*climate*⟩

Gemäuer [gəˈmɔyɐ] **das;** ~s, ~: walls *pl.*; *(Ruine)* ruin

Gemauschel das; ~s *(ugs. abwertend)* underhand dealing

Gemecker[e] das; ~s **a)** *(von Schafen, Ziegen)* bleating; **b)** *(abwertend: Lachen)* cackling; **c)** *(ugs. abwertend: Nörgelei)* griping *(coll.)*; grousing *(sl.)*; moaning

gemein 1. *Adj.* **a)** *(abstoßend)* coarse, vulgar ⟨*joke, expression*⟩; nasty ⟨*person*⟩; **b)** *(niederträchtig)* mean; base, dirty ⟨*lie*⟩; mean, dirty ⟨*trick*⟩; **du bist ~!/das ist ~ [von dir]!** you're mean *or* nasty!/that's mean *or* nasty [of you]!; **c)** *(ärgerlich)* infuriating; damned annoying *(coll.)*; **d)** *nicht präd. (Bot., Zool., sonst veralt.: allgemein vorkommend)* common; **der ~e Mann** the ordinary man; the man in the street; **ein ~er Soldat** a common soldier; **e)** *(veralt.: allgemein)* general; **das ~e Wohl** the common good; **etw. mit jmdm./etw. ~ haben** have sth. in common with sb./sth.; **sich mit jmdm. ~ machen** associate with sb.; **das ist ihnen ~:** they have that in common; they share that. **2.** *adv.* **a)** *(niederträchtig)* **jmdn. ~ behandeln** treat sb. in a mean *or* nasty way; **b)** *(ugs.: sehr)* **sich ~ verletzen** injure oneself badly; **es hat ganz ~ weh getan** it hurt like hell *(coll.)*; **~ kalt** terribly *or* hellish cold *(coll.)*

Gemein·besitz der common property

Gemeinde [gəˈmaində] **die;** ~, ~n **a)** *(staatliche Verwaltungseinheit)* municipality; *(ugs.: ~amt)* local authority; **die ~ X** the municipality of X; **einen Zug durch die ~ machen** *(fig. ugs.)* go an a pub crawl *(Brit. coll.)*; go bar-hopping *(Amer. coll.)*; **b)** *(Seelsorgebezirk) (christlich)* parish; *(nichtchristlich)* community; *(Mitglieder)* parish; parishioners *pl.*; **c)** *(Bewohner)* community; local population; **d)** *(Gottesdienstteilnehmer)* congregation; **e)** *(Anhängerschaft)* body of followers; **die ~ seiner Anhänger** his following

gemeinde-, Gemeinde-: ~abgaben *Pl.* rates [and local taxes] *(Brit.)*; local taxes *(Amer.)*; **~amt das** local authority; *(Gebäude)* municipal offices *pl.*; **~beamte der** local government official; **~behörde die** local authority; **~bezirk der a)** municipality; district; **b)** *(österr.)* ward; **~diener der** *(veralt.)* beadle; **~eigen** *Adj.* municipal ⟨*swimming pool, sports centre, etc.*⟩; **~eigen sein** be municipally owned; **~haus das** parish hall; **~mitglied das** parishioner; **~ordnung die** [state] law governing local authorities; **~pflege die** parish welfare work; **~rat der a)** *(Gremium)* local council; **b)** *(Mitglied)* local councillor; **~schwester die** district nurse; **~steuer die** local tax

gemein·deutsch *Adj.* standard German

Gemeinde-: ~verwaltung die local administration; **~vor·stand der** local council; **~wahl die** *s.* **Kommunalwahl; ~zentrum das** community centre

gemein-, Gemein-: ~eigentum das *(Politik, Wirtsch.)* public property; **~gefährlich** *Adj.* dangerous to the public; **~gefährlich sein** be a danger to the public; **ein ~gefährlicher Verbrecher** a dangerous criminal; **~gültig** *Adj. s.* **allgemeingültig; ~gültigkeit die** *s.* **Allgemeingültigkeit; ~gut das;** *o. Pl. (geh.)* common property

Gemein·heit die; ~, ~en **a)** *o. Pl. (niederträchtige Gesinnung)* meanness; nastiness; **etw. aus ~ tun/sagen** do/say sth. out of meanness *or* nastiness; **b)** *(gemeine Handlung)* mean *or* nasty *or* dirty trick; **das war eine ~:** that was a mean *or* nasty thing to do/say; **c)** *(unerfreulicher Umstand)* **so eine ~!** *(ugs.)* what a damned nuisance!

gemein-, Gemein-: ~hin *Adv.* commonly; generally; **wie man ~hin vermutet/annimmt** as is commonly *or* generally supposed/assumed; **~kosten** *Pl. (Wirtsch.)* overheads; overhead expenses; **~nutz der; ~es** public good; **~nutz geht vor Eigennutz** the public interest comes first; **~nützig** [-nʏtsɪç] *Adj.* serving the public good *postpos., not pred.*; *(wohltätig)* charitable; **eine ~nützige Institution** a charitable *or* non-profit-making institution; **~platz der** platitude; commonplace

gemeinsam 1. *Adj.* **a)** common ⟨*interests, characteristics*⟩; mutual ⟨*acquaintance, friend*⟩; joint ⟨*property, account*⟩; shared ⟨*experience*⟩; **der Gemeinsame Markt** the Common Market; **~e Interessen/Merkmale haben** have interests/characteristics in common; **~e Kasse machen** pool funds *or* resources; **größter ~er Teiler** *(Math.)* highest common denominator; **kleinstes ~es Vielfaches** *(Math.)* lowest common multiple; **b)** *nicht präd. (miteinander unternommen)* joint ⟨*undertaking, consultations*⟩; joint, concerted ⟨*efforts, action, measures*⟩; **[mit jmdm.] ~e Sache machen** join forces *or* up [with sb.]; **c)** *nicht attr. (übereinstimmend)* **ihnen ist nur das ~:** that's the only thing they have in common; **das blonde Haar ist ihnen ~:** they both have blond hair; **viel Gemeinsames haben** have a lot in common. **2.** *adv.* together; **es gehört ihnen ~:** it is owned by them jointly

Gemeinsamkeit die; ~, ~en **a)** *(gemeinsames Merkmal)* common feature; point in common; **zwischen den beiden Parteien gab es keine ~en** there was no common ground between the two parties; **b)** *o. Pl. (Einheit)* community of interest; **ein Gefühl der ~:** a sense of community

Gemeinschaft die; ~, ~en **a)** community; **die ~ der Heiligen** *(Rel.)* the communion of saints; **die Europäische ~:** the European Community; **b)** *o. Pl. (Verbundenheit)* coexistence; **in unserer Klasse herrscht keine echte ~:** there is no real sense of community in our class; **in ~ mit jmdm.** together *or* jointly with sb.

gemeinschaftlich 1. *Adj.*; *nicht präd.* common ⟨*interests, characteristics*⟩; joint ⟨*property, undertaking*⟩; mutual ⟨*acquaintance, friend*⟩; joint, concerted ⟨*efforts, action*⟩. **2.** *adv.* together; **wir führen die Firma ~:** we run the firm jointly *or* together

Gemeinschafts-: ~an·schluß der *(Fernspr.)* party line; **~antenne die** community aerial *(Brit.) or (Amer.)* antenna; **~arbeit die a)** *o. Pl. (gemeinschaftliches Arbeiten)* joint work; **etw. in ~arbeit tun** do sth. jointly; **sozialistische ~arbeit** *(DDR)* collective socialist work *or* efforts *pl.*; **b)** *(Ergebnis der Zusammenarbeit)* joint product *or* effort; **~auf·gabe die a)** common *or* shared task; **b)** *(Bundesrepublik Deutschland) major project for which Land and Federation are jointly responsible*; **~beichte die** *(christl. Rel.)* public confession; **~gefühl das;** *o. Pl.* community spirit; **~küche die** *(in einem Wohnheim usw.)* shared kitchen; **~kunde die;** *o. Pl.* social studies *sing.*; **~leben das;** *o. Pl.* communal life; **~produktion die** *(von einem Film, Buch usw.)* co-production; **~raum der** common-room *(Brit.)*; **~schule die** non-denominational school; **~sendung die** *(Rundf., Ferns.)* joint transmission; **~sinn der;** *o. Pl.* community spirit; **~werbung die** joint advertising; **~werbung machen** run a joint advertisement; **~wesen das** social being *or* animal; **~zelle die** shared cell

gemein-, Gemein-: ~schuldner der *(Rechtsw.)* [declared] bankrupt; **~sinn der;** *o. Pl.* public spirit; **~sprache die** *(Sprachw.)* standard language; ordinary language; **~verständlich 1.** *Adj.* generally comprehensible *or* intelligible; **2.** *adv.* **sich ~verständlich ausdrücken** make oneself generally comprehensible *or* intelligible; **~wesen das** community; *(staatlich)* political unit; polity; **~wohl das** public *or* common good; **etw./jmd. dient dem ~wohl** sth. is/sb. acts in the public interest

Gemenge das; ~s, ~ **a)** *(Gemisch)* mixture **(aus, von** of); **b)** *(Durcheinander)* jumble; *(von Menschen)* crowd; **c)** *(Landw.)* mixed crop

Gemengsel [gəˈmɛŋzl] **das;** ~s, ~: mixture; *(von Gerüchten, Düften)* medley

gemessen 1. *2. Part. v.* **messen. 2.** *Adj.* **a)** *(würdevoll)* measured ⟨*steps, tones, language*⟩; deliberate ⟨*words, manner of speaking*⟩; **~en Schrittes** with measured tread *or* steps *pl.*; **b)** *nicht präd. (an~)* **in ~em Abstand** *od.* **~er Entfernung** at a respectful distance; **in ~er Bescheidenheit** with due modesty; **c)** *(veralt.: zurückhaltend)* reserved. **3.** *adv.* **~ schreiten** walk with measured tread *or* steps *pl.*; **~ sprechen** speak in measured tones

Gemessenheit die; ~ **a)** *(Würde) s.* **gemessen 2a:** measuredness; deliberateness; **in aller ~:** slowly and with all due solemnity; **b)** *(An~)* respectfulness; **c)** *(veralt.: Zurückhaltung)* reserve

Gemetzel das; ~s, ~ *(abwertend)* bloodbath; massacre

gemieden [gəˈmi:dn̩] *2. Part. v.* **meiden**

Gemisch das; ~[e]s, ~e *(auch fig.)* mixture **(aus, von** of); mix *(coll.)*; *(Kfz-W.)* mixture

gemischt 1. *2. Part. v.* **mischen. 2.** *Adj.* **a)** mixed; **~e Kost** a varied diet; **eine ~e Klasse** a mixed *or* coeducational *or (coll.)* coed class; **b)** *(abwertend: anrüchig)* **eine ~e Gesellschaft** a disreputable crowd. **3.** *adv. (abwertend: anrüchig)* **es geht sehr ~ zu** there are all sorts of goings-on

gemischt-, Gemischt-: ~rassig, ~rassisch *Adj.* multiracial; **~rassige Badestrände** desegregated bathing-beaches; **~waren·handlung die** *(veralt.)* general store

Gemme [ˈgɛmə] **die;** ~, ~n **a)** *(Edelstein)* engraved gem; *(Intaglio)* intaglio; *(Kamee)* cameo; **b)** *meist Pl. (Biol.: Zelle)* gemma

gemocht [gəˈmɔxt] *2. Part. v.* **mögen**

gemolken *2. Part. v.* **melken**

gemoppelt [gəˈmɔpl̩t] *s.* **doppelt 2a**

Gemotze das; ~s *(salopp)* grumbling; fault-finding; crabbing *(coll.)*

Gems-: ~bart der *s.* **Gamsbart; ~bock der** chamois buck

Gemse [ˈgɛmzə] **die;** ~, ~n chamois

Gemunkel das; ~s rumours *pl.*; whispers *pl.*

Gemurmel das; ~s murmuring

Gemüse [gəˈmy:zə] **das;** ~s, ~: vegetables *pl.*; **ein ~:** a vegetable; **frisches/gekochtes ~:** fresh/cooked vegetables; **junges ~** *(fig. ugs.)* youngsters *pl.*; **dieses junge ~ kann man doch nicht ernst nehmen** *(fig. ugs.)* these young whippersnappers *pl.* can't be taken seriously

Gemüse-: ~anbau der; *o. Pl.* growing of vegetables; *(Handelsgärtnerei)* market gardening; **~beet das** vegetable patch *or* plot; **~beilage die** vegetables *pl.*; **~eintopf der** vegetable stew; **~frau die** vegetable seller; **~garten der** vegetable *or* kitchen garden; *(Teil eines Gartens)* vegetable patch *or* plot; **~händler der** greengrocer; **~konserve die** canned *or (Brit.)* tinned vegetables *pl.*; *(in einem Glas)* preserved vegetables *pl.*; **~laden der** greengrocer's [shop]; **~pflanze die** vegetable; **~platte die** vegetable dish; *(als Beilage)* dish of assorted vegetables; **~saft der** vegetable juice; **~suppe die** vegetable soup

gemußt [gə'mʊst] *2. Part. v.* **müssen**

Gemüt [gə'my:t] **das; ~[e]s, ~er a)** *(Gefühlsleben)* nature; disposition; **ein sonniges/kindliches ~ haben** *(iron.)* be [really] naive; **b)** *(Empfindungsvermögen)* heart; soul; **viel/wenig ~ haben** be soft-hearted/hard-hearted; **das rührt ans** *od.* **ist etw. fürs ~:** that touches the heart *or* tears at one's heart-strings; **jmdm. aufs ~ schlagen** *od.* **gehen** make sb. depressed; **sich** *(Dat.)* **etw. zu ~e führen** *(beherzigen)* take sth. to heart; *(essen od. trinken)* treat oneself to sth.; **c)** *(Mensch)* soul; **einfache/romantische ~er** simple/romantic souls; **etw. erhitzt/erregt die ~er** sth. makes feelings run high; **die ~er haben sich beruhigt** feelings have cooled down

gemütlich 1. *Adj.* **a)** *(behaglich)* snug; cosy; gemütlich *(literary); (bequem)* comfortable; **mach es dir ~!** make yourself comfortable *or* at home!; **b)** *(ungezwungen)* informal; **ein ~es Beisammensein** an informal get together; **c)** *(umgänglich)* sociable; friendly; *(gelassen)* easygoing; **d)** *(gemächlich)* leisurely; **ein ~es Tempo** a leisurely *or* comfortable pace. **2.** *adv.* **a)** *(behaglich)* cosily; *(bequem)* comfortably; **b)** *(ungezwungen)* **~ beisammensitzen** sit pleasantly together; **sich ~ unterhalten** have a pleasant chat; **c)** *(gemächlich)* at a leisurely *or* comfortable pace; unhurriedly

Gemütlichkeit die; ~ a) *(Behaglichkeit)* snugness; **b)** *(Zwanglosigkeit)* informality; **die ~ stören** disturb the atmosphere *or* mood of informality; **c)** *(Gemächlichkeit)* **in aller ~:** quite unhurriedly; **da hört [sich] doch die ~ auf** *(fig. ugs.)* that's going too far

gemüts-, Gemüts-: ~arm *Adj.* insensitive; cold; **~art die** nature; disposition; **~bewegung die** emotion; **~krank** *Adj.* *(Med., Psych.)* emotionally disturbed; **~krankheit die** emotional disorder; **~lage die** emotional state; **~mensch der** *(ugs.) (gutmütiger Mensch)* good-natured *or* even-tempered person; *(etwas langsamer Mensch)* phlegmatic person; **du bist [vielleicht] ein ~mensch!** *(iron. abwertend)* you're the soul of tact, I must say!; *(du bist naiv)* you'll be lucky!; **~regung die** emotion; **~ruhe die** peace of mind; **in aller ~ruhe** *(ugs.) (ohne Sorge)* completely unconcerned; *(ohne Hast)* as if there were all the time in the world; **~verfassung die, ~zustand der** emotional state

gemüt·voll *Adj.* warm-hearted; *(empfindsam)* sentimental

gen [gɛn] *Präp. + Akk. (veralt., bibl., noch dichter.)* towards; toward; **~ Süden/Osten** *usw.* southwards, eastwards, *etc.*; **einen Blick ~ Himmel werfen** throw a glance heavenwards

Gen [ge:n] **das; ~s, ~e** *(Biol.)* gene

genagelt [gə'na:glt] **1.** *2. Part. v.* **nageln. 2.** *Adj.* **~e Schuhe** hobnailed boots

genannt [gə'nant] *2. Part. v.* **nennen**

genant [ʒe'nant] *Adj.* **a)** *(veralt.: peinlich)* embarrassing; **b)** *(bes. südd.: schüchtern)* shy; bashful

genas [gə'na:s] *1. u. 3. Pers. Sg. Prät. v.* **genesen**

genäschig [gə'nɛʃɪç] *Adj. s.* **naschhaft**

genau [gə'nau] **1.** *Adj.* **a)** *(exakt)* exact; precise; **eine ~e Waage** accurate scales *pl.*; **die ~e Uhrzeit** the exact *or* right time; **~e Untersuchungen** accurate *or* precise investigations; **Genaues/Genaueres wissen** know the/more exact *or* precise details; **ich weiß nichts Genaues/Genaueres** I don't know anything definite/more definite; **b)** *(sorgfältig, gründlich)* meticulous, painstaking ⟨*person*⟩; careful ⟨*study*⟩; precise ⟨*use of language*⟩; detailed, thorough ⟨*knowledge*⟩. **2.** *adv.* **a)** exactly; precisely; **~ um 8⁰⁰** at 8 o'clock precisely; at exactly 8 o'clock; **die Uhr geht [auf die Minute] ~:** the watch/clock keeps perfect time; **die Schuhe paßten ihm ~:** the shoes fitted him perfectly; **b)** *(gerade, eben)* just; **~ reichen** be just enough; **c)** *(als Verstärkung)* just; exactly; precisely; **~ das habe ich gesagt** that's just *or* exactly what I said; **d)** *(als Zustimmung)* exactly; precisely; quite [so]; **e)** *(sorgfältig)* **~ arbeiten/etw. ~ durchdenken** work/think sth. out carefully *or* meticulously; **jmdn. ~ kennen** know exactly what sb. is like; **etw. ~ beachten** observe sth. meticulously *or* painstakingly; **es mit etw. [nicht so] ~ nehmen** be [not too] particular about sth.

genau·genommen *Adv.* strictly speaking

Genauigkeit die; ~ a) *(Exaktheit)* exactness; exactitude; precision; *(einer Waage)* accuracy; **b)** *(Sorgfalt)* meticulousness

genau·so *Adv.* **a)** *mit Adjektiven* just as; **~so schlecht wie ...:** just as bad/badly as ...; **b)** *mit Verben* in exactly the same way; *(in demselben Maße)* just as much; **ich werde es ~ machen wie du** I'll do exactly the same as you; *s. auch* **ebenso**

genauso-: *s.* **ebenso-**

genaustens *Adv.* **etw. ~ durchdenken/beachten** think sth. out/observe sth. most meticulously

Gendarm [ʒan'darm] **der; ~en, ~en** *(österr., sonst veralt.)* village *or* local policeman *or* constable

Gendarmerie [ʒandarmə'ri:] **die; ~, ~n** *(österr., sonst veralt.)* village *or* local constabulary

Genealoge [genea'lo:gə] **der; ~n, ~n** genealogist

Genealogie [genealo'gi:] **die; ~, ~n** genealogy

genealogisch *Adj.; nicht präd.* genealogical

genehm [gə'ne:m] *Adj.* **in jmdm. ~ sein** *(geh.) (jmdm. passen)* be convenient to *or* suit sb.; *(jmdm. angenehm sein)* be acceptable to sb.

genehmigen *tr. V.* approve ⟨*plan, alterations*⟩; grant, approve ⟨*application*⟩; authorize ⟨*stay*⟩; grant, agree to ⟨*request*⟩; give permission for ⟨*demonstration*⟩; **sich** *(Dat.)* **etw. ~** *(ugs.)* treat oneself to sth.; **sich** *(Dat.)* **einen ~** *(ugs.)* have a drink

Genehmigung die; ~, ~en a) *(eines Plans, Antrags, einer Veränderung)* approval; *(eines Aufenthalts)* authorization; *(einer Bitte)* granting; *(einer Demonstration)* permission (*Gen.* for); **jmdm. die ~ zur Eröffnung einer Gaststätte verweigern** refuse [to grant] sb. a licence to open a restaurant/pub; **b)** *(Schriftstück)* permit; *(Lizenz)* licence

genehmigungs-, Genehmigungs-: ~pflicht die; *o. Pl. (Rechtsspr.)* obligation to obtain official approval; **der ~pflicht unterliegen** require official approval; **~pflichtig** *Adj.* requiring official approval *postpos.*; **~pflichtig sein** require official approval; **Demonstrationen sind ~pflichtig** demonstrations require official permission

geneigt [gə'naikt] **1.** *2. Part. v.* **neigen. 2.** *Adj.* **in ~ sein** *od.* **sich ~ zeigen, etw. zu tun** be inclined to do sth.; *(bereit sein)* be ready *or* willing to do sth.; **jmdm./einer Sache ~ sein** *(geh.)* be well-disposed towards sb./sth.; **~er Leser** *(veralt.)* gentle reader

Geneigtheit die; ~ a) inclination; disposition; *(Bereitschaft)* readiness; willingness; **b)** *(Wohlwollen)* goodwill **(gegenüber, für** towards)

Genera *s.* **Genus**

General [genə'ra:l] **der; ~s, ~e** *od.* **Generäle** [genə'rɛ:lə] *(auch kath. Rel.)* general; **Herr ~:** General

General-: ~amnestie die general amnesty; **~angriff der** general offensive; **~baß der** *(Musik)* [basso] continuo; thorough-bass; **~beichte die** *(kath. Rel.)* general confession; **~bevollmächtigte der/die** *(Rechtsw.)* general agent; universal agent [with full powers of attorney]; *(Politik)* plenipotentiary; *(in einer Firma)* general manager; **~bundes·anwalt der** Chief Federal Prosecutor; **~direktion die** top management; **~direktor der** chairman; president *(Amer.)*; **~feld·marschall** [---'---] **der** *(Milit.) s.* **Feldmarschall; ~gouverneur der** Governor-General; **~inspekteur der** *(Milit.)* inspector general; **~intendant der** artistic director

generalisieren *tr., itr. V.* generalize

Generalisierung die; ~, ~en generalization

Generalissimus [genəra'lɪsimʊs] **der; ~, ~se** *od.* **Generalissimi** [-'lɪsimi] *(Milit.)* generalissimo

Generalist der; ~en, ~en generalist

Generalität [genərali'tɛ:t] **die; ~, ~en** *(Milit.)* **die ~:** the generals *pl.*

general-, General-: ~klausel die *(Rechtsw.)* blanket *or* general clause; **~konsul der** consul general; **~konsulat das** consulate general; **~leutnant der** *(Milit.)* lieutenant-general; *(Luftw.)* air marshal *(Brit.)*; **~major der** *(Milit.)* major-general; *(Luftw.)* air vice-marshal *(Brit.)*; **~musik·direktor** [----'----] **der** musical director; **~nenner der** *s.* **Hauptnenner; ~präventiv** *Adj. (Rechtsspr.)* ⟨*judgement*⟩ acting as a general deterrent; **~probe die a)** *(auch fig.)* dress *or* final rehearsal; **b)** *(Sport: letztes Testspiel)* final trial; **~sekretär der** Secretary General; *(einer Partei)* general secretary; **~staatsanwalt** [---'---] **der** chief public prosecutor *(in a Higher Regional Court)*

General·stab der *(Milit.)* general staff

Generalstabs-: ~chef der chief of the general staff; **~karte die** *(hist.)* ordnance survey map *(scale 1:100,000)*; **~offizier der** general staff officer

Generals·rang der rank of general

general-, General-: ~streik der general strike; **~überholen** *tr. V.; nur im Inf. und 2. Part. gebr. (bes. Technik)* **etw. ~überholen** give sth. a general overhaul; **etw. ~überholen lassen** have sth. generally overhauled; **~überholung die** general overhaul; **~versammlung die** general meeting; **die ~versammlung der Vereinten Nationen** the General Assembly of the United Nations; **~vertreter der** general representative; **~vertretung die** *s.* **Alleinvertretung; ~vollmacht die** *(Rechtsw.)* full *or* unlimited power of attorney

Generation [genəra'tsio:n] **die; ~, ~en** generation

Generations-: ~konflikt der generation gap; **~problem das** generation problem; **~unterschied der** generation gap; **~wechsel der a)** new generation; **ein ~wechsel ist notwendig** new blood is needed; **b)** *(Biol.)* alternation of generations

generativ [genəra'ti:f] *Adj.* **a)** *(Biol.)* generative ⟨*cell, nucleus, etc.*⟩; sexual ⟨*reproduction*⟩; **b)** *(Sprachw.)* generative

Generator [genə'ra:tɔr] **der; ~s, ~en** [---'--] **a)** generator; **b)** *(Gas~)* producer

Generator·gas das producer gas

generell [genə'rɛl] **1.** *Adj.* general. **2.** *adv.* generally; **man kann ganz ~ sagen, daß ...:** generally speaking *or* in general, it can be said that ...; **es sollte sonnabends ~ schulfrei sein** all schools should close on Saturdays

generieren *tr. V. (geh.; Sprachw.)* generate

Generikum [ge'ne:rikʊm] **das; ~s, Generika** generic product

generös [genə'rø:s] *(geh.)* **1.** *Adj.* generous. **2.** *adv.* generously

Generosität [genərozi'tɛ:t] **die; ~** *(geh.)* generosity

Genese [ge'ne:zə] **die; ~, ~n** genesis

genesen [gə'ne:zn̩] *unr. itr. V.; mit sein* **a)**

(geh.) recover; recuperate; *(fig.)* recover; **von einer Krankheit ~:** recover from an illness; **b)** *(veralt. dichter.)* **eines Knaben ~:** be delivered of a son
Genesende der/die; *adj. Dekl.* convalescent
Genesis ['genezɪs] **die; ~:** genesis; **die ~** *(bibl.)* [the Book of] Genesis
Genesung die; ~, ~en *(geh.)* recovery
Genesungs-: ~heim das convalescent home; **~prozeß der** [process of] recovery; **~urlaub der** *(Milit.)* convalescent leave
Genetik [ge'ne:tɪk] **die; ~** *(Biol.)* genetics *sing., no art.*
Genetiker der; ~s, ~: geneticist
genetisch *(Biol.)* **1.** *Adj.* genetic. **2.** *adv.* genetically
Genezareth [ge'ne:tsarɛt] **(das); ~s** Gennesaret; **der See ~:** the Sea of Galilee
Genf [gɛnf] **(das); ~s** Geneva
Gẹnfer 1. der; ~s, ~: Genevese. **2.** *Adj.* Genevese; **der ~ See** Lake Geneva; **die ~ Konvention** the Geneva Convention; *s. auch* **Kölner**
Gẹnfer·see der; *o. Pl. (schweiz.)* Lake Geneva
genial [ge'nia:l] **1.** *Adj.* brillant ⟨*idea, invention, solution, etc.*⟩; **ein ~er Mensch** a [man/woman of] genius; **ein ~er Künstler/Musiker** an inspired artist/musician; an artist/musician of genius. **2.** *adv.* brilliantly
genialisch 1. *Adj.* **a)** brilliant; **ein ~er Musiker** a brilliant musician; a musical genius; **b)** *(exaltiert)* **ein ~er Hauch** a touch of the eccentric genius. **2.** *adv.* **a)** like a genius; **b)** *(exaltiert)* like an eccentric genius
Genialität [geniali'tɛ:t] **die; ~:** genius
Genick [gə'nɪk] **das; ~[e]s, ~e** back *or* nape of the neck; **sich das ~ brechen** *(auch fig.)* break one's neck; **jmdn. beim ~ packen** grab sb. by the scruff of the neck; **ein Schlag ins ~:** a blow to the back of the neck; **jmdm./einer Sache das ~ brechen** *(ugs.)* ruin sb./sth.; **jmdm. im ~ sitzen** *(ugs.)* haunt sb.
Genịck-: ~schlag der blow to the back of the neck; rabbit punch; **~schuß der** shot through the base of the skull; **~starre die** stiffness of the neck
[1]Genie [ʒe'ni:] **das; ~s, ~s** genius; **sie ist ein ~ im Kochen** she is a brilliant cook
[2]Genie [-] **die; ~, ~s** *(schweiz. Milit.)* *s.* **Genietruppe**
genieren [ʒe'ni:rən] **1.** *refl. V.* be *or* feel embarrassed **(wegen** about); **sich vor jmdm. ~:** be *or* feel embarrassed *or* shy in sb.'s presence; **greifen Sie zu, ~ Sie sich nicht!** help yourself – don't be shy! **2.** *tr. V. (veralt.)* disturb
genierlich *Adj. (ugs.)* **a)** *(peinlich)* embarrassing; **b)** *(schüchtern)* shy
genießbar *Adj. (eßbar)* edible; *(trinkbar)* drinkable; **er ist heute nicht ~** *(fig. ugs.)* he is unbearable today
genießen [gə'ni:sn̩] *unr. tr. V.* **a)** enjoy; **er hat eine gute Ausbildung genossen** he had [the benefit of] a good education; **er genießt Vertrauen in der Partei** he has the confidence of the Party; **b)** *(geh.: essen/trinken)* eat/drink; **das Fleisch ist nicht/nicht mehr zu ~:** the meat is inedible/no longer edible; **er ist heute nicht zu ~** *(fig. ugs.)* he is unbearable today
Genießer der; ~s, ~: er ist ein richtiger ~: he is a regular 'bon viveur'; he really knows how to enjoy life [to the full]; **er ist ein stiller ~:** he enjoys life [to the full] in his own quiet way
genießerisch 1. *Adj.* appreciative; sensuous ⟨*lips*⟩. **2.** *adv.* appreciatively; ⟨*drink, eat*⟩ with relish
Genie-: ~streich der *(auch iron.)* stroke of genius; **~truppe die** *(schweiz. Milit.)* engineer corps; **~zeit die** *(Literaturw.)* Storm and Stress Period
genital [geni'ta:l] *Adj.; nicht präd.* genital
Genital·apparat der *s.* **Geschlechtsapparat**
Genitale das; ~s, Genitalien [geni'ta:li̯ən], **Genital·organ das** genital organ; **die männlichen/weiblichen Genitalien** the male/female genitals *or* genital organs *or* genitalia
Genitiv ['ge:niti:f] **der; ~s, ~e** *(Sprachw.)* genitive [case]; *(Wort im ~)* genitive; **im/mit dem ~ stehen** be in/take the genitive [case]
Genitiv-: ~attribut das genitive attribute; **~objekt das** genitive object
Genius ['ge:ni̯ʊs] **der; ~, Genien** ['ge:ni̯ən] **a)** *(Geist)* guardian spirit; genius; **~ loci** [~ 'lo:tsi] *(geh.)* genius loci; **b)** *o. Pl. (geh.: Schöpferkraft)* [creative] genius; **c)** *(Mensch, Gottheit)* genius
Gen-: ~manipulation die genetic manipulation; **~mutation die** gene mutation
Genom [ge'no:m] **das; ~s, ~e** *(Biol.)* genome
genommen [gə'nɔmən] *2. Part. v.* **nehmen**
genoppt [gə'nɔpt] **1.** *2. Part. v.* **noppen. 2.** *Adj.* knop ⟨*yarn, wool*⟩; pimpled ⟨*rubber*⟩; ⟨*suit*⟩ made of knop yarn
Genörgel [gə'nœrgl̩] **das; ~s** *(abwertend)* grumbling; moaning; *(Krittelei)* carping
genoß [gə'nɔs] *1. u. 3. Pers. Sg. Prät. v.* **genießen**
Genosse [gə'nɔsə] **der; ~n, ~n a)** comrade; **„~ General/Professor"** *usw.* 'Comrade General/Professor' *etc;* **er ist kein ~ der Partei** he is not a party member; **b)** *(veralt.: Kamerad)* comrade; companion; **... und ~n** *(abwertend)* ... and his/her/their ilk; **c)** *(Wirtsch. veralt.)* member of a/the co-operative
genossen [gə'nɔsn̩] *2. Part. v.* **genießen**
Genọssenschaft die; ~, ~en co-operative
Genọssenschaftler der; ~s, ~: member of a/the co-operative
genọssenschaftlich 1. *Adj.* co-operative; collective ⟨*ownership*⟩; jointly owned ⟨*property*⟩. **2.** *adv.* on a co-operative basis
Genọssenschafts-: ~bank die credit co-operative *or* union; **~bauer der** *(bes. DDR)* member of a/the farming co-operative; **~betrieb der** co-operative
Genọssin die; ~, ~nen a) *s.* **Genosse a:** comrade; **b)** *(veralt.: Kameradin)* companion
Geno·typ [geno-], **Geno·typus der** *(Biol.)* genotype
Genozid [-'tsi:t] **der** *od.* **das; ~[e]s, ~e** *od.* **~ien** [-'tsi:di̯ən] genocide; **der** *od.* **das ~ der Nazis an den Juden** the genocide perpetrated by the Nazis against the Jews
Genre ['ʒã:rə] **das; ~s, ~s** genre
Genre-: ~bild das genre-picture; genre-painting; **~malerei die;** *o. Pl.* genre-painting
[1]Gent [dʒɛnt] **der; ~s, ~s** *(iron.)* dandy
[2]Gent [gɛnt] **(das); ~s** Ghent
Gen-: ~technik die, ~technologie die genetic engineering *no art.*
Genua ['ge:nu̯a] **(das); ~s** Genoa
Genuese [ge'nue:zə] **der; ~n, ~n** Genoese
Genueser 1. der; ~s, ~: Genoese. **2.** *Adj.* Genoese; *s. auch* **Kölner**
Genueserin die; ~, ~nen Genoese
genuesisch *Adj.* Genoese
genug [gə'nu:k] *Adv.* enough; **er hat ~ Geld/Geld ~:** he has enough *or* sufficient money; **das ist ~:** that's enough *or* sufficient; **er hat ~ gearbeitet** he has done enough work; **ich habe jetzt ~ [davon]** now I've had enough [of it]; **~ davon!** enough of that!; **nicht ~ damit, daß er faul ist, er ist auch frech** not only is he lazy, he is cheeky as well; **~ der Worte** *(geh.)* I/we/you have talked long enough; **er ist Manns ~, um zu ...:** he is man enough to ...; **das ist ihm nicht gut ~:** that is not good enough for him; **sich** *(Dat.)* **selbst ~ sein** be quite happy in one's own company; **er kann nicht ~ kriegen** *(ugs.)* he is very greedy; **davon kann er nicht ~ kriegen** *(ugs.)* he can't get enough of it *(fig. coll.)*; **von Bach kann ich nicht ~ kriegen** *(ugs.)* I can always listen to Bach's music
Genüge [gə'ny:gə] *(geh.) in* **jmdm. ~ tun** *od.* **leisten** satisfy sb.; **einer Anordnung/einer Pflicht ~ tun** *od.* **leisten** comply with an order; fulfil a duty *or* an obligation; **der Gerechtigkeit wurde ~ getan** justice was done; **zur ~** *(ausreichend)* enough; sufficiently; *(im Übermaß)* quite enough; **etw. zur ~ kennen** know sth. only too well; be only too familiar with sth.
genügen *itr. V.* **a)** be enough *or* sufficient; **diese Wohnung genügt für uns** this flat is adequate for us; **das genügt mir** that is enough *or* sufficient [for me]; that will do [for me]; *(das befriedigt mich)* that satisfies me; **b)** *(erfüllen)* satisfy; **den Anforderungen ~:** satisfy *or* meet *or* fulfil the requirements; **den Bestimmungen ~:** comply with the regulations; **einer Pflicht ~:** fulfil a duty *or* an obligation
genügend 1. *Adj.* **a)** enough; sufficient; **b)** *(befriedigend)* satisfactory. **2.** *adv.* enough; sufficiently; **~ lange** long enough; **~ Geld/Zeit haben** have enough *or* sufficient money/time
genugsam *Adv. (geh.)* sufficiently; **das Thema dürfte ~ diskutiert sein** the subject has probably been adequately discussed
genügsam [gə'ny:kza:m] **1.** *Adj.* modest ⟨*life*⟩; **ein ~er Mensch** a person who lives modestly; **Schafe sind sehr ~e Tiere** sheep can live *or* subsist on very little; **in bezug auf Kleidung ist sie sehr ~:** she does not spend a great deal on clothes. **2.** *adv.* **~ leben** live modestly
Genügsamkeit die; ~: sie weiß, was ~ heißt she knows what it means to live modestly; **wegen ihrer ~ sind Schafe ...:** as they can live *or* subsist on very little, sheep are ...
genug|tun *unr. itr. V. (veralt.) in* **er konnte sich** *(Dat.)* **nicht ~, sie/es zu loben** he couldn't praise her/it enough
Genugtuung [-tu:ʊŋ] **die; ~, ~en** satisfaction; **es ist mir eine ~, das zu hören** it gives me satisfaction to hear that; **~ über etw.** *(Akk.)* **empfinden** feel satisfied *or* a sense of satisfaction about sth.; **[für etw.] ~ verlangen** demand satisfaction [for sth.]
genuin [genu'i:n] *(geh.) Adj.* genuine
Genus ['gɛnʊs] **das; ~, Genera** ['gɛnera] *(Sprachw.)* gender
Genuschel [gə'nʊʃl̩] **das; ~s** *(meist abwertend)* mumbling
Genuß [gə'nʊs] **der; Genụsses, Genüsse** [gə'nʏsə] **a)** *o. Pl.* consumption; **der ~ von schmerzstillenden Mitteln/Heroin** the use *or* taking of pain-killers/heroin; **b)** *(Wohlbehagen)* **etw. mit/ohne ~ essen/trinken** eat/drink sth. with/without relish; **etw. mit ~ lesen** enjoy reading sth.; **das Konzert/der Kuchen ist ein ~:** the concert is thoroughly enjoyable/the cake is delicious; **die Genüsse des Lebens** the pleasures *or* good things of life; **in den ~ von etw. kommen** enjoy sth.; **in den ~ einer Rente kommen** receive a pension
genụß·freudig *Adj.* pleasure-loving
Genụß·gift das *(Amtsspr.) stimulant etc.* (*see* **Genußmittel**) *dangerous to health*
genüßlich [gə'nʏslɪç] **1.** *Adj.* appreciative; comfortable ⟨*feeling*⟩; *(schadenfroh)* gleeful. **2.** *adv.* appreciatively; ⟨*eat, drink*⟩ with relish; *(schadenfroh)* ⟨*smile*⟩ gleefully; **sich ~ im Sessel zurücklehnen** lie back luxuriously in the armchair
genụß-, Genụß-: ~mensch der hedonist; **~mittel das** *tea, coffee, alcoholic drinks, tobacco, etc.;* **~reich** *Adj.* very *or* highly enjoyable; **~sucht die;** *o. Pl. (oft abwertend)* craving for pleasure; **~süchtig**

Adj. (oft abwertend) pleasure-seeking; **~voll 1.** *Adj. (erfreulich)* very *or* highly enjoyable; *(genüßlich)* appreciative; **2.** *adv.* appreciatively; ⟨*eat, drink*⟩ with relish

Geodäsie [-dɛ'zi:] **die; ~:** geodesy *no art.*

Geodät der; ~en, ~en geodesist

geodätisch *Adj.* geodetic

Geo·dreieck Ⓦ **das** geometry set square

Geograph [-'gra:f] **der; ~en, ~en** geographer

Geographie die; ~: geography *no art.*

geographisch 1. *Adj.* geographic[al]. **2.** *adv.* geographically

Geologe [-'lo:gə] **der; ~n, ~n** geologist

Geologen·hammer der geologist's hammer

Geologie die; ~: geology *no art.*

geologisch 1. *Adj.; nicht präd.* geological; **2.** *adv.* geologically

Geo·meter der; ~s, ~ a) *s.* **Geodät; b)** *(veralt.)* geometer; geometrician

Geometrie die; ~: geometry *no art.*

geometrisch 1. *Adj.* geometric[al] **2.** *adv.* geometrically

Geo·morphologie die geomorphology *no art.*

Geo·physik die geophysics *sing., no art.*

Geo·politik die geopolitics *sing., no art.*

geo·politisch *Adj.; nicht präd.* geopolitical

geordnet 1. *2. Part. v.* **ordnen. 2.** *Adj.* **in ~en Verhältnissen leben** live a settled life; **~e Verhältnisse schaffen** put things on a proper footing; **ein ~er Rückzug** *(Milit.)* an orderly retreat

Georg [ge'ɔrk, 'ge:ɔrk] **(der)** George

Georgien [ge'ɔrgi̯ən] **(das); ~s** Georgia

Georgier [ge'ɔrgi̯ɐ] **der; ~s, ~, Georgierin die; ~, ~nen** Georgian

Geo·wissenschaft die geoscience *no art.*

Geozentrik [geo'tsɛntrɪk] **die; ~** *(Astron.)* geocentric system

geozentrisch *Adj. (Astron.)* geocentric

Gepäck [gə'pɛk] **das; ~[e]s a)** luggage *(Brit.)*; baggage *(Amer.)*; *(am Flughafen)* baggage; **mit leichtem ~ reisen** travel light; **das ~ aufgeben/einchecken** hand in *or* check in the luggage; check the baggage *(Amer.)*; **b)** *(Milit.)* kit

Gepäck-: ~ab·fertigung die a) *o. Pl. s.* **Gepäck a:** checking in the luggage/baggage; **b)** *(Schalter) (am Bahnhof)* luggage office *(Brit.)*; baggage office *(Amer.)*; *(am Flughafen)* baggage check-in; **~ab·lage die** luggage rack *(Brit.)*; baggage rack *(Amer.)*; **~annahme die a)** *o. Pl. s.* **Gepäck a:** checking in the luggage/baggage; **bei der ~annahme** when checking in the luggage/baggage; **b)** *(Schalter)* [in-counter of the] luggage office *(Brit.) or* baggage office *(Amer.)*; *(zur Aufbewahrung)* [in-counter of the] left-luggage office *(Brit.) or* checkroom *(Amer.)*; *(am Flughafen)* baggage check-in; **~auf·bewahrung die a)** *o. Pl.* **Schäden, die während der ~aufbewahrung entstanden sind** damage to items in left-luggage *(Brit.) or* the checkroom *(Amer.)*; **b)** *(Schalter)* left-luggage office *(Brit.)*; checkroom *(Amer.)*; *(Schließfächer)* luggage lockers *(Brit.)*; baggage lockers *(Amer.)*; **~aufbewahrungs·schein der** left-luggage ticket *(Brit.)*; baggage check *(Amer.)*; **~auf·gabe die** *s.* **~abfertigung a, b; ~aus·gabe die a)** *o. Pl. (am Bahnhof)* returning the luggage *(Brit.) or (Amer.)* baggage; *(am Flughafen)* reclaiming of baggage; **b)** *(Schalter)* [out-counter of the] luggage office *(Brit.) or (Amer.)* baggage office; *(zur Aufbewahrung)* [out-counter of the] left-luggage office *(Brit.) or (Amer.)* checkroom; *(am Flughafen)* baggage reclaim; **~beförderung die** *(mit der Bahn)* conveyance of luggage *(Brit.) or (Amer.)* baggage; *(mit einem Flugzeug)* conveyance of baggage; **~karren der** *s.* **Gepäck a:** luggage/baggage trolley; **~kontrolle die** baggage check; **~marsch der** *(Milit.)* route march with full kit; **~netz das** *s.* **~ablage; ~raum der** *s.* **Gepäck a:** luggage/baggage compartment; **~schalter der** *s.* **~annahme b; ~schein der** luggage ticket *(Brit.)*; baggage check *(Amer.)*; **~schließ·fach das** luggage locker *(Brit.)*; baggage locker *(Amer.)*; **~stück das** *s.* **Gepäck a:** piece *or* item of luggage/baggage; **~träger der a)** porter; **b)** *(am Fahrrad)* carrier; rack; **~versicherung die** *s.* **Gepäck a:** luggage/baggage insurance; **~wagen der** luggage van *(Brit.)*; baggage car *(Amer.)*

Gepard ['ge:part] **der; ~s, ~e** cheetah; hunting leopard

gepfeffert 1. *2. Part. v.* **pfeffern. 2.** *Adj. (ugs.)* **a)** *(unverschämt)* steep *(coll.)* ⟨*price, rent, etc.*⟩; **b)** *(hart)* tough ⟨*question, problem, speech*⟩; tough, harsh ⟨*words, criticism*⟩; **c)** *(derb)* crude ⟨*joke, oath, language, talk*⟩; spicy ⟨*story*⟩

Gepfeife das; ~s *(ugs. abwertend)* [continuous, tuneless] whistling

gepfiffen [gə'pfɪfn̩] *2. Part. v.* **pfeifen**

gepflegt 1. *2. Part. v.* **pflegen. 2.** *Adj.* **a)** well-groomed, spruce ⟨*appearance*⟩; neat ⟨*clothing*⟩; cultured ⟨*conversation*⟩; cultured, sophisticated ⟨*atmosphere, environment*⟩; stylish ⟨*living*⟩; well-kept, well-tended ⟨*garden, park*⟩; well-kept ⟨*street*⟩; well cared-for ⟨*hands, house*⟩; **b)** *(hochwertig)* choice ⟨*food, drink*⟩. **3.** *adv.* **~ essen** dine in style; **~ essen gehen** dine at a good restaurant; **sich ~ ausdrücken** express oneself in a cultured manner

Gepflegtheit die; ~ a) die [äußere] ~: a well-groomed appearance; smartness of appearance; **b)** *(Kultiviertheit)* **die ~ seines Stils** his cultured style

gepflogen [gə'pflo:gn̩] *2. Part. v.* **pflegen 4**

Gepflogenheit die; ~, ~en *(geh.) (Sitte, Brauch)* custom; tradition; *(Gewohnheit)* habit; *(Verfahrensweise)* practice

Geplänkel [gə'plɛŋkl̩] **das; ~s, ~ a)** *(Wort~)* banter *no indef. art.*; **b)** *(Milit. veralt.)* skirmish

Geplapper das; ~s *(ugs., oft abwertend)* prattling; **das ~ des Babys** the baby's babbling

Geplärr[e] das; ~s *(ugs. abwertend)* bawling

Geplätscher das; ~s splashing; **das seichte ~ der Unterhaltung** *(fig.)* the superficial *or* polite exchange of pleasantries

geplättet 1. *2. Part. v.* **plätten. 2.** *Adj. (salopp)* flabbergasted

Geplauder das; ~s *(geh.)* chatting

Gepolter das; ~s a) clatter; **sie rannten mit ~ die Treppe hinunter** they clattered down the stairs; **b)** *(Schimpfen)* grumbling; moaning

Gepräge das; ~s, ~ a) *(Münzk.)* strike; **b)** *(geh.: Merkmal)* [special] character; *(Aura, Ambiente)* aura; **einer Sache** *(Dat.)* **ihr ~ geben** give sth. its character

Geprahle das; ~s *(abwertend)* bragging; boasting

Gepränge [gə'prɛŋə] **das; ~s** *(geh.)* pomp; splendour; **mit festlichem/feierlichem ~:** with pomp and pageantry/in solemn splendour

Geprassel das; ~s *(von Kies usw.)* rattle; *(von Feuer)* crackle; crackling

gepriesen *2. Part. v.* **preisen**

gepunktet 1. *2. Part. v.* **punkten. 2.** *Adj.* spotted ⟨*tie, blouse, etc.*⟩; *(regelmäßig)* polka-dot; dotted ⟨*line*⟩

Gequake das; ~s *(ugs.)* croaking; *(von Enten)* quacking

Gequäke das; ~s *(ugs.)* bawling

gequält 1. *2. Part. v.* **quälen. 2.** *Adj.* forced ⟨*smile, gaiety*⟩; pained ⟨*expression*⟩

Gequassel, Gequatsche das; ~s *(ugs. abwertend)* jabbering

Gequengel[e] das; ~s *(ugs. abwertend)* whimpering; *(Drängelei)* nagging; *(Nörgelei)* carping

Gequieke das; ~s *(ugs.)* squealing

Gequietsche das; ~s *(ugs.)* squeaking; *(von Bremsen, Reifen, Kränen)* squealing; screeching; *(von Menschen)* squealing, shrieking

gequollen *2. Part. v.* **quellen**

Ger [ge:ɐ̯] **der; ~[e]s, ~e** *(hist.)* spear, javelin *(of ancient Germanic peoples)*

gerade [gə'ra:də], *(ugs.)* **grade** ['gra:də] **1.** *Adj.* **a)** straight; **~ geschnitten** cut straight; **in ~r Linie von jmdm. abstammen** *(fig.)* be descended in a direct line from sb.; **den ~n Weg verfolgen** *(fig.)* keep to the straight and narrow; **b)** *(nicht schief)* upright; **~ gewachsen sein** ⟨*plant*⟩ have grown straight; ⟨*person*⟩ have grown up straight; **~ sitzen/stehen** sit up/stand up straight; **c)** *(aufrichtig)* forthright; direct; **d)** *nicht präd. (genau)* **das ~ Gegenteil** the direct *or* exact opposite; **e)** *(Math.)* even ⟨*number*⟩. **2.** *Adv.* **a)** *(soeben, ugs.: für kurze Zeit)* just; **halt ~ [mal] fest!** just hold this [for a moment]; **haben Sie ~ Zeit?** do you have time just now?; **~ erst** only just; **wir wollten diese Sache ~ noch besprechen** we were just going to discuss the matter; **b)** *(direkt)* right; **~ gegenüber/um die Ecke** right opposite/just round the corner; **jmdm. ~ in die Augen schauen** look sb. straight in the eyes; **c)** *(knapp)* just; **~ noch** only just; **er hat das Examen ~ so bestanden** he just scraped through the examination; **~ so viel, daß ...:** just enough to ...; **~ noch rechtzeitig** only just in time; **d)** *(eben)* just; **~ diese Angelegenheit** precisely *or* just this matter; **e)** *(ausgerechnet)* **~ du/dieser Idiot** you/this idiot, of all people; **warum ~ ich/heute?** why me of all people/today of all days?; **~ seine Toleranz wurde ihm als Schwäche angerechnet** it was precisely his tolerance which was regarded as a weakness. **3.** *Partikel* **a)** *(besonders)* particularly; **nicht ~:** not exactly; **b)** *(ugs.: erst recht)* **nun** *od.* **jetzt [tue ich es] ~:** [you] just watch me; [you] just try and stop me now; **nun** *od.* **jetzt [tue ich es] ~ nicht** now I certainly shan't [do it]

Gerade die; ~n, ~n a) *(Geom.)* straight line; **b)** *(Leichtathletik)* straight; **c)** *(Boxen)* straight-arm punch; **linke/rechte ~:** straight left/right

gerade·aus *Adv.* straight ahead; ⟨*walk, drive*⟩ straight on, straight ahead; **immer ~ gehen/fahren** carry straight on; **er ist sehr ~** *(fig.)* he is very straightforward *or* direct

gerade-, Gerade-: ~|biegen *unr. tr. V.* **a)** bend straight; straighten [out]; **b)** *(ugs.: bereinigen)* straighten out; put right; **~|halten 1.** *unr. tr. V.* **etw. ~halten** hold sth. straight; **den Kopf ~halten** hold one's head up; **2.** *unr. refl. V.* hold oneself [up] straight; **sich bei Tisch ~halten** sit up straight at the table; **~halter der** shoulder brace; **~heraus** [----'-] *(ugs.)* **1.** *Adv.* **etw. ~heraus sagen** say sth. straight out; **jmdm. ~heraus sagen/jmdn. ~heraus fragen** tell/ask sb. straight; **~heraus gesagt** quite frankly; to be quite frank; **2.** *adj.; nicht präd.* straightforward; direct; **~|klopfen** *tr. V.* hammer straight; **~|legen** *tr. V.* put *or* set straight; **~|machen** *tr. V. (ugs.)* straighten [out]

geraden·wegs *s.* **geradewegs**

gerade|richten *tr. V.* straighten [out]; put or set straight

gerädert 1. *2. Part. v.* **rädern. 2.** *Adj. (ugs.)* whacked *(coll.)*; tired out; **wie ~ sein/sich wie ~ fühlen** be/feel whacked *(coll.) or* tired out

gerade-: ~|sitzen *unr. itr. V.* sit up straight; **~so** *Adv.* **etw. ~ machen wie jmd. anderes** do sth. just like sb. else; **~so groß/lang wie ...:** just as big/long as ...; **~so·gut**

Adv. just as well; equally well; **~sogut wie...:** just as well as...; **~so·viel** *Indefinitpron.* just as much; **~|stehen** *unr. itr. V.* **a)** stand up straight; **b)** *(fig.: einstehen)* **für etw. ~stehen** accept responsibility for sth.; **für jmdn. ~stehen** answer for sb.; **~wegs** *Adv.* **a)** straight; **b)** *(ohne Umschweife)* straight away; directly; **er kam ~wegs zum Thema** he came straight to the point; **~zu 1.** *Adv.* **a)** really; perfectly; *(beinahe)* almost; **das ist ~zu lächerlich** that is downright ridiculous; **ein ~zu ideales Beispiel** an absolutely perfect example; **b)** *(landsch.: unverblümt)* bluntly; directly; **2.** *adj., nicht attr. (landsch.: unverblümt)* blunt; direct

Gerad·heit die; ~: straightforwardness

gerad-, Gerad-: **~linig** [~li:nıç] **1.** *Adj.* **a)** straight; direct, lineal ⟨*descent, descendant*⟩; **b)** *(aufrichtig)* straightforward; **2.** *adv.* **a)** **~linig verlaufen** run in a straight line; **b)** *(aufrichtig)* **~linig handeln/denken** be straightforward; **~linigkeit die;** ~ **a)** straightness; **b)** *(Aufrichtigkeit)* straightforwardness; **~sinnig** *Adj.* straightforward; honest

gerammelt 1. *2. Part. v.* **rammeln. 2.** *Adv. in* ~ **voll** *(ugs.)* [jam-]packed *(coll.)*; packed out *(coll.)*

geändert *Adj.* **rot ~e Augen** red-rimmed eyes; **schwarz ~es Papier** black-edged paper

Gerangel [gəˈraŋl̩] **das;** ~s *(ugs.)* **a)** scrapping *(coll.)*; **b)** *(abwertend: Kampf)* free-for-all; scramble; **ein ~ um etw.** a scramble for sth.; a free-for-all for sth.

Geranie [geˈra:ni̯ə] **die;** ~, ~n geranium

gerann [gəˈran] *3. Pers. Sg. Prät. v.* **gerinnen**

gerannt [gəˈrant] *2. Part. v.* **rennen**

Geraschel das; ~s *(ugs.)* rustling

Gerassel [gəˈrasl̩] **das;** ~s rattling; rattle

gerät [gəˈrɛ:t] *3. Pers. Sg. Präsens v.* **geraten**

Gerät [gəˈrɛ:t] **das;** ~[e]s, ~e **a)** piece of equipment; *(Fernseher, Radio)* set; *(Garten~)* tool; *(Küchen~)* utensil; *(Meß~)* instrument; **landwirtschaftliche ~e** agricultural implements; **elektrische ~e** electrical appliances; **b)** *(Turnen)* piece of apparatus; **an den ~en turnen** do gymnastics on the apparatus; **c)** *o. Pl. (Ausrüstung)* equipment *no pl.; (des Anglers)* tackle; *(des Handwerkers)* tools *pl.*

Geräte·haus das *(Feuerwehr)* appliance room

[1]**geraten** *unr. itr. V.; mit sein* **a)** get; **in ein Unwetter ~:** be caught in a storm; **unter ein Auto ~:** be run over by a car; **an jmdn. ~:** meet sb.; **an den Richtigen/Falschen ~:** come to the right/wrong person; **in Panik/Wut/Ekstase ~:** panic *or* get into a panic/fly into a rage/go into a state of ecstasy; *s. auch* **Gesellschaft a; Verdacht; Verruf** *usw.*; **b)** *(gelingen)* turn out well; **das Essen ist [ihr] gut ~:** the meal [she cooked] turned out well; **sie ist zu kurz/lang ~** *(scherzh.)* she has turned out on the short/tall side; **die Tapeten sind zu bunt ~:** the wallpaper turned out to be too colourful; **c)** *(ähneln)* **nach jmdm. ~:** take after sb.; **d)** *(werden)* **zu etw. ~:** turn into *or* become sth.

[2]**geraten 1.** *2. Part. v.* **raten,** [1]**geraten. 2.** *Adj.; nicht attr.* advisable; **es scheint mir ~, ...:** I think it advisable ...

Geräte-: **~raum der a)** [sports] equipment store; **b)** *(für Gartengeräte usw.)* tool shed; **~schuppen der** tool shed; **~turnen das** apparatus gymnastics *sing.*

Geratewohl *in* **wir fuhren aufs ~ los** *(ugs.)* we went for a drive just to see where we ended up; **er hat sich aufs ~ einige Firmen ausgewählt** *(ugs.)* he selected a few firms at random; **sie ist aufs ~ in die Prüfung gegangen** *(ugs.)* she took the examination on the off-chance [of passing]

Gerätschaften [gəˈrɛ:tʃaftn̩] *Pl. (Werkzeug)* tools; *(Küchengeräte)* utensils

gerätst *2. Pers. Sg. Präsens v.* **geraten**

Geratter das; ~s *(ugs.)* clatter; *(von Schüssen)* rattle

Geräucherte [gəˈrɔyçɐtə] **das;** ~n; *adj. Dekl.* smoked *or* cured meat *(usually ham or bacon)*

geraum *Adj.; nicht präd. (geh.)* considerable; **nach ~er Zeit** after some [considerable] time

geräumig [gəˈrɔymıç] *Adj.* spacious ⟨*room*⟩; roomy ⟨*cupboard, compartment*⟩

Geräumigkeit die; ~ *(eines Zimmers)* spaciousness; *(eines Schrankes, Kofferraums)* roominess

Geraune das; ~s *(geh.)* whispering; *(Gemurmel)* murmuring

Geraunze das; ~s *(österr., südd. abwertend)* grumbling; moaning; grousing *(coll.)*

Geräusch [gəˈrɔyʃ] **das;** ~[e]s, ~e sound; *(unerwünscht)* noise

geräusch-, Geräusch-: **~arm 1.** *Adj.* quiet; **2.** *adv.* quietly; **~empfindlich** *Adj.* sensitive to noise *pred.*; **~empfindliche Menschen** people who are sensitive to noise; **~kulisse die a)** background noise; **b)** *(akustische Untermalung)* [background] sound effects; **~los 1.** *Adj.* silent; noiseless; **2.** *adv.* **a)** silently; without a sound; noiselessly; **b)** *(fig. ugs.: ohne Aufsehen)* without [any] fuss; quietly; **~losigkeit die;** ~: quietness; noiselessness; **~pegel der** noise level; **~voll 1.** *Adj.* noisy; **2.** *adv.* noisily

Geräusper [gəˈrɔyspɐ] **das;** ~s noise of throat-clearing

gerben [ˈgɛrbn̩] *tr. V.* tan ⟨*hides, skins*⟩; **von Wind und Wetter gegerbte Haut** *(fig.)* skin tanned by wind and sun

Gerber der; ~s, ~: tanner

Gerbera [ˈgɛrbəra] **die;** ~, ~[s] gerbera

Gerberei die; ~, ~en **a)** tannery; **b)** *(das Gerben)* tanning

Gerber·lohe die tanning bark

Gerbung die; ~, ~en tanning

gerecht 1. *Adj.* **a)** just ⟨*verdict, punishment*⟩; *(unparteiisch)* just; fair; **ein ~er Richter/Lehrer** an impartial judge/a just teacher; **~ gegen jmdn. sein** be fair *or* just to sb.; **eine ~e Sache** a just cause; **~er Zorn** righteous anger; **jmdm./einer Sache ~ werden** do justice to sb./sth.; **einer Aufgabe/der Belastung ~ werden** cope with a task/the strain; **b)** *(bibl.)* **der ~e Gott** our righteous Lord; **die Gerechten** the righteous. **2.** *adv.* justly; ⟨*judge, treat*⟩ fairly

-gerecht *Adj.* **a)** *(passend)* **kind~/behinderten~:** suitable for children/the disabled *postpos.*; **umwelt~:** harmless to the environment *postpos.*; **b)** *(entsprechend)* **protokoll~:** in accordance with protocol *postpos.*; **leistungs~:** productivity- *or* output-related

gerechterweise *Adv.* in [all] fairness; to be fair

gerechtfertigt 1. *2. Part. v.* **rechtfertigen. 2.** *Adj.* justified

Gerechtigkeit die; ~ **a)** justice; **~ üben** *(geh.)* act justly; be just; **jmdm. ~ widerfahren lassen** *(geh.)* treat sb. justly; **um der ~ willen** in order that justice be done; **b)** *(Recht)* **die ~ nimmt ihren Lauf** the law takes its course; **c)** *(christl. Rel.)* **die ~ Gottes** the righteousness of God; **d)** *(geh.: Justiz)* **jmdn. den Händen der ~ übergeben** hand sb. over to be dealt with by the courts

gerechtigkeits-, Gerechtigkeits-: **~fanatiker der** stickler for the law; **~fimmel der** *(ugs. abwertend)* exaggerated concern for justice; **~gefühl das** sense of justice; **~liebend** *Adj.* **~liebend sein** have a love of justice; **ein ~liebender Mensch** a person with a love of justice; **~sinn der** sense of justice

Gerede das; ~s *(abwertend)* **a)** *(ugs.)* talk; **das ewige ~ darüber ändert doch nichts** talking about it all the time won't change anything; **b)** *(Klatsch)* gossip; **jmdn. ins ~ bringen** bring sb. into disrepute; **ins ~ kommen** get into disrepute

geregelt 1. *2. Part. v.* **regeln. 2.** *Adj.; nicht präd.* regular, steady ⟨*job*⟩; orderly, well-ordered ⟨*life*⟩; **~er Katalysator** computer-controlled catalytic converter

gereichen *itr. V. (geh.)* **jmdm. zur Ehre/zum Vorteil ~:** redound to sb.'s honour *or* credit/advantage

gereift 1. *2. Part. v.* **reifen. 2.** *Adj.; nicht präd.* mature; **sie ist jetzt geistig ~:** she has now matured as a person

gereizt 1. *2. Part. v.* **reizen. 2.** *Adj.* irritable; touchy. **3.** *adv.* irritably; **~ reagieren** react angrily; **~ lächeln** smile wearily

Gereiztheit die; ~: irritability; touchiness

Gerenne [gəˈrɛnə] **das;** ~s *(ugs.)* running *or* racing about

gereuen *tr. V. (geh. veralt.)* **sein Zornesausbruch gereute ihn** he regretted his angry outburst; *(unpers.)* **es gereute ihn, daß...:** he regretted that...; **es gereute ihn** he was sorry

Geriater [geˈri̯a:tɐ] **der;** ~s, ~ *(Med.)* geriatrician; geriatrist

Geriatrie die; ~: geriatrics *sing., no art.*

geriatrisch *Adj.* geriatric

[1]**Gericht** [gəˈrıçt] **das;** ~[e]s, ~e **a)** *(Institution)* court; **jmdn. dem ~** *od.* **den ~en übergeben** *od.* **ausliefern** hand sb. over to be dealt with by the courts; **jmdn. vor ~ laden** *od.* **zitieren** summon sb. to appear in court; **vor ~ erscheinen/aussagen** appear/testify in court; **vor ~ stehen** be on *or* stand trial; **mit einem Fall vor ~ gehen** take a case to court; **b)** *(Richter)* bench; **Hohes ~!** Your Honour!; **das ~ zieht sich zur Beratung zurück** the bench retires for discussion; **c)** *(Gebäude)* court[-house]; **d)** *in* **das Jüngste** *od.* **Letzte ~** *(Rel.)* the Last Judgement; **mit jmdm. [hart** *od.* **scharf] ins ~ gehen** *(zurechtweisen)* take sb. [severely] to task; *(bestrafen)* punish sb. [severely]; **über jmdn. ~ halten** *od.* **zu ~ sitzen** sit in judgement on sb.

[2]**Gericht das;** ~[e]s, ~e dish; **~e aus der Dose** canned *or (Brit.)* tinned food *sing.*

gerichtlich 1. *Adj.; nicht präd.* judicial; forensic ⟨*psychology, medicine*⟩; legal ⟨*proceedings*⟩; court ⟨*order*⟩; **~e Zuständigkeit** [legal] jurisdiction; **eine ~e Vorladung** a summons from the court; **ein ~es Nachspiel haben** have legal consequences; **die Sache wird ein ~es Nachspiel haben** the matter will end up in court. **2.** *adv.* **jmdn. ~ verfolgen** prosecute sb.; take sb. to court; **gegen jmdn. ~ vorgehen** take legal action against sb.; take sb. to court; **etw. ~ bezeugen/beeiden** testify/swear to sth. in court; **jmdn. ~ für tot erklären** pronounce sb. legally dead

gerichts-, Gerichts-: **~akte die** court record; **~arzt der** specialist in forensic medicine; **~ärztlich** *Adj.; nicht präd.* forensic medical ⟨*report, test, investigation*⟩; **~assessor der** *law student appointed as judge or court official for trial period after his second state examination*

Gerichtsbarkeit die; ~, ~en jurisdiction; **der staatlichen ~ nicht unterliegen** be immune from legal proceedings by the State

gerichts-, Gerichts-: **~beschluß der** decision of the/a court; the/a court's decision; **~bezirk der** jurisdictional district; **~diener der** *(veralt.)* court usher; **~dolmetscher der** court interpreter; **~entscheid der, ~entscheidung die** decision of the/a court; the/a court's decision; **~ferien** *Pl.* recess *sing.*; vacation *sing.*; **~gebäude das** court-house; **~herr der** *(hist.)* [highest] judicial authority; **der oberste ~herr** the supreme judicial authority; **~hof der a)** Court of Justice; **der Oberste/Internationale/Europäische ~hof** the Supreme/International/European Court of Justice; **b)** *(früher: Kollegialgericht)* tribunal, Court of Justice *(with more than one judge)*; **Hoher ~hof!** if it please the court; **~hoheit die** supreme legal authority; **~kosten** *Pl.* legal costs; costs of the case; **~kundig** *Adj. s.* **~notorisch; ~medizin die** forensic medicine *no art.*; **~mediziner der** specialist in forensic medicine; **~medizinisch 1.** *Adj.* forensic medical ⟨*examination, report*⟩; **2.** *adv.* **etw. ~medizinisch feststellen** establish sth. by forensic medical tests; **~notorisch** *(Rechtsspr.) Adj.* ⟨*person, event, fact*⟩ known to the court; **~präsident der** senior judge; **~referendar der** *law student who has passed his/her first state examination;* **~reporter der** legal correspondent; **~saal der** courtroom; **Ruhe im ~saal!** silence in court!; **~schreiber der** clerk of the court; **~stand der** *(Rechtsspr.)* place of jurisdiction; **~tag der** court-day; **Mittwoch ist ~tag** the court sits on Wednesdays; **~termin der** *(strafrechtlich)* date of the/a trial; *(zivil)* date of the/a hearing; **~urteil das** judgement [of the court]; **~verfahren das** legal proceedings *pl.*; **ein ~verfahren einleiten** institute legal *or* court proceedings; **ohne ~verfahren** without trial; **~verfassung die** constitution of the courts; **~verhandlung die** *(strafrechtlich)* trial; *(zivil)* hearing; **~verwaltung die** administration of the courts; **~vollzieher der; ~s, ~:** bailiff; **~weg der: auf dem ~weg** through the courts; by taking legal proceedings; **~weibel der** *(schweiz.) s.* **~diener; ~wesen das;** *o. Pl.* judicial system

gerieben 1. *2. Part. v.* **reiben. 2.** *Adj. (ugs.)* artful

Geriebenheit die; ~ *(ugs.)* artfulness

gerieren [ge'ri:rən] *refl. V. (geh.)* **sich als etw. ~:** talk and act as if one were sth.

Geriesel das; ~s trickling; trickle; *(von Schnee)* gentle fall

geriffelt 1. *2. Part. v.* **riffeln. 2.** *Adj.* corrugated ⟨*surface, sheet metal*⟩; fluted ⟨*column*⟩; ribbed ⟨*glass*⟩

gering [gə'rɪŋ] **1.** *Adj.* **a)** *(nicht groß, niedrig)* low ⟨*temperature, pressure, price*⟩; low, small ⟨*income, fee*⟩; little ⟨*value*⟩; small ⟨*quantity, amount*⟩; short ⟨*distance, time*⟩; **in ~er Entfernung** a short distance away; **von/in ~er Höhe** low/low down; **der Abstand wird ~er** the gap is closing *or* getting smaller; **um ein ~es** *(veralt.)* a little [bit]; *(um wenig Geld)* for a trifle *or* a mere bagatelle; *(fast)* nearly; almost; **b)** *(unbedeutend)* slight; minor ⟨*role*⟩; **meine ~ste Sorge** the least of my worries; **das Geringste** the least; **nicht das ~ste** nothing at all; **nicht im ~sten** not in the slightest *or* least; **c)** *(veralt.: niedrigstehend)* humble ⟨*origin, person*⟩; **kein Geringerer als ...:** no less a person than ...; **d)** *(geh.: schlecht)* poor, low, inferior ⟨*quality, opinion*⟩; poor ⟨*knowledge*⟩. **2.** *adv.* **~ von jmdm. sprechen/denken** speak badly/have a low opinion of sb.

gering|achten *tr. V.: s.* **geringschätzen**

Gering·achtung die *s.* **Geringschätzung**

geringelt 1. *2. Part. v.* **ringeln. 2.** *Adj.* curly; ⟨*hair*⟩ in ringlets; ⟨*pattern, socks, jumper*⟩ with horizontal stripes

gering·fügig [-fy:gɪç] **1.** *Adj.* slight ⟨*difference, deviation, improvement*⟩; slight, minor ⟨*alteration, injury*⟩; small, trivial ⟨*amount*⟩; minor, trivial ⟨*detail*⟩. **2.** *adv.* slightly

Geringfügigkeit die; ~, ~en a) *o. Pl.* triviality; insignificance; **eine Beschwerde wegen ~ ablehnen** dismiss a complaint because of its trivial nature; **b)** *(Kleinigkeit)* triviality; trifle; *(Angelegenheit auch)* trivial matter

gering|schätzen *tr. V.* **a)** *(verachten)* have a low opinion of, think very little of ⟨*person, achievement*⟩; set little store by ⟨*success, riches*⟩; **b)** *(mißachten)* disregard ⟨*warning*⟩; make light of ⟨*danger*⟩; **sein eigenes Leben ~:** have scant regard for one's own life

gering·schätzig [-ʃɛtsɪç] **1.** *Adj.* disdainful; contemptuous; disparaging ⟨*remark*⟩. **2.** *adv.* disdainfully; contemptuously; **von jmdm. ~ sprechen** speak disparagingly of sb.

Geringschätzigkeit die; ~: disdain[fulness]; contempt[uousness]

Gering·schätzung die; *o. Pl.* **a)** *(Verachtung)* disdain; contempt; **b)** *(Mißachtung)* disregard; **die ~ des Lebens** a scant regard for life

geringsten·falls *Adv. (geh.)* at the very least

gerinnen *unr. itr. V.; mit sein* **a)** coagulate; ⟨*blood*⟩ coagulate, clot; ⟨*milk*⟩ curdle; *s. auch* **Blut; b)** *(fig. geh.)* **zu etw. ~:** develop into *or* become sth.

Gerinnsel [gə'rɪnzl] **das; ~s, ~ a)** *(Blut)* clot; **b)** *(veralt.: Rinnsal)* streamlet; rivulet

Gerinnung die; ~, ~en coagulating; *(von Blut auch)* clotting; *(von Milch)* curdling

gerinnungs-: ~fähig *Adj.* coagulable; **sein Blut ist nicht ~fähig** his blood does not clot properly; **~hemmend** *Adj.* anticoagulant

Gerippe das; ~s, ~ a) skeleton; **sie ist bis zum ~ abgemagert** *(fig.)* she has lost so much weight that she is only skin and bones; **b)** *(fig.)* framework; *(von Schiffen, Gebäuden)* skeleton; *(Grundriß, Entwurf)* outline

gerippt [gə'rɪpt] *Adj.* ribbed ⟨*fabric, garment*⟩; fluted ⟨*glass, column*⟩; laid ⟨*paper*⟩

gerissen [gə'rɪsn̩] **1.** *2. Part. v.* **reißen. 2.** *Adj. (ugs.)* crafty

Gerissenheit die; ~: craftiness

geritten *2. Part. v.* **reiten**

geritzt 1. *2. Part. v.* **ritzen. 2.** *Adj. (salopp)* **in etw. ist ~:** sth. is [all] settled; **ist ~!** will do! *(coll.)*

Germ [gɛrm] **der; ~[e]s,** *österr. auch:* **die; ~** *(südd., österr.)* yeast

Germane [gɛr'ma:nə] **der; ~n, ~n** *(hist.)* ancient German; Teuton; *(scherzh.)* Teutonic type; **die alten ~n** the ancient Germanic peoples *or* Teutons; **die Skandinavier sind ~n** the Scandinavians are of Germanic *or* Teutonic origin

Germanentum das; ~s *(Kultur)* Germanic *or* Teutonic culture; *(germanische Völker)* Germanic *or* Teutonic world

Germania [gɛr'ma:ni̯a] **(die)** Germania

Germanien [gɛr'ma:ni̯ən] **(das); ~s** *(hist.)* Germania

Germanin die; ~, ~nen ancient German; Teuton

germanisch *Adj. (auch fig.)* Germanic; Teutonic; **Germanisches Seminar** Institute of Germanic Studies

germanisieren *tr. V.* Germanize

Germanisierung die; ~: Germanization

Germanismus der; ~, Germanismen *(Sprachw.)* Germanism

Germanist der; ~en, ~en Germanist; German scholar

Germanistik die; ~: German studies *pl., no art.*

Germanistin die; ~, ~nen Germanist; German scholar

germanistisch *Adj.; nicht präd.* **~e Studien** German studies; **eine ~e Zeitschrift** a periodical on *or* devoted to German studies; **Germanistisches Seminar** Institute of German Studies

Germanium [gɛr'ma:ni̯ʊm] **das; ~s** *(Chemie)* germanium

germanophil [gɛrmano'fi:l] *Adj.* Germanophile

germanophob [gɛrmano'fo:p] *Adj.* Germanophobe

gern[e] ['gɛrn(ə)]; **lieber** ['li:bɐ], **am liebsten** [-'li:pstn̩] *Adv.* **a)** *(mit Vergnügen)* **etw. ~ tun** like *or* enjoy *or* be fond of doing sth.; **er spielt lieber Tennis als Golf** he prefers playing tennis to golf; **etw. ~ essen/trinken** like sth.; **am liebsten trinkt er Wein** he likes wine best; **ja, ~/aber ~:** yes, of course; certainly!; **Kommst du mit? – Ja, ~!** Are you coming too? – Yes I'd like to!; **[das ist] ~ geschehen** it is *or* was a pleasure; **jmdn. ~ haben** like *or* be fond of sb.; **er hat sie lieber als dich** he likes her more than he does you; **sie hat ihn am liebsten** she likes him best; **sie hat** *od.* **sieht es lieber/am liebsten, wenn ...:** she likes it better/likes it best if ...; **~ gesehen sein/werden** be welcome; **der kann mich ~ haben!** *(ugs.)* he can go to hell! *(coll.)*; he can get stuffed *(sl.)*; **b)** *(drückt Billigung aus: durchaus)* **das glaube ich ~:** I can quite *or* well believe that; **das kannst du ~ tun/haben** you are welcome to do/have that; **c)** *(drückt Wunsch aus)* **ich hätte ~ einen Apfel** I would like an apple; **er wäre ~ mitgekommen** he would have liked to come along; **ich wäre lieber [zu Fuß] gegangen** I would rather have walked; **das hättest du lieber nicht tun sollen** it would have been better if you had not done that; **laß das lieber** better not do that; **noch ein Stück Kuchen? – Lieber nicht** Another piece of cake? – I'd rather not; *(aus Vernunftsgründen)* I'd better not; **ich bleibe heute lieber im Bett** I'd better stay in bed today; **d)** *(gewöhnlich)* **etw. ~ tun** usually do sth.; **e)** *(ugs.: leicht, oft)* soon

Gerne·groß der; ~, ~e *(ugs. scherzh.)* **er ist ein [kleiner] ~:** he likes to act big *(coll.)*

Geröchel das; ~s rattle in the throat; *(eines Sterbenden)* [death-]rattle

gerochen *2. Part. v.* **riechen**

Geröll [gə'rœl] **das; ~s, ~e** detritus; debris; *(größer)* boulders *pl.*; *(im Gebirge auch)* scree

Geröll-: ~halde die scree [slope]; **~schutt der** detritus; debris; **~wüste die** boulder-strewn wilderness; *(Geogr.)* rock desert

geronnen [gə'rɔnən] *2. Part. v.* **rinnen, gerinnen**

Gerontokratie [gerɔntokra'ti:] **die; ~, ~n** *(hist., Völkerk.)* gerontocracy

Gerontologie die; ~ *(Med.)* gerontology *no art.*

Geröstete [gə'rø:stətə, gə'rœstətə] *Pl.; adj. Dekl. (südd., österr.)* sauté potatoes

Gerste ['gɛrstə] **die; ~:** barley

Gersten-: ~grütze die a) barley groats; **b)** *(Brei)* porridge *or* gruel made from barley; **~kaffee der** *coffee substitute produced from malted barley;* **~korn das a)** *(Frucht)* barleycorn; **b)** *(Augenentzündung)* sty; **~saft der** *(scherzh.)* beer; **~schrot der** *od.* **das** bruised *or* ground barley; **~zucker der** barley sugar

Gerte ['gɛrtə] **die; ~, ~n** switch

gerten·schlank *Adj.* slim *or* slender and willowy

Geruch [gə'rʊx] **der; ~[e]s, Gerüche** [gə'rʏçə] **a)** smell; odour; *(von Blumen)* scent; fragrance; *(von Brot, Kuchen)* smell; aroma; **ein ~ nach/der ~ von frischem Brot** a/the smell of freshly-baked bread; **einen unangenehmen ~ verbreiten** give off an unpleasant smell *or* odour *or* a stench; **b)** *o. Pl. (Geruchssinn)* sense of smell; **c)** *o. Pl. (geh.: Ruf)* reputation; **im ~ stehen, etw. zu sein/getan zu haben** be reputed to be sth./to have done sth.

geruch·los *Adj.* odourless; *(ohne Duft)* unscented, scentless ⟨*flower etc.*⟩

geruchs-, Geruchs-: ~belästigung die nuisance caused by the smell *or* stench; **~bindend** *Adj.* deodorant; **~empfindlich** *Adj.* sensitive to smells *postpos.*; **~empfindung die a)** olfactory sensation; **b)** *s.* **~sinn; ~nerv der** olfactory nerve; **~organ das** olfactory organ; **~sinn der;** *o. Pl.* sense of smell; olfactory sense; **~stoff der** aromatic essence; *(von Tieren)* scent; **~verschluß der** [anti-siphon] trap

Gerücht [gəˈrʏçt] **das; ~[e]s, ~e** rumour; **ein ~ in die Welt** *od.* **in Umlauf setzen** start a rumour; **es geht das ~, daß ...:** there's a rumour going round that ...; **das halte ich für ein ~!** *(ugs.)* I can't believe that!

Gerüchte-: ~küche die *(ugs. abwertend)* hotbed of rumours; **~macher der** *(abwertend)* rumour-monger

geruch·tilgend *Adj.* deodorant

gerücht·weise *Adv.* **ich habe ~ vernommen** *od.* **gehört, daß ...:** I've heard a rumour that ...; I've heard it rumoured that ...; **~ verlautet, er sei ...:** rumour has it *or* it is rumoured that he is ...

gerufen *2. Part. v.* **rufen**

geruhen *tr. V. (geh. veralt.; sonst iron.)* **~, etw. zu tun** condescend *or* deign to do sth.

gerührt 1. *2. Part. v.* **rühren. 2.** *Adj.* touched *(also iron.)*; moved

geruhsam 1. *Adj.* peaceful; quiet; leisurely ‹*stroll*›; **jmdm. eine ~e Nacht wünschen** wish sb. a restful night. **2.** *adv.* leisurely; *(ungestört)* quietly

Geruhsamkeit die; ~: peacefulness; quietness; *(eines Spaziergangs)* leisureliness

Gerumpel das; ~s bumping and banging; *(von Lastwagen usw.)* rumbling

Gerümpel [gəˈrʏmpl] **das; ~s** *(abwertend)* junk; [useless] rubbish

Gerundium [geˈrʊndiʊm] **das; ~s, Gerundien** *(Sprachw.)* gerund

Gerundiv [gerʊnˈdi:f] **das; ~s, ~e** [-ˈdi:və] *(Sprachw.)* gerundive

gerundivisch *Adj. (Sprachw.)* gerundival

gerungen [gəˈrʊŋən] *2. Part. v.* **ringen**

Gerüst [gəˈrʏst] **das; ~[e]s, ~e** scaffolding *no pl., no indef. art.*; *(fig.: eines Romans usw.)* framework

Gerüst-: ~bau der; *o. Pl.* erection of the scaffolding; **„~bau: H. Müller, Mannheim"** 'scaffolding by H. Müller, Mannheim'; **~bauer der; ~s, ~:** scaffolder

gerüttelt 1. *2. Part. v.* **rütteln. 2.** *Adj. in* **~ voll** *(veralt.)* [jam-]packed; **ein ~ Maß** *(veralt.)* a good measure

ges, Ges [gɛs] **das; ~, ~** *(Musik)* [key of] G flat; *s. auch* **a, A**

Gesabber [gəˈzabɐ] **das; ~s a)** slavering; slobbering; *(eines Babys)* dribbling; **b)** *(salopp: Gerede)* rabbiting *(Brit. sl.)*; babbling

Gesalbte [gəˈzalptə] **der/die;** *adj. Dekl. (Rel., hist.)* **er/sie kehrte als ~r/~ von Rom zurück** he/she returned anointed from Rome; **Christus, der ~:** Christ, the Lord's Anointed

gesalzen 1. *2. Part. v.* **salzen. 2.** *Adj. (salopp)* **a)** *(sehr hoch)* steep *(coll.)* ‹*price, bill*›; **b)** *(derb ausgedrückt)* crude ‹*joke, language*›; spicy ‹*story*›

Gesalzene das; *adj. Dekl.; o. Pl.* salt[ed] meat

gesammelt 1. *2. Part. v.* **sammeln. 2.** *Adj.* concentrated ‹*attention, energy*›; intense ‹*fear*›; **~e Werke** collected works

gesamt *Adj.; nicht präd.* whole; entire; **das ~e Vermögen** the entire *or* total wealth; **die ~en Werke** the complete works

Gesamt das; ~s *s.* **Gesamtheit**

gesamt-, Gesamt-: ~ansicht die general *or* overall view; **~auflage die** *(Druckw.)* total edition; *(einer Zeitung)* total circulation; **~ausgabe die** *(Druckw.)* complete edition; **~betrag der** total amount; **~bild das** general *or* overall view; *(fig.)* general *or* overall picture; **~darstellung die** general account *or* description; **~deutsch** *Adj.; nicht präd.* all-German; **~deutschland das** all Germany; **~eindruck der** general *or* overall impression; **~einkommen das** total income; **~ergebnis das** overall result; **~erscheinung die** general appearance; **~fläche die** total area; **~gesellschaftlich** *Adj.; nicht präd. (Soziol.)* of society *or* the community as a whole *postpos.*; **~gewicht das** total weight; **das zulässige ~gewicht** the permissible maximum weight

gesamthaft *(schweiz.)* **1.** *Adj.; nicht präd. s.* **gesamt. 2.** *adv. s.* **insgesamt**

Gesamtheit die; ~ a) die ~ der Beamten all civil servants; **die ~ der Bevölkerung** the whole of the *or* the entire population; **die Verleger in ihrer ~:** publishers as a whole; **b)** *s.* **Allgemeinheit**

gesamt-, Gesamt-: ~hoch·schule die *(Hochschulw.) institution with colleges teaching at various levels, so that students can more readily extend their courses;* **die integrierte ~hochschule** *centrally administrated, fully integrated ~hochschule;* **~kapital das** total capital; **~katalog der** complete catalogue; *(Katalog der Bestände mehrerer Bibliotheken)* union catalogue; **~lage die** general *or* overall situation; **~note die** overall mark; **~produktion die** total production *or* output; **~schaden der** total damage; **ein ~schaden von 1000 DM** total damage amounting to 1,000 marks; **~schuldner** *Pl. (Rechtsw.)* joint debtors; **~schule die** comprehensive [school]; **eine integrierte ~schule** an all-ages comprehensive [school]; **eine kooperative ~schule** *a comprehensive [school] which retains ability bands corresponding to the traditional types of school: Hauptschule, Realschule, and Gymnasium;* **~sieg der** *(Sport)* overall victory; **~sieger der** *(Sport)* overall winner; **~stärke die** total strength; **~strafe die** *(Rechtsw.)* concurrent sentence; **~summe die** *s.* **~betrag; ~um·satz der** total turnover; **~unterricht der** *(Schulw.)* interdisciplinary teaching *no art.*; **~verband der** *(Wirtsch.)* general *or* national association; **~volumen das** *(Wirtsch.)* total volume; **das ~volumen des Verteidigungsetats** the total size of the defence budget; **~werk das** œuvre; *(Bücher)* complete works *pl.*; **~wert der** total value; **~wirtschaft die** economy as a whole; national economy; **~wirtschaftlich 1.** *Adj.; nicht präd.* overall economic ‹*development etc.*›; ‹*development etc.*› of the economy as a whole; **2.** *adv.* **~wirtschaftlich vertretbar** justifiable from the point of view of the economy as a whole; **~zahl die** total number; **~zusammenhang der** general *or* overall context

gesandt [gəˈzant] *2. Part. v.* **senden**

Gesandte der/die; *adj. Dekl.* envoy; **der päpstliche ~:** the papal legate *or* nuncio

Gesandtin die; ~, ~nen envoy

Gesandtschaft die; ~, ~en legation

Gesandtschafts·rat der counsellor at a/the legation

Gesang [gəˈzaŋ] **der; ~[e]s, Gesänge** [gəˈzɛŋə] **a)** *o. Pl.* singing; **b)** *(Lied)* song; *s. auch* **Gregorianisch; c)** *(Literaturw.)* canto

Gesang·buch das hymn-book; **das richtige/falsche ~buch haben** *(ugs. scherzh.)* belong to the right/wrong [religious] denomination; *(in der Politik)* belong to the right/wrong [political] party

gesanglich 1. *Adj.* vocal; **großes ~es Talent haben** have great talent as a singer. **2.** *adv.* vocally

Gesang[s]-: ~lehrer der, ~lehrerin die singing-teacher; **~stunde die** singing-lesson; **~unterricht der** singing instruction; **~unterricht nehmen/geben** take/give singing-lessons *pl.*

Gesang·verein der choral society; **mein lieber Herr ~!** *(salopp)* my godfathers!; ye gods [and little fishes]!

Gesäß [gəˈzɛ:s] **das; ~es, ~e** backside; buttocks *pl.*

Gesäß-: ~falte die *(Anat.)* gluteal fold; gluteal furrow; **~muskel der** *(Anat.)* gluteal muscle; **~tasche die** back pocket

gesättigt 1. *2. Part. v.* **sättigen. 2.** *Adj. (Chemie)* **~e Fettsäuren** saturated fatty acids

Gesäusel [gəˈzɔyzl̩] **das; ~s** *(von Wind)* whispering; murmuring; *(von Blättern)* rustling; whispering; *(ugs. abwertend: Schmeichelei)* flannel *(coll.)*

gesch. *Abk.* **geschieden**

Geschädigte [gəˈʃɛ:dɪçtə] **der/die;** *adj. Dekl.* injured party

geschaffen *2. Part. v.* **schaffen 1**

geschafft 1. *2. Part. v.* **schaffen 2, 3. 2.** *Adj.; nicht attr. (ugs.)* all in *(coll.)*

Geschäft [gəˈʃɛft] **das; ~[e]s, ~e a)** business; *(Abmachung)* [business] deal *or* transaction; **die ~e gehen gut** business is good; **mit jmdm. ~e/ein ~ machen** do business with sb.; strike a bargain *or* do a deal with sb.; **in ein ~ einsteigen** go into a business; **in ~en reisen/unterwegs sein** travel/be travelling on business; **mit jmdm. ins ~ kommen** go into business with sb.; **~ ist ~:** business is business; **das ~ mit der Angst** trading on people's fears; **b)** *o. Pl. (Absatz)* business *no art.*; **das ~ blüht** business *or* trade is booming; **c)** *o. Pl. (Profit)* profit; **mit etw. ein gutes/schlechtes ~ machen** make a good/poor profit on sth.; **diese Unternehmung war für uns [k]ein ~:** this venture was [not] a financial success for us; **d)** *(Firma)* business; **ein ~ führen** run *or* manage a business; **ins ~ gehen** *(südd.)* go to work; **e)** *(Laden)* shop; store *(Amer.)*; *(Kaufhaus)* store; **f)** *(Aufgabe)* task; duty; **seinen ~en nachgehen** go about one's business; **g) sein großes/kleines ~ erledigen** *od.* **machen** *(ugs. verhüll.)* do big jobs *or* number two/small jobs *or* number one *(child language)*

-geschäft das a) *(Laden)* **Schuh~/Lebensmittel~/Feinkost~:** shoe shop/food shop/delicatessen [shop]; shoe store/food store/delicatessen [store] *(Amer.)*; **b)** *(Transaktion)* **Bank~/Kompensations~:** bank/barter transaction; *(Absatz)* **Weihnachts~:** Christmas trade; **c)** *(Aufgabe)* **Amts~e/Staats~e** official/state duties

geschäfte-, Geschäfte-: ~halber *Adv. (in Geschäften)* on business; *(wegen Geschäften)* because of business; **~macher der** *(abwertend)* profit-seeker; **~macherei die** *(abwertend)* profit-seeking *no pl.*

geschäftig 1. *Adj.* bustling; **ein ~es Treiben** bustling activity; hustle and bustle. **2.** *adv.* **~ hin und her laufen** bustle about

Geschäftigkeit die; ~: bustle

Geschaftlhuber [gəˈʃaftl̩hu:bɐ] **der; ~s, ~** *(bes. südd., österr. abwertend)* officious meddler

geschäftlich 1. *Adj.* **a)** business *attrib.* ‹*conference, appointment*›; **das Geschäftliche besprechen** discuss business [matters]; **b)** *(sachlich, kühl)* business-like. **2.** *adv.* **a)** on business; **er hat dort ~ zu tun** he has [some] business to do there; **ich habe nächste Woche ~ in Hamburg zu tun** I have to be in Hamburg next week on business; **Wie geht es Ihnen? – Meinen Sie ~ oder privat?** How are you doing? – Do you mean how's business or how am I personally?; **b)** *(sachlich, kühl)* in a business-like way *or* manner

geschäfts-, Geschäfts-: ~ablauf der business *no art.*; **~abschluß der** conclusion of the/a business transaction *or* deal; **einen ~abschluß tätigen** conclude a business transaction *or* deal; **~anteil der** share in the/a business; **~aufgabe die** closure of the/a business; **zur ~aufgabe gezwungen werden** be forced to close down; **„Ausverkauf wegen ~aufgabe!"** 'closing-down sale'; 'going-out-of-business sale' *(Amer.)*; **~auto das** *s.* **~wagen; ~bedingungen** *Pl.* terms [and conditions] of trade; **~beginn der** opening-time; **eine Schlange hatte sich vor ~beginn gebildet** a queue *(Brit.)* or *(Amer.)* line had formed before the shop opened; **~bereich der** portfolio; **Minister ohne ~bereich** Minister without portfolio; **~bericht der** company report; *(jährlich)* annual report; **~beziehungen** *Pl.* business dealings; **in ~beziehungen mit einer Firma stehen** have business dealings with a firm; **~beziehungen zu China** business contacts with China; **~brief der** business letter; **~bücher** *Pl.* books; accounts; **~eröffnung die** opening of a/the shop *or (Amer.)* store; **~fähig** *Adj. (Rechtsspr.)* legally competent; **~fähigkeit die** *(Rechtsspr.)* legal competence; **~frau die** businesswoman; **~freund der** business associate; **~führend** *Adj.; nicht präd.* managing ⟨*director*⟩; executive ⟨*chairman*⟩; *(leitend)* acting; **die ~führende Regierung** the caretaker government; **~führer der a)** *(leitender Angestellter)* manager; **b)** *(Vereinswesen)* secretary; **~führung die;** *o. Pl.* management; **~gang der a)** business *no art.*; **b)** *(Dienstweg)* **den normalen ~gang gehen** go through the normal channels; **c)** *(Besorgung)* errand; **~gebaren das** business *no art.*; business practices *pl.*; **~geheimnis das** business secret; **~geist der;** *o. Pl.* business acumen *or* sense; **~haus das a)** business [house]; firm; **b)** *(Gebäude)* office-block *(with or without shops)*; **~inhaber der** owner *or* proprietor of the/a business; **~interesse das;** *meist Pl.* **das ~interesse/die ~interessen** the interests *pl.* of the business; **~jahr das** financial year; **~jubiläum das** anniversary of the firm; **die Firma feiert ihr fünfzigjähriges ~jubiläum** the firm is celebrating its fiftieth anniversary; **~kapital das** working capital; **~kosten** *Pl. in* **auf ~kosten [gehen]** [be] on expenses; **~kundig** *Adj.* ⟨*person*⟩ with business experience; **~lage die a)** *(wirtschaftliche Lage)* **die ~lage der Firma** the [business] position of the firm; **die allgemeine ~lage** the general business situation; **b)** *(Ort)* **in guter ~lage** well situated [for business]; **~leben das** business [life]; **er steht seit vierzig Jahren im ~leben** he's been active in business [life] for forty years; **~leitung die** *s.* **~führung; ~leute** *s.* **~mann; ~mann der;** *Pl.* **~leute** businessman; **~mäßig** *Adj.* business-like; **~methoden** *Pl.* business methods; **~ordnung die** standing orders *pl.*; *(im Parlament)* [rules *pl.* of] procedure; **Antrag zur ~ordnung** procedural motion; **Fragen zur ~ordnung** questions on points of order; **zur ~ordnung!** point of order!; **~papiere** *Pl.* business documents *or* papers; **~partner der** business partner; **~politik die** business *or* trading policy; **~räume** *Pl.* business premises; *(Büroräume)* offices; **~reise die** business trip; **auf ~reise sein** be on a business trip; **~rück·gang der** decline *or* fall-off in business; **~schädigend** *Adj.* bad for business; ⟨*conduct*⟩ damaging to the interests of the company; **~schluß der** closing-time; **nach ~schluß** after business hours; *(im Büro)* after office hours; **~sinn der;** *o. Pl.* business sense *or* acumen; **~sitz der** place of business; **eingetragener ~sitz** registered office[s]; **~stelle die a)** *(einer Bank, Firma)* branch; *(einer Partei, eines Vereins)* office; **b)** *(Rechtsspr.)* court office; **~straße die** shopping-street; **~stunden** *Pl.* business hours; *(im Büro)* office hours; **~tätigkeit die** business activity *no indef. art.*; **~träger der** *(Dipl.)* chargé d'affaires; **~tüchtig** *Adj.* able, capable, efficient ⟨*businessman, landlord, etc.*⟩; **eine ~tüchtige Frau** an able *or* capable businesswoman; **~tüchtigkeit die** business ability *or* efficiency; **~über·gabe die** transfer of the business; **~übernahme die** take-over of the business; **~unfähig** *Adj. (Rechtsspr.)* legally incompetent; **~unfähigkeit die** *(Rechtsspr.)* legal incompetence; **~verbindung die** business connection; **~verkehr der** business; business dealings *pl.*; **~viertel das** business quarter; *(Einkaufszentrum)* shopping district; **~wagen der** company car; **~welt die;** *o. Pl.* **a)** business world *or* community; **b)** *s.* **~leben; ~zeit die** business hours *pl.*; *(im Büro)* office hours *pl.*; **~zentrum das** *s.* **~viertel; ~zimmer das** office; **~zweig der** branch of the/a business

geschah [gəˈʃaː] *3. Pers. Sg. Prät. v.* **geschehen**

Geschäker [gəˈʃɛːkɐ] **das; ~s** flirting

Geschạrre das; ~s *(abwertend)* scraping; *(mit den Füßen)* scraping of feet; *(von Hühnern)* scratching

Geschaukel das; ~s rocking; *(auf See)* rolling

gescheckt [gəˈʃɛkt] *Adj.* spotted ⟨*cow, bull, rabbit, etc.*⟩; skewbald ⟨*horse*⟩; *(mit weißen Flecken auf schwarzem Fell)* piebald ⟨*horse*⟩

geschehen [gəˈʃeːən] *unr. itr. V.; mit sein* **a)** *(passieren)* happen; occur; **so tun, als wäre nichts ~:** act as if nothing had happened; **~ ist ~:** what's done is done; **so ~ ...** *(veralt.)* this came to pass ...; **b)** *(ausgeführt werden)* be done; **die Tat/der Mord geschah aus Eifersucht** the deed was done/the murder was committed out of jealousy; **es muß etwas ~:** something must be done; **was geschieht damit?** what's to be done with it?; **er ließ es ~:** he let it happen; **c)** *(widerfahren)* **jmdm. geschieht etw.** sth. happens to sb.; **es geschieht dir nichts** nothing will happen to you; **das geschieht ihm recht** it serves him right; **ihm ist ein Unrecht ~:** he's been wronged; **e) es ist um ihn ~:** it's all up with him; **es ist um seine Gesundheit/Stellung ~:** his health is ruined/he has lost his job; **als er sie sah, war es um ihn ~:** he was lost the moment he saw her

Geschehen das; ~s, ~ *(geh.)* **a)** *(Ablauf der Ereignisse)* events *pl.*; happenings *pl.*; **das politische ~:** political events *pl.*; **b)** *(Vorgang)* action

Geschehnis das; ~ses, ~se *(geh.)* event

gescheit [gəˈʃait] **1.** *Adj.* **a)** *(intelligent)* clever; **daraus werde ich nicht ~:** I can't make head or tail of it; **b)** *(ugs.: vernünftig)* sensible; **sei doch ~:** be sensible; **nichts/etwas Gescheites** nothing/something sensible; **gibt es etwas Gescheites zu essen?** is there anything decent to eat?; **du bist wohl nicht ganz** *od.* **nicht recht ~:** you can't be quite right in the head; you must be off your head *(coll.)*. **2.** *adv.* cleverly

Gescheitheit die; ~: cleverness

Geschenk [gəˈʃɛŋk] **das; ~[e]s, ~e** present; gift; **jmdm. ein ~ machen** give sb. a present; **jmdm. etw. zum ~ machen** make sb. a present of sth.; give sth. to sb. as a present; **kleine ~e erhalten die Freundschaft** *(Spr.)* small gifts preserve friendships; **ein ~ des Himmels** a godsend

Geschẹnk-: ~artikel der gift; **~packung die** gift pack; **~papier das** gift wrapping-paper; **~sendung die** *(Postw.)* parcel containing a gift/gifts; **„~sendung"** 'gift [only]'

Gescherr [gəˈʃɛr] *s.* **Herr c**

geschert [gəˈʃeːɐ̯t] *Adj. (südd., österr. salopp)* stupid; idiotic

Geschẹrte der; *adj. Dekl. (südd., österr. salopp)* stupid git *(sl.)*

Geschichte [gəˈʃɪçtə] **die; ~, ~n a)** *o. Pl. (auch Wissenschaft, Darstellung)* history; **die ~ Frankreichs** the history of France; **die englische ~:** English history; **Alte/Mittlere/Neue ~:** ancient/medieval/modern history; **~ machen** make history; **in die ~ eingehen** *(geh.)* go down in history; **etw. gehört der ~** *(Dat.)* **an** sth. belongs to *or* is part of history; **b)** *(Erzählung)* story; *(Fabel, Märchen)* story; tale; **c)** *(ugs.: Sache)* **das sind alte ~n** that's old hat *(coll.)*; **das ist [wieder] die alte ~:** it's the [same] old story [all over again]; **das sind ja schöne ~n!** *(iron.)* that's a fine thing *or* state of affairs! *(iron.)*; **die ganze ~:** the whole business *or* thing; **mach keine ~n!** don't do anything silly; **Du wirst doch nicht krank werden. Mach keine ~n!** You won't fall ill. Don't be [so] silly!; **mach keine langen ~n** don't make a [great] fuss

Geschịchten-: ~buch das story-book; **~erzähler der** story-teller

geschịchtlich 1. *Adj.* **a)** historical; **b)** *(bedeutungsvoll)* historic. **2.** *adv.* historically; **etw. ~ betrachten** consider sth. from a historical point of view *or* perspective

Geschịchtlichkeit die; ~ *(Philos.)* historicity

geschịchts-, Geschịchts-: ~atlas der historical atlas; **~auffassung die** conception *or* view of history; **~bewußtsein das** awareness of history; historical awareness; **~bild das** *s.* **~auffassung; ~buch das** history book; **~drama das** *(Literaturw.)* historical drama; **~epoche die** historical epoch; **~fälschung die** falsification of history; **~forscher der** historian; **~forschung die** historical research; **~klitterung die** deliberately biased account of history; **~lehrer der** history teacher; **~los** *Adj.* ⟨*country, society, people, etc.*⟩ without a history *or* past; *(ohne Geschichtsbewußtsein)* with no sense of its own history; **~philosophie die** philosophy of history; **~philosophisch 1.** *Adj.* ⟨*writings*⟩ on/⟨*studies*⟩ in/⟨*interpretation*⟩ according to/⟨*view of the world*⟩ based on the philosophy of history; **2.** *adv.* **etw. ~philosophisch interpretieren** interpret sth. from the point of view of the philosophy of history; **~schreiber der** historian; *(Chronist)* chronicler; **~schreibung die** historiography; **~unterricht der** history teaching; *(Unterrichtsstunde)* history lesson; **im ~unterricht nehmen sie den Dreißigjährigen Krieg durch** in history they are doing the Thirty Years War; *s. auch* **Englischunterricht; ~werk das** historical work; **~wissenschaft die** [science of] history; **~wissenschaftler der** [academic] historian; **~zahl die** [historical] date

[1]**Geschick** [gəˈʃɪk] **das; ~[e]s, ~e a)** *(geh.: Schicksal)* fate; **ihn ereilte sein ~:** he met his fate; **ein glückliches/gutes ~:** a kindly Providence; **b)** *Pl. (Lebensumstände)* destiny *sing.*

[2]**Geschịck das; ~[e]s** skill; **ein ~ für etw. haben** be skilful at sth.

Geschịcklichkeit die; ~: skilfulness; skill; **es zu großer ~ in etw.** *(Dat.)* **bringen** become very skilful at sth.

Geschịcklichkeits-: ~fahren das *(Motorsport)* manoeuvring tests *pl.*; **~spiel das** game of skill

geschịckt 1. *2. Part. v.* **schicken. 2.** *Adj.* **a)** *(gewandt)* skilful; *(fingerfertig)* skilful; dexterous; **~ im Klettern sein** be an agile climber; **b)** *(klug)* clever; adroit; **c)** *(südd.: geeignet)* suitable **(für** for). **3.** *adv.* **a)** *(gewandt)* skilfully; *(fingerfertig)* skilfully; dexterously; **b)** *(klug)* cleverly; adroitly

Geschịcktheit die; ~: *s.* **Geschicklichkeit**

Geschiebe das; ~s, ~ a) *(ugs.)* pushing and shoving; **b)** *(Geol.)* debris

geschieden *2. Part. v.* **scheiden**

Geschiedene der/die; *adj. Dekl.* divorcee; **seine ~:** his ex-wife; **ihr ~r** her ex-husband

geschienen *2. Part. v.* **scheinen**

Geschịmpfe das; ~s *(ugs.)* cursing; *(das Tadeln)* scolding

Geschirr [gəˈʃɪr] **das; ~[e]s, ~e a)** *(Riemenzeug)* harness; **dem Pferd das ~ anlegen** harness the horse; put the harness on the horse; **sich ins ~ legen** *(kräftig ziehen)* pull hard; *(angestrengt arbeiten)* work like a slave; **b)** *(Teller, Tassen usw.)* crockery; *(benutzt)* dishes *pl.*; *(zusammenpassend)* [dinner/tea] service; *(Küchen~)* pots and pans *pl.*; kitchenware; **das gute/beste ~:** the good/best china; **feuerfestes ~:** ovenware set; **das ~ abwaschen** wash up *or* do the dishes; **c)** *(veralt.: Gefäß)* pot

Geschirr-: ~**aufzug der** dumb waiter; ~**schrank der** china cupboard; ~**spülen das;** ~s washing-up; ~**spüler der a)** washer-up; **b)** *s.* ~**spülmaschine;** ~**spül·maschine die** dish-washing machine; dishwasher; ~**tuch das;** *Pl.* **-tücher** tea-towel; drying-up cloth *(Brit.);* dish towel *(Amer.)*
Geschiß [gəˈʃɪs] **das; Geschisses** *(derb)* fuss and bother *(coll.)*
geschissen [gəˈʃɪsn̩] *2. Part. v.* **scheißen**
Geschlabber das; ~s *(ugs.)* **a)** *(das Schlabbern)* slurping *(coll.);* **b)** *(bei Kleidern)* **das ~ ihres langen Rocks** the flapping of her long skirt; **c)** *(Brei, Pudding usw.)* mush
geschlafen *2. Part. v.* **schlafen**
geschlagen *2. Part. v.* **schlagen**
Geschlecht das; ~[e]s, ~er **a)** sex; **männlichen/weiblichen ~s sein** be male/female; **Jugendliche beiderlei ~s** young people of both sexes; **das starke ~** *(ugs. scherzh.)* the stronger sex; **das schwache/schöne/zarte ~** *(ugs. scherzh.)* the weaker/fair/gentle sex; **b)** *(Generation)* generation; **die nachfolgenden ~er** future generations; **c)** *(Sippe)* family; **von altem ~:** of ancient lineage; **das ~ der Habsburger** the house of Habsburg; **ein edles ~:** a noble house; **d)** *(Sprachw.)* gender; **e)** *o. Pl. (Geschlechtsteil)* sex; **f)** *(dichter.: Gattung)* **das menschliche ~** *od.* **das ~ der Menschen** the human race; **das ~ der Götter** the gods
Geschlechter-: ~**folge die** succession of generations; **die ~folgen** the generations; ~**trennung die** segregation of the sexes
geschlechtlich 1. *Adj.* sexual. **2.** *adv.* **mit jmdm. ~ verkehren** have sexual intercourse with sb.
Geschlechtlichkeit die; ~: sexuality
geschlechts-, Geschlechts-: ~**akt der** sex[ual] act; ~**apparat der** *(Fachspr.)* genital organs *pl.;* genitals *pl.;* ~**bestimmung die a)** *(Festlegung)* sex determination; **b)** *(Feststellung)* determination of sex; *(von Tieren auch)* sexing; **eine ~bestimmung vornehmen** determine the sex of a baby/an animal; ~**chromosom das** *(Biol.)* sex chromosome; ~**drüse die** *(Anat., Zool.)* gonad; ~**erziehung die** sex education; ~**gebunden 1.** *Adj.* sex-linked; **2.** *adv.* **~gebunden weitervererbt werden** be passed on in a way which shows sex-linkage; ~**hormon das** sex hormone; ~**krank** *Adj.* ⟨*person*⟩ suffering from VD *or* a venereal disease; **~krank sein** have VD; be suffering from a venereal disease; ~**krankheit die** venereal disease; ~**leben das** sex life; ~**los** *Adj. (Biol.)* asexual; *(fig.)* sexless; ~**lust die** sexual desire *or* lust; ~**merkmal das** sex[ual] characteristic; ~**organ das** sex[ual] organ; genital organ; ~**partner der** sex partner; ~**reif** *Adj.* sexually mature; ~**reife die** sexual maturity; ~**rolle die** *(Soziol.)* sex role; ~**spezifisch** *Adj. (Soziol.)* sex-specific; ~**teil das: die ~teile/das ~teil** the genitals *pl.;* ~**trieb der** sex[ual] drive *or* urge; ~**umwandlung die** sex change; change of sex; ~**unterschied der** difference between the sexes; ~**verkehr der** sexual intercourse; ~**wort das** *s.* **Artikel;** ~**zelle die** gamete
geschlichen *2. Part. v.* **schleichen**
geschliffen 1. *2. Part. v.* **schleifen. 2.** *Adj.* polished, refined ⟨*style, manners, etc.*⟩; polished ⟨*sentence*⟩. **3.** *adv.* in a polished manner
Geschliffenheit die; ~, ~en refinement; *(des Stils)* polish
geschlissen [gəˈʃlɪsn̩] *2. Part. v.* **schleißen**
geschlossen 1. *2. Part. v.* **schließen. 2.** *Adj.* **a)** *(gemeinsam)* united ⟨*action, front*⟩; unified ⟨*procedure*⟩; *s. auch* **Gesellschaft; b)** *(zusammenhängend)* **eine ~e Ortschaft** a built-up area; **eine ~e Linie von Demonstranten** a solid line of demonstrators; **c)** *(abgerundet)* **eine [in sich] ~e Persönlichkeit** a well-rounded personality; **ein ~es Bild/~er Eindruck** a full *or* complete picture/impression. **3.** *adv.* **~ für etw. stimmen/sein** vote/be unanimously in favour of sth.; **wir verließen ~ unser Büro** we walked out in a body *or* en masse; **~ gegen etw. vorgehen** take concerted action against sth.; **~ hinter jmdm. stehen** be solidly behind sb.; **die ganze Gruppe stand ~ auf** the whole group rose with one accord
Geschlossenheit die; ~ **a)** *(Gemeinschaft)* unity; **b)** *(Einheitlichkeit)* unity; uniformity; **c) die ~ der Handlung** the tight construction of the plot
Geschluchze das; ~s *(ugs.)* sobbing; **hör mit dem ~ auf!** stop your blubbering *or (sl.)* blubbing
Geschlürfe das; ~s *(ugs. abwertend)* slurping
geschlungen [gəˈʃlʊŋən] *2. Part. v.* **schlingen**
Geschmack [gəˈʃmak] **der;** ~[e]s, **Geschmäcke** [gəˈʃmɛkə] *od. ugs. scherzh.:* **Geschmäcker** [gəˈʃmɛkɐ]) **a)** taste; **einen schlechten ~ im Munde haben** have a bad *or* nasty taste in one's mouth; **einen guten/schlechten ~ haben** have good/bad taste; **das ist [nicht] mein** *od.* **nach meinem ~:** that is [not] to my taste; **jmds. ~** *(Akk.)* **treffen** guess sb.'s taste exactly; **das verstößt gegen den guten ~:** that offends against good taste; **im ~ jener Zeit eingerichtet** furnished in the style of that period; **von erlesenem ~:** exquisitely tasteful; showing exquisite taste; **die Geschmäcker sind verschieden** *(ugs. scherzh.)* tastes differ; **über ~ läßt sich nicht streiten** there's no accounting for taste[s]; **an etw.** *(Akk.)* **~ finden** *od.* **gewinnen** acquire a taste for sth.; take a liking to sth.; **einer Sache** *(Dat.)* **~ abgewinnen** come *or* grow to like sth.; **sie kann solchen Bildern keinen ~ abgewinnen** she cannot appreciate such pictures; **auf den ~ kommen** acquire the taste for it; get to like it; **b)** *o. Pl. (Geschmackssinn)* sense of taste
geschmacklich 1. *Adj.; nicht präd.* as regards taste *postpos.;* **zur ~en Verfeinerung** to improve the taste *or* flavour. **2.** *adv.* as regards taste
geschmacklos 1. *Adj.* **a)** *(ohne Geschmack)* tasteless; insipid; **b)** *(unschön, taktlos)* tasteless; **~ sein** be in bad taste; ⟨*person*⟩ be lacking in taste. **2.** *adv.* tastelessly
Geschmacklosigkeit die; ~, ~en **a)** lack of [good] taste; bad taste; **diese Gebäude sind ~en** these buildings are examples of bad taste; **b)** *o. Pl. (Unverschämtheit)* tastelessness; bad taste; **das ist eine ~ ersten Ranges!** that is the height of bad taste!; **c)** *(Äußerung)* tasteless remark; *(Handlung)* tasteless behaviour *sing., no indef. art.*
geschmacks-, Geschmacks-: ~**empfindung die** sense of taste; ~**frage die** question *or* matter of taste; ~**knospe die** *(Zool., Anat.)* taste-bud; ~**neutral** *Adj.* tasteless; flavourless; ~**richtung die a)** flavour; **b)** *(Geschmack, Vorliebe)* taste
Geschmack[s]·sache die *in* **das ist ~:** that is a question *or* matter of taste
Geschmacks-: ~**sinn der;** *o. Pl.* sense of taste; ~**stoff der** flavouring; ~**verirrung die** *(abwertend)* lapse of taste; **an** *od.* **unter ~verirrung** *(Dat.)* **leiden** *(ugs.)* suffer from a lapse in taste
geschmack·voll 1. *Adj.* tasteful; **die Bemerkung war nicht sehr ~:** the remark was not in very good taste. **2.** *adv.* tastefully
Geschmatze das; ~s *(ugs. abwertend)* smacking one's lips *no art.; (beim Essen)* noisy eating *no art.;* **hör mit dem ~ auf!** stop making so much noise when you're eating!
Geschmeide [gəˈʃmaidə] **das;** ~s, ~ *(geh.)* jewellery *no pl.; (einzelnes Schmuckstück)* piece of jewellery
geschmeidig 1. *Adj.* **a)** *(schmiegsam)* sleek ⟨*hair, fur*⟩; supple, soft ⟨*leather, boots, skin*⟩; smooth ⟨*dough*⟩; **b)** *(gelenkig)* supple ⟨*fingers*⟩; supple, lithe ⟨*body, movement, person*⟩; **c)** *(fig.: anpassungsfähig)* adaptable. **2.** *adv.* **a)** *(gelenkig)* agilely; **b)** *(fig.)* adaptably
Geschmeidigkeit die; ~: *s.* **geschmeidig 1:** sleekness; suppleness; softness; smoothness; litheness; adaptability
Geschmeiß das; ~es **a)** *(veralt., auch fig.)* vermin; **b)** *(Jägerspr.)* droppings *pl.*
Geschmiere das; ~s *(ugs. abwertend)* **a)** [filthy] mess; **b)** *(Geschriebenes)* scribble; scrawl; **c)** *(Machwerk)* rubbish; bilge *(sl.)*
geschmissen [gəˈʃmɪsn̩] *2. Part. v.* **schmeißen**
geschmolzen *2. Part. v.* **schmelzen**
Geschmorte [gəˈʃmoːɐ̯tə] **das;** *adj. Dekl. (ugs.)* braised meat
Geschmunzel das; ~s *(ugs.)* smiling; **allgemeines ~ auslösen** make everyone smile
Geschmuse das; ~s *(ugs.)* cuddling; *(eines Pärchens)* kissing and cuddling
Geschnäbel das; ~s *(ugs.)* **a)** *(von Vögeln)* billing; **b)** *(ugs. scherzh.: Geküsse)* billing and cooing
Geschnatter das; ~s *(ugs.)* **a)** *(das Schnattern)* cackling; cackle; **b)** *(abwertend: das Sprechen)* chatter[ing]; nattering *(coll.)*
Geschnetzelte das; *adj. Dekl. small, thin slices of meat [cooked in sauce]*
geschniegelt 1. *2. Part. v.* **schniegeln. 2.** *Adj. (ugs. abwertend)* nattily dressed; **~ und gebügelt** *od.* **gestriegelt** all spruced up
geschnitten [gəˈʃnɪtn̩] *2. Part. v.* **schneiden**
geschnoben *2. Part. v.* **schnauben**
geschoben [gəˈʃoːbn̩] *2. Part. v.* **schieben**
geschollen *2. Part. v.* **schallen**
gescholten [gəˈʃɔltn̩] *2. Part. v.* **schelten**
Geschöpf [gəˈʃœpf] **das;** ~[e]s, ~e **a)** creature; **ein ~ Gottes** one of God's creatures; **b)** *(erfundene Gestalt)* creation
geschoren *2. Part. v.* **scheren**
[1]Geschoß das; Geschosses, Geschosse projectile; *(Kugel)* bullet; *(Rakete)* rocket; missile; *(Granate)* shell: grenade
[2]Geschoß das; Geschosses, Geschosse *(Etage)* floor; *(Stockwerk)* storey; **im ersten ~:** on the first *(Brit.) or (Amer.)* second floor
Geschoß·bahn die trajectory
geschossen [gəˈʃɔsn̩] *2. Part. v.* **schießen**
Geschoß·hagel der hail of bullets
-geschossig 1. *Adj.* -storey; **ein~/zwei~/mehr~:** single-storey/two-storey/multi-storey; **unser Wohnhaus ist zwei~:** our house has two storeys. **2.** *adv.* **drei~ bauen** build three storeys high
geschraubt 1. *2. Part. v.* **schrauben. 2.** *Adj. (ugs. abwertend)* stilted ⟨*language, construction*⟩; *(schwülstig)* affected, pretentious ⟨*way of speaking, style*⟩. **3.** *adv.* **sich ~ ausdrücken** express oneself in an affected *or* a pretentious manner *or* way
Geschraubtheit die; ~: stiltedness; *(Schwulst)* affectedness; pretentiousness
Geschrei das; ~s **a)** shouting; shouts *pl.; (durchdringend)* yelling; yells *pl.; (schrill)* shrieking; shrieks *pl.; (von Verletzten, Tieren)* screaming; screams *pl.;* **hört mit dem ~ auf** stop that shouting *or* yelling; **b)** *(ugs.: das Lamentieren)* fuss; to-do; **ein großes ~ wegen etw. machen** make *or* kick up a great fuss about sth.; make a great to-do about sth.
Geschreibsel [gəˈʃraipsl̩] **das;** ~s *(ugs. abwertend)* rubbish; bilge *(sl.)*
geschrieben *2. Part. v.* **schreiben**
geschrie[e]n [gəˈʃriː(ə)n] *2. Part. v.* **schreien**
geschritten *2. Part. v.* **schreiten**
geschunden *2. Part. v.* **schinden**
Geschütz das; ~es, ~e [big] gun; piece of

artillery; die ~e the artillery sing.; the [big] guns; grobes od. schweres ~ auffahren (fig. ugs.) bring up the big guns or heavy artillery (fig.)

Geschütz-: ~bedienung die (Milit.) gun crew; ~donner der roar or booming of the [big] guns or the artillery; ~feuer das artillery-fire; shell-fire; ~stand der, ~stellung die (Milit.) gun-emplacement

geschützt 1. 2. Part. v. schützen. 2. Adj. a) sheltered; b) (unter Naturschutz) protected

Geschwader [gə'ʃva:dɐ] das; ~s, ~ (Marine) squadron; (Luftwaffe) wing (Brit.); group (Amer.)

Geschwafel das; ~s (ugs. abwertend) waffle

Geschwätz das; ~es (ugs. abwertend) a) (Gerede) prattle; prattling; b) (Klatsch) gossip; tittle-tattle

Geschwatze, Geschwätze das; ~s (ugs. abwertend) chatter[ing]; nattering (coll.)

geschwätzig Adj. (abwertend) talkative

Geschwätzigkeit die; ~ (abwertend) talkativeness; sie neigt ein bißchen zur ~: she tends to be rather talkative

geschweift 1. 2. Part. v. schweifen. 2. Adj. (gebogen) curved; ~e Klammern (Druckw.) braces

geschweige Konj. ~ [denn] let alone; never mind

geschwiegen 2. Part. v. schweigen

geschwind [gə'ʃvɪnt] (bes. südd.) 1. Adj. swift; quick. 2. adv. swiftly; quickly; ~! be quick!; ich laufe ~ zum Kaufmann I'm just dashing to the grocer's

Geschwindigkeit die; ~, ~en speed: mit großer/hoher ~: at great/high speed; mit einer ~ von 50 km/h at a speed of 50 km/h; überhöhte ~: excessive speed; die ~ erhöhen/drosseln od. verringern increase/reduce speed; speed up/slow down

Geschwindigkeits-: ~abfall der loss of speed; drop in speed; ~begrenzung die, ~beschränkung die speed limit; die ~beschränkung nicht beachten exceed the speed limit; ~kontrolle die speed check; ~messer der speedometer; ~überschreitung die exceeding the speed limit no art.; speeding; ~zunahme die increase in speed; increase in velocity (Phys.)

Geschwirr das; ~s (von Pfeilen) whizzing; (von Insekten) buzzing

Geschwister [gə'ʃvɪstɐ] das; ~s, ~ a) Pl. brothers and sisters; Hans und Maria sind ~: Hans and Maria are brother and sister; b) (bes. Biol., Psych.) sibling

Geschwister·kind das (veralt.) a) (Neffe/Nichte) nephew/niece; b) (Cousin/Cousine) cousin

geschwisterlich 1. Adj. brotherly/sisterly ⟨affection, love⟩. 2. adv. das Geld ~ teilen divide the money fairly among everybody

Geschwister-: ~liebe die a) brotherly/sisterly love or affection; b) (Inzest) love affair between a brother and [a] sister; ~paar das brother and sister; zwei ~paare two sets of brother and sister

geschwollen 1. 2. Part. v. schwellen. 2. Adj. a) swollen; b) (fig. abwertend) pompous; bombastic. 3. adv. pompously; bombastically

geschwommen [gə'ʃvɔmən] 2. Part. v. schwimmen

geschworen 1. 2. Part. v. schwören. 2. Adj. in ein ~er Feind od. Gegner von etw. sein be a sworn enemy of sth.

Geschworene, (österr.:) **Geschworne** der/die; adj. Dekl. juror; die ~n the jury

Geschworenen-: ~bank jury-box; (fig.) jury; ~gericht das s. Schwurgericht

Geschwulst [gə'ʃvʊlst] die; ~, Geschwülste [gə'ʃvʏlstə] tumour

geschwunden 2. Part. v. schwinden

geschwungen 1. 2. Part. v. schwingen. 2. Adj. curved

Geschwür [gə'ʃvy:ɐ̯] das; ~s, ~e ulcer; (Furunkel) boil; (fig.) running sore

Ges-Dur [auch: '-'-] das; ~ (Musik) G major; s. auch C-Dur

gesehen [gə'ze:ən] 2. Part. v. sehen

Geselchte [gə'zɛlçtə] das; adj. Dekl.; o. Pl. (südd., österr.) smoked meat

Gesell [gə'zɛl] der; ~en, ~en (veralt.), **Geselle** [gə'zɛlə] der; ~n, ~n a) journeyman; b) (Kerl) fellow

-geselle der: Tischler~/Fleischer~: journeyman-carpenter/-butcher

gesellen refl. V. sich zu jmdm. ~: join sb.; (fig.: hinzukommen) dazu gesellten sich noch Krankheit und finanzielle Unsicherheit together with this came illness and financial insecurity

Gesellen-: ~brief der journeyman's diploma or certificate; ~prüfung die examination to become a journeyman; apprentice's final examination; ~stück das piece of work produced by an apprentice in order to qualify as a journeyman

gesellig 1. Adj. a) sociable; gregarious; ein ~er Abend/~es Beisammensein a convivial or sociable evening/a friendly get-together; b) (Biol.) gregarious. 2. adv. ~ leben live gregariously; be gregarious; ~ zusammensitzen sit [together] and chat [sociably]

Geselligkeit die; ~, ~en a) o. Pl. (Umgang) die ~ lieben enjoy [good] company; b) (geselliger Abend) social gathering

Gesellschaft die; ~, ~en a) society; eine geschlossene ~: a closed community or society; die ~ verändern change society; ~ bekommen get company; in schlechte ~ geraten get into bad company; jmdm. ~ leisten keep sb. company; die Damen der ~: society ladies; zur ~ gehören belong to society; jmdn. in die ~ einführen introduce sb. into society; die ~ Jesu (kath. Rel.) the Society of Jesus; zur ~: to be sociable; sich in guter ~ befinden (fig. scherzh.) be in good company; b) (Veranstaltung) party; eine ~ geben give a party; eine geschlossene ~: a private function or party; c) (Kreis von Menschen) group of people; crowd; (abwertend) crew; lot (coll.); d) (Wirtschaft) company; ~ mit beschränkter Haftung limited liability company

Gesellschafter der; ~s, ~ a) (Unterhalter) ein glänzender ~: a brilliant conversationalist; ein guter ~ sein be good company; b) (verhüll.: Callboy) [male] escort (euphem.); c) (Wirtsch.) partner; (Teilhaber) shareholder; stiller ~: sleeping partner; silent partner (Amer.)

Gesellschafterin die; ~, ~nen a) [lady] companion; b) (verhüll.: Callgirl) escort (euphem.); c) (Wirtsch.) partner; (Teilhaber) shareholder

gesellschaftlich 1. Adj.; nicht präd. a) social; die ~en Verhältnisse social conditions; b) (Soziol.) society; die ~e Produktion production by society; ~es Eigentum an etw. (Dat.) social ownership of sth.; c) (DDR) ⟨work etc.⟩ in the service of the community. 2. adv. a) socially; sich ~ unmöglich machen put oneself beyond the pale of society; b) (DDR) ~ nützliche Tätigkeit socially useful activity; ~ aktiv sein od. sich ~ betätigen be actively involved in service to the community

gesellschafts-, Gesellschafts-: ~abend der social evening; ~anzug der dress-suit; ~dame die (veralt.) s. Gesellschafterin a; ~fähig Adj. (auch fig.) socially acceptable; ~feindlich Adj. antisocial; ~form die form of society; social system; ~formation die (Soziol.) social system; ~kapital das (Wirtsch.) capital of a/the company; ~klasse die social class; ~kritik die social criticism; ~kritiker der critic of society; ~kritisch 1. Adj. critical of society postpos.; die ~kritischen Elemente bei Fontane the elements of social criticism in Fontane; 2. adv. etw. ~kritisch interpretieren interpret sth. from the point of view of social criticism; ~lehre die (veralt.) sociology; (Schulfach) social studies pl., no art.; ~ordnung die social order; ~politik die social policy; ~politisch 1. Adj. socio-political; 2. adv. socio-politically; ~raum der function room; (auf Schiffen) saloon; ~reise die group tour; ~roman der social novel; ~schicht die stratum of society; ~spiel das parlour or party game; ~struktur die structure of society; die japanische ~struktur the structure of Japanese society; ~stück das a) (Theater) comedy of manners; b) (Malerei) genre painting; ~system das social system; ~tanz der ballroom dance; (das Tanzen) ballroom dancing; ~vertrag der a) (Philos.) social contract; b) (Rechtsw.) memorandum or articles of association; ~wissenschaften Pl. social sciences; ~wissenschaftlich Adj. sociological ⟨studies, analyses⟩; ~wissenschaftliche Fächer social-science subjects

gesessen [gə'zɛsn̩] 2. Part. v. sitzen

Gesetz [gə'zɛts] das; ~es, ~e a) law; (geschrieben) statute; ein ~ verabschieden/einbringen pass/introduce a bill; [zum] ~ werden become law; vor dem ~: in [the eyes of the] law; das ~ der Serie the expectation that future events will continue the pattern of past ones; das ~ des Handelns the need or necessity to act; das ~ des Handelns an sich reißen seize the initiative; etw. hat seine eigenen ~e (fig.) sth. is a law unto itself; b) (Regel) rule; law; jmdm. höchstes ~ sein be sb.'s golden rule; s. auch aufheben c; einhalten 1

Gesetz-: ~blatt das law gazette; ~buch das statute-book; das Bürgerliche ~buch the Civil Code; ~entwurf der bill

gesetzes-, Gesetzes-: ~brecher der law-breaker; ~hüter der (iron.) guardian of the law; ~kraft die force of law; legal force; ~kraft haben have the force of law or legal force; ~kraft erlangen become law; be placed on the statute-book; ~kundig Adj. well versed in the law postpos.

gesetzes-, Gesetzes-: ~lücke die loophole in the law; ~novelle die amendment; ~sammlung die legal digest; ~tafel die (hist.) tablet on which laws are written; die ~tafeln (bibl.) the Tables of the Law; the Two Tables; ~text der wording of the/a law; ~treu 1. Adj. law-abiding; 2. adv. in accordance with the law; ~treue die law-abidingness; ~übertretung die violation of the law; ~vorlage die bill; ~werk das corpus or body of laws

gesetz-, Gesetz-: ~gebend Adj. legislative; die ~gebende Versammlung/Gewalt the legislative assembly or the legislature/the legislative power; ~geber der legislator; law-maker; (Organ) legislature; ~gebung die; ~: legislation; law-making; ~gebungs·hoheit die supreme authority to make or enact laws; supreme legislative power or authority; ~kundig Adj.: s. gesetzeskundig

gesetzlich 1. Adj. legal ⟨requirement, definition, respresentative, interest⟩; legal, statutory ⟨obligation⟩; statutory ⟨holiday⟩; lawful, legitimate ⟨heir, claim⟩; ~es Zahlungsmittel legal tender; ~e Kündigungsfrist statutory period of notice. 2. adv. legally; ~ verankert sein be established in law; ~ geschützt registered ⟨patent, design⟩; ⟨symbol⟩ registered as a trade mark; ~ geschützt/verboten sein be protected/forbidden by law

Gesetzlichkeit die; ~ a) (Gesetzmäßigkeit) conformity to a [natural] law/[natural] laws; einer ~ folgen obey a law/laws; b) (geregelter Zustand) ~ wiederherstellen re-

store law and order; **außerhalb der ~ liegen** be illegal
gesetz-, Gesetz-: ~los *Adj.* lawless; **~losigkeit die; ~:** lawlessness; **~mäßig 1.** *Adj.* **a)** law-governed ⟨*development, process*⟩; **~mäßig sein** be governed by *or* obey a [natural] law/ [natural] laws; **b)** *(gesetzlich)* legal; *(rechtmäßig)* lawful; legitimate; **2.** *adv.* in accordance with a [natural] law/ [natural] laws; **~mäßigkeit die a)** conformity to a [natural] law/[natural] laws; **~mäßigkeiten im Verhalten von Tieren entdecken** discover laws governing animal behaviour; **b)** *(Gesetzlichkeit)* legality; *(Rechtmäßigkeit)* lawfulness; legitimacy
gesetzt 1. *2. Part. v.* **setzen. 2.** *Adj.* staid; **eine Dame ~en Alters** a woman of mature years
Gesetztheit die; ~: staidness
gesetz·widrig 1. *Adj.* illegal; unlawful. **2.** *adv.* illegally; unlawfully
Gesetz·widrigkeit die a) illegality; unlawfulness; **b)** *Pl. (Handlungen)* unlawful acts
Geseufze das; ~s sighing
[1]**Gesicht** [gəˈzɪçt] **das; ~[e]s, ~er a)** face; **das ~ abwenden** turn one's face away; **ein fröhliches ~ machen** look pleasant *or* cheerful; **über das ganze ~ strahlen** *(ugs.)* beam all over one's face; **sich** *(Dat.)* **eine Zigarette ins ~ stecken** *(ugs.)* stick a cigarette in one's mouth *(coll.)*; *(fig.)* **sein wahres ~ zeigen** show oneself in one's true colours; show one's true character; **jmdm. wie aus dem ~ geschnitten sein** be the [very *or* dead] spit [and image] of sb.; **ihm fiel das Essen aus dem ~** *(ugs. scherzh.)* he threw up *(coll.)*; **das ist ein Schlag ins ~:** that is a slap in the face; **jmdm. ins ~ lachen** laugh in sb.'s face; **jmdm. ins ~ lügen** lie to sb.'s face; **jmdm. etw. ins ~ sagen** say sth. to sb.'s face; **jmdm. nicht ins ~ sehen können** be unable to look sb. in the face; **den Tatsachen ins ~ sehen** face the facts; **jmdm. [nicht] zu ~[e] stehen** [not] become sb.: **solche Unhöflichkeit steht dir nicht zu ~[e]** such impoliteness ill becomes you; **jmdm. ins ~ springen** *(ugs.)* go for sb.; **ein bekanntes/fremdes ~:** a familiar *or* well-known/unknown *or* strange face; **ein anderes ~ aufsetzen** *od.* **machen** put on a different expression; **das ~ wahren** *od.* **retten** save one's face; **das ~ verlieren** lose face; **ein ~ machen wie drei** *od.* **acht** *od.* **vierzehn Tage Regenwetter** look as miserable as sin; **ein langes ~/lange ~er machen** pull a long face; **ein schiefes ~ machen** make a wry face; **ein ~ ziehen** *od.* **machen** make *or* pull a face; **~er schneiden** pull *or* make faces; **das stand ihm im ~ geschrieben** it was written all over his face; **b)** *(fig.: Aussehen)* **das ~ einer Stadt** the appearance of a town; **die vielen ~er Chinas** the many faces of China; **diese Pläne haben noch kein ~:** these plans still have no definite shape *or* form; **ein anderes ~ bekommen** take on a different complexion *or* character; **c)** *o. Pl. (geh., veralt.: Sehvermögen)* sight; **das Zweite ~ [haben]** [have] second sight; **jmdn./etw. aus dem ~ verlieren** lose sight of sb./sth.; **jmdn./etw. zu ~ bekommen** set eyes on *or* see sb./sth.; **jmdm. zu ~ kommen** *(Amtsspr.)* be seen by sb.
[2]**Gesicht das; ~[e]s, ~e** *(geh.)* vision; **ein ~/~e haben** have a vision/visions
gesichts-, Gesichts-: ~ausdruck der expression; look; **~creme die** face-cream; **~erker der** *(ugs. scherzh.)* conk *(sl.)*; hooter *(Brit. sl.)*; schnozzle *(Amer. sl.)*; **~farbe die** complexion; **~feld das** field of vision *or* view; **~hälfte die** side of the face; **seine rechte ~hälfte** the right side of his face; **~haut die** facial skin; **~kontrolle die** identity check *(before granting admittance to night-club etc.)*; **~kreis der** *(veralt.)* **a)** field of view; field *or* range of vision; **jmdn. aus dem ~kreis verlieren** *(fig.)* lose touch with sb.; **b)** *(Horizont)* horizon; outlook; **seinen ~kreis erweitern** broaden one's horizons *pl.*; **~lähmung die** facial paralysis; **~los** *Adj.* faceless; **~lotion die** face lotion; **~maske die a)** *(Larve)* mask; **b)** *(Med.)* face-mask; **c)** *(Kosmetik)* face-mask; face-pack; **d)** *(Sport)* face-guard; **~muskel der** facial muscle; **~nerv der** facial nerve; **~partie die** part of the face; **ihre untere ~partie** the lower part of her face; **~pflege die** care of one's face; **ihre tägliche ~pflege** her daily facial; **zur ~pflege benutzt sie nur Wasser und Seife** all she uses on her face is soap and water; **~plastik die** *(Med.)* plastic surgery *no art.* on the face; **~puder der** face-powder; **~punkt der** point of view; **etw. unter einem anderen/neuen ~punkt betrachten** consider sth. from a different/new point of view; **~rose die** *(Med.)* facial erysipelas; **~schnitt der** [cast *sing.* of] features *pl.*; **~sinn der;** *o. Pl.* visual faculty; **~verlust der** loss of face; **~wasser das** face-lotion; **~winkel der a)** angle of vision; visual angle; **b)** *s.* **~punkt; ~züge** *Pl.* features
Gesims das; ~es, ~e cornice
Gesinde [gəˈzɪndə] **das; ~s, ~** *(veralt.)* [domestic] servants *pl.*; *(auf einem Bauernhof)* [farm-]hands *pl.*
Gesindel [gəˈzɪndl] **das; ~s** *(abwertend)* rabble; riff-raff *pl.*; **lichtscheues ~:** shady characters *pl.*
Gesinde·stube die *(veralt.)* servants' quarters *pl.*; *(auf einem Bauernhof)* quarters *pl.* for the farm-hands
Gesinge das; ~s *(ugs. abwertend)* singing
gesinnt [gəˈzɪnt] *Adj.* **christlich/sozial ~ [sein]** [be] Christian-minded/public-spirited; **jmdm. freundlich/übel ~ sein** be well-disposed/ill-disposed towards sb.
Gesinnung die; ~, ~en [basic] convictions *pl.*; [fundamental] beliefs *pl.*; **eine niedrige ~:** a low cast of mind
gesinnungs-, Gesinnungs-: ~freund der, ~genosse der like-minded person; **seine ~freunde** *od.* **~genossen** people of the same mind as himself; **~los** *(abwertend)* **1.** *Adj.* unprincipled; **2.** *adv.* in an unprincipled manner; **~losigkeit die; ~:** lack of principle; **~lump der** *(ugs. abwertend)* time-server; **~schnüffelei die** *(abwertend)* snooping around to find out people's political convictions; political snooping; **~täter der** law-breaker motivated by moral *or* political convictions; **~treu** *Adj.* loyal; **~treue die** loyalty; **~wandel der, ~wechsel der** change *or* shift of attitude *or* views
gesittet [gəˈzɪtət] **1.** *Adj.* **a)** well-behaved; well-mannered ⟨*behaviour*⟩; **b)** *(zivilisiert)* civilized. **2.** *adv.* **a) sich ~ benehmen** *od.* **aufführen** be well-behaved; **b)** *(zivilisiert)* in a civilized manner
Gesittung die; ~ *(geh.)* cultured behaviour
Gesocks [gəˈzɔks] **das; ~** *(salopp abwertend)* riff-raff; rabble
Gesöff [gəˈzœf] **das; ~[e]s, ~e** *(salopp abwertend)* muck *(coll.)*; awful stuff *(coll.)*
gesogen [gəˈzo:gn̩] *2. Part. v.* **saugen**
gesondert [gəˈzɔndɐt] **1.** *Adj.* separate. **2.** *adv.* separately
gesonnen [gəˈzɔnən] **1.** *2. Part. v.* **sinnen. 2.** *Adj.* **~ sein, etw. zu tun** feel disposed to do sth.
gesotten [gəˈzɔtn̩] *2. Part. v.* **sieden**
Gesottene das; *adj. Dekl.; o. Pl. (landsch.)* boiled meat
Gespann [gəˈʃpan] **das; ~[e]s, ~e a)** *(Zugtiere)* team; **ein ~ Ochsen** a yoke *or* team of oxen; **b)** *(Wagen)* horse and carriage; *(zur Güterbeförderung)* horse and cart; **c)** *(Menschen)* couple; pair
gespannt 1. *2. Part. v.* **spannen. 2.** *Adj.* **a)** *(erwartungsvoll)* eager; expectant; rapt ⟨*attention*⟩; **ich bin ~, ob ...:** I'm keen *or* eager to know/see whether ...; *s. auch* **Flitz[e]bogen; b)** *(konfliktbeladen)* tense ⟨*situation, atmosphere*⟩; strained ⟨*relations, relationships*⟩. **3.** *adv.* eagerly; expectantly; **die Kinder hörten seinen Erzählungen ~ zu** the children listened with rapt attention to his stories
Gespanntheit die a) eager expectancy; **voller ~ die Entwicklung verfolgen** follow the developments with tense interest; **b)** *(Gereiztheit)* tenseness
gespaßig *(bayr., österr.) s.* **spaßig**
Gespenst [gəˈʃpɛnst] **das; ~[e]s, ~er a)** ghost; **~er sehen** *(fig.)* be imagining things; **b)** *(geh.: Gefahr)* spectre
Gespenster-: ~geschichte die ghost story; **~glaube der** belief in ghosts
gespensterhaft *Adj.* ghostly
gespenstern *itr. V.* **in etw.** *(Dat.)* **~:** haunt sth.
Gespenster·stunde die witching hour
gespenstig, gespenstisch *Adj.* ghostly; ghostly, eerie ⟨*appearance*⟩; eerie ⟨*building, atmosphere*⟩
gespie[e]n [gəˈʃpi:(ə)n] *2. Part. v.* **speien**
Gespiele der; ~n, ~n, Gespielin die; ~, ~nen *(geh. veralt.)* **a)** playmate; **b)** *(abwertend: Geliebte[r])* lover
Gespinst [gəˈʃpɪnst] **das; ~[e]s, ~e** gossamer-like material; **das ~ der Seidenraupe** the cocoon of the silkworm; **ein ~ von Lügen** *(fig.)* a tissue of lies
gesplissen [gəˈʃplɪsn̩] *2. Part. v.* **spleißen**
gesponnen [gəˈʃpɔnən] *2. Part. v.* **spinnen**
[1]**Gespons** [gəˈʃpɔns] **der; ~es, ~e** *(veralt., noch scherzh.)* spouse; *(Bräutigam)* bridegroom
[2]**Gespons das; ~es, ~e** *(veralt., noch scherzh.)* spouse; *(Braut)* bride
gespornt 1. *2. Part. v.* **spornen. 2.** *Adj. s.* **gestiefelt**
Gespött [gəˈʃpœt] **das; ~[e]s** mockery; ridicule; **jmdn./sich zum ~ machen** make sb./oneself a laughing-stock
Gespräch [gəˈʃprɛ:ç] **das; ~[e]s, ~e a)** conversation; *(Diskussion)* discussion; **das ~ auf etw.** *(Akk.)* **bringen** bring *or* steer the conversation round to sth.; **ein ~ über etw.** *(Akk.)* a conversation *or* talk about sth.; **~e** *(Politik)* talks; discussions; **der Gegenstand des ~[e]s** the subject *or* topic under discussion; **ein ~ mit jmdm. führen** have a conversation *or* talk with sb.; **jmdn. in ein ~ verwickeln** engage sb. in conversation; **mit jmdm. ins ~ kommen** *(sich unterhalten)* get into *or* engage in conversation with sb.; *(fig.: sich annähern)* enter into a dialogue with sb.; **im ~ sein** be under discussion; **als neuer Vorsitzender ist Herr X im ~:** Mr X's name is being discussed in connection with the chairmanship; **b)** *(Telefon~)* call **(mit** to); **ein ~ anmelden** make *or* place a call; **ein ~ für Sie!** there's a call for you!; **c)** *(ugs.: Gesprächsgegenstand)* **das ~ der Stadt/der Familie** the talk of the town/the whole family; **das ~ der letzten Wochen** the talking-point for the last few weeks
gesprächig *Adj.* talkative; **der Alkohol machte ihn ~:** the alcohol loosened his tongue
Gesprächigkeit die; ~: talkativeness
gesprächs-, Gesprächs-: ~bereit *Adj.* ready to talk *postpos.*; *(zu Verhandlungen bereit auch)* ready for discussions *postpos.*; *(Telefon)* **sind Sie jetzt ~bereit?** are you ready to speak now?; **~bereitschaft die** readiness for discussions; **~dauer die** *(Fernspr.)* call-time; **~einheit die** *s.* **Gebühreneinheit; ~fetzen der** fragment *or* snatch of conversation; **~form die;** *o. Pl.* **in ~form** in the form of a dialogue; in dialogue form; **~gegenstand der** topic of conversation; *(Diskussionsgegenstand)* subject of the discussion; **~gegenstand war ...:**

the subject *or* topic of conversation/the subject of the discussion was ...; **~kreis der** discussion group; **~leiter der** discussion leader; chairman; **~partner der: wer war ihr ~partner?** who was she talking to?; **mein heutiger ~partner wird der Innenminister sein** today I shall be talking to the Minister of the Interior; **der Kanzler und seine ~partner** the Chancellor and his partners in the talks; **~pause die** break in the discussions *or* talks; **~stoff der** subjects *pl. or* topics *pl.* of conversation; **ihr geht nie der ~stoff aus** she never runs out of things to talk about; **~teilnehmer der** participant in the discussion; **~thema das** topic of conversation; **~therapie die** *(Psych.)* therapy by means of conversation; **~weise** *Adv.* in [the course of] conversation; **~zeit die** *(Fernspr.)* call-time; **Ihre ~zeit ist abgelaufen** the time allowed for your call has run out

gespreizt 1. *2. Part. v.* **spreizen. 2.** *Adj. (abwertend)* stilted; affected. **3.** *adv. (abwertend)* in a stilted *or* an affected manner

Gespreiztheit die; ~ *(abwertend)* stiltedness; affectedness

gesprenkelt 1. *2. Part. v.* **sprenkeln. 2.** *Adj.* mottled; speckled ⟨*egg*⟩

Gespritzte der; *adj. Dekl. (südd.)* wine with soda water

gesprochen [gəˈʃprɔxn̩] *2. Part. v.* **sprechen**

gesprossen [gəˈʃprɔsn̩] *2. Part. v.* **sprießen**

Gesprudel das; ~s bubbling

gesprungen *2. Part. v.* **springen**

Gespür [gəˈʃpyːɐ̯] **das;** ~s feel; **sie hat ein feines ~ für Unaufrichtigkeiten** she quickly senses when somebody is being insincere

gest. *Abk.* **gestorben** d.

Gestade [gəˈʃtaːdə] **das;** ~s, ~ *(dichter.)* shore(s)

Gestagen [gɛstaˈgeːn] **das;** ~s, ~e *(Med.)* gestagen

Gestalt [gəˈʃtalt] **die;** ~, ~en **a)** build; **von kräftiger ~, kräftig von ~:** of powerful *or* strong build; **zierlich von ~:** petite; **klein von ~:** small in stature; of small build; **b)** *(Mensch, Persönlichkeit)* figure; **eine zwielichtige ~:** a shady character; **c)** *(in der Dichtung)* character; **d)** *(Form)* form; **die ~ des neuen Hochhauses** the shape of the new tower block; **~ annehmen** *od.* **gewinnen** take shape; **einer Sache** *(Dat.)* **~ geben** *od.* **verleihen** give shape [and form] to sth.; *(etw. ausdrücken)* express sth.; **in ~ von einer Sache** *od.* **einer Sache** *(Gen.)* in the form of sth.; **sich in seiner wahren ~ zeigen** show one's true character; show [oneself in] one's true colours

gestalten 1. *tr. V.* fashion, shape, form ⟨*vase, figure, etc.*⟩; design ⟨*furnishings, stage-set, etc.*⟩; lay out ⟨*public gardens*⟩; dress ⟨*shop-window*⟩; mould, shape ⟨*character, personality*⟩; arrange ⟨*party, conference, etc.*⟩; frame ⟨*sentence, reply, etc.*⟩; **etw. moderner ~:** modernize sth.; **etw. künstlerisch/literarisch ~:** give artistic/literary form to sth. **2.** *refl. V.* turn out; **sich schwieriger ~ als erwartet** turn out *or* prove to be more difficult than had been expected; **er fragte sich, wie sich seine Zukunft ~ würde** he wondered what the future would hold for him

Gestalter der; ~s, ~, **Gestalterin die;** ~, ~nen creator

gestalterisch *Adj.; nicht präd.* creative; artistic; **vom ~en Standpunkt** creatively; artistically

gestalt·los *Adj.* shapeless; formless; **eine ~e Masse** an amorphous mass

Gestalt·psychologie die Gestalt psychology

Gestaltung die; ~, ~en **a)** *s.* **gestalten:** fashioning; shaping; forming; designing; laying out; dressing; moulding; shaping; arranging; framing; **die literarische ~ dieses historischen Ereignisses** the literary representation of this historic event; **Hochschule für ~:** academy of art and design; **die künstlerische ~ des Films** the artistic direction of the film; **b)** *(Gestaltetes)* form

Gestaltungs-: ~form die form; **~kraft die** creative power; **~prinzip das** formal principle

Gestammel das; ~s stammering; stuttering; **seine Antwort war nur ein ~:** he was only able to stammer *or* stutter out a reply

Gestampfe das; ~s stamping; **das ~ der Baumaschinen** the pounding *or* thumping of the construction plant

gestand *1. u. 3. Pers. Sg. Prät. v.* **gestehen**

gestanden 1. *2. Part. v.* **stehen, gestehen. 2.** *Adj.; nicht präd.* **ein ~er Mann** a grown man; **ein ~er Parlamentarier** an experienced *or* seasoned parliamentarian

geständig *Adj.* **~ sein** have confessed; **wenn Sie ~ wären** if you confessed; **der ~e Entführer** the self-confessed kidnapper

Geständnis [gəˈʃtɛntnɪs] **das;** ~ses, ~se confession; **ein ~ ablegen** make a confession; **ich muß dir ein ~ machen** I must make a confession to you

Gestänge [gəˈʃtɛŋə] **das;** ~s, ~ **a)** *(Stangen)* struts *pl.;* **b)** *(Technik)* linkage; *(des Kolbens)* connecting rod

Gestank [gəˈʃtaŋk] **der;** ~[e]s *(abwertend)* stench; stink

Gestänker [gəˈʃtɛnkɐ] **das;** ~s *(ugs.)* trouble-making

Gestapo [geˈstaːpo] **die;** ~ *(ns.)* Gestapo

Gestapo·methoden *Pl. (abwertend)* Gestapo methods

gestatten [gəˈʃtatn̩] **1.** *tr., itr. V.* permit; allow; **jmdm. ~, etw. zu tun** permit *or* allow sb. to do sth.; **„Rauchen nicht gestattet!"** 'no smoking'; **~ Sie eine Bemerkung** allow *or* permit me to make a remark; **~ Sie, daß ich ...:** may I ...?; **wenn Sie ~:** if I may; **wenn es die Umstände ~:** if circumstances permit *or* allow; circumstances permitting. **2.** *refl. V. (geh.)* **sich** *(Dat.)* **etw. ~:** allow oneself sth.; **wenn ich mir eine Bemerkung ~ darf** if I may be so bold as to make a remark; **sich** *(Dat.)* **~, etw. zu tun** take the liberty of doing sth.; **ich gestatte mir, Sie zu diesem Fest einzuladen** I have pleasure in inviting you to this celebration

Geste [ˈgɛstə, ˈgeːstə] **die;** ~, ~n *(auch fig.)* gesture

Gesteck [gəˈʃtɛk] **das;** ~[e]s, ~e flower arrangement

gestehen *tr., itr. V.* confess; **die Tat** *usw.* **~:** confess to the deed *etc.*; **jmdm. seine Gefühle ~:** confess one's feelings to sb.; **ich muß ~, daß ...:** I must confess that ...; **offen gestanden ...:** frankly *or* to be honest ...

Gestehungs·kosten *Pl. (Wirtsch.)* production costs

Gestein das; ~[e]s, ~e rock

Gesteins-: ~ader die rock seam; **~art die** type of rock; **~brocken der** rock; **~formation die** rock formation; **~kunde die** petrology; **~masse die** rock mass; mass of rock; **~probe die** rock sample; **~schicht die** stratum *or* layer of rock

Gestell [gəˈʃtɛl] **das;** ~[e]s, ~e **a)** *(für Weinflaschen)* rack; *(zum Wäschetrocknen)* horse; *(für Pflanzen)* planter; **b)** *(Unterbau)* frame; *(eines Wagens)* chassis; *(fig. salopp)* legs *pl.;* **c)** *(salopp: dünne Person)* scarecrow; **sie ist ein dünnes ~:** she's as skinny as a rake

Gestellung die; ~, ~en **a)** *(Milit., hist.)* reporting *no art.* for military service; **b)** *(Amtsspr.)* provision; **er bat um die ~ weiterer LKWs** he requested that more trucks *or (Brit.)* lorries be made available

Gestellungs·befehl der *(Milit., hist.)* call-up papers *pl.*

gestelzt 1. *2. Part. v.* **stelzen. 2.** *Adj.* stilted; affected. **3.** *adv.* in a stilted *or* an affected manner

gestern [ˈgɛstɐn] *Adv.* **a)** yesterday; **~ morgen/abend/mittag** yesterday morning/evening/[at] midday yesterday; **seit ~:** since yesterday; **~ vor einer Woche** a week ago yesterday; **die Zeitung von ~:** yesterday's [news]paper; **die Welt/die Mode von ~:** the world of yesterday *or* yesteryear/yesterday's fashions *pl.;* **das Gestern** yesterday; the past; **im Gestern leben** live in the past; **von ~ sein** be outdated *or* outmoded; **sie ist nicht von ~** *(ugs.)* she wasn't born yesterday *(coll.)*

Gestichel [gəˈʃtɪçl̩] **das;** ~s *(ugs. abwertend)* snide remarks *pl. or* comments *pl. (coll.)*

gestiefelt *Adj.* booted; **der gestiefelte Kater** Puss in Boots; **~ und gespornt** *(ugs. scherzh.)* ready and waiting

gestiegen *2. Part. v.* **steigen**

gestielt *Adj. (Bot.)* stemmed, petiolate ⟨*leaf*⟩; stemmed, pedunculate ⟨*flower*⟩; stalked ⟨*fruit*⟩

Gestik [ˈgɛstɪk] **die;** ~: gestures *pl.*

Gestikulation [gɛstikulaˈtsi̯oːn] **die;** ~, ~en gesticulation

gestikulieren [gɛstikuˈliːrən] *itr. V.* gesticulate

gestimmt 1. *2. Part. v.* **stimmen. 2.** *Adj.* **freudig/heiter ~:** in a joyful/cheerful mood *pred.*

Gestimmtheit die; ~, ~en mood

Gestirn das; ~[e]s, ~e heavenly body; *(Stern)* star

gestirnt *Adj. (geh.)* starry

gestoben [gəˈʃtoːbn̩] *2. Part. v.* **stieben**

Gestöber [gəˈʃtøːbɐ] **das;** ~s, ~: snowstorm

gestochen [gəˈʃtɔxn̩] **1.** *2. Part. v.* **stechen. 2.** *Adj.* **eine ~e Handschrift** extremely neat *or* careful handwriting. **3.** *adv.* **~ scharfe Bilder** crystal-clear photographs

gestohlen [gəˈʃtoːlən] **1.** *2. Part. v.* **stehlen. 2.** *Adj.* **der/das kann mir ~ bleiben** *(ugs.)* he can get lost *(sl.)*/you can keep it *(coll.)*

Gestöhne das; ~s groaning

gestorben [gəˈʃtɔrbn̩] *2. Part. v.* **sterben**

gestört [gəˈʃtøːɐ̯t] **1.** *2. Part. v.* **stören. 2.** *Adj.* disturbed; **ein ~es Verhältnis zu jmdm./etw. haben** have a disturbed relationship with sb./sth.; **geistig ~ sein** be mentally disturbed *or* unbalanced

gestoßen *2. Part. v.* **stoßen**

Gestotter [gəˈʃtɔtɐ] **das;** ~s *(ugs., meist abwertend)* stuttering; stammering; **das ~ des Motors** *(fig.)* the spluttering of the engine

Gestrampel das; ~s *(ugs.)* kicking about; *(beim Radfahren)* pedalling

Gesträuch [gəˈʃtrɔyç] **das;** ~[e]s, ~e shrubbery; bushes *pl.*

gestreckt 1. *2. Part. v.* **strecken. 2.** *Adj.* full ⟨*gallop*⟩; 180° ⟨*angle*⟩; flat ⟨*trajectory*⟩

gestreift 1. *2. Part. v.* **streifen. 2.** *Adj.* striped

Gestreite das; ~s *(ugs.)* quarrelling; squabbling; bickering

gestreng *Adj. (veralt.)* strict; severe; stern

gestrichen 1. *2. Part. v.* **streichen. 2.** *Adj.* level ⟨*measure*⟩; **ein ~er Teelöffel [Zucker** *usw.*] a level teaspoon[ful] [of sugar *etc.*]. **3.** *adv.* **~ voll** full to the brim; *s. auch* **Hose b; Nase b**

gestrig [ˈgɛstrɪç] *Adj.; nicht präd.* yesterday's; **der ~e Abend** yesterday evening; *(spät)* last night; **der ~e Tag** yesterday; **unser ~es Gespräch** our conversation yesterday; **die ewig Gestrigen** *(fig.)* those who live in the past

gestritten [gəˈʃtrɪtn̩] *2. Part. v.* **streiten**

Gestrüpp [gəˈʃtrʏp] **das;** ~[e]s, ~e undergrowth

gestuft 1. *2. Part. v.* **stufen. 2.** *Adj.* stepped ⟨*gable, façade*⟩; terraced ⟨*landscape, slope*⟩; graduated ⟨*colours, shades*⟩; *(fig.: abgestuft)* staggered ⟨*working hours*⟩

Gestühl [gəˈʃtyːl] **das;** ~[e]s, ~e seats *pl.;* *(Kirchen~)* pews *pl.*

Gestümper [gəˈʃtʏmpɐ] **das;** ~s *(ugs. abwertend)* ham-fisted performance; **das ist kein literarisches Kunstwerk, das ist abgeschmacktes** ~: that's no work of literature, it's banal rubbish; **ihr** ~ **auf der Violine** her amateurish efforts *pl.* on the violin
gestunken [gəˈʃtʊŋkn̩] *2. Part. v.* **stinken**
Gestus [ˈgɛstʊs] **der;** ~ *(geh.)* **a)** *(Attitüde)* air; **b)** *s.* **Gestik**
Gestüt [gəˈʃtyːt] **das;** ~[e]s, ~e stud[-farm]
Gesuch [gəˈzuːx] **das;** ~[e]s, ~e request (**um** for); *(Antrag)* application (**um** for); **ein** ~ **einreichen/zurückziehen** submit/withdraw a request/an application
Gesuch·steller [-ʃtɛlɐ] **der;** ~s, ~ *(Amtsspr. veralt.)* petitioner
gesucht 1. *2. Part. v.* **suchen. 2.** *Adj.* **a)** *(begehrt)* [much] sought-after; **einer der ~esten Dirigenten** one of the most sought-after conductors; **b)** *(gekünstelt)* affected ⟨*style*⟩; laboured ⟨*expression*⟩; far-fetched ⟨*comparison*⟩. **3.** *adv.* ⟨*express oneself*⟩ affectedly
Gesudel [gəˈzuːdl̩] **das;** ~s *(abwertend)* scrawl; *(fig.: schlechte Literatur)* rubbish
Gesülze [gəˈzʏltsə] **das;** ~s *(salopp)* drivel (**von** about ⟨*topic*⟩, from ⟨*speaker*⟩)
Gesumm [gəˈzʊm] **das;** ~[e]s buzzing; humming
Gesums [gəˈzʊms] **das;** ~es *(ugs.)* fuss (**um** about); **dein** ~: the fuss you make
gesund [gəˈzʊnt]; **gesünder** [gəˈzʏndɐ], *seltener:* **gesunder, gesündest...** [gəˈzʏndəst...], *seltener:* **gesundest...** *Adj.* **a)** healthy; healthy, strong ⟨*constitution*⟩; *(fig.)* viable, financially sound ⟨*company, business*⟩; **wieder** ~ **werden** get better; recover; ~ **sein** ⟨*person*⟩ be healthy; *(im Augenblick)* be in good health; **jmdn.** ~ **pflegen** nurse sb. back to health; **jmdn.** ~ **schreiben** pass sb. fit; ~ **und munter** hale and hearty; **frisch und** ~: fit and well; **aber sonst bist du** ~**?** *(ugs. iron.)* [are] you sure you're feeling all right? *(coll.)*; **bleib** ~! look after yourself!; **das ist** ~ **für ihn** *(fig.)* that will do him good; **b)** *(natürlich, normal)* healthy ⟨*mistrust, ambition, etc.*⟩; sound ⟨*construction*⟩; healthy, sound ⟨*attitude, approach*⟩; **der ~e Menschenverstand** common sense
gesund-, Gesund-: ~|**beten** *tr. V.* **jmdn. ~beten** heal sb. *or* restore sb. to health by prayer; **~beten das;** ~s faith-healing *no art.*; healing by prayer; **~beter der** faith-healer; **~beterei die;** ~: *s.* **~beten; ~brunnen der** *(geh.)* **die Beschäftigung mit der Jugend/dieser Urlaub ist für mich der reinste ~brunnen** working with young people keeps me young and healthy/this holiday is doing wonders to restore me to health
Gesunde [gəˈzʊndə] **der/die;** *adj. Dekl.* healthy person
gesunden *itr. V.; mit sein* ⟨*person*⟩ recover, get well, regain one's health; ⟨*tissue*⟩ heal; *(fig.)* ⟨*economy etc.*⟩ recover
Gesundheit die; ~: health; **von zarter** ~ **sein** have a delicate constitution; **bei bester** ~ **sein** be in the best of health; **auf jmds.** ~ *(Akk.)* **trinken/anstoßen** drink sb.'s health; ~ **und ein langes Leben!** your very good health!; *(als Geburtstagswunsch)* many happy returns!; ~! *(ugs.: Zuruf beim Niesen)* bless you!
gesundheitlich 1. *Adj.; nicht präd.* **~e Betreuung** health care; **sein ~er Zustand** [the state of] his health; **aus ~en Gründen** for reasons of health. **2.** *adv.* **wie geht es Ihnen** ~? how are you?; ~ **geht es ihm nicht sehr gut** he is not in very good health
gesundheits-, Gesundheits-: **~amt das** [local] public health department; **~apostel der** *(spött.)* health fanatic; **~attest das** certificate of health; health certificate; **~behörde die;** *meist Pl.* public health authority; **~fabrik die** *(abwertend) large, impersonal hospital dispensing assembly-line treatment;* **~fördernd** *Adj.* conducive to health *postpos.*; good for one's health *postpos.*; healthy ⟨*food, diet, climate, etc.*⟩; **~fürsorge die** medical welfare services *pl.*; **~gefährdung die** risk to health; **~halber** *Adv.* for reasons of health; for health reasons; **~lehre die** *s.* **Hygiene c; ~lenker der** *(ugs. scherzh.)* 'sit up and beg' handlebars; **~pflege die** health care; **~schaden der** damage *no pl., no indef. art.* to [one's] health; **das kann ~schäden bewirken** that can damage one's health; **einen bleibenden ~schaden davontragen** suffer permanent damage to one's health as a result; **trotz eines leichten ~schadens ...:** despite a slight disability ...; **~schädlich** *Adj.* detrimental to [one's] health *postpos.*; unhealthy; **Rauchen ist ~schädlich** smoking can damage your health; **~schutz der** *(DDR)* [system of] preventive health care; **~wesen das** [public] health service; **~zeugnis das** certificate of health; health certificate; **~zustand der** state of health
gesund-: ~|**machen** *refl. V. (ugs.)* make a pile *(coll.)*; ~|**schrumpfen** *itr. (auch refl.) V. (ugs.)* ⟨*industry, firm*⟩ be slimmed down; **eine Firma ~schrumpfen lassen** slim a firm down; ~|**stoßen** *unr. refl. V. (salopp)* grow fat *(coll.)*
Gesundung die; ~ *(geh., auch fig.)* recovery
gesungen [gəˈzʊŋən] *2. Part. v.* **singen**
gesunken [gəˈzʊŋkn̩] *2. Part. v.* **sinken**
Gesurre [gəˈzʊrə] **das;** ~s *(von Insekten)* buzzing; *(einer Filmkamera)* whirring
Getäfel [gəˈtɛːfl̩] **das;** ~s panelling
getäfelt *2. Part. v.* **täfeln**
getan [gəˈtaːn] *2. Part. v.* **tun**
Getändel das; ~s *(veralt.)* dalliance
geteilt 1. *2. Part. v.* **teilen. 2.** *Adj. (Bot.)* **~e Blätter** compound leaves
Getier das; ~[e]s *(geh.)* **a)** *(Tiere)* animals *pl.*; wildlife; **b)** *(einzelnes Tier)* animal/insect
getigert [gəˈtiːgɐt] *Adj.* **a)** *(mit ungleichen Flecken)* patterned like a tiger *postpos.*; **b)** *(mit Querstreifen)* striped
Getobe das; ~s romping *or* charging about
Getose das; ~s roar
Getöse das; ~s [thunderous] roar; *(von vielen Menschen)* din; **mit** ~: with a roar
getragen 1. *2. Part. v.* **tragen. 2.** *Adj.* solemn ⟨*music, voice, etc.*⟩. **3.** *adv.* solemnly
Geträller das; ~s *(von Vögeln)* trilling; *(von Menschen)* warbling
Getrampel das; ~s *(ugs.)* tramping; *(als Zeichen des Beifalls, der Ablehnung)* stamping
Getränk [gəˈtrɛŋk] **das;** ~[e]s, ~e drink; beverage *(formal)*
Getränke-: **~automat der** drinks machine *or* dispenser; **~bude die** drinks stand *or* kiosk; **~karte die** list of beverages; *(in einem Restaurant)* wine list; **~stand der** drinks stand *or* kiosk; **~steuer die** *tax on alcoholic drinks*
Getrappel das; ~s *(von Hufen, Pferden)* clatter; *(von Füßen)* patter; **das** ~ **der Tänzer** the patter of the dancers' feet
Getratsch[e] das; ~s *(ugs. abwertend)* gossip; gossiping
getrauen *refl. V.* dare; **sich [nicht]** *od. (seltener:)* **sich** *(Dat.)* **es [nicht]** ~, **etw. zu tun** [not] dare to do sth.; **ich getraue mich nicht über die Straße** I dare not cross the road; **ich getraue mir den doppelten Salto noch nicht** I dare not attempt the double somersault yet
Getreide [gəˈtraidə] **das;** ~s grain; corn; ~ **anbauen** grow cereals *pl. or* grain
Getreide-: **~anbau der** growing of cereals *or* grain; **~art die** kind of grain *or* cereal; **~börse die** corn exchange; **~ernte die** grain harvest; **~feld das** cornfield; **~halm der** corn-stalk; **~handel der** corn-trade; **~korn das** [cereal] grain; **~land das a)** corn-growing country; **b)** *o. Pl. (Ackerland)* corn-land; **~produkt das** cereal *or* grain product; **~schädling der** grain pest; **~speicher der** grain silo
getrennt 1. *2. Part. v.* **trennen. 2.** *Adj.* separate; **~e Kasse führen** pay separately. **3.** *adv.* ⟨*pay*⟩ separately; ⟨*sleep*⟩ in separate rooms; **[von jmdm.]** ~ **leben** live apart [from sb.]
Getrennt·schreibung die *writing a lexical item as two or more separate words;* **beachten Sie bitte die** ~ **von „so daß"** please remember that 'so daß' is written as two words
getreten *2. Part. v.* **treten**
getreu 1. *Adj. (geh.)* **a)** *(genau entsprechend)* exact ⟨*wording*⟩; true, faithful ⟨*image*⟩; **b)** *(treu)* faithful, loyal ⟨*friend, servant*⟩; ~ **bis in den Tod** faithful unto death. **2.** *adv. (geh.)* **a)** *(genau entsprechend)* ⟨*report, describe*⟩ faithfully, accurately; **b)** *(treu)* faithfully, loyally. **3.** *präpositional (geh.)* ~ **einem Versprechen/einer Abmachung handeln** act in accordance with a promise/an agreement
Getreue der/die; *adj. Dekl.* faithful *or* loyal follower
getreulich *Adv. s.* **getreu 2**
Getriebe das; ~s, ~ **a)** gears *pl.*; *(in einer Maschine)* gear system; *(~kasten)* gearbox; **b)** *(Betriebsamkeit)* hustle and bustle
Getriebe-: **~bremse die** transmission brake; **~gehäuse das** gearbox casing; **~kasten der** gearbox
getrieben *2. Part. v.* **treiben**
Getriebe·schaden der gearbox damage
Getriller [gəˈtrɪlɐ] **das;** ~s trilling
getroffen *2. Part. v.* **treffen, triefen**
getrogen [gəˈtroːgn̩] *2. Part. v.* **trügen**
Getrommel das; ~s *(ugs.)* drumming
getrost 1. *Adj.* confident; **sei** ~! take heart! **2.** *adv.* **a)** *(zuversichtlich)* confidently; **b)** *(ruhig)* **du kannst das Kind** ~ **allein lassen** you need have no qualms about leaving the child on its own; **du kannst mir** ~ **glauben, daß ...:** you can take my word for it that ...; **man kann** ~ **behaupten, daß ...:** one can safely say that ...
getrüffelt *Adj.* ⟨*pheasant etc.*⟩ [served *or* garnished] with truffles
getrunken *2. Part. v.* **trinken**
Getto [ˈgɛto] **das;** ~s, ~s ghetto
Getto·bildung die creation of a ghetto/of ghettos
Getue [gəˈtuːə] **das;** ~s *(ugs. abwertend)* fuss (**um** about); **ein** ~ **machen** kick up *or* make a fuss; *(sich wichtig machen)* put on airs
Getümmel [gəˈtʏml̩] **das;** ~s tumult; **das fröhliche/dichte** ~: the merry/crowded bustle; **mitten im dichtesten** *od.* **dicksten** ~: in the thick of it
getupft 1. *2. Part. v.* **tupfen. 2.** *Adj.* speckled ⟨*garment, fabric, etc.*⟩
Getuschel das; ~s *(ugs.)* whispering
geübt [gəˈ|yːpt] **1.** *2. Part. v.* **üben. 2.** *Adj.* experienced, accomplished, proficient ⟨*horseman, speaker, etc.*⟩; trained, practised ⟨*eye, ear*⟩; **in etw.** *(Dat.)* ~ **sein** be proficient at sth.
Gevatter [gəˈfatɐ] **der;** ~s *od. (älter:)* ~n, ~n *(veralt.)* **a)** *(Pate)* godfather; **[bei jmdm.] zu** ~ **stehen** act as *or* be [sb.'s] godfather; **jmdn. zu** ~ **bitten** ask sb. to act as *or* be godfather; ~ **Tod** *(dicht. veralt.) (im Märchen)* Godfather Death; *(fig.)* the Grim Reaper; **bei etw.** ~ **stehen** *(scherzh.)* be the inspiration behind sth.; **b)** *(veralt., noch scherzh.)* **Grüß Gott,** ~! greetings, friend!
Gevatterin die; ~, ~nen **a)** *(Patin)* godmother; **b)** *(veralt., noch scherzh.) s.* **Gevatter b**
Geviert das; ~[e]s, ~e **a)** *(veralt.) s.* **Quadrat; b)** *(Druckw.)* quadrat; quad
GEW *Abk.* **Gewerkschaft Erziehung und Wissenschaft** Educators' Union
Gewächs [gəˈvɛks] **das;** ~es, ~e **a)** *(Pflanze)*

plant; **b)** *(Weinsorte)* wine; *(Weinjahrgang)* vintage; **c)** *(Med.: Geschwulst)* growth

gewạchsen 1. *2. Part. v.* **wachsen. 2.** *in* **jmdm./einer Sache ~ sein** be a match for sb./be equal to sth.

Gewä̱chs·haus das greenhouse; glasshouse; *(Treibhaus)* hothouse

gewạgt 1. *2. Part. v.* **wagen. 2.** *Adj.* **a)** *(kühn)* daring; *(gefährlich)* risky; **b)** *(fast anstößig)* risqué ⟨*joke, song, etc.*⟩; daring ⟨*neckline etc.*⟩

gewä̱hlt 1. *2. Part. v.* **wählen. 2.** *Adj.* refined, elegant ⟨*style, manner of expression, etc.*⟩; refined ⟨*taste*⟩. **3.** *adv.* in a refined manner; elegantly

Gewä̱hltheit die; ~ *(des Ausdrucks)* refinement; *(der Kleidung)* elegance

gewahr [gəˈvaːɐ̯] *in* **jmdn./etw.** *od. (geh.)* **jmds./einer Sache ~ werden** catch sight of sb./sth.; **etw.** *(Akk.) od. (geh.)* **einer Sache** *(Gen.)* **~ werden** *(etw. erkennen, feststellen)* become aware of sth.

Gewähr [gəˈvɛːɐ̯] **die; ~:** guarantee; **für etw. ~ leisten/die ~ geben** guarantee sth.; **die ~ für etw. übernehmen/bieten** guarantee sth.; **keine ~ übernehmen** be unable to guarantee sth.; **die Angaben erfolgen ohne ~:** no responsibility is accepted for the accuracy of this information; **ohne ~** *(auf Fahrplänen usw.)* subject to change

gewa̱hren *tr. V. (geh.)* become aware of

gewä̱hren 1. *tr. V.* **a)** *(zugestehen)* give; grant, give ⟨*asylum, credit, loan*⟩; **jmdm. einen Aufschub ~:** grant *or* allow sb. a period of grace; **b)** *(erfüllen)* grant; **jmdm. seinen Wunsch/seine Bitte** *usw.* **~:** grant sb.'s wish/request *etc.*; **c)** *(bieten)* offer ⟨*advantage*⟩; give ⟨*pleasure, joy*⟩. **2.** *itr. V.* **in jmdn. ~ lassen** let sb. do as he/she likes; **laß ihn nur ~:** leave him alone

gewä̱hr·leisten *tr. V.* guarantee; ensure ⟨*safety*⟩

Gewä̱hr·leistung die a) guarantee; *(von Sicherheit)* ensuring; **b)** *s.* **Mängelhaftung**

Gewahrsam [gəˈvaːɐ̯zaːm] **der; ~s a)** *(Obhut)* safe-keeping; **etw. in ~ nehmen/behalten** take sth. into safe-keeping/keep sth. safe; **jmdm. etw. in ~ geben** give sth. to sb. for safe-keeping; **b)** *(Haft)* custody; **jmdn. in ~ bringen** take sb. into custody; **jmdn. in polizeilichen ~ bringen** hand sb. over to the police; **sich in [polizeilichem] ~ befinden** be in [police] custody

Gewä̱hrs-: ~mann der; *Pl.* **~männer** *od.* **~leute, ~person die** informant; source

Gewä̱hrung die; ~: *s.* **gewähren 1:** granting; giving; offering

Gewalt [gəˈvalt] **die; ~, ~en a)** *(Macht, Befugnis)* power; **die elterliche/richterliche ~:** parental/judicial power *or* authority; **jmdn. in seiner ~ haben** have sb. in one's power; **jmdn./ein Land in seine ~ bekommen/bringen** catch sb./bring a country under one's control; **in** *od.* **unter jmds. ~** *(Dat.)* **stehen** be in sb.'s power; **die ~ über sein Fahrzeug verlieren** *(fig.)* lose control of one's vehicle; **sich/seine Beine in der ~ haben** have oneself under control/have control over one's legs; **b)** *o. Pl. (Willkür)* force; **der ~ weichen** yield to force; **etw. mit ~ zu erreichen suchen** try to achieve sth. by force; **sich** *(Dat.)* **~ antun [müssen]** [have to] force oneself; **er versuchte mit aller ~, seinen Ehrgeiz zu befriedigen** he did everything he could to achieve his ambition; **etw. mit [aller] ~ wollen** want sth. desperately; **c)** *o. Pl. (körperliche Kraft)* force; violence; **~ anwenden** use force *or* violence; **etw. mit ~ öffnen** force sth. open; **mit roher/brutaler ~:** with brute force; **einer Frau ~ antun** *(geh. verhüll.)* violate a woman; **d)** *(geh.: elementare Kraft)* force; **die ~ der Leidenschaft/Rede** *(fig.)* the power of passion/oratory; **höhere ~ [sein]** [be] an act of God; **im Falle höherer ~:** in the case of an act of God/acts of God

Gewạlt-: ~akt der act of violence; **~androhung die** threat of violence; **~anwendung die** use of force *or* violence; **~einwirkung die: keinerlei Spuren von ~einwirkung aufweisen** show no signs of violence; **durch ~einwirkung sterben** die as a result of violence

Gewạlten-: ~teilung die, ~trennung die separation of powers

Gewạlt-: ~herrschaft die; *o. Pl.* tyranny; despotism; **~herrscher der** tyrant; despot

gewạltig 1. *Adj.* **a)** *(immens)* enormous, huge ⟨*sum, amount, difference, loss*⟩; tremendous ⟨*progress*⟩; **b)** *(imponierend)* mighty, huge, massive ⟨*wall, pillar, building, rock*⟩; monumental ⟨*literary work etc.*⟩; mighty ⟨*spectacle of nature*⟩; **c)** *(mächtig; auch fig.)* powerful. **2.** *adv. (ugs.: sehr, überaus)* **sich ~ irren/täuschen** be very much mistaken; **es wundert mich/imponiert mir ~:** I'm amazed/tremendously impressed; **etw. ist ~ gestiegen/gesunken** sth. has risen/dropped sharply

-gewaltige der/die; *adj. Dekl.* boss; **die Zeitungs~n** the press barons

Gewạltigkeit die; ~ *(von Mauern, Felsen, Gebäuden usw.)* mightiness; massiveness

gewạlt-, Gewạlt-: ~kur die *(ugs.)* drastic measures *pl. or* methods *pl.*; drastic treatment *no indef. art.*; **~los 1.** *Adj.* non-violent; **2.** *adv.* without violence; **~losigkeit die; ~:** non-violence; **~marsch der** forced march; **~maßnahme die** violent measure; **er schreckte vor ~maßnahmen nicht zurück** he was not afraid to use force; **~mensch der** brutal person; brute

gewạltsam 1. *Adj.* forcible ⟨*expulsion*⟩; enforced ⟨*separation*⟩; violent ⟨*death*⟩; **ein ~es Ende nehmen** meet a violent death. **2.** *adv.* forcibly; **~ die Tür öffnen** open the door by force; **sich ~ zurückhalten/wach halten** exercise the utmost restraint/force oneself to keep awake; **~ ums Leben kommen** meet a violent death

Gewạltsamkeit die; ~: violence

gewạlt-, Gewạlt-: ~streich der bold surprise action; **~tat die** *s.* **~verbrechen; ~tätig** *Adj.* violent; **~tätigkeit die a)** *o. Pl. (gewalttätige Art)* violence; **b)** *s.* **~akt; ~verbrechen das** crime of violence; **~verbrecher der** violent criminal; **~verzicht der** renunciation of the use of force; **~verzichts·abkommen das** non-aggression treaty

Gewạnd das; ~[e]s, Gewänder [gəˈvɛndɐ] *(geh.)* robe; gown; *(Abendkleid)* gown; **geistliche Gewänder** vestments; **im neuen ~** *(fig.)* dressed up as new; **ab nächster Woche erscheint die Zeitung in einem neuen ~** *(fig.)* from next week the newspaper will have a new look

gewạndet *Adj.; nicht präd. (veralt./scherzh.)* clad; apparelled *(arch.)*

Gewạnd-: ~haus das *(hist.)* cloth-hall; **~meister der** wardrobe master/mistress

gewandt [gəˈvant] **1.** *2. Part. v.* **wenden. 2.** *Adj.* skilful; *(körperlich)* agile; expert ⟨*skier*⟩; **ein ~es Auftreten/~e Umgangsformen** an easy, confident manner/easy social manners. **3.** *adv.* skilfully; *(körperlich)* agilely

Gewạndtheit die; ~: *s.* **gewandt 2:** skill; skilfulness; agility; expertness; easiness

gewạnn [gəˈvan] *1. u. 3. Pers. Sg. Prät. v.* **gewinnen**

gewärtig [gəˈvɛrtɪç] *in einer Sache (Gen.)* **~ sein** *(geh.)* be prepared for sth.; **~ sein, daß ...:** expect that ...

gewä̱rtigen *tr. V. (geh.) (erwarten)* expect; *(gefaßt sein auf)* be prepared for

Gewäsch [gəˈvɛʃ] **das; ~[e]s** *(ugs. abwertend)* twaddle; garbage *(Amer. coll.)*

gewạschen *2. Part. v.* **waschen**

Gewässer [gəˈvɛsɐ] **das; ~s, ~:** stretch of water; **ein fließendes/stehendes ~:** a stretch of running/standing water; **sich in arktische ~ wagen** venture into Arctic waters

Gewạ̈sser-: ~kunde die hydrography *no art.*; **~schutz der** prevention of water pollution

Gewẹbe das; ~s, ~ a) *(Stoff)* fabric; **b)** *(Med., Biol.)* tissue

Gewẹbs-: ~transplantation die, ~verpflanzung die *(Med.)* tissue graft

Gewehr [gəˈveːɐ̯] **das; ~[e]s, ~e** rifle; *(Schrot~)* shotgun; **mit dem ~ auf jmdn./etw. zielen** aim [one's rifle/shotgun] at sb./sth.; **~ ab!** *(Milit.)* order arms!; **das ~ über!** *(Milit.)* shoulder arms!; **präsentiert das ~!** *(Milit.)* present arms!; **~ bei Fuß stehen** be at the ready

Gewẹhr-: ~feuer das; *o. Pl.* rifle fire; **~kolben der** rifle/shotgun butt; **~kugel die** rifle bullet; **~lauf der** rifle/shotgun barrel; **~riemen der** rifle/shotgun sling; **~schloß das** lock of a rifle/shotgun; **~schuß der** rifle shot

Geweih [gəˈvai̯] **das; ~[e]s, ~e** antlers *pl.*; **~e/ein ~:** sets of antlers/a set of antlers

Gewei̱h·stange die *(Jägerspr.)* beam; main trunk

Gewẹrbe das; ~s, ~ a) business; *(Handel, Handwerk)* trade; **ein dunkles/schmutziges ~:** a shady/dirty business; **in einem ~ tätig sein** be in a trade/business; **das horizontale ~** *(ugs. scherzh.)*, **das älteste ~ der Welt** *(verhüll. scherzh.)* the oldest profession [in the world] *(joc.)*; **b)** *o. Pl. (kleine Betriebe)* [small and medium-sized] businesses and industries

Gewẹrbe·aufsicht die *enforcement of laws governing health and safety and conditions of work*

Gewẹrbe·aufsichts·amt das ≈ factory inspectorate (*authority with responsibility for* **Gewerbeaufsicht**)

Gewẹrbe-: ~betrieb der *(des Handels)* commercial enterprise; business; *(der Industrie)* industrial enterprise; business; **~freiheit die** right to carry on a business *or* trade; **~lehrer der** teacher in a trade school; **~ordnung die** laws *pl.* governing trade and industry; **~schein der** licence to carry on a business *or* trade; **~schule die** trade school; **~steuer die** trade tax; **~tätigkeit die** business activities *pl.*; **~treibende der/die;** *adj. Dekl.* tradesman/tradeswoman; **~zweig der** branch of trade

gewẹrblich 1. *Adj.; nicht präd.* commercial; business *attrib.*; *(industriell)* industrial; trade *attrib.* ⟨*union, apprentice*⟩; **~e Nutzung** use for commercial *or* business/industrial purposes. **2.** *adv.* **~ tätig sein** work; **etw. ~ nutzen** use sth. for commercial *or* business/industrial purposes

gewẹrbs·mäßig 1. *Adj.; nicht präd.* professional; **~e Unzucht** prostitution; **ein ~er Hehler** a receiver of stolen goods. **2.** *adv.* **etw. ~ betreiben** do sth. professionally *or* for gain

Gewerkschaft [gəˈvɛrkʃaft] **die; ~, ~en a)** trade union; **b)** *(veralt.: Bergbauunternehmen) mining company whose capital is divided into shares of no par value*

Gewẹrkschaft[l]er der; ~s, ~, Gewẹrkschaft[l]erin die; ~, ~nen trade unionist

gewẹrkschaftlich 1. *Adj.* [trade] union *attrib.*; ⟨*rights, duties*⟩ as a [trade] union member; **~er Vertrauensmann/~e Vertrauensfrau** shop steward; **der ~e Kampf** the struggle of the trade union movement. **2.** *adv.* **~ organisiert sein** belong to a [trade] union; **sich ~ engagieren** devote oneself to trade union work

gewẹrkschafts-, Gewẹrkschafts-: ~arbeit die; *o. Pl.* work for *or* on behalf of the/a [trade] union; **~bank die; ~, ~en** trade union bank; **~bewegung die;** *o. Pl.* [trade] union movement; **~boß der** *(ugs. abwertend)* [trade] union boss; **~bund der**

federation of trade unions; ≈ Trades Union Congress *(Brit.)*; ≈ AFL–CIO *(Amer.)*; **~eigen** *Adj.* owned by a [trade] union *postpos.*; **~führer der** [trade] union leader; **~funktionär der** [trade] union official; **~kongreß der** *s.* **~tag**; **~mitglied das** member of a [trade] union; **~tag der** [trade] union conference

Gewese das; ~s *(ugs.)* fuss; **ein großes ~ um etw. machen** kick up *or* make a lot of fuss about sth.

gewesen 1. *2. Part. v.* **¹sein. 2.** *Adj.; nicht präd. (bes. österr.)* former

gewichen *2. Part. v.* **weichen**

gewichst [gəˈvɪkst] **1.** *2. Part. v.* **wichsen. 2.** *Adj. (ugs.)* smart

Gewicht [gəˈvɪçt] **das; ~[e]s, ~e** *(auch Physik, auch fig.)* weight; **ein ~ von 75 kg/ein großes ~ haben** weigh 75 kg/be very heavy; **das zulässige ~:** the maximum permitted weight; the weight limit; **das spezifische ~** *(Physik)* the specific gravity; **sein ~ halten** stay the same weight; **etw. nach ~ verkaufen** sell sth. by weight; **seine Meinung/eine adlige Abstammung hat noch großes ~:** his opinion still carries a great deal of weight/it still counts for a great deal to be of noble descent; **einer Sache** *(Dat.)* **[kein] ~ beimessen** *od.* **beilegen** attach [no] importance to sth.; **sein ganzes ~ in die Waagschale werfen** throw one's whole weight behind it; **auf etw.** *(Akk.)* **~ legen** attach importance to sth.; **[nicht] ins ~ fallen** be of [no] consequence

gewichten *tr. V.* **a)** *(Statistik)* weight; **b)** *(Schwerpunkte festsetzen)* evaluate

Gewicht-: ~heben das; ~s weight-lifting; **~heber der; ~s, ~:** weight-lifter

gewichtig *Adj.* **a)** *(veralt.: schwer)* heavy; weighty; **jmd. ist ~** *(scherzh.)* sb. is impressively large; **b)** *(bedeutungsvoll)* weighty, important ⟨*reason, question, decision, etc.*⟩; **eine ~e Persönlichkeit** an important person *or* figure; **~ tun** act pompously; **ein ~es Gesicht machen** *(iron.)* put on *or* assume an air of importance

Gewichtigkeit die; ~: *s.* **gewichtig b:** importance; weightiness

gewichts-, Gewichts-: ~abnahme die decrease *or* reduction in weight; *(~verlust)* loss of weight; **~angabe die** indication of weight; **~klasse die a)** *(Sport)* weight [division *or* class]; **b)** *(Kaufmannsspr.)* weight class; **Eier nach ~klassen sortieren** grade eggs according to weight; **~los** *Adj.* **a)** *s.* **schwerelos 1; b)** *(bedeutungslos)* lacking in substance *postpos.*; **~verlagerung die** shift *or* transfer of weight; *(fig.)* shift in *or* of emphasis; **~verlust der** loss of weight; **~zunahme die** increase in weight

Gewichtung die; ~, ~en evaluation

gewieft [gəˈviːft] *Adj. (ugs.)* cunning; wily

gewiegt 1. *2. Part. v.* **²wiegen. 2.** *Adj. s.* **gewieft**

Gewieher [gəˈviːɐ] **das; ~s a)** *(Wiehern)* neighing; **b)** *(salopp: Gelächter)* guffawing; braying laughter

gewiesen *2. Part. v.* **weisen**

gewillt [gəˈvɪlt] *Adj. in* **~/nicht ~ sein, etw. zu tun** be willing/unwilling to do sth.

Gewimmel das; ~s throng; milling crowd; *(von Insekten)* teeming mass

Gewimmer das; ~s whimpering

Gewinde das; ~s, ~ a) *(Technik)* thread; **b)** *(veralt.: Girlande)* garland

Gewinde-: ~bohrer der [screw] tap; **~gang der** turn [of a thread]; **~schneiden das; ~s** thread-cutting; *(innen)* tapping; **~stift der** grub-screw

Gewinn [gəˈvɪn] **der; ~[e]s, ~e a)** *(Reinertrag)* profit; **aus etw. ~ schlagen** *od.* **ziehen** make a profit out of sth.; **mit ~ wirtschaften** operate at a profit *or* profitably; **etw. mit ~ verkaufen** sell sth. at a profit; **b)** *(Preis einer Lotterie)* prize; *(beim Wetten, Kartenspiel usw.)* winnings *pl.*; **die ~e auslosen** draw the winners *or* winning numbers; **jedes zweite Los ist ein ~:** every other ticket is a winner; **c)** *(Nutzen)* gain; profit; **das war ein großer ~ für uns** we gained a great deal *or* profited greatly from it; **der neue Spieler ist ein [großer] ~ für unsere Mannschaft** the new player is a valuable addition to our team; **d)** *(Sieg)* win; **auf ~ stehen** *(Schach)* be in a winning position

gewinn-, Gewinn-: ~anteil der *(Wirtsch.)* share of the profits; **~beteiligung die** *(Wirtsch.)* profit-sharing; *(Betrag)* profit-sharing bonus; **gegen ~beteiligung** in return for a share of the profits; **~bringend** *Adj.* **a)** profitable; lucrative; **b)** *(nutzbringend)* profitable; valuable ⟨*knowledge, information*⟩; **~chance die** chance of winning

gewinnen [gəˈvɪnən] **1.** *unr. tr. V.* **a)** *(siegen in)* win ⟨*contest, race, etc.*⟩; **es [nicht] über sich ~, etw. zu tun** *(geh. veralt.)* [not] bring oneself to do sth.; *s. auch* **Spiel b; b)** *(erringen, erreichen, erhalten)* gain, win ⟨*respect, sympathy, etc.*⟩; gain ⟨*time, lead, influence, validity, confidence*⟩; win ⟨*prize*⟩; **Klarheit über etw.** *(Akk.)* **~:** become clear in one's mind about sth.; **wie gewonnen, so zerronnen** *(Spr.)* easy come, easy go; *s. auch* **Abstand c; Oberhand; c)** *(Unterstützung erlangen)* **jmdn. für etw. ~:** win sb. over [to sth.]; **jmdn. als Kunden/Freund ~:** win sb. as a customer/friend; **d)** *(abbauen, fördern)* mine, extract ⟨*coal, ore, metal*⟩; recover ⟨*oil*⟩; **e)** *(erzeugen)* produce **(aus** from); *(durch Recycling)* reclaim; recover. **2.** *unr. itr. V.* **a)** win **(bei** at); **in der Lotterie ~:** win [a prize] in the lottery; **jedes zweite Los gewinnt!** every other ticket [is] a winner!; **b)** *(sich vorteilhaft verändern)* improve; **c)** *(zunehmen)* **an Höhe/Fahrt ~:** gain height/gain *or* pick up speed; **an Bedeutung ~:** gain in importance

gewinnend 1. *Adj.* winning, engaging, winsome ⟨*manner, smile, way*⟩; charming ⟨*manners*⟩. **2.** *adv.* ⟨*smile*⟩ winningly, engagingly, winsomely

Gewinner der; ~s, ~ , Gewinnerin die; ~, ~nen winner

Gewinner·straße die *(Sport, Jargon)* **auf der ~straße sein** be set *or* heading for victory

gewinn-, Gewinn-: ~los das winning ticket; **~nummer die** *s.* **Gewinnummer; ~quote die** share of prize money; **~satz der** *(Sport)* **über fünf ~sätze spielen** *(Tennis)* play the best of five sets; *(Tischtennis)* play the best of five games; **der fünfte Satz war ihr ~satz** *(Tennis)* she won in the fifth set; *(Tischtennis)* she won in the fifth game; **~spanne die** profit margin; **~streben das** pursuit of profit; **~sucht die;** *o. Pl.* greed for profit; **~süchtig** *Adj.* greedy for profits *pred.*; **in ~süchtiger Absicht** *(Rechtsspr.)* with the intention of making unreasonably high profits; **~trächtig** *Adj.* profitable; lucrative

Gewinnummer die winning number

Gewinn-und-Verlust-Rechnung die *(Wirtsch.)* profit and loss account

Gewinnung die; ~ a) *(von Kohle, Erz usw.)* mining; extraction; *(von Öl)* recovery; *(von Metall aus Erz)* extraction; **b)** *(Erzeugung)* production

Gewinn·zahl die winning number

Gewinsel das; ~s *(abwertend)* **a)** whimpering; whining; **b)** *(das Klagen, Bitten)* whining

Gewirr das; ~[e]s a) *(wirres Knäuel)* tangle; **b)** *(Durcheinander)* **ein ~ von Ästen** a maze of branches; **ein ~ von Paragraphen** a maze *or* jungle of regulations; **ein ~ von Stimmen** a [confused] babble of voices

Gewisper das; ~s whispering

gewiß [gəˈvɪs] **1.** *Adj.* **a)** *nicht präd. (nicht sehr viel/groß)* certain; **in gewisser Beziehung** in some respects; **eine gewisse Ähnlichkeit/Distanz** a certain resemblance/distance; *s. auch* **Etwas; ¹Maß d; b)** *(sicher)* certain (+ *Gen.* of); **etw. ist jmdm. ~:** sb. is certain *or* sure of sth.; **wir können seiner Hilfe ~ sein** we can be certain *or* sure of his help; we can count on his help; **man weiß nichts Gewisses** nothing certain *or* definite is known. **2.** *adv.* certainly; **ja** *od.* **aber ~ [doch]!** but of course!; **du hast ~ nichts dagegen, wenn ...:** I'm sure you won't mind if ...; **ich weiß es ganz ~:** I'm sure *or* certain of it

Gewissen das; ~s, ~: conscience; **ein gutes/schlechtes ~:** a clean/guilty *or* bad conscience; **ruhigen ~s etw. tun** do sth. with a clear conscience; **mit gutem ~:** with a clear conscience; **ein gutes ~ ist ein sanftes Ruhekissen** *(Spr.)* one can sleep more easily with a clear conscience; **sich** *(Dat.)* **kein ~ daraus machen, etw. zu tun** have no scruples *or* qualms about doing sth.; **etw./jmdn. auf dem ~ haben** have sth./sb. on one's conscience; **jmdm. ins ~ reden [, etw. zu tun]** have a serious talk with sb. [and persuade him/her to do sth.]; *s. auch* **Wissen**

gewissenhaft 1. *Adj.* conscientious. **2.** *adv.* conscientiously

Gewissenhaftigkeit die; ~: conscientiousness

gewissen·los 1. *Adj.* conscienceless; unscrupulous; **er ist vollkommen ~:** he is completely without conscience. **2.** *adv.* **~ handeln** act with a complete lack of conscience

Gewissenlosigkeit die; ~ a) *(gewissenloses Wesen)* lack of conscience; **b)** *(gewissenloses Handeln)* unscrupulous act; **wie konntest du eine solche ~ begehen?** how could you show such a lack of conscience?

Gewissens-: ~bisse *Pl.* pangs of conscience; **sich** *(Dat.)* **~bisse über etw.** *(Akk.)* **machen** have a guilty conscience about sth.; **~entscheidung die** decision on a matter of conscience; **~frage die** question *or* matter of conscience; matter for one's conscience; **~freiheit die;** *o. Pl.* freedom of conscience; **~gründe** *Pl.* reasons of conscience; **aus ~gründen** for reasons of conscience; **~konflikt der** moral conflict; **~not die** moral dilemma; **~qual die: ~qual[en]** agonies *pl.* of conscience

gewissermaßen *Adv. (sozusagen)* as it were; *(in gewissem Sinne)* to a certain extent

Gewißheit die; ~, ~en certainty; **wir haben noch keine ~, ob ...:** we still do not know for certain whether ...; **sich** *(Dat.)* **~ verschaffen** find out for certain; **zur ~ werden** turn into certainty

gewißlich *Adv. (veralt.) s.* **gewiß 2**

Gewitter [gəˈvɪtɐ] **das; ~s, ~:** thunderstorm; *(fig.)* storm

Gewitter·front die storm front

gewitterig *Adj. s.* **gewittrig**

gewittern *itr. V. (unpers.)* **es gewitterte/wird bald ~:** there was/will soon be thunder and lightning

Gewitter-: ~neigung die; *o. Pl.* likelihood of thunderstorms; **~regen der, ~schauer der** thundery shower; **~sturm der** thunderstorm; **~wolke die** thundercloud

gewittrig [gəˈvɪtrɪç] *Adj.* thundery; **~e Schwüle** sultry heat

gewitzigt [gəˈvɪt͜sɪçt] *Adj.* **a)** *(klüger geworden)* wiser; **durch Erfahrung/Schaden ~ sein** have learnt from experience/one's mistakes; **b)** *s.* **gewitzt**

gewitzt [gəˈvɪt͜st] *Adj.* shrewd; **ein ~er Junge** a smart lad

gewoben [gəˈvoːbn̩] *2. Part. v.* **weben**

Gewoge das; ~s *(von einem Kornfeld usw.)* waving; *(von Gedanken)* surge; **das ~ der Menschenmenge** the surging back and forth of the crowd

gewogen 1. *2. Part. v.* **wiegen. 2.** *Adj. (geh.)* well disposed, favourably inclined (+ *Dat.* towards)

Gewogenheit die; ~ *(geh.)* favourable attitude; **bei aller ~, die ich Ihnen entgegenbringe, kann ich nicht ...:** although I'm favourably disposed towards you, I can't ...

gewöhnen [gəˈvøːnən] **1.** *tr. V.* **jmdn. an jmdn./etw. ~:** get sb. used *or* accustomed to sb./sth.; accustom sb. to sb./sth.; **Kinder an Sauberkeit ~:** get children used to being clean and tidy; **an jmdn./etw. gewöhnt sein** be used *or* accustomed to sb./sth.. **2.** *refl. V.* **sich an jmdn./etw. ~:** get used *or* get *or* become accustomed to sb./sth.; accustom oneself to sb./sth.; **sich daran ~ müssen, daß ...:** have to get used to the fact that ...

Gewohnheit [gəˈvoːnhait] **die;** ~, ~**en** habit; **die ~ haben, etw. zu tun** be in the habit of doing sth.; **das ist ihm zur ~ geworden** this has become a habit with him; **sich** *(Dat.)* **etw. zur ~ machen** make a habit of sth.; **nach alter ~:** from long-established habit; **etw. aus ~ tun** do sth. out of habit *or* from force of habit; **die Macht der ~:** the force of habit

gewohnheits-, Gewohnheits-: ~gemäß *Adv.* as is/was his/her *etc.* custom; **~mäßig 1.** *Adj.* habitual ⟨*drinker etc.*⟩; automatic ⟨*reaction etc.*⟩; **2.** *adv.* **a)** *(regelmäßig)* habitually; **b)** *(einer Gewohnheit folgend)* as is/was my/his *etc.* habit; **~mensch der** creature of habit; **~recht das** *(Rechtsw.)* **a)** *o. Pl. (System)* common law; **b)** *(einzelnes Recht)* established right; **~sache die** matter *or* question of habit; **~tier das** *(scherzh.)* creature of habit; **der Mensch ist ein ~tier** man is a creature of habit; **~trinker der** habitual drinker; **~verbrecher der** *(Rechtsw.)* habitual criminal

gewöhnlich [gəˈvøːnlɪç] **1.** *Adj.* **a)** *nicht präd. (alltäglich)* normal; ordinary; **im ~en Leben** in ordinary *or* everyday life; **ein ~er Sterblicher** an ordinary mortal; **b)** *nicht präd. (gewohnt, üblich)* usual; normal; customary; **c)** *(abwertend: ordinär)* common. **2.** *adv.* **a) [für] ~:** usually; normally; **wie ~:** as usual; **b)** *(abwertend: ordinär)* in a common way

Gewöhnlichkeit die; ~ *(abwertend)* commonness

gewohnt 1. *2. Part. v.* **wohnen. 2.** *Adj.* **a)** *nicht präd. (vertraut)* usual; **zur ~en Zeit/Stunde** at the usual *or* normal *or* customary time; **in ~er** *od.* **auf ~e Weise** in the/one's usual manner *or* way; **b) etw.** *(Akk.)* **~ sein** be used *or* accustomed to sth.; **es ~ sein, etw. zu tun** be used *or* accustomed to doing sth.

gewohntermaßen *Adv.* as usual

Gewöhnung die; ~ **a)** habituation **(an** + *Akk.* to); **b)** *(Sucht)* habit; addiction

Gewölbe [gəˈvœlbə] **das;** ~**s,** ~**:** vault; **das blaue ~ des Himmels** *(fig.)* the blue vault of the sky; **das ~ der Burg** the vaults *pl.* of the castle

Gewölk [gəˈvœlk] **das;** ~**[e]s** clouds *pl.*

gewonnen [gəˈvɔnən] *2. Part. v.* **gewinnen**

geworben [gəˈvɔrbn̩] *2. Part. v.* **werben**

geworfen [gəˈvɔrfn̩] *2. Part. v.* **werfen**

gewrungen [gəˈvrʊŋən] *2. Part. v.* **wringen**

Gewühl das; ~**[e]s a)** milling crowd; **das ~ der Menschenmassen** the milling crowd [of people]; **b)** *(das Wühlen)* rooting about

gewunden *2. Part. v.* **winden**

gewunken [gəˈvʊŋkn̩] *2. Part. v.* **winken**

gewürfelt 1. *2. Part. v.* **würfeln. 2.** *Adj. (kariert)* check; checked

Gewürm [gəˈvʏrm] **das;** ~**[e]s,** ~**e** *(oft abwertend)* worms *pl.*; *(fig. geh.)* swarm of diminutive creatures

Gewürz das; ~**es,** ~**e** spice; *(würzende Zutat)* seasoning; condiment; *(Kraut)* herb; **verschiedene ~e** various herbs *or* spices

Gewürz-: ~essig der *s.* **Kräuteressig; ~gurke die** pickled gherkin; **~mischung die** mixed spices *pl.*/herbs *pl.*; **~nelke die** clove; **~traminer der** Gewürztraminer

Gewusel [gəˈvuːzl̩] **das;** ~**s** *(landsch.) s.* **Gewimmel**

gewußt *2. Part. v.* **wissen**

Geysir [ˈgaizɪr] **der;** ~**s,** ~**e** geyser

gez. *Abk.* **gezeichnet** sgd.

gezähnt [gəˈtsɛːnt] *Adj. (Bot.)* dentate

Gezänk [gəˈtsɛŋk] **das;** ~**[e]s, Gezanke** [gəˈtsaŋkə] **das;** ~**s** *(abwertend)* quarrelling

Gezappel das; ~**s** *(ugs., oft abwertend)* wriggling

Gezeiten *Pl.* tides

Gezeiten-: ~kraft·werk das tidal power-station; **~strom der** tidal current; **~tafel die** tide table

Gezeter das; ~**s** *(abwertend)* scolding; nagging

Geziefer [gəˈtsiːfɐ] **das;** ~**s** *(veralt.) s.* **Ungeziefer**

geziehen [gəˈtsiːən] *2. Part. v.* **zeihen**

gezielt 1. *2. Part. v.* **zielen. 2.** *Adj.* specific ⟨*questions, measures, etc.*⟩; deliberate ⟨*insult, indiscretion*⟩; well-directed ⟨*advertising campaign*⟩. **3.** *adv.* ⟨*proceed, act*⟩ purposefully, in a purposeful manner; **~ nach etw. forschen** search specifically for sth.

geziemen *(geh. veralt.)* **1.** *itr. V.* **jmdm. [nicht] ~:** [ill] befit sb. **2.** *refl. V.* be proper *or* right; **sich für jmdn. ~:** befit sb.; **es geziemt sich nicht, so mit deiner Mutter zu reden** it isn't proper *or* right for you to talk to your mother like that

geziemend *(geh.)* **1.** *Adj.* fitting; proper, due ⟨*respect*⟩; **in ~er Weise** in a proper manner; **mit ~en Worten** with a few fitting remarks; **mit der ihr ~en Bescheidenheit** with fitting modesty. **2.** *adv.* in a fitting manner

geziert 1. *2. Part. v.* **zieren. 2.** *Adj. (abwertend)* affected. **3.** *adv. (abwertend)* affectedly

Geziertheit die; ~ *(abwertend)* affectedness

Gezirp[e] das; ~**s** *(oft abwertend)* chirping; chirruping

gezogen [gəˈtsoːgn̩] *2. Part. v.* **ziehen**

Gezücht das; ~**[e]s,** ~**e** *(geh. abwertend)* riff-raff *pl.*; rabble

Gezüngel [gəˈtsʏŋl̩] **das;** ~**s: das ~ der Schlange/Schlangen** the flicking *or* darting of the snake's tongue/snakes' tongues; **das ~ der Flammen** *(fig.)* the flickering of the flames

Gezweig das; ~**[e]s** *(geh.)* branches *pl.*

Gezwitscher das; ~**s** twittering; chirping; chirruping

gezwungen [gəˈtsvʊŋən] **1.** *2. Part. v.* **zwingen. 2.** *Adj.* forced ⟨*laugh, smile, etc.*⟩; stiff ⟨*behaviour*⟩. **3.** *adv.* ⟨*laugh*⟩ in a forced way *or* manner; ⟨*behave*⟩ stiffly

gezwungenermaßen *Adv.* of necessity; **etw. ~ machen** be forced to do sth.

GG *Abk.* **Grundgesetz**

ggf. *Abk.* **gegebenenfalls**

Ghana [ˈgaːna] **(das);** ~**s** Ghana

Ghanaer der; ~**s,** ~**:** Ghanaian

Ghetto *s.* **Getto**

Ghostwriter [ˈgoʊstraitə] **der;** ~**s,** ~**:** ghost-writer; **von ~n geschrieben werden** be ghosted

gib [giːp] *Imperativ Sg. Präsens v.* **geben**

Gibbon [ˈgɪbɔn] **der;** ~**s,** ~**s** *(Zool.)* gibbon

gibst [giːpst] *2. Pers. Sg. Präsens v.* **geben**

gibt [giːpt] *3. Pers. Sg. Präsens v.* **geben**

[1]**Gicht** [gɪçt] **die;** ~, ~**en** *(Metall.)* **a)** *(Öffnung)* throat [of the/a furnace]; **b)** *(Oberteil des Hochofens)* top [of the/a furnace]; **c)** *(Menge)* charge

[2]**Gicht die;** ~**:** gout

gicht·brüchig *Adj. (veralt.)* gouty; **die Gichtbrüchigen** *(bibl.)* those that had the palsy

gichtig, gichtisch *Adj.* gouty

Gicht·knoten der gouty concretion

gicht·krank *Adj.* gouty

gicksen [ˈgɪksn̩] *(bes. md.)* **1.** *itr. V. (einen Schrei ausstoßen)* squeak. **2.** *tr. V. (stechen, stoßen)* **jmdn. ~:** jab sb.; **jmdn.** *od.* **jmdm. in die Seite ~:** jab sb. in the side

Giebel [ˈgiːbl̩] **der;** ~**s,** ~ **a)** gable; **b)** *(von Portalen)* pediment

Giebel-: ~dach das gable roof; **~feld das** *(Archit.)* tympanum; **~fenster das** gable-window; **~seite die** gable end; **~wand die** gable wall

Gier [giːɐ̯] **die;** ~ **a)** greed **(nach** for); **mit solcher ~:** so greedily; **~ nach Macht/Ruhm** lust *or* craving for power/craving for fame; **~ nach Zigaretten** greedy desire for cigarettes; **~ nach Leben** passionate desire for life; **b)** *(Lüsternheit)* lust

[1]**gieren** *itr. V. (geh.)* **nach etw. ~:** crave for sth.; **nach Macht/Rache ~:** lust for power/revenge

[2]**gieren** *itr. V. (Seemannsspr.)* yaw

gierig 1. *Adj.* greedy; avid ⟨*reader, desire*⟩; **nach etw. ~ sein** be greedy for sth. **2.** *adv.* greedily

Gieß·bach der [mountain] torrent; *(nach starkem Regen)* swollen [mountain] stream

gießen [ˈgiːsn̩] **1.** *unr. tr. V.* **a)** *(rinnen lassen/schütten)* pour **(in** + *Akk.* into, **über** + *Akk.* over); **b)** *(verschütten)* spill **(über** + *Akk.* over); **c)** *(begießen)* water ⟨*plants, flowers, garden*⟩; **d)** cast ⟨*machine part, statue, candles, etc.*⟩; cast, found ⟨*metal*⟩; found ⟨*glass*⟩; **Blei zu Kugeln ~:** cast lead into bullets. **2. a)** *unr. itr. V.* **ich muß im Garten noch ~:** I still have to water the garden; **b)** *(unpers., ugs.)* pour [with rain]; **es gießt in Strömen** it is coming down in buckets; it's raining cats and dogs

Gießer der; ~**s,** ~**:** caster; founder

Gießerei die; ~, ~**en a)** *(Betrieb)* foundry; **b)** *o. Pl. (Zweig der Metallindustrie)* casting; founding

Gieß-: ~form die *(Gießerei)* [casting-]mould; **~grube die** *(Gießerei)* casting-pit; **~harz das** *(Technik)* cast resin; **~kanne die** watering-can

Gießkannen·prinzip das; *o. Pl. (scherzh.)* principle of 'equal shares for all'

Gieß-: ~kelle die *(Gießerei)* casting ladle; **~pfanne die** *(Gießerei)* pouring *or* teeming ladle

Gift [gɪft] **das;** ~**[e]s,** ~**e a)** poison; *(Schlangen~)* venom; **jmdm. ~ [ein]geben** poison sb.; **~ [aus]legen** put poison down; **b)** *(fig.)* **~ für jmdn./etw. sein** be extremely bad for sb./sth.; **sein ~ verspritzen** *(ugs.)* spit venom *(fig.)*; **~ und Galle speien** *od.* **spucken** *(sehr wütend sein)* be in a terrible rage; *(gehässig reagieren)* give vent to one's spleen; **du kannst ~ darauf nehmen** *(ugs.)* you can bet your life on it; *s. auch* **blond**

Gift-: ~becher der *(hist.)* cup of poison; **~drüse die** *(Zool.)* poison gland

giften *(ugs.)* **1.** *tr. V. (böse machen)* rile *(coll.)*; infuriate. **2.** *refl. V. (sich ärgern)* be furious. **3.** *itr. V. (gehässig reden)* **gegen jmdn./etw. ~:** be nasty about sb./sth.

gift-, Gift-: ~frei *Adj.* non-toxic; non-poisonous; **~gas das** poison gas; **~grün** *Adj.* garish green

giftig *Adj.* **1. a)** poisonous; venomous, poisonous ⟨*snake*⟩; toxic, poisonous ⟨*substance, gas, chemical*⟩; **b)** *(ugs.: bösartig)* venomous, spiteful ⟨*remark, person, words, etc.*⟩; venomous ⟨*look*⟩; **~ werden** turn nasty; **c)** *(grell, schreiend)* garish, loud ⟨*colour*⟩. **2.** *adv.* venomously

Gift-: ~küche die *(scherzh.)* chemical laboratory *(with its unpleasant products)*; **~mischer der a)** *(ugs. abwertend)* maker of poisons; **b)** *(ugs. scherzh.: Apotheker)* chemist; **~mord der** [murder by] poisoning; **~mörder der** poisoner; **~müll der**

toxic waste; ~**müll·deponie die** toxic [waste] tip *or* dump; ~**pfeil der** poisoned arrow; ~**pflanze die** poisonous plant; ~**pilz der** poisonous mushroom; [poisonous] toadstool; ~**schlange die** poisonous *or* venomous snake; ~**schrank der** poison cabinet *or* cupboard; ~**spinne die** poisonous spider; ~**stachel der** poisonous sting; ~**stoff der** poisonous *or* toxic substance; ~**trank der** *(geh.)* poisoned drink; ~**zahn der** poison fang; ~**zwerg der** *(ugs. abwertend)* [nasty] spiteful little man

Giga- [giga-] giga‹*hertz etc.*›

Gigant [gi'gant] **der; ~en, ~en a)** *(geh.: Riese)* giant; **b)** *(sehr beeindruckende Sache, Person)* giant; titan; **~en der Landstraße/des Meeres** *(fig.)* juggernauts of the road/leviathans of the ocean

gigạntisch *Adj.* gigantic; huge ‹*success*›

Gigantomanie [gigantoma'ni:] **die;** ~ *(geh.)* craze for the huge and spectacular

Gigerl ['gi:gɐl] **der** *od.* **das; ~s, ~n** *(südd., österr. ugs.)* dandy; fop

Gigolo ['ʒi:golo] **der; ~s, ~s** gigolo

Gilde ['gɪldə] **die; ~, ~n a)** *(hist.)* guild; **b)** *(Interessengruppe)* fraternity

gilt [gɪlt] *3. Pers. Sg. Präsens v.* **gelten**

Gimpel ['gɪmpl̩] **der; ~s, ~ a)** *(Vogel)* bullfinch; **b)** *(ugs. abwertend: einfältiger Mensch)* ninny; simpleton

Gin [dʒɪn] **der; ~s,** *(Sorten:)* **~s** gin

Gin-Fizz ['dʒɪnfɪs] **der; ~, ~:** gin-fizz

ging [gɪŋ] *1. u. 3. Pers. Sg. Prät. v.* **gehen**

Ginseng ['gɪnzɛŋ] **der; ~s, ~s** ginseng

Ginster ['gɪnstɐ] **der; ~s, ~:** broom; *(Stech~)* gorse; furze

Gipfel ['gɪpfl̩] **der; ~s, ~ a)** peak; *(höchster Punkt des Berges)* summit; **den ~ besteigen/bezwingen** climb the peak/conquer the peak *or* summit; **b)** *(Höhepunkt)* height; *(von Begeisterung, Glück, Ruhm, Macht auch)* peak; **auf dem ~ der Macht/des Ruhmes** at the height of one's power/fame; **der ~ der Geschmacklosigkeit/Dummheit** *(ugs.)* the height of bad taste/stupidity; **das ist [doch] der ~!** *(ugs.)* that's the limit!; **c)** *(veralt.: Wipfel)* top; **d)** *(~konferenz)* summit

Gịpfel-: ~**gespräch das** summit talks *pl.;* ~**konferenz die** summit conference; ~**kreuz das** cross on the summit of a/the mountain

gịpfeln *itr. V.* **in etw.** *(Dat.)* **~:** culminate in sth.

Gịpfel·punkt der highest point; top; *(fig.)* high point; **der ~ seines künstlerischen Schaffens** the peak of his artistic powers

Gips [gɪps] **der; ~es,** *(Sorten:)* **~e** plaster; gypsum *(Chem.)*; *(zum Modellieren)* plaster of Paris; **einen Arm in ~ legen** put an arm in plaster; **drei Monate im ~ liegen** be laid up in plaster for three months

Gịps-: ~**abdruck der,** ~**abguß der** plaster cast; ~**bein das** *(ugs.)* **ich komme mit meinem ~bein nicht mit** I can't keep up, with this plaster on my leg; **durch ein ~bein behindert werden** be hindered by having one's leg in plaster

gịpsen *tr. V.* **a)** plaster ‹*wall, ceiling*›; put ‹*leg, arm, etc.*› in plaster; **b)** *(ausbessern)* repair with plaster

Gịpser der; ~s, ~: plasterer

Gịps-: ~**figur die** plaster [of Paris] figure; ~**korsett das** *(Med.)* plaster jacket; ~**modell das** plaster model; ~**verband der** plaster cast

Giraffe [gi'rafə] **die; ~, ~n** giraffe

Girant [ʒi'rant] **der; ~en, ~en** *(Finanzw.)* endorser

girieren [ʒi'ri:rən] *tr. V. (Finanzw.)* endorse

Girl [gø:ɐ̯l] **das; ~s, ~s a)** *(ugs., oft scherzh.: Mädchen)* girl; **b)** *(Tänzerin)* chorus-girl

Girlande [gɪr'landə] **die; ~, ~n** festoon

Giro ['ʒi:ro] **das; ~s, ~s,** *österr. auch* **Giri** *(Finanzw.)* **a)** *(Überweisung)* giro; **b)** *(Vermerk)* endorsement

Gịro-: ~**bank die** *(Finanzw.)* clearing bank; ~**konto das** *(Finanzw.)* current account

girren ['gɪrən] *itr. V. (auch fig.)* coo

Gis, gis [gɪs] **das; ~, ~** *(Musik)* G sharp

Gischt [gɪʃt] **der; ~[e]s, ~e** *od.* **die; ~, ~en a)** *(Schaumkronen)* foam; surf; **b)** *(Sprühwasser)* spray

gịschten *itr. V. (geh.)* spray up

Gịs-Dur [*auch:* '-'-] **das; ~** *(Musik)* G sharp major; *s. auch* **A-Dur**

gịs-Moll [*auch:* '-'-] **das; ~** *(Musik)* G sharp minor; *s. auch* **a-Moll**

Gitarre [gi'tarə] **die; ~, ~n** guitar

Gitạrren·spieler der guitar player; guitarist

Gitarrịst der; ~en, ~en guitarist

Gitter ['gɪtɐ] **das; ~s, ~ a)** *(parallele Stäbe)* bars *pl.*; *(Drahtgeflecht vor Fenster-, Türöffnungen)* grille; *(in der Straßendecke, im Fußboden)* grating; *(Geländer)* railing[s *pl.*]; *(Spalier)* trellis; *(feines Draht~)* mesh; *(Kamin~)* [fire-]guard; **hinter ~n** *(ugs.)* behind bars; **b)** *(Physik, Chemie)* lattice; **c)** *(Math., Elektronik, auf Landkarten)* grid

Gịtter-: ~**bett das** cot; ~**fenster das** barred window; ~**mast der** *(Technik)* pylon; lattice tower; ~**netz das** *(Kartographie)* grid; ~**rost der** grating; ~**stab der** bar; ~**struktur die** *(Physik)* lattice structure; ~**tor das** iron-barred gate; ~**werk das;** *o. Pl.* ironwork; *(kunstvoller)* wrought-iron work; ~**zaun der** railing[s *pl.*]; *(mit gekreuzten Stäben)* lattice[-work] fence

Glace ['glasə] **die; ~, ~n** *(schweiz.)* ice cream

Glacé- [gla'se:]: ~**hand·schuh der** kid glove; **jmdn./etw. mit ~handschuhen anfassen** *(ugs.)* handle sb./sth. with kid gloves; ~**leder das** glacé leather

glacieren [gla'si:rən] *tr. V. (Kochk.)* glaze

Glacis [gla'si:] **das; ~, ~** *(Milit.)* glacis

Gladiator [gla'di̯a:tɔr] **der; ~s, ~en** [-'to:rən] gladiator

Gladiole [gla'di̯o:lə] **die; ~, ~n** gladiolus

Glamour ['glæmə] **der** *od.* **das; ~s** glamour

Glạmour·girl das glamour girl

Glanz [glants] **der; ~es a)** *(von Licht, Sternen)* brightness; brilliance; *(von Haar, Metall, Perlen, Leder usw.)* shine; lustre; sheen; *(von Augen)* shine; brightness; lustre; **den ~ verlieren** ‹*diamonds, eyes*› lose their sparkle; ‹*metal, leather*› lose its shine; **etw. auf ~ polieren** polish sth. till it shines; **welch ~ in meiner Hütte!** *(scherzh. iron.)* to what do I owe the honour of this visit? *(iron.)*; **b)** *(der Jugend, Schönheit)* radiance; *(des Adels usw.)* splendour; **zu neuem ~ kommen** acquire new splendour; **mit ~** *(ugs.)* with flying colours; **mit ~ und Gloria** *(ugs. iron.)* in grand style

Glạnz·abzug der *(Fot.)* glossy print

glänzen ['glɛntsn̩] *itr. V.* **a)** *(Glanz ausstrahlen)* shine; ‹*car, hair, metal, paintwork, etc.*› gleam; ‹*elbows, trousers, etc.*› be shiny; **vor Sauberkeit ~:** be so clean [that] it shines; **sein Gesicht glänzte vor Freude** his face shone with joy *or* pleasure; **b)** *(Bewunderung erregen)* shine **(bei** at); **durch Wissen/Können ~:** be outstanding for one's knowledge/ability; **in einer Rolle ~:** shine in a role; **durch Abwesenheit ~** *(iron.)* be conspicuous by one's absence

glạ̈nzend *(ugs.)* **1.** *Adj.* **a)** shining; gleaming ‹*car, hair, metal, paintwork, etc.*›; shiny ‹*elbows, trousers, etc.*›; **b)** *(bewundernswert)* brilliant ‹*idea, career, victory, pupil, prospects, etc.*›; splendid, excellent, outstanding ‹*references, marks, results, etc.*›; **in ~er Laune/Form sein** be in a splendid mood/in splendid form. **2.** *adv.* **~ mit jmdm. auskommen** get on very well with sb.; **es geht mir/uns ~:** I am/we are very well; *(finanziell)* I am/we are doing very well *or* very nicely; **eine Aufgabe ~ lösen** solve a problem brilliantly

glạnz-, Glạnz-: ~**kohle die** glance coal; ~**leistung die** *(auch iron.)* brilliant performance; ~**licht das** *(bild. Kunst)* highlight; **einer Sache** *(Dat.)* **[noch einige] ~lichter aufsetzen** give sth. [more] sparkle; ~**los** *Adj.* dull; lacklustre; ~**nummer die** star turn; **diese Rezitation ist seine ~nummer** this recitation is his pièce de résistance; ~**papier das** glossy paper; ~**parade die** *(Sport)* superb *or* outstanding save; ~**politur die** high-gloss polish; ~**punkt der** high spot; highlight; ~**rolle die** star role; ~**stück das a)** *(Meisterwerk)* pièce de résistance; **b)** *(der kostbarste Gegenstand)* show-piece; ~**voll 1.** *Adj.* **a)** *(ausgezeichnet)* brilliant; sparkling ‹*variety number*›; **b)** *(prachtvoll)* magnificent; **2.** *adv.* **a)** *(ausgezeichnet)* brilliantly; **eine Prüfung ~voll bestehen** pass an examination with flying colours; do brilliantly in an examination; **b)** *(prachtvoll)* **Louis XIV pflegte ~voll Hof zu halten** Louis XIV used to hold court in glittering style; ~**zeit die** heyday; **ihre ~zeit ist vorüber** she's had her day

[1]**Glas** ['gla:s] **das; ~es, Gläser** ['glɛ:zɐ] **a)** *o. Pl.* glass; **unter ~:** behind glass; ‹*plants*› under glass; **„Vorsicht, ~!"** 'glass – handle with care'; **du bist nicht aus ~** *(ugs.)* you make a better door than you do window *(coll.)*; **b)** *(Trinkgefäß)* glass; **zwei ~** *od.* **Gläser Wein/Bier** two glasses of wine/beer; **ein ~ über den Durst trinken** *(ugs. scherzh.)*, **zu tief ins ~ gucken** *(ugs. scherzh.)* have one too many *or* one over the eight; **c)** *(Behälter aus ~)* jar; **ein ~ Marmelade/Honig** a jar of jam/honey; **d)** *(geh.: Brillen~)* lens; **Gläser** *(veralt.: Brille)* spectacles; glasses; **e)** *(Fern~)* binoculars *pl.*; [field-]glasses *pl.*; *(Opern~)* opera-glasses *pl.*

[2]**Glas das; ~es, ~en** *(Seemannsspr.)* bell; **es schlug acht ~en** it struck eight bells

glas-, Glas-: ~**artig** *Adj.* vitreous; glassy; ~**auge das** glass eye; ~**ballon der** carboy; ~**baustein der** glass brick *or* block; ~**bläser der** glass-blower; ~**bläserei** [~blɛ:zə'rai] **die; ~, ~en a)** *o. Pl.* glass-blowing; **b)** *(Betrieb)* glass-blowing works *sing. or pl.*

Gläschen ['glɛ:sçən] **das; ~s, ~ a)** *(kleines Trinkglas)* [little] glass; **b)** *(kleines Gefäß aus Glas)* [little] [glass] jar

Glas·dach das glass roof

Glaser der; ~s, ~: glazier

Glaserei die; ~, ~en a) *(Betrieb)* glazing business; *(Werkstatt)* glazier's workshop; **b)** *o. Pl.* glazier's trade

gläsern ['glɛ:zɐn] *Adj.* **a)** *nicht präd. (aus Glas)* glass; **ein ~er Abgeordneter** *(fig.)* a member of parliament who has no secrets; **b)** *(dichter.: wie Glas)* glassy

glas-, Glas-: ~**fabrik die** glassworks *sing. or pl.*; ~**faser die;** *meist Pl.* glass fibre; ~**fenster das** [glass] window; **bemalte ~fenster** stained glass windows; ~**fiber die** *s.* ~**faser;** ~**fiber·stab der** *(Leichtathletik)* glass-fibre pole; ~**flasche die** glass bottle; ~**flügler der; ~s, ~** *(Zool.)* clearwing; ~**fluß der** paste; ~**geschirr das** glassware; ~**hart 1.** *Adj.* **a)** ['--] *(hart)* solid ‹*ice*›; rigid ‹*plastic*›; *(spröde)* brittle; **b)** ['-'-] *(Sport)* cracking ‹*shot*›; solid ‹*punch*›; **2.** *adv.* **a)** ~**hart gefroren** frozen hard; **b)** *(Sport)* **seine Rechte ~hart schlagen** have a solid right; ~**haus das** greenhouse; glasshouse; **wer [selbst] im ~haus sitzt, soll nicht mit Steinen werfen** *(Spr.)* those who live in glass houses shouldn't throw stones *(prov.)*; ~**hütte die** glassworks *sing. or pl.*

glasieren *tr. V.* **a)** *(glätten und haltbar machen)* glaze; **b)** *(Kochk.)* ice ‹*cake etc.*›; glaze ‹*meat*›

glasig *Adj.* **a)** *(starr)* glassy ‹*stare, eyes, etc.*›; **b)** *(Kochk.: durchsichtig)* transparent

glas-, Glas-: ~**kasten der a)** glass case; *(kleiner)* glass box; **b)** *(ugs.: Raum)* glass box; ~**keramik die** devitrified glass;

~**kinn das** *(Sportjargon)* vulnerable chin; ~**klar** *Adj. (auch fig.)* crystal clear; ~**kolben der** glass flask; *(einer Glühbirne)* glass bulb; ~**körper der** *(Anat.)* vitreous body; ~**kugel die** glass ball; *(einer Wahrsagerin)* crystal ball; *(Murmel)* marble; ~**malerei die** stained glass; *(Verfahren)* glass-staining; ~**papier das** glass *or* sand paper; ~**perle die** glass bead; ~**platte die** glass plate; *(eines Tisches)* glass top; *(im Fenster)* pane of glass; ~**röhrchen das** small glass tube; ~**scheibe die** sheet of glass; *(im Fenster)* pane of glass; ~**scherbe die** piece of broken glass; ~**scherben** [pieces of] broken glass; ~**schleifer der a)** glass cutter; **b)** *(Optik)* glass grinder; ~**schneider der** glass-cutter; ~**schrank der** glass-fronted cabinet; *(mit Wänden aus Glas)* glass cabinet; ~**splitter der** splinter of glass; ~**stein der** *s.* ~**baustein;** ~**tür die** glass door

Glasur [gla'zu:ɐ] **die;** ~, ~**en a)** *(Schmelz)* glaze; **b)** *(Kochk.) (auf Kuchen)* icing; *(auf Fleisch)* glaze

glas-, Glas-: ~**veranda die** glassed-in veranda; ~**vitrine die** glass showcase; ~**ware die;** *meist Pl.* piece of glassware; ~**waren** glassware *sing.;* ~**watte die** *s.* ~**wolle;** ~**weise** *Adv.* by the glass; ~**wolle die** glass wool; ~**ziegel der** glass tile

glatt [glat] **1.** *Adj.* **a)** smooth; straight ⟨*hair*⟩; **eine ~e Eins/Fünf** a clear A/E; **b)** *(rutschig)* slippery; **c)** *nicht präd. (komplikationslos)* smooth ⟨*landing, journey*⟩; clean, straightforward ⟨*fracture*⟩; **d)** *nicht präd. (ugs.: offensichtlich)* downright, outright ⟨*lie*⟩; outright ⟨*deception, fraud*⟩; sheer, utter ⟨*nonsense, madness, etc.*⟩; pure, sheer ⟨*invention*⟩, flat ⟨*refusal*⟩; complete ⟨*failure*⟩; ~**er Mord sein** be tantamount to murder; **e)** *(allzu gewandt)* smooth. **2.** *adv.* **a) die Rechnung geht ~ auf** the calculation works out exactly; **stricken Sie die ersten zehn Reihen ~ rechts** start with ten rows of plain knitting; **b)** *(komplikationslos)* smoothly; **jmdn. ~ schlagen/besiegen** beat/defeat sb. decisively; **c)** *(ugs.: rückhaltlos)* **jmdm. etw. ~ ins Gesicht sagen** tell sb. sth. straight to his/her face; **etw. ~ ablehnen/leugnen** reject/deny sth. flatly; **etw. ~ vergessen** completely *or* clean forget sth.; **d)** *(abwertend: allzu gewandt)* smoothly

glatt|bügeln *tr. V.* iron smooth

Glätte ['glɛtə] **die;** ~ **a)** *(ebene Beschaffenheit)* smoothness; **b)** *(Rutschigkeit)* slipperiness; **c)** *(abwertend: allzu große Gewandtheit)* smoothness

Glatt·eis das glaze; ice; *(auf der Straße)* black ice; **jmdn. aufs ~ führen** *(fig.)* catch sb. out; **aufs ~ geraten** *(fig.)* get on to tricky ground

Glatteis·bildung die formation of black ice

Glätt·eisen das *(schweiz.) s.* **Bügeleisen**

Glatteis·gefahr die; *o. Pl.* danger of black ice

glätten 1. *tr. V.* smooth out ⟨*piece of paper, banknote, etc.*⟩; smooth [down] ⟨*feathers, fur, etc.*⟩; plane ⟨*wood etc.*⟩; **jmds. Zorn/aufgebrachte Stimmung ~** *(fig.)* calm sb.'s anger/smooth sb.'s ruffled feathers. **2.** *refl. V.* ⟨*waves*⟩ subside; ⟨*sea*⟩ become calm *or* smooth; *(fig.)* subside; die down; **ihre Stirn glättete sich** her frown vanished. **3.** *tr., itr. V. (schweiz.) s.* **bügeln**

Glätterin die; ~, ~**nen** *(schweiz.) s.* **Büglerin**

glatt-: ~**|gehen** *unr. itr. V.; mit sein (ugs.)* go smoothly; ~**|hobeln** *tr. V.* plane smooth; ~**|kämmen** *tr. V.* **seine Haare ~kämmen** comb one's hair straight; ~**|machen** *tr. V.* **a)** *(ebnen, glätten)* smooth out; level ⟨*ground*⟩; **b)** *(ugs.: begleichen)* settle ⟨*account etc.*⟩; ~**rasiert** *Adj.* clean-shaven; ~**weg** *Adv. (ugs.)* **etw. ~weg ablehnen/ignorieren** turn sth. down flat/just *or* simply ignore sth.; **das ist ~weg erlogen/erfunden** that's a downright lie/that's pure invention; ~**|ziehen** *unr. tr. V.* pull straight; ~**züngig** [~tsʏŋɪç] *Adj. (geh. abwertend)* smooth-tongued; glib

Glatze ['glatsə] **die;** ~, ~**n** bald head; *(kahle Stelle)* bald patch; **eine ~ haben/bekommen** be/go bald; **sich eine ~ schneiden lassen** *(ugs.)* have one's hair cropped very short all over; **ein Mann mit ~:** a man with a bald head; a bald-headed man

Glatz·kopf der a) *(Kopf)* bald head; **b)** *(ugs.: Person)* baldhead

glatz·köpfig *Adj.* bald[-headed]

Glaube ['glaubə] **der;** ~**ns a)** *(gefühlsmäßige Bindung)* faith **(an** + *Akk.* in); *(Überzeugung, Meinung)* belief **(an** + *Akk.* in); **den ~n an jmdn./etw. verlieren** lose faith in sb./sth.; **jmdm./jmds. Worten ~n schenken** believe sb./what sb. says; **[bei jmdm.] ~n finden** be believed [by sb.]; **guten ~ns sein, daß ...:** be quite convinced that ...; **in dem ~n leben, daß ...:** live in the belief that ...; **laß ihn in seinem ~n** don't disillusion him; **jmdn. bei** *od.* **in dem ~n lassen, daß ...:** let sb. believe that ...; **[der] ~ versetzt Berge** *od.* **kann Berge versetzen** faith can move mountains; **sich in dem ~n wiegen, daß ...:** labour under the illusion that ...; **in gutem** *od.* **im guten ~n** in good faith; **b)** *(religiöse Überzeugung, Religion, Bekenntnis)* faith; **den ~n verlieren** lose one's [religious] faith; **den ~n an Gott verlieren** lose one's faith *or* belief in God

glauben 1. *tr. V.* **a)** *(annehmen, meinen)* think; believe; **ich glaube, ja** I think *or* believe so; **ich glaube, nein** *od.* **nicht** I don't think so; I think *or* believe not; **jmdn. etw. ~ machen wollen** try to make sb. believe sth.; **b)** *(für wahr halten)* believe; **jmdm. [etw.] ~:** believe sb.; **ich glaube ihm seine Geschichte** I believe his story; **das glaubst du doch selbst nicht!** [surely] you can't be serious; **sie glaubt ihm jedes Wort** she believes every word he says; **ob du es glaubst oder nicht ...:** believe it or not ...; **wer hätte das [je] geglaubt?** who would [ever] have thought it?; **wer hätte [je] geglaubt, daß ...:** who would [ever] have believed *or* thought that ...; **du glaubst [gar] nicht, wie ...:** you have no idea how ...; **wer's glaubt, wird selig** *(ugs. scherzh.)* if you believe that, you'll believe anything; **das ist doch kaum zu ~** *(ugs.)* it's incredible; **c)** *(fälschlich annehmen)* **wir glaubten ihn tot/in Sicherheit** we thought *or* believed him [to be] dead/safe; **sich allein/unbeobachtet ~:** think *or* believe oneself [to be] alone/unobserved. **2.** *itr. V.* **a)** *(vertrauen)* **an jmdn./etw./sich [selbst] ~:** believe in *or* have faith in sb./sth./oneself; **b)** *(gläubig sein)* hold religious beliefs; believe; **fest/unbeirrbar ~:** have a strong/unshakeable religious belief; **c)** *(von der Existenz von etw. überzeugt sein)* believe **(an** + *Akk.* in); **an Gott ~:** believe in God; **d) dran ~ müssen** *(salopp: getötet werden)* buy it *(sl.)*; *(salopp: sterben)* peg out *(sl.)*; kick the bucket *(sl.)*; **heute muß sie dran ~ und Küchendienst machen** *(ugs.: ist an der Reihe)* today it is her turn to be lumbered with working in the kitchen *(coll.)*

Glauben der; ~**s** *s.* **Glaube**

glaubens-, Glaubens-: ~**artikel der** article of faith; ~**bekenntnis das a)** *o. Pl. (auch fig.: Überzeugung)* creed; *s. auch* **apostolisch a; b)** *(Konfessionsangehörigkeit)* religion; ~**bruder der** co-religionist; fellow-believer; ~**dinge** *Pl.* matters of faith; ~**eifer der** religious zeal; ~**frage die** question of faith *or* belief; ~**freiheit die;** *o. Pl.* religious freedom; freedom of worship; ~**gemeinschaft die** religious sect; denomination; ~**kampf der** religious war; war of religion; ~**lehre die** doctrine; *(Dogma)* dogma; *(Dogmatik)* dogmatics *sing.;* ~**sache die** *(ugs.)* matter of faith *or* belief; ~**satz der** doctrine; dogma; ~**spaltung die** schism; ~**stark** *Adj.* deeply religious; ~**streit der** religious dispute; ~**wahrheit die** religious truth; ~**wechsel der** change of religion

Glauber·salz ['glaubɐ-] **das;** ~**es** *(Chemie)* Glauber's salt

glaubhaft 1. *Adj.* credible; believable. **2.** *adv.* convincingly

Glaubhaftigkeit die; ~: credibility

Glaubhaft·machung die; ~ *(Rechtsspr.)* substantiation

gläubig ['glɔybɪç] **1.** *Adj.* **a)** *(religiös)* devout; **sehr/zutiefst ~ sein** be very/deeply religious; **b)** *(vertrauensvoll)* trusting; **~e Anhänger** faithful followers. **2.** *adv.* **a)** *(religiös)* devoutly; **b)** *(vertrauensvoll)* trustingly

-gläubig *Adj.* having a blind trust in ⟨*authority, drugs, Hitler, the Party, etc.*⟩

Gläubige der/die; *adj. Dekl.* believer; **die ~n** the faithful

Gläubiger der; ~**s,** ~, **Gläubigerin die;** ~, ~**nen** creditor

Gläubigkeit die; ~ **a)** *(religiose Überzeugung)* religious faith; **b)** *(Vertrauen)* trustfulness

glaublich *Adj. in:* **es ist kaum ~:** it is scarcely *or* hardly credible

glaub·würdig 1. *Adj.* credible; believable; **von ~er Seite/aus ~er Quelle** from reliable quarters/a reliable source. **2.** *adv.* convincingly

Glaubwürdigkeit die credibility

Glaukom [glau'ko:m] **das;** ~**s,** ~**e** *(Med.)* glaucoma

glazial [gla'tsia:l] *Adj. (Geol.)* glacial

Glazial das; ~**s,** ~**e** *(Geol.)* glacial epoch

gleich [glaiç] **1.** *Adj.* **a)** *(identisch, von derselben Art)* same; *(~berechtigt, ~wertig, Math.)* equal; **zur ~en Zeit/im ~en Augenblick** at the same time/at the same moment; **~er Lohn für ~e Arbeit** equal pay for equal work; **~es Recht für alle** equal rights for all; **dreimal zwei [ist] ~ sechs** three times two equals *or* is six; **das ~e wollen/beabsichtigen** have the same objective[s *pl.*]/intentions *pl.*; **das ~e gilt auch für dich** the same applies to *or* goes for you too; **das kommt auf das ~e** *od.* **aufs ~e heraus** it amounts *or* comes to the same thing; **der/die ~e bleiben** remain *or* stay the same; **~es mit ~em vergelten** pay sb. back in his/her own coin *or* in kind; **~ und ~ gesellt sich gern** *(Spr.)* birds of a feather flock together *(prov.)*; **b)** *(ugs.: gleichgültig)* **es ist mir völlig** *od.* **ganz ~:** it's all the same to me; I couldn't care less *(coll.)*; **ganz ~, wer anruft, ...:** no matter who calls, ... **2.** *adv.* **a)** *(übereinstimmend)* **~ groß/alt** *usw.* **sein** be the same height/age *etc.*; **~ gut/schlecht** *usw.* equally good/bad *etc.*; **b)** *(in derselben Weise)* **~ aufgebaut/gekleidet** having the same structure/wearing identical clothes; **alle Menschen ~ behandeln** treat everyone alike; **c)** *(sofort)* at once; right *or* straight away; *(bald)* in a moment *or* minute; **ich komme ~:** I'm just coming; **es muß nicht ~ sein** there's no immediate hurry; **ich bin ~ wieder da** I'll be back in a moment *or* minute; I'll be right back; **es ist ~ zehn Uhr** it is almost *or* nearly ten o'clock; **das habe ich [euch] ~ gesagt** I told you so; what did I tell you?; **warum nicht ~ so?** why didn't you do that/say so in the first place?; **bis ~!** see you later!; **d)** *(räumlich)* right; immediately; just; **~ rechts/links** just *or* immediately on the right/left; **~ um die Ecke** just round the corner; **e)** *(geh.: schon, auch)* **wenn er ~ reich war, ...:** rich though he was, ...; **ob er ~ unschuldig war, ...:** although he was innocent, ... **3.** *Präp.* + *Dat. (geh.)* like; **einem silbernen Band ~:** like a silver ribbon. **4.** *Partikel* **a) nun wein' nicht ~/sei nicht ~ böse** don't start crying/don't get cross; **da könnte**

man doch ~ in die Luft gehen/aus der Haut fahren it's enough to drive you up the wall *(coll.)*; **b)** *(in Fragesätzen)* **wie hieß er ~?** what was his name [again]?; **was wollte ich ~ sagen?** what was I going to say?

gleich-, Gleich-: ~alt[e]rig [~alt[ə]rıç] *Adj.* of the same age (**mit** as); **die beiden sind ~alt[e]rig** they are both the same age; **Gleichalt[e]rige** *Pl.* people/children of the same age; **~artig 1.** *Adj.* of the same kind *postpos.* (+ *Dat.* as); *(sehr ähnlich)* very similar (+ *Dat.* to); **2.** *adv.* in the same way; **~artigkeit die;** *o. Pl.* great similarity; **~bedeutend** *Adj.* **~bedeutend mit** synonymous with; ‹*action*› tantamount to; **~berechtigt** *Adj.* having *or* enjoying *or* with equal rights *postpos.*; **~berechtigte Partner/Mitglieder** equal partners/members; **~berechtigt sein** have *or* enjoy equal rights; **~berechtigt mit jmdm. sein** have the same rights as sb.; **Gleichberechtigte** *Pl.* people who have *or* enjoy equal rights; **~berechtigung die** equal rights *pl.*; equality; **für die ~berechtigung der Frauen kämpfen** fight for equal rights *or* equality for women; **~|bleiben** *unr. itr. V.; mit sein* remain *or* stay the same; ‹*speed, temperature, etc.*› remain *or* stay constant *or* steady; ‹*prices*› remain unchanged, stay the same; **sich** *(Dat.)* **~bleiben** remain the same; **das bleibt sich [doch] gleich** *(ugs.)* it makes no difference; **~bleibend** *Adj.* constant, steady ‹*temperature, speed, etc.*›; **~bleibend sein** remain *or* stay the same; ‹*temperature, speed, etc.*› remain *or* stay constant *or* steady; **in ~bleibendem Abstand** at a steady distance; **~denkend** *Adj.; nicht präd. s.* **~gesinnt**

gleichen *unr. itr. V.* **jmdm./einer Sache ~:** be like *or* resemble sb./sth.; *(sehr ähnlich aussehen)* closely resemble sb./sth.; **sich** *(Dat.)* **~:** be alike; *(sehr ähnlich aussehen)* closely resemble each other; **nichts gleicht dem Zauber dieser Musik** nothing can equal *or* there is nothing to equal the enchanting quality of this music

gleichen·orts *Adv. (schweiz.)* in the same place

gleichermaßen *Adv.* equally

gleich-, Gleich-: ~falls *Adv. (auch)* also; *(ebenfalls)* likewise; **danke ~falls!** thank you, [and] the same to you; **~farbig** *Adj.* of the same colour *postpos.*; **~förmig 1.** *Adj.* **a)** *(einheitlich)* uniform; uniform, even ‹*light*›; steady ‹*development*›; **b)** *(langweilig, monoton)* monotonous; **2.** *adv.* **a)** *(einheitlich)* uniformly; **b)** *(langweilig, monoton)* monotonously; **~förmig sprechen** speak in a monotone; **~förmigkeit die; ~ a)** *(Einheitlichkeit)* uniformity; **b)** *(Monotonie)* monotony; **~geschlechtlich** *Adj.* homosexual; **~gesinnt** *Adj.; nicht präd.* like-minded; **Gleichgesinnte** *Pl.* like-minded people

Gleich·gewicht das; *o. Pl.* **a)** balance; **das ~ halten/verlieren** keep/lose one's balance; **aus dem ~ kommen** lose one's balance; **im ~ sein** be in equilibrium; **ihr ~ ist leicht gestört** her sense of balance is slightly impaired; **b)** *(Ausgewogenheit)* balance; **das europäische ~:** the balance of power in Europe; **das ~ der Kräfte** the balance of power; **c)** *(innere Ausgeglichenheit)* equilibrium; **aus dem ~ geraten** lose one's equilibrium; **sein ~ bewahren/verlieren** keep *or* retain/lose one's equilibrium; **jmdn. aus dem ~ bringen** throw sb. off balance

Gleichgewichts-: ~lage die equilibrium; **~organ das** *(Anat.)* organ of equilibrium; **~sinn der** sense of balance; **~störung die** disturbance of one's sense of balance; **~störungen** impaired balance *sing.*

gleich·gültig 1. *Adj.* **a)** *(teilnahmslos)* indifferent (**gegenüber** towards); **sie war ihm [nicht] ~** *(verhüll.)* he was [by no means] indifferent to her; **b)** *(belanglos)* trivial, unimportant ‹*matter, question, etc.*›; trivial ‹*conversation*›; **es ist ~, ob ...:** it does not matter whether ...; **das ist mir [vollkommen] ~:** it's a matter of [complete] indifference to me. **2.** *adv.* indifferently; ‹*look on*› with indifference

Gleich·gültigkeit die indifference (**gegenüber** towards)

Gleichheit die; ~, ~en a) *(Identität)* identity; *(Ähnlichkeit)* similarity; **bei ~ der Punktzahl** if the teams/players *etc.* are level on points; **b)** *o. Pl. (gleiche Rechte)* equality

Gleichheits-: ~[grund]satz der principle of equality before the law; **~zeichen das** equals sign

gleich-, Gleich-: ~klang der harmony; **~|kommen** *unr. itr. V.; mit sein* **a)** *(entsprechen)* amount to; be tantamount to; **b)** *(die gleiche Leistung erreichen)* **jmdm./einer Sache [an etw.** *(Dat.)***] ~kommen** equal sb./sth. [in sth.]; **jmdm. an Erfolg/Schnelligkeit ~kommen** equal *or* match sb.'s success/match sb. for speed; **~lauf der;** *o. Pl. (Technik)* synchronism; **~laufend** *Adj.* parallel (**mit** with); **~lautend** *Adj.* **a)** *(im Klang, Laut gleich)* identical ‹*sound, syllable, etc.*›; ‹*words*› with the same pronunciation; homonymous ‹*words*› *(Ling.)*; **b)** *(mit gleichem Wortlaut)* identical; identically worded; **~|machen** *tr. V.* make equal; **der Tod macht alle Menschen gleich** Death is the great leveller; *s. auch* **Erdboden; ~macherei die; ~, ~en** *(abwertend)* levelling down *(derog.)*; egalitarianism; **~macherisch** *Adj. (abwertend)* egalitarian; **~maß das;** *o. Pl.* **a)** *(Ebenmaß) (von Bewegung, Strophen)* regularity; *(von Zügen, Proportionen)* symmetry; **b)** *(Ausgeglichenheit)* equilibrium; **~mäßig 1.** *Adj.* regular ‹*interval, rhythm*›; uniform ‹*acceleration, distribution*›; even ‹*heat*›; **~mäßige Atemzüge** regular breathing *sing.*; **2.** *adv.* ‹*breathe*› regularly; **etw. ~mäßig verteilen/auftragen** distribute sth. equally/apply sth. evenly; **~mäßig hohe Temperaturen** constantly high temperatures; **~mäßigkeit die** *s.* **~mäßig:** regularity; uniformity; evenness; **~mut der** (*veralt., landsch. auch:* **die; ~**) equanimity; calmness; composure; **etw. mit ~mut hinnehmen/ertragen** accept/bear sth. with equanimity; **~mütig 1.** *Adj.* calm; composed; unruffled ‹*calm*›; **2.** *adv.* with equanimity; calmly; **~mütigkeit die; ~:** *s.* **~mut; ~namig** [-na:mıç] *Adj.* **a)** of the same name *postpos.*; **b)** *(Math.)* **~namige Brüche** fractions with a common denominator; **Brüche ~namig machen** reduce fractions to a common denominator; **c)** *(Physik)* like ‹*charges, poles*›

Gleichnis das; ~ses, ~se *(Allegorie)* allegory; *(Parabel)* parable

gleichnishaft 1. *Adj. (allegorisch)* allegorical; *(parabolisch)* parabolic. **2.** *adv.* allegorically/parabolically

gleich-, Gleich-: ~rangig [-raŋıç] **1.** *Adj.* ‹*principle, problem, etc.*› of equal importance *or* status; equally important ‹*principle, problem, etc.*›; ‹*official, job*› of equal rank; **2.** *adv.* **alle Punkte ~rangig behandeln** give all points equal treatment; **~|richten** *tr. V. (Elektrot.)* rectify; **~richter der** *(Elektrot.)* rectifier

gleichsam *Adv. (geh.)* as it were; so to speak; **~ als [ob] ...:** just as if ...

gleich-, Gleich-: ~|schalten *tr. V. (abwertend)* force *or* bring into line; **~schaltung die** *(abwertend)* Gleichschaltung; **~schenk[e]lig** *Adj. (Math.)* isosceles; **~schritt der;** *o. Pl.* marching in step; **im ~schritt** in step; **im ~schritt marsch!** forward march!; **~schritt halten** keep in step; **~|sehen** *unr. itr. V.* **jmdm./einer Sache ~sehen** look like sb./sth.; **~seitig** *Adj. (Math.)* equilateral; **~|setzen** *tr. V.* **zwei Dinge ~setzen** equate two things; **etw. einer Sache** *(Dat.) od.* **mit etw. ~setzen** equate sth. with sth.; **sich mit jmdm. ~setzen** put oneself on the same level as *or* on a level with sb.; **Ludwig XIV. setzte sich mit seinem Staat ~:** Ludwig XIV identified himself with his state; **~setzung die; ~, ~en: die ~setzung von sozialistischen und fortschrittlichen Ideen** equating socialist and progressive ideas; **die ~setzung der Arbeiter mit den Vertretern der Intelligenz** placing the workers on the same level as the members of the intelligentsia; **~silbig** *Adj.* having the same number of syllables *postpos., not pred.*; **~silbig sein** have the same number of syllables; **~sinnig 1.** *Adj.* ‹*fluctuations etc.*› in the same direction; **2.** *adv.* in the same direction; **~stand der;** *o. Pl.* **a)** *(Sport: gleicher Spielstand)* **den ~stand herstellen/erzielen** level the score; **beim ~stand von 1:1** with the scores level at 1 all; **das Spiel wurde beim ~stand von 1:1 beendet** the match ended in a 1 all draw; **b)** *(Politik)* balance of forces; **~|stehen** *unr. itr. V.* be equal (*Dat.* to, with); *(Sport)* be level; **~|stellen** *tr. V.* **zwei Dinge ~stellen** equate two things; **etw. einer Sache** *(Dat.) od.* **mit etw. ~stellen** equate sth. with sth.; **jmd. [mit] jmdm. ~stellen** put sb. on the same level *or* on a level with sb.; *(gleiche Rechte zugestehen)* put sb. on an equal footing with sb.; **~stellung die: die rechtliche ~stellung unehelicher Kinder** giving equal rights to illegitimate children; **soziale ~stellung** social equality; **~strom der** *(Elektrot.)* direct current; **~|tun** *unr. tr. V.* **es jmdm. ~tun** match *or* equal sb.; *(nachahmen)* copy sb.; **es jmdm. an** *od.* **in etw.** *(Dat.)* **~tun** match *or* equal sb. in sth.; **es jmdm. an Schnelligkeit ~tun** match *or* equal sb. for speed

Gleichung die; ~, ~en equation; **die ~ ging nicht auf** *(fig.)* things did not work out as planned

gleich-, Gleich-: ~viel [-'- *od.* '--] *Adv.* no matter; **~viel wohin** no matter where; **~viel ob es leicht oder schwer geht/du darüber böse bist** regardless of whether it's easy or difficult/even if you are angry about it; **~wertig** *Adj.* **a)** *(Sport: gleich stark)* evenly matched ‹*opponents, teams*›; **b)** *(von gleichem Wert)* of equal *or* the same value *postpos.*; ‹*performances*› of the same standard; **c)** *(Chemie)* equivalent; **~wertigkeit die: wie ist ~wertigkeit der Arbeit zu definieren?** how can you define what constitutes equal work?; **die ~wertigkeit beider Inszenierungen steht außer Frage** that the two productions are of an equal standard is beyond question; **~wink[e]lig** *Adj. (Geom.)* equiangular; **~wohl** [-'- *od.* '--] **1.** *Adv.* nevertheless; nonetheless; **2.** *Konj. (selten, noch landsch.)* although; **~zeitig 1.** *Adj.; nicht präd.* simultaneous; **2.** *adv.* **a)** *(zur gleichen Zeit)* simultaneously; at the same time; **b)** *(auch noch)* at the same time; **~zeitigkeit die** simultaneity; simultaneousness; *(von historischen Ereignissen)* contemporaneity; contemporaneousness; **~|ziehen** *unr. itr. V.* catch up; draw level

Gleis [glais] **das; ~es, ~e a)** *(Fahrspur)* track; line; rails *pl.*; permanent way *as Brit. tech. term*; *(Bahnsteig)* platform; *(einzelne Schiene)* rail; **auf ~ 5 einlaufen** ‹*train:*› arrive at platform 5; **„das Überschreiten der ~e ist verboten!"** 'passengers must not cross the line'; **aus dem ~ springen/kommen** jump/leave the rails; **ein totes ~:** an unused siding; **b)** *(fig.)* **auf** *od.* **in ein falsches ~ geraten** get on [to] the wrong track; **jmdn. aufs tote ~ schieben** put sb. out of harm's way *(fig.)*; **etw. auf ein totes ~ schieben** shelve sth. indefinitely; **jmdn. aus dem ~ bringen** *od.* **werfen** put sb. off [his/her stroke]; *(von jmdm. psychisch nicht bewältigt werden)* upset *or* affect sb. deeply; **sie/alles wird**

wieder ins rechte ~ kommen she'll be all right/everything will sort itself out; **alles wieder ins [rechte] ~ bringen** put things *or* matters right again; **aus dem ~ kommen** go off the rails *(fig.)*; **er/alles ist wieder im ~:** he's/everything's all right again; **sich in ausgefahrenen ~en bewegen** be in a rut
Gleis-: ~an·lage die [railway] lines *pl. or* tracks *pl.*; **~an·schluß der** siding; **~bau der;** *o. Pl.* track-laying; construction of permanent way *(Brit.)*; **~bremse die** *(Eisenb.)* rail brake; **~kette die** *(Technik)* caterpillar track
Gleisner ['glaisnɐ] **der; ~s, ~** *(veralt.)* hypocrite
gleisnerisch *Adj. (veralt.)* hypocritical
gleißen ['glaisn̩] *itr. V. (dichter.)* blaze
Gleis-: ~sperre die *(Eisenb.)* scotch block; **~waage die** weighbridge
Gleit-: ~bahn die *(Flugw.)* glide path; **~boot das** hydroplane
gleiten ['glaitn̩] *unr. itr. V.; mit sein* **a)** glide; ⟨*hand*⟩ slide; **ein Lächeln glitt über ihr Gesicht** a smile passed over her face; **aus dem Sattel/ins Wasser ~:** slide out of the saddle/slide *or* slip into the water; **jmdm. aus den Händen ~:** slip from sb.'s hands; **er ließ das Geld in seine Tasche ~:** he slipped the money into his pocket; **b)** *(ugs.: in bezug auf Arbeitszeit)* work flexitime
gleitend *Adj.; nicht präd.* **~e Arbeitszeit** flexitime; flexible working hours *pl.*; **~e Lohnskala** index-linked wage scale
Gleiter der; ~s, ~: glider
gleit-, Gleit-: ~fläche die slide; *(für Schiffe)* slipway; *(am Ski)* sole [of the ski]; **~flug der** glide; **im ~flug landen** glide-land; **zum ~flug ansetzen** go into a glide; **~flugzeug das** glider; **~klausel die** *(Rechtsw.)* escalator clause; **~kufe die** *(Fliegerspr.)* skid; **~laut der** *(Sprachw.)* glide; **~schiene die** guide *or* slide rail; **~schutz der** *(Kfz-W.)* anti-skid protection; *(Bauteil)* anti-skid device; **~sicher** *Adj.* non-slip ⟨*shoe, surface, etc.*⟩; non-skid ⟨*tyre*⟩; **~zeit die a)** *(Zeitspanne)* flexible working hours *pl. or* starting and finishing times *pl.*; **b) drei Stunden ~zeit** three hours flexitime; **c)** *o. Pl. (ugs.: gleitende Arbeitszeit)* flexitime; flexible working hours *pl.*
Glencheck ['glɛntʃɛk] **der; ~[s], ~s a)** *(Material)* glen-check cloth; **b)** *(Anzug)* glen-check suit
Gletscher ['glɛtʃɐ] **der; ~s, ~:** glacier
Gletscher-: ~bach der glacial stream; **~brand der** glacier burn; **~eis das** glacial ice; **~mühle die** glacier mill; moulin; **~spalte die** crevasse; **~tisch der** *(Geol.)* glacier table; **~tor das** *(Geol.)* glacier snout
glibberig ['glıbərıç] *Adj. (bes. nordd.)* slippery; *(schleimig)* slimy
glich [glıç] *1. u. 3. Pers. Sg. Prät. v.* **gleichen**
Glied [gli:t] **das; ~[e]s, ~er a)** *(Körperteil)* limb; *(Finger~, Zehen~)* joint; phalanx *(Anat.)*; **kein ~ rühren können** be unable to move a muscle; **der Schreck sitzt** *od.* **steckt ihm noch in den ~ern** he is [still] shaking with the shock; **der Schreck fuhr ihr in die** *od.* **durch alle ~er** the shock made her shake all over; **b)** *(Ketten~, auch fig.)* link; **c)** *(Teil eines Ganzen)* section; part; *(Mitglied)* member; *(eines Satzes)* part; *(einer Gleichung)* term; **ein nützliches ~ der Gesellschaft** a useful member of society; **d)** *(Penis)* penis; **e)** *(Mannschaftsreihe)* rank; **f)** *(geh. veralt.: Generation)* generation
glieder-, Glieder-: ~bau der; *o. Pl.* limb structure; **~füßer der** *(Zool.)* arthropod; **~lahm** *Adj.* stiff-limbed
gliedern ['gli:dɐn] **1.** *tr. V.* structure; organize ⟨*thoughts*⟩; **nach Eigenschaften ~:** classify according to properties; **in Teile ~:** arrange in parts; **einen Aufsatz in drei Teile ~:** divide an essay into three sections; **hierarchisch gegliedert** hierarchically structured. **2.** *refl. V.* **sich in Gruppen/Abschnitte** *usw.* **~:** divide *or* be divided into groups/sections *etc.*
Glieder-: ~puppe die jointed doll; *(als Modell für Maler o. ä.)* lay figure; **~reißen das; ~s** *(ugs.)*, **~schmerz der** rheumatic pains *pl.*; **~tier das** *(Zool.)* member of the Articulata; **die ~tiere** the Articulata
Gliederung die; ~, ~en a) *(Aufbau, Einteilung)* structure; **in militärischer ~:** in military formation; **die ~ eines Buches in Kapitel** the division of a book into chapters; **b)** *(das Gliedern)* structuring; *(von Gedanken)* organization; *(nach Eigenschaften)* classification; *(in Teile)* arrangement; **c)** *(ns.: Gruppe)* section
Glieder·zucken das; ~s twitching of the limbs
glied-, Glied-: ~maße [-ma:sə] **die; ~, ~n** limb; **~satz der** *(Sprachw.)* subordinate clause; **~staat der** member *or* constituent state; **~weise** *Adv.* in ranks
glimmen ['glımən] *unr. od. regelm. itr. V.* glow; **in seinen Augen glomm ein gefährlicher Funke** *(fig.)* there was a dangerous glint in his eyes
Glimmer der; ~s, ~: mica
glimmern *itr. V.* glimmer; ⟨*lake etc.*⟩ glisten
Glimm-: ~lampe die *(Elektrot.)* glow lamp; **~stengel der** *(ugs. scherzh.)* fag *(sl.)*; ciggy *(coll.)*
glimpflich ['glımpflıç] **1.** *Adj.* **a) der Unfall nahm ein ~es Ende** the accident turned out not to be too serious; **sie war über den ~en Ausgang der Angelegenheit erfreut** she was glad to have got off so lightly; **b)** *(mild)* lenient ⟨*sentence, punishment*⟩. **2.** *adv.* **a)** *(ohne Schaden)* **~ davonkommen** get off lightly; **es ist ~ abgegangen** it turned out not to be too bad; **b)** *(mild)* mildly; leniently
glitschen ['glıtʃn̩] *itr. V.; mit sein (ugs.)* slip; **jmdm. aus der Hand ~:** slip out of sb.'s hand
glitschig ['glıtʃıç] *Adj. (ugs.)* slippery
glitt [glıt] *1. u. 3. Pers. Sg. Prät. v.* **gleiten**
glitz[e]rig ['glıts(ə)rıç] *Adj. (ugs.)* glistening ⟨*snow*⟩; sparkling, glittering ⟨*diamond, decorations*⟩
glitzern ['glıtsɐn] *itr. V.* ⟨*star*⟩ twinkle; ⟨*diamond, decorations*⟩ sparkle, glitter; ⟨*snow, eyes, tears*⟩ glisten
glitzrig *s.* **glitz[e]rig**
global [glo'ba:l] **1.** *Adj.* **a)** *(weltweit)* global; world-wide; **b)** *(umfassend)* general, all-round ⟨*education*⟩; overall ⟨*control, planning, etc.*⟩; **c)** *(allgemein)* general. **2.** *adv.* **a)** *(weltweit)* world-wide; globally; **b)** *(umfassend)* in overall terms; **~ gesteuert werden** be subject to overall control; **c)** *(allgemein)* in general terms; **~ gerechnet** in round figures
Global-: ~steuerung die *(Wirtsch.)* overall control; **~strategie die** global *or* world-wide strategy
Globen *s.* **Globus**
Globetrotter ['glo:bətrɔtɐ] **der; ~s, ~:** globetrotter
Globus ['glo:bʊs] **der; ~** *od.* **~ses, Globen** ['glo:bn̩] **a)** globe; **b)** *(salopp: Kopf)* nut *(sl.)*; bonce *(Brit. sl.)*
Glöckchen ['glœkçən] **das; ~s, ~:** [little] bell
Glocke ['glɔkə] **die; ~, ~n a)** *(auch: Tür~, Taucher~, Blüte)* bell; **etw. an die große ~ hängen** *(ugs.)* tell the whole world about sth.; **wissen, was die ~ geschlagen hat** *(ugs.)* know what one is in for *(coll.)*; **b)** *(Hut)* cloche; **c)** *(Käse~, Butter~, Kuchen~)* cover; bell; **d)** *(Fechten)* coquille
glocken-, Glocken-: ~balken der [bell] yoke; **~blume die** *(Bot.)* bell-flower; campanula; **~förmig 1.** *Adj.* bell-shaped; widely flared ⟨*skirt etc.*⟩; **2.** *adv.* **~förmig geschnitten** widely flared; **~geläute das** pealing *or* ringing of bells; **~gießer der** bell-founder; **~gießerei** [----'-] **die** bell-foundry; **~guß der** bell-founding *no art.*; **~heide die** *(Bot.)* bell-heather; **~hell 1.** *Adj.* bell-like; **eine ~helle Stimme** a high, clear voice; **2.** *adv.* **~hell lachen** give a high, clear laugh; **~klang der** pealing *or* ringing of bells; **~klöppel der** [bell-]clapper; **~läuten das** pealing *or* ringing of bells; **~mantel der** *(Gußform)* cope; **~rein 1.** *Adj.* as clear as a bell *postpos.*; **2.** *adv.* as clear as a bell; **~rock der** widely flared skirt; **~schlag der** stroke; **beim ~schlag um acht Uhr** on the stroke of eight o'clock; **mit dem** *od.* **auf den ~schlag** *(ugs.)* on the dot *(coll.)*; **~seil das** bell-rope; **~spiel das a)** carillon; *(mit einer Uhr gekoppelt auch)* chimes *pl.*; **b)** *(Instrument)* glockenspiel; **~strang der** *s.* **~seil**; **~stube die** belfry; **~stuhl der** bell-cage; **~ton der** stroke of a/the bell; **~töne** the sound of a/the bell/of bells; **~turm der** bell tower; belfry; **~weihe die** *(kath. Rel.)* baptism *or* blessing of a/the bell; **~zeichen das** ring of a/the bell; **auf das ~zeichen** when the bell rings/rang; **~zug der** *(Klingelschnur)* bell-pull; *(~strang)* bell-rope
glockig ['glɔkıç] *s.* **glockenförmig**
Glöckner ['glœknɐ] **der; ~s, ~** *(veralt.)* bell-ringer; **der ~ von Notre Dame** the Hunchback of Notre Dame
glomm [glɔm] *1. u. 3. Pers. Sg. Prät. v.* **glimmen**
¹Gloria ['glo:ri̯a] **das; ~s** *od.* **die; ~** *(iron.)* glory
²Gloria das; ~s, ~s *(Rel.)* gloria; **das große/kleine ~:** the greater/lesser doxology
Glorie ['glo:ri̯ə] **die; ~, ~n a)** *(geh.: Ruhm)* glory; **b)** *(geh.: Lichtschein)* glory; *(um den Kopf, um einen Stern)* halo
Glorien·schein der glory; *(um den Kopf, fig.)* halo
Glorifikation [glorifika'tsi̯o:n] **die; ~, ~en** glorification
glorifizieren [glorifi'tsi:rən] *tr. V.* glorify
Glorifizierung die; ~, ~en glorification
Gloriole [glo'ri̯o:lə] **die; ~, ~n a)** *(auch fig.)* glory; **b)** *(um den Kopf)* halo; aura
glorios [glo'ri̯o:s] *(iron.)* **1.** *Adj.* brilliant. **2.** *adv.* brilliantly
glor·reich ['glo:ɐ̯-] **1.** *Adj.* glorious. **2.** *adv.* gloriously
glosen ['glo:zn̩] *itr. V. (landsch./dichter.) s.* **glimmen**
Glossar [glɔ'sa:ɐ̯] **das; ~s, ~e** glossary
Glosse ['glɔsə] **die; ~, ~n a)** *(in den Medien)* commentary; **b)** *(spöttische Bemerkung)* sneering *or (coll.)* snide comment; **c)** *(Sprachw., Literaturw.)* gloss
Glossen·schreiber der commentator
glossieren *tr. V.* **a)** commentate on; **b)** *(bespötteln)* sneer at; **c)** *(Sprachw., Literaturw.)* gloss
Glottal [glɔ'ta:l] **der; ~s, ~e** *(Phon.)* glottal stop
Glottis ['glɔtıs] **die; ~, Glottides** ['glɔtide:s] *(Anat.)* glottis
Glotz·auge das a) *Pl. (salopp abwertend)* goggle eyes; **~augen machen/bekommen** go goggle-eyed; goggle; **b)** *(Med.)* exophthalmus
glotz·äugig *Adj.* goggle-eyed
Glotze ['glɔtsə] **die; ~, ~n** *(salopp)* box *(coll.)*; goggle-box *(Brit. sl.)*
glotzen *itr. V. (abwertend)* goggle; gawk, gawp *(coll.)*
Glotz·kiste die *(salopp)* box *(coll.)*; goggle-box *(Brit. sl.)*
Glotzophon [glɔtso'fo:n] **das; ~s, ~e** *(salopp scherzh.) s.* **Glotze**
Gloxinie [glɔ'ksi:ni̯ə] **die; ~, ~n** *(Bot.)* gloxinia
Glubsch·augen ['glʊpʃ-] *Pl. (nordd.) s.* **Glupschaugen**
gluck [glʊk] *Interj.* **a)** *(für das Glucken)* cluck; **b)** *(für das Gluckern)* glug; **~, ~, weg**

war er *(scherzh.)* glug, glug, and he went under; ~, ~ **machen** *(ugs. scherzh.)* have a few *(sl.)*
Glück [glʏk] **das; ~[e]s a)** luck; **ein großes/unverdientes ~:** a great/an undeserved stroke of luck; **[es ist/war] ein ~, daß ...:** it's/it was lucky that ...; **er hat [kein] ~ gehabt** he was [un]lucky; **sie hatte das ~, zu ...:** she was lucky enough to ...; **bei jmdm. ~ mit etw. haben** succeed in getting sb. to agree to sth.; **bei jmdm. kein ~ haben** get no joy out of sb.; ~ **bei Frauen haben** be successful with women; **bei der Auslosung kein ~ haben** have no luck in the draw; ~ **im Unglück haben** be quite lucky in the circumstances; **jmdm. ~ wünschen** wish sb. [good] luck; **jmdm. viel ~ zum Geburtstag wünschen** wish sb. a very happy birthday; **viel ~!** [the] best of luck!; good luck!; ~ **bringen** bring [good] luck; ~ **muß der Mensch haben** my/his *etc.* luck must have been in; **mehr ~ als Verstand haben** have more luck than judgement; **er weiß noch nichts von seinem ~** *(iron.)* he doesn't know what's in store for him yet; **sein ~ versuchen** *od.* **probieren** try one's luck; **sein ~ machen** make one's fortune; **auf gut ~:** trusting to luck; **er hatte sich auf gut ~ beworben** he had applied on the off-chance; **sie wählte ein Buch auf gut ~:** she chose a book at random; **von ~ sagen** *od.* **reden können** consider *or* count oneself lucky; **zum ~** *od.* **zu meinem/seinem** *usw.* **~:** luckily *or* fortunately [for me/him *etc.*]; ~ **auf!** *(Bergmannsgruß)* good luck!; ~ **ab!** *(Fliegergruß)* happy landings!; good luck!; **b)** *(Hochstimmung)* happiness; **das häusliche ~:** domestic bliss; **sie ist sein ganzes ~:** she means everything to him; **jmdn. zu seinem ~ zwingen** make sb. do what is good for him/her; **man kann niemanden zu seinem ~ zwingen** you can lead a horse to water but you can't make him drink; **du hast/das hat mir gerade noch zu meinem ~ gefehlt** *(iron.)* you're/that's all I needed; **jeder ist seines ~es Schmied** *(Spr.)* life is what you make it; ~ **und Glas, wie leicht bricht das** *(Spr.)* happiness is such a fragile thing; **c)** *(Fortuna)* fortune; luck; **das ~ ist launisch** fortunes change; **er ist ein Liebling des ~s** fortune has always smiled upon him; **das ~ war ihm hold** *(geh.)* fortune smiled [up]on him
glück·bringend *Adj.* lucky
Glucke ['glʊkə] **die; ~, ~n** brood-hen; mother hen
glucken *itr. V.* **a)** *(brüten)* brood; **b)** *(ugs.: herumsitzen)* sit around; **c)** *(Laut hervorbringen)* cluck
glücken *tr. V.; mit sein* succeed; be successful; **etw. glückt jmdm.** sb. is successful with sth.; **ein geglückter Versuch** a successful attempt; **die Flucht ist nicht geglückt** the escape[-attempt] failed; **es glückt jmdm., etw. zu tun** sb. manages to do sth.
gluckern ['glʊkɐn] *itr. V.* gurgle; glug
glück·haft *Adj. (geh.)* happy
Gluck·henne die *s.* **Glucke**
glücklich 1. *Adj.* **a)** *(von Glück erfüllt)* happy (**über** + *Akk.* about); **wunschlos/unsagbar ~ sein** be perfectly happy; **Geld allein macht nicht ~:** money by itself won't bring happiness; **du Glücklicher!** you lucky thing!; lucky you!; **wer ist denn der/die Glückliche?** who is the lucky man/woman/girl *etc.?;* **b)** *(erfolgreich)* lucky ⟨*winner*⟩; successful ⟨*outcome*⟩; safe ⟨*journey*⟩; happy ⟨*ending*⟩; **c)** *(vorteilhaft)* fortunate; **ein ~er Zufall** a happy coincidence; a lucky chance; *s. auch* **Hand f. 2.** *adv.* **a)** *(erfolgreich)* successfully; **b)** *(vorteilhaft, zufrieden)* happily ⟨*chosen, married*⟩; **c)** *(endlich)* eventually; at last
glücklicher·weise *Adv.* fortunately; luckily
glück·los *Adj.* luckless ⟨*enterprise*⟩; unhappy ⟨*existence etc.*⟩
Glück·sache *s.* **Glücks·sache**
Glücks-: ~bote der bearer of good news *or* glad tidings; **~botschaft die** good news *sing.;* glad tidings *pl.;* **~bringer der** lucky *or* good-luck charm; [lucky] mascot; *(Person)* [lucky] mascot
glück·selig 1. *Adj.* blissfully happy ⟨*person*⟩; blissfully happy, blissful ⟨*time, experience, etc.*⟩. **2.** *adv.* blissfully
Glück·seligkeit die; ~: bliss; blissful happiness
glucksen ['glʊksn̩] *itr. V.* **a)** *s.* **gluckern; b)** *(lachen)* chuckle; ⟨*baby*⟩ gurgle
Glücks-: ~fall der piece *or* stroke of luck; **~fee die: sie war seine ~fee** she [always] brought him good luck; **~gefühl das** feeling of happiness; **~göttin die** goddess of fortune; Fortune *no art.;* **~güter** *Pl. (geh.)* riches; **~käfer der** *s.* **Marienkäfer; ~kind das** lucky person; **er/sie ist ein ~kind** he/she was born lucky; **~klee der** four-leaf *or* four-leaved clover; **~linie die** line of fortune; **~pfennig der** lucky penny; **~pilz der** *(ugs.)* lucky devil *(coll.) or* beggar *(coll.);* **~rad das** wheel of fortune; **~ritter der** *(abwertend)* adventurer; fortune-hunter
Glück[s]·sache die: das ist ~: it's a matter of luck
Glücks-: ~schwein[chen] das *model of a pig as a symbol of good luck or as a good-luck charm;* **~spiel das a)** game of chance; **dem ~spiel verfallen sein** be addicted to gambling; **b)** *(fig.)* matter of luck; lottery; **~spieler der** gambler; **~stern der** lucky star; **~strähne die** lucky streak; **eine ~strähne haben** have hit a lucky streak; have a run of good luck; **~tag der** lucky day
glück·strahlend 1. *Adj.* radiant; radiantly happy. **2.** *adv.* **sie verkündete uns ~, daß sie heiraten werde** she was radiant with happiness *or* radiantly happy as she told us she was going to get married
Glücks-: ~treffer der a) *(Gewinn)* bit *or* piece of luck; **b)** *(beim Schießen)* lucky hit; fluke; **~umstand der** fortunate circumstance; **~zahl die** lucky number
glück·verheißend *Adj. (geh.)* auspicious, propitious ⟨*sign, omen*⟩; ⟨*smile*⟩ which holds/held out the promise of happiness
Glück·wunsch der congratulations *pl.;* **herzlichen ~ zur Beförderung!** [many] congratulations on your promotion!; **herzlichen ~ zum Geburtstag!** happy birthday!; many happy returns of the day!; **jmdm. die herzlichsten Glückwünsche übermitteln/senden** convey/send one's congratulations to sb.
Glückwunsch-: ~adresse die message of congratulation; congratulatory message; **~karte die** congratulations card; *(zum Geburtstag, zu Weihnachten usw.)* greetings card; **~schreiben das** letter of congratulation; congratulatory letter; **~telegramm das** telegram of congratulations; congratulatory telegram; *(zum Geburtstag, zu Weihnachten usw.)* greetings telegram
Glucose [glu'ko:ze] **die; ~** *(Chemie)* glucose
Glüh-: ~birne die light-bulb; **~draht der** filament
glühen ['gly:ən] **1.** *itr. V.* **a)** *(leuchten)* glow; *(fig.)* ⟨*eyes, cheeks, etc.*⟩ be aglow, glow; **heiß glühte die Sonne über der Wüste** *(fig.)* the sun was burning down on the desert; **ihr Körper glühte im Fieber** *(fig.)* her body was burning with fever; **b)** *(geh.: erregt sein)* burn; **in Liebe/Leidenschaft ~:** burn with love/passion; **vor Begeisterung ~:** be fired with enthusiasm. **2.** *tr. V. (zum Leuchten bringen)* heat until red-hot
glühend 1. *Adj.* **a)** *(heiß)* red-hot ⟨*metal etc.*⟩; *(fig.)* blazing ⟨*heat*⟩; burning ⟨*hatred*⟩; flushed, burning ⟨*cheeks*⟩; **b)** *(begeistert)* ardent ⟨*admirer etc.*⟩; passionate ⟨*words, letter, etc.*⟩. **2.** *adv.* **a)** *(heiß)* ~ heiß scorching *or* blazing hot; ~ **rot** red-hot; **b)** *(begeistert)* ⟨*love*⟩ passionately; ⟨*admire*⟩ ardently; **jmdn. ~ beneiden** be intensely envious of sb.
glühend-: ~heiß *Adj. (präd. getrennt geschrieben)* scorching *or* blazing hot; **~rot** *Adj. (präd. getrennt geschrieben)* red-hot
Glüh-: ~faden der filament; **~kerze die** *(Kfz-W.)* glow plug; **~lampe die** light bulb; **~ofen der** *(Technik)* annealing furnace; **~strumpf der** gas mantle; **~wein der** mulled wine; glühwein; **~würmchen das** *(ugs.) (weiblich)* glow-worm; *(männlich)* firefly
Glukose *s.* **Glucose**
Glupsch·augen ['glʊpʃ-] *Pl. (nordd.)* goggle-eyes; ~ **machen** *od.* **bekommen** go goggle-eyed; goggle
Glut [glu:t] **die; ~, ~en a)** embers *pl.; (von einer Zigarette)* [burning] ash; *(fig.)* [blazing] heat; *(des Fiebers)* [burning] heat; **die ~ ihrer Wangen** the flush on her cheeks; **die ~ des Abendhimmels** the glow of the evening sky; **b)** *(geh.: Leidenschaft)* passion; **die ~ seiner Leidenschaft** the ardour of his passion; **die ~ seines Hasses** the fire of his hatred
Glutamat [gluta'ma:t] **das; ~[e]s, ~e** *(Chemie)* glutamate
Glutamin [gluta'mi:n] **das; ~s, ~e** *(Chemie)* glutamine
Glutamin·säure die *(Chemie)* glutamic acid
glut-, Glut-: ~äugig *Adj.* fiery-eyed; **~hauch der** *(dichter.)* scorching *or* sweltering heat; **~heiß** *Adj.* blazing *or* swelteringly hot; **~hitze die** blazing *or* sweltering heat; **~rot** *Adj.* fiery red; **~voll 1.** *Adj.* passionate; **2.** *adv.* passionately
Glycerin *(fachspr.) s.* **Glyzerin**
Glykogen [glyko'ge:n] **das; ~s** *(Med., Biol.)* glycogen
Glykol [gly'ko:l] **das; ~s, ~e** *(Chemie)* [ethylene] glycol
Glyzerin [glytse'ri:n] **das; ~s** glycerine; glycerol *(Chem.)*
Glyzerin·creme die glycerine cream
Glyzine, Glyzinie [gly'tsi:n(i)ə] **die; ~, ~n** wistaria
GmbH *Abk.* **Gesellschaft mit beschränkter Haftung** ≈ Plc, plc
g-Moll ['ge:mɔl] **das; ~** *(Musik)* G minor; *s. auch* **a-Moll**
Gnade ['gna:də] **die; ~, ~n a)** *(Gewogenheit)* favour; **die ~ [des Königs] erlangen/verlieren** gain/lose [the king's] favour; **die ~ haben, etw. zu tun** *(iron.)* graciously consent to do sth. *(iron.);* **vor jmdm.** *od.* **vor jmds. Augen ~ finden** find favour with sb. *or* in sb.'s eyes; **jmdm. auf ~ und** *od.* **oder Ungnade ausgeliefert sein** be [completely] at sb.'s mercy; **etw. aus ~ [und Barmherzigkeit] tun** do sth. out of the kindness of one's heart; **in ~n wieder aufgenommen werden** be restored to favour; **bei jmdm. in [hohen] ~n stehen** *(geh.)* stand high in sb.'s favour; **von jmds. ~n** by the grace of sb.; **b)** *(Rel.: Güte)* grace; **c)** *(Milde)* mercy; ~ **walten lassen** show mercy; be lenient; ~ **vor** *od.* **für Recht ergehen lassen** temper justice with mercy; **d)** *(veraltete Anrede)* **Euer** *od.* **Ihro** *od.* **Ihre ~n** Your Grace
gnaden *itr. V. in* **gnade mir/dir Gott!** God *or* Heaven help me/you!
gnaden-, Gnaden-: ~akt der act of mercy; **~beweis der, ~bezeigung die** token of [his/her *etc.*] favour; **~bild das** *(kath. Rel.) picture of Christ, the Virgin Mary, or a saint, possessing miraculous powers;* **~brot das: jmdm./einem Tier das ~brot geben** keep sb./an animal in his/her/its old age; **einem Pferd das ~brot geben** put a horse out to grass; **~erweis der** *(Rechtsw.)* pardon; **~frist die** reprieve; **jmdm. eine ~frist von 4 Wochen gewähren** give sb. four weeks' grace; **ihm bleibt eine**

~**frist von einer Woche** he has a week left; ~**gesuch das** plea for clemency; ~**instanz die** *person in whom or authority in which the right of pardon is vested;* ~**los** *(auch fig.)* **1.** *Adj.* merciless; **2.** *adv.* mercilessly; ~**losigkeit die;** ~: mercilessness; ~**reich** *Adj. (geh.)* gracious; ~**schuß der** coup de grâce *(by shooting);* **einem Pferd den** ~**schuß geben** put a horse out of its misery [by shooting it]; ~**stoß der** coup de grâce *(with sword etc.);* ~**tod der** euthanasia; mercy killing; **jmdm. den** ~**tod gewähren** allow sb. to die; ~**voll** *Adj. (geh.)* gracious; ~**weg der: auf dem** ~**weg** by a pardon; **ihm steht der** ~**weg offen** he can ask *or* has the right to ask for a pardon

gnädig ['gnɛːdɪç] **1.** *Adj.* **a)** *(oft iron.)* gracious; **er war so** ~, **mich nach Hause zu begleiten** *(iron.)* he condescended to take me home; *(Anrede)* ~**es Fräulein/**~**e Frau** madam; ~**er Herr** *(veralt.)* sir; **die** ~**e Frau/das** ~**e Fräulein/der** ~**e Herr** *(veralt.)* madam/the young lady/the master; **die Gnädige** *(spött.)* her ladyship; **b)** *(glimpflich)* lenient, light ⟨*sentence etc.*⟩; **c)** *(Rel.)* gracious ⟨*God*⟩; **Gott ist allen Sündern** ~: God is merciful to *or* has mercy on all sinners; **Gott sei uns** ~: [may] the good Lord preserve us. **2.** *adv.* **a)** *(oft iron.)* graciously; **b)** *(glimpflich)* **das ist** ~ **abgegangen** it turned out not to be too bad; **machen Sie es** ~ **mit mir** *(scherzh.)* have mercy on me *(joc.)*

Gneis [gnais] **der;** ~**es,** ~**e** *(Geol.)* gneiss

Gnom [gnoːm] **der;** ~**en,** ~**en** gnome; *(fig.: ugs.)* little twerp *(sl.)*

gnomen·haft *Adj.* gnome-like

Gnosis ['gnoːzɪs] **die;** ~ *(Rel.)* gnosis

Gnostiker ['gnɔstikɐ] **der;** ~**s,** ~ *(Rel.)* gnostic

gnostisch *Adj. (Rel.)* gnostic

Gnostizismus [gnɔsti'tsɪsmʊs] **der;** ~ *(Rel.)* gnosticism *no art.*

Gnu [gnuː] **das;** ~**s,** ~**s** gnu

Go [goː] **das;** ~: go

Goal [goːl] **das;** ~**s,** ~**s** *(österr., schweiz. Sport)* goal

Goal-: ~**getter** [-gɛtɐ] **der;** ~**s,** ~ *(Sport)* goal-scorer; ~**keeper** [-kiːpɐ] **der;** ~**s,** ~ *(Sport, bes. österr. u. schweiz.)* goalkeeper

Gobelin [gobə'lɛ̃ː] **der;** ~**s,** ~**s** Gobelin [tapestry]

Gobelin·stickerei die Gobelin embroidery

Go-cart *s.* **Go-Kart**

Gockel ['gɔkl̩] **der;** ~**s,** ~ *(bes. südd., sonst ugs. scherzh.)* cock; **stolz wie ein** ~: [as] proud as a peacock; **ein verliebter alter** ~ *(fig.)* an amorous old goat *(coll.)*

Gockel·hahn der *s.* **Gockel**

Godemiché [goːdmi'ʃeː] **der;** ~, ~**s** dildo

Goetheana [gøte'aːna] *Pl.* works by and on Goethe

goethesch ['gøːtəʃ], **goethisch** ['gøːtɪʃ] *Adj.* Goethean

Goethesch, Goethisch *Adj.* Goethe's ⟨*poems etc.*⟩; ⟨*poems etc.*⟩ of Goethe

Go-go-Girl ['goːgogøːɐ̯l] **das** go-go girl *or* dancer

Go-in [goː'ɪn] **das;** ~**s,** ~**s: ein** ~ **veranstalten** disrupt the/a meeting

Goi ['goːi] **der;** ~**[s], Gojim** ['goːjɪm] goy

Go-Kart ['goːkart] **der;** ~**[s],** ~**s** go-kart *(Brit.);* kart

Golan·höhen [go'laːn-] *Pl.* Golan Heights

gold [gɔlt] *Adj. in* **uns geht's ja noch** ~ *(ugs.)* we're still doing just marvellously

Gold das; ~**[e]s** gold; **etw. ist aus** ~: sth. is [made of] gold; **ein Barren** ~: a gold bar *or* ingot; **das schwarze** ~ *(fig.)* black gold *(fig.);* **das flüssige** ~ *(fig.)* liquid gold *(fig.);* **es ist nicht alles** ~, **was glänzt** *(Spr.)* all that glitters *or* glistens is not gold *(prov.);* **treu wie** ~ **sein** be absolutely loyal *or* faithful; **etw. in** ~ **bezahlen** pay for sth. in gold; ~ **in der Kehle haben** *(fig.)* have a golden voice; **jmd. ist nicht mit** ~ **zu bezahlen** sb. is worth his/her weight in gold *(fig.);* **etw. ist nicht mit** ~ **zu bezahlen** *od.* **aufzuwiegen** sth. is invaluable; **olympisches** ~: Olympic gold; **er hat bereits dreimal olympisches** ~ **geholt** he has already won three Olympic gold medals *or* golds

gold-, Gold-: ~**ader die** vein of gold; ~**ammer die** yellowhammer; ~**arbeit die** goldwork; *(Gegenstand)* piece of goldwork; ~**auflage die** gold plating *no indef. art.;* ~**barren der** gold bar *or* ingot; ~**barsch der** *s.* **Rotbarsch;** ~**bestand der** gold reserves *pl.;* ~**bestickt** *Adj.* embroidered with gold [thread] *postpos.;* ~**betreßt** *Adj.* trimmed with gold braid *postpos.;* ~**blech das** rolled gold; ~**blond** *Adj.* golden ⟨*hair etc.*⟩; ~**borte die** gold braid; ~**braun** *Adj.* golden brown; ~**broiler der** *(DDR)* spit-roasted chicken; ~**brokat der** gold brocade; ~**deckung die** gold cover; ~**doublé das** *s.* ~**dublee;** ~**druck der** gold tooling; ~**dublee das** rolled gold; ~**echt** *Adj. (ugs.)* completely genuine ⟨*person*⟩

golden 1. *Adj.* **a)** gold ⟨*bracelet, watch, etc.*⟩; **das Goldene Kalb** *(bibl.)* the golden calf; **der Tanz ums Goldene Kalb** the worship of the golden calf *or* Mammon; **eine** ~**e Schallplatte** a gold disc; **die Goldene Bulle** *(hist.)* the Golden Bull; **das Goldene Vlies** *(Myth.)* the Golden Fleece; *(Orden)* the [order of the] Golden Fleece; **das Goldene Buch [der Stadt]** the [town's] visitors' book; **die Goldene Stadt** the Golden City *(Prague);* **b)** *(dichter.: goldfarben)* golden; **c)** *(herrlich)* golden ⟨*days, memories, etc.*⟩; blissful ⟨*freedom etc.*⟩; **der** ~**e Westen** the promised land in the West; ~**e Worte/Lehren** words of wisdom/wise teachings; **einen** ~**en Humor haben** have a wonderful sense of humour; **ein** ~**es Herz haben** have a heart of gold; **die** ~**e Mitte** *od.* **den** ~**en Mittelweg finden/wählen** find/strike a happy medium; **das Goldene Zeitalter** the Golden Age; **die goldenen zwanziger [Jahre]** the roaring twenties; **der Goldene Schnitt** *(Math.)* the golden section. **2.** *adv.* like gold

gold-, Gold-: ~**esel der** *(ugs.)* **ich bin auch kein** ~**esel** I'm not made of money *(coll.);* ~**faden der** gold thread; ~**farben,** ~**farbig** *Adj.* gold-coloured; golden; ~**fasan der** golden pheasant; ~**feder die** gold nib; ~**fieber das** gold fever; ~**folie die** gold foil; ~**fuchs der a)** *(Pferd)* golden chestnut [horse]; **b)** *(veralt.: Goldstück)* gold coin *or* piece; ~**füllung die** gold filling; ~**fund der** gold find *or* strike; ~**gefaßt** *Adj.* gold-rimmed ⟨*glasses*⟩; ⟨*jewel*⟩ mounted in gold; ~**gehalt der** gold content; ~**gelb** *Adj.* golden yellow; ~**gerändert** *Adj.* ⟨*plate etc.*⟩ edged with gold; gold-rimmed ⟨*glasses*⟩; ~**glänzend** *Adj.* shining gold; ~**gräber der** gold-digger; ~**grube die** *(auch fig.)* gold-mine; ~**haltig** *Adj.* gold-bearing; auriferous; ~**hamster der** golden hamster

goldig 1. *Adj. (niedlich, landsch.: nett)* sweet. **2.** *adv.* sweetly

Gold-: ~**junge der a)** *(Kosewort)* good [little] boy; **b)** *(Sportjargon)* gold medallist; gold-medal winner; ~**käfer der a)** rose chafer; rose beetle; **b)** *(ugs.: reiches Mädchen)* rich girl; ~**kette die** gold chain; ~**kind das** *(ugs. Kosew.)* little treasure *(coll.);* **mein** ~**kind** my precious *(coll.);* my pet; ~**klumpen der** gold nugget; ~**krone die** *(Zahnmed.)* gold crown; ~**kurs der** *(Börsenw.)* price of gold; gold price; ~**küste die;** ~ *(Geogr.)* Gold Coast; ~**lack der a)** gold lacquer; **b)** *(Bot.)* wallflower; ~**lager·stätte die** gold deposit; ~**legierung die** gold alloy; ~**leiste die** gilt strip *or* fillet; ~**macher der** alchemist; ~**mädchen das** *(Sportjargon)* gold medallist; gold-medal winner; ~**mark die** *(hist.)* gold mark

Gold·medaille die gold medal

Goldmedaillen-: ~**gewinner der,** ~**gewinnerin die** gold medallist; gold-medal winner

gold-, Gold-: ~**mine die** gold mine; ~**münze die** gold coin; ~**papier das** gold[-coloured] paper; ~**parität die** *(Wirtsch.)* gold parity; ~**pool der** *(Wirtsch.)* gold pool; ~**preis der** price of gold; gold price; ~**probe die** gold assay; ~**rahmen der** gold *or* gilt frame; ~**rausch der** gold fever; ~**regen der a)** *(Bot.)* laburnum; golden rain; **b)** *(Feuerwerk)* golden rain; **c)** *(Reichtum)* riches *pl.;* wealth; ~**reif der** *(geh.)* gold ring; *(Armband)* gold bracelet; ~**reserve die** gold reserve; ~**richtig** *(ugs.)* **1.** *Adj.* absolutely *or* dead right; **du bist** ~**richtig, so wie du bist** you're perfectly all right as you are; **2.** *adv.* absolutely right; ~**schatz der a)** *(Schatz)* gold treasure; *(verborgen auch)* hoard of gold; **b)** *(Kosew.)* treasure

Gold·schmied der goldsmith

Goldschmiede-: ~**arbeit die** piece of goldwork; ~**handwerk das** goldsmith's craft; goldwork *no art.;* ~**kunst die;** *o. Pl.* goldsmith's art; goldwork *no art.*

Gold-: ~**schmuck der** gold jewelry *or* *(Brit.)* jewellery; ~**schnitt der** gilt edging; ~**schrift die** gold lettering; ~**staub der** gold dust; ~**stück das** *(hist.)* gold piece; **sie ist ein** ~**stück** *(fig.)* she is a [real] treasure; ~**sucher der** gold prospector; ~**ton der** golden colour; ~**topas der** yellow topaz; ~**tresse die** gold braid; ~**überzug der** layer of gold plate; ~**uhr die** gold watch; ~**vorkommen das** gold deposit; ~**waage die** gold balance; **alles** *od.* **jedes Wort auf die** ~**waage legen** *(wörtlich nehmen)* take everything *or* every word [too] literally; *(vorsichtig äußern)* weigh one's words very carefully; ~**währung die** *(Wirtsch.)* currency tied to the gold standard; ~**waren** *Pl.* gold articles; ~**wäscher der** gold washer; ~**wert der a)** *(Wert des Goldes)* value of gold; **b)** *(Wert in Gold)* value in gold; ~**zahn der** *(ugs.)* gold tooth

Golem ['goːlɛm] **der;** ~**s** golem

[1]Golf [gɔlf] **der;** ~**[e]s,** ~**e** gulf; **der** ~ **von Neapel** the Bay of Naples

[2]Golf das; ~**s** *(Sport)* golf

Golf·ball der golf ball

Golfer der; ~**s,** ~, **Golferin die;** ~, ~**nen** golfer

Golf-: ~**hose die** golf[ing] trousers *pl.;* ~**mütze die** golf[ing] cap; ~**platz der** golf-course; ~**schläger der** golf club; ~**schuh der** golf[ing] shoe; ~**spieler der,** ~**spielerin die** golfer; ~**staat der** Gulf State; ~**strom der** Gulf Stream; ~**turnier das** golf tournament

Golgatha ['gɔlgata] **das;** ~**[s]** *(bibl.)* Golgotha; **für ihn war diese Niederlage/dieser Verlust ein** ~ *(fig. geh.)* this defeat/loss caused him much pain and suffering

Goliath ['goːliat] **der;** ~**s,** ~**s** Goliath

Gomorrha [go'mɔra] *s.* **Sodom**

Gondel ['gɔndl̩] **die;** ~, ~**n** gondola

Gondel-: ~**bahn die a)** *(Seilbahn)* cable railway; **b)** *(schweiz.) s.* **Sessellift;** ~**fahrt die** trip in a gondola; gondola trip

gondeln *itr. V.; mit sein (ugs.)* **a)** *(mit einem Boot)* cruise; **b)** *(reisen)* travel around; **c)** *(herumfahren)* drive *or* cruise around; **durch die Stadt** ~: drive *or* cruise around town

Gondoliere [gɔndo'li̯eːrə] **der;** ~**s, Gondolieri** gondolier

Gong [gɔŋ] **der;** ~**s,** ~**s** gong

gongen *itr. V.* **es hat gegongt** the gong has sounded; **der Butler gongte zum Abendessen** the butler sounded the gong for dinner

Gong·schlag der stroke of the/a gong; **beim** ~: when the gong sounds/sounded

gönnen ['gœnən] *tr. V.* **a)** *(zugestehen)*

jmdm. etw. ~: not begrudge sb. sth.; **ich gönne ihm diesen Erfolg von ganzem Herzen** I'm delighted *or* very pleased for him that he has had this success; **jmdm. den Mißerfolg ~** *(iron.)* delight in sb.'s misfortune; **b)** *(zukommen lassen)* **sich/jmdm. etw. ~:** give *or* allow oneself/sb. sth.; **sie gönnte sich** *(Dat.)* **einen großen Cognac** she treated herself to a large cognac; **sie gönnte ihm keinen Blick/kein Wort** she didn't spare him a single glance/she didn't say a single word to him

Gönner der; ~s, ~: patron

gönnerhaft *(abwertend)* **1.** *Adj.* patronizing; **mit ~er Miene** with a patronizing expression [on his/her face]. **2.** *adv.* patronizingly; in a patronizing manner

Gönnerin die; ~, ~nen patroness

Gönner·miene die *(abwertend)* patronizing expression; **mit ~:** with a patronizing expression [on his/her face]

Gonokokkus [gono'kɔkʊs] **der; ~, Gonokokken** *(Med.)* gonococcus

Gonorrhö[e] [gonɔ'rø:] **die; ~, Gonorrhöen** [gonɔ'rø:ən] *(Med.)* gonorrhoea

Goodwill ['gʊd'wɪl] **der; ~s a)** *(Ansehen)* good name; **b)** *(Wohlwollen)* goodwill

Goodwill-: ~reise die goodwill trip **(nach** to); **~tour die** goodwill tour **(durch** of)

Göpel ['gø:pl] **der; ~s, ~:** whim

gor [go:ɐ̯] *3. Pers. Sg. Prät. v.* **gären**

Gör [gø:ɐ̯] **das; ~[e]s, ~en** *(nordd., oft abwertend) s.* **Göre**

gordisch ['gɔrdɪʃ] *Adj.* **der Gordische Knoten** the Gordian knot; **ein ~er Knoten** *(fig.)* a Gordian knot *(fig.)*

Göre ['gø:rə] **die; ~, ~n** *(nordd., oft abwertend)* **a)** *(Kind)* child; kid *(coll.)*; brat *(coll. derog.)*; **b)** *(freches Mädchen)* [cheeky *or* saucy] little madam *(coll.)*

Gorilla [go'rɪla] **der; ~s, ~s a)** gorilla; **b)** *(ugs.: Leibwächter)* heavy *(coll.)*

Gosch[e] ['gɔʃ(ə)], **Goschen** ['gɔʃn̩] **die; ~, Goschen** *(südd., österr. meist abwertend)* mouth; **eine große/freche ~ haben** *(derb)* have a big mouth *(coll.)*/be a cheeky so-and-so *(coll.)*; **die ~ halten** *(derb)* shut one's gob *or* trap *(sl.)*

Gospel ['gɔspl] **das** *od.* **der; ~s, ~s, Gospel·song der; ~s, ~s** gospel song

goß [gɔs] *1. u. 3. Pers. Sg. Prät. v.* **gießen**

Gosse ['gɔsə] **die; ~, ~n** gutter; *(fig. abwertend)* **aus der ~ kommen** come from the gutter; **in der ~ enden** end up in the gutter; **jmdn.** *od.* **jmds. Namen durch die ~ ziehen** drag sb.'s name through the mud

Gossen-: ~jargon der, ~sprache die *(abwertend)* gutter language; language of the gutter

¹Gote ['go:tə] **der; ~n, ~n** Goth

²Gote der; ~n, ~n *(bes. südd.: Pate)* godfather

³Gote die; ~, ~n *(bes. südd.: Patin)* godmother

Gotha ['go:ta] **der; ~:** *almanac containing information on the nobility of Europe*

Gotik ['go:tɪk] **die; ~** *(Stil)* Gothic [style]; *(Epoche)* Gothic period

gotisch *Adj.* Gothic; **die ~e Schrift** Gothic [script]

Gott [gɔt] **der; ~es, Götter** ['gœtɐ] **a)** *o. Pl.; o. Art.* God; **~ Vater** God the Father; **hier ruht in ~ ...:** here lies ...; **~ segne dich!** God bless you!; **~es Mühlen mahlen langsam** *(Spr.)* the mills of God grind slowly; **bei ~ ist kein Ding unmöglich** *(Spr.)* with God all things are possible; **grüß [dich] ~!** *(landsch.)* hello!; **behüt' dich ~!** *(südd., österr.)* goodbye! God bless!; **vergelt's ~!** *(landsch.)* thank you! God bless you!; **großer** *od.* **mein ~!** good God!; **o** *od.* **ach [du lieber] ~!** goodness me!; **weiß ~:** God *or* heaven knows; **~ behüte** God *or* Heaven forbid; **~ steh mir bei** God help me; **gebe ~, daß alles gut ausgeht** please God, may everything turn out all right; **wie ~ ihn/sie geschaffen hat** *(scherzh.)* in his/her birthday suit *(joc.)*; in the altogether *(joc.)*; **~ und die Welt** all the world and his wife; **über ~ und die Welt quatschen** *(ugs.)* talk about everything under the sun *(coll.)*; **~ sei Dank!** *(ugs.)* thank God!; **~ sei's geklagt!** alas; **um ~es Willen** *(bei Erschrecken)* for God's sake; *(bei einer Bitte)* for heaven's *or* goodness' sake; **tue es in ~es Namen** *(ugs.)* do it and have done with it; **da sei ~ vor!** God forbid!; **~ soll mich strafen, wenn ...:** may God strike me down if ...; **so ~ will** *(ugs.)* God willing; **~ hab' ihn selig** God rest his soul; **wie ~ in Frankreich leben** *(ugs.)* live in the lap of luxury; **den lieben ~ einen guten Mann sein lassen** *(ugs.)* take things as they come; **ein Wetter, daß [es] ~ erbarm'** *(ugs.)* abominable weather; **er spielt/kocht, daß [es] ~ erbarm'** his playing/cooking is abominable; **dem lieben ~ den Tag stehlen** laze the day away; **er/sie ist ganz und gar von ~ verlassen** *(ugs.)* he/she has quite taken leave of his/her senses; **b)** *(übermenschliches Wesen)* god; **wie ein junger ~ spielen/tanzen** play/dance divinely; **das wissen die Götter** *(ugs.)* God *or* heaven only knows; **es war ein Bild für die Götter** *(ugs.)* it was priceless *(coll.)*

gott·ähnlich *Adj.* godlike

Gottchen *in* **[ach] ~!** oh dear!

Gott·erbarmen das *in* **zum ~ sein** *(mitleiderregend)* be pitiful; *(schlecht)* be pathetic; **zum ~ schreien** cry out pitifully; **zum ~ spielen/singen** play/sing pathetically

Götter-: ~bild das idol; **~bote der** messenger of the gods; **~dämmerung die** *(nord. Myth.)* twilight of the gods; *(fig.)* end of civilization; götterdämmerung; **~gatte der** *(ugs. scherzh.)* lord and master *(coll. joc.)*

gott·ergeben 1. *Adj.* meek. **2.** *adv.* meekly

Gott·ergebenheit die meekness

götter-, Götter-: ~gestalt die god; **~gleich** *Adj.* godlike; **~sage die a)** *(Myth.)* mythology of the gods; **b)** *(Sage von einem Gott)* myth about a god/the gods; **~speise die a)** *o. Pl. (Myth.)* food of the gods; **b)** *(Kochk.)* jelly; **~trank der;** *o. Pl. (Myth.)* drink of the gods; **~vater der** *(Myth.)* father of the gods

gottes-, Gottes-: ~acker der *(geh.)* God's Acre *no art. (literary)*; graveyard; **~begriff der** conception of God; **~beweis der** proof of the existence of God; **~dienst der** service; **den ~dienst besuchen** go to church; **~erkenntnis die;** *o. Pl.* knowledge of God; **~friede der** *(hist.)* Truce of God; **~furcht die** fear of God; **~fürchtig** *Adj.* god-fearing; **~gabe die** gift from God; **~gelehrte der** *(veralt.)* theologian; **~gnadentum das; ~s** *(hist.)* divine right [of kings]; **~haus das** *(geh.)* house of God; **~lästerer der** blasphemer; **~lästerlich 1.** *Adj.* blasphemous; **2.** *adv.* blasphemously; **~lästerung die** blasphemy; **~lohn der** God's reward; **um ~lohn** for love; **~mann der;** *Pl.* **~männer** *(geh.)* man of God; **~mutter die;** *o. Pl.* Mother of God; **~sohn der;** *o. Pl.* Son of God; **~staat der** theocracy; **~urteil das** *(hist.)* trial by ordeal

gott-: ~gefällig *Adj. (geh.)* pleasing to God *postpos.*; **~gegeben** *Adj.* God-given; **~gesandt** *Adj.* sent by God *postpos.*; **~geweiht** *Adj.* dedicated to God *postpos.*; **~gewollt** *Adj.* ordained by God *postpos.*; **~gläubig** *Adj.* **a)** *(veralt.)* religious; **b)** *(ns.)* **~gläubig sein** be a theist but of no particular denomination

Gottheit die; ~, ~en a) *(Gott, Göttin)* deity; **b)** *o. Pl. (geh.: Gottsein)* divinity; **c)** *o. Pl. (geh.: Gott)* **die ~:** the Godhead

Göttin ['gœtɪn] **die; ~, ~nen** goddess

göttlich ['gœtlɪç] **1.** *Adj.* **a)** *(Gott eigen od. ähnlich; herrlich)* divine ⟨*grace, beauty, etc.*⟩; **die ~e Gerechtigkeit** divine justice; **b)** *(einem Gott zukommend)* god-like ⟨*status etc.*⟩; **jmdm. ~e Verehrung entgegenbringen** worship sb. as if he/she were a God. **2.** *adv. (herrlich)* divinely

gott-, Gott-: ~lob *adv.* thank goodness; **es hat ~lob nicht geschneit** it didn't snow, thank goodness; **~los 1.** *Adj.* **a)** *(verwerflich)* ungodly, wicked ⟨*life etc.*⟩; impious ⟨*words, speech, etc.*⟩; *(pietätlos)* irreverent; **b)** *(Gott leugnend)* godless ⟨*theory etc.*⟩; **2.** *adv. (verwerflich)* irreverently; **~losigkeit die; ~ a)** *(Verwerflichkeit)* ungodliness; wickedness; *(von der Rede)* impiety; **b)** *(Unglauben)* godlessness; **~mensch der** God-man; **~sei·bei·uns der; ~** *(verhüll.)* **der ~seibeiuns** the Evil One

gotts·erbärmlich, gotts·jämmerlich 1. *Adj. (salopp)* **a)** *(erbärmlich)* dreadful *(coll.)*; **b)** *(stark)* dreadful *(coll.)*; terrible *(coll.)*; God-awful *(sl.)*. **2.** *adv.* terribly *(coll.)*; dreadfully *(coll.)*

gott-, Gott-: ~vater der; *o. Pl.* God the Father; **~verdammich** [~fɛɐ̯'damɪç] *Interj. (derb)* God damn it *(sl.)*; God Almighty *(sl.)*; **~verdammt** *Adj.; nicht präd. (salopp)*, **~verflucht** *Adj.; nicht präd. (salopp)* goddamn[ed] *(sl.)*; **~vergessen** *Adj.* **a)** *(gottlos)* godless; **b)** *s.* **~verlassen; ~verlassen** *Adj.* **a)** *(ugs.: abseits)* godforsaken; **b)** *(von Gott verlassen)* forsaken by God *postpos.*; **sich ~verlassen fühlen** feel that God has forsaken one; **~vertrauen das** trust in God; **~voll 1.** *Adj.* **a)** *(ugs.: komisch)* priceless *(coll.)*; **b)** *(herrlich)* divine; **2.** *adv.* divinely

Götze ['gœtsə] **der; ~n, ~n** *(auch fig.)* idol

Götzen-: ~anbeter der *s.* **~diener; ~bild das** idol; graven image *(bibl.)*; *(fig.)* idol; **~diener der** idolater; *(fig.)* worshipper; **~dienerin die** idolatress; *(fig.)* worshipper; **~dienst der;** *o. Pl.* idolatry *no art.*; *(fig.)* worship; **~dienst leisten** practise idolatry; **~verehrung die;** *o. Pl.* idolatry *no art.*

Götz·zitat ['gœts-] **das** *the insulting remark 'du kannst mich am Arsch lecken' or the like, frequently used in altercations; a verbal equivalent of the V-sign*

Gouache [gua(:)ʃ] **die; ~, ~n** gouache

Gouda ['gauda] **der; ~s, ~s, Gouda·käse der** Gouda [cheese]

Goulasch *s.* **Gulasch**

Gourmand [gʊr'mã:] **der; ~s, ~s** gourmand

Gourmet [gʊr'mɛ] **der; ~s, ~s** gourmet

goutieren [gu'ti:rən] *tr. V. (geh.)* appreciate

Gouvernante [guvɛr'nantə] **die; ~, ~n** governess

gouvernanten·haft 1. *Adj.* schoolmarmish *(coll.)*. **2.** *adv.* like a schoolmarm *(coll.)*

Gouvernement [guvɛrnə'mã:] **das; ~s, ~s a)** *(Regierung)* government; *(Verwaltung)* administration; **b)** *(Verwaltungsbezirk)* province

Gouverneur [guvɛr'nø:ɐ̯] **der; ~s, ~e** governor

GPU [ge:pe:'|u:] **die; ~:** Ogpu

Grab [gra:p] **das; ~[e]s, Gräber** ['grɛ:bɐ] grave; **das ~ meiner Träume/Hoffnungen** *(fig.)* the end of my dreams/hopes; **er würde sich im ~[e] herumdrehen** *(fig. ugs.)* he would turn in his grave; **das Heilige ~:** the Holy Sepulchre; **das ~ des Unbekannten Soldaten** the tomb of the Unknown Soldier *or* Warrior; **verschwiegen wie ein** *od.* **das ~ sein** *(ugs.)* keep absolutely mum *(coll.)*; **ein feuchtes** *od.* **nasses ~ finden,** *(geh.)* **sein ~ in den Wellen finden** go to a watery grave; meet a watery end; **sich** *(Dat.)* **selbst sein ~ schaufeln** *(fig.)* dig one's own grave *(fig.)*; **mit einem Fuß** *od.* **Bein im ~[e] stehen** *(fig.)* have one foot in the grave *(fig.)*; **jmdn. an den Rand des ~es bringen** *(fig. geh.)* drive sb. to distraction; jmdn. ins ~ bringen be the death of sb.; jmdm. ins ~ folgen (geh.) follow sb. to the grave; etw. mit ins ~ nehmen (geh.) take sth. with one to the grave; bis ins od. ans ~ (fig. geh.) [right up] to the end; jmdn. zu ~e tragen (geh.) bury sb.; seine Pläne/Hoffnungen zu ~e tragen (fig. geh.) abandon one's plans/hopes

Grab·beigabe die burial object

grabbeln ['grabḷn] itr. V. (ugs., bes. nordd.) grope [about]; rummage [about]

Grab·denkmal das s. Grabmal

graben 1. unr. tr. V. a) dig ⟨hole, grave, etc.⟩; dig, carve ⟨groove⟩; Furchen/Falten in jmds. Gesicht ~ (fig.) carve or etch lines/wrinkles in sb.'s face; b) (gewinnen) cut ⟨turf⟩; mine ⟨coal etc.⟩; c) (geh.: eingraben) carve; engrave. 2. unr. itr. V. dig (nach for); seine Zähne/Hände in etw. (Akk.) ~ (geh.) sink or bury one's teeth/hands in sth. 3. unr. refl. V. (geh.) sich in etw. ~: dig into sth.; es grub sich ihm ins Gedächtnis (fig.) it became imprinted or engraved in his memory

Graben der; ~s, Gräben ['grɛ:bn̩] a) ditch; b) (Schützengraben) trench; im ~ liegen lie in the trenches; c) (Festungsgraben) moat; d) (Geol.) rift valley; graben

Graben-: ~bruch der (Geol.) graben; ~kampf der, ~krieg der trench warfare no pl., no indef. art.

Gräber-: ~feld das [large] cemetery; ~fund der grave find

Grabes-: ~kälte die (geh.) deathly cold; ~luft die (geh.) grave-like or tomb-like air no pl., no indef. art.; ~ruhe die, ~stille die deathly silence or hush; ~stimme die (ugs.) sepulchral voice

Grab-: ~fund der s. Gräberfund; ~geläut[e] das [death-]knell; ~gesang der dirge; funeral hymn; (fig.) death-knell; ~gewölbe das vault; (in Kirche, Dom) crypt; ~hügel der grave mound; ~inschrift die inscription [on a/the gravestone]; epitaph; ~kammer die burial chamber; ~kreuz das cross [on the/a grave]; ~legung die; ~, ~en a) o. Pl. (christl. Rel.) entombment of Christ; b) (Kunst) die ~legung Christi the Entombment of Christ; ~licht das; Pl. ~lichter grave-light; ~mal das; Pl. ~mäler, geh. ~male monument; (~stein) gravestone; das ~mal des Unbekannten Soldaten the tomb of the Unknown Soldier or Warrior; ~platte die memorial slab; (aus Metall) memorial plate; ~rede die funeral oration or speech; ~schänder der desecrator of a/the grave/of [the] graves; ~schändung die desecration of a/the grave/of [the] graves

grabschen ['grapʃn̩] 1. tr. V. grab; snatch. 2. itr. V. nach etw. ~: grab at sth.

Grab-: ~spruch der epitaph; ~stätte die tomb; grave; ~stein der gravestone; tombstone; ~stelle die burial plot

gräbst [grɛ:pst] 2. Pers. Sg. Präsens v. graben

gräbt 3. Pers. Sg. Präsens v. graben

Grabung die; ~, ~en (bes. Archäol.) excavation

Grab·urne die funeral urn

Grabungs·fund der archaeological find

Gracht [graxt] die; ~, ~en canal

Grad [gra:t] der; ~[e]s, ~e a) degree; Verbrennungen ersten/zweiten ~es first-/second-degree burns; ein Verwandter ersten/zweiten ~es an immediate relation/a relation once removed; Vettern ersten ~es first cousins; bis zu einem gewissen ~[e] to a [certain] degree; in hohem ~e to a great or large extent; er ist mir in höchstem ~e unsympathisch I dislike him intensely; in geringem ~e to a slight extent; slightly; b) (akademischer ~) degree; (Milit.) rank; c) (Maßeinheit, Math., Geogr.) degree; 20 ~ Celsius/Fahrenheit usw. 20 degrees Centigrade or Celsius/Fahrenheit etc.; 10 ~ Wärme/Kälte 10 degrees above zero/below [zero]; 39 ~ Fieber haben have a temperature of 39 degrees; minus 5 ~/5 ~ minus minus 5 degrees; null ~: zero; etw. auf 90 ~ erhitzen heat sth. to [a temperature of] 90 degrees; Gleichungen zweiten ~es equations of the second degree; quadratic equations; sich um hundertachtzig ~ drehen (fig.) completely change [one's views]; der 50. ~ nördlicher Breite [latitude] 50 degrees North; die Insel liegt auf dem 42. ~ östlicher Länge the longitude of the island is 42 degrees East

grad. Abk. graduiert

grad-, ¹Grad- s. gerad[e]-, Gerad[e]-

²Grad-: ~bogen der graduated arc; ~einteilung die graduation

Gradient [gra'di̯ɛnt] der; ~en, ~en (bes. Math., Physik) gradient

gradieren tr. V. graduate; calibrate

Gradier·werk das thorn-house; graduation-house

grad-, Grad-: ~mäßig s. graduell; ~messer der gauge, yardstick (für of); ~netz das network of parallels and meridians

graduell [gra'du̯ɛl] 1. Adj. gradual ⟨development etc.⟩; slight ⟨difference etc.⟩. 2. adv. gradually; by degrees; ⟨different⟩ in degree

graduieren 1. tr. V. a) (an Hochschulen) award a degree to; graduate (Amer.); b) ⟨in Grade einteilen⟩ graduate; calibrate. 2. itr. V. (an Hochschulen) graduate

graduiert Adj. graduate; ein ~er Ingenieur/eine ~e Ingenieurin an engineering graduate

Graduierte der/die; adj. Dekl. graduate

Graduierung die; ~, ~en graduation

Grad·unterschied der difference of or in degree

grad·weise Adv. gradually; by degrees

Graecum ['grɛ:kʊm] das; ~s (Prüfung) examination in Greek; (Qualifikation) qualification in Greek

Graf [gra:f] der; ~en, ~en a) count; (britischer ~) earl; b) o. Pl. (Titel) Count; (britischer ~) Earl; ~ Koks [von der Gasanstalt] (salopp scherzh.), ~ Rotz [von der Backe] (salopp abwertend) Lord Muck (Brit. joc.)

Grafen·stand der a) (Rang eines Grafen) rank of count; (in Großbritannien) rank of earl; earldom; jmdn. in den ~stand erheben confer the rank of count/earl upon sb.; b) (Gesamtheit der Grafen) counts pl.; (in Großbritannien) earls pl.

Graffito [gra'fi:to] der od. das; ~[s], Graffiti a) (Kunst) graffito; b) Pl. (Kritzelei) graffiti

Grafik s. Graphik

Grafiker s. Graphiker

Gräfin ['grɛ:fɪn] die; ~, ~nen countess; (Titel) Countess

grafisch s. graphisch

gräflich ['grɛ:flɪç] Adj. count's attrib.; of the count postpos., not pred.; (in Großbritannien) earl's; of the earl

Grafschaft die; ~, ~en a) (Amtsbezirk des Grafen) count's land; (in Großbritannien) earldom; b) (Verwaltungsbezirk) county

Graham·brot ['gra:ham-] das wholemeal (Brit.) or (Amer.) wheatmeal bread

gräko- ['grɛ:ko-] Graeco-; ~-lateinisch Graeco-Latin

Gral [gra:l] der; ~[e]s: der [Heilige] ~: the [Holy] Grail

Grals-: ~hüter der keeper of the [Holy] Grail; (fig.) guardian; ~ritter der knight of the [Holy] Grail

gram [gra:m] in jmdm. ~ sein be aggrieved at sb.

Gram der; ~[e]s (geh.) grief; sorrow; aus ~ um od. über etw. (Akk.) out of grief or sorrow at sth.; vom od. von ~ gebeugt sein be bowed down with grief or sorrow

grämen ['grɛ:mən] 1. tr. V. grieve. 2. refl. V. grieve (über + Akk., um over); sich wegen etw. ~: worry about sth.

gram·erfüllt 1. Adj. grief-stricken; sorrowful. 2. adv. sorrowfully

Gram-Färbung die (Bakteriol.) Gram's method

gram·gebeugt Adj. bowed down with grief or sorrow postpos.

grämlich ['grɛ:mlɪç] 1. Adj. morose; sullen; morose ⟨thought⟩. 2. adv. morosely; sullenly

Gramm [gram] das; ~s, ~e gram; 250 ~ Käse 250 grams of cheese

Grammatik [gra'matɪk] die; ~, ~en a) grammar; b) (Lehrbuch) grammar [book]

grammatikalisch [gramati'ka:lɪʃ] Adj. s. grammatisch

Grammatik·regel die grammatical rule; rule of grammar

grammatisch 1. Adj. grammatical. 2. adv. grammatically

Gramm·atom das (Chemie, Physik) gram-atom

Grammel ['graml̩] die; ~, ~n (bayr., österr.) s. Griebe

Grammophon ⓦ [gramo'fo:n] das; ~s, ~e gramophone; phonograph (Amer.); auf dem ~ spielen (ugs.) play records

Grammophon·trichter der gramophone or (Amer.) phonograph horn

gram-: ~negativ Adj. (Bakteriol.) Gram-negative; ~positiv Adj. (Bakteriol.) Gram-positive

Gran [gra:n] das; ~[e]s, ~e; bei Maßangaben ungebeugt (veralt.) grain

Grän [grɛ:n] das; ~[e]s, ~e; bei Maßangaben ungebeugt grain

Granat [gra'na:t] der; ~[e]s, ~e a) (Schmuckstein) garnet; b) (Garnele) [common] shrimp

Granat·apfel der pomegranate

Granat·[apfel]baum der pomegranate [tree]

Granate [gra'na:tə] die; ~, ~n shell; (Hand~) grenade

granaten·voll Adj. (ugs.) absolutely plastered (sl.); totally canned (Brit. sl.)

Granat-: ~feuer das shell-fire no pl., no indef. art.; ~splitter der shell splinter; ~trichter der shell crater; ~werfer der (Milit.) mortar

Grand [grã: od. graŋ] der; ~s, ~s (Skat) grand; ~ Hand grand solo; ~ ouvert open grand

Grande ['grandə] der; ~n, ~n (hist.) grandee

Grandeur [grã'dø:ɐ̯] die; ~: grandeur

Grandezza [gran'dɛtsa] die; ~: grandeur; mit ~: with a grand air

Grand·hotel ['grã:-] das luxury or five-star hotel

grandios [gran'di̯o:s] 1. Adj. magnificent. 2. adv. magnificently

Grand Prix [grã'pri:] der; ~ ~ [- pri:(s)], ~ ~ [- pri:s] Grand Prix

Grandseigneur [grãsɛn'jø:ɐ̯] der; ~s, ~s od. ~e (geh.) grand seigneur

Granit [gra'ni:t] der; ~s, ~e granite; auf ~ beißen (fig.) bang one's head against a brick wall (fig.); bei jmdm. auf ~ beißen (fig.) get nowhere with sb. (fig.)

Granit·block der; Pl. -blöcke block of granite; granite block

graniten Adj. a) granite; granitic (Geol.); b) (geh.: hart) granitic; granite; (fig.) rigid; inflexible; granitic

Granit·gestein das granitic rock

Granne ['granə] die; ~, ~n awn; beard

Grant [grant] der; ~s (südd., österr. ugs.) [wegen etw.] einen ~ haben/bekommen be in/get into a bad mood [because of sth.]

grantig ['grantɪç] (südd., österr. ugs.) 1. Adj. bad-tempered; grumpy. 2. adv. bad-temperedly; grumpily

Granulat [granu'la:t] das; ~[e]s, ~e (bes. Chemie) granules pl.

granulieren *itr., tr. V. (bes. Chemie)* granulate
Grapefruit ['gre:pfru:t] **die;** ~, ~s grapefruit
Grapefruit·saft der grapefruit juice
[1]**Graph** [gra:f] **der;** ~en, ~en *(Math., Naturw.)* graph
[2]**Graph das;** ~s, ~e *(Sprachw.)* graph
Graphem [gra'fe:m] **das;** ~s, ~e *(Sprachw.)* grapheme
Graphie [gra'fi:] **die;** ~, ~n *(Sprachw.)* written form
Graphik ['gra:fɪk] **die;** ~, ~en **a)** *o. Pl. (Gestaltung, graphisches Schaffen)* graphic art[s *pl.*]; **b)** *(Kunstwerk)* graphic; *(Druck)* print; **c)** *(Illustration)* diagram
Graphiker der; ~s, ~, **Graphikerin die;** ~, ~nen [graphic] designer; *(Künstler[in])* graphic artist
graphisch 1. *Adj.* **a)** graphic; **das ~e Gewerbe** *(veralt.)* the printing trade; **b)** *(schematisch)* graphic; diagrammatic; **eine ~e Darstellung** a diagram; *(Math.: ein Graph)* a graph; **c)** *(Sprachw.)* graphic. **2.** *adv.* graphically
Graphit [gra'fi:t] **der;** ~s, ~e graphite
graphit·grau *Adj.* dark grey
Graphit·stift der lead pencil
Graphologe [grafo'lo:gə] **der;** ~n, ~n graphologist
Graphologie die; ~: graphology *no art.*
Graphologin die; ~, ~nen graphologist
graphologisch 1. *Adj.* graphological. **2.** *adv.* graphologically; ‹*analysed, interpreted*› by a graphologist
grapschen ['grapʃn̩] *s.* **grabschen**
Gras [gra:s] **das;** ~es, **Gräser** ['grɛ:zɐ] grass; **wo er hinhaut, da wächst kein ~ mehr** *(fig. ugs.)* one blow from him and you'd be out cold *(coll.)*; **das ~ wachsen hören** *(ugs. spött.)* read too much into things; **über etw.** *(Akk.)* **~ wachsen lassen** *(ugs.)* let the dust settle on sth.; **ins ~ beißen [müssen]** *(salopp)* bite the dust *(coll.)*
gras-, Gras-: ~**bahn die** *(Sport)* grass track; ~**bedeckt,** ~**bewachsen** *Adj.* grass-covered; grassy; ~**büschel das** tuft of grass; ~**decke die** covering of grass
grasen *itr. V.* **a)** graze; **b)** *(ugs.: suchen)* **nach etw. ~:** search for sth.
gras-, Gras-: ~**fläche die** area of grass; *(Rasen)* lawn; ~**fleck der a)** patch of grass; **b)** *(auf der Kleidung)* grass stain; ~**fresser der** *(Zool.)* herbivore; ~**frosch der** grass frog; ~**grün** *Adj.* grass-green; ~**halm der** blade of grass; ~**hüpfer der** *(ugs.)* grasshopper; ~**land das;** *o. Pl.* grassland; ~**mäher der,** ~**mäh·maschine die** grass-mower; [grass-]mowing machine; ~**mücke die** warbler; ~**narbe die** turf; ~**nelke die** thrift; ~**pflanze die** gramineous plant *(Bot.)*; grass
Grass [gra:s] **das;** ~ *(Drogenjargon)* grass *(sl.)*
grassieren [gra'si:rən] *itr. V.* ‹*disease etc.*› rage, be rampant; ‹*craze etc.*› be [all] the rage; ‹*rumour*› be rife
Gras·ski der grass ski
gräßlich ['grɛslɪç] **1.** *Adj.* **a)** *(abscheulich)* horrible; terrible ‹*accident*›; **b)** *(ugs.: unangenehm)* dreadful *(coll.)*; awful; **c)** *(ugs.: sehr stark)* terrible *(coll.)*; awful. **2.** *adv.* **a)** *(abscheulich)* horribly; terribly; **b)** *(ugs.: unangenehm)* terribly *(coll.)*; **c)** *(ugs.: sehr)* terribly *(coll.)*; dreadfully *(coll.)*; ~ **frieren** be terribly *or* dreadfully cold *(coll.)*
Gräßlichkeit die; ~, ~en **a)** *o. Pl. (Abscheulichkeit)* horribleness; *(eines Unfalls)* terribleness; **b)** *o. Pl. (unangenehme Art)* dreadfullness *(coll.)*; awfulness; **c)** *(gräßliche Handlung)* atrocity
Gras-: ~**steppe die** *(Geogr.)* [grassy] steppe; ~**streifen der** strip of grass; *(längs einer Straße)* grass verge; ~**teppich der** *(geh.)* sward *(literary)*

Grat [gra:t] **der;** ~[e]s, ~e **a)** *(Bergrücken)* ridge; **b)** *(Archit.)* hip; **c)** *(Technik)* burr
Gräte ['grɛ:tə] **die;** ~, ~n **a)** [fish-]bone; **b)** *(salopp: Knochen)* bone; **sich** *(Dat.)* **die ~n brechen** get badly smashed up *(sl.)*; **jmdm. alle** *od.* **sämtliche ~n brechen** break every bone in sb.'s body *(coll.)*
gräten-, Gräten-: ~**los** *Adj.* boneless; ~**muster das** herring-bone [pattern]; **ein Jackett mit ~muster** a herring-bone jacket; ~**schritt der** *(Skifahren)* herring-bone [step]
Gratifikation [gratifika'tsio:n] **die;** ~, ~en bonus
gratinieren [grati'ni:rən] *tr. V. (Gastr.)* brown [the top of]; **gratinierter Blumenkohl** cauliflower au gratin
gratis ['gra:tɪs] *Adv.* free [of charge]; gratis; ~ **und franko** *(ugs.)* for free *(coll.)*
Gratis-: ~**aktie die** *(Börsenw.)* bonus share; ~**anzeiger der** *(schweiz.)* [free] advertisement paper; ~**exemplar das** free copy; ~**muster das,** ~**probe die** free sample; ~**vorstellung die** free performance
Grätsche ['grɛ:tʃə] **die;** ~, ~n *(Turnen)* straddle; *(Sprung)* straddle-vault; **in die ~ gehen** go into the straddle position
grätschen 1. *tr. V.* **die Beine ~:** straddle one's legs. **2.** *itr. V.; mit sein* straddle; do *or* perform a straddle; **über ein Gerät ~:** do a straddle-vault over a piece of apparatus
Grätsch-: ~**sitz der** *(Turnen)* straddle-position; ~**sprung der** *(Turnen)* astride jump; *(über ein Gerät)* straddle-vault; ~**stellung die** *(Turnen)* straddle-position
Gratulant [gratu'lant] **der;** ~en, ~en, **Gratulantin die;** ~, ~nen well-wisher; **sie war die erste Gratulantin** she was the first to offer her congratulations
Gratulation [gratula'tsio:n] **die;** ~, ~en **a)** *(Glückwunsch)* congratulations *pl.*; **~en entgegennehmen** receive congratulations; **meine [herzliche] ~!** [many] congratulations!; **b)** *(das Gratulieren)* **sie kamen zur ~:** they came to congratulate him/her/them
Gratulations-: ~**besuch der** congratulatory visit; ~**cour die** reception; ~**schreiben das** letter of congratulation[s]; congratulatory letter
gratulieren *itr. V.* **jmdm. ~:** congratulate sb.; **jmdm. zum Geburtstag ~:** wish sb. many happy returns [of the day]; **jmdm. zum Examen ~:** congratulate sb. on passing his/her exam; **[ich] gratuliere!** congratulations!; **zu dieser Tochter kann ich Ihnen/er sich nur ~:** you are/he is lucky to have a daughter like her
Grat·wanderung die ridge walk; *(fig.)* balancing act
grau [grau] *Adj.* **a)** grey; ~ **werden** go grey; ~ **im Gesicht** grey- *or* ashen-faced; **eine ~e Stadt** *(fig.)* a grey *or* drab town; **deine ~en Zellen** *(ugs.)* your grey matter *(coll.)*; ~ **in ~:** grey and drab; **b)** *(trostlos)* dreary; drab; depressing; **der ~e Alltag** the dull routine *or* monotony of daily life; **alles ~ in ~ sehen** always see the gloomy side of things; **alles ~ in ~ malen** paint a gloomy *or* bleak picture of things; **c)** *(zwischen legal und illegal)* grey; **der ~e Markt** the grey market; **d)** *(unbestimmt)* vague; **in ~er Vorzeit/Ferne** in the dim and distant past/future
Grau das; ~s, ~ **a)** grey; **b)** *o. Pl. (Trostlosigkeit)* dreariness; drabness
grau-, Grau-: ~**äugig** *Adj.* grey-eyed; ~**bart der** *(ugs.)* greybeard; ~**bärtig** *Adj.* grey-bearded; ~**blau** *Adj.* grey-blue; ~**brot das** *bread made with rye- and wheat-flour*
Grau·bünden [-'bʏndn̩] **(das);** ~s the Grisons
[1]**grauen** *itr. V. (geh.)* **der Morgen/der Tag graut** morning is breaking; day is dawning *or* breaking

[2]**grauen** *itr. V. (unpers.)* **ihm graut [es] davor/vor ihr** he dreads [the thought of] it/he's terrified of her; **mir graut es, wenn ich nur daran denke** I dread the [mere] thought of it
Grauen das; ~s, ~ **a)** *o. Pl.* horror (**vor** + *Dat.* of); **ein Bild des ~s** a scene of horror; **b)** *(Schreckbild)* horror
grauen·erregend *Adj.* horrifying
grauen·haft, grauen·voll 1. *Adj.* **a)** horrifying; **b)** *(ugs.: sehr unangenehm)* terrible *(coll.)*; dreadful *(coll.)*. **2.** *adv.* **a)** horrifyingly; **b)** *(ugs.: sehr unangenehm)* terribly *(coll.)*; dreadfully *(coll.)*
grau-, Grau-: ~**gans die** grey goose; greylag [goose]; ~**grün** *Adj.* grey-green; ~**guß der** *(Technik)* grey iron; ~**haarig** *Adj.* grey-haired; ~**kopf der** *(ugs.)* **a)** *(graues Haar)* grey hair; **einen ~kopf haben** have grey hair; **b)** *(Mensch)* grey-headed man/woman
graulen ['graulən] **1.** *tr. V.* drive out; **jmdn. aus dem Haus ~:** drive sb. out of the house. **2.** *refl. V.* **sich [vor jmdm./etw.] ~:** be scared *or* frightened [of sb./sth.]. **3.** *tr., itr. V. (unpers.)* **davor graulte [es] ihm/ihn** he dreaded it; **mir/mich grault bei dem Gedanken, daß ...:** I shudder at the thought that ...
graulich *Adj.* scary
gräulich ['grɔylɪç] *Adj.* greyish
grau·meliert *Adj. (präd. getrennt geschrieben)* greying ‹*hair*›
Graupe ['graupə] **die;** ~, ~n **a)** *(Gerstenkorn)* grain of pearl barley; *(Weizenkorn)* grain of hulled wheat; **~n** pearl barley *sing.*/hulled wheat *sing.*; **b)** *Pl. (Gericht)* pearl barley *sing.*
Graupel ['graupl̩] **die;** ~, ~n soft hail pellet; **~n** soft hail; graupel
graupeln *itr. V. (unpers.)* **es graupelt** there's soft hail falling
Graupel-: ~**regen der** shower of soft hail; **der ~regen behinderte den Verkehr** the soft hail impeded the flow of traffic; ~**schauer der** shower of soft hail; **der Regen ging in ~schauer über** the rain turned to soft hail
Graupen·suppe die barley soup *or* broth
Graus [graus] **der;** ~es **a) es ist ein ~:** it's terrible; **es ist ein ~ mit dem Jungen** the boy's impossible *(coll.)*; **o ~!** *(ugs. scherzh.)* oh horror! *(joc.)*; **b)** *(veralt.: Grausen)* horror
grausam 1. *Adj.* **a)** cruel; ~ **gegen jmdn. sein** be cruel to sb.; **b)** *(furchtbar)* terrible; dreadful; **c)** *(ugs.: sehr schlimm)* terrible *(coll.)*; dreadful *(coll.)*. **2.** *adv.* **a)** cruelly; **sich ~ für etw. rächen** take cruel revenge for sth.; **b)** *(furchtbar)* terribly, dreadfully; **~ ums Leben kommen** die a horrible death; **c)** *(ugs.: sehr stark)* terribly *(coll.)*; dreadfully *(coll.)*
Grausamkeit die; ~, ~en **a)** *o. Pl.* cruelty; **b)** *(Handlung)* act of cruelty; *(Greueltat)* atrocity
grau-, Grau-: ~**schimmel der a)** *(Pferd)* grey [horse]; **b)** *(Pilz)* grey mould; ~**schwarz** *Adj.* grey-black
grausen 1. *tr., itr. V. (unpers.)* **es grauste ihm** *od.* **ihn davor/vor ihr** he dreaded [the thought of] it/he was terrified of her; **es graust ihr** *od.* **sie, wenn sie nur an die Prüfung denkt** she dreads the [mere] thought of the exam; **uns grauste vor der langen Fahrt** we were dreading the long journey. **2.** *refl. V.* **sich vor etw./jmdm. ~:** be terrified by *or* dread sth./be terrified of sb.
Grausen das; ~s horror; **das kalte ~ kriegen** *(ugs.)* be scared stiff *or* to death *(coll.)*
grausig *s.* **grauenhaft**
grauslich *(bes. bayr., österr.)* *s.* **gräßlich**
grau-, Grau-: ~**specht der** grey-headed woodpecker; ~**tier das** *(ugs. scherzh.)* *(Esel)* ass; donkey; *(Maultier)* mule; ~**ton der** [shade of] grey; ~**wal der** grey whale; ~**weiß** *Adj.* greyish white; ~**zone die** grey area *(fig.)*
Graveur [gra'vø:ɐ] **der;** ~s, ~e, **Graveurin die;** ~, ~nen engraver

Gravier-: ~anstalt die engraving establishment; engraver's; **~arbeit die** engraving
gravieren [gra'vi:rən] *tr. V.* engrave; **etw. auf etw.** *(Akk.)* **~:** engrave sth. on sth.
gravierend *Adj.* serious, grave ‹*matter, accusation, error, etc.*›; important ‹*difference, decision, etc.*›; **~e Beweise** very strong evidence
Gravier·nadel die engraving needle
Gravierung die; ~, ~en engraving
Gravimetrie [gravime'tri:] **die; ~** *(Chemie, Physik)* gravimetry *no art.*
Gravis ['gra:vɪs] **der; ~, ~** *(Sprachw.)* grave [accent]
Gravitation [gravita'tsio:n] **die; ~** *(Physik, Astron.)* gravitation
Gravitations-: ~feld das *(Physik, Astron.)* gravitational field; **~gesetz das** *(Physik, Astron.)* law of gravitation
gravitätisch 1. *Adj.* grave; solemn. **2.** *adv.* gravely; solemnly
gravitieren [gravi'ti:rən] *itr. V. (Physik, Astron.)* gravitate
Gravur [gra'vu:ɐ̯] **die; ~, ~en, Gravüre** [gra'vy:rə] **die; ~, ~n** engraving
Grazie ['gra:tsiə] **die; ~, ~n a)** *o. Pl. (Anmut)* grace; gracefulness; **b)** *Pl. (Myth.)* Graces; **c)** *Pl. (scherzh.: junge Mädchen)* beauties
grazil [gra'tsi:l] *Adj. (auch fig.)* delicate
graziös [gra'tsiø:s] **1.** *Adj.* graceful; *(anmutig)* charming. **2.** *adv.* gracefully; *(anmutig)* charmingly
Gräzismus [grɛ'tsɪsmʊs] **der; ~, Gräzismen** Graecism
Gräzist der; ~en, ~en, Gräzistin die; ~, ~nen expert on/student of ancient Greece
Greenhorn ['gri:nhɔ:n] **das; ~s, ~s** greenhorn
Gregor ['gre:gɔr] **(der)** Gregory
Gregorianisch [grego'ria:nɪʃ] *Adj.* Gregorian; **~er Gesang** Gregorian chant; **der ~e Kalender** the Gregorian calendar
Greif [graif] **der; ~[e]s** *od.* **~en, ~en a)** *(Wappentier)* griffin; gryphon; **b)** *s.* **~vogel**
Greif-: ~arm der *(Technik)* grasping arm; **~bagger der** grab-dredger
greif·bar 1. *Adj.* **a) etw. ~ haben** have sth. to hand; **~ sein** be within reach; **in ~er Nähe** *(fig.)* within reach; **der Urlaub ist in ~e Nähe gerückt** *(fig.)* the holiday is just coming up [now]; **b)** *(deutlich)* tangible; concrete; **c)** *nicht attr. (ugs.: verfügbar)* available. **2.** *adv.* **~ nahe** *(fig.)* within reach
Greif·bewegung die grasping movement
greifen 1. *unr. tr. V.* **a)** *(er~)* take hold of; grasp; *(rasch ~)* grab; seize; **sich** *(Dat.)* **etw. ~:** help oneself to sth.; **jmdn. an den Händen ~:** take sb. by the hand; **aus dem Leben gegriffen sein** be taken from real life; **von hier scheint der See zum Greifen nah[e]** from here the lake seems close enough to reach out and touch; **zum Greifen nahe sein** ‹*end, liberation*› be imminent; ‹*goal, success*› be within sb.'s grasp; **b)** *(fangen)* catch; **den werde ich mir mal ~** *(ugs.)* I'll sort *(Brit.) or (Amer.)* straighten him out *(coll.)*; **Greifen spielen** play tag; **c) einen Akkord ~** *(auf dem Klavier usw.)* play a chord; *(auf der Gitarre usw.)* finger a chord; **er kann noch keine Oktave ~:** he can't reach an octave yet; **d)** *(schätzen)* **tausend ist zu hoch/niedrig gegriffen** one thousand is an overestimate/underestimate; **sein Ziel ist zu hoch gegriffen** *(fig.)* he has set his sights too high *(fig.)*. **2.** *unr. itr. V.* **a) in/unter/hinter etw./sich** *(Akk.)* **~:** reach into/under/behind sth./one; **nach etw. ~:** reach for sth.; *(hastig)* make a grab for sth.; **zu Drogen/zur Zigarette ~:** turn to drugs/reach for a cigarette; **zu strengen Maßnahmen ~** *(fig.)* resort to *or* use tough measures; **nach der Macht ~** *(fig.)* try to seize power; **[jmdm.] ans Herz ~** *(fig. geh.)* tug at sb.'s heartstrings; **seine Argumentation greift zu kurz** *(fig.)* his arguments do not go far enough; **etw. greift um sich** sth. is spreading; **b)** *(Technik)* grip; **c)** *(ugs.: spielen)* **in die Tasten/Saiten ~:** sweep one's hand over the keys/across the strings; **d)** *(wirken)* take effect; **nicht mehr ~:** be no longer effective
Greifer der; ~s, ~ a) *(Technik)* grab[-bucket]; **b)** *(salopp abwertend: Polizist)* cop *(sl.)*
Greif-: ~fuß der *(Zool.)* prehensile foot; **~vogel der** *(Zool.)* diurnal bird of prey; **~zange die** tongs *pl.*; **~zirkel der** [outside] callipers *pl.*
greinen ['grainən] *itr. V. (ugs. abwertend)* grizzle *(coll. derog.)*; *(weinerlich klagen)* whine
greis [grais] *Adj. (geh.)* aged; white ‹*hair, head*›; **~ werden** grow old
Greis der; ~es, ~e old man
Greisen·alter das old age; **im [hohen] ~:** in old age
greisen·haft 1. *Adj.* old man's/woman's *attrib.*; aged; *(von jüngerem Menschen)* ‹*face etc.*› like that of an old man/woman. **2.** *adv.* like an old man/woman
Greisen·haupt das *(geh.)* old head
Greisin die; ~, ~nen old woman *or* lady
grell [grɛl] **1.** *Adj.* **a)** *(hell)* glaring, dazzling ‹*light, sun, etc.*›; **b)** *(auffallend)* garish, gaudy ‹*colour etc.*›; flashy, loud ‹*dress, pattern, etc.*›; **c)** *(schrill)* shrill, piercing ‹*cry, voice, etc.*›. **2.** *adv.* **a)** *(hell)* with glaring *or* dazzling brightness; **b)** *(auffallend)* **gegen** *od.* **von etw. ~ abstechen** contrast sharply with sth.; **c)** *(schrill)* shrilly; piercingly
grell-: ~beleuchtet *Adj. (präd. getrennt geschrieben)* dazzlingly lit; **~bunt** *Adj.* gaudily coloured
Grelle ['grɛlə] **die; ~, Grellheit die; ~ a)** *(Helligkeit)* dazzling brightness; **b)** *(Auffälligkeit)* garishness; gaudiness; **c)** *(Schrillheit)* shrillness; piercing quality
grell·rot *Adj.* garish *or* bright red
Gremium ['gre:miʊm] **das; ~s, Gremien** committee
Grenadier [grena'di:ɐ̯] **der; ~s, ~e** *(Milit.)* **a)** *(Infanterist)* infantryman; **er kam zu den ~en** he went into *or* joined the infantry; **b)** *(hist.)* grenadier
Grenz-: ~abfertigung die *(Zollw.)* passport control and customs clearance [at the/a border]; **~baum der** *s.* **Schlagbaum; ~beamte der** border official; **~befestigung die** *(Milit.)* border fortification; **~bereich der a)** *o. Pl. (Umkreis der Grenze)* border or frontier zone or area; **b)** *(äußerster Bereich)* limit[s *pl.*]; **~berichtigung die** adjustment to a/the border; **~bewohner der** inhabitant of a/the border *or* frontier zone; **die ~bewohner** [the] people living near the border *or* frontier; **~bezirk der** border *or* frontier district
Grenze ['grɛntsə] **die; ~, ~n a)** *(zwischen Staaten)* border; frontier; **die ~ zu Italien** the border with Italy; **die ~ passieren/überschreiten** cross the border *or* frontier; **über die ~n hinaus** beyond the borders of this country; **an der ~ wohnen** live on the border *or* frontier; **über die grüne ~ gehen** *(ugs.)* cross the border *or* frontier illegally; **b)** *(zwischen Gebieten)* boundary; **die ~ des Grundstücks** the boundary of the property; **c)** *(gedachte Trennungslinie)* borderline; dividing line; **d)** *(Schranke)* limit; **jmdm. [keine] ~n setzen** impose [no] limits on sb.; **einer Sache** *(Dat.)* **[keine] ~n setzen** set [no] limits to sth.; **alles hat seine ~n** there is a limit *or* are limits to everything; one must draw the line somewhere; **an seine ~n stoßen** reach its limit[s]; **an ~n stoßen** come up against limiting factors; **keine ~n kennen** know no bounds; **seine ~n kennen** know one's limitations; **jmdn. in seine ~n verweisen** put sb. in his/her place; **sich in ~n halten** *(begrenzt sein)* keep *or* stay within limits; **seine Leistungen hielten sich in ~n** his achievements were not [all that *(coll.)*] outstanding; **die ~n des Möglichen** the bounds of possibility
grenzen *itr. V.* **an etw.** *(Akk.)* **~:** border [on] sth.; *(fig.)* verge on sth.
grenzen·los 1. *Adj.* boundless; endless; *(fig.)* boundless, unbounded ‹*joy, wonder, jealousy, grief, etc.*›; unlimited ‹*wealth, power*›; limitless ‹*patience, ambition*›; extreme ‹*tiredness, anger, foolishness*›. **2.** *adv.* endlessly; *(fig.)* beyond all measure
Grenzen·losigkeit die; ~: boundlessness; immensity; **bis zur ~ steigern** *(fig.)* increase beyond all measure
Grenzer der; ~s, ~ *(ugs.)* **a)** *s.* **Grenzbewohner; b)** *s.* **Grenzsoldat**
grenz-, Grenz-: ~fall der *(nicht eindeutiger Fall)* borderline case; *(Sonderfall)* limiting case; **~fluß der** river forming a/the border *or* frontier; **~formalitäten** *Pl.* passport and customs formalities [at the/a border]; **~gänger der; ~s, ~:** [regular] commuter across the border *or* frontier; **~gebiet das a)** border *or* frontier area *or* zone; **b)** *(Sachgebiet zwischen Disziplinen)* adjacent field; **die Biochemie ist ein ~gebiet der Medizin** biochemistry is a field bordering on medicine; **im ~gebiet zwischen zwei Wissenschaften** in the area where two sciences meet; **~konflikt der** border *or* frontier conflict; **~kontrolle die a)** border *or* frontier check; **b)** *(Personen)* border officials *pl.*; **~land das** border *or* frontier area; **~linie die a)** *(Grenze)* border; **b)** *(Sport)* line *(marking edge of playing area)*; **~mark die** *(hist.)* marches *pl.*; **~nah** *Adj.*; *nicht präd.* close to the border *or* frontier *postpos.*; **~nutzen der** *(Wirtsch.)* marginal utility; **~polizei die** border *or* frontier police; **~posten der** border *or* frontier guard; **~schutz der a)** border *or* frontier protection; **b)** *(ugs.: Bundesgrenzschutz)* border *or* frontier police; **~situation die** borderline situation; **~soldat der** border *or* frontier guard; **~stadt die** border *or* frontier town; **~stein der** boundary stone; **~streitigkeit die** boundary dispute; *(wegen einer Staatsgrenze)* border *or* frontier dispute; **~übergang der a)** border crossing-point; frontier crossing-point; [border] checkpoint; **b)** *(das Passieren der Grenze)* crossing of the border *or* frontier; **~überschreitend** *Adj.*; *nicht präd.* across the/a border *or* frontier/across the borders *or* frontiers *postpos., not pred.*; **~verkehr der** [cross-]border traffic; frontier traffic; **der kleine ~verkehr** local [cross-]border *or* frontier traffic; **~verlauf der** frontier line; **~verletzung die** border *or* frontier violation; **~wacht die** *(schweiz.)* border *or* frontier guard[s *pl.*]; **~wall der** border *or* frontier rampart; **~wert der** *(Math.)* limit; **~zwischenfall der** border incident
Gretchen-: ~frage die; ~: crucial question; sixty-four-thousand-dollar question *(coll.)*; **~frisur die** chaplet hairstyle
Greuel ['grɔyəl] **der; ~s, ~** *(geh.)* **a)** *o. Pl. (Abscheu)* horror; **~ vor etw.** *(Dat.)* **empfinden** have a horror of sth.; **er/sie/es ist mir ein ~:** I loathe *or* detest him/her/it; **es ist ihm ein ~, das zu tun** he loathes *or* detests doing it; **b)** *meist Pl. (~tat)* atrocity
Greuel-: ~geschichte die, ~märchen das horror story; **~meldung die** report of an/the atrocity/of atrocities; **~propaganda die** atrocity propaganda; stories *pl.* of atrocities; **~tat die** atrocity
greulich ['grɔylɪç] **1.** *Adj.* **a)** *(entsetzlich)* horrifying; **b)** *(unangenehm)* awful. **2.** *adv.* **a)** *(entsetzlich)* horrifyingly; **b)** *(unangenehm)* terribly
Greyerzer ['graiɐtsɐ] **der; ~s, ~:** Gruyère
Griebe ['gri:bə] **die; ~, ~n** crackling *no indef. art.*; greaves *pl.*

Grieben-: ~fett das bacon dripping; **~schmalz das** dripping with crackling *or* greaves
Grieche ['gri:çə] **der; ~n, ~n** Greek
Griechen·land (das); ~s Greece
Griechentum das; ~s *(Zivilisation)* Hellenism *no art.;* Greek civilization; *(Kultur)* Greek culture
Griechin die; ~, ~nen Greek
griechisch 1. *Adj.* Greek ‹*language, mythology, island, etc.*›; Grecian, Greek ‹*vase, style, etc.*›; **die ~e Tragödie** Greek tragedy. **2.** *adv.* **~ sprechen/schreiben** speak/write in Greek; *s. auch* **deutsch**
Griechisch das; ~[s] Greek *no art.; s. auch* **Deutsch**
Griechische das; ~n a) *(Sprache)* Greek *no art.;* **b)** *(Eigenart)* things Greek *pl.;* **alles ~:** all things *pl. or* everything Greek
griechisch-: ~-orthodox *Adj.* Greek Orthodox; **~-römisch** *Adj. (Ringen)* Graeco-Roman
grienen ['gri:nən] *itr. V. (bes. nordd.)* grin
Griesgram ['gri:sgra:m] **der; ~[e]s, ~e** *(abwertend)* grouch *(coll.)*
griesgrämig ['gri:sgrɛ:mɪç] **1.** *Adj.* grouchy *(coll.); grumpy.* **2.** *adv.* in a grouchy *(coll.) or* grumpy manner
Grieß [gri:s] **der; ~es, ~e** semolina
Grieß-: ~brei der semolina; **~kloß der, ~klößchen das** semolina dumpling
griff [grɪf] *1. u. 3. Pers. Sg. Prät. v.* **greifen**
Griff der; ~[e]s, ~e a) grip; grasp; **mit eisernem/festem ~:** with a grip of iron/a firm grip; **der ~ nach etw./in etw.** *(Akk.)***/an etw.** *(Akk.)* reaching for sth./dipping into sth./taking hold of *or* grasping sth.; **der ~ zum Alkohol/zu Drogen** turning to alcohol/drugs; **[mit jmdm./etw.] einen guten/glücklichen ~ tun** make a good choice [with sb./sth.]; **einen ~ in die Ladenkasse tun** *(verhüll.)* put one's hand in the till; **der ~ nach der Macht** *(fig.)* the bid for *or* attempt to seize power; **b)** *(beim Ringen, Bergsteigen)* hold; *(beim Turnen)* grip; *(bei der Arbeit)* **jeder ~ muß sitzen** every movement must be exactly right; **mit wenigen ~en** with very little effort; **~e kloppen** *(Soldatenspr.)* do rifle drill; **etw. im ~ haben** *(etw. routinemäßig beherrschen)* have the hang of sth. *(coll.); (etw. unter Kontrolle haben)* have sth. under control; **etw. in den ~ bekommen** *od. (ugs.)* **kriegen** get the hang *or* knack of sth. *(coll.);* acquire a grasp of *or* hold on sth.; **c)** *(Knauf, Henkel)* handle; *(eines Gewehrs, einer Pistole)* butt; *(eines Schwerts)* hilt; **d)** *(Musik)* finger-placing; **schwierige ~e beherrschen** master difficult fingering; **e)** *(Weberei)* hand; handle
griff·bereit *Adj.* ready to hand *postpos.*
Griff·brett das *(Musik)* finger-board
Griffel ['grɪfl̩] **der; ~s, ~ a)** *(Schreibgerät)* slate-pencil; **b)** *(Bot.)* style; **c)** *(salopp: Finger)* finger
Griffel·kasten der *(veralt.)* pencil-box
griffig *Adj.* **a)** *(handlich)* handy; ‹*tool etc.*› that is easy to handle; *(fig.)* handy, useful ‹*word, expression, etc.*›; **b)** *(gut greifend)* that grips well *postpos., not pred.;* non-slip ‹*surface, floor*›; **ein ~er Reifen** a tyre with good road-holding characteristics; **c)** *(festgewebt)* ‹*cloth*› with a firm handle; **d)** *(österr.: grobkörnig)* coarse ‹*flour*›
Griffigkeit die; ~ a) *(Handlichkeit)* handiness; **b)** *(von Reifen, Straßen)* grip; **c)** *(Festigkeit des Gewebes)* firm handle; **d)** *(österr.: von Mehl)* coarseness
Griff·loch das *(Musik)* fingerhole
Grill [grɪl] **der; ~s, ~s a)** *(Feuerstelle)* grill; *(Rost)* barbecue; **b)** *(Kfz-W.)* radiator grille
Grille ['grɪlə] **die; ~, ~n a)** *(Insekt)* cricket; **b)** *(sonderbarer Einfall)* whim; fancy; **er hat ~n im Kopf** *(hat seltsame Ideen)* his head is [stuffed] full of silly ideas; *(hat trübselige Gedanken)* he's in low spirits *or (coll.)* [down] in the dumps; *(fig.)* **~n fangen** *(veralt.)* be in low spirits *or (coll.)* down in the dumps; **jmdm. die ~n vertreiben** *od.* **austreiben** *(fig. veralt.)* knock some sense into sb.
grillen 1. *tr. V.* grill. **2.** *itr. V.* **im Garten ~:** have a barbecue in the garden. **3.** *refl. V. (ugs.: bräunen)* **sich in der Sonne ~:** soak up the sun
Grill-: ~platz der barbecue area; **~spieß der** ≈ souvlaki
Grimasse [gri'masə] **die; ~, ~n** grimace; **eine ~ schneiden** *od.* **machen** grimace; pull a face
Grimm [grɪm] **der; ~[e]s** *(geh.)* fury
Grimm·darm der *(Anat.)* colon
grimmen *tr., itr. V. (unpers.) (veralt.)* **es grimmt mir** *od.* **mich im Bauch/Magen** I have griping pains in my stomach
Grimmen das; ~s colic; griping pains *pl.*
grimmig 1. *Adj.* **a)** *(zornig)* furious ‹*person*›; grim ‹*face, expression*›; fierce ferocious ‹*enemy, lion, etc.*›; **b)** *(heftig)* fierce, severe ‹*cold, hunger, pain, etc.*›. **2.** *adv.* **a)** *(wütend)* furiously; **~ lachen** laugh grimly; **b)** *(heftig)* fiercely; **~ kalt** bitterly *or* fiercely cold
Grind [grɪnt] **der; ~[e]s, ~e a)** *(Flechte)* impetigo; **b)** *(Wundschorf)* scab
grindig *Adj.* scabby
grinsen ['grɪnzn̩] *itr. V.* grin; *(höhnisch)* smirk
Grinsen das; ~s: ein fröhliches/unverschämtes ~: a happy grin/an insolent smirk
grippal [grɪ'pa:l] *Adj.; nicht präd.* influenzal; grippal
Grippe ['grɪpə] **die; ~, ~n a)** influenza; flu *(coll.);* **b)** *(volkst.: Erkältung)* cold
Grippe-: ~epidemie die influenza epidemic; **~impfung die** influenza *or (coll.)* flu immunization; **~welle die** wave of influenza *or (coll.)* flu
Grips [grɪps] **der; ~es** *(bes. nordd. u. md. ugs.)* brains *pl.;* nous *(coll.);* **streng deinen ~ an** use your brains *or* nous
Grisly·bär, Grizzly·bär ['grɪslɪ-] **der** grizzly bear
grob [gro:p] **1.** *Adj.* **a)** coarse ‹*sand, gravel, paper, sieve, etc.*›; thick ‹*wire*›; rough, dirty ‹*work*›; **~e Gesichtszüge** coarse features; **b)** *(ungefähr)* rough; **in ~en Umrissen** in rough outline; **c)** *(schwerwiegend)* gross; flagrant ‹*lie*›; **ein ~er Fehler/Irrtum** a bad mistake *or* gross error; **~er Unfug** disorderly conduct; **das Gröbste** the worst; **aus dem Gröbsten heraussein** *(ugs.)* be over the worst; **d)** *(barsch)* coarse; rude; **~ werden** become abusive *or* rude; **e)** *(nicht sanft)* rough; **~ [zu jmdm.] sein** be rough [with sb.]; **f)** *(heftig)* fierce ‹*gust of wind*›; **~e See** *(Seemannsspr.)* rough sea. **2.** *adv.* **a)** coarsely; **ein ~ geschnittenes Gesicht haben** have coarse features *pl.;* **b)** *(ungefähr)* roughly; **~ gerechnet** *od.* **geschätzt** at a rough estimate; **etw. ~ umreißen/darlegen** present a rough outline/exposition of sth.; **c)** *(schwerwiegend)* grossly; **~ fahrlässig handeln** *(Rechtsspr.)* be guilty of gross negligence; **d)** *(barsch)* coarsely; rudely; **jmdm. ~ kommen** *(ugs.)* get rude with sb.; **e)** *(nicht sanft)* roughly
grob-, Grob-: ~blech das thick *or* heavy [steel] plate; **~einstellung die** rough adjustment; **~faserig** *Adj.* coarse-fibred; **~gemahlen** *Adj. (präd. getrennt geschrieben)* coarsely ground; coarse-ground; **~gesponnen** *Adj. (präd. getrennt geschrieben)* coarsely spun; coarse-spun
Grobheit die; ~, ~en a) *o. Pl. (Wesensart)* rudeness; coarseness; **b)** *(Äußerung)* rude remark; *(Handlung)* [piece of] rudeness; **jmdm. ~en sagen/***(ugs.)* **an den Kopf werfen** be extremely rude to sb.; **c)** *o. Pl. (derbe Beschaffenheit)* coarseness
Grobian ['gro:bi̯a:n] **der; ~[e]s, ~e** boor; lout
grob-: ~knochig *Adj.* big-boned; **~körnig** *Adj.* coarse ‹*sand, flour, etc.*›; *(Fot.)* coarse-grained ‹*film*›
gröblich ['grø:plɪç] *(geh.)* **1.** *Adj.; nicht präd.* gross. **2.** *adv.* grossly
grob-, Grob-: ~maschig *Adj.* wide-meshed ‹*sieve, net, etc.*›; loose-knit ‹*pullover etc.*›; **~schlächtig** [~ʃlɛçtɪç] *Adj.* heavily built; **eine ~schlächtige Darstellung** *(fig.)* a simplistic account; **~schmied der** *(veralt.)* blacksmith
Grog [grɔk] **der; ~s, ~s** grog
groggy ['grɔgi] *Adj.; nicht attr.* **a)** *(Boxen)* groggy; **b)** *(ugs.: erschöpft)* whacked [out] *(coll.);* all in *(coll.)*
grölen ['grø:lən] **1.** *tr. V. (ugs. abwertend)* bawl [out]; roar, howl ‹*approval*›. **2.** *itr. V.* bawl; **eine ~de Menge** a roaring crowd
Groll [grɔl] **der; ~[e]s** *(geh.)* rancour; resentment; **einen ~ auf jmdn./etw. haben** *od.* **gegen jmdn./etw. hegen** harbour resentment *or* a grudge against sb./sth.; **aus ~ über jmdn./etw.** from a grudge against sb./out of resentment at sth.; **ohne ~:** without rancour; with no ill feelings
grollen *itr. V. (geh.)* **a)** *(verstimmt sein)* be sullen; **[mit] jmdm. ~:** bear a grudge against sb.; bear sb. a grudge; **b)** *(dröhnen)* rumble; ‹*thunder*› roll, rumble; **das Grollen des Donners** the roll *or* rumble of thunder
Grön·land ['grø:n-] **(das); ~s** Greenland
Grön·länder der; ~s, ~: Greenlander
[1]**Gros** [gro:] **das; ~** [gro:(s)], **~** [gro:s] bulk; main body; **das ~ der Betriebe** the greater *or* major part of industry
[2]**Gros** [grɔs] **das; ~ses, ~se** *(bei Maßangaben ungebeugt)* gross
Groschen ['grɔʃn̩] **der; ~s, ~ a)** *(österreichische Münze)* groschen; **b)** *(ugs.: Zehnpfennigstück)* ten-pfennig piece; *(fig.)* penny; cent *(Amer.);* **Bonbons für einen** *od.* **zu einem ~:** ten pfennigs' worth of sweets; **[sich** *(Dat.)***] ein paar ~ verdienen** *(ugs.)* earn [oneself] a few pennies *or* pence; **die ~ zusammenhalten müssen** *(ugs.)* have to count every penny [one spends]; **der ~ ist [bei ihm] gefallen** *(fig.)* the penny has dropped; **bei ihr fällt der ~ pfennigweise** *(fig.)* she's a bit slow on the uptake
Groschen-: ~blatt das *(abwertend)* tabloid; cheap rag *(derog.);* **~roman der** *(abwertend)* cheap novel; dime novel *(Amer.)*
groß [gro:s] **größer** ['grø:sɐ], **größt...** ['grø:st...] **1.** *Adj.* **a)** big; big, large ‹*house, window, area, room, etc.*›; large ‹*pack, size, can, etc.*›; great ‹*length, width, height*›; tall ‹*person*›; **~e Eier/Kartoffeln** large eggs/potatoes; **der ~e Zeiger** the big *or* minute hand; **ein ~er Buchstabe** a big *or* capital letter; **eine ~e Terz/Sekunde** *(Musik)* a major third/second; **ein ~es Bier, bitte** a pint, please; **im Großen einkaufen** buy in bulk; **die Großen Seen/der Große Salzsee** the Great Lakes/Great Salt Lake; **ein/zwei Nummern zu ~:** one size/two sizes too big; **b)** *(eine bestimmte Größe aufweisend)* **1 m²/2 ha ~:** 1 m²/2 ha in area; **sie ist 1,75 m ~:** she is 1.75 m tall; **doppelt/dreimal so ~ wie ...:** twice/three times the size of ...; **c)** *(älter)* big ‹*brother, sister*›; **seine größere Schwester** his elder sister; **unsere Große/unser Großer** our eldest *or* oldest daughter/son; *(von zwei Kindern)* our elder *or* older daughter/son; **d)** *(erwachsen)* grown-up ‹*children, son, daughter*›; **[mit etw.] ~ werden** grow up [with sth.]; **die Großen** *(Erwachsene)* the grown-ups; *(ältere Kinder)* the older children; **~ und klein** old and young [alike]; **e)** *(lange dauernd)* long, lengthy ‹*delay, talk, explanation, pause*›; **ein ~er Zeitraum** a long period of time; **die ~en Ferien** *(Schulw.)* the summer holidays *or (Amer.)* long vacation *sing.;* **die ~e Pause** *(Schulw.)* [mid-morning] break; **f)** *(beträchtlich)* **eine ~e Zuhörerschaft/Kundschaft** a large audi-

ence/clientele; ~e **Summen/Kosten** large sums/heavy costs; **eine ~e Familie** a big *or* large family; **eine ~e Auswahl** a wide selection *or* range; **~es Geld** notes *pl.*; **das ~e Geld machen** *(ugs.) od.* **verdienen** make big money; **g)** *(außerordentlich)* great ⟨*pleasure, pain, hunger, anxiety, hurry, progress, difficulty, mistake, importance*⟩; intense ⟨*heat, cold*⟩; high ⟨*speed*⟩; **mit dem größten Vergnügen** with the greatest of pleasure; **eine ~e Freude empfinden** feel great pleasure; **ein ~er Lärm** a lot of noise; **~en Hunger haben** be very hungry; **ein ~er Esser/Bastler** a great *or* heavy eater/great handyman; **ihre/seine ~e Liebe** her/his great love; **~ im Geschäft sein** be in great demand; **h)** *(gewichtig)* great; major ⟨*producer, exporter*⟩; great, major ⟨*event*⟩; **ein ~er Augenblick/Tag** a great moment/day; **~e Worte/Gesten** grand *or* fine words/grand gestures; **[k]eine ~e Rolle spielen** [not] play a great *or* an important part; **sie hat Großes geleistet** she has achieved great things; **die Großen [der Welt]** the great figures [of our world]; **i)** *nicht präd. (glanzvoll)* grand ⟨*celebration, ball, etc.*⟩; **in ~er Aufmachung/Garderobe** in all one's finery; **die ~e Dame/den ~en Herrn spielen** *(iron.)* play the fine lady/gentleman; **j)** *(bedeutend)* great, major ⟨*artist, painter, work*⟩; **Otto der Große/Katharina die Große** Otto/Catherine the Great; *s. auch* **Karl**; **k)** *(wesentlich)* **die ~e Linie/der ~e Zusammenhang** the basic line/the overall context; **in ~en Zügen** *od.* **Umrissen** in broad outline; **im ~en [und] ganzen** by and large; on the whole; **l)** *(geh.: selbstlos)* noble ⟨*deed etc.*⟩; **ein ~es Herz haben** be great-hearted; **m)** *(ugs.: ~artig)* great *(coll.)*; **das finde ich** *od.* **das ist ganz ~** *(iron.)* that's just great *(coll. iron.)*; **~ in etw.** *(Dat.)* **sein** be a great one for sth.; **n)** *(ugs.: ~spurig)* **~e Reden schwingen** *od. (salopp)* **Töne spucken** talk big *(coll.)*. **2.** *adv.* **a) die Heizung** *usw.* **~/größer einstellen** turn the heating *etc.* up high/higher; **ein Wort ~ schreiben** write a word with a capital [initial] letter *or* a capital; **jmdn. ~ ansehen** stare hard at sb.; **~ machen** *(Kinderspr.)* do number two *(child lang.)*; **~ und breit** at great length; **b)** *(ugs.: aufwendig)* **~ ausgehen** go out for a big celebration; **etw. ~ feiern** celebrate sth. in a big way; **jmdn./etw. ~ herausbringen** publicize sb./sth. with a big splash; **c)** *(ugs.: besonders)* greatly; particularly; **es lohnt [sich] nicht ~, das zu tun** there is not much point in doing that; **sich nicht ~ um jmdn./etw. kümmern** not bother *or* concern oneself greatly about sb./sth.; **wir haben nicht ~ darauf geachtet** we didn't pay much attention to it; **was gibt es da noch ~ zu diskutieren?** why do we need all this long discussion?; **niemand freute sich ~**: nobody was very pleased *or (coll.)* exactly overjoyed; **d)** *(geh.: selbstlos)* **~ handeln** act nobly; **fähig sein, ~ zu fühlen** be capable of noble sentiments; **e)** *(ugs.: ~artig)* **sie steht ganz ~ da** she has made it big *(coll.) or* made the big time *(coll.)*; **f)** *(ugs.: ~spurig)* **~ daherreden/auftreten** talk/act big *(coll.)*

groß-, Groß-: **~abnehmer der** bulk buyer *or* purchaser; **~admiral der** *(Milit. hist.)* Grand Admiral; **~aktion die** major campaign; big drive; **~aktionär der** *(Wirtsch.)* principal *or* major shareholder; **~alarm der** full-scale alarm; **~angelegt** *Adj.; nicht präd.* large-scale ⟨*project, plan, etc.*⟩; full-scale ⟨*attack, investigation*⟩; **~angriff der** *(Milit.)* full-scale attack; **~artig 1.** *Adj.* magnificent; splendid; wonderful ⟨*person*⟩; **2.** *adv.* magnificently; splendidly; **wir haben uns ~artig amüsiert** we had a marvellous time; **~artigkeit die** magnificence; splendour; **~aufnahme die a)** *(Film)* close-up; **in ~aufnahme** in close-up; **b)** *(Fot.) s.* **Nahaufnahme**; **~auftrag der** *(Wirtsch.)* large order; **~bank die**; *Pl.* **~banken** *(Finanzw.)* big bank; **die fünf ~banken** the Big Five; **~bauer der** big farmer; **~betrieb der** large *or* big concern; large-scale enterprise; **~bourgeoisie die** *(marx.)* haute bourgeoisie; **~brand der** large fire *or* blaze

Groß·britannien (das) the United Kingdom; [Great] Britain

groß-, Groß-: **~buchstabe der** capital [letter]; upper-case letter *(Printing)*; **~bürgerlich** *Adj.* upper middle-class; **~bürgertum das** upper middle class; **~deutsch** *Adj. (bes. ns.)* Pan-German; **~deutschland (das)** *(bes. ns.) Germany after the anschluss of Austria*

Größe ['grø:sə] **die**; **~, ~n a)** size; *(Kleider~)* **in ~ 38** in size 38; **sie trägt ~ 44** she is *or* takes size 44; **b)** *(Höhe, Körper~)* height; **der ~ nach** by height; **c)** *(Bedeutsamkeit, sittlicher Wert)* greatness; **d)** *(Ausmaß)* **die ~ der Katastrophe** the [full] scale *or* extent of the catastrophe; **e)** *(Genie)* outstanding *or* important figure; **f)** *(Math., Physik)* quantity; **eine gegebene/** *(auch fig.)* **unbekannte ~**: a given/an unknown quantity

Groß-: **~ein·kauf der** bulk purchase; **~einkauf machen** do all one's shopping at one time; **~ein·satz der** large-scale operation; **~eltern** *Pl.* grandparents; **~enkel der** great-grandchild; *(Junge)* great-grandson; **~enkelin die** great-granddaughter

Größen-: **~klasse die a)** size [group]; **Eier der ~klasse 2** class 2 eggs; **b)** *(Astron.)* magnitude; **~ordnung die a)** *(Dimension)* order [of magnitude]; **in einer ~ordnung von einer Milliarde Mark** in the order of a thousand million marks; **b)** *(Physik, Math.)* order of magnitude

großen·teils *Adv.* largely; for the most part

größen-, Größen-: **~verhältnis das a)** *(Maßstab)* scale; **im ~verhältnis 1:10** on a scale of 1:10; **b)** *(Proportion)* proportions *pl.*; **~wahn der** *(abwertend)* megalomania; delusions *pl.* of grandeur; **~wahnsinnig** *Adj.* megalomaniacal; **er ist ~wahnsinnig** he's a megalomaniac

größer *s.* **groß**

Groß·erzeuger der large *or* big producer

groß-, Groß-: **~fahndung die** large-scale search *or* manhunt; **~familie die** *(Soziol.)* extended family; *(mehrere Kleinfamilien)* composite family; **~feuer das** large fire *or* blaze; **~flug·hafen der** large *or* major airport; **~folio das** *(Buchw.)* large folio; **~format das** large size; *(bei Büchern)* large format *or* size; **~fürst der** *(hist.)* Grand Duke; **~fürstin die** *(hist.)* Grand Duchess; **~grund·besitz der** ownership of large estates; **~grund·besitzer der** big landowner; **~handel der** wholesale trade; **~händler der** wholesaler; **~handlung die** wholesale business; **~herzig** *(geh.)* **1.** *Adj.* magnanimous; **2.** *adv.* magnanimously; **~herzigkeit die** *(geh.)* magnanimity; **~herzog der** Grand Duke; **~herzogin die** Grand Duchess; **~herzoglich** *Adj.; nicht präd.* grand-ducal; **~herzogtum das** grand duchy; **~herzogtum Luxemburg** Grand Duchy of Luxembourg; **~hirn das** *(Anat.)* cerebrum; **~hirn·rinde die** *(Anat.)* cerebral cortex; **~industrie die** big industry; **~industrielle der/die**; *adj. Dekl.* big industrialist; **~inquisitor der** *(hist.)* Grand Inquisitor

Grossist der; **~en, ~en** *(Kaufmannsspr.)* wholesaler

groß-, Groß-: **~jährig** *Adj. (veralt.)* ⟨*person*⟩ who is of age; **~jährig werden/sein** come/be of age; **~jährigkeit die**; **~** *(veralt.)* majority; **die ~jährigkeit erlangen** reach the age of majority; **~kampf·schiff das** *(Milit. veralt.)* capital ship; **~kapital das** *(Wirtsch.)* big business *or* capital; **~kapitalist der** big capitalist; **~katze die** *(Zool.)* big cat; **~kaufmann der** merchant; **~kind das** *(schweiz.)* grandchild; **~klima das** *(Met.)* macroclimate; **~konzern der** big *or* large combine; **~kopfe[r]te** [-kɔpfətə] **der**; *adj. Dekl. (ugs. abwertend)* high-up *(coll.)*; *(Intellektueller)* egghead *(coll.)*; **~kotzig** [~kɔtsɪç] **1.** *Adj. (salopp abwertend)* pretentious ⟨*style*⟩; swanky *(coll.)* ⟨*present etc.*⟩; boastful ⟨*tone etc.*⟩; **2.** *adv.* boastfully; **~kreuz das** Grand Cross; **~küche die** large kitchen *(of hotel, hospital, etc.)*; **~kundgebung die** mass rally *or* meeting; **~macht die** great power; **die ~macht USA** the USA, one of the great powers; **~macht·stellung die** great power status; **~mama die** *(ugs.)* grandma *(coll./child lang.)*; granny *(coll./child lang.)*; **~manns·sucht die** *(abwertend)* craving for status; **~markt der** central market; **~maschig** *Adj.* wide-meshed; **~mast der** *(Seemannsspr.)* mainmast; **~maul das** *(ugs. abwertend)* big-mouth *(coll.)*; braggart; **~mäulig** [~mɔylɪç] *Adj. (ugs. abwertend)* big-mouthed *(coll.)*; **~meister der** Grand Master; *(Schach)* grand master; **~mut die**; **~**: magnanimity; generosity; **~mütig** [~my:tɪç] **1.** *Adj.* magnanimous; generous; **2.** *adv.* magnanimously; generously; **~mutter die a)** grandmother; **~mutter werden** become a grandmother; **das kannst du deiner ~mutter erzählen** *(ugs.)* tell that to the marines; **b)** *(ugs.: alte Frau)* old lady; **~mütterlich** *Adj.; nicht präd.* **a)** grandmother's; **das ~mütterliche Haus** one's grandmother's house; **jmds. ~mütterliches Erbe** sb.'s inheritance from his/her/their grandmother; **b)** *(wie eine ~mutter)* grandmotherly; **~neffe der** great-nephew; grandnephew; **~nichte die** great-niece; grandniece; **~offensive die** *(Milit.)* major *or* full-scale offensive; **~oktav das** *(Buchw.)* royal octavo; **~onkel der** great-uncle; granduncle; **~papa der** *(ugs.)* grandpa *(coll./child lang.)*; granddad *(coll./child lang.)*; **~rat der** *(schweiz.) member of a cantonal great council*; **~raum der** area; **im ~raum Hamburg** in the [Greater] Hamburg area; **~raum·abteil das** *(Eisenb.)* open carriage; **~raum·büro das** open-plan office; **~raum·flugzeug das** wide-bodied aircraft

großräumig [-rɔymɪç] **1.** *Adj.* extensive; over a wide *or* large area *postpos., not pred.*; *(viel Platz bietend)* spacious, roomy ⟨*office, house, etc.*⟩; wide-bodied ⟨*aircraft*⟩. **2.** *adv.* over a wide *or* large area; **eine ~ gebaute Stadt** a town [built] with plenty of open space; **ein ~ konzipiertes Flugzeug** an aircraft designed for high-capacity air transport

groß-, Groß-: **~raum·wagen der** *(Verkehrsw.)* open car; **~rechner der** *(DV)* mainframe [computer]; **~reinemachen das** *(ugs.)* thorough cleaning; spring-clean; **ein ~reinemachen veranstalten** spring-clean the house; **~schanze die** *(Skisport)* ninety-metre hill; **~schnauze die** *(salopp)* big-mouth *(coll.)*; **~schnauzig** *Adj. (salopp)* big-mouthed *(coll.)*; **~|schreiben** *unr. tr. V. (ugs.)* **in ~geschrieben werden** be stressed *or* emphasized; **bei ihm wird Verdienen ~geschrieben** earning money comes high on his list of priorities; *s. auch* **groß 2a**; **~schreibung die** capitalization; **~segel das** *(Seemannsspr.)* mainsail; **~sprecher der** *(abwertend)* braggart; boaster; **~sprecherisch** *Adj. (abwertend)* boastful ⟨*person*⟩; bragging *attrib.*, boastful ⟨*words, manner, etc.*⟩; **~spurig** *(abwertend)* **1.** *Adj.* boastful; *(hochtrabend)* pretentious ⟨*word, language*⟩; grandiose ⟨*plan*⟩; **2.** *adv.* boastfully; *(hochtrabend)* pretentiously; **~stadt die** city; large town;

~städter der city-dweller; urbanite; **~städtisch** *Adj.* [big-]city *attrib.* ‹*life*›; **der ~städtische Autoverkehr** traffic in the [big] cities; **Genf ist in vielem ~städtischer als Bern** in many ways Geneva is more of a big city than Berne; **~stadt·luft die** city air; *(fig. ugs.: Atmosphäre)* atmosphere of the big city *(fig.)*; **~stadt·verkehr der** [big-] city traffic

größt... *s.* **groß**

Groß-: ~tante die great-aunt; grandaunt; **~tat die** *(geh.)* great feat; **~teil der a)** *(Hauptteil)* major part; **zum ~teil** mostly; for the most part; **b)** *(nicht unerheblicher Teil)* large part; **zu einem ~teil** largely

größten·teils *Adv.* for the most part

Größt·maß das a) *(zulässiges Maß)* maximum size *or* dimensions *pl.*; **b)** *(größtmöglicher Anteil)* maximum amount

größt·möglich *Adj.; nicht präd.* greatest possible

groß-, Groß-: ~tuer [~tu:ɐ] **der; ~s, ~** *(abwertend)* braggart; boaster; **~tuerei die** *(abwertend)* bragging; boasting; **~tuerisch** *Adj. (abwertend)* boastful; bragging; **~|tun 1.** *unr. itr. V.* boast; brag; **mit jmdm./etw. ~tun** boast *or* brag about sb./sth.; **mit seinen Kenntnissen ~tun** show off one's knowledge; **2.** *unr. refl. V.* **sich mit jmdm./etw. ~tun** boast *or* brag about sb./sth.; **~unternehmen das** *(Wirtsch.)* large-scale enterprise; big concern; **~unternehmer der** *(Wirtsch.)* big businessman; **~vater der** grandfather; **~väterlich a)** *Adj.; nicht präd.* grandfather's; **das ~väterliche Haus** one's grandfather's house; **jmds. ~väterliches Erbe** sb.'s inheritance from his/her/their grandfather; **b)** *(wie ein ~vater)* grandfatherly; **~vater·stuhl der** *(ugs.)* easy chair; wing chair; **~veranstaltung die** mass rally *or* meeting; **~verbraucher der** bulk *or* large consumer; **~verdiener der** big earner; **~versandhaus das** [large] mail-order firm *or* house; **~vieh das** cattle and horses *pl.*; **~wesir der** *(hist.)* grand vizier; **~wetter·lage die** *(Met.)* macro weather situation; *(fig.)* general political situation; **~wild das** big game; **~wild·jagd die** big-game hunting *no art.*; **~wild·jäger der** big-game hunter; **~-ziehen** *unr. tr. V.* bring up; raise; rear ‹*animal*›; **~zügig 1.** *Adj.* generous; generous, handsome ‹*tip*›; **b)** *(in großem Stil)* grand and spacious ‹*building, gardens, etc.*›; generous, liberal ‹*working conditions*›; large-scale ‹*measures*›; **2.** *adv.* **a)** generously; **sich ~zügig über etw.** *(Akk.)* **hinwegsetzen** be broadminded enough to disregard sth.; **b)** *(in großem Stil)* **ein ~zügig eingerichtetes Büro** a handsomely equipped office; **die ~zügig angelegten Schloßgärten** the palace gardens, laid out on a grand scale; **~zügigkeit die a)** generosity; **b)** *(großes Ausmaß)* grand scale

grotesk [gro'tɛsk] **1.** *Adj.* grotesque. **2.** *adv.* grotesquely

Grotesk die; ~ *(Druckw.)* Grotesque; sanserif

Groteske die; ~, ~n a) *(Ornamentik)* grotesque; **b)** *(Literaturwiss.)* grotesque tale

grotesker·weise *Adv.* absurdly [enough]

Grotte ['grɔtə] **die; ~, ~n** grotto

Grotten·olm der olm

grub [gru:p] *1. u. 3. Pers. Sg. Prät. v.* **graben**

Grubber ['grʊbɐ] **der; ~s, ~** *(Landw.)* cultivator

Grübchen ['gry:pçən] **das; ~s, ~:** dimple

Grube die; ~, ~n a) pit; hole; **wer andern eine ~ gräbt, fällt selbst hinein** *(Spr.)* take care that you are not hoist with your own petard; **b)** *(Bergbau)* mine; pit; **in der ~ arbeiten/in die ~ einfahren** work/go down the mine; **c)** *(veralt.: offenes Grab)* grave; **in die** *od.* **zur ~ fahren** *(veralt.)* yield up the ghost *(arch.)*

Grübelei die; ~, ~en pondering; *(Melancholie)* brooding

grübeln ['gry:bl̩n] *itr. V.* ponder **(über +** *Dat.* on, over); *(brüten)* brood **(über +** *Dat.* over, about)

Gruben-: ~arbeiter der miner; mine-worker; **~bahn die** mine *or* pit tram *or* train; **~brand der** pit fire; **~gas das** fire-damp; **~lampe die** miner's lamp; **~unglück das** pit *or* mine disaster; **~wasser das** pit *or* mine water

Grübler der; ~s, ~, Grüblerin die; ~, ~nen meditative person; *(Melancholiker)* brooder; brooding person

grüblerisch *Adj.* meditative; *(melancholisch)* brooding

grüezi ['gry:ɛtsi] *Adv. (schweiz.)* hallo

Gruft [grʊft] **die; ~, Grüfte** ['grʏftə] **a)** *(Gewölbe)* vault; *(in einer Kirche)* crypt; **b)** *(offenes Grab)* grave

grummeln ['grʊml̩n] *itr. V.* **a)** *(dröhnen)* rumble; **man hörte den Donner/die Geschütze ~:** one could hear the rumble of thunder/the guns; **b)** *(murmeln)* mumble

Grummet ['grʊmət] **das; ~s, Grumt** [grʊmt] **das; ~[e]s** aftermath

grün [gry:n] *Adj.* **a)** green; **~er Salat** lettuce; **die Ampel ist ~** *(ugs.)* the lights are green; **wir haben ~e Weihnachten gehabt** we didn't have a white Christmas; **die Grüne Insel** the Emerald Isle; **~e Bohnen/Erbsen** French beans/green peas; **~es Holz** green timber; **~e Heringe** fresh herrings; **ein ~er Junge** *(abwertend)* a greenhorn; **~es Licht geben** give the go-ahead; **jmdn. ~ und blau** *od.* **gelb schlagen** *(ugs.)* beat sb. black and blue; **sich ~ und blau** *od.* **gelb ärgern** *(ugs.)* be livid *(coll.) or* furious; **du bist noch [zu] ~ hinter den Ohren** *(abwertend)* you're still [too] wet behind the ears *(coll.)*; *s. auch* **Welle a; b)** *(ugs.: wohlgesinnt)* **ich bin ihr nicht ~:** she's not someone I care for; **die beiden sind sich** *(Dat.)* **nicht ~:** there's no love lost between them; **c)** *(Politik)* ecological; **ein ~er Abgeordneter** a Member belonging to the Green party

Grün das; ~s, ~ *od. (ugs.)* **~s a)** green; **die Ampel steht auf** *od.* **zeigt ~:** the lights *pl.* are at green; **das ist dasselbe in ~** *(ugs.)* it makes *or* there is no real difference; **b)** *o. Pl. (Pflanzen)* greenery; **c)** *(Golf)* green; **d)** *(Spielkartenfarbe)* spades *pl.*; *s. auch* **²Pik**

Grün·anlage die green space; *(Park)* park

grün·blau *Adj.* greenish blue

Grund [grʊnt] **der; ~[e]s, Gründe** ['grʏndə] **a)** *(Erdoberfläche)* ground; **etw. bis auf den ~ abreißen** raze sth. to the ground; **etw. von ~ auf neu bauen** rebuild sth. from scratch; **den ~ zu etw. legen** *(fig.)* lay the foundations *pl.* of *or* for sth. *(fig.)*; **sich in ~ und Boden schämen** be utterly ashamed; **etw. in ~ und Boden verdammen** condemn sth. outright; **jmdn. in ~ und Boden reden** shoot every one of sb.'s arguments to pieces; **etw. in ~ und Boden wirtschaften** bring *or* reduce sth. to rack and ruin; **b)** *o. Pl. (eines Gewässers, geh.: eines Gefäßes)* bottom; **auf ~ laufen** run aground; **ein Glas bis auf den ~ leeren** *(geh.)* drain a glass [to the dregs]; **im ~e seines Herzens/seiner Seele** *(fig. geh.)* at heart *or* deep down/in his innermost soul; **der Sache** *(Dat.)* **auf den ~ gehen/kommen** get to the bottom *or* root of the matter; **im ~e [genommen]** basically; **c)** *(Ursache, Veranlassung)* reason; *(Beweg~)* grounds *pl.*; reason; **es gibt keinen/nicht den geringsten ~ zu etw.** there is no/not the slightest reason for sth.; **allen ~ haben, etw. zu tun** have every *or* good reason to do *or* for doing sth.; **[k]einen ~ zum Feiern/Klagen haben** have [no] cause for [a] celebration/to complain *or* for complaint; **aus Gründen der Geheimhaltung/Sicherheit** for reasons of secrecy/security; **aus dem einfachen ~, weil ...** *(ugs.)* for the simple reason that ...; **ohne ersichtlichen ~:** for no obvious *or* apparent reason; **auf ~ ihrer Aussagen/dieser Lage** on the basis *or* strength of their statements/in view of this situation; **Gründe und Gegengründe** pros and cons; arguments for and against; **d)** *(veralt., noch landsch.: Erdreich)* soil; ground; **e)** *(bes. österr.: ~besitz)* land *no indef. art., no pl.*; *(Bau~)* plot [of land]; **~ und Boden** land; **f)** *(veralt.: kleines Tal)* valley; **g)** *o. Pl. (Unter~)* ground

grund-, Grund-: ~anschauung die fundamental ideas *pl. or* attitudes *pl.*; **seine politische ~anschauung** his basic political outlook; **~anständig** *Adj.* thoroughly decent; **~anstrich der** priming coat; **~ausbildung die** *(Milit.)* basic training; **~ausstattung die** basic equipment; **~bedeutung die a)** fundamental *or* basic *or* essential meaning; **b)** *(Sprachw.)* original meaning; **~bedingung die** basic condition; **~begriff der** basic *or* fundamental concept; **die ~begriffe der lateinischen Sprache** the rudiments of Latin; **~besitz der a)** *(Eigentum an Land)* ownership of land; **b)** *(Land)* land; landed property; **~besitzer der** landowner; **~bestand·teil der** [basic] element; **~buch das** land register; **~buch·amt das** land registry; **~ehrlich** *Adj.* thoroughly honest; **~eigentum das** *s.* **~besitz a; ~eigentümer der** *s.* **~besitzer; ~einheit die a)** *(Physik)* fundamental unit; **b)** *(DDR: organisatorische Einheit)* local group; **~einstellung die** fundamental *or* basic attitude; **~eis das** anchor ice; ground ice; *s. auch* **Arsch a**

gründen ['grʏndn̩] **1.** *tr. V.* **a)** *(neu schaffen)* found, set up, establish ‹*organization, party, etc.*›; set up, establish ‹*business*›; start [up] ‹*club*›; **eine Familie/ein Heim ~:** start a family/set up home; **b)** *(aufbauen)* base ‹*plan, theory, etc.*› **(auf +** *Akk.* on). **2.** *itr. V.* **auf** *od.* **in etw.** *(Dat.)* **~:** be based on sth. **3.** *refl. V.* **sich auf etw.** *(Akk.)* **~:** be based on sth.

Gründer der; ~s, ~, Gründerin die; ~, ~nen: founder

Gründer·jahre *Pl.: period (1871–1873) when many industrial firms were founded in Germany*

Grund-: ~erwerb der *(Rechtsw.)* acquisition of land; *(Kauf)* purchase of land; **~erwerb[s]·steuer die** *(Steuerw.)* land transfer tax

Gründer·zeit die; *o. Pl. s.* **Gründerjahre**

grund-, Grund-: ~falsch *Adj.* utterly wrong; **~farbe die a)** *(Malerei, Druckw.)* primary colour; **b)** *(Untergrundfarbe)* ground colour; **~fehler der** basic *or* fundamental mistake *or* error; **~festen** *Pl. in* **an den ~festen von etw. rütteln** shake the [very] foundations of sth.; **etw. in seinen** *od.* **bis in seine ~festen erschüttern** shake sth. to its [very] foundations; **~fläche die a)** *(eines Zimmers)* [floor] area; **b)** *(Math.)* base; **~form die a)** *(Hauptform)* basic form; **b)** *(Urform)* original form; **c)** *(Sprachw.)* infinitive; *(Satzbauplan)* basic [grammatical] structure of a/the sentence; **~frage die** basic *or* fundamental issue *or* question; **die politischen ~fragen** the basic *or* fundamental political issues *or* questions; **~gebühr die** basic *or* standing charge; **~gedanke der** basic idea; **¹~gehalt der** *(einer Theorie)* basic idea; *(eines Dramas)* basic theme; **²~gehalt das** basic salary; **~gescheit** *Adj.* extremely clever *or* bright; **~gesetz das a)** *(Verfassung)* Basic Law; **b)** *(wichtiges Gesetz)* fundamental *or* basic law; **~haltung die a)** *(Sport: Körperhaltung)* basic position; **b)** *(Einstellung)* basic *or* fundamental attitude; **~herr der** *(hist.)* lord of the manor

Grundier·anstrich der priming coat

grundieren [grʊn'di:rən] *tr. V.* prime; *(Ölmalerei)* ground; apply the ground to

Grundier·farbe die primer
Grundierung die; ~, ~en a) *(das Grundieren)* priming; *(Ölmalerei)* grounding; applying the ground (*Gen.* to); **b)** *(erster Anstrich)* priming coat; *(Ölmalerei)* ground coat
Grund-: ~kapital das *(Wirtsch.)* equity *or* share capital; **~kenntnis die;** *meist Pl.* basic knowledge *no pl.* **(in** + *Dat.* of); **~konzeption die** basic *or* fundamental conception; **~kurs der** basic course
Grund·lage die basis; foundation; **auf der ~:** on the basis; **jeder ~ entbehren** be completely unfounded *or* without any foundation; **die geistigen/theoretischen ~n** the intellectual/theoretical foundations; **die ~n einer Wissenschaft** the basic principles of a science; **auf breiter ~ arbeiten** work *or* operate on a broad basis; **iß mal tüchtig, damit du eine gute ~ hast** *(ugs.)* get a good meal inside you to line your stomach with *(coll.)*
Grundlagen·forschung die basic research
grund·legend 1. *Adj.* fundamental, basic **(für** to); seminal ‹*idea, work*›. **2.** *adv.* fundamentally; **sich ~ zu etw. äußern** make a statement of fundamental importance on sth.
Grund·legung die; ~ *(fig.)* laying of the foundations (*Gen.* for)
gründlich ['grʏntlɪç] **1.** *Adj.* thorough. **2.** *adv.* **a)** *(gewissenhaft)* thoroughly; **b)** *(ugs.: gehörig)* **sich ~ täuschen** be sadly *or* greatly mistaken; **sich ~ langweilen** be bored to tears *(coll.)*; **~ mit etw. aufräumen** do away completely with sth.; **~ mit jmdm. abrechnen** really get even with sb.
Gründlichkeit die; ~: thoroughness
Gründling ['grʏntlɪŋ] **der; ~s, ~e** *(Zool.)* gudgeon
grund-, Grund-: ~linie die a) *(Math.)* base; **b)** *(Sport)* baseline; **c)** *(Hauptzug)* main *or* principal feature *or* characteristic; **~linien·spiel das** *(Tennis)* baseline play; **~lohn der** basic salary; **~los 1.** *Adj.* **a)** *(unbegründet)* groundless; unfounded; **b)** *(ohne festen Boden)* bottomless ‹*sea, depths, etc.*›; **2.** *adv.* **sich ~los aufregen/ängstigen** be needlessly agitated/alarmed; **~los lachen** laugh for no reason [at all]; **jmdn. ~los verdächtigen** be suspicious of sb. without reason; **~mauer die** foundation wall; **das Haus war bis auf die ~mauern abgebrannt** the house had burnt to the ground; **~nahrungs·mittel das** basic food[stuff]; **~norm die** basic standard
Grün·donnerstag der Maundy Thursday
Grund-: ~ordnung die basic fundamental [constitutional] order; **~pfeiler der** foundation *or* main pillar; *(einer Brücke)* main pier; *(fig.)* main pillar; **~prinzip das** fundamental *or* basic principle; **~rechen·art, ~rechnungs·art die** fundamental *or* basic arithmetical operation; **~recht das** basic *or* fundamental *or* constitutional right; **~regel die** fundamental *or* basic rule; **~rente die a)** *(Wirtsch.: Bodenrente)* ground rent; **b)** *(Sozialw.)* basic pension; **~riß der a)** *(Bauw.)* [ground-] plan; **b)** *(Leitfaden)* outline; **~satz der** principle; **aus ~satz** on principle; **sich** *(Dat.)* **etw. zum ~satz machen** make sth. a matter of principle; **ein Mann von ~sätzen** a man of principle; **~satz·entscheidung die** decision on fundamental principles; *(Rechtsw.)* ruling; **~satz·erklärung die** declaration of principle
grund·sätzlich 1. *Adj.* **a)** fundamental ‹*difference, question, etc.*›; **b)** *(aus Prinzip)* ‹*rejection, opponent, etc.*› on principle; **c)** *(allgemein)* ‹*agreement, readiness, etc.*› in principle. **2.** *adv.* **a)** fundamentally; **zu etw. ~ Stellung nehmen** make a statement of principle on sth.; **b)** *(aus Prinzip)* as a matter of principle; on principle; **es ist ~ verboten** it is absolutely forbidden; **c)** *(allgemein)* in principle; **~ habe ich nichts dagegen einzuwenden, aber ...:** basically *or* in principle I've nothing against it, but ...
Grund-: ~satz·programm das political programme; **~schnelligkeit die** *(Sport)* **a)** maximum speed; **b)** *(angeboren)* basic speed capability; **~schuld die** *(Rechtsw., Finanzw.)* land charge; encumbrance; **~schule die** primary school; **~schüler der** primary school pupil; **~schul·lehrer der** primary-school teacher; **~stein der** foundation-stone; *(fig.)* foundation[-stone]; **den ~stein zu etw. legen** lay the foundation-stone of sth.; *(fig.)* lay the foundation[s *pl.*] for *or* of sth.; **~stein·legung die; ~, ~en** laying of the foundation-stone; **~stellung die** *(Sport)* basic position; **~steuer die** *(Steuerw.)* property tax [under German law]; **~stimmung die** prevailing mood; **eine pessemistische ~stimmung** a prevailing mood of pessimism; **~stock der** basis; foundation; *(einer Sammlung)* basis; nucleus; **~stoff der a)** *(Chemie: Element)* element; **b)** *(Rohstoff)* [basic] raw material; **~stoff·industrie die** basic industry
Grund·stück das plot [of land]; *(Bau~)* plot of land; site; **ein bebautes ~:** a developed site *or* property; **Grundstücke kaufen/erben** buy/inherit property *sing.*
Grundstücks-: ~makler der estate agent; **~spekulant der** property speculator
Grund-: ~studium das basic course; **~tendenz die** basic trend; **~text der** original text; **~ton der a)** *(Farbton)* basic colour; **b)** *(~stimmung)* basic *or* prevailing tone *or* mood; **ein optimistischer ~ton** a basic *or* prevailing mood of optimism; **c)** *(Musik)* fundamental [tone]; root; **~übel das** basic evil; **~umsatz der** *(Physiol.)* basal metabolic rate
Gründung die; ~, ~en *(Partei~, Vereins~)* foundation; establishment; setting up; *(Geschäfts~)* setting up; establishing; *(Klub~)* starting [up]; **die ~ einer Familie** starting a family
Gründungs-: ~feier die foundation ceremony; **~jahr das** year of foundation *or* establishment; **das ~jahr unseres Vereins** the year of the foundation of our organization; **~kapital das** *(Wirtsch.)* original *or* initial capital
grund-, Grund-: ~verkehrt *Adj.* completely *or* entirely wrong; **~vermögen das** *(Finanzw.)* [landed] property; real estate; **~verschieden** *Adj.* totally *or* completely different; **~wahrheit die** fundamental *or* basic truth; **~wasser das** *(Geol.)* ground water; **~wasser·spiegel der** water table; ground-water level; **~wehr·dienst der** basic military service; national service; **~wissen das** basic *or* elementary knowledge; **~wissenschaft die** basic discipline; **~wort das;** *Pl.* **~wörter** *(Sprachw.)* basic component; **~wort·schatz der** *(Sprachw.)* basic vocabulary; **~zahl die** cardinal [number]; **~zug der** essential feature; **etw. in seinen ~zügen darstellen** outline the essential features *or* essentials of sth.
[1]**Grüne das;** *adj. Dekl.* **a)** green; **b) im ~n/ins ~:** [out] in/into the country; **c)** *meist o. Art. (ugs.: grüne Pflanzen)* greenery; *(Salat)* green salad; *(Gemüse)* greens *pl.*; green vegetables *pl.*
[2]**Grüne der/die;** *adj. Dekl. (Politik)* member of the Green Party; **die ~n** the Greens
[3]**Grüne der;** *adj. Dekl. (ugs.)* **a)** *(Polizist)* cop *(sl.)*; **b)** *(20-Mark-Schein)* 20-mark note
grünen *itr. V. (geh.)* be green; *(grün werden)* turn green; *(fig. dichter.)* spring up anew
grün-, Grün-: ~fink der greenfinch; **~fläche die** green space; *(im Park)* lawn; **~futter das** *(Landw.)* green fodder; **~gelb** *Adj.* greenish yellow; **~gürtel der** green belt; **~kern der** *dried unripe spelt grains (used to thicken soup)*; **~kohl der** curly kale; **~land das** *(Landw.) (Wiese)* meadow land; *(Weide)* pasture land; *(mit Grünfutter bebaut)* land used for growing green fodder
grünlich *Adj.* greenish
grün-, Grün-: ~pflanze die foliage plant; **~schnabel der** *(abwertend)* [young] whippersnapper; *(Neuling)* greenhorn; **~span der** verdigris; **~specht der** green woodpecker; **~stichig** *Adj. (Fot.)* with a green cast *postpos., not pred.*; **~stichig sein** have a green cast; **~streifen der** central reservation; centre strip *(grassed and often with trees and bushes)*; *(am Straßenrand)* grass verge
grunzen ['grʊntsn̩] *tr., itr. V.* grunt
Grün·zeug das *(ugs.) s.* [1]**Grüne c**
Grunz·laut der grunt
Grüppchen ['grʏpçən] **das; ~s, ~:** small group
Gruppe ['grʊpə] **die; ~, ~n a)** *(auch Sport, Math., Musik)* group; **eine ~ Jugendlicher/Erwachsener** *od.* **von Jugendlichen/Erwachsenen** a group of juveniles/adults; **b)** *(Klassifizierung)* class; category; **die ~ der starken/schwachen Verben** the class of strong/weak verbs; **c)** *(Milit.: kleine Einheit)* section; *(Luftwaffe)* ≈ squadron
gruppen-, Gruppen-: ~arbeit die; *o. Pl.* group work; **~aufnahme die** *s.* **~bild a; ~bild das a)** *(Fot.)* group photograph; **b)** *(Gemälde)* group portrait; **~dynamik die** *(Sozialpsych.)* group dynamics *sing., no art.*; **~führer der a)** *(Milit.)* ≈ section commander *or* leader; **b)** *(Wirtsch.)* team *or* group leader; **c)** *(ns.)* SS lieutenant-general; **~mitglied das** member of the/a group; **~reise die** *(Touristik)* group travel *no pl., no art.*; **eine ~reise nach London machen** travel to London with a group; **~sex der** group sex; **~sieg der** *(Sport)* top place in the group; **den ~sieg erreichen** win the group; **~sieger der** *(Sport)* winner of the/a group; **~therapie die** *(Psych.)* group therapy; **~unterricht der a)** *(Päd.)* teaching of groups; **etw. im ~unterricht lernen** learn sth. as part of a group; **b)** *(erteilter Unterricht)* group instruction; **~versicherung die** *(Versicherungsw.)* group insurance; **~weise** *Adv.* in groups
gruppieren 1. *tr. V.* arrange; **die Stühle um den Tisch ~:** arrange *or* set the chairs round the table; **Pflanzen nach verschiedenen Gesichtspunkten ~:** group plants according to different criteria. **2.** *refl. V.* form a group/groups; **sie gruppierten sich um den Tisch** they arranged themselves in a group around the table
Gruppierung die; ~, ~en a) *(Personengruppe)* grouping; group; *(Politik)* faction; **b)** *(Anordnung)* arrangement; grouping
Grus [gru:s] **der; ~es, ~e a)** *(Kohlenstaub)* breeze; slack; **b)** *(Geol.)* detritus
Grusel-: ~effekt der horror effect; **~film der** horror film; **~geschichte die** horror story
gruselig ['gru:zəlɪç], **gruslig** ['gru:slɪç] *Adj.* eerie; creepy; blood-curdling ‹*apparition, scream*›; spine-chilling ‹*story, film*›
gruseln 1. *tr., itr. V. (unpers.)* **es gruselt jmdn.** *od.* **jmdm.** sb.'s flesh creeps; **es hat mich** *od.* **mir vor diesem Anblick gegruselt** this sight made my flesh creep *or (coll.)* gave me the creeps. **2.** *refl. V.* be frightened; get the creeps *(coll.)*; **mit leichtem Gruseln** with a small shiver of fear
gruslig *s.* **gruselig**
Gruß [gru:s] **der; ~es, Grüße** ['gry:sə] **a)** greeting; *(Milit.)* salute; **jmdm. die Hand zum ~ reichen** *(geh.)* shake hands with sb.; **jmdm. herzliche Grüße senden** send sb. one's best regards *or* wishes; **viele Grüße** best wishes **(an** + *Akk.* to); **bestell Barbara**

bitte viele Grüße von mir please give Barbara my regards; please remember me to Barbara; einen [schönen] ~ an jmdn./von jmdm. [best] regards *pl.* to/from sb.; der Deutsche ~ *(ns.)* the Nazi salute; b) *(im Brief)* mit herzlichen Grüßen [with] best wishes; viele liebe Grüße Euer Hans love, Hans; mit bestem ~/freundlichen Grüßen Yours sincerely

Gruß·adresse die message of greetings

grüßen ['gry:sn̩] 1. *tr. V.* a) greet; *(Milit.)* salute; grüß [dich] Gott! *(südd.)* hello; er hat mich nie gegrüßt he never said hello to me; grüß dich! *(ugs.)* hello *or (coll.)* hi [there]!; b) *(Grüße senden)* grüße deine Eltern [ganz herzlich] von mir please give your parents my [kindest] regards; jmdn. ~ lassen send one's regards to sb.; grüß mir die Familie remember me to your family. 2. *itr. V.* say hello; *(Milit.)* salute; Franz läßt ~: Franz sends his regards

gruß-, Gruß-: ~**formel die** salutation; *(am Briefende)* [complimentary] close; ~**los** *Adv.* without a word of greeting/farewell; ~**wort das;** *Pl.* ~worte a) *s.* ~adresse; b) *(Ansprache)* [short] welcoming speech *or* address; einige ~worte a few words of welcome

Grütz·beutel der sebaceous cyst

Grütze ['grvtsə] **die;** ~, ~n a) groats *pl.*; rote ~: red fruit pudding *(made with fruit juice, fruit and cornflour, etc.)*; b) *o. Pl. (ugs.: Verstand)* brains *pl.*; nous *(coll.)*; die hat [keine] ~ im Kopf she's got [no] nous *(coll.)*

G-Saite ['ge:-] **die** *(Musik)* G-string

Gschaftlhuber *s.* Geschaftlhuber

gschert, Gscherte *s.* geschert, Gescherte

G-Schlüssel ['ge:-] **der** *(Musik) s.* Violinschlüssel

Gspusi ['kʃpu:zi] **das;** ~s, ~s *(südd., österr. ugs.)* a) *(Liebschaft)* [love] affair; b) *(Geliebte[r])* sweetheart

Guatemala [guate'ma:la] **(das);** ~s Guatemala

Guatemalteke [guatemal'te:kə] **der;** ~n, ~n, **Guatemaltekin die;** ~, ~nen Guatemalan

Guayana [gua'ja:na] *s.* Guyana

gucken ['gʊkn̩] 1. *itr. V. (ugs.)* a) look; *(heimlich)* peep; jmdm. über die Schulter ~: look *or* peer over sb.'s shoulder; laß [mich] mal ~! let's have a look! *(coll.)*; *s. auch* Karte g; b) *(hervorsehen)* stick out; c) *(dreinschauen)* look; finster/freundlich ~: look grim/affable. 2. *tr. V. (ugs.)* Fernsehen ~: watch TV *or (coll.)* telly *or (coll.)* the box

Guck·fenster das judas [window]

Gucki ['gʊki] **der;** ~s, ~s *(Fot.)* [slide] viewer

Guck-: ~**in·die·luft der;** ~ *(ugs.) s.* Hans; ~**kasten der** peep-show; ~**loch das** spy-hole; peep-hole

[1]**Guerilla** [ge'rɪlja] **die;** ~, ~s a) *(Krieg)* guerrilla war; b) *(Einheit)* guerrilla unit

[2]**Guerilla der;** ~s, ~s *(Kämpfer)* guerrilla

Guerilla-: ~**kämpfer der** guerrilla; ~**krieg der** guerrilla war; eine Spezialausbildung für den ~krieg special training in guerrilla warfare

Guerillero [-'je:ro] **der;** ~s, ~s guerrilla

Gugel·hupf [-hʊpf] **der;** ~[e]s, ~e *(südd., österr.)* gugelhupf

Güggeli ['gvgəli] **das;** ~s, ~ *(schweiz.)* roast chicken

Guillotine [gijo'ti:nə] **die;** ~, ~n guillotine

guillotinieren *tr. V.* guillotine

Guinea [gi'ne:a] **(das);** ~s Guinea

Guineer [gi'ne:ɐ] **der;** ~s, ~: Guinean

Gulasch ['gʊlaʃ, 'gu:laʃ] **das** *od.* **der;** ~[e]s, ~e *od.* ~s goulash

Gulasch-: ~**kanone die** *(Soldatenspr. scherzh.)* field kitchen; ~**suppe die** goulash soup

Gulden ['gʊldn̩] **der;** ~s, ~: guilder; florin

gülden ['gvldn̩] *Adj. (dichter.)* golden

Gulli, Gully ['gʊli] **der;** ~s, ~s drain

gültig ['gvltɪç] *Adj.* valid; current ⟨*note, coin*⟩; ein ~er Beweis a valid proof; das bisher ~e Gesetz the law previously/hitherto in force; diese Münze/dieser Geldschein ist nicht mehr ~: this coin/note is no longer legal tender; der Fahrplan ist ab 1. Oktober ~: the timetable comes into operation on 1 October; einen Vertrag als ~ anerkennen recognize a contract as valid *or* legally binding; eine Ehe für ~ erklären declare a marriage [to be] legal *or* valid; ~ für zwanzig Fahrten sein be valid *or* good for twenty journeys

Gültigkeit die; ~: validity; *(eines Gesetzes)* [legal] force; ~ haben/erlangen be/become valid; ⟨*law*⟩ be in/come into force; die ~ verlieren become invalid; wann verliert diese Münze ihre ~? when does this coin cease to be legal tender?; einem Dokument ~ verleihen validate a document

Gültigkeits-: ~**dauer die** period of validity; ~**erklärung die** validation

[1]**Gummi** ['gʊmi] **der** *od.* **das;** ~s, ~[s] a) [india] rubber; b) *(~ring)* rubber *or* elastic band

[2]**Gummi der;** ~s, ~s a) *(Radier~)* rubber; eraser; b) *(salopp: Präservativ)* rubber *(sl.)*

[3]**Gummi das;** ~s, ~s *(~band)* elastic *no indef. art.*

gummi-, Gummi-: ~**arabikum** [~a'ra:bikʊm] **das;** ~s gum arabic; ~**artig** *Adj.* rubbery; rubber-like ⟨*material*⟩; ~**ball der** rubber ball; ~**band das;** *Pl.* ~bänder a) rubber *or* elastic band; b) *(in Kleidung)* elastic *no indef. art.*; ein ~band einziehen insert a piece of elastic; ~**bär der,** ~**bärchen das** jelly baby; ~**baum der** *(Zimmerpflanze)* rubber plant; ~**bereifung die** rubber tyres *pl.*; ~**bonbon das** gumdrop; ~**druck der;** *o. Pl. (Druckw.)* flexography

gummieren *tr. V.* a) gum; b) *(Textilw.)* rubberize

Gummierung die; ~, ~en a) *(gummierte Fläche)* gummed surface; *(Textilw.)* rubberized surface; b) *(das Gummieren)* gumming; *(Textilw.)* rubberizing

Gummi-: ~**gutt das;** ~s gamboge; ~**hand·schuh der** rubber glove; ~**harz das** gum resin; ~**knüppel der** [rubber] truncheon; ~**lack der** shellac; ~**linse die** *(Fot.)* zoom lens; ~**lösung die** rubber solution; ~**mantel der** mackintosh *(Brit.)*; raincoat; ~**paragraph der** *(ugs.)* paragraph *or* section with an elastic interpretation; ~**reifen der** rubber tyre; ~**ring der** a) rubber band; b) *(Spielzeug)* rubber ring; quoit; c) *(Weckglasring)* rubber seal; ~**sauger der** rubber teat; ~**schlauch der** rubber hose; ~**schuh der** a) rubber shoe; b) *s.* ~überschuh; ~**schutz der** *(veralt.)* sheath; condom; ~**sohle die** rubber sole; ~**stiefel der** rubber boot; *(für Regenwetter)* wellington [boot] *(Brit.)*; *(bis zum Oberschenkel)* wader; ~**strumpf der** elastic stocking; ~**tier das** rubber animal; *(aufblasbar)* inflatable animal; ~**über·schuh der** galosh; rubber overshoe; ~**waren** *Pl.* rubber goods; ~**zelle die** padded cell; ~**zug der** *s.* ~band b

Gunder·mann ['gʊndɐ-] **der;** ~[e]s *(Bot.)* ground ivy

Gunst [gʊnst] **die;** ~: favour; goodwill; jmds. ~ erlangen win *or* gain sb.'s favour; in jmds. ~ *(Dat.) od.* bei jmdm. in ~ *(Dat.)* stehen *(geh.)* enjoy sb.'s favour; be in favour with sb.; jmdm. seine ~ bezeugen show one's favour to sb.; die ~ der Stunde/Lage nutzen *(fig.)* take advantage of the favourable *or* propitious moment/situation; zu jmds. ~en in sb.'s favour

Gunst·bezeigung die mark of favour *or* goodwill

günstig ['gvnstɪç] 1. *Adj.* a) *(vorteilhaft)* favourable; propitious ⟨*sign*⟩; auspicious ⟨*moment*⟩; beneficial ⟨*influence*⟩; good, reasonable ⟨*price*⟩; bei ~em Wetter if the weather is favourable; weather permitting; der Zug um 10 Uhr ist ~er the 10 o'clock train is better *or* more convenient; b) *(wohlwollend)* well-disposed; favourably disposed; das Glück war uns ~: luck was on our side. 2. *adv.* a) *(vorteilhaft)* favourably; etw. ~ beeinflussen have *or* exert a beneficial influence on sth.; etw. ~ kaufen/verkaufen buy/sell sth. at a good price; das trifft sich ~: that's a piece of luck; b) *(wohlwollend)* jmdn./etw. ~ aufnehmen receive sb./sth. well *or* favourably; jmdn. ~ stimmen put sb. in a favourable mood; jmdn. für etw. ~ stimmen make sb. well-disposed towards sth.; jmdm./einer Sache ~ gesinnt sein be well *or* favourably disposed towards sb./sth.

günstig[st]en·falls *Adv.* at best

Günstling ['gvnstlɪŋ] **der;** ~s, ~e favourite

Günstlings·wirtschaft die; *o. Pl. (abwertend)* favouritism

Guppy ['gʊpi] **der;** ~s, ~s *(Zool.)* guppy

Gurgel ['gʊrgl̩] **die;** ~, ~n throat; jmdm. die ~ zudrücken strangle *or* throttle sb.; jmdm. die ~ durchschneiden cut sb.'s throat; jmdm. an die ~ springen/fahren jump *or* leap at/go for sb.'s throat; jmdm. an die ~ wollen fly at sb.; jmdm. die ~ abdrehen *od.* zudrücken *(fig. salopp)* force *or* send sb. to the wall; sein ganzes Geld durch die ~ jagen *(ugs.)* drink all one's money away *(coll.)*; sich *(Dat.)* die ~ ölen *od.* schmieren *(ugs.)* wet one's whistle *(coll.)*

gurgeln *itr. V.* a) *(spülen)* gargle; b) *(blubbern)* gurgle

Gürkchen ['gvrkçən] **das;** ~s, ~: [cocktail] gherkin

Gurke ['gʊrkə] **die;** ~, ~n a) cucumber; *(eingelegt)* gherkin; saure ~n pickled gherkins; b) *(salopp scherzh.: Nase)* hooter *(sl.)*; snout *(coll.)*; c) *(salopp abwertend: Auto)* [old] banger *(sl.)*

Gurken-: ~**hobel der** cucumber-slicer; ~**salat der** cucumber salad; ~**truppe die** *(salopp)* useless *or* feeble bunch *(coll.)*

gurren ['gʊrən] *itr. V. (auch fig.)* coo

Gurt [gʊrt] **der;** ~[e]s, ~e strap; *(Gürtel)* belt; *(im Auto, Flugzeug)* [seat-]belt

Gürtel ['gvrtl̩] **der;** ~s, ~: belt; den ~ enger schnallen *(fig. ugs.)* tighten one's belt *(fig.)*

Gürtel-: ~**linie die** waist[line]; ein Schlag unter die ~linie *(Boxen)* a punch *or* blow below the belt; das war ein Schlag unter die ~linie *(fig. ugs.)* that was hitting below the belt *(fig. coll.)*; ~**reifen der** radial[-ply] tyre; ~**rose die;** *o. Pl. (Med.)* shingles *sing. or pl.*; ~**schnalle die** belt buckle; ~**tier das** armadillo

gürten ['gvrtn̩] *(geh. veralt.)* 1. *tr. V.* gird *(arch./literary)*; jmdn. mit dem Schwert ~: gird sb. with his sword. 2. *refl. V.* sich [zum Kampf] ~: gird oneself; sich mit dem Schwert ~: gird on one's sword

Gurt·muffel der *(ugs.)* person not wearing a safety-belt

Guru ['gʊru] **der;** ~s, ~s guru

Guß [gʊs] **der;** Gusses, Güsse ['gvsə] a) *(das Gießen)* casting; founding; [wie] aus einem ~: forming a unified *or* an integrated whole; fully co-ordinated ⟨*plan*⟩; b) *(ugs.: Regenschauer)* downpour; ein heftiger/wolkenbruchartiger ~: a violent downpour/a cloudburst; c) *(gegossenes Erzeugnis)* casting; cast; d) *(das Begießen)* stream; *(Med.)* affusion; e) *(auf Backwaren)* icing; eine Torte mit ~ überziehen ice a gateau

guß-, Guß-: ~**asphalt der** [poured] asphalt; ~**beton der** cast concrete; ~**eisen das** cast iron; ~**eisern** *Adj.* cast-iron; ~**form die** casting mould; ~**naht die** *(Gießerei)* [casting] fin *or* flash; ~**stahl der** cast steel

Gusto ['gʊsto] **der;** ~s, ~s a) *(Neigung)* taste; liking; nach jmds. ~/nach eigenem ~

sein be to sb.'s/one's own taste *or* liking; **b)** *(Appetit)* ~ **auf etw.** *(Akk.)* **haben** feel like *or* fancy sth.

Gụsto·stückerl das *(österr.)* star turn

gut [gu:t]; **besser** ['bɛsɐ], **best...** ['bɛst...] **1.** *Adj.* **a)** good; fine ⟨*wine*⟩; **in Französisch ~ sein** be good at French; **ist der Kuchen ~ geworden?** did the cake turn out all right?; **es wäre ~, wenn ...:** it would be as well if ...; **also ~:** very well; all right; **schon ~:** [it's] all right *or (coll.)* OK; **nun ~:** very well *or* all right [then]; **wie ~, daß ...:** it's good that ...; **jetzt ist es aber ~!** *(ugs.)* that's enough!; **das ist ja alles ~ und schön** that's all very well *or* all well and good; **etwas Gutes zu essen/trinken** something good to eat/drink; **es ~ sein lassen** *(ugs.)* leave it at that; **laß es ~ sein** *(ugs.)* let's say no more about it; **das ist ~ gegen** *od.* **für Kopfschmerzen** it's good for headaches; **wer weiß, wozu das ~ ist** perhaps it's for the best; **das ist so ~ wie gewonnen** it's as good as won; **dieser Stürmer ist immer ~ für ein Tor** *(ugs.)* this forward is always likely to score goals; **~en Tag!** good morning/afternoon!; **~en Morgen!** good morning!; **~en Abend!** good evening!; **~e Nacht!** good night!; **etw. zu einem ~en Ende führen** bring sth. to a happy conclusion; **ein ~es neues Jahr** a happy new year; **Sie haben es noch nie so ~ gehabt** you've never had it so good; **er hat es doch ~ bei uns** he's well enough off with us; **ihr habt es ~:** it's all right for 'you; **mir ist nicht ~:** I'm not feeling well; I don't feel well; **alles Gute!** all the best!; **das bedeutet nichts Gutes** that's an ominous sign; **das ist zuviel des Guten** *(iron.)* that's overdoing it; **das Gute daran** the good thing about it; **~en Appetit!** enjoy your lunch/dinner *etc.!*; **es dürfte eine ~e Stunde [von hier] sein** it must be a good hour [from here]; **ein ~ Teil von etw.** a good deal *or* part of sth.; **~e Frau/~er Mann** *(iron. Anrede)* dear lady/my good man; **sich** *(Dat.)* **zu ~ für etw. sein** consider sth. beneath one *or* beneath one's dignity; **du bist ~!** *(iron.)* you're joking!; you must be joking!; **im ~en wie im bösen haben wir uns bemüht ...:** we've done everything we can to try ...; **jmdm. ~ sein** *(ugs.)* feel a lot of affection for sb.; **wieder ~ [mit jmdm.] sein** be friends [with sb.] again; **sei [bitte] so ~ und reich mir das Buch** would you be good *or* kind enough to pass me the book?; **im ~en auseinandergehen** part amicably *or* on amicable terms; **b)** *(besonderen Anlässen vorbehalten)* best; **sein ~er Anzug** his best suit; **die ~e Stube** the best room; **für ~** *(ugs.)* for best; for special occasions. **2.** *adv.* **a)** well; **~ reiten/schwimmen** be a good rider/swimmer; **etw. ~ können** be good at sth.; **seine Sache ~ machen** do well; **~ hören/sehen** [be able to] hear/see well *or* clearly; **[das hast du] ~ gemacht!** well done!; **du tätest ~ daran, darüber zu schweigen** you would do well *or* be wise to say nothing about it; **der Laden/das Geschäft geht ~:** the shop/business is doing well; **~ eine Stunde [von hier] entfernt** a good hour [from here]; **~ zwei Pfund wiegen** weigh a good two pounds; **~ und gern** *(ugs.)* easily; at least *(ugs.)*; **so ~ wie nichts** next to nothing; **so ~ ich kann** as best I can; **~ und richtig handeln** do the right thing; **jmdm. ~ zureden** coax sb. [gently]; **mit jmdm. ~ stehen** *od.* **auskommen** be on good *or* friendly terms with sb.; get on well with sb.; **es ~ meinen** mean well; **es ~ mit jmdm. meinen** have sb.'s interests at heart; *s. auch* **anschreiben 1 b**; **b)** *(mühelos)* easily; **~ zu Fuß sein** *(ugs.)* be a strong walker; **hinterher hat** *od.* **kann man ~ reden** it's easy to be wise after the event; **du hast ~ lachen** it's all right for you to laugh; **es kann ~ sein, daß ...:** it may well be that ...; **ich kann das nicht ~ tun** I can't very well do that; *s. auch* **besser, best...**

Gụt das; ~[e]s, Güter ['gy:tɐ] **a)** *(Eigentum)* property; *(Besitztum, auch fig.)* possession; **ererbtes/gestohlenes ~:** inherited/stolen property; **irdische Güter** earthly goods *or* possessions; **die geistigen Güter des Volkes** the intellectual wealth *sing.* of the people; **bewegliche/unbewegliche Güter** movables/immovables; **das höchste ~** *(fig.)* the greatest good; **unrecht ~ gedeihet nicht** *od.* **tut selten gut** *(Spr.)* ill-gotten goods *or* gains never *or* seldom prosper; **b)** *(landwirtschaftlicher Grundbesitz)* estate; **c)** *(Fracht~, Ware)* item; **Güter** goods; *(Fracht~)* freight *sing.*; goods *(Brit.)*; **d)** *(das Gute)* **~ und Böse** good and evil; **jenseits von ~ und Böse sein** *(iron.)* be past it *(coll.)*; **e)** *(veralt.: Material)* material [to be processed]

gut-, Gut-: ~achten *itr. V.* give an expert opinion; *(in einem Prozeß)* act as an expert witness; **der ~achtende Arzt** the medical expert; **~achten das; ~s, ~:** [expert's] report; **~achter der; ~s, ~:** expert; *(in einem Prozeß)* expert witness; **~achtlich 1.** *Adj.*; *nicht präd.* expert; **2.** *adv.* **etw. ~achtlich prüfen/untersuchen lassen** commission an expert report on sth.; **~artig** *Adj.* **a)** good-natured; **b)** *(nicht gefährlich)* benign; **~artigkeit die;** *o. Pl.* **a)** good nature; goodnaturedness; **b)** *(Ungefährlichkeit)* benignity; **~aussehend** *Adj.*; *nicht präd.* good-looking; **~bezahlt** *Adj.*; *nicht präd.* well-paid; **~|bringen** *unr. tr. V.* *(Kaufmannsspr.) s.* **~schreiben**; **~bürgerlich 1.** *Adj.* good middle-class; **~bürgerliche Küche** good plain cooking; **~bürgerliches Zuhause** comfortable middle-class home; **2.** *adv.* in a good middle-class way; ⟨*grow up*⟩ in good middle-class circumstances; **~bürgerlich essen** eat good plain food; **~dünken das; ~s** discretion; judgement; **nach [eigenem] ~dünken** at one's own discretion; **nach [eigenem/seinem] ~dünken mit jmdm./etw. verfahren** use one's own discretion in dealing with sb./sth.

Güte ['gy:tə] **die; ~ a)** goodness; kindness; *(~ Gottes)* loving-kindness; goodness; **er ist die ~ selbst** he is goodness *or* kindness itself; **sich mit jmdm. in ~ einigen** come to an amicable agreement with sb.; **ein Vorschlag zur ~:** a suggestion for an amicable agreement; **hätten Sie die ~, mir zu helfen?** *(geh.)* would you be kind *or* good enough to help me?; **[ach] du meine** *od.* **liebe ~!** *(ugs.)* my goodness!; goodness me; **b)** *(Qualität)* quality

Güte·klasse die grade; class

Gute·nạcht·kuß der good-night kiss

Güter-: ~abfertigung die a) *(Abfertigung von Waren)* dispatch of freight *or (Brit.)* goods; **b)** *(Annahmestelle)* freight *or (Brit.)* goods office; **~austausch der** exchange of goods *or* commodities; **~bahnhof der** freight depot; goods station *(Brit.)*; **~fern·verkehr** [--'---] **der** long-distance haulage *no art.*; **~gemeinschaft die** *(Rechtsw.)* community of property; **~nah·verkehr** [--'---] **der** short-distance haulage *no art.*; **~recht das** *(Rechtsw.)* law of property; **~schuppen der** goods shed *(Brit.)*; freight house *(Amer.)*; **~transport der** transport *or* carriage of goods *(Brit.) or* freight; **~trennung die** *(Rechtsw.)* separation of property; **~verkehr der** freight *or (Brit.)* goods traffic; **~wagen der** goods wagon *(Brit.)*; freight car *(Amer.)*; **~zug der** goods train *(Brit.)*; freight train *(Amer.)*

Güte-: ~siegel das *s.* **~zeichen**; **~verfahren das** *(Rechtsw.)* conciliation procedure; *(Verhandlung)* conciliation meeting; **~zeichen das** quality mark

gut-, Gụt-: ~|gehen *unr. itr. V.; mit sein* **a)** *(unpers.)* **es geht jmdm. gut** *(gesundheitlich)* sb. is well *or (coll.)* fine; *(geschäftlich, beruflich)* sb. is doing well; **b)** *(~ ausgehen)* turn out well; **es ist noch einmal ~gegangen** it worked out all right again this time; **~gehend** *Adj.*; *nicht präd.* flourishing; thriving; **~gekleidet** *Adj.* *(präd. getrennt geschrieben)* well-dressed; **~gelaunt** *Adj.* *(präd. getrennt geschrieben)* good-humoured; cheerful; **~gemeint** *Adj.* *(präd. getrennt geschrieben)* well-meant; **~gläubig** *Adj.* innocently trusting; **~gläubigkeit die** innocent trust; **~|haben** *unr. tr. V.* **etw. bei jmdm. ~haben** be owed sth. by sb.; **~haben das; ~s, ~:** credit balance; **Sie haben ein ~haben von 450 DM auf Ihrem Konto** your account is 450 marks in credit; **~|heißen** *unr. tr. V.* approve of; **~herzig** *Adj.* kind-hearted; good-hearted; **~herzigkeit die** kind-heartedness; good-heartedness

gütig ['gy:tɪç] **1.** *Adj.* kindly; kind ⟨*heart*⟩; **mit Ihrer ~en Erlaubnis** *(geh./iron.)* with your kind permission. **2.** *adv.* **~ lächeln/nicken** give a kindly smile/nod

gütlich ['gy:tlɪç] **1.** *Adj.*; *nicht präd.* amicable. **2.** *adv.* amicably; **sich ~ an etw.** *(Dat.)* **tun** regale oneself with sth.

gut-, Gut-: ~|machen *tr. V.* **a)** *(in Ordnung bringen)* make good ⟨*damage*⟩; put right, correct ⟨*omission, mistake, etc.*⟩; **an jmdm. viel ~zumachen haben** have a lot to make up *or* make amends to sb. for; **wie soll/kann ich das ~machen?** how can I ever repay you?; **b)** *(Überschuß erzielen)* make [a profit of] **(bei** on); *(aufholen)* **gegenüber der führenden Mannschaft fünf Sekunden ~machen** make up five seconds on the leading team; **~mütig 1.** *Adj.* good-natured; **2.** *adv.* good-naturedly; **~mütig veranlagt sein** be good-natured; **~mütigkeit die; ~:** good nature; goodnaturedness; **~nạchbarlich 1.** *Adj.* good-neigbourly ⟨*relations etc.*⟩; **2.** *adv.* as good neighbours; **~|sagen** *itr. V.* **für jmdn./etw. ~sagen** vouch for sb./sth.

Gụts·besitzer der owner of a/the estate; landowner

gut-, Gụt-: ~schein der voucher, coupon **(für, auf +** *Akk.* for); **~|schreiben** *unr. tr. V.* credit; **etw. jmdm./jmds. Konto ~schreiben** credit sb./sb.'s account with sth.; **~schrift die a)** *(Betrag)* credit; **b)** *(Bescheinigung)* credit slip *or* note; **c)** *(Vorgang)* crediting

Gụts-: ~haus das manor house; **~herr der** lord of the manor; **~herrin die** lady of the manor; **~hof der** estate; manor

Gụts·verwalter der steward; bailiff

Guttapercha [gʊta'pɛrça] **die; ~** *od.* **das; ~[s]** gutta-percha

gụt·tun *unr. itr. V.* do good; **etw. tut jmdm. gut** sth. does sb. good; **es tut ihm gut, das zu machen** it'll do him good to do that; **ein Schnaps tut gut bei der Kälte** schnapps is good for you when it's cold

Guttural[laut] [gʊtu'ra:l(-)] **der; ~s, ~e** *(Sprachw. veralt.)* guttural

gut-, Gụt-: ~unterrichtet *Adj.* *(präd. getrennt geschrieben)* well-informed; **~willig 1.** *Adj.* willing; *(entgegenkommend)* obliging; **sich ~willig zeigen** be obliging; show willing *(coll.)*; **2.** *adv.* **etw. ~willig herausgeben/versprechen** hand sth. over voluntarily/promise sth. willingly *or* freely; **~willigkeit die** willingness; *(Entgegenkommen)* obligingness

Guyana [gu'ja:na] **(das); ~s** Guyana

gymnasial [gʏmna'zi̯a:l] *Adj.*; *nicht präd.* ≈ grammar-school ⟨*education, syllabus*⟩

Gymnasiạl- ≈ grammar-school ⟨*education, teacher*⟩

Gymnasiast [gʏmna'zi̯ast] **der; ~en, ~en, Gymnasiạstin die; ~, ~nen** ≈ grammar-school pupil

Gymnasium [gʏm'na:zi̯ʊm] **das; ~s, Gymnạsien a)** *(höhere Schule)* ≈ grammar school; **neusprachliches ~:** ≈ grammar

school stressing modern languages; **aufs ~ gehen** ≈ be at *or* attend grammar school; **b)** *(in der Antike)* gymnasium
Gymnastik [gym'nastık] **die; ~:** physical exercises *pl.; (Turnen)* gymnastics *sing.*
Gymnastik-: ~lehrer der teacher of physical exercises; **~saal der** gymnasium; gym *(coll.)*
gymnastisch *Adj.* gymnastic
Gynäkologe [gynɛko'lo:gə] **der; ~n, ~n** gynaecologist
Gynäkologie die; ~: gynaecology *no art.*
Gynäkologin die; ~, ~nen gynaecologist
gynäkologisch *Adj.; nicht präd.* gynaecological
Gyroskop [gyro'sko:p] **das; ~s, ~e** gyroscope

H

h, H [ha:] **das; ~, ~ a)** *(Buchstabe)* h/H; **b)** *(Musik)* [key of] B; *s. auch* **a, A**
h *Abk.* **a) Uhr** hrs; **b) Stunde** hr[s]
H *Abk.* **a) Herren; b) Haltestelle**
H. *Abk.* **Heft** No.
[1]**ha** [ha(:)] *Interj.* **a)** *(Überraschung)* ha!; oh!; ah!; **b)** *(Triumph)* aha!
[2]**ha** *Abk.* **Hektar** ha
Haag [ha:k] **(das)** *od.* **der; ~s** The Hague; *s. auch* **Den Haag**
Haar [ha:ɐ̯] **das; ~[e]s, ~e a)** *(auch Zool., Bot.)* hair; **blonde ~e** *od.* **blondes ~ haben** have fair hair; **echtes ~:** real hair; **sein echtes ~:** his own hair; **[sich** *(Dat.)***] das ~** *od.* **die ~e waschen** wash one's hair; **sich** *(Dat.)* **das ~** *od.* **die ~e schneiden lassen** have *or* get one's hair cut; **ihm geht das ~ aus** he's losing his hair; **sich** *(Dat.)* **die ~e [aus]raufen** *(ugs.)* tear one's hair [out]; **b)** *(fig.)* **ihr stehen die ~e zu Berge** *od.* **sträuben sich die ~e** *(ugs.)* her hair stands on end; **ein ~ in der Suppe finden** *(ugs.)* find something to quibble about *or* find fault with; **kein gutes ~ an jmdm./etw. lassen** *(ugs.)* pull sb./sth. to pieces *(fig. coll.)*; **jmdm. die ~e vom Kopf fressen** *(ugs. scherzh.)* eat sb. out of house and home; **~e auf den Zähnen haben** *(ugs. scherzh.)* be a tough customer; **sich** *(Dat.)* **über** *od.* **wegen** *od.* **um etw. keine grauen ~e wachsen lassen** not lose any sleep over sth.; not worry one's head about sth.; **er wird dir kein ~ krümmen** *(ugs.)* he won't harm a hair of your head; **an einem ~ hängen** *(ugs.)* be touch-and-go; **das ist an den ~en herbeigezogen** *(ugs.)* that's far-fetched; **jmdm. aufs ~ gleichen** be the spitting image of sb.; **sie gleichen sich aufs ~:** they're as alike as two peas in a pod; **sich in die ~e geraten** *od.* **kriegen** *(ugs.)* quarrel, squabble **(wegen** over); **sich** *(Dat.)* **in den ~en liegen** *(ugs.)* be at loggerheads; **um ein ~** *(ugs.)* very nearly; **sie wäre um ein ~ abgestürzt** *(ugs.)* she came within an inch *or* an ace *or* a whisker of falling; **ich hätte sie um ein ~ verfehlt** *(ugs.)* I just missed her by a hair's breadth; **nicht [um] ein ~** *od.* **[um] kein ~ besser** *(ugs.)* not a whit *or* bit better

Haar-: ~ansatz der a) hairline; **b)** *(unmittelbar an der Kopfhaut)* roots *pl.*; **~ausfall der** loss of hair; hair loss; **~balg der;** *Pl.* **~bälge** hair follicle; **~band das;** *Pl.* **~bänder** hair-band; **~besen der** broom; **~breit das** *in* **nicht [um] ein** *od.* **[um] kein ~breit** not an inch; **~bürste die** hairbrush; **~büschel das** tuft of hair
haaren *itr. V.* moult; lose *or* shed its hair
Haar-: ~entferner der; ~s, ~: hair-remover; depilatory; **~ersatz der** hair-piece
Haares·breite die *in* **um ~:** by a hair's breadth; **nicht um ~ von etw. abweichen** not budge an inch from sth.
haar-, Haar-: ~farbe die hair colour; **mit seiner ~farbe nicht zufrieden sein** be unhappy with the colour of one's hair; **welche ~farbe hatte der Dieb?** what colour hair did the thief have?; **~färbe·mittel das** hair dye; **~fein** *Adj.* fine as a hair *postpos.*; **ein ~feiner Sprung** a hair-line crack; **~festiger der** setting lotion; **~garn das** *(Textilw.)* hair yarn; **~gefäß das;** *meist Pl. (Med.)* capillary [vessel]; **~genau** *(ugs.)* **1.** *Adj.* exact; **2.** *adv.* exactly; **die Beschreibung trifft ~genau auf sie zu** the description fits her to a T *(coll.)*; **etw. ~genau erzählen** relate sth. in great detail; **das stimmt ~genau** that is absolutely right
haarig *Adj.* **a)** *(behaart)* hairy; **b)** *(ugs.: heikel)* tricky
haar-, Haar-: ~klammer die hair-grip; **~kleid das** *(geh.)* coat; **~klein 1.** *Adj.* minute; **2.** *adv.* in minute detail; **~klemme die** hair-grip; **~kranz der a)** fringe *or* circle of hair; **b)** *(Frisur)* chaplet [of plaited hair]; **~künstler der** *(oft scherzh.)* hair stylist; tonsorial artist *(joc.)*; **~lack der** hair lacquer; **~los** *Adj.* hairless; *(glatzköpfig)* bald; **~mode die** hair-style; **~nadel die** hairpin; **~nadel·kurve die** hairpin bend; **~netz das** hair-net; **~öl das** hair oil; **~pflege die** hair care; **~pflege·mittel das** hair-care product; **~pinsel der** fine animal-hair brush; **~pracht die** *(scherzh.)* magnificent head of hair; **~riss der** hair-line crack; **~röhrchen das** *(Physik)* capillary tube; **~scharf 1.** *Adj. (sehr genau)* razor-sharp ⟨*remark*⟩; very fine ⟨*distinction*⟩; very good ⟨*memory*⟩; **2.** *adv.* **a)** *(sehr nah)* **das Auto blieb ~scharf vor dem Kind stehen** the car stopped only a hair's breadth from the child; **die Kugel flog ~scharf an ihm vorbei** the bullet missed him by a hair's breadth; **~scharf an jmdm. vorbeizielen** aim to just miss sb.; **b)** *(sehr genau)* with great precision; **~schleife die** bow; hair-ribbon; **~schmuck der** hair ornaments *pl.*; **~schneide·maschine die** electric clippers *pl.*; **~schnitt der** haircut; *(modisch)* hair-style; **jmdm. einen ~schnitt machen** cut sb.'s hair; give sb. a haircut; **~schopf der** mop *or* shock of hair; **~schwund der** loss of hair; hair loss; **~seite die a)** *(Textilw.)* right side; front; **b)** *(Gerberei)* hair side; *(eines Pelzes)* fur side; **~sieb das** hair sieve; **~spalter der; ~s, ~** *(abwertend)* hair-splitter; **~spalterei die; ~** *(abwertend)* hair-splitting; **das ist doch ~spalterei** that's splitting hairs; **~spalterisch** *Adj.* *(abwertend)* hair-splitting; **~spange die** hair-slide; **~spitze die** end of a hair; **die ~spitzen** the ends of the hairs; **~spray der** *od.* **das** hair spray; **~sträubend** *Adj.* **a)** *(grauenhaft)* hair-raising; horrifying; **b)** *(empörend)* outrageous; shocking; **~teil das** hair-piece; **~tracht die** *(veralt.)* hair-style; **~trockner der** hair-dryer; **~wäsche die** shampoo; [hair-] wash; **~wasch·mittel das** shampoo; **~wasser das;** *Pl.* **~wässer** hair lotion; **~wild das** *(Jägerspr.)* ground game; **~wuchs der** hair growth; growth of hair; **einen spärlichen/starken ~wuchs haben** have little/a lot of hair; **~wuchs·mittel das** hair-restorer; **~wurzel die** root [of the/a hair]
Hab [ha:p] *in* **~ und Gut** *(geh.)* possessions *pl.*; belongings *pl.*
Habacht·stellung die *s.* **Habtachtstellung**
Habe ['ha:bə] **die; ~** *(geh.)* possessions *pl.*; belongings *pl.*; **bewegliche ~:** movables *pl.*
Habeaskorpus·akte [ha:beas'kɔrpʊs-] **die;** *o. Pl. (hist.)* Habeas Corpus Act
haben 1. *unr. tr. V.* **a)** have; have got; **er hat nichts** *(ugs.)* he has nothing; **von ihm kannst du dir kein Geld borgen: er hat selber nichts** you can't borrow money from him: he hasn't got any himself; **wer hat, der hat** *(scherzh./iron.)* I/you *etc.* can afford it; **was man hat, das hat man** *(scherzh./iron.)* I'd rather have something than nothing; **da hast du das Geld** there's the money; **die ~'s ja** *(ugs.)* they can afford it; **gute Kenntnisse ~:** be knowledgeable; **ich habe Zeit/keine Zeit** I have [got] [the] time/I have [got] no time *or* I haven't [got] any time; **die Sache hat Zeit** it's not urgent; it can wait *(coll.)*; **heute ~ wir schönes Wetter/30°** the weather is fine/it's 30° today; **wann hast du Urlaub?** when is your holiday?; *s. auch* **Datum a; Schuld b; b)** *(empfinden)* **Hunger/Durst ~:** be hungry/thirsty; **Sehnsucht nach etw. ~:** long for sth.; **Heimweh/Furcht ~:** be homesick/afraid; **Husten/Fieber/Schmerzen ~:** have [got] a cough/a temperature/ have pain; **es an der Leber/auf der Brust ~** *(ugs.)* have [got] liver trouble *or* something wrong with one's liver/have [got] a bad chest; **was hast du denn?** *(ugs.)* what's the matter?; what's wrong?; **hast du was?** *(ugs.)* is [there] something the matter?; is [there] something wrong?; **ich kann das nicht ~** *(ugs.)* I can't stand it; **dich hat's wohl** *(ugs.)* you must be mad *or* crazy; **c)** *mit Adj. u.* „**es**" **es gut/schlecht/schwer/eilig ~:** have it good *(coll.)*/have a bad time [of it]/have a difficult *or* tough time/be in a hurry; **wir ~ es sehr gemütlich hier** we are very comfortable here; **möchten Sie es etwas wärmer ~?** are you warm enough?; **d)** *mit „zu" u. Inf.* **nichts zu essen/trinken ~:** have nothing to eat/drink; **habt ihr nichts zu trinken?** haven't you got anything to drink?; **er hat nichts mehr zu erwarten** he can expect nothing more; *(müssen)* **du hast zu gehorchen** you must obey; **etw. zu tun/erledigen ~:** have [got] sth. to do *or* that one must do; **er hat zu tun** he's busy; *(dürfen)* **er hat mir nichts zu befehlen** he has [got] no right to order me about; **du hast dich hier nicht einzumischen** you should mind your own business; **e)** *(sich zusammensetzen aus)* **das Jahr hat 12 Monate** there are 12 months in a year; **ein Kilometer hat 1000 Meter** there are 1,000 metres in a kilometre; **diese Stadt hat 10 000 Einwohner** this town has 10,000 inhabitants; **die USA haben 50 Bundesstaaten** the USA is made up of 50 states; **f)** *(bekommen)* have; **kann ich heute dein Auto ~?** can I have your car today?; **sind diese Puppen noch zu ~?** can you still get these dolls?; **zu ~ sein** *(ugs.)* be unattached; *(zum Beischlaf bereit sein)* be available; **dafür ist er immer zu ~:** he's always game for that; **er ist immer für ein gutes Essen zu ~:** he always likes *or* enjoys a good meal; **für so etw. bin ich nicht zu ~:** I'm not one for *or* keen on things like that; **da hast du's** *(ugs.)* there you are; **g)** *(ugs.: in der Schule)* **morgen ~ wir Geschichte** we've got history tomorrow; **wir ~ schon seit Monaten keine Chemie** we haven't done [any] chemistry for months; **h)** *(ugs.: gebrauchen)* **man hat das nicht mehr** it is no longer in use/in fashion; **hat man bei euch noch die alten Karbidlampen?** are you still using the old carbide lamps?; **i)** *(ugs.: gefaßt ~)* have ⟨*thief etc.*⟩; **jetzt hab' ich dich** now I've got you; **j)** *(be-*

kommen ~) **Nachricht von jmdm. ~:** have heard from sb.; **was** *(ugs.)***/welche Note hast du diesmal in Physik?** what did you get in *or* for physics this time?; **k)** *(gefunden ~)* **~ Sie den Fehler?** have you found the mistake?; **ich hab's!** *(ugs.)* I've got it!; **das werden wir gleich ~** *(ugs.)* we'll soon find out; **l)** *(ugs.: repariert, beendet ~)* **noch zwei Minuten, dann hab' ich's** I'll be finished in a couple of minutes; **das werden wir gleich ~:** we'll soon fix that; **m)** *mit Präp.* **sie hat einen guten Freund an ihm** he is a good friend to her; **er weiß ja gar nicht, was er an dir hat** he doesn't realize how lucky he is to have you; **wir ~ viele Bilder an der Wand [hängen]** we have quite a lot of pictures up; **er hat immer Blumen auf dem Tisch [stehen]** he has always [got] flowers on the table; **ich habe meinen Wagen auf dem Parkplatz [stehen]** I've got my car in the car park; **etwas/nichts gegen jmdn.** *od.* **etw. ~:** have something/nothing against sb. *or* sth.; **sie hat alle Kollegen gegen sich** all her colleagues are against her; **etwas mit jmdm. ~** *(ugs.)* have a thing *or* something going with sb. *(coll.)*; **hast du es schon einmal mit einer Frau gehabt?** *(salopp)* have you ever had it off with a woman? *(sl.)*; **viel/wenig von jmdm. ~:** see a lot/little of sb.; **er hat etwas von einem Tyrannen/Faulpelz** he is a bit of a tyrant/lazybones; **etw. von etw. ~:** get sth. out of sth.; **ihn würde ich gerne zum Freund ~:** I would like [to have] him as a friend; **er hat eine Adlige zur Frau** he has [got] an aristocratic wife; *s. auch* **an, auf, bei** *usw.*; **n)** *unpers. (bes. österr., südd.: vorhanden sein)* **es hat ...:** there is/are ... **2.** *refl. V.* **a)** *(ugs. abwertend: sich aufregen)* make a fuss; **hab dich nicht so!** don't make *or* stop making such a fuss!; **b)** *(ugs.: sich erledigt ~)* **und damit hat es sich** *od.* **hat sich die Sache** then that's that; **hat sich was!** far from it! **3.** *Hilfsverb* have; **ich habe/hatte ihn eben gesehen** I have *or* I've/I had *or* I'd just seen him; **sie ~ gelacht** they laughed; **er hat das gewußt** he knew it; **wir suchten, bis wir ihn gefunden hatten** we kept looking until we [had] found him; **das hättest du früher machen können** you could have done that earlier

Haben das; ~s, ~ *(Kaufmannsspr.)* credit; *(~seite)* **etw. im ~ verbuchen** credit sth.; *s. auch* **Soll a**

Habe·nichts der; ~, ~e pauper

Haben-: ~seite die *(Kaufmannsspr.)* credit side; **~zinsen** *Pl.* interest *sing.* on deposits

Haber der; ~s *(südd., österr., schweiz.) s.* **Hafer**

Hab·gier die *(abwertend)* greed

hab·gierig 1. *Adj. (abwertend)* greedy. **2.** *adv.* greedily

habhaft *in* **jmds./einer Sache ~ werden** catch *or* apprehend sb./get hold of sth.

Habicht ['ha:bɪçt] **der; ~s, ~e a)** hawk; **b)** *(Hühner~)* goshawk

Habichts-: ~kraut das *(Bot.)* hawkweed; **~nase die** hooked *or* aquiline nose

Habilitand [habili'tant] **der; ~en, ~en, Habilitandin die; ~, ~nen** person working on his/her habilitation thesis

Habilitation [habilita'tsio:n] **die; ~, ~en** habilitation *(qualification as a university lecturer)*

Habilitations·schrift die *postdoctoral thesis required in order to qualify as a university lecturer*

habilitieren [habili'ti:rən] **1.** *itr., refl. V.* habilitate *(qualify as a university lecturer)*; **[sich] in Berlin/bei Prof. Schumacher ~:** habilitate at Berlin/under Professor Schumacher. **2.** *tr. V.* **jmdn. ~:** habilitate sb.; confer on sb. his/her qualification as a university lecturer

¹Habit [ha'bi:t] **das** *od.* **der; ~s, ~e a)** *(abwertend, iron.)* outfit; **b)** *(Amtskleidung)* habit

²Habit ['hæbɪt] **das** *od.* **der; ~s, ~s** *(Psych.: Gewohnheit)* habit

Habitat [habi'ta:t] **das; ~s, ~e** *(Biol.)* habitat

habituell [habi'tu̯ɛl] *Adj.* habitual

Habitus ['ha(:)bitʊs] **der; ~** *(geh.)* **a)** *(Gesamterscheinungsbild)* appearance and manner *or* bearing; **b)** *(Haltung)* attitude; **c)** *(Benehmen)* behaviour; **d)** *(Med.)* habitus

Habsburger ['ha:psbʊrgɐ] **der; ~s, ~** *(hist.)* Habsburg

hab-, Hab-: ~seligkeiten *Pl.* [meagre] possessions *or* belongings; **~sucht die; ~** *(abwertend)* greed; avarice; **~süchtig** *(abwertend)* **1.** *Adj.* greedy; avaricious; **2.** *adv.* greedily; avariciously

Hab[t]·acht·stellung die attention; **in ~ stehen** stand to attention

hach [hax] *Interj.* oh!

Haché [[h]a'ʃe:] *s.* **Haschee**

Hachse ['haksə] **die; ~, ~n** *(südd.)* **a)** knuckle; **~ vom Kalb** knuckle of veal; **b)** *(ugs. scherzh.)* leg

Hack [hak] **das; ~s** *(ugs., bes. nordd.)* mince; minced meat

Hack-: ~beil das chopper; cleaver; **~braten der** *(Kochk.)* meat loaf; **~brett das** *(Musik)* dulcimer

¹Hacke die; ~, ~n hoe; *(Pickel)* pick[axe]

²Hacke die; ~, ~n *(bes. nordd. u. md.)* heel; **sich** *(Dat.)* **die ~n nach etw. ablaufen** *od.* **abrennen** wear oneself out running around looking for sth.; *s. auch* **Ferse**

hacken 1. *itr. V.* **a)** *(mit der Hacke arbeiten)* hoe; **sich** *(Dat. od. Akk.)* **ins Bein ~:** cut one's leg [with a hoe/an axe *etc.*]; **b)** *(picken)* peck; **nach jmdm./etw. ~:** peck at sb./sth.; **der Papagei hat mir in den Finger gehackt** the parrot pecked my finger. **2.** *tr. V.* **a)** *(mit der Hacke bearbeiten)* hoe ‹*garden, flower-bed, etc.*›; **b)** *(mit der Axt zerkleinern)* chop ‹*wood etc.*›; **etw. in Stücke ~:** chop sth. up; **c)** *(ein Loch machen)* chop, hack ‹*hole*›; **d)** *(zerkleinern)* chop [up] ‹*meat, vegetables, etc.*›

Hacker der; ~s ~ *(DV-Jargon)* hacker

Hack-: ~fleisch das minced meat; mince; **aus jmdm. ~fleisch machen** *(fig. ugs.)* make mincemeat of sb.; **~frucht die;** *meist Pl. (Landw.)* root crop; **~klotz der** chopping-block; **~messer das** chopper; cleaver; **~ordnung die** *(Verhaltensf.)* pecking order

Häcksel ['hɛksl] **der** *od.* **das; ~s** *(Landw.)* chaff

Häcks[e]ler der; ~s, ~, Häcksel·maschine die *(Landw.)* chaff-cutter

häckseln *tr. V.* chop [up] ‹*straw, hay, etc.*›

Hader ['ha:dɐ] **der; ~s** *(geh.)* discord

hadern *itr. V. (geh.)* **a)** *(streiten)* quarrel; **b)** *(unzufrieden sein)* **mit etw. ~:** be at odds with sth.; **er haderte mit seinem Schicksal** he railed against his fate

Hadern·papier das *(fachspr.)* rag paper

Hades ['ha:dɛs] **der; ~** *(griech. Myth.)* Hades *no art.*

Hadschi ['ha:dʒi] **der; ~s, ~s** hadji

¹Hafen ['ha:fn̩] **der; ~s, Häfen** harbour; port; *(~anlagen)* docks *pl.*; **der Hamburger ~:** the port of Hamburg; **ein Schiff läuft den ~ an/aus dem ~ aus/in den ~ ein** a ship is putting into/leaving/entering port *or* harbour; **in den ~ der Ehe einlaufen** *(fig. scherzh.)* taste the joys of married *or* wedded bliss

²Hafen der; ~s, ~ *(südd., schweiz., österr.)* pot; *(Schüssel)* bowl

Hafen-: ~amt das port *or* harbour authority; **~anlagen** *Pl.* docks; **~arbeiter der** dock-worker; docker; **~aus·fahrt die** harbour mouth; **~bahn die** harbour railway; **~becken das** harbour basin; dock; **~behörde die** port *or* harbour authority; **~blockade die** blockade of a/the harbour *or* port; **~ein·fahrt die** harbour entrance *or* mouth; **~gebühren** *Pl.*, **~geld das** harbour charges *pl.*; port dues *pl.*; **~kneipe die** dockland pub *(Brit. coll.) or (Amer.)* bar; **~meister der** harbour-master; **~polizei die** port *or* dock police; **~rund·fahrt die** trip round the harbour; **~stadt die** port; **~viertel das** dock area; dockland *no art.*

Hafer ['ha:fɐ] **der; ~s** oats *pl.*; **jmdn. sticht der ~** *(ugs.)* sb. is feeling his oats

Hafer-: ~brei der porridge; **~flocken** *Pl.* rolled oats; porridge oats; **~grütze die a)** oat groats; **b)** *(Brei)* porridge; **~mehl das** oatmeal; **~sack der** nosebag; **~schleim der** gruel

Haff [haf] **das; ~[e]s, ~s** *od.* **~e** lagoon

Haflinger ['ha:flɪŋɐ] **der; ~s, ~:** Haflinger [horse]

Hafner der; ~s, ~ *(südd., österr., schweiz.)* **a)** *(Töpfer)* potter; **b)** *(Ofensetzer)* stove-fitter

Haft [haft] **die; ~ a)** *(Gewahrsam)* custody; *(aus politischen Gründen)* detention; **jmdn. aus der ~ entlassen** release sb. from custody/detention; **sich in ~ befinden** be [held] in custody/detention; **jmdn. in ~ nehmen** take sb. into custody; *(aus politischen Gründen)* detain sb.; **b)** *(Freiheitsstrafe)* imprisonment; **jmdn. zu zwei Jahren ~ verurteilen** sentence sb. to two years in prison *or* two years' imprisonment

-haft *Adj., adv.* -like

Haft-: ~anstalt die prison; **~aussetzung die** *(Rechtsspr.)* **der Verteidiger beantragte ~aussetzung** the defence counsel requested that the defendant be released from custody

haftbar *Adj. (bes. Rechtsspr.)* **in für etw. ~ sein** be [legally] responsible *or* liable for sth.; **jmdn. für etw. ~ machen** make *or* hold sb. [legally] liable for sth.

Haft-: ~befehl der *(Rechtsw.)* warrant [of arrest]; **einen ~befehl gegen jmdn. ausstellen** issue a warrant for sb.'s arrest; **~beschwerde die** *(Rechtsw.)* appeal against a remand in custody; **~creme die** *(Pharm.)* fixative cream; **~dauer die** term of imprisonment

¹haften *itr. V.* **a)** *(festkleben)* stick; **an/auf etw.** *(Dat.)* **~:** stick to sth.; **b)** *(sich festsetzen)* ‹*smell, dirt, etc.*› cling **(an +** *Dat.* to); **in der Erinnerung ~** *(fig.)* stick in one's memory *or* mind; **~de Eindrücke** lasting impressions; **an ihm haftet ein Makel** *(fig.)* he carries a stigma; **seine Augen hafteten/sein Blick haftete an ...** *(Dat.) (fig.)* his eyes were/gaze was fixed on ...; **c)** ‹*tyre*› grip

²haften *itr. V.* **a)** *(einstehen)* **für jmdn./etw. ~:** be responsible for sb./liable for sth.; *(verantwortlich sein)* **jmdn. für etw. ~:** be responsible *or* answerable to sb. for sth.; **für etw. nicht ~:** ‹*company*› not accept liability for sth.; *s. auch* **Garderobe a; b)** *(Rechtsw., Wirtsch.)* be liable

haften|bleiben *unr. itr. V.; mit sein* **a)** *(festkleben)* stick **(an/auf +** *Dat.* to); **b)** *(sich festsetzen)* ‹*mud, clay, dirt, etc.*› stick, cling **(an/auf +** *Dat.* to); ‹*smell, smoke*› cling **(an/auf +** *Dat.* to); **c)** *(ugs.: im Gedächtnis bleiben)* stick

haft-, Haft-: ~erleichterung die special privilege; **¹~fähig** *Adj. (Rechtsw.)* fit to be kept in prison *postpos.*; **²~fähig** *Adj. (klebend)* adhesive; **¹~fähigkeit die;** *o. Pl. (Rechtsw.)* fitness to be kept in prison; **²~fähigkeit die;** *o. Pl. (von Materialien)* adhesion

Häftling ['hɛftlɪŋ] **der; ~s, ~e** prisoner

Häftlings·kleidung die prison clothing

Haft·pflicht die a) liability **(für** for); **b)** *s.* **Haftpflichtversicherung**

haftpflichtig *Adj.* liable **(für** for)

Haftpflicht·versicherung die personal liability insurance; *(für Autofahrer)* third party insurance

haft-, Haft-: ~prüfung die *(Rechtsw.)* review of a/the remand in custody; **~psy-**

chose die prison psychosis; **~reibung die** *(Physik)* static friction; **~richter der** *(Rechtsw.)* magistrate; **~schale die;** *meist Pl.* contact lens; **~strafe die** *(Rechtsspr. veralt.)* prison sentence; **~unfähig** *Adj.* unfit to be kept in prison *postpos.*; **~unfähigkeit die** unfitness to be kept in prison

[1]**Haftung die; ~:** adhesion; *(von Reifen)* grip

[2]**Haftung die; ~, ~en a)** *(Verantwortlichkeit)* liability; responsibility; *s. auch* **Garderobe; b)** *(Rechtsw., Wirtsch.)* liability; **Gesellschaft mit [un]beschränkter ~:** [un]limited [liability] company

Haft·verschonung die *(Rechtsw.)* suspended sentence

Hag [ha:k] **der; ~[e]s, ~e** *(veralt., noch schweiz.)* **a)** *(Hecke)* hedge; **b)** *(Wald)* grove

Hagebutte ['ha:gəbʊtə] **die; ~, ~n a)** *(Frucht)* rose-hip; **b)** *(ugs.: Heckenrose)* dog-rose

Hagebutten·tee der rose-hip tea

Hage·dorn der; *Pl.* **~e** hawthorn

Hagel ['ha:gl̩] **der; ~s, ~** *(auch fig.)* hail; **ein ~ von Drohungen** a stream of threats

Hagel·korn das hailstone

hageln 1. *itr., tr. V. (unpers.)* hail; **es hagelt** it is hailing; **es hagelte Steine und leere Bierdosen** *(fig.)* there was a hail of stones and empty beer-cans; **es hagelte Drohungen/Fragen** *(fig.)* there was a stream of threats/flood of questions. **2.** *itr. V.; mit sein (fig.)* **auf jmdn./etw. ~:** ⟨*stones, bombs, etc.*⟩ rain down on sb./sth.

Hagel-: ~schaden der the damage *no pl.* caused by hail; **~schauer der** [short] hailstorm; **~schlag der** hail; **~sturm der** hailstorm; **~zucker der** sugar crystals *pl.*

hager ['ha:gɐ] *Adj.* gaunt ⟨*person, figure, face*⟩; thin ⟨*neck, arm, fingers*⟩

Hagerkeit die; ~ *s.* **hager:** gauntness; thinness

Hage·stolz der; ~es, ~e *(veralt.)* confirmed bachelor

haha [ha'ha(:)] *Interj.* ha ha

Häher ['hɛ:ɐ] **der; ~s, ~:** jay

[1]**Hahn** [ha:n] **der; ~[e]s, Hähne** ['hɛ:nə] **a)** cock; *(junger ~)* cockerel; **~ im Korb sein** *(ugs.)* be cock of the walk; **nach ihr/danach kräht kein ~** *(ugs.)* no one could care less about her/it; **jmdm. den roten ~ aufs Dach setzen** *(veralt.)* set sb.'s house on fire; **b)** *(Wetter~)* weathercock; **c)** *Pl.* **~en** *(Jägerspr.)* cock

[2]**Hahn der; ~[e]s, Hähne,** *fachspr.:* **~en a)** tap; faucet *(Amer.)*; *(eines Fasses)* tap; spigot; *s. auch* **abdrehen 1 a; b)** *(bei Waffen)* hammer; **den ~ spannen** cock a/the gun

Hähnchen ['hɛ:nçən] **das; ~s, ~:** chicken; *(junger Hahn)* cockerel

Hahnen-: ~fuß der buttercup; **~fuß·gewächs das** ranunculus; **~kamm der** cockscomb; **~kampf der a)** cock-fighting; *(einzelner Wettkampf)* cock-fight; **b)** *(Gymnastik) hopping-game in which players barge each other and attempt to push each other off balance;* **~schrei der** cock-crow; **beim ersten ~schrei** at cock-crow; **~tritt·muster das** dog-tooth *or* dog's tooth check

Hahnrei ['ha:nrai] **der; ~s, ~e** *(geh., veralt.)* cuckold

Hai [hai] **der; ~s, ~e** *(auch fig.)* shark

Hai·fisch der shark

Haifisch·flossen·suppe die *(Kochk.)* shark-fin soup

Hain [hain] **der; ~[e]s, ~e** *(dichter. veralt.)* grove

Hain·buche die hornbeam

Haiti [ha'i:ti] **(das); ~s** Haiti

Haitianer [hai'tia:nɐ] **der; ~s, ~, Haitianerin die; ~, ~nen** Haitian

haitianisch *Adj.* Haitian

Häkchen ['hɛ:kçən] **das; ~s, ~ a)** [small] hook; **was ein ~ werden will, krümmt sich beizeiten** *(Spr.)* there's nothing like starting young; **b)** *(Zeichen)* mark; *(beim Abhaken)* tick

Häkel-: ~arbeit die crocheting; crochet-work; *(etw. Gehäkeltes)* a piece of crochet-work *or* crocheting; **~decke die** crocheted table-cloth; *(für ein Sofa, einen Stuhl usw.)* crocheted cover

Häkelei die; ~, ~en *s.* **Häkelarbeit**

Häkel-: ~garn das crochet thread *or* yarn; **~muster das** crochet pattern

hakeln ['ha:kl̩n] **1.** *itr. V.* **a)** *(landsch.)* finger-wrestle; **b)** *(Fußball)* trip the/an opposing player. **2.** *tr. V.* **a)** *(Fußball)* trip; **b)** *(Ringen)* **jmds. Bein/Fuß ~:** get sb. in a leg-lock/foot-lock

häkeln ['hɛ:kl̩n] *tr., itr. V.* crochet

Häkel·nadel die crochet-hook

haken ['ha:kn̩] **1.** *tr. V.* **a)** hook **(an + Akk.** on to); **b)** *([Eis]hockey)* hook; **c)** *(Fußball) s.* **hakeln 2. 2.** *itr. V. (klemmen)* be stuck

Haken der; ~s, ~ a) hook; **~ und Öse** hook and eye; **einen ~ schlagen** dart sideways; **mit ~ und Ösen** *(fig. ugs.)* by fair means or foul; **b)** *(Zeichen)* tick; **c)** *(ugs.: Schwierigkeit)* catch; snag; **wo ist der ~?** where's the catch?; **der ~ an etw.** *(Dat.)* the catch in sth.; **d)** *(Boxen)* hook

haken-, Haken-: ~förmig 1. *Adj.* hooked; hook-shaped; **2.** *adv.* **~förmig gebogen** hooked; hook-shaped; **~kreuz das** swastika; **~leiter die** hook-ladder; **~nase die** hooked nose; hook-nose

Halali [hala'li:] **das; ~s, ~[s]** *(Jägerspr.)* **a)** *(Signal)* mort; **b)** *(Ende der Jagd)* mort; kill

halb [halp] **1.** *Adj. u. Bruchz.* **a)** *(die Hälfte von)* half; **eine ~e Stunde/ein ~er Meter/ein ~es Glas** half an hour/a metre/a glass; **zum ~en Preis** [at] half price; **~ Europa/die ~e Welt** half of Europe/half the world; **es ist ~ eins** it's half past twelve; **5 Minuten vor/nach ~:** 25 [minutes] past/to; *s. auch* **Arm c; Höhe b; Note a; Weg d; b)** *(unvollständig, vermindert)* **die ~e Wahrheit** half [of] *or* part of the truth; **er macht keine ~en Sachen** he doesn't do things by halves; **er hat [nur] ~e Arbeit getan** he hasn't done the job properly; **nichts Halbes und nichts Ganzes [sein]** [be] neither one thing nor the other; **c)** *(fast)* **[noch] ein ~es Kind sein** be hardly *or* scarcely more than a child; **eine ~e Ewigkeit warten** wait [for] ages; **die ~e Stadt** half the town. **2.** *adv.* **a)** *(zur Hälfte)* **~ voll/leer** half-full/-empty; **~ lachend, ~ weinend** half laughing, half crying; **b)** *(unvollständig)* **~ gar/angezogen/wach** half-done *or* -cooked/half dressed/half awake; **die Pflaumen sind erst ~ reif** the plums aren't fully ripe; **er hat seine Arbeit ~ getan** he has done some of his work; **die Verletzung war nur ~ so schlimm, wie er erst dachte** the injury was not as serious as he at first thought; **etw. nur ~ verstehen** only half understand sth.; **nur ~ zuhören** be only half listening; **nur ~ bei der Sache sein** be only half with it *(coll.)*; *s. auch* **schlimm 1 b; c)** *(fast)* **~ blind/verhungert/tot** half blind/starved/dead; **ich bin schon ~ fertig** I'm nearly *or* almost finished; **~ so klug** half as clever; **~ und ~** *(ugs.)* more or less; **Gefällt es dir? – Halb und ~** *(ugs.)* Do you like it? – Sort of *(coll.)*

halb-, Halb-: ~affe der *(Zool.)* half-ape; prosimian; **~amtlich** *Adj.* semi-official; **~automatisch 1.** *Adj.* semi-automatic; **2.** *adv.* semi-automatically; **~bekleidet** *Adj.; nicht präd.* half-dressed; **~bildung die** *(abwertend)* superficial education; **~bitter** *Adj.* plain ⟨*chocolate*⟩; **~blind** *Adj. (präd. getrennt geschrieben)* half-blind; **~blut das a)** *(bei Pferden)* cross-breed; **b)** *(Mischling)* half-caste; half-breed; **~bruder der** half-brother; **~dunkel** *Adj. (präd. getrennt geschrieben)* half-dark; **~dunkel das** semi-darkness

Halbe der *od.* **die** *od.* **das;** *adj. Dekl. (ugs.)* half litre *(of beer etc.)*; **ein ~s** a half litre

Halb·edelstein der *(veralt.)* semi-precious stone

halbe-halbe *in* **[mit jmdm.] ~ machen** *(ugs.)* go halves [with sb.]

halber ['halbɐ] *Präp. mit Gen. (wegen)* on account of; *(um ... willen)* for the sake of; **der Ordnung ~:** as a matter of form; **der Wahrheit ~:** to tell the truth

halb-, Halb-: ~erfroren *Adj. (präd. getrennt geschrieben)* half-frozen; **~erwachsen** *Adj. (präd. getrennt geschrieben)* teenage; adolescent; **~fabrikat das** *(Wirtsch.)* semi-finished product; **~fertig** *Adj. (präd. getrennt geschrieben)* half-finished; **~fett 1.** *Adj.* **a)** *(Druckw.)* bold ⟨*type*⟩; *(schmaler, kleiner)* semibold; **b)** medium-fat ⟨*cheese*⟩; **2.** *adv.* **etw. ~fett drucken** print sth. in bold/semibold [type]; **~finale das** *(Sport)* semi-final; **~gar** *Adj.* half-cooked; half-done; **~gebildet 1.** *Adj.* *(abwertend)* half-educated; **2.** *adv.* in a half-educated way; **~gebildete der/die;** *adj. Dekl. (abwertend)* half-educated person; **~gefror[e]ne das;** *adj. Dekl.* soft ice cream; **~geschoß das** *(Archit.)* mezzanine [floor]; **~geschwister** *Pl.* half-brothers/half-sisters/half-brother[s] and -sister[s]; **~gott der** *(Myth., fig. iron.)* demigod; **~götter in Weiß** *(ugs. iron.)* [hospital] doctors

Halbheit die; ~, ~en *(abwertend)* half-measure

halb-, Halb-: ~herzig 1. *Adj.* half-hearted; **2.** *adv.* half-heartedly; **~herzigkeit die; ~:** half-heartedness; **~hoch 1.** *Adj. (bes. Sport)* shoulder-high ⟨*shot, pass, etc.*⟩; low ⟨*shelf etc.*⟩; calf-length ⟨*boot*⟩; **2.** *adv.* **der Ball kam ~hoch** the ball came at shoulder-height

halbieren *tr. V.* cut/tear ⟨*object*⟩ in half; halve ⟨*amount, number*⟩; *(Math.)* bisect

halb-, Halb-: ~insel die peninsula; **~jahr das** six months *pl.*; half year; **im ersten/zweiten ~jahr** in the first/last six months [of the year]; **~jahres·bilanz die** half-yearly figures *pl. or* results *pl.*; **~jahres·zeugnis das** half-yearly report; **~jährig** *Adj.; nicht präd.* **a)** *(ein halbes Jahr alt)* six-months-old ⟨*baby, pony, etc.*⟩; **b)** *(ein halbes Jahr dauernd)* six-month ⟨*contract, course, etc.*⟩; **~jährlich 1.** *Adj.* half-yearly; six-monthly; **2.** *adv.* every six months; twice a year; **~jude der** *(bes. ns.)* half-Jew; **~jude sein** be half Jewish; **~kanton der** demicanton; **~kreis der** semicircle; **sich im ~kreis aufstellen** form a semicircle; **im ~kreis sitzen** sit in a semicircle; **~kreis·förmig 1.** *Adj.* semicircular; **2.** *adv.* in a semicircle; **~kugel die** hemisphere; **~kugel·förmig** *Adj.* hemispherical; **~lang** *Adj.* mid-length ⟨*hair*⟩; mid-calf length ⟨*coat, dress, etc.*⟩; **[nun] mach [aber mal] ~lang!** *(ugs.)* hang on a minute! *(coll.)*; **~laut 1.** *Adj.* low; quiet; **2.** *adv.* in a low voice; in an undertone; **~leder das** *(Buchw.)* half-leather; **~leer** *Adj. (präd. getrennt geschrieben)* half empty; **~leinen das a)** *(Gewebe)* fifty-per-cent linen material; **b)** *(Buchw.)* half-cloth; **~leiter der** *(Elektronik)* semiconductor; **~link...** [-'-] *Adj.; nicht präd. (bes. Fußball)* inside left; **~linke** [-'--] **der** *(bes. Fußball)* inside left; **~links** [-'-] *Adv.* **a)** *(Fußball)* ⟨*play*⟩ [at] inside left; **b) ~links abbiegen** fork left; **~mast** *Adv.* at half-mast; **~mast flaggen** fly a flag/the flags at half-mast; **~matt** *Adj. (Fot.)* semi-matt; **~messer der** *(Math.)* radius; **~metall das** *(Chemie)* semi-metal; **~militärisch** *Adj.* paramilitary; **~monatlich 1.** *Adj.* fortnightly; twice-monthly; **2.** *adv.* fortnightly; twice monthly; **~monatsschrift die** fortnightly periodical; **~mond der a)** *(Mond)* half-moon; **heute ist ~mond** there's a half-moon tonight; **b)** *(Figur)* crescent; **c)** *(an Fingernägeln)* half-moon; **~mond·förmig** *Adj.* crescent-shaped; **~nackt** *Adj.*

(präd. getrennt geschrieben) half-naked; **~offen** *Adj. (präd. getrennt geschrieben)* **a)** half-open ⟨*door etc.*⟩; **b)** open ⟨*prison*⟩; **~offiziell** *Adj.* semi-official; **~part** *Adv. in* **[mit jmdm.] ~part machen** *(ugs.)* go halves [with sb.]; **~pension die;** *o. Pl., meist o. Art.* half-board; **~recht...** [-'-] *Adj.; nicht präd. (bes. Fußball)* inside right; **~rechte** [-'--] **der** *(bes. Fußball)* inside right; **~rechts** [-'-] *Adv.* **a)** *(Fußball)* ⟨*play*⟩ [at] inside right; **b) ~rechts abbiegen** fork right; **~reif** *Adj. (präd. getrennt geschrieben)* half-ripe; **~rock der** waist petticoat; **~roh** *Adj. (präd. getrennt geschrieben)* half-cooked; half-done; **~rund** *Adj. (präd. getrennt geschrieben)* semicircular; **~rund das** semicircle; **~schatten der a)** half shadow; **b)** *(Optik, Astron.)* penumbra; **~schlaf der** light sleep; **im ~schlaf liegen** be half asleep; doze; **~schuh der** shoe; **~schwer·gewicht das** *(Schwerathletik)* **a)** *o. Pl.* light-heavyweight; *s. auch* **Fliegengewicht a; b)** *s.* **~schwergewichtler; ~schwergewichtler** [-gəvɪçtlɐ] **der; ~s, ~** *(Schwerathletik)* light-heavyweight; **~schwester die** half-sister; **~seide die** fifty-per-cent silk [mixture]; **~seiden** *Adj.* **a)** fifty-per-cent silk; **b)** *(ugs. abwertend: unmännlich)* poofy *(coll.)*; pansyish *(coll.)*; **c)** *(ugs. abwertend: anrüchig)* dubious ⟨*business practice etc.*⟩; fast ⟨*woman*⟩; **~seitig 1.** *Adv.* **a)** *(Med.)* **~seitig gelähmt sein** be hemiplegic; be paralysed down one side; **b) ein Blatt ~seitig beschreiben** write on the left-hand/right-hand side of a sheet only; **2.** *adj.* half-page ⟨*article etc.*⟩; **~staatlich** *Adj. (präd. getrennt geschrieben) (DDR)* partially state-controlled *or* state-run; **~stark** *Adj.; nicht präd. (ugs. abwertend)* rowdy; **~starke der;** *adj. Dekl. (ugs. abwertend)* young rowdy; [young] hooligan; **~stiefel der** half-boot; ankle boot; **~stündig** *Adj.; nicht präd.* half-hour; lasting half an hour *postpos., not pred.*; **eine ~stündige Fahrt** a half-hour journey; half an hour's journey; **~stündlich 1.** *Adj.; nicht präd.* half-hourly; **2.** *adv.* half-hourly; every half an hour; **~stürmer der** *(bes. Fußball)* mid-field player; **~tägig 1.** *Adj.; nicht präd.* half-day ⟨*excursion etc.*⟩; part-time ⟨*work, worker, etc.*⟩; *(morgens/nachmittags)* morning/afternoon ⟨*work etc.*⟩; **2.** *adv.* ⟨*work*⟩ part-time; *(morgens/nachmittags)* ⟨*work*⟩ [in the] mornings/afternoons; **~täglich 1.** *Adj.* twice daily; **2.** *adv.* twice a day; twice daily

halb·tags *Adv.* ⟨*work*⟩ part-time; *(morgens/nachmittags)* ⟨*work*⟩ [in the] mornings/afternoons

Halbtags-: ~arbeit die; *o. Pl.*, **~beschäftigung die;** *o. Pl.* part-time job; *(morgens/nachmittags)* morning/afternoon job; **~kraft die** part-time worker; part-timer; **~schule die** half-day school

halb-, Halb-: ~ton der; *Pl.* **~töne a)** *(Musik)* semitone; halftone *(Amer.)*; **b)** *(Malerei)* half-tone; **~tot** *Adj. (präd. getrennt geschrieben)* half-dead; **~totale die** *(Film)* medium shot; **~trauer die** half mourning; **~trauer tragen** be in half mourning; **~verdaut** *Adj. (präd. getrennt geschrieben) (auch fig.)* half-digested; **~verhungert** *Adj. (präd. getrennt geschrieben)* half-starved; **~verwest** *Adj. (präd. getrennt geschrieben)* partially decomposed; **~vokal der** *(Phon.)* semivowel; **~voll** *Adj. (präd. getrennt geschrieben)* half-full; half-filled; *s. auch* **voll 1 a; ~wach** *Adj. (präd. getrennt geschrieben)* half-awake; **in ~wachem Zustand** half awake; **~wahrheit die** half-truth; **~waise die** fatherless/motherless child; **er/sie ist ~waise** he/she has lost one of his/her parents; **~wegs** ['~'ve:ks] *Adv.* **a)** to some extent; reasonably ⟨*good, clear, comprehensible, etc.*⟩; **es geht mir ~wegs besser** I'm feeling a bit better; **kannst du dich nicht wenigstens ~wegs ordentlich benehmen?** can't you behave at all properly?; **ich kann ~wegs von meinem Einkommen leben** I can live fairly well on my income; **b)** *(veralt.: auf halbem Weg)* half-way; **~welt die;** *o. Pl.* demi-monde; **~welt·dame die** demi-mondaine; **~welter·gewicht das a)** *o. Pl. (Klasse)* light-welterweight; **b)** *(Sportler)* light-welterweight; **~werts·zeit die** *(Physik)* half-life; **~wild** *Adj. (präd. getrennt geschrieben)* half-wild ⟨*animal, country*⟩; half-savage ⟨*person*⟩; **wie die ~wilden** like [a bunch of] savages; **~wissen das** *(abwertend)* superficial knowledge; smattering of knowledge; **sein medizinisches ~wissen** his smattering of medical knowledge; **~wüchsig** [~vy:ksɪç] *Adj.* adolescent; teenage; **~wüchsige der/die;** *adj. Dekl.* adolescent; teenager; **~zeit die** *(bes. Fußball)* **a)** half; **die erste/zweite ~zeit** the first/second half; **während der ersten ~zeit seiner Amtsperiode** *(fig.)* during the first half of his period of office; **b)** *(Pause)* half-time; **zur ~zeit seiner Regierungszeit** *(fig.)* half-way through his period of office; **~zeit·pause die** *(Sport)* half-time; **~zeit·pfiff der** *(Sport)* half-time whistle; **~zeug das** *(Wirtsch.)* semi-finished product

Halde ['haldə] **die; ~, ~n a)** *(Bergbau)* slag-heap; *(von Vorräten)* pile; *(fig.)* mountain; pile; **neue Wagen liegen massenhaft auf ~:** there are piles of unsold new cars; **Kartoffeln werden jetzt für die ~ produziert** the potatoes now being produced will simply go to swell existing stocks; **b)** *(geh.: Hang)* slope

half [half] *1. u. 3. Pers. Sg. Prät. v.* **helfen**

Hälfte ['hɛlftə] **die; ~, ~n a)** half; **die ~ einer Sache** *(Gen.) od.* **von etw.** half [of] sth.; **Studenten bezahlen die ~ des Preises** students pay *or (coll.)* are half-price; **etw. in zwei gleiche ~n teilen** divide sth. in half *or* into two equal parts; **er füllte sein Glas nur bis zur ~:** he only half-filled his glass; **über die ~:** more than *or* over half; **um die ~ größer/kleiner** half as big/small again; **um die ~ zuviel/mehr** too much by half/half as much again; **etw. um die ~ steigern** increase sth. by half; **etw. zur ~ zahlen** pay half of sth.; **die gegnerische ~** *(Sport)* the opponents' half; **ich habe die ~ vergessen** I've forgotten half of it; **meine bessere ~** *(ugs. scherzh.)* my better half *(coll. joc.)*; **b)** *(ugs.: Teil)* part; **die größere ~ ihres Gehalts/des Publikums** the greater part of her salary/the majority of the audience

[1]Halfter ['halftɐ] **der** *od.* **das; ~s, ~;** *veralt. auch* **die; ~, ~n** halter

[2]Halfter die; ~, ~n; *auch* **das; ~s, ~:** holster

halftern *tr. V.* halter

Halfter·riemen der halter-strap

Hall [hal] **der; ~[e]s, ~e a)** *(geh.)* reverberation; **b)** *(Echo)* echo

Halle ['halə] **die; ~, ~n** *(Saal, Gebäude)* hall; *(Fabrik~)* shed; *(Hotel~, Theater~)* lobby; foyer; *(Sport~)* [sports] hall; *(Schwimm~)* pool; **Tennis in der ~ spielen** play tennis indoors *or* on an indoor court; **in diesen heiligen ~n** *(iron.)* within these sacred halls *(iron.)*

halleluja [hale'lu:ja] *Interj.* hallelujah!; *(scherzh.: hurra)* hurrah!

Halleluja das; ~s, ~s hallelujah; **das ~ aus Händels „Messias"** the Hallelujah Chorus from Handel's 'Messiah'

hallen *itr. V.* **a)** reverberate; ring; ⟨*shot, bell, cry*⟩ ring out; **b)** *(widerhallen)* echo; **von etw. ~:** reverberate *or* echo with sth.

Hallen- indoor ⟨*swimming-pool, handball, football, hockey, tennis, championship, record, sport, etc.*⟩

Hallig ['halɪç] **die; ~, ~en** small low island *(particularly one of those off Schleswig-Holstein)*

Hallimasch ['halimaʃ] **der; ~[e]s, ~e** *(Bot.)* honey agaric; honey mushroom

hallo *Interj.* **a)** *meist* ['halo] *(am Telefon)* hello; **~, warte doch mal auf mich!** hey! wait for me!; **~, gehört Ihnen diese Tasche?** excuse me! is this your bag?; **b)** *meist* [ha'lo:] *(überrascht)* hello; **c)** *(ugs., bes. Jugendspr. als Gruß)* hi *(coll.)*; hello

Hallo [ha'lo:] **das; ~s, ~s a)** cheering; cheers *pl.*; **mit großem ~:** with loud cheering *or* cheers; **b)** *(Aufsehen)* hullabaloo

Hallodri [ha'lo:dri] **der; ~s, ~[s]** *(bayr., österr. ugs. abwertend)* rogue

Hallstatt·zeit ['halʃtat-] **die; ~** *(Archäol.)* Hallstatt period

Halluzination [halutsina'tsio:n] **die; ~, ~en** hallucination; **du hast wohl ~en** you must be seeing things

halluzinatorisch [halutsina'to:rɪʃ] *Adj. (Med., Psych.)* hallucinatory

halluzinieren *itr. V. (Med., Psych.)* hallucinate; have hallucinations

halluzinogen [halutsino'ge:n] *Adj. (Med., Psych.)* hallucinogenic

Halluzinogen das; ~s, ~e *(Med., Psych.)* hallucinogen

Halm [halm] **der; ~[e]s, ~e** stalk; stem; **das Getreide/die Ernte auf dem ~:** the standing corn

Halma ['halma] **das; ~s** halma

Hälmchen ['hɛlmçən] **das; ~s, ~:** [small] stalk *or* stem

Halm·frucht die; *meist Pl.* cereal

Halo ['ha:lo] **der; ~[s], ~s** *od.* **~nen** [-'--] *(Physik)* halo

Halogen [halo'ge:n] **das; ~s, ~e** *(Chemie)* halogen

Halogen- halogen ⟨*lamp, headlamp*⟩

Hals [hals] **der; ~es, Hälse** ['hɛlzə] **a)** neck; **sich** *(Dat.)* **den ~ brechen** break one's neck; **jmdm. um den ~ fallen** throw *or* fling one's arms around sb.['s neck]; **~ über Kopf** *(ugs.)* in a rush *or* hurry: **sich ~ über Kopf verlieben** fall head over heels in love; **sich** *(Dat.)* **nach jmdm./etw. den ~ verrenken** crane one's neck to see sb./sth.; **einen langen ~/lange Hälse machen** *(ugs.)* crane one's neck/their necks; **jmdm. den ~ abschneiden** *od.* **umdrehen** *od.* **brechen** *(ugs.)* drive sb. to the wall; **das kostete ihn** *od.* **ihm den ~** *(ugs.)* that did for him *(coll.)*; **jmdn./etw. auf dem** *od.* **am ~ haben** *(ugs.)* be saddled with sb./sth. *(coll.)*; **zuviel am ~ haben** *(ugs.)* have too much on one's plate *(coll.)*; **sich jmdm. an den ~ werfen** *(ugs.)* throw oneself at sb.; **jmdm. jmdn. auf den ~ schicken** *od.* **hetzen** *(ugs.)* get *or* put sb. on [to] sb.; **sich** *(Dat.)* **jmdn./etw. auf den ~ laden** *(ugs.)* lumber *or* saddle oneself with sb./sth. *(coll.)*; **bis über den ~ in etw.** *(Dat.)* **stecken** *(ugs.)* be up to one's ears *or* eyes in sth.; **jmdm. steht** *od.* **geht das Wasser bis zum** *od.* **an den ~** *(ugs.: jmd. hat Schulden)* sb. is up to his/her eyes in debt; *(ugs.: jmd. hat Schwierigkeiten)* sb. is up to his/her neck in it; **jmdm. mit etw. vom ~[e] bleiben** *(ugs.)* not bother sb. with sth.; **sich** *(Dat.)* **jmdn. vom ~[e] halten** *(ugs.)* keep sb. away: **dem Chef alle Besucher vom ~e halten** *(ugs.)* keep all visitors away from the boss; **b)** *(Kehle)* throat; **aus vollem ~[e]** at the top of one's voice; **er hat es in den falschen** *od.* **verkehrten ~ bekommen** *(ugs.: falsch verstanden)* he took it the wrong way; *(ugs.: sich verschluckt)* it went down [his throat] the wrong way; **er kann den ~ nicht voll [genug] kriegen** *(ugs.)* he can't get enough; he's insatiable; **das hängt/wächst mir zum ~[e] heraus** *(ugs.)* I'm sick and tired of it *(coll.)*; **c)** *(einer Flasche)* neck; **einer Flasche** *(Dat.)* **den ~ brechen** *(ugs.)* crack [open] a bottle; **d)** *(Musik) (einer Note)* stem; *(eines Saiteninstruments)* neck; **e)** *(Anat.)* neck; collum

(Anat.); *(Gebärmutter~)* neck; cervix *(Anat.)*
hals-, Hals-: ~ab·schneider der *(ugs. abwertend)* shark; **~abschneiderisch** *Adj.* cutthroat ⟨*practice etc.*⟩; extortionate ⟨*interest etc.*⟩; **~aus·schnitt der** neckline; **~band das**; *Pl.* **~bänder a)** *(für Tiere)* collar; **b)** *(Samtband)* choker; neck-band; **c)** *(veralt.: Halskette)* necklace; **~brecherisch** [~brɛçərɪʃ] *Adj.* dangerous, risky ⟨*climb, action, etc.*⟩; hazardous ⟨*road*⟩; breakneck *attrib.* ⟨*speed*⟩; **~bruch der** *s.* **~- und Beinbruch**
Hälschen ['hɛlsçən] **das; ~s, ~:** [little] neck
¹halsen *tr. V. (veralt.)* embrace
²halsen *itr. V. (Seemannsspr.)* wear
hals-, Hals-: ~entzündung die inflammation of the throat; **~kette die** necklace; *(für Hunde)* chain; **~kragen der** collar; **~krause die** ruff; **~länge die** *(Pferdesport)* neck; **um eine ~länge** by a neck; **~-Nasen-Ohren-Arzt der** ear, nose, and throat specialist; **~-Nasen-Ohren-Krankheiten** *Pl. (Med.)* diseases of the ear, nose, and throat; **Facharzt für ~-Nasen-Ohren-Krankheiten** ear, nose, and throat specialist; **~schlagader die** carotid [artery]; **~schmerzen** *Pl.* sore throat *sing.*; **[starke] ~schmerzen haben** have a[n extremely] sore throat; **~starrig** [~ʃtarɪç] **1.** *Adj. (abwertend)* stubborn; obstinate; **2.** *adv.* stubbornly; obstinately; **~starrigkeit die** *(abwertend)* stubbornness; obstinacy; **~stück das** *(Kochk.)* neck; **~tuch das** cravat; *(des Cowboys)* neckerchief; **~- und Beinbruch** *Interj. (scherzh.)* good luck!; best of luck!; **~weh das**; *o. Pl. (ugs.) s.* **~schmerzen**; **~wickel der** *(Med.)* compress *(applied to the throat)*; **~wirbel der** *(Anat.)* cervical vertebra
¹halt [halt] *Partikel (südd., österr., schweiz.) s.* **eben 3b**
²halt *Interj.* stop; *(Milit.)* halt; **~, ich habe etwas vergessen** wait a minute *or (coll.)* hold on, I've forgotten something
Halt der; ~[e]s, ~e a) *o. Pl. (Stütze)* hold; **seine Füße/Hände fanden keinen ~:** he couldn't find *or* get a foothold/handhold; **in diesen Schuhen haben meine Füße keinen ~:** these shoes don't give my feet any support; **den ~ verlieren** lose one's hold; **inneren ~ haben** be secure; **ohne jeden ~:** totally insecure; **er hat einen festen ~ an seinem Glauben** his faith gives him *or* provides him with a great sense of security; **b)** *(Anhalten)* stop; **einen ~ machen** make a stop; **zum ~ kommen** come to a stop *or* halt; **ohne ~:** non-stop; without stopping
haltbar *Adj.* **a)** *(nicht verderblich)* **~ sein** ⟨*food*⟩ keep [well]; **etw. ~ machen** preserve sth.; **~ bis 5. 3.** use by 5 March; **b)** *(nicht verschleißend)* hard-wearing, durable ⟨*material, clothes*⟩; **c)** *(aufrechtzuerhalten)* tenable ⟨*hypothesis etc.*⟩; **d)** *(Ballspiele)* stoppable, savable ⟨*shot*⟩; **der Ball war nicht ~:** the shot was unstoppable; **e)** *(beizubehalten)* maintainable ⟨*position etc.*⟩; **die Position war nicht ~:** the position could not be maintained
Haltbarkeit die; ~ a) Lebensmittel von beschränkter ~: perishable foods; **eine längere ~ haben** keep longer; **b)** *(Strapazierfähigkeit)* durability; **ein Teppich von größter ~:** an extremely hard-wearing carpet; **c)** *(Glaubhaftigkeit)* tenability
Haltbarkeits·dauer die: Sahne, die eine ~ von 3 Monaten hat cream which keeps for three months; **die ~ von verpackten Lebensmitteln muß auf der Packung angegeben werden** the date by which packed foodstuffs should be eaten must be shown on the pack
Halte-: ~bogen der *(Musik)* tie; **~bucht die** *(Verkehrsw.)* lay-by *(Brit.)*; turn-out *(Amer.)*; **~griff der a)** [grab] handle; *(Riemen)* [grab] strap; **b)** *(Budo, Ringen)* pinning hold; **~gurt der** seat belt; **~linie die** *(Verkehrsw.)* stop line
halten 1. *unr. tr. V.* **a)** *(auch Milit.)* hold; **etw. an einem Ende/am Griff ~:** hold one end of sth./hold sth. by the handle; **jmdm. den Mantel ~:** hold sb.'s coat [for him/her]; **sich** *(Dat.)* **den Kopf/den Bauch ~:** hold one's head/stomach; **jmdn. an** *od.* **bei der Hand ~:** hold sb.'s hand; hold sb. by the hand; **jmdn./etw. im Arm ~:** hold sb./sth. in one's arms; **die Hand vor den Mund ~:** put one's hand in front of one's mouth; **etw. ins Licht/gegen das Licht ~:** hold sth. to/up to the light; **b)** *(Ballspiele)* save ⟨*shot, penalty, etc.*⟩; **c)** *(bewahren)* keep; *(beibehalten, aufrechterhalten)* keep up ⟨*speed etc.*⟩; maintain ⟨*temperature, equilibrium*⟩; **einen Ton ~:** stay in tune; *(lange an~)* sustain a note; **den Takt ~:** keep time; **Diät ~:** keep to a diet; **den Kurs ~:** stay on course; **diese Forderungen lassen sich nicht ~** *od.* **sind nicht zu ~:** these demands cannot be kept up *or* maintained; **diese Behauptung läßt sich nicht ~:** this statement does not hold up; **mit jmdm. Kontakt** *od.* **Verbindung ~:** keep in touch *or* contact with sb.; **Ordnung/Frieden ~:** keep order/the peace; **Ruhe in der Klasse ~:** ⟨*teacher*⟩ keep the class quiet; ⟨*pupils*⟩ keep quiet in class; **d)** *(erfüllen)* keep; **sein Wort/ein Versprechen ~:** keep one's word/a promise; **das Buch hielt nicht, was das Titelbild versprach** *(fig.)* the book didn't live up to the promise of the picture on its cover; **e)** *(besitzen, beschäftigen, beziehen)* keep ⟨*chickens etc.*⟩; take ⟨*newspaper, magazine, etc.*⟩; **ein Auto ~:** run a car; **sich** *(Dat.)* **eine Putzfrau ~:** have a woman to come in and clean; **f)** *(einschätzen)* **jmdn. für reich/ehrlich ~:** think sb. is *or* consider sb. to be rich/honest; **jmdn. für tot ~:** think sb. is dead; **ich halte es für das beste/möglich/meine Pflicht** I think it best/possible/my duty; **viel/nichts/wenig von jmdm./etw. ~:** think a lot/nothing/not think much of sb./sth.; **g)** *(ab~, veranstalten)* give, make ⟨*speech*⟩; give, hold ⟨*lecture*⟩; **Unterricht ~:** give lessons; teach; **seinen Winterschlaf ~:** hibernate; **seinen Mittagsschlaf ~:** have one's *or* an afternoon nap; **eine Mahlzeit ~** *(veralt.)* have a meal; **h)** *(Halt geben)* hold up, support ⟨*bridge etc.*⟩; hold back ⟨*curtain, hair*⟩; fasten ⟨*dress*⟩; **i)** *(zurück~)* keep; **ihn hält hier nichts** there's nothing to keep him here; **es hält dich niemand** nobody's stopping you; **j)** *(bei sich be~)* **das Wasser ~:** hold one's water; **k)** *(nicht aufgeben)* **ein Geschäft** *usw.* **~:** keep a business *etc.* going; **l)** *(behandeln)* treat; **jmdn. streng ~:** be strict with sb.; **m)** *(vorziehen)* **es mit jmdm./etw. ~:** like sb./sth.; **es mehr od. lieber mit jmdm./etw. ~:** prefer sb./sth.; **n)** *(verfahren)* **es mit einer Sache so/anders ~:** deal with *or* handle sth. like this/differently; **wie haltet ihr es in diesem Jahr mit eurem Urlaub?** what are you doing about holidays this year?; **o)** *(lassen, be~)* keep; **für jmdn. das Essen warm ~:** keep sb.'s meal hot; **jmdn. jung/fit ~:** keep sb. young/fit; **jmdn. bei Laune/in Bewegung/in Atem ~:** keep sb. happy/on the go/in suspense; **p)** *(gestalten)* **das Badezimmer ist in Grün ge~:** the bathroom is decorated in green; **sie wollten das Eßzimmer ganz in Eiche ~:** they wanted all oak furniture in the dining room; **die Rede war sehr allgemein ge~:** the speech was very general. **2.** *unr. itr. V.* **a)** *(stehenbleiben)* stop; **etw. zum Halten bringen** stop sth.; bring sth. to a stop; **halt [mal]** *(fig. ugs.)* hang *or* hold on [a minute] *(coll.)*; **b)** *(unverändert, an seinem Platz bleiben)* last; **der Nagel/das Seil hält nicht mehr länger** the nail/rope won't hold much longer; **die Tapete hält nicht** the wallpaper won't stay on; **diese Freundschaft hält nicht [lange]** *(fig.)* this friendship won't last [long]; **c)** *(Sport)* save; **er hat gut ge~:** he made some good saves; **d)** *(beistehen)* **zu jmdm. ~:** stand *or* stick by sb.; **e)** *(zielen)* aim **(auf +** *Akk.* at); **f)** *(Seemannsspr.)* head; **auf etw.** *(Akk.)* **~:** head for *or* towards sth.; **g)** *(sich beherrschen)* **an sich** *(Akk.)* **~:** control oneself; **h)** *(achten)* **auf Ordnung ~:** attach importance to tidiness; **auf sich** *(Akk.)* **~:** take a pride in oneself. **3.** *unr. refl. V.* **a)** *(sich durchsetzen, behaupten)* **wir werden uns/die Stadt wird sich nicht länger ~ können** we/the town won't be able to hold out much longer; **das Geschäft wird sich nicht ~ können** the shop won't keep going [for long]; **der neue Regisseur konnte sich nicht ~:** the new director didn't last; **b)** *(sich bewähren)* **sich gut ~:** do well; make a good showing; **halte dich tapfer** be brave; **c)** *(unverändert bleiben)* ⟨*weather, flowers, etc.*⟩ last; ⟨*milk, meat, etc.*⟩ keep; **d)** *(Körperhaltung haben)* **sich schlecht/gerade/aufrecht ~:** hold *or* carry oneself badly/straight/erect; **e)** *(bleiben)* **sich auf den Beinen/im Sattel ~:** stay on one's feet/in the saddle; **f)** *(gehen, bleiben)* **sich links/rechts ~:** keep [to the] left/right; **sich südwärts/in Richtung Bahnhof ~:** keep going south/towards the station; **sich an jmds. Seite** *(Dat.)***/hinter jmdm. ~:** stay *or* keep next to/behind sb.; **g)** *(befolgen)* **sich an etw.** *(Akk.)* **~:** keep to *or* follow sth.; **der Film hat sich nicht eng an den Roman ge~:** the film didn't keep *or* stick closely to the book; **h)** *(sich wenden)* **sich an jmdn. ~:** ask sb.; **halte dich an Peter, der ist immer hilfsbereit** stay *or* stick with Peter – he's always helpful; **i)** *(ugs.: jung, gesund bleiben)* **sie hat sich gut ge~:** she is well preserved for her age *(coll.)*
Halte-: ~platz der [taxi-]rank *(Brit.)*; [cab-]stand *(Amer.)*; **~punkt der** stop
Halter der; ~s, ~ a) *(Fahrzeug~)* keeper; **b)** *(Tier~)* owner; **c)** *(Vorrichtung)* holder; *(Handtuch~)* towel-rail; **d)** *(ugs.: Feder~)* pen; **e)** *(österr.) s.* **Viehhirt**
Halterin die; ~, ~nen *s.* **Halter a, b**
Halterung die; ~, ~en support
Halte-: ~seil das supporting cable; *(eines Ballons)* mooring cable; **~signal das** stop signal; **~stelle die** stop; **~verbot das a)** **„~verbot"** 'no stopping'; **auf dieser Straße besteht ~verbot** stopping is prohibited in this street; **„absolutes/eingeschränktes ~verbot"** 'no stopping/no waiting'; **b)** *(Stelle)* no-stopping zone; **hier ist ~verbot** this is a no-stopping zone; **~verbots·schild das** no-stopping sign; **~vorrichtung die** *s.* **Halterung**
-haltig [-haltɪç], *(österr.)* **-hältig** [-hɛltɪç] **vitamin~/silber~** *usw.* containing vitamins/silver *etc. postpos., not pred.*; **vitamin~ sein** contain vitamins
halt-, Halt-: ~los *Adj.* **a)** *(labil)* **~los sein** be a weak character; **ein ~loser Mensch** a weak character; **b)** *(unbegründet)* unfounded; **~losigkeit die; ~ a)** *(Labilität)* weakness of character; **b)** *(mangelnde Begründung)* unfoundedness; **~|machen** *itr. V.* stop; **vor jmdm./etw. nicht ~machen** not spare sb./sth.; **vor nichts [und niemandem] ~machen** stop at nothing
Haltung die; ~, ~en a) *(Körper~)* posture; *(Sport)* stance; *(in der Bewegung)* style; **~ annehmen** *(Milit.)* stand to attention; **b)** *(Pose)* manner; **c)** *(Einstellung)* attitude; **d)** *o. Pl. (Fassung)* composure; **~ zeigen/bewahren** keep one's composure; **e)** *(Tier~)* keeping
Haltungs-: ~fehler der a) *(Med.)* bad posture; **b)** *(Sport)* style fault; **~schaden der** *(Med.)* bad posture; **~schäden** bad posture
Halt·verbot das *s.* **Halteverbot**
Halunke [ha'lʊnkə] **der; ~n, ~n a)** *(Schurke)* scoundrel; villain; **b)** *(scherzh.: Lausbub)* rascal; scamp

Hämatit [hɛma'ti:t] der; ~s, ~e (Geol.) haematite
Hämatologe [hɛmato'lo:gə] der; ~n, ~n (Med.) haematologist
Hämatologie die; ~ (Med.) haematology no art.
Hämatom [hɛma'to:m] das; ~s, ~e (Med.) haematoma
Hamburg ['hambʊrk] (das); ~s Hamburg
¹Hamburger 1. der; ~s, ~: native of Hamburg; (Einwohner) inhabitant of Hamburg; Schmidt ist ~: Schmidt comes from Hamburg. 2. indekl. Adj. Hamburg; der ~ Hafen the harbour at Hamburg; Hamburg harbour; s. auch Kölner
²Hamburger der; ~s, ~ od. ~s (Frikadelle) hamburger
hamburgern itr. V. speak Hamburg dialect
hamburgisch Adj. Hamburg attrib.; of Hamburg postpos.
Häme ['hɛ:mə] die; ~: malice
Hameln ['ha:mḷn] (das); ~s Hamelin; der Rattenfänger von ~: the Pied Piper of Hamelin
hämisch ['hɛ:mɪʃ] 1. Adj. malicious. 2. adv. maliciously
Hammel ['hamḷ] der; ~s, ~ a) wether; b) (Fleisch) mutton; c) (salopp abwertend) oaf; dolt
Hammel-: ~bein das in jmdm. die ~beine langziehen (ugs.) give sb. a good telling-off; ~fleisch das mutton; ~herde die (salopp abwertend) flock of sheep; ~keule die leg of mutton; ~sprung der (Parl.) division
Hammer ['hamɐ] der; ~s, Hämmer ['hɛmɐ] a) hammer; (Holz~) mallet; (Eis~) hammer axe; (eines Auktionators) hammer; gavel; ~ und Sichel hammer and sickle; ~ und Zirkel hammer and compasses (on the GDR national flag); unter den ~ kommen come under the hammer; etw. unter den ~ bringen auction sth.; b) (Technik) tup; ram; c) (Musik) hammer; d) (Leichtathletik) hammer; e) (ugs.: Fehler) bad mistake; (in einer Aufgabe) howler (coll.); ein dicker ~: an awful blunder; er hat einen ~: he must be round the bend (coll.) or (sl.) twist; f) (ugs.: Überraschung, Clou) real surprise; das ist ein ~! (großartig) that's fantastic! (coll.); (unerhört) that's quite outrageous!; g) (Anat.) hammer; malleus
Hämmerchen ['hɛmɐçən] das; ~s, ~: [small] hammer
hammer-, Hammer-: ~förmig Adj. hammer-shaped; ~hai der hammer-head [shark]; ~klavier das (veralt.) pianoforte; ~kopf der (auch Leichtathletik, Musik) hammerhead
hämmern ['hɛmɐn] 1. itr. V. a) hammer; es hämmert sb. is hammering; b) (schlagen) hammer; (mit der Faust) hammer; pound; gegen die Wand/die Tür ~: hammer/pound on the wall/door; c) (klopfen) pound; ⟨pulse⟩ race. 2. tr. V. a) hammer; beat, hammer ⟨tin, silver, etc.⟩; beat ⟨jewellery⟩; b) (ugs.) hammer or pound out ⟨melody etc.⟩; c) (ugs.: einprägen) jmdm. etw. in den Schädel ~: hammer or knock sth. into sb.'s head (coll.); d) (Fußballjargon) hammer, slam ⟨ball⟩
Hammer-: ~schlag der a) hammer-blow; blow from a/the hammer; b) (Boxen) rabbit punch; c) (Faustball) smash; d) (Technik) hammer scale; ~stiel der handle or shaft of a/the hammer; ~werfen das (Leichtathletik) throwing the hammer; er ist Weltmeister im ~werfen he's world champion in the hammer; ~werfer der; ~s, ~ (Leichtathletik) hammer-thrower; ~werk das a) (veralt.) hammer-mill; b) (Musik) striking mechanism; ~wurf der (Leichtathletik) a) s. ~werfen; b) (einzelner Wurf) hammer throw; ~zehe die hammer-toe
Hammond·orgel ['hæmənd-] die Hammond organ
Hämoglobin [hɛmoglo'bi:n] das; ~s (Physiol.) haemoglobin
Hämorrhoiden [hɛmɔro'i:dṇ] Pl. (Med.) haemorrhoids; piles
Hämozyt [hɛmo'tsy:t] der; ~en, ~en (Physiol.) haemocyte
Hampelei die; ~ (ugs. abwertend) fidgeting
Hampel·mann ['hampḷ-] der; ~[e]s, Hampelmänner a) jumping jack; b) (ugs. abwertend) puppet; jmdn. zu einem/seinem ~ machen make sb. one's puppet; c) (Gymnastik) side-straddle hop; jumping jack
hampeln itr. V. (ugs.) jump about
Hamster ['hamstɐ] der; ~s, ~: hamster
Hamster·backen Pl. chubby cheeks
Hamsterer der; ~s, ~, **Hamsterin** die; ~, ~nen (ugs.) hoarder
Hamster-: ~fahrt die foraging trip; auf ~fahrt gehen go foraging; ~kauf der panic-buying no pl.; ~käufe machen panic-buy
hamstern tr., itr. V. a) (horten) hoard; (Hamsterkäufe machen) panic-buy; b) (Lebensmittel tauschen) barter goods for [food]
Hand [hant] die; ~, Hände ['hɛndə] a) hand; mit der rechten/linken ~: with one's right/left hand; jmdm. die ~ geben od. (geh.) reichen shake sb.'s hand; shake sb. by the hand; jmdm. die ~ drücken/schütteln press/shake sb.'s hand; eine ~ frei haben have a free hand; ich habe keine ~ frei my hands are full; Hände hoch! hands up!; jmdm. die ~ küssen kiss sb.'s hand; jmdn. an die od. (geh.) bei der ~ nehmen take sb. by the hand; jmdm. etw. aus der ~ nehmen take sth. out of sb.'s hand/hands; etw. aus der ~ legen put sth. down; jmdm. aus der ~ lesen read sb.'s hand or palm; etw. in die/zur ~ nehmen pick sth. up; etw. in der ~/den Händen haben od. (geh.) halten have got or hold sth. in one's hand/hands; in die Hände klatschen clap one's hands; mit Händen und Füßen reden use gestures to make oneself understood; etw. mit der ~ schreiben/nähen write/sew sth. by hand; von ~: by hand; ~ in ~ gehen go or walk hand-in-hand; eine Sonate für vier Hände od. zu vier Händen a four-handed sonata; jmdm. etw. in die ~ versprechen promise sb. sth. faithfully; b) o. Pl. (Fußball) handball; c) (Boxen) punch; d) (veralt., geh.: ~schrift) hand; e) (österr. ugs.: Arm) arm; f) (in Wendungen) was hältst du davon – ~ aufs Herz! what do you think? – be honest; ~ aufs Herz, ich habe ihn nicht gesehen I haven't seen him, word of honour or (coll.) cross my heart; eine ~ wäscht die andere you scratch my back and I'll scratch yours; Zuschüsse von öffentlicher ~: subsidies from government funds or from the government; die öffentlichen Hände the local/regional authorities; jmds. rechte ~: sb's right-hand man; ihm rutschte die ~ aus (ugs.) he couldn't stop himself [hitting her/him etc.]; jmdm. sind die Hände gebunden sb.'s hands are tied; ~ und Fuß/weder ~ noch Fuß haben (ugs.) make sense/no sense; [bei etw. selbst mit] ~ anlegen lend a hand [with sth.]; die od. seine ~ aufhalten od. hinhalten (ugs.) hold out one's hand; jmds. ~ ausschlagen (veralt. geh.) reject sb.; keine ~ rühren (ugs.) not lift a finger; ~ an sich legen (geh.) take one's own life; letzte ~ an etw. (Akk.) legen put the finishing touches pl. to sth.; jmdm. die ~ [zum Bund] fürs Leben reichen (geh.) marry sb.; sich (Dat.) od. (geh.) einander die ~ reichen können be tarred with the same brush; dann können wir uns die ~ reichen snap!; shake!; alle od. beide Hände damit voll haben, etw. zu tun (ugs.) have one's hands full doing sth.; er hat alle Hände voll zu tun he's got his hands full; sich (Dat.) die ~ für jmdn./etw. abhacken od. abschlagen lassen (ugs.) do anything for sb./stake one's life on sth.; jmdm. auf etw. (Akk.) die ~ geben promise sb. sth.; die Hände in den Schoß legen sit back and do nothing; bei etw. die od. seine Hände [mit] im Spiel haben have a hand in sth.; überall seine ~ od. Hände im Spiel haben have a finger in every pie; die Hände über dem Kopf zusammenschlagen (ugs.) throw up one's hands in horror; die od. seine ~ über jmdn. halten (geh.) protect sb.; zwei linke Hände haben (ugs.) have two left hands (coll.); eine lockere od. lose ~ haben (ugs.) hit out at the slightest provocation; eine offene ~ haben be open-handed; eine glückliche ~ bei etw. haben have a feel for the right choice in sth.; dabei hat er eine glückliche ~ gehabt he intuitively made the right choice; eine glückliche ~ in etw. (Dat.) haben have the right knack for sth.; im Umgang mit Kindern hat er eine glückliche ~: he's very good or has a way with children; sie hat in solchen Dingen eine glückliche ~: she has a [natural] flair for such things; eine grüne ~ haben (ugs.) have green fingers; linker/rechter ~: on or to the left/right; an ~ (+ Gen.) with the help of; an ~ dieses Berichts from this report; jmdm. etw. an die ~ geben make sth. available to sb.; jmdn. an der ~ haben (ugs.) know [of] sb.; [klar] auf der ~ liegen (ugs.) be obvious; jmdn. auf Händen tragen lavish every kind of care and attention on sb.; ein Auto/Möbel aus erster ~: a car/furniture which has/had had one [previous] owner; etw. aus erster ~ wissen know sth. at first hand; have first-hand knowledge of sth.; Kleidung aus zweiter ~: second-hand clothes pl.; das Auto ist aus zweiter ~: the car has had two [previous] owners; Leihgaben aus od. von privater ~: loans from private collections; jmdm. aus der ~ fressen eat out of sb.'s hand (fig.); etw. aus der ~ geben (weggeben) let sth. out of one's hands; (aufgeben) give sth. up; [aus der] ~ spielen (Skat) play without using the widow or skat; jmdm. etw. aus der ~ nehmen relieve sb. of sth.; etw. bei der ~ haben (greifbar haben) have sth. handy; (parat haben) have sth. ready; mit etw. schnell od. rasch bei der ~ sein (ugs.) be ready [with sth.]; [schon od. bereits] durch viele Hände gegangen sein have been or have [been] passed through many hands; die Vera ist schon durch viele Hände gegangen (ugs.) she's been around a bit, has Vera (coll.); ~ in ~ arbeiten work hand in hand; Regierung und Rauschgifthändler arbeiteten ~ in ~: the government and the drug-dealers were working hand in glove; mit etw. ~ in ~ gehen go hand in hand with sth.; hinter vorgehaltener ~: off the record; in die Hände spucken spit on one's hands; (fig. ugs.) roll up one's sleeves (fig.); jmdm./einer Sache in die Hände arbeiten play into sb.'s hands/help bring sth. about; jmdn./etw. in die ~ od. Hände bekommen od. kriegen lay or get one's hands on sb./get one's hands on sth.; jmdm. in die Hände fallen fall into sb.'s hands; etw. in der ~ haben have sth.; jmdn. in der ~ haben have or hold sb. in the palm of one's hand; etw. in Händen halten hold sth.; etw. in jmds. ~ od. Hände legen (geh.) put sth. in sb.'s hands; etw. in die ~ nehmen take sth. in hand; in jmds. ~ (Dat.) sein od. (geh.) liegen be in sb.'s hands; in festen Händen sein (ugs.) be spoken for or attached; in sicheren od. guten Händen sein, sich in guten Händen befinden be in safe or good hands; jmdm. Informationen usw. in die ~ od. Hände spielen pass information etc. to sb.; in jmds. ~ od. Hände übergehen pass into sb.'s hands; mit Händen zu greifen sein be as plain as a pikestaff; be perfectly obvious; mit beiden Händen zugreifen grab or seize the opportunity with both hands; sich mit Händen und Füßen gegen etw. sträuben od. wehren (ugs.) fight tooth and nail against sth.; mit leeren Händen empty-

handed; **das mache ich mit der linken ~** *(ugs.)* I could do that with my eyes closed; **mit starker** *od.* **fester ~:** with a firm hand; **das Geld mit vollen Händen ausgeben** spend money like water; **um jmds. ~ anhalten** *od.* **bitten** *(geh. veralt.)* ask for sb.'s hand [in marriage]; **etw. unter den Händen haben** be working on sth.; **von jmds. ~ [sterben]** *(geh.)* [die] at sb.'s hand; **das geht ihm gut/leicht von der ~:** he finds that no trouble; **etw. von langer ~ vorbereiten** plan sth. well in advance; **die Nachteile/seine Argumente lassen sich nicht von der ~ weisen** *od.* **sind nicht von der ~ zu weisen** the disadvantages cannot be denied/his arguments cannot [simply] be dismissed; **von der ~ in den Mund leben** live from hand to mouth; **von ~ zu ~ gehen** be passed from hand to hand; **etw. zu treuen Händen nehmen** take sth. into one's care; **jmdm. etw. zu treuen Händen geben** give sth. to sb. for safe keeping; **zur linken/rechten ~:** on *or* to the left/right[-hand side]; **etw. zur ~ haben** have sth. handy; **ich habe kein Kleingeld zur ~:** I haven't got any change on me; **jmdm. zur ~ gehen** lend sb. a hand; **zu Händen [von] Herrn Müller** for the attention of Herr Müller; attention Herr Müller; *s. auch* **öffentlich 1**

hạnd-, Hạnd-: ~ab·zug der a) *(Druckw.)* proof pulled by hand; **b)** *(Fot.)* print made by hand; **~akte die** file; **~apparat der a)** *(Fernspr.)* handset; **b)** *(Bücher)* set of reference books; reference collection; **~arbeit die a)** *o. Pl.* handicraft; craft work; **etw. in ~arbeit herstellen** make sth. by hand; **b)** *(Gegenstand)* handmade article; **das ist eine ~arbeit** that is handmade *or* made by hand; **c)** *(Arbeit aus Stoff, Wolle usw.)* [piece of] needlework; *(gestrickt)* [piece of] knitting; *(gehäkelt)* [piece of] crocheting; **sie macht gerne ~arbeiten** she likes doing needlework/knitting/crocheting; **d)** *o. Pl. (ugs.: ~arbeitsunterricht)* needlework; **~arbeiten** *itr. V.* do needlework; **ich kann nicht gut ~arbeiten** I am not very good at needlework; **~arbeiter der** manual worker

Hạndarbeits-: ~geschäft das wool and needlework shop; **~korb der** workbasket; **~lehrerin die** needlework teacher

Hạnd-: ~aufheben das; ~s *(bei einer Wahl)* show of hands; **sich durch ~aufheben melden** put one's hand up to speak/answer; **~auflegen das; ~s** *(bes. Rel.)* laying on *or* imposition of hands

Hạnd·ball der a) *o. Pl. (Spiel)* handball; **b)** *(Ball)* handball

Hạnd·ballen der ball of the thumb

Hạnd·baller der; ~s, ~ *(ugs.)* handball player

Hạndball-: ~mannschaft die handball team; **~spiel das a)** handball match; **b)** *o. Pl. (Sportart)* **das ~spiel** the game of handball; **~spieler der** handball player

hạnd-, Hạnd-: ~bedienung die; *o. Pl.* manual operation; **eine Maschine mit ~bedienung** a manually operated *or* hand-operated machine; **~besen der** brush; **~betrieb der;** *o. Pl.* manual operation; **mit ~betrieb** manually operated *or* hand-operated; **~betrieben** *Adj.* manually operated; hand-operated; **~bewegung die a)** movement of the hand; **b)** *(Geste)* gesture; **~bibliothek die a)** reference library; **b)** *(~apparat)* set of reference books; reference collection; **~bohrer der** *(mit Kurbel)* hand-drill; *(zum Vorbohren)* gimlet; **~bohr·maschine die** hand-drill; *(elektrisch)* drill; **~brause die** shower handset; **~breit 1.** *Adj.* ‹*seam etc.*› a few inches wide; **ein ~breiter Abstand** a gap of a few inches; **2.** *adv.* a few inches; **~breit die; ~, ~: eine/zwei ~breit** a few/several inches; **keine ~breit** barely an inch; **~breite die: ein Abstand/Streifen von einer ~breite** a gap of a few inches/a strip a few inches wide; **~bremse die** handbrake; **~buch das** handbook; *(technisches ~buch)* manual

Händchen ['hɛntçən] **das; ~s, ~:** [little] hand; **~ halten** *(ugs. scherzh.)* hold hands; **für etw. ein ~ haben** *(fig. ugs.)* have a knack for sth.; be good at sth.

Hạ̈ndchen·halten das; ~s *(ugs. scherzh.)* holding hands *no art.*

hạ̈ndchen·haltend 1. *Adj.; nicht präd. (ugs. scherzh.)* **ein ~es junges Paar** a young couple holding hands. **2.** *adv.* holding hands

Hạnd·creme die hand cream

Hände *s.* **Hand**

Hạ̈nde-: ~druck der; *Pl.* **~drücke** handshake; **~klatschen das; ~s** clapping; applause

[1]Handel ['handḷ] **der; ~s a)** *(Wirtschaft)* trade; commerce; **~ und Industrie/~ und Gewerbe** trade and industry; **b)** *(Handeln)* trade; **der ~ mit Waffen/Drogen** the traffic in arms/drugs; **c)** *(Geschäftsverkehr)* trade; **der internationale/überseeische ~:** international/overseas trade; **ein Produkt aus dem ~ ziehen** take a product off the market; **in den ~ kommen** come on [to] the market; **das ist [nicht mehr] im ~:** it is [no longer] on the market; **~ und Wandel** *(veralt.)* commercial and social life; **d)** *(veralt.: Geschäft)* business; **e)** *(Vereinbarung)* deal

[2]Hạ̈ndel der; ~s, Händel ['hɛndḷ]; *meist Pl. (geh.)* quarrel; **einen ~ [mit jmdm.] austragen** settle a quarrel [with sb.]; **Händel anfangen/suchen** start/ [try to] pick a quarrel

Hạnd·elfmeter der *(Fußball)* penalty for handball

hạndeln 1. *itr. V.* **a)** trade; deal; **mit** *od.* **in Gemüse/Gebrauchtwagen ~:** deal in vegetables/second-hand cars; **mit Waffen/Drogen ~:** traffic in arms/drugs; **mit jmdm. ~:** trade *or* deal with sb.; **en gros/en detail ~:** be in the wholesale/retail trade; **wir ~ en gros mit Spielwaren** we are toy-wholesalers; **b)** *(feilschen)* haggle; bargain; **um den Preis ~:** haggle over the price; **mit ihm läßt sich [nicht] ~:** he is [not] open to negotiation; **er läßt nicht mit sich ~:** it's impossible to bargain with him; **c)** *(eingreifen)* act; **auf Befehl/aus Überzeugung ~:** act on orders/out of conviction; **im Affekt/in Notwehr ~:** act in the heat of the moment/in self-defence; **d)** *(verfahren)* act; **eigenmächtig/richtig/fahrlässig ~:** act on one's own authority/correctly/carelessly; **e)** *(sich verhalten)* behave; **gut/schlecht an jmdm.** *od.* **gegen jmdn. ~:** behave well/badly towards sb.; **f) von etw.** *od.* **über etw.** *(Akk.)* **~** ‹*book, film, etc.*› be about *or* deal with sth. **2.** *refl. V. (unpers.)* **bei dem Besucher handelte es sich um einen entfernten Verwandten** the visitor was a distant relative; **es handelt sich um ...:** it is a matter of ...; *(es dreht sich um)* it's about *or* it concerns ...; **es handelt sich darum, daß die Presse nichts davon erfährt** the important thing is that the press should not get wind of it. **3.** *tr. V.* sell **(für** at, for); **diese Papiere werden nicht an der Börse gehandelt** these securities are not traded on the stock exchange; **der US-Dollar wird jetzt zu 2 DM gehandelt** the US dollar is now valued at 2 marks

Hạndeln das; ~s a) *(das Feilschen)* haggling; bargaining; **b)** *(das Eingreifen)* action; **c)** *(Verhalten)* action[s *pl.*]

hạndels-, Hạndels-: ~abkommen das trade agreement; **~agent der** *(österr.) s.* **~vertreter; ~akademie die** *(österr.)* commercial college; **~artikel der** commodity; **~attaché der** commercial attaché; **~bank die** merchant bank; **~beschränkung die** trade restriction; **~beziehungen** *Pl.* trade relations; **~bilanz die a)** *(eines Betriebes)* balance-sheet; **b)** *(eines Staates)* balance of trade; **eine aktive/passive ~bilanz** a balance of trade surplus/deficit; **~boykott der** trade boycott; **~delegation die** trade delegation; **~einig, ~eins** *in* **mit jmdm. ~einig** *od.* **~eins werden/sein** agree/have agreed terms *or* come/have come to an agreement with sb.; **~firma die** [business *or* commercial] firm; business concern; **~flagge die** merchant flag; **~flotte die** merchant fleet; **~geist der;** *o. Pl.* business acumen *or* sense; **~gericht das** commercial court; **~gesellschaft die** company; **offene ~gesellschaft** general partnership; **~gesetz das** commercial law; **~gesetz·buch das;** *o. Pl.* commercial code; **~größe die** *(Kaufmannsspr.)* commercial size; **~hafen der** commercial *or* trading port; **~haus das** *(veralt.)* business-house; firm; **~kammer die** *s.* **Industrie- und ~kammer; ~kette die** *(Kaufmannsspr.)* **a)** *(Weg der Ware)* channel of distribution; **b)** *(Zusammenschluß von Händlern)* voluntary chain; **~klasse die** grade; **~kontor das** *(hist.)* branch; **~korrespondenz die** business correspondence; **~lehrer der** teacher of commercial subjects; **~macht die** trading power; **~marine die** merchant navy; **~marke die** trade mark; **~messe die** trade fair; **~metropole die** commercial metropolis *or* centre; **~minister der** minister of trade; *(in UK)* Secretary of State for Trade; Trade Secretary *(coll.)*; **~ministerium das** ministry of trade; *(in UK)* Department of Trade; **~mission die** trade mission; **~monopol das** trading monopoly; **~name der** trade *or* business name; **~nation die** trading nation; **~niederlassung die** branch; **~organ das** *(DDR)* branch; **~organisation die a)** trading organization; **b)** *(DDR) [state-owned] commercial concern running shops, hotels, etc.*; **~partner der** trading partner; **~politik die** trade *or* commercial policy; **~politisch 1.** *Adj.; nicht präd.* relating to trade *or* commercial policy *postpos.*; **vom ~politischen Standpunkt** from the point of view of trade *or* commercial policy; **2.** *adv.* as far as trade *or* commercial policy is concerned; **~recht das;** *o. Pl.* commercial law; **~rechtlich 1.** *Adj.; nicht präd.* relating to commercial law *postpos.*; ‹*offence*› against commercial law; **2.** *adv.* from the point of view of commercial law; **es ist ~rechtlich nicht erlaubt** it is not allowed under commercial law; **~register das** register of companies; **~reisende der/die;** *adj. Dekl. s.* **~vertreter; ~schiff das** merchant ship; trading vessel; **~schiffahrt die** merchant shipping; *(Schiffsverkehr)* movement of merchant shipping; **~schranke die;** *meist Pl.* trade barrier; **~schule die** commercial college; **~schüler der** student at a commercial college; **~schul·lehrer der** teacher at a commercial college; **~spanne die** *(Kaufmannsspr.)* margin; **~sperre die** trade embargo; **~sprache die** trade language; language of commerce; **~stadt die** trading town; *(Großstadt)* trading city; **~straße die** *(hist.)* trade route; **~üblich** *Adj.* **~übliche Praktiken/Größen** normal *or* standard business practices/standard [commercial] sizes; **~üblich sein** be normal *or* standard business practice

Hạ̈ndel·sucht die *(geh. veralt.)* quarrelsomeness

hạ̈ndel·süchtig *Adj. (geh. veralt.)* quarrelsome

Hạndels-: ~unternehmen das trading concern; **~verbindung die;** *meist Pl.* trade link; **~vertrag der** trade agreement; **~vertreter der** [sales] representative; travelling salesmann/saleswoman; commercial traveller; **~vertretung die** *s.* **~mission; ~volumen das** *(Wirtsch.)* volume of trade; **~ware die** commodity;

„keine ~ware" *(Postw.)* 'no commercial value'; **~weg der a)** commercial artery; **b)** *(Weg der Ware)* channel of distribution; **~wert der** *(Kaufmannsspr.)* commercial value; **~zentrum das** trading *or* commercial centre

handel·treibend *Adj.; nicht präd.* trading ⟨*nation*⟩; ⟨*tribe*⟩ engaged primarily in trade

hände-, Hände-: ~ringend *Adv.* **a)** wringing one's hands; **b)** *(ugs.: dringend)* **~ringend suchen** need urgently; **~ringend nach jmdm./etw. suchen** search desperately for sb./sth.; **~schütteln das; ~s** handshaking *no pl.*; **die ersten zehn Minuten vergingen mit ~schütteln** the first ten minutes were spent shaking hands; **~trockner der** hand-drier; **~waschen das; ~s** washing *no art.* one's hands; **sie ging zum ~waschen ins Bad** she went to the bathroom to wash her hands

hand-, Hand-: ~feger der brush; **herumlaufen wie ein wild gewordener ~feger** *(salopp) (zerzaust)* go round looking like a scarecrow; *(aufgeregt)* run around madly; **~fertigkeit die;** *o. Pl.* [manual] dexterity; **~fest 1.** *Adj.* **a)** *(kräftig)* robust; sturdy; **b)** *(deftig)* substantial ⟨*meal etc.*⟩; **etwas Handfestes** something substantial; **c)** *(gewichtig)* solid, tangible ⟨*proof*⟩; concrete ⟨*suggestion*⟩; full-blooded, violent ⟨*row*⟩; complete ⟨*lie*⟩; well-founded ⟨*argument*⟩; real, thorough ⟨*beating*⟩; **2.** *adv. (deutlich)* ⟨*criticize*⟩ severely; **er hat mich ~fest belogen/betrogen** he told me a complete lie/it was an out-and-out deception; **~feuerlöscher der** hand fire-extinguisher; **~feuer·waffe die** hand-gun; **~feuerwaffen** small arms; **~fläche die** palm [of one's/the hand]; flat of one's/the hand; **~galopp der** *(Reiten)* canter; hand gallop; **~gas das** *(Kfz-W.)* hand throttle; **mit ~gas fahren** drive using the hand throttle; **~gearbeitet** *Adj.* handmade ⟨*furniture, jewellery, etc.*⟩; **~gefertigt** *Adj.* hand-made; **~geknüpft** *Adj.* hand-woven; **~geld das** lump sum [payment]; **~gelenk das** wrist; **ein loses** *od.* **lockeres ~gelenk haben** *(ugs.)* lash out at the slightest provocation; **aus dem ~gelenk [heraus]** *(ugs.) (unvermittelt)* offhand; *(ohne Mühe)* effortlessly; as easily as anything *(coll.)*; **etw. aus dem ~gelenk schütteln** *(ugs.)* do sth. just like that *(coll.)*; **~gemacht** *Adj.* handmade; **~gemalt** *Adj.* hand-painted; **~gemenge das a)** fight; **b)** *(Milit.)* hand-to-hand fighting *no indef. art.*; **~gepäck das** hand-baggage; **~geschliffen** *Adj.* hand-cut; **~geschmiedet** *Adj.* hand-wrought; **~geschöpft** *Adj.* handmade; **~geschrieben** *Adj.* handwritten; **~gesponnen** *Adj.* hand-spun; **~gesteuert** *Adj.* manually operated; manually controlled ⟨*vehicle*⟩; **~gestrickt** *Adj.* hand-knitted; *(fig. abwertend)* half-baked ⟨*idea, theory, etc.*⟩; **~gewebt** *Adj.* hand-woven; **~granate die** hand-grenade; **~greiflich 1.** *Adj.* **a)** *(tätlich)* **eine ~greifliche Auseinandersetzung** a scuffle; **~greiflich werden** start using one's fists; **b)** tangible ⟨*success, advantage, proof, etc.*⟩; palpable ⟨*contradiction, error*⟩; obvious ⟨*fact*⟩; **2.** *adv.* **a)** *(tätlich)* **sich ~greiflich auseinandersetzen** come to blows; **b)** *(konkret faßbar)* clearly; **~greiflichkeit die; ~, ~en a)** *(eines Beweises)* tangibility; *(eines Widerspruchs, Fehlers)* palpability; **b)** *(Tätlichkeit)* scuffle; fight; **es kam zu/nicht zu ~greiflichkeiten** a fight broke out/there was no violence; **~griff der a) ein falscher ~griff** a false move; **ein geschickter ~griff, und ...:** one deft action and ...; **mit einem ~griff/wenigen ~griffen** in one movement/without much trouble; *(schnell)* in no time at all/next to no time; **jeder ~griff muß sitzen** every movement must be exactly right; **keinen ~griff [für jmdn.] tun** *(fig.)* not do anything to help sb.; **b)** *(am Koffer, an einem Werkzeug)* handle; **c)** *(Haltegriff)* grab handle; **~groß** *Adj.* ⟨*hole, wound, etc.*⟩ the size of a hand; **~habbar** [~ha:pba:ɐ̯] *Adj.* handy; **kaum ~habbar** very difficult *or* awkward to manage; very unwieldy; **~habe die; ~, ~n: eine [rechtliche] ~habe [gegen jmdn.]** a legal handle [against sb.]; **~haben** *tr. V.* **a)** handle; operate ⟨*device, machine*⟩; **b)** *(praktizieren)* implement ⟨*law etc.*⟩; **~habung die; ~, ~en a)** handling; *(eines Gerätes, einer Maschine)* operation; **b)** *(Durchführung)* implementation; **~harmonika die** accordion

Handikap ['hɛndikɛp] **das; ~s, ~s** *(auch Sport)* handicap

handikapen ['hɛndikɛpn̩] *tr. V.* handicap

händisch ['hɛndɪʃ] *(österr. ugs.)* **1.** *Adj.* manual. **2.** *adv.* manually; by hand

Hand-: ~kamera die hand camera; **~kante die** edge of the/one's hand

Handkanten·schlag der chop

hand-, Hand-: ~karre die, ~karren der handcart; **~käse der** *(landsch.) small, hand-formed curd cheese;* **~käse mit Musik** *(landsch.)* marinaded hand-formed curd cheese; **~koffer der** [small] suitcase; **~koloriert** *Adj.* hand-coloured; **~kurbel die** [hand-]crank; **~kuß der** kiss on sb.'s hand; **etw. mit ~kuß [an]nehmen/tun** accept/do sth. with [the greatest of] pleasure; **~lampe die** hand-lamp; inspection-lamp

Hand·langer der; ~s, ~ a) *(ungelernter Arbeiter)* labourer; *(abwertend)* lackey; general dogsbody; **c)** *(abwertend: Büttel)* henchman

Handlanger·dienst der; *meist Pl. (abwertend)* **für jmdn. ~e leisten** do sb.'s dirty work for him/her

Hand·lauf der handrail

Händler ['hɛndlɐ] **der; ~s, ~:** trader; tradesman/tradeswoman; **ein fliegender ~:** a hawker *or* street-trader

-händler der ⟨*cattle-, furniture-, scrap-, stamp-*⟩dealer; ⟨*coal-, corn-, scrap-, timber-, wine-*⟩merchant

Händlerin die; ~, ~nen *s.* **Händler**

Hand-: ~lese·kunst die palmistry *no art.*; **~lexikon das** concise encyclopaedia

handlich ['hantlɪç] **1.** *Adj.* handy; easily carried ⟨*parcel, suitcase*⟩; easily portable ⟨*television, camera*⟩; manœuvrable ⟨*car*⟩. **2.** *adv.* **~ verpackt** wrapped as a manageable parcel

Handlichkeit die; ~: handiness; *(eines Buches)* handy size; *(eines Autos)* manœuvrability

Hand-: ~linie die line of the hand; **~linien·deutung die;** *o. Pl.* palmistry

Handlung die; ~, ~en a) *(Vorgehen)* action; *(Tat)* act; **eine symbolische/feierliche ~:** a symbolic/ceremonial act; **b)** *(Fabel)* plot; **Einheit der ~:** unity of action; **c)** *(veralt.: Geschäft)* business

handlungs-, Handlungs-: ~ablauf der action; **~arm** *Adj.* short on action *pred.*; **~bevollmächtigte der/die** authorized representative; **~fähig** *Adj.* **a)** able to act *pred.*; working *attrib.* ⟨*majority*⟩; **b)** *(Rechtsw.)* able to act on one's own account *pred.*; **~fähigkeit die;** *o. Pl.* **a)** ability to act; **b)** *(Rechtsw.)* ability to act on one's own account; **~freiheit die;** *o. Pl.* freedom of action *or* to act; **~gehilfe der** *(Kaufmannsspr.)* employee *(on the business side of a firm)*; **~reich** *Adj.* action-packed; **~reisende der/die** *s.* **Handelsvertreter; ~schema das** plot structure; **~spiel·raum der** scope for action; **~unfähig** *Adj.* **a)** unable to act *pred.*; **b)** *(Rechtsw.)* unable to act on one's own account *pred.*; **~unfähigkeit die a)** inability to act; **b)** *(Rechtsw.)* inability to act on one's own account; **~vollmacht die** authority to act; **~weise die** behaviour; conduct

Hand-: ~mixer der hand-mixer; **~mühle die** hand-mill

Handout ['hɛndaut] **das; ~s, ~s** hand-out

Hand-: ~presse die hand-press; **~pumpe die** hand-pump; **~puppe die** glove *or* hand puppet; **~puppen·spiel das** glove puppet *or* hand puppet show; *(Technik)* glove *or* hand puppetry; **~rad das** handwheel; **~reichung die: eine ~reichung/~reichungen machen** lend a hand; **sie konnte nur einige ~reichungen machen** she couldn't help very much; **~rücken der** the back of the/one's hand; **auf beiden ~rücken tätowiert** with tattoos on the back of both hands; **~säge die** hand-saw; **~satz der;** *o. Pl.* *(Druckw.)* hand-setting; **etw. im ~satz herstellen** hand-set sth.; **~schelle die** handcuff; **jmdm. ~schellen anlegen** handcuff sb.; put handcuffs on sb.; **~schlag der a)** handshake; **jmdn. mit ~schlag begrüßen** greet sb. by shaking hands; **etw. durch einen ~schlag besiegeln** shake hands on sth.; **b)** *in* **er tat keinen ~schlag** *(ugs.)* he did not lift a finger

Hand·schrift die a) handwriting; **eine deutliche/unleserliche ~schrift** clear/illegible handwriting; **b)** *(Ausdrucksweise)* personal style; **c)** *(Text)* manuscript

Handschriften-: ~deutung die graphology *no art.*; analysis of handwriting; **~kunde die** palaeography; **~probe die** sample of handwriting

Handschrift·leser der *(DV) optical character reader for reading handwritten block letters and numerals*

hand·schriftlich 1. *Adj.* hand-written; **~schriftliche Quellen/Urkunden** manuscript sources/texts. **2.** *adv.* by hand

Hand·schuh der glove

Handschuh-: ~fach das glove compartment *or* box; **~größe die** glove size; **welche ~größe haben Sie?** what size glove do you take?; **~macher der** glove-maker

hand-, Hand-: ~schutz der hand guard; **~setzer der** *(Druckw.)* hand compositor; **~signiert** *Adj.* signed; **~skizze die** free-hand sketch; **~spiegel der** hand-mirror; **~spiel das** *(Fußball)* handball

Hand·stand der *(Turnen)* handstand; **einen ~ machen** do a handstand

Handstand·überschlag der *(Turnen)* handspring

Hand-: ~steuerung die a) *o. Pl.* manual operation *or* control; **b)** *(Apparatur)* manual control; **~streich der** *(bes. Milit.)* lightning *or* surprise attack; **in einem** *od.* **im ~streich** in a surprise *or* lightning attack; **~tasche die** handbag; **~teller der** palm [of the/one's hand]; **~trommel die** hand-drum

Hand·tuch das; *Pl.* **-tücher** towel; *(Geschirrtuch)* tea-towel; tea-cloth; **dieser Raum ist nicht mehr als ein ~** *(ugs.)* this room is nowhere near wide enough; **das ~ werfen** *od.* *(ugs.)* **schmeißen** *(Boxen, fig.)* throw in the towel

Handtuch·halter der towel-rail

hand-, Hand-: ~umdrehen *in* **im ~umdrehen** in no time at all; **~verlesen** *Adj.* hand-picked; **~vermittlung die** *(Fernspr.)* connection by the operator; **über ~vermittlung laufen** be connected by the operator; **~voll die; ~** *(auch fig.)* handful; **ein paar ~voll** a couple of handfuls; **~waffe die** hand weapon; **~wagen der** handcart; **~warm 1.** *Adj.* hand-hot; **2.** *adv.* **etw. ~warm waschen** wash sth. in hand-hot water; **~wäsche die** washing by hand; **diese Pullover kommen in die ~wäsche** these pullovers will have to be washed by hand

Handwerk das a) craft; *(als Beruf)* trade; **ein ~ ausüben/betreiben** carry on/ply a trade; **b)** *(Beruf)* **sein ~ kennen** *od.* **verstehen/beherrschen** know one's job; ⟨*tradesman*⟩ know/be master of one's trade;

jmdm. das ~ legen put a stop to sb.'s activities; **jmdm. ins ~ pfuschen** try to do sb.'s job for him/her; **c)** *o. Pl. (Berufsstand)* craft professions *pl.*

-handwerk das: Töpfer~/Bäcker~/Schuhmacher~: potter's/baker's/shoemaker's trade

Handwerker der; ~s, ~: tradesman; craftsman; **die ~ im Haus haben** have the workmen in; **er ist ein guter ~:** he's a good craftsman

Handwerkerschaft die; ~: skilled tradesmen *pl. or* craftsmen *pl.*

Handwerker·stand der artisan class

handwerklich *Adj.; nicht präd.* **a)** ⟨*training, skill, ability*⟩ as a craftsman; **ein ~er Beruf** a [skilled] trade; **b)** *(fig.)* technical

Handwerks-: ~beruf der [skilled] trade; **~betrieb der** workshop; **~bursche der** *(veralt.)* travelling journeyman *(arch.)*; **~kammer die** Chamber of Crafts; **~meister der** master craftsman; **~rolle die** register of qualified craftsmen; **~zeug das** tools *pl.*; *(fig.)* tools *pl.* of the trade

Hand·wörter·buch das concise dictionary

Hand·wurzel die wrist; carpus *(Anat.)*

Handwurzel·knochen der *(Anat.)* wristbone; carpal bone *(Anat.)*

Hand-: ~zeichen das a) sign [with one's hand]; *(eines Autofahrers)* hand signal; **darf ich die Betroffenen um Ihr ~zeichen bitten?** will those concerned please raise their hands; **b)** *(Abstimmung)* show of hands; **durch ~zeichen** by a show of hands; **~zeichnung die** drawing; *(Skizze)* sketch; **~zettel der** handbill; leaflet

hanebüchen ['ha:nəby:çn̩] **1.** *Adj.* outrageous. **2.** *adv.* outrageously; **~ lügen** tell the most outrageous lies

Hanf [hanf] **der; ~[e]s a)** *(Pflanze, Faser)* hemp; **b)** *(Samen)* hempseed

Hanf·anbau der growing *or* cultivation of hemp

hanfen, hänfen ['hɛnfn̩] *Adj.; nicht präd.* hempen; hemp

Hänfling ['hɛnflɪŋ] **der; ~s, ~e a)** *(Vogel)* linnet; **b)** *(abwertend)* weakling

Hanf-: ~seil das, ~strick der hempen *or* hemp rope

Hang [haŋ] **der; ~[e]s, Hänge** ['hɛŋə] **a)** *(Berg~)* slope; hillside/mountainside; *(Ski~)* slope; **das Haus am ~:** the house on the hillside; **das Haus ist an einen ~ gebaut** the house is built on a slope; **b)** *(Neigung)* tendency; **einen ~ zum Träumen/Lügen** *usw.* **haben** have a tendency to dream/lie *etc.*; **einen ~ haben, etw. zu tun** tend to do sth.; **c)** *(Turnen)* hang

Hangar ['haŋga:ɐ̯] **der; ~s, ~s** hangar

Hänge-: ~arsch der *(derb)* sagging backside *(coll.)*; **~backe die** flabby cheek; **~bauch der** paunch; **~bauch·schwein das** pot-bellied pig; **~boden der** false *or* drop ceiling; **~brücke die** suspension bridge; **~brust die, ~busen der** sagging breasts *pl.*; **~dach das** suspended roof; **~gleiter der** hang-glider; **~kleid das** tent dress; **~lampe die** pendant-light; drop-light

hangeln ['haŋl̩n] **1.** *itr. V.; meist mit sein* make one's way hand over hand; **an einem Seil über die Schlucht ~:** make one's way hand over hand along a rope over the ravine. **2.** *refl. V.* **sich aufwärts/abwärts ~:** climb up/down hand over hand

Hänge·matte die hammock

hangen ['haŋən] *(schweiz., landsch.) s.* ^{1}**hängen**

Hangen das; ~s *in* **mit ~ und Bangen** *(geh.)* in fear and trepidation

^{1}**hängen** ['hɛŋən] *unr. itr. V.; südd., österr., schweiz. mit sein* **a)** hang; **die Bilder ~ [schon]** the pictures are [already] up; **der Schrank hängt voller Kleider** the wardrobe is full of clothes; **der Weihnachtsbaum hängt voller Süßigkeiten** the Christmas tree is laden with sweets; **sein Zimmer hängt voller Plakate** the walls of his room are covered with posters; **an einem Faden ~:** be hanging by a thread; **die Nachbarn hingen aus den Fenstern** *(fig.)* the neighbours were hanging out of the windows; **b)** *(sich festhalten)* hang, dangle (**an** + *Dat.* from); **jmdm. am Hals ~:** hang round sb.'s neck; **der Junge hing an ihrem Arm** the boy hung on to her arm; *s. auch* **Rockzipfel; c)** *(erhängt werden)* hang; be hanged; **d)** *(an einem Fahrzeug)* be hitched *or* attached (**an** + *Dat.* to); **e)** *(herab~)* hang down; **bis auf den Boden ~:** hang down to the ground; **die Pflanzen ließen ihre Blätter ~:** the leaves of the plants drooped; **die Beine ins Wasser ~ lassen** let one's legs dangle in the water; **der Anzug hängt ihm am Leib** the suit hangs loosely on him; **f)** *(unordentlich sitzen)* **im Sessel ~** *(erschöpft, betrunken)* be *or* sit slumped in one's/the chair; *(flegelhaft)* lounge in one's/the chair; **g)** *(geh.: schweben, auch fig.)* hang (**über** + *Dat.* over); **h)** *(haften)* cling, stick (**an** + *Dat.* to); **ihre Augen hingen an seinen Lippen** *(fig.)* her eyes were fixed on his lips; **i)** *(fest~)* **sie hing mit dem Rock am Zaun/in der Fahrradkette** her skirt was caught on the fence/in the bicycle chain; **j)** *(ugs.: sich aufhalten, sein)* hang around *(coll.)*; **[schon wieder] am Radio/Telefon/vorm Fernseher ~:** have got the radio on [again]/be on the telephone [again]/be in front of the television [again]; **k)** *(sich nicht trennen wollen)* **an jmdm./etw. ~:** be very attached to sb./sth.; **am Geld/Leben ~:** love money/life; **l)** *(sich neigen)* lean; ⟨*road*⟩ slope to one side; **m)** *(ugs.: angeschlossen sein)* **an etw.** *(Dat.)* **~:** be on sth.; **n)** *(ugs.: nicht weiterkommen)* be stuck; **die Verhandlungen ~:** the talks are deadlocked; **o)** *(ugs.: zurück sein)* be behind; **p)** *(verschuldet sein)* **bei ihr hänge ich mit 2 000 DM** I owe her 2,000 marks; **q)** *(entschieden werden)* **an/bei jmdm./etw. ~:** depend on sb./sth.; **r)** *(Schach)* ⟨*man*⟩ be en prise; *(nicht beendet sein)* ⟨*game*⟩ be adjourned; **s)** *(ugs.: verbunden sein)* **etw. hängt an etw.** *(Dat.)* sth. involves sth.

^{2}**hängen 1.** *tr. V.* **a) etw. in/über etw.** *(Akk.)* **~:** hang sth. in/over sth.; **etw. an/auf etw.** *(Akk.)* **~:** hang sth. on sth.; **den Hörer in die Gabel ~:** replace the receiver; **b)** *(befestigen)* hitch up (**an** + *Akk.* to); couple on ⟨*railway carriage, trailer, etc.*⟩ (**an** + *Akk.* to); **c)** *(~ lassen)* hang; **seinen Arm aus dem Fenster ~:** put one's arm out of the window; **die Beine ins Wasser ~:** let one's legs dangle in the water; **d)** *(er~)* hang; **Tod durch Hängen** death by hanging; **mit Hängen und Würgen** by the skin of one's teeth; **e)** *(ugs.: aufwenden)* **an/in etw.** *(Akk.)* **~:** put ⟨*work, time, money*⟩ into sth.; spend ⟨*time, money*⟩ on sth.; **f)** *(ugs.: anschließen)* **jmdn./etw. an etw.** *(Akk.)* **~:** put sb./sth. on sth.; *s. auch* **Glocke a; Nagel b. 2.** *refl. V.* **a)** *(ergreifen)* **sich an etw.** *(Akk.)* **~:** hang on to sth.; **sich jmdm. an den Hals ~:** cling to sb.'s neck; **sich ans Telefon ~** *(fig. ugs.)* get on the telephone; **sich an den Wasserhahn ~** *(ugs. fig.)* turn the tap on and drink thirstily from it; **b)** *(sich festsetzen)* ⟨*smell*⟩ cling (**an** + *Akk.* to); ⟨*burr, hairs, etc.*⟩ cling, stick (**an** + *Akk.* to); **c)** *(anschließen)* **sich an jmdn. ~:** attach oneself to sb.; latch on to sb. *(coll.)*; **sie hängt sich zu sehr an mich** she clings to me too much; **d)** *(verfolgen)* **sich an jmdn./ein Auto ~:** follow *or (coll.)* tail sb./a car; **e)** *(binden)* **sich an jmdn./etw. ~:** get *or* become attached to sb./sth.; **sie hängt sich zu sehr an materielle Werte** she's too attached to material values

hängen|bleiben *unr. itr. V.; mit sein (ugs.)* **a)** *(festgehalten werden)* **[mit dem Ärmel** *usw.***] an/in etw.** *(Dat.)* **~:** get one's sleeve *etc.* caught on/in sth.; **der Angriff blieb im Mittelfeld hängen** *(fig.)* the attack broke down in mid-field; **sein Blick blieb an der Uhr hängen** *(fig.)* his gaze rested on the clock; **b)** *(verweilen)* get stuck *(coll.)*; **ich bin bei Freunden hängengeblieben** I got stuck talking to friends *(coll.)*; **c)** *(haften)* **an/auf etw.** *(Dat.)* **~:** stick to sth.; **das bleibt an mir hängen** *(fig.)* I've been stuck *or* landed with it *(coll.)*; **von dem Vortrag blieb [bei ihm] nicht viel hängen** *(fig.)* not much of the lecture stuck *(coll.)*; **ein Verdacht bleibt an ihr hängen** *(fig.)* suspicion rests on her; **d)** *(ugs.: sitzenbleiben)* stay down; have to repeat a year

hängend *Adj.* hanging; **die Hängenden Gärten der Semiramis** the Hanging Gardens of Babylon; **mit ~em Kopf** with head hanging; **mit ~er Zunge** *(fig.)* gasping for breath

hängen|lassen 1. *unr. tr. V.* **a)** *(vergessen)* **etw. ~:** leave sth. behind; **b)** *(ugs.: nicht helfen)* **jmdn. ~:** let sb. down. **2.** *unr. refl. V.* let oneself go; **laß dich nicht so hängen!** [you must] pull yourself together!

Hänge-: ~ohr das lop ear; **~partie die** *(Schach)* adjourned game; **~pflanze die** trailing plant

Hänger der; ~s, ~ a) *s.* **Anhänger b; b)** *s.* **Hängekleid; c)** *(weiter Mantel)* loose[-fitting] coat; tent coat

Hänge-: ~schrank der wall-cupboard; **~schultern** *Pl.* round shoulders

hängig *Adj.* **a)** *(schweiz. Rechtsspr.)* **~ sein** be in progress; continue; **ein ~er Prozeß** a trial that is in progress; **b)** *(fachspr.)* sloping; **in ~er Lage** on a slope *or* an incline

Hang·lage die hillside location; **in ~:** in a hillside location

Hängolin [hɛŋo'li:n] **das; ~s** *(salopp scherzh.) substance allegedly used in order to diminish sb.'s sex drive*

Hang-: ~täter der *(Rechtsspr.)* compulsive criminal; **~wind der** slope wind

Hannover [ha'no:fɐ] **(das); ~s** Hanover

Hannoveraner 1. der; ~s, ~ *(Einwohner, Pferd)* Hanoverian. **2.** *indekl. Adj.* Hanover; *s. auch* **Kölner**

hannoversch [ha'no:fɐʃ] *Adj.* Hanoverian; **im Hannoverschen** in the Hanover area

Hans [hans] **der; ~, Hänse** ['hɛnzə] **~ im Glück** lucky devil; *(Märchenfigur)* Hans in Luck; **~ Guckindieluft** dreamer; *(Märchenfigur)* Johnny-Head-in-Air; **jeder ~ findet seine Grete** every Jack shall have his Jill

Hansaplast Ⓦⓩ [hanza'plast] **das; ~[e]s** sticking plaster; Elastoplast **(P)**

Hänschen ['hɛnsçən] **das; ~s, ~: was ~ nicht lernt, lernt Hans nimmermehr** what you don't learn as a child, you'll never learn as an adult

Hans·dampf der; ~[e]s, ~e: ~ [in allen Gassen] Jack of all trades

Hanse ['hanzə] **die; ~** *(hist.)* Hanse; Hanseatic league

Hanseat [hanze'a:t] **der; ~en, ~en a)** citizen of a Hanseatic city; **ein typischer ~:** *someone with the dignified bearing regarded as typical of upper-class citizens of the Hanseatic cities;* **b)** *(hist.)* member of the Hanseatic League

hanseatisch *Adj.* Hanseatic

Hanse-: ~bund der *s.* **Hanse; ~kogge die** *(hist.)* Hansa cog

Hänselei die; ~, ~en a) *o. Pl.* teasing; **b)** *(Bemerkung)* teasing remark

hänseln ['hɛnzl̩n] *tr. V.* tease

Hanse·stadt die Hanseatic city

Hans·wurst der; ~[e]s, ~e a) *(dummer Mensch)* clown; **b)** *(Theater)* fool; hanswurst

Hans·wurstiade [hansvʊrs'tja:də] **die; ~, ~n a)** *(Scherz)* clowning; buffoonery; **b)** *(Theater)* harlequinade

Hantel ['hantl] **die; ~, ~n** *(Sport) (kurz)* dumb-bell; *(lang)* barbell
hanteln *itr. V.* exercise with dumb-bells/barbells
hantieren [han'ti:rən] *itr. V.* be busy; **sie hantierte mit einem Schraubenschlüssel an ihrem Auto** she was busy doing something to her car with a spanner
hapern ['ha:pɐn] *itr. V. (unpers.)* **a)** *(fehlen)* **es hapert an etw.** *(Dat.)* there's a shortage of sth.; **es hapert bei jmdm. an etw.** sb. is short of sth.; **ich wäre gerne mitgefahren, aber es hapert an der Zeit** I'd like to have gone, but I haven't got the time; **b)** *(nicht klappen)* **es hapert mit etw.** there's a problem with sth.; **bei ihr hapert es in Latein** she's poor at *or* weak in Latin
haploid [haplo'i:t] *Adj. (Biol.)* haploid
Häppchen ['hɛpçən] **das; ~s, ~ a)** [small] morsel; **b)** *(Appetithappen)* canapé
Happen ['hapn̩] **der; ~s, ~:** morsel; **einen ~ essen** have a bite to eat; **ein fetter ~** *(fig.)* a real plum
Happening ['hɛpənɪŋ] **das; ~s, ~s** happening
happig ['hapɪç] *Adj. (ugs.)* steep *(coll.)*; **~e Preise** fancy prices *(coll.)*; **das ist aber [ein bißchen] ~:** that's a bit much *(coll.)*
happy ['hɛpi] *(ugs.)* **1.** *Adj.; nicht attr.* happy. **2.** *adv.* happily
Happy-End ['hɛpi'|ɛnt] **das; ~[s], ~s** happy ending
Harakiri [hara'ki:ri] **das; ~[s], ~s** hara-kiri *no art.*; **politisches ~ begehen** *(fig.)* commit political suicide; **gesellschaftliches ~ begehen** *(fig.)* ruin one's reputation
Härchen ['hɛ:ɐ̯çən] **das; ~s, ~:** little *or* tiny hair; **die feinen ~ in ihrem Nacken** the fine down on her neck
Hard cover ['ha:d'kʌvə] **das; ~ ~s, ~ ~s** *(Buchw.)* hardback
Hardtop ['ha:dtɔp] **das** *od.* **der; ~s, ~s** hardtop
Hardware ['ha:dwɛə] **die; ~, ~s** *(DV)* hardware
Harem ['ha:rɛm] **der; ~s, ~s** *(auch ugs. scherzh.)* harem
Harems-: ~dame die lady of the harem; **~wächter der** guardian of the harem
hären ['hɛ:rən] *Adj.; nicht präd. (geh.)* [made] of hair *postpos.*; hair
Häresie [hɛre'zi:] **die; ~, ~n** [-i:ən] heresy
Häretiker [hɛ're:tikɐ] **der; ~s, ~:** heretic
häretisch *Adj.* heretical
Harfe ['harfə] **die; ~, ~n** harp
harfen 1. *itr. V.* play the harp; harp. **2.** *tr. V.* **ein Lied** *usw.* **~:** play a song *etc.* on the harp
Harfenist der; ~en, ~en, Harfenistin die; ~, ~nen harpist; harp-player
Harfen·spiel das harp-playing; *(Musik)* harp music
Harke ['harkə] **die; ~, ~n** rake; **jmdm. zeigen, was eine ~ ist** *(fig. salopp)* give sb. what for *(coll.)*
harken *tr. V.* rake
Harlekin ['harleki:n] **der; ~s, ~e** harlequin
Harlekinade [harleki'na:də] **die; ~, ~n** *s.* **Hanswurstiade**
Harm [harm] **der; ~[e]s** *(geh. veralt.)* distress; *(über Verlorenes)* grief
härmen ['hɛrmən] *refl. V. (geh.)* grieve **(um** over)
harm·los 1. *Adj.* **a)** *(ungefährlich)* harmless; slight ⟨*injury, cold, etc.*⟩; mild ⟨*illness*⟩; safe ⟨*medicine, bend, road, etc.*⟩; **eine ~e Grippe** a mild bout of flu; **b)** *(arglos)* innocent; harmless ⟨*fun, pastime, etc.*⟩. **2.** *adv.* **a)** *(ungefährlich)* harmlessly; **b)** *(arglos)* innocently; **ich bin ganz ~ hingegangen** I went there quite innocently; **er hatte nur ~ gefragt** he only asked an innocent *or* inoffensive question; **ganz ~ tun** act innocent
Harmlosigkeit die; ~ a) *(Ungefährlichkeit)* harmlessness; *(einer Krankheit)* mildness; *(eines Medikamentes)* safety; **b)** *(Arglosigkeit, harmloses Verhalten)* innocence; **in aller ~:** in all innocence
Harmonie [harmo'ni:] **die; ~, ~n** *(auch fig.)* harmony
Harmonie-: ~lehre die; *o. Pl.* theory of harmony; **~musik die** music for wind instruments
harmonieren *itr. V.* **a)** *(zusammenpassen)* harmonize; go together; match; **mit etw. ~:** harmonize *or* go together with sth.; **b)** *(miteinander auskommen)* get on well
Harmonik [har'mo:nɪk] **die; ~:** harmony
Harmonika [har'mo:nika] **die; ~, ~s** *od.* **Harmoniken** harmonica
Harmonika-: ~spieler der harmonica player; **~tür die** folding door; accordion door
harmonisch 1. *Adj.* **a)** *(Musik)* harmonic ⟨*tone, minor*⟩; **b)** *(wohlklingend, zusammenpassend, übereinstimmend)* harmonious; **c)** *(Math.)* **~e Teilung** harmonic division. **2.** *adv.* **a)** *(Musik)* harmonically; **b)** *(wohlklingend, zusammenpassend, übereinstimmend)* harmoniously; **~ zusammenleben** live together in harmony
harmonisieren *tr. V.* **a)** *(Musik)* harmonize; **b)** *(in Einklang bringen)* coordinate; **etw. mit etw. ~** *(Wirtsch.)* bring sth. into line with sth.
Harmonisierung die; ~, ~en *(Wirtsch.)* harmonization
Harmonium [har'mo:nɪ̯ʊm] **das; ~s, Harmonien** harmonium
Harn [harn] **der; ~[e]s, ~e** *(Med.)* urine; **~ lassen** *(ugs.)* pass water; urinate
Harn-: ~blase die bladder; **~drang der** desire to urinate *or* pass water
Harnisch ['harnɪʃ] **der; ~s, ~e a)** armour; **b) in ~ sein** be in a furious temper; **jmdn. in ~ bringen** get sb.'s hackles up; make sb. see red; **in ~ geraten** get up in arms **(über +** *Akk.* over, about)
harn-, Harn-: ~lassen das urination *no pl., no art.*; **Schmerzen beim ~lassen haben** find it painful to urinate *or* pass water; **~leiter der** *(Med.)* ureter; **~röhre die** *(Anat.)* urethra; **~säure die** *(Med., Chemie)* uric acid; **~stein der** *(Med.)* urinary calculus; **~stoff der** *(Med., Chemie)* urea; **~treibend 1.** *Adj.* diuretic; **2.** *adv.* **~treibend wirken** have a diuretic effect; **~vergiftung die** *(Med.)* uraemia; **~wege** *Pl. (Med.)* urinary tract *sing.*
Harpune [har'pu:nə] **die; ~, ~n** harpoon
Harpunier [harpu'ni:ɐ̯] **der; ~s, ~e** harpooner
harpunieren 1. *tr. V.* harpoon. **2.** *itr. V.* throw/fire the harpoon
Harpyie [har'py:jə] **die; ~, ~n** *(Myth.)* harpy
harren ['harən] *itr. V. (geh.)* **jmds./einer Sache** *od.* **auf jmdn./etw. ~:** wait for *or* await sb./sth.; *(fig.)* await sb./sth.; **der Dinge ~, die da kommen sollen** wait and see what happens
harsch [harʃ] **1.** *Adj.* **a)** *(vereist)* crusted ⟨*snow*⟩; **b)** *(barsch)* harsh. **2.** *adv.* harshly
Harsch der; ~[e]s crusted *or* hard snow
harschen *itr. V.* ⟨*snow*⟩ freeze [over]
harschig *Adj.* ⟨*snow*⟩ frozen hard [on top]
Harsch·schnee der *s.* **Harsch**
hart [hart]; **härter** ['hɛrtɐ], **härtest...** ['hɛrtəst...] **1.** *Adj.* **a)** hard ⟨*wood, bread, cheese, etc.*⟩; **~e Eier** hard-boiled eggs; **Eier ~ kochen** hard-boil eggs; **~ gefroren** frozen solid; **~ werden** go hard; harden; ⟨*cheese etc.*⟩ go hard; *s. auch* **Brocken b; Nuß a; Schädel a; b)** *(abgehärtet)* tough; **~ im Nehmen sein** *(Schläge ertragen können)* be able to take a punch; *(Enttäuschungen ertragen können)* be able to take the rough with the smooth; **c)** *(schwer erträglich)* hard ⟨*work, life, fate, lot, times*⟩; tough ⟨*childhood, situation, job*⟩; harsh ⟨*reality, truth*⟩; bitter ⟨*disappointment*⟩; heavy, severe ⟨*loss*⟩; severe ⟨*hardship*⟩; **jmds. Geduld** *usw.* **auf eine ~e Probe stellen** sorely try sb.'s patience *etc.*; **ein ~er Schlag für jmdn. sein** be a heavy *or* severe blow for sb.; **es war ~ für ihn, darauf zu verzichten** it was hard for him to go without; **es ist sehr ~ für ihn, daß er nicht mitkommen darf** it's very hard on him that he can't come too; **d)** *(streng)* severe, harsh ⟨*penalty, punishment, judgement*⟩; tough ⟨*measure, law, course*⟩; hard, harsh ⟨*words*⟩; harsh ⟨*treatment*⟩; severe, hard ⟨*features*⟩; **durch eine ~e Schule gegangen sein** have been through a hard school; **~ gegen jmdn. sein** be hard on sb.; **e)** *(heftig)* hard, violent ⟨*impact, jolt*⟩; heavy ⟨*fall*⟩; violent ⟨*argument*⟩; **f)** *(rauh)* rough ⟨*game, opponent*⟩; **g)** *(stabil)* hard ⟨*currency*⟩; **h)** *(kalkig)* hard ⟨*water*⟩; **i)** hard, severe ⟨*winter, frost*⟩; harsh ⟨*accent, light, colour, contrast*⟩; hard ⟨*consonant, drink, drug, pornography*⟩; **j)** *(Physik)* hard ⟨*rays etc.*⟩. **2.** *adv.* **a) ~ schlafen/sitzen** sleep on a hard bed/sit on a hard chair; **b)** *(mühevoll)* ⟨*work*⟩ hard; **es kommt mich ~ an** it is hard for me; **c)** *(streng)* severely; harshly; **~ durchgreifen** take tough measures; **jmdn. ~ anfassen** be tough with sb.; **d)** *(heftig)* **~ aneinandergeraten** have a violent argument; have a real set-to *(coll.)*; **jmdm. ~ zusetzen, jmdn. ~ bedrängen** press sb. hard; **jmdn. ~ treffen** hit sb. hard; **es geht ~ auf ~:** the chips are down; **e)** *(nahe)* close **(an +** *Dat.* to); **die Kugel ging ~ an seinem Kopf vorbei** the bullet just missed his head; **das ist ~ an der Grenze der Legalität/des Machbaren** that is very close to being illegal/that's nearing the limits of what's possible; **~ am Wind segeln** *(Seemannsspr.)* sail near *or* close to the wind; **~ auf ein Ziel zuhalten** *(Seemannsspr.)* hold steady on course for sth.
hart·bedrängt *Adj. (präd. getrennt geschrieben)* hard-pressed
Hart·beton der granolithic concrete
Härte ['hɛrtə] **die; ~, ~n a)** *(auch Physik)* hardness; **b)** *o. Pl. (Widerstandsfähigkeit)* toughness; **c)** *(schwere Belastung)* hardship; **eine soziale ~:** a case of social hardship; **d)** *o. Pl. (Strenge)* severity; **e)** *o. Pl. (Heftigkeit) (eines Aufpralls usw.)* force; *(eines Streits)* violence; **f)** *(Rauheit)* roughness; **g)** *o. Pl. (Stabilität)* hardness; **h)** *(von Wasser)* hardness; **i)** *(von Licht, Farbe)* harshness; *(von Frost)* hardness
Härte-: ~ausgleich der *(Sozialw.)* hardship payment; **~fall der a)** case of hardship; **b)** *(ugs.: Person)* hardship case; **~fonds der** hardship fund; **~grad der** degree of hardness; **~mittel das** hardener
härten 1. *tr. V.* harden; harden, temper ⟨*steel*⟩; cure ⟨*plastic*⟩. **2.** *itr. V.* harden
härter *s.* **hart**
Härter der; ~s, ~ *(Chemie)* hardener
Härte·skala die *(Mineral.)* scale of hardness; hardness scale
härtest... *s.* **hart**
Hart·faser·platte die hardboard
hart-, Hart-: ~gefroren *Adj. (präd. getrennt geschrieben)* frozen; frozen hard *pred.*; **~gekocht** *Adj.* **a)** hard-boiled ⟨*egg*⟩; **b)** *s.* **~gesotten; ~geld das** coins *pl.*; small change; **~gesotten** *Adj.* **a)** *(gefühllos)* hard-bitten; hard-boiled; **b)** *(unbelehrbar)* hardened; **~gummi das** hard rubber; **~herzig 1.** *Adj.* hard-hearted; **2.** *adv.* hard-heartedly; **~herzigkeit die; ~:** hard-heartedness; **~holz das** hardwood; **~käse der** hard cheese; **~laub·gewächs das** *(Bot.)* sclerophyll [plant]; sclerophyllous plant; **~löten** *tr., itr. V.* hard-solder; **~metall das** hard metal; **~näckig** [~nɛkɪç] **1.** *Adj.* **a)** *(eigensinnig)* obstinate; stubborn; **b)** *(ausdauernd)* persistent; dogged; inveterate ⟨*liar*⟩; stubborn, dogged ⟨*resistance*⟩; persistent ⟨*questioning, ques-*

tioner〉; c) (langwierig) stubborn 〈illness, stain〉; 2. adv. a) (eigensinnig) obstinately; stubbornly; b) (ausdauernd) persistently; doggedly; ~näckigkeit die; ~ a) (Eigensinn) obstinacy; stubbornness; b) (Ausdauer) persistence; doggedness; c) (Langwierigkeit) stubbornness; ~packung die cardboard packet; ~papier das (Technik) laminated paper; ~pappe die fibreboard; ~platz der (Sport) (Tennis) hard court; (Fußball) asphalt pitch; ~schalig [~ʃa:lıç] Adj. hardshell; hard-shelled; thick-skinned 〈apple, pear, etc.〉; ~umkämpft Adj. (präd. getrennt geschrieben) bitterly contested

Härtung die; ~, ~en hardening; (von Stahl auch) tempering; (von Kunststoffen) curing

Hart- ~ware die (fachspr.) household article; ~waren household goods; ~weizen·grieß der semolina; ~wurst die dry sausage

Harz [ha:ɐ̯ts] **das; ~es, ~e** resin

harzen 1. itr. V. exude resin. **2.** tr. V. resin; resinate 〈wine〉

Harzer der; ~s, ~, Harzer Käse der; ~ ~s, ~ ~: Harz [Mountain] cheese

Harzer Roller der; ~ ~s, ~ ~ a) s. Harzer Käse; **b)** (Kanarienvogel) Harz mountain roller

Harz·geruch der smell of resin

harzig Adj. **a)** resinous; **b)** (schweiz.: zähflüssig) slow-moving 〈traffic, queue〉

Harz·säure die resin acid

Hasard [ha'zart] **das; ~s: ~ spielen** (auch fig.) gamble

Hasardeur [hazar'dø:ɐ̯] **der; ~s, ~e** (abwertend) gambler

Hasard·spiel das a) (Glücksspiel) game of chance; **b)** (Wagnis) gamble

Hasch [haʃ] **das; ~s** (ugs.) hash (coll.)

Haschee [ha'ʃe:] (Kochk.) **das; ~s, ~s** hash

[1]haschen (veralt.) **1.** tr. V. catch. **2.** itr. V. **nach etw. ~:** make a grab for sth.; **nach Komplimenten/Beifall ~** (fig.) fish or angle for compliments/applause

[2]haschen itr. V. (ugs.) smoke [hash] (coll.)

Haschen das; ~s tag

Häschen ['hɛ:sçən] **das; ~, ~:** bunny

Hascher der; ~s, ~ (ugs.) hash-smoker (coll.)

Häscher ['hɛʃɐ] **der; ~s, ~** (geh. veralt.) pursuer

Hascherl ['haʃɐl] **das; ~s, ~n** (südd., österr. ugs.) **armes ~!** poor thing or soul!; (Kind) poor little thing or soul!

Haschisch ['haʃıʃ] **das od. der; ~[s]** hashish

Haschmich ['haʃmıç] **in einen ~ haben** (salopp) have a screw loose (coll.)

Hase ['ha:zə] **der; ~n, ~n a)** hare; (männlicher ~) hare; buck; **ängstlich wie ein ~:** timid as a mouse; **ein alter ~ sein** (ugs.) be an old hand; **falscher ~** (Kochk.) meat loaf; **da liegt der ~ im Pfeffer** (ugs.) that's the real trouble; **sehen/wissen wie der ~ läuft** (ugs.) see/know which way the wind blows; **mein Name ist ~** (ugs. scherzh.) I'm not saying anything; **b)** (landsch.) s. **Kaninchen**

Hasel-: ~busch der hazel [tree]; ~huhn das hazel grouse or hen; ~kätzchen das hazel catkin; ~nuß die a) hazel-nut; b) hazel [tree]; ~[nuß]·strauch der hazel [tree]

hasen-, Hasen-: ~braten der roast hare; ~fuß der (spöttisch abwertend) coward; chicken (sl.); ~füßig Adj. (spöttisch abwertend) cowardly; ~herz das s. ~fuß; ~jagd die hare shoot; **auf ~jagd gehen** go on a hare-shoot; go hare-shooting; ~klein das; ~s trimmings pl. of hare; ~panier in **das ~panier ergreifen** take to one's heels; ~pfeffer der (Kochk.) marinaded and stewed trimmings pl. of hare; ~rein Adj. (Jagdw.) steady from hare; **er/das ist nicht ganz ~rein** (fig.) there's something fishy (coll.) about him/it; ~scharte die (Med.) harelip

Häsin ['hɛ:zın] **die; ~, ~nen** doe [hare]

Haspel ['haspl̩] **die; ~, ~n** (Technik) **a)** (für Garn) reel; bobbin; (für ein Seil, Kabel) drum; **b)** (Seilwinde) windlass

haspeln 1. tr. V. wind. **2.** itr. V. (ugs.: hastig reden) gabble

Haß [has] **der; Hasses** hate, hatred (**auf** + Akk., **gegen** of, for); **~ auf** od. **gegen jmdn. empfinden** feel hatred of or for sb.; **sich** (Dat.) **jmds. ~ zuziehen** incur sb.'s hatred

hassen tr., itr. V. hate; s. auch **Pest**

hassens·wert Adj. hateful; odious

haß·erfüllt 1. Adj. filled with hatred or hate postpos. **2.** adv. **jmdn. ~ ansehen** look at sb. with [one's] eyes full of hatred or hate

Haß·gefühl das feeling of hatred

häßlich ['hɛslıç] **1.** Adj. **a)** ugly; **~ wie die Nacht** as ugly as sin (coll.); **b)** (gemein) nasty; hateful; **~ zu jmdm. sein** be mean or hateful to sb.; **das war ~ von dir** that was mean or nasty of you; **c)** (unangenehm) terrible (coll.), awful 〈weather, cold, situation, etc.〉. **2.** adv. **a)** 〈dress〉 unattractively; **b)** (gemein) nastily; hatefully; **~ von jmdm. sprechen** be mean or nasty about sb.; **c)** (unangenehm) terribly (coll.); awfully

Häßlichkeit die; ~, ~en a) o. Pl. (Aussehen) ugliness; **b)** o. Pl. (Gesinnung) meanness; nastiness; hatefulness; **c)** (Äußerung) mean remark

haß-, Haß-: ~liebe die love-hate relationship; ~tirade die (abwertend) tirade of hatred or hate; ~verzerrt Adj. twisted with hatred or hate postpos.

hast [hast] 2. Pers. Sg. Präsens v. **haben**

Hast die; ~: haste; **etw. in** od. **mit größter ~ tun** do sth. in great haste; **ohne ~:** unhurriedly; without hurrying or haste

haste ['hastə] (ugs.) = **hast du; [was] ~ was kannste** as fast as he/you/they etc. can/could; **~ was, biste was** money talks

hasten itr. V.; mit sein hurry; hasten

hastig 1. Adj. hasty; hurried. **2.** adv. hastily; hurriedly; **sein Essen ~ herunterschlingen** gobble [down] one's food; **nur nicht so ~!** not so fast!

hat [hat] 3. Pers. Sg. Präsens v. **haben**

Hätschelei die; ~, ~en (abwertend) **a)** ~[en] fondling; caressing; **b)** o. Pl. (das Verwöhnen) pampering

Hätschel·kind das pampered child; (fig.) darling

hätscheln ['hɛtʃl̩n] tr. V. **a)** (liebkosen) fondle; caress; **b)** (verwöhnen) pamper; (fig.) lionize; **c)** (sich widmen) cherish 〈idea, hope, etc.〉; nurse 〈pain etc.〉

hatschen ['ha:tʃn̩] itr. V.; mit sein (bayr., österr. ugs.) **a)** (schlendern) stroll; saunter; **b)** (hinken) hobble; limp; **c)** (mühselig gehen) trudge

hatschi [ha'tʃi:] Interj. atishoo; atchoo; **~ machen** (Kinderspr.) sneeze

hatte ['hatə] 1. u. 3. Pers. Sg. Prät. v. **haben**

hätte ['hɛtə] 1. u. 3. Pers. Sg. Konjunktiv II v. **haben**

Hat-Trick, Hattrick ['hættrık] **der; ~s, ~s a)** (Fußball, Handball) three successive goals by the same player in the same half; **b)** (Sport) hat trick

Hatz [hats] **die; ~, ~en a)** (Hetzjagd, auch fig. ugs.) hunt; **b)** (ugs., bes. bayr.: Eile, Streß) mad rush

hatzi [ha'tsi:] s. **hatschi**

Hau [hau] **in einen ~ haben** (salopp) have a screw loose (coll.)

Häubchen ['hɔypçən] **das; ~s, ~:** s. **Haube a, e**

Haube ['haubə] **die; ~, ~n a)** bonnet; (einer Krankenschwester) cap; **unter die ~ kommen** (ugs. scherzh.) get hitched (coll.); **unter der ~ sein** (ugs. scherzh.) be married; **jmdn. unter die ~ bringen** (ugs. scherzh.) marry sb. off; **b)** (Kfz-W.) bonnet (Brit.); hood (Amer.); **c)** s. **Trocken~; d)** (südd., österr.: Mütze) [woollen] cap; **e)** (Zool.) crest; **f)** (Bedeckung) cover; (über Teekanne, Kaffeekanne, Ei) cosy

Hauben-: ~lerche die crested lark; ~taucher der great crested grebe

Haubitze [hau'bıtsə] **die; ~, ~n** (Milit.) howitzer; **voll wie eine ~ sein** (derb) be as pissed as a newt (coarse)

Hauch [haux] **der; ~[e]s, ~e** (geh.) **a)** (Atem, auch fig.) breath; **b)** (Luftzug) breath of wind; breeze; **c)** (leichter Duft) delicate smell; waft; **d)** (dünne Schicht) [gossamer-] thin layer; **ein ~ von Reif** a [thin] film of hoar-frost; **e)** (Atmosphäre) air; feeling; **f)** (Anflug) hint; trace; **der ~ eines Lächelns** a ghost or hint of a smile

hauch·dünn 1. Adj. gossamer-thin 〈material, dress〉; wafer-thin, paper-thin 〈layer, slice, majority〉; **ein ~er Sieg** (fig.) the narrowest of victories. **2.** adv. **etw. ~ auftragen** apply sth. very sparingly; **etw. ~ schneiden** cut sth. wafer-thin or into wafer-thin slices

hauchen 1. itr. V. breathe (**gegen, auf** + Akk. on). **2.** tr. V. (auch fig.: flüstern) breathe; **jmdm. etw. ins Ohr ~:** breathe sth. in sb.'s ear

hauch-, Hauch-: ~fein Adj. extremely fine; ~laut der (Phon.) aspirate; ~zart Adj. extremely delicate; gossamer-thin

Hau·degen der: [alter] ~: old soldier or warhorse

Haue ['hauə] **die; ~, ~n a)** (südd., österr.: Hacke) hoe; **b)** o. Pl. (ugs.: Prügel) a hiding (coll.); **..., sonst gibt's ~:** ... or you'll get a hiding

hauen 1. unr. tr. V. **a)** (ugs.: schlagen) belt; clobber (coll.); beat; **jmdn. windelweich/grün und blau ~:** beat sb. black and blue; **jmdn. zu Brei ~** (salopp) beat sb.'s brains in (sl.); **b)** (ugs.: auf einen Körperteil) belt (coll.); hit; (mit der Faust auch) smash (sl.); punch; (mit offener Hand auch) slap; smack; **jmdn. ins Gesicht ~:** hit/belt/slap sb. in the face; **jmdm. das Heft um die Ohren ~:** clout (coll.) or hit sb. round the ears with the exercise-book; **c)** (ugs.: hineinschlagen) knock; **einen Nagel in die Wand ~:** knock a nail into the wall; **d)** (herstellen) carve 〈figure, statue, etc.〉 (**in** + Akk. in); cut, chop 〈hole〉; (mit einem Hammer) knock 〈hole〉; **Stufen in den Fels ~:** cut steps in the rock; **e)** (mit einer Waffe schlagen) **jmdn. aus dem Sattel/vom Pferd ~:** knock sb. out of the saddle/off his/her horse; **das haut mich vom Stuhl** od. **aus dem Anzug** (salopp) I'm [absolutely] staggered (coll.); **f)** (salopp: schleudern) sling (coll.); fling; (nachlässig schreiben) stick (coll.), scrawl 〈comments, signature〉 (**in** + Akk. in, **unter** + Akk. underneath); **jmdm. eine 6 ins Zeugnis ~** (fig.) stick a 6 on sb.'s report (coll.); **g)** (landsch.: fällen) fell; cut down; **h)** (Bergbau) cut 〈coal, ore〉. **2.** unr. itr. V. **a)** (ugs.: prügeln) **hau doch nicht schon wieder!** don't belt me again!; **er haut immer gleich** he's quick to hit out; **b)** (auf einen Körperteil) belt; hit; (mit der Faust auch) punch; (mit offener Hand auch) slap; smack; **jmdm. auf die Schulter ~:** slap or clap sb. on the shoulder; **jmdm. ins Gesicht ~:** belt/slap sb. in the face; **c)** (ugs.: auf/gegen etw. schlagen) thump; **mit der Faust auf den Tisch ~:** thump the table [with one's fist]; **auf die Tasten ~:** thump on the keys; **auf den Putz** od. **Pudding ~** (fig. salopp) run riot; **d)** mit sein (ugs.: stoßen) bump; **mit dem Kopf/Bein gegen etw. ~:** bang or hit or bump one's head/leg against sth.; **e)** mit sein (ugs.: auftreffen) **auf etw.** (Akk.) **~:** hit sth. **3.** unr. refl. V. **a)** (ugs.: sich prügeln) have a punch-up (coll.) or a fight; fight; **b)** (salopp: sich setzen, legen) fling or throw oneself; **sich ins Bett ~:** hit the sack (sl.)

Hauer der; ~s, ~ a) (Bergmannsspr.) faceworker; **b)** (Jägerspr.) tusk; (fig.) fang; **c)** (südd., österr.: Winzer) wine-grower

Häufchen ['hɔyfçən] **das; ~s, ~:** [small or

little] pile *or* heap; **wie ein ~ Unglück** *od.* **Elend aussehen/dasitzen** *(ugs.)* look a/sit there looking a picture of misery; **nur noch ein ~ Unglück** *od.* **Elend sein** *(ugs.)* be nothing but a small bundle of misery

Haufe ['haufə] **der; ~ns, ~n** *(veralt.) s.* **Haufen**

häufeln ['hɔyfl̩n] *tr. V.* **a)** *(Gartenbau)* earth *or* hill up; **b)** *(zu Häufchen schichten)* pile *or* heap up

Haufen ['haufn̩] **der; ~s, ~ a)** heap; pile; **ein ~ Erde/trockenes Stroh** *od.* **trockenen Strohs** a heap *or* pile of earth/dry straw; **etw. zu ~ aufschichten** stack sth. up in piles; **alles auf einen ~ werfen** throw everything in a heap; **der Hund hat da einen ~ gemacht** *(ugs.)* the dog has done his business there *(coll.)*; **etw. über den ~ werfen** *(ugs.)* *(aufgeben)* chuck sth. in *(coll.)*; *(zunichte machen)* mess sth. up; **jmdn. über den ~ fahren/rennen** *(ugs.)* knock sb. down; run sb. over; **jmdn. über den ~ schießen** *od.* **knallen** *(ugs.)* gun *or* shoot sb. down *(coll.)*; **b)** *(ugs.: große Menge)* heap *(coll.)*; pile *(coll.)*; load *(coll.)*; **ein ~ Arbeit/Bücher** a load *or* heap *or* pile of work/books *(coll.)*; loads *or* heaps *or* piles of work/books *(coll.)*; **ein ~ Unsinn** a load of rubbish *or* nonsense *(coll.)*; **ein ~ Geld** loads of money *(coll.)*; **einen ~ Geld machen** make a packet *(coll.)*; **c)** *(Ansammlung von Menschen)* crowd; **so viele Idioten auf einem ~** *(ugs.)* so many idiots in one place; **d)** *(Gruppe)* crowd *(coll.)*; bunch *(coll.)*; **e)** *(Soldatenspr.)* troop

häufen ['hɔyfn̩] **1.** *tr. V.* heap, pile (**auf** + *Akk.* on to); *(aufheben)* hoard ‹*money, supplies*›. **2.** *refl. V.* *(sich mehren)* pile up; *s. auch* **gehäuft**

haufen-, Haufen-: ~dorf das Haufendorf *(irregular conglomerate village)*; **~weise** *Adv. (ugs.)* **~weise Geld ausgeben/Eis essen** spend loads of money/eat heaps *or* loads of ice cream *(coll.)*; **~wolke die** *(Met.)* cumulus [cloud]

häufig ['hɔyfɪç] **1.** *Adj.* frequent. **2.** *adv.* frequently; often

Häufigkeit die; ~, ~en frequency

Häufigkeits·zahl die, Häufigkeits·ziffer die frequency

Häuflein ['hɔyflain] **das; ~s, ~ a)** *(kleine Menge) s.* **Häufchen; b)** *(kleine Gruppe)* handful

Häufung die; ~, ~en increasing frequency; **in dieser ~:** in these large numbers; *(so oft)* with this high frequency

Haupt [haupt] **das; ~[e]s, Häupter** ['hɔyptɐ] **a)** *(geh.: Kopf)* head; **bloßen** *od.* **entblößten ~es** with one's head bared; **erhobenen ~es** with one's head [held] high; **gesenkten ~es** with head bowed; **gekrönte Häupter** crowned heads; **an ~ und Gliedern** completely; **zu jmds. Häupten** *(in Kopfhöhe)* at head height; *(bei einem Liegenden)* at sb.'s head; **jmdn. aufs ~ schlagen** vanquish sb.; **b)** *(geh.: wichtigste Person)* head

haupt-, Haupt-: ~abnehmer der main *or* principal *or* chief customer; **der ~abnehmer eines Produktes** the main buyer of a product; **~achse die a)** *(beim Fahrzeug)* main axle; **b)** *(Geom.)* principal axis; **~aktion die** *s.* **~- und Staatsaktion; ~aktionär der** principal shareholder; **~akzent der** *(Phon.)* main *or* primary stress; *(fig.)* main emphasis; **~altar der** high altar; **~amtlich 1.** *Adj.* full-time; **2.** *adv.* **~amtlich tätig sein** work full-time *or* on a full-time basis; **~angeklagte der/die** *(Rechtsw.)* main *or* principal defendant; **~anschluß der** *(Fernspr.)* main exchange line; **~arbeit die** main part of the work; **~argument das** main *or* principal argument; **~augenmerk das** closest attention; **sein ~augenmerk galt ...** (+ *Dat.*) he paid closest attention to ...; **~bahnhof der** main station; **Amsterdam ~bahnhof** Amsterdam Central; **~belastungs·zeuge der** *(Rechtsw.)* principal *or* main *or* chief prosecution witness; **~beruf der** main occupation *or* job; **er ist im ~beruf Schreiner** his main occupation *or* job is that of carpenter; **~beruflich 1.** *Adj.* **seine ~berufliche Tätigkeit** his main occupation; **2.** *adv.* **er ist ~beruflich als Elektriker tätig** his main occupation is that of electrician; **~beschäftigung die** main occupation; **~buch das** *(Kaufmannsspr.)* ledger; **~darsteller der** *(Theater, Film)* leading man; male lead; **~darstellerin die** *(Theater, Film)* leading lady; female lead; **~deck das** main deck; **~eingang der** main entrance; **~einnahme·quelle die** main *or* principal source of income; *(eines Staates)* main *or* principal source of revenue

Häuptel ['hɔyptl̩] **das; ~s, ~[n]** *(südd., österr.)* head *(of cabbage/lettuce)*; **ein ~ Salat/Kohl** a [head of] lettuce/cabbage

Haupt·erbe der principal heir

Hauptes·länge die *in* **jmdn. um ~ überragen** *(geh.)* be a head taller than sb

Haupt-: ~fach das a) *(Universität)* main subject; major; **etw. im ~fach studieren** study sth. as one's main subject; **b)** *(Schule)* main subject; **~farbe die** main *or* principal colour; **~fehler der** main *or* principal *or* chief mistake/*(im Charakter)* fault/*(in einer Theorie, einem Argument)* flaw; **~feind der** main *or* principal *or* chief enemy; **~feld das** *(Sport)* [main] bunch; **~feldwebel der** *(Milit.)* **a)** ≈ staff sergeant *(Brit.)*; ≈ sergeant first class *(Amer.)*; **b)** *(hist.)* company sergeant-major; **~figur die** main *or* principal character; **~film der** main feature *or* film; **~forderung die** main *or* principal *or* chief demand; **~frage die** main question; *(Angelegenheit)* main question *or* issue; **~gang der a)** main corridor; **b)** *s.* **~gericht; ~gas·leitung die** gas main; **~gebäude das** main building; **~gegenstand der** main *or* principal *or* chief subject; **~gericht das** main course; **~geschäft das a)** *(Laden)* main branch; **b)** *(größter Umsatz)* peak sales *pl.*; *(wichtigster Geschäftszweig)* main line; **~geschäfts·stelle die** head office; **~geschäfts·straße die** main shopping street; **~geschäfts·zeit die** peak shopping hours *pl.*; **~gewicht das** main emphasis; **~gewinn der** first *or* top prize; **~grund der** main *or* principal *or* chief reason; **~hahn der** mains stopcock; **~interesse das** main interest; **~kampf·linie die** *(Milit.)* front [line]; **~kasse die** main cash desk; **~katalog der** main catalogue; **~last die** main burden; **~lehrer der** *(veralt.)* head teacher; **~leitung die** *(Gas-, Wasserleitung)* main; *(Stromleitung)* main[s *pl.*]; **~leute** *s.* **~mann**

Häuptling ['hɔyptlɪŋ] **der; ~s, ~e** chief[tain]; *(iron. abwertend)* bigwig *(coll.)*

haupt-, Haupt-: ~macht die *(veralt.)* main body [of the army]; **~mahlzeit die** main meal; **~mangel der** main *or* principal defect; **~mann der;** *Pl.* **~leute a)** *(Milit.)* captain; **b)** *(hist.)* leader; **~masse die** bulk; **~merkmal das** main *or* principal *or* chief characteristic; **~mieter der** [main] tenant; **~motiv das a)** *(Gegenstand)* main *or* principal motif; **b)** *(Beweggrund)* main *or* principal *or* chief motive; **~nahrung die** staple *or* main food; **~nenner der** *(Math.)* common denominator; **~person die** central figure; **sie will immer und überall die ~person sein** *(fig.)* she always wants to be the centre of everything *or* of attention; **~portal das** main portal; **~post die, ~post·amt das** main post office; **~probe die** *s.* **Generalprobe a; ~problem das** main *or* chief problem; **~produkt das** main *or* chief product; **~punkt der** main point; **~quartier das** *(Milit., auch fig.)* headquarters *sing. or pl.*; **~quelle die** main *or* principal *or* primary source; **~redner der** main *or* principal speaker; **~reise·zeit die** high season; peak [holiday] season; **~rolle die** leading *or* main role; lead; **die ~rolle spielen** play the leading role *or* the lead (**in** + *Dat.* in); **die ~rolle [in** *od.* **bei etw.] spielen** *(fig.)* play the leading role [in sth.]; **~runde die** *(Fußball)* main round; **~sache die** main *or* most important thing; **~sache, du bist gesund** *(ugs.)* the main thing is, you're in good health; **in der ~sache** mainly; in the main; **~sächlich 1.** *Adv.* mainly; principally; chiefly; **2.** *Adj.; nicht präd.* main; principal; chief; **~saison die** high season; **~satz der a)** *(Sprachw.)* main clause; *(alleinstehend)* sentence; **b)** *(Musik)* first subject; **c)** *(grundlegender Satz)* first *or* basic principle; **~schalter der a)** *(Elektrot.)* mains switch; **b)** *(in der Bank, Post)* main counter; **~schiff das** *(Archit.)* nave; **~schlag·ader die** aorta; **~schlüssel der** master key; pass key; **~schrift·leiter der** *(veralt.) s.* **Chefredakteur; ~schul·abschluß der** ≈ secondary school leaving certificate; **~schuld die** main share of the blame; **die ~schuld an etw.** *(Dat.)* **haben** bear the main part of the blame for sth.; **~schuldige der/die** person mainly to blame; *(an einem Verbrechen)* main *or* chief offender; **~schule die** ≈ secondary modern school; **~schüler der** ≈ secondary modern school pupil; **~schul·lehrer der** ≈ secondary modern school teacher; **~schwierigkeit die** main *or* chief difficulty; **~segel das** *(Seemannsspr.)* mainsail; **~seminar das** *(Hochschulw.)* advanced seminar; **~sicherung die** *(Elektrot.)* mains fuse; **~sitz der** head office; headquarters *pl.*; **~sorge die** main worry; **~stadt die** capital [city]; **~städter der, ~städterin die** citizen *or* inhabitant of the capital; **~städtisch** *Adj.* metropolitan; **~straße die a)** *(wichtigste Geschäftsstraße)* high *or* main street; **b)** *(Durchgangsstraße)* main road; **~strecke die** *(Eisenb.)* main line; **~stütze die** main support; *(fig.)* mainstay; **~sünde die** *(kath. Rel.)* cardinal sin; **~tätigkeit die** main *or* principal activity; **~teil der** major part; **~thema das** main topic *or* theme; *(Musik)* main theme; **~ton der a)** *(Musik)* principal note; **b)** *s.* **~akzent; ~treffer der** *s.* **~gewinn; ~tribüne die** *(Sport)* main stand; **~übel das** main *or* chief evil; **~- und Staatsaktion die** *in* **eine ~- und Staatsaktion aus etw. machen** make a big thing *or* a meal of sth. *(coll.)*; **~unterschied der** main *or* principal *or* chief difference; **~ursache die** main *or* principal *or* chief cause; **~verantwortliche der/die** person mainly responsible; **~verdiener der** principal *or* main wage-earner; bread-winner; **~verhandlung die** *(Rechtsw.)* main hearing

Haupt·verkehr der bulk of the traffic

Hauptverkehrs-: ~straße die main road; **~zeit die** rush hour

Haupt-: ~versammlung die *(Wirtsch.)* shareholders' meeting; **~verwaltung die** head office; **~wache die** main police station; **~wacht·meister der a)** *(Polizist) s.* **Polizeihauptwachtmeister; b)** *(hist.) s.* **~feldwebel b; ~werk das a)** *(eines Künstlers)* major *or* most important work; **b)** *(zentrales Werk mit mehreren Teilbetrieben)* main works *sing. or pl.*; **c)** *(an der Orgel)* great organ; **~wohn·sitz der** main place of residence; **~wort das** *(Sprachw.)* noun; **~zeuge der** principal *or* main *or* chief witness; **~zug der a)** *(Eisenbahnw.)* scheduled train; **b)** *(wichtigste Eigenschaft)* main *or* principal feature; **~zweck der** main *or* chief purpose *or* aim

hau ruck ['hau'rʊk] *Interj.* heave[-ho]

Haus [haus] **das; ~es, Häuser** ['hɔyzɐ] **a)**

house; *(Firmengebäude)* building; **~ an ~ wohnen** be next-door neighbours; **~ an ~ mit jmdm. wohnen** live next door to sb.; **er ist gerade aus dem ~ gegangen** he has just gone out; **im ~ spielen** play indoors; **kommt ins ~, es regnet** come inside, it's raining; **Herrn X, im ~e** *(auf Briefen)* to Mr X *(living in the same block of flats, working in the same firm, etc.)*; **das ~ Gottes** *(geh.)* the house of God; **das Weiße ~:** the White House; **~ und Hof** house and home; **jmdm. ins ~ stehen** *(ugs.)* be in store for sb.; *s. auch* **öffentlich 1; b)** *(Heim)* home; **jmdm. das ~ verbieten** not allow sb. in one's *or* the house; **etw. ins ~/frei ~ liefern** deliver sth. to sb.'s door/free of charge; **das ~ auf den Kopf stellen** *(ugs.)* turn the place upside down; **außer ~[e] sein/essen** be/eat out; **ist Ihre Frau im ~[e]?** is your wife at home?; **nach ~e** home; **zu ~e** at home; **fühlt euch wie zu ~e** make yourselves at home; **sich zu ~e fühlen** *(fig.)* feel at home; **schon dreißig, und er wohnt noch zu ~e** he's already thirty and he's still living with his parents; **bei ihnen zu ~e** in their house/flat; *(in ihrer Heimat)* where they come from; **dieser Brauch ist in Holstein zu ~e** this custom comes from Holstein; **zu ~e spielen** *(Sport)* play at home; *s. auch* **daheim a; das ~ hüten** stay at home *or* indoors; **jmdm. das ~ einrennen** *(ugs.)* be constantly on sb.'s doorstep; **jmdm. ins ~ schneien** *(ugs.)* descend on sb.; **auf einem Gebiet/in etw.** *(Dat.)* **zu ~e sein** *(ugs.)* be at home in a field/in sth.; **c)** *(Theater)* theatre; *(Publikum)* house; **das große/kleine ~:** the large/small theatre; **vor vollen/ausverkauften Häusern spielen** play to full *or* packed houses; **d)** *(Gasthof, Geschäft)* **das erste ~ am Platze** the best shop of its kind/hotel in the town/village *etc.*; **eine Spezialität des ~es** a speciality of the house; **e)** *(Firma)* firm; business house; **das ~ Meyer** the firm of Meyer; **f)** *(geh.: Parlament)* **das Hohe ~:** the House; **beide Häuser [im Parlament]** both Houses [of Parliament]; **Hohes ~!** ≈ Mr Speaker, Sir; **g)** *(geh.: Familie)* household; **der Herr/die Dame des ~es** the master/lady of the house; **aus gutem ~e kommen** come from a *or* be of good family; **der Herr im eigenen ~ sein** be master in one's own house; **Grüße von ~ zu ~:** regards from all of us to all of you; **von ~[e] aus** *(von der Familie her)* by birth; *(eigentlich)* really; actually; **h)** *(~halt)* household; **jmdm. das ~ führen** keep house for sb.; **jmdn. ins ~ nehmen** take sb. in and look after him/her; **i)** *(Dynastie)* house; **das ~ Tudor/[der] Hohenzollern** the House of Tudor/Hohenzollern; **j)** *(ugs.: die ~bewohner)* occupants *pl.* [of the house]; **das ganze ~:** the whole house; **k)** *(ugs. scherzh.: Mensch)* **ein gelehrtes/lustiges** *usw.* **~:** a scholarly/amusing *etc.* sort *(coll.)*; **l)** *(Schnecken~)* shell; **m)** *(Astrol.)* house

haus-, Haus-: ~altar der domestic altar; **~angestellte der/die** domestic servant; **~antenne die** external aerial *(Brit.) or (Amer.)* antenna; **~anzug der** *(für Männer)* leisure suit; *(für Frauen)* pyjama suit; **~apotheke die** medicine cabinet; **~arbeit die a)** housework; **b)** *(Schulw.)* item of homework; **~arbeiten aufhaben** *(ugs.)* have homework *sing.*; **~arrest der a)** house arrest; **b)** *(in der Familie)* **er bestraft seinen Sohn mit ~arrest** he punishes his son by keeping him in; **mein Bruder hat ~arrest** my brother is being kept in; **~arzt der a)** family doctor; **b)** *(eines Hotels, Heims)* resident doctor; **~aufgabe die** piece of homework; **~aufgaben aufhaben** *(ugs.)* have homework *sing.*; **~aufsatz der** homework essay; **~backen 1.** *Adj.* plain; unadventurous, boring ⟨*clothes*⟩; **2.** *adv.* ⟨*dress*⟩ unadventurously; **~ball der** [private] dance *(held at sb.'s house)*; **~bar die a)** *(Möbelstück)* cocktail cabinet; **b)** *(kleine Bar)* [home] bar; **~bau der** house-building; **beim ~bau** when building a/one's house; **mit dem ~bau beginnen** start building a/one's house; **~besetzer der** squatter; **~besetzung die** *(Vorgang)* squatting; *(Ergebnis)* squat; **~besitzer der** house-owner; *(Vermieter)* landlord; **~besitzerin die** house-owner; *(Vermieterin)* landlady; **~besorger der, ~besorgerin die** *(österr.) s.* **~meister[in]; ~besuch der** house-call; **~bewohner der** occupant [of the house]; **~boot das** houseboat; **~brand der;** *o. Pl.* **a)** *(Material)* domestic fuel; **b)** *(Prozeß)* domestic heating; **~bursche der** page-boy

Häuschen ['hɔysçən] **das; ~s, ~: a)** little *or* small house; **b) [ganz** *od.* **rein] aus dem ~ sein** *(ugs.)* be [completely] over the moon *(coll.)*; **[ganz** *od.* **rein] aus dem ~ geraten** *od.* **fahren** *(ugs.)* go wild with excitement; **jmdn. aus dem ~ bringen** *(ugs.)* get sb. wildly excited; **c)** *(ugs.: Toilette)* privy

haus-, Haus-: ~dame die housekeeper; **~detektiv der** house detective; **~diener der** domestic servant; **~drachen der** *(ugs. abwertend)* dragon *(coll.)*; **~durchsuchung die** *(österr.) s.* **~suchung; ~ecke die** corner of the house; **~eigen** *Adj.* **der ~eigene Kindergarten** the company's/hotel's *etc.* own kindergarten; **das Hotel hat einen ~eigenen Swimming-pool/Strand** the hotel has its own swimming-pool/[private] beach; **~eigentümer der** *s.* **~besitzer; ~einfahrt die a)** drive[way] [of the house]; **b)** *(österr.) s.* **~eingang; ~eingang der** entrance [to the house]

hausen *itr. V.* **a)** *(ugs. abwertend: wohnen)* live; **b)** *(ugs. abwertend: Verwüstungen anrichten)* **[furchtbar] ~:** cause *or* wreak havoc; **wie die Wandalen ~:** behave like vandals; **c)** *(schweiz.: sparen)* be economical

Häuser-: ~block der block [of houses]; **~makler der** estate agent; **~meer das** mass of houses; **~reihe die** row of houses; *(aneinandergebaut)* terrace [of houses]

Haus-: ~fassade die house-front; **~flagge die** *(Seew.)* house-flag; **~flur der** hall[way]; entrance-hall; *(im Obergeschoß)* landing

Haus·frau die a) housewife; **b)** *(südd., österr.) s.* **~besitzerin**

Hausfrauen-: ~art die *in* **nach** *od.* **auf ~art** home-made-style *attrib.*; **~pflicht die;** *meist Pl.* housewifely duty

hausfraulich *Adj.* housewifely; **ihre ~en Fähigkeiten** her abilities as a housewife

Haus·freund der a) friend of the family; family friend; **b)** *(verhüll.: Liebhaber)* manfriend *(euphem.)*

Haus·friede[n] der *(in der Familie)* domestic peace; *(zwischen Hausbewohnern)* good relationships *pl.* between the tenants

Hausfriedens·bruch der *(Rechtsw.)* trespass

haus-, Haus-: ~gans die domestic goose; **~gast der** resident; guest; **~gebrauch der** domestic use; **das reicht für den ~gebrauch** *(ugs.)* it's good enough to get by *(coll.)*; **Spielst du Klavier? – Ja, aber nur für den ~gebrauch** Do you play the piano? – Yes, but only well enough to get by *(coll.)*; **~gehilfin die** [home] help; **~geist der a)** *(Gespenst)* [resident] ghost; **b)** *(scherzh.: ~angestellte)* **unser guter ~geist** our faithful housekeeper; **~gemacht** *Adj.* home-made; **~gemeinschaft die a)** *(gemeinsamer ~halt)* household; **in einer ~gemeinschaft mit jmdm. leben** live together with sb.; **b)** *(Bewohner eines Hauses)* occupants *pl.* of the block; **~genosse der** *(veralt.)* member of the household; **~gerät das a)** *o. Pl.* *(veralt.)* household articles *pl.*; **b)** *s.* **Haushalts·gerät**

Haus·halt der a) household; **einen ~ gründen/auflösen** set up home/break up a household; **b)** *(Arbeit im ~)* housekeeping; **jmdm. den ~ führen** keep house for sb.; **im ~ helfen** help with the housework; **c)** *(Politik)* budget

-haushalt der *(bes. Biol., Med.)* balance

haus|halten *unr. itr. V.* **a)** *(sparsam wirtschaften)* be economical **(mit** with); **mit seinen Kräften ~:** conserve one's strength; **b)** *(veralt.: den Haushalt führen)* keep house

Haushälterin die; ~, ~nen housekeeper

haushälterisch 1. *Adj.* economical. **2.** *adv.* **~ mit etw. umgehen** be economical with sth.; use sth. economically

haushalts-, Haushalts-: ~artikel der household article; **billige ~artikel** cheap household articles *or* goods; **~auflösung die** house clearance; **bei einer ~auflösung** when a house/flat is cleared; **~ausgleich der** *(Politik)* **den ~ausgleich garantieren** guarantee a balanced budget; **einen ~ausgleich herbeiführen** balance the budget; **~buch das** housekeeping book; **~debatte die** *(Politik)* budget debate; **~defizit das** budgetary deficit; **~frage die** budgetary question *or* issue; **~führung die** housekeeping; **~geld das;** *o. Pl.* housekeeping money; **~gerät das** household appliance; **~gesetz das** *(Amtsspr.)* budget legislation; **~hilfe die** home help; **~jahr das a)** *(Rechnungsjahr)* financial year; **b)** *(Lehrzeit in einem Haushalt)* **sie machte ein ~jahr** she spent a year with a family, learning how to keep house; **~kasse die** housekeeping money; **die ~kasse war leer** there was no housekeeping money left; **diese alte Schachtel dient uns als ~kasse** we use this old box to keep the housekeeping money in; **~mittel** *Pl.* budgetary funds; **~packung die** family pack; **~plan der** budget; **~politik die** budgetary policy; **~politisch 1.** *Adj.; nicht präd.* related to budgetary policy *postpos.*; **~politische Erwägungen** considerations of budgetary policy; **2.** *adv.* **~politisch gesehen** from the point of view of the budget; **~volumen das** total budget; **~waage die** kitchen scales *pl.*; **~waren** *Pl.* household goods

Haushaltung die a) *s.* **Haushalt a; b)** *(Haushaltsführung)* housekeeping

Haushaltungs-: ~kosten *Pl.* housekeeping costs; **~vorstand der** head of the household

haus-, Haus-: ~herr der a) *(Familienoberhaupt)* head of the household; **b)** *(als Gastgeber)* host; **c)** *(Rechtsspr.) (Eigentümer)* owner; *(Mieter)* occupier; **d)** *(südd., österr.) s.* **~besitzer; e)** *(Sportjargon)* **die ~herren** the hosts; the home team *sing.*; **~herrin die a)** *(Familienoberhaupt)* lady of the house; **b)** *(als Gastgeberin)* hostess; **c)** *(südd., österr.) s.* **~besitzerin; ~hoch 1.** *Adj.* ⟨*flames/waves etc.*⟩ as high as a house; *(fig.)* overwhelming ⟨*superiority etc.*⟩; **die ~hohe Favoritin** the hot favourite; **2.** *adv.* **~hoch türmten sich die Wellen** the waves were mountainous; *(fig.)* **~hoch gewinnen/jmdn. ~hoch schlagen** win hands down/beat sb. hands down; **jmdm. ~hoch überlegen sein** be vastly superior to sb.; **~huhn das** domestic chicken; **~hund der** domestic dog

hausieren *itr. V.* **[mit etw.] ~:** hawk [sth.]; peddle [sth.]; **mit einer Idee ~ [gehen]** *(ugs. abwertend)* hawk an idea around; **„Hausieren verboten"** 'no hawkers'

Hausierer der; ~s, ~: pedlar; hawker

haus-, Haus-: ~intern 1. *Adj.* internal ⟨*regulations, purposes, information*⟩; ⟨*agreement, custom*⟩ within the company; **2.** *adv.* internally; within the company; **~jacke die** casual [wrapover] jacket *(worn at home)*; **~jurist der** firm's lawyer; company lawyer; **¹~kapelle die** private chapel; **²~ka-**

pelle die resident band; **~katze die** domestic cat; **~kleid das** house dress; **~konzert das** concert given at home; **~lehrer der** private tutor

häuslich ['hɔyslɪç] **1.** *Adj.* **a)** *nicht präd.* domestic ⟨*bliss, peace, affairs, duties, etc.*⟩; **am ~en Kaminfeuer** at one's own fireside; *s. auch* **Herd a**; **b)** *(das Zuhause liebend)* home-loving. **2.** *adv.* **sich [bei jmdm./irgendwo] ~ niederlassen** *od.* **einrichten** *(ugs.)* make oneself at home [in sb.'s house/somewhere]

Häuslichkeit die; ~: domesticity

Hausmacher-: ~art die *in* **nach ~art** home-made-style *attrib.*; **~wurst die** home-made sausage

Haus-: ~macht die *(hist.)* allodium; *(fig.)* power base; **~mädchen das** [home] help

Haus·mann der *man who stays at home and does the housework; (Ehemann)* househusband

Hausmanns·kost die plain cooking

Haus-: ~mantel der housecoat; **~märchen das** folk tale; **die märchen der Brüder Grimm** Grimms' Fairy Tales; **~marke die a)** *(Wein, Sekt)* house wine; **b)** *(ugs.: bevorzugtes Getränk)* usual *or* favourite tipple *(coll.)*; **c)** *(Markenfabrikat einer Firma)* own brand; **~maus die** house mouse; **~meier der** *(hist.)* mayor of the palace; **~meister der, ~meisterin die a)** caretaker; **b)** *(schweiz.) s.* **~besitzer[in]**; **~mitteilung die a)** *(im Büro)* [internal] memo; **b)** *(für Kunden)* company newsletter; **~mittel das** household remedy; **~musik die** music at home; **~musik machen** play music at home; **~mutter die** house-mother; **~mütterchen das** *(ugs. scherzh.)* little housewife; **~nummer die** house number; **ihre ~nummer** the number of her house; **~ordnung die** house rules *pl.*; **~partei die** *(österr.)* tenant; **~postille die** *(hist.) collection of religious and devotional sayings and stories for the family; (fig. ugs.)* organ; **~putz der** spring-clean; *(regelmäßig)* clean-out; **beim ~putz helfen** help with the regular cleaning-out; **~putz halten** *od.* **machen** spring-clean the house

Haus·rat der household goods *pl.*

Hausrat·versicherung die [household *or* home] contents insurance

Haus-: ~recht das *(Rechtsw.) right of a householder or owner of a property to forbid sb. entrance or order sb. to leave;* **von seinem ~recht Gebrauch machen** forbid sb. entrance/order sb. to leave; **~rind das** domestic ox; **~sammlung die** house-to-house *or* door-to-door collection; **~schaf das** domestic sheep; **~schlachtung die** home slaughtering; **aus eigener ~schlachtung stammen** be home-slaughtered; **~schlüssel der** front-door key; house-key; **~schneiderin die** visiting seamstress; **~schuh der** slipper; **~schwamm der** *(Pilz)* dry rot; **~schwein das** domestic pig

Hausse ['ho:s(ə)] **die; ~, ~n** *(Börsenw.)* rise [in prices]; *(fig.)* boom; **~ haben** rise [on the Stock Exchange]; **auf ~ spekulieren** bull; speculate for a rise

Haus·segen der house blessing *(devotional inscription placed in a house);* **bei ihnen hängt der ~ schief** *(ugs. scherzh.)* they've been having a row

Haussier [(h)o'si̯e:] **der; ~s, ~s** *(Börsenw.)* bull

Haus·stand der household; **einen [eigenen] ~stand gründen** set up home [on their own]; **sie führt einen eigenen ~stand** she lives independently

Haussuchung die; ~, ~en house search

Haussuchungs·befehl der search warrant

Haus-: ~telefon das internal telephone; **~tier das a)** pet; **b)** *(Nutztier)* domestic animal; **~tochter die** *young girl living with a family in order to learn how to keep house;* **~tor das** front entrance; **~tür die** front door; **etw. direkt vor der ~tür haben** *(ugs. fig.)* have sth. on one's doorstep; **~tyrann der** *(ugs.)* tyrant [in one's own home]; **~vater der a)** *(in einem Heim)* house-father; *(in einer Jugendherberge)* warden; **b)** *(veralt.: Familienvater)* paterfamilias; **~verbot das** ban on entering the house/pub/restaurant *etc.*; **~verbot haben/bekommen** be banned [from the house/pub/restaurant *etc.*]; **jmdm. ~verbot erteilen** ban sb. [from the house/pub/restaurant *etc.*]; **~versammlung die** *(DDR)* tenants' meeting; **~verwalter der** manager [of the block]; **~verwaltung die** management [of the block]; **~wand die** [house] wall; **~wart der** *(landsch.)* caretaker; **~wesen das;** *o. Pl. (veralt.)* household; **~wirt der** landlord; **~wirtin die** landlady

Haus·wirtschaft die; *o. Pl.* **a)** domestic science and home economics; **b)** *(DDR Landw.)* **individuelle** *od.* **persönliche ~:** *co-operative farmer's personal holding of land, buildings livestock, and equipment*

hauswirtschaftlich 1. *Adj.; nicht präd.* domestic; **~e Kenntnisse** knowledge of domestic matters. **2.** *adv.* **~ interessiert/begabt** interested/talented in domestic matters

Hauswirtschafts-: ~lehrerin die home economics and domestic science teacher; **~leiterin die** housekeeper; **~schule die** college of domestic science and home economics

Haus-: ~zelt das ridge tent; **~zins der** *(südd., schweiz.) s.* **¹Miete a**

Haut [haut] **die; ~, Häute** ['hɔytə] **a)** skin; **sich** *(Dat.)* **die ~ abschürfen** graze oneself; **viel ~ zeigen** *(ugs. scherzh.)* show a lot of bare flesh *(coll.)*; **naß bis auf die ~:** soaked to the skin; wet through; **nur noch ~ und Knochen sein** *(ugs.)*, **nur noch aus ~ und Knochen bestehen** *(ugs.)* be nothing but skin and bone; **seine eigene ~ retten** save one's own skin; **seine ~ zu Markte tragen** *(ugs.)* risk one's neck *(coll.)*; **seine ~ so teuer wie möglich verkaufen** *(ugs.)* sell oneself as dearly as possible; **sich seiner ~** *(Gen.)* **wehren** *(ugs.)* stand up for oneself; **aus der ~ fahren** *(ugs.)* go up the wall *(coll.)*; **es ist zum Aus-der-~-Fahren** it's enough to drive *or* send you up the wall *(coll.)*; **er/sie kann nicht aus seiner/ihrer ~ heraus** *(ugs.)* a leopard cannot change its spots *(prov.)*; **sich in seiner ~ nicht wohl fühlen** *(ugs.)* feel uneasy; *(unzufrieden sein)* feel discontented [with one's lot]; **sich in seiner ~ wohl fühlen** *(ugs.)* feel contented [with one's lot]; **ich möchte nicht in deiner ~ stecken** *(ugs.)* I shouldn't like to be in your shoes *(coll.)*; **mit heiler ~ davonkommen** *(ugs.)* get away with it; **jmdm. mit ~ und Haar[en] verfallen sein** *(ugs.)* be head over heels in love with sb.; **sich einer Aufgabe** *(Dat.)* **mit ~ und Haar[en] verschreiben** *(ugs.)* devote oneself completely *or* wholeheartedly to a task; **jmdm. unter die ~ gehen** *(ugs.)* get under sb.'s skin *(coll.)*; **b)** *(Fell)* skin; *(von größerem Tier auch)* hide; **auf der faulen ~ liegen** *(ugs.)* sit around and do nothing; **sich auf die faule ~ legen** *(ugs.)* sit back and do nothing; **c)** *(Schale)* skin; **d)** *(dünne Schicht, Bespannung)* skin; **e)** *(Mensch)* **eine gute/ehrliche ~:** a good/honest sort *(coll.)*

Haut-: ~abschürfung die graze; **~arzt der** skin specialist; dermatologist; **~atmung die** *(Med., Zool.)* cutaneous respiration; **~ausschlag der** [skin-]rash

Häutchen ['hɔytçən] **das; ~s, ~ a)** *s.* **Haut c:** piece of skin; **b)** *s.* **Haut d:** thin skin

Haut·creme die skin cream

Haute Couture [(h)o:tku'ty:ɐ̯] **die; ~ ~:** haute couture

häuten ['hɔytn̩] **1.** *tr. V.* skin, flay ⟨*animal*⟩; skin ⟨*tomato, almond, etc.*⟩. **2.** *refl. V.* shed its skin/their skins; ⟨*snake*⟩ shed *or* slough its skin

haut·eng *Adj.* skin-tight

Hautevolee [(h)o:tvo'le:] **die; ~** *(abwertend)* upper crust *(coll.)*

haut-, Haut-: ~falte die fold [of skin]; **~farbe die** [skin] colour; **wegen seiner ~farbe** because of the colour of his skin; **~farben** *Adj.* skin-coloured; flesh-coloured; **~freundlich** *Adj.* kind to the/one's skin *pred.*

-häutig [-'hɔytɪç] *Adj.* -skinned

haut-, Haut-: ~jucken das itching *no indef. art.*; **~krankheit die** skin disease; **~nah 1.** *Adj.* **a)** *(unmittelbar)* immediate ⟨*contact*⟩; eyeball-to-eyeball ⟨*confrontation*⟩; **b)** *(ugs.: packend, anschaulich)* realistic and gripping ⟨*description*⟩; **c)** *(Anat.)* close to *or* immediately below the skin *postpos.*; **2.** *adv.* **a)** *(unmittelbar)* **mit etw. ~nah in Berührung/Kontakt kommen** come into very close contact with sth.; **jmdn. ~nah decken** *od.* **bewachen** *(Sport Jargon)* mark sb. very tightly *or* closely; *(sehr eng)* **~nah tanzen** dance very close together; **b)** *(ugs.: packend, anschaulich)* **etw. ~nah beschreiben** describe sth. in a realistic and gripping way; **~öl das** body oil; **~pflege die** skin care; **~pilz der** fungus parasitic on the skin; cutaneous fungus *(Med.)*; **~reizung die** skin irritation; **~schere die** cuticle scissors *pl.*; **~schicht die** layer of skin; **~schonend** *Adj.* kind to the/one's skin *pred.*; **~transplantation die** *(Med.)* skin graft; **~typ der** skin type

Häutung die; ~, ~en a) *s.* **häuten 1:** skinning; flaying; **b)** *(das Sichhäuten)* **Schlangen machen viele ~en durch** snakes shed *or* slough their skin many times; **eine Eidechse bei der ~:** a lizard shedding its skin

haut·verträglich *Adj.* kind to the/one's skin *pred.*

¹Havanna [ha'vana] **(das); ~s** Havana

²Havanna die; ~, ~[s], Havanna·zigarre die Havana [cigar]

Havarie [hava'ri:] **die; ~, ~n** *(Seew., Flugw., österr. auch: ~ eines Autos)* accident; *(Schaden)* damage *no indef. art.*; average *(Ins.)*; *(fig.)* breakdown

havarieren *itr. V. (Seew., Flugw.)* ⟨*aircraft*⟩ crash; ⟨*ship*⟩ have an accident; **zwei Militärmaschinen/***(österr.)* **Autos havarierten** two military planes/cars collided; **ein havariertes Schiff** a damaged ship

Havarist der; ~en, ~en *(Seew.)* **a)** *(Schiff)* damaged ship; **b)** *(Eigentümer)* owner of a/the damaged ship

Hawaii [ha'vai̯] **(das); ~s** Hawaii

Hawaii-: ~gitarre die Hawaiian guitar; **~-Inseln** *Pl.* Hawaiian Islands

hawaiisch *Adj.* Hawaiian

Haxe die; ~, ~n *s.* **Hachse**

H-Bombe ['ha:-] **die** H-bomb

H-Dur ['ha:-] **das; ~** *(Musik)* B major; *s. auch* **A-Dur**

he [he:] *Interj. (ugs.)* **a)** *(Zuruf, Ausruf)* hey; **~ [du], komm mal her!** hey [you], come here!; **b)** *(zur Verstärkung einer Frage)* eh

Hearing ['hɪərɪŋ] **das; ~[s], ~s** *(bes. Politik)* hearing

Heb·amme die midwife

Hebe-: ~balken der, ~baum der lever; **~bühne die** hydraulic lift; **~figur die** *(Eis-, Rollkunstlauf)* lift

Hebel ['he:bl̩] **der; ~s, ~** *(auch Griff, Physik)* lever; **den ~ ansetzen** position the lever; **da müssen wir den ~ ansetzen** *(fig.)* that's where we've got to start *(coll.)*; **alle ~ in Bewegung setzen** *(ugs.)* move heaven and earth; **am längeren ~ sitzen** *(ugs.)* have the whip hand

Hebel-: ~arm der *(Physik)* lever arm; **~gesetz das** *(Physik)* principle of the lever; **~griff der** *(Ringen)* lever [hold]; **~kraft die** leverage; **~wirkung die** leverage

heben ['he:bn̩] **1.** *unr. tr. V.* **a)** *(nach oben bewegen)* lift; raise; raise ⟨*baton, camera, glass*⟩; **eine Last ~:** lift a load; **die Hand/den Arm ~:** raise one's hand/arm; **schlurft nicht, hebt die Füße!** pick your feet up!; **100 kg/einen Rekord ~** *(Sport)* lift 100 kg./a record weight; **die Stimme ~** *(geh.)* raise one's voice; **einen ~** *(ugs.)* have a drink; **b)** *(an eine andere Stelle bringen)* lift; **jmdn. auf die Schulter/von der Mauer ~:** lift sb. [up] on to one's shoulders/[down] from the wall; **c)** *(heraufholen)* dig up ⟨*treasure etc.*⟩; raise ⟨*wreck*⟩; **d)** *(verbessern)* raise, improve ⟨*standard, level*⟩; increase ⟨*turnover, self-confidence*⟩; improve ⟨*mood*⟩; enhance ⟨*standing*⟩; boost ⟨*morale*⟩; **e)** *(unpers.)* **es hebt jmdm. den Magen** sb.'s stomach heaves; **es hebt mich, wenn ich das sehe** it turns me over to see it *(coll.)*. **2.** *unr. refl. V.* **a)** *(geh.: sich recken, sich er~)* rise; **sich auf die Zehenspitzen ~:** stand on tiptoe; **b)** *(hochgehen, hochsteigen)* rise; ⟨*curtain*⟩ rise, go up; ⟨*mist, fog*⟩ lift; **sich ~ und senken** rise and fall; ⟨*sea, chest*⟩ rise and fall, heave; **d)** *(sich verbessern)* ⟨*mood*⟩ improve; ⟨*trade*⟩ pick up; ⟨*standard, level*⟩ rise, improve, go up; **e)** *(geh.: emporragen)* rise [up]

Heber der; ~s, ~ a) *(Technik)* jack; **b)** *(Chemie)* pipette; **c)** *(Sport: Gewicht~)* weightlifter

-hebig [-he:bɪç] *(Verslehre)* ~-footed

Hebräer [he'brɛ:ɐ] **der; ~s, ~, Hebräerin die; ~, ~nen** Hebrew

Hebraicum [he'bra:ikʊm] **das; ~s** qualifying examination in Hebrew *(taken by theology students)*; **das ~ haben** have passed the Hebrew examination

hebräisch *Adj.* Hebrew

Hebung die; ~, ~en a) *(Bergung)* **die ~ eines Schiffes** the raising of a ship; **bei der ~ des Schatzes ...:** when the treasure is/was dug up ...; **b)** *o. Pl. (Verbesserung)* raising; improvement; **zur ~ des Selbstvertrauens/der Moral** to improve sb.'s self-confidence/morale; **c)** *(Geol.)* uplift; **d)** *(Verslehre)* stressed syllable

Hechel ['hɛçl̩] **die; ~, ~n** *(Landw.)* card; hackle; heckle

Hechelei die; ~, ~en *(ugs. abwertend)* backbiting *no pl.*; *(Klatsch)* gossip *no pl.*

¹hecheln 1. *itr. V. (ugs. abwertend)* gossip. **2.** *tr. V. (Landw.)* card; hackle; heckle

²hecheln *itr. V.* pant [for breath]

Hecht [hɛçt] **der; ~[e]s, ~e a)** pike; **der ~ im Karpfenteich sein** *(ugs.)* be a new broom; be a live wire full of new ideas; *(die erste Rolle spielen)* be the kingpin; **b)** *(ugs.: Bursche)* **ein toller ~:** an incredible fellow; **c)** *(Tabaksqualm)* fug *(coll).*

hechten *itr. V.; mit sein* dive headlong; make a headlong dive; *(schräg nach oben)* throw oneself sideways; *(Schwimmen)* perform *or* do a racing dive; *(vom Sprungturm)* perform *or* do a pike-dive; *(Turnen)* do a long-fly

Hecht-: ~rolle die *(Turnen)* piked roll; **~sprung der a)** *(Turnen)* Hecht vault; **b)** *(Schwimmen)* racing dive; *(vom Sprungturm)* pike-dive; **~suppe die** *in* **es zieht wie ~suppe** *(ugs.)* there's a terrible draught *(coll.)*

¹Heck [hɛk] **das; ~[e]s, ~e** *od.* **~s a)** *(Schiffs~)* stern; **b)** *(Flugzeug~)* tail; **im ~ der Maschine** at the rear of the plane; **c)** *(Auto~)* rear; back

²Heck das; ~[e]s, ~e *(nordd.)* gate

Heck·antrieb der *(Kfz-W.)* rear-wheel drive

Hecke die; ~, ~n a) hedge; **b)** *(wildwachsend)* thicket

Hecken-: ~landschaft die landscape of fields and hedgerows; **~rose die** dogrose; **~schere die** hedge shears *pl.*; *(elektrisch)* hedge trimmer; **~schütze der** sniper

heck-, Heck-: ~fenster das rear *or* back window; **~flosse die** tail-fin; **~lastig** [~lastɪç] **1.** *Adj.* tail-heavy; **2.** *adv.* **das Auto reagiert ~lastig** the car tends to be tail-heavy

Heckmeck ['hɛkmɛk] **der; ~s** *(ugs. abwertend)* **a)** *(Getue)* fuss; **b)** *(Unsinn)* rubbish

Heck-: ~motor der rear engine; **~scheibe die** rear *or* back window; **~tür die** back

heda ['he:da] *Interj. (veralt.)* I say

Hederich ['he:dərɪç] **der; ~s, ~e** *(Bot.)* jointed charlock

Hedonismus [hedo'nɪsmʊs] **der; ~** *(Philos.)* hedonism *no art.*

Hedonist der; ~en, ~en *(Philos.)* hedonist

hedonistisch *Adj.* hedonistic

Hedschra ['hɛdʒra] **die; ~:** Hegira

Heer [he:ɐ] **das; ~[e]s, ~e a)** *(Gesamtheit der Streitkräfte)* armed forces *pl.*; **das stehende ~:** the standing army; **in das ~ eintreten** join the services; **b)** *(für den Landkrieg)* army; **c)** *(fig.: große Anzahl)* army

Heeres-: ~bericht der *(Milit.)* military communiqué; **~bestände** *Pl.* army supplies *or* stores; **~dienst der** military service; **~leitung die** *(Milit.)* army command staff; **die oberste ~leitung** the high command; **~reform die** army reform

Heer-: ~führer der army commander; **~lager das** army camp; **~schar die** *(veralt., noch fig.)* host *(arch.)*; *s. auch* **himmlisch 1a**; **~straße die** *(veralt.)* military road; **~wesen das** armed forces *pl.*

Hefe ['he:fə] **die; ~, ~n a)** yeast; *(fig.)* driving force; **b)** *(geh. abwertend: Abschaum)* scum

Hefe-: ~gebäck das pastry *(made with yeast dough)*; **~kloß der** dumpling made with yeast dough; **aufgehen** *od.* **auseinandergehen wie ein ~kloß** *(ugs. scherzh.)* blow up like a balloon; **~kuchen der** yeast cake; **~pilz der** yeast fungus; **~teig der** yeast dough; **~zopf der** plaited bun

¹Heft [hɛft] **das; ~[e]s, ~e** *(geh.) (am Dolch, Messer)* haft; handle; *(am Schwert)* hilt; **das ~ ergreifen** *od.* **in die Hand nehmen** *(geh.)* take control; **das ~ in der Hand haben/behalten** *(geh.)* be in/keep control; **jmdm. das ~ aus der Hand nehmen** *(geh.)* take control from sb.

²Heft das; ~[e]s, ~e a) *(bes. Schule)* exercise-book; **b)** *(Nummer einer Zeitschrift)* issue; **Jahrgang 10, Heft 12** Volume 10, No. 12; **c)** *(kleines Buch) (small stapled)* book

Heftchen das; ~s, ~ a) *(Comic)* comic; *(Groschenroman)* novelette; **b)** *(Block)* book [of tickets/stamps *etc.*]

heften 1. *tr. V.* **a)** *(mit einer Nadel)* pin; fix; *(mit einer Klammer)* clip; fix; *(mit Klebstoff)* stick; **etw. an/in etw.** *(Akk.)* **~:** pin/stick/clip sth. to/into sth.; **etw. in einen Ordner ~:** put *or* insert sth. in[to] a file; **b)** *(richten)* **die Augen/den Blick auf jmdn./etw. ~:** fasten one's eyes/gaze on sb./sth.; **c)** *(Schneiderei)* tack; baste; **d)** *(Buchbinderei)* stitch; *(mit Klammern)* staple. **2.** *refl. V.* **a)** *(verfolgen)* **sich an jmds. Fersen** *(Akk.)* **~:** stick hard on sb.'s heels; **sich an jmds. Spur** *(Akk.)* **~:** get on the track of sb.; **b)** *(geh.: knüpfen)* **sich an etw.** *(Akk.)* **~:** be linked with sth.; **c)** *(richten)* ⟨*eyes, look*⟩ be fixed **(auf +** *Akk.* on)

Hefter der; ~s, ~: [loose-leaf] file

Heft·garn das tacking-thread; basting-thread

heftig 1. *Adj.* **a)** violent ⟨*storm, explosion, struggle, collision, argument, movement, passion*⟩; heavy ⟨*rain, shower, blow*⟩; intense, burning ⟨*hatred, desire*⟩; fierce ⟨*controversy, criticism, competition*⟩; severe ⟨*pain, cold*⟩; loud ⟨*bang*⟩; rapid ⟨*breathing*⟩; bitter ⟨*weeping*⟩; **b)** *(unbeherrscht)* violent ⟨*reaction, manner*⟩; ⟨*person*⟩ with a violent temper; heated, vehement ⟨*tone, words*⟩; **~ werden/gleich ~ sein** fly into a temper/flare up. **2.** *adv.* **a)** ⟨*rain, snow, breathe*⟩ heavily; ⟨*hit*⟩ hard; ⟨*hurt*⟩ a great deal; ⟨*quarrel, shiver*⟩ violently; **~ weinen** bawl; cry loudly; **sich ~ verlieben** fall passionately *or (coll.)* madly in love; **b)** *(unbeherrscht)* ⟨*answer*⟩ angrily, heatedly; ⟨*react*⟩ angrily, violently

Heftigkeit die; ~ a) *s.* **heftig a:** violence; heaviness; intensity; fierceness; severity; loudness; rapidity; bitterness; **b)** *(Unbeherrschtheit)* vehemence

Heft-: ~klammer a) staple; **b)** *s.* **Büroklammer; ~maschine die** stapler; *(Buchbinderei)* stitcher; **~pflaster das** sticking plaster; **~zwecke die** *s.* **Reißzwecke**

Hege ['he:gə] **die; ~** *(Forstw., Jagdw.)* care and protection; *(fig.)* care

Hegelianer [he:gə'li̯a:nɐ] **der; ~s, ~:** Hegelian

hegelianisch *Adj.* Hegelian

Hegelianismus der; ~: Hegelianism *no art.*

Hegelsch ['he:gl̩ʃ] *Adj.* Hegelian; **die ~e Staatsphilosophie** Hegel's political philosophy

hegemonial [hegemo'ni̯a:l] *Adj.* hegemonic

Hegemonie [hegemo'ni:] **die; ~, ~n** [-ən] hegemony

hegen *tr. V.* **a)** *(bes. Forstw., Jagdw.)* look after, tend ⟨*plants, animals*⟩; **b)** *(geh.: umsorgen)* look after; take care of; preserve ⟨*old customs*⟩; **jmdn./etw. ~ und pflegen** lavish care and attention on sb./sth.; **c)** *(in sich tragen)* feel ⟨*contempt, hatred, mistrust*⟩; cherish ⟨*hope, wish, desire*⟩; harbour, nurse ⟨*grudge, suspicion*⟩; **eine Abneigung gegen/eine gewisse Achtung für jmdn. ~:** have a dislike/a certain respect for sb.; **ich hege den Verdacht, daß ...:** I have a suspicion that ...; **große Zweifel [an etw.** *(Dat.)*] **~:** have *or* entertain grave doubts [about sth.]

Hehl [he:l] *in* **kein[en] ~ aus etw. machen** make no secret of sth.; **er macht kein[en] ~ daraus, daß ...:** he makes no secret of the fact that ...

Hehler der; ~s, ~: receiver [of stolen goods]; fence *(coll.)*

Hehlerei die; ~, ~en *(Rechtsw.)* receiving [stolen goods] *no art.*

hehr [he:ɐ] *Adj. (geh.)* majestic ⟨*sight*⟩; glorious ⟨*moment*⟩; noble ⟨*ideal*⟩

hei [hai̯] *Interj.* **~, war das eine Fahrt!** wow, what a trip; **~, ist das ein Spaß!** oh *or* hey, what fun!

heia ['hai̯a] *(Kinderspr.) in* **~ machen** go bye-byes *or* beddy-byes *(child lang.)*

Heia die; ~, ~[s], Heia·bett das *(Kinderspr.)* bye-byes, beddy-byes *(child lang.)*; **ab in die ~:** off to bye-byes *or* beddy-byes

heiapopeia *Interj. s.* **eiapopeia**

¹Heide ['hai̯də] **der; ~n, ~n** heathen; pagan; **das Kind ist ein kleiner ~:** the child is a little heathen

²Heide die; ~, ~n a) moor; heath; *(~landschaft)* moorland; heathland; **die Lüneburger ~:** the Luneburg Heath; **b)** *s.* **~kraut**

Heide-: ~kraut das; *o. Pl.* heather; ling; **~land das** moorland; heathland

Heidel·beere ['hai̯dl̩-] **die** bilberry; blueberry; whortleberry; **in die ~n gehen** *(ugs.)* go picking bilberries *etc.*

Heiden-: ~angst die; *o. Pl. (ugs.)* **eine ~angst vor etw.** *(Dat.)* **haben** be scared stiff of sth. *(coll.)*; **er hatte eine ~angst vor der Fahrprüfung** he was in a blue funk about the driving test *(sl.)*; **~arbeit die;** *o. Pl. (ugs.)* a heck of a lot of work *(coll.)*; **~geld das;** *o. Pl. (ugs.)* a packet *(coll.)*; a heck of a lot of money *(coll.)*; **~krach der;** *o. Pl. (ugs.)* **a)** *s.* **~lärm; b)** *(Streit)* flaming row *(coll.)*; **~lärm der** *(ugs.)* unholy *or* dreadful din *or* row *(coll.)*; dreadful racket *(coll.)*; **~mission die** missionary work; **~respekt der** *(ugs.)* healthy respect **(vor +** *Dat.* for); **~röschen das** *s.* **Heideröschen**

b; ~schreck der; *o. Pl. (ugs.)* terrible fright *(coll.)*; **ihr habt mir einen ~schreck eingejagt** you frightened the life out of me *(coll.)*; ~**spaß der**; *o. Pl. (ugs.)* terrific fun *(coll.)*; **es macht einen ~spaß** it's terrific fun *(coll.)*; ~**spektakel der** *(ugs.) (Lärm)* unholy *or* dreadful din *or* row *(coll.)*; *(Aufregung)* great *or (coll.)* dreadful commotion; ~**tempel der** heathen *or* pagan temple
Heidentum das; ~s a) *(Zustand)* heathenism; paganism; **b)** *(die Heiden)* the heathen *pl. or* pagans *pl.*; **das westliche ~:** the infidels *pl.* in the West
Heide·röschen das a) rock-rose *(of genus Fumana)*; **b)** *(veralt.: Hundsrose)* dogrose
heidi [hai'di:] *Interj.* **[und] ~ begann die wilde Fahrt** away he/they *etc.* went; **~ ging's den Berg hinunter** away he/they *etc.* went down the hill
Heidin die; ~, ~nen heathen; pagan
heidnisch 1. *Adj.* heathen; pagan. **2.** *adv.* **~ leben** live a heathen *or* pagan life
Heid·schnucke die; ~, ~n German Heath [sheep]
heikel ['haikl] *Adj.* **a)** *(schwierig)* delicate, ticklish ⟨*matter, subject*⟩; ticklish, awkward, tricky ⟨*problem, question, situation*⟩; **b)** *(wählerisch, empfindlich)* finicky, fussy, fastidious (**in bezug auf** + *Akk.* about); **in allen Dingen der Hygiene ist sie sehr ~:** she is very particular in all matters of hygiene
heil [hail] *Adj.* **a)** *(unverletzt)* unhurt, unharmed ⟨*person*⟩; **ein Wunder, daß seine Knochen ~ geblieben sind** it's a wonder he didn't break any bones; **~ ankommen** arrive safely *or* safe and sound; **etw. ~ überstehen** survive sth. unscathed; **sollte ich diese Angelegenheit ~ überstehen** *(fig.)* if I come out of this affair without getting my fingers burned; **aus etw. ~ herauskommen** come through sth. safely *or* unscathed; *(fig.)* survive sth.; *s. auch* **Haut a; b)** *nicht attr. (wieder gesund)* **~ werden/wieder ~ sein** ⟨*injured part*⟩ heal [up]/have healed [up]; **c)** *(nicht entzwei)* intact; in one piece; **er hat nicht ein einziges ~es Hemd** he hasn't got a single shirt that doesn't need mending; **es gab nur noch wenige ~e Häuser** only a few houses were undamaged; **eine ~e Welt** *(fig.)* an ideal *or* a perfect world
Heil das; ~s a) *(Wohlergehen)* benefit; **sein ~ in etw.** *(Dat.)* **suchen** seek one's salvation in sth.; **bei jmdm./irgendwo sein ~ versuchen** try one's luck with sb./somewhere; **~ Hitler!** *(ns.)* heil Hitler!; **sein ~ in der Flucht suchen** seek refuge in flight; *s. auch* **Berg a; Petri Heil; Ski; b)** *(Rel.)* salvation
Heiland ['hailant] **der; ~[e]s, ~e a)** *o. Pl. (Christus)* Saviour; Redeemer; **b)** *(geh.: Retter)* saviour
Heil-: ~anstalt die a) *(Anstalt für Kranke od. Süchtige)* sanatorium; **b)** *(psychiatrische Klinik)* mental hospital *or* home; **~bad das a)** *(Kurort)* spa; watering-place; **b)** *(medizinisches Bad)* medicinal bath
heilbar *Adj.* curable
Heilbarkeit die; ~: curability
heil·bringend *Adj.* saving; redeeming; **die ~e Botschaft** the message of salvation *or* redemption
Heil·butt der halibut
heilen 1. *tr. V.* **a)** cure ⟨*disease*⟩; heal ⟨*wound*⟩; **jmdn. ~:** cure sb.; restore sb. to health; **b)** *(befreien)* **jmdn. von etw. ~:** cure sb. of sth.; **davon/von ihm bin ich geheilt** *(ugs.)* I've been cured of it/my attachment to him. **2.** *itr. V.; mit sein* ⟨*wound*⟩ heal [up]; ⟨*infection*⟩ clear up; ⟨*fracture*⟩ mend
heil-, Heil-: ~erde die *pulverized earth with therapeutic properties, used in treating skin diseases and intestinal complaints*; **~erfolg der** success *(of cure etc.)*; **zum ~erfolg führen** lead to a successful cure; **~froh** *Adj.; nicht attr.* very *or (Brit. coll.)* jolly glad; **~gymnastik die** *s.* **Krankengymnastik**

heilig *Adj.* **a)** holy; **der Heilige Vater** the Holy Father; **der Heilige Stuhl** the Holy See; **die Heilige Jungfrau** the Blessed Virgin; **die ~e Barbara/der ~e Augustinus** Saint Barbara/Saint Augustine; **die Heilige Familie/Dreifaltigkeit** the Holy Family/Trinity; **der Heilige Geist** the Holy Spirit; **die Heiligen Drei Könige** the Three Kings *or* Wise Men; the Magi; **die ~e Taufe/Messe** Holy Baptism/Mass; **der ~e Sonntag** the Sabbath; **die Heilige Schrift** the Holy Scriptures *pl.*; **die Heilige Allianz** *(hist.)* the Holy Alliance; **das Heilige Römische Reich** *(hist.)* the Holy Roman Empire; **b)** *(besonders geweiht)* holy; sacred; **~e Stätten** holy *or* sacred places; **der Heilige Abend/die Heilige Nacht** Christmas Eve/Night; **das Heilige Land** the Holy Land; **c)** *(geh.: unantastbar)* sacred ⟨*right, tradition, cause, etc.*⟩; sacred, solemn ⟨*duty*⟩; gospel ⟨*truth*⟩; solemn ⟨*conviction, oath*⟩; righteous ⟨*anger, zeal*⟩; awed ⟨*silence*⟩; **etw. ist jmdm. ~:** sth. is sacred to sb.; **bei allem, was mir ~ ist** by all that I hold sacred; *s. auch* **hoch 2d; d)** *(ugs.: groß)* incredible *(coll.)*; healthy ⟨*respect*⟩; **seine ~e Not mit jmdm. haben** have a lot of trouble *or* a hard time with sb.; **e)** *(veralt.: fromm)* [extremely] devout *or* pious
Heilig·abend der Christmas Eve
Heilige der/die; *adj. Dekl.* saint; **ein sonderbarer** *od.* **komischer ~r** *(ugs. iron.)* a queer fish *(coll.)*
heiligen *tr. V.* **a)** keep, observe ⟨*tradition, Sabbath, etc.*⟩; **die geheiligten Räume** *(auch iron.)* the inner sanctum; the holy of holies; **der Zweck heiligt die Mittel** the end justifies the means; **b)** *(geh.: weihen)* consecrate ⟨*church*⟩; bless ⟨*house, field, etc.*⟩
Heiligen-: ~bild das picture of a saint; **~figur die** figure of a saint; **~legende die** life of a saint; **~schein der** gloriole; aureole; *(um den Kopf)* halo; **jmdn. mit einem ~schein umgeben** *(fig.)* be unable to see sb.'s faults; **~verehrung die** veneration of the saints
heilig|halten *unr. tr. V.* keep; observe
Heiligkeit die; ~ a) holiness; **Seine/Euere ~** *(Anrede)* His/Your Holiness; **b)** *(der Ehe, Taufe usw.)* sanctity; sacredness; *(geh.: des Zornes)* righteousness; **die ~ des Eigentums** *(geh.)* the sanctity *or* inviolability of property
heilig-, Heilig-: ~mäßig 1. *Adj.* saintly; **2.** *adv.* **~mäßig leben** lead a saintly life; **~|sprechen** *unr. tr. V. (kath. Kirche)* canonize; **~sprechung die; ~, ~en** *(kath. Kirche)* canonization
Heiligtum das; ~s, Heiligtümer shrine; **ein ~ für jmdn. sein** *(fig.)* be a sacred object to sb.; **sein Arbeitszimmer ist sein ~** *(fig.)* his study is his sanctuary *or* sanctum
Heiligung die; ~, ~en *(geh.)* **a)** *(das Heilighalten)* observance; **b)** *(Rechtfertigung)* justification
heil-, Heil-: ~klima das healthy climate; **ein gutes ~klima** a healthy climate; **~kraft die** healing *or* curative power; **~kräftig** *Adj.* medicinal ⟨*herb, plant, etc.*⟩; curative ⟨*effect*⟩; **~kraut das** medicinal *or* officinal herb; **~kunde die** medicine; **~kundig** *Adj.* skilled in medicine *or* the art of healing *postpos.*; **~los 1.** *Adj.* hopeless, awful ⟨*mess, muddle*⟩; utter, *(coll.)* terrible ⟨*confusion*⟩; **eine ~lose Angst haben** be terrified *or (coll.)* terribly frightened; **2.** *adv.* hopelessly; **~massage die** curative massage; **~massagen** massage treatment *sing., no indef. art.*; **~methode die** curative treatment; method of treatment; **~mittel das** *(auch fig.)* remedy (**gegen** for); *(Medikament)* medicament; **~pädagoge der** teacher of children with special needs; **~pädagogik die** special education *no art.*; **~pflanze die** medicinal *or* officinal plant *or* herb; **~praktiker der** non-medical practitioner; **~quelle die** mineral spring
heilsam *Adj.* salutary ⟨*lesson, effect, experience, etc.*⟩
Heils-: ~armee die Salvation Army; **~botschaft die** message of salvation
Heil-: ~schlaf der *(Med.)* healing sleep; **~serum das** *(Med.)* [antitoxic] serum
Heils-: ~geschichte die *(Theol.)* Heilsgeschichte; salvation-history; **~lehre die** *(auch fig.)* doctrine of salvation
Heil·stätte die sanatorium; clinic
Heilung die; ~, ~en a) *(einer Wunde)* healing; *(von Krankheit, Kranken)* curing; **wenig Hoffnung auf ~ haben** have little hope of being cured; **~ suchen** seek a cure; **b)** *(das Gesundwerden)* **die ~ dieser Fraktur dauert mehrere Wochen** this fracture will take several weeks to mend; **diese Salbe wird die ~ der Wunde beschleunigen** this ointment will help the wound to heal faster
Heilungs-: ~prozeß der, ~verlauf der healing process; *(Rekonvaleszenz)* process of recovery
Heil-: ~verfahren das [course of] treatment; **~wirkung die** therapeutic *or* curative effect; **~zweck der** *in* **zu ~zwecken** for therapeutic *or* medicinal purposes
heim [haim] *Adv.* home
Heim das; ~[e]s, ~e a) *(Zuhause)* home; **ein eigenes ~:** a home of his/their *etc.* own; **b)** *(Anstalt, Alters~)* home; *(für Obdachlose)* hostel; *(für Studenten)* hall of residence; hostel; **c)** *s.* **Erholungs~**
Heim-: ~abend der social evening; **~arbeit die** outwork; **eine ~arbeit suchen/bekommen** look for/get outwork; **etw. in ~arbeit herstellen lassen** have sth. produced by home-workers; **~arbeiter der, ~arbeiterin die** home-worker; out-worker
Heimat ['haima:t] **die; ~, ~en a)** *(~ort)* home; home town/village; *(~land)* home; homeland; **ihr ist Frankreich zur zweiten ~ geworden** France has become her second home; **b)** *(Ursprungsland)* natural habitat; **Frankreich ist die ~ des Champagners** France is the home of champagne
Heimat-: ~an·schrift die home address; **~dichter der** regional writer; **~dichtung die** regional literature; **~erde die** native soil; **~film der** [sentimental] film in a[n idealized] regional setting; **~forschung die** research into local history; **~front die** *(bes. ns.)* home front; **~hafen der** home port; **~kunde die** local history, geography, and natural history; **~land das** homeland; native land; *(fig.)* home
heimatlich *Adj.* **a)** *(zur Heimat gehörend)* native ⟨*dialect*⟩; **die ~en Berge** the mountains of [one's] home; **die ~e Landschaft/die ~en Bräuche** the landscape/customs of one's native land/district; *s. auch* **Gefilde; b)** *(an die Heimat erinnernd)* nostalgic ⟨*emotions*⟩; **~e Klänge** sounds which evoke memories of home
heimat-, Heimat-: ~lied das song of one's homeland; **~los** *Adj.* homeless; **durch den Krieg ~los werden** be displaced by the war; **~lose der/die;** *adj. Dekl.* homeless person; **die ~losen** the homeless; **~museum das** museum of local history; **~ort der a)** home town/village; **b)** *s.* **~hafen; ~recht das** right of domicile; **~sprache die** native language; *(Mundart)* native dialect; **~stadt die** home town; **~verein der** local history society; **~vertrieben** *Adj.* expelled from his/her homeland *postpos.*; **~vertriebene der/die;** *adj. Dekl.* expellee [from his/her homeland]
heim-: ~|begeben *unr. refl. V. (geh.)* make one's way home; go home; **~|begleiten** *tr. V.* **jmdn. ~begleiten** take *or* see sb. home; **~|bringen** *unr. tr. V.* **a)** *s.* **~begleiten; b)** bring home

Heimchen das; ~s, ~ **a)** *(ugs. abwertend: Frau)* ~ **[am Herd]** little hausfrau *or* housewife; **b)** *(Grille)* house cricket

Heim·computer der home computer

heim|dürfen *unr. itr. V.* be allowed [to go] home; **darf ich heim?** may I go home?

heimelig ['haiməlɪç] *Adj.* cosy

heim-, Heim-: **~erzieher der** *counsellor in a home for children or young people;* **~|fahren 1.** *unr. itr. V.; mit sein* drive home; **2.** *unr. tr. V.* drive home; *s. auch* **fahren 1 a, 2 c; ~fahrt die** journey home; *(mit dem Auto)* drive home; **~|finden** *unr. itr. V.* find one's way home; **~|führen** *tr. V.* **a)** *(geleiten)* take home; **b)** *(geh. veralt.: heiraten)* **eine Frau ~führen** take a wife; **er führte sie ~:** he took her to wife *(arch.)*; **er führte sie als seine Braut ~:** he took her for his bride; **~gang der** *(geh. verhüll.)* passing away; **nach dem ~gang ihres Mannes** after her husband passed away; **~gegangene der/die;** *adj. Dekl. (geh. verhüll.)* departed; **unser lieber ~gegangener** our dear departed friend/brother *etc.;* **~|gehen** *unr. itr. V.; mit sein* **a)** go home; **b)** *(geh. verhüll.: sterben)* pass away; **c)** *(unpers.)* **es geht heim** I/we *etc.* are going home; **~geschädigt** *Adj.* institutionalized; **~|holen** *tr. V.* **a)** fetch home; **b)** *(geh. verhüll.)* **Gott hat ihn [zu sich] ~geholt** he has been called to his Maker; **~industrie die** cottage industry

heimisch *Adj.* **a)** *(einheimisch)* indigenous, native ⟨*plants, animals, etc.*⟩ **(in** + *Dat.* to); domestic, home ⟨*industry*⟩; **die ~en Flüsse und Seen** the rivers and lakes of his/her *etc.* native land; **vor ~em Publikum** *(Sport)* in front of a home crowd; **b)** *nicht präd. (zum Heim gehörend)* **an den ~en Herd zurückkehren** go back home; **vom ~en Herd flüchten** get away from the house; **c)** ~ **sein/sich ~ fühlen** be/feel at home; ~ **werden** settle in; ~ **werden in** (+ *Dat.*) settle into

heim-, Heim-: **~kehr die;** ~: return home; homecoming; **~|kehren** *itr. V.; mit sein* return home **(aus** from); **~kehrer der** home-comer; **die ~kehrer aus dem Krieg/Urlaub** the soldiers returning from the war/the holidaymakers returning home; **~kind das** child brought up in a home; **ein ~kind adoptieren** adopt a child from a home; **~kino das a)** home movies *pl.*; **eine Vorführung im ~kino** a home-movie show; **b)** *(ugs. scherzh.: Fernsehen)* box *(coll.)*; goggle-box *(Brit. sl.)*; **~|kommen** *unr. itr. V.; mit sein* come *or* return home; **~|laufen** *unr. itr. V.; mit sein* run [back] home; **schnell ~laufen** dash home; **~leiter der** warden; *(eines Kinder-/Jugendheims)* superintendent; *(eines Pflegeheims)* director; **~leiterin die** warden; *(eines Kinder-/Jugendheims)* superintendent; *(eines Pflegeheims)* matron; **~leitung die a)** warden's office; *(eines Kinder-/Jugendheims)* superintendent's office; *(eines Pflegeheims)* director's/matron's office; **b)** *(Person) s.* **~leiter, ~leiterin; ~|leuchten** *itr. V. (salopp)* **jmdm. ~leuchten** give sb. a piece of one's mind *(coll.)*

heimlich 1. *Adj.* **a)** secret; secret, clandestine ⟨*agreement, meeting*⟩; **b)** *(österr.) s.* **heimelig. 2.** *adv.* secretly; ⟨*meet*⟩ secretly, in secret; **sie schaute ~ auf die Uhr** she looked furtively at her watch; **er ist ~ weggelaufen** he slipped *or* stole away; **~, still und leise** *(ugs.)* on the quiet; quietly

Heimlichkeit die; ~, ~en; *meist Pl.* secret; **in aller ~:** in secret; secretly

Heimlichtuer [-tu:ɐ] **der;** ~s, ~ *(abwertend)* secretive person

heim-, Heim-: **~mannschaft die** *(Sport)* home team *or* side; **~|müssen** *unr. itr. V.* have to go home; **~niederlage die** *(Sport)* home defeat; **~ordnung die** rules of the/a home/hostel *etc.;* **~orgel die** home organ; **~platz der** place in a home/hostel *etc.;* **~recht das** *(Sport)* **~recht haben** be playing at home; **die Mannschaft mit ~recht** the home team *or* side; **~reise die** journey home; **~|schicken** *tr. V.* send home; **~schwach** *Adj. (Sport)* **~schwach sein** have a poor home record; **~sieg der** *(Sport)* home win; **~spiel das** *(Sport)* home match *or* game; **~stark** *Adj. (Sport)* **~stark sein** have a very good home record; **~statt die** *(geh.)* home; **~stätte die a)** *s.* **Heimstatt; b)** *(Grundbesitz für Vertriebene)* homestead *(for refugees etc.)*; **~|suchen** *tr. V.* **a)** *(überfallen)* ⟨*storm, earthquake, epidemic*⟩ strike; ⟨*disease*⟩ afflict; ⟨*nightmares, doubts*⟩ plague; ⟨*catastrophe, fate*⟩ overtake; **von Streiks/Dürre ~gesucht** strike-torn/drought-ridden; **b)** *(aufsuchen)* ⟨*visitor, salesman, etc.*⟩ descend [up]on; **~suchung die;** ~, ~en affliction; visitation; **~|trauen** *refl. V.* dare to go home

Heim·tücke die; ~ *(Bösartigkeit)* [concealed] malice; *(Hinterlistigkeit, fig.: einer Krankheit)* insidiousness

heim·tückisch 1. *Adj. (bösartig)* malicious; *(fig.)* insidious ⟨*disease*⟩; *(hinterlistig)* insidious. **2.** *adv.* maliciously

heim-, Heim-: **~vorteil der** *(Sport)* advantage of playing at home; home advantage; **~wärts** [~vɛrts] *(nach Hause zu)* home; *(in Richtung Heimat)* homeward[s]; **~weg der** way home; **sich auf den ~weg machen** set off [for] home; **haben Sie einen weiten ~weg?** have you got a long way to go to get home?

Heim·weh das homesickness; **nach jmdm./einem Ort ~ haben** pine for sb./be homesick for a place; **~ bekommen** get homesick

heimweh·krank *Adj.* homesick

heim-, Heim-: **~werker der** handyman; do-it-yourselfer; **~|wollen** *unr. itr. V.* want to go home; **~|zahlen** *tr. V.* **jmdm. etw. ~zahlen** pay sb. back *or* get even with sb. for sth.; **jmdm. in gleicher Münze ~zahlen** pay sb. back in the same coin; **~|ziehen 1.** *unr. itr. V.; mit sein* return home; **2.** *unr. tr. V. (unpers.)* **es zog ihn ~:** he wanted to go home; **~zögling der** *s.* **~kind**

Hein [hain] *in* **Freund ~** *(verhüll.)* [Angel of] Death

Heini ['haini] **der;** ~s, ~s *(ugs. Schimpfwort)* idiot; half-wit; clot *(sl.)*

Heinzel·männchen ['haintsl̩-] **das;** ~s, ~: brownie

Heirat ['haira:t] **die;** ~, ~en marriage

heiraten 1. *itr. V.* marry; get married; **~ müssen** *(verhüll.)* have to get married; **das Heiraten** marriage *no art.;* getting married *no art.;* **sie hat nach Amerika geheiratet** she got married and settled in America. **2.** *tr. V.* marry

heirats-, Heirats-: **~absichten** *Pl.* marriage plans; **ernsthafte ~absichten haben** seriously intend to marry *or* get married; **~alter das** marrying age; **im ~alter sein** be of an age to marry; **~annonce die** advertisement for a marriage partner; **~antrag der** proposal *or* offer of marriage; **jmdm. einen ~antrag machen** propose to sb.; **~anzeige die a)** *(Anzeige, daß jemand heiratet)* announcement of a/the forthcoming marriage; **b)** *s.* **~annonce; ~fähig** *Adj.* ⟨*person*⟩ of marriageable age; **im ~fähigen Alter** of marriageable age; **~institut das** marriage bureau; **~kandidat der** *(scherzh.)* **a)** *(jmd., der heiraten will)* husband-to-be; **b)** *(unverheirateter Mann)* eligible bachelor; **~lustig** *Adj. (scherzh.)* eager *or* keen to get married *postpos.;* **~markt der** *(scherzh.)* **a)** *(Zeitungsrubrik)* matrimonial advertisements *pl.;* **b)** *(Veranstaltung)* marriage market; **~schwindel der** fraud involving a spurious offer of marriage; **~schwindler der** *person who makes a spurious offer of marriage for purposes of fraud;* **~urkunde die** marriage certificate; **~vermittler der** marriage broker; **~versprechen das** promise of marriage; **Bruch eines ~versprechens** *(Rechtsw.)* breach of promise

heisa ['haiza *od.* 'haisa] *Interj. (veralt.)* hooray

heischen ['haiʃn̩] *tr. V. (geh.)* **a)** *(fordern)* demand; **b)** *(veralt.: bitten um)* ask for; *(inständig)* beg

heiser ['haizɐ] **1.** *Adj.* hoarse; *(rauchig)* husky; **sich ~ schreien/reden** shout/talk oneself hoarse. **2.** *adv.* hoarsely; in a hoarse voice

Heiserkeit die; ~: *s.* **heiser:** hoarseness; huskiness

heiß [hais] **1.** *Adj.* **a)** hot; hot, torrid ⟨*zone*⟩; **brennend/glühend ~:** burning/scorching hot; **jmdm. ist ~:** sb. feels hot; **etw. ~ machen** heat sth. up; **ein Paar Heiße** *(ugs.)* a couple of hot sausages; **es überläuft mich ~ und kalt, es läuft mir ~ und kalt den Rücken hinunter** I feel hot and cold all over; **sie haben sich die Köpfe ~ geredet** the conversation/debate became heated; **dich haben sie wohl zu ~ gebadet?** *(salopp)* you must be off your rocker *(sl.)*; **b)** *(heftig)* heated ⟨*debate, argument*⟩; impassioned ⟨*anger*⟩; burning, fervent ⟨*desire*⟩; fierce ⟨*fight, battle*⟩; **c)** *(innig)* ardent, passionate ⟨*wish, love*⟩; **~e Tränen weinen** weep bitterly; cry one's heart out; **~en Dank** *(ugs.)* thanks a lot! *(coll.)*; **d)** *(aufreizend)* hot ⟨*rhythm etc.*⟩; sexy ⟨*blouse, dress, etc.*⟩; **eine ~e Nummer** *(ugs.)* a [red-]hot number *(coll.)*; **was für'n ~er Typ!** *(salopp)* what a guy! *(coll.)*; *s. auch* **Sohle a; e)** *(ugs.: gefährlich)* hot *(coll.)* ⟨*goods, money*⟩; **das wird ein ~es Jahr** things are going to get pretty hot this year *(coll.)*; **ein ~es Thema** a controversial subject; **ein ~es Geschäft** a risky business; **eine ~e Gegend** a rough district; *s. auch* **Eisen b; f)** *nicht präd. (ugs.: Aussichten habend)* hot ⟨*favourite, tip, contender, etc.*⟩; **auf einer ~en Spur sein** be hot on the scent; **g)** *nicht präd. (ugs.: schnell)* hot; *s. auch* **Ofen e; h)** *(ugs.: brünstig)* on heat; **i)** *(salopp: aufgereizt)* **jmdn. ~ machen** turn sb. on *(coll.)*; **j)** *(Physik)* hot *(sl.)*. **2.** *adv.* **a)** *(heftig)* ⟨*fight*⟩ fiercely; **die Stadt wurde ~ umkämpft** the town was the object of fierce fighting; **es ging ~ her** things got heated; sparks flew *(coll.)*; *(auf einer Party usw.)* things got wild; **b)** *(innig)* **jmdn. ~ und innig lieben** love sb. dearly *or* with all one's heart; **etw. ~ ersehnen** long fervently for sth.

heißa ['haisa] *s.* **heisa**

heiß·blütig *Adj. (leidenschaftlich)* hot-blooded; ardent, passionate ⟨*lover*⟩; *(leicht erregbar)* hot-tempered

¹heißen 1. *unr. itr. V.* **a)** *(den Namen tragen)* be called; **ich heiße Hans** I am called Hans; my name is Hans; **er heißt mit Nachnamen Müller** his surname is Müller; **früher hat sie anders geheißen** she used to have a different name; **nach jmdm. ~:** be named *or* called after sb.; **und wie sie alle ~:** and the rest [of them]; **wie kann man nur Traugott ~?** how can anyone have a name like Traugott?; **so wahr ich ... heiße** *(ugs.)* as sure as I'm standing here; **dann will ich Emil ~** *(ugs.)* then I'm a Dutchman *(coll.)*; **b)** *(bedeuten)* mean; **was heißt „danke" auf Französisch?** what's the French for 'thanks'?; **das will viel/nicht viel ~:** that means a lot/doesn't mean much; **was soll das denn ~?** what's that supposed to mean?; **was heißt hier: morgen?** what do you mean, tomorrow?; **das heißt** that is [to say]; **c)** *(lauten)* ⟨*saying*⟩ go; **wie heißt das Buch?** what's [the title *or* name of] the book?; **der Titel/sein Motto heißt ...:** the title/his motto is ...; **d)** *(unpers.) (man sagt)* **es heißt, daß ...:** they say *or* it is said that ...; **es heißt, daß sie unheilbar krank ist** she is said to be incurably ill; **wie es hieß, war sie unheilbar krank** they said *or* it was said [that] she was incurably ill; **es hieß allgemein, daß ...:** everybody said that ...; **es soll nicht ~, daß ...:** never let it be said that ...; **e)** *(unpers.) (ist zu lesen)* **in dem Gedicht/Roman/Artikel heißt es ...:** in the poem/novel/article it says that ...; **wie heißt es doch gleich bei Goethe?** what was it Goethe said?; **f)** *(unpers.) (geh.: es gilt)* **jetzt heißt es aufgepaßt!** you'd better watch out now!; **jetzt heißt es handeln!** now it's time to act *or* for action! **2.** *unr. tr. V.* **a)** *(geh.: auffordern)* tell; bid; **jmdn. etw. tun ~:** tell sb. to do sth.; bid sb. do sth.; **b)** *(geh.: bezeichnen)* call; **jmdn. einen Lügner ~:** call sb. a liar; **jmdn. willkommen ~:** bid sb. welcome; **c)** *(veralt.: einen Namen geben)* name; call

²heißen *tr. V. s.* **hissen**

heiß-, Heiß-: ~ersehnt *Adj.; präd. getrennt geschrieben* **das ~ersehnte Fahrrad** the bicycle he/she has/had longed for so fervently; **~geliebt** *Adj.; präd. getrennt geschrieben* dearly beloved ⟨*husband, son, etc.*⟩; beloved ⟨*doll, car, etc.*⟩; **~getränk das** hot drink; **~getränke** *(auf Speisekarten)* hot beverages; **~hunger der: einen ~hunger auf etw.** *(Akk.)* *od.* **nach etw. [haben]** [have] a craving for sth.; **etw. mit [wahrem] ~hunger verschlingen** devour sth. ravenously; [absolutely *(coll.)*] wolf sth. down; **sich mit [wahrem] ~hunger auf etw.** *(Akk.)* **stürzen** *(fig.)* [absolutely *(coll.)*] devour sth.; **~hungrig 1.** *Adj.* ravenous; **2.** *adv.* ravenously; voraciously; **~|laufen 1.** *unr. itr. V.; mit sein* run hot; ⟨*engine*⟩ run hot, overheat; **sie hat soviel telefoniert, daß die Drähte heißliefen** she made so many telephone calls that the wires were buzzing; **2.** *unr. refl. V.* run hot; ⟨*engine*⟩ run hot, overheat

Heiß·luft die hot air

Heißluft-: ~bad das hot-air bath; **~ballon der** hot-air balloon; **~gerät das** *(Trockner)* hot-air dryer; *(Herd)* hot-air oven

heiß-, Heiß-: ~mangel die rotary ironer; **~sporn der** hothead; **~umkämpft** *Adj.* *(präd. getrennt geschrieben)* fiercely contested *or* disputed; **~umstritten** *Adj.* *(präd. getrennt geschrieben)* hotly debated ⟨*matter, subject, etc.*⟩; highly controversial ⟨*figure, director, etc*⟩

Heiß·wasser-: ~bereiter der water heater; **~speicher der** hot-water tank with an immersion heater

heiter ['haitɐ] *Adj.* **a)** *(fröhlich)* cheerful, happy ⟨*person, nature*⟩; happy, merry ⟨*laughter*⟩; **~ und zufrieden** happy and contented; **b)** *(froh stimmend)* cheerful ⟨*music etc.*⟩; cheerful, bright ⟨*colour, wallpaper, room, etc.*⟩; *(amüsant)* funny, amusing ⟨*story etc.*⟩; **einer Sache** *(Dat.)* **die ~e Seite abgewinnen** look on the bright side of sth.; **das ist ja ~!** *(ugs. iron.)* that's just great *or* wonderful *(iron.)*; **das kann ja ~ werden!** *(ugs. iron.)* that'll be fun *(iron.)*; **c)** *(sonnig)* fine ⟨*weather*⟩; bright, fine ⟨*day*⟩; **~ bis wolkig** generally fine, though cloudy in places

Heiterkeit die; ~ a) *(Frohsinn)* cheerfulness; **b)** *(Belustigung)* merriment; **allgemeine ~ erregen** provoke *or* cause general merriment; **c)** *(sonniges Wetter)* brightness

Heiterkeits·ausbruch der burst of merriment

heizbar *Adj.* heated ⟨*windscreen, room, etc.*⟩; **das Zimmer ist nicht/schwer ~:** the room has no heating/is difficult to heat

Heiz·decke die electric blanket

heizen ['haitsn̩] **1.** *itr. V.* have the heating on; **der Ofen heizt gut** the stove gives off *or* throws out a good heat; **mit Kohle** *usw.* **~:** use coal *etc.* for heating. **2.** *tr. V.* **a)** *(warm machen)* heat ⟨*room etc.*⟩; **b)** *(anheizen)* stoke ⟨*furnace, boiler, etc.*⟩; **den Badeofen ~:** heat the bath-water; **sie ~ ihre Öfen mit Öl** their boilers are oil-fired; **c)** *(als Brennstoff verwenden)* burn. **3.** *refl. V.* **sich gut/schlecht ~:** be easy/difficult to heat

Heizer der; ~s, ~ *(einer Lokomotive)* fireman; stoker; *(eines Schiffes)* stoker

Heiz-: ~fläche die heating surface; **~gerät das** heater; **~kessel der** boiler; **~kissen das** heating pad; **~körper der** radiator; **~kosten** *Pl.* heating costs; **~lüfter der** fan heater; **~material das** fuel [for heating]; **~ofen der** stove; heater; **ein elektrischer ~ofen** an electric heater; **~öl das** heating oil; fuel oil; **~periode die** heating period; **~platte die** hotplate; **~rohr das** heating pipe; **~sonne die** bowl fire; parabolic heater; **~strahler der** radiant heater

Heizung die; ~, ~en a) [central] heating *no pl., no indef. art.*; **b)** *(ugs.: Heizkörper)* radiator

Heizungs-: ~anlage die heating system; **~keller der** boiler-room *(in the basement)*; **~monteur der** heating engineer; **~technik die** heating engineering

Heiz·wert der calorific value

Hektar ['hɛkta:ɐ̯] **das** *od.* **der; ~s, ~e** hectare

Hektar·ertrag der *(Landw.)* yield per hectare

Hektik ['hɛktɪk] **die; ~:** hectic rush; *(des Lebens)* hectic pace; **wozu die ~?** *(ugs.)* what's the rush?; **nur keine ~!** *(ugs.)* take it easy!

hektisch 1. *Adj.* **a)** *(fieberhaft)* hectic; **sie ist immer furchtbar ~:** she is always in a hectic rush; **nun mal nicht so ~!** take it easy!; **b)** *(Med. veralt.)* hectic; **~e Flecken** *(fig.)* red blotches. **2.** *adv.* ⟨*work, run to and fro*⟩ frantically; **~ zugehen** be hectic; **~ leben** lead a hectic life

Hektographie [hɛktogra'fi:] **die; ~, ~n a)** *o. Pl. (veralt.: Verfahren)* hectography *no art.*; **b)** *(Kopie)* hectographed *or* hectographic copy

hektographieren *tr. V.* **a)** *(veralt.)* hectograph; **b)** *(vervielfältigen)* duplicate; copy

Hekto-: ~liter der *od.* **das** hectolitre; **~watt das** hundred watts

Helanca Ⓦⓩ [he'laŋka] **das; ~:** nylon stretch fabric

helau [he'lau] *Interj.: cheer or greeting used at Carnival time*

Held [hɛlt] **der; ~en, ~en** hero; **du bist mir ein schöner** *od.* **netter ~** *(scherzh.)* a fine one you are!; **den ~en spielen** *(abwertend)* play the hero; **kein ~ in etw.** *(Dat.)* **sein** *(ugs. scherzh. od. spött.)* be no great shakes at sth. *(coll.)*; **du bist nicht gerade ein ~ in der Schule** *(ugs.)* you're not exactly doing brilliantly at school; **der ~ des Tages/des Abends** the hero of the hour; **~ der Arbeit** *(DDR)* Hero of Labour

Helden-: ~brust die *(scherzh./iron.)* manly chest; **~darsteller der** *(Theater)* actor of heroic roles; **~dichtung die** *(Literaturw.)* epic *or* heroic poetry; **~epos das** *(Literaturw.)* heroic epic; **~friedhof der** military *or* war cemetery; **~gedenktag der** *(veralt.)* ≈ Remembrance Day *(Brit.)*; Memorial Day *(Amer.)*; **~gestalt die** hero

heldenhaft 1. *Adj.* heroic. **2.** *adv.* heroically

helden-, Helden-: ~lied das *(Literaturw.)* heroic song *or* lay; **~mut der** heroism; **~mütig 1.** *Adj.* heroic; **2.** *adv.* heroically; **~pose die** *(abwertend)* heroic pose; **~rolle die** *(Theater)* part *or* role of the hero; **~sage die** *(Literaturw.)* heroic legend; *(aus Norwegen, Island)* heroic saga; **~stück das** *(iron.)* **das war kein ~stück** that was nothing to be proud of; **~tat die** heroic feat *or* deed; **das war keine ~tat** *(spött.)* that was nothing to be proud of; **~tenor der a)** *(Sänger)* heroic *or* dramatic tenor; Heldentenor; **b)** *(Stimmlage)* Heldentenor; **~tod der** *(geh. verhüll.)* death in action; **den ~tod sterben/finden** be killed in action

Heldentum das; ~s heroism

Heldin die; ~, ~nen heroine

helfen ['hɛlfn̩] *unr. itr. V.* **a)** *(behilflich sein)* **jmdm. ~ [etw. zu tun]** help *or* assist sb. [to do sth.]; lend *or* give sb. a hand [in doing sth.]; **jmdm. bei etw. ~:** help *or* assist sb. with sth.; **jmdm. in den/aus dem Mantel ~:** help sb. into *or* on with/out of *or* off with his/her coat; **jmdm. über die Straße/in den Bus ~:** help sb. across the road/on to the bus; **dem Kranken war nicht mehr zu ~:** the patient was beyond [all] help; **dir ist nicht zu ~** *(ugs.)* you're a hopeless case; **sich** *(Dat.)* **nicht mehr zu ~ wissen** be at one's wits' end; **sich immer zu ~ wissen** be able to take care of oneself; **dem werde ich ~, einfach die Schule zu schwänzen!** *(ugs.)* I'll teach him to play truant; **ich kann mir nicht ~, aber ...:** I'm sorry, but [I have to say that] ...; **b)** *(nützlich sein)* help; **ein paar Tage Ruhe werden Ihnen sicher ~:** a couple of days' rest will certainly do you good; **das hilft gegen** *od.* **bei Kopfschmerzen** it is good for *or* helps to relieve headaches; **das hilft mir auch nichts** that's no help *or* good to me either; **hilf dir selbst, so hilft dir Gott** *(Spr.)* God helps those who help themselves; **da hilft alles nichts** there's nothing *or* no help for it; **da hilft kein Jammern und kein Klagen** it's no good *or* use moaning and groaning; **c)** *(unpers.)* **es hilft nichts** it's no use *or* good; **was hilft's?** what's the use *or* good?; **damit ist uns nicht geholfen** that is no help to us; that doesn't help us; **es hilft dir wenig zu jammern** it's not much good *or* use moaning

Helfer der; ~s, ~: helper; *(Mitarbeiter)* assistant; *(eines Verbrechens)* accomplice; **ein ~ in der Not** a friend in need

Helferin die; ~, ~nen *s.* **Helfer**

Helfers·helfer der; ~s, ~ *(abwertend)* accomplice

Helikopter [heli'kɔptɐ] **der; ~s, ~:** helicopter

helio-, Helio- [helio-] helio-

Heliograph [-'gra:f] **der; ~en, ~en** *(Astron., Nachrichtenw.)* heliograph

Heliographie [-gra'fi:] **die; ~** *(Druckw., Nachrichtenw.)* heliography *no art.*

Helioskop [-'sko:p] **das; ~s, ~e** *(Astron.)* helioscope

Heliostat [-'sta:t] **der; ~[e]s** *od.* **~en, ~en** *(Astron.)* heliostat

¹Heliotrop das; ~s, ~e *(Pflanze, Farbe, Farbstoff)* heliotrope

²Heliotrop der; ~s, ~e *(Schmuckstein)* bloodstone; heliotrope

Helium ['he:liʊm] **das; ~s** helium

Helix ['he:lɪks] **die; ~, Helices** ['he:litse:s] *(Chemie)* helix

hell [hɛl] **1.** *Adj.* **a)** *(von Licht erfüllt)* light ⟨*room etc.*⟩; well-lit ⟨*stairs*⟩; **es wird ~:** it's getting light; **es war schon ~er Morgen/Tag** it was already broad daylight; **am ~en Tag** *(ugs.)* in broad daylight; **in ~en Flammen stehen** be in flames *or* ablaze; **b)** *(klar)* bright ⟨*day, sky, etc.*⟩; **eine ~ere Zukunft** *(fig. ugs.)* a brighter *or* more promising future; **c)** *(viel Licht spendend)* bright ⟨*light, lamp, star, etc.*⟩; **d)** *(blaß)* light ⟨*colour*⟩; fair ⟨*skin, hair*⟩; light-coloured ⟨*clothes*⟩; **~es Bier** ≈ lager; **e)** *(akustisch)* **ein ~er Ton/Klang** a high, clear sound; **eine ~e Stimme** a high, clear voice; **ein ~es Lachen** a ringing laugh; **f)** *(klug)* bright; intelligent; **ein ~er Kopf sein** be bright; **dort fehlt ein ~er Kopf** what is needed there is somebody with brains; **g)** *(voll bewußt)* lucid ⟨*moment, interval*⟩; **h)** *nicht präd. (ugs.: absolut)* sheer, utter ⟨*madness, foolishness, despair, nonsense*⟩; unbounded, boundless ⟨*enthusiasm*⟩; unrestrained ⟨*jubilation*⟩; **in ~e Wut geraten** fly into a blind rage; **er hat seine ~e Freude an ihr/daran** she/it is his great joy; **daran wirst du deine ~e Freude haben** *(iron.)* you'll soon find out what you've let yourself in for; *s. auch* **Schar. 2.** *adv.* **a)** brightly

⟨*lit*⟩; ⟨*shine, blaze*⟩ brightly; **b)** *(in hoher Tonlage)* ~ **läuteten die Glocken** the bells rang out high and clear; ~ **lachen** give a ringing laugh; **c)** *(sehr)* highly ⟨*enthusiastic, delighted, indignant, etc.*⟩; *(laut)* **über diesen Unsinn mußte er ~ lachen** he had to laugh heartily at this nonsense

hẹll-, Hẹll-: ~auf *Adv.* highly ⟨*enthusiastic, indignant, etc.*⟩; **~auf lachen** laugh out loud; **~äugig** *Adj.* ⟨*person*⟩ with light-coloured eyes; **~blau** *Adj.* light blue; **~blond** *Adj.* very fair; light blonde; **~braun** *Adj.* light brown; **~-Dụnkel-Adap[ta]tion die** the adaptation to light and dark; **~-dụnkel·malerei die** chiaroscuro

hẹlle *Adj.; nicht attr. (landsch.)* bright; intelligent; **sei ~!** use your head!

¹Hẹlle die; ~ *(geh.) s.* **Helligkeit**

²Hẹlle das; *adj. Dekl.* ≈ lager

Hellebarde [hɛlə'bardə] **die;** ~, **~n** *(hist.)* halberd

hellenisieren [hɛleni'zi:rən] *tr. V.* Hellenize *no art.*

Hellenịsmus der; ~: Hellenism *no art.*

Hellenịst der; **~en, ~en** Hellenist

Hellenịstik die; ~: classical Greek studies *pl., no art.*

hellenịstisch *Adj.* Hellenistic; **die ~en Staaten** the states of Ancient Greece

Hẹller der; **~s,** ~: heller; **bis auf den letzten ~/bis auf ~ und Pfennig** *(ugs.)* down to the last penny *or (Amer.)* cent; **das ist keinen [roten** *od.* **lumpigen] ~ wert** *(ugs.)* it's not worth a penny *or (Amer.)* one red cent; **sie hat keinen [roten** *od.* **lumpigen] ~** *(ugs.)* she doesn't have a penny to her name *or (Amer.)* have one [red] cent; **keinen [roten] ~ für jmdn./etw. geben** *(ugs.)* not care tuppence about sb./sth.

hẹll·erleuchtet *Adj. (präd. getrennt geschrieben)* brightly-lit

helleuchtend ['hɛlɔyçtn̩t] *Adj.* (*präd. getrennt geschrieben:* **hell leuchtend**) bright

hẹll-: ~farben, ~farbig *Adj.* light-coloured; **~gekleidet** *Adj. (präd. getrennt geschrieben)* [dressed] in light-coloured clothes *postpos.*; **~gelb** *Adj.* light yellow; **~gestreift** *Adj. (präd. getrennt geschrieben)* with light-coloured stripes *postpos.*; **~grau** *Adj.* light grey; **~grün** *Adj.* light green; **~haarig** *Adj.* fair[-haired]; **~häutig** *Adj.* fair[-skinned]; fair-skinned, pale-skinned ⟨*race*⟩; **~hörig** *Adj.* **a)** *(aufmerksam)* **~hörig werden** sit up and take notice *(coll.)*; **jmdn. ~hörig machen** make sb. sit up and take notice *(coll.)*; **b)** *(schalldurchlässig)* badly *or* poorly sound-proofed; **c)** *(veralt.: gut hörend)* **~hörig sein** have keen hearing *or* sharp ears

hellicht ['hɛl'lɪçt] *Adj. in* **es ist ~er Tag** it's broad daylight; **am ~en Tag** in broad daylight

Hẹlligkeit die; ~, **~en** *(auch Physik)* brightness; **eine Lampe von größerer ~:** a brighter lamp

Hẹlligkeits·regler der *(Elektrot.)* dimming control; dimmer; *(beim Fernsehgerät)* brightness-control; **Lichtschalter mit ~:** dimmer-switch

hellodernd ['hɛlo:dɐnt] *Adj.; nicht präd.* blazing; **~e Flammen** raging flames

hẹll-, Hẹll-: ~rot *Adj.* light red; **~sehen** *unr. itr. V.; nur im Inf.* **~sehen können** have second sight; be clairvoyant; **~seher der, ~seherin die** clairvoyant; **~seherisch** *Adj.* clairvoyant; **~seherische Begabung haben** have the gift of second sight; **~sichtig** *Adj.* **a)** *(durchschauend)* perceptive; **b)** *(weitblickend)* far-sighted; **~sichtigkeit die;** ~: perceptiveness; **~wach** *Adj.* **a)** *(ganz wach)* wide awake; **b)** *(ugs.: klug)* bright; **~werden das;** **~s** daybreak *no art.*

¹Hẹlm [hɛlm] **der;** **~[e]s, ~e a)** *(Kopfschutz)* helmet; ~ **ab zum Gebet!** *(Milit.)* helmets off for prayers!; **b)** *(Archit.)* *(pyramidenförmig)* helm *or* pyramidal roof; *(kegelförmig)* conical roof

²Hẹlm der; **~[e]s, ~e** *(einer Axt, eines Hammers usw.)* helve; *(eines Messers)* haft; handle

Hẹlm-: ~busch der plume; crest; **~dach das** *s.* **¹Helm b; ~zier die** crest

Helot [he'lo:t] **der;** **~en, ~en** *(hist.)* Helot

Helo̱tentum das; **~s** *(hist.)* helotism; helotry

hem [həm] *Interj.* hem

Hẹmd [hɛmt] **das;** **~[e]s, ~en a)** *(Oberhemd)* shirt; **b)** *(Unterhemd)* [under]vest; undershirt; **c)** *in* **etw. wechseln wie das** *od.* **sein ~** *(ugs. abwertend)* change sth. as often as one changes one's clothes; **naß bis aufs ~ sein** be soaked to the skin; be wet through; **das ~ ist mir näher als der Rock** for me charity begins at home; **mach dir nicht ins ~** *(salopp)* don't get [all] uptight *(coll.)*; **das zieht einem [ja] das ~ aus** *(ugs.)* that's terrible!; **für sie gibt er sein letztes** *od.* **das letzte ~ her** *(ugs.)* he'd sell the shirt off his back to help her; **jmdn. bis aufs ~ ausziehen** *(ugs.)* have the shirt off sb.'s back *(coll.)*; **alles bis aufs ~ verlieren** *(ugs.)* lose almost everything

Hẹmd-: ~ärmel der *(österr.)* *s.* **Hemdsärmel; ~bluse die** shirt; **~blusen·kleid das** shirt-waist dress; **~brust die** shirt-front; dicky *(coll.)*

Hẹmden·matz der *(ugs. scherzh.)* *small child wearing only a shirt or vest;* little bare-bum *(coll.)*

Hẹmd-: ~knopf der shirt-button; **~kragen der** shirt-collar

Hẹmds·ärmel der shirt-sleeve; **in ~n** in [one's] shirt-sleeves

hẹmdsärmelig [~ɛrməlɪç] *Adj.* **a)** *(im Hemd)* shirt-sleeved *attrib.*; in [one's] shirt-sleeves *postpos.*; **b)** *(ugs.: leger)* casual ⟨*manner*⟩; informal ⟨*style*⟩; **sich ~ geben** behave in a casual manner; **er ist mir zu ~:** he's too pally for my liking *(coll.)*

Hẹmd·zipfel der shirt-tail

Hemisphäre [hemi'sfɛ:rə] **die;** ~, **~n** hemisphere

hẹmmen ['hɛmən] *tr. V.* **a)** *(verlangsamen)* slow [down]; retard; **seinen Schritt ~:** slow one's pace; slow down; **b)** *(aufhalten)* check; stem ⟨*flow*⟩; **c)** *(beeinträchtigen)* hinder; hamper; **jmdn. in seiner Entwicklung ~:** inhibit sb.'s development; **d)** *(behindern)* impede, hamper ⟨*person*⟩; **die Verletzung hemmte sie beim Laufen** her injury made walking difficult

Hẹmmnis das; **~ses, ~se** obstacle, hindrance **(für** to)

Hẹmm·schuh der a) *(Hemmnis)* obstacle, hindrance **(für** to); **b)** *(Eisenb.)* slipper [brake]; **c)** *(Bremsklotz)* chock; **d)** *(Bremse)* skid; drag

Hẹmmung die; ~, **~en a)** *(Gehemmtheit)* inhibition; **~en haben** have inhibitions; be inhibited; **ich hatte ~en, sie darum zu bitten** I felt awkward about asking her for it; **b)** *(Bedenken)* scruple; **keine ~en haben, etw. zu tun** have no scruples about doing sth.; **c)** *(Hemmen) (des Wachstums, einer Entwicklung)* inhibition

hẹmmungs·los 1. *Adj.* unrestrained; unrestrained, unbridled ⟨*passion*⟩; *(skrupellos)* unscrupulous; **ein ~er Mensch** a person lacking in all restraint/an unscrupulous person. **2.** *adv.* unrestrainedly; without restraint; ⟨*cry, laugh, scream*⟩ uncontrollably; *(skrupellos)* unscrupulously

Hẹmmungslosigkeit die; ~: lack of restraint; *(Skrupellosigkeit)* unscrupulousness

Hendl ['hɛndl̩] **das;** **~s, ~[n]** *(bayr., österr.)* chicken; *(Brathähnchen)* [roast] chicken

Hẹngst [hɛŋst] **der;** **~[e]s, ~e** *(Pferd)* stallion; *(Kamel)* male; *(Esel)* male; jackass

Hẹngst-: ~fohlen das, ~füllen das colt; [male] foal

Henkel ['hɛŋkl̩] **der;** **~s,** ~: handle; *(einer Kanne)* handle; ear

Hẹnkel-: ~kanne die jug; *(größer)* pitcher; **~kreuz das** ansate cross; ankh; **~mann der** *(ugs.)* *portable set of stacked containers for taking a hot meal to one's work*

henken ['hɛŋkn̩] *tr. V. (veralt.)* hang

Hẹnker der; **~s, ~ a)** hangman; *(Scharfrichter, auch fig.)* executioner; **b)** *(salopp)* **sich den ~ um etw. scheren** not give a damn about sth. *(coll.)*; **scher dich** *od.* **geh zum ~!** go to blazes *or* to the devil! *(coll.)*; **hol's der ~!** damn [it]! *(coll.)*; the devil take it! *(coll.)*; **weiß der ~!** the devil only knows *(coll.)*; **beim** *od.* **zum ~!** damn it! *(coll.)*; hang it all! *(coll.)*

Hẹnker[s]-: ~beil das executioner's axe; **~hand die:** **durch** *od.* **von ~hand** *(geh.)* at the hand of the executioner

Hẹnkers-: ~knecht der hangman's assistant; *(eines Scharfrichters)* executioner's assistant; *(fig.)* henchman; **~mahlzeit die** last meal *(before execution)*; *(scherzh.)* last slap-up meal *(before examination, operation, departure, etc.)*

Henna ['hɛna] **die;** ~ *od.* **das;** **~[s]** henna

Henne ['hɛnə] **die;** ~, **~n** hen

Hepatitis [hepa'ti:tɪs] **die;** ~, **Hepatitịden** *(Med.)* hepatitis

her [he:ɐ̯] *Adv.* **a)** ~ **damit** give it to me; give it here *(coll.)*; ~ **mit dem Geld** hand over *or* give me the money; **Bier ~!** bring me/us some beer!; **vom Fenster ~:** from the window; **von weit ~:** from far away *or* a long way off; **b)** *(zeitlich)* **von ihrer Kindheit ~:** since childhood; **jmdn. von früher/von der Schulzeit ~ kennen** know sb. from earlier times/from one's school-days; *s. auch* **früher 2; hersein; c) von der Konzeption ~:** as far as the basic design is concerned; **das ist von der Sache ~ nicht vertretbar** it is unjustifiable in the nature of the matter

herab [hɛ'rap] *Adv.* **vom Gipfel ~ bis ins Tal** from the summit down to the valley; **bis ~ auf etw.** *(Akk.)* down to sth.; **die Treppe/den Berg ~:** down the stairs/the mountain; **von oben ~** *(fig.)* condescendingly; **er ist immer so von oben ~:** he's always so superior

herạb-, Herạb- *(s. auch* **herunter-**): **~|blicken** *itr. V. (geh.) s.* **~sehen; ~|flehen** *tr. V. (geh.)* **Gottes Hilfe ~flehen** beseech God's help; **Gottes Segen auf jmdn. ~flehen** call down God's blessing on sb.; **~|fließen** *unr. itr. V.; mit sein (geh.)* flow down; **~|hängen** *unr. itr. V.* **a)** *(nach unten hängen)* hang [down] **(von** from); *(fig.)* ⟨*clouds*⟩ hang low [in the sky]; **b)** *(schlaff hängen)* ⟨*hair, arms, etc.*⟩ hang down; **~hängende Schultern** drooping shoulders; **~|klettern** *itr. V.; mit sein (geh.)* climb down; descend; **~|kommen** *unr. itr. V.; mit sein (geh.)* come down; descend; **~|lassen 1.** *unr. tr. V.* let down; lower; **2.** *unr. refl. V.* **a)** *(iron.: bereit sein)* **sich ~lassen, etw. zu tun** condescend *or* deign to do sth.; **b)** *(iron. veralt.: leutselig sein)* **sich zu jmdm. ~lassen** come down to sb.'s level; **~lassend 1.** *Adj.* condescending; patronizing **(zu** towards); **2.** *adv.* condescendingly; patronizingly; in a condescending *or* patronizing manner; **~lassung die;** ~: condescension; **~|mindern** *tr. V.* **a)** reduce; **b)** *(schlechtmachen)* belittle, disparage ⟨*achievement, qualities, etc.*⟩; **~minderung die** belittlement; disparagement; **~|regnen** *itr. V.; mit sein* ⟨*drops of rain*⟩ fall; *(fig.)* rain down; **~|rieseln** *itr. V.; mit sein (geh.)* trickle down; ⟨*snow*⟩ fall gently; ⟨*snowflakes*⟩ float down; **~|sehen** *unr. itr. V.* **a)** *(nach unten sehen)* look down **(auf** + *Akk.* on); **b)** *(geringschätzig betrachten)* **auf jmdn. ~sehen** look down on sb.; **~|senken** *refl. V. (geh.)* ⟨*night, evening*⟩ fall; ⟨*mist, fog*⟩ settle, descend **(auf** + *Akk.* on, over);

~|**setzen** *tr. V.* **a)** *(reduzieren)* reduce, cut ⟨*cost, price, working hours, etc.*⟩; reduce ⟨*speed*⟩; **zu ~gesetzten Preisen** at reduced prices; **~gesetzte Waren** *(ugs.)* cut-price goods; **b)** *(abwerten)* belittle; disparage; **~setzung die; ~:** *s.* **~setzen: a)** reduction, cut (*Gen.* in); **b)** belittling; disparagement; ~|**sinken** *unr. itr. V.; mit sein* **a)** *(nach unten sinken)* sink [down]; *(fig.)* ⟨*night*⟩ fall; descend; ⟨*mist, fog*⟩ settle, descend (**auf +** *Akk.* on, over); **b)** *(moralisch absinken)* sink; ~|**steigen** *unr. itr. V.; mit sein (geh.)* descend; climb down; *(vom Pferd)* dismount; ~|**stoßen** *(geh.)* **1.** *unr. tr. V.* push down; **er hat ihn von der Klippe ~gestoßen** he pushed him off the cliff; **2.** *unr. itr. V.; mit sein* swoop down; ~|**stürzen 1.** *itr. V.; mit sein* plummet down; **er stürzte vom Gerüst ~:** he fell from *or* off the scaffolding; **~stürzende Felsbrocken** falling rocks; **2.** *refl. V.* throw oneself (**von** from *or* off); ~|**würdigen** *tr. V.* belittle; disparage; **~würdigung die;** *o. Pl.* belittling; disparagement; ~|**ziehen** *unr. tr. V. (geh.)* **a)** pull down; **b)** *(moralisch)* **jmdn. zu sich/auf sein eigenes Niveau ~ziehen** drag sb. down to one's own level

Heraklit [hera'kli:t] **(der)** Heraclitus

Heraldik [he'raldɪk] **die; ~:** heraldry *no art.*

Heraldiker der; ~s, ~: heraldist; expert in heraldry

heraldisch *Adj.* heraldic

heran [hɛ'ran] *Adv.* **an etw.** *(Akk.)* **~:** close to *or* right up to sth.; **nur ~ zu mir!, immer ~!** come closer!

heran-, Heran-: ~|**arbeiten** *refl. V.* **sich an etw.** *(Akk.)* **~arbeiten** work one's way towards sth.; ~|**bilden 1.** *tr. V.* train [up]; *(auf der Schule, Universität)* educate; **2.** *refl. V. (sich entwickeln)* develop; ~|**bringen** *unr. tr. V.* **a)** *(zu jmdm. bringen)* bring [up] (**an +** *Akk.*, **zu** to); **b)** *(vertraut machen)* **jmdn. an etw.** *(Akk.)* **~bringen** introduce sb. to sth.; ~|**fahren** *unr. itr. V.; mit sein* drive up (**an +** *Akk.* to); ~|**führen 1.** *tr. V.* **a)** *(in die Nähe führen)* lead up; bring up ⟨*troops*⟩; **aus dem Osten wird Kaltluft ~geführt** there is/will be a cold easterly air-stream; **b)** *(nahe bringen)* bring up (**an +** *Akk.* to); **c)** *(vertraut machen)* **jmdn. an etw.** *(Akk.)* **~führen** introduce sb. to sth.; **2.** *itr. V.* **an etw.** *(Akk.)* **~führen** lead to sth.; ~|**gehen** *unr. itr. V.; mit sein* **a)** go up (**an +** *Akk.* to); **näher ~gehen** go [up] closer; **b)** *(anpacken)* **an ein Problem/eine Aufgabe/die Arbeit** *usw.* **~gehen** tackle a problem/a task/the work *etc.*; **an die Lösung eines Problems ~gehen** set about solving a problem; ~|**holen** *tr. V.* fetch; ~|**kommen** *unr. itr. V.; mit sein* **a) an etw.** *(Akk.)* **~kommen** come *or* draw near to sth.; approach sth.; **laß es erst an dich ~kommen** *(ugs.)* cross that bridge when you get to it; **wir waren fast an den Fluß ~gekommen** we had almost reached the river; **ganz nahe an etw.** *(Akk.)* **~kommen** come right up to sth.; **b)** *(zeitlich)* **der große Tag kam näher ~/war ~gekommen** the big day drew nearer/had arrived; **c) an etw.** *(Akk.)* **~kommen** *(erreichen)* reach sth.; *(erwerben)* obtain sth.; get hold of sth.; **an den Motor** *usw.* **~kommen** get at the engine *etc.*; **an jmdn. ~kommen** *(fig.)* get hold of sb.; **er ist so verschlossen, man kommt nur schwer an ihn ~:** he's so reserved, it's very hard to get to know him; **an diesen Wissenschaftler kommt keiner ~** *(fig.)* there is no one who can compare with this scientist; **an jmds. Erfolg/Rekord ~kommen** *(fig.)* equal sb.'s success/record; ~|**machen** *refl. V. (ugs.)* **a)** *(beginnen)* **sich an etw.** *(Akk.)* **~machen** get down to *or (coll.)* get going on sth.; **b)** *(nähern)* **sich an jmdn. ~machen** chat sb. up *(coll.)*; ~|**nahen** *itr. V.; mit sein (geh.)* approach; draw near; ~|**nehmen** *unr. tr. V.* **die Lehrlinge werden ganz schön ~genommen** the apprentices are really made to work [hard]; **der Lehrer nahm den Schüler tüchtig ~:** the teacher took the boy firmly in hand; ~|**reichen** *itr. V.* **a)** *(erreichen)* reach; **an die oberen Schrankfächer ~reichen** reach [up to] the top shelves; **b)** *(von gleicher Qualität sein)* **an jmdn./etw. ~reichen** come *or* measure up to the standard of sb./sth.; ~|**reifen** *itr. V.; mit sein* ⟨*fruit, crops*⟩ ripen; *(fig.)* ⟨*plan*⟩ mature; **zur Frau/zum Mann/zu einer großen Malerin ~reifen** mature into a woman/man/great painter; **in ihm reifte der Entschluß ~, ins Ausland zu gehen** *(fig.)* he became increasingly resolved to go abroad; ~|**rücken 1.** *tr. V.* pull up ⟨*table*⟩; draw *or* pull *or* bring up ⟨*chair*⟩; **2.** *itr. V.; mit sein* move *or* come closer *or* nearer; ⟨*troops*⟩ advance (**an +** *Akk.* towards); **dicht** *od.* **nah ~rücken** move up close (**an +** *Akk.* to); **mit seinem Stuhl ~rücken** draw *or* pull *or* bring one's chair up closer; ~|**schaffen** *tr. V.* bring; *(liefern)* supply; ~|**schleichen** *unr. itr. V. mit sein; refl. V.* **[sich an etw./jmdn.] ~schleichen** creep *or* sneak up [to sth./on sb.]; ~|**tasten** *refl. V.* **sich [an etw.** *Akk.* **] ~tasten** grope *or* feel one's way [over to sth.]; *(fig.)* feel one's way [towards sth.]; ~|**tragen** *unr. tr. V.* **a)** bring [over]; **b)** *(vorbringen)* **eine Bitte/Beschwerde an jmdn. ~tragen** go/come to sb. with a request/complaint; ~|**treten** *unr. itr. V.; mit sein* **a)** *(an eine Stelle treten)* come/go up (**an +** *Akk.* to); **treten Sie nur näher ~!** come along!; [just] stop this way!; **b)** *(sich ergeben)* **Probleme/Fragen/Anfechtungen treten an jmdn. ~:** sb. is faced with problems/questions/accusations; **Zweifel treten an ihn ~:** he is assailed by doubts; **c)** *(sich wenden)* **an jmdn. ~treten** approach sb.; ~|**wachsen** *unr. itr. V.; mit sein* grow up; *(fig.)* develop; **zum Mann/zur Frau ~wachsen** grow up into *or* to be a man/woman; **die ~wachsende Generation** the rising *or* up-and-coming generation; **~wachsende der/die;** *adj. Dekl.* **a)** young person; **viele ~wachsende** many young people; **b)** *(Rechtsw.)* adolescent; ~|**wagen** *refl. V.* venture near; dare to go near; **sich an etw.** *(Akk.)* **~wagen** venture near sth.; dare to go near sth.; *(fig.)* venture *or* dare to tackle *or* attempt sth.; **er wagte sich nicht an das Mädchen ~:** he did not dare to approach the girl; ~|**ziehen 1.** *unr. tr. V.* **a)** *(an eine Stelle ziehen)* pull *or* draw over; pull *or* draw up ⟨*chair*⟩; **etw. zu sich ~ziehen** pull *or* draw sth. towards one; **etw. näher ~ziehen** pull *or* draw sth. closer *or* near (**an +** *Akk.* to); **b)** *(beauftragen)* call *or* bring in; **weitere Arbeitskräfte ~ziehen** bring in more labour; **c)** *(in Betracht ziehen)* refer to; *(geltend machen)* invoke; quote; **d)** *(großziehen)* rear, raise ⟨*animal*⟩; grow ⟨*plant*⟩; *(ugs.)* rear, raise ⟨*child*⟩; **e)** *(ausbilden)* **jmdn. zu etw. ~ziehen** make *or* turn sb. into sth.; **2.** *unr. itr. V.; mit sein (auch fig.)* approach; *(Milit.)* advance

herauf [hɛ'rauf] *Adv.* up; **~ ist es beschwerlich** it's hard work coming up; **vom Tal ~:** up from the valley

herauf-: ~|**arbeiten** *refl. V.* **a)** work one's/its way up; **b)** *(hocharbeiten)* work one's way up; ~|**bemühen 1.** *tr. V.* **jmdn. ~bemühen** trouble sb. to come up; **2.** *refl. V.* take the trouble to come up; **würden Sie sich bitte ~bemühen?** *(geh.)* would you mind coming up?; ~|**beschwören** *tr. V.* **a)** *(verursachen)* cause, bring about ⟨*disaster, war, crisis*⟩; cause, provoke ⟨*dispute, argument*⟩; give rise to ⟨*criticism*⟩; **b)** *(erinnern)* evoke ⟨*memories etc.*⟩; ~|**bitten** *unr. tr. V.* **jmdn. ~bitten** ask sb. [to come] up; ~|**bringen** *unr. tr. V.* bring up; ~|**dämmern** *itr. V.; mit sein* ⟨*day, morning*⟩ dawn, break; *(fig.)* dawn; ~|**dringen** *unr. itr. V.; mit sein* rise up [from below]; ⟨*smell*⟩ drift up [from below]; **von/aus etw. ~dringen** rise/drift up from sth.; **Lachen drang zu uns ~:** [the sound of] laughter reached our ears from below; ~|**fahren 1.** *unr. itr. V.; mit sein* drive up; *(mit einem Motorrad, Rad)* ride up; **2.** *unr. tr. V.* **jmdn. ~fahren** drive sb. up; ~|**führen 1.** *itr. V.* **es führen zwei Wege ~:** there are two paths up; **2.** *tr. V.* show ⟨*person*⟩ up; ~|**kommen** *unr. itr. V.; mit sein* **a)** *(nach oben kommen)* come up; **auf den Baum/die Mauer ~kommen** climb *or* get up the tree/up on the wall; **in das obere Stockwerk ~kommen** come up to the top floor; **b)** *(aufsteigen)* rise; come up; **c)** *(bevorstehen)* ⟨*storm*⟩ be approaching *or* gathering *or* brewing; ~|**lassen** *unr. tr. V. (ugs.)* **jmdn. ~lassen** allow sb. [to come] up; let sb. [come] up; ~|**reichen 1.** *tr. V.* hand *or* pass up; **2.** *itr. V. (ugs.: erreichen)* **bis zu etw. ~reichen** reach up to sth.; ~|**sehen** *unr. itr. V.* look up; ~|**setzen** *tr. V.* increase, raise, put up ⟨*prices, rents, interest rates, etc.*⟩; ~|**steigen** *unr. itr. V.; mit sein* **a)** *(nach [hier] oben kommen)* climb [up]; **b)** *(aufsteigen)* rise; come up; ⟨*mist, smoke*⟩ rise; **c)** *(geh.: beginnen)* ⟨*day, morning*⟩ dawn, break; ⟨*night*⟩ come on, fall; ⟨*dawn*⟩ break; ⟨*new age*⟩ dawn; ~|**ziehen 1.** *unr. tr. V.* pull up; **2.** *unr. itr. V.; mit sein* **a)** *(näher kommen)* ⟨*storm*⟩ be approaching *or* gathering *or* brewing; *(fig.)* ⟨*disaster*⟩ be approaching; **b)** *s.* **~steigen c**

heraus [hɛ'raus] *Adv.* **~ aus den Federn!/dem Bett!** rise and shine!/out of bed!; **~ mit dir!** get out of here!; **~ damit!** *(gib her!)* hand it over!; *(weg damit!)* get rid of it!; **~ mit der Sprache!** out with it!; **nach vorn ~ wohnen** live at the front; **aus einem Gefühl der Einsamkeit ~:** out of a feeling of loneliness

heraus-, Heraus-: ~|**arbeiten 1.** *tr. V.* **a)** *(aus Stein, Holz)* fashion, carve (**aus** out of); **b)** *(hervorheben)* bring out ⟨*difference, aspect, point of view, etc.*⟩; develop ⟨*observation, remark*⟩; **2.** *refl. V.* work one's way out (**aus** of); ~|**bekommen 1.** *unr. tr. V.* **a)** *(entfernen)* get out (**aus** of); **b)** *(ugs.: lösen)* work out ⟨*problem, answer, etc.*⟩; solve ⟨*puzzle*⟩; **c)** *(ermitteln)* find out; **etw. aus jmdm. ~bekommen** get sth. out of sb.; **d)** *(als Wechselgeld bekommen)* **5 DM ~bekommen** get back 5 marks change; **ich bekomme noch 5 DM ~:** I still have 5 marks [change] to come; **e)** *(von sich geben) s.* **~bringen h; 2.** *unr. itr. V. (Wechselgeld bekommen)* **richtig/falsch ~bekommen** *(ugs.)* get the right/wrong change; ~|**bilden** *refl. V.* develop; ~|**bitten** *unr. tr. V.* **jmdn. ~bitten** ask sb. to come out[side]; **darf ich Sie einen Moment ~bitten?** would you mind coming outside for a moment?; ~|**boxen** *tr. V.* **a)** *(Fußball, Handball)* punch out; **b)** *(befreien)* bail out; ~|**brechen 1.** *unr. tr. V.* knock out; *(mit brutaler Gewalt)* wrench out; pull up ⟨*paving-stone*⟩; **eine Tür/ein paar Fliesen aus der Wand ~brechen** knock out a hole [in the wall] for a doorway/knock a few tiles off the wall; **2.** *unr. itr. V.; mit sein* ⟨*anger, hatred*⟩ burst forth, erupt; **aus dem Glas ist ein großer Splitter ~gebrochen** there's a large chip out of the glass; ~|**bringen** *unr. tr. V.* **a)** *(nach außen bringen)* bring out (**aus** of); **b)** *(nach draußen begleiten)* show out; **c)** *(veröffentlichen)* bring out; publish; *(aufführen)* put on, stage ⟨*play*⟩; screen ⟨*film*⟩; **d)** *(auf den Markt bringen)* bring out; launch; **e)** *(populär machen)* make widely known; **jmdn./etw. ganz groß ~bringen** launch sb./sth. in a big way; **f)** *(ugs.: ermitteln) s.* **~bekommen 1 c; g)** *(ugs.: lösen) s.* **~bekommen 1 b; h)** *(von sich geben)* utter; say; ~|**drehen** *tr. V.* unscrew; ~|**drücken** *tr. V.* **a) etw. ~drücken** squeeze sth. out (**aus** of); squeeze *or* press ⟨*juice, oil*⟩ out (**aus** of); **b)** *(vorwölben)* stick out ⟨*chest etc.*⟩;

~|**dürfen** *unr. itr. V.* be allowed [to come/go] out; ~|**fahren 1.** *unr. itr. V.; mit sein* **a)** *(nach außen fahren)* **aus etw. ~fahren** drive out of sth.; *(mit dem Rad, Motorrad)* ride out of sth.; **der Zug fuhr aus dem Bahnhof ~**: the train pulled out of the station; **b)** *(fahrend ~kommen)* come out; **c)** *(ugs.: schnell ~kommen)* **aus dem Bett ~fahren** shoot *or* leap out of bed; **eilig fuhr sie aus dem Mantel ~**: she whipped off her coat; **d)** *(ugs.: entschlüpfen)* ‹*word, remark, etc.*› slip out; **2.** *unr. tr. V.* **a) den Wagen/das Fahrrad [aus dem Hof] ~fahren** drive the car/ride the bicycle out [of the yard]; **jmdn. ~fahren** drive sb. out (**zu** to); **b)** *(Sport)* **eine gute Zeit/einen Sieg ~fahren** record a good *or* fast time/a victory; **den zweiten Platz ~fahren** take second place; ~|**finden 1.** *unr. tr. V.* **a)** *(entdecken)* find out; trace ‹*fault*›; **man fand ~, daß ...**: it was found *or* discovered that ...; **b)** *(aus einer Menge)* pick out (**aus** from [among]); find (**aus** among); **2.** *unr. itr. V.* find one's way out (**aus** of); **3.** *unr. refl. V.* find one's way out (**aus** of); ~|**fischen** *tr. V. (ugs.)* fish out *(coll.)* (**aus** of); **sie hat sich** *(Dat.)* **einige hübsche Sachen ~gefischt** she picked out some nice things [for herself]; ~|**fliegen 1.** *unr. itr. V.; mit sein* **a)** fly out (**aus** of); **b)** *(aus etw. fallen)* be thrown out (**aus** of); **c)** *(ugs.: entlassen werden)* be fired *or (coll.)* sacked (**bei** from); **2.** *unr. tr. V.* fly out (**aus** of); **~forderer der; ~s, ~** *(auch Sport)* challenger; ~|**fordern 1.** *tr. V.* **a)** *(auch Sport)* challenge; **b)** *(heraufbeschwören)* provoke ‹*person, resistance, etc.*›; invite ‹*criticism*›; court ‹*danger*›; **sein Schicksal ~fordern** tempt fate *or* providence; **2.** *itr. V. (provozieren)* **zu etw. ~fordern** provoke sth.; **~fordernd 1.** *Adj.* provocative; *(verlockend)* provocative, inviting ‹*glance, smile, etc.*›; *(Streit suchend)* challenging, defiant ‹*words, speech, look*›; **2.** *adv.: s. Adj.:* provocatively; invitingly; challengingly; defiantly

Heraus·forderung die *(auch Sport)* challenge; *(Provokation)* provocation

heraus-, Heraus-: ~|**fühlen** *tr. V.* sense; feel; ~|**führen 1.** *tr. V.* **a)** *(nach außen führen)* lead out; **b)** *(nach draußen führen)* bring out; **was führt dich denn zu uns ~?** what brings you out to see us, then?; **2.** *itr. V.* lead out (**aus** of); **~gabe die;** *o. Pl.* **a)** *(von Eigentum, Personen, Geiseln usw.)* handing over; *(Rückgabe)* return; **b)** *(das Veröffentlichen)* publication; *(Redaktion)* editing; ~|**geben 1.** *unr. tr. V.* **a)** *(nach außen geben)* hand *or* pass out; **b)** *(aushändigen)* hand over ‹*property, person, hostage, etc.*›; *(zurückgeben)* return; give back; **c)** *(als Wechselgeld zurückgeben)* **5 DM/zuviel ~geben** give 5 marks/too much change; **d)** *(veröffentlichen)* publish; *(für die Veröffentlichung bearbeiten)* edit [for publication]; **e)** issue ‹*stamp, coin, etc.*›; **f)** *(erlassen)* issue; **2.** *itr. V.* give change; **können Sie [auf 100 DM] ~geben?** do you have *or* can you give me change [for 100 marks]?; **jmdn. falsch/richtig ~geben** give sb. the wrong/right change; **~geber der, ~geberin die** publisher; *(Redakteur)* editor; ~|**gehen** *unr. itr. V.; mit sein* **a)** *(nach außen gehen)* go out; leave; **aus dem Saal ~gehen** go out of the hall; **aus sich ~gehen** come out of one's shell; **b)** *(sich entfernen lassen)* ‹*stain, cork, nail, etc.*› come out; ~|**greifen** *unr. tr. V.* pick out; select; **sich** *(Dat.)* **jmdn. ~greifen** pick *or* single sb. out (**aus** from); *(fig.)* take ‹*example, aspect, etc.*› (**aus** from); ~|**haben** *unr. tr. V. (ugs.)* **a)** *(entfernt haben)* have got ‹*stain, nail, cork, etc.*› out; **ich will ihn aus dem Verein ~haben** I want him out of the club; **b)** *(verstanden haben)* have found out; **den Bogen** *od.* **Dreh ~haben[, wie man es macht]** have got the knack [of doing it]; **c)** *(gelöst haben)* have worked out *or* solved ‹*problem*›; have solved ‹*puzzle*›; **er hat etwas anderes ~ als ich** we arrived at *or* got different answers; **ich hab's ~!** I've done it!; **d)** *(ermittelt haben)* know; have found out; ~|**halten 1.** *unr. tr. V.* **a)** *(nach außen halten)* put *or* stick out (**aus** of); **b)** *(ugs.: fernhalten, nicht verwickeln)* keep out (**aus** of); **2.** *unr. refl. V.* keep *or* stay out; **halte du dich da ~!** you keep *or* stay out of this *or* it!; [1]~|**hängen** *unr. itr. V.* hang out (**aus** of); [2]~|**hängen** *tr. V.* hang out (**aus** of); ~|**hauen** *unr. tr. V.* **a)** chop *or* cut down and clear ‹*tree*›; **b)** *(durch Hauen fertigen)* carve ‹*figure, letters, relief, etc.*› (**aus** from, out of); **c)** *(ugs.: befreien)* get out; *(aus Schwierigkeiten)* bail out; ~|**heben 1.** *unr. tr. V.* **a)** *(nach außen heben)* lift out (**aus** of); **b)** *(hervorheben)* bring out; **es ist diese Eigenschaft, die ihn aus der Masse ~hebt** it is this quality that raises him above *or* sets him apart from the rest; **etw. durch Fettdruck aus dem übrigen Text ~heben** make sth. stand out from the rest of the text with bold type; **2.** *unr. refl. V.* stand out (**aus** from); ~|**helfen** *unr. itr. V.* **jmdm. ~helfen** *(auch fig.)* help sb. out (**aus** of); **er half ihr aus dem Zug ~**: he helped her off the train; ~|**holen** *tr. V.* **a)** *(nach außen holen)* bring out; **etw. aus einem brennenden Haus ~holen** get sth. out of a burning house; **b)** *(ugs.: abgewinnen)* get out; gain, win ‹*victory, points*›; gain, take ‹*place*›; **er holte das Letzte aus sich ~**: he made an all-out *or* supreme effort; **c)** *(ugs.: erwirken)* gain, win ‹*wage increase, advantage, etc.*›; get, achieve ‹*result*›; **d)** *(ugs.: durch Fragen)* get out; **etw. aus jmdm. ~holen** get sth. out of sb.; **e)** *(ugs.: ~arbeiten)* bring out ‹*difference, aspect, point of view*›; **f)** *(ausgleichen)* make up ‹*time, points deficit, etc.*›; **g)** *(ugs.)* **Geld aus jmdm. ~holen** get money out of *or* extract money from sb.; ~|**hören** *tr. V.* **a)** hear; **b)** *(erkennen)* detect, sense (**aus** in); ~|**kehren** *tr. V.* parade; **den Vorgesetzten ~kehren** parade the fact that one is in charge; **die Dame der Gesellschaft ~kehren** act the society lady; **~kehren, daß ...**: parade the fact that ...; ~|**kommen** *unr. itr. V.; mit sein* **a)** *(nach außen kommen)* come out (**aus** of); **nach/in zwei Jahren wieder ~kommen** *(ugs.)* be let out after/in two years; **b)** *(ein Gebiet verlassen)* **er ist nie aus seiner Heimatstadt ~gekommen** he's never been out of *or* never left his home town; **du kommst viel zu wenig ~**: you don't get out nearly enough; **wir kamen aus dem Staunen/Lachen nicht ~** *(fig.)* we couldn't get over our surprise/stop laughing; **c)** *(ugs.: einen Ausweg finden)* get out (**aus** of); **aus einer Situation/den Sorgen ~kommen** get out of a situation/get over one's worries; **aus den Schulden ~kommen** get out of debt; **d)** *(ugs.: auf den Markt kommen)* come out; **mit einem Produkt ~kommen** bring out *or* launch a product; **e)** *(erscheinen)* ‹*book, timetable, etc.*› come out, be published, appear; ‹*coin, postage stamp*› be issued; ‹*play*› be staged; **f)** *(ugs.: bekannt werden)* come out; **g)** *(ugs.: zur Sprache kommen)* **mit etw. ~kommen** come out with sth.; **h)** *(ugs.: sich erfolgreich produzieren)* **ganz groß ~kommen** make a big splash; **i)** *(deutlich werden)* come out; ‹*colour*› show up; **j)** *(ugs.: ausgedrückt werden)* sound; **k)** *(ugs.: sich als Resultat ergeben)* **bei etw. ~kommen** come out of *or* emerge from sth.; **auf dasselbe ~kommen** amount to the same thing; **was kommt bei der Aufgabe ~?** what is the answer to the question?; **dabei kommt nichts ~**: nothing will come of it; **was soll dabei ~kommen?** what's that supposed to achieve?; **l)** *(ugs.: aus der Übung kommen)* get out of practice; **m)** *(ugs.: ausspielen)* lead; **wer kommt ~?** whose lead is it?; **mit etw. ~kommen** lead sth.; **n)** *(ugs.: gewinnen)* ‹*number, person*› come up; **o)** *(schweiz.: ausgehen, enden)* turn out; ~|**kriegen** *tr. V. (ugs.) s.* **~bekommen;** ~|**kristallisieren 1.** *tr. V.* **a)** *(Chemie)* crystallize [out]; **b)** *(zusammenfassen)* extract; **2.** *refl. V.* **a)** *(Chemie)* crystallize [out]; ‹*crystal*› form; **b)** *(entwickeln)* crystallize (**aus** out of); ~|**lassen** *unr. tr. V. (ugs.)* **a)** *(nach außen kommen lassen)* let out (**aus** of); release (**aus** from); **abends lassen sie den Wachhund ~**: they let the guard-dog loose in the evenings; **b)** *(weglassen)* leave out (**aus** of); ~|**laufen 1.** *unr. itr. V.; mit sein* **a)** run out (**aus** of); *(Fußball)* ‹*goalkeeper*› come out; **b)** *(nach außen fließen)* run out (**aus** of); **2.** *unr. tr. V.* *(Sport)* win ‹*victory*›; build up ‹*lead*›; take ‹*first place etc.*›; **eine gute Zeit ~laufen** run *or* record a good time; ~|**lesen** *unr. tr. V.* **a)** *(entnehmen)* tell (**aus** from); **b)** *(interpretieren)* **etw. aus etw. ~lesen** read sth. into sth.; **c)** *(auswählen)* pick out (**aus** from); ~|**locken** *tr. V.* **a)** entice out (**aus** of); lure ‹*enemy, victim, etc.*› out (**aus** of); **b)** *(durch List)* **Geld/ein Geheimnis aus jmdm. ~locken** wheedle money/worm a secret out of sb.; **jmdn. aus seiner Reserve ~locken** draw sb. out of his/her shell; ~|**lügen** *unr. refl. V.* **sich aus etw. ~lügen** lie one's way out of sth.; ~|**machen** *(ugs.)* **1.** *tr. V.* take out; get out ‹*stain*›; **2.** *refl. V.* come on well; *(nach einer Krankheit)* pick up; *(finanziell)* do well; ~|**müssen** *unr. itr. V. (ugs.)* **a) aus etw. ~müssen** have to leave sth.; **dieser Zahn muß ~**: this tooth has to come out; **b)** *(aufstehen müssen)* have to get up; **c)** *(gesagt werden müssen)* have to come out; **das mußte einfach ~!** I simply had to get that off my chest *(coll.)*; **~nehmbar** *Adj.* removable; detachable ‹*lining*›; ~|**nehmen** *unr. tr. V.* **a)** take out (**aus** of); **b)** *(ugs.: entfernen)* take out, remove ‹*appendix, tonsils, tooth, etc.*›; **jmdm. den Blinddarm ~nehmen** take out *or* remove sb.'s appendix; **sich** *(Dat.)* **die Mandeln ~nehmen lassen** have one's tonsils out; **den Gang ~nehmen** *(fig.)* put the car into neutral; **ein Kind aus einer Schule ~nehmen** take a child away *or* remove a child from a school; *(Ballspiele)* take off ‹*player*›; **c)** *(ugs.: erlauben)* **sich** *(Dat.)* **Freiheiten ~nehmen** take liberties; **was nimmst du dir ~, mich so zu kritisieren!** how dare you criticize me like that!; **sich** *(Dat.)* **zuviel ~nehmen** go too far; ~|**picken** *tr. V. (fig.)* pick out (**aus** of); ~|**platzen** *itr. V.; mit sein (ugs.)* **a)** *(~lachen)* burst out laughing; **b)** *(spontan äußern)* **mit etw. ~platzen** blurt sth. out; ~|**pressen** *tr. V.* **a)** *(aus etw. pressen) s.* **~drücken a; b)** *(erpressen)* squeeze out ‹*money*› (**aus** from); wring out ‹*confession, concession*› (**aus** from); ~|**putzen** *tr. V.* **a)** *(festlich kleiden)* dress up; **sich ~putzen** get dressed up; **b)** *(festlich schmücken)* deck out; **sich ~putzen** be decked out; ~|**ragen** *itr. V.* **a)** jut out, project (**aus** from); *(sich erheben über)* **aus etw. ~ragen** rise above sth.; **b)** *(hervortreten)* stand out (**aus** from); **~ragend** *Adj.* outstanding; ~|**reden** *refl. V. (ugs.)* talk one's way out (**aus** of); ~|**reißen** *unr. tr. V.* **a)** tear *or* rip out (**aus** of); pull up *or* out ‹*plant*›; pull out ‹*hair*›; pull up ‹*floor*›; rip out ‹*tiles*›; **b)** *(aus der Umgebung, der Arbeit)* tear away (**aus** from); **die Krankheit hat ihn aus der Arbeit ~gerissen** the illness had interrupted his work; **jmdn. aus einem Gespräch/seiner Lethargie ~reißen** drag sb. away from a conversation/jolt *or* shake sb. out of his/her lethargy; **jmdn. aus seiner Traurigkeit ~reißen** take sb. out of himself/herself; **c)** *(ugs.: befreien)* save; ~|**rücken 1.** *tr. V.* **a)** *(nach außen rücken)* move out (**aus** of); **b)** *(ugs.: hergeben)* hand over; cough up *(coll.)* ‹*money*›; **2.** *itr. V.; mit sein* **mit etw./der**

Sprache ~rücken come out with sth./it; **~|rufen 1.** *unr. itr. V.* call *or* shout out (**aus** of); **2.** *unr. tr. V.* call out; **jmdn. aus einer Sitzung ~rufen** call sb. out of a meeting; **das Publikum rief den Sänger mehrmals ~:** the audience called the singer back several times; **~|rutschen** *itr. V.; mit sein* **a)** slip out (**aus** of); **ihm rutscht immer das Hemd aus der Hose ~:** his shirt is always coming out of his trousers; **b)** *(ugs.: entschlüpfen)* ⟨*remark etc.*⟩ slip out; **die Bemerkung war ihr nur so ~gerutscht** the remark just slipped out somehow; **~|saugen** *unr. (auch regelm.) tr. V.* suck out (**aus** of); **~|schälen** *refl. V.* **a)** *(erkennbar werden)* emerge (**aus** from); **b)** *(sich erweisen)* **sich als etw. ~schälen** turn out *or* prove to be sth.; **~|schauen** *itr. V. (landsch.)* **a)** look out (**aus/zu** of); **b)** *(hervorschauen)* ⟨*petticoat etc.*⟩ be showing; ⟨*shirt*⟩ be hanging out; **c)** *(ugs.: zu erwarten sein)* **dabei schaut etwas/nicht viel für ihn ~:** there's something/not much in it for him; **es schaut nichts dabei ~:** there's nothing to be gained by it; **~|schießen** *unr. itr. V.* **a)** **aus einem Fenster/Auto ~schießen** shoot *or* fire from a window/car; **b)** *mit sein (sich schnell bewegen)* shoot out (**aus** of); **ein Blutstrahl schoß aus der Wunde ~:** blood spurted from the wound; **~geschossen kommen** *(ugs.)* shoot out (**aus** of); **~|schlagen 1.** *unr. tr. V.* **a)** knock out; **b)** *(ugs.: gewinnen)* get ⟨*discount, advantage, etc.*⟩; make ⟨*money, profit*⟩; **2.** *unr. itr. V.; mit sein* ⟨*flames*⟩ leap out (**aus** of); **~|schleichen 1.** *unr. itr. V.; mit sein* sneak *or* steal out (**aus** of); **2.** *unr. refl. V.* sneak *or* steal out (**aus** of); **~|schleudern** *tr. V.* hurl *or* fling out (**aus** of); hurl ⟨*accusations etc.*⟩; **die Straßenbahn wurde aus den Schienen ~geschleudert** the tram *(Brit.) or (Amer.)* streetcar was flung *or* thrown off the rails; **~|schlüpfen** *itr. V.; mit sein* slip out (**aus** of); **eine Bemerkung schlüpfte ihm ~:** a remark slipped out; **~|schmecken 1.** *tr. V.* **etw. ~schmecken [können]** be able to taste sth.; **2.** *itr. V.* taste; **~|schmeißen** *s.* **rausschmeißen; ~|schmuggeln** *tr. V.* smuggle out (**aus** of); **~|schneiden** *unr. tr. V.* cut out (**aus** of); **~|schrauben** *tr. V.* unscrew ⟨*light bulb, screw*⟩; unscrew, screw off ⟨*door handle, table leg, etc.*⟩; **~|schreiben** *unr. tr. V.* copy out (**aus** from); **~|schreien** *unr. tr. V.* **seine Wut/seinen Zorn/seinen Haß ~schreien** vent *or* give vent to one's anger/rage/hatred in a loud outburst; **~|sein** *unr. itr. V. mit sein (nur im Inf. u. Part. zusammengeschrieben) (ugs.)* **a)** *(draußen sein)* be out; **b)** *(entfernt sein)* ⟨*tooth, appendix, nail, etc.*⟩ be out; **c)** *(hervorgekommen sein)* ⟨*flowers, stars, etc.*⟩ be out; **d)** *(hinter sich gelassen haben)* **aus etw. ~sein** be out of sth.; **aus der Schule ~sein** have left school; **e)** *(überstanden haben)* **aus den Schulden/einem Dilemma** *usw.* **~sein** have got *or* be out of debt/a dilemma *etc.*; **aus dem Gröbsten ~sein** be over the worst; **f)** *(veröffentlicht sein)* ⟨*book, banknote, timetable, etc.*⟩ be out; **g)** *(bekannt sein)* be known; **h)** *(ausgesprochen sein)* ⟨*truth*⟩ be out, have come out; ⟨*words*⟩ have been said; **i)** *(ugs.)* **fein ~sein** be sitting pretty *(coll.)*

heraußen [hɛˈrausn̩] *Adv. (südd., österr.)* out here

heraus-: ~|springen *unr. itr. V.; mit sein* **a)** jump *or* leap out (**aus** of); **b)** *(sich lösen)* come out; **c)** *s.* **~schauen c; ~|sprudeln 1.** *itr. V.; mit sein* bubble out (**aus** of); **2.** *tr. V.* **sie sprudelte die Worte heraus** the words tumbled from her lips; **~|stehen** *unr. itr. V.* protrude; stick out; **~|stellen 1.** *tr. V.* **a)** put out[side]; **sie stellte das Geschirr zum Abendessen ~:** she got the china out ready for dinner; **einen Spieler ~stellen** *(Sport)* send a player off; **b)** *(hervorheben)* emphasize; bring out; present, set out ⟨*principles etc.*⟩; **eine Nebenfigur ~stellen** give prominence to a minor character; **2.** *refl. V.* **es stellte sich ~, daß ...:** it turned out *or* emerged that ...; **wie sich später ~stellte, hatte er ...:** it turned out later that he had ...; **wer recht hat, wird sich erst noch ~stellen müssen** it remains to be seen who is right; **es wird sich bald ~stellen, ob ...:** we shall soon know *or* find out whether ...; **sich als falsch/wahr** *usw.* **~stellen** turn out *or* prove to be wrong/true *etc.*; **~|strecken** *tr. V.* stick out (**aus** of); **jmdm. die Zunge ~strecken** stick *or* put one's tongue out at sb.; **seinen Arm/Kopf zum Fenster ~strecken** stick *or* put one's arm/head out of the window; **~|streichen** *unr. tr. V.* **a)** *(ausstreichen)* cross out; delete (**aus** from); **b)** *(hervorheben)* point out; **er streicht gerne ~, daß ...:** he likes everyone to know that ...; **~|strömen** *itr. V.; mit sein* **a)** *(ausströmen)* ⟨*water etc.*⟩ pour out (**aus** of); ⟨*gas*⟩ escape (**aus** from); **b)** *(~kommen)* ⟨*Menschenmenge*⟩ pour out (**aus** of); **~|stürzen** *itr. V.; mit sein* **a)** *(~fallen)* fall out (**aus** of); **b)** *(eilen)* rush *or* dash out (**aus** of); **~|suchen** *tr. V.* pick out; look out ⟨*file*⟩; **~|tragen** *unr. tr. V.* carry outside; **die Kisten aus dem Haus ~tragen** carry the boxes out of the house; **~|treten** *unr. itr. V.; mit sein* **a)** come out (**aus** of); **auf den Balkon ~treten** come *or* step out onto the balcony; **b)** *(sich abzeichnen)* ⟨*veins etc.*⟩ stand out; **~|trommeln** *tr. V. (ugs.)* get out; **~|wachsen** *unr. itr. V.; mit sein* grow out (**aus** of); **~|werfen** *unr. tr. V.* **a)** throw out (**aus** of); **b)** *s.* **hinauswerfen; ~|winden** *unr. refl. V.* wriggle out (**aus** of); **~|wirtschaften** *tr. V.* make ⟨*profit etc.*⟩ (**aus** out of); **~|wollen** *unr. itr. V.* want to come/go out (**aus** of); **er wollte nicht mit der Sprache ~:** he did not want to come out with it; **~|ziehen 1.** *unr. tr. V.* **a)** pull out (**aus** of); **b)** *(wegbringen)* pull out, withdraw ⟨*troops etc.*⟩; **c)** *(exzerpieren, extrahieren)* extract (**aus** from); **2.** *unr. itr. V.; mit sein* move out (**aus** of)

herb [hɛrp] **1.** *Adj.* **a)** [slightly] sharp *or* astringent ⟨*taste*⟩; dry ⟨*wine*⟩; [slightly] sharp *or* tangy ⟨*smell, perfume*⟩; **b)** bitter ⟨*disappointment, loss*⟩; severe ⟨*face, features*⟩; austere ⟨*beauty*⟩; **c)** *(unfreundlich)* harsh ⟨*words, criticism*⟩; curt ⟨*greeting*⟩. **2.** *adv.* bitterly ⟨*disappointed*⟩

Herbarium [hɛrˈbaːri̯ʊm] **das; ~s, Herbarien** [-ˈ-ri̯ən] herbarium

herbei [hɛɐ̯ˈbai̯] *Adv.* **~ [zu mir]!** come [over] here!; **alle Mann** *od. (ugs.)* **alles ~!** come [over] here, everybody!

herbei-: ~|bringen *unr. tr. V.* bring [over]; **~|eilen** *itr. V.; mit sein* hurry over; come hurrying up; **~|führen** *tr. V.* produce, bring about ⟨*decision*⟩; bring about, cause ⟨*downfall*⟩; cause ⟨*accident*⟩; **wenn nicht bald eine Entscheidung ~geführt wird** if no decision is reached soon; **den Tod ~führen** cause death; **~|holen** *tr. V.* fetch; **sich** *(Dat.)* **etw. ~holen lassen** have sth. brought to one; **einen Arzt ~holen/~holen lassen** fetch/send for a doctor; **~|kommen** *unr. itr. V.; mit sein* come up *or* along; **die Menschen kamen aus allen Richtungen ~:** people came from all directions; **~|lassen** *unr. refl. V. (iron.)* **sich ~lassen, etw. zu tun** condescend *or* deign to do sth.; **~|laufen** *unr. itr. V.; mit sein* come running up; **~|rufen** *unr. tr. V.* call over; **Hilfe/einen Arzt ~rufen** summon help/call a doctor; **~|schaffen** *tr. V.* bring; *(besorgen)* get; **~|sehnen** *tr. V.* long for; **sie hatte den Urlaub sehr ~gesehnt** she had been longing for the holidays to arrive; **~|strömen** *itr. V.; mit sein* come in crowds; come flocking; **~|winken** *tr. V.* **jmdn. ~winken** beckon sb. over; **~|wünschen** *tr. V.* long for; **jmdn. ~wünschen** long for sb. to come; **~|ziehen** *unr. tr. V.* **etw. ~ziehen** pull *or* draw sth. up; draw ⟨*crowd etc.*⟩; **jmdn. ~ziehen** draw sb. to one; **sich** *(Dat.)* **etw. ~ziehen** pull *or* draw sth. to one; *s. auch* **Haar b; ~|zitieren** *tr. V.* **jmdn. ~zitieren** send for *or* summon sb.

her-: ~|bekommen *unr. tr. V.* get; **~|bemühen** *(geh.)* **1.** *tr. V.* **jmdn. ~bemühen** trouble sb. to come; **2.** *refl. V.* take the trouble to come; **~|beordern** *tr. V.* summon; send for

Herberge [ˈhɛrbɛrgə] **die; ~, ~n a)** *(veralt.: Gasthaus)* inn; **b)** *(Jugend~)* [youth] hostel; **c)** *(veralt.: Unterkunft)* accommodation *no indef. art.*

Herbergs-: ~mutter die, ~vater der warden [of the/a youth hostel]

her-: ~|bestellen *tr. V.* **jmdn. ~bestellen** ask sb. to come; *(~beordern)* summon sb.; **~|beten** *s.* **herunterbeten**

Herbheit die; ~: *s.* **herb 1a, b:** [slight] sharpness *or* astringency; dryness; [slight] sharpness *or* tanginess; bitterness; severity; austerity

her|bitten *unr. tr. V.* **jmdn. ~:** ask sb. to come

Herbizid [hɛrbiˈtsiːt] **das; ~s, ~e** herbicide

her|bringen *unr. tr. V.* **etw. ~:** bring sth. [here]

Herbst [hɛrpst] **der; ~[e]s, ~e** autumn; fall *(Amer.)*; *s. auch* **Frühling**

Herbst-: ~anfang der beginning of autumn; **~blume die** autumn flower

herbsten *itr. V. (unpers.) (geh.)* **es herbstet** autumn is coming *or* approaching

Herbst·ferien *Pl.* autumn half-term holiday *sing.*

herbstlich 1. *Adj.* autumn *attrib.*; autumnal; *(wie im Herbst)* autumnal; **es wird ~:** autumn is coming. **2.** *adv.* **sich ~ färben** take on the colours of autumn; **~ kühle Tage** cool autumn days; **es ist schon ~ kühl** there's already an autumn chill in the air

Herbst-: ~monat der a) autumn month; **b)** *(veralt.)* **der ~monat** September; **~tag der** autumn day; **~wetter das** autumnal weather; **~zeit·lose die; ~, ~n** *(Bot.)* meadow saffron

Herd [heːɐ̯t] **der; ~[e]s, ~e a)** *(Kochstelle)* cooker; stove; **das Essen auf dem ~ haben** *(ugs.)* be cooking something; **den ganzen Tag am ~ stehen** *(ugs.)* slave over a hot stove all day; **am heimischen** *od.* **häuslichen ~:** by one's own fireside; **eigener ~ ist Goldes wert** there's no place like home *(prov.)*; **b)** *(Ausgangspunkt)* centre *(of disturbance/rebellion)*; *(Geol.)* focus; **c)** *(Med.)* focus; seat; **d)** *(Technik)* hearth

Herd·buch das *(Landw.)* herd-book

Herde [ˈheːɐ̯də] **die; ~, ~n a)** *(von Tieren)* herd; **eine ~ Rinder** a herd of cattle; **eine ~ Schafe** a flock of sheep; **b)** *(abwertend: Menschenmenge)* crowd; **mit der ~ laufen, der ~ folgen** follow the herd *or* crowd; **c)** *(fig.: kirchliche Gemeinde)* flock

Herden-: ~mensch der *(abwertend) s.* **~tier b; ~tier das a)** gregarious animal; **b)** *(abwertend: Mensch)* sheep; **~trieb der** *(auch fig. abwertend)* herd instinct

Herd·platte die *(eines Elektroherdes)* hotplate; *(eines Kohlenherds)* top

herein [hɛˈrai̯n] *Adv.* **~!** come in!; **[immer] nur ~ mit dir!** come on in!

herein-: ~|bekommen *unr. tr. V. (ugs.)* get in ⟨*fresh stocks*⟩; pick up ⟨*radio station*⟩; recover ⟨*investment*⟩; **~|bemühen** *(geh.)* **1.** *tr. V.* **jmdn. ~bemühen** trouble sb. to come in; **2.** *refl. V.* take the trouble to come in; **~|bitten** *unr. tr. V.* **jmdn. ~bitten** ask *or* invite sb. in; **~|brechen** *unr. itr. V.; mit sein* **a)** *(geh.: hart treffen)* **über jmdn./etw. ~brechen** ⟨*fate, disaster, misfortune, etc.*⟩ befall *or* overtake sb./sth.; **b)** *(geh.: beginnen)* ⟨*night, evening, dusk*⟩ fall; ⟨*winter*⟩ set in; ⟨*storm*⟩ strike, break; **c)** *(überfluten)* **über etw.** *(Akk.)* **~brechen** break over sth.;

eine Flut von Beschimpfungen brach über ihn ~ *(fig.)* he was engulfed in a flood of abuse; **~|bringen** *unr. tr. V.* **a)** bring in; **etw. in etw.** *(Akk.)* **~bringen** bring sth. into sth.; **b)** *(wettmachen)* make up ⟨*loss*⟩*;* make up for ⟨*delay*⟩; recoup ⟨*costs*⟩; **~|drängen** *itr. V.; mit sein* push one's way in; **in etw.** *(Akk.)* **~drängen** push one's way into sth.; **~|dürfen** *unr. itr. V. (ugs.)* be allowed in; **in etw.** *(Akk.)* **~dürfen** be allowed into sth.; **darf er ~?** may *or* can he come in?; **~|fallen** *unr. itr. V.; mit sein* **a)** ⟨*light*⟩ shine in; **b)** *(ugs.: betrogen werden)* be taken for a ride *(coll.);* be done *(coll.);* **bei/mit etw. ~fallen** be taken for a ride with sth.; **auf jmdn./etw. ~fallen** be taken in by sb./sth.; **~|führen** *tr. V.* **jmdn. ~führen** show sb. in; **~|holen** *tr. V.* **a)** bring in; **b)** *(ugs.: verdienen)* make *(coll.);* **~|kommen** *unr. itr. V.; mit sein* come in; **in das Haus/zur Tür ~kommen** come into the house/in through the door; **wie sind sie ~gekommen?** how did they get in?; **~|kriegen** *tr. V. (ugs.) s.* **~bekommen; ~|lassen** *unr. tr. V.* let *or* allow in; **jmdn. ins Zimmer ~lassen** let *or* allow sb. into the room; **~|legen** *tr. V. (ugs.)* **jmdn. ~legen** take sb. for a ride *(coll.)* **(mit, bei** with); **~|nehmen** *unr. tr. V.* **a)** bring in; **etw. ins Haus ~nehmen** bring sth. into the house; **b)** *(in eine Liste)* include; **etw. in sein Sortiment ~nehmen** start selling sth. as well; **~|platzen** *itr. V.; mit sein (ugs.)* burst in; come bursting in; **in den Saal ~platzen** burst *or* come bursting into the hall; **~|rasseln** *itr. V.; mit sein (salopp)* **a)** *(betrogen werden)* **mit/bei etw. ~rasseln** be taken for a ride *(coll.);* **b)** *(in Schwierigkeiten geraten)* get into deep water *(coll.);* **~|regnen** *itr. V. (unpers.)* **es regnet ~:** the rain's coming in; **~|reichen 1.** *tr. V.* hand *or* pass in; **2.** *itr. V.* **etw. reicht in das Zimmer ~:** sth. comes [right] in to the room; **~|reißen** *unr. tr. V. (ugs.) s.* **reinreißen; ~|reiten 1.** *unr. itr. V.; mit sein* ride in; **in den Hof ~reiten** ride into the yard; **2.** *s.* **reinreiten; ~|rufen** *unr. tr. V.* **jmdn. ~rufen** call sb. in; **~|schauen** *itr. V. (landsch.) s.* **~sehen; ~|schleichen** *unr. itr. V. mit sein; refl. V.* creep *or* steal in; **[sich] ins Haus ~schleichen** creep *or* steal into the house; **~|schneien** *unr. itr. V.* **a)** *mit sein (ugs.)* turn up out of the blue *(coll.);* **b)** *(unpers.)* **es schneit ~:** the snow's coming in; **~|sehen** *unr. itr. V.* **a)** see in; *(hereinblicken)* look in; **in etw.** *(Akk.)* **~sehen** see/look into sth.; **b)** *(kurz besuchen)* look *or* drop in **(bei** on); **~|spazieren** *itr. V.; mit sein (ugs.)* walk in; stroll in; **er ist einfach in das Zimmer ~spaziert** he simply walked straight into the room; **nur ~spaziert!** come right in!; **~|stecken** *tr. V.* **den Kopf zur Tür ~stecken** *s.* **Tür; ~|strömen** *itr. V.; mit sein* ⟨*water etc.*⟩ pour in; ⟨*people*⟩ pour *or* stream in; **in etw.** *(Akk.)* **~strömen** pour *or* stream into sth.; **~|stürmen** *itr. V.; mit sein* rush *or* dash in; come rushing *or* dashing in; *(wütend)* storm in; come storming in; **ins Zimmer ~stürmen** rush/storm into the room; **~|stürzen** *itr. V.; mit sein* rush in; burst in; **ins Zimmer ~stürzen** rush *or* burst into the room; **~|tragen** *unr. tr. V.* carry in; **etw. ins Haus ~tragen** carry sth. into the house; **~|wagen** *refl. V.* venture to come in; **~|wollen** *unr. itr. V. (ugs.)* want to come in; **ins Haus ~wollen** want to come into the house

her-, Her-: ~|fahren 1. *unr. itr. V.; mit sein* come here; *(mit einem Auto)* drive *or* come here; *(mit einem [Motor]rad)* ride *or* come here; **hinter/vor jmdm./etw. ~fahren** drive/ride along behind/in front of sb./sth.; **2.** *unr. tr. V.* **jmdn. ~fahren** drive sb. here; **~fahrt die** journey here; **~|fallen** *unr. itr. V.; mit sein* **a) über jmdn. ~fallen** set upon *or* attack sb.; ⟨*animal*⟩ attack sb.; **mit Fragen/Vorwürfen über jmdn. ~fallen** *(fig.)* besiege sb. with questions/hurl reproaches at sb.; **b)** *(gierig zu essen beginnen)* **über etw.** *(Akk.)* **~fallen** fall upon sth.; **~|finden** *unr. itr. V.* find one's way here; **~|führen** *tr. V.* **a)** *(geleiten)* **jmdn. ~führen** bring sb. here; **ein Tier hinter/vor jmdm. ~führen** lead an animal along in front of/behind sb.; **b)** *(an einen Ort gelangen lassen)* **was führt dich ~?** what brings you here?; **~gang der: der ~gang der Ereignisse** the sequence of events; **jmdn. über den ~gang befragen** question sb. about what happened; **schildern Sie den ~gang des Überfalls** describe what happened during the attack; **~|geben** *unr. tr. V.* **a)** hand over; *(weggeben)* give away; **sein Geld für etw. ~geben** put one's money into sth.; **seinen Namen für etw. ~geben** lend one's name to sth.; allow one's name to be associated with sth.; **er hat sein letztes ~gegeben** he gave everything he had; **sich für etw. ~geben** get involved in sth.; **dazu gebe ich mich nicht ~:** I won't have anything to do with it; **b)** *(reichen)* give; **gib es ~!** hand it over!; **c)** *(erbringen)* **der Boden gibt wenig ~:** the soil is poor; **das Thema wird viel ~geben** there's a lot to this topic; **was seine Beine ~gaben** as fast as his legs could carry him; **~gebracht 1.** *2. Part. v.* **~bringen; 2.** *Adj.; nicht präd.* time-honoured; **~|gehen** *unr. itr. V.; mit sein* **a)** *(begleiten)* **neben/vor/hinter jmdm. ~gehen** walk along beside/in front of/behind sb.; **b)** *(ugs.)* **~gehen und etw. tun** just [go and] do sth.; **c)** *(südd., österr.: herkommen)* come [here]; **d)** *(unpers.) (ugs.)* **auf der Party ging es hoch/lustig ~:** everyone had a whale of a time *(coll.)*/great fun at the party; **bei der Debatte ging es heiß ~:** the sparks really flew in the debate; **~|gehören** *s.* **hierhergehören; ~gelaufen 1.** *2. Part. v.* **~laufen; 2.** *Adj.; nicht präd.* **dieser ~gelaufene Strolch** this good-for-nothing rascal from Heaven knows where; **~|haben** *unr. tr. V. (ugs.)* **wo hat er/sie das ~?** where did he/she get that from?; **~|halten 1.** *unr. itr. V.* **~halten müssen [für jmdn./etw.]** be the one to suffer [for sb./sth.]; **als Beweis für die Theorie ~halten** serve as proof of the theory; **der Mantel wird diesen Winter noch einmal ~halten müssen** the coat will have to do for one more winter; **2.** *unr. tr. V.* hold out; **~|holen** *tr. V.* fetch; **etw. von weit ~holen** get sth. from a long way away; **weit ~geholt** far-fetched; **~|hören** *itr. V.* listen; **alle mal ~hören!** listen everybody

Hering ['he:rɪŋ] **der; ~s, ~e a)** herring; **wie die ~e** *(fig.)* packed together like sardines; **b)** *(Zeltpflock)* peg; **c)** *(ugs.: sehr dünne Person)* **ein [richtiger] ~ sein** be as thin as a rake

Herings-: ~fänger der *(Schiff)* herring-boat; **~filet das** herring fillet; **~fischerei die** herring fishing; **~salat der** herring salad

herinnen [hɛ'rɪnən] *Adv. (südd., österr.)* in here

her-, Her-: ~|jagen 1. *tr. V.* **ein Tier ~jagen** drive *or* chase an animal here; **jmdn./ein Tier vor sich** *(Dat.)* **~jagen** drive *or* chase sb./an animal along ahead of one; **2.** *itr. V.; mit sein* **hinter jmdm. ~jagen** chase *or* pursue sb.; **hinter etw. ~jagen** *(fig.)* pursue sth.; **~|kommen** *unr. itr. V.; mit sein* **a)** come here; **komm [mal] ~!** come here!; **sie wird mit Sicherheit ~kommen** she'll definitely come; **b)** *(abstammen)* come; **wer weiß, wo das ~kommt** *(ugs.: warum das so ist)* who can tell the reason?; **c)** *(~genommen werden)* **wo soll das Geld ~kommen?** where is the money coming from?; **~kommen das; ~s a)** *(Brauch, Sitte)* tradition; **b)** *s.* **Herkunft a; ~kömmlich** [~kœmlɪç] *Adj.* conventional; traditional ⟨*custom*⟩

Herkules ['hɛrkulɛs] **der; ~, ~se** Hercules

Herkules·arbeit die Herculean task

herkulisch [hɛr'ku:lɪʃ] *Adj. (geh.)* Herculean

Herkunft ['he:ɐ̯kʊnft] **die; ~, Herkünfte** ['he:ɐ̯kʏnftə] **a)** *(soziale Abstammung)* origin[s *pl.*]; **einfacher** *(Gen.)* **od. von einfacher ~ sein** be of humble origin *or* stock; **sie ist ihrer ~ nach Amerikanerin** she is of American descent *or* extraction; **b)** *(Ursprung)* origin

Herkunfts-: ~bezeichnung die indication of country of origin; **~land das** country of origin

her-: ~|laufen *unr. itr. V.; mit sein* **a) vor/hinter/neben jmdm. ~laufen** run [along] in front of/behind/alongside sb.; **b)** *(nachlaufen)* **hinter jmdm. ~laufen** run after sb.; *(fig.)* chase sb. up; **c)** *(zum Sprechenden laufen)* come on foot; *(schneller)* come running up; **ich bin ~gelaufen** I walked here; *(schneller)* I ran here; **~|leiten 1.** *tr. V.* derive **(aus, von** from); **etw. von jmdm. ~leiten** derive sth. from sb.; **2.** *refl. V.* **sich von/aus etw. ~leiten** derive *or* be derived from sth.; **~|locken** *tr. V.* **jmdn./ein Tier ~locken** live *or* entice sb./an animal here; **ein Tier hinter sich** *(Dat.)* **~locken** entice an animal to follow one along; **~|machen** *(ugs.)* **1.** *refl. V.* **a) sich über etw.** *(Akk.)* **~machen** get stuck into sth. *(coll.);* **sich über das Essen/die Geschenke ~machen** fall upon the food/presents; **b)** *(~fallen)* **sich über jmdn. ~machen** set on *or* attack sb.; **2.** *tr. V.* **wenig ~machen** not look much *(coll.);* **viel ~machen** look great *(coll.);* **nichts ~machen** not look much at all *(coll.);* **viel von jmdm./etw. ~machen** make a lot of fuss about sb./sth.; **wenig/nichts von jmdm./etw. ~machen** not make a lot of/any fuss about sth.

Hermaphrodit [hɛrm|afro'di:t] **der; ~en, ~en** *(Biol., Med.)* hermaphrodite

[1]Hermelin [hɛrmə'li:n] **das; ~s, ~e** *(Tier)* ermine; *(im Sommerfell)* stoat

[2]Hermelin der; ~s, ~e *(Pelz)* ermine

Hermeneutik [hɛrme'nɔytɪk] **die; ~:** hermeneutics *sing., no art.*

hermeneutisch *Adj.* hermeneutic

hermetisch [hɛr'me:tɪʃ] **1.** *Adj.* hermetic. **2.** *adv.* hermetically; **ein Dorf** *usw.* **~ abriegeln** seal a village *etc.* off completely

her|müssen *unr. itr. V. (ugs.)* **das muß her** I/we have to *or* must have it

her·nach *Adv. (veralt.)* after that

her|nehmen *unr. tr. V.* **a)** *(beschaffen)* **wo soll ich das Geld ~?** where am I supposed to get the money from *or* find the money?; **b)** *(bes. österr.: stark beanspruchen)* **die Arbeit/Krankheit/der Schicksalsschlag hat sie hergenommen** the work/illness/blow of fate took it out of her; **c)** *(ugs.: scharf tadeln)* **jmdn. ~:** give sb. a good talking-to

her·nieder- *in Zus. (geh.)* down

heroben [hɛ'ro:bn̩] *Adv. (südd., österr.)* up here

Heroe [he'ro:ə] **der; ~n, ~n** *(geh.)* hero

Heroen·kult der *(geh.)* hero-worship

Heroin [hero'i:n] **das; ~s** heroin

Heroine [hero'i:nə] **die; ~, ~n** *(Theater)* actress who plays heroine roles

heroin·süchtig *Adj.* addicted to heroin *postpos.*

heroisch *Adj.* heroic

heroisieren *tr. V.* make a hero of, heroize ⟨*person*⟩; glorify ⟨*deed*⟩

Heroismus der; ~: heroism

Herold ['he:rɔlt] **der; ~[e]s, ~e** herald

Herr [hɛr] **der; ~n** *(selten:* **~en), ~en a)** *(Mann)* gentleman; **ein feiner ~:** a refined gentleman; **ein feiner/sauberer ~** *(iron.)* a fine one; **das Kugelstoßen/Finale der ~en** *(Sport)* the men's shot-put/singles final; **mein Alter ~** *(ugs. scherzh.: Vater)* my old man *(coll.);* **Alter ~** *(Studentenspr.)* former member; *(Sport)* veteran; **b)** *(Titel, Anrede)* **~ Schulze** Mr Schulze; **~ Professor/Dr.**

Schulze Professor/Dr Schulze; ~ **Minister/Direktor/Studienrat Schulze** Mr Schulze; ~ **Minister/Professor/Doktor** Minister/Professor/doctor; ~ **Vorsitzender/Präsident** Mr Chairman/President; **Sehr geehrter ~ Schulze!** Dear Sir; *(bei persönlicher Bekanntschaft)* Dear Mr Schulze; **Sehr geehrte ~en!** Dear Sirs; ~ **Ober!** waiter!; **mein ~:** sir; **meine ~en** gentlemen; **meine ~en!** *(salopp)* my God!; **bitte sehr, der ~!** there you are, sir; **womit kann ich dem ~n dienen?** *(veralt.)* can I help you, sir?; **Ihr ~ Vater/Sohn/Gemahl** *(geh.)* your father/son/husband; **c)** *(Gebieter)* master; **~! Gebt uns die Freiheit** Sire, give us our freedom; **er ist ~ über alle Menschen auf der Insel** he rules over the whole population of the island; **mein ~ und Gebieter** *(scherzh.)* my lord and master *(joc.)*; **die ~en der Schöpfung** *(ugs. scherzh.)* their lordships *(coll. joc.)*; **in diesem Land ist der König ~ über Leben und Tod** in this country the king has the power of life and death; **wie der ~, so's Gescherr** like master, like man; **sein eigener ~ sein** be one's own master; ~ **der Lage sein/bleiben** be/remain master of the situation; **einer Sache** *(Gen.)* ~ **werden** get sth. under control; **nicht mehr ~ seiner Sinne sein** be no longer in control of oneself; **aus aller ~en Länder[n]** *(geh.)* from the four corners of the earth; from all over the world; **d)** *(Besitzer)* master (**über** + *Akk.* of); **e)** *(christl. Rel.: Gott)* Lord; **Gott der ~:** Lord God; **Brüder und Schwestern im ~n** brothers and sisters in the Lord; **der ~ der Heerscharen** the Lord of Hosts; **er ist ein großer Jäger/Angler vor dem ~n** *(scherzh.)* he loves his hunting/angling

Herrchen das; ~s, ~: master

her|reichen 1. *tr. V.* pass; hand. **2.** *itr. V.* *(bes. südd.)* reach; be long enough

Her·reise die journey here

herren-, Herren-: **~abend der** stag evening; **~artikel der a)** *Pl. (Kleidung)* menswear *sing.*; **b)** *(kleinere Bedarfsartikel)* accessories for men; **~ausstatter der** [gentle]men's outfitter; **~begleitung die: in/ohne ~begleitung** in the company of a gentleman/unaccompanied; with/without a male companion; **~bekanntschaft die** gentleman acquaintance; **eine ~bekanntschaft machen** make the acquaintance of a gentleman; **~besuch der** gentleman visitor/visitors; **~besuch haben** have a gentleman visitor/gentlemen visitors; **~besuch ist ab 20⁰⁰ untersagt** no male visitors after 8 p.m.; **~doppel das** *(Sport)* men's doubles *pl.*; **~einzel das** *(Sport)* men's singles *pl.*; **~fahrrad das** gent's *or* man's bicycle; **~friseur der** men's hairdresser; **~haus das a)** *(großes Wohnhaus)* manor house; **b)** *(hist.)* upper chamber; **~hemd das** *s.* **Oberhemd; ~konfektion die** menswear *no pl., no indef. art.*; **~leben das** life of luxury and ease; **~los** *Adj.* abandoned ‹*car, luggage*›; stray ‹*dog, cat*›; **~magazin das** men's magazine; magazine for men; **~mensch der** masterful person; *(ns.)* member of the master race; **~mode die** men's fashion; **~partie die** stag outing; **~rasse die** *(ns.)* master race; **~reiter der** *(Reiten)* amateur rider; **~salon der** men's hairdressing salon; **~schnitt der** Eton crop; **~schuh der** man's shoe; **~schuhe** men's shoes; **~toilette die** [gentle]men's toilet; **~unter·wäsche die** men's underwear; **~volk das** *(bes. ns.)* master race; **~zimmer das** smoking-room

Herr·gott der; ~s a) *(ugs.: Gott)* **der [lieber]/unser ~:** the Lord [God]; God; **~ noch mal!** for Heaven's sake!; for God's sake!; **b)** *(südd., österr.: Kruzifix)* crucifix

Herrgotts-: **~frühe die** *in* **in aller ~frühe** at the crack of dawn; **~schnitzer der** *(südd., österr.)* carver of crucifixes *(and figures of Christ and saints)*

her·richten 1. *tr. V.* **a)** *(bereitmachen)* get ‹*room, refreshments, etc.*› ready; dress ‹*shop-window*›; arrange ‹*table*›; **b)** *(in Ordnung bringen)* renovate; do up *(coll.)*. **2.** *refl. V.* get ready

Herrin die; ~, ~en mistress; *(als Anrede)* my lady

herrisch 1. *Adj.* overbearing; peremptory; imperious. **2.** *adv.* peremptorily; imperiously; ~ **auftreten** have a peremptory *or* imperious manner

herr·je, herrjemine [hɛr'je:mine] *Interj.* *(ugs.)* goodness gracious [me]; heavens [above]

herrlich 1. *Adj.* marvellous; marvellous, glorious ‹*weather*›; magnificent, splendid ‹*view*›; magnificent, gorgeous ‹*clothes*›; marvellous, wonderful, splendid ‹*meal*›; ‹*sth. tastes, looks, sounds*› wonderful, marvellous. **2.** *adv.* marvellously; ~ **und in Freuden leben** live in clover

Herrlichkeit die; ~, ~en a) *o. Pl.* *(Schönheit)* magnificence; splendour; **die ~ Gottes** the glory of God; **Ist das die ganze ~?** *(iron.)* is that all [there is]?; **b)** *meist Pl.* *(herrliche Sache)* marvellous *or* wonderful thing; *(einer Sammlung)* treasure

Herrschaft die; ~, ~en a) *o. Pl.* rule; *(Macht)* power; **unter jmds. ~** *(Dat.)* **stehen** be under sb.'s rule; **die ~ an sich reißen/erringen** seize/gain power; **die ~ über jmdn./etw. ausüben/innehaben** rule over *or* hold sway over sb./sth.; **die ~ über sich/das Auto verlieren** *(fig.)* lose control of oneself/the car; **b)** *Pl.* *(Damen u. Herren)* ladies and gentlemen; **die älteren/jüngeren ~en** the older/younger people; **meine ~en!** ladies and gentlemen!; **darf ich die ~en bitten, Platz zu nehmen** ladies and gentlemen/ladies/gentlemen, would you please take your seats; *(Mann und Frau)* would sir and madam care to take their seats, please; **Ruhe bitte, ~!** *(ugs.)* quiet please, all of you!; **meine Alten ~en** *(ugs. scherzh.)* my old man and old woman *(coll.)*; **c)** *(veralt.: Dienstherr[in])* master/mistress; **d)** ~ **[noch mal]!** *(ugs.)* for Heaven's sake!

herrschaftlich *Adj.* **a)** *(zu einer Herrschaft gehörend)* master's/mistress's ‹*coach etc.*›; **b)** *(einer Herrschaft gemäß)* grand

Herrschafts-: **~an·spruch der** claim to power; **~form die** system of government; **~system das** system of rule

herrschen ['hɛrʃn̩] *itr. V.* **a)** *(regieren)* rule; ‹*monarch*› reign, rule; **allein über jmdn./etw. ~:** have absolute power over sb./sth.; **b)** *(vorhanden sein)* **draußen ~ 30° Kälte** it's 30° below outside; **überall herrschte große Freude/Trauer** there was great joy/sorrow everywhere; **in der Stadt herrschte reges Leben** the town was bustling with life; **jetzt herrscht hier wieder Ordnung** order has been restored here; **c)** *(unpers.)* prevail; **es herrscht jetzt Einigkeit** there is now agreement; **es herrscht die Meinung, daß ...:** the prevailing opinion is that ...

herrschend *Adj., nicht präd.* **a)** ruling ‹*power, party, etc.*›; reigning ‹*monarch*›; **die Herrschenden** the rulers; those in power; **b)** *(vorhanden)* prevailing ‹*opinion, view, conditions, etc.*›

Herrscher der; ~s, ~: ruler; **~ über ein Volk sein** be [the] ruler of a people

Herrscher-: **~geschlecht das** ruling dynasty; **~haus das** ruling house

Herrscherin die; ~, ~nen *s.* **Herrscher**

Herrscher·paar das ruler and his/her consort

Herrsch·sucht die thirst for power; *(herrisches Wesen)* domineering nature

herrsch·süchtig *Adj.* domineering

her-: **~|rufen** *unr. tr. V.* call ‹*dog*›; **jmdn. ~rufen** call sb. [over]; **etw. hinter jmdm. ~rufen** call sth. after sb.; **~|rühren** *itr. V.* **von jmdm./etw. ~rühren** come from sb./stem from sth.; **~|sagen** *tr. V.* **etw. ~sagen** recite sth. mechanically; **~|schaffen** *tr. V.* **jmdn./etw. ~schaffen** bring sb./sth. here; **das Geld ~schaffen** get the money; **~|schenken** *tr. V.* *(landsch.)* give away; **~|schicken** *tr. V.* **jmdn./etw. ~schicken** send sb./sth. here; **jmdn./etw. hinter jmdm. ~schicken** send sb./sth. after sb.; **~|schieben** *unr. tr. V.* **etw. ~schieben** push sth. here; **etw. vor sich** *(Dat.)* **~schieben** push sth. along in front of one; *(fig.)* put sth. off; **~|schleichen 1.** *unr. itr. V.; mit sein* creep [over] here; **2.** *unr. refl. V.* **sich hinter jmdm. ~schleichen** creep along behind sb.; **~|sehen** *unr. itr. V.* look [over] here *or* this way; **seht mal alle ~!** look here *or* this way, everyone!; **hinter jmdm. ~sehen** follow sb. with one's eyes; **~|sein** *unr. itr. V.; mit sein* **a) einen Monat/einige Zeit/lange ~sein** be a month/some time/a long time ago; **es ist lange ~, daß wir ...:** it is a long time since we ...; **es ist schon einem Monat her** it was a month ago; **es muß 5 Jahre ~sein, daß wir ...:** it must be five years since we ...; **b)** *(stammen)* **von Köln ~sein** be *or* come from Cologne; **c) es ist nicht weit ~ mit jmdm./etw.** *(ugs.)* sb./sth. isn't all that hot *(coll.)*; **hinter jmdm.** *(ugs.)*/**etw. ~sein** be after sb./sth.; **~|stellen** *tr. V.* **a)** *(anfertigen)* produce; manufacture; make; **ein Auto von Hand ~stellen** build a car by hand; **in Deutschland ~gestellt** made in Germany; **etw. serienmäßig ~stellen** mass-produce sth.; **b)** *(zustande bringen)* establish ‹*contact, relationship, etc.*›; bring about ‹*peace, order, etc.*›; **eine Verbindung zwischen der Insel und dem Festland ~stellen** connect the island to the mainland; **c)** *(gesund machen)* **sie** *od.* **ihre Gesundheit ist [ganz] ~gestellt** she has [quite] recovered; **d)** *(zum Sprechenden stellen)* **etw. ~stellen** put sth. [over] here; **stell dich ~ [zu mir]** [come and] stand over here [next to *or* by me]

Her·steller der; ~s, ~ a) *(Produzent)* producer; manufacturer; **b)** *(Buchw.: Berufsbez.)* production department worker

Hersteller·firma die manufacturer

Her·stellung die a) *(Anfertigung)* production; manufacture; **b)** *s.* **herstellen b:** establishment; bringing about

Herstellungs-: **~kosten** *Pl.* production *or* manufacturing costs; **~land das** country of manufacture; **~verfahren das** production *or* manufacturing process

her-: **~|stürzen** *itr. V.; mit sein* **a)** *(nachlaufen)* **hinter jmdm. ~stürzen** rush after sb.; **b)** *(zum Sprecher)* rush *or* come rushing here; **~|tragen** *unr. tr. V.* **a)** *(zum Sprecher)* **etw. ~tragen** carry sth. here; **b)** *(begleiten und tragen)* **etw. hinter/vor jmdm. ~tragen** carry sth. along behind/in front of sb.; **~|treiben** *unr. tr. V.* **a)** *(zum Sprecher)* drive ‹*animal*› here; **jmdn. ~treiben** ‹*yearning, hunger, worry, etc.*› drive sb. here; **b)** *(antreiben)* **etw. vor sich** *(Dat.)* **~treiben** drive sth. along in front of one; **der Spieler trieb den Ball vor sich** *(Dat.)* **~:** the player dribbled the ball; **der Wind trieb die Wolken vor sich** *(Dat.)* **~:** the wind drove *or* blew the clouds along

Hertz [hɛrts] **das; ~, ~** *(Physik)* hertz

herüben [hɛ'ry:bn̩] *Adv.* *(südd., österr.)* over here

herüber [hɛ'ry:bɐ] *Adv.* over; **die Fahrt von Amerika ~:** the journey over from America; **~ und hinüber** back and forth

herüber-: **~|bitten** *unr. tr. V.* **jmdn. ~bitten** ask sb. [to come] over; **~|bringen** *unr. tr. V.* **jmdn./etw. ~bringen** bring sb./sth. over; **~|fahren 1.** *unr. itr. V.; mit sein* drive *or* come over; *(mit dem Motorrad, Rad)* come *or* ride over; **2.** *unr. tr. V.* **jmdn./etw. ~fahren** drive sb./sth. over; **~|fliegen 1.** *unr. itr. V.; mit sein* fly over; **2.** *unr. tr. V.* **jmdn./etw. ~fliegen** fly sb./sth. over; **~|ge-**

ben *unr. tr. V.* pass *or* hand over; ~|**grüßen** *itr. V.* **[zu jmdm.]** ~**grüßen** call across to sb. in greeting; ~|**holen** *tr. V.* **jmdn./etw.** ~**holen** bring sb./sth. over; ~|**kommen** *unr. itr. V.; mit sein* come over; **über den Zaun/Fluß ~kommen** get over the fence/ across the river; **kommt doch ~!** come over!; ~|**lassen** *unr. tr. V.* **jmdn. ~lassen** let sb. come over; allow sb. to come over; ~|**laufen** *unr. itr. V.; mit sein* run *or* come running over; ~|**reichen 1.** *tr. V. s.* ~**geben; 2.** *itr. V.* **[über etw.** *(Akk.)***]** ~**reichen** reach across [sth.]; ~|**retten 1.** *tr. V.* retain; **etw. in die Gegenwart ~retten** preserve sth. [until the present day]; **2.** *refl. V.* ⟨*customs, hopes, etc.*⟩ survive; ~|**schicken** *tr. V.* **jmdn./etw. ~schicken** send sb./sth. over; ~|**schwimmen** *unr. itr. V.; mit sein* swim over *or* across; ⟨*boat*⟩ float over *or* across; ~|**sehen** *unr. itr. V.* **[zu jmdm.]** ~**sehen** look across [at sb.]; ~|**wechseln** *itr. V.; mit sein od. haben* cross over; **er ist in unsere Partei ~gewechselt** he has swapped parties and joined ours; ~|**wehen 1.** *itr. V.* **a)** *(zum Sprecher)* **von Osten/Westen ~wehen** blow across from the East/West; **zu uns ~wehen** blow in our direction *or* towards us; **b)** *mit sein* ⟨*scent*⟩ waft across; ⟨*sound*⟩ be blown across; **2.** *tr. V.* **Blätter/den Duft ~wehen** blow leaves/waft the scent across here; ~|**wollen** *unr. itr. V.* want to come over; **über den Zaun ~wollen** want to get over the fence; ~|**ziehen 1.** *unr. tr. V.* **etw. ~ziehen** pull sth. over; **jmdn. ~ziehen** *(fig.)* win sb. over; **2.** *unr. itr. V.; mit sein* ⟨*clouds, troops*⟩ move across; *(umziehen)* move here

herum [hɛˈrʊm] *Adv.* **a)** *(Richtung)* round; **im Kreis ~:** round in a circle; **verkehrt/richtig ~:** the wrong/right way round; *(mit Ober- und Unterseite)* upside down/the right way up; **etw. falsch** *od.* **verkehrt ~ anziehen** put sth. on back-to-front/*(Innenseite nach außen)* inside-out; **b)** *(Anordnung)* **um jmdn./etw. ~:** around sb./sth.; **um die Stadt ~ zog sich ein Grüngürtel** the town was surrounded by a green belt; **c)** *(in enger Umgebung)* **um jmdn. ~:** around sb.; **um München/Berlin ~:** around Munich/Berlin; **d)** *(ugs.: ungefähr)* **um Weihnachten/Ostern ~:** around Christmas/Easter; **um 100 DM/das Jahr 1050 ~:** around *or* about 100 marks/ the year 1050

herum-, Herum-: ~|**albern** *itr. V. (ugs.)* fool around *or* about; ~|**ärgern** *refl. V. (ugs.)* **sich mit jmdm./etw. ~ärgern** keep getting annoyed with sb./sth.; **sich mit einem Problem ~ärgern müssen** be plagued by a problem; ~|**balgen** *refl. V.* **sich [mit jmdm.] ~balgen** keep scrapping *(coll.)* [with sb.]; ~|**basteln** *itr. V. (ugs.)* **an etw.** *(Dat.)* **~basteln** mess about with sth.; ~|**bekommen** *unr. tr. V. (ugs.)* **a)** *(überreden)* **jmdn. ~bekommen** talk sb. into it; **jmdn. ~bekommen, etw. zu tun** talk sb. into doing sth.; **b)** *(hinter sich bringen)* [manage to] pass *or* spend ⟨*time*⟩; ~|**blättern** *itr. V.* **in etw.** *(Dat.)* **~blättern** keep leafing through sth.; ~|**bohren** *itr. V. (ugs.)* **[in etw.** *(Dat.)***]** ~**bohren** keep poking [in sth.]; ~|**brüllen** *itr. V. (ugs.)* go on shouting one's head off *(coll.)*; ~|**bummeln** *itr. V. (ugs.)* **a)** *mit sein (spazieren)* stroll *or* wander around; **in der Stadt ~bummeln** stroll *or* wander around the town; **b)** *(trödeln)* **[mit etw.] ~bummeln** dawdle [over sth.]; ~|**doktern** *itr. V. (ugs.)* **an jmdm./etw. ~doktern** have a go at treating sb./sth.; **an etw.** *(Dat.)* **~doktern** *(fig.)* fiddle *or* tinker around *or* about with sth.; ~|**drehen 1.** *tr. V. (ugs.)* turn ⟨*key*⟩; turn over ⟨*coin, mattress, hand, etc.*⟩; **den Kopf ~drehen** turn one's head; **2.** *refl. V.* turn [a]round; **sich im Kreis ~drehen** turn right round; **sich [auf die andere Seite] ~drehen** turn over [on to one's other side]; **3.** *itr. V. (ugs.)* **an etw.** *(Dat.)* **~drehen** fiddle [around *or* about] with sth.; ~|**drücken** *refl. V.* **a)** *(ugs.: vermeiden)* **sich um etw. ~drücken** get out of *or (coll.)* dodge sth.; **b)** *(ugs.: sich aufhalten)* hang around; **wo hast du dich ~gedrückt?** where have you been?; ~|**drucksen** *itr. V. (ugs.)* hum and haw *(coll.)*; ~|**erzählen** *tr. V. (ugs.)* **etw. ~erzählen** spread sth. around; **er erzählte überall ~, daß ...:** he went around telling everyone that ...; ~|**experimentieren** *itr. V.* **[an jmdm./ etw.]** ~**experimentieren** carry out experiments [on sb./sth.]; ~|**fahren** *(ugs.)* **1.** *unr. itr. V.; mit sein* **a)** **um etw. ~fahren** drive *or* go round sth.; *(mit einem Motorrad, Rad)* ride *or* go round sth.; *(mit einem Schiff)* sail round sth.; **b)** *(irgendwohin fahren)* drive/ ride/sail around; **c)** *(sich plötzlich herumdrehen)* spin round; **d)** *(hin und her bewegen)* **mit den Armen/dem Schirm** *usw.* **~fahren** wave one's arms/umbrella *etc.* about; **2.** *unr. tr. V.* **jmdn. [in der Stadt] ~fahren** drive sb. around the town; ~|**flattern** *itr. V.; mit sein (ugs.)* **[um jmdn./etw.] ~flattern** flutter around [sb./sth.]; ~|**fliegen** *(ugs.)* **1.** *unr. itr. V.; mit sein* **a)** **[um etw.] ~fliegen** fly around [sth.]; **b)** *(salopp: herumliegen) s.* **rumfliegen 1 b; 2.** *unr. tr. V.* **jmdn. ~fliegen** fly sb. around; ~|**fragen** *itr. V. (ugs.)* ask around **(bei** among); ~|**fuchteln** *itr. V. (ugs.)* **mit den Armen/einem Messer** *usw.* **~fuchteln** wave one's arms/a knife *etc.* around *or* about; ~|**führen 1.** *tr. V.* **a)** **jmdn. [in der Stadt] ~führen** show sb. around the town; *s. auch* **Nase; b)** *(rund um etw. führen)* **jmdn. um etw. ~führen** lead *or* take sb. round sth.; **c)** *(um etw. bauen)* **die Straße um die Stadt ~führen** take the road round the town; **2.** *itr. V.* **um etw. ~führen** ⟨*road etc.*⟩ go round sth.; ~|**fuhr·werken** *itr. V. (ugs.)* mess about; **mit einem Schraubenzieher an der Uhr ~fuhrwerken** fiddle around with the clock with the aid of a screwdriver; ~|**fummeln** *itr. V. (ugs.)* **a)** **an etw.** *(Dat.)* **~fummeln** fiddle about with sth.; **b)** *(sich handwerklich beschäftigen)* fiddle *or* mess around with sth.; **c)** *(betasten)* **an jmdm. ~fummeln** touch sb. up *(sl.)*; ~|**geben** *unr. tr. V.: s.* ~**reichen 1**; ~|**gehen** *unr. itr. V.; mit sein* **a)** **um etw. ~gehen** go *or* walk round sth.; **b)** *(ziellos gehen)* walk around; **im Garten ~gehen** walk around the garden; **c)** *(die Runde machen)* go around; *(~gereicht werden)* be passed *or* handed around; **etw. ~gehen lassen** circulate sth.; **d)** *(vergehen)* pass; go by; ~|**geistern** *itr. V.; mit sein (ugs.)* wander around *or* about; *(fig.)* ⟨*idea, rumour, etc.*⟩ go round; **im Haus ~geistern** wander around the house [like a ghost]; **jmdm. im Kopf ~geistern** go round in sb.'s mind; ~|**gondeln** *itr. V.; mit sein (salopp)* travel around; **in der Weltgeschichte ~gondeln** travel around all over the place; ~|**hacken** *itr. V. (ugs.)* **a)** *(kritisieren)* **auf jmdm. ~hacken** keep getting at sb. *(coll.)*; **b)** *(mit einer Hacke bearbeiten)* **auf etw.** *(Dat.)* **~hacken** hack away at sth.; ~|**hängen** *unr. itr. V. (ugs.)* **a)** *(aufgehängt sein)* **überall ~hängen** be hung up all over the place; **b)** *s.* **rumhängen a**; ~|**hantieren** *itr. V. (ugs.)* mess about; **an etw.** *(Dat.)* **~hantieren** mess about with sth.; ~|**hetzen** *(ugs.)* **1.** *tr. V.* **jmdn. ~hetzen** rush sb. off his/her feet; **2.** *itr. V.; mit sein* rush *or* chase around *or* about; ~|**horchen** *itr. V. (ugs.)* keep one's ears open; **horch mal ~, ob ...:** keep your ears open and try and find out whether ...; ~|**irren** *itr. V.; mit sein* wander around *or* about; **im Wald ~irren** wander about the wood; ~|**kommandieren** *(ugs.)* **1.** *tr. V.* **jmdn. ~kommandieren** boss *(coll.) or* order sb. around *or* about; **2.** *itr. V.* boss *(coll.) or* order people around *or* about; ~|**kommen** *unr. itr. V.; mit sein (ugs.)* **a)** *(vorbeikommen können)* get round; **[mit etw.** *(Dat.)***] um die Ecke** *usw.* **~kommen** get [sth.] round the corner *etc.*; **b)** *(sich herumbewegen)* come round; **um die Ecke ~kommen** come round the corner; **c)** *(vermeiden können)* **um etw. [nicht] ~kommen** [not] be able to get out of sth.; **um eine Operation/Entscheidung ~kommen** avoid having an operation/coming to a decision; **wir kommen nicht um die Tatsache ~, daß ...:** we cannot get away *or* there is no getting away from the fact that ...; **d)** *(viel reisen)* get around *or* about; **in der Welt ~kommen** see a lot of the world; **viel ~kommen** get around *or* about a lot *or* a great deal; **e)** *(umschließen können)* **mit den Armen/der Hand/dem Seil um etw. ~kommen** get one's arms/hand/the rope [a]round sth.; ~|**kramen** *itr. V. (ugs.)* keep rummaging around *or* about; ~|**krebsen** *itr. V. (ugs.)* struggle; ~|**kriechen** *unr. itr. V.; mit sein* crawl around *or* about; **um etw. ~kriechen** crawl round sth.; ~|**kriegen** *tr. V.* **a)** *(salopp)* **jmdn. ~kriegen** talk sb. into it; *(verführen)* get sb. into bed *(coll.)*; **b)** *(ugs.) s.* **~bekommen b**; ~|**kritisieren** *itr. V. (ugs.)* **an jmdm./etw. ~kritisieren** pick holes in sb./sth.; run sb./sth. down; ~|**kutschieren** *(ugs.)* **1.** *itr. V.; mit sein* drive around [aimlessly]; **2.** *tr. V.* drive ⟨*person*⟩ about [with no particular destination]; ~|**laborieren** *itr. V. (ugs.)* **an etw.** *(Dat.)* **~laborieren** try to get over sth.; ~|**laufen** *unr. itr. V.; mit sein* **a)** walk/*(schneller)* run around *or* about; **in der Stadt ~laufen** walk/*(schneller)* run around the town; **b)** *(umrunden)* **um etw. ~laufen** walk *or* go round sth.; **c)** *(gekleidet sein)* **wie ein Hippie ~laufen** go about looking *or* dressed like a hippie; **wie läufst du wieder ~!** what do you look like!; ~|**liegen** *unr. itr. V. (ugs.)* lie around *or* about; ~|**lümmeln** *refl. V. (ugs.)* lounge around; ~|**lungern** *itr. V. (salopp)* loaf around; ~|**machen** *itr. V. (ugs.)* be busy; *(abwertend)* mess about *or* around; **er fing an, an mir/meiner Bluse ~zumachen** he started trying to fondle me/undo my blouse; ~|**mäkeln** *itr. V. (ugs.)* **[an jmdm./ etw.]** ~**mäkeln** pick holes [in sb./sth.]; **am Essen ~mäkeln** moan *(coll.) or* grumble about the food; ~|**nörgeln** *itr. V. (ugs. abwertend)* moan; grumble; **an jmdm./etw. ~nörgeln** moan *or* grumble about sb./sth.; ~|**pfuschen** *itr. V. (ugs. abwertend)* **[an jmdm./etw.]** ~**pfuschen** mess about [with sb./sth.]; ~|**posaunen** *tr. V. (ugs.)* broadcast; **sie posaunte im ganzen Dorf ~, daß ...:** she broadcast to the whole village the fact that ...; ~|**quälen** *refl. V. (ugs.)* **sich [mit einem Problem] ~quälen** struggle [with a problem]; **sich mit Rheuma/finanziellen Sorgen ~quälen** be plagued by rheumatism/ financial worries; ~|**rätseln** *itr. V. (ugs.)* **an etw.** *(Dat.)* **~rätseln** try to figure *or* puzzle sth. out; ~|**reden** *itr. V. (ugs.)* **um etw. ~reden** talk round sth.; **red nicht lange um die Sache ~!** don't beat about the bush!; ~|**reichen** *(ugs.)* **1.** *tr. V.* **etw. ~reichen** pass sth. round; **jmdn. [überall] ~reichen** *(fig.)* introduce sb. everywhere; **2.** *itr. V.* **[um etw.] ~reichen** reach round [sth.]; ~|**reisen** *itr. V.; mit sein (ugs.)* travel around *or* about; ~|**reißen** *unr. tr. V.* **den Wagen/das Pferd ~reißen** swing the car/horse round; *s. auch* [1]**Steuer**; ~|**reiten** *unr. itr. V.; mit sein* **a)** *(ziellos reiten)* ride around *or* about; **in der Gegend ~reiten** ride around the area; **b)** *(salopp; auf dasselbe zurückkommen)* **auf etw.** *(Dat.)* **~reiten** go on about sth. *(coll.)*; harp on sth.; **c)** *(salopp: kritisieren)* **auf jmdm. ~reiten** keep getting at sb. *(coll.)*; ~|**rennen** *unr. itr. V.; mit sein (ugs.)* **a)** *(ziellos rennen)* run around *or* about; **b)** *(im Bogen rennen)* **um etw. ~rennen** run round sth.; **im Kreis ~rennen** run round in a circle; ~|**rutschen** *itr. V.; mit sein (ugs.)* slide around *or* about; ~|**scharwenzeln** *itr. V.;*

mit sein (ugs. abwertend) **um jmdn. ~scharwenzeln** dance attendance on sb.; **~|schlagen 1.** *unr. tr. V.* **Papier/eine Decke** *usw.* **um etw. ~schlagen** wrap paper/a blanket *etc.* round sth.; **2.** *unr. refl. V. (ugs.)* **a)** *(sich schlagen)* **sich mit jmdm. ~schlagen** keep fighting *or* getting into fights with sb.; **b)** *(sich auseinandersetzen)* **sich mit Problemen/Einwänden ~schlagen** grapple with problems/battle against objections; **sich mit jmdm. [wegen etw.] ~schlagen** conduct a running battle with sb. [about sth.]; **~|schleichen** *unr. itr. V.; mit sein (ugs.)* creep around *or* about; **um etw. ~schleichen** creep round sth.; **~|schlendern** *itr. V.; mit sein (ugs.)* stroll around *or* about; **in der Stadt ~schlendern** stroll around *or* about the town; **~|schleppen** *tr. V. (ugs.)* **etw. um etw. ~schleppen** lug sth. round sth.; **eine Erkältung/ein Problem mit sich** *(Dat.)* **~schleppen** *(fig.)* go around with a cold/be worried by a problem; **die Probleme anderer mit sich** *(Dat.)* **~schleppen** *(fig.)* worry about other people's problems; **~|schnüffeln** *itr. V. (ugs. abwertend)* nose *or* snoop around *or* about *(coll.)*; **in jmds. Schreibtisch ~schnüffeln** poke around *or* about in sb.'s desk *(coll.)*; **in anderer Leute Angelegenheiten ~schnüffeln** poke one's nose into other people's affairs; **~|schubsen** *tr. V. (ugs.)* **jmdn. ~schubsen** push sb. around; **~|sein** *unr. itr. V.; mit sein; Zusammenschreibung nur im Inf. und Part. (ugs.)* **a)** *(vergangen sein)* have passed; have gone by; **seine Probezeit ist noch nicht ~:** his probationary period is not yet over; **b)** *(bekannt geworden sein)* have got around; **c)** *(sich in der Nähe aufhalten)* **immer um jmdn. ~sein** be always around sb; **~|sitzen** *unr. itr. V. (ugs.)* sit around *or* about; **um etw. ~sitzen** sit round sth.; **tatenlos ~sitzen** sit around *or* about doing nothing; **~|spielen** *itr. V. (ugs.)* **an/mit etw. ~spielen** keep playing [around *or* about] with sth.; **an seinen Knöpfen ~spielen** fiddle with one's buttons; **~|spionieren** *itr. V. (ugs.)* snoop *or* nose around *or* about *(coll.)*; **~|sprechen** *unr. refl. V.* get around *or* about; **schnell hatte sich ~gesprochen, daß ...:** it had quickly got around that ...; **~|spuken** *itr. V. (ugs.)* **in/auf etw.** *(Dat.)* **~spuken** haunt sth.; **ich möchte wissen, was in seinem Kopf ~spukt** *(fig.)* I'd like to know what's going on in his mind; **~|stänkern** *itr. V. (ugs.)* keep complaining; **~|stehen** *unr. itr. V. (ugs.)* stand around *or* about; **um etw. ~stehen** stand round sth.; **~|stöbern** *itr. V. (ugs.) (in einem Schreibtisch usw.)* keep rummaging around *or* about (**in** + *Dat.* in); **die Jagdhunde stöberten im Dickicht ~:** the hounds were hunting around in the thicket; **ich habe in der ganzen Wohnung ~gestöbert** I've hunted all over the house; **~|stochern** *itr. V.* poke around *or* about; **im Essen ~stochern** pick at one's food; **~|stoßen** *unr. tr. V. (ugs.)* **jmdn. ~stoßen** push sb. around; **~|streichen** *unr. itr. V.; mit sein (abwertend)* **a)** *(umherstreifen)* roam around *or* about; **b)** *(lauernd umkreisen)* **um jmdn./etw. ~streichen** prowl round sb./sth.; **~|streifen** *itr. V.; mit sein (ugs.)* roam around *or* about; **auf den Straßen ~streifen** roam the streets; **~|streiten** *unr. refl. V. (ugs.)* **sich [mit jmdm.] ~streiten** keep quarrelling *or* wrangling [with sb.]; **~|streunen** *itr. V.; mit sein (abwertend)* roam around *or* about; **auf den Feldern ~streunen** roam the fields; **~|stromern** *itr. V.; mit sein (salopp abwertend)* roam around *or* about; **~|tanzen** *itr. V.; mit sein (ugs.)* **a)** dance around *or* about; **im Zimmer ~tanzen** dance around *or* about the room; **b)** *(im Bogen um etw. tanzen)* **um jmdn./etw. ~tanzen** dance round sb./sth.; **um jmdn. ~tanzen** *(fig.)* dance attendance on sb.; *s. auch* **Kopf a; Nase b; ~|tollen** *itr. V.; mit sein* romp around *or* about; **auf dem Hof ~tollen** romp around the yard; **~|tragen** *unr. tr. V. (ugs.)* **a)** *(überallhin tragen)* **jmdn./etw. ~tragen** carry sb./sth. around *or* about; **jmdn./etw. mit sich ~tragen** carry sb./sth. around with one; **b) eine Idee/einen Plan mit sich ~tragen** nurse an idea/a plan; **c)** *(abwertend: weitererzählen)* **etw. ~tragen** spread sth. around; **~|trampeln** *itr. V.; mit haben od. sein* **auf etw.** *(Dat.)* **~trampeln** trample [around] on sth.; trample all over sth.; **auf jmdm. ~trampeln** *(fig.)* walk all over sb.; **auf jmds. Nerven/Gefühlen ~trampeln** *(fig.)* really get on sb.'s nerves/trample on sb.'s feelings; **~|treiben** *unr. refl. V. (ugs. abwertend)* **a)** *(kein geordnetes Leben führen)* **sich auf den Straßen/in Spelunken ~treiben** hang around the streets/*(coll.)* in dives; **sich mit Männern ~treiben** hang around with men; **b)** *(sich irgendwo aufhalten)* **sich in der Welt ~treiben** roam *or* move about the world; **wo hast du dich nur ~getrieben?** where have you been?; **Ich möchte wissen, wo er sich ~treibt** I'd like to know where he's got to; **~treiber der, ~treiberin die** *(ugs.)* layabout; *(Streuner)* vagabond; **~|trödeln** *itr. V. (ugs.)* dawdle around *or* about (**mit** over); **~|wälzen** *(ugs.)* **1.** *tr. V.* **etw. ~wälzen** roll sth. over; **2.** *refl. V.* roll around *or* about; **sich im Bett ~wälzen** toss and turn in bed; **sich im Schlamm ~wälzen** wallow in the mud; **~|wandern** *itr. V.; mit sein* **a)** *(ugs.: umhergehen)* wander around *or* about; **im Garten ~wandern** wander around *or* about the garden; **b)** *(im Bogen um etw. wandern)* **um den Berg/See** *usw.* **~wandern** hike around the mountain/the lake *etc.*; **~|werfen 1.** *unr. tr. V.* **a)** *(ugs.: umherwerfen)* **etw. ~werfen** chuck *(coll.) or* throw sth. around *or* about; **etw. im Zimmer ~werfen** chuck *(coll.) or* throw sth. around *or* about the room; **b)** *(in eine andere Richtung drehen)* throw ⟨*helm, steering-wheel, etc.*⟩ [hard] over; **den Kopf ~werfen** turn one's head quickly; **2.** *unr. refl. V.* **sich im Bett ~werfen** toss and turn in bed; **~|wickeln** *tr. V.* **etw. um etw. ~wickeln** wrap sth. round sth.; **~|wirbeln 1.** *tr. V.* **jmdn./etw. ~wirbeln** whirl *or* spin sb./sth. [a]round; **der Wind wirbelte die Blätter ~:** the wind whirled the leaves around *or* about; **2.** *itr. V.; mit sein* spin *or* whirl [a]round; **~|wühlen** *itr. V.* **in etw.** *(Dat.)* **~wühlen** rummage *or* root around *or* about in sth.; **in jmds. Vergangenheit ~wühlen** *(fig.)* dig into sb.'s past; **~|wurschteln, ~|wursteln** *itr. V. (salopp)* **mit etw. ~wurschteln** *od.* **~wursteln** mess *or* fiddle around *or* about with sth.; **~|zanken** *refl. V. (ugs.) s.* **~streiten; ~|zeigen** *tr. V. (ugs.)* **etw. ~zeigen** show sth. round; **~|ziehen 1.** *unr. itr. V.* move around *or* about; **im Land ~ziehen** move around *or* about the country; **um etw. ~ziehen** go round sth.; **2.** *unr. tr. V. (ugs.: mit sich ziehen)* **jmdn./etw. ~ziehen** drag sb./sth. round *(coll.)*; **3.** *unr. refl. V.* **sich um etw. ~ziehen** ⟨*fence, wall, river, etc.*⟩ go *or* run round sth.; ⟨*wood etc.*⟩ surround sth.

herunten [hɛˈrʊntn̩] *Adv. (südd., österr.)* down here

herunter [hɛˈrʊntɐ] *Adv.* **a)** *(nach unten)* down; **von Kiel nach München ~** *(fig.)* from Kiel down to Munich; **b)** *(fort)* off; **~ vom Sofa!** [get] off the sofa!; **~ vom Baum/von der Mauer!** get *or* come down from that tree/wall!

herunter-: ~|bekommen *unr. tr. V. (ugs.)* **a)** *(essen können)* be able to eat; *(~schlucken)* swallow; **b)** *(entfernen können)* **etw. [von etw.] ~bekommen** be able to get sth. off [sth.]; **~|bemühen 1.** *tr. V.* **jmdn. ~bemühen** trouble sb. to come down; **2.** *refl. V.* take the trouble to come down; **würden Sie sich bitte ~bemühen?** would you mind coming down?; **~|beten** *tr. V. (abwertend)* **etw. ~beten** recite sth. mechanically; **~|bitten** *unr. tr. V.* ask sb. [to come] down; **~|brennen** *unr. itr. V.* **a)** *mit sein (vollkommen abbrennen)* ⟨*house, fire, etc.*⟩ burn down; **b)** ⟨*sun*⟩ burn *or* beat down; **~|bringen** *unr. tr. V.* **a)** *(nach unten bringen)* bring down; **b)** *(zugrunde richten)* ruin; **c)** *(ugs.: herunterschlucken) s.* **~bekommen a; ~|drücken** *tr. V.* **a)** *(nach unten drücken)* **etw. ~drücken** press sth. down; **b)** *(auf ein niedriges Niveau bringen, verringern)* force down ⟨*prices, wages, etc.*⟩; bring down ⟨*temperature*⟩; reduce ⟨*marks*⟩; **~|fahren 1.** *unr. itr. V.; mit sein* drive *or* come down; ⟨*skier*⟩ ski down; *(mit einem Motorrad, Rad)* ride down; **2.** *unr. tr. V.* **jmdn./etw. ~fahren** drive *or* bring sb. down/bring sth. down; **~|fallen** *unr. itr. V.; mit sein* fall down; **vom Tisch/Stuhl ~fallen** fall off the table/chair; **die Treppe ~fallen** fall down the stairs; **jmdm. fällt etw. herunter** sb. drops sth.; **~|fliegen** *unr. itr. V.; mit sein* **a)** *(nach unten fliegen)* fly down; **b)** *(ugs.) s.* **~fallen; ~|geben** *unr. tr. V. (ugs.)* pass *or* hand down; **~|gehen** *unr. itr. V.; mit sein* **a)** *(nach unten gehen)* come down; **b)** *(niedriger werden)* ⟨*temperature*⟩ go down, drop, fall; ⟨*prices*⟩ come down, fall; **im Preis ~gehen** come down in price; **c)** *(die Höhe senken)* **auf eine Flughöhe von 2 000 m ~gehen** descend to 6,000 ft.; **auf eine geringere Geschwindigkeit ~gehen** slow down; reduce speed; **mit den Preisen ~gehen** reduce one's/its prices; **d) von etw. ~gehen** *(ugs.: räumen)* get off sth.; **e)** *(ugs.: sich lösen)* come off; **~gekommen 1.** *2. Part. v.* **~kommen; 2.** *Adj.* poor ⟨*health*⟩; dilapidated, run-down ⟨*building*⟩; run-down ⟨*area*⟩; down and out ⟨*person*⟩; **ein [völlig] ~gekommenes Subjekt** a down-and-out; **~|handeln** *tr. V. (ugs.)* **einen Preis ~handeln** beat down a price; **100 DM vom Kaufpreis ~handeln** get 100 marks knocked off the price *(coll.)*; **~|hängen** *unr. itr. V.* hang down; **~|hauen** *unr. tr. V. (ugs.)* **a)** *(ohrfeigen)* **jmdm. eine ~hauen** give sb. a clout round the ear *(coll.)*; **b)** *(schlecht ausführen)* dash off; **~|heben** *unr. tr. V.* **etw. [von etw.] ~heben** lift sth. down [from sth.]; **~|helfen** *unr. itr. V. (ugs.)* **jmdm. ~helfen** help sb. down; **~|holen** *tr. V.; mit sein* **a)** *(nach unten holen)* **jmdn./etw. ~holen** fetch sb./sth. down; **b)** *(ugs.: abschießen)* bring down; **~|klappen** *tr. V.* pull *or* put down ⟨*seat*⟩; close ⟨*lid*⟩; **seinen Kragen ~klappen** turn down one's collar; **~|klettern** *itr. V.; mit sein* climb down; **~|kommen** *unr. itr. V.; mit sein* **a)** *(kommen)* come down; *(nach unten kommen können)* manage to come down; **b)** *(ugs.: verfallen)* go to the dogs *(coll.)*; **er ist so weit ~gekommen, daß ...:** he has sunk so low that ...; **er ist gesundheitlich ~gekommen** his health has deteriorated; **c)** *(ugs.: wegkommen)* **von Drogen/vom Alkohol ~kommen** come off drugs/alcohol; kick the habit *(sl.)*; **von einer [schlechten] Note ~kommen** improve on a [bad] mark; **~|können** *unr. itr. V. (ugs.)* be able to get down; **~|kriegen** *tr. V. (ugs.) s.* **runterkriegen; ~|lassen** *unr. tr. V. (schließen)* let down, lower ⟨*blind, shutter*⟩; lower ⟨*barrier*⟩; shut ⟨*window*⟩; *(nach unten gleiten lassen)* wind down ⟨*car window*⟩; **jmdn./etw. an etw.** *(Dat.)* **~lassen** lower sb./sth. by sth.; **die Hose ~lassen** take one's trousers down; **~|leiern** *tr. V. (salopp)* **a)** *(abwertend)* drone out *(coll.)*; **b)** wind down ⟨*car window*⟩; **~|machen** *tr. V. (salopp)* **a)** *(zurechtweisen)* **jmdn. ~machen** give sb. a rocket *(sl.)*; tear sb. off a strip *(coll.)*; **b)** *(herabsetzen)* slate *(coll.)*; run down *(coll.)*; **~|nehmen** *unr. tr. V.* take down; **die Arme ~nehmen** put one's arms down; **etw. von etw.**

~nehmen take sth. off sth.; **~|purzeln** *itr. V.; mit sein (ugs.)* **die Treppe ~purzeln** tumble down the stairs; **vom Stuhl ~purzeln** topple off the chair; **~|putzen** *tr. V. (salopp) s.* **~machen a**; **~|rasseln** *(ugs.)* **1.** *tr. V.* rattle off; **2.** *itr. V.; mit sein* rattle down; come rattling down; **~|reißen** *unr. tr. V. (ugs.)* **a)** *(nach unten reißen)* pull down; **b)** *(abreißen)* pull off ‹*plaster, wallpaper*›; tear down ‹*poster*›; **c)** *(salopp: ableisten)* get through; **~|rutschen** *itr. V.; mit sein (ugs.)* slide down; ‹*trousers, socks*› slip down; **~|schalten** *itr. V. (Kfz-Jargon)* change down; **~|schießen 1.** *unr. tr. V.* shoot down ‹*bird, aircraft, etc.*›; **2.** *unr. itr. V.* **a) von einem Fenster aus ~schießen** shoot *or* fire down from a window; **b)** *mit sein (~stürzen)* hurtle down; come hurtling down; **~|schlagen** *unr. tr. V.* **a)** knock off; **den Stuck von der Wand ~schlagen** knock the stucco off the wall; **b)** *(nach unten wenden)* turn ‹*collar etc.*› down; **~|schlucken** *tr. V.* swallow; **~|schrauben** *tr. V.* turn down ‹*wick etc.*›; **seine Ansprüche/Erwartungen ~schrauben** *(fig.)* reduce one's requirements/lower one's expectations; **~|sehen** *unr. itr. V.* **a)** *(nach unten sehen)* look down; **b)** *(geringschätzig betrachten)* **auf jmdn. ~sehen** look down [up]on sb.; **~|sein** *unr. itr. V.; mit sein; Zusammenschreibung nur im Inf. und Part. (ugs.)* **a)** *(unten sein)* be down; **b)** *(am Ende der Kräfte sein)* **[körperlich] ~sein** be in poor health; **er ist mit seiner Gesundheit/seinen Nerven ~:** he's in poor health/his nerves are in a bad state; **~|setzen** *tr. V. (ugs.) s.* **herabsetzen**; **~|spielen** *tr. V. (ugs.)* **a)** *(als unbedeutend darstellen)* play down *(coll.)*; **b)** *(ausdruckslos spielen)* **etw. ~spielen** play sth. through mechanically; **~|steigen** *unr. itr. V.; mit sein* climb down; **~|stürzen 1.** *itr. V.; mit sein* fall down; *(steil herabfallen)* ‹*aircraft, person, etc.*› plunge down; *(~eilen)* rush down; **vom Dach ~stürzen** fall off the roof; **2.** *tr. V.* **a)** *(schnell trinken)* gulp down; **b) jmdn. ~stürzen** throw sb. down; **~|tragen** *unr. tr. V.* **etw. ~tragen** carry sth. down; **~|werfen** *unr. tr. V.* **a)** *(nach unten werfen)* **etw. ~werfen** throw sth. down; **b)** *(ugs.: herunterfallen lassen)* drop; **~|wirtschaften** *tr. V. (ugs.)* **etw. ~wirtschaften** ruin sth./bring sth. to the brink *or* edge of ruin [by mismanagement]; **~|ziehen 1.** *unr. tr. V.* pull down; **jmdn. [auf seine Ebene] ~ziehen** *(fig.)* drag sb. down [to one's own level]; **2.** *unr. itr. V.; mit sein* go *or* move down; *(umziehen)* move down

her·vor *Adv.* **aus etw. ~:** out of sth.; **aus der Ecke ~ kam ...:** from out of the corner came ...

hervor-, Hervor-: ~|brechen *unr. itr. V.; mit sein (geh.)* **a)** *(zum Vorschein kommen)* ‹*animal etc.*› burst out; ‹*sun*› break through; ‹*plant*› come up *or* through; **b)** *(sich äußern)* ‹*feelings*› burst forth *or* out; **~|bringen** *unr. tr. V.* **a)** *(zum Vorschein bringen)* bring out **(aus** from); produce **(aus** from); **b)** *(wachsen, entstehen lassen; auch fig.)* produce; **c)** *(von sich geben)* say; produce ‹*sound*›; **er brachte kein Wort/keinen Ton ~:** he could not utter a word/sound; **~|dringen** *unr. itr. V.; mit sein (geh.)* ‹*plant*› come up *or* through; **~|gehen** *unr. itr. V.; mit sein (geh.)* **a)** *(seinen Ursprung haben)* **viele große Musiker gingen aus dieser Stadt ~:** this city produced many great musicians; **drei Kinder gingen aus der Ehe ~:** the marriage produced three children; there were three children of the marriage; **eines geht aus dem andern ~:** one thing evolves from another; **b)** *(herauskommen, sich ergeben)* emerge **(aus** from); **aus etw. siegreich/als Sieger ~gehen** emerge victorious from sth.; **aus seinem Brief geht klar ~, daß ...:** it is clear from his letter that ...; **d)** *(zu folgern sein)* follow; **daraus geht ~, daß ...:** from this it follows that ...; **~|gucken** *itr. V. (ugs.)* look out; **unter etw.** *(Dat.)* **~gucken** peep out from under sth.; **~|heben** *unr. tr. V.* emphasize; stress; **etw. durch Kursivdruck ~heben** make sth. stand out by using italics; **~|holen** *tr. V.* take out **(aus of)**; **ich muß meine alten Schulbücher ~holen** I must get out my old school-books; **~|kehren** *tr. V. s.* **herauskehren**; **~|kommen** *unr. itr. V.; mit sein* come out **(aus** of, **unter +** *Dat.* from under); **~|locken** *tr. V.* lure *or* entice ‹*person, animal*› out **(aus** of); **~|quellen** *unr. itr. V.; mit sein* well up; ‹*smoke*› pour out; **aus etw. ~quellen** stream from sth.; **unter dem Hut quoll ihr Haar ~:** her hair spilled out from under her hat; **~quellende Augen** bulging eyes; **~|ragen** *itr. V.* **a)** *(aus etw. ragen)* project; jut out; ‹*cheekbones*› stand out; **aus dem Häusermeer ragte der Kirchturm ~:** the church spire stood out above the sea of houses; **b)** *(sich auszeichnen)* stand out; **~ragend 1.** *Adj.* outstanding[ly good]; **2.** *adv.* **~ragend geschult** outstandingly well trained; **~ragend spielen/arbeiten** play/work outstandingly well *or* excellently; **~ruf der** curtain-call; **~|rufen** *unr. tr. V.* **a)** *(nach vorn rufen)* **jmdn. ~rufen** call for sb. to come out; *(Theater usw.)* call sb. back; **sie wurde sechsmal ~gerufen** she had to take six curtain-calls; **b)** *(verursachen)* elicit, provoke ‹*response*›; arouse ‹*admiration*›; cause ‹*unease, disquiet, confusion, merriment, disease*›; provoke ‹*protest, displeasure*›; **~|sehen** *unr. itr. V.* be visible; *(unerwünscht)* show; **~|springen** *unr. itr. V.; mit sein* **a)** *(springend hervorkommen)* leap *or* jump out **(hinter +** *Dat.* from behind); **b)** *(vorspringen)* project; jut out; ‹*nose*› stick out; **~|stechen** *unr. itr. V.* **a)** *(herausstehen)* stick out **(aus** of); **b)** *(sich abheben)* stand out; **~stechend** *Adj.* outstanding; striking; **~|stehen** *unr. itr. V.* protrude; stick out; ‹*cheekbones*› stand out; **~|stürzen** *itr. V.; mit sein* rush *or* burst out **(hinter +** *Dat.* from behind); **~|suchen** *tr. V.* look out; **~|treten** *unr. itr. V.; mit sein* **a)** emerge, step out **(hinter +** *Dat.* from behind); ‹*veins, ribs, etc.*› stand out; ‹*similarity etc.*› become apparent *or* evident; ‹*eyes*› bulge, protrude; **die Sonne trat aus den Wolken ~** *(fig. geh.)* the sun emerged *or* came out from behind the clouds; **b)** *(bekannt werden)* make one's mark; make a name for oneself; **~|tun** *unr. refl. V.* **a)** *(Besonderes leisten)* distinguish oneself; **sie hat sich nicht sonderlich ~getan** she did not exactly distinguish herself; **sich mit/als etw. ~tun** make one's mark with/as sth.; **b)** *(wichtig tun)* show off; **~|wagen** *refl. V.* dare to come out **(aus** of); **du kannst dich wieder ~wagen** you can come out again; **~|zaubern** *tr. V.* conjure up; **er zauberte ein Päckchen Zigaretten ~:** as if by magic he produced a packet of cigarettes; **~|ziehen** *unr. tr. V.* pull out **(hinter +** *Dat.* from behind, **unter +** *Dat.* from under)

her|wagen *refl. V. (ugs.)* dare to come here

Her·weg der: auf dem ~weg on the way here

Herz [hɛrts] **das; ~ens, ~en a)** *(auch: herzförmiger Gegenstand, zentraler Teil)* heart; **sie hat es am ~en** *(ugs.)* she has a bad heart; *(fig.)* **komm an mein ~, Geliebter** come into my arms, my darling; **jmdm. das ~ zerreißen** break sb.'s heart; **dabei dreht sich mir das ~ im Leib[e] um** it makes my heart bleed; **mir blutet das ~** *(auch iron.)* my heart bleeds; **mir lacht das ~ im Leibe** my heart sings; **ihm rutschte** *od.* **fiel das ~ in die Hose[n]** *(ugs., oft scherzh.)* his heart sank into his boots; **jmds. ~ höher schlagen lassen** make sb.'s heart beat faster; **jmdm. das ~ brechen** *(geh.)* break sb.'s heart; **das ~ auf dem rechten Fleck haben** have one's heart in the right place; **das ~ in die Hand** *od.* **in beide Hände nehmen** take one's courage in both hands; **jmdn./etw. auf ~ und Nieren prüfen** *(ugs.)* grill sb./go over sth. with a fine tooth-comb; **ein Kind unter dem Herzen tragen** *(dichter.)* be with child; be great with child *(arch.)*; *s. auch* **drücken a; klopfen 1 b; b)** *(meist geh.: Gemüt)* heart; **ein treues ~ haben** be true-hearted; **ein warmes/gutes ~ haben** have a warm/good *or* kind heart; **die ~en bewegen/rühren** touch people's hearts; **von ~en kommen** come from the heart; **im Grunde seines Herzens** in his heart of hearts; **man kann einem Menschen nicht ins ~ sehen** one cannot see *or* look into another man's heart; **wes das ~ voll ist, des geht der Mund über** *(prov.)* when you're excited about something, it's difficult to stop talking about it; **ein ~ und eine Seele sein** be bosom friends; **jmds. ~ hängt an etw.** *(Dat.)* *(jmd. möchte etw. sehr gerne behalten)* sb. is attached to sth.; *(jmd. möchte etw. sehr gerne haben)* sb.'s heart is set on sth.; **sein ~ gehört der Musik/Literatur** *usw. (geh.)* music/literature *etc.* is his first love; **ihm war/wurde das ~ schwer** his heart was/grew heavy; **alles, was das ~ begehrt** everything one's heart desires; **nicht das ~ haben, etw. zu tun** not have the heart to do sth.; **sich** *(Dat.)* **ein ~ fassen** pluck up one's courage; take one's courage in both hands; **sein ~ an jmdn./etw. hängen** *(geh.)* give one's heart to sb./devote oneself to sth.; **sein ~ für etw. entdecken** *(geh.)* discover a passion for sth.; **ein ~ für die Armen und Kranken haben** feel for the sick and the poor; **ein ~ für Kinder/die Kunst haben** have a love of children/art; **jmdm. sein ~ ausschütten** pour out one's heart to sb.; **jmdm. das ~ schwermachen** sadden sb.'s heart; **das ~ auf der Zunge haben** wear one's heart on one's sleeve; **die** *od.* **alle ~en im Sturm erobern** *(geh.)* capture everybody's heart; **seinem ~en einen Stoß geben** [suddenly] pluck up courage; **seinem ~en Luft machen** *(ugs.)* give vent to one's feelings; **leichten ~ens** easily; happily; **schweren ~ens** with a heavy heart; **jmd./etw. liegt jmdm. am ~en** sb. has the interests of sb./sth. at heart; **jmdm. etw. ans ~ legen** entrust sb. with sth.; **jmd./etw. ist jmdm. ans ~ gewachsen** sb. has grown very fond of sb./sth.; **etw. auf dem ~en haben** have sth. on one's mind; **aus seinem ~en keine Mördergrube machen** speak freely *or* frankly; **aus tiefstem ~en** *(geh.)* from the bottom of one's heart; **jmdn. ins** *od.* **in sein ~ schließen** take to sb.; **jmdn. ins ~ treffen** cut sb. to the quick; **mit halbem ~en** *(geh.)* half-heartedly; **es nicht übers ~ bringen, etw. zu tun** not have the heart to do sth.; **von ~en gern** [most] gladly; **von ganzem ~en** *(aufrichtig)* with all one's heart; *(aus voller Überzeugung)* whole-heartedly; **sich** *(Dat.)* **etw. zu ~en nehmen** take sth. to heart; **habt ein ~ [mit dem armen Kerl]!** have pity [on the poor fellow]!; **mit ganzem ~en** *(geh.)* whole-heartedly; **ein Mann** *usw.* **nach jmds. ~en** a man *etc.* after sb.'s own heart; **jmdm. aus dem ~en sprechen** express just what sb. is/was thinking; **jmdm. sein ~ schenken** *(geh.)* give sb. one's heart; **die Dame seines ~ens** *(geh., oft scherzh.)* the woman of his heart; **von ~en kommen** ‹*present*› be given with cordial feeling; ‹*congratulations, thanks, etc.*› come from the heart; **jmdm. zu ~en gehen** upset sb. deeply; *s. auch* **golden 1 c; Luft c; Stein b; Stich e; Zentnerlast; c)** *o. Art., o. Pl. (Kartenspiel)* hearts *pl.*; *s. auch* **[2]Pik; d)** *(Speise)* heart; **ein Pfund ~ vom Schwein** a pound of pig's heart[s]; **e)** *(Kosewort)* **mein ~:** my dear

herz-, Herz-: ~allerliebste der/die; *adj. Dekl. (veralt.)* beloved; **~allerliebster mein** my beloved; my darling; **~an·fall der**

ns|heart attack; **~as das** ace of hearts; **~asthma das** *(Med.)* cardiac asthma; cardiasthma; **~beklemmend** *Adj.* oppressive; **~beklemmung die** angina; **~beschwerden** *Pl.* heart trouble *sing.*; **~beutel der** *(Anat.)* pericardium; **~binkerl** [~bɪŋkɐl] **das; ~s, ~** *(bayr., österr. ugs.)* pet *(coll.)*; darling; **~blatt das a)** *(Gartenbau)* new, inner leaf; **b)** *(Kosewort)* darling; **~blut das** *in* **sein ~blut für jmdn./etw. hingeben** *(geh. veralt.)* sacrifice everything for sb./sth.; **~bube der** jack of hearts

Herzchen das; ~s, ~ a) *(abwertend: naive/unzuverlässige Person)* simpleton/unreliable person; **b)** *(Kosewort)* darling; sweetheart; **c)** *(kleines Herz)* little heart

Herz-: ~chirurgie die heart *or* cardiac surgery; **~dame die** queen of hearts

her|zeigen *tr. V. (ugs.)* show; **zeig [es] mal her!** let me see [it]!

Herze·leid das *(veralt.)* heartbreak

herzen *tr. V. (veralt.)* hug

herzens-, Herzens-: ~angelegenheit die *(Liebesangelegenheit)* affair of the heart; *(Leidenschaft)* passion; **~angst die** *(geh.)* deep anxiety; *(bei unmittelbarer Bedrohung)* [mortal] fear; **~bedürfnis das** *in* **jmdm. ein ~bedürfnis sein** *(geh.)* be very important to sb.; **~bildung die;** *o. Pl. (geh.)* sensitivity; **~brecher der** lady-killer; **~grund der** *in* **aus ~grund** from the bottom of one's heart; **~gut** ['--'-] *Adj.* kind-hearted; good-hearted; **~güte die** *(geh.)* kindness of heart; kind-heartedness; goodness of heart; **~lust die** *in* **nach ~lust** to one's heart's content; **~wunsch der** dearest *or* fondest wish

herz-, Herz-: ~entzündung die *(Med.) s.* **Karditis; ~erfreuend** *Adj.* heart-warming; **~erfrischend 1.** *Adj.* refreshing; **2.** *adv.* refreshingly; **~ergreifend 1.** *Adj.* heart-rending; **2.** *adv.* heart-rendingly; **~erquickend** *Adj. s.* **~erfrischend; ~fehler der** heart defect; **~flimmern das** *(Med.) (Kammerflimmern)* ventricular fibrillation; *(Vorhofflimmern)* auricular fibrillation; **~förmig** *Adj.* heart-shaped; heart-shaped, cordate ‹*leaf*›; **~gegend die** area *or* region of the heart; **~geräusch das** *(Med.)* heart murmur

herzhaft 1. *Adj.* **a)** *(kräftig)* hearty; **b)** *(nahrhaft)* hearty, substantial ‹*meal*›; *(von kräftigem Geschmack)* tasty; **ein ~er Eintopf** a substantial/tasty stew; **c)** *(veralt.: mutig)* bold. **2.** *adv.* **a)** *(kräftig)* heartily; **~ gähnen** give a wide yawn; **b)** *(nahrhaft)* **er ißt gern ~:** he likes to have a hearty meal; **c)** *(veralt.: mutig)* boldly

her|ziehen 1. *unr. itr. V.* **a)** *mit sein od. haben (ugs.: abfällig reden)* **über jmdn./etw. ~:** run sb./sth. down; pull sb./sth. to pieces; **b)** *mit sein (mitgehen)* **vor/hinter/neben jmdm./etw. ~:** walk along in front of/behind/beside sb./sth.; *(marschieren)* march along in front of/behind/beside sb./sth.; **c)** *(umziehen) mit sein* move here. **2.** *unr. tr. V.* **a)** *(ugs.: zum Sprechenden bewegen)* **etw. ~:** pull sth. over [here]; **b)** *(mit sich führen)* **jmdn./etw. hinter sich** *(Dat.)* **~:** pull sb./sth. along behind one

herzig 1. *Adj.* sweet; dear; delightful. **2.** *adv.* sweetly; delightfully

herz-, Herz-: ~infarkt der heart attack; cardiac infarction *(Med.)*; **~innig** *(veralt.)*, **~inniglich** *(veralt.)* **1.** *Adj.* heartfelt; **2.** *adv.* with heartfelt emotion; **jmdn. ~innig lieben** love sb. with all one's heart; **~insuffizienz die** *(Med.)* cardiac insufficiency; **~kammer die** *(Anat.)* ventricle; **~kirsche die** heart cherry; sweet cherry; **~klappe die** *(Anat.)* heart-valve; **~klappen·fehler der** *(Med.)* valvular defect *or* insufficiency; **~klopfen das; ~s: jmd. hat ~klopfen** sb.'s heart is pounding; **jmd. bekommt ~klopfen** sb.'s heart starts to pound; **mit ~klopfen** with a pounding heart; **~kollaps der** *s.* **~versagen; ~könig der** king of hearts; **~krampf der** heart spasm; **~krank** *Adj.* ‹*person*› with *or* suffering from a heart condition; **[sehr] ~krank sein/werden** have/get a [serious] heart condition; **~kranke Patienten** cardiac patients; **~kranke der/die** person with *or* suffering from a heart condition; *(Patient)* cardiac patient; **~kranz·gefäß das;** *meist Pl.* coronary vessel; **~leiden das** heart condition

herzlich 1. *Adj.* **a)** *(warmherzig)* warm ‹*smile, reception*›; kind ‹*words*›; **~ zu jmdm. sein** be cordial towards sb.; **b)** *(ehrlich gemeint)* sincere; **~e Grüße/~en Dank** kind regards/many thanks; **sein ~es Beileid zum Ausdruck bringen** express one's sincere condolences *pl.*; **~[st] Dein/Euer Julius** *(als Briefschluß)* kind[est] regards, Julius; *s. auch* **Glückwunsch. 2.** *adv.* **a)** *(warmherzig)* warmly; **der Empfang fiel sehr ~ aus** the reception was very cordial; **b)** *(ehrlich gemeint)* sincerely; ‹*congratulate*› heartily; **es grüßt euch ~ Eure Viktoria** *(als Briefschluß)* kind regards, Victoria; **c)** *(sehr)* **~ wenig** very *or (coll.)* precious little; **~ schlecht** dreadful; **~ gern!** gladly; **etw. ~ satt haben** be heartily sick of sth.

Herzlichkeit die a) *s.* **herzlich a:** warmth; kindness; **b)** *(Aufrichtigkeit)* sincerity

herz-, Herz-: ~liebste der/die *s.* **~allerliebste; ~los 1.** *Adj.* heartless; callous; **2.** *adv.* heartlessly; callously; **~losigkeit die; ~, ~en a)** *o. Pl.* heartlessness; callousness; **b)** *(herzlose Tat/Bemerkung)* heartless act/remark; **~-Lungen-Maschine die** heart-lung machine; **~massage die** cardiac massage; heart massage; **~mittel das** *(ugs.)* heart pills *pl.*; **~muskel der** *(Anat.)* heart muscle; cardiac muscle

Herzog ['hɛrtso:k] **der; ~s, Herzöge** ['hɛrtsø:gə] duke; **[Herr] Friedrich ~ von Meiningen** Frederick, Duke of Meiningen

Herzogin die; ~, ~nen duchess

herzoglich *Adj.; nicht präd.* ducal; of the duke *postpos., not pred.*; **die ~e Familie** the family of the duke

Herzogtum das; ~s, Herzogtümer duchy

Herz·rhythmus der *(Med.)* heart rhythm; cardiac rhythm

Herzrhythmus·störung die *(Med.)* disturbance of the heart *or* cardiac rhythm

herz-, Herz-: ~schlag der a) heartbeat; **einen ~schlag lang** *(geh.)* for a *or* one fleeting moment; **b)** *o. Pl. (Abfolge der Herzschläge, auch fig. geh.)* pulse; **c)** *(Herzversagen)* heart failure; **an einem ~schlag sterben** die of heart failure; **~schmerz der;** *meist Pl.* pain in the region of the heart; **~schrittmacher der** *(Anat., Med.)* [cardiac] pacemaker; **~schwäche die** cardiac insufficiency; **~spender der** heart donor; **~spezialist der** heart specialist; **~stärkend** *Adj.* **ein ~stärkendes Mittel** a cardiac tonic; **~stärkend sein/wirken** act as a cardiac tonic; **~still·stand der** *(Med.)* cardiac arrest; **~stück das** *(geh.)* heart; **~tätigkeit die** action of the heart; **~ton der;** *meist Pl. (Med.)* heart sound; cardiac sound; **~transplantation die** *(Med.)* heart transplantation

herzu [hɛɐ'tsu:] *Adv. (geh.) s.* **herbei**

herz-, Herz-: ~verfettung die fatty degeneration of the heart; **~verpflanzung die** *s.* **~transplantation; ~versagen das; ~s** heart failure; **~zerreißend 1.** *Adj.* heart-rending; **2.** *adv.* heart-rendingly

Hesse ['hɛsə] **der; ~n, ~n** Hessian

Hessen (das) Hesse

hessisch *Adj.* Hessian

Hetäre [he'tɛ:rə] **die; ~, ~n** hetaera

hetero-, Hetero- [hetero-] *in Zus.* hetero-

heterodox [-'dɔks] *Adj. (Rel.)* heterodox

Heterodoxie [-dɔ'ksi:] **die; ~, ~n** *(Rel.)* heterodoxy

heterogen [-'ge:n] *Adj.* heterogeneous

Heterogenität [-geni'tɛ:t] **die; ~:** heterogeneity

heteronom [-'no:m] *Adj. (geh.; Zool.)* heteronomous

Hetero·sexualität die; ~: heterosexuality *no art.*

hetero·sexuell *Adj.* heterosexual

Hethiter [he'ti:tɐ] **der; ~s, ~:** Hittite

Hetz [hɛts] **die; ~, ~en** *(österr. ugs.)* **das war eine ~!** that was a [good] laugh; **seine ~ haben** have some fun; **aus ~:** for fun

Hetz·blatt das *(abwertend)* political smear-sheet

Hetze ['hɛtsə] **die; ~ a)** *(große Hast)* [mad] rush; **in großer ~:** in a mad rush *or* hurry; **heute war eine fürchterliche ~:** today was one mad rush; **b)** *o. Pl. (abwertend: Aufhetzung)* smear campaign; *(gegen eine Minderheit)* hate campaign; **eine ~ betreiben** mount *or* run a smear/hate campaign; **c)** *(Jägerspr.) s.* **Hetzjagd a**

hetzen 1. *tr. V.* **a)** hunt; **ein Tier zu Tode ~:** hunt an animal to death; **die Hunde/die Polizei auf jmdn. ~:** set the dogs on [to] sb./get the police on to sb.; **b)** *(antreiben)* rush; hurry. **2.** *itr. V.* **a)** *(in großer Eile sein)* rush; **den ganzen Tag ~:** be in a rush all day long; **b)** *mit sein (hasten)* rush; hurry; *(rennen)* dash; race; **c)** *(abwertend: Haß entfachen)* stir up hatred; *(schmähen)* say malicious things; **gegen jmdn./etw. ~:** smear sb./agitate against sth.; **gegen eine Minderheit ~:** stir up hatred against minorities; **zum Krieg ~:** engage in warmongering; **bei jmdm. gegen jmdn. ~:** try to turn sb. against sb.

Hetzer der; ~s, ~: malicious agitator

Hetzerei die; ~, ~en a) *o. Pl. (Hast)* [mad] rush; **b)** *o. Pl. (ugs. abwertend: Aufwiegelei)* malicious agitation; **c)** *(ugs. abwertend: hetzerische Handlung/hetzerisches Wort)* inflammatory act/word

hetzerisch *Adj.* inflammatory

Hetz-: ~hund der hound; hunting dog; **~jagd die a)** *(Jagdw.)* hunting *(with hounds)*; *(einzelne Jagd)* hunt *(with hounds)*; **b)** *(Hast)* [mad] rush; **~kampagne die** *(abwertend)* smear campaign; *(gegen eine Minderheit)* hate campaign; **~rede die** *(abwertend)* inflammatory speech

Heu [hɔy] **das; ~[e]s a)** hay; **~ machen** make hay; **b)** *(ugs.: Geld)* dough *(sl.)*; **der hat vielleicht ~:** he's rolling in money *or* it *(coll.)*; *s. auch* **Geld a**

Heu-: ~blume die; *meist Pl.*; **~blume[n** *Pl.*] *mixture of seeds, flowers, and grasses sieved from hay and used for medical purposes;* **~boden der** hayloft

Heuchelei die; ~, ~en *(abwertend)* **a)** *o. Pl. (Verstellung)* hypocrisy; **b)** *(Äußerung)* piece of hypocrisy; hypocritical remark

heucheln ['hɔyçl̩n] **1.** *itr. V.* be a hypocrite. **2.** *tr. V.* feign ‹*joy, sympathy, etc.*›

Heuchler der; ~s, ~, Heuchlerin die; ~, ~nen hypocrite

heuchlerisch 1. *Adj.* **a)** *(unaufrichtig)* hypocritical; **b)** *(geheuchelt)* feigned ‹*interest, sympathy, etc.*›. **2.** *adv.* hypocritically

heuen *itr. V. (landsch.)* make hay

heuer ['hɔyɐ] *Adv. (südd., österr., schweiz.)* this year

Heuer die; ~, ~n *(Seemannsspr.)* **a)** *(Lohn)* pay; wages *pl.*; **b)** *(Anstellung)* **auf einem Schiff [als Funker] ~ nehmen** join a ship [as wireless operator]; **auf einem Frachter ~ nehmen** ship on board a freighter; **eine ~ bekommen** get hired

Heu·ernte die a) hay harvest; haymaking; **b)** *(Ertrag)* hay crop

Heuer·vertrag der *(Seemannsspr.)* contract of employment

Heu-: ~fieber das *s.* **~schnupfen; ~forke die** *(nordd.)*, **~gabel die** hay-fork; **~haufen der** haystack; hayrick; *s. auch* **Stecknadel**

Heul·boje die a) *(Seew.)* whistling-buoy; **b)** *(ugs. abwertend: Sänger)* caterwauler
heulen ['hɔylən] *itr. V.* **a)** ‹*wolf, dog, jackal, etc.*› howl; *(fig.)* ‹*wind, gale*› howl; ‹*storm*› roar; **b)** ‹*siren, buoy, etc.*› wail; **c)** *(ugs.: weinen)* howl; bawl; **vor Wut/Schmerz/Freude ~:** howl and weep with rage/pain/howl with delight; **das ist zum Heulen** *(ugs.)* it's enough to make you weep; **Heulen und Zähneklappern** *od.* **Zähneknirschen** wailing and gnashing of teeth
Heuler der; ~s, ~ a) *(ugs.: Heulton)* whine; **b)** *(Feuerwerkskörper)* wailing banshee; **c)** *(salopp: tolle Sache)* **das ist wirklich ein ~:** it's really great *or* fantastic *(coll.)*; **das ist [ja] der letzte ~!** *(iron.)* it's bloody awful! *(Brit. sl.)*; **d)** *(ugs.: Seehund)* seal
Heulerei die; ~, ~en; *Pl. selten (abwertend)* **a)** *(einer Sirene, Boje)* wailing; **b)** *(ugs.: heftiges Weinen)* howling; bawling
Heulsuse ['hɔylzu:zə] **die; ~, ~n** *(ugs. abwertend)* cry-baby
Heu-: ~monat der, ~mond der *(veralt.)* July; **~pferd das** grasshopper; **~reiter** *(österr.)*, **~reuter** *(südd.)* **der** drying-rack for hay
heureka ['hɔyreka] *Interj. (geh.)* eureka
heurig ['hɔyrɪç] *Adj.; nicht präd. (südd., österr., schweiz.)* this year's ‹*harvest, crop, etc.*›; new ‹*potatoes, wine*›; **der ~e Sommer** this summer
Heurige der; *adj. Dekl. (bes. österr.)* **a)** *(Wein)* new wine; **sie saßen beim ~n** they sat drinking the new wine; **b)** *(Weinlokal)* inn with new wine on tap
Heuristik [hɔy'rɪstɪk] **die; ~:** heuristics *sing.*
heuristisch *Adj.* heuristic
Heu-: ~schnupfen der hay fever; **~schober der** *(südd., österr.)* haystack; hayrick; **~schrecke die** grasshopper; *(in Afrika, Asien)* locust; grasshopper; **~stadel der** *(südd., österr., schweiz.)* [hay] barn
heut [hɔyt] *(ugs.)*, **heute** ['hɔytə] *Adv.* today; **~ früh** early this morning; **~ morgen/abend** this morning/evening; **~ mittag** [at] midday today; **~ nacht** tonight; *(letzte Nacht)* last night; **~ in einer Woche** a week [from] today; today week; **~ vor einer Woche** a week ago today; **seit ~:** from today; **ab ~, von ~ an** from today [on]; **bis ~:** until today; **bis ~ nicht** *(erst ~)* not until today; *(überhaupt noch nicht)* not to this day; *(bis jetzt noch nicht)* not as yet; **für ~:** for today; **die Zeitung von ~:** today's paper; **das Brot ist von ~:** it is today's bread; **das kann sich ~ oder morgen schon ändern** *(ugs.)* that can change at any time; **lieber ~ als morgen** *(ugs.)* the sooner, the better; **von ~ auf morgen** from one day to the next; **von ~ auf morgen sterben** die suddenly; **das geht nicht von ~ auf morgen** it can't be done at such short notice; **das Heute** the present; today; **der Bauernhof/die Frau von ~:** the farm/woman of today
heutig *Adj.; nicht präd.* **a)** *(von diesem Tag)* today's; **die ~e Post/Zeitung/Vorstellung** today's post/newspaper/performance; **der ~e Tag/am ~en Tage** today; **am ~en Abend** this evening; **bis zum ~en Tag** until the present day *or* today; **b)** *(gegenwärtig)* today's; of today *postpos.*; **die ~e Jugend/Generation** today's youth/generation; the youth/generation of today; **der ~e Stand der Forschung** the present state of research; **in der ~en Zeit** today; nowadays
heut·zu·tage *Adv.* nowadays
Heu-: ~wagen der hay-cart; **~wender der** *(Landw.)* tedder; tedding machine
Hexagon [hɛksa'go:n] **das; ~s, ~e** *(Math.)* hexagon
Hexa·gramm [hɛksa-] **das** hexagram
Hexameter [hɛ'ksa:metɐ] **der; ~s, ~** *(Verslehre)* hexameter
Hexe ['hɛksə] **die; ~, ~n a)** witch; **b)** *(abwertend)* **diese kleine ~:** this little minx
hexen 1. *itr. V.* work magic; **ich kann doch nicht ~** *(ugs.)* I'm not a magician *(coll.)*. **2.** *tr. V.* conjure up
Hexen-: ~einmaleins das magic formula; **~haus das** witch's cottage; **~jagd die** *(auch fig.)* witch-hunt; **~kessel der: ein [wahrer] ~kessel sein** be [absolute] bedlam; **das Fußballstadion glich einem ~kessel** there was pandemonium *or* bedlam in the football-ground; **~meister der** sorcerer; **~prozeß der** *(hist.)* witch trial; **~ring der a)** *(von Pilzen)* fairy ring; **b)** *(Jägerspr.)* *circular run trodden by roedeer in the mating season;* **~sabbat der a)** *(Zusammenkunft der Hexen)* witches' sabbath; **b)** *(wüstes Treiben)* orgy; **~schuß der;** *o. Pl.* lumbago *no indef. art.*; **~verbrennung die** *(hist.)* burning of a witch/of witches; **~verfolgung die** *(hist.)* witch-hunt
Hexer der; ~s, ~: sorcerer
Hexerei die; ~, ~en sorcery; witchcraft; *(von Kunststücken usw.)* magic; **das ist doch keine ~:** there's no magic about it
Hexode [hɛ'kso:də] **die; ~, ~n** *(Elektrot.)* hexode
HGB *Abk.* **Handelsgesetzbuch**
hick [hɪk] *Interj. (ugs.)* hic
Hickhack ['hɪkhak] **das** *od.* **der; ~s, ~s** *(ugs.)* squabbling; bickering
hie [hi:] *Adv.* **in ~ und da** *(stellenweise)* here and there; *(von Zeit zu Zeit)* now and then; from time to time; **~ ..., da ...:** on the one hand ..., on the other [hand] ...
hieb [hi:p] *1. u. 3. Pers. Sg. Prät. v.* **hauen**
Hieb der; ~[e]s, ~e a) *(Schlag)* blow; *(mit der Peitsche)* lash; *(im Fechten)* cut; *(fig.)* dig **(gegen** at); **jmdm. einen ~ mit der Faust/einem Beil versetzen** punch sb./strike sb. with an axe; **b)** *Pl. (ugs.: Prügel)* hiding *sing.*; beating *sing.*; walloping *sing. (sl.)*; **~e bekommen/kriegen** get a hiding *or* beating *or (sl.)* walloping; **es gibt/setzt ~e!** you'll get a hiding *or* beating *or (sl.)* walloping
hieb·fest *Adj.* **in hieb- und stichfest** watertight; cast-iron
Hieb·waffe die cutting weapon
hielt [hi:lt] *1. u. 3. Pers. Sg. Prät. v.* **halten**
hienieden [hi:'ni:dn̩] *Adv. (bes. österr., sonst veralt.)* here below; here in this world [below]
hier [hi:ɐ] *Adv.* **a)** *(an diesem Ort)* here; **[von] ~ oben/unten** [from] up/down here; **~ vorn** here in front; **~ draußen/drinnen** out/in here; **~ entlang** along here; **von ~ [aus]** from here; **wo ist ~ die nächste Tankstelle?** where is the nearest petrol station *(Brit.) or (Amer.)* gas station around here?; **er ist nicht von ~:** he's not from this area *or* around here; **das Buch ~:** this book [here]; **~ spricht Hans Schulze** this is Hans Schulze [speaking]; **~ und da** *od.* **dort** *(an manchen Stellen)* here and there; *(manchmal)* [every] now and then; **~ und jetzt** *od.* **heute** *(geh.)* here and now; **das Hier und Jetzt** *od.* **Heute** *(geh.)* the here and now; **b)** *(zu diesem Zeitpunkt)* now; **von ~ an** from now on; **c)** *(in diesem Zusammenhang, Punkt)* here; **was gibt es ~ zu lachen?** what's funny [about this]?
hier-: *Bei den aus* **hier** *und einer Präposition gebildeten Adverbien* **(hieran, hierauf, hierbei** *usw.) werden im folgenden* this, these *oder* here *zur Übersetzung verwendet* (hold on to this; on here; among these; about this). *Dies ist im allgemeinen die angemessene Form der Übersetzung. Wenn der Bestandteil* **hier-** *weniger stark betont ist, kann man* this *oder* here *durch* it *ersetzen* (hold on to it; on it; about it). *Beispiele:* **er suchte einen starken Ast und lehnte die Leiter hieran** he looked for a strong branch and leaned the ladder against it; **sie ging zum Schuppen, um ihr Fahrrad hierhinter zu stellen** she went to the shed to put her bicycle behind it. *Ähnlich:* **hierunter befanden sich auch einige Deutsche** there were some Germans among them.
hieran ['hi:'ran] *Adv.* **a)** *(an dieser/diese Stelle)* here; **sich ~ festhalten** hold on to this; **b)** *(fig.)* **im Anschluß ~:** immediately after this; **~ wird deutlich, daß ...:** this shows clearly that ...; *s. auch* **hier-**
Hierarchie [hierar'çi:] **die; ~, ~n** hierarchy
hierarchisch 1. *Adj.* hierarchical. **2.** *adv.* hierarchically
hierauf ['hi:'rauf] *Adv.* **a)** *(auf dieser/diese Stelle)* on here; **b)** *(darauf)* on this; **wir werden ~ zurückkommen** we'll come back to this; **c)** *(danach)* after that; then; **d)** *(infolgedessen)* whereupon; *s. auch* **hier-**
hierauf·hin *Adv.* hereupon
hieraus ['hi:'raus] *Adv.* **a)** *(aus dem eben Erwähnten)* out of *or* from here; **b)** *(aus dieser Tatsache, Quelle)* from this; **c)** *(aus diesem Material)* out of this; *s. auch* **hier-**
hier|behalten *unr. tr. V.* **jmdn./etw. ~:** keep sb./sth. here
hier·bei *Adv.* **a)** *(bei dieser Gelegenheit)* **Diese Übung ist sehr schwierig. Man kann sich ~ leicht verletzen.** This exercise is very difficult. You can easily injure yourself doing it; **Ich habe ihn gestern getroffen. Hierbei habe ich gleich ...:** I met him yesterday, and straightaway I ...; **b)** *(bei der erwähnten Sache)* here; *s. auch* **hier-**
hier|bleiben *unr. itr. V.; mit sein* stay here
hier·durch *Adv.* **a)** *(hier hindurch)* through here; **b)** *(auf Grund dieser Sache)* because of this; as a result of this; **c)** *s.* **hiermit**; *s. auch* **hier-**
hierein ['hi:rain] *Adv.* in here; *s. auch* **hier-**
hier·für *Adv.* for this; **ich habe kein Interesse ~:** I have no interest in this; *s. auch* **hier-**
hier·gegen *Adv.* **a)** *(gegen die erwähnte Sache)* against this; **b)** *(gegen diese Stelle)* against here; **c)** *(im Gegensatz hierzu)* in *or* by comparison with this; compared with this; *s. auch* **hier-**
hier·her *Adv.* here; **ich gehe bis ~ und nicht weiter** I'm going this far and no further; **bis ~ und nicht weiter** *(als Warnung)* so far and no further
hierher-: ~|bemühen 1. *tr. V.* **jmdn. ~bemühen** trouble sb. to come here; **2.** *refl. V.* take the trouble to come here; **~|bitten** *unr. tr. V.* **jmdn. ~bitten** ask sb. [to come] here; **darf ich Sie ~bitten?** would you come here, please?; **~|bringen** *unr. tr. V.* **jmdn./etw. ~bringen** bring sb./sth. here; **~|fahren 1.** *unr. itr. V.; mit sein* drive here; *(mit einem Motorrad, Rad)* ride here; **2.** *unr. tr. V.* **jmdn. ~fahren** drive sb. here; **~|führen** *tr. V.* **jmdn. ~führen** bring sb. here; **~|gehören** *itr. V.* **a)** *(an diesen Ort gehören)* belong here; **b)** *(hierfür wichtig sein)* be relevant [here]; **~|kommen** *unr. itr. V.; mit sein* come here; **wie bist du ~gekommen?** how did you get here?; **~|laufen** *unr. itr. V.; mit sein* walk/*(schneller)* run here; **~|schicken** *tr. V.* **jmdn./etw. ~schicken** send sb./sth. here; **~|stellen** *tr. V.* **etw. ~stellen** put sth. here
hier·herum *Adv.* **a)** *(an dieser Stelle herum)* round here; *(in diese Richtung)* round this way; **b)** *(ugs.: hier irgendwo)* around here
hierher-: ~|wagen *refl. V.* dare to come here; **~|ziehen 1.** *unr. tr. V.* **etw. ~ziehen** pull sth. here; **2.** *unr. itr. V.; mit sein (umziehen)* move here
hier·hin *Adv.* here; **sie blickte bald ~, bald dorthin** she looked this way and that; **bis ~:** up to here *or* this point
hier·hinab *Adv.* down here
hier·hinauf *Adv.* up here
hier·hinaus *Adv.* **a)** *(an dieser Stelle)* out here; **b)** *(aus diesem Raum)* out of here
hier·hinein *Adv.* in here
hier·hinter *Adv.* behind here; *s. auch* **hier-**
hier·hinunter *Adv.* **a)** *(unter diesen Gegen-*

stand) under here; **b)** *(an dieser Stelle)* down here
hierin ['hi:'rɪn] *Adv.* **a)** *(in diesem Gegenstand)* in here; **b)** *(in dieser Angelegenheit)* in this; *s. auch* **hier-**
hier|lassen *unr. tr. V.* **etw. ~:** leave sth. here
hier·mit *Adv.* with this/these; **~ ist der Fall erledigt** that puts an end to the matter; **~ erkläre ich, daß ...** *(Amtsspr.)* I hereby declare that ...; **~ wird bestätigt/bescheinigt, daß ...** *(Amtsspr.)* this is to confirm/certify that ...; *s. auch* **hier-**
hier·nach *Adv.* **a)** *(einer Sache entsprechend)* in accordance with this/these; **b)** *(demnach)* according to this/these; **c)** *(anschließend)* after that; *s. auch* **hier-**
hier·neben *Adv.* beside this; next to this; *s. auch* **hier-**
Hieroglyphe [hiero'gly:fə] **die; ~, ~n** hieroglyph; **~n** hieroglyphics
hier·orts *Adv.* here
hier|sein *unr. itr. V.; mit seln; Zusammenschreibung nur im Inf. und Part.* be here
hierüber ['hi:'ry:bɐ] *Adv.* **a)** *(über dem Erwähnten)* above here; **b)** *(über das Erwähnte)* over here; **c)** *(das Erwähnte betreffend)* about this/these; **d)** *(geh.: währenddessen)* **er war ~ eingeschlafen** he had fallen asleep while doing so; *s. auch* **hier-**
hierum ['hi:'rʊm] *Adv.* about this; *(um ... herum)* round here; **~ geht es gar nicht** that's not the point; it's not a question of that; *s. auch* **hier-**
hierunter ['hi:'rʊntɐ] *Adv.* **a)** *(unter diese[r] Stelle)* under here; **b)** *(unter der erwähnten Sache)* **~ leiden** suffer from this; **etw. ~ verstehen** *od.* **sich** *(Dat.)* **etw. ~ vorstellen** understand sth. by this; **c)** *(unter die genannte/der genannten Gruppe)* among these; *s. auch* **hier-**
hier·von *Adv.* **a)** *(von dieser Stelle)* from here; **b)** *(von dieser Sache)* of this; **~ zeugen** bear witness to this; **c)** *(dadurch)* because of this; **d)** *(aus dieser Menge)* of this/these; **e)** *(aus diesem Material)* out of this; *s. auch* **hier-**
hier·vor *Adv.* **a)** *(vor dieser/diese Stelle)* in front of this *or* here; **b)** *(vor der erwähnten Sache)* **Respekt ~ haben** have respect for this; **Angst ~ haben** be afraid of this; *s. auch* **hier-**
hier·zu *Adv.* **a)** *(zu dieser Sache)* with this; **vgl. ~:** cf.; **b)** *(zu dieser Gruppe)* **~ gehört/gehören ...:** this includes/these include; **c)** *(zu diesem Zweck)* **ich kann dir ~ nur raten** I can only recommend you to do this/buy this/go *etc.*; **ich wünsche dir ~ viel Erfolg** I wish you every success with this; **~ reicht mein Geld nicht** I haven't got enough money for that; **d)** *(hinsichtlich dieser Sache)* about this; *s. auch* **hier-**
hierzu·lande *Adv. (in diesem Land)* [here] in this country; [here] in these parts; *(in dieser Gegend)* [here] in these parts
hiesig ['hi:zɪç] *Adj.; nicht präd.* local; **die ~e Gegend** this locality; **meine ~en Verwandten** my relatives here
hieß [hi:s] *1. u. 3. Pers. Sg. Prät. v.* **heißen**
hieven ['hi:vn̩] *tr. V.* heave
Hi-Fi-Anlage ['haifi-] **die** *(Rundf.)* hi-fi system
high [haɪ] *Adj.; nur präd. (ugs.)* high *(coll.)*
Highlife ['hailaif] **das; ~[s]** *(ugs.)* high life; **bei uns ist heute ~:** we're living it up today; **~ machen** live it up
High-Society [-sə'saɪətɪ] **die; ~:** high society; **zur ~ gehören** be a member of high society
High-Tech- ['hai'tɛk-] *in Zus.* high-tech
hihi [hi'hi:], **hihihi** [hihi'hi:] *Interj.* hehe[-he]
Hilfe ['hɪlfə] **die; ~, ~n a)** help; *(für Notleidende)* aid; relief; **wirtschaftliche/finanzielle ~:** economic aid/financial assistance; **jmdm. ~ leisten** help sb.; **mit ~** (+ *Gen.*) with the help *or* aid of; **ohne fremde ~:** unaided; without help *or* assistance; **jmdn. um ~ bitten/***(geh.)* **ersuchen** ask sb. for help *or* assistance/request sb.'s help *or* assistance; **um ~ rufen** shout for help; **jmdn. zu ~ rufen** call on sb. for help; **jmdm. zu ~ kommen/eilen** come/hurry to sb.'s aid *or* assistance; **zu ~!** help!; **jmds. Gedächtnis zu ~ kommen** *(fig.)* refresh sb.'s memory [for him/her]; **etw. zu ~ nehmen** use sth.; make use of sth.; **jmdm. eine große ~ sein** be a great help to sb.; **jmdm. ~n geben** give sb. some help; **einem Pferd ~n geben** give a horse aids; **Erste ~:** first aid; **b)** *(Hilfskraft)* help; *(im Geschäft)* assistant
hilfe-, Hilfe-: ~leistung die help; assistance; **finanzielle ~leistung** financial aid *or* assistance; **unterlassene ~leistung** *(Rechtsspr.)* failure to render assistance in an emergency; **~ruf der** cry for help; *(Notsignal)* distress signal; **~stellung die** *(Turnen)* **a) jmdm. ~stellung geben** act as spotter for sb.; **b)** *(Person)* spotter; **~suchend 1.** *Adj.* **sein ~suchender Blick ging zum Fenster** he looked towards the window, seeking help; **2.** *adv.* **sich ~suchend umschauen** look round for help; **sich ~suchend an jmdn. wenden** turn to sb. for help
hilf-, Hilf-: ~los 1. *Adj.* **a)** helpless; **b)** *(unbeholfen)* awkward; **2.** *adv.* **a)** helplessly; **b)** *(unbeholfen)* awkwardly; **~losigkeit die; ~ a)** helplessness; **b)** *(Unbeholfenheit)* awkwardness; **~reich** *(geh.)* **1.** *Adj.* helpful; **2.** *adv.* **jmdm. ~reich zur Seite stehen** lend support to sb.; stand by sb.
hilfs-, Hilfs-: ~aktion die relief programme; **~arbeiter der** labourer; *(in einer Fabrik)* unskilled worker; **~bedürftig** *Adj.* **a)** *(schwach)* in need of help *postpos.*; **b)** *(notleidend)* in need; needy; **~bedürftigkeit die** need; neediness; **~bereit** *Adj.* helpful; **~bereitschaft die** helpfulness; readiness *or* willingness to help; **~dienst der a)** *(Dienst zu Hilfszwecken)* community work; **b)** *(Organisation)* emergency service; *(bei Katastrophen)* [emergency] relief service; *(für Autofahrer)* [emergency] breakdown service; **~fonds der** aid *or* relief fund; **~geistliche der** *(ev. u. kath. Kirche)* curate; **~gelder** *Pl.* aid money *sing.*; **~konstruktion die** *(Geom.)* auxiliary construction; **~kraft die** assistant; **~lehrer der, ~lehrerin die** assistant teacher; **~maßnahme die** aid *or* relief measure; **~mittel das a)** *(Mittel zur Erleichterung)* aid; **b)** *Pl. (finanzielle Mittel)* [financial] aid *sing.*; *(materielle Mittel)* aid *sing.*; supplies; **~motor der** auxiliary engine; **ein Fahrrad mit ~motor** a motor-assisted bicycle; **~organisation die** aid *or* relief organization; **~personal das** auxiliary staff; **~polizist der** reserve policeman; **~programm das** aid *or* relief programme; **~quelle die**; *meist Pl.* **a)** *(Material)* source; **b)** *(finanziell)* source of [financial] aid; **~schule die** *(veralt., noch ugs.)* special school; **~schüler der** *(veralt., noch ugs.)* pupil at a special school; **~schul·lehrer der** *(veralt., noch ugs.)* teacher at a special school; **~schwester die** nursing auxiliary; auxiliary nurse; **~sheriff der** deputy sheriff; **~truppe die**; *meist Pl. (Milit.)* reserve unit; **~verb das** *(Sprachw.)* auxiliary [verb]; **~willig** *Adj.* helpful; willing to help *postpos.*; **~willige der/die**; *adj. Dekl.* **a)** person willing to help; **die ~willigen** the people willing to help; **b)** *(hist.) volunteer from German occupied territory serving in German army in Second World War;* **~wissenschaft die** ancillary science; **~zeit·wort das** *s.* **~verb**
Himalaja [hi'ma:laja] **der; ~[s]: der/im ~:** the/in the Himalayas *pl.*
Him·beere ['hɪm-] **die** raspberry
Himbeer-: ~eis das raspberry ice [cream]; **~marmelade die** raspberry jam; **~saft der** raspberry juice; **~strauch der** raspberry bush
Himmel ['hɪml̩] **der; ~s, ~ a)** sky; **hoch am ~ stehen** be high in the sky; **eher stürzt der ~ ein, als daß er dir Geld leiht** *(ugs.)* never in a million years will he lend you any money *(coll.)*; **unter freiem ~:** in the open [air]; outdoors; **~ und Erde** *(Kochk.) dish of puréed potato and apple with fried blood sausage and liver sausage;* **aus heiterem ~** *(ugs.)* out of the blue; **jmdn./etw. in den ~ heben** *(ugs.)* praise sb./sth. to the skies; **Fortschritte fallen nicht vom Himmel** advances don't come overnight; **b)** *(Aufenthalt Gottes)* heaven; **in den ~ kommen** go to heaven; **im ~ sein** *(verhüll.)* be in heaven; **zum ~** *od.* **in den ~ auffahren,** *(geh.)* **gen ~ fahren** ascend into heaven; **Sohn des ~s** *(hist.: Titel des chinesischen Kaisers)* Son of Heaven; **~ und Hölle** *(Kinderspiel)* ≈ hopscotch; **jmdm. hängt der ~ voller Geigen** *(geh.)* sb. is walking on air; **~ und Hölle** *od.* **Erde in Bewegung setzen** move heaven and earth; **sie hat den ~ auf Erden** *(geh.)* life is heaven on earth for her; **jmdm. den ~ auf Erden versprechen** promise sb. the earth; **im sieb[en]ten ~ sein/sich [wie] im sieb[en]ten ~ fühlen** *(ugs.)* be in the seventh heaven; **etw. schreit zum ~:** sth. is scandalous *or* a scandal; **etw. stinkt zum ~** *(salopp)* sth. stinks to high heaven; **c)** *(verhüll.: Schicksal)* Heaven; **gerechter/gütiger/[ach] du lieber ~!** good Heavens!; Heavens above!; **dem ~ sei Dank** thank Heaven[s]; **das weiß der [liebe] ~** *od.* **das mag der liebe ~ wissen** Heaven [only] knows; **weiß der ~!** *(ugs.)* Heaven knows; **weiß der ~, wer .../wie .../wo .../wann ...** *(ugs.)* Heaven [only] knows who .../how.../where .../when ...; **um [des] ~s willen!** *(Ausruf des Schreckens)* good Heavens!; good God!; *(inständige Bitte)* for Heaven's sake; **~ noch [ein]mal!** for Heaven's *or* goodness' sake!; **~, Herrgott, Sakrament!** for Heaven's sake!; **~, Kreuz, Donnerwetter!** *(salopp)* damn and blast! *(sl.)*; **~, Arsch und Zwirn!** *(derb)* bloody hell! *(Brit. sl.)*; **d)** *(Baldachin)* canopy
himmel-, Himmel-: ~an *Adv. (dichter.)* heavenwards *(poet.)*; up towards the sky; **~angst** *Adj.* **in mir ist/wird ~angst** I am scared to death; **~bett das** four-poster bed; **~blau** *Adj.* sky-blue; azure; clear blue ‹*eyes*›; **~donner·wetter** *Interj.* **in ~donnerwetter noch [ein]mal!** *(salopp)* hell's bells! *(sl.)*
Himmel·fahrt die *(Rel.)* **a)** *(Auffahrt in den Himmel)* ascent to heaven; **Christi/Mariä ~:** the Ascension of Christ/the Assumption of the Virgin Mary; **b)** *(Festtag)* **[Christi] ~:** Ascension Day *no art.*
Himmelfahrts-: ~kommando das a) *(Unternehmen)* suicide mission *or* operation; **b)** *(Personen)* suicide squad; **~nase die** *(ugs. scherzh.)* turned-up nose; **~tag der** Ascension Day *no art.*
himmel-, Himmel-: ~herr·gott *Interj.* **in ~herrgott noch [ein]mal!** *(salopp)* hell's bells! *(sl.)*; **~herr·gott·sakra** *Interj.* *(österr., südd. salopp)* bloody hell! *(Brit. sl.)*; **~hoch 1.** *Adj.* soaring; towering; **2.** *adv.* ‹*rise up etc.*› high into the sky; **~hoch jauchzend, zu Tode betrübt** up one minute, down the next; on top of the world one minute, down in the dumps the next; **~hund der** *(derb)* unscrupulous bastard *(coll.)*; *(Draufgänger)* daredevil; **~reich das** *(christl. Rel.)* kingdom of heaven; **ein ~reich für ...:** I'd give anything for ...; *s. auch* **[1]Mensch b**
Himmels-: ~achse die; *o. Pl. (Astron.)* celestial axis; **~äquator der** *(Astron.)* celestial equator; **~bahn die** *(dichter.)* path across the heavens
himmel·schreiend *Adj.* scandalous; out-

rageous; scandalous, appalling ⟨*conditions, disgrace*⟩; arrant *attrib.* ⟨*nonsense*⟩; **ihre Dummheit ist ~:** she is appallingly stupid; **eine ~e Ungerechtigkeit** an injustice that cries out to heaven

Hịmmels-: ~erscheinung die celestial phenomenon; **~fürst der** *(christl. Rel.)* King of heaven; **~gabe die** *(geh.)* gift from heaven; **~gegend die** *s.* **~richtung; ~gewölbe das a)** *(dichter.)* firmament; vault of heaven *or* the heavens; **b)** *(Astron.)* sky; **~globus der** celestial globe; **~karte die** *(Astron.)* star map; **~königin die** *(kath. Rel.)* Queen of heaven; **~körper der** celestial body; **~kugel die** celestial sphere; **~kunde die** astronomy; **~kuppel die** *s.* **~gewölbe a; ~labor das** *(Raumf., bes. DDR)* space lab[oratory]; **~macht die** *(geh.)* heavenly power; **~pforte die** *(dichter.)* gates *pl.* of heaven; Pearly Gates *(also joc.)*; **~pol der** *(Astron.)* celestial pole; **~richtung die** point of the compass; cardinal point; **die vier ~richtungen** the four points of the compass; **aus allen ~richtungen** from all directions; **in alle ~richtungen verstreut sein** be scattered to all four corners of the earth; **von hier aus führen Wege in alle ~richtungen** from this point paths radiate in all directions; **~schlüssel der, ~schlüsselchen das** cowslip; *(Waldschlüsselblume)* oxlip; **~sphäre die** celestial sphere; **~spion der** *(ugs.)* spy-in-the-sky satellite *(coll.)*; **~stürmer der** *(geh.)* unshakeable idealist; **~tor das, ~tür die** *(dichter.)* gates *pl.* of heaven

hịmmel·stürmend *Adj.; nicht präd. (geh.)* boundless ⟨*enthusiasm*⟩; unbridled ⟨*feelings*⟩; wildly ambitious ⟨*plan*⟩

Hịmmels·zelt das *(dichter.)* firmament

hịmmel-: ~wärts *Adv. (geh.)* heavenwards; **~weit 1.** *Adj.* enormous, vast ⟨*difference*⟩; **zwischen uns besteht ein ~weiter Unterschied** there's a world of difference between us; **2.** *adv.* **~weit voneinander entfernt sein** be poles apart; **~weit von etw. entfernt sein** be nowhere near sth.

hịmmlisch 1. *Adj.* **a)** *nicht präd. (den Himmel betreffend)* heavenly; **der ~e Vater** our Heavenly Father; **die ~en Heerscharen** the heavenly host[s]; **b)** *nicht präd. (göttlich)* divine; **eine ~e Fügung** divine providence; **c)** *(herrlich)* heavenly; divine; wonderful ⟨*weather, day, view*⟩. **2.** *adv.* divinely; wonderfully, gloriously ⟨*comfortable, warm*⟩

hin [hɪn] *Adv.* **a)** *(räumlich)* **zur Straße ~ liegen** face the road; **nach rechts ~ verlaufen** ⟨*road*⟩ go off to the right; **nach Frankfurt ~:** in the direction of Frankfurt; **bis zu dieser Stelle ~:** [up] to this point; as far as here; **sich zu etw. ~ erstrecken** stretch as far as sth.; **zur Straße ~ sind es 500 m** *(landsch.)* it's 500 m to the road; **über die ganze Welt ~** *(veralt.)* all over the world; throughout the world; **b)** *(zeitlich)* **gegen Mittag ~:** towards midday; **zum Herbst ~:** towards the autumn; as autumn approaches/approached; **über einen Monat ~:** for a whole month; **durch viele Jahre ~:** for many years; **c)** *(in Verbindungen)* **nach außen ~:** outwardly; **auf meine Anweisung/meinen Rat ~:** on *or* in response to my instructions/advice; **auf seine Bitte/seinen Anruf/eine Annonce ~:** at his request/in response to his [telephone] call/an advertisement; **selbst/auch auf die Gefahr ~, einen Fehler zu begehen** even at the risk of making a mistake; **etw. auf eine spätere Erweiterung ~ planen** plan sth. with a view to future expansion; *s. auch* **vor 2; d)** *(in Wortpaaren)* **~ und zurück** there and back; **einmal Köln ~ und zurück** a return [ticket] to Cologne; **Hin und zurück? – Nein, nur ~:** Return? – No, just a single; **~ und her** to and fro; back and forth; **~ und her beraten/reden** go backwards and forwards over the same old ground; **das Hin und Her** the toing and froing; **nach langem Hin und Her** after a great deal of argument; **das reicht/langt nicht ~ und nicht her** *(ugs.)* it's nowhere near enough; **Regen ~, Regen her** rain or no rain; **~ und wieder** [every] now and then; **e)** *(elliptisch)* **nichts wie ~!** what are we waiting for?; **~ zu ihm!** [hurry up,] to him!; *s. auch* **hinsein**

hinab [hɪˈnap] *Adv.* down; **den Hang ~:** down the slope; **ins Tal ~:** down into the valley; **den Fluß ~:** downstream; down the river; **bis ~ zu** down to

hinab- (*s. auch* **hinunter-**): **~|blicken** *itr. V.* look down; **~|senken 1.** *tr. V.* lower; sink ⟨*foundations*⟩; **2.** *refl. V.* slope down; **~|steigen** *unr. itr. V.; mit sein* climb down; *(hinuntergehen)* go down; **~|ziehen 1.** *unr. tr. V. (auch fig.)* **jmdn. ~ziehen** drag sb. down; **2.** *unr. itr. V.; mit sein (geh.)* move down

hinan [hɪˈnan] *Adv. (geh.) s.* **hinauf**

hịn|arbeiten *itr. V.* **auf etw.** *(Akk.)* **~:** work towards sth.; **auf eine Prüfung ~:** work for an examination; **auf einen Krieg ~:** work to bring about war

hinauf [hɪˈnauf] *Adv.* up; **den Hügel ~:** up the hill; **die Treppe ~:** up the stairs; upstairs; **bis ~ zu** up to

hinauf-: ~|arbeiten *refl. V. s.* **hocharbeiten; ~|begeben** *unr. refl. V. (geh.)* go up[stairs]; **~|begleiten** *tr. V.* **jmdn. ~begleiten** accompany sb. up[stairs]; **~|bemühen 1.** *tr. V.* **jmdn. ~bemühen** trouble sb. to go up; **2.** *refl. V.* take the trouble to go up; **~|bitten** *unr. tr. V.* **jmdn. ~bitten** ask sb. to go up; **~|blicken** *itr. V.* look up; **~|bringen** *unr. tr. V.* **jmdn./etw. ~bringen** take sb./sth. up[stairs]; **~|fahren 1.** *unr. itr. V.; mit sein* go up; *(im Auto)* drive up; *(mit einem Motorrad)* ride up; **2.** *unr. tr. V.* **jmdn. ~fahren** drive *or* take sb. up; **~|fallen** *unr. itr. V.; mit sein s.* **Treppe a; ~|führen 1.** *itr. V.* lead up; **2.** *tr. V.* **jmdn. ~führen** show sb. up; **~|gehen** *unr. itr. V.; mit sein* **a)** *(nach oben gehen)* go up; **die Treppe ~gehen** go up the stairs *or* upstairs; **auf 1000 Meter ~gehen** ⟨*aircraft, pilot*⟩ climb to 1,000 metres; **b)** *(nach oben führen)* lead up; **es geht steil ~:** the road/path climbs steeply; **c)** *(ugs.: steigen)* ⟨*prices, taxes, etc.*⟩ go up; rise; **d) mit dem Preis/der Miete ~gehen** *(ugs.)* put the price/rent up; **~|gelangen** *itr. V.; mit sein* [manage to] get up; **auf etw.** *(Akk.)* **~gelangen** [manage to] get up sth.; **~|helfen** *unr. itr. V.* **jmdm. [die Treppe] ~helfen** help sb. up [the stairs]; **~|klettern** *itr. V.; mit sein* climb up; **[auf] den Baum ~klettern** climb up the tree; **~|kommen** *unr. itr. V.; mit sein* **a)** *(nach oben kommen)* come up; **b)** *(nach oben kommen können)* [manage to] get up; **~|lassen** *unr. tr. V.* **jmdn. ~lassen** allow sb. to go up; let sb. go up; **~|laufen** *unr. itr. V.; mit sein* run up; **die Treppe ~laufen** run up the stairs; **~|reichen 1.** *tr. V.* hand *or* pass up; **jmdm. etw. ~reichen** hand *or* pass sth. up to sb.; **2.** *itr. V.* **bis zu etw. ~reichen** reach up to sth.; **~|schauen** *itr. V. (südd.)* look up; **~|schicken** *tr. V.* send up; **~|schnellen** *itr. V.; mit sein* shoot up; **~|sehen** *unr. itr. V.* look up; **~|setzen** *tr. V.* **a)** *(erhöhen)* raise; increase; put up; **die Preise ~setzen** increase *or* raise prices; **b)** *(nach oben setzen)* **etw. auf etw.** *(Dat.)* **~setzen** put sth. up on sth.; **~|steigen** *unr. itr. V.; mit sein* climb up; *(hinaufgehen)* go up; **~|tragen** *unr. tr. V.* carry *or* take up; **~|werfen** *unr. tr. V.* **etw. ~werfen** throw sth. up **(auf +** *Akk.* on to); **~|winden** *unr. refl. V.* **a) sich [an etw.** *(Dat.)***] ~winden** ⟨*plant*⟩ creep *or* climb up [sth.]; **b)** *(nach oben verlaufen)* wind up; **~|ziehen 1.** *unr. tr. V.* pull up; **2.** *unr. itr. V.; mit sein* move up; **3.** *unr. refl. V. (sich erstrecken)* stretch up; ⟨*pain*⟩ spread up

hinaus [hɪˈnaus] *Adv.* **a)** *(räumlich)* out; **~ [mit dir]!** out you go!; out with you!; **zum Fenster ~:** out of the window; **hier/dort ~:** this/that way out; **nach hinten/vorne ~ wohnen/liegen** live/be situated at the back/front; **durch die Tür ~:** out through the door; **über die Grenze ~:** beyond the frontier; **b)** *(zeitlich)* **auf Jahre ~:** for years to come; **bis über die Achtzig ~:** well past *or* over eighty; well into one's eighties; **c)** *(etw. überschreitend)* **über etw.** *(Akk.)* **~:** over and above *or* in addition to sth.; **über das Grab ~:** beyond the grave; *s. auch* **darüber**

hinaus-, Hinaus-: ~|befördern *tr. V.* **jmdn. ~befördern** throw *or (coll.)* chuck sb. out; **~|begeben** *unr. refl. V.* go out; **~|begleiten** *tr. V.* **jmdn. ~begleiten** see sb. out; **~|beugen** *refl. V.* lean out; **sich zum Fenster ~beugen** lean out of the window; **~|bitten** *unr. tr. V.* **jmdn. ~bitten** ask sb. to go *or* step outside; **~|blicken** *itr. V.* look out **(aus** of); **~|bringen** *unr. tr. V.* **a) jmdn./etw. ~bringen** take *or* see sb. out/take sth. out **(aus** of); **b)** *(weiterbringen)* **es nie über den untersten Dienstgrad ~bringen** never make it *or* get beyond the lowest grade; **~|bugsieren** *tr. V. (ugs.)* **jmdn. ~bugsieren** *(mit Geschick)* steer sb. out **(aus** of); *(hinausbefördern)* hustle sb. out **(aus** of); **~|drängen 1.** *itr. V.; mit sein* push one's way out **(aus** of); ⟨*crowd*⟩ push its way out **(aus** of); **2.** *tr. V.* **jmdn. ~drängen** push sb. out **(aus** of); *(fig.)* push sb. out **(aus** of); oust sb. **(aus** from); **~|dürfen** *unr. itr. V.* be allowed out **(aus** of); **darf ich bitte ~?** may I go out?; **~|eilen** *itr. V.; mit sein* hurry out **(aus** of); **~|ekeln** *tr. V. (ugs.)* **jmdn. ~ekeln** drive sb. out; **~|fahren 1.** *unr. itr. V.; mit sein* **a) aus etw. ~fahren** *(mit dem Auto)* drive out of sth.; *(mit dem Zweirad)* ride out of sth.; ⟨*car, bus*⟩ go out of sth.; ⟨*train*⟩ pull out of sth.; **zum Flugplatz ~fahren** drive out to the airport; **aufs Meer ~fahren** head for the sea; **b)** *(herauskommen)* shoot out **(aus** of); **c)** *(weiterfahren)* **über etw.** *(Akk.)* **~fahren** go past sth.; **2.** *unr. tr. V.* **jmdn./etw. ~fahren** drive *or* take sb./take sth. out; **~|fallen** *unr. itr. V.; mit sein* fall out **(aus** of); ⟨*light*⟩ come out **(aus** of); **~|finden** *unr. itr. V.* find one's way out **(aus** of); **er wird alleine ~finden** he'll find his own way out; **~|fliegen 1.** *unr. itr. V.; mit sein* **a)** fly out **(aus** of); **b)** *(geworfen werden)* be thrown out **(aus** of); fly out; **c)** *(ugs.: ~fallen)* fall out **(aus** of); **d)** *(ugs.: hinausgeworfen werden)* be chucked out *(coll.)*; *(als Arbeitnehmer)* get the sack *(coll.)*; be fired *(coll.)*; *(als Mieter)* be thrown out *(coll.)*; **2.** *unr. tr. V.* fly out **(aus** of); **~|führen 1.** *tr. V.* **a) jmdn. ~führen** show sb. out; **b)** *(retten)* **die Partei aus der Krise ~führen** lead the party out of the crisis; **den Betrieb aus den roten Zahlen ~führen** get the business out of the red; **c)** *(weiterführen)* **jmdn. über etw.** *(Akk.)* **~führen** take sb. beyond sth.; **2.** *itr. V.* **a)** *(verlaufen)* lead out **(aus** of); **b)** *(nach draußen gerichtet sein)* lead out; **c)** *(weiter verlaufen, überschreiten)* **über etw.** *(Akk.)* **~führen** go beyond sth.; **~|gehen** *unr. itr. V.; mit sein* **a)** go out; **aus dem Zimmer ~gehen** go *or* walk out of *or* leave the room; **b)** *(gerichtet sein)* **das Zimmer geht zum Garten/nach Westen ~:** the room looks out on to *or* faces the garden/faces west; **die Tür geht auf den Hof ~:** the door leads *or* opens into the yard; **die Schlafzimmer gehen nach hinten ~:** the bedrooms are at the back; **c)** *(verlaufen)* lead; **d)** *(überschreiten)* **über etw.** *(Akk.)* **~gehen** go beyond sth.; **e)** *(gesendet werden)* go out; be sent out; **f)** *(unpers.)* **wo geht es ~?** which is the way out?; **hier/da geht es ~:** this/that is the way out; **~|gelangen** *itr. V.; mit sein* **a)** *(nach draußen gelangen, auch fig.)* [manage to] get out **(aus** of); **b)**

(weiter gelangen) **über etw.** *(Akk.)* **~gelangen** progress *or* get beyond sth.; **~|greifen** *unr. itr. V.* **über etw.** *(Akk.)* **~greifen** go beyond sth.; **~|gucken** *itr. V. (ugs.) s.* **~blicken; ~|halten** *unr. tr. V.* hold ‹*lamp, flag, etc.*› out; **den Kopf/die Hand [zum Fenster] ~halten** put *or* stick one's head/hand out [of the window]; **¹~|hängen** *unr. itr. V.* hang out **(aus** of); **²~|hängen** *tr. V.* hang out **(aus** of); **~|heben** *unr. tr. V.* **a) jmdn./etw. ~heben** lift sb./sth. out **(aus** of); **etw. aus dem Bus ~heben** lift sth. down from the bus; **b)** *(geh.: erheben)* **jmdn. über die anderen ~heben** raise sb. above the others; **~|jagen 1.** *tr. V.* drive *or* chase out; **jmdn. ~jagen** *(fig.: aus dem Haus)* drive *or* turn sb. out; **2.** *itr. V.; mit sein* rush *or* race out **(aus** of); **~|katapultieren** *tr. V.* **a)** *(mit dem Schleudersitz)* eject; **b)** *(salopp: verdrängen)* **jmdn. ~katapultieren** push sb. out **(aus** of); **~|kommen** *unr. itr. V.; mit sein* **a)** come out **(aus** of); **ich bin schon seit zwei Tagen nicht mehr ~gekommen** I've not got *or* been out of the house for two days; **b)** *(ein Gebiet verlassen)* **er ist nie aus dem Dorf/aus Europa ~gekommen** he has never been out of *or* outside his village/Europe; **c)** *(ugs.: einen Ausweg finden)* get out **(aus** of); **d) über etw.** *(Akk.)* **~kommen** *(auch fig.)* get beyond sth.; **e)** *s.* **~laufen b; ~|komplimentieren** *tr. V.* **jmdn. ~komplimentieren** show sb. the door; *(verabschieden)* usher sb. out [with a great show of courtesy]; **~|lassen** *unr. tr. V.* **jmdn. ~lassen** let sb. out; **~|laufen** *unr. itr. V.; mit sein* **a)** run out **(aus** of); **zur Tür ~laufen** run out of the door; **b)** *(als Ergebnis haben)* **auf etw.** *(Akk.)* **~laufen** lead to sth.; **das läuft auf dasselbe ~:** it comes to the same thing; **~|lehnen** *refl. V.* lean out; **sich zum Fenster ~lehnen** lean out of the window; **~|manövrieren** *tr. V.* **sich/jmdn./etw. aus etw. ~manövrieren** manoeuvre oneself/sb./sth. out of sth.; **~|müssen** *unr. itr. V. (ugs.)* have to get out **(aus** of); **~|nehmen** *unr. tr. V.* **jmdn./etw. ~nehmen** take sb./sth. out **(aus** of); **nimm den Mülleimer mit ~:** put *or* take the dustbin out when you go; **~|posaunen** *tr. V. (ugs.)* broadcast; **~posaunen, daß ...:** broadcast the fact that ...; **~|ragen** *itr. V.* **a)** *(vertikal)* rise up **(über +** *Akk.* above); *(horizontal)* jut out; project; **b)** *(übertreffen)* **über seine Kollegen/die anderen Werke ~ragen** stand out from one's colleagues/the other works; **~|reden** *refl. V. (südd., österr., schweiz.)* talk one's way out **(aus** of); **~|reichen 1.** *tr. V.* **etw. ~reichen** hand *or* pass sth. out **(aus** of); **etw. zum** *od.* **aus dem Fenster ~reichen** hand *or* pass sth. out through the window; **2.** *itr. V.* **a)** *(bis nach draußen reichen)* reach *or* stretch **(bis zu** as far as); **b)** *(weiter reichen)* **über etw.** *(Akk.)* **~reichen** go beyond sth.; **~|rennen** *unr. itr. V.; mit sein* run out; **aus etw. ~rennen** run out of sth.; **~|rücken** *tr. V.* **a)** move out; **b)** *(verschieben)* put off; postpone; **~|schaffen** *tr. V.* **jmdn./etw. ~schaffen** get sb./sth. out **(aus** of); **~|schauen** *itr. V. (südd.) s.* **~blicken; ~|scheren** *refl. V.* **scher dich ~!** get out of here!; **~|scheuchen** *tr. V.* chase out; **~|schicken** *tr. V.* **a) jmdn. ~schicken** send sb. out; **b)** *(senden)* send out; **~|schieben 1.** *unr. tr. V.* **a)** *(nach draußen schieben)* **jmdn./etw. ~schieben** push sb./sth. out **(aus** of); **b)** *(aufschieben)* put off; postpone; **eine Entscheidung [um einen Tag] ~schieben** put off *or* postpone *or* defer a decision [by one day]; **2.** *unr. refl. V.* **a)** *(sich nach draußen schieben)* push one's/its way out **(aus** of); **b)** *(sich verschieben)* be put off *or* postponed; **~|schießen** *unr. itr. V.* **a) aus dem Auto/zum Fenster ~schießen** fire from the car/the window; **b)** *mit sein (sich schnell hinausbewegen)* shoot out **(aus** of); ‹*water*› rush out **(aus** of); **c)** *(weiter bewegen)* **über etw.** *(Akk.)* **~schießen** shoot past sth.; **über das Ziel ~schießen** *(fig.)* go too far; **~|schleichen** *unr. itr. V. mit sein; unr. refl. V.* creep *or* steal out **(aus** of); **~|schmeißen** *unr. tr. V. (ugs.) s.* **rausschmeißen; ~|schmuggeln** *tr. V.* smuggle out **(aus** of); **~|schreien 1.** *unr. itr. V.* shout out; **2.** *unr. tr. V. (geh.)* **seinen Haß/Zorn ~schreien** vent *or* give vent to one's hate/rage in a loud outburst; **~|schwimmen** *unr. itr. V.; mit sein* ‹*person*› swim out; ‹*object*› float out; **~|sehen** *unr. itr. V.* look out; **zum Fenster ~sehen** look out of the window; **~|sein** *unr. itr. V.; mit sein; nur im Inf. u. Part. zusammengeschrieben* **a) über etw.** *(Akk.)* **~sein** be past *or* beyond sth.; **b)** *(ugs.: fortsein)* have gone out; **~|setzen 1.** *tr. V.* **etw. ~setzen** put sth. out[side]; **2.** *refl. V.* go and sit outside; **~|stehlen** *unr. refl. V.* sneak *or* steal out **(aus** of); **~|steigen** *unr itr. V.; mit sein* climb out **(aus** of); **zum Fenster ~steigen** climb out of the window; **~|stellen 1.** *tr. V.* **a)** put out[side]; **b)** *(Sport)* **einen Spieler ~stellen** send a player off; **2.** *refl. V.* go and stand outside; **~stellung die** *(Sport)* sending-off; **~|strecken** *tr. V.* stick *or* put out **(aus** of); **den Arm/Kopf zum Fenster ~strecken** put *or* stick one's arm/head out of the window; **~|strömen** *itr. V.; mit sein* pour out **(aus** of); **~|stürzen 1.** *itr. V.; mit sein* **a)** *(hinausfallen)* fall **(aus** out of); **zum Fenster ~stürzen** fall out of the window; **b)** *(hinauseilen)* rush *or* dash out **(aus** of); **zur Tür ~stürzen** rush *or* dash out of the door; **2.** *refl. V.* throw oneself out **(aus** of); **~|tragen** *unr. tr. V.* **a)** *(nach draußen tragen)* **jmdn./etw. ~tragen** carry sb./sth. out; **b)** *(verbreiten)* **etw. in alle Welt ~tragen** spread sth. throughout the world; **c)** *(weiter tragen)* **über etw.** *(Akk.)* **~getragen werden** be carried across sth.; **aufs Meer ~getragen werden** be carried out to sea; **~|trauen** *refl. V.* venture out; dare to go out; **~|treiben 1.** *unr. tr. V.* drive out **(aus** of); **es treibt jmdn. in fremde Länder/die Welt ~:** sb. has an urge to travel to *or* see other countries/see the world; **2.** *unr. itr. V.; mit sein* drift out; **~|treten** *unr. itr. V.; mit sein* step out **(aus** of); **ins Leben ~treten** go out into the world; **~|trompeten** *tr. V. s.* **~posaunen; ~|wachsen** *unr. itr. V.; mit sein* **a)** *(größer werden)* **über etw.** *(Akk.)* **~wachsen** grow taller than *or* up above sth.; **b)** *(hinauskommen)* **über etw.** *(Akk.)* **~wachsen** outgrow sth.; **über jmdn./sich ~wachsen** surpass sb./rise above oneself; **~|wagen** *refl. V.* **a)** venture out **(aus** of); **sich in die Dunkelheit ~wagen** dare [to] go out into the dark; **b)** *(sich weiter wagen)* **sich über etw.** *(Akk.)* **~wagen** venture beyond *or* dare [to] go beyond sth.; **~|weisen 1.** *unr. tr. V.* **jmdn. ~weisen** order sb. out **(aus** of); **2.** *unr. itr. V.* **ein Symbol weist über sich ~** *(fig.)* a symbol implies something more than itself; **~|werfen** *unr. tr. V.* **a)** *(nach draußen werfen)* throw out **(aus** of); **etw. zur Tür ~werfen** throw sth. out of the door; **b)** *(nach draußen richten)* **einen Blick ~werfen** take *or* have a look *or* glance outside; **c)** *(ugs.: entfernen)* throw out; **d)** *(ugs.: ausschließen, die Wohnung kündigen)* **jmdn. ~werfen** throw sb. out **(aus** of); *(ugs.: entlassen)* sack sb. *(coll.)*; **~|wollen** *unr. itr. V. (ugs.)* want to get *or* go out **(aus** of); **[zu] hoch ~wollen** *(fig.)* aim [too] high; set one's sights [too] high; **worauf willst du ~?** *(fig.)* what are you getting *or* driving at?; **auf etwas Bestimmtes ~wollen** *(fig.)* have something particular in mind; **~wurf der** *(ugs.)* throwing out; *(eines Angestellten)* sacking *(coll.)*; **~|ziehen 1.** *unr. tr. V.* **a)** *(nach draußen ziehen)* **jmdn./etw. ~ziehen** pull *or* drag sb./sth. out **(aus** of); tow ‹*ship*› out; **b)** *(in die Ferne ziehen)* **das Fernweh zog ihn in die Welt ~:** his wanderlust drove him out into the world; **c)** *(hinziehen)* draw *or* drag out; prolong; protract; **d)** *(verzögern)* put off; delay; **e)** *(unpers.)* **es zog sie in die Natur ~:** she felt the urge to get out into the countryside; **2.** *unr. itr. V.; mit sein* **a)** *(umziehen)* move out; **b)** *(in die Ferne ziehen)* go out **(aus** of); ‹*group, troops*› move out **(aus** of); **c)** *(nach draußen dringen)* get out; **3.** *unr. refl. V.* **a)** *(sich erstrecken)* extend; **b)** *(sich hinziehen)* drag on; **c)** *(sich verzögern)* be delayed; **~|zögern 1.** *tr. V.* delay; put off; **2.** *refl. V.* be delayed; be put off

hin-, Hin-: ~|bauen *tr. V.* build; put up; **~|begeben** *unr. refl. V.* **sich irgendwo ~begeben** go *or* proceed somewhere; **sich zu jmdm. ~begeben** go to see sb.; **~|begleiten** *tr. V.* **jmdn. ~begleiten** accompany sb. [there]; **~|bekommen** *unr. tr. V. (ugs.)* **a)** *(fertigbringen)* **das hast du gut ~bekommen** you made a good job of that; **b)** *(in Ordnung bringen)* **etw. ~bekommen** straighten sth. out; get sth. straightened out; put sth. right; **~|bemühen 1.** *tr. V.* **jmdn. ~bemühen** trouble sb. to go; **2.** *refl. V.* take the trouble to go; **~|beordern** *tr. V.* **jmdn. ~beordern** order sb. [to go] there; **~|bestellen** *tr. V.* **jmdn. ~bestellen** tell sb. to be there; **~|biegen** *unr. tr. V. (ugs.)* **etw. ~biegen** sort sth. out; **wie hat er das bloß ~gebogen?** how did he manage *or (sl.)* wangle that?; **den werden wir schon ~biegen** we'll lick *or* knock him into shape *(coll.)*; **~|blättern** *tr. V. (ugs.)* fork *or* shell out *(sl.)*, pay out ‹*sum of money*›; **~blick der** *in* **im** *od.* **in ~blick auf etw.** *(Akk.)* *(wegen)* in view of; *(hinsichtlich)* with regard to; **~|blicken** *itr. V.* look; **zu jmdm. ~blicken** look [across] at sb.; **~|bringen** *unr. tr. V.* **a) jmdn./etw. ~bringen** take sb./sth. [there]; **b)** *(verbringen)* while away; *(müßig)* spend; **c)** *(ugs.: fertigbringen)* manage

Hinde ['hɪndə] **die**; **~, ~n** *(veralt.)* hind

hin|denken *unr. itr. V.* **wo denkst du hin?** *(ugs.)* whatever are you thinking of?; what an idea!

hinderlich *Adj.* **~ sein** get in the *or* sb.'s way; **ein ~er Verband/Mantel** a bandage a coat that gets in the way *or* is restricting; **jmds. Karriere** *(Dat.)***/für jmds. Karriere ~ sein** be an obstacle to sb.'s career; **jmdm.** *od.* **für jmdn. ~ sein** be a nuisance to sb.; **sich als ~ erweisen** prove to be a hindrance

hindern ['hɪndɐn] *tr. V.* **a)** *(abhalten)* **jmdn. ~:** stop *or* prevent sb.; **jmdn. [daran] ~, etw. zu tun** prevent *or* stop sb. [from] doing sth.; **jmdn. am Sprechen ~:** prevent *or* stop sb. [from] speaking; **ich werde dich nicht ~** *(iron.)* I'm not stopping you; **b)** *(behindern)* hinder, hamper ‹*person*›; impede, hamper, hinder ‹*growth, progress, etc.*›

Hindernis das; ~ses, ~se a) obstacle; **jmdm. ~se in den Weg legen** *(fig.)* put obstacles in sb.'s way; **b)** *(Leichtathletik, Geländeritt)* obstacle; *(Springreiten)* jump; obstacle; *(Pferderennen)* fence; **c)** *(Golf)* hazard

Hindernis-: ~lauf der, ~laufen das *(Leichtathletik)* steeplechase; **~rennen das** *(Pferdesport)* steeplechase

Hinderung die; ~, ~en hindrance

Hinderungs·grund der: das ist kein ~ für mich it does not prevent *or* stop me; **darin sehe ich keinen ~ für den Weiterbau** I do not see it as any reason why we should not continue with the construction

hin|deuten *itr. V.* **a) auf jmdn./etw.** *od.* **zu jmdm./etw. ~:** point to sb./sth.; **b)** *(aufmerksam machen)* **auf etw.** *(Akk.)* **~:** draw *or* call attention to sth.; point sth. out; **darauf ~, daß ...:** draw *or* call attention to the fact that ...; point out that ...; **c)** *(anzeigen)* suggest; point to; **alles deutet darauf hin, daß ...:** everything suggests that ...

Hindi ['hɪndi] **das; ~:** Hindi

Hindin die; ~, ~nen *(veralt.)* hind

hịn|drängen 1. *tr. V.* **jmdn. zu etw. ~:** force sb. towards sth. **2.** *itr. V.; mit sein* **zu jmdm. ~:** push one's way towards sb. **3.** *refl. V.* **sich zu jmdm./etw. ~:** push [one's way] towards sb./sth.

Hindu ['hındu] **der; ~[s], ~[s]** Hindu

Hinduịsmus der; ~: Hinduism *no art.*

hinduịstisch *Adj.* Hindu

hin·dụrch *Adv.* **a)** *(räumlich)* **durch den Wald ~:** through the wood; **mitten/quer durch etw. ~:** straight through sth.; **b)** *(zeitlich)* **das ganze Jahr ~:** throughout the year; **den ganzen Tag/die ganze Nacht ~:** all day/night [long]; throughout the day/night; all through the day/night; **die ganze Zeit ~:** all the time; **durch all die Schwierigkeiten ~** *(fig.)* through all the difficulties

hindụrch-: ~|finden *unr. itr., refl. V.* **[sich] durch etw. ~finden** find one's way through sth.; **~|gehen** *unr. itr. V.; mit sein* **a)** walk *or* go through; **durch etw. ~gehen** walk *or* go through sth.; *(fig.)* go through sth.; **unter der Brücke ~gehen** walk *or* go under the bridge; **b) durch etw. ~gehen** *(dringen)* go through sth.; *(verlaufen, auch fig.)* run through sth.; *(passen)* ⟨*person, vehicle*⟩ go *or* get through sth.; ⟨*object*⟩ go through sth.; **~|müssen** *unr. itr. V.* **durch etw. ~müssen** have to go through sth.; **~|sehen** *unr. itr. V.* **a) [durch etw.] ~sehen** see through [sth.]; **b)** *(sichtbar sein)* peep through; **~|ziehen 1.** *unr. tr. V.* **etw. [durch etw.] ~ziehen** pull *or* draw sth. through [sth.]; **2.** *unr. itr. V.; mit sein* move through; **3.** *unr. refl. V.* **sich durch etw. ~ziehen** run through sth.

hịn-: ~|dürfen *unr. itr. V. (ugs.)* be allowed to go (**zu** to); **dort dürft ihr nicht mehr ~:** you're not to go there any more; **~|eilen** *itr. V.; mit sein* **a)** hurry (**zu** to); **alle eilten ~:** everyone hurried there; **b)** *(sich schnell bewegen)* ⟨*train etc.*⟩ speed (**über +** *Akk.* across); ⟨*person*⟩ rush (**über +** *Akk.* across)

hinein [hı'nain] *Adv.* **a)** *(räumlich)* in; **~ mit euch!** in you go!; in with you!; **in etw.** *(Akk.)* **~:** into sth.; **nur ~!** go *or* walk right in!; **b)** *(zeitlich)* **bis in den Morgen/tief in die Nacht ~:** till morning/far into the night

hinẹin-: ~|begeben *unr. refl. V.* go in[side]; **sich in etw.** *(Akk.)* **~begeben** enter sth.; **~|bekommen** *unr. tr. V. (ugs.)* **etw. [in etw.** *(Akk.)***] ~bekommen** get sth. in[to sth.]; **~|bemühen 1.** *tr. V.* **jmdn. ~bemühen** trouble sb. to go in; **2.** *refl. V.* take the trouble to go in; **~|bitten** *unr. tr. V.* **jmdn. ~bitten** ask *or* invite sb. in; **~|blicken** *itr. V.* look in; **in etw.** *(Akk.)* **~blicken** look into sth.; **~|bohren 1.** *tr. V.* **Löcher in die Wand ~bohren** drill holes in the wall; **den Finger in den Kuchen ~bohren** stick *or* poke one's finger into the cake; **2.** *refl. V.* **sich in etw.** *(Akk.)* **~bohren** bore one's/its way into sth.; **~|bringen** *unr. tr. V.* **a)** take in; **bringen Sie mir die Unterlagen ~:** bring me in the documents; **Ordnung in etw. ~bringen** *(fig.)* bring [some] order into sth.; **etw. in die Diskussion ~bringen** *(fig.)* introduce sth. into the discussion; **Schwung in etw.** *(Akk.)* **~bringen** put [some] life into sth.; liven sth. up; **b)** *(ugs.) s.* **~bekommen; ~|denken** *unr. refl. V.* **sich in jmdn./in jmds. Lage ~denken** put oneself in sb.'s position; **sich in ein Problem ~denken** think one's way into a problem; **~|drängen 1.** *itr. V. mit sein; refl. V.* **[sich] in etw.** *(Akk.)* **~drängen** push one's way into sth.; **[sich] in den Bus ~drängen** push one's way on to the bus; **2.** *tr. V.* **jmdn. in etw.** *(Akk.)* **~drängen** push sb. into sth.; **jmdn. in eine Rolle ~drängen** *(fig.)* force sb. into a role; **~|dürfen** *unr. itr. V.* be allowed in; **in etw.** *(Akk.)* **~dürfen** be allowed into sth.; **~|fahren 1.** *unr. itr. V.; mit sein* **a)** *(mit dem Auto)* drive in; *(mit dem Zweirad)* ride in; **in etw.** *(Akk.)* **~fahren** drive/ride into sth.; **der Zug fuhr [in den Bahnhof] ~:** the train pulled in[to the station]; **b)** *(ugs.)* **in ein anderes Auto ~fahren** run into another car; **c) in seine Kleider ~fahren** slip into one's clothes; **2.** *unr. tr. V.* **a) den Wagen in etw.** *(Akk.)* **~fahren** drive one's car into sth.; **b) jmdn. in die Stadt ~fahren** drive sb. into town; **~|fallen** *unr. itr. V.; mit sein* fall in; **in etw.** *(Akk.)* **~fallen** fall into sth.; **sich in einen Sessel ~fallen lassen** drop into a chair; **~|finden** *unr. refl. V.* **sich in etw.** *(Akk.)* **~finden** *(sich vertraut machen)* get used to sth.; *(sich abfinden)* come to terms with sth.; **~|fliegen 1.** *unr. itr. V.; mit sein* **a)** fly in; **in etw.** *(Akk.)* **~fliegen** fly into sth.; **zum Fenster ~fliegen** fly in through the window; **b)** *(geworfen werden)* **in etw.** *(Akk.)* **~fliegen** be thrown into sth.; **2.** *unr. tr. V.* fly in; **etw. in etw.** *(Akk.)* **~fliegen** fly sth. into sth.; **~|fressen 1.** *unr. tr. V.* **etw. in sich ~fressen** ⟨*animal, (derb) person*⟩ gobble sth. down *or* up, wolf sth. down; **seine Sorgen/seinen Ärger in sich ~fressen** *(fig.)* bottle up one's worries/anger; **2.** *unr. refl. V.* **sich in etw.** *(Akk.)* **~fressen** eat into sth.; **~geboren** *Adj.* **in eine Zeit/Umwelt ~geboren** born into an age/environment; **~|geheimnissen** *tr. V.* **etw. in etw.** *(Akk.)* **~geheimnissen** read sth. into sth.; **~|gehen** *unr. itr. V.; mit sein* go in; **in etw.** *(Akk.)* **~gehen** go into sth.; **in den Eimer gehen 3 l ~:** the bucket holds three litres; **~|geraten** *unr. itr. V.; mit sein* **in eine Schlägerei ~geraten** get into a fight; **~|gießen** *unr. tr. V.* pour in; **etw. in etw.** *(Akk.)* **~gießen** pour sth. into sth.; **~|grätschen** *itr. V.; mit sein (bes. Fußball)* **[in jmdn.] ~grätschen** make a sliding tackle [on sb.]; **~|gucken** *itr. V. (ugs.)* look in; **in etw.** *(Akk.)* **~gucken** look in[to] sth.; take a look in sth.; **~|halten 1.** *unr. tr. V.* **etw. in etw.** *(Akk.)* **~halten** put sth. into sth.; **2.** *unr. itr. V. (schießen)* **in die Menge ~halten** fire into the crowd; **~|helfen** *unr. itr. V.* **jmdm. in den Mantel ~helfen** help sb. on with his/her coat; **jmdm. in den Bus ~helfen** help sb. on to the bus; **~|interpretieren** *tr. V.* **etw. in etw.** *(Akk.)* **~interpretieren** read sth. into sth.; **~|jagen** *tr. V.* drive *or* chase in; **jmdn./ein Tier in etw. ~jagen** drive *or* chase sb./an animal into sth.; **~|knien** *refl. V. (ugs.)* **sich in etw.** *(Akk.)* **~knien** get one's teeth into sth.; **~|kommen** *unr. itr. V.; mit sein* **a)** come in; **in etw.** *(Akk.)* **~kommen** come into sth.; **b)** *(gelangen, auch fig.)* get in; **in etw.** *(Akk.)* **~kommen** get into sth.; **c)** *(sich hineinfinden)* **[wieder] in eine Sprache/ein Fach ~kommen** get [back] into a language/subject; **d)** *(ugs.: hinzugefügt werden)* **in etw.** *(Akk.)* **~kommen** go into sth.; **~|kriechen** *unr. itr. V.; mit sein* crawl in; **in etw.** *(Akk.)* **~kriechen** crawl into sth.; *s. auch* **reinkriechen; ~|kriegen** *tr. V. (ugs.) s.* **~bekommen; ~|lachen** *itr. V.* **in sich ~lachen** laugh to oneself; **~|lassen** *unr. tr. V.* let *or* allow in; **jmdn. ins Zimmer ~lassen** let *or* allow sb. into the room; **~|laufen** *unr. itr. V.; mit sein* **a)** run in; *(zu Fuß gehen)* walk in; **in etw.** *(Akk.)* **~laufen** run/walk into sth.; **in sein Verderben ~laufen** *(fig.)* be heading [straight] for disaster; **in ein Fahrzeug ~laufen** run under a vehicle; **b)** *(fließen)* **in etw.** *(Akk.)* **~laufen** run into sth.; **~|legen** *tr. V.* **a) etw. [in etw.** *(Akk.)***] ~legen** put sth. in[to sth.]; **seine ganze Liebe/sein ganzes Gefühl in etw. ~legen** put all one's love/feeling into sth.; **b)** *s.* **~interpretieren; c)** *(ugs.) s.* **hereinlegen; ~|lesen 1.** *unr. refl. V. s.* **einlesen 1; 2.** *unr. tr. V. s.* **~interpretieren; ~|leuchten** *itr. V.* **a)** shine in; **in etw.** *(Akk.)* **~leuchten** shine into sth.; **b)** *(Licht hineinwerfen)* **mit einer Lampe in den Keller ~leuchten** shine a light into the cellar; **c)** *(fig.)* **in etw.** *(Akk.)* **~leuchten** throw light on sth.; **~|manövrieren** *tr. V.* **a) etw. in etw.** *(Akk.)* **~manövrieren** manoeuvre sth. into sth.; **b)** *(in etw. bringen)* **jmdn./sich in eine verzwickte Lage ~manövrieren** get *or* put sb./oneself into a tricky situation; **~|passen** *itr. V.* fit in; **in etw.** *(Akk.)* **~passen** fit into sth.; *(fig.)* fit in with sth.; **~|pfuschen** *itr. V.* **jmdm. in seine Arbeit ~pfuschen** meddle *or* interfere in sb.'s work; **~|platzen** *itr. V.; mit sein (ugs.)* burst in; **in etw.** *(Akk.)* **~platzen** burst into sth.; **~|pressen** *tr. V.* **a)** *(durch Pressen erzeugen)* **etw. in etw.** *(Akk.)* **~pressen** stamp sth. into sth.; **b)** *(in etw. pressen)* **etw. in etw.** *(Akk.)* **~pressen** press sth. into sth.; **etw. in ein Schema ~pressen** *(fig.)* force sth. into a pattern; **~|projizieren** *tr. V.* **etw. in etw.** *(Akk.)* **~projizieren** project sth. into sth.; **~|pumpen** *tr. V.* **a)** pump in; **etw. in etw.** *(Akk.)* **~pumpen** pump sth. into sth.; **b)** *(fig. ugs.)* **Geld in etw./Drogen in jmdn. ~pumpen** pump money into sth./drugs into sb.; **~|ragen** *itr. V.* **in den Himmel ~ragen** rise up into the sky; **~|reden** *itr. V.* **a) ins Leere ~reden** talk to an empty hall/lecture theatre *etc.*; **in die Stille ~reden** break the silence with a remark/exclamation *etc.*; **b)** *(abwertend: sich einmischen)* **jmdm. in seine Angelegenheiten/Entscheidungen** *usw.* **~reden** meddle *or* interfere in sb.'s affairs/decisions *etc.*; **~|regnen** *itr. V. (unpers.)* **es regnet [ins Zimmer] ~:** the rain is coming in[to the room]; **es regnet bei uns ~:** the rain is coming in through our roof; **~|reichen 1.** *tr. V.* **etw. [zum Fenster] ~reichen** hand *or* pass sth. in [through the window]; **2.** *itr. V.* **a)** *(lang genug sein)* **in etw.** *(Akk.)* **~reichen** reach into sth.; **b)** *(sich erstrecken)* **in etw.** *(Akk.)* **~reichen** extend into sth.; **~|reißen** *unr. tr. V.* **jmdn. in etw.** *(Akk.)* **~reißen** *(auch fig.)* drag sb. into sth.; **~|reiten 1.** *unr. itr. V.; mit sein* ride in; **in etw.** *(Akk.)* **~reiten** ride into sth.; **2.** *unr. tr. V. (ugs.) s.* **reinreiten; ~|rennen** *unr. itr. V.; mit sein (ugs.)* run in; race in; **in etw.** *(Akk.)* **~rennen** run *or* race into sth.; **in sein Verderben ~rennen** *(fig.)* be heading [straight] for disaster; **~|riechen** *unr. itr. V. (ugs.)* **in eine Arbeit/eine Firma ~riechen** get a taste of a job/a firm; **~|rufen 1.** *unr. tr. V.* **jmdn./etw. ~rufen** call sb./sth. in; **2.** *unr. itr. V.* **in etw.** *(Akk.)* **~rufen** call into sth.; **~|schaffen** *tr. V.* **jmdn./etw. [in etw.** *(Akk.)***] ~schaffen** get sb./sth. in[to sth.]; **~|schauen** *itr. V.* **a)** *(bes. südd., österr.) s.* **~sehen; b)** *(bes. südd., österr.: kurz besuchen)* **bei jmdm. ~schauen** look in on sb.; **~|schießen** *unr. itr. V.* **a) in etw.** *(Akk.)* **~schießen** fire into sth.; **in die Menge ~schießen** fire into the crowd; **b)** *mit sein (sich schnell hineinbewegen)* ⟨*person, car*⟩ shoot in; ⟨*water*⟩ rush in; **in etw.** *(Akk.)* **~schießen** shoot/rush into sth.; **~|schlagen** *unr. tr. V.* **einen Nagel/Pfahl [in etw.** *(Akk.)***] ~schlagen** knock *or* drive a nail/stake in[to sth.]; **ein Loch in etw.** *(Akk.)* **~schlagen** knock *or* cut a hole in sth.; **~|schleichen 1.** *unr. itr. V.; mit sein* **[in etw.** *(Akk.)***] ~schleichen** creep *or* steal in[to sth.]; **2.** *unr. refl. V.* **sich [in etw.** *(Akk.)***] ~schleichen** creep *or* steal in[to sth.]; *(fig.)* ⟨*error*⟩ creep in[to sth.]; **~|schlingen** *unr. tr. V.* **etw. in sich ~schlingen** devour sth.; **~|schlittern** *itr. V.; mit sein (ugs.)* **in eine Situation** *usw.* **~schlittern** stumble into a situation *etc.*; **~|schlüpfen** *itr. V.; mit sein* slip in; **ins Zimmer/in seinen Mantel ~schlüpfen** slip into the room/one's coat; **~|schmuggeln** *tr. V.* smuggle in; **jmdn./etw. [in etw.** *(Akk.)***] ~schmuggeln** smuggle sb./sth. in[to sth.]; **~|schneien** *itr. V.* **a)** *(unpers.)* **es schneit [in die Hütte] ~:** the snow is coming in[to the hut]; **b)** *mit sein s.* **hereinschneien a; ~|schreiben** *unr. tr. V.* write in; **etw. in etw.** *(Akk.)* **~schreiben** write sth. in sth.; **~|schütten** *tr. V.* pour in; **etw. in etw.** *(Akk.)* **~schütten** pour sth. into sth.; **etw. in sich ~schütten** *(fig.)* knock sth. back *(sl.)*; pour sth. down one's throat; **~|sehen**

unr. itr. V. look in; **in etw.** *(Akk.)* **~sehen** look into sth.; **in jmds. Zeitung ~sehen** have a look at sb.'s paper; **~|setzen 1.** *tr. V. (auch ugs.: zuweisen)* **jmdn./etw. [in etw.** *(Akk.)***] ~setzen** put sb./sth. in[to sth.]; **2.** *refl. V.* **a) sich in etw.** *(Akk.)* **~setzen** sit down in sth.; **b)** *(festsetzen)* **sich in die Ecken/die Teppiche ~setzen** ⟨*dust, dirt*⟩ get right into the corners/the carpet; **~|spazieren** *itr. V.; mit sein* walk *or* stroll in; **nur ~spaziert!** walk right [on] in!; **~|spielen 1.** *itr. V.* **da spielen viele Dinge/Faktoren ~:** there are a lot of contributory factors; **2.** *tr. V. (Sport)* **den Ball [in den Strafraum** *usw.***] ~spielen** play the ball in[to the penalty area *etc.*]; **~|sprechen** *unr. itr. V.* **in etw.** *(Akk.)* **~sprechen** speak into sth.; **~|stecken** *tr. V.* **a) etw. [in etw.** *(Akk.)***] ~stecken** put sth. in[to sth.]; **b)** *(ugs.: in etw. bringen)* **etw. [in etw.** *(Akk.)***] ~stecken** stick *(coll.) or* put sth. in sth.; **c) viel Geld in etw.** *(Akk.)* **~stecken** *(ugs.)* put *or* sink a lot of money into sth.; **viel Arbeit in etw.** *(Akk.)* **~stecken** *(ugs.)* put a lot of work into sth.; **~|steigern** *refl. V.* **sich in große Erregung/seine Ängste/seine Wut ~steigern** work oneself up into a state of great excitement/anxiety/into a rage; **~|stoßen 1.** *unr. tr. V.* **a)** thrust in; **etw. in etw.** *(Akk.)* **~stoßen** thrust sth. into sth.; **b)** *(hineinbringen)* **jmdn. in etw.** *(Akk.)* **~stoßen** push sb. into sth.; *(fig.)* plunge sb. into sth.; **2.** *unr. itr. V.; mit sein* **in etw.** *(Akk.)* **~stoßen** *(vordringen)* push *or* thrust into sth.; *(hineinsteuern)* drive *or* turn into sth.; **~|stürzen 1.** *itr. V.; mit sein* **a)** *(hineinfallen)* **in etw.** *(Akk.)* **~stürzen** fall *or* plunge into sth.; **b)** *(nach innen eilen)* rush *or* burst in; **ins Zimmer ~stürzen** rush *or* burst into the room; **2.** *tr. V.* **jmdn. in etw.** *(Akk.)* **~stürzen** hurl sb. into sth.; **3.** *refl. V.* **sich in etw.** *(Akk.)* **~stürzen** throw oneself *or* plunge into sth.; **sich in die Arbeit ~stürzen** *(fig.)* throw oneself into one's work; **~|tappen** *itr. V.; mit sein (ugs.)* **in etw.** *(Akk.)* **~tappen** grope one's way into sth.; *(hineingeraten)* walk [right] into sth.; **~|tragen** *unr. tr. V.* **a)** carry in; **etw. in etw.** *(Akk.)* **~tragen** carry sth. into sth.; **Schmutz ins Haus ~tragen** bring dirt into the house; **b)** *(verbreiten)* **etw. in etw.** *(Akk.)* **~tragen** bring sth. into sth.; **Unruhe in einen Betrieb ~tragen** spread unrest in a firm; **~|treiben** *unr. tr. V.* **a) jmdn./etw. in etw.** *(Akk.)* **~treiben** drive sb./sth. into sth.; ⟨*tide*⟩ carry sb./sth. into sth.; **b)** *(verwickeln)* **jmdn. in etw.** *(Akk.)* **~treiben** force sb. into sth.; **c)** *(in etw. schlagen)* **etw. [in etw.** *(Akk.)***] ~treiben** drive sth. in[to sth.]; **~|tun** *unr. tr. V.* **a)** *(ugs.: in etw. tun)* **etw. [in etw.** *(Akk.)***] ~tun** put sth. in[to sth.]; **b)** *(vollführen)* **einen Blick [in etw.** *(Akk.)***] ~tun** take a look in[to sth.]; **~|versetzen** *refl. V.* **sich in jmdn.** *od.* **jmds. Lage ~versetzen** put oneself in sb.'s position; **~|wachsen** *unr. itr. V.; mit sein* **a) in das Haus/das Fleisch ~wachsen** grow into the house/the *or* one's flesh; **b)** *(ugs.: hineinpassen)* **in ein Kleid** *usw.* **~wachsen** grow into a dress *etc.*; **in die Uniform ~wachsen** *(fig.)* come to identify with the *or* one's uniform; **c)** *(vertraut werden)* **in eine Aufgabe/Rolle ~wachsen** get to know a job/get into *or* inside a part; **~|wagen** *refl. V.* venture in; dare to go in; **sich in etw.** *(Akk.)* **~wagen** venture into sth.; dare to go into sth.; **~|werfen** *unr. tr. V.* **a) etw. [in etw.** *(Akk.)***] ~werfen** throw sth. in[to sth.]; **b)** *(fallen lassen)* **einen Blick [in etw.** *(Akk.)***] ~werfen** glance at sth.; **~|wollen** *unr. itr. V. (ugs.: ~gelangen wollen)* want to get *or* go in; **in etw.** *(Akk.)* **~wollen** want to go/get into sth.; **das will mir nicht in den Kopf ~:** I just *or* simply can't understand it; **~|ziehen 1.** *unr. tr. V.* **a)** *(nach drinnen ziehen)* pull *or* draw in; **etw./jmdn. in etw.** *(Akk.)* **~ziehen** pull *or* draw sth./sb. into sth.; **b)** *(verwickeln)* **jmdn. in eine Angelegenheit/einen Streit/Skandal ~ziehen** drag sb. into an affair/a dispute/scandal; **2.** *unr. itr. V.; mit sein* **a)** march in; **in etw.** *(Akk.)* **~ziehen** march into sth.; **b)** *(nach innen ziehen)* ⟨*smoke, fumes, etc.*⟩ drift in; **in etw.** *(Akk.)* **~ziehen** drift into sth.; **~|zwängen 1.** *tr. V.* **etw. [in etw.** *(Akk.)***] ~zwängen** squeeze *or* force sth. in[to sth.]; **2.** *refl. V.* squeeze in; **sich in die Hose ~zwängen** squeeze [oneself] into one's trousers; **~|zwingen** *unr. tr. V.* **jmdn. [in etw.** *(Akk.)***] ~zwingen** force sb. to go in[to sth.]; **jmdn. in ein Schema/eine Rolle ~zwingen** force sb. into rigid pattern/a role

hin-, Hin-: ~|fahren 1. *unr. itr. V.; mit sein* **a)** *(an einen Ort fahren)* go there; *(mit einem Auto)* drive *or* go there; *(mit einem Fahrrad, Motorrad)* ride *or* go there; **wo ist er ~gefahren?** where has he gone?; **b)** *(streichen)* **mit der Hand/den Fingern über etw.** *(Akk.)* **~fahren** run one's hand/fingers over sth.; **2.** *unr. tr. V.* **jmdn. ~fahren** drive *or* take sb. there; **jmdn. zum Bahnhof ~fahren** drive *or* take sb. to the station; **~fahrt die** journey there; *(Seereise)* voyage out; **auf der ~fahrt** on the way *or* journey there/the voyage out; **~|fallen** *unr. itr. V.; mit sein* **a)** *(stürzen)* fall down *or* over; **lang ~fallen** fall flat [on one's face/back]; **b)** *(herunterfallen)* **jmdm. fällt etw. ~:** sb. drops sth.; **etw. ~fallen lassen** drop sth.; **~fällig** *Adj.* **a)** *(schwächlich)* infirm; frail; **b)** *(ungültig)* invalid; **~fälligkeit die; ~ a)** *(Schwäche)* infirmity; frailty; **b)** *(Ungültigkeit)* invalidity; **~|finden** *unr. itr. V.* find one's way there; **zu jmdm./zu einem Ort ~finden** find one's way to sb./a place; **~|fläzen, ~|flegeln** *refl. V. (ugs. abwertend)* loll around *or* about; **~|fliegen 1.** *unr. itr. V.; mit sein* **a)** fly there; **er fliegt heute ~:** he's flying [out] there today; **wo fliegt sie ~?** where is she flying to?; **b)** *(ugs.: fallen)* come a cropper *(coll.)*; fall over; **mit dem Fahrrad ~fliegen** come a cropper on one's bicycle *(coll.)*; fall off one's bicycle; **2.** *unr. tr. V.* **jmdn./etw. ~fliegen** fly sb./sth. [out] there; **~flug der** outward flight

hin·fort *Adv. (geh.)* henceforth; henceforward

hin|führen 1. *tr. V.* **a) jmdn. ~:** lead *or* take sb. there; **b)** *(zu etw. bringen)* **jmdn. zu etw. ~:** lead sb. to sth. **2.** *itr. V.* **zu etw. ~:** lead to sth.; **wo soll das ~?** what will it lead to?

hing [hɪŋ] *1. u. 3. Pers. Sg. Prät. v.* **hängen**

Hin·gabe die; ~ a) devotion; *(Eifer)* dedication; **etw. mit ~ tun** do sth. with dedication; **mit ~ tanzen** put one's whole soul into one's dancing; **b)** *(geh.: das Opfern)* **unter ~ des Lebens** at the cost of one's life

hin-, Hin-: ~gang der *(geh.)* decease; demise; **~|geben 1.** *unr. tr. V. (geh.)* give; sacrifice; **sein Leben ~geben** lay down *or* sacrifice one's life; **2.** *unr. refl. V.* **a) sich einer Illusion/einem Genuß ~geben** entertain an illusion/abandon oneself to a pleasure; **b)** *(verhüll.)* **sich einem Mann ~geben** give oneself to a man; **~gebend** *Adj.* devoted

Hingebung die; ~: devotion

hingebungs·voll 1. *Adj.* devoted. **2.** *adv.* devotedly; with devotion; ⟨*listen*⟩ raptly, with rapt attention; ⟨*dance, play*⟩ with abandon

hin·gegen *Konj., Adv. (jedoch)* however; *(andererseits)* on the other hand

hin-: ~gegossen *Adj. (ugs. scherzh.)* **wie ~gegossen auf der Couch liegen/sitzen** have draped oneself over the couch; **~|gehen** *unr. itr. V.; mit sein* **a)** go [there]; **zu jmdm./etw. ~gehen** go to sb./sth.; **wo gehst du ~?** where are you going?; **b)** *(verstreichen)* ⟨*years, time*⟩ pass, go by; **darüber gingen Jahre ~:** it took years; **c)** *(hingleiten)* **sein Blick ging über die Landschaft ~:** he *or* his eyes scanned the landscape; **d)** *(tragbar sein)* pass; **diesmal mag das noch ~gehen** I'll/we'll *etc.* let it pass this time; **~|gehören** *itr. V. (ugs.)* go; belong; ⟨*person*⟩ belong; **wo gehört das ~?** where does this go *or* belong *or (coll.)* live?; **~|gelangen** *itr. V.; mit sein* get there; **zu jmdm./etw. ~gelangen** get to sb./sth.; **~|geraten** *unr. itr. V.; mit sein* get there; **wie sind wir dort ~geraten?** how did we get there?; **wo ist er/der Brief ~geraten?** where has he/the letter got to?; **~gerissen 1.** *2. Part. v.* **hinreißen; 2.** *Adj.; nicht attr.* carried away; spellbound; **~gerissen der Musik lauschen** listen spellbound to the music; **~|gleiten** *unr. itr. V.; mit sein* **a)** glide along; **die Hand über etw.** *(Akk.)* **~gleiten lassen** run one's hand over sth.; **den Blick über etw. ~gleiten lassen** *(fig.)* let one's gaze sweep over sth.; **b)** *(geh.: vergehen)* slip away; **~|halten** *unr. tr. V.* **a)** hold out; **jmdm. etw. ~halten** hold sth. out to sb.; **b)** *(warten lassen)* **jmdn. ~halten** put sb. off; keep sb. waiting; **c)** *(Milit.: aufhalten)* hold off

Hin·halte-: ~politik die policy of procrastination; **~taktik die** delaying tactics *pl.*

hin-: ~|hängen *tr. V. (ugs.)* hang up; **~|hauen 1.** *unr. tr. V.* **a)** *(salopp: aufgeben)* chuck in *(sl.)*; **den ganzen Kram ~hauen** chuck the whole thing in *(sl.)*; **b)** *(salopp abwertend: flüchtig anfertigen)* knock off *(coll.)*; dash off; **c)** *(unpers. salopp)* **es hat mich ~gehauen** I came a cropper *(coll.)*; **d)** *(salopp: hinwerfen)* chuck down *(coll.)*; **2.** *unr. itr. V.* **a)** *(ugs.: schlagen)* **[mit etw.] ~hauen** take a swipe [with sth.] *(coll.)*; **b)** *mit sein (hinfallen)* fall [down] heavily; **c)** *(salopp: gutgehen)* ⟨*plan*⟩ work [all right]; **es wird schon ~hauen** it'll work out *or* be all right *or (coll.)* OK; **d)** *(salopp: richtig sein)* ⟨*calculation*⟩ be right; **so haut das nicht ~:** it's wrong as it stands; **3.** *unr. refl. V. (salopp)* lie down and have a kip *(coll.)*; **~|hören** *itr. V.* listen

Hinke·bein ['hɪŋkə-] **das** *(ugs.)* **a)** stiff *or (sl.)* gammy leg; **b)** *(jmd., der hinkt)* person with a limp *or (sl.)* a gammy leg

Hinkel·stein der menhir; standing stone

hinken ['hɪŋkn̩] *itr. V.* **a)** limp; walk with a limp; **auf** *od.* **mit dem rechten Bein ~:** have a limp in one's right leg; **b)** *mit sein (hinkend gehen)* limp; hobble; **c)** *(fig.)* ⟨*line*⟩ be clumsy *or* halting; ⟨*rhyme*⟩ be clumsy; ⟨*comparison*⟩ be poor *or* feeble

hin-, Hin-: ~|knallen *(ugs.)* **1.** *tr. V.* slam down; **2.** *itr. V.; mit sein* fall [down] heavily; come a cropper *(coll.)*; **~|knien** *refl. V.* kneel [down]; **~|kommen** *unr. itr. V.; mit sein* **a)** get there; **nach Madrid ~kommen** get to Madrid; **wie kommt man zu ihm ~?** how do you get to his place?; **b)** *(an einen Ort gehören)* go; belong; **wo kommen die Gläser ~?** where do the glasses go *or* belong?; **wo ist meine Uhr ~gekommen?** where has my watch got to *or* gone?; **wo kommen** *od.* **kämen wir ~, wenn ...** *(fig.)* where would we be if ...; **c)** *(ugs.: auskommen)* **mit etw. ~kommen** manage with sth.; **d)** *(ugs.: in Ordnung kommen)* work out *or* turn out all right *or (coll.)* OK; **e)** *(ugs.: stimmen)* be right; **~|kriegen** *tr. V. (ugs.)* **a)** *(fertigbringen)* **das hat sie toll ~gekriegt** she made a great job of that *(coll.)*; **so genau wie auf der Vorlage kriege ich das nicht ~:** I won't be able to get it as accurate as it is on the pattern; **das wird er schon ~kriegen** he'll manage it all right *or (coll.)* OK; **b)** *(in Ordnung bringen)* fix ⟨*radio etc.*⟩; **jmdn. wieder ~kriegen** put sb. right; **~kunft die** *in* **in ~kunft** *(österr.)* in future; **~|langen** *itr. V.* **a)** *(ugs.: fassen)* **er langte ~ und steckte einige Uhren in seine Tasche** he reached over and stuck some watches in his pocket *(coll.)*; **b)** *(salopp: zuschlagen)* **[kräftig] ~langen** take a [hefty] swipe *(coll.)*; **c)** *(salopp: sich bedienen)* help oneself; **schön/**

ordentlich ~langen help oneself in a big way *(coll.)*; **d)** *(ugs.: ausreichen)* be enough; **e)** *(ugs.: auskommen)* manage; **~länglich 1.** *Adj.* sufficient; *(angemessen)* adequate; **2.** *adv.* sufficiently; *(angemessen)* adequately; **etw. ist ~länglich bekannt** sth. is sufficiently well known; **~|lassen** *unr. tr. V. (ugs.)* **jmdn. ~lassen** allow sb. to go there; let sb. go there; **jmdn. zu etw. ~lassen** allow sb. to go to sth.; let sb. go to sth.; **~|laufen** *unr. itr. V.; mit sein* **a)** *(an einen Ort laufen)* run there; **zu jmdm./zu einer Stelle ~laufen** run to sb./a place; **b)** *(zu Fuß gehen)* walk [there]; **c)** *(zu jmdm./etw. gehen)* **zum Anwalt/Arzt/Chef ~laufen** run to *or* rush off to the lawyer/doctor/boss; **~|legen 1.** *tr. V.* **a)** *(an eine Stelle legen)* put; **sie legte den Kindern frische Wäsche ~:** she put out clean underwear for the children; **b)** *(weglegen)* put down; **c)** *(zu Bett bringen)* **jmdn. ~legen** lay sb. down; **d)** *(ugs.: bezahlen)* pay *or (sl.)* shell out; **e)** *(salopp: ausführen)* **eine hervorragende Rede ~legen** do a brilliant speech; **eine gekonnte Übung auf dem Trampolin ~legen** turn in a splendid performance on the trampoline; **2.** *refl. V.* **a)** lie down; **da legst du dich [lang] ~** *(ugs.)* you won't believe your ears; **b)** *(sich schlafen legen)* lie down; **sich zeitig ~legen** have an early night; **sich zum Sterben ~legen** *(geh.)* lie down to die; **c)** *(ugs.: hinfallen)* come a cropper *(coll.)*; fall [down *or* over]; **~|leiten** *tr. V.* lead there; **etw. zu etw. ~leiten** lead sth. to sth.; **~|lenken** *tr. V.* **a) etw. [zu etw.] ~lenken** steer sth. [to sth.]; **seine Schritte zum Bahnhof ~lenken** direct one's steps towards the station; **b)** *(fig.)* steer ⟨*conversation*⟩ **(auf +** *Akk.* round to); direct ⟨*attention*⟩ **(auf +** *Akk.* towards); turn ⟨*gaze*⟩ **(auf +** *Akk.* towards); **~|machen** *(salopp)* **1.** *tr. V.* **a)** put up ⟨*curtain, picture, fence, etc.*⟩; put on ⟨*paint, oil, cream*⟩; put in ⟨*comma etc.*⟩; put ⟨*cross, ring, etc.*⟩; make ⟨*dirty mark etc.*⟩; **b)** *(töten)* do in *(sl.)*; rub out *(sl.)*; bump off *(sl.)*; **2.** *itr. V.* **a)** *(seine Notdurft verrichten)* do one's/its business *(coll.)*; **b)** *(landsch.: sich beeilen)* hurry up; get a move on *(coll.)*; **~|marschieren** *itr. V.; mit sein* march there; **~|metzeln, ~|morden** *tr. V. (geh.)* massacre; slaughter; butcher; **~nahme die; ~:** acceptance; **~|nehmen** *unr. tr. V.* **a)** *(annehmen)* accept; take; put up with, swallow, accept ⟨*insult*⟩; **etw. als gegeben ~nehmen** take sth. for granted; accept sth. as a fact; **b)** *(ugs.: mitnehmen)* **kannst du das Buch mit ~nehmen** can you take the book with you?; **~|neigen 1.** *tr. V.* incline; **den Kopf zu jmdm. ~neigen** incline *or* bend one's head towards sb.; **2.** *refl. V.* lean [over]; **3.** *itr. V.* **zu einer Auffassung** *usw.* **~neigen** incline to a point of view *etc.*

hinnen ['hɪnən] *in* **von ~** *(veralt. geh.)* [from] hence; **von ~ scheiden** *(verhüll.)* depart this life; pass away *or* on

hin-, Hin-: ~|passen *itr. V. (ugs.)* **a)** *(an eine Stelle passen)* fit *or* go in; **b)** *(in die Umgebung passen)* fit in; go; **~|pfeffern** *tr. V. (ugs.)* **a)** *(hinwerfen)* fling *or* slam down; **b)** *(äußern)* rap out; **~|pflanzen 1.** *tr. V.* plant; **2.** *refl. V. (ugs.)* **sich vor jmdn. ~pflanzen** plant oneself in front of sb.; **~|reichen 1.** *tr. V.* hand; pass; **jmdm. etw. ~reichen** hand *or* pass sth. to sb.; **2.** *itr. V.* **a)** *(erstrecken)* reach; **bis zu etw. ~reichen** reach to *or* as far as sth.; **b)** *(ausreichen)* be enough *or* sufficient; **c)** *(ugs.: auskommen)* manage; **mit etw. ~reichen** manage on sth.; **~reichend 1.** *Adj.* sufficient; *(angemessen)* adequate; **2.** *adv.* sufficiently; *(angemessen)* adequately; **~reise die** journey there; outward journey; *(mit dem Schiff)* voyage out; outward voyage; **die ~reise nach Rom** the journey to Rome; **[die] Hin- und Rückreise** the journey there and back; **~|reisen** *itr. V.; mit sein* travel there; **~|reißen** *unr. tr. V.* **a) jmdn. zu sich ~reißen** pull sb. to one; **b)** *(begeistern)* enrapture; **das Publikum zu Beifallsstürmen ~reißen** elicit thunderous *or* rapturous applause from the audience; **c)** *(verleiten)* **jmdn. zu etw. ~reißen** drive sb. to sth.; **sich ~reißen lassen** let oneself get *or* be carried away; **~reißend 1.** *Adj.* enchanting ⟨*person, picture, view*⟩; captivating ⟨*speaker, play*⟩; **2.** *adv.* enchantingly; **~|richten** *tr. V.* execute; **~richtung die** execution

Hinrichtungs-: ~kommando das firing-squad; **~stätte die** place of execution

hin-, Hin-: ~|rücken 1. *tr. V.* **etw. ~rücken** move *or* push sth. over; **2.** *itr. V.; mit sein* move over; **~|sagen** *tr. V.* say without thinking; *(nur beiläufig sagen)* say casually; **das hat er nur so ~gesagt** he just said it without thinking; **~|schaffen** *unr. tr. V.* **etw. ~schaffen** get sth. there; **etw. zum Bahnhof ~schaffen** get sth. to the station; **~|schauen** *itr. V. (bes. südd., österr.) s.* **~sehen; ~|scheiden** *unr. itr. V.; mit sein (geh. verhüll.)* pass away *or* over; **der Hingeschiedene** the deceased *or* departed; **~|scheiden das; ~s** *(geh. verhüll.)* decease; demise; **~|scheißen** *unr. itr. V. (derb)* crap *(vulg.)*; **~|schicken** *tr. V.* send; **~|schieben** *unr. tr. V.* **jmdm. etw. ~schieben** push sth. over to sb.; **~schied der; ~[e]s, ~e** *(schweiz.) s.* **~scheiden; ~|schielen** *itr. V.* steal a glance/glances **(zu** at); **~|schlachten** *tr. V. (geh.)* massacre; slaughter; butcher; **~|schlagen** *unr. itr. V.* **a)** *(auf eine Stelle schlagen)* strike; hit; **b)** *mit sein (ugs.: fallen)* **[der Länge nach** *od.* **lang] ~schlagen** fall flat on one's face/back; **da schlag einer lang ~!** *(ugs.)* well I never *(coll.)*; would you believe it! *(coll.)*; **~|schleichen** *unr. itr. V. mit sein; unr. refl. V.* creep *or* steal over; **~|schleppen 1.** *refl. V.* **a)** *(mühsam gehen)* drag oneself along; **sich zu etw. ~schleppen** drag oneself to sth.; **b)** *(sich hinziehen)* drag on; **2.** *tr. V.* **a)** *(an einen Ort schleppen)* **etw. ~schleppen** drag sth. there; **etw. zu etw. ~schleppen** drag sth. to sth.; **b)** *(verzögern)* drag out; **~|schmeißen** *unr. tr. V. (salopp)* **a)** *(werfen)* chuck down *(coll.)*; **b)** *(aufgeben)* chuck in *(coll.)*; **~|schmelzen** *unr. itr. V.; mit sein* **a)** *s.* **zerschmelzen; b)** *(ugs. scherzh.: vergehen)* swoon; **vor Rührung ~schmelzen** be overcome with emotion; **~|schmieren** *tr. V. (ugs.) (~schreiben)* scrawl; scribble; *(~malen)* daub; **~|schreiben 1.** *unr. tr. V.* write down; **2.** *unr. itr. V. (an eine Firma o. ä. schreiben)* write; **~|schwinden** *unr. V. s.* **dahinschwinden; ~|sehen** *unr. itr. V.* look; **ich kann nicht ~sehen** I can't [bear to] look; **bei genauerem Hinsehen** on closer inspection; **~|sein** *unr. itr. V.; mit sein (nur im Inf. u. Part. zusammengeschrieben) (ugs.)* **a)** *(verloren sein)* be *or* have gone; **was ~ ist, ist ~:** what's done is done; **b)** *(nicht mehr brauchbar sein)* have had it *(coll.)*; ⟨*car*⟩ be a write-off; **c)** *(salopp: tot sein)* have snuffed it *(sl.)*; have pegged out *(sl.)*; **wenn er richtig zuschlägt, bist du ~:** if he really hits you you've had it *(coll.)*; **d)** *(ugs.: hingerissen sein)* **von jmdm./etw. ganz ~sein** be mad about sb./bowled over by sth.; **e)** *(zugrunde gerichtet sein)* be ruined *or* in ruins; **f)** *(~gegangen/~gefahren sein)* have gone; **g)** *(in Verbindung mit bis)* **bis zu dem Termin ist es noch einige Zeit ~:** there's some time to go before the deadline; **~|setzen 1.** *tr. V.* **a)** *(an eine Stelle setzen)* put; seat, put ⟨*person*⟩; **das Kind ~setzen** sit the child/baby down; **b)** *(absetzen)* put *or* set down; **2.** *refl. V.* **a)** sit down; **setzen Sie sich doch ~!** do sit down!; **wo soll ich mich ~setzen?** where should I sit?; **sich gerade ~setzen** sit up straight; **sich ~setzen und etw. tun** *(fig.)* sit down and do sth.; get down to doing sth.; **b)** *(ugs.: fallen)* land on one's backside; **c)** *(salopp: überrascht sein)* **er wird sich ~setzen** he won't believe his ears; **~sicht die;** *o. Pl.* **in gewisser ~sicht** in a way/in some respect *or* ways; **in mancher ~sicht** in some respects *or* ways; **in jeder ~sicht** in every respect; **in finanzieller ~sicht** financially; **in ~sicht auf** (+ *Akk.*) with regard to; **~sichtlich** *Präp. mit Gen. (Amtsspr.)* with regard to; *(in Anbetracht)* in view of; **~|sinken** *unr. itr. V.; mit sein (geh.)* sink down; sink to the ground; **~|sollen** *unr. itr. V. (ugs.)* **wo sollen die Sachen ~?** where do these things go?; where do you want these things [to go]?; **wo soll ich mit den Büchern ~?** where should I put the books?; what should I do with the books?; **sie weiß nicht, wo sie ~soll** she doesn't know where to go; **~spiel das** *(Sport)* first leg; **~|starren** *itr. V.* stare **(zu, nach** at); **~|stellen 1.** *tr. V.* **a)** *(an eine Stelle stellen)* put; put up ⟨*building*⟩; put, park ⟨*car*⟩; **b)** *(absetzen)* put down; **c)** *(bezeichnen)* **etw. als falsch ~stellen** make sth. out to be *or* represent sth. as false; **jmdn. als Lügner ~stellen** make sb. out to be *or* represent sb. as a liar; **jmdn. als Vorbild ~stellen** hold sb. up as an example; **er hat die Sache so ~gestellt, als seien wir die Schuldigen** he made it look as though it was our fault; **2.** *refl. V.* **a)** *(sich an eine Stelle stellen)* stand; ⟨*driver*⟩ park; **sich gerade ~stellen** stand up straight; **sich vor jmdn. ~stellen** stand in front of sb.; **b)** *(sich bezeichnen)* **sich als unschuldig ~stellen** make out that one is innocent; **~|steuern 1.** *tr. V.* steer; **das Boot zum Ufer ~steuern** steer the boat towards the bank; **2.** *itr. V.; mit sein* **a) zu etw. ~steuern** make *or* head for sth.; **b)** *(eine Absicht verfolgen)* **auf etw.** *(Akk.)* **~steuern** aim at sth.; **~|strecken 1.** *tr. V.* **a)** stretch out; hold out; **jmdm. die Hand ~strecken** hold out one's hand to sb.; **b)** *(geh. veralt.: töten)* fell; slay *(liter.)*; **2.** *refl. V.* **a)** *(sich ausgestreckt hinlegen)* stretch [oneself] out; lie down full length; **b)** *(sich erstrecken)* extend, stretch **(bis an +** *Akk.* as far as); **~|strömen** *itr. V.; mit sein* **a)** ⟨*river*⟩ flow; **b)** ⟨*people*⟩ flock there; **zu etw. ~strömen** flock to sth.; **~|stürzen** *itr. V.; mit sein* **a)** *(hinfallen)* fall down [heavily]; **b)** *(hineilen)* rush *or* dash there; **zum Ausgang ~stürzen** rush *or* dash towards the exit

hintan-, Hintan- [hɪnt'|an-]: **~|setzen** *tr. V.* **etw. ~setzen** put sth. last; **Differenzen ~setzen** put *or* set aside differences; **~setzung die; ~: nur unter ~setzung persönlicher Interessen** only by putting personal interests last; **~|stellen** *tr. V. s.* **~setzen**

hinten ['hɪntn̩] *Adv.* **a)** *(am rückwärtigen Ende)* at the back; in *or* at the rear; **~ im Bus sitzen** sit in the back of the bus; **~ in die Straßenbahn einsteigen** get on at the back of the tram *(Brit.) or (Amer.)* streetcar; **ganz ~ im Garten/in der Garage/im Schrank** right at the back of the garden/the garage/the cupboard; **sich ~ anstellen** join the back of the queue *(Brit.) or (Amer.)* line; **nach ~ abgehen** move [off] towards the back; exit upstage *(Theatre)*; **~ im Buch** at the back *or* end of the book; **weiter ~:** further back; *(in einem Buch)* further on; **von ~ anfangen** start from the end; **von ~ nach vorne** backwards; *(in einem Buch)* from back to front; *(Bewegung)* towards the front; **nach ~ gehen** go *or* walk to the back/into the room behind; **b)** *(an/auf/von der Rückseite)* **die Adresse steht ~ auf dem Brief** the address is on the back of the envelope; **~ auf der Münze** on the back *or* reverse of the coin; **~ am Haus** at the back *or* rear of the house; **nach ~ hinaus liegen/gehen** be at the back *or* rear; **von ~ kommen/jmdn. von ~ erstechen** come from behind/stab sb. from behind; **von ~ sah sie jünger aus** she looked younger from the back; **jmdn. von ~ erken-**

nen recognize sb. from the back; jmdm. ~ drauffahren *(ugs.)* run into the back of sb.; ~ und vorn[e] nichts haben *(salopp)* be as flat as an ironing-board *(coll.)*; c) *(entfernt)* die anderen sind ganz weit ~: the others are a long way back *or* behind; ~ in Sibirien far away in Siberia; ~ im Wald in the depths of the forest; deep in the forest; ganz weit ~ konnte man die Bergspitzen erkennen far away in the distance you could make out the mountain peaks; d) *(in Wendungen)* jetzt heißt es Herr Meier ~, Herr Meier vorn now it's Herr Meier this, and Herr Meier that; ~ und vorn[e] bedient werden be waited on hand and foot; das kann ~ und vorn[e] nicht stimmen that cannot possibly be true; there is no way that can be true; ~ und vorn[e] betrogen werden be cheated right, left and centre; nicht [mehr] wissen, wo ~ und vorn[e] ist *(ugs.)* not know whether one is coming or going; ~ nicht mehr hochkönnen *(ugs.)* be in desperate straits; jmdn. am liebsten von ~ sehen *(ugs.)* be glad to see the back of sb.; von ~ durch die Brust ins Auge *(salopp scherzh.)* in a roundabout fashion *or* way

hinten-: ~**dran** *Adv. (ugs.)* at the back; ~dran einen Anhänger hängen hitch a trailer on behind; ~**drauf** *Adv. (ugs.)* on the back; jmdm. eins *od.* ein paar ~drauf geben *(ugs.)* smack sb.'s bottom; ~**drein** *Adv. s.* hinterher; ~**heraus** ['----] *Adv.* ~heraus liegen/wohnen be/live at the back; ~**herum** ['----] *Adv. (ugs.)* a) *(um die hintere Seite herum)* round the back; b) *(am Rücken)* mir ist ~herum kalt my back's cold; c) *(ugs.: heimlich)* etw. ~herum erfahren hear sth. indirectly; Waren ~herum besorgen get goods under the counter; ~**nach** *Adv. (südd., österr.) s.* hinterher

hinten·über *Adv.* backwards

hintenüber-: ~**|fallen** *unr. itr. V.; mit sein* fall [over] backwards; ~**|kippen** *itr. V.; mit sein* tip [over] backwards; ~**|stürzen** *itr. V.; mit sein s.* ~fallen

hinter ['hɪntɐ] 1. *Präp. mit Dat.* a) behind; ~ dem Haus sein be behind *or* at the back of the house; ~ jmdm. zurückbleiben lag behind sb.; eine große Strecke ~ sich haben have put a good distance behind one; ~ der Mauer hervortreten step out from behind the wall; ~ jmdm. stehen *(fig.)* be behind sb.; back *or* support sb.; ~ etw. *(Dat.)* stehen *(fig.)* support sth.; jmdn. ~ sich haben *(fig.)* have sb.'s backing; sich ~ etw. verbergen *(fig.)* ⟨*person*⟩ hide behind sth.; ⟨*danger*⟩ lie concealed behind sth.; ⟨*purpose*⟩ lie behind sth.; b) *(nach)* after; 3 km ~ der Grenze 3 km beyond the frontier; die nächste Station ~ Mannheim the next stop after Mannheim; c) *(in der Rangfolge)* ~ jmdm. zurückstehen lag behind sb.; ~ der Entwicklung/der Zeit zurückbleiben lag behind in development/be behind in times; er ist ~ unseren Erwartungen zurückgeblieben he has fallen short of our expectations; d) *(bewältigt)* eine Prüfung/Aufgabe ~ sich haben *(fig.)* have got an examination/a job over [and done] with; viele Enttäuschungen/eine Krankheit ~ sich haben have experienced many disappointments/have got over an illness; wenn er das Studium ~ sich hat when he's finished his studies. 2. *Präp. mit Akk.* a) behind; ~ das Haus gehen go behind the house; sich ~ jmdn./etw. stellen *(fig.)* stand *or* get behind sb./support sth.; b) ~ jmdn. zurückfallen fall behind sb.; c) etw. ~ sich bringen get sth. over [and done] with; d) *(zeitlich)* ~ etw. gehen/reichen go back to before sth.; e) *(fig.)* ~ ein Geheimnis/die Wahrheit/seine Geschichte kommen find out a secret/get to the truth/get to the bottom of his story

hinter... *Adj.; nicht präd.* back; das ~e Ende des Ganges/des Zimmers the far end of the corridor/the far end *or* the back of the room; das ~e Ende des Zuges the back *or* rear [end] of the train; die ~ste Reihe the back row; die Hinter[st]en those [right] at the back

Hinter-: ~**achse** die rear *or* back axle; ~**an·sicht** die rear *or* back view; ~**ausgang** der rear *or* back exit; ~**backe** die *(ugs.)* buttock; auf seine ~backen fallen fall over on one's backside; ~**bänkler** [~bɛŋklɐ] der; ~s, ~ *(ugs.)* inconspicuous back-bencher; ~**bein** das hind leg; sich auf die ~beine stellen *(ugs.)* put up a fight; sich auf die ~beine setzen *(ugs.)* get *or* knuckle down and do some work

Hinterbliebene [-'bli:bənə] der/die; *adj. Dekl.* a) *(Familienangehörige)* die ~n the bereaved [family]; b) *(jur.)* surviving dependant

Hinterbliebenen·rente die [surviving] dependant's pension

hinter-, Hinter-: [1]~**bringen** [--'--] *unr. tr. V.* jmdm. etw. ~bringen inform sb. [confidentially] of sth.; [2]~**|bringen** *unr. tr. V. (landsch.)* bring to the back; ~**deck** das *(Seew.)* after-deck

hinter·einander *Adv.* a) *(räumlich)* one behind the other; sie liefen dicht ~: they were running close behind one another; b) *(zeitlich)* one after another *or* the other; an drei Tagen ~: for three days running *or* in succession

hintereinander-: ~**|fahren** *unr. itr. V.; mit sein (mit dem Auto/Fahrrad)* drive/ride one behind the other; ~**|gehen** *unr. itr. V.; mit sein* walk in single file; walk one behind the other; ~**|schalten** *tr. V. (Elektrot.)* Widerstände *usw.* ~schalten connect resistances *etc.* in series; ~**weg** *Adv. (ugs.)* one after the other

hinter-, Hinter-: ~**ein·gang** der rear *or* back entrance; ~**fotzig** [~fɔtsɪç] *Adj. (bayr.; sonst derb)* underhand[ed]; ~**fragen** [--'--] *tr. V.* examine; analyse; ~**fuß** der hind foot; ~**gebäude** das *s.* ~haus; ~**gedanke** der ulterior motive; einen ~gedanken bei etw. haben have an ulterior motive for sth.; [1]~**gehen** [--'--] *unr. tr. V.* deceive; sie hat ihren Mann mit seinem besten Freund ~gangen she deceived her husband by having an affair with his best friend; [2]~**|gehen** *unr. itr. V.; mit sein (landsch.)* go to the back; ins Lager ~gehen go to the back of the store room

Hinterglas·malerei die *(Kunst)* a) *o. Pl. (Herstellung)* verre églomisé; b) *(Bild)* verre églomisé picture

Hinter·grund der background; *(der Bühne)* back; *(Theater: Kulisse)* backcloth; backdrop; der akustische/musikalische ~: the background sounds/music; im ~ der Bühne at the back of the stage; die Hintergründe dieser Verhaltensweise *(fig.)* the background *sing.* to this behaviour; jmdn./etw. in den ~ drängen push sb./sth. into the background; in den ~ treten/geraten recede *or* fade into the background; sich im ~ halten keep in the background; etw. im ~ haben have sth. up one's sleeve

hinter·gründig 1. *Adj.* enigmatic; cryptic. 2. *adv.* enigmatically; cryptically

Hintergründigkeit die; ~, ~en a) *o. Pl. (Eigenschaft)* enigmaticness; crypticness; b) *(Äußerung)* enigmatic *or* cryptic remark

Hintergrund-: ~**information** die item *or* piece of background information; ~informationen [items *or* pieces of] background information *sing.*; ~**musik** die background music

hinter-, Hinter-: ~**halt** der ambush; in einen ~halt geraten be ambushed; jmdn. aus dem ~halt überfallen ambush sb.; im ~halt lauern lie in ambush; jmdn. aus dem ~halt angreifen *(fig.)* attack sb. without warning; make a surprise attack on sb.; etw. im ~halt haben have sth. up one's sleeve *or* in reserve; ~**hältig** 1. *Adj.* underhand; 2. *adv.* in an underhand fashion *or* manner; ~**hältigkeit** die; ~, ~en a) *o. Pl. (Eigenschaft)* underhandedness; b) *(Handlung)* underhand act; ~**hand** die a) *(bei Tieren)* hindquarters *pl.*; b) etw. in der ~hand haben have sth. up one's sleeve *or* in reserve; in der ~hand sein *od.* sitzen *(Kartenspiel)* play last; ~**haus** das *dwelling situated at or forming the rear of a house [and accessible only from a courtyard]*

hinter·her *Adv.* a) *(räumlich)* behind; nichts wie ihm ~! quick, after him!; *s. auch* nichts; b) *(nachher)* afterwards; es ~ besser wissen be wise after the event

hinterher-: ~**|blicken** *itr. V.* jmdm. ~blicken follow sb. with one's eyes; gaze after sb.; ~**|fahren** *unr. itr. V.; mit sein (mit dem Auto/Fahrrad)* drive/ride [along] behind (jmdm. sb.); *(folgen)* follow (jmdm. sb.); ~**|gehen** *unr. itr. V.; mit sein* walk [along] behind (jmdm. sb.); *(folgen)* follow (jmdm. sb.); ~**|hinken** *itr. V.; mit sein* a) limp *or* hobble [along] behind (jmdm. sb.); b) *(fig.)* einer Sache *(Dat.)* ~hinken lag behind sth.; mit etw. ~hinken be behind with sth.; ~**|kommen** *unr. itr. V.; mit sein* a) *(dahinter ankommen)* follow behind; b) *(danach kommen)* follow; come after; ~**|laufen** *unr. itr. V.; mit sein* a) run [along] behind (jmdm. sb.); b) *s.* ~gehen; c) *(ugs.: für sich zu gewinnen suchen)* jmdm./etw. ~laufen run after sb./sth.; ~**|schicken** *tr. V.* jmdm. jmdn./etw. ~schicken send sb. after sb./send sth. on to sb.; ~**sein** *unr. itr. V.; mit sein (nur im Inf. u. Part. zusammengeschrieben) (ugs.)* a) *(zurückgeblieben sein)* be behind (mit with); b) *(verfolgen)* jmdm. ~sein be after sb.; ~**|spionieren** *itr. V.* jmdm. ~spionieren spy on sb.

hinter-, Hinter-: ~**hof** der courtyard; ~**kopf** der back of the/one's head; etw. im ~kopf haben/behalten *(ugs.)* have/keep sth. at the back of one's mind; ~**lader** der *(Waffenkunde)* breech-loader; ~**land** das hinterland; *(Milit.)* back area; ~**lassen** [--'--] *unr. tr. V.* a) leave; *(testamentarisch)* leave; bequeath; die ~lassenen Schriften the posthumous works; b) *(zurücklassen)* leave ⟨*message, telephone number, etc.*⟩; ein Zimmer in Unordnung ~lassen leave a room in a muddle; c) *(verursachen)* leave ⟨*fingerprints, impression, etc.*⟩; keine Spuren ~lassen leave no trace[s] [behind]; ~**lassene** [--'---] der/die; *adj. Dekl. (schweiz.) s.* ~bliebene; ~**lassenschaft** [--'---] die; ~, ~en estate; jmds. ~lassenschaft antreten inherit sb.'s estate; *(ugs. scherzh.)* take over from sb.; jmds. literarische ~lassenschaft the writings that sb. has left to posterity; ~**lastig** *Adj.* tail-heavy ⟨*aircraft*⟩; stern-heavy ⟨*ship*⟩; ~**lauf** der *(Jägerspr.)* hind leg; ~**legen** [--'--] *tr. V.* deposit (bei with); *(als Pfand)* deposit, leave (bei with)

Hinterlegung die; ~, ~en *s.* hinterlegen: depositing; leaving; jmdn. gegen ~ einer Kaution freilassen release sb. on bail

Hinterlegungs·schein der deposit receipt

hinter-, Hinter-: ~**list** die guile; deceit; *(Verrat)* treachery; eine ~list an underhand trick; a piece of deceit; ~**listig** *Adj.* deceitful; *(verräterisch)* treacherous

hinterm ['hɪntɐm] *(ugs.) Präp. + Art.* = hinter dem

Hinter-: ~**mann** der; *Pl.* ~männer a) person behind; sein ~mann the person behind [him]; b) *(Gewährsmann)* [secret] informant; c) *(jmd., der aus dem Hintergrund lenkt)* der ~mann/die ~männer the brains behind the operation; ~**mannschaft** die *(Sport)* defence

hintern *(ugs.) Präp. + Art.* = hinter den

Hintern ['hɪntɐn] der; ~s, ~ *(ugs.)* behind;

backside; bottom; **jmdm. den ~ verhauen** *od.* **versohlen** tan sb.'s hide; **jmdn.** *od.* **jmdm. in den ~ treten** kick sb. in the pants *(coll.) or* up the backside; *(fig.)* kick sb. in the teeth *(fig.)*; **sich [vor Wut** *od.* **Ärger] in den ~ beißen** *(salopp)* kick oneself; **jmdm. in den ~ kriechen** *(derb)* lick sb.'s arse *(coarse)*; suck up to sb. *(sl.)*; **sich auf den ~ setzen** *(salopp) (sich anstrengen)* get *or* knuckle down to it; *(aufs Gesäß fallen)* fall on one's behind; *(überrascht sein)* be flabbergasted; **Hummeln** *od.* **Pfeffer im ~ haben** *(salopp)* have ants in one's pants *(sl.)*; *s. auch* **abwischen b**

Hinter-: ~pfote die hind paw; **~rad das** back *or* rear wheel; **~rad·antrieb der** rear-wheel drive; **~reifen der** back *or* rear tyre

hinter·rücks ['hɪntɐrʏks] *Adv.* **a)** *(von hinten)* from behind; **b)** *(veralt.: hinter jmds. Rücken)* behind sb.'s back

hinters ['hɪntɐs] *(ugs.) Präp. + Art.* = **hinter das**

hinter-, Hinter-: ~schiff das stern; **~seite die** *s.* **Rückseite**; **~sinn der** deeper meaning; **~sinnig** *Adj.* ‹*remark, story, etc.*› with a deeper meaning; subtle ‹*sense of humour*›

hinterst... ['hɪntɐst...] *s.* **hinter...**

hinter-, Hinter-: ~steven der a) *(Seemannsspr.)* stern-post; **b)** *(ugs. scherzh.: Gesäß)* backside; behind; **~teil das** *(ugs.: Gesäß)* backside; behind; *(eines Tieres)* rump; **~treffen das** *(ugs.) in* **ins ~treffen geraten** *od.* **kommen** fall behind; **jmdn./etw. ins ~treffen bringen** put sb./sth. behind; **~treiben** [--'--] *unr. tr. V.* foil, thwart, frustrate ‹*plan*›; prevent ‹*marriage, promotion*›; block ‹*law, investigation, reform*›; **~treibung die**; **~, ~en** *s.* **~treiben:** foiling; thwarting; frustration; prevention; blocking; **~treppe die** back stairs *pl.*; **~treppen·roman der** *(abwertend)* trashy novel; **~tupfingen** [~'tʊpfɪŋən] **(das)**; **~s** *(ugs. spött.)* the back of beyond; **~tür die** back door; **durch die** *od.* **durch eine ~tür** *(auch fig.)* by the back door; **sich** *(Dat.)* **eine ~tür offenhalten** *(fig.)* leave oneself a way out *(fig.)*; **~wäldler** [~vɛltlɐ] **der**; **~s, ~** *(spött.)* backwoodsman; **~wäldlerisch** *Adj.* *(spött.)* backwoods *attrib.* ‹*views, attitudes, manners, etc.*›; **~ziehen** [--'--] *unr. tr. V.* misappropriate ‹*materials, goods*›; **Steuern ~ziehen** evade [payment of] tax; **~ziehung die** *s.* **~ziehen:** misappropriation; evasion; **~zimmer das** back room

hintnach [hɪnt'na:x] *Adv. (österr. ugs.) s.* **hinterher**

hin-: ~|tragen *unr. tr. V.* **jmdn./etw. ~tragen** carry sb./take *or* carry sth. there; **etw. zu jmdm.** *od.* **jmdm. etw. ~tragen** take sth. to sb.; **~|treiben 1.** *unr. tr. V.* **a)** *(an eine Stelle treiben)* **die Schafe ~treiben/zur Weide ~treiben** drive the sheep there/to the pasture; **die Strömung/der Wind trieb das Boot zum Ufer ~:** the current carried/the wind blew the boat to the shore; **b)** *(unpers.)* **es trieb ihn immer wieder zu ihr ~:** something always drove him back to her; **2.** *unr. itr. V.; mit sein* drift *or* float there; **~|treten** *unr. itr. V.* **a)** *mit sein* **zu jmdm./etw. ~treten** step over to sb./sth.; **vor jmdn. ~treten** go up to sb.; **b)** *(gegen jmdn./etw. treten)* kick him/her/it *etc.*

hintüber [hɪnt'|y:bɐ] *Adv. s.* **hintenüber**

hin|tun *unr. tr. V. (ugs.)* put; **wo soll ich ihn bloß ~?** *(fig.)* I can't place him

hinüber [hɪ'ny:bɐ] *Adv.* over; across; **bis zur anderen Seite ~:** over *or* across to the other side; **~ und herüber** back and forth

hinüber- *(s. auch* **rüber-): ~|blicken** *itr. V.* look across; **zu** *od.* **nach jmdm. ~blicken** look across at sb.; **~|bringen** *unr. tr. V.* **jmdn./etw. ~bringen** take sb./sth. across *or* over **(auf +** *Akk.*, **zu** to); **~|dämmern** *itr. V.; mit sein* **a)** *(einschlafen)* drift off; **b)** *(geh. verhüll.: sterben)* pass away in one's sleep; **~|fahren 1.** *unr. itr. V.; mit sein (mit dem Auto/Fahrrad)* drive/ride *or* go over *or* across; **über den Fluß ~fahren** cross the river; **2.** *unr. tr. V.* **jmdn./ein Auto ~fahren** drive *or* take sb./drive a car over *or* across; **~|führen 1.** *tr. V.* **jmdn. über die Straße/die Grenze/in den Saal ~führen** take sb. across the road/guide sb. over *or* across the frontier/take *or* show sb. across to the hall; **2.** *itr. V.* ‹*street, path, etc.*› lead *or* go over *or* across **(an +** *Akk.*, **nach** to); **über etw.** *(Akk.)* **~führen** lead *or* go over sth.; **~|gehen** *unr. itr. V.; mit sein* **a)** walk *or* go over *or* across; **zu jmdm. ~gehen** go across *or* over to sb.; **ins Nebenzimmer ~gehen** go across into the next room; **b)** *(geh. verhüll.: sterben)* pass away; **~|helfen** *unr. itr. V.* **jmdm. [über etw.** *(Akk.)*] **~helfen** help sb. over *or* across [sth.]; **jmdm. auf die andere Seite ~helfen** help sb. over *or* across to the other side; **~|kommen** *unr. itr. V.; mit sein* **a)** *(nach drüben kommen)* come over *or* across; *(~kommen können)* get across; **über etw.** *(Akk.)* **~kommen** get across sth.; **b)** *(ugs.: Besuch machen)* come over; pop over *(coll.)*; **~|lassen** *unr. tr. V.* **jmdn. ~lassen** allow *or* let sb. over *or* across; **~|reichen 1.** *tr. V.* **[jmdm.] etw. ~reichen** pass *or* hand sth. across [to sb.]; **2.** *itr. V.* **a)** *(sich erstrecken)* extend [over *or* across]; **b)** *(lang genug sein)* reach over *or* across; **über die Mauer ~reichen** reach over the wall; **~|retten 1.** *tr. V.* **a)** *(in Sicherheit bringen)* **sein Vermögen in die Schweiz ~retten** save one's fortune by getting it over *or* across the border into Switzerland; **b)** *(bewahren)* keep alive, preserve ‹*tradition etc.*›; **2.** *refl. V.* **a)** *(sich in Sicherheit bringen)* **sich ins Ausland ~retten** reach safety abroad; **b)** *(sich erhalten)* ‹*customs, hopes, etc.*› survive; **~|rufen 1.** *unr. tr. V.* **jmdn. ~rufen** call sb. over; **2.** *unr. itr. V.* call over; **~|schauen** *itr. V.* **a)** *(landsch.) s.* **~blicken; b)** *(ugs.: besuchen)* **zu jmdm. ~schauen** look in on sb.; **~|schicken** *tr. V.* **jmdn./etw. ~schicken** send sb./sth. over; **~|schwimmen** *unr. itr. V.; mit sein* swim over *or* across; **~|sehen** *unr. itr. V. s.* **~blicken; ~|sein** *unr. itr. V.; mit sein (nur im Inf. u. 2. Part. zusammengeschrieben) (ugs.)* **a)** *(tot, unbrauchbar sein)* have had it *(coll.)*; **er ist ~:** he's had it *(coll.)*; **b)** *(verdorben sein)* be off; have gone off; **c)** *(eingeschlafen sein)* have dropped off; *(bewußtlos sein)* be out for the count *(coll.)*; **d)** *(betrunken sein)* be well away *(coll.) or* plastered *(sl.)*; **~|spielen 1.** *tr. V.* *(Sport)* cross ‹*ball*›; **2.** *itr. V.* **das Weiß spielt ins Gelbliche ~:** the white is tinged with yellow *or* has a yellow tinge; **~|springen** *unr. itr. V.; mit sein* **über etw.** *(Akk.)***/ein Hindernis ~springen** jump over sth./clear an obstacle; **~|steigen** *unr. itr. V.; mit sein* **[über etw.** *(Akk.)*] **~steigen** climb over [sth.]; **~|wechseln** *itr. V.; mit haben od. sein* cross over; **zu einer anderen Partei ~wechseln** go over *or* switch to another party; **~|werfen** *unr. tr. V.* **etw. ~werfen** throw sth. over *or* across; **einen Blick ~werfen** *(fig.)* glance over *or* across; **~|ziehen 1.** *unr. tr. V.* **jmdn./etw. ~ziehen** draw sb. over/pull *or* draw sth. over *or* across; **2.** *unr. itr. V.; mit sein* **a)** *(wandern)* **über etw. ~ziehen** go over *or* across sth.; cross sth.; **b)** *(umziehen)* move across

hin- und her-: ~|bewegen *tr. V.* **etw. hin- und herbewegen** move sth. to and fro *or* back and forth; **~|fahren 1.** *unr. itr. V.; mit sein* travel *or* go to and fro *or* back and forth; *(mit dem Auto)* drive to and fro *or* back and forth; *(mit dem Fahrrad)* ride to and fro *or* back and forth; **2.** *unr. tr. V.* **jmdn. ~fahren** drive sb. to and fro *or* back and forth; **~|gehen** *unr. itr. V.; mit sein* walk up and down *or* to and fro; *(aufgeregt)* pace up and down *or* to and fro; **im Zimmer ~gehen** walk/pace up and down the room

Hinundher·gerede das: bei diesem ~ kommt doch nichts heraus we're going backwards and forwards over the same old ground and getting nowhere

hin- und her|pendeln *itr. V.; mit sein* ‹*person*› commute; ‹*bus*› shuttle to and fro

Hin- und Rück-: ~fahrt die journey there and back; round trip *(Amer.)*; **~flug der** outward and return flight; **~reise die, ~weg der** journey there and back

hinunter [hɪ'nʊntɐ] *Adv.* down; **den Berg ~:** down the mountain; **~ mit der Medizin!** *(ugs.)* get the medicine down!

hinunter-: ~|begeben *unr. refl. V.* **sich ~begeben** go down; **sich die Treppe ~begeben** go downstairs; **~|blicken** *itr. V.* look down; **auf jmdn. ~blicken** *(fig.)* look down on sb.; **~|bringen** *unr. tr. V.* **jmdn./etw. ~bringen** take sb./sth. down; **~|fahren 1.** *unr. itr. V.; mit sein* go down; *(mit dem Auto)* drive down; *(mit dem Fahrrad)* ride down; **2.** *unr. tr. V.* **jmdn./ein Auto/eine Ladung ~fahren** drive *or* take sb. down/drive a car down/take a load down; **~|fallen** *unr. itr. V.; mit sein* fall down; **die Treppe ~fallen** fall down the stairs; **mir ist die Vase ~gefallen** I dropped the vase; **~|führen 1.** *tr. V.* **jmdn. ~führen** lead *or* guide sb. down; **2.** *itr. V.* ‹*path, road, etc.*› lead *or* run down; **den Berg ~führen** lead *or* run down the mountain; **~|gehen** *unr. itr. V.; mit sein* **a)** go down; *(zu Fuß)* go *or* walk down; ‹*aircraft*› descend; **b)** ‹*path, road, etc.*› go *or* run down; **~|jagen 1.** *tr. V.* **jmdn. ~jagen** chase sb. down; **2.** *itr. V.; mit sein* **die Treppe/Straße ~jagen** race down the stairs/street; **~|kippen** *tr. V.* **a) etw. ~kippen** tip sth. down; **b)** *(ugs.: trinken)* knock back *(sl.)*; down; **~|klettern** *itr. V.; mit sein* climb down; **~|kommen** *unr. itr. V.; mit sein* come down; **die Treppe ~kommen** come downstairs; **~|lassen** *unr. tr. V.* **a)** *(mit einem Seil usw.)* **jmdn./etw. ~lassen** lower sb./sth.; let sb./sth. down; **b)** *(erlauben)* **jmdn. ~lassen** let sb. [go] down; **~|laufen** *unr. itr. V.; mit sein* **a)** run down; *(zu Fuß ~gehen)* walk down; **die Treppe ~laufen** run/walk down the stairs *or* downstairs; **b)** *(nach unten fließen)* run down; **an der Wand ~laufen** run down the wall; **c)** *(fig.)* **ein Schauer lief ihm den Rücken ~:** a shiver ran down his spine; **~|reichen 1.** *tr. V.* pass *or* hand down; **2.** *itr. V.* **a)** *(sich bis hinunter erstrecken)* reach down **(bis auf +** *Akk.* to); **b)** *(bis zu einer Stufe reichen)* **bis zu jmdm. ~reichen** reach *or* extend down to sb.; **~|rutschen** *itr. V.; mit sein* slide down; **~|schauen** *itr. V. (landsch.) s.* **~blicken; ~|schlingen** *unr. tr. V.* gulp *or* gobble down; **~|schlucken** *tr. V.* **a)** swallow; **b)** *(hinnehmen)* swallow ‹*insult etc.*›; **c)** *(unterdrücken)* bite back ‹*remark, oath, etc.*›; choke back ‹*tears, anger*›; **~|sehen** *unr. itr. V. s.* **~blicken; ~|springen** *unr. itr. V.; mit sein* **a)** jump down; **b)** *(ugs.: schnell ~laufen)* run down; **die Treppe ~springen** run down the stairs *or* downstairs; **~|spülen** *tr. V.* **a) etw. [den Ausguß] ~spülen** swill sth. down [the sink]; **etw. [die Toilette] ~spülen** flush sth. down [the toilet]; **b)** *(ugs.: hinunterschlucken)* wash down ‹*tablets etc.*›; **seinen Kummer [mit Alkohol] ~spülen** *(fig.)* drown one's sorrows [in drink]; **~|stürzen 1.** *itr. V.; mit sein* **a)** fall *or* plunge down; **die Treppe ~stürzen** fall down the stairs *or* downstairs; **b)** *(ugs.: eilen)* rush *or* race down; **2.** *refl. V.* throw *or* fling oneself down; **sich von etw. ~stürzen** throw *or* fling oneself off sth.; **3.** *tr. V.* **a) jmdn. ~stürzen** throw *or* hurl sb. down; **jmdn. von den Klippen/in den Abgrund ~stürzen** push sb. off the cliff/over the precipice; **b)** *(ugs.: schnell trinken)* gulp down; knock back *(sl.)*; **~|tragen** *unr. tr. V.* **etw. ~tragen** carry sth. down; **~|werfen** *unr. tr. V.* throw down; **einen Blick ~werfen** *(fig.)* glance down; **~|ziehen 1.** *unr. itr. V.; mit sein* **a)** *(umziehen)* move down; **b)** *(sich nach unten bewegen)* move *or* go down; **2.** *unr. tr. V.* **jmdn./etw. ~ziehen** pull sb./sth. down; **3.** *unr. refl. V.* stretch *or* extend down

hin-, Hin-: ~|wagen *refl. V.* dare [to] go there; venture there; **~wärts** *Adv.* on the way there; **~weg der** way there; **auf dem ~weg** on the way there; **für den ~weg** for the journey there

hin·weg *Adv.* **a)** *(geh.)* **~ mit diesem Unrat!** away with this rubbish!; **~ mit dir!** away with you!; **b) über etw. ~:** over sth.; **über den Brillenrand ~:** over [the top of] his/her spectacles; **über alle Schwierigkeiten** *usw.* **~** *(fig.)* in spite of *or* despite all the difficulties *etc.*; **über jmdn. ~** *(fig.)* over sb.'s head; **über Jahre/lange Zeit ~:** for many years/a long time

hinweg-: ~|brausen *itr. V.; mit sein* **über etw.** *(Akk.)* **~brausen** roar over sth.; **~|gehen** *unr. itr. V.; mit sein (nicht beachten)* **über etw.** *(Akk.)* **~gehen** pass over sth.; *(sich über etw. fortbewegen, auch fig.)* pass *or* sweep over sth.; **~|helfen** *unr. itr. V.* **jmdm. über etw.** *(Akk.)* **~helfen** help sb. [to] get over sth.; **~|kommen** *unr. itr. V.; mit sein* **über etw.** *(Akk.)* **~kommen** get over sth.; **~|lesen** *unr. itr. V.* **über etw.** *(Akk.)* **~lesen** read past sth. without noticing it; **~|raffen** *tr. V. (geh.)* carry off; **~|sehen** *unr. itr. V.* **a) über jmdn./etw. ~sehen** see over sb. *or* sb.'s head/sth.; **b)** *(übersehen)* **über jmdn. ~sehen** look past sb.; **c)** *(unbeachtet lassen)* **über etw.** *(Akk.)* **~sehen** overlook sth.; **~|setzen 1.** *itr. V.; auch mit sein* **über etw.** *(Akk.)* **~setzen** leap *or* jump over sth.; **2.** *refl. V.* **sich über etw.** *(Akk.)* **~setzen** ignore *or* disregard sth.; **~|täuschen** *tr. V.* **jmdn. über etw.** *(Akk.)* **~täuschen** blind sb. to sth.; deceive *or* mislead sb. about sth.; **darüber ~täuschen, daß ...:** hide *or* obscure the fact that ...; **~|trösten** *tr. V.* **jmdn. über etw.** *(Akk.)* **~trösten** console sb. for sth.

Hinweis ['hɪnvais] **der; ~es, ~e a)** *(Wink)* hint; tip; **jmdm. einen ~ geben** give sb. a hint; **wenn ich mir den ~ erlauben darf** if I may [just] point something out *or* draw your attention to something; **~e für den Benutzer** notes for the user; **~e aus der Bevölkerung** leads provided by the public; **b) unter ~ auf** (+ *Akk.*) with reference to; **c)** *(Anzeichen)* hint; indication

hin-: ~|weisen 1. *unr. itr. V.* **a)** *(zeigen)* **auf jmdn./etw. ~weisen** point to *or* indicate sb./sth.; **b) auf etw.** *(Akk.)* **~weisen** *(anzeigen)* point to *or* indicate sth.; *(verweisen)* point sth. out; refer to sth.; **darauf ~weisen, daß ...:** point to the fact that *or* indicate that/point out that; **2.** *unr. tr. V.* **jmdn. auf etw.** *(Akk.)* **~weisen** point sth. out to sb.; draw sb.'s attention to sth.; **~weisend** *Adj. (Grammatik)* demonstrative ⟨*pronoun, adjective, etc.*⟩

Hinweis-: ~schild das sign; *(Straßenschild)* [road] sign; **~tafel die** information board

hin-, Hin-: ~|wenden 1. *unr. tr. V.* turn **(zu** towards); **2.** *unr. refl. V.* turn **(zu** to, towards); **wo soll ich mich jetzt noch ~wenden?** *(ugs. fig.)* where shall I turn now?; **~wendung die;** *o. Pl.* change of direction **(zu** towards); **~|werfen 1.** *unr. tr. V.* **a)** *(an eine Stelle werfen)* throw down; **b)** *(von sich werfen)* throw *or* fling down; **c)** *(ugs.: aufgeben)* chuck in *(coll.)*; **d)** *(flüchtig schreiben)* jot down; *(flüchtig zeichnen)* dash off; **e)** *(beiläufig äußern)* drop [casually] ⟨*remark*⟩; ask casually ⟨*question*⟩; make casually ⟨*accusation*⟩; say casually ⟨*words*⟩; **eine [beiläufig] ~geworfene Bemerkung** a casual remark; **f)** *(ugs.: fallen lassen)* drop; **2.** *unr. refl. V.* **sich [vor jmdm.] ~werfen** throw oneself down [before sb.]

hin·wieder, hin·wiederum *Adv. (veralt.)* on the other hand

hin|wirken *itr. V.* **auf etw.** *(Akk.)* **~:** work towards sth.; **bei jmdm. darauf ~, daß er seine Meinung ändert** try to persuade sb. to change his opinion

Hinz [hɪnts] *in* **~ und Kunz** *(ugs. abwertend)* every Tom, Dick and Harry

hin-: ~|zählen *tr. V.* count out; **~|zaubern** *tr. V. (ugs.)* **etw. ~zaubern** produce sth. as if by magic; **~|zeigen** *itr. V.* point **(zu** to, towards); **~|ziehen 1.** *unr. tr. V.* **a)** pull, draw **(zu** to, towards); **b)** *(zu etw., jmdm. treiben)* draw, attract **(zu** to); **sich zu jmdm./etw. ~gezogen fühlen** be *or* feel attracted to sb./sth.; **c)** *(in die Länge ziehen)* draw out; protract; **d)** *(verzögern)* delay; put off; **2.** *unr. itr. V.; mit sein* **a)** *(umziehen)* move there; **wo ist sie ~gezogen?** where did she move to?; **b)** *(an einen Ort ziehen)* move **(zu** towards); **am Himmel ~ziehen** *(dichter.)* sail across the sky; **3.** *unr. refl. V.* **a)** *(sich erstrecken)* drag on **(über** + *Akk.* for); **b)** *(sich verzögern)* be delayed; **~|zielen** *itr. V.* **auf etw.** *(Akk.)* **~zielen** aim at sth.; ⟨*policies, efforts, etc.*⟩ be aimed at sth.

hin·zu *Adv.* in addition; besides; **dieses Gehalt und noch das Doppelte ~, dann wäre ich zufrieden** I'd be content with this salary and twice as much again *or* on top

hinzu-, Hinzu-: ~|bekommen *unr. tr. V.* get in addition; **~|denken** *unr. refl. V.* **sich** *(Dat.)* **etw. ~denken** add sth. in one's imagination; **~|dichten** *tr. V.* **~dichten** make sth. up and add it; add sth. out of one's head; **~|fügen** *tr. V.* add; **~fügung die** addition; **unter ~fügung** *(Dat.)* **einer Sache** *(Gen.)* *od.* **von etw.** with the addition of sth.; **~|geben** *unr. tr. V.* **a)** *(dazugeben)* **jmdm. etw. ~geben** give sth. to sb. in addition; **b)** *(hineingeben)* add; **~|gesellen** *refl. V.* **sich [zu] jmdm./etw. ~gesellen** join sb./sth.; **~|gewinnen** *unr. tr. V.* gain in addition; **~|kommen** *unr. itr. V.; mit sein* **a)** *(zufällig kommen)* arrive *or* appear [on the scene]; come along; **er kam gerade** *od.* **genau in dem Moment ~, als ...:** he arrived *or* happened to arrive at the very moment when *or* just as ...; **b)** *(hinkommen)* come along *or* up; **c)** *(sich anschließen)* join; **zu etw. ~kommen** join sth.; **d)** *(hinzugefügt werden)* **zu etw. ~kommen** be added to sth.; **zu der Grippe kam noch eine Lungenentzündung ~:** in addition to the flu he/she also contracted a lung infection; **es kommt noch ~, daß ...:** there is also the fact that ...; **~|nehmen** *unr. tr. V.* add; **~|setzen 1.** *refl. V.* **sich zu jmdm./einer Gruppe** *usw.* **~setzen** join sb./a group *etc.*; **2.** *tr. V.* add; **~|treten** *unr. itr. V.; mit sein* **a)** come up; **zu jmdm./den anderen ~treten** come up to sb./join the others; **b)** *s.* **~kommen d**; **~|tun** *unr. tr. V. (ugs.)* add; *s. auch* **dazutun**; **~|verdienen** *tr. V.* **etwas ~verdienen** earn a bit extra; **~|zählen** *tr. V.* add [on]; **~|ziehen** *unr. tr. V.* consult; call in; **~ziehung die; ~:** consultation; **unter ~ziehung einschlägiger Literatur** by consulting the relevant literature

Hiob ['hi:ɔp] **(der)** Job

Hiobs·botschaft die bad news

¹Hippe ['hɪpə] **die; ~, ~n** pruning-knife; *(des Todes)* scythe

²Hippe die; ~, ~n *(ugs. abwertend)* bitch *(derog.)*

hipp, hipp, hurra ['hɪp'hɪphʊ'ra:] *Interj.* hip, hip, hooray *or* hurrah

Hipphipphurra [hɪphɪphʊ'ra:] **das; ~s, ~s** cheer; **dem Sieger ein dreifaches ~:** three cheers for the winner

Hippie ['hɪpi] **der; ~s, ~s** hippie *(coll.)*

Hippodrom [hɪpo'dro:m] **der** *od.* **das; ~s, ~e** hippodrome

hippokratisch [hɪpo'kra:tɪʃ] *Adj.; nicht präd.* **der ~e Eid** the Hippocratic oath

Hirn [hɪrn] **das; ~[e]s, ~e a)** brain; **b)** *(Speise; ugs.: Verstand)* brains *pl.*; **sein ~ anstrengen** exercise one's mental faculties; **sich** *(Dat.)* **das ~ zermartern** rack one's brains; **welchem ~ ist das entsprungen?** whose brainchild is that?

hirn-, Hirn-: ~anhangs·drüse die *(Anat.)* pituitary gland *or* body; **~gespinst das** *(abwertend)* fantasy; **~hautentzündung die** *(Med.)* meningitis; **~kasten der** *(salopp scherzh.) s.* **Gehirnkasten**; **~los** *(abwertend)* **1.** *Adj.* brainless; **2.** *adv.* brainlessly; **~rinde die** *(Anat.)* cerebral cortex; **~rissig** *Adj. (abwertend)* crazy; crack-brained *(coll.)*; **~stamm der** *(Anat.)* brain-stem; **~tumor der** *(Med.)* brain tumour; **~tod der** *(Med.)* brain death; **~verbrannt** *Adj. (abwertend)* crazy; crack-brained *(coll.)*; **~windung die** *(Med.)* convolution *or (Med.)* gyrus of the brain

Hirsch [hɪrʃ] **der; ~[e]s, ~e a)** deer; **b)** *(Rothirsch)* red deer; **c)** *(männlicher Rothirsch)* stag; hart; **d)** *(Speise)* venison; **e)** *(Schimpfwort)* bastard *(coll.)*

Hirsch-: ~brunft, ~brunst die rut [of the stags]; **während der ~brunft** *od.* **~brunst** while the stags are in rut; **~fänger der** *(Jägerspr.)* [double-edged] hunting knife; **~geweih das** [stag's] antlers *pl.*; **ein ~geweih** a set of antlers; **~horn das** stag-horn; **~horn·salz das** salt of hartshorn; ammonium carbonate; **~käfer der** stag-beetle; **~kalb das** [male] deer calf; [male] fawn; **~kuh die** hind; **~leder das** buckskin; **~ragout das** *(Kochk.)* ragout of venison; **~steak das** *(Kochk.)* venison steak

Hirse ['hɪrzə] **die; ~, ~n** millet

Hirse·brei der millet gruel

Hirt [hɪrt] **der; ~en, ~en** herdsman; *(Schaf~)* shepherd

Hirte der; ~n, ~n *(geh.) s.* **Hirt; der Gute ~:** the Good Shepherd

Hirten-: ~amt das *(kath. Rel.)* pastorate; pastoral office; **~brief der** *(kath. Rel.)* pastoral letter; **~dichtung die** *(Literaturw.)* pastoral *or* bucolic poetry; **~hund der** sheep-dog; **~junge der, ~knabe der** *(dicht.)* shepherd boy; **~mädchen das** shepherd girl; **~spiel das** pastoral [play]; **~stab der a)** *(geh.)* shepherd's crook; **b)** *(kath. Rel.)* pastoral staff; crosier; **~täschel[kraut] das; ~s** *(Bot.)* shepherd's purse; **~volk das** pastoral people

Hirtin die; ~, ~nen *(veralt. selten)* shepherdess

his, His [hɪs] **das; ~, ~** *(Musik)* B sharp; *s. auch* **a, A**

hispanisieren [hɪspani'zi:rən] *tr. V.* Hispanicize

Hispanist der; ~en, ~en Hispanicist

Hispanistik die; ~: study of Hispanic languages and literature; ≈ Hispanic studies

hissen ['hɪsn̩] *tr. V.* hoist ⟨*sail*⟩; hoist, run up ⟨*flag*⟩

Histamin [hɪsta'mi:n] **das; ~s** *(Chemie)* histamine

Histologie [hɪstolo'gi:] **die; ~** *(Med.)* histology *no art.*

histologisch *Adj. (Med.)* histological

Histörchen [hɪs'tø:ɐ̯çən] **das; ~s, ~** *(scherzh.)* anecdote

Historie [hɪs'to:ri̯ə] **die; ~, ~n** *(veralt.)* **a)** *o. Pl.* history; **b)** *(Erzählung)* story; tale

Historien-: ~maler der painter of historical scenes; historical painter; **~malerei die** painting of historical scenes; historical painting

Historiker [hɪs'to:rikɐ] **der; ~s, ~:** historian

historisch 1. *Adj.* **a)** historical; **b)** *(geschichtlich bedeutungsvoll)* historic. **2.** *adv.*

a) das ist ~ belegt this is historically attested; there is historical evidence for this; **etw. ~ erklären** explain sth. in historical terms; **~ erwiesen sein** be historically proven; **etw. ~ betrachten** see sth. in the light of history *or* in historical terms; **b) ~ höchst bedeutsam** of historic importance

historisieren *itr. V. (geh.)* historicize

Historismus der; ~: historicism

Hit [hɪt] **der; ~[s], ~s** *(ugs.)* hit

Hitler- ['hɪtlɐ-]: **~bärtchen das** *(ugs.)* Hitler moustache; **~faschismus der** Hitlerite fascism; **~gruß der** Nazi salute; **~jugend die** Hitler Youth; **~junge der** member of the Hitler Youth; **~zeit die** Hitler era

Hit-: ~liste die top ten/twenty/thirty *etc.*; **~parade die** hit parade

Hitze ['hɪtsə] **die; ~,** *(fachspr.:)* **~n** heat; **bei dieser ~:** in this heat; **etw. bei mittlerer/mäßiger ~ backen** bake sth. in a medium/moderate oven; **die fliegende ~ haben** *(fig.)* have [got] the hot flushes; **sich in ~** *(Akk.)* **reden** *(fig.)* get more and more excited as one talks; **in der ~ des Gefechts** in the heat of the moment

hitze-, Hitze-: ~abweisend *Adj.* heat-reflecting; **~beständig** *Adj.* heat-resistant, heat-resisting ⟨*metal etc.*⟩; heat-proof, heat-resistant ⟨*glass etc.*⟩; **~bläschen das** heat spot; **~empfindlich** *Adj.* sensitive to heat *postpos.*; heat-sensitive ⟨*material*⟩; **~frei** *Adj.* **~frei haben/bekommen** have/be given the rest of the day off [school/work] because of excessively hot weather; **~periode die** hot spell; spell *or* period of hot weather; *(~welle)* heat wave; **~schild der** *(Raumf.)* heat shield; **~wallung die** hot flush; **~welle die** heat wave

hitzig *Adj.* **a)** *(heftig)* hot-tempered; quick-tempered; **~ werden** flare up; fly into a temper; **b)** *(leidenschaftlich)* hot-blooded ⟨*person, race, etc.*⟩; hot ⟨*blood*⟩; passionate ⟨*supporter, advocate, etc.*⟩; **c)** *(erregt)* heated ⟨*discussion, argument, words, etc.*⟩; **d)** *nicht präd. (veralt.: fiebrig)* fevered ⟨*brow, cheeks, etc.*⟩; feverish ⟨*red*⟩; **e)** *(läufig)* on *or* in heat *pred.*

Hitzigkeit die; ~ a) *(Heftigkeit)* hot *or* quick temper; **b)** *(Leidenschaftlichkeit)* hot-bloodedness

hitz-, Hitz-: ~kopf der hothead; **~köpfig** *Adj.* hot-headed; **~pocke die** *s.* **Hitzebläschen; ~schlag der** heat-stroke

HIV *Abk.* **humanes Immundefizienzvirus** HIV

Hiwi ['hi:vi] **der; ~s, ~s** laboratory *or (coll.)* lab/departmental/library assistant

HJ die; ~ *Abk. (ns.)* **Hitlerjugend**

hl *Abk.* **Hektoliter** hl

hl. *Abk.* **heilig** St.

hm [hm̩] *Interj.* h'm; hem

H-Milch ['ha:-] **die; ~:** long-life *or* UHT milk

h-Moll ['ha:mɔl] **das; ~** *(Musik)* B minor; *s. auch* **a-Moll**

HNO-Arzt [ha:|ɛn'|o:-] **der** ENT specialist

HO [ha:'|o:] **die; ~** *(DDR)* **a)** *s.* **Handelsorganisation b; b)** *s.* **HO-Geschäft**

hob [ho:p] *1. u. 3. Pers. Sg. Prät. v.* **heben**

Hobby ['hɔbi] **das; ~s, ~s** hobby

Hobby- amateur ⟨*gardener, archaeologist, astronomer, etc.*⟩

Hobby·raum der hobby room

Hobel ['ho:bl̩] **der; ~s, ~ a)** plane; **b)** *(Küchengerät)* [vegetable] slicer

Hobel-: ~bank die carpenter's *or* woodworker's bench; **~eisen das, ~messer das** plane iron

hobeln *tr., itr. V.* **a)** plane; **an etw.** *(Dat.)* **~:** plane sth.; **b)** *(schneiden)* slice

Hobel·span der shaving

hoch [ho:x]; **höher** ['hø:ɐ], **höchst...** ['hø:çst...] **1.** *Adj.* **a)** *(von beträchtlicher Höhe)* high; high, tall ⟨*building*⟩; tall ⟨*tree, mast*⟩; long ⟨*grass*⟩; deep ⟨*snow, water*⟩; long, tall ⟨*ladder*⟩; high-ceilinged ⟨*room*⟩; **10 m ~:** 10 m high; **eine hohe Stirn** a high forehead; **er bekommt eine hohe Stirn** he's receding; **von hoher Gestalt** *(geh.)* tall in stature; of tall stature; **hohe Absätze** high heels; **hohe Schuhe** *(mit hohem Schaft)* high boots; *(mit hohen Absätzen)* high-heeled shoes; **b)** *(mengenmäßig groß)* high ⟨*price, wage, rent, speed, pressure, temperature, sensitivity*⟩; heavy ⟨*fine*⟩; great ⟨*weight*⟩; large ⟨*sum, amount*⟩; high, large, big ⟨*profit*⟩; severe, extensive ⟨*damage*⟩; **einen hohen Blutdruck haben** have high blood pressure; **c)** *(zeitlich fortgeschritten)* great ⟨*age*⟩; **ein hohes Alter erreichen** live to *or* reach a ripe old age; **es ist höchste Zeit, daß ...:** it is high time that ...; **d)** *(oben in einer Rangordnung)* high ⟨*birth, office*⟩; high-ranking ⟨*officer, civil servant*⟩; senior ⟨*official, officer, post*⟩; high-level ⟨*diplomacy, politics*⟩; important ⟨*guest, festival*⟩; **Verhandlungen auf höchster Ebene** top-level negotiations; **der hohe Adel** the higher ranks of the nobility; **eine hohe Ehre** a great honour; **mit höchster Diskretion/Eile** with the greatest discretion/urgency; **das Höchste Wesen** the Supreme Being; **sich zu Höherem berufen fühlen** feel called to higher things; **höchste Gefahr** extreme danger; **im höchsten Fall[e]** at the most; *s. auch* **Blödsinn; Gefühl b; Gewalt d; Haus f; Jagd a; Tier; Tochter a; e)** *(qualitativ ~stehend)* high ⟨*standard, opinion*⟩; great ⟨*responsibility, concentration, talent, happiness, good, importance*⟩; **die Hohe Schule** *(Reiten)* haute école; **f)** *(Musik)* high ⟨*voice, note*⟩; **das hohe C** top C; **g)** *(Math.)* **vier ~ zwei** four to the power [of] two; four squared; **h)** *(in großer Höhe)* high ⟨*cloud, branch, etc.*⟩; **der hohe Norden** *(fig.)* the far North; **i)** *(auf dem Höhepunkt)* **das hohe Mittelalter** the High Middle Ages; **j)** *in* **das ist mir zu ~** *(ugs.)* that's beyond me; that went over my head. **2.** *adv.* **a)** *(in großer Höhe)* high; **~ oben am Himmel** high up in the sky; **~ über uns** high above us; **die Sonne steht ~:** the sun is high in the sky; **wenn die Sonne am höchsten steht** when the sun is [at its] highest; **~ zu Roß** *(geh.)* on horseback; **er wohnt drei Treppen ~:** he lives on the third *(Brit.) or (Amer.)* fourth floor; **~ auf etw.** *(Dat.)* **sitzen** sit high up on sth.; **b)** *(nach oben)* up; **Kopf ~!** chin up! **die Flammen loderten ~:** the flames leapt up high; **zu ~ zielen** aim too high; **ein ~ aufgeschossener Junge** a very tall lad; **einen Ball ~ in die Luft werfen** throw a ball high in the air; **die Nase ~ tragen** walk around with one's nose in the air; **c)** *(zahlenmäßig viel)* highly ⟨*taxed, paid*⟩; heavily ⟨*taxed*⟩; **~ verschuldet/versichert** heavily in debt/insured for a large sum [of money]; **~ gewinnen/verlieren** *(Sport)* win/lose by a large margin; **wenn es ~ kommt** at [the] most; **d)** *(dem Rang nach oben)* **etw. ~ und heilig versprechen** promise sth. faithfully; **~ hinauswollen** *(ugs.)* aim high; have great ambitions; **zu ~ hinauswollen** *(ugs.)* aim too high; be too ambitious; **e)** *(sehr)* highly ⟨*gifted, delighted, satisfied*⟩; most ⟨*welcome*⟩; highly, greatly ⟨*esteemed*⟩; **jmdm. etw. ~ anrechnen** consider sth. [to be] greatly to sb.'s credit; **jmdn. ~ verehren** esteem sb. highly *or* greatly; **f)** *(zeitlich fortgeschritten)* **~ in den Siebzigern** well into his/her seventies; **g)** *(Musik)* high; **h)** *(in Wendungen)* **das Herz höher schlagen lassen** make sb.'s heart beat faster; **es ging ~ her** things were pretty lively; **sie kamen drei Mann ~:** three of them came; there were three of them; *s. auch* **höchst**

Hoch das; ~s, ~s a) *(Hochruf)* **ein [dreifaches] ~ auf jmdn. ausbringen** give three cheers for sb.; **ein ~ dem Gastgeber!** three cheers for the host!; **b)** *(Met.)* high

hoch-: ~achtbar *Adj.* highly respectable; **~|achten** *tr. V. (geh.)* **jmdn./etw. ~achten** respect sb./sth. greatly; have a high regard for sb./sth.

Hoch·achtung die great respect; high esteem; **~ vor jmdm. haben** have a great respect for sb.; hold sb. in high esteem; **meine ~!** may I congratulate you; **mit vorzüglicher ~** *(veralt.: Briefschluß)* most respectfully yours *(dated)*; yours faithfully

hochachtungs·voll *Adv.* *(Briefschluß)* yours faithfully

hoch-, Hoch-: ~adel der higher ranks *pl.* of the nobility; **~aktuell** *Adj.* highly topical; **~alpin** *Adj.* high alpine *attrib.* ⟨*landscape, flora, fauna, etc.*⟩; **~altar der** high altar; **~amt das** *(kath. Rel.)* high mass; **~angesehen** *Adj. (präd. getrennt geschrieben)* highly respected *or* regarded; **~anständig 1.** *Adj.* very decent; **2.** *adv.* very *or* most decently; **~antenne die** roof aerial *(Brit.) or (Amer.)* antenna; **~|arbeiten** *refl. V.* work one's way up; **~bahn die** overhead railway; elevated railroad *(Amer.)*; **~barren der** *(Sport)* parallel bars *pl. (set at international height of 180 cm.)*; **~bau der;** *o. Pl.* [building] construction *no art.*; **~- und Tiefbau** [building] construction and civil engineering *no art.*; **~befriedigt** *Adj. (präd. getrennt geschrieben)* highly satisfied; **~begabt** *Adj. (präd. getrennt geschrieben)* highly gifted *or* talented; **~beglückt** *Adj. (präd. getrennt geschrieben)* blissfully happy; **~beinig** *Adj.* long-legged ⟨*person, animal*⟩; ⟨*table, sofa, etc.*⟩ with long legs; **~bejahrt** *Adj. (geh.) s.* **~betagt; ~|bekommen** *unr. tr. V.* [manage to] lift; [manage to] do up ⟨*zip*⟩; **~beladen** *Adj. (präd. getrennt geschrieben)* heavily laden; **~berühmt** *Adj.* very famous; **~betagt** *Adj.* aged; ⟨*person*⟩ advanced in years *postpos.*; **~betrieb der;** *o. Pl. (ugs.)* **es herrschte ~ betrieb im Geschäft** the shop was at its busiest; **heute herrschte ~betrieb im Büro** the office was very busy today; **~bezahlt** *Adj. (präd. getrennt geschrieben)* highly paid; **~|biegen 1.** *unr. tr. V.* **etw. ~biegen** bend sth. up[wards]; **2.** *unr. refl. V.* bend up; **~|binden** *unr. tr. V.* tie up ⟨*plant*⟩; put up ⟨*hair*⟩; **~|blicken** *itr. V.* look up; **~blüte die** golden age; **~|bringen** *unr. tr. V.* **a)** *(nach oben bringen)* bring up; **b)** *(ugs.: in die Wohnung bringen)* bring in[to the flat *(Brit.) or (Amer.)* apartment]; **c)** *(gesund machen)* **jmdn. ~bringen** put sb. on his/her feet; **d)** *(ugs.: ärgern)* **jmdn. ~bringen** put sb.'s back up; **~burg die** stronghold; **~busig** *Adj.* high-bosomed; **~dekoriert** *Adj. (präd. getrennt geschrieben)* much decorated; **~deutsch** *Adj.* standard *or* High German; **die ~deutsche Lautverschiebung** the High German *or* second sound shift; **mit jmdm. ~deutsch sprechen** *od.* **reden** *(ugs.)* give sb. a piece of one's mind; **~deutsch das, ~deutsche das** standard *or* High German; **~|dienen** *refl. V.* work one's way up; **~dotiert** *Adj. (präd. getrennt geschrieben)* highly paid; **~|drehen** *tr. V.* **a)** *(in die Höhe drehen)* wind up ⟨*window, barrier, etc.*⟩; **b)** *(Technik)* rev [up] *(coll.)* ⟨*engine*⟩

¹Hoch·druck der a) *(Physik, Met.)* high pressure; **b)** *(Geschäftigkeit)* **mit** *od.* **unter ~ arbeiten** *(ugs.)* work flat out *or* at full stretch; **in allen Abteilungen herrschte ~:** all departments were at full stretch; **c)** *(Med.)* high blood pressure; hypertension *(Med.)*

²Hoch·druck der *(Druckw.)* **a)** *(Verfahren)* relief *or* letterpress printing; **etw. im ~ herstellen/drucken** produce/print sth. by letterpress; **b)** *(Erzeugnis)* piece of letterpress work; **~e** letterpress work

Hochdruck·gebiet das high-pressure area

hoch-, Hoch-: ~ebene die plateau; tableland; **~empfindlich** *Adj.* highly sensitive ⟨*instrument, device, material, etc.*⟩; high-speed, fast ⟨*film*⟩; extremely delicate ⟨*fabric*⟩; **~entwickelt** *Adj. (präd. getrennt geschrieben)* highly developed ⟨*country etc.*⟩; [highly] sophisticated ⟨*method, device, etc.*⟩; **~erhoben** *Adj. (präd. getrennt geschrieben)* **mit ~erhobenen Armen** with arms raised *or* held high; **~erhobenen Hauptes** with head held high; **~explosiv** *Adj. (auch fig.)* highly explosive; **~|fahren 1.** *unr. itr. V.; mit sein* **a)** *(ugs.: nach oben fahren)* go up; *(mit dem Auto)* drive up; *(mit dem Fahrrad, Motorrad)* ride up; **b)** *(ugs.: nach Norden fahren)* drive up; **c)** *(auffahren)* start up; **aus dem Sessel ~fahren** start [up] from one's chair; **aus dem Schlaf ~fahren** wake up with a start; **d)** *(aufbrausen)* flare up; **2.** *unr. tr. V. (ugs.)* **jmdn./etw. ~fahren** take sb./sth. up; **das Auto ~fahren** drive the car up; **~fahrend** *Adj.* arrogant; supercilious; **~fein** *Adj.* of the finest quality *postpos.*; **aus ~feiner Schokolade/~feinem Batist** of the finest chocolate/batiste; **~finanz die** high finance; **~fläche die** plateau; tableland; **~|fliegen** *unr. itr. V.; mit sein* fly up [into the air]; **~fliegend** *Adj.* ambitious ⟨*plan, idea, etc.*⟩; **~flut die** high water *or* tide; *(fig.)* flood; **~form die** peak *or* top form; **~format das** upright format; **ein Bild/Blatt in ~format** a picture/sheet with an upright format; **~frequenz die** *(Physik)* high frequency; **~frequenz·technik die** radio-frequency engineering *no art.*; **~frisur die** upswept hair-style; **~garage die** multi-storey car park; **~geachtet** *Adj. (präd. getrennt geschrieben)* highly respected *or* regarded; **~gebildet** *Adj. (präd. getrennt geschrieben)* highly cultured; **~gebirge das** [high] mountains *pl.*; **~gebirgs·landschaft die** high-mountain region; **~geboren** *Adj. (veralt.)* high-born; **~geehrt** *Adj.; nicht präd.* highly honoured; **~gefühl das** [feeling of] elation; **im ~gefühl des Erfolges/Sieges** in his/her *etc.* elation at success/victory; **~|gehen** *unr. itr. V.; mit sein* **a)** *(steigen)* go up; rise; **b)** *(ugs.: hinaufgehen)* go up; **die Treppe ~gehen** go up the stairs *or* upstairs; **c)** *(ugs.: zornig werden)* blow one's top *(coll.)*; explode; **d)** *(ugs.: explodieren)* ⟨*bomb, mine*⟩ go off; ⟨*bridge, building, etc.*⟩ go up; **etw. ~gehen lassen** *(salopp)* blow sth. up; **e)** *(ugs.: aufgedeckt werden)* get caught *or (sl.)* nabbed; **jmdn. ~gehen lassen** ⟨*informer*⟩ grass *or* squeal on sb. *(sl.)*; **die Polizei ließ den Rauschgiftring ~gehen** the police smashed the drug ring; **~geistig** *Adj.* highly intellectual; **~gelegen** *Adj. (präd. getrennt geschrieben)* high-lying; **~gelehrt** *Adj.* extremely *or* very learned *or* erudite; **~gemut** [~gəmu:t] *(geh.)* **1.** *Adj.* cheerful; **2.** *adv.* cheerfully; in good spirits; **~genuß der** *in* **ein ~genuß sein** be a real delight; ⟨*meal, concert, etc.*⟩ be a real treat; **ihm zuzuhören ist ein ~genuß** he is a real delight to listen to; **~geschätzt** *Adj. (präd. getrennt geschrieben)* highly esteemed *or* respected; **~geschlossen** *Adj.* high-necked ⟨*dress*⟩; **~gesinnt** *Adj. (geh.)* high-minded; noble-minded; **~gescheit** *Adj. s.* **~intelligent; ~gespannt** *Adj.* great, high ⟨*expectations*⟩; **~gesteckt** *Adj.* ambitious ⟨*goal, plan*⟩; **~gestellt** *Adj.; nicht präd.* ⟨*person*⟩ in a high position; important ⟨*person*⟩; *s. auch* **~stellen; ~gestimmt** *Adj. (geh.)* elated; **~gestochen** *(ugs. abwertend)* **1.** *Adj.* **a)** *(anspruchsvoll)* highbrow *(coll.)*; *(geschraubt)* stilted ⟨*style*⟩; **b)** *(eingebildet)* conceited; stuck-up; **2.** *adv.* in a highbrow way *(coll.)*; **~gewachsen** *Adj.* tall; **~gezüchtet** *Adj.* highly-bred ⟨*animal*⟩; **ein ~gezüchteter Motor** a very finely tuned engine

Hoch·glanz der: ein Foto in ~ *(Dat.)* a high-gloss print; **etw. auf ~** *(Akk.)* **polieren** polish sth. until it shines *or* gleams; **etw. auf ~** *(Akk.)* **bringen** give sth. a high polish; *(fig.)* make sth. spick and span

Hochglanz·folie die glazing sheet

hoch-, Hoch-: ~gradig 1. *Adj.; nicht präd.* extreme; **2.** *adv.* extremely; **~hackig** *Adj.* high-heeled ⟨*shoe*⟩; **~|halten** *unr. tr. V.* **a)** hold up ⟨*arms*⟩; **b)** *(geh.: schützen)* uphold ⟨*truth, tradition, etc.*⟩; **jmds. Andenken ~halten** honour sb.'s memory; **~haus das** high-rise-building; **~|heben** *unr. tr. V.* lift up; raise ⟨*arm, leg, etc.*⟩; raise, hold up ⟨*hand*⟩; **~herrschaftlich** *Adj.* palatial ⟨*house, apartment*⟩; **~herzig** *Adj. (geh.)* magnanimous; generous; **~herzigkeit die; ~:** magnanimity; generosity; **~intelligent** *Adj.* highly intelligent; **~interessant** *Adj.* extremely *or* most interesting; fascinating; **~|jagen** *tr. V.* **a)** scare up ⟨*birds*⟩; forcibly rouse ⟨*sleeper*⟩; **b)** *(Jargon)* race, *(coll.)* rev up ⟨*engine*⟩; **c)** *(ugs.: sprengen)* blow up; **~|jubeln** *tr. V. (ugs.)* **jmdn./etw. ~jubeln** build sb. up as a star/sth. up as a hit; **~kant** *Adv.* **a)** on end; **b)** *(ugs.)* **in jmdn. ~kant hinauswerfen** *od. (salopp)* **rausschmeißen** chuck sb. out *(sl.)*; throw sb. out on his/her ear *(coll.)*; **~kant hinausfliegen** *od. (salopp)* **rausfliegen** be chucked out *(sl.)*; be thrown out on one's ear *(coll.)*; **~kantig** *Adv. s.* **~kant; ~karätig** [~karɛ:tıç] *Adj.* **a)** high-carat ⟨*gold, diamond*⟩; **b)** *(fig.)* top-flight *(coll.)*; **~kirche die** High Church; **~|klappen 1.** *tr. V.* fold up ⟨*chair, table*⟩; raise, lift up ⟨*lid, car-bonnet*⟩; turn up ⟨*collar*⟩; **2.** *itr. V.; mit sein* fold up; **~|klettern** *itr. V.; mit sein (ugs.)* climb up; **den Baum ~klettern** climb [up] the tree; **~|kommen** *unr. itr. V.; mit sein (ugs.)* **a)** come up; **b)** *(vorwärtskommen)* get on; **c)** *(aus dem Magen)* **ihr kam das Essen ~:** she threw up *(coll.) or* brought up her meal; **es kommt einem ~, wenn ...** *(fig.)* it makes you sick when ...; **d)** *(sich erheben)* get up; *(sich erheben können)* be able to get up; **e)** *(fig.)* **in jmdm. ~kommen** rise up in sb.; **~konjunktur die** *(Wirtsch.)* boom; **auf dem Automarkt herrscht ~konjunktur** the car market is booming; there's a boom in car sales; **~|können** *unr. V. (ugs.)* be able to get up; **~konzentriert** *Adj.* highly concentrated; **~|krempeln** *tr. V.* roll up ⟨*sleeve, trouserleg*⟩; **~|kriegen** *tr. V. (ugs.) s.* **~bekommen; einen ~kriegen** *(salopp)* get it up *(sl.)*; **~kultur die** advanced civilization *or* culture; **~lage die;** *meist Pl.* higher region; **~land das;** *Pl.* **~länder** highlands *pl.*; **~|leben** *itr. V.* **in jmdn./etw. ~leben lassen** cheer sb./sth.; **er/unser Verein lebe ~!** three cheers for him/our club!; **der König lebe ~!** long live the king!; **~|legen** *tr. V.* **ein gebrochenes Bein ~legen** support a broken leg in a raised position; **die Beine ~legen** put one's feet up

Hoch·leistung die outstanding performance

Hochleistungs·sport der top-level sport

höchlich[st] ['hø:çlıç(st)] *Adv. (veralt.)* highly; greatly; most

hoch-, Hoch-: ~mittel·alter das High Middle Ages; **~modern 1.** *Adj.* ultramodern; **2.** *adv.* **~modern gekleidet/eingerichtet sein** be extremely fashionably dressed *or* dressed in the very latest fashions/be furnished in the very latest style; **~moor das** *(Geogr.)* high-moor bog; **~motiviert** *Adj.* highly motivated; **~mut der** arrogance; **~mut kommt vor dem Fall** *(Spr.)* pride goes before a fall *(prov.)*; **~mütig** *Adj.* arrogant; **~näsig** [~nɛ:zıç] *Adj. (abwertend)* stuck-up; conceited; **~näsigkeit die; ~** *(abwertend)* conceitedness; **~nebel der** low stratus [cloud]; **~|nehmen** *unr. tr. V.* **a)** lift *or* pick up; **b)** *(ugs.: verspotten)* **jmdn. ~nehmen** pull sb.'s leg; **c)** *(ugs.: nach oben nehmen)* **jmdn./etw. mit ~nehmen** take sb./sth. up with one; **d)** *(salopp: verhaften)* run in; **~not·peinlich** *Adj. (veralt.)* ⟨*interrogation*⟩ under torture; **ein ~notpeinliches Verhör** *(fig.: scherzh.)* an inquisition; **~ofen der** blast furnace; **~offiziell** *Adj.* extremely formal; **~|päppeln** *tr. V. (salopp)* feed up; **~parterre das** upper ground floor; **~plateau das** high plateau; **~politisch** *Adj.* highly political; **~prozentig** *Adj.* high-proof ⟨*spirits*⟩; **~punkt der** *(Math.)* maximum; **~qualifiziert** *Adj. (präd. getrennt geschrieben)* highly qualified; **~rädrig** *Adj.* large-wheeled; **~|ragen** *itr. V.* rise *or* tower up; **~|rappeln** *refl. V. s.* **aufrappeln; ~rechnung die** *(Statistik)* projection; **~reck das** *(Turnen)* high *or* horizontal bar; **~|reißen** *unr. tr. V.* whip up; pull up ⟨*aircraft*⟩; **die Arme ~reißen** throw one's arms up; **~relief das** high relief; **~rot** *Adj.* bright red; **~rot im Gesicht werden** *(aus Verlegenheit)* go as red as a beetroot; **~ruf der** cheer; **~|rutschen** *itr. V.; mit sein (ugs.)* ⟨*dress, shirt, etc.*⟩ ride up; **~saison die** high season; **~|schaukeln** *(ugs.) tr. V.* blow up ⟨*problem, incident, etc.*⟩; **sich [gegenseitig] ~schaukeln** goad each other; **~|scheuchen** *tr. V. s.* **aufscheuchen; ~|schieben** *unr. tr. V. (ugs.)* push up; **~|schießen 1.** *unr. tr. V.* send up, launch ⟨*rocket, space probe, etc.*⟩; **2.** *unr. itr. V.; mit sein (auch fig.)* shoot up; **~|schlagen 1.** *unr. tr. V.* turn up ⟨*collar, brim*⟩; **2.** *unr. itr. V.; mit sein* ⟨*water, waves*⟩ surge up; ⟨*flames*⟩ leap up; **Wellen der Begeisterung schlugen ~** *(fig.)* there was a great surge of enthusiasm; **~|schnellen** *itr. V.; mit sein* leap up; **~schrank der** wardrobe; **~|schrauben 1.** *tr. V.* **a)** raise ⟨*seat*⟩ *(by screwing)*; **b)** *(fig.)* force up ⟨*prices*⟩; step up, increase ⟨*demands*⟩; raise ⟨*expectations*⟩; **2.** *refl. V.* circle up[wards]; **~|schrecken** *s.* **aufschrecken**

Hochschul·bildung die college/university education

Hoch-: ~schule die college; *(Universität)* university; **~schüler der** college/university student

Hochschul-: ~lehrer der college/university lecturer *or* teacher; **~studium das** college/university studies *pl., no art.*; **~wesen das** university and college system; *(Bereich)* higher education

hoch·schwanger *Adj.* in an advanced stage of pregnancy *postpos.*; very pregnant *(coll.)*

Hoch·see die; *o. Pl.* open sea

hochsee-, Hochsee-: ~fischerei die deep-sea fishing *no art.*; **~flotte die** deep sea fleet; **~jacht die** ocean-going yacht; **~tüchtig** *Adj.* seaworthy

Hoch·seil das high wire

Hochseil-: ~akrobat, ~artist der performer on the high wire

hoch-, Hoch-: ~sicherheits·trakt der high-security wing; **~sitz der** *(Jagdw.)* raised hide; **~sommer der** high summer; midsummer; **~sommerlich** *Adj.* very summery ⟨*weather etc.*⟩

Hoch·spannung die a) *(Elektrot.)* high voltage *or* tension; **Vorsicht, ~spannung!** danger – high voltage; **b)** *o. Pl. (gespannte Stimmung)* high tension; **es herrscht ~spannung** there's a great deal of tension

Hochspannungs-: ~leitung die high voltage *or* high tension [transmission] line; power line; **~mast der** electricity pylon

hoch-, Hoch-: ~|spielen *tr. V.* blow up ⟨*incident, affair, etc.*⟩; **~sprache die** standard language; **~sprachlich 1.** *Adj.* standard; **2.** *adv.* **sich ~sprachlich ausdrücken** speak the standard language; **~|springen** *unr. itr. V.; mit sein* **a)** jump *or* leap up; **an jmdm. ~springen** ⟨*dog etc.*⟩ jump up at sb.;

b) *nur im Inf. u. Part. gebr. (Sport)* do the high jump; **~springer der** *(Sport)* high jumper; **~sprung der** *(Sport)* high jump; *(einzelner Sprung)* jump; **~sprung·anlage die** *(Sport)* high jump apparatus

höchst [hø:çst] *Adv.* extremely; most

höchst... *s.* **hoch**

Höchstädt ['hø:çʃtɛt] **(das); ~s: die Schlacht bei ~:** the Battle of Blenheim

hoch-, Hoch-: ~stämmig *Adj.* standard ‹*rose*›; **~stand der** *(Jagdw.)* raised stand; **~stapelei** [~ʃta:pə'lai] **die; ~, ~en a)** fraud; **eine ~stapelei** a confidence trick; **b)** *(Aufschneiderei)* empty boasting; **~|stapeln** *itr. V.* **a)** perpetrate a fraud/frauds; **b)** *(aufschneiden)* make empty boasts; **~stapler** [~ʃta:plɐ] **der; ~s, ~ a)** confidence trickster; con-man *(coll.)*; **b)** *(Aufschneider)* fraud

Höchst-: ~belastung die extreme strain *or* stress *no indef. art.*; *(Technik)* maximum [safe] load; **~betrag der** maximum amount; **~bietende der/die;** *adj. Dekl.* highest bidder

hoch-: ~stehend *Adj.* ‹*person*› of high standing; **geistig ~stehend** intellectually distinguished; ‹*person*› of high intellect; **sittlich ~stehend** high-minded; **~|steigen** *unr. itr. V.; mit sein* **a)** climb; **die Treppe/Stufen ~steigen** climb the stairs/steps; **b)** ‹*bubbles, smoke, etc.*› rise; ‹*rocket*› go up; **c)** *(langsam entstehen)* rise up; ‹*tears*› well up; **Freude/Wut stieg in ihr ~:** joy rose in her heart/rage rose [up] inside her

höchst·eigen *Adj.; nicht präd. (veralt.; noch scherzh.)* **in ~er Person** in person

hoch-: ~|stellen *tr. V.* **a)** put up; **b)** *(hochklappen)* turn up ‹*collar*›; **c)** *(Math.)* **eine ~gestellte Zahl** a superior number; *s. auch* **~gestellt; ~|stemmen** *tr. V.* **a)** lift; **b)** *(aufrichten)* **sich/seinen Oberkörper ~stemmen** raise oneself [up]

höchsten·falls ['hø:çstn̩-] *Adv.* at [the] most *or* the outside; at the very most

höchstens *Adv.* **a)** *(nicht mehr als)* at most; *(bestenfalls)* at best; **in ~** *od.* **~ in drei Fällen** in three cases at most; **b)** *(außer)* **sie verreist nicht, ~ daß sie einmal zu ihren Verwandten fährt** she never goes away anywhere, apart from *or* except for visiting her relations once in a while

Höchst-: ~fall der *in* **im ~fall** at [the] most *or* the outside; at the very most; **~form die** *(bes. Sport)* peak *or* top form; **~gebot das** highest bid *or* offer; **etw. gegen ~gebot verkaufen** sell sth. to the highest bidder; **„große Briefmarkensammlung gegen ~gebot zu verkaufen"** 'offers invited for large stamp collection'; **~geschwindigkeit die** top *or* maximum speed; *(Geschwindigkeitsbegrenzung)* speed limit; **~grenze die** maximum

hoch|stilisieren *tr. V. (abwertend)* build up **(zu** into)

Hoch·stimmung die festive mood; high spirits *pl.*; **in ~ sein** be in a festive mood

höchst-, Höchst-: ~leistung die supreme performance; *(Ergebnis)* supreme achievement; *(Technik)* maximum performance; **~maß das: ein ~maß an etw.** *(Dat.)* a very high degree of sth.; **ein ~maß von etw.** *(Dat.)* a maximum [amount] of sth.; **~möglich** *Adj.; nicht präd.* highest possible; **~persönlich 1.** *Adj.; nicht präd.* personal; **2.** *adv.* in person; **~preis der** *(höchstmöglicher Preis)* highest price; *(höchstzulässiger Preis)* maximum price

Hoch·straße die overpass; flyover *(Brit.)*

hoch|streifen *tr. V.* pull up

höchst-, Höchst-: ~richterlich *Adj.; nicht präd.* **eine ~richterliche Entscheidung** a ruling of the supreme court; **~satz der** maximum *or* top rate; **~stand der** highest level; **~strafe die** maximum penalty; **~wahrscheinlich** *Adv.* very probably; **~wert der** maximum value; **~zulässig** [auch: '-'---] *Adj.; nicht präd.* maximum [permissible] ‹*weight, speed, etc.*›

hoch-, Hoch-: ~tal das high[-lying] valley; **~tour die** *in* **auf ~touren laufen** run at top *or* full speed; *(intensiv betrieben werden)* be in full swing; **einen Motor auf ~touren bringen** rev an engine up to full speed *(coll.)*; **~tourig** [~tu:rɪç] *(Technik)* **1.** *Adj.* fast-revving *(coll.)* ‹*engine*›; **2.** *adv.* **~tourig fahren** drive at high revs *(coll.)*; **~trabend** *(abwertend)* **1.** *Adj.* pretentious; high-flown; **2.** *adv.* pretentiously; in a high-flown manner; **~|tragen** *unr. tr. V.* carry up; **~|treiben** *unr. tr. V.* **a)** *(ugs.: hinauftreiben)* drive up; **die Schafe den Berg ~treiben** drive the sheep up the mountain; **b)** *(fig.)* force *or* push up ‹*prices etc.*›; **~verdient** *Adj. (präd. getrennt geschrieben)* ‹*scientist etc.*› of outstanding merit; richly deserved ‹*victory, success, etc.*›; **~verehrt** *Adj.; nicht präd.* highly respected *or* esteemed; *(als Anrede)* **meine ~verehrten Damen und Herren!** ladies and gentlemen!; **~verehrte Frau Schmidt** my dear Mrs Schmidt; **~verrat der** high treason; **~verräter der** traitor; person guilty of high treason; **~verräterisch** *Adj.* traitorous; treasonable; **~verschuldet** *Adj. (präd. getrennt geschrieben)* heavily *or* deep in debt *postpos.*; **~verzinslich** *Adj. (Finanzw.)* ‹*security etc.*› yielding a high rate of interest; **~wald der** *(Forstw.)* high forest

Hoch·wasser das *(Flut)* high tide *or* water; *(Überschwemmung)* flood; **der Fluß hat** *od.* **führt ~:** the river is in flood; **er hat ~:** *(ugs. scherzh.)* his trousers are at half-mast *(coll.)*

Hochwasser-: ~gefahr die flood danger; danger of flooding; **~hose[n] die** *(scherzh.)* trousers *pl.* at half-mast *(coll.)*; **~schaden der** flood damage

hoch-, Hoch-: ~|werfen *unr. tr. V.* **etw. ~werfen** throw sth. up; **eine Münze ~werfen** toss a coin; **~wertig** *Adj.* high-quality ‹*goods*›; highly nutritious ‹*food*›; **~wild das** *(Jägerspr.) larger game animals, eg. deer, boar, chamois;* **~willkommen** *Adj. (präd. getrennt geschrieben)* very *or* most welcome; **~|winden 1.** *unr. tr. V.* wind up; weigh ‹*anchor*›; **2.** *unr. refl. V.* wind one's/its way up; **~wirksam** *Adj. (präd. getrennt geschrieben)* highly *or* extremely effective; **~wohlgeboren** *Adj. (veralt.)* high-born; **Euer Hochwohlgeboren** Your Honour; **~|wollen** *unr. itr. V. (ugs.)* want to get up; **~|wuchten** *tr. V. (ugs.)* heave up; **~würden** *o. Art.;* **~[s]** *(veralt.)* Reverend Father; **~zahl die** *(Math.)* exponent

[1]**Hoch·zeit die** *(geh.)* Golden Age

[2]**Hochzeit** ['hɔxtsait] **die; ~, ~en** wedding; **~ halten** *od.* **machen** *(veralt.)* get married; **grüne ~:** wedding day; **silberne/goldene ~:** silver/golden wedding [anniversary]; **man kann nicht auf zwei ~en tanzen** *(fig. ugs.)* you can't be in two places at once

Hochzeiter der; ~s, ~ *(landsch.)* [bride]groom; **die ~:** the bride and groom

Hochzeiterin die; ~, ~nen *(landsch.)* bride

Hochzeits-: ~anzeige die wedding announcement; **~bitter der** *(veralt.) person who invites guests to a wedding;* **~feier die** wedding; **~flug der** *(Zool.)* nuptial flight; **~geschenk das** wedding gift *or* present; **~kleid das a)** *(Brautkleid)* wedding dress; **b)** *(Zool.) (von Vögeln)* nuptial plumage; *(von Tieren)* nuptial coloration; **~kuchen der** wedding cake; **~nacht die** wedding night; **~reise die** honeymoon [trip]; **wir haben unsere ~reise nach Berlin gemacht** we went to Berlin for our honeymoon; **~tag der a)** wedding day; **b)** *(Jahrestag)* wedding anniversary; **~zug der** wedding procession

hoch-, Hoch-: ~|ziehen 1. *unr. tr. V.* **a)** *(nach oben ziehen)* pull up; pull up, raise ‹*shutters, blind*›; hoist, raise, run up ‹*flag*›; hoist ‹*sail*›; **die Schultern/Brauen ~ziehen** hunch one's shoulders/raise one's eyebrows; **die Nase ~ziehen** sniff [loudly]; **b) ein Flugzeug ~ziehen** put an aircraft into a steep climb; **c)** *(mauern)* put up, build ‹*wall, building*›; **2.** *unr. refl. V.* **sich [an etw.** *(Dat.)*] **~ziehen** pull oneself up [by hanging on to sth.]; **sich an etw.** *(Dat.)* **~ziehen** *(fig.)* latch on to sth.; **~zins·politik die** policy of keeping interest rates high

Hocke ['hɔkə] **die; ~, ~n a)** *(Körperhaltung)* squat; crouch; **in der ~ sitzen** squat; crouch; **in die ~ gehen** squat [down]; crouch down; **b)** *(Turnen)* squat vault

hocken 1. *itr. V.* **a)** *mit haben od. (südd.) sein* squat; crouch; **b)** *mit haben od. (südd.) sein (ugs.: sich aufhalten)* sit around; **hinter einem Schreibtisch ~:** sit behind a desk; **c)** *mit sein (südd.: sitzen)* sit; **d)** *mit sein (Turnen)* perform *or* do a squat vault **(über +** *Akk.* over). **2.** *refl. V.* **a)** crouch down; squat [down]; **b)** *(südd.: sich setzen)* sit down

Hocker der; ~s, ~: stool

Höcker ['hœkɐ] **der; ~s, ~ a)** hump; *(auf der Nase)* bump; *(auf dem Schnabel)* knob; **er hat einen ~:** he's humpbacked; **b)** *(Hügel)* hillock; hump

Hocker·grab das *(Archäol.)* crouched burial

höckerig *Adj.* bumpy

Höcker·schwan der mute swan

Hockey ['hɔki] **das; ~s** hockey

Hockey-: ~schläger der hockey stick; **~spieler der** hockey player

Hock-: ~sitz der *(Turnen)* squat; **~stand der** *(Turnen)* crouch

Hoden ['ho:dn̩] **der; ~s, ~:** testicle

Hoden-: ~bruch der *(Med.)* scrotal hernia; **~sack der** scrotum

Hoek van Holland ['hʊk 'fan 'hɔlant] **(das); Hoeks van Holland** Hook of Holland

Hof [ho:f] **der; ~[e]s, Höfe** ['hø:fə] **a)** courtyard; *(Schul~)* playground; *(Gefängnis~)* [prison] yard; **b)** *(Bauern~)* farm; **in einen ~ einheiraten** marry into a farming family; **c)** *(Herrscher, Hofstaat)* court; **am ~ leben/verkehren** live at court/move in court circles; **die europäischen Höfe** the European royal courts; **jmdn. bei ~e einführen/vorstellen** present sb. at court; **d) jmdm. den ~ machen** *(veralt.)* pay court to sb.; **f)** *(Aureole)* corona; aureole; **g)** *(in Namen von Hotels, z. B. „Bayerischer Hof") (implying or suggesting a particular, e.g. Bavarian, style and a superior standard of accommodation)*

hof-, Hof-: ~amt das *(hist.)* [hereditary] office at court; **~ball der** court ball; **~dame die** lady of the court; *(Begleiterin der Königin)* lady-in-waiting; **~dichter der** *(hist.)* court poet; **~etikette die** court etiquette; **~fähig** *Adj.* presentable at court *pred.*; *(fig.)* [socially] acceptable

Hoffart ['hɔfart] **die; ~** *(veralt. abwertend)* overweening pride; haughtiness

hoffärtig ['hɔfɛrtɪç] *(veralt. abwertend)* **1.** *Adj.* haughty. **2.** *adv.* haughtily

hoffen ['hɔfn̩] **1.** *tr. V.* hope; **ich hoffe es/will es ~:** I hope so/can only hope so; **ich will es [doch wohl] ~:** I should hope so; **ich will nicht ~, daß sie das macht** I hope she doesn't do that; **ich will es nicht ~:** I hope not; **es bleibt zu ~, daß ...:** let us hope that ...; **das wollen wir ~:** let's hope so; **~ wir das Beste** let's hope for the best. **2.** *itr. V.* **a)** *(vertrauen)* **auf etw.** *(Akk.)* **~:** hope for sth.; *(Vertrauen setzen auf)* **auf jmdn./etw. ~:** put one's trust *or* faith in sb./sth.; **b)** *(Hoffnung haben)* hope

hoffentlich ['hɔfn̩tlɪç] *Adv.* hopefully; **~!** let's hope so; **~ ist ihr nichts passiert** I do hope nothing's happened to her; **es ist dir doch ~ recht** I hope it's all right with you

-höffig [-hœfɪç] *adj.* promising to be rich in ‹*oil, gas, uranium, etc.*›

Hoffnung ['hɔfnʊŋ] **die; ~, ~en** hope; **seine ~ auf jmdn./etw. setzen** pin one's hopes *pl.* on sb./sth.; **keine ~ mehr haben, die ~ aufgegeben haben** have given up [all] hope; **sich** *(Dat.)* **[falsche] ~en machen** have [false] hopes; **jmdm. ~en machen** raise sb.'s hopes; **jmdm. auf etw.** *(Akk.)* **~en machen** lead sb. to expect sth.; **guter ~ sein** *(veralt.)* be expecting [a baby]; be with child *(dated)*; **in der ~ auf etw.** *(Akk.)* in the hope of sth.

hoffnungs-, Hoffnungs-: ~froh *(geh.)* **1.** *Adj.* hopeful; **2.** *adv.* hopefully; ⟨*smile etc.*⟩ in happy anticipation; **~funke[n] der;** *o. Pl. (geh.)* spark *or* glimmer of hope; **~lauf der** *(Sport)* repêchage; **~los 1.** *Adj.* hopeless; despairing ⟨*person*⟩; **2.** *adv.* hopelessly; **~losigkeit die; ~:** despair; *(der Lage)* hopelessness; **~schimmer der** *(geh.)* glimmer of hope; **~strahl der** *(geh.)* ray of hope; **~voll 1.** *Adj.* **a)** hopeful; full of hope *pred.*; **jmdn. ~voll stimmen** give sb. cause to hope *or* make sb. hopeful; **b)** *(erfolgversprechend)* promising; **2.** *adv.* **a)** full of hope; **b)** *(erfolgversprechend)* promisingly

Hof·gang der exercise; **während des ~es** during the exercise period

hof-, Hof-: ~gesellschaft die court; **~|halten** *unr. itr. V.* hold court; **~haltung die** running of the court; *(Haushalt)* court; **~hund der** watchdog

hofieren [ho'fi:rən] *tr. V. (geh.)* pay court to

höfisch ['hø:fɪʃ] *Adj.* courtly

Hof-: ~knicks der curtsy; **~kreise** *Pl.* **in in/aus ~kreisen** in/from court circles; **~leben das** life at court; court life

höflich ['hø:flɪç] **1.** *Adj.* polite; courteous; **etw. in ~em Ton fragen/sagen** ask/say sth. politely. **2.** *adv.* politely; courteously

Höflichkeit die; ~, ~en a) *o. Pl.* politeness; courteousness; **etw. [nur] aus ~ tun/sagen** do/say sth. [only] to be polite *or* out of politeness; **b)** *meist Pl. (höfliche Redensart)* civility; courtesy

höflichkeits-, Höflichkeits-: ~besuch der courtesy visit; **~floskel, ~formel die** polite phrase; **~halber** *Adv.* to be polite; out of politeness

Hof·lieferant der *(veralt.)* supplier to the court; **königlicher ~:** supplier to the royal court; *(von Lebensmitteln)* purveyor to the royal court

Höfling ['hø:flɪŋ] **der; ~s, ~e** courtier

Hof-: ~marschall der major-domo; **~meister der** *(veralt.)* court tutor and master of ceremonies; **~narr der** *(hist.)* court jester; **~prediger der** court chaplain; **~rat der** *(veralt., noch österr.) honorary title conferred on senior civil servant;* **~sänger der a)** *(hist.)* court minstrel; **b)** *(ugs.)* courtyard busker; **~schranze die** *od.* **der** *(veralt. abwertend)* fawning courtier; **~staat der;** *o. Pl.* court; **~theater das** court theatre; **~tor das** courtyard gate; **~tür die** courtyard door

HO-Geschäft [ha:|'o:-] **das** *(DDR) shop owned by the Handelsorganisation*

hoh... ['ho:ə...] *s.* **hoch**

Höhe ['hø:ə] **die; ~, ~n a)** *(Ausdehnung nach oben)* height; **das ist ja die ~!** *(ugs.)* that's the limit!; **b)** *(Entfernung nach oben)* height; altitude; **in einer ~ von 4000 m fliegen/eine ~ von 4000 m erreichen** fly at/reach a height *or* altitude of 4,000 m.; **an ~ gewinnen/verlieren** gain/lose height *or* altitude; **in großen ~n** at great heights *or* high altitudes; **auf halber ~:** at mid-altitude; **c)** *(Richtung)* **etw. in die ~ heben** lift sth. up; **in die ~ [auf]steigen** rise up[wards]; **d)** *(Gipfelpunkt)* height; **auf der ~ seines Ruhmes/Könnens/Erfolges sein** be at the height of one's fame/ability/success; **auf der ~ sein** *(fig. ugs.) (gesund sein)* be fit; *(sich wohl fühlen)* feel fine; **nicht [ganz] auf der ~ sein** *(fig. ugs.)* be/feel a bit under the weather *(coll.)*; not be/feel quite oneself; **e)** *(meßbare Größe)* level; *(von Einkommen)* size; level; **die ~ der Geschwindigkeit/Temperatur** the speed/temperature level; **Unkosten/ein Stipendium in ~ von 5000 DM** expenses/a grant of 5,000 DM; **f)** *(Linie)* **auf gleicher ~ sein/fahren** be in line abreast *or* be level/travel in line abreast; **die Pferde waren auf gleicher ~:** the horses were neck and neck; **auf ~ des Leuchtturms/von Hull sein** *(Seemannsspr.)* be level with *or* abreast of the lighthouse *etc.*/be off Hull; **g)** *(hoher Grad)* high level; **h)** *(Anhöhe)* hill; **die ~n und Tiefen des Lebens** *(fig.)* the ups and downs of life; **i)** *(Math., Astron.)* altitude; **j)** *Pl. (Akustik)* treble *sing.*

Hoheit ['ho:hait] **die; ~, ~en a)** *o. Pl. (Souveränität)* sovereignty (**über** + *Akk.* over); **unter der ~ eines Staates stehen** be under the sovereignty of a state; **b) Seine/Ihre ~:** His/Your Highness; **c)** *o. Pl. (geh.: Würde)* majestic dignity; majesty

hoheitlich *Adj.* **a)** sovereign; **b)** *(selten) s.* **hoheitsvoll**

hoheits-, Hoheits-: ~ab·zeichen das national emblem; **~gebiet das** [sovereign] territory; **~gewässer das;** *meist Pl.* territorial waters; **~recht das;** *meist Pl.* right of the state; **~voll** *Adj.* majestic; stately ⟨*gesture*⟩; **~zeichen das** national emblem

Hohe·lied das; Hohenlied[e]s a) *(bibl.)* **das ~:** The Song of Songs; **b)** *(fig. geh.)* song of praise; **ein ~ der Liebe** a song in praise of love

höhen-, Höhen-: ~an·gabe die altitude reading; *(auf Karten)* altitude marking; **~angst die;** *o. Pl.* fear of heights; **~flug der** *(Flugw.)* high-altitude flight; *(fig.)* flight; **im ~flug** at high altitude; **~gleich** *(Verkehrsw.)* **1.** *Adj.* level ⟨*crossing*⟩; **2.** *adv.* at the same level; **~klima das** mountain climate; **~krankheit die** altitude sickness; **~lage die** altitude; **in ~lage** at high altitude; **in ~lagen über 1500 m** at altitudes over 1,500 m.; **~leitwerk das** *(Flugw.)* tailplane; **~linie die** *(Geogr.)* contour [line]; **~luft die;** *o. Pl.* mountain air; air at high altitude; **~marke die** *(Vermessungsw.)* bench-mark; **~messer der** altimeter; **~messung die** measurement of height; **~rekord der** altitude record; **~ruder das** *(Flugw.)* elevator; **~sonne die a)** *(Med.: Quarzlampe)* ultra-violet lamp; sun lamp; **b)** *(Med.: Bestrahlung)* ultra-violet radiation treatment; sun lamp treatment; **c)** *(Met.)* high-altitude solar radiation; **~steuer das** *(Flugw.)* elevator control; **~strahlung die** *(Physik)* cosmic radiation; **~training das** *(Sport)* [high-]altitude training; **~unterschied der** altitude difference; difference in altitude; **~weg der** ridge path; **~winkel der** *(Geom.)* angle of elevation; **~zug der** *(Geogr.)* range of hills; *(Bergkette)* range of mountains; mountain range

Hohe·priester der; Hohenpriesters, Hohenpriester *(bibl.)* high priest

Höhepunkt der high point; *(einer Veranstaltung)* high spot; highlight; *(einer Laufbahn, des Ruhms)* peak; pinnacle; *(einer Krankheit)* crisis; critical point; *(einer Krise)* turning-point; *(der Macht)* summit; pinnacle; *(des Glücks)* height; *(Orgasmus; eines Stückes)* climax; **auf dem ~ seiner Laufbahn stehen** be at the peak of one's career

höher ['hø:ɐ] *s.* **hoch**

höher-, Höher-: ~gestellt *Adj. (präd. getrennt geschrieben)* senior ⟨*official, civil servant*⟩; **die ~gestellten Persönlichkeiten** the more prominent public figures; **~|schrauben** *tr. V.* force *or* push up ⟨*prices*⟩; **~stufung die** upgrading

hohl [ho:l] **1.** *Adj.* **a)** *(leer)* hollow; **sich innerlich ~ fühlen** *(fig.)* feel empty inside; **b)** *(nach innen gebogen)* cupped ⟨*hand*⟩; sunken, hollow ⟨*cheeks, eyes*⟩; concave ⟨*lens, mirror*⟩; **ein ~es Kreuz** a hollow back; **c)** *(dumpf)* hollow ⟨*sound, voice, etc.*⟩; **d)** *(abwertend: geistlos)* hollow, empty ⟨*phrases, slogans*⟩; empty ⟨*talk, chatter*⟩; shallow ⟨*person*⟩. **2.** *adv.* **a)** *(dumpf)* hollowly; **b)** *(abwertend: geistlos)* inanely

hohl·äugig *Adj.* hollow-eyed; sunken-eyed

Hohl·block·stein der *(Bauw.)* hollow block

Höhle ['hø:lə] **die; ~, ~n a)** cave; *(größer)* cavern; **b)** *(Tierbau)* den; lair; *(von Höhlenbrütern)* nest; **sich in die ~ des Löwen begeben** *(scherzh.)* enter the lion's den; **c)** *(abwertend: Wohnung)* hole; **d)** *meist Pl. (Augen~)* socket

Hohl·eisen das *(Handw.)* gouge; hollow chisel

höhlen ['hø:lən] *tr. V.* hollow out; **steter Tropfen höhlt den Stein** *(Spr.)* these things take their toll eventually

Höhlen-: ~bär der cave-bear; **~brüter der** *(Zool.)* bird that nests in holes; hole-nester; **~forscher der** speleologist; *(Sportler)* caver; **~forschung die** speleology; *(als Sport)* caving; **~malerei die** cave-painting; **~mensch der** cave-dweller; cave-man; **~zeichnung die** cave-painting

Hohlheit die; ~ a) hollowness; **b)** *(innere Leere, auch fig. abwertend)* emptiness

hohl-, Hohl-: ~kopf der *(abwertend)* idiot *(coll.)*; dimwit; **~köpfig** *Adj. (abwertend)* idiotic *(coll.)*; blockheaded; **~körper der** hollow body; **~kreuz das** hollow back; lordosis *(Med.)*; **~kugel die** hollow sphere; **~maß das a)** *(Maßeinheit)* measure of capacity; **b)** *(Gefäß)* dry/liquid measure; **~nadel die** *(Med.)* cannula; *(für Einspritzungen)* hypodermic needle; **~raum der** cavity; [hollow] space; **~raum·versiegelung die** *(Kfz-W.)* body-cavity sealing; **~saum der** *(Handarb.)* hem-stitch; **~schliff der** hollow grinding; **eine Klinge mit ~schliff** a hollow-ground blade; **~spiegel der** concave mirror; **~tier das** coelenterate

Höhlung die; ~, ~en a) *(das Aushöhlen)* excavation; **b)** *(Vertiefung)* hollow

hohl-, Hohl-: ~wangig *Adj.* hollow-cheeked; sunken-cheeked; **~weg der** defile; *(Durchstich)* cutting; **~ziegel der** perforated tile; *(Dachziegel)* concave tile

Hohn [ho:n] **der; ~[e]s** scorn; derision; **jmdn. mit ~ und Spott überschütten** pour *or* heap scorn on sb.; **das ist der reine** *od.* **der blanke ~** *(fig.)* it is just grotesque

höhnen ['hø:nən] *(geh.) itr. V.* jeer; sneer

Hohn·gelächter das derisive *or* scornful laughter

höhnisch ['hø:nɪʃ] **1.** *Adj.* scornful; derisive. **2.** *adv.* scornfully; derisively

hohn-: ~lächeln, ~|lächeln *itr. V.* **er ~lächelte** *od.* **lächelte ~:** he smiled scornfully *or* derisively; **ein Hohnlächeln** a scornful *or* derisive smile; **~lachen, ~|lachen** *itr. V.* **a)** laugh scornfully *or* derisively; **ein Hohnlachen** a scornful *or* derisive laugh; **b)** *(geh.: zuwiderlaufen)* **einer Sache** *(Dat.)* **~lachen** fly in the face of sth.; **~|sprechen** *unr. itr. V.* **einer Sache** *(Dat.)* **~sprechen** fly in the face of sth.

Höker ['hø:kɐ] **der; ~s, ~, Hökerin die; ~, ~nen** *(veralt.) (auf dem Markt)* stallholder; *(auf der Straße)* street trader; street pedlar *(Amer.)*

hökern *itr. V. (auf dem Markt)* run a market-stall; *(auf der Straße)* run a street-stall

Hokuspokus [ho:kʊs'po:kʊs] **der; ~:** hocus-pocus; *(abwertend: Drum und Dran)* fuss

hold [hɔlt] **1.** *Adj.* **a)** *(dichter. veralt.: anmutig)* fair; lovely; lovely ⟨*sight*⟩; sweet, lovely ⟨*smile*⟩; **die ~e Weiblichkeit** *(scherzh.)* the fair sex; **mein ~er Gatte/mei-**

ne ~e Gattin *(scherzh.)* my beloved spouse *(joc.)*; **b)** *in* **jmdm./einer Sache ~ sein** *(geh.)* be well-disposed towards sb./sth.; *(jmdn./etw. gern haben)* be fond of sb./sth.; **das Glück war uns** *(Dat.)* **~:** fortune smiled upon us. **2.** *adv.* sweetly

Holder der; ~s, ~ *(bes. südd.) s.* **Holunder**

Holding·gesellschaft ['ho:ldıŋ-] **die** *(Wirtsch.)* holding company

Holdrio ['hɔldrio] **das; ~s, ~s** halloo

hold·selig *(dichter. veralt.)* **1.** *Adj.* sweet; lovely; lovely ‹*sight, appearance*›. **2.** *adv.* sweetly

holen ['ho:lən] **1.** *tr. V.* **a)** fetch; get; **jmdn. aus dem Bett ~:** get *or (coll.)* drag sb. out of bed; **da/bei ihr ist nichts/nichts mehr zu ~** *(fig.)* you won't get anything/any more there/out of her; **b)** *(ab~)* fetch; pick up; collect; take away ‹*suspect, prisoner, etc.*›; **c)** *(ugs.: erlangen)* get, win ‹*prize*›; get, carry off, win ‹*medal, trophy, etc.*›; get, score ‹*points*›; **den Sieg ~:** win; **d)** *(landsch.: kaufen)* buy; get; **e)** *(Seemannsspr.: herabziehen)* take in ‹*sail*›; haul ‹*boat*› alongside. **2.** *refl. V.* **a)** *(sich verschaffen)* get; **sich** *(Dat.)* **Hilfe/Rat** *usw.* **~:** get [some] help/advice *etc.*; **b)** *(erlangen)* win, take ‹*championship, prize, etc.*›; **sich** *(Dat.)* **eine Niederlage ~:** be beaten; lose; **c)** *(ugs.: sich zuziehen)* catch; **sich** *(Dat.)* **[beim Baden** *usw.***] einen Schnupfen/die Grippe ~:** catch a cold/the flu [swimming *etc.*]; **sich** *(Dat.)* **den Tod ~** *(fig.)* catch one's death [of cold]

holla ['hɔla] *Interj.* hallo; hello; hey

Holland ['hɔlant] **(das); ~s** Holland

Holländer ['hɔlɛndɐ] **1. der; ~s, ~ a)** Dutchman; **er ist ~:** he is Dutch *or* a Dutchman; **die ~:** the Dutch; **b)** *(Käse)* Dutch cheese; **c)** *(Papierherstellung)* Hollander. **2.** *indekl. Adj.; nicht präd.* **~ Käse** Dutch cheese

Holländerin die; ~, ~nen Dutchwoman/Dutch girl

holländisch *Adj.* Dutch; *s. auch* **deutsch; Deutsch**

Holle *in* **Frau Holle schüttelt die Betten [aus]** *(veralt.)* it is snowing; the old woman is plucking her geese *(dated)*

Hölle ['hœlə] **die; ~, ~n a)** hell *no art.*; **in die ~ kommen** go to hell; **zur ~ fahren** *(geh.)* descend into hell; **jmdn. zur ~ wünschen** *(geh.)* wish sb. to hell; **zur ~ mit ihm/damit!** to hell with him/it *(coll.)*; **b)** *(fig.)* **die ~ ist los** *(ugs.)* all hell has broken loose *(coll.)*; **es war die reinste ~:** it was pure hell *(coll.)*; **die ~ auf Erden haben** suffer hell on earth; **jmdm. das Leben zur ~ machen** make sb.'s life hell *(coll.)*; **jmdm. die ~ heiß machen** give sb. hell *(coll.)*; **die grüne ~:** the jungle; *s. auch* **Vorsatz**

Höllen-: ~angst die *(salopp)* terror; **eine ~angst vor etw.** *(Dat.)* **haben** be scared to death of sth. *(coll.)*; be terrified of sth.; **~fahrt die** *(Myth., Rel.)* descent into hell; **~feuer das** hellfire; **das ~feuer** the fires *pl.* of hell; **~fürst der;** *o. Pl.* Prince of Darkness; **~hund der** *(Myth.)* hell-hound; hound of hell; **~lärm der** *(ugs.)* diabolical noise *or* row *(coll.)*; **~maschine die** infernal machine *(arch.)*; time bomb; **~pein, ~qual die** agony; **~qualen erleiden** suffer the torments of hell *(fig.)*; suffer terrible agony *sing.*; **~spektakel das** *(ugs.) s.* **~lärm**; **~stein der** lunar caustic; **~tempo das (ugs.)** breakneck speed; **in einem ~tempo** at breakneck speed

Holler ['hɔlɐ] **der; ~s, ~** *(bes. südd., österr.) s.* **Holunder**

höllisch ['hœlıʃ] **1.** *Adj.* **a)** *nicht präd.* infernal; ‹*spirits, torments*› of hell; **b)** *(schrecklich)* terrible ‹*war, situation*›; fiendish, diabolical ‹*invention, laughter*›; **~e Schmerzen** terrible agony *sing.*; **c)** *(ugs.: sehr groß)* tremendous *(coll.)* ‹*noise, shock, respect*› *(coll.)*; enormous *(coll.)* ‹*pleasure*›; **~e Angst vor etw.** *(Dat.)* **haben** be scared stiff of sth. *(coll.)*. **2.** *adv.* *(ugs.: sehr)* terribly, hellishly *(coll.)*‹*cold, difficult*›; **sich ~ zusammennehmen** make a tremendous effort to control oneself *(coll.)*; **~ [genau] aufpassen** be tremendously careful *(coll.)*; **es tut ~ weh** it hurts like hell *(coll.)*

Hollywood·schaukel ['hɔlıwʊd-] **die** swinging garden hammock

Holm [hɔlm] **der; ~[e]s, ~e a)** *(Turnen)* bar; **b)** *(Leiter~)* upright; side-piece; **c)** *(Geländer~)* [banister] rail; **d)** *(Flugw.)* spar

Holocaust [holo'kaust] **der; ~[s], ~s** Holocaust

Hologramm [holo'gram] **das** *(Physik)* hologram

Holographie [hologra'fi:] **die; ~** *(Physik)* holography *no art.*

Holozän [holo'tsɛ:n] **das; ~s** *(Geol.)* Holocene

holperig *s.* **holprig**

holpern ['hɔlpɐn] *itr. V.* **a)** *mit sein (fahren)* jolt; bump; **b)** *(schütteln)* jolt; **c)** *(stockend lesen)* stumble [over one's words]

holprig ['hɔlprıç] **1.** *Adj.* **a)** *(uneben)* bumpy; uneven; rough; **b)** *(stockend)* stumbling, halting ‹*speech*›; clumsy ‹*verses*›; broken, halting ‹*English etc.*›. **2.** *adv.* haltingly; **~ lesen** stumble over one's words when reading

Hol·schuld ['ho:l-] **die** *(Rechtsw.) debt to be collected at the debtor's residence*

Holster ['hɔlstɐ] **das; ~s, ~:** holster

holterdiepolter [hɔltɐdi'pɔltɐ] *Adv.* *(ugs.)* helter-skelter; **alles ging ~:** there was a mad rush

holüber [ho:l'|y:bɐ] *Interj.* **[Fährmann] ~!** ferry[man]!

Holunder [ho'lʊndɐ] **der; ~s, ~ a)** *(Strauch)* elder; **b)** *o. Pl. (Früchte)* elderberries *pl.*

Holunder-: ~beere die elderberry; **~strauch der** elder[berry] bush; **~tee der** elder tea

Holz [hɔlts] **das; ~es, Hölzer** ['hœltsɐ] **a)** *o. Pl.* wood; *(Bau~, Tischler~)* timber; wood; **bearbeitetes ~:** timber *(Brit.)*; lumber *(Amer.)*; **ein Stück/Festmeter ~:** a piece of wood *or* timber/cubic metre of timber; **viel ~** *(fig. ugs.)* a hell of a lot *(coll.)*; **[viel] ~ vor der Hütte** *od.* **Tür haben** *(fig. ugs. scherzh.)* be well stacked *(coll.) or* well endowed; **ich bin nicht aus ~:** I've got feelings, you know; **b)** *(~art)* wood; **aus dem ~ sein, aus dem man Minister/Helden macht** be cut out to be a minister/be of the stuff heroes are made of; **aus dem gleichen ~ [geschnitzt] sein** *(fig.)* be cast in the same mould; **aus anderem ~ [geschnitzt] sein** *(fig.)* be cast in a different mould; **c)** *(Forstw.)* felled trunk; **d)** *(Golf)* wood; **e) den Ball mit dem ~ schlagen/treffen** *(Tennis, Badminton)* hit the ball with the wood; **f)** *Pl.* **~** *(Kegeln)* skittles; ninepins; **gut ~!** have a good game! *(skittle-players' greeting)*; **g)** *o. Pl. (Musik)* woodwind; **h)** *(Streich~)* match; **i)** *o. Pl. (veralt., Jägerspr.: Wald)* wood

holz-, Holz-: ~apfel der a) crab-apple; **b)** *(Baum)* crab-apple tree; **~arbeiter der** *s.* **~fäller; ~arm** *Adj.* ‹*country*› with little timber of its own; **~arm sein** have little timber of its own; **~art die** kind of wood *or* timber; **~auge das** *in* **~auge sei wachsam!** *(scherzh.)* better be careful; **~bearbeitung die** processing of timber; timber processing; *(in der Tischlerei)* woodworking; **~bein das** wooden leg; **~bläser der** woodwind player; **~blas·instrument das** woodwind instrument; **~block der;** *Pl.* **~blöcke** block of wood; **~bock der a)** *(Gestell)* wooden stand *or trestle*; **b)** *(Zecke)* castor-bean tick; **c)** *(Käfer)* poplar longhorn; **~bohrer der a)** wood drill; **b)** *(Schmetterling)* goat moth; carpenter moth; **~bündel das** bundle of wood

Hölzchen ['hœltsçən] **das; ~s, ~ a)** small piece of wood; *(Stöckchen)* stick; **b)** *(Streichholz)* match

Holz-: ~diele die plank; *(für Fußböden)* [floor]board; **~dübel der** wooden dowel; *(in der Wand)* wooden plug

holzen *itr. V.* *(Fußballjargon)* play dirty *(coll.)*

Holzerei die; ~, ~en a) *(Fußballjargon)* dirty play; **eine ~:** a dirty game *or* match; **b)** *(Prügelei)* brawl; free-for-all

hölzern ['hœltsṇ] *Adj.; nicht präd. (auch fig.)* wooden

holz-, Holz-: ~essig der wood vinegar; **~fäller der** woodcutter; lumberjack *(Amer.)*; **~feuer das** wood fire; **~frei** *Adj.* wood-free ‹*paper*›; **~gas das** wood-gas; **~geist der** wood spirit; **~geschnitzt** *Adj.* carved wooden *attrib.*; carved in wood *pred.*; **~hacker der a)** *(bes. österr.) s.* **~fäller; b)** *(Fußballjargon)* dirty player; **~haltig** *Adj.* woody ‹*paper*›; ‹*paper*› containing mechanical wood pulp

Holz·hammer der [wooden] mallet

Holzhammer·methode die *(ugs.)* sledgehammer method

Holz-: ~handel der timber trade; **~haus das** timber *or* wooden house

holzig *Adj.* woody

holz-, Holz-: ~industrie die timber industry; **~kitt der** plastic wood; **~klotz der** block of wood; *(als Spielzeug)* wooden block; **dasitzen wie ein ~klotz** *(fig.)* sit there like a stuffed dummy; **~kohle die** charcoal; **~kohlen·grill der** charcoal grill; **~kopf der a)** wooden head; **b)** *(salopp abwertend)* blockhead; numskull; **~kreuz das** wooden cross; **~lager das** timber yard; **~leim der** wood-glue; **~leiste die** batten; **~malerei die** painting on wood; wood painting; **~nagel der** wooden nail; **~pantine die** *(landsch.)*, **~pantoffel der** clog; **~pflock der** wooden stake; **~sandale die** wooden sandal; **~schädling der** wood pest; **~schale die** wooden bowl; **~scheit das** piece of wood; *(Brenn~)* piece of firewood; **~schläger der** *(Golf)* wood; **~schneider der** wood-engraver; **~schnitt der a)** *o. Pl.* woodcutting *no art.*; **b)** *(Blatt)* woodcut; **~schnitt·artig** *Adj.* *(fig.)* simplistic; **~schnitzer der** woodcarver; **~schnitzerei die** wood-carving; **~schraube die** wood screw; **~schuh der** clog; **~schuh·tanz der** clog-dance; **~schuppen der a)** *(aus Holz)* wooden shed; **b)** *(für Holz)* wood-shed; **~span der a)** *(zum Feueranzünden)* stick of firewood; *(zum Rühren usw.)* small stick [of wood]; **b)** *meist Pl. (Hobelspan)* [wood] shaving; **~spielzeug das** wooden toy; **~spiritus der** wood alcohol; **~splitter der** splinter of wood; **~stab der** wooden rod; **~stich der** wood-engraving; **~stift der** *s.* **~nagel; ~stock der a)** [wooden] stick; **b)** *(Graphik)* wood-block; **~stoß der** pile of wood; **~täfelung die** wood[en] panelling; **~teer der** wood tar; **~treppe die** wooden steps *pl.*; **~verarbeitend** *Adj.; nicht präd.* timber processing ‹*industry etc.*›; **~verschlag der a)** area divided off by a wooden partition; **b)** *(Schuppen)* wooden shed; **~waren** *Pl.* wooden articles; **~weg der** *(fig.) in* **auf dem ~weg sein** *od.* **sich auf dem ~weg befinden** be on the wrong track *(fig.)*; be barking up the wrong tree *(fig.)*; **wenn du glaubst, du kannst das verhindern, so bist du auf dem ~weg** if you think you can prevent it, you're very much mistaken *or (coll.)* you've got another think coming; **~wirtschaft die** timber industry; **~wolle die;** *o. Pl.* wood-wool; **~wurm der** woodworm

Homburg ['hɔmbʊrk] **der; ~s, ~s** Homburg

homerisch [ho'me:rıʃ] *Adj.* Homeric; **ein ~es Gelächter** Homeric laughter

Home·trainer ['hoʊm-] **der** exerciser
Hommage [ɔ'ma:ʒ] **die;** ~, ~**n** *(geh.)* tribute (**für** to)
homo *Adj.; nur präd. (ugs.)* queer *(coll.)*
Homo ['ho:mo] **der;** ~**s,** ~**s** *(ugs.)* queer *(coll.),* homo *(coll.)*
homo-, Homo-: ~**erotisch** *Adj. (geh.)* homo-erotic *(Psych.);* homosexual; ~**gen** [~'ge:n] *Adj.* homogeneous; ~**genisieren** *tr. V.* **a)** *(Chemie, Metallbearb.)* homogenize; **b)** *(geh.)* homogenize; integrate ⟨*groups*⟩; ~**genität** [~geni'tɛ:t] **die;** ~ *(geh.)* homogeneity; ~**log** [~'lo:k] *Adj. (Biol., Math., Chemie)* homologous; ~**logieren** *tr. V. (Motorsport)* homologate; ~**nym** [~'ny:m] *Adj. (Sprachw.)* homonymous; ~**nym das;** ~**s,** ~**e** *(Sprachw.)* homonym; ~**nymie** [homony'mi:] **die;** ~ *(Sprachw.)* homonymy
homöo-, Homöo- [homøo-]: ~**path** [~'pa:t] **der;** ~**en,** ~**en** homoeopath; ~**pathie die;** ~: homoeopathy *no art.;* ~**pathisch** *Adj.* homoeopathic
homo-, Homo-: ~**phil** [~'fi:l] *Adj. (geh.)* homophile; ~**phon das;** ~**s,** ~**e** *(Sprachw.)* homophone; ~**sexualität die;** ~: homosexuality; ~**sexuell 1.** *Adj.* homosexual; **2.** *adv.* ~**sexuell veranlagt sein** have homosexual tendencies; ~**sexuelle der/die;** *adj. Dekl.* homosexual
Homunkulus [ho'mʊŋkulʊs] **der;** ~, ~**se** *od.* **Homunkuli** homunculus
Honduras [hɔn'du:ras] **(das); Honduras'** Honduras
honen ['ho:nən] *tr. V. (Technik)* hone
honett [hɔ'nɛt] *Adj. (geh.) (rechtschaffen)* honest; upright; *(anständig)* decent; *(ehrenhaft)* honourable
Hongkong ['hɔŋkɔŋ] **(das);** ~**s** Hong Kong
Honig ['ho:nɪç] **der;** ~**s,** ~**e** honey; **jmdm. ~ um den Bart** *(ugs.) od. (salopp)* **ums Maul schmieren** *(fig.)* butter sb. up
honig-, Honig-: ~**biene die** honey-bee; ~**brot das** bread and honey; **ein ~brot** a slice of bread and honey; ~**farben** *Adj.* honey-coloured; ~**gelb** *Adj.* honey-yellow; ~**kuchen der** honey cake; ~**kuchen·pferd das** *in* **lachen** *od.* **grinsen** *od.* **strahlen wie ein ~kuchenpferd** *(ugs. scherzh.)* grin like a Cheshire cat; ~**lecken das** *in* **das ist kein ~lecken** *(ugs.)* it is not a bed of roses; ~**melone die** honeydew melon; ~**schlecken das** *s.* ~**lecken;** ~**süß 1.** *Adj.* ⟨*grapes, taste, etc.*⟩ as sweet as honey; *(fig.)* honey-sweet ⟨*voice*⟩; **ein ~süßes Lächeln** *(fig.)* the sweetest of smiles; **mit ~süßer Stimme** *(fig.)* in honeyed tones; **2.** *adv. (fig.)* ~**süß lächeln/antworten** smile a honey-sweet smile/answer in honeyed tones; ~**tau der** honeydew; ~**wabe die** honeycomb; ~**wein der** mead; ~**zelle die** honey[comb] cell
Honneur [(h)ɔ'nø:ɐ̯] *in* **die ~s machen** *(veralt.)* do the honours
Honorar [hono'ra:ɐ̯] **das;** ~**s,** ~**e** fee; *(Autoren~)* royalty
Honorar·professor der *professor who is not primarily an academic and has no voice in faculty matters*
Honoratioren [honora'tsio:rən] *Pl.* notabilities
honorieren *tr. V.* **a) jmdn. ~:** pay sb. [a/his/her fee]; **jmds. Leistung/Buch ~:** pay sb. [a/his/her fee] for his/her work/book; **b)** *(würdigen)* appreciate; *(belohnen)* reward; **c)** *(Finanzw.)* honour ⟨*cheque*⟩
Honorierung die; ~, ~**en a)** payment; **b)** *(Würdigung)* appreciation; *(Belohnung)* rewarding; **c)** *(Finanzw.)* honouring
honorig *Adj.* honourable; respectable
honoris causa [ho'no:rɪs 'kauza] *Adv.* honoris causa; **Doktor ~ ~:** honorary doctor
hopfen ['hɔpfn̩] *tr. V.* hop ⟨*beer*⟩
Hopfen der; ~**s,** ~: hop; **bei ihm ist ~ und Malz verloren** *(ugs.)* he's a hopeless case
Hopfen-: ~**garten der** hop-garden; ~**stange die** hop-pole
hopp [hɔp] **1.** *Interj.* quick; look sharp. **2.** *Adv.* in double-quick time; **bei ihm muß alles ~ gehen** he likes everything done in double-quick time
hoppe ['hɔpə] *Interj. in* ~, ~, **Reiter machen** *(Kindersp r.)* play gee-gees *(on sb.'s knee)*
hoppeln ['hɔpl̩n] *itr. V.; mit sein* hop **(über** + *Akk.* across, over); *(fig.)* bump, jolt **(über** + *Akk.* across, over)
Hoppelpoppel ['hɔpl̩'pɔpl̩] **das;** ~**s,** ~ **a)** *(bes. berlin.) s.* **Bauernfrühstück; b)** *(Getränk)* ≈ egg-nog
hoppla ['hɔpla] *Interj.* oops; whoops
hopp|nehmen *unr. tr. V. (salopp)* nab *(sl.);* nick *(sl.)*
hops [hɔps] **1.** *Interj.* up; jump. **2.** *Adj.; nicht attr. (salopp)* ~ **sein** be gone; ⟨*money*⟩ have gone down the drain *(coll.); (entzweigegangen sein)* be broken
Hops der; ~**es,** ~**e** [little] jump
hopsala ['hɔpsala], **hopsasa** ['hɔpsasa] *Interj. (Kindersp r.)* oops-a-daisy *(coll.);* *whoops-a-daisy (coll.)*
hopsen *itr. V.; mit sein (ugs.) (springen)* jump; *(hüpfen)* ⟨*animal*⟩ hop; ⟨*child*⟩ skip; ⟨*ball*⟩ bounce
Hopser der; ~**s,** ~ *(ugs.)* **a)** *(kleiner Sprung)* [little] jump; **b)** *(Tanz)* écossaise
Hopserei die; ~, ~**en** *(ugs. abwertend)* jumping about *or* around; *(Tanzen)* leaping about *or* around
hops-: ~**|gehen** *unr. itr. V.; mit sein (salopp)* **a)** *(umkommen)* buy it *(sl.);* **b)** *(entzweigehen)* get broken; *(abhanden kommen)* go missing; *(unbrauchbar werden)* ⟨*car, machine, etc.*⟩ pack up *(coll.);* ~**|nehmen** *unr. tr. V. s.* **hoppnehmen**
Hör·apparat der hearing-aid
hörbar 1. *Adj.* audible. **2.** *adv.* audibly; *(geräuschvoll)* noisily
Hör-: ~**bereich der** audible range; range of hearing; ~**bild das** radio feature *(combining documentary and dramatic techniques);* ~**brille** hearing-aid spectacles *pl.*
horchen ['hɔrçn̩] *itr. V.* listen **(auf** + *Akk.* to); *(heimlich zuhören)* eavesdrop; listen; **an der Tür/Wand ~:** listen at the door/through the wall
Horcher der; ~**s,** ~: *s.* **Lauscher a**
Horch-: ~**gerät das** sound locator; *(Marine)* hydrophone; ~**posten der** *(Milit., auch fig. scherzh.)* listening-post
[1]**Horde** ['hɔrdə] **die;** ~, ~**n** *(auch Völkerk.)* horde; *(von Halbstarken)* mob; crowd; **eine ~ Kinder** *od.* **von Kindern** a horde of children
[2]**Horde die;** ~, ~**n** *(Gestell)* rack
hören ['hø:rən] **1.** *tr. V.* **a)** hear; **jmdn. kommen/sprechen ~:** hear sb. coming/speaking; **ich habe sagen ~, daß ...:** I have heard it said that ...; **ich höre nichts** I can't hear anything; *s. auch* **Gras; b)** *(anhören)* listen to, hear ⟨*programme, broadcast, performance, etc.*⟩; hear ⟨*singer, musician*⟩; **Rundfunk** *od.* **Radio ~:** listen to the radio; **den Angeklagten/Zeugen ~:** hear the accused/witness; **eine Vorlesung bei jmdm. ~:** go to *or* attend a lecture by sb.; **das läßt sich ~:** that's good news; **c)** *(erfahren)* hear; **etw. von jmdm. ~:** hear sth. from sb.; **er läßt nichts von sich ~:** I/we *etc.* haven't heard from him; **laß mal etwas von dir ~!** keep in touch; **etw. von jmdm. zu ~ bekommen** *od. (ugs.)* **kriegen** get a good talking-to from sb. *(coll.);* **d)** *(erkennen)* **an etw.** *(Dat.)* ~, **daß ...:** hear *or* tell by sth. that ... **2.** *itr. V.* **a)** hear; **gut ~:** have good hearing; **schlecht ~:** have bad hearing; be hard of hearing; **nur auf einem Ohr ~:** be deaf in one ear; **höre ich recht?** am I hearing things?; **ich geb' dir gleich eine, daß dir Hören und Sehen vergeht** *(ugs.)* I'll give you such a clout in a minute that you'll be seeing stars for a week *(coll.);* **er raste über die Autobahn, daß uns Hören und Sehen verging** *(ugs.)* he tore along the motorway so fast that we were scared out of our wits *(coll.);* **b)** *(aufmerksam verfolgen)* **auf etw.** *(Akk.)* ~: listen to sth.; **c)** *(zuhören)* listen; **ich höre** I'm listening; **hörst du!** listen [here]!; **hörst du?** are you listening?; **man höre und staune** would you believe it!; wonders will never cease *(iron.);* **hör mal!/~ Sie mal!** listen [here]!; **hört, hört!** aha, listen to this!; **d)** *(befolgen)* **auf jmdn./jmds. Rat ~:** listen to *or* heed sb./sb.'s advice; **alles hört auf mein Kommando!** *(Milit.)* I'm taking command; *(scherzh.)* everyone do as I say; **auf den Namen Monika ~:** answer to the name [of] Monika; **e)** *(Kenntnis erhalten)* **von jmdm./etw. ~:** hear of sb./sth.; **davon ~, daß ...:** hear that ...; **von jmdm. ~** *(Nachricht bekommen)* hear from sb.; **Sie hören noch von mir** you'll be hearing from me again; you haven't heard the last of this; **ich lasse wieder von mir ~:** I'll be in touch; **f)** *(ugs.: gehorchen)* do as one is told; **nicht ~ wollen** not do as one's told; **wer nicht ~ will, muß fühlen** *(Spr.)* if you don't do as you're told, you'll suffer for it
Hören·sagen das; ~**s** *in* **vom ~:** by *or* from hearsay
Hörer der; ~**s,** ~ **a)** listener; **b)** *(Telefon~)* receiver
Hörer·brief der listener's letter; ~**e** listeners' letters
Hörerin die; ~, ~**nen** listener
Hörer·kreis der audience
Hörerschaft die; ~, ~**en** audience
Hör-: ~**fehler der a) das war ein ~fehler** he/she *etc.* misheard; ~**fehler ausschließen** exclude the possibility of mishearing [sth.]; **b)** *(Schwerhörigkeit)* hearing defect; ~**folge die** radio series; *(in Fortsetzungen)* radio serial; ~**funk der** radio; **im ~funk** on the radio; ~**gerät das** hearing-aid
hörig *Adj.* **a) in jmdm. ~ sein** be submissively dependent on sb.; *(sexuell)* be sexually dependent on *or* enslaved to sb.; be sb.'s sexual slave; **b)** *(hist.)* **die ~en Bauern** the serfs; ~ **sein** be in bondage
Hörige der/die; *adj. Dekl. (hist.)* serf; bondsman/bondswoman
Hörigkeit die; ~ **a)** enslavement; *(sexuell)* sexual dependence; **b)** *(hist.)* bondage; serfdom
Horizont [hori'tsɔnt] **der;** ~**[e]s,** ~**e** *(auch Geol., fig.)* horizon; **am ~:** on the horizon; **einen engen** *od.* **kleinen ~ haben** *(fig.)* have narrow horizons *pl.;* **seinen ~ erweitern** *(fig.)* widen *or* expand one's horizons *pl.;* **hinter dem ~:** below the horizon; **über jmds. ~** *(Akk.)* **gehen** *(fig.)* be beyond sb.; go over sb.'s head
horizontal [horitsɔn'ta:l] **1.** *Adj.* horizontal; *s. auch* **Gewerbe a. 2.** *adv.* horizontally
Horizontale die; ~, ~**n a)** *(Linie)* horizontal line; **b)** *o. Pl. (Lage)* **die ~:** the horizontal; **etw. in die ~ bringen** lay sth. flat; **sich in die ~ begeben** *(scherzh.)* lie down
Hormon [hɔr'mo:n] **das;** ~**s,** ~**e** hormone
hormonal [hɔrmo'na:l] **1.** *Adj.* hormonal. **2.** *adv.* hormonally
Hormon·behandlung die hormone treatment; **eine ~:** a course of hormone treatment
hormonell [hɔrmo'nɛl] *Adj., adv. s.* **hormonal**
Hormon-: ~**haushalt der** hormone balance; ~**präparat das** hormone preparation; ~**spiegel der** hormone level
Hör·muschel die ear-piece
Horn [hɔrn] **das;** ~**[e]s, Hörner** ['hœrnɐ] **a)** horn; **jmdm. Hörner aufsetzen** *(fig. ugs.)* cuckold sb.; **sich** *(Dat.)* **die Hörner ablaufen** *od.* **abstoßen** *(fig.)* sow one's wild oats; **b)** *(Blasinstrument)* horn; *(Milit.)* bugle; **ins gleiche ~ stoßen** *(fig.)* take the same line; **c)** *Pl.* ~**e** *(Substanz)* horn; **d)** *(Signal~) (eines*

Autos usw.) horn; hooter *(Brit.)*; *(eines Zuges)* horn
horn·artig *Adj.* hornlike
Hornberger ['hɔrnbɛrgɐ] *in* **wie das ~ Schießen ausgehen** all come to nothing
Horn-: **~blende die** *(Mineral.)* hornblende; **~brille die** horn-rimmed spectacles *pl. or* glasses *pl.*
Hörnchen ['hœrnçən] **das; ~s, ~ a)** small *or* little horn; **b)** *(Gebäck)* croissant; **c)** *(Nagetier)* squirrel
Hörner·klang der sound of horns
hörnern *Adj.; nicht präd.* horn ⟨*handle etc.*⟩; ⟨*handle etc.*⟩ [made] of horn
Horn·haut die a) callus; hard *or* callused skin *no indef. art.*; **b)** *(am Auge)* cornea
Hornhaut-: **~entzündung die** inflammation of the cornea; corneitis *no indef. art. (Med.)*; keratitis *no indef. art. (Med.)*; **~trübung die** corneal opacity; opacity of the cornea; **~übertragung die** corneal grafting
hornig *Adj.* horny
Hornisse [hɔr'nɪsə] **die; ~, ~n** hornet
Hornist der; ~en, ~en a) horn player; **b)** *(Milit.)* bugler
Horn-: **~kamm der** horn comb; **~ochse der** *(ugs.)* stupid ass; **~signal das** blast on a/the horn; **~tier das** horned animal; **die ~tiere** the Bovidae
Hornung der; ~s, ~e *(veralt.)* February
Hör·organ das *s.* **Gehörorgan**
Horoskop [horo'sko:p] **das; ~s, ~e** horoscope; **jmdm. das ~ stellen** cast sb.'s horoscope
horrend [hɔ'rɛnt] *Adj.* shocking *(coll.)*, horrendous *(coll.)* ⟨*price*⟩; colossal *(coll.)* ⟨*sum, amount, rent*⟩; shocking *(coll.)* ⟨*blunder, mistake, lack of discipline*⟩
horrido [hɔri'do:] *Interj. (Jägerspr.)* hurrah
Hör·rohr das a) *(Stethoskop)* stethoscope; **b)** *(Hörgerät)* ear-trumpet
Horror ['hɔrɔr] **der; ~s** horror; **einen ~ vor jmdm./etw. haben** loathe and fear sb./have a horror of sth.
Horror-: **~film der** horror film; **~trip der** *(ugs.)* bad trip; **der reinste ~trip sein** *(fig.)* be a nightmare
Hör-: **~saal der a)** lecture theatre *or* hall *or* room; **b)** *o. Pl. (Zuhörerschaft)* audience; **~schwelle die** *(Akustik)* threshold of audibility *or* hearing
Horsd'oeuvre [ɔr'dœ:vr] **das; ~s, ~s** *(Gastr.)* hors-d'oeuvre
Hör·spiel das a) radio play; **b)** *(Gattung)* radio drama *no art.*
Horst [hɔrst] **der; ~[e]s, ~e a)** *(Nest)* eyrie; **b)** *(Forstw.) (Bäume)* group of trees; *(Gebüsch)* group of bushes; **c)** *(Geol.)* horst; **d)** *s.* **Fliegerhorst**
horsten *itr. V.* nest
Hör·sturz der *(Med.)* acute hearing loss
Hort [hɔrt] **der; ~[e]s, ~e a)** *(dichter.: Goldschatz)* hoard [of gold]; **b)** *(geh.: Schutz)* refuge; sanctuary; **ein ~ der Freiheit** a stronghold *or* bulwark of liberty; **c)** *(geh.: Stätte)* **ein ~ des Lasters/des Geistes** a hotbed of vice/a centre of intellectual activity; **d)** *s.* **Kinderhort**
horten *tr. V.* hoard; stockpile ⟨*raw materials*⟩
Hortensie [hɔr'tɛnzi̯ə] **die; ~, ~n** hydrangea
Hör·test der hearing test
Hortnerin ['hɔrtnərɪn] **die; ~, ~nen** *supervisor in a day-home for schoolchildren*
Hortung die; ~: hoarding; *(von Rohstoffen)* stockpiling
ho ruck ['ho:'rʊk] *s.* **hau ruck**
Hör-: **~vermögen das;** *o. Pl.* hearing; **~weite die** hearing range; **in/außer ~weite** in/out of hearing range *or* of earshot
hosanna [ho'zana] *s.* **hosianna**
Höschen ['hø:sçən] **das; ~s, ~ a)** trousers *pl.*; pair of trousers; *(kurzes ~)* short trousers *pl.*; shorts *pl.*; pair of shorts; **heiße ~** *(ugs. scherzh.)* hot pants; **b)** *(Slip)* panties *pl.*; pair of panties
Hose ['ho:zə] **die; ~, ~n a)** trousers *pl.*; pants *pl. (Amer.)*; *(Unter~)* pants *pl.*; *(Freizeit~)* slacks *pl.*; *(Bund~)* breeches *pl.*; *(Reit~)* jodhpurs *pl.*; riding breeches *pl.*; **eine ~:** a pair of trousers/pants/slacks *etc.*; **eine kurze/lange ~:** [a pair of] short trousers *or* shorts/long trousers; **ein/zwei Paar ~n** one/two pairs of trousers; **in die ~n schlüpfen/steigen** slip/get one's trousers on; slip/get into one's trousers; **das Kind hat in die ~[n] gemacht/die ~ vollgemacht** the child has made a mess in its pants; **b)** *(fig.)* **[zu Hause** *od.* **daheim] die ~n anhaben** *(ugs.)* wear the trousers [at home]; **die ~n runterlassen** *(salopp)* come clean *(coll.)*; **die ~[n] [gestrichen] voll haben** *(salopp)* be shitting oneself *(coarse)*; be in a blue funk *(sl.)*; **die ~n voll kriegen** *(ugs.)* get a good hiding *(coll.)*; **jmdm. die ~n strammziehen** *(ugs.)* give sb. a good hiding *(coll.)*; **in die ~[n] gehen** *(salopp)* be a [complete] flop *(coll.)*; **sich [vor Angst] in die ~[n] machen** *(salopp)* shit oneself *(coarse)*; get into a blue funk *(sl.)*; **es ist tote ~** *(Jugendspr.)* there's nothing doing *(coll.)*
Hosen-: **~an·zug der** trouser suit *(Brit.)*; pant suit; **~aufschlag der** [trouser *or (Amer.)* pants] turn-up; **~band·orden der** Order of the Garter; **~bein das** trouser-leg; pants leg *(Amer.)*; **~boden der** seat of the/one's/sb.'s trousers *or (Amer.)* pants; **ein paar auf den ~boden bekommen** get a smacked bottom; **sich auf den ~boden setzen** *(fig.)* knuckle down to it; **jmdm. den ~boden strammziehen** *(fig. ugs.)* give sb. a good hiding *(coll.)*; **~boje die** *(Seew.)* breeches-buoy; **~bügel der** trouser-hanger; **~bund der** waistband; **~klammer die** bicycle-clip; **~knopf der** trouser-button; pants button *(Amer.)*; **~latz der a)** *(an Lederhosen)* flap; *(an Trachten~, Matrosen~)* bib; **b)** *(landsch.) s.* **~schlitz; ~matz der** *(ugs. scherzh.)* toddler; [tiny] tot; **~naht die** trouser-seam; pants seam *(Amer.)*; **Hände an die ~naht!** *(Milit.)* thumbs on your trouser-seams!; **~rock der** culottes *pl.*; divided skirt; **~rolle die** *(Theater)* breeches part; **~scheißer der a)** *(derb: Feigling)* chicken *(coll.)*; **b)** *(ugs. scherzh.) s.* **~matz; ~schlitz der** fly; flies *pl.*; **~spanner der** *s.* **~bügel; ~stall der** *(ugs. scherzh.) s.* **~schlitz; ~tasche die** trouser-pocket; pants pocket *(Amer.)*; **etw. wie seine ~tasche kennen** *(fig. ugs.)* know sth. like the back of one's hand; **~träger** *Pl.* braces; suspenders *(Amer.)*; pair of braces/suspenders
hosianna [ho'zi̯ana] *Interj. (christl. Rel.)* hosanna
Hospital [hɔspi'ta:l] **das; ~s, ~e** *od.* **Hospitäler** [hɔspi'tɛ:lɐ] **a)** hospital; **b)** *(veralt.: Pflegeheim)* nursing home *(Brit.)*
Hospitalismus der; ~ *(Psych., Päd., Med.)* hospitalism *no art.*
Hospitant [hɔspi'tant] **der; ~en, ~en, Hospitantin die; ~, ~nen a)** *person sitting in on a class/lecture*; **b)** *s.* **Gasthörer**
hospitieren *itr. V.* **bei jmdm. ~:** sit in on sb.'s lectures/seminars; **in einem Seminar/einer Vorlesung ~:** sit in on a seminar/lecture
Hospiz [hɔs'pi:ts] **das; ~es, ~e a)** hospice; **b)** *(Hotel)* **[christliches] ~:** *private hotel run in accordance with Protestant principles*
Hostess, Hosteß [hɔs'tɛs] **die; ~, Hostessen** hostess
Hostie ['hɔsti̯ə] **die; ~, ~n** *(christl. Rel.)* host
Hostien-: *(christl. Religion)* **~schrein der** tabernacle; **~teller der** paten
Hotel [ho'tɛl] **das; ~s, ~s** hotel
Hotel-: **~bar die** hotel bar; **~boy der** page[-boy]; bellboy *(Amer.)*; **~direktor der** hotel manager; **~fach das;** *o. Pl.* hotel trade; **~fach·schule die** school of hotel management; **~führer der** hotel guide
Hotel garni [~ gar'ni:] **das; ~ ~, ~s ~s** bed-and-breakfast hotel
Hotel-: **~gast der** hotel guest; **~halle die** hotel lobby
Hotelier [hotɛ'li̯e:] **der; ~s, ~s** hotelier
Hotel-: **~page der** *s.* **~boy; ~portier der** [hotel] commissionaire; **~zimmer das** hotel room
hott [hɔt] *Interj.* gee[-up]; *s. auch* **hü**
HQ *Abk.* **Hauptquartier** HQ.
HR *Abk.* **Hessischer Rundfunk** Hesse Radio
hrsg. *Abk.* **herausgegeben** ed.
Hrsg. *Abk.* **Herausgeber** ed.
Hs. *Abk.* **Handschrift** MS.
hu [hu:] *Interj.* **a)** ugh; **b)** *(bei Kälte)* brrr; **c)** *(zum Erschrecken)* boo
hü [hy:] *Interj.* **a)** *(vorwärts)* giddap; gee[-up]; **b)** *(halt)* whoa; **einmal sagt sie ~ und einmal hott** *(fig. ugs.)* first she says one thing, then another
Hub [hu:p] **der; ~[e]s, Hübe** ['hy:bə] *(Technik)* **a)** *(das Heben)* lifting; **in einem ~:** in one lift; *(bei einem Bagger)* in one load; **b)** *(Weg des Kolbens)* stroke
Hubbel ['hʊbl̩] **der; ~s, ~** *(bes. südd.)* bump
hubbelig *Adj. (bes. südd.)* bumpy
Hub·brücke die *(Technik)* lift bridge
hüben ['hy:bn̩] *Adv.* on this side; over here; **~ und** *od.* **wie drüben** on both sides
Hubertus·jagd [hu'bɛrtʊs-] **die; ~, ~en** *(Jagdw.)* St. Hubert's Day hunt
Hub-: **~höhe die** *(Technik) (eines Krans)* lifting height; *(einer Schleuse)* lift; *(eines Kolbens)* length of stroke; **~raum der** *(Technik)* piston displacement; swept volume; *(Meßgröße für die Leistungsfähigkeit eines Motors)* cubic capacity
hübsch [hʏpʃ] **1.** *Adj.* **a)** pretty; nice-looking ⟨*boy, person*⟩; *(reizvoll)* nice, pleasant ⟨*area, flat, voice, tune, etc.*⟩; nice ⟨*phrase, idea, present*⟩; **ihr Hübschen** *(ugs.)* my pretty ones; **sich ~ machen** make oneself look nice; **b)** *nicht präd. (ugs.: ziemlich groß)* **eine ~e Stange Geld kosten** cost a pretty penny; **ein ~es Sümmchen** a tidy sum *(coll.)*; a nice little sum; **ein ~es Stück Arbeit** a fair amount *or* quite a lot of work; **c)** *(ugs. iron.: unangenehm)* **das ist eine ~e Geschichte/hier herrschen ~e Zustände** this is a fine *or* pretty kettle of fish *(coll.) or* a fine state of affairs. **2.** *adv.* **a)** prettily; **sich ~ anziehen** dress nicely; wear nice clothes; **~ eingerichtet/gekleidet** nicely *or* attractively furnished/dressed; **~ singen/spielen** sing/play nicely; **b)** *(ugs.: sehr)* **~ kalt** perishing cold; **c)** *(ugs.: ordentlich)* **immer ~ der Reihe nach** everybody must take his turn; **sei ~ brav** be a good boy/girl; **immer ~ langsam** take it nice and slowly
Hub·schrauber der; ~s, ~: helicopter
Hubschrauber·lande·platz der heliport; *(kleiner)* helicopter pad; landing pad
Hub-: **~stapler der a)** stacker truck; **b)** *s.* **Gabelstapler; ~volumen das** *s.* **~raum**
huch [hʊx] *Interj.* ugh; *(bei Kälte)* brrr
Hucke ['hʊkə] **die; ~, ~n** pannier; **jmdm. die ~ voll hauen** *(fig. ugs.)* give sb. a good hiding *(coll.)*; *(bei einer Prügelei)* beat hell out of sb. *(coll.)*; **jmdm. die ~ voll lügen** *(fig. ugs.)* tell sb. a pack of lies; **die ~ voll kriegen** *(fig. ugs.)* get a good hiding *(coll.)*; *(bei einer Prügelei)* get a proper beating *(coll.)*; *s. auch* **saufen 3**
huckepack ['hʊkəpak] *Adv. (ugs.)* **in jmdn. ~ tragen** carry sb. piggyback; give sb. a piggyback; **etw. ~ tragen** carry sth. piggyback; **jmdn./etw. ~ nehmen** take sth. up on one's back
Hudelei die; ~, ~en *(bes. südd., österr.)* **a)** *(Arbeitsweise)* sloppiness; **b)** *(Pfuscharbeit)* sloppy *or* slipshod *or* slapdash work *no indef. art.*

hudelig *(bes. südd., österr.)* **1.** *Adj.* sloppy; slapdash; slipshod ⟨*work*⟩. **2.** *adv.* sloppily; in a sloppy *or* slipshod *or* slapdash manner
hudeln ['hu:dl̩n] *itr. V. (bes. südd., österr.)* work sloppily; be sloppy *or* slapdash (**bei** in); **nur nicht ~!** don't be in such a hurry!; take it easy!
hudlig *s.* **hudelig**
Huf [hu:f] **der; ~[e]s, ~e** hoof; **einem Pferd die ~e beschlagen** shoe a horse
huf-, Huf-: ~eisen das horseshoe; **~eisen·form die: in ~eisenform** in [the shape of] a horseshoe; **~eisenförmig 1.** *Adj.* horseshoe-shaped; **2.** *adv.* in [the shape of] a horseshoe
Hufen·dorf das *linear village in which each house has its own fields behind it*
Huf-: ~lattich der coltsfoot; **~nagel der** horseshoe nail; **~schlag der a)** *(Klang)* hoofbeats *pl.;* **b)** *(Stoß)* kick [from a/the horse]; **~schmied der** farrier; blacksmith; **~schmiede die** farrier's *or* blacksmith's workshop
Hüft·bein das *(Anat.)* hip bone; innominate bone *(Anat.)*
Hüfte ['hʏftə] **die; ~, ~n** hip; **sie stand da, die Arme in die ~n gestemmt ...:** she stood there, hands on hips *or* with arms akimbo; **sich in den ~n wiegen** swing one's hips; **aus der ~ schießen/feuern** shoot/fire from the hip
hüft-, Hüft-: ~gelenk das *(Anat.)* hip-joint; **~gelenk·entzündung die** coxitis; **~gürtel der, ~halter der** girdle; **~hoch 1.** *Adj.* **~hoch sein** ⟨*grass, wall*⟩ be almost waist-high; ⟨*water, snow, mud*⟩ be almost waist-deep; **2.** *adv.* **~hoch im Schlamm stehen** stand waist-deep in mud
Huf·tier das hoofed animal; ungulate *(Zool.)*
Hüft-: ~knochen der *s.* **Hüftbein; ~nerv der** sciatic nerve; **~schwung der** *(Ringen)* cross-buttock; **~um·fang der, ~weite die** *(Schneiderei)* hip size
Hügel ['hy:gl̩] **der; ~s, ~ a)** hill; *(fig.)* heap; pile; **b)** *(dichter.)* grave mound
hügel-, Hügel-: ~ab *Adv. (geh.)* downhill; **~an, ~auf** *Adv. (geh.)* uphill; **~grab das** *(Archäol.)* barrow; tumulus
hügelig *Adj.* hilly
Hügel-: ~kette die chain *or* range of hills; **~land das;** *Pl.* **~länder** hill country
Hugenotte [hugə'nɔtə] **der; ~n, ~n** Huguenot
hüglig *s.* **hügelig**
huh *s.* **hu**
hüh *s.* **hü**
Huhn [hu:n] **das; ~[e]s, Hühner** ['hy:nɐ] **a)** chicken; [domestic] fowl; *(Henne)* chicken; hen; **gebratenes ~:** roast chicken; **herumlaufen wie ein aufgescheuchtes ~** *(ugs.)* run about in a great panic *(coll.);* **da lachen [ja] die Hühner** *(ugs.)* you/he/she *etc.* must be joking *(coll.);* **ein blindes ~ findet auch mal ein Korn** *(Spr.)* anyone can have a stroke of luck once in a while; **mit den Hühnern aufstehen/zu Bett gehen** *(scherzh.)* get up with the lark/go to bed early; **b)** *(ugs.: Mensch)* **ein verrücktes/dummes/fideles ~:** a nutcase *(sl.) or* idiot/stupid twit *(Brit. sl.) or* idiot/cheerful sort *(coll.);* **c)** *(Jägerspr.) s.* **Rebhuhn**
Hühnchen ['hy:nçən] **das; ~s, ~:** little *or* small chicken; **mit jmdm. [noch] ein ~ zu rupfen haben** *(ugs.)* [still] have a bone to pick with sb.
Hühner-: ~auge das *(am Fuß)* corn; **jmdm. auf die ~augen treten** *(fig. ugs.)* tread on sb.'s corns *or* toes; **~augen·pflaster das** corn plaster; **~brühe die** chicken broth; **~brust die a)** *(Med.)* chicken-breast; pigeon-breast; **b)** *(ugs.: flacher Brustkorb)* scrawny chest; **~dieb der** chicken-thief; **~dreck der** *(ugs.)* chicken dirt; **~ei das** hen's egg; **~farm die** chicken farm; **~frikassee das** chicken fricassee; fricassee of chicken; **~futter das** chicken-feed; **~habicht der** [northern] goshawk; **~hof der** chicken-run; **~hund der** *s.* **Vorstehhund; ~klein das** trimmings *pl.* of chicken *(in stew etc.);* **~leiter die** chicken-ladder; **~mist der** chicken droppings *pl.;* **~pest die** *(Tiermed.)* fowl pest; **~stall der** chicken-coop; hen-coop; **~suppe die** chicken soup; **~vogel der;** *meist Pl. (Zool.)* gallinaceous bird; **~zucht die a)** *o. Pl.* chicken-rearing *no art.;* chicken-farming *no art.;* **b)** *(Betrieb)* chicken farm
hui [hui̯] *Interj.* whoosh; **außen ~ und innen pfui** *(von Geräten usw.)* the outside's fine but inside it's a different story; *(von Personen)* he/she seems very nice on the surface, but underneath it's a different story
Huld [hʊlt] **die; ~** *(geh., veralt., noch iron.) (Gunst)* favour; *(Güte)* graciousness; **jmdm. seine ~ schenken** bestow one's favour on sb.
huldigen ['hʊldɪgn̩] *itr. V.* **a) jmdm. ~:** pay tribute to *or* honour sb.; **b)** *(geh.: anhängen)* **einem Grundsatz/einer Ansicht/Mode ~:** hold [devotedly] to a principle/a point of view/follow a fashion; **dem Kartenspiel/Alkohol ~:** be addicted to cards/enjoy a few drinks; **c)** *(hist.: Treue geloben)* **jmdm. ~:** pay *or* render homage to sb.
Huldigung die; ~, ~en a) *(Ehrung)* tribute; homage; **einer Dame seine ~ darbringen** pay one's addresses *pl.* to a lady; **b)** *(hist.: Treuegelöbnis)* homage
Huldigungs·gedicht das panegyric
huld·reich, huld·voll *(geh. veralt.)* **1.** *Adj.* gracious. **2.** *adv.* graciously
Hülle ['hʏlə] **die; ~, ~n a)** *(Umhüllung)* cover; *(für Ausweis, Zeitkarte)* cover; holder; *(für Füllhalter)* case; *(Schallplatten~)* cover; sleeve; *(fig.: eines Menschen)* **die leibliche ~** *(dicht.)* this mortal frame *(literary);* **die sterbliche ~** *(geh. verhüll.)* the mortal remains *pl.;* **b)** *(ugs. scherzh.: Kleidung)* **seine** *od.* **die ~ fallen lassen** strip off [one's clothes]; **c) in ~ und Fülle,** *(geh.)* **die ~ und Fülle** in abundance; in plenty; **d)** *(Bot.)* involucre
hüllen *tr. V. (geh.)* wrap; **jmdn./sich in etw.** *(Akk.)* **~:** wrap sb./oneself in sth.; **in Dunkel** *(Akk.)* **gehüllt** *(fig.)* shrouded *or* veiled in obscurity; **in Wolken** *(Akk.)* **gehüllt** *(fig.)* enveloped in clouds
hüllenlos *Adj.* **a)** *nicht präd. (unverhüllt)* plain; clear; **b)** *(scherzh.: nackt)* naked; in one's birthday suit *pred. (joc.)*
Hülse ['hʏlzə] **die; ~, ~n a)** *(Hülle) (für Füllhalter, Thermometer, Patrone)* case; *(für Film)* [cassette] container; *(für Impfstoff)* capsule; **b)** *(Bot.)* pod; hull
Hülsen·frucht die; *meist Pl.* **a)** *(Frucht)* fruit of a leguminous plant; **Hülsenfrüchte** pulse *sing.;* **b)** *(Pflanze)* legume; leguminous plant
human [hu'ma:n] **1.** *Adj.* **a)** *(menschenwürdig)* humane; **die modernen Großstädte müssen ~er werden** modern cities must provide a more humane environment for people to live in; **b)** *(nachsichtig)* considerate; **c)** *(Med.)* human. **2.** *adv.* **a)** *(menschenwürdig)* humanly; **b)** *(nachsichtig)* considerately
Human-: ~biologie die human biology *no art.;* **~genetik die** human genetics *sing., no art.*
humanisieren *tr. V.* humanize
Humanisierung die; ~: humanization
Humanismus der; ~: humanism; *(Epoche)* Humanism *no art.*
Humanist der; ~en, ~en a) humanist; *(hist.)* Humanist; **b)** *(Altsprachler)* classical scholar; *(Student)* classics student
humanistisch *Adj.* **a)** humanist[ic]; *(hist.)* Humanist; **b)** *(altsprachlich)* classical; **ein ~es Gymnasium** *secondary school emphasizing classical languages*
humanitär [humani'tɛ:ɐ̯] *Adj.* humanitarian
Humanität [humani'tɛ:t] **die; ~:** respect for humanity
Humanitäts·duselei [-du:zəlai̯] **die; ~, ~en** *(abwertend)* **[eine] ~/~en** *Pl.* sentimental humanitarianism *sing.*
Human-: ~medizin die human medicine *no art.;* **~mediziner der** practitioner of human medicine; **~versuch der** *(Med.)* test on a human being/on human beings
Humbug ['hʊmbʊk] **der; ~s** *(ugs. abwertend)* humbug
Hummel ['hʊml̩] **die; ~, ~n** bumble-bee; humble-bee; **eine wilde ~** *(scherzh.)* a proper tomboy; *s. auch* **Hintern**
Hummer ['hʊmɐ] **der; ~s, ~:** lobster
Hummer-: ~cocktail der *(Kochk.)* lobster cocktail; **~krabbe die** king prawn; **~mayonnaise die** *(Kochk.)* lobster mayonnaise
Humor [hu'mo:ɐ̯] **der; ~s, ~e a)** humour; *(Sinn für ~)* sense of humour; **etw. mit ~ tragen/nehmen** bear/take sth. with a sense of humour *or* cheerfully; **keinen [Sinn für] ~ haben** have no sense of humour; **er hat ~ – läßt mich mit der ganzen Arbeit allein hier sitzen** he's got a strange sense of humour, leaving me sitting here on my own with all the work; **~ ist, wenn man trotzdem lacht** it's not the end of the world; **der rheinische/englische ~:** Rhenish/English humour; the Rhinelander's/Englishman's sense of humour; **schwarzer ~:** black humour; **b)** *o. Pl. (gute Laune)* **den ~ nicht verlieren** remain good-humoured
Humoreske [humo'rɛskə] **die; ~, ~n a)** *(Literaturwiss.)* humorous sketch; **b)** *(Musik)* humoresque
humorig *Adj.* humorous
Humorist der; ~en, ~en a) *(Autor)* humorist; **b)** *(Vortragskünstler)* comedian
humoristisch 1. *Adj.* humorous; **er ist ein großes ~es Talent** he has great talent to amuse. **2.** *adv.* with humour
humor-, Humor-: ~los 1. *Adj.* humourless; **2.** *adv.* without humour; **~losigkeit die; ~:** humourlessness; lack of humour; **~voll 1.** *Adj.* humorous; **2.** *adv.* humorously; in a humorous way
Humpelei die; ~ *(ugs.)* hobbling; **er übertreibt ein bißchen mit seiner ~:** he's overdoing the limp a bit
humpeln ['hʊmpl̩n] *itr. V.* **a)** *auch mit sein* walk with *or* have a limp; **b)** *mit sein (sich ~d fortbewegen)* hobble; limp
Humpen ['hʊmpn̩] **der; ~s, ~:** tankard; [beer-]mug; *(aus Ton auch)* stein
Humus ['hu:mʊs] **der; ~:** humus
humus-, Humus-: ~boden der, ~erde die humus soil; **~reich** *Adj.* ⟨*soil*⟩ rich in humus; rich ⟨*soil*⟩
Hund [hʊnt] **der; ~es, ~e a)** dog; *(Jagd~)* hound; dog; **ein junger ~:** a puppy *or* pup; **bei diesem Wetter würde man keinen ~ vor die Tür schicken** I wouldn't turn a dog out in weather like this; **da liegt der ~ begraben** *(fig. ugs.) (Ursache)* that's what's causing it; *(Grund)* that's the real reason; **da wird der ~ in der Pfanne verrückt** *(salopp)* it's quite incredible; **das ist zum Junge-Hunde-Kriegen** *(ugs.)* it's enough to drive you to despair; it's enough to drive you spare *(Brit. sl.);* **viele ~e sind des Hasen Tod** *(Spr.)* it's one against many; **~e, die bellen, beißen nicht** *(Spr.)* barking dogs seldom bite; **den letzten beißen die ~e** *(fig.)* late-comers must expect to be unlucky; **ein dicker ~** *(ugs.: grober Fehler)* a real bloomer *(Brit. sl.) or (sl.)* goof; **das ist ein dicker ~** *(ugs.: Frechheit)* that's a bit thick *(coll.);* **kalter ~** *(ugs.) gateau consisting of layers of biscuit and chocolate-flavoured filling;* **der Große ~/der Kleine ~** *(Astron.)* the Great[er] Dog/the Little *or* Lesser Dog; **bekannt sein wie ein**

bunter *od.* scheckiger ~: be a well-known figure; **wie ~ und Katze leben** *(ugs.)* lead a cat-and-dog life; **damit kannst du keinen ~ hinter dem Ofen hervorlocken** that won't tempt anybody; **auf den ~ kommen** *(ugs.)* go to the dogs *(coll.)*; **mit allen ~en gehetzt sein** *(ugs.)* be up to *(coll.) or* know all the tricks; **vor die ~e gehen** *(ugs.)* go to the dogs *(coll.)*; *(sterben)* die; kick the bucket *(sl.)*; **b)** *(salopp: Mann)* bloke *(Brit. coll.)*; *(abwertend)* bastard *(coll.)*; **so ein blöder ~!** [what a] stupid bastard!; **c)** *(Bergmannsspr.)* [mine-]car; tub

Hundchen, Hündchen ['hʏntçən] **das; ~s,** ~ *(kleiner Hund)* little dog; *(Koseform)* doggie *(coll.)*; *(junger Hund)* puppy; pup

hunde-, Hunde-: ~art die *s.* **~rasse; ~artige** *Pl.; adj. Dekl. (Zool.)* canines; **die ~artigen** the Canidae; **~aus·stellung die** dog show; **~blick der** *(fig. ugs.)* doglike look; *(ergeben)* look of doglike devotion; **~blume die** dandelion; **~deckchen das a)** dog-coat; **b)** *(scherzh.: Gamasche)* gaiter; **~dreck der** dog's mess *or* muck; **~elend** *Adj.; nicht attr.* [really] wretched *or* awful; **~fänger der** dog-catcher; **~futter das** dog food; **~gespann das** dog-team; **~halsband das** dog-collar; **~halter der** *(Amtsspr.)* dog-owner; **~hütte die** *(auch fig. abwertend)* [dog-]kennel; **~kalt** *Adj.; nicht attr. (ugs.)* freezing cold; **~kälte die** *(ugs.)* freezing cold; **~klo[sett] das** dogs' toilet *or* lavatory; **~kot der** *(geh.)* dog-dirt; **~kuchen der** dog-biscuit; **~leben das** *(ugs.)* dog's life; **~marke die a)** dog-licence disc; dog-tag; **b)** *(salopp scherzh.: Erkennungsmarke) (bei Soldaten)* identity disc; dog-tag *(Amer. sl.)*; *(bei der Polizei) s.* **Kennmarke; ~müde** *Adj.; nicht attr. (ugs.)* dog-tired; **~narr der** fanatical dog-lover; **~rasse die** breed of dog; **~rennen das** dog-racing; greyhound-racing; **ein Vermögen beim ~rennen verlieren** lose a fortune at the dog-track *or (coll.)* on the dogs *pl.*

hundert ['hʊndɐt] *Kardinalz.* **a)** a *or* one hundred; **mehrere/einige ~ Menschen** several/a few hundred people; **auf ~ kommen/sein** *(ugs.)* blow one's top *(coll.)*/be in a raging *or (coll.)* flaming temper; *s. auch* **acht; b)** *(ugs.: viele)* hundreds of; **~ Neuigkeiten** lots of news

[1]**Hundert das; ~s, ~e** *od. (nach unbest. Zahlwörtern)* ~ **a)** hundred; **ein halbes ~:** fifty; **fünf vom ~:** five per cent; **b)** *Pl. (große Anzahl)* **~e von Menschen** hundreds of people; **von solchen Menschen gibt es unter ~en nur einen** people like that are few and far between; **in die ~e gehen** *(ugs.)* run into hundreds

[2]**Hundert die; ~, ~en** hundred

hundert·ein[s] *Kardinalz.* a *or* one hundred and one

Hunderter der; ~s, ~ a) *(ugs.)* hundred-mark/-dollar *etc.* note; **das wird mich einige ~ kosten** that will cost me a few hundred [marks/dollars *etc.*]; **b)** *(Math.)* hundred

hunderterlei *Gattungsz.; indekl. (ugs.)* **a)** *(von verschiedener Art)* a hundred and one different ⟨*answers, kinds, etc.*⟩; **b)** *(viele)* a hundred and one; **ich muß noch ~ besorgen** I still have a hundred and one things to see to

hundert·fach *Vervielfältigungsz.* hundredfold; **die ~e Menge/der ~e Preis** a hundred times the amount/price; *s. auch* **achtfach**

Hundert·fünf·und·siebziger der; ~s, ~ *(ugs. veralt.)* homo *(coll.)*; queer *(sl.)*

hundert·fünfzig·prozentig *Adj. (ugs. iron.)* over-zealous ⟨*official*⟩; fanatical ⟨*nationalist, communist, etc.*⟩

Hundert·jahr·feier die centenary; centennial; **die ~ unserer Organisation** the centenary *or* centennial of our organization

hundert·jährig *Adj.* **a)** *(100 Jahre alt)* [one-]hundred-year-old; **ein ~er Greis** a centenarian; **b)** *(100 Jahre dauernd)* **nach ~em Kampf** after a hundred years of war; **ihr/sein ~es Bestehen feiern** celebrate its centenary; **der Hundertjährige Krieg** *(hist.)* the Hundred Years' War; **der Hundertjährige Kalender** the Century Almanac

hundert·mal *Adv.* a hundred times; **auch wenn du dich ~ beschwerst** *(ugs.)* however much *or* no matter how much you complain; *s. auch* **achtmal**

Hundert-: ~mark·schein der hundred-mark note; **~meter·hürden·lauf der** *(Leichtathletik)* hundred-metres hurdles *sing.*; **~meter·lauf der** *(Leichtathletik)* hundred metres *sing.*; **sie gehört zu den Weltbesten im ~meterlauf** she is among the world's best at a *or* the hundred metres

hundert·prozentig 1. *Adj.* **a)** *(von 100%)* [one-]hundred per cent *attrib.*; **~er Alkohol** pure alcohol; **b)** *(ugs.: völlig)* a hundred per cent, complete, absolute ⟨*certainty, agreement, etc.*⟩; **c)** *(ugs.: ganz sicher)* completely *or* absolutely reliable; **d)** *(ugs.: typisch)* **ein ~er Konservativer/eine ~e Amerikanerin** a conservative/an American through and through. **2.** *adv. (ugs.)* **ich bin nicht ~ sicher** I'm not a hundred per cent sure; **du kannst dich ~ auf ihn/darauf verlassen** you can rely on him/it absolutely *or* one hundred per cent; **~ recht haben** be absolutely right; **etw. ~ wissen** know sth. for sure; **er wird das tun, ~:** he will do it, you can be a hundred per cent sure of that

Hundertschaft die; ~, ~en group of a hundred; **einige ~en der Polizei** several hundred police

hundertst... ['hʊndɐtst...] *Ordinalz.* hundredth; **zum ~en Mal fragen** *(ugs.)* ask for the hundredth time; **vom Hundertsten ins Tausendste kommen** get carried away so that one subject just leads another

hundertstel ['hʊndɐtstl̩] *Bruchz.* hundredth; *s. auch* **achtel**

Hundertstel das *(schweiz. meist* **der**); **~s, ~:** hundredth

Hundertstel·sekunde die hundredth of a second

hundert·tausend *Kardinalz.* a *or* one hundred thousand; **mehrere/viele ~ Menschen** several hundred thousand people/many hundreds of thousands of people

hundert·und·ein[s] *Kardinalz.* a *or* one hundred and one

hundert·zehn *Kardinalz.* a *or* one hundred and ten

Hundert·zehn·meter·hürden·lauf der *(Leichtathletik)* 110 metres hurdles *sing.*

Hunde-: ~salon der poodle *or* dog parlour; **~scheiße die** *(derb)* dog-shit *(coarse)*; **~schlitten der** dog-sledge; dog-sled *(Amer.)*; **~schnauze die** dog's muzzle *or* snout; **kalt wie eine ~schnauze sein** *(fig. ugs.)* be as cold as ice *(fig.)*; **~sohn der** *(abwertend)* cur; **~steuer die** dog-licence fee; **~streife die** dog-patrol; **~wetter das** *(ugs.)* filthy *or (sl.)* lousy weather; **~zucht die a)** *o. Pl.* dog-breeding *no art.*; **b)** *(Betrieb)* [breeding] kennels *pl.*; **~zwinger der** dog run

Hündin ['hʏndɪn] **die; ~, ~nen** bitch

hündisch ['hʏndɪʃ] **1.** *Adj.* **a)** *(würdelos)* doglike, servile ⟨*obedience*⟩; doglike ⟨*devotion*⟩; fawning, abject ⟨*submissiveness*⟩; **b)** *(gemein)* mean; nasty. **2.** *adv.* **jmdm. ~ ergeben sein** have a doglike devotion to sb.; **sich einer Sache** *(Dat.)* **~ unterwerfen** submit abjectly to sth.

hunds-, Hunds-: ~erbärmlich *(ugs.)* **1.** *Adj.* **a)** [really] dreadful *(coll.)*; **b)** *(verabscheuenswürdig)* dirty *attrib.* ⟨*lie, coward*⟩; **eine ~erbärmliche Gemeinheit** a dirty low-down thing to do/say; **2.** *adv.* **a)** *(sehr)* terribly *(coll.)*, dreadfully *(coll.)*⟨*cold*⟩; **b)** *(sehr schlecht)* [really] abysmally *(coll.) or* dreadfully *(coll.)*; **~fott** [~fɔt] **der; ~[e]s, ~e** *od.* **~fötter** [fœtɐ] *(derb abwertend)* low-down bastard *(coll.)*; **~föttisch** [~fœtɪʃ] *Adj. (derb abwertend)* low-down *attrib.*; dirty *attrib.* ⟨*coward*⟩; **~gemein** *(ugs.)* **1.** *Adj.* **a)** *(abwertend: überaus gemein)* really mean *or* shabby; dirty ⟨*liar*⟩; **es war ~gemein, uns so hereinzulegen** it was a really mean *or* shabby trick to take us for a ride *(sl.)* like that; **b)** *(sehr stark)* terrible *(coll.)*, dreadful *(coll.)* ⟨*cold, weather, pain, etc.*⟩; **2.** *adv.* **a)** *(gemein)* ⟨*deceive, behave*⟩ really meanly *or* shabbily; **b)** *(sehr stark)* **das tut ~gemein weh** it hurts like hell *(coll.) or* terribly *(coll.)*; **~gemeinheit die** *(abwertend)* really mean *or* shabby trick; **~miserabel** *(salopp abwertend)* **1.** *Adj.* [really] lousy *(sl.) or* dreadful *(coll.)*; **2.** *adv.* ⟨*behave*⟩ [really] appallingly *(coll.) or* dreadfully *(coll.)*; **~rose die** *(Bot.)* dog-rose; wild briar; **~stern der** *(Astron.)* dog-star; **~tage** *Pl.* dog-days; **~veilchen das** dog violet; **~wut die** *(veralt.) s.* **Tollwut**

Hüne ['hy:nə] **der; ~n, ~n** giant

Hünen·grab das megalithic tomb; *(Hügelgrab)* barrow; tumulus

hünenhaft *Adj.* gigantic ⟨*build, stature*⟩

Hunger ['hʊŋɐ] **der; ~s a) ~ bekommen/haben** get/be hungry; **ich habe ~ wie ein Bär** *od.* **Wolf** I'm so hungry I could eat a horse; **sein ~ war groß** he was very hungry; **~ auf etw.** *(Akk.)* **haben** fancy sth.; feel like sth. *(coll.)*; **~ leiden** go hungry; starve; **wissen, was ~ ist** know what it is to go hungry; **vor ~ sterben** die of starvation *or* hunger; starve to death; **seinen ~ stillen** satisfy one's hunger; **~ ist der beste Koch** *(Spr.)* hunger is the best sauce *(prov.)*; **der ~ treibt's rein** *(ugs. scherzh.)* if you're hungry enough, you'll eat anything; **b)** *(Hungersnot)* famine; **c)** *(geh.: Verlangen)* hunger; *(nach Ruhm, Macht)* craving; thirst; **~ nach Gerechtigkeit** powerful desire to see justice done

Hunger-: ~blockade die food-blockade; **~da·sein das** existence at starvation level *or* below subsistence level; **~gefühl das** feeling of hunger; **~jahr das** hungry year; **~kur die** starvation diet; **eine ~kur machen** go on a starvation diet; **~leider der** *(ugs. abwertend)* starving pauper; **~lohn der** *(abwertend)* starvation wage[s *pl.*]

hungern ['hʊŋɐn] **1.** *itr. V.* **a)** go hungry; starve; **~, um schlank zu werden** be on a starvation diet in order to get slim; **jmdn. ~ lassen** let sb. starve; *(als Strafe)* starve sb.; **b)** *(verlangen)* **nach etw. ~:** hunger *or* be hungry for sth.; *(nach Macht, Ruhm)* crave sth.; thirst for sth. **2.** *refl. V.* **sich schlank ~:** go on a [slimming] diet; *(mit totalem Verzicht auf Nahrung)* slim by going on a starvation diet; **sich zu Tode ~:** starve oneself to death. **3.** *tr. V. (unpers.) (dichter.: verlangen)* **jmdn. hungert nach etw.** sb. craves [for] sth. *or* hungers for sth.

Hunger-: ~ödem das *(Med.)* famine-oedema; nutritional oedema; **~ration die** *(ugs.)* starvation rations *pl.*

Hungers·not die famine

Hunger-: ~streik der hunger-strike; **in den ~streik treten** go on hunger-strike; **~tod der** death from starvation; **den ~tod sterben** die of starvation; **~tuch das** *in* **am ~tuch nagen** *(ugs. scherzh.)* be on the breadline; **~turm der** *(hist.) dungeon in which prisoners were starved to death*

hungrig *Adj.* **a)** hungry; **das macht [einen] ~:** it makes you hungry *or* gives you an appetite; **~ nach etw. sein** fancy sth.; feel like sth. *(coll.)*; **b)** *(geh.: begierig)* hungry **(nach** for); **~ nach Anerkennung sein** crave recognition

Hunne ['hʊnə] **der; ~n, ~n** *(hist.)* Hun

Hupe ['hu:pə] **die; ~, ~n** horn; **auf die ~ drücken** sound the/one's horn

hupen *itr. V.* sound the *or* one's horn; **drei-**

mal ~: hoot three times; give three toots on the horn
Huperei die; ~: honking; hooting
Hupf·dohle die *(salopp)* chorus-girl
hupfen ['hʊpfn̩] *itr. V.; mit sein (südd., österr.)* hop; **das ist gehupft wie gesprungen** *(ugs.)* it doesn't make any difference; it doesn't matter either way
hüpfen ['hʏpfn̩] *itr. V.; mit sein* hop; ⟨*ball*⟩ bounce; ⟨*lamb*⟩ gambol; **über die Straße ~:** skip across the road; **Hüpfen spielen** play [at] hopscotch; **mein Herz hüpfte vor Freude** my heart leapt for joy; **das ist gehüpft wie gesprungen** *(ugs.) s.* **hupfen**
Hupfer der; ~s, ~ *(bes. südd., österr.),* **Hüpfer der; ~s, ~:** skip; *(auf einem Bein)* hop
Hup-: ~konzert das *(ugs. scherzh.)* chorus of hooting; **~signal das** hoot; toot; **~verbot das** ban on sounding one's horn
Hürde ['hʏrdə] **die; ~, ~n a)** *(Leichtathletik, Reitsport, fig.)* hurdle; **eine ~ nehmen/reißen** clear/knock over a hurdle; **eine ~ nehmen** *(fig.)* get over a hurdle
Hürden-: ~lauf der *(Leichtathletik)* hurdling; *(Wettbewerb)* hurdles *pl.;* hurdle race; **~läufer der** *(Leichtathletik)* hurdler; **~rennen das** *(Reitsport)* hurdle race; **~rennen reiten** ride in a hurdle race
Hure ['hu:rə] **die; ~, ~n** *(abwertend)* whore
huren *itr. V. (abwertend)* whore; fornicate; **mit jmdm. ~:** fornicate with sb.
Huren-: ~bock der *(abwertend)* whoremonger; fornicator; **~kind das** *(Druckw.)* widow; **~sohn der** *(abwertend)* bastard *(coll.);* son of a bitch *(derog.)*
Hurerei die; ~, ~en *(abwertend)* **~/~en** *Pl.* whoring *sing.;* fornication *sing.*
Huri ['hu:ri] **die; ~, ~s** *(islam. Rel.)* houri
hurra [hʊ'ra:] *Interj.* hurray; hurrah; **~ schreien** cheer; *s. auch* **hipp, hipp, ~**
Hurra das; ~s, ~s cheer; **ein dreifaches ~:** three cheers *pl.;* **jmdn. mit ~ begrüßen** greet sb. with cheering *or* cheers *pl.*
hurra-, Hurra-: ~gebrüll das, ~geschrei das [loud] cheering *or* cheers *pl.;* **~patriot der** *(ugs. abwertend)* flag-waving patriot; **~patriotisch** *Adj. (ugs. abwertend)* flag-waving ⟨*speech etc.*⟩; **~patriotismus der** *(ugs. abwertend)* flag-waving patriotism; **~ruf der** cheering; cheers *pl.*
Hurrikan ['hʌrɪkən] **der; ~s, ~s** hurricane
hurtig ['hʊrtɪç] **1.** *Adj.; nicht präd.* rapid. **2.** *adv.* quickly; ⟨*work*⟩ fast, quickly
Husar [hu'za:ɐ̯] **der; ~en, ~en** *(hist.)* hussar
Husaren-: ~streich der, ~stück das daring coup
husch [hʊʃ] **1.** *Interj.* quick; quickly; **~, ~!** away with you!; be off with you!; *(zu einem Tier)* shoo! **2.** *Adv.* **das geht nicht so ~, ~:** it can't be rushed; **bei ihr muß alles ~, ~ gehen** she wants everything done in a hurry
Husch der; ~[e]s, ~e *in* **in einem ~** *(ugs.)* in a flash; in no time at all
Husche ['hʊʃə] **die; ~, ~n** *(ostmd.)* [sudden] shower
huschen *itr. V.; mit sein (lautlos u. leichtfüßig)* ⟨*person*⟩ slip, steal; *(lautlos u. schnell)* flit, dart; ⟨*mouse, lizard, etc.*⟩ dart; ⟨*smile*⟩ flit; ⟨*light*⟩ flash; ⟨*shadow*⟩ slide *or* glide quickly
hussa ['hʊsa], **hussasa** ['hʊsasa] *Interj. (bei der Jagd)* tally-ho; halloo; *(zum Pferd)* gee-up
hüsteln ['hy:stl̩n] *itr. V.* cough slightly; give a slight cough; **verlegen/vornehm ~:** cough with embarrassment/politely
husten ['hu:stn̩] **1.** *itr. V.* **a)** cough; **auf etw.** *(Akk.)* **~** *(salopp)* not give a damn for sth.; **b)** *(Husten haben)* have a cough; be coughing. **2.** *tr. V.* cough up ⟨*blood, phlegm*⟩; **jmdm. etwas ~** *(salopp spött.)* tell sb. where he/she can get off *(coll.)*
Husten der; ~s, ~: cough; **~ haben** have a cough
Husten-: ~an·fall der coughing-fit; fit of coughing; **~bonbon das** cough sweet *(Brit.);* cough-drop; **~mittel das** cough medicine *or* mixture; **~reiz der** tickling in the throat; **den ~reiz nicht unterdrücken können** be unable to suppress the urge *or* need to cough; **~saft der** cough-syrup; cough mixture; **~tee der** *herb-tea which soothes coughs;* **~tropfen** *Pl.* cough-drops
¹Hut [hu:t] **der; ~es, Hüte** ['hy:tə] **a)** hat; **den ~ abnehmen/aufsetzen** take off/put on one's hat; **vor jmdm. den ~ ziehen** *(abnehmen)* take off one's hat to sb.; *(zum Gruß)* raise one's hat to sb.; **in ~ und Mantel** wearing one's hat and coat; with one's hat and coat on; **b)** *(fig.)* **da geht einem/mir der ~ hoch** *(ugs.)* it makes you/me mad *or* wild *(coll.);* **~ ab!** *(ugs.)* hats off to him/her *etc.;* I take my hat off to him/her *etc.;* **ein alter ~ sein** *(ugs.)* be old hat; **seinen ~ nehmen [müssen]** *(ugs.)* [have to] pack one's bags and go; **vor jmdm./etw. den ~ ziehen** *(ugs.)* take off one's hat to sb./sth.; **das kann er sich** *(Dat.)* **an den ~ stecken** *(ugs. abwertend)* he can keep it *(coll.) or (sl.)* stick it; **mit etw. nichts am ~ haben** *(ugs.)* have nothing to do with sth.; **jmdm. eins auf den ~ geben** *(ugs.)* give sb. a dressing down *or (Brit. sl.)* rocket; **eins auf den ~ kriegen** *(ugs.)* get a dressing down *or (sl.)* rocket; **verschiedene Interessen/Personen unter einen ~ bringen** *(ugs.)* reconcile different interests/the interests of different people; **c)** *(Bot.)* cap
²Hut die; ~ *(geh.)* keeping; care; **bei jmdm. in guter ~ sein** be in good hands with sb.; **auf der ~ sein** be on one's guard
Hut-: ~ab·lage die hat rack; **~band das** hat-band; *(eines Damenhutes)* hat-ribbon
Hüte·junge der shepherd boy
hüten ['hy:tn̩] **1.** *tr. V.* look after; take care of; tend, keep watch over ⟨*sheep, cattle, etc.*⟩; **etw. eifersüchtig ~:** guard sth. jealously; **ein Geheimnis ~** *(fig.)* keep *or* guard a secret; *s. auch* **Bett a. 2.** *refl. V. (vorsehen)* be on one's guard; **sich vor jmdm./etw. ~:** be on one's guard against sb./sth.; **sich ~, etw. zu tun** take [good] care not to do sth.; **ich werde mich ~!** *(ugs.)* no fear! *(coll.);* not likely! *(coll.)*
Hüter der; ~s, ~: guardian; custodian; **soll ich meines Bruders ~ sein?** *(bibl.)* am I my brother's keeper?; **ein ~ des Gesetzes** *(scherzh.)* a custodian of the law *(coll.)*
Hüterin die; ~, ~nen guardian; custodian
Hut-: ~feder die hat feather; *(größer)* plume; **~geschäft das** hat shop; hatter's [shop]; *(für Damen)* hat shop; milliner's (shop); **~größe die** hat size; size of hat; **~krempe die** [hat] brim; **~macher der** hatter; hat maker; *(für Damen)* milliner; **~macherin die; ~, ~nen** *s.* **~macher;** **~mode die** *(der Herren)* fashion in gents' *or* gentlemen's hats; *(der Damen)* fashion in ladies' hats; **~nadel die** hat-pin; **~schachtel die** hat-box
Hutsche ['hʊtʃə] **die; ~, ~n** *(südd., österr. ugs.) s.* **Schaukel**
Hut·schnur die *in* **das geht mir über die ~** *(ugs.)* that's going too far
Hutsch·pferd das *(südd., österr.) s.* **Schaukelpferd**
Hütte ['hʏtə] **die; ~, ~n a)** hut; *(Holz~)* cabin; hut; *(ärmliches Haus)* shack; hut; **b)** *(Eisen~)* iron [and steel] works *sing. or pl.;* *(Glas~)* glassworks *sing. or pl.;* *(Blei~)* lead works *sing. or pl.;* **c)** *(Jagd~)* [hunting-]lodge; **d)** *(Seemannsspr.)* poop
Hütten-: ~abend der *evening social gathering or party in a mountain hut;* **~arbeiter der** *(in der Eisenhütte)* worker in a/the iron/steel works; ironworker/steelworker; *(in der Glashütte)* glass worker; **~industrie die** iron and steel industry; **~käse der** cottage cheese; **~kombinat das** *(DDR)* metallurgical combine; **~schuh der** slipper-sock; **~werk das** *s.* **Hütte b;** **~wesen das;** *o. Pl. (Technik)* metallurgical engineering *no art.;* *(~industrie)* iron and steel industry
Hutzel ['hʊtsl̩] **die; ~, ~n** *(bes. südd.)* dried fruit; *(Birne)* dried pear
Hutzel·brot das *(bes. südd.)* fruit bread; **ein ~:** a fruit loaf
hutzelig *Adj. (ugs.)* wizened ⟨*person, face*⟩; shrivelled, dried-up ⟨*fruit*⟩
Hutzel-: ~männchen das brownie; **~weib[lein] das** wizened old woman
Hut·zucker der loaf sugar *(in the shape of a cone)*
Hyäne ['hyɛ:nə] **die; ~, ~n** *(auch fig. ugs.)* hyena
Hyazinthe [hya'tsɪntə] **die; ~, ~n** hyacinth
hybrid [hy'bri:t] *Adj. (bes. Biol.)* hybrid
Hybride der; ~n, ~n *(Biol.)* hybrid
Hybrid-: ~rechner der *(DV)* hybrid computer; **~züchtung die** *(Biol.)* cross-breeding; crossing
Hybris ['hy:brɪs] **die; ~** *(geh.)* hubris
Hydra ['hy:dra] **die; ~, Hydren** hydra
Hydrant [hy'drant] **der; ~en, ~en** hydrant
Hydrat [hy'dra:t] **das; ~[e]s, ~e** *(Chemie)* hydrate
Hydra[ta]tion [hydra[ta]'tsio:n] **die; ~** *(Chemie)* hydration
Hydraulik [hy'draulɪk] **die; ~** *(Technik)* **a)** *(Theorie)* hydraulics *sing., no art.;* **b)** *(Vorrichtungen)* hydraulics *pl.;* hydraulic system
hydraulisch *(Technik)* **1.** *Adj.* hydraulic. **2.** *adv.* hydraulically
Hydrid [hy'dri:t] **das; ~[e]s, ~e** *(Chemie)* hydride
hydrieren [hy'dri:rən] *tr. V. (Chemie)* hydrogenate
Hydrierung die; ~ *(Chemie)* hydrogenation
hydro-, Hydro- [hydro-]: **~biologie die** hydrobiology *no art.;* **~dynamik die** *(Physik)* hydrodynamics *sing., no art.;* **~dynamisch** *Adj. (Physik)* hydrodynamic; **~kultur die; ~, ~en** *(Gartenbau)* hydroponics *sing.;* **~lyse** [~'ly:zə] **die; ~, ~n** *(Chemie)* hydrolysis; **~meter das; ~s, ~** current meter; *(Senkwaage)* hydrometer; **~phil** [~'fi:l] *Adj.* **a)** *(Biol.)* hydrophilous ⟨*plant, insect*⟩; water-loving ⟨*animal*⟩; **b)** *(Chemie)* hydrophilic; **~phob** [~'fo:p] *Adj.* **a)** *(Biol.)* ⟨*plant, animal*⟩ that avoids water; **b)** *(Chemie)* hydrophobic; **~pneumatisch** *Adj. (Technik)* hydropneumatic; **~technik die; ~:** hydraulic engineering *no art.;* **~therapie die; ~, ~n** *(Med.)* hydrotherapy
Hydroxid, Hydroxyd das; ~[e]s, ~e *(Chemie)* hydroxide
Hygiene [hy'gie:nə] **die; ~ a)** *(Gesundheitspflege)* health care; **b)** *(Sauberkeit)* hygiene; **c)** *(Med.)* hygiene *no art.;* hygienics *sing., no art.*
hygienisch 1. *Adj.* hygienic. **2.** *adv.* hygienically
hygro-, Hygro- [hygro-]: **~meter das; ~s, ~** *(Met.)* hygrometer; **~skop** [~'sko:p] **das; ~s, ~e** *(Met.)* hygroscope; **~skopisch** *Adj. (Chemie)* hygroscopic
Hymen ['hy:mən] **das** *od.* **der; ~s, ~** *(Anat.)* hymen
Hymne ['hʏmnə] **die; ~, ~n a)** hymn; **b)** *(Nationalhymne)* national anthem
hymnisch *Adj.* hymnic; **ein ~er Gesang** a paean [of praise]
Hymnus ['hʏmnʊs] **der; ~, Hymnen** *(geh.) s.* **Hymne a**
Hyperbel [hy'pɛrbl̩] **die; ~, ~n a)** *(Geom.)* hyperbola; **b)** *(Rhet.)* hyperbole
Hyperbel·funktion die *(Math.)* hyperbolic function
hyperbolisch [hypɐ'bo:lɪʃ] *(Math., Rhet.)* hyperbolic
hyper-, Hyper- [hypɐ-]: **~korrekt** *(ugs. abwertend, Sprachw.)* **1.** *Adj.* hypercorrect;

2. *adv.* in a hypercorrect way; ~**kritisch** *Adj. (abwertend)* hypercritical; ~**modern** 1. *Adj.* ultra-modern; ultra-fashionable ⟨*clothes*⟩; 2. *adv.* ultra-modernly; ⟨*dress*⟩ ultra-fashionably; ~**sensibel** *Adj.* hypersensitive; ~**tonie** [~to'ni:] **die; ~, ~n** *(Med.)* **a)** hypertension; **b)** *(im Auge, Muskel)* hypertonia; ~**toniker** [~'to:nikɐ] **der; ~s, ~** *(Med.)* hypertensive; ~**troph** [~'tro:f] *Adj. (Med.)* hypertrophic; ~**trophie** [~tro'fi:] **die; ~** *(Med.)* hypertrophy

Hypnose [hʏp'no:zə] **die; ~, ~n** hypnosis; **jmdn. in ~ versetzen** put sb. under hypnosis; **unter ~ stehen** be under hypnosis

Hypno·therapie die hypnotherapy

Hypnotikum [hʏp'no:tikʊm] **das; ~s, Hypnotika** *(Med.)* hypnotic; soporific

hypnotisch *Adj.* hypnotic; hypnotic, soporific ⟨*drug*⟩

Hypnotiseur [hʏpnoti'zø:ɐ̯] **der; ~s, ~e** hypnotist

hypnotisieren *tr. V.* hypnotize

Hypnotismus der; ~: hypnotism *no art.*

Hypochonder [hypo'xɔndɐ] **der; ~s, ~:** hypochondriac

Hypochondrie die; ~, ~n *(Med.)* hypochondria *no art.*

hypochondrisch *Adj.* hypochondriac

hypo-, Hypo- [hypo-]: ~**nym** [~'ny:m] **das; ~s, ~e** *(Sprachw.)* hyponym; ~**physe** [~'fy:zə] **die; ~, ~n** *(Anat.)* hypophysis; ~**stase** [~'sta:zə] **die; ~, ~n a)** *(Philos.)* hypostasis; **b)** *(Sprachw.)* establishment as an independent word; ~**taktisch** [~'taktɪʃ] *Adj. (Sprachw.)* hypotactic; ~**taxe** [~'taksə] **die; ~, ~n** *(Sprachw.)* hypotaxis; ~**tenuse** [~te'nu:zə] **die; ~, ~n** *(Math.)* hypotenuse; ~**thalamus der** *(Anat.)* hypothalamus

Hypothek [-'te:k] **die; ~, ~en a)** *(Bankw.)* mortgage; **eine ~ aufnehmen** take out a mortgage; **etw. mit einer ~ belasten** encumber sth. with a mortgage; mortgage sth.; **b)** *(Bürde)* burden

hypothekarisch [-te'ka:rɪʃ] **1.** *Adj.* **~e Sicherheiten bieten** offer a mortgage [on property] as security; **~e Belastungen** mortgage *sing.* **2.** *adv.* **etw. ~ belasten** mortgage sth.

Hypotheken-: ~**brief der** *(Bankw.)* mortgage deed; ~**gläubiger der** *(Bankw.)* mortgagee; ~**pfand·brief der** *(Bankw.)* mortgage bond; ~**schuldner der** *(Bankw.)* mortgagor; ~**zins der;** *meist Pl.* mortgage interest

hypo-, Hypo-: ~**these** [~'te:zə] **die; ~, ~n** hypothesis; **das ist eine reine ~these** that's pure hypothesis; ~**thetisch 1.** *Adj.* hypothetical; **2.** *adv.* hypothetically; ~**tonie** [~to'ni:] **die; ~, ~n** *(Med.)* **a)** *(niedriger Blutdruck)* hypotension; **b)** *(im Auge, Muskel)* hypotonia; ~**toniker** [~'to:nikɐ] **der; ~s, ~:** hypotensive; ~**zykloide die** *(Math.)* hypocycloid

Hysterie [hʏste'ri:] **die; ~, ~n** [-i:ən] hysteria

Hysteriker [hʏs'te:rikɐ] **der; ~s, ~, Hysterikerin die; ~, ~nen** hysterical person; hysteric

hysterisch 1. *Adj.* hysterical; **einen ~en Anfall bekommen** have [a fit of] hysterics. **2.** *adv.* hysterically

Hz *Abk.* **Hertz** Hz

I

i, I [i:] **das; ~, ~:** i/I; **das Tüpfelchen** *od.* **der Punkt auf dem i** *(fig.)* the final touch; *s. auch* **a, A**

i *Interj.* ugh; **i bewahre, i wo** *(ugs.)* [good] heavens, no!

i. A. *Abk.* **im Auftrag[e]** p.p.

iah ['i:'a:] *Interj.* hee-haw

iahen ['i:'a:ən] *itr. V.* hee-haw; bray

IAO *Abk.* **Internationale Arbeitsorganisation** ILO

ibd. *Abk.* **ibidem** ibid.

iberisch [i'be:rɪʃ] *Adj.* Iberian; **Iberische Halbinsel** Iberian Peninsula

Ibero·amerika [i'be:ro-] Latin America

IBFG *Abk.* **Internationaler Bund Freier Gewerkschaften** ICFTU *(International Confederation of Free Trade Unions)*

ibidem [i'bi:dɛm] *Adv.* ibidem

Ibis ['i:bɪs] **der; ~ses, ~se** *(Zool.)* ibis

IC *Abk.* **Intercity** IC

ich [ɪç] *Personalpron.; 1. Pers. Sg. Nom.* I; **Wer ist da? – Ich bin's!** Who's there? – It's me!; **Wer hat nun das gemacht? – Ich war's** Who did that? – I did *or* It was me; **Hat sie mich gerufen? – Nein, ~:** Was it she who called me? – No, I did; **und ~ Esel/Idiot habe es gemacht** and I, silly ass/idiot that I am, did it; and, like a fool, I did it; **~ Idiot/Esel!** what an idiot I am!; I 'am an idiot!; **immer ~** *(ugs.)* [it's] always me; **~ selbst** I myself; **~ nicht** not me; **Menschen wie du und ~:** people like you and I *or* me; *s. auch (Gen.)* **meiner,** *(Dat.)* **mir,** *(Akk.)* **mich**

Ich das; ~[s], ~[s] a) self; **das eigene ~:** one's own self; **b)** *(Psych.)* ego

ich-, Ich-: ~**bewußt·sein das** self-awareness; ~**bezogen 1.** *Adj.* egocentric; *(in der Kommunikation)* egotistic; **2.** *adv.* **~bezogen denken** think in an egocentric way; ~**bezogenheit die; ~:** egocentricity; *(in der Kommunikation)* egotism; ~**-Erzähler der** first-person narrator; ~**-Form die;** *o. Pl.* first person; ~**-Laut der** *(Sprachw.)* palatal fricative; ich-laut; ~**sucht die;** *o. Pl. (geh.)* egoism; ~**süchtig** *Adj. (geh.)* egoistic[al]

Ichthyo·saurier [ɪçtʏo-] **der** ichthyosaurus

ideal [ide'a:l] **1.** *Adj.* ideal. **2.** *adv.* ideally; **das Haus liegt ~:** the house is ideally situated

Ideal das; ~s, ~e ideal; **er ist das ~ eines Vorgesetzten** he is the ideal *or* perfect boss *(coll.)*

Ideal-: ~**besetzung die a)** *(Film, Theater)* ideal cast; **b)** *(Sport)* ideal line-up; ~**bild das** ideal; ~**fall der** ideal case; **im ~fall** in ideal circumstances *pl.*; ~**figur die** ideal figure; ~**gestalt die** ideal; ~**gewicht das** ideal weight

idealisieren *tr. V.* idealize; **ein ~des Bild von etw.** an idealized picture of sth.

Idealisierung die; ~, ~en idealization

Idealismus der; ~ *(auch Philos.)* idealism

Idealist der; ~en, ~en *(auch Philos.)* idealist

idealistisch *(auch Philos.)* **1.** *Adj.* idealistic. **2.** *adv.* idealistically

ideal-, Ideal-: ~**konkurrenz die** *(Rechtsw.) s.* **Tateinheit;** ~**linie die** *(Sport)* ideal line; ~**typisch** *Adj. (Soziol.)* ideal-typical; idealized; ~**typus der** *(Soziol.)* ideal type; ~**vorstellung die** ideal

Idee [i'de:] **die; ~, ~n a)** idea; **du hast [vielleicht] ~n** *(iron.)* you do get some ideas, don't you!; **auf eine ~ kommen** hit [up]on an idea; **wie bist du nur auf die ~ gekommen?** whatever gave you 'that idea?; **jmdn. auf eine ~ bringen** give sb. an idea; **eine fixe ~:** an obsession; an idée fixe; **er ist von der fixen ~ besessen, Rennfahrer zu werden** he is obsessed with the idea of becoming a racing driver; **b)** *(ein bißchen)* **eine ~:** a shade *or* trifle; **eine ~ [Salz/Pfeffer]** a touch [of salt/pepper]

ideell [ide'ɛl] **1.** *Adj.* non-material; *(geistig-seelisch)* spiritual. **2.** *adv.* **etw. ~ unterstützen** support sth. in non-material ways

ideen-, Ideen-: ~**arm** *Adj.* lacking in ideas *postpos.*; ~**armut die** lack of ideas; ~**aus·tausch der** exchange of ideas; ~**drama das** *(Literaturw.)* drama of ideas; ~**gut das;** *o. Pl.* ideas *pl.*; ~**los** *Adj.* devoid of *or* [completely] lacking in ideas *postpos.*; ~**losigkeit die; ~:** [complete] lack of ideas; ~**reich** *Adj.* full of ideas *postpos.*; inventive; ~**reichtum der;** *o. Pl.* inventiveness

Iden ['i:dn̩] *Pl. (hist.)* **die ~ des März** the ides of March

Identifikation [idɛntifika'tsio:n] **die; ~, ~en** *(auch Psych.)* identification

identifizierbar *Adj.* identifiable; recognizable ⟨*handwriting*⟩

identifizieren [idɛntifi'tsi:rən] **1.** *tr. V.* identify. **2.** *refl. V. (auch Psych.)* **sich mit jmdm./etw. ~:** identify with sb./sth.

Identifizierung die; ~, ~en *(auch Psych.)* identification

identisch [i'dɛntɪʃ] *Adj.* identical; **möglicherweise sind der Einbrecher und der entsprungene Häftling ~:** it's possible that the intruder and the escaped prisoner are one and the same person

Identität [idɛnti'tɛ:t] **die; ~:** identity; **jmds. ~ feststellen** establish sb.'s identity; **die ~ dieser beiden Begriffe** the identity between these two concepts

Identitäts-: ~**krise die** identity crisis; ~**nachweis der** proof of identity; ~**verlust der** loss of identity

Ideogramm [ideo'gram] **das; ~s, ~e** ideogram

Ideologe [ideo'lo:gə] **der; ~n, ~n** ideologue

Ideologie die; ~, ~n [-i:ən] ideology

Ideologie-: ~**begriff der** conception of ideology; ~**kritik die** *(Soziol.)* ideological criticism

Ideologin die; ~, ~nen ideologue

ideologisch 1. *Adj.* ideological. **2.** *adv.* ideologically; **jmdn. ~ schulen** give sb. ideological instruction

ideologisieren *tr. V.* ideologize

Ideologisierung die; ~, ~en ideologization

Idiom [i'dio:m] **das; ~s, ~e** *(Sprachw.)* idiom

Idiomatik [idio'ma:tɪk] **die; ~** *(Sprachw.)* idioms *pl.*; *(Gebiet der Lexikologie)* idiomology *no art.*

idiomatisch 1. *Adj.* idiomatic. **2.** *adv.* idiomatically

Idiosynkrasie [idiozʏnkra'zi:] **die; ~, ~n a)** *(Med.)* idiosyncrasy; **b)** *(Psych.)* pathological aversion

Idiot [i'dio:t] **der; ~en, ~en a)** idiot; **b)** *(ugs. abwertend)* fool; *(stärker)* idiot *(coll.)*

Idioten-: ~**hang der,** ~**hügel der** *(ugs. scherzh.)* nursery slope

idioten·sicher *Adj. (ugs. scherzh.)* foolproof

Idiotie [idio'ti:] **die; ~, ~n** [-i:ən] **a)** idiocy; **b)** *(ugs. abwertend: Dummheit)* lunacy; madness; **seine ~n** his idiocies

Idiotikon [i'dio:tikɔn] **das; ~s, Idiotiken** *od.* **Idiotika** dialect dictionary

Idiotin die; ~, ~nen a) idiot; **b)** *(ugs. abwertend)* fool; *(stärker)* idiot

idiotisch 1. *Adj.* **a)** *(Psych.)* severely subnormal; idiotic *(as tech. term);* **b)** *(ugs. abwertend: unsinnig)* stupid; *(stärker)* idiotic. **2.** *adv.* **a)** *(schwachsinnig)* idiotically; **b)** *(ugs. abwertend: unsinnig)* stupidly; *(stärker)* idiotically

Idiotismus der; ~, Idiotismen a) *(Krankheit)* idiocy; **b)** *(Äußerung der Idiotie)* symptom of idiocy

Idol [i'do:l] **das; ~s, ~e** *(auch bild. Kunst)* idol; **jmdn. als ~ vergöttern** idolize sb.

Idolatrie die; ~, ~n [-i:ən] *(geh.)* idolatry

Idyll [i'dʏl] **das; ~s, ~e** idyll; **ein ~ für Erholungssuchende** an idyllic place *or* spot for those seeking relaxation and recreation

Idylle die; ~, ~n *(auch Literaturw.)* idyll

idyllisch 1. *Adj. (auch Literaturw.)* idyllic. **2.** *adv.* **~ gelegen** in an idyllic spot

i. e. *Abk.* **id est** i.e.

IG *Abk.* **Industriegewerkschaft**

Igel ['i:gl̩] **der; ~s, ~:** hedgehog

Igel-: ~schnitt der crew cut; **~stellung die** *(Milit.)* hedgehog position

igitt[igitt] [i'gɪt(i'gɪt)] *Interj.* ugh

Iglu ['i:glu] **der** *od.* **das; ~s, ~s** igloo

ignorant [ɪgno'rant] *Adj. (abwertend)* ignorant

Ignorant der; ~en, ~en *(abwertend)* ignoramus

Ignoranz [ɪgno'rants] **die; ~** *(abwertend)* ignorance

ignorieren *tr. V.* ignore

ihm [i:m] *Dat. der Personalpron.* **er, es: a)** *(nach Präpositionen) (bei Personen)* him; *(bei Dingen, Tieren)* it; *(bei männlichen Tieren)* him; it; **b) gib es ~:** give it to him; give him it; *(dem Tier)* give it to it/him; **ich sagte ~, daß ...:** I told him that ...; I said to him that ...; **~ geht es gut** he's well; **~ war, als habe man ~ ins Gesicht geschlagen** he felt as if somebody had punched him in the face; **sie sah ~ ins Gesicht** she looked him in the face; **sie hat ~ etwas zu essen gekocht** she cooked him a meal; she cooked a meal for him; **sie kämmte ihm das Haar** she combed his hair [for him]; **ich bin zu ~ gegangen** I went to see him; **Freunde von ~:** friends of his

ihn [i:n] *Akk. des Personalpron.* **er** *(bei Personen)* him; *(bei Dingen, Tieren)* it; *(bei männlichen Tieren)* him; it

ihnen ['i:nən] *Dat. des Personalpron.* **sie,** *Pl.* **a)** *(nach Präpositionen)* them; **b) gib es ~:** give it to them; give them it; **~ geht es gut** they're well; **Freunde von ~:** friends of theirs; *s. auch* **ihm**

Ihnen *Dat. von* **Sie** *(Anrede)* **a)** *(nach Präpositionen)* you; **b) ich habe es ~ gegeben** I gave it to you; I gave you it; **geht es ~ gut?** are you well?; **Freunde von ~:** friends of yours; *s. auch* **ihm**

¹ihr [i:ɐ̯] *Dat. des Personalpron.* **sie,** *Sg. (nach Präpositionen) (bei Personen)* her; *(bei Dingen, Tieren)* it; *(bei weiblichen Tieren)* her; it; *s. auch* **ihm**

²ihr, *(in Briefen)* **Ihr** *Personalpron.; 2. Pers. Pl. Nom. (Anrede an vertraute Personen)* you; **Ihr Lieben** *(im Brief)* dear all; *s. auch (Gen.)* **euer/Euer,** *(Dat., Akk.)* **euch/Euch**

³ihr *Possessivpron.* **a)** *(einer Person)* her; **Ihre Majestät** Her Majesty; **das Buch dort, ist das ~[e]s?** that book there, is it hers?; is that book hers?; **das ist nicht mein Mann, sondern ~er** that is not my husband, but hers; **der/die/das ~e** hers; **die ~en** hers; **die Ihren** her family; **b)** *(eines Tieres, einer Sache)* its; *(eines weiblichen Tieres)* her; its; **die Lok fährt glatt ~e 200 Sachen** *(ugs.)* the locomotive does a good 200 kilometres an hour; **c)** *(mehrerer Personen, Tiere, Sachen)* their; **das Haus am Ende der Straße ist ~es** the house at the end of the street is theirs; **der/die/das ~e** theirs; **die ~en** theirs; **die Ihren** their family; **sie haben das Ihre getan** they did their bit; **sie haben das Ihre bekommen** they got their due *or* what was due to them

Ihr *Possessivpron. (Anrede)* your; **~ Hans Meier** *(Briefschluß)* yours, Hans Meier; **welcher Mantel ist ~er?** which coat is yours?; **der/die/das ~e** yours; **die ~en** yours; **Sie haben das ~e getan** you have done your bit; *s. auch* **³ihr**

ihrer ['i:rɐ] **a)** *Gen. des Personalpron.* **sie,** *Sg. (geh.)* **wir gedachten ~:** we remembered her; **b)** *Gen. des Personalpron.* **sie,** *Pl. (geh.)* **wir werden ~ gedenken** we will remember them; **es waren ~ zwölf** there were twelve of them

Ihrer *Gen. von* **Sie** *(Anrede) (geh.)* **wir werden ~ gedenken** we will remember you

ihrerseits [-zaits] *Adv.* **a)** *Sg. (von ihrer Seite)* on her part; *(auf ihrer Seite)* for her part; **b)** *Pl. (von ihrer Seite)* on their part; *(auf ihrer Seite)* for their part

Ihrerseits *Adv. (von Ihrer Seite)* on your part; *(auf Ihrer Seite)* for your part

ihres·gleichen *indekl. Pron.* **a)** *Sg.* people *pl.* like her; *(abwertend)* the likes of her; her sort *or* kind; **sie fühlt sich nur unter ~ wohl** she only feels at home among people like herself *or* her own kind; **b)** *Pl.* people like them; *(abwertend)* the likes of them; their sort *or* kind; **sie sollten unter ~ bleiben** they should stay among their own kind

Ihresgleichen *indekl. Pron.* people *pl.* like you; *(abwertend)* the likes of you; your sort *or* kind; **Sie sollten besser unter ~ bleiben** you should stay among your own kind

ihret·halben *(veralt.),* **ihret·wegen** *Adv.* **a)** *Sg. (wegen ihr)* because of her; on her account; *(für sie)* on her behalf; *(ihr zuliebe)* for her sake; **mach dir ~ keine Sorgen** don't worry about her; **b)** *Pl. (wegen ihnen)* because of them; on their account; *(für sie)* on their behalf; *(ihnen zuliebe)* for their sake[s]; *(um sie)* about them

Ihrethalben *(veralt.),* **Ihretwegen** *Adv. (wegen Ihnen)* because of you; on your account; *(für Sie)* on your behalf; *(Ihnen zuliebe)* for your sake; *Pl.* for your sake[s]; *(um Sie)* about you

ihret·willen *Adv.* **in um ~** *(Sg.)* for her sake; *(Pl.)* for their sake[s]

Ihret·willen *Adv.* **in um ~** *(Sg.)* for your sake; *(Pl.)* for your sake[s]

ihrige ['i:rɪgə] *Possessivpron. (geh. veralt.)* **a)** *Sg.* **der/die/das ~:** hers; **b)** *Pl.* **der/die/das ~:** theirs; s. auch **deinige**

Ihrige *Possessivpron. (Anrede) (geh. veralt.)* **der/die/das ~:** yours

Ihro ['i:ro] *indekl. Pron. (veralt.)* your; **~ Gnaden** Your Grace

Ikebana [ike'ba:na] **das; ~[s]** ikebana

Ikone [i'ko:nə] **die; ~, ~n** icon

Ikonoklasmus [ikono'klasmʊs] **der; ~, Ikonoklasmen** *(geh.)* iconoclasm

Ikosaeder [ikoza'|e:dɐ] **das; ~s, ~** *(Math.)* icosahedron

Ilex ['i:lɛks] **die** *od.* **der; ~, ~** *(Bot.)* holly

Ilias ['i:li̯as] **die; ~:** Iliad

illegal ['ɪlega:l] **1.** *Adj.* illegal. **2.** *adv.* illegally

Illegalität [ɪlegali'tɛ:t] **die; ~, ~en** illegality

illegitim ['ɪlegiti:m] *Adj. (geh.)* illegitimate

Illegitimität die; ~ *(geh.)* illegitimacy

illiquid ['ɪlikvi:t] *Adj. (Wirtsch.)* insolvent

Illiquidität die; ~ *(Wirtsch.)* insolvency

illoyal ['ɪloaja:l] *Adj. (geh.)* disloyal

Illoyalität die; ~ *(geh.)* disloyalty

Illumination [ɪlumina'tsi̯o:n] **die; ~, ~en a)** *(Beleuchtung)* illumination; **die Stadt zeigte sich in festlicher ~:** the town was festively lit; **b)** *(von Handschriften)* illumination

Illuminator [ɪlumi'na:tɔr] **der; ~s, ~en** [-'to:rən] illuminator

illuminieren *tr. V.* illuminate

Illuminierung die; ~, ~en illumination

Illusion [ɪlu'zi̯o:n] **die; ~, ~en** illusion; **sich** *(Dat.)* **~en machen** delude oneself; **jmdm. die ~en rauben** rob sb. of his/her illusions; **gib dich doch nicht der ~ hin, du könntest damit irgend etwas erreichen** do not delude yourself that you could achieve anything by that

illusionär [ɪluzi̯o'nɛ:ɐ̯] *Adj. (geh.)* illusory ⟨*conception, expectation, thing*⟩; fanciful ⟨*demand, procedure, attempt*⟩

Illusionist der; ~en, ~en a) *(geh.)* dreamer; **b)** *(Zauberkünstler)* illusionist

illusionistisch *Adj. (Kunstw.)* illusionistic

illusions·los 1. *Adj.* [sober and] realistic; **~ sein** have no illusions. **2.** *adv.* without any illusions

illusorisch [ɪlu'zo:rɪʃ] *Adj.* **a)** *(trügerisch)* illusory; **b)** *(zwecklos)* pointless

illuster [ɪ'lʊstɐ] *Adj. (geh.)* illustrious

Illustration [ɪlʊstra'tsi̯o:n] **die; ~, ~en** illustration; **zur ~ von etw. [dienen]** *(fig.)* [serve] to illustrate sth.

illustrativ [ɪlʊstra'ti:f] **1.** *Adj. (auch fig.)* illustrative; **ein sehr ~er Vortrag** *(fig.)* a very illuminating lecture. **2.** *adv.* **etw. ~ schildern** describe sth. graphically

Illustrator [ɪlʊs'tra:tɔr] **der; ~s, ~en** [-'to:rən] illustrator

illustrieren *tr. V. (auch fig.)* illustrate; **eine illustrierte Zeitschrift** a magazine; **jmdm. etw. ~:** illustrate sth. for sb.

Illustrierte die; *adj. Dekl.* magazine

Illustrierung die; ~, ~en *(auch fig.)* illustration

Iltis ['ɪltɪs] **der; ~ses, ~se** polecat; *(Pelz)* fitch

im [ɪm] *Präp.* + *Art.* **a) = in dem; b)** *(räumlich)* in the; **er wohnt im vierten Stock** he lives on the fourth floor; **im Theater** at the theatre; **er tritt im Zirkus auf** he is appearing in *or* performing with the circus; **im Fernsehen** on television; **im Bett** in bed; **im Spessart/Schwarzwald** in the Spessart/the Black Forest; **c)** *(zeitlich)* **im Mai/Januar** in May/January; **im Jahre 1648** in [the year] 1648; **im letzten Jahr** last year; **im Alter von 50 Jahren** at the age of 50; **d)** *(Verlauf)* **etw. im Sitzen tun** do sth. [while] sitting down; **noch im Laufen** while still running; **im Gehen/Kommen sein** be going/coming

i. m. *Abk. (Med.)* **intramuskulär** IM

Image ['ɪmɪtʃ] **das; ~[s], ~s** ['ɪmɪtʃs] image

Image·pflege die; *o. Pl.* cultivation of one's image

imaginär [imagi'nɛ:ɐ̯] *Adj. (geh., Math.)* imaginary

Imagination [imagina'tsi̯o:n] **die; ~, ~en** *(geh.)* imagination

imaginativ [imagina'ti:f] *Adj. (geh.)* imaginative

Imagismus [ima'gɪsmʊs] **der; ~** *(Literaturw.)* imagism *no art.*

Imago [i'ma:go] **die; ~, Imagines** [-gine:s] **a)** *(Psych., Biol.)* imago; **b)** *(Kunstwiss.) wax death mask of an ancestor*

Imam [i'ma:m] **der; ~s, ~s** *od.* **~e** imam

imbezil [ɪmbe'tsi:l], **imbezill** [ɪmbe'tsɪl] *Adj. (Med.)* imbecile

Imbiß ['ɪmbɪs] **der; Imbisses, Imbisse a)** *(kleine Mahlzeit)* snack; **b)** *s.* **Imbißlokal**

Imbiß-: ~bude die *(ugs.)* ≈ hot-dog stall *or* stand; **~lokal das** café; **~stand der** *s.* **~bude; ~stube die** *s.* **~lokal**

-imitat das; ~s, ~e imitation ⟨*leather, wood, etc.*⟩

Imitation [imita'tsi̯o:n] **die; ~, ~en** imitation

Imitator [imi'ta:tɔr] **der; ~s, ~en** [-ta'to:rən] imitator; mimic; *(im Kabarett usw.)* impressionist

imitieren *tr. V.* imitate

Imker ['ɪmkɐ] **der; ~s, ~:** bee-keeper; apiarist *(formal)*

Imkerei die; ~, ~en a) *o. Pl. (Bienenzucht)* bee-keeping *no art.; (as tech. term)* apiculture *no art.;* **b)** *(Betrieb)* apiary

imkern *itr. V.* keep bees

immanent [ɪma'nɛnt] *Adj.* **a)** *(geh.)* inherent; **einer Sache** *(Dat.)* **~ sein** be inherent in sth.; **b)** *(Philos.)* immanent

Immanenz [ɪma'nɛnts] **die;** ~ *(Philos.)* immanence

immateriell [ɪmate'ri̯ɛl] *Adj. (geh.)* non-material

Immatrikulation [ɪmatrikula'tsi̯o:n] **die;** ~, **~en a)** *(Hochschulw.)* registration; **b)** *(schweiz.: eines Fahrzeugs)* registration

immatrikulieren 1. *tr. V.* **a)** *(Hochschulw.)* register; **b)** *(schweiz.)* register ⟨*vehicle*⟩. **2.** *refl. V. (Hochschulw.)* register

Imme ['ɪmə] **die;** ~, **~n** *(dichter.)* bee

immens [ɪ'mɛns] **1.** *Adj.* immense. **2.** *adv.* immensely; enormously ⟨*expensive*⟩

immer ['ɪmɐ] *Adv.* **a)** always; **wie ~:** as always; as usual; **mach es wie ~!** do it the way you've/we've always done it; **~ dieser Nebel/dieser Streit** this fog never seems to lift/you're/they're *etc.* always arguing; **~ diese Kinder!** these wretched children!; **schon ~:** always; **~ und ewig** for ever; *(jedesmal)* always; **auf** *od.* **für ~ [und ewig]** for ever [and ever]; **sie haben sich für ~ getrennt** they've split up for good; **~ wieder** again and again; time and time again; **~ wieder von vorne anfangen** keep on starting from the beginning again; **~, wenn** every time that; whenever; **er ist ~ der Dumme** *(ugs.)* he's always the loser; **~ ich!** *(ugs.)* [it's] always me; **b) ~ +** *Komp. (nach u. nach)* **~ dunkler/häufiger** darker and darker/more and more often; **~ mehr** more and more; **~ mehr zunehmen** keep on increasing; **c)** *(ugs.: jeweils)* **es durften ~ zwei auf einmal eintreten** we/they were allowed in two at a time; **~ drei Stufen auf einmal** three steps at a time; **d)** *(auch)* **wo/wer/wann/wie [auch] ~:** wherever/whoever/whenever/however; **e)** *(verstärkend)* **~ noch, noch ~:** still; **f)** *(ugs.: bei Aufforderung)* **~ langsam!/mit der Ruhe!** take it easy!; **nur ~ zu!** keep it up!; **~ geradeaus!** keep [going] straight on; **~ der Nase nach!** keep following your nose!; **was treibst du denn ~?** what are you doing these days?; **g)** *(irgend)* **so schnell er ~ konnte** as fast as he possibly could

immer-, Immer-: ~dar [~'da:ɐ̯] *Adv. (geh.)* forever; [for] evermore; **~fort** *Adv.* all the time; constantly; **~grün** *Adj.* evergreen; **~grün das** periwinkle; **~hin** *Adv.* **a)** *(wenigstens)* at any rate; anyhow; at least; **er hat es ~hin versucht** he tried, anyhow *or* at any rate; at least he tried; **er ist zwar nicht reich, aber ~hin!** he's not rich, it's true, but still; **b)** *(trotz allem)* nevertheless; all the same; **c)** *(schließlich)* after all

Immersion [ɪmɛr'zi̯o:n] **die;** ~, **~en** *(Physik, Astron.)* immersion

immer-: ~während 1. *Adj.; nicht präd.* perpetual; eternal, everlasting ⟨*bliss, friendship, memory*⟩; **der ~währende Kalender** the perpetual calendar; **2.** *adv.* perpetually; **~zu** *Adv. (ugs.)* the whole time; all the time; constantly

Immigrant [ɪmi'grant] **der;** ~**en,** ~**en, Immigrantin die;** ~, **~nen** immigrant

Immigration [ɪmigra'tsi̯o:n] **die;** ~, **~en** immigration

immigrieren *itr. V.; mit sein* immigrate

imminent [ɪmi'nɛnt] *Adj. (veralt.)* imminent

Immission [ɪmi'si̯o:n] **die;** ~, **~en** *(fachspr.)* *air pollution, noise, noxious substances, radiation, etc. constituting a private nuisance*

Immissions·schutz der *protection against the effects of air pollution, noise, noxious substances, radiation, etc.*

immobil ['ɪmobi:l] *Adj.* **a)** *(geh.)* immobile; **~es Vermögen** immovable property; real estate *or* property; **b)** *(Milit.)* not on a war footing *postpos.*

Immobilien [ɪmo'bi:li̯ən] *Pl.* [real] property *sing.*; real estate *sing.*; *(Rubrik in Zeitungen)* property *sing.*

Immobilien-: ~handel der dealing *no art.* in real estate *or* in property; **~händler der** estate agent

immobilisieren *tr. V. (Med.)* immobilize

Immoralismus [ɪmora'lɪsmʊs] **der;** ~ *(geh.)* immoralism

Immortelle [ɪmɔr'tɛlə] **die;** ~, **~n** everlasting [flower]; immortelle

immun [ɪ'mu:n] **a)** *(Med., fig.)* immune (**gegen** to); **b)** *(Rechtsspr.)* **~ sein** have *or* enjoy immunity

immunisieren *tr. V.* immunize (**gegen** against)

Immunisierung die; ~, **~en** immunization (**gegen** against)

Immunität [ɪmuni'tɛ:t] **die;** ~, **~en a)** *(Med.)* immunity (**gegen** to); **b)** *(Rechtsspr.)* immunity (**gegen** from)

Immunologie [ɪmunolo'gi:] **die;** ~**:** immunology

Imp. *Abk.* **a) Imperfekt** imperf.; **b) Imperativ** imper.

Impedanz [ɪmpe'dants] **die;** ~, **~en** *(Elektrot.)* impedance

Imperativ ['ɪmperati:f] **der;** ~**s,** ~**e a)** *(Sprachw.)* imperative; **b)** *(Philos.)* **[kategorischer] ~:** [categorical] imperative

imperativisch *(Sprachw.)* **1.** *Adj.* imperative. **2.** *adv.* in the imperative

Imperativ·satz der imperative sentence

Imperator [ɪmpe'ra:tɔr] **der;** ~**s,** ~**en** [-'to:rən] *(hist.)* **a)** *(römischer Oberfeldherr)* imperator; **b)** *(Kaiser)* emperor; **~ Rex** King Emperor

Imperfekt ['ɪmpɛrfɛkt] **das;** ~**s,** ~**e, Imperfektum** [ɪmpɛr'fɛktʊm] **das;** ~**s, Imperfekta** *(Sprachw.)* imperfect [tense]

Imperialismus [ɪmperi̯a'lɪsmus] **der;** ~**:** imperialism *no art.*

Imperialist der; ~**en,** ~**en** imperialist

imperialistisch *Adj.* imperialistic

Imperium [ɪm'pe:ri̯ʊm] **das;** ~**s, Imperien** *(hist., fig.)* empire

impertinent [ɪmpɛrti'nɛnt] **1.** *Adj.* impertinent; impudent. **2.** *adv.* impertinently; impudently

Impertinenz [ɪmpɛrti'nɛnts] **die;** ~, **~en** impertinence; impudence; **diese ~en** this impertinence *or* impudence *sing.*

Impetus ['ɪmpetʊs] **der;** ~ **a)** *(Antrieb)* impetus; **b)** *(Schwung)* verve; zest

Impf-: ~aktion die vaccination *or* inoculation programme; **~arzt der** vaccinator; inoculator; **~ausweis der** vaccination certificate

impfen ['ɪmpfn̩] *tr. V.* **a)** vaccinate, inoculate; **sich ~ lassen** be vaccinated *or* inoculated; **b)** *(Biol., Landw.)* inoculate

Impfling ['ɪmpflɪŋ] **der;** ~**s,** ~**e** person who has been vaccinated; *(zu impfende Person)* person waiting to be vaccinated

Impf-: ~paß der vaccination certificate; **~pflicht die: die ~pflicht für die Pockenimpfung wurde aufgehoben** compulsory vaccination for smallpox was abolished; **~pistole die** inoculation injector; **~schaden der** vaccine damage *no pl., no indef. art.*; **~schutz der** protection given by vaccination; **~stoff der** vaccine

Impfung die; ~, **~en** vaccination; inoculation

Impf-: ~zeugnis das *s.* **~ausweis; ~zwang der** *s.* **~pflicht**

Implantat [ɪmplan'ta:t] **das;** ~**[e]s,** ~**e** *(Med.)* implant

Implantation [ɪmplanta'tsi̯o:n] **die;** ~, **~en** *(Med.)* implantation

implantieren *tr. V. (Med.)* implant; **jmdm. etw. implantieren** implant sth. in sb.

Implikation [ɪmplika'tsi̯o:n] **die;** ~, **~en** *(geh., Logik)* implication

implizieren [ɪmpli'tsi:rən] *tr. V. (geh.)* imply

implizit [ɪmpli'tsi:t] *(geh.)* **1.** *Adj.* implicit. **2.** *adv.* implicitly

implizite [ɪm'pli:tsite] *Adv. (geh.)* **implicitly**

implodieren [ɪmplo'di:rən] *itr. V.; mit sein (fachspr.)* implode

Implosion [ɪmplo'zi̯o:n] **die;** ~, **~en** *(fachspr.)* implosion

Imponderabilien [ɪmpɔndəra'bi:li̯ən] *Pl. (geh.)* imponderables

imponieren [ɪmpo'ni:rən] *itr. V.* impress; **jmdm. durch etw./mit etw. ~:** impress sb. by sth.; **am meisten imponiert uns an ihm seine Ruhe** what impresses us most about him is his calmness

imponierend 1. *Adj.* impressive. **2.** *adv.* impressively

Imponier·gehabe[n] das *(Verhaltensf.)* display

Import [ɪm'pɔrt] **der;** ~**[e]s,** ~**e** import; **den ~ erhöhen** increase imports; **eine Firma für ~ und Export** an import/export firm

Importeur [ɪmpɔr'tø:ɐ̯] **der;** ~**s,** ~**e** importer

Import·geschäft das a) import business; **b)** *(geschäftlicher Abschluß)* import deal

importieren *tr., itr. V.* import

Import-: ~kaufmann der importer; **~über·schuß der** import surplus

imposant [ɪmpo'zant] **1.** *Adj.* imposing; impressive ⟨*achievement*⟩. **2.** *adv.* imposingly

impotent ['ɪmpotɛnt] *Adj.* impotent

Impotenz ['ɪmpotɛnts] **die;** ~**:** impotence

imprägnieren [ɪmprɛ'gni:rən] *tr. V.* **a)** impregnate; *(wasserdicht machen)* waterproof; **b)** *(fachspr.)* carbonate ⟨*wine*⟩

Imprägnierung die; ~, **~en** *s.* **imprägnieren a, b:** impregnation; waterproofing; carbonation

im·praktikabel *Adj.* impracticable

Impresario [ɪmpre'za:ri̯o] **der;** ~**s,** ~**s** *od.* **Impresari** *(veralt.)* impresario

Impressen *s.* **Impressum**

Impression [ɪmprɛ'si̯o:n] **die;** ~, **~en** impression

Impressionismus der; ~**:** impressionism *no art.*

Impressionist der; ~**en,** ~**en** impressionist

impressionistisch *Adj.* impressionistic

Impressum [ɪm'prɛsum] **das;** ~**s, Impressen** imprint

Imprimatur [ɪmpri'ma:tʊr] **das;** ~**s,** *(österr.:)* [---'-] **die;** ~ **a)** *(Buchw.)* **das** *od.* *(österr.)* **die ~ [für etw.] erteilen** pass sth. for press; **b)** *(kath. Kirche)* imprimatur

Improvisation [ɪmproviza'tsi̯o:n] **die;** ~, **~en** improvisation

Improvisations·talent das gift *or* talent for improvisation

improvisieren *tr., itr. V.* improvise; **über ein Thema ~** *(Musik)* improvise on a theme

Impuls [ɪm'pʊls] **der;** ~**es,** ~**e a)** *(Anstoß)* stimulus; **von etw. gehen wichtige ~e aus** sth. is an important stimulus *sing.*; **einer Sache** *(Dat.)* **neue ~e geben** give sth. fresh stimulus *sing. or* impetus *sing.*; **b)** *(innere Regung)* impulse; **einem ~ folgen** act on [an] impulse; **etw. aus einem ~ heraus tun** do sth. on impulse; **c)** *(Elektrot.)* pulse; **d)** *(Physik)* impulse; *(Produkt aus Masse u. Geschwindigkeit)* momentum

Impuls-: ~geber der, ~generator der *(Elektrot.)* pulse generator

impulsiv [ɪmpʊl'zi:f] **1.** *Adj.* impulsive. **2.** *adv.* impulsively

Impulsivität [ɪmpʊlzivi'tɛ:t] **die;** ~**:** impulsiveness

Impuls·satz der *(Physik)* principle of the conservation of momentum

imstande [ɪm'ʃtandə] *Adv.* **~ sein, etw. zu tun** *(fähig sein)* be able to do sth.; be capable of doing sth.; *(die Möglichkeit haben)* be in a position to do sth.; **zu etw. ~ sein** be capable of sth.; **er ist ~ und schiebt mir die Schuld in die Schuhe** he's [quite] capable of putting the blame on to me

¹in [ɪn] **1.** *Präp. mit Dat.* **a)** *(auf die Frage: wo?)* in; **er hat ~ Tübingen studiert** he studied at Tübingen; ~ **Deutschland/der Schweiz** in Germany/Switzerland; **sind Sie schon mal ~ China gewesen?** have you ever been to China?; ~ **der Schule/Kirche** at school/church; ~ **der Schule/Kirche steht noch eine alte Orgel** there's still an old organ in the school/church; ~ **einer Partei** in a party; **b)** *(auf die Frage: wann?)* in; ~ **zwei Tagen/einer Woche** in two days/a week; ~ **diesem Sommer** this summer; **[gerade] ~ dem Moment, als er kam** the [very] moment he came; ~ **diesem Jahr/Monat** this/that year/month; **c)** *(auf die Frage: wie?)* in; ~ **Farbe/Schwarzweiß** in colour/black and white; ~ **deutsch/englisch** in German/English; **d)** *(fig.)* ~ **Mathematik/Englisch** in mathematics/English; **sich ~ jmdm. täuschen** be wrong about sb.; **e)** *in* **er hat es ~ sich** *(ugs.)* he's got what it takes *(coll.)*; **der Schnaps/diese Übersetzung hat es ~ sich** *(ugs.)* this schnapps packs a punch *(coll.)*/this translation is a tough one; **f)** *(Kaufmannsspr.)* ~ **etw. handeln** deal in sth.; **er macht ~ Spirituosen** *(ugs.)* he deals in spirits; *s. auch* **im. 2.** *Präp. mit Akk.* **a)** *(auf die Frage: wohin?)* into; ~ **die Stadt/das Dorf** into town/the village; ~ **die Schweiz** to Switzerland; ~ **die Kirche/Schule gehen** go to church/school; ~ **eine Partei eintreten** join a party; **b)** *(auf die Frage: [bis] wann?)* into; **bis ~ den Herbst** into the autumn; **c)** *(fig.)* ~ **die Millionen gehen** run into millions; **sich ~ jmdn. verlieben** fall in love with sb.; ~ **etw. einwilligen** agree *or* consent to sth.; *s. auch* **ins**

²in *Adj. in* ~ **sein** *(ugs.)* be in

-in *Bei der Übersetzung ins Englische wird das deutsche Suffix* **-in**, *mit dem feminine Substantive wie* **Lehrerin** *oder* **Kanadierin** *als Ableitungen von Maskulina gebildet werden, im allgemeinen nicht übersetzt* (**Lehrerin** = teacher). *Soll jedoch betont werden, daß es sich um weibliche Personen im Gegensatz zu männlichen handelt, bieten sich folgende Übersetzungsmöglichkeiten an:* **Lehrerinnen gehen mit 60 in den Ruhestand** women teachers retire at sixty; **sie ist die bekannteste Kanadierin** she is the best-known Canadian woman; *gelegentlich sind Formulierungen wie* lady teachers *oder* Canadian lady *angebracht, wenn eine besonders höfliche Ausdrucksweise angestrebt wird. Sofern es sich um eine Nationalitätenbezeichnung handelt und die betreffende Person noch recht jung ist, findet man auch häufig die Form* Canadian girl. *In diesem Wörterbuch wurde aus Platzgründen auf die Darstellung solcher Möglichkeiten beim jeweiligen Einzelstichwort meist verzichtet*

in·adäquat 1. *Adj. (geh.)* inadequate. **2.** *adv.* inadequately

in·aktiv 1. *Adj. (geh., auch Chemie, Med.)* inactive. **2.** *adv.* **sich ~ verhalten** be inactive

In·aktivität die; ~ *(geh., auch Chemie, Med.)* inactivity

in·akzeptabel *Adj. (geh.)* unacceptable

In·angriffnahme [-na:mə] **die;** ~, ~**n** *(Amtsspr.)* commencement; *(eines Problems)* tackling

In·anspruchnahme die; ~, ~**n a)** *(Amtsspr.)* use; **bei häufiger ~ der Versicherung** if frequent [insurance] claims are made; **auf ~ seiner Rechte verzichten** waive one's rights; **b)** *(starke Belastung)* demands *pl.*; **die große berufliche ~:** the heavy demands made on him/her by his/her job; **c)** *(von Maschinen, Material)* use; *(von Einrichtungen)* utilization

in·artikuliert *(geh.)* **1.** *Adj.* inarticulate. **2.** *adv.* inarticulately

In·augenscheinnahme die; ~, ~**n** *(Amtsspr.)* inspection; **nach ~ mehrerer Wohnungen** after inspecting several flats

Inaugural·dissertation [ɪnlaugu'ra:l-] **die** *(doctoral)* thesis

Inauguration [ɪnlaugura'tsio:n] **die;** ~, ~**en** *(geh.)* inauguration

In·begriff der quintessence; **der ~ des Gelehrten/Spießers** the epitome of the scholar/petit bourgeois; the quintessential scholar/petit bourgeois; **der ~ der Schönheit/des Schreckens** the quintessence of beauty/terror; **sie ist der ~ der Tugend/des Bösen** she is virtue personified *or* itself/the embodiment of evil

inbegriffen *Adj.* included

In·besitznahme die; ~, ~**n** *(Amtsspr.)* appropriation

In·betriebnahme die; ~, ~**n, In·betriebsetzung** [-zɛtsʊŋ] **die;** ~, ~**en** *(Amtsspr.)* **a)** *(von [öffentlichen] Einrichtungen)* opening; **b)** *(von Maschinen)* bringing into service; **vor ~ der Maschine** before bringing the machine into service; **c)** *(eines Kraftwerks)* commissioning

In·brunst die; ~ *(geh.)* fervour; *(der Liebe)* ardour; **mit ~:** with fervour; **jmdn. mit ~ lieben** love sb. ardently

in·brünstig *(geh.)* **1.** *Adj.* fervent; ardent ‹*love*›. **2.** *adv.* fervently; ‹*love*› ardently

Inbus·schlüssel ⓦ ['ɪnbʊs-] **der** *(Technik)* Allen key

Indanthren ⓦ [ɪndan'tre:n] **das;** ~**s,** ~**e** *(Textilind.)* indanthrene

Indefinit·pronomen [ɪndefi'ni:t-] **das** *(Sprachw.)* indefinite pronoun

in·deklinabel *Adj. (Sprachw.)* indeclinable

in·dem *Konj.* **a)** *(während)* while; *(gerade als)* as; **b)** *(dadurch, daß)* ~ **man etw. tut** by doing sth.; **c)** *(bes. südd.)* ~ **daß** because

Indemnität [ɪndɛmni'tɛ:t] **die;** ~**:** ≈ parliamentary privilege

Inder ['ɪndɐ] **der;** ~**s,** ~, **Inderin die;** ~, ~**nen** Indian

in·des *(selten),* **in·dessen 1.** *Konj. (geh.)* **a)** *(während)* while; **b)** *(wohingegen)* whereas. **2.** *Adv.* **a)** *(inzwischen)* meanwhile; in the mean time; **b)** *(jedoch)* however

Index ['ɪndɛks] **der;** ~ *od.* ~**es,** ~**e** *od.* **Indizes** ['ɪnditse:s] **a)** *Pl.* ~**e** *od.* **Indizes** *(Register)* index; **b)** *Pl.* ~**e** *(kath. Kirche)* Index; **c)** *Pl.* **Indizes** *(Math., Physik, Wirtsch.)* index

Index·zahl die *(Wirtsch.)* index [number]

in·dezent *Adj. (geh.)* indelicate

Indianer [ɪn'dia:nɐ] **der;** ~**s,** ~**:** [American] Indian

Indianer-: ~**geheul das** *(scherzh.)* **mit ~geheul** whooping and yelling like a Red Indian/[Red] Indians; ~**häuptling der** Indian chief

Indianerin die; ~, ~**nen** [American] Indian

Indianer-: ~**krapfen der** *(österr.) s.* **Mohrenkopf a**; ~**reservat das** Indian reservation

indianisch *Adj.* Indian

Indien ['ɪndiən] **(das)** India

In·dienst·stellung die; ~, ~**en** *(Amtsspr.)* commissioning

in·different 1. *Adj. (geh., fachspr.)* indifferent. **2.** *adv. (geh.)* indifferently

In·differenz die; ~, ~**en** *(geh., auch Chemie, Med.)* indifference

Indignation [ɪndɪgna'tsio:n] **die;** ~ *(geh.)* indignation

indigniert [ɪndɪ'gni:ɐt] *Adj.* indignant

Indigo ['ɪndigo] **der** *od.* **das;** ~**s,** *(Arten:)* ~**s** indigo

indigo·blau *Adj.* indigo [blue]

Indikation [ɪndika'tsio:n] **die;** ~, ~**en a)** *(Med.: Heilanzeige)* indication; **b)** *(Rechtsw.)* **[medizinische/soziale/ethische] ~:** [medical/social/ethical] grounds *pl.* for abortion

Indikativ ['ɪndikati:f] **der;** ~**s,** ~**e** [-i:və] *(Sprachw.)* indicative [mood]

indikativisch *Adj. (Sprachw.)* indicative

Indikator [ɪndi'ka:tɔr] **der;** ~**s,** ~**en** [-ka'to:rən] *(auch Chemie, Technik)* indicator

Indio ['ɪndio] **der;** ~**s,** ~**s** *(Central/South American)* Indian

in·direkt 1. *Adj.; nicht präd.* indirect; ~**e Rede/eine ~e Frage** *(Sprachw.)* indirect *or* reported speech/an indirect question; **ein ~er Freistoß** *(Sport)* an indirect free kick. **2.** *adv.* indirectly; **einen Freistoß ~ ausführen** *(Sport)* take an indirect free kick

indisch ['ɪndɪʃ] **1.** *Adj.* Indian. **2.** *adv.* **sie hat gestern ~ gekocht** she cooked an Indian meal yesterday

in·diskret *Adj.* indiscreet

In·diskretion die; ~, ~**en** indiscretion

in·diskutabel *Adj. (abwertend)* unworthy of discussion *pred.*

in·disponiert *Adj. (geh.)* indisposed

In·disposition die *(geh.)* indisposition

individualisieren *tr. V. (geh.)* individualize

Individualismus [ɪndividua'lɪsmʊs] **der;** ~ *(Philos., geh.)* individualism

Individualist der; ~**en,** ~**en** *(geh.)* individualist

individualistisch *Adj. (geh.)* individualistic

Individualität [ɪndividuali'tɛ:t] **die;** ~, ~**en** *(geh.)* **a)** *o. Pl.* individuality; **b)** *(Persönlichkeit)* personality

Individual·verkehr der private vehicle traffic; private vehicles *pl.*

Individuation [ɪndividua'tsio:n] **die;** ~, ~**en** *(Psych.)* individuation

individuell [ɪndivi'duɛl] **1.** *Adj.* **a)** individual; **b)** *nicht präd. (einem einzelnen gehörend)* private ‹*property, vehicle, etc.*›. **2.** *adv.* individually; **etw. ~ gestalten** give sth. one's own personal touch; **das ist ~ verschieden** it varies from case to case

Individuum [ɪndi'vi:duʊm] **das;** ~**s, Individuen** *(auch Chemie, Biol.)* individual; **ein fragwürdiges/verdächtiges ~** *(abwertend)* a dubious/suspicious individual *or* character

Indiz [ɪn'di:ts] **das;** ~**es,** ~**ien a)** *(Rechtsw.)* piece of circumstantial evidence; ~**ien** circumstantial evidence *sing.*; **b)** *(Anzeichen)* sign **(für** of)

Indizien·beweis der *(Rechtsw.)* piece of circumstantial evidence; ~**e** circumstantial evidence *sing.*

indizieren [ɪndi'tsi:rən] *tr. V.* **a)** *(Med.)* indicate; **b)** *(kath. Kirche)* **ein Buch ~:** place a book on the Index

indo-, Indo- [ɪndo-]: ~**china (das)** Indo-China; ~**europäer** *Pl. s.* ~**germanen;** ~**europäisch** *Adj. s.* ~**germanisch;** ~**germanen** *Pl.* Indo-Europeans; ~**germanisch** *Adj.* Indo-European; Indo-Germanic

Indoktrination [ɪndɔktrina'tsio:n] **die;** ~, ~**en** indoctrination

indoktrinieren *tr. V.* indoctrinate

indolent ['ɪndolɛnt] *Adj. (geh., Med.)* indolent

Indonesien [ɪndo'ne:ziən] **(das)** Indonesia

Indonesier der; ~**s,** ~, **Indonesierin die;** ~, ~**nen** Indonesian

indonesisch *Adj.* Indonesian

Indossament [ɪndɔsa'mɛnt] **das;** ~**[e]s,** ~**e** *(Finanzw.)* endorsement

Indossant [ɪndɔ'sant] **der;** ~**en,** ~**en** *(Finanzw.)* endorser

Indossat [ɪndɔ'sa:t] **der;** ~**en,** ~**en, Indossator** [ɪndɔ'sa:tɔr] **der;** ~**s,** ~**e** *(Finanzw.)* endorsee

indossieren *tr. V. (Finanzw.)* endorse

Induktanz [ɪndʊk'tants] **die;** ~ *(Elektrot.)* inductance

Induktion [ɪndʊk'tsio:n] **die;** ~, ~**en** *(Philos., Elektrot., Biol.)* induction

Induktions-: ~**maschine die** *(Elektrot.)* induction machine; ~**ofen der** *(Technik)* induction furnace; ~**schleife die** *(Elektrot.)* induction control loop; ~**spule die** *(Elektrot.)* induction coil; ~**strom der** *(Elektrot.)* induced current

induktiv [ɪndʊk'ti:f] *Adj.* *(Philos., Elektrot.)* inductive

Induktivität [ɪndʊktivi'tɛ:t] **die;** ~, ~**en** *(Elektrot.)* self-inductance; coefficient of self-induction

industrialisieren [ɪndʊstriali'zi:rən] *tr. V.* industrialize

Industrialisierung die; ~: industrialization

Industrie [ɪndʊs'tri:] **die;** ~, ~**n** industry; **in die** ~ **gehen** *(ugs.)* go into industry; **in der** ~ **arbeiten** work in industry

Industrie-: ~**aktie die** industrial share; ~**an·lage die** industrial plant; ~**an·sied·lung die** setting-up of industry; ~**arbeiter der** industrial worker; ~**archäologie die** industrial archaeology *no art.*; ~**ausstel·lung die** industrial exhibition; ~**betrieb der** industrial company *or* firm; ~**erzeug·nis das** industrial product; ~**gebiet das** industrial area; ~**gesellschaft die** *(Soziol.)* industrial society; ~**gewerkschaft die** industrial union; ~**kapitän der** captain of industry; ~**kaufmann der** *person with three years' business training employed on the business side of an industrial company;* ~**laden der** *(DDR) shop owned and operated by an enterprise or combine for the sale of its own goods direct to the customer;* ~**landschaft die** industrial landscape

industriell [ɪndʊstri'ɛl] **1.** *Adj.; nicht präd.* industrial; **die** ~**e Revolution** *(hist.)* the Industrial Revolution. **2.** *adv.* industrially; ~ **überlegen/rückständig** industrially more/less advanced

Industrielle der/die; *adj. Dekl.* industrialist

Industrie-: ~**magnat der** industrial magnate; ~**müll der** industrial waste; ~**pro·dukt das** industrial product; ~**spionage die** industrial espionage; ~**staat der** industrial nation; ~**stadt die** industrial town; *(größer)* industrial city

Industrie- und Handels·kammer die Chamber of Industry and Commerce

Industrie-: ~**unternehmen das** industrial concern *or* company; ~**zweig der** branch of industry

induzieren [ɪndu'tsi:rən] *tr. V.* *(Philos., Elektrot.)* induce

in·effektiv *Adj.* ineffective

in·effizient *Adj.* *(geh.)* inefficient

In·effizienz die *(geh.)* inefficiency

in·einander *Adv.* ~ **verliebt sein** be in love with each other *or* one another; ~ **verschlungene Ornamente** intertwined decorations; **ganz** ~ **aufgehen** be totally wrapped up in each other *or* one another; ~ **übergehen** merge

ineinander-: ~**|fließen** *unr. itr. V.; mit sein* flow together; ‹*rivers etc.*› flow into each other *or* one another; ‹*dyes, colours*› run into each other *or* one another; ‹*lines*› run together; ~**|fügen 1.** *tr. V.* fit into each other *or* one another; fit together; **2.** *refl. V.* fit into each other *or* one another; fit together; ~**|greifen** *unr. itr. V.* mesh *or* engage [with each other *or* one another]; mesh together *(lit. or fig.)*; ~**|laufen** *unr. itr. V.; mit sein* run into each other *or* one another; run together; ~**|passen** *itr. V.* fit into each other *or* one another; fit together; ~**|schieben 1.** *unr. tr. V.* telescope ‹*vehicles*›; **die Teile der Tischplatte lassen sich leicht** ~**schieben** the leaves of the table can easily be pushed in; **2.** *unr. refl. V.* ‹*vehicles*› telescope

in·existent *Adj.* *(geh.)* non-existent

infam [ɪn'fa:m] **1.** *Adj.* disgraceful; ~**e Schmerzen** *(ugs.)* dreadful pain *sing. (coll.)*. **2.** *adv.* disgracefully; ~ **weh tun** *(ugs.)* hurt like mad *or* hell *(coll.)*

Infamie [ɪnfa'mi:] **die;** ~, ~**n a)** *o. Pl.* disgracefulness; **b)** *(Äußerung)* disgraceful remark; *(Handlung)* disgraceful action

Infant [ɪn'fant] **der;** ~**en,** ~**en** *(hist.)* infante; *(Thronfolger)* principe

Infanterie ['ɪnfant(ə)ri:] **die;** ~, ~**n** *(Milit.)* infantry

Infanterie-: ~**regiment das** *(Milit.)* infantry regiment; ~**stellung die** *(Milit.)* infantry position

Infanterist der; ~**en,** ~**en** *(Milit.)* infantryman

infantil [ɪnfan'ti:l] *(Psych., Med., sonst abwertend)* **1.** *Adj.* infantile. **2.** *adv.* in an infantile way

Infantilismus der; ~, **Infantilismen** *(Psych., Med.)* infantilism

Infantilität [ɪnfantili'tɛ:t] **die;** ~ **a)** *(abwertend)* infantility; **b)** *(Psych., Med.)* infantilism

Infantin die; ~, ~**nen** *(hist.)* infanta

Infarkt [ɪn'farkt] **der;** ~**[e]s,** ~**e** *(Med.)* infarct; infarction

infarkt·gefährdet *Adj.* *(Med.)* ‹*person*› with a high risk of suffering a cardiac infarction

Infekt [ɪn'fɛkt] **der;** ~**[e]s,** ~**e** *(Med.)* infection; **ein grippaler** ~: an influenzal infection

Infektion [ɪnfɛk'tsio:n] **die;** ~, ~**en** *(Med.)* **a)** *(Ansteckung)* infection; **b)** *(ugs.: Entzündung)* inflammation

Infektions-: ~**gefahr die** *(Med.)* danger *or* risk of infection; ~**herd der** *(Med.)* seat of the/an infection; ~**krankheit die** *(Med.)* infectious disease

infektiös [ɪnfɛk'tsiø:s] *Adj.* *(Med.)* infectious

Inferiorität [ɪnferiori'tɛ:t] **die;** ~ *(geh.)* inferiority

Inferioritäts·komplex der *(Psych.)* *s.* **Minderwertigkeitskomplex**

infernalisch [ɪnfɛr'na:lɪʃ] *(geh.)* **1.** *Adj.* infernal; ~ **schmecken** taste dreadful. **2.** *adv.* infernally; ~ **stinken** stink dreadfully

Inferno [ɪn'fɛrno] **das;** ~**s** *(geh.)* inferno

Infiltrat [ɪnfɪl'tra:t] **das;** ~**[e]s,** ~**e** *(Med.)* infiltrate

Infiltration [ɪnfɪltra'tsio:n] **die;** ~, ~**en** *(auch Med.)* infiltration

infiltrieren *tr. V.* *(auch Med.)* infiltrate; **jmdm. etw.** ~ *(Med.)* infiltrate sth. into sb.

in·finit *Adj.* *(Sprachw.)* infinite

Infinitesimal·rechnung [ɪnfinitezi'ma:l-] **die** *(Math.)* infinitesimal calculus

Infinitv ['ɪnfiniti:f] **der;** ~**s,** ~**e** [-ti:və] *(Sprachw.)* infinitive

Infinitiv·satz der *(Sprachw.)* infinitive clause

infizieren [ɪnfi'tsi:rən] **1.** *tr. V.* *(auch fig.)* infect. **2.** *refl. V.* become *or* get infected; **sich bei jmdm.** ~: be infected by sb.; catch an infection from sb.

in flagranti [ɪn fla'granti] *Adv.* *(geh.)* in flagrante [delicto]

Inflation [ɪnfla'tsio:n] **die;** ~, ~**en** *(Wirtsch.)* inflation; *(Zeit der* ~*)* period of inflation; **eine schleichende** ~: creeping inflation

inflationär [ɪnflatsio'nɛ:ɐ̯], **inflationistisch** *Adj.* inflationary

Inflations-: ~**ausgleich der** increase to allow for inflation; ~**politik die** policy of inflation; ~**rate die** inflation rate; rate of inflation

in·flexibel *Adj.* **a)** *(auch fig.)* inflexible; **b)** *(Sprachw.)* uninflected

In·flexibilität die; ~ *(auch fig.)* inflexibility

Influenz [ɪnflu'ɛnts] **die;** ~, ~**en** *(Elektrot.)* [electrostatic] induction

Influenza [ɪnflu'ɛntsa] **die;** ~ *(veralt.)* influenza

Info ['ɪnfo] **das;** ~**s,** ~**s** *(ugs.)* hand-out

in·folge 1. *Präp. + Gen.* as a result of; owing to. **2.** *Adv.* ~ **von etw.** *(Dat.)* as a result of *or* owing to sth.

infolge·dessen *Adv.* consequently; as a result of this

Informant [ɪnfɔr'mant] **der;** ~**en,** ~**en** *(auch Sprachw.)* informant

Informatik [ɪnfɔr'ma:tɪk] **die;** ~: computer science *no art.*

Informatiker der; ~**s,** ~: computer scientist

Information [ɪnfɔrma'tsio:n] **die;** ~, ~**en a)** *(auch Kybernetik)* information *no pl., no indef. art.* (**über** + *Akk.* about, on); **eine** ~: [a piece of] information; **eine umfassende** ~ **der Öffentlichkeit zu diesen Vorfällen ist unbedingt notwendig** it is vital to inform the public fully about these incidents; **zu Ihrer** ~: for your information; **nach neuesten** ~**en** according to the latest information; **nähere** ~**en erhalten Sie ...:** you can obtain more information ...; **b)** *(Büro)* information bureau; *(Stand)* information desk

Informations-: ~**aus·tausch der** exchange of information; ~**büro das** information bureau *or* office; ~**fluß der;** *o. Pl.* flow of information; ~**gespräch das** mutual briefing session; ~**material das** informational literature; ~**quelle die** source of information; ~**stand der a)** information stand; **b)** *(Zustand)* **bei meinem jetzigen** ~**stand** with the information I have at present; ~**theorie die** information theory *no art.*; ~**vor·sprung der** superior knowledge

informativ [ɪnfɔrma'ti:f] **1.** *Adj.* informative. **2.** *adv.* informatively

informatorisch [ɪnfɔrma'to:rɪʃ] *Adj.* informatory

in·formell *Adj.* informal

informieren 1. *tr. V.* inform (**über** + *Akk.* about); **falsch/einseitig informiert sein** be misinformed/have biased information; **aus gut informierten Kreisen** from well-informed circles. **2.** *refl. V.* inform oneself, find out (**über** + *Akk.* about); **sich aus der Presse/in der Zeitung über etw.** *(Akk.)* ~: inform oneself *or* find out about sth. from the press/the newspaper

infra·rot ['ɪnfra-] *Adj.* *(Physik)* infra-red

Infra·rot das; ~**s** *(Physik)* infra-red radiation; **im** ~: in the infra-red

Infrarot-: ~**film der** infra-red film; ~**strahler der a)** *(Heizgerät)* infra-red heater; **b)** *(Med.)* infra-red lamp

Infra-: ~**schall der** *(Physik)* infrasound; ~**struktur die** infrastructure

Infusion [ɪnfu'zio:n] **die;** ~, ~**en** *(Med.)* infusion; *(durch den After)* enema

Infusions·tierchen das, Infusorium [ɪnfu'zo:riʊm] **das;** ~**s, Infusorien;** *meist Pl.* *(Biol.)* infusorium

Ing. *Abk.* **Ingenieur**

In·gebrauch·nahme die; ~: **vor** ~ **des Geräts** before operating the appliance

Ingenieur [ɪnʒe'niø:ɐ̯] **der;** ~**s,** ~**e** [qualified] engineer

Ingenieur-: ~**bau der;** ~**[e]s,** ~**ten** civil engineering structure; ~**büro das** firm of consulting engineers

Ingenieurin die; ~, ~**nen** [qualified] engineer

Ingenieur·schule die college of engineering

ingeniös [ɪnge'niø:s] *(geh.)* **1.** *Adj.* ingenious. **2.** *adv.* ingeniously

Ingeniosität [ɪngeniozi'tɛ:t] **die;** ~ *(geh.)* ingenuity

Ingredienz [ɪngre'diɛnts] **die;** ~, ~**en;** *meist Pl.* *(bes. Pharm., Kochk.)* ingredient

In·grimm der *(geh.)* inward rage *or* wrath

in·grimmig *(geh.)* **1.** *Adj.* wrathful ‹*look, expression*›. **2.** *adv.* wrathfully

Ingwer ['ɪŋvɐ] **der;** ~**s,** ~ **a)** ginger; **b)** *(Likör)* ginger liqueur

Ingwer·bier das ginger beer

Inhaber ['ɪnha:bɐ] **der;** ~**s,** ~ **a)** *(einer Aktie, einer Lizenz, eines Rekords, eines Patents, eines Passes)* holder; *(eines Schecks)* bearer; *(eines Amtes)* holder; incumbent; **b)**

(Besitzer) owner; *(eines Hotels, Restaurants, Ladens)* owner; proprietor
Inhaberin die; ~, ~nen a) *s.* **Inhaber a; b)** *s.* **Inhaber b:** owner; proprietress
Inhaber·papier das *(Wirtsch.)* bearer security
inhaftieren [ɪnhafˈtiːrən] *tr. V.* take into custody; detain; **jmdn. zwei Tage lang ~:** keep sb. in custody *or* detain sb. for two days
Inhaftierte der/die; *adj. Dekl.* prisoner
Inhaftierung die; ~, ~en detention
Inhalation [ɪnhalaˈtsi̯oːn] **die; ~, ~en** *(Med.)* inhalation
inhalieren 1. *tr. V. (Med./ugs.)* inhale. **2.** *itr. V. (Med.)* use an inhalant
In·halt der; ~[e]s, ~e a) contents *pl.*; **b)** *(das Dargestellte/geistiger Gehalt)* content; **etw. zum ~ haben** deal with *or* concern sth.; **ein Buch politischen ~s** a political book; **der ~ eines Wortes** the meaning of a word; **wir erhielten eine Nachricht des ~s, daß ...** *(geh.)* we received a message to the effect that ...; **c)** *(bes. Math.) (Flächen~)* area; *(Raum~)* volume
inhaltlich 1. *Adj.* **die ~e Struktur des Dramas** the plot-structure of the drama; **an ~en Gesichtspunkten gemessen** from the point of view of content. **2.** *adv.* **~ ist der Aufsatz gut** the essay is good as regards content; **~ übereinstimmen** be the same in content
inhalts-, Inhalts-: ~an·gabe die summary [of contents]; synopsis; *(eines Films, Dramas)* [plot] summary; synopsis; **~bezogen** *Adj. (Sprachw.)* **~bezogene Grammatik** content[-oriented] grammar; **~erklärung die** declaration of contents; **~leer, ~los** *Adj.* lacking in content *postpos.*; meaningless ⟨*word, phrase*⟩; empty ⟨*life*⟩; **~reich** *Adj.* full ⟨*life, discussion*⟩; **~schwer** *Adj.* weighty; **~übersicht die** summary [of contents]; **~verzeichnis das** table of contents; *(auf einem Paket)* list of contents; *(als Überschrift)* [table of] contents; **~voll** *Adj. s.* **~reich**
inhärent [ɪnhɛˈrɛnt] *Adj. (geh., Philos.)* inherent (+ *Dat.* in)
Inhärenz [ɪnhɛˈrɛnts] **die; ~** *(Philos.)* inherence
in·homogen *Adj. (geh., fachspr.)* inhomogeneous
In·homogenität die; ~ *(geh., fachspr.)* inhomogeneity
in·human *Adj.* **a)** *(unmenschlich)* inhuman; **b)** *(rücksichtslos)* inhumane
In·humanität die; ~: inhumanity
Initial [iniˈtsi̯aːl] **das; ~s, ~e** *(selten),* **Initiale die; ~, ~n** initial [letter]
Initial-: ~zünder der detonator; **~zündung die** detonation
Initiation [initsi̯aˈtsi̯oːn] **die; ~, ~en** *(Soziol., Völkerk.)* initiation
Initiations·ritus der *(Soziol., Völkerk.)* initiation rite
initiativ [initsi̯aˈtiːf] *Adj.* **~ werden** take the initiative
Initiative die; ~, ~n a) *(erster Anstoß)* initiative; **die ~ ergreifen** take the initiative; **auf jmds. ~** *(Akk.)* **[hin]** on sb.'s initiative; **b)** *o. Pl. (Entschlußkraft)* initiative; **~ entwickeln/entfalten** develop initiative; **nur der ~** *(Dat.)* **der Opposition ist es zu verdanken, daß ...:** it is only thanks to the Opposition that ...; **c)** *s.* **Bürgerinitiative; d)** *(Parl.)* right to table *or* introduce a bill; *(das Einbringen)* tabling *or* introduction of a bill; **e)** *(schweiz.) s.* **Volksbegehren**
Initiator [iniˈtsi̯aːtɔr] **der; ~s, ~en, Initiatorin die; ~, ~nen** initiator; *(einer Organisation)* founder
initiieren [initsiˈiːrən] *tr. V. (geh.)* initiate
Injektion [ɪnjɛkˈtsi̯oːn] **die; ~, ~en** *(Med.)* injection
Injektions-: ~nadel die hypodermic needle; **~spritze die** hypodermic syringe

injizieren [ɪnjiˈtsiːrən] *tr. V. (Med.)* inject; **jmdm. etw. ~:** inject sb. with sth.
Injurie [ɪnˈjuːri̯ə] **die; ~, ~n** *(geh., Rechtsw.)* injury
Inka [ˈɪŋka] **der; ~[s], ~[s]** Inca
Inkarnation [ɪnkarnaˈtsi̯oːn] **die; ~, ~en** incarnation
Inkasso [ɪnˈkaso] **das; ~s, ~s** *od.* **Inkassi** *(Finanzw.)* collection
In·kaufnahme die; ~ *(Amtsspr.)* acceptance; **er konnte den Vertrag nur unter ~ von Verlusten abschließen** he could complete the contract only by accepting the losses involved
inkl. *Abk.* **inklusive** incl.
inklusive [ɪnkluˈziːvə] **1.** *Präp.* + *Gen. (bes. Kaufmannsspr.)* inclusive of; including; **der Preis versteht sich ~ der Verpackung** the price includes *or* is inclusive of packing; **wir bezahlten ~ Frühstück 40 DM** we paid 40 DM, breakfast included *or* including breakfast. **2.** *Adv.* inclusive
inkognito [ɪnˈkɔgnito] *Adv. (geh.)* incognito
Inkognito das; ~s, ~s incognito
in·kommensurabel *Adj. (geh., Math.)* incommensurable
in·kommodieren [ɪnkɔmoˈdiːrən] *(geh.)* **1.** *tr. V.* inconvenience; trouble; **jmdn. mit etw. ~:** trouble sb. with sth. **2.** *refl. V.* trouble oneself
in·kompatibel *Adj. (fachspr.)* incompatible
In·kompatibilität die *(fachspr.)* incompatibility
in·kompetent *Adj.* **a)** *(unfähig)* incompetent; **b)** *(bes. Rechtsspr.: nicht befugt)* not competent *postpos.*; incompetent
In·kompetenz die incompetence
In·kongruenz die *(Math.)* incongruence
in·konsequent 1. *Adj.* inconsistent. **2.** *adv.* inconsistently
In·konsequenz die inconsistency
in·konsistent *Adj. (geh.)* inconsistent
in·konstant *Adj.* **a)** *(Physik)* inconstant; **b)** *(geh.)* inconsistent; [constantly] shifting ⟨*balance of power*⟩
in·konvertibel *Adj. (Wirtsch.)* inconvertible ⟨*currency*⟩
in·korrekt 1. *Adj.* incorrect; incorrect, improper ⟨*dress, behaviour*⟩. **2.** *adv.* incorrectly; **sich ~ kleiden/benehmen** dress/behave incorrectly *or* inproperly
Inkorrektheit die; ~, ~en a) *o. Pl. (Fehlerhaftigkeit)* incorrectness; *(des Benehmens)* incorrectness; impropriety; **b)** *(Fehler)* mistake; *(inkorrektes Benehmen)* breach of propriety; impropriety
In·kraftsetzung [-zɛtsʊŋ] **die; ~, ~en** *(Amtsspr.)* **mit ~ dieses Gesetzes** when this law is/was brought *or* put into force
In·kraft·treten das; ~s: das ~ des Gesetzes erfolgt dann, wenn ...: the law comes into effect *or* force when ...
In·kreis der *(Geom.)* inscribed circle
inkriminieren [ɪnkrimiˈniːrən] *tr. V. (bes. Rechtsspr.)* incriminate
Inkubation [ɪnkubaˈtsi̯oːn] **die; ~, ~en** *(Med., Biol.)* incubation
Inkubations·zeit die; ~, ~en *(Med.)* incubation period
Inkubator [ɪnkuˈbaːtɔr] **der; ~s, ~en** *(Med.)* incubator
Inkubus [ˈɪnkubʊs] **der; ~, Inkuben** incubus
in·kulant *Adj. (Kaufmannsspr.)* unaccommodating; disobliging
Inkulanz [ˈɪnkulants] **die; ~** *(Kaufmannsspr.)* disobligingness
Inkunabel [ɪnkuˈnaːbl] **die; ~, ~n;** *meist Pl. (Buchw., Literaturw.)* incunabulum
In·land das; ~[e]s a) *(das eigene Land)* **im ~:** at home; **im ~ hergestellte Waren, Produktionen des ~es** home-produced goods; **für das ~ bestimmte Waren** goods for the home market; **wir werden unseren Urlaub diesmal im ~ verbringen** we're not going abroad for our holidays this year; **im In- und Ausland** at home and abroad; **b)** *(Binnenland)* interior; inland; **im/ins ~:** inland
Inland·eis das; ~es inland ice
Inländer [ˈɪnlɛndɐ] **der; ~s, ~, Inländerin die; ~, ~nen** native citizen
inländisch *Adj.* domestic; internal, domestic ⟨*trade, traffic*⟩; home, domestic ⟨*market*⟩; home-produced, domestic ⟨*goods*⟩
Inlands-: ~ab·satz der *(Wirtsch.)* domestic sales *pl.*; **~markt der** home *or* domestic market; **~porto das** inland postage; **~presse die** domestic press; **~verkehr der** internal *or* domestic traffic
In·laut der; ~[e]s, ~e *(Sprachw.)* **im ~ stehen/vorkommen** occur in [word-]medial position *or* [word-]medially
Inlett [ˈɪnlɛt] **das; ~[e]s, ~e** *od.* **~s** *(Stoff)* tick; ticking; *(Hülle)* tick
in·liegend *Adj. (Amtsspr., bes. österr.) s.* **einliegend**
in·mitten 1. *Präp.* + *Gen. (geh.)* in the midst of; surrounded by. **2.** *Adv.* **~ von** in the midst of; surrounded by
inne- [ˈɪnə-]: **~|haben** *unr. tr. V.* **a)** *(einnehmen)* hold, occupy ⟨*position*⟩; hold ⟨*office*⟩; **die Führung/Leitung ~haben** be in charge; **einen Lehrstuhl ~haben** hold a [professorial] chair; **b)** *(geh.: besitzen)* own; possess; **~|halten** *unr. itr. V.* pause; **in** *od.* **mit etw. ~halten** stop sth. for a moment; **er hielt in seiner Arbeit/im Laufen ~:** he stopped work/running for a moment; **er hielt mitten im Satz ~:** he stopped *or* paused in the middle of his sentence *or* in mid-sentence
innen [ˈɪnən] *Adv.* **a)** inside; *(auf/an der Innenseite)* on the inside; **etw. von ~ nach außen kehren** turn sth. inside out; **die Leitung verlief von ~ nach außen** the cable ran from the inside to the outside; **~ und außen** inside and out[side]; **nach ~ aufgehen** open inwards; **etw. von ~ besichtigen/ansehen** look round/at the inside of sth.; **die Füße nach ~ setzen** turn one's feet in[wards]; **~ laufen** *(Sport)* run on the inside; **von ~ heraus** from within; **b)** *(österr.: drinnen)* inside; *(im Haus)* indoors
innen-, Innen-: ~ansicht die interior view; **~antenne die** indoor aerial; **~arbeiten** *Pl.* interior work *sing.*; **~architekt der** interior designer; **~aufnahme die** *(Fot.)* indoor photo[graph]; *(Film)* indoor *or* interior shot; **~ausstattung die: [eine] ~ausstattung** decoration and furnishings; *(eines Autos)* [an] interior trim; **~bahn die** *(Sport)* inside lane; **~beleuchtung die a)** *(eines Fahrzeugs)* interior light; *(beim Türöffnen aufleuchtend)* courtesy light; **b)** *(im Zug, Flugzeug)* interior lighting; **~dienst der: ~dienst haben** be working in the office; ⟨*policeman*⟩ be on station duty; **im ~dienst tätig sein** work in the office; ⟨*policeman*⟩ do station duty; **~durchmesser der** internal diameter; **~einrichtung die** furnishings *pl.*; **~fläche die** inner surface; *(der Hand)* palm; **~geleitet** *Adj. (Soziol.)* self-directed; **~hof der** inner courtyard; *(eines Klosters, Colleges)* quadrangle; **~kurve die** inside bend; **die ~kurve nehmen** ⟨*driver*⟩ cut the corner; **~leben das;** *o. Pl.* **a)** [inner] thoughts and feelings *pl.*; **b)** *(oft scherzh.: Ausstattung)* inside; *(eines Hauses)* interior; *(eines Autos, Fernsehers usw.)* inner workings *pl.*; **~minister der** Minister of the Interior; ≈ Home Secretary *(Brit.)*; ≈ Secretary of the Interior *(Amer.)*; **~ministerium das** Ministry of the Interior; ≈ Home Office *(Brit.)*; ≈ Department of the Interior *(Amer.)*; **~pfosten der** *(Ballspiele)* inside of the post; **der rechte ~pfosten** the inside of the right-hand post; **~politik die** *(eines Staates)* home affairs *pl.*; *(einer Regierung)* domestic policy/policies *pl.*; **~politiker der** politician con-

cerned with home affairs; **~politisch** *s.* **~politik: 1.** *Adj.* **~politische Fragen** matters of domestic policy; **der ~politische Kurs der Regierung** the government's domestic policy; **eine ~politische Debatte** a debate on home affairs/domestic policy; **2.** *adv.* as regards home affairs/domestic policy; **~politisch betrachtet** from the point of view of home affairs/domestic policy; **~raum der a)** inner room; **die ~räume des Hauses** the interior of the house; **b)** *o. Pl. (Platz im Innern)* room inside; **ein Auto/Haus mit großem ~raum** a car/house with a spacious interior; **~rist der** *(bes. Fußball)* inside of the *or* one's foot; **~rolle die** hair curled under *no pl., no indef. art.;* **~seite die** inside; *(eines Stoffes)* wrong side; **~senator der** *minister for internal affairs (in Bremen, Hamburg, West-Berlin);* **~spiegel der** rearview mirror; **~stadt die** town centre; downtown *(Amer.); (einer Großstadt)* city centre; **~stürmer der** *(Ballspiele)* inside forward; **~tasche die** inside pocket; **~temperatur die** inside temperature; **bei 22 °C ~temperatur** when the temperature inside is 22 °C; when it's 22 °C inside; **wir haben eine ~temperatur von 22 °C** the temperature inside is 22 °C; **~wand die** interior wall; **~welt die** inner world; **sie hat sich ganz in ihre ~welt zurückgezogen** she withdrew completely into her own private world; **~winkel der** interior angle

inner... ['ɪnɐ...] *Adj.; nicht präd.* **a)** inner; inside ⟨*pocket, lane*⟩; **die ~e Seite** the inside; **b)** *(Med.)* internal; **die ~en Organe** the internal organs; **eine ~e Blutung/~e Blutungen** *Pl.* internal bleeding; **die ~e Medizin** internal medicine; **die Innere** *(Med. Jargon)* the medical ward; **c)** *(im Innern gefühlt)* inner ⟨*calm, impatience, etc.*⟩; **d)** *(einer Sache innewohnend)* internal ⟨*structure, stability, etc.*⟩; **e)** *(inländisch)* internal

inner-: ~betrieblich 1. *Adj.* internal ⟨*problem, question, regulation, agreement*⟩; **2.** *adv.* internally; **~deutsch** *Adj.* **a)** *(Deutschland betreffend)* **~deutsche Angelegenheiten** the internal *or* domestic affairs of Germany; Germany's internal *or* domestic affairs; **b)** *(die beiden deutschen Staaten betreffend)* ⟨*trade, relations, border*⟩ between the two German states; **der Bundesminister für ~deutsche Beziehungen** the Federal Minister for Intra-German Relations

Innere ['ɪnərə] **das;** *adj. Dekl.; o. Pl.* **a)** inside; *(eines Gebäudes, Wagens, Schiffes)* interior; inside; *(eines Landes)* interior; **im ~n des Waldes** deep within the forest; **der Minister des Innern** the Minister of the Interior; *s. auch* **Innenminister; b)** *(Empfindung)* inner being; **in seinem tiefsten ~n** in his heart of hearts; deep [down] inside; **wenn wir nur wüßten, was in ihrem ~n vorgeht** if only we knew what's going on inside her; **c)** *(Kern)* heart

Innereien [ɪnə'raiən] *Pl.* entrails; *(Kochk.)* offal *sing.*

inner·halb 1. *Präp. + Gen.* **a)** *(im Innern)* within, inside; **~ der Familie/Partei** *(fig.)* within the family/party; **b)** *(binnen)* within; **~ einer Woche** within a week; **~ der Arbeitszeit** during *or* in working hours. **2.** *Adv.* **a)** *(im Innern)* **~ von** within; inside; **b)** *(im Verlauf)* **~ von zwei Jahren** within two years

innerlich 1. *Adj.* **a)** *(geistig-seelisch)* inner; *(nicht nach außen gezeigt)* inward; **b)** *(geh.) (nach innen gewandt)* introvert[ed]; *(nicht oberflächlich)* inwardly directed; **c)** *(im Körper)* internal ⟨*use, effect*⟩. **2.** *adv.* **a)** *(geistig-seelisch)* inwardly; **~ lachen** laugh inwardly *or* to oneself; **b)** *(im Körper)* **die Arznei muß ~ wirken/wird ~ angewendet** the medicine must work/is used internally

Innerlichkeit die; ~: inwardness

inner-: ~parteilich *Adj.* **~parteiliche Auseinandersetzungen** internal [party] disputes; disputes within the party; **~parteiliche Diskussionen** discussions within the party; **~staatlich** *Adj.* internal; domestic; **~städtisch** *Adj.* urban

innerst... *Adj.; nicht präd.* inmost; innermost; **ihre ~e Überzeugung** her deepest *or* most profound conviction

Innerste das; *adj. Dekl.; o. Pl.* innermost being; **in meinem ~n** in my heart of hearts; deep [down] inside

innert ['ɪnɐt] *Präp. + Gen. od. Dat. (schweiz., österr.)* within

inne-: ~|sein *unr. itr. V.; mit sein (Zusammenschreibung nur im Inf. u. Part.) (geh.)* **einer Sache** *(Gen.)* **~sein** be [fully] aware of sth.; **~|werden** *unr. itr. V.; mit sein (Zusammenschreibung nur im Inf. u. Part.) (geh.)* **einer Sache** *(Gen.)* **~werden** become [fully] aware of sth.; **~|wohnen** *itr. V. (geh.)* **etw. wohnt jmdm./einer Sache ~:** sb./sth. possesses sth.

innig ['ɪnɪç] **1.** *Adj.* **a)** heartfelt, deep ⟨*affection, sympathy*⟩; heartfelt, fervent ⟨*wish*⟩; intimate ⟨*relation, relationship, friendship*⟩; **mein ~ster Dank** my sincerest thanks; **unsere ~sten Wünsche begleiten euch** our warmest wishes go with you; **b)** *(Chemie)* intimate. **2.** *adv.* ⟨*hope*⟩ fervently; ⟨*love*⟩ deeply, with all one's heart; **~ verbunden sein** ⟨*friends, families*⟩ be very close

Innigkeit die; ~: depth; *(einer Beziehung, Freundschaft)* intimacy; **die ~ seiner Worte** the depth of feeling in his words

inniglich ['ɪnɪklɪç] *Adj., adv. (geh.) s.* **innig**

Innovation [ɪnova'tsi̯o:n] **die;** ~, **~en** *(Soziol., Wirtsch.)* innovation

Innung ['ɪnʊŋ] **die;** ~, **~en** [trade] guild; **die ganze ~ blamieren** *(ugs. scherzh.)* let the side down

-innung die: Fleischer~/Bäcker~: butchers'/bakers' guild

in·offiziell 1. *Adj.* unofficial. **2.** *adv.* unofficially

in·operabel *Adj. (Med.)* inoperable

in·opportun *Adj. (geh.)* inopportune

in petto [ɪn 'pɛto] *in etw.* **~ ~ haben** *(ugs.)* have sth. up one's sleeve

in puncto [ɪn 'pʊŋkto] **~ ~ Pünktlichkeit** *usw.* as regards punctuality *etc.;* where punctuality *etc.* is concerned

Input ['ɪnpʊt] **der** *od.* **das;** ~s, ~s *(Wirtsch., Datenverarb.)* input

Inquisition [ɪnkvizi'tsi̯o:n] **die;** ~, **~en** *(hist.)* **a)** *o. Pl.* Inquisition; **b)** *(Untersuchung vor der ~)* inquisition

Inquisitions·gericht das *(hist.)* court of the Inquisition

Inquisitor [ɪnkvi'zi:tɔr] **der;** ~s, **~en** [-zi-'to:rən] *(hist.)* inquisitor

ins [ɪns] *Präp. + Art.* **a)** = **in das; b) ~ Bett/Theater gehen** go to bed/the theatre; **er geriet ~ Stottern** he began to stutter; **etw. ins Englische übersetzen** translate sth. into English

Insasse ['ɪnzasə] **der;** ~n, ~n **a)** *(Fahrgast)* passenger; **die ~n eines Autos/Flugzeuges** the passengers in a car/an aircraft; **b)** *(Bewohner)* inmate

Insassen·versicherung die passenger insurance

Insassin die; ~, **~nen** *s.* **Insasse**

ins·besond[e]re *Adv.* especially; particularly; in particular

In·schrift die inscription

Insekt [ɪn'zɛkt] **das;** ~s, **~en** insect

insekten-, Insekten-: ~bekämpfung die; *o. Pl.* insect control; **~fressend** *Adj.; nicht präd.* insectivorous; insect-eating; **~fresser der** insectivore; insect-eater; **~kunde die** entomology *no art.;* **~plage die** plague of insects; **~pulver das** insect-powder; **~stich der** *(einer Wespe, Biene)* insect-sting; *(einer Mücke)* insect-bite; **~vertilgungs·mittel das** insecticide

Insektizid [ɪnzɛkti'tsi:t] **das;** ~s, ~e *(fachspr.)* insecticide

Insel ['ɪnzl̩] **die;** ~, ~n *(auch fig.)* island; **die ~ Helgoland** the island of Heligoland; **die ~ Man** the Isle of Man

Insel·bewohner der islander

Inselchen das; ~s, ~: islet; little island

Insel-: ~gruppe die group of islands; **~lage die** island position; position as an island; **~reich das** island kingdom; **~republik die** island republic; **~staat der** island state; **~volk das** island race *or* people; **~welt die** islands *pl.*

Inserat [ɪnze'ra:t] **das;** ~[e]s, ~e advertisement *(in a newspaper);* **sich auf ein ~ melden** reply to an advertisement; **ein ~ aufgeben** put in an advertisement; **am besten gibst du ein ~ auf** the best thing you can do is to put an advertisement in the paper

Inseraten·teil der advertisement section

Inserent [ɪnze'rɛnt] **der;** ~en, ~en advertiser

inserieren *itr., tr. V.* advertise; **[wegen etw.] in einer Zeitung ~:** advertise [sth.] in a newspaper

ins·geheim *Adv.* secretly

ins·gemein *Adv. (veralt.)* **die Naturwissenschaften ~ waren seine Leidenschaft** he had a passion for the natural sciences as a whole

ins·gesamt *Adv.* **a)** in all; altogether; **es waren ~ 500** there were 500 in all *or* altogether; **b)** *(alles in allem)* all in all; **~ gesehen** all in all

Insider ['ɪnsaɪdə] **der;** ~s, ~: insider; **~ der Rock-Szene** those in on the rock scene

Insigne [ɪn'zɪgnə] **das;** ~s, **Insignien;** *meist Pl.* insignia

in·signifikant *Adj. (geh.)* insignificant

insistieren [ɪnzɪs'ti:rən] *itr. V. (geh.)* **auf etw.** *(Dat.)* **~:** insist on sth.

inskribieren [ɪnskri'bi:rən] *(österr.)* **1.** *itr. V.* register; **in Wien ~:** register at [the university of] Vienna. **2.** *tr. V.* **Germanistik ~:** register to study German; **bei jmdm. Vorlesungen ~:** register to attend sb.'s lectures

Inskription [ɪnskrɪp'tsi̯o:n] *(österr.)* **die;** ~, **~en** registration

insofern 1. *Adv.* [ɪn'zo:fɛrn] *(in dieser Hinsicht)* in this respect; to this extent; **~, als** in so far as; **die Vorstellung ist ~ irrig, als ...:** this notion is wrong in so far as ... **2.** *Konj.* [ɪnzo'fɛrn] *(falls)* provided [that]; so *or* as long as

in·solvent *Adj.* insolvent

In·solvenz die; ~, **~en** *(bes. Wirtsch.)* insolvency

insonderheit [ɪn'zɔndɐhai̯t] *Adv. (geh.)* particularly; in particular

insoweit [ɪn'zo:vai̯t/ɪnzo'vai̯t] *Adv./Konj. s.* **insofern**

in spe [ɪn 'spe:] future *attrib.;* **mein Schwiegersohn ~ ~:** my future son-in-law

Inspekteur [ɪnspɛk'tø:ɐ̯] **der;** ~s, ~e *(Milit.)* Chief of Staff

Inspektion [ɪnspɛk'tsi̯o:n] **die;** ~, **~en a)** *(Kontrolle)* inspection; **b)** *(Kfz-W.)* service; **das Auto zur ~ bringen** take the car in for a service; **c)** *(Behörde)* inspectorate

Inspektions·reise die tour of inspection

Inspektor [ɪn'spɛktɔr] **der;** ~s, **~en** [-'to:rən], **Inspektorin die;** ~, **~nen** inspector; **das Gutachten des Inspektors Müller, Inspektor Müllers Gutachten** Inspector Müller's report; *s. auch* **-in**

Inspiration [ɪnspira'tsi̯o:n] **die;** ~, **~en** inspiration

inspirieren *tr. V.* inspire; **das inspirierte ihn zu einem Roman** it inspired him to write a novel; **sich von jmdm./etw. ~ lassen** be inspired by sb./sth.

Inspizient [ɪnspi'tsi̯ɛnt] **der;** ~en, ~en *(Theater)* stage-manager; *(Ferns., Rundf.)* studio manager

inspizieren *tr. V.* inspect
Inspizierung die; ~, ~**en** inspection
in·stabil *Adj. (auch Physik, Technik)* unstable
In·stabilität die; ~, ~**en** *(auch Physik, Technik)* instability
Installateur [ɪnstala'tø:ɐ] **der;** ~**s,** ~**e a)** *(Klempner)* plumber; **b)** *(Gas~)* [gas-]fitter; **c)** *(Heizungs~)* heating engineer; **d)** *(Elektro~)* electrician
Installation [ɪnstala'tsi̯o:n] **die;** ~, ~**en a)** *o. Pl.* installation; **b)** *(Anlage)* installation; *(Rohre)* plumbing *no pl.*; **c)** *(schweiz., sonst veralt.: Amtseinführung)* installation
installieren 1. *tr. V.* **a)** *(einbauen)* install; **b)** *(geh.: in ein Amt einführen)* install; **c)** *(einrichten)* set up. **2.** *refl. V.* settle in
in·stand *Adv.* **etw. ist gut/schlecht** ~: sth. is in good/poor condition; **etw.** ~ **halten** keep sth. in good condition *or* repair *or (funktionsfähig)* in working order; **etw.** ~ **setzen/bringen** repair sth.; *(funktionsfähig machen)* get sth. into working order; **jmdn.** ~ **setzen, etw. zu tun** enable sb. to do sth.
instand-, Instand-: ~**besetzen** *tr. V.* **ein Haus** ~**besetzen** occupy and renovate a house *(illegally, to prove that its demolition is not desirable)*; ~**besetzung die** *illegal occupation and renovation*; ~**haltung die** maintenance; upkeep; ~**haltungs·kosten** *Pl.* maintenance costs
in·ständig 1. *Adj.* urgent; insistent ⟨*invitation*⟩. **2.** *adv.* urgently; ~ **um etw. bitten** beg for sth.; **jmdn.** ~ **bitten, etw. zu tun** beg *or* implore *or* beseech sb. to do sth.; ~ **auf etw.** *(Akk.)* **hoffen** hope fervently for sth.
Instandsetzung die; ~, ~**en** *(Amtsspr.)* repair; *(Renovierung)* renovation; **eine** ~ **der Brücke hätte sich nicht gelohnt** it would not have been worth repairing the bridge
Instanz [ɪn'stants] **die;** ~, ~**en a)** authority; **durch alle** ~**en gehen** *od.* **alle** ~**en durchlaufen** go *or* pass through all the official channels; **in letzter** ~ **ist ... entscheidend** *(fig.)* in the final analysis, ... is decisive; **b)** *(Rechtsw.)* **[die] erste/zweite/dritte** ~: the court of first instance *or* court of original jurisdiction/the appeal court/the court of final appeal; **durch alle** ~**en gehen** go through all the courts
Instanzen·weg der official channels *pl.*; *(Rechtsspr.)* stages *pl.* of appeal; **den** ~ **nehmen** go through the official channels/the various stages of appeal
Instinkt [ɪn'stɪŋkt] **der;** ~**[e]s,** ~**e** instinct; **etw. aus** ~ **tun** do sth. instinctively; **den richtigen** ~ **für etw. haben** have a flair for sth.; **seinem** ~ **folgen** follow one's instincts *pl.*
Instinkt·handlung die instinctive action
instinktiv [ɪnstɪŋk'ti:f] **1.** *Adj.* instinctive. **2.** *adv.* instinctively
instinkt·los 1. *Adj.* insensitive. **2.** *adv.* insensitively; **politisch** ~ **handeln** act with political insensitivity
Instinktlosigkeit die; ~, ~**en** insensitivity; **eine** ~ **sein** be insensitive
Institut [ɪnsti'tu:t] **das;** ~**[e]s,** ~**e a)** institute; **das** ~ **für Kernphysik** the Institute of Nuclear Physics; **b)** *(Rechtsspr.)* institution
Institution [ɪnstitu'tsi̯o:n] **die;** ~, ~**en** *(auch fig.)* institution
institutionalisieren [ɪnstitutsi̯onali'zi:rən] *tr. V. (geh.)* institutionalize
institutionell [ɪnstitutsi̯o'nɛl] *Adj.* institutional
Instituts-: ~**bibliothek die** institute library; ~**leiter der** director of the/an institute
instruieren [ɪnstru'i:rən] *tr. V.* **a)** *(in Kenntnis setzen)* inform; **jmdn. über etw.** *(Akk.)* ~: inform sb. about sth.; **b)** *(anleiten)* instruct; **jmdn. genau** ~: give sb. precise instructions
Instrukteur [ɪnstrʊk'tø:ɐ] **der;** ~**s,** ~**e** instructor
Instruktion [ɪnstrʊk'tsi̯o:n] **die;** ~, ~**en** instruction
instruktiv [ɪnstrʊk'ti:f] **1.** *Adj.* instructive; informative. **2.** *adv.* instructively; informatively
Instrument [ɪnstru'mɛnt] **das;** ~**[e]s,** ~**e** instrument
instrumental [ɪnstrumɛn'ta:l] *(Musik)* **1.** *Adj.* instrumental. **2.** *adv.* instrumentally; ~ **musizieren** play instrumental music
Instrumental·begleitung die instrumental accompaniment
Instrumentalismus der; ~ *(Philos.)* instrumentalism
Instrumental·musik die instrumental music
Instrumentarium [ɪnstrumɛn'ta:ri̯ʊm] **das;** ~**s, Instrumentarien a)** *(Technik)* equipment; instruments *pl.*; **b)** *(Musik)* instruments *pl.*; **diese Oper verlangt ein großes** ~: this opera calls for a large number and range of instruments; **c)** *(geh.: Gesamtheit der Mittel)* apparatus
instrumentell [ɪnstrumɛn'tɛl] **1.** *Adj. (mit Instrumenten)* using instruments *postpos.*; ~**e Hilfsmittel/Ausrüstung** equipment; instruments *pl.* **2.** *adv.* **etw.** ~ **untersuchen** investigate sth. using instruments; ~ **gut/schlecht ausgerüstet** well/poorly equipped
Instrumenten-: ~**bau der** making of musical instruments; ~**brett das** instrument panel; ~**flug der** *(Flugw.)* flying on instruments; instrument-flying; ~**kasten der** instrument housing; *(tragbar)* instrument case
instrumentieren 1. *tr. V.* **a)** *(Musik: für das Orchester ausarbeiten)* instrument; *(für das Orchester umarbeiten)* orchestrate; **b)** *(Technik)* instrument; equip with instruments. **2.** *itr. V. (Med.)* **bei jmdm.** ~: assist sb. by handing him/her the instruments
In·subordination die; ~, ~**en** *(geh.)* insubordination; **eine** ~: an act of insubordination
Insuffizienz ['ɪnzʊfitsi̯ɛnts] **die;** ~, ~**en** *(Med.)* insufficiency
Insulaner [ɪnzu'la:nɐ] **der;** ~**s,** ~ *(veralt., noch scherzh.)* islander
insular [ɪnzu'la:ɐ] *Adj.* insular
Insulin [ɪnzu'li:n] **das;** ~**s** insulin
Insulin·schock der *(Med.)* insulin shock
inszenatorisch [ɪnstsena'to:rɪʃ] *Adj.; nicht präd.* directorial; **eine** ~**e Meisterleistung** a masterpiece of directing
inszenieren [ɪnstse'ni:rən] *tr. V.* **a)** stage, put on ⟨*play, opera*⟩; *(Regie führen bei)* direct; *(Ferns.)* direct; produce; **b)** *(oft abwertend) (einfädeln)* engineer; *(organisieren)* stage
Inszenierung die; ~, ~**en a)** staging; *(Regie)* direction; **b)** *(Aufführung)* production; **Rigoletto in neuer** ~: a new production of 'Rigoletto'; **c)** *(oft abwertend) (das Einfädeln)* engineering; *(das Organisieren)* staging
intakt [ɪn'takt] *Adj.* **a)** *(unbeschädigt)* intact; undamaged; unspoiled ⟨*region*⟩; **b)** *(funktionsfähig)* in [proper] working order *postpos.*; healthy ⟨*economy*⟩; **einen** ~**en Organismus haben** be physically healthy
Intarsie [ɪn'tarzi̯ə] **die;** ~, ~**n** intarsia
integer [ɪn'te:gɐ] *Adj.* **eine integre Persönlichkeit** a person of integrity; ~ **sein** be a person of integrity
integral [ɪnte'gra:l] *Adj.* integral
Integral das; ~**s,** ~**s** *(Math.)* integral; *(Zeichen)* integral sign
Integral-: ~**helm der** integral helmet; ~**rechnung die a)** integral calculus; **b)** *(einzelne Rechnung)* problem in integral calculus
Integration [ɪntegra'tsi̯o:n] **die;** ~, ~**en** *(auch Math.)* integration
integrieren *tr. V. (auch Math.)* integrate; *s. auch* **Gesamthochschule; Gesamtschule**
integrierend *Adj.* integral ⟨*part, component, element*⟩
Integrierung die; ~, ~**en** *(auch Math.)* integration
Integrität [ɪntegri'tɛ:t] **die;** ~: integrity
Intellekt [ɪntɛ'lɛkt] **der;** ~**[e]s** intellect
intellektuell [ɪntɛlɛk'tu̯ɛl] *Adj.* intellectual
Intellektuelle der/die; *adj. Dekl.* intellectual
intelligent [ɪntɛli'gɛnt] **1.** *Adj.* intelligent. **2.** *adv.* intelligently
Intelligenz [ɪntɛli'gɛnts] **die;** ~, ~**en a)** *o. Pl.* intelligence; **b)** *o. Pl. (Gesamtheit der Intellektuellen)* intelligentsia; **c)** *(veralt.: intelligentes Wesen)* intelligence
Intelligenz·bestie die *(ugs.)* **a)** egghead *(coll.)*; brain *(coll.)*; **b)** *(abwertend)* clever-clever type
Intelligenzija [ɪntɛli'gɛntsi̯ja] **die;** ~: intelligentsia
Intelligenz·leistung die instance of intelligent behaviour; **das war mal eine** ~ **von dir!** *(iron.)* that was bright of you, I must say
Intelligenzler der; ~**s,** ~ *(abwertend)* intellectual
Intelligenz-: ~**quotient der** intelligence quotient; ~**test der** intelligence test
intelligibel [ɪntɛli'gi:bl̩] *(Philos.) Adj.* intelligible
Intendant [ɪntɛn'dant] **der;** ~**en,** ~**en a)** *(Theater)* manager and artistic director; *(Fernseh~, Rundfunk~)* director-general
Intendantur [ɪntɛndan'tu:ɐ] **die;** ~, ~**en** *s.* **Intendanz a**
Intendanz [ɪntɛn'dants] **die;** ~, ~**en a)** *(Amt)* management and artistic directorship; *(Ferns., Rundf.)* director-generalship; **b)** *(Büro)* office of the manager and artistic director; *(Ferns., Rundf.)* director-general's office
intendieren [ɪntɛn'di:rən] *tr. V. (geh.)* intend
Intensität [ɪntɛnzi'tɛ:t] **die;** ~ *(auch Physik)* intensity
intensiv [ɪntɛn'zi:f] **1.** *Adj.* **a)** *(gründlich)* intensive ⟨*research, efforts, etc.*⟩; **b)** *(kräftig)* intense; strong ⟨*smell, taste*⟩; **c)** *(Landw.)* intensive ⟨*cultivation etc.*⟩. **2.** *adv.* **a)** *(gründlich)* intensively; ⟨*think*⟩ hard; **sich** ~ **mit etw. beschäftigen** be deeply involved with sth.; **b)** *(kräftig)* intensely; ⟨*smell, taste*⟩ strongly; ~ **leuchten** shine with intense brightness; **c)** *(Landw.)* ⟨*farm etc.*⟩ intensively
-intensiv -intensive; **geruchs~:** strong-smelling
Intensiv-: ~**anbau der** *(Landw.)* intensive cultivation; ~**haltung die** *(Landw.)* intensive rearing
intensivieren *tr. V.* intensify; increase ⟨*exports*⟩; strengthen ⟨*connections*⟩
Intensivierung die; ~, ~**en** intensification; **bei einer** ~ **des Exports** by increasing exports *pl.*
Intensiv-: ~**kurs der** intensive course; ~**station die** intensive-care unit
Intention [ɪntɛn'tsi̯o:n] **die;** ~, ~**en** intention; **das liegt nicht in seinen** ~**en** that is not his intention
intentional [ɪntɛntsi̯o'na:l] *(Philos.)* **1.** *Adj.* intentional. **2.** *adv.* intentionally
Inter- [ɪntɐ-]: ~**aktion die** *(Psych., Soziol.)* interaction; ~**brigaden** *Pl. (hist.)* International Brigades
Inter·city der; ~**s,** ~**s** *(ugs.)* inter-city [train]
Intercity-: ~**-Verkehr der** inter-city [railway] traffic; ~**-Zug der** inter-city train
inter-, Inter-: ~**dependent** *Adj. (geh.)* interdependent; ~**dependenz die;** ~, ~**en** *(geh.)* interdependence *no pl.*; ~**disziplinär 1.** *Adj.* interdisciplinary; **2.** *adv.* ~**disziplinär forschen** do interdisciplinary research

interessant [ɪntərɛ'sant] **1.** *Adj.* interesting; **sich ~ machen** attract attention to oneself; **das ist ja ~:** that's [very] interesting; **das Angebot ist für uns nicht ~:** the offer is of no interest to us *or* doesn't interest us. **2.** *adv.* **~ schreiben** write in an interesting way

interessanterweise *Adv.* interestingly enough

Interesse [ɪntə'rɛsə] **das; ~s, ~n a)** *o. Pl.* interest; **[großes] ~ an jmdm./etw. haben** be [very] interested in sb./sth.; **~ für jmdn./etw. haben/zeigen** have/show an interest in sb./sth.; **b)** *(Neigung)* interest; **gemeinsame ~n haben** have interests in common; **im eigenen ~ handeln** act in one's own interest; **jmds. ~n wahrnehmen** look after *or* represent sb.'s interests; **in jmds. ~ (Dat.) liegen** be in sb.'s interest; **es liegt in unser aller ~:** it's in all our interests *pl.*

interesse-, Interesse-: ~halber [~halbɐ] *Adv.* out of interest; **~los 1.** *Adj.* uninterested; **2.** *adv.* without interest; uninterestedly; **~losigkeit die; ~:** lack of interest

Interessen-: ~ausgleich der reconciliation of [conflicting] interests; **~bereich der, ~gebiet das** field of interest; **~gegensatz der** *s.* **~konflikt; ~gemeinschaft die a) sich in einer ~gemeinschaft zusammenfinden** join together with sb. to pursue common interests; **b)** *(Wirtsch.)* syndicate; **~gruppe die** interest group; **~kollision die** clash of interests; **~konflikt der** conflict of interests; **~lage die** interests *pl.*; **~sphäre die** sphere of influence

Interessent [ɪntərɛ'sɛnt] **der; ~en, ~en a)** interested person; **wenn es genug ~en gibt** if enough people are interested; **auf die Anzeige haben sich zahlreiche ~en gemeldet** the advertisement attracted a large response; **~en werden gebeten ...:** those interested are asked ...; **b)** *(möglicher Käufer)* potential buyer

Interessenten·kreis der market

Interessentin die; ~, ~nen *s.* **Interessent**

Interessen-: ~verband der [organized] interest group; **~vertretung die a)** representation; **b)** *(Vertreter von Interessen)* representative body

interessieren 1. *refl. V.* **sich für jmdn./etw. ~:** be interested in sb./sth. **2.** *tr. V.* interest; **interessiert dich denn nicht, was passiert ist?** aren't you interested to know what happened?; **das interessiert mich nicht** I'm not interested [in it]; it doesn't interest me; **das hat dich zu ~:** you can't just ignore it; **das hat dich nicht zu ~:** it's none of your business; it's no concern of yours

interessiert *Adj.* interested; **an jmdm./etw. ~ sein** be interested in sb./sth.; **er ist daran ~, daß sie nichts davon erfahren** he doesn't want them to find out anything about it; **vielseitig ~ sein** have a wide range of interests; **~ zuhören** listen with interest

Interessiertheit die; ~: das Prinzip der materiellen ~ *(DDR) principle that the individual can directly improve his own standard of living by working harder and more efficiently to achieve the goals of socialism*

inter-, Inter-: ~ferenz [~fe'rɛnts] **die; ~ferenz, ~ferenzen** *(Physik, Med., Sprachw.)* interference *no pl.*; **~feron** [~fe'ro:n] **das; ~ferons, ~ferone** *(Med.)* interferon; **~fraktionell** [~fraktsi̯o'nɛl] **1.** *Adj.* inter-party *attrib.*; **2.** *adv.* **etw. ~fraktionell besprechen** discuss sth. on an inter-party basis; hold inter-party discussions about sth.; **~hotel** ['----] **das** *(DDR)* Interhotel *(hotel intended mainly for visitors to the GDR)*

Interieur [ɛ̃te'ri̯ø:ɐ̯] **das; ~s, ~s** *od.* **~e** *(auch bild. Kunst)* interior

Interim ['ɪnterɪm] **das; ~s, ~s** *(geh.)* interim measure

interimistisch 1. *Adj. (geh.)* interim *attrib.*; temporary; provisional. **2.** *adv.* on an interim basis

Interims-: ~lösung die interim solution; **~regierung die** caretaker government; **~schein der** *(Wirtsch.)* scrip; **~trainer der** *(Sport)* temporary trainer

Interjektion [ɪntɐjɛk'tsi̯o:n] **die; ~, ~en** *(Sprachw.)* interjection

inter-, Inter-: ~kantonal 1. *Adj.* intercantonal; **2.** *adv.* on an inter-cantonal basis; **~konfessionell** *Adj. (geh.)* interdenominational; interconfessional; **~kontinental** *Adj. (geh.)* intercontinental; **~kontinental·rakete die** *(Milit.)* intercontinental ballistic missile; **~linear** *Adj. (Literaturw.)* interlinear; **~linear·version die** interlinear version *or* translation; **~ludium** [~'lu:di̯ʊm] **das; ~ludiums, ~ludien** *(Musik)* interlude; **~mezzo** [~'mɛtso] **das; ~mezzos, ~mezzos** *od.* **~mezzi** *(Theat., Musik)* intermezzo; *(fig.)* interlude; intermezzo; **~ministeriell 1.** *Adj.* interministerial; **2.** *adv.* on an inter-ministerial basis; **~mittierend** [~mɪ'ti:rənt] *Adj. (geh.)* intermittent; lightning ⟨*strike*⟩

intern [ɪn'tɛrn] **1.** *Adj.* **a)** internal; **diese Dinge müssen ~ bleiben** these matters must not become public knowledge; **b)** *(im Internat wohnend)* **ein ~er Schüler** a boarder. **2.** *adv.* internally; **wir haben das Jubiläum nur ~ gefeiert** we only celebrated the anniversary among ourselves

-intern 1. *Adj.* **firmen~e/klub~e/abteilungs~e Dinge** internal [company/club/departmental] matters; **eine firmen~e/klub~e Regelung** an arrangement within the company/club. **2.** *adv.* **firmen~/klub~/abteilungs~:** within the company/club/department; internally

Interna *s.* **Internum**

internalisieren [ɪntɐnali'zi:rən] *tr. V. (Soziol., Psych.)* internalize

Internalisierung die; ~, ~en *(Soziol., Psych.)* internalization

Internat [ɪntə'na:t] **das; ~[e]s, ~e a)** boarding-school; **b)** *(einer Schule angeschlossenes Heim)* dormitory block

inter-, Inter-: ~national 1. *Adj.* international; **2.** *adv.* internationally; **~nationale die; ~, ~n a)** *(Internationale Arbeiterassoziation)* International; Internationale; **b)** *(Lied)* Internationale; **~nationalisieren** *tr. V.* internationalize; **~nationalismus der a)** *o. Pl. (Politik)* internationalism; **sozialistischer ~nationalismus** *(DDR)* socialist internationalism; **b)** *(Sprachw.)* internationalism; **~nationalistisch** *Adj. (Politik)* internationalistic

Internats-: ~schule die boarding-school; **~schüler der, ~schülerin die** boarding-school pupil; boarder

Interne der/die; *adj. Dekl.* boarder

internieren *tr. V.* **a)** *(Milit.)* intern; **b)** *(Med.)* **jmdn. [in einem Krankenhaus] ~:** confine sb. to [a] hospital

Internierte der/die; *adj. Dekl.* **a)** *(Milit.)* internee; **b)** *(Med.)* patient confined to hospital

Internierung die; ~, ~en internment

Internierungs·lager das internment camp

Internist der; ~en, ~en *(Med.)* internist

Internum [ɪn'tɛrnʊm] **das; ~s, Interna;** *meist Pl. (geh.)* internal matter

inter-, Inter-: ~parlamentarisch *(Politik) Adj.* inter-parliamentary; **~pellation** [~pɛla'tsi̯o:n] **die; ~pellation, ~pellationen** *(Politik)* interpellation; **~pellieren** *itr. V. (Politik)* interpellate; **~planetar[isch]** *Adj. (Astron.)* interplanetary; **~pol** ['---] **die; Interpol** Interpol *no art.*; **~polation** [~pola'tsi̯o:n] **die; ~polation, ~polationen** *(Math., Sprachw.)* interpolation; **~polieren** *itr. (auch tr.) V. (Math., Sprachw.)* interpolate

Interpret [ɪntɐ'pre:t] **der; ~en, ~en** interpreter *(of music, text, events, etc.)*

Interpretation [ɪntɐpreta'tsi̯o:n] **die; ~, ~en** interpretation *(of music, text, events, etc.)*

interpretieren *tr. V.* interpret ⟨*music, texts, events, etc.*⟩; **etw. falsch ~:** misinterpret sth.; interpret sth. wrongly

Interpretin die; ~, ~nen *s.* **Interpret**

interpunktieren *tr., itr. V. (Sprachw.)* punctuate

Interpunktion [ɪntɐpʊŋk'tsi̯o:n] **die; ~** *(Sprachw.)* punctuation

Interpunktions-: ~regel die punctuation rule; **~zeichen das** punctuation mark

Interrail·karte ['ɪntəreɪl-] **die** *(Eisenbahnw.)* Interrail card

Interregnum [ɪntɐ'rɛgnʊm] **das; ~s, Interregnen** *od.* **Interregna** *(Politik)* interregnum

interrogativ [ɪntɐroga'ti:f] *Adj. (Sprachw.)* interrogative

Interrogativ-: ~pronomen das interrogative pronoun; **~satz der** interrogative sentence

Interruptus [ɪntɐ'rʊptʊs] **der; ~** *(ugs.)* withdrawal

Intershop ['ɪntɐʃɔp] **der; ~s, ~s** *(DDR)* Intershop *(shop where foreign goods and top-quality GDR goods are sold for freely convertible currency)*

inter-: ~stellar [~stɛ'la:ɐ̯] *Adj. (Astron.)* interstellar; **~subjektiv** *(Psych.) Adj.* intersubjective

Intervall [ɪntɐ'val] **das; ~s, ~e** *(Musik, Math.)* interval

Intervall·training das *(Sport)* interval training

intervenieren [ɪntɐve'ni:rən] *itr. V. (geh., Politik)* intervene; **bei jmdm. gegen etw. ~:** make representations to sb. about sth.; **für jmdn. ~:** intervene on sb.'s behalf

Intervention [ɪntɐvɛn'tsi̯o:n] **die; ~, ~en** *(geh., Politik)* intervention; *(Protest)* representations *pl.*

Interventions·krieg der war of intervention

Interview [ɪntɐ'vju:] **das; ~s, ~s** interview

interviewen [ɪntɐ'vju:ən] *tr. V.* interview

Interviewer [ɪntɐ'vju:ɐ] **der; ~s, ~, Interviewerin die; ~, ~nen** interviewer

Intervision die; ~: Intervision *(alliance of Eastern European television corporations for pooling of programmes)*

Inter·zonen-: ~auto·bahn die interzonal autobahn; **~handel der** interzonal trade; **~verkehr der** interzonal traffic; **~zug der** interzonal train

Inthronisation [ɪntroniza'tsi̯o:n] **die; ~, ~en** enthronement

inthronisieren *tr. V.* enthrone

intim [ɪn'ti:m] **1.** *Adj.* **a)** intimate; **im ~en Kreis** among close friends; **~e Beziehungen mit jmdm. haben** *(verhüll.)* have intimate relations with sb. *(euphem.)*; **mit jmdm. ~ sein/werden** *(verhüll.)* be/become intimate with sb. *(euphem.)*; **~e Hygiene/Körperpflege** intimate personal hygiene; **b)** *(tiefinnerlich)* intimate; innermost. **2.** *adv.* **~ befreundet sein** be intimate friends; **mit jmdm. ~ verkehren** *(verhüll.)* have intimate relations with sb. *(euphem.)*

Intim-: ~bereich der a) *s.* **~sphäre; b)** *(Genitalbereich)* genital area; **~feind der** *person whom one knows well and dislikes intensely*; **~hygiene die** intimate personal hygiene

Intimität [ɪntimi'tɛ:t] **die; ~, ~en** intimacy; **es ist zu ~en gekommen** *(verhüll.)* intimacy took place *(euphem.)*; **~en austauschen** *(verhüll.)* be engaged in intimacy *(euphem.)*

Intim-: ~kenner der: ein ~kenner von etw. sein have an intimate knowledge of sth.; **von einem ~kenner der politischen Szene stammen** come from someone with an intimate knowledge of the political scene;

~leben das *(verhüll.)* intimate life; **~pflege die** *s.* **~hygiene; ~sphäre die** private life; **jmds. ~sphäre verletzen** invade sb.'s privacy; **jmdn. wegen Verletzung seiner ~sphäre verklagen** sue sb. for invasion of privacy; **~spray der** *od.* **das** intimate deodorant

Intimus ['ɪntimʊs] **der; ~, Intimi** intimate friend; *(Vertrauter)* confidant

Intim·verkehr der *(verhüll.)* intimate relations *pl. (euphem.)*

in·tolerant 1. *Adj.* intolerant **(gegenüber** of); **sich ~ zeigen** display *or* show intolerance. **2.** *adv.* intolerantly

In·toleranz die; ~, ~en intolerance **(gegenüber** of)

Intonation [ɪntona'tsi̯o:n] **die; ~, ~en** *(Sprachw., Musik)* intonation

intonieren 1. *tr. V.* **a)** *(Musik) (anstimmen)* **etw. ~:** sing/play the first few bars of sth.; start to sing/play sth.; *(Ton angeben)* play/sing; **bitte intoniere ein a** please give me/us an A; **b)** *(Musik: hervorbringen)* **die Melodie sauber/weich ~:** play/sing the melody with clean/soft intonation; **c)** *(Sprachw.)* **etw. richtig/falsch/anders ~:** say sth. with the right/wrong/a different intonation. **2.** *itr. V.* **a)** *(Musik)* **er hat sauber/weich intoniert** he played/sang with clean/soft intonation; **b)** *(Sprachw.)* **richtig/falsch ~:** use the right/wrong intonation

Intoxikation [ɪntɔksika'tsi̯o:n] **die; ~, ~en** *(Med.)* intoxication *(Med.)*

intramuskulär [ɪntramʊsku'lɛ:ɐ̯] *(Med.)* **1.** *Adj.* intramuscular. **2.** *adv.* intramuscularly

intransitiv 1. *Adj. (Sprachw.)* intransitive. **2.** *adv.* intransitively

Intrauterin·pessar [ɪntra|ute'ri:n-] **das** *(Med.)* intra-uterine device

intravenös [ɪntrave'nø:s] *(Med.)* **1.** *Adj.* intravenous. **2.** *adv.* intravenously

intrigant [ɪntri'gant] *Adj.* scheming

Intrigant der; ~en, ~en, Intrigantin die; ~, ~nen schemer; intriguer

Intrige [ɪn'tri:gə] **die; ~, ~n** intrigue

Intrigen-: ~spiel das intrigue; **~wirtschaft die;** *o. Pl. (abwertend)* constant scheming and intriguing

intrigieren *itr. V.* intrigue; scheme; **gegen jmdn. ~:** intrigue *or* scheme against sb.; **er intrigierte beim Chef gegen sie** he attempted to turn the boss against her with hints and insinuations

intro-, Intro- [ɪntro-]: **~duktion** [~dʊk'tsi̯o:n] **die; ~duktion, ~duktionen** *(geh., Musik)* introduction; **~spektion** [~spɛk'tsi̯o:n] **die; ~spektion** *(Psych.)* introspection; **~vertiert** [~vɛr'ti:ɐ̯t] *Adj. (Psych.)* introverted; **ein Introvertierter/eine Introvertierte** an introvert; **~vertiertheit die; ~vertiertheit** *(Psych.)* introversion

Intuition [ɪntui̯'tsi̯o:n] **die; ~, ~en** intuition

intuitiv [ɪntui̯'ti:f] **1.** *Adj.* intuitive. **2.** *adv.* intuitively

intus ['ɪntʊs] *in* **etw. ~ haben** *(ugs.) (begriffen haben)* have got sth. into one's head; *(gegessen od. getrunken haben)* have put sth. away *(coll.)*; **einen ~ haben** *(ugs.)* have had a few *(coll.)*

invalid [ɪnva'li:t], **invalide** [ɪnva'li:də] *Adj.* invalid *attrib.*; **~ sein** be an invalid

Invalide der; *adj. Dekl.* invalid

Invaliden-: ~heim das home for the disabled and infirm; **~rente die** *(veralt./schweiz.)* invalidity *or* disability pension; **~versicherung die** *(veralt., schweiz.)* invalidity *or* disability insurance

Invalidität [ɪnvalidi'tɛ:t] **die; ~:** invalidity

in·variabel *Adj.* invariable

Invasion [ɪnva'zi̯o:n] **die; ~, ~en** *(auch fig. scherzh.)* invasion

Invasions·krieg der war of invasion

Invasor [ɪn'va:zɔr] **der; ~s, ~en** invader

Invektive [ɪnvɛk'ti:və] **die; ~, ~n** *(geh.)* invective

Inventar [ɪnvɛn'ta:ɐ̯] **das; ~s, ~e a) [totes] ~** *(einer Firma)* fittings and equipment *pl.*; *(eines Hauses, Büros)* furnishings and fittings *pl.*; *(eines Hofes)* machinery and equipment; **lebendes ~:** livestock; **zum ~ gehören** *(fig.)* ⟨*person*⟩ be part of the scenery; **b)** *(Verzeichnis)* inventory

inventarisieren *tr. V.* inventory; draw up *or* make an inventory of

Inventar·stück das [inventoried] item

Inventur [ɪnvɛn'tu:ɐ̯] **die; ~, ~en** stock-taking; **~ machen** carry out a stock-taking; stock-take; *(fig.)* take stock

Inventur·liste die stock list; inventory list

Inversion [ɪnvɛr'zi̯o:n] **die; ~, ~en** *(fachspr.)* inversion

Invest- [ɪn'vɛst-] *(DDR) s.* **Investitions-**

investieren *tr., itr. V. (auch fig.)* invest **(in** + *Akk.* in); **Gefühle in jmdn. ~** *(fig.)* become emotionally involved with sb.

Investition [ɪnvɛsti'tsi̯o:n] **die; ~, ~en** investment; **die privaten ~en sind zurückgegangen** private investment has fallen

Investitions-; ~güter *Pl. (Wirtsch.)* capital goods; **~güter·industrie die** capital-goods industry; **~lenkung die** investment control; **~tätigkeit die** investment activity

Investitur [ɪnvɛsti'tu:ɐ̯] **die; ~, ~en** investiture

Investiv·lohn [ɪnvɛs'ti:f-] **der** *(Wirtsch.) portion of worker's wages set aside for investment in the company's investment savings scheme*

Investment [ɪn'vɛstmɛnt] **das; ~s, ~s** *(Finanzw.) s.* **Investition**

Investment-: ~fonds der investment fund; **~gesellschaft die** investment trust; **~papier das;** *meist Pl.*, **~zertifikat das** investment fund certificate

Investor [ɪn'vɛstɔr] **der; ~s, ~en** [-'to:rən] *(Wirtsch.)* investor

involvieren [ɪnvɔl'vi:rən] *tr. V. (geh.)* involve

in·wendig 1. *Adj.* inside ⟨*pocket*⟩; inner ⟨*part*⟩; *(fig.)* inner, inward ⟨*happiness, strength*⟩. **2.** *adv.* [on the] inside; *(fig.)* inwardly; deep down [inside]; **etw./jmdn. in- und auswendig kennen** *(ugs.)* know sb./sth. inside out

in·wie·fern *Adv. (in welcher Hinsicht)* in what way; *(bis zu welchem Grade)* to what extent; how far

in·wie·weit *Adv.* to what extent; how far

In·zahlungnahme die; ~, ~n part-exchange; trade in *(Amer.)*; **durch ~ Ihres Altgerätes ...:** by taking your old appliance in part-exchange ...; if you trade in your old appliance ...

Inzest [ɪn'tsɛst] **der; ~[e]s, ~e** incest

Inzest·tabu das *(Völkerk.)* incest-taboo

inzestuös [ɪntsɛs'tu̯ø:s] *Adj.* incestuous

In·zucht die; ~: inbreeding

in·zwischen *Adv.* **a)** *(seither)* in the meantime; since [then]; **es hatte sich ~ nichts geändert** nothing had changed in the meantime *or* since; **b)** *(bis zu einem Zeitpunkt) (in der Gegenwart)* by now; *(in der Vergangenheit)* by then; *(in der Zukunft)* by then; by that time; **er hat/hatte sich ~ daran gewöhnt** he has/had got used to it by now/then; **bestell ihm ~ einen schönen Gruß!** *(ugs.)* till then, give him my regards; **c)** *(währenddessen)* meanwhile; in the meantime

IOK [i:o:'ka:] **das; ~[s] Internationales Olympisches Komitee** IOC

Ion [i̯o:n] **das; ~s, ~en** *(Physik, Chemie)* ion

Ionen-: ~austauscher der *(Physik, Chemie)* ion exchanger; **~beschleuniger der** *(Elektronik)* ion accelerator; **~bindung die** *(Physik, Chemie)* ionic bond; **~gitter das** *(Chemie)* ionic lattice; **~strahl der** *(Physik, Chemie)* ion beam

Ionien ['i̯o:ni̯ən] **(das); ~s** Ionia

Ionisation [i̯oniza'tsi̯o:n] **die; ~, ~en** *(Physik, Chemie)* ionization

ionisch *Adj.* **a)** Ionic ⟨*dialect, order, column*⟩; **das Ionische Meer** the Ionian Sea; **b)** *(Musik)* Ionian ⟨*mode*⟩

ionisieren *tr. V. (Physik, Chemie)* ionize

Ionisierung die; ~, ~en *s.* **Ionisation**

Iono·sphäre [i̯ono-] **die** ionosphere

Ionosphären- ionospheric

ionosphärisch *Adj.* ionospheric

I-Punkt ['i:-] **der** dot over *or* on the i; **ein i ohne ~:** a dotless i; **bis auf den ~** *(fig.)* down to the last detail

IQ [i:'ku: *od.* aɪ'kju:] **der; ~[s], ~[s]** IQ

i. R. [i:'ɛr] *Abk.* retd.

IRA [i:|ɛr'|a:] **die; ~:** IRA

Irak [i'ra:k] **(das); ~s** *od.* **der; ~[s]** Iraq; **in/nach/aus** *od.* **im/in den/aus dem ~:** in/to/from Iraq

Iraker der; ~s, ~, Irakerin die; ~, ~nen Iraqi; *s. auch* **-in**

irakisch Iraqi

Iran [i'ra:n] **(das); ~s** *od.* **der; ~[s]** Iran; *s. auch* **Irak**

Iraner der; ~s, ~, Iranerin die; ~, ~nen Iranian; *s. auch* **-in**

iranisch *Adj.* Iranian; **Iranisch/das Iranische** Iranian; *s. auch* **Deutsch**

Iranistik die; ~: Iranian studies *pl., no art.*

irden ['ɪrdn̩] *Adj.* earthen[ware] ⟨*bowl, pot, jug*⟩; **~es Geschirr** earthenware

Irden·ware die earthenware

irdisch *Adj.* **a)** earthly ⟨*joys, paradise, love*⟩; mortal, earthly ⟨*creature, being*⟩; temporal ⟨*power, justice*⟩; worldly ⟨*goods, pleasures, possessions*⟩; **dieses ~e Jammertal** this vale of tears; **die Irdischen** *(dichter.)* the mortals; **den Weg alles Irdischen gehen** go the way of all flesh; ⟨*object*⟩ go the way of all things; **alles Irdische ist vergänglich** all earthly things must fade; **b)** *(zur Erde gehörig)* terrestrial; **das ~e Leben** life on earth

Ire ['i:rə] **der; ~n, ~n** Irishman; **die ~n** the Irish; **er ist ~:** he is Irish *or* an Irishman

irgend ['ɪrgn̩t] *Adv.* **a) ~ jemand** someone; somebody; somebody or other *(coll.)*; *(fragend, verneinend)* anyone; anybody; **Haben Sie an jemand Bestimmtes gedacht? – Ach wo, ~ jemand** Did you have anyone particular in mind? – Oh, anyone *or* anybody [will do]; **warum hast du nicht ~ jemanden gefragt?** why didn't you ask someone *or* somebody?; **~ etwas** something; *(fragend, verneinend)* anything; **~ so ein Politiker** *(ugs.)* some politician [or other]; **~ so etwas** something like that; something of the sort *or* kind; **führen Sie ~ so etwas?** do you stock anything like that?; **b)** *(irgendwie)* **wenn ~ möglich** if at all possible; **wenn ich Ihnen ~ helfen kann** if I can help you in any way

irgend-: ~ein *Indefinitpron.* **a)** *(attr.)* some; *(fragend, verneinend)* any; **~ein Idiot** some idiot [or other]; **in ~einer Zeitung habe ich neulich gelesen, daß ...:** I read in one of the papers recently that ...; **Welche Zeitung soll es sein? – Irgendeine** What newspaper do you want? – Just any; **~ein anderer Redakteur/~eine andere Zeitung/~ein anderes Buch** some other editor/newspaper/book; *(fragend, verneinend)* any other editor/newspaper/book; **~ein anderer/~eine andere** someone *or* somebody else; *(fragend, verneinend)* anyone *or* anybody else; **mehr als ~ein anderer** more than anyone *or* anybody else; **b)** *(subst.)* **~einer/~eine** someone; somebody; *(fragend, verneinend)* anyone; anybody; **~eines** *od.* *(ugs.)* **~eins** any one; **~einer muß es machen** someone *or* somebody [or other] must do it; **nicht ~einer** not just anyone; **~einmal** *Adv.* sometime; [at] some time [or other]; **hast du schon ~einmal solchen Unsinn gehört?** have you ever heard such nonsense before?; **~wann** *Adv.* [at] some time [or other]; somewhen; *(zu jeder beliebigen Zeit)* [at] any time; **~wann einmal** [at] some time [or other]; ~**wạs** *Indefinitpron. (ugs.)* something [or other]; *(fragend, verneinend)* anything; **[nimm] ~was** [take] anything [you like]; **ist ~was?** is [there] something wrong *or* the matter?; ~**wẹlch** *Indefinitpron.* some; *(fragend, verneinend)* any; **er raucht nicht ~welche Zigarren** he doesn't smoke just any *or (coll.)* any old cigars; ~**wẹr** *Indefinitpron. (ugs.)* somebody or other *(coll.)*; someone; somebody; *(fragend, verneinend)* anyone; anybody; ~**wịe** *Adv.* **a)** somehow; somehow or other *(coll.)*; **ich glaube nicht, daß ihr das noch ~wie schaffen könnt** I don't think there's any way you could do it; **wer ~wie kann, sollte helfen** anyone who can help in any way should do so; **kann man das ~wie anders/besser machen?** is there some other/better way of doing this?; **er tut mir ~wie leid, aber ...:** I feel sorry for him in a way, but ...; **ihr Lächeln war ~wie kalt** her smile was somehow *or (coll.)* sort of cold; **b)** *(ugs.: als Füllwort)* **sie will ~wie auch kommen** I somehow think she wants to come too; ~**wọ** *Adv.* **a)** somewhere; some place [or other] *(coll.)*; *(fragend, verneinend)* anywhere; **ist hier ~wo ein Lokal?** is there a pub anywhere around here?; **~wo anders** somewhere/anywhere else; **b)** *(ugs.: irgendwie)* **er tut mir ~wo leid, aber ...:** I feel sorry for him in a way, but ...; ~**wohẹr** *Adv.* from somewhere; from some place; from somewhere or other *(coll.)*; *(fragend, verneinend)* from anywhere; from any place; **Woher soll ich das nehmen? – [Von] ~woher** Where shall I get it from? – From anywhere *or* wherever you like; ~**wohịn** *Adv.* somewhere; somewhere or other *(coll.)*; *(fragend, verneinend)* anywhere; **wollen wir ~wohin gehen?** shall we go out somewhere?; **Wohin soll ich die Socken werfen? – Irgendwohin** Where should I throw these socks? – Anywhere [will do *or* you like]; ~**wo·mịt** *Adv.* with something; with something or other *(coll.)*; ~**worạn** *Adv.* **~woran erinnert mich dieses Gebäude** this building reminds me of something; **~woran werden wir es schon erkennen** we'll recognize it by something

Iridium [i'ri:dịum] **das; ~s** *(Chemie)* iridium

Irin die; ~, ~nen Irishwoman; **sie ist ~:** she is Irish *or* an Irishwoman

Iris ['i:rɪs] **die; ~, ~** *(Bot., Anat.)* iris

Ịris·blende die *(Fot.)* iris [diaphragm]

ịrisch *Adj.* Irish; **die Irische See** the Irish Sea; **Irisch-Republikanische Armee** Irish Republican Army; **~-römisches Bad** Turkish bath; **Irisch/das Irische** Irish; *s. auch* **Deutsch**

Ịris·diagnostik die *(Med.)* iridodiagnosis

irisịeren *itr. V.* iridesce; be iridescent; **~d** iridescent

Irland ['ɪrlant] **(das); ~s** Ireland; *(die Republik)* Ireland; Eire

Ironie [iro'ni:] **die; ~, ~n** irony; **etw. mit ~ sagen** say sth. ironically; **das war ~:** that was meant ironically *or* meant to be ironic; **die ~ des Lebens hat es mit sich gebracht, daß ...:** it was one of life's ironies that ...; **die ~ des Schicksals wollte es, daß ...:** it was one of the ironies of fate *or* an irony of fate that ...

irọnisch 1. *Adj.* ironic; ironical; **das Ironische in der Literatur** irony *or* the ironic in literature; **sie zieht alles ins Ironische** she tends to be ironic about everything. **2.** *adv.* ironically

irọnischer·wẹise *Adv.* ironically

ironisịeren *tr. V.* ironize

Ironisịerung die; ~, ~en ironizing

irr [ɪr] *Adj. s.* **irre 1**

irrational ['ɪratsiona:l] **1.** *Adj.* irrational. **2.** *adv.* irrationally

Irrationalịsmus der; ~, Irrationalịsmen irrationalism

Irrationalitạ̈t die; ~: irrationality

irre ['ɪrə] **1.** *Adj.* **a)** *(geistesgestört)* mad, insane ⟨*person*⟩; insane ⟨*laughter*⟩; demented ⟨*grin, look*⟩; insane, crazy ⟨*idea, thought, suggestion*⟩; **davon kann man ja ~ werden** it's enough to drive you mad *or* crazy; **sich wie ~ gebärden** act *or* behave like a madman/madwoman; **b)** *nicht präd. (salopp: stark)* terrific *(coll.)*; terrible *(coll.)*; **eine ~ Arbeit** a hell of a job *(coll.)*; **c)** *(salopp: faszinierend)* amazing *(coll.)*; **d)** *(geh.)* **an jmdm. ~ werden** lose faith in sb.; **an sich** *(Dat.)* **selbst ~ werden** doubt oneself; **am Glauben ~ werden** begin to have agonizing doubts about one's faith. **2.** *adv. (salopp)* terrifically *(coll.)*; terribly *(coll.)*; **sich ~ freuen** be thrilled to bits *(coll.)*

¹Irre ['ɪrə] **der/die;** *adj. Dekl.* madman/madwoman; lunatic; *(fig.)* fool; idiot; lunatic; **das sind alles ~:** they're all crazy *or* mad; **er fährt wie ein ~r** he drives like a maniac *or* lunatic; **er schreit/arbeitet wie ein ~r** he shouts/works like mad

²Irre die *(geh.)* **in die ~ gehen** *(sich verirren)* go astray; *(fig.: sich irren)* make a mistake; **in die ~ führen** *(fig.)* be misleading; *(täuschen)* be deceptive; **jmdn. in die ~ führen** mislead sb.; *(täuschen)* deceive sb.

irreal ['ɪrea:l] *Adj.* **a)** *(unwirklich)* unreal; **b)** *(unrealistisch)* unrealistic

Irrealis ['ɪrea:lɪs] **der; ~, Irreales** [-le:s] *(Sprachw.)* hypothetical subjunctive

Irrealität die; ~ a) unreality; **b)** *(Sprachw.)* **als Ausdruck der ~:** as an expression of the unreal *or* hypothetical

ịrre-, Ịrre-: ~|führen *tr. V.* mislead; *(täuschen)* deceive; **lassen Sie sich durch ... nicht ~führen** don't be misled *or* deceived by ...; **~führend** *Adj.* misleading; *(täuschend)* deceptive; **~führung die: das war eine bewußte ~führung** that was a deliberate attempt to mislead; **~führung der Öffentlichkeit** misleading the public; **~|gehen** *unr. V.; mit sein (geh.)* **a)** *(sich irren)* be mistaken; **b)** *(sich verirren)* go astray

irregulär ['ɪregulɛ:ɐ̯] *Adj.* **a)** *(regelwidrig, Milit.)* irregular; **b)** *(abnorm)* abnormal

ịrre|leiten *tr. V. (geh.)* **a)** *(verführen, täuschen)* lead astray; **irregeleitete Emotionen/Jugend** misguided emotions/youth; **b)** *(falsch leiten)* **ein irregeleiteter Brief** a misdirected letter

irrelevant ['ɪrelevant] *Adj.* irrelevant **(für** to)

Ịrrelevanz die irrelevance **(für** to)

ịrreligiös *Adj.* non-religious; unreligious ⟨*person, science, country*⟩

ịrre|machen *tr. V.* **a)** *(verwirren)* disconcert; put off; **laß dich durch ihn nicht ~:** don't be disconcerted *or (coll.)* put off by him; **b)** *(zweifeln lassen)* **jmdn. in seinem Glauben ~:** shake sb.'s faith; **sie ließ sich in ihrer Hoffnung/ihrem Plan nicht ~:** she would not let anything confound her hopes/her plan

irren ['ɪrən] **1.** *refl. V.* be mistaken; **man kann sich auch mal ~:** everybody makes *or* we all make mistakes [sometimes]; **Sie ~ sich, wenn ...:** you are making a mistake if ...; **ich irre mich oft bei Namen** I often get names mixed up; **er hat sich in einigen Punkten geirrt** he got a few things wrong; **Sie haben sich in der Person/Hausnummer geirrt** you've got the wrong person/number; **sich um 1 DM ~:** be out by 1 DM; be 1 DM out; **ich habe mich in dir geirrt** I was wrong about you. **2.** *itr. V.* **a)** *(sich irren)* **da ~ Sie** you are mistaken *or* wrong there; **die Zeitungsberichte ~ in diesem Punkt alle** the newspaper reports are all wrong on this point; **Irren ist menschlich** to err is human *(prov.)*; **b)** *mit sein (ziellos umherstreifen)* wander; **durch die Straßen/den Park ~:** wander the streets/about in the park

ịrren-, Ịrren-: ~anstalt die *(veralt. abwertend)* mental home; madhouse *(derog.)*; **~arzt der** *(veralt. abwertend)* mad-doctor *(arch.)*; **~haus das** *(abwertend)* [lunatic] asylum; madhouse *(derog.)*; **das war das reinste ~haus** *(ugs.)* it was bedlam *or* an absolute madhouse; **er ist reif fürs ~haus** *(ugs.)* he'll crack up soon *(coll.)*; **~häusler der** *(veralt. abwertend)* lunatic *(derog.)*; **~haus·reif** *Adj. (ugs.)* **sie ist bald ~hausreif** she'll crack up before long *(coll.)*; **~wärter der** *(veralt. abwertend)* keeper *(arch.)*; mad-nurse; **~witz der** *(ugs.)* loony joke *(coll.)*; joke about lunatics

irreparabel [ɪrepa'ra:bl̩] *Adj. (nicht reparabel)* irreparable; beyond repair *pred.*; *(nicht zu beheben, Med.)* irreparable ⟨*loss, damage, etc.*⟩

Ịrre·sein das *s.* **manisch-depressiv**

ịrreversibel *Adj. (fachspr.)* irreversible

ịrr-, Ịrr-: ~fahrt die wandering; **meine Reise wurde zu einer endlosen ~fahrt** my journey turned into an endless series of wanderings; **~flug der** aimless flight; **~garten der** maze; labyrinth; **~glaube[n] der a)** misconception; **b)** *(Rel.)* heresy; heterodoxy; **~gläubige der/die** heretic

irrig ['ɪrɪç] *Adj.* erroneous ⟨*impression, belief, assumption, etc.*⟩; false ⟨*premise*⟩

Irrigation [ɪriga'tsi̯o:n] **die; ~, ~en** irrigation; *(Med.: Spülung)* douche

Irrigator [ɪri'ga:tɔr] **der; ~s, ~en** [-ga'to:ren] *(Med.)* irrigator

ịrrigerwẹise *Adv.* mistakenly; erroneously

Irritation [ɪrita'tsi̯o:n] **die; ~, ~en** *(Med., geh.)* irritation

irritịeren *tr., itr. V.* **a)** *(verwirren)* bother; put off; **das irritiert** it's off-putting; **laß dich nicht dadurch ~:** don't be put off by it; **b)** *(stören)* disturb; **c)** *(befremden)* annoy; irritate

ịrr-, Ịrr-: ~läufer der *(Postw.)* misdirected letter/parcel; **~lehre die** *(Rel.)* heresy; heterodoxy; *(fig.)* false doctrine; **~licht das** will o' the wisp; jack o' lantern; **~lichter entstehen durch ...:** will o' the wisp *or* jack o' lantern is caused by ...; **~sinn der;** *o. Pl.* **a)** *(Wahnsinn)* insanity; madness; **er war dem ~sinn nahe** he was on the brink of madness; **b)** *(ugs. abwertend)* madness; lunacy; **so ein ~sinn!** what lunacy!; **~sinnig 1.** *Adj.* **a)** *(geistig gestört)* insane; mad; *(absurd)* idiotic; **bist du ~sinnig?** are you mad?; **wie ~sinnig schreien/rasen** scream/rush like mad; **b)** *(ugs.: extrem)* terrible *(coll.)*, horrific *(coll.)* ⟨*pain, screams, prices, etc.*⟩; terrific *(coll.)* ⟨*speed, heat, cold*⟩; **2.** *adv. (ugs.)* terribly *(coll.)*; frightfully *(coll.)*; **~sinnig schuften** slog away like mad *or (coll.)* crazy; **~sinnige der/die;** *adj. Dekl.* madman/madwoman; lunatic; **sie schrie wie eine ~sinnige** she screamed like mad

Ịrrtum der; ~s, Irrtümer ['ɪrty:mɐ] **a)** *(falsche Vorstellung, Fehlhandlung)* fallacy; misconception; **im ~ sein** *od.* **sich im ~ befinden** be wrong *or* mistaken; **b)** *(Fehler)* mistake; error; **~!** wrong!

irrtümlich ['ɪrty:mlɪç] **1.** *Adj.*; *nicht präd.* incorrect; wrong. **2.** *adv.* by mistake; **~ gemachte Angaben** inaccuracies; incorrect information *sing.*

ịrrtümlicherwẹise *Adv.* by mistake; **wie man oft ~ meint** as is often erroneously *or* mistakenly thought

Ịrrung die; ~, ~en *(geh.)* **die ~en und Wirrungen seiner verfehlten Jugend** the vagaries of his misspent youth

ịrr-, Ịrr-: ~weg der error; **diese Methode hat sich als ~weg erwiesen** this method has proved to be wrong; **auf ~wege geraten** *(gedanklich)* go off on the wrong track; *(moralisch)* depart from the straight and narrow; **~wisch** [~vɪʃ] **der; ~s, ~e** flibbertigibbet; **~witz der** *(geh.)* madness; lunacy; **~witzig** *Adj. (geh.)* mad

Ischias ['ɪʃi̯as] **der** *od.* **das** *od. Med.* **die; ~:** sciatica

Ischias·nerv der sciatic nerve

Isegrim ['i:zəgrɪm] **der; ~s, ~e a)** *o. Pl. (Myth.)* **[Meister] ~:** Isegrim; Isgrin; **b)** *(mürrischer Mann)* crusty old man

Islam [ɪs'la:m *od.* 'ɪslam] **der; ~[s]: der ~:** Islam; **die Welt des ~[s]** the Islamic world; the world of Islam

islamisch *Adj.* Islamic; Islamitic

islamisieren *tr. V.* Islamize

Is·land ['i:s-] **(das); ~s** Iceland

Isländer ['i:slɛndɐ] **der; ~s, ~, Isländerin die; ~, ~nen** Icelander

isländisch ['i:slɛndɪʃ] *Adj.* Icelandic; **Isländisch/das Isländische** Icelandic; *s. auch* **Deutsch**

Ismailit [ɪsmai'li:t] **der; ~en, ~en** Ismaili

Ismus ['ɪsmʊs] **der; ~, Ismen** *(abwertend)* ism

iso-, Iso-, *(vor Vokalen auch:)* **is-, Is-** [iz(o)-] iso-

Iso·bar das; ~s, ~e *(Physik)* isobar

Iso·bare die; ~, ~n *(Met.)* isobar

Isogamie [izoga'mi:] **die; ~, ~n** [-i:ən] *(Biol.)* isogamy *no art.*

Isolation [izola'tsi̯o:n] **die; ~, ~en** *s.* **Isolierung**

Isolations-: ~folter die torture by solitary confinement; **~haft die** solitary confinement

Isolator [izo'la:tɔr] **der; ~s, ~en** [-'to:ren] insulator

Isolier·band das; *Pl.* **~bänder** insulating tape

Isolier·baracke die isolation ward

isolieren *tr. V.* **a)** isolate ⟨*prisoner, patient, bacterium, element*⟩; **von der Umwelt isoliert** cut off from the outside world; **etw. isoliert betrachten** look at sth. out of context; **b)** *(Technik)* insulate ⟨*wiring, wall, etc.*⟩; lag ⟨*boilers, pipes, etc.*⟩; *(gegen Schall)* soundproof; insulate ⟨*room, door, window, etc.*⟩

Isolierer der; ~s, ~: insulation engineer

Isolier-: ~kanne die Thermos jug **(P)**; vacuum jug; **~schicht die** insulating layer; **~station die** *(Med.)* isolation ward

Isolierung die; ~, ~en a) *(Absonderung, auch fig.)* isolation; **in der ~:** in isolation; **in die ~ geraten** *(fig.)* become isolated *or* detached; **b)** *(Technik) (das Isolieren)* insulation; insulating; *(von Kesseln, Röhren)* lagging; *(gegen Schall)* soundproofing; **c)** *(Isoliermaterial)* insulation; *(für Kessel, Röhren)* lagging

Isomer [izo'me:ɐ̯] **das; ~s, ~e, Isomere das;** *adj. Dekl. (Chemie)* isomer

Isometrie [izome'tri:] **die; ~** *(Biol., Geodäsie)* isometry

isometrisch 1. *Adj.* isometric. **2.** *adv.* isometrically

Isotherme [izo'tɛrmə] **die; ~, ~n** *(Met.)* isotherm

Isotop [izo'to:p] **das; ~s, ~e** isotope

Isotopen·therapie die *(Med.)* radiotherapy

Israel ['ɪsrae:l] **(das); ~s** Israel; **das Volk ~** *(bibl.)* the Israelites; the people of Israel; **die Kinder ~[s]** *(bibl.)* the Children of Israel

Israeli der; ~[s], ~[s]/die; ~, ~[s] Israeli

israelisch *Adj.* Israeli

Israelit der; ~en, ~en, Israelitin die; ~, ~nen Israelite; *s. auch* **-in**

israelitisch *Adj.* Israelite

iß [ɪs] *Imperativ Sg. v.* **essen**

ißt [ɪst] *2. u. 3. Pers. Sg. Präsens v.* **essen**

ist [ɪst] *3. Pers. Sg. Präsens v.* **sein**

Ist-: ~-Aufkommen das *(Steuerw.)* actual *or* real yield; **~-Bestand der** *(Kaufmannsspr.)* actual stocks *pl.*; **~-Stärke die** *(Milit.)* actual strength

Isthmus ['ɪstmʊs] **der; ~, Isthmen** isthmus

Itaker ['i:takɐ] **der; ~s, ~** *(salopp abwertend)* Eyetie *(sl. derog.)*; dago *(sl. derog.)*

Italien [i'ta:li̯ən] **(das); ~s** Italy

Italiener [ita'li̯e:nɐ] **der; ~s, ~, Italienerin die; ~, ~nen** Italian; *s. auch* **-in**

italienisch *Adj.* Italian; **Italienisch/das Italienische** Italian; *s. auch* **Deutsch**

Italo·western ['i:talo-] **der** Italian-made Western; spaghetti western *(derog.)*

iterativ [itera'ti:f] *Adj. (Sprachw., Math.)* iterative

I-Tüpfel[chen] das; ~s, ~, *(österr.)* **I-Tüpferl** ['i:typfɐl] **das; ~s, ~n** final *or* finishing touch; **bis aufs [letzte] ~:** down to the last *or* smallest detail

I-Tüpfel-Reiter der *(österr. ugs.)* nit-picker *(coll.)*

i. v. *Abk. (Med.)* **intravenös** IV

i. V. [i:'fau̯] *Abk.* **in Vertretung**

Iwan ['i:va(:)n] **der; ~s, ~s** *(salopp abwertend)* Russki *(derog.)*; Ivan *(derog.)*; **der ~:** the Russkis *pl.*; Ivan

i. w. S. *Abk.* **im weiteren Sinne**

J

j, J [jɔt, *österr.:* je:] **das; ~, ~:** j/J; *s. auch* **a, A**

ja [ja:] *Partikel* **a)** *(zustimmend)* yes; **Wohnen Sie hier? – Ja** Do you live here? – Yes [, I do]; **Hast du ihm Bescheid gesagt? – Ja** Have you told him? – Yes [, I have]; **ja zu etw. sagen** say yes to sth.; **b)** *(bekräftigend)* yes; **ja natürlich** *od.* **sicher!** [yes,] of course; [yes,] certainly; **o ja!** oh, yes!; **aber ja doch!** yes, of course [I/you *etc.* can/do *etc.*]; **c)** *(betont, nachgestellt)* won't you/doesn't it *etc.*?; **du bleibst doch noch ein bißchen, ja?** but you'll stay on a bit, won't you *or* surely?; **das Kleid sieht doch gut aus, ja?** the dress looks nice, doesn't it?; **d)** *(unbetont)* **ich komme ja schon** I'm [just] coming; **Sie wissen ja, daß ...:** you know, of course, that ...; **du kennst ihn ja:** you know what he's like; you know him; **es schneit ja!** it's [actually] snowing!; **da seid ihr ja!** there you are!; **e)** *(einschränkend)* **er mag ja recht haben** he may [well] be right; **f)** *(betont: unbedingt)* **laß ja die Finger davon!** [just you] leave it alone!; **sag das ja nicht weiter!** don't [you dare] pass it on, whatever you do!; **damit er ja alles mitbekommt** to make sure he knows all *or* everything that's going on; **damit wir ja nicht zu spät kommen** so that there's no risk of us being late; **g)** *(unbetont: sogar)* indeed; even; **ich schätze, ja bewundere ihn** I like him, indeed admire him *or* admire him even; **h)** *(allerdings)* oh; **ja, das waren noch Zeiten!** [yes], those were the days!; **i)** *(fragend) (am Telefon usw.)* **ja [bitte]?** yes?; **Sie kommen. – Ja?** They're coming. – Are they?; *(ungläubig)* **Der König ist tot. – Ja?** The King is dead. – [Is he] really?

Ja das; ~[s], ~[s] yes; **mit ~ stimmen** vote yes

Jacht [jaxt] **die; ~, ~en** yacht

Jacht-: ~hafen der yacht harbour; marina; **~klub der** yacht club

Jäckchen ['jɛkçən] **das; ~s, ~:** jacket; *(gestrickt)* cardigan

Jacke ['jakə] **die; ~, ~n** jacket; *(gestrickt)* cardigan; **das ist ~ wie Hose** *(ugs.)* it makes no odds *(coll.)*; *s. auch* **saufen 3**

Jacken-: ~kleid das dress and jacket combination; **~tasche die** jacket pocket

Jacket·krone ['dʒɛkɪt-] **die** *(Zahnmed.)* jacket crown

Jackett [ʒa'kɛt] **das; ~s, ~s** jacket

Jade ['ja:də] **der; ~[s]** *od.* **die; ~:** jade

jade·grün *Adj.* jade-green

Jagd [ja:kt] **die; ~, ~en a)** *o. Pl. (Weidwerk)* **die ~:** shooting; hunting; *(Hetzjagd)* hunting; **die ~ auf Hasen** hare-hunting; *(mit Hunden)* hare-coursing; **die ~ auf Federwild** shooting game birds; **~ auf Fasanen/Wildschweine machen** shoot pheasant/hunt wild boar; **auf der ~ sein** be hunting/shooting; **auf die ~ gehen** go hunting/shooting; **die hohe/niedere ~** *(Jägerspr.)* hunting for Hochwild/Niederwild; **b)** *(Veranstaltung)* shoot; *(Hetzjagd)* hunt; **c)** *(Revier)* preserve; shoot; **eine ~ pachten** rent a hunting-preserve *or* shoot; **d)** *(Verfolgung)* hunt; *(Verfolgungsjagd)* chase; **auf jmdn./etw. ~ machen** hunt for sb./sth.; **die ~ nach Geld/Besitz** *(fig.)* the constant pursuit of money/possessions; **e)** *(~gesellschaft)* shooting party; *(bei einer Hetzjagd)* hunt; field; **die Wilde ~:** the Wild Hunt

Jagd-: ~aufklärer der *(Luftwaffe)* fighter-reconnaissance aircraft; **~aufseher der** game warden

jagdbar *Adj.* **~e Tiere** animals that can be hunted/shot

Jagd-: ~beute die bag; kill; **eine reiche/magere ~beute** a good/poor bag; **~bomber der** *(Luftwaffe)* fighter-bomber; **~falke der** falcon; **~fieber das** hunting-fever; **vom ~fieber gepackt** in the fever of the hunt; **~flieger der** *(Luftwaffe)* fighter pilot; **~flugzeug das** *(Luftwaffe)* fighter aircraft; **~frevel der** poaching; **~gebiet das** hunting-ground[s *pl.*]; **~geschwader das** *(Luftwaffe)* fighter wing; **~gesellschaft die** shooting-party; hunting-party; *(bei Hetzjagden)* hunting-party; **~gewehr das** sporting gun; **~glück das: ~glück/kein ~glück haben** be lucky/unlucky [in the hunt]; **~grund der;** *meist Pl.* hunting-ground; **in die ewigen Jagdgründe eingehen** go to the happy hunting-grounds; **~haus das** hunting *or* shooting lodge; hunting *or* shooting box; **~herr der** owner of a/the preserve *or* shoot; **~horn das** hunting-horn; **~hund der** gun-dog; *(bei Hetzjagden)* hunting-dog; hound; **~hütte die** hunting *or* shooting box; **~messer das** hunting-knife; **~pächter der** game-tenant; **~panzer der** *(Milit.)* anti-tank vehicle; tank destroyer; **~rennen das** *(Pferdesport)* steeplechase; **~revier das** preserve; shoot; *(fig.)* hunting-ground; **~schein der** game licence; **er hat den** *od.* **einen ~schein** *(fig. ugs.)* he's certified – the courts can't do anything about him; **~schloß das** hunting seat *or* lodge; **~springen das** *(Pferdesport)* show-jumping; **~staffel die** *(Luftwaffe)* fighter squadron; **~stock der** shooting stick; **~stück das** *(Malerei)* hunting-piece; **~stuhl der** *s.* **~stock**; **~szene die** *(bild. Kunst)* hunting-scene; **~waffe die** hunting weapon; **~wesen das** hunting; **~wurst die** chasseur sausage; **~zeit die** open *or* hunting *or* shooting season

jagen ['ja:gn̩] **1.** *tr. V.* **a)** *(verfolgen)* hunt ⟨*game, fugitive, criminal, etc.*⟩; shoot ⟨*game, game birds*⟩; *(hetzen)* chase, pursue ⟨*fugitive, criminal, etc.*⟩; *(wegscheuchen)* chase; run after; **von Todesfurcht/Gewissensbissen gejagt** stricken by the fear of death/by pangs of conscience; **ein Gedanke jagte den anderen** thoughts raced through his/her *etc.* mind; **b)** *(in eine bestimmte Richtung treiben)* drive ⟨*animals*⟩; **den Ball ins Netz ~** *(Fußballjargon)* drive the ball into the net; **c)** *(weg-, vertreiben)* **den Feind aus dem Land ~:** drive the enemy out of *or* from the country; **jmdn. aus dem Haus ~:** throw sb. out of the house; **jmdn. aus dem Bett ~:** turn sb. out of bed; **jmdn. in die Flucht ~:** put sb. to flight; **damit kannst du mich ~** *(ugs.)* I can't stand it/that/them; *s. auch* **Gurgel; d)** *(ugs.)* **sich/jmdm. eine Spritze in den Arm ~:** jab *or* stick a needle in one's/sb.'s arm; **sich/jmdm. eine Kugel durch den Kopf ~:** blow one's/sb.'s brains out. **2.** *itr. V.* **a)** *(Jägerspr.)* **auf Rebhühner ~:** shoot partridge; **auf Hasen ~:** hunt *or* shoot hare; **b)** *(die Jagd ausüben)* go shooting *or* hunting; *(auf Hetzjagd gehen)* go hunting; **c) nach Geld/Glück ~:** chase after money/happiness; **d)** *mit sein (eilen)* race; rush; **Wolken ~ am Himmel** *(fig.)* clouds race *or* scud across the sky; **mit ~dem Puls** *(fig.)* with his/her *etc.* pulse racing

Jagen das; ~s, ~ *(Forstw.)* compartment

Jäger ['jɛ:gɐ] **der; ~s, ~: a)** hunter; *(bei Hetzjagden)* huntsman; **~ und Sammler** *(Prähist.)* hunters and gatherers; **b)** *(Milit.)* rifleman; jaeger; **c)** *(Soldatenspr.: Jagdflugzeug)* fighter

Jäger·art die *(Kochk.)* **Schnitzel nach ~:** escalope chasseur

Jägerei die; ~ a) *(das Jagen)* shooting; hunting; *(Hetzjagd)* hunting; **b)** *(Jagdwesen)* hunting

Jäger·hut der huntsman's hat

Jägerin die; ~, ~nen huntress; huntswoman

Jäger-: ~latein das *(scherzh.)* [hunter's *or* huntsman's] tall story/stories; **das ist das reinste ~latein** that's all wild exaggeration; **~rock der** hunting jacket; **~schnitzel das** *(Kochk.)* escalope chasseur

Jägers·mann der; *Pl.* **~leute** *(ugs. veralt.) s.* **Jäger a**

Jäger·sprache die hunting language

Jag·hund ['ja:k-] **der** *(schweiz.) s.* **Jagdhund**

Jaguar ['ja:gua:ɐ] **der; ~s, ~e** jaguar

jäh [jɛ:] **1.** *Adj. (geh.)* **a)** *(plötzlich, heftig)* sudden; sudden, abrupt ‹*change, movement, stop*›; sudden, sharp ‹*pain*›; **er fand einen ~en Tod** he met his death suddenly; **ein ~es Erwachen** a sudden awakening; *(fig.)* a rude awakening; **b)** *(steil)* steep; precipitous ‹*slope, ravine, ridge*›. **2.** *adv.* **a)** *(plötzlich)* **die Stimmung schlug ~ um** the mood changed suddenly *or* abruptly; **b)** *(steil)* **dort ging es ~ in die Tiefe** the ground fell *or* dropped away steeply *or* abruptly at that point

jählings ['jɛ:lɪŋs] *Adv. (geh.)* **a)** *(plötzlich)* ‹*change, end, stop*› suddenly, abruptly; ‹*die, understand, wake up*› suddenly; **b)** *(steil)* steeply; precipitously

Jahr [ja:ɐ] **das; ~[e]s, ~e a)** *(12 Monate)* year; **ein halbes ~:** six months; **anderthalb ~e** eighteen months; a year and a half; **im ~[e] 1908** in [the year] 1908; **jedes ~:** every year; **jedes zweite ~:** [once] every two years; **alle halbe[n] ~ [mal]** *(ugs.)* [once] every six months; **alle ~e** every year; **1000 Tonnen pro ~:** 1,000 tonnes per *or* a year; **100 000 DM pro ~:** DM 100,000 per annum; **lange ~e [hindurch]** for many years; **nach langen ~en** after many years; **vor langen ~en** many years ago; **~ für** *od.* **um ~:** year after year; **von ~ zu ~:** from one year to the next; from year to year; **ich war seit ~ und Tag nicht mehr dort** I haven't been there for many years; **zwischen den ~en** between Christmas and the New Year; **das Buch/der Sportler des ~es** the book/sportsman *or* sports personality of the year; **zu zehn ~en [Gefängnis] verurteilt werden** be sentenced to ten years' imprisonment; **er ist Lehrling im zweiten ~:** he is an apprentice in his second year; **auf ~ und Tag** to the exact day; **nach ~ und Tag** after many years; **vor ~ und Tag** *(mit Präteritum)* many years ago; *(mit Plusquamperfekt)* many years before; **b)** *(Lebens~)* year; **er ist zwanzig ~e [alt]** he is twenty years old *or* of age; **Kinder bis zu zwölf ~en** children up to the age of twelve *or* up to twelve years of age; **Kinder über 14 ~e** children over the age of 14 *or* over 14 years of age; **Kinder ab zwei ~en** children of two years and over; **alle Männer zwischen 18 und 45 ~en** all men between the ages of 18 and 45; **mit 65 ~en** *od.* **im Alter von 65 ~en** at the age of 65; **seine ~e spüren** feel one's age; **das hat er schon in jungen ~en gelernt** he learned that at an early age *or* while he was still young; **für seine achtzig ~e ist er noch erstaunlich rüstig** he's amazingly sprightly for [a man of] eighty; **mit den ~en** as he/she *etc.* grows/grew older; **er ist um ~e gealtert** he's put on years; **in die ~e kommen** reach middle age

jahr·aus *Adv.* **~, jahrein** year in, year out

Jahr·buch das year-book

Jährchen ['jɛ:ɐçən] **das; ~s, ~** *(scherzh.)* year; **die paar ~, die ich noch zu leben habe!** the few short years I have left to live; **einige ~ auf dem Buckel haben** be knocking on a bit *(coll.)*

jahr·ein *Adv.; s.* **jahraus**

jahre·lang 1. *Adj.; nicht präd.* [many] years of ‹*practice, imprisonment, experience, etc.*›; long-standing ‹*feud, friendship*›; **mit ~er Verspätung** years late. **2.** *adv.* for [many] years; **sie ist schon ~ tot** she has been dead for [many] years; **man sprach noch ~ darüber** people were talking about it for years afterwards

jähren ['jɛ:rən] *refl. V.* **heute jährt sich [zum fünften Male] sein Todestag** today is the [fifth] anniversary of his death; **heute jährt sich zum zehntenmal, daß ...:** it is ten years ago today that ...; it is ten years since ...

jahres-, Jahres-: ~abonnement das annual *or* yearly subscription; **~abrechnung die** annual accounts *pl.*; *(Abrechnungsblatt)* annual [statement of] account; **~ab·schluß der a)** *(Wirtsch., Kaufmannsspr.)* annual accounts *pl.*; **b)** *s.* **~ende; ~anfang der** beginning *or* start of the year; **~ausgleich der** *(Steuerw.)* end-of-year adjustment; **den ~ausgleich beantragen** send in one's tax return; **~aus·klang der** close of the year; **Musik zum ~ausklang** music at the close of the year; **~aus·stoß der** *(Wirtsch.)* annual production; **~beginn der** beginning *or* start of the new year; **den ~beginn feiern** celebrate New Year; **~beitrag der** annual *or* yearly subscription; **~best·leistung die** *(Sport)* best performance of the season; **~best·zeit die** *(Sport)* fastest *or* best time of the season; **~bezüge** *Pl.* annual income *sing.*; **~bilanz die** *(Wirtsch., Kaufmannssspr.)* annual balance [of accounts]; *(Dokument)* annual balance sheet; **~durch·schnitt der** yearly *or* annual average; **~einkommen das** annual income; **~ende das** end of the year; **~etat der** annual budget; **~frist;** *o. Art.; o. Pl.* **in** *od.* **innerhalb** *od.* **binnen ~frist** within [a period of] a *or* one year; **vor ~frist** in less than a year; within [a period of] a *or* one year; *(vor einem Jahr)* a year ago; **nach ~frist** after [a period of] a *or* one year; **~gehalt das** annual salary; **zwei ~gehälter** two years' salary; **~hälfte die** half of *or* six months of the year; **die erste/zweite ~hälfte** the first/second half *or* six months of the year; **~haupt·versammlung die** *(Wirtsch.)* annual general meeting; **~kapazität die** *(Wirtsch.)* annual *or* yearly capacity; **~karte die** yearly season ticket; **~miete die** annual *or* yearly rent; **eine Kaution in Höhe einer ~miete** a deposit equivalent to a year's rent; **~mittel das** annual mean; **im ~mittel fallen 3,2 cm Niederschlag** the mean annual precipitation is 3.2 cm; **~plan der** [economic, financial] plan for the year; **~produktion die** annual *or* yearly production; **~ring der;** *meist Pl.* *(Bot.)* annual ring; **~rück·blick der** end-of-the-year review; **~schluß der** *s.* **~ende; ~schluß·bilanz die** *s.* **~abschluß a; ~schrift die** annual; **~soll das** *(DDR Wirtsch.)* production target for the year; **~tag der** anniversary; **~tagung die** annual congress *or* conference *or* convention; **~temperatur die: die höchste/tiefste ~temperatur** the highest/lowest temperature of the year; **die mittlere ~temperatur** the mean temperature during the year; **eine mittlere ~temperatur von 9 °C** a mean annual temperature of 9 °C; **~um·satz der** annual turnover; **~urlaub der** annual holiday *or (formal)* leave *or (Amer.)* vacation; **~versammlung die** annual [general] meeting; **~vertrag der** one-year contract; **~wechsel der** turn of the year; **zum ~wechsel die besten Wünsche** best wishes for the New Year; **~wende die a)** *(geh.) s.* **~wechsel; b)** turn of the year; **um die ~wende 1976/1977** around the end of 1976; around the beginning of 1977; **~zahl die** date; **ohne Angabe der ~zahl** with no indication of the date *or* year; **~zeit die** season; **für die ~zeit ist es kalt** it's cold for the time of the year; **trotz der vorgerückten ~zeit** although it is/was late in the year; **~zeitlich 1.** *Adj.; nicht präd.* seasonal; **2.** *adv.* **~zeitlich schwanken** vary with the seasons *or* according to the time of year; **~zeitlich bedingt sein** be governed by seasonal factors

Jahr·gang der a) *(Altersklasse)* year; **der ~ 1900** those *pl.* born in 1900; **der ~ 1900 hat viele Gelehrte hervorgebracht** the year 1900 produced many scholars; **sie ist ~ 1943** she was born in 1943; **er ist mein ~:** he was born in the same year as I was; **welcher ~ sind Sie?** which year were you born in?; **b)** *(eines Weines)* vintage; **der 81er soll ein guter ~ werden** 81 should be a vintage year; **ein Edelzwicker ~ 1978** a 1978 Edelzwicker; **c)** *(einer Zeitschrift)* set [of issues] for a/the year; **die beiden letzten Jahrgänge** the sets of back numbers for the past two years; **d)** *(eines Autos usw.)* year; **ein Modell ~ 1950** a 1950 model

Jahr·gänger der; ~s, ~, Jahr·gängerin die; ~, ~nen *(südd., schweiz.)* **er ist mein Jahrgänger** he was born in the same year as I was

Jahr·hundert das century; **das 18. ~:** the 18th century; **im 19. und 20. ~:** in the 19th and 20th centuries; **durch die ~e** over *or* through the centuries; **im ersten ~ vor/nach Christi Geburt** in the first century BC/AD; **die Literatur des 19. ~s** 19th-century literature; the literature of the 19th century

jahrhunderte-: ~alt *Adj.* centuries-old; **~lang 1.** *Adj.; nicht präd.* age-long. **2.** *adv.* for centuries; **das dauert noch ~lang** that will take centuries

Jahrhundert-: ~hälfte die: die erste/zweite ~hälfte the first/second half of the century; **~mitte die** middle of the century; **~sommer der** summer of the century; **~wein der** exceptional vintage wine; **~wende die** turn of the century; **aus der Zeit um die ~wende** from the turn of the century

-jährig ['jɛ:rɪç] **a)** *(... Jahre alt)* **ein elfjähriges/halbjähriges Kind** an eleven-year-old/a six-month-old child; **kaum acht~:** hardly eight years old; **b)** *(... Jahre dauernd)* ... year's/years'; -year; **nach vierjähriger/halbjähriger Vorbereitung** after four years'/six months' preparation; **mit dreijähriger/halbjähriger Verspätung** three years/six months late

jährlich ['jɛ:ɐlɪç] **1.** *Adj.; nicht präd.* annual; yearly. **2.** *adv.* annually; yearly; **einmal/zweimal ~:** once/twice a *or* per year; **ein Umsatz von 5 Millionen ~:** a turnover of five million per annum

Jahr·markt der fair; fun-fair; **ein ~ der Eitelkeit[en]** *(fig.)* a Vanity Fair
Jahrmarkts·bude die fair-ground booth
Jahr·millionen *Pl.* millions of years
Jahr·schießet das *(schweiz.) s.* **Schützenfest**
Jahr·tausend das thousand years; millennium; **vor ~en** thousands of years ago; **das dritte ~ nach Christi Geburt** the third millennium AD
jahrtausende-: ~alt *Adj.* age-old; **ein ~altes Gebäude** a building dating back thousands of years; **~lang 1.** *Adj.; nicht präd.* age-long; **2.** *adv.* for thousands of years; **das dauert ~lang** that will take thousands of years
Jahrtausend·wende die turn of the millennium
Jahr·zahl die *(schweiz.) s.* **Jahreszahl**
Jahr·zehnt das decade
jahrzehnte·lang 1. *Adj.; nicht präd.* **das macht die ~e Übung** that's the result of decades of practice; **mit ~er Verspätung** decades late; **nach ~er Abwesenheit** after being away for decades. **2.** *adv.* for decades
Jahve, *(ökum.:)* **Jahwe** ['ja:və] **(der); ~s** Jehova; Yahweh
Jäh·zorn der violent anger; **er neigt zum ~:** he tends towards violent fits *or* outbursts of temper *or* anger; **in wildem ~ zuschlagen** lash out in blind anger *or* a blind rage
jäh·zornig 1. *Adj.* violent-tempered; **ein ~er Charakter, ein ~es Temperament** a violent temper. **2.** *adv.* in blind anger; in a blind rage
ja·ja *Part. (ugs.)* **a)** *(seufzend)* **~[, so ist das Leben]** o well[, that's life]; **b)** *(ungeduldig)* **~[, ich komme schon]!** OK, OK *or* all right, all right[, I'm coming]!
Jak [jak] **der; ~s, ~s** yak
Jakob ['ja:kɔp] **(der)** James; *(in der Bibel)* Jacob; **ich weiß ja nicht, ob das der wahre ~ ist** I don't know if that is really quite the thing; **der billige ~:** the/a cheap jack
Jakobi [ja'ko:bi] **(das);** *indekl. s.* **Jakobstag**
Jakobiner [jako'bi:nɐ] **der; ~s, ~** *(hist.)* Jacobin
Jakobiner·mütze die *(hist.)* cap of liberty; Phrygian cap
Jakobinertum das Jacobinism *no art.*
jakobinisch *Adj.* Jacobin; Jacobinic
Jakobit [jako'bi:t] **der; ~en, ~en** *(hist.)* Jacobite
Jakobi·tag der *s.* **Jakobstag**
Jakobs·leiter die *(Seemannsspr., Bot.)* Jacob's ladder
Jakobs·tag der St. James's Day; Feast of St. James
Jalousette [ʒalu'zɛtə] **die; ~, ~n, Jalousie** [ʒalu'zi:] **die; ~, ~n** venetian blind
Jalta ['jalta] **(das); ~s** Yalta
Jamaika [ja'maika] **(das); ~s** Jamaica
Jamaikaner der; ~s, ~, Jamaikanerin die; ~, ~nen Jamaican; *s. auch* **-in**
jamaikanisch *Adj.* Jamaican
Jamaika·rum der Jamaica rum
Jambe ['jambə] **die; ~, ~n** *s.* **Jambus**
jambisch *Adj. (Verslehre)* iambic
Jamboree [dʒæmbə'ri:] **das; ~[s], ~s** jamboree
Jambus ['jambʊs] **der; ~, Jamben** *(Verslehre)* iambus; iamb; **ein Drama in Jamben** a drama in iambic verse *or* in iambics
Jammer ['jamɐ] **der; ~s a)** *(Wehklagen)* [mournful] wailing; **b)** *(Elend)* misery; **ein Bild des ~s** a picture of misery; **es ist ein ~, daß ...** *(ugs.)* it's a crying shame that ...
Jammer-: ~bild das miserable sight; **~geschrei das** *(von Menschen)* wailing; moaning; *(von Vögeln)* squawking; squawks; **~gestalt die a)** *(elender Mensch)* pitiful creature; **b)** *(ugs. abwertend)* miserable wretch; **~lappen der** *(ugs. abwertend)* *(Feigling)* coward; *(Schwächling)* sniveller
jämmerlich ['jɛmɐlɪç] **1.** *Adj.* **a)** *(Jammer ausdrückend)* pathetic; pitiful; **b)** *(beklagenswert)* miserable ‹*existence, conditions, etc.*›; wretched ‹*appearance, existence, etc.*›; **c)** *(ärmlich)* pathetic; pitiful ‹*conditions, clothing, housing*›; paltry, meagre ‹*quantity*›; pitiful, sorry ‹*state*›; **d)** *(abwertend: minderwertig)* contemptible ‹*person*›; pathetic, paltry ‹*wages, sum*›; pathetic, useless ‹*piece of work etc.*›; **e)** *nicht präd. (sehr groß, stark)* awful; terrible *(coll.)*. **2.** *adv.* **a)** *(Jammer ausdrückend)* pathetically; pitifully; **b)** *(beklagenswert)* miserably; hopelessly; pitifully; **~ versagen** fail miserably *or* hopelessly; **c)** *(ärmlich)* pitifully; miserably; **d)** *(abwertend: schlecht)* pathetically; hopelessly; **e)** *(sehr, stark)* terribly *(coll.)*; **~ frieren** be frozen stiff
Jämmerlich·keit die; ~: a) *(Jammer)* mournfulness; **b)** *(Elend)* wretchedness; **c)** *(Ärmlichkeit)* pitifulness; wretchedness; **d)** *(abwertend) (eines Menschen)* contemptibility; *(einer Arbeit usw.)* uselessness
Jämmerling ['jɛmɐlɪŋ] **der; ~s, ~e** *(ugs. abwertend) (Feigling)* chicken *(coll.)*; *(Schwächling)* weakling
jammern 1. *itr. V.* **a)** wail; **ohne zu ~:** without so much as a groan; **Jammern und Klagen** groans and cries *pl.*; **b)** *(sich beklagen)* moan; grumble; **über sein Schicksal ~:** bemoan one's fate; **c)** *(verlangen)* cry [out]; **die Kinder jammerten nach einem Stück Brot** the children were crying out for *or* crying after a piece of bread. **2.** *tr. V. (geh.: Mitleid erregen)* grieve; distress; **er/sein Elend jammert mich** his distress grieves me; my heart goes out to him in his distress
jammer-, Jammer-: ~schade *Adj.; nicht attr. (ugs.)* **es ist ~schade, daß ...:** it's a crying shame that ...; **es ist ~schade um ihn** it's a great pity about him; **~tal das;** *o. Pl. (geh.)* vale of tears; **dieses irdische ~tal** this earthly vale of tears; **~voll 1.** *Adj.* **a)** *(Jammer ausdrückend)* pathetic; pitiful ‹*cry etc.*›; **b)** *(beklagenswert)* miserable; **2.** *adv.* **a)** *(Jammer ausdrückend)* pathetically; pitifully; **b)** *(beklagenswert)* miserably; wretchedly
Jan. *Abk.* **Januar**
Janker ['jaŋkɐ] **der; ~s, ~** *(südd., österr.)* Alpine jacket
Jänner ['jɛnɐ] **der; ~s, ~** *(österr.),* **Januar** ['janʊa:ɐ̯] **der; ~[s], ~e** January; *s. auch* **April**
janus-, Janus- ['ja:nʊs-]: **~gesicht das, ~kopf der** Janus face; **~köpfig** *Adj.* Janus-faced
Japan ['ja:pan] **(das); ~s** Japan
Japaner der; ~s, ~, Japanerin die; ~, ~nen Japanese; *s. auch* **-in**
japanisch *Adj.* Japanese; **das Japanische Meer** the Sea of Japan; **Japanisch/das Japanische** Japanese; *s. auch* **Deutsch**
Japan·lack der Chinese *or* Japanese lacquer
Japan·papier das rice paper
Japs [japs] **der; ~es, ~e** *(ugs. abwertend)* Jap *(derog.)*
japsen ['japsn̩] *itr. V. (ugs.)* pant; **ich kann kaum noch ~:** I'm gasping for breath
Japser der; ~s, ~ *(ugs.)* gasp of breath
Jargon [jar'gõ:] **der; ~s, ~s a)** *(Gruppensprache)* jargon; **der ~ der Juristen/Mediziner** legal/medical jargon; **der ~ der Journalisten** journalese; **der Berliner ~:** Berlin slang; **im „Spiegel"-~:** in the jargon of the 'Spiegel'; **b)** *(abwertend: ungepflegte Ausdrucksweise)* language; **er redet in einem ganz ordinären ~:** he uses very vulgar language
Ja·sager [-za:gɐ] **der; ~s, ~** *(abwertend)* yes-man
Jasmin [jas'mi:n] **der; ~s, ~e a)** *(Echter ~)* jasmine; **b)** *(Falscher ~)* mock orange; syringa
Jasmin·tee der jasmine-tea
Jaspis ['jaspɪs] **der; ~** *od.* **~ses, ~se** jasper
Jaß [jas] **der; Jasses** *(schweiz.)* jass
jassen *itr. V. (schweiz.)* play jass
Ja·stimme die yes-vote; **die ~n** the votes in favour; the ayes *(Brit. Parl.)*
jäten ['jɛ:tn̩] *tr., itr. V.* weed; **Unkraut ~:** weed; **Brennesseln ~:** pull out *or* weed out stinging nettles
Jauche ['jauxə] **die; ~, ~n a)** liquid manure; **b)** *(ugs. abwertend)* muck
jauchen *tr., itr. V. (Landw.)* manure
Jauche·grube die liquid-manure reservoir
jauchzen ['jauxtsn̩] *itr. V.* **a)** *(laut jubeln)* cheer; **vor Freude ~:** shout for joy; **der Säugling jauchzte laut** the baby gurgled with pleasure; **das Publikum jauchzte** the audience was in raptures; **b)** *(veralt.)* rejoice; **jauchzet dem Herrn** rejoice in the Lord
Jauchzer der; ~s, ~: cry of delight
jaulen ['jaulən] *itr. V.* ‹*dog, cat, etc.*› howl, yowl; ‹*wind*› howl; ‹*engine*› scream
Jause ['jauzə] **die; ~, ~n** *(österr.)* **a)** snack; **eine ~ machen** have a snack; **b)** *(Nachmittagskaffee)* [afternoon] tea
Jausen·station die *(österr.)* café
jausnen *itr. V. (österr.)* have a snack
Java ['ja:va] **(das); ~s** Java
ja·wohl *Part.* **a)** certainly; **~, Herr Oberst!** yes, sir!; **b)** *(verstärkend)* **Kant, ~ Kant** Kant, no less
jawoll [ja'vɔl] *(ugs.) s.* **jawohl**
Ja·wort das consent; **jmdm. das ~ geben** consent to marry sb.; **sich** *(Dat.)* **das ~ geben** accept each other in marriage
Jazz [dʒæz *od.* dʒɛs *od.* jats] **der; ~:** jazz
Jazz·band die jazz band
jazzen ['dʒɛsn̩ *od.* 'jatsn̩] *itr. V.* play jazz
Jazzer ['dʒɛsɐ *od.* 'jatsɐ] **der; ~s, ~:** jazz musician
Jazz·fan der jazz-fan
jazzig ['jatsɪç] *Adj. (ugs.)* jazzy
Jazz-: ~kapelle die jazz band; **~keller der** jazz cellar; **~musik die** jazz music
[1]je [je:] **1.** *Adv.* **a)** *(jemals)* ever; **mehr/besser denn je** more/better than ever; **seit** *od.* **von je** always; for as long as anyone can remember; *s. auch* **[2]eh b**; **b)** *(jeweils)* **je zehn Personen** ten people at a time; **die Gruppen bestehen aus je acht Mitgliedern** the groups consist of eight members each; **die Kinder stellen sich je zwei und zwei auf** the children arrange themselves in twos *or* in pairs; **die Schränke sind je zwei Meter breit** the wardrobes are each two metres wide; **sie kosten je 30 DM** they cost 30 DM each; **er gab den Mädchen je eine Birne** he gave each of the girls a pear; **in Schachteln mit** *od.* **zu je 10 Stück verpackt** packed in boxes of ten; **c)** *(entsprechend)* **je nach Gewicht/Geschmack** according to weight/taste. **2.** *Präp. mit Akk.* per; for each; **je angebrochene Stunde** for each *or* per hour or part of an hour. **3.** *Konj.* **a) je länger, je lieber** the longer the better; **je früher du kommst, desto** *od.* **um so mehr Zeit haben wir** the earlier you come, the more time we'll have; **b) je nachdem** it all depends; **wir gehen hin, je nachdem [ob] wir Zeit haben oder nicht** we'll go, depending on whether we have the time or not; **Willst du mitgehen? – Je nachdem** *(ugs.)* Do you want to come too? – I'll see
[2]je 1. *Interj.* **ach je, wie schade!** oh dear *or* dear me, what a shame!; *s. auch* **oje. 2.** *Adv. (veralt.)* **je nun** well now
Jeans [dʒi:nz] *Pl. od.* **die; ~, ~ a)** *(Hose)* jeans *pl.*; denims *pl.*; **b)** *(Stoff)* denim; jean[s] material
Jeans-: ~hose die [pair of] jeans; **~jacke die** denim jacket; **~stoff der** denim; jean[s] material
jeck [jɛk] *Adj. (rhein., meist abwertend) (leicht verrückt)* stupid; daft; *(wahnsinnig)* crazy
Jeck der; ~en, ~en *(rhein.)* **a)** *(abwertend:*

Verrückter) idiot; **b)** *(Fastnachter)* carnival clown

jede *s.* **jeder**

jeden·falls *Adv.* **a)** *(gewiß)* certainly; definitely; **b)** *(zumindest)* at any rate; **ich ~ habe keine Lust mehr** I at any rate *or* for one have had enough; **c)** *(soviel steht fest)* in any case; at any rate; anyway; **das steht ~ fest** that much is certain, in any case *or* at any rate *or* anyway

jeder ['je:dɐ], **jede, jedes** *Indefinitpron. u. unbest. Zahlwort* **1.** *attr.* **a)** *(alle)* every; **jeder einzelne Schüler** every single pupil; **jeder zweite Bürger** one out of *or* in every two citizens; **der Zug fährt jeden Tag/viermal jeden Tag** the train runs every day/four times a day; **b)** *(verstärkend)* **das kann Ihnen jedes Kind sagen** any child could tell you that; **ohne jeden Zweifel** without any doubt; **ohne jeden Grund** without any reason whatever; for no reason whatever; **c)** *(alle einzeln)* each; **jeder Mitspieler bekommt sechs Karten** each player receives six cards; **d)** *(jeglicher)* all; **jede Hilfe kam zu spät** all help came too late; **hier wurde jedes Maß überschritten** that went beyond all bounds; **Menschen jeden** *od.* **jedes Alters** people of all ages; **„nehme jede Arbeit an"** 'all offers of work accepted'. **2.** *alleinstehend* **a)** *(alle)* everyone; everybody; **jeder** *od. (geh.)* **ein jeder darf mitkommen** everyone *or* everybody can come; **hier kennt jeder jeden** everybody knows everybody else here; *(verstärkend)* **jeder, der Lust hat, ist willkommen** anyone who wants to come is welcome; **das kann ja jeder** anyone can do that; **b)** *(alle einzeln)* **jedes der Kinder** every one *or* each of the children; **jeder für sich hat recht** each of us/you/them *etc.* is right in his own way; **jeder von uns kann helfen** each *or* every one of us can help; **jedem nach seinem Verdienst** to each according to his merits

jeder-: **~art** *unbest. Gattungsz.; indekl.; nicht präd.* any kind *or* sort *or* type of; **er ist bereit, ~art Arbeit anzunehmen** he is prepared to take any kind of work; **~lei** *unbest. Gattungsz.; indekl.; nicht präd. (geh.)* all kinds *or* sorts of; **~mann** *Indefinitpron. u. unbest. Zahlwort; nur alleinstehend* everyone; everybody; **hier kann ~mann mitmachen** everyone *or* everybody *or* anyone *or* anybody can come along and join in; **das ist ~manns Pflicht** that is everyone's *or* everybody's duty; **Schnecken sind nicht ~manns Sache/Geschmack** snails are not to everyone's *or* everybody's taste; **~zeit** *Adv.* [at] any time; **natürlich, ~zeit!** of course, any time!

jedes *s.* **jeder**

jedes·mal *Adv.* every time; **er kommt ~ zu spät** he arrives late every time; he always arrives late; **~, wenn das Telefon klingelt, ...:** every time the telephone rings ...

je·doch *Konj., Adv.* however; **es war ~ zu spät** it was too late, however; it was, however, too late

jedweder ['je:t've:dɐ], **jedwede, jedwedes** *Indefinitpron. u. unbest. Zahlwort (nachdrücklich, veralt.)* **a)** *attr.* every; **ohne jedwede Rücksicht** without any consideration whatsoever; **b)** *alleinstehend* everyone; everybody

Jeep Ⓦ [dʒi:p] **der; ~s, ~s** jeep **(P)**

jeglicher ['je:klɪçɐ], **jegliche, jegliches** *Indefinitpron. u. unbest. Zahlw. s.* **jeder 1c, 2b**

je·her [od. '-'-] *Adv.* **seit** *od.* **von ~:** always; since *or* from time immemorial; **es wurde seit** *od.* **von ~ so gehandhabt, daß ...:** the procedure has always been that ...

Jehova [je'ho:va] *s.* **Zeuge**

jein [jain] *Adv. (scherzh.)* yes and no

Je·länger·je·lieber das; ~s, ~ *(Bot.)* honeysuckle; woodbine

jemals ['je:ma:ls] *Adv.* ever

jemand ['je:mant] *Indefinitpron.* someone; somebody; *(fragend, verneinend)* anyone; anybody; **ich kenne ~[en], der ...:** I know someone *or* somebody who ...; **sich mit ~[em] treffen** to meet someone *or* somebody; **ist da ~?** is anybody there?; **ich glaube nicht, daß da ~ ist** I don't think there's anybody there; **~ anders/Fremdes** someone *or* somebody else/strange; **ein gewisser Jemand** *(scherzh.)* a certain somebody; **kaum ~:** hardly *or* scarcely anyone *or* anybody; *s. auch* **irgend a**

Jemen ['je:mən] **(das); ~s** *od.* **der; ~[s]** Yemen; *s. auch* **Irak**

Jemenit [jemə'ni:t] **der; ~en, ~en, Jemenitin die; ~, ~nen** Yemenite; Yemeni

jemenitisch *Adj.* Yemenite; Yemeni

jemine ['je:mine] *Interj. (veralt.)* **ach ~!** oh dear; dear me!

jener ['je:nɐ], **jene, jenes** *Demonstrativpron. (geh.)* **1.** *attr.* that; *(im Pl.)* those; **in jenem Haus dort** in that house [over] there; **vergleichen Sie dieses mit jenem Bild** compare this picture and that one; **zu jenem Zeitpunkt** at that time; **in jenen Tagen** in those days. **2.** *alleinstehend* that one; *(im Pl.)* those; **jene, die ...:** those who ...; **ein Roman Bölls, in dem jener schildert, wie ...:** a novel by Böll in which he describes how ...

jenseitig ['je:n- *od.* 'jɛn-] *Adj.; nicht präd.* **a)** *(gegenüberliegend)* opposite; far, opposite ‹*bank, shore*›; **b)** *(geh.)* **die ~e Welt** *od.* **das Jenseitige** the next world; the hereafter

jenseits ['je:n-] **1.** *Präp. mit Gen.* on the other side of; *(in größerer Entfernung)* beyond; **~ des Urals** beyond the Urals; **~ des Flusses** on the other *or* far *or* opposite side of the river; **sie ist schon ~ der Vierzig** she's already over *or (coll.)* the wrong side of forty. **2.** *Adv.* beyond; on the other side; **~ vom Rhein** on the other side of *or* beyond the Rhine; **eine Welt ~ von Haß und Gewalt** a world free from hatred and violence; *s. auch* **gut 4b**

Jenseits das; ~: hereafter; beyond; **ins ~ abgerufen** *od.* **abberufen werden** *(geh. verhüll.)* pass away; **jmdn. ins ~ befördern** *(salopp)* bump sb. off *(sl.)*

Jeremia [jere'mi:a] **(der); ~s** Jeremiah

Jeremiade [jere'mia:də] **die; ~** *(geh., veralt.)* jeremiad

[1]**Jersey** ['dʒø:ɐ̯zi] **der; ~[s], ~s** *(Textilind.)* jersey

[2]**Jersey das; ~s, ~s** *(Sport: Trikot)* jersey

Jersey·kleid das jersey dress

jerum ['je:rʊm] *Interj. s.* **ojerum**

Jesaja [je'za:ja] **(der); ~s** Isaiah

Jessas [na] ['jɛsas (na:)] *Interj. (österr.)* my goodness

Jesuit [je'zui:t] **der; ~en, ~en** *(Rel., auch abwertend)* Jesuit

Jesuiten-: **~general der** General of the Jesuits; **~orden der** order of Jesuits; Society of Jesus; **~schule die** Jesuit school

Jesuitentum das Jesuitism

Jesus ['je:zʊs] **(der); Jesu** ['je:zu] Jesus; **~ Christus** Jesus Christ

Jesus[, Maria und Josef] *Interj. (veralt.)* oh [my] Lord

Jesus-: **~kind das: das ~:** the Infant Jesus; baby Jesus *(child lang.)*; **~knabe der** *s.* **~kind; ~latschen der** *(scherzh.)* Jesus sandal *(joc.)*

Jet [dʒɛt] **der; ~[s], ~s** jet; **mit einem ~ fliegen/reisen** fly/travel by jet

Jet·flug der flight by jet

Jeton [ʒə'tõ:] **der; ~s, ~s a)** *(Spielmarke)* gaming chip *or* token; **b)** *(für das Telefon usw.)* token

Jet-set ['dʒɛtsɛt] **der; ~[s], ~s** jet set

jetten ['dʒɛtn̩] *itr. V.; mit sein (ugs.)* jet

jetzig ['jɛtsɪç] *Adj.; nicht präd.* present; current; **in der ~en Zeit** at present; in present times

jetzo ['jɛtso] *(veralt.) s.* **jetzt**

jetzt [jɛtst] *Adv.* **a)** *(im Augenblick)* at the moment; just now; **bis ~:** up to now; **bis ~ noch nicht** not yet; not so far; **von ~ an** *od.* **ab** from now on[wards]; **~ noch** still; **was, ~ [so spät] noch?** what, now?; **das geht nicht von ~ auf nachher** *(ugs.)* it can't be done at a moment's notice; **~ oder nie!** it's now or never; **~ ist aber Schluß!** that's [quite] enough!; **b)** *(nun, nunmehr)* now; **~ ist es aus mit uns** we've had it now; **sie ist gerade ~ weggegangen** she has just left; **~ endlich** [now,] at last; **~ erst [einmal]** just; **erst ~** *od.* **~ erst** only just; **schon ~:** already; **er ist ~ schon drei Wochen krank** he has been ill for three weeks now; **c)** *(heutzutage)* now; these days; nowadays; **d)** *(landsch.: wohl)* **von wem wird ~ der Brief sein?** now, who will that letter be from, I wonder?

Jetzt das; ~ *(geh.)* **das ~:** the present

Jetzt·zeit die; *o. Pl.* present times *pl.*; **in der ~:** in present times; in our times

je·weilen *Adv. (schweiz.)* occasionally; once in a while

jeweilig ['je:vailɪç] *Adj.; nicht präd.* **a)** *(in einem bestimmten Fall)* particular; **nach den ~en Umständen** according to the particular circumstances; **b)** *(zu einer bestimmten Zeit)* current; of the time *postpos., not pred.*; **nach der ~en Mode** in the current fashion; in the fashion of the time; **c)** *(zugehörig, zugewiesen)* respective

jeweils ['je:vails] *Adv.* **a)** *(jedesmal)* **~ am ersten/letzten Mittwoch des Monats** on the first/last Wednesday of each month; **b)** *(zur Zeit)* currently; at the time; **die ~ amtierende Regierung** the government of the day

Jg. *Abk.* **Jahrgang**

Jh. *Abk.* **Jahrhundert** c.

jiddeln ['jɪdl̩n] *s.* **jüdeln**

jiddisch ['jɪdɪʃ] *Adj.* Yiddish; **Jiddisch/das Jiddische** Yiddish; *s. auch* **Deutsch**

Jitterbug [dʒɪtəbʌg] **der; ~:** jitterbug

Jiu-Jitsu ['dʒi:u'dʒɪtsu] **das; ~[s]** j[i]u-jitsu

Jive [dʒaɪv] **der; ~:** jive; **~ tanzen** jive

[1]**Job** [jo:p] *s.* **Hiob**

[2]**Job** [dʒɔp] **der; ~s, ~s** *(ugs.; auch DV)* job

jobben *itr. V. (ugs.)* do a job/jobs; **als Taxifahrer ~:** do [some] taxi-driving

Jobber der; ~s, ~ *(Börsenw.)* [stock] jobber; *(ugs. abwertend)* jobber *(derog.)*

Joch [jɔx] **das; ~[e]s, ~e** *(bei Maßangaben ungebeugt)* **a)** *(bei Zugtieren)* yoke; **Ochsen/Kühe ins/unters ~ spannen** yoke oxen/cows; **das ~ der Tyrannei abschütteln** *(fig. geh.)* throw *or* cast off the yoke of tyranny; **b)** *(Gespann, Feldmaß)* **zwei ~ Ochsen/Land** two yoke of oxen/land; **c)** *(Geogr.)* col; saddle; **d)** *(Archit.)* bay

Joch·bein das *(Anat.)* zygomatic bone; malar bone

Jockei, Jockey ['dʒɔke *od.* 'dʒɔki] **der; ~s, ~s** jockey

Jockey·mütze die jockey cap

Jod [jo:t] **das; ~[e]s** iodine

Jodel·lied das yodelling song

jodeln ['jo:dl̩n] *itr., tr. V.* yodel

jod·haltig *Adj.* iodiferous

Jodler der; ~s, ~: a) *(Person)* yodeller; **b)** *(kurzes Jodeln)* yodel; **c)** *s.* **Jodellied**

Jodlerin die; ~, ~nen yodeller

Jod-: **~tinktur die** tincture of iodine; iodine tincture; **~zahl die** *(Chemie)* iodine number; iodine value

Joga ['jo:ga] **der** *od.* **das; ~[s]** yoga; **~ betreiben** *od. (ugs.)* **machen** practise *or (coll.)* do yoga

Joga·übung die yoga exercise

joggen ['dʒɔgn̩] *itr. V.; mit Richtungsangabe mit sein* jog; **[zwei Kilometer] ~:** go jogging [for two km]

Jogging ['dʒɔgɪŋ] **das; ~s** jogging *no art.*

Joghurt ['jo:gʊrt] **der** *od.* **das; ~[s], ~[s]** yoghurt

Joghurt·becher der yoghurt pot *(Brit.) or (Amer.)* container

Jogi ['jo:gi], **Jogin** ['jo:gɪn] **der; ~s, ~s** yogi
Johann ['jo:han] **(der)** John
Johanna [jo'hana] **(die): ~ von Orléans** Joan of Arc
Johannes [jo'hanəs] **1. (der); Johannes'** John; **~ der Täufer** John the Baptist. **2. der; ~, ~se** *(salopp) s.* **Jonny**
Johannes·evangelium das St John's Gospel; Gospel according to St John
Johanni [jo'hani] **(das);** *indekl. s.* **Johannistag**
Johannis·beere die a) *(Frucht)* currant; **rote/weiße/schwarze ~n** redcurrants/white currants/blackcurrants; **b)** *(Strauch)* currant [bush]; **rote/weiße/schwarze ~n** redcurrant/white currant/blackcurrant bushes
Johannisbeer-: ~saft der currant juice; **~strauch der** currant bush
Johannis-: ~brot das *(Bot.)* Saint-John's-bread; carob [bean]; **~brot·baum der** *(Bot.)* Saint-John's-bread; carob [tree]; **~feuer das** Saint John's fire; **~käfer der** *(südd.) s.* **Leuchtkäfer; ~kraut das** Saint John's wort; **~tag der** Saint John's the Baptist's day; **~trieb der** *(Bot.)* **a)** *(das Austreiben)* Lammas growth; **b)** *(Trieb)* Lammas shoot
Johanniter [jo:ha'ni:tɐ] **der; ~s, ~:** Knight of St. John of Jerusalem
Johanniter·orden der Order of [the Hospital of] St. John of Jerusalem
johlen ['jo:lən] **1.** *itr. V.* yell; *(vor Wut)* howl. **2.** *tr. V.* **die Menge johlte Beifall/Pfuirufe** the crowd yelled *or* roared its approval/howled *or* roared its disapproval
Joint [dʒɔɪnt] **der; ~s, ~s** *(ugs.)* joint *(sl.)*; **einen ~ kreisen lassen** pass a joint round
Jo-Jo [jo(:)'jo:] **das; ~s, ~s** yo-yo
Joker ['jo:kɐ *od.* dʒo:kɐ] **der; ~s, ~** *(Kartensp.)* joker
Jokus ['jo:kʊs] **der; ~, ~se** *(veralt.)* **seinen ~ mit etw./jmdm. haben** tease sth./sb.; make fun of sth./sb.
Jolle ['jɔlə] **die; ~, ~n a)** *(Sportboot)* [sailing] yacht; **b)** *(mit Schwert)* keel-centre-board yawl; **c)** *(Beiboot)* yawl; jolly[-boat]
Jollen·kreuzer der dinghy cruiser
Jongleur [ʒɔŋ'lø:ɐ] **der; ~s, ~e** juggler
jonglieren *tr., itr. V.* juggle; **Bälle** *od.* **mit Bällen ~:** juggle with balls; **mit Zahlen ~:** juggle [about] with figures; **ich werde das schon irgendwie ~** *(ugs.)* I'll wangle *(coll.) or* work it somehow
Jonny ['dʒɔni] **der; ~s, ~s** *(salopp: Penis)* John Thomas *(sl.)*
Joppe ['jɔpə] **die; ~, ~n** heavy jacket
Jordan ['jɔrdan] **der; ~[s]** Jordan; **über den ~ gehen** *(verhüll.)* go the way of all flesh
Jordanien [jɔr'da:ni̯ən] **(das); ~s** Jordan
Jordanier der; ~s, ~, Jordanierin die; ~, ~nen Jordanian; *s. auch* **-in**
jordanisch *Adj.* Jordanian
Josef, Joseph ['jo:zɛf] **(der)** Joseph
Joseph[s]·ehe die unconsumated marriage
Jot [jɔt] **das; ~, ~:** j, J; *s. auch* **a, A**
Jota ['jo:ta] **das; ~[s], ~s** iota; **kein/nicht ein/um kein ~** *(geh.)* not an iota; not one jot
Joule [dʒu:l *od.* dʒau̯l] **das; ~[s], ~** *(Physik)* joule
Jour [ʒu:ɐ] **der; ~s, ~s** *(veralt.)* open house; **~ fixe** at-home
Journaille [ʒʊr'nalјə *od.* ʒʊr'nai̯l] **die; ~** *(veralt. abwertend)* **a)** *(verantwortungslose Presse)* yellow *or* gutter press; **b)** *(Sensationsjournalisten)* hacks *pl. (derog.)*
Journal [ʒʊr'na:l] **das; ~s, ~e a)** *(veralt.: Tageszeitung)* journal *(dated)*; newspaper; **b)** *(geh.: Zeitschrift)* journal; periodical; **ein ~ für Mode/Kunst** a fashion/an art journal *or* periodical; **c)** *(veralt.: Tagebuch)* journal *(dated)*; diary; **d)** *(Schiffstagebuch)* log[-book]; **e)** *(Kaufmannsspr.)* day-book
Journal·beamte der *(österr.)* official *or* officer [on duty]
Journalismus der; ~: journalism *no art.*
Journalist der; ~en, ~en journalist
Journalisten·deutsch das *(oft abwertend)* journalese
Journalistik die; ~: journalism *no art.*
Journalistin die; ~, ~nen journalist
journalistisch 1. *Adj.; nicht präd.* journalistic; **eine ~e Ausbildung** a training in journalism. **2.** *adv.* journalistically; **~ tätig sein** work as *or* be a journalist
jovial [jo'vi̯a:l] *Adj.* jovial
Jovialität [jovi̯ali'tɛ:t] **die; ~:** joviality
jr. *Abk.* **junior** Jr.
Jubel ['ju:bl̩] **der; ~s** *(das Jauchzen)* rejoicing; jubilation; *(laut)* cheering; **ein großer ~ brach aus** a loud cheer went up; **unter dem ~ der Zuschauer** amid the cheering *or* cheers of the spectators; **~, Trubel, Heiterkeit** an atmosphere of eat, drink, and be merry
Jubel-: ~feier die jubilee; anniversary; *(Feierlichkeiten)* jubilee *or* anniversary celebrations *pl.*; **~greis der** *(scherzh.)* old swinger *(coll. joc.)*; **~jahr das** jubilee; **alle ~jahre [einmal]** once in a blue moon
jubeln 1. *itr. V.* cheer; **über etw.** *(Akk.)* **~:** rejoice over sth.; celebrate sth.; **~de Instrumente/Klänge** *(dichter.)* joyful instruments/sounds. **2.** *tr. V.* **Beifall ~:** applaud; give applause; **„Hurra!" jubelte er** 'hurrah!' he cried delightedly
Jubel-: ~paar das couple celebrating their wedding anniversary; **~perser der** *(ugs. abwertend)* person hired to cheer in the/a crowd; **~ruf der** cheer; joyful shout; *(religiös)* exultation; shout of praise
Jubilar [jubi'la:ɐ] **der; ~s, ~e** man celebrating his anniversary/birthday
Jubilarin die; ~, ~nen woman celebrating her anniversary/birthday
Jubilate [jubi'la:tə] *o. Art., indekl. (ev. Kirche)* Jubilate
Jubiläum [jubi'lɛ:ʊm] **das; ~s, Jubiläen** anniversary; *(eines Monarchen)* jubilee; **fünfundzwanzig-/fünfzigjähriges ~:** twenty-fifth/fiftieth anniversary/jubilee; **hundertjähriges ~:** hundredth anniversary; centenary; **500jähriges/1000jähriges ~:** quincentenary/millenary; **sein 25jähriges ~ bei der Firma begehen** celebrate 25 years with the firm
Jubiläums-: ~aus·gabe die jubilee edition; **~aus·stellung die** jubilee exhibition; **~heft das** jubilee issue
jubilieren *itr. V. (geh. veralt.)* jubilate *(literary)*; rejoice; **die Lerche trällerte ~d** the lark sang joyfully
juchhe [jʊx'he:], **juchhei** [jʊx'hai̯], **juchheirassa[ssa]** [jʊx'hai̯rasa(sa)] *(veralt.)*, **juchheißa** [jʊx'hai̯sa] *(veralt.) Interj.* hurrah
Juchten ['jʊxtn̩] **der** *od.* **das; ~s a)** *(Leder)* Russia [leather]; **b)** *(Duftstoff)* Russian leather
juchzen ['jʊxtsn̩] *itr. V. (ugs.)* shout with glee
Juchzer der; ~s, ~ *(ugs.)* shout of glee; **einen ~ ausstoßen** shout with glee
jucken ['jʊkn̩] **1.** *tr., itr. V.* **a) mir juckt die Haut** I itch; **es juckt mir** *od.* **mich auf dem Kopf** my head itches; **es juckt mich am ganzen Körper** I itch all over; **es juckt mich hier** I've got an itch here; **wen's juckt, der kratze sich** *(fig.)* anybody who does not like it should say something; **b)** *(Juckreiz verursachen)* irritate; **die Wolle juckt ihn** *od.* **ihm auf der Haut** the wool makes him itch; the wool irritates his skin; **ein ~der Hautausschlag** an itching rash; **c)** *(bes. nordd. salopp)* **laß ~!** get a rove on! *(coll.)*. **2.** *tr. V. (reizen, verlocken)* **es juckt mich, das zu tun** I am itching *or* dying to do it; **ihn juckt das Geld** he is tempted by the money; **das juckt mich nicht** *(ugs.)* I couldn't care less *(coll.)*. **3.** *refl. V. (ugs.: sich kratzen)* scratch
Jucken das; ~s itching; **ein ~ verspüren** feel an itch
Juck-: ~pulver das itching powder; **~reiz der** itch
Judäa [ju'dɛ:a] **(das); ~s** Jud[a]ea
Judaika [ju'da:ika] *Pl.* Judaica
Judaist der; ~en, ~en, Judaistin die; ~, ~nen specialist in Jewish studies; *(Student)* student of Jewish studies
Judaistik die; ~: Jewish studies *pl., no art.*
Judas ['ju:das] **1. (der); Judas'** Judas; **~ Ischariot** Judas Iscariot. **2. der; ~, ~se** *(fig.)* Judas
Jude ['ju:də] **der; ~n, ~n** Jew; **er ist ~:** he is a Jew; he is Jewish
jüdeln ['jy:dl̩n] *itr. V.* speak half Yiddish
Juden-: ~frage die *(ns. verhüll.)* Jewish question; **~haß der** anti-Semitism; hatred of [the] Jews; **~hetze die** Jew-baiting; **~pogrom der** *od.* **das** pogrom against the Jews; **~stern der** *(ns.)* Star of David
Judentum das; ~s a) *(Volk)* Jewry; Jews *pl.*; **das gesamte ~:** the whole of Jewry; **b)** *(Kultur u. Religion)* Judaism; **c)** *(jüdisches Wesen)* Jewishness
Juden-: ~verfolgung die persecution of [the] Jews; **~viertel das** Jewish quarter; *(hist.)* Jewry
Judikative [judika'ti:və] **die; ~, ~n** *(Rechtsw., Politik)* judiciary
Judikatur [judika'tu:ɐ] **die; ~, ~en** *(Rechtsw.)* judicature
Jüdin ['jy:dɪn] **die; ~, ~nen** Jewess; **sie ist ~:** she is Jewish *or* a Jewess
jüdisch *Adj.* Jewish; **~ fühlen/denken** feel/think like a Jew
judizieren [judi'tsi:rən] *itr. V. (Rechtsspr.)* administer justice
Judo ['ju:do] **das; ~[s]** judo *no art.*
Judo·griff der judo throw; *(Haltegriff)* judo hold
Judoka [ju'do:ka] **der; ~[s], ~[s]** judoka; judoist
Jugend ['ju:gn̩t] **die; ~ a)** youth; **in ihrer ~:** in her youth; when she was young; **schon in früher ~:** at an early age; **seit früher ~, schon von ~ auf** from an early age; from his/her *etc.* youth; **b)** *(Jugendliche)* young people; **die ~ der Welt** the youth *or* the young people of the world; **die weibliche/männliche ~:** girls *pl.*/boys *pl.*; **er spielt in der ~** *(Sport)* he plays in the youth side *or* team; **die reifere ~** *(scherzh.)* the over-forties *pl.*; **c)** *(Biol., Med.)* immature stage [of development]
jugend-, Jugend-: ~alkoholismus der alcoholism among young people; **~alter das** adolescence; **~amt das** youth office *(agency responsible for education and welfare of young people)*; **~arbeit die** *o. Pl.* **a)** *(Bildung und Erziehung)* youth work; **b)** *(Erwerbstätigkeit)* youth employment; employment of young people; **~arbeitslosigkeit die** youth unemployment; **~arbeits·schutz der** protection of young people at work; **~arrest der** detention in a community home; **zu vier Wochen ~arrest verurteilt werden** be sentenced to four weeks in a community home; **~bewegt** *Adj. (meist scherzh.)* boy-scoutish; **~bewegung die** *(hist.)* [German] youth Movement; **~bild das: ein ~bild seines Vaters/seiner Mutter** a picture of his father/mother as a young man/woman; **~brigade die** *(DDR)* youth brigade; **~buch das** book for young people; **~erinnerung die** memory of one's youth; *(Foto usw.)* memento of one's youth; **~film der** film for young people; **~frei** *Adj.* ⟨*film, book, etc.*⟩ suitable for persons under 18; **nicht ~frei** ⟨*film*⟩ not U-certificate *pred.*; *(scherzh.)* ⟨*joke, story, etc.*⟩ not for young ears *pred.*; **~freund der a)** friend of [the days of] one's youth; **er ist ein ~freund von ihr** he used to be a friend of hers when she was young; **b)** *(DDR)* FDJ

member; **~frische die** youthfulness; **~funk der** programmes *pl.* for young people; **~gefährdend** *Adj.* liable to have an undesirable influence on the moral development of young people *postpos.*; **~gericht das** juvenile court; **~gruppe die** youth group; **~heim das** youth centre; **~herberge die** youth hostel; **~klub der** youth club; **~kriminalität die** juvenile delinquency

jugendlich ['ju:gn̩tlɪç] **1.** *Adj.* **a)** *nicht präd.* young ⟨*offender, customer, etc.*⟩; **noch in ~em Alter sein** still be a youngster; still be young; **b)** *(für Jugendliche charakteristisch)* youthful; **in ~er Begeisterung** fired by the spirit of youth *or* by youthful enthusiasm; **c)** *(jung wirkend)* youthful ⟨*person, appearance*⟩; **sie ist/wirkt noch sehr ~:** she still is/looks very young; **d)** *(bes. Werbespr.)* young ⟨*fashions, dress, hairstyle, etc.*⟩. **2.** *adv.* **sich ~ kleiden** dress young

Jugendliche ['ju:gn̩tlɪçə] **der/die;** *adj. Dekl.* **a)** young person; **die ~n** the young people; **b)** *(Rechtsspr.)* juvenile; young person; **zwei ~:** two juveniles; two young persons; **ein 16jähriger ~r/eine 16jährige ~:** a 16-year-old youth/girl

Jugendlichkeit die youth; *(jugendliche Wirkung)* youthfulness

Jugend-: ~liebe die love *or* sweetheart of one's youth; **seine/ihre [alte] ~liebe** the love *or* sweatheart of his/her youth; **~mannschaft die** *(Sport)* youth team *or* side; **~meister der** youth champion; *(Mannschaft)* youth champions; **~meisterschaft die** youth championship; **~objekt das** *(DDR)* youth project; **~pfleger der** youth worker; **~psychologie die** psychology of adolescence; adolescent psychology *no art.*; **~recht das** laws *pl.* relating to young persons; **~schutz der** protection of young people; **~schutz·gesetz das** laws *pl.* protecting young people; **~sprache die** young people's language *no art.*; **~stil der** art nouveau; *(in Deutschland)* Jugendstil; **Möbel im ~stil** art nouveau/Jugendstil furniture; **~straf·anstalt die** detention centre; **~strafe die** youth custody sentence; **sechs Monate ~strafe bekommen** get six months in a detention centre; **~sünde die, ~torheit die** youthful folly; **~traum der** youthful dream; **es war sein ~traum gewesen, zu ...:** when he was young, it had been his ambition to ...; **~verband der** youth organization; **~vor·stellung die** performance for young people; **~weihe die a)** *(DDR) ceremony in which fourteen-year-olds are given adult social status;* **b)** *Free Church ceremony for child of primary school-leaving age, in place of confirmation;* **~werk das** early *or* youthful work; *(gesamtes)* early *or* youthful works *pl.*; juvenilia *pl.*; **~zeit die** youth; younger days *pl.*; **~zeit·schrift die** magazine for young people; **~zentrum das** youth centre

Jugo·slawe [jugo-] **der** Yugoslav

Jugo·slawien (das); ~s Yugoslavia

Jugo·slawin die Yugoslav; *s. auch* **-in**

jugo·slawisch *Adj.* Yugoslav[ian]

juhu *Interj.* **a)** [ju'hu:] *(Ausruf des Jubels)* yippee; hooray; **b)** ['ju'hu:] *(Zuruf)* yoo-hoo

Juice [dʒu:s] **der** *od.* **das;** ~, ~s ['dʒu:sɪs] *(bes. österr., DDR: Fruchtsaft) (esp. citrus)* [fruit] juice; *(DDR: Gemüsesaft)* vegetable juice

Julei [ju:'lai] **der;** ~[s], ~s *s.* **Juli**

Jul·fest ['ju:l-] **das** yule-tide festival

Juli ['ju:li] **der;** ~[s], ~s July; *s. auch* **April**

Jumbo-Jet ['jʊmbo-] **der;** ~s, ~s jumbo jet

Jumelage [ʒym'la:ʒ] **die;** ~, ~n: **zwischen Bonn und Oxford besteht eine ~:** Bonn and Oxford are twinned *(Brit.) or (Amer.)* are sister cities

Jumper ['dʒampɐ] **der;** ~s, ~: jumper *(Brit.)*; pullover

jun. *Abk.* **junior** Jr.

jung [jʊŋ] *Adj.*; **jünger** ['jʏŋɐ], **jüngst...** ['jʏŋst...] **a)** young; **in ~en Jahren** at an early age; **er ist ~ gestorben** he died young; **in seinen ~en Jahren** in the days of his youth; **~ an Jahren sein** be young [in years]; **der jüngere Bruder** the younger brother; **die jüngste Tochter** the youngest daughter; **der ~e Meier** *(ugs.)* Meier junior; **Sport erhält ~:** sport keeps you young; **b)** *(neu)* young ⟨*state, country, firm, foliage*⟩; new ⟨*project, undertaking, sport, marriage, etc.*⟩; **die Nacht ist noch ~:** the night is young; **der ~e Tag** *(geh.)* the new day; **c)** *(letzt...)* recent; **in jüngster Zeit** recently; lately; **ein Ereignis der jüngeren/jüngsten Geschichte** an event in recent/very recent history; **die jüngsten Geschehnisse** the latest *or* [most] recent happenings; **d)** *(ugs. scherzh.)* **er ist ganze 30 Jahre ~:** he's 30 years young; **e) der Jüngste Tag** doomsday; *s. auch* [1]**Gericht d; jünger**

Jung-: ~akademiker der newly-qualified [university] graduate; **~arbeiter der** young worker; **~bauer der** young farmer; **~brunnen der** Fountain of Youth; **das ist ein wahrer ~brunnen** *(fig.)* that's a real tonic; **~bürger der** *(bes. österr.)* first-time voter; new voter

Jungchen das; ~s, ~ *(bes. ostd.)* little boy; little lad; **mein ~:** my boy *or* lad

Jung·demokrat der Young Democrat

[1]**Junge** ['jʊŋə] **der;** ~n, ~n *od. (ugs.)* **Jung[en]s a)** boy; *(Lauf~, Lehr~)* boy; lad; **Tag, alter ~!** *(ugs.)* hello, old pal! *(coll.)*; **jmdn. wie einen dummen ~n behandeln** *(ugs.)* treat sb. like a child; **~, ~!** *(ugs.)* [boy], oh boy!; *s. auch* **schwer 1e; b)** *(ugs.: beim Kartenspiel)* jack; knave

[2]**Junge das;** *adj. Dekl.* **ein ~s** one of the young; **~ kriegen** give birth to young; **eine Löwin und ihr ~s** a lioness and her cub

Jüngelchen ['jʏŋl̩çən] **das;** ~s, ~ *(ugs. abwertend)* young puppy *or* cub

jungen *itr. V.* give birth; produce young; ⟨*cat*⟩ have kittens; ⟨*dog*⟩ have pups

jungenhaft 1. *Adj.* boyish. **2.** *adv.* **seine Stimme klang ~ hell** his voice was high and clear like a boy's; **sie kleidet sich ~:** she dresses boyishly

Jungen-: ~klasse die boys' class; **wir waren eine reine ~klasse** our class was all boys; **~schule die** boy's school; school for boys; **~streich der** boyish prank

jünger ['jʏŋɐ] *Adj.* youngish; **sie ist noch ~:** she is still quite young; *s. auch* **jung**

Jünger der; ~s, ~: follower; disciple; *(der Kunst, Literatur)* devotee; **Jesus und seine ~:** Jesus and his disciples

Jüngere der/die; *adj. Dekl.* **die ~n unter Ihnen** the younger ones amongst you; **die ~n werden das nicht mehr wissen** younger people won't remember it; **Lucas Cranach der ~:** Lucas Cranach the younger

Jüngerin die; ~, ~nen *s.* **Jünger**

Jungfer ['jʊŋfɐ] **die;** ~, ~n **a)** *(veralt.) (Fräulein)* young lady; *(als Anrede)* Mistress; **b)** *(abwertend: ältere ledige Frau)* spinster; **eine alte ~:** an old maid

Jungfern-: ~fahrt die maiden voyage; **~flug der** maiden flight; **~häutchen das** hymen; **~kranz der** *(veralt.) s.* **Brautkranz; ~rede die** maiden speech; **~zeugung die** *(Biol.)* parthenogenesis

Jung·frau die a) virgin; **sie ist noch ~:** she is still a virgin; **die Heilige ~:** the Holy Virgin; **die ~ Maria** the Virgin Mary; **die eiserne ~:** the iron maiden; **zu etw. kommen wie die ~ zum Kind[e]** get sth. by sheer chance or luck; **wir sind zu den Büchern gekommen wie die ~ zum Kind[e]** we have no idea how the books got here; **b)** *(Astrol.)* Virgo; *s. auch* **Fisch c; c)** *(veralt.: junges Mädchen)* young maid *or* maiden *(arch.)*

jung·fräulich [-frɔylɪç] *Adj. (geh., auch fig.)* virgin; virginal ⟨*innocence, appearance*⟩; **~ in die Ehe gehen** be a virgin bride; **ihr ~er Leib** *(dichter.)* her chaste body

Jungfräulichkeit die *(geh.)* virginity; *(fig.: von Wald, Erde usw.)* virgin state

Jung·geselle der bachelor; **~ bleiben** remain a bachelor

Jung·gesellen-: ~bude die *(ugs.)* bachelor pad *(coll.)*; **~leben das** bachelor['s] life; **~wirtschaft die;** *o. Pl. (ugs., oft scherzh.)* **ich habe die ~wirtschaft satt** I've had enough of looking after myself; **~wohnung die** bachelor flat; **~zeit die** bachelor days *pl.*; bachelorhood

Jung-: ~gesellin die bachelor girl; **sie ist ~gesellin geblieben** she never married; **~grammatiker der;** *meist Pl. (Sprachw.)* neogrammarian; **~lehrer der** probationary teacher *(teaching before second Staatsexamen)*

Jüngling ['jʏŋlɪŋ] **der;** ~s, ~e *(geh./spött.)* youth; boy; **ein grüner** *od.* **unreifer ~** *(spött.)* a raw youth

Jünglings-: ~alter das; *o. Pl. (geh.)* youth; **im zarten ~alter** as a tender youth; **~jahre** *Pl. (geh.)* years of one's youth; young years

Jung-: ~mädel das *(ns.) girl member of the Hitler Youth, aged 10–14;* **~mann der** *(veralt.)* young man; **~sozialist der** Young Socialist

jüngst [jʏŋst] *Adv. (geh.)* recently

jüngst... *s.* **jung**

Jüngste der/die; *adj. Dekl.* youngest [one]; **die ~n** the youngest ones

Jung-: ~stein·zeit die Neolithic period; New Stone Age; **~tier das** young animal; **~trieb der** new growth; **~verheiratete der/die;** *adj. Dekl.*, **~vermählte der/die;** *adj. Dekl. (geh.)* young married man/woman; **die ~verheirateten** the newlyweds; **~volk das;** *o. Pl.* **a)** *(veralt.)* young folk; **b)** *(ns.) 10–14 year-old members of the Hitler Youth;* **~wähler der** first-time voter; new voter; **~wald der** *(Forstw.)* young forest/wood

Juni ['ju:ni] **der;** ~[s], ~s June; *s. auch* **April**

Juni·käfer der summer chafer

junior ['ju:niɔr] *indekl. Adj.; nach Personennamen* junior

Junior der; ~s, ~en [-'nio:rən] **a)** *(oft scherzh.)* junior *(joc.)*; **mit seinem ~:** with junior; **b)** *(Kaufmannsspr.)* junior partner; **c)** *(Sport)* junior

Junior·chef der owner's *or (coll.)* boss's son

Junioren-: ~mannschaft die youth team; **~meister der** junior champion; *(Mannschaft)* junior champions; **~meisterschaft die** junior championship

Juniorin die; ~, ~nen junior partner

Junior·partner der *(Kaufmannsspr.)* junior partner

Junker ['jʊŋkɐ] **der;** ~s, ~: **a)** *(hist.)* junker; young nobleman; *(als Anrede)* young sir; **b)** *(oft abwertend: Landadliger)* junker; squire

Junkertum das; ~s *(hist.)* junkerdom; squirearchy

Junkie [dʒʌŋki] **der;** ~s, ~s *(Drogenjargon)* junkie *(sl.)*

Junktim das; ~s, ~s package [deal]; **zwischen den beiden Abkommen besteht ein ~:** the two agreements form one package

Juno [ju'no:] **der;** ~[s], ~s *s.* **Juni**

Junta ['xʊnta] **die;** ~, **Junten** junta

[1]**Jupiter** ['ju:pitɐ] **der;** ~s *(Astron.)*, [2]**Jupiter (der)** *(Myth.)* Jupiter

Jupon [ʒy'põ:] **der;** ~[s], ~s *(schweiz.)* petticoat; slip

[1]**Jura** ['ju:ra] *o. Art., o. Pl.* law; **~ studieren** read *or* study Law

[2]**Jura der;** ~s *(Geol.)* Jurassic [period/system]

juridisch [ju'ri:dɪʃ] *Adj. (österr./veralt.) s.* **juristisch**

Jurisdiktion [jʊrɪsdɪk'tsio:n] **die; ~, ~en** *(Rechtsw., kath. Kirche)* jurisdiction
Jurisprudenz [jʊrɪspru'dɛnts] **die;** ~ *(geh.)* jurisprudence *no art.*
Jurist der; ~en, ~en lawyer; jurist
Juristen·deutsch das *(oft abwertend)* legal jargon
Juristerei die; ~ *(abwertend, oft scherzh.)* law *no art.*
Juristin die; ~, ~nen lawyer; jurist; *s. auch* **-in**
juristisch 1. *Adj.* legal ‹*wrangle, term, training, career*›; **eine ~e Staatsprüfung** a state law examination; **die Juristische Fakultät** the Law Faculty. **2.** *adv.* **~ denken** think in legal terms; **~ argumentieren** use legal arguments
Juror ['ju:rɔr] **der; ~s, ~en** [-'ro:rən], **Jurorin die; ~, ~nen** judge
Jurte ['jʊrtə] **die; ~, ~n** yurt
Jury [ʒy'ri:] **die; ~, ~s a)** *(Preisrichter)* panel [of judges]; jury; **b)** *(Sachverständige)* panel [of experts]
[1]**Jus** [ju:s] **das;** ~ *(österr., schweiz.) s.* [1]**Jura**
[2]**Jus** [ʒy:] **die** *od.* **das** *od.* **der; ~: a)** *(Fleischsaft)* meat juices *pl.*; meat stock; **b)** *(schweiz.) (Fruchtsaft)* fruit juice; *(Gemüsesaft)* vegetable juice
Juso ['ju:zo] **der; ~s, ~s** Young Socialist
just [jʊst] *Adv. (veralt., noch scherzh.)* just; **~ in diesem Augenblick** just at that moment; at that very moment; **~ an jenem Tag** on that very day
justieren *tr. V.* adjust
Justierung die; ~, ~en adjustment
Justitia [jʊs'ti:tsia] **die; ~:** Justice *no art.*; *(Statue)* statue of Justice
justitiabel [jʊsti'tsia:bl̩] *(geh.)* justiciable
Justitiar [jʊstitsia:ɐ̯] **der; ~s, ~e** company lawyer
Justiz [jʊs'ti:ts] **die; ~: a)** justice; **b)** *(Behörden)* judiciary; **ein Vertreter der ~:** a representative of justice *or* of the law
Justiz-: ~beamte der court official; **~behörde die** judicial authority; **~irrtum der** miscarriage of justice; **~minister der** Minister of Justice; **~ministerium das** Ministry of Justice; **~mord der** judicial murder; **~vollzugs·anstalt die** *(Amtsspr.)* penal institution *(formal)*; prison; **~wacht·meister der** court usher
Jute ['ju:tə] **die; ~:** jute
Jute·sack der jute *or* gunny sack
Jüt·land ['jy:t-] **(das); ~s** Jutland
[1]**Juwel** [ju've:l] **das** *od.* **der; ~s, ~en** piece *or* item of jewellery; *(Edelstein)* jewel; gem; **Schmuck und ~en** jewellery
[2]**Juwel das; ~s, ~e** *(Kostbarkeit)* gem; **ein ~ gotischer Baukunst** a gem *or* jewel of Gothic architecture
Juwelen-: ~händler der dealer in precious stones; **~raub der** jewel robbery *or* theft
Juwelier [juvə'li:ɐ̯] **der; ~s** jeweller; *s. auch* **Bäcker**
Juwelier·geschäft das jeweller's shop
Jux [jʊks] **der; ~es, ~e** *(ugs.)* joke; **aus ~:** as a joke; for fun; **sie machten sich** *(Dat.)* **einen ~ daraus, das zu tun** they did it as a joke *or* for a lark; **sich** *(Dat.)* **einen ~ mit jmdm. machen** play a [practical] joke on sb.; **aus [lauter] ~ und Tollerei** just for the fun *or (coll.)* hell of it
Juxta·position ['juksta-] **die** *(Sprachw.)* juxtaposition
jwd [jɔtve:'de:] *Adv. (ugs. scherzh.)* in *or* at the back of beyond; miles out

K

k, K [ka:] **das; ~, ~:** k/K; *s. auch* **a, A**
K *Abk. (Physik)* **Kelvin** K
Kabale [ka'ba:lə] **die; ~, ~n** *(veralt.)* cabal
Kabarett [kaba'rɛt] **das; ~s, ~s** *od.* **~e a)** satirical cabaret [show]; satirical revue; **ein politisches ~:** a satirical political revue; **b)** *(Ensemble)* cabaret act; **c)** *(Speiseplatte)* [revolvable] partitioned dish
Kabarettist der; ~en, ~en, Kabarettistin die; ~, ~nen revue performer
kabarettistisch *Adj.* [satirical] revue *attrib.*; **~e Szenen** scenes in the style of a [satirical] revue
Kabäuschen [ka'bɔysçən] **das; ~s, ~** *(ugs.) (Zimmer)* cubby-hole; *(Häuschen)* little hut
Kabbala ['kabala] **die; ~:** cabbala
Kabbalistik die; ~: cabbalism *no art.*
Kabbelei die; ~, ~en squabble
kabbelig *Adj. (Seemannsspr.)* choppy
kabbeln ['kabl̩n] *refl. V. (ugs.)* squabble, bicker **(mit** with)
Kabel ['ka:bl̩] **das; ~s, ~: a)** *(elektrische Leitung)* cable; *(für kleineres Gerät)* flex; **b)** *(Stahltrosse)* cable; **c)** *(veralt.: Telegramm)* cable
Kabel-: ~bericht der *(veralt.)* cabled dispatch; **~fernsehen das** cable television
Kabeljau ['ka:bl̩jau] **der; ~s, ~e** *od.* **~s** cod
Kabel-: ~länge die *(Seew.)* cable['s length]; **~leger der** cable ship; **~mantel der** cable-sheath
kabeln *tr., itr. V. (veralt.)* cable
Kabel-: ~rolle die cable drum; **~schacht der** cable duct; *(in der Straße)* cable pit
Kabine [ka'bi:nə] **die; ~, ~en a)** *(auf Schiffen, in Flugzeugen)* cabin; **b)** *(Umkleideraum, abgeteilter Raum)* cubicle; **in die ~n gehen** *(Fußball)* go back into the dressing-rooms; **c)** *(einer Seilbahn)* [cable-]car
Kabinen-: ~bahn die cableway; **~roller der** bubble car
Kabinett [kabi'nɛt] **das; ~s, ~e a)** *(Gesamtheit der Minister)* Cabinet; **b)** *(veralt.: Arbeitszimmer)* cabinet *(arch.)*; **c)** *(österr.: kleines Zimmer)* small room with one window; box-room *(Brit.)*
Kabinetts-: ~beschluß der Cabinet decision; **~bildung die** formation of a/the Cabinet; **~justiz die** *interference by ruler or government in the process of law;* **~krise die** Cabinet crisis; **~liste die** list of Cabinet members; **~sitzung die** Cabinet meeting
Kabinett-: ~stück[chen] das tour de force; **~wein der** Kabinett wine
Kabis ['ka:bɪs] **der; ~** *(südd., schweiz.)* cabbage
Kabrio ['ka:brio] **das; ~s, ~s, Kabriolett** [kabrio'lɛt] **das; ~s, ~s a)** convertible; **b)** *(veralt.: Kutsche)* cabriolet
Kabuff [ka'bʊf] **das; ~s, ~s** *(ugs., oft abwertend)* [poky little] cubby-hole
Kachel ['kaxl̩] **die; ~, ~n** [glazed] tile; **etw. mit ~n auslegen** tile sth.
Kachel·bad das tiled bathroom
kacheln *tr. V.* tile; **eine grün gekachelte Wand** a wall covered with green tiles
Kachel·ofen der tiled stove
kack·braun *Adj. (derb)* dirty brown; shit-coloured *(coarse)*
Kacke ['kakə] **die;** ~ *(derb; auch fig.)* shit *(coarse)*; crap *(coarse)*; **so eine ~!** shit! *(coarse)*; **dann/jetzt ist die ~ am Dampfen** then/now there'll be hell to pay *(coll.)*
kacken ['kakn̩] *itr. V. (derb)* shit *(coarse)*; crap *(coarse)*
Kacker der; ~s, ~ *(derb)* shit *(coarse)*
Kadaver [ka'da:vɐ] **der; ~s, ~** *(auch fig., abwertend)* carcass
Kadaver·gehorsam der *(abwertend)* blind obedience
Kadenz [ka'dɛnts] **die; ~, ~en a)** *(Musik)* cadence; *(solistische Paraphrasierung)* cadenza; **b)** *(Verslehre)* cadence
Kader ['ka:dɐ] **der** *od. (schweiz.)* **das; ~s, ~: a)** cadre; **b)** *(Sport)* squad
kader-, Kader-: ~abteilung die *(DDR)* personnel department; **~akte die** *(DDR)* personal file; **~arbeit die** *(DDR)* cadre work; **~armee die** cadre army; **~leiter der** *(DDR)* [chief] personnel officer; **~partei die** cadre party; **~politisch** *Adj. (DDR)* ‹*matters, problems, measures, etc.*› relating to the political development and function of the cadres; **~schmiede die** *(ugs.)* training-ground for new cadres
Kadett [ka'dɛt] **der; ~en, ~en a)** *(hist., Milit.)* cadet; **b)** *(ugs.: Bursche)* lad
Kadetten·anstalt die *(hist.)* cadet school
Kadi ['ka:di] **der; ~s, ~s a)** *(islam. Richter)* cadi; **b)** *(ugs.: Gericht)* **jmdn. vor den ~ schleppen** haul sb. up before a judge *or (Brit. sl.)* the beak; **zum ~ laufen** go to court
Kadmium ['katmiʊm] **das; ~s** *(Chemie)* cadmium
Käfer ['kɛ:fɐ] **der; ~s, ~: a)** *(Insekt; auch ugs.: VW)* beetle; **b)** *(ugs.: junges Mädchen)* lass; girl; **ein flotter ~:** a nice bit of fluff *(coll.)*
Kaff [kaf] **das; ~s, ~s** *od.* **Käffer** ['kɛfɐ] *(ugs. abwertend)* dump *(coll.)*; [dead-and-alive] hole *(coll.)*
Kaffee ['kafe *od. (österr.)* ka'fe:] **der; ~s, ~s a)** coffee; **~ kochen** make coffee; **~ mit Milch** white coffee *(Brit.)*; coffee with milk/cream; **mir kam der ~ hoch** *(ugs.)* I felt like puking *(coarse)*; **dir haben sie wohl was in den ~ getan?** *(ugs.)* have you gone soft in the head? *(coll.)*; **das ist kalter ~** *(ugs.) (ist längst bekannt)* that's old hat *(coll.)*; *(ist Unsinn)* that's a load of old rubbish *(coll.)*; **b)** *(Nachmittags~)* afternoon coffee; **~ trinken** have afternoon coffee; **jmdn. zum ~ einladen** invite sb. round for afternoon coffee
kaffee-, Kaffee-: ~automat der coffee-maker; **~bohne die** coffee-bean; **~braun** *Adj.* coffee-coloured; **~durst der: ~durst haben** feel like a [cup of] coffee; **~-Ersatz der** coffee substitute; **~-Extrakt der** coffee essence; **~fahrt die a)** *(Fahrt)* trip [out] for afternoon coffee; **b)** *(Werbefahrt) free trip for afternoon coffee during which goods are offered for sale to participants by sponsoring firm;* **~filter der** coffee filter; *(Filtertüte)* filter [paper]; **~geschirr das** coffee-service *or* -set *(including small plates)*; **~haube die** *s.* **~wärmer**
Kaffee·haus das *(bes. österr.)* coffee-house
Kaffee·haus-: ~atmosphäre die coffee-house atmosphere; **~musik die** *(oft abwertend)* palm-court music
Kaffee-: ~kanne die coffee-pot; **~kirsche die** coffee cherry; **~klatsch der** *(ugs. scherzh.)* get-together and a chat over coffee; coffeeklatsch *(Amer.)*; **heute ist bei ihr ~klatsch** she's having people round today for coffee and a chat; **~kränzchen das** *(veralt.)* **a)** *(Zusammentreffen)* coffee afternoon; **b)** *(Gruppe)* coffee circle; **~löffel der** coffee-spoon; **~maschine die** coffee-maker; **~mühle die** coffee-grinder; **~pause die** coffee-break; **~pflanze die** coffee plant; **~plantage die** coffee plantation; **~pulver das** coffee powder; **~rösterei die** coffee-roasting establishment; **~sahne**

die coffee cream; **~satz der** coffee-grounds *pl.;* **sich aus dem ~satz wahrsagen lassen** have one's fortune told from the coffee-grounds; **~schale die** *(österr.)* coffee-cup; **~service das** coffee-service *or* -set; **~sieb das** coffee-strainer; **~strauch der** coffee tree *or* plant; **~stube die** coffee shop; **~tante die** *(ugs. scherzh.)* coffee addict; **~tasse die** coffee-cup; **~tisch der: sie saßen gerade am ~tisch** they were [sitting] having coffee and cakes; **den ~tisch decken** lay the table for coffee and cakes; **~trinker der** coffee drinker; **~wärmer der** coffee-pot cosy *or* cover; **~wasser das** water for the coffee; **ich werde ~wasser/das ~wasser aufsetzen** I'll put on some water for coffee/the water for the coffee

Kaffer ['kafɐ] **der; ~s, ~n a)** Xhosa; **b)** *(Schimpfwort)* blockhead; thickhead

Kaffern·büffel der; ~s, ~: African *or* Cape buffalo

Käfig ['kɛːfɪç] **der; ~s, ~e** cage; **in einem goldenen ~ sitzen** *(fig.)* be a bird in a gilded cage

Käfig-: ~haltung die battery farming *no art.;* **~vogel der** cage-bird

kafkaesk [kafka'ɛsk] *Adj. (geh.)* Kafkaesque

Kaftan ['kaftan] **der; ~s, ~e** caftan

kahl [kaːl] *Adj.* **a)** *(ohne Haare)* bald; *(ohne Federn)* bald; featherless; **~ werden** go bald; **b)** *(ohne Grün, schmucklos)* bare

Kahl·fraß der [complete] defoliation [by insects]

kahl|fressen *unr. tr. V.* **etw. ~fressen** strip sth. bare

Kahlheit die; ~: *s.* **kahl a, b:** baldness; bareness

kahl-, Kahl-: ~hieb der *s.* **Kahlschlag a; ~kopf der a)** bald head; **b)** *(ugs.: Person)* baldhead; **~köpfig** *Adj.* bald[-headed]; **~köpfig werden** go bald; **~köpfigkeit die** baldness; bald-headedness; **~|scheren** *unr. tr. V.* **jmdn. ~scheren** shave sb.'s hair off; shave sb.'s head; **ein Schaf ~scheren** shear a sheep completely bald; **sein ~geschorener Kopf** his shaven head; **~schlag der a)** clear-felling *no indef. art.;* clear-cutting *no indef. art.;* **b)** *(Waldfläche)* clear-felled area; **c)** *(fig.) (Beseitigung)* clearance; *(Kürzung)* massive cutbacks *pl.;* **~|schlagen** *unr. tr. V.* clear-fell; clear-cut

Kahm·haut ['kaːm-] **die** *(Biol.)* film of mould

Kahn [kaːn] **der; ~[e]s, Kähne** ['kɛːnə] **a)** *(Ruder~)* rowing-boat; *(Stech~)* punt; **~ fahren** go rowing/punting; **b)** *(Lastschiff)* barge; **c)** *(ugs., oft abwertend: Schiff)* tub; **d)** *Pl. (ugs.: ausgetretene Schuhe)* old, worn-out shoes; **e)** *o. Pl. (Soldatenspr.: Gefängnis)* glasshouse *(Mil. sl.);* **f)** *(ugs. scherzh.: Bett)* bed; **in den ~ gehen** hit the hay *(coll.)*

Kahn·fahrt die; ~, ~en trip in a rowing-boat/punt

Kai [kai] **der; ~s, ~s** quay

Kai·anlage die quays *pl.*

Kaiman ['kaiman] **der; ~s, ~e** *(Zool.)* cayman

Kai·mauer die quay wall

Kains·mal ['kains-] **das, Kains·zeichen das** mark of Cain

Kairo ['kairo] **(das); ~s** Cairo

Kaiser ['kaizɐ] **der; ~s, ~:** emperor; **sich um des ~s Bart streiten** engage in pointless argument; **dem ~ geben, was des ~s ist** render unto Caesar the things which are Caesar's; **er ist da/da hingegangen, wo auch der ~ zu Fuß hingeht** *(ugs. scherzh. verhüll.)* he's paying/he's gone to pay a call *(coll.)*

Kaiser-: ~adler der imperial eagle; **~haus das** imperial house *or* family

Kaiserin die; ~, ~nen empress

Kaiserin·mutter die dowager empress

Kaiser·krone die a) imperial crown; **b)** *(Zierpflanze)* crown imperial

kaiserlich 1. *Adj.* imperial; **der ~e Hof** the imperial court. **2.** *adv.* **~ gesinnt sein** be loyal to the emperor; *(monarchistisch sein)* be monarchistic *or* imperialistic

kaiserlich-königlich *Adj.; nicht präd.* imperial and royal; **die ~e Monarchie** the Austro-Hungarian monarchy

Kaiser-: ~krönung die imperial coronation; **~pinguin der** emperor penguin; **~reich das** empire; **~schmarren der** *(österr., südd.) pancake pulled to pieces and sprinkled with powdered sugar and raisins;* **~schnitt der** Caesarean section

Kaisertum das; ~s empire

Kaiser·wetter das *(scherzh.)* glorious, sunny weather *(for an event)*

Kajak ['kaːjak] **der; ~s, ~s** kayak

Kajüt·boot das cabin cruiser

Kajüte [ka'jyːtə] **die; ~, ~n** *(Seemannsspr.)* cabin

Kakadu ['kakadu] **der; ~s, ~s** cockatoo

Kakao [ka'kau] **der; ~s, ~s** cocoa; **jmdn./etw. durch den ~ ziehen** *(ugs.)* make fun of sb./sth.; take the mickey out of sb./sth. *(Brit. sl.)*

Kakao-: ~baum der cacao-tree; **~bohne die** cocoa bean; **~pulver das** cocoa powder

kakeln ['kaːkl̩n] *itr. V. (nordd.)* **a)** *(gackern)* cluck; **b)** *(schwatzen)* chat; natter *(sl.)*

Kakerlak ['kaːkɐlak] **der; ~s** *od.* **~en, ~en** cockroach; black-beetle

Kakophonie [kakofo'niː] **die; ~, ~n** cacophony

Kaktee [kak'teːə] **die; ~, ~n, Kaktus** ['kaktʊs] **der; ~, Kakteen** cactus

Kalamität [kalami'tɛːt] **die; ~, ~en** calamity; **sich in einer ~/in ~en befinden** be in [serious] difficulties *pl.*

Kalander [ka'landɐ] **der; ~s, ~** *(Technik)* calender

Kalauer ['kaːlauɐ] **der; ~s, ~:** laboured *or (coll.)* corny joke; *(Wortspiel)* atrocious *or (coll.)* corny pun

kalauern *itr. V.* tell laboured *or (coll.)* corny jokes; *(mit Wortspielen)* make atrocious *or (coll.)* corny puns

Kalb [kalp] **das; ~[e]s, Kälber** ['kɛlbɐ] **a)** calf; *(Hirsch~)* fawn; **glotzen** *od.* **Augen machen wie ein [ab]gestochenes ~** *(ugs.)* look pop-eyed; **das Goldene ~ anbeten/ um das Goldene ~ tanzen** *(geh.)* worship the golden calf; **b)** *(ugs.: ~fleisch)* veal; **c)** *(dummer, alberner Mensch)* [silly] idiot

Kälbchen ['kɛlpçən] **das; ~s, ~:** little calf; *(Hirsch~)* little fawn

kalben *itr. V.* **a)** *(ein Kalb gebären)* calve; **b)** *(Geogr.)* ⟨*glacier, iceberg*⟩ calve

Kalberei die; ~, ~en *(ugs.)* messing *or* fooling about *or* around *no pl.*

kalbern ['kalbɐn] *itr. V. (ugs.)* mess *or* fool about *or* around

Kalb-: ~fell das *s.* **Kalbsfell; ~fleisch das** veal; **~leder das** *s.* **Kalbsleder**

Kalbs-: ~braten der *(Kochk.)* roast veal *no indef. art.; (Gericht)* roast of veal; **~brust die** breast of veal; **~fell das** calfskin; **~frikassee das** *(Kochk.)* fricassee of veal; **~hachse,** *(südd.:)* **~haxe die** *(Kochk.)* knuckle of veal; **~kotelett das** veal cutlet *(with bone);* **~leder das** calfskin; calf-leather; **~nieren·braten der** *(Kochk.)* loin of veal with kidneys; **~schnitzel das** veal cutlet

Kaldaune [kal'daunə] **die; ~, ~n** entrails *pl.*

Kalebasse [kale'basə] **die; ~, ~n** calabash

Kaleidoskop [kalaido'skoːp] **das; ~s, ~e** *(auch fig.)* kaleidoscope

kalendarisch [kalɛn'daːrɪʃ] *Adj.* ⟨*age etc.*⟩ according to the calendar; **der ~e Beginn einer Jahreszeit** the beginning of a season according to the calendar

Kalender [ka'lɛndɐ] **der; ~s, ~: a)** calendar; **sich** *(Dat.)* **etw./einen Tag im ~ [rot] anstreichen** *(oft iron.)* mark sth. in red on the calendar/mark a day as a red-letter day; **der Julianische ~:** the Julian calendar; *s. auch* **Gregorianisch; b)** *(Taschen~)* diary

Kalender-: ~blatt das calendar sheet; **~block der;** *Pl.* **~blocks** calendar pad; **~geschichte die** *edifying story or fable published on a calendar;* **~jahr das** calendar year; **~uhr die** calendar watch

Kalesche [ka'lɛʃə] **die; ~, ~n** *(hist.)* barouche

Kalfaktor [kal'faktɔr] **der; ~s, ~en** *(veralt., oft abwertend)* **a)** general factotum; general dogsbody *(coll. derog.);* **b)** *(Strafgefangener)* trusty

kalfatern [kal'faːtɐn] *tr., itr. V. (Seemannsspr.)* caulk

Kali ['kaːli] **das; ~s, ~s** potash

Kaliber [ka'liːbɐ] **das; ~s, ~: a)** *(Technik, Waffenkunde)* calibre; **b)** *(ugs., oft abwertend)* sort; kind; **älteren/jüngeren ~s sein** be older/younger

Kali·dünger der potash fertilizer

Kalif [ka'liːf] **der; ~en, ~en** *(hist.)* caliph

Kalifat [kali'faːt] **das; ~[e]s, ~e** *(hist.)* caliphate

Kalifornien [kali'fɔrni̯ən] **(das); ~s** California

kalifornisch *Adj.* Californian

Kaliko ['kaliko] **der; ~s, ~s** calico

Kali-: ~lauge die caustic potash solution; **~salpeter der** saltpetre; potassium nitrate; **~salz das;** *meist Pl.* potassium *or* potash salt

Kalium ['kaːli̯ʊm] *(Chemie)* **das; ~s** potassium

Kali·werk das potash works *sing. or. pl.*

Kalk [kalk] **der; ~[e]s, ~e a)** *(Kalziumkarbonat)* calcium carbonate; **b)** *(Baustoff)* lime; quicklime; burnt lime; **die Wände mit ~ streichen** whitewash *or* lime-wash the walls; **bei ihm rieselt schon der ~** *(salopp)* he's going a bit senile; **c)** *(Knochensubstanz)* calcium

Kalk-: ~ablagerung die deposit of calcium carbonate; **~boden der** limy soil; lime soil; **~bruch der** *s.* **~steinbruch**

kalken ['kalkn̩] *tr. V.* **a)** *(tünchen)* whitewash; **b)** *(Kalk zuführen)* lime

kalk-, Kalk-: ~erde die a) *(gebrannter Kalk)* lime; quicklime; burnt lime; **b)** *(kalkhaltige Erde)* lime *or* limy soil; **~grube die** lime-pit; **~haltig** *Adj. (bes. Geol., Mineral.)* limy ⟨*soil*⟩; calcareous ⟨*soil, rock*⟩ *(Geol., Min.);* ⟨*water*⟩ containing calcium carbonate; **das Wasser ist sehr ~haltig** the water is high in calcium carbonate; **~mangel der;** *o. Pl.* **a)** *(Mangel an Kalzium)* calcium deficiency; **b)** *(Mangel an Kalk)* deficiency of lime; **~milch die** lime-wash; **~sand·stein der** sand-lime brick; **~spat der** calcite; **~stein der** limestone; **~stein·bruch der** limestone quarry

[1]**Kalkül** [kal'kyːl] **das** *od.* **der; ~s, ~e** *(geh.)* calculation

[2]**Kalkül der; ~s, ~e** *(Math.)* calculus

Kalkulation [kalkula'tsi̯oːn] **die; ~, ~en** *(auch Wirtsch.)* calculation; **die ~ der Herstellungskosten eines Buches** the costing of a book; **in der ~ liegt ein Fehler** there's an error in the costings *pl.;* **nach meiner ~:** according to my calculations *pl.*

Kalkulator [kalku'laːtɔr] **der; ~s, ~en** [-la'toːrən] cost accountant

kalkulieren 1. *tr. V.* **a)** *(Kaufmannsspr.: veranschlagen)* calculate ⟨*cost, price*⟩; cost ⟨*product, article*⟩; **die Herstellungskosten eines Buches ~:** cost a book; **b)** *(abschätzen)* calculate; **c)** *(ugs.: annehmen)* reckon. **2.** *itr. V.* calculate; **falsch ~:** miscalculate

Kalkutta [kal'kʊta] **(das); ~s** Calcutta

kalk·weiß *Adj.* **a)** *(weiß wie Kalk)* chalk-white; **b)** *(sehr bleich)* deathly pale; chalky white; **~ sein** be as white as a sheet

Kalligraphie [kaligra'fiː] **die; ~:** calligraphy *no art.*

Kalme ['kalmə] **die;** ~, ~**n** *(Met.)* calm
Kalmen·gürtel der *(Met.)* calm belt
Kalorie [kalo'ri:] **die;** ~, ~**n** calorie
kalorien-, Kalorien-: ~arm 1. *Adj.* low-calorie *attrib.*; ~**arm sein** be low in calories; **2.** *adv.* ~**arm kochen/essen** cook low-calorie meals/eat low-calorie foods; ~**bewußt 1.** *Adj.* calorie-conscious; **2.** *adv.* in a calorie-conscious way; ~**gehalt der** calorie content; ~**reich 1.** *Adj.* high-calorie *attrib.*; ~**reich sein** be high in calories; **2.** *adv.* ~**reich kochen/essen** cook high-calorie meals/eat high-calorie foods
Kalori·meter [kalori-] **das;** ~**s,** ~ *(Physik)* calorimeter
kalt [kalt]; **kälter** ['kɛltɐ], **kältest...** ['kɛltəst...] **1.** *Adj.* cold; chilly, frosty ‹*atmosphere, smile*›; **ein ~es Buffet** a cold buffet; **mir ist/wird** ~: I am/am getting cold; **das Essen wird** ~: the food is getting cold; **im Kalten sitzen** sit in the cold; ~ **und berechnend sein** be cold and calculating; **es packte uns das ~e Grausen/Entsetzen** our blood ran cold; **jmdm. die ~e Schulter zeigen** give sb. the cold shoulder; cold-shoulder sb. **2.** *adv.* **a)** ~ **duschen** have *or* take a cold shower; ~ **schlafen** sleep in a cold room; **Getränke/Sekt ~ stellen** cool drinks/chill champagne; ~ **Zigarre/Pfeife rauchen** *(ugs.)* have an unlit cigar/pipe in one's mouth; **jmdn. ~ erwischen** *(bes. Sportjargon)* catch sb. on the hop; **b)** *(nüchtern)* coldly; **c)** *(abweisend, unfreundlich)* coldly; frostily; **jmdn. ~ anblicken** look at sb. coldly; ~ **lächeln** smile coldly *or* frostily; **d) mich überlief** *od.* **durchrieselte es** ~: cold shivers ran down my spine
kalt-, Kalt-: ~|bleiben *unr. itr. V.; mit sein* remain unmoved; ~**blut das** heavy draught-horse; ~**blüter** [-bly:tɐ] **der** *(Zool.)* cold-blooded animal; ~**blütig 1.** *Adj.* **a)** *(beherrscht)* cool-headed; **b)** *(abwertend: skrupellos)* cold-blooded; **c)** *(Zool.)* cold-blooded; **2.** *adv.* **a)** *(beherrscht)* coolly; calmly; **einer Gefahr ~blütig ins Auge sehen** face a danger coolly *or* calmly; **b)** *(abwertend: skrupellos)* cold-bloodedly; ~**blütigkeit die;** ~: *s.* ~**blütig a, b:** coolheadedness; cold-bloodedness
Kälte ['kɛltə] **die;** ~: **a)** cold; **10 Grad** ~: 10 degrees of frost; 10 degrees below freezing; **vor ~ zittern** *od. (ugs.)* **bibbern** shiver with cold; **bei dieser** ~: in this cold; when it's as cold as this; **b)** *(Teilnahmslosigkeit, Unbehaglichkeit)* coldness
kälte-, Kälte-: ~beständig *Adj.* cold-resistant; ~**beständig sein** be resistant to cold; ~**ein·bruch der** *(Met.)* sudden onset of cold weather; ~**empfindlich** *Adj.* sensitive to cold *pred.*; ~**empfindliche Pflanzen** plants which are sensitive to cold; ~**gefühl das** sensation *or* feeling of cold; chill; ~**grad der** degree of frost; ~**maschine die** *(Technik)* refrigerating machine; ~**pol der** cold pole
kälter *s.* **kalt**
kältest... *s.* **kalt**
Kälte-: ~sturz der *(Met.)* sudden drop in temperature; ~**technik die** refrigeration engineering *no art.*; ~**tod der: den ~tod erleiden** freeze to death; die of cold; ~**welle die** cold wave *or* spell
kalt-, Kalt-: ~front die *(Met.)* cold front; ~**haus das** *(Gartenbau)* cold house; ~**herzig** *Adj.* cold-hearted; ~**lächelnd** *Adv. (ugs. abwertend)* **etw. ~lächelnd tun** take callous pleasure in doing sth.; ~**|lassen** *unr. tr. V. (ugs.)* **jmdn. ~lassen** leave sb. unmoved; *(nicht interessieren)* leave sb. cold *(coll.)*; ~**leim der** [cold] woodworking adhesive; ~**luft die;** *o. Pl. (Met.)* cold air; **polare ~luft** cold polar air; ~**|machen** *tr. V. (salopp)* **jmdn. ~machen** do sb. in *(sl.)*; ~**mamsell die** *girl/woman who prepares and serves cold dishes in a restaurant, hotel, etc.*; ~**miete die** rent exclusive of heating; ~**schale die** *cold sweet soup made with fruit, beer, wine, or milk*; ~**schnäuzig** [~ʃnɔytsɪç] *(ugs.)* **1.** *Adj.* cold and insensitive; *(frech)* insolent; **2.** *adv.* coldly and insensitively; *(frech)* insolently; ~**schnäuzigkeit die;** ~ *(ugs.)* coldness and insensitivity; *(Frechheit)* insolence; ~**start der** *(Kfz-W.)* cold start; **beim ~start** when starting from cold; ~**|stellen** *tr. V. (ugs.)* **jmdn. ~stellen** put sb. out of the way *(coll. joc.)*; **den Mittelstürmer ~stellen** cut the centre-forward out of the game
Kalvarien·berg [kal'va:riən-] **der:** [Mount] Calvary
Kalvinismus [kalvi'nɪsmʊs] **der;** ~: Calvinism *no art.*
Kalvinist der; ~**en,** ~**en, Kalvinistin die;** ~, ~**nen** Calvinist
kalvinistisch *Adj.* Calvinist
Kalzium ['kaltsiʊm] **das;** ~**s** calcium
kam [ka:m] *1. u. 3. Pers. Prät. v.* **kommen**
Kamarilla [kama'rɪlja] **die;** ~, **Kamarillen** *(geh.)* camarilla
Kambodscha [kam'bɔdʒa] **(das);** ~**s** Cambodia
Kambodschaner [kambo'dʒa:nɐ] **der;** ~**s,** ~: Cambodian
käme ['kɛ:mə] *1. u. 3. Pers. Konjunktiv II v.* **kommen**
Kamel [ka'me:l] **das;** ~**s,** ~**e a)** camel; **eher geht ein ~ durch ein Nadelöhr, als daß das geschieht** that will never happen in a million years; **b)** *(salopp: dummer Mensch)* clot *(Brit. sl.)*; twit *(Brit. sl.)*; fathead
Kamel-: ~haar das; *o. Pl.* camel-hair; ~**haar·mantel der** camel-hair coat
Kamelie [ka'me:liə] **die;** ~, ~**n** camellia
Kamellen [ka'mɛlən] *Pl. (ugs.) in* **das sind alte** *od.* **olle** ~: that's old hat *(coll.)*; **es wurden nur alte** *od.* **olle ~ aufgewärmt** the same old stuff was dished up *(coll.)*
Kamel·treiber der a) camel-driver; **b)** *(salopp abwertend)* smelly Arab *(sl. derog.)*
Kamera ['kamərа] **die;** ~, ~**s** camera; **vor der ~ stehen** appear in front of the cameras *pl.*
Kamera·assistent der camera assistant; assistant cameraman
Kamerad [kamə'ra:t] **der;** ~**en,** ~**en** *(Lebens~, Gefährte)* companion; *(Freund)* friend; *(Mitschüler)* mate; friend; *(Soldat)* comrade; *(Sport)* team-mate
Kameraderie [kamərado'ri:] **die;** ~ *(meist abwertend)* loyalty to a/the clique; **falschverstandene** ~: mistaken sense of comradeship and loyalty
Kameradin die; ~, ~**nen** *s.* **Kamerad**
Kameradschaft die; ~, ~**en a)** *o. Pl.* comradeship; **die ~ zwischen ihnen** the sense of comradeship between them; **b)** *(Gruppe)* association
kameradschaftlich 1. *Adj.* comradely. **2.** *adv.* in a comradely way
Kameradschaftlichkeit die; ~: comradeliness
Kameradschafts-: ~abend der social evening *(of youth group, ex-servicemen's association, etc.)*; ~**ehe die** *marriage based on feelings of companionship*; ~**geist der;** *o. Pl.* spirit of comradeship
Kamera-: ~führung die *(Film)* camerawork *no indef. art.*; ~**mann der** *Pl.* ~**männer** *od.* ~**leute** cameraman
Kamerun ['kaməru:n] **(das);** ~**s** Cameroon; the Cameroons *pl.*
Kameruner der; ~**s,** ~: native of Cameroon *or* the Cameroons; Cameroonian
Kamille [ka'mɪlə] **die;** ~, ~**n** camomile
Kamillen·tee der camomile tea
Kamin [ka'mi:n] **der,** *schweiz.:* **das;** ~**s,** ~**e a)** *(Feuerstelle)* fireplace; **sie saßen am** ~: they sat by the hearth *or* the fireside; **b)** *(bes. südd.: Schornstein)* chimney; **er kann/muß das in den ~ schreiben** *(ugs.)* he can/will have to kiss goodbye to that *(coll.)*; **c)** *(Bergsteigen: Felsspalt)* chimney
Kamin-: ~feger der *(bes. südd.) s.* **Schornsteinfeger;** ~**feuer das** [open] fire; ~**kehrer der** *(bes. südd.) s.* **Schornsteinfeger;** ~**sims der** mantelpiece; mantelshelf
Kamm [kam] **der;** ~**[e]s, Kämme** ['kɛmə] **a)** comb; **alle/alles über einen ~ scheren** lump everyone/everything together; **b)** *(bei Hühnern usw.)* comb; *(bei Reptilien, Amphibien)* crest; **ihm schwillt der ~** *(ugs.)* his hackles rise; *(er wird überheblich)* he gets cocky and big-headed *(coll.)*; **c)** *(Gebirgs~)* ridge; crest; **d)** *(Wellen~)* crest; **e)** *(Rinder~)* neck; *(Schweine~)* spare rib; **f)** *(beim Pferd)* crest
kämmen ['kɛmən] *tr. V.* **a)** comb; **jmdm./sich die Haare ~, jmdn./sich ~:** comb sb.'s/one's hair; **jmdm. einen Scheitel/Pony ~:** put a parting in sb.'s hair/comb sb.'s hair into a fringe; **b)** *(Textilind.)* comb
Kammer ['kamɐ] **die;** ~, ~**n a)** store-room; *(veralt.: Schlafraum)* chamber; **b)** *(Biol., Med., Technik, Waffenkunde)* chamber; **c)** *(Parl.)* chamber; House; **die erste/zweite ~:** the upper/lower chamber *or* House; **d)** *(Rechtsw.)* court *(dealing with a particular branch of judicial business)*; **e)** *(gewerbliche Vereinigung)* professional association; **f)** *(Milit.)* stores *pl.*
Kammer·chor der chamber choir
Kämmerchen ['kɛmɐçən] **das;** ~**s,** ~: small room; *(Abstellkammer)* [small] store-room
Kammer·diener der *(veralt.)* valet
Kämmerer ['kɛmɐrɐ] **der;** ~**s,** ~ *(veralt.)* [town/city] treasurer
Kammer-: ~frau die *(veralt.)* lady's maid; **die ~frau der Fürstin** the princess's maid; ~**gericht das** *(hist.)* Supreme Court; ~**herr der** *(hist.)* chamberlain; ~**jäger der** pest controller; ~**konzert das** chamber concert
Kämmerlein ['kɛmɐlain] **das;** ~**s,** ~ *(oft scherzh.) in* **ich muß mal im stillen ~ darüber nachdenken** I must [go away by myself and] think about that in peace and quiet; **das hat er sich im stillen ~ ausgedacht** he thought that up all by himself without anyone realizing
Kammer-: ~musik die; *o. Pl.* chamber music; ~**orchester das** chamber orchestra; ~**sänger der** *title awarded to singer of outstanding merit*; ~**spiel das a)** *(kleines Theaterstück)* intimate chamber-drama; **b)** *Pl. (kleines Theater)* studio theatre *sing.*; ~**ton der** *(Musik)* standard pitch; ~**zofe die** *(veralt.)* lady's maid
Kamm-: ~garn das worsted; ~**griff der** *(Turnen)* undergrasp; ~**muschel die** *s.* **Kammuschel**
Kammuschel ['kammʊʃl] **die;** ~, ~**n** scallop
Kamm·wolle die *(Textilw.)* worsted
Kamp [kamp] **der;** ~**s, Kämpe** ['kɛmpə] *(Forstw.)* [small] tree-nursery
Kampagne [kam'panjə] **die;** ~, ~**n a)** *(größere Aktion)* campaign **(für** for, on behalf of; **gegen** against); **b)** *(bestimmte Zeitspanne)* busy season; **c)** *(Archäol.)* phase *(of an excavation)*
Kampanile [kampa'ni:lə] **der;** ~, ~: campanile
Kämpe ['kɛmpə] **der;** ~**n,** ~**n** *(veralt.)* [brave] warrior *or* fighter; **ein alter ~** *(scherzh.)* an old campaigner; a seasoned veteran
Kampf [kampf] **der;** ~**[e]s, Kämpfe a)** *(militärisch)* battle **(um** for); **nach wochenlangen erbitterten Kämpfen** after weeks of bitter fighting; **den ~ einstellen** stop fighting; **er ist im ~ gefallen** he fell *or* was killed in action *or* combat; **b)** *(zwischen persönlichen Gegnern)* fight; *(fig.)* struggle; **ein ~ aller gegen alle** a free-for-all; **ein ~ Mann gegen Mann** a hand-to-hand fight; **ein ~ auf Le-**

ben und Tod a fight to the death; **den ~ aufgeben** *od.* **verloren geben** give up the fight; **aus einem ~ als Sieger/Verlierer hervorgehen** emerge as victor *or* winner/loser from a fight; **sich dem ~ stellen** be prepared to fight; **c)** *(Wett~)* contest; *(Boxen)* contest; fight; bout; **sich einen spannenden ~ liefern** produce an exciting contest; **d)** *(Einsatz aller Mittel)* struggle, fight (**um, für** for; **gegen** against); **der ~ ums Dasein** the struggle for existence; **jmdm./einer Sache den ~ ansagen** declare war on sb./sth.; **~ dem Faschismus/Atomtod!** fight fascism/the nuclear menace!; **e)** *(heftig ausgetragene Kontroverse)* battle; **der ~ zwischen den Geschlechtern** the battle of the sexes; **auf in den ~!** *(scherzh.)* into the fray!; **f)** *(innerer Zwiespalt)* **ein ~ mit sich selbst** a struggle *or* battle with oneself

kampf-, Kampf-: ~ab·schnitt der *(Milit.)* combat *or* battle sector; **~ab·stimmung die** *(Politik)* crucial vote; **~an·sage die** declaration of war; **~an·zug der** combat uniform; **~bahn die** *(für Gladiatoren)* arena; *(für Stiere)* ring; *(veralt.: Sportstadion)* stadium; **~bereit** *Adj.* willing to fight *postpos.*; *(fertig)* ready to fight *postpos.*; ⟨*army*⟩ ready for battle; ⟨*troops*⟩ ready for battle *or* action; **~bereitschaft die** willingness to fight; *(eines Heeres)* readiness for battle; *(einer Truppe)* readiness for battle *or* action; **~boot das** fighting ship; warship; **~bündnis das** alliance; **~einheit die** *(Milit.)* combat unit

kämpfen ['kɛmpfn̩] **1.** *itr. V.* **a)** fight; **mit jmdm. ~:** fight [with] sb.; **gegen jmdn. ~:** fight [against] sb.; **um die Vorherrschaft/eine Stadt/Frau ~:** fight for supremacy/a town/over a woman; **um einen Titel ~:** compete for a title; **um seine Existenz ~:** fight *or* struggle for one's existence; **für jmdn./etw. ~:** fight for sb./sth.; **mit den Tränen ~** *(fig.)* fight back one's tears; **mit dem Schlaf ~** *(fig.)* struggle to keep awake; **mit dem Tod ~** *(fig.)* fight for one's life *or* to stay alive; **mit etw. zu ~ haben** *(fig.)* have to contend with sth.; **[lange] mit sich** *(Dat.)* **~:** have a [long] struggle with oneself; **b)** *(Sport: sich messen)* ⟨*team*⟩ play; ⟨*wrestler, boxer*⟩ fight; **gegen jmdn. ~:** play/fight sb. **2.** *refl. V. (auch fig.)* fight one's way. **3.** *tr. V.* **einen Kampf ~** *(auch fig.)* fight a battle

Kampfer ['kampfɐ] **der; ~s** camphor

[1]**Kämpfer** ['kɛmpfɐ] **der; ~s, ~:** fighter

[2]**Kämpfer der; ~s, ~: a)** *(Archit.)* impost; **b)** *(Bauw.)* transom

Kämpferin die; ~, ~nen fighter

kämpferisch 1. *Adj.* **a)** fighting ⟨*spirit, mood*⟩; ⟨*person*⟩ full of fighting spirit; **eine ~e Natur sein** be full of fighting spirit; **b)** *(Sport: mit großem Einsatz)* spirited. **2.** *adv.* **a)** *(voller Kampfgeist)* in a fighting spirit; **b)** *(Sport: mit großem Einsatz)* spiritedly

Kämpfer·natur die fighter

kampf·erprobt *Adj.* battle-tried; battle-tested ⟨*equipment*⟩

Kampfes-: ~grüße *Pl. (bes. DDR)* greetings; **~lust die** eagerness for the fray; **in wilder ~lust** lusting for battle

kampf-, Kampf-: ~fähig *Adj.* ⟨*troops*⟩ fit for action *or* battle; ⟨*boxer etc.*⟩ fit to fight; **~fahrzeug das** *(Milit.)* combat vehicle; **~flieger der** *(Milit.)* bomber pilot; **~flugzeug das** bomber; **~gas das** war gas; **~gebiet das** battle area; combat zone; **~gefährte der, ~gefährtin die** *(im militärischen Kampf)* comrade in arms; *(im politischen Kampf)* comrade in the struggle; **~geist der;** *o. Pl.* fighting spirit; **~gemeinschaft die** action group; **~gericht das** *(Sport)* [panel of] judges *pl.*; **~geschehen das** fighting *no indef. art.*; **~gruppe die** *(Milit.)* task force; **~hahn der a)** *(Hahn für Kämpfe)* fighting cock; **b)** *(ugs.)* fighter; brawler; **~handlungen** *Pl.* fighting *sing.*; **die ~handlungen einstellen** cease hostilities *or* fighting; **~kraft die** fighting power *or* strength; *(einer Mannschaft)* strength; **~lied das** battle song; *(einer Bewegung)* battle anthem; **~los 1.** *Adj.* peaceful; **an eine ~lose Übergabe der Stadt war nicht zu denken** to hand over the town without a fight was unthinkable; **2.** *adv.* without a fight; **~lustig 1.** *Adj.* belligerent; **2.** *adv.* belligerently; **~maßnahme die;** *meist Pl.* active measure; **~maßnahmen [beschließen]** [decide to take] action *sing.*; **~moral die** morale; **~panzer der** [battle-]tank; **~platz der** battlefield; **~preis der** *(Wirtsch.)* cut price; **~richter der** *(Sport)* judge; **~schiff das** fighting ship; warship; **~schrift die** polemical document; **~spiel das** *(Sport)* contact sport; **~stark** *Adj.* powerful ⟨*army*⟩; efficient ⟨*troops*⟩; strong, powerful ⟨*team*⟩; **~stärke die** *(eines Feindes, Heeres)* fighting strength *or* power; *(einer Mannschaft)* strength; **~stier der** fighting bull; **~stoff der;** *meist Pl.* warfare agent; **~tag der** day of action; **~truppe die** *(Milit.)* fighting *or* combat unit; **~truppen** fighting *or* combat troops; **~unfähig** *Adj.* ⟨*troops*⟩ unfit for action *or* battle; ⟨*boxer etc.*⟩ unfit to fight; **jmdn./etw. ~unfähig machen** put sb./sth. out of action; **der Boxer schlug seinen Gegner ~unfähig** the boxer put his opponent out of the fight; **~verband der** *(Milit.)* combat unit; **~wagen der** chariot; **~ziel das** objective; **~zone die** *(Milit.)* battle zone; combat zone

kampieren [kam'pi:rən] *itr. V.* camp; *(ugs.: wohnen)* camp down *or* out; **du kannst bei uns im Wohnzimmer ~:** you can bed down *or (Brit. sl.)* doss down in our living room

Kamputschea [kampʊ'tʃe:a] **(das); ~s** Kampuchea

Kamuffel [ka'mʊfl̩] **das; ~s, ~** *(Schimpfwort)* [silly] fool

Kanada ['kanada] **(das); ~s** Canada

Kanadier [ka'na:di̯ɐ] **der; ~s, ~ a)** *(Einwohner Kanadas)* Canadian; **b)** *(Boot)* Canadian canoe

Kanadierin die; ~, ~nen Canadian; *s. auch* **-in**

kanadisch [ka'na:dɪʃ] *Adj.* Canadian

Kanaille [ka'naljə] **die; ~, ~n** *(abwertend)* **a)** *(gemeiner Mensch)* scoundrel; villain; **b)** *o. Pl. (Mob, Pöbel)* rabble; mob

Kanake [ka'na:kə] **der; ~n, ~n a)** *(Polynesier)* kanaka; **b)** *(derb abwertend: Südländer, Orientale)* dago *(sl. derog.)*

Kanal [ka'na:l] **der; ~s, Kanäle** [ka'nɛ:lə] **a)** *(künstlicher Wasserlauf)* canal; **b)** *(Geogr.)* **der ~:** the [English] Channel; **c)** *(für Abwässer)* sewer; **d)** *(zur Entwässerung, Bewässerung)* channel; *(Graben)* ditch; **e)** *(Rundf., Ferns., Weg der Information)* channel; **f)** *(salopp)* **den ~ voll haben** *(betrunken sein)* be canned *or* plastered *(sl.)*; *(überdrüssig sein)* have had a bellyful *or* as much as one can take

Kanal-: ~arbeiter der a) sewerage worker; **b)** *(Politik Jargon)* back-room boy; **~bau der** canal/sewer building *or* construction; **~deckel der** manhole cover; **~gebühr die** canal toll; canal dues *pl.*; **~inseln** *Pl.* Channel Islands

Kanalisation [kanaliza'tsi̯o:n] **die; ~, ~en a)** *(System der Abwasserkanäle)* sewerage system; sewers *pl.*; **b)** *(Bau der Abwasserkanäle)* installation of a/the sewerage system; **c)** *(Ausbau eines Flusses)* canalization

Kanalisations·system das sewerage system; [system of] sewers *pl.*

kanalisieren *tr. V.* **a)** *(mit Kanalisation versehen)* install a sewerage system in ⟨*area, village, etc.*⟩; **b)** *(lenken)* channel ⟨*energies, goods, etc.*⟩; **c)** *(schiffbar machen)* canalize

Kanalisierung die; ~, ~en a) installation of a/the sewerage system; **die ~ des Dorfes** the installation of a/the sewerage system in the village; **b)** *(Lenkung)* channelling; **c)** *(Schiffbarmachen)* canalization

Kanal-: ~tunnel der Channel Tunnel; **~zone die** Canal Zone

Kanapee ['kanape] **das; ~s, ~s a)** *(veralt., noch scherzh.: Sofa)* sofa; settee; **b)** *(belegtes Weißbrotschnittchen)* canapé

Kanaren [ka'na:rən] *Pl.* Canaries

Kanari [ka'na:ri] **der; ~s, ~** *(südd., österr. ugs.)*, **Kanarien·vogel** [ka'na:ri̯ən-] **der** canary

Kanarische Inseln *Pl.* Canary Islands

Kandare [kan'da:rə] **die; ~, ~n** curb bit; **jmdn. an die ~ nehmen** *(fig.)* take sb. in hand; **jmdn. an der ~ haben** *(fig.)* keep sb. on a tight rein

Kandelaber [kande'la:bɐ] **der; ~s, ~:** candelabrum

Kandidat [kandi'da:t] **der; ~en, ~en a)** candidate; **jmdn. als ~en aufstellen** nominate sb. *or* put sb. forward as a candidate; **b)** *(beim Quiz usw.)* contestant; **c)** *(an Hochschulen) person studying for the final examination for a doctorate;* **~ der Medizin/Philosophie** *usw.* 'Kandidat' in medicine/philosophy *etc.*

Kandidatenliste die list of candidates

Kandidatin die; ~, ~nen *s.* **Kandidat;** *s. auch* **-in**

Kandidatur [kandida'tu:ɐ̯] **die; ~, ~en** candidature (**auf** + *Akk.* for)

kandidieren *itr. V.* stand [as a candidate] (**für** for)

kandieren [kan'di:rən] *tr. V.* candy; **kandiert** crystallized ⟨*orange, petal*⟩; glacé ⟨*cherry, pear*⟩; candied ⟨*peel*⟩

Kandis ['kandɪs] **der; ~, Kandis·zucker der** rock candy

Kaneel [ka'ne:l] **der; ~s, ~e** cinnamon

Känguruh ['kɛŋguru] **das; ~s, ~s** kangaroo

Kanin [ka'ni:n] **das; ~s, ~e** *(fachspr.)* rabbit [fur]

Kaninchen [ka'ni:nçən] **das; ~s, ~:** rabbit

Kaninchen-: ~bau der; *Pl.* **~baue** rabbit-burrow; rabbit-hole; **~fell das** rabbit fur; **~fleisch das** rabbit [meat]; **~stall der** rabbit-hutch

Kanister [ka'nɪstɐ] **der; ~s, ~:** can; [metal/plastic] container

kann [kan] *1. u. 3. Pers. Sg. Präsens v.* **können**

Kann-Bestimmung die authorization

Kännchen ['kɛnçən] **das; ~s, ~:** [small] pot; *(für Milch)* [small] jug; **ein ~ Kaffee/Milch** a [small] pot of coffee/jug of milk

Kanne ['kanə] **die; ~, ~n a)** *(Krug) (Tee~, Kaffee~)* pot; *(Milch~, Wein~, Wasser~)* jug; **b)** *(Henkel~)* can; *(für Milch)* pail; *(beim Melken)* churn; *(für Essen)* container; *(Gieß~)* watering-can; **c)** *(Jazzjargon: Saxophon)* sax *(coll.)*

Kannelierung die; ~, ~en *(Archit.)* fluting

kannen·weise *Adv.* by the jugful

Kannibale [kani'ba:lə] **der; ~n, ~n** cannibal

kannibalisch *Adj.* cannibalistic

Kannibalismus der; ~ *(auch Zool.)* cannibalism *no art.*

kannst [kanst] *2. Pers. Sg. Präsens v.* **können**

kannste ['kanstə] *(ugs.)* = **kannst du;** *s. auch* **haste**

kannte ['kantə] *1. u. 3. Pers. Sg. Prät. v.* **kennen**

Kanon ['ka:nɔn] **der; ~s, ~s** *(Musik, Lit., Theol., geh.)* canon

Kanonade [kano'na:də] **die; ~, ~n** *(Milit.)* cannonade; **eine ~ aufs Tor** *(fig.)* a barrage of shots [at goal]; **eine ~ von Flüchen** *usw.* *(fig. ugs.)* a barrage of curses *or* oaths *etc.*

Kanone [ka'no:nə] **die; ~, ~n a)** *(Geschütz)* cannon; big gun; **mit ~n auf Spatzen** *(Akk.)* **schießen** *(fig.)* take a sledgehammer to crack a nut; **das ist unter aller ~** *(ugs.)* it's appallingly bad *or* indescribably dreadful *(coll.)*; **unter aller ~ spielen** *(ugs.)* play appallingly badly *(coll.)*; **b)** *(ugs.: Kön-*

ner) ace; **c)** *(salopp: Revolver)* shooting-iron *(sl.)*; rod *(Amer. sl.)*

Kanonen·boot das gunboat

Kanonenboot-: ~diplomatie die, ~politik die gunboat diplomacy

Kanonen-: ~donner der [rumble of] gunfire; **~futter das** *(ugs.)* cannon-fodder; **~kugel die** cannon-ball; **~ofen der** cylindrical [iron] stove; **~rohr das** gun-barrel; **[ach du] heiliges ~rohr!** *(ugs.)* good grief!; **~schlag der** thunder-flash; cannon cracker

Kanonier [kano'ni:ɐ̯] **der; ~s, ~e** *(Milit.)* gunner; artilleryman

Kanoniker [ka'no:nikɐ] **der; ~s, ~, Kanonikus** [ka'no:nikʊs] **der; ~, Kanoniker** *(christl. Kirche)* canon

kanonisch 1. *Adj.* **a)** *(kath. Kirche)* canonical; **~es Recht** canon law; **b)** *(mustergültig, klassisch)* canonical. **2.** *adv.* canonically

kanonisieren *tr. V.* canonize

Kanossa [ka'nɔsa] **das; ~s** *(geh.)* humiliation; **nach ~ gehen** eat humble pie; go to Canossa *(literary)*

Kanossa·gang der *(geh.)* humiliation; **einen ~ antreten/machen** eat humble pie; go to Canossa *(literary)*

[1]**Kantate** [kan'ta:tə] **die; ~, ~n** *(Musik)* cantata

[2]**Kantate** *o. Art., indekl. (ev. Kirche)* fourth Sunday after Easter; Cantate Sunday

Kante ['kantə] **die; ~, ~n a)** *(Schnittlinie zweier Flächen, Rand)* edge; *(bei Stoffen)* selvedge; **etw. auf die hohe ~ legen** *(ugs.)* put sth. away *or* by; **etw. auf der hohen ~ haben** *(ugs.)* have sth. put away *or* by; *s. auch* **Ecke a; b)** *(landsch.: Gegend)* part

kanten 1. *tr. V.* **a)** tilt; *(auf die Kante stellen)* stand on edge; **„Nicht ~!"** 'do not tilt!'; **b)** *(Skisport)* edge ‹*ski*›. **2.** *itr. V.* *(Skisport)* edge

Kanten der; ~s, ~ *(nordd.) (Anfangs- oder Endstück von Brot)* crust

Kanter der; ~s, ~ *(Reiten)* canter

Kanter·sieg der *(Sport)* runaway *or* easy victory

Kant-: ~haken der a) jmdn. beim ~haken nehmen *od.* **kriegen** *(salopp)* give sb. what for *(sl.)*; **jetzt haben wir ihn beim ~haken** *(salopp)* now we've got him *(coll.)*; **b)** canthook; **~holz das** squared timber; *(Stück)* piece of squared timber

Kantianer [kan'ti̯a:nɐ] **der; ~s, ~** *(Philos.)* Kantian

kantig *Adj.* square-cut ‹*timber, stone*›; rough-edged ‹*rock*›; angular ‹*face, figure, etc.*›; sharp ‹*nose*›; square ‹*chin*›; jerky, awkward ‹*movement*›

Kantine [kan'ti:nə] **die; ~, ~n** canteen

Kantinen·essen das canteen food *no indef. art.*

kantisch *Adj.* Kantian

Kanton [kan'to:n] **der; ~s, ~e** canton

kantonal [kanto'na:l] **1.** *Adj.* cantonal. **2.** *adv.* on a cantonal basis

Kantonist [kanto'nɪst] **der; ~en, ~en** *in* **ein unsicherer ~ sein** *(ugs.)* be an unreliable type; be unreliable

Kantons-: ~rat der *(schweiz.)* cantonal great council; **~regierung die** *(schweiz.)* cantonal government

Kantor ['kantɔr] **der; ~s, ~en** [-'to:rən] choirmaster and organist

Kantorei die; ~, ~en [church] choir

Kant·stein der kerb

Kanu ['ka:nu] **das; ~s, ~s** canoe

Kanu·fahrer der canoeist

Kanüle [ka'ny:lə] **die; ~, ~n** *(Med.)* cannula; *(einer Injektionsspritze)* [hypodermic] needle

Kanu·sport der canoeing *no art.*

Kanute [ka'nu:tə] **der; ~n, ~n** *(Sport)* canoeist

Kanzel ['kants̮l] **die; ~, ~n a)** pulpit; **auf der ~:** in the pulpit; **von der ~ herab** from the pulpit; **b)** *(Flugw.)* cockpit; **c)** *(Bergsteigen)* spur; **d)** *(Jägerspr.)* raised hide; high seat

Kanzel-: ~mißbrauch der abuse *or* misuse of the pulpit [for political ends]; **~redner der** preacher

kanzerogen [kants̮ero'ge:n] *Adj. (Med.)* carcinogenic

kanzerös [kants̮e'rø:s] *Adj. (Med.)* cancerous

Kanzlei [kants̮'lai] **die; ~, ~en a)** *(veralt.: Büro)* office; **b)** *(Anwalts~)* chambers *pl. (of barrister)*; office *(of lawyer)*; **c)** *s.* **Staatskanzlei**

Kanzlei-: ~diener der *(veralt.)* messenger; **~kraft die** *(österr.) s.* **Bürokraft; ~sprache die;** *o. Pl.* language of officialdom; officialese; **~stil der** *(abwertend)* officialese

Kanzler ['kants̮lɐ] **der; ~s, ~ a)** chancellor; **b)** *(an Hochschulen)* vice-chancellor; **c)** *(in diplomatischen Vertretungen)* chief secretary

Kanzler-: ~amt das a) *(~büro)* chancellor's office; **b)** *(Amt des Kanzlers)* chancellorship; office of chancellor; **~kandidat der** candidate for the chancellorship

Kanzlerschaft die chancellorship

Kanzlist der; ~en, ~en *(veralt.)* clerk

Kaolin [kao'li:n] **das,** *(fachspr.:)* **der; ~s, ~e** kaolin

Kap [kap] **das; ~s, ~s** cape; **~ der Guten Hoffnung** Cape of Good Hope; **~ Hoorn** Cape Horn

Kapaun [ka'pa̲un] **der; ~s, ~e** capon

Kapazität [kapats̮i'tɛ:t] **die; ~, ~en a)** *(Wirtsch.: Leistung)* capacity; **b)** *meist Pl. (Wirtsch.: Gesamtheit der Einrichtungen)* capacity *no pl.*; **c)** *(Fassungsvermögen)* capacity; **d)** *(Experte)* expert; **e)** *(Physik)* capacitance

Kapazitäts·auslastung die *(Wirtsch.)* use *or* utilization of capacity

Kapee [ka'pe] *in* **schwer von ~ sein** *(salopp)* be slow on the uptake

[1]**Kapelle** [ka'pɛlə] **die; ~, ~n** *(Archit.)* chapel

[2]**Kapelle die; ~, ~n** *(Musik~)* band; [light] orchestra

Kapell·meister der band-leader; bandmaster; *(im Orchester)* conductor; *(im Theater usw.)* musical director

[1]**Kaper** ['ka:pɐ] **die; ~, ~n** caper *usu. in pl.*

[2]**Kaper der; ~s, ~** *(hist.: Schiff, Freibeuter)* privateer

Kaper·brief der *(hist.)* letter[s *pl.*] of marque

Kaperei die; ~, ~en *(hist.)* privateering *no art.*

kapern *tr. V.* **a)** *(hist.)* capture; seize; **b)** *(ugs.)* **jmdn. [für etw.] ~:** rope sb. in[to sth.]; **sich** *(Dat.)* **eine Frau/einen Mann ~:** hook [oneself] a wife/husband

Kapern·soße die caper sauce

Kaper·schiff das *(hist.)* privateer

kapieren [ka'pi:rən] *(ugs.)* **1.** *tr. V. (ugs.)* get *(coll.)*; understand; **kapier das endlich!** get that into your thick skull! *(coll.)*. **2.** *itr. V.* **kapiert?** got it? *(coll.)*; **sie hat schnell kapiert** she was quick to catch on *(coll.)*

Kapillare [kapɪ'la:rə] **die; ~, ~n** *(Biol., Med.)* capillary

Kapillar·gefäß das *(Biol., Med.)* capillary vessel

kapital [kapi'ta:l] *Adj.; nicht präd.* **a)** *(außergewöhnlich)* major ‹*error, blunder, etc.*›; **eine ~e Dummheit begehen** do something exceedingly foolish; **b)** *(Jägerspr.: sehr groß und stark)* large and powerful; royal ‹*stag*›; **c)** *(schwerwiegend)* serious, bad ‹*accident etc.*›

Kapital das; ~s, ~e *od.* **~ien a)** capital; **b)** *(fig.)* asset; **seine Hände sind sein einziges ~:** his capable hands are his only asset; **~ aus etw. schlagen** make capital out of sth.; capitalize on sth.; **c)** *o. Pl. (Kapitalisten)* capital

Kapital-: ~abwanderung die *(Wirtsch.)* exodus of capital; **~anlage die** *(Wirtsch.)* capital investment; **~anteil der** *(Wirtsch.)* share; stake

Kapitale die; ~, ~n *(geh.)* capital [city]

Kapital-: ~eigner der *(Wirtsch.)* shareowner; **~ertrag der** *(Wirtsch.)* return on capital; **~ertrag[s]·steuer die** *(Steuerw.)* tax on capital income; **~flucht die** flight of capital; **~geber der** investor; **~gesellschaft die** joint-stock company

kapitalisieren *tr. V. (Wirtsch.)* capitalize

Kapitalismus der; ~, Kapitalismen; *Pl. selten* capitalism *no art.*

Kapitalist der; ~en, ~en capitalist

kapitalistisch 1. *Adj.* capitalistic. **2.** *adv.* capitalistically

kapital-, Kapital-: ~konto das *(Wirtsch.)* capital account; **~kräftig** *Adj. (Wirtsch.)* financially strong; **~markt der** *(Wirtsch.)* capital market; **~verbrechen das** serious offence *or* crime; *(mit Todesstrafe bedroht)* capital offence *or* crime; **~verbrecher der** serious/capital offender; **~verflechtung die** interlacing of capital interests

Kapitän [kapi'tɛ:n] **der; ~s, ~e a)** *(Seew.)* captain; *(auf einem Handelsschiff)* master; captain; *(auf einem kleineren Schiff)* skipper; captain; **~ der Landstraße** *(ugs.)* knight of the road; [long-distance] truck-driver *or (Brit.)* lorry-driver; **b)** *(Flugw.)* captain; **c)** *(Sport)* captain; skipper

Kapitän·leutnant der *(Marine)* lieutenant-commander

Kapitäns·patent das master's certificate

Kapitel [ka'pɪtl̩] **das; ~s, ~ a)** *(Abschnitt, auch fig.)* chapter; **das ist ein anderes ~** *(fig.)* that's another story; **ein dunkles ~ in jmds. Geschichte** *(fig.)* a black period in sb.'s history; **das ist ein ~ für sich** *(fig.)* that's an awkward subject; *(etwas Unklares)* that's a complicated subject; **b)** *(Geistliche einer Dom- oder Stiftskirche)* chapter

Kapitell [kapi'tɛl] **das; ~s, ~e** capital

Kapitulation [kapitula'ts̮i̯o:n] **die; ~, ~en a)** surrender; capitulation; **seine ~ erklären** admit defeat; **b)** *(fig.: das Aufgeben)* giving up; **c)** *(Vertrag)* surrender *or* capitulation document

kapitulieren *itr. V.* **a)** surrender; capitulate; **vor dem Feind ~:** surrender to the enemy; **b)** *(fig.: aufgeben)* give up; **vor etw.** *(Dat.)* **~:** give up in the face of sth.

Kaplan [ka'pla:n] **der; ~s, Kapläne** *(kath. Kirche)* **a)** *(Hilfsgeistlicher)* curate; **b)** *(Geistlicher mit besonderen Aufgaben)* chaplain

Kapo ['kapo] **der; ~s, ~s a)** *(Soldatenspr.)* NCO; **b)** *(Lagerjargon)* prisoner acting as an overseer

Kapok ['kapɔk] **der; ~s** kapok

Kapott·hut [ka'pɔt-] **der** capote; *(ugs. abwertend: old or old-fashioned)* hat

Kappe ['kapə] **die; ~, ~n a)** *(Kopfbedeckung)* cap; *(Flieger~)* helmet; **etw. auf seine [eigene] ~ nehmen** *(ugs.)* take the responsibility for sth.; **b)** *(Abdeckung)* cover; *(eines Rades)* hub-cap; **c)** *(Verschluß)* cap; top; *(eines Füllers)* cap; **d)** *(am Schuh)* *(vorn)* [toe-]cap; *(hinten)* counter

kappen *tr. V.* **a)** *(Seemannsspr.)* cut; **b)** *(beschneiden)* cut back ‹*hedge etc.*›; *(fig.)* cut; **c)** *(abschneiden)* cut off ‹*branches, shoots, crown, etc.*›; **d)** *(kastrieren)* caponize, castrate ‹*cockerel*›

Kappen·abend der *(landsch.)* carnival party *(at which funny hats are worn)*

Kappes ['kapəs] **der; ~** *(bes. westd.)* **a)** *(Weißkohl)* cabbage; **b)** *(ugs.: Unsinn)* rubbish; nonsense

Käppi ['kɛpi] **das; ~s, ~s** overseas cap; garrison cap

Kapp·naht die *(Schneiderei)* flat-fell seam

Kaprice [ka'pri:sə] **die; ~, ~n** *(geh.)* caprice; whim

Kapriole [kapri'o:lə] **die;** ~, ~**n a)** *(Luftsprung)* caper; capriole; ~**n schlagen** cut capers; **b)** *(Streich)* trick; **c)** *(Reiten)* capriole

Kaprize [ka'pri:tsə] **die;** ~, ~**n** *(österr.) s.* **Kaprice**

kaprizieren *refl. V.* **sich darauf** ~, **etw. zu tun** be intent on doing sth.; **sich auf ein Land** ~: be utterly committed to a country

kapriziös [kapri'tsiø:s] **1.** *Adj.* capricious. **2.** *adv.* capriciously

Kapsel ['kapsl̩] **die;** ~, ~**n** capsule

Kapstadt ['kap-ʃtat] **(das)** Cape Town

kaputt [ka'pʊt] *Adj.* **a)** *(entzwei)* broken ⟨*toy, cup, plate, arm, leg, etc.*⟩; **die Maschine/das Auto ist** ~: the machine/car has broken down; *(ganz und gar)* the machine/car has had it *(coll.)*; **irgend etwas ist am Auto** ~: there's something wrong with the car; **diese Jacke ist** ~: this jacket needs mending; *(ist zerrissen)* this jacket's torn; **die Birne ist** ~: the bulb has gone; *(ist zerbrochen)* the bulb is smashed; **das Telefon ist** ~: the phone is not working *or* is out of order; **der Fernseher ist** ~: the television has gone wrong; **sein Leben ist** ~: his life is in ruins; **eine** ~**e Ehe** *(ugs.)* a marriage that has broken up; **ein** ~**er Typ** *(fig. ugs.)* a down-and-out; **eine** ~**e Lunge/ein** ~**es Herz haben** *(ugs.)* have bad lungs/a bad heart; **die Ehe ist** ~: the marriage has failed *or (coll.)* is on the rocks; **was ist denn jetzt** ~**?** *(salopp)* what's wrong *or* the matter now?; **bei dir ist was** ~ *(salopp)* there must be something wrong with you *(coll.)*; **b)** *(ugs.: erschöpft)* shattered *(coll.)*; whacked *(Brit. coll.)*; pooped *(coll.)*; **c)** *(salopp: krankhaft, abartig)* sick

kaputt-: ~**|arbeiten** *refl. V. (ugs.)* work oneself into the ground *(coll.)*; ~**|fahren** *unr. tr. V. (ugs.)* run over ⟨*animal*⟩; smash up ⟨*car etc.*⟩; ~**|gehen** *unr. itr. V.; mit sein (ugs.)* **a)** *(entzweigehen)* break; ⟨*machine*⟩ break down, *(sl.)* pack up; ⟨*clothes, shoes*⟩ fall to pieces; ⟨*light-bulb*⟩ go; *(zerbrechen)* be smashed; *(eingehen)* ⟨*plant*⟩ die; *(verderben)* ⟨*fish, fruit, etc.*⟩ go off; *(fig.)* ⟨*marriage*⟩ fail; ⟨*community, relationship, etc.*⟩ break up; **b)** *(zugrunde gehen)* ⟨*firm*⟩ go bust *(coll.)*; ⟨*person*⟩ go to pieces; **er ist an Drogen** ~**gegangen** he was destroyed by drugs; ~**|kriegen** *tr. V. (ugs.)* break; **wie hast du das** ~**gekriegt?** how did you [manage to] break it?; ~**|lachen** *refl. V. (ugs.)* kill oneself [laughing] *(coll.)*; **das ist ja zum Kaputtlachen!** that's a laugh!; ~**|machen** (ugs.) **1.** *tr. V.* **a)** *(zerstören)* break ⟨*watch, spectacles, plate, etc.*⟩; spoil ⟨*sth. made with effort*⟩; ruin ⟨*clothes, furniture, etc.*⟩; burst ⟨*balloon*⟩; **b)** *(ruinieren)* drive ⟨*business, company*⟩ to the wall; destroy ⟨*political party*⟩; finish ⟨*person*⟩ off; **2.** *refl. V.* wear oneself out; ~**|schlagen** *unr. tr. V. (ugs.)* smash; ~**|schmeißen** *unr. tr. V. (ugs.)* smash

Kapuze [ka'pu:tsə] **die;** ~, ~**n** hood; *(bei Mönchen)* cowl; hood

Kapuzen·mantel der coat with a hood

Kapuziner [kapu'tsi:nɐ] **der;** ~**s,** ~ **a)** *(Mönch)* Capuchin [friar]; **b)** *(österr.: Kaffee)* cappuccino

Kapuziner·kresse die nasturtium

Kar [ka:ɐ̯] *(Geol.)* **das;** ~**[e]s,** ~**e** cirque; corrie; kar

Karabiner [kara'bi:nɐ] **der;** ~**s,** ~ **a)** *(Gewehr)* carbine; **b)** *(österr.) s.* **Karabinerhaken**

Karabiner·haken der snap hook; spring hook; *(Bergsteigen)* karabiner

Karacho [ka'raxo] **das;** ~**s** *in* **mit** ~ *od.* **in vollem** ~ *(ugs.)* hell for leather *(coll.)*

Karaffe [ka'rafə] **die;** ~, ~**n** carafe; *(mit Glasstöpsel)* decanter

Karakul·schaf [kara'kʊl-] **das** caracul [sheep]

Karambolage [karambo'la:ʒə] **die;** ~, ~**n a)** *(ugs.)* crash; collision; **b)** *(Billard)* cannon

Karambole [karam'bo:lə] **die;** ~, ~**n** *(Billard)* red [ball]

karambolieren *itr. V.* **a)** *(Billard)* cannon; **b)** *mit haben od. sein (zusammenstoßen)* crash; **mit etw.** ~: crash into sth.; collide with sth.

Karamel [kara'mɛl] **der** *(schweiz.:* **das);** ~**s** caramel

Karamel-: ~**bonbon der** *od.* **das** caramel [toffee]; ~**creme die** crème caramel

Karamelle [kara'mɛlə] **die;** ~, ~**n** caramel [toffee]

Karat [ka'ra:t] **das;** ~**[e]s,** ~**e** carat; **ein Diamant von 5** ~: a 5-carat diamond; **reines Gold hat 24** ~: pure gold is 24 carats

Karate [ka'ra:tə] **das;** ~**[s]** karate

-karäter [-karɛ:tɐ] **der Zehnkaräter/Fünfkaräter** ten-carat/five-carat diamond/stone

Karate·schlag der karate chop

-karätig [-karɛ:tɪç] **zehnkarätig/fünfkarätig** ten-carat/five-carat

Karavelle [kara'vɛlə] **die;** ~, ~**n** *(hist.)* caravel

Karawane [kara'va:nə] **die;** ~, ~**n** caravan; ~**n von Autos** *(fig.)* long lines of cars

Karawanen·straße die caravan route

Karawanserei [karavanzə'rai] **die;** ~, ~**en** caravanserai

Karbid [kar'bi:t] **das;** ~**[e]s,** ~**e** *(Chem.)* carbide

Karbid·lampe die carbide lamp

Karbol [kar'bo:l] **das;** ~**s, Karbol·säure die;** *o. Pl.* carbolic acid

Karbol·seife die carbolic soap

Karbonat [karbo'na:t] **das;** ~**[e]s,** ~**e** *(Chem.)* carbonate

Karbunkel [kar'bʊŋkl̩] **der;** ~**s,** ~ *(Med.)* carbuncle

Kardamom [karda'mo:m] **der** *od.* **das;** ~**s,** ~**e[n]** cardamom

Kardan- [kar'da:n-]: ~**an·trieb der** *(Technik)* cardan drive; ~**aufhängung die** *(Technik)* cardanic suspension; ~**gelenk das** *(Technik)* cardan joint

kardanisch *Adj. in* ~**e Aufhängung** cardanic suspension

Kardan-: ~**tunnel der** *(Kfz-W.)* cardan tunnel; cardan-shaft housing; ~**welle die** *(Technik)* cardan shaft

Kardätsche [kar'dɛ:tʃə] **die;** ~, ~**n** dandy-brush; body brush

kardinal [kardi'na:l] *Adj.* cardinal

Kardinal der; ~**s, Kardinäle** [kardi'nɛ:lə] **a)** *(kath. Kirche)* cardinal; **b)** *(Vogel)* cardinal [bird]

Kardinal-: ~**bischof der** cardinal bishop; ~**fehler der** cardinal error

Kardinals·kollegium das college of cardinals; Sacred College

Kardinal-: ~**tugend die;** *meist Pl.* cardinal virtue; ~**zahl die** cardinal [number]

Kardiogramm [kardi̯o'gram] **das;** ~**s,** ~**e** *(Med.)* **a)** *s.* **Elektrokardiogramm; b)** *(Bild der Herzstoßkurven)* cardiogram

Kardiologie die; ~ *(Med.)* cardiology *no art.*

Karditis [kar'di:tɪs] **die;** ~, **Karditiden** [kardi'ti:dn̩] *(Med.)* carditis

Karenz [ka'rɛnts] **die;** ~, ~**en, Karenz·zeit die** waiting period

Karfiol [kar'fi̯o:l] **der;** ~**s** *(südd., österr.)* cauliflower

Kar·freitag [ka:ɐ̯-] **der** Good Friday

Karfunkel [kar'fʊŋkl̩] **der;** ~**s,** ~ *(Edelstein; volkst.: Geschwür)* carbuncle

karg [kark] **1.** *Adj.* meagre ⟨*wages, pay, etc.*⟩; frugal ⟨*meal etc.*⟩; poor ⟨*light, accommodation*⟩; scanty ⟨*supply*⟩; meagre, scant ⟨*applause*⟩; sketchy ⟨*report*⟩; sparse ⟨*furnishings*⟩; *(wenig fruchtbar)* barren, poor ⟨*soil*⟩; barren ⟨*desert, land*⟩; ~ **mit Lob sein** be grudging *or* sparing in one's praise. **2.** *adv.* ~ **bemessen sein** ⟨*helping*⟩ be mingy *(Brit. coll.)*; ⟨*supply*⟩ be scanty; ~ **leben** live frugally; ~ **möbliert** sparsely furnished; ~ **ausgestattet** scantily equipped

kargen *itr. V.* **mit Geld** ~: be mean with one's money; **mit seinen Worten** ~: be a person of few words

Kargheit die; ~ *(geh.) s.* **karg 1:** meagreness; frugality; poorness; scantiness; sketchiness; sparseness; barrenness

kärglich ['kɛrklɪç] **1.** *Adj.* meagre, poor ⟨*wages, pension, etc.*⟩; poor ⟨*light*⟩; frugal ⟨*meal*⟩; scanty ⟨*supply*⟩; meagre ⟨*existence*⟩; meagre, scant ⟨*applause*⟩; sparse ⟨*furnishing*⟩. **2.** *adv.* sparsely ⟨*furnished*⟩; poorly ⟨*lit, paid, rewarded*⟩

Kargo ['kargo] **der;** ~**s,** ~**s** *(Seemannsspr.)* cargo

Karibik [ka'ri:bɪk] **die;** ~: Caribbean; **in die** ~: to the Caribbean

karibisch *Adj.* Caribbean; **die** ~**en Inseln** the Caribbean Islands

kariert [ka'ri:ɐ̯t] **1.** *Adj.* check, checked ⟨*material, pattern*⟩; check ⟨*jacket etc.*⟩; squared ⟨*paper*⟩. **2.** *adv. (ugs.)* ~ **reden** *od.* **quatschen** talk rubbish

Karies ['ka:ri̯ɛs] **die;** ~ *(Zahnmed.)* caries

Karikatur [karika'tu:ɐ̯] **die;** ~, ~**en a)** cartoon; *(Porträt)* caricature; **b)** *(abwertend: Zerrbild)* caricature

Karikaturist der; ~**en,** ~**en** cartoonist; *(Porträtist)* caricaturist

karikaturistisch 1. *Adj.* caricatural; **der Film gibt eine** ~**e Darstellung des Familienlebens** the film is a caricature of family life. **2.** *adv.* **etw.** ~ **überzeichnen** caricature sth.

karikieren [kari'ki:rən] *tr. V.* caricature

kariös [ka'ri̯ø:s] *Adj. (Zahnmed.)* carious

Karitas ['ka:ritas] **die;** ~ *(geh.)* charity

karitativ [karita'ti:f] **1.** *Adj.* charitable. **2.** *adv.* **sich** ~ **betätigen** do work for charity

Karkasse [kar'kasə] **die;** ~, ~**n** *(Technik, Kochk.)* carcass

Karl [karl] **(der)** Charles; ~ **der Große** Charlemagne

Karmeliter [karme'li:tɐ] **der;** ~**s,** ~**:** Carmelite [friar]

Karmelit[er]in die; ~, ~**nen** Carmelite [nun]

Karmesin [karme'zi:n] **das;** ~**s** *s.* **Karmin**

karmesin·rot *Adj. s.* **karminrot**

Karmin [kar'mi:n] **das;** ~**s** carmine

karmin·rot *Adj.* carmine

Karneol [karne'o:l] **der;** ~**s,** ~**e** cornelian

Karneval ['karnəval] **der;** ~**s,** ~**e** *od.* ~**s** carnival; **im** ~**:** at carnival time; ~ **feiern** join in the carnival festivities

Karnevalist der; ~**en,** ~**en** carnival reveller; *(Vortragender bei Karnevalssitzungen)* carnival performer

karnevalistisch 1. *Adj.* carnival *attrib.* ⟨*time, festivities, etc.*⟩. **2.** *adv.* **sich** ~ **verkleiden** dress up in a carnival costume/carnival costumes

Karnevals-: ~**kostüm das** carnival costume; ~**sitzung die** carnival convention *(variety show organized by carnival society)*; ~**verein der** carnival society; ~**zug der** carnival procession

Karnickel [kar'nɪkl̩] **das;** ~**s,** ~ **a)** *(landsch.)* rabbit; **b)** *(ugs.: Sündenbock)* **immer bin ich das** ~**!** I always get the blame!

Karnickel-: ~**bock der** *(bes. nordd.)* buck rabbit; ~**stall der** *(bes. nordd.)* rabbit-hutch

karnivor [karni'vo:ɐ̯] *Adj. (Biol.)* carnivorous

Kärnten ['kɛrntn̩] **(das);** ~**s** Carinthia

Kärnt[e]ner der; ~**s,** ~, **Kärntnerin die;** ~, ~**nen** Carinthian

Karo ['ka:ro] **das;** ~**s,** ~**s a)** *(Viereck)* square; *(auf der Spitze stehend)* diamond; **b)** *o. Pl.* *(~muster)* check; **c)** *o. Art.; o. Pl. (Kartenspiel: Farbe)* diamonds *pl.*; **d)** *(Kartenspiel: Karte)* diamond; *s. auch* [2]**Pik**

Karo-: ~**as das** ace of diamonds; ~**bube**

der jack of diamonds; ~**dame die** queen of diamonds; ~**könig der** king of diamonds; ~**muster das** check; check[ed] pattern
Karolinger ['ka:rolɪŋɐ] **der; ~s, ~** *(hist.)* Carolingian
Karosse [ka'rɔsə] **die; ~, ~n a)** *(Prunkwagen)* [state-]coach; **b)** *(scherzh. iron.: Auto)* limousine
Karosserie [karɔsə'ri:] **die; ~, ~n** bodywork; coachwork
Karosserie·bauer der coachbuilder
Karotin [karo'ti:n] **das; ~s** carotene
Karotte [ka'rɔtə] **die; ~, ~n** small carrot
Karpaten [kar'pa:tn̩] *Pl.* Carpathians; Carpathian Mountains
Karpfen ['karpfn̩] **der; ~s, ~:** carp
Karpfen·teich der carp pond; *s. auch* **Hecht a**
Karre ['karə] **die; ~, ~n** *(bes. nordd.)* **a)** *s.* **Karren; b)** *(abwertend: Fahrzeug)* [old] heap *(coll.)*
Karree [ka're:] **das; ~s, ~s a)** *(Viereck)* rectangle; *(Quadrat)* square; *(bes. Milit.: Formation)* square; **b)** *(Häuserblock)* **ums ~ gehen/fahren** walk/drive round the block
karren 1. *tr. V.* **a)** *(mit einer Karre)* cart; **etw./jmdn. nach Hause ~:** bring/take sth./sb. home in a cart; **b)** *(salopp: mit einem Auto)* run *(coll.)*. **2.** *itr. V.; mit sein (ugs.)* drive [around]
Karren der; ~s, ~ *(bes. südd., österr.)* cart; *(zweirädrig)* barrow; *(Schubkarren)* [wheel]barrow; *(für Gepäck usw.)* trolley; **ein ~ voll Sand** a cartload/barrowload of sand; *(fig.)* **den ~ in den Dreck fahren** *(ugs.)* get things into a mess; mess things up; **den ~ [für jmdn.] aus dem Dreck ziehen** *(ugs.)* sort out the mess [for sb.]; **jmdm. an den ~ fahren** *(ugs.)* tell sb. where he/she gets off *(coll.)*
Karrette [ka'rɛtə] **die; ~, ~n** *(schweiz.)* **a)** handcart; *(Schubkarren)* [wheel]barrow; **b)** *(Einkaufswagen)* [shopping-]trolley
Karriere [ka'ri̯e:rə] **die; ~, ~n a)** career; **~ machen** make a [successful] career for oneself; **b)** *(Reiten)* [full *or* extended] gallop
Karriere-: ~frau die career woman/girl; **~macher der** *(abwertend)* careerist
Karrierist der; ~en, ~en *(abwertend)* careerist
karriolen *itr. V.; mit sein (ugs.)* ride around
Kärrner ['kɛrnɐ] **der; ~s, ~** *(veralt.)* labourer
Kar·samstag [ka:ɐ̯-] **der** Easter Saturday; Holy Saturday
[1]**Karst** [karst] **der; ~[e]s, ~e** *(landsch.)* [two-pronged] hoe
[2]**Karst der; ~[e]s, ~e** *(Geol.)* karst
karstig *Adj.* karstic
Karst·landschaft die karst landscape
Kartätsche [kar'tɛ:tʃə] **die; ~, ~n** *(hist.)* case-shot
Kartäuser [kar'tɔyzɐ] **der; ~s, ~ a)** *(Mönch)* Carthusian [monk]; **b)** *(Likör)* chartreuse
Karte ['kartə] **die; ~, ~n a)** *(Kartei~, Loch~ usw.)* card; **die gelbe/rote ~** *(Fußball)* the yellow/red card; **die grüne ~** *(Verkehrsw.)* the green card; **b)** *(Ansichts~, Post~, Glückwunsch~, Visiten~)* card; *(Einladungs~)* invitation[-card]; **c)** *(Speise~)* menu; *(Wein~)* wine-list; **nach der ~ essen** eat à la carte; **d)** *(Fahr~, Flug~, Eintritts~)* ticket; **e)** *(Lebensmittel~)* ration-card; **auf ~n** on coupons; **f)** *(Land~)* map; *(See~)* chart; **~n lesen** map-read; **g)** *(Spiel~)* card; **jmdm. die ~n legen** read sb.'s fortune from the cards; *(fig.)* **diese ~ sticht nicht [mehr]** that won't work [any more]; **die** *od.* **seine ~n aufdecken** *od.* **[offen] auf den Tisch legen** *od.* **offenlegen** put one's cards on the table; **alles auf eine ~ setzen** stake everything on one chance; **auf die falsche ~ setzen** back the wrong horse; **jmdm. in die ~n sehen** *od. (ugs.)* **gucken** find out *or* see what sb. is up to; **sich** *(Dat.)* **nicht in die ~n sehen** *od. (ugs.)* **gucken lassen** play one's cards close to one's chest; not show one's hand; **mit offenen/verdeckten ~n spielen** put one's cards on the table/play one's cards close to one's chest; **h)** *o. Pl. (Anzahl von Spielkarten)* hand; **eine schlechte ~ [auf der Hand] haben** have a poor hand
Kartei [kar'tai̯] **die; ~, ~en** card file *or* index
Kartei-: ~karte die file *or* index card; **~kasten der** file-card *or* index-card box; **~leiche die** *(scherzh.)* **a)** dead card; **b)** *(ugs.: passives Mitglied)* inactive member
Kartell [kar'tɛl] **das; ~s, ~e** *(Wirtsch., Politik)* cartel
Kartell-: ~amt das, ~behörde die *government body concerned with the control and supervision of cartels;* ≈ Monopolies and Mergers Commission *(Brit.)*; **~gesetz das, ~recht das** law relating to cartels; ≈ monopolies law *(Brit.)*
Karten-: ~bestellung die [ticket] reservation; booking; **~brief der** letter-card; **~gruß der** greeting *or* short message on a [post-]card; **an jmdn. einen ~gruß verschicken** send sb. a card; **~haus das** house of cards; **~kunst·stück das** card trick; **~legen das; ~s** reading the cards *no art.*; cartomancy; **~leger der, ~legerin die** fortune-teller *(who tells fortunes by reading the cards)*; **~lesen das** map-reading; **~spiel das a)** *(Spiel mit Karten)* card-game; **b)** *(Satz Spielkarten)* pack *or (Amer.)* deck [of cards]; **c)** *(das Kartenspielen)* card-playing *no art.*; **~spieler der** card-player; **~ständer der** map-stand; **~tisch der a)** *(bes. Milit.)* map-table; *(Seew.)* chart-table; **b)** *(Spieltisch)* card-table; **~verkauf der;** *o. Pl.* sale of tickets; **~vor·verkauf der;** *o. Pl.* advance booking; **im ~vorverkauf sind die Karten billiger** the tickets are cheaper if you buy them in advance
kartesianisch [karte'zi̯a:nɪʃ], **kartesisch** [kar'te:zɪʃ] *Adj.* Cartesian
Karthager [kar'ta:gɐ] **der; ~s, ~:** Carthaginian
Karthago [kar'ta:go] **(das); ~s** Carthage
Kartoffel [kar'tɔfl̩] **die; ~, ~n a)** potato; **rin in die ~n, raus aus die ~n** *(salopp scherzh.)* it's 'do this' one minute and 'do that' the next; **jmdn. wie eine heiße ~ fallenlassen** *(ugs.)* drop sb. just like that *(coll.)*; **b)** *(ugs. scherzh.: Nase)* conk *(sl.)*; hooter *(Brit. sl.)*; **c)** *(ugs. scherzh.: Loch im Strumpf)* large hole; potato *(coll.)*
Kartoffel-: ~acker der potato-field; **~brei der** mashed *or* creamed potatoes *pl.*; mash *(coll.)*; **~chips** *Pl.* [potato] crisps *(Brit.) or (Amer.)* chips; **~ernte die** potato harvest; **~ferien** *Pl. (ugs.)* autumn [school] holiday *sing.*; **~feuer das** fire to dispose of potato leaves *(after the potato harvest)*; **~käfer der** Colorado beetle; potato-beetle; **~kloß der, ~knödel der** *(südd.)* potato dumpling; **~mehl das;** *o. Pl.* potato flour; **~puffer der** potato pancake *(made from grated raw potatoes)*; **~püree das;** *s.* **~brei; ~sack der** potato-sack; **~salat der** potato salad; **~schale die** potato skin; *(abgeschält)* potato peel *or* peelings *pl.*; **~suppe die** potato soup
Kartograph [karto'gra:f] **der; ~en, ~en** cartographer
Kartographie die; ~: cartography *no art.*
kartographieren *tr. V.* map
kartographisch *Adj.* cartographic
Karton [kar'tɔŋ] **der; ~s, ~s a)** *(Pappe)* card[board]; **b)** *(Behälter)* cardboard box; *(kleiner und dünner)* carton; **zwei ~[s] Seife/Batterien** two boxes *or* packs of soap/batteries; **c)** *(Kunstwiss.)* cartoon
Kartonage [karto'na:ʒə] **die; ~, ~n** cardboard boxes [and cartons] *pl.*; cardboard packaging
kartonieren [karto'ni:rən] *tr. V. (Buchw.)* bind in [paper] boards
Kartothek [karto'te:k] **die; ~, ~en** *s.* **Kartei**
Kartusche [kar'tʊʃə] **die; ~, ~n a)** *(Metallhülse)* cartridge; **b)** *(Kunstwiss.)* cartouche
Karussell [karʊ'sɛl] **das; ~s, ~s** *od.* **~e** merry-go-round; carousel *(Amer.)*; *(kleineres)* roundabout; **~ fahren** have a ride on *or* go on the merry-go-round/roundabout; **mit jmdm. ~ fahren** *(fig. ugs.)* give sb. a good telling-off
Kar·woche ['ka:ɐ̯vɔxə] **die** Holy Week; Passion Week
Karyatide [karya'ti:də] **die; ~, ~n** *(bild. Kunst)* caryatid
Karzer ['kartsɐ] **der; ~s, ~** *(hist.)* **a)** *(Arrestraum)* detention room *(in university, school)*; **b)** *o. Pl. (Strafe)* detention *(often lasting several days)*
karzinogen [kartsino'ge:n] *Adj.* *(Med.)* carcinogenic
Karzinologie die *(Med.)* oncology *no art.*
Karzinom [kartsi'no:m] **das; ~s, ~e** *(Med.)* carcinoma
Kasack ['ka:zak] **der; ~s, ~s** *(österr.:* **die; ~, ~s)** tunic
Kaschemme [ka'ʃɛmə] **die; ~, ~n** *(abwertend)* [low] dive *(coll.)*
kaschen ['kaʃn̩] *tr. V. (salopp)* **a)** *(verhaften)* nab *(sl.)*; nick *(sl.)*; **b)** *(sich aneignen)* pinch *(sl.)*; nick *(Brit. sl.)*
kaschieren [ka'ʃi:rən] *tr. V.* **a)** *(verhüllen)* conceal; hide; disguise ⟨*fault*⟩; **b)** *(Buchw.)* laminate ⟨*jacket etc.*⟩; line ⟨*cover etc.*⟩ [with paper]; **c)** *(Textilw.)* bond [together]
[1]**Kaschmir** ['kaʃmi:ɐ̯] **(das); ~s** Kashmir
[2]**Kaschmir der; ~s, ~e** *(Textilw.)* cashmere; **ein Pullover/Kleid aus ~:** a cashmere sweater/dress
Käse ['kɛ:zə] **der; ~s, ~ a)** cheese; **b)** *(ugs. abwertend: Unsinn)* rubbish; nonsense; codswallop *(Brit. sl.)*
Käse-: ~blatt das *(salopp abwertend)* rag; **~brot das** slice of bread and cheese; *(zugeklappt)* cheese sandwich; **~fondue das** cheese fondue; **~fuß der;** *meist Pl. (salopp abwertend)* cheesy *or* smelly foot; **~gebäck das** cheese savouries *pl.*; **~glocke die** cheese dome
Kasein [kaze'i:n], *(Chemie:)* **Casein das; ~s** casein
Käse·kuchen der cheesecake
Kasematte [kazə'matə] **die; ~, ~n** *(Milit., Marine)* casemate
Käse·platte die *(Platte)* cheeseboard; *(Gericht)* [selection of] assorted cheeses *pl.*
Käserei [kɛ:zə'rai̯] **die; ~, ~en a)** *o. Pl. (Herstellen von Käse)* cheese-making *no art.* **b)** *(Betrieb)* cheese-factory
Kaserne [ka'zɛrnə] **die; ~, ~n** barracks *sing. or pl.*
Kasernen-: ~hof der barrack square; **~sprache die** *(abwertend)* army lingo
kasernieren *tr. V.* quarter in barracks; *(fig.)* keep in isolation
Kasernierung die; ~, ~en quartering in barracks *no art.*; *(fig.)* keeping in isolation *no art.*
käse-, Käse-: ~stange die cheese straw; **~torte die** cheesecake; **~weiß** *Adj. (ugs.)* [as] white as a sheet; **sie war ~weiß im Gesicht** her face was as white as a sheet
käsig *Adj.* **a)** *(ugs.: bleich)* pasty; pale; *(vor Schreck)* as white as a sheet; **b)** *(wie Käse)* cheesy; cheeselike
Kasino [ka'zi:no] **das; ~s, ~s a)** *(Spiel~)* casino; **b)** *(Offiziers~)* [officers'] mess; **c)** *(Speiseraum)* canteen
Kaskade [kas'ka:də] **die; ~, ~n a)** *(Wasserfall, auch fig.)* cascade; **in ~n fallen** cascade [down]; **eine ~ von Verwünschungen/Flüchen** *(fig.)* a barrage of curses; **b)** *(Sprung)* acrobatic leap *(in which the acrobat pretends to fall)*; **c)** *(Elektrot.)* cascade
kasko·versichern *tr. V.; nur im Inf. u. 2. Part. gebr. (mit Vollkasko)* insure comprehensively; *(mit Teilkasko) insure against theft, fire, or act of God*

Kasko·versicherung die *(Voll~)* comprehensive insurance; *(Teil~) insurance against theft, fire, or act of God*

Kasper ['kaspɐ] **der; ~s, ~ a)** ≈ Punch; **b)** *(ugs.: alberner Mensch)* clown; fool

Kasperl ['kaspɐl] **das; ~s, ~[n]** *(österr.)*, **Kasperle** ['kaspɐlə] **das** *od.* **der; ~s, ~:** *s.* **Kasper**

Kasperle-: ~puppe die ≈ Punch and Judy puppet; **~theater das** ≈ Punch and Judy show; *(Puppenbühne)* ≈ Punch and Judy theatre

kaspern *itr. V. (ugs.)* clown *or* fool around

Kasper·theater das *s.* **Kasperletheater**

Kaspische Meer ['kaspɪʃə -] **das** Caspian Sea

Kassa ['kasa] **die; ~, Kassen** *(österr.) s.* **Kasse**

Kassa-: ~geschäft das a) *(Börsenw.)* spot transaction; **b)** *(Wirtsch.)* cash transaction; **~kurs der** *(Börsenw.)* spot price; **~markt der** *(Börsenw.)* spot market

Kassandra·ruf [ka'sandra-] **der** *(geh.)* prophecy of doom

Kassation [kasa'tsi̯o:n] **die; ~, ~en a)** *(von Urkunden)* annulment; **b)** *(von Urteilen)* quashing; setting aside; **c)** *(veralt.: unehrenhafte Entlassung)* cashiering

Kassations·gericht das *(schweiz. Rechtsw.)* court of appeal *(in a canton)*

Kasse ['kasə] **die; ~, ~n a)** *(Kassette)* cashbox; *(Registrier~)* till; cash register; **in die ~ greifen** *od.* **einen Griff in die ~ tun** *(ugs.; auch fig.)* help oneself from the till; **er wurde beim Griff in die ~ ertappt** *(auch fig.)* he was caught with his fingers in the till; **die ~ klingelt** *(fig.)* the tills are ringing merrily; **b)** *(Ort zum Bezahlen)* cash *or* pay desk; *(im Supermarkt)* check-out; *(in einer Bank)* counter; **~ machen** *(Kaufmannsspr.)* cash up; **jmdn. zur ~ bitten** *(ugs.)* ask sb. to pay up; **c)** *(Bargeld)* cash; **gemeinsame ~ führen** *od.* **machen** share expenses; **getrennte ~ haben** pay separately; **gut/knapp bei ~ sein** be well-off *or* flush/be short of cash *or* money; **bei ~ sein** be in the money; **etw. reißt ein Loch in die ~** *(ugs.)* sth. makes a hole in sb.'s pocket *or* a dent in sb.'s finances; **die ~ führen** be in charge of the money *or* finances *pl.;* **d)** *(in Behörde, Unternehmen)* cashier's office; **e)** *(Kassenraum)* cashier's office; *(in einer Bank)* counter hall; **f)** *(Theater~, Kino~, Stadion~)* box-office; **g)** *(Spar~)* [savings] bank; **h)** *s.* **Krankenkasse; i)** *(Kaufmannsspr.: Barzahlung)* [payment in] cash; **wir liefern nur gegen ~:** we deliver only if payment is made in cash

Kasseler ['kasəlɐ] **das; ~s** smoked loin of pork; *s. auch* **Rippenspeer**

kassen-, Kassen-: ~arzt der *doctor who treats members of health insurance schemes;* **~ärztlich** *Adj.; nicht präd.* **~ärztliche Behandlung** treatment under a health insurance scheme; **~bericht der** *(Wirtsch.)* financial report *or* statement; **~bestand der** cash [in hand]; **~bon der** sales slip; receipt; **~brille die** *(ugs.) glasses provided under a health insurance scheme;* ≈ National Health glasses *pl. (Brit.);* **~buch das** cashbook; **~erfolg der** box-office success; **~führer der** treasurer; **~gestell das** *(ugs.) spectacle frame provided under a health insurance scheme;* ≈ National Health frame *(Brit.);* **~magnet der** *(ugs.)* box-office draw; **~patient der** *patient who is a member of a health insurance scheme;* **~raum der** counter hall; **~schlager der** *(ugs.)* **a)** *(Film, Theater)* box-office hit; **b)** *(von Waren)* top seller; **~schrank der** safe; **~stunden** *Pl.* hours of business, business hours *(of bank, cashier's office, etc.);* **~sturz der** *(ugs.)* **~sturz machen** check up on one's ready cash; **~wart der** treasurer; **~zettel der a)** *(Quittung)* receipt; **b)** *(~bon)* sales slip

Kasserolle [kasə'rɔlə] **die; ~, ~n** saucepan

Kassette [ka'sɛtə] **die; ~, ~n a)** *(für Geld u. Wertsachen)* box; case; **b)** *(mit Büchern, Schallplatten)* boxed set; **c)** *(Tonband~)* cassette; **etw. auf ~ aufnehmen** record *or* tape sth. on cassette; **d)** *(Filmrolle)* cartridge; **e)** *(Behälter für Filmrollen)* can; **f)** *(Archit.)* coffer; lacunar

Kassetten-: ~deck das cassette deck; **~film der** cartridge film; **~recorder der** cassette recorder *or* player

Kassiber [ka'si:bɐ] **der; ~s, ~** *(Gaunerspr.)* [secret] message

Kassier [ka'si:ɐ̯] **der; ~s, ~e** *(südd., österr., schweiz.) s.* **Kassierer**

[1]kassieren 1. *tr. V.* **a)** *(einziehen)* collect ⟨*rent etc.*⟩; **b)** *(ugs.: einnehmen)* collect ⟨*money, fee, etc.*⟩; *(fig.)* receive, get ⟨*recognition, praise, etc.*⟩; **dafür hat er viel Geld kassiert** he got a lot of money for it *or* made a lot of money out of it; **bei der Transaktion hat er 100 000 DM kassiert** he made 100,000 marks on the deal; **c)** *(ugs.: hinnehmen müssen)* receive, get ⟨*penalty points, scorn, ingratitude, etc.*⟩; **d)** *(ugs.: wegnehmen)* confiscate; take away ⟨*driving licence*⟩; **er hat das Erbteil seiner Schwester kassiert** he appropriated his sister's share of the inheritance; **e)** *(ugs.: verhaften/gefangennehmen)* pick up; nab *(sl.);* nick *(Brit. sl.).* **2.** *itr. V.* **a)** *(abkassieren)* **bei jmdm. ~:** give sb. his/her bill *or (Amer.)* check; *(ohne Rechnung)* settle up with sb.; **darf ich bei Ihnen ~?** would you like your bill?/can I settle up with you?; **b)** *(ugs.: Geld einnehmen)* collect the money; *(bezahlt werden)* make money; **[bei einem Geschäft] ganz schön ~:** make a packet *(coll.) or (sl.)* a bomb [on a deal]

[2]kassieren *tr. V. (Rechtsw.)* quash ⟨*judgement etc.*⟩

Kassierer der; ~s, ~, Kassiererin die; ~, ~nen a) *(in Geschäften, Banken)* cashier; teller; **b)** *(bei einem Verein)* treasurer

Kastagnette [kastan'jɛtə] **die; ~, ~n** castanet

Kastanie [kas'ta:ni̯ə] **die; ~, ~n** chestnut; **[für jmdn.] die ~n aus dem Feuer holen** *(ugs.)* pull the chestnuts out of the fire [for sb.]

kastanien-, Kastanien-: ~baum der chestnut-tree; **~braun** *Adj.* chestnut

Kästchen ['kɛstçən] **das; ~s, ~ a)** small box; **b)** *(vorgedrucktes Quadrat)* square; *(auf Fragebögen)* box

Kaste ['kastə] **die; ~, ~n** caste

kasteien [kas'tai̯ən] *refl. V.* **a)** *(als Bußübung)* chastise oneself; **b)** *(sich Entbehrungen auferlegen)* deny oneself

Kasteiung die; ~, ~en a) *(als Bußübung)* self-chastisement; **b)** *(Auferlegung von Entbehrungen)* self-denial

Kastell [kas'tɛl] **das; ~s, ~e a)** *(hist.: röm. Lager)* fort; **b)** *(Burg)* castle

Kastellan [kastɛ'la:n] **der; ~s, ~e** *(hist.)* castellan

Kasten ['kastn̩] **der; ~s, Kästen** ['kɛstn̩] **a)** box; **b)** *(für Flaschen)* crate; **c)** *(ugs.: Briefkasten)* post-box; letter-box; **d)** *(ugs. abwertend: Gebäude)* barracks *sing. or pl.;* **das ist ja ein furchtbarer alter ~:** that's a terrible old barracks of a place; **e)** *(ugs. abwertend) (Flugzeug)* crate *(sl.); (Schiff)* tub; *(Auto)* heap *(coll.); (Fernseher, Radio)* box *(coll.);* **f)** *(ugs.: Kamera)* **ein Bild im ~ haben** have got a picture; **eine Szene im ~ haben** have a picture in the can; **g)** *in* **etw. auf dem ~ haben** *(ugs.)* have got it up top *(coll.);* have plenty of grey matter; **h)** *(Schaukasten)* show-case; display case; **i)** *(Soldatenspr.)* glasshouse *(Milit. sl.);* **vier Tage ~:** four days in the glasshouse *or* the cooler; **j)** *(Turnen)* box; **k)** *(Ballspiele Jargon)* goal; **l)** *(bes. nordd.: Schublade)* drawer; **m)** *(südd., österr., schweiz.: Schrank)* cupboard

Kasten-: ~brot das tin[-loaf]; **~form die** [rectangular] tin; **~geist der;** *o. Pl.* caste spirit; **~wagen der** cart; *(Lieferwagen)* van; **~wesen das;** *o. Pl.* caste system

Kastilien [kas'ti:li̯ən] **(das); ~s** Castile

kastilisch *Adj.* Castilian

Kastrat [kas'tra:t] **der; ~en, ~en a)** *(Eunuch)* eunuch; **b)** *(Musik hist.)* castrato

Kastraten·stimme die a) *(Musik)* castrato voice; **b)** *(abwertend)* falsetto voice

Kastration [kastra'tsi̯o:n] **die; ~, ~en** castration

Kastrations-: ~angst die *(Psych.)* castration anxiety; **~komplex der** *(Psych.)* castration complex

kastrieren *tr. V.* castrate; **eine Kastrierte** *(salopp scherzh.)* a filter cigarette

Kasuistik [ka'zu̯ɪstɪk] **die; ~** *(Philos., geh.)* casuistry

kasuistisch *Adj. (Philos., geh.)* casuistic

Kasus ['ka:zʊs] **der; ~, ~** ['ka:zu:s] *(Sprachw.)* case

Kasus-: ~bildung die *(Sprachw.)* case formation; **~endung die** *(Sprachw.)* case ending

Kat [kat] **der; ~s, ~s** *(ugs.) s.* **Katalysator b**

Katafalk [kata'falk] **der; ~s, ~e** catafalque

Katakombe [kata'kɔmbə] **die; ~, ~n;** *meist Pl.* catacomb

katalanisch [kata'la:nɪʃ] *Adj.* Catalan

Katalog [kata'lo:k] **der; ~[e]s, ~e** *(auch fig.)* catalogue

katalogisieren *tr. V.* catalogue

Katalonien [kata'lo:ni̯ən] **(das); ~s** Catalonia

Katalysator [kataly'za:tɔr] **der; ~s, ~en** [-za'to:rən] **a)** *(Chemie, fig. geh.)* catalyst; **b)** *(Kfz-W.)* catalytic converter; *s. auch* **geregelt 2**

Katalyse [kata'ly:zə] **die; ~, ~n** *(Chemie)* catalysis

katalytisch [kata'ly:tɪʃ] *Adj. (Chemie)* catalytic

Katamaran [katama'ra:n] **der** *od.* **das; ~s, ~e** catamaran

Katapult [kata'pʊlt] **das** *od.* **der; ~[e]s, ~e** catapult

katapultieren *tr. V. (auch fig.)* catapult; eject ⟨*pilot*⟩

Katapult-: ~sitz der ejector seat; **~start der** catapult launch

Katarakt [kata'rakt] **der; ~[e]s, ~e** *(Stromschnelle)* rapids *pl.; (Wasserfall)* cataract

Katarrh [ka'tar] **der; ~s, ~e** *(Med.)* catarrh; **einen ~ haben** have catarrh

Kataster [ka'tastɐ] **der** *od.* **das; ~s, ~:** land register

Kataster·amt das land registry

katastrophal [katastro'fa:l] **1.** *Adj.* disastrous; *(stärker)* catastrophic; *(entsetzlich)* appalling; atrocious. **2.** *adv.* disastrously; *(stärker)* catastrophically; **sich ~ auswirken** have a disastrous/catastrophic effect; **~ enden** end in disaster/catastrophe

Katastrophe [katas'tro:fə] **die; ~, ~n a)** *(Unglück)* disaster; *(stärker)* catastrophe; **jmd. ist eine ~** *(ugs.)* sb. is a disaster; **b)** *(Literaturw.)* catastrophe

Katastrophen-: ~alarm der emergency *or* disaster alert; **~dienst der** emergency services *pl.;* **~einsatz der: den ~einsatz üben** practise procedures in case of a disaster; **~fall der** disaster [situation]; **~gebiet das** disaster area; **~schutz der a)** *(Organisation)* emergency services *pl.;* **b)** *(Maßnahmen)* disaster procedures *pl.;* **dem ~schutz dienen** be useful in the event of a disaster

Kate ['ka:tə] **die; ~, ~n** *(bes. nordd.)* small cottage

Katechese [katɛ'çe:zə] **die; ~, ~n** *(christl. Kirche)* catechesis

Katechet [katɛ'çe:t] **der; ~en, ~en** *(christl. Kirche)* catechist

Katechismus [katɛ'çɪsmʊs] **der; ~, Katechismen** *(christl. Kirche)* catechism

Katechist der; ~en, ~en catechist

kategorial [katego'ri̯a:l] *Adj. (geh.)* categorial
Kategorie [katego'ri:] **die; ~, ~n** [-i:ən] category; **diese ~ Mensch** that sort of person
kategorisch 1. *Adj.* categorical; *s. auch* **Imperativ b. 2.** *adv.* categorically
kategorisieren *tr. V.* categorize
Kater ['ka:tɐ] **der; ~s, ~ a)** tom-cat; **wie ein verliebter ~:** like an amorous tom-cat; *s. auch* **gestiefelt; b)** *(ugs.: schlechte Verfassung)* hangover; **einen ~ haben** have a hangover; be hung-over
Kater-: ~frühstück das *breakfast, usually of pickled herrings and gherkins, supposed to cure a hangover;* **~stimmung die** morning-after feeling; **er ist in der fürchterlichsten ~stimmung** he's got a terrible hangover
Katharina [kata'ri:na] **(die)** Catherine; Katherine
Katharsis ['ka(:)tarzıs] **die; ~** *(Literaturw.)* catharsis
kathartisch [ka'tartıʃ] *(geh.)* **1.** *Adj.* cathartic. **2.** *adv.* cathartically
Katheder [ka'te:dɐ] **das** *od.* **der; ~s, ~:** lectern; *(Pult des Lehrers)* teacher's desk
Kathederweisheit die theoretical *or* academic knowledge *no pl., no indef. art.*
Kathedrale [kate'dra:lə] **die; ~, ~n** cathedral
Kathete [ka'te:tə] **die; ~, ~n** *(Math.)* leg *(of a right-angled triangle)*
Katheter [ka'te:tɐ] **der; ~s, ~** *(Med.)* catheter
Kathode [ka'to:də] **die; ~, ~n** *(Physik)* cathode
Katholik [kato'li:k] **der; ~en, ~en, Katholikin die; ~, ~nen** [Roman] Catholic
katholisch *Adj.* [Roman] Catholic; **die Katholischen** *(ugs.)* the Catholics; *s. auch* **taufen a**
Katholizismus [katoli'tsısmʊs] **der; ~:** [Roman] Catholicism *no art.*
Katholizität [katolitsi'tɛ:t] **die; ~:** Catholicism
Katode [ka'to:də] **die; ~, ~n** *s.* **Kathode**
Kattun [ka'tu:n] **der; ~s, ~e** calico
Kattunkleid das calico dress
Katz [kats] **die** *in* **~ und Maus [mit jmdm.] spielen** *(ugs.)* play cat and mouse [with sb.]; **für die ~ sein** *(salopp)* be a waste of time
katzbalgen *refl. V. (ugs.)* scrap; fight
katzbuckeln *itr. V. (abwertend)* bow and scrape; **vor jmdm. ~:** bow and scrape to sb.
Kätzchen ['kɛtsçən] **das; ~s, ~ a)** *(kleine Katze)* little cat; *(liebkosend)* pussy; *(junge Katze)* kitten; **b)** *meist Pl. (Blüte der Birke, Erle u. a.)* catkin; **c)** *(ugs.: Mädchen)* kitten
Kätzchenzweig der catkin twig
Katze ['katsə] **die; ~, ~n a)** cat; **die ~ läßt das Mausen nicht** *(Spr.)* a leopard cannot change its spots *(prov.);* **bei Nacht** *od.* **nachts sind alle ~n grau** it's impossible to see any details in the dark; **wenn die ~ aus dem Haus ist, tanzen die Mäuse [auf dem Tisch]** *(Spr.)* when the cat's away the mice will play *(prov.);* **da beißt sich die ~ in den Schwanz** *(fig.)* we've come round in a circle; **die ~ aus dem Sack lassen** *(ugs.)* let the cat out of the bag; **die ~ im Sack kaufen** *(ugs.)* buy a pig in a poke; **um etw. herumgehen wie die ~ um den heißen Brei** *(ugs.)* beat about the bush; *s. auch* **Katz; b)** *(Jägerspr.)* female; **c)** *(temperamentvolle Frau)* cat
Katzelmacher der; ~s, ~ *(südd., österr.: salopp abwertend)* wop *(sl. derog.)*
katzen-, Katzen-: ~auge das a) *(ugs.: Rückstrahler)* reflector; **b)** *(Mineral.)* cat's-eye; **~buckel der** hunched back; **einen ~buckel machen** hunch one's back; **~fell das** cat's skin; **~freundlich** *Adj.* ingratiatingly friendly; **~haft** *Adj.* catlike; **~jammer der a)** *(Kater)* hangover; **b)** *(fig.)* mood of depression; **~klo das** *(ugs.)* cat's [litter] tray; **~kopf der** *(ugs.)* cobble[-stone]; **~musik die** *(ugs. abwertend)* terrible row *(coll.);* cacophony; **~sprung der** stone's throw; **bis zum Strand ist es nur ein ~sprung** the beach is only a stone's throw away; **~tisch der** *(ugs. scherzh.)* children's table; **~wäsche die** *(ugs.)* lick and a promise *(coll.);* catlick *(coll.);* **~wäsche machen** have a lick and a promise *or* a catlick; **~zunge die** langue de chat
Kaubewegung die chewing movement
Kauderwelsch ['kaudɐvɛlʃ] **das; ~[s]** gibberish *no indef. art.;* double Dutch *no indef. art.;* **juristisches/medizinisches ~:** legal/medical jargon; **ein ~ aus Deutsch, Englisch und Französisch** an incomprehensible hotchpotch of German, English, and French
kauderwelschen *itr. V.* talk gibberish *or* double Dutch
kauen ['kauən] **1.** *tr. V.* chew; masticate *(Med., formal);* **[die] Nägel ~:** bite *or* chew one's nails. **2.** *itr. V.* **a)** chew; **an etw.** *(Dat.)* **~:** chew [on] sth.; **an einem Problem ~** *(fig.)* wrestle *or* struggle with a problem; **un dieser Niederlage wird er noch einige Zeit zu ~ haben** *(fig.)* it will take him some time to get over this defeat; **mit vollen Backen ~** *(ugs.)* chew with one's mouth [stuffed] full; **b)** *(nagen, knabbern)* chew; bite; **an einem Bleistift/den Fingernägeln ~:** chew a pencil/bite *or* chew one's nails
kauern ['kauɐn] **1.** *itr. V.* crouch [down]; *(ängstlich)* cower. **2.** *refl. V.* crouch [down]; *(ängstlich)* cower; **sich an jmdn. ~:** huddle up to sb.
Kauf [kauf] **der; ~[e]s, Käufe** ['kɔyfə] **a)** *(das Kaufen)* buying; purchasing *(formal);* **den ~ vermitteln** arrange the purchase; **einen ~ abschließen/tätigen** complete/make a purchase; **jmdn. zum ~ ermuntern/veranlassen** encourage/induce sb. to buy; **jmdm. etw. zum ~ anbieten** offer sb. sth. for sale; **etw. in ~ nehmen** *(fig.)* accept sth.; **jmdn. in ~ nehmen** *(fig. ugs.)* put up with sb.; **b)** *(das käuflich Erworbene)* purchase
Kauf-: ~auftrag der order to buy *or* purchase; **~brief der** bill of sale; *(beim Hauskauf)* title deed
kaufen 1. *tr. V.* **a)** *(erwerben)* buy; purchase; **etw. billig/zu teuer ~:** buy sth. cheaply/pay too much for sth.; **sich/jmdm. etw. ~:** buy sth. for oneself/sb.; buy oneself/sb. sth.; **etw. auf Raten** *od.* **Abzahlung ~:** buy sth. on hire-purchase *(Brit.) or (Amer.)* the installment plan; **etw. auf Stottern** *od.* **Pump ~** *(ugs.)* buy sth. on the never-never *(Brit. coll.) or (Amer. coll.)* on time; **etw. für viel** *od.* **teures Geld ~:** pay a lot of money for sth.; **das wird viel** *od.* **gern gekauft** it sells well; **dafür kann ich mir nichts ~** *(ugs.)* a [fat] lot of use that is to me *(coll.);* **sich** *(Dat.)* **jmdn. ~** *(ugs.)* give sb. what for *(sl.);* let sb. have *or* give sb. a piece of one's mind; **b)** *(ugs.: bestechen)* buy. **2.** *itr. V. (einkaufen)* shop; **in diesem Laden kaufe ich nicht mehr** I'm not getting anything in that shop again
Käufer ['kɔyfɐ] **der; ~s, ~, Käuferin die; ~, ~nen** buyer; purchaser; *(Kunde/Kundin)* customer; *s. auch* **-in**
Käuferschicht die class of customer *or* consumer
kauf-, Kauf-: ~fahrer der *(veralt.),* **~fahrteischiff** [~fa:ɐ̯'tai̯-] **das** *(veralt.)* merchantman; **~frau die** businesswoman; *(Händlerin)* trader; merchant; **~haus das** department store; **~hausdetektiv der** store detective; **~kraft die** *(Wirtsch.)* **a)** *(Wert des Geldes)* purchasing power; **b)** *(Zahlungsfähigkeit)* spending power; **~kräftig** *Adj.* **ein ~kräftiger Kunde/Interessent** a customer with money to spend/a wealthy potential buyer; **~kräftig sein** have money to spend; **~laden der a)** *(veralt.) (kleiner Laden)* [small] shop; *(Lebensmittelladen)* [small] grocer's shop; **b)** *(Kinderspielzeug)* toy shop
käuflich ['kɔyflıç] **1.** *Adj.* **a)** *(gegen Bezahlung erhältlich)* for sale *postpos.;* **~e Liebe** *(fig.)* prostitution; **ein ~es Mädchen** *(fig.)* a woman/girl of easy virtue; **b)** *(bestechlich)* venal; **~ sein** be easily bought. **2.** *adv.* **etw. ~ erwerben/erstehen** buy *or* purchase sth.; **~ zu erwerben sein** be for sale
kauf-, Kauf-: ~lust die inclination *or* desire to buy; **~lustig** *Adj.* eager to buy *pred.;* **die Kauflustigen** the eager shoppers
Kaufmann der; *Pl.* **Kaufleute a)** *(Geschäftsmann)* businessman; *(Händler)* trader; merchant; **gelernter ~:** *person who has completed a course of training in some branch of business;* **b)** *(Besitzer eines Kaufladens)* shopkeeper; *(Besitzer eines Lebensmittelladens)* grocer; **zum ~ gehen** go to the shop/grocer's
kaufmännisch 1. *Adj.* commercial; business *attrib.;* commercial ⟨*bookkeeping*⟩; **~er Angestellter** clerk; employee in business; **einen ~en Beruf ergreifen/erlernen** go into business/receive a business training; **~es Geschick/~e Erfahrung haben** possess business skill/experience. **2.** *adv.* **~ tätig sein** be in business; **~ denken** think along commercial lines
Kaufmanns-: ~sprache die business parlance; **~stand der** *(veralt.)* merchant class
Kauf-: ~objekt das article for sale; *(Haus usw.)* property for sale; **~preis der** purchase price; **~rausch der** frantic urge to spend; **~summe die** purchase price; **~vertrag der** contract of sale; *(beim Hauskauf)* title-deed; **~zwang der** obligation to buy *or* purchase; **ohne ~zwang** without obligation [to buy *or* purchase]
Kaugummi der *od.* **das; ~s, ~s** chewing gum
Kaukasien [kau'ka:zi̯ən] **(das); ~s** Caucasia
Kaukasier der; ~s, ~: Caucasian
kaukasisch *Adj.* Caucasian
Kaukasus ['kaukazʊs] **der; ~:** the Caucasus
Kaulquappe ['kaulkvapə] **die; ~, ~n** tadpole
kaum [kaum] *Adv.* **a)** *(fast gar nicht)* hardly; scarcely; **~ jemand/etwas** hardly anybody *or* anyone/anything; **~ älter/größer/besser** hardly *or* scarcely any older/bigger/better; **wir haben ~ noch Zeit** we really haven't the time; **das war ~ noch zu erwarten** it was really too late to expect that; **b)** *(nur mit Mühe)* hardly; scarcely; barely; **ich kann es ~ glauben/erwarten** I can hardly believe it/wait; **ich konnte ~ rechtzeitig damit fertig werden** I could hardly *or* barely finish it in time; **diese Schrift ist ~ zu entziffern** this writing is barely decipherable; **c)** *(vermutlich nicht)* hardly; scarcely; **er wird [wohl] ~ zustimmen** he is hardly likely to agree; **ich glaube ~:** I hardly *or* scarcely think so; **es wird sich ~ lohnen** it is unlikely to be profitable; **d)** *(in dem Augenblick)* **~ hatte er Platz genommen, als ...:** no sooner had he sat down than ...; **e)** *(nicht lange nachdem)* **~ daß er aus dem Gefängnis gekommen war ...:** hardly *or* scarcely had he left prison when ...; **der Regen war, ~ daß er angefangen hatte, auch schon wieder vorüber** the rain had stopped almost as soon as it had started; **f)** *(geh.)* **~ daß ich mich an die Landschaft erinnere** I can hardly even remember the scenery
Kaumuskel der *(Anat.)* masticatory muscle; **[äußerer] ~:** masseter
kausal [kau'za:l] *Adj. (geh., Sprachw.)* causal
Kausalgesetz das; *o. Pl. (bes. Philos., Logik)* law of causality
Kausalität [kauzali'tɛ:t] **die; ~, ~en** causality

Kausalitäts·gesetz das *s.* **Kausalgesetz**
Kausal-: ~**kette die** *(bes. Philos., Logik)* causal chain; ~**satz der** *(Sprachw.)* causal clause; ~**zusammenhang der** *(bes. Philos., Logik)* causal connection
Kausativ ['kauzati:f] **das;** ~**s,** ~**e** [-i:və] *(Sprachw.)* causative verb
Kau·tabak der chewing tobacco
Kautel [kau'te:l] **die;** ~**,** ~**en;** *meist Pl. (Rechtsw.)* proviso
Kaution [kau'tsio:n] **die;** ~**,** ~**en a)** *(bei Freilassung eines Gefangenen)* bail; **eine ~ für jmdn. stellen** stand bail *or* surety for sb.; **gegen ~:** on bail; **jmdn. gegen ~ freibekommen** bail sb. out; **b)** *(beim Mieten einer Wohnung)* deposit
Kautschuk ['kautʃʊk] **der;** ~**s,** ~**e** [india] rubber
Kautschuk-: ~**milch die** rubber latex; ~**paragraph der** *(ugs.) s.* **Gummiparagraph**
Kauz [kauts] **der;** ~**es, Käuze** ['kɔytsə] **a)** *(Wald~)* tawny owl; *(Stein~)* little owl; **b)** *(Sonderling)* odd *or* strange fellow; oddball *(coll.)*; **ein komischer ~:** an odd *or* a queer bird *(coll.)*
Käuzchen ['kɔytsçən] **das;** ~**s,** ~**:** *s.* **Kauz a**
kauzig *Adj.* odd; queer; funny *(coll.)*
Kavalier [kava'li:ɐ] **der;** ~**s,** ~**e a)** *(höflicher Mann)* gentleman; **der ~ genießt und schweigt** a gentleman never talks about his amours; **b)** *(veralt., noch scherzh.: Freund)* beau *(dated)*; young man; **c)** *(hist.: Edelmann)* cavalier; nobleman
kavaliers-, Kavaliers-: ~**delikt das** trifling offence; peccadillo; ~**mäßig 1.** *Adj.* gentlemanly; **2.** *adv.* like a gentleman; in a gentlemanly manner; ~**start der** racing start
Kavalkade [kaval'ka:də] **die;** ~**,** ~**n** *(veralt.)* cavalcade
Kavallerie [kavalə'ri:] **die;** ~**,** ~**n** *(Milit. hist.)* cavalry
Kavallerie·pferd das cavalry horse
Kavallerist der; ~**en,** ~**en** cavalryman; trooper
Kavents·mann [ka'vɛnts-] **der** *(bes. nordd.) (übergroßes Exemplar)* monster
Kaverne [ka'vɛrnə] **die;** ~**,** ~**n a)** *(unterirdischer Hohlraum)* [artificial] cavern; **b)** *(Med.)* cavern
Kaviar ['ka:viar] **der;** ~**s,** ~**e** caviare
Kaviar·brot das French bread; **ein ~:** a French loaf
kcal *Abk.* **Kilo[gramm]kalorie** kcal
KdF *Abk. (ns.)* **Kraft durch Freude** Strength through Joy [movement]
Kebse ['ke:psə] **die;** ~**,** ~**n** *(hist.),* **Kebs·weib das** *(hist.)* concubine
keck [kɛk] **1.** *Adj.* **a)** *(respektlos)* impertinent; cheeky; saucy *(Brit.)*; **b)** *(veralt.: verwegen)* bold; **c)** *(flott)* jaunty, pert ⟨*hat etc.*⟩. **2.** *adv.* **a)** *(respektlos)* impertinently; cheekily; saucily *(Brit.)*; **b)** *(veralt.: verwegen)* boldly; **c)** *(flott)* jauntily
Keckheit die; ~**,** ~**en a)** *(Respektlosigkeit)* impertinence; cheek; sauce *(Brit.)*; **b)** *(veralt.: Kühnheit)* boldness
Keeper ['ki:pɐ] **der;** ~**s,** ~ *(Fußball, bes. österr.)* [goal]keeper
Kefir ['ke:fɪr] **der;** ~**s** kefir
Kegel ['ke:gl̩] **der;** ~**s,** ~ **a)** *(geometrischer Körper)* cone; **b)** *(Spielfigur)* skittle; *(beim Bowling)* pin; **~ schieben** *s.* **kegelschieben; c)** *(Berg~)* peak; **d)** *(Licht~)* beam; **e)** *(Druckw.)* body size; point size
kegel-, Kegel-: ~**abend der** skittles night; ~**bahn die** skittle alley; ~**bruder der** skittle-club friend; ~**förmig** *Adj.* conical; cone-shaped; ~**klub der** skittle club; ~**kugel die** [skittle] ball; ~**mantel der** *(Geom.)* lateral surface of a/the cone
kegeln 1. *itr. V.* **a)** *(eine Kegelpartie machen)* play skittles *or* ninepins; *(beim Bowling)* bowl; **b)** *mit sein (ugs.: hinfallen)* tumble. **2.** *tr. V.* **a)** *(durch Kegeln ausführen)* play; **b)** *(durch Kegeln erzielen)* bowl; score
kegel-, Kegel-: ~**rad das** *(Technik)* bevel wheel; ~**|schieben** *unr. itr. V.; Zusammenschreibung nur im Inf.* play skittles *or* ninepins; ~**schieben das** skittles *sing.;* ninepins *sing.;* ~**schnitt der** *(Geom.)* conic section; ~**sport der** skittles *sing.;* ninepins *sing.;* ~**stumpf der** truncated cone; frustum of a cone
Kegler der; ~**s,** ~**:** skittle player; *(bei Bowling)* [ten-pin] bowler
Kehle ['ke:lə] **die;** ~**,** ~**n a)** throat; **jmdm. an die ~ springen/fahren** leap at sb.'s throat; **sich** *(Dat.)* **die ~ schmieren** *od.* **ölen** *od.* **anfeuchten** wet one's whistle *(coll.)*; **sich** *(Dat.)* **die ~ aus dem Hals schreien** *(ugs.)* shout *or* yell one's head off; **aus voller ~:** at the top of one's voice; **sein ganzes Geld durch die ~ jagen** pour all one's money down one's throat; **etw. bleibt jmdm. in der ~ stecken** sth. sticks in sb.'s throat *or* gullet; **etw. in die falsche ~ bekommen** *(ugs.) (fig.: etw. mißverstehen)* take sth. the wrong way; *(sich an etw. verschlucken)* have sth. go down the wrong way; *s. auch* **Messer a; b)** *(Archit.)* hollow moulding; *(Dach~)* [roof] valley
kehlig 1. *Adj.* guttural ⟨*language, speech, sound, etc.*⟩; throaty, guttural ⟨*voice, laugh, etc.*⟩. **2.** *adv.* throatily; gutturally; in a throaty *or* guttural voice
Kehl·kopf der *(Anat.)* larynx
Kehlkopf-: ~**entzündung die** laryngitis *no indef. art.;* ~**krebs der** *(Med.)* cancer of the larynx; ~**mikrophon das** throat microphone; ~**spiegel der** *(Med.)* laryngoscope
Kehl·laut der a) guttural sound; **b)** *(Sprachw.)* guttural
Kehr-: ~**aus der;** ~ **a)** *(letzter Tanz)* last dance; **b)** *(Schluß einer Veranstaltung)* **den ~aus machen** finish; call it a day *(coll.)*; *(zumachen)* close; ~**besen der** broom; *(Handfeger)* brush; ~**blech das** *(bes. südd.)* small shovel *(used as dustpan)*
Kehre ['ke:rə] **die;** ~**,** ~**n a)** *(scharfe Kurve)* sharp bend *or* turn; *(Haarnadelkurve)* hairpin bend; **b)** *(geh.: Wende)* [abrupt] change of direction; **c)** *(Turnen)* back *or* rear vault
[1]**kehren 1.** *tr. V.* turn; **die Innenseite von etw. nach außen ~:** turn sth. inside out; **jmdm. den Rücken ~:** turn one's back on sb.; **die Augen zum Himmel ~:** raise one's eyes to the sky *or* heavenwards; **etw./alles zum Besten ~:** make sure sth./everything turns out for the best. **2.** *refl. V.* turn; **sich gegen jmdn./etw. ~:** turn against sb./sth.; **etw./alles wird sich zum Besten ~:** sth./everything will turn out all right; **sich an etw.** *(Dat.)* **nicht ~:** pay no attention to *or* not care about sth. **3.** *itr. V.* **a)** *(selten: umkehren)* turn [round]; **Abteilung kehrt!** *(Milit.)* squad, about turn *or (Amer.)* face!; **rechtsum/linksum kehrt!** right/left turn *or (Amer.)* face!; **b)** *mit sein (geh.: zurück~/ein~)* return; **in sich** *(Akk.)* **gekehrt** lost in thought; in a brown study; **ein in sich** *(Akk.)* **gekehrter Mensch** an introverted person
[2]**kehren 1.** *itr. V. (bes. südd.)* sweep; do the sweeping. **2.** *tr. V.* sweep; *(mit einem Handfeger)* brush; **den Staub von etw./auf etw.** *(Akk.)* **~:** sweep/brush the dust off sth./on to sth.
Kehricht ['ke:rɪçt] **der** *od.* **das;** ~**s a)** *(geh.: Schmutz, Unrat)* rubbish; **das geht dich einen feuchten ~ an!** *(salopp)* mind your own damned business!; **b)** *(schweiz.: Müll)* refuse; garbage *(Amer.)*
Kehricht-: ~**eimer der** dustbin; garbage can *(Amer.)*; ~**haufen der** pile *or* heap of rubbish; ~**schaufel die** *s.* **Kehrschaufel**
Kehr-: ~**maschine die** [mechanical] road sweeper; ~**reim der** refrain; ~**schaufel die** dustpan; ~**seite die a)** *(Rückseite)* back; *(einer Münze, Medaille)* reverse; *(eines Stoffes)* back; wrong side; **die ~seite der Medaille** *(fig.)* the other side of the coin; **b)** *(scherzh.) (Gesäß)* backside; *(Rücken)* back; **c)** *(nachteiliger Aspekt)* drawback; disadvantage
kehrt|machen *itr. V. (ugs.) (sich umdrehen)* do an about-turn; *(umkehren)* turn [round and go] back; *(plötzlich)* turn in one's tracks; **auf dem Absatz ~:** turn on one's heel
Kehrt·wendung die *(bes. Milit. od. fig.)* about-turn; about-face *(Amer.)*; **eine ~ machen** make *or* do an about-turn *or (Amer.)* about-face
Kehr·wert der *(Math.)* reciprocal
keifen ['kaifn̩] *itr. V. (abwertend)* nag; scold; **das Keifen der Marktfrauen** the squabbling *or* bickering of the market women
Keiferei [kaifə'rai] **die;** ~**,** ~**en** *(abwertend)* nagging; scolding
Keil [kail] **der;** ~**[e]s,** ~**e a)** *(zum Spalten)* wedge; **einen ~ in etw.** *(Akk.)* **treiben** drive a wedge into sth.; **einen ~ zwischen die beiden Freunde treiben** *(fig.)* drive a wedge between the two friends; **b)** *(zum Festklemmen)* chock; *(unter einer Tür)* wedge; **c)** *(bes. Milit.: keilförmige Formation)* wedge; **d)** *(Schneiderei)* [wedge-shaped] gusset
Keil·absatz der wedge [heel]
Keile ['kailə] **die;** ~ *(nordd.)* walloping *(sl.)*; thrashing; **~ bekommen** *od.* **kriegen** get a walloping *(sl.) or* thrashing
keilen 1. *refl. V. (ugs.: sich prügeln)* fight; scrap; **sich um etw. ~:** fight over sth. **2.** *tr. V.* **a)** *(fachspr.: mit einem Keil spalten)* split with a wedge; **b)** *(fachspr.: als Keil hineinschlagen)* **etw. in etw.** *(Akk.)* **~:** drive sth. into sth.; **c)** *(ugs.: anwerben)* rope in *(coll.)*; recruit. **3.** *itr. V. (ausschlagen)* kick
Keiler der; ~**s,** ~ *(Jägerspr.)* wild boar
Keilerei die; ~**,** ~**en** *(ugs.)* punch-up *(coll.)*; brawl; fight; **eine allgemeine ~:** a free-for-all
keil-, Keil-: ~**förmig** wedge-shaped; cuneiform ⟨*lettering, script*⟩; ~**hose die** tapering trousers; *(Skihose)* tapering skipants; ~**kissen das** wedge-shaped bolster; ~**riemen der** *(Technik)* V-belt; ~**schrift die** cuneiform script
Keim [kaim] **der;** ~**[e]s,** ~**e a)** *(Bot.: erster Trieb)* shoot; **b)** *(Biol.: befruchtete Eizelle)* embryo; **c)** *(Ursprung, Ausgangspunkt)* seed[s *pl.*]; **etw. im ~ ersticken** nip sth. in the bud; **den ~ zu etw. legen** sow the seeds *pl.* of sth.; **d)** *meist Pl. (Biol., Med.: Krankheitserreger)* germ; **e)** *(Physik)* nucleus
Keim-: ~**blatt das a)** *(Bot.)* cotyledon; seed leaf; **b)** *(Biol., Med.)* germ layer; ~**drüse die** *(Zool., Med.)* gonad; ~**drüsen·hormon das** sex hormone
keimen *itr. V.* **a)** *(zu sprießen beginnen)* germinate; sprout; **b)** *(innerlich entstehen)* ⟨*hope*⟩ stir; ⟨*thought, belief, decision*⟩ form; ⟨*love, yearning*⟩ awaken
keim-, Keim-: ~**fähig** *Adj.* viable; capable of germinating *postpos.;* ~**fähigkeit die;** *o. Pl.* viability; ability to germinate; ~**frei** *Adj.* germ-free; sterile; **etw. ~frei machen** sterilize sth.; **~freie Milch** sterilized milk; **~frei verpackt/gelagert** packed in sterile containers/stored in sterile conditions
keimhaft 1. *Adj. (geh.)* incipient; *(noch nicht ausgeprägt)* embryonic. **2.** *adv.* **~ angelegt** embryonically present
Keimling ['kaimlɪŋ] **der;** ~**s,** ~**e** *(Bot.)* embryo
keim-, Keim-: ~**scheibe die** *(Biol.)* blastodisc; germinal disc; ~**tötend** *Adj.* germicidal; ~**träger der** *(Med.)* carrier
Keimung die; ~**,** ~**en** germination
Keim·zelle die a) *(Ausgangspunkt)* nucleus; **b)** *(Bot.)* germ-cell; **c)** *s.* **Gamet**

kein [kain] *Indefinitpron.* **a)** no; *(bei abstrakten Begriffen)* no; not any; **er hat ~ Wort gesagt** he didn't say a word; he said not a word; **er konnte ~e Arbeit finden** he could find no work; he could not find any work; **ich habe ~ Geld/~e Zeit** I have no money/time; I don't have any money/time; **hat er ~e Kinder?** has he no children?; **kennst du ~e Deutschen/~en Deutschen, der ...?** don't you know any Germans/a German who ...?; **~ Mensch/~ einziger** nobody *or* no one/not a single one; **in ~er Weise/unter ~en Umständen** in no way/in *or* under no circumstances; **das ist ~ dummer Vorschlag** that's not a bad suggestion; **er ist ~ Dichter** he is not a poet; *(er dichtet schlecht)* he is no poet; **zwischen den beiden Vorgängen besteht ~ großer Unterschied** there's no great difference between the two processes; **~ anderer als er kann es gewesen sein** it can't have been anybody else but him; **b)** *(ugs.: nicht ganz, nicht einmal)* less than; **es ist ~e drei Tage her, daß ich zuletzt dort war** it's not *or* it's less than three days since I was last there; **sie ist noch ~e zehn Jahre alt** she's not ten years old yet; **es dauert ~e fünf Minuten** it won't take five minutes; **c)** *alleinstehend (niemand/nichts)* nobody; no one; **~er von uns** not one of us; none of us; **ich kenne ~en, der dir helfen kann** I don't know anyone who can help you; **keins von beiden** neither [of them]; **ich wollte ~es von beiden** I didn't want either of them; **mir kann ~er!** *(salopp)* I can look after myself!; **Kannst du mir Geld geben? – Ich habe selbst ~[e]s mehr** Can you give me some money? – No, I haven't any left either; **d)** *alleinstehend (überhaupt nicht)* **Post kam ~e** there was no *or* wasn't any post *or* mail; **Lust habe ich ~e** I don't feel like it

keinerlei *indekl. unbest. Gattungsz.* no ... at all; no ... what[so]ever

keiner·seits *Adv. (selten)* **ihr Vorschlag fand ~ Zustimmung** her suggestion met with no support anywhere *or* from any side

keines·falls *Adv.* on no account; **die Aufgabe ist schwer, aber ~ unlösbar** the problem is difficult but by no means insoluble

keines·wegs *Adv.* by no means; not by any means; not at all; **sein Einfluß darf ~ unterschätzt werden** his influence must in no way be underestimated; **ich nehme euch eure Offenheit ~ übel** I'm not in any way *or* not in the least offended by your frankness

kein·mal *Adv.* not [even] once; *s. auch* **einmal a**

Keks [ke:ks] **der;** ~ *od.* **~es,** ~ *od.* **~e** (*österr.:* **~, ~[e]**) biscuit *(Brit.)*; cookie *(Amer.)*; **~[e] essen/backen** eat/bake biscuits/cookies; **das/er geht mir auf den ~** *(salopp)* it/he gets up my nose *(sl.)*

Kelch [kɛlç] **der; ~[e]s, ~e a)** *(Trinkgefäß)* goblet; **den [bitteren] ~ bis auf den Grund** *od.* **bis zur Neige leeren [müssen]** *(geh.)* [have to] drain the [bitter] cup to the dregs; **der ~ ist an uns/ihm vorübergegangen** *(geh.)* we were/he was spared that ordeal; **b)** *(Rel.)* chalice; communion cup; **c)** *(Bot.)* calyx

kelch-, Kelch-: ~blatt das *(Bot.)* sepal; **~förmig** *Adj.* goblet-shaped; **~glas das** goblet

Kelim ['ke:lɪm] **der; ~s, ~s** Kilim

Kelle ['kɛlə] **die; ~, ~n a)** *(Schöpflöffel)* ladle; **b)** *(Signalstab)* signalling disc; **c)** *(Maurer~)* trowel; **d)** *(ugs.)* *(Tischtennisschläger)* bat; *(Tennisschläger)* racket

Keller ['kɛlɐ] **der; ~s, ~ a)** cellar; *(einer Burg usw.)* cellars *pl.*; *(~geschoß)* basement; **der Dollar/der Kurs des Dollars ist in den ~ gefallen** *(fig.)* the dollar has gone through the floor *(fig.)*; **im ~ sein** *(Skat Jargon)* have a minus score *or* minus points; **b)** *(~raum)* cellar; **c)** *(ugs.: Weinvorrat)* cellar; **d)** *(Luftschutz)* [air-raid] shelter; **e)** *s.* **Kellerlokal**

Keller·assel die wood-louse

Kellerei die; ~, ~en a) *(~betrieb)* winery; wine producer's; **b)** *(Kellerräume)* [wine] cellars *pl.*

Keller-: ~fenster das cellar window; *(von ~geschoß)* basement window; **~geschoß das** basement; **~gewölbe das** underground vault; **~kind das** *(ugs.)* slum child *or (sl.)* kid; **~lokal das** cellar bar/disco *etc.*; *(Restaurant)* cellar restaurant; **~meister der** maître de chai; **~treppe die** cellar stairs *pl.*; *(zum ~geschoß)* basement stairs *pl.*; **~wohnung die** basement flat *(Brit.) or (Amer.)* apartment

Kellner ['kɛlnɐ] **der; ~s, ~:** waiter

Kellnerin die; ~, ~nen waitress

kellnern *itr. V. (ugs.)* work as a waiter/waitress

Kelte ['kɛltə] **der; ~n, ~n** Celt

Kelter ['kɛltɐ] **die; ~, ~n** *(für Weintrauben)* winepress; *(für andere Obstarten)* fruit-press

Kelterei die; ~, ~en *(für Weintrauben)* grape crushing and pressing plant; *(für andere Obstarten)* fruit crushing and pressing plant

keltern *tr. V.* press ‹*grapes etc.*›

keltisch *Adj.* Celtic

Keltisch das; ~[s] Celtic; *s. auch* **Deutsch**

Kelvin ['kɛlvɪn] **das; ~s, ~** *(Phys.)* kelvin

Kemenate [keme'na:tə] **die; ~, ~n** [ladies'] heated apartments *pl. (in a medieval castle)*

Kenia ['ke:nia] **(das); ~s** Kenya

Kenianer [ke'nia:nɐ] **der; ~s, ~, Kenianerin die; ~, ~nen** Kenyan; *s. auch* **-in**

Kenn·daten ['kɛn-] *Pl. (fachspr.)* personal data *or* details

kennen ['kɛnən] *unr. tr. V.* **a)** know; **das Leben ~:** know about life; know the ways of the world; **das ~ wir gar nicht anders** *(haben es nie anders gemacht)* we've always done it that way; *(haben es erfahren)* it's always been like that; **jmdn. als Schriftsteller/Feigling ~:** know sb. as a writer/know sb. to be a coward; **kennst du den?** *(diesen Mann)* do you know who he is?; *(bist du mit ihm bekannt)* are you acquainted with him?; *(diesen Witz)* have you heard this one?; **jmds. Bücher/Werk ~:** know *or* be acquainted with sb.'s books/work; **da kennst du mich aber schlecht** *(ugs.)* that just shows you don't know me very well; **das kennen wir [schon]** *(ugs. abwertend) (das ist nichts Neues)* we've heard all that before; *(diese Ausrede kennen wir)* we've heard that one before; **sich nicht mehr ~ [vor ...]** be beside oneself [with ...]; **einen guten Arzt/ein gutes Restaurant ~:** know [of] a good doctor/restaurant; **da kenne ich/da kennt er nichts** *(ugs.)* and to hell with everything else *(coll.)*; **b)** *(bekannt sein mit)* know; be acquainted with; **jmdn. flüchtig/persönlich ~:** know sb. slightly/personally; **die beiden ~ sich nicht mehr** the two are no longer on speaking terms; **ich glaube, wir beide ~ uns noch nicht** I don't think we've been introduced; **er will mich nicht mehr ~:** he doesn't want to know me any more; **c)** *(haben)* have; **keinen Winter/Sommer ~:** have no winter/summer; **er kennt keine Kopfschmerzen** he never gets a headache; **kein Mitleid ~:** know *or* have no pity; **d)** *(wiedererkennen)* know; recognize; **na, kennst du mich noch?** well, do you remember me?; **jmdn. am Gang/an der Stimme ~:** know *or* recognize sb. by his/her walk/voice

kennen|lernen *tr. V.* **a)** *(Kenntnis erlangen)* get to know; acquaint oneself with; **jmdn./etw. näher ~:** get to know sb./sth. better; become better acquainted with sb./sth.; **jmdn. von einer bestimmten Seite ~:** see a particular side of sb.; **jmdn. als einen bescheidenen Menschen** *usw.* **~:** come to know sb. as a modest person *etc.*; **b)** *(bekannt werden mit)* get to know; become acquainted with; *(erstmals begegnen)* meet; **freut mich, Sie kennenzulernen** pleased to meet you; pleased to make your acquaintance *(formal)*; **c)** *(in Berührung gebracht werden mit)* come to know; **du wirst mich noch ~!** you'll find out I don't stand for any nonsense

Kenner der; ~s, ~ a) *(Fachmann)* expert, authority (+ *Gen.* on); **b)** *(von Wein, Speisen)* connoisseur; **dieser Wein ist etwas für den ~:** this is a wine for the connoisseur

Kennerblick der expert eye; **mit ~:** with an expert eye; **er warf ~e auf die Ausstellungsstücke** he cast an expert eye over the exhibits

Kennerin die; ~, ~nen *s.* **Kenner**

Kenner·miene die air of an expert/connoisseur; **mit ~:** with the air of an expert/connoisseur

Kennerschaft die; ~: connoisseurship; *(Sachkenntnis)* expertise

Kenn-: ~karte die identity card; **~marke die** [police] identification badge; ≈ [police] warrant card *or (Amer.)* ID card; **~melodie die** *(Rundf.)* signature tune; **~nummer die** *s.* **Kennummer**

kenntlich ['kɛntlɪç] *Adj.* **~ sein** be recognizable *or* distinguishable **(an** by); **etw./jmdn. ~ machen** mark sth./make sb. [easily] identifiable; **etw. als Gift ~ machen** mark *or* label sth. as a poison

Kenntnis ['kɛntnɪs] **die; ~, ~se a)** *o. Pl. (das Kennen, Wissen)* knowledge; **von etw. ~ haben/erhalten** be informed on sth. *or* have knowledge of sth./learn *or* hear about sth.; **das entzieht sich meiner ~** *(geh.)* I have no knowledge of that; **von etw. ~ nehmen, etw. zur ~ nehmen** take note of sth.; **jmdn. von etw. in ~ setzen** inform *or* notify sb. of sth.; **jmdn. zur ~ nehmen** take notice of sb.; **b)** *Pl. (Sach- und Erfahrungswissen)* knowledge *sing.*; **oberflächliche/gründliche ~se von etw. haben** have a superficial/thorough knowledge of sth.; **~se in Mathematik** *od.* **auf dem Gebiet der Mathematik** a knowledge of mathematics

Kenntnisnahme die; ~ *(Papierdt.)* **jmdm. etw. zur ~ vorlegen** submit sth. to sb. for his/her attention; **wir bitten um gefällige ~ der Akten** please give these documents your kind attention; **nach ~ der Akten** after giving the documents my/his *etc.* attention

kenntnis·reich *Adj.* well-informed; knowledgeable

Kennummer die; ~, ~n reference number; code number; *(eines Agenten)* code number

kenn-, Kenn-: ~wort das; *Pl.* **~wörter a)** *(Erkennungszeichen)* code-word; reference; **b)** *(Parole)* password; code-word; **~zahl die a)** *(charakteristischer Zahlenwert)* index; **b)** *(Fernspr.)* code; **~zeichen das a)** *(Merkmal)* sign; mark; **ein ~zeichen für einen Witterungsumschlag** a sign of a change in the weather; **ein ~zeichen eines Genies** a [hall]mark of a genius; **besondere ~zeichen** distinguishing marks; **b)** *(Erkennungszeichen)* badge; *(auf einem Behälter, einer Ware usw.)* label; **etw. als ~zeichen tragen** carry/wear sth. as a means of identification; *(einer Gruppe)* carry/wear sth. as an indication of membership; **c)** *(am Fahrzeug)* registration number; **~zeichnen** *tr. V.* **a)** *(mit einem Kennzeichen versehen)* mark; label ‹*container, goods, etc.*›; mark, signpost ‹*way*›; tag ‹*bird, animal*›; **etw. als ... ~zeichnen** mark *or* identify sth. as ...; **b)** *(charakterisieren)* characterize; **jmdn. als ... ~zeichnen** characterize sb. as ...; **c)** *(in seiner Eigenart erkennen lassen)* typify; **jmdn. als ... ~zeichnen** mark sb. out as ...; **~zeichnend** *Adj.* typical, characteristic **(für** of); **~zeichnung die a)** marking; *(von Behältern, Waren)* labelling; *(von Vögeln, Tieren)* tagging; **b)** *(Charakterisierung)* characterization; **c)** *(Kennzeichen)* label;

eine auffällige ~zeichnung von Fußgängerüberwegen a conspicuous means of marking pedestrian crossings; **d)** *(Logik)* definite description; **~ziffer die a)** *(Ziffer zur Unterscheidung)* reference number; *(bei einem Zeitungsinserat)* box number; **b)** *(Math.)* characteristic

Kenotaph [keno'ta:f] **das; ~s, ~e** cenotaph

Kentaur [kɛn'tau̯ɐ] **der; ~en, ~en** *s.* **Zentaur**

kentern ['kɛntɐn] *itr. V.* **a)** *mit sein* ‹*boat, ship, etc.*› capsize; **b)** *(Seemannsspr.)* ‹*tide, wind*› turn

Keramik [ke'ra:mɪk] **die; ~, ~en a)** *o. Pl. (gebrannter Ton)* ceramics *pl.;* pottery; **b)** *(~gegenstand)* ceramic; piece of pottery; **c)** *(Material)* fired clay; **d)** *o. Pl. (Technik)* ceramics *sing.;* pottery

keramisch *Adj.; nicht präd.* ceramic

Kerbe ['kɛrbə] **die; ~, ~n** notch; **in dieselbe** *od.* **die gleiche ~ hauen** *od.* **schlagen** *(ugs.)* take the same line

Kerbel ['kɛrbl̩] **der; ~s** chervil

kerben *tr. V.* **a)** *(mit Kerben versehen)* notch; cut a notch/notches in; **b)** carve ‹*pattern etc.*›

Kerb-: ~holz das *in* **etwas/einiges auf dem ~holz haben** *(ugs.)* have done a job/a job or two *(sl.)*; **~tier das** insect

Kerker ['kɛrkɐ] **der; ~s, ~ a)** *(hist.: Gefängnis)* dungeons *pl.;* *(einzelne Zelle)* dungeon; **b)** *(österr., hist.: Freiheitsstrafe)* imprisonment

Kerker-: ~haft die *(hist.)* imprisonment; **~meister der** *(hist.)* jailer; **~strafe die** *(österr., hist.)* *s.* **Gefängnisstrafe**

Kerl [kɛrl] **der; ~s, ~e** *(nordd., md. auch: ~s)* **a)** *(ugs.: männliche Person)* fellow *(coll.)*; chap *(coll.)*; bloke *(Brit. sl.)*; **ein ganzer** *od.* **richtiger ~:** a splendid fellow *(coll.) or* chap *(coll.)*; **ein gemeiner/frecher ~** *(abwertend)* a nasty so-and-so *(coll.)*/an impudent fellow *(coll.)*; **b)** *(ugs.: sympathischer Mensch)* **er ist ein feiner ~:** he's a fine chap *(coll.) or (sl.)* a good bloke; **sie ist ein netter/feiner ~:** she's a nice/fine woman

Kern [kɛrn] **der; ~[e]s, ~e a)** *(Fruchtsamen)* pip; *(von Steinobst)* stone; *(von Nüssen, Mandeln usw.)* kernel; **der ~ eines Problems/Vorschlags** *(fig.)* the crux *or* gist of a problem/gist of a suggestion; **er hat einen guten** *od.* **in ihm steckt ein guter ~** *(fig.)* he is good at heart; **das birgt einen wahren ~** *(fig.)* it contains a core of truth; **zum ~ einer Sache** *(Gen.)* **kommen** *(fig.)* get to the heart of a matter; **b)** *(wichtigster Teil einer Gruppe)* core; nucleus; **der harte ~:** the hard core; **c)** *(Physik: Atom~)* nucleus; **d)** *(einer elektrischen Spule, eines Reaktors)* core; **e)** *(Gießerei)* core; **f)** *(Biol.: Zell~)* nucleus; *(Anat., Biol.: Nerven~)* centre; **g)** *(Zentrum)* city/town centre; **h)** *(Met.)* **mit seinem ~ über Schottland liegend** ‹*depression etc.*› centred over Scotland

kern-, Kern-: ~beißer der hawfinch; **~brenn·stoff der** nuclear fuel; **~chemie die** nuclear chemistry; **~energie die** nuclear energy *no art.;* **~explosion die a)** *(von atomaren Sprengkörpern)* nuclear explosion; **b)** *(Physik)* [complete] fragmentation of the nucleus; **~fach das** *(Schulw.)* core subject; **~fäule die** *(Forstw.)* heart-rot; **~forschung die** nuclear research; **~frage die** central question; **~frucht die** *(Bot.)* pome; **~fusion die** *(Phys., Biol.)* nuclear fusion *no art.;* **~gedanke der** central idea; **~gehäuse das** core; **~gesund** *Adj.* fit as a fiddle *pred.;* sound as a bell *pred.;* **~haus das** *s.* **~gehäuse; ~holz das** *(Holzverarb.)* heartwood

kernig 1. *Adj.* **a)** *(urwüchsig, markig)* robust, earthy ‹*language*›; down-to-earth ‹*remarks*›; *(kraftvoll)* powerful, forceful ‹*speech*›; pithy ‹*saying*›; **ein ~er Mann/Typ** *(ugs.)* a robust and athletic man/type; **b)** *(fest, haltbar)* robust, stout, sturdy ‹*boots, shoes*›; sound ‹*wood*›; robust ‹*leather*›; **c)** *(gehaltvoll, kräftig)* full-bodied ‹*wine*›; **d)** *(ugs.: vortrefflich)* great *(coll.)*; **e)** *(voller Kerne)* full of pips *pred.* **2.** *adv.* **a)** *(urwüchsig, markig)* robustly; *(kraftvoll)* forcefully; *(knapp)* pithily ‹*expressed*›; **b)** *(ugs.: vortrefflich)* **wir haben ~ gezecht und geschwoft** we had a whale of a time drinking and dancing *(coll.)*

Kern·kraft die a) *Pl. (Physik)* nuclear forces; **b)** nuclear power *no art.*

Kernkraft-: ~gegner der opponent of nuclear power; **~werk das** nuclear power station *or* plant

Kern·ladungszahl die atomic number

kern-, Kern-: ~los *Adj.* seedless; **~obst das** pomaceous fruit; pomes *pl.;* **~pflicht·fach das** *(Schulw.)* core-curriculum subject; **~physik die** nuclear physics *sing., no art.;* **~physiker der** nuclear physicist; **~punkt der** central point; **~reaktion die** *(Physik)* nuclear reaction; **~reaktor der** nuclear reactor; **~satz der a)** *(wesentlicher Satz)* key sentence *or* statement; **b)** *(Sprachw.) basic structural form of the sentence, with the finite verb as the second idea;* kernel sentence; **~schatten der** *(Optik, Astron.)* umbra; total shadow; **~seife die** washing soap; hard soap; **~spaltung die** *(Physik)* nuclear fission *no art.;* **~spruch der** wise saw *or* saying; **~stück das** centre-piece; *(einer Diskussion, eines Programms)* central *or* main item; *(eines Plans)* main point; **~technik die** nuclear engineering *no art.;* **~truppe die** crack unit; **~verschmelzung die** *(Physik, Biol.)* nuclear fusion *no art.;* **~waffe die;** *meist Pl.* nuclear weapon; **~waffen·frei** *Adj.* nuclear-free; **~waffen·versuch der** nuclear [weapons] test; **~zeit die** core time

Kerosin [kero'zi:n] **das; ~s** kerosene

Kerze ['kɛrtsə] **die; ~, ~n a)** candle; **elektrische ~:** candle bulb; **b)** *(Zünd~)* sparkplug; sparking-plug; **c)** *(Turnen Jargon)* shoulder stand; **d)** *(Physik veralt.)* candela

kerzen-, Kerzen-: ~beleuchtung die candle-light *no indef. art.;* **~docht der** [candle] wick; **~gerade,** *(ugs.)* **~grade 1.** *Adj.* dead straight ‹*tree, post, etc.*›; very stiff ‹*bow*›; **2.** *adv.* bolt upright; ‹*rise*› straight upwards; **~halter der** candle-holder; **~leuchter der** candlestick; *(für mehrere Kerzen)* candelabrum; **~licht das;** *o. Pl.* the light of a candle/of candles; **bei ~licht** by candle-light; **~schein der;** *o. Pl.* candle-light *no pl.;* **~schlüssel der** *(Kfz-W.)* plug spanner; **~stummel der, ~stumpf der** stump of a/the candle

Kescher ['kɛʃɐ] **der; ~s, ~** *(für Fische)* hand-net; fishing-net; *(für Schmetterlinge)* butterfly-net

keß [kɛs] **1.** *Adj.* **a)** *(hübsch, flott)* pert; pert, jaunty ‹*hat, dress, etc.*›; *s. auch* **Sohle a; b)** *(frech, vorlaut)* cheeky; **c)** *(salopp)* **kesser Vater** bulldyke *(sl.)*; butch *(sl.)*. **2.** *adv.* **a)** *(hübsch, flott)* jauntily; **b)** *(frech, vorlaut)* cheekily

Kessel ['kɛsl̩] **der; ~s, ~ a)** *(Tee~)* kettle; **b)** *(zum Kochen)* pot; *(für offenes Feuer)* cauldron; *(in einer Brauerei)* vat; *(Wasch~)* copper; wash-boiler; **c)** *(Berg~)* basin-shaped valley; **d)** *(Milit.)* encircled area; *(kleiner)* pocket; **e)** *(Jägerspr.)* ring of hunters and beaters; **f)** *(Dampf~, Heiz~)* boiler

Kessel-: ~fleisch das *s.* **Wellfleisch; ~flicker der** *(veralt.)* tinker; **~haus das** boiler-house; **~jagd die** *s.* **~treiben a; ~pauke die** kettledrum; **~raum der** boiler-room; **~schlacht die** battle of encirclement; **~schmied der** boilermaker; **~schmiede die** boiler shop; **~stein der;** *o. Pl.* fur; scale; **~treiben das a)** *(Jägerspr.: Treibjagd)* battue *(using a circle of hunters and beaters)*; **b)** *(Hetzkampagne)* witch-hunt; **~wagen der** *(Kfz-W.)* road tanker; tanker lorry *(Brit.)*; tank truck *(Amer.)*; *(Eisenbahn)* tank-wagon; tank-car

Ketchup ['kɛtʃap] **der** *od.* **das; ~[s], ~s** ketchup

Ketsch [kɛtʃ] **die; ~, ~en** *(Segeln)* ketch

Kettchen ['kɛtçən] **das; ~s, ~:** [neck-]chain *(with cross etc. attached)*; *(Fuß~)* anklet; *(Arm~)* bracelet

Kette ['kɛtə] **die; ~, ~n a)** chain; *(von Kettenfahrzeugen)* track; **die ~ [an der Tür] vorlegen** put the chain across [the door]; **an der ~ liegen** ‹*dog*› be chained up; **jmdn. in ~n legen** put sb. in chains; **die ~n abwerfen/sprengen** *od.* **zerreißen** *(fig. geh.)* cast off *or* throw off/break one's chains *or* shackles; **jmdn. an die ~ legen** *(fig.)* keep sb. on a [tight *or* short] leash; **b)** *(Halsschmuck)* necklace; *(eines Bürgermeisters usw.)* chain; **c)** *(Reihe)* chain; *(von Autos)* line; **eine ~ bilden** form a chain; **eine ~ von Beweisen** a chain of evidence; **die ~ der Berge** the chain of mountains; **~ rauchen** *(ugs.)* chain-smoke; **d)** *(von Ereignissen)* string; series; **e)** *(Weberei)* warp

Kettel·maschine ['kɛtl̩-] **die** *(Textilw.)* looper

ketten *tr. V.* **a)** *(mit einer Kette anbinden)* chain **(an** + *Akk.* to); **b)** *(unauflösbar binden)* bind; **jmdn. an sich** *(Akk.)* **~:** bind sb. to oneself; **sich an jmdn. ~:** tie oneself to sb.

Ketten-: ~antrieb der chain drive; chain transmission; **~armband das** *(für eine Armbanduhr)* [mesh-link/open-link] bracelet; *(Schmuck)* [chain] bracelet; **~brücke die** chain bridge; **~fahrzeug das** *s.* **Raupenfahrzeug; ~glied das** [chain-]link; **~hemd das** *(hist.)* coat of chain mail; **~hund der a)** watch-dog *or* guard-dog *(kept on a chain)*; **b)** *(Milit. Jargon)* Military Policeman; **~laden der** chain store; **~panzer der** chain mail; chain-armour; **~rauchen das; ~s** chain-smoking *no art.;* **~raucher der** chain-smoker; **~reaktion die** chain reaction; **eine ~reaktion auslösen** trigger a chain reaction; **~säge die** chain saw; **~schluß der** *(Logik)* chain syllogism; sorites; **~schutz der** chain guard; **~stich der** *(Handarb.)* chain stitch

Ketzer ['kɛtsɐ] **der; ~s, ~** *(auch fig.)* heretic

Ketzerei die; ~, ~en *(auch fig.)* heresy

Ketzer·gericht das *(hist.)* Inquisition

Ketzerin die; ~, ~nen *(auch fig.)* heretic

ketzerisch *(auch fig.)* **1.** *Adj.* heretical. **2.** *adv.* heretically

keuchen ['kɔyçn̩] *itr. V.* **a)** *(schwer atmen)* pant; gasp for breath; *(fig.)* ‹*locomotive*› chug; **mit ~dem Atem** gasping *or* panting for breath; **b)** *mit sein (sich keuchend fortbewegen)* puff *or* pant one's way; come/go puffing *or* panting along

Keuch·husten der whooping cough *no art.*

Keule ['kɔylə] **die; ~, ~n a)** *(Schlagwaffe)* club; cudgel; **chemische ~:** Chemical Mace **(P); b)** *(Gymnastik)* [Indian] club; **c)** *(Kochk.)* leg; *(Reh~, Hasen~)* haunch; *(Gänse~, Hühner~)* drumstick; leg

Keulen-: ~hieb der, ~schlag der blow with a club *or* cudgel; *(fig.)* terrible blow; **~schwingen das** *(Gymnastik)* club swinging; swinging [Indian] clubs

keusch [kɔyʃ] **1.** *Adj.* **a)** *(sexuell enthaltsam)* chaste; pure; **b)** *(geh. veralt.) (sittsam)* modest; demure; *(sittlich und moralisch rein)* pure. **2.** *adv.* **a)** *(sexuell enthaltsam)* **~ leben** lead a chaste life; **b)** *(sittsam)* modestly; demurely; *(sittlich und moralisch rein)* in a pure manner

Keuschheit die; ~ a) *(sexuelle Enthaltsamkeit)* chastity; **b)** *(geh. veralt.) (Sittsamkeit)* modesty; *(sittliche und moralische Reinheit)* purity

Keuschheits-: ~gelübde das vow of chastity; **~gürtel der** chastity belt
Kfz [ka:|ɛf'tsɛt] *Abk.* **Kraftfahrzeug**
kg *Abk.* **Kilogramm** kg
KG *Abk.* **Kommanditgesellschaft**
K-Gruppe ['ka:-] **die** *(Politik) [anti-Soviet] Communist organization*
¹Khaki ['ka:ki] **der; ~[s]** *(Stoff)* khaki
²Khaki das; ~[s] *(Farbe)* khaki
khaki·farben *Adj.* khaki[-coloured]
kHz *Abk.* **Kilohertz** kHz
Kibbuz [kɪ'bu:ts] **der; ~, ~im** [kɪbu'tsi:m] *od.* ~e kibbutz
Kibbuznik [kɪ'bu:tsnɪk] **der; ~s, ~s** kibbutznik
Kicher·erbse die chick-pea
kichern ['kɪçn̩] *itr. V.* giggle; **in sich hinein/vor sich hin ~:** giggle to oneself; **daß ich nicht kichere!** *(iron.)* don't make me laugh!
Kick [kɪk] **der; ~[s], ~s** *(Fußball, ugs.)* kick
Kick·down [kɪk'daʊn] **das; ~s, ~s** *(Kfz-W.)* kick-down
kicken *(ugs.)* **1.** *itr. V.* play football. **2.** *tr. V.* kick
Kicker der; ~s, ~[s] *(ugs.)* footballer; [football-]player
Kick·starter der *(Kfz-W.)* kick-starter; kick-start
kidnappen ['kɪtnɛpn̩] *tr. V.* kidnap
Kidnapper der; ~s, ~: kidnapper
Kidnapping ['kɪtnɛpɪŋ] **das; ~s, ~s** kidnapping
kiebig ['ki:bɪç] *Adj. (bes. nordd.) (frech)* cheeky; impertinent; *(gereizt)* touchy
Kiebitz ['ki:bɪts] **der; ~es, ~e a)** *(Vogel)* lapwing; peewit; **b)** *(ugs.: Zuschauer beim Spiel)* kibitzer *(coll.)*
kiebitzen *itr. V. (ugs. scherzh.)* **a)** *(bei einem Spiel zuschauen)* kibitz *(coll.)*; **b)** *(neugierig beobachten)* look on
¹Kiefer ['ki:fɐ] **der; ~s, ~:** jaw; *(~knochen)* jaw-bone
²Kiefer die; ~, ~n a) *(Nadelbaum)* pine-[tree]; **b)** *o. Pl. (Holz)* pine[-wood]
Kiefer-: ~bruch der *(Med.)* fracture of the jaw; fractured jaw; **~chirurgie die** oral surgery *no art.*; **~höhle die** *(Anat.)* maxillary sinus; **~höhlen·entzündung die** maxillary sinusitis *no art.*; **~klemme die** *(Med.)* lockjaw; trismus *(Med.)*; **~knochen der** jaw-bone
Kiefern-: ~holz das pine[-wood]; **~nadel die** pine-needle; **~wald der** pinewood; *(größer)* pine forest; **~zapfen der** pine-cone
Kiefer·orthopädie die orthodontics *sing., no art.*
kieken ['ki:kn̩] *itr. V. (nordd.)* look
Kieker ['ki:kɐ] **der; ~s, ~ a)** *(Seemannsspr.) (Fernglas)* binoculars *pl.*; *(Fernrohr)* telescope; **b)** *in* **jmdn. auf dem ~ haben** *(ugs.)* have it in for sb. *(coll.)*; *(mißtrauisch beobachten)* keep a careful eye *or* watch on sb.
kieksen ['ki:ksn̩] *s.* **gicksen**
¹Kiel [ki:l] **der; ~[e]s, ~e** keel; **ein Schiff auf ~ legen** *(Schiffsbau)* lay down a ship; lay the keel of a ship
²Kiel der; ~[e]s, ~e a) *(Teil einer Vogelfeder)* quill; **b)** *(hist.: Schreibfeder)* quill[-pen]
kiel-, Kiel-: ~feder die quill-feather; **~holen** *tr. V. (Seemannsspr.)* **a)** *(auf die Seite legen)* careen ⟨*ship*⟩; **b)** *(unter dem Schiff hindurchziehen)* keel-haul; **~oben** [-'--] *Adv.* bottom up; **~raum der** bilge; **~wasser das** wake; **in jmds. ~wasser segeln** *od.* **schwimmen** *(fig.)* follow in sb.'s wake
Kieme ['ki:mə] **die; ~, ~n;** *meist Pl.* gill
Kiemen-: ~atmer [~|a:tmɐ] **der; ~s, ~** *(Zool.)* gill-breathing animal; gill-breather; **~spalte die;** *meist Pl. (Zool.)* gill slit
Kien [ki:n] **der; ~[e]s** resinous wood; *(Kiefernholz)* resinous pine-wood
Kien-: ~apfel der *s.* **Kiefernzapfen; ~fackel die** pine[-wood] torch; **~span der** pine-wood chip; *(zum Anzünden)* pine-wood spill
Kiepe ['ki:pə] **die; ~, ~n** *(nordd., md.)* dosser; pannier
Kies [ki:s] **der; ~es, ~e a)** *(kleine, runde Steine)* gravel; *(auf dem Strand)* shingle; **b)** *(Mineral.)* pyrites *sing.*; **c)** *(salopp: Geld)* dough *(sl.)*; bread *(sl.)*
Kiesel ['ki:zl̩] **der; ~s, ~:** pebble
Kiesel-: ~erde die siliceous earth; **~säure die** *(Chemie)* silicic acid; **~stein der** pebble
kiesen ['ki:zn̩] *unr., auch regelm. tr. V. (dichter. veralt.)* choose; select
Kies·grube die gravel pit
Kies·weg der gravel path
Kiez [ki:ts] **der; ~es, ~e a)** *(nordostd., bes. berlin.) (Stadtteil)* neighbourhood; **b)** *(Jargon: Bordellgegend)* red-light district
Kif [kɪf] **der; ~[s]** *(ugs.)* pot *(sl.)*; grass *(sl.)*
kiffen ['kɪfn̩] *itr. V. (ugs.)* smoke pot *(sl.) or* grass *(sl.)*
Kiffer der; ~s, ~ *(ugs.)* pot-head *(sl.)*
kikeriki [kikəri'ki:] *Interj. (Kinderspr.)* cock-a-doodle-doo
Kikeriki das; ~s, ~s cock-a-doodle-doo
Kilbi ['kɪlbi] **die; ~, Kilbenen** ['kɪlbənən] *(schweiz.) s.* **Kirchweih**
killekille ['kɪlə'kɪlə] *Interj. (Kinderspr.)* tickle-tickle; **bei jmdm. ~ machen** tickle sb.
¹killen ['kɪlən] *tr. V. (salopp)* do in *(sl.)*; bump off *(sl.)*
²killen *itr. V. (Seemannsspr.)* ⟨*sail*⟩ shiver
Killer der; ~s, ~ *(salopp)* killer; *(gegen Bezahlung)* hit man *(sl.)*
Killer·satellit der *(ugs.)* hunter-killer satellite
Kilo ['ki:lo] **das; ~s, ~[s]** kilo
Kilo-: ~gramm das kilogram; **~hertz das; ~, ~** *(Physik)* kilohertz; **~kalorie die** *(Physik veralt.)* kilocalorie
Kilometer der; ~s, ~: kilometre; **75 ~ in der Stunde** 75 kilometres per hour
kilometer-, Kilometer-: ~fresser der *(ugs. scherzh. od. abwertend)* **er ist ein ~fresser** he really burns up the miles *(coll.)*; **~geld das** mileage allowance; **~lang 1.** *Adj.* miles long *pred.*; **eine ~lange Autoschlange** a traffic jam stretching [back] for miles; **2.** *adv.* for miles [and miles]; **~pauschale die** *(Steuerw.)* mileage allowance *(to taxpayer driving to and from work)*; **~stand der** mileage reading; **~stein der** milestone; **~weit 1.** *Adj.; nicht präd.* **in ~weiter Entfernung** miles away in the distance; **eine ~weite Aussicht** a view for miles; **2.** *adv.* for miles [and miles]
Kilowatt·stunde die *(Physik; bes. Elektrot.)* kilowatt-hour
Kimbern ['kɪmbɐn] *Pl.* Cimbri
Kimm [kɪm] **die; ~** *(Seemannsspr.)* **a)** *(Horizontlinie)* apparent *or* visible horizon; **b)** *(von Schiffen)* bilge
Kimme ['kɪmə] **die; ~, ~n a)** *(Einschnitt im Visier)* sighting notch; **b)** *(salopp: Gesäßspalte)* cleft between the buttocks
Kimmung die; ~ *(Seemannsspr.)* mirage
Kimono [ki'mo:no] **der; ~s, ~s** kimono
Kind [kɪnt] **das; ~[e]s, ~er a)** child; *(Kleinkind)* child; infant; *(Baby)* child; baby; **ein ~ erwarten/bekommen** *od. (ugs.)* **kriegen** be expecting/have a baby; **ich glaube, ihre Tochter kriegt ein ~:** I think her daughter's going to have a baby; **ein ~ zur Welt bringen** *(geh.)* give birth to a child; **ein ~/~er in die Welt setzen** bring a child/children into the world; **von einem ~ entbunden werden** be delivered of a child; **das ~ beim [rechten] Namen nennen** *(fig.)* call a spade a spade; **das ~ muß doch einen Namen haben** *(ugs.)* we need a good name for it; *(wir müssen einen Vorwand dafür finden)* we've got to dress it up somehow; **wir werden das ~ schon [richtig] schaukeln** *(ugs.)* we'll soon sort things out *or* have things sorted out; **unschuldig wie ein neugeborenes ~ sein** be as innocent as a new-born babe; **jmdm. ein ~ machen** *od.* **andrehen** *(ugs.)* put sb. in the family way *(coll.) or* in the club *(sl.)*; **das ~ mit dem Bade ausschütten** *(fig.)* throw the baby out with the bath-water; **jmdn. wie ein [kleines] ~ behandeln** treat sb. like a [small] child; **das weiß/kann doch jedes ~:** any child *or* five-year old knows/can do that; **von ~ an** *od.* **auf** from childhood; **er ist ein großes ~:** he is a big baby; **sich wie ein ~ freuen** be [as] pleased as Punch; **über schöne Dinge kann er sich wie ein ~ freuen** he takes a childlike pleasure in beautiful things; **du bist als ~ [wohl] zu heiß gebadet worden** *(ugs.)* you [must] have a screw loose *(coll.)*; **wie sag' ich's meinem ~e?** I don't know the best way to put it; *(bei einer unangenehmen Nachricht)* how do I break the news?; **aus ~ern werden Leute** childhood passes [all too soon]; **dann kommt bei ihm das ~ im Manne durch** *(scherzh.)* then he shows that he is [still] a child at heart; **[seine/deine** *usw.*] **~er und Kindeskinder** [his/your *etc.*] children and [his/your *etc.*] children's children; **bei jmdm. lieb ~ sein** *(ugs.)* be a favourite with sb.; **sich bei jmdm. lieb ~ machen** *(ugs.)* get on the right side of sb.; **einziges ~ sein** be an only child; **armer/reicher Leute ~ sein** be the child of poor/wealthy parents; come from a poor/wealthy family; **ein ~ seiner Zeit** *(fig.)* a child of one's times; **~er Gottes** *(fig.)* God's children; **ein ~ des Todes sein** *(fig. geh.)* be as good as dead; **ein [echtes] Wiener/Berliner ~:** a [true] Viennese/Berliner; **ein ~ der Liebe** *(geh. verhüll.)* a love-child; **er ist/du bist** *usw.* **kein ~ von Traurigkeit** *(ugs.)* he knows/you know *etc.* how to enjoy himself/yourself *etc.*; **jmds. liebstes ~ sein** ⟨*person*⟩ be sb.'s pet; **das Auto/die Oberstufenreform ist sein liebstes ~:** the car is his first love/reform of the sixth form is his pet project; **jmdn. an ~es Statt annehmen** *(veralt.)* adopt sb.; *s. auch* **totgeboren; b)** *(ugs.: als Anrede)* **mein [liebes] ~:** my [dear] child; **~er, hört mal alle her!** listen to this, all of you *(coll.)*; **[~er,] ~er!** my goodness!
Kind·bett das *(veralt.) s.* **Wochenbett**
Kindbett·fieber das childbed *or* puerperal fever
Kindchen ['kɪntçən] **a)** *(kleines Kind)* [small *or* little] child; **b)** *(Anrede)* dear child
kinder-, Kinder-: ~arbeit die; *o. Pl.* child labour; **~arm** *Adj.* with few children *postpos., not pred.*; **~arzt der** paediatrician; **~auge das;** *meist Pl.* **mit sehnsüchtigen ~augen auf etw.** *(Akk.)* **blicken** look at sth. with the wistful eyes of a child; **~beihilfe die** *(österr.) s.* **~geld; ~bekleidung die** children's wear; **~besteck das** children's cutlery; **ein ~besteck** a set of children's cutlery; **~bett das** cot; *(für größeres Kind)* child's bed; **~bewahr·anstalt die** *(veralt.)* children's home; **~bild das** *(Foto)* photograph of a child; *(Malerei usw.)* portrait of a child; **~buch das** children's book; **~chor der** children's choir; **~dorf das** children's village; **~ehe die** child marriage
Kinderei die; ~, ~en childishness *no indef. art., no pl.*; **eine ~:** a childish prank; **~en** childishness *sing.*; childish behaviour *sing.*
kinder-, Kinder-: ~ermäßigung die reduction for children; **~erziehung die** bringing up of children; **~fahrrad das** child's bicycle; **~feindlich 1.** *Adj.* hostile to children *pred.*; anti-children *pred.*; *(für Kinder nicht förderlich)* ⟨*planning, policy*⟩ which does not cater for the needs of children; **2.** *adv.* **sich ~feindlich verhalten** act in a manner hostile to children; **~feindlichkeit die;** *o. Pl.* hostility to children; *(von Planung, Politik)* failure to cater for children; **~fest das** children's party; children's fête; **~film der** children's film;

~**fräulein das** *s.* **Gouvernante;** ~**freund der: ein [großer] ~freund/[große] ~freunde sein** be [very] fond of children; ~**freundlich 1.** *Adj.* fond of children *pred.;* ‹*town, resort*› which caters for children; ‹*planning, policy*› which caters for the needs of children; **2.** *adv.* **sich ~freundlich verhalten** act in a manner friendly to children; ~**freundlich geplant werden** be planned with children in mind; ~**freundlichkeit die** fondness for children; ~**funk der** children's programme; *(Abteilung)* Children's Programmes *sing., no art.;* ~**garten der** kindergarten; nursery school; ~**gärtnerin die** kindergarten teacher; nursery-school teacher; ~**geld das** child benefit; ~**geschrei das** *(oft abwertend)* screaming *or* shouting of children; noise of children screaming *or* shouting; ~**gesicht das** child's face; *(eines Erwachsenen)* childlike face; baby-face; ~**glaube der** childlike belief *or* faith; *(abwertend)* childish belief *or* faith; ~**gottes·dienst der** children's service; ~**heil·kunde die** paediatrics *sing., no art.;* ~**heim das** children's home; ~**hort der** day-home for schoolchildren; ~**jahre** *Pl.* childhood years; ~**karussell das** children's roundabout; ~**kleidung die** children's clothes *pl.;* children's wear; ~**krankheit die a)** *(Infektionskrankheit bei Kindern)* children's disease *or* illness; **welche ~krankheiten hatten Sie?** what childhood diseases have you had?; **b)** *Pl. (Anfangsschwierigkeiten)* teething troubles; ~**kreuzzug der** *(hist.)* Children's Crusade; ~**kriegen das;** ~**s** *(ugs.)* having children; ~**krippe die** crèche; day nursey; ~**lähmung die** poliomyelitis; infantile paralysis *no art.;* ~**leicht** *(ugs.)* **1.** *(Adj.)* childishly simple *or* easy; dead easy; **das ist ~leicht** it's child's play *or (coll.)* kid's stuff; **2.** *adv.* **das kann ~leicht bedient werden** it's childishly simple to use; ~**lieb** *Adj.* fond of children *pred.;* ~**liebe die** love of children; ~**lied das** nursery rhyme; ~**los** *Adj.* childless; ~**losigkeit die** childlessness; ~**mädchen das** nursemaid; nanny; ~**märchen das** [children's] fairy-tale; ~**mord der** child-murder; ~**mund der** child's mouth; ~**mund tut Wahrheit kund** *(Prov.)* it takes a child to point out the truth; ~**narr der: er ist ein ~narr** he adores children; ~**pflegerin die** children's nurse; ~**popo der** *(ugs.)* [baby's] bottom; **glatt wie ein ~popo** [as] smooth as a baby's bottom; ~**psychologie die** child psychology *no art.;* ~**puder der** baby powder; ~**reich** *Adj.* with many children *postpos., not pred.;* **eine ~reiche Familie** a large family; ~**reichtum der;** *o. Pl.* large number of children; ~**reim der** nursery rhyme; ~**schar die** crowd of children; ~**schreck der;** *o. Pl.* bogyman; ~**schuh der** child's shoe; **ich bin/du bist den ~schuhen entwachsen** *(fig.)* I'm/you're not a child any more; **noch in den ~schuhen stecken** ‹*process, technique, etc.*› be still in its infancy; ~**schutz der** child protection legislation; ~**schwester die** children's nurse; ~**segen der;** *o. Pl. (oft scherzh.)* **eine Familie mit reichem ~segen** a family blessed with a large number of children; ~**sitz der** child's seat; *(an einem Fahrrad)* child-carrier [seat]; *(im Auto)* child's safety seat; ~**spiel das** children's game; **[für jmdn.] ein ~spiel sein** be child's play [to sb.]; ~**spiel·platz der** [children's] playground; ~**spiel·zeug das** [children's] toys *pl. or* playthings *pl.; (einzeln)* [child's] toy *or* plaything; ~**sprache die;** *o. Pl.* **a)** *(Sprache eines Kindes)* child language; children's language; **b)** *(kindliche Sprechweise Erwachsener)* nursery language; ~**sterblichkeit die** child mortality; ~**stimme die** child's voice; ~**stube die;** *o. Pl.* **eine gute/schlechte ~stube gehabt** *od.* **genossen haben** have been well/badly brought up; **hast du gar keine ~stube?** didn't you ever learn any manners?; ~**stuhl der** child's chair; *(Hochstuhl)* high chair; ~**tages·heim das,** ~**tages·stätte die** day nursery; ~**teller der a)** child's plate; **b)** *(auf der Speisekarte)* children's menu; ~**trommel die** toy drum; ~**wagen der** pram *(Brit.);* baby carriage *(Amer.); (Sportwagen)* push-chair *(Brit.);* stroller *(Amer.);* ~**wäsche die** [children's] underwear; *(für Neugeborene)* baby linen; ~**zahl die** number of children per family; ~**zeit die** childhood; ~**zimmer das a)** children's room; *(für Kleinkinder)* nursery; **b)** *(Einrichtung)* furniture for the children's room/nursery; ~**zuschlag der** child benefit

Kịndes-: ~**alter das;** *o. Pl.* childhood; **im ~alter** at an early age; ~**annahme die** *s.* **Adoption;** ~**aussetzung die** abandonment of [new-born] children; ~**beine** *Pl.* **in von ~beinen an** from *or* since childhood; from an early age; ~**entführung die** kidnapping [of a child]; child abduction; ~**kind das** *(veralt.)* grandchild; *s. auch* **Kind a;** ~**liebe die** *(geh.)* filial love *or* affection; ~**mißhandlung die** *(Rechtsw.)* child abuse; ~**mord der** child murder; *(Mord am eigenen Kind)* infanticide; ~**mörderin die** infanticide; ~**nöte** *Pl. (veralt.)* labour pains; **in ~nöten liegen** *od.* **sein** be in labour *sing.;* ~**pflicht die** filial duty; ~**raub der** *s.* ~**entführung;** ~**tötung die** *(Rechtsw.)* infanticide

Kịnd·frau die a) *(frühreifes Mädchen)* precocious young lady; **b)** *(kindliche Frau)* childlike woman

kịnd·gemäß *Adj.* suitable for children *postpos.*

kịndhaft *Adj.* childlike

Kịndheit die; ~**:** childhood; **seit frühester ~:** from earliest childhood; from infancy

Kịndheits·erinnerung die childhood memory

kịndisch 1. *Adj.* childish, infantile ‹*behaviour, enjoyment*›; naïve ‹*ideas*›; ~ **werden** become childish; **werd nicht ~!** do behave sensibly. **2.** *adv.* childishly; **sich ~ über etw.** *(Akk.)* **freuen** be absurdly pleased about sth.; **sich ~ an etw.** *(Dat.)* **freuen** take childish pleasure in sth.

kịndlich 1. *Adj.* childlike; ~**er Gehorsam** filial obedience; **im ~en Alter** at an early age. **2.** *adv.* ‹*behave*› in a childlike way *or* manner; **sich ~ über etw.** *(Akk.)* **freuen** take a childlike pleasure in sth.

Kịndlichkeit die; ~**:** childlike quality

Kịnds·kopf der overgrown child; **sei doch kein ~!** don't be so childish!; act your age!

Kịnd·taufe die christening

Kinematographie [kınematogra'fi:] **die;** ~**:** cinematography *no art.*

Kinetik [ki'ne:tık] **die;** ~ **a)** *(Physik)* kinetics *sing., no art.;* **b)** *(bild. Kunst)* kinetic art

kinetisch *Adj. (Physik, bild. Kunst)* kinetic

King [kıŋ] **der;** ~**s,** ~**s** *(ugs.)* boss *(coll.);* top dog *(coll.)*

Kinkerlitzchen ['kıŋkelıtsçən] *Pl. (ugs.)* trifles

Kinn [kın] **das;** ~**[e]s,** ~**e** chin

Kịnn-: ~**backe die,** ~**backen der** *(südd.)* cheek; ~**bart der** chin-beard; chin-tuft; ~**haken der** hook to the chin; ~**lade die** jaw; ~**riemen der** chin-strap

Kino ['ki:no] **das;** ~**s,** ~**s a)** *(Filmtheater)* cinema *(Brit.);* movie theatre *or* house *(Amer.);* **in die [deutschen] ~s kommen** go on general release [in Germany]; **b)** *Pl. selten (Filmvorstellung)* film; movie *(Amer.);* **ins ~ gehen** go to the cinema *(Brit.) or* pictures *(Brit.) or (Amer.)* movies *pl.;* **c)** *o. Pl. (Film als Medium)* cinema

Kịno-: ~**besuch der** visit to the cinema *(Brit.) or (Amer.)* movies; ~**besucher der** cinema-goer *(Brit.);* moviegoer *(Amer.);* ~**film der** cinema film *(Brit.);* movie film *(Amer.);* ~**gänger der** cinema-goer *(Brit.);* moviegoer *(Amer.);* ~**karte die** cinema ticket *(Brit.);* movie ticket *(Amer.);* ~**kasse die** cinema *(Brit.) or (Amer.)* movie box-office; ~**programm das a)** *(Programm zu einem Film)* film programme; **b)** *(Programmvorschau)* cinema guide; ~**reklame die a)** *(Reklame für einen Film)* publicity *no indef. art.* for the/a film; **b)** *(Werbung vor einer Vorstellung)* cinema advertisements *pl.;* screen commercials *pl.;* ~**vorstellung die** *s.* **Filmvorstellung**

Kintopp ['ki:ntɔp] **der** *od.* **das;** ~**s,** ~**s** *od.* **Kintöppe** ['ki:ntœpə] *(ugs.)* cinema

Kiosk [kị̣ɔsk] **der;** ~**[e]s,** ~**e** kiosk

Kipf [kıpf] **der;** ~**[e]s,** ~**e** *(südd.)* long loaf

Kipfel ['kıpfl] **das;** ~**s,** ~**, Kipferl** ['kıpfəl] **das;** ~**s,** ~**n** *(bayr., österr.) s.* **Hörnchen b**

[1]Kippe ['kıpə] **die;** ~**,** ~**n** *(ugs.)* cigarette end; fag-end *(sl.);* dog-end *(sl.)*

[2]Kịppe die; ~**,** ~**n a)** *(Bergmannsspr.: Abraumhalde)* slag-heap; **b)** *in* **auf der ~ stehen** *(ugs.)* be balanced precariously; **etw. steht auf der ~** *(fig.) (etw. befindet sich in einer kritischen Lage)* it's touch and go with sth.; *(etw. ist noch nicht entschieden)* sth. hangs in the balance; **c)** *(Turnen)* upstart; kip *(Amer.);* **d)** *(Müll~)* tip; dump

kippelig ['kıpəlıç] *Adj. (ugs.)* wobbly; rickety, wobbly ‹*chair, table*›

kippeln ['kıpln] *itr. V. (ugs.)* **a)** *(leicht wackeln)* wobble; ‹*chair, table*› wobble; be wobbly *or* rickety; **b)** *(mit dem Stuhl wackeln)* **[mit seinem Stuhl] ~:** rock one's chair backwards and forwards

kịppen 1. *tr. V.* **a)** *(schräg stellen, neigen)* tip [up]; tilt; **b)** *(ausschütten)* tip [out]; **c)** *(ugs.: trinken)* knock back *(sl.);* **einen ~:** have a quick one *(coll.) or* a drink; **d)** *(ugs.: abbrechen)* give ‹*project, series*› the chop *(coll.).* **2.** *itr. V.; mit sein* tip over; ‹*top-heavy object*› topple over; ‹*person*› fall, topple; ‹*boat*› overturn; ‹*car*› roll over; **von etw. ~:** topple *or* fall off sth.

Kịpper der; ~**s,** ~**:** tipper lorry *or* truck; dump truck; *(Eisenb.)* tipper *or* tipping wagon; dump car *(Amer.)*

Kịpp-: ~**fenster das** horizontally pivoted window; ~**lore die** tipper *or* tipping wagon; ~**schalter der** tumbler *or* toggle switch; ~**wagen der** *s.* ~**lore**

Kirche ['kırçə] **die;** ~**,** ~**n a)** *(Gebäude)* church; **die ~ im Dorf lassen** *(fig.)* keep a sense of proportion; **mit der ~ ums Dorf laufen** *(einen unnötigen Umweg machen)* go all round the houses; *(unnötig kompliziert vorgehen)* do things in a roundabout way; **b)** *o. Pl. (Gottesdienst)* church *no art.;* **in der ~ sein** be at church; **in die ~ gehen** go to church; **c)** *(Institution)* Church

kịrchen-, Kịrchen-: ~**älteste der** *(ev. Kirche)* [church-]elder; ~**amt das a)** *(Stellung)* ecclesiastical office; **b)** *(Verwaltungsstelle)* Church administrative offices *pl.;* ~**austritt der** secession from the Church; **die Zahl der ~austritte** the number of people seceding from *or* leaving the Church; ~**bank die** [church-]pew; ~**bann der** *(kath. Kirche)* excommunication; ~**besuch der** attendance at church; ~**besucher der** church-goer; worshipper; ~**blatt das** parish magazine; ~**buch das** parish register; ~**chor der** church choir; ~**diebstahl der** theft from a/the church; ~**diener der** sexton; ~**feindlich** *Adj.* hostile to the Church *postpos.;* ~**fenster das** church window; ~**fest das** religious festival; church festival; ~**fürst der** *(geh.)* high ecclesiastical dignitary; high dignitary of the Church; *(kath. Kirche: Kardinal)* Prince of the Church; ~**gebet das** *(veralt.)* collect; ~**gemeinde die** parish; *(beim Gottesdienst)* congregation; ~**geschichte die** ecclesiastical history *no art.;* Church history *no art.*; **~gestühl das** [church-]pews *pl.*; **~glocke die** church bell; **~jahr das** ecclesiastical year; Church year; **~kampf der** struggle between the Church and the State *(e.g. in the period of Nazi rule)*; **~leitung die** governing body of the Church; **~licht das**; *Pl.* **~lichter** *in* **kein** *od.* **nicht gerade ein [großes] ~licht sein** *(ugs. scherzh.)* be not too *or* not all that bright; **~lied das** hymn; **~maus die** *in* **arm sein wie eine ~maus** *(ugs. scherzh.)* be as poor as a church mouse; **~musik die** church music; sacred music; **~politik die** policy of the State towards the Church; **~portal das** portal *or* main door of the/a church; **~rat der** *(ev. Kirche)* **a)** *(Verwaltungsorgan)* ecclesiastical council; **b)** *o. Pl. (Titel)* member of the/an ecclesiastical council; **~raub der** *s.* **~diebstahl**; **~räuber der** church-robber; **~recht das** ecclesiastical law; **~schändung die** sacrilege *no indef. art.*; profanation of a/the church; **~schiff das** *(Archit.)* nave; **~spaltung die** schism; **~staat der** *(hist.)* Papal States *pl.*; **~steuer die** church tax; **~tag der** Church congress; **~ton·art die** *(Musik)* ecclesiastical *or* church mode; **~tür die** church door; **~vater der** Father of the Church; **~vor·stand der** parochial church council

Kirch-: ~gang der: der sonntägliche ~gang going to church on Sunday; **~gänger der** church-goer; **~hof der** *(veralt.)* churchyard; graveyard

kirchlich 1. *Adj.* **a)** *(die Kirche betreffend)* ecclesiastical; Church *attrib.*; ecclesiastical ‹*law, building*›; religious, church ‹*music, festival*›; **b)** *(den Riten der Kirche entsprechend)* church *attrib.* ‹*wedding, funeral*›. **2.** *adv.* **~ getraut/begraben werden** have a church wedding *or* be married in church/ have a church funeral

Kirch·spiel das *(veralt.)* parish

Kirch·turm der *(mit Turmspitze)* [church] steeple; *(ohne Turmspitze)* church tower

Kirchturm-: ~politik die parish-pump politics *sing.*; **~spitze die** church spire; **~uhr die** church clock

Kirch-: ~weih die; ~, **~en** fair *(held on the anniversary of the consecration of a church)*; **~weihe die** consecration of a/the church

Kirmes ['kɪrməs] **die**; ~, **Kirmessen** ['kɪrmɛsn̩] *(bes. md., niederd.) s.* **Kirchweih**

kirre ['kɪrə] *Adj.*; *nicht attr. (ugs.)* compliant; obedient; **jmdn. ~ machen/kriegen** bring sb. to heel

Kirsch [kɪrʃ] **der**; **~[e]s, ~:** *s.* **Kirschwasser**

Kirsch-: ~baum der a) cherry[-tree]; **b)** *(Holz) o. Pl.* cherry[-wood]; **~blüte die a)** *(Blüte des ~baums)* cherry blossom; **b)** *(Zeit der ~blüte)* cherry blossom time

Kirsche ['kɪrʃə] **die**; ~, **~n a)** cherry; **mit ihm ist nicht gut ~n essen** *(ugs.)* it's best not to tangle with him; **b)** *s.* **Kirschbaum**

kirsch-, Kirsch-: ~kern der cherry stone; **~kuchen der** cake with cherry topping; **~likör der** cherry liqueur; *(Weinbrand)* cherry brandy; **~rot** *Adj.* cherry[-red]; **~saft der** cherry juice; **~stein der** *s.* **~kern**; **~torte die** cherry gateau; *(mit Tortenboden)* cherry flan; **Schwarzwälder ~torte** Black Forest gateau; **~wasser das** kirsch

Kissen ['kɪsn̩] **das**; **~s, ~:** cushion; *(Kopf~)* pillow

Kissen-: ~bezug der cushion cover; *(für Kopfkissen)* pillow-case; pillow-slip; **~schlacht die** *(ugs.)* pillow-fight

Kiste ['kɪstə] **die**; ~, **~n a)** *(Behälter)* box; *(Truhe)* chest; *(Latten~)* crate; *(für Obst)* case; box; **eine ~ Wein/ Zigarren** a case of wine/box of cigars; **in die ~ gehen** *(fig. ugs.)* hit the hay *(sl.)*; go to bed; **b)** *(salopp) (Flugzeug, Auto)* bus *(coll.)*; *(Boot)* tub; **c)** *(ugs., bes. berlin.: Sache, Angelegenheit)* affair; business

kisten·weise *Adv.* **Wein/Obst ~ kaufen** buy wine by the case/fruit by the case *or* box; **Obst ~ wegwerfen** throw away fruit by the caseful *or* boxful

Kitsch [kɪtʃ] **der**; **~[e]s** kitsch

kitschig *Adj.* kitschy

Kitt [kɪt] **der**; **~[e]s**, *(Arten:)* **~e** *(Fenster~)* putty; *(für Porzellan, Kacheln usw.)* cement; *(Füllmasse)* filler

Kittchen das; **~s**, ~ *(ugs.)* clink *(sl.)*; jug *(sl.)*; jail; **im ~ sitzen** be inside *(coll.)*; be in clink *or* jug *(sl.)*

Kittel ['kɪtl̩] **der**; **~s**, **~ a)** overall; *(eines Arztes, Krankenpflegers, Laboranten)* white coat; **b)** *(hemdartige Bluse)* smock; **c)** *(südd.: Jackett)* jacket

Kittel-: ~kleid das [simple] button-through dress; **~schürze die** sleeveless overall

kitten *tr. V.* cement [together]; stick [together] with cement; *(fig.)* mend ‹*breach*›; patch up ‹*broken marriage, friendship*›

Kitz [kɪts] **das**; **~es, ~e** *(Reh~)* fawn; *(Ziegen~, Gemsen~)* kid

Kitzel ['kɪtsl̩] **der**; **~s**, **~ a)** *Pl. selten (Juckreiz)* tickle; tickling feeling *or* sensation; **b)** *(Reiz, Antrieb)* itch; urge; *(freudige Erregung)* thrill

kitzelig *s.* **kitzlig**

kitzeln 1. *tr. V.* **a)** tickle; **es kitzelt mich in der Nase** my nose tickles; **b)** *(einen Sinnenreiz hervorrufen)* tickle; **der Duft kitzelte sie in der Nase** the aroma tickled her nose; **jmds. Eitelkeit ~:** tickle sb.'s vanity; **c)** *(reizen)* prompt; *(in freudige Erregung versetzen)* thrill; **es kitzelt jmdn., etw. zu tun** sb. is itching to do sth.; sb. feels an urge to do sth. **2.** *itr. V.* tickle; **auf der Haut ~:** tickle [the skin]

Kitzler der; **~s**, ~ *(Anat.)* clitoris

kitzlig *Adj.* **a)** *(empfindlich gegen Kitzeln)* ticklish; **b)** *(empfindlich reagierend)* touchy (**in** + *Dat.* about); **c)** *(schwierig, heikel)* ticklish

Kiwi ['ki:vi] **die**; ~, **~s** kiwi [fruit]

KKW *Abk.* **Kernkraftwerk**

Kl. *Abk.* **Klasse**

Klabauter·mann [kla'bautɐ-] **der** *(nordd.)* protective spirit of a/the ship

klack [klak] *Interj.* **a)** click; **b)** *(von Tropfen)* tap

klacken *itr. V. (ugs.)* click

klackern ['klakɐn] *itr. V. (landsch.)* clatter

Klacks [klaks] **der**; **~es, ~e** *(ugs.)* *(~ Schlagsahne, Kartoffelbrei)* dollop *(coll.)*; *(~ Senf)* blob; dab; **etw. ist nur ein ~ [für jmdn.]** *(fig.)* sth. is no trouble at all [for sb.]

Kladde ['kladə] **die**; ~, **~n a)** *(Heft für erste Niederschrift)* rough book; **etw. in ~ schreiben** write sth. in rough; **b)** *(dickes Schreibheft)* thick notebook

kladderadatsch [kladəra'da:tʃ] *Interj.* crash-bang-wallop

Kladderadatsch der; **~[e]s, ~e** *(ugs.)* **a)** *(Chaos, Durcheinander)* unholy mess *(coll.)*; **b)** *(Skandal)* scandal

klaffen ['klafn̩] *itr. V.* gape; yawn; ‹*hole, wound*› gape; ‹*gap*› yawn; **in der Mauer klaffte ein großes Loch** there was a gaping hole in the wall

kläffen ['klɛfn̩] *itr. V. (abwertend)* yap

klaffend *Adj.* gaping; yawning; gaping ‹*hole, wound*›; yawning ‹*gap*›

Kläffer der; **~s**, ~ *(ugs. abwertend)* yapping dog; yapper

Klafter ['klaftɐ] **der** *od.* **das**; **~s**, **~ a)** *(frühere Längeneinheit)* fathom; **b)** *(Raummaß für Holz)* cord

klafter·tief *Adj.* six feet deep; ‹*water*› a fathom deep; *(fig.)* very deep

klagbar *Adj. (Rechtsw.)* actionable ‹*matter*›; enforceable ‹*claim*›

Klage ['kla:gə] **die**; ~, **~n a)** *(Äußerung der Trauer)* lamentation; lament; *(Äußerung des Schmerzes)* complaint; **die ~n um jmdn./über den Verlust von etw.** the lamentations *pl.* for sb./over the loss of sth.; **b)** *(Beschwerde, Äußerung des Unmuts)* complaint; **~n werden laut** complaints are being voiced; **keinen Grund zur ~ geben/haben** give/have no grounds *pl. or* reason for complaint; **bei jmdm. über jmdn./etw. ~ führen** make a complaint to sb. *or* lodge a complaint with sb. about sb./sth.; **c)** *(Rechtsw.) (im Zivilrecht)* action; suit; *(im Strafrecht)* charge; **eine ~ auf etw.** *(Akk.)* an action for sth.; **eine ~ auf Scheidung** a petition for divorce; **[öffentliche] ~ gegen jmdn. einreichen/erheben** bring an action against sb.; institute [criminal] proceedings against sb.

Klage-: ~ab·weisung die *(Rechtsw.)* dismissal of the action *or* suit; **~erhebung die** *(Rechtsw.)* institution of [legal] proceedings; bringing of an action *or* a suit; **~frau die** *s.* **~weib**; **~laut der** plaintive cry; *(von Schmerzen verursacht)* cry of pain; *(stöhnend)* moan; **~lied das** lament; **ein ~lied [über jmdn./etw.] anstimmen/singen** start to moan/moan [about sb./sth.]; **~mauer die** Wailing Wall

klagen 1. *itr. V.* **a)** *(geh.: jammern)* wail; *(stöhnend)* moan; ‹*animal*› cry plaintively; **der klagende Ruf des Käuzchens** the plaintive cry of the little owl; **b)** *(sich beschweren)* complain; **über etw.** *(Akk.)* **~:** complain about sth.; **über Rückenschmerzen/Kopfschmerzen ~:** complain of backache *sing.*/a headache; **[ich] kann nicht ~:** [I] can't complain; [I] mustn't grumble; **c)** *(geh.)* **um jmdn./jmds. Tod ~:** mourn sb./sb.'s death; **über den Verlust seines Vermögens ~:** lament *or* bewail the loss of one's fortune; **d)** *(bei Gericht)* sue; take legal action; **auf Schadenersatz ~:** sue for damages; bring an action for damages; **auf Scheidung ~:** petition for divorce; **gegen jmdn. ~:** sue sb.; take legal action against sb. **2.** *tr. V.* **a) jmdm. sein Leid/seine Not/sein Mißgeschick ~:** pour out one's sorrows *pl.*/troubles *pl.*/tale of misfortune to sb.; **Gott sei's geklagt** *(veralt.)* alas, alack *(arch.)*; **b)** *(österr.: verklagen)* sue; take legal action against

Klage·punkt der *(Rechtsw.) (im Zivilrecht)* particular of the/a claim; *(im Strafrecht)* count of the/a charge

Kläger ['klɛ:gɐ] **der**; **~s**, ~, **Klägerin die**; ~, **~nen** *(im Zivilrecht)* plaintiff; *(im Strafrecht)* prosecuting party; *(bei einer Scheidung)* petitioner; **wo kein ~ ist, ist auch kein Richter** *(Spr.)* if there's no law against it/if nobody complains, he/we *etc.* needn't worry

Klage-: ~ruf der plaintive cry; *(von Schmerz verursacht)* cry of pain; *(stöhnend)* moan; **~schrift die** *(Rechtsw.) (im Zivilrecht)* statement of claim; *(im Strafrecht)* charge/list of charges; *(bei einer Scheidung)* petition; **~weg der** *(Rechtsw.)* **auf dem ~weg** *od.* **im ~weg** by [taking] legal action *or* proceedings; through the courts; **~weib das** [professional] mourner

kläglich ['klɛ:klɪç] **1.** *Adj.* **a)** *(mitleiderregend)* pitiful ‹*expression, voice, cry*›; pitiful, wretched ‹*condition, appearance*›; **ein ~es Ende nehmen** come to a miserable end; **b)** *(minderwertig)* pathetic ‹*achievement, result, etc.*›; **ein ~er Rest** a few pathetic remains *pl.*; **c)** *(erbärmlich)* despicable, wretched ‹*behaviour, role, compromise*›; pathetic ‹*result, defeat*›. **2.** *adv.* **a)** ‹*weep, sob*› pitifully; **b)** *(erbärmlich)* ‹*behave*› wretchedly, despicably; ‹*fail*› miserably

Kläglichkeit die; ~ *s.* **kläglich 1a–c:** pitifulness; wretchedness; patheticness; despicableness

klaglos 1. *Adj.* uncomplaining. **2.** *adv.* uncomplainingly; without complaint

Klamauk [kla'mauk] **der**; **~s** *(ugs. abwertend)* fuss; to-do; *(Lärm, Krach)* row *(coll.)*;

racket; *(Reklamewirbel)* fuss; hullabaloo; *(im Theater)* slapstick

klamm [klam] *Adj.* **a)** *(feucht)* cold and damp; **b)** *(steif)* numb; ~ **vor Kälte** numb with cold; **c)** ~ **sein** *(salopp)* be hard-up

Klamm die; ~, ~**en** [deep and narrow] gorge; ravine

Klammer die; ~, ~**n a)** *(Wäsche~)* peg; **b)** *(Haar~)* [hair-]grip; **c)** *(Zahn~)* brace; **d)** *(Wund~)* clip; **e)** *(Büro~)* paper-clip; *(Heft~)* staple; **f)** *(Bau~)* cramp[-iron]; [timber-]dog; **g)** *(Schriftzeichen)* bracket; **runde** ~**n** round brackets; parentheses; **eckige/spitze** ~**n** square/angle *or* pointed brackets; **geschweifte** ~**n** braces; ~ **auf/zu** open/close brackets; **h)** *(Text in* ~*n)* bracketed material; material in [the] brackets; *(Math.)* bracket; bracketed expression; **die** ~**n auflösen** remove the brackets; **i)** *(Griff)* grip; **j)** *(fig.) (Verbindung)* bond; link; *(Fessel)* shackle; tie

Klammer-: ~**affe der** *(Zool.)* spider-monkey; ~**aus·druck der** *(Math.)* bracket; bracketed expression; ~**beutel der** peg-bag; **dich haben sie wohl mit dem** ~**beutel gepudert!** *(berlin. salopp)* you must be off your rocker! *(sl.)*

klammern 1. *refl. V.* **sich an jmdn./etw.** ~ *(auch fig.)* cling to sb./sth.; **sich an Worte** ~: be pedantic about the words used. **2.** *tr. V.* **a) er klammerte seine Hände um das Geländer** he grasped the railing [with both hands]; **b)** *(zusammenhalten)* **eine Wunde** ~: close a wound with a clip/clips; **c)** *(befestigen) (mit einer Büroklammer)* clip; *(mit einer Heftmaschine)* staple; *(mit einer Wäscheklammer)* peg. **3.** *itr. V. (Boxen)* clinch

klamm·heimlich 1. *Adj.; nicht präd. (ugs.)* on the quiet *postpos.*; ⟨*meeting*⟩ held on the quiet. **2.** *adv.* on the quiet

Klamotte [kla'mɔtə] **die;** ~, ~**n a)** *Pl. (salopp: Kleidung)* clobber *sing. (sl.)*; gear *sing. (sl.)*; **b)** *Pl. (salopp: Kram)* junk *sing.*; stuff *sing.*; **c)** *(ugs. abwertend: Schwank)* rubbishy play/film *etc.*

Klamotten·kiste die *(ugs.)* *in* **etw. aus der** ~ **hervorholen** dig sth. up again; **ein Witz/eine Anekdote aus der** ~: an old chestnut

Klampfe ['klampfə] **die;** ~, ~**n a)** *(volkst.: Gitarre)* guitar; **b)** *(österr.) s.* **Klammer f**

Klan [kla:n] **der;** ~**s,** ~**e** *s.* **Clan**

klang [klaŋ] *1. u. 3. Pers. Sg. Prät. v.* **klingen**

Klang der; ~**[e]s, Klänge** ['klɛŋə] **a)** *(Ton)* sound; **b)** *(~farbe)* tone; **der Name dieser Familie/Firma hat einen guten/schlechten** ~ *(fig.)* this family/firm has a good/bad name; **ihre Worte hatten einen bitteren** ~ *(fig.)* there was a bitter note in *or* edge to her words; **c)** *Pl. (Melodie)* **das Orchester spielte alte, wohlbekannte Klänge** the orchestra played old familiar tunes; **nach den Klängen eines Walzers tanzen** dance to the strains of a waltz

Klang-: ~**bild das** *(fachspr.)* sound; ~**effekt der** sound effect; ~**farbe die** tone colour *or* quality; *(einer Stimme)* tone; ~**fülle die** *(eines Instruments)* richness *or* fullness of tone; *(eines Orchesters)* richness *or* fullness of sound; *(einer Stimme)* sonority

klanglich 1. *Adj.; nicht präd.* tonal ⟨*beauty, quality, etc.*⟩; tonal, tone *attr.* ⟨*characteristics*⟩. **2.** *adv.* tonally

klanglos 1. *Adj.* toneless; **mit** ~**er Stimme** in a toneless voice; tonelessly. **2.** *adv.* tonelessly; *s. auch* **sanglos**

klang-, Klang-: ~**regler der** *(Technik) s.* **Tonblende;** ~**rein 1.** *Adj.* ~**rein sein** have a pure tone *or* sound; **2.** *adv.* **er spielte so** ~**rein, daß ...:** he played with such [a] purity of tone that ...; ~**schön** *Adj.* **ein** ~**schönes Instrument** an instrument with a beautiful tone *or* sound; ~**treu** *Adj.* faithful ⟨*reproduction*⟩; high-fidelity ⟨*receiver, reception*⟩; ~**voll** *Adj.* **a)** sonorous ⟨*voice, language*⟩; **b)** *(berühmt)* illustrious ⟨*name, title*⟩

klapp [klap] *Interj.* click

Klapp-: ~**bett das** folding bed; ~**brücke die** bascule bridge; ~**deckel der** hinged lid

Klappe die; ~, ~**n a)** [hinged] lid; *(am Fenster)* [hinged] vent; *(am Briefkasten)* flap; *(am Tisch)* leaf; ~ **zu, Affe tot** *(salopp)* there's an end to it; **b)** *(am LKW)* tail-board; tail-gate; *(seitlich)* side-gate; *(am Kombiwagen)* back; **c)** *(an Kleidertaschen)* flap; **d)** *(am Ofen)* [drop-]door; **e)** *(an Musikinstrumenten)* key; *(an einer Trompete)* valve; **f)** *(Herz~)* valve; **g)** *(Augen~)* [eye-]patch; **h)** *(Achselstück)* shoulder-strap; **i)** *(Filmjargon)* clapper-board; **das war die letzte** ~: that was the last take; **j)** *(salopp: Mund)* trap *(sl.)*; **die** *od.* **seine** ~ **halten** shut one's trap *(sl.)*; **eine große** *od.* **freche** ~ **haben** *(abwertend)* have a big mouth; **k)** *(ugs.: Bett)* **sich in die** ~ **hauen** hit the hay *(sl.)*; get one's head down

klappen 1. *tr. V.* **nach oben/unten** ~: turn up/down ⟨*collar, hat-brim*⟩; lift up/put down *or* lower ⟨*lid*⟩; **nach vorne/hinten** ~: tilt forward/back ⟨*seat*⟩. **2.** *itr. V.* **a)** ⟨*door, shutter*⟩ bang; **mit der Tür** ~: bang the door; **b)** *(stoßen)* bang; **c)** *(ugs.: gelingen)* work out all right; ⟨*rehearsal, performance, etc.*⟩ go [off] all right; **die Sache wird schon** ~: it *or* things will work out all right; **hat es mit den Karten geklappt?** did you get the tickets all right?

Klappen-: ~**fehler der** *s.* **Herzklappenfehler;** ~**text der** *(Buchw.)* blurb

Klapper die; ~, ~**n** rattle

klapper-, Klapper-: ~**dürr** *(ugs.)* all skin and bone *pred.*; ~**gestell das** *(ugs.)* **a)** *(dünner Mensch)* bag of bones; **b)** *(scherzh.: Fahrzeug)* rattletrap; ~**kasten der,** ~**kiste die** *(ugs.)* rattletrap

klappern *itr. V.* **a)** rattle; ⟨*heels, knitting-needles*⟩ click; **vor Kälte** ~ **ihr die Zähne** her teeth are chattering with cold; **b)** *(ein Klappern erzeugen)* make a clatter; **vor Angst/Kälte klapperte er mit den Zähnen** his teeth were chattering with fear/cold; **auf der Schreibmaschine** ~ *(ugs.)* clatter away on the typewriter; **mit den Augen** ~ *(ugs.)* keep blinking; *(kokettieren)* flutter one's eyelashes; **c)** *mit sein (sich klappernd fortbewegen)* ⟨*car*⟩ rattle along; ⟨*person*⟩ clatter along

Klapper-: ~**schlange die** rattlesnake; ~**storch der** *(Kinderspr.)* stork; **glaubst du noch an den** ~**storch?** do you still believe that babies are brought by the stork?

Klapp-: ~**fahr·rad das** folding bicycle; ~**fenster das** top-hung window; ~**laden der** folding shutter; ~**liege die** [folding] lounger *or* sunbed; ~**messer das** clasp-knife; ~**rad das** folding bicycle

klapprig *Adj.* **a)** *(alt)* rickety; ramshackle; **b)** *(wenig stabil)* rickety; wobbly; **c)** *(ugs.: hinfällig)* decrepit; **er ist noch etwas** ~: he's still a bit shaky

Klapp-: ~**sitz der** folding seat; tip-up seat; ~**stuhl der** folding chair; ~**stulle die** *(berlin.)* sandwich; ~**tisch der** folding table; ~**tür die** hinged door; ~**verdeck das** collapsible *or* folding hood *or* top; ~**zylinder der** opera-hat; crush hat

Klaps [klaps] **der;** ~**es,** ~**e a)** *(ugs.: leichter Schlag)* smack; slap; **jmdm. einen** ~ **geben** give sb. a slap *or* smack; **b)** *(salopp)* **einen** ~ **haben** have a screw loose *(coll.)*; be a bit bonkers *(sl.)*

Klaps·mühle die *(salopp)* loony-bin *(sl.)*; nut-house *(sl.)*

Klar das; ~**s,** ~ *(österr.) s.* **Eiweiß a**

klar [kla:ɐ̯] **1.** *Adj.* **a)** clear; ~**e Brühe** clear soup; **mit** ~**en Augen** clear-eyed; **bei** ~**er Sicht** when it's clear; on a clear day; **einen** ~**en Moment haben** *(fig.)* have a lucid moment; **ein** ~**er Verstand** clear judgement *no art.*; **er ist nicht bei** ~**em Verstand** he's not in his right mind; he's not in full possession of his faculties; ~ **[im Kopf] sein** have a clear head; be able to think clearly *or* straight; **er ist nicht ganz** ~ **im Kopf** *(salopp)* he's not quite right in the head *(sl.)*; **b)** *(eindeutig)* clear ⟨*decision*⟩; straight ⟨*question, answer*⟩; **ein** ~**es Ziel vor Augen haben** have a clear aim *or* objective; ~**e Verhältnisse schaffen** set things straight; **[ist] alles** ~**?** [is] everything clear?; **jetzt ist mir alles** ~: now I understand; **na** ~**!** *(ugs.)*, **aber** ~**!** *(ugs.)* of course!; ~**, daß ...:** naturally, ...; **Das werdet ihr nicht tun. Ist das** ~**?** You must not do that. Is that clear *or* Do I make myself clear?; **ist dir** ~**, daß ...?** are you aware that ...?; **das ist** ~ **wie Klärchen** *od.* **Kloßbrühe** *od.* **dicke Tinte** *(ugs.)* it's as plain as a pikestaff *(Brit.)* *or* as the nose on your face; **sich** *(Dat.)* **über etw.** *(Akk.)* **im** ~**en sein** realize *or* be aware of sth.; **c)** *nicht attr. (fertig)* ready; ~ **zum Auslaufen** ready to sail. **2.** *adv.* clearly; **sie haben die gegnerische Mannschaft** ~ **besiegt** they won a clear[-cut] victory over the opposing team; **nicht** ~ **denken können** be unable to think clearly *or* straight; ~ **auf der Hand liegen** *(ugs.)* be blindingly obvious; **etw.** ~ **und deutlich sagen** say sth. clearly and unambiguously

Klär·anlage die sewage treatment plant; *(einer Fabrik)* wastewater treatment plant

klar-, Klar-: ~**apfel der** *type of early dessert apple;* ≈ White/Yellow Transparent; ~**blick der** clear-sightedness; ~**blickend** *Adj.* clear-sighted; ~**denkend** *Adj.* clear-thinking

Klare der; ~**n,** ~**n** schnapps

klären ['klɛ:rən] **1.** *tr. V.* **a)** *(aufklären)* settle, resolve ⟨*question, issue, matter*⟩; clarify ⟨*situation*⟩; clear up ⟨*case, affair, misunderstanding*⟩; **b)** *(reinigen)* purify; treat ⟨*effluent, sewage*⟩; clear ⟨*beer, wine*⟩. **2.** *refl. V.* **a)** *(klar werden)* ⟨*situation*⟩ become clear; ⟨*question, issue, matter*⟩ be settled *or* resolved; **b)** *(rein werden)* ⟨*liquid, sky*⟩ clear; ⟨*weather*⟩ clear [up]. **3.** *itr. V. (Ballspiele)* clear [the ball]; **auf der Linie** ~: clear [the ball] off the line

klar|gehen *unr. itr. V.; mit sein (ugs.)* go OK *(coll.)*; **geht das klar mit dem Antrag?** is the application going OK? *(coll.)*; **es wird schon** ~: it'll be OK *(coll.)*

Klarheit die; ~, ~**en a)** *o. Pl.* clarity; **b)** *o. Pl. (Eindeutigkeit)* clarity; *(von Ausführungen, Rede usw.)* clarity; lucidity; **c)** *o. Pl. (Gewißheit)* **sich** *(Dat.)* **über etw.** *(Akk.)* ~ **verschaffen** clarify sth.; **völlige** ~ **verlangen** demand full information *or* all the facts **(über** + *Akk.* about); **d)** *(ugs. scherzh.)* **jetzt sind alle** ~**en beseitigt** now I'm/everyone's *etc.* totally confused

klarieren *tr. V. (Seemannsspr.)* **etw.** ~: clear sth. [through customs]

Klarinette [klari'nɛtə] **die;** ~, ~**n** clarinet

Klarinettist der; ~**en,** ~**en, Klarinettistin die;** ~, ~**nen** clarinettist

Klarisse [kla'rɪsə] **die;** ~, ~**n, Klarissin die;** ~, ~**nen** nun of the order of St. Clare; **die Klarissen** *od.* **Klarissinnen** the poor Clares

klar-, Klar-: ~**|kommen** *unr. itr. V.; mit sein (ugs.)* manage; cope; **mit jmdm.** ~**kommen** get on with sb.; **ich komme mit der neuen Waschmaschine/der Matheaufgabe nicht** ~: I can't get on with my new washing machine/sort out this maths exercise; ~**lack der** clear varnish; ~**|legen** *tr. V. (ugs.)* make clear; explain; ~**|machen** *tr. V.* **a)** *(ugs.: erklären)* make clear; **jmdm./sich etw.** ~**machen** make sth. clear to sb./realize sth.; **b)** *(Seemannsspr.)* get ready; prepare

Klär·schlamm der *(Technik)* sludge

Klar·schrift·leser der *(DV)* optical character reader

klar|sehen *unr. itr. V.* understand the matter

Klarsicht-: ~**folie die** transparent film;

~packung die transparent pack; **~um·schlag der** transparent cover

klar-, Klar-: ~|spülen *itr. V.* rinse; **~|stellen** *tr. V.* clear up; clarify; **ich möchte ~stellen, daß ...:** I should like to make it clear that ...; **~stellung die** clarification; **~text der** *(auch DV)* clear *or* plain text; text in clear; **im ~text** *(fig.)* in plain language

Klärung die; ~, ~en a) *(Beseitigung von Mißverständnissen)* clarification; **b)** *(Reinigung)* purification; *(von Abwässern)* treatment

klar|werden *unr. V.; mit sein; nur im Inf. und Part. zusammengeschrieben* **1.** *refl. V.* **sich** *(Dat.)* **über etw.** *(Akk.)* **~:** realize *or* grasp sth.; **ich muß mir über meine Pläne für die Zukunft erst ~:** I must first get my plans for the future clear in my own mind. **2.** *itr. V.* **jmdm. wird etw. klar** sth. becomes clear to sb.

Klär·werk das sewage works *sing. or pl.; (einer Fabrik)* wastewater treatment works *sing. or pl.*

klaß [klas] *(südd., österr.) s.* **klasse**

klasse ['klasə] *(ugs.)* **1.** *indekl. Adj.* great *(coll.);* marvellous. **2.** *adv.* marvellously

Klasse die; ~, ~n a) *(Schul~)* class; form *(esp. Brit.); (Raum)* class-room; *(Stufe)* year; grade *(Amer.);* **die vierte ~ besuchen** be in the fourth year *or (Amer.)* grade; **b)** *(Bevölkerungsgruppe)* class; **die ~ der Werktätigen/der Besitzlosen** the working/propertyless class; **c)** *(Sport)* league; *(Boxen)* division; class; **d)** *(Fahrzeug~)* class; **PKWs der gehobenen ~:** up-market cars; **ein Führerschein der ~ 1/2/3/4/5** ≈ a driving licence for a motor cycle/a heavy goods vehicle/a private car/a moped/a motor-assisted bicycle; **e)** *(Boots~)* class; **f)** *(Qualitätsstufe)* class; **ein Wagen/eine Fahrkarte erster ~:** a first-class carriage/ticket; **zweiter ~ liegen** occupy a second-class hospital-bed; **er ist ein Künstler erster ~** *(ugs.)* he is a first-class *or* first-rate artist; **das ist [einsame** *od.* **ganz große] ~!** *(ugs.)* that's [just] great *(coll.) or* marvellous!; **der Verdienstorden erster ~:** the Order of Merit first-class; **g)** *(Biol.)* class

Klasse-: ~frau die *(ugs.)* stunner *(coll.);* smasher *(coll.);* **~mann der a)** *(ugs.)* marvellous man; fantastic guy *(sl.);* **b)** *(Sportjargon)* top-class *or* first-rate player; **~mannschaft die** *(Sportjargon)* top-class *or* first-rate team

Klassement [klasə'mã:] **das; ~s, ~s** *(Sport)* [list *sing.* of] rankings *pl.*

klassen-, Klassen-: ~arbeit die *(Schulw.)* [written] class test; **~auf·satz der** *(Schulw.)* essay written in class; class essay; **~aus·flug der** *(Schulw.)* class outing; **~beste der/die;** *adj. Dekl.* top pupil in the class; **wer ist denn bei euch der oder die ~beste?** who is top of your class?; **~bewußt·sein das** *(Soziol.)* class-consciousness; **~buch das** *(Schulw.) book recording details of pupils' attendance, behaviour, and of topics covered in each lesson* ≈ [class-]register; **~durch·schnitt der** *(Schulw.)* class-average; **~erhalt der** *(Sport)* **um den ~erhalt kämpfen** struggle *or* battle to avoid relegation; **~fahrt die** *(Schulw.)* class outing; **~feind der** *(marx.)* class enemy; **~gegen·satz der** class difference; **~geist der** *(Schulw.)* class spirit; **~gemeinschaft die** *(Schulw.) (~kollektiv)* class; *(~geist)* class spirit; **~gesellschaft die** *(Soziol.)* class society; **~haß der** *(Sozialpsych.)* class hatred *no art.;* **~herrschaft die** *(Soziol.)* class rule *no art.;* **~justiz die** *(Soziol.)* legal system with a built-in class bias; **~kamerad der, ~kameradin die** *(Schulw.)* class-fellow; class-mate; **~kampf der** *(marx.)* class struggle; **~kämpferisch** *(marx.) Adj.* **~kämpferische Parolen** slogans supporting the class struggle; **~keile die** *(Schülerspr.)* **~keile beziehen** *od.* **bekommen** be punched and pushed by the rest of the class; **~lehrer der, ~lehrerin die, ~leiter der, ~leiterin die** *(Schulw.)* class *or* form teacher; form master/mistress; **~los** *Adj. (Soziol.)* classless; **~lotterie die** *lottery in which draws are made on a number of different days and for which tickets can be bought for each individual draw;* **~raum der** *s.* **~zimmer; ~schranke die** *(Soziol.)* class barrier; **~sprecher der, ~sprecherin die** *(Schulw.)* class spokesman; ≈ form leader *or* captain; **~stärke die** *(Schulw.)* size of the/a class/of classes; **~treffen das** *(Schulw.)* class reunion; **~unterschied der a)** *(Soziol.)* class difference; **b)** *(Sport)* difference in class; **~wahl·recht das** *(hist.)* class-based electoral system; class[-based] system of franchise; **~weise** *(Schulw.) Adv.* class by class; **~ziel das** *(Schulw.)* required standard *(for pupils in a particular class);* **das ~ziel erreichen** reach the required standard; *(fig.)* make the grade; come up to scratch; **~zimmer das** *(Schulw.)* class-room

Klasse-: ~spieler der *(Sport Jargon)* [top-]class *or* first-rate player; **~weib das** *(ugs.)* stunner *(coll.);* smasher *(coll.)*

Klassifikation [klasifika'tsio:n] **die; ~, ~en** classification

klassifizieren [klasifi'tsi:rən] *tr. V.* classify **(als as)**

Klassifizierung die; ~, ~en classification

-klassig *Adj.* -class; **mehr~/zwei~:** with a number of/two classes

Klassik ['klasık] **die; ~ a)** *(Antike)* classical antiquity *no art.;* **b)** *(Zeit kultureller Höchstleistung)* classical period *or* age

Klassiker der; ~s, ~ a) *(der antiken Klassik)* classic; classical writer; **b)** *(einer Epoche)* classic; classical writer/composer *etc.;* **c)** *(Künstler, dessen Werk als mustergültig gilt)* classical exponent; classic

klassisch *Adj.* **a)** classical; **b)** *(vollendet, zeitlos; auch iron.)* classic; **c)** *(herkömmlich)* classical; conventional ‹*warfare*›

Klassizismus [klasi'tsısmʊs] **der; ~, Klassizismen a)** *o. Pl. (Stilform)* classicism; **b)** *(Stilmerkmal)* feature of the classical style

klassizistisch *Adj.* classical

-kläßler [-klɛslɐ] **der; ~s, ~:** -former; **Erst~/Zweit~:** first-former/second-former

klatsch *Interj.* smack; *(wenn etw. Weiches auf den Boden fällt)* splosh

Klatsch [klatʃ] **der; ~[e]s, ~e a)** *o. Pl. (ugs. abwertend: Gerede)* gossip; tittle-tattle; **b)** *(Geräusch)* smack; **es gab einen lauten ~, als er auf dem Wasser aufschlug** there was a loud splash *or (lauter und schärfer)* smack as he hit the water

Klatsch·base die *(ugs. abwertend)* gossip

Klatsche die; ~, ~n a) *(Fliegen~)* fly-swatter; **b)** *(Schülerspr.: Übersetzung)* crib; **c)** *(abwertend) s.* **Klatschbase**

klatschen 1. *itr. V.* **a)** *auch mit sein* ‹*waves, wet sails*› slap **(gegen** against); **der Regen klatscht gegen die Scheiben** the rain beats against the windows; **sie gab ihm eine Ohrfeige, daß es nur so klatschte** she gave him a resounding smack *or* slap round the face; **b)** *(mit den Händen; applaudieren)* clap; **in die Hände ~:** clap one's hands; **lautes Klatschen** loud applause; **c)** *(schlagen)* slap; **sich** *(Dat.)* **auf die Schenkel/gegen die Stirn ~:** slap one's thighs/clap one's hand to one's forehead; **d)** *(ugs. abwertend: reden)* gossip **(über** + *Akk.* about). **2.** *tr. V.* **a)** *(ugs.: werfen)* slap; chuck *(coll.)* ‹*book etc.*›; **b) den Takt ~** ‹*teacher*› clap time; ‹*audience*› clap in time; **jmdm. Beifall ~:** clap *or* applaud sb.; **c)** *(ugs.: schlagen)* **jmdm. eine ~:** slap sb. across the face; give sb. a slap across the face

Klatscherei die; ~, ~en *(ugs. abwertend)* gossiping

Klatsch·geschichte die *(abwertend)* piece of gossip; **~n** gossip *sing.*

klatschhaft *Adj.* gossipy; fond of gossip *pred.*

Klatschhaftigkeit die; ~: fondness for gossip

klatsch-, Klatsch-: ~kolumnist der *(abwertend)* gossip columnist; **~maul das** *(ugs. abwertend)* gossip; **~mohn der** corn-poppy; field poppy; **~naß** *Adj.* *(ugs.)* soaking *or* sopping wet ‹*clothes*›; dripping wet ‹*hair*›; **wir sind ~naß geworden** we got soaked [to the skin] *or* drenched; **~spalte die** *(ugs. abwertend)* gossip column; **~sucht die;** *o. Pl. (abwertend)* passion for gossip *or* tittle-tattle; **~süchtig** *Adj.* extremely gossipy; **~süchtig sein** be a compulsive gossip/compulsive gossips; **~tante die** *(ugs. abwertend),* **~weib das** *(ugs. abwertend) s.* **~base**

klauben ['klaubn̩] *tr. V. (landsch.)* **a)** *(entfernen)* **die Flusen vom Teppich/die Rosinen aus dem Kuchen ~:** pick the fluff *sing.* off the carpet/the raisins out of the cake; **b)** *(auslesen)* pick over; **c)** *(bes. südd., österr. ugs.: sammeln)* pick ‹*berries*›; gather, collect ‹*wood*›; dig ‹*potatoes*›

Klaue ['klauə] **die; ~, ~n a)** claw; *(von Raubvögeln)* talon; *(fig. geh.)* **in den ~n eines Erpressers** in the clutches of a blackmailer; **jmdn. den ~n des Todes entreißen** snatch sb. from the jaws of death; **b)** *(Huf)* hoof; **c)** *(salopp: Hand)* mitt *(sl.);* paw *(coll.);* **d)** *o. Pl. (salopp abwertend: Handschrift)* handwriting; **seine ~ kann ich nicht entziffern** I can't decipher his scrawl

klauen *(ugs.)* **1.** *tr. V.* pinch *(sl.);* nick *(Brit. sl.); (fig.)* pinch *(sl.),* nick *(Brit. sl.),* crib ‹*idea*›; **jmdm. etw. ~:** pinch *or (Brit.)* nick/crib sth. from sb. **2.** *itr. V.* pinch *(sl.) or* nick *(Brit. sl.)* things

Klauen·seuche die *s.* **Maul- und Klauenseuche**

Klause ['klauzə] **die; ~, ~n a)** *(Einsiedelei)* hermitage; **b)** *(Klosterzelle)* cell; *(fig.)* den; **c)** *s.* **Klus**

Klausel ['klauzl̩] **die; ~, ~n** clause; *(Bedingung)* stipulation; condition; *(Vorbehalt)* proviso

Klausner ['klausnɐ] **der; ~s, ~:** hermit; recluse

Klaustrophobie [klaustrofo'bi:] **die; ~, ~n** *(Psych.)* claustrophobia

Klausur [klau'zu:ɐ̯] **die; ~, ~en a)** *o. Pl. (Abgeschlossenheit)* **in ~ leben/tagen** live in seclusion/meet in private; **b)** *(Klausurarbeit)* [examination] paper; *(Examen)* examination; **eine ~ schreiben** take a[n examination] paper/an examination; **c)** *(Klosterbereich)* enclosure

Klausur-: ~arbeit die [examination] paper; **~tagung die** private meeting

Klaviatur [klavia'tu:ɐ̯] **die; ~, ~en a)** keyboard; **b)** *(Vielfalt)* [whole] gamut *or* range

Klavichord [klavi'kɔrt] **das; ~[e]s, ~s** clavichord

Klavier [kla'vi:ɐ̯] **das; ~s, ~e** piano

Klavier-: ~aus·zug der piano score; **~bauer der** piano-maker; **~bearbeitung die** piano arrangement; arrangement for the piano; **~begleitung die** piano accompaniment; **~hocker der** piano-stool; **~konzert das a)** *(Musikstück)* piano concerto; **b)** *(Veranstaltung)* piano recital; **~lehrer der, ~lehrerin die** piano teacher; **~schemel der** piano-stool; **~schule die** piano tutor; **~sonate die** piano sonata; **~spiel das** piano-playing; **~spieler der** pianist; piano-player; **~stimmer der; ~s, ~:** piano-tuner; **~stunde die** piano-lesson; **~unterricht der** piano-lessons *pl.*

Klebe ['kle:bə] **die; ~** *(ugs.)* glue

Klebe-: ~band das adhesive *or* sticky tape;

~bindung die *(Buchw.)* adhesive *or* perfect binding; **~folie die** adhesive film; *(für Regale)* self-adhesive plastic sheeting

kleben 1. *itr. V.* **a)** stick (**an** + *Dat.* to); **an allen Hauswänden klebten riesige Plakate** there were huge posters stuck on the walls of all the houses; **das Hemd klebte ihm am Körper** his shirt stuck *or* clung to his body; **an seinen Händen klebt Blut** *(fig.)* he has blood on his hands *(fig.)*; his hands are stained with blood *(fig.)*; **am Berghang ~** ⟨*hut etc.*⟩ cling to the mountainside; **jmdm. an der Stoßstange ~** *(fig. salopp)* ⟨*driver, vehicle*⟩ hang on sb.'s tail; **an jmdm. ~** *(salopp)* cling to sb.; **b)** *(ugs.: klebrig sein)* be sticky (**von, vor** + *Dat.* with); **c)** *(ugs.: an sich hängen haben)* **voller Fliegen/Kletten usw. ~**: be covered in flies/burrs; **d)** *(ugs.: sich klammern)* **an seinem Stuhl/an der Theke ~**: stay put in one's chair *(coll.)*/prop the bar up *(coll.)*; **klebt nicht so an der Textvorlage** *(fig.)* don't stick so closely to the original text; **e)** *(verbunden sein)* **daran klebt ein Makel** there's a stigma attached to it; **f)** *(ugs.: Sozialversicherungsbeiträge entrichten)* pay stamps. **2.** *tr. V.* **a)** *(befestigen)* stick; *(mit Klebstoff)* stick; glue; *(mit Leim)* stick; paste; **jmdm. eine ~** *(salopp)* belt sb. one *(coll.)*; **b)** *(mit Klebstoff reparieren)* stick *or* glue ⟨*vase etc.*⟩ back together; **c)** *(zusammenfügen)* splice ⟨*tape, film*⟩

kleben|bleiben *unr. itr. V.; mit sein* **a)** *(haftenbleiben)* stick; remain stuck; **b)** *(salopp: nicht versetzt werden)* stay down; repeat a year; **er wird in diesem Jahr ~**: he will be staying down this year; **c)** *(ugs.: sich nicht trennen können; auch fig.)* get stuck; **d)** *(verbunden sein)* **diese Schande wird an ihr ~**: this disgrace will remain with her

Klebe·pflaster das adhesive plaster; sticking-plaster

Kleber der; ~s, ~: adhesive; glue

Klebe-: ~streifen der *s.* **Klebstreifen; ~verband der** *(Med.)* adhesive bandage

Kleb-: ~fläche die adhesive surface; sticky side; **~kraft die** adhesive strength; **~pflaster das** *s.* **Klebepflaster**

klebrig *Adj.* **a)** *(klebend)* sticky; *(von Schweiß)* clammy ⟨*hands etc.*⟩; **b)** *(abwertend: schmierig)* slimy

Klebrigkeit die; ~ *s.* **klebrig:** stickiness; clamminess; sliminess

Kleb-: ~stelle die join; *(eines Films, Tonbandes)* splice; **~stoff der** adhesive; glue; **~streifen der** adhesive *or* sticky tape; *(zum Befeuchten auch)* gummed tape

Kleckerei die; ~, ~en *(ugs.)* mess

Klecker·kram der *(ugs. abwertend)* peanuts *(sl.)*

kleckern ['klɛkɐn] *(ugs.)* **1.** *itr. V.* **a)** *(Flecken machen)* make a mess; **oje, jetzt habe ich gekleckert** oh dear, now I've gone and spilled something *(coll.)*; **b)** *mit sein (heruntertropfen)* drip; spill; **c)** *(zögernd verlaufen)* ⟨*orders*⟩ come in dribs and drabs; **d)** *(ugs.: halbherzig investieren u. ä.)* mess about with half-measures; **nicht ~, sondern klotzen** stop messing about with half-measures, and do the thing properly, whatever the cost. **2.** *tr. V.* spill; splash ⟨*paint*⟩

kleckerweise *Adv. (ugs.)* in dribs and drabs; **der Umzug ging nur ~ vonstatten** the move went ahead in fits and starts

Klecks [klɛks] **der; ~es, ~e a)** stain; *(nicht aufgesogen)* blob; *(Tintenfleck)* [ink-]blot; **b)** *(ugs.: kleine Menge)* spot; *(von Senf, Mayonnaise)* dab

klecksen 1. *itr. V.* **a)** *(Klecks[e] machen)* make a stain/stains; *(mit Tinte)* make a blot/blots; ⟨*pen*⟩ blot; **er hat auf den Teppich gekleckst** he has made a stain/stains on the carpet; **b)** *(ugs. abwertend: schlecht malen)* daub. **2.** *tr. V. (ugs.)* daub ⟨*paint*⟩; **Marmelade aufs Brot ~**: smear blobs of jam on the bread

Kleckser der; ~s, ~ *(ugs.)* **a)** *(abwertend) (Maler)* dauber; *(Schriftsteller)* scribbler; **b)** *s.* **Klecks**

Kleckserei die; ~, ~en *(ugs. abwertend)* **a)** *o. Pl. (dauerndes Klecksen)* making stains *no art.*; *(mit Tinte)* making blots *no art.*; **b)** *(Hingeschmiertes)* scribble; scrawl; *(schlecht gemaltes Bild)* daub; daubing

Kledage [kle'da:ʒə], **Kledasche** [kle'da:ʃə] **die; ~** *(nordd., md. salopp)* clobber *(sl.) no indef. art.*

Klee [kle:] **der; ~s** clover; **jmdn./etw. über den grünen ~ loben** *(ugs.)* praise sb./sth. to the skies

Klee·blatt das a) *(Blatt des Klees)* clover-leaf; *(als Symbol Irlands)* shamrock; **ein vierblättriges ~**: a four-leaf *or* four-leaved clover; **b)** *(ugs.: drei Personen)* trio; threesome; **c)** *(Verkehrsw.: Straßenkreuz)* clover-leaf [intersection *or* junction]

Kleiber ['klaibɐ] **der; ~s, ~:** nuthatch

Kleid [klait] **das; ~es, ~er a)** dress; **ein zweiteiliges ~**: a two-piece [suit]; **die Natur trägt ein weißes ~** *(fig. geh.)* Nature is dressed *or* covered in a mantle of white *(literary)*; **b)** *Pl. (Kleidung)* clothes; **in den ~ern schlafen** sleep in one's clothes; **~er machen Leute** *(Spr.)* clothes make the man; the apparel oft proclaims the man *(literary)*; **c)** *(geh.) (Gefieder)* plumage; *(Fell)* coat; **d)** *(veralt. geh.: Uniform)* uniform; **e)** *(schweiz.: Anzug)* suit

Kleidchen das; ~s, ~ a) little dress; **b)** *(ugs.: leichtes Kleid)* plain little dress

kleiden 1. *refl. V.* dress. **2.** *tr. V.* **a)** dress; **die Armen ~**: clothe the poor; **b)** suit; look well on; **die Farbe kleidet dich gut** the colour suits you *or* looks well on you; **c) etw. in Worte ~**: express sth. in words; put sth. into words; **etw. in schöne Worte ~**: clothe sth. in fine language

Kleider-: ~ab·lage die a) *(Ablage)* coat rack; **b)** *(Raum)* cloakroom; checkroom *(Amer.)*; **~bad das** *dry-cleaning process in which the article is simply dipped in the cleaning fluid and not given any finishing treatment*; **~bügel der** clothes-hanger; coat-hanger; **~bürste die** clothes-brush; **~größe die** size; **~haken der** coat-hook; **~kammer die** *(bes. Milit.)* clothing-store; **~kasten der** *(südd., österr., schweiz.) s.* **~schrank; ~macher der** *(österr./veralt.) s.* **Schneider; ~ordnung die** *(hist.)* laws *pl.* governing dress; **~puppe die** tailor's dummy; **~rock der** pinafore dress; **~sack der** *(bes. Milit.)* kitbag; **~schrank der** wardrobe; **er ist ein ~schrank** *(fig. ugs.)* he is a great hulk *or* a giant of a man; **~ständer der** coat-stand; **~stange die** clothes-rail; **~stoff der** *(Stoff für ein Kleid)* dress-material; *(Stoff für Kleidungsstücke)* clothes-material

kleidsam *Adj.* becoming

Kleidung die; ~: clothes *pl.*; **leichte/warme ~**: light/warm clothes *pl. or* clothing

Kleidungs·stück das garment; article of clothing; **~e** clothes

Kleie ['klaiə] **die; ~:** bran

klein [klain] **1.** *Adj.* **a)** little; small; small ⟨*format, letter*⟩; little ⟨*finger, toe*⟩; **das Kleid ist mir zu ~**: the dress is too small for me; **ein ~es Bier** a small beer; ≈ a half[-pint]; **ein ~es Export** ≈ a half[-pint] of Export; **eine ~e Terz/Sekunde** *(Musik)* a minor third/second; **~e Schritte machen** take small *or* short steps; **sich ~ machen** make oneself small; **auf ~stem Raum** in the minimum of space; **sie ist ~ [von Gestalt/für ihr Alter]** she is small [in stature/for her age]; **er ist [einen Kopf] ~er als ich** he is [a head] shorter than me *or* shorter than I am [by a head]; **im ~en** in miniature; on a small scale; **Pippin der Kleine** *(hist.)* Pippin the Short; **~, aber oho** he/she may be small, but he/she certainly makes up for it; **~, aber fein** little, but very nice; **b)** *(jung)* little; **sein ~er Bruder** his little brother; **als ich [noch] ~ war** when I was small *or* little; **unsere Kleine/unser Kleiner** our little girl/boy; **für die Kleinen** for the little ones; **von ~ auf** from an early age; **c)** *(von kurzer Dauer)* little, short ⟨*while*⟩; short ⟨*walk, break, holiday*⟩; short, brief ⟨*delay, introduction*⟩; brief ⟨*moment*⟩; **d)** *(von geringer Menge)* small ⟨*family, amount, audience, staff*⟩; small, low ⟨*salary*⟩; low ⟨*price*⟩; **das Gas auf ~ stellen** turn the gas down [low]; **~es Geld haben** have some [small] change; **haben Sie es ~?** *(ugs.)* do you have the right money?; **~er habe ich es nicht** I don't have anything smaller; **e)** *(von geringem Ausmaß)* light ⟨*refreshment*⟩; small ⟨*party, gift*⟩; scant, little ⟨*attention*⟩; slight ⟨*cold, indisposition*⟩; slight, small ⟨*mistake, irregularity*⟩; minor ⟨*event, error*⟩; **die ~en Dinge des Alltags** the little everyday things; **einen ~en Schreck bekommen** get a bit of a shock; **das ~ere Übel** the lesser evil; the lesser of the two evils; **das ist meine ~ste Sorge** that's the least of my worries; **du ~er Schwindler!** you little twister!; **ein ~es Spielchen** a little game; **ein ~[es] bißchen** a little *or* tiny bit; **ein ~ wenig** a little bit; **ein ~ wenig Rücksichtnahme** a little bit of consideration; **im Kleinen wie im Großen** in little things as well as in big ones; **bis ins Kleinste** down to the smallest *or* tiniest detail; **f)** *(unbedeutend)* lowly ⟨*employee, sales assistant*⟩; minor ⟨*official*⟩; **der ~e Mann** the ordinary citizen; the man in the street; **die ~en Leute** ordinary people; the man *sing.* in the street; **in ~en Verhältnissen leben** live in humble *or* modest circumstances; **~ anfangen** *(ugs.)* start off in a small way; **die Kleinen hängt man, die Großen läßt man laufen** it's always the small fry that get caught, while the big fish get away; **g) ganz ~ [und häßlich] werden** become meek and subdued; **den mache ich so ~ mit Hut!** *(ugs.)* I'll bring him down a peg or two; **jetzt ist sie so ~**: she's come down a peg or two; **h) ein ~er Geist** *(engstirnig)* a narrow-minded person; *(beschränkt)* a person of limited intellect. **2.** *adv.* **a) die Heizung ~/~er einstellen** turn the heating down low/lower; **ein Wort ~ schreiben** write a word with a small initial letter; **~ machen** *(Kinderspr.)* do number one *(child lang.)*; **b)** *(engstirnig)* **~ von jmdm./etw. denken** think little *or* have a low opinion of sb./sth.; *s. auch* **beigeben 2**

Klein das; ~s *(Kochk.) (von Geflügel)* giblets *pl.*; *(von Hasen)* trimmings *pl.*

klein-, Klein-: ~aktie die *(Wirtsch.) minimum par-value (50-mark) share*; **~aktionär der** *(Wirtsch.)* small shareholder; **~anzeige die** *(Zeitungsw.)* small *or* classified advertisement *or (coll.)* ad; **~arbeit die;** *o. Pl.* painstaking and detailed work; **~asien (das)** Asia Minor; **~bahn die** light [narrow-gauge] railway; **~bauer der** small farmer; smallholder; **~|bekommen** *unr. tr. V.: s.* **~kriegen; ~betrieb der a)** *(Industrie)* small business; **ein industrieller/handwerklicher ~betrieb** a small factory/small workshop; **b)** *(Landw.)* small farm; smallholding; **~bild·kamera die** *(Fot.)* miniature camera; 35 mm camera; **~buchstabe der** small letter; lower-case letter *(Printing)*; **~bürger der** lower middle-class person; *(abwertend: Spießbürger)* petit bourgeois; **die ~bürger** lower middle-class people; **~bürgerlich 1.** *Adj.* **a)** *(das Kleinbürgertum betreffend)* lower middle-class; **b)** *(abwertend: spießbürgerlich)* petit bourgeois; **2.** *adv. (abwertend: spießbürgerlich)* **~bürgerlich denken** have a petit-bourgeois way of thinking; **~bürgerlichkeit die** *(abwertend)* petit bourgeois nature; **~bürgertum das** lower middle class; petite bourgeoisie; **~bus der** minibus; **~dar-**

steller der small-part *or (coll.)* bit-part actor

[1]**Kleine der;** *adj. Dekl.* **a)** *(kleiner Junge)* little boy; **b)** *(ugs. Anrede)* little man; **na, ~r** *(Prostituierte zum Passanten)* hello, dearie

[2]**Kleine die;** *adj. Dekl.* **a)** *(kleines Mädchen)* little girl; **b)** *(ugs. Anrede)* love; *(abwertend)* little madam; **c)** *(ugs.: Freundin)* girl[-friend]

[3]**Kleine das;** *adj. Dekl.* **a)** *(ugs. scherzh.)* little boy/girl *(joc.)*; **das ~ der Familie** the baby of the family; **b)** *(von Tieren)* baby; little one

Kleine·leute·milieu das world of simple, ordinary people

Klein-: ~familie die *(Soziol.)* nuclear family; **~format das** small size; *(bei Büchern)* small format *or* size

Klein·garten der ≈ allotment *(cultivated primarily as a garden)*; **in ihrem ~** on her allotment

Kleingarten·anlage die ≈ allotments *pl.*

klein-, Klein-: ~gärtner der ≈ allotment-holder; **~gebäck das** biscuits *(Brit.) or (Amer.)* cookies and small pastries; **~geblümt** *Adj. (präd. getrennt geschrieben)* ⟨*dress, wallpaper, etc.*⟩ with a small floral pattern; **~gedruckt** *Adj. (präd. getrennt geschrieben)* in small print *postpos.*; **die ~gedruckten Passagen in Verträgen** the [sections *pl.* in] small print *sing.* in contracts; **~gedruckte das;** *adj. Dekl.* small print; **~geist der** *(abwertend)* small-minded person; **~geistig** *Adj.* small-minded; petty-minded ⟨*official*⟩; **~geld das;** *o. Pl.* [small] change; **würden Sie mir für 10 DM ~geld geben?** can you change a *or* give me change for a ten-mark note?; **über das nötige ~geld verfügen** *(iron.)* have the wherewithal *(coll.)*; **~gemustert** *Adj. (präd. getrennt geschrieben)* small-patterned; **~gläubig** *Adj. (unfähig zum festen Glauben)* of little faith *postpos.*; sceptical; *(ängstlich-zweifelnd)* faint-hearted; **o ihr Kleingläubigen!** *(bibl.)* o ye of little faith; **die Kleingläubigen** the doubters/faint-hearts; **~gläubigkeit die** *s.* **~gläubig:** lack of faith; scepticism; faint-heartedness; **~|hacken** *tr. V.* chop up

Kleinheit die; ~ a) *(geringe Größe)* smallness; small size; **b)** *(selten: Beschränktheit)* limitedness; restrictedness

Klein-: ~hirn das *(Anat.)* cerebellum; little brain; **~holz das** chopped wood; **~holz machen** chop wood; **~holz aus etw. machen, etw. zu ~holz machen** *(ugs.)* smash sth. to pieces; **~holz aus jmdm. machen, jmdn. zu ~holz machen** *(ugs.)* make mincemeat of sb.

Kleinigkeit die; ~, ~en a) *(kleine Sache)* small thing; *(Einzelheit)* [small] detail; minor point; **bis auf einige ~en habe ich alle Einkäufe gemacht** apart from a few small items *or* a few odds and ends I've done all the shopping; **ich habe noch eine ~ zu erledigen** I still have a small matter to attend to; **jmdm. eine ~ schenken** give sb. a small *or* little gift *or* present; **eine ~ essen** have a [small] bite to eat; **das kostet eine ~** *(ugs. iron.)* that costs a bob or two *(Brit. coll.) or* a tidy sum *(coll.)*; **die ~ von 50 000 DM** *(ugs. iron.)* the small *or* little matter of 50,000 marks; **sich nicht mit ~en abgeben** not concern oneself with details *or* trifles; **b)** *(leichte Aufgabe)* **eine ~ für jmdn. sein[, etw. zu tun]** be no trouble for sb. [to do sth.]; be a simple matter for sb. [to do sth.]; **es war eine ~ für sie, ihren Mann zu überreden** she had no trouble in persuading her husband; **es war keine ~ für ihn** it was no small matter for him; **das war eine ~:** it was nothing; **c)** *(ugs.: ein Stückchen)* a little bit; *(noch kleiner)* a fraction; a shade

Kleinigkeits·krämer der *(abwertend)* pettifogger; pettifogging individual

Kleinigkeits·krämerei die *(abwertend)* pettifoggery; pettifogging

klein-, Klein-: ~kaliber·gewehr das small-bore rifle; **~kalibrig** *Adj.* small-bore *attrib.*; **~kariert 1.** *Adj.* **a)** *(mit kleinen Karos)* ⟨*skirt, shirt, etc.*⟩ with a small check *or* with a small-checked pattern; **b)** *(ugs. abwertend: engstirnig)* narrow-minded; **2.** *adv. (ugs. abwertend)* narrow-mindedly; in a narrow-minded way; **~kind das** small child; **~kleckers·dorf** [~'klɛkɐs-] **(das)** *(ugs. spött.)* somewhere in the back of beyond *(coll.)*; some tiny little place way out in the sticks *(sl.)*; **~klima das** *(Met.)* microclimate; **~kram der** *(ugs.)* **a)** *(kleine Dinge)* odds and ends *pl.*; **b)** *(unbedeutende Dinge)* trivial matters *pl.*; *(Einzelheiten)* trivial details; *(kleinere Arbeiten)* trivial little jobs; **der tägliche ~kram** the trivial concerns *pl.* of everyday life; **~kredit der** *(Bankw.)* personal loan *(repayable within two years)*; **~krieg der a)** *(Guerillakrieg)* guerrilla warfare; **ein ~krieg** a guerrilla war; **b)** *(ständiger Streit)* running battle; **~|kriegen** *tr. V. (ugs.)* **a)** *(zerkleinern)* crush [to pieces]; get one's teeth through ⟨*tough meat*⟩; **b)** *(zerstören)* smash; break; **nicht ~zukriegen sein** be indestructible; **c)** *(aufbrauchen)* get through, *(sl.)* blow ⟨*money*⟩; get through, *(joc.)* demolish ⟨*sweets, cakes, etc.*⟩; **d)** *(entmutigen)* **jmdn. ~kriegen** get sb. down *(coll.)*; *(durch Drohungen)* intimidate sb.; *(gefügig machen)* bring sb. into line; **sich nicht ~kriegen lassen** not allow oneself to be got down/intimidated

Klein·kunst die; *o. Pl.* cabaret

Kleinkunst·bühne die cabaret ensemble

klein·laut 1. *Adj.* subdued; *(verlegen)* sheepish. **2.** *adv.* in a subdued fashion; *(verlegen)* sheepishly

kleinlich *(abwertend)* **1.** *Adj.* pernickety; *(ohne Großzügigkeit)* mean; *(engstirnig)* small-minded; petty; *(in bezug auf Sauberkeit und Ordnung)* pernickety; fussy; petty ⟨*regulations*⟩. **2.** *adv.* meticulously; punctiliously; **~ denken** have a mean and petty cast of mind

Kleinlichkeit die; ~ *(abwertend) s.* **kleinlich:** pernicketiness; meanness; small-mindedness; pettiness; fussiness

klein-, Klein-: ~|machen *tr. V.* **a)** *(zerkleinern)* cut up small; chop up ⟨*wood*⟩; **b)** *(ugs.: aufbrauchen)* get through, *(sl.)* blow ⟨*money*⟩; **c)** *(ugs.: wechseln)* change; **kann mir jemand ein 5-Mark-Stück ~machen?** can anyone give me change for a five-mark piece?; **~möbel das** smaller item of furniture; **~mut der** *(geh.)* faint-heartedness; timidity; **~mütig** *Adj. (geh.)* faint-hearted; timid

Kleinod ['klaino:t] **das; ~[e]s, ~e** *od.* **~ien** [-'no:di̯ən] *(geh.)* **a)** *(Schmuckstück)* piece of jewellery; *(Edelstein)* jewel; **b)** *(Kostbarkeit)* gem

klein-, Klein-: ~rentner der person living on a small pension; **~|schneiden** *unr. tr. V.* cut up small; cut into small pieces; chop up ⟨*onion*⟩ [small]; **~|schreiben** *unr. tr. V.* in **~geschrieben werden** *(ugs.)* count for [very] little **(bei** with); *s. auch* **klein 2a**; **~schreibung die** use of small initial letters; **~sparer der** *(Finanzw.)* small saver; **~staat der** small state; **~stadt die** small town; **~städter der** small-town dweller; **~städtisch** *Adj.* small-town *attrib.*

Kleinst·betrag der minimum *or* smallest sum *or* amount

Kleinst·bild·kamera die subminiature camera

Kleinste der/die/das; *adj. Dekl.* smallest *or* youngest boy/girl/child

klein|stellen *tr. V.* turn down [low]

kleinst-, Kleinst-: ~kind das very small child *(up to two years old)*; **~lebe·wesen das** micro-organism; **~möglich** *Adj.; nicht präd.* smallest possible

Klein·tier das pet; *(Nutztier)* small domestic animal

Kleintier-: ~halter der breeder of small animals; **~haltung die** breeding of small animals; **~zucht die** [professional] breeding of small animals; *(Betrieb)* establishment for breeding small animals

Klein·verdiener der person on a low income

Klein·vieh das small farm *or* domestic animals *pl.*; small livestock; **~ macht auch Mist** *(ugs.)* many a mickle makes a muckle *(prov.)*; every little helps

Kleinvieh·zucht die breeding of small farm *or* domestic animals

Klein·wagen der small car

klein·wüchsig [-vy:ksɪç] *Adj.* ⟨*person*⟩ of small stature; small, short ⟨*person, race*⟩; small ⟨*variety, species*⟩

Kleister ['klaistɐ] **der; ~s, ~:** paste; *(ugs. abwertend: Brei)* goo *(coll.)*

kleist[e]rig *Adj. (ugs.)* gooey *(coll.)*

kleistern *tr. V. (ugs.)* **a)** *(kleben)* paste, stick **(an +** *Akk.* on); **b)** *(reparieren)* stick; **c)** *(dick auftragen)* plaster **(auf +** *Akk.* on); **d) jmdm. eine ~:** belt sb. one *(coll.)*

Klementine [klemɛn'ti:nə] **die; ~, ~n** clementine

Klemmappe ['klɛmmapə] **die; ~, ~n** spring *or* springback binder

Klemme ['klɛmə] **die; ~, ~n a)** *(Haar~)* [hair-]clip; *(Papier~)* paper-clip; *(Technik)* clip; *(Elektrot.)* terminal; *(Med.)* clip; **b)** *(ugs.: schwierige Lage)* **in der ~ sein** *od.* **sitzen** be in a fix *or* jam *(coll.)*; **jmdm. aus der ~ helfen** help sb. out of a fix *or* jam *(coll.)*

klemmen 1. *tr. V.* **a)** *(befestigen)* tuck; stick *(coll.)*; **etw. unter den Arm ~:** tuck *or (coll.)* stick sth. under one's arm; **b)** *(quetschen)* **sich** *(Dat.)* **den Fuß/die Hand ~:** get one's foot/hand caught *or* trapped; catch *or* trap one's foot/hand; **c)** *(salopp: stehlen)* swipe *(sl.)*; pinch *(sl.)*; nick *(Brit. sl.)*. **2.** *refl. V.* **sich hinter etw.** *(Akk.)* **~:** wedge oneself behind sth.; *(fig. ugs.: sich einsetzen)* put some hard work into sth.; **sich hinter jmdn. ~:** squeeze in behind sb.; *(fig. ugs.: antreiben)* get to work on sb. *(coll.)*; **sich hinters Lenkrad ~** *(ugs.)* get behind the wheel. **3.** *itr. V.* ⟨*door, drawer, etc.*⟩ stick

Klemm-mappe *getrennte Schreibung von Klemmappe*

Klempner ['klɛmpnɐ] **der; ~s, ~:** tinsmith; *(~ und Installateur)* plumber

Klepper ['klɛpɐ] **der; ~s, ~** *(abwertend)* broken-down nag

Kleptomane [klɛpto'ma:nə] **der; ~n, ~n** *(Psych.)* kleptomaniac; **~ sein** be a kleptomaniac

Kleptomanie [klɛptoma'ni:] **die; ~** *(Psych.)* kleptomania *no art.*

Kleptomanin die; ~, ~nen kleptomaniac

kleptomanisch *Adj. (Psych.)* kleptomaniac

klerikal [kleri'ka:l] *Adj. (auch abwertend)* clerical; church ⟨*property*⟩

Klerikale der/die; *adj. Dekl. (auch abwertend)* cleric; **die ~n** the clergy *sing.*

Klerikalismus der; ~ *(oft abwertend)* clericalism

Kleriker ['kle:rikɐ] **der; ~s, ~:** cleric

Klerus ['kle:rʊs] **der; ~:** clergy

Klette ['klɛtə] **die; ~, ~n** bur; *(Pflanze)* burdock; **sich wie eine ~ an jmdn. hängen** *(ugs.)* stick like a bur to sb.

Kletter·affe der: ein ~ sein be able to climb like a monkey

Kletterei die; ~, ~en *(ugs.)* **a)** *(Herumklettern)* climbing [about]; **b)** *(Bergsteigen)* climbing

Kletterer der; ~s, ~: climber

Kletter-: ~gerüst das climbing-frame; **~maxe der** *(ugs. scherzh.)* **a)** *(Kind, das*

gerne klettert) climbing-mad child; **b)** *(Fassadenkletterer)* cat burglar

klettern ['klɛtɐn] *itr. V.; mit sein (auch fig.)* climb; *(mit Mühe)* clamber; **auf einen Baum ~:** climb a tree; **aus dem Bett/Auto ~** *(ugs.)* climb out of bed/the car *(coll.)*

Kletter-: ~partie die a) *(Bergsteigen)* climb; **b)** *(ugs.: anstrengende Wanderung)* climbing expedition; **~pflanze die** creeper; *(Bot.)* climbing plant; climber; **~rose die** climbing *or* rambling rose; **~seil das** climbing-rope; **~stange die** *(Turnen)* climbing-pole; **~tau das** *s.* **~seil; ~tour die** *s.* **~partie; ~wand die** *(Turnen)* climbing-wall

Klett·verschluß der Velcro **(P)** fastening

Kletze ['klɛtsə] **die; ~, ~n** *(österr.)* dried pear

klick [klɪk] *Interj.* click; **~ machen** click; go click; **da machte es bei ihm ~** *(fig. ugs.)* and then the penny dropped *(coll.)*

klicken *itr. V.* click; **es klickte** there was a click

Klicker der; ~s, ~ *(westmd.)* marble

klickern *itr. V. (westmd.)* play marbles

Klient [kli'ɛnt] **der; ~en, ~en** client

Klientel [kliɛn'te:l] **die; ~, ~en** clientele

Klientin die; ~, ~nen client

klieren ['kli:rən] *tr., itr. V. (nordd.)* scrawl

Kliff [klɪf] **das; ~[e]s, ~e** cliff

Kliff·küste die cliffed coast; cliffs *pl.*

Klima ['kli:ma] **das; ~s, ~s** *od.* **Klimate** [kli'ma:tə] climate; **das politische/soziale ~** *(fig.)* the political/social climate; **im Büro herrscht ein angenehmes ~** *(fig.)* there's a pleasant atmosphere in the office

Klima-: ~an·lage die air-conditioning *no indef. art.;* air-conditioning system; **mit ~anlage** air-conditioned; **~kammer die** *(Med., Biol.)* climatic chamber; **~karte die** climatic map; **~kunde die** climatology *no art.;* **~technik die;** *o. Pl.* air-conditioning engineering *no art.*

Klimakterium [klimak'te:ri̯ʊm] **das; ~s** *(Med.)* menopause; change of life

klimatisch [kli'ma:tɪʃ] **1.** *Adj.; nicht präd.* climatic. **2.** *adv.* climatically

klimatisieren *tr. V.* air-condition

Klimatologie [klimatolo'gi:] **die; ~:** climatology *no art.*

Klima·wechsel der change of climate

Klimax ['kli:maks] **die; ~:** climax

Klima·zone die climatic zone

Klimbim [klɪm'bɪm] **der; ~s** *(ugs.)* **a)** *(Kram)* junk; odds and ends *pl.;* **b)** *(Wirbel)* fuss; **~ um etw. machen** make a fuss about sth.

klimmen ['klɪmən] *unr. itr. V.; mit sein (geh.)* clamber; climb

Klimm·zug der *(Turnen)* pull-up; **geistige Klimmzüge machen** *(fig. ugs.)* do mental gymnastics

Klimperei die; ~, ~en *(ugs. abwertend)* [awful] plunking

Klimper·kasten der *(ugs. abwertend)* joanna *(sl.);* piano

klimpern ['klɪmpɐn] **1.** *itr. V.* jingle; tinkle; ⟨*coins, keys*⟩ jingle; **mit den Geldstücken/Schlüsseln ~:** jingle the coins/keys; **mit den Wimpern ~** *(scherzh.)* flutter one's eyelashes [seductively]; **auf dem Klavier/der Gitarre/dem Banjo ~** *(ugs.)* plunk away on the piano/guitar/banjo. **2.** *tr. V. (ugs. abwertend)* plunk out ⟨*tune etc.*⟩

kling [klɪŋ] *Interj. (einer Glocke)* ding; *(von Gläsern)* chink; clink; **~ machen** ding/chink *or* clink

Klinge die; ~, ~n a) blade; **b)** *(geh. veralt.: Waffe)* blade *(literary);* **mit jmdm. die ~n kreuzen** *(geh.)* cross swords with sb.; **eine [gute] ~ schlagen** *(geh.)* be a good swordsman; **eine scharfe ~ führen** *(fig. geh.)* be hard-hitting in debate; **jmdn. über die ~ springen lassen** *(fig.) (töten)* dispose of *or* kill sb.; *(ugs.: ruinieren)* ruin sb.; *(beruflich)* put paid to sb.'s career *(coll.)*

Klingel ['klɪŋl̩] **die; ~, ~n a)** bell; **b)** *(kleine Glocke)* small bell

Klingel-: ~beutel der offertory-bag; collection-bag; **~draht der** bell-wire

klinge[linge]ling [klɪŋə(lɪŋə)'lɪŋ] *Interj.* ting-a-ling

Klingel·knopf der bell-button; bell-push

klingeln *itr. V.* **a)** ring; ⟨*alarm clock*⟩ go off; ring; **es klingelt** *(an der Tür)* somebody is ringing the doorbell; there is a ring at the door; *(Telefon)* the telephone is ringing; **es hat bei ihm/ihr** *usw.* **geklingelt** *(ugs.)* the penny's dropped *(coll.); s. auch* **Kasse a; b)** *(die Klingel betätigen)* ring [the bell]; **nach jmdm. ~:** ring for sb.; **der Radfahrer klingelte** the cyclist rang his/her bell; **es klingelte zur Pause** the bell went for the break; **jmdn. aus dem Schlaf ~:** ring [the bell] and wake sb. up; **c)** *(Kfz-W.)* ⟨*engine*⟩ pink

Klingel-: ~putzen das; ~s *(ugs.)* ringing doorbells [and running away]; **~schnur die** bell-pull; **~zeichen das** ring; **das ist das ~zeichen für das Ende der Pause** that is the bell for the end of break/the interval *(Brit.) or (Amer.)* intermission; **~zug der** bell-pull

klingen *unr. itr. V.* **a) die Glocken klangen** the bells were ringing; **aus dem Haus klangen fröhliche Stimmen** the sound of merry voices came from the house; **aus dem Wald klang der Ruf des Kuckucks** from the forest could be heard the call of the cuckoo; **die Gläser ~ lassen** clink glasses [in a toast]; **b)** *(einen bestimmten Klang haben)* sound; **seine Worte klangen wie ein Vorwurf** his words sounded like a reproach; **es klang, als ob geschossen wurde** it sounded as if a shot had been fired

klingend 1. *s.* **klingen. 2.** *Adj.* **ein ~er Reim** *(Verslehre)* a feminine rhyme; **~e Münze** [hard] cash; **mit ~em Spiel** with the band playing

kling, klang *Interj.* ding dong

klingling [klɪŋ'lɪŋ] *Interj.* ting-a-ling

Klinik ['kli:nɪk] **die; ~, ~en a)** hospital; *(spezialisiert)* clinic; **b)** *o. Pl. (Med.: klinisches Studium)* clinical training

Kliniker der; ~s, ~ *(Med.)* **a)** *(Arzt)* clinician; doctor teaching at a university hospital; **b)** *(Student)* medical student doing his/her clinical training

Klinikum ['kli:nikʊm] **das; ~s, Klinika** *od.* **Kliniken a)** *(Med.: Ausbildung)* clinical training; **b)** *(Zusammenschluß mehrerer Kliniken)* hospital complex *(usually teaching hospitals and clinics, with central administration)*

klinisch 1. *Adj.; nicht präd. (Med.)* clinical; **sie ist jetzt im 5. ~en Semester** she is now in the fifth term of her clinical training. **2.** *adv.* **~ tot** clinically dead

Klinke ['klɪŋkə] **die; ~, ~n a)** *(an der Tür)* door-handle; **sich** *(Dat.)* **die ~ in die Hand geben** *(ugs.)* come and go in a continuous stream; **~n putzen** *(ugs. abwertend) (als Vertreter)* peddle one's goods from door to door; *(betteln)* go begging from door to door; **b)** *(Technik)* catch; pawl

Klinken·putzer der *(ugs. abwertend) (Vertreter)* door-to-door salesman; *(Bettler)* beggar

Klinker der; ~s, ~: [Dutch] clinker

Klinker-: ~bau der building of clinker brick; **~stein der** *s.* **Klinker**

klipp [klɪp] *Adv.* **~ und klar** *(ugs.)* quite plainly *or* clearly

Klippe die; ~, ~n rock; **alle ~n umschiffen** *(fig.)* negotiate every obstacle [successfully]

Klipper der; ~s, ~ *(hist.)* clipper

Klipp·fisch der *cod etc. split open, salted, and partly dried;* klipfish

klipp, klapp *Interj.* click-clack

Klipp·schule die *(nordd. abwertend)* second-rate school

klirren ['klɪrən] *itr. V.* ⟨*glasses, ice-cubes*⟩ clink; ⟨*weapons in fight*⟩ clash; ⟨*windowpane*⟩ rattle; ⟨*chains, spurs*⟩ clank, rattle; ⟨*harness*⟩ jingle; **mit der Kette/den Sporen ~:** clank *or* rattle the chain/one's spurs; **~der Frost** *(fig.)* sharp frost

Klirr·faktor der *(Elektrot.)* distortion factor

Klischee [kli'ʃe:] **das; ~s, ~s a)** cliché; **das ~ vom braven Hausmütterchen** the conventional picture *or* stereotype of the good little housewife; **b)** *(Druckw.)* block; plate

klischeehaft 1. *Adj.* stereotyped, hackneyed ⟨*picture, description*⟩; cliché-ridden ⟨*style*⟩. **2.** *adv.* in a stereotyped *or* hackneyed way *or* manner

Klischee·vorstellung die stereotyped idea

klischieren *tr. V. (Druckw.)* stereotype

Klistier [klɪs'ti:ɐ̯] **das; ~s, ~e** *(Med.)* enema

Klitoris ['kli:torɪs] **die; ~, ~** *od.* **Klitorides** [kli'to:ride:s] *(Anat.)* clitoris

Klitsch [klɪtʃ] **der; ~[e]s, ~e** *(landsch.)* **a)** *(Brei)* soggy mass; mush; **b)** *(Schlag)* slap; smack

Klitsche die; ~, ~n *(ugs.)* **a)** *(ärmlicher Bauernhof)* poor, run-down farm; **b)** *(armseliges Dorf)* wretched little village *or* place; **c)** *(kleiner Betrieb)* little shoestring outfit *(coll.);* **d)** *(Schmierentheater)* third-rate little theatre

klitsch, klatsch *Interj.* smack; **~, ~, schlug der Regen gegen die Scheiben** pitter-patter went the rain on the window panes

klitsch·naß *Adj. (ugs.)* soaking *or* sopping wet; *(tropfnaß)* dripping wet; **wir sind ~ geworden** we got soaked [to the skin] *or* drenched

klitze·klein ['klɪtsə-] *Adj. (ugs.)* teeny[-weeny] *(coll.)*

Klivie ['kli:vi̯ə] **die; ~, ~n** *(Bot.)* clivia

Klo [klo:] **das; ~s, ~s** *(ugs.)* loo *(Brit. coll.);* john *(Amer. coll.);* **aufs ~ müssen** have to go to the loo; **etw. ins ~ schütten** tip sth. down the loo

Kloake [klo'a:kə] **die; ~, ~n** *(Senkgrube, auch fig.)* cesspit; *(Kanal)* sewer

Kloben ['klo:bn̩] **der; ~s, ~** *(Holz~)* log

klobig *Adj.* **a)** *(kantig)* heavy and clumsy[-looking] ⟨*shoes, furniture*⟩; heavily-built, bulky ⟨*figure*⟩; **b)** *(plump)* clumsy; boorish; boorish ⟨*behaviour*⟩

Klo-: ~bürste die *(ugs.)* loo-brush *(Brit. coll.);* toilet-brush; **~frau die** *(ugs.)* loo-attendant *(Brit. coll.);* bathroom attendant *(Amer.)*

klomm [klɔm] *1. u. 3. Pers. Sg. Prät. v.* **klimmen**

Klon [klo:n] **der; ~s, ~e** *(Biol.)* clone

klönen ['klø:nən] *itr. V. (nordd.)* chat

Klo·papier das *(ugs.)* loo-paper *(Brit. coll.);* toilet-paper

klopfen ['klɔpfn̩] **1.** *itr. V.* **a)** *(schlagen)* knock; **an die Tür ~:** knock at the door; **es hat geklopft** there's somebody knocking at the door; **jmdm.** *od.* **jmdn. auf die Schulter ~:** slap sb. on the shoulder; **„bitte ~!"** 'please knock'; **„bitte zweimal ~!"** 'please give two knocks'; **b)** *(pulsieren)* ⟨*heart*⟩ beat; ⟨*pulse*⟩ throb; **sein Herz schien ihm bis zum Hals zu ~:** his heart was in his mouth *or* was pounding wildly; **mit ~dem Herzen** with pounding *or* beating heart; **ein ~der Schmerz** a throbbing pain; **c)** *(Kfz-W.)* ⟨*engine*⟩ knock. **2.** *tr. V.* beat ⟨*carpet*⟩; **Beifall ~:** applaud by banging *or* rapping on the desk/table with one's fist; **den Takt [zur Musik] ~:** beat time [to the music]; **Fleisch ~:** beat *or* tenderize meat; **Steine ~:** break stones; *(pflastern)* lay cobbles; **Staub vom Mantel ~:** beat dust from one's coat; **die Asche aus der Pfeife ~:** knock *or* tap the ash out of one's pipe; **einen Nagel in die Wand ~:** knock *or* hammer a nail into the wall; **jmdn. aus dem Schlaf ~:** knock sb. up *(Brit.);* awaken sb. by knocking

Klopfer der; ~s, ~ a) *(Teppich~)* carpet-beater; **b)** *(Tür~)* [door-]knocker; **c)** *(Fleisch~)* meat mallet *or* tenderizer

klopf-, Klopf-: ~fest *Adj.* antiknock ⟨*petrol, fuel*⟩; **~festigkeit die** antiknock properties *pl.*; **~zeichen das** knock; *(leiser)* tap

Kloppe ['klɔpə] **die; ~** *(nordd., md.)* [good] hiding *(coll.) or* thrashing; **~ kriegen** get a [good] hiding *(coll.) or* thrashing

Klöppel ['klœpl̩] **der; ~s, ~ a)** *(Glocken~)* clapper; **b)** *(Musik)* beater; **c)** *(Handarbeiten: Spule)* bobbin

Klöppel·arbeit die a) *o. Pl.* bobbin-lace *or* pillow-lace making *no art.*; **b)** *(Erzeugnis)* piece of pillow-lace *or* bobbin-lace

klöppeln *tr., itr. V.* **[etw.] ~:** make *or* work [sth. in] pillow-lace *or* bobbin-lace

Klöppel·spitze die pillow-lace; bobbin-lace

kloppen *(nordd., md.)* **1.** *tr. V.* hit. **2.** *refl. V.* fight; scrap *(coll.)*

Klopperei die; ~, ~en *(nordd., md.)* fight; scrap *(coll.)*

Klöppler der; ~s, ~, Klöpplerin die; ~, ~nen pillow-lace *or* bobbin-lace maker

Klops [klɔps] **der; ~es, ~e** *(nordostd.)* meat ball

Klosett [klo'zɛt] **das; ~s, ~s** *od.* **~e** lavatory; **etw. ins ~ schütten** tip sth. down the lavatory

Klosett-: ~becken das lavatory pan; toilet bowl; **~brille die** *(ugs.)* loo-seat *(Brit. coll.)*; toilet-seat; **~bürste die** lavatory-brush; toilet-brush; **~deckel der** toilet-lid; **~frau die** lavatory attendant; **~papier das** toilet-paper; lavatory-paper; **~sitz der** toilet-seat; lavatory-seat

Kloß [klo:s] **der; ~es, Klöße** ['klø:sə] dumpling; *(Fleisch~)* meat ball; **ihm sitzt ein ~ im Hals, er hat einen ~ im Hals** *(ugs.)* he has a lump in his throat

Kloster ['klo:stɐ] **das; ~s, Klöster** ['klø:stɐ] *(Mönchs~)* monastery; *(Nonnen~)* convent; nunnery; **ins ~ gehen** enter a monastery/convent

Kloster-: ~bruder der lay brother; *(veralt.: Mönch)* monk; **~frau die** *(geh. veralt.)* nun; **~kirche die** monastery/convent church

klösterlich 1. *Adj.* **a)** monastic; monastic/convent ⟨*life*⟩; **b)** *(zum Kloster gehörend)* of the monastery/convent *postpos., not pred.*; monastery/convent *attrib.* **2.** *adv.* **~ abgeschieden leben** live in monastic seclusion

Kloster-: ~regel die rules *pl.* of the monastery/convent; **~schule die** monastery-school/convent-school; **~schüler der** monastery-school/convent-school pupil

Klotz [klɔts] **der; ~es, Klötze** ['klœtsə] **a)** *(Stück Holz)* block [of wood]; *(Stück eines Baumstamms)* log; **schlafen wie ein ~** *(fig.)* sleep like a log; **ein ~ aus Beton [und Glas]** *(fig.)* a concrete [and glass] monstrosity; **jmdm. ein ~ am Bein sein** *(ugs.)* be a millstone round sb.'s neck; **mit ihm hast du dir einen ~ ans Bein gebunden** *(ugs.)* you have tied a millstone round your neck by getting involved with him; **auf einen groben ~ gehört ein grober Keil** *(Spr.)* rudeness can only be answered with rudeness; **b)** *(salopp abwertend) (ungehobelter Mensch)* clod; oaf; *(roher Mensch)* lout

Klötzchen ['klœtsçən] **das; ~s, ~:** small block of wood

klotzen *(ugs.)* **1.** *itr. V.* **a)** *(großzügig vorgehen)* lash out in a big way *(coll.)*; *s. auch* **kleckern 1 d**; **b)** *(hart arbeiten)* graft *(sl.)*. **2.** *tr. V.* stick up *(coll.)* ⟨*building, town*⟩

klotzig *Adj.* **a)** *(abwertend: unförmig)* large and ugly[-looking] ⟨*building*⟩; large and clumsy[-looking] ⟨*furniture*⟩; **b)** *(ugs.: gewaltig)* massive great *(coll.)* ⟨*car, villa, etc.*⟩

Klub [klʊp] **der; ~s, ~s a)** *(Vereinigung)* club; **b)** *(Gebäude)* club; **im ~:** at the club; **c)** *(Clique)* crowd

klub-, Klub-: ~eigen *Adj.* club's *attrib.*; the club's *pred.*; **~garnitur die** thickly upholstered three-piece suite; **~haus das** club-house; **~jacke die** blazer; **~mitglied das** club-member; **~sessel der** club chair; **~zwang der** *(österr.) s.* **Fraktionszwang**

¹Kluft [klʊft] **die; ~, ~en** *(ugs.)* rig-out *(coll.)*; gear *(coll.)*; *(Uniform)* uniform; garb; **sich in seine beste ~ werfen** put on one's Sunday best *or* one's best things

²Kluft die; ~, Klüfte ['klʏftə] **a)** *(veralt.) (Spalte)* cleft; fissure; *(im Gletscher)* crevasse; *(Abgrund)* chasm; **b)** *(Gegensatz)* gulf

klug [klu:k]; **klüger** ['kly:gɐ], **klügst...** ['kly:kst...] **1.** *Adj.* **a)** *(intelligent)* clever; intelligent; clever, bright ⟨*child, pupil*⟩; intelligent ⟨*eyes*⟩; **er ist ein ~er Kopf** he's clever *or* bright; he's got brains; **b)** *(gelehrt, weise)* wise; **so ~ wie vorher** *od.* **zuvor sein** be none the wiser; **so ~ waren wir auch!** we know that as well as you do; **hinterher ist man immer klüger** it's easy to be wise after the event; **daraus werde ich nicht ~, daraus soll ein Mensch ~ werden** I can't make head or tail of it; **aus jmdm. nicht ~ werden** not know what to make of sb.; **c)** *(vernünftig)* wise; wise, sound ⟨*advice*⟩; wise, prudent ⟨*remark, course of action*⟩; *(geschickt)* clever, shrewd ⟨*politician, negotiator, question*⟩; shrewd, astute ⟨*businessman*⟩; great ⟨*foresight*⟩; **es wäre das klügste, wenn wir ...:** the wisest course *or* thing would be for us to ...; **der Klügere gibt nach** *(Spr.)* discretion is the better part of valour *(prov.)*; **der ~e Mann baut vor** it pays to be prepared. **2.** *adv.* **a)** *(intelligent)* cleverly; intelligently; **~ daherreden** talk as if one knows it all; **~ daherreden kann jeder!** anyone can talk!; **b)** *(vernünftig)* wisely; *(geschickt)* cleverly; shrewdly

Klügelei die; ~, ~en *(abwertend)* **~[en** *Pl.***]** over-subtle reasoning *no pl.*

klügeln [kly:gl̩n] *itr. V.* **an etw.** *(Dat.)* **~:** ponder [over] sth.

klüger *s.* **klug**

klugerweise *Adv.* wisely

Klugheit die; ~, ~en a) *o. Pl.*; *s.* **klug a, b, c:** cleverness; intelligence; brightness; wisdom; soundness; prudence; shrewdness; astuteness; **b)** *Pl. (iron.: weise Sprüche)* clever remarks

klüglich *Adv. (geh.)* wisely

klug|reden *itr. V. (ugs.)* talk as if one knows it all

Klug·scheißer der *(salopp abwertend)* know-it-all *(coll.)*; smart aleck *(coll.)*

klügst... *s.* **klug**

Klump [klʊmp] **der; ~s** *in* **einen Wagen zu** *od.* **in ~ fahren** *(salopp)* smash up *or* write off a car; **jmdn. zu ~ schlagen** *(salopp)* beat the living daylights out of sb. *(sl.)*

Klumpatsch ['klʊmpatʃ] **der; ~[e]s** *(salopp abwertend)* junk

klumpen ['klʊmpn̩] *itr. V.* go lumpy

Klumpen der; ~s, ~ a) lump; **ein ~ Erde** a lump or clod of earth; **ein ~ Gold** a gold nugget; **b)** *(rhein.: Holzschuh)* clog

Klump·fuß der club foot

klumpig *Adj.* lumpy

Klüngel ['klʏŋl̩] **der; ~s, ~** *(abwertend)* **a)** *(Clique)* clique; **b)** *(Cliquenwesen)* cliquism *no indef. art.*

Klüngelei die; ~, ~en *(abwertend)* cliquism *no pl.*; *(Vetternwirtschaft)* nepotism *no pl.*

klüngeln *itr. V. (ugs.) s.* **Klüngelei:** indulge in cliquism/nepotism

Klunker ['klʊŋkɐ] **die; ~, ~n** *od.* **der; ~s, ~** *(ugs.)* rock *(sl.)*

Klus [klu:s] **die; ~, ~en** *(schweiz.)* narrow gorge; cluse *(Geol.)*

Klüse ['kly:zə] **die; ~, ~n** *s.* **Ankerklüse**

Klüver ['kly:vɐ] **der; ~s, ~** *(Seemannsspr.)* jib

Klüver·baum der *(Seemannsspr.)* jib-boom

km *Abk.* **Kilometer** km.

knabbern ['knabɐn] **1.** *tr. V.* nibble; **etw. zum Knabbern** sth. to nibble; **nichts mehr zu ~ haben** *(ugs. verhüll.)* be broke *(coll.) or* skint *(sl.)*. **2.** *itr. V.* **an etw.** *(Dat.)* **~:** nibble *or* gnaw [at] sth.; **an etw.** *(Dat.)* **[noch lange] zu ~ haben** *(ugs.) (sich anstrengen müssen)* have sth. to think about *or* chew on; *(leiden müssen)* take a long time to get over sth.; **an dieser Übersetzung hatten die Schüler ganz schön zu ~:** this translation really gave the pupils something to think about *or* chew on

Knabe ['kna:bə] **der; ~n, ~n a)** *(geh. veralt./südd., österr., schweiz.)* boy; **b)** *(ugs.: Bursche)* chap *(coll.)*; **Na, alter ~! Wie geht's?** well, old boy *or* old chap, how are you? *(coll.)*

Knaben-: ~alter das *(geh.)* boyhood; **~chor der** boys' choir

knabenhaft 1. *Adj.* boyish. **2.** *adv.* boyishly

Knaben-: ~kraut das orchis; wild orchid; **~liebe die** *(geh.)* pederasty; **~schule die** *(veralt.)* boys' school; **~stimme die** boy's voice; **~streich der** *(geh.)* boyish prank

knack [knak] *Interj.* crack

Knack der; ~[e]s, ~e crack

Knäcke·brot ['knɛkə-] **das** crispbread; *(Scheibe)* slice of crispbread

knacken 1. *itr. V.* **a)** *(krachen)* ⟨*bed, floor, etc.*⟩ creak; **es knackt im Telefon** the [telephone-]line is crackling; **es knackte im Gebälk** the beams creaked; **mit den Fingern ~:** crack one's fingers; **b)** *mit sein (ugs.: zerbrechen)* snap; ⟨*window*⟩ crack; **c)** *in* **an etw.** *(Dat.)* **zu ~ haben** *(ugs.)* take a long time to get over sth.. **2.** *tr. V.* **a)** *(zerbrechen)* crack ⟨*nut, shell*⟩; **b)** *(salopp: zerquetschen)* squash; **c)** *(aufbrechen)* crack ⟨*safe*⟩ [open]; break into ⟨*car, bank, vending-machine, etc.*⟩; crack, break ⟨*code*⟩

Knacker der; ~s, ~ a) *in* **alter ~** *(salopp)* old fogey; **b)** *(ugs.: Geldschrankknacker)* safe-cracker; **c)** *s.* **Knackwurst**

knack·frisch *Adj. (ugs.)* crispy fresh ⟨*rolls, crisps, etc.*⟩; crisp fresh ⟨*fruit, vegetables*⟩

Knacki ['knaki] **der; ~s, ~s** *(salopp)* con *(coll.)*; jailbird

knackig *Adj.* **a)** *(knusprig)* crisp; crisp, crunchy ⟨*apple*⟩; **b)** *(ugs.: attraktiv)* luscious, delectable ⟨*girl*⟩

Knack·laut der *(Phon.)* glottal stop

knacks *Interj.* crack

Knacks der; ~es, ~e *(ugs.)* **a)** *(Ton)* crack; **b)** *(Sprung)* crack; **c)** *(fig.: Defekt)* **einen ~ bekommen** ⟨*person*⟩ have *or* suffer a breakdown; ⟨*health*⟩ suffer; **die Ehe hatte einen ~:** the marriage was in difficulties

Knack·wurst die *[smoked] sausage filled with minced meat and pieces of fat, the tight skin of which makes a cracking sound when bitten*; knackwurst

Knall [knal] **der; ~[e]s, ~e** bang; *(fig.)* big row; **einen ~ haben** *(salopp)* be barmy *(sl.) or* off one's rocker *(sl.)*; **auf ~ und Fall, ~ auf Fall** *(ugs.)* without warning

knall-, Knall-: ~bonbon der *od.* **das** cracker; **~bunt** *Adj.* gaudy; ⟨*car*⟩ painted in gaudy colours; **~effekt der** *(ugs.) (Überraschendes)* astonishing part; *(Sensation)* sensational part

knallen 1. *itr. V.* **a)** *(einen Knall verursachen)* ⟨*shot*⟩ ring out; ⟨*firework*⟩ go bang; ⟨*cork*⟩ pop; ⟨*door*⟩ bang, slam; ⟨*whip, rifle*⟩ crack; **die Peitsche ~ lassen** crack the whip; **mit der Tür ~:** bang *or* slam the door; **an der Kreuzung hat es geknallt** *(ugs.)* there was a crash at the crossroads; **sei ruhig, oder es knallt!** *(fig. ugs.)* be quiet, or you'll get a good hiding; **b)** *(ugs.: schießen)* shoot, fire **(auf +** *Akk.* at); *(mehrere Male)* blaze *or (coll.)* bang away **(auf +** *Akk.* at); **Hände hoch, oder es knallt!** hands up, or I'll shoot!; **c)** *(Ballspiele ugs.)* **aufs Tor ~:** belt the ball/puck at the goal *(coll.)*; **d)** *mit sein (ugs.: prallen)* **die Tür knallte ins Schloß** the door slammed *or* banged shut; **sie knallte mit dem Fahrrad gegen einen Laternenpfahl** she crashed into a lamp-post on her bicycle; **mit dem Kopf gegen die Windschutzscheibe ~:** bang one's head against the windscreen; **der Ball knallte gegen die Latte** the ball slammed against the crossbar; **e)** *(ugs.: scheinen)* blaze *or* beat down. **2.** *tr. V.* **a)** *(ugs.) (hart aufsetzen)* slam *or* bang down; *(werfen)* sling *(coll.)*; **den Hörer auf die Gabel ~:** slam *or* bang down the receiver; **b)** *(ugs.: schlagen)* **du kriegst gleich eine geknallt!** you're going to get a clout any minute *(coll.)*; **jmdm. eine ~** *(salopp)* belt *or* clout sb. one *(coll.)*; **c)** *(Ballspiele ugs.)* belt ‹*ball*›

knạll·ẹng *Adj. (ugs.)* skin-tight

Knạller der; ~s, ~: banger

Knạll·erbse die ≈ cap-bomb

Knallerei die; ~, ~en *(ugs.) (von Korken)* popping; *(einer Peitsche)* cracking; *(von Gewehren)* banging, shooting; *(von Feuerwerk)* banging

knạll-, Knạll-: ~frosch der jumping jack; **~gas das** *(Chemie)* oxy-hydrogen; **~gẹlb** *Adj. (ugs.)* bright *or* vivid yellow; **~hạrt** *(ugs.)* **1.** *Adj.* **a)** very tough ‹*job, demands, action, measures, etc.*›; ‹*person*› as hard as nails; hard[-core] ‹*pornography*›; very sharp ‹*criticism*›; **ein ~harter Bursche** a thug; **b)** *(kraftvoll)* fierce ‹*serve*›; crashing ‹*blow*›; **2.** *adv.* **a)** *(rücksichtslos, brutal)* brutally; **gegen etw. ~hart vorgehen** take very tough action against sth.; **jmdm. etw. ~hart sagen** say sth. to sb. quite brutally; **b)** *(kraftvoll)* ‹*serve, hit*› really hard; **~heiß** *Adj. (ugs.)* boiling *or* baking hot *(coll.)*

knạllig *Adj. (ugs.)* loud; gaudy

knạll-, Knạll-: ~kopf, ~kopp der *(salopp)* [stupid] berk *(Brit. sl.) or (Amer. sl.)* jerk; **~körper der** banger; *(bei Aufprall explodierend)* ≈ cap-bomb; **~rọt** *Adj.* bright *or* vivid red; **sie bekam einen ~roten Kopf** she *or* her face turned [bright] scarlet *or* as red as a beetroot; **~tüte die** *(ugs.)* nitwit *(coll.)*; clot *(Brit. sl.)*

knapp [knap] **1.** *Adj.* **a)** *(kaum ausreichend)* meagre, low ‹*pension, wage, salary*›; meagre ‹*pocket-money*›; **Kaffee war ~:** coffee was scarce *or* in short supply; **das Geld wird ~:** money is getting tight; **die Vorräte wurden ~:** supplies ran short; **sie bekam nur ein sehr ~es Haushaltsgeld** she received very little housekeeping money; **~ mit etw. sein** be short of sth.; **..., und nicht zu ~! ...** and how!; **b)** *(gerade ausreichend)* narrow ‹*victory, lead*›; narrow, bare ‹*majority*›; close ‹*result*›; **c)** *(nicht ganz)* **vor einer ~en Stunde** almost *or* just under an hour ago; **d)** *(eng)* tight-fitting ‹*garment*›; *(zu eng)* tight ‹*garment*›; **e)** *(kurz)* terse ‹*reply, greeting*›; concise, succinct ‹*description, account, report*›; **mit ~en Worten** in a few brief words. **2.** *adv.* **a)** *(kaum ausreichend)* **~ bemessen sein** be meagre; **seine Zeit war ~ bemessen** his time was limited; **~ gerechnet** at the lowest estimate; **b)** *(gerade ausreichend)* **~ gewinnen/verlieren** win/lose narrowly *or* by a narrow margin; **eine Prüfung ~ bestehen** just pass an examination; **c)** *(sehr nahe)* just; **~ über dem Knie enden** come to just above the knee; **d)** *(nicht ganz)* just under; not quite; **vor ~ einer Stunde** just under *or* not quite an hour ago; **er ist ~ fünfzig** he is not quite fifty *or* just this side of fifty; **e)** *(eng)* **~ sitzen** fit tightly; *(zu eng)* be a tight fit; **~ geschnitten/sitzend** tight-fitting; **f)** *(kurz)* ‹*reply*› tersely; ‹*describe, summarize*› concisely, succinctly

Knạppe der; ~n, ~n **a)** *(Bergmann)* miner *(who has completed his apprenticeship)*; **b)** *(hist.)* squire

knạpp|halten *unr. tr. V. (ugs.)* keep ‹*goods etc.*› in short supply; **jmdn. [mit Geld] ~:** keep sb. short [of money]

Knạppheit die; ~ **a)** *(Mangel)* shortage, scarcity (**an** + *Dat.* of); *(von Geld, Zeit)* shortage; **b)** *(Kürze) (einer Antwort, eines Grußes)* terseness; *(einer Beschreibung, eines Berichts)* conciseness, succinctness

Knạppschaft die; ~, ~en *(Bergmannsspr.)* **a)** *(Gesamtheit der Knappen)* miners *pl.*; **b)** *(Organisation)* miners' guild

knapsen ['knapsn̩] *itr. V. (ugs.)* skimp; scrimp

Knarre ['knarə] **die;** ~, ~n **a)** *(Rassel)* rattle; **b)** *(salopp: Gewehr)* shooting-iron *(sl.)*

knạrren *itr. V.* creak; **mit ~der Stimme** in a rasping *or* grating voice

Knast [knast] **der;** ~[e]s, **Knäste** ['knɛstə] *od.* ~e *(ugs.)* **a)** *o. Pl. (Strafe)* bird *(sl.)*; time; **man hat ihm zwei Jahre ~ gegeben** he got two years' bird *(sl.)*; **~ schieben** *(salopp)* do bird *(sl.) or* time; **b)** *(Gefängnis)* clink *(sl.)*; jug *(sl.)*; prison; **im ~ sitzen** be in clink *or* jug *(sl.)*

Knạst·bruder der *(ugs.)* **a)** jailbird; old lag *(sl.)*; **b)** *(Mitgefangener)* fellow jailbird

Knạster der; ~s, ~ **a)** *(veralt.: Tabak)* weed *(arch.)*; **b)** *(ugs. abwertend: schlechter Tabak)* evil-smelling tobacco

Knastologe [knasto'lo:gə] **der;** ~n, ~n *(ugs. scherzh.)* jailbird; old lag *(sl.)*

Knatsch [kna:tʃ] **der;** ~[e]s *(ugs.: Ärger)* trouble; **die beiden haben schon wieder ~ miteinander** the two of them are already rowing again

knạtschig *Adj. (ugs.)* grumpy; *(weinerlich)* fretful

knattern ['knatərn] *itr. V.* **a)** ‹*machine-gun*› rattle, clatter; ‹*sail*› flap; ‹*radio*› crackle; ‹*motor vehicle, engine*› clatter; **b)** *mit sein (~d fahren)* clatter

Knäuel ['knɔyəl] **der** *od.* **das;** ~s, ~ **a)** ball; *(wirres ~)* tangle; **er knüllte den Brief zu einem ~ zusammen** he screwed the letter into a ball; **b)** *(fig.) (von Menschen)* knot; *(größer)* [milling] crowd; *(von Widersprüchen, Ereignissen)* tangle

Knauf [knauf] **der;** ~[e]s, **Knäufe** ['knɔyfə] *(einer Tür, eines Gehstocks)* knob; *(eines Schwertes, Dolches)* pommel

Knauser der; ~s, ~ *(ugs. abwertend)* Scrooge; skinflint; miser

Knauserei die; ~,~en *(ugs. abwertend)* **a)** *o. Pl. (knauseriges Wirtschaften)* stinginess; penny-pinching; miserliness; **b)** *(Fall von ~)* piece of stinginess *or* miserliness

knauserig *Adj. (ugs. abwertend)* stingy; tight-fisted; close-fisted

Knauserigkeit die; ~, ~en *s.* **Knauserei**

knausern ['knauzərn] *itr. V. (ugs. abwertend)* be stingy; skimp; scrimp; **mit etw. ~:** be stingy with sth.

Knaus-Ogino-Methode ['knaus|o'gi:no-] **die** rhythm method *(with calendar-marking)*

knautschen ['knautʃn̩] *(ugs.)* **1.** *tr. V.* crumple; crumple, crease ‹*dress*›. **2.** *itr. V.* ‹*dress, material*› crease, get creased

knautschig *Adj. (ugs.)* crumpled ‹*suit, dress, etc.*›

Knautsch-: ~lack der, ~lack·leder das, ~leder das patterned patent leather; *(Imitat)* imitation patterned patent leather; **~zone die** *(Kfz-W.)* crumple zone

Knebel ['kne:bl̩] **der;** ~s, ~ **a)** *(zum Knebeln)* gag; **b)** *(Griff)* toggle; *(am Schraubstock)* handle

Knebel-: ~bart der Vandyke beard; *(Schnurrbart)* twisted moustache; **~knopf der** toggle

knebeln *tr. V.* gag; *(fig.)* gag, muzzle ‹*the press, a people*›

Knecht [knɛçt] **der;** ~[e]s, ~e **a)** farm-labourer; farm-hand; *(fig.)* slave; vassal; **b)** **~ Ruprecht** *helper to St. Nicholas [≈ to Santa Claus]*

knẹchten *tr. V. (geh.) (versklaven)* reduce to servitude *or* slavery; enslave; *(unterdrücken)* oppress ‹*people, nation*›

knẹchtisch *(geh.)* **1.** *Adj.* servile, slavish ‹*obedience, submissiveness*›; servile, submissive ‹*person, character*›. **2.** *adv.* servilely; submissively

Knẹchtschaft die; ~, ~en *(geh.)* bondage; servitude; slavery

Knẹchtung die; ~, ~en *(geh.) s.* **knechten:** enslavement; oppression

kneifen ['knaifn̩] **1.** *unr. tr., itr. V.* pinch; **jmdm.** *od.* **jmdn. in den Arm ~:** pinch sb.'s arm. **2.** *unr. itr. V.* **a)** *(drücken)* ‹*clothes*› be too tight; **b)** *(ugs. abwertend: sich drücken)* chicken *(sl.)* or back out (**vor** + *Dat.* of); **vor einer Prüfung/Verantwortung ~:** funk an examination *(sl.)*/*(coll.)* duck [out of] a responsibility

Kneifer der; ~s, ~: pince-nez

Kneif·zange die pincers *pl.*; **eine ~:** a pair of pincers

Kneip·abend der [students'] drinking evening

Kneipe ['knaipə] **die;** ~, ~n **a)** *(ugs.)* pub *(Brit. coll.)*; bar *(Amer.)*; **b)** *(Studentenspr. veralt.)* [students'] drinking evening

Kneipen·wirt der, Kneipier [knai'pie:] **der;** ~s, ~s *(salopp)* [pub *(coll.)*] landlord *(Brit.)*; bar-keeper *(Amer.)*

kneippen ['knaipn̩] *itr. V. (ugs.)* take *or* undergo a Kneipp cure

Kneipp·kur die Kneipp cure

knẹtbar *Adj.* workable; kneadable ‹*dough*›

Knete die; ~ **a)** *(ugs.) s.* **Knetmasse; b)** *(salopp: Geld)* dough *(sl.)*

kneten ['kne:tn̩] *tr. V.* **a)** *(bearbeiten)* knead ‹*dough, muscles*›; work ‹*clay*›; **b)** *(formen)* model ‹*figure*›; **eine Figur aus Ton ~:** mould *or* fashion a figure in clay

Knet-: ~maschine die kneading machine; **~masse die** plastic modelling-material; Plasticine (P)

Knick [knɪk] **der;** ~[e]s, ~e **a)** *(Biegung)* sharp bend; *(in einem Draht)* kink; **du hast wohl einen ~ in der Optik!** *(ugs. scherzh.)* are you blind?; **b)** *(Falz)* crease; **c)** *Pl.* ~s *(nordd.: Hecke)* boundary hedge [with ditches and rampart]

Knickebein ['knɪkəbain] **der;** ~s *egg liqueur used as a filling in sweets, Easter eggs, etc.*

Knịck·ei das cracked egg

knịcken 1. *tr. V.* **a)** *(brechen)* snap; **b)** *(falten)* crease ‹*page, paper, etc.*›; **„Bitte nicht ~!"** *(auf einem Umschlag)* 'please do not bend'; *(auf einem Formular)* 'please do not fold'. **2.** *itr. V.; mit sein* snap

Knịcker der; ~s, ~ **a)** *(ugs. abwertend)* Scrooge; skinflint; miser; **b)** *(niederd.: Murmel)* marble

Knịckerbocker [-bɔkɐ] *Pl.* knickerbockers; *(länger und breiter)* plus-fours

knịck[e]rig *Adj. (ugs. abwertend)* stingy; tight-fisted

Knịck[e]rigkeit die; ~ *(ugs. abwertend)* stinginess; tight-fistedness

Knịck·fuß der club-foot

Knịcks [knɪks] **der;** ~es, ~e curtsy; **einen ~ machen** make *or* drop a curtsy (**vor** + *Dat.* to)

knịcksen *itr. V.* curtsy (**vor** + *Dat.* to)

Knie [kni:] **das;** ~s, ~ ['kni:(ə)] **a)** knee; **jmdm. auf [den] ~n danken** go down on one's knees and thank sb.; **jmdn. auf ~n bitten** beg sb. on bended knees; **vor jmdm. auf die ~ fallen** go down on one's knees before sb.; **er hatte/bekam weiche ~** *(ugs.)* his knees trembled/started to tremble; **vor lauter Aufregung hatte ich ganz weiche ~:** I was weak at the knees with sheer excitement; **jmdn. auf** *od.* **in die ~ zwingen** *(geh.)* force sb. to his knees; **in die ~ gehen** *(umfallen)* sink to one's knees; *(eine Kniebeuge machen)* bend one's knees; *(sich unterordnen)* submit, bow (**vor** + *Dat.* to); **jmdn. übers ~**

legen *(ugs.)* put sb. across one's knee; **etw. übers ~ brechen** *(ugs.)* rush sth.; **b)** *(an Hosen, Strümpfen)* knee; **c)** *(Biegung)* sharp bend; *(eines Rohres)* elbow

Knie·beuge die knee-bend

Knie·bund·hose die knee-breeches *pl.*; **eine ~:** a pair of knee-breeches

knie-, Knie-: ~fall der: einen ~fall tun *od.* **machen** *(auch fig.)* go down on one's knees (**vor** + *Dat.* before); **~fällig 1.** *Adj.; nicht präd.* **sein ~fälliges Bitten** his pleading on bended knee; **2.** *adv.* on bended knees; on one's knees; **~frei** *Adj.* ‹*skirt*› worn above the knee; **wird die Mode wieder ~frei?** is the above-the-knee look coming back again?; **~gelenk das** knee-joint; **~hoch** *Adj.* knee-deep ‹*water, snow*›; knee-high ‹*grass*›; knee-length ‹*boots*›; **~hose die** knee-breeches *pl.*; **~kehle die** hollow of the knee; popliteal space *(Anat.)*; **~lang** *Adj.* knee-length

knien ['kni:(ə)n] **1.** *itr. V.* kneel; **diese Arbeit muß man ~d verrichten** this work has to be done on one's knees *or* kneeling. **2.** *refl. V.* kneel [down]; get down on one's knees; **sich in die Arbeit/die Akten ~** *(fig. ugs.)* get stuck into one's work/the files *(sl.)*

Knies [kni:s] **der; ~es** *(ugs.)* **a)** *(Schmutzschicht)* layer of muck *(coll.) or* dirt; **b)** *(Unstimmigkeit)* quarrel; **ständig ~ mit jmdm. haben** always be quarrelling with sb.

knie-, Knie-: ~scheibe die kneecap; patella *(Anat.)*; **~schützer der** *(Sport)* knee-pad; **~strumpf der** knee-length sock; knee-sock; **~tief** *Adj.* knee-deep

Kniff [knɪf] **der; ~[e]s, ~e a)** *(das Kneifen)* pinch; **b)** *(Falte)* crease; *(in Papier)* crease; fold; **c)** *(Kunstgriff)* trick; dodge; **den ~ [bei etw.] heraushaben** have got the knack [of sth.]

Kniffelei die; ~, ~en *(ugs.)* fiddly job *(coll.)*

kniff[e]lig *Adj.* **a)** *(schwierig)* fiddly *(coll.)*; tricky ‹*problem, crossword-puzzle*›; **b)** *(heikel)* tricky

Knigge ['knɪgə] **der; ~[s], ~:** book on etiquette

Knilch [knɪlç] **der; ~s, ~e** *(salopp abwertend)* bastard *(coll.)*

knipsen ['knɪpsn̩] **1.** *tr. V.* **a)** *(entwerten)* clip; punch; **b)** *(fotografieren)* snap; take a snap[shot] of; **c)** *(wegschnellen)* flick. **2.** *itr. V.* **a)** *(fotografieren)* take snapshots; **b) mit den Fingern ~:** snap one's fingers

Knipser der; ~s, ~, Knips·schalter der *(ugs.)* snap switch

Knirps [knɪrps] **der; ~es, ~e a)** (Wz) *Taschenschirm)* telescopic umbrella; **b)** *(ugs.: Junge)* nipper *(coll.)*; **c)** *(ugs. abwertend: kleiner Mann)* [little] squirt *(coll.)*

knirschen ['knɪrʃn̩] *itr. V.* **a)** crunch; **b) mit den Zähnen ~:** grind one's teeth; *(fig.)* gnash one's teeth

knistern ['knɪstɐn] *itr. V.* rustle; ‹*wood, fire*› crackle; **mit etw. ~:** rustle sth.; **eine ~de Atmosphäre** *(fig.)* a tense *or* charged atmosphere; *s. auch* **Gebälk**

Knittel·vers ['knɪtl̩-] **der** *(Metrik)* rhyming couplets of four-stress lines

Knitter ['knɪtɐ] **der; ~s, ~;** *meist Pl.* crease

knitter·frei *Adj.* non-crease; **[vollkommen] ~ sein** not crease [at all]

knitt[e]rig *Adj.* creased; crumpled; *(fig.)* wrinkled ‹*face*›

knittern *tr., itr. V.* crease; crumple

Knobel·becher der a) *(Würfelbecher)* dice-cup; **b)** *(Soldatenspr.: Stiefel)* army boot

knobeln *itr. V.* **a)** *(mit Würfeln)* play dice; *(mit Streichhölzern)* play spoof; *(mit Handzeichen)* play scissors, paper, stone; **um etw. ~:** play dice *etc.* to decide sth.; **b)** *(ugs.: nachdenken)* puzzle (**an** + *Dat.* over)

Knob·lauch ['kno:p-] **der** garlic

Knoblauch-: ~butter die *(Kochk.)* garlic butter; **~zehe die** clove of garlic; **~zwiebel die** garlic bulb

Knöchel ['knœçl̩] **der; ~s, ~ a)** *(am Fuß)* ankle; **bis an/über die ~:** up to the *or* one's ankles/to above ankle level; **das Kleid reicht bis an die ~:** the dress reaches [down] to the ankles; **b)** *(am Finger)* knuckle

knöchel-, Knöchel-: ~bruch der broken ankle; **~lang** *Adj.* ankle-length; **~tief** *Adj.* ankle-deep

Knochen ['knɔxn̩] **der; ~s, ~ a)** bone; **Fleisch mit/ohne ~:** meat on/off the bone; **jmdm. alle ~ [einzeln] brechen** *(salopp)* break every [single] bone in sb.'s body; **die Wunde geht bis auf den ~:** the wound reaches to the bone; **mir tun sämtliche ~ weh** *(ugs.)* every bone in my body aches; **der Schreck fuhr ihm in die ~** *(ugs.)* he was shaken to the core; **eine Grippe in den ~ haben** *(ugs.)* feel the flu coming on *(coll.)*; **keinen Mumm in den ~ haben** *(ugs.)* be a weed; **sich** *(Dat.)* **die ~ brechen** break something; **seine ~ für etw. hinhalten [müssen]** *(ugs.)* [have to] risk one's neck fighting for sth.; **die ~ zusammenreißen** *(Soldatenspr.)* stand up straight; **das geht auf die ~** *(salopp)* it's knackering *(Brit. sl.)*; it burns you out *(Amer. coll.)*; **sie hat mich bis auf die ~ blamiert** *(ugs.)* she made a complete *or* proper fool of me; **b)** *(ugs. abwertend: Kerl)* so-and-so *(coll.)*; **c)** *(ugs.: Schraubenschlüssel)* double-ended ring spanner

knochen-, Knochen-: ~arbeit die *(ugs.)* back-breaking work; **~bau der;** *o. Pl.* bone structure; **ein sehr kräftiger ~bau** a very powerful frame; **~bruch der** fracture; **sich** *(Dat.)* **einen ~bruch zuziehen** sustain a fracture; **~erweichung die** *(Med.)* softening of the bones; osteomalacia *(Med.)*; **~gerüst das a)** skeleton; **b)** *(ugs. abwertend: magere Person)* bag of bones *(coll.)*; **~hart** *Adj. (ugs.)* rock-hard; **der Kuchen ist ja ~hart** the cake is as hard as a rock; **~haut die** *(Med.)* periosteum; **~haut·entzündung die** *(Med.)* periostitis; **~mann der** *(veralt.)* Death; **~mark das** bone marrow; **~mehl das** bone-meal; **~mühle die** *(ugs.)* **diese Fabrik ist die reinste ~mühle** working in this factory is worse than the chain-gang! *(joc.)*; **~schinken der** ham on the bone; **~schwund der** *(Med.)* bone atrophy; osteoporosis *(Med.)*; **~trocken** *Adj. (ugs.)* bone-dry; **~tuberkulose die** *(Med.)* tuberculosis of the bones

knöchern ['knœçɐn] *Adj.; nicht präd.* bony, *(formal)* osseous ‹*material etc.*›; bone *attrib.* ‹*handle, tool, etc.*›

knochig 1. *Adj.* bony. **2.** *adv.* **sehr ~ gebaut sein** be very bony

Knockdown [nɔk'daun] **der; ~[s], ~** *(Boxen)* knock-down

Knockout [nɔk'aut] **der; ~[s], ~s** *(Boxen)* knock-out

Knödel ['knø:dl̩] **der; ~s, ~** *(bes. südd., österr.)* dumpling

Knöllchen ['knœlçən] **das; ~s, ~ a)** *s.* **Knolle; Knollen; b)** *(ugs.: Strafzettel)* [parking-]ticket

Knolle ['knɔlə] **die; ~, ~n a)** *(einer Pflanze)* tuber; **b)** *(ugs.: Auswuchs)* large round lump; *(Nase)* big fat conk *(sl.) or (Amer.)* schnozzle

Knollen der; ~s, ~ a) *(Klumpen)* lump; clod; **b)** *(ugs.: Strafzettel)* [parking-]ticket

Knollen-: ~begonie die tuberous begonia; **~blätter·pilz der** amanita; **~nase die** large bulbous nose

knollig *Adj.* bulbous

Knopf [knɔpf] **der; ~[e]s, Knöpfe** ['knœpfə] **a)** *(an Kleidungsstücken, Geräten, Anlagen)* button; **[sich** *(Dat.)***] etw. an den Knöpfen abzählen** *(ugs. scherzh.)* decide sth. by counting off one's buttons; **b)** *(Knauf)* knob; *(eines Schwertes, Dolches)* pommel; **c)** *(ugs. abwertend: kleiner Mann)* [little] squirt *(coll.)*; **d)** *(ugs.: Kind)* little thing *(coll.)*; **e)** *(südd., österr., schweiz.: Knoten)* knot; **f)** *(südd., österr., schweiz.: Knospe)* bud

Knopf·auge das; *meist Pl.* [boot-]button eye

knöpfen ['knœpfn̩] *tr. V.* button [up]; **der Rock wird seitlich/vorn/hinten geknöpft** the skirt buttons up at the side/in front/at the back

Knopf-: ~leiste die button-facing; **ein Mantel mit verdeckter ~leiste** a coat with a fly front; **~loch das** buttonhole; **aus allen** *od.* **sämtlichen ~löchern platzen** *(ugs.)* be bursting at the seams; **aus allen** *od.* **sämtlichen ~löchern stinken** *(salopp)* stink *or* smell to high heaven *(coll.)*; stink *or* smell something terrible *(sl.)*

knorke ['knɔrkə] *Adj.; meist präd. (berlin. veralt.)* super *(coll.)*; terrific *(coll.)*

Knorpel ['knɔrpl̩] **der; ~s, ~ a)** *(Anat.)* cartilage; **b)** *(im Steak o. ä.)* gristle

knorpelig, knorplig *Adj.* **a)** *(Anat.)* cartilaginous; **b)** gristly ‹*meat*›

Knorren ['knɔrən] **der; ~s, ~ a)** *(Teil eines Astes)* gnarl; knot; **b)** *(Baumstumpf)* [tree] stump; **c)** *(im Holz)* knot

knorrig *Adj.* **a)** *(krumm gewachsen)* gnarled ‹*tree, branch*›; **b)** *(wenig umgänglich)* gruff

Knospe ['knɔspə] **die; ~, ~n** bud; **~n ansetzen** put forth buds; bud; **eine zarte ~** *(fig.)* a tender young bloom *(literary)*

knospen *itr. V.* bud; *(fig.)* burgeon

Knötchen ['knø:tçən] **das; ~s, ~ a)** *(scherzh.: Haartracht)* [little] bun *or* knot; **b)** *(Med.)* nodule; tubercle

knoten ['kno:tn̩] *tr. V.* **a)** *(zu einem Knoten schlingen)* knot; tie a knot in; **sich** *(Dat.)* **ein Tuch um den Hals ~:** tie a scarf round one's neck; **b)** *(durch einen Knoten verknüpfen)* knot together; do *or* tie up ‹*shoelace*›

Knoten der; ~s, ~ a) knot; **sich** *(Dat.)* **einen ~ ins Taschentuch machen** tie a knot in one's handkerchief; **der ~ der Handlung schürzt sich** *(fig.)* the plot thickens; *s. auch* **gordisch; b)** *(Haartracht)* bun; knot; **c)** *(Maßeinheit)* knot; **d)** *(Bot.)* node; **e)** *(Med.)* node *(Med.)*; lump; *(Gicht~)* tophus *(Med.)*; **f)** *(Astron., Physik, Elektrot., Anat., Math., Sprachw.)* node; **g)** *s.* **Knotenpunkt a**

Knoten-: ~punkt der a) *(Verkehrs~)* junction; intersection; **b)** *s.* **Knoten f; ~stock der** knobby *or* knobbly *or* gnarled [walking-]stick

Knöterich ['knø:tərɪç] **der; ~s, ~e** *(Gattung)* Polygonum; *(Vogel~)* knot-grass; *(Wiesen~)* bistort

knotig *Adj.* **a)** *(Knoten aufweisend)* knobby; knobbly; gnarled; knobbly ‹*fabric*›; **b)** *(knotenförmig)* nodular

Know-how [noʊ'hau] **das; ~[s]** know-how

Knubbel ['knʊbl̩] **der; ~s, ~** *(bes. nordd.) (Verdickung)* small lump

knubbelig *Adj. (bes. nordd.)* podgy *(coll.)*

knuddeln ['knʊdl̩n] *tr. V. (bes. nordd.)* hug and squeeze

Knuff [knʊf] **der; ~[e]s, Knüffe** ['knʏfə] *(ugs.)* poke

knuffen ['knʊfn̩] *tr. V.* poke; **jmdn. in den Arm/in die Rippen ~:** poke sb. in the arm/in the ribs

knülle ['knʏlə] *Adj.; nur präd. (ugs.)* tight *(coll.)*; pie-eyed *(sl.)*

knüllen 1. *tr. V.* crumple [up] ‹*paper*›; crease, crumple ‹*clothes, fabrics*›. **2.** *itr. V.* crease; crumple

Knüller der; ~s, ~ *(ugs.)* sensation; *(Film, Buch usw.)* sensation; sensational success; *(Angebot, Verkaufsartikel)* sensational offer

knüpfen ['knʏpfn̩] **1.** *tr. V.* **a)** tie (**an** + *Akk.* to); **Bande der Freundschaft ~** *(fig.)* establish ties *or* bonds of friendship; **b)** *(durch Knoten herstellen)* knot; make ‹*net*›; **c)** *(gedanklich verbinden)* **große Erwartungen/Hoffnungen an etw.** *(Akk.)* **~:** have great expectations/hopes of sth.; **Bedingungen an etw.** *(Akk.)* **~:** attach conditions to sth. **2.**

refl. V. **sich an etw.** *(Akk.)* **~:** be connected with sth.; **an dieses Haus ~ sich nette Erinnerungen für mich** this house has pleasant memories for me

Knüppel ['knʏpl̩] **der; ~s, ~ a)** cudgel; club; *(Polizei~)* truncheon; **da möchte man doch gleich mit dem ~ dreinschlagen** *(ugs.)* sb. ought to bang *or* knock their heads together; *s. auch* **Bein; b)** *s.* **Steuerknüppel; c)** *s.* **Schaltknüppel**

knüppel-, Knüppel-: ~damm der log road; corduroy road; **~dick** *Adv. (ugs.)* **es kam ~dick** it was one disaster after the other; **~dick voll** full to bursting; **~hart** *Adj.: s.* **knochenhart**

knüppeln 1. *tr. V.* cudgel; club; beat with a cudgel *or* club/*(Polizeiknüppel)* truncheon. **2.** *itr. V.* **a)** use a/one's cudgel *or* club/truncheon; **b)** *(Sport Jargon)* play rough; **c)** *(unpers.) (ugs.)* **heute knüppelt es wieder** things are hectic again today

Knüppel·schaltung die *(Kfz-W.)* floor-[-type] gear-change

knurren ['knʊrən] **1.** *itr. V.* **a)** ⟨*animal*⟩ growl; *(wütend)* snarl; **jmdm. knurrt der Magen** *(fig.)* sb.'s stomach is rumbling; **mit knurrendem Magen** *(fig.)* with one's stomach rumbling; **b)** *(murren)* grumble **(über +** *Akk.* about); **c)** *(verärgert reden)* growl. **2.** *tr. V. (verärgert sagen)* growl

Knurr·hahn der *(Zool.)* gurnard

knurrig 1. *Adj.* grumpy. **2.** *adv.* grumpily

Knusper·häuschen das gingerbread house

knusperig *s.* **knusprig**

knuspern ['knʊspɐn] *tr., itr. V.* nibble; *(geräuschvoll)* crunch; **an etw.** *(Dat.)* **~:** nibble [at] sth.

knusprig 1. *Adj.* **a)** crisp; crisp, crusty ⟨*roll*⟩; crusty ⟨*bread*⟩; **etw. ~ braten** roast/fry sth. crisp and brown; **b)** *(ugs.: frisch u. adrett)* delightfully fresh and attractive. **2.** *adv.* **~frisch** crunchy fresh ⟨*crisps, nuts*⟩; crispy fresh ⟨*rolls*⟩

Knust [knu:st] **der; ~[e]s, ~e** *od.* **Knüste** ['kny:stə] *(bes. nordd.)* crust

Knute ['knu:tə] **die; ~, ~n** knout; **unter jmds. ~ [stehen]** *(fig.)* [be] under sb.'s heel

knutschen ['knu:tʃn̩] *(ugs.)* **1.** *tr. V.* smooch with *(coll.)*; neck with *(sl.)*; *(sexuell berühren)* pet; **sich ~:** smooch *(coll.) or* neck *(sl.)*/pet. **2.** *itr. V.* smooch *(coll.)*, neck *(sl.)* **(mit** with); *(sich sexuell berühren)* pet

Knutscherei die; ~, ~en *(ugs.)* **~[en]** smooching *(coll.)*; necking *(sl.)*; *(sexuelle Berührung)* petting

Knutsch·fleck der *(ugs.)* love bite

Knüttel ['knʏtl̩] **der; ~s, ~** *s.* **Knüppel**

Knüttel·vers der *s.* **Knittelvers**

k. o. [ka:'|o:] *Adj.; nicht attr.* **a)** *(Boxen)* **jmdn. k. o. schlagen** knock sb. out; **stehend k. o. sein** be counted out on one's feet; **k. o. gehen** be knocked out; **b)** *(ugs.: übermüdet)* all in *(coll.)*; whacked *(coll.)*

K. o. der; ~, ~ *(Boxen)* knock-out; **[Sieger] durch K. o.** [the winner] by a knock-out

koagulieren [ko|agu'li:rən] *(Chemie)* **1.** *itr. V.; auch mit sein* coagulate. **2.** *tr. V.* coagulate

Koala [ko'a:la] **der; ~s, ~s** koala [bear]

koalieren [ko|a'li:rən] *itr. V. (Politik)* form a coalition **(mit** with)

Koalition [ko|ali'tsi̯o:n] **die; ~, ~en** coalition; **die große/kleine ~:** the grand/little coalition

Koalitions-: ~freiheit die; *o. Pl.* freedom of association *(of workers or employers)*; **~partner der** coalition partner; **~recht das;** *o. Pl.* right of freedom of association *(of workers or employers)*; **~regierung die** coalition government

Koaxial·kabel [ko|a'ksi̯a:l-] **das** *(Technik)* coaxial cable

Kob [kɔp] **der; ~s, ~s** *(ugs.) s.* **Kontaktbereichsbeamte**

Kobalt ['ko:balt] **das; ~s** *(Chemie)* cobalt

kobalt·blau *Adj.* cobalt blue

Kobalt·bombe die cobalt bomb

Koben ['ko:bn̩] **der; ~s, ~** *(Schweinestall)* pigsty; *(Verschlag)* pen

Kober ['ko:bɐ] **der; ~s, ~** *(ostmd.)* food-basket

Kobold ['ko:bɔlt] **der; ~[e]s, ~e** goblin; kobold; *(fig.)* imp

Kobolz [ko'bɔlts] **der** *in* **~ schießen** *od.* **schlagen** *(bes. nordd.)* turn *or* do a somersault/somersaults

Kobra ['ko:bra] **die; ~, ~s** cobra

Koch [kɔx] **der; ~[e]s, Köche** ['kœçə] cook; *(Küchenchef)* chef; **viele Köche verderben den Brei** *(Spr.)* too many cooks spoil the broth *(prov.)*

koch-, Koch-: ~an·leitung die cooking instructions *pl.*; **~apfel der** cooking apple; **~buch das** cookery book; cookbook; **~echt** *Adj.* ⟨*fabric, garment*⟩ that is washable in boiling water; ⟨*colour, dye*⟩ that is fast in boiling water

Köchel·verzeichnis ['kœçl̩-] **das;** *o. Pl. (Musik)* Köchel Catalogue

kochen 1. *tr. V.* **a)** boil; *(zubereiten)* cook ⟨*meal*⟩; make ⟨*purée, jam*⟩; **Suppe/Kaffee/Tee/Kakao ~:** make some soup/coffee/tea/cocoa; **sich** *(Dat.)* **einen Tee ~:** make some tea; **die Eier hart/weich ~:** hard-/soft-boil the eggs; **etw. weich/gar ~:** cook sth. until it is soft/[properly] done; **gar gekocht sein** be done; *s. auch* **Flamme a; b)** *(waschen)* boil; **c)** *(verflüssigen)* heat ⟨*tar, glue, etc.*⟩ *(till it melts)*. **2.** *itr. V.* **a)** *(Speisen zubereiten)* cook; *(das Kochen übernehmen)* do the cooking; **gerne/gut ~:** like cooking/be a good cook; **fett/fettarm ~:** use a lot of fat/little fat in cooking; **b)** *(sieden)* ⟨*water, milk, etc.*⟩ boil; *(fig.)* ⟨*sea*⟩ boil, seethe; **das Wasser/die Milch kocht** the water/the milk is boiling; **~d heißes Wasser** boiling hot water; **am Kochen sein** *(landsch.)* be on the boil; be boiling; **etw. zum Kochen bringen** bring sth. to the boil; **c)** *(in ~dem Wasser liegen)* be boiled; **d)** *(ugs.: wütend sein)* **vor Wut/innerlich ~:** be boiling *or* seething with rage/inwardly

kochend·heiß *Adj.; nicht präd.* boiling hot; piping hot ⟨*soup etc.*⟩

Kocher der; ~s, ~ a) [small] stove; *(Kochplatte)* hotplate; **b)** *(Technik)* boiler

Köcher ['kœçɐ] **der; ~s, ~ a)** *(für Pfeile)* quiver; **b)** *(für Fernglas o. ä.)* case

Kocherei die; ~ *(ugs.)* cookery

koch-, Koch-: ~fertig *Adj.* ready-to-cook *attrib.*; ready to cook *pred.*; **~fest** *Adj.: s.* **~echt; ~fleisch das** stewing meat; **~gelegenheit die** cooking facilities *pl.*; **~geschirr das** *(Milit.)* mess-tin; **~herd der** *s.* **Herd a**

Köchin ['kœçɪn] **die; ~, ~nen** cook

Koch-: ~käse der *(type of)* processed curd cheese; **~kunst die a)** culinary art; **b)** *Pl.* **~künste** *(ugs.: Fertigkeit im Kochen)* culinary skill[s *pl.*]; **~kurs[us] der** cookery course; **~löffel der** wooden spoon; **den ~löffel schwingen** *(scherzh.)* do the cooking; **~nische die** kitchenette; **~platte die a)** hotplate; **b)** *(Kocher)* [small] stove; **~rezept das** recipe

Koch·salz das common salt; sodium chloride *(Chem.)*

Kochsalz·lösung die salt solution; sodium chloride solution *(Chem.)*

Koch-: ~schinken der boiled ham; **~topf der** [cooking] pot; **~wäsche die;** *o. Pl.* washing that is to be boiled; **~zeit die** cooking time

kodderig ['kɔd(ə)rɪç] *Adj. (nordd.)* **a)** *in* **jmdm. ist ~:** sb. feels sick; **b)** *nicht präd. (frech)* impertinent; impudent

Kode [ko:t] **der; ~s, ~s** code

Kodein [kode'i:n] **das; ~s** *(Pharm.)* codeine

Köder ['kø:dɐ] **der; ~s, ~:** bait; *(fig.)* bait; lure; **einen/mehrere ~ auslegen** put out bait/a number of baits

ködern *tr. V.* lure; **jmdn. für eine Show ~** *(fig. ugs.)* entice sb. to appear on a show; **sich von jmdm./etw. nicht ~ lassen** *(fig. ugs.)* not be tempted by sb.'s offer/by sth.

Kodex ['ko:dɛks] **der; ~es** *od.* **~, ~e** *od.* **Kodizes** ['ko:ditse:s] **a)** *(Handschrift)* codex; **b)** *(hist.: Gesetzbuch)* code; codex; **c)** *(Verhaltensregel)* code

kodieren *tr. V.* code; encode

kodifizieren [kodifi'tsi:rən] *tr. V. (bes. Rechtsw.)* codify

Kodizes *s.* **Kodex**

Koedukation [ko|eduka'tsi̯o:n] **die; ~:** coeducation

Koeffizient [ko|ɛfi'tsi̯ɛnt] **der; ~en, ~en** *(Math., Physik)* coefficient

Koexistenz die; ~: coexistence

Koffein [kɔfe'i:n] **das; ~s** caffeine

koffein·frei *Adj.* decaffeinated

Koffer ['kɔfɐ] **der; ~s, ~ a)** [suit]case; *(Schrank~)* wardrobe trunk; **die ~ packen** pack one's bags [and leave]; **aus dem ~ leben** live out of a suitcase; **b)** *(Soldatenspr.)* heavy shell; **c)** *(Straßenbau)* road-bed

Koffer·anhänger der luggage tag *or* label

Köfferchen ['kœfɐçən] **das; ~s, ~:** small [suit]case

Koffer-: ~gerät das portable [radio/gramophone *etc.*]; **~kuli der** luggage trolley; **~radio das** portable radio; **~raum der** boot *(Brit.)*; trunk *(Amer.)*; **~schreib·maschine die** portable typewriter

Kogel ['ko:gl̩] **der; ~s, ~** *(südd., österr.)* rounded, wooded mountain top

Kogge ['kɔgə] **die; ~, ~n** cog

Kognak ['kɔnjak] **der; ~s, ~s** brandy; *s. auch* **Cognac**

Kognak-: ~bohne die *bean-shaped brandy-filled chocolate;* **~schwenker der** brandy glass

kognitiv [kɔgni'ti:f] *Adj.; nicht präd. (bes. Psych., Päd.)* cognitive

kohärent [kohɛ'rɛnt] *Adj. (Phys.)* coherent

Kohäsion [kohɛ'zi̯o:n] **die; ~** *(geh., Physik)* cohesion

Kohl [ko:l] **der; ~[e]s a)** cabbage; **das macht den ~ [auch] nicht fett** *(ugs.)* that doesn't help a lot; **b)** *(ugs. abwertend: Unsinn)* rubbish; rot *(sl.)*; **red/mach keinen ~!** don't talk rot! *(sl.)*/stop messing around *(coll.)*

Kohl·dampf der; *o. Pl. (salopp)* **[einen] ~ haben** be ravenously hungry; **~ schieben [müssen]** [have to] go hungry

Kohle ['ko:lə] **die; ~, ~n a)** *(Brennstoff)* coal; **glühende ~n** live coals; embers; **wir haben keine ~n mehr** we have run out of coal; **[wie] auf [glühenden] ~n sitzen** *(gespannt warten)* be on tenterhooks; *(ungeduldig warten)* suffer agonies of impatience; **feurige ~n auf jmds. Haupt** *(Akk.)* **sammeln** *(geh.)* heap coals of fire upon sb.'s head; **b)** *Pl. (salopp: Geld)* dough *sing. (sl.)*; **Hauptsache, die ~n stimmen!** as long as the money's right; **c)** *(Elektrot.) s.* **Bürste c; d)** *(Chemie) s.* **Aktivkohle; e)** *s.* **Zeichenkohle**

Kohle-: ~filter der charcoal filter; **~hydrat** *s.* **Kohlenhydrat; ~kraft·werk das** coal-fired power station

[1]kohlen *itr. V.* smoulder; ⟨*wick*⟩ smoke

[2]kohlen *itr. V. (fam.) (lügen)* tell fibs; *(übertreiben)* exaggerate; *(prahlen)* boast

kohlen-, Kohlen-: ~bergbau der coal-mining *no art.*; **~berg·werk das** coal-mine; colliery; **~bunker der** coal bunker; **~dioxid** *(fachspr.)*, **~dioxyd** [--'---] **das** *(Chemie)* carbon dioxide; **~eimer der** coal-scuttle; **~grube die** coal-mine; [coal-]pit; **~grus der** breeze; slack; **~halde die** coal heap; **~händler der** coal merchant; **~handlung die** coal merchant's; **~heizung die** coal-fired central heating *no indef. art.*; **~hydrat das** *(Chemie)* carbohydrate; **~kasten der** coal-box; **~keller der**

coal-cellar; ~**monoxid** *(fachspr.)*, ~**monoxyd** [--'---] **das** *(Chemie)* carbon monoxide; ~**monoxyd·vergiftung** [--'------] **die** carbon monoxide poisoning; ~**ofen der** coal-burning stove; ~**pott der**; *o. Pl. (abwertend)* Ruhr [area]; ~**sauer** *Adj. (Chemie)* carbonic; ~**saures Natron/Kalzium** sodium/calcium carbonate; ~**säure die** carbonic acid; ~**säure·haltig** *Adj.* carbonated; ~**schaufel die** coal-shovel; ~**staub der** coal-dust; ~**stoff der**; *o. Pl.* carbon; ~**trimmer der** *(Seew. hist.)* [coal-]trimmer; ~**wasserstoff** [--'---] **der** *(Chemie)* hydrocarbon; ~**zange die** coal tongs *pl.*

Kohle-: ~**ofen** *s.* **Kohlenofen**; ~**papier das** carbon paper

Köhler ['kø:lɐ] **der**; ~s, ~: charcoal burner

Köhlerei die; ~: charcoal burning *no art.*

Köhler·glaube der *(geh. abwertend)* blind faith

Kohle-: ~**stift der a)** *(Elektrot.)* carbon rod; **b)** *(zum Zeichnen)* charcoal stick; ~**tablette die** charcoal tablet; ~**zeichnung die** charcoal drawing

kohl-, Kohl-: ~**kopf der** [head of] cabbage; ~**meise die** great tit; ~**räbchen** [-'--] **das** young kohlrabi; ~**raben·schwarz** *Adj.* raven *attrib.*, raven-black, jet-black ⟨*hair*⟩; jet-black ⟨*eyes*⟩; ⟨*face, hands, etc.*⟩ as black as soot; ~**rabi** [~'ra:bi] **der**; ~[s], ~[s] kohlrabi; ~**roulade die** *(Kochk.)* stuffed cabbage; ~**rübe die** swede; ~**sprosse die** *(österr.)* [Brussels] sprout; ~**weißling der** cabbage white; cabbage butterfly

Kohorte [ko'hɔrtə] **die**; ~, ~n *(hist., Soziol.)* cohort

Koinzidenz [koǀɪntsi'dɛnts] **die**; ~ *(geh.)* coincidence

koitieren [koi'ti:rən] *itr. V. (geh.)* engage in *or* have sexual intercourse

Koitus ['ko:itʊs] **der**; ~, **Koitus** *(geh.)* sexual intercourse; coitus *(formal)*

Koje ['ko:jə] **die**; ~, ~n **a)** *(Seemannsspr.)* bunk; berth; **b)** *(Ausstellungsstand)* stand; **c)** *(ugs. scherzh.: Bett)* bed

Kojote [ko'jo:tə] **der**; ~n, ~n coyote

Kokain [koka'i:n] **das**; ~s cocaine

kokain·süchtig *Adj.* addicted to cocaine *postpos.*

Kokarde [ko'kardə] **die**; ~, ~n cockade

Koka·strauch ['ko:ka-] **der** coca

kokeln ['ko:kl̩n] *itr. V. (ugs.)* play with fire

Kokerei [ko:kə'rai] **die**; ~, ~en coking plant

kokett [ko'kɛt] **1.** *Adj.* coquettish. **2.** *adv.* coquettishly

Koketterie [kokɛtə'ri:] **die**; ~: coquetry; coquettishness

kokettieren *itr. V.* **a)** play the coquette; flirt; **b)** *(kokett erwähnen)* **mit etw.** ~: make much play with sth.; **c)** *(fig.)* **mit der Gefahr** ~: flirt with danger

Kokke ['kɔkə] **die**; ~, ~n *(Biol.)* coccus

Kokolores [koko'lo:rɛs] **der**; ~ *(ugs.)* **a)** *(Unsinn)* rubbish; nonsense; rot *(sl.)*; **b)** *(Getue)* fuss

Kokon [ko'kõ:] **der**; ~s, ~s cocoon

Kokos- ['ko:kɔs-]: ~**fett das** coconut oil; ~**faser die** coconut fibre; ~**flocken** *Pl.* coconut ice *sing.*; *(als Füllung)* desiccated coconut *sing.*; ~**läufer der** runner made of coconut-matting; ~**milch die** coconut milk; ~**nuß die** coconut; ~**palme die** coconut palm; coconut tree

Kokotte [ko'kɔtə] **die**; ~, ~n *(geh. veralt.)* cocotte *(arch.)*

[1]**Koks** [ko:ks] **der**; ~es **a)** coke; **b)** *(salopp scherzh.: Geld)* dough *(sl.)*

[2]**Koks der**; ~es *(Drogenjargon: Kokain)* coke *(sl.)*; snow *(sl.)*

[3]**Koks der**; ~es *(salopp: Unsinn)* rubbish; nonsense; rot *(sl.)*

koksen *itr. V. (Jargon)* take coke *(sl.)*

Kokser der; ~s, ~ *(Drogenjargon)* [cocaine-]sniffer; snow-bird *(Amer. sl.)*

Koks-: ~**heizung die** coke-fired heating; ~**ofen der a)** *(mit Koks geheizt)* coke-burning stove; **b)** *(für die Koksherstellung)* coke oven

Kola *s.* **Kolon**

Kola·baum ['ko:la-] **der** cola *or* kola [tree]

Kolben ['kɔlbn̩] **der**; ~s, ~ **a)** *(Technik)* piston; **b)** *(Chemie: Glasgefäß)* flask; **c)** *(Teil des Gewehrs)* butt; **d)** *(Bot.)* spadix; *(Mais~)* cob; **e)** *(salopp: dicke Nase)* hooter *(Brit. sl.)*; conk *(sl.)*; **f)** *(der Glühlampe)* glass

Kolben-: ~**fresser der** *(ugs.)* piston seize-up; **einen ~fresser haben** have piston seizure *or* a seized[-up] piston; ~**hub der** *(Technik)* piston stroke; ~**ring der** *(Technik)* piston ring

Kolchos·bauer ['kɔlçɔs-] **der** kolkhoznik; worker on a Soviet collective farm

Kolchose [kɔl'ço:zə] **die**; ~, ~n kolkhoz; Soviet collective farm

Kolibri ['ko:libri] **der**; ~s, ~s humming-bird

Kolik ['ko:lɪk] **die**; ~, ~en colic

Kolk·rabe ['kɔlk-] **der** *(Zool.)* raven

kollabieren [kɔla'bi:rən] *itr. V.*; *mit sein (Med.)* collapse

Kollaborateur [kɔlabora'tø:ɐ̯] **der**; ~s, ~e collaborator

Kollaboration [kɔlabora'tsio:n] **die**; ~: collaboration

kollaborieren *itr. V.* collaborate (**mit** with)

Kollagen [kɔla'ge:n] **das**; ~s, ~e *(Med., Biol.)* collagen

Kollaps ['kɔlaps] **der**; ~es, ~e *(Med., fig.)* collapse; **einen ~ erleiden** collapse

kollationieren [kɔlatsio'ni:rən] *tr. V.* **a)** *(vergleichen)* collate, compare (**mit** with); *(Druckw.)* read (**mit** against); **b)** *(bes. Buchbinderei)* collate

Kolleg [kɔ'le:k] **das**; ~s, ~s **a)** *(Vorlesung)* lecture; *(Vorlesungsreihe)* course of lectures; **b)** *(Institut) college offering full-time courses to prepare qualified adults for university entrance*; **c)** *(kath. Kirche)* theological college

Kollege [kɔ'le:gə] **der**; ~n, ~n **a)** colleague; *(Arbeiter)* workmate; **die ~n vom Fach** professional colleagues; ~ **kommt gleich!** *(im Restaurant)* somebody [else] will be with you in a moment; **Herr ~!** Mr. Smith/Jones *etc.!*; **Herr ~ [Müller** *usw.*] *(Abgeordneter)* ≈ the Honourable Gentleman; *(als Anrede)* **Herr ~ [Müller], Sie müssen ...** ≈ the Honourable Gentleman must ...; **b)** *(Gewerkschaftsmitglied)* [union] member; **c)** *(DDR: Werktätiger)* worker; **der ~ Werkleiter/Ober** the works manager/the waiter; **d)** *(salopp: Freund)* mate *(coll.)*

Kollegen-: ~**kreis der**: **im ~kreis** among colleagues; ~**rabatt der** trade discount *(in the publishing trade)*

Kolleg-: ~**geld das**; *meist Pl. (Hochschulw.)* lecture fee; ~**heft das** lecture notebook

kollegial [kɔle'gia:l] **1.** *Adj.* helpful and considerate. **2.** *adv.* ⟨*act etc.*⟩ like a good colleague/good colleagues

Kollegialität [kɔlegiali'tɛ:t] **die**; ~: helpfulness and consideration

Kollegin die; ~, ~nen *s.* **Kollege a, b, c**; *s. auch* **-in**

Kollegium [kɔ'le:giʊm] **das**; ~s, **Kollegien a)** *(Gruppe)* group; *(unmittelbar zusammenarbeitend)* team; **b)** *(Lehrkörper)* [teaching] staff; **c)** *(Komitee)* committee

Kolleg-: ~**mappe die** document case; ~**stufe die** *(Schulw.)* sixth-form college *(offering academic and vocational courses)*

Kollekte [kɔ'lɛktə] **die**; ~, ~n collection

Kollektion [kɔlɛk'tsio:n] **die**; ~, ~en **a)** *(Sortiment)* range; *(Mode)* collection; **b)** *(Sammlung, Zusammenstellung)* collection

kollektiv [kɔlɛk'ti:f] **1.** *Adj.* collective; joint ⟨*collaboration*⟩. **2.** *adv.* collectively

Kollektiv das; ~s, ~e *od.* ~s **a)** group; **als ~ auftreten** put up a united front; **b)** *(bes. DDR: Arbeitsgruppe)* collective; **c)** *(Statistik)* population

Kollektiv-: ~**arbeit die** joint work; ~**bewußt·sein das** collective consciousness; ~**geist der**; *o. Pl.* collective spirit; ~**gesellschaft die** *(schweiz. Wirtsch.)* general partnership

kollektivieren *tr. V.* collectivize

Kollektivismus der; ~: collectivism *no art.*

kollektivistisch *Adj.* collectivist

Kollektiv-: ~**schuld die**; *o. Pl.* collective guilt; ~**strafe die** collective punishment

Kollektivum [kɔlɛk'ti:vʊm] **das**; ~s, **Kollektiva** *(Sprachw.)* collective noun; collective

Kollektiv·wirtschaft die collective farm

Kollektor [kɔ'lɛktɔr] **der**; ~s, ~en [-'to:rən] *(Elektrot., Physik)* collector

[1]**Koller** ['kɔlɐ] **der**; ~s, ~ *(ugs.)* rage; **einen ~ haben/bekommen** be in/fly *or* get into a rage

[2]**Koller das**; ~s, ~ *(hist.)* cape collar

[1]**kollern** *itr. V.*; *mit sein* roll

[2]**kollern** *itr. V.* ⟨*turkey etc.*⟩ gobble; ⟨*stomach*⟩ rumble

kollidieren [kɔli'di:rən] *itr. V.* **a)** *mit sein (zusammenstoßen)* collide, be in collision (**mit** with); **b)** *(im Widerspruch stehen)* clash, conflict (**mit** with); **miteinander** ~: ⟨*meetings etc.*⟩ clash

Kollier [kɔ'lie:] **das**; ~s, ~s **a)** *(Halskette)* necklace; **b)** *(schmaler Pelz)* necklet

Kollision [kɔli'zio:n] **die**; ~, ~en **a)** *(Zusammenstoß)* collision; **b)** *(Widerstreit)* conflict, clash (+ *Gen.* between); **mit etw. in ~ geraten** come into conflict with sth.

Kollisions·kurs der; *o. Pl.* collision course; **gegen jmdn./etw. auf ~ gehen** *(fig.)* be heading for a confrontation with sb./sth.

Kolloid [kɔlo'i:t] **das**; ~[e]s, ~e *(Chemie)* colloid

Kolloquium [kɔ'lɔkviʊm] **das**; ~s, **Kolloquien a)** *(Hochschulw.)* seminar; **b)** *(Zusammenkunft)* colloquium; **c)** *(österr.: Prüfung)* test

Köln [kœln] **(das)**; ~s Cologne

Kölner 1. *indekl. Adj.*; *nicht präd.* Cologne *attrib.*; *(in Köln)* in Cologne *postpos.*, *not pred.*; ⟨*suburb, archbishop, mayor, speciality*⟩ of Cologne; ⟨*car factory, river bank*⟩ at Cologne; **der ~ Dom/Karneval** Cologne Cathedral/the Cologne carnival; **meine ~ Freunde** *(in Köln)* my friends in Cologne; *(aus Köln)* my friends from Cologne; **seine ~ Heimat** his native Cologne; **meine ~ Zeit** my time in Cologne; **die ~ Innenstadt** Central Cologne; **alle ~ Bahnhöfe** every station in Cologne; **die 2000jährige ~ Geschichte** Cologne's 2000-year history. **2. der**; ~s, ~: inhabitant of Cologne; *(von Geburt)* native of Cologne; **er ist ~**: he is a native of Cologne; he comes from Cologne; **ein echter ~**: someone born and bred in Cologne; *(dem Naturell nach)* a true native of Cologne; **der ~** *(bestimmter Mann)* the man from Cologne; that chap from Cologne *(coll.)*; *(das ~ Auto usw.)* the car/bus *etc.* with the Cologne number-plate; *(ugs.: die ~)* people *pl.* from Cologne; **wir ~**: we citizens of Cologne; **die ~**: the people of Cologne; *(die ~ Mannschaft usw.)* Cologne *pl.*; *(die ~ Fans usw.)* the Cologne supporters; *(die ~ Firma usw.)* the Cologne works *sing. or pl.*/group *etc. sing.*; **die ~ haben einen Oberbürgermeister gewählt** Cologne has elected a mayor; ~ *Pl.* Cologne people; *(außerhalb Kölns)* people from Cologne; **das sind ~**: they are from Cologne; **er hatte als ~ eine tiefe Abneigung gegen Düsseldorf** coming from Cologne, he had a great dislike for Düsseldorf; **Sie als ~ mögen den Karneval nicht?** you come from Cologne, and you don't like the carnival?

Kölnerin die; ~, ~nen *s.* **Kölner 2**; *s. auch* **-in**

kölnisch *Adj.* Cologne *attrib.*; of Cologne *postpos., not pred.*; **Kölnisch Wasser** eau-de-Cologne

Kolombine [kolɔm'bi:nə] **die; ~, ~n** Columbine

Kolon ['ko:lɔn] **das; ~s, ~s** *od.* **Kola a)** *(antike Metrik, Rhet.)* colon; **b)** *(veralt.: Doppelpunkt)* colon

Kolonel [kolo'nɛl] **die;** ~ *(Druckw.)* minion

kolonial [kolo'nia:l] *Adj.; nicht präd.* colonial

kolonialisieren *tr. V.* colonialize

Kolonialisierung die; ~, ~en colonialization

Kolonialismus der; ~: colonialism *no art.*

kolonialistisch *Adj.* colonialist

Kolonial-: ~macht die colonial power; **~politik die;** *o. Pl.* colonial policy; **~stil der;** *o. Pl.* colonial style; **~waren** *Pl. (veralt.)* groceries *pl.*; **~waren·händler der** *(veralt.)* grocer; **~zeit die;** *o. Pl.* colonial era *or* period

Kolonie [kolo'ni:] **die; ~, ~n a)** *(auch Gruppe von Ausländern, Biol.)* colony; **b)** *(Siedlung)* colony; settlement

Kolonisation [koloniza'tsio:n] **die; ~, ~en** colonization

kolonisieren *tr. V.* **a)** *(zur Kolonie machen)* colonize; **b)** *(besiedeln, erschließen)* settle and develop; *(urbar machen)* clear and cultivate ‹*land*›; reclaim ‹*swampland*›

Kolonisierung die; ~, ~en colonization

Kolonist der; ~en, ~en colonist; *(früher Siedler)* settler

Kolonnade [kolɔ'na:də] **die; ~, ~n** colonnade

Kolonne [ko'lɔnə] **die; ~, ~n a)** *(Truppe, Gruppe von Menschen, Zahlenreihe)* column; **die fünfte ~:** the fifth column; **b)** *(Fahrzeuge)* column; *(Schlange)* [long] line of traffic; *(Konvoi)* convoy; **~ fahren** drive in a [long] line of traffic; **c)** *(Arbeits~)* gang

Kolonnen-: ~fahren das driving in a [long] line of traffic; **~springer der** *(ugs.)* *motorist who dodges in and out of a line of traffic in order to overtake*

Kolophonium [kolo'fo:niʊm] **das; ~s** colophony; rosin

Koloratur [kolora'tu:ɐ̯] **die; ~, ~en** *(Musik)* coloratura

Koloratur·sängerin die *(Musik)* coloratura

kolorieren [kolo'ri:rən] *tr. V.* **a)** *(ausmalen)* colour; **b)** *(Musik)* decorate; embellish

Kolorit [kolo'ri:t] **das; ~[e]s, ~e** *od.* **~s a)** *(Farbgebung)* colouring; **b)** *(Musik: Klangfarbe)* [tone] colour; **c)** *(Atmosphäre)* colour

Koloß [ko'lɔs] **der; Kolosses, Kolosse a)** *(Standbild)* colossus; **der ~ von Rhodos** the Colossus of Rhodes; **b)** *(riesiges Gebilde, ugs. scherzh.: große Person)* colossus; giant

kolossal [kolɔ'sa:l] **1.** *Adj.* **a)** *(riesenhaft)* colossal; gigantic; enormous; **b)** *(ugs.: sehr groß)* tremendous *(coll.)*; incredible *(coll.)* ‹*rubbish, nonsense*›; **eine ~e Dummheit begehen** do something incredibly stupid; **~es Glück haben** be incredibly lucky *(coll.)*. **2.** *adv. (ugs.)* tremendously *(coll.)*; **~ viel Geld** a tremendous *or* vast amount of money *(coll.)*

Kolossal-: ~film der [film] epic; **~gemälde das** huge painting; **~schinken der** *(salopp abwertend)* **a)** *(Film)* massive great epic *(coll.)*; **b)** *(Gemälde)* whacking great painting *(sl.)*

Kolportage [kɔlpɔr'ta:ʒə] **die; ~, ~n a)** *(minderwertiger Bericht)* trashy writing; trash; **b)** *(Verbreitung von Gerüchten)* rumour-mongering

Kolportage-: ~literatur die trashy literature; **~roman der** trashy novel

Kolporteur [kɔlpɔr'tø:ɐ̯] **der; ~s, ~e** *(geh.)* rumour-monger

kolportieren *tr. V. (geh.)* spread, circulate ‹*rumour, story*›

kölsch [kœlʃ] *s.* **kölnisch**

Kölsch das; ~[s] a) *strong very pale beer brewed in Cologne;* **b)** Cologne dialect; *s. auch* **Deutsch a**

Kolumbianer [kolʊm'bia:nɐ] **der; ~s, ~:** Colombian

kolumbianisch *Adj.* Colombian

Kolumbien [ko'lʊmbiən] **(das); ~s** Colombia

Kolumbus [ko'lʊmbʊs] **(der)** Columbus; *s. auch* **Ei a**

Kolumne [ko'lʊmnə] **die; ~, ~n** *(Druckw., Meinungsbeitrag)* column

Kolumnen·titel der *(Druckw.)* running title *or* head

Kolumnist der; ~en, ~en, Kolumnistin die; ~, ~nen columnist

Koma ['ko:ma] **das; ~s, ~s** *od.* **~ta** *(Med.)* coma

Kombattant [kɔmba'tant] **der; ~en, ~en** *(Völkerr.; geh. veralt.)* combatant

Kombi ['kɔmbi] **der; ~[s], ~s** *s.* **Kombiwagen**

Kombinat [kɔmbi'na:t] **das; ~[e]s, ~e** *(bes. DDR)* combine

Kombination [kɔmbina'tsio:n] **die; ~, ~en a)** *(Verbindung)* combination; **b)** *(gedankliche Verknüpfung)* deduction; piece of reasoning; **unsere ~en** our reasoning *sing. or* deductions; **c)** *(Kleidungsstücke)* ensemble; suit; *(Herren~)* suit; *(Flieger~)* flying-suit; **d)** *(Ballspiele)* combined move; **e)** *(Schach)* combination; **f)** *(Ski) s.* **alpin; nordisch**

Kombinations-: ~gabe die; *o. Pl.* powers *pl.* of deduction *or* reasoning; **~schloß das** combination lock; **~sprung·lauf der** *(Ski)* jumping event *(of Nordic combination)*

Kombinatorik [kɔmbina'to:rɪk] **die; ~:** *(Math.)* combinatorial analysis *no art.*

kombinatorisch *Adj.* deductive; **~e Fähigkeiten** powers of deduction *or* reasoning; deductive powers

kombinieren [kɔmbi'ni:rən] **1.** *tr. V.* combine; **zwei Dinge zu etw. ~:** combine two things into sth.; **etw. mit etw. ~:** combine sth. with sth. **2.** *itr. V.* **a)** *(Zusammenhänge herstellen)* deduce; reason; **falsch/richtig ~:** come to the wrong/right conclusion; **b)** *(Ballspiele)* combine

Kombi-: ~wagen der estate [car]; station wagon *(Amer.)*; **~zange die** combination pliers *pl.*; **eine ~zange** a pair of combination pliers

Kombüse [kɔm'by:zə] **die; ~, ~n** *(Seemannsspr.)* galley

Komet [ko'me:t] **der; ~en, ~en** comet

kometen·haft *Adj.* meteoric ‹*rise, career*›; extremely rapid ‹*upturn, development*›

Komfort [kɔm'fo:ɐ̯] **der; ~s** comfort; **mit allem ~** ‹*flat, house*› with all modern conveniences *pl.*; ‹*car*› with all the latest luxury features *pl.*

komfortabel [kɔmfɔr'ta:bl̩] **1.** *Adj.* comfortable. **2.** *adv.* comfortably

Komfort·wohnung die [comfortable] flat *(Brit.) or (Amer.)* apartment with all modern conveniences

Komik ['ko:mɪk] **die; ~:** comic effect; *(komisches Element)* comic element *or* aspect; **die ~ der Situation** the funny side of the situation; **Sinn für ~ haben** have a sense of the comic; **etw. entbehrt nicht einer gewissen ~:** sth. is not without an element of comedy; **~ und Tragik** comedy and tragedy; the comic and the tragic

Komiker der; ~s, ~ a) *(Vortragskünstler)* comedian; comic *(coll.)*; **b)** *(Darsteller)* comic actor; **c)** *(salopp abwertend)* clown

Kominform [komɪn'fɔrm] **das; ~s** *(hist.)* Cominform

Komintern [komɪn'tɛrn] **die; ~** *(hist.)* Comintern

komisch ['ko:mɪʃ] *Adj.* **a)** *(lustig)* comical; funny; **ich finde das gar nicht ~** *(ugs.)* I don't think that's at all funny; **b)** *(seltsam)* funny; strange; odd; **~, was?** *(ugs.)* [it's] funny *or* strange *or* odd, isn't it?; **~ [zu jmdm.] sein** act *or* behave strangely [towards sb.]; **~ [ist nur], daß ...:** it's [just] funny *or* strange *or* odd that ...; **mir ist/wird so ~:** I'm feeling funny *or* peculiar; **c)** *(Theater)* comic ‹*part*›

komischer·weise *Adv. (ugs.)* strangely enough

Komitee [komi'te:] **das; ~s, ~s** committee

Komma ['kɔma] **das; ~s, ~s** *od.* **~ta a)** *(Satzzeichen)* comma; **b)** *(Math.)* decimal point; **zwei ~ acht** two point eight; **zwei Stellen hinter dem ~:** two decimal places

Komma·fehler der mistake involving the use of the comma

Kommandant [kɔman'dant] **der; ~en, ~en** *(einer Stadt, Festung)* commandant; *(eines Panzers, Raumschiffs)* commander; *(einer Militäreinheit)* commander; commanding officer; *(eines Flugzeugs, Schiffs)* captain

Kommandantur [kɔmandan'tu:ɐ̯] **die; ~, ~en** commandant's headquarters *sing. or pl.*

Kommandeur [kɔman'dø:ɐ̯] **der; ~s, ~e** *(Milit.)* commander; commanding officer

kommandieren 1. *tr. V.* **a)** *(befehligen)* command; be in command of; **b)** *(abkommandieren)* **jmdn. an die Front ~:** order sb. to the front; **c)** order ‹*retreat, advance*›; **d)** *(ugs.: herumkommandieren)* **jmdn. ~:** order *or (sl.)* boss sb. about. **2.** *itr. V.* **a)** *(Milit.)* **Kommandierender General** Corps commander; **b)** *(ugs.)* order *or (sl.)* boss people about

Kommandit·gesellschaft [kɔman'di:t-] **die** *(Wirtsch.)* limited partnership

Kommanditist der; ~en, ~en *(Wirtsch.)* limited partner

Kommando [kɔ'mando] **das; ~s, ~s,** *österr. auch:* **Kommanden a)** *(Befehl)* command; **das ~ zum Schießen geben** give the command *or* order to shoot; **auf ~ gehorchen** obey [immediately] on command; **wie auf ~:** as if by command; *s. auch* **hören 2d; b)** *o. Pl. (Befehlsgewalt)* command; **das ~ haben** *od.* **führen/übernehmen** be in/assume *or* take command; **c)** *(Milit.) (Einheit)* detachment; *(Stoßtrupp)* commando; *(Dienststelle)* headquarters *sing. or pl.*

Kommando-: ~brücke die bridge; **~sache die** *in* **geheime ~sache** *(bes. Milit.)* military secret; **~stab der** *(Milit.)* headquarters *or* command staff; **~stand der** *(Milit.)* command post; **~stelle die** *(Milit.)* command post; **~stimme die** commanding [tone of] voice

Kommata *s.* **Komma**

kommen ['kɔmən] *unr. itr. V.; mit sein* **a)** come; *(eintreffen)* come; arrive; **der Kellner kommt sofort** the waiter will be with you directly; **zu spät ~:** be late; **zu Fuß/mit dem Auto ~:** come on foot/by car; **in einer halben Stunde/zwei Monaten ~:** come in half an hour/two months' time; **durch eine Gegend ~:** pass through a region; **von der Arbeit ~:** come [back] from work; **nach Hause ~:** come *or* get home; **ins Zimmer ~:** come into the room; **ich komme schon!** I'm coming!; **ich komme, Sie abzuholen** I've come to fetch you; **komm' ich heut nicht, komm' ich morgen** *(spött.)* you'll/he'll *etc.* get there eventually!; **b)** *(gelangen)* get; **ans Ufer/Ziel ~:** reach the bank/finishing-line; **komme ich hier zum Bahnhof?** can I get to the station this way?; **wie komme ich nach Paris?** how do I get to Paris?; **kaum noch aus dem Haus/ins Kino ~:** hardly ever get out of the house/to the cinema; **auf etw.** *(Akk.)* **zu sprechen ~** *(fig.)* turn to the discussion of sth.; **zum Schluß seiner Ausführungen ~** *(fig.)* come to the end of one's remarks; **c)** + *Bewegungsverb im 2. Part.* **angelaufen/angebraust ~:** come running/roaring along; *(auf jmdn. zu)* come running/roaring up; **angekrochen** ~ *(fig.)* come crawling up; **d)** *(teilnehmen)* come; attend; **zu einer Tagung** ~: come to/attend a meeting; **e)** *(besuchen)* come; **zu jmdm.** ~: come and see sb.; **er kommt zu uns zum Abendbrot** he's coming [to us] for supper; **f)** *(gebracht werden)* come; **die Post/ein Paket ist ge~**: the post/a parcel has come; **ist keine Post für mich ge~?** is/was there no post for me?; **g)** ~ **lassen** *(bestellen)* order ⟨*taxi*⟩; **den Arzt/die Polizei** ~ **lassen** send for *or* call a doctor/the police; **Getränke** *usw.* **aufs Zimmer** ~ **lassen** have drinks *etc.* sent up to one's room; **h)** *(aufgenommen werden)* **zur Schule/aufs Gymnasium** ~: go to *or* start school/grammar school; **ins Krankenhaus/Gefängnis** ~: go into hospital/to prison; **in die Lehre** ~: start an apprenticeship; **in den Himmel/in die Hölle** ~ *(fig.)* go to heaven/hell; **i)** *(auftauchen)* ⟨*seeds, plants*⟩ come up; ⟨*buds, flowers*⟩ come out; ⟨*peas, beans*⟩ form; ⟨*teeth*⟩ come through; **zur Welt** ~: be born; **ihr ist ein Gedanke/eine Idee ge~**: she had a thought/an idea; a thought/an idea came to her; **die Tränen** ~ **jmdm. in die Augen** tears come to sb.'s eyes; *s. auch* **Herz b**; **j)** *(seinen festen Platz haben)* go; belong; **in die Schublade/ins Regal** ~: go *or* belong in the drawer/on the shelf; **k)** *(seinen Platz erhalten)* **in die Mannschaft** ~: get into the team; **auf den ersten Platz** ~: go into first place; **l)** *(geraten)* get; **in Gefahr/Not/Verlegenheit** ~: get into danger/serious difficulties/get *or* become embarrassed; **unter ein Auto/zu Tode** ~: be knocked down by a car/be *or* get killed; **ins Schleudern** ~: go into a skid; *s. auch* **Schwung; Stimmung; m)** *(Gelegenheit haben)* **dazu** ~, **etw. zu tun** get round to doing sth.; **zum Einkaufen/Waschen** ~: get round to doing the shopping/washing; **kaum noch zum Schlafen** ~: hardly be able to find time to sleep; **n)** *(nahen)* **ein Gewitter/die Flut kommt** a storm is approaching/the tide's coming in; **den Zeitpunkt für gekommen halten** think *or* consider the moment has come; **der Tag/die Nacht kommt** *(geh.)* day is breaking/night is falling; **dieses Unglück habe ich schon lange** ~ **sehen** I saw this disaster coming a long time ago; **im Kommen sein** ⟨*fashion etc.*⟩ be coming in; ⟨*person*⟩ be on the way up; **o)** *(sich ereignen)* come about; happen; **was auch immer** ~ **mag** come what may; **das durfte [jetzt] nicht** ~ *(ugs. spött.)* that's hardly the thing to say now; **es kam, wie es** ~ **mußte** the inevitable happened; **es kam zum Streit/Kampf** there was a quarrel/fight; **es kam alles ganz anders** it all *or* everything turned out quite differently; **wie's kommt, so kommt's** *od.* **wie's kommt, so wird's genommen** *(ugs.)* what will be will be; **so weit kommt es noch[, daß ich euern Dreck wieder wegräume]!** *(ugs. iron.)* that really is the limit[, expecting me to clear up your rubbish after you]!; **p)** *(ugs.: erreicht werden)* **wann kommt der nächste Bahnhof?** when do we get to the next station? *(coll.)*; **jetzt kommt gleich Mannheim** we'll be at Mannheim any moment; **da vorn kommt eine Tankstelle** there's a petrol station coming up *(coll.)*; **q)** **zu Geld** ~: become wealthy; **zu Erfolg/Ruhm** *usw.* ~: gain success/fame *etc.*; **nie zu etwas** ~ *(ugs.)* never get anywhere; **wieder zu Kräften** ~: regain one's strength; **[wieder] zu sich** ~: regain consciousness; come round; **zu sich** ~ *(sich fassen)* become one's normal self again; **r)** **jmdm. auf die Spur/Schliche** ~: get on sb.'s trail/get wise to sb.'s tricks; **wie kommst du darauf?** what gives you that idea?; **hinter jmds. Geheimnis/Pläne** ~: find out sb.'s secret/plans; **s)** *(an der Reihe sein; folgen)* **zuerst/zuletzt kam ...**: first/last came ...; **als erster/letzter** ~: come first/last; **jetzt komme ich an die Reihe** it is my turn now; **wann** ~ **wir an die Reihe?** when do we get a turn?; **t)** *(sich darstellen)* **gelegen/ungelegen** ~ ⟨*offer, opportunity*⟩ come/not come at the right moment; ⟨*visit*⟩ be/not be convenient; **überraschend [für jmdn.]** ~: come as a surprise [to sb.]; **u)** *(ugs.: sich verhalten)* **jmdm. frech/unverschämt/grob** ~: be cheeky/impertinent/rude to sb.; **so lasse ich mir nicht** ~! I don't stand for that sort of thing!; **so können Sie mir nicht** ~! don't take that line with me! *(coll.)*; **v)** *(ugs.: sich an jmdn. wenden)* **komm mir nicht mit ...!** don't give me ...; **da könnte ja jeder** ~! who do you think you are?/who does he think he is? *etc.*; **komm mir nicht damit, du hättest keine Zeit!** don't try and tell me you don't have the time!; **mit so etw. darfst du mir nicht** ~: don't try that sort of thing on with me *(coll.)*; **w)** **ich lasse auf ihn** *usw.* **nichts** ~: I won't hear anything said against him *etc.*; **x)** + *Inf.* **mit zu** *(in eine Lage geraten)* **neben jmdn. zu sitzen** ~: get to sit next to sb.; **y)** **über jmdn.** ~ *(erfassen)* ⟨*feeling*⟩ come over sb.; **z)** *(verlieren)* **um etw.** ~: lose sth.; **ums Leben** ~: lose one's life; **wir sind um unseren Theaterbesuch gekommen** we missed out on our visit to the theatre; **aa)** *(entfallen)* **auf hundert Berufstätige** ~ **vier Arbeitslose** for every hundred people in employment, there are four people unemployed; **bb)** **woher** ~ **diese Sachen?** where do these things come from?; **seine Eltern** ~ **aus Sachsen** his parents come *or* are from Saxony; **cc)** **daher kommt es, daß ...**: that's [the reason] why ...; **das kommt davon, daß ...**: that's because ...; **vom vielen Rauchen/vom Vitaminmangel** ~: be due to smoking/vitamin deficiency; **wie kommt es, daß du/er** *usw.* **...**: how is it that you/he *etc.* ...; how come that you/he *etc.* ... *(coll.)*; **das kommt davon!** see what happens!; **das kommt davon, wenn du nicht aufpaßt!** that's what happens when you don't pay attention; that's what comes of not paying attention; **dd)** *(ugs.: kosten)* **auf 100 Mark** ~: cost 100 marks; **alles zusammen kam auf ...**: altogether it came to ...; **wie teuer kommt der Stoff?** how much *or* dear is that material?; **etw. kommt [jmdn.] teuer** sth. comes expensive [for sb.]; **ee)** *(ugs.: starten)* start; **ff)** *(salopp: Orgasmus haben)* come *(sl.)*; **es kommt jmdm.** sb. is coming *(sl.)*; **gg)** *(im Funkverkehr)* **[bitte]** ~! come in[, please]; **hh)** *(ugs.: als Aufforderung, Ermahnung)* **komm/kommt/kommen Sie** come on, now; **komm, komm** oh, come on; **ii)** *(Sportjargon: gelingen)* **[gut]** ~/**nicht** ~ ⟨*serve, backhand, forehand, etc.*⟩ be going/not be going well; **jj)** *in festen Wendungen s.* **Ausbruch b; Einsatz c; Entfaltung a; [1]Fall a; [1]Gesicht c** *usw.*

kommend *Adj.; nicht präd.* **a)** *(folgend)* next; **das ~e Wochenende/am ~en Sonntag** next weekend/Sunday; **in der ~en Saison/Woche** next season/week; **~e Generationen** generations to come; future generations; **in den ~en Jahren** in years to come; **b)** *(mit großer Zukunft)* **der ~e Mann/Meister** the coming man/future champion

kommensurabel [kɔmɛnzu'ra:bl] *Adj. (Physik, Math.)* commensurable

Komment [kɔ'mã:] **der; ~s, ~s** *(Studentenspr.)* code of conduct *(in student fraternities)*

Kommentar [kɔmɛn'ta:ɐ̯] **der; ~s, ~e** **a)** *(Erläuterung)* commentary; **b)** *(Stellungnahme)* commentary; comment; **kein ~!** no comment!; **c)** *(oft abwertend: Anmerkung)* comment; ~ **überflüssig** no comment needed; **sich** *(Dat.)* **jedes ~s enthalten** refrain from commenting; **seinen ~ zu etw. geben** comment on sth.

kommentarlos **1.** *Adj.* without comment *postpos.* **2.** *adv.* without comment

Kommentator [kɔmɛn'ta:tɔr] **der; ~s, ~en** [-ta'to:rən] commentator

kommentieren *tr. V.* **a)** *(erläutern)* furnish with a commentary, annotate ⟨*text, work*⟩; **eine kommentierte Ausgabe** an annotated edition; **b)** *(Stellung nehmen zu; ugs.: Anmerkungen machen zu)* comment on

Kommers [kɔ'mɛrs] **der; ~es, ~e** *(Studentenspr.)* students' drinking evening *(to celebrate a particular occasion)*

Kommers·buch **das** book of students' drinking songs

Kommerz [kɔ'mɛrts] **der; ~es** *(abwertend)* business interests *pl.*

kommerzialisieren [kɔmɛrtsiali'zi:rən] *tr. V.* commercialize

Kommerzial·rat [kɔmɛr'tsia:l-] **der** *(österr.) s.* **Kommerzienrat**

kommerziell [kɔmɛr'tsiɛl] **1.** *Adj.* commercial. **2.** *adv.* commercially

Kommerzien·rat [kɔ'mɛrtsiən-] **der** *(hist.) honorary title conferred on business magnates and financiers*

Kommilitone [kɔmili'to:nə] **der; ~n, ~n,** **Kommilitonin** **die; ~, ~nen** *(Studentenspr.)* [one's] fellow student; **der ~/die ~ Meyer** ≈ Mr/Ms Meyer

Kommis [kɔ'mi:] **der; ~** [kɔ'mi:(s)], **~** [kɔ'mi:s] *(veralt.) employee on the business side of a commercial firm; (in einem Laden)* [shop] assistant

Kommiß [kɔ'mɪs] **der; Kommisses** *(Soldatenspr.)* army; **beim ~ sein** be in the army

Kommissar [kɔmɪ'sa:ɐ̯] **der; ~s, ~e** **a)** *(Beamter der Polizei)* detective superintendent; **b)** *(staatlicher Beauftragter)* commissioner; **der Hohe ~**: the High Commissioner

Kommissariat [kɔmɪsa'ria:t] **das; ~s, ~e** **a)** *(Dienststelle) (der Polizei)* detective superintendent's office; *(allgemein)* commissioner's office; **b)** *(Amt) (der Polizei)* rank of detective superintendent; *(allgemein)* commissionership; **c)** *(österr.: Polizeistation)* police station

kommissarisch **1.** *Adj.; nicht präd.* acting. **2.** *adv.* in an acting capacity

Kommiß·brot **das** [coarse] wholemeal bread

Kommission [kɔmɪ'sio:n] **die; ~, ~en** **a)** *(Gremium)* committee; *(Prüfungs~)* commission; **b)** *(Kaufmannsspr. veralt.: Bestellung)* order; **c)** **etw. in ~ nehmen/haben/geben** *(Wirtsch.)* take/have sth. on commission/give sth. to a dealer for sale on commission; **d)** *(veralt.: Einkauf)* **~en machen** *od.* **tätigen** do some shopping

Kommissionär [kɔmɪsio'nɛ:ɐ̯] **der; ~s, ~e** **a)** *(Wirtsch.)* commission agent *or* merchant; **b)** *(Buchhändler)* wholesale bookseller

Kommissions-: **~buch·handel** **der** *(Wirtsch.)* wholesale book trade; **~geschäft das** *(Wirtsch.)* commission business

Kommiß-: **~stiefel der** army boot; **~ton der;** *o. Pl. (abwertend)* peremptory tone [of voice]

kommod [kɔ'mo:t] *Adj. (bes. österr.) s.* **bequem 1 a, 2 a**

Kommode [kɔ'mo:də] **die; ~, ~n** chest of drawers

Kommodore [kɔmo'do:rə] **der; ~s, ~n** *od.* **~s** *(Marine, Handelsmarine)* commodore; *(Luftwaffe)* wing commander

kommunal [kɔmu'na:l] **1.** *Adj.* local; *(bei einer städtischen Gemeinde)* municipal; local. **2.** *adv.* **etw. wird ~ verwaltet** sth. comes under local government

Kommunal-: **~abgaben** *Pl.* rates [and local taxes]; **~anleihe die** municipal bond; **~politik die** local politics *sing.*; **~verwaltung die** local government; **~wahl die** local [government] elections *pl.*

Kommunarde [kɔmu'nardə] **der; ~n, ~n** **a)** *(hist.)* Communard; **b)** *(einer Wohngemeinschaft)* member of a/the commune

Kommune [kɔ'mu:nə] **die; ~, ~n** **a)** *(politische Gemeinde)* local authority area; *(städ-*

tische Gemeinde) municipality; **b) die Pariser** ~ *(hist.)* the Paris Commune; **c)** *(Wohngemeinschaft)* commune
Kommunikant [kɔmuni'kant] **der;** ~**en,** ~**en, Kommunikantin die;** ~, ~**nen a)** *(kath. Kirche)* communicant; **b)** *(Sprachw., Soziol.)* participant in the communicative process
Kommunikation ['kɔmunika'tsio:n] **die;** ~, ~**en** *(Sprachw., Soziol.)* communication
Kommunikations-: ~**mittel das** communication medium; ~**satellit der** communications satellite; ~**schwierigkeit die;** *meist Pl.* difficulty in communicating; ~**wissenschaft die** communication science *no art.;* ~**zentrum das** central meeting-place *(for social and cultural activities)*
kommunikativ [kɔmunika'ti:f] *Adj.* communicative
Kommunion [kɔmu'nio:n] **die;** ~, ~**en** *(kath. Kirche)* [Holy] Communion
Kommunion-: ~**bank die: auf der** ~**bank knien** ≈ kneel at the Communion rail; ~**kleid das** *dress worn to first Communion;* ~**unterricht der** *preparation for first Communion*
Kommuniqué [kɔmyni'ke:] **das;** ~**s,** ~**s** communiqué
Kommunismus der; ~: communism; *(Bewegung)* Communism *no art.*
Kommunist der; ~**en,** ~**en, Kommunistin die;** ~, ~**nen** communist; *(Parteimitglied)* Communist
kommunistisch 1. *Adj.* communist; *(die* ~*e Partei betreffend)* Communist; **das Kommunistische Manifest** the Communist Manifesto. **2.** *adv.* Communist-⟨*influenced, led, ruled, etc.*⟩
kommunizieren [kɔmuni'tsi:rən] *itr. V.* **a)** *(geh.)* communicate; ~**de Röhren** *(Physik)* communicating tubes; **b)** *(kath. Kirche)* receive [Holy] Communion
Kommutation [kɔmuta'tsio:n] **die;** ~, ~**en** *(Math., Sprachw., Astron.)* commutation
kommutativ [kɔmuta'ti:f] *Adj.* *(Math., Sprachw.)* commutative
Komödiant [komø'diant] **der;** ~**en,** ~**en a)** *(veralt.: Schauspieler)* actor; player; **b)** *(abwertend: Heuchler)* play-actor
komödiantenhaft *Adj.* theatrical
Komödiantin die; ~, ~**nen a)** *(veralt.: Schauspielerin)* actress; **b)** *(abwertend: Heuchlerin)* play-actor
komödiantisch *Adj.* theatrical; acting ⟨*talent*⟩
Komödie [ko'mø:diə] **die;** ~, ~**n a)** comedy; *(fig.)* farce; **b)** *(Theater)* comedy theatre; **c)** *(Heuchelei)* play-acting; ~ **spielen** put on an act
Kompagnon [kɔmpan'jõ:] **der;** ~**s,** ~**s** *(Wirtsch.)* partner; associate
kompakt [kɔm'pakt] *Adj.* **a)** *(massiv)* solid; **b)** *(ugs.: gedrungen)* stocky
Kompakt-: ~**an·lage die** music centre; *(bei übereinander angeordneten Geräten)* compact stereo system; ~**bau·weise die** compact design
Kompanie [kɔmpa'ni:] **die;** ~, ~**n** *(Milit., veralt.: Handelsgesellschaft)* company
Kompanie·chef der, Kompanie·führer der *(Milit.)* company commander
Komparation [kɔmpara'tsio:n] **die;** ~, ~**en** *(Sprachw.)* comparison
Komparatistik [kɔmpara'tɪstɪk] **die;** ~: comparative literature *no art.*
Komparativ ['kɔmparati:f] **der;** ~**s,** ~**e** *(Sprachw.)* comparative
Komparse [kɔm'parzə] **der;** ~**n,** ~**n** *(Theater)* supernumerary; super *(coll.);* *(Film)* extra
Komparserie [kɔmparzə'ri:] **die;** ~, ~**n** *(Theater)* supernumeraries *pl.;* supers *pl. (coll.);* *(Film)* extras *pl.*
Kompaß ['kɔmpas] **der; Kompasses, Kompasse** compass; **nach dem** ~ **marschieren** march by the compass
Kompaß-: ~**häuschen das** *(Seew. hist.)* binnacle; ~**nadel die** compass needle; ~**rose die** compass card
kompatibel [kɔmpa'ti:bl̩] *Adj.* *(Nachrichtenw., Sprachw.)* compatible
Kompendium [kɔm'pɛndium] **das;** ~**s, Kompendien** *(geh.)* compendium
Kompensation [kɔmpɛnza'tsio:n] **die;** ~, ~**en** *(Wirtsch., Physik, geh.)* compensation
kompensatorisch *Adj.* *(Päd., Psych.)* compensatory
kompensieren *tr. V.* **a)** *(ausgleichen)* **etw. mit etw.** *od.* **durch etw.** ~: compensate for *or* make up for sth. by sth.; **b)** *(Wirtsch.: gegeneinander aufrechnen)* offset; **etw. durch etw.** ~: offset sth. against sth.
kompetent [kɔmpe'tɛnt] *Adj.* **a)** *(sachverständig)* competent; **ein** ~**er Sprecher** *(Sprachw.)* a person with native-speaker competence; **für diese Probleme/Fragen ist er nicht** ~: he's not competent to deal with these problems/answer these questions; **b)** *(bes. Rechtsw.: zuständig)* competent, responsible ⟨*authority*⟩; **das dafür** ~**e Gericht/der dafür** ~**e Kollege** the court which has jurisdiction in/the colleague who deals with these matters
Kompetenz [kɔmpe'tɛnts] **die;** ~, ~**en a)** *(Sachverstand)* competence; **b)** *(bes. Rechtsw.: Zuständigkeit)* authority; powers *pl.;* *(eines Gerichts)* jurisdiction; competence; **in jmds.** ~ *(Dat.)* **liegen/in jmds.** ~ *(Akk.)* **fallen** be/come within sb.'s authority *or* powers; **das liegt außerhalb meiner** ~: that doesn't lie within my authority *or* powers; **seine** ~ **überschreiten** exceed one's authority *or* powers; **die** ~ **haben/erhalten, etw. zu tun** have/receive the authority to do sth.; **c)** *(Sprachw.)* competence
Kompetenz-: ~**bereich der** area of authority *or* responsibility/jurisdiction; ~**konflikt der,** ~**streitigkeit die;** *meist Pl.* dispute over respective areas of authority *or* responsibility/jurisdiction
Kompilation [kɔmpila'tsio:n] **die;** ~, ~**en** *(geh., meist abwertend)* [mere] compilation
kompilieren *tr. V.* *(geh., meist abwertend)* [merely] compile
Komplement [kɔmple'mɛnt] **das;** ~**[e]s,** ~**e** *(Math.)* complement
komplementär [kɔmplemɛn'tɛ:ɐ̯] **1.** *Adj.* complementary. **2.** *adv.* **sich** ~ **verhalten/zueinander stehen** complement one another; be complementary
Komplementär der; ~**s,** ~**e** *(Wirtsch.)* general partner
Komplementär·farbe die *(Optik)* complementary colour
Komplement·winkel der *(Math.)* complementary angle
¹Komplet [kõ'ple:] **das;** ~**s,** ~**s** dress and matching jacket/coat
²Komplet [kɔm'ple:t] **die;** ~, ~**e** *(kath. Kirche)* compline
komplett [kɔm'plɛt] **1.** *Adj.* **a)** *(vollständig)* complete; **das kostet** ~ **1500 Mark** it costs 1,500 marks complete; **heute sind wir** ~ *(ugs.)* today we are all here; **b)** *nicht präd.* *(ugs.: ganz und gar)* complete; utter; **c)** *(österr.: voll)* full ⟨*hotel, tram, etc.*⟩. **2.** *adv.* **a)** *(vollständig)* ~ **möbliert/ausgerüstet** fully furnished/equipped; **b)** *(ugs.: ganz und gar)* completely; totally
komplettieren *tr. V.* complete
komplex [kɔm'plɛks] *(geh.)* **1.** *Adj.* **a)** complex; ~**e Zahl** *(Math.)* complex number; **b)** *(bes. DDR: allseitig)* full, complete ⟨*automation*⟩; comprehensive ⟨*reconstruction, planning, provision*⟩; ⟨*analysis, treatment*⟩ by several methods. **2.** *adv.* *(bes. DDR)* **etw.** ~ **vorbereiten** make comprehensive preparations for sth.
Komplex der; ~**es,** ~**e a)** *(Bereich)* complex; **Fragen im** ~ **lösen** *(DDR)* solve questions as parts of an integrated whole; **b)** *(Gebäudeblock)* complex; **in diesem** ~ **des Schlosses** in this complex of buildings in the castle; **c)** *(Psych.)* complex
Komplexität [kɔmplɛksi'tɛ:t] **die;** ~: complexity
Komplikation [kɔmplika'tsio:n] **die;** ~, ~**en** *(auch Med.)* complication
Kompliment [kɔmpli'mɛnt] **das;** ~**[e]s,** ~**e a)** compliment; **jmdm. ein** ~ **machen** pay sb. a compliment **(über** + *Akk.* on); **mein** ~**!** permit me to compliment you; my compliments!; **nicht gerade ein** ~ **für jmdn. sein** *(fig.)* not exactly do sb. credit; **b)** *(veralt.: Gruß)* **meine** ~**e an die gnädige Frau** give my respects to your good wife
komplimentieren *tr. V.* *(geh.)* **jmdn. ins Haus/in den Sessel** ~: usher *or* show sb. into the house/help sb. into his/her seat with a great show of courtesy; **jmdn. aus dem Zimmer** ~ *(verhüll.)* usher sb. out of the room
Komplize [kɔm'pli:tsə] **der;** ~**n,** ~**n** *(abwertend)* accomplice
komplizieren *tr. V.* complicate; **sich** ~: become more complicated
kompliziert 1. *Adj.* complicated; complicated, intricate ⟨*device, piece of apparatus*⟩; complicated, involved ⟨*problem, procedure*⟩; **ein** ~**er Bruch** *(Med.)* a compound fracture. **2.** *adv.* ~ **aufgebaut sein** have a complicated *or* complex structure; **sich** ~ **ausdrücken** express oneself in a complicated *or* an involved way *or* manner; *s. auch* **einfach 1 b**
Kompliziertheit die; ~: complexity; complicatedness
Komplizin die; ~, ~**nen** *s.* **Komplize**
Komplott [kɔm'plɔt] **das;** ~**[e]s,** ~**e** plot; conspiracy; **ein** ~ **zur Ermordung des Diktators** a plot *or* conspiracy to assassinate the dictator; **ein** ~ **schmieden** hatch a plot
Komponente [kɔmpo'nɛntə] **die;** ~, ~**n a)** *(Bestandteil)* component; **b)** *(Aspekt)* component; element
komponieren 1. *tr. V.* *(auch geh.: gestalten)* compose. **2.** *itr. V.* compose
Komponist der; ~**en,** ~**en, Komponistin die;** ~, ~**nen** composer
Komposition [kɔmpozi'tsio:n] **die;** ~, ~**en** *(Musik, geh.)* composition; **eine** ~ **kostbarer Essenzen** *(geh.)* a fusion *or* blend of expensive essential oils
Kompositions·lehre die *(Musik)* [theory of] composition
kompositorisch [kɔmpozi'to:rɪʃ] *Adj.* compositional
Kompositum [kɔm'po:zitʊm] **das;** ~**s, Komposita** *(Sprachw.)* compound [word]
Kompost [kɔm'pɔst] **der;** ~**[e]s,** ~**e** compost
Kompost-: ~**erde die** [well-rotted] compost; ~**haufen der** compost heap
Kompott [kɔm'pɔt] **das;** ~**[e]s,** ~**e** stewed fruit; compote; **Pflaumen~/Himbeer~:** stewed plums/raspberries *pl.*
Kompott·schale die fruit dish *or* bowl
kompreß [kɔm'prɛs] *(Druckw.)* **1.** *Adj.* solid. **2.** *adv.* ⟨*set*⟩ in solid type
Kompresse [kɔm'prɛsə] **die;** ~, ~**n** *(Med.)* **a)** *(Umschlag)* [wet] compress; **b)** *(Mull)* [gauze] pad
Kompression [kɔmprɛ'sio:n] **die;** ~, ~**en** *(Physik, Technik, Med.)* compression
Kompressions·verband der *(Med.)* *s.* **Druckverband**
Kompressor [kɔm'prɛsɔr] **der;** ~**s,** ~**en** [-'so:rən] *(Technik)* compressor
komprimieren [kɔmpri'mi:rən] *tr. V.* *(auch Physik, Technik)* compress; *(fig.)* condense ⟨*book, text*⟩
komprimiert 1. *Adj.* condensed ⟨*account etc.*⟩. **2.** *adv.* **etw.** ~ **darstellen** present sth. in a condensed form
Kompromiß [kɔmpro'mɪs] **der; Kompro-**

misses, **Kompromisse** compromise; **einen ~ schließen** make a compromise; compromise; **zu einem/keinem ~ bereit sein** be/not be ready to compromise; **ein fauler ~** *(ugs.)* a poor sort of compromise *(coll.)*

kompromiß-, Kompromiß-: ~bereit *Adj.* ready *or* willing to compromise *pred.*; **~bereitschaft die;** *o. Pl.* readiness *or* willingness to compromise; **~los 1.** *Adj.* uncompromising; **2.** *adv.* uncompromisingly; **~lösung die** compromise solution; **~vor·schlag der** compromise proposal *or* suggestion

kompromittieren [kɔmpromɪ'ti:rən] *tr. V.* compromise; **sich ~:** compromise oneself

Komsomolze [kɔmzo'mɔltsə] **der; ~n, ~n** Komsomol member

Komteß, Komtesse [kɔm'tɛs(ə)] **die; ~, Komtessen** *(veralt.)* count's [unmarried] daughter

Komtur [kɔm'tu:ɐ] **der; ~s, ~e** *(hist.)* commander *(of an honorary or a religious military order)*

Kondensat [kɔndɛn'za:t] **das; ~[e]s, ~e** *(Physik, Chemie)* condensate

Kondensation [kɔndɛnza'tsio:n] **die; ~, ~en** *(Physik, Chemie)* condensation

Kondensations·punkt der *(Physik, Chemie)* condensation point

Kondensator [kɔndɛn'za:tɔr] **der; ~s, ~en** [-za'to:rən] **a)** *(Elektrot.)* capacitor; condenser; **b)** *(Technik)* condenser

kondensieren *tr., itr. V. (itr. auch mit sein) (Physik, Chemie)* condense

Kondens-: ~milch die condensed milk; **~streifen der** condensation trail; vapour trail; **~wasser das** condensation

Kondition [kɔndi'tsio:n] **die; ~, ~en a)** *meist Pl. (bes. Kaufmannsspr., Finanzw.)* condition; **die ~en** the terms *or* conditions; **zu günstigen ~en** on favourable terms; **b)** *o. Pl. (körperlich-seelische Verfassung, Leistungsfähigkeit)* condition; **eine gute/schlechte ~ haben** be/not be in good condition *or* shape; **keine ~ haben** be out of condition; *(fig.)* have no stamina

konditional [kɔnditsio'na:l] *Adj. (bes. Sprachw.)* conditional

Konditional·satz der *(Sprachw.)* conditional clause

konditionieren *tr. V. (Technik, Psych.)* condition

Konditions-: ~mangel der, ~schwäche die lack of condition *or* fitness; **~training das** fitness training

Konditor [kɔn'di:tɔr] **der; ~s, ~en** [-di'to:rən] confectioner; pastry-cook; **beim ~:** at the cake-shop

Konditorei die; ~, ~en a) cake-shop; *(Lokal)* café; **b)** *o. Pl. (Herstellung)* confectionery

Konditor·waren *Pl.* cakes and pastries

Kondolenz- [kɔndo'lɛnts-]: **~besuch der** visit of condolence; **~buch das** book of condolence

kondolieren [kɔndo'li:rən] *itr. V.* offer one's condolences; **jmdm. [zu jmds. Tod] ~:** offer one's condolences to sb. *or* condole with sb. [on sb.'s death]

Kondom [kɔn'do:m] **das** *od.* **der; ~s, ~e** condom; [contraceptive] sheath

Kondominium [kɔndo'mi:niʊm] **das; ~s, Kondominien** *(Völkerr.)* condominium

Kondor ['kɔndɔr] **der; ~s, ~e** condor

Kondukteur [kɔndʊk'tø:ɐ] **der; ~s, ~e** *(schweiz.) (in der Straßenbahn)* conductor; *(in der Eisenbahn)* ticket-collector

Kondukteurin die; ~, ~nen *(schweiz.) s.* **Kondukteur:** conductress/ticket-collector

Konen *s.* **Konus**

Konfekt [kɔn'fɛkt] **das; ~[e]s a)** *(Süßigkeiten)* confectionery; sweets *pl. (Brit.)*; candies *pl. (Amer.)*; **b)** *(bes. südd., österr., schweiz.: Teegebäck)* [small] fancy biscuits *pl. (Brit.) or (Amer.)* cookies *pl.*

Konfektion [kɔnfɛk'tsio:n] **die; ~, ~en a)** *(Anfertigung)* manufacture of ready-made *or* off-the-peg *(Brit.) or (Amer.)* off-the-rack clothes *or* garments; **b)** *(Kleidung)* ready-made *or* off-the-peg *(Brit.) or (Amer.)* off-the-rack clothes *pl. or* garments *pl.*; **c)** *(Industrie)* clothing industry

Konfektionär [kɔnfɛktsio'nɛ:ɐ] **der; ~s, ~e** manufacturer of ready-made *or* off-the-peg *(Brit.) or (Amer.)* off-the-rack clothing; clothing manufacturer; *(Angestellter)* employee in a clothing factory

Konfektions-: ~an·zug der ready-made *or* off-the-peg *(Brit.) or (Amer.)* off-the-rack suit; **~geschäft das** [ready-made *or* off-the-peg *(Brit.) or (Amer.)* off-the-rack] clothes shop; **~größe die** size; **~ware die** ready-made *or* off-the-peg *(Brit.) or (Amer.)* off-the-rack clothes *pl. or* garments *pl.*

Konferenz [kɔnfe'rɛnts] **die; ~, ~en** conference; *(Besprechung)* meeting

Konferenz-: ~saal der conference hall; **~schaltung die** *(Rundf., Ferns., Fernspr.)* conference circuit; **~teilnehmer der** conference participant; **~tisch der** conference table

konferieren [kɔnfe'ri:rən] **1.** *itr. V.* **a)** *(beraten)* confer **(über + Akk.** on, about); **b)** *(ansagen)* act as compère. **2.** *tr. V. (ansagen)* compère

Konfession [kɔnfɛ'sio:n] **die; ~, ~en a)** denomination; religion; **die katholische ~:** the Catholic religion; **welche ~ haben Sie?** what denomination *or* religion are you?; **b)** *(geh.: Geständnis)* confession

Konfessionalismus [kɔnfɛsiona'lɪsmʊs] **der; ~** *(geh.)* denominationalism *no art.*

konfessionell [kɔnfɛsio'nɛl] **1.** *Adj.; nicht präd.* denominational. **2.** *adv.* as regards denomination; **~ [un]gebunden sein/sich ~ [un]gebunden fühlen** have/feel [no] denominational ties

konfessions·los *Adj.* not belonging to any denomination *or* religion *postpos., not pred.*

Konfessions·schule die denominational school

Konfetti [kɔn'fɛti] **das; ~[s]** confetti

Konfident [kɔnfi'dɛnt] **der; ~en, ~en** *(österr.: Spitzel)* [police] informer

Konfiguration [kɔnfigura'tsio:n] **die; ~, ~en** *(Physik, Chemie, Sprachw.)* configuration

Konfirmand [kɔnfɪr'mant] **der; ~en, ~en** *(ev. Rel.)* confirmand

Konfirmanden·unterricht der confirmation classes *pl.*

Konfirmandin die; ~, ~nen *s.* **Konfirmand**

Konfirmation [kɔnfɪrma'tsio:n] **die; ~, ~en** *(ev. Rel.)* confirmation

konfirmieren *tr. V. (ev. Rel.)* confirm

Konfiserie [kɔnfizə'ri:] **die; ~, ~n** *(schweiz.) s.* **Konditorei**

Konfiskation [kɔnfɪska'tsio:n] **die; ~, ~en** *(Rechtsw.)* confiscation

konfiszieren [kɔnfɪs'tsi:rən] *tr. V. (bes. Rechtsw.)* confiscate

Konfitüre [kɔnfi'ty:rə] **die; ~, ~n** jam *(made from whole fruit)*

Konflikt [kɔn'flɪkt] **der; ~[e]s, ~e** conflict; **ein offener/bewaffneter ~:** open/armed conflict; **mit etw. in ~ geraten** *od.* **kommen** come into conflict with sth.

konflikt-, Konflikt-: ~fall der: im ~fall in the event of conflict; **~forschung die** conflict studies *pl.*; **~los** *Adj.* conflict-free; **~situation die** conflict situation; **~stoff der** cause for conflict *or* dispute

Konföderation [kɔnfødera'tsio:n] **die; ~, ~en** confederation; *(von kürzerer Dauer)* confederacy

Konföderierte der/die; *adj. Dekl.* confederate; **die ~n** *(hist.)* the Confederates

konform [kɔn'fɔrm] *Adj.* concurring *attrib.* ‹*views*›; **mit jmdm./etw. ~ gehen** be in agreement with sb./sth.; **in etw.** *(Dat.)* **~ sein** agree *or* be in agreement on sth.

Konformismus der; ~: conformism

Konformist der; ~en, ~en *(auch Rel.)* conformist

konformistisch 1. *Adj.* conformist. **2.** *adv.* in a conformist way

Konformität [kɔnfɔrmi'tɛ:t] **die; ~:** conformity

Konfrater [kɔn'fra:tɐ] **der; ~s, Konfratres** *(kath. Kirche)* fellow clergyman; brother-priest

Konfrontation [kɔnfrɔnta'tsio:n] **die; ~, ~en** confrontation

konfrontieren *tr. V.* confront; **sich mit etw. konfrontiert sehen** be confronted with sth.

konfus [kɔn'fu:s] **1.** *Adj.* confused; muddled; **jmdn. ~ machen** confuse *or* muddle sb. **2.** *adv.* in a confused *or* muddled fashion; confusedly

Konfusion [kɔnfu'zio:n] **die; ~, ~en** confusion

konfuzianisch [kɔnfu'tsia:nɪʃ] *Adj.* Confucian

Konfuzianismus der; ~: Confucianism *no art.*

kongenial [kɔnge'nia:l] *(geh.) Adj.* congenial, kindred ‹*spirits*›; ideally matched ‹*translation*›

Kongenialität [kɔngeniali'tɛ:t] **die; ~** *(der Geister)* congeniality; *(einer Übersetzung)* well-matched quality

Konglomerat [kɔnglome'ra:t] **das; ~[e]s, ~e a)** conglomeration; **b)** *(Geol.)* conglomerate

[1]Kongo ['kɔŋgo] **der; ~[s]** *(Fluß)* Congo

[2]Kongo ['kɔŋgo] **(das); ~s** *od.* **der; ~[s]** *(Staat)* the Congo

Kongolese [kɔŋgo'le:zə] **der; ~n, ~n, Kongolesin die; ~, ~nen** Congolese

Kongregation [kɔngrega'tsio:n] **die; ~, ~en** *(kath. Kirche)* congregation

Kongreß [kɔn'grɛs] **der; Kongresses, Kongresse a)** *(Tagung)* congress; conference; **b)** *o. Pl. (USA)* **der ~:** Congress

Kongreß-: ~halle die conference hall; **~mit·glied das** *(USA)* Congressman/Congresswoman; **~teilnehmer der** congress *or* conference participant; **~zentrum das** conference centre

kongruent [kɔngru'ɛnt] *Adj.* **a)** *(geh.)* identical; **b)** *(Math.)* congruent

Kongruenz [kɔngru'ɛnts] **die; ~, ~en a)** *(geh.)* identity; **b)** *(Math.)* congruence; **c)** *(Sprachw.)* agreement; concord

kongruieren *itr. V.* **a)** *(geh.)* coincide; **b)** *(Math.)* be congruent; **c)** *(Sprachw.)* agree

K.-o.-Nieder·lage die *(Boxen)* defeat by a knock-out; **durch eine ~:** by a knock-out

Konifere [koni'fe:rə] **die; ~, ~n** *(Bot.)* conifer

König ['kø:nɪç] **der; ~s, ~e** *(auch Schach, Kartenspiele, fig.)* king; **der ~ der Wüste/Lüfte** *(dicht.)***/des Jazz** the king of beasts/birds/jazz; **der Kunde ist ~:** the customer is always right

Königin die; ~, ~nen *(auch Bienen~)* queen; **die ~ des Festes/Balles** *(geh.)* the belle of the ball; **~ der Nacht** *(Bot.)* queen of the night

Königin·mutter die; *Pl.* **Königinmütter** queen mother

königlich 1. *Adj.* **a)** *nicht präd.* royal; **b)** *(vornehm)* regal; **c)** *(reichlich)* princely ‹*gift, salary, wage*›; lavish ‹*hospitality*›; **d)** *(ugs.: außerordentlich)* tremendous *(coll.)* ‹*fun*›. **2.** *adv.* **a)** *(reichlich)* ‹*entertain*› lavishly; ‹*pay*› handsomely; **~ beschenkt werden** be showered with lavish presents; **b)** *(ugs.: außerordentlich)* ‹*enjoy oneself*› immensely *(coll.)*; **sich über etw. (Akk.) ~ freuen** be as pleased as Punch about sth.

König·reich das kingdom

königs-, Königs-: ~blau *Adj.* royal blue;

~**haus** das royal house; ~**hof** der royal court; king's court; ~**kerze** die *(Bot.)* mullein; ~**kind** das prince/princess; king's son/daughter; ~**krone** die royal crown; ~**macher** der *(ugs.)* kingmaker; ~**paar** das royal couple; ~**sohn** der prince; king's son; ~**thron** der royal throne; ~**tiger** der Bengal tiger; ~**tochter** die princess; king's daughter; ~**treu** *Adj.* loyal to the king *postpos.; (der Monarchie treu)* royalist; ~**wasser** das *(Chemie, Technik)* aqua regia; ~**weg** der *(geh.)* ideal way

Königtum das; ~s, Königtümer a) *o. Pl. (Monarchie)* monarchy; b) *(veralt.: Reich)* kingdom

konisch ['ko:nɪʃ] 1. *Adj.* conical. 2. *adv.* conically; ~ zugespitzt sein taper to a point

Konjektur [kɔnjɛk'tu:ɐ̯] die; ~, ~en *(Literaturw.)* conjecture

Konjugation [kɔnjuga'tsio:n] die; ~, ~en *(Sprachw.)* conjugation

konjugieren *tr. V. (Sprachw.)* conjugate

Konjunktion [kɔnjʊŋk'tsio:n] die; ~, ~en *(Sprachw.)* conjunction

Konjunktional·satz der *(Sprachw.)* conjunctional clause

Konjunktiv ['kɔnjʊŋkti:f] der; ~s, ~e *(Sprachw.)* subjunctive; ~ I/II present/imperfect subjunctive

konjunktivisch 1. *Adj. (Sprachw.)* subjunctive. 2. *adv.* in the subjunctive

Konjunktur [kɔnjʊŋk'tu:ɐ̯] die; ~, ~en *(Wirtsch.)* a) *(wirtschaftliche Lage)* [level of] economic activity; economy; *(Tendenz)* economic trend; **eine rückläufige/steigende ~**: declining/increasing economic activity; **die ~ beleben/bremsen** stimulate/slow down the economy; b) *(Hoch~)* boom; *(Aufschwung)* upturn [in the economy]; ~ **haben** *(fig.)* be in great demand

konjunktur-, Konjunktur-: ~**abhängig** *Adj. (Wirtsch.)* dependent on economic trends *postpos.*; ~**ab·schwächung** die *(Wirtsch.)* economic downturn; ~**aufschwung** der *(Wirtsch.)* economic upturn; upturn in the economy; ~**barometer** das *(Wirtsch.)* graph of leading economic indicators; *(fig.)* economic barometer; ~**bedingt** *Adj. (Wirtsch.)* due to economic trends *postpos.*; cyclical; ~**bericht** der *(Wirtsch.)* report on the economy

konjunkturell [kɔnjʊŋktu'rɛl] 1. *Adj.; nicht präd.* economic; **die ~e Entwicklung** the development of the economy. 2. *adv.* ~ **bedingt** due to economic trends *postpos.*

konjunktur-, Konjunktur-: ~**entwicklung** die *(Wirtsch.)* economic trends *pl.*; ~**flaute** die *(Wirtsch.)* [economic] recession; ~**gerecht** *Adj. (Wirtsch.)* in keeping with the needs of the economy *postpos.*; ~**politik** die *(Wirtsch.)* stabilization policy; measures *pl.* aimed at avoiding violent fluctuations in the economy; ~**ritter** der *(Wirtsch. abwertend)* opportunist; ~**rückgang** der *(Wirtsch.)* [economic] recession; decline in economic activity; ~**schwankung** die *(Wirtsch.)* fluctuation in the level of economic activity; ~**spritze** die *(Wirtsch. ugs.)* boost to the economy; ~**zyklus** der *(Wirtsch.)* trade cycle

konkav [kɔn'ka:f] *(Optik)* 1. *Adj.* concave. 2. *adv.* concavely

Konkav·spiegel der *(Optik)* concave mirror

Konklave [kɔn'kla:və] das; ~s, ~n *(kath. Kirche)* conclave

Konklusion [kɔnklu'zio:n] die; ~, ~en *(bes. Philos.)* conclusion

Konkordanz [kɔnkɔr'dants] die; ~, ~en *(Wissensch.)* concordance

Konkordat [kɔnkɔr'da:t] das; ~[e]s, ~e concordat

konkret [kɔn'kre:t] 1. *Adj.* concrete; **~e Literatur/Musik** concrete poetry/music. 2. *adv.* a) *(nicht abstrakt)* in concrete terms; **kannst du mal ~ sagen, was du damit meinst?** could you tell me exactly what you mean by that?; **kannst du dich etwas ~er ausdrücken?** could you be a bit move specific [about that]?; b) *(in der Praxis)* in practice

konkretisieren *tr. V.* **etw. ~**: put sth. in concrete terms

Konkubinat [kɔnkubi'na:t] das; ~[e]s, ~e *(Rechtsw.)* concubinage; **mit jmdm. im ~ leben** live in concubinage with sb.

Konkubine [kɔnku'bi:nə] die; ~, ~n a) *(hist.)* concubine; b) *(abwertend: Geliebte)* mistress

Konkurrent [kɔnkʊ'rɛnt] der; ~en, ~en, **Konkurrentin** die; ~, ~nen rival; *(Sport, Wirtsch.)* competitor

Konkurrenz [kɔnkʊ'rɛnts] die; ~, ~en a) *o. Pl. (Rivalität)* rivalry *no indef. art.; (Sport, Wirtsch.)* competition *no indef. art.*; **jmdm. ~ machen** compete with sb.; **mit jmdm. in ~ treten/stehen** enter into/be in competition with sb.; b) *(Wettbewerb)* competition; **außer ~ starten/teilnehmen** take part as an unofficial competitor; c) *o. Pl. (die Konkurrenten)* competition

konkurrenz-, Konkurrenz-: ~**druck** der; *o. Pl.* pressure of competition; ~**fähig** *Adj.* competitive; ~**kampf** der competition; *(zwischen zwei Menschen)* rivalry; ~**los** *Adj.* ‹*product, firm, etc.*› that has no competition *or* competitors; *(unvergleichlich)* unrivalled; ~**los sein** have no competition *or* competitors; ~**unternehmen** das rival company *or* concern; **zwei ~unternehmen** two rival *or* competing companies *or* concerns

konkurrieren *itr. V.* compete; **mit jmdm./etw. [um etw.] ~**: compete with sb./sth. [for sth.]

Konkurs [kɔn'kʊrs] der; ~es, ~e a) *(Bankrott)* bankruptcy; ~ **machen** *od.* **in ~ gehen** go bankrupt; **[den] ~ anmelden** file for bankruptcy; have oneself declared bankrupt; b) *(gerichtliches Verfahren)* bankruptcy proceedings *pl.*

Konkurs-: ~**masse** die *(Wirtsch.)* bankrupt's assets *pl.*; ~**verfahren** das *(Wirtsch.)* bankruptcy proceedings *pl.*; ~**verwalter** der *(Wirtsch.)* receiver

können ['kœnən] 1. *unr. Modalverb; 2. Part.* ~ a) *(vermögen)* be able to; **er hat/hätte es machen ~**: he was able to *or* he could do it/he could have done it; **er kann es machen/nicht machen** he can do it *or* is able to do it/cannot *or (coll.)* can't do it *or* is unable to do it; **er kann gut reden/tanzen** he can talk/dance well; he is a good talker/dancer; **Auto fahren/Klavier spielen ~**: be able to drive [a car]/play the piano; **er kann Auto fahren** he can drive; **ich kann nicht schlafen** I cannot *or (coll.)* can't sleep; **er konnte das genau hören/sehen** he could hear/see everything; **er konnte nicht bleiben** he couldn't stay; **ich kann das nicht mehr hören/sehen** I can't stand *or* bear to hear it/can't stand *or* bear the sight of it any longer *(coll.)*; **ich kann dir sagen!** *(ugs.)* I can tell you; **nirgends kann man besser jagen als in ...**: nowhere is the hunting *or* shooting better than in ...; b) *(die Möglichkeit haben)* **kann das explodieren?** could it explode?; **er kann jeden Moment kommen** he could *or* might come at any moment; **wer kann es sein/gewesen sein?** who can it be/could it have been?; **man kann nie wissen** you never know; one never knows; **es kann sein, daß ...**: it could *or* might be that ...; **das könnte [gut] sein** that could [well] be the case; **das kann nicht sein** that's not possible; **kann ich Ihnen helfen?** can I help you?; **können Sie mir sagen, ...?** can you tell me ...?; **~ Sie nicht grüßen?** don't you know how to salute?; **kannst du nicht aufpassen?** can't you be more careful?; **kann sein** *(ugs.)* could be *(coll.)*; **kann sein, kann nicht sein** *(ugs.)* might be, might not be *(coll.)*; **Kommst du morgen? – Kann sein** Are you coming tomorrow? – Might do; c) *(Grund haben)* **du kannst ganz ruhig sein** you don't have to worry; **wir ~ uns/er kann sich freuen, daß ...**: we can/he should be glad that ...; **er kann sie/es nicht leiden** he can't stand her/it; **er kann einem leid tun** *(ugs.)* you have to feel sorry for him; **das kann man wohl sagen!** you could well say that; d) *(dürfen)* **kann ich gehen?** can I go?; ~ **wir mit[kommen]?** can we come too? 2. *unr. tr. V.* a) *(beherrschen)* know ‹*language*›; be able to play, know how to play ‹*game*›; **sie kann das [gut]** she can do that [well]; **sie kann/kann keine Mathe** she can/can't do maths; **er kann etwas auf seinem Gebiet** he has quite a lot of know-how in his field; **hast du die Hausaufgabe gekonnt?** could you do the homework?; **ein Gedicht ~**: know a poem [by heart]; **er lief, was er konnte** he ran as fast as he could; b) **du kannst mich [mal]!** *(salopp verhüll.)* you can get stuffed *(sl.)*; you know what you can do *(coll.)*. 3. *unr. itr. V.* a) *(fähig sein)* **er kann nicht anders** there's nothing else he can do; *(es ist seine Art)* he can't help it *(coll.)*; ~ **vor Lachen** *(ugs.)* I would if I could; b) *(Zeit haben)* **ich kann heute nicht** I can't today *(coll.)*; c) *(ugs.: Kraft haben)* **kannst du noch [weiter]?** can you go on?; **der Läufer konnte nicht mehr** the runner could not go on; d) *(ugs.: essen ~)* **für mich keinen Nachtisch, ich kann nicht mehr** no dessert for me, I couldn't manage any more; e) *(ugs.: umgehen ~)* **[gut] mit jmdm. ~**: get on *or* along [well] with sb.; f) **dafür kann er nichts** he can't do anything about it *(coll.)*; **was kann ich dafür?** what am I supposed to do about it?

Können das; ~s ability; *(Kunstfertigkeit)* skill

Könner der; ~s, ~, **Könnerin** die; ~, ~nen expert

Konnex [kɔ'nɛks] der; ~es, ~e *(geh.)* a) *(Zusammenhang)* connection; link; b) *(Kontakt)* contact

Konnossement [kɔnɔsə'mɛnt] das; ~[e]s, ~e *(Seew.)* bill of lading

Konnotation [kɔnota'tsio:n] die; ~, ~en *(Sprachw.)* connotation

konnte ['kɔntə] *1. u. 3. Pers. Sg. Prät. v.* **können**

könnte ['kœntə] *1. u. 3. Pers. Sg. Konjunktiv II v.* **können**

Konrektor ['kɔnrɛktɔr] der; ~s, ~en [-'to:rən] *(Schulw.)* deputy head[master]

Konsekration [kɔnzekra'tsio:n] die; ~, ~en *(kath. Kirche)* consecration

konsekutiv [kɔnzeku'ti:f] *Adj. (auch Sprachw.)* consecutive; **~es Dolmetschen** consecutive interpreting

Konsekutiv·satz der *(Sprachw.)* consecutive clause

Konsens [kɔn'zɛns] der; ~es, ~e a) *(Übereinstimmung)* consensus; b) *(veralt.: Zustimmung)* consent

konsequent [kɔnze'kvɛnt] 1. *Adj.* a) *(folgerichtig)* logical; logically consistent, logical ‹*thinking, argumentation*›; b) *(unbeirrbar)* consistent; c) *(Sport)* close, tight ‹*marking*›. 2. *adv.* a) *(folgerichtig)* logically; b) *(unbeirrbar)* consistently; **ein Ziel ~ verfolgen** resolutely and single-mindedly pursue a goal; ~ **durchgreifen** take rigorous action; c) *(Sport)* ‹*mark*› closely, tightly

konsequenter·maßen, konsequenter·weise *Adv.* to be consistent

Konsequenz [kɔnze'kvɛnts] die; ~, ~en a) *(Folge)* consequence; **die ~en tragen** take the consequences; **[aus etw.] die ~en ziehen** draw the obvious conclusion [from sth.]; *(gezwungenermaßen)* accept the obvious consequences [of sth.]; b) *o. Pl. (Unbeirrbar-*

keit) resolution; determination; **einer Sache** *(Dat.)* **mit ~ nachgehen** investigate sth. rigorously; **c)** *o. Pl. (Folgerichtigkeit)* logicality; *(eines Gedankenganges, einer Argumentation)* logical consistency; logicality
konservativ [kɔnzɛrva'ti:f] **1.** *Adj. (auch Med.)* conservative; *(die ~e Partei betreffend)* Conservative. **2.** *adv. (althergebracht)* conservatively
Konservative der/die; *adj. Dekl.* conservative; **die ~n** *(Politik)* the Conservatives
Konservativismus der; ~: conservativism
Konservator [kɔnzɛr'va:tɔr] **der; ~s, ~en** [-'to:rən] curator; keeper
Konservatorium [kɔnzɛrva'to:riʊm] **das; ~s, Konservatorien** conservatoire; conservatory *(Amer.)*
Konserve [kɔn'zɛrvə] **die; ~, ~n a)** *(Büchse)* can; tin *(Brit.)*; **Musik aus der ~** *(fig. ugs.)* canned music *(coll.)*; **b)** *(konservierte Lebensmittel)* preserved food; *(in Dosen)* canned *or (Brit.)* tinned food; **von ~n leben** eat out of cans *or (Brit.)* tins; live on canned *or (Brit.)* tinned food; **c)** *(Med.: Blut~)* stored blood
Konserven-: ~büchse die, ~dose die can; tin *(Brit.)*; **~fabrik die** canning factory; cannery; **~nahrung die** canned *or (Brit.)* tinned food
konservierbar *Adv.* preservable
konservieren *tr. V.* preserve; conserve, preserve ‹*building, work of art*›
Konservierung die; ~, ~en preservation; *(von Gebäuden, Kunstwerken usw.)* conservation; preservation
Konservierungs-: ~mittel das, ~stoff der preservative
konsistent [kɔnzɪs'tɛnt] *Adj.* **a)** *(zähflüssig)* stiff; **b)** *(beständig)* stable; **c)** *(widerspruchsfrei)* consistent
Konsistenz [kɔnzɪs'tɛnts] **die; ~, ~en a)** *(Beschaffenheit)* consistency; **b)** *(Stabilität)* stability
Konsistorium [kɔnzɪs'to:riʊm] *(kath. Kirche)* **das; ~s, Konsistorien** consistory
Konsole [kɔn'zo:lə] **die; ~, ~n a)** *(Archit.)* console; **b)** *(Brett)* shelf; *(Tischchen)* console [table]
konsolidieren [kɔnzoli'di:rən] **1.** *tr. V.* **a)** *(festigen)* consolidate; **b)** *(Wirtsch.) (in Anleihen umwandeln)* fund ‹*debts*›; *(vereinigen)* consolidate ‹*debts*›. **2.** *refl. V.* become consolidated
Konsolidierung die; ~, ~en a) *(Festigung)* consolidation; **b)** *(Wirtsch.) (Umwandlung in Anleihen)* funding; *(Vereinigung)* consolidation
Konsonant [kɔnzo'nant] **der; ~en, ~en** consonant
konsonantisch *(Sprachw.)* **1.** *Adj.* consonantal. **2.** *adv.* ‹*pronounce*› as a consonant
Konsorten [kɔn'zɔrtn̩] *Pl. (abwertend)* **Meier und ~:** Meier and his lot *or* crowd *(coll.)*; Meier and Co. *(coll.)*
Konsortium [kɔn'zɔrtsiʊm] **das; ~s, Konsortien** *(Wirtsch.)* consortium
Konspekt [kɔn'spɛkt] **der; ~[e]s, ~e** *(DDR)* synopsis; summary
Konspiration [kɔnspira'tsio:n] **die; ~, ~en** conspiracy
konspirativ [kɔnspira'ti:f] **1.** *Adj.* conspiratorial; **eine ~e Wohnung** a flat *(Brit.) or (Amer.)* an apartment used by persons engaged in subversive activities. **2.** *adv.* **sich ~ zusammenschließen** form a conspiracy
konspirieren *itr. V.* conspire, plot **(gegen** against)
konstant [kɔn'stant] **1.** *Adj.* **a)** *(gleichbleibend, ständig)* constant; **eine ~e Größe** *(Math.)* a constant quantity; **eine ~e Leistung zeigen** maintain a consistent standard; **b)** *(beharrlich)* consistent; persistent. **2.** *adv.* **a)** *(gleichbleibend)* constantly; **wir hatten ~ schlechtes Wetter** we had consistently bad weather; **b)** *(beharrlich)* consistently; persistently
Konstante die; ~[n], ~n *(Math., Physik)* constant; *(fig.)* constant factor (+ *Gen.* in)
Konstantin ['kɔnstanti:n] **(der)** Constantine
Konstantinopel [kɔnstanti'no:pl̩] **(das); ~s** *(hist.)* Constantinople
Konstanz [kɔn'stants] **die; ~:** constancy
konstatieren [kɔnsta'ti:rən] *tr. V.* **a)** *(feststellen)* establish ‹*facts*›; *(wahrnehmen)* detect ‹*changes etc.*›; **b)** *(erklären)* state
Konstellation [kɔnstɛla'tsio:n] **die; ~, ~en a)** *(von Parteien usw.)* grouping; *(von Umständen)* combination; **die gesamte ~:** the whole situation; **b)** *(Astron., Astrol.)* constellation
konsternieren [kɔnstɛr'ni:rən] *tr. V.* **jmdn. ~:** fill sb. with consternation
konsterniert 1. *s.* **konsternieren. 2.** *Adj.* filled with consternation *pred.* **3.** *adv.* with consternation; **sie blickte ihn ~ an** she looked at him in consternation
Konstituente [kɔnsti'tuɛntə] **die; ~, ~n** *(Sprachw.)* constituent
konstituieren [kɔnstitu'i:rən] **1.** *tr. V.* *(gründen)* constitute; set up; *(für etw. konstitutiv sein)* constitute; **die ~de Versammlung** the constituent assembly. **2.** *refl. V.* be constituted
Konstitution [kɔnstitu'tsio:n] **die; ~, ~en** *(auch Politik, Chemie)* constitution
konstitutionell [kɔnstitutsio'nɛl] *(Politik, Med.)* **1.** *Adj.* constitutional. **2.** *adv.* constitutionally
konstitutiv [kɔnstitu'ti:f] *Adj. (geh.)* constitutive; **für etw. ~ sein** be a[n essential] constitutive element of sth.
konstruieren [kɔnstru'i:rən] *tr. V.* **a)** *(entwerfen)* design; *(entwerfen und zusammenbauen)* design and construct; **b)** *(aufbauen, Geom.)* construct; **c)** *(Sprachw.)* construct; **dieses Verb wird mit dem Dativ konstruiert** this verb takes the dative *or* is construed with the dative; **d)** *(abwertend: künstlich aufbauen)* fabricate; **ein konstruierter Fall** a hypothetical *or* fictitious case; **die Handlung/seine Begründung wirkt sehr konstruiert** the plot seems/his reasons *pl.* seem very contrived
Konstrukteur [kɔnstrʊk'tø:ɐ̯] **der; ~s, ~e, Konstrukteurin die; ~, ~nen** designer; design engineer
Konstruktion [kɔnstrʊk'tsio:n] **die; ~, ~en a)** *(Aufbau, Geom., Sprachw.)* construction; *(das Entwerfen)* designing; *(das Entwerfen und Zusammenbauen)* designing and construction; **b)** *(Entwurf)* design; *(Bau)* construction; structure
Konstruktions-: ~büro das drawing-office; **~fehler der** design fault
konstruktiv [kɔnstrʊk'ti:f] **1.** *Adj.* **a)** constructive; **ein ~es Mißtrauensvotum** *(Parl.)* a constructive vote of no confidence; **b)** *(Technik)* constructional. **2.** *adv.* **a)** constructively; **b)** *(Technik)* with regard to construction
Konstruktivismus der; ~ *(bild. Kunst)* constructivism *no art.*
Konsul ['kɔnzʊl] **der; ~s, ~n** *(Dipl., hist.)* consul
konsularisch *Adj. (Dipl.)* consular
Konsulat [kɔnzu'la:t] **das; ~[e]s, ~e** *(Dipl., hist.: Amt)* consulate
Konsultation [kɔnzʊlta'tsio:n] **die; ~, ~en** consultation; **sich zu ~en treffen** meet for consultations
konsultieren *tr. V. (auch fig.)* consult
[1]**Konsum** [kɔn'zu:m] **der; ~s** consumption **(an** + *Dat.* of); **der ~ von Alkohol steigt** alcohol consumption is on the increase
[2]**Konsum** ['kɔnzʊm] **der; ~s, ~s a)** *o. Pl.* *(Genossenschaft)* co-operative society; **b)** *(Laden)* co-operative shop *or* store; co-op *(coll.)*
-konsum der; ~s ... consumption
Konsum·artikel der *(Wirtsch.)* consumer item *or* article; **~** *Pl.* consumer goods
Konsumation [kɔnzuma'tsio:n] **die; ~, ~en** *(österr., schweiz.)* consumption
Konsument [kɔnzu'mɛnt] **der; ~en, ~en** consumer
Konsum-: ~genossenschaft die *(Wirtsch.)* co-operative society; **~gesellschaft die** consumer society; **~gewohnheiten** *Pl. (Wirtsch.)* consumer habits
Konsum·gut das; *meist Pl. (Wirtsch.) s.* **Konsumartikel**
Konsumgüter·industrie die *(Wirtsch.)* consumer goods industry
konsumieren *tr. V.* consume; *(fig.)* devour ‹*book*›
Konsum-: ~terror der *(abwertend)* pressure to buy *(generated in a consumer society)*; **~verzicht der** reduction in consumption; **~zwang der;** *o. Pl.* pressure to buy *(generated in a consumer society)*
Kontakt [kɔn'takt] **der; ~[e]s, ~e a)** *(auch fachspr.)* contact; **mit** *od.* **zu jmdm. ~ haben/halten** be/remain in contact *or* touch with sb.; **mit jmdm. [keinen] ~ bekommen** [not] get to know sb.; **[den] ~ mit jmdm./etw. finden/suchen** establish/try to establish contact with sb./sth.; **er findet keinen ~ zu seinen Zuhörern** he cannot establish a rapport with his audience; **in ~ mit jmdm. stehen** be in contact *or* touch with sb.; **den ~ zu jmdm. abbrechen/verlieren** break off contact/lose contact *or* touch with sb.; **mit jmdm. ~ aufnehmen** get into contact with sb.; contact sb.; **b)** *(Elektrot.)* contact; **die Klingel hat/die Drähte haben keinen ~:** the bell is not connected up properly/the wires are not making contact
kontakt-, Kontakt-: ~ab·zug der *(Fot.)* contact print; **~anzeige die** contact advertisement; **~arm** *Adj.* **~arm sein** not make friends easily; find it difficult to make friends; **~aufnahme die: unsere erste ~aufnahme mit dieser Firma** our first approach to this firm; **~bereichs·beamte der** community policeman
kontakten 1. *tr. V.* contact. **2.** *itr. V.* make contacts
kontakt-, Kontakt-: ~fähig *Adj.* **ein ~fähiger Mensch** a good mixer; **ein ~fähiger Mitarbeiter** a colleague who is able to communicate easily with people; **~feder die** *(Elektrot.)* contact spring; **~freudig** *Adj.* sociable; **~freudig sein** make friends easily; **~hof der** *[inner] courtyard of an eros centre etc. where prostitutes wait for clients*
kontaktieren *tr. V.* contact
kontakt-, Kontakt-: ~linse die contact lens; **~los** *Adj.* friendless; lonely; **~mangel der** lack of social contact; **~mann der;** *Pl.:* **~männer** *od.* **~leute** *(Agent)* contact; **~nahme die** *s.* **~aufnahme; ~person die** *(Med.)* contact; **~pflege die: ~pflege betreiben** be sociable; mix socially; **~schale die** *s.* **~linse; ~schwelle die** *(Verkehrsw.)* vehicle detector pad; **~schwierigkeiten** *Pl.* problems in mixing with others; **~sperre die** *(Rechtsw.)* ban on visits and letters; **~sperre über jmdn. verhängen** ban all sb.'s visits and letters; **~studium das** *(Hochschulw.) in-service study undertaken to keep up with the latest developments in one's field*
Kontamination [kɔntamina'tsio:n] **die; ~, ~en a)** *(bes. Med., Biol., Milit.)* contamination; **b)** *(Sprachw.)* contamination; blending; *(Wort)* blend
kontaminieren *tr. V.* **a)** *(bes. Med., Biol., Milit.)* contaminate; **b)** *(Sprachw.)* blend
Kontemplation [kɔntɛmpla'tsio:n] **die; ~, ~en** *(geh.)* contemplation
kontemplativ [kɔntɛmpla'ti:f] *(geh.)* **1.** *Adj.* contemplative. **2.** *adv.* contemplatively

Konten *s.* **Konto**
Kontenance *s.* **Contenance**
Konten·bewegung die *(Bankw.)* change in the state of the/an account
Konter ['kɔntɐ] **der; ~s, ~ a)** *(Boxen)* counter; **b)** *(Ballspiele)* counter-attack
Konter-: ~admiral der *(Marine)* rear-admiral; **~bande die;** *o. Pl.* **a)** *(Völkerrecht)* contraband [of war]; **b)** *(veralt.: Schmuggelware)* contraband
Konterfei ['kɔntɐfai] **das; ~s, ~s** *od.* **~e** *(veralt., noch scherzh.)* likeness
konterfeien *tr. V. (veralt., noch scherzh.)* paint/draw a likeness of
kontern *tr., itr. V. (Boxen)* counter; *(Ballspiele)* counter-attack; *(fig.)* counter **(mit** with)
konter-, Konter-: ~revolution die counter-revolution; **~revolutionär** *Adj.* counter-revolutionary; **~revolutionär der** counter-revolutionary; **~schlag der** *(Boxen)* counter; *(Ballspiele, fig.)* counter-attack
Kontext [kɔn'tɛkst] **der; ~[e]s, ~e** *(auch Sprachw.)* context
Konti *s.* **Konto**
Kontinent [kɔnti'nɛnt] **der; ~[e]s, ~e** continent
kontinental [kɔntinɛn'ta:l] *Adj.* continental
Kontinental-: ~klima das *(Geogr.)* continental climate; **~sockel der** *(Geogr.)* continental shelf; **~sperre die;** *o. Pl. (hist.)* Continental System; **~verschiebung die** *(Geol.)* continental drift
Kontingent [kɔntɪŋ'gɛnt] **das; ~[e]s, ~e a)** *(Menge)* quota; *(fig.)* contingent; **b)** *(Truppen~)* contingent
kontingentieren *tr. V. (bes. Wirtsch.)* limit by quotas; impose quotas on; *(rationieren)* ration
Kontingentierung die; ~, ~en *(bes. Wirtsch.)* imposition of quotas (*Gen.* on)
kontinuierlich [kɔntinu'i:ɐlɪç] **1.** *Adj.* steady; continuous; **eine ~e Außenpolitik** a consistent foreign policy. **2.** *adv.* steadily
Kontinuität [kɔntinui'tɛ:t] **die; ~:** continuity
Kontinuum [kɔn'ti:nuʊm] **das; ~s, Kontinua** *od.* **Kontinuen** continuum
Konto ['kɔnto] **das; ~s, Konten** *od.* **Konti** account; **ein laufendes ~:** a current account; **die nächste Runde geht auf mein ~** *(ugs.)* the next round is on me *(coll.)*; **etw. geht auf jmds. ~** *(ugs.: jmd. ist schuld an etw.)* sb. is to blame *or* is responsible for sth.
Konto-: ~aus·zug der *(Bankw.)* [bank] statement; statement of account; **~buch das** *(Buchf.)* account-book; **~führungs·gebühr die** *(Bankw.)* bank charges *pl.*; **~inhaber der** *(Bankw.)* account-holder; holder of an/the account; **~korrent** [~kɔ'rɛnt] **das; ~s, ~e a)** *(Wirtsch.)* open account; **b)** *o. Pl. (Buchf.)* open accounting *no art.*; **~nummer die** account number
Kontor [kɔn'to:ɐ] **das; ~s, ~e a)** *(Niederlassung) (eines Handelsunternehmens)* branch; *(einer Reederei)* office; **b)** *(DDR: Handelszentrale)* wholesale organization; **c)** *(veralt.: Büro)* office; *s. auch* **Schlag a**
Kontorist der; ~en, ~en, Kontoristin die; ~, ~nen [office] clerk; *s. auch* **-in**
Konto·stand der *(Bankw.)* balance; state of an/one's account
kontra ['kɔntra] **1.** *Präp. mit Akk. (Rechtsspr., auch fig.)* versus. **2.** *Adv.* against; **ich bin dazu ~ eingestellt** I am against it
Kontra das; ~s, ~s *(Kartenspiele)* double; **~ sagen** *od.* **geben** double; **jmdm. ~ geben** *(fig. ugs.)* flatly contradict sb.
Kontra·baß der *(Musik)* double-bass
kontradiktorisch [kɔntradɪk'to:rɪʃ] **1.** *Adj.* contradictory. **2.** *adv.* in a contradictory way
Kontra·fagott das *(Musik)* double bassoon; contrabassoon
Kontrahent [kɔntra'hɛnt] **der; ~en, ~en a)** *(Gegner)* adversary; opponent; **b)** *(Rechtsw., Kaufmannsspr.: Vertragspartner)* contracting party
kontrahieren 1. *itr., refl. V. (Biol., Med.)* contract. **2.** *tr. V.* **a)** *(Biol., Med.)* contract; **b)** *(Rechtsw., Kaufmannsspr.)* **Erdgaslieferungen ~:** contract to supply natural gas
Kontrakt [kɔn'trakt] **der; ~[e]s, ~e** contract
Kontraktion [kɔntrak'tsio:n] **die; ~, ~en** *(Med., Sprachw.)* contraction
kontraktlich 1. *Adj.* contractual. **2.** *adv.* contractually; by contract
Kontra·punkt der *(Musik, fig.)* counterpoint
kontrapunktisch *(Musik, fig.)* **1.** *Adj.* contrapuntal. **2.** *adv.* contrapuntally
konträr [kɔn'trɛ:ɐ] **1.** contrary; opposite. **2.** *adv.* **zwei so ~ gesinnte Politiker** two politicians with such opposing views; **sich ~ entwickeln** develop in contrary *or* opposite ways
Kontrast [kɔn'trast] **der; ~[e]s, ~e** *(auch Fot., Film, Fernsehen)* contrast; **etw. steht im/in ~ zu etw. anderem** sth. is in contrast with sth. else
Kontrast-: ~brei der *(Med.)* opaque *or* test meal; **~farbe die** contrasting colour; **~filter der** *(Fot.)* contrast filter
kontrastieren *tr., itr. V.* contrast
kontrastiv [kɔntras'ti:f] *Adj. (Sprachw.)* constrastive
kontrast-, Kontrast-: ~mittel das *(Med.)* contrast medium; **~programm das** *(Rundf., Fernsehen)* alternative programme; **~reich** *Adj.* rich in *or* full of contrasts *pred.*; richly varied
Kontrazeptivum [kɔntratsɛp'ti:vʊm] **das; ~s, Kontrazeptiva** *(Med.)* contraceptive
Kontribution [kɔntribu'tsio:n] **die; ~, ~en** *(hist.)* contribution
Kontroll·abschnitt der stub
Kontrollampe die pilot-light; indicator light; *(Warnleuchte)* warning light
Kontroll-: ~apparat der supervisory apparatus; *(Polizei, Geheimdienst o. ä.)* surveillance and control apparatus; **~beamte der** inspector; *(an der Paß-/Zollkontrolle)* passport/customs officer; **~behörde die** monitoring authority
Kontrolle [kɔn'trɔlə] **die; ~, ~n a)** *(Überwachung)* surveillance; **unter ~ stehen** be under surveillance; **der ~ durch das Parlament unterliegen** be under the scrutiny of Parliament; **eine gegenseitige ~ ausüben** keep a check on each other; **b)** *(Überprüfung)* check; *(bei Waren)* check; inspection; *(bei Lebensmitteln)* inspection; **~n durchführen** carry out checks/inspections; **jmdn./etw. einer ~ unterziehen** check sb./sth.; **Anwärter auf eine Stelle einer ~ unterziehen** screen candidates for a post; **in eine ~ kommen** be stopped at a police check; **zur ~:** as a check; **c)** *(Herrschaft)* control; **die ~ über etw.** *(Akk.)* **verlieren** lose control of sth.; **die ~ über sich** *(Akk.)* **verlieren** lose control of oneself; **außer ~ geraten** get out of control; **etw. unter ~** *(Akk.)* **bringen/halten** get *or* bring/keep sth. under control; **d)** *(~punkt)* check-point; *(an der Paß~/Zoll~)* passport control/customs
Kontrolleur [kɔntrɔ'lø:ɐ] **der; ~s, ~e** inspector
Kontroll-: ~funktion die monitoring function; **~gang der** tour of inspection; *(eines Nachtwächters)* round; *(eines Polizisten)* patrol; **~gruppe die** *(Med., Psych., Soziol.)* control group
kontrollierbar *Adj.* ‹*authority, body, decision, etc.*› that is open to scrutiny; ‹*statement, statistic, etc.*› that is verifiable *or* checkable; demonstrable ‹*progress*›
kontrollieren 1. *tr. V.* **a)** *(überwachen)* check; monitor; **die Regierung ~:** scrutinize the actions of the government; **die Lebensmittelproduktion wird streng kontrolliert** strict checks are kept *or* made on the production of food; **b)** *(überprüfen)* check; check, inspect ‹*goods*›; inspect ‹*food*›; **jmdn. auf etw.** *(Akk.)* **[hin] ~:** check sb. for sth.; **etw. auf etw.** *(Akk.)* **[hin] ~:** check/inspect sth. for sth.; **c)** *(beherrschen)* control. **2.** *itr. V.* carry out a check/checks
Kontrolliste die check-list
Kontroll-: ~lampe *s.* **Kontrollampe; ~liste** *s.* **Kontrolliste; ~organ das** monitoring body; **~punkt der** check-point; *(bei einer Rallye)* control [point]; **~rat der;** *o. Pl.* **Alliierter ~rat** Allied Control Commission; **~stempel der** *(auf Waren, Lebensmitteln)* inspection stamp; *(bei einer Rallye)* control stamp; **~turm der** control tower; **~uhr die** time clock; *(für Wächter)* tell-tale clock
kontrovers [kɔntro'vɛrs] **1.** *Adj.* conflicting; *(strittig)* controversial. **2.** *adv.* **sich ~ zu etw. äußern** express conflicting opinions on sth.; **etw. ~ schildern** give conflicting accounts of sth.
Kontroverse die; ~, ~n controversy **(um, über +** *Akk.* about)
Kontur [kɔn'tu:ɐ] **die; ~, ~en;** *meist Pl.* contour; outline; **~ gewinnen/an ~ verlieren** *(fig.)* become clearer/fade
Konturen·stift der lip pencil
konturieren *tr. V. (auch fig.)* outline
Konus ['ko:nʊs] **der; ~, ~se** *od.* **Konen** *(Math., Technik)* cone
Konvektor [kɔn'vɛktɔr] **der; ~s, ~en** [-'to:rən] convector [heater]
konvenieren [kɔnve'ni:rən] *itr. V. (österr.)* **jmdm. ~:** be convenient for sb.; suit sb.
Konvent [kɔn'vɛnt] **der; ~es, ~e a)** *(kath. Kirche) (von Nonnen)* convent; *(von Mönchen)* monastery; **b)** *(Hochschulw.) qualified academic staff of a university*
Konvention [kɔnvɛn'tsio:n] **die; ~, ~en** *(Verhaltensnorm, Völkerr.)* convention
Konventional·strafe die *(Rechtsw.)* liquidated damages *pl.*
konventionell 1. *Adj.* **a)** *(herkömmlich)* conventional; **~e Waffen** *(Milit.)* conventional weapons; **b)** *(förmlich)* formal. **2.** *adv.* **a)** *(herkömmlich, Milit.)* conventionally; in a conventional way; **b)** *(förmlich)* formally; **hier geht es sehr ~ zu** things are very formal here
konvergent [kɔnvɛr'gɛnt] *(geh., Math.)* **1.** *Adj.* convergent. **2.** *adv.* convergently
Konvergenz [kɔnvɛr'gɛnts] **die; ~, ~en** *(geh., Math.)* convergence
Konvergenz·theorie die *(Politik)* theory of convergence
konvergieren *tr. V. (geh., Math.)* converge
Konversation [kɔnvɛrza'tsio:n] **die; ~, ~en** conversation; **~ in Französisch treiben** hold a conversation in French; **~ machen** make conversation
Konversations·lexikon das encyclopaedia
Konversion die; ~, ~en *(Kirche, Sprachw., Psych., Kerntechnik, Börsenw.)* conversion
Konverter [kɔn'vɛrtɐ] **der; ~s, ~ a)** *(Hüttenw., Rundfunk)* converter; **b)** *(Fot.)* converter [lens]
konvertibel [kɔnvɛr'ti:bl̩], **konvertierbar** *Adj. (Wirtsch.)* convertible
Konvertierbarkeit die; ~ *(Wirtsch.)* convertibility
konvertieren 1. *itr. V.; auch mit sein (Rel.)* be converted. **2.** *tr. V.* **a)** *(Wirtsch.)* convert; **sein Geld in Franken ~:** convert one's money into francs; **b)** *(DV)* convert
Konvertit [kɔnvɛr'ti:t] **der; ~en, ~en, Konvertitin die; ~, ~nen** convert
konvex [kɔn'vɛks] *(Optik)* **1.** *Adj.* convex. **2.** *adv.* convexly
Konvex·spiegel der *(Optik)* convex mirror

Konvikt [kɔn'vɪkt] **das;** ~**[e]s,** ~**e a)** *(Stift)* seminary; *(Wohnheim)* hall of residence *(for theology students);* **b)** *(österr.: kath. Internat)* [Roman Catholic] boarding-school
Konvoi [kɔn'vɔy] **der;** ~**s,** ~**s** *(bes. Milit.)* convoy; **im ~ fahren** travel in convoy
Konvolut [kɔnvo'lu:t] **das;** ~**[e]s,** ~**e** bundle *(of letters, papers, etc.)*
Konvulsion [kɔnvʊl'zio:n] **die;** ~, ~**en** *(Med.)* convulsion
konvulsiv [kɔnvʊl'zi:f], **konvulsivisch** *(Med.)* **1.** *Adj.* convulsive. **2.** *adv.* convulsively
konzedieren [kɔntse'di:rən] *tr. V. (geh.)* concede; **jmdm. etw.** ~: concede sb. sth.
Konzentrat [kɔntsɛn'tra:t] **das;** ~**[e]s,** ~**e** *(bes. Chemie)* concentrate; **ein ~ seiner früheren Werke** *(fig.)* a collection of his most important writings, chosen from his earlier works
Konzentration [kɔntsɛntra'tsio:n] **die;** ~, ~**en** *(auch Chemie)* concentration
Konzentrations-: ~**fähigkeit die;** *o. Pl.* ability to concentrate; powers *pl.* of concentration; ~**lager das** *(bes. ns.)* concentration camp; ~**mangel der** *(Med., Psych.)* lack of concentration; ~**schwäche die** *(Med., Psych.)* poor powers *pl.* of concentration
konzentrieren 1. *refl. V.* **a)** concentrate; **sich auf etw.** *(Akk.)* ~: concentrate on sth.; **b)** *(richten)* be concentrated. **2.** *tr. V.* concentrate; **seine Gedanken auf etw.** *(Akk.)* ~: concentrate one's thoughts on sth.
konzentriert 1. *s.* **konzentrieren. 2.** *Adj. (auch Chemie)* concentrated. **3.** *adv.* with concentration; **sehr ~ arbeiten** work with great concentration
konzentrisch *(Math., fig.)* **1.** *Adj.* concentric. **2.** *adv.* concentrically
Konzept [kɔn'tsɛpt] **das;** ~**[e]s,** ~**e a)** *(Rohfassung)* [rough] draft; **es ist im ~ fertig** the [rough] draft is finished; **aus dem ~ kommen** *od.* **geraten** lose one's thread; **jmdn. aus dem ~ bringen** put sb. off his/her stroke; **b)** *(Programm)* programme; *(Plan)* plan; **jmdm. das ~ verderben** *(ugs.)* ruin sb.'s plans; **jmdm. nicht ins ~ passen** *(ugs.)* not suit sb.'s plans
Konzeption [kɔntsɛp'tsio:n] **die;** ~, ~**en a)** central idea; *(Entwurf)* conception; **b)** *(Med.)* conception
konzeptionslos 1. *Adj.* haphazard. **2.** *adv.* haphazardly; with no clear plan
Konzeptionslosigkeit die; ~: haphazardness; lack of any clear plan
Konzept·papier das; *o. Pl.* rough paper
Konzern [kɔn'tsɛrn] **der;** ~**[e]s,** ~**e** *(Wirtsch.)* group [of companies]
-konzern der; ~**[e]s,** ~**e ...** group
Konzert [kɔn'tsɛrt] **das;** ~**[e]s,** ~**e a)** *(Komposition)* concerto; **b)** *(Veranstaltung)* concert; **ins ~ gehen** go to a concert; **c)** *o. Pl. (geh.: Zusammenspiel)* concert
Konzert-: ~**abend der** concert evening; ~**agentur die** concert artists' agency
konzertant [kɔntsɛr'tant] *Adj., nicht präd. (Musik)* concert ⟨*performance etc.*⟩; ~**e Sinfonie** [sinfonia] concertante
Konzert-: ~**direktion die** concert promotion agency; ~**flügel der** concert grand; ~**führer der** concert guide
konzertieren *itr. V. (geh.)* give a concert
konzertiert 1. *s.* **konzertieren. 2.** *Adj.; nicht präd.* concerted; **die ~e Aktion** concerted action
Konzertina [kɔntsɛr'ti:na] **die;** ~, ~**s** concertina
Konzert-: ~**meister der,** ~**meisterin die** leader [of a/the orchestra]; concert-master; ~**pavillon der** bandstand; ~**pianist der** concert pianist; ~**reise die** concert tour; ~**saal der** concert-hall; ~**sänger der,** ~**sängerin die** concert singer
Konzession [kɔntsɛ'sio:n] **die;** ~, ~**en a)** *(Amtsspr.)* licence; **b)** *(Zugeständnis)* concession; ~**en [an jmdn./etw.] machen** make concessions [to sb./sth.]
Konzessionär [kɔntsɛsio'nɛ:ɐ̯] **der;** ~**s,** ~**e** *(Amtsspr.)* licensee
konzessions·bereit *Adj.* ready *or* willing *or* prepared to make concessions *pred.*
konzessiv [kɔntsɛ'si:f] *Adj. (Sprachw.)* concessive
Konzessiv·satz der *(Sprachw.)* concessive clause
Konzil [kɔn'tsi:l] **das;** ~**s,** ~**e** *od.* ~**ien a)** *(kath. Kirche)* council; **b)** *(Hochschulw.)* ≈ senate
konziliant [kɔntsi'liant] *(geh.)* **1.** *Adj.* accommodating; obliging. **2.** *adv.* accommodatingly; obligingly
Konzilianz [kɔntsi'liants] **die;** ~ *(geh.)* obligingness
konzipieren [kɔntsi'pi:rən] **1.** *tr. V.* draft ⟨*speech, essay*⟩; draw up, draft ⟨*plan, policy, etc.*⟩; design ⟨*device, car, etc.*⟩. **2.** *itr. V. (Med.)* conceive
konzis [kɔn'tsi:s] **1.** *Adj.* concise. **2.** *adv.* concisely
Koog [ko:k] **der;** ~**[e]s, Köge** ['kø:gə] *(niederd.)* polder
Kooperation die; ~, ~**en** co-operation *no indef. art.*
kooperations·bereit *Adj.* ready *or* willing *or* prepared to co-operate *pred.*
kooperativ 1. *Adj.* co-operative. **2.** *adv.* co-operatively
Kooperativ das; ~**s,** ~**e, Kooperative die;** ~, ~**n** co-operative
kooperieren *tr. V.* co-operate
Koordinate die; ~, ~**n a)** *(Geogr.)* co-ordinate; **b)** *(Math.)* coordinate
Koordinaten-: ~**achse die** *(Math.)* coordinate axis; ~**kreuz das** *(Math.)* coordinate axes *pl.;* ~**system das** *(Math.)* system of coordinates
Koordination die; ~, ~**en** co-ordination
Koordinations·störung die *(Med.)* impaired co-ordination *no indef. art., no pl.*
Koordinator [ko|ɔrdi'na:tɔr] **der;** ~**s,** ~**en** [-'to:rən], **Koordinatorin die;** ~, ~**nen** co-ordinator
koordinieren *tr. V.* co-ordinate
Koordinierung die; ~, ~**en** co-ordination
Kopeke [ko'pe:kə] **die;** ~, ~**n** copeck
Kopenhagen [ko:pn̩'ha:gn̩] **(das);** ~**s** Copenhagen
Köpenickiade [kø:pənɪ'kia:də] **die;** ~, ~**n** hoax *(involving impersonation of a uniformed official or military officer)*
Köper ['kø:pɐ] **der;** ~**s,** ~: twill
kopernikanisch [kopɛrni'ka:nɪʃ] *Adj.; nicht präd.* Copernican
Kopernikus [ko'pɛrnikʊs] **(der)** Copernicus
Kopf [kɔpf] **der;** ~**[e]s, Köpfe** ['kœpfə] **a)** head; **jmdm. den ~ waschen** wash sb.'s hair; *(fig. ugs.: jmdn. zurechtweisen)* give sb. a good talking-to *(coll.);* give sb. what for *(sl.);* **[um] einen ganzen/halben ~ größer sein** be a good head/a few inches taller; **die Köpfe zusammenstecken** go into a huddle; **sie haben sich die Köpfe heiß geredet** the conversation/debate became heated; **~ an ~** *(dicht gedrängt)* shoulder to shoulder; *(im Wettlauf)* neck and neck; **~ weg!** *(ugs.)* mind your head!; **den ~ einziehen** duck; *(fig.: sich einschüchtern lassen)* be intimidated; **und wenn du dich auf den ~ stellst** you can talk until you're blue in the face; **~ ab!** off with his head!; **ich werde/er wird dir nicht gleich den ~ abreißen** *(ugs.)* I'm/he's not going to bite your head off; **auf dem ~ stehen** *(Kopfstand machen)* stand on one's head; *(ugs.: umgedreht sein)* be upside down; *(fig.)* **auf seinen ~ ist eine Belohnung ausgesetzt** there is a price on his head; **jmdm. schwirrt/***(ugs.)* **raucht der ~:** sb.'s head is spinning; **nicht wissen, wo einem der ~ steht** not know whether one is coming or going; **einen dicken** *od.* **schweren ~ haben** have a headache; *(vom Alkohol)* have a thick head *(coll.) or* a hangover; **jmdm.** *od.* **jmdn. den ~ kosten** cost sb. dearly; *(jmdn. das Leben kosten)* cost sb. his/her life; **~ hoch!** chin up!; **den ~ hängen lassen** become disheartened; **~ und Kragen riskieren** risk one's neck; **den ~ hinhalten [müssen]** *(ugs.)* [have to] face the music; [have to] take the blame *or (sl.)* rap; **sich** *(Dat.)* **[an etw.** *(Dat.)***] den ~ einrennen** beat *or* run one's head against a brick wall [with sth.]; **den ~ aus der Schlinge ziehen** avoid any adverse consequences *or (sl.)* the rap; **den ~ in den Sand stecken** bury one's head in the sand; **den ~ hoch tragen** hold one's head high; **es gibt keinen Grund dafür, daß er den ~ so hoch trägt** *(überheblich ist)* there is no reason for him to act so superior; **jmdm. den ~ zurechtrücken** *(ugs.)* bring sb. to his/her senses; **sich [gegenseitig]** *od.* **einander die Köpfe einschlagen** be at each other's throats; **jmdn. [um] einen ~ kürzer** *od.* **kleiner machen** *(ugs.)* chop sb.'s head off; **sich** *(Dat.)* **an den ~ fassen** *od.* **greifen** *(ugs.)* throw up one's hands in despair; **jmdm. Beleidigungen an den ~ werfen** hurl insults at sb.; **sein Geld auf den ~ hauen** *(ugs.)* blow one's money *(sl.);* **etw. auf den ~ stellen** *(ugs.)* turn sth. upside down; **die Tatsachen/den Ablauf der Ereignisse auf den ~ stellen** get the facts/the order of events completely *or* entirely wrong; **jmdm. auf dem ~ herumtanzen** *(ugs.)* treat sb. just as one likes; do what one likes with sb.; **sich** *(Dat.)* **nicht auf den ~ spucken lassen** *(salopp)* not let people walk all over one *(coll.);* **jmdm. auf den ~ spucken können** *(salopp scherzh.)* be head and shoulders taller than sb.; **er ist nicht auf den ~ gefallen** *(ugs.)* there are no flies on him *(coll.);* **jmdm. etw. auf den ~ zusagen** say sth. to sb.'s face; **das hältst du im ~ nicht aus!** *(ugs.)* he/she/it really is the limit! *(coll.);* **jmdm. in den** *od.* **zu ~ steigen** go to sb.'s head; **mit dem ~ durch die Wand wollen** *(ugs.)* beat *or* run one's head against a brick wall; **etw. über jmds. ~ [hin]weg entscheiden** decide sth. over sb.'s head; **über die Köpfe der Zuhörer** *usw.* **hinwegreden** talk over the heads of the audience *etc.;* **jmdm. über den ~ wachsen** *(ugs.)* outgrow sb.; *(überfordern)* become too much for sb.; **bis über den ~ in etw. stecken** *(ugs.)* be up to one's ears in sth.; **es geht um ~ und Kragen** *(ugs.)* it's a matter of life and death; **sich um ~ und Kragen reden** *(ugs.)* risk one's neck with careless talk; *(sich belasten)* incriminate oneself as soon as one opens one's mouth; **von ~ bis Fuß** from head to toe *or* foot; **jmdn. vor den ~ stoßen** *(ugs.)* offend sb.; **wie vor den ~ geschlagen sein** *(ugs.)* be stunned; *s. auch* **Hand f; b)** *(Person)* person; **ein kluger/fähiger ~ sein** be a clever/able man/woman; **pro ~:** per head *or* person; **eine Familie mit acht Köpfen** a family of eight; **c)** *(geistige Leitung)* **er ist der ~ der Firma** he's the brains of the firm; **die führenden Köpfe der Wirtschaft** the leading minds in the field of economics; **d)** *(Wille)* **seinen ~ durchsetzen** make sb. do what one wants; **einen dicken ~ haben** have a mind of one's own; **muß es immer nach deinem ~ gehen?** why must you always decide?; **e)** *(Verstand)* mind; head; **hast du noch im ~, wie ...?** can you still remember how ...?; **er hat die Zahlen im ~** *(ugs.)* he has the figures in his head; **er hat nur Autos im ~** *(ugs.)* all he ever thinks about is cars; **was wohl in ihrem ~ vorgeht?** what's going on in her mind?; **sie ist nicht ganz richtig im ~** *(ugs.)* she's not quite right in the head; **einen klaren/kühlen ~ bewahren** *od.* **behalten** keep a cool head; keep one's head; **ich habe den ~ voll mit anderen**

Dingen I've got a lot of other things on my mind; **den ~ verlieren** lose one's head; **jmdm. den ~ verdrehen** *(ugs.)* steal sb.'s heart [away]; **sich** *(Dat.)* **den ~ zerbrechen** *(ugs.)* rack one's brains (**über** + *Akk.* over); *(sich Sorgen machen)* worry (**über** + *Akk.* about); **aus dem ~:** off the top of one's head; **das geht** *od.* **will ihm nicht aus dem ~:** he can't get it out of his mind; **sich** *(Dat.)* **etw. aus dem ~ schlagen** put sth. out of one's head; **sich** *(Dat.)* **etw. durch den ~ gehen lassen** think sth. over; **der Gedanke geht mir gerade durch den ~:** it just occurs to me; **jmdm. [plötzlich] durch den ~ schießen** [suddenly] occur to sb.; **jmdm. im ~ herumgehen** *(ugs.)* go round and round in sb.'s mind; **jmdm./sich etw. in den ~ setzen** put sth. into sb.'s head/get sth. into one's head; **etw. im ~ [aus]rechnen** work sth. out in one's head; **was man nicht im ~ hat, muß man in den Beinen haben** a short memory makes work for the legs; **jmdm. geht** *od.* **will etw. nicht in den ~ [hinein]** *(ugs.)* sb. can't get sth. into his/her head; **f)** *(von Nadeln, Nägeln, Blumen)* head; *(von Pfeifen)* bowl; **g) ein ~ Salat/Blumenkohl/Rotkohl** a lettuce/cauliflower/red cabbage; **h)** *(oberer Teil) (eines Briefes, einer Tafel)* head; *(einer Zeitung)* heading; head; **i)** *(auf Münzen)* **~ [oder Zahl?]** heads [or tails?]

kọpf-, Kọpf-: ~-an-Kọpf-Rennen das *(Sport, auch fig.)* neck-and-neck race (+ *Gen.* between); **~arbeit die** brainwork; intellectual work; **~arbeiter der** brain-worker; **~bahn·hof der** terminal station; **~ball der** *(Fußball)* header; **durch ~ball** with a header; **~ball·spiel das;** *o. Pl. (Fußball)* heading; **~ball·stark** *Adj. (Fußball)* good at heading *pred.*; **der einzige ~ballstarke Spieler** the only good header of the ball; **~ball·tor das** *(Fußball)* headed goal; **ein ~balltor von Fischer** a goal headed by Fischer; **~bedeckung die** headgear; **ohne ~bedeckung** without anything on one's head; without a hat

Köpfchen ['kœpfçən] **das; ~s, ~ a)** little head; **b)** *(Findigkeit)* brains *pl.*; **~ muß man haben** you've got to have it up here *(coll.)*; **~ haben** have brains *pl.*; **~, ~!** clever, eh? *(coll.)*

köpfeln ['kœpfl̩n] *(südd., österr., schweiz.)* **1.** *tr. V.: s.* **köpfen b. 2.** *itr. V.* dive head first

köpfen ['kœpfn̩] *tr. V.* **a)** decapitate; *(hinrichten)* behead; *(fig.)* break *or* crack open ⟨*bottle*⟩; slice the top off ⟨*egg*⟩; **b)** *(Fußball)* head; **das 2:0 ~:** head [in] the goal to make it 2–0

Kọpf-: ~ende das head end; **~form die** head shape; shape of the head; **~freiheit die** headroom; **~füßer der** *(Zool.)* cephalopod; **~geld das** reward; bounty; **~grippe die** *(volkst.)* headachy cold; **~haar das** hair on the head; **~haltung die: die/eine ~haltung** the way one holds one's head; **~haut die** [skin of the] scalp; **~höhe die: in ~höhe** at head height; **~hörer der** headphones *pl.*

-köpfig *Adj.* -headed; **drei~/fünf~:** three-headed/five-headed ⟨*monster*⟩; **eine dreiköpfige/fünfköpfige Familie** a family of three/five

kọpf-, Kọpf-: ~jäger der head-hunter; **~kissen das** pillow; **~kissen·bezug der** pillow-case; **~lage die** *(Med.)* cephalic *or* head presentation; **~länge die** head; **mit einer ~länge Vorsprung** by a head; **~lastig** *Adj.* down by the head *pred.*; nose-heavy ⟨*aircraft*⟩; *(fig.)* top-heavy; **~laus die** head louse; **~los 1.** *Adj.* **a)** rash; *(in Panik)* panic-stricken; **seine ~lose Flucht** his headlong *or* panic-stricken flight; **b)** *(ohne Kopf)* headless; **2.** *adv.* rashly; **~los davonrennen/umherrennen** flee in panic/run round in a panic; **~losigkeit die; ~:** rashness; *(Panik)* panic; **~nicken das; ~s** nod [of the head]; **durch ~nicken** by nodding [one's head]; **~nuß die** *(ugs.)* rap on the head with one's *or* the knuckles; **~rechnen** *itr. V.; nur im Inf. gebr.* do mental arithmetic; **gut ~rechnen können** be good at mental arithmetic; **~rechnen das** mental arithmetic; **~salat der** cabbage *or* head lettuce; **~scheu** *Adj.* in **jmdn. ~scheu machen** *(ugs.)* unnerve sb.; **~scheu werden** lose one's nerve; **~schmerz der;** *meist Pl.* headache; **~schmerzen haben** have a headache *sing.*; **sich** *(Dat.)* **über etw.** *(Akk.) od.* **wegen etw. keine ~schmerzen machen** *(ugs.)* not worry about *or* concern oneself about sth.; **etw. bereitet** *od.* **macht jmdm. ~schmerzen** *(ugs.)* sth. weighs on sb.'s mind; **~schmuck der** head-dress; **~schuppe die;** *meist Pl.* flake of dandruff; **~schuppen** dandruff; **~schuß der** bullet wound in the head; **er wurde durch einen ~schuß getötet** he was killed by a bullet in the head; **~schütteln das; ~s** shake of the head; **ein allgemeines ~schütteln auslösen** cause everyone to shake their heads; **durch ~schütteln** by shaking one's head; **nicht ohne ~schütteln** not without some head-shaking; **~schüttelnd** *Adj.* **sich ~schüttelnd abwenden** turn away, shaking one's head; **~schutz der** *(Sport)* protective headgear; **~sprung der** header; **einen ~sprung machen** dive head first; **~stand der** headstand; **~|stehen** *unr. itr. V.* **a)** stand on one's head; **b)** *(ugs.: überrascht sein)* be bowled over; **~stein·pflaster das** cobblestones *pl.*; **~steuer die** *(hist.)* poll tax; **~stimme die** head voice; *(Falsett)* falsetto [voice]; **~stoß der a)** *(Fußball)* header; **b)** *(Boxen)* butt; **~stück das** *(Kochk.)* head end; **~stütze die** head-rest; **~tuch das** headscarf; **~über** [-'--] *Adv.* head first; *(fig.) (voller Tatendrang)* with a will; *(ohne Zögern)* headlong; **~verband der** head bandage; **~verletzung die** head injury; **~wäsche die a)** hair-wash; shampoo; **b)** *(fig. ugs.)* dressing down; **~weh das;** *o. Pl. (ugs.)* headache; **~weh haben** have a headache; **~zerbrechen das; ~s: etw. bereitet** *od.* **macht jmdm. ~zerbrechen** sb. has to rack his/her brains about sth.; *(etw. macht jmdm. Sorgen)* sth. is a worry to sb.; **sich** *(Dat.)* **über etw.** *(Akk.)* **[kein] ~zerbrechen machen** [not] worry about sth.

Kopie [ko'pi:] **die; ~, ~n a)** copy; *(Durchschrift)* carbon copy; *(Fotokopie)* photocopy; **b)** *(Fot., Film)* print; **c)** *(Nachbildung)* copy; **d)** *(Abklatsch) (Werk)* pastiche; *(Person)* likeness

Kopier·anstalt die *(Fot.)* [photographic] processing laboratory

kopieren *tr. V.* **a)** copy; *(fotokopieren)* photocopy; **etw. mit Blaupapier ~:** take a carbon copy of sth.; **b)** *(Fot., Film)* print; **c)** *(nachbilden)* copy; *(imitieren)* imitate

Kopierer der; ~s, ~ *(ugs.)* [photo]copier

Kopier-: ~gerät das photocopier; photocopying machine; **~papier das a)** *(Fot.)* printing paper; **b)** *(zum Fotokopieren)* photocopying paper; **~stift der** indelible pencil

Kọpilot der; ~en, ~en, Kọpilotin die; ~, ~nen *(Flugw.)* co-pilot; *(Motorsport)* co-driver

Kopịst der; ~en, ~en a) *(Kunst)* copier; copyist; **b)** *(Vervielfältiger)* photocopying-machine operator; photocopier; *(Fot.)* [darkroom] printer

[1]**Koppel** ['kɔpl̩] **das; ~s, ~,** *österr.:* **die; ~, ~n** *(Gürtel)* [leather] belt *(as part of a uniform)*

[2]**Kọppel die; ~, ~n a)** *(Weide)* paddock; **auf** *od.* **in der ~:** in the paddock; **b)** *(Hunde~)* pack; *(Pferde~)* string; **c)** *(Musik)* coupler

kọppeln *tr. V.* **a)** *(aneinanderbinden)* string together ⟨*horses*⟩; leash together ⟨*dogs*⟩; couple ⟨*hounds*⟩; **b)** *(aneinanderhängen)* dock ⟨*spacecraft*⟩; couple [up] ⟨*railway carriage, trailers, etc.*⟩ (**an** + *Akk.* to); **c)** *(verbinden)* link; couple ⟨*circuits, systems, etc.*⟩; **etw. an etw.** *(Dat.)* **~:** link sth. to sth.; **mit etw. gekoppelt sein** be associated with sth.; **d)** *(Sprachw.)* link

Kọppel-: ~rick das a) *(Zaun)* paddock fence; **b)** *(Hindernis)* post and rails; **~schloß das** belt buckle *(as part of a uniform)*

Kọppelung *s.* **Kopplung**

Köpper ['kœpɐ] **der; ~s, ~** *(ugs.)* header

koppheister [kɔp'haistɐ] *Adv. (nordd.) s.* **kopfüber**

Kọpplung die; ~, ~en a) *(Raumf.)* docking; *(von Eisenbahnwagen, Anhängern usw.)* coupling [up]; **b)** *(Verbindung)* linking; *(von Schaltungen, Systemen)* coupling; **c)** *(Sprachw.)* linking

Kọpplungs-: ~geschäft das *(Wirtsch.)* package deal; tie-in deal *(Amer.)*; **~manöver das** *(Raumf.)* docking manoeuvre

Kopra ['ko:pra] **die; ~:** copra

Koproduktion die; ~, ~en co-production; joint production

Koproduzent der; ~en, ~en co-producer

Kopte ['kɔptə] **der; ~n, ~n** Copt

kọptisch *Adj.* Coptic

Kopula ['ko:pula] **die; ~, ~s** *od.* **Kopulae** ['ko:pulɛ] *(Sprachw.)* copula

Kopulation [kopula'tsio:n] **die; ~, ~en a)** *(Biol.)* copulation; **b)** *(Gartenbau)* splice graft

kopulativ [kopula'ti:f] *Adj. (Sprachw.)* copulative

Kopulativum [kopula'ti:vʊm] **das; ~s, Kopulativa** *(Sprachw.)* copulative conjunction; copulative

kopulieren 1. *itr. V.* copulate. **2.** *tr. V. (Gartenbau)* splice-graft

kor [ko:ɐ] *s.* **küren; kiesen**

Koralle [ko'ralə] **die; ~, ~n** coral

korạllen-, Korạllen-: ~bank die; *Pl.* **~bänke** coral reef; **~bäumchen das** *(Bot.)* Jerusalem cherry; **~fischer der** coral fisherman; **~insel die** coral island; **~riff das** coral reef; **~rot** *Adj.* coral-red; **~schmuck der** coral jewellery

Koran [ko'ra:n] **der; ~s, ~e** Koran

Korb [kɔrp] **der; ~es, Körbe** ['kœrbə] **a)** basket; *(für ein Baby)* wicker cradle; *(Last~ auf einem Tier)* pannier; *(Bienen~)* hive; *(Förder~)* cage; **ein ~ Kartoffeln** a basket[ful] of potatoes; **b)** *(Gondel)* basket; **c)** *(~ball)* net; *(Basketball)* basket; *(Treffer)* goal; **d)** *o. Pl. (Flechtwerk)* wicker[work]; **e)** *(Ablehnung)* **jmdm. einen ~ geben** turn sb. down; **einen ~ bekommen, sich** *(Dat.)* **einen ~ holen** be turned down

Kọrb-: ~ball der; *o. Pl.* netball; **~blütler der** *(Bot.)* composite flower; composite

Körbchen ['kœrpçən] **das; ~s, ~ a)** [little] basket; **husch, husch ins ~** *(fam.)* time for bye-bye[s] *or* beddy-byes *(child lang.)*; **b)** *(des Büstenhalters)* cup

körbeweise ['kœrbə-] *Adv.* by the basketful

Kọrb-: ~flasche die wicker bottle; **~geflecht das** wicker[work]; **~macher der** basket-maker; **~möbel das** piece of wicker[work] furniture; **~möbel** *Pl.* wickerwork furniture *sing.*; **~wagen der** wicker pram; **~ware die;** *meist Pl.* wickerwork article; **~waren** wickerwork *sing.*; basketry *sing.*; wickerwork articles; **~weide die** osier; basket willow; **~wurf der** *(Basketball)* throw *or* shot at goal *or* the basket

Kord [kɔrt] **der; ~[e]s a)** corduroy; cord; **b)** *s.* **Kordsamt**

Kọrd·anzug der corduroy suit

Kordel ['kɔrdl̩] **die; ~, ~n a)** cord; **b)** *(landsch.: Bindfaden)* string

Kọrd-: ~hose die corduroy *or* cord trousers *pl.*; **~jeans** *Pl.* corduroy *or* cord jeans

Kordon [kɔr'dõ, *österr.:* -'do:n] **der; ~s, ~s** *od. österr.:* **~e a)** *(Absperrung)* cordon; **b)** *(Ordensband)* cordon; ribbon
Kord·samt der cord velvet
Korea [ko're:a] **(das); ~s** Korea
Korea·krieg der Korean War
Koreaner [kore'a:nɐ] **der; ~s, ~, Koreanerin die; ~, ~nen** Korean; *s. auch* **-in**
koreanisch *Adj.* Korean; *s. auch* **deutsch; Deutsch; ²Deutsche**
Koreferat *s.* **Korreferat**
kören ['kø:rən] *tr. V. (Landw.)* rank *or* classify ⟨*males*⟩ for breeding
Korfu ['kɔrfu] **(das); ~s** Corfu
Koriander [ko'ri̯andɐ] **der; ~s, ~:** coriander
Korinth [ko'rɪnt] **(das); ~s** Corinth
Korinthe [ko'rɪntə] **die; ~, ~n** currant
Korinthen-: ~brot das currant bread; **~kacker der** *(derb abwertend)* stupid rule-bound bastard *(sl.)*; *(Pfennigfuchser)* pettifogger *(coll.)*
Korinther der; ~s, ~: Corinthian
korinthisch *Adj. (Kunstwiss.)* Corinthian ⟨*column, order, etc.*⟩
Kork [kɔrk] **der; ~s, ~e** cork
Kork·eiche die cork-oak
Korken der; ~s, ~: cork
Korken·zieher der corkscrew
Korkenzieher·locke die corkscrew *or* spiral curl
korkig *Adj.* corked, corky ⟨*wine*⟩
Kork·sohle die cork sole
Kormoran [kɔrmo'ra:n] **der; ~s, ~e** cormorant
¹Korn [kɔrn] **das; ~[e]s, Körner** ['kœrnɐ] **a)** *(Frucht)* seed; grain; *(Getreide~)* grain [of corn]; *(Pfeffer~)* corn; **b)** *o. Pl. (Getreide)* corn; grain; **das ~ steht gut** the grain harvest looks promising; **c)** *(Salz~, Sand~)* grain; *(Hagel~)* stone; **d)** *Pl.* **~e** *(an Handfeuerwaffen)* front sight; foresight; **etw. aufs ~ nehmen** take aim at *or* draw a bead on sth.; *(fig. ugs.)* attack sth.; **jmdn. aufs ~ nehmen** take aim at *or* draw a bead on sb.; *(fig. ugs.)* start to keep close tabs on sb. *(coll.)*; **e)** *(Fot.; von Papier, Stoff)* grain
²Korn der; ~[e]s, ~ *(ugs.)* corn schnapps; corn liquor *(Amer.)*
korn-, Korn-: ~ähre die ear of corn; **~blume die** cornflower; **~blumen·blau** *Adj.* cornflower [blue]; *(fig. salopp)* paralytic *(sl.)*; **~brannt·wein der** corn schnapps; corn liquor *(Amer.)*
Körnchen ['kœrnçən] **das; ~s, ~** *(Frucht)* tiny seed *or* grain; *(von Sand usw.)* [tiny] grain; granule; **an etw.** *(Dat.)* **ist ein ~ Wahrheit** *(fig.)* there's a grain of truth in sth.
körnen ['kœrnən] *tr. V.* **a)** *(zerkleinern, körnig machen)* granulate; **gekörnte Brühe** stock granules *pl. (for soup)*; **b)** *(Handw.: markieren)* punch
Körner *s.* **Korn**
Körner-: ~fresser der *(Ornith.)* seed-eater; granivore; **~futter das** grain [feed]; *(für Vögel)* seed
Kornett [kɔr'nɛt] **das; ~[e]s, ~e** *od.* **~s** *(Musik)* cornet
Korn·feld das cornfield
körnig ['kœrnɪç] *Adj.* granular; *(Fot.)* grainy
-körnig *Adj.* -grained
Korn-: ~kammer die granary; **~rade die** corn cockle; corn campion; **~silo der** *od.* **das** grain silo
Körnung die; ~, ~en a) *(Korngröße)* grain size; *(von Papier)* grain; **b)** *(Jägerspr.) s.* **Körnerfutter**
Korona [ko'ro:na] **die; ~, Koronen a)** *(Astron.)* corona; **b)** *(fig.)* crowd *(coll.)*
Koronar·insuffizienz [koro'na:ɐ̯-] **die** *(Med.)* coronary insufficiency
Körper ['kœrpɐ] **der; ~s, ~ a)** body; **~ und Geist** body and mind; **am ganzen ~ frieren/zittern** be [freezing] cold/shake all over; **b)** *(Rumpf)* trunk; body; **c)** *(Gegenstand)* object; **d)** *(Physik, Chemie)* body; **e)** *(Geom.)* solid body; solid; **f)** *(von Wein, Farbe)* body; **g)** *s.* **Körperschaft**
körper-, Körper-: ~bau der; *o. Pl.* physique; **~behaarung die** body hair *no indef. art.*; **~beherrschung die** body control; **~behindert** *Adj.* physically handicapped *or* disabled; **~behinderte der/die** physically handicapped *or* disabled person; **~behinderte** *Pl.* physically handicapped *or* disabled people; **die ~behinderten** *(als Kategorie)* the physically handicapped *or* disabled; **~behinderung die** physical handicap *or* disability; **~beschädigte der/die** *(Amtsspr.)* disabled person; **~betont 1.** *Adj.* figure-hugging ⟨*clothes*⟩; ⟨*clothes*⟩ that emphasize the figure; **2.** *adv.* **~betont geschnitten** cut to emphasize the figure; **~eigen** *Adj. (Biol.)* endogenous; **~erzieher der** *(bes. DDR)* physical education teacher; **~fremd** *Adj. (Biol.)* foreign; **~fülle die** corpulence; **~funktion die** bodily function; **~gerecht** *Adj.* shaped to fit the contours of the body *postpos.*; **~geruch der** body odour; BO *(coll.)*; **~gewicht das** body weight; **~größe die** height; **~hälfte die** side of the body; **~haltung die** posture; **~hygiene die** *s.* **~pflege**; **~kontakt der** *(Psych.)* physical contact; **~kraft die** physical strength; **~kultur die** *(bes. DDR)* physical education *no art.*; **~länge die** *(bei Menschen)* height; *(bei Tieren)* length
körperlich 1. *Adj.* physical; **~e Ertüchtigung** physical training; **~e Züchtigung** corporal punishment; **~e Liebe** carnal love. **2.** *adv.* physically; **~ [hart] arbeiten** do [hard] physical work
körper-, Körper-: ~los *Adj.* incorporeal; **~maße** *Pl.* measurements; **~öffnung die** orifice of the body; **~pflege die** body care *no art.*; *(Reinigung)* personal hygiene; **~saft der;** *meist Pl.* body fluid
Körperschaft die; ~, ~en a) *(Rechtsw.)* corporation; corporate body; **~ des öffentlichen Rechts** public corporation; **b)** *(Politik)* body
Körperschaft[s]·steuer die *(Steuerw.)* corporation tax
Körper-: ~schwäche die; *o. Pl.* physical weakness; **~sprache die** body language; **~spray der** *od.* **das** aerosol deodorant; deodorant spray; **~stärke die;** *o. Pl.* physical strength; **~teil der** part of the/one's body; **~temperatur die** body temperature; **~verletzung die** *(Rechtsw.)* bodily harm *no indef. art.*; **schwere/leichte ~verletzung** grievous/actual bodily harm; **~verletzung mit Todesfolge** *bodily harm resulting in death*; **~verletzung im Amt** bodily harm caused by a public servant when executing his/her duty; **~wärme die** body heat
Korpora *s.* **²Korpus**
Korporal [kɔrpo'ra:l] **der; ~s, ~e** *od.* **Korporäle** [kɔrpo'rɛ:lə] *(Milit. veralt.)* corporal
Korporation [kɔrpora'tsi̯o:n] **die; ~, ~en a)** *(veralt.: Körperschaft)* corporation; **b)** *(Studentenverbindung)* student society
korporiert [kɔrpo'ri:ɐ̯t] *Adj.* ⟨*student*⟩ belonging to a student society
Korporierte der; *adj. Dekl.* member of a student society
Korps [ko:ɐ̯] **das; ~** [ko:ɐ̯(s)], **~** [ko:ɐ̯s] **a)** *(Milit.)* corps; **b)** *(Studentenverbindung)* student duelling society
Korps-: ~bruder der *(Studentenspr.)* fellow member of a student duelling society; **~geist der** *(geh.)* esprit de corps; **~student der** student belonging to a duelling society
korpulent [kɔrpu'lɛnt] *Adj.* corpulent
Korpulenz [kɔrpu'lɛnts] **die; ~:** corpulence
¹Korpus ['kɔrpʊs] **der; ~, ~se a)** *(scherzh.)* body; **b)** *(bild. Kunst)* figure of Christ *(on crucifix)*; **c)** *(fachspr.)* carcass
²Korpus das; ~, Korpora ['kɔrpora] **a)** *(Sprachw.)* corpus; **b)** *o. Pl. (Musik)* body
³Korpus die; ~ *(Druckw.)* long primer
Korpuskel [kɔr'pʊskl̩] **das; ~s, ~n** *od.* **die; ~, ~n** *(Physik)* corpuscle; particle
Korreferat [kɔrefe'ra:t] **das; ~s, ~e** *scholarly paper which supplements the main paper;* supplementary paper *(to a paper read at a seminar etc.)*
Korreferent [kɔrefe'rɛnt] **der; ~en, ~en, Korreferentin die; ~, ~nen a)** *(Redner)* reader of a/the supplementary paper; **b)** *(Prüfer)* second examiner
korrekt [kɔ'rɛkt] **1.** *Adj.* correct; **es wäre ~ gewesen, ...:** the correct thing would have been to ...; **ein ~er Beamter** a very correct civil servant. **2.** *adv.* correctly
korrekter·weise *Adv.* to be [strictly] correct
Korrektheit die; ~: correctness
Korrektiv [kɔrɛk'ti:f] **das; ~s, ~e** corrective **(gegen** to)
Korrektor [kɔ'rɛktɔr] **der; ~s, ~en** [-'to:rən] proof-reader
Korrektur [kɔrɛk'tu:ɐ̯] **die; ~, ~en a)** correction; *(von Ansichten usw.)* revision; **b)** *(Druckw.)* proof-reading; *(Verbesserung)* proof-correction; **~ lesen** read/correct the proofs
Korrektur-: ~ab·zug der, ~fahne die galley [proof]; **~zeichen das** proof-correction mark
Korrelat [kɔre'la:t] **das; ~[e]s, ~e** correlate
Korrelation [kɔrela'tsi̯o:n] **die; ~, ~en** *(auch Math.)* correlation
korrelieren *itr. V.* correlate **(mit** with, to)
Korrepetitor [kɔrepe'ti:tɔr] **der; ~s, ~en** [-ti'to:rən] *(Musik)* répétiteur
Korrespondent [kɔrɛspɔn'dɛnt] **der; ~en, ~en, Korrespondentin die; ~, ~nen a)** *(Zeitungsw., veralt.: Briefpartner)* correspondent; **b)** *(Wirtsch.)* correspondence clerk
Korrespondenz [kɔrɛspɔn'dɛnts] **die; ~, ~en a)** correspondence; **die ~ erledigen** deal with the correspondence; **in ~ mit jmdm. stehen** correspond with sb.; **b)** *(Brief)* letter; **~en** correspondence *sing.*
Korrespondenz-: ~büro das press agency; **~karte die** *(österr., schweiz.) prestamped postcard*
korrespondieren *itr. V.* **a)** *(schreiben)* correspond **(mit** with); **b)** *(geh.: übereinstimmen)* **mit etw. ~:** correspond to *or* with sth.; ⟨*colour*⟩ match sth.
Korridor ['kɔrido:ɐ̯] **der; ~s, ~e** corridor; **der Polnische ~:** the Polish Corridor
korrigierbar *Adj.* correctable
korrigieren [kɔri'gi:rən] *tr. V.* correct; revise ⟨*opinion, view*⟩
korrodieren [kɔro'di:rən] *(bes. Chemie, Geol.) tr., itr. V. (itr. mit sein)* corrode
Korrosion [kɔro'zi̯o:n] **die; ~, ~en** *(auch Geol., Med.)* corrosion
korrosions-, Korrosions-: ~beständig *Adj.*, **~fest** *Adj.* corrosion-resistant; **~schutz der** protection against corrosion
korrosiv [kɔro'zi:f] *Adj.* **a)** corrosive; **b)** *(korrosionsbedingt)* ⟨*damage etc.*⟩ caused by corrosion
korrumpieren [kɔrʊm'pi:rən] *tr. V.* corrupt
Korrumpierung die; ~, ~en corruption
korrupt [kɔ'rʊpt] *Adj.* corrupt
Korruption [kɔrʊp'tsi̯o:n] **die; ~, ~en** corruption
Korsage [kɔr'za:ʒə] **die; ~, ~n** strapless, tight-fitting corsage *or* bodice
Korsar [kɔr'za:ɐ̯] **der; ~en, ~en a)** *(hist.)* corsair; **b)** *(Segeln)* Korsar
Korse ['kɔrzə] **der; ~n, ~n** Corsican
Korselett [kɔrzə'lɛt] **das; ~s, ~s** *od.* **~e** corselette
Korsett [kɔr'zɛt] **das; ~s, ~s** *od.* **~e** corset; *(fig.)* strait-jacket
Korsett·stange die corset bone

Korsika ['kɔrzika] **(das); ~s** Corsica
korsisch *Adj.* Corsican
Korso ['kɔrzo] **der; ~s, ~s** procession
Kortison [kɔrti'zo:n] **das; ~s** *(Med.)* cortisone
Korund [ko'rʊnt] **der; ~[e]s, ~e** corundum
Körung die; ~, ~en *(Landw.)* ranking *or* classification for breeding
Korvette [kɔr'vɛtə] **die; ~, ~n** *(auch hist.)* corvette
Korvetten·kapitän der lieutenant-commander
Koryphäe [kory'fɛ:ə] **die; ~, ~n** eminent authority; distinguished expert
Kosak [ko'zak] **der; ~en, ~en** *(hist.)* Cossack
Kosaken·mütze die Cossack hat
Koschenille [kɔʃə'nɪljə] **die; ~:** cochineal
koscher ['ko:ʃɐ] *Adj.* **a)** kosher; **b)** *(ugs.: einwandfrei)* kosher *(coll.)*
K.-o.-Schlag der *(Boxen)* knock-out punch
Kose·form die familiar form
Kosekans ['ko:zekans] **der; ~, ~** *(Math.)* cosecant
kosen ['ko:zn̩] *(dichter. veralt.)* **1.** *tr. V.* caress. **2.** *itr. V.* **mit jmdm. ~:** caress sb.
Kose·name der pet name
Kose·wort das; *Pl.* **-wörter** term of endearment; **jmdm. Kosewörter ins Ohr flüstern** whisper endearments in sb.'s ear
K.-o.-Sieg der *(Boxen)* knock-out victory; victory by a knock-out
Kosinus ['ko:zinʊs] **der; ~, ~** *od.* **~se** *(Math.)* cosine
Kosmetik [kɔs'me:tɪk] **die; ~ a)** beauty culture *no art.*; **b)** *(fig.)* cosmetic procedures *pl.*
Kosmetik·abteilung die cosmetics department
Kosmetiker der; ~s, ~, Kosmetikerin die; ~, ~nen a) cosmetician; beautician; **b)** *(Chemiker/Chemikerin)* cosmetics chemist
Kosmetik-: ~salon der beauty salon; **~tasche die** make-up bag; *(groß)* vanity case
Kosmetikum [kɔs'me:tikʊm] **das; ~s, Kosmetika;** *meist Pl.* cosmetic
kosmetisch 1. *Adj. (auch fig.)* cosmetic. **2.** *adv.* **jmdn. ~ beraten** give sb. advice on beauty care; **sich ~ behandeln lassen** have beauty treatment
kosmisch ['kɔsmɪʃ] *Adj.* cosmic ⟨*ray, dust, etc.*⟩; space ⟨*age, station, research, etc.*⟩; meteoric ⟨*iron*⟩
Kosmodrom [kɔsmo'dro:m] **das; ~s, ~e** cosmodrome
Kosmologie [kɔsmolo'gi:] **die; ~, ~n** cosmology
Kosmonaut [kɔsmo'naut] **der; ~en, ~en, Kosmonautin die; ~, ~nen** cosmonaut
Kosmopolit [kɔsmopo'li:t] **der; ~en, ~en** *(geh.)* cosmopolitan
kosmopolitisch *Adj.* cosmopolitan
Kosmos ['kɔsmɔs] **der; ~ a)** *(Weltall)* cosmos; **b)** *(geh.: Welt)* world
Kost [kɔst] **die; ~ a)** *(Nahrung)* food; **vegetarische ~:** vegetarian food; a vegetarian diet; **geistige ~** *(fig.)* intellectual nourishment; **leichte/schwere ~** *(fig.)* easy/heavy going; **b)** *(Verpflegung)* **~ und Logis** board and lodging
kostbar 1. *Adj.* **a)** *(erlesen)* valuable; **b)** *(wichtig)* precious; **die Zeit ist ~:** time is precious. **2.** *adv.* expensively ⟨*dressed*⟩; luxuriously ⟨*decorated*⟩
Kostbarkeit die; ~, ~en a) *(Sache)* treasure; precious object; **b)** *o. Pl.* *(Eigenschaft)* value
[1]**kosten 1.** *tr. V.* **a)** *(probieren)* taste; try; sample; **jmdm. etw. zum Kosten geben** give sb. sth. to taste *or* try *or* sample; **b)** *(geh.: empfinden)* taste; *(fig. iron.)* have a taste of. **2.** *itr. V. (probieren)* have a taste; **von etw. ~:** have a taste of *or* taste sth.
[2]**kosten 1.** *tr. V.* **a)** cost; **wieviel kostet .../was kostet ...?** how much/what does ... cost?; how much is ...?; **koste es** *od.* **es koste, was es wolle** whatever the cost; **sich** *(Akk. od. Dat.)* **eine Sache etw. ~ lassen** *(ugs.)* spend a fair bit of money on sth.; **b)** *(erfordern)* take; cost ⟨*lives*⟩; **es kostet mich nur ein Wort** it would only take a word from me; **viel Arbeit ~:** take a great deal of work; **c)** *(Verlust nach sich ziehen)* **jmdn.** *od.* **jmdm. etw. ~:** cost sb. sth.; **jmdn. den Sieg ~:** cost sb. victory. **2.** *itr. V.* *(Geld ~)* **das kostet!** that will cost a bit!
Kosten *Pl.* cost *sing.*; costs; *(Auslagen)* expenses; *(Rechtsw.)* costs; **die ~ tragen, für die ~ aufkommen** bear the cost[s]; **keine ~ scheuen** spare no expense; **laufende ~:** running costs; **auf seine ~ kommen** cover one's costs; *(fig.)* get one's money's worth; **auf jmds. ~:** at sb.'s expense; **auf ~ von jmdm./etw.** at the expense of sb./sth.
kosten-, Kosten-: ~aufwand der expense; cost; **mit einem ~aufwand von ...:** at a cost of ...; **~berechnung die** costing; **~beteiligung die** sharing of expenses; **~deckend 1.** *Adj.* that covers/cover [one's] costs *postpos., not pred.*; **2.** *adv.* **~deckend kalkulieren** ensure that the estimates cover the true costs; **~druck der;** *o. Pl.* *(Wirtsch.)* pressure of costs; **~ersparnis die** cost saving; **~erstattung die** reimbursement of costs; **~explosion die** cost explosion; **~frage die** question of cost; **~intensiv** *Adj. (Wirtsch.)* cost-intensive; **~los 1.** *Adj* free; **2.** *adv.* free of charge; **~pflichtig** *(Rechtsw.)* **1.** *Adj.* **eine ~pflichtige Verwarnung** a fine and a caution; **2.** *adv.* **eine Klage ~pflichtig abweisen** dismiss a case with costs; **ein Auto ~pflichtig abschleppen** tow a car away at the owner's expense; **~punkt der** *(ugs.)* **~punkt?** how much is it/are they?; **~punkt 25 DM** it costs/they cost 25 marks; **~rechnung die** *(Wirtsch.)* cost accounting; **~sparend** *Adj.* *(Wirtsch.)* cost-saving; **~stelle die** *(Wirtsch.)* cost centre; **~träger der** *(Wirtsch.)* cost unit; **~vor·an·schlag der** estimate
Kost-: ~gänger der *(veralt.)* boarder; **~geld das** payment for [one's] board; **er gab seinen Eltern ~geld** he paid his parents for his board
köstlich ['kœstlɪç] **1.** *Adj.* **a)** delicious; **b)** *(unterhaltsam)* delightful; **der Witz war einfach zu ~:** the joke was simply priceless *(coll.)*. **2.** *adv.* **a)** ⟨*taste*⟩ delicious; **b) sich ~ amüsieren/unterhalten** enjoy oneself enormously *(coll.)*
Köstlichkeit die; ~, ~en a) *(Sache)* delicacy; **eine literarische ~:** a literary gem; **b)** *o. Pl.* *(geh.: Eigenschaft)* deliciousness
Kost·probe die; ~, ~n taste; *(fig.)* sample
kost·spielig [-ʃpi:lɪç] **1.** *Adj.* expensive; costly. **2.** *adv.* expensively
Kostüm [kɔs'ty:m] **das; ~s, ~e a)** suit; **b)** *(historisches ~, Theater~, Verkleidung)* costume
Kostüm-: ~ball der fancy-dress ball; **~bildner der** *(Theater, Film)* costume-designer; **~film der** period picture *or* film
kostümieren *tr. V.* **a)** *(verkleiden)* **jmdn./sich ~:** dress sb. up/dress [oneself] up; **wie hatte er sich kostümiert?** what was he dressed [up] as?; **alle erschienen kostümiert** they all came in fancy dress; **b)** *(ugs. abwertend: unpassend anziehen)* **jmdn./sich ~:** get sb./oneself up
Kostüm-: ~jacke die jacket; **~probe die** *(Theater)* dress rehearsal; **~rock der** skirt; **~verleih der** [theatrical] costume agency
Kost·verächter der *in* **kein ~ sein** *(scherzh.)* be fond of one's food; *(die Frauen lieben)* be one for the ladies
K.-o.-System das *(Sport)* knock-out system
Kot [ko:t] **der; ~[e]s, ~e a)** *(Exkrement)* excrement; **b)** *(veralt.: Schmutz)* mud; dirt
Kotangens ['ko:taŋɛns] **der; ~, ~** *(Math.)* cotangent
Kotau [ko'tau] **der; ~s, ~s** kowtow; **[vor jmdm.] einen** *od.* **seinen ~ machen** kowtow [to sb.]
Kotelett [kɔt'lɛt] **das; ~s, ~s a)** chop; *(vom Nacken)* cutlet; **b)** *(Teil des Tieres) (eines Schweins)* loin; *(eines Kalbs)* loin and rib
Koteletten *Pl.* side-whiskers
koten ['ko:tn̩] *itr. V.* *(Zool.)* defecate
Köter ['kø:tɐ] **der; ~s, ~** *(abwertend)* cur; tyke
Kot·flügel der *(Kfz-W.)* wing
Kothurn [ko'tʊrn] **der; ~s, ~e** cothurnus
kotig ['ko:tɪç] *Adj.* **a)** dirty ⟨*nappy, underpants*⟩; **b)** *(schmutzig)* muddy; filthy
Kotz·brocken der *(derb)* shit *(coarse)*; turd *(coarse)*
[1]**Kotze** ['kɔtsə] **die; ~** *(derb)* vomit; puke *(coarse)*
[2]**Kotze die; ~, ~n** *(südd., österr.)* **a)** coarse woollen blanket; **b)** *(Umhang)* cape
kotzen *itr. V. (derb)* puke *(coarse)*; throw up *(coll.)*; **das ist/ich finde ihn zum Kotzen** it/he makes me sick; it/he makes me want to puke *(coarse)*; **da kann man das [große] ~ kriegen** *od.* **bekommen** it makes you want to puke *(coarse)*
kotz-: ~langweilig *Adj. (derb abwertend)* bleeding boring *(coarse)*; **~übel** *Adj. (derb)* **mir ist ~übel** I feel as if I'm going to throw up *(coll.) or (coarse)* puke
KP *Abk.* **Kommunistische Partei** CP
KPdSU *Abk.* **Kommunistische Partei der Sowjetunion**
Krabbe ['krabə] **die; ~, ~n a)** *(Zool.)* crab; **b)** *(ugs.: Garnele)* shrimp; *(größer)* prawn; **c)** *(ugs. scherzh.: Kind)* [little] mite; *(älter)* kid *(coll.)*; **d)** *(bild. Kunst)* crochet
Krabbel·alter das *(ugs.)* crawling stage
krabbeln ['krabl̩n] **1.** *itr. V.; mit sein* crawl. **2.** *tr. V. (ugs.: kraulen)* tickle
krach *Interj.* crash; bang; *(wenn etw. zerbricht, einstürzt)* crash
Krach [krax] **der; ~[e]s, Kräche** ['krɛçə] **a)** *o. Pl. (Lärm)* noise; row; **~ machen** make a noise *or (coll.)* a row; be noisy; **b)** *(lautes Geräusch)* crash; bang; *(wenn etw. zerbricht, einstürzt)* crash; **mit** *od.* **unter lautem ~:** with a loud crash *or* bang/crash; **c)** *(ugs.: Streit)* row; **mit jmdm. ~ anfangen/kriegen** start/have a row with sb. *(coll.)*; **~ machen** *od.* **schlagen** *(ugs.)* kick up *or* make a fuss; **es gibt oft ~:** there are frequent rows; **d)** *(ugs.: Börsen~)* crash
krachen 1. *itr. V.* **a)** *(Krach auslösen)* ⟨*thunder*⟩ crash; ⟨*shot*⟩ ring out; ⟨*floorboard*⟩ creak; **in allen Fugen ~:** creak at the joints; **~de Kälte/~der Frost** *(fig.)* bitter cold/heavy frost; **b)** *mit sein (ugs.: bersten)* ⟨*ice*⟩ crack; ⟨*bed*⟩ collapse; ⟨*trousers, dress, etc.*⟩ split; **c)** *mit sein (ugs.: mit Krach auftreffen)* crash; **die Tür krachte ins Schloß** the door banged *or* slammed shut; **d)** *(ugs.: Bankrott machen)* crash; **e)** *(unpers.)* **an der Kreuzung kracht es dauernd** there are frequent crashes at that junction; **sonst kracht's!** *(fig. ugs.)* or there'll be trouble; *(es gibt Schläge)* or you'll get a beating; **etw. tun, daß es nur so kracht** *(ugs.)* do sth. with a vengeance. **2.** *refl. V. (ugs.)* row *(coll.)*; have a row *(coll.)*
Kracher der; ~s, ~ *(ugs.: Knallkörper)* banger
Kracherl ['kraxɐl] **das; ~s, ~n** *(südd., österr.)* fizzy lemonade; pop *(coll.)*
krach·ledern *Adj.* rustic
Krach·lederne die; ~n, ~n *(südd.)* Lederhosen *pl.*; leather shorts *pl.*
Krach·macher der *(ugs.) (Person)* noisy so-and-so *(coll.)*; *(Gerät)* noise-maker
krächzen ['krɛçtsn̩] *itr. V.* ⟨*raven, crow*⟩ caw; ⟨*parrot*⟩ squawk; ⟨*person*⟩ croak; *(fig.)* ⟨*loudspeaker etc.*⟩ crackle and splutter

kracken ['krakn̩] *tr. V. (Chemie)* crack
Kräcker ['krɛkɐ] **der; ~s, ~:** *s.* **Cracker**
Krad [kra:t] **das; ~[e]s, Kräder** ['krɛ:dɐ] *(bes. Milit.) s.* **Kraftrad**
Krad-: ~fahrer der *(bes. Milit.)* motorcyclist; motor-cycle rider; **~melder der** *(Milit.)* [motor-cycle] despatch rider
kraft [kraft] *Präp. + Gen. (Amtsspr.)* **~ [meines] Amtes** by virtue of my office; **~ Gesetzes** by law; **~ [des] Gesetzes hat der Richter ihn zum Tode verurteilt** as empowered by the law, the judge sentenced him to death
Kraft die; ~, Kräfte ['krɛftə] **a)** strength; **geistige/schöpferische Kräfte** mental/creative powers; **unter Aufbietung aller Kräfte** applying all one's energies; **jmds. Kräfte übersteigen** be too much for sb.; **wieder bei Kräften sein** have [got] one's strength back; **bei Kräften bleiben** keep one's strength up; **mit letzter ~:** with one's last ounce of strength; **mit frischer ~:** with renewed energy; **aus eigener ~:** by oneself *or* one's own efforts; **ich werde tun, was in meinen Kräften steht** I shall do everything [with]in my power; **mit vereinten Kräften sollte es gelingen** if we join forces *or* combine our efforts we should succeed; **nach [besten] Kräften** to the best of one's ability; **die militärische/wirtschaftliche ~ eines Landes** *(fig.)* the military/economic strength of a country; **b)** *(Wirksamkeit)* power; **die treibende ~:** the driving force; **c)** *(Arbeits~)* employee; *(in einer Fabrik)* employee; worker; **Kräfte** employees/workers; personnel *pl.*; *(Angestellte auch)* staff *pl.*; **d)** *Pl. (Gruppe)* forces; **e)** *(Physik)* force; **f)** *(Seemannsspr.)* **mit voller/halber ~:** at full/half speed; **volle/halbe ~ voraus!** full/half speed ahead!; **g)** *in* **außer ~ setzen** repeal ⟨*law*⟩; countermand ⟨*order*⟩; **außer ~ sein/treten** no longer be/cease to be in force; **in ~ treten/sein/bleiben** come into/be in/remain in force
Kraft-: ~akt der feat of strength; *(im Zirkus usw.)* strong-man act; *(fig.)* show of strength; **~arm der** *(Physik)* [lever] arm to which force is applied; **~aufwand der** effort; **~aus·druck der** swear-word; **~brühe die** strong meat broth; **~droschke die** *(veralt.)* hackney carriage; taxi
Kräfte-: ~parallelogramm das *(Physik)* parallelogram of forces; **~verhältnis das** *(bes. Politik)* balance of power; **~verschleiß der** loss of strength
Kraft·fahrer der *(bes. Amtsspr.)* driver; motorist; *(Beruf)* driver
Kraftfahrer·gruß der *s.* **Autofahrergruß**
Kraft·fahrzeug das; ~[e]s, ~e *(bes. Amtsspr.)* motor vehicle
Kraftfahrzeug-: ~bau der; *o. Pl.* automobile construction; **~brief der** vehicle registration document; log-book *(Brit.)*; **~industrie die** motor industry; **~mechaniker der** motor mechanic; **~schein der** vehicle registration document *(containing detailed technical description of the vehicle and details of the owner)*; **~steuer die** vehicle *or* road tax; **~zulassungs·stelle die** vehicle registration office
Kraft-: ~feld das *(Physik)* force field; **~futter das** concentrated feed
kräftig ['krɛftɪç] **1.** *Adj.* **a)** *(stark)* strong ⟨*person*⟩; strong, powerful ⟨*arms, voice*⟩; vigorous ⟨*plant, shoot*⟩; **b)** *(fest)* powerful, hefty, hard ⟨*blow, kick, etc.*⟩; firm ⟨*handshake*⟩; **c)** *(ausgeprägt)* strong ⟨*breeze, high-pressure area*⟩; deep ⟨*depression*⟩; considerable ⟨*increase*⟩; **einen ~en Schluck nehmen** take a deep drink *or (coll.)* good swig; **eine ~e Tracht [Prügel]** a good hiding *(coll.)*; a sound beating; **d)** *(intensiv)* strong, powerful ⟨*smell, taste, etc.*⟩; bold ⟨*pattern*⟩; strong ⟨*colour*⟩; **e)** *(kräftigend)* nourishing ⟨*soup, bread, meal, etc.*⟩; **etw. Kräftiges essen** eat a good nourishing meal; **f)** *(grob)* strong ⟨*language*⟩; coarse ⟨*expression, oath, etc.*⟩. **2.** *adv.* **a)** strongly, powerfully ⟨*built*⟩; ⟨*hit, kick, press, push*⟩ hard; ⟨*sneeze*⟩ loudly; **~ entwickelt sein** strong, vigorous ⟨*plant*⟩; sturdy ⟨*child*⟩; **b)** *(tüchtig)* ⟨*rain, snow*⟩ heavily; ⟨*eat*⟩ heartily; ⟨*sing*⟩ lustily; **etw. ~ schütteln** shake sth. vigorously; give sth. a good shake; **die Preise sind ~ gestiegen** prices have risen steeply; **der Flasche/dem Alkohol ~ zusprechen** hit the bottle in a big way *(coll.)*; **c)** *(mit Nachdruck)* **jmdm. ~ die** *od.* **seine Meinung sagen** give sb. a piece of one's mind
kräftigen *tr. V.* ⟨*holiday, air, etc.*⟩ invigorate; ⟨*food etc.*⟩ fortify; **sich ~:** build up one's strength; **~de Nahrung/Luft** nourishing food/bracing air
Kräftigung die; ~, ~en strengthening
Kräftigungs·mittel das tonic
kraft-, Kraft-: ~linien *Pl. (Physik)* lines of force; **~los** *Adj.* weak; feeble; *(fig.)* weak ⟨*sun*⟩; **~losigkeit die; ~:** weakness; feebleness; **~maschine die** *(Technik)* engine; prime mover; **~meier der; ~s, ~** *(ugs.: abwertend)* muscleman; **~meierei die; ~** *(ugs. abwertend)* playing the muscleman; **~mensch der** strong man; muscleman; **~messer der a)** *(Physik)* dynamometer; **b)** *(auf dem Jahrmarkt)* try-your-strength machine; **~paket das** *(Spieler)* powerhouse; *(Pferd)* powerful animal; *(Auto)* powerful machine; **ein ~paket von Spieler** a powerhouse of a player; **~post die** post-bus service; **~probe die** trial of strength; **~protz der** *(abwertend)* muscleman; **~rad das** *(Amtsspr.)* motorcycle; **~reserven** *Pl.* reserves of strength; **~sport der** *s.* **Schwerathletik; ~stoff der** *(Kfz-W.)* fuel; **~stoff·anzeiger der** *(Kfz-W.)* fuel gauge; **~stoff-Luft-Gemisch das** *(Kfz-W.)* air-fuel mixture; **~stoff·verbrauch der** fuel consumption; **~strotzend** *Adj.* vigorous; bursting with vigour *postpos.*; **~vergeudung die** waste of energy; **~verkehr der** *(Amtsspr.)* [motor] traffic; **~verschwendung die** *s.* **~vergeudung; ~voll 1.** *Adj.* powerful; **2.** *adv.* powerfully; **~wagen der** motor vehicle; **~werk das** power station; **~wort das** *s.* **~ausdruck**
Kragen ['kra:gn̩] **der; ~s, ~,** *südd., österr. u. schweiz. auch:* **Krägen** ['krɛ:gn̩] **a)** collar; **b)** *in* **ihm platzte der ~** *(salopp)* he blew his top *(coll.)*; **jetzt platzt mir aber der ~!** *(salopp)* that's the last straw!; **es geht ihm an den ~** *(ugs.)* he's in for it now; **jmdn. am** *od.* **beim ~ packen** *od.* **nehmen** *(ugs.)* collar sb.; **jmdm. an den ~ wollen** *(ugs.)* get at *or* be after sb.; *(jmdn. verantwortlich machen)* try to hang sth. on sb. *(coll.)*; *s. auch* **Kopf a; c)** *(Jägerspr.)* collar
Kragen-: ~bär der [Himalayan] black bear; **~knopf der** collar-stud *(Brit.)*; *(oberster Knopf am Hemd)* top button; **~weite die** collar size; **[nicht] jmds. ~weite sein** *(salopp)* [not] be sb.'s cup of tea *(coll.)*
Krag·stein der *(Archit.)* bracket; *(Konsole)* console
Krähe ['krɛ:ə] **die; ~, ~n** crow; **eine ~ hackt der anderen kein Auge aus** *(Spr.)* dog does not eat dog *(prov.)*
krähen *itr. V. (auch fig.)* crow; *s. auch* **Hahn**
Krähen-: ~füße *Pl. (ugs.)* **a)** *(Hautfalten)* crow's feet; **b)** *(aus Eisen) devices with many sharp points scattered on the road to burst the tyres of a vehicle*; ≈ [tin] tacks; **~nest das** *(auch Seemannsspr.)* crow's nest
Kräh·winkel *o. Art.; o. Pl. (spött.)* provincial backwater
Krakau ['kra:kau̯] **(das); ~s** Cracow; Krakow
[1]**Krakauer der; ~s, ~:** Cracovian
[2]**Krakauer die; ~, ~** *(Wurst) highly spiced, smoked beef and pork sausage*
Krake ['kra:kə] **der; ~n, ~n a)** *(Tintenfisch)* octopus; **b)** *(Meeresungeheuer)* kraken
Krakeel [kra'ke:l] **der; ~s** *(ugs. abwertend)* row *(coll.)*
krakeelen 1. *itr. V. (ugs. abwertend)* kick up a row *(coll.)*. **2.** *tr. V.* scream
Krakeeler der; ~s, ~ *(ugs. abwertend)* rowdy
Krakel ['kra:kl̩] **der; ~s, ~** *(ugs. abwertend)* scrawl; scribble
krakelig *s.* **kraklig**
krakeln *tr., itr. V. (ugs. abwertend)* scrawl; scribble
kraklig *Adj. (ugs. abwertend)* scrawly
Kral [kra:l] **der; ~s, ~e** *od.* **~s** kraal
Kralle ['kralə] **die; ~, ~n** claw; *(von Raubvögeln)* claw; talon; **die ~n des Todes** *(fig.)* the jaws of death; **jmdm. die ~n zeigen** *(ugs.)* show sb. one's claws; **etw. in die ~n bekommen** *od.* **kriegen** *(ugs.)* get sth. in one's clutches
krallen 1. *refl. V.* **sich an etw.** *(Akk.)* **~** ⟨*cat*⟩ dig its claws into sth.; ⟨*bird*⟩ dig its claws *or* talons into sth.; ⟨*person*⟩ clutch sth. [tightly]; **sich in/um etw.** *(Akk.)* **~:** dig into/clutch sth. **2.** *tr. V.* **a)** *(fest greifen)* **die Finger in/um etw.** *(Akk.)* **~:** dig one's fingers into sth./clutch sth. [tightly] with one's fingers; **b)** *(krümmen)* **er krallte seine Finger/seine Hand** he bent his fingers into [the shape of] a claw; **c)** *(salopp: stehlen)* pinch *(sl.)*; nick *(Brit. sl.)*; **d)** *(salopp: ergreifen)* collar; *(verhaften)* nab *(sl.)*
Kram [kra:m] **der; ~[e]s** *(ugs.)* **a)** stuff; *(Gerümpel)* junk; **den ganzen ~ hinschmeißen** *(fig. ugs.)* chuck the whole thing in *(coll.)*; **b)** *(Angelegenheit)* business; affair; **mach deinen ~ alleine!** do it yourself!; **jmdm. [genau] in den ~ passen** suit sb. [down to the ground *(coll.)*]
kramen 1. *itr. V.* **a)** *(ugs.: herumwühlen)* **in etw.** *(Dat.)* **~:** rummage about in *or* rummage through sth.; **nach etw. ~:** rummage about looking for sth.; **b)** *(schweiz.: einkaufen)* do some *or* a bit of shopping. **2.** *tr. V.* *(ugs.)* **etw. aus etw. ~:** fish *(coll.) or* get sth. out of sth.
Krämer ['krɛ:mɐ] **der; ~s, ~ a)** *(veralt.: Lebensmittelhändler)* grocer; **b)** *(abwertend) (geiziger Mensch)* skinflint; stingy person; *(engstirniger Mensch)* petty-minded *or* small-minded person
Krämer·seele die *(abwertend)* **a)** *(Geiz)* stingy nature; *(Engstirnigkeit)* petty-mindedness; small-mindedness; **b)** *(geiziger Mensch)* skinflint; *(engstirniger Mensch)* petty-minded *or* small-minded person
Kram·laden der *(ugs. abwertend)* junk shop
Krampe ['krampə] **die; ~, ~n** staple
Krampen der; ~s, ~ a) *s.* **Krampe; b)** *(bayr., österr.: Spitzhacke)* pick[-axe]
Krampf [krampf] **der; ~[e]s, Krämpfe** ['krɛmpfə] **a)** cramp; *(Zuckung)* spasm; *(bei Anfällen)* convulsion; **sich in Krämpfen winden** curl up in convulsions; **einen ~ bekommen** *od. (ugs.)* **kriegen** get cramp; **einen ~** *od.* **Krämpfe kriegen** *(fig. ugs.)* have a fit; **b)** *o. Pl. (gequältes Tun)* painful strain; *(sinnloses Tun)* senseless waste of effort; **das ist doch alles ~:** it's all a senseless waste of effort
Krampf·ader die varicose vein
krampf·artig 1. *Adj.* convulsive. **2.** *adv.* convulsively
krampfen 1. *itr. V.* **a)** be affected with cramp; *(bei Anfällen)* be convulsed; **sein Magen krampfte** he got stomach cramp; **b)** *(schweiz.: sich anstrengen)* slave away. **2.** *refl. V.* **a)** be affected with cramp; *(bei Anfällen)* be convulsed; **b)** *(umklammern)* **sich um/in etw.** *(Akk.)* **~:** clench sth./dig into sth. **3.** *tr. V.* **a)** *(schließen)* **die Fäuste/Finger um/in etw.** *(Akk.)* **~:** clench sth./dig one's hands/fingers into sth.; **b)** *(ugs.: an sich bringen)* **sich** *(Dat.)* **etw. ~:** grab sth.

krampfhaft 1. *Adj.* **a)** convulsive; **b)** *(verbissen)* desperate; forced ‹*cheerfulness*›. **2.** *adv.* **a)** convulsively; **b)** *(verbissen)* desperately

krampf-, Krampf-: ~husten der *(Med.)* whooping cough; **~lösend** *Adj.*, **~stillend** *Adj.* antispasmodic

Kran [kra:n] **der; ~[e]s, Kräne** ['krɛ:nə] **a)** crane; **b)** *Pl.:* **Kräne** *od.* **~en** *(südwestd.: Wasserhahn)* tap; faucet *(Amer.)*

Kran-: ~brücke die *(Technik)* gantry; **~führer der** crane-operator; *(~fahrer)* crane-driver

Kranich ['kra:nɪç] **der; ~s, ~e** crane

krank [kraŋk]; **kränker** ['krɛŋkɐ], **kränkst...** ['krɛŋkst...] *Adj.* **a)** ill *usu. pred.*; sick; bad ‹*leg, tooth*›; diseased ‹*plant, organ*›; *(fig.)* sick, ailing ‹*economy, business*›; **ein ~es Herz/eine ~e Leber haben** have a bad heart/a liver complaint; **[schwer] ~ werden** be taken *or* fall [seriously *or* very] ill; **er wurde immer kränker** he got steadily worse; **du siehst ~ aus** you don't look well; **sie liegt ~ zu/im Bett** she is ill in bed; **auf den Tod ~ sein** be critically *or* dangerously ill; **jmdn. ~ machen** make sb. ill; *(fig.)* get on sb.'s nerves; **vor Heimweh/Liebe ~ sein** be homesick/lovesick; **sich ~ melden** let the office/boss *etc.* know that one is off sick; **jmdn. ~ schreiben** give sb. a medical certificate; **b)** *(Jägerspr.: angeschossen)* wounded

Kranke ['kraŋkə] **der/die;** *adj. Dekl.* sick man/woman; *(Patient)* patient; **die ~n** the sick *pl.*; the patients

kränkeln ['krɛŋkl̩n] *itr. V.* be in poor health; not be well; *(fig.)* be in poor shape; **er kränkelt leicht** he is always ailing

kranken *itr. V. (leiden)* **an etw.** *(Dat.)* **~** ‹*firm, project, etc.*› suffer from sth.

kränken ['krɛŋkn̩] **1.** *tr. V.* **jmdn. ~:** hurt *or* wound sb. *or* sb.'s feelings; **jmdn. in seiner Ehre/seinem Stolz/seiner Eitelkeit ~:** wound sb.'s honour/injure *or* wound sb.'s pride/vanity; **~d sein** be hurtful; **tief/schwer gekränkt sein** be deeply hurt. **2.** *refl. V. (geh. veralt.)* **sich über jmdn./etw. ~:** be *or* feel hurt by sb./sth.

kranken-, Kranken-: ~anstalten *Pl. (Amtsspr.)* hospital complex *sing.*; **~auto das** *s.* **~wagen; ~bericht der** case report; **~besuch der** visit to a sick person; **~blatt das** medical report [card]; **~fahrstuhl der** *(Amtsspr.)* wheelchair; **~geld das** sickness benefit; **~geschichte die** case history; **~gymnastik die** remedial *or* medical gymnastics *sing.*; physiotherapy; **~gymnastin die** remedial gymnast; medical gymnast; physiotherapist; **~haus das** hospital; **jmdn. ins ~haus einliefern/aus dem ~haus entlassen** take sb. to hospital/discharge sb. from hospital; **im ~haus liegen** be in hospital; **ins ~haus [gehen] müssen** have to go [in]to hospital; **~haus·arzt der** hospital doctor; **~haus·aufenthalt der** stay in hospital; **~haus·reif** *Adj. (salopp)* **~hausreif aussehen** look like a hospital case; **jmdn. ~hausreif schlagen** make a real mess of sb. *(coll.)*; **~kassa die** *(österr.)*, **~kasse die** health insurance scheme; *(Körperschaft)* health insurance institution; *(privat)* health insurance company; **~kassen·beitrag der** health insurance contribution; **~lager das** *(geh.)* **a)** *(Zeit des Krankseins)* illness; **b)** *(Krankenbett)* sickbed; **~pflege die** nursing; **in der ~pflege tätig sein** be a nurse; **~pfleger der** male nurse; **~saal der** ward; **~salbung die** *(kath. Kirche)* extreme unction *no art.*; **~schein der** health insurance certificate; **~schwester die** nurse; **~stand der** number of staff away sick; **im ~stand sein** *(österr.)* be away sick; **~stuhl der** *s.* **~fahrstuhl; ~transport der** transportation of sick/injured persons; **~versicherung die a)** *(Versicherung)* health insurance; **b)** *(Unternehmen)* health insurance company; **~versicherungs·pflichtig** *Adj.* ‹*person*› who is required to join a health insurance scheme; **~wagen der** ambulance; **~zimmer das** sick-room; *(im Krankenhaus)* patients' room

krank|feiern *itr. V. (ugs.)* skive off work *(sl.)* [pretending to be ill]; **ich glaube, ich feiere mal krank** I think I might just [have to] go sick *(joc.)*

kränker *s.* **krank**

krankhaft 1. *Adj.* **a)** *(pathologisch)* pathological ‹*change etc.*›; morbid ‹*growth, state, swelling, etc.*›; **b)** *(abnorm gesteigert)* pathological; pathological, morbid ‹*fear, obsession*›. **2.** *adv.* **a)** *(pathologisch)* pathologically; morbidly ‹*swollen*›; **b)** *(abnorm gesteigert)* pathologically; pathologically, morbidly ‹*obsessed, sensitive*›

Krankheit die; ~, ~en a) illness; *(bestimmte Art, von Pflanzen, Organen)* disease; **von einer ~ befallen werden** contract *or* catch an illness/a disease; **an einer ~ leiden/sterben** suffer from/die of an illness/a disease; **eine ~ heilen/einer ~ vorbeugen** cure/prevent an illness/a disease; **das ist doch kein Auto, das ist eine ~** *(fig. ugs. scherzh.)* that's just an apology for a car; **b)** *o. Pl. (Zeit des Krankseins)* illness; **nach langer/schwerer ~:** after a long/serious illness

krankheits-, Krankheits-: ~bild das clinical picture; **~erreger der** pathogen; disease-causing agent; **~fall der** case of illness; **im ~fall** in the event of illness; **~halber** *Adv.* due to illness; **~keim der** germ [causing the/a disease]

krank|lachen *refl. V. (ugs.)* laugh one's head off; laugh oneself silly

kränklich ['krɛŋklɪç] *Adj.* sickly; ailing

krank-, Krank-: ~|machen *itr. V. (ugs.) s.* **~feiern;** *s. auch* **krank a; ~meldung die** notification of absence through illness

kränkste *s.* **krank**

Kränkung die; ~, ~en: eine ~: an injury to one's/sb.'s feelings; **etw. als ~ empfinden** be hurt by sth.; take offence at sth.

Kranz [krants] **der; ~es, Kränze** ['krɛntsə] **a)** wreath; garland; *(auf einem Grab, Sarg, an einem Denkmal)* wreath; **einen ~ niederlegen** lay a wreath; **b)** *(Haar~)* chaplet *(of plaited hair)*; **c)** *(Kuchen)* ring cake; **d)** *(geh.: Kreis)* circle; **ein ~ von Sagen** a cycle of legends

Kränzchen ['krɛntsçən] **das; ~s, ~ a)** *(zum Kaffeetrinken)* coffee circle; coffee klatch *(Amer.)*; *(zum Handarbeiten)* sewing circle; **b)** *(kleiner Kranz)* small wreath *or* garland

Kranz-: ~gefäß das *s.* **Herzkranzgefäß; ~geld das** *(Rechtsw.) damages for loss of virginity awarded against a woman's fiancé if he breaks off the engagement without good cause;* **~kuchen der** *s.* **Kranz c; ~niederlegung die** laying of a wreath; **~spende die** wreath; **„von ~spenden bitten wir abzusehen"** 'no flowers please'

Krapfen ['krapfn̩] **der; ~s, ~ a)** *(Berliner)* doughnut; **b)** *(Kochkunst)* fritter

kraß [kras] **1.** *Adj.* blatant ‹*case*›; gross, flagrant ‹*injustice*›; rank, complete ‹*outsider*›; glaring, stark ‹*contrast*›; complete ‹*contradiction*›; sharp ‹*difference*›; gross ‹*discrepancy, imbalance*›; out-and-out ‹*egoist*›. **2.** *adv.* **sich ~ ausdrücken** put sth. bluntly; **sich von etw. ~ unterscheiden** be in stark contrast to sth.

Krater ['kra:tɐ] **der; ~s, ~:** crater

Krater-: ~landschaft die cratered landscape; **~see der** crater lake

Kratz·bürste die *(ugs. scherzh.)* stroppy *(Brit. sl.) or* prickly so-and-so

kratzbürstig *Adj. (ugs. scherzh.)* stroppy *(Brit. sl.)*; prickly

Kratze die; ~, ~n scraper

Krätze ['krɛtsə] **die; ~:** scabies *sing.*

kratzen ['kratsn̩] **1.** *tr. V.* **a)** scratch; **jmdm./sich den Arm blutig ~:** scratch sb.'s/one's arm and make it bleed; **b)** *(scharren)* scratch; **seinen Namen in die Wand ~:** scratch one's name on the wall; **c)** *(entfernen)* scrape; **etw. aus/von etw. ~:** scrape sth. out of/off sth.; **d)** *(ugs.: stören)* bother; **jmdn. wenig ~:** not bother sb. all that much; **wen kratzt das schon?** who cares *or* who's bothered [about that]?. **2.** *itr. V.* **a)** scratch; *(aus~)* scrape; **das Kratzen** scratching; **an jmds. Ehre/Vormachtstellung** *(Dat.)* **~** *(fig.)* chip away at sb.'s honour/supremacy; **b)** *(jucken)* itch; be scratchy *or* itchy; **c)** *(brennen)* **im Hals ~** ‹*wine*› taste rough; ‹*tobacco*› be rough on the throat; ‹*smoke*› irritate the throat. **3.** *refl. V.* scratch [oneself]; **sich hinter dem Ohr/am Kopf ~:** scratch oneself behind the ear/scratch one's head

Kratzer der; ~s, ~ a) *(ugs.)* scratch; **b)** *(Schaber)* scraper

Krätzer ['krɛtsɐ] **der; ~s, ~** *(abwertend)* rough wine; plonk *(Brit. sl.)*

kratz·fest *Adj.* scratch-proof; non-scratch

Kratz·fuß der *(veralt.)* leg *(arch.)*; **einen ~ machen** make a leg *(arch.)*

kratzig *Adj.* scratchy, itchy ‹*material, pullover, etc.*›; scratchy, rough ‹*voice*›

krätzig ['krɛtsɪç] *Adj.* scabious ‹*skin*›; mangy ‹*dog*›

Krätz·milbe die *(Zool.)* itch-mite

Kratz-: ~putz der sgraffito; **~spur die** scratch[-mark]; **~wunde die** scratch

krauchen ['krauxn̩] *itr. V.; mit sein (md.) s.* **kriechen**

krauen ['krauən] *tr. V. s.* **²kraulen**

Kraul [kraul] **das; ~s** *(Sport)* crawl

¹kraulen 1. *itr. V.* **a)** do *or* swim the crawl; **b)** *mit sein* **über den See/ans Ufer ~:** swim across the lake/to the bank using the crawl. **2.** *tr. V.; auch mit sein* **eine Strecke ~:** cover a distance using the crawl

²kraulen *tr. V.* **jmdm. das Kinn ~:** tickle sb. under the chin; **jmdn. in den Haaren ~:** run one's fingers through sb.'s hair; **seinen Bart ~:** finger one's beard

Kraul·schwimmen das crawl; **beim ~:** when doing the crawl

kraus [kraus] *Adj.* **a)** frizzy ‹*hair, beard*›; creased ‹*skirt etc.*›; wavy ‹*sea*›; wrinkled ‹*brow*›; **die Stirn ~ ziehen** wrinkle one's brow; *(unmutig)* frown; **die Nase ~ ziehen** wrinkle one's nose; **b)** *(abwertend: verworren)* muddled; confused

Krause die; ~, ~n a) *(Kragen)* ruff; *(am Ärmel)* ruffle; frill; **b)** *(im Haar)* frizziness; **eine [starke] ~ haben/bekommen** ‹*hair*› be/go [very] frizzy; ‹*person*› be/go [very] frizzy-haired

Kräusel-: ~band das Rufflette [tape] **(P); ~krepp der** crêpe

kräuseln ['krɔyzl̩n] **1.** *tr. V.* ruffle ‹*water, surface*›; gather ‹*material etc.*›; frizz ‹*hair*›; pucker [up] ‹*lips*›. **2.** *refl. V.* ‹*hair*› go frizzy; ‹*water*› ripple; ‹*smoke*› curl up; ‹*material*› pucker up

krausen 1. *tr. V.* gather ‹*material etc.*›; frizz ‹*hair*›; wrinkle [up] ‹*forehead, nose*›. **2.** *itr. V.* ‹*material, clothes*› crease

kraus·haarig *Adj.* frizzy-haired ‹*person*›; curly-coated ‹*dog etc.*›

Kraus·kopf der frizzy hair; **einen ~ haben** have frizzy hair; be frizzy-haired; *s. auch* **Wuschelkopf**

Kraut [kraut] **das; ~[e]s, Kräuter** ['krɔytɐ] **a)** herb; **dagegen ist kein ~ gewachsen** *(ugs.)* there's nothing anyone can do about it; **b)** *o. Pl. (Blätter)* foliage; stems and leaves *pl.*; *(von Kartoffeln, Bohnen usw.)* haulm; *(von Möhren, Rüben)* tops *pl.*; **ins ~ schießen** put on too much foliage; bolt; *(fig.)* run wild; **wie ~ und Rüben** *(ugs.)* all over the place; in a complete muddle; **c)** *o. Pl. (bes. südd., österr.: Kohl)* cabbage; **d)** *(ugs. abwertend: Tabak)* tobacco; **er raucht ein ganz elendes ~:** he is smoking some really foul stuff

Kräutchen ['krɔytçən] **das;** ~s, ~: [small] herb; **ein** ~ **Rührmichnichtan sein** *(veralt.)* be over-sensitive and easily upset

Kräuter-: ~**buch das** herbal; ~**butter die** herb butter; ~**essig der** herb vinegar; ~**frau die** herbwoman; ~**käse der** cheese flavoured with herbs; ~**kissen das** herb pillow; ~**likör der** herb liqueur; ~**sammler der** herbalist; ~**tee der** herb tea; ~**weib das** *(veralt.) s.* ~**frau**

krautig *Adj.* herbaceous

Kraut-: ~**junker der** *(hist. abwertend)* large landowner; ~**kopf der** *s.* **Kohlkopf**

Kräutlein das; ~s, ~ *s.* **Kräutchen**

Kraut-: ~**salat der** coleslaw; ~**wickel der** *(südd., österr.) s.* **Kohlroulade**

Krawall [kra'val] **der;** ~s, ~e **a)** *(Tumult)* riot; **b)** *o. Pl. (ugs.: Lärm)* row *(coll.)*; racket; **es gab** ~: there was a row *(coll.) or* racket; ~ **machen** kick up *or* make a row *(coll.) or* racket; ~ **schlagen** kick up *or* make a fuss

Krawall·macher der rowdy

Krawatte [kra'vatə] **die;** ~, ~n **a)** tie; **b)** *(Catchen)* headlock; chancery

Krawatten-: ~**halter der** tie-clip; ~**knoten der** knot [of the/a/one's tie]; ~**muffel der** *(ugs.)* stick-in-the-mud where ties are concerned; ~**nadel die** tie-pin; ~**zwang der: hier herrscht [kein]** ~**zwang** you [do not] have to wear a tie here

kraxeln ['kraksl̩n] *itr. V.; mit sein (bes. südd., österr. ugs.)* climb; *(mit Mühe)* clamber; **auf etw.** *(Akk.)* ~: climb [up] sth.; *(mit Mühe)* clamber up sth.

Kreation [krea'tsio:n] **die;** ~, ~en *(bes. Mode)* creation

kreativ [krea'ti:f] **1.** *Adj.* creative. **2.** *adv.* ~ **veranlagt sein** have a creative bent

Kreativität [kreativi'tɛ:t] **die;** ~: creativity

Kreativ·urlaub der [arts and crafts] activity holiday

Kreatur [krea'tu:ɐ̯] **die;** ~, ~en **a)** *(Geschöpf)* creature; **b)** *o. Pl. (alle Lebewesen)* creation; **alle** ~: all creation; **Gott schuf alle** ~: God made all creatures *pl.*; **c)** *(Mensch)* creature; wretch; **d)** *(abwertend: willenloser Mensch)* minion; creature

kreatürlich [krea'ty:ɐ̯lɪç] *Adj. (geh.)* creaturely, natural ⟨*feeling, love, etc.*⟩; animal *attrib.* ⟨*fear*⟩

Krebs [kre:ps] **der;** ~es, ~e **a)** crustacean; *(Fluß~)* crayfish; *(Krabbe)* crab; **rot wie ein** ~: as red as a lobster; **einen** ~ **fangen** *(Ruderjargon)* catch a crab; **b)** *(Krankheit)* cancer; **c)** *(Astrol.)* Cancer; the Crab; *s. auch* **Fisch**

krebs·artig 1. *Adj.* cancerous. **2.** *adv.* cancerously; in the manner of a cancer

krebsen *itr. V.* **a)** *(Flußkrebse fangen)* catch crayfish; *(Krabben fangen)* catch crabs; **b)** *(ugs.: sich abmühen)* **mit etw. zu** ~ **haben** find sth. a real *or* uphill struggle

krebs-, Krebs-: ~**erregend,** ~**erzeugend** *Adj.* carcinogenic; cancer-producing *usu. attrib.*; **das Rauchen kann** ~**erregend** *od.* ~**erzeugend sein** smoking can cause cancer; ~**forschung die** cancer research; ~**gang der a)** *o. Pl. (rückläufige Entwicklung)* retrogression; **den** ~**gang gehen** ⟨*business*⟩ go downhill; **im** ~**gang gehen** go backwards; **b)** *(Musik)* retrograde movement; retrogression; ~**geschwulst die** cancerous growth *or* tumour; ~**geschwür das** *(volkst.)* cancerous ulcer; *(fig. geh.)* cancer; ~**krank** *Adj.* cancer *attrib.* ⟨*patient etc.*⟩; ~**krank sein** suffer from *or* have cancer; ~**kranke der/die** person suffering from cancer; *(Patient)* cancer patient; ~**leiden das** cancer *no def. art.*; ~**rot** *Adj.* as red as a lobster *postpos.*; *(aus Verlegenheit)* as red as a beetroot *postpos.*; ~**rot werden** *od.* **anlaufen** go *or* turn as red as a beetroot; ~**suppe die** crab soup; *(aus Flußkrebsen)* crayfish soup; ~**tier das;** *meist Pl. (Zool.)* crustacean; ~**vorsorge die** *(bes. Amtsspr.)* **[Maßnahmen zur]** ~**vorsorge** precautions *pl.* against cancer; ~**zelle die** cancer cell

Kredenz [kre'dɛnts] **die;** ~, ~en *(veralt.)* sideboard

kredenzen *tr. V. (geh.)* **[jmdm.] etw.** ~: serve [sb. with] sth.

[1]**Kredit** [kre'di:t] **der;** ~[e]s, ~e **a)** *(Darlehen)* loan; credit; **jmdm. einen** ~ **gewähren** *od.* **einräumen** *od.* **geben** give *or* grant sb. a loan *or* a credit; **einen** ~ **kündigen** call in a loan; **b)** *o. Pl. (Zahlungsaufschub)* credit; **er hat bei uns** ~: his credit is good with us; **jmdm.** ~ **geben** give *or* grant sb. credit; **auf** ~: on credit; **c)** *o. Pl. (Kaufmannsspr.: Vertrauenswürdigkeit)* good reputation *or* name; **jmdm. großen politischen** ~ **verschaffen** give sb. considerable political standing

[2]**Kredit** ['kre:dɪt] **das;** ~s, ~s *(Finanzw.)* credit side

kredit-, Kredit-: ~**abteilung die** credit department; ~**anstalt die** credit institution; ~**aufnahme die: durch** ~**aufnahme** by means of a loan/loans; ~**brief der** *(Finanzw.)* letter of credit; ~**fähig** *Adj. (Finanzw.)* credit-worthy; ~**geber der** lender; ~**geschäft das** credit transaction; ~**hai der** *(ugs. abwertend)* loan shark *(coll.)*

kreditieren *tr. V. (Kaufmannsspr.)* **jmdm. einen Betrag** ~**/jmdn. für einen Betrag** ~: advance sb. an amount *or* give sb. an amount on credit/credit sb. with an amount

kredit-, Kredit-: ~**institut das** credit institution; ~**karte die** credit card; **mit** ~**karte bezahlen** pay by credit card; ~**kauf der** credit purchase; ~**linie die** *(Finanzw.)* credit limit; ~**nehmer der** borrower; ~**schutz der** *(Finanzw.)* credit protection; ~**würdig** *Adj. (Finanzw.)* credit-worthy

Kredo ['kre:do] **das;** ~s, ~s **a)** *(kath. Kirche)* creed; credo; **b)** *(fig. geh.)* credo

kregel ['kre:gl̩] *Adj. (bes. nordd., md.)* lively

Kreide ['kraidə] **die;** ~, ~n **a)** *o. Pl. (Kalkstein)* chalk; **b)** *(zum Schreiben)* chalk; **mit** ~ **zeichnen/schreiben** draw/write in *or* with chalk; **ein Stück** ~: a piece of chalk; **bei jmdm. [tief] in der** ~ **stehen** *od.* **sitzen** *od.* **sein** be [deep] in debt to sb.; owe sb. [a lot of] money; **c)** *o. Pl. (Geol.)* Cretaceous [period]

kreide-, Kreide-: ~**bleich** *Adj.* as white as a sheet *postpos.*; ~**felsen der** chalk cliff; ~**haltig** *Adj.* chalky; cretaceous *(Geol.)*; ~**stift der** [piece of] chalk; *(bild. Kunst)* chalk; crayon; ~**weiß** *Adj.*: *s.* ~**bleich**; ~**zeichnung die** chalk drawing; ~**zeit die** *s.* **Kreide c**

kreidig *Adj.* **a)** *(voller Kreide)* chalky; **b)** *(kreidehaltig)* chalky; cretaceous *(Geol.)*; **c)** *(geh.: bleich)* deathly pale ⟨*face*⟩

kreieren [kre'i:rən] *tr. V. (auch Theater)* create

Kreis [krais] **der;** ~es, ~e **a)** circle; **einen** ~ **schlagen** *od.* **beschreiben** describe a circle; **jmds.** ~**e stören** *(geh.)* disturb sb.; **b)** *(Handball: Wurfkreis)* goal area; **c)** *(Ring)* circle; **einen** ~ **bilden** *od.* **schließen** form *or* make a circle; **in einem** *od.* **im** ~ **stehen/sitzen** stand/sit in a circle; **sich im** ~ **drehen** *od.* **bewegen** go *or* turn round in a circle; *(fig.)* go round in circles; **mir dreht sich alles im** ~: everything's going round and round; **der** ~ **hat sich geschlossen** the last piece has fallen into place; ~**e ziehen** ⟨*court case*⟩ have [wide] repercussions; ⟨*movement*⟩ grow in size and influence; **d)** *(Gruppe)* circle; **der** ~ **meiner Freunde** my circle of friends; **im** ~**e der Freunde/Familie** among *or* with friends/within the family; **im kleinen** *od.* **engsten** ~: with a few close friends [and relatives]; **der** ~ **seiner Leser/Anhänger** his readers *pl.*/followers *pl.*; **e)** *(Teil der Gesellschaft)* circle; **in seinen** ~**en** in the circles in which he moves/moved; **in weiten** *od.* **breiten** ~**en der Bevölkerung** amongst wide sections of the population; **die besseren/besten** ~**e** the best circles; **f)** *(von Problemen, Lösungen usw.)* range; **g)** *(Verwaltungsbezirk)* district; *(Wahl~)* ward; **der** ~ **Heidelberg** the Heidelberg district *or* district of Heidelberg; **h)** *(Elektrot.)* circuit

Kreis-: ~**ab·schnitt der** *(Geom.)* segment [of a/the circle]; ~**arzt der** district medical officer; ~**aus·schnitt der** *(Geom.)* sector [of a/the circle]; ~**bahn die** orbit; ~**bewegung die** circular movement; ~**bogen der** *(Geom.)* arc [of a/the circle]

kreischen ['kraiʃn̩] *regelm. (veralt. auch unr.) itr. V.* ⟨*person*⟩ screech, shriek; ⟨*bird*⟩ screech; ⟨*brakes*⟩ squeal, screech; ⟨*door*⟩ creak; ⟨*saw*⟩ screech; **mit** ~**den Bremsen** with a squeal *or* screech of brakes

Kreisel ['kraizl̩] **der;** ~s, ~ **a)** *(Technik)* gyroscope; **b)** *(Kinderspielzeug)* top; **den** ~ **schlagen** spin *or* whip the top; **c)** *(ugs.: Kreisverkehr)* roundabout

Kreisel-: ~**bewegung die** gyration; spinning movement; ~**kompaß der** *(Schifffahrt)* gyro-compass

kreiseln *itr. V.* **a)** *auch mit sein (sich drehen)* spin [round]; gyrate; **b)** *(mit einem Kreisel spielen)* play with a top; spin a top

Kreisel·pumpe die *(Technik)* centrifugal pump

kreisen *itr. V.* **a)** *auch mit sein* ⟨*planet*⟩ revolve (**um** around); ⟨*satellite etc.*⟩ orbit; ⟨*aircraft, bird*⟩ circle; **der Satellit kreist um die Erde** the satellite orbits the Earth ; **das Blut kreiste schneller in seinen Adern** *(fig.)* the blood coursed faster in his veins; **die Flasche [in der Runde]** ~ **lassen** *(fig.)* pass the bottle round; **seine Gedanken kreisten immer um dasselbe Thema** *(fig.)* his thoughts always revolved around the same subject; **b)** *(Sport)* **die Arme** ~ **lassen** swing one's arms round [in a circle]

kreis-, Kreis-: ~**fläche die** *(Geom.)* area of a/the circle; ~**förmig 1.** *Adj.* circular; **2.** *adv.* **ein** ~**förmig gebogenes Stück Draht** a piece of wire bent into a circle; ~**frei** *Adj. (Amtsspr.)* **eine** ~**freie Stadt** a town that is administered as a district in its own right; ~**klasse die** *(Sport)* district league; ~**kolben·motor der** *s.* **Wankelmotor;** ~**lauf der a)** *(der Natur, der Wirtschaft, des Lebens usw.)* cycle; *(des Geldes; Technik)* circulation; **b)** *(Physiol.)* circulation; ~**läufer der** *(Hallenhandball) s.* ~**spieler;** ~**lauf·kollaps der** *(Med.)* circulatory collapse; ~**lauf·mittel das a)** remedy to prevent faintness; **b)** *(Med.)* circulatory preparation; *(den* ~*lauf anregend)* circulatory stimulant; ~**lauf·störung die a)** *bes. im Pl.* faintness; **b)** *(Med.)* cardio-vascular disorder; circulatory disturbance; ~**lauf·störungen** *Pl.* circulatory trouble *sing.*; ~**leitung die** *(DDR)* district committee; ~**linie die** *(Geom.)* circumference [of a/the circle]; ~**ring der** *(Geom.)* annulus; ~**rund 1.** *Adj.* [perfectly] circular *or* round; **2.** *adv.* ⟨*bent etc.*⟩ in[to] a [perfect] circle; ~**säge die a)** *(Werkzeug)* circular saw; **b)** *(ugs. scherzh.: Strohhut)* boater

kreißen ['kraisn̩] *itr. V. (veralt.)* be in labour

Kreis·spieler der *(Hallenhandball)* pivot player

Kreiß·saal der *(Med.)* delivery room

Kreis-: ~**stadt die** chief town of a/the district; ~**tag der** district assembly; ~**verkehr der** traffic on *or* going round a/the roundabout; *(Platz)* roundabout; ~**verwaltung die** administration of a/the district; *(Behörde)* district authority; ~**wehrersatz·amt das** district recruiting office; ~**zahl die** *(Math.)* pi *no art.*

Krem [kre:m] **die;** ~, ~s *s.* **Creme**

Krematorium [krema'to:riʊm] **das;** ~s, **Krematorien** crematorium

kremig *s.* **cremig**

Kreml ['krɛml] **der;** ~s Kremlin
Krempe ['krɛmpə] **die;** ~, ~n brim
[1]**Krempel** ['krɛmpl] **der;** ~s *(ugs. abwertend)* stuff; *(Gerümpel)* junk; **den ganzen ~ hinwerfen** *(fig.)* chuck the whole thing in *(coll.)*
[2]**Krempel die;** ~, ~n *(Textilind.)* carding machine
[1]**krempeln** *tr. V.* roll
[2]**krempeln** *tr. V. (Textilind.)* card
Kremser ['krɛmzɐ] **der;** ~s, ~ *(veralt.)* [covered] charabanc *(Brit. dated)*
Kren [kre:n] **der;** ~[e]s *(südd., bes. österr.) s.* **Meerrettich**
Kreole [kre'o:lə] **der;** ~n, ~n, **Kreolin die;** ~, ~nen Creole
kreolisch *Adj.* Creole
krepieren [kre'pi:rən] *itr. V.; mit sein* **a)** *(zerplatzen)* explode; go off; **b)** *(salopp: sterben)* ‹*animal*› die; ‹*person*› snuff it *(sl.)*
Krepp [krɛp] **der;** ~s, ~s *od.* ~e crêpe
Kreppapier das crêpe paper
Krepp-: ~papier *s.* **Kreppapier; ~sohle die** crêpe sole
Kresse ['krɛsə] **die;** ~, ~n *(Bot.)* cress
Kreta ['kre:ta] **(das);** ~s Crete
Kreter ['kre:tɐ] **der;** ~s, ~, **Kreterin die;** ~, ~nen Cretan
Krethi und Plethi *o. Art., o. Gen.; Pl., auch Sg. (abwertend)* every Tom, Dick and Harry *sing.*
Kretin [kre'tɛ̃:] **der;** ~s, ~s **a)** *(Med.)* cretin; **b)** *(fig. abwertend)* imbecile
Kretinismus [kreti'nɪsmʊs] **der;** ~ *(Med.)* cretinism *no art.*
kreucht [krɔyçt] *in* **alles, was da ~ und fleucht** all living creatures *or* things
kreuz: ~ **und quer durch die Stadt fahren** drive all over/round the town; **in die Kreuz und [in die] Quere fahren** drive all over the place
Kreuz [krɔyts] **das;** ~es, ~e **a)** cross; *(Symbol)* cross; crucifix; **etw. über ~ legen/falten** lay sth. down/fold sth. crosswise; **das ~ des Südens** *(Astron.)* the Southern Cross; **zu ~e kriechen** humble oneself; *s. auch* **eisern 1 a; rot 1; b)** *(hist.)* cross; **jmdn. ans ~ schlagen** *od.* **nageln** nail sb. to the cross; **c)** *(Kreuzzeichen)* sign of the cross; **das/ein ~ schlagen** make the sign of the cross; *(sich bekreuzigen)* cross oneself; **drei ~e machen** *(ugs.)* heave a sigh of relief; **d)** *o. Pl. (Leid)* cross; **sein ~ auf sich nehmen/tragen** take up/bear one's cross; **es ist ein ~ mit jmdm./etw.** *(ugs.)* sb. is a real strain *or* is really trying/sth. is a real problem; **e)** *(Teil des Rückens)* small of the back; **ein steifes ~ haben** have a stiff back; **Schmerzen im ~:** pain in the small of the back; **ich hab's im ~** *(ugs.)* I've got back trouble *or* a bad back; **jmdn. aufs ~ legen** *(salopp)* take sb. for a ride *(sl.)*; **eine Frau aufs ~ legen** *(salopp: mit ihr schlafen)* lay a woman *(sl.)*; **fast** *od.* **beinahe aufs ~ fallen** *(fig.)* almost fall through the floor; **jmdm. etw. aus dem ~ leiern** *(salopp)* talk sb. into handing sth. over; **f)** *o. Art., o. Pl. (Kartenspiel) (Farbe)* clubs *pl.*; *(Karte)* club; *s. auch* [2]**Pik; h)** *(Autobahn)* interchange; **i)** *(Musik)* sharp
kreuz-, Kreuz-: ~abnahme die *(bild. Kunst)* Descent *or* Deposition from the Cross; **~as das** ace of clubs; **~band das** *(Anat.)* cruciate ligament; **~bein das** *(Anat.)* sacrum; **~blume die a)** *(Bot.)* milkwort; **b)** *(Archit.)* finial; **~blütler der** *(Bot.)* cruciferous plant; crucifer; **~brav** *Adj.* thoroughly good and honest ‹*person*›; very good *or* well-behaved ‹*child*›; **~bube der** jack of clubs; **~dame die** queen of clubs
kreuzen 1. *tr. V. (auch Biol.)* cross; **die Arme/Beine [übereinander] ~:** cross *or* fold one's arms/cross one's legs; *s. auch* **Klinge b. 2.** *refl. V.* **a)** *(überschneiden)* cross; intersect; **ihre Wege ~ sich** *(fig.)* their paths cross; **ihre Blicke ~ sich** *(fig.)* their eyes meet; **b)** *(zuwiderlaufen)* clash **(mit** with). **3.** *itr. V.* **a)** *mit haben od. sein (hin und her fahren)* cruise; **b)** *(Seemannsspr.)* tack
Kreuzer der; ~s, ~ **a)** *(Milit.: Kriegsschiff)* cruiser; **b)** *(Segelsport)* cruising yacht; cruiser; **c)** *(hist.: Münze)* kreuzer
Kreuzes·tod der [death by] crucifixion; **den ~ sterben** die on the cross
kreuz-, Kreuz-: ~fahrer der *(hist.)* crusader; **~fahrt die a)** *(Seereise)* cruise; **eine ~fahrt machen** go on a cruise; **b)** *(hist.) s.* **~zug; ~feuer das** *(Milit., auch fig.)* crossfire; **etw. unter ~feuer nehmen** direct crossfire at sth.; **im ~feuer stehen** be under fire from all sides; **ins ~feuer geraten** come under fire from all sides; **~fidel** *Adj. (ugs.) (sehr gut gelaunt)* very cheerful; *(sehr lustig)* very jolly; **~förmig 1.** *Adj.* cross-shaped; cruciform; **2.** *adv.* ‹*built, arranged, etc.*› in the shape of a cross; **~gang der** cloister; **~gelenk das** *s.* **Kardangelenk; ~gewölbe das** *(Archit.)* cross vault; **~griff der** *(Turnen)* cross grip; **~hacke die** pickaxe
kreuzigen ['krɔytsɪgn̩] *tr. V.* crucify; **der Gekreuzigte** Christ crucified
Kreuzigung die; ~, ~en **a)** *(das Kreuzigen)* crucifixion; **b)** *(bild. Kunst)* Crucifixion
kreuz-, Kreuz-: ~knoten der *(Seemannsspr.)* reef-knot; **~könig der** king of clubs; **~lahm** *Adj.* broken-backed ‹*horse etc.*›; **ich bin ganz ~lahm** *(ugs.)* my back is killing me *(coll.)*; **~mast der** *(Seemannsspr.)* mizen-mast; **~otter die** adder; [common] viper; **~reim der** *(Verslehre)* alternate rhyme; **~rippen·gewölbe das** *(Archit.)* ribbed vault; **~ritter der** *(hist.)* **a)** crusader; **b)** *(vom deutschen Ritterorden)* Teutonic Knight; knight of the Teutonic Order; **~schlitz·schraube die** Phillips screw **(P); ~schlitz·schrauben·dreher der** Phillips screwdriver **(P); ~schlüssel der** four-way wheel-brace; **~schmerzen** *Pl.* pain *sing.* in the small of the back; **~schnabel der** *(Zool.)* crossbill; **~spinne die** cross spider; garden spider; **~stich der** *(Handarb.)* cross-stitch
Kreuzung die; ~, ~en **a)** junction; crossroads *sing.*; **b)** *(Biol.)* crossing; crossbreeding; *(Ergebnis)* cross; cross-breed; **eine ~ aus** *od.* **von ... und ...:** a cross between ... and ...
kreuz·unglücklich *Adj. (ugs.)* terribly miserable *(coll.)*
kreuzungs·frei *Adj. (Verkehrsw.)* without [any] junctions *postpos.*
Kreuzungs·punkt der junction; *(von Autobahnen)* intersection
kreuz-, Kreuz-: ~verband der *(Bauw.)* English cross bond; **~verhör das** cross-examination; **jmdn. ins ~verhör nehmen** *(fig.)* cross-examine sb.; **~weg der a)** *(Wegkreuzung)* crossroads *sing.*; **am ~weg stehen/an einen ~weg gekommen sein** *(geh.)* stand *or* be at/have reached a crossroads; **b)** *(kath. Kirche: Darstellung, Gebete)* stations of the Cross, way of the Cross; **~weise** *Adv.* crosswise; crossways; **du kannst mich mal ~weise!** *(derb)* [you can] get stuffed! *(sl.)*; **~wort·rätsel das** crossword [puzzle]; **~zeichen das** *(bes. kath. Kirche)* sign of the cross; **das ~zeichen machen** make the sign of the cross; *(sich bekreuzigen)* cross oneself; **~zug der a)** *(hist.)* crusade; **b)** *(Kampagne)* crusade
Krevette [kre'vɛtə] **die;** ~, ~n palaemon prawn; leander
kribbelig *Adj. (ugs.)* **a)** *(vor Ungeduld)* fidgety; *(nervös)* edgy; **b)** *(kribbelnd)* **ein ~es Gefühl in der Hand** pins and needles in one's hand
kribbeln ['krɪbl̩n] *itr. V.* **a)** *(jucken)* tickle; *(prickeln)* tingle; **es kribbelt mir** *od.* **mich in der Nase/in den Füßen/unter der Haut** I've got a tickle in my nose/my feet are tingling *or* I've got pins and needles in my feet/my skin is itching *or* prickling; **es kribbelt mir in den Fingern, es zu tun** *(fig.)* I'm just itching to do it; **b)** *(wimmeln)* swarm [about]; **in dem Ameisenhaufen kribbelte und krabbelte** es the ants were swarming about in the anthill
kribblig *s.* **kribbelig**
Krickelkrakel ['krɪkl̩krakl̩] **das;** ~s *(ugs.)* scribble; scrawl
Kricket ['krɪkət] **das;** ~s cricket
Krida ['kri:da] **die;** ~ *(österr. Rechtsw.)* fraudulent bankruptcy; *(fahrlässig)* bankruptcy through negligence
kriechen ['kri:çn̩] *unr. itr. V.* **a)** *mit sein* ‹*insect, baby*› crawl; ‹*plant*› creep; ‹*person, animal*› creep, crawl; ‹*car, train, etc.*› crawl *or* creep [along]; **aus dem Ei/der Puppe ~:** hatch [out]/emerge from the chrysalis; **~de Pflanzen** creepers; **erschöpft ins Bett ~:** crawl exhausted into bed; **auf allen vieren/auf dem Bauch ~:** crawl on all fours/crawl [along] on one's stomach; **die Zeit/der Zeiger kriecht** *(fig.)* time creeps by/the hand creeps [around the dial]; *s. auch* **Kreuz a; b)** *mit sein (ugs.: sich fortbewegen)* walk; get about; **kaum noch ~ können** hardly be able to get about *or* walk; *(alt und gebrechlich sein)* be old and decrepit; **c)** *auch mit sein (abwertend: sich unterwürfig verhalten)* crawl, grovel **(vor + Dat.** to)
Kriecher der; ~s, ~ *(abwertend)* crawler; groveller
kriecherisch *Adj. (abwertend)* crawling; grovelling
Kriech-: ~spur die *(Verkehrsw.)* crawler lane; **~strom der** *(Elektrot.)* leakage current; **~tempo das** *(abwertend)* **im ~tempo** at a snail's pace; **~tier das** *(Zool.)* reptile
Krieg [kri:k] **der;** ~[e]s, ~e war; *(~sführung)* warfare; **[gegen jmdn.] ~ führen** wage war [on sb.]; **einem Land den ~ erklären** declare war on a country; **sich im ~ befinden** *od.* **im ~ stehen [mit ...]** be at war [with ...]; **in den ~ ziehen** go to war; **im ~ bleiben** *od.* **fallen** be killed in the war; **der kalte ~:** the cold war
kriegen *tr. V. (ugs.)* **a)** *(bekommen)* get; **noch Geld von jmdm. ~:** be owed money by sb.; **Bescheid ~:** be told; **Schläge** *od.* **sie ~:** get a good hiding *(coll.) or* beating; **du kriegst gleich eine/ein paar!** I'll clout you in a moment!; **ein Jahr [Gefängnis] ~:** get a *or* one year [in prison]; **einen Schnupfen ~:** catch [a] cold; **Besuch ~:** have a visitor/visitors; **seinen Willen ~:** get one's own way; **ich kriege keine Verbindung** *od.* **keinen Anschluß** I can't get through; **am Ende des Films ~ sie sich** at the end of the film boy gets girl; **was ~ Sie?** what can I get you?; **ein Baby/Kind ~:** have a baby/child; **Junge ~:** have puppies/kittens *etc.*; **jmdn. dazu ~, etw. zu tun** get sb. to do sth.; **er ist nicht aus dem Haus** *od.* **vor die Tür zu ~:** nothing will get him out of the house *or* front door; **jmdn. satt/frei ~:** feed sb./get sb. free; **wir werden das** *od.* **es schon ~:** we'll soon sort it out; *s. auch* **genug; Motte a; zuviel 1 a; b)** *(befallen werden)* get; **die Wut/Angst/einen Schrecken ~:** get angry scared/have *or* get a shock; **Hunger/Durst ~:** get hungry/thirsty; **Heimweh/Fernweh ~:** get homesick/start suffering from wanderlust; **einen roten Kopf ~:** go red; blush; **Falten/eine Glatze ~:** get wrinkles/go bald; **c)** *(erreichen)* catch ‹*train, bus, etc.*›; **d)** *(fangen)* catch; **e)** + *Inf. mit „zu" (die Möglichkeit haben)* **etw. zu essen ~:** get sth. to eat; **er kriegte den Ast zu fassen** he was able to *or* he managed to grab hold of the branch; **f)** + *Inf. mit „zu" (ertragen müssen)* **etw. zu spüren/hören ~:** feel the force of sth./get a good talking-to; **es mit jmdm. zu tun ~:** have sb. to reckon with; **g)** + *2. Part.* **etw. geschenkt ~:** get sth. as a present; **ein gutes Essen vorgesetzt ~:** get served with a good meal; **h)** *in* **es nicht über sich ~, etw. zu tun** *(ugs.)* not be able to bring oneself to do sth.

Krieger der; ~s, ~: warrior; *(nordamerikanischer Indianer)* brave; **die alten ~:** the veterans; **ein müder ~** *(fig.)* a tired old thing

Krieger·denkmal das *(veralt.)* war memorial

kriegerisch *Adj.* **a)** *(kampflustig)* warlike; **b)** *nicht präd. (militärisch)* military; **eine ~e Auseinandersetzung** an armed conflict

Krieger·witwe die war widow

krieg·führend *Adj.; nicht präd.* warring; belligerent

Krieg·führung die warfare *no art.; (Leitung)* conduct of the war

kriegs-, Kriegs-: ~anleihe die war loan; **~aus·bruch der** outbreak of war; **bei/vor ~ausbruch** at/before the outbreak of war; **~bedingt** *Adj.* caused by the war *postpos.;* **~beginn der;** *o. Pl.* beginning *or* start of the war; **~beil das** tomahawk; **das ~beil ausgraben/begraben** *(scherzh.)* start fighting/bury the hatchet; **~bemalung die** *(Völkerk.)* war-paint; **in voller ~bemalung** *(scherzh.)* in full war-paint; **~berichterstatter der** war correspondent; **~berichterstattung die** war reporting *no art.;* **~beschädigt** *Adj.* war-disabled; **~beschädigte der/die** war-disabled person; war invalid; **~beute die** spoils *pl.* of war; **~blinde der/die** person blinded in the war; **~dienst der a)** *(im Krieg)* active service; **b)** *(Wehrdienst)* military service; **den ~dienst verweigern** be a conscientious objector; **~dienst·verweigerer der** conscientious objector; **~dienst·verweigerung die** conscientious objection; **~einwirkung die: infolge von ~einwirkungen** as a result of the war; **~ende das** end of the war; **bei/vor ~ende** at/before the end of the war; **~entschädigung die** reparations *pl.;* **~entscheidend** *Adj.* decisive for the outcome of the war *postpos.;* **~erklärung die** declaration of war; **~erlebnis das** wartime experience; **~fall der: im ~fall[e]** in the event of war; **~film der** war film; **~flagge die** naval ensign; **~flotte die** navy; fleet; **~freiwillige der** [war] volunteer; **~führung die** *s.* **Kriegführung; ~fuß der** *in* **mit jmdm. auf [dem] ~fuß stehen** *od.* **leben** *(scherzh.)* be at loggerheads with sb.; **mit etw. auf [dem] ~fuß stehen** *(scherzh.)* be totally lost when it comes to sth.; **~gebiet das** war zone; **~gefahr die;** *o. Pl.* danger of war; **~gefangen** *Adj.* captured; **~gefangene der** prisoner of war; POW; **~gefangenschaft die** captivity; **in ~gefangenschaft sein/geraten** be a prisoner of war/be taken prisoner; **aus der ~gefangenschaft entlassen werden** be released from captivity; **~gegner der a)** *(Gegner im Krieg)* enemy; **b)** *(Gegner des Krieges)* opponent of the/a war; *(Pazifist)* opponent of war; **~gericht das** court martial; **jmdn. vor ein ~gericht stellen** court-martial sb.; **~geschrei das** war cries *pl.;* **~gewinnler** [~gəvınlɐ] **der; ~s, ~** *(abwertend)* war profiteer; **~glück das** *(geh.)* fortune *or* luck in war; **~gott der** *(Myth.)* god of war; **~gräber·fürsorge die a)** care of war graves; **b)** *(Institution)* war graves commission; **~greuel der** wartime atrocity; **~hafen der** naval port; **~handwerk das** *(geh. veralt.)* art of warfare; **~held der** *(geh.)* war hero; **~herr der** *(geh. veralt.)* commander; **oberster ~herr** supreme commander; commander-in-chief; **~hetze die;** *o. Pl. (abwertend)* warmongering; **~hetze betreiben** stir up war; **~hinterbliebene der/die** war orphan/widow; **die ~hinterbliebenen** war widows and orphans; **~industrie die** armaments industry; **~invalide der** war-disabled person; war invalid; **~jahr das: im ersten/dritten ~jahr** in the first/third year of the war; **während der ~jahre/der letzten ~jahre** during the war years/the last years of the war; **~kamerad der** wartime comrade; **~knecht der** *(veralt.)* soldier; *(Söldner)* mercenary; **~kunst die** *(geh., veralt.)* art of war *or* warfare; **~list die** military stratagem; *(fig. scherzh.)* ruse; **~lüstern** *Adj.* bellicose; warlike; **~marine die** navy; **~maschine die** *(hist.)* engine [of war]; **~maschinerie die** *(abwertend)* machinery of war; **~minister der** *(hist.)* minister of *or* for war; **~ministerium das** *(hist.)* war ministry; *(in Großbritannien)* War Office *(Hist.);* **~müde** *Adj.* war-weary; **~opfer das** war victim; **~pfad der** *in* **auf dem ~pfad** *(auch fig.)* on the war-path; **~propaganda die** wartime propaganda; **~rat der** *in* **~rat [ab]halten** *(scherzh.)* have a pow-wow; **~recht das;** *o. Pl.* **a)** laws *pl.* of war; **b) das ~recht verhängen** impose martial law; **~schaden der** *(bes. Amtsspr.)* war damage *no art.;* **~schäden** *Pl.* war damage *sing., no art.;* **~schau·platz der** theatre of war; **~schiff das** warship; **~schuld die** war guilt; **~schulden** *Pl.* war debts; **~spiel das a)** *(Milit.)* war game; **b)** *(Kinderspiel)* [game of] soldiers *sing.;* **~spiel·zeug das** war toys *pl.; (einzelnes)* war toy; **~stärke die;** *o. Pl.* wartime strength; **~tanz der** *(Völkerk.)* war-dance; **~tauglich** *Adj.* fit for active service *postpos.;* **~teilnehmer der** combatant; *(ehemaliger Soldat)* ex-serviceman; war veteran *(Amer.);* **~trauung die** war-marriage; **~treiber der** *(abwertend)* war-monger; **~untauglich** *Adj.* unfit for active service *postpos.;* **~verbrechen das** *(Rechtsw.)* war crime; **~verbrecher der** war criminal; **~verbrecher·prozeß der** war crimes trial; **~verbündet** *Adj.* co-belligerent; **~verbündete der** co-belligerent; **~verletzung die** war wound *or* injury; **~versehrt** *Adj.: s.* **~beschädigt; ~versehrte der/die** *s.* **~beschädigte; ~verwendungs·fähig** *Adj. (Amtsspr.)* fit for active service *postpos.;* **~waise die** war orphan; **~wichtig** *Adj.* essential to the war effort *postpos.;* **~wirren** *Pl.* chaos *sing.* of war; **~wirtschaft die** war[time] economy; **~zeit die** wartime; **in ~zeiten** *Pl.* in wartime; **~ziel das** war aim; aim of a/the war; **~zu·stand der** state of war; **sich im ~zustand befinden** be at war

Krill [krıl] **der; ~[e]s** krill

Krim [krım] **die; ~: die ~:** the Crimea

Krimi ['kri:mi] **der; ~[s], ~[s]** *(ugs.)* **a)** *(Film, Stück)* crime thriller; whodunit *(coll.); (fig.: Fußballspiel, Quizsendung usw.)* thriller; cliff-hanger; **b)** *(Roman)* crime thriller; whodunit *(coll.); (mit Detektiv als Held)* detective story

Kriminal·beamte [krimi'na:l-] **der** [plain-clothes] detective

Kriminale der; *adj. Dekl.,* **Kriminaler der; ~s, ~** *(ugs.)* detective

Kriminal-: ~fall der criminal case; crime; **~film der** crime film *or* thriller; **~gericht das** *(veralt.) s.* **Strafgericht; ~hör·spiel das** radio crime thriller

kriminalisieren *tr. V.* **a)** *(kriminell machen)* **jmdn. ~:** make sb. turn to crime; **b)** *(als kriminell hinstellen)* **jmdn./etw. ~:** present sb. as a criminal/sth. as [being] criminal *or* a criminal act

Kriminalist der; ~en, ~en detective

Kriminalistik die; ~: criminalistics *sing., no art.*

kriminalistisch 1. *Adj.* ⟨*methods, practice*⟩ of criminalistics; ⟨*abilities*⟩ in the field of criminalistics. **2.** *adv.* ⟨*proceed etc.*⟩ using the methods of criminalistics

Kriminalität [kriminali'tɛ:t] **die; ~ a)** crime *no art.;* **ein Absinken der ~:** a drop in the level of crime *or* in the crime rate; **b)** *(Straffälligkeit)* criminality

Kriminal-: ~kommissar der ≈ detective superintendent; **~komödie die** comedy thriller; **~polizei die** criminal investigation department; **~roman der** crime novel *or* thriller; *(mit Detektiv als Held)* detective novel

kriminell [krimi'nɛl] **1.** *Adj. (auch ugs.: rücksichtslos)* criminal; **~ werden/sein** become a criminal *or* turn to crime/be a criminal. **2.** *adv.* **a) ~ veranlagt sein** have criminal tendencies; **~ handeln** act illegally; break the law; **b)** *(ugs.: rücksichtslos)* criminally; ⟨*drive*⟩ with criminal recklessness

Kriminelle der/die; *adj. Dekl.* criminal

Kriminologie [kriminolo'gi:] **die** criminology *no art.*

Krim·krieg ['krım-] **der; ~[e]s** Crimean War

Krimskrams ['krımskrams] **der; ~[es]** *(ugs.)* stuff; **einigen ~ kaufen** buy a few bits and pieces

Kringel ['krıŋl̩] **der; ~s, ~ a)** *(Kreis)* [small] ring; *(Kritzelei)* round squiggle; **b)** *(Gebäck)* [ring-shaped] biscuit; ring

kringelig *Adj.* crinkly ⟨*hair*⟩; squiggly ⟨*shape, line, etc.*⟩; **sich ~ lachen** *(ugs.)* laugh one's head off; kill oneself [laughing] *(coll.)*

kringeln 1. *tr. V.* curl [up] ⟨*tail*⟩; **jmds. Haar ~:** curl sb.'s hair; ⟨*wind, rain*⟩ make sb.'s hair go curly. **2.** *refl. V.* curl [up]; ⟨*hair*⟩ go curly; **sich [vor Lachen] ~** *(ugs.)* laugh one's head off; kill oneself [laughing] *(coll.)*

Krinoline [krino'li:nə] **die; ~, ~n** *(hist.)* crinoline

Kripo ['kri:po] **die; ~** *(ugs.)* **die ~:** ≈ the CID

Krippe ['krıpə] **die; ~, ~n a)** *(Futtertrog)* manger; crib; *s. auch* **Futterkrippe; b)** *(Weihnachten)* model of a nativity scene; crib; **c)** *(Kinder~)* crèche; day nursery

Krippen·spiel das nativity play

Kris [kri:s] **der; ~es, ~e** kris

Krise ['kri:zə] **die; ~, ~n** *(auch Med.)* crisis; **eine ~ durchmachen/überwinden** go through/overcome a crisis; **in eine ~ geraten** enter a state of crisis

kriseln ['kri:zl̩n] *itr. V. (unpers.)* **es kriselt in ihrer Ehe/in der Partei** *(eine Krise droht)* their marriage is running into trouble/there is a crisis looming in the party; *(eine Krise ist vorhanden)* their marriage is in trouble/the party is in a state of crisis

krisen-, Krisen-: ~anfällig *Adj.* crisis-prone; **~fest** *Adj.* that is/are unaffected by crises *postpos., not pred.;* **~fest sein** be unaffected by crises; **~gebiet das** crisis area; **~herd der** trouble spot; **~management das** crisis management; **~stab der** crisis team

Krisis ['kri:zıs] **die; ~, Krisen** *(veralt., Med.) s.* **Krise**

[1]Kristall [krıs'tal] **der; ~s, ~e** crystal

[2]Kristall das; ~s a) *(Material)* crystal *no indef. art.;* **Gläser aus ~:** crystal glasses; **b)** *(Gegenstände)* crystal *no indef. art.*

Kristall·bildung die *s.* **Kristallisation**

kristallen *Adj.; nicht präd.* crystal

Kristalleuchter der crystal chandelier

Kristall-: ~gitter das *(Chemie)* crystal lattice; **~glas das a)** crystal glass; **b)** *(Bleikristall)* crystal

kristallin [krısta'li:n] *Adj. (bes. Mineral.)* crystalline

Kristallisation [krıstaliza'tsi̯o:n] **die; ~, ~en** *(bes. Chemie)* crystallization

kristallisieren *(bes. Chemie)* **1.** *itr. V.* crystallize. **2.** *refl. V. (auch fig.)* crystallize

kristall-, Kristall-: ~klar *Adj. (auch fig.)* crystal-clear; **~leuchter** *s.* **Kristalleuchter; ~lüster** *s.* **Kristallüster; ~nacht die** *(ns.)* crystal night; kristallnacht; *National Socialist pogrom against Jews in November 1938;* **~schale die** crystal bowl

Kristallüster der *(veralt.)* crystal chandelier

Kristall-: ~waren *Pl.* crystal [glass] *sing.;* **~zucker der** *(bes. fachspr.)* refined sugar in crystals

Kriterium [kri'te:ri̯ʊm] **das; ~s, Kriterien a)** criterion; **b)** *(bes. Skisport)* race; **c)** *(Radsport)* criterium
Kritik [kri'ti:k] **die; ~, ~en a)** criticism *no indef. art.* **(an** + *Dat.* of); **an jmdm./etw. ~ üben** criticize sb./sth.; **auf ~ stoßen** meet with *or* come in for criticism; **unter aller** *od.* **jeder ~ sein** *(ugs.)* be absolutely hopeless; **b)** *(Besprechung)* review; notice; **eine gute/schlechte ~** *od.* **gute/schlechte ~en bekommen** get good/bad reviews *or* notices; **c)** *o. Pl. (die Kritiker)* critics *pl.*; reviewers *pl.*; **d)** *(Philos., Analyse)* critique
Kritikaster [kriti'kastɐ] **der; ~s, ~** *(geh. abwertend)* criticaster; caviller
Kritiker ['kri:tikɐ] **der; ~s, ~, Kritikerin die; ~, ~nen** critic
Kritik·fähigkeit die critical faculties *pl.*
kritik·los 1. *Adj.* uncritical; **2.** *adv.* uncritically; **etw. ~ hinnehmen** accept sth. without criticism
kritisch ['kri:tɪʃ] **1.** *Adj.* **a)** *(auch Kernphysik)* critical; **ein ~er Apparat** *(Wissensch.)* critical apparatus; **eine ~e Ausgabe** *(Wissensch.)* a critical edition; **b)** *(entscheidend)* critical; **~er Punkt** *(Skisport)* critical point; **~e Temperatur** *(Physik, Chemie)* critical temperature. **2.** *adv.* critically; **sich mit etw. ~ auseinandersetzen** make a critical study of sth.; **jmdm./etw. ~ gegenüberstehen** be critical of sb./sth.
kritisieren [kriti'zi:rən] *tr. V.* criticize; review ⟨*book, play, etc.*⟩; **immer etw. zu ~ haben** always find sth. to criticize
Kritizismus [kriti'tsɪsmʊs] **der; ~** *(Philos.)* critical philosophy
Krittelei die; ~, ~en *(abwertend)* fault-finding; carping
kritteln ['krɪtl̩n] *itr. V. (abwertend)* find fault **(an** + *Dat.*, **über** + *Akk.* with); carp **(an** + *Dat.*, **über** + *Akk.* at)
Kritzelei die; ~, ~en a) *o. Pl. (das Schreiben)* scribbling; *(das Zeichnen)* doodling; **b)** *(Schrift)* scribble; *(Zeichnung)* doodle; *(an Wänden)* graffiti *sing. or pl.*
kritzeln ['krɪtsl̩n] **1.** *itr. V. (schreiben)* scribble; *(zeichnen)* doodle. **2.** *tr. V.* scribble; **etw. auf/in etw.** *(Akk.)* **~:** scribble sth. on/in sth.
Kroate [kro'a:tə] **der; ~n, ~n** Croat; Croatian
Kroatien [kro'a:tsi̯ən] **(das)** Croatia
Kroatin die; ~, ~nen *s.* **Kroate**; *s. auch* **-in**
kroatisch *Adj.* Croatian
Kroatz·beere [kro'ats-] **die; ~, ~n** *(ostmd.) s.* **Brombeere**
kroch *1. u. 3. Pers. Sg. Prät. v.* **kriechen**
Krocket ['krɔkət] **das; ~s** croquet
Krokant [kro'kant] **der; ~s** praline
Krokette [kro'kɛtə] **die; ~, ~n** *(Kochk.)* croquette
Kroki [kro'ki:] **das; ~s, ~s** sketch-map; *(künstlerische Skizze)* sketch
Kroko ['kro:ko] **das; ~[s]** crocodile [leather]
Krokodil [kroko'di:l] **das; ~s, ~e** crocodile
Krokodil·leder das crocodile skin *or* leather
Krokodils·tränen *Pl. (ugs.)* crocodile tears
Kroko·tasche die crocodile[-skin] [hand]bag
Krokus ['kro:kʊs] **der; ~, ~** *od.* **~se** crocus
Krönchen ['krø:nçən] **das; ~s, ~:** small crown; *(einer Welle)* small crest
Krone ['kro:nə] **die; ~, ~n a)** crown; *(kleinere, eines Herzogs, eines Grafen)* coronet; **einer Sache** *(Dat.)***/allem die ~ aufsetzen** cap sth./cap it all; **das setzt doch allem die ~ auf** that beats everything; **jmdm. in die ~ steigen** *(ugs.)* go to sb.'s head; **einen in der ~ haben** *(ugs.)* have had a drop too much *(coll.)*; **die ~** *(fig.: Herrscherhaus)* the Crown; **dir wird keine Perle** *od.* **kein Stein aus der ~ fallen, wenn du uns mal hilfst** *(ugs.)* it won't hurt you to help us occasionally; **b)** *(Spitze) (eines Baumes)* top; crown; *(einer Welle)* crest; **c)** *o. Pl. (das Beste)* **die ~ der Schöpfung/meiner Sammlung** the pride of creation/my collection; **die ~ der Literatur** the highest form of literature; **d)** *(Zahnmed.)* crown; **e)** *(Jägerspr.) (beim Hirsch)* surroyals *pl.*; surroyal antlers *pl.*; *(beim Rehbock)* antlers *pl.*; **f)** *(Rad an Uhren)* winder; [winding] crown; **g)** *(Währungseinheit) (hist.)* crown; *(in Schweden, Island)* krona; *(in Dänemark, Norwegen)* krone; *(in der Tschechoslowakei)* koruna
krönen ['krø:nən] *tr. V.* **a)** crown; **jmdn. zum König/Kaiser ~:** crown sb. king/emperor; **gekrönte Häupter** crowned heads; **b)** *(den Höhepunkt bilden)* crown; **von Erfolg gekrönt sein** *od.* **werden** be crowned with success; **der ~de Abschluß** the culmination; **c)** *(oben abschließen)* crown
Kronen-: ~korken der crown cap *or* cork; **~mutter die** castle nut; castellated nut
Kron-: ~erbe der *s.* **Thronfolger; ~gut das** royal demesne; **~juwel das** *od.* **der;** *meist Pl.* **a) die ~juwelen** the crown jewels; **b)** *(fig.)* gem; **~kolonie die** crown colony; **~land das** *(österr. hist.)* crownland; **~leuchter der** chandelier; **~prinz der** crown prince; **~prinzessin die** crown princess
Krönung die; ~, ~en a) coronation; **b)** *(Höhepunkt)* culmination
Kron·zeuge der *(Rechtsw.)* person who turns Queen's/King's evidence; **als ~ auftreten** turn Queen's/King's evidence
Kropf [krɔpf] **der; ~[e]s, Kröpfe** ['krœpfə] **a)** *(Med.)* goitre; **b)** *(von Vögeln)* crop
Kropf·taube die pouter
Kroppzeug ['krɔp-] **das; ~s** *(ugs. abwertend)* **a)** *(Gesindel)* rabble; riff-raff; **b)** *(unnützes Zeug)* junk
kroß [krɔs] *(nordd.) Adj.: s.* **knusprig**
Krösus ['krø:zʊs] **der; ~** *od.* **~ses, ~se** *(oft scherzh.)* Croesus; **ich bin doch kein ~:** I'm not made of money
Kröte ['krø:tə] **die; ~, ~n a)** toad; **b)** *Pl. (salopp: Geld)* **ein paar/eine ganze Menge ~n verdienen** earn a few bob *(Brit. sl.)*/a fair old whack *(sl.)*; **meine letzten paar ~n** my last few bob *(Brit. sl.)*/bucks *(Amer. sl.)*; **c)** *(ugs. scherzh.: Kind)* **du kleine ~:** you little rascal; **eine süße kleine ~:** a sweet little thing; **d)** *(abwertend: Mensch)* creature
Kröten·test der *(Med.) s.* **Froschtest**
Krücke ['krʏkə] **die; ~, ~n a)** *(Stock)* crutch; **an** *od.* **auf ~n** *(Dat.)* **gehen** walk on crutches; **b)** *(Griff)* crook; handle; **c)** *(ugs. abwertend) (Versager)* dead loss *(coll.)*; wash-out *(sl.)*; *(Gegenstand)* dead loss *(coll.)*; **meine ~ von Auto** my old junk-heap of a car *(sl.)*
Krück·stock der walking-stick; *s. auch* **Blinde**
krude ['kru:də] **1.** *Adj.* rude. **2.** *adv.* rudely
Krug [kru:k] **der; ~[e]s, Krüge** ['kry:gə] **a)** *(Gefäß für Flüssigkeiten)* jug; *(größer)* pitcher; *(Bier~)* mug; *(aus Ton)* mug; stein; *(Honig~)* jar; pot; **der ~ geht so lange zum Brunnen, bis er bricht** *(Spr.)* one day you'll come unstuck; you'll try it once too often; **b)** *(bes. nordd.: Wirtshaus)* inn
Kruke ['kru:kə] **die; ~, ~n** *(bes. nordd.)* **a)** *(Krug)* [earthenware] jug; *(zum Einlegen usw.)* [earthenware] jar; *(größer)* [earthenware] pitcher; **b)** *(kauziger Mensch)* **eine seltsame** *od.* **schrullige ~:** a queer fish
Krüll·schnitt ['krʏl-] **der** shag
Krümchen ['kry:mçən] **das; ~s, ~:** [tiny] crumb; **ein ~ Erde** a grain of soil
Krume ['kru:mə] **die; ~, ~n a)** crumb; **b)** *s.* **Ackerkrume**
Krümel ['kry:ml̩] **der; ~s, ~ a)** crumb; **ein ~ Zucker** a grain of sugar; **b)** *(scherzh.: kleines Kind)* little one
krümelig *Adj.* **a)** crumbly; **b)** *(voller Krümel)* covered in crumbs *postpos.*
krümeln *itr. V.* **a)** *(zerfallen)* crumble; be crumbly; **b)** *(Krümel machen)* make crumbs
krumm [krʊm] **1.** *Adj.* **a)** bent ⟨*nail etc.*⟩; crooked ⟨*stick, branch, etc.*⟩; bandy ⟨*legs*⟩; bent ⟨*back*⟩; **eine ~e Nase** a crooked nose; *(Hakennase)* a hooked nose; **~ sein/werden** ⟨*person*⟩ stoop/develop a stoop; **etw. ~ biegen** bend sth.; **mach nicht so einen ~en Buckel** *od.* **Rücken** don't sit/stand with such a bent back; **~e Beine haben** have bandy legs; be bow-legged; **jmdn. ~ und lahm schlagen** beat sb. black and blue; **sich ~ und schief lachen** fall about laughing; laugh one's head off; **b)** *nicht präd. (ugs.: unrechtmäßig)* crooked; **ein ~es Ding drehen** get up to sth. crooked; **auf die ~e Tour versuchen, etw. zu tun** try to do sth. by crooked means. **2.** *adv.* crookedly; **~ gewachsen** crooked ⟨*tree etc.*⟩; **~ dasitzen/gehen** slouch/walk with a stoop; **sitz nicht so ~ da!** sit up straight!; *s. auch* **Finger b**
krumm·beinig *Adj.* bandy[-legged]; bow-legged
Krumm·darm der *(Anat.)* ileum
krümmen ['krʏmən] **1.** *tr. V.* bend; **in gekrümmter Haltung** stooping. **2.** *refl. V.* **a)** *(sich winden)* writhe; **sich vor Schmerzen/in Krämpfen ~:** double up with pain/cramp; **sich vor Lachen ~:** double up with laughter; **sich ~ wie ein Wurm** wriggle like a worm; **das Blech krümmte sich in der Hitze** the metal warped *or* buckled in the heat; **b)** *(krumm verlaufen)* ⟨*road, path, river*⟩ bend, curve; **eine gekrümmte Fläche** a curved surface
krumm-, Krumm-: ~horn das *(Musik)* krummhorn; **~|lachen** *refl. V. (ugs.)* **sich über etw.** *(Akk.)* **~lachen** fall about laughing *(Brit.) or* laugh one's head off over sth.; **~|legen** *refl. V. (ugs.)* scrimp and scrape; pinch and scrape; **~nasig** *Adj.* crooked-nosed; *(mit Hakennase)* hook-nosed; **~|nehmen** *unr. tr. V. (ugs.)* **etw. ~nehmen** take offence at sth.; take sth. the wrong way; **~säbel der** scimitar; **~stab der** *s.* **Bischofsstab**
Krümmung die; ~, ~en a) *(Biegung) (der Wirbelsäule)* curvature; *(der Nase usw.)* curve; *(eines Weges, Flusses usw.)* bend; turn; **b)** *(Geom.)* curvature
krumpelig ['krʊmpəlɪç] *Adj. (westmd.)* creased
krumpfen ['krʊmpf̩n] *tr. V. (Textilind.)* pre-shrink
Kruppe ['krʊpə] **die; ~, ~n** croup
Krüppel ['krʏpl̩] **der; ~s, ~:** cripple; **zum ~ werden** be crippled; **jmdn. zum ~ schlagen** beat sb. and leave him/her a cripple
krüppelig *Adj.* crippled ⟨*person*⟩; stunted ⟨*tree, growth, etc.*⟩
Kruste ['krʊstə] **die; ~, ~n a)** crust; *(vom Braten)* crisp; *(vom Schweinebraten)* crackling; **b)** *(Überzug)* coating; **mit ~:** with a coating; **eine ~ aus** *od.* **von Blut und Dreck/Blut** a crust of blood and dirt/a scab
Krux *s.* **Crux**
Kruzifix ['kru:tsifɪks] **das; ~es, ~e** crucifix
Krypta ['krʏpta] **die; ~, Krypten** *(Archit.)* crypt
krypto-, Krypto- ['krʏpto-] crypto-
Krypton ['krʏptɔn] **das; ~s** *(Chemie)* krypton
KSZE *Abk.* **Konferenz für Sicherheit und Zusammenarbeit in Europa** CSCE
Kuba ['ku:ba] **(das); ~s** Cuba
Kubaner [ku'ba:nɐ] **der; ~s, ~, Kubanerin die; ~, ~nen** Cuban; *s. auch* **-in**
kubanisch *Adj.* Cuban
Kübel ['ky:bl̩] **der; ~s, ~ a)** pail; *(Wasser~, Abfall~)* pail; bucket; *(Pflanzen~)* tub; **Palmen in ~n** potted palms; **~ voll** *od.* **von Bosheit über jmdn. ausgießen** *(fig.)* pour torrents of abuse over sb.; **es gießt wie aus ~n** *(ugs.)* it's bucketing down; **b)** *(Toiletteneimer)* [latrine] bucket

kübeln *itr. V. (salopp: trinken)* booze *(coll.)*
Kuben *s.* **Kubus**
Kubik- [ku'bi:k-] cubic ⟨*metre, foot, etc.*⟩
Kubik-: ~wurzel die *(Math.)* cube root; **~zahl die** *(Math.)* cube number
kubisch ['ku:bɪʃ] *Adj.* **a)** *(würfelförmig)* cubical; cube-shaped; **b)** *(Math.)* cubic ⟨*equation etc.*⟩
Kubismus der; ~ *(Kunstw.)* cubism *no art.*
Kubist der; ~en, ~en *(Kunstw.)* cubist
kubistisch *Adj. (Kunstw.)* cubist
Kubus ['ku:bʊs] **der; ~, Kuben** cube
Küche ['kʏçə] **die; ~, ~n a)** *(Raum)* kitchen; *(klein)* kitchenette; **was ~ und Keller zu bieten haben** the best food and drink in the house; **b)** *(Einrichtung)* kitchen furniture *no indef. art.*; **~n** kitchen furniture *sing.*; **c)** *(Kochk.)* cooking; cuisine; **die chinesische/französische** *usw.* **~:** Chinese/French *etc.* cooking; **kalte/warme ~:** cold/hot meals *pl. or* food; *s. auch* **gutbürgerlich**
Kuchen ['ku:xn̩] **der; ~s, ~:** cake; *(Obst~)* flan; *(Torte)* gateau; cake
Küchen-: ~abfälle *Pl.* kitchen scraps; **~bank die;** *Pl.* **~bänke** kitchen bench-seat; **~benutzung die: Zimmer mit ~benutzung** room and shared kitchen *or* use of kitchen
Kuchen·blech das baking-sheet *or* -tray; *(mit höherem Rand)* baking-tin
Küchen-: ~bulle der *(Soldatenspr. salopp)* cookhouse wallah *(Mil. sl.)*; **~chef der** chef; **~dienst der** kitchen duty; **~dienst haben** be on kitchen duty; **~fee die** *(ugs. scherzh.)* cook
Kuchen-: ~form die cake-tin; **~gabel die** pastry-fork
Küchen-: ~gerät das kitchen utensil; *(als Kollektivum)* kitchen utensils *pl.*; **~geschirr das** kitchen crockery; **~hand·tuch das** kitchen towel; **~herd der** cooker; *(mit Holz- od. Kohlefeuer)* kitchen-range; **~hilfe die** kitchen help; **~junge der** *(veralt.)* apprentice cook; **~latein das** *(iron.)* dog Latin; **~maschine die** food-processor; **~meister der** chef; *s. auch* **Schmalhans; ~messer das** kitchen knife; **~möbel** *Pl.* kitchen furniture *sing.*; **~personal das** kitchen staff; **~schabe die** cockroach; **~schrank der** kitchen cupboard; **~schürze die** kitchen apron
Kuchen-: ~teig der cake mixture; **~teller der a)** *(mit Kuchen)* plate of cakes; **b)** *(für Kuchen)* cake-plate
Küchen-: ~tisch der kitchen table; **~uhr die** kitchen clock; **~waage die** kitchen scales *pl.*; **~zeile die** *kitchen fittings along one wall of a room;* **~zettel der** menu
[1]**Küchlein das; ~s, ~** *(veralt.: Küken)* chick
[2]**Küchlein das; ~s, ~** *(kleiner Kuchen)* small cake
kucken ['kʊkn̩] *(nordd.) s.* **gucken**
Kücken ['kʏkn̩] *(österr.) s.* **Küken**
kuckuck ['kʊkʊk] *Interj.* cuckoo; *(beim Versteckspiel mit Kindern)* yoo-hoo
Kuckuck der; ~s, ~e a) cuckoo; **[das] weiß der ~** *(salopp)* heaven [only] knows; it's anybody's guess; **hol dich der ~!, der ~ soll dich holen!** *(salopp)* go to blazes! *(sl.)*; **zum ~ [noch mal]!** *(salopp)* for crying out loud! *(coll.)*; **wo, zum ~, hast du nur die Zeitung hingelegt?** *(salopp)* where the hell did you put the newspaper? *(coll.)*; **das Geld ist zum ~** *(salopp)* the money's all gone; **b)** *(scherzh.: Siegel des Gerichtsvollziehers)* bailiff's seal *(placed on distrained goods)*
Kuckucks-: ~ei das a) cuckoo's egg; **b)** *(ugs.: zweifelhafte Gabe)* **sich als ~ei erweisen** turn out to be more of a liability than an asset; **jmdm./sich ein ~ei ins Nest legen** do sb./oneself a dubious service; **c)** *(salopp: Kind eines anderen Vaters)* **ein ~ei** somebody else's *or* another man's child; **~uhr die** cuckoo clock
Kuddelmuddel ['kʊdl̩mʊdl̩] **der** *od.* **das; ~s** *(ugs.)* muddle; confusion

[1]**Kufe** ['ku:fə] **die; ~, ~n a)** *(von Schlitten, Schlittschuhen)* runner; **b)** *(von Flugzeugen, Hubschraubern)* skid
[2]**Kufe** *(landsch.)* **die; ~, ~n** tub; *(zum Keltern, Brauen)* tun; vat
Küfer ['ky:fɐ] **der; ~s, ~ a)** *(südwestd., schweiz. Böttcher)* cooper; **b)** *(Wein~)* cellarman
Kugel ['ku:gl̩] **die; ~, ~n a)** ball; *(Geom.)* sphere; *(Kegeln)* bowl; *(beim Kugelstoßen)* shot; *(eines ~lagers)* ball[-bearing]; **die Erde ist eine ~:** the Earth is a sphere; **der Croupier ließ die ~ rollen** the croupier spun the wheel; **eine ruhige ~ schieben** *(ugs.)* take it *or* things easy; *(keine anstrengende Stellung haben)* have a cushy number *(coll.)*; **b)** *(ugs.: Geschoß)* bullet; *(Kanonen~)* [cannon-]ball; *(Luftgewehr~)* pellet; **sich** *(Dat.)* **eine ~ durch** *od.* **in den Kopf schießen** *od. (ugs.)* **jagen** blow one's brains out
Kugel-: ~ab·schnitt der *(Geom.)* spherical segment [of one base]; **~aus·schnitt der** *(Geom.)* spherical sector; **~blitz der** ball lightning
Kügelchen ['ky:gl̩çən] **das; ~s, ~:** small ball; *(aus Papier)* pellet
kugel-, Kugel-: ~fang der butt; **ein Kind/eine Frau als ~fang benutzen** *(fig.)* use a child/woman as a shield; **~fest** *Adj.* bullet-proof; **~förmig** *Adj.* spherical; **~gelenk das** *(Anat., Technik)* ball-and-socket joint; **~hagel der** hail of bullets
kugelig *Adj.* spherical; ⟨*head*⟩ as round as a football; *(fig. scherzh.: dick)* rotund; plump; tubby; **sich ~ lachen** *(ugs.)* double *or* roll up [laughing *or* with laughter]; **ich hätte mich ~ lachen können** *(ugs.)* I could have died laughing
Kugel-: ~kopf der golf ball; **~kopf·maschine die** golf-ball typewriter; **~lager das** *(Technik)* ball-bearing
kugeln 1. *tr. V.* roll. **2.** *refl. V.* roll [about]; **sich [vor Lachen] ~** *(ugs.)* double *or* roll up [laughing *or* with laughter]. **3.** *itr. V.; mit sein* roll
kugel-, Kugel-: ~ober·fläche die *(Geom.)* surface of a sphere; *(Flächeninhalt)* surface area of a sphere; **~regen der** *s.* **~hagel; ~rund** [-'-] *Adj.* **a)** round as a ball *postpos.*; **b)** *(scherzh.: dick)* rotund; plump; tubby; **~schreiber der** ball-point [pen]; ball-pen; Biro **(P)**; **~schreiber·mine die** refill for a ball-point [pen]; **~sicher** *Adj.* bullet-proof; **~stoßen das; ~s** shot[-put]; *(Disziplin)* shot-putting *no art.*; putting the shot *no art.*; **~stoßer,** *(schweiz.)* **~stößer** [~ʃtœ:sɐ] **der; ~s, ~, ~stoßerin,** *(schweiz.)* **~stößerin die; ~, ~nen** shot-putter; **~wechsel der;** *o. Pl.* exchange of shots
Kuh [ku:] **die; ~, Kühe** ['ky:ə] **a)** cow; **heilige ~** *(ugs.)* sacred cow; **ich bin doch keine ~, die man melken kann** *(ugs.)* I am not made of money; *s. auch* **dastehen a; b)** *(Elefanten~, Giraffen~, Flußpferd~)* cow; *(Hirsch~)* hind; **c)** *(salopp abwertend: Frau)* cow *(sl. derog.)*
kuh-, Kuh-: ~augen *Pl. (salopp)* cow-eyes; **~dorf das** *(salopp abwertend)* one-horse town *(sl.)*; **~fladen der** cow-pat; **~fuß der** *(Technik)* crowbar; **~glocke die** cow-bell; **~handel der** *(ugs. abwertend)* shady horse-trading *no indef. art.*; **ein ~handel** a bit of shady horse-trading; **~haut die** cowhide; **das geht auf keine ~haut** *(fig. salopp)* it's absolutely staggering *or* beyond belief; **~herde die** herd of cows; **~hirt der** cowherd
kühl [ky:l] **1.** *Adj.* **a)** cool; **mir ist/wird ~:** I feel/I'm getting chilly; **etw. ~ lagern** *od.* **aufbewahren** keep sth. in a cool place; **b)** *(abweisend, nüchtern)* cool; **ein ~er Rechner** a cool, calculating person; **aus diesem ~en Grunde** *(scherzh.)* for this simple reason. **2.** *adv. (abweisend, nüchtern)* coolly

Kühl-: ~aggregat das refrigeration unit; **~an·lage die** refrigeration plant; cold-storage plant; **~box die** cool box
Kuhle ['ku:lə] **die; ~, ~n** *(ugs.)* hollow
Kühle ['ky:lə] **die; ~ a)** *(Frische)* coolness; **die ~ des Morgens/Abends** the cool of the morning/evening; **b)** *(Nüchternheit)* coolness
kühlen 1. *tr. V.* cool; chill, cool ⟨*wine*⟩; **seinen Zorn/seine Rache [an jmdm.] ~:** vent one's rage/revenge oneself [on sb.]. **2.** *itr. V.* ⟨*cold compress, ointment, breeze, etc.*⟩ have a cooling effect
Kühler der; ~s, ~ a) *(am Auto)* radiator; *(~haube)* bonnet *(Brit.)*; hood *(Amer.)*; **jmdn. auf den ~ nehmen** *(ugs.)* drive *or* run into *or* hit sb.; **b)** *(Sekt~)* ice-bucket; **c)** *(Chem.)* condenser
Kühler-: ~figur die radiator mascot; **~haube die** bonnet *(Brit.)*; hood *(Amer.)*
Kühl-: ~fach das frozen food compartment; **~haus das** cold store; **~kette die** *(Wirtsch.)* cold chain; **~mittel das** *(Technik)* coolant; **~raum der** cold store; cold-storage room; **~rippe die** cooling fin *or* rib; **~schiff das** refrigerator ship; refrigerated ship; **~schlange die** *(Technik)* cooling coil; **~schrank der** refrigerator; fridge *(Brit. coll.)*; icebox *(Amer.)*; **~tasche die** cool bag; **~theke die** cold shelves *pl.*; **~truhe die** [chest] freezer; deep-freeze; *(im Lebensmittelgeschäft)* freezer [cabinet]; **~turm der** *(Technik)* cooling tower
Kühlung die; ~, ~en a) cooling; **zur ~ der entzündeten Stellen** to cool the inflamed areas; **auch bei ~ sind die Waren nur begrenzt haltbar** even when refrigerated, the goods will keep only for a limited time; **b)** *(Vorrichtung)* cooling system; *(für Lebensmittel)* refrigeration system; **c)** *o. Pl. (Frische)* coolness; **sich** *(Dat.)* **~ verschaffen** cool down *or* off
Kühl-: ~wagen der a) *(Eisenb.)* refrigerated *or* refrigerator car *or (Brit.)* wagon; **b)** *(Lastwagen)* refrigerated *or* refrigerator truck *or (Brit.)* lorry; **~wasser das** cooling water
Kuh-: ~milch die cow's milk; **~mist der** cow dung
kühn [ky:n] **1.** *Adj.* **a)** *(mutig, eigenwillig)* bold; *(gewagt)* daring; brave, fearless ⟨*warrior*⟩; **das übertraf meine ~sten Träume** that exceeded my wildest dreams; **b)** *(dreist)* audacious; impudent. **2.** *adv.* **a)** *(mutig, eigenwillig)* boldly; *(gewagt)* daringly; **eine ~ geschwungene Nase** an aquiline nose; **b)** *(dreist)* audaciously; impudently
Kühnheit die; ~ a) *(Mut, Eigenwilligkeit)* boldness; *(Gewagtheit)* daringness; **b)** *(Dreistigkeit)* audacity; impudence
kuh-, Kuh-: ~pocken *Pl.* cowpox *sing., no art.*; **~schelle die** *(Bot.)* pasque-flower; **~stall der** cowshed; **~warm** *Adj.* ⟨*milk*⟩ warm *or* fresh from the cow
Kujon [ku'jo:n] **der; ~s, ~e** *(veralt. abwertend)* scoundrel; rogue
kujonieren *tr. V. (veralt. abwertend)* bully; harass
k. u. k. ['ka:|ʊnt'ka:] *Abk. (österr. hist.)* **kaiserlich und königlich** imperial and royal
Küken ['ky:kn̩] **das; ~s, ~ a)** *(von Hühnern)* chick; **b)** *(ugs.) (kleines Kind)* kiddie *(sl.)*; *(junges Mädchen)* young girl
Ku-Klux-Klan [kuklʊks'kla:n] **der; ~[s]** Ku-Klux-Klan
kulant [ku'lant] **1.** *Adj.* obliging; accommodating; fair ⟨*terms*⟩. **2.** *adv.* **sich ~ verhalten** be obliging *or* accommodating
Kulanz [ku'lants] **die; ~:** readiness *or* willingness to oblige; **aus ~:** out of good will; **eine Reparatur auf ~:** repair done free of charge out of good will
Kuli ['ku:li] **der; ~s, ~s a)** coolie; *(fig.)* slave; **b)** *(ugs.: Kugelschreiber)* ball-point; Biro **(P)**

kulinarisch [kuli'na:rɪʃ] *Adj.* culinary; **ein rein ~es Interesse an der Musik haben** *(fig.)* be interested in music purely as entertainment

Kulisse [ku'lɪsə] **die; ~, ~n** piece of scenery; flat; wing; *(Hintergrund)* backdrop; **die ~n** the scenery *sing.*; **~n schieben** be a scene-shifter; **aus der ~ treten** step out from the wings *pl.*; **die ~ für etw. bilden** *(fig.)* form the backdrop to sth.; **hinter den ~n** *(fig.)* behind the scenes

kulissenhaft *Adj.* like a stage-setting *pred.*

Kulissen-: **~schieber der** *(ugs. scherzh.)* scene-shifter; **~wechsel der** scene-change

Kuller die; ~, ~n *(ostmd.: Murmel)* marble

Kuller·augen *Pl. (ugs. scherzh.)* big, round eyes; **er machte ~:** his eyes nearly popped out of his head

kullern ['kʊlɐn] *(ugs.)* **1.** *itr. V.* **a)** *mit sein* roll; **b) mit den Augen ~:** roll one's eyes. **2.** *tr. V.* roll

Kuller·pfirsich der *(ugs.)* peach served in a glass of champagne

Kulmination [kʊlmina'tsi̯o:n] **die; ~, ~en** *(auch Astron.)* culmination

Kulminations·punkt der a) culmination; culminating point; **b)** *(Astron.)* point of culmination

kulminieren [kʊlmi'ni:rən] *itr. V. (auch Astron.)* culminate (**in** + *Dat.* in)

Kult [kʊlt] **der; ~[e]s, ~e a)** cult; **der ~ der Ahnen** ancestor-worship; **b)** *(fig.)* cult (**mit** of); **mit jmdm./etw. einen ~ treiben** make a cult [figure] out of sb./make a cult out of sth.

-kult der: Motorrad~/Star~/Wagner~ *usw.* motor cycle/star/Wagner *etc.* cult

Kult-: **~bild das** devotional image; **~figur die** cult figure; **~film der** cult film; **~handlung die** ritual; ritualistic act

kultisch 1. *Adj.* cultic; ritual, cultic ⟨*object*⟩. **2.** *adv.* ⟨*worship*⟩ cultically

Kultivator [kʊlti'va:tɔr] **der; ~s, ~en** [-va'to:rən] *(Landw.)* cultivator

kultivierbar *Adj.* **a)** cultivable; cultivatable; **leicht/schwer ~:** easy/hard to cultivate

kultivieren [kʊlti'vi:rən] *tr. V. (auch fig.)* cultivate

kultiviert 1. *s.* **kultivieren. 2.** *Adj.* **a)** *(gepflegt)* cultivated; cultured; **b)** *(vornehm)* refined. **3.** *adv.* in a cultivated *or* cultured manner; *(vornehm)* in a refined manner; with refinement; **~ essen** get a civilized meal

Kultiviertheit die; ~: refinement

Kultivierung die; ~, ~en *(auch fig.)* cultivation; improvement

Kult·stätte die centre of cult worship

Kultur [kʊl'tu:ɐ̯] **die; ~, ~en a)** *o. Pl. (geistiger und moralischer Überbau)* culture; **b)** *(Zivilisation, Lebensform)* civilization; **c)** *o. Pl. (Kultiviertheit, geistiges Niveau)* **ein Mensch von ~:** a cultured person; **sie hat [keine] ~:** she is [un]cultured; **d)** *o. Pl. (kultivierte Lebensart, Verfeinerung)* refinement; **~ haben** be refined; **e)** *(Landw., Gartenbau)* young crop; *(Forstw.)* young plantation; **f)** *(Biol., Med.)* culture; **g)** *o. Pl. (Landw., Gartenbau: Kultivierung)* cultivation

Kultur-: **~ab·gabe die** *(DDR)* culture tax; **~abkommen das** cultural agreement; **~anthropologie die** cultural anthropology *no art.*; **~arbeit die**; *o. Pl.* cultural activity *or* activities; **~attaché der** cultural attaché; **~aus·tausch der** cultural exchange; **~banause der** *(abwertend, oft scherzh.)* philistine; **~bei·lage die** arts supplement; **~betrieb der**; *o. Pl.* culture industry; **~beutel der** sponge-bag *(Brit.)*; toilet-bag; **~boden der a)** *(bearbeiteter Boden)* cultivated land; **b)** *(Gebiet mit bedeutender ~)* **[ur]alter ~boden** the site of an ancient civilization; **~denkmal das** cultural monument

kulturell [kʊltu'rɛl] **1.** *Adj.* cultural. **2.** *adv.* culturally; **die ehemals ~ führende Metropole** the metropolis, once cultural centre

kultur-, Kultur-: **~epoche die** cultural epoch; **~erbe das** cultural heritage; **~feindlich** *Adj.* ⟨*atmosphere, policy, etc.*⟩ that is hostile to culture; **~feindlich sein** be hostile to culture; **~film der** documentary film; **~flüchter der; ~s, ~** *(Biol.)* plant/animal that does not survive in areas developed by man; **~föderalismus der** *system of separate ministries for education and cultural affairs*; **~folger der; ~s, ~** *(Biol.)* plant/animal that survives in areas developed by man; **~geschichte die a)** *o. Pl.* history of civilization; *(einer bestimmten Kultur)* cultural history; **die ~geschichte des Menschen** the history of human civilization; **b)** *(Buch)* cultural history; **~geschichtlich 1.** *Adj.* ⟨*importance*⟩ for *or* in the history of civilization/cultural history; ⟨*question, factor*⟩ connected with the history of civilization/cultural history; ⟨*essay, reflections*⟩ on the history of civilization/cultural history; *(die ~geschichte eines bestimmten Landes betreffend)* historico-cultural ⟨*law, phenomenon, standpoint, study, etc.*⟩; **2.** *adv.* from the standpoint of the history of civilization/of cultural history; **~gut das** cultural possessions *pl.*; **~haus das** arts and leisure centre; **~historisch** *Adj., adv.: s.* **~geschichtlich**; **~hoheit die** autonomy *or* independence in cultural and educational matters; **~industrie die** *(meist abwertend)* culture industry; **~kampf der** *(hist.)* kulturkampf *(struggle between the Prussian state and the Church 1872–87)*; **~kreis der a)** *(~raum)* cultural area; **b)** *(Verein)* arts society; **~kritik die**; *o. Pl.* critique of contemporary civilization *or* culture; **~kritiker der** critic of contemporary civilization *or* culture; **~landschaft die a)** *(Agrargebiet)* cultivated area; area cultivated by man; *(Industrie-, Bergbaugebiet)* area developed by man; **b)** *(kulturelles Leben)* cultural scene; **~leben das**; *o. Pl.* cultural life; **~los** *Adj.* uncultured; lacking in culture *postpos.*; **~magazin das** *(Ferns.)* arts magazine; **~minister der** *(bes. DDR)* minister for the arts; **~ministerium das** *(bes. DDR)* ministry for the arts; **~palast der** *(bes. DDR)* palace of culture; **~pessimismus der** cultural pessimism; **~pessimist der** cultural pessimist; **~pflanze die** cultivated plant; **~politik die** cultural and educational policy; **~politisch 1.** *Adj.* ⟨*area, questions, aims, principles*⟩ of cultural and educational policy; ⟨*programme*⟩ of cultural and educational policies; ⟨*periodical*⟩ devoted to matters of cultural and educational policy; **2.** *adv.* in regard to cultural and educational policy; **~preis der** arts prize; **~psychologie die** psychology of culture; **~raum der** cultural area; **~revolution die** cultural revolution; **~schaffende der/die**; *adj. Dekl. (DDR)* creative artist; *(Intellektueller)* intellectual; **~schande die** *(abwertend)* disgrace in a civilized society; **~schock der** *(Soziol.)* culture shock; **~soziologie die** cultural sociology; **~sprache die** language of a civilized people; **in fast alle ~sprachen übersetzt** translated into nearly every civilized language; **~stätte die** *(geh.)* site of archaeological and cultural interest; **~steppe die** *(Geogr.)* cultivated steppe land; steppe [land] created by excessive cultivation of the soil; **~stufe die** level of civilization; **~szene die**; *o. Pl. (ugs.)* cultural scene; **~träger der** vehicle of culture; **~volk das** civilized people *sing.*; **~voll** *Adj. (DDR)* rich in culture *postpos.*; *(niveauvoll)* sophisticated; **~wissenschaften** *Pl.: s.* **Geisteswissenschaften**; **~zentrum das a)** cultural centre; centre of cultural life; **b)** *(Anlage)* arts centre

Kultus ['kʊltʊs] **der; ~ a)** *(geh.) s.* **Kult a**; **b)** *(Amtsspr.)* **Ministerium für Unterricht und ~:** *s.* **Kultusministerium**

Kultus-: **~minister der** minister for education and cultural affairs; **~ministerium das** ministry of education and cultural affairs; **~senator der** minister for education and cultural affairs *(in Bremen, Hamburg, and West Berlin)*

Kumarin [kuma'ri:n] **das; ~s** coumarin

Kumaron [kuma'ro:n] **das; ~s** *(Chemie)* coumarone

Kumme ['kʊmə] **die; ~, ~n** *(nordd.)* bowl

Kümmel ['kʏml̩] **der; ~s, ~ a)** *(Pflanze)* caraway; **b)** *(Gewürz)* caraway [seed]; **c)** *(Branntwein)* kümmel

Kümmel-: **~brannt·wein der** caraway brandy; **~brötchen das** caraway[-seed] roll; **~käse der** caraway-seed[-flavoured] cheese; **~öl das** caraway oil; **~schnaps der** *s.* **~branntwein**; **~türke der a)** *(salopp abwertend) (Türke)* Turkish bastard *(derog.)*; **b) schuften wie ein ~türke/die ~türken** *(ugs.)* work like a slave/like slaves

Kummer ['kʊmɐ] **der; ~s** sorrow; grief; *(Ärger, Sorgen)* trouble; **~ um** *od.* **über jmdn.** grief for *or* over sb.; **hast du ~?** is there a problem?; **viel** *od.* **großen ~ haben** have a lot of trouble; **was hast du denn für ~?** what's bothering *or* troubling you?; **jmdm. ~ machen** give sb. trouble *or* bother; **ich bin ~ gewohnt** *(ugs.)* it happens all the time; I'm used to it

Kummer·falte die wrinkle [caused by worry]; **~n** lines of worry

Kümmer·form die *(Biol.)* degenerate form

Kummer-: **~kasten der** *(scherzh.)* complaints-box; **~kasten·tante die** *(scherzh.)* agony columnist *or* aunt *(coll.)*

kümmerlich 1. *Adj.* **a)** *(schwächlich)* puny; stunted ⟨*vegetation, plants*⟩; **b)** *(ärmlich)* wretched; miserable; **c)** *(abwertend: gering)* miserable; meagre, scanty ⟨*knowledge, leftovers*⟩; very poor ⟨*effort*⟩. **2.** *adv.* **sich ~ ernähren** live on a poor *or* meagre diet; **sich ~ durchschlagen** eke out a bare/miserable existence

Kümmerling der; ~s, ~e stunted plant/animal

kümmern ['kʏmɐn] **1.** *refl. V.* **a) sich um jmdn./etw. ~:** take care of *or* look after sb./sth.; **du solltest dich mal darum ~, daß ...:** you should see to it that ...; **du kümmerst dich aber auch um gar nichts!** you don't bother to do anything!; **b)** *(sich befassen mit)* **sich nicht um das Geschwätz** *usw.* **~:** not worry *or* mind about the gossip *etc.*; **sich nicht um Politik ~:** not care about *or* be interested in politics; **kümmere dich um deine eigenen Angelegenheiten** mind your own business. **2.** *tr. V.* concern; **was kümmert dich das?** what concern *or* business is it of yours?; what's it to you?; **Mach doch, was du willst! Was kümmert's mich?** Do what you like! What do I care? **3.** *itr. V. (verkümmern)* become stunted

Kümmernis die; ~, ~se *(geh.)* trouble; worry

Kummer·speck der *(ugs.)* over-weight caused by overeating as a result of emotional stress; **sie hat ~ angesetzt** all the worrying has made her eat too much, and she's [really] put on weight

kummer·voll 1. *Adj.* sorrowful; sad; sad ⟨*face*⟩. **2.** *adv.* sorrowfully; sadly

Kummet ['kʊmət] **das,** *schweiz. auch* **der; ~s, ~e** [horse-]collar

Kümo ['ky:mo] **das; ~s, ~s** [motor-]coaster

Kumpan [kʊm'pa:n] **der; ~s, ~e** *(ugs.)* **a)** pal *(coll.)*; mate; buddy *(coll.)*; **b)** *(abwertend: Mittäter)* accomplice

Kumpanei die; ~ *(ugs.)* chumminess *(coll.)*

Kumpel ['kʊmpl̩] **der; ~s, ~,** *ugs. auch:* **~s**

a) *(Bergmannsspr.)* miner; collier; **b)** *(salopp: Kamerad)* pal; mate; buddy *(coll.)*
kumpelhaft 1. *Adj.* matey; chummy *(coll.)*. **2.** *adv.* matily; chummily *(coll.)*
Kumpen ['kʊmpn̩] **der; ~s, ~** *(nordd.)* bowl; basin
Kumt [kʊmt] **das; ~[e]s, ~e** *s.* **Kummet**
Kumulation [kumula'tsio:n] **die; ~, ~en** cumulation; *(von Ämtern)* plurality
kumulativ [kumula'ti:f] *Adj.* cumulative
kumulieren [kumu'li:rən] *tr. V.* cumulate; **eine ~de Bibliographie** a cumulative bibliography
Kumulierung die; ~, ~en cumulation
Kumulus ['ku:mulʊs] **der; ~, Kumuli** *(Met.)* cumulus [cloud]
Kumulus·wolke die *(Met.)* cumulus cloud
kund [kʊnt] *Adj. in* **jmdm. etw. ~ und zu wissen tun** *(veralt.)* make sth. known to sb.
kündbar *Adj.* terminable ⟨*contract*⟩; redeemable ⟨*loan, mortgage*⟩; **er hat eine nicht ~e Stellung** his employment cannot be terminated; **Beamte sind nicht ~:** established civil servants cannot be dismissed *or* given their notice
Kündbarkeit die; ~ *(von Verträgen)* terminability; *(von Anleihen, Hypotheken)* redeemability
¹Kunde ['kʊndə] **der; ~n, ~n a)** customer; *(eines Architekten-, Anwaltbüros, einer Versicherung usw.)* client; **Dienst am ~n sein** be a service to the customer; *s. auch* **König; b)** *(ugs.: Kerl)* customer *(coll.)*
²Kunde die; ~ a) *(geh.)* tidings *pl.* *(literary)*; **jmdm. von etw. ~ geben** *(veralt.)* bring sb. tidings of sth.; **b)** *(Lehre)* science
³Kunde die; ~ *(österr.) s.* **Kundschaft a**
-kunde die science of ...; **Metall~/Vogel~:** metallurgy/ornithology
künden ['kʏndn̩] **1.** *tr. V. (geh.: ver~)* proclaim; **diese Zeichen ~ Unglück** these omens herald misfortune. **2.** *itr. V. (geh.)* **von etw. ~:** bear witness to *or* tell of sth.
Kunden-: ~beratung die a) customer advisory service; **~beratungen durchführen** advise customers; **b)** *(Stelle)* customer advisory department; **~besuch der** call on a/the customer/client; **~dienst der a)** *o. Pl.* service to customers; *(Wartung)* after-sales service; **b)** *(Abteilung)* service department; **~fang der** *(abwertend)* touting for custom *or* customers; **auf ~fang gehen** go touting for custom *or* customers; **~kredit der** *(Wirtsch.)* credit terms *pl.*; **einen ~kredit in Anspruch nehmen** use the credit facilities which are available; **~kreis der** customers *pl.*; *(eines Architekten-, Anwaltbüros, einer Versicherung usw.)* clientele; **~stamm der** regular clientele *or* trade; **~werbung die** advertising aimed at attracting customers; **zu Zwecken der ~werbung** to attract custom *or* customers
Künder der; ~s, ~ *(geh.)* herald
Kund·gabe die; *o. Pl. (geh.)* announcement; *(von Gefühlen, Erfahrungen)* expression
kund|geben *(geh.) unr. tr. V.* declare; announce; express, make known ⟨*opinion, feelings*⟩
Kundgebung die; ~, ~en a) rally; **b)** *(geh.: Äußerung)* expression
kundig 1. *Adj. (kenntnisreich)* knowledgeable; well-informed; *(sachverständig)* expert; **mit ~er Hand** with an expert hand; **sich über etw.** *(Akk.)* **~ machen** *(Amtsdt.)* inform oneself about sth.; **einer Sache** *(Gen.)* **~/nicht ~ sein** *(geh.)* know about sth./have no knowledge of sth. **2.** *adv.* expertly
kündigen ['kʏndɪgn̩] **1.** *tr. V.* call in, cancel ⟨*loan*⟩; foreclose ⟨*mortgage*⟩; cancel, discontinue ⟨*magazine subscription, membership*⟩; terminate ⟨*contract, agreement*⟩; denounce ⟨*treaty*⟩; **seine Stellung ~:** give in *or* hand in one's notice **(bei** to); **jmdm. die Stellung** *od.* **jmds. Arbeitsverhältnis ~:** give sb. his/her notice; **ich bin gekündigt worden** *(ugs.)* I've been given my notice; **der Vermieter hat ihm die Wohnung gekündigt** the landlord gave him notice to quit the flat *(Brit.) or (Amer.)* apartment; **er hat seine Wohnung gekündigt** he's given notice that he's leaving his flat *(Brit.) or (Amer.)* apartment; **jmdm. die Freundschaft ~** *(fig.)* break off a friendship with sb. **2.** *unr. itr. V.* **a)** *(ein Mietverhältnis beenden)* ⟨*tenant*⟩ give notice [that one is leaving]; **jmdm. ~** ⟨*landlord*⟩ give sb. notice to quit; **zum 1. Juli ~:** give notice for 1 July; **b)** *(ein Arbeitsverhältnis beenden)* ⟨*employee*⟩ give in *or* hand in one's notice **(bei** to); **jmdm. ~** ⟨*employer*⟩ give sb. his/her notice
Kündigung die; ~, ~en a) *(eines Kredits)* calling-in; cancellation; *(einer Hypothek)* foreclosure; *(der Mitgliedschaft, eines Abonnements)* cancellation; discontinuation; *(eines Vertrags)* termination; **die Bank droht mit der ~ der Kredite** the bank is threatening to call in *or* cancel the loans; **b)** *(eines Arbeitsverhältnisses)* **jmdm. die ~ aussprechen** give sb. his/her notice; dismiss sb.; **mit ~ drohen** ⟨*employee*⟩ threaten to give in *or* hand in one's notice *or* to quit; ⟨*employer*⟩ threaten dismissal; **ihm droht die ~:** he is threatened with dismissal; **eine fristlose ~:** dismissal without notice; **c)** *(eines Mietverhältnisses)* **sie mußte mit ~ rechnen** she had to reckon on being given notice to quit; **ich sah mich zur ~ gezwungen** I felt compelled to give notice; **d)** *s.* **Kündigungsschreiben; e)** *(Kündigungsfrist)* [period *or* term of] notice; **bei jährlicher ~ betragen die Zinsen 9,5 %** with one year's notice of withdrawal, interest is at 9.5 %
Kündigungs-: ~frist die period of notice; **~grund der** *(Arbeitsrecht)* grounds *pl.* for dismissal; grounds *pl.* for giving sb. his/her notice; *(Mietrecht)* grounds *pl.* for giving sb. notice to quit; **~schreiben das** written notice; notice in writing; **~schutz der** protection against wrongful dismissal
Kundin die; ~, ~nen customer/client; *s. auch* **¹Kunde a**
kund|machen *tr. V. (österr. Amtsspr.)* announce; make known; *(feierlich)* proclaim; promulgate ⟨*law*⟩
Kundschaft die; ~, ~en a) *o. Pl.; s.* **¹Kunde a:** customers *pl.*; clientele; **~!** service!; **ich habe gerade ~:** I've got a customer/customers at the moment; **b)** *(veralt.: Erkundung)* **auf ~ ausgehen/jmdn. auf ~ ausschicken** go out on/send sb. out on reconnaissance *or* to reconnoitre; **c)** *(veralt.: Nachricht)* news *sing.*; tidings *pl.* *(literary)*
Kundschafter der; ~s, ~: scout
kund|tun *(geh.)* **1.** *unr. tr. V.* announce; make known. **2.** *unr. refl. V.* be revealed; show itself
kund|werden *unr itr. V.; mit sein (veralt.)* become known; **ihm wurde der Verrat kund** he learned of the betrayal
künftig ['kʏnftɪç] **1.** *Adj.* future; **ihr ~er Mann** her future husband; her husband-to-be; **am 15. ~en Monats** *(geh.)* on the 15th of next month. **2.** *adv.* in future
künftig·hin *Adv. (geh.)* henceforth; henceforward; in future
Kungelei die; ~, ~en *(abwertend)* wheeling and dealing; **eine ~ um etw.** bargaining over sth.; **große ~en** a great deal *sing.* of wheeling and dealing
kungeln ['kʊŋl̩n] *itr. V.* **[mit jmdm.] um etw. ~:** bargain [with sb.] over sth.; **dort wird viel gekungelt** there is a lot of wheeling and dealing there
Kunst [kʊnst] **die; ~, Künste** ['kʏnstə] **a)** art; **die Schwarze ~** *(Magie)* the black art; *(Buchdruck)* [the art of] printing; **die schönen Künste** [the] fine arts; fine art *sing.*; **was macht die ~?** *(ugs.)* how are things?; how's tricks? *(sl.)*; *s. auch* **bilden a; darstellen 1 a; ²sieben; b)** *(das Können)* skill; **die ärztliche ~:** medical skill; **die ~ des Reitens/der Selbstverteidigung** the art of riding/self-defence; **nach einer Vorlage zu stricken ist keine ~:** it's easy enough *or* it doesn't take anything to knit from a pattern; **~ kommt von können** *(meist iron.)* either you've got it or you haven't; **das ist keine/die ganze ~!** *(ugs.)* there's nothing 'to it/nothing more to it than that; **mit seiner ~ am Ende sein** be at a complete loss; *s. auch* **brotlos; Regel a**
Kunst-: ~akademie die *s.* **~hochschule; ~aus·stellung die** art exhibition; **~banause der** *(abwertend)* philistine; **~band der** *(high-quality)* art book; **~besitz der** art collection; **~blatt das** art print; **~buch das** art book; **~darm der** artificial *or* synthetic sausage-skin; **~denkmal das** artistic and cultural monument; **~denkmäler der Kelten/Griechen** *usw.* monuments of Celtic/Greek *etc.* art; **~diebstahl der** art theft; **~druck der a)** [fine] art print; **b)** *o. Pl. (Druckw.)* fine-art printing; **etw. im ~druck herstellen** produce sth. by fine-art printing methods; **~druck·papier das** art paper; **~dünger der** chemical *or* artificial fertilizer; **~eis·bahn die** artificial ice-rink
Künstelei die; ~ *(abwertend)* affectation
künsteln *s.* **gekünstelt**
kunst-, Kunst-: ~erzieher der, ~erzieherin die art teacher; **~erziehung die** art education; *(Schulfach)* art; **~fälschung die** art forgery; **~faser die** man-made *or* synthetic fibre; **~fehler der** professional error; *(fig. scherzh.: Versehen)* mistake; **ein ärztlicher ~fehler** a professional error on the part of a doctor; **~fertig 1.** *Adj.* skilful; **2.** *adv.* skilfully; **~fertigkeit die** skill; skilfulness; **~flieger der** aerobatic pilot; stunt pilot *(coll.)*; **~flug der** aerobatics *sing.*; stunt-flying *(coll.)*; **ein ~flug** a piece of aerobatic flying *or (coll.)* stunt-flying; **~form die** art form; **~freund der** art lover; lover of the arts; **~führer der** guide to cultural and artistic monuments [of an/the area]; **~galerie die** art gallery; **~gegenstand der** work of art; **~genuß der** enjoyment of art; *(Ereignis)* artistic treat; **~gerecht 1.** *Adj.* expert; skilful; **2.** *adv.* expertly; skilfully; **~geschichte die a)** *o. Pl.* art history; history of art; **b)** *(Buch)* art history book; book on the history of art; **~geschichtlich 1.** *Adj.* art historical ⟨*studies, evidence, expertise, etc.*⟩; ⟨*work*⟩ on art history *or* the history of art; ⟨*interest*⟩ in art history *or* the history of art; **~geschichtliches Museum** art-history museum; museum of art history; **2.** *adv.* **~geschichtlich interessiert/versiert** interested/well versed in art history *or* the history of art; **~geschichtlich bedeutsam** significant from an art-historical point of view; **~gewerbe das** arts and crafts *pl.*; **~gewerblich 1.** *Adj.* craft *attrib.* ⟨*objects, skills, etc.*⟩; **~gewerbliche Arbeiten** craftwork *sing.*; **2.** *adv.* **~gewerblich hergestellte Produkte** craft products; **~glied das** artificial limb; **~griff der** move; *(fig.)* trick; dodge; **~halle die** art gallery; **~handel der** [fine-]art trade; **~händler der** [fine-]art dealer; **~handwerk das** craftwork; **Erzeugnisse des ~handwerks** craft products; craftwork *sing.*; **~harz das** *(Chemie)* synthetic resin; **~historiker der** art historian; **~historisch** *s.* **~geschichtlich; ~hoch·schule die** art college; college of art; **~honig der** artifical honey; honey substitute; **~kalender der** art calendar; **~kenner der** art connoisseur *or* expert; **~kopf der** *(Tontechnik)* dummy head; **~kraft·sport der** sports acrobatics *sing.*; **~kritik die** art criticism; *(die Kritiker)* art critics *pl.*; **~kritiker der** art critic; **~lauf der** *(Sport)* figure-skating; **~leder das** artificial *or* imitation leather

Künstler ['kynstlɐ] **der;** ~s, ~, **Künstlerin die;** ~, ~nen **a)** artist; *(Zirkus~, Varieté~)* artiste; **ein bildender** ~: a visual artist; **b)** *(Könner)* genius (**in** + *Dat.* at); **ein** ~ **in seinem Fach** a genius in one's field/at one's trade

Künstler-: ~**atelier das** studio; ~**beruf der** artistic career; ~**hand die** *in* **von** ~**hand** by the artist's hand

künstlerisch 1. *Adj.* artistic. **2.** *adv.* artistically; **etw.** ~ **darstellen** express sth. in artistic form; **ein** ~ **wertvoller Film** a film of great artistic worth

Künstler-: ~**kneipe die** pub *(Brit. coll.) or (Amer.)* bar frequented by artists; ~**kolonie die** artists' colony; colony of artists; ~**mähne die** *(ugs. veralt. scherzh.)* mane of hair; ~**name der** stage-name; ~**pech das** *(ugs. scherzh.)* hard luck

Künstlertum das; ~s artistic genius

künstlich ['kynstlɪç] **1.** *Adj.* **a)** artificial; artificial, glass ⟨*eye*⟩; false ⟨*teeth, eyelashes, hair*⟩; synthetic, man-made ⟨*fibre*⟩; imitation, synthetic ⟨*diamond*⟩; **b)** *(gezwungen)* forced ⟨*laugh, cheerfulness, etc.*⟩; enforced ⟨*rest*⟩. **2.** *adv.* **a)** artificially; **jmdn.** ~ **ernähren** feed sb. artificially; **b)** *(gezwungen)* **sich** ~ **aufregen** *(ugs.)* get worked up *or* excited about nothing

Künstlichkeit die; ~: artificiality

kunst-, Kunst-: ~**licht das;** *o. Pl.* artificial light; **bei** ~**licht** in artificial light; ~**liebhaber der** art lover; lover of the arts; ~**lied das** art song; Kunstlied; ~**los 1.** *Adj.* plain; **2.** *adv.* plainly; ~**maler der** artist; painter; ~**märchen das** *(Literaturw.)* literary fairy-tale; ~**pause die** pause for effect; *(iron.: Stockung)* awkward pause; **eine** ~**pause machen** pause for effect/pause awkwardly; ~**post·karte die** art postcard; ~**rasen der** artificial turf; ~**reich** *s.* ~**voll**; ~**reiter der** circus rider; bareback rider; ~**richtung die** trend in art; **neue** ~**richtungen** new directions in art; ~**sammler der** art collector; ~**sammlung die** art collection; ~**schaffende der/die;** *adj. Dekl.* artist; ~**schatz der** art treasure; ~**schmied der** wrought-iron craftsman; ~**schwimmen das** *(Sport)* synchronized swimming *no art.*; ~**seide die** artificial silk; rayon; ~**sinn der** artistic sense; feeling for art; ~**sprache die** artificial language; ~**springen das** *(Sport)* springboard diving; ~**stein der** artificial stone

Kunst·stoff der synthetic material; plastic

Kunst·stoffaser die synthetic fibre

Kunst·stoff-: ~**bahn die** *(Sport)* synthetic track; ~**faser** *s.* **Kunststoffaser;** ~**karosserie die** plastic body

kunst-, Kunst-: ~**stopfen** *tr. V. (nur im Inf. u. 2. Part. gebr.)* repair by invisible mending; invisibly mend; ~**stück das** trick; **das ist kein** ~**stück** *(ugs.)* it's no great feat *or* achievement; ~**stück!** *(ugs. iron.)* that's no great achievement; *(ist nicht verwunderlich)* it's hardly surprising; ~**turnen das** gymnastics *sing.*; ~**verstand der** artistic sense; feeling for art; ~**voll 1.** *Adj.* ornate *or* elaborate and artistic; *(kompliziert)* elaborate; **2.** *adv.* **a)** ornately *or* elaborately and artistically; **b)** *(geschickt)* skilfully; ~**werk das** *(auch fig.)* work of art; ~**wissenschaft die** aesthetics and art history; ~**wort das;** *Pl.* ~**wörter** *(Sprachw.)* made-up *or* invented word; ~**szene die** art world

kunter·bunt ['kʊntɐ-] **1.** *Adj.* **a)** *(vielfarbig)* multi-coloured; **b)** *(abwechslungsreich)* varied; **wir laden Sie zu unserem** ~**en Abend mit ... ein** you are invited to our evening of varied entertainment with ...; **c)** *(ungeordnet)* jumbled ⟨*confusion, muddle, rows, etc.*⟩. **2.** *adv.* **a)** ⟨*painted, printed*⟩ in many colours; **b)** *(abwechslungsreich)* **ein** ~ **gestalteter Abend** an evening of varied entertainment; **sein Leben verlief recht** ~: he had a very varied life; **c)** *(ungeordnet)* ~ **durcheinander sein** be higgledy-piggledy *or* all jumbled up; **es ging** ~ **durcheinander** it was completely chaotic

Kunterbunt das; ~s **a)** *(von Farben)* riotous profusion of colour; **b)** *(Gemisch)* potpourri; **c)** *(Durcheinander)* muddle

Kunz [kʊnts] *s.* **Hinz**

Kupfer ['kʊpfɐ] **das;** ~s **a)** copper; **etw. in** ~ *(Akk.)* **stechen** engrave *or* etch sth. on copper; **b)** *(~geschirr)* copperware; *(~geld)* coppers *pl.*; **c)** *s.* **Kupferstich b**

kupfer-, Kupfer-: ~**blech das** copper sheeting; **ein** ~**blech** a copper sheet; ~**draht der** copper wire; ~**druck der a)** *o. Pl.* copperplate printing *no art.*; **etw. in** ~**druck herstellen** produce sth. by copperplate printing; **b)** *(Abbildung)* copperplate [print]; ~**erz das** copper ore; ~**geld das** coppers *pl.*; ~**haltig** *Adj.* containing copper *postpos., not pred.*; cupriferous; ~**kessel der** copper kettle; *(zum Bierbrauen)* copper vat; ~**legierung die** copper alloy; ~**münze die** copper coin; copper

kupfern *Adj. (geh.)* **a)** *nicht präd.* copper; **die** ~**e Hochzeit** the seventh wedding anniversary; **b)** *(wie Kupfer)* coppery

kupfer-, Kupfer-: ~**rot** *Adj.* copper-red; copper-coloured; ~**schmied der** coppersmith; ~**stecher der** copper[plate] engraver; **mein lieber Freund und** ~**stecher** *(ugs. scherzh.)* now then, my friend; ~**stich der a)** *o. Pl.* copperplate engraving *no art.*; **b)** *(Blatt)* copperplate print *or* engraving; ~**sulfat das** *(Chemie)* copper sulphate; ~**vitriol das** *(Chemie)* blue vitriol

kupieren [ku'pi:rən] *tr. V.* **a)** crop, dock ⟨*tail*⟩; crop ⟨*ears, hedge*⟩; clip ⟨*wings*⟩; prune ⟨*bush etc.*⟩; **b)** *(Med.)* arrest; check

Kupon *s.* **Coupon**

Kuppe ['kʊpə] **die;** ~, ~n **a)** [rounded] hilltop; **b)** *(Finger~)* tip; end

Kuppel ['kʊpl̩] **die;** ~, ~n dome; *(kleiner)* cupola; **die** ~ **der Bäume** the domed canopy of trees

Kuppel-: ~**bau der;** *Pl.* ~**bauten** domed building; ~**dach das** domed *or* dome-shaped roof

Kuppelei die; ~, ~en **a)** *(veralt. abwertend)* match-making; **b)** *o. Pl. (Rechtsspr.)* procuring; procuration

Kuppel·mutter die *(abwertend)* procuress

kuppeln 1. *itr. V.* **a)** *(bei einem Kfz)* operate the clutch; **hier muß man viel** ~: you have to use the clutch a great deal here; **b)** *(veralt.: Kuppelei betreiben)* match-make; play the match-maker. **2.** *tr. V.* **a)** *(koppeln)* couple (**an** + *Akk.*, **zu** [on] to); **b)** *(Technik)* couple; **gekuppelt** coupled ⟨*exposure meter, range-finder*⟩; **mit etw. gekuppelt sein** *(fig.)* be linked with sth.

Kuppel·pelz der *in* **sich** *(Dat.)* **den** ~ **verdienen** *(abwertend)* arrange a/the match; play the match-maker

Kuppelung *s.* **Kupplung**

Kuppler der; ~s, ~ *(abwertend)* procurer

Kupplerin die; ~, ~nen *(abwertend)* procuress

Kupplung die; ~, ~en **a)** *(Kfz-W.)* clutch; **b)** *(Technik: Vorrichtung zum Verbinden)* coupling; **c)** *o. Pl. (das Verbinden)* coupling; *(fig.)* linking

Kupplungs-: ~**pedal das** *(Kfz-W.)* clutch-pedal; ~**scheibe die** *(Kfz-W.)* clutch-plate; ~**seil das** *(Kfz-W.)* clutch-cable

Kur [ku:ɐ̯] **die;** ~, ~en [health] cure; *(ohne Aufenthalt im Badeort)* course of treatment; **eine** ~ **machen** take a cure/a course of treatment; **in** ~ **gehen** go to a health resort *or* spa [to take a cure]

Kür [ky:ɐ̯] **die;** ~, ~en **a)** *(Eiskunstlauf)* free programme; *(Turnen)* optional exercises *pl.*; **eine** ~ **laufen/tanzen** skate/dance one's free programme; **eine** ~ **turnen** perform one's optional exercises; **die beste** ~ **laufen** skate the best free programme; **b)** *(veralt.: Wahl)* choosing

Kurant [ku'rant] **das;** ~[e]s, ~e *(veralt.) coin whose face value is equal to the value of its constituent metals*

Küraß ['ky:ras] **der;** **Kürasses, Kürasse** *(hist.)* cuirass

Kürassier [kyra'si:ɐ̯] **der;** ~s, ~e *(Milit. hist.)* cuirassier

Kurat [ku'ra:t] **der;** ~en, ~en *(kath. Kirche)* curate

Kuratel [kura'te:l] **die;** ~, ~en *(Rechtsspr. veralt.)* guardianship; **unter** ~ **stehen** be under the care of a guardian; **jmdn. unter** ~ **stellen** place sb. under the care of a guardian; *(jmdn. stärker kontrollieren)* place sb. under closer supervision

Kurator [ku'ra:tɔr] **der;** ~s, ~en [-ra'to:rən] **a)** *(einer Stiftung)* trustee; **b)** *(einer Universität) university officer dealing with financial and legal matters;* **c)** *(veralt.: Vormund)* guardian

Kuratorium [kura'to:ri̯ʊm] **das;** ~s, **Kuratorien** board of trustees

Kur-: ~**aufenthalt der** stay at a health resort *or* spa; **ein** ~**aufenthalt am Meer** a stay at a seaside health resort; ~**bad das** health resort; spa

Kurbel ['kʊrbl̩] **die;** ~, ~n *(bei Autos, Maschinen)* crank [handle]; *(an Fenstern, Spieldosen, Grammophonen)* winder; *(an einem Brunnen)* [winding-]handle

kurbeln 1. *tr. V.* **a)** **etw. nach oben/unten** ~: wind sth. up/down; **den Eimer aus dem Brunnen** ~: wind the bucket up out of the well; **sie kurbelte den Tisch so tief es ging** she wound the table down as far as it would go; **b)** *(ugs.: filmen)* film; shoot ⟨*film*⟩. **2.** *itr. V.* turn *or* wind a/the handle; *(bei Autos)* turn a/the crank [handle]; crank; **er mußte ziemlich** ~, **um aus der Parklücke herauszukommen** *(fig. ugs.)* he had to use a lot of lock *(Brit.)* to get out of the parking space

Kurbel·welle die *(Technik)* crankshaft

Kürbis ['kyrbɪs] **der;** ~ses, ~se **a)** pumpkin; **b)** *(salopp: Kopf)* nut *(sl.)*; bonce *(Brit. sl.)*

Kürbis-: ~**flasche die** gourd; ~**kern der** pumpkin seed

Kurde ['kʊrdə] **der;** ~n, ~n, **Kurdin die;** ~, ~nen Kurd

kurdisch *Adj.* Kurdish; **das Kurdische** Kurdish; *s. auch* **deutsch; Deutsch**

Kurdistan ['kʊrdɪsta:n] **(das);** ~s Kurdistan

kuren *itr. V. (ugs.)* take a cure

küren *regelm. (veralt. auch unr.) tr. V.* choose (**zu** as)

Kürettage [kyrɛ'ta:ʒə] **die;** ~, ~n *(Med.)* curettage

Kürette [ky'rɛtə] **die;** ~, ~n *(Med.)* curette

kur-, Kur-: ~**fürst der** *(hist.)* Elector; ~**fürstentum das** *(hist.)* electorate; ~**fürstlich** *Adj. (hist.)* electoral; ~**gast der** visitor to a/the health resort *or* spa; *(Patient)* patient at a/the health resort *or* spa; ~**haus das** assembly rooms [at a health resort *or* spa]; ~**heim das** sanatorium

Kurie ['ku:ri̯ə] **die;** ~, ~n *(kath. Kirche)* Curia

Kurien·kardinal der *(kath. Kirche)* cardinal of the Roman Curia

Kurier [ku'ri:ɐ̯] **der;** ~s, ~e courier; messenger

Kurier·dienst der courier *or* messenger service; ~**e leisten** act as a courier/as couriers

kurieren *tr. V. (auch fig.)* cure (**von** of)

Kurier·gepäck das diplomatic bags *pl.*

kurios [ku'ri̯o:s] **1.** *Adj.* curious; strange; odd. **2.** *adv.* curiously; strangely; oddly

Kuriosa *s.* **Kuriosum**

kurioser·weise *Adv.* curiously *or* strangely *or* oddly enough

Kuriosität [kuri̯ozi'tɛ:t] **die;** ~, ~en **a)** *o. Pl.*

strangeness; oddity; peculiarity; **b)** *(Gegenstand)* curiosity; curio; *(Ereignis)* curious occurrence
Kuriositäten·kabinett das gallery of curios
Kuriosum [ku'ri̯o:zʊm] **das; ~s, Kuriosa** *(Gegenstand)* curiosity; curio; oddity; *(Situation)* curious *or* odd *or* strange situation
Kur-: ~kapelle die spa orchestra; **~karte die** [visitor's] pass *or* season ticket *(allowing use of the facilities of a health resort or spa)*; **~klinik die** health clinic; **~konzert das** concert [at a health resort *or* spa]; spa concert
Kurkuma ['kʊrkuma] **das; ~[s]** turmeric
Kurlaub ['ku:ɐ̯lau̯p] **der; ~[e]s, ~e** holiday [combined with cure] at a health resort *or* spa
Kür·lauf der *(Eiskunstlauf)* free programme; **er zeigte einen hervorragenden ~:** he gave an excellent display of free skating
kur-, Kur-: ~mittel das spa-treatment; **~mittel·haus das** spa-house; **~ort der** health resort; spa; **~park der** gardens *pl.* [of a/the health resort *or* spa]; **~pfalz die** *(hist.)* Electoral Palatinate; **~pfälzisch** *Adj. (hist.)* of the Electoral Palatinate *postpos., not pred.*; **~pfuscher der** *(ugs. abwertend)* quack; doctor; **~pfuscherei die** *(ugs. abwertend)* quackery; **~promenade die** [spa] promenade
Kurrende [kʊ'rɛndə] **die; ~, ~n** *(ev. Kirche)* young people's choir
Kurrent·schrift [kʊ'rɛnt-] **die a)** *(österr.)* Gothic handwriting *or* script; **b)** *(veralt.: Schreibschrift)* cursive writing *or* script; running hand
Kurrikulum *s.* **Curriculum**
Kurs [kʊrs] **der; ~es, ~e a)** *(Richtung)* course; **auf [nördlichen] ~ gehen** set [a northerly] course; **ein harter/weicher ~** *(fig.)* a hard/soft line; **den ~ ändern** *(auch fig.)* change *or* alter course; **seinen ~ beibehalten** *(auch fig.)* maintain course; **vom ~ abkommen** deviate from one's/its course; **den ~ halten** hold *or* maintain course; **~ auf Hamburg** *(Akk.)* **nehmen** set course for *or* head for Hamburg; **~ haben auf** (+ *Akk.*) be heading for; *s. auch* **einschlagen 1d; b)** *(von Wertpapieren)* price; *(von Devisen)* rate of exchange; exchange rate; **zum ~ von ...:** at a rate of ...; **die ~e steigen/fallen** prices/ rates are rising/falling; **der ~ des Dollars** the dollar rate; **hoch im ~ stehen** ⟨*securities*⟩ be high; *(fig.)* be very popular (**bei** with); **er steht hoch im ~ bei seinem Chef** his boss thinks very highly of him; **etw. außer ~ setzen** withdraw sth. from circulation; **c)** *(Lehrgang)* course; **ein ~ in Spanisch** *(Dat.)* a course in Spanish; a Spanish course; **d)** *(die Teilnehmer eines Kurses)* class; **e)** *(Sport: Rennstrecke)* course
Kurs-: ~änderung die *(auch fig.)* change of course; **~anstieg der** *(Börsenw.)* rise in prices/price; price rise; *(an Devisenbörsen)* rise in exchange rates/the exchange rate
Kursant [kʊr'zant] **der; ~en, ~en** *(DDR) s.* **Kursteilnehmer**
Kurs-: ~bericht der *(Börsenw.) s.* **~zettel; ~buch das** *(Eisenb.)* timetable
Kur·schatten der *(ugs. scherzh.)* lady-friend/boy-friend at/from the spa
Kürschner ['kʏrʃnɐ] **der; ~s, ~:** furrier
Kürschnerei die; ~, ~en a) *o. Pl.* furriery; **b)** *(Werkstatt)* furrier's workroom
Kürschnerin die; ~, ~nen furrier
Kurs-: ~ein·buße die *(Börsenw.)* fall in prices/price; price fall; *(bes. bei Devisen)* fall *or* decline in value; **~gewinn der** *(Börsenw.)* **a)** market profit; *(bei Devisen)* profit on the foreign exchange market; **b)** *(Wertzuwachs)* market gain
kursieren *itr. V.; auch mit sein* circulate
Kursist der; ~en, ~en *(DDR) s.* **Kursteilnehmer**
kursiv [kʊr'zi:f] *(Druckw.)* **1.** *Adj.* italic. **2.** *adv.* **etw. ~ drucken** print sth. in italics; *(zur Hervorhebung)* italicize sth.
Kursive die; ~, ~n, Kursiv·schrift die *(Druckw.)* italics *pl.*; **in ~:** in italics
Kurs-: ~korrektur die *(auch fig.)* course correction; **~leiter der** course-leader
kursorisch [kʊr'zo:rɪʃ] **1.** *Adj.* cursory. **2.** *adv.* cursorily
Kurs-: ~rück·gang der *(Börsenw.)* fall in prices/price; price fall; *(bei Devisen)* fall in exchange rates/the exchange rate; **~schwankung die** *(Börsenw.)* fluctuation in prices/price; *(bei Devisen)* fluctuation in exchange rates/the exchange rate; **~system das** *(Schulw.)* course system; **~teilnehmer der** course participant
Kursus ['kʊrzʊs] **der; ~, Kurse** *s.* **Kurs c, d**
Kurs-: ~verlust der *(Börsenw.)* market loss; *(bei Devisen)* loss on the foreign exchange market; **~wagen der** *(Eisenb.)* through carriage *or* coach; **~wechsel der** *(auch fig.)* change of course; **~wert der** *(Börsenw.)* market value *or* price; **~zettel der** *(Börsenw.)* stock exchange list; list of [market] quotations; *(bei Devisen)* list of foreign exchange rates
Kur·taxe die visitors' tax *(at a health resort)*
Kurtisane [kʊrti'za:nə] **die; ~, ~n** *(hist.)* courtesan
Kurve ['kʊrvə] **die; ~, ~n a)** *(einer Straße)* bend; curve; *(sehr scharf)* corner; **in dieser ~:** on this bend *or* curve; **die Straße macht eine [scharfe] ~:** the road bends *or* curves [sharply]; **die ~ kratzen** *(ugs.)* quickly make oneself scarce *(coll.)*; **die ~ kriegen** *(ugs.)* manage to do it; *(etw. überwinden)* manage to do something decisive about it; *s. auch* **schneiden; b)** *(Geom.)* curve; **c)** *(in der Statistik, Temperatur~ usw.)* graph; curve; **d)** *(Bogenlinie)* curve; **eine ~ fliegen** do a banking turn; **e)** *Pl. (ugs.: Körperformen)* curves
kurven *itr. V.; mit sein* **a)** ⟨*aircraft*⟩ circle; ⟨*tanks etc.*⟩ circle [round]; **um die Ecke ~:** turn the corner; **b)** *(ugs.: fahren)* drive around; *(mit dem Motorrad, Fahrrad)* ride around; **durch ganz Frankreich ~:** drive/ ride all round France
kurven-, Kurven-: ~diskussion die *(Math.)* curve-tracing; **~lineal das** French curve; **~reich** *Adj.* **a)** winding; twisting; **„~reiche Strecke"** 'series of bends'; **b)** *(ugs. scherzh.)* curvaceous; **~schreiber der** *(Technik)* graphic recording instrument; *(DV)* plotter; **~verhalten das** *(Kfz-W.)* cornering characteristics *pl.*; **~vor·gabe die** *(Leichtathletik)* stagger
Kur·verwaltung die administrative office/offices of a/the health resort *or* spa
kurvig *Adj.* curved; winding, twisting ⟨*path, road, etc.*⟩
kurz [kʊrts]; **kürzer** ['kʏrtsɐ], **kürzest...** ['kʏrtsəst...] **1.** *Adj.* **a)** *(räumlich)* short; **~e Hosen** short trousers; shorts; **etw. kürzer machen** make sth. shorter; shorten sth.; **ein kürzerer Weg** a shorter *or* quicker way; **die Hundeleine ~ halten** keep the dog on a short lead; **etw./alles ~ und klein schlagen** *od.* **hauen** *(ugs.)* smash sth./everything to bits *or* pieces; **den kürzeren ziehen** come off worst *or* second-best; get the worst of it; **nicht zu ~/zu ~ kommen** get one's/less than one's fair share; **b)** *(zeitlich)* short, brief ⟨*trip, journey, visit, reply*⟩; short ⟨*life, break, time*⟩; quick ⟨*look*⟩; **nach einer ~en Weile** after a short *or* little while; **es ~ machen** make *or* keep it short; be brief; **c)** *(knapp)* short, brief ⟨*outline, note, report, summary, introduction*⟩; **etw. in ~en Worten sagen** say sth. in a few brief words; **~ und bündig** *od.* **knapp** brief and succinct. **2.** *adv.* **a)** *(zeitlich)* briefly; for a short time *or* while; **die Freude währte nur ~** *(geh.)* his/her *etc.* joy was short-lived; **binnen ~em** shortly; soon; **er hatte binnen ~em das ganze Vermögen verjubelt** before long he had frittered away the entire fortune; **über ~ oder lang** sooner or later; **vor ~em** a short time *or* while ago; recently; **sie lebt erst seit ~em in Bonn** she's only been living in Bonn [for] a short time *or* while; **b)** *(knapp)* **~ gesagt** in a word; **~ angebunden sein** be curt *or* brusque (**mit** with); **sich ~ fassen** be brief; **~ und bündig** *od.* **knapp** briefly and succinctly; **~ und gut** in a word; **c)** *(rasch)* **ich muß mal ~ weg** I must leave you for a few minutes; **er schaute ~ herein** he looked *or* dropped in for a short while; **kann ich Sie ~ sprechen?** can I speak to you *or* have a word with you for a moment?; **ich muß ~ etwas in der Stadt erledigen** I've just got something to do in town. I won't be long; **~ und schmerzlos** *(ugs.)* quickly and smoothly *or* without any hitches; *s. auch* **entschlossen 3; d)** *(in geringer Entfernung)* **~ vor/hinter der Kreuzung** just before/past the crossroads; **~ vor Bremen hatten wir eine Panne** just before we reached Bremen, we broke down; **e)** *(mit geringem zeitlichen Abstand)* **~ vor/nach Pfingsten** just *or* shortly before/after Whitsun; **~ bevor .../nachdem ...:** just *or* shortly before .../after ...; *s. auch* **Atem; Kopf a; Prozeß c**
kurz-, Kurz-: ~arbeit die short time; short-time working; **~|arbeiten** *itr. V.* work short time; **~arbeiter der** short-time worker; worker on short time; **~ärm[e]lig** [~lɛrm(ə)lɪç] *Adj.* short-sleeved; **~atmig** [~a:tmɪç] **1.** *Adj. (auch fig.)* short-winded; **~atmig sein** be short of breath; be short-winded; **2.** *adv.* ⟨*speak*⟩ breathlessly; **~atmigkeit die; ~:** short-windedness; **~beinig** *Adj.* short-legged ⟨*breed, dog, etc.*⟩; ⟨*person*⟩ with short legs; **~bericht der** brief *or* short report; **~biographie die** short *or* potted biography
Kurze der; *adj. Dekl. (ugs.)* **a)** *(Kurzschluß)* short *(coll.)*; **b)** *(Schnaps)* schnapps
Kürze ['kʏrtsə] **die; ~, ~n a)** *o. Pl.* shortness; **b)** *o. Pl. (geringe Dauer)* shortness; short duration; brevity; **in ~:** shortly; soon; **c)** *o. Pl. (Knappheit)* brevity; **in aller/gebotener ~:** very briefly/with due brevity; **in der ~ liegt die Würze** *(Spr.)* brevity is the soul of wit *(prov.)*; **d)** *(Verslehre)* short syllable; short
Kürzel ['kʏrtsl̩] **das; ~s, ~ a)** shorthand symbol; **b)** *(Abkürzung)* abbreviation
kürzen *tr. V.* **a)** shorten; shorten, take up ⟨*garment*⟩; **ein Kleid um 5 cm ~:** shorten a dress by 5 cm; take a dress up 5 cm; **b)** *(verringern)* shorten ⟨*speech*⟩; shorten, abridge ⟨*article, book*⟩; reduce, cut ⟨*pension, budget, etc.*⟩; **jmdm. das Gehalt ~:** reduce *or* cut sb.'s salary; **eine gekürzte Fassung** a shortened *or* an abridged version; **c)** *(Math.)* cancel
kürzer *s.* **kurz**
kurzer·hand *Adv.* without more ado; **jmdn. ~ vor die Tür setzen** *(ugs.)* unceremoniously throw sb. out; **etw. ~ ablehnen** flatly reject sth.; reject sth. out of hand; **sich ~ entschließen, etw. zu tun** decide there and then to do sth.
kürzer|treten *unr. itr. V. (sich mehr schonen)* take things *or* it easier; *(sparsamer sein)* cut back; spend less
kürzest... *s.* **kurz**
kurz-, Kurz-: ~fassung die shortened *or* abridged version; **~film der** short; short film; **~form die** *(Sprachw.)* shortened *or* abbreviated form; **~fristig 1.** *Adj.* **a)** *(plötzlich)* ⟨*refusal, resignation, etc.*⟩ at short notice; **b)** *(für kurze Zeit)* short-term; **eine ~fristige Freiheitsstrafe** a short period of imprisonment; **c)** *(rasch)* quick ⟨*solution*⟩; **2.** *adv.* **a)** *(plötzlich)* at short notice; **sich ~fristig entschließen, etw. zu tun** make up one's mind within a short time to do sth.; **b)**

(für kurze Zeit) for a short time *or* period; *(auf kurze Sicht)* in the short term; **~fristig gesehen** looked at *or* viewed in the short term; **c)** *(in kurzer Zeit)* without delay; **~gebraten** *Adj.* ⟨*meat*⟩ fried on high heat for a very short time; **~gefaßt** *Adj.* terse; succinct; briefly-worded; **~geschichte die** *(Literaturw.)* short story; **~geschnitten** *Adj.* cropped short *postpos.*; **~haarfrisur die** bob; bobbed hair-style; **~haardackel der** short-haired dachshund; **~haarig** *Adj.* short-haired ⟨*dog, breed, etc.*⟩; ⟨*person*⟩ with short hair; **~|halten** *unr. tr. V.* **jmdn. ~halten** *(wenig Geld geben)* keep sb. short of money; *(wenig erlauben)* keep sb. on a tight rein; **~lebig** [~le:bɪç] *Adj. (auch fig.)* short-lived; *(wenig haltbar)* non-durable ⟨*goods, materials*⟩; with a short life *postpos.*; **~lebigkeit die** short-livedness; *(von Gebrauchsgütern)* lack of durability; **~lehrgang der** short course

kụ̈rzlich *Adv.* recently; not long ago; **erst ~:** just *or* only recently; only a short time ago

kụrz-, Kụrz-: ~meldung die brief report; *(während einer anderen Sendung)* news flash; **~nachrichten** *Pl.* news *sing.* in brief; news summary *sing.*; **~parker der** short-stay *(Brit.) or* short-term parker; **„nur für ~parker“** 'short-stay *(Brit.) or* short-term parking only'; **~referat das** short paper; **~|schließen 1.** *unr. tr. V.* short-circuit; **ein Auto ~schließen** short-circuit a car's ignition; **2.** *unr. refl. V.* **sich mit jmdm./etw. ~schließen** contact sb./sth. directly; **~schluß der a)** *(Elektrot.)* short-circuit; **b)** *(fig. ugs.)* brainstorm; **c)** *(falscher Schluß)* fallacy; **~schluß·handlung die** sudden irrational act; **~schrift die** shorthand; **~sichtig** *(auch fig.)* **1.** *Adj.* short-sighted; **2.** *adv.* short-sightedly; **~sichtigkeit die;** ~ *(auch fig.)* short-sightedness; **~stielig** *Adj.* short-stemmed ⟨*glass, flower*⟩; short-handled ⟨*axe, hammer, etc.*⟩; **~strecke die a)** short haul *or* distance; **auf ~strecken** over short distances; **b)** *(Sport)* sprint distance; sprint; **auf [den] ~strecken** over sprint distances; in sprinting

Kụrzstrecken-: ~flug der short-haul flight; **~lauf der** *(Sport)* short-distance race; sprint; *(Disziplin)* sprinting *no art.*; **~läufer der** *(Sport)* sprinter; **~rakete die** short-range missile

kụrz-: ~|treten *unr. itr. V.* **a)** take things *or* it easy; *(sparsam sein)* retrench; cut back; **b)** *(Milit.)* march with shortened steps; **~um** [-'-] *Adv.* in short; in a word

Kụ̈rzung die; ~, **~en a)** cut; reduction; **eine ~ des Gehaltes** a cut *or* reduction in salary; a salary cut; **b)** *(Streichung)* cut; *(das Streichen)* abridgement

kụrz-, Kụrz-: ~urlaub der short holiday; *(Milit.)* short leave; **~waren** *Pl.* haberdashery *sing. (Brit.)*; notions *(Amer.)*; **~waren·abteilung die** haberdashery department *(Brit.)*; notions department *(Amer.)*; **~weg** [-'-] *Adv. s.* **kurzerhand**; **~weil die;** ~ *(veralt.)* amusement; **allerlei ~weil treiben** have fun; amuse oneself; **~weilig** *Adj.* entertaining; **~welle die** *(Physik, Rundf.)* short wave; **auf** *od.* **über ~welle** on short wave; **~wellen·empfänger der** *(Funkt., Rundf.)* short-wave receiver; **~wellen·sender der** *(Funkt., Rundf.)* short-wave transmitter; **~wort das** *(Sprachw.)* abbreviation; **~zeit·gedächtnis das;** *o. Pl. (Psych.)* short-term memory; **~zeitig 1.** *Adj.* brief; **2.** *adv.* briefly; for a short time

kụsch *Interj.* [lie] down; *(sei still)* quiet

kụschelig *Adj.* cosy

kuscheln ['kʊʃl̩n] *refl. V.* **sich an jmdn. ~:** snuggle up *or* cuddle up to sb.; ⟨*cat etc.*⟩ snuggle up to sb.; **sich in etw.** *(Akk.)* **~:** snuggle up in sth.

Kụschel·tier das cuddly toy

kụschel·weich *Adj.* beautifully soft

kụschen ['kʊʃn̩] *itr. V.* **a)** knuckle under **(vor** + *Dat.* to); **b)** ⟨*dog*⟩ lie down

Kusine [ku'zi:nə] **die;** ~, **~n** *s.* **Cousine**

Kuß [kʊs] **der; Kụsses, Küsse** ['kʏsə] kiss; **Gruß und ~ [Dein ...]** love and kisses [from ...]

Küßchen ['kʏsçən] **das;** ~s, ~: little kiss; **ein ~ in Ehren kann niemand verwehren** *(Spr.)* a friendly kiss can do no harm

kụß·echt *Adj.* kissproof

küssen ['kʏsn̩] *tr., itr. V.* kiss; **jmdm. die Hand ~:** kiss sb.'s hand; **küss' die Hand** *(südd., österr.) (beim Kommen)* how do you do?; good day; *(beim Gehen)* goodbye; **sich** *od. (geh.)* **einander ~:** kiss [each other]

kụß·fest *Adj.*: *s.* **~echt**

Kụß·hand die: jmdm. eine ~ zuwerfen blow sb. a kiss; **mit ~** *(ugs.)* gladly; with [the greatest] pleasure; **jmdn./etw. mit ~ nehmen** *(ugs.)* be only too glad *or* pleased to take sb./sth.

Küste ['kʏstə] **die;** ~, **~n** coast

Küsten-: ~bewohner *Pl.* coastal inhabitants; **die deutschen ~bewohner** those living on the German coast; **~fischerei die** inshore fishing; **~gewässer das, ~meer das** coastal waters *pl.*; **~schiffahrt die** coastal shipping *no art.*; **~strich der** stretch of coast; coastal strip; **~wache die** coastguard [service]

Küster ['kʏstɐ] **der;** ~s, ~: sexton

Kustos ['kʊstɔs] **der;** ~, **Kustoden** [kʊs'to:dn̩] curator

Kụtsch·bock der coach-box

Kutsche ['kʊtʃə] **die;** ~, **~n a)** coach; carriage; **b)** *(salopp: Auto)* jalopy *(coll.)*

kụtschen *s.* **kutschieren**

Kụtschen·schlag der coach-door; carriage-door

Kụtscher der; ~s, ~: coachman; coach-driver

kutschieren 1. *itr. V.; mit sein* **a)** drive, ride [in a coach *or* carriage]; **b)** *(ugs.)* **durch die Gegend/durch Europa ~:** drive around/drive around Europe. **2.** *tr. V.* **a) jmdn. ~:** drive sb. [in a coach *or* carriage]; **b)** *(ugs.)* **jmdn. nach Hause ~:** run sb. home; **c)** *(ugs.: lenken)* drive ⟨*car, lorry*⟩

Kụtsch·pferd das coach-horse; carriage-horse

Kutte ['kʊtə] **die;** ~, **~n a)** [monk's/nun's] habit; **b)** *(Jugendspr.) (Jacke)* jacket; *(Mantel)* coat

Kutteln ['kʊtl̩n] *Pl. (südd., österr., schweiz.)* tripe *sing.*

Kutter ['kʊtɐ] **der;** ~s, ~: cutter

Kuvert [ku've:ɐ̯] **das;** ~s, **~s a)** *(landsch., veralt.: Umschlag)* envelope; **b)** *(geh.: Gedeck)* cover

kuvertieren [kuvɛr'ti:rən] *tr. V.* **etw. ~:** put sth. into an envelope

Kuvertüre [kuvɛr'ty:rə] **die;** ~, **~n** chocolate coating

Kuwait [ku'vait] **(das);** ~s Kuwait

Kuwaiter der; ~s, ~, **Kuwaiterin die;** ~, **~nen** Kuwaiti

kuwaitisch *Adj.* Kuwaiti

kV [ka:'fau] *(Physik) Abk.* **Kilovolt** kV

kW [ka:'ve:] *(Physik) Abk.* **Kilowatt** kW

KW *Abk.* **Kurzwelle** SW

Kwaß [kvas] **der;** ~ *od.* **Kwạsses** kvass

kWh *(Physik) Abk.* **Kilowattstunde** kWh

Kybernetik [kybɛr'ne:tɪk] **die;** ~: cybernetics *sing.*

Kybernetiker der; ~s, ~, **Kybernetikerin die;** ~, **~nen** cybernetician; cyberneticist

kybernetisch *Adj.* cybernetic

Kyrie ['ky:ri̯ə] **das;** ~, **~s** kyrie; **~ eleison!** [e'laizɔn] kyrie eleison

kyrillisch [ky'rɪlɪʃ] *Adj.* Cyrillic

KZ [ka:'tsɛt] **das;** ~[s], ~[s] *Abk.* **Konzentrationslager**

KZ-Häftling der, KZler der; ~s, ~, **KZlerin die;** ~, **~nen** concentration-camp prisoner

L

l, L [ɛl] **das;** ~, ~: l/L; *s. auch* **a, A**

l *Abk.* **Liter** l.

la [la:] la; **etw. auf la la singen** la-la sth.

Lab [la:p] **das;** ~[e]s, ~e **a)** *(Enzym)* rennin; **b)** *(zur Käseherstellung)* rennet

labberig ['labərɪç] *Adj. (ugs. abwertend)* **a)** *(fade)* wishy-washy; **~ schmecken** taste of nothing; **b)** *(weich)* floppy, limp ⟨*material*⟩; floppy ⟨*trousers, dress, etc.*⟩; slack ⟨*elastic*⟩; **c)** *(flau)* queasy

labbern ['labɐn] *(nordd. abwertend)* **1.** *tr. V.* slurp. **2.** *itr. V.* ⟨*sail*⟩ flap [about]

lạbbrig *s.* **labberig**

Labe die; ~ *(dichter. veralt.)* refreshment *no indef. art.*; *(~trunk)* refreshing draught

Label ['le:bl̩] **das;** ~s, **~s** label

laben ['la:bn̩] *(geh.)* **1.** *tr. V.* **jmdn. ~:** give sb. refreshment; **ein ~der Trunk** a refreshing drink; **das Auge ~** *(fig.)* delight the eye. **2.** *refl. V.* refresh oneself **(an** + *Dat.*, **mit** with)

labern ['la:bɐn] *(ugs. abwertend)* **1.** *tr. V.* talk; **was laberst du da?** what are you rabbiting *(Brit. coll.) or* babbling on about? **2.** *itr. V.* rabbit *(Brit. coll.) or* babble on

labial [la'bi̯a:l] *(Phon.)* **1.** *Adj.* labial. **2.** *adv.* labially

Labial der; ~s, ~e, **Labial·laut der** *(Sprachw.)* labial [sound]

labil [la'bi:l] *Adj.* **a)** *(Med.)* delicate, frail ⟨*constitution, health*⟩; poor ⟨*circulation*⟩; **b)** *(auch Psych.)* unstable ⟨*person, character, situation, equilibrium, etc.*⟩

Labilität [labili'tɛ:t] **die;** ~, **~en** *s.* **labil a, b:** delicateness; frailness; poorness; instability

Labiodental [labi̯o-] **der** *(Sprachw.)* labiodental

Lab-: ~kraut das *(Bot.)* bedstraw; **~magen der** *(Zool.)* abomasum; rennet stomach

Labor [la'bo:ɐ̯] **das;** ~s, ~s, *auch:* **~e** laboratory

Laborant [labo'rant] **der;** ~en, ~en, **Laborạntin die;** ~, **~nen** laboratory *or (coll.)* lab assistant *or* technician

Laboratorium [labora'to:ri̯ʊm] **das;** ~s, **Laboratorien** laboratory

laborieren *itr. V. (ugs.)* **a)** *(leiden)* suffer **(an** + *Dat.* from); **er laboriert schon seit Wochen an einer Grippe** he's been trying to shake off the flu for weeks *(coll.)*; **b)** *(sich abmühen)* **an etw.** *(Dat.)* **~:** labour *or* toil away at sth.

Labor-: ~platz der place in a/the laboratory; **~versuch der** laboratory experiment

Labsal ['la:pza:l] **das;** ~[e]s, ~e *od. (südd., österr.)* **die;** ~, ~e *(geh.)* refreshment; **ein ~ für jmdn. sein** refresh sb.

Labskaus ['lapskaus] **das;** ~ *(Kochk.)* ≈

lobscouse; *stew made with beef, potatoes, onions, gherkins, and beetroot, eaten with a fried egg*
Labung die; ~, ~en *(geh.)* refreshment
Labyrinth [laby'rɪnt] **das; ~[e]s, ~e a)** maze; labyrinth; **b)** *(Anat.)* labyrinth
labyrinthisch 1. *Adj.* labyrinthine. **2.** *adv.* **~ verschlungene Wege** a maze of winding paths
Lach·anfall der laughing-fit; fit of laughing
[1]**Lache** ['laxə] **die; ~, ~n** *(ugs.)* laugh
[2]**Lache** ['la(:)xə] **die; ~, ~n** puddle; *(von Blut, Öl)* pool
lächeln ['lɛçl̩n] *itr. V.* smile **(über** + *Akk.* at); **freundlich/verlegen ~:** give a friendly/an embarrassed smile
Lächeln das; ~s smile
lachen 1. *itr. V.* **a)** laugh; **da kann man** *od.* **ich doch nur ~:** that's a laugh; **jmdn. zum Lachen bringen** make sb. laugh; **die Clowns waren zum Lachen** the clowns were very amusing; **platzen/sterben vor Lachen** *(fig.)* split one's sides laughing/die laughing; **die Sonne** *od.* **der Himmel lacht** *(fig.)* the sun is shining brightly; **ihm lacht das Glück** *(dichter.)* Fortune smiled upon *or* favoured him; **wer zuletzt lacht, lacht am besten** *(Spr.)* he who laughs last, laughs longest; **zum Lachen sein** *(ugs. abwertend)* be laughable *or* ridiculous; **daß ich nicht lache!** *(ugs.)* don't make me laugh *(coll.)*; **b)** *(sich lustig machen)* laugh, make *or* poke fun **(über** + *Akk.* at); *s. auch* **dritt...**; [2]**Erbe. 2.** *tr. V.* **was gibt es denn zu ~?** what's so funny?; **es** *od.* **das wäre ja** *od.* **doch gelacht, wenn ...** *(ugs.)* it would be ridiculous if ...; **wenn dein Vater das erfährt, hast du nichts zu ~:** you won't think it funny if your father finds out about it; **da gibt es gar nichts zu ~:** it's no laughing matter; **nichts zu ~ haben** *(ugs.)* have a hard time of it **(bei** with); *s. auch* **scheckig**
Lachen das; ~s laughter; **ein lautes ~:** a loud laugh; **sie konnte sich das ~ kaum verbeißen** she could hardly stop herself laughing; **ihm wird das ~ noch vergehen** he'll be laughing on the other side of his face
Lacher der; ~s, ~ a) laugher; **die ~:** those who are/were laughing; **die ~ auf seiner Seite haben** score by making everybody laugh; **b)** *(kurzes Lachen)* laugh
Lach·erfolg der: einen ~ haben, ein ~ sein make everybody laugh; **einen großen ~ haben, ein großer ~ sein** bring the house down
lächerlich ['lɛçɐlɪç] *(abwertend)* **1.** *Adj.* **a)** *(komisch)* ridiculous; **jmdn./sich [vor jmdm.] ~ machen** make a fool of sb./oneself *or* make sb./oneself look silly [in front of sb.]; **sich** *(Dat.)* **~ vorkommen** feel ridiculous; **etw. ins Lächerliche ziehen** make a joke out of sth.; **b)** *(töricht)* ridiculous; ludicrous ⟨*argument, statement*⟩; **c)** *(gering)* derisory, ridiculously *or* ludicrously small ⟨*sum, amount*⟩; ridiculously low ⟨*price, payment*⟩; **d)** *(geringfügig)* ridiculously trivial *or* trifling; **~e Kleinigkeiten** ridiculous trivialities. **2.** *adv.* ridiculously; **~ wenig** ridiculously *or* ludicrously little
lächerlicher·weise *Adv. (abwertend)* ridiculously enough
Lächerlichkeit die; ~, ~en *(abwertend)* **a)** *o. Pl.* ridiculousness; *(von Argumenten, Behauptungen usw.)* ridiculousness; ludicrousness; **jmdn. der ~ preisgeben** make a laughing-stock of sb.; make sb. look ridiculous; **b)** *meist Pl.* ridiculous triviality
Lach-: ~fältchen das; *meist Pl.* laughter-line; **~gas das** laughing-gas
lachhaft *(abwertend)* **1.** *Adj.* ridiculous; laughable. **2.** *adv.* ridiculously
Lach·krampf der paroxysm of laughter; violent fit of laughter; **einen ~ bekommen** go [off] into fits of laughter; **einen ~ haben** be in fits of laughter; be convulsed with laughter
Lach·möwe die laughing gull; peewit gull
Lachs der; ~es, ~e salmon
Lach·salve die roar *or* peal of laughter
lachs-, Lachs-: ~ersatz der rock salmon; **~farben** *Adj.* salmon-pink; salmon-coloured; **~schinken der** lachsschinken *(rolled, smoked, and cured loin of pork)*
Lack [lak] **der; ~[e]s, ~e a)** varnish; *(für Metall, Lackarbeiten)* lacquer; *(Auto~)* paint; *(transparent)* lacquer; *(Nagel~)* varnish; **der ~ ist ab** *(salopp: etw. hat seinen Reiz verloren)* the novelty has worn off; *(salopp: jmd. ist nicht mehr ganz jung)* he/she's no spring chicken any more; *s. auch* **fertig**
Lack-: ~affe der *(ugs. abwertend)* dandy; **~arbeit die** piece of lacquerwork
Lackel ['lakl̩] **der; ~s, ~** *(bes. südd., österr. abwertend)* oaf; **so ein ~!** stupid oaf!
lacken *tr. V.: s.* **lackieren a**
Lack·farbe die lacquer paint; *(für Autos)* paint; *(Emaillelack)* enamel paint
lackieren *tr. V.* **a)** varnish ⟨*wood*⟩; varnish, paint ⟨*finger-nails*⟩; spray ⟨*car*⟩; *(mit Emaillelack)* paint ⟨*metal*⟩; **einen Wagen neu ~:** respray a car; **b)** *(ugs.: täuschen)* **jmdn. ~:** take sb. for a ride *(sl.)*; dupe sb.; **der Lackierte sein** have to carry the can *(sl.)*
Lackierer der; ~s, ~ *(Möbel~)* varnisher; *(Metall~)* painter; *(Auto~)* [paint-]sprayer
Lackiererei die; ~, ~en varnisher's; *(für Autos)* paint shop
Lackiererin die; ~, ~nen *s.* **Lackierer**
Lackierung die; ~, ~en a) *(von Holz)* varnishing; *(von Autos)* [paint-]spraying; **b)** *(Lackschicht) (auf Holz)* varnish; *(auf Metall, Autos)* paintwork; *(auf Lackarbeiten)* lacquer; **die zweite ~:** the second coat [of varnish/paint/lacquer]
Lack·leder das patent leather
lackmeiern *s.* **gelackmeiert**
Lackmus ['lakmʊs] **das** *od.* **der; ~** *(Chemie)* litmus
Lackmus·papier das *(Chemie)* litmus paper
Lack-: ~reiniger der original-colour restorer; **~schaden der** damage to the paintwork; **~schuh der** patent-leather shoe
Lade ['la:də] **die; ~, ~n** *(landsch.)* **a)** *(Schub~)* drawer; **b)** *(veralt.: Truhe)* chest
Lade-: ~baum der derrick boom; cargo boom; **~bühne die** *s.* **~rampe; ~fläche die** payload area; **~gerät das** *(Elektrot.)* charger; **~gewicht das** carrying capacity; maximum [permitted] load; **~hemmung die** jam; stoppage; **[eine] ~hemmung haben** *(fig. scherzh.)* have a mental block; **~klappe die** *(an einem LKW)* tail-board; tail-gate; *(an einem Flugzeug)* tail-door; **~kran der** loading crane; **~luke die** cargo hatch; loading hatch; **~mast der** derrick mast
[1]**laden 1.** *unr. tr. V.* **a)** *(ver~, be~)* load; **b)** *(aufnehmen)* **die Schiffe ~ Getreide** the ships are taking on *or* are being loaded with grain; **der LKW hat Sand ge~:** the truck is loaded up with sand; **der Tanker hat Flüssiggas ge~:** the tanker has a cargo of *or* is carrying liquid gas; **c)** *(legen)* load; **sich** *(Dat.)* **einen Sack auf die Schultern ~:** load a sack on one's shoulders; **schwere Schuld auf sich ~** *(fig.)* incur a heavy burden of guilt; **eine ziemliche Verantwortung auf sich ~:** shoulder quite a bit of responsibility; **d)** *(Munition einlegen)* load ⟨*gun, pistol, etc.*⟩; **e)** *(Physik)* charge; **er ist ge~** *(ugs.)* he's livid *(coll.)*; he's hopping mad *(coll.)*; **f)** *(aus~)* unload **(aus** from). **2.** *unr. itr. V.* load [up]; **der LKW hat schwer ge~:** the truck is heavily loaded; **schwer** *od.* **ganz schön ge~ haben** *(ugs. scherzh.)* be well tanked up *(sl.)*; have had a skinful
[2]**laden** *unr. tr. V.* **a)** *(Rechtsspr.)* summon; **b)** *(geh.: ein~)* invite
Laden der; ~s, Läden ['lɛ:dn̩] **a)** shop; store *(Amer.)*; **b)** *(ugs.: Unternehmung)* **der ~** läuft business is good; **wie ich den ~ kenne** *(fig.)* if I know how things go in this outfit *(coll.)*; **den ~ dichtmachen** shut up shop; **den ~ schmeißen** manage *or* handle everything with no problem; **den ~ hinwerfen** *od.* **hinschmeißen** chuck the whole thing in *(coll.)*; **c)** *Pl. auch ~ (Fenster~)* shutter
Laden-: ~besitzer der shopkeeper; storekeeper *(Amer.)*; **~dieb der** shop-lifter; **~diebstahl der** shop-lifting; **[die] ~diebstähle** shop-lifting offences; **~front die** shop-front; **~glocke die** shop-bell; **~hüter der** *(abwertend) (sich schlecht verkaufend)* slow seller; slow-moving article/line; *(sich nicht verkaufend)* non-seller; article/line which isn't/wasn't selling; **~inhaber der** *s.* **~besitzer; ~kasse die** till; **~preis der** shop price; **~schild das** shop sign
Laden·schluß der shop *or (Amer.)* store closing-time; **kurz vor/nach ~:** shortly before/after the shops *or (Amer.)* stores close/closed; **samstags ist um 14 Uhr ~:** the shops *or (Amer.)* stores close at two o'clock on Saturdays
Ladenschluß-: ~gesetz das law regulating shop *or (Amer.)* store closing-times; **~zeit die** shop *or (Amer.)* store closing-time
Laden-: ~schwengel der *(ugs. abwertend)* shop-boy; **~straße die** shopping-street; **~tisch der** [shop-]counter; **unterm ~tisch** *(ugs.)* under the counter; **~tochter die** *(schweiz.)* salesgirl; shop *or* sales assistant
Lade-: ~platz der loading area; **~rampe die** loading ramp; **~raum der a)** *(beim Auto)* luggage-space; **b)** *(beim Flugzeug, Schiff)* hold; **c)** *(bei LKWs)* payload space; **~stock der;** *Pl.* **~stöcke** *(hist.)* ramrod
lädieren [lɛ'di:rən] *tr. V.* damage; *(fig.)* damage, harm ⟨*reputation etc.*⟩; undermine ⟨*confidence*⟩; **lädiert aussehen** *(ugs., scherzh.)* look battered
lädst [lɛ:tst] *2. Pers. Sg. Präsens v.* **laden**
lädt [lɛ:t] *3. Pers. Sg. Präsens v.* **laden**
Ladung die; ~, ~en a) *(Schiffs~, Flugzeug~)* cargo; *(LKW~)* load; **eine ~ Kohle** a cargo/load of coal; **b)** *(beim Sprengen, Schießen)* charge; **eine ~ Dynamit/Schrot** a charge of dynamite/shot; **c)** *(ugs.: Menge)* load *(coll.)*; **eine ganze ~ Sand** a whole load of sand; **d)** *(Physik)* charge; **e)** *(Rechtsspr.: Vor~)* summons *sing.*
Lady ['leɪdɪ] **die; ~, ~s** *od.* **Ladies a)** *(Adlige)* Lady; **b)** *(Dame)* lady
Lafette [la'fɛtə] **die; ~, ~n** gun-carriage
Laffe ['lafə] **der; ~n, ~n** *(veralt. abwertend)* fop; dandy
lag [la:k] *1. u. 3. Pers. Sg. Prät. v.* **liegen**
Lage ['la:gə] **die; ~, ~n a)** situation; location; **in ruhiger ~:** in a quiet location; **eine gute ~ haben** be peacefully/well situated; be in a good/peaceful location; **in höheren/tieferen ~n** *(Met.)* on high/low ground; **b)** *(Art des Liegens)* position; **jetzt habe ich eine bequeme ~:** now I'm lying comfortably; now I'm [lying] in a comfortable position; **c)** *(Situation)* situation; **jmdn./sich in eine dumme ~ bringen** get sb./get [oneself] into a stupid situation; **er war nicht in der ~, das zu tun** he was not in a position to do that; **versetzen Sie sich in meine ~:** put yourself in my position *or* place; **jmdn. in die ~ versetzen, etw. zu tun** put somebody in a position to do sth.; **nach ~ der Dinge** as matters stand/stood; **die ~ der Dinge erfordert es, daß ...:** the situation requires that ...; **die ~ peilen** *od.* **spannen** *(ugs.)* see how the land lies; find out the lie of the land; *s. auch* **Herr; d)** *meist Pl. (Schwimmen)* **die 400 m ~n** the 400 m. individual medley; **die 4 × 100 m ~n** the 4 × 100 m. medley relay; **e)** *(Schicht)* layer; **f)** *(Stimm~)* register; **g)** *(Musik: Stellung der Hand)* position; **h)** *(ugs.: Runde)* round; **eine ~ ausgeben** *(ugs.) od.* **schmeißen** *(salopp)* get *or* stand a round

Lage-: ~**bericht der** report; *(Milit.)* situation report; ~**besprechung die** discussion of the situation; **eine ~besprechung abhalten** discuss the situation

Lagen-: ~**schwimmen das** *(Schwimmen)* individual medley; ~**staffel die** *(Schwimmen)* **a)** *(Wettbewerb)* medley relay; **b)** *(Mannschaft)* medley relay team

Lage·plan der map of the area

Lager ['la:gɐ] **das;** ~**s,** ~ **a)** camp; **ein ~ aufschlagen** set up *or* pitch camp; **b)** *(Gruppe, politischer Block)* camp; **ins andere ~ überwechseln** change camps *or* sides; join the other side; **c)** *(Raum)* store-room; *(in Geschäften, Betrieben)* stock-room; **etw. auf** *od.* **am ~ haben** have sth. in stock; **am ~ sein** be in stock; **etw. auf ~ haben** *(fig. ugs.)* be ready with sth.; **d)** *(Warenbestand)* stock; **wir müssen das ~ auffüllen** we must replenish our stocks; **e)** *(geh.)* bed; **jmdn. aufs ~ werfen** force sb. to take to his/her bed; put sb. in bed; **an jmds. ~ treten** step up to sb.'s bedside; **f)** *(Geol.)* bed; **g)** *(Technik)* bearing

lager-, Lager-: ~**bestand der** *(Wirtsch.)* stock; **den ~bestand aufnehmen** do a stocktaking; **die ~bestände räumen** clear stocks; ~**bier das** lager [beer]; ~**fähig** *Adj.* suitable for storage *or* storing *postpos.*; ~**feuer das** camp-fire; ~**feuer·romantik die** romance of the great outdoors; ~**gebühr die** *(Wirtsch.)* storage charge; ~**halle die** warehouse; ~**haltung die a)** storage; **b)** *(Wirtsch.)* holding stocks *no art.*; ~**haus das** warehouse

Lagerist der; ~**en,** ~**en** storeman; storekeeper

Lageristin die storekeeper

Lager-: ~**koller der: einen ~koller bekommen** *od.* **kriegen** be driven to a frenzy by life in the camp; ~**leben das** camp-life *no art.*; *(im Straf~, KZ usw.)* life in the camp; ~**leiter der** *(im Jugend~, Ferien~)* camp leader; *(im Straf~, KZ usw.)* camp director

lagern 1. *tr. V.* **a)** store; **etw. kühl/trocken ~:** keep *or* store sth. in a cool/dry place; **b)** *(hinlegen)* lay down; **jmdn. flach/bequem ~:** lay sb. flat/in a comfortable position; **die Beine hoch ~:** rest one's legs in a raised position; **c)** *(Technik)* support; mount ‹*machine-part, workpiece*›; **drehbar gelagert sein** be mounted on a pivot. **2.** *itr. V.* **a)** camp; be encamped; **auf Luftmatratzen ~:** use air-mattresses; **b)** *(liegen)* lie; ‹*foodstuffs, medicines, etc.*› be stored *or* kept; *(sich ab~)* have settled; *(fig.)* ‹*mist, fog, stillness, heat, etc.*› lie, hang; **ein guter Wein muß mehrere Jahre ~:** a good wine must be kept for several years; **c)** *(Geol.)* **hier ~ Eisenerze/Ölvorräte** there are deposits of iron ore/oil here; **d)** *(Technik)* be supported; ‹*machine-part, workpiece*› be mounted; **e)** *(beschaffen sein, sich verhalten)* **ganz ähnlich/anders gelagert sein** be quite similar/different [in nature]. **3.** *refl. V.* settle oneself/itself down; *(fig.)* ‹*mist, fog*› lie, hang

Lager-: ~**obst das** fruit for storing; **gutes ~obst sein** be good [fruit] for storing; [be fruit that] keep well; ~**platz der** campsite; ~**raum a)** store-room; *(im Geschäft, Betrieb)* stock-room; **b)** *o. Pl. (Fläche)* storage space; *(in Lagerhallen)* warehouse space; ~**schein der** *(Wirtsch.)* warehouse receipt; ~**statt die** *(geh.)* bed; couch *(literary)*; ~**stätte die a)** *(Geol.)* deposit; **b)** *s.* ~**statt**

Lagerung die; ~, ~**en a)** storage; **bei ~ im Tiefkühlfach** if *or* when stored in a deep-freeze; **b)** *(von Kranken)* **bei richtiger/falscher ~ des Verletzten** if the injured person is placed in the correct/wrong position

Lager·verwalter der storekeeper; stores supervisor

Lagune [la'gu:nə] **die;** ~, ~**n** lagoon

Lagunen·stadt die: die ~ Venedig Venice with its lagoons and islands

lahm [la:m] **1.** *Adj.* **a)** *(gelähmt)* lame; crippled, useless ‹*wing*›; **ein ~es Bein haben** be lame in one leg; **auf dem linken Bein ~ sein** be lame in the *or* one's left leg; **b)** *(ugs.: unbeweglich)* stiff; **ihm wurde der Arm ~:** his arm became *or* got stiff; **c)** *(ugs. abwertend: unzureichend)* lame, feeble ‹*excuse, explanation, etc.*›; **d)** *(ugs. abwertend: matt)* dreary; dull; feeble ‹*protest*›; dull, dreary, lifeless ‹*discussion*›; **ein ~er Typ** a dull, lethargic [sort of] bloke *(Brit. coll.) or (sl.)* guy; *s. auch* **Ente a. 2.** *adv.* **a)** *(kraftlos)* feebly; **b)** *(ugs. abwertend)* lethargically

lahm-, Lahm-: ~**arsch der** *(derb)* boring, lethargic old sod *(Brit. coarse) or (coll.)* bastard; ~**arschig** *(derb)* **1.** *Adj.* bloody *(Brit. sl.) or* damned lethargic; **2.** *adv.* bloody *(Brit. sl.) or* damned lethargically; ~**arschigkeit die;** ~**:** bloody *(Brit. sl.) or* damned lethargy

Lahme der/die; *adj. Dekl.* cripple

lahmen *itr. V.* be lame; **auf der rechten Hinterhand ~:** be lame in the right hind leg

lähmen ['lɛ:mən] *tr. V.* **a)** paralyse; **an beiden Beinen gelähmt sein** be paralysed in both legs; **er ist durch einen Unfall gelähmt** he was paralysed in an accident; **einseitig gelähmt sein** be paralysed down one side of one's body; **vor Angst wie gelähmt sein** be paralysed with fear; **b)** *(fig.)* cripple, paralyse ‹*economy, industry*›; bring ‹*traffic*› to a standstill; deaden ‹*enthusiasm*›; numb ‹*will*›; **die Angst lähmte seine Schritte** *(geh.)* he was rooted to the spot with fear; **von ~der Müdigkeit/~dem Entsetzen befallen werden** be completely numbed with fatigue/paralysed with horror

lahm|legen *tr. V.* bring ‹*traffic, production, industry*› to a standstill; paralyse ‹*industry*›

Lahmlegung die; ~**: eine ~ des Verkehrs/der Wirtschaft zur Folge haben** bring traffic to a standstill/paralyse the economy

Lähmung die; ~, ~**en a)** paralysis; **eine halbseitige ~:** paralysis down one side of the body; **b)** *(fig.) (der Wirtschaft, Industrie)* paralysis; *(der Begeisterung)* deadening; *(des Willens)* numbing; **zu einer ~ des Verkehrs führen** bring traffic to a standstill

Lähmungs·erscheinung die; *meist Pl.* symptom *or* sign of paralysis

Lahn [la:n] **die;** ~, ~**en** *(bayr., österr.) s.* **Lawine**

Laib [laip] **der;** ~**[e]s,** ~**e** loaf; **ein [halber] ~ Brot** [half] a loaf of bread; **ein ~ Käse** a whole cheese

Laibung die; ~, ~**en** *(Archit., Bauw.)* reveal; *(eines Bogens)* intrados; soffit

Laich [laiç] **der;** ~**[e]s,** ~**e** spawn

laichen *itr. V.* spawn

Laich-: ~**platz der** spawning-ground; ~**zeit die** spawning-time

Laie ['laiə] **der;** ~**n,** ~**n a)** *(Mann)* layman; *(Frau)* laywoman; **da staunt der ~ [und der Fachmann wundert sich]** it's incredible; **b)** *(Kirche) (Mann)* layman; *(Frau)* laywoman; **die ~n** the laity *pl.*

Laien-: ~**apostolat das,** *fachspr. auch:* **der** *(kath. Theol.)* lay apostolate; ~**bruder der** *(kath. Kirche)* lay brother; ~**bühne die** amateur theatre group

laienhaft 1. *Adj.* amateurish; unprofessional; inexpert. **2.** *adv.* amateurishly; unprofessionally; inexpertly

Laien-: ~**investitur die** *(MA.)* lay investiture; ~**prediger der** *(Rel.)* lay preacher; ~**richter der** lay judge; ~**schau·spieler der** amateur actor; ~**schwester die** *(kath. Kirche)* lay sister; ~**spiel das;** *o. Pl.* amateur performance; ~**stand der** *(Rel.)* laity *pl.*; ~**theater das a)** amateur theatre group; **b)** *s.* ~**spiel**

laisieren [lai'zi:rən] *tr. V. (kath. Kirche)* unfrock; defrock

Laisierung die; ~, ~**en** unfrocking; defrocking

Laisser-faire [lɛse'fɛ:r] **das;** ~**:** laisser-faire *no art.*

Laizismus [lai'tsɪsmʊs] **der;** ~ *(Politik, Geschichte)* laicism *no art.*

Lakai [la'kai] **der;** ~**en,** ~**en a)** lackey; liveried footman; **b)** *(abwertend)* lackey

lakaienhaft *(abwertend)* **1.** *Adj.* servile. **2.** *adv.* servilely

Lake ['la:kə] **die;** ~, ~**n** brine

Laken ['la:kn̩] **das;** ~**s,** ~ *(bes. nordd.)* sheet

lakonisch [la'ko:nɪʃ] **1.** *Adj.* laconic. **2.** *adv.* laconically

Lakritz [la'krɪts] **der** *od.* **das;** ~**es,** ~**e,**

Lakritze die; ~, ~**n** liquorice

Laktation [lakta'tsio:n] **die;** ~, ~**en** *(Biol.)* lactation

Laktose [lak'to:zə] **die;** ~ *(Biochemie)* lactose

la la [la'la] *in* **so ~ ~** *(ugs.)* so-so; **es geht ihm so ~ ~:** he's so-so *or* not too bad

lallen ['lalən] *tr., itr. V.* ‹*baby*› babble; ‹*drunk/drowsy person*› mumble

[1]Lama ['la:ma] **das;** ~**s,** ~**s** *(Zool.)* llama

[2]Lama der; ~**[s],** ~**s** *(Rel.)* lama

Lamaismus der; ~**:** lamaism

Lama·kloster das lamasery

Lamäng [la'mɛŋ] **die** *in* **aus der Lamäng** *(ugs.)* just like that; off the top of one's head *(sl.)*; *(ohne Besteck)* with one's fingers

Lama·wolle die llama [wool]

Lambda·sonde ['lambda-] **die** *(Technik)* lambda probe

Lambris [lã'bri:] **der;** ~, ~**:** wainscoting

Lamé [la'me:] **der;** ~**[s],** ~**s** lamé

Lamelle [la'mɛlə] **die;** ~, ~**n a)** *(einer Jalousie)* slat; **b)** *(eines Heizkörpers)* rib; **c)** *(eines Pilzes)* lamella *(Bot.)*; gill

Lamellen·kupplung die *(Technik)* multiplate clutch; multiple-disc clutch

lamentieren [lamɛn'ti:rən] *itr. V. (ugs.)* moan, complain (**über** + *Akk.* about)

Lamento [la'mɛnto] **das;** ~**s,** ~**s** *(ugs. abwertend)* loud regrets *pl.*; **ein [lautes** *od.* **großes] ~ [über etw.** *(Akk.)* *od.* **um etw.** *od.* **wegen etw.] anstimmen** kick up *or* make a [great] fuss [about sth.]

Lametta [la'mɛta] **das;** ~**s a)** lametta; **b)** *(ugs. iron.: Orden)* gongs *pl. (coll.)*

laminieren [lami'ni:rən] *tr. V.* **a)** *(Buchw.)* laminate ‹*material, book-cover*›; **b)** *(Textilw.)* draw ‹*fibres*›

Lamm [lam] **das;** ~**[e]s, Lämmer** ['lɛmɐ] **a)** lamb; **das ~ Gottes** the Lamb of God; **b)** *(o. Pl. ~fell)* lambskin

Lamm·braten der roast lamb *no indef. art.*; *(Gericht)* roast of lamb

Lämmchen ['lɛmçən] **das;** ~**s,** ~**:** little lamb

lammen *itr. V.* lamb

Lämmer-: ~**geier der** bearded vulture; ~**wolke die;** *meist Pl.* [light] fleecy cloud; cotton-wool cloud

lamm-, Lamm-: ~**fell das** lambskin; ~**fleisch das** lamb; ~**fromm 1.** *Adj.* ‹*horse*› as gentle as a [little] lamb; ‹*person*› as meek as a [little] lamb; **2.** *adv.* ~**fromm antworten** answer like a lamb; ~**kotelett das** lamb chop

Lämpchen ['lɛmpçən] **das;** ~**s,** ~**:** small *or* little light; **ein rotes ~:** a little red light

Lampe ['lampə] **die;** ~, ~**n a)** light; *(Tisch~, Öl~, Signal~)* lamp; *(Straßen~)* lamp; light; **[sich** *(Dat.)***] einen auf die ~ gießen** *(fig. ugs.)* wet one's whistle *(coll.)*; **b)** *(bes. fachspr.: Glüh~)* bulb; *s. auch* **Meister**

Lampen~: ~**fieber das** stage fright; ~**licht das;** *o. Pl.* lamplight; **bei ~licht** by lamplight; by the light of a lamp/lamps; ~**schirm der** [lamp]shade

Lampion [lam'piɔŋ] **der;** ~**s,** ~**s** Chinese lantern

Lampion·blume die Chinese-lantern plant; winter cherry

lancieren [lã'si:rən] *tr. V.* **a)** [deliberately] spread ‹*report, rumour, etc.*›; **eine Nachricht in die Presse ~:** get a report into the papers;

b) jmdn. in eine Stellung ~: get sb. into a position by pulling strings; **c)** *(bes. Wirtsch., Werbung)* launch

Land [lant] **das; ~es, Länder** ['lɛndɐ] *od. (veralt.)* **~e a)** *o. Pl. (Festland)* land *no indef. art.;* **an ~:** ashore; **~ in Sicht!** *(Seemannsspr.)* land [ahead]!; **„~ unter!" melden** report that the land is flooded *or* under water; **auf dem ~ leben** live on [dry] land; **festes ~ unter den Füßen haben** be on dry land *or* terra firma; **[wieder] ~ sehen** *(fig.)* be able to see light at the end of the tunnel *(fig.);* **kein ~ mehr sehen** *(fig.)* be getting deeper and deeper into the mire *(fig.);* **[sich** *(Dat.)***] eine Millionärin/antike Truhe/einen fetten Auftrag an ~ ziehen** *(ugs., oft scherzh.)* hook a millionairess/get one's hands on an antique chest/land a fat contract; **b)** *o. Pl. (Ackerboden, Gelände)* land; **ein Stück/5 Hektar ~:** a plot *or* piece of land *or* ground/five hectares of land; **das ~ bebauen/bestellen** farm/till the land; **c)** *Pl.* **~e** *(veralt.) (Gegend)* country; land; **dies ist das ~ van Goghs** this is van Gogh country; **in deutschen ~en** *(veralt.)* in Germany; **Wochen/Jahre waren ins ~ gegangen** *od.* **gezogen** weeks/years had passed *or* gone by; **d)** *o. Pl. (dörfliche Gegend)* country *no indef. art.;* **auf dem ~ wohnen** live in the country; **aufs ~ ziehen** move into the country; **über ~ fahren** *(veralt.)* travel from village to village; **e)** *Pl.* **Länder** *(Staat)* country; **andere Länder, andere Sitten** *(Spr.)* every nation has its own ways of behaving; **~ und Leute kennenlernen** get to know the country and its people *or* inhabitants; **außer ~es gehen/sich außer ~es befinden** leave the country/be out of the country; **das ~ der unbegrenzten Möglichkeiten** the land of opportunity; **das ~ der aufgehenden Sonne** the land of the rising sun; **das ~ der tausend Seen** the land of a thousand lakes; **wieder im ~e sein** *(ugs.)* be back again; **das ~ meiner/seiner Väter** *(geh.)* the land of my/his fathers *(literary;* **f)** *(Bundesland)* Land; state; *(österr.)* province; **das ~ Bayern/Kärnten** the Land *or* state of Bavaria/the province of Carinthia

-land das *(geh.)* **[das] Bayern~:** Bavaria's fair land; **das große Sowjet~:** the mighty Soviet nation; **das schöne Schweizer~:** the lovely country of Switzerland

land-, Land-: ~ab [-'-] *s.* **~auf; ~adel der** *(hist.)* landed aristocracy; **~arbeit die** agricultural work; farm work; **~arbeiter der** agricultural worker; farm worker; **~arzt der** country doctor

Landauer ['landauɐ] **der; ~s, ~** *(hist.)* landau

land-, Land-: ~auf [-'-] *Adv. in* **~auf, ~ab** *(geh.)* throughout the land; far and wide; **~aus** [-'-] *Adv. in* **~aus, ~ein** throughout the [length and breadth of the] country; **~bau der** *s.* **Ackerbau; ~besitz der** *s.* **Grundbesitz; ~bevölkerung die** rural population; **~brot das** farm-baked bread; *(Laib) round loaf of farm-baked type;* **~brücke die** *(Geogr.)* land bridge; **~butter die** farm butter

Lande-: ~an·flug der *(Flugw.)* [landing] approach; **~bahn die** *(Flugw.)* [landing] runway; **~erlaubnis die** *(Flugw.)* permission to land *no art.*

land-, Land-: ~ei das farm egg; **~ein** [-'-] *s.* **~aus; ~einwärts** [-'--] *Adv.* inland

Lande·klappe die *(Flugw.)* landing flap

landen 1. *itr. V.; mit sein* **a)** land; *(Schiff im Hafen)* arrive; **weich ~:** make a soft landing; **bei jmdm. nicht ~ [können]** *(fig. ugs.)* not get anywhere *or* very far with sb.; **b)** *(ugs.: ankommen)* **zu Hause/in Paris ~:** get home/to Paris; **c)** *(ugs.: gelangen)* land *or* end up; **im Krankenhaus/Zuchthaus/Papierkorb ~:** land up in hospital/end up in prison/the waste-paper basket. **2.** *tr. V.* **a)** land ‹*aircraft, troops, passengers, fish, etc.*›; **b)** *(ugs.: zustande bringen)* pull off ‹*victory, coup*›; have ‹*smash hit*›; **c)** *(Boxen)* land ‹*punch*›

länden ['lɛndn̩] *tr. V.* recover ‹*corpse, wreck, etc.*›

Land·enge die *(Geogr.)* isthmus

Lande-: ~piste die landing-strip; **~platz der a)** *(Flugw.)* landing-strip; airstrip; *(für Hubschrauber)* landing-pad; *(nicht ausgebaut)* place to land; **b)** *s.* **Landungsplatz**

Ländereien [lɛndə'raiən] *Pl.* estates

Länder-: ~kammer die second *or* upper chamber *(composed of representatives of the member states of a federation);* **~kampf der** *(Sport)* international match; **~kunde die;** *o. Pl.* regional geography *no art.;* **~spiel das** *(Sport)* international [match]

landes-, Landes-: ~bank die; *Pl.* **~banken** regional bank; **~behörde die** regional authority; **~brauch der** custom of the country; national custom; **~ebene die: auf [hessischer] ~ebene** at regional level [in Hessen]; at the level of the Land [of Hessen]; **~farben** *Pl.* national colours; *(eines Bundeslandes)* colours of a Land/province; **~fürst der** *(hist.) s.* **~herr; ~gericht das** *(österr.)* district court *(at a provincial capital);* **~grenze die** national border *or* frontier; **die ~grenzen** the borders of the country; **~haupt·mann der;** *Pl.* **~hauptleute** *od.* **~hauptmänner** *(österr.)* prime minister of a province; **~haupt·stadt die** capital; **~herr der** *(hist.)* sovereign prince; *(scherzh.)* the leading figure in his Land; **~innere das** interior [of the country]; **~kind das** *(veralt., noch scherzh.)* citizen [of the country]; **~kirche die** Land church; **~kunde die;** *o. Pl.* regional studies *pl., no art.; study of the geography, history, and civilization of a country/region;* **~kundig** *Adj.* knowledgeable about country *postpos.;* **~kundlich** *Adj.; nicht präd.* **~kundliche Forschungen** research into the geography, history, and civilization of a/the country/region; **~liste die** *(Politik)* regional list; **~mutter die** *(geh. veralt.)* sovereign lady; **~recht das** *(Rechtsw.)* law of a/the Land/province; **~regierung die** government of a/the Land/province; **~rekord der** *(Sport)* national record; **~sprache die** language of the country; **die drei belgischen ~sprachen** the three national languages of Belgium

Lande·steg der landing stage; jetty

landes-, Landes-: ~tracht die national costume *or* dress; **~üblich** *Adj.* usual *or* customary in a/the country; **die ~übliche Kleidung** the costume of the country; **~vater der** *(veralt.)* sovereign lord; **~verrat der** *(Rechtsw.)* treason; **~verteidigung die;** *o. Pl.* national defence; **~verweisung die** *(bes. österr.) s.* **Ausweisung; ~währung die** currency of a/the country; **~wappen das** national coat of arms

land-, Land-: ~fahrer der *(veralt.)* vagrant; **~fahrzeug das** land vehicle; **~fein** *in* **sich ~fein machen** *(Seemannsspr.)* get spruced up *or* dressed up to go ashore; **~flucht die** migration from the land *or* countryside [to the towns]; **~frau die** countrywoman

Land·friede[n] der *(hist.)* general peace

Landfriedens·bruch der *(Rechtsw.)* breach of the peace

land-, Land-: ~funk der farming programme [on the radio]; *(Sendefolge)* farming programmes *pl.* [on the radio]; **~gang der** *(Seemannsspr.)* shore leave; **~gericht das** regional court; Land court; **~gestützt** *Adj. (Milit.)* land-based; **~gewinnung die** reclamation of land; **~graf der** *(hist.)* landgrave; **~gut das** country estate; **~haus das** country house; **~jäger der a)** *(veralt.: Polizist)* country policeman; **b)** *(Wurst) small, highly seasoned, smoked, hard, flat sausage;* **~karte die** map; **~klima das** continental climate; **~kreis der** district; **~krieg der** land warfare; **~läufig** *Adj.* widely held *or* accepted; *(nicht fachlich)* popular; **~leben das;** *o. Pl.* country life

Ländler ['lɛntlɐ] **der; ~s, ~:** ländler

Land·leute *Pl.* **a)** *(veralt.)* country folk *or* people; **b)** *s.* **Landmann**

ländlich ['lɛntlɪç] *Adj.* rural; country *attrib.* ‹*life*›; **die ~e Ruhe** the quiet of the countryside

ländlich-sittlich *(scherzh.) Adj.* countrified; rustic; **hier herrschen noch ~e Zustände** people are still very countrified in their ways around here

Land-: ~luft die country air; **~macht die** land power; **~mann der;** *Pl.* **~leute** *(geh. veralt.)* husbandman *(arch.);* farmer; **~maschine die** agricultural machine; farm machine; **~maschinen** agricultural machinery; farm machinery; **~messer der** [land] surveyor; **~nahme** [~na:mə] **die;** *o. Pl.* occupation and settlement of land; **~partie die** *(veralt.)* outing into the country; **~pfarrer der** country parson; **~pfleger der** *(bibl.)* governor; **~plage die** plague [on the country]; *(fig.)* pest; nuisance; **dieses Jahr sind die Wespen eine wahre ~plage** there is an absolute plague of wasps all over the country this year; **~pomeranze die** *(ugs. abwertend)* country cousin *(derog.);* **~rat der a)** chief administrative officer of a/the district; **b)** *(schweiz.)* parliament of a/the canton; **~ratte die** *(ugs., oft scherzh.)* landlubber; **~recht das** *(hist.)* common law; **~regen der** steady rain; **~rücken der** *(Geogr.)* ridge of land

Landschaft die; ~, ~en a) landscape; *(ländliche Gegend)* countryside; **in die politische ~ passen** *(fig.)* fit in with the political mood; **in der ~ herumstehen** *(ugs.)* stand around; **die politische ~** *(fig.)* the political scene; **b)** *(Gemälde)* landscape; **c)** *(Gegend)* region

-landschaft die *(fig.)* scene; **in der Banken~:** on the banking scene

landschaftlich 1. *Adj.* regional ‹*accent, speech, expression, custom, usage, etc.*›; **die ~en Gegebenheiten** the nature *sing.* of the landscape; the topography *sing.* **2.** *adv.* **~ herrlich gelegen sein** be in a glorious natural setting; **die Umgebung der Stadt ist ~ sehr schön** the town is in *or* has a beautiful natural setting; **eine ~ gefärbte Aussprache** an accent with a regional tinge; **~ verschieden sein** differ from one part of the country to another

Landschafts-: ~bild das a) *(Gemälde)* landscape [painting]; **b)** *(Aussehen)* landscape; **~gärtner der** landscape gardener; **~maler der** landscape painter; **~malerei die;** *o. Pl.* landscape painting; **~pflege die;** *o. Pl.* landscape conservation *no art.;* **~schutz·gebiet das** conservation area

Land·schild·kröte die land tortoise

Landser ['lantsɐ] **der; ~s, ~** *(veralt.)* [ordinary] soldier

Land·sitz der country seat

Lands-: ~knecht der *(hist.)* lansquenet; **~mann der;** *Pl.* **~leute** fellow-countryman; compatriot; **~männin die; ~, ~nen** fellow-countrywoman; compatriot; **~mannschaft die a)** *(studentische Verbindung) association of students from the same country or region;* **b)** *(von Heimatvertriebenen) association of refugees and displaced persons from a particular region*

Land-: ~straße die country road; *(im Gegensatz zur Autobahn)* ordinary road; **~streicher der** tramp; vagrant; **~streicherei die;** *o. Pl.* vagrancy *no art.;* **~streicherin die** tramp; vagrant; **~streitkräfte** *Pl.* land forces; **~strich der** area; **ein bewaldeter ~strich** a wooded tract of land; a wooded area; **~sturm der a)** *(hist.)* landsturm; territorial reserve; **b)** *(schweiz.) territorial reserve consisting of men between the ages of 49 and 60;* **~tag der** Landtag; state parliament; *(österr.)* provincial parliament; **~technik die** *(DDR)* agricultural engineering *no art.*

Landung die; ~, ~en landing; **zur ~ ansetzen** begin one's/its landing approach; **den Piloten/das Flugzeug zur ~ zwingen** force the pilot/aircraft to land

Landungs-: ~boot das landing-craft; **~brücke die** [floating] landing-stage; **~platz der** landing-place; **~steg der** landing-stage

land-, Land-: ~urlaub der shore leave; **~vermesser der** *s.* **~messer; ~vermessung die** [land] surveying; **~vogt der** governor *(of an imperial province);* landvogt; **~wärts** *Adv.* landward; towards the land; **~weg der a)** *(über das Festland)* overland route; **auf dem ~weg** overland; by the overland route; **b)** *(Feldweg)* track across the fields; **~wehr die** *(hist.: Reserveeinheit)* territorial reserve; **~wein der** ordinary local wine; vin du pays; **~wind der** land *or* offshore breeze; **~wirt der** farmer

Land·wirtschaft die a) *o. Pl.* agriculture *no art.;* farming *no art.;* **b)** *(Betrieb)* [small] farm

land·wirtschaftlich 1. *Adj.; nicht präd.* agricultural; agricultural, farm *attrib.* ⟨*machinery*⟩. **2.** *adv.* **~ genutzt werden** be used for agricultural *or* farming purposes

Landwirtschafts-: ~ministerium das ministry of agriculture; **~schule die** agricultural college

Land·zunge die *(Geogr.)* tongue of land

¹lang [laŋ]; **länger** ['lɛŋɐ], **längst...** ['lɛŋst...] **1.** *Adj.* **a)** *(räumlich)* long; **eine Bluse mit ~en Ärmeln** a long-sleeved blouse; **etw. länger machen** make sth. longer; lengthen sth.; **b)** *(von bestimmter Länge)* **ein fünf Meter ~es Seil** a rope five metres long *or* in length; **c)** *(ugs.: groß)* tall; **komm mal her, Langer** come here, lofty *(coll.); s. auch* **Latte a; Lulatsch; d)** *(ausführlich)* long; **des ~en und breiten** *(geh.)* at great length; in great detail; **e)** *(zeitlich)* long; long, lengthy ⟨*speech, lecture, etc.*⟩; prolonged ⟨*thought*⟩; **seit ~er Zeit, seit ~em** for a long time; **f)** *nicht präd.* **ein vier Wochen ~es Seminar** a four-week seminar; **sein sechs Jahre ~es Studium** his six years of study. **2.** *adv.* **a)** *(zeitlich)* [for] a long time; **der ~ anhaltende Beifall** the lengthy *or* prolonged applause; **etw. nicht länger ertragen können** be unable to bear *or* stand sth. any longer; **~ und breit** at great length; in great detail; **b)** *(von bestimmter Dauer)* **eine Sekunde/einen Augenblick/mehrere Stunden ~:** for a second/a moment/several hours; **den ganzen Winter ~:** all through the winter; **sein Leben ~:** all one's life; **ich werde das mein Leben ~ nicht vergessen** I won't forget it as long as I live; *s. auch* **länger 2, 3**

²lang *(bes. nordd.)* **1.** *Präp.: s.* **entlang. 2.** *Adv.* **[nicht] wissen, wo es ~ geht** *(fig.)* [not] know what it's all about; *s. auch* **entlang**

lang-, Lang-: ~ärm[e]lig [~ɛrm(ə)lɪç] *Adj.* long-sleeved; **~atmig** [~a:tmɪç] **1.** *Adj.* long-winded; **2.** *adv.* long-windedly; **etw. ~atmig erzählen** relate sth. at great length; **~atmigkeit die; ~:** long-windedness; **~beinig** *Adj.* long-legged

lange; länger, am längsten *Adv.* **a)** a long time; **er ist schon ~ fertig** he finished long ago; **~ schlafen/arbeiten** sleep/work late; **bist du schon ~ hier?** have you been here long?; **es ist schon ~/länger her, daß ...:** it's a long time/some time since ...; **es ist noch gar nicht ~ her, daß ich ihn gesehen habe** it's not long since I saw him; I saw him not long ago; **[es dauert] nicht mehr ~, und es gibt Ärger** it won't be long before there's trouble; **da kannst du ~ warten** you can wait for ever; **sie wird es nicht mehr ~ machen** *(ugs.)* she won't last much longer; **was fragst du noch ~?** why do you keep asking questions?; *s. auch* **länger 3; b)** *(bei weitem)* **das ist [noch] ~ nicht alles** that's not all by any means; that's not all, not by a long chalk *or* shot *(coll.);* **er spielt ~ nicht so gut Tennis wie du** he doesn't play tennis nearly *or* anything like as well as you; **er ist noch ~ nicht soweit** he's got a long time to go till then

Länge ['lɛŋə] **die; ~, ~n a)** *(räumliche Ausdehnung)* length; **eine ~ von zwei Metern haben** be two metres in length; **auf einer ~ von zwei Kilometern** for two kilometres; **etw. der ~ nach falten** fold sth. lengthways; **der ~ nach hinschlagen** fall flat on one's face; measure one's length on the ground/floor; **sich der ~ nach hinwerfen** throw oneself flat on the ground/floor; **b)** *(hoher Wuchs)* tallness; **sich zu seiner ganzen ~ aufrichten** draw oneself up to one's full height; **c)** *(Ausführlichkeit)* length; **d)** *(Geogr.)* longitude; **die Insel liegt auf** *od.* **unter] 15° östlicher ~:** the longitude of the island is 15° east; **e)** *(zeitliche Ausdehnung)* length; **ein Film von einer Stunde ~:** a film one hour in length; an hour-long film; **etw. in die ~ ziehen** drag sth. out; **sich in die ~ ziehen** drag on; go on and on; **f)** *(Sport)* length; **mit einer ~ [Vorsprung] siegen** win by a length; **um ~n gewinnen** *(ugs.)* win easily; **g)** *Pl. (in einem Film, Theaterstück usw.)* long drawn-out *or* tedious scene; *(in einem Buch)* long drawn-out *or* tedious passage; **h)** *(Verslehre)* long syllable; long

länge·lang *Adv.* at full length

langen *(ugs.)* **1.** *itr. V.* **a)** *(ausreichen)* be enough; **das Geld langt nicht** I/we *etc.* haven't got enough money; **das langt mir** that's enough for me; that'll do for me; **jetzt langt's mir aber!** now I've had enough!; that's enough of that!; **b)** *(greifen)* reach **(in + *Akk.*** into; **auf + *Akk.*** on to; **nach** for); **c)** *(sich erstrecken)* **bis zu etw. ~:** reach sth.; **d)** *(erreichen)* reach; **bis zu etw. ~:** reach sth.. **2.** *tr. V.* **jmdm. etw. ~:** pass *or* hand sb. sth.; **jmdm. eine ~:** give sb. a clout [around the ear] *(coll.)*

längen *tr. V.* **a)** lengthen ⟨*garment*⟩; **b)** *(strecken)* thin ⟨*soup, sauce*⟩

Längen-: ~grad der *(Geogr.)* degree of longitude; **dieser Ort liegt auf dem 20. ~grad der östlichen Halbkugel** the longitude of this place is 20° east; **~kreis der** *s.* **Meridian; ~maß das** unit of length

länger ['lɛŋɐ] **1.** *s.* **¹lang, lange. 2.** *Adj.* **eine ~e Abwesenheit/Behandlung** a fairly long *or* prolonged absence/period of treatment; **seit ~er Zeit** for quite some time; **es ist doch eine ~e Strecke** it's quite a long way; it's a longish way. **3.** *adv.* for some time; **es hat etwas ~ gedauert** it took/has taken some time

länger·fristig [-frɪstɪç] **1.** *Adj.* fairly long-term. **2.** *adv.* on a fairly long-term basis

lang·ersehnt *Adj.; nicht präd.* long-awaited; longed-for

Lange·weile die; ~ *od.* **Langenweile** boredom; **~ haben** be bored; **aus ~** *od.* **Langerweile** out of boredom

lang-, Lang-: ~fädig [~fɛ:dɪç] *Adj.* *(schweiz.)* long-winded; **~finger der** *(oft scherzh.) (Dieb)* thief; *(Taschendieb)* pickpocket; **~fristig** [~frɪstɪç] **1.** *Adj.* long-term; long-dated ⟨*loan*⟩; **2.** *adv.* on a long-term basis; **~fristig gesehen** in the long term; **~gehegt** *Adj.; nicht präd.* long-cherished; **~|gehen** *unr. itr. V.; mit sein (ugs.)* **an etw.** *(Dat.)* **~gehen** go along sth.; *s. auch* **²lang; ~gestreckt** *Adj.* long; **~gezogen** *Adj.* long drawn-out; **~haardackel der** long-haired dachshund; **~haarig** *Adj.* long-haired; **~haus das** nave; *(mit Seitenschiffen)* nave and side aisles; **~holz das;** *o. Pl. (Forstw.)* long timber; **~jährig** *Adj.; nicht präd.* ⟨*customer, friend*⟩ of many years' standing; long-standing ⟨*friendship*⟩; **~jährige Erfahrung** many years of experience; many years' experience; **eine ~jährige Strafe** a long sentence; **einer unserer ~jährigen Mitarbeiter** a colleague who has been with us for many years; **~lauf der** *(Skisport)* cross-country; **~läufer der** cross-country skier

Langlauf·ski der cross-country ski

lang-, Lang-: ~lebig [~le:bɪç] *Adj.* long-lived ⟨*animals, organisms*⟩; durable ⟨*goods, materials*⟩; **~lebige Gebrauchsgüter** consumer durables; **~lebigkeit die; ~** *(von Tieren, Organismen)* longevity; long-livedness; *(von Gebrauchsgütern)* durability; **~|legen** *refl. V. (ugs.)* **a) sich eine Stunde/etwas ~legen** lie down *or* have a lie down for an hour/a bit; **b)** *(salopp: hinfallen)* fall flat [on one's face/back]

länglich ['lɛŋlɪç] *Adj.* oblong; long narrow ⟨*opening*⟩; long [narrow] ⟨*envelope*⟩; long ⟨*box*⟩; oval ⟨*roll*⟩

länglich·rund *Adj.: s.* **oval**

lang-, Lang-: ~mähnig [~mɛ:nɪç] *Adj.* long-maned ⟨*animal*⟩; long-haired ⟨*person*⟩; **~mut die; ~:** forbearance; **~mütig** [~my:tɪç] *Adj.* forbearing; **~mütigkeit die; ~:** forbearance

Langobarde [laŋgo'bardə] **der; ~n, ~n** Lombard

langobardisch *Adj.* Lombardic

Lang-: ~ohr das *(scherzh.)* **a)** *(Hase)* hare; *(Kaninchen)* rabbit; bunny *(child lang.);* **b)** *(Esel)* donkey; **~pferd das** *(Turnen)* long horse

längs [lɛŋs] **1.** *Präp. + Gen. od. (selten) Dat.* along; **~ des Flusses** *od.* **dem Fluß** along the river [bank]; **~ der Straße standen Apfelbäume** the road was lined with apple-trees. **2.** *Adv.* **a)** lengthways; **stellt das Sofa hier ~ an die Wand** put the sofa along here against the wall; **b)** *(nordd.) s.* **entlang**

Längs·achse die longitudinal axis

langsam 1. *Adj.* **a)** slow; low ⟨*speed*⟩; **b)** *(allmählich)* gradual. **2.** *adv.* **a)** slowly; **geh [etwas] ~er!** go [a bit] more slowly; slow down [a bit]!; **~, aber sicher** *(ugs.)* slowly but surely; **b)** *(allmählich)* gradually; **es wird ~ Zeit, daß du gehst** it's about time you left *or* went

Langsamkeit die; ~: slowness

Lang-: ~schäfter [~ʃɛftɐ] **der; ~s, ~:** high boot; **~schläfer der** late riser; **~seite die** long side

längs·gestreift *Adj.* with vertical stripes; vertically striped; ⟨*material*⟩ with lengthwise stripes

Langspiel·platte die long-playing record; LP

längs-, Längs-: ~richtung die longitudinal direction; **in der ~richtung** lengthways; **~schnitt der** longitudinal section; **~seite die** long side; **~seits** *(Seemannsspr.)* **1.** *Präp. + Gen.* alongside; **2.** *Adv.* alongside; **~seits am Kai** alongside the quay

längst [lɛŋst] *Adv.* **a)** *(schon lange)* a long time ago; long since; **ich wußte das ~:** I've known that for a long time; I knew that long ago; **er ist ~ gestorben** he's been dead for a long time; he is long since dead; **seine ~ fälligen Schulden** his long overdue debts; **b)** *(bei weitem)* **hier ist es ~ nicht so schön** it isn't nearly as nice here; **sie singt ~ nicht so gut wie du** she doesn't sing anything like as well as you; **ich bin ~ noch nicht fertig** I'm nowhere near finished

längst... *s.* **¹lang**

längstens ['lɛŋstns] *Adv. (ugs.)* **a)** *(höchstens)* at [the] most; **~ eine Woche** a week at the most; **b)** *(spätestens)* at the latest

lang·stielig *Adj.* long-stemmed ⟨*glass, flower*⟩; long-handled ⟨*axe, hammer, etc.*⟩

Lang·strecke die a) long haul *or* distance; **auf ~n** over long distances; **b)** *(Sport)* long distance; **auf [den] ~n** over long distances; in long-distance running

Langstrecken-: ~flug der long-haul flight; **~lauf der** *(Sport)* long-distance race; *(Disziplin)* long-distance running *no art.*; **~läufer der** *(Sport)* long-distance runner; **~rakete die** long-range missile

Languste [laŋ'gʊstə] **die; ~, ~n** spiny lobster; langouste

lang-, Lang-: ~weile die: *s.* **Langeweile; ~weilen 1.** *tr. V.* bore; **er sah gelangweilt aus dem Fenster** he gazed out of the window, feeling bored. **2.** *refl. V.* be bored; **sich tödlich** *od.* **zu Tode ~weilen** be bored to death; **~weiler der** *(ugs. abwertend)* **a)** bore; **b)** *(schwerfälliger Mensch)* slowcoach; **~weilig 1.** *Adj.* **a)** boring; dull ⟨*place*⟩; **b)** *(ugs.: schleppend)* slow ⟨*person*⟩; tedious ⟨*business*⟩; **ein ~weiliger Kerl** a slowcoach; **2.** *adv.* boringly; **~weiligkeit die; ~ a)** boringness; **b)** *(Langsamkeit)* slowness; **~welle die** *(Physik, Rundf.)* long wave; **auf** *od.* **über ~welle** on long wave; **~wierig** [~vi:rɪç] *Adj.* lengthy; prolonged ⟨*search*⟩; protracted, lengthy, long ⟨*negotiations, treatment*⟩; **~wierigkeit die; ~:** lengthiness; **~zeile die** *(Verslehre)* long line; **~zeit·gedächtnis das** long-term memory; **~zeit·programm das** long-term programme

Lanolin [lano'li:n] **das; ~s** lanolin

Lanze ['lantsə] **die; ~, ~n** lance; *(zum Werfen)* spear; **für jmdn. eine ~ brechen** *(fig.)* take up the cudgels on sb.'s behalf

Lanzen-: ~spitze die lance-head; *(der Wurflanze)* spearhead; **~stoß der** lance thrust; *(mit der Wurflanze)* spear thrust

Lanzette [lan'tsɛtə] **die; ~, ~n** *(Med.)* lancet

Lanzett·fischchen das *(Zool.)* lancelet

Laos ['la:ɔs] **(das)** Laos

Laote [la'o:tə] **der; ~n, ~n** Laotian

laotisch *Adj.* Laotian

lapidar [lapi'da:ɐ̯] **1.** *Adj. (kurz, aber wirkungsvoll)* succinct; *(knapp)* terse; **in ~er Kürze** succinctly/tersely. **2.** *adv.* succinctly/tersely

Lapislazuli [lapɪs'la:tsuli] **der; ~, ~:** lapis lazuli

Lappalie [la'pa:li̯ə] **die; ~, ~n** trifle

Lappe ['lapə] **der; ~n, ~n** Lapp; Laplander

Lappen der; ~s, ~ a) cloth; *(Fetzen)* rag; *(Wasch~)* flannel; **b)** *(salopp: Geldschein)* [large] note; **ein blauer ~:** a hundred-mark note; **c)** *(Zool.)* flap of skin; *(eines Hahns)* wattle; **d)** *in* **jmdm. durch die ~ gehen** *(ugs.)* slip through sb.'s fingers; **e)** *(Anat.)* lobe

läppen ['lɛpn̩] *tr. V. (Technik)* lap

läppern ['lɛpɐn] *tr. V. (ugs.) in* **es läppert jmdn. nach etw.** *(landsch.)* sb. has a sudden craving for sth.; **es läppert sich** it's mounting up

lappig *Adj. (ugs.)* limp; loosely sagging ⟨*skin*⟩

läppisch ['lɛpɪʃ] *Adj.* silly

Lapp·land (das) Lapland

lappländisch *Adj.* lapp

Lapp·maschine die *(Technik)* lapping machine

Lapsus ['lapsʊs] **der; ~, ~** *(geh.)* slip; *(gesellschaftlich)* faux pas; **mir ist ein ~ unterlaufen** I made a slip/committed a faux pas

Laptop ['lɛptɔp] **der; ~s, ~s** *(DV)* lap-top

Lärche ['lɛrçə] **die; ~, ~n** larch

Largo ['largo] **das; ~[s], ~s** *od.* **Larghi** ['largi] *(Musik)* largo

larifari [lari'fa:ri] *(ugs.)* **1.** *Interj.* nonsense; rubbish; fiddlesticks. **2.** *Adj.; nicht attr.* slipshod. **3.** *adv.* sloppily

Larifari das; ~s *(ugs.)* nonsense; rubbish

Lärm [lɛrm] **der; ~[e]s** noise; *(Krach)* din; row *(coll.)*; *(fig.)* fuss; to-do; **um jmdn./etw. ~ machen** *(fig.)* make a fuss about sb./sth.; **„Viel ~ um Nichts"** 'Much Ado about Nothing'; **viel ~ um nichts machen** *(fig.)* make a big fuss *or* to-do about nothing; **~ schlagen** kick up *or* make a fuss

lärm-, Lärm-: ~bekämpfung die; *o. Pl.* noise abatement; **~belästigung die** disturbance caused by noise; **~belastung die** noise pollution; **~empfindlich** *Adj.* sensitive to noise *postpos.*

lärmen *itr. V.* make a noise *or (coll.)* row; ⟨*radio*⟩ blare; **die ~de Menge** the noisy crowd; **~d vorbeigehen** go noisily past

larmoyant [larmo̯a'jant] *(geh.)* **1.** *Adj.* maudlin; tearfully sentimental. **2.** *adv.* in a maudlin way; in a tearful and sentimental manner

Larmoyanz [larmo̯a'jants] **die; ~** *(geh.)* maudlin *or* tearful sentimentality

Lärm-: ~pegel der noise level; **~quelle die** source of noise; **~schutz der a)** protection against noise; **b)** *(Vorrichtung)* noise barrier; noise *or* sound insulation *no indef. art.*; **~schutz·wand die** sound-insulating wall

Larve ['larfə] **die; ~, ~n a)** grub; larva; **b)** *(veralt.: Maske)* mask; **c)** *(abwertend veralt.: Gesicht)* mask

las [la:s] *1. u. 3. Pers. Sg. Prät. v.* **lesen**

lasch [laʃ] **1.** *Adj.* limp ⟨*handshake*⟩; feeble ⟨*action, measure*⟩; listless ⟨*movement, gait*⟩; lax ⟨*upbringing*⟩. **2.** *adv. s. Adj.:* limply; feebly; listlessly; laxly; **~ gewürzt sein** be insipid *or* tasteless

Lasche die; ~, ~n a) *(Gürtel~)* loop; *(eines Briefumschlags)* flap; *(Schuh~)* tongue; **b)** *(Technik) (von Eisenbahnschienen)* fishplate; *(Stoßplatte)* butt strap

Laschheit die; ~ *s.* **lasch 1:** limpness; feebleness; listlessness; laxness

Laser ['leɪzə] **der; ~s, ~** *(Physik)* laser

Laser-: ~strahl der *(Physik)* laser beam; **~ziel·gerät das** laser sight

lasieren [la'zi:rən] *tr. V.* varnish

laß [las] *Imperativ Sg. v.* **lassen**

lassen ['lasn̩] **1.** *unr. tr. V.* **a)** *mit Inf. + Akk. (2. Part. ~) (veranlassen)* **etw. tun/machen/bauen/waschen ~:** have *or* get sth. done/made/built/washed; **von welcher Baufirma haben Sir Ihr Haus bauen ~?** which builder did you get to build your house?; **Essen kommen ~:** have some food sent in; **Wasser in die Wanne laufen ~:** run water into the bath; **das Licht über Nacht brennen ~:** keep the light on overnight; **sie ließ mir eine Nachricht zukommen** she sent me a message; **jmdn. warten/erschießen ~:** keep sb. waiting/have sb. shot; **jmdn. grüßen ~:** send one's regards to sb.; **jmdn. kommen/rufen ~:** send for sb.; **jmdm. etw. mitteilen/jmdn. etw. wissen ~:** let sb. know sth.; **b)** *mit Inf. + Akk. (2. Part. ~) (erlauben)* **jmdn. etw. tun ~:** let sb. do sth.; allow sb. to do sth.; **jmdn. ausreden ~:** let sb. finish speaking; allow sb. to finish speaking; **er läßt sich** *(Dat.)* **nichts sagen** you can't tell him anything; **ich lasse mich nicht beleidigen/einschüchtern** I won't be insulted/intimidated; **das lasse ich mir nicht gefallen** I'm not standing for that; **alles mit sich geschehen ~:** put up with anything and everything; **c)** *(zugestehen, belassen)* **laß den Kindern den Spaß** let the children enjoy themselves; **jmdn. in Frieden ~:** leave sb. in peace; **laß ihn in seinem Glauben** don't disillusion him; **nichts unversucht ~:** try everything; **etw. ungesagt ~:** leave sth. unsaid; **jmdn. kalt/unbeeindruckt ~:** leave sb. cold/unimpressed; **das muß man ihm/ihr ~:** one must grant *or* give him/her that; **d)** *(hinein~/heraus~)* let *or* allow **(in** + *Akk.* into, **aus** out of); **jmdn. in die Wohnung ~:** let *or* allow sb. into the flat *(Brit.) or (Amer.)* apartment; **e)** *(unterlassen)* stop; *(Begonnenes)* put aside; **laß das!** stop that *or* it!; **etw. nicht ~ können** be unable to stop sth.; **es nicht ~ können, etw. zu tun** be unable to stop doing sth.; **tu, was du nicht ~ kannst** go ahead and do what you want to do; **die Arbeit Arbeit sein ~** *(ugs.)* forget about work *(coll.)*; **laß das Grübeln!** stop brooding!; **f)** *(zurück~; bleiben ~)* leave; **jmdn. allein ~:** leave sb. alone *or* on his/her own; **g)** *(überlassen)* **jmdm. etw. ~:** let sb. have sth.; **jmdm. etw. als** *od.* **zum Pfand ~:** leave sb. sth. as security; **jmdm. etw. billig/für 10 Mark ~:** let sb. have sth. cheaply/for ten marks; **h)** *(als Aufforderung)* **laß/laßt uns gehen/fahren!** let's go!; **i)** *(verlieren)* lose; *(ausgeben)* spend; **sein Leben für eine Idee ~:** lay down one's life for an idea; **er hat zwei Söhne im Krieg ~ müssen** he lost two sons in the war; **er hat im Kasino viel Geld gelassen** he lost/*(langfristig)* has lost a lot of money at the casino; **j)** *(abwarten, bis ...)* **laß sie nur erst einmal erwachsen sein** wait till she's grown up. **2.** *unr. refl. V.* **a) die Tür läßt sich leicht öffnen** the door opens easily; **dieses Material läßt sich gut verarbeiten** this material is easy to work with; **das läßt sich nicht beweisen** it can't be proved; **das läßt sich machen** that can be done; *s. auch* **hören 1 b, c; b)** *(unpers.)* **es läßt sich nicht leugnen/verschweigen, daß ...:** it cannot be denied *or* there's no denying that .../we/you *etc.* cannot hide the fact that ...; **hier läßt es sich leben/wohl sein** it's a good life here. **3.** *unr. itr. V.* **a)** *(ugs.)* **Laß mal. Ich mache das schon** Leave it. I'll do it; **Laß doch! Du kannst mir das Geld später zurückgeben** That's all right. You can pay me back later; **b)** *(veranlassen)* **ich lasse bitten** would you ask him/her/them to come in; **einspannen ~:** have the horses harnessed; **ich habe mir sagen ~, daß ...:** I've been told *or* informed that ...; **c)** *(veralt.: aufgeben)* **von jmdm./etw. ~:** part from sb./sth.; **vom Alkohol nicht ~ können** be unable to give up alcohol

lässig ['lɛsɪç] **1.** *Adj.* casual. **2.** *adv.* **a)** *(ungezwungen)* casually; **b)** *(ugs.: leicht)* easily; effortlessly

Lässigkeit die; ~ a) casualness; **b)** *(ugs.: Leichtigkeit)* effortlessness

läßlich ['lɛslɪç] *Adj. (kath. Kirche, auch fig.)* venial, pardonable ⟨*sin*⟩

Lasso ['laso] **das** *od.* **der; ~s, ~s** lasso

läßt [lɛst] *3. Pers. Sg. Präsens v.* **lassen**

Last [last] **die; ~, ~en a)** load; *(Trag~)* load; burden; **b)** *(belastendes Gewicht)* weight; **c)** *(Bürde)* burden; **die ~ des Amtes/der Verantwortung** the burden of office/responsibility; **die ~ auf andere abwälzen** shift the burden on to others; **jmdm. zur ~ fallen/werden** be/become a burden on sb.; **jmdm. etw. zur ~ legen** charge sb. with sth.; accuse sb. of sth.; **d)** *Pl. (Abgaben)* charges; *(Kosten)* costs; **die steuerlichen ~en** the tax burden *sing.*; **die Verpackungskosten gehen zu ~en der Kunden** the cost of packaging will be charged to the customer; **die Einsparungsmaßnahmen gehen vor allem zu ~en der Minderheiten** the burden of the economy measures falls heaviest on the minorities

Last-: ~arm der *(Physik)* load arm; weight arm; **~auto das** *s.* **~kraftwagen**

lasten *itr. V.* **a)** be a burden; **auf jmdm./etw. ~:** weigh heavily [up]on sb./sth.; **das Amt lastet auf seinen Schultern** *(fig.)* the burden of office rests on his shoulders; **auf seinen Schultern lastet die ganze Arbeit** *(fig.)* all the work falls on his shoulders; **eine ~de Stille/Hitze** *(fig.)* an oppressive silence/heat; **b)** *(belastet sein mit)* **auf dem Haus ~ zwei Hypotheken** the house is encumbered with two mortgages

Lasten-: ~auf·zug der goods lift *(Brit.)*; freight elevator *(Amer.)*; **~ausgleich der** *(Bundesrepublik Deutschland): compensation paid to individuals for damage and losses during and immediately after the Second World War*

[1]Lạster der; ~s, ~ *(ugs.: Lkw)* truck; lorry *(Brit.)*

[2]Lạster das; ~s, ~: vice; **ein langes ~** *(fig. ugs.)* a beanpole

Lặsterer der; ~s, ~ a) ein ~ sein have a malicious tongue; be constantly making malicious remarks; **b)** *(veralt.: Gottes~)* blasphemer

lạsterhaft *Adj. (abwertend)* depraved

Lạsterhaftigkeit die; ~: depravity

Lạster-: ~höhle die *(ugs. abwertend)* den of vice *or* iniquity; **~leben das;** *o. Pl. (oft scherzh.)* life of depravity

lặsterlich 1. *Adj.* malicious ‹*remark*›; malevolent ‹*curse, oath*›. **2.** *adv.* ‹*curse*› malevolently; ‹*speak*› maliciously

Lặster·maul das *(abwertend salopp)* **ein ~ sein/haben** have a malicious tongue; be constantly making malicious remarks; **halt dein ~!** keep your malicious remarks to yourself!

lästern ['lɛstɐn] **1.** *itr. V. (abwertend)* **über jmdn./etw. ~:** make malicious remarks about sb./sth. **2.** *tr. V. (veralt.: schmähen)* blaspheme against ‹*God, God's law, etc.*›

Lặsterung die; ~, ~en malicious remark; *(gegen Gott)* blasphemy

Lạst·esel der pack-donkey

Lastex Ⓦⓩ ['lastɛks] **das; ~:** Lastex **(P);** stretch fabric

Lạstex·hose die stretch trousers *or (coll.)* pants *pl.*

lästig ['lɛstɪç] *Adj.* tiresome ‹*person*›; tiresome, irksome ‹*task, duty, etc.*›; troublesome ‹*illness, cough, etc.*›; **jmdm. ~ sein** *od.* **fallen/werden** be/become a nuisance to sb.

Lạst-: ~kahn der [cargo] barge; **~kraft·wagen der** heavy goods *(Brit.) or (Amer.)* freight vehicle; **~pferd das** pack-horse; **~schiff das** cargo ship; freighter; **~schrift die a)** *(Betrag)* debit; **b)** *(Bescheinigung)* debit advice; **c)** *(Vorgang)* debiting; **d)** *(Verkehr)* direct debit; **~tier das** pack-animal; **~träger der** porter; bearer; **~wagen der** truck; lorry *(Brit.)*; **~wagen·fahrer der** truck driver; lorry driver *(Brit.)*; **~zug der** truck *or (Brit.)* lorry and trailer/trailers

Lasur [la'zu:ɐ̯] **die; ~, ~en** varnish; *(farbig)* glaze

lasziv [las'tsi:f] *Adj.* lascivious

Laszivität [lastsivi'tɛ:t] **die; ~:** lasciviousness

Latein [la'tain] **das; ~s** Latin; **mit seinem ~ am Ende sein** be at one's wit's end; *s. auch* **Deutsch**

Latein-: ~amerika (das) Latin America; **~amerikaner der** Latin American; **~amerikanisch** *Adj.* Latin-American

Lateiner [la'tainɐ] **der; ~s, ~:** Latin scholar; Latinist; *(Schüler)* Latin pupil

lateinisch *Adj.* Latin; *s. auch* **deutsch; [2]Deutsche**

Latein-: ~schule die *(hist.)* grammar school; **~unterricht der** latin teaching; *s. auch* **Englischunterricht**

latent [la'tɛnt] **1.** *Adj.* latent. **2.** *adv.* **~ vorhanden sein** be latent

Latenz [la'tɛnts] **die** *(geh.)* latency

Latẹnz·periode die *(Psych.)* latency period

Laterna magica [la'tɛrna 'ma:gika] **die; ~ ~, Laternae magicae** [-nɛ -tsɛ] magic lantern

Laterne [la'tɛrnə] **die; ~, ~n a)** *(Leuchte)* lamp; lantern *(Naut.)*; **gute Handwerker/so ein Auto kann man mit der ~ suchen** *(fig.)* good craftsmen/cars like that are few and far between; **b)** *(Straßen~)* street light; street lamp; **c) die rote ~ übernehmen/an eine andere Elf abgeben** *(Sport Jargon)* drop to/move off the bottom of the table; **d)** *(Bauw.)* lantern

Latẹrnen-: ~licht das light of the street lamp/lamps; **~parker der** *(scherzh.)* driver who regularly parks in the road; **~pfahl der** lamppost

Latex ['la:tɛks] **der; ~, Latizes** ['la:titse:s] latex

Latifundium [lati'fʊndi̯ʊm] **das; ~s, Latifụndien** *(hist.)* latifundium

latinisieren [latini'zi:rən] *tr. V.* latinize

Latinịsmus der; ~, Latinịsmen *(Sprachw.)* Latinism

Latinịst der; ~en, ~en Latinist; Latin scholar

Latinum [la'ti:nʊm] **das; ~s: das kleine/große ~:** ≈ GCSE/'A' level Latin [examination]

Latizes *s.* **Latex**

Latrine [la'tri:nə] **die; ~, ~n** latrine

Latrịnen·parole die *(ugs. abwertend)* empty rumour

[1]Latsche ['latʃə] **die; ~, ~n** *(variety of)* [Swiss] mountain pine

[2]Latsche ['la:tʃə] **die; ~, ~n:** *s.* **Latschen**

latschen ['la:tʃn̩] *itr. V.; mit sein (salopp)* trudge; *(schlurfend)* slouch

Lạtschen der; ~s, ~ *(ugs.)* old worn-out shoe; *(Hausschuh)* old worn-out slipper; **wenn ich nicht bald etwas zu essen kriege, kippe ich noch aus den ~** *(salopp)* if I don't get something to eat soon, I shall keel over; **er ist bald aus den ~ gekippt, als er hörte, daß ich im Lotto gewonnen hatte** *(salopp)* he was flabbergasted when he heard I'd got a prize in the lottery

Lạtschen·kiefer die: *s.* **[1]Latsche**

Latte ['latə] **die; ~, ~n a)** lath; slat; *(Zaun~)* pale; **eine lange ~** *(ugs.)* a beanpole; **b)** *(Sport: Quer~ des Tores)* [cross]bar; **c)** *(Leichtathletik)* bar; **d)** *in eine* **[lange] ~ von Schulden/Vorstrafen** *(ugs.)* a [large] pile of debts/a [long] list *or* string of previous convictions

Lạtten-: ~kiste die crate; **~kreuz das** *(Fuß-, Handball)* angle of the [cross]bar and the post; **im ~kreuz** in the top corner of the net; **~rost der** *(auf dem Boden)* duckboards *pl.*; *(eines Bettes)* slatted frame; **~schuß der** *(Ballspiele)* **es war nur ein ~schuß** the shot only hit the [cross]bar; **~zaun der** paling fence

Lattich ['latɪç] **der; ~s, ~e** lettuce

Latüchte [la'tʏçtə] **die; ~, ~n** *(ugs. scherzh.)* lamp; **geh mir aus der ~!** *(salopp)* get out of the light!

Latwerge [lat'vɛrgə] **die; ~, ~n a)** *(Med. veralt.)* confection; **b)** *(bes. südwestd.: Mus)* [fruit] purée

Latz [lats] **der; ~es, Lätze** ['lɛtsə] **a)** bib; **jmdm. eine[n] vor den ~ knallen** *od.* **ballern** *(salopp)* sock *(sl.) or* thump sb.; **b)** *s.* **Hosenlatz**

Lätzchen ['lɛtsçən] **das; ~s, ~:** bib

Lạtz-: ~hose die bib and brace; *(für Kinder)* dungarees *pl.*; **~rock der** bib-top pinafore dress

lau [lau] *Adj.* **a)** *(mäßig warm)* tepid, lukewarm ‹*water etc.*›; *(nicht mehr kalt)* warm ‹*beer etc.*›; **b)** *(mild)* mild ‹*wind, air, evening, etc.*›; mild and gentle ‹*rain*›; **c)** *(unentschlossen)* lukewarm; half-hearted

Laub [laup] **das; ~[e]s** leaves *pl.*; **dichtes/neues ~:** thick/new foliage

Laub-: ~baum der broad-leaved tree; **~blatt das** [broad] leaf; **~dach das** *(dicht.)* leafy canopy *(poet.)*; canopy of leaves

Laube die; ~, ~n a) summer-house; *(überdeckter Sitzplatz)* bower; arbour; *s. auch* **fertig; b)** *(Archit.)* porch

Lauben-: ~kolonie die group of allotment gardens; **~pieper der** *(berlin. scherzh.)* allotment gardener

Laub-: ~frosch der tree frog; **~hölzer** *Pl.* broad-leaved trees and shrubs; **~hütten·fest das** *(jüd. Rel.)* Feast of Tabernacles; Succoth; **~krone die a)** *(geh.: Wipfel)* tree-top; **b)** *(Krone)* crest coronet

Laub·säge die fretsaw

Laubsäge·arbeit die fretsaw work; **eine ~:** a piece of fretsaw work

laub-, Laub-: ~sänger der *(Zool.)* leaf warbler; **~tragend** *Adj.; nicht präd.* bearing [broad] leaves *postpos., not pred.*; **~wald der** deciduous wood/forest; **~werk das a)** *(Archit., Kunst)* foliage; **b)** *(geh.) s.* **Belaubung b**

Lauch [laux] **der; ~[e]s, ~e** *(Bot.)* allium; *(Porree)* leek

Laudatio [lau'da:tsi̯o] **die; ~, ~nes** [-'tsi̯o:ne:s] *od.* **~nen** [-'tsi̯o:nən] eulogy; encomium

Laue[ne] ['lau̯ə(nə)] **die; ~, ~n** *(schweiz.) s.* **Lawine**

Lauer ['lauɐ] **die; ~** *in* **auf der ~ liegen** *od.* **sein** *(ugs.) (jmdm. auflauern)* lie in wait; *(etw. erfahren wollen)* be on the look-out; *(um zu hören)* be listening out; **sich auf die ~ legen** settle down to lie in wait

lauern *itr. V.* **a)** *(auch fig.)* lurk; **auf jmdn./etw. ~:** lie in wait for sb./sth.; **er wartete ~d auf unsere Antwort** he slyly awaited our reply; **ein ~der Blick** a sly look; **b)** *(ugs.: ungeduldig warten)* **auf jmdn./etw. ~:** wait [impatiently] for sb./sth.

Lauf [lauf] **der; ~[e]s, Läufe** ['lɔyfə] **a)** *o. Pl.* running; **b)** *(Sport: Wettrennen)* heat; **c)** *o. Pl. (Ver~, Entwicklung)* course; **im ~[e] der Zeit** in the course of time; **im ~[e] der Jahre** over the years; as the years go/went by; **im ~[e] des Tages** during the day; **[irgendwann] im ~[e] des Sommers** [some time] during the summer; **im ~[e] seines Lebens** in the course of *or* during his life; **einer Sache** *(Dat.)* **ihren** *od.* **freien ~ lassen** give free rein to sth.; **seinem Zorn freien ~ lassen** give vent to one's anger; **seiner Phantasie freien ~ lassen** give free rein to one's imagination; *(zu sehr)* indulge in flights of fancy; **laß doch den Dingen ihren ~!** let matters *or* things take their course; **der ~ der Geschichte/Welt** the course of history/the way of the world; **seinen ~ nehmen** take its course; **d)** *(von Schußwaffen)* barrel; **etw. vor den ~ bekommen** get a shot at sth.; **e)** *o. Pl. (eines Flusses, einer Straße)* course; **der obere/untere ~ eines Flusses** the upper/lower reaches *pl.* of a river; **der ~ der Straße** the route followed by the road; **dem ~ der Straße/Bahnschienen folgen** follow the road/railway lines; **f)** *(Musik)* run; **g)** *(Jägerspr.)* leg; **h)** *o. Pl. (von Maschinen)* running

Lauf-: ~bahn die a) *(Werdegang)* career; **eine wissenschaftliche/künstlerische ~bahn einschlagen** take up a career in the sciences/as an artist; **b)** *(Leichtathletik)* running-track; **~buchse die** *(Technik)* cylinder liner; **~bursche der** errand boy; messenger boy

laufen 1. *unr. itr. V.; mit sein* **a)** run; **ge~ kommen** come running up; **er lief, was er konnte** *(ugs.)* he ran as fast as he could; **b)** *(gehen)* go; *(zu Fuß gehen)* walk; **auf und ab/hin und her ~:** walk up and down/back and forth; **wir sind im Urlaub viel ge~:** we did a lot of walking while on holiday; **es sind noch/nur fünf Minuten zu ~:** it's another/only five minutes' walk; **das Kind lernt ~:** the child is learning to walk; **c)** *(stoßen)* **in** *(Akk.)***/gegen etw. ~:** walk into sth.; **d)** *(ugs.: ständig hingehen)* **dauernd zum Arzt/ins Kino/in die Kirche ~:** keep running to the doctor/be always going to the cinema *(Brit.) or (Amer.)* the movies/to church; **in jede Veranstaltung der Partei ~:** go to every event organized by the party; **e)** *(in einem Wettkampf)* run; *(beim Eislauf)* skate; *(beim Ski~)* ski; **ein Pferd ~ lassen** run a horse; **f)** *(im Gang sein)* ‹*machine*› be running; ‹*radio, television, etc.*› be on; *(funktionieren)* ‹*machine*› run; ‹*radio, television, etc.*› work; **ruhig/auf Hochtouren ~:** be running quietly/at full speed; **g)** *(sich bewegen, [aus]fließen; auch fig.)* **auf Schienen/**

über Rollen ~: run on rails/over pulleys; **von den Fließbändern ~:** come off the conveyor belts; **es lief mir eiskalt über den Rücken** a chill ran down my spine; **ihm lief der Schweiß über das Gesicht** the sweat ran down his face; **Wasser in die Wanne ~ lassen** run the bathwater; **deine Nase läuft** your nose is running; you've got a runny nose; **der Käse läuft** the cheese has gone runny *(coll.)*; **h)** *(gelten)* ⟨*contract, agreement, engagement, etc.*⟩ run; **der Vertrag läuft noch bis ...:** the contract runs until ...; **i)** *(gespielt werden)* ⟨*programme, play*⟩ be on; ⟨*film*⟩ be on *or* showing; ⟨*show*⟩ be on *or* playing; **im dritten Programm ~:** be on the regional programme; **der Hauptfilm läuft schon** the main film has already started; **j)** *(fahren)* run; **auf Grund ~:** run aground; **k)** *(vonstatten gehen)* **parallel mit etw. ~:** run in parallel with sth.; **ich möchte wissen, wie der Prozeß ge~ ist** I'd like to know the outcome of the trial; **der Laden läuft/die Geschäfte ~ gut/schlecht** *(ugs.)* the shop is doing well/badly/business is good/bad; **wie geplant/nach Wunsch ~:** go as planned *or* according to plan; **die Sache ist ge~** *(ugs.: daran ist nichts mehr zu ändern)* it's too late now; **l)** *(eingeleitet sein)* ⟨*negotiations, investigations*⟩ be in progress *or* under way; ⟨*application*⟩ be under consideration; **m)** *(registriert sein)* **auf jmds. Namen** *(Akk.)* **~:** be in sb.'s name; **n)** *(ugs.: gut verkäuflich sein)* go *or* sell well; **o)** *(verlaufen)* run. **2.** *unr. tr. u. itr. V.* **a)** *mit sein (zurücklegen) (zu Fuß gehen)* walk; *(rennen)* run; **die 800 m/einige Runden/sechs Rennen ~** *(Sport)* run the 800 m./a few laps/[in] six races; **b)** *mit sein (erzielen)* **einen Rekord ~:** set up a record; **über die 100 m 9,9 Sekunden ~:** run the 100 m. in 9.9 seconds; **c)** *mit haben od. sein* **Ski/Schlittschuh/Rollschuh ~:** ski/skate/roller-skate; **d) sich** *(Dat.)* **die Füße wund ~:** get sore feet from running/walking; **sich** *(Dat.)* **ein Loch in die Schuhsohle ~:** wear a hole in one's shoe *or* sole. **3.** *unr. refl. V.* **a) sich warm ~:** warm up; *s. auch* **müde; b)** *(unpers.)* **in diesen Schuhen läuft es sich sehr bequem** these shoes are very comfortable for running/walking in *or* to run/walk in; **auf dem steinigen Weg lief es sich nicht gut** the stony path was not good for walking/running on

laufend 1. *Adj.; nicht präd.* **a)** *(ständig)* regular ⟨*interest, income*⟩; recurring ⟨*costs*⟩; **die ~en Arbeiten/Geschäfte** the day-to-day *or* routine work *sing.* /business *sing.*; **b)** *(gegenwärtig)* current ⟨*issue, year, month, etc.*⟩; **c)** *(aufeinanderfolgend)* **zehn Mark der ~e Meter** ten marks a *or* per metre; **d) auf dem ~en sein/bleiben** be/keep *or* stay up-to-date *or* fully informed; **jmdn. auf dem ~en halten** keep sb. up-to-date *or* informed; **mit etw. auf dem ~en sein** be up-to-date with sth. **2.** *adv.* constantly; continually; ⟨*increase*⟩ steadily

laufen|lassen *unr. tr. V. (ugs.)* **jmdn. ~:** let sb. go

Läufer ['lɔyfɐ] **der; ~s, ~ a)** *(Sport)* runner; *(Handball)* half-back; **b)** *(Fußball veralt.)* half-back; **c)** *(Teppich) (long narrow)* carpet; **d)** *(Schach)* bishop; **e)** *(Landw.: junges Schwein)* young pig; **f)** *(Bauw.: Mauerstein)* stretcher

Lauferei die; ~, ~en *(ugs.)* running around *no pl.*; **die ~ zu den Ärzten kostet viel Zeit** it takes a lot of time to go the rounds of all the doctors

Läuferin die; ~, ~nen runner

läuferisch 1. *Adj.* athletic; *(beim Eislaufen)* skating *attrib.* **2.** *adv.* as regards the skating

Läufer·reihe die *(Fußball veralt.)* half-back line

Lauf-: ~feuer das brush fire; **wie ein ~feuer** like wildfire; **~fläche die** *(am Reifen)* tread; *(am Ski)* sole [of the ski]; **~gewicht das** sliding weight; **~graben der** *(Milit.)* communications trench

läufig ['lɔyfɪç] *Adj.* on heat *postpos.*; in season *postpos.*

Lauf-: ~junge der: *s.* **~bursche; ~katze die** *(Technik)* crab; **~kran der** *(Technik)* travelling crane; **~kundschaft die** passing trade; **~kundschaft haben** have a passing trade; **~masche die** ladder; **~paß der: der Präsident gab seinem Berater den ~paß** *(ugs.)* the president gave his adviser his marching orders *(coll.)*; **er hat seiner Freundin den ~paß gegeben** *(ugs.)* he finished with his girl-friend *(coll.)*; **~pensum das** *(Sport)* **der Verteidiger bewältigte** *od.* **absolvierte ein ungeheures ~pensum** the defender never stopped running; **~planke die** gangplank; gangway; **~rad das** *(Technik)* **a)** running wheel; non-driven wheel; **b)** *(an Turbinen)* runner; **~rolle die** *(Technik) (von Toren, Türen)* roller; *(von Panzern)* road wheel; *(von Möbeln)* castor; **~schiene die** *(Technik)* track; rail; **~schrift die** newscaster; **~schritt der a) wir haben die ganze Strecke im ~schritt zurückgelegt** we ran all the way; **im ~schritt, marsch, marsch!** at the double, quick march!; **b)** *(Leichtathletik)* running step

läufst [lɔyfst] *2. Pers. Sg. Präsens v.* **laufen**

Lauf-: ~stall der playpen; **~steg der** catwalk

läuft [lɔyft] *3. Pers. Sg. Präsens v.* **laufen**

Lauf-: ~vogel der *(Zool.)* ratite *(Zool.)*; flightless bird; **~werk das** *(Technik)* **a)** mechanism; **b)** *(Uhrwerk)* clockwork; mechanism; **c)** *(Eisenb.)* running gear; **d)** *(DV)* drive; **~zeit die a)** term; **der Vertrag hatte eine ~zeit von zwei Jahren** the agreement ran for two years; **ein Kredit mit befristeter ~zeit** a limited-term loan; **b)** *(Film, Theater)* run; **c)** *(Sport)* time; **~zettel der** *(Bürow., Verwaltung)* **a)** *(Rundschreiben)* circular; **b)** *(Empfangsbestätigung)* distribution slip; circulation slip; **c)** *(Passierschein)* pass; permit; **d)** *(an Werkstücken)* work progress slip; control tag

Lauge ['laugə] **die; ~, ~n a)** soapy water; soapsuds; **b)** *(Chemie)* alkaline solution

Laugen·brezel die *(südd.)* pretzel

Lauheit die; ~: half-heartedness

Lau·mann der; ~[e]s, *Pl.* **-männer** *(ugs. abwertend)* shilly-shallyer

Laune ['launə] **die; ~, ~n a)** *(momentane Stimmung)* mood; **schlechte/gute ~ haben** be in a bad/good mood *or* temper; **[nicht] in** *od.* **bei ~ sein** [not] be in a good mood; **jmdn. bei guter ~ halten** keep sb. in a good mood; keep sb. happy *(coll.)*; **bringt gute ~ mit!** come ready to enjoy yourselves; **b)** *meist Pl. (wechselnde Stimmung)* mood; **sie hat nur selten ~n** she is rarely moody; **die ~n des Wetters/Zufalls** *(fig.)* the vagaries of the weather/of chance; **c)** *(spontane Idee)* whim; **aus einer ~ heraus** on a whim; on the spur of the moment

launenhaft *Adj.* temperamental; *(unberechenbar)* capricious

Launenhaftigkeit die; ~: moodiness; *(Unberechenbarkeit)* capriciousness

launig 1. *Adj.* witty. **2.** *adv.* wittily

launisch *Adj.: s.* **launenhaft**

Laus [laus] **die; ~, Läuse** ['lɔyzə] louse; **ihm ist eine ~ über die Leber gelaufen** *(ugs.)* he has got out of bed on the wrong side; **was ist ihm für eine ~ über die Leber gelaufen?** *(ugs.)* what's eating him? *(coll.)*; **jmdm./sich eine ~ in den Pelz setzen** *(ugs.)* let sb./oneself in for something

Laus·bub der little rascal *or* devil; scamp

Lausbuben·streich der prank

laus·bübisch 1. *Adj.* impish. **2.** *adv.* impishly

Lausch·aktion die bugging operation *(coll.)*

lauschen ['lauʃn̩] *itr. V.* **a)** *(horchen)* listen *(so as to overhear sth.)*; **an der Tür ~:** eavesdrop at the door; **b)** *(zuhören)* listen [attentively]; **jmds. Worten** *usw.* **~:** listen [attentively] to sb.'s words *etc.*

Lauscher der; ~s, ~ a) eavesdropper; **der ~ an der Wand hört seine eigene Schand** *(Spr.)* eavesdroppers never hear any good of themselves; **b)** *(Jägerspr.: Ohr)* ear

lauschig *Adj.* cosy, snug ⟨*corner*⟩; **ein ~es Plätzchen im Grünen** a quiet *or* secluded spot in the country

Lause-: ~bengel, ~junge, ~lümmel der *(salopp)* little rascal *or* devil; scamp

lausen *tr. V.* delouse; **ich denk', mich laust der Affe!** *(salopp)* well, I'll be damned *or* blowed!

Lauser der; ~s, ~ *(landsch. ugs.)* little rascal *or* devil; scamp

lausig 1. *Adj. (ugs.)* **a)** *(abwertend: unangenehm, schäbig)* lousy *(sl.)*; rotten *(coll.)*; **~e Zeiten** hard times; **b)** *(sehr groß)* perishing *(Brit. sl.)*, freezing ⟨*cold*⟩; terrible *(coll.)*, awful ⟨*heat*⟩. **2.** *adv.* terribly *(coll.)*; awfully; **draußen ist es ~ kalt** it's perishing cold outside *(Brit. sl.)*

¹laut [laut] **1.** *Adj.* **a)** loud; *(fig.)* loud, garish ⟨*colour*⟩; garish ⟨*advertisement*⟩; **der Motor ist zu ~:** the engine is too noisy; **spreche ich jetzt ~ genug?** can you hear me now?; **er wußte sich ohne ein ~es Wort Respekt zu verschaffen** he was able to gain respect without raising his voice; **werden Sie bitte nicht ~!** there's no need to shout; **~ werden** *(fig.: bekannt werden)* be made known; **es sind Zweifel an der Gültigkeit dieser Aussage ~ geworden** doubts have been raised *or* expressed *or* voiced as to the validity of this statement; **b)** *(geräuschvoll)* noisy. **2.** *adv.* **a)** loudly; **~er sprechen** speak louder; speak up; **~ lachen** laugh out loud; **etw. nicht ~ sagen dürfen** not be allowed to say sth. out loud; **~ denken** think aloud; **das kannst du aber ~ sagen** *(ugs.)* you can say that again; **b)** *(geräuschvoll)* noisily; **geht es hier immer so ~ zu?** is it always this noisy here?

²laut *Präp. + Gen. od. Dat. (Amtsspr.)* according to; *(gemäß)* in accordance with; **~ Vertrag** according to/in accordance with the contract

Laut der; ~[e]s, ~e a) *(Geräusch)* sound; **keinen ~ von sich geben** not make a sound; **~ geben** ⟨*dog, hound*⟩ give tongue; **b)** *(sprachliche Einheit)* sound; **fremde/heimatliche ~e** sounds of a foreign/familiar tongue

Laut·bildung die *(Sprachw.)* articulation; formation of sounds

Laute die; ~, ~n lute

lauten 1. *itr. V.* ⟨*answer, instruction, slogan*⟩ be, run; ⟨*letter, passage, etc.*⟩ read, go; ⟨*law*⟩ state; **die Anklage/das Urteil lautet auf ...:** the charge/sentence is ...; **auf jmds. Namen** *(Akk.)* **~:** be in sb.'s name. **2.** *tr. V. (Sprachw.: aussprechen)* pronounce

läuten [lɔytn̩] **1.** *tr., itr. V.* ring; ⟨*alarm clock*⟩ go off; **12 Uhr/Mittag ~:** strike 12 o'clock/midday; **Feuer/Sturm ~** *(hist.)* ring the fire-bell/storm-bell; **ich habe davon ~ gehört** *od.* **hören, daß ...:** I have heard rumours that ... **2.** *itr. V. (bes. südd.: klingeln)* ring; **nach jmdm. ~:** ring for sb.; **es läutete** the bell rang *or* went (**zu** for)

Lautenist [lautə'nɪst] **der; ~en, ~en** lutenist

Lauten·spieler der lute-player

¹lauter *Adj. (geh.)* **a)** honourable ⟨*person, intentions, etc.*⟩; honest ⟨*truth*⟩; **b)** *(rein)* pure ⟨*gold, silver, etc.*⟩; clear ⟨*water*⟩

²lauter *indekl. Adj.* nothing but; sheer, pure ⟨*nonsense, joy, etc.*⟩; **das sind ~ Lügen** that's nothing but lies; that's a pack of lies; **das sind ~ Kunden unserer Firma** they are all customers of our firm; **aus ~ kleinen Quadraten zusammengesetzt** made up entirely of little squares; **vor ~ Arbeit komme ich nicht ins Theater** I can't go to the theatre because of all the work I've got

Lauterkeit die; ~: honourableness
läutern ['lɔytɐn] *tr. V. (geh.)* **a)** reform ⟨*character*⟩; purify ⟨*soul*⟩; **b)** *(reinigen)* purify (**von** of)
Läuterung die; ~, ~en *(geh.)* **a)** *(des Charakters)* reformation; *(der Seele)* purification; **b)** *(Reinigung)* purification
laut-, Laut-: ~gesetz das *(Sprachw.)* phonetic law; **~getreu 1.** *Adj.* phonetically accurate; **2.** *adv.* with phonetic accuracy; **~hals** *Adv.* ⟨*sing, shout, etc.*⟩ at the top of one's voice; **~hals lachen** roar with laughter
Laut·lehre die *(Sprachw.)* phonetics and phonology *no art.*
lautlich 1. *Adj.* phonetic. **2.** *adv.* phonetically
laut-, Laut-: ~los 1. *Adj.* silent; soundless; *(wortlos)* silent; **~lose Stille** utter *or* complete silence; **2.** *adv.* silently; soundlessly; **~losigkeit die; ~:** silence; soundlessness; *(Wortlosigkeit)* silence; **~malend** *Adj. (Sprachw.)* onomatopoeic; **~schrift die** *(Phon.)* phonetic alphabet; *(Umschrift)* phonetic transcription
Laut·sprecher der loudspeaker; loud hailer *(esp. Naut.)*; *(einer Stereoanlage usw.)* speaker; **über ~:** over the loudspeaker[s]
Lautsprecher-: ~an·lage die public address *or* PA system; loudspeaker system; **~box die** speaker cabinet; **~wagen der** loudspeaker car/van
laut-, Laut-: ~stark 1. *Adj.* loud; vociferous, loud ⟨*protest*⟩; **2.** *adv.* loudly; ⟨*protest*⟩ vociferously, loudly; **~stärke die a)** volume; **in/bei voller ~stärke** at full volume; **das Radio auf volle ~stärke drehen** turn the radio right up; **b)** *(Lärm)* **die ~stärke in diesem Raum** the volume of noise in this room; **~stärke·regler der** volume control
Lautung die; ~, ~en *(Sprachw.)* pronunciation
Laut-: ~verschiebung die *(Sprachw.)* sound shift; **die erste** *od.* **germanische/zweite** *od.* **hochdeutsche ~verschiebung** the first *or* Germanic/second *or* High German sound shift; **~wandel der** *(Sprachw.)* sound change
Läut·werk das a) *(Eisenb.)* bell; **b)** *(des Weckers)* alarm
lau·warm *Adj.* lukewarm ⟨*food*⟩; lukewarm, tepid ⟨*drink*⟩; *(nicht mehr kalt)* warm ⟨*beer etc.*⟩
Lava ['la:va] **die; ~, Laven** *(Geol.)* lava
Lavabo [la'va:bo] **das; ~[s], ~s** *(schweiz.) s.* **Waschbecken**
Lava·strom der lava stream; *(ausströmende Lava)* lava flow
Lavendel [la'vɛndl̩] **der; ~s, ~:** lavender
Lavendel·öl das lavender oil
¹lavieren [la'vi:rən] *tr. V., itr. V.* manœuvre
²lavieren *tr. V. (bild. Kunst)* wash; **eine lavierte Zeichnung** a wash drawing
Lavoir [la'vo̯a:ɐ̯] **das; ~s, ~s** *(österr.) s.* **Waschbecken**
Lawine [la'vi:nə] **die; ~, ~n** *(auch fig.)* avalanche; **eine ~ von Protesten** *(fig.)* a storm of protest
lawinen-, Lawinen-: ~artig *Adv.* like an avalanche; **~artig anschwellen** ⟨*political etc. movement, number of accidents etc.*⟩ snowball; **~gefahr die** danger of avalanches; **~[such]hund der** avalanche dog
lax [laks] **1.** *Adj.* lax. **2.** *adv.* laxly
Laxativ [laksa'ti:f] **das; ~s, ~e** *(Med.)* laxative
Laxheit die; ~: laxness; laxity
Layout [leɪ'aʊt] **das; ~s, ~s** *(Druckw., Elektronik)* layout
Layouter ['le:|aʊtɐ] **der; ~s, ~:** layout man
Lazarett [latsa'rɛt] **das; ~[e]s** military hospital
Lazarett·schiff das hospital ship
leasen ['li:zn̩] *tr. V.* rent; *(für längere Zeit mieten)* lease ⟨*car etc.*⟩
Leasing ['li:zɪŋ] **das; ~s, ~s** *(Wirtsch.)* leasing
Lebe-: ~dame die *(abwertend)* good-time girl; **~hoch** [--'-] **das; ~s, ~s** cheer; **ein dreifaches ~hoch** three cheers *pl.*; **~mann der;** *Pl.* **~männer** playboy
leben ['le:bn̩] **1.** *itr. V.* live; *(lebendig sein)* be alive; **anständig/sorgenfrei ~:** live a respectable/carefree life; **auf dem Land/im Wasser ~de Tiere** animals which live on land/in water; **für jmdn./etw. ~** *od. (geh.)* **jmdm./einer Sache ~:** live for sb./sth.; **leb[e] wohl!** farewell!; **so [et]was lebt, und Schiller mußte sterben!** *(scherzh.)* why do we have to put up with people like that?; **nicht mehr ~ wollen** not want to go on living; have lost the will to live; **er wird nicht mehr lange zu ~ haben** he will not live much longer; **lebst du noch?** *(ugs. scherzh.)* are you still in the land of the living? *(joc.)*; **lang lebe der König!** long live the king!; **von seiner Rente/seinem Gehalt ~:** live on one's pension/salary; **von seiner Hände Arbeit ~:** live by the work of one's hands; **Wie geht es dir? – Man lebt!** *(ugs.)* How are you? – Oh, surviving *(coll.)*; **~ und ~ lassen** live and let live; **davon kann ich/sie/er** *usw.* **nicht ~ und nicht sterben** it's hardly enough to keep body and soul together; **fleischlos ~:** not eat meat; **von Kartoffeln ~:** live on potatoes; **er lebt in seinen Werken** he lives on in his works; *s. auch* **Brot; diät. 2.** *tr. V.* live; **ein glückliches Leben ~:** live a happy life
Leben das; ~s, ~ a) life; **das ~:** life; **jmdm. das ~ retten** save sb.'s life; **sein ~ für etw. wagen/***(geh.)* **hingeben** risk/give one's life for sth.; **sich** *(Dat.)* **das ~ nehmen,** *(geh.)* **[freiwillig] aus dem ~ scheiden** take one's [own] life; **am ~ sein/bleiben** be/stay alive; **seines ~s nicht [mehr] sicher sein** not be safe [any more]; **um sein ~ rennen** run for one's life; **ums ~ kommen** lose one's life; **das nackte ~ retten** barely escape with one's life; **sein ~ teuer verkaufen** sell one's life dearly; **seinem ~ ein Ende setzen** *od.* **machen** *(verhüll.)* take one's [own] life; **auf Tod und ~ kämpfen** be engaged in a life-and-death struggle; **etw. für sein ~ gern tun** love doing sth.; **etw. für sein ~ gern essen** love sth.; **etw. ins ~ rufen** bring sth. into being; **mit dem ~ davonkommen** escape with one's life; **jmdm. nach dem ~ trachten** try to kill sb.; **wie das blühende ~ aussehen** *(ugs.)* look the picture of health; **ein/sein [ganzes] ~ lang** one's whole life long; **zeit seines ~s** all his life; **noch nie im ~/zum erstenmal im ~:** never in/for the first time in one's life; **jmdm. das ~ sauer machen** make sb.'s life a misery; **sich durchs ~ schlagen** struggle through life; **mit beiden Beinen** *od.* **Füßen im ~ stehen** have one's feet firmly on the ground; **nie im ~, im ~ nicht!** *(ugs.)* not on your life! *(coll.)*; never in your life! *(coll.)*; **ein ~ in Wohlstand/Armut** a life of affluence/poverty; **das süße ~:** la dolce vita; **wie das ~ so spielt** it's funny the way things turn out; **im öffentlichen ~ stehen** be in public life; **so ist das ~:** such is life; that's the way things go; **die Musik ist ihr ~:** music is her [whole] life; **b)** *(Betriebsamkeit)* **auf dem Markt herrschte ein reges ~:** the market was bustling with activity; **das ~ auf der Straße** the comings and goings in the street; **~ ins Haus bringen** bring some life into the house
lebend *Adj.* living; live ⟨*animal*⟩; **~e Sprachen** living languages; **tot oder ~:** dead or alive; **nicht mehr unter den Lebenden weilen** *(geh.)* have passed away
lebend·gebärend *Adj. (Zool.)* viviparous
Lebend·gewicht das a) live weight; **b)** *(scherzh.: Gewicht eines Menschen)* **100 kg ~ auf die Waage bringen** turn the scales at 100 kg
lebendig [le'bɛndɪç] **1.** *Adj.* **a)** *(lebend)* living; **jmdn. ~** *od.* **bei ~em Leibe verbrennen** burn sb. alive; **man fühlt sich hier wie ~ begraben** being stuck here is like being buried alive *(coll.)*; **ich kann ihn nicht wieder ~ machen** I can't bring him back to life [again]; **mehr tot als ~:** more dead than alive; **es von den Lebendigen nehmen** be unduly grasping; **b)** *(wirksam)* living ⟨*tradition etc.*⟩; **die Erinnerung daran wurde in ihm wieder ~:** the memory of it came back to him vividly; **c)** *(lebhaft)* lively ⟨*account, imagination, child, etc.*⟩; gay, bright ⟨*colours*⟩; **auf der Straße wurde es allmählich ~:** the street began to fill with life. **2.** *adv. (lebhaft)* in a lively fashion *or* way; **etw. ~ schildern** give a lively description of sth.
Lebendigkeit die; ~: liveliness
lebens-, Lebens-: ~abend der *(geh.)* evening *or* autumn of one's life *(literary)*; **~ab·schnitt der** stage of *or* chapter in one's life; **~ader die** vital line of communication; **~alter das** age; **ein hohes ~alter erreichen** live to a considerable age *or (coll.)* a ripe old age; **~angst die** unwillingness to face life's problems; *(Angst um die Existenz)* worry about one's ability to survive; **~art die a)** way of life; **b)** *o. Pl. (Umgangsformen)* manners *pl.*; **keine ~art haben** have no manners; be ill-mannered; **~auf·gabe die** life's work; **sich** *(Dat.)* **etw. zur ~aufgabe machen** make sth. one's life's work; **~baum der a)** arbor vitae; **b)** *(Rel., Kunstwiss.)* tree of life; **~bedingungen** *Pl.* conditions of life; **~bejahend** *Adj.* ⟨*person*⟩ with a positive attitude *or* approach to life; **~bejahung die** positive attitude *or* approach to life; affirmation of life; **~bereich der** area of life; **~beschreibung die** biography; *(Buch)* biography; life; **~dauer die a)** life-span; **b)** *(von Maschinen)* [useful] life; **~echt 1.** *Adj.* true-to-life; **2.** *adv.* in a true-to-life way; **~elixier das** *(Volksk.; auch fig.)* elixir of life; **~ende das** end [of one's life]; **bis an sein** *od.* **bis ans ~ende** to the end of one's life *or* days; **~erfahrung die** experience *no indef. art.* of life; **~erinnerungen** *Pl.* memories of one's life; *(aufgezeichnet)* memoirs; **~erwartung die** life expectancy; **~fähig** *Adj. (auch fig.)* viable; **~fähigkeit die** viability; **~form die a)** *(Biol.)* life-form; **b)** *(~weise)* way of life; **~frage die** vital matter *or* question; **~fremd** *Adj.* out of touch with *or* remote from everyday life *postpos.*; **~freude die;** *o. Pl.* zest for life; joie de vivre; **~froh** *Adj.* full of zest for life *or* joie de vivre *postpos.*; **~führung die** life-style; **eine moralisch einwandfreie ~führung** a completely blameless life; **~gefahr die** mortal danger; **für jmdn. besteht [keine] ~gefahr** sb.'s life is [not] in danger; **„Achtung, ~gefahr!"** 'danger'; **sie schwebt in ~gefahr** she is in danger of dying; *(von einer Kranken)* her condition is critical; **außer ~gefahr sein** be out of danger; **etw. unter ~gefahr** *(Dat.)* **tun** risk one's life to do sth.; **~gefährlich 1.** *Adj.* highly *or* extremely dangerous; critical ⟨*injury*⟩; **2.** *adv.* critically ⟨*injured, ill*⟩; **jmdn. ~gefährlich verletzen** cause sb. critical injuries; **~gefährte der, ~gefährtin die** *(geh.)* companion through life *(literary)*; **~gefühl das** awareness of life; **~geister** *Pl.* **jmds. ~geister [wieder] wecken** put new life into sb.; **~gemeinschaft die a)** *(von Menschen)* long-term relationship; **b)** *(Biol.: von Tieren, Pflanzen)* biocoenosis; **~geschichte die** life-story; **~groß** *Adj.* life-size; **~größe die: eine Statue in ~größe** a life-size statue; **ein Porträt von jmdm. in ~größe malen** paint a life-size portrait of sb.
Lebens·haltung die a) *(~skosten)* cost of living; **die ~ ist teurer geworden** the cost of living has risen; **b)** *(Lebensführung)* lifestyle

Lebenshaltungs-: ~index der *(Wirtsch.)* cost-of-living index; **~kosten** *Pl.* cost of living *sing.*

lebens-, Lebens-: ~hilfe die counselling; **~hunger der** desire to live life to the full; **~hungrig** *Adj.* ⟨*person*⟩ who is eager to live life to the full; **~inhalt der** purpose in life; **die Musik/ihre Familie ist ihr ~inhalt** music/her family is her whole life; **~jahr das** year of [one's] life; **die letzten ~jahre** the last years of one's life; one's last years; **in seinem 12. ~jahr** in his twelfth year; **mit dem vollendeten 18. ~jahr** on reaching the age of eighteen; **~kampf der** struggle for existence *or* life; **~kraft die** vitality; vital energy; **~kreis der: in jmds. ~kreis** *(Akk.)* **treten** come into *or* enter sb.'s life; **~künstler der: ein [echter/wahrer] ~künstler** a person who always knows how to make the best of things; **~lage die** situation [in life]; **in allen ~lagen** in any situation; **~lang 1.** *Adj.* lifelong; **2.** *adv.* all one's life; **~länglich 1.** *Adj.* **~länglicher Freiheitsentzug** life imprisonment; **„~länglich" bekommen** *od.* *(ugs.)* **kriegen** get life imprisonment *or* *(coll.)* life; **2.** *adv.* **jmdn. ~länglich gefangenhalten** keep sb. imprisoned for life; **~längliche der/die;** *adj. Dekl.* *(salopp)* lifer *(sl.)*; **~lauf der a)** curriculum vitae; c.v.; **b)** *(Verlauf eines Lebens)* life; **~licht das** *(geh.)* flame of life *(literary)*; **jmdm. das ~licht ausblasen** *od.* **auspusten** *(ugs.)* send sb. to kingdom-come *(coll.)*; **~linie die** life line; **~lüge die** lifelong illusion; **~lust die;** *o. Pl.: s.* **~freude; ~lustig** *Adj.* ⟨*person*⟩ full of the joys of life; **~mitte die** middle years *pl.* of one's life; **die Krise in der ~mitte** mid-life crisis

Lebens·mittel das; *meist Pl.* food[stuff]; **~** *Pl.* food *sing.*; foods *(formal)*; foodstuffs *(formal)*; *(als Ware)* food *sing.*

Lebensmittel-: ~abteilung die food department; **~chemie die** food chemistry *no art.*; **~geschäft das** food shop; **~karte die** food ration card; **~vergiftung die** *(Med.)* food poisoning

lebens-, Lebens-: ~müde *Adj.* weary of life *pred.*; **du bist wohl ~müde?** *(scherzh.)* you must be tired of living; **~müdigkeit die** weariness of life; **~mut der** courage to go on living; **~nah 1.** *Adj.* true-to-life ⟨*film, description, etc.*⟩; **~naher Unterricht** teaching that is closely related to life; **2.** *adv.* **etw. ~nah schildern** describe sth. in a true-to-life way; **~nerv der: eine Industrie/Firma in ihrem ~nerv treffen** hit a vital nerve of an industry/a firm; **~notwendig** *Adj.* essential; vital; vital ⟨*organ*⟩; essential ⟨*foodstuff*⟩

leben·spendend *Adj.* *(geh.)* life-giving

lebens-, Lebens-: ~philosophie die philosophy of life; *(Lehre)* life philosophy *no art.*; Lebensphilosophie *no art.*; **~qualität die;** *o. Pl.* quality of life; **~raum der a)** *(Umkreis)* lebensraum; **b)** *(Biol.) s.* **Biotop; ~regel die** rule [of life]; maxim; **sich** *(Dat.)* **etw. zur ~regel machen** make sth. a rule [in life] *or* a maxim; **~retter der** rescuer; **sein ~retter** the person who saved his life; **du bist mein ~retter** you saved my life; **~rhythmus der** rhythm of life; **sein ~rhythmus** the rhythm of his life; **~standard der** standard of living; **~stellung die** permanent position *or* job; job for life; **~stil der** life-style; **~tüchtig** *Adj.* able to cope with life *postpos.*; **~überdruß der** weariness of life; world-weariness; **~umstände** *Pl.* circumstances; **~unfähig** *Adj.* non-viable; **~unterhalt der: seinen ~unterhalt verdienen/bestreiten** earn one's living/support oneself; **für jmds. ~unterhalt sorgen** support sb.; **~untüchtig** *Adj.* unable to cope with life *postpos.*; **~versicherung die** life insurance; life assurance; **eine ~versicherung abschließen** take out a life insurance *or* assurance policy; **~wandel der** way of life; **einen zweifelhaften/einwandfreien ~wandel führen** lead a dubious/an irreproachable life; **~weg der** [journey through] life; **jmdm. etw. mit auf den ~weg geben** give sb. sth. to take with him/her on his/her journey through life; **alles Gute für den weiteren ~weg** all the best for the future; **~weise die** way of life; **die sitzende ~weise** the sedentary life; **~weisheit die a)** *(Erfahrung)* wisdom; **b)** *(weiser Ausspruch)* wise saying *or* maxim; **~werk das** life's work; **~wert** *Adj.* **ein ~wertes Leben** a life worth living; **das ist kein ~wertes Dasein mehr** that's no kind of life any more; **das Leben ist ~wert** life is worth living; **~wert der** basic human value; **~wichtig** *s.* **~notwendig; ~wille der** will to live; **~zeichen das** sign of life; **kein ~zeichen [von sich] geben** show no sign of life; **kein ~zeichen von jmdm. bekommen** *(fig.)* have no sign of life from sb.; **~zeit die** life[-span]; **auf ~zeit** for life; **ein Beamter auf ~zeit** an established civil servant; **~ziel das** aim in life; **~zweck der** purpose in life

Leber ['le:bɐ] **die; ~, ~n** liver; **es an der ~ haben** *(ugs.)* have [got] liver trouble; **frisch** *od.* **frei von der ~ weg sprechen** *od.* **reden** *(ugs.)* speak one's mind; **sich** *(Dat.)* **etw. von der Leber reden** *(ugs.)* get sth. off one's chest *(coll.)*; *s. auch* **Laus**

leber-, Leber-: ~blümchen das liverwort; **~entzündung die** inflammation of the liver; hepatitis *(Med.)*; **~fleck der** liver spot; **~haken der** *(Boxen)* hook to the liver; **~käse der;** *o. Pl.* *meat loaf made with mincemeat, [minced liver,] eggs, and spices;* **~knödel der** *(südd., österr.)* *meat ball made from minced liver, onions, eggs, and flour;* **~krank** *Adj.* ⟨*patient etc.*⟩ suffering from a liver complaint *or* disorder; **~krank sein** have a liver complaint *or* disorder; **~krebs der** *(Med.)* cancer of the liver; **~leiden das** *(Med.)* liver complaint *or* disorder; **~pastete die** *(Kochk.)* liver pâté; **~schaden der** liver damage; damage to the liver; **~schrumpfung die** *s.* **~zirrhose; ~tran der** fish-liver oil; *(des Kabeljaus)* cod-liver oil; **~wurst die** liver sausage; **die gekränkte** *od.* **beleidigte ~wurst spielen** *(ugs.)* get all huffy *(coll.)*; **~zirrhose die** *(Med.)* cirrhosis of the liver

Lebe-: ~welt die playboy set; **~wesen das** living being *or* thing *or* creature; **einzellige ~wesen** single-celled creatures; unicellular organisms *(Biol.)*; **~wohl** [--'-] **das; [e]s, ~** *od.* **~e** *(geh.)* farewell; **jmdm. ~wohl sagen** bid sb. farewell

lebhaft 1. *Adj.* **a)** *(lebendig)* lively ⟨*person, gesture, imagination, bustle, etc.*⟩; lively, animated ⟨*conversation, discussion*⟩; lively, brisk ⟨*activity*⟩; busy ⟨*traffic*⟩; brisk ⟨*business*⟩; **b)** *(deutlich)* vivid ⟨*idea, picture, etc.*⟩; **etw. in ~er Erinnerung haben** remember sth. vividly; **c)** *(kräftig)* lively ⟨*interest*⟩; lively, gay ⟨*pattern*⟩; bright, gay ⟨*colour*⟩; vigorous ⟨*applause, opposition*⟩. **2.** *adv.* **a)** *(lebendig)* in a lively way *or* fashion; **sich ~ unterhalten/~ diskutieren** have a lively *or* animated conversation/discussion; **b)** *(deutlich)* vividly; **sich ~ an etw.** *(Akk.)* **erinnern können** be able to remember sth. vividly; **sich** *(Dat.)* **etw. ~ vorstellen können** have a vivid picture of sth.; **c)** *(kräftig)* brightly, gaily ⟨*coloured*⟩; gaily ⟨*patterned*⟩; **etw. ~ bedauern** deeply regret sth.; **sich ~ für etw. interessieren** take a lively *or* keen interest in sth.

Lebhaftigkeit die; ~ a) *(reges Wesen)* liveliness; *(einer Unterhaltung, Diskussion)* liveliness; animation; **b)** *(Intensität)* liveliness; *(eines Musters)* liveliness; gaiety; *(von Farben)* brightness; gaiety

Leb·kuchen der ≈ gingerbread

leb-, Leb-: ~los *Adj.* lifeless ⟨*body, eyes*⟩; **[wie] ~los daliegen** lie there as if dead; **~losigkeit die; ~:** lifelessness; **~tag der** *in* **[all] mein/dein** *usw.* **~tag** *(ugs.)* all my/your *etc.* life; **so was habe ich mein ~tag nicht erlebt** *(ugs.)* I've never seen anything like it in all my life *or* in all my born days; **~zeiten** *Pl. in* **bei** *od.* **zu ~zeiten** while still alive; **bei** *od.* **zu jmds. ~zeiten** while sb. is/was still alive; during sb.'s lifetime

lechzen ['lɛçtsn̩] *itr. V.* *(geh.)* **nach einem Trunk/nach Kühlung ~:** long for a drink/to be able to cool off; **nach Rache/Macht** *usw.* **~:** thirst for revenge/power *etc.*

Lecithin [letsi'ti:n] *s.* **Lezithin**

leck [lɛk] *Adj.* leaky; **~ sein** leak

Leck das; ~[e]s, ~s leak

Lecke ['lɛkə] *s.* **Salzlecke**

[1]lecken 1. *tr. V.* lick; **sich** *(Dat.)* **die Wunden/Lippen** *usw.* **~:** lick one's wounds/lips *etc.*; **jmdm. die Hand** *usw.* **~:** lick sb.'s hand *etc.*; **sich** *(Dat.)* **etw. von etw. ~:** lick sth. off sth.; **leck mich [doch]!** *(derb)* [why don't you] piss off! *(coarse)*; *s. auch* **Arsch a; Finger b. 2.** *itr. V.* **an etw.** *(Dat.)* **~:** lick sth.

[2]lecken *itr. V.* *(leck sein)* leak

lecker *Adj.* tasty ⟨*meal*⟩; delicious ⟨*cake etc.*⟩; good ⟨*smell, taste*⟩; *(fig.: ansprechend)* lovely ⟨*girl*⟩; **hier riecht es aber ~:** there's a delicious smell around here

Lecker·bissen der delicacy; **ein musikalischer ~** *(fig.)* a musical treat

Leckerei die; ~, ~en *(ugs.)* dainty; *(Süßigkeit)* sweet [meat]

Lecker-: ~maul, ~mäulchen das: ein ~maul *od.* **~mäulchen sein** have a sweet tooth

leck|schlagen *unr. itr V.; mit sein* *(Seemannsspr.)* be holed

led. *Abk.* **ledig**

Leder ['le:dɐ] **das; ~s, ~ a)** leather; **in ~ [gebunden]** leather-bound; **ein Gürtel aus ~:** a leather belt; **zäh wie ~ sein** be as tough as leather; ⟨*person*⟩ be as hard as nails; **jmdm. ans ~ gehen/wollen** *(ugs.)* go for sb./be out to get sb.; **gegen jmdn./etw. vom ~ ziehen** *(ugs.)* speak one's mind about sb./sth.; **b)** *(Fenster~)* leather; chamois *or* chammy [leather]; **c)** *(Fußballjargon: Ball)* ball; leather *(dated sl.)*

leder-, Leder-: ~artig *Adj.* leathery; leather-like ⟨*material*⟩; **~band der;** *Pl.* **~bände** leather-bound volume; **~fetischist der** leather fetishist; **~garnitur die** leather-upholstered suite; **~hand·schuh der** leather glove; **~haut die** *(Anat., Zool.)* dermis; **~hose die** leather shorts *pl.*; lederhosen *pl.*; *(lang)* leather trousers; **~jacke die** leather jacket; **~mantel der** leather [over]coat

[1]ledern *tr. V.* leather

[2]ledern *Adj.* **a)** *nicht präd.* *(aus Leder)* leather; **b)** *(wie Leder)* leathery

Leder-: ~nacken der leather-neck *(sl.)*; **~riemen der** [leather] strap; **~schuh der** leather shoe; **~schurz der** leather apron; **~sessel der** leather[-upholstered] armchair; **~sohle die** leather sole; **~waren** *Pl.* leather goods

ledig ['le:dɪç] *Adj.* **a)** *(nicht verheiratet)* unmarried; single; **eine ~e Mutter** an unmarried mother; **b)** *in* **einer Sache** *(Gen.)* **~ sein** *(geh.)* be free of sth.

Ledige der/die; *adj. Dekl.* single person

lediglich *Adj.* only; merely; simply

Lee [le:] **die** *od.* **das; ~** *(Seemannsspr.)* **nach ~ drehen** turn to leeward; **in ~ liegen** lie to leeward

leer [le:ɐ̯] *Adj.* **a)** empty; blank, clean ⟨*sheet of paper*⟩; **die Kasse ist ~** *(ugs.)* there's no money left; **sein Glas ~ trinken** empty *or* drain one's glass; **seinen Teller ~ essen** clear one's plate; **die Schachtel ~ machen** *(ugs.)* finish the box; **den Laden/die Regale ~ kaufen** strip every shelf in the shop/strip the shelves bare; **die Warnungen gingen ins Leere** the warnings fell on deaf ears; **~ ausge-**

hen come away empty-handed; ~ **laufen** ‹*machine*› idle; ‹*business*› be at a standstill; *s. auch* **leerlaufen; b)** *(menschenleer)* empty; empty, deserted ‹*streets*›; **vor ~en Bänken spielen** play to an empty house/empty houses; **die Wohnung steht ~:** the house is standing empty *or* is unoccupied; **c)** *(abwertend: oberflächlich)* empty ‹*words, promise, talk, display*›; vacant ‹*expression*›; **mit ~en Augen/~em Blick starren** stare vacantly

Leere die; ~ *(auch fig.)* emptiness; **eine gähnende ~:** a gaping void; **im Restaurant/Theatersaal herrschte ~:** the restaurant/theatre was completely empty; **eine innere ~** *(fig.)* a feeling of emptiness inside

leeren 1. *tr. V.* **a)** empty; empty, clear ‹*post-box*›; **b)** *(österr.: gießen)* pour ‹*water, milk, etc.*›; empty ‹*bucket*›. **2.** *refl. V.* ‹*hall, theatre, etc.*› empty

leer-, Leer-: ~formel die *(geh.)* empty formula; **~gefegt** *Adj.* deserted ‹*street, town*›; **wie ~gefegt** deserted; **~gewicht das** unladen weight; **~gut das** empties *pl.*; **~lauf der;** *o. Pl.* **a) im ~lauf den Berg hinunterfahren** ‹*driver*› coast down the hill in neutral; ‹*cyclist*› freewheel *or* coast down the hill; **eine Maschine auf ~lauf stellen** let a machine idle; **b)** *(fig.)* **es gab [viel] ~lauf im Büro** there were [long] slack periods in the office; **zwischen den Hauptdarbietungen gab es viel ~lauf** between the main acts there were long periods when nothing happened; **~|laufen** *unr. itr. V.; mit sein* **a)** *(auslaufen)* **die Badewanne läuft ~:** the bathwater is running out; **der Tank lief ~:** the oil/wine *etc.* was running *or* draining out of the tank; **das Faß ist ~gelaufen** the barrel has run dry; **b)** *in* **jmdn. ~laufen lassen** *(Ballspiele)* send sb. the wrong way; sell sb. a dummy *(coll.)*; *s. auch* **leer a; ~packung die** dummy; display package; **~stehend** *Adj.* empty, unoccupied ‹*house, flat*›; **~taste die** space-bar

Leerung die; ~, **~en** emptying; **die ~ der Mülltonnen erfolgt einmal wöchentlich** the dustbins are emptied once a week; **nächste ~ um 12 Uhr** *(auf Briefkästen)* next collection at 12.00

Lefze ['lɛftsə] **die;** ~, **~n** lip; **die ~n eines Jagdhundes** the flews of a hound

legal [le'ga:l] **1.** *Adj.* legal; **auf ~em Wege** by legal means; legally. **2.** *adv.* legally

legalisieren *tr. V.* legalize

Legalität [legali'tɛ:t] **die;** ~: legality; **außerhalb der ~:** outside the law; **am Rande der ~:** just within the bounds of legality

Legalitäts·prinzip das *(Rechtsw.) principle that all complaints must be investigated and that, where an offence appears to have been committed, a charge must be brought*

Legasthenie [legaste'ni:] **die;** ~, **~n** *(Psych., Med.)* difficulty in learning to read and write

Legastheniker [legas'te:nikɐ] **der;** **~s,** ~ *(Psych., Med.)* one who has difficulty with reading and writing

[1]**Legat** [le'ga:t] **der;** **~en, ~en** *(kath. Kirche)* legate

[2]**Legat das;** **~[e]s, ~e** *(Rechtsw.)* legacy

Legations·rat [lega'tsi̯o:ns-] **der** counsellor

legato [le'ga:to] *Adv. (Musik)* legato

Lege-: ~batterie die laying battery; **~henne die** laying hen

Legel ['le:gl̩] **der** *od.* **das;** **~s,** ~ *(Seemannsspr.)* **a)** *(aus Tauwerk)* cringle; **b)** *(aus Holz)* mast hoop

legen ['le:gn̩] **1.** *tr. V.* **a)** lay [down]; **jmdn. auf den Rücken ~:** lay sb. on his/her back; **einen Gegenspieler ~** *(Sportjargon)* bring down an opposing player; **etw. auf den Tisch/Boden ~:** lay sth. on the table/floor; **etw. aus der Hand ~:** put sth. down; **etw. in Spiritus ~:** preserve sth. in alcohol; **etw. beiseite ~:** put sth. aside *or* down; **das Fleisch in den Kühlschrank ~:** put the meat in the refrigerator; **die Hand an die Mütze ~:** raise one's hand to one's cap; **die Füße auf den Tisch ~:** put one's feet on the table; **etw. auf den Abend ~:** arrange sth. for the evening; **b)** *(verlegen)* lay ‹*pipe, cable, railway track, carpet, tiles, etc.*›; plant ‹*potatoes*›; *s. auch* **Fundament a; Grundstein; Karte g; c)** *(in eine bestimmte Form bringen)* **etw. in Falten ~:** fold sth.; **sich** *(Dat.)* **die Haare ~ lassen** have one's hair set; *s. auch* **Falte c; d)** *(schräg hinstellen)* lean; **etw. an etw.** *(Akk.)* **~:** lean sth. [up] against sth. **2.** *tr., itr. V.* ‹*hen*› lay; **die Hühner ~ fleißig/schlecht** the hens are laying/not laying well. **3.** *refl. V.* **a)** lie down; **sich auf etw.** *(Akk.)* **~:** lie down on sth.; **sich in die Sonne ~:** lie in the sun; **das Schiff/Flugzeug legte sich auf die Seite** the ship keeled over/the aircraft banked steeply; **sich in die Kurve ~:** lean into the bend; *s. auch* **Bett a; Ohr b; b)** *(nachlassen)* ‹*wind, storm*› die down, abate, subside; ‹*noise*› die down, abate; ‹*enthusiasm*› wear off, subside, fade; ‹*anger*› abate, subside; ‹*excitement*› die down, subside; **c)** *(sich herabsenken)* **sich auf** *od.* **über etw.** *(Akk.)* **~:** ‹*mist, fog*› descend *or* settle on sth., [come down and] blanket sth.

legendär [legɛn'dɛ:ɐ̯] *Adj.* legendary

Legende [le'gɛndə] **die;** ~, **~n a)** legend; **zur ~ werden** *(fig.)* ‹*event, incident, etc.*› become legendary; **[schon zu Lebzeiten] zur ~ werden** *(fig.)* ‹*person*› become a legend [in one's own lifetime]; **b)** *(Zeichenerklärung)* legend; key

legenden·umwoben *Adj.* ‹*person, figure, etc.*› surrounded by legends

leger [le'ʒe:ɐ̯] **1.** *Adj.* **a)** *(ungezwungen)* casual; relaxed; *(oberflächlich)* casual; **b)** *(bequem)* casual ‹*jacket etc.*›. **2.** *adv.* **a)** *(ungezwungen)* casually; in a casual *or* relaxed manner; *(oberflächlich)* casually; **b)** *(bequem)* ‹*dress*› casually

Leg·henne ['le:k-] **die** *s.* **Legehenne**

legieren [le'gi:rən] *tr. V.* **a)** alloy; **Kupfer und** *od.* **mit Zinn ~:** alloy copper and tin; **b)** *(Kochk.)* thicken

Legierung die; ~, **~en** alloy

Legion [le'gi̯o:n] **die;** ~, **~en a)** *(Milit.)* legion; *(Fremden~)* Legion; **b)** *(Menge)* horde (**von** of); **~ sein** *(geh.)* be legion

Legionär [legi̯o'nɛ:ɐ̯] **der;** **~s, ~e** legionary

Legionärs·krankheit die *(Med.)* legionnaire's disease

legislativ [legɪsla'ti:f] **1.** *Adj. (Politik)* legislative. **2.** *adv.* by legislation

Legislative [legɪsla'ti:və] **die;** ~, **~n** *(Politik)* legislature

Legislatur [legɪsla'tu:ɐ̯] **die;** ~, **~en a)** *o. Pl.* legislature; **b)** *s.* **Legislaturperiode**

Legislatur·periode die *(Politik)* parliamentary term; legislative period; *(Amtsdauer einer Regierung)* term of office

legitim [legi'ti:m] **1.** *Adj.* legitimate. **2.** *adv.* legitimately

Legitimation [legitima'tsi̯o:n] **die;** ~, **~en a)** *(auch Rechtsw.: Ehelicherklärung)* legitimation; **b)** *(Ausweis)* proof of identity; *(Bevollmächtigung)* authorization

legitimieren 1. *tr. V.* **a)** *(rechtfertigen)* justify; **b)** *(bevollmächtigen)* authorize; **c)** *(für legitim erklären)* legitimize ‹*child, relationship*›. **2.** *refl. V.* show proof of one's identity

Legitimität [legitimi'tɛ:t] **die;** ~: legitimacy; *(Rechtfertigung)* justification

Leguan [le'gu̯a:n] **der;** **~s, ~e** *(Zool.)* iguana

Lehen ['le:ən] **das;** **~s,** ~ *(hist.)* fief; **jmdm. etw. zu ~ geben** grant sb. sth. in fee

Lehm [le:m] **der;** **~s** loam; *(Ton)* clay

lehm-, Lehm-: ~bau der; *Pl.* **~bauten** clay *or* mud building; **~bau·weise die** building with clay; *(~flechtwerk)* wattle and daub construction; **~boden der** loamy soil; *(Tonerde)* clay soil; **~farben, ~farbig** *Adj.* clay-coloured; **~grube die** claypit; **~haltig** *Adj.* loamy; *(tonartig)* clayey; **~hütte die** mud hut

lehmig *Adj.* loamy ‹*soil, earth*›; *(tonartig)* clayey ‹*soil, shoes, etc.*›

Lehm·ziegel der clay brick

Lehn [le:n] *s.* **Lehen**

Lehn- *(Sprachw.)*: **~bedeutung die** loan-meaning; **~bildung die** loan-formation

Lehne ['le:nə] **die;** ~, **~n a)** *(Rücken~)* back; *(Arm~)* arm; **b)** *(südd., österr., schweiz.: Abhang)* slope

lehnen 1. *tr. V.* lean (**an** + *Akk.*, **gegen** against); **den Kopf/Arm an etw.** *(Akk.)* **~:** lean one's head/arm on sth. **2.** *refl. V.* lean (**an** + *Akk.*, **gegen** against; **über** + *Akk.* over); **sich aus dem Fenster ~:** lean out of the window; **sich zu weit aus dem Fenster ~** *(fig.)* stick one's neck out *(coll.)*; go too far. **3.** *itr. V.* be leaning (**an** + *Dat.* against)

Lehns·dienst der *(hist.)* feudal service *no pl., no art.*

Lehn·sessel der armchair

Lehns- *(hist.)*: **~herr der** feudal lord; **~mann der;** *Pl.* **~männer** *od.* **~leute** vassal; **~pflicht die** feudal duty

Lehn·stuhl der armchair

Lehns·wesen das *(hist.)* system of feudal tenure; feudal system

Lehn- *(Sprachw.)*: **~übersetzung die** loan-translation; **~wort das** loan-word

Lehr-: ~amt das *(Schulw.)* teaching post; *(Beruf)* **das ~amt** the teaching profession; **das höhere ~amt** *teaching at Gymnasien or vocational schools;* **~amts·anwärter der** *(Schulw.)* trainee primary-school teacher; **~amts·kandidat der** trainee grammar-school teacher/vocational school teacher; **~anstalt die** *(Amtsspr.)* educational establishment; **höhere ~anstalt** *(veralt.)* secondary education establishment; **~auftrag der** lectureship *(not giving full status as member of a department or as a permanent civil servant)*; **~beauftragte der/die** lecturer *(not having full status as member of a department or as a permanent civil servant)*; **~befähigung die** *(Amtsspr.)* teaching qualification; **~behelf der** *(österr.) s.* **~mittel; ~berechtigung die** teaching qualification; **~beruf der a)** *s.* **Ausbildungsberuf; b)** *(Lehrerberuf)* **der ~beruf** the teaching profession; **den ~beruf ausüben** teach; be a teacher/teachers; **~betrieb der** teaching programme; **~bub der** *(südd., österr., schweiz.) s.* **~junge; ~buch das** textbook; **~dichtung die** *(Literaturw.)* **a)** *o. Pl.* didactic poetry; **b)** *(Gedicht)* didactic poem

[1]**Lehre** ['le:rə] **die;** ~, **~n a)** *(Berufsausbildung)* apprenticeship; **eine ~ machen** serve an apprenticeship (**als** as); **bei einem Handwerker in die ~ gehen** be apprenticed to a craftsman; **bei jmdm. in die ~ gegangen sein** *(fig.)* have learnt a lot from sb.; **b)** *(Weltanschauung)* doctrine; **die christliche ~:** Christian doctrine; **die ~ Kants/Hegels/Buddhas** the teachings *pl.* of Kant/Hegel/Buddha; **c)** *(Theorie, Wissenschaft)* theory; **die ~ vom Schall** the science of sound *or* acoustics; **d)** *(Erfahrung)* lesson; **laß dir das eine ~ sein!** let that be a lesson to you; **jmdm. eine [heilsame] ~ erteilen** teach sb. a [salutary] lesson; **aus etw. seine ~ ziehen** learn one's lesson from sth.; **e)** *(Verhaltensregel)* precept

[2]**Lehre die;** ~, **~n** *(Bauw., Technik)* gauge

lehren *tr., itr. V.* teach; **jmdn. lesen/schreiben ~:** teach sb. to read/write; **ich bin das gelehrt worden** I was taught that; **ich werde dich ~, so bockig zu sein!** *(ugs.)* I'll teach you to be so contrary *(coll.)*; **die Geschichte lehrt, daß ...:** history teaches *or* shows us that ...; **erst die Zukunft wird uns ~, ...:** time alone will tell ...

Lehrende der/die; *adj. Dekl. (Hochschulw.)* **~ und Lernende** teaching staff and students
Lehrer der; ~s, ~ a) *(auch fig.)* teacher; **er ist ~ für Geschichte** he teaches history; he is a history teacher; **b)** *(Ausbilder)* instructor
-lehrer der: Türkisch~/Ski~: teacher of Turkish/skiing instructor; **unser Französischlehrer** our French teacher
lehrer-, Lehrer-: ~aus·bildung die teacher training *no art.*; **~haft** *Adj. (abwertend)* schoolmasterly; *(von Frauen)* schoolmarmish *(coll.)*
Lehrerin die; ~, ~nen teacher; *s. auch* **-in; Lehrer; -lehrer**
Lehrer-: ~kollegium das teaching staff; faculty *(Amer.)*; **~mangel der** shortage of teachers
Lehrerschaft die; ~, ~en teachers *pl.*; *(einer Schule)* teaching staff; faculty *(Amer.)*
Lehrer-: ~schwemme die *(ugs.)* glut of teachers; **~zimmer das** staff-room
Lehr-: ~fach das a) subject; **b)** *(Beruf des Lehrens)* teaching profession; **im ~fach tätig sein** be a teacher; be in teaching; **~film der** educational film; **~freiheit die** academic freedom *no art.*; **~gang der** course **(für, in + *Dat.* in)**; **einen ~gang machen, an einem ~gang teilnehmen** take a course; **~gebäude das** *(geh.)* **das Hegelsche ~gebäude** the edifice of Hegelian teachings; **~gegen·stand der** *(österr.) s.* **~fach a; ~geld das a)** *(hist.)* apprenticeship premium; **b)** *(fig.)* **du kannst dir dein ~geld zurückgeben lassen!** your education was wasted on you; **~geld geben** *od.* **[be]zahlen [müssen]** learn the hard way
lehrhaft *Adj. (belehrend)* instructive; didactic ⟨*intention*⟩
Lehr-: ~herr der *(geh. veralt.)* master *(of an apprentice)*; **~jahr das** year as an apprentice; **sie ist im zweiten ~jahr** she is in the second year of her apprenticeship; **~jahre sind keine Herrenjahre** *(Spr.)* we all have to start at the bottom of the ladder; **~junge der** apprentice; **~kanzel die** *(österr.) s.* **~stuhl; ~körper der** *(Amtsspr.)* teaching staff; faculty *(Amer.)*; **~kraft die** teacher
Lehrling ['le:ɐ̯lɪŋ] **der; ~s, ~e** apprentice; *(in kaufmännischen Berufen)* trainee
Lehrlings-: ~aus·bildung die training of apprentices; **~heim das** apprentices' hostel
lehr-, Lehr-: ~mädchen das [girl] apprentice; *(in kaufmännischen Berufen)* [girl] trainee; **~meinung die** *(geh.)* [expert] opinion; **~meister der** teacher; *(Vorbild)* mentor; **~methode die** teaching method; **~mittel das** *(Schulw.)* teaching aid; **~mittel** *Pl.* teaching materials; **~mittel·freiheit die;** *o. Pl. (Schulw.)* free provision of teaching materials; **~pfad der** trail; *(Naturpfad)* nature trail; **~plan der** *(Schulw.)* syllabus; *(Gesamtlehrgang)* curriculum; **~probe die** *(Schulw.)* teaching practice; **eine ~probe geben** *od.* **machen** do a teaching practice; **~reich** *Adj.* instructive, informative ⟨*book, film, etc.*⟩; **es war eine ~reiche Erfahrung für ihn** the experience taught him a lot; **~satz der** proposition; *(in der Geometrie, Logik)* theorem; **die Euklidischen ~sätze** the propositions of Euclid; **~schwimm·becken das** learners' [swimming-]pool; **~stelle die** apprenticeship; *(in kaufmännischen Berufen)* trainee post; **~stoff der** *(Schulw.)* syllabus; **~stück das** *(Literaturw.)* didactic play; **~stuhl der** *(Hochschulw.)* chair **(für** of); **~stuhl·inhaber der** holder of a/the chair; **~veranstaltung die** *(Hochschulw.)* class; *(Vorlesung)* lecture; **~vertrag der** indentures *pl.*; **~werk das** course; *(Buch)* textbook; **~werkstatt die** apprentices' *or* training workshop; **~zeit die** [period of] apprenticeship
Leib [laip] **der; ~[e]s, ~er** *(geh.)* **a)** body; **ich hatte keinen trockenen Faden mehr am ~[e]** I was wet through *or* soaked to the skin; **am ganzen ~ zittern** shiver all over; **bleib mir vom ~[e]!** keep away from me!; keep your distance!; **der ~ Christi/des Herrn** *(christl. Rel.)* the Body of Christ; **etw. am eigenen ~ erfahren** *od.* **erleben** experience sth. for oneself; **er hat sich mit ~ und Seele der Musik verschrieben** he dedicated himself heart and soul to music; **mit ~ und Seele Arzt/Krankenschwester** *usw.* **sein** be a dedicated doctor/nurse *etc.*; **mit ~ und Seele dabei sein** put one's whole heart into it; **jmdm. auf den ~** *od.* **zu ~e rücken** *(ugs.)* chivvy sb.; *(mit Kritik)* get at sb. *(coll.)*; **jmdm. so zu ~e rücken, daß ...:** go on at sb. until ...*(coll.)*; **sich** *(Dat.)* **jmdn. vom ~e halten** *(ugs.)* keep sb. at arm's length; **jmdm. mit einer Sache vom ~e bleiben** *(ugs.)* not pester sb. with sth.; **einer Sache** *(Dat.)* **zu ~e gehen** *od.* **rücken** tackle sth.; set about sth.; **jmdm. auf den ~ geschnitten sein** be tailor-made for sb.; suit sb. down to the ground; **die Rolle ist ihm [wie] auf den ~ geschrieben** the part could have been written for him; *(fig.)* the role fits him like a glove; **was hast du für einen Ton am ~?** *(salopp)* what a way to talk!; *s. auch* **lebendig 1a; b)** *(geh., fachspr.: Bauch)* belly; *(Magen)* stomach; **gesegneten ~es sein** *(veralt.)* be with child *(dated)*; **c)** *(veralt.)* **~ und Gut wagen/hingeben** risk/give one's all; **eine Gefahr für ~ und Leben** a danger to life and limb; **~ und Leben opfern** sacrifice one's life
Leib-: ~arzt der personal physician; **~binde die** [warm] body belt
Leibchen ['laipçən] **das; ~s, ~ a)** *(Trachten~)* bodice; **b)** *(landsch.: Unterhemd)* vest *(Brit.)*; undershirt *(Amer.)*
leib-, Leib-: ~diener der valet; **~eigen** *Adj. (hist.)* in serfdom *postpos.*; **~eigene der/die;** *adj. Dekl. (hist.)* serf; *(fig.)* slave; **~eigenschaft die;** *o. Pl. (hist.)* serfdom *no def. art.*
leiben *itr. V. in* **wie er/sie** *usw.* **leibt und lebt** to a T
Leibes-: ~ertüchtigung die *(veralt.)* keeping fit *or* in trim *no art.*; physical training *no art.*; **~erziehung die** *(Schulw.)* physical education; PE; **~frucht die** *(Med.)* embryo; *(nach 8 Wochen)* foetus; *(Rechtsspr.)* unborn child; **~fülle die** *(geh.)* corpulence; *(Umfang)* girth; **~kräfte** *Pl. in* **aus** *od.* **nach ~kräften** with all one's might; **aus ~kräften schreien** shout for all one is worth; **~übungen** *Pl. (Schulw.)* physical education *sing.*; PE; **~visitation** [~vizitatsio:n] **die; ~, ~en** body search
Leib-: ~garde die bodyguard; **die ~garde der Königin** *(in Großbritannien)* the Queen's Life Guards *pl.*; **~gardist der** [member of the/a] bodyguard; *(der britischen Monarchen)* Life Guard; **~gericht das** favourite dish
leibhaftig [laip'haftɪç] **1.** *Adj.* **a)** *(persönlich)* in person *postpos.*; **da stand er ~ vor uns** there he was, as large as life; **der ~e Beweis dafür, daß ...:** the living proof that ...; **b)** *(echt)* real; **ein ~er Herzog** a real live duke; **der ~e Teufel,** *(scherzh.)* **der Leibhaftige** the devil incarnate. **2.** *adv. (ugs.)* actually; believe it or not
leiblich *Adj.* **a)** physical ⟨*well-being*⟩; **b)** *(blutsverwandt)* real ⟨*mother, parents, etc.*⟩; **er liebte ihn wie seinen ~en Sohn** he loved him like his own son
Leib-: ~rente die life annuity; **~riemen der** *(veralt.)* belt; **~schmerzen** *Pl.* abdominal pain *sing.*; **~speise die** *s.* **~gericht; ~wache die** bodyguard; **~wächter der** bodyguard; **~wäsche die** underwear; underclothes *pl.*
Leiche ['laiçə] **die; ~, ~n a)** [dead] body; *(bes. eines Unbekannten)* corpse; **er sieht aus wie eine lebende** *od.* **wandelnde ~** *(salopp)* he looks like death warmed up *(sl.)*; **nur über meine ~!** over my dead body!; **über ~n gehen** *(abwertend)* be utterly ruthless *or* unscrupulous; **um seine Interessen durchzusetzen, geht er über ~n** he will stick at nothing to attain his own ends; **eine ~ im Keller haben** *(fig. ugs.)* have a skeleton in the cupboard; **b)** *(landsch. veralt.: Begräbnis)* funeral; **c)** *(Druckw.)* out *(Printing)*; omission
leichen-, Leichen-: ~begängnis das *(geh.)* funeral; **~beschauer der** *doctor who performs a post-mortem;* autopsist *(Amer.)*; **~bestatter der** undertaker; mortician *(Amer.)*; **~bitter·miene die** *(iron.)* doleful expression; **~blaß** *Adj.* deathly pale; white as a sheet *postpos.*; **~fledderei die** *(Rechtsw.) robbery of a dead or unconscious person;* **~fledderer der** *(Rechtsw.) one who robs a dead or unconscious person;* **~frau die** layer-out; **~halle die** mortuary; **~hemd das** burial garment; **~öffnung die** post-mortem *or* autopsy *(with dissection)*; **~rede die** *(geh.)* funeral oration; **~schänder der** desecrator of a/the corpse; *(sexuell)* necrophiliac; **~schändung die** desecration of a corpse; *(sexuell)* necrophilia *no art.*; **der zweite Schlag ist ~schändung** *(salopp, scherzh.)* these fists are lethal weapons *(joc.)*; **~schau die** post-mortem; autopsy; **~schau·haus das** morgue; **~schmaus der** *(scherzh.)* funeral meal; **~starre die** rigor mortis; **~tuch das** *(veralt.)* winding-sheet; shroud; **~verbrennung die** cremation; **~wagen der** hearse; **~wäscher der** *person who washes corpses for burial;* **~zug der** *(geh.)* cortège; funeral procession
Leichnam ['laiçna:m] **der; ~s, ~e** *(geh.)* body; **jmds. ~:** sb.'s body *or* mortal remains *pl.*
leicht [laiçt] **1.** *Adj.* **a)** light; lightweight ⟨*suit, material*⟩; **~e Waffen** small-calibre arms; **~e Kleidung** thin clothes; *(luftig)* light *or* cool clothes; **gewogen und zu ~ befunden** tried and found wanting; **jmdn. um etw. ~er machen** *(ugs.)* relieve sb. of sth.; **mit ~er Hand** with ease; **etw. auf die ~e Schulter** *od.* **Achsel nehmen** *(ugs.)* take sth. casually; make light of sth.; **b)** *(einfach)* easy ⟨*task, question, job, etc.*⟩; *(nicht anstrengend)* light ⟨*work, duties, etc.*⟩; **ein ~es Leben haben** have an easy life; **es ~/nicht ~ haben** have/not have it easy *or* an easy time of it; **nichts ~er als das** nothing could be simpler *or* easier; **du machst dir die Sache zu ~:** you're making it too easy for yourself *or* not taking it seriously enough; **es wäre ihm ein ~es zu helfen** it would be an easy *or* simple matter for him to help; **keinen ~en Stand haben** not have an easy time of it; **mit jmdm. [kein] ~es Spiel haben** find sb. is [not] easy meat; **man hat's nicht ~, aber ~ hat's einen** *(salopp)* it's a hard *or* tough life; **c)** *(schwach)* slight ⟨*accent, illness, wound, doubt, etc.*⟩; light ⟨*wind, rain, sleep, perfume*⟩; **ein ~er Stoß [in die Rippen]** a gentle nudge [in the ribs]; **eine ~e Grippe** a mild attack of flu *(coll.)*; **d)** *(bekömmlich)* light ⟨*food, wine*⟩; mild ⟨*cigar, cigarette*⟩; **e)** *(heiter)* light-hearted; **ihr wurde ~ ums Herz** *(geh.)* a weight was lifted from her heart; **ihr wurde es etwas/viel ~er** she felt somewhat/much easier *or* relieved; **f)** *(unterhaltend)* light ⟨*music, reading, etc.*⟩; **g)** *(veralt. abwertend)* **ein ~es Mädchen** a loose-living girl. **2.** *adv.* **a)** lightly ⟨*built*⟩; **~ bekleidet sein** be lightly *or* thinly dressed; *(fast nackt)* be scantily clad; **b)** *(einfach, schnell, spielend)* easily; **~ verständlich** *od.* **zu verstehen sein** be easy to understand; be easily understood; **~ zerbrechlich sein** be very fragile; **~ entzündlich sein** be highly inflammable; **sie hat ~ reden** it's easy *or* all very well for her to talk; **das ist ~er gesagt als getan** that's easier said than done; **jemanden wie ihn wer-**

den Sie nicht so ~ wiederfinden you won't find someone like him again in a hurry *(coll.)*; sie wird ~ böse she has a quick temper; das ist ~ möglich that is perfectly possible; ihr wird ~ schlecht the slightest thing makes her sick; c) *(geringfügig)* slightly; ~ gewürzt sein be lightly seasoned; es regnete ~: there was a light rain falling; es hat ~ gefroren there was a slight frost; d) *(bekömmlich)* ~ essen eat light food

leicht-, Leicht-: ~**athlet der** [track/field] athlete; ~**athletik die** [track and field] athletics *sing.*; ~**bau·platte die** *(Bauw.)* lightweight building board; ~**bau·weise die** lightweight construction; etw. in ~bauweise herstellen *od.* produzieren make sth. with lightweight materials; ~**bekleidet** *Adj.; präd. getrennt geschrieben* lightly dressed; *(fast nackt)* scantily clad; ~**benzin das** benzine; ~**beschwingt** *Adj.; präd. getrennt geschrieben* carefree; ⟨*music*⟩ with a gay lilt; ~**bewaffnet** *Adj.; präd. getrennt geschrieben* lightly armed; ~**blütig** *Adj. (geh.)* happy-go-lucky; *(leichtsinnig)* frivolous; ~**entzündlich** *Adj.; präd. getrennt geschrieben* highly inflammable

Leichter der; ~s, ~ *(Seew.)* lighter

leicht-, Leicht-: ~|**fallen** *unr. itr. V.; mit sein* be easy; das fällt mir ~: it is easy for me; I find it easy; ~**fertig 1.** *Adj.* **a)** careless ⟨*behaviour, person*⟩; rash ⟨*promise*⟩; ill-considered, slapdash ⟨*plan*⟩; **b)** *(veralt.: moralisch bedenkenlos)* promiscuous; loose ⟨*woman*⟩; **2.** *adv.* carelessly; ~**fertigkeit die;** *o. Pl.* carelessness; ~**fuß der** *(abwertend)* Casanova; lady-killer; ~**füßig** *(geh.)* **1.** *Adj.* nimble; **2.** *adv.* with light *or* nimble steps; ~**füßigkeit die;** *o. Pl.* lightness *or* nimbleness of foot; ~**geschürzt** [~gəʃʏrtst] *Adj.; präd. getrennt geschrieben (scherzh.)* scantily clad; ~**gewicht das** *(Schwerathletik)* **a)** *o. Pl.* lightweight; *s. auch* Fliegengewicht; **b)** *s.* ~gewichtler; **c)** *(ugs. scherzh.) (Mädchen)* sylph; *(Mann)* featherweight; ~**gewichtler** [~gəvɪçtlɐ] **der;** ~s, ~ *(Schwerathletik)* lightweight; ~**gläubig** *Adj.* gullible; credulous; ~**gläubigkeit die** gullibility; credulity; ~**hin** *Adv.* **a)** *(ohne Überlegung)* without [really] thinking; *(lässig)* casually; etw. ~hin sagen say sth. casually *or* unthinkingly; **b)** *(nebenbei)* in an offhand *or* casual manner

Leichtigkeit ['laiçtɪçkait] **die;** ~ **a)** *(geringes Gewicht, Schwerelosigkeit)* lightness; **b)** *(Mühelosigkeit)* ease; es ist eine ~ [für ihn], das zu tun it is a simple matter [for him] to do it; mit ~: with ease; easily

leicht-, Leicht-: ~**industrie die** light industry; ~**lebig** *Adj.* happy-go-lucky; ~**lebigkeit die;** *o. Pl.* happy-go-lucky attitude; ~**lohn·gruppe die** *(verhüll.)* low-wage group; ~|**machen** *tr. V.* jmdm./sich etw. ~machen make sth. easy for sb./oneself; es sich *(Dat.)* *od.* sich *(Dat.)* die Sache ~machen make it *or* things easy for oneself; take the easy way out; ~**matrose der** ordinary seaman; ~**metall das** light metal; *(Legierung)* [light] alloy; ~|**nehmen** *unr. tr. V.* etw. ~nehmen make light of sth.; seine Aufgabe nicht ~nehmen take one's task seriously; nimm's ~: don't worry about it; ~**öl das** light oil; ~**schwer·gewicht das** *(Schwerathletik)* light heavyweight; Weltmeister im ~schwergewicht world light heavyweight champion; ~**sinn der;** *o. Pl.* carelessness *no indef. art.*; *(mit Gefahr verbunden)* recklessness *no indef. art.*; *(Fahrlässigkeit)* negligence *no indef. art.*; das sagst du so in deinem jugendlichen ~sinn *(ugs.)* that's easier said than done; ~**sinnig 1.** *Adj.* careless; *(sich, andere gefährdend)* reckless; *(fahrlässig)* negligent; **2.** *adv.* carelessly; *(gefährlich)* recklessly; ⟨*promise*⟩ rashly; ~sinnig mit seinem Geld umgehen be careless with one's money; ~**sinnigerweise** *Adv.* carelessly; *(gefährlicherweise)* recklessly; ⟨*promise*⟩ rashly; ~**sinnigkeit die;** *o. Pl.: s.* Leichtsinn; ~|**tun** *unr. refl. V. (ugs.)* sich *(Dat., auch Akk.)* mit etw. ~tun/nicht ~tun manage sth. easily/have a hard time with sth.; ~**verdaulich** *Adj.; präd. getrennt geschrieben* [easily] digestible; ~**verkäuflich** *Adj.; präd. getrennt geschrieben* fast-selling; ~**verletzt** *Adj.; präd. getrennt geschrieben* slightly injured; ~**verletzte der/die** slightly injured man/woman/person; 200 ~verletzte two hundred slightly injured; ~**verwundet** *Adj.; präd. getrennt geschrieben* slightly wounded; ~**verwundete der/die** slightly wounded man/woman/person; die ~verwundeten those with slight wounds

leid [lait] *Adj.; nicht attr.* **a)** es tut mir ~[, daß ...] I'm sorry [that ...]; das braucht dir nicht ~ zu tun you needn't feel sorry *or (coll.)* bad about that; so ~ es mir tut, aber ...: I'm very sorry, but ...; er tut mir ~: I feel sorry for him; es tut mir ~ darum/um ihn I feel sorry *or (coll.)* bad about it/sorry for him; **b)** *(überdrüssig)* etw./jmdn. ~ sein/werden *(ugs.)* be/get fed up with *(coll.)* or tired of sth./sb.; wird sie es nie ~, das zu tun? will she never tire of doing this?; jmdm. ~ sein/werden *(veralt.)* be/become wearisome to sb.; die Arbeit ist ihm längst ~: he wearied of the work long ago

Leid das; ~[e]s **a)** *(Schmerz)* suffering; *(Kummer)* grief; sorrow; großes *od.* schweres ~ erfahren suffer greatly; *(Kummer)* suffer great sorrow; geteiltes ~ ist halbes ~ *(Spr.)* a sorrow shared is a sorrow halved; jmdm. sein ~ klagen tell sb. all one's woes; **b)** *(Unrecht)* wrong; *(Böses)* harm; jmdm. ein ~ zufügen wrong/harm sb.; do sb. wrong/harm; ihm soll kein ~ *od.* *(veralt.)* ~s geschehen he shall come to no harm; sich *(Dat.)* ein ~s antun *(ugs. veralt.)* take one's own life

Leide·form die *(Sprachw.) s.* Passiv

leiden 1. *unr. itr. V.* **a)** suffer (an, unter + *Dat.* from); unter jmdm. ~: suffer because of sb.; **b)** *(Schaden nehmen)* suffer (durch, unter + *Dat.* from); durch den Frost ~: suffer from *or* be harmed by the frost. **2.** *unr. tr. V.* **a)** jmdn. [gut] ~ können *od.* mögen like sb.; ich kann sie/das nicht ~: I can't stand her/it; **b)** *(geh.: ertragen müssen)* suffer ⟨*hunger, thirst, want, torment, etc.*⟩; **c)** *(dulden)* tolerate; sie ist überall/bei ihren Vorgesetzten wohl gelitten *(geh.)* she is liked by everybody/by her superiors; **d)** *(veralt.: aushalten)* sie litt es nicht mehr zu Hause she could endure it no longer at home

Leiden das; ~s, ~ **a)** *(Krankheit)* illness; *(Gebrechen)* complaint; nach langem, schwerem ~ sterben die after a long and painful illness; [es ist] immer das alte ~: [it's] the same old story; **b)** *(Qual)* suffering; Freud[en] und ~[en] joy[s] and sorrow[s]; das *od.* die ~ Christi Christ's Passion; **c)** ein langes ~ [von Sohn] *(ugs. scherzh.)* a beanpole [of a son]

-leiden das: ein Asthma~/Herz~ haben have an asthmatic condition/a heart condition

leidend *Adj.* **a)** *(krank)* ailing; in poor health *postpos.*; ~ aussehen look sickly *or* poorly; **b)** *(schmerzvoll)* strained ⟨*voice*⟩; martyred ⟨*expression*⟩; ⟨*look*⟩ full of suffering

Leidenschaft die; ~, ~en passion (zu, für for); mit ~: fervently; passionately; Reiten ist seine [ganze] ~: riding is his great love; seine ~ für etw. entdecken realize one's great love for sth.; er ist Sammler aus ~: he is a dedicated collector; ein Thema frei von jeder ~ diskutieren discuss a subject dispassionately

leidenschaftlich 1. *Adj.* passionate; ardent, passionate ⟨*lover*⟩; passionate[ly keen] ⟨*skier, collector, etc.*⟩; violent, passionate ⟨*hatred, quarrel*⟩; vehement ⟨*protest*⟩. **2.** *adv.* **a)** passionately; *(eifrig)* dedicatedly; ~ diskutiert werden be discussed heatedly; etw. ~ ablehnen/verneinen reject/deny sth. vehemently; er treibt ~ Sport/sammelt ~ Briefmarken he is a passionately keen sportsman/stamp-collector; **b)** *(intensivierend)* etw. ~ gern tun adore doing sth.; sie ißt ~ gerne Schokolade she adores *or* has a passion for chocolate

Leidenschaftlichkeit die; ~ **a)** passion; *(in der Liebe)* ardour; *(bei einer Diskussion)* heat; *(bei der Darlegung eines Standpunkts)* vehemence; **b)** *(Begeisterung)* passionate dedication; mit ungeheurer ~: with tremendous enthusiasm

leidenschaftslos 1. *Adj.* dispassionate; detached. **2.** *adv.* dispassionately; in a detached way

Leidenschaftslosigkeit die; ~: detachment; mit völliger ~: in an entirely detached manner; *(ohne Nachdruck)* without any expression

leidens-, Leidens-: ~**druck der** *(Psych.)* strain imposed by suffering; psychological strain (+ *Gen.* on); ~**fähig** *Adj.* with a great capacity for suffering *postpos., not pred.*; ~**fähigkeit die;** *o. Pl.* capacity for suffering; ~**gefährte der,** ~**gefährtin die;** ~**genosse der,** ~**genossin die** fellow-sufferer; ~**geschichte die;** *o. Pl.* *(christl. Rel.)* die ~geschichte Christi Christ's Passion; seine ~geschichte *(fig.)* his tale of woe; ~**miene die** woeful *or* martyred expression; ~**weg der** *(geh.)* life of suffering *or* hardship

leider *Adv.* unfortunately; ich habe ~ keine Zeit unfortunately *or* I'm afraid I haven't any time; ~ ja/nein I'm afraid so/afraid not; ~ Gottes ist es nun einmal so *(ugs.)* that's how it is, I'm afraid *or* worse luck; *(in förmlichen Briefen)* wir müssen Ihnen ~ mitteilen ...: we regret to inform you ...

leid-: ~**erfüllt** *Adj.* full of suffering *postpos.*; wretched; ⟨*look*⟩ of suffering; ~**geprüft** *Adj.* sorely tried; long-suffering

leidig *Adj.* tiresome; wretched; das ist ein ~er Trost that's not much comfort

leidlich 1. *Adj.* reasonable; passable. **2.** *adv.* reasonably; fairly; es geht mir [ganz] ~ *(ugs.)* I'm quite well *or* not too bad; sie kann ~ Klavier spielen she can play the piano reasonably well

leid-, Leid-: ~**tragende der/die;** *adj. Dekl.* victim; der *od.* die ~tragende/die ~tragenden [dabei] sein be the one/ones to suffer [in this]; ~**voll** *Adj. (geh.)* ⟨*life, youth, look*⟩ full of suffering; painful ⟨*experience*⟩; in der langen, ~vollen Geschichte Afrikas in the long history of Africa with all its suffering; ~**wesen das** *in* zu jmds. ~wesen to sb.'s regret; ja, sehr zu meinem ~wesen yes, much to my regret

Leier ['laiɐ] **die;** ~, ~n lyre; [es ist] immer die alte/dieselbe ~ *(ugs. abwertend)* [it's] always the same old story

Leier·kasten der *(ugs.)* barrel-organ; hurdy-gurdy *(coll.)*

Leierkasten·mann der organ-grinder; hurdy-gurdy man *(coll.)*

leiern *(ugs.)* **1.** *tr. V.* **a)** *(kurbeln)* [nach oben/unten] ~: wind [up/down]; *s.* Kreuz e; **b)** *(auf der Drehorgel spielen)* grind out ⟨*tune*⟩; **c)** *(monoton aufsagen)* drone through; *(schnell)* reel *or* rattle off. **2.** *itr. V.* **a)** an etw. *(Dat.)* ~: wind away at sth.; **b)** *(monoton sprechen)* drone [on]

Leih-: ~**arbeit die;** *o. Pl. (Wirtsch.)* subcontracted labour; ~**arbeiter der** subcontracted worker; ~**bibliothek die,** ~**bücherei die** lending library

leihen ['laiən] *unr. tr. V.* **a)** jmdm. etw. ~:

lend sb. sth.; lend sth. to sb.; **leihst du es mir?** will you lend it to me?; **b)** *(entleihen)* borrow; **[sich** *(Dat.)***] [von** *od.* **bei jmdm.] etw. ~:** borrow sth. [from sb.]; **ein geliehener Wagen** a borrowed car; **c)** *(geh.: gewähren)* lend, give ‹*support*›; give ‹*attention*›

Leih-: ~frist die loan period; *(bei Wagen, Frack usw.)* hire period; rental period *(Amer.)*; **~gabe die** loan (*Gen.* from); **~gebühr die** hire *or (Amer.)* rental charge; *(bei Büchern)* lending charge; borrowing fee; **~haus das** pawnbroker's; pawnshop; **im ~haus sein** ‹*possession*› be at the pawnbroker's; be pawned; **~mutter die** surrogate mother; **~schein der a)** *(im Leihhaus)* pawn-ticket; **b)** *(in der Bibliothek)* borrowing slip; **~verkehr der** [inter-library] loan service; **~wagen der** hire *or (Amer.)* rental car; **[sich** *(Dat.)***] einen ~wagen nehmen** hire *or (Amer.)* rent a car; **~weise 1.** *Adv.* on loan; **das hat er mir ~weise überlassen** he has lent it to me; **hier hast du das Buch, aber nur ~weise** I'll give you the book, but only to borrow; **2.** *adj.* **„~weise Überlassung durch die Nationalgalerie"** 'on loan from the National Gallery'

Leim [laim] **der; ~[e]s** glue; **aus dem ~ gehen** *(ugs.) (entzweigehen)* come apart; ‹*marriage, friendship*› break up; *(dick werden)* put on a lot of weight; ‹*woman*› lose one's figure; **jmdm. auf den ~ gehen** *od.* **kriechen** *(ugs.)* be taken in by sb.; fall for sb.'s trick/tricks; **jmdn. auf den ~ führen** *(ugs.)* take sb. in

leimen *tr. V.* **a)** glue (**an** + *Akk.* to); *(zusammen~)* glue [together]; **b)** *(ugs.: hereinlegen)* **jmdn. ~:** take sb. in

Leim·farbe die distemper

leimig *Adj.* gluey; *(noch nicht trocken)* tacky

Leim·rute die [bird]lime-twig

Lein [lain] **der; ~[e]s, ~e** *(Bot.)* flax

-lein das; ~s, ~: little ...; **sein schwarzes Büchlein** his little black book

Leine ['lainə] **die; ~, ~n a)** rope; *(Zelt~)* guy-rope; **die ~n losmachen** *(Seemannsspr.)* cast off; **~ ziehen** *(ugs.)* clear off; **b)** *(Wäsche~, Angel~)* line; **einen Fisch an die ~ kriegen** hook a fish; **c)** *(Hunde~)* lead *(esp. Brit.)*; leash; **den Hund an die ~ nehmen** put the dog on the lead/leash; **„Hunde sind an der ~ zu führen"** 'dogs must be kept on a lead/leash'; **jmdm. ~/mehr ~ lassen** *(ugs.)* give sb. plenty of/more leeway; **jmdn. an der [kurzen] ~ haben** *od.* **halten** *(ugs.)* keep sb. on a tight rein; **jmdn. an die ~ legen** *(ugs.)* get sb. under one's thumb

leinen *Adj.* linen ‹*tablecloth, sheet, etc.*›; cloth[-covered] ‹*cushion etc.*›; **~es Verdeck** canvas [car-]hood

Leinen das; ~s a) *(Gewebe)* linen; **b)** *(Buchw.)* cloth; **Ausgabe in ~:** cloth edition

Leinen-: ~band der; *Pl.* **~bände** cloth-bound volume; **~ein·band der** cloth binding; **~kleid das** linen dress; **~tuch das** linen sheet; *(Tischtuch)* linen [table]cloth; **~zeug das;** *o. Pl.* linen

Leine·weber der linen-weaver

Lein-: ~kraut das toadflax; **~öl das** linseed oil; **~pfad der** tow-path; **~samen der** linseed

Lein·wand die a) *o. Pl.* linen; *(grob)* canvas; **b)** *(des Malers)* canvas; **c)** *(für Filme und Dias)* screen; **einen Roman** *usw.* **auf die ~ bringen** *(fig.)* film a novel *etc.*; **jmdn. von der ~ kennen** *(fig.)* know sb. from films

Leinwand-: ~bindung die *(Textilind.)* plain weave; **~größe die** *(scherzh.)* famous film star; film great; **~held der** *(iron.)* hero of the silver screen

Lein·zeug das *s.* Leinenzeug

leis *s.* leise

leise ['laizə] **1.** *Adj.* **a)** quiet; soft ‹*steps, music, etc.*›; faint ‹*noise*›; **sei ~!** be quiet!; **könnt ihr nicht ~r sein?** can't you make less noise?; **das Radio/die Musik ~[r] stellen** turn the radio/music down; **b)** *nicht präd. (leicht; kaum merklich)* faint; slight; slight, gentle ‹*touch*›; light ‹*rain*›; **ich habe ~ Bedenken** I have my doubts; **eine ~ Andeutung machen** give a gentle hint; **nicht die ~ste Ahnung haben, nicht im ~sten ahnen** not have the faintest *or* slightest idea; **ich zweifle nicht im ~sten daran, daß ...:** I haven't the slightest doubt that .... **2.** *adv.* **a)** quietly; **sprich doch etwas ~r** lower your voice; **~ weinend** crying softly; **b)** *(leicht; kaum merklich)* slightly; ‹*touch, rain*› gently; **~ kochen** simmer gently; **~ zweifeln/hoffen/ahnen** have a slight doubt/hope/suspicion

Leise-: ~treter der *(abwertend)* pussy-footer; **~treterei die; ~** *(abwertend)* pussyfooting

Leiste ['laistə] **die; ~, ~n a)** strip; *(Holz~)* batten; *(profiliert)* moulding; *(halbrund)* beading; *(am Auto)* trim; *(Tapeten~)* [picture-]rail; picture moulding *(Amer.)*; *(eines Bilderrahmens)* frame wood; **eine ~:** a piece *or* strip of moulding/beading/trim/frame wood; *(Holz~)* a batten; **b)** *(Knopf~)* facing; **c)** *(Anat.)* groin; **d)** *(Weberei)* selvage

leisten 1. *tr. V.* **a)** do ‹*work*›; *(schaffen)* achieve ‹*a lot, nothing*›; **gute** *od.* **ganze Arbeit ~:** do good work *or* a good job; *(gründlich arbeiten)* do a thorough job; **der Motor leistet 80 PS** the engine develops *or* produces 80 b.h.p.; **der Wagen leistet 220 km/h** the car will do 220 k.p.h.; **die Produktionsstraße leistet 30 Einheiten pro Stunde** the production line has an output of 30 units per hour; **b)** *(verblaßt od. als Funktionsverb)* **jmdm. Hilfe ~:** help sb.; **einen Eid ~:** swear *or* take an oath; *s. auch* **Abbitte; Beistand a; Beitrag a; Folge c; Gehorsam; Gewähr; Widerstand a** *usw.* **2.** *refl. V. (ugs.)* **a) sich** *(Dat.)* **etw. ~:** treat oneself to sth.; **wer leistet sich** *(Dat.)* **denn heute noch diesen Luxus?** who nowadays is prepared to spend the money on such a luxury?; **b)** *(mit „können")* **sich** *(Dat.)* **etw. [nicht] ~ können** [not] be able to afford sth.; **er kann es sich** *(Dat.)* **~, das zu tun** he can afford to do it; *(etw. Riskantes)* he can get away with doing it; **c)** *(wagen)* **sich** *(Dat.)* **etw. ~:** get up to sth.; **was der sich** *(Dat.)* **leistet!** the things he gets away with!; **sich** *(Dat.)* **einen groben Schnitzer ~:** make a great blunder; **wer hat sich** *(Dat.)* **diese Frechheit geleistet?** who was it who had the cheek to do/say *etc.* that?; **ich habe mir heute vielleicht was [Schönes] geleistet** *(ugs.)* I really excelled myself today *(iron.)*; I did something really brilliant today *(iron.)*

Leisten der; ~s, ~: last; **alles/alle über einen ~ schlagen** *(ugs.)* lump everybody/everything together

Leisten-: ~bruch der rupture; **~gegend die** *(Anat.)* [area of the] groin

Leistung die; ~, ~en a) *o. Pl. (Qualität bzw. Quantität der Arbeit)* performance; **Bezahlung nach ~:** payment according to performance *or* results; *(in der Industrie)* payment according to productivity; **b)** *(Errungenschaft)* achievement; *(im Sport)* performance; **reife ~!** *(Jugendspr.)* not bad!; **gute/hervorragende/außergewöhnliche ~en vollbringen** achieve good/outstanding/exceptional results; **eine große sportliche/technische ~:** a great sporting/technical feat; **die schulischen ~en** results at school; **c)** *o. Pl. (Leistungsvermögen, Physik: Arbeits~)* power; *(Ausstoß)* output; **die ~ einer Fabrik** the output *or* [production] capacity of a factory; **d)** *(Zahlung, Zuwendung)* payment; *(Versicherungsw.)* benefit; **die sozialen ~en der Firma** the firm's fringe benefits; **e)** *(Dienst~)* service; **f)** *o. Pl. (das Leisten)* carrying out; *(Eides~)* swearing; **jmdn. auf ~ verklagen** *(Rechtsspr.)* sue sb. for specific performance

leistungs-, Leistungs-: ~berechtigt *Adj. (Amtsspr.)* entitled to benefits *postpos.*; **~bilanz die** *(Wirtsch.)* balance of trade; **~druck der** *(bei Arbeitnehmern)* pressure to work harder; *(bei Sportlern, Schülern)* pressure to achieve *or* to do well; **~fähig** *Adj.* **a)** capable ‹*person*›; *(körperlich)* able-bodied; *(gute Arbeit leistend)* efficient ‹*worker, factory, industry, etc.*›; powerful ‹*engine, computer, etc.*›; *(konkurrenzfähig)* competitive ‹*firm, industry*›; **b)** *(zahlungsfähig)* capable of paying *postpos.*; solvent; **~fähigkeit die** *(eines Menschen)* capability; *(bei guter Arbeitsleistung)* efficiency; *(eines Betriebs, der Industrie)* productivity; *(Wirtschaftlichkeit)* efficiency; *(eines Motors, eines Computers usw.)* power; performance; **die Grenze seiner ~fähigkeit erreicht haben** have reached the limit of what one can do; **~gerecht 1.** *Adj.* ‹*salary, income*› based on performance *or* results; *(in der Industrie)* based on productivity; **2.** *adv.* **~gerecht bezahlt werden** receive a performance-related salary; **~gesellschaft die** [highly] competitive society; performance-oriented society; **~grenze die;** *o. Pl.* maximum potential; *(eines Sportlers)* performance limit; *(von Maschinen, Fabriken)* maximum output; **seine ~grenze erreichen** reach the limit of one's/its capacity; **~klage die** *(Rechtsw.)* action for specific performance; **~kontrolle die** *(Schulw.)* **a)** *o. Pl.* **der ~kontrolle dienen** be used as a check on the standard reached; **b)** *(Test)* [performance] test; **~kraft die** *s.* **~fähigkeit; ~kurs der** *(Schulw.)* extension course *(going beyond the basic course, based on a university form of study)*; **~kurve die** performance curve; *(eines Motors)* power curve; **~lohn der** pay based on productivity; **~motivation die** *(Psych.)* achievement motivation; **~nachweis der** evidence of [academic] achievement; **~niveau das** *(Schulw.)* level of achievement; *(Sport)* standard of performance; **~orientiert** *Adj.* **a)** achievement-oriented; [highly] competitive ‹*society*›; **b)** *s.* **~gerecht; ~prämie die** *(Arbeitswelt)* productivity bonus; **~prinzip das;** *o. Pl.* achievement principle; competitive principle; **~prüfung die a)** *(Schulw.)* achievement test; **b)** *(Sport)* trial; test [of performance]; **~schau die** *(Wirtsch., Landw.)* [product] exhibition; **~schwach** *Adj.* not performing well *pred.*; low-achieving *attrib.* ‹*worker, pupil*›; *(minderbegabt)* less able, lower-ability *attrib.* ‹*pupil*›; weak ‹*team*›; low-powered ‹*engine*›; **~schwächer** lower-achieving *attrib.* ‹*worker, pupil*›; lower-ability *attrib.* ‹*pupil*›; less powerful ‹*engine*›; **~schwäche die** poor performance; *(Schulw.)* low achievement; *(eines Motors)* low power; **~sport der** competitive sport *no art.*; **~sportler der** competitive sportsman; **~stand der** level of performance; *(Schulw.)* standard of work; *(Ausstoß)* level of output; **~stark** *Adj.* high-performing *attrib.* ‹*athlete*›; able ‹*pupil, athlete, etc.*›; high-performance *attrib.*, powerful ‹*engine, car*›; highly efficient ‹*business, power-station*›; *(sehr konkurrenzfähig)* highly competitive ‹*business, athlete*›; **~stärke die** level of performance; *(Schulw.)* standard of work; *(Ausstoß)* level of output; **~steigerung die** improvement in performance; *(eines Schülers)* improvement [in his/her work]; *(eines Unternehmens)* improvement in efficiency; *(in der Produktion)* improvement in output; **~test der** *(bei Motoren, Maschinen)* performance test; *(bei Schülern)* achievement test; **~träger der** *(Sport)* key player; **~vergleich der** competition; **~vermögen das** *s.* **~fähigkeit; ~verweigerung die** *(bes. Soziol., Päd.)* refusal to work; *(allgemein)* refusal to be part of competitive society; **~wettbewerb der** *(Wirtsch.)* competition [for high output and efficiency]; **~zentrum das** *(Sport)* intensive training centre; **~zu·lage die, ~zu·schlag der** bonus *(for additional work, responsibility, etc.)*; **~zwang der** *(Soziol.) (bei Arbeitnehmern)* compulsion to work hard; *(bei Sportlern/Schülern)* compulsion to achieve *or* to do well

Leit-: ~antrag der *(Politik)* motion put forward by the party leadership; **~artikel der** *(Zeitungsw.)* leading article; leader; **~artikler der** *(Zeitungsw.)* leader-writer; **~bild das** model; **~bilder der Mode** leaders of fashion

leiten ['laitn̩] *tr. V.* **a)** *(anführen)* lead, head ⟨*expedition, team, discussion, etc.*⟩; be head of ⟨*school*⟩; *(verantwortlich sein für)* be in charge of ⟨*project, expedition, etc.*⟩; manage ⟨*factory, enterprise*⟩; *(den Vorsitz führen bei)* chair ⟨*meeting, discussion, etc.*⟩; *(Musik: dirigieren)* conduct ⟨*orchestra, choir*⟩; direct ⟨*small orchestra etc.*⟩; *(Sport: als Schiedsrichter)* referee ⟨*game, match*⟩; **~der Angestellter** executive; manager; **~de Angestellte** senior *or* managerial staff; **~der Beamte** senior civil servant; **eine ~de Position** a position in [senior] management; a managerial position; **b)** *(begleiten, führen)* lead; **jmdn. auf die richtige Spur ~:** put sb. on the right track; **sich von etw. ~ lassen** [let oneself] be guided by sth.; **er läßt sich nur von seinen Gefühlen ~:** he is governed solely by his feelings; **sich schwer/leicht ~ lassen** be hard/easy to manage; **die ~de Hand/der ~de Gedanke** the guiding hand/principle; **c)** *(lenken)* direct; route ⟨*traffic*⟩; *(um~)* divert ⟨*traffic, stream*⟩; **Erdöl durch Rohre ~:** pipe oil; **den Verkehr über eine Umgehungsstraße ~:** route/divert traffic along a bypass; **etw. an die zuständige Stelle ~:** pass on *or* forward sth. to the competent authority; **d)** *auch itr. (Physik)* conduct ⟨*heat, current, sound*⟩; **etw. leitet gut/schlecht** sth. is a good/bad conductor

[1]Leiter der; ~s, ~ a) *(einer Delegation, Gruppe)* leader; head; *(einer Abteilung)* head; manager; *(eines Instituts)* director; *(einer Schule)* head teacher; headmaster *(Brit.)*; principal *(esp. Amer.)*; *(einer Diskussion)* leader; *(Vorsitz)* chair[man]; *(eines Chors)* choirmaster; *(Dirigent)* conductor; **kaufmännischer ~:** marketing manager; *(Verkaufs~)* sales manager; **technischer/künstlerischer ~:** technical/artistic director; **b)** *(Physik)* conductor

[2]Leiter die; ~, ~n ladder; *(Steh~)* step-ladder; **die ~ des Erfolgs** *(fig.)* the ladder of success

Leiterin die; ~, ~nen *s.* **[1]Leiter;** *(einer Schule)* head teacher; headmistress *(Brit.)*; principal *(esp. Amer.)*; *(eines Chors)* choirmistress

Leiter-: ~sprosse die rung [of a/the ladder]; **~wagen der** open-frame wooden handcart

leit-, Leit-: ~faden der a) [basic] textbook; **~faden der Physik** basic course in physics; introduction to physics; **b)** *(Leitgedanke)* main idea *or* theme; **das durchzieht sein Werk wie ein ~faden** it runs through his works like a connecting thread; **~fähig** *Adj. (Physik)* conductive; **~fähigkeit die** *(Physik)* conductivity; **~feuer das** *(Schiffahrt)* leading light; **~fossil das** *(Geol.)* index fossil; **~gedanke der** dominant *or* central theme; **~hammel der a)** bellwether; **b)** *(abwertend: Führer)* leader [of the herd]; boss-figure; **~linie die a)** *(Richtlinie)* guideline; **b)** *(Verkehrsw.)* lane marking; **c)** *(Geom.)* directrix; **~motiv das** *(Musik, Literaturw., fig.)* **a)** leitmotiv; **b)** *(Leitgedanke)* dominant *or* central theme; **~planke die** crash barrier; guardrail *(Amer.)*; **~satz der** guiding principle; **~spruch der** motto; **~stelle die** control room; *(Büro)* central office; **~stern der** *(auch fig. geh.)* lodestar; **~strahl der a)** *(Flugw., Milit.)* radio guidance beam; **b)** *(Geom.)* radius vector; **~tier das** *(Zool.)* leader [of the herd]; **~ton der** *(Musik)* leading note

Leitung die; ~, ~en a) *o. Pl. s.* **leiten a:** leading; heading; being in charge; management; chairing; *(Schulw.)* working as a/the head; *(Musik)* conducting; directing; *(Sport)* refereeing; **b)** *o. Pl. (einer Expedition usw.)* leadership; *(Verantwortung)* responsibility (*Gen.* for); *(eines Betriebes, Unternehmens)* management; *(einer Sitzung, Diskussion)* chairmanship; *(Schulw.)* headship; *(Musik)* conductorship; *(Sport)* [task of] refereeing; **unter der ~ eines Managers stehen** be headed by a manager; **unter jmds. ~ (Dat.) arbeiten** work under sb. *or* under sb.'s direction; *(Musik)* **unter der ~ von X/des Komponisten** conducted by X/the composer; **die ~ hatte Otto Klemperer** the conductor was Otto Klemperer; **die ~ der Sendung/Diskussion hat X** the programme is presented/the discussion is chaired by X; **bei einem Spiel die ~ haben** referee a match; **c)** *(leitende Personen)* management; *(einer Schule)* head and senior staff; **d)** *(Rohr~)* pipe; *(Haupt~)* main; **Wasser aus der ~ trinken** drink tap-water; **e)** *(Draht, Kabel)* cable; *(für ein Gerät)* lead; *(einzelne od. ohne Isolierung)* wire; **die ~en [im Haus/Auto usw.]** the wiring *sing.* [of the house/car etc.]; **f)** *(Telefon~)* line; **es ist jemand in der ~** *(ugs.)* there's somebody on the line; **gehen Sie aus der ~!** get off the line!; **auf einer anderen ~ sprechen** be [talking] on another line; **eine lange ~ haben** *(ugs.)* be slow on the uptake; **er steht** *od.* **sitzt auf der ~** *(salopp)* he's not really with it *(coll.)*

Leitungs-: ~draht der [electrical] wire; *(größer)* [electrical] cable; **~gremium das** [executive] committee; **~mast der** *(für Strom)* pylon; *(Telefonmast)* telegraph-pole; **~netz das a)** *(für Wasser, Gas)* mains network; mains *pl.*; *(für Fernwärme usw.)* network of pipes; **b)** *(Elektrizität)* mains network *or* grid; **c)** *(Telefonnetz)* telephone network; **~rohr das** [water/gas] pipe; *(Haupt~)* main; **~wasser das** tap-water

Leit-: ~währung die *(Wirtsch.)* base *or* key currency; **~werk das a)** *(Flugw., Waffent.)* control surfaces *pl.*; *(am Heck)* tail unit; **b)** *(Seew.)* approach pier; **c)** *(DV)* control unit; **~wert** *(Physik, Elektrot.)* conductance; **~wort das a)** *Pl.* **~wörter** catchword; motto; **b)** *Pl.* **~worte** *s.* **Leitspruch; ~zahl die** *(Fot.)* guide number; **~zins[satz] der** *(Finanzw.)* **a)** *(Diskontsatz)* discount rate; ≈ base rate; **b)** *s.* **Eckzins**

Lektion [lɛk'tsio:n] **die; ~, ~en** lesson; **jmdm. eine ~ erteilen** *(fig.)* teach sb. a lesson

Lektor ['lɛktɔr] **der; ~s, ~en** [lɛk'to:rən] **a)** *(Hochschulw.) junior university teacher in charge of practical or supplementary classes etc.*; **b)** *(Verlags~)* [publisher's] editor

Lektorat [lɛkto'ra:t] **das; ~[e]s, ~e a)** *(Hochschulw.)* post of 'Lektor'; **b)** *(im Verlag)* editorial department

Lektorin die; ~, ~nen *s.* **Lektor**

Lektüre [lɛk'ty:rə] **die; ~, ~n a)** *o. Pl.* reading; **bei der ~ des Romans** when reading the novel; **b)** *(Lesestoff)* reading [matter]; **etw. als ~/als leichte ~ empfehlen** recommend sth. as a good read/as light reading; **nicht die richtige ~ für den Urlaub** not the right thing to read while on holiday; **das ist keine passende ~ für dich** that is not suitable reading for you

Lemma ['lɛma] **das; ~s, ~ta** *(Sprachw.)* lemma; headword

Lemming ['lɛmɪŋ] **der; ~s, ~e** *(Zool.)* lemming

Lemure [le'mu:rə] **der; ~n, ~n a)** *(Myth.)* **die ~n** the lemures; **b)** *(Zool.)* lemur

Lende ['lɛndə] **die; ~, ~n** loin

lenden-, Lenden-: ~braten der *(Kochk.)* roast loin; *(vom Rind)* sirloin steak; **~gegend die** loins *pl.*; lumbar region *(Anat.)*; **~lahm** *Adj.* **a)** *(kreuzlahm)* **[furchtbar] ~lahm sein** be bent double with backache; **b)** *(fig.)* crippled; feeble, lame ⟨*excuse*⟩; **~schurz der** loincloth; **~stück das** *(Kochk.)* piece of loin; **~wirbel der** *(Anat.)* lumbar vertebra

Leninismus [leni'nɪsmʊs] **der; ~:** Leninism *no art.*

Leninist der; ~en, ~en Leninist

leninistisch *Adj.* Leninist

Lenk·achse die *(Eisenb.)* pivot axle

lenkbar *Adj.* **a)** *(Technik)* **leicht/schwer ~ sein** be easy/difficult to steer; *(kontrollierbar)* be easy/difficult to control; **b)** *(von Menschen)* acquiescent; obedient; manageable, controllable ⟨*child*⟩

lenken ['lɛŋkn̩] *tr. V.* **a)** *auch itr.* steer ⟨*car, bicycle, etc.*⟩; be at the controls of ⟨*aircraft*⟩; guide ⟨*missile*⟩; *(fahren)* drive ⟨*car etc.*⟩; **wenn du geschickt lenkst** if you do some crafty steering; **b)** direct, guide ⟨*thoughts etc.*⟩ (**auf** + *Akk.* to); turn ⟨*attention*⟩ (**auf** + *Akk.* to); steer ⟨*conversation*⟩; **die Diskussion auf etw./jmdn. ~:** steer *or* bring the discussion round to sth./sb.; **den Verdacht auf jmdn. ~:** throw suspicion on sb.; **seine Blicke auf jmdn. ~:** turn one's gaze on sb.; **seine Schritte gen Bahnhof/heimwärts ~** *(geh., scherzh.)* direct one's steps towards the station/wend one's way homewards; **c)** *(kontrollieren)* control ⟨*person, press, economy*⟩; rule, govern ⟨*state*⟩; **die ~de Hand** the guiding hand; **eine gelenkte Wirtschaft** a planned economy

Lenker der; ~s, ~ a) *(Lenkstange)* handlebars *pl.*; *(Lenkrad)* steering wheel; **sich** *(Dat.)* **den goldenen ~ verdienen** *(ugs. spött.)* win the prize for bootlicking; **b)** *(Fahrer)* driver; **c)** *(fig. geh.)* director; controller; *(eines Staates)* captain

Lenkerin die; ~, ~nen *s.* **Lenker b, c**

Lenk-: ~flug·körper der *(Waffent.)* guided missile; **~rad das** steering-wheel; **jmdm. ins ~rad greifen** grab the steering-wheel from sb.; **~rad·schaltung die** *(Kfz-W.)* steering-column gear-change *(Brit.)* *or (Amer.)* gearshift; **~rad·schloß das** *(Kfz-W.)* steering[-wheel] lock; **~säule die** *(Kfz-W.)* steering-column; **~stange die** handlebars *pl.*

Lenkung die; ~, ~en a) *o. Pl. (Leitung)* control; *(eines Staates)* ruling *no indef. art.*; governing *no indef. art.*; **b)** *(Kfz-W.)* steering

Lenz [lɛnts] **der; ~es, ~e** *(dichter. veralt.)* spring; **der ~ ist da!** spring is here!; **der ~ des Lebens** *(fig.)* the springtime of life; **einen sonnigen** *od.* **ruhigen** *od.* **faulen ~ haben** *od.* **schieben** *(salopp)* have an easy time of it; *(eine leichte Arbeit haben)* have a cushy job *(coll.)*; **sich** *(Dat.)* **einen schönen ~ machen** *(salopp)* take it easy; **sie zählt erst 15 ~e** she is a girl of only 15 summers *(literary)*

lenzen *(Seemannsspr.)* **1.** *tr. V.* bail out ⟨*boat, water*⟩; *(mit Pumpe)* pump out ⟨*water, bilge*⟩. **2.** *itr. V.* scud [under light sail]

Lenz·pumpe die *(Seemannsspr.)* bilge-pump

Leopard [leo'part] **der; ~en, ~en** leopard

Lepra ['le:pra] **die; ~:** leprosy *no art.*

Lepra·kranke der/die leper

leprös [le'prø:s] *Adj.* leprous

leptosom [lɛpto'zo:m] *Adj. (Med., Anthrop.)* leptosome; leptosomatic

Lerche ['lɛrçə] **die; ~, ~n** lark

lernbar *Adj.* learnable; **das ist [für jeden] ~:** that can be learnt [by anybody]; **leicht ~:** easy to learn *pred.*

lern-, Lern-: ~begier die, ~begierde die

eagerness to learn; ~**begierig** *Adj.* eager to learn *postpos.*; ~**behindert** *Adj.* *(Päd.)* educationally subnormal; with learning difficulties *postpos., not pred.*; ~**behinderte der/die** slow learner; child with learning difficulties; ~**eifer der** eagerness to learn

lernen ['lɛrnən] **1.** *itr. V.* study; *(als Berufsausbildung)* train; **gut/schlecht** ~: be a good/poor learner *or* pupil; *(fleißig/nicht fleißig sein)* work hard/not work hard [at school]; **leicht** ~: find it easy to learn; find school-work easy; **mit jmdm.** ~ *(ugs.)* help sb. with his/her [school-]work; **auf etw.** *(Akk.)* ~ *(ugs.)* train to be sth.. **2.** *tr. V.* **a)** learn (**aus** from); **schwimmen/sprechen** ~: learn to swim/talk; **Trompete/Klavier** ~: learn to play the trumpet/piano; **er/mancher lernt es nie** *(ugs.)* he/some people [will] never learn; **von ihm kann man noch was** ~: you can learn a thing or two from him; **das will gelernt sein** that is something one has to learn; **gelernt ist gelernt** once learnt, never forgotten; **das Fürchten** ~: find out what it is to be afraid; **b) einen Beruf** ~: learn a trade; **Maurer/Bäcker** *usw.* ~: train to be *or* as a bricklayer/baker *etc.*; **sie hat Friseuse gelernt** she trained as a hairdresser

Lernende der/die; *adj. Dekl. s.* **Lehrende**

Lerner der; ~**s,** ~ *(Sprachw.)* learner

lern-, Lern-: ~**fabrik die** *(abwertend)* swotting factory *(Brit.)*; cramming mill *(Amer.)*; ~**fähig** *Adj.* able to learn *pred.*; capable of learning *pred.*; ~**hilfe die** aid to learning; ~**mittel das** learning aid; *(Lehrmittel)* teaching aid; ~**mittel** *Pl.* teaching materials; ~**mittel·freiheit die;** *o. Pl.* free provision of teaching materials; ~**prozeß der** learning process; ~**psychologie die** psychology of learning; ~**schwester die** student nurse; ~**ziel das** [educational] aim

Les·art ['le:s-] **die a)** *(Fassung)* variant; **b)** *(Deutung)* interpretation; reading

lesbar *Adj.* **a)** legible; **b)** *(klar)* lucid ⟨*style*⟩; *(verständlich)* comprehensible; **gut** ~: easy to read; very readable

Lesbe ['lɛsbə] **die;** ~, ~**n** *(ugs.)* Lesbian; dike *(sl.)*

Lesben·bewegung die gay women's movement

Lesbierin ['lɛsbiərɪn] **die;** ~, ~**nen** Lesbian

lesbisch *Adj.* Lesbian; ~ **sein** be a Lesbian/Lesbians

Lese ['le:zə] **die;** ~, ~**n a)** *(Weinernte)* grape-harvest; **b)** *(geh.: Auswahl)* selection

Lese-: reading ...

Lese-: ~**abend der** [evening] reading; **einen** ~**abend geben** read from one's works; ~**automat der** *s.* ~**gerät;** ~**brille die** reading-glasses *pl.*; ~**buch das** reader; ~**exemplar das** reading copy; *(noch ungebunden)* proof copy; ~**gerät das** *(DV)* reader; ~**hunger der** appetite for reading matter; ~**lampe die** reading-lamp; ~**maschine die** *s.* **Lesegerät**

[1]**lesen 1.** *unr. tr., itr. V.* **a)** read; **sie las in der Zeitung/in einem Buch** she was reading the paper/a book; **er hat wochenlang an dem Buch gelesen** he has been reading the book for weeks; **er liest aus seinem neuesten Werk** he is reading from his latest work; **ein Gesetz [zum ersten Mal]** ~ *(Parl.)* give a bill a [first] reading; **die/eine Messe** ~: say Mass/a Mass; **hier ist zu** ~, **daß ...:** it says here that ...; **der Text ist so zu** ~, **daß ...:** the text is to be taken as meaning that ...; *s. auch* **Leviten; b)** *(entnehmen)* tell (**in** + *Dat.*, **aus** from); **in seiner Miene war Verbitterung zu** ~: there were signs of bitterness in his expression; **aus den Zeilen konnte man gewisse Zweifel** ~: reading between the lines, one could make out certain doubts; **Gedanken** ~ **können** be a mind-reader; **jmds. Gedanken** ~: read sb.'s mind *or* thoughts; **aus der Hand** ~: read palms; **sich** *(Dat.)* **aus der Hand** ~ **lassen** have one's palm *or* hand read; **c)** *(Hochschulw.)* lecture (**über** + *Akk.* on); **er liest neue Geschichte/Völkerrecht** he lectures on modern history/international law. **2.** *unr. refl. V.* read; **es liest sich leicht/schnell** it is easy/quick to read; **es liest sich sehr unterhaltsam** it's a very entertaining read

[2]**lesen** *unr. tr. V.* **a)** *(sammeln, pflücken)* pick ⟨*grapes, berries, fruit*⟩; gather ⟨*firewood*⟩; **Ähren** ~: glean [ears of corn]; **b)** *(aussondern)* pick over

lesens·wert *Adj.* worth reading *postpos.*

Leser der; ~**s,** ~: reader

Leser·analyse die readership survey

Lese·ratte die *(ugs. scherzh.)* bookworm; voracious reader

Leser·brief der reader's letter; ~**e** readers' letters; „~**e**" *(Zeitungsrubrik)* 'Letters to the editor'

Leserin die; ~, ~**nen** *s.* **Leser**

Leser·kreis der readership

leserlich 1. *Adj.* legible. **2.** *adv.* legibly

Leserschaft die; ~: readership

Leser-: ~**wunsch der** reader's request; ~**wünsche** readers' requests; ~**zahl die** circulation; *(~kreis)* readership; ~**zuschrift die** reader's letter; ~**zuschriften** readers' letters (**zu** in response to)

Lese-: ~**saal der** reading-room; ~**stoff der** reading matter; ~**wut die** craving to read; ~**zeichen das** bookmark; ~**zirkel der** *commercial enterprise which supplies a selection of magazines on a regular loan basis to subscribers*

Lesung die; ~, ~**en a)** *(auch Parl.)* reading; **b)** *(christl. Kirche)* lesson

Lethargie [letar'gi:] **die;** ~: lethargy

lethargisch 1. *Adj.* lethargic. **2.** *adv.* lethargically

Lette ['lɛtə] **der;** ~**n,** ~**n** Latvian; Lett

Letter die; ~, ~**n a)** letter; **b)** *(Druckw.)* character; sort *(as tech. term)*

lettisch *Adj.* Latvian; Lettish ⟨*language*⟩

Lett·land (das); ~**s** Latvia

Lettner ['lɛtnɐ] **der;** ~**s,** ~ *(Archit.)* choir-screen

Letzt ['lɛtst] *in* **zu guter** ~: in the end; *(endlich)* at long last

letzt... *Adj.* **a)** last; **die** ~**e Reihe** the back row; **auf dem** ~**en Platz sein** be [placed] last; *(während des Rennens)* be in last place; *(in einer Tabelle)* be in bottom place; **er war** *od.* **wurde** ~**er, er ging als** ~**er durchs Ziel** he came last; ~**er Mann** *(bes. Fußball)* back; **der/die** ~**e sein** be the last; **als** ~**er aussteigen** be the last [one] to get off; **er ist der** ~**e, dem ich das sagen würde** he's the last person I would tell [about it]; **am Letzten [des Monats]** on the last day of the month; **im** ~**en Moment** at the last moment; **die Letzten werden die Ersten sein** *(Spr.)* the last shall be first; **das ist mein** ~**es Wort/Angebot** that is my last word [on the subject]/my final offer; **mein** ~**es Geld** the last of my money; **ist das dein** ~**es Geld?** is that all the money you have left?; **mit** ~**er Kraft** gathering all his/her remaining strength; ~**en Endes** in the end; when all is said and done; **jmds./die** ~**e Rettung sein** *(fig.)* be sb.'s/the last hope; *s. auch* **Ölung; Wille; b)** *(äußerst...)* ultimate; **jmdm. das Letzte an ...** *(Dat.)* **abverlangen** demand of sb. the utmost *or* maximum ...; **das Letzte hergeben** give one's all; **bis aufs** ~**e** totally; *(finanziell)* down to the last penny; **bis ins** ~**e** down to the last detail; **bis zum** ~**en** to the utmost; **c)** *(gerade vergangen)* last; *(neuest...)* latest ⟨*news*⟩; **in den** ~**en Wochen/Jahren** in the last few weeks/in recent years; **in der** ~**en Zeit** recently; *s. auch* **Schrei; c)** *(ugs. abwertend) (schlechtest...)* worst; *(entsetzlichst...)* most dreadful; **er ist der** ~**e Mensch** he is the lowest of the low; **die Show war das Letzte** *(ugs.)* the show was the end *(coll.) or* the pits *(coll.)*; **das ist doch das Letzte!** *(ugs.)* that really is the limit!; *s. auch* **Dreck b**

letzte·mal *in* **das** ~: [the] last time

letzt·endlich *Adv.* in the end; *(schließlich doch)* ultimately

letzten·mal *in* **beim** ~: last time; **zum** ~: for the last time

letztens ['lɛtstn̩s] *Adv.* **a)** *(kürzlich)* recently; **b) drittens/viertens und letztens** thirdly/fourthly and lastly

letzter... *Adj.* latter; ~**es** *od.* **das** ~**e trifft hier zu** the latter is the case here

letzt·genannt *Adj.*; *nicht präd.* last-mentioned; last-named ⟨*person*⟩

letzt·hin *Adv.* **a)** *(kürzlich)* recently; **b)** *(schließlich doch)* ultimately

letztlich *Adv.* ultimately; in the end

letzt-: ~**mals** *Adv.* the last time; **er hat** ~**mals vor fünf Jahren teilgenommen** the last time he took part was five years ago; ~**möglich** *Adj.*; *nicht präd.* latest possible; ~**willig 1.** *Adj.*; *nicht präd.* in his/her/the will *postpos.*; ~**willige Verfügung** last will and testament; **2.** *adv.* in his/her/the will

Leu [lɔy] **der;** ~**en,** ~**en** *(dichter. veralt.)* lion

Leucht-: ~**boje die** *(Seew.)* light-buoy; ~**bombe die** parachute flare; ~**buchstabe der** neon-sign letter

Leuchte ['lɔyçtə] **die;** ~, ~**n a)** light; **hast du eine** ~**?** have you got a torch?; **b)** *(fig. ugs.)* **[in Mathe** *usw.***] eine** ~ **sein** be brilliant *or* shine [at maths *etc.*]; **er ist eine** ~ **auf diesem Gebiet** he is a leading light in this field

leuchten *itr. V.* **a)** ⟨*moon, sun, star, etc.*⟩ be shining; ⟨*fire, face*⟩ glow; **grell** ~: give a glaring light; glare; **in der Sonne** ~: ⟨*hair, sea, snow*⟩ gleam in the sun; ⟨*mountains etc.*⟩ glow in the sun; **golden** ~: have a golden glow; **seine Augen leuchteten vor Freude** *(fig.)* his eyes were shining *or* sparkling with joy; **b)** shine a/the light; **jmdm.** ~: light the way for sb.; **mit etw. in etw.** *(Akk.)* ~: shine sth. into sth.; **jmdm. mit etw. ins Gesicht** ~: shine sth. into sb.'s face

leuchtend *Adj.*; *nicht präd.* **a)** shining ⟨*eyes*⟩; brilliant, luminous ⟨*colours*⟩; bright ⟨*blue, red, etc.*⟩; **grell** ~: glaring; **sanft** ~: softly glowing; **etw. in den** ~**sten Farben schildern** *(fig.)* paint sth. in glowing colours; **b)** *(großartig)* shining ⟨*example*⟩

Leuchter der; ~**s,** ~ candelabrum; *(für eine Kerze)* candlestick; *(Kron~)* chandelier

Leucht-: ~**farbe die** luminous paint; ~**feuer das** *(Seew.)* beacon; light; *(Flugw.)* runway light; ~**gas das** *s.* **Stadtgas;** ~**geschoß das** *s.* ~**kugel;** ~**käfer der** firefly; *(Glühwürmchen)* glow-worm; ~**kraft die a)** brilliance; **b)** *(Astron.)* luminosity; ~**kugel die** flare; ~**pistole die** flare pistol; ~**rakete die** rocket flare; ~**reklame die** neon [advertising] sign; ~**röhre die** neon tube; ~**schrift die** neon letters *pl.*; *(Schild)* neon sign; ~**spur·geschoß das** tracer bullet; ~**stoff der** *(Physik)* fluorescent substance; *(nachleuchtend)* luminous substance; ~**stoff·lampe die** fluorescent light *or* lamp; ~**stoff·röhre die** fluorescent tube; *(für ~reklame)* neon tube; ~**tonne die** light-buoy; ~**turm der** lighthouse; ~**turm·wärter der** lighthouse-keeper; ~**zeiger der** luminous hand; ~**ziffer die** luminous numeral; ~**ziffer·blatt das** luminous dial

leugnen ['lɔygnən] **1.** *tr. V.* deny; **er leugnete die Tat/das Verbrechen** he denied doing the deed/committing the crime; **er leugnet, daran beteiligt zu sein** *od.* **daß er daran beteiligt ist** he denies being involved *or* that he is involved in it; **es ist nicht zu** ~: it is undeniable. **2.** *itr. V.* deny it; *(alles* ~*)* deny everything; **er leugnet noch** he still denies doing it *or* that he did it

Leugnung die; ~, ~**en** denial

Leukämie [lɔykɛ'mi:] **die;** ~, ~n *(Med.)* leukaemia
leukämisch *Adj. (Med.)* leukaemic; ‹*symptoms*› of leukaemia
Leukoplast ⓦ [lɔyko'plast] **das** sticking-plaster *(containing zinc oxide)*
Leukozyt [lɔyko'tsy:t] **der;** ~en, ~en *(Anat.)* leucocyte
Leumund ['lɔymʊnt] **der;** ~[e]s *(geh.)* reputation; **den guten ~ verlieren** lose one's good name; **jmdm. einen guten ~ bescheinigen** vouch for sb.'s good character
Leumunds·zeugnis das a) *(geh.)* character reference (**über** + *Akk.* for); **b)** *(schweiz. Rechtsspr.) s.* **Führungszeugnis**
Leutchen ['lɔytçn̩] *Pl. (ugs.)* people; *s. auch* **Leute b**
Leute ['lɔytə] *Pl.* **a)** people; **die reichen/alten ~:** the rich/the old; **wir sind hier bei feinen ~n** we are in a respectable household; **die kleinen ~:** the ordinary people; the man *sing.* in the street; **was werden die ~ sagen?** *(ugs.)* what will people say?; **wir sind geschiedene ~:** our ways have parted; we have parted company; *(in Zukunft)* I will have no more to do with you/him *etc.*; **unter ~ gehen** mix with people; **vor allen ~n** in front of everybody; **hier ist es ja nicht wie bei armen ~n** *(scherzh.)* we're not in the poor-house *or (Amer.)* on the breadline yet; **unter die ~ bringen** *(ugs.)* spread ‹*rumour*›; tell everybody about ‹*suspicions etc.*›; *s. auch* **Kind; b)** *(ugs.: als Anrede)* **auf, [ihr] ~!** come on, everybody! *(coll.)*; c'mon, folks! *(Amer.)*; **~, ~!** oh dear!; **c)** *(ugs.: Arbeiter)* people; *(Milit.: Soldaten)* men; **die Hälfte der ~:** half the staff; **d)** *(landsch. ugs.: Familie)* **meine ~:** my family *sing. or (coll.)* folks; **e)** *(veralt.: Gesinde)* servants
Leute·schinder der *(abwertend)* slave-driver
Leutnant ['lɔytnant] **der;** ~s, ~s *od. selten:* ~e second lieutenant *(Milit.)*; **~ zur See** sub-lieutenant *(Brit.)*; lieutenant junior grade *(Amer.)*
leut·selig 1. *Adj.* affable. **2.** *adv.* affably
Leut·seligkeit die; *o. Pl.* affability
Levante [le'vantə] **die;** ~ *(geh.)* the Levant
Leviat[h]an [le'vi̯a:tan] **der;** ~s, ~e *(Myth.)* leviathan
Leviten [le'vi:tn̩] *Pl.* **in jmdm. die ~ lesen** *(ugs.)* read sb. the Riot Act *(coll.)*
Levkoje [lɛf'ko:jə] **die;** ~, ~n *(Bot.)* stock
Lex [lɛks] **die;** ~, **Leges** ['le:ge:s] *(Parl.)* **die ~ Heinze** the Heinze Act
Lexem [lɛ'kse:m] **das;** ~s, ~e *(Sprachw.)* lexeme
Lexik ['lɛksɪk] **die;** ~ *(Sprachw.)* lexicon
lexikalisch [lɛksi'ka:lɪʃ] *(auch Sprachw.)* **1.** *Adj.* lexical. **2.** *adv.* lexically
lexikalisieren *tr. V. (Sprachw.)* lexicalize
Lexikograph [lɛksiko'gra:f] **der;** ~en, ~en lexicographer
Lexikographie [leksikogra'fi:] **die;** ~: lexicography *no art.*
Lexikographin die; ~, ~nen lexicographer; *s. auch* **-in**
lexikographisch 1. *Adj.* lexicographical. **2.** *adv.* lexicographically; **~ gesehen** looked at from a lexicographical point of view; **~ arbeiten** work as a lexicographer
Lexikologie [lɛksikolo'gi:] **die;** ~: lexicology *no art.*
Lexikon ['lɛksikɔn] **das;** ~s, **Lexika** *od.* **Lexiken a)** encyclopaedia (+ *Gen.*, **für** of); **ein wandelndes ~ sein** *(ugs. scherzh.)* be a walking encyclopaedia; **b)** *(veralt.: Wörterbuch)* dictionary; **c)** *(Sprachw.)* lexicon
Lezithin, *(fachspr.:)* **Lecithin** [letsi'ti:n] **das;** ~s, ~e *(Chemie, Biol.)* lecithin
lfd. *Abk.:* **laufend**
Lfg. *Abk.:* **Lieferung**
Liaison [li̯ɛ'zõ:] **die;** ~, ~s *(geh.)* liaison; *(fig.: zwischen Staaten, Firmen)* link; tie-up; **eine ~ eingehen** enter into a liaison
Liane ['li̯a:nə] **die;** ~, ~n *(Bot.)* liana
Libanese [liba'ne:zə] **der;** ~n, ~n Lebanese; **roter ~** *(Drogenjargon)* Lebanese red
Libanesin die; ~, ~nen Lebanese; *s. auch* **-in**
libanesisch *Adj.* Lebanese
¹**Libanon** ['li:banɔn] **(das)** *od.* **der;** ~s Lebanon
²**Libanon der;** ~s *(Gebirge)* Lebanon Mountains *pl.*
Libelle [li'bɛlə] **die;** ~, ~n **a)** dragon-fly; **b)** *(Haarspange)* winged hair-slide; **c)** *(an Meßinstrumenten)* bubble tube; *(Wasserwaage)* spirit-level
liberal [libə'ra:l] **1.** *Adj.* liberal; **~ wählen** vote liberal. **2.** *adv.* liberally; **jmdn. ~ erziehen** give sb. a liberal education; **~ ausgerichtet** following liberal principles *postpos., not pred.*
Liberale der/die; *adj. Dekl.* liberal
liberalisieren *tr. V.* liberalize; relax ‹*import controls*›
Liberalisierung die; ~, ~en liberalization; *(von Kontrollen)* relaxation
Liberalismus [libəra'lɪsmʊs] **der;** ~: liberalism
Liberalität [libərali'tɛ:t] **die;** ~ **a)** liberalism; liberality; **b)** *(Großzügigkeit)* liberality
Liberia [li:'be:ria] **(das);** ~s Liberia
Liberianer der; ~s, ~, **Liberianerin die;** ~, ~nen Liberian; *s. auch* **-in**
liberianisch *Adj.* Liberian
Libero ['li:bəro] **der;** ~s, ~s *(Fußball)* sweeper
libidinös [libidi'nø:s] *Adj. (Psych.)* libidinal
Libido ['li:bido] **die;** ~ *(Psych.)* libido
Librettist [librɛ'tɪst] **der;** ~en, ~en, **Librettistin die;** ~, ~nen librettist; *s. auch* **-in**
Libretto [li'brɛto] **das;** ~s, ~s *od.* **Libretti** libretto
Libyen ['li:bӯən] **(das);** ~s Libya
libysch ['li:bʏʃ] *Adj.* Libyan
licht [lɪçt] *Adj.* **a)** *(geh.)* light; light, pale ‹*colour*›; **es war ~er Tag** it was broad daylight; **einen ~en Moment** *od.* **Augenblick/~e Momente haben** *(fig.)* have a lucid moment/lucid moments; *(scherzh.)* have a bright moment/bright moments; **b)** *(dünn bewachsen)* sparse; thin; **~es Haar haben** be thin on top; **die Reihen der alten Kameraden/der Zuschauer werden ~er** *(fig.)* the ranks of old comrades are dwindling/the rows of spectators are emptying; **c)** *(bes. Technik)* **die ~e Höhe/Weite** the [overall] internal height/width; **die ~e Höhe/Weite einer Brücke** the headroom/span of a bridge
Licht das; ~[e]s, ~er **a)** *o. Pl.* light; **das ~ des Tages** the light of day; **etw. gegen das ~ halten** hold sth. up to the light; **etw. bei ~ sehen** see sth. in daylight; **bei ~ besehen** *(fig.)* seen in the light of day; **jmdm. das [ganze] ~ [weg]nehmen** take [all] sb.'s light; **jmdm. im ~ stehen** stand in sb.'s light; **das ~ der Welt erblicken** *(geh.)* see the light of day; **ein zweifelhaftes/ungünstiges ~ auf jmdn. werfen** *(fig.)* throw a dubious/unfavourable light on sb.; **~ in etw.** *(Akk.)* **bringen** *(fig.)* shed some light on sth.; **jmdn. hinters ~ führen** *(fig.)* fool sb.; pull the wool over sb.'s eyes; **jmdn./etw./sich ins rechte ~ rücken** *od.* **setzen** *od.* **stellen** *(fig.)* show sb./sth. in the correct light/appear in the correct light; **in einem guten** *od.* **günstigen/schlechten ~ erscheinen** *(fig.)* appear in a good *or* a favourable/a bad *or* an unfavourable light; **etw. in einem besseren ~ erscheinen lassen** *(fig.)* put a better complexion on sth.; **etw. in einem milderen ~ sehen** *(fig.)* take a more lenient view of sth.; **in ein falsches ~ geraten** *(fig.)* give the wrong impression; **das ~ scheuen** *(fig.)* shun the light; **ans ~ kommen** *(fig.)* come to light; be revealed; **b)** *(elektrisches ~)* light; **das ~ anmachen/ausmachen** switch *or* turn the light on/off; **mach doch ~!** turn the light on[, will you]!; **c)** *Pl. auch* ~e *(Kerze)* candle; **kein** *od.* **nicht gerade ein großes ~ sein** *(ugs.)* be no genius; be not exactly brilliant; **mir ging ein ~ auf** *(ugs.)* it dawned on me; I realized what was going on; **sein ~ [nicht] unter den Scheffel stellen** [not] hide one's light under a bushel; **jmdm. ein ~ aufstecken** *(ugs.)* enlighten sb.; put sb. wise; **d)** *o. Pl. (ugs.: Strom)* electricity; **e)** *(Jägerspr.)* eye
licht-, Licht-: ~an·lage die lighting installation; **~behandlung die** *(Med.)* phototherapy; *(mit Sonnenlicht)* sunlight treatment; **~beständig** *Adj.* light-fast; **~bild das a)** [small] photograph *(for passport etc.)*; **b)** *(veralt.) (Diapositiv)* slide; *(Fotografie)* photograph; **~bilder·vortrag der** slide lecture; **~blick der** bright spot; **~bogen der** *(Elektrot.)* arc; **~brechung die** *(Optik)* refraction of light; **~bündel das** beam [of light]; **~druck der a)** *o. Pl. (Physik)* light pressure; **b)** *o. Pl. (Druckw.)* collotype; **c)** *Pl.* **~drucke** *(Druckw.: Bild)* collotype [print]; **~durchflutet** *Adj. (geh.)* flooded with light *postpos.*; **~durchlässig** *Adj.* translucent; **~echt** *Adj.* light-fast; **~echtheit die** light-fastness; **~effekt der** light effect; **~einwirkung die** effects *pl.* of light; **~elektrisch** *Adj. (Physik)* photoelectric; **~empfindlich** *Adj.* sensitive to light; *(Chemie)* photosensitive ‹*film, solution, etc.*›; **~empfindlichkeit die** sensitivity to light; *(Chemie)* photosensitivity
¹**lichten 1.** *tr. V.* thin out ‹*trees etc.*›; *(fig.)* reduce ‹*number*›. **2.** *refl. V.* **a)** ‹*trees*› thin out; ‹*hair*› grow thin; ‹*fog, mist*› clear, lift; **die Reihen ~ sich** *(fig.)* the numbers are dwindling; *(im Theater usw.)* the rows are emptying; **b)** *(geh.) (heller werden)* become lighter; lighten; *(fig.)* ‹*mystery etc.*› be cleared up
²**lichten** *tr. V. (Seemannsspr.)* **den/die Anker ~:** weigh anchor
Lichter-: ~baum der Christmas tree; **~fest das** *(jüd. Rel.)* Hanukkah; Festival of Lights; **~glanz der** blaze of lights; *s. auch* **erstrahlen; ~kette die** chain of lights
lichterloh ['lɪçtɐ'lo:] **1.** *Adj.; nicht präd.* blazing ‹*fire*›; fierce, leaping ‹*flames*›. **2.** *adv.* **~ brennen** be blazing fiercely; *(fig.)* ‹*heart*› be aflame
Lichter-: ~·meer das sea of lights; **das ~meer der Stadt** the sea of lights formed by the city; **~stadt die** city of light
licht-, Licht-: ~filter der light-filter; **~geschwindigkeit die** speed of light; **~hof der a)** *(Bauw.)* light-well; **b)** *(Fot.)* halation; **~hupe die** headlight flasher; **die ~hupe betätigen** flash [one's lights]; **~jahr das** *(Astron.)* light-year; **~kegel der** beam; *(Physik)* cone of light; **~leitung die** *(ugs.)* lighting wire; **die ~leitungen** the wiring for the lights; **~los** *Adj.* dark; poorly lit; **~mangel der** lack of light; **~maschine die** *(Kfz-W.) (mit Gleichstrom)* dynamo; *(mit Wechselstrom)* alternator; generator *(esp. Amer.)*; **~mast der** lamp-standard; **~meß (das),** ~ *(kath. Kirche)* Candlemas; **[das Fest] Mariä ~meß** [the Feast of the] Purification of the Virgin Mary; **~nelke die** campion; **~orgel die** colour organ; clavilux; **~pause die** photostat (*Brit.* P) *(of transparent original)*; **~punkt der** spot of light; **~quant** *(Physik)* light quantum; **~quelle die** light-source; **~reklame die** neon [advertising] sign; **~satz der;** *o. Pl. (Druckw.)* filmsetting; **~schacht der** light-shaft; **~schalter der** light-switch; **~schein der** gleam [of light]; *(~strahl)* beam of light; **~scheu** *Adj.* **a)** shade-loving ‹*plant*›; ‹*animal*› that shuns the light; **b)** *(fig.)* shady ‹*riff-raff*›; **~schranke die** photoelectric beam; **~schutz·faktor der** protection factor *(against sunburn)*; **~seite die** bright *or* good side; **alles hat seine**

Licht- und Schattenseiten everything has its good and bad sides; **~setz·maschine die** *(Druckw.)* filmsetting machine; **~spiel·haus das, ~spiel·theater das** *(geh.)* cinema; picture-theatre *(dated);* movie house *(Amer.);* **~stark** *Adj. (Fot.)* fast ⟨*lens*⟩; **~stärke die a)** *(Physik)* luminous intensity; **b)** *(Fot.)* speed *(of a lens);* **~strahl der** beam [of light]; **~undurch·lässig** *Adj.* light-proof

Lichtung die; ~, ~en clearing; **auf dieser ~:** in this clearing

Licht-: ~verhältnisse *Pl.* light conditions; **~wechsel der** *(Astron.)* light-variation; **~zeichen das** light signal

Lid [li:t] **das; ~[e]s, ~er** eyelid

Lid-: ~schatten der eye-shadow; **~strich der** line drawn with eyeliner pencil; eyelining *no indef. art.*

lieb [li:p] **1.** *Adj.* **a)** *(liebevoll)* kind ⟨*words, gesture*⟩; **viele ~e Grüße [an ... (Akk.)]** much love [to ...] *(coll.);* **sei so ~ und hilf mir beim Aufräumen** be a dear and help me clear up; **das ist ~ von dir** it's sweet of you; **b)** *(liebenswert)* likeable; nice; *(stärker)* lovable, sweet ⟨*child, girl, pet*⟩; **seine Frau/ihr Mann ist sehr ~:** his wife/her husband is a dear; **sie hat ein ~es Gesicht** she has a sweet *or* charming face; **~ aussehen** look sweet *or (Amer.)* cute; **c)** *(artig)* good, nice ⟨*child, dog*⟩; **die Kinder könnten etwas ~er sein** the children could be a little better behaved; **sei schön ~!** be a good girl/boy!; **sich bei jmdm. ~ Kind machen** *(ugs. abwertend)* get on the right side of sb.; **bei jmdm. ~ Kind sein** *(ugs. abwertend)* be sb.'s pet *or* favourite; **d)** *(geschätzt)* dear; **sein liebstes Spielzeug** his favourite toy; **~er Hans/~e Else/~e Oma!** *(am Briefanfang)* dear Hans/Else/Grandma; **~e Karola, ~er Ernst!** *(am Briefanfang)* dear Karola and Ernst; **~er Gott** dear God; **der ~e Gott** the Good Lord; **die ~e Verwandtschaft** *(iron.)* my/our/your/their *etc.* dear relations *(iron.);* **sie ist mir ~ und teuer** *od.* **wert** she is very dear to me; **wenn dir dein Leben ~ ist, ...:** if you value your life ...; **das ~e Geld** *(iron.)* the wretched money; **den ~en langen Tag** *(ugs.)* all the livelong day; **so manches ~e Mal, so manch ~es Mal** *(veralt.)* many a time; **meine Lieben** *(Familie)* my people; my nearest and dearest *(joc.); (als Anrede)* [you] good people; *(an Familie usw.)* my dears; **meine Liebe** my dear; *(herablassend)* my dear woman/girl; **mein Lieber** *(Mann an Mann)* my dear fellow; *(Frau/Mann an Jungen)* my dear boy; *(Frau an Mann)* my dear man; *(als Publikumsanrede)* **~e Mitbürgerinnen und Mitbürger** fellow citizens; **~e Kinder/Freunde/Genossen!** children/friends/comrades; **~e Hörerinnen und Hörer/~e Zuschauer!** *Anreden dieser Art sind im Englischen ungebräuchlich und werden deshalb nicht übersetzt;* **~ Gemeinde, ~e Schwestern und Brüder!** *(christl. Kirche)* dearly beloved; **[ach] du ~e Güte** *od.* **~e Zeit** *od.* **~er Himmel** *od.* **~es Lieschen** *od.* **~es bißchen** *(ugs.) (erstaunt)* good grief!; good heavens!; [good] gracious!; *(entsetzt)* good grief!; heavens above!; **mit jmdm./etw. seine ~e Not haben** have no end of trouble with sb./sth.; **e)** *(angenehm)* welcome; **er ist uns** *(Dat.)* **ein ~er Gast** he is a welcome visitor [with us]; **unser Besuch war ihr nicht ~:** our visit was unwelcome [to her]; **es wäre mir ~/~er, wenn ...:** I should be glad *or* should like it/should prefer it if ...; **am ~sten wäre mir, ich könnte heute noch abreisen** I should like it best if I could leave today; **wir hatten mehr Schnee, als mir ~ war** we had too much snow for my liking; **das wirst du noch früher erfahren, als dir ~ ist** you'll hear about it sooner than you've bargained for. **2.** *adv.* **a)** *(liebenswert)* kindly; **das hast du aber ~ gesagt** you 'did put that nicely; **sie hat sich sehr ~ um die alten Leute gekümmert** it was very sweet the way she looked after the old people; **b)** *(artig)* nicely; **er ist ganz ~ ins Bett gegangen** he went off to bed as good as gold

lieb·äugeln *itr. V.* **a) mit etw. ~:** have one's eye on sth.; fancy sth.; **er liebäugelt mit dem Gedanken, das zu tun** he's toying *or* flirting with the idea of doing it; **b)** *(geh.: flirten)* **mit jmdm. ~:** make eyes at sb.

lieb|behalten *unr. tr. V.* **jmdn. ~:** [continue to] be fond of sb.; *(lieben)* go on loving sb.

Liebchen ['li:pçən] **das; ~s, ~** *(veralt.)* **a) [mein] ~:** my darling; my sweet[heart]; **b)** *(abwertend)* lady-love

Liebe ['li:bə] **die; ~, ~n a)** *o. Pl.* love **(zu** for); **~ zu Gott** love of God; **aus ~ zu jmdm.** for love of sb.; **aus ~ heiraten** marry for love; **was macht die ~?** how's your love-life?; **bei aller ~, aber das geht zu weit** much as I sympathize, that's going too far; **bei aller ~, aber ich kann das nicht** much as I'd like to, I can't do it; *(Briefschluß)* **in ~ Dein Egon** [with] all my love, yours, Egon; **~ geht durch den Magen** *(scherzh.)* the way to a man's heart is through his stomach; **~ macht blind** *(Spr.)* love is blind *(prov.);* **wo die ~ hinfällt!** *(ugs.)* the ways of love are strange indeed; **~ auf den ersten Blick** love at first sight; **b)** *o. Pl.* **~ zu etw.** love of sth.; **seine ganze ~ gehört dem Meer** he adores the sea; **mit ~:** lovingly; with loving care; **c)** *(ugs.: geliebter Mensch)* love; **seine große ~:** his great love; the [great] love of his life; **d)** *(Gefälligkeit)* favour; **tu mir die ~ und warte noch** do me a favour and wait a while

liebe-, Liebe-: ~bedürftig *Adj.* in need of love *or* affection *postpos.;* **~dienerei** [-di:nə'rai] **die;** *o. Pl. (abwertend)* toadying; sycophancy; **~dienern** *itr. V.* toady **(bei, vor + Dat.** to)

Liebelei [li:bə'lai] **die; ~, ~en** *(abwertend)* flirtation

liebeln *itr. V. (veralt.)* flirt

lieben 1. *tr. V.* **a) jmdn. ~:** love sb.; *(verliebt sein)* be in love with *or* love sb.; *(koitieren)* make love to sb.; **sich ~:** be in love; *(sexuell)* make love; **was sich liebt, das neckt sich** *(Spr.)* lovers always tease each other; **b) etw. ~:** be fond of sth.; like sth.; *(stärker)* love sth.; **es ~, etw. zu tun** like *or* enjoy doing sth.; *(stärker)* love doing sth.; **diese Pflanzen ~ Schatten** these plants like shade. **2.** *itr. V.* be in love; *(sexuell)* make love; **er ist unfähig zu ~:** he is incapable of love

liebend 1. *Adj.; nicht präd.* loving; **der/die Liebende** the lover; **eine Liebende** a woman in love; **Liebende** *pl.* lovers. **2.** *adv.* **etw. ~ gerne tun** [simply] love doing sth.

lieben|lernen *tr. V.* learn to love

liebens-; Liebens-: ~wert *Adj.* likeable ⟨*person*⟩; *(stärker)* loveable ⟨*person*⟩; attractive, endearing ⟨*trait*⟩; **~würdig** *Adj.* kind; charming ⟨*smile*⟩; **seien Sie doch so ~würdig und öffnen Sie das Fenster** would you be so kind as to open the window?; **~würdigerweise** *Adv.* kindly; **~würdigkeit die; ~, ~en a)** *o. Pl.* kindness; **würden Sie die ~würdigkeit haben, das Fenster zu schließen?** would you be so kind as to shut the window?; **b)** *(Handlung, Äußerung)* kindness; **jmdm. einige ~würdigkeiten sagen** *(iron.)* say a few choice words to sb. *(iron.)*

lieber 1. *Adj.: s.* **lieb. 2.** *Adv.: s.* **gern**

liebes-, Liebes~: ~abenteuer das amorous adventure; **~affäre die** love affair; amour; **~akt der** *(geh.)* act of love; **ein Paar beim ~akt** a couple engaged in sexual intercourse; **~bande** *Pl. (dichter. veralt.)* bonds of love; **~bedürfnis das** need for love; **~beweis der** proof *or* token of love; **~beziehung die** [love] affair **(zu, mit** with); **~brief der** love-letter; **~dichtung die** love-poetry; **~dienerin die** *(verhüll. scherzh.)* lady of pleasure; **~dienst der** [act of] kindness; favour; **jmdm. einen ~dienst erweisen** do sb. a kindness *or* favour; **~entzug der** *(Psych.)* withdrawal of love; **~erklärung die** declaration of love; **~fähig** *Adj.* capable of love *postpos.;* **~fähigkeit die** capacity for love; **~film der** romantic film; **~gabe die** charitable gift; *(Spende)* donation; **~gedicht das** love-poem; **~geschichte die a)** love-story; **b)** *(~affäre)* [love] affair; **~gott der** god of love; **~göttin die** goddess of love; **~heirat die** love-match; **~knochen der** *(landsch.)* eclair; **~kummer der** lovesickness; **~kummer haben** be lovesick; be unhappily in love; **sich aus ~kummer umbringen** kill oneself for love; **~kunst die** art of love; **~laube die** *(scherzh.)* love-nest; **~leben das;** *o. Pl.* love-life; **~lied das** love-song; **~müh[e] die** *in* **das ist vergebliche** *od.* **verlorene ~müh[e]** that is a waste of effort; **~nacht die** night of love; **~nest das** love-nest; **~paar das** courting couple; [pair of] lovers; **~perlen** *Pl.* hundreds and thousands; **~roman der** romantic novel; **~spiel das** love-play; **~szene die** love-scene; **~toll** *Adj.* love-crazed; **~töter** *Pl. (ugs. scherzh.)* passion-killers *(sl. joc.);* **~trank der** love-potion; **~trunken** *Adj. (dichter.)* intoxicated with love *postpos.;* **~verhältnis das** [love] affair; **~verlust der** *(Psych.)* loss of love

liebe·voll 1. *Adj.* loving *attrib.* ⟨*care*⟩; affectionate ⟨*embrace, gesture, person*⟩. **2.** *adv.* **a)** lovingly; affectionately; **b)** *(mit Sorgfalt)* lovingly; with loving care; **sehr ~ dekoriert** decorated with much loving care

lieb|gewinnen *unr. tr. V.* grow fond of

lieb·geworden *Adj.; nicht präd.* ⟨*habit, object*⟩ of which one has grown very fond; much loved ⟨*object*⟩

lieb|haben *unr. tr. V.* love; *(gern haben)* be fond of

Liebhaber ['li:pha:bɐ] **der; ~s, ~ a)** lover; **b)** *(Interessierter, Anhänger)* enthusiast (+ *Gen.* for); *(Sammler)* collector; **ein ~ von schönen Teppichen/Oldtimern** a lover of beautiful carpets/a vintage-car enthusiast; **ein Stück für ~:** a collector's item

Liebhaber·ausgabe die collector's edition; bibliophile edition

Liebhaberei die; ~, ~en hobby

Liebhaberin die; ~, ~nen *s.* **Liebhaber**

Liebhaber-: ~preis der collector's price; **~stück das** collector's item; **~wert der ~wert haben** be valuable as a collector's item/collectors' items

lieb·kosen *tr. V. (geh.)* caress

Liebkosung die; ~, ~en *(geh.)* caress

lieblich 1. *Adj.* **a)** charming; appealing; *(friedlich)* peaceful; gentle ⟨*landscape*⟩; **b)** *(angenehm)* sweet ⟨*scent, sound*⟩; fragrant ⟨*flower*⟩; melodious ⟨*sound*⟩; mellow ⟨*red wine*⟩; [medium] sweet ⟨*white wine*⟩; **c)** *(ugs. iron: unangenehm)* **das kann ja ~ werden** this is going to be just great *(coll. iron.).* **2.** *adv.* **a)** charmingly; sweetly; **b)** *(angenehm)* pleasingly; **eine ~ klingende Stimme** a sweet and melodious voice

Lieblichkeit die; ~ a) charm; sweetness; *(einer Landschaft)* gentleness; **b)** *(angenehme Wirkung)* sweetness; *(des Klangs)* melodiousness; *(des Dufts)* fragrance; *(des Rotweins)* mellowness; **c)** *(Karnevalsprinzessin)* **Ihre ~** *title given to carnival queen*

Liebling der; ~s, ~e a) *(geliebte Person; bes. als Anrede)* darling; **b)** *(bevorzugte Person)* favourite; *(des Publikums)* darling; **der ~ des Lehrers** teacher's pet; **ein ~ der Götter** *(fig.)* a darling of the gods

Lieblings- favourite

lieb·los 1. *Adj.* loveless; *(grausam)* heartless, unfeeling ⟨*treatment, behaviour*⟩. **2.** *adv.* **a)** without affection; **~ von jmdm. spre-**

chen speak unkindly of sb.; **b)** *(ohne Sorgfalt)* carelessly; without proper care
Lieblosigkeit die; ~, ~en a) *(Handlung/Äußerung)* unkind *or* unfeeling act/word; **b)** *o. Pl. (lieblose Art)* unkindness; lack of feeling; *(Mangel an Sorgfalt)* lack of care
Lieb·reiz der; *o. Pl. (geh.)* beguiling charm
Liebschaft die; ~, ~en [casual] affair; *(Flirt)* flirtation
liebst... [li:pst...] **1.** *Adj.: s.* **lieb. 2.** *Adv.* **am ~en** *s.* **gern**
Liebste der/die; *adj. Dekl. (veralt.)* loved one; sweetheart; **meine ~:** my dearest
Liebstöckel ['li:p-ʃtœkl] **das** *od.* **der; ~s, ~** *(Bot.)* lovage
Liechtenstein (das); ~s Liechtenstein; *s. auch* **Fürstentum**
Lied [li:t] **das; ~[e]s, ~er** song; *(Kirchen~)* hymn; *(deutsches Kunst~)* lied; **und das Ende vom ~ ist dann, daß ...** *(ugs.)* and the upshot *or* net result is that; **es ist immer das alte** *od.* **gleiche** *od.* **dasselbe ~** *(ugs.)* it's always the same old story; **davon kann ich ein ~ singen** I can tell you a thing or two about that; **das ~ der ~er** *(bibl.)* the Song of Songs
Lieder-: ~abend der [evening] song recital; *(mit deutschen Kunstliedern)* [evening] lieder recital; **~buch das** song-book; **~hand·schrift die** [medieval] song-manuscript
Liederjan ['li:dɐja:n] **der; ~[e]s, ~e** *(ugs.)* messy devil
liederlich ['li:dɐlɪç] **1.** *Adj.* **a)** *(schlampig)* slovenly; messy ⟨*hair-style, person*⟩; slipshod, slovenly ⟨*work*⟩; **b)** *(verwerflich)* dissolute; **ein ~es Weibsstück** *(salopp abwertend)* a floozie *(coll.)* . **2.** *adv.* sloppily; messily; **~ angezogen sein** be slovenly dressed; **~ geschrieben** written in a slipshod manner
Liederlichkeit die; ~ a) *(Schlampigkeit)* slovenliness; **b)** *(Verwerflichkeit)* dissoluteness
Lieder-: ~macher der; ~macherin die singer-song-writer *(writing satirical songs mainly on topical/political subjects)*; **~zyklus der** song-cycle
lief [li:f] *1. u. 3. Pers. Sg. Prät. v.* **laufen**
Lieferant [lifə'rant] **der; ~en, ~en** *(Firma)* supplier; *(Auslieferer)* delivery man; **~en werden gebeten, den Eingang im Hof zu benutzen** all deliveries via the entrance in the yard
Lieferanten·eingang der goods entrance; *(bei Wohnhäusern)* tradesmen's entrance
lieferbar *Adj.* available; *(vorrätig)* in stock; **sofort ~:** available for immediate delivery; **~ zum 1. 10. 89** for delivery by 1. 10. 89
Liefer-: ~bedingungen *Pl.* terms of delivery; **~betrieb der, ~firma die** supplier; **~frist die** delivery time; **bei Möbeln besteht eine ~frist von 6–8 Wochen** there is 6–8 weeks delivery on furniture
liefern ['li:fɐn] *tr. V.* **a)** *(bringen)* deliver (**an** + *Akk.* to); *(zur Verfügung stellen)* supply; **wir ~ auch ins Ausland** we also supply our goods abroad *or* deliver to foreign destinations; **wir ~ nicht an Privat** we do not supply private individuals; **jmdm. etw. ~:** supply sb. with sth.; deliver sth. to sb.; **b)** *(hervorbringen)* produce; *(geben)* provide ⟨*eggs, honey, examples, raw material, etc.*⟩; **den Nachweis** *od.* **Beweis für etw. ~:** provide proof of sth.; **c)** *(austragen)* **sich** *(Dat.)* **eine Schlacht ~:** fight a battle [with each other]; **jmdm. ein gutes Spiel ~:** give sb. a good game *or* match; **d)** *(ugs.:)* **geliefert sein** be sunk *(coll.)*; have had it *(coll.)*
Liefer-: ~schein der acknowledgement of delivery; delivery note; **~termin der** delivery date
Lieferung die; ~, ~en a) *o. Pl. (das Liefern)* delivery; **Zahlung bei ~:** payment on delivery; **b)** *(Ware)* consignment [of goods]; delivery; **c)** *(Buchw.)* instalment; *(eines Wörterbuchs usw.)* fascicle
Liefer-: ~vertrag der supply contract; **~wagen der** [delivery] van; *(offen)* pick-up; **~zeit die** delivery time
Liege ['li:gə] **die; ~, ~n** day-bed; *(zum Ausklappen)* bed-settee; sofa bed; *(als Gartenmöbel)* sun-lounger
Liege·geld das *(Schiffahrt)* demurrage
liegen *unr. itr. V.; (südd., österr., schweiz. mit sein)* **a)** lie; ⟨*person*⟩ be lying down; *(sich hinlegen)* lie down; **während der Krankheit mußte er ~:** while he was ill he had to lie down all the time; **Weinflaschen sollen ~:** wine-bottles should lie flat *or* on their sides; **die Beine sollen höher ~ als der Kopf** your legs should be [placed] higher than your head; **auf dem Boden ~:** lie on the floor; ⟨*carpet*⟩ be on the floor; **im Bett ~:** lie in bed; *(das Bett hüten)* be *or* stay in bed; **auf den Knien ~:** be prostrate on one's knees; **im Krankenhaus/auf Station 6 ~:** be in hospital/in ward 6; **krank im Bett ~:** be ill in bed; **der Wagen liegt gut auf der Straße** the car holds the road well; **richtig ~:** be in the right position; ⟨*hair*⟩ stay in place; **die Säge liegt gut/fest in der Hand** the saw rests comfortably/firmly in the hand; **b)** *(vorhanden sein)* lie; **es liegt Schnee auf den Bergen** there is snow [lying] on the hills; **der Schnee liegt meterhoch** the snow is more than a metre deep; **der Stoff liegt 80 cm breit** the material is 80 cm wide; **c)** *(sich befinden)* be; ⟨*object*⟩ be [lying]; ⟨*town, house, etc.*⟩ be [situated]; **etw. im Keller** *usw.* **~ haben** have sth. [lying] in the cellar *etc.*; **die Preise ~ höher** prices are higher; **die Verhältnisse ~/die Sache liegt anders** circumstances are/the situation is different; **wie die Dinge ~:** as things are or stand [at the moment]; **die Stadt liegt an der Küste** the town is *or* lies on the coast; **das Dorf liegt sehr hoch** the village is very high up; **das liegt an meinem Weg** it is on my way; **schön ~:** be beautifully situated; **ein einsam liegender Hof** an isolated farm; **verkehrsgünstig ~:** be well placed for transport; ⟨*town, city*⟩ have good communications; **etw. rechts/links ~ lassen** leave sth. on one's right/left; **das Fenster liegt nach vorn/nach Süden/zum Garten** the window is at the front/faces south/faces the garden; **es liegt nicht in meiner Absicht, das zu tun** it is not my intention to do that; **nichts liegt uns ferner, als ...:** nothing could be further from our intentions than ...; **die Betonung liegt auf der ersten Silbe** the stress is on the first syllable; **das Essen lag mir schwer im Magen** the food/meal lay heavy on my stomach; **auf ihm liegt eine große Verantwortung** a heavy responsibility rests on his shoulders; **d)** *(zeitlich)* be; **das liegt noch vor mir/schon hinter mir** I still have that to come/that's all behind me now; **die Stunden, die zwischen den Prüfungen lagen** the hours between the examinations; **das liegt so weit** *od.* **lange zurück** it is so long ago; **e) das liegt an ihm** *od.* **bei ihm** it is up to him; *(ist seine Schuld)* it is his fault; **die Verantwortung/Schuld liegt bei ihm** it is his responsibility/fault; **an mir soll es nicht ~:** don't let me stop you; I won't stand in your way; *(ich werde mich beteiligen)* I'm easy *(coll.)*; **es liegt daran, daß ...:** it is because ...; **ich weiß nicht, woran es liegt** I don't know what the reason is; **woran mag es nur ~, daß ...?** why ever is it that ...?; **f)** *(gemäß sein)* **es liegt mir nicht** it doesn't suit me; it isn't right for me; *(es spricht mich nicht an)* it doesn't appeal to me; *(ich mag es nicht)* I don't like it *or* care for it; **Physik liegt ihr sehr** physics is right up her street *(coll.)*; **solche Tätigkeiten ~ ihm [sehr]** this kind of activity suits him [down to the ground]; **es liegt ihm nicht, das zu tun** he does not like doing that; *(so etwas tut er nicht)* it is not his way to do that; **mit Kindern umzugehen scheint ihr nicht zu ~:** handling children doesn't seem to be her cup of tea *(coll.)*; **g) daran liegt ihm viel/wenig/nichts** he sets great/little/no store by that; it means a lot/little/nothing to him; **ihr liegt [einiges] daran, anerkannt zu werden** it is of [some] importance to her to be recognized; **an ihm liegt mir schon etwas** I do care about him [a bit]; **h)** *(bedeckt sein)* **der Tisch liegt voller Bücher** the desk is covered with books; **i)** *(bes. Milit.: verweilen)* be; ⟨*troops*⟩ be stationed; ⟨*ship*⟩ lie; **vor Verdun ~:** be stationed *or* positioned outside Verdun; **irgendwo [in Quartier] ~:** be quartered *or* billeted somewhere; *s. auch* **Straße**
liegen|bleiben *unr. itr. V.; mit sein* **a)** stay [lying]; **[im Bett] ~:** stay in bed; **bewußtlos/bewegungslos ~:** lie unconscious/motionless; **verletzt ~:** end up lying on the ground injured; **b)** *(nicht tauen)* ⟨*snow*⟩ lie; **c)** *(bleiben)* ⟨*things*⟩ stay, be left; *(vergessen werden)* be left behind; *(nicht verkauft werden)* remain unsold; **d)** *(nicht erledigt werden)* be left undone; **diese Briefe können bis morgen ~:** these letters can wait until tomorrow; **e)** *(mit dem Auto)* break down
liegend reclining, recumbent ⟨*figure, posture*⟩; prone ⟨*position*⟩; horizontal ⟨*position, engine*⟩; **etw. ~ aufbewahren** store sth. flat/on its side
liegen|lassen *unr. tr. V.* leave; *(vergessen)* leave [behind]; **er ließ die Papiere auf dem Tisch liegen** he left the papers [lying] on the desk; **alles liegen- und stehenlassen** drop everything; **b)** *(unerledigt lassen)* leave ⟨*work*⟩ undone; leave ⟨*letters*⟩ unposted/unopened; *s. auch* **links 1 a**
Liegenschaft die; ~, ~en; *meist Pl. (bes. Rechtsspr.)* land holding; *(Gebäude)* property
Liege-: ~platz der mooring; **~sitz der** reclining seat; **~statt die** *(geh.)* resting-place; *(Bett)* bed; **~stuhl der** *(einfach, mit Holzgestell)* deck-chair; *(Luxusausstattung, mit Metallgestell)* lounger; **~stütz der** press-up; **~stütz machen** do press-ups; **in den ~stütz gehen** get into a press-up position; **~wagen der** couchette car; **wollen Sie Schlafwagen oder ~wagen?** do you want a sleeper or a couchette?; **der ~wagen ist hinten** the couchettes are at the back of the train; **~wiese die** sunbathing lawn
lieh [li:] *1. u. 3. Pers. Sg. Prät. v.* **leihen**
lies [li:s] *Imperativ Sg. v.* **lesen**
Lieschen ['li:sçən] **~ Müller** *(ugs.)* the average girl/woman *(coll.)*; **Fleißiges ~** *(Bot.)* busy Lizzie; *s. auch* **lieb d**
Liese die; ~, ~n *(ugs. abwertend)* **eine dumme ~:** a stupid cow *(sl.)*; **eine liederliche ~:** a slovenly Sue; a messy Jessie
ließ [li:s] *1. u. 3. Pers. Sg. Prät. v.* **lassen**
liest [li:st] *3. Pers. Sg. Präsens v.* **lesen**
Lift [lɪft] **der; ~[e]s, ~e** *od.* **~s a)** lift *(Brit.)*; elevator *(Amer.)*; **b)** *Pl.:* **~e** *(Ski~, Sessel~)* lift
Lift·boy der lift-boy *(Brit.)*; elevator boy *(Amer.)*
¹liften ['lɪftn̩] *itr. V.; mit sein* take the [ski-] lift
²liften *tr. V.* **die Gesichtshaut ~:** tighten the skin of the face; **sich ~ lassen** *(ugs.)* have a face-lift
Liga ['li:ga] **die; ~, Ligen** league; *(Sport)* division; **~ für Menschenrechte** League of Human Rights
Ligament [liga'mɛnt] **das; ~[e], ~e** *(Anat.)* ligament
Ligatur [liga'tu:ɐ̯] **die; ~, ~en** *(Druckw., Musik, Med.)* ligature; *(Musik: in der modernen Notenschrift)* ligature; tie
Liguster [li'gʊstɐ] **der; ~s, ~** *(Bot.)* privet
liieren [li'i:rən] **1.** *refl. V.* **a) sich mit jmdm. ~:** start an affair with sb.; **mit jmdm. liiert sein** be having an affair with sb.; **b)** *(bes.*

Wirtsch., Politik) ⟨*firm*⟩ form links (**mit** with); **sich [miteinander]** ~ ⟨*firms, countries*⟩ form links; **mit einer Firma liiert sein** have links with a firm. **2.** *tr. V. (bes. Wirtsch.)* **zwei Betriebe miteinander ~:** establish links between two businesses

Likör [li'kø:ɐ̯] **der; ~s, ~e** liqueur

lila ['li:la] *indekl. Adj.* mauve; *(dunkel~)* purple

Lila das; ~s *od. (ugs.)* **~s** mauve; *(Dunkel~)* purple

Lilie ['li:li̯ə] **die; ~, ~n a)** lily; **b)** *(Her.)* fleur-de-lis

Liliput- ['li:lipʊt-] miniature ⟨*railway, format*⟩; tiny ⟨*house, country*⟩

Liliputaner [lilipu'ta:nɐ] **der; ~s, ~:** dwarf; midget

Limburger ['lɪmbʊrgɐ] **der; ~s, ~, Limburger Käse der** Limburger [cheese]

Limerick ['lɪmərɪk] **der; ~[s], ~s** limerick

Limes ['li:mɛs] **der; ~, ~ a)** *(hist.)* limes; **b)** *(Math.)* limit

Limit ['lɪmɪt] **das; ~s, ~s** limit; **das äußerste ~:** the top limit; *(Termin)* the latest possible date; **das ~ überschreiten** exceed the limit; *(fig.)* go too far; **dieses ~ kann nicht unterschritten werden** one cannot go below this minimum; **jmdm. ein ~ [bis Ende der Woche** *usw.***] setzen** set sb. a limit [of the end of the week *etc.*]

limitieren *tr. V.* limit; restrict

Limo ['lɪmo] **die,** *auch:* **das; ~, ~[s]** *(ugs.)* fizzy drink; **die Kinder kriegen ~:** the children can have pop *(coll.)*

Limonade [limo'na:də] **die; ~, ~n** fizzy drink; mineral; *(Zitronen~)* lemonade

Limone [li'mo:nə] **die; ~, ~n** lime

Limousine [limu'zi:nə] **die; ~, ~n** [large] saloon *(Brit.) or (Amer.)* sedan; *(mit Trennwand)* limousine

lind [lɪnt] *Adj. (dichter.)* **a)** *(mild)* balmy ⟨*night, air*⟩; **b)** *(sanft)* gentle ⟨*wind, voice*⟩

Linde ['lɪndə] **die; ~, ~n a)** *(Baum)* lime[-tree]; **b)** *o. Pl. (Holz)* limewood

Linden-: ~baum der lime-tree; **~blüten·honig der** lime-blossom honey; **~blüten·tee der** lime-blossom tea

lindern ['lɪndɐn] *tr. V.* alleviate, relieve ⟨*suffering*⟩; ease, relieve ⟨*pain*⟩; quench, slake ⟨*thirst*⟩

Linderung die; ~ *(der Not)* relief; alleviation; *(des Schmerzes)* relief; **jmdm. [vorübergehend/sofort] ~ bringen** bring sb. [temporary/immediate] relief

lind·grün *Adj.* lime-green

Lind·wurm ['lɪnt-] **der** *(Myth.)* lindworm

Lineal [line'a:l] **das; ~s, ~e** ruler; **Striche mit einem ~ ziehen** rule lines; **er ging, als ob er ein ~ verschluckt hätte** he walked as stiff as a poker

linear [line'a:ɐ̯] **1.** *Adj.* **a)** *(Math., Physik; auch geh.: geradlinig)* linear; **b)** *(Arbeitswelt)* **~e Lohnerhöhung** phased pay rise in a series of equal steps; **~e Abschreibung** straight-line depreciation. **2.** *adv.* **a)** *(Phys., geh.)* linearly; in a linear manner; **b)** *(Arbeitswelt)* **die Gehälter ~ erhöhen/eine Lohnerhöhung ~ vornehmen** increase salaries/implement a pay increase in a series of equal steps

Linguist [lɪŋ'guɪst] **der; ~en, ~en** linguist

Linguistik die; ~: linguistics *sing., no art.*

Linguistin die; ~, ~nen linguist

linguistisch 1. *Adj.* linguistic. **2.** *adv.* linguistically

Linie ['li:ni̯ə] **die; ~, ~n a)** line; **ein Kleid in modischer/strenger ~:** a dress in a fashionable/severe style *or* with fashionable/severe lines; **auf die [schlanke] ~ achten** *(ugs. scherzh.)* watch one's figure; **in einer ~ stehen/sich in einer ~ aufstellen** stand in line/line up; **die feindliche[n] ~[n]** *(Milit.)* [the] enemy lines *pl.;* **in der vordersten** *od.* **in vorderster ~ kämpfen** *(Milit.)* fight in the front line; **in vorderster ~ stehen** *(fig.)* be in the front line; **in ~ antreten** *(Milit.)* fall in; *(Sport)* line up; **b)** *(Verkehrsstrecke)* route; *(Eisenbahn~, Straßenbahn~)* line; route; **die ~ Frankfurt-London** the Frankfurt-London route; **eine ~ stillegen** stop a service; **c)** *(Verkehrsmittel)* **fahren Sie mit der ~ 4** take a *or* the number 4; **die ~ 12** the number 12; **d)** *(allgemeine Richtung)* line; policy; **eine ~ vertreten** take a line; **die große ~ wahren** stick to the broad principle; **eine/keine klare ~ erkennen lassen** reveal a/no clear policy; **sich auf der gleichen ~ bewegen** be on *or* along the same lines *pl.;* **e)** *(Verwandtschaftszweig)* line; **in direkter ~ von jmdm. abstammen** be directly descended from *or* a direct descendant of sb.; **f)** *in* **in erster ~ geht es darum, daß das Projekt beschleunigt wird** the first priority is to speed up the project; **in erster ~ kommt sein Stellvertreter in Frage** his deputy is first in line; **wir müssen in erster ~ darauf bedacht sein, daß ...:** our prime concern must be that ...; **Geld spielt in dieser Sache erst in zweiter ~ eine Rolle** money is only of secondary importance *or* plays only a secondary role in this matter; **auf der ganzen ~:** all along the line; **g)** *(Seemannsspr.: Äquator) o. Pl.* **die ~ passieren** *od.* **kreuzen** cross the line

linien-, Linien-: ~blatt das line guide; guide sheet; **~bus der** regular bus; **~dienst der** regular service; *(Flugw.)* scheduled *or* regular service; **im ~dienst fahren/fliegen** ⟨*bus, coach/aircraft*⟩ be used on regular routes; **~flug der** scheduled flight; **~flugzeug das** scheduled plane *or* aircraft; **~führung die a)** *(Art des Zeichnens)* line-work; **b)** *(Gestaltung der Umrißlinien)* lines *pl.;* **~maschine die** *s.* **~flugzeug; ~netz das** route network; **~papier das** ruled *or* lined paper; **~richter der** *(Fußball usw.)* linesman; *(Tennis)* line judge; *(Rugby)* touch judge; **~schiff das a)** liner; **b)** *(hist.)* ship of the line; **~treu** *(abwertend)* **1.** *Adj.* loyal to the party line *postpos.;* **2.** *adv.* ⟨*act*⟩ in accordance with the party line; **~verkehr der** regular services *pl.; (Flugw.)* scheduled *or* regular services *pl.;* **im ~verkehr fahren/fliegen** ⟨*aircraft*⟩ be used on regular *or* scheduled routes

linieren [li'ni:rən], **liniieren** [lini'i:rən] *tr. V.* rule; rule lines on; **lini[i]ertes Papier** ruled *or* lined paper

Linierung, Liniierung die; ~, ~en a) *(Vorgang)* ruling; **b)** *(Linien)* [ruled] lines *pl.*

link [lɪŋk] *(salopp)* **1.** *Adj.* underhand; shady, underhand ⟨*deal*⟩; **ein ~er Vogel** a shady customer *(coll.) or* character; **komm mir bloß nicht auf die ~e Tour!** just don't try and pull a fast one on me *(sl.).* **2.** *adv.* in an underhand way

link... *Adj.* **a)** left; left[-hand] ⟨*edge*⟩; **die ~e Spur** the left-hand lane; **~er Hand, zur ~en Hand** on the left-hand side; on the left; **auf der ~en Seite** on the left-hand side; **auf der ~en Seite gehen** walk on the left; **der ~e Außenstürmer/Verteidiger** *(Ballspiele)* the outside left/the left back; **mit dem ~en Fuß** *od.* **Bein zuerst aufgestanden sein** *(fig. ugs.)* have got out of bed on the wrong side; *s. auch* **Ehe; b)** *(außen, sichtbar)* wrong, reverse ⟨*side*⟩; **~e Maschen** *(Handarb.)* purl stitches; **eine ~e Masche stricken** purl one; **c)** *(in der Politik)* left-wing; leftist *(derog.);* **der ~e Flügel einer Partei** the left wing of a party

[1]**Linke der/die** *adj. Dekl.* left-winger; leftist *(derog.);* **von den ~n organisiert sein** be organized by the left

[2]**Linke die; ~n, ~n a)** *(Hand)* left hand; **seine ~ einsetzen** *(Boxen)* use one's left; **zur ~n des Königs** on *or* to the left of the king; on the king's left; **jmdm. zur ~n** on sb.'s left; to the left of sb.; **zur ~n** on the left; **b)** *(Politik)* left

linker·seits *Adv.* on the left[-hand side]

linkisch 1. *Adj.* awkward. **2.** *adv.* awkwardly

links [lɪŋks] **1.** *Adv.* **a)** *(auf der linken Seite)* on the left; *(Theater)* stage right; **die zweite Straße ~:** the second street *or* turning on the left; **~ von jmdm/etw.** on sb.'s left *or* to the left of sb./on *or* to the left of sth.; **von ~ kommen** come from the left; **nach ~ gehen/sich nach ~ wenden** go/turn to the left; **er wandte sich nach ~:** he turned to his *or* the left; **sich ~ halten** keep to the left; **weder nach ~ noch nach rechts schauend verließ sie den Saal** looking neither [to the] left nor [to the] right she walked out of the room; **er blickte weder nach ~ noch nach rechts, sondern rannte einfach über die Straße** he didn't look left or right, but just ran straight across the road; **sich ~ einordnen** move *or* get into the left-hand lane; **jmdn./etw. ~ liegenlassen** *(fig.)* ignore sb./sth.; **ich weiß/sie wissen** *usw.* **nicht [mehr], was ~ und [was] rechts ist** *(fig.)* I don't know 'where I am/they don't know 'where they are *etc.;* **b)** *(Politik)* on the left wing; **~ stehen** *od.* **sein** be left-wing *or* on the left; **~ eingestellt sein** have left-wing leanings; **weit ~ stehen** be on the far left; **c)** *(ugs.: ~händig)* left-handed; **mit ~** *(fig.)* easily; with no trouble; **d)** *(Handarb.)* **zwei ~, zwei rechts** two purl, two plain; purl two, knit two; **ein ~ gestrickter Pullover** a purl[-knit] pullover; **e)** *(~seitig)* **etw. von ~ bügeln** iron sth. on the wrong side *or* reverse side; **nach ~ wenden** turn ⟨*dress, skirt, etc.*⟩ inside out. **2.** *Präp. mit Gen.* **~ des Rheins/der Straße** on the left side *or* bank of the Rhine/on the left-hand side of the road *or* to the left of the road

links-, Links-: ~abbieger der *(Verkehrsw.)* motorist/cyclist/car *etc.* turning left; **die ~abbieger** the traffic *sing.* turning left; **als ~abbieger mußte er ...:** since he was turning left he had to ...; **~abbieger·spur die** *(Verkehrsw.)* left-hand turn lane; **~abweichler der** *(Politik)* left deviationist; **~ausleger der** *(Boxen)* orthodox boxer; **~außen** *Adv.* **a)** *(Ballspiele)* ⟨*run, break through*⟩ down the left wing; **nach ~außen spielen** play the ball out to the left wing; **b)** *(Politik ugs.)* ⟨*move, drift*⟩ to the extreme left; **ganz ~außen stehen** be on the extreme left [wing]; be an extreme left-winger; **~außen der; ~, ~ a)** *(Ballspiele)* left wing; outside left; **b)** *(Politik ugs.)* extreme left-winger; **~drall der a)** pull to the left; **der Tennisspieler gab dem Ball einen ~drall** the tennis player swerved the ball to the left; **b)** *(Waffent.)* left-handed twist; **c)** *(Politik ugs.)* tendency to the left; left-wing tendency; **~drehend** *Adj.* **a)** *(bes. Technik)* left-hand ⟨*thread*⟩; **b)** *(Chemie, Physik)* laevorotatory; **~drehung die** *(Chemie, Physik)* laevorotation; **~extremismus der** *(Politik)* left-wing extremism; **~extremist der** *(Politik)* left-wing extremist; **~gängig** *Adj. s.* **~drehend a; ~gerichtet** *Adj. (Politik)* left-wing orientated; **~gewinde das** *(Technik)* left-hand thread; **~händer** [~hɛndɐ] **der; ~s, ~, ~händerin die; ~, ~nen** left-hander; **~händer[in] sein** be left-handed; **~händig 1.** *Adj.* left-handed; **2.** *adv.* with one's left hand; **~händigkeit die; ~:** left-handedness; **~herum** *Adv.* [round] to the left; **etw. ~herum drehen** turn sth. anticlockwise *or* [round] to the left; **~intellektuelle der/die** the left-wing intellectual; **~kurve die** left-hand bend; **~lastig** *Adj.* **a)** ⟨*ship*⟩ listing to the left; ⟨*car*⟩ down at the left, leaning to the left; **~lastig sein** ⟨*ship*⟩ list to the left, have a list to the left; ⟨*car*⟩ be down at the left, lean to the left; **b)** *(Politik ugs.)* leftist; **~läufig** *Adj.* running from right to left *postpos., not pred.;* **~liberal** *Adj.* left-wing liberal; **~liberale der/die** left-wing liberal; **~partei die** *(Politik)* left-wing party; **~ra-**

dikal *(Politik)* **1.** *Adj.* radical left-wing; **2.** *adv.* **eine ~radikal orientierte Gruppe** a group with a radical left-wing orientation; **~radikale der/die** left-wing radical; **~radikalismus der** left-wing radicalism; **~rheinisch 1.** *Adj.; nicht präd.* on *or* to the left of the Rhine *postpos.*; **auf der ~rheinischen Seite** on the left side of the Rhine; **2.** *adv.* on *or* to the left of the Rhine; **~ruck der** *(Politik ugs.)* shift to the left; **~rum** *Adv. (ugs.) s.* **~herum; ~seitig 1.** *Adj.* ‹*paralysis*› of the left side; **2.** *adv.* on the left [side]; **~seitig gelähmt sein** be paralysed on *or* down the *or* one's left side; **~stehend** *Adj. (Politik)* left-wing; **~steuerung die** left-hand drive; **~um** [*auch:* -'-] *Adv. (bes. Milit.)* to the left; **~um kehrt!** to the left about turn!; **~um machen** do a left turn; **~verkehr der** driving *no art.* on the left

linnen ['lɪnən] *Adj.; nicht präd. (veralt.)* linen

Linnen das; ~s, ~ *(veralt.)* linen

Linoleum [li'no:leʊm] **das;** ~s linoleum; lino

Linol·schnitt der linocut

Linse ['lɪnzə] **die;** ~, ~n **a)** *(Bot., Kochk.)* lentil; **b)** *(Med., Optik)* lens; **c)** *(ugs.: Objektiv)* lens; **jmdn. vor die ~ bekommen** get sb. in front of the camera

linsen *itr. V. (ugs.)* peep; peek

Linsen-: ~gericht das lentil dish; **für ein ~gericht** *(geh.)* for a mess of pottage; **~suppe die** lentil soup

Lippe ['lɪpə] **die;** ~, ~n lip; **jmdm. nicht über die ~n kommen, nicht über jmds. ~n** *(Akk.)* **kommen** not pass sb.'s lips; **sie brachte es nicht über die ~n** she couldn't bring herself to say it; **jmdm. glatt von den ~n gehen** come easily to sb.'s lips; **ein fröhliches Lied auf den ~n** singing merrily; **an jmds. Lippen** *(Dat.)* **hängen** hang on sb.'s every word; **eine [dicke** *od.* **große] ~ riskieren** *(salopp)* shoot one's mouth off *(sl.)*

Lippen-: ~bekenntnis das *(abwertend)* empty talk *no pl.*; **~bekenntnisse für etw. ablegen** pay lip-service to sth.; **~blütler der** *(Bot.)* labiate; **~laut der** *(Phon.)* labial; **~stift der** lipstick

liquid [li'kvi:t] *Adj. (Wirtsch.)* liquid ‹*funds, resources*›; solvent ‹*business*›; **ich bin zur Zeit nicht ~:** I'm out of funds at the moment

Liquida ['li:kvida] **die;** ~, **Liquidä** *od.* **Liquiden** *(Phon.)* liquid

Liquidation [likvida'tsi̯o:n] **die;** ~, ~en **a)** *(verhüll.: Tötung)* liquidation; **b)** *(Wirtsch.)* liquidation *no indef. art.*; **c)** *(Rechnung)* account; **d)** *(geh.: Tilgung)* elimination; *(eines Systems)* abolition

liquide *s.* **liquid**

liquidieren [likvi'di:rən] **1.** *tr. V.* **a)** *(verhüll.: töten)* liquidate; **b)** *(Wirtsch.)* liquidate; **c)** *(Rechnung ausstellen)* charge; **d)** *(geh.: tilgen)* eliminate; abolish ‹*system of government*›. **2.** *itr. V. (Wirtsch.)* go into liquidation

Liquidierung die; ~, ~en *s.* **Liquidation**

Liquidität [likvidi'tɛ:t] **die;** ~, ~en *(Wirtsch.)* liquidity; solvency; *(flüssige Mittel)* liquid assets *pl.*

Liquiditäts·schwierigkeiten *Pl.* **in ~ sein** *(Wirtsch.)* have liquidity problems

lispeln ['lɪspl̩n] *itr. V.* **a)** lisp; **er hat schon immer gelispelt** he's always had a lisp; **b)** *auch tr. (flüstern)* whisper

Lissabon ['lɪsabɔn] **(das);** ~s Lisbon

Lissabonner ['lɪsabɔnɐ] **1.** *Adj.; nicht präd.* Lisbon; *s. auch* **Kölner 1. 2. der;** ~s, ~: inhabitant/native of Lisbon; *s. auch* **Kölner 2**

List [lɪst] **die;** ~, ~en **a)** [cunning] trick *or* ruse; **zu einer ~ greifen** resort to a [cunning] trick *or* ruse; use a little cunning; **b)** *(listige Art) o. Pl.* cunning; **mit ~ und Tücke** *(ugs.)* by cunning and trickery

Liste die; ~, ~n list; **eine ~ über etw.** *(Akk.)* **anlegen/führen** draw up/keep a list of sth.; **jmdn./etw. auf eine ~ setzen** put sb./sth. on a list; **jmdn./etw. von einer ~ streichen** take *or* cross sb./sth. off a list; **eine schwarze ~:** a blacklist

Listen-: ~platz der *(Politik)* place on the [party] list; **~preis der** list price; **~wahl die** *(Parl.)* list system

listig 1. *Adj.* cunning; crafty. **2.** *adv.* cunningly; craftily; **jmdn. ~ ansehen/angrinsen** look/grin at sb. slyly.

Litanei [lita'nai̯] **die;** ~, ~en *(Rel., auch fig. abwertend)* litany; **eine ~ beten/***(abwertend)* **herbeten** recite a litany

Litauen ['li:tau̯ən] **(das);** ~s Lithuania

Litauer der; ~s, ~: Lithuanian

litauisch *Adj.* Lithuanian

Liter ['li:tɐ] **der,** *auch:* **das;** ~s, ~: litre

literar·historisch *s.* **literaturgeschichtlich**

literarisch [lɪtə'ra:rɪʃ] **1.** *Adj.* literary. **2.** *adv.* **~ hervortreten** emerge as a writer; **sich ~ betätigen** write; do some writing; **~ interessiert/gebildet sein** be interested in literature/be well-read

Literat [lɪtə'ra:t] **der;** ~en, ~en, **Literatin die;** ~, ~nen writer; literary figure

Literatur [lɪtəra'tu:ɐ̯] **die;** ~, ~en literature; **belletristische ~:** belles-lettres *pl.*; **in die ~ eingehen** find one's place in literature

literatur-, Literatur-: ~an·gabe die [bibliographical] reference; **~denkmal das** literary monument; **~gattung die** literary genre; **~geschichte die** literary history; history of literature; **~geschichtlich 1.** *Adj.; nicht präd.* literary-historical; **2.** *adv.* **~geschichtlich interessiert/beschlagen sein** interested/versed in literary history; **~geschichtlich gesehen** from the point of view of literary history; **~hinweis der** reference to further reading; **~historiker der** literary historian; **~kritik die** literary criticism; **~kritiker der** literary critic; **~papst der** *(iron.)* leading literary pundit; **~preis der** prize for literature; literary prize; **~verzeichnis das** list of references; **~wissenschaft die** literary studies *pl., no art.*; study of literature; **vergleichende ~wissenschaft** comparative literature; **~zeitschrift die** literary magazine; *(Fachzeitschrift)* literary journal

Liter·flasche die litre bottle

liter·weise *Adv.* by the litre; in litres

Litfaß·säule ['lɪtfas-] **die** advertising column *or* pillar

Lithograph [lito'gra:f] **der;** ~en, ~en lithographer

Lithographie [litogra'fi:] **die;** ~, ~n **a)** *o. Pl. (Verfahren)* lithography *no art.*; **b)** *(Druck)* lithograph

lithographisch *Adj.* lithographic

Litotes [li'to:tɛs] **die;** ~, ~ *(Rhet.)* litotes

litt [lɪt] *1. u. 3. Pers. Sg. Prät. v.* **leiden**

Liturgie [litʊr'gi:] **die;** ~, ~n *(christl. Kirche)* liturgy

liturgisch 1. *Adj.* liturgical. **2.** *adv.* liturgically

Litze ['lɪtsə] **die;** ~, ~n **a)** braid; **b)** *(Elektrot.)* flex *(Brit.)*; cord *(Amer.)*

live [laif] *(Rundf., Ferns.)* **1.** *Adj.* live. **2.** *adv.* live; **in dieser Sendung wird nur ~ gesungen** in this programme all the singing is live

Live-: ~-Sendung die *(Rundf., Ferns.)* live programme; *(Übertragung)* live broadcast; **~-Show die** live show

Livius ['li:vi̯ʊs] **(der)** Livy

Livree [li'vre:] **die;** ~, ~n livery; **ein Diener in ~:** a liveried servant

livriert *Adj.* liveried

¹Lizentiat [litsɛn'tsi̯a:t] **der;** ~en, ~en *(schweiz.)* licentiate

²Lizentiat das; ~s, ~e *(schweiz.)* licentiate

Lizenz [li'tsɛnts] **die;** ~, ~en licence; **etw. in ~ herstellen** manufacture sth. under licence

Lizenz-: ~aus·gabe die *(Buchw.)* licensed edition; **~gebühr die** licence fee; *(Verlagsw.)* royalty

lizenzieren [litsɛn'tsi:rən] *tr. V.* license

Lizenz-: ~spieler der *(Sport)* licensed professional; **~träger der** licensee; **~vertrag der** licence agreement

Lkw, LKW [ɛlka:'ve:] **der;** ~[s], ~[s] *Abk.* **Lastkraftwagen**

Lkw-Fahrer der truck *or (Brit.)* lorry driver; trucker *(Amer.)*

¹Lob [lo:p] **das;** ~[e]s, ~e praise *no indef. art.*; **ein ~ bekommen** receive praise; come in for praise; **[ein] ~ für etw. verdienen** deserve praise for sth.; **jmdm. ~ spenden** *(geh.)* bestow praise on sb.; **über jedes ~ erhaben sein** be beyond praise; **voll des ~es** *od.* **des ~es voll über jmdn./etw. sein** *(geh.)* be full of praise for sb./sth.; **Gott sei ~ und Dank!** *(geh.)* praise and thanks be to God; **ein ~ dem Küchenchef/der Hausfrau** my compliments to the chef/the hostess

²Lob [lɔp] **der;** ~s, ~s *(Tennis)* lob

Lobby ['lɔbi] **die;** ~, ~s *od.* **Lobbies** lobby

Lobbyismus der; ~: lobbyism *no art.*

Lobbyist der; ~en, ~en, **Lobbyistin die;** ~, ~nen lobbyist

loben *tr., auch itr. V.* praise; **jmdn. für** *od.* **wegen etw. ~:** praise sb. for sth.; **jmdn./etw. ~d erwähnen** commend sb./sth.; **da lob' ich mir ...:** give me ... any day; what I like is ...; **das lob' ich mir** good for you/him *etc. (coll.)*; **„Bravo", lobte er [seinen Sohn]** 'Bravo', he said approvingly [to his son]; **er lobt gern** he is generous with his praise

lobens·wert 1. *Adj.* praiseworthy; laudable; commendable. **2.** *adv.* laudably; commendably

lobesam *Adj. (veralt.)* **Kaiser Rotbart ~:** the good Emperor Redbeard *or* Barbarossa

Lobes·hymne die *(oft iron.)* hymn of praise; **~n auf jmdn./etw. singen** *od.* **anstimmen** *(fig.)* sing sb.'s praises/the praises of sth.; praise sb./sth. to the skies

Lob-: ~gesang der song *or* hymn of praise; **~hudelei die** *(abwertend)* extravagant praise *no pl.* **(auf +** *Akk.* **of)**

löblich ['lø:plɪç] *Adj. (oft iron.)* laudable; commendable

lob-, Lob-: ~lied das song of praise; **ein ~lied auf jmdn./etw. anstimmen** *(fig.)* sing sb.'s praises/the praises of sth.; **~preisen** *unr. od. regelm. tr. V. (dichter.)* praise; **~preisung die** *(dichter.)* praise; **zur ~preisung Gottes** in praise of God; **~rede die** eulogy; panegyric; **eine ~rede auf jmdn. halten** make a speech in praise of sb.; eulogize sb.

Loch [lɔx] **das;** ~[e]s, **Löcher** ['lœçɐ] **a)** hole; **ein ~ im Zahn/Kopf haben** have a hole *or* cavity in one's tooth/gash on one's *or* the head; **sich** *(Dat.)* **ein ~ in den Kopf** *usw.* **stoßen** gash one's head *etc.*; **das ~ in etw.** *(Dat.)* **stopfen** *(fig.)* plug the gap in sth.; **ein großes ~ in jmds. Geldbeutel reißen** *(fig.)* make a big hole in sb.'s pocket; **jmdm. ein ~** *od.* **Löcher in den Bauch fragen** *(salopp)* drive sb. up the wall with [all] one's questions *(coll.)*; **Löcher in die Luft gucken** *od.* **starren** *(ugs.)* gaze into space; **ein ~** *od.* **Löcher in die Luft schießen** *(ugs.)* shoot wide; miss completely; **auf** *od.* **aus dem letzten ~ pfeifen** be on one's/its last legs; *s. auch* **saufen 1 b; b)** *(salopp abwertend: Wohnraum)* hole; **c)** *(salopp: Gefängnis)* nick *(sl.)*; clink *(sl.)*; **ins ~ kommen/im ~ sitzen** be put in/be in the nick *or* clink; **d)** *(derb: Vagina)* cunt *(vulg.)*; hole *(coarse)*; **e)** *(ugs.: im Billardtisch)* pocket

Loch-: ~beitel der mortise chisel; **~billard das** pocket billiards; pool; **~eisen das** punch

lochen *tr. V.* **a)** punch holes/a hole in; punch, clip ‹*ticket*›; punch [holes in] ‹*invoice, copy, bill*› *(for filing)*; *(perforieren)* perforate; **b)** *(DV)* punch

Locher der; ~s, ~ a) *(auch DV)* punch; **b)** *(Beruf)* keypunch operator
löcherig *Adj.* holey; full of holes *pred.*; **die Abwehr war ~** *(fig.)* the defence was full of gaps *or* was wide open; **sein Alibi/seine Argumentation war recht ~** *(fig.)* his alibi/argument was full of holes
Locherin die; ~, ~nen keypunch operator
löchern *tr. V. (ugs.)* **jmdn. ~:** pester sb. to death; **jmdn. ~, etw. zu tun** pester sb. to do sth.
Loch-: ~kamera die pinhole camera; **~karte die** *(Technik, DV)* punch[ed] card
Loch·karten·verfahren das; *o. Pl.* punch[ed]-card system
löchrig *Adj. s.* **löcherig**
Loch-: ~säge die compass saw; keyhole saw; **~stickerei die** broderie anglaise; **~streifen der** *(Technik, DV)* punch[ed] tape; **~zange die** [ticket] punch; **~ziegel der** *(Bauw.)* perforated brick
Locke ['lɔkə] **die; ~, ~n** curl; **~n haben** have curly hair
¹locken *tr. V.* **a)** lure, *(fig.)* entice **(aus** out of, **in +** *Akk.* into); **die Henne lockte die Küken** the hen called her chicks; **ein Tier aus dem Bau/in den Käfig ~:** lure an animal out of its hole/into its cage; **jmdn. in einen Hinterhalt/auf eine falsche Fährte ~:** lure sb. into an ambush/put sb. on the wrong track; **b)** *(reizen)* tempt; **es lockt mich sehr** I am very tempted; **ein ~des Angebot/Abenteuer** a tempting offer/alluring adventure
²locken 1. *tr. V.* curl; **jmdm. das Haar ~:** curl sb.'s hair; **gelocktes Haar** curly hair. **2.** *refl. V.* ⟨*hair*⟩ curl
löcken ['lœkn̩] *itr. V.* **wider** *od.* **gegen den Stachel ~** *(geh.)* kick against the pricks
Locken-: ~haar das curly hair; **~kopf der a)** curly hair; **b)** *(Mensch)* curly head; **~köpfig** *Adj.* curly haired; **~pracht die** *(scherzh.)* magnificent head of curls; **~wickler der** [hair] curler *or* roller; **sich** *(Dat.)* **~wickler ins Haar drehen** put one's hair in curlers
locker 1. *Adj.* **a)** loose ⟨*tooth, nail, chair-leg, etc.*⟩; **etw. ~ machen** loosen sth.; *s. auch* **Schraube; b)** *(durchlässig, leicht)* loose ⟨*soil, snow, fabric*⟩; light ⟨*mixture, cake*⟩; **c)** *(entspannt)* relaxed ⟨*position, muscles*⟩; slack ⟨*rope, rein*⟩; *(fig.: unverbindlich)* loose ⟨*relationship, connection, etc.*⟩; **das Seil/die Zügel ~ lassen** slacken the rope [off]/slacken the reins; **~ werden** ⟨*person*⟩ loosen up; **d)** *(leichtfertig)* loose ⟨*morals, life*⟩; frivolous ⟨*jokes, remarks*⟩; **sein ~es Mundwerk** *(salopp)* his big mouth *(coll.)*; **ein ~er Vogel** *(ugs.)* a bit of a lad *(coll.)*; *s. auch* **Hand f. 2.** *adv.* **a) ~ sitzen** ⟨*tooth, screw, nail*⟩ be loose; **ein ~ sitzender Zahn** a loose tooth; **bei ihm sitzt das Geld ~ [in der Tasche]** *(fig.)* money burns a hole in his pocket; **b)** *(durchlässig)* loosely; ⟨*bake*⟩ lightly; **c)** *(entspannt, ungezwungen)* loosely; **etw. ganz ~ machen** *(ugs.)* do sth. without any trouble; **sich ~ geben** be relaxed; **~ vom Hocker** *(ugs.)* coolly; **dieses Gesetz wird ~ gehandhabt** this law is not strictly enforced
locker-: ~|lassen *unr. itr. V. (ugs.)* **nicht ~lassen** not give *or* let up; **~|machen** *tr. V. (ugs.)* fork up *or* out *(sl.)*; shell out *(sl.)*; **bei jmdm. etw. ~machen** get sb. to fork up *or* fork out sth.
lockern 1. *tr. V.* **a)** loosen ⟨*screw, tie, collar, etc.*⟩; slacken [off] ⟨*rope, dog-leash, etc.*⟩; *(fig.)* relax ⟨*regulation, law, etc.*⟩; **seinen Griff ~:** loosen *or* relax one's grip; **b)** *(entspannen)* loosen up, relax ⟨*muscles, limbs*⟩; *(fig.)* relax ⟨*attitude*⟩; **c)** *(auf~)* loosen, break up ⟨*soil*⟩. **2.** *refl. V.* **a)** ⟨*brick, tooth, etc.*⟩ work itself loose; **bei mir hat sich ein Zahn gelockert** one of my teeth has worked itself loose; **sein Griff lockerte sich** his grip loosened; **b)** *(entspannen)* ⟨*person*⟩ loosen up; *(vor Spielbeginn)* loosen *or* limber up; *(fig.)* ⟨*tenseness, tension*⟩ ease; **die Sitten haben sich gelockert** *(fig.)* morals have become *or* grown lax
Lockerung die; ~, ~en a) loosening; *(fig.: von Bestimmung, Gesetz usw.)* relaxation; **b)** *(Entspannung)* loosening up; relaxation
Lockerungs·übung die loosening-up *or* limbering-up exercise
lockig *Adj.* curly
Lock-: ~mittel das enticement; **~ruf der** call; **~speise die** *(geh.)* bait; **~spitzel der** *(abwertend)* agent provocateur
Lockung die; ~, ~en *(geh.)* temptation; **die ~ der Ferne** the lure of distant lands; **jmds. ~en** *(Dat.)* **widerstehen** resist sb.'s enticements
Lock·vogel der decoy; *(fig.)* lure; decoy
Loden ['lo:dn̩] **der; ~s, ~:** loden
Loden·mantel der loden coat
lodern *itr. V. (geh., auch fig.)* blaze; **die Flammen loderten zum Himmel** the flames leapt up to the sky; **ihre Augen loderten vor Zorn** *(fig.)* her eyes blazed with anger
Löffel ['lœfl̩] **der; ~s, ~ a)** spoon; *(als Maßangabe)* spoonful; **ein ~ Zucker** a spoonful of sugar; **den ~ abgeben** *(fig. salopp)* kick the bucket *(sl.)*; **mit einem goldenen** *od.* **silbernen ~ im Mund geboren sein** *(fig. ugs.)* be born with a silver spoon in one's mouth; **jmdn. über den ~ barbieren** *od.* **balbieren** *(fig. ugs.)* do *(sl.) or* swindle sb.; **b)** *(Jägerspr.)* ear; *(fig.)* **sperr doch die ~ auf!** *(ugs.)* pin your lugholes *(Brit.) or* ears back! *(coll.)*; **jmdm. eins** *od.* **ein paar hinter die ~ geben** *(ugs.)* give sb. a clout round the ear; **sich** *(Dat.)* **etw. hinter die ~ schreiben** *(ugs.)* get sth. into one's head
Löffel·bagger der mechanical shovel; excavator
löffeln *tr. V.* spoon [up]; **sie löffelte Suppe aus der Terrine** she ladled soup from the tureen
Löffel·stiel der [spoon] handle
löffel·weise *Adv.* by the spoonful
log [lo:k] **1.** *u.* **3.** *Pers. Sg. Prät. v.* **lügen**
Log [lɔk] **das; ~s, ~e** *(Seew.)* log
Logarithmen·tafel die *(Math.)* log[arithmic] table
logarithmieren *(Math.)* **1.** *tr. V.* find the log[arithm] of. **2.** *itr. V.* do logs *or* logarithms
logarithmisch *Adj. (Math.)* logarithmic
Logarithmus [loga'rɪtmʊs] **der; ~, Logarithmen** *(Math.)* logarithm; log
Log·buch das *(Seew.)* log [book]
Loge ['lo:ʒə] **die; ~, ~n a)** *(Theater)* box; **b)** *(Freimaurer~, Pförtner~)* lodge
Logen-: ~bruder der brother mason; **~platz der** *(Theater)* seat in a box; **~schließer der** box attendant
Logger ['lɔgɐ] **der; ~s, ~** *(Seew.)* lugger
Loggia ['lɔdʒia] **die; ~, Loggien a)** *(Balkon)* balcony; **b)** *(Archit.)* loggia
Logier·besuch der *(veralt.)* house-guest/-guests
logieren *(veralt.)* **1.** *itr. V.* stay. **2.** *tr. V. (schweiz.)* **jmdn. bei sich ~:** put sb. up [at one's house/flat *(Brit.) or (Amer.)* apartment *etc.*]
Logier·gast *der (veralt.)* house-guest
Logik ['lo:gɪk] **die; ~:** logic; **in der ~:** in logic
Logiker ['lo:gikɐ] **der; ~s, ~, Logikerin die; ~, ~nen a)** *(Philos.)* logician; **b)** *(logisch Denkende/Denkender)* logical thinker
Logis [lo'ʒi:] **das; ~** [lo'ʒi:(s)], **~** [lo'ʒi:s] **a)** lodgings *pl.*; room/rooms *pl.*; *s. auch* **Kost; b) [***auch:* 'lo:gɪs**]** *(Seemannsspr.)* **das ~ [der Matrosen]** the crew's quarters *pl.*
logisch ['lo:gɪʃ] **1.** *Adj.* logical; **in keinem ~en Zusammenhang stehen** have no logical connection; **[ist doch] ~** *(ugs.)* yes, of course. **2.** *adv.* logically
logischerweise *Adv.* logically; *(selbstverständlich)* naturally
Logistik die; ~ a) *(Math.)* mathematical *or* symbolic logic *no art.*; **b)** *(Milit.)* logistics *sing., no art.*; *(fig.)* logistics *pl.*
Log·leine die *(Seew.)* log line
logo ['lo:go] *Adj. (salopp)* **[ist doch] ~!** you bet! *(coll.)*; of course!
Logopäde [logo'pɛ:də] **der; ~n, ~n** speech therapist
Logopädie [logopɛ'di:] **die; ~:** speech therapy *no art.*
Logopädin die; ~, ~nen speech therapist
¹Lohe ['lo:ə] **die; ~, ~n** *(dichter.: Flamme)* blaze; **die ~n** the raging flames
²Lohe die; ~, ~n tan [bark]
¹lohen *itr. V. (dichter.)* blaze
²lohen *tr. V.* tan ⟨*hides etc.*⟩ [with tanbark]
Loh-: ~gerber der [vegetable] tanner; **~gerberei die a)** *(Betrieb)* [vegetable] tannery; **b)** *(~gerbung)* [vegetable] tanning
Lohn [lo:n] **der; ~[e]s, Löhne** ['lø:nə] **a)** wage[s *pl.*]; pay *no indef. art., no pl.*; **die Löhne drücken/einfrieren** *(ugs.)* lower/freeze wages; **bei jmdm./einer Firma in ~ und Brot stehen** be employed by sb./a firm; work for sb./a firm; **jmdn. um ~ und Brot bringen** deprive sb. of his/her livelihood; **b)** *o. Pl. (Belohnung, auch fig.)* reward; **als** *od.* **zum ~ für ...:** as a reward for ...; **der Verbrecher hat seinen ~ bekommen** *(fig.)* the criminal got his deserts *pl.*
lohn-, Lohn-: ~abbau der reduction in wages; **~abhängig** *Adj.* wage-earning *attrib.*; **~abhängig sein** be a wage-earner; **~abhängige der/die** wage-earner; **~abrechnung die** wage-slip; pay-slip; **~arbeit die** *(Soziol.)* wage-labour; **~aus·fall der** loss of earnings; **~ausgleich der** making-up of wages; **[eine] kürzere Arbeitszeit bei vollem ~ausgleich** shorter working hours with no loss of pay; **~buch·halter der** payroll clerk; **~buch·haltung die a)** *o. Pl.* payroll accounting; **b)** *(Abteilung)* payroll office; **~büro das** payroll office; **~empfänger der** wage-earner
lohnen 1. *refl., itr. V.* be worth it; be worthwhile; **die Anstrengung hat sich gelohnt** it was worth the effort; **das lohnt [sich] nicht** it's not worth it; **es lohnt [sich], den Versuch zu machen** it's worth making the attempt; **das lohnt sich nicht für mich** it's not worth my while; **die Mühe hat [sich] gelohnt** it was worth the trouble *or* effort; **lohnt [sich] das?** is it worth it?; **der Film lohnt sich sehr** the film is well worth seeing. **2.** *tr. V.* **a)** *(rechtfertigen)* be worth; **die Ausstellung lohnt einen Besuch** the exhibition is worth a visit *or* is worth visiting; **das lohnt die Mühe nicht** it is not worth the trouble; **b) jmdm. etw. ~:** reward sb. for sth.; *(vergelten)* repay sb. for sth.; **Gott wird dir deine Hilfe ~** *(geh.)* God will reward you for your help
löhnen *tr., itr. V.* **a)** *(Lohn auszahlen)* pay; **b)** *(salopp: bezahlen)* pay; fork out *or* up *(sl.)*
lohnend *Adj.* rewarding ⟨*task*⟩; worthwhile, rewarding ⟨*occupation*⟩; worthwhile ⟨*aim*⟩; *(einträglich)* financially rewarding; lucrative; **das Studium dieses Buches ist wirklich ~:** this book is really worth studying; it is really worth studying this book; **die Ausstellung ist wirklich ~:** the exhibition is really worth seeing
lohnens·wert *Adj.* worthwhile *attrib.*; worth while *pred.*
lohn-, Lohn-: ~erhöhung die wage *or* pay increase *or (Brit.)* rise; **~forderung die** wage demand *or* claim; **~fort·zahlung die** continued payment of wages; **~gruppe die** wage group; **~intensiv** *Adj. (Wirtsch.)* wage-intensive; **~kampf der** wage dispute; **~kosten** *Pl.* wage costs; **~kürzung die** wage cut *or* reduction; **~liste die** payroll; **~pause die** pay pause; **~pfändung die** garnishment [of wages]; **~politik die** *(Politik, Wirtsch.)* pay policy;

policy on wages; ~-**Preis-Spirale die** wage-price spiral; ~**raub der** *(abwertend)* wage exploitation; ~**runde die** wage *or* pay round; ~**skala die** wage *or* pay scale

Lohn·steuer die income tax

Lohnsteuer-: ~**jahres·ausgleich der** annual adjustment of income tax; ~**karte die** income-tax card

Lohn-: ~**stopp der** wage *or* pay freeze; ~**streifen der** pay-slip; ~**tarif der** wage rate; ~**tüte die** pay-packet *(Brit.);* wage packet

Löhnung die; ~, ~en a) *(Auszahlung)* payment of wages; **b)** *(Lohn)* pay

Lohn-: ~**zettel der** pay-slip; ~**zuwachs der** pay increase

Loipe ['lɔypə] **die; ~, ~n** *(Skisport)* [cross-country] course

Lok [lɔk] **die; ~, ~s** engine; locomotive

lokal [lo'ka:l] **1.** *Adj.* **a)** *(örtlich)* local; **Lokales** *(Zeitungsw.)* local news *sing.;* **b)** *(Gram.)* of place *postpos.* **2.** *adv.* **jmdn. ~ betäuben** give sb. a local anaesthetic

Lokal das; ~s, ~e pub *(Brit. coll.);* bar *(Amer.); (Speise~)* restaurant

Lokal-: ~**anästhesie die** *(Med.)* local anaesthesia; ~**augen·schein der** *(österr.) s.* **Lokaltermin;** ~**blatt das** *(Zeitungsw.)* local paper

lokalisieren *tr. V.* locate; *(eingrenzen, Med.)* localize; limit, contain ⟨*fire*⟩

Lokalisierung die; ~, ~en location; *(Eingrenzung, Med.)* localization

Lokalität [lokali'tɛ:t] **die; ~, ~en** locality; **die ~en kennen** know the locality *or* district *or* area; **wo sind hier die ~en?** *(verhüll.)* where is the cloakroom? *(Brit. euphem.);* where's the rest-room? *(esp. Amer. euphem.)*

Lokal-: ~**kolorit das** local colour; ~**matador der** *(bes. Sport)* local hero *or* favourite; ~**patriotismus der** local patriotism; ~**politik die** local politics *sing., no art.;* ~**politiker der** local politician; ~**presse die** local press; ~**redakteur der** *(Zeitungsw.)* local-news editor; editor of the local[-news] section; ~**redaktion die** *(Rundf., Ferns., Zeitungsw.)* local-news section; ~**runde die** round for everyone [in the pub *(Brit. coll.) or (Amer.)* bar]; **eine ~runde ausgeben** *od. (salopp)* **schmeißen** buy a round *or* drink for everyone in the pub *(Brit. coll.) or (Amer.)* bar; ~**seite die** *(Zeitungsw.)* local page; ~**teil der** *(Zeitungsw.)* local section; ~**termin der** *(Rechtsspr.)* visit to the scene [of the crime]; ~**verbot das: [in einer Gaststätte] ~verbot haben/bekommen** be/get banned [from a pub *(Brit. coll.) or (Amer.)* bar]; **jmdm. ~verbot erteilen** ban sb. [from the/a pub *(Brit. coll.) or (Amer.)* bar]; ~**zeitung die** local [news]paper

Lok·führer der *s.* **Lokomotivführer**

Lokomotive [lokomo'ti:və] **die; ~, ~n** locomotive; [railway] engine

Lokomotiv·führer der engine-driver *(Brit.);* engineer *(Amer.)*

Lokus ['lo:kʊs] **der; ~** *od.* **~ses, ~** *od.* **~se** *(salopp)* loo *(Brit. coll.);* john *(Amer. coll.)*

Lokus·papier das *(salopp)* loo paper *(Brit. coll.);* toilet paper

Lombardei [lɔmbar'dai] **die; ~:** Lombardy

lombardisch *Adj.* Lombardic

Lombard·satz der *(Bankw.)* Lombard rate

London ['lɔndɔn] **(das); ~s** London

Londoner 1. *indekl. Adj.; nicht präd.* London. **2. der; ~s, ~:** Londoner; *s. auch* **Kölner**

Long·drink ['lɔŋdrɪŋk] **der** long drink

Longe ['lõ:ʒə] **die; ~, ~n a)** *(Reiten)* lunge; **b)** *(Turnen, Schwimmen)* harness

Look [lʊk] **der; ~s, ~s** look

Looping ['lu:pɪŋ] **der; ~s, ~s** *(Fliegerspr.)* loop; **einen ~ drehen** loop the loop

Lorbeer ['lɔrbe:ɐ̯] **der; ~s, ~en a)** *(Baum)* laurel; **b)** *(Gewürz)* bay-leaf; **c)** *(~kranz)* laurel wreath; **mit etw. keine ~en ernten können** *(fig.)* get no credit for sth.; **[sich] auf seinen ~en ausruhen** *(fig. ugs.)* rest on one's laurels

Lorbeer-: ~**baum der** laurel[-tree]; ~**blatt das** bay-leaf; ~**kranz der** laurel wreath

Lord [lɔrt] **der; ~s, ~s** lord

Lord·kanzler der Lord Chancellor

Lordschaft die: Eure ~: Your Lordship

Lord·siegel·bewahrer der; ~s, ~: Lord Privy Seal

Lore ['lo:rə] **die; ~, ~n** car; *(kleiner)* tub

Lorenz ['lo:rɛnts] **(der)** Lawrence; Laurence

Lorgnette [lɔrn'jɛtə] **die; ~, ~n** lorgnette

Lorgnon [lɔen'jõ:] **das; ~s, ~s** lorgnon

los [lo:s] **1.** *Adj.; nicht attr.* **a)** *(abgetrennt)* **der Knopf ist ~:** the button has come off; **der Hund ist [von der Leine] ~:** the dog is off the leash; **jmdn./etw. ~ sein** *(befreit sein von)* be rid *or (coll.)* shot of sb./sth.; *(verloren haben)* have lost sth.; **einer Sache** *(Gen.)* **~ und ledig sein** *(geh.)* be totally free *or* well and truly rid of sth.; **b) es ist etwas ~:** something is *or* there is something going on; **hier ist viel/wenig/immer etw. ~:** there is a lot/not much/always sth. going on here; **was ist hier ~?** *(was geschieht?)* what's going on here?; *(was ist nicht in Ordnung?)* what's the matter here?; what's up here? *(coll.);* **mit jmdm./etw. ist nichts/nicht viel ~** *(ugs.)* sb./sth. isn't up to much *(coll.);* **was ist denn mit dir ~?** what's up *or* wrong *or* the matter with you? **2.** *Adv.* **a)** come on!; *(geh schon!)* go on!; **auf die Plätze** *od.* **Achtung, fertig, ~!** on your marks, get set, go; **~ doch!** go on!; **nun aber ~!** [come on,] let's get moving *or* going!; **nichts wie ~!** *(ugs.)* let's scarper *(Brit. sl.);* let's beat it *(sl.);* **b)** *(ugs.: ~gehen, ~fahren usw.);* **er ist mit dem Wagen ~:** he's gone off in the car; *s. auch* **losmüssen; lossollen; loswollen; c)** *(ugs.: gelöst)* **ich habe die Schraube/das Brett/das Rad ~:** I have got the screw out/the board/wheel off; *s. auch* **loshaben; loskriegen** *usw.*

Los das; ~es, ~e a) lot; **etw. durch [das] ~ entscheiden** decide sth. by drawing lots; **das ~ soll entscheiden** it shall be decided by drawing lots; **das ~ hat mich getroffen** it has fallen to my lot; **b)** *(Lotterie~)* ticket; **ein halbes/ganzes ~:** a half ticket/full ticket; **das Große ~:** [the] first prize; **mit jmdm./etw. das Große ~ ziehen** *(fig.)* hit the jackpot with sb./sth.; **c)** *(geh.: Schicksal)* lot; **ihm war ein schweres ~ beschieden** his was a hard lot; **d)** *(Wirtsch.: Maßeinheit)* batch; lot; *(bei Versteigerungen)* lot; **e)** *(Bau~)* section

-los *Adj.* -less

los|ballern *itr. V. (salopp)* start blazing away

lösbar *Adj.* **a)** soluble, solvable ⟨*problem, equation, etc.*⟩; **b)** *(löslich)* soluble ⟨*substance, gas*⟩

los-: ~**|bekommen** *unr. tr. V.* get ⟨*string, tape, ribbon, etc.*⟩ off; get ⟨*screw, nail, etc.*⟩ out; **die Hände ~bekommen** get one's hands free; ~**|binden** *unr. tr. V.* untie; ~**|brechen 1.** *unr. itr. V.; mit sein* **a)** *(beginnen)* ⟨*storm*⟩ break; ⟨*cheering, laughter, etc.*⟩ break out; **b)** *(abbrechen)* break off. **2.** *unr. tr. V.* break off

Lösch-: ~**arbeit die** fire-fighting operations *pl.;* **wir halfen bei den ~arbeiten** we helped to fight *or* to put out the fire; ~**blatt das** piece of blotting-paper; ~**boot das** fire-boat; ~**eimer der** fire-bucket

[1]löschen ['lœʃn̩] *tr. V.* **a)** *(aus~)* put out, extinguish ⟨*fire, candle, flames, etc.*⟩; **seinen Durst ~** *(fig.)* quench one's thirst; **b)** *(tilgen)* close ⟨*bank account*⟩; delete, strike out ⟨*entry*⟩; extinguish, wipe out, pay off ⟨*debt*⟩; erase, wipe out ⟨*recording, memory, etc.*⟩; **die Schrift auf der Tafel ~:** clean *or (Amer.)* erase the blackboard; **im Register gelöscht werden** ⟨*firm, name, etc.*⟩ be removed from the register; **c)** *(geh.: ausschalten)* switch off, turn off *or* out ⟨*light, lamp*⟩; **d)** *(trocknen)* blot ⟨*ink etc.*⟩; **e)** *(vermischen)* slake ⟨*lime*⟩

[2]löschen *tr. V. (Seemannsspr.)* unload

Löscher der; ~s, ~ a) *(Tinten~)* blotter; **b)** *(Feuer~)* [fire] extinguisher

Lösch-: ~**fahrzeug das** fire-engine; ~**kalk der** slaked lime; ~**kopf der** *(Elektronik)* erase head; ~**mannschaft die** fire-fighting team; ~**papier das** blotting paper; ~**taste die** erase button; ~**trupp der** *s.* **~mannschaft**

[1]Löschung die; ~, ~en *(eines Kontos)* closing; *(einer Eintragung)* deletion; striking out; *(einer Schuld)* extinguishing; wiping out; paying off

[2]Löschung *(Seemannsspr.)* **die; ~:** unloading

Lösch·zug der set of fire-fighting appliances

los|donnern *(ugs.)* **1.** *itr. V.; mit sein* roar off. **2.** *tr. V.* **„...", donnerte er los** '...', he bellowed

lose 1. *Adj.* **a)** *(nicht fest, auch fig.)* loose; **zwischen ihnen besteht nur eine ~ Bekanntschaft** *(fig.)* they are not closely acquainted; **b)** *(nicht verpackt)* loose ⟨*sugar, cigarettes, sweets, sheets of paper, nails, etc.*⟩; unbottled ⟨*drink*⟩; **etw. ~ verkaufen** sell sth. loose/unbottled; **c)** *(locker)* loose[-fitting] ⟨*clothes*⟩; **d)** *(ugs.: leichtfertig)* **ein ~s Mädchen** *(veralt.)* a loose woman; **er ist ein ~er Vogel** he is a bit of a lad; **e)** *(ugs.: vorlaut, frech)* cheeky; impudent; **einen ~n Mund haben** be a cheeky *or* impudent so-and-so *(coll.);* **~e Reden führen** be cheeky; **f)** *(geh.: aufgelockert)* loose ⟨*group, line, etc.*⟩. **2.** *adv.* **a)** *(nicht fest, auch fig.)* loosely; **~ herunterhängen** hang down loosely *or* loose; **b)** *(locker)* ⟨*hang, drape, etc.*⟩ loosely

Loseblatt·sammlung die: als ~ *od.* **in Form einer ~ herauskommen** be published in loose-leaf form

Löse·geld das ransom; **1 Million Pfund ~:** a ransom of one million pounds; **das ~ wurde in einer Telefonzelle hinterlegt** the ransom money was left in a telephone kiosk

los|eisen *tr. V. (ugs.)* **jmdn./etw. von jmdm./etw. ~:** prise *or* get sb./sth. away from sb./sth.; **sich von jmdm./etw. ~:** get away from sb./sth.; **etw. bei jmdm. ~:** get sth. out of sb.

losen *itr. V.* draws lots **(um** for); **~, wer anfangen soll** draw lots to decide who will start

lösen ['lø:zn̩] **1.** *tr. V.* **a)** remove, take *or* get off ⟨*stamp, wallpaper*⟩; **etw. von etw. ~:** remove sth. from sth.; **das Fleisch von den Knochen ~:** take the meat off the bones; **den Blick von etw. nicht ~ können** *(fig.)* not be able to take one's eyes off sth.; **b)** *(lockern)* take *or* let ⟨*handbrake*⟩ off; release ⟨*handbrake*⟩; undo ⟨*screw, belt, tie*⟩; let ⟨*hair*⟩ down; remove, untie ⟨*string, rope, knot, bonds*⟩; loosen ⟨*phlegm*⟩; ease ⟨*cramp*⟩; *(fig.)* ease, relieve ⟨*[mental] pain, tension, etc.*⟩; remove ⟨*inhibitions*⟩; **jmds. Zunge ~** *(fig.)* loosen sb.'s tongue; **c)** *(klären)* solve ⟨*problem, puzzle, equation, etc.*⟩; resolve ⟨*contradiction, conflict*⟩; solve, resolve ⟨*difficulty*⟩; **d)** *(annullieren)* break off ⟨*engagement*⟩; cancel ⟨*contract*⟩; sever ⟨*connection, relationship*⟩; **sein Arbeitsverhältnis ~:** terminate one's employment *(formal);* **e)** *(zergehen lassen)* **etw. in etw.** *(Dat.)* **~:** dissolve sth. in sth.; **f)** *(kaufen)* buy; obtain ⟨*ticket*⟩. **2.** *refl. V.* **a)** *(lose werden)* come off; ⟨*avalanche*⟩ start; **sich von etw. ~:** come off sth.; **b)** *(sich trennen)* **sich aus etw. ~:** free oneself from sth.; **das Flugzeug löste sich vom Boden** the plane left the ground; **ein Läufer hat sich vom Feld gelöst** a runner broke away from the field; **sich von seinem**

Elternhaus ~ *(fig.)* break away from one's parental home; **sich aus einer Verpflichtung ~:** free *or* rid oneself of an obligation; **c)** *(sich lockern)* ⟨*wallpaper, plaster*⟩ come off *or* away; ⟨*packing, screw*⟩ come loose *or* undone; ⟨*paint, book-cover*⟩ come off; ⟨*phlegm, cough*⟩ get looser; ⟨*cramp*⟩ ease; ⟨*muscle*⟩ loosen up; **d)** *(sich klären, entwirren)* ⟨*puzzle, problem*⟩ be solved; **sich von selbst ~** ⟨*problem*⟩ solve *or* resolve itself; **e)** *(zergehen)* **sich in etw.** *(Dat.)* **~:** dissolve in sth.; **f) aus seiner Pistole löste sich ein Schuß** *(geh.)* his pistol went off

Los·entscheid der: durch ~: by drawing lots; *(bei einem Preisausschreiben)* by [making *or* having] a draw

los-: ~|fahren *unr. itr. V.; mit sein* **a)** *(starten)* set off; *(wegfahren)* move off; **b)** *(zufahren)* **auf jmdn./etw. ~fahren** drive/ride towards sb./sth.; **direkt auf jmdn./etw. ~fahren** drive/ride straight at sb./sth.; **~|gehen** *unr. itr. V.; mit sein* **a)** *(aufbrechen)* set off; **auf ein Ziel ~gehen** *(fig.)* go straight for a goal; **~ geht's!** let's be off; **b)** *(ugs.: beginnen)* start; **es geht ~:** it's starting; *(fangen wir an)* let's go; **~ geht's!** let's get started; **gleich geht es wieder ~ mit dem Lärm** the noise will soon start up again; **ich glaube, es geht ~!** *(salopp)* you/he, *etc.* must be kidding *(coll.)*; **c)** *(ugs.: abgehen)* ⟨*button, handle, etc.*⟩ come off; **d)** *(angreifen)* **auf jmdn. ~gehen** go for sb.; **e)** *(abgefeuert werden)* ⟨*gun, mine, firework, etc.*⟩ go off; **~|haben** *unr. tr. V. (ugs.)* **in seinem Beruf hat er was ~:** he's very good at his job; **~|heulen** *itr. V. (ugs.)* burst out crying; burst into tears; **~|kaufen** *tr. V.* **jmdn. ~kaufen** buy sb.'s freedom *or* release; **~|kommen** *unr. itr. V.; mit sein (ugs.)* **a)** *(fortkommen)* get away; **b)** *(freikommen)* get free; free oneself; *(freigelassen werden)* be freed; **von jmdm./etw. ~kommen** *(fig.)* get away from sb./get rid of sth.; **vom Alkohol ~kommen** *(fig.)* get off *or* give up alcohol; **er kam von dem Gedanken nicht ~:** he couldn't get the thought out of his mind; **~|kriegen** *tr. V. (ugs.)* **a)** *(lösen können)* get ⟨*screw, nail, etc.*⟩ out; get ⟨*lid*⟩ off; **b)** *(loswerden)* get rid *or* *(sl.)* shot of; **c)** *(verkaufen können)* get rid of; **~|lachen** *itr. V.* burst out laughing; **~|lassen** *unr. tr. V.* **a)** *(nicht festhalten)* let go of; **der Gedanke/das Bild ließ sie nicht mehr ~** *(fig.)* she could not get the thought/image out of her mind; **b)** *(freilassen)* let ⟨*person, animal*⟩ go; **c)** *(ugs. abwertend: hetzen)* **jmdn. auf jmdn./etw. ~lassen** let sb. loose on sb./sth.; **d)** *(ugs.: äußern)* come out with ⟨*remark, joke, etc.*⟩; let out ⟨*curse*⟩; **e)** *(abschicken)* send off ⟨*letter, telegram, etc.*⟩; **~|laufen** *unr. itr. V.; mit sein (weglaufen)* run off; *(anfangen zu laufen)* start running; **lauf schnell los und hol Brot** run out and get some bread; **~|legen** *itr. V. (ugs.)* **a)** *(sich stürmisch äußern)* let rip; **mit Fragen ~legen** start firing questions; **wenn er ~legt** *(zu reden anfängt)* when *or* once he gets going *or* started; **b)** *(anfangen)* get going *or* started; **mit der Arbeit ~legen** get down to work

löslich *Adj.* soluble; **leicht/schwer ~:** readily/not readily *or* only slightly soluble

Löslichkeit die; ~: solubility

los-: ~|lösen 1. *tr. V.* remove; take off; **2.** *refl. V.* ⟨*wallpaper*⟩ come off; ⟨*trailer*⟩ become uncoupled *or* detached; **~|machen 1.** *tr. V. (ugs.)* let ⟨*animal*⟩ loose; untie, undo ⟨*string, line, rope*⟩; take out ⟨*plank*⟩; unhitch ⟨*trailer*⟩; **das Boot ~machen** cast off; **2.** *refl. V. (ugs.: sich befreien, auch fig.)* free oneself **(von** from); **3.** *itr. V.* **a)** *(Seemannsspr.: ablegen)* cast off; **b)** *(ugs.: sich beeilen)* get a move on *(coll.)*; **nun mach ~, daß du fertig wirst** hurry up and get ready; **~|müssen** *unr. itr. V. (ugs.)* have to be off; have to go; **ich muß ~:** I must be off

Los·nummer die [lottery] ticket number

los-: ~|platzen *itr. V.; mit sein (ugs.)* **a)** burst out; **sofort platzte sie damit ~:** she blurted it out immediately; **b)** *(plötzlich lachen)* burst out laughing; **~|rasen** *itr. V.; mit sein* race *or* tear off; **auf etw.** *(Akk.)* **~rasen** race towards sth.; **~|reißen 1.** *unr. tr. V.* tear off; *(schneller, gewaltsamer)* rip off; pull ⟨*plank*⟩ off; ⟨*wind*⟩ rip ⟨*tile*⟩ off; **er konnte seine Augen nicht von der Statue ~reißen** *(fig.)* he couldn't take his eyes off the statue; **2.** *unr. refl. V.* break free *or* loose; **sich von etw.** *(Dat.)* **~reißen** break free *or* loose from sth.; *(fig.)* tear oneself away from sth.

Löß [lœs] **der; Lösses, Lösse** *(Geol.)* loess

los-, Los-: ~|sagen *refl. V.* **sich von jmdm./etw. ~sagen** renounce sb./sth.; break with sb./sth.; **~sagung die; ~, ~en** renunciation **(von** of); break **(von** with)

Löß·boden der loess soil; loessial soil

los-: ~|schicken *tr. V. (ugs.)* send off ⟨*letter, telegram, etc.*⟩; **jmdn. ~schicken, um etw. zu holen** send sb. out to get sth.; **~|schießen** *unr. itr. V. (ugs.)* **a)** start shooting; **b)** *mit sein (sich schnell bewegen)* shoot *or* race off; **auf jmdn./etw. ~schießen** race towards sb./sth.; *(direkt)* race up to sb./sth.; **~|schlagen 1.** *unr. tr. V.* **a)** *(abschlagen)* knock off; knock ⟨*board, plank*⟩ out; **den Verputz von der Wand ~schlagen** knock the rendering off the wall; **b)** *(ugs.: verkaufen)* get rid of; flog *(Brit. sl.)*; **2.** *unr. itr. V.* **a)** *(einschlagen)* **auf jmdn. ~schlagen** let fly at sb.; **b)** *(bes. Milit.)* attack; launch one's attack; **~|schnallen** *tr. V.* unfasten; **~|sollen** *unr. itr. V.* **wann sollen wir ~?** what time should we be off?; **~|sprechen** *unr. tr. V. (bes. Rel.)* absolve **(von** from); **jmdn. von aller Schuld ~sprechen** absolve sb. of all guilt; **~|steuern** *itr. V.; mit sein* **auf etw.** *(Akk.)* **~steuern** head *or* make for sth.; **auf ein Ziel ~steuern** *(fig.)* aim for a goal; **~|tigern** *itr. V.; mit sein (ugs.)* march off; **~|trennen** *tr. V.* undo; unpick ⟨*seam, hem*⟩

Los·trommel die [lottery] drum

¹Losung die; ~, ~en a) *(Wahlspruch)* slogan; **b)** *(Milit.: Kennwort)* password; **die ~ nennen** give the password

²Losung die; ~, ~en *(Jägerspr.)* droppings *pl.*

Lösung die; ~, ~en a) *(Bewältigung)* solution *(Gen.* to); *(eines Konflikts, Widerspruchs)* resolution; *(einer Aufgabe, eines Problems, usw.)* solution *(Gen.,* **für** to); **des Rätsels ~:** the answer to the mystery; **das also ist des Rätsels ~:** so 'that's it *or* the answer; **b)** *(Annullierung) (einer Verlobung)* breaking off; *(eines Vertrags)* cancellation; *(einer Verbindung, eines Verhältnisses)* severing; *(eines Arbeitsverhältnisses)* termination; **c)** *(Physik, Chemie) (Flüssigkeit)* solution; *(das Auflösen)* dissolution; dissolving

Lösungs-: ~mittel das *(Physik, Chemie)* solvent; **~vorschlag der** proposed solution **(für** to); **ich hätte einen ~vorschlag für euer Problem** I think I might have a solution to your problem; I've got a suggestion as to how you might solve your problem

Losungs·wort das password

Los·verkäufer der [lottery-]ticket seller

los-: ~|werden *unr. tr. V.; mit sein* **a)** *(sich befreien können von)* get rid of; **ich werde den Gedanken/Verdacht nicht ~, daß ...:** I can't get the thought/suspicion/impression out of my mind that ...; **b)** *(ugs.: aussprechen, mitteilen)* tell; **er wollte etwas ~werden** he wanted to tell me/us *etc.* something; **... konnte ich endlich meine Frage ~werden:** ... I finally got the chance to put my question; **c)** *(ugs.: verkaufen)* get rid of; flog *(Brit. sl.)*; **d)** *(ugs.: verlieren)* lose; **~|wollen** *unr. itr. V. (ugs.)* want to be off; **~|ziehen** *unr. itr. V.; mit sein (ugs.)* **a)** *(losgehen)* set off; **b)** *(abwertend: herziehen)* **über jmdn. ~ziehen** pull sb. to pieces

Los·ziehung die draw

Lot [lo:t] **das; ~[e]s, ~e a)** *(Bauw.)* plumb[-bob]; **b)** *(Bauw.: Senkrechte) o. Pl.* **im ~ stehen** be plumb; **nicht im ~ sein, außer ~ sein** be out of plumb; **nicht im ~ sein** *(fig.)* not be straightened *or* sorted out; **[wieder] ins ~ kommen** *(fig.)* be all right [again]; **c)** *(Seew.)* sounding-line; lead-line; **d)** *(Geom.)* perpendicular; **das ~ fällen** drop a perpendicular; **e)** *(veralt.: Maßeinheit) measure varying between 15.5 g and 16.6 g*

loten *tr. V.* **a)** *(Bauw.)* plumb; **b)** *(Seew.)* sound; take soundings of; plumb

löten ['lø:tn̩] *tr. V. (Technik)* solder

Lothringen ['lo:trɪŋən] **(das); ~s** Lorraine

¹Lothringer *indekl. Adj.; nicht präd.* Lorraine *attrib.*; **das ~ Kreuz** the Cross of Lorraine

²Lothringer der; ~s, ~, Lothringerin die; ~, ~nen Lorrainer

lothringisch *Adj.* Lorraine *attrib.*; Lorrainese

Lotion [lo'tsio:n] **die; ~, ~en** *od.* **~s** lotion

Löt-: ~kolben der soldering-iron; **~lampe die** blowlamp

Lot·leine die *(Seew.)* sounding-line; lead-line

Löt·mittel das [soldering] flux

Lotos ['lo:tɔs] **der; ~, ~:** lotus

Lotos-: ~blume die lotus-flower; **~sitz der** *o. Pl. (Joga)* lotus position

lot·recht 1. *Adj.* perpendicular; vertical. **2.** *adv.* perpendicularly; vertically

Lot·rechte die perpendicular; vertical; **in der ~ stehen** be perpendicular *or* vertical

Lotse ['lo:tsə] **der; ~n, ~n** *(Seew.)* pilot; *(fig.)* guide; **ich mache den ~n** *(fig.)* I'll guide you; I'll show you the way

lotsen *tr. V.* **a)** *(Seew.)* pilot; *(Flugw.)* guide; **b)** *(leiten)* guide; **c)** *(ugs.: führen, leiten)* drag

Lotsen-: ~boot das pilot boat; **~dienst der a)** pilot service; **b)** *(Verkehrsw.)* driver-guide service; **~zwang der** *o. Pl.* compulsory pilotage *no art.*

Löt·stelle die soldered joint

Lotterie [lɔtə'ri:] **die; ~, ~n** lottery; **[in der] ~ spielen** take part in *or* do the lottery

Lotterie-: ~einnehmer der; ~s, ~: lottery-ticket seller; **~gewinn der** win in the lottery; *(gewonnenes Geld)* lottery winnings *pl.*; **~los das** lottery-ticket; **~spiel das** *(auch fig.)* lottery

lotterig ['lɔtərɪç] *Adj. (ugs. abwertend)* slovenly, sloppy ⟨*work*⟩; scruffy ⟨*appearance, house, clothes, etc.*⟩

Lotter·leben das *o. Pl. (abwertend)* dissolute life

Lotter·wirtschaft die *o. Pl. (abwertend)* [slovenly] mess *or* muddle; shambles *(coll.)*

Lotto ['lɔto] **das; ~s, ~s a)** national lottery; **4 Richtige im ~ haben** have four correct numbers in the national lottery; **~ spielen** do the [national] lottery; **b)** *(Gesellschaftsspiel)* lotto

Lotto-: ~annahme·stelle die acceptance point for national-lottery coupons; *(Stand)* national-lottery kiosk; **~gewinn der** win in the national lottery; *(gewonnenes Geld)* winnings *pl.* in the national lottery; **~schein der** national-lottery coupon; **~zahlen** *Pl.* winning national-lottery numbers

Lotung die; ~, ~en a) *(Bauw.)* plumbing; **b)** *(Seew.)* sounding; plumbing; **die ~ der Wassertiefe** sounding *or* plumbing the depth of the water

Lotus ['lo:tʊs] **der; ~, ~** lotus

Löt·zinn der [tin-lead] solder

Louis ['lu:i] **der; ~** ['lu:i(:s)], **~** ['lu:i:s] *(ugs.)* pimp

Louisdor [lu̯i'do:ɐ̯] der; ~s, ~e louis-d'or
Löwe ['lø:və] der; ~n, ~n a) lion; b) *(Astrol.)* Leo; the Lion; *s. auch* Fisch
Löwen-: ~an·teil der lion's share; sich den ~anteil [von etw. *(Dat.)*] sichern get the lion's share [of sth.]; ~bändiger der; ~s, ~: *(veralt.)* lion-tamer; ~jagd die lion-hunting; *(Veranstaltung)* lion-hunt; ~mähne die a) lion's mane; b) *(ugs.: fülliges Haar)* [flowing] mane; ~maul, ~mäulchen das *o. Pl. (Bot.)* snapdragon; antirrhinum; ~mut der courage of a lion; ~zahn der; *o. Pl. (Bot.)* dandelion; *(Herbstlöwenzahn)* hawkbit
Löwin ['lø:vɪn] die; ~, ~nen lioness
loyal [lo̩a'ja:l] 1. *Adj.* loyal (gegenüber to). 2. *adv.* loyally; einen Vertrag ~ erfüllen/einhalten faithfully fulfil/keep to an agreement
Loyalität [lo̩ajali'tɛ:t] die; ~: loyalty (gegenüber to)
LP [ɛl'pe:] die; ~, ~[s] *Abk.* Langspielplatte LP
LPG [ɛlpe:'ge:] die; ~, ~[s] *Abk. (DDR)* Landwirtschaftliche Produktionsgenossenschaft; *s.* Produktionsgenossenschaft
LSD [ɛllɛs'de:] das; ~[s] LSD
lt. *Abk.* [2]laut
Luchs [lʊks] der; ~es, ~e *(auch ~fell)* lynx; wie ein ~ aufpassen watch like a hawk
Luchs·auge das *(fig.)* eagle eye; den ~augen meiner Wirtin entgeht nichts my lynx-eyed landlady misses nothing
Lücke ['lʏkə] die; ~, ~n a) gap; *(Park~, auf einem Formular, in einem Text)* space; eine ~ füllen/schließen fill/close a gap; b) *(Mangel)* gap; *(in der Versorgung)* break; *(im Gesetz)* loophole
Lücken·büßer der *(ugs.)* stopgap; den ~ spielen act as a stopgap
lückenhaft 1. *Adj.* ⟨teeth⟩ full of gaps; gappy ⟨*teeth*⟩; sketchy ⟨*knowledge*⟩; sketchy, vague ⟨*memory*⟩; incomplete, sketchy ⟨*report, account, etc.*⟩; incomplete ⟨*statement*⟩; ⟨*alibi*⟩ full of holes; sein Wissen/seine Erinnerung ist ~: there are gaps in his knowledge/memory. 2. *adv.* ⟨*remember*⟩ vaguely, sketchily; einen Fragebogen [sehr] ~ ausfüllen fill in a questionnaire leaving [many] gaps
Lückenhaftigkeit die; ~ *(von Wissen, Kenntnissen)* sketchiness; *(eines Berichts)* incompleteness; sketchiness
lücken-, Lücken-: ~los 1. *Adj.* unbroken ⟨*line, row, etc.*⟩; complete ⟨*account, report, curriculum vitae*⟩; solid, cast-iron ⟨*alibi*⟩; comprehensive, perfect ⟨*knowledge*⟩; sie hat ein strahlend weißes, ~loses Gebiß she has gleaming white teeth without any gaps; eine ~lose Beweiskette a solid chain of evidence. 2. *adv.* without any gaps; ein ~los nachgewiesenes Alibi a cast-iron alibi; ~losigkeit die *(einer Darstellung)* completeness; *(eines Alibis)* solidness
lud [lu:t] *1. u. 3. Pers. Sg. Prät. v.* laden
Lude ['lu:də] der; ~n, ~n *(salopp)* pimp; ponce
Luder das; ~s, ~ *(salopp)* so-and-so *(coll.)*; ein armes/freches ~: a poor/cheeky so-and-so *(coll.)*
Luft [lʊft] die; ~, Lüfte ['lʏftə] a) *o. Pl.* air; an die frische ~ gehen/in der frischen ~ sein get out in[to]/be out in the fresh air; jmdn. an die [frische] ~ setzen *od.* befördern *(ugs.) (hinauswerfen)* show sb. the door; *(entlassen)* give sb. the sack *(coll.) or (sl.)* push; etw. mit ~ kühlen air-cool sth.; die ~ anhalten hold one's breath; halt die ~ an! *(ugs.) (hör auf zu reden!)* pipe down *(coll.)*; put a sock in it *(Brit. sl.)*; *(übertreib nicht so!)* come off it! *(coll.)*; tief ~ holen take a deep breath; ~ schnappen *(ugs.)* get some fresh air; nach ~ schnappen *(fig. ugs.)* struggle to keep one's head above water *(fig.)*; er kriegte keine/kaum ~: he couldn't breathe/could hardly breathe; die ~ ist rein *(fig.)* the coast is clear; hier/im Büro ist dicke ~ *(fig. ugs.)* there's a bad atmosphere here/in the office *(fig.)*; aus der Sache ist die ~ raus *(fig. ugs.)* it's/the whole thing has gone flat; sich in ~ auflösen *(ugs.)* vanish into thin air; ⟨*plans*⟩ go up in smoke *(fig.)*; er ist ~ für mich *(ugs.)* I ignore him completely; jmdn. wie ~ behandeln *(ugs.)* treat sb. as if he/she didn't exist; die ~ aus jmds. Glas lassen *(ugs. scherzh.)* fill sb. up; da bleibt einem die ~ weg *(ugs.)* it takes your breath away; ihm/der Firma geht die ~ aus *(fig. ugs.)* he's/the firm's going broke *(coll.)*; von ~ und Liebe kann man nicht leben *(ugs.)* you can't live on nothing at all; b) *(Himmelsraum)* air; Aufnahmen aus der ~ machen take pictures from the air; in die ~ ragen soar *or* rise up into the sky; sich in die Lüfte schwingen *(geh.)* soar into the air; etw. in die ~ sprengen *od.* jagen *(ugs.)* blow sth. up; aus der ~ gegriffen sein *(fig.)* ⟨*story, accusation, etc.*⟩ be pure invention; in der ~ liegen *(fig.)* ⟨*crisis, ideas, etc.*⟩ be in the air; in der ~ hängen *od.* schweben *(fig. ugs.)* ⟨*plans, etc.*⟩ be up in the air; ⟨*person*⟩ be left dangling *(fig.)*; in die ~ gehen *(fig. ugs.)* blow one's top *(coll.)*; etw. in der ~ zerreißen *(fig. ugs.)* tear sth. to pieces; ich könnte ihn in der ~ zerreißen *(ugs.)* I could murder him *(coll.)*; c) *o. Pl. (fig.: Spielraum)* space; room; ~ schaffen *od.* machen create *or* make space *or* room; sich *(Dat.)* ~ [ver]schaffen take the pressure off oneself; deine 300 Mark haben mir erst mal ~ verschafft your 300 marks have given me a breathing space; in den Preisen ist noch ~ [drin] *(ugs.)* there's some leeway in the prices; sich *(Dat.) od.* seinem Herzen ~ machen get it off one's chest *(coll.)*; ich hatte eine solche Wut, ich mußte mir einmal ~ machen I was so angry I had to give vent to my feelings; seinem Zorn/Ärger *usw.* ~ machen *(ugs.)* give vent to one's anger; d) *(Brise)* breeze; sich *(Dat.)* ~ zufächeln fan oneself
Luft-: ~abwehr die *(Milit.)* air defence; anti-aircraft defence; ~akrobat der trapeze artist; ~an·griff der *(Milit.)* air raid; ~armee die *(DDR)* air force unit; ~auf·klärung die *(Milit.)* air reconnaissance; aerial reconnaissance; ~aufnahme die aerial photograph; ~ballon der balloon; ~befeuchter der humidifier; ~betankung die in-flight refuelling; ~bild das aerial photograph; ~blase die air bubble; ~-Boden-Rakete die air-to-ground missile; ~brücke die airlift
Lüftchen ['lʏftçən] das; ~s, ~: breeze; kein ~ regte sich there was not the slightest breath of wind
luft-, Luft-: ~dicht *Adj.* airtight; etw. ~ abpacken/abschließen pack sth. in an airtight container/put an airtight seal around sth.; ~dichte die *(Physik., Met.)* air density; ~druck der a) *(Physik)* air pressure; atmospheric pressure; b) *(Druckwelle)* blast; ~druck·messer der barometer; ~durchlässig *Adj.* pervious *or* permeable to air *postpos.*; well-ventilated ⟨*shoes*⟩; ~durchlässigkeit die perviousness *or* permeability to air
lüften 1. *tr. V.* a) air; *(ständig; mit Klimaanlage usw.)* ventilate; das Lüften airing/ventilation; b) *(aus~)* air ⟨*clothes, bed. etc.*⟩; c) *(hochheben)* raise, lift ⟨*hat, lid, veil, etc.*⟩; d) *(enthüllen)* reveal; disclose ⟨*secret*⟩; jmds. Inkognito ~: reveal sb.'s identity. 2. *itr. V.* air the room/house/flat *(Brit.) or (Amer.)* apartment *etc.*; wir müssen hier mal ~: we must let some [fresh] air in here
Lüfter der; ~s, ~: fan
Luft·fahrt die; *o. Pl.* aeronautics *sing.*, *no art.*; *(mit Flugzeugen)* aviation *no art.*
Luft-und-Raumfahrt- aerospace
Luftfahrt·gesellschaft die airline
luft-, Luft-: ~fahrzeug das aircraft; ~feuchte, ~feuchtigkeit die [atmospheric] humidity; ~filter der *od.* das *(Technik)* air filter; ~flotte die *(Milit.)* air fleet; ~fracht die air freight; ~geist der *(Myth.)* spirit of the air; ~gekühlt *Adj.* air-cooled; ~getrocknet *Adj.* air-dried; ~gewehr das air rifle; airgun; ~hauch der *(geh.)* breath of air; ~herrschaft die *o. Pl. (Milit.)* air supremacy; ~hoheit die air sovereignty; ~hülle die atmosphere
luftig 1. *Adj.* airy ⟨*room, building, etc.*⟩; well ventilated ⟨*cellar, store*⟩; light, cool ⟨*clothes*⟩; auf der Terrasse ist es etwas ~er there's more air out on the terrace. 2. *adv.* ~/zu ~ angezogen sein be lightly/not warmly enough dressed
Luftikus ['lʊftikʊs] der; ~[ses], ~se *(ugs. abwertend)* careless and unreliable sort *(coll.)*
Luft-: ~kampf der air battle; aerial battle; ~kissen das *(Technik)* air-cushion
Luftkissen-: ~boot das hovercraft; ~fahrzeug das hovercraft; air-cushion vehicle
luft-, Luft-: ~klappe die ventilation flap; ~korridor der *(Flugw.)* air corridor; ~krieg der air warfare *no art.*; aerial warfare *no art.*; ~kühlung die *(Technik)* air cooling; ein Motor mit ~kühlung an air-cooled engine; ~kur·ort der climatic health resort; ~lande·truppe die *(Milit.)* airborne troops *pl.*; ~leer *Adj.* ein ~leerer Raum a vacuum; im ~leeren Raum *(fig.)* in a vacuum; ~linie die *o. Pl.* 1000 km ~linie 1,000 km. as the crow flies; ~loch das a) *(Öffnung)* air-hole; b) *(ugs.: Windbö)* air pocket; ~-Luft-Rakete die *(Milit.)* air-to-air missile; ~mangel der; *o. Pl.* a) lack of air; b) *(Atembeschwerden)* shortness of breath; ~masche die *(Handarb.)* chain-stitch; ~massen *Pl. (Met.)* air masses; ~matratze die air-bed; air mattress; Lilo (P); ~mine die aerial mine; air mine; ~pirat der [aircraft] hijacker
Luft·post die airmail; etw. per *od.* mit ~ schicken send sth. [by] airmail
Luftpost-: ~brief der airmail letter; ~leicht·brief der aerogramme; ~papier das *o. Pl.* airmail paper
Luft-: ~pumpe die air pump; *(für Fahrrad)* [bicycle-]pump; ~raum der airspace; ~röhre die *(Anat.)* windpipe; trachea *(Anat.)*; ~sack der a) *(Kfz-W.)* airbag; b) *(Zool.)* air sac; ~schacht der ventilation shaft; *(einer Klimaanlage)* ventilation duct; ~schaukel die swing-boat; ~schiff das airship; ~schiffahrt die *o. Pl.* airship travel; ~schlacht die air battle; aerial battle; die ~schlacht um England the Battle of Britain; ~schlange die *meist Pl.* [paper] streamer; ~schleuse die *(Technik)* air-lock; ~schloß das; *meist Pl.* castle in the air; Luftschlösser bauen build castles in the air; ~schraube die *(Technik)* airscrew; propeller
Luft·schutz der air-raid protection *no art.*
Luftschutz-: ~bunker, ~keller, ~raum der air-raid shelter; ~sirene die air-raid siren; ~übung die air-raid drill; ~wart der *(hist.)* air-raid warden
luft-, Luft-: ~sieg der air victory; ~spiegelung die mirage; ~sprung der jump in the air; vor Freude ~sprünge/einen ~sprung machen *od.* vollführen jump for joy; ~streitkräfte *Pl. (Milit.)* air force *sing.*; ~strom der stream of air; ~strömung die *(Met.)* airstream; air current; ~stützpunkt der *(Milit.)* air base; ~taxe die, ~taxi das air taxi; ~temperatur die *(Met.)* air temperature; ~überlegenheit die *(Milit.)* air superiority
Lüftung die; ~, ~en a) *(das Lüften)* ventilation; b) *(Anlage)* ventilation system
Lüftungs-: ~an·lage die ventilation system; ~klappe die ventilation flap

Luft-: ~veränderung die change of air; **~verflüssigung die** *(Physik)* liquefaction of air; **~verkehr der** air traffic; **~verpestung die** *(abwertend).* **~verschmutzung die** air pollution; **~verteidigung die** *(Milit.)* air defence; **~waffe die** air force; **bei der ~waffe** in the air force; **~waffen·helfer der** *(hist.)* air-force auxiliary; **~weg der a) etw. auf dem ~weg verschicken/befördern** send/transport sth. by air; **auf dem ~weg reisen** travel by air; **b)** *Pl. (Anat.: Atemwege)* airways; air passages; respiratory tract *sing.; **~wider·stand der** (Physik)* air resistance; **~wurzel die** *(Bot.)* aerial root; **~zufuhr die** air supply; **~zug der** *o. Pl.* [gentle] breeze; *(in Zimmern, Gebäuden)* draught

Lug [lu:k] *in* **~ und Trug** lies *pl.* and deception

Luganer See, *(schweiz.)* **Luganer·see der** Lake Lugano

Lüge ['ly:gə] **die; ~, ~n** lie; **eine barmherzige ~:** a compassionate falsehood; **jmdn. der ~ bezichtigen** accuse sb. of lying; call sb. a liar; **jmdm. ~n auftischen** *(ugs.)* serve sb. up a lot *or* load of lies *(coll.);* **~n haben kurze Beine** *(Spr.)* [the] truth will out; **jmdn./etw. ~n strafen** prove sb. a liar/give the lie to sth.; *s. auch* **fromm 1c**

lugen *itr. V. (südwestd.) (auch fig.)* peep; *(hervorgucken)* **aus etw. ~:** poke out of sth.

lügen 1. *itr. V.* lie; **hier wird nur gelogen und betrogen** there's nothing but lies and deception here; **~ wie gedruckt** lie like mad; be a terrible liar *(coll.);* **ich müßte ~, wenn ...:** I should be lying if ...; **das Lügen** lying; **die Sterne ~ nicht** *(fig.)* the stars never lie; **wer einmal lügt, dem glaubt man nicht, und wenn er auch die Wahrheit spricht** *(Spr.)* a liar is never believed, even when he's telling the truth; *s. auch* **Tasche. 2.** *tr. V.* **er hat das alles gelogen** that was all a lie *or* all lies; **das ist gelogen!** that's a lie!

Lügen-: ~bold [~bolt] **der; ~[e]s, ~e** liar; **~detektor der** lie-detector; **~gebäude das** tissue of lies; **~gespinst das** *(geh.)* web *or* tissue of lies

lügenhaft *(abwertend)* **1.** *Adj.* untruthful, mendacious ⟨*statement, account, report, etc.*⟩ **2.** *adv.* untruthfully; mendaciously

Lügen-: ~kampagne die campaign of lies; **~märchen das** tall story; cock-and-bull story; **~maul das** *(derb)* filthy liar

Lügner der; ~s, ~, Lügnerin die; ~, ~nen liar

lügnerisch *Adj.* untruthful; mendacious; lying *attrib.* ⟨*scoundrel*⟩

[1]**Lukas** ['lu:kas] **(der)** *(Evangelist)* Luke

[2]**Lukas der; ~, ~** *(Maschine)* try-your-strength machine; **hau den ~!** try your strength!

Lukas·evangelium das St Luke's Gospel; Gospel according to St Luke

Luke ['lu:kə] **die; ~, ~n a)** *(Dach~)* skylight; **b)** *(bei Schiffen)* hatch; *(Keller~)* trap-door

lukrativ [lukra'ti:f] **1.** *Adj.* lucrative. **2.** *adv.* lucratively

lukullisch [lu'kʊlɪʃ] *(geh.)* **1.** *Adj.* Lucullan; epicurean. **2.** *adv.* **~ essen** *od.* **speisen** eat *or* have a Lucullan *or* an epicurean meal/meals

Lulatsch ['lu:la(:)tʃ] **der; ~[e]s, ~e** *(ugs.)* [long] lanky fellow; **ein langer ~:** a beanpole

Lulle ['lʊlə] **die; ~, ~n** *(ugs.)* cig *(coll.);* fag *(Brit. sl.)*

lullen *tr. V.* lull; **ein Kind in den Schlaf ~:** lull a child to sleep

Lumme ['lʊmə] **die; ~, ~n** *(Zool.)* guillemot

Lümmel ['lʏml̩] **der; ~s, ~ a)** *(abwertend: Flegel)* lout; **b)** *(ugs., fam.: Bengel)* rascal; **c)** *(salopp: Penis)* willy *(sl.)*

Lümmelei die; ~, ~en *(abwertend) s.* **Flegelei**

lümmelhaft *(abwertend) s.* **flegelhaft**

lümmeln *refl. V. (ugs. abwertend) s.* **flegeln**

Lump [lʊmp] **der; ~en, ~en** scoundrel; rogue

lumpen *(ugs.)* **1.** *tr. V. in* **sich nicht ~ lassen** splash out *(coll.).* **2.** *itr. V.* be out on the tiles *(sl.)*

Lumpen der; ~s, ~ a) rag; **b)** *meist Pl. (abwertend: Kleidung)* rags *pl.*

Lumpen-: ~gesindel das *(abwertend)* rabble; riff-raff; **~händler der** rag-and-bone man; **~hund, ~kerl der** *(abwertend)* scoundrel; bastard *(coll.);* **~pack das** *(abwertend) s.* **~gesindel; ~proletariat das** *(Soziol.)* lumpenproletariat; **~sammler der a)** rag-and-bone man; **b)** *(scherzh.: letztes Verkehrsmittel)* last bus/tram *(Brit.) or (Amer.)* streetcar/train

Lumperei die; ~, ~en *(abwertend)* dirty *or* mean trick; **eine große ~:** a very dirty *or* mean trick

lumpig *(abwertend)* **1.** *Adj.* **a)** *nicht präd. (kümmerlich)* paltry, miserable ⟨*pay, wages, etc.*⟩; **b)** *(niederträchtig)* mean, shabby ⟨*behaviour, attitude*⟩; mean ⟨*person*⟩. **2.** *adv.* ⟨*act, behave*⟩ shabbily

lunar [lu'na:ɐ̯] *Adj.; nicht präd.* lunar

Lunch [lanʃ] **der; ~[e]s** *od.* **~, ~[e]s** *od.* **~e** lunch; luncheon *(formal)*

lunchen ['lanʃn̩] *itr. V.* have lunch *or (formal)* luncheon; lunch

Lüneburger Heide ['ly:nəbʊrgə -] **die; ~:** Lüneburg Heath

Lunge ['lʊŋə] **die; ~, ~n** lungs *pl.; (Lungenflügel)* lung; **er hat es auf der ~** *(ugs.)* he has got lung trouble *(coll.);* **auf ~** *od.* **über die ~ rauchen** inhale; **die grüne ~ einer Großstadt** *(fig.)* the lungs *pl.* of a city; **sich** *(Dat.)* **die ~ aus dem Hals** *od.* **Leib schreien** *(ugs.)* yell one's head off *(coll.)*

lungen-, Lungen-: ~bläschen das *(Anat.)* pulmonary alveolus; **~braten der** *(österr.) s.* **Lendenbraten; ~embolie die** *(Med.)* pulmonary embolism; **~entzündung die** pneumonia *no indef. art.;* **~flügel der** lung; **~haschee das** *(Kochk.)* chopped lights *pl.* in sauce; **~krank** *Adj.* suffering from a lung disease *postpos.; (an Tuberkulose leidend)* suffering from tuberculosis *postpos.;* **~kranke der/die** person with *or* suffering from a lung disease; *(an Tuberkulose leidend)* tuberculosis sufferer; **~krebs der** lung cancer; **~tuberkulose die** tuberculosis [of the lung]; pulmonary tuberculosis; **~zug der** inhalation; **einen tiefen ~zug machen** inhale deeply

lungern *itr. V. s.* **herumlungern**

Lunte ['lʊntə] **die; ~, ~n a)** *(veralt.: Zündschnur)* fuse; match; **~ riechen** *(ugs.)* smell a rat; **b)** *(Jägerspr.: Schwanz)* brush

Lupe ['lu:pə] **die; ~, ~n** magnifying glass; **jmdn./etw. unter die ~ nehmen** *(ugs.)* examine sb./sth. closely; take a close look at sb./sth.; **so etwas/solche Leute kann man mit der ~ suchen** *(ugs.)* things/people like that are very hard to find *or* are few and far between

lupenrein *Adj.* **a)** flawless ⟨*diamond, stone, etc.*⟩; ⟨*diamond*⟩ of the first water; **b)** *(musterhaft)* genuine ⟨*amateur*⟩; unimpeachable ⟨*record, reputation*⟩; perfect ⟨*forgery, gentleman*⟩

lupfen ['lʊpfn̩] *(südd., schweiz., österr.),* **lüpfen** ['lʏpfn̩] *tr. V.* raise; lift

Lupine [lu'pi:nə] **die; ~, ~n** *(Bot.)* lupin

Lurch [lʊrç] **der; ~[e]s, ~e** amphibian

Lure ['lu:rə] **die; ~, ~n** *(hist.)* lur

Lusche ['lʊʃə] **die; ~, ~n** *(ugs.)* low card

Lust [lʊst] **die; ~, Lüste** ['lʏstə] *o. Pl. (Bedürfnis)* **~ haben** *od.* **verspüren, etw. zu tun** feel like doing sth.; **große/keine ~ haben, etw. zu tun** really/not feel like doing sth.; **wir hatten nicht die geringste ~, das zu tun** we didn't feel in the least *or* slightest like doing it; **plötzlich ~ bekommen, etw. zu tun** suddenly feel like doing sth.; **auf etw.** *(Akk.)* **~ haben** fancy sth.; **ich hätte große ~ auf ...** *(Akk.)* I could really fancy ...; **ich habe jetzt keine ~:** I'm not in the mood at the moment; **das kannst du machen, wie du ~ hast** you can do it however you like *or* whatever way you like; **mir ist die ~ dazu vergangen** I've lost [all] enthusiasm for it; **ich mache das nach ~ und Laune** I do it when I feel like it; **ich hätte ~ dazu** I'd like to; **b)** *o. Pl. (Vergnügen)* pleasure; joy; **~ an etw.** *(Dat.)* **haben** take great pleasure in *or* really enjoy sth.; **die ~ an etw.** *(Dat.)* **verlieren** lose interest in *or* stop enjoying sth.; **aus purer ~ am Töten** out of sheer pleasure in killing; **er hat an allem die ~ verloren** he no longer takes pleasure in anything; **etw. mit ~ und Liebe tun** love doing sth.; **c)** *(Begierde)* desire; *(geschlechtlich)* desire; lust *(usu. derog.);* **die ~ des Fleisches** *(geh.)* the desires *pl. or* lusts *pl.* of the flesh

Lustbarkeit die; ~, ~en *(geh. veralt.)* entertainment; festivity

lust·betont *Adj.* pleasure-orientated ⟨*behaviour*⟩; fun-loving, pleasure-loving ⟨*person*⟩; **~es Spielen** fun-orientated play

Luster ['lʊstɐ] **der; ~s, ~** *(österr.) s.* **Lüster a**

Lüster ['lʏstɐ] **der; ~s, ~ a)** *(veralt.: Kronleuchter)* chandelier; **b)** *(Überzug)* lustre

lüstern 1. *Adj.* **a)** lecherous; lascivious; **nach jmdm. ~ sein** lust after sb.; **b)** *(begierig)* **mit ~en Augen/Blicken** with greedy eyes. **2.** *adv.* **a)** lecherously; lasciviously; **b)** *(begierig)* greedily

Lust-: ~fahrt die *(veralt.)* excursion; **~garten der** *(hist.)* pleasance *(arch.);* pleasure-ground; **~gefühl das** feeling of pleasure; **~gewinn der** *o. Pl.* pleasure; **~greis der** *(abwertend)* [old] lecher; **~haus das** *(hist.)* summer-house

lustig 1. *Adj.* **a)** *(vergnügt)* merry; jolly; merry, jolly, jovial ⟨*person*⟩; happy, enjoyable ⟨*time*⟩; **dort war es immer sehr ~:** it was always a lot of fun there; **das kann ja ~ werden!** *(ugs. iron.)* this/that is going to be fun! **sich über jmdn./etw. ~ machen** make fun of sb./sth.; **b)** *(komisch)* funny; amusing; **etw. Lustiges** sth. funny; **c)** *(ugs.) in* **wie du ~ bist** *(ugs.)* however you fancy; whatever way you fancy; **solange du ~ bist** *(ugs.)* for as long as you like. **2.** *adv.* **a)** *(vergnügt)* ⟨*laugh, play*⟩ merrily, happily; **bei euch scheint es sehr ~ zuzugehen** you seem to be really enjoying yourselves *or* having a lot of fun; **~ brennen/flattern** *(fig.)* burn/flutter merrily; **b)** *(komisch)* funnily; amusingly; **sie kann so ~ erzählen** she can tell such funny *or* amusing stories; **c)** *(unbekümmert)* gaily

-lustig ['lʊstɪç] *adj.* **[sehr] tanz~/sanges~/lese~ sein** be very fond of *or* keen on dancing/singing/reading; **der wanderlustige Urlauber** the holidaymaker who is keen on hiking

Lustigkeit die; ~ a) *(Fröhlichkeit)* merriness; jolliness; *(Frohsinn auch)* joviality; **b)** *(Komik)* funniness

Lust·knabe der *(veralt., scherzh.)* catamite

Lüstling ['lʏstlɪŋ] **der; ~s, ~e** *(veralt. abwertend, scherzh.)* lecher

lust-, Lust-: ~los 1. *Adj.* **a)** *(unlustig)* listless; *(ohne Begeisterung)* unenthusiastic [and uninterested]; **b)** *(Börsenw.)* slack; dull; **2.** *adv.* listlessly; *(ohne Begeisterung)* without enthusiasm [or interest]; **sie stocherte ~los in ihrem Essen herum** she picked at her food with no real [interest or] enthusiasm; **~losigkeit die;** *o. Pl.* **a)** *(Unlust)* listlessness; *(mangelnde Begeisterung)* lack of [interest and] enthusiasm; **b)** *(Börsenw.)* slackness; dullness; **~molch der** *(ugs. scherzh.)* sex maniac; **ein alter ~molch** an old lecher; **~mord der** sex murder; **~mörder der** sex killer; **~objekt das** sex object; **~prinzip das** *(Psych.)* pleasure principle; **~schloß das** summer residence; **~schrei der** cry of pleasure; **~seuche die a)** *(veralt.: Syphilis)* syphilis *no art.*; **b)** *(geh.: Geschlechtskrankheit)* sexual scourge; **~spiel das** comedy; **~spiel·dichter der** comic dramatist; **~wandeln** *itr. V.; mit sein od. haben (geh. veralt.)* stroll; take a stroll

Lutheraner [lʊtəˈraːnɐ] **der; ~s, ~; Lutheranerin die; ~, ~nen** Lutheran

Luther·bibel die Luther's Bible; Lutheran Bible

lutherisch 1. *Adj.* Lutheran. **2.** *adv.* ‹*think etc.*› as a Lutheran; **jmdn. ~ erziehen** bring sb. up in the Lutheran religion

Lutherisch *Adj.* Luther's; **das berühmte ~e Wort** Luther's famous words *pl.*

Luthersch [ˈlʊtɐʃ] *Adj. s.* **Lutherisch**

Luthertum das; ~s Lutheranism *no art.*

lutschen [ˈlʊtʃn̩] **1.** *tr. V.* suck. **2.** *itr. V.* suck **an etw.** *(Dat.)* **~:** suck sth.; **am Daumen ~:** suck one's thumb

Lutscher der; ~s, ~ a) lollipop; **b)** *(Schnuller)* dummy *(Brit.)*; pacifier *(Amer.)*

Lüttich [ˈlʏtɪç] **(das); ~s** Liège

Luv [luːf] **die,** *auch* **das; ~** *(Seemannsspr.)* **in in/nach ~:** to windward

luven [ˈluːvn̩] *itr. V. (Seemannsspr.)* luff

Lux [lʊks] **das; ~, ~:** *(Physik)* lux

Luxation [lʊksaˈtsi̯oːn] **die; ~, ~en** *(Med.)* luxation *(Med.)*; dislocation

Luxemburg [ˈlʊksm̩bʊrk] **(das); ~s** Luxembourg; *s. auch* **Großherzogtum**

Luxemburger 1. *Adj.; nicht präd.* Luxembourg; **die ~ EG-Behörden** the EEC authorities in Luxembourg. **2. der; ~s, ~:** Luxembourger; *s. auch* **Kölner**

Luxemburgerin die; ~, ~nen Luxembourger; *s. auch* **-in**

luxemburgisch *Adj.* Luxembourgian

luxuriös [lʊksuˈri̯øːs] **1.** *Adj.* luxurious; **ein ~es Leben führen** lead a life of luxury. **2.** *adv.* luxuriously; **[sehr] ~ leben/wohnen** live in [great] luxury

Luxus [ˈlʊksʊs] **der; ~** *(auch fig.)* luxury; **etw. ist reiner ~:** sth. is sheer extravagance; **den ~ lieben** love luxury; **im ~ leben** live in [the lap of] luxury; **sich (Dat.) den ~ leisten, etw. zu tun** *(fig.)* allow oneself the luxury of doing sth.

Luxus-: ~artikel der luxury article; **dieses Geschäft führt nur ~artikel** this shop sells only luxury goods; **~aus·führung die** de luxe version; **~aus·gabe die** de luxe edition; **~dampfer der** luxury cruiser; **~hotel das** luxury hotel; **~jacht die** luxury yacht; **~kabine die** luxury cabin; **~klasse die** luxury class; **Automobile der ~klasse** luxury cars; **~limousine die** luxury limousine; **~schlitten der** *(ugs.)* classy car *or* job *(sl.)*; **~weibchen das** *(abwertend)* woman who expects to live in luxury

Luzern [luˈtsɛrn] **(das); ~s** Lucerne

Luzerne [luˈtsɛrnə] **die; ~, ~n** *(Bot.)* alfalfa; lucerne *(Brit.)*

luzid [luˈtsiːt] *Adj.* lucid

Luzidität [lutsidiˈtɛːt] **die; ~:** lucidity

Luzifer [ˈluːtsifɛr] **(der)** Lucifer

luziferisch *(geh.) Adj.* diabolical; vicious ‹*sarcasm*›

LW *Abk.* **Langwelle** LW

Lymph·drüse die *(veralt.) s.* **Lymphknoten**

Lymphe [ˈlʏmfə] **die; ~, ~n** lymph

Lymph·knoten der lymph node *or* gland

lynchen [ˈlʏnçn̩] *tr. V.* lynch; *(scherzh.)* lynch; kill

Lynch-: ~justiz die lynch-law; **~mord der** lynching

Lyoner [Wurst] [ˈli̯oːnɐ-] **die; ~ [~], ~ [Würste]** bologna [sausage]

Lyra [ˈlyːra] **die; ~, Lyren a)** *(Mus.)* lyre; **b)** *(Astron.)* Lyra; the lyre

Lyrik [ˈlyːrɪk] **die; ~:** lyric poetry

Lyriker der; ~s, ~, Lyrikerin die; ~, ~nen lyric poet; lyricist

lyrisch 1. *Adj.* **a)** lyric ‹*poem, poetry, epic, drama*›; lyrical ‹*passage, style, description, etc.*›; **b)** *(gefühlvoll)* lyrical; **c)** *nicht präd. (Mus.)* lyric. **2.** *adv.* lyrically

Lyzeum [lyˈtseːʊm] **das; ~s, Lyzeen** [lyˈtseːən] girls' high school

M

m, M [ɛm] **das; ~, ~:** m/M; *s. auch* **a, A**

m *Abk.* **Meter** m

M *(DDR) Abk.* ¹**Mark**

MA *Abk.* **Mittelalter**

Mäander [mɛˈandɐ] **der; ~s, ~** *(Geogr., Kunstwiss.)* meander

Maar [maːɐ̯] **das; ~[e]s ~e** *(Geogr.)* maar; *(See)* crater lake

Maas [maːs] **die; ~:** Meuse

Maat [maːt] **der; ~[e]s, ~e[n] a)** *(Seemannsspr.)* [ship's] mate; **b)** *(Dienstgrad)* petty officer

Mach [max] **das; ~[s], ~** *(Physik)* Mach

Machandel [maˈxandl̩] **der; ~s, ~** *(nordd.) s.* **Wacholder**

Mach·art die style; *(Schnitt)* cut

machbar *Adj.* feasible

Mache die; ~ *(ugs.)* **a)** *(abwertend)* sham; **das ist reine** *od.* **nichts als ~:** it's pure sham; it's all put on; **b) etw. in der ~ haben** have sth. on the stocks; be working on sth.; **jmdn. in der ~ haben/in die ~ nehmen** *(salopp) (jmdm. zusetzen)* be working/work on sb.; *(jmdn. verprügeln)* be working/work sb. over *(coll.)*

machen [ˈmaxn̩] **1.** *tr. V.* **a)** *(herstellen)* make; **aus Plastik/Holz** *usw.* **gemacht** made of plastic/wood *etc.*; **aus diesen Äpfeln ~ wir Saft** we will make juice from these apples; **aus diesem Zimmer ~ wir gerade ein Büro** we are making *or* turning this room into an office; **sich** *(Dat.)* **etw. ~ lassen** have sth. made; **Geld/ein Vermögen/einen Gewinn ~:** make money/a fortune/a profit; **dafür ist er wie gemacht/nicht gemacht** *(fig.)* that's just his line/that's not his line; **etw. aus jmdm. ~:** make sb. into sth.; *(verwandeln)* turn sb. into sth.; **jmdn. zum Präsidenten** *usw.* **~:** make sb. president *etc.*; **er machte sie zu seiner Frau** *(geh. veralt.)* he made her his wife; **b)** *(geben)* **jmdm. einen Kostenvoranschlag ~:** let sb. have *or* give sb. an estimate; **jmdm. einen guten Preis ~** *(ugs.) (beim Kauf)* make sb. a good offer; *(beim Verkauf)* name a good price; **c)** *(zubereiten)* get, prepare ‹*meal*›; **den Salat ~** *(ugs.)* do the salad *(coll.)*; **was machst du heute zum Abendessen?** what are you getting/doing for supper tonight?; **jmdm./sich [einen] Kaffee ~:** make [some] coffee for sb./oneself; **jmdm. einen Cocktail ~:** get *or* mix sb. a cocktail; **d)** *(verursachen)* **jmdm. Arbeit ~:** cause *or* make [extra] work for sb.; **jmdm. Sorgen ~:** cause sb. anxiety; worry sb.; **jmdm. Mut/Hoffnung ~:** give sb. courage/hope; **das macht Durst/Hunger** *od.* **Appetit** this makes one thirsty/hungry; this gives one a thirst/an appetite; **das macht das Wetter** that's [because of] the weather; **das macht das viele Rauchen** that comes from smoking a lot; **mach, daß er gesund wird!** make him get well!; **mach, daß du nach Hause kommst!** *(ugs.)* off home with you!; **ich muß ~, daß ich zum Bahnhof komme** *(ugs.)* I must see that I get to the station; **e)** *(ausführen)* do ‹*job, repair, etc.*›; **seine Hausaufgaben ~:** do one's homework; **ein Foto** *od.* **eine Aufnahme ~:** take a photograph; **ein Examen ~:** take an exam; **einen Spaziergang ~:** go for *or* take a walk; **eine Reise ~:** go on a journey *or* trip; **einen Besuch [bei jmdm.] ~:** pay [sb.] a visit; **wie man's macht, macht man's falsch** *od.* **verkehrt** *(ugs.)* [however you do it,] there's always something wrong; *(jmdm. ist nichts recht)* there's no pleasing some people; **er macht es nicht unter 100 DM** he won't do it for under *or* less than 100 marks; **f)** (+ *Adj. od. V.: Zustand verändern*) **jmdn. glücklich/eifersüchtig** *usw.* **~:** make sb. happy/jealous *etc.*; **etw. größer/länger/kürzer ~:** make sth. bigger/longer/shorter; **mach es dir gemütlich** *od.* **bequem!** make yourself comfortable *or* at home; **das Kleid macht sie älter** the dress makes her look older; **jmdn. lachen/weinen/leiden ~** *(geh.)* make sb. laugh/cry/suffer; **g)** *(tun)* do; **was machst du da?** what are you doing?; **mußt du noch viel ~?** do you still have a lot to do?; **mach doch etwas!** 'do something!; **mach' ich, wird gemacht!** *(ugs.)* will do!; **was ~ Sie [beruflich]?** what do you do [for a living]?; **da ist nichts zu machen, dagegen kann man nichts ~:** there's nothing one can do [about it]; **was soll ich nur ~?** what am I to do?; **was macht der Fußball in der Küche?** what is the football doing in the kitchen?; **was hat er nur wieder gemacht [, daß alle so wütend sind]?** what has he been up to this time [to make everyone so angry]?; **so etwas macht man nicht** that [just] isn't done; **mach was dran!** *(ugs.)* what can you do?; **mit mir könnt ihr es ja ~** *(ugs.)* you can get away with it with me; **sie läßt alles mit sich ~:** she is very long-suffering; **h) was macht ...?** *(wie ist um ... bestellt?)* how is ...?; **was macht die Arbeit?** how is the job [getting on]?; how are things at work?; **was macht die Gesundheit?** how are you keeping?; **i)** *(ergeben) (beim Rechnen)* be; *(bei Geldbeträgen)* come to; **zwei mal zwei macht vier** two times two is four; **was** *od.* **wieviel macht das [alles zusammen]?** how much does that come to?; **das macht 12 DM** that is *or* costs 12 marks; *(Endsumme)* that comes to 12 marks; **j)** *(schaden)* **was macht das schon?** what does it matter?; **macht das was?** does it matter?; do you mind?; **macht nichts!** *(ugs.)* never mind!; it doesn't matter; **k)** *(teilnehmen an)* **einen Kursus** *od.* **Lehrgang ~:** take a course; **ein Seminar ~** *(ugs.)* take part in a seminar; **l)** *(ugs.: veranstalten)* organize, *(coll.)* do ‹*trips, meals, bookings, etc.*›; **ein Fest ~:** give a party; **m) mach's gut!** *(ugs.)* look after yourself!; *(auf Wiedersehen)* so long!; **er macht es nicht mehr lange** *(ugs.)* he won't last much longer; **n)** *(ugs.: ordnen, saubermachen, renovieren);* do ‹*room, stairs, washing, etc.*›; **das Bett ~:** make the bed; **die Haare/Fingernägel ~:** do one's hair/nails; **den Garten ~:** do the garden *(coll.)*; **o)** *(ugs. verhüll.: seine Notdurft verrichten)* **sein Geschäft ~:** relieve oneself; **groß/klein ~:** do big jobs/small jobs *(child language)*; **p)** *(ugs.: spielen, sein)* play, act ‹*part, the clown, etc.*› **wer macht hier den Vorarbeiter?** who is the foreman here?; **q) es [mit jmdm.] ~** *(ugs. verhüll.)* have it off [with sb.] *(sl.)*; **es jmdm. ~** *(derb)* give it to sb. *(sl.)*. **2.** *refl. V.* **a)** *mit Adj.* **sich ... ~:** make oneself ...; **sich hübsch ~:** smarten [oneself] up; **sich schmutzig ~:** get [oneself] dirty; **sich verständlich ~:** make oneself clear; **das macht sich bezahlt!** it's worth it!;

sie macht sich besser, als sie ist she pretends to be better than she is; **b)** *(beginnen)* **sich an etw.** *(Akk.)* **~:** get down to sth.; **mach dich ans Werk/an die Arbeit** get down to work; get on with it; **c)** *(ugs.: sich entwickeln)* do well; get on; **du hast dich aber gemacht!** you've made great strides!; **d)** *(passen)* **das macht sich gut hier** this fits in well; this looks good here; **e) mach dir nichts daraus!** *(ugs.)* don't let it bother you; **ich mache mir nichts daraus** it doesn't bother me; **sich** *(Dat.)* **nichts/wenig aus jmdm./etw. ~** *(ugs.)* not care at all/much for sb./sth.; **f)** *(gestalten)* **wir wollen uns** *(Dat.)* **einen schönen Abend ~:** we want to have an enjoyable evening; **macht euch ein paar schöne Stunden** enjoy yourselves for a few hours; **g) sich** *(Dat.)* **Feinde ~:** make enemies; **sich** *(Dat.)* **jmdn. zum Freund/Feind ~:** make a friend/an enemy of sb.; **sich** *(Dat.)* **etw. zum Grundsatz/zur Aufgabe ~:** make sth. a principle/one's task; **h) das macht sich von selbst** it takes care of itself; **wenn es sich [irgendwie] ~ läßt** if it can [somehow] be done; if it is [at all] possible. **3.** *itr. V.* **a)** *(ugs.: sich beeilen)* **mach schon!** get a move on! *(coll.)*; look snappy! *(coll.)*; **mach schneller!** hurry up!; **b) das macht müde** it makes you tired; it is tiring; **das macht hungrig** it makes you hungry; **das macht durstig** it makes you thirsty; **das Kleid macht dick** the dress makes one look fat; **c)** *(tun)* **laß mich nur ~** *(ugs.)* leave it to me; **d)** *(ugs. verhüll.)* ‹*child, pet*› perform *(coll.)*; **ins Bett/in die Hose ~:** wet one's bed/pants; **e)** *(salopp: tätig sein)* **er macht in Lederwaren** he is in leather goods; **der Konzern macht auch in Versicherungen** the group also does insurance; **f)** *(salopp abwertend: mimen)* **auf naiv** *usw.* **~:** pretend to be naïve *etc.*; act naïve *etc.*; **auf feine Dame/großen Geschäftsmann ~:** act the fine lady/big business man; **auf vornehm ~:** give oneself airs; **g)** *mit sein (landsch. ugs.: sich begeben)* go; **in den Westen ~:** go to the west

Machenschaften *Pl. (abwertend)* machinations; wheeling and dealing *sing.*

Macher der; ~s, ~ *(ugs.)* doer; **der Typ des ~s** the dynamic type who just gets on with things

-macher der, -macherin die; ~, ~nen ...-maker; **Filme~/Besen~/Bücher~** film-maker/broom-maker/maker of books

Macher·lohn der *(Schneiderei)* making-up charge

Machete [ma'xe:tə] **die; ~, ~n** machete

Machiavellismus [makjavɛ'lɪsmʊs] **der; ~** *(Philos., Politik)* machiavellianism *no art.*

machiavellistisch *(Philos., Politik) Adj.* machiavellian

Machismo [ma'tʃɪsmo] **der; ~[s]** *(abwertend)* machismo

Macho ['matʃo] **der; ~s, ~s** *(abwertend)* macho

Macht [maxt] **die; ~, Mächte** ['mɛçtə] **a)** *o. Pl. (Kraft, Einfluß)* power; *(Stärke)* strength; *(Befugnis)* authority; power; **mit aller ~:** with all one's might; **alles, was in seiner ~ steht, tun** do everything in one's power; **seine ~ ausspielen** use one's authority *or* power; **das liegt nicht in ihrer ~:** that is not within her power; that is outside her authority; **~ über jmdn. haben** have a hold over sb.; **eine unwiderstehliche ~ auf** *od.* **über jmdn. ausüben** exert an irresistible influence over sb.; **die ~ der Gewohnheit/der Verhältnisse** the force of habit/circumstances; **der Frühling kommt mit ~:** spring is coming with a vengeance; **b)** *o. Pl. (Herrschaft)* power *no art.*; **die ~ ergreifen** *od.* **an sich reißen** seize power; **an die ~ kommen** come to power; **c)** *(Staat)* power; **d)** *(~gruppe; geheimnisvolle Kraft)* power; force; **die Mächte der Reaktion** the forces of reaction; **die Mächte der Finsternis** the powers of darkness; **böse Mächte** evil forces; **e)** *(geh., veralt.: Heer)* forces *pl.*; **mit großer ~:** with a large force *or* army

Macht-: ~an·spruch der claim *or* pretension to power; **~apparat der** power structure; **~aus·übung die** exercise of power *(Gen.* by); **~befugnis die** authority *no pl., no art.*; power *no art.*; **~bereich der** sphere of influence; **~block der** power bloc

Mächte·gruppierung die *(Politik)* power grouping

macht-, Macht-: ~entfaltung die expansion of power; **~ergreifung die** *(Politik)* seizure of power *(Gen.* by); **~gier die** *(abwertend)* craving for power; **~gierig** *Adj.* with a craving for power *postpos., not pred.*; **~gierig sein** crave power; **~haber** [-ha:bɐ] **der; ~s, ~:** ruler; **die gegenwärtigen ~haber** those at present in power; **~hunger der** hunger for power; **~hungrig** *Adj.* power-hungry

mächtig ['mɛçtɪç] **1.** *Adj.* **a)** powerful; **die Mächtigen dieser Welt** the high and mighty; the wielders of power; **b) seiner Sinne** *od* **seiner selbst** *(Gen.)* **[nicht] ~ sein** [not] be in control of oneself; **einer Sprache** *(Gen.)* **/des Lesens und Schreibens ~ sein** *(geh.)* have a command of a language/be capable of reading and writing; **c)** *(beeindruckend groß)* mighty; powerful, mighty ‹*voice, blow*›; tremendous, powerful ‹*effect*›; *(ugs.)* terrific *(coll.)* ‹*luck*›; terrible *(coll.)* ‹*fright*›; **~en Hunger/~e Angst haben** be terribly hungry/afraid; **d)** *(landsch.: schwer)* heavy ‹*food*›; *(sättigend)* filling ‹*food*›. **2.** *adv. (ugs.)* terribly *(coll.)*; extremely; **~ viel** an awful lot *(coll.)*; **~ groß** tremendously large *(coll.)*; **er ist ~ gewachsen** he has grown a lot; **ihr müßt euch ~ beeilen** you'll really have to step on it *(coll.)*

Mächtigkeit die; ~ a) *(Einfluß)* power; **b)** *(Größe)* massive size; *(Gewalt)* force

macht-, Macht-: ~instrument das *(Politik)* instrument of power; **~kampf der** *(bes. Politik)* power struggle; **~los** *Adj.* powerless; impotent; **gegen etw. ~los sein, einer Sache** *(Dat.)* **~los gegenüberstehen** be powerless in the face of sth.; **gegenüber jmdm. ~los sein** be powerless against sb.; **gegen so viel Frechheit/Dummheit bin ich/ist man einfach ~los** there is nothing one can do in the face of such impudence/stupidity; **~losigkeit die** impotence **(gegen, gegenüber** in the face of); **~miß·brauch der** abuse of power; **~mittel** *das* instrument of power; **~politik die** power politics *sing., no art.*; **~position die** *(bes. Politik)* position of power; **~probe die** trial of strength; **~stellung die** *s.* **~position**; **~streben das** ambition for power; **~übernahme die** *(Politik)* take-over [of power] *(Gen.* by); **~verhältnisse** *Pl.* balance of power *sing.*; *(innerhalb einer Organisation)* power structure *sing.*; **~voll 1.** *Adj.* powerful; *(imponierend)* impressive ‹*demonstration, appearance*›; **2.** *adv.* powerfully; *(imponierend)* impressively; **~vollkommenheit die** absolute power; **aus eigener ~vollkommenheit** on one's own authority *or* initiative; **~wechsel der** *(Politik)* change of government; **~wort das** word of command; decree; **ein ~wort sprechen** put one's foot down; lay down the law

Mach·werk das *(abwertend)* shoddy effort

Macke ['makə] **die; ~, ~n a)** *(salopp: Tick)* fad; **'ne ~ haben** have a fad; *(verrückt sein)* be off one's rocker *(sl.)*; **b)** *(ugs.: Defekt)* defect; *(optisch)* mark; blemish

Macker der; ~s, ~ a) *(Jugendspr.: Freund, Kerl)* guy *(sl.)*; bloke *(Brit. sl.)*; **b)** *(abwertend)* macho

MAD [ɛm/a:'de:] **der; ~s** *Abk.* **Militärischer Abschirmdienst** Military Counter Intelligence [Service]

Madagaskar [mada'gaskar] **(das); ~s** Madagascar

Madagasse [mada'gasə] **der; ~n, ~n, Madagassin die; ~, ~nen** Madagascan; Madagasy

madagassisch *Adj.* Madagascan; Madagasy

Madam [ma'dam] **die; ~, ~s a)** *(ugs. scherzh.)* [portly] matron; **b)** *(landsch. scherzh.: Ehefrau)* better half *(joc.)*

Mädchen ['mɛ:tçən] **das; ~s, ~ a)** girl; *(ugs. veralt.: Freundin)* girl[-friend]; **für kleine ~ müssen** *(fam. scherzh. verhüll.)* need to spend a penny *(Brit. coll.)*; **b)** *(Haus~)* maid; **~ für alles** *(ugs.)* maid of all work; *(im Büro usw.)* girl Friday; *(Mann)* man Friday

Mädchen·alter das girlhood years *pl.*; **im [zarten] ~alter** when still a [young] girl

mädchenhaft 1. *Adj.* girlish; **~ aussehen** ‹*boy*› have a girlish look; look like a girl; ‹*girl*› look childlike. **2.** *adv.* **sich ~ kleiden** dress in a girlish manner; ‹*older woman*› wear young clothes, dress like a young girl

Mädchen-: ~handel der; *o. Pl.* white-slave traffic; **~händler der** white-slave trader; **~klasse die** girls' class; **~kleidung die** girls' clothes *pl.*; **~name der a)** *(Vorname)* girl's name; **b)** *(Name vor der Ehe)* maiden name; **~pensionat das** girls' boarding-school; **~schule die** girls' school; school for girls; **~zimmer das a)** *(für ein ~)* girl's room; *(für mehrere)* girls' room; **b)** *(für Hausmädchen)* maid's room

Made ['ma:də] **die; ~, ~n** maggot; *(Larve)* larva; **leben wie die ~ im Speck** be living in the lap of luxury *or* off the fat of the land

Madeira [ma'de:ra] **der; ~s, ~s, Madeira·wein der** Madeira

Madel [ma:dl̩] **das; ~s, ~n,** *(südd., österr. mundartl.),* **Mädel** ['mɛ:dl̩] **das; ~s, ~,** *nordd.*: **~s** *s.* **Mädchen a**

Maderl, Mäderl ['mɛ:dɐl], **das; ~s, ~n** *(österr. ugs.) s.* **Mädchen a**

madig *Adj.* maggoty; **jmdm. etw./ein Vergnügen ~ machen** *(ugs.)* spoil sb.'s pleasure in sth./spoil a pleasure for sb.; **jmdn./etw. ~ machen** *(ugs.)* run sb./sth. down

Madonna [ma'dɔna] **die; ~, Madonnen a)** *(christl. Rel.) o. Pl.* **die ~:** Our Lady; the Virgin Mary; **b)** *(Kunst)* madonna

madonnen-, Madonnen-: ~gesicht das madonna-like features *pl.*; **~haft 1.** *Adj.* madonna-like; **2.** *adv.* in a madonna-like manner; **~scheitel der** centre parting

Madrigal [madri'ga:l] **das; ~s, ~e** *(Literaturw., Musik)* madrigal

Maestro [ma'ɛstro] **der; ~s, ~s** *od.* **Maestri** maestro

Maf[f]ia ['mafi̯a] **die; ~, ~s a)** *o. Pl.* Mafia; **b)** *(fig.)* mafia

Mafioso [ma'fi̯o:zo] **der; ~s, Mafiosi** mafioso

mag [ma'k] *1. u. 3. Pers. Sg. Präsens v.* **mögen**

Magazin [maga'tsi:n] **das; ~s, ~e a)** *(Lager)* store; *(für Waren)* stock-room; *(für Waffen u. Munition)* magazine; *(in der Bibliothek)* stack[-room]; stacks *pl.*; **b)** *(für Patronen, Dias, Film usw.)* magazine; *(an Werkzeugmaschinen)* feeder; **c)** *(Zeitschrift)* magazine; *(Rundf., Ferns.)* magazine programme

Magazineur [magatsi'nø:ɐ̯] **der; ~s, ~e** *(österr.)* storekeeper; stores supervisor

magazinieren *tr. V.* [put in] store; put ‹*explosives, weapons*› in a/the magazine

Magd [ma:kt] **die; ~, Mägde** ['mɛ:kdə] **a)** *(veralt.) (Landarbeiterin)* [female] farmhand; *(Vieh~)* milkmaid; *(Dienst~)* maidservant; **b)** *(dichter. veralt.: Jungfrau)* maid; damsel; **Maria, die reine ~** *(christl. Rel.)* Mary, the pure Virgin

Mägdelein ['mɛ:kdəlai̯n], **Mägdlein** ['mɛ:ktlai̯n] **das; ~s, ~** *(dichter. veralt.)* maiden

Magellan·straße [magɛ'la:n-] **die** Straits *pl.* of Magellan

Magen ['ma:gn̩] **der; ~s, Mägen** ['mɛ:gn̩] *od.* **~:** stomach; **mir knurrt der ~** *(ugs.)* my tummy is rumbling *(coll.)*; **sich** *(Dat.)* **den ~ verderben** get an upset stomach; **etw. auf nüchternen** *od.* **leeren ~ essen/trinken** eat/drink sth. on an empty stomach; **etwas/nichts im ~ haben** have had something/nothing to eat; **jmdm. auf den ~ schlagen** upset sb.'s stomach; **jmdm. schwer im ~ liegen** lie heavy on sb.'s stomach; **diese Sache liegt mir schwer auf dem** *od.* **im ~** *(fig. ugs.)* this business is preying on my mind; **mit leerem ~:** with an empty stomach; **da dreht sich einem/mir der ~ um** *(ugs.)* it's enough to make *or* it makes one's/my stomach turn; *(fig.)* it makes you/me sick; *s. auch* **Liebe a**

magen-, Magen-: ~ausheberung die; ~, ~en *(Med.)* pumping-out of the stomach; **~beschwerden** *Pl.* stomach trouble *sing.*; **~bitter der; ~s, ~:** bitters *pl.*; **~blutung die** gastric haemorrhage; **~-Darm-Kanal der** *(Anat.)* gastro-intestinal tract; **~-Darm-Katarrh der** *(Med.)* gastroenteritis; **~drücken das** feeling of pressure in the stomach; *(~schmerzen)* stomach-ache; **~durch·bruch der** *(Med.)* *s.* **~perforation; ~fahr·plan der** *(ugs. scherzh.)* menu; eating schedule; **~freundlich** *adj.* kind to the stomach *pred.*; **~gegend die** region of the stomach; **ein unangenehmes Gefühl in der ~gegend** an unpleasant feeling in the [pit of the] stomach; **~geschwür das** stomach ulcer; **~grube die** pit of the stomach; **~inhalt der** contents *pl.* of the stomach; **~katarrh der** *(Med.)* gastritis; **~knurren das** *(ugs.)* tummy rumbles *pl.* *(coll.)*; **~krampf der** stomach cramp; **~krämpfe** stomach spasms; **~krank** *Adj.* ⟨*person*⟩ suffering from a stomach disorder *or* complaint; **~krank sein/werden** have/get a stomach disorder *or* complaint; **~krankheit die** stomach complaint; **~krebs der** cancer of the stomach; **~leiden das** *s.* **~krankheit; ~leidend** *Adj.*: *s.* **~krank; ~mittel das** medicine for the stomach; stomachic *(Pharm.)*; **~perforation die** *(Med.)* perforation of the stomach; **~saft der** gastric juice; **~säure die** gastric acid; **~schleim·haut die** lining of the stomach; **~schleimhaut·entzündung die** gastritis; **~schmerzen** *Pl.* stomach-ache *sing.*; **~spiegelung die** *(Med.)* gastroscopy; **~spülung die** *(Med.)* gastric irrigation; **~verstimmung die** stomach upset

mager ['ma:gɐ] **1.** *Adj.* **a)** *(dünn)* thin; **b)** *(fettarm)* low-fat; low in fat *pred.*; lean ⟨*meat*⟩; **ein ~es Benzingemisch** *(Kfz-W.)* a lean mixture; **c)** *(nicht ertragreich)* poor ⟨*soil, harvest*⟩; infertile ⟨*field*⟩; lean ⟨*years*⟩; *(fig.: dürftig)* meagre ⟨*profit, increase, success, report, etc.*⟩; thin ⟨*programme*⟩; **d)** *(Druckw.)* light-face ⟨*type, characters*⟩. **2.** *adv.* **~ essen** follow a low-fat diet; eat low-fat foods

Mager·käse der low-fat cheese

Magerkeit die; ~ a) thinness; **b)** *(Ertragsarmut)* poorness; *(fig.: Dürftigkeit)* meagreness

Mager-: ~milch die skim[med] milk; **~quark der** low-fat curd cheese; **~sucht die** *o. Pl.* *(Med.)* wasting disease; *(Anorexie)* anorexia

Magie [ma'gi:] **die; ~:** magic; **Schwarze/Weiße ~:** black/white magic

Magier ['ma:giɐ] **der; ~s, ~** *(auch fig.)* magician; **die drei ~** *(bibl.)*: the Three Magi

magisch 1. *Adj.* **a)** magic ⟨*powers*⟩; **~es Quadrat** magic square; **b)** *(geheimnisvoll)* magical ⟨*attraction, light, force, etc.*⟩; *(unwirklich)* eerie ⟨*light, half-light*⟩. **2.** *adv.* *(durch Zauber)* by magic; *(wie durch Zauber)* as if by magic; magically; *(unwirklich)* eerily; **~ beleuchtet** with magical/eerie lighting *postpos., not pred.*

Magister [ma'gɪstɐ] **der; ~s, ~ a)** Master's degree; **den ~ haben/machen** ≈ have/work for an MA *or (Amer.)* a Master's; **~ Artium** [~ 'artsiʊm] Master of Arts; **b)** *(Inhaber des Titels)* person holding a Master's degree; **~ sein** have a Master's degree

[1]**Magistrat** [magɪs'tra:t] **der; ~[e]s, ~e** City Council

[2]**Magistrat der; ~en, ~en** *(schweiz.)* Federal Councillor

Magma ['magma] **das; ~s, Magmen** *(Geol.)* magma

Magna Charta ['magna 'karta] **die; ~ ~** *(hist.)* Magna Carta

magna cum laude ['magna kʊm 'laudə] *(Hochschulw.)* with great distinction; *second of four grades of succesful doctoral examination*

Magnat [ma'gna:t] **der; ~en, ~en a)** magnate; **b)** *(hist.)* great nobleman

Magnesia [ma'gne:zia] **die; ~ a)** *(Chemie, Med.)* magnesia; **b)** *(Turnen)* chalk

Magnesium [ma'gne:ziʊm] **das; ~s** *(Chemie)* magnesium

Magnet [ma'gne:t] **der; ~en** *od.* **~[e]s, ~e** *(auch fig.)* magnet

Magnet-: ~auf·zeichnung die [magnetic] tape recording; **~band das** *Pl.*: **~bänder** magnetic tape; **~berg der** Magnetic Mountain; **~bild·verfahren das;** *o. Pl.* *(Technik)* videotape technique; **~eisen·stein der** *(Mineral.)* magnetite; **~feld das** *(Physik)* magnetic field

magnetisch 1. *Adj.* *(auch fig.)* magnetic. **2.** *adv.* magnetically; **~ gespeichert/aufgezeichnet** stored/recorded on magnetic tape; **jmdn. ~ anziehen** *(fig.)* have a magnetic attraction for sb.

Magnetiseur [magneti'sø:ɐ] **der; ~s, ~e** mesmerist

magnetisieren *tr. V.* **a)** *(Physik)* magnetize; **b)** *(Psych. veralt.)* treat ⟨*patient*⟩ by mesmerism

Magnetisierung die; ~, ~en *(Physik)* magnetization

Magnetismus der; ~ a) *(Physik)* magnetism; **b)** *(Psych. veralt.)* mesmerism *no art.*

Magnet-: ~kern der *(Physik)* core [of a/the magnet]; **~kompaß der** magnetic compass; **~nadel die** [compass] needle

Magneton ['magnetɔn] **das; ~s, ~[s]** *(Kernphysik)* magneton

Magnetophon ⓦ [magneto'fo:n] **das; ~s, ~e** tape recorder

Magnetosphäre die; ~: magnetosphere

Magnetron ['magnetrɔn] **das; ~s, ~e** [-'tro:nə] *(Physik)* magnetron

Magnet-: ~schalter der *(Kfz-W.)* solenoid switch; *(im Spannungsregler)* [magnetic] cut-out; **~spule die a)** coil [of an/the electromagnet]; **b)** *(Solenoid)* solenoid; **~zündung die** *(Kfz-W.)* magneto ignition

Magnifikat [ma'gni:fikat] **das; ~s** *(kath. Kirche)* magnificat

Magnifizenz [magnifi'tsɛnts] **die; ~, ~en** *(Hochschulw.)* **Seine/Eure ~:** His/Your Magnificence *(mode of address or title of German university rector)*; **die ~en** the rectors

Magnolie [ma'gno:liə] **die; ~, ~n** magnolia

mäh [mɛ:] *Interj.* baa

Mahagoni [maha'go:ni] **das; ~s** mahogany

Maharadscha [maha'ratʃa] **der; ~s, ~s** maharaja

Maharani [maha'ra:ni] **die; ~, ~s** maharanee

Mäh·binder der harvester[-binder]

[1]**Mahd** [ma:t] **die; ~, ~en** *(landsch.)* **a)** *(Mähen)* mowing; **b)** *(das Gemähte)* mown grass; (Heu) [new-mown] hay

[2]**Mahd das; ~[e]s, Mähder** ['mɛ:dɐ] *(österr., schweiz.)* high pasture

Mäh·drescher der combine harvester

[1]**mähen** ['mɛ:ən] **1.** *tr. V.* mow ⟨*grass, lawn, meadow*⟩; cut, reap ⟨*corn*⟩. **2.** *itr. V.* mow; *(Getreide ~)* reap

[2]**mähen** *itr. V.* ⟨*sheep*⟩ bleat

Mäher der; ~s, ~ a) mower; *(von Getreide)* reaper; **b)** *(ugs.)* *s.* **Mähmaschine**

Mahl [ma:l] **das; ~[e]s, Mähler** [mɛ:lɐ] *(geh.)* meal; repast *(formal)*; **beim ~ sitzen** sit at table

mahlen *unr. tr., itr. V.* grind; **etw. fein/grob ~:** grind sth. fine/coarsely; **wer zuerst kommt, mahlt zuerst** *(Spr.)* the early bird catches the worm *(prov.)*

Mahl-: ~gang der *(Technik)* grinding-machine; *(~steine)* set of millstones; **~gut das** grist

mählich ['mɛ:lɪç] *(geh. veralt.)* **1.** *Adj.* gradual. **2.** *adv.* gradually

Mahl-: ~stein der a) grinding-stone; **b)** *(Mühlstein)* millstone; **~strom der** *(geh.)* maelstrom; **~zahn der** molar; **~zeit die** meal; **sich an die ~en halten** eat meals at regular times; **~!** *(ugs.)* have a good lunch; bon appetit; **[na dann] prost ~!** *(ugs.)* what a delightful prospect! *(iron.)*; *(an einen anderen)* [in that case] the best of British! *(Brit. coll.)*

Mäh·maschine die [power] mower; *(für Getreide)* reaper

Mahn-: ~bescheid der writ for payment; **~brief der** *s.* **~schreiben**

Mähne ['mɛ:nə] **die; ~, ~n** mane; *(scherzh.: Haarschopf)* mane [of hair]

mahnen ['ma:nən] **1.** *tr., itr. V.* **a)** *(auffordern)* urge; **zur Eile/Vorsicht ~:** urge haste/caution; **jmdn. zur Eile/Vorsicht~:** urge sb. to hurry/to be careful; **jmdn. eindringlich ~:** give sb. an urgent warning; **jmdn. ~d ansehen** look admonishingly at sb.; **b)** *(erinnern)* remind **(an** + *Akk.* of); **einen Schuldner [schriftlich] ~:** send a debtor a [written] demand for payment *or* a reminder. **2.** *itr. V.* *(geh.)* **an etw.** *(Akk.)* **~:** be reminiscent of sth.

Mahner der; ~s, ~ *(geh.)* admonisher; *(Unheilsprophet)* Cassandra

Mahn-: ~gebühr die reminder fee; **~mal das** memorial *(erected as a warning to future generations)*; **~ruf der** *(geh.)* warning cry; admonition; **~schreiben das** reminder (+ *Gen.* from); *(an einen Schuldner)* demand [for payment]; reminder

Mahnung die; ~, ~en a) *(Aufforderung)* exhortation; *(Warnung)* admonition; **b)** *(Erinnerung)* reminder; **c)** *s.* **Mahnschreiben**

Mahn·verfahren das summary proceedings *pl.* [for the payment of a debt]

Mähre ['mɛ:rə] **die; ~, ~n** *(veralt. abwertend)* jade *(dated)*

Mähren (das); ~s Moravia

mährisch *Adj.* Moravian

Mai [mai] **der; ~[e]s** *od.* **~,** *dichter.*: **~en, ~e** May; **der Erste ~:** the first of May; May Day; **Kundgebungen zum Ersten ~:** May Day rallies; **im ~ des Lebens** *(geh.)* in the springtime of life; **wie einst im ~:** as in the days of my/their *etc.* youth

Mai-: ~andacht die *(kath. Kirche)* May devotion; **~baum der a)** maypole; **b)** *(Birkenbäumchen) small birch-tree traditionally tied to doorpost for May festival*; **~blume die a)** mayflower; **b)** *(~glöckchen)* lily of the valley; **~bowle die** *cup made of white wine and champagne with fresh woodruff*

Maid [mait] **die; ~, ~en** *(veralt.)* maiden

Mai·demonstration die May Day demonstration

Maie die; ~, ~n *(veralt.) young birch-tree or birch leaves traditionally tied to doorpost for May celebrations*

Maien·nacht die *(dichter. veralt.)* May night

Mai-: ~feier die May Day celebration; **~feier·tag der** May Day *no def. art.*; **~glöckchen das** lily of the valley; **~käfer der** May-bug; **~königin die** *(Volksk.)*

Queen of the May; **~kundgebung die** May Day rally

Mailand (das); ~s Milan

Mailänder ['mailɛndɐ] **1.** *indekl. Adj.; nicht präd.* Milan; Milanese ⟨*climate, spring, etc.*⟩ **die ~ Scala** La Scala, Milan. **2. der; ~s, ~:** Milanese; *s. auch* **Kölner**

Mailänderin die; ~, ~nen Milanese

mailändisch *Adj.* Milanese

Mai·parade die May Day parade

Mais [mais] **der; ~es** maize; corn *(esp. Amer.); (als Gericht)* sweet corn

Mais-: ~birne die *(Sport)* [suspended] punch-ball *(Brit.) or (Amer.)* punching-bag; **~brei der** maize *or (Amer.)* corn [meal] porridge; **~brot das** corn bread

Maische ['maiʃə] **die; ~, ~n** *(bei Bier, Spiritus)* mash; *(bei Wein)* must

maischen *tr. V.* mash ⟨*malt*⟩; crush ⟨*grapes*⟩

Mais-: ~kolben der corn-cob; *(als Gericht)* corn on the cob; **~korn das** grain of maize *or (Amer.)* corn; **~mehl das** maize *or (Amer.)* corn flour

Maison[n]ette [mɛzɔ'nɛt] **die; ~, ~s, Maison[n]ette·wohnung die** maisonette

Mais·stärke die cornflour *(Brit.);* cornstarch *(esp. Amer.)*

Maître de plaisir [mɛtrəplɛ'zi:r] **der; ~ ~ ~, ~s** [mɛtrə-] **~ ~** *(veralt., noch scherzh.)* Master of Ceremonies

Majestät [majɛs'tɛ:t] **die; ~, ~en a)** *(Titel)* Majesty; **Seine/Ihre/Eure** *od.* **Euer ~:** His/Her/Your Majesty; **b)** *o. Pl. (geh.: Erhabenheit)* majesty

majestätisch 1. *Adj.* majestic. **2.** *adv.* majestically

Majestäts·beleidigung die lèse-majesté

Majolika [ma'jo:lika] **die; ~, Majoliken** majolica; **Majoliken** pieces of majolica

Major [ma'jo:ɐ̯] **der; ~s, ~e** *(Milit.)* major; *(der Luftwaffe)* squadron leader *(Brit.);* major *(Amer.)*

Majoran ['ma:joran] **der; ~s, ~e** marjoram

Majorette [majɔ'rɛt] **die; ~, ~s** *od.* **~n** majorette

Majorin die; ~, ~nen a) *(in der Heilsarmee)* major; **b)** *(veralt.)* major's wife

majorisieren *tr. V. (geh.)* outvote

Majorität [majori'tɛ:t] **die; ~, ~en** majority; **die ~ haben** have a majority

Majoritäts-: ~beschluß der majority decision; **~prinzip das** principle of a majority vote; majority principle

Majuskel [ma'jʊskl̩] **die; ~, ~n** *(Druckw.)* capital [letter]

makaber [ma'ka:bɐ] *Adj.* macabre

Makedonien [make'do:ni̯ən] **(das); ~s** Macedonia

Makedonier der; ~s, ~: Macedonian

makedonisch *Adj.* Macedonian

Makel ['ma:kl̩] **der; ~s, ~** *(geh.)* **a)** *(Schmach)* stigma; taint; **an ihm haftet ein ~:** a stain *or* taint clings to him; **b)** *(Fehler)* blemish; flaw; **ohne ~:** without a [single] flaw

Mäkelei die; ~ *(abwertend)* carping

mäkelig *Adj. (abwertend)* carping; *(beim Essen)* fussy; particular

makel·los 1. *Adj.* flawless, perfect ⟨*skin, teeth, figure, stone*⟩; spotless, immaculate ⟨*white, cleanness, clothes*⟩; impeccable ⟨*accent*⟩; *(fig.)* spotless, unblemished ⟨*reputation, character*⟩. **2.** *adv.* immaculately; spotlessly ⟨*clean*⟩; *(fehlerfrei)* flawlessly

Makellosigkeit die; ~ *s.* **makellos:** flawlessness; perfection; spotlessness; immaculateness; impeccability; *(fig.)* spotlessness

makeln *(ugs.) tr. V.* be a broker for ⟨*stocks, shares*⟩; be an agent for ⟨*houses, building-sites, etc.*⟩

mäkeln ['mɛ:kl̩n] *itr. V. (abwertend)* carp; **an etw.** *(Dat.) od.* **über etw.** *(Akk.)* **~:** carp at *or* find fault with sth.

Make-up [me:k'|ap] **das; ~s, ~s a)** make-up; **b)** *(Präparate)* make-up; **die ~s** the make-up products; **c)** *(Tönungscreme)* liquid make-up; foundation

Makkaroni [maka'ro:ni] *Pl.* macaroni *sing.*

Makkaroni·fresser der *(derb abwertend)* Eyetie *(sl. derog.);* wop *(sl. derog.)*

Makler ['ma:klɐ] **der; ~s, ~ a)** *(Häuser~)* estate agent *(Brit.);* realtor *(Amer.);* **b)** *(Börsen~)* broker

Makler-: ~firma die estate agents *pl. (Brit.); (Amer.)* realtors *pl.;* **~gebühr die, ~provision die** agent's fee *or* commission; *(eines Börsenmaklers)* brokerage charges *pl.*

Mako ['mako] **die; ~, ~s** *od.* **der** *od.* **das; ~[s], ~s** Egyptian cotton

Makramee [makra'me:] **das; ~[s]** macramé

Makrele [ma'kre:lə] **die; ~, ~n** mackerel

makro-, Makro- [makro-]: **~biotik** [~'bio:tɪk] **die; ~:** macrobiotics *sing., no art.;* **~biotisch 1.** *Adj.* macrobiotic; **2.** *adv.* on macrobiotic principles; **~klima das** *(Met.)* macroclimate; **~kosmos der** macrocosm; **~molekül das** macromolecule

Makrone [ma'kro:nə] **die; ~, ~n** macaroon

Makulatur [makula'tu:ɐ̯] **die; ~, ~en a)** *(Druckw.)* spoilt sheets *pl.;* spoilage *no pl.;* **b)** *(Altpapier)* waste paper; **~ reden** *(ugs. abwertend)* talk rubbish

mal [ma:l] **1.** *Adv.* **a)** *(Math.)* times; *(bei Flächen)* by; **zwei ~ zwei** twice two; two times two; **der Raum ist 5 ~ 6 Meter groß** the room is five metres by six. **2.** *Partikel (ugs.)* **komm ~ her!** come here!; **hör ~ zu!** listen!; *s. auch* **einmal 2**

¹Mal das; ~[e]s, ~e time; **ein anderes ~:** another time; **nur dies eine ~:** just this once; **kein einziges ~:** not once; not a single time; **beim ersten/letzten ~:** the first/last time; **zum zweiten/x-ten ~:** for the second/n-th time; **mit einem ~[e]** all at once; all of a sudden; **von ~ zu ~ heftiger werden/nachlassen** become more and more violent/decrease more and more [each time]

²Mal das; ~[e]s, ~e *od.* **Mäler** ['mɛ:lɐ] **a)** mark; *(Muttermal)* birthmark; *(braun)* mole; **b)** *(geh.: Denk~, Mahn~)* memorial; **c)** *(Baseball)* base; **d)** *(Rugby)* goal; *(~feld)* in-goal

Malachit [mala'xi:t] **der; ~s, ~e** malachite

malad[e] [ma'la:d(ə)] *Adj. (veralt., landsch.)* ill; sick *(esp. Amer.)*

Malaga ['malaga] **der; ~s, ~s, Malaga·wein der** Malaga [wine]

Malaie [ma'laiə] **der; ~n, ~n, Malaiin die; ~, ~nen** Malay

malaiisch *Adj.* Malayan

Malaise [ma'lɛ:zə] **die; ~, ~n,** *schweiz.:* **das; ~s, ~s a)** malaise; sense of unease; **b)** *(Misere)* unhappy situation

Malaria [ma'la:ri̯a] **die; ~:** malaria

malaria·krank *Adj.* suffering from malaria *postpos.*

Malaria·mücke die malaria mosquito

Malawi [ma'la:vi] **(das); ~s** Malawi

Malawier der; ~s, ~, Malawierin die; ~, ~nen Malawian

malawisch *Adj.* Malawian

Malaysia [ma'laizi̯a] **(das); ~s** Malaysia

malaysisch *Adj.* Malaysian

Mal·buch das colouring-book

malen 1. *tr., itr. V.* **a)** paint ⟨*picture, portrait, person, etc.*⟩; *(mit Farbstiften)* draw with crayons; *(ausmalen)* colour; **sich ~ lassen** have one's portrait painted; **etw. in düsteren Farben ~** *(fig.)* paint *or* portray sth. in gloomy colours; **etw. allzu rosig/schwarz ~** *(fig.)* paint far too rosy/black a picture of sth.; **b)** *(sauber schreiben)* write carefully; **c)** *(anstreichen)* paint ⟨*door, window, etc.*⟩; decorate ⟨*flat, room, walls*⟩. **2.** *refl. V.* **a)** paint one's self-portrait; **b)** *(geh.)* **auf seinem Gesicht malte sich Erstaunen/Entsetzen** astonishment/horror was mirrored in his face

Maler ['ma:lɐ] **der; ~s, ~** painter

Maler·arbeit die; *meist Pl.* painting and decorating *no pl.*

Malerei die; ~, ~en a) *o. Pl.* painting *no art.;* **b)** *(Gemälde)* painting

Malerin die; ~, ~nen [woman] painter

malerisch 1. *Adj.* **a)** picturesque ⟨*village, house, etc.*⟩; **einen ~en Anblick bieten** look as pretty as a picture; **b)** *(zur Malerei gehörend)* artistic ⟨*skill, talent*⟩; ⟨*skill, talent*⟩ as a painter; ⟨*motif, subject*⟩ for painters; **sein ~es Werk** his paintings *pl.* **2.** *adv.* **a)** picturesquely ⟨*situated*⟩; **b)** ⟨*train*⟩ as a painter; **ihr ~ geschultes Auge** her trained artist's eye

Maler-: ~lein·wand die [artist's] canvas; **~meister der** master painter [and decorator]

Malesche [ma'lɛʃə] **die; ~, ~n** *(nordd. ugs.)* mess; **in der ~ sitzen/in ~n kommen** be/land in the soup *(sl.)*

Mal·feld das *(Rugby)* in-goal

Malheur [ma'lø:ɐ̯] **das; ~s, ~e** *od.* **~s** mishap; **das ist doch kein ~!** it's not the end of the world!

Mali ['ma:li] **(das); ~s** Mali

maligne [ma'lɪgnə] *Adj. (Med.)* malignant

maliziös [mali'tsi̯ø:s] *(geh.)* **1.** *Adj.* malicious. **2.** *adv.* maliciously

Mal·kasten der paintbox

mall [mal] *Adj. (ugs., bes. nordd.)* barmy *(Brit. sl.);* crazy

Mallorca [ma'lɔrka] **(das); ~s** Majorca

mallorquinisch [malɔr'ki:nɪʃ] *Adj.* Majorcan

mal|nehmen *unr. tr., itr. V.* multiply **(mit** by); **das Malnehmen** multiplication

Maloche [ma'lo:xə] **die; ~** *(salopp)* drudgery *no indef. art.;* slog; **auf ~ sein** be at work; *(schwer arbeiten)* slog away

malochen *itr. V. (salopp)* slog *or* slave [away]

Mal-: ~pinsel der paintbrush; **~stift der** crayon; **~strom der** *s.* **Mahlstrom**

Malta [malta] **(das); ~s** Malta

Mal·technik die painting technique

Malteser [mal'te:zɐ] **1.** *indekl. Adj.; nicht präd.* Maltese. **2. der; ~s, ~ a)** Maltese; *s. auch* **Kölner 2; b)** *s.* **~ritter**

Malteser-: ~hilfs·dienst der ≈ St John Ambulance Brigade; **~kreuz das** *(auch Technik)* Maltese cross; **~orden der** *o. Pl.* Order of the Knights of St John; **~ritter der** Knight of St John

maltesisch *Adj.* Maltese

Maltesisch das; ~ *(Sprachw.)* Maltese

Maltose [mal'to:zə] **die; ~** *(Biochemie)* maltose

malträtieren [maltrɛ'ti:rən] *tr. V.* maltreat; ill-treat

Malus ['ma:lʊs] **der; ~** *od.* **~ses, ~** *od.* **~se a)** *(Versicherungsw.)* supplementary premium *(imposed after a number of claims);* **b)** *(Schulw.)* negative weighting; handicap; **einen ~ von ... bekommen** be marked down by ...

Mal·utensilien *Pl.* painting equipment *sing. or (coll.)* things

Malve ['malvə] **die; ~, ~n** mallow

malven-: ~farben, ~farbig *Adj.* [pale] mauve

Malwinen [mal'vi:nən] *Pl.* **die ~:** the Falkland Islands

Malz [malts] **das; ~es** malt

Malz-: ~bier das malt beer; **~bonbon das** malted cough lozenge

Mal·zeichen das multiplication sign

mälzen ['mɛltsn̩] *tr., itr. V. (Brauereiwesen)* malt

Mälzerei die; ~, ~en *(Brauereiwesen)* **a)** *(Gebäude)* malt-house; malting; **b)** *(Malzbereitung)* malting

Malz-: ~extrakt der malt extract; **~kaf-**

fee der *coffee substitute made from germinated, dried, and roasted barley;* **~zucker der** *(Biochemie)* maltose

Mama ['mama, *geh. veralt.:* ma'ma:] **die;** ~, ~s *(fam.)* mamma

Mama-: **~puppe die** talking doll *(saying 'Mama');* **~söhnchen das** *(abwertend)* mummy's boy *(coll.)*

Mameluck [mamə'lʊk] **der;** ~en, ~en *(hist.)* Mameluke

Mami ['mami] **die;** ~, ~s *(fam.)* mummy *(Brit. coll.);* mommy *(Amer. coll.)*

Mammographie [mamogra'fi:] **die;** ~, ~n *(Med.)* mammography *no art.*

Mammon ['mamɔn] **der;** ~s *(abwertend)* Mammon; **dem ~ nachjagen** devote oneself to the pursuit of Mammon *or* of riches; **der schnöde ~:** filthy lucre

Mammut ['mamʊt] **das;** ~s, ~e *od.* ~s mammoth

Mammut- mammoth; *(sehr lange dauernd)* marathon

Mammut-: **~baum der** mammoth tree; sequoia; **~film der** mammoth [screen] epic; blockbuster; **~konzern der** mammoth concern; **~prozeß der** marathon trial; **~sitzung die** marathon session

mampfen ['mampfn̩] *tr., itr. V. (salopp)* munch; nosh *(sl.)*

Mamsell [mam'zɛl] **die;** ~, ~en *od.* ~s *(veralt.: Hauswirtschafterin)* housekeeper

[1]**man** [man] *Indefinitpron. im Nom.* **a)** one; you; **~ hat von dort eine herrliche Aussicht** one has *or* there is a magnificent view from there; **~ kann nie wissen** one *or* you never can tell; **dagegen muß ~ etwas unternehmen** something has to be done about it; **~ nehme 250 g Butter** take 250 grams of butter; **für weitere Auskünfte wende ~ sich an ...:** for further information apply to ...; **b)** *(irgend jemand)* somebody; *(die Behörden; die Leute dort)* they; **~ hat mir gesagt ...:** I was told ...; they told me ...; **hat ~ dir das nicht mitgeteilt?** didn't anybody/they tell you that?; **~ vermutet/hat herausgefunden, daß ...:** it is thought/has been discovered that ...; they think/have discovered that ...; **c)** *(die Menschen im allgemeinen)* people *pl.;* **das trägt ~ heute** that's what people wear *or* what is worn nowadays; **so etwas tut ~ [einfach] nicht** that's [just] not done; **d)** *(ich)* one; **~ versteht sein eigenes Wort nicht** you can't hear yourself speak

[2]**man** *Adv. (bes. nordd.)* **laß ~ gut sein!** forget it!; **na, denn ~ los** let's be off then

Management ['mænɪdʒmənt] **das;** ~s, ~s management

managen ['mɛnɪdʒn̩] *tr. V.* **a)** *(ugs.)* fix; organize; **ich manage das schon** I'll fix it; *(durch Tricks)* I'll fiddle it *(sl.);* **b)** *(betreuen)* manage, act as manager for ⟨*singer, artist, player*⟩; **von seiner Frau gemanagt werden** have one's wife as one's manager

Manager ['mɛnɪdʒɐ] **der;** ~s, ~, **Managerin die;** ~, ~nen manager; *(eines Fußballvereins)* club secretary

Manager·krankheit die *(volkst.)* stress disease *no def. art.*

manch [manç] *Indefinitpron.* **a)** many a; **[so] ~er Beamte, ~ ein Beamter** many an official; **in [so] ~er Beziehung** in many respects; **[so] ~ schöne[n] Stunden** many a happy hour; **~ einer** *od.* **~er** many a person/man; **~ eine** *od.* **~e** many a woman; **b)** *substantivisch* **~e** some; *(viele)* many; **[so] ~er mußte das erleben** many people had to go through this; **[so] ~es** a number of things; *(allerhand Verschiedenes)* all kinds of things; **[so] ~es von dem, was wir lernten** much of what we learnt

manchenorts *s.* **mancherorts**

mancherlei *unbest. Gattungsz.; indekl.* **a)** various; a number of; **~ Käse** various kinds of cheese; **b)** *(Verschiedenes)* various things; a number of things

mancherorten, mancherorts *Adv. (geh.)* in some places; *(an verschiedenen Orten)* in various places

Manchester ['mɛntʃɛstɐ] **der;** ~s [heavy] corduroy

manch·mal *Adv.* sometimes

Mandant [man'dant] **der;** ~en, ~en, **Mandantin die;** ~, ~nen *(Rechtsw.)* client

Mandarin [manda'ri:n] **der;** ~s, ~e *(hist.)* mandarin

Mandarine [manda'ri:nə] **die;** ~, ~n mandarin [orange]; tangerine

Mandat [man'da:t] **das;** ~[e]s, ~e **a)** *(Parlamentssitz)* [parliamentary] seat; **sein ~ niederlegen** resign one's seat; **b)** *(Auftrag) (eines Abgeordneten)* mandate; *(eines Anwalts)* brief; **das politische ~ der Studentenausschüsse** the right of student committees to make political statements on behalf of members; **c)** *(Treuhandgebiet)* mandate; mandated territory

Mandatar [manda'ta:ɐ̯] **der;** ~s, ~e **a)** mandatary; **b)** *(österr.: Abgeordneter)* member [of parliament]; deputy

Mandats-: **~gebiet das** mandated territory; mandate; **~träger der** *(Politik)* member of parliament; deputy

Mandel ['mandl̩] **die;** ~, ~n **a)** almond; **b)** *(Anat.)* tonsil

mandel-, Mandel-: **~augen** *Pl. (geh.)* almond eyes; **~äugig** *Adj. (geh.)* almond-eyed; **~baum der** almond[-tree]; **~entzündung die** tonsillitis *no indef. art.;* **~förmig** *Adj.* almond-shaped; **~operation die** tonsillectomy

Mandoline [mando'li:nə] **die;** ~, ~n mandolin

Mandrill [man'drɪl] **der;** ~s, ~e *(Zool.)* mandrill

Mandschure [man'dʒu:rə] **der;** ~n, ~n Manchu; Manchurian

Mandschurei die; ~: Manchuria *no art.*

mandschurisch *Adj.* Manchurian

Manege [ma'ne:ʒə] **die;** ~, ~n *(im Zirkus)* ring; *(in der Reitschule)* arena

mang [maŋ(k)] *Präp. mit Dat. od. Akk. (nordd., berlin.)* among

Mangan [maŋ'ga:n] **das;** ~s *(Chemie)* manganese

Mangan-: **~erz das** manganese ore; **~säure die** manganic acid

[1]**Mangel** ['maŋl̩] **der;** ~s, **Mängel** ['mɛŋl̩] **a)** *o. Pl. (Fehlen)* lack **(an** + *Dat.* of); *(Knappheit)* shortage, lack **(an** + *Dat.* of); **es herrscht** *od.* **besteht ~ an etw.** *(Dat.)* there is a lack *or* shortage of sth.; sth. is in short supply; **~ an Vitaminen** vitamin deficiency; **aus ~** *od.* **wegen ~s an Beweisen** for lack of evidence; **aus ~ an Erfahrung** from *or* owing to lack of experience; **keinen ~ leiden** not go short [of anything]; not want for anything; **b)** *(Fehler)* defect; **geringfügige Mängel** minor flaws *or* imperfections; **die Mängel eines Nachschlagewerkes/Drehbuchs** the shortcomings *or* deficiences of a reference work/film script

[2]**Mangel die;** ~, ~n *(Wäsche~)* [large] mangle; **jmdn. durch die ~ drehen** *od.* **in die ~ nehmen** *od.* **in der ~ haben** *(fig. salopp)* put sb. through the hoop

Mangel·bericht der *(Technik)* defect report (+ *Gen.* on); list of faults

Mangel-: **~beruf der** understaffed profession; **~erscheinung die** *(Med.)* deficiency symptom

mangelhaft **1.** *Adj. (fehlerhaft)* defective ⟨*goods, memory*⟩; faulty ⟨*goods, German, English, etc.*⟩; *(schlecht)* poor ⟨*memory, lighting*⟩; bad ⟨*road conditions, German*⟩; *(unzulänglich)* inadequate ⟨*knowledge, lighting*⟩; incomplete ⟨*reports*⟩; *(Schulw.)* **die Note „~"** the mark 'unsatisfactory'; *(bei Prüfungen)* the fail mark. **2.** *adv. (fehlerhaft)* defectively; faultily; *(schlecht)* poorly; *(unzulänglich)* inadequately; **~ befestigte Straßen** badly made roads; **Französisch beherrsche ich nur ~:** I have only an imperfect command of French

Mängel·haftung die *(Rechtsw.)* liability for defects

Mangel·krankheit die *(Med.)* deficiency disease

[1]**mangeln** *itr. V.* **es mangelt an etw.** *(Dat.) (ist nicht vorhanden)* there is a lack of sth.; *(ist unzureichend vorhanden)* there is a shortage of sth.; sth. is in short supply; **jmdm./einer Sache mangelt etw.** *od.* **es an etw.** *(Dat.)* sb./sth. lacks sth.; **es mangelt mir an Platz** I am short of space; **seine ~de Menschenkenntnis** his inadequate understanding of people; **die ~de Kompromißbereitschaft** the unwillingness to compromise

[2]**mangeln** **1.** *tr. V.* mangle. **2.** *itr. V.* do the mangling

Mängel·rüge die *(Rechtsw.)* complaint *(about quality, service, etc.)*

mangels ['maŋls] *Präp. mit Gen.* in the absence of; **~ eines eigenen Büros** having no office of his *etc.* own; **~ Beweisen** *(Dat.)* owing to lack of evidence

Mangel·ware die: **~ sein** be scarce *or* in short supply; ⟨*article*⟩ be a scarce commodity; **erfahrene Fachkräfte sind ~** *(fig. ugs.)* experienced skilled workers are thin on the ground *(coll.)*

Mangel·wäsche die [laundry for] mangling

Mango ['maŋgo] **die;** ~, ~s mango

Mangold ['maŋgɔlt] **der;** ~[e]s [Swiss] chard

Mangrove [maŋ'gro:və] **die;** ~, ~n mangrove forest

Mangrove[n]-: **~baum der** mangrove [tree]; **~küste die** mangrove coastline

Manichäismus [manɪçɛ'ɪsmʊs] **der;** ~: Manichaeism *no art.*

Manie [ma'ni:] **die;** ~, ~n mania; **bei jmdm. zur ~ werden** become an obsession with sb.

Manier [ma'ni:ɐ̯] **die;** ~, ~en **a)** manner; **in gewohnter ~:** in his/her usual way *or* manner; **auf eine bravouröse ~:** brilliantly; in a masterly fashion; **in der ~ Dalis** in Dali's manner *or* style; in the manner of Dali; **b)** *Pl. (Umgangsformen)* manners; **keine ~en haben** have no manners; **ich werde dir ~en beibringen!** I'll teach you some manners!; **c)** *(veralt.)* **das ist doch keine ~!** that's no way to behave

manieriert [mani'ri:ɐ̯t] *(geh.)* **1.** *Adj.* mannered. **2.** *adv.* in a mannered fashion

Manieriertheit die; ~, ~en *(geh.)* mannerism

Manierismus der; ~ *(Kunstwiss., Literaturw.)* mannerism

manierlich **1.** *Adj.* **a)** *(fam.)* well-mannered; well-behaved ⟨*child*⟩; **b)** *(ugs.: einigermaßen gut)* reasonable; decent. **2.** *adv.* **a)** *(fam.)* properly; nicely; **b)** *(ugs.: einigermaßen gut)* **ganz/recht ~:** quite/really nicely *or* decently

manifest [mani'fɛst] *Adj. (geh.)* manifest; **es wird an diesem Beispiel ~:** it is made manifest by this example

Manifest das; ~[e]s, ~e manifesto

Manifestant [manifɛs'tant] **der;** ~en, ~en *(schweiz.)* demonstrator

Manifestation [manifɛsta'tsi̯o:n] **die;** ~, ~en **a)** *(Med., Psych. usw.)* manifestation; **b)** *(schweiz.: Kundgebung)* demonstration

manifestieren *(geh.)* **1.** *refl. V.* be manifested; manifest itself. **2.** *tr. V.* demonstrate. **3.** *itr. V. (veralt.)* demonstrate

Maniküre [mani'ky:rə] **die;** ~, ~n **a)** *o. Pl.* manicure; **~ machen** manicure oneself; **b)** *(Person)* manicurist

Maniküre·etui das manicure set

maniküren *tr. V.* manicure

Manila·faser [ma'ni:la-] **die, Manilahanf der** Manila [hemp]

Maniok [ma'ni̯ɔk] **der;** ~s, ~s manioc; cassava

Manipulant [manipu'lant] der; ~en, ~en (geh.) manipulator
Manipulation [manipula'tsio:n] die; ~, ~en (geh.) manipulation
manipulativ [manipula'ti:f] (geh.) 1. Adj. manipulative. 2. adv. by manipulation
Manipulator [manipu'la:tɔr] der; ~s, ~en [-to:ren] a) (Technik, geh. fig.) manipulator; b) (Zauberkünstler) sleight-of-hand performer; (Jongleur) conjuror
manipulierbar Adj. (geh.) manipulable; susceptible to manipulation postpos.; leicht ~: easy to manipulate
Manipulierbarkeit die; ~ (geh.) manipulability; susceptibility to manipulation; die ~ der öffentlichen Meinung the extent to which public opinion can be manipulated
manipulieren [manipu'li:rən] tr. V. manipulate; rig ‹election result, composition of a committee›
Manipulierung die; ~, ~en manipulation
manisch ['ma:nɪʃ] (geh., Psych.) 1. Adj. manic. 2. adv. maniacally
manisch-depressiv Adj. (Psych.; Med.) manic-depressive; ~es Irresein (veralt.) manic depression
Manitu ['ma:nitu] der; ~s manitou
Manko ['maŋko] das; ~s, ~s a) (Mangel) shortcoming; deficiency; (Nachteil) handicap; b) (Fehlbetrag) deficit; ein ~ von 1200 DM haben be 1,200 marks short
Mann [man] der; ~[e]s, Männer ['mɛnɐ]; s. auch Mannen a) man; alle erwachsenen Männer wurden festgenommen all adult males were arrested; ein ~, ein Wort a man's word is his bond; ein ~ der Tat a man of action; ein ~ des Todes (geh.) a doomed man; ein ~ der Feder/der Wissenschaft (geh.) a man of letters/of science; ein ~ aus dem Volk a man of humble origins; ein ~ des Volkes a man of the people; der ~ am Klavier the pianist; the man at the piano; der geeignete od. richtige ~ sein be the right man; der böse od. schwarze ~: the bogy man; der ~ des Tages/Jahres the man of the moment/year; der ~ auf der Straße the man in the street; auf den ~ dressiert sein ‹dog› be trained to attack people; der ~ im Mond the man in the moon; ; [mein lieber] ~! (ugs.) (überrascht, bewundernd) my goodness!; (verärgert) for goodness sake!; ~ [Gottes]! (ugs.) my God!; wie ein ~: to a man; with one voice; der Geschäftsleitung wie ein ~ entgegentreten approach the management like one man or with a united front; [nicht] ~s genug sein, etw. zu tun [not] be man enough to do sth.; [nicht] der ~ sein, etw. zu tun [not] be the right man to do sth.; er ist nicht der ~, der kurz entschlossen eine Entscheidung treffen kann he is not the sort who can make a decision at the drop of a hat; seinen ~ stehen (seine Pflicht tun) do one's duty; (selbständig sein) stand on one's own two feet; (sich durchsetzen) stand up for oneself; seinen ~ gefunden haben have met one's match; dieser Beruf ernährt seinen ~: you can make a good living in that job; du hast wohl einen kleinen ~ im Ohr (salopp) you must be out of your tiny mind (sl.); etw. an den ~ bringen (ugs.) (verkaufen) flog sth. (Brit. sl.); push sth. (Amer.); find a taker/takers for sth.; seine Ansicht/seine Witze an den ~ bringen (ugs.) find an audience for one's view/one's jokes; seine Tochter an den ~ bringen (ugs. scherzh.) find a taker for or marry off one's daughter; ~ für ~: one by one; Kämpfe od. der Kampf ~ gegen ~: hand-to-hand fighting; von ~ zu ~: [from] man to man; laß dir mal von ~ zu ~ sagen, ...: let me tell you straight, ...; s. auch Welt a; b) (Besatzungsmitglied) man; mit 1000 ~ Besatzung with a crew of 1,000 [men]; an Bord des Düsenjägers waren 4 ~: there were four men on board the jet fighter; bis zum letzten ~: to the last man; alle ~ an Deck! (Seemannsspr.) all hands on deck!; ~ über Bord! (Seemannsspr.) man overboard!; mit ~ und Maus untergehen (Seemannsspr.) go down with all on board; c) (Teilnehmer) pro ~ (ugs.) per person; per head; alle ~ [hoch] (ugs.) in force; all together; wir gingen noch alle ~ [hoch] in eine Kneipe (ugs.) afterwards the whole lot of us went into a pub (Brit. coll.) or (Amer.) bar; uns fehlt der dritte/vierte ~ zum Skatspielen we need a third/fourth person or player for a game of skat; ~ decken mark [an/one's opponent]; an od. in den ~ gehen (bes. Fußball) go in hard; s. auch frei 1 o; Gott a; letzt... a; Not f; d) (Ehemann) husband; als od. wie ~ und Frau leben (geh.) live as man and wife; ~ und Frau werden (geh.) become man and wife
Manna ['mana] das; ~[s], auch: die; ~ (bibl.) manna
mannbar Adj. (geh. veralt.) a) marriageable ‹daughter, girl›; ~ werden become of marriageable age; b) (geschlechtsreif) sexually mature ‹youth›; das ~e Alter sexual maturity
Männchen ['mɛnçən] das; ~s, ~ a) little man; ein altes, verhutzeltes ~: a little wizened old man; ~ malen draw matchstick men; b) (Tier~) male; (Vogel~) male; cock; ~ machen ‹animal› sit up and beg; (fig. ugs.: salutieren) ‹soldier› salute smartly
Mann·deckung die (Ballspiele) man-to-man marking
Männe ['mɛnə] der; ~, ~s (ugs.) hubby (coll.)
Männeken ['mɛnəkn̩] das; ~s, ~s (niederd., bes. berlin.) little chap; kleines ~: tiny fellow
Mannen Pl. (dichter. veralt.) vassals; der Trainer und seine ~ (scherzh.) the manager and his troops
Mannequin ['manəkɛ̃] das; ~s, ~s mannequin; [fashion] model
männer-, Männer-: ~arbeit die a man's work; work for a man; ~bekanntschaft die male or gentleman friend; von ~bekanntschaften leben earn one's living from prostitution; ~beruf der all-male profession; (überwiegend von Männern ausgeübt) male-dominated profession; ~bund der; Pl. ~bünde male society; ~chor der male voice choir; ~fang der in auf ~fang gehen/aussein (ugs.) go/be after the men; ~feindlich 1. Adj. anti-male; 2. adv. in an anti-male way; ~freundschaft die friendship between men; ~gesang·verein der male choral society; ~gesellschaft die male-dominated society; ~geschichten Pl. (ugs.) affairs with men; ~haus das (Völkerk.) men's house; ~herz das man's heart; ~herzen men's hearts; ~kleider Pl. men's clothes; ~mordend Adj. (ugs. scherzh.) man-eating (fig.); ~sache die in das ist ~sache that's men's business; ~station die men's ward; ~stimme die man's voice; male voice; ~treu die; ~, ~ (Bot.) (Veronica) speedwell; veronica; (Eryngium) eryngo; sea holly; ~über·schuß der surplus of men; ~welt die o. Pl. (scherzh.) men pl.; ~wirtschaft die (scherzh.) male housekeeping no art.; ~wohn·heim das men's hostel
Mannes-: ~alter das manhood no art.; im besten ~alter sein be in the prime of life or in one's prime; ~jahre Pl. [years of] manhood sing.; ~kraft die (geh.) virility; ~tugend die (geh. veralt.) manly virtue; ~wort das; Pl. ~e (geh.) word as a gentleman; ~würde die; o. Pl. (geh.) honour as a gentleman; ~zucht die (geh. veralt.) manly self-control or discipline
mannhaft 1. Adj. manful; (tapfer) courageous ‹decision etc.›; (entschlossen) resolute ‹behaviour›; stout ‹resistance›. 2. adv. manfully; (tapfer) courageously; (entschlossen) resolutely; ~ Widerstand leisten offer stout resistance
Mannhaftigkeit die; ~: manfulness; (Mut) [manly] courage
mannig·fach 1. Adj.; nicht präd. multifarious; manifold (literary). 2. adv. in a whole variety of ways; etw. ~ gestalten give sth. many different forms
mannig·faltig (geh.) 1. Adj. multifarious; manifold (literary); (verschiedener Art) diverse. 2. adv. in a large variety of different ways; das ~ gestaltete Programm the programme with its diversity of different items
Mannig·faltigkeit die; ~: [great] diversity
Männin ['mɛnɪn] die; ~ (bibl., dichter.) woman; (Gefährtin) spouse
Männlein ['mɛnlain] das; ~s, ~ a) [kleines] ~: little man; b) (ugs. scherzh.) ~ und/oder Weiblein men and/or women; (bei jüngeren) boys and/or girls
männlich 1. Adj. a) male ‹sex, line, descendant, flower, etc.›; ~er Vorname boy's or man's name; das ~e Tier the male [animal]; b) (für den Mann typisch) masculine ‹behaviour, characteristic, etc.›; male ‹vanity›; ausgesprochen ~ wirken have a decidedly masculine appearance; eine ~e Haltung a manly attitude; ~e Stärke/Energie the strength/energy of a man; c) (Sprachw.) masculine; (Verslehre) male ‹rhyme›. 2. adv. in a masculine way
Männlichkeit die; ~ a) masculinity; manliness; b) (Potenz) virility; c) (scherzh.: Geschlechtsteile) privates pl.; private parts pl.
Männlichkeits·wahn der obsession with masculinity
Mann·loch das (Technik) manhole
Mannomann ['mano'man] Interj. (salopp) boy, oh boy!
Manns·bild das (ugs., bes. südd., österr.) man
Mannschaft die; ~, ~en a) (Sport, auch fig.) team; die erste/zweite ~ (Fußball) the first/second eleven; b) (Schiffs-, Flugzeugbesatzung) crew; c) (Milit.: Einheit) unit; vor versammelter ~: in front of all the men; (fig.) in front of everybody; d) Pl. (Milit.: einfache Soldaten) other ranks
mannschaftlich (Sport) 1. Adj.; nicht präd. as a team postpos.; das ~e Zusammenwirken the teamwork. 2. adv. as a team
Mannschafts-: ~auf·stellung die (Sport) a) [composition of the] team; team line-up; b) (das Aufstellen) selection of the team; ~dienst·grad der (Milit.) [lower] non-commissioned rank; ~führer der (Sport) team captain; ~geist der; o. Pl. (Sport) team spirit; ~kampf der (Sport) team contest or event; ~kapitän der (Sport) team captain; ~meisterschaft die (Sport) team championship; ~raum der (Seew.) crew's quarters pl.; ~spiel das (Sport) a) team game; b) (Zusammenspiel) team play; teamwork; ~sport der team sport; ~stärke die a) (Sport) team strength; b) (Milit.) personnel; ~wagen der personnel carrier; ~wertung die (Sport) team placings pl. or classification
manns-, Manns-: ~hoch Adj. as tall as a man postpos.; six-foot-high; ~leute Pl. (veralt.) menfolk; ~person die (veralt.) male personage; ~toll Adj. (ugs. abwertend) man-mad (coll.); nymphomaniac; ~tollheit die (ugs. abwertend) nymphomania no art.; ~volk das (veralt.) menfolk pl.
Mann·weib das (abwertend) amazon
Manometer [mano'me:tɐ] das; ~s, ~ a) (Physik) manometer; pressure-gauge; b) Interj. (salopp) ~! boy, oh boy!
Manöver [ma'nø:vɐ] das; ~s, ~ a) (Milit.) exercise; ~ Pl. manœuvres; ins ~ gehen od. ziehen go on manœuvres; b) (Bewegung: fig. abwertend: Trick) manœuvre

Manöver-: ~gelände das manœuvre area; **~gelände der amerikanischen Truppen** area used for manœuvres by the American troops; **~kritik die** *(Milit.)* exercise evaluation; *(fig.)* post-mortem *(coll.)*; **~kritik üben** *(fig.)* hold a post-mortem; **~schaden der** damage *no pl.* caused by manœuvres/an exercise

manövrieren 1. *itr. V.* manœuvre; **politisch klug/unklug ~** *(fig.)* perform clever/imprudent political manœuvres. **2.** *tr. V.* manœuvre ‹*vehicle*›; **jmdn. in eine einflußreiche Position ~** *(fig.)* wangle sb. into an influential position *(sl.)*

manövrier-, Manövrier-: ~fähig *Adj.* manœuvrable; **~fähigkeit die;** *o. Pl.* manœuvrability; **~un·fähig** *Adj.* unmanœuvrable

Mansarde [man'zardə] **die; ~, ~n** attic; *(Zimmer)* attic room

Mansarden-: ~dach das mansard roof; **~fenster das** mansard dormer window; **~wohnung die** attic flat *(Brit.)* or *(Amer.)* apartment

Mansch [manʃ] **der; ~[e]s** *(ugs.)* sloshy mess *(coll.)*; *(Schneematsch)* slush

manschen *itr. V. (ugs.)* slosh about *(coll.)*

Manschette [man'ʃɛtə] **die; ~, ~n a)** cuff; **[vor etw.** *(Dat.)***] ~n haben** *(fig. ugs.)* have got the willies *(sl.)* or have got the wind up *(Brit. sl.)* [about sth.]; **jetzt, wo es ernst wird, hat sie ~n** *(fig. ugs.)* now it's serious she's got cold feet; **sag bloß, du hast ~n vor ihm!** *(fig. ugs.)* don't say you're scared of him!; **b)** *(Umhüllung)* paper frill; **c)** *(Ringen: Würgegriff)* stranglehold; **d)** *(Technik: Dichtungsring)* sealing ring; ring seal

Manschetten·knopf der cuff-link

Mantel ['mantl̩] **der; ~s, Mäntel** ['mɛntl̩] **a)** coat; *(schwerer)* overcoat; **der ~ des Schweigens/Vergessens** *(fig.)* the cloak or mantle of silence/oblivion; **den ~ des Schweigens über etw.** *(Akk.)* **breiten** od. **decken** *(fig.)* observe a strict silence about sth.; **b)** *(Technik)* *(Isolier~, Kühl~)* jacket; *(Ofen~)* casing; *(Rohr~)* sleeve; *(Kabel~)* sheath; *(Geschoß~)* [bullet-]casing; *(einer Granate)* [shell-]case; *(Glocken~)* cope; *(Reifen~)* [outer] cover; casing; **c)** *(Geom.: Zylinder~, Kegel~)* curved surface; **d)** *(Finanzw.)* share or *(Amer.)* stock certificate; **e)** *(Arbeitswelt ugs.)* s. **~tarifvertrag**

Mäntelchen ['mɛntlçən] **das, ~s, ~:** little coat; *(für Kinder)* [child's] coat; **einer Sache** *(Dat.)* **ein ~ umhängen** cover up sth.; *(etw. beschönigen)* gloss over sth.; *s. auch* **Wind**

Mantel-: ~futter das [over]coat-lining; **~kleid das** coat dress; **~pavian der** hamadryas baboon; **~sack der** *(veralt.)* saddle-bag; **~tarif der** *(Arbeitswelt)* terms of the **Manteltarifvertrag**; **~tarif·vertrag der** *(Wirtsch.)* framework collective agreement [on working conditions]; **~tiere** *Pl. (Zool.)* tunicates

Mantisse [man'tɪsə] **die; ~, ~n** *(Math.)* mantissa

Mantsch [mantʃ] **der; ~[e]s** *s.* **Mansch**

mantschen *itr. V. s.* **manschen**

Manual [ma'nu̯a:l] **das; ~s, ~e, Manuale das; ~[s], ~[n]** *(Musik)* keyboard; manual

manuell [ma'nu̯ɛl] **1.** *Adj.* manual. **2.** *adv.* manually; by hand

Manufaktur [manufak'tu:ɐ̯] **die; ~, ~en a)** [small] factory *(where goods are produced largely by hand)*; **b)** *(veralt.: handgearbeitete Ware)* hand-made or handcrafted article

Manus ['ma:nʊs] **das; ~, ~** *(österr., schweiz.)*, **Manuskript** [manu'skrɪpt] **das; ~[e]s, ~e a)** *(auch hist.)* manuscript; *(Typoskript)* typescript; *(zu einem Film/Fernsehspiel/Hörspiel)* script; **als ~ gedruckt** printed for private circulation; **b)** *(Notizen eines Redners usw.)* notes *pl.*

Maoismus [mao'ɪsmʊs] **der; ~:** Maoism *no art.*

Maoist der; ~en, ~en Maoist

maoistisch 1. *Adj.* Maoist. **2.** *adv.* on Maoist lines

Mäppchen ['mɛpçən] **das; ~s, ~:** pencil-case

Mappe ['mapə] **die; ~, ~n a)** folder; *(größer, für Zeichnungen usw.)* portfolio; **b)** *(Aktentasche)* briefcase; *(Schul~)* school-bag

Mär [mɛ:ɐ̯] **die; ~, ~en** *(dichter.)* fable; *(fig.)* myth

Marabu ['ma:rabu] **der; ~s, ~s** *(Zool.)* marabou

Marathon- ['ma(:)ratɔn]: **~lauf der** marathon; **~läufer der** marathon runner; **~sitzung die** marathon session

-marathon das; ~s, ~s *(ugs.)* **Verhandlungs~/Sitzungs~:** marathon negotiations *pl.* /session

Märchen ['mɛ:ɐ̯çən] **das; ~s, ~ a)** fairy story; fairy-tale; **b)** *(ugs.: Lüge)* [tall] story *(coll.)*; **erzähl doch keine ~!** don't give me that story! *(coll.)*

Märchen-: ~buch das book of fairy stories; **~dichtung die** fairy-tale literature; **~erzähler der** teller of fairy stories; **~figur die** fairy-tale figure; **~film der** film of a fairy story

märchenhaft 1. *Adj.* **a)** fairy-story *attrib.*; *(wie ein Märchen)* fairy-story-like; as in a fairy story *postpos.*; **b)** *(zauberhaft)* magical; *(feenhaft)* fairy-like; **~ sein** be sheer magic; be like a dream; **c)** *(ugs.)* *(großartig)* fabulous; *(sehr groß)* fantastic *(coll.)*, incredible *(coll.)* ‹*speed, wealth*›. **2.** *adv. s. Adj.:* **a)** as in a fairy story; **~ gestaltet** in the form of a fairy story; **b)** magically; **~ schön** bewitchingly beautiful; **c)** *(ugs.)* fantastically *(coll.)*; incredibly *(coll.)*; **~ spielen** play like a dream or fabulously

Märchen-: ~land das: das ~land the world of fairy-tale; fairyland; **~onkel der** *(fam.)* story-hour presenter; **~prinz der** fairy-tale prince; *(fig.)* Prince Charming; **~schloß das** fairy-tale castle; **~stunde die** [children's] story hour; **~tante die** *(fam.)* [female] story-hour presenter

Marder ['mardɐ] **der; ~s, ~:** marten

Mare ['ma:rə] **das; ~, ~** od. **Maria** *(Astron.)* mare

Margarete [marga're:tə] **(die)** Margaret

Margarine [marga'ri:nə] **die; ~:** margarine

Marge ['marʒə] **die; ~, ~n** *(Wirtsch.)* margin; *(Preisdifferenz)* difference in price; *(bei Aktien)* increase in price *(over issue price)*

Margerite [margə'ri:tə] **die; ~, ~n** ox-eye daisy; *(als Zierpflanze)* marguerite

marginal [margi'na:l] *(geh.)* **1.** *Adj.* marginal. **2.** *adv.* marginally

Marginalie [margi'na:li̯ə] **die; ~, ~n** marginal note; **~n** marginalia

Maria [ma'ri:a] **(die); ~s** od. **Mariens** od. *(Rel.)* **Mariä** Mary; **Mariä Empfängnis/Geburt** Conception/Nativity of the Blessed Virgin Mary; **Mariä Himmelfahrt** Assumption

marianisch [ma'ri̯a:nɪʃ] *Adj. (kath. Kirche)* Marian

Marianne [ma'ri̯anə] **(die)** Marianne; *(fig.: Frankreich)* France; the French *pl.*

Marie [ma'ri:] **die; ~** *(salopp: Geld)* dough *(sl.)*; lolly *(Brit. sl.)*

Marien-: ~altar der Lady-altar; **~bild das** madonna; **~dichtung die** *(Literaturw.)* Marian literature; **~käfer der** ladybird; **~kult der** Marian cult; Mariolatry; **~leben das** *(Literaturw., Kunstw.)* life of our Lady; **~legende die** legend of the Virgin Mary; Marian legend; **~verehrung die** worship of the Virgin Mary; Mariolatry

Marihuana [mari'hu̯a:na] **das; ~s** marijuana

Marille [ma'rɪlə] **die; ~, ~n** *(bes. österr.)* apricot

marin [ma'ri:n] *Adj.* marine

Marinade [mari'na:də] **die; ~, ~n a)** *(Beize)* marinade; **b)** *(Salatsauce)* [marinade] dressing; **c)** *(Fischkonserve)* marinaded fish

Marine [ma'ri:nə] **die; ~, ~n a)** *(Flotte)* fleet; **b)** *(Kriegs~)* navy

marine-, Marine-: ~blau *Adj.* navy [blue]; **~flieger der** naval airman; **~infanterie die** marines *pl.*; **~infanterist der** marine; **~luft·waffe die** Fleet Air Arm *(Brit.)*; Navy Air Force *(Amer.)*; **~maler der** *(Kunst)* marine painter

Mariner der; ~s, ~ *(ugs.)* sailor

Marine-: ~schule die naval academy; **~soldat der** marine; **~stütz·punkt der** naval base; **~truppen** *Pl.* marines; **~uniform die** naval uniform

marinieren *tr. V.* marinade; **marinierte Heringe** soused herrings

Marionette [mario'nɛtə] **die; ~, ~n** puppet; marionette; *(fig. abwertend)* puppet

Marionetten-: ~regierung die *(abwertend)* puppet government; **~spieler der** puppet-master; puppeteer; **~theater das** puppet theatre

maritim [mari'ti:m] *Adj.* maritime

¹Mark [mark] **die; ~, ~** od. *(ugs. scherzh.:)* **Märker** ['mɛrkɐ] mark; **Deutsche ~:** Deutschmark; West German mark; **~ der DDR** GDR or East German mark; **zwei ~ fünfzig** two marks fifty; **die paar Märker** *(ugs.)* those few measly marks *(sl.)*; **keine müde ~** *(ugs.)* not a penny; not a cent *(Amer.)*; *s. auch* **umdrehen 1**

²Mark das; ~[e]s a) *(Knochen~)* marrow; medulla *(Anat.)*; **jmdm. das ~ aus den Knochen saugen** *(fig. ugs.)* *(finanziell)* bleed sb. white; *(arbeitsmäßig)* work sb. to death; **das ging mir durch ~ und Bein** od. *(scherzh.)* **durch ~ und Pfennig** *(fig.)* it put my teeth on edge; it went right through me; **jmdn. bis ins ~ treffen** *(fig.)* cut or sting sb. to the quick; **b)** *(Bot.)* *(Frucht~)* pulp; *(inneres Gewebe)* medulla *(as techn. term)*; pith

³Mark die; ~, ~en *(hist.)* march; **die ~ Brandenburg** the Mark [of] Brandenburg

markant [mar'kant] *Adj.* striking; distinctive; prominent ‹*figure, nose, chin*›; clear-cut, distinctive ‹*features, profile*›; **ein ~er Punkt in der Stadt** a landmark in the town

mark·durch·dringend 1. *Adj.* spine-chilling; blood-curdling. **2.** *adv.* **~ schreien** utter a spine-chilling scream

Marke die; ~, ~n a) *(Waren~)* brand; *(Fabrikat)* make; **Tabak der ~ Erinmore** the Erinmore brand of tobacco; **b)** *(Brief~, Rabatt~, Beitrags~)* stamp; **zehn ~n zu 60 Pfennig** ten 60-pfennig stamps; **c)** *(Garderoben~)* [cloakroom or *(Amer.)* checkroom] counter or tag; *(Zettel)* [cloakroom or *(Amer.)* checkroom] ticket; *(Essen~)* meal-ticket; **d)** *(Erkennungs~)* [identification] disc; *(Dienst~)* [police] identification badge; ≈ warrant card *(Brit.)* or *(Amer.)* ID card; **e)** *(Lebensmittel~)* coupon; **auf ~n verkauft werden** be on coupons; **f)** *(Markierung)* mark; *(Sport: Rekord)* record [height/distance]; **g)** *(salopp)* **du bist mir vielleicht eine ~!** you are a fine one! *(iron.)*

Märke ['mɛrkə] **die; ~, ~n** *(österr.)* monogram

Marken-: ~artikel der proprietary or *(Brit.)* branded article; **~artikel** *Pl.* proprietary or *(Brit.)* branded goods; **~butter die** best butter *(legally defined first grade of butter)*; **~erzeugnis das, ~fabrikat das** proprietary or *(Brit.)* branded product; **~name der** brand name; **~schutz der** protection of trade marks; **~zeichen das** trade mark

mark·erschütternd 1. *Adj.* heart-rending. **2.** *adv.* heart-rendingly

Marketender [markə'tɛndɐ] **der; ~s, ~, Marketenderin die; ~, ~nen** *(hist.)* sutler

Marketender·ware die troops' personal supplies *pl.*; ≈ NAAFI *(Brit.)* or *(Amer.)* PX goods *pl.*

Marketing ['markətɪŋ] **das**; ~s *(Wirtsch.)* marketing

mark-, Mark-: ~**graf der** margrave; ~**gräfin die** margravine; ~**gräflich** *Adj.; nicht präd.* margrave's; of the margrave *postpos.*

markieren 1. *tr. V.* **a)** *(auch fig.)* mark; *(Sport)* mark out ‹*course*›; **b)** *(ugs.)* sham ‹*illness, breakdown, etc.*›; **den Dummen** ~: act stupid; **c)** *(Sport)* mark ‹*player*›. **2.** *itr. V. (ugs.)* sham; put it on *(coll.)*

Markierung die; ~, ~en **a)** *(Zeichen)* marking; **ein Flugzeug mit fremder** ~: an aircraft with foreign markings *pl.*; **b)** *o. Pl.* marking [out]

Markierungs-: ~**fähnchen das** course-marker; marker flag; ~**linie die** line

markig 1. *Adj. (kernig)* pithy ‹*saying, style*›; *(kraftvoll)* vigorous, breezy ‹*commands, manner*›; powerful ‹*voice*›; ~**e Worte** strong words; *(iron.: große Reden)* big words. **2.** *adv.* pithily

märkisch *Adj.* of the Mark [of] Brandenburg *postpos.*; ‹*food, produce, etc.*› from the Mark [of] Brandenburg; *s. auch* **badisch**

Markise [mar'ki:zə] **die**; ~, ~n awning

mark-, Mark-: ~**klößchen das** *(Kochk.)* bone-marrow dumpling; ~**knochen der** marrowbone; ~**scheide die** *(Bergmannsspr.)* boundary *(of a mining area)*; ~**stein der** *(fig.)* milestone; ~**stück das** one-mark piece; ~**stück·groß** *Adj.* the size of a one-mark piece *postpos.*

Markt [markt] **der**; ~[e]s, **Märkte** ['mɛrktə] **a)** market; **heute/freitags ist** ~: today/Friday is market-day; **zum** *od.* **auf den** ~ **gehen** go to the market; **auf dem** ~: at the market; **b)** *s.* ~**platz**; **c)** *(Super~)* supermarket; **d)** *(Warenverkehr, Absatzgebiet)* market; **der** ~ **für Gebrauchtwagen** the used-car market; **eine Ware auf den** ~ **bringen** *od.* **werfen** market a product; *(mit viel Werbung)* launch a product; **auf dem** *od.* **am** ~ **sein** ‹*firm*› be in the market; ‹*article*› be on the market; *s. auch* **gemeinsam 1a; grau c; schwarz 1c**

markt-, Markt-: ~**ab·sprache die** *(Wirtsch.)* marketing agreement; ~**analyse die** *(Wirtsch.)* market analysis; ~**an·teil der** share of the market; ~**anteile zurückgewinnen** regain parts of the market; ~**beherrschend** *Adj.* market-dominating *attrib.*; ~**beherrschend sein** have a dominant position in the market; ~**bewußt 1.** *Adj.* aware of products and prices *postpos.*; **2.** *adv.* with a knowledge of products and prices; ~**fähig** *Adj. (Wirtsch.)* marketable; ~**fähig werden** become a marketable proposition; ~**flecken der** *(veralt.)* small market town; ~**forschung die** market research *no def. art.*; ~**frau die** market-woman; ~**gängig** *Adj. (Wirtsch.)* with a ready sale *postpos., not pred.*; *(fig.: üblich)* customary; usual; ~**gerecht 1.** *Adj.* ‹*product*› geared to market requirements; ‹*price*› in line with market conditions; **2.** *adv.* in accordance with market conditions; ~**halle die** covered market; ~**lage die** market situation; state of the market; ~**leiter der** supermarket manager; ~**lücke die** gap in the market; **in eine** ~**lücke [vor]stoßen** fill a gap in the market; ~**ordnung die a)** *(Wirtsch.)* [Common] Market regulations *pl.*; **b)** *(bei Wochenmärkten)* market regulations *pl.*; ~**platz der** market-place *or* -square; ~**recht das** *(hist.)* right to hold a market; market right; ~**schreier der** barker; stall-holder who cries his wares; *(fig. abwertend)* vociferous propagandist; ~**schreierisch** *(abwertend, auch fig.)* **1.** *Adj.* vociferous; **2.** *adv.* vociferously; ~**stand der** market stall; ~**tag der** market-day; ~**üblich** *Adj.* customary [in the market] *postpos.*; ~**übliche Zinsen** customary market rates; ~**weib das** *(salopp)* market-woman; **wie ein** ~**weib** like a fishwife; ~**wert der** market value; ~**wirtschaft die**: **[freie]** ~**wirtschaft** [free] market economy; **die soziale** ~**wirtschaft** the social market economy *(with State intervention safeguarding social justice and free competition)*; ~**wirtschaftlich 1.** *Adj.; nicht präd.* market-economy; free-market; **2.** *adv.* on market-economy lines

Markus·evangelium ['markʊs-] **das** St Mark's Gospel; Gospel according to St Mark

Marmara·meer ['marmara-] **das** Sea of Marmara

Marmelade [marmə'la:də] **die**; ~, ~n jam; *(Orangen~)* marmalade

Marmelade[n]-: ~**brot** [piece of] bread and jam; *(zugeklappt)* jam sandwich; ~**glas das** jam-jar

Marmor ['marmɔr] **der**; ~s marble

Marmor-: ~**bild das** *(veralt.)* marble statue; ~**block der**; *Pl.* ~**blöcke** block of marble; marble block; ~**bruch der** marble-quarry; ~**büste die** marble bust

marmorieren *tr. V.* **etw.** ~: give sth. a marbled effect; marble sth.; **eine marmorierte Platte** a marbled slab

Marmorierung die; ~, ~en marbling; marbled effect

Marmor·kuchen der marble cake

marmorn *Adj.* marble; *(fig.)* pale as marble *postpos.*; ashen ‹*pallor*›

marode *Adj. (ugs. abwertend)* clapped-out *(Brit. sl.)*

Marodeur [maro'dø:ɐ̯] **der**; ~s, ~e *(Soldatenspr.)* looter

Marokkaner [marɔ'ka:nɐ] **der**; ~s, ~, **Marokkanerin die**; ~, ~nen Moroccan

marokkanisch *Adj.* Moroccan

Marokko [ma'rɔko] **(das)**; ~s Morocco

Marone [ma'ro:nə] **die**; ~, ~n **a)** [sweet] chestnut; **b)** *s.* **Maronenpilz**

Maronen·pilz der chestnut boletus

Maronit [maro'ni:t] **der**; ~en, ~en *(Rel.)* Maronite

Marotte [ma'rɔtə] **die**; ~, ~n fad

Marquis [mar'ki:] **der**; ~ [mar'ki:(s)], ~ [mar'ki:s] marquis

Marquise [mar'ki:zə] **die**; ~, ~n marquise

[1]**Mars** [mars] **der**; ~ *(Astron.)*, [2]**Mars (der)** *(Myth.)* Mars *no def. art.*

[3]**Mars der**; ~, ~e *od.* **die**; ~, ~en *(Seemannsspr.)* crow's nest

Marsala [mar'za:la] **der**; ~s, ~s, **Marsalawein der** Marsala

Mars·bewohner der Martian

marsch [marʃ] *Interj.* **a)** *(Milit.)* [forward] march; **kehrt** – ~! about turn *or (Amer.)* face! forward march!; *s. auch* **Gleichschritt**; **b)** *(ugs.)* ~ ~! off with you!; *(beeil dich!)* move it! *(coll.)*; look snappy! *(coll.)*; ~ **ins Bett!** off to bed [with you]!; ~ **an die Arbeit!** get down to work!

[1]**Marsch der**; ~[e]s, **Märsche** ['mɛrʃə] **a)** *(Milit.)* march; *(Wanderung)* [long] walk; hike; **ein** ~ **von einer Stunde** an hour's march/walk; **einen** ~ **[von einer Stunde] machen** go for *or* take a long walk [lasting an hour]; **jmdn. in** ~ **setzen** *(Milit.)* march sb. off; *(fig.)* mobilize sb.; **sich in** ~ **setzen** make a move; get moving; *(Milit.)* march off; **b)** *(Musikstück)* march; **jmdm. [gehörig] den** ~ **blasen** *(fig. salopp)* give sb. a real rocket *(Brit. sl.) or (coll.)* bawling out

[2]**Marsch die**; ~, ~en fertile marshland

Marschall ['marʃal] **der**; ~s, **Marschälle** ['marʃɛlə] *(hist.)* marshal

Marschall[s]·stab der marshal's baton; **den** ~ **im Tornister tragen** *(fig.)* have what it takes to achieve high rank

marsch-, Marsch-: ~**befehl der** *(Milit.)* marching orders *pl.*; **der** ~**befehl** one's marching orders; ~**bereit** *Adj. (Milit.)* ready to march *or* move *pred.*; *(ugs.)* ready to go *pred.*; ~**boden der** [fertile] marshy soil; ~**flug·körper der** cruise missile; ~**gepäck das** *(Milit.)* marching pack; **unser** ~**gepäck** our marching packs *pl.*

marschieren *itr. V.; mit sein* **a)** march; **b)** *(ugs.: mit großen Schritten gehen)* march; stalk; *(wandern)* walk; hike; **c)** *(ugs.: vorankommen)* **[richtig]** ~: progress smoothly; **der Fortschritt marschiert** the march of progress is inexorable

Marsch-: ~**kolonne die** *(Milit.)* marching column; ~**land das** [fertile] marshland; ~**lied das** marching song; ~**musik die** march music; ~**ordnung die** *(Milit.)* marching order; ~**pause die** halt [on the march]; **eine** ~**pause einlegen** make a halt; ~**richtung die** *(Milit.)* direction of march; ~**route die** *(Milit.)* route; *(fig.)* line [of approach]; **die** ~**route für die Verhandlungen** *(fig.)* the line to be taken in the negotiations; ~**säule die** column of marchers; ~**tempo das** marching pace; *(Musik)* march tempo; **im** ~**tempo** at a quick march; *(Musik)* in march tempo; ~**verpflegung die** *(Milit.)* marching rations *pl.*; *(fig. ugs.)* rations *pl.* [for the journey]

Marseillaise [marzɛ'jɛ:zə] **die**; ~: Marseillaise

Marseille [mar'zɛ:j] **(das)**; ~s Marseilles

Marshall·plan ['marʃal-] **der** *(hist.)* Marshall Plan

Mars-: ~**mensch der** Martian; ~**segel das** *(Seemannsspr.)* main topsail; ~**sonde die** *(Raumfahrt)* Mars probe

Mar·stall ['mar-] **der** *(hist.)* [royal *or* princely] stables *pl.*

Marter ['martɐ] **die**; ~, ~n *(geh.) (Folter)* torture; *(fig.: seelisch)* torment; **jmdm.** ~**n bereiten** *od.* **zufügen** *(körperlich)* subject sb. to torture; *(seelisch)* inflict torment on sb.

Marter·instrument das instrument of torture

Marterl ['martɐl] **das**; ~s, ~n *(bayr., österr.)* wayside shrine

martern *tr. V. (geh.)* torture; *(fig.: seelisch)* torment; **jmdn. zu Tode** ~: torture sb. to death

Marter-: ~**pfahl der** stake; ~**tod der** *(geh.)* death by torture; *(Märtyrertod)* death of a martyr

Marterung die; ~, ~en *(geh.)* torture; *(seelisch)* torment

martialisch [mar'tsi̯a:lɪʃ] *(geh.)* **1.** *Adj.* warlike ‹*appearance, figure, etc.*›; martial ‹*music*›. **2.** *adv.* in a warlike manner; *(drohend)* threateningly; aggressively

Martin-Horn Ⓦⓩ **das** *s.* **Martinshorn**

Martini [mar'ti:ni] **(das)**; *indekl.* **zu** ~: on St Martin's Day; at Martinmas

Martins-: ~**gans die** Martinmas goose; ~**horn das** *(volkstümlich)* siren *(of emergency vehicle)*; **mit** ~**horn** sounding its siren; ~**tag der** St Martin's Day

Märtyrer ['mɛrtyrɐ] **der**; ~s, ~, **Märtyrerin die**; ~, ~nen martyr

Märtyrer-: ~**krone die** martyr's crown; **die** ~**krone tragen** be a martyr/martyrs; ~**tod der** death of a martyr; **den** ~**tod sterben** die a martyr's death

Märtyrin ['mɛrtyrɪn] **die**; ~, ~nen *s.* **Märtyrerin**

Martyrium [mar'ty:ri̯ʊm] **das**; ~s, **Martyrien** martyrdom; **das war ein** ~ *(fig.)* it was sheer martyrdom

Marxismus [mar'ksɪsmʊs] **der**; ~: Marxism *no art.*

Marxismus-Leninismus der Marxism-Leninism *no art.*

Marxist der; ~en, ~en, **Marxistin die**; ~, ~nen Marxist

marxistisch 1. *Adj.* Marxist. **2.** *adv.* ‹*view, interpret*› from a Marxist point of view; ‹*think, act*› in line with Marxism

marxistisch-leninistisch 1. *Adj.* Marxist-Leninist. **2.** *adv.* ‹*view, interpret*› from a Marxist-Leninist point of view; ‹*think, act*› in line with Marxism-Leninism

März [mɛrts] **der;** ~**[es],** *dichter.:* ~**en** March; *s. auch* **April**
März[en]-: ~**becher der a)** Spring Snowflake; **b)** *(volkstümlich: Narzisse)* daffodil; ~**bier das** *kind of dark bock beer*
Marzipan [martsi'pa:n, *österr.* '---] **das;** ~**s,** *österr.:* **der;** ~**s** marzipan
Marzipan-: ~**kartoffel die** marzipan ball; ~**schwein das** marzipan pig
Mascara [mas'ka:ra] **der;** ~, ~**s** mascara brush/pencil
Masche ['maʃə] **die;** ~, ~**n a)** stitch; *(Lauf~)* run; ladder *(Brit.)*; *(beim Netz)* mesh; **die** ~**n eines Netzes** the mesh *sing.* of a net; **durch die** ~**n des Gesetzes schlüpfen** *(fig.)* slip through a loophole in the law; **b)** *(ugs.: Trick)* trick; **das ist die** ~: that's the way *or* trick; **c)** *(ugs.: Mode, Gag)* **die neueste** ~: the latest fad *or* craze; **d)** *(österr.: Schleife)* bow
Maschen-: ~**draht der** wire netting; ~**draht·zaun der** wire-netting fence; ~**probe die** *(Handarb.)* tension check
Maschine [ma'ʃi:nə] **die;** ~, ~**n a)** machine; *(Näh~/Wasch~)* [sewing-/washing-]machine; **ich bin doch keine** ~: I'm not a machine; **b)** *(ugs.: Automotor)* engine; **c)** *(Flugzeug)* [aero]plane; **die erste** ~ **nach Zürich** the first plane *or* flight to Zurich; **d)** *(ugs.: Motorrad)* machine; **e)** *(Schreib~)* typewriter; **einen Brief in die** ~ **diktieren** dictate a letter straight on to the typewriter; ~ **schreiben** type; **f)** *(ugs. abwertend: dicke Frau)* great hulk of a woman
maschine·geschrieben 1. *2. Part. v.* **maschineschreiben. 2.** *Adj.* typed; typewritten
maschinell [maʃi'nɛl] **1.** *Adj.* **a)** *nicht präd.* machine *attrib.*; by machine *postpos.*; ~**e Herstellung** machine production; **b)** *(wie eine Maschine)* mechanical. **2.** *adv.* **a)** by machine; ~ **hergestellt** machine-made; **b)** *(wie eine Maschine)* mechanically
maschinen-, Maschinen-: ~**bau der;** *o. Pl.* **a)** machine construction *no art.*; mechanical engineering *no art.*; **b)** *(Lehrfach)* mechanical engineering *no art.*; ~**bauer der** machine-builder; ~**bau·ingenieur der** mechanical engineer; ~**fabrik die** engineering works *sing. or pl.*; ~**geschrieben** *Adj. s.* **maschinegeschrieben 2**; ~**gewehr das** machine-gun; ~**halle die** machine-shop; ~**haus das** power house; *(auf Schiffen)* engine-room; ~**kraft die** mechanical power; engine power; **mit** ~**kraft** by mechanical *or* engine power; ~**lesbar 1.** *Adj.* machine-readable; **2.** *adv.* in machine-readable form; ~**park der** plant; ~**pistole die** sub-machine-gun; ~**raum der** engine-room; ~**satz der** *(Druckw.)* machine composition; ~**schaden der** engine trouble *no indef. art.*; ~**schlosser der** fitter; ~**schreiben das** typing; **das** ~**schreiben lernen** learn to type; ~**schreiber der,** ~**schreiberin die** typist; ~**schrift die** typing; *(Schriftart)* typeface; type; **in** ~**schrift** typed; ~**schriftlich** *Adj.* typewritten; typed; ~**stürmer** *Pl.* *(hist.)* machine-breakers; machine-wreckers; ~**stürmerei die;** ~: machine-breaking; machine-wrecking; ~**zeit·alter das** machine age
Maschinerie [maʃinə'ri:] **die;** ~, ~**n** machinery; **die gnadenlose** ~ **der Justiz** *(fig. geh.)* the merciless wheels *pl.* of justice
maschine·schreiben *unr. itr. V.; Zusschr. nur im Inf. u. Part.* type
Maschinist der; ~**en,** ~**en, Maschinistin die;** ~, ~**nen a)** machinist; **b)** *(Schiffs~)* engineer
Maser ['ma:zɐ] **die;** ~, ~**n** figure
maserig *Adj.* figured
masern *tr. V.* grain ‹*wood*›
Masern *Pl.* measles *sing. or pl.*
Maserung die; ~, ~**en** *(in Holz, Leder)* [wavy] grain; *(in Marmor)* vein; *(in Fell)* patterning

Maske ['maskə] **die;** ~, ~**n a)** *(auch fig.)* mask; **ihr Gesicht erstarrte zur** ~: her features froze into a mask; **die** ~ **fallen lassen** *od.* **abwerfen** *(fig.)* drop one's mask; **jmdm. die** ~ **vom Gesicht reißen** *(fig.)* unmask sb.; **b)** *(Theater)* make-up; ~ **machen** make up; **d)** *(Mensch)* masker
Masken-: ~**ball der** masked ball; masquerade; ~**bildner der** make-up artist
maskenhaft 1. *Adj.* mask-like. **2.** *adv.* like a mask; **ein** ~ **starres Gesicht** a face frozen into a mask
Maskerade [maskə'ra:də] **die;** ~, ~**n a)** [fancy-dress] costume; ~ **sein** *(fig.)* be a masquerade; **b)** *(veralt.: Maskenball)* masquerade; *(Kostümfest)* fancy-dress ball
maskieren 1. *tr. V.* **a)** mask; **b)** *(verkleiden)* dress up. **2.** *refl. V.* **a)** put on a mask/masks; **b)** *(sich verkleiden)* dress up
Maskierung die; ~, ~**en a)** *(das Verkleiden)* dressing up; **b)** *(Verkleidung)* disguise; *(beim Kostümball)* [fancy-dress] costume; **c)** *(Tarnung)* masking; disguising
Maskottchen [mas'kɔtçən] **das;** ~**s,** ~: [lucky] mascot
maskulin [masku'li:n, *auch* '---] **1.** *Adj.* *(auch Sprachw.)* masculine. **2.** *adv.* in a masculine way
Maskulinum ['maskuli:nʊm] **das;** ~**s, Maskulina** *(Sprachw.)* masculine noun
Masochismus [mazɔ'xɪsmʊs] **der;** ~ *(Psych.)* masochism *no art.*
Masochist [mazɔ'xɪst] **der;** ~**en,** ~**en, Masochistin die;** ~, ~**nen** *(Psych.)* masochist
masochistisch *(Psych.)* **1.** *Adj.* masochistic. **2.** *adv.* masochistically; ~ **veranlagt sein** have masochistic tendencies
maß *1. u. 3. Pers. Sg. Prät. v.* **messen**
[1]Maß [ma:s] **das;** ~**es,** ~**e a)** measure **(für** of); ~**e und Gewichte** weights and measures; **b)** *(fig.)* **ein gerüttelt** ~ **[an** *(Dat.) od.* **von etw.]** *(geh.)* a good measure [of sth.]; **das** ~ **ist voll** enough is enough; **das** ~ **vollmachen** go too far; **mit zweierlei** ~ **messen** apply different [sets of] standards; **c)** *(Größe)* measurement; *(von Räumen, Möbeln)* dimension; measurement; **ihre** ~**e sind ...:** her measurements *or* vital statistics are ...; **[bei] jmdm.** ~ **nehmen** take sb.'s measurements; measure sb. [up]; **d)** *(Grad)* measure, degree **(an** + *Dat.* of); **in solchem** ~**e** *od.* **in einem** ~**e, daß ...:** to such an extent that ...; **in großem/gewissem** ~**e** to a great/certain extent; **im höchsten** ~**[e]** extremely; exceedingly; **in vollem** ~**e** fully; **im gleichen** ~**[e]** to the same extent; **e)** *(Mäßigung)* **weder** ~ **noch Ziel kennen** know no restraint; **ohne** ~ **und Ziel** immoderately; **in** *od.* **mit** ~**en** in moderation; **über die** *od.* **alle** ~**en** *(geh.)* beyond [all] measure
[2]Maß die; ~, ~**[e]** *(bayr., österr.)* litre [of beer]; **zwei** ~ **Bier** two litres of beer
Massage [ma'sa:ʒə] **die;** ~, ~**n** massage; **zur** ~ **gehen** go for a massage
Massage-: ~**gerät das** massager; ~**institut das** *(auch verhüll.)* massage parlour; ~**öl das** massage oil; ~**salon der** *(verhüll.)* massage parlour *(euphem.)*; ~**stab der** vibrator
Massaker [ma'sa:kɐ] **das;** ~**s,** ~: massacre
massakrieren *tr. V.* massacre
Maß-: ~**analyse die** *(Chemie)* volumetric analysis; ~**an·gabe die** stated dimensions *pl. or* measurements *pl.*; *(bei Hohlmaßen)* stated capacity; ~**an·zug der** made-to-measure suit; tailor-made suit; ~**arbeit die a)** custom-made item; *(Kleidungsstück)* made-to-measure item; **[eine]** ~**arbeit sein** be custom-made/made-to-measure; **b)** *(genaue Arbeit)* neat work
Masse ['masə] **die;** ~, ~**n a)** mass; *(Kochk.)* mixture; **b)** *(Menge)* mass; ~**n an** *(Dat.) od.* **von Autos** masses of cars; **riesige** ~**n Papier** huge piles *or* heaps of paper; **die** ~ **der Befragten** the bulk of those questioned; **die** ~ **macht's** *(ugs.)* it's quantity that's important; **sie kamen in** ~**n** they came in their masses *or* in droves; **das ist eine ganze** ~: that's a lot *(coll.) or* a great deal; **c)** *(Menschen~)* **eine große** ~ **[an] Menschen** *(Dat.)* a great mass of people; **die namenlose** ~: the anonymous masses *pl.*; **die breite** ~: the bulk *or* broad mass of the population; **die [werktätigen]** ~**n** the [working] masses; **d)** *(Physik)* mass; **e)** *(Wirtsch.)* assets *pl.*; *(Erb~)* estate; **mangels** ~: for lack of assets
Maß-: ~**einheit die** unit of measurement; ~**ein·teilung die** calibrations *pl.*
Massel ['masl̩] **der;** ~**s** *(ugs.)* ~ **haben** be dead lucky *(coll.)*
Massen-: ~**ab·fertigung die** *(oft abwertend)* mass processing *no indef. art.*; ~**absatz der** mass sale; **für den** ~**absatz gefertigt** produced for mass sale; ~**an·drang der** crush; ~**an·ziehung die** *(Physik)* gravitation; ~**arbeitslosigkeit die** mass unemployment; ~**artikel der** mass-produced article; ~**auf·gebot das** large body *or* contingent; ~**bedarf der** mass demand; ~**bedarfs·artikel der** mass consumer commodity; ~**bewegung die** mass movement; ~**blatt das** mass-circulation paper; ~**demonstration die** mass demonstration; ~**entlassungen** *Pl.* mass redundancies *pl.*; ~**fabrikation die** mass production; ~**gesellschaft die** *(Soziol.)* mass society; ~**grab das** mass grave; ~**güter** *Pl.* **a)** mass-produced goods; **b)** *(Frachtgut)* bulk goods
massenhaft 1. *Adj.; nicht präd.* in huge numbers *postpos.*; **das** ~**e Auftreten dieser Schädlinge** the appearance of huge numbers of these pests. **2.** *adv.* on a huge *or* massive scale; ~ **kommen** come in vast *or* huge numbers; ~ **Geld haben** *(ugs.)* have pots of money *(coll.)*; ~ **Schulden haben** have a pile of debts *(coll.)*
massen-, Massen-: ~**her·stellung die** *s.* ~**produktion;** ~**hin·richtung die** mass execution; ~**hysterie die** mass hysteria; ~**initiative die** *(DDR)* mass initiative; ~**karambolage die** multiple crash; [multiple] pile-up; ~**kommunikations·mittel das** medium of mass communication; mass medium; ~**kundgebung die** mass rally; ~**medium das** mass medium; ~**mord der** mass murder; ~**mörder der** mass murderer; ~**organisation die** *(bes. DDR)* mass organisation; ~**produktion die** mass production; **etw. in** ~**produktion herstellen** mass-produce sth.; ~**psychologie die** mass psychology *no art.*; ~**psychose die** mass psychosis *no indef. art.*; ~**quartier das** *(abwertend)* mass accommodation *no indef. art.*; ~**schlägerei die** [grand] free-for-all; pitched battle *(fig.)*; ~**sport der** mass sport; ~**sterben das: das** ~**sterben von ...:** the death of huge numbers of ...; **ein** ~**sterben begann** people/animals *etc.* began to die in huge numbers; ~**szene die** crowd scene; ~**tourismus der** mass tourism *no art.*; ~**verhaftung die** mass arrest; ~**verkehrsmittel das** means *sing.* of mass transportation; ~**vernichtung die** mass extermination; ~**vernichtungs·waffen** *Pl.* weapons of mass destruction; ~**wahn der** mass hysteria; ~**ware die** mass-produced article; ~**waren** mass-produced goods; ~**weise** *Adv.* in huge numbers *or* quantities; ~**wirksam** *Adj.* with mass impact *postpos., not pred.*; ~**wirksam sein** have mass impact; ~**wirkung die** mass impact
Masseur [ma'søːɐ̯] **der;** ~**s,** ~**e** masseur
Masseurin die; ~, ~**nen** masseuse
Masseuse [ma'sø:zə] **die;** ~, ~**n** *(auch verhüll.)* masseuse
Maß·gabe die *in* **nach** ~ (+ *Gen.*) *(geh.)* in accordance with; **mit der** ~, **etw. zu tun** with instructions to do sth.

maß·gearbeitet *Adj.* custom-made; made-to-measure ⟨*clothes*⟩

maß·gebend, maß·geblich 1. *Adj.* authoritative ⟨*book, expert, opinion*⟩; definitive ⟨*text*⟩; important, influential ⟨*person, circles, etc.*⟩; decisive ⟨*factor, influence, etc.*⟩; *(zuständig)* competent ⟨*authority, person, etc.*⟩; **sein Urteil ist nicht ~:** his opinion carries no weight. **2.** *adv.* ⟨*influence*⟩ considerably, to a considerable extent; *(entscheidend)* decisively; **~ an etw.** *(Dat.)* **beteiligt sein** play a leading role in sth.

maß-, Maß-: ~gerecht 1. accurate; **genau ~gerecht für etw. sein** be just the right size for sth.; **2.** *adv.* accurately; **~gerecht zugeschnittene Regalbretter** shelves cut to size; **~geschneidert** *Adj.* made-to-measure; *(fig.)* tailor-made; **~halte·appell der** call *or* appeal for moderation; **~|halten** *unr. itr. V.* exercise moderation

¹massieren 1. *tr. V.* massage. **2.** *itr. V.* **gut ~ können** be a good masseur/masseuse

²massieren 1. *tr. V.* mass ⟨*troops etc.*⟩. **2.** *refl. V.* ⟨*troops etc.*⟩ mass

massig 1. *Adj.* massive; bulky, massive ⟨*figure*⟩. **2.** *adv. (ugs.)* **~ Geld verdienen** earn pots of money *(coll.)*; **~ zu tun haben** have loads *or* tons to do *(coll.)*

mäßig ['mɛːsɪç] **1.** *Adj.* **a)** moderate; **im Essen ~ sein** eat in moderation; be a moderate eater; **b)** *(gering)* moderate, modest ⟨*interest, income, talent, attendance*⟩; **c)** *(mittel~)* mediocre; indifferent; indifferent ⟨*health*⟩; **seine Leistungen sind mehr als ~:** his performance is worse than mediocre. **2.** *adv.* **a)** in moderation; **~, aber regelmäßig** *(scherzh.)* in moderation but regularly; **b)** *(gering)* moderately ⟨*gifted, talented*⟩; **nur ~ verkauft worden sein** have had only a modest sale; **c)** *(mittel~)* indifferently

mäßigen *(geh.)* **1.** *tr. V.* moderate ⟨*language, demands*⟩; curb, check ⟨*anger, impatience*⟩; slacken, reduce ⟨*speed*⟩. **2.** *refl. V.* **a)** practise *or* exercise moderation **(bei** in); *(sich beherrschen)* control *or* restrain oneself; **b)** *(nachlassen)* ⟨*storm*⟩ abate; ⟨*heat*⟩ grow less intense

Mäßigkeit die; ~ a) moderation; **jmdm. ~ empfehlen** advise sb. to exercise moderation; **b)** *(Mittel~)* mediocrity

Mäßigung die; ~: moderation; restraint; **jmdn. zur ~ mahnen** urge sb. to control *or* restrain himself/herself

massiv [ma'siːf] **1.** *Adj.* **a)** solid; **~ bauen** build solidly; **b)** *(heftig)* massive ⟨*demand*⟩; crude ⟨*accusation, threat*⟩; heavy, strong ⟨*attack, criticism, pressure*⟩; **~ werden** *(ugs.)* get tough. **2.** *adv.* ⟨*attack*⟩ heavily, strongly; ⟨*accuse, threaten*⟩ crudely

Massiv das; ~s, ~e massif

Massiv-: ~bau der, ~bau·weise die massive construction; **in ~bauweise errichtet sein** be of massive construction

Massivität [masivi'tɛːt] **die; ~** *s.* **massiv b:** massiveness; crudeness; heaviness; strength

Maß·krug der *(südd., österr.)* litre tankard *or* beer-mug; *(aus Steingut)* stein

Maß·liebchen das daisy

maß·los 1. *Adj. (äußerst)* extreme; *(übermäßig)* inordinate; gross ⟨*exaggeration, insult*⟩; excessive ⟨*demand, claim*⟩; *(grenzenlos)* boundless ⟨*ambition, greed, sorrow, joy*⟩; extravagant ⟨*spendthrift*⟩; **~ im Essen/Trinken sein** eat/drink to excess; **~ in seinen Ansprüchen sein** be excessive in one's demands. **2.** *adv. (äußerst)* extremely; *(übermäßig)* inordinately; ⟨*exaggerate*⟩ grossly; **sie ist ~ ehrgeizig** her ambition knows no bounds

Maßlosigkeit die; ~ *s.* **maßlos:** extremeness; inordinateness; grossness; excessiveness; boundlessness

Maßnahme die; ~, ~n measure; **~n gegen etw. einleiten/treffen** introduce/take measures against sth.; **~n zur Verhütung von Unfällen treffen** take measures *or* steps to prevent accidents; **eine abschreckende ~:** a deterrent

Maß·regel die regulation; *(Maßnahme)* measure

maßregeln *tr. V. (zurechtweisen)* reprimand; *(bestrafen)* discipline

Maß·reg[e]lung die *(Zurechtweisung)* reprimand; *(Bestrafung)* disciplinary measure

Maß·schneider der bespoke tailor *(Brit.)*; custom tailor *(Amer.)*

Maß·stab der a) standard; **einen hohen ~ anlegen/setzen** apply/set a high standard; **sich** *(Dat.)* **jmdn./etw. zum ~ nehmen** take sb./sth. as one's model; **b)** *(Geogr.)* scale; **diese Karte hat einen großen/kleinen ~:** this is a large-/small-scale map; **den ~ 1:150 000 haben** be drawn to a scale of 1:150,000; **im ~ 1:100** to a scale of 1:100; **c)** *(Zollstock)* rule; *(Lineal)* ruler

maßstäblich ['-ʃtɛːplɪç], **maßstab[s]·gerecht, maßstab[s]·getreu 1.** *Adj.* scale *attrib.* ⟨*model, drawing, etc.*⟩; [true] to scale *pred.*; **2.** *adv.* to scale

maß-, Maß-: ~system das system of measuring units; **~voll 1.** *Adj.* moderate; **2.** *adv.* in moderation; **~voll urteilen** be moderate in one's judgements; **~vor·lage die** *(Fußballjargon)* accurate pass; **~werk das;** *o. Pl. (Archit.)* tracery

¹Mast [mast] **der; ~[e]s, ~en,** *auch:* **~e** *(Schiffs~, Antennen~)* mast; *(Stange, Fahnen~)* pole; *(Hochspannungs~)* pylon

²Mast die; ~, ~en *(Landw.)* fattening; **für die ~ geeignet** suitable for fattening

Mast-: ~baum der mast; **~bulle der** *(gemästet)* fattened bull; *(für die Mast vorgesehen)* fattening bull; **~darm der** *(Anat.)* rectum

mästen ['mɛstn̩] *tr. V.* fatten; *(fig. ugs.)* overfeed; **sich ~** *(ugs.)* fatten oneself up

Mast·futter das fattening feed[stuff]

Mastiff ['mastɪf] **der; ~s, ~s** *(Zool.)* mastiff

Mast-: ~korb der crow's-nest; **~schwein das** *(gemästet)* fattened pig; *(für die Mast vorgesehen)* fattening pig

Mästung die; ~: fattening

Masturbation [mastʊrba'tsioːn] **die; ~, ~en** masturbation

masturbieren [mastʊr'biːrən] *itr., tr. V.* masturbate

Matador [mata'doːɐ̯] **der; ~s, ~e a)** matador; **b)** *(fig.)* star

Match [mɛtʃ] **das** *od.* **der; ~[e]s, ~s** *od.* **~e** match

Match-: ~ball der *([Tisch]tennis)* match point; **~beutel der, ~sack der** duffle bag

Mate ['maːtə] **der; ~, Mate·tee der** maté

Mater ['maːtɐ] **die; ~, ~n** *(Druckw.) s.* **Matrize**

material *Adj. (Philos.)* material

Material [mate'ri̯aːl] **das; ~s, ~ien a)** material; *(Bau~)* materials *pl.*; **b)** *(Hilfsmittel, Utensilien)* materials *pl.*; *(für den Bau)* equipment; **das rollende ~** *(Eisenb.)* the rolling stock; **c)** *(Beweis~)* evidence

Material-: ~aus·gabe die a) issue of materials; **b)** *(Raum)* stores *pl.*; store-room; **~beschaffung die** obtaining of materials; *(Kauf)* purchasing of materials; **~fehler der** material defect

Materialisation [materializa'tsioːn] **die; ~, ~en** *(Parapsych., Physik)* materialization

materialisieren *tr., refl. V. (Parapsych., Physik)* materialize

Materialismus der; ~ *(auch abwertend)* materialism

Materialist der; ~en, ~en, Materialistin die; ~, ~en *(auch abwertend)* materialist

materialistisch *(auch abwertend)* **1.** *Adj.* materialistic. **2.** *adv.* materialistically

Materialität [materi̯ali'tɛːt] **die; ~** *(Philos.)* materiality

Material-: ~kosten *Pl.* cost *sing.* of materials; **~ökonomie die** *(DDR)* economical use of materials; economy in the use of materials; **~prüfung die** materials testing; **~prüfungen** tests on materials; **~sammlung die** collection *or* gathering of material; **~schlacht die** *(Milit.)* battle of matériel

Materie [ma'teːri̯ə] **die; ~, ~n a)** *(geh.)* subject; **b)** *(Physik, Philos.)* matter

materiell [mate'ri̯ɛl] **1.** *Adj.* **a)** *(stofflich)* material; physical; **b)** *(wirtschaftlich)* material ⟨*value, damage*⟩; *(finanziell)* financial; **c)** *(abwertend: materialistisch)* materialistic. **2.** *adv.* **a)** *(wirtschaftlich)* materially; *(finanziell)* financially; **b)** *(abwertend)* materialistically; **~ eingestellt sein** be materialistic

Mate·tee der *s.* **Mate**

Mathe ['matə] **die; ~** *(ugs.)* maths *sing.* *(Brit. coll.)*; math *(Amer. coll.)*

Mathe·arbeit die *(ugs.)* maths test *(coll.)*

Mathematik [matəma'tiːk] **die; ~:** mathematics *sing., no art.*

Mathematiker der; ~s, ~, Mathematikerin die; ~, ~nen mathematician

Mathematik·unterricht der mathematics teaching/lesson; *s. auch* **Englischunterricht**

mathematisch 1. *Adj.* mathematical. **2.** *adv.* mathematically

Matinee [mati'neː] **die; ~, ~n** morning performance

Matjes ['matjəs] **der; ~, ~:** matie [herring]

Matjes-: ~filet das filleted matie [herring]; **~hering der** salted matie [herring]

Matratze [ma'tratsə] **die; ~, ~n** mattress; **er horcht an der ~** *(fig. scherzh.)* he's [in bed] having a kip *(Brit. sl.) or (coll.)* snooze

Matratzen·lager das mattress/mattresses on the floor

Mätresse [mɛ'trɛsə] **die; ~, ~n** *(geh. veralt.)* mistress

matriarchalisch [matriar'çaːlɪʃ] *Adj.* matriarchal

Matriarchat [matriar'çaːt] **das; ~[e]s, ~e** matriarchy

Matrikel [ma'triːkl̩] **die; ~, ~n a)** *(Hochschulw.)* student register; **b)** *(österr.: Personenstandsregister)* register of births, deaths, and marriages

Matrix ['maːtrɪks] **die; ~, Matrizes** [ma'triːtseːs] *(Biol., Math., Sprachw.)* matrix

Matrize [ma'triːtsə] **die; ~, ~n** *(Druckw.)* **a)** matrix; **b)** *(Folie)* stencil; **einen Text auf ~** *(Akk.)* **schreiben** make a stencil of a text

Matrone [ma'troːnə] **die; ~, ~n** matron

matronenhaft *(abwertend)* **1.** *Adj.* matronly. **2.** *adv.* in a matronly fashion

Matrose [ma'troːzə] **der; ~n, ~n a)** sailor; seaman; **b)** *(Dienstgrad)* ordinary seaman

Matrosen-: ~an·zug der sailor suit; **~mütze die** sailor's cap

Matsch der; ~[e]s *(ugs.)*, **Matsche** ['matʃə] **die; ~** *(nordd.)* **a)** *(aufgeweichter Boden)* mud; *(breiiger Schmutz)* sludge; *(Schnee~)* slush; **b)** *(Brei)* mush

matschen *itr. V. (ugs.)* **in etw.** *(Dat.)* **~:** splash about in sth.; **im Essen ~:** mess about with one's food

matschig *Adj. (ugs.)* **a)** muddy; slushy ⟨*snow*⟩; **b)** *(weich)* mushy; squashy ⟨*fruit*⟩

Matsch·wetter das *(ugs.)* **bei diesem ~:** when it's muddy like this; *(bei Schneematsch)* when it's slushy like this; **dieses widerliche ~:** this revolting weather, when there's mud/slush everywhere

matt [mat] **1.** *Adj.* **a)** weak; weary ⟨*limbs, spirit, etc.*⟩; weak, faint ⟨*voice, smile, pulse*⟩; feeble ⟨*applause, reaction*⟩; limp, feeble ⟨*handshake*⟩; faint ⟨*echo*⟩; **vor Hunger/Durst ~ sein** be faint *or* weak with hunger/thirst; **sich ~ fühlen** feel weak and listless; **ein ~es Echo finden** find a lukewarm response; **b)** *(glanzlos)* matt ⟨*paper, polish,* etc.⟩; dull ⟨*metal, mirror, etc.*⟩; dull, lustreless ⟨*eyes, look*⟩; **c)** *(undurchsichtig)* frosted ⟨*glass*⟩; pearl ⟨*light-bulb*⟩; **d)** *(gedämpft)* soft, subdued ⟨*light*⟩; soft, pale ⟨*colour*⟩; **e)** *(unbeherzt, nicht überzeugend)* feeble; weak; feeble, lame ⟨*excuse, joke*⟩; **f)** *(beim Schachspiel)* **[Schach und] ~!** checkmate!; **~ sein** be checkmated; **jmdn. ~ setzen** *(auch fig.)* checkmate sb. **2.** *adv.* **a)** *(kraftlos)* weakly; ⟨*smile*⟩ weakly, faintly; ⟨*applaud, react*⟩ feebly; **b)** *(gedämpft)* softly ⟨*lit*⟩; **der Mond schien ~ durch die Bäume** the moon shone wanly through the trees; **c)** *(mäßig)* ⟨*protest, contradict*⟩ feebly, weakly

Matt das; ~s *(Schach)* [check]mate

matt·blau *Adj.* pale blue

[1]Matte ['matə] **die; ~, ~n** *(auch Sport)* mat; **um 7 Uhr hier/dort auf der ~ stehen** *(fig. ugs.)* be here/there at 7 o'clock; **bei jmdm. auf der ~ stehen** *(fig. ugs.)* turn up on sb.'s doorstep

[2]Matte die; ~, ~n *(schweiz., dichter. veralt.)* meadow

Matt-: ~glass das frosted glass; *(Fot.)* ground glass; **~gold das** dull gold

Matthäi [ma'tɛ:i] *in* **bei ihm ist ~ am letzten** *(ugs.)* it's all up with him; *(finanziell)* he hasn't got a penny to his name

Matthäus [ma'tɛ:ʊs] **(der); Matthäus'** Matthew

Matthäus·evangelium das St Matthew's Gospel; the Gospel according to St Matthew

mattieren *tr. V.* give a matt finish to; matt; frost ⟨*glass*⟩

Mattigkeit die; ~ *(Schwäche)* weakness; *(Erschöpfung)* weariness

Matt-: ~lack der matt varnish; **~scheibe die a)** *(ugs.)* telly *(Brit. coll.)*; box *(coll.)*; **b)** *(Fot.)* matt screen; ground-glass screen; **ich habe ~scheibe** *(fig. ugs.)* I'm not with it *(coll.)*

Matur [ma'tu:ɐ̯] *(schweiz.)*, **Matura die; ~** *(österr., schweiz.) s.* **Abitur**

Maturand [matu'rant] **der; ~en, ~en, Maturandin die; ~, ~nen** *(schweiz.) s.* **Abiturient, Abiturientin**

Maturant [matu'rant] **der; ~en, ~en, Maturantin die; ~, ~nen** *(österr.) s.* **Abiturient, Abiturientin**

Maturität [maturi'tɛ:t] **die; ~ a)** *(veralt.: Reife)* maturity; **b)** *(schweiz.) s.* **Abitur**

Matz [mat͜s] **der; ~es, ~e** *od.* **Mätze** ['mɛt͜sə] *(fam.)* **kleiner ~:** little man

Mätzchen ['mɛt͜sçən] **das; ~s, ~** *(ugs.)* *(Posse)* antic; *(Kniff)* trick; **laßt die ~:** stop fooling about *or* around; stop your antics; **~ machen** fool about *or* around; **Hände hoch, und keine ~!** *(salopp)* stick 'em up, and no tricks! *(sl.)*

Matze ['mat͜sə] **die; ~, ~n, Matzen** ['mat͜sn̩] **der; ~s, ~:** matzo

mau [mau̯] *(ugs.)* **1.** *Adj.; nicht attr.* *(flau)* queasy; *(unwohl)* poorly. **2.** *adv.* badly; **die Geschäfte gehen ~:** business is bad

mauen *itr. V.* *(südwestd., schweiz.)* miaow

Mauer ['mauɐ] **die; ~, ~n** *(auch Sport)* wall; **in den ~n einer Stadt** *(geh.)* in a town/city; **die [Berliner] ~** *(hist.)* the [Berlin] Wall; **die Chinesische ~:** the Great Wall of China; **eine ~ des Schweigens** *(fig.)* a wall of silence

Mauer-: ~ab·satz der offset; **~arbeit die** *s.* **Maurerarbeit**; **~bau der;** *o. Pl.* construction *or* building of the wall/walls; *(Bau der Berliner ~)* building of the Wall; **~blümchen das** *(ugs.)* *(beim Tanz)* wallflower *(coll.)*; *(unscheinbares Mädchen, auch fig.)* Cinderella; **~brecher der** *(hist.)* battering-ram; **~kelle die** *s.* **Maurerkelle**; **~krone die** coping [of a/the wall]

mauern 1. *tr. V.* build; **ein gemauerter Schornstein** a brick chimney. **2.** *itr. V.* **a)** lay bricks; **b)** *(Sportjargon)* *(Ballspiele)* play defensively; *(Kricket, fig.)* stonewall; **c)** *(Kartenspiele)* hold back one's good cards

Mauer-: ~schwalbe die, ~segler der swift; **~stein der** building brick; **~verband der** *(Bauw.)* masonry bond; **~vorsprung der** projecting section of a/the wall; **~werk das a)** *(aus Stein)* stonework; masonry; *(aus Ziegeln)* brickwork; **b)** *(Mauern)* walls *pl.*; **~ziegel der** [building] brick

Mauke ['maukə] **die; ~, ~n** *(Tiermed.)* mallenders *pl.*

Mauken *Pl.* *(berlin. salopp)* hooves *(coll.)*; feet

Maul [maul] **das; ~[e]s, Mäuler** ['mɔylɐ] **a)** *(von Tieren)* mouth; **b)** *(derb: Mund)* gob *(sl.)*; **ein freches** *od.* **loses ~ haben** have a cheeky tongue; **ein gottloses ~ haben** have an insolent tongue; **jmdn. aufs ~ hauen** smack sb. in the gob *(sl.)*; **er hat fünf hungrige Mäuler zu stopfen** *(fig.)* he's got five hungry mouths to feed; **das** *od.* **sein ~ aufmachen** *(fig.)* say something; **dein/sein** *usw.* **ungewaschenes ~** *(fig.)* your/his *etc.* filthy trap *(sl.)* *or* mouth; **das ~ aufreißen** *od.* **voll nehmen, ein großes ~ haben** *(fig.)* shoot one's mouth off *(fig. sl.)*; **sich** *(Dat.)* **das ~ [über jmdn.] zerreißen** *(fig.)* gossip maliciously [about sb.]; **ein schiefes ~ ziehen** *(fig.)* pull a long face; **das ~ halten** keep one's trap shut *(sl.)*; **halt's** *od.* **halt dein ~:** shut your trap *(sl.)*; shut up *(coll.)*; **das** *od.* **sein ~ nicht aufkriegen** *(fig.)* not dare [to] open one's mouth; **jmdm. übers ~ fahren** *(fig.)* cut sb. short; *s. auch* **stopfen 1 d**; **verbrennen 2 b**

Maul-: ~affe der a) *in* **~affen feilhalten** *(abwertend)* stand gaping *or* *(coll.)* gawping; **b)** *(veralt.)* gaping fool; **~beer·baum der** mulberry tree; **~beere die** mulberry

maulen *itr. V.* *(salopp)* grouse *(coll.)*; moan; grumble

maul-, Maul-: ~esel der mule; *(Zool.)* hinny; **~faul** *Adj.* *(ugs. abwertend)* uncommunicative; taciturn; **sei doch nicht so ~faul!** come on, haven't you got any more to say for yourself than that?; **~held der** *(ugs. abwertend)* loudmouth; braggart

Maul·korb der *(auch fig.)* muzzle; **einem Hund/*(fig.)* jmdm. einen ~ anlegen** muzzle a dog/sb.; **einen ~ tragen** *(auch fig.)* be muzzled

Maulkorb·erlaß der *(ugs.)* decree muzzling freedom of speech

Maul-: ~schelle die *(ugs. veralt.)* slap round the face; **~schlüssel der** open-ended spanner; **~sperre die** *(salopp)* **die ~sperre kriegen** *od.* **bekommen** *(fig.)* gape in surprise; **~tasche die** *(Kochk.)* *filled pasta case served in soup*; **~tier das** mule; **~trommel die** Jew's harp; **~- und Klauen·seuche die** *(Tiermed.)* foot-and-mouth disease

Maul·wurf der mole

Maulwurfs-: ~haufen der, ~hügel der molehill

Mau-Mau [mau'mau] **das; ~[s]** *(Kartenspiele)* Mau-Mau

maunzen ['maunt͜sn̩] *itr. V.* *(ugs.)* ⟨*cat*⟩ miaow plaintively; ⟨*baby*⟩ mewl

Maure ['maurə] **der; ~n, ~n, Maurin die; ~, ~nen** Moor

Maurer ['maurɐ] **der; ~s, ~:** bricklayer; **pünktlich wie die ~** *(ugs. scherzh.)* bang on time *(coll.)*

Maurer-: ~arbeit die bricklaying [work] *no pl.*; **~geselle der** journeyman bricklayer; **~handwerk das;** *o. Pl.* bricklaying [trade]; **~kelle die** brick[layer's] trowel; **~kolonne die** bricklaying gang; **~meister der** master bricklayer; **~polier der** foreman bricklayer

Mauretanien [maure'ta:niən] **(das); ~s** Mauritania

Mauretanier [maure'ta:niɐ] **der; ~s, ~, Mauretanierin die; ~, ~nen** Mauritanian

Mauritius [mau'ri:tsiʊs] **(das); Mauritius'** Mauritius

Maus [maus] **die; ~, Mäuse** ['mɔyzə] **a)** mouse; **da beißt die ~ keinen Faden ab** *(ugs.)* there's nothing to be done about it; **die weißen Mäuse** *(fig. ugs. scherzh.)* the traffic police; **weiße Mäuse sehen** *(fig. ugs.)* see pink elephants; **eine graue ~** *(fig. ugs. abwertend)* a colourless nondescript sort of [a] person; *s. auch* **Katze**; **b)** *Pl.* *(salopp: Geld)* bread *sing.* *(sl.)*; dough *sing.* *(sl.)*; **ein paar Mäuse** a few marks/quid *(Brit. sl.)*/bucks *(Amer. sl.)* *etc.*

Mauschelei die; ~, ~en *(ugs. abwertend)* shady wheeling and dealing *no indef. art.*

mauscheln ['mauʃl̩n] *itr. V.* *(ugs. abwertend)* engage in shady wheeling and dealing; **da wird viel gemauschelt** a lot of shady wheeling and dealing goes on there

Mauscheln das; ~s *card-game similar to four-card loo*

Mäuschen ['mɔysçən] **das; ~s, ~ a)** little mouse; **~ sein** *od.* **spielen** *(fig. ugs.)* be a fly on the wall *(coll.)*; **b)** *(fig. ugs.)* **mein ~:** my sweet

mäuschen·still 1. *Adj.* **~ sein** ⟨*person*⟩ be as quiet as a mouse; **es war ~:** it was so quiet you could have heard a pin drop. **2.** *adv.* **~ dort sitzen bleiben/sich ~ verhalten** sit there/keep as quiet as a mouse

Mäuse·bussard der *(Zool.)* [common] buzzard

Mause-: ~falle die mousetrap; *(fig.)* trap; **~loch das** mouse-hole; **ich hätte mich am liebsten in ein ~loch verkrochen** *(ugs.)* I wished the ground would open and swallow me up

Mäuse·melken das *in* **es ist zum ~** *(ugs.)* it's enough to send *or* drive you up the wall *(coll.)*

mausen 1. *tr. V.* *(ugs. veralt.)* pinch *(sl.)*. **2.** *itr. V.* *(veralt.: Mäuse fangen)* catch mice; mouse

Mauser die; ~: moult; **in der ~ sein** be moulting

Mäuserich ['mɔyzərɪç] **der; ~s, ~e** *(ugs.)* [male] mouse

mausern *refl. V.* moult; **sich zur Dame ~** *(fig. ugs.)* blossom into a lady

Mauser·pistole die Mauser [pistol]

mause·tot *Adj.* *(ugs.)* [as] dead as a doornail *pred.*; stone-dead

Mause·zähnchen *Pl.* *(Handarb.)* picot edging *sing.*

maus·grau *Adj.* mouse-grey

mausig *Adj.* *in* **sich ~ machen** *(salopp)* be cheeky and make a nuisance of oneself

Mäuslein ['mɔyslain] **das; ~s, ~** *s.* **Mäuschen**

Mausoleum [mauzo'le:ʊm] **das; ~s, Mausoleen** mausoleum

maus·tot *Adj.* *(österr.) s.* **mausetot**

Maut [maut] **die; ~, ~en** toll; **~ bezahlen/erheben** pay/levy a toll

Maut-: ~gebühr die toll; **~straße die** toll road

m.a.W. *Abk.* **mit anderen Worten** in other words

Max [maks] *in* **strammer Max** *(Kochk.)* fried egg on ham and bread

maxi ['maksi] *Adj.; nicht attr.* *(Mode)* **~ tragen/gehen** wear a maxi *(coll.)*

Maxi das; ~s, ~s *(Mode)* maxi *(coll.)*; **im ~:** in a maxi *(coll.)*; **ein Rock in ~:** a maxi-length skirt

maximal [maksi'ma:l] **1.** *Adj.; nicht präd.* maximum. **2.** *adv.* **~ zulässige Geschwindigkeit** maximum permitted speed; **bis zu ~ 85 °C/20 t** up to a maximum of 85 °C/20 t; **dieses Boot ist für ~ vier Personen zugelassen** this boat is licensed to carry a maximum of four people

Maximal-: ~forderung die maximum demand; **~wert der** maximum value

Maxime [ma'ksi:mə] **die; ~, ~n** maxim

maximieren *tr. V.* maximize

Maximierung die; ~, ~en maximization

Maximum ['maksimʊm] **das; ~s, Maxima** maximum (**an** + *Dat.* of)
Maxi·single die maxi-single
Mayonnaise [majɔ'nɛ:zə] **die; ~, ~n** mayonnaise
MAZ [mats] **die; ~** *(Ferns.)* VTR
Mazedonien [matse'do:niən] *s.* **Makedonien**
Mäzen [mɛ'tse:n] **der; ~s, ~e** *(geh.)* patron
Mäzenatentum [mɛtse'na:tntu:m] **das; ~s** *(geh.)* patronage
Mäzenin die; ~, ~nen *(geh.)* patron[ess]
Mazurka [ma'zʊrka] **die; ~, Mazurken** *u.* **~s** mazurka
MdB, M.d.B. *Abk.* **Mitglied des Bundestages** Member of the Bundestag
MdL, M.d.L. *Abk.* **Mitglied des Landtages** Member of the Landtag
MdNR *Abk.* **Mitglied des Nationalrates** *(Österr.)* Member of the Nationalrat
MdV, M.d.V. *Abk.* **Mitglied der Volkskammer** *(DDR)* Member of the Volkskammer
m.E. *Abk.* **meines Erachtens** in my opinion *or* view
Mechanik [me'ça:nɪk] **die; ~ a)** *(Physik)* mechanics *sing., no art.;* **b)** *(Bauelement)* mechanism; *(eines Klaviers)* action; **c)** *(Funktion)* mechanics *sing. or pl.*
Mechaniker der; ~s, ~, Mechanikerin die; ~, ~nen mechanic
mechanisch 1. *Adj.* mechanical; power *attrib.* ⟨*loom, press*⟩. **2.** *adv.* mechanically
mechanisieren *tr. V.* mechanize
Mechanisierung die; ~: mechanization
Mechanismus der; ~, Mechanismen *(auch fig.)* mechanism; *(fig.: einer Organisation, Bürokratie)* machinery
meck [mɛk] *(Interj.)* me-e-eh *(of goat)*
Mecker·ecke die *(ugs.)* grumbles section *(Brit. coll.);* complaints column
Meckerei die; ~, ~en *(ugs. abwertend)* moaning; grousing *(sl.);* grumbling
Meckerer der; ~s, ~ *(ugs. abwertend)* moaner; grouser *(sl.);* grumbler
Mecker-: ~fritze der *(salopp abwertend)* grouser *(sl.);* moaner; grumbler; **~liese die** *(salopp abwertend)* moaning Minnie *(Brit. coll.);* grouser *(sl.);* grouch *(coll.)*
meckern ['mɛkɐn] *itr. V.* **a)** *(auch fig.)* bleat; **b)** *(ugs. abwertend: nörgeln)* grumble; moan; grouse *(sl.);* **etw. zu ~ haben** have sth. to grumble *etc.* about
Mecklenburg ['me:klənbʊrk] **(das); ~s** Mecklenburg
mecklenburgisch *Adj.* Mecklenburg *attrib.; s. auch* **badisch**
med. *Abk.* **medizinisch** med.
Medaille [me'daljə] **die; ~, ~n** medal; *s. auch* **Kehrseite a**
Medaillen-: ~gewinner der medallist; medal winner; **~spiegel der** medal table
Medaillon [medal'jõ:] **das; ~s, ~s a)** locket; **b)** *(Kochk., bild. Kunst)* medallion
Media- ['mɛ:dia-]: *(Werbespr.) s.* **Medien-**
medial [me'dia:l] *Adj.* *(Parapsych.)* mediumistic
Mediävist [medie'vɪst] **der; ~en, ~en** medievalist
Mediävistik die; ~: medieval studies *pl., no art.*
Mediävistin die; ~, ~nen medievalist
medien-, Medien-: ~fach·mann der media expert; **~forschung die** media research; **~konzern der** media concern; **~landschaft die** media scene; **~politik die** media policy; **~politisch** *Adj.* media-policy *attrib.* ⟨*spokesman, measure, etc.*⟩; **~verbund der a)** *(für den Unterricht)* multi-media system; **im ~verbund** using the multi-media system; **b)** *(kommerziell)* media syndicate; *(Ergebnis einer Fusion)* media group
Medikament [medika'mɛnt] **das; ~[e]s, ~e** medicine; *(Droge)* drug; **ein ~ gegen Kopfschmerzen** a remedy for headaches
Medikamenten·schrank der medicine cabinet
medikamentös [medikamɛn'tø:s] **1.** *Adj.* ⟨*treatment*⟩ with drugs. **2.** *adv.* ⟨*treat, cure*⟩ with drugs
Medikus ['me:dikʊs] **der; ~, Medizi** ['me:ditsi] *(scherzh.)* doctor; doc *(coll.)*
mediokер [me'dio:kɐ] *Adj. (geh.)* mediocre
Mediothek [medio'te:k] **die; ~, ~en** audio-visual library
Meditation [medita'tsio:n] **die; ~, ~en** meditation
Meditations·übung die meditation exercise
meditativ [medita'ti:f] *(geh.)* **1.** *Adj.* meditative. **2.** *adv.* through meditation
mediterran [medite'ra:n] *Adj.* Mediterranean
meditieren [medi'ti:rən] *itr. V.* meditate (**über** + *Akk.* [up]on)
Medium ['me:diʊm] **das; ~s, Medien** medium; **das ~ Presse** the medium of the press
Medizin [medi'tsi:n] **die; ~, ~en a)** *o. Pl.* medicine *no art.;* **b)** *(Heilmittel)* medicine (**gegen** for); **eine bittere ~ für jmdn. sein** *(fig.)* be a bitter pill for sb. to swallow
Medizinal- [meditsi'na:l-]: **~assistent der** houseman *(Brit.);* intern *(Amer.);* **~rat der** ≈ medical officer
Medizin·ball der *(Sport)* medicine ball
Mediziner [medi'tsi:nɐ] **der; ~s, ~, Medizinerin die; ~, ~nen** doctor; *(Student)* medical student; **seine Brüder sind alle Mediziner** his brothers are all medical men
medizinisch 1. *Adj.* **a)** medical ⟨*journal, problem, etc.*⟩; **~e Fakultät** faculty of medicine; **b)** *(heilend)* medicinal ⟨*bath etc.*⟩; medicated ⟨*toothpaste, soap, etc.*⟩. **2.** *adv.* medically
medizinisch-technisch *Adj.* **~e Assistentin** medical laboratory assistant
Medizin-: ~mann der; *Pl.* **~männer** medicine man; **~schränkchen das** medicine cabinet; **~student der, ~studentin die** medical student
Meduse [me'du:zə] **die; ~, ~n a)** *(Myth.)* Medusa; **b)** *(Zool.)* medusa *(Zool.);* jellyfish
Medusen·haupt das a) *(geh.)* head of Medusa; **b)** *(Med.)* caput medusae; cirsomphalos
Meer [me:ɐ] **das; ~[e]s, ~e a)** *(auch fig.)* sea; *(Welt~)* ocean; **die sieben Meere** the seven seas; **ans ~ fahren** go to the seaside; **am ~:** by the sea; **im ~:** in the sea; **aufs ~ hinausfahren** go out to sea; **übers ~ fahren** cross the sea; **1 000 m über dem ~:** 1 000 m above sea-level
Meer-: ~busen der gulf; **der Finnische/Bottnische ~busen** the Gulf of Finland/Bothnia; **~enge die** straits *pl.;* strait
Meeres-: ~algen *Pl.* marine algae; **~biologie die** marine biology *no art.;* **~boden der** sea bed *or* bottom *or* floor; **~bucht die** bay; **~fauna die** marine fauna; **~flora die** marine flora; **~forschung die** marine research; **~früchte** *Pl. (Kochk.)* seafood *sing.;* **ein Salat mit ~früchten** a seafood salad; **~grund der** *s.* **~boden; ~klima das** maritime climate; **~kunde die** oceanography *no art.;* **~luft die** *(Met.)* maritime air; **~ober·fläche die** surface of the sea; **~rauschen das** sound of the sea; **~spiegel der** sea-level; **200 m über/unter dem ~spiegel** 200 m above/below sea-level; **~strand der** *(geh., dichter.)* sea-shore; strand *(poet.);* **~straße die** straits *pl.;* strait; **~strömung die** current; *(im Weltmeer)* ocean current; **~tiefe die** depth of the sea; *(im Weltmeer)* depth of the ocean; **~ufer das** shore
meer-, Meer-: ~forelle die salmon *or* sea trout; **~gott der** sea-god; **~göttin die** sea-goddess; **~grün** *Adj.* sea-green; **~jungfrau die** mermaid; **~katze die** guenon; **~rettich der** horse-radish; **~salz das** sea-salt; **~schaum der** meerschaum; **~schaum·pfeife die** meerschaum [pipe]; **~schweinchen das** guinea-pig; **~ungeheuer das** *(Myth.)* sea monster; **~wasser das** sea water
Meeting ['mi:tɪŋ] **das; ~s, ~s** *(bes. DDR)* meeting
mega-, Mega- [mɛga-] mega-
Mega·hertz das *(Phys.)* megahertz
Megalith [mɛga'li:t] **der; ~s** *od.* **~en, ~e[n]** megalith
Megalith·grab das megalithic tomb
megaloman [megalo'ma:n] *Adj. (Psych.)* megalomaniac[al]; **~ sein** be a megalomaniac
Megalomanie die *(Psych.)* megalomania *no art.*
Megaphon das; ~s, ~e megaphone; loud hailer
Megäre [me'gɛ:rə] **die; ~, ~n** *(geh.)* fury
Mega-: ~tonne die megaton[ne]; **~tote der** *(milit. Jargon)* mega death; **~watt das** *(Physik)* megawatt
Mehl [me:l] **das; ~[e]s a)** flour; *(gröber)* meal; **b)** *(Pulver)* powder; *(Knochen~, Fisch~)* meal
Mehl-: ~beere die whitebeam; **~brei der** flour [and water/milk] paste
mehlig *Adj.* **a)** floury; **b)** *(wie Mehl)* powdery ⟨*sand etc.*⟩; **c)** *(nicht saftig)* mealy ⟨*potato, apple, etc.*⟩
Mehl-: ~sack der *(Sack für Mehl)* flour sack; *(Sack voll Mehl)* sack of flour; **wie ein ~sack hinfallen** fall like a sack of potatoes; **~schwalbe die** house martin; **~schwitze die** *(Kochk.)* roux; **~speise die a)** *dish with flour as the main ingredient;* **b)** *(österr.)* sweet; dessert; *(Kuchen)* cake; **~tau der** mildew; **~wurm der** meal-worm
mehr [me:ɐ] **1.** *Indefinitpron.* more; **~ als genug** more than enough; **~ als die Hälfte** more than half; **ein Grund ~, es zu tun** one more *or* an additional reason for doing it; **das war ~ als unverschämt** that was impertinent, to say the very least; **das schmeckt nach ~** *(ugs.)* it's very moreish *(coll.);* **~ nicht?** is that all?; **~ und ~:** more and more; **~ oder minder** *od.* **weniger** more or less. **2.** *adv.* **a)** *(in größerem Maße)* more; **das sagt ihr ~ zu** it appeals to her more; she likes it better; **b)** *(eher)* **~ tot als lebendig** more dead than alive; **~ schlecht als recht** after a fashion; **er ist ~ Künstler als Gelehrter** he is more of an artist than a scholar; **c)** (+ *Negation*) **es war niemand ~ da** there was no one left; **es hat sich keiner ~ gemeldet** there was not another word from anyone; **ich erinnere mich nicht ~:** I no longer remember; **nicht ~ über etw.** *(Akk.)* **sprechen** not discuss sth. any more *or* further; **das wird nie ~ vorkommen** it will never happen again; **davon will ich nichts ~ hören** I don't want to hear any more about it; **da ist nichts ~ zu machen** there is nothing more to be done; **ich habe keine Lust/kein Interesse ~:** I have lost all desire/interest; **du bist doch kein Kind ~:** you're no longer a child; you're not a child any more; **er mußte nicht ~ an die Front** he never had to go to the front; **sie hat ihren Großvater nicht ~ gekannt** she never had the chance to know her grandfather; **d)** *(südd.)* **nur ~ 5 Mark** only 5 marks
Mehr das; ~s increase (**an** + *Dat.* in); **mit einem ~ an Zeit** with more time
mehr-, Mehr-: ~arbeit die; *o. Pl.* extra *or* additional work; *(Überstunden)* overtime; **das bedeutet ~arbeit für mich** that means more *or* extra work for me; **~aufwand der** additional expenditure *no pl.;* **~aus·gabe die** additional expenditure *no pl.;* **~bändig** *Adj.* in several volumes *postpos.;* **~bedarf der** *(Wirtsch.)* increased demand (**an** + *Dat.* for); **~belastung die** extra *or* additional burden (*Gen.* on); **~bereichs·öl**

das *(Technik)* multi-purpose oil; ~**betrag der** extra *or* additional amount; *(Überschuß)* surplus; ~**deutig 1.** *Adj.* ambiguous; **2.** *adv.* ambiguously; ~**deutigkeit die;** ~, ~**en** ambiguity; ~**dimensional** *Adj.* multidimensional; ~**einnahme die** additional revenue

mehren *(geh.)* **1.** *tr. V.* increase. **2.** *refl. V.* **a)** increase; **diese Vorfälle ~ sich** these incidents are increasing in number; **b)** *(veralt.)* **seid fruchtbar und mehret euch** *(bibl.)* be fruitful and multiply

mehrer... *Indefinitpron.* **a)** *attr.* several; a number of; *(verschieden)* various; several; ~**e hundert Bücher** several hundred[s of] books; **b)** *alleinstehend* ~**e** several people; ~**es** several things *pl.*; **sie kamen zu ~en** several of them came

Mehrer ['me:rɐ] **der;** ~**s,** ~ *(geh. veralt.)* increaser *(arch.)*

mehrerlei *indekl. unbest. Gattungsz. (ugs.)* several [different]; various; *alleinstehend* several *or* various things

Mehr-: ~**erlös der** extra *or* additional proceeds *pl.*; ~**ertrag der** additional profit

mehr·fach 1. *Adj.; nicht präd.* multiple; *(wiederholt)* repeated; **ein Bericht in ~er Ausfertigung** several copies *pl.* of a report; **der ~e deutsche Meister** the player/sprinter *etc.* who has been German champion several times; **ein ~er Millionär** a multimillionaire; **er verdient ein Mehrfaches von dem, was ich bekomme** he earns several times as much as I do. **2.** *adv.* several times; *(wiederholt)* repeatedly; ~ **vorbestraft sein** have several previous convictions

Mehrfach-: ~**impf·stoff der** polyvalent *or* mixed vaccine; ~**spreng·kopf der** multiple warhead

mehr-, Mehr-: ~**familien·haus das** multiple dwelling *(formal)*; large house with several flats *(Brit.) or (Amer.)* apartments; ~**farben·druck der** [multi-]colour printing; ~**farbig** *Adj.* multi-coloured; [multi-]colour *attrib.*; ~**gebot das** higher bid; ~**geschossig** *Adj. s.* ~**stöckig**; ~**gewicht das** additional weight; *(Übergewicht)* excess weight

Mehrheit die; ~, ~**en** majority; **in der ~ sein** be in the majority; **die ~ haben/erringen** have/win a majority; **die ~ verlieren** lose one's majority; **er wurde mit großer ~ gewählt** he was elected by a large majority; **die ~ der Stimmen auf sich vereinigen** secure a majority of votes; **die/eine absolute ~** *(Politik)* an absolute majority; **die einfache/relative ~** *(Politik)* a simple/relative majority; **eine qualifizierte ~** *(Politik)* a qualified majority

mehrheitlich 1. *Adj.; nicht präd.* majority; of the majority *postpos.* **2.** *adv.* by a majority

mehrheits-, Mehrheits-: ~**beschluß der,** ~**entscheidung die** majority decision; ~**fähig** *Adj.* ~**fähig sein** ⟨*law*⟩ be capable of securing a majority; ⟨*party*⟩ be capable of forming a majority; ~**partei die** majority party; ~**prinzip das** principle of majority rule; ~**wahl·recht das** first-past-the-post electoral system

mehr-, Mehr-: ~**jährig** *Adj.; nicht präd.* **a)** lasting several years *postpos.*; **eine ~jährige Erfahrung** several years' experience; several years of experience; **eine ~jährige Freundschaft** a friendship of several years' standing; **b)** *(Bot.)* perennial; ~**kampf der** *(Sport)* multi-discipline event; ~**klassig** *Adj. (Schulw.)* ⟨*school*⟩ with several classes; ~**kosten** *Pl.* additional *or* extra costs; ~**malig** *Adj.; nicht präd.* repeated; ~**mals** *Adv.* several times; *(wiederholt)* repeatedly; ~**parteien·system das** multi-party system; ~**produktion die** increased production; *(Überproduktion)* surplus *or* excess production; ~**seitig** *Adj.* consisting of several pages *postpos., not pred.*; several pages long *postpos.*; ~**silbig** *Adj.* polysyllabic; ~**sprachig** *Adj.* multilingual; ~**sprachig aufwachsen** grow up speaking several languages; ~**sprachigkeit die** multilingualism; ~**stimmig** *(Musik)* **1.** *Adj.* for several voices *postpos.*; **ein ~stimmiges Lied** a part-song; **2.** *adv.* ~**stimmig singen** sing in harmony; **etwas ~stimmig singen** sing sth. as a part-song; ~**stöckig 1.** *Adj.* several storeys high *postpos.*; *(vielstöckig)* multi-storey; **2.** *adv.* ~**stöckig bauen** erect multi-storey buildings/a multi-storey building; ~**stufig** *Adj.* consisting of several steps *postpos., not pred.*; multi-stage ⟨*rocket*⟩; ~**stündig** *Adj.; nicht präd.* lasting several hours *postpos., not pred.*; ⟨*delay*⟩ of several hours; ~**stündige Verhandlungen** several hours of negotiations; ~**tägig** *Adj.; nicht präd.* lasting several days *postpos., not pred.*; ~**teiler der** serial; *(Dokumentarfilm etc.)* series; ~**teilig** *Adj.* in several parts *postpos.*

Mehrung die; ~ *(geh.)* increase

mehr-, Mehr-: ~**wert der** *(Wirtsch.)* surplus value; ~**wert·steuer die** *(Wirtsch.)* value added tax *(Brit.)*; VAT *(Brit.)*; sales tax *(Amer.)*; ~**wöchig** *Adj.; nicht präd.* lasting several weeks *postpos., not pred.*; ⟨*absence*⟩ of several weeks; ~**zahl die;** *o. Pl.* **a)** *(Sprachw.)* plural; **b)** *(Mehrheit)* majority; ~**zeilig** *Adj.* of several lines *postpos.*

Mehr·zweck-: multi-purpose ...

meiden ['maidn̩] *unr. tr. V. (geh.)* avoid

Meier ['maiɐ] **der;** ~**s,** ~ *(hist.)* bailiff; steward

Meierei die; ~, ~**en a)** *(hist.)* feudal estate; **b)** *(Molkerei)* dairy

Meile ['mailə] **die;** ~, ~**n** mile; **das riecht man drei ~n gegen den Wind** *(abwertend)* you can smell it a mile off; *(fig.)* you can tell that a mile off; it stands out a mile

Meilen·stein der *(auch fig.)* milestone

meilen·weit 1. *Adj.* ⟨*distance*⟩ of many miles. **2.** *adv.* for miles; ~ **entfernt** *(auch fig.)* miles away **(von** from)

Meiler der; ~**s,** ~ **a)** *(Kohlen~)* charcoal kiln; **b)** *(Atom~)* [atomic] pile

[1]**mein** [main] *Possessivpron.* my; **ich trinke so ~e acht Tassen Kaffee am Tag** I drink my eight cups of coffee a day; ~**e Damen und Herren** ladies and gentlemen; **das Buch dort, ist das ~[e]s?** that book over there, is it mine?; **das ist nicht ihr Vater, sondern ~er** that's not her father but mine; **was ~ ist, ist auch dein** what's mine is yours; **das ist nicht sein Auto, sondern das ~e** that's not his car but mine; **die Meine** *(geh.)* my wife; **die Meinen** *(geh.)* my family *sing.*; **das Meine** *(geh.: Eigentum)* my possessions *pl. or* property; **ich habe das Meine getan** *(was ich konnte)* I have done what I could; *(meinen Teil)* I have done my share; **sie kann ~ und dein nicht unterscheiden** *(scherzh.)* she doesn't understand that some things don't belong to her

[2]**mein** *Gen. des Personalpronomens* **ich** *(dichter. veralt.) s.* **meiner**

Mein·eid der perjury *no indef. art.*; **einen ~ schwören** perjure oneself; commit perjury

meineidig *Adj.* perjured; ~ **werden** perjure oneself; commit perjury

Meineidige der/die; *adj. Dekl.* perjurer

meinen 1. *itr. V.* think; **[ganz] wie Sie ~!** whatever you think; *(wie Sie möchten)* [just] as you wish; ~ **Sie?** do you think so?; **wie ~ Sie?** I beg your pardon?; **wie ~?** *(scherzh.)* beg your pardon?; **ich meine ja nur [so]** *(ugs.)* it was just an idea *or* a thought. **2.** *tr. V.* **a)** *(denken, glauben)* think; **meinst du, das weiß ich nicht?** do you think I don't know that?; **man könnte ~, ...:** one might [almost] think ...; **man sollte ~, ...:** one would think *or* would have thought ...; **das meine ich auch** I think so too; **b)** *(sagen wollen, im Sinn haben)* mean; **was meint er damit?** what does he mean by that?; **das habe ich nicht gemeint** that's not what I meant; **was ~ Sie?** what do you mean?; **c)** *(beabsichtigen)* mean; intend; **er meint es gut/ehrlich** he means well *or* his intentions are good/his intentions are honest; **es gut mit jmdm. ~:** mean well by sb.; **etw. wörtlich/ironisch ~:** mean sth. literally/ironically; **es war nicht böse gemeint** no harm was meant *or* intended; **er hat es nicht so gemeint** *(ugs.)* he didn't mean it like that; **das Wetter/die Sonne meint es gut mit uns** *(fig. ugs.)* the weather is [being] kind to us/the sun is certainly doing its best for us; **d)** *(sagen)* say; **e)** *(geh.)* **sie meinte zu träumen** she thought she was dreaming

meiner *Gen. des Personalpronomens* **ich** *(geh.)* **gedenke ~:** remember me; **erbarme dich ~:** have mercy upon me

meinerseits *Adv.* for my part; **ganz ~:** the pleasure is [all] mine

meinesgleichen *indekl. Pron.* people *pl.* like me *or* myself; *(abwertend)* the likes *pl.* of me; my sort *or* kind

meinesteils *Adv.* for my part

meinethalben *Adv. (veralt.),* **meinetwegen** *Adv.* **a)** because of me; *(für mich)* on my behalf; *(mir zuliebe)* for my sake; *(um mich)* about me; **b)** [*auch* --'--] *(ugs.)* as far as I'm concerned; ~**!** if you like; ~ **soll er sich den Hals brechen** he can break his neck for all I care; **also gut, ~!** fair enough!; **Darf ich heute abend ausgehen? – Meinetwegen!** May I go out tonight? – It's all right with me; **c)** *(zum Beispiel)* for instance

meinetwillen *Adv.* in **um ~:** for my sake

meinige ['mainɪgə] *Possessivpron., adj. Dekl. (geh. veralt.)* **der/die/das ~:** mine; **ich habe das Meinige getan** *(was ich konnte)* I have done what I could; *(meinen Teil getan)* I have done my share; **die Meinigen** my family *sing.*

Meinung die; ~, ~**en** opinion; *(Ansicht, Auffassung)* opinion; view; **eine vorgefaßte/gegenteilige ~ haben** have preconceived ideas *pl.*/hold an opposite opinion; **eine ~ zu etw./über jmdn./etw. haben** have an opinion on/about sb./sth.; **was ist deine** *od.* **was hast du für eine ~?** what is your opinion?; **die ~en sind geteilt** *od.* **gehen auseinander** opinions are divided; **anderer/geteilter ~ sein** be of a different opinion/differing opinions *pl.*; hold a different view/differing views *pl.*; **seine ~ ändern** change one's opinion *or* mind; **er ist der ~, daß ...:** he is of the opinion *or* takes the view that ...; **nach meiner ~, meiner ~ nach** in my opinion *or* view; **ganz meine ~:** I agree entirely; **einer ~ sein** be of *or* share the same opinion; **eine hohe ~ von jmdm. haben** have a high opinion of sb.; think highly of sb.; **die öffentliche ~:** public opinion; **jmdm. [gehörig] die ~ sagen** give sb. a [good] piece of one's mind

meinungs-, Meinungs-: ~**äußerung die** [expression of] opinion; **das Recht auf freie ~äußerung** the right of free speech; ~**aus·tausch der** exchange of views; **in einem ~austausch mit jmdm. stehen** exchange views with sb.; ~**bildend** *Adj.* opinion-forming; ~**bildung die: die öffentliche ~bildung** the shaping of public opinion; **der Prozeß der ~bildung ist bei uns noch im Gange** we have not yet formed an opinion; ~**forscher der** opinion pollster *or* researcher; ~**forschung die** opinion research; ~**forschungs·institut das** opinion research institute; ~**freiheit die** freedom to form and express one's own opinions; *(Redefreiheit)* freedom of speech; ~**mache die** *(abwertend)* attempted manipulation of people's opinions; ~**macher der** opinion-maker; ~**monopol das** *(abwertend)* monopolizing influence over public opinion; ~**um·frage die** [public] opinion poll; ~**um·schwung der** swing of opinion; ~**verschiedenheit die** *(auch verhüll.: Streit)* difference of opinion

Meise ['maizə] **die; ~, ~n** tit[mouse]; **eine ~ haben** *(salopp)* be nuts *(sl.)*; be off one's head *(coll.)*

Meißel ['maisl̩] **der; ~s, ~:** chisel

meißeln 1. *tr. V.* chisel; carve ‹*statue, sculpture*› with a chisel. **2.** *itr. V.* chisel; work with a chisel; carve; **an einer Statue ~:** be working on *or* carving a statue with a chisel

Meiß[e]ner ['maisənɐ] *Adj.* **~ Porzellan** Meissen china *or* porcelain

meist [maist] *Adv.* mostly; usually; *(zum größten Teil)* mostly; for the most part; **er hat ~ keine Zeit** he doesn't usually have any time; **er ist ~ betrunken** he's drunk most of the time

meist... *Indefinitpron. u. unbest. Zahlw.* most; **das ~e Geld haben** have [the] most money; **die ~e Angst haben** be [the] most afraid; **seine ~e Zeit** most of his time; **am ~en arbeiten** work [the] most; **die ~en Leute haben ...:** most people have; **die ~en Leute, die da waren** most of the people who were there; **darüber habe ich mich am ~en gefreut** that pleased me [the] most; **die ~e Zeit des Jahres** most of the year; **die ~en meiner Kollegen** most of my colleagues; **er hat das ~e vergessen** he has forgotten most of it; **die am ~en befahrene Straße** the most used road; **das am ~en verkaufte Buch** the best-selling book

meist·bietend 1. *Adj.; nicht präd.* highest-bidding; **der ~bietende Käufer** the highest bidder. **2.** *adv.* **etw. ~bietend versteigern/verkaufen** *usw.* auction sth. off/sell sth. *etc.* to the highest bidder

Meist·bietende der/die; *adj. Dekl.* highest bidder

meistens ['maistn̩s] *Adv. s.* **meist**

meistenteils *Adv.* for the most part

Meister ['maistɐ] **der; ~s, ~ a)** master craftsman; **~ im Kürschnerhandwerk sein** be a master furrier; **seinen ~ machen** *(ugs.)* get one's master craftsman's diploma *or* certificate; **b)** *(Vorgesetzter) (in der Fabrik, auf der Baustelle)* foreman; *(in anderen Betrieben)* boss *(coll.)*; **in Ordnung, ~!** OK, chief *or* boss *(coll.)*; **c)** *(geh.: Könner)* master; **es ist noch kein ~ vom Himmel gefallen** *(Spr.)* you can't always expect to get it right first time; **früh übt sich, was ein ~ werden will** *(Spr.)* there's nothing like starting young; **[in jmdm.] seinen ~ gefunden haben** have met one's match [in sb.]; **d)** *(Künstler, geh.: Lehrer)* master; **die alten ~:** the old masters; **e)** *(Sport)* champion; *(Mannschaft)* champions *pl.*; **f)** *(salopp: Anrede)* chief *(coll.)*; guv *(Brit. sl.)*; **g)** *(in Märchen)* **~ Lampe** Master Hare; **~ Petz** Bruin the Bear; *(Anrede)* Master Bruin; **~ Grimbart** Brock the Badger; *(Anrede)* Master Brock; **~ Urian** Old Nick

Meister-: ~brief der master craftsman's diploma *or* certificate; **~dieb der** master thief; **~elf die** *(Fußball)* **die ~elf aus München/die Münchner ~elf** the champions Munich; **~gesang der;** *o. Pl.* Meistergesang; art and music of the Meistersingers

meisterhaft 1. *Adj.* masterly. **2.** *adv.* in a masterly manner; **es ~ verstehen, etw. zu tun** be a [past-]master *or* an expert at doing sth.; **die Gitarre ~ beherrschen** be a masterly guitar-player

Meister·hand die master-hand; **von ~:** by a master-hand

Meisterin die; ~, ~nen a) master craftswoman; **b)** *(geh.: Könnerin)* master; **im Erfinden von Ausreden ist sie eine ~:** she is a [past] master *or* an expert at inventing excuses; **c)** *(Sport)* [women's] champion

Meister-: ~klasse die a) *(Sport)* championship class; **b)** *(Musik, Kunst)* master class; **~leistung die** masterly performance; *(Meisterstück)* masterpiece; *(geniale Tat)* master-stroke

meisterlich *(geh. veralt.) s.* **meisterhaft**

Meister-: ~macher der *(Sportjargon)* champion-maker; **~mannschaft die** champions *pl.*; title-holders *pl.*

meistern *tr. V.* master; master, overcome ‹*problem, difficulty*›; control ‹*anger, excitement, etc.*›; **sein Schicksal/Leben ~:** cope with one's fate/with life

Meister·prüfung die examination for the/one's master craftsman's diploma *or* certificate

Meisterschaft die; ~, ~en a) *o. Pl.* mastery; **b)** *(Sport)* championship; *(Veranstaltung)* championships *pl.*; **die ~ erringen** take the championship

Meisterschafts-: ~kampf der *(Sport)* championship; **~spiel das** *(Sport)* championship match *or* game

Meister-: ~schüler der *(Musik, Kunst)* master-class student; **~singer der** Meistersinger; mastersinger; **~stück das a)** *piece of work executed to qualify as a master craftsman*; **b)** *(Meisterleistung)* masterpiece (**an** + *Dat.* of); *(geniale Tat)* master-stroke; **~titel der a)** *(Sport)* championship [title]; **b)** *(im Handwerksberuf)* title of master craftsman

Meisterung die; ~: mastering

Meister-: ~werk das masterpiece (**an** + *Dat.* of); **~würde die** title of master craftsman

Meist·gebot das highest bid

Mekka ['mɛka] **(das); ~s** Mecca; *(fig.)* Mecca (+ *Gen.* for)

Melamin·harz [mela'mi:n-] **das** melamine resin

Melancholie [melaŋko:'li:] **die; ~, ~** *(Psych.:)* **~n** *(Gemütszustand)* melancholy; *(Psych.)* melancholia

Melancholiker [melaŋ'ko:likɐ] **der; ~s, ~, Melancholikerin die; ~, ~nen** melancholic

melancholisch 1. *Adj.* melancholy; melancholy, melancholic ‹*person, temperament*›. **2.** *adv.* melancholically

Melanesien [mela'ne:ziən] **(das); ~s** Melanesia

Melange [me'lã:ʒ(ə)] **die; ~, ~n a)** *(österr.) s.* **Milchkaffee; b)** *(Gemisch)* blend

Melanom [mela'no:m] **das; ~s, ~e** *(Med.)* melanoma

Melasse [me'lasə] **die; ~:** molasses *sing.*

Melde-: ~amt das registration office *(for registering with the authorities on changing one's place of residence)*; **~fahrer der** *(Milit.)* dispatch-rider; **~frist die** *(bei der Anmeldung, Abmeldung)* registration period; *(Versicherungsw.)* notification period; **~gänger der** *(Milit.)* runner; messenger

melden ['mɛldn̩] **1.** *tr. V.* **a)** report; *(registrieren lassen)* register ‹*birth, death, etc.*› (*Dat.* with); **wie soeben gemeldet wird** *(Fernseh., Rundf.)* according to reports just coming in; **etw. den Behörden ~:** report sth. to the authorities; **jmdn. als vermißt ~:** report sb. missing; **melde gehorsamst, ...** *(Milit. veralt.)* beg to report ...; **nichts/nicht viel zu ~ haben** *(ugs.)* have no/little say; **b)** *(ankündigen)* announce; **wen darf ich ~?** what name shall I say?; who shall I say is here?; **c)** *(Schülerspr.)* **jmdn. ~:** tell on sb; **das wird gemeldet!** I'll tell! **2.** *refl. V.* **a)** report; **sich polizeilich ~:** register with the police; **sich auf dem Polizeipräsidium ~:** report to police headquarters; **sich zum Militär ~:** enlist [in the armed forces]; **sich freiwillig ~:** volunteer (**zu** for); **sich auf eine Anzeige ~:** reply to *or* answer an advertisement; **sich zu einem Lehrgang ~:** sign on *or* enrol for a course; **sich zu einer Prüfung ~:** enter for an examination; **sich zum Dienst ~:** report for duty; *s. auch* **krank a; b)** *(am Telefon)* answer; **der Teilnehmer meldet sich nicht/es meldet sich niemand** there is no answer *or* reply; **c)** *(ums Wort bitten)* put one's hand up; **d)** *(von sich hören lassen)* get in touch (**bei** with); **wenn du etwas brauchst, melde dich** if you need anything let me/us know; **Otto 2, bitte ~!** Otto 2, come in please!; **e)** *(sich ankündigen)* ‹*old age, rheumatism, etc.*› make itself *or* its presence felt. **3.** *itr. V.* ‹*dog*› start barking

Melde·pflicht die a) *(Gesundheitsw.)* obligation *(on doctor)* to notify the authorities; **Thypus unterliegt der ~** cases of typhoid must be notified to the authorities; **b)** *(Verwaltung)* obligation to register with the authorities; **polizeiliche ~** obligation to register with the police

melde·pflichtig *Adj.* **a)** *(Gesundheitsw.)* notifiable ‹*disease*›; **b)** *(Verwaltung)* ‹*accident*› which must be reported

Melder der; ~s, ~ *(Milit.)* runner; messenger

Melde-: ~schluß der; *o. Pl.* closing date; **~wesen das;** *o. Pl.* system of registration; **~zettel der** registration form

Meldung die; ~, ~en a) report; *(Nachricht)* piece of news; *(Ankündigung)* announcement; **~en aus dem Ausland** news from abroad; **~en vom Sport** sports news *sing.*; **~en in Kürze** news headlines; **b) ~ machen** *od.* **erstatten** *(Milit.)* report; make a report; **c)** *(Anzeige)* report; **über etw.** *(Akk.)* **~ machen** report sth.; **d)** *(Anmeldung) (bei einem Wettbewerb, Examen)* entry; *(bei einem Kurs)* enrolment; **wir bitten um freiwillige ~en** we are asking *or* calling for volunteers; **seine ~ [zu etw.] zurückziehen** withdraw [from sth.]; **e)** *(Wort~)* request to speak; **gibt es noch weitere ~en?** does anyone else wish to speak?

meliert [me'li:ɐt] *Adj.* mottled; **grün/braun ~:** mottled green/brown; **[grau] ~es Haar** hair streaked with grey

Melioration [meliora'tsio:n] **die; ~, ~en** *(Landw.)* melioration; land improvement

Melisse [me'lɪsə] **die; ~, ~n** melissa; balm

Melk-: ~an·lage die *(Landw.)* milking equipment *no indef. art.*; **~eimer der** *(Landw.)* milking-pail

melken ['mɛlkn̩] **1.** *regelm. (auch unr.) tr. V. (auch fig. salopp)* milk. **2.** *regelm. (auch unr.) itr. V. (veralt.: Milch geben)* give milk; **eine ~de Kuh** a cow in milk; a milch cow

Melker der; ~s, ~: milker

Melkerin die; ~, ~nen milkmaid

Melk-: ~maschine die milking machine; **~schemel der** milking-stool

Melodei [melo'dai] **die; ~, ~en** *(dichter. veralt.) s.* **Melodie a**

Melodie [melo'di:] **die; ~, ~n a)** melody; *(Weise)* tune; melody; **nach einer ~:** to a melody/tune; **b)** *(Satz~)* intonation

Melodien-: ~folge die, ~reigen der medley [of tunes]; musical medley

Melodik [me'lo:dɪk] **die; ~** *(Musik)* **a)** *(Lehre)* theory of melody; **b)** *(melodische Merkmale)* melodic characteristics *pl.*

melodiös [melo'diø:s] **1.** *Adj.* melodious. **2.** *adv.* melodiously

melodisch 1. *Adj.* melodic; melodious. **2.** *adv.* melodically; melodiously; **~ sprechen** speak in a melodic *or* melodious voice

Melodram [melo'dra:m] **das; ~s, Melodramen, Melodrama das; ~s, Melodramen** melodrama

melodramatisch 1. *Adj.* melodramatic. **2.** *adv.* melodramatically

Melone [me'lo:nə] **die; ~, ~n a)** melon; **b)** *(ugs. scherzh.)* bowler [hat]

Membran [mɛm'bra:n] **die; ~, ~en, Membrane die; ~, ~n a)** *(Technik)* diaphragm; **b)** *(Biol., Chemie)* membrane

Memento [me'mɛnto] **das; ~s, ~s a)** *(kath. Rel.)* Memento; **b)** *(geh.: Mahnung)* warning reminder

Memme ['mɛmə] **die; ~, ~n** *(veralt. abwertend)* [craven] coward

Memoiren [me'mo̯a:rən] *Pl.* memoirs

Memorandum [memo'randʊm] **das; ~s, Memoranden** *od.* **Memoranda** memorandum

Memorial [memo'ri̯a:l] **das; ~s, ~s** *(geh.)* memorial event; *(Rennen)* memorial race

memorieren [memo'ri:rən] *tr. V. (geh. veralt.)* memorize

Menage [me'na:ʒə] **die; ~, ~n** cruet[-stand]

Menagerie [menaʒə'ri:] **die; ~, ~n** *(veralt.)* menagerie

menagieren [mena'ʒi:rən] *itr. V. (österr. Milit.)* draw rations

mendeln ['mɛndl̩n] *itr. V. (Biol.)* Mendelize

Mendelsche Gesetze ['mɛndl̩ʃə-] *Pl. (Biol.)* Mendel's laws

Menetekel [mene'te:kl̩] **das; ~s, ~** *(geh.)* warning sign *or* portent

Menge ['mɛŋə] **die; ~, ~n a)** *(Quantum)* quantity; amount; **die dreifache ~:** three times *or* triple the amount; three times as much; **in ausreichender ~:** in sufficient quantities *pl.*; **in ~n zu ...:** in quantities of ...; **b)** *(große Anzahl)* large number; lot *(coll.)*; **eine ~ Leute** a lot *or* lots *pl.* of people *(coll.)*; **eine ~** *(ugs.)* a lot *or* lots [of it/them] *(coll.)*; **eine ~ Zeit** *(ugs.)* a lot *or* lots of time; plenty of time; **Kuchen/Blumen in ~n** cakes/flowers in abundance; lots of cakes/flowers *(coll.)*; **er weiß eine [ganze] ~** *(ugs.)* he knows [quite] a lot *(coll.) or* a great deal; **sie bildet sich eine ~ ein** *(ugs.)* she is very conceited **(auf +** *Akk.* about); **eine ~ trinken/essen** *(ugs.)* drink/eat a hell of a lot *(coll.)*; **jede ~ Arbeit/Alkohol** *usw. (ugs.)* masses *pl. or* loads *pl.* of work/alcohol *etc. (coll.)*; *s. auch* **rauh 1h; c)** *(Menschen~)* crowd; throng; **d)** *(Math.)* set

mengen *(veralt.)* **1.** *tr. V.* mix; **Rosinen unter den Teig ~:** mix raisins into the dough. **2.** *refl. V. (ugs.)* mingle **(unter +** *Akk.* with)

mengen-, Mengen-: ~an·gabe die indication of quantity/quantities; **~lehre die;** *o. Pl. (Math., Logik)* set theory *no art.*; **~mäßig 1.** *Adj.* quantitative; **2.** *adv.* quantitatively; as far as quantity is/was concerned; **~rabatt der** *(Wirtsch.)* bulk discount

Menhir ['mɛnhɪr] **der; ~s, ~e** menhir

Meningitis [menɪŋ'gi:tɪs] **die; ~, Meningitiden** *(Med.)* meningitis

Meniskus [me'nɪskʊs] **der; ~, Menisken** *(Anat., Optik)* meniscus

Meniskus·riß der *(Med.)* torn meniscus

Menkenke [mɛŋ'kɛŋkə] **die; ~** *(md. ugs.)* fuss; **mach keine ~:** don't make a fuss

Mennige ['mɛnɪgə] **die; ~:** red lead

Menopause [meno'pa̯uzə] **die; ~, ~n** *(Physiol.)* menopause

Menora [mɛno'ra:] **die; ~, ~:** menorah

Mensa ['mɛnza] **die; ~, ~s** *od.* **Mensen** refectory, canteen *(of university, college)*

Mensa·essen das refectory *or* canteen food

[1]**Mensch** [mɛnʃ] **der; ~en, ~en a)** *(Gattung)* **der ~:** man; **die ~en** man *sing.*; human beings; **das Gute im ~en** the good in man; **das sind starrköpfige ~en** they are stubborn people; **alle ~en müssen sterben** we are all mortal; **der ~ lebt nicht vom Brot allein** *(Spr.)* man does not live by bread alone *(prov.)*; **ich bin auch nur ein ~:** I'm only human; **der ~ denkt, Gott lenkt** *(Spr.)* man proposes, God disposes *(prov.)*; **das sind doch keine ~en mehr!** they are a pack of animals; **nur noch ein halber ~ sein** be just about all in; **wieder ein ~ sein** *(ugs.)* feel like a human being again; **b)** *(Person)* person; man/woman; **~en** people; **kein ~:** no one; **es war kein ~ da** there was no one *or* not a soul there; **unter die ~en gehen** mix with people; **des ~en Wille ist sein Himmelreich** you/he *etc.* must do whatever makes you/him *etc.* happy; **wie der erste ~/die ersten ~en:** extremely awkwardly; **ein neuer ~ werden** become a new man/woman; **von ~ zu ~:** man to man/woman to woman; **~, ärgere dich nicht** *(Gesellschaftsspiel)* ludo; **c)** *Pl. (Menschheit)* mankind *sing., no art.*; man *sing., no art.*; **d)** *(salopp: Anrede) (bewundernd)* wow; *(erstaunt)* wow; good grief; *(vorwurfsvoll)* for heaven's sake; **~, war das ein Glück!** boy, that was a piece of luck!; **~, hast du dich verändert!** good Lord, haven't you changed!; **~, das habe ich ganz vergessen!** damn *or (Brit.)* blast, I completely forgot!; **~ Meier!** good grief!

[2]**Mensch das; ~[e]s, ~er** *(abwertend: Frau)* slut; trollop

menschen-, Menschen-: ~affe der anthropoid [ape]; **~ähnlich** *Adj.* manlike; like a human being/human beings *postpos.*; **~alter das** lifetime; **~an·sammlung die** gathering [of people]; *(~menge)* crowd [of people]; **~arm** *Adj.* sparsely populated; **~auf·lauf der** crowd [of people]; **~bild das** conception of man; **~feind der** misanthropist; **~feindlich 1.** *Adj.* **a)** misanthropic; **b)** *(unmenschlich)* inhuman ⟨*system, policy etc.*⟩; ⟨*environment*⟩ hostile to man; **2.** *adv.* **a)** misanthropically; **b)** *(unmenschlich)* inhumanly; **~feindlich konzipierte Trabantenstädte** satellite towns designed in a way that creates an environment hostile to man; **~feindlichkeit die** *s.* **menschenfeindlich 1:** misanthropy; inhumanity; hostility to man; **~fleisch das** human flesh; **~fressend** *Adj., nicht präd.* man-eating; **~fresser der** *(ugs.)* cannibal; *(Mythol.)* man-eater; **er ist doch kein ~fresser** *(scherzh.)* he won't eat *or* bite you; **~freund der** philanthropist; **~freundlich 1.** *Adj.* **a)** philanthropic; **b)** *(human)* ⟨*environment*⟩ catering for human needs; ⟨*architecture*⟩ designed with [the needs of] people in mind; **2.** *adv.* **a)** philanthropically; **b) ~freundlich gestaltet/konstruiert** designed with [the needs of] people in mind; **~freundlichkeit die;** *o. Pl.* philanthropy; **aus reiner ~freundlichkeit** out of the sheer goodness of one's heart; **~führung die** leadership; **~gedenken das: das wird seit ~gedenken so gemacht** it has been done that way for as long as anyone can remember; **der heißeste Sommer seit ~gedenken** the hottest summer in living memory; **~geschlecht das** *(geh.)* human race; **~gestalt die** human form; **ein Engel/Teufel** *od.* **Satan in ~gestalt sein** be an angel in human form/the devil incarnate; **~gewühl das** milling crowd; **~haar das** human hair; **~hand die** *(geh.)* hand of man; human hand; **von ~hand geschaffen** created by the hand of man *or* by human hand; **~handel der a)** trade *or* traffic in human beings; *(Sklavenhandel)* slave-trade; **b)** *(DDR) illegal smuggling of GDR citizens out of the country;* **~händler der a)** trafficker [in human beings]; *(Sklavenhändler)* slave-trader; **b)** *(DDR) person who engages in illegal smuggling of GDR citizens out of the country;* **~haß der** misanthropy; **~hasser der** *s.* **~feind; ~jagd die** *(abwertend)* man-hunting; man-hunts *pl.*; *(Verfolgung)* persecution; **eine ~jagd** a man-hunt; **~jäger der** *(abwertend)* man-hunter; **~kenner der** judge of character *or* human nature; **~kenntnis die;** *o. Pl.* ability to judge character *or* human nature; **~kette die** human chain; **~kind das** creature; soul; **~leben das** life; **ein ~leben lang währen** *(geh.)* last a whole lifetime; **der Unfall forderte vier ~leben** *(geh.)* the accident claimed four lives; **~leben waren nicht zu beklagen** *(geh.)* there was no loss of life; **~leer** *Adj.* deserted; **~liebe die** philanthropy; love of humanity *or* mankind; **~masse die** crowd [of people]; **~material das;** *o. Pl. (Militärjargon)* [human] material; **~menge die** crowd [of people]; **~möglich** *Adj.; nicht attr.* humanly possible; **das ist doch nicht ~möglich!** but that's impossible!; **alles ~mögliche tun** do all that is/was humanly possible; **~opfer das a)** human sacrifice; **b)** *(~leben)* **es waren hunderte von ~opfern zu beklagen** hundreds of lives were lost; **~raub der** kidnapping; abduction; **~recht das** human right; **~rechts·konvention die** Human Rights Convention; **~scheu** *Adj.* afraid of people; *(ungesellig)* unsociable; **~scheu die** fear of people; **~schinder der** *(abwertend)* cruel and ruthless slave-driver; **~schlag der** race *or* breed [of people]; **~seele die** human soul; **keine ~seele** not a [living] soul

Menschens·kind *Interj. (salopp) (erstaunt)* good heavens; good grief; *(vorwurfsvoll)* for heaven's sake

Menschen·sohn der; *o. Pl. (christl. Rel.)* Son of Man

menschen-, Menschen-: ~unwürdig 1. *Adj.* degrading and inhumane ⟨*treatment*⟩; ⟨*accommodation*⟩ unfit for human habitation; ⟨*conditions*⟩ unfit for human beings; ⟨*behaviour*⟩ unworthy of a human being; **2.** *adv.* ⟨*treat*⟩ in a degrading and inhumane way; ⟨*live, be housed*⟩ in conditions unfit for human beings; **~verächter der** despiser of humanity *or* mankind; **~verachtung die** contempt for humanity *or* mankind; **~verstand der** human intelligence *or* intellect; *s. auch* **gesund; ~werk das** *(geh.)* work of man; **alles ~werk ist vergänglich** the works *pl.* of men are ephemeral; **~würde die** human dignity *no art.*; **~würdig 1.** *Adj.* humane ⟨*treatment*⟩; ⟨*accommodation*⟩ fit for human habitation; ⟨*conditions*⟩ fit for human beings; ⟨*behaviour*⟩ worthy of a human being; **2.** *adv.* ⟨*treat*⟩ humanely; ⟨*live, be housed*⟩ in conditions fit for human beings

Menschewik [mɛnʃe'vɪk] **der; ~en, ~en** *u.* **~i** *(hist.)* Menshevik

Menschheit die; ~ mankind *no art.*; humanity *no art.*; human race

Menschheits-: ~entwicklung die evolution of man; **~geschichte die** history of mankind *or* of the human race; **~traum der** dream of mankind

menschlich 1. *Adj.* **a)** human; **~es Versagen** human error; **das ~e Leben** human life; *s. auch* **irren a; b)** *(annehmbar)* civilized; **wieder ganz ~ aussehen** *(ugs.)* look quite presentable again; **c)** *(human)* humane ⟨*person, treatment, etc.*⟩; human ⟨*trait, emotion, etc.*⟩; **sich von der ~en Seite zeigen** show one's human side. **2.** *adv.* **a) er ist ~ sympathisch** I like him as a person; **sich ~ näherkommen** get on closer [personal] terms [with one another]; **b)** *(human)* humanely; in a humane manner

Menschliche das; ~n: nichts ~s war ihr fremd she was familiar with every aspect of human experience; **er hat nichts ~s an sich** he shows no human traits; there's nothing human about him

Menschlichkeit die humanity *no art.*; **etw. aus reiner ~ tun** do sth. for purely humanitarian reasons

Mensch·werdung [-ve:ɐ̯dʊŋ] **die; ~** *(christl. Rel.)* incarnation

Mensen *s.* **Mensa**

Menstruation [mɛnstrua'ts̮i̯o:n] **die; ~, ~en** *(Physiol.)* menstruation; *(Periode)* [menstrual] period

menstruieren *itr. V. (Physiol.)* menstruate

Mensur [mɛn'zu:ɐ̯] **die; ~, ~en a)** students' duel; **eine ~ schlagen** fight a duel; **b)** *(Fechten)* [fencing] measure *or* distance

mental [mɛn'ta:l] *(geh.)* **1.** *Adj.* mental. **2.** *adv.* mentally

Mentalität [mɛntali'tɛ:t] **die; ~, ~en** mentality

Menthol [mɛn'to:l] **das; ~s** menthol
Mentor ['mɛntɔr] **der; ~s, ~en** [-'to:rən] **a)** *(geh.)* mentor; **b)** *(veralt.: Lehrer)* tutor; **c)** *(Schulw.)* supervisor
Menu [me'ny] *(schweiz.)*, **Menü** [me'ny:] **das; ~s, ~s** *(auch DV)* menu; *(im Restaurant)* set meal *or* menu
Menuett [me'nuɛt] **das; ~s, ~e** *od.* **~s** minuet
mephistophelisch [mefɪsto'fe:lɪʃ] *(geh.)* Mephistophelian
Mercator·projektion [mɛr'ka:tɔr-] **die** *(Geogr.)* Mercator's projection
Mergel ['mɛrgl̩] **der; ~s** *(Geol.)* marl
Meridian [meri'di̯a:n] **der; ~s, ~e** *(Geogr., Astron.)* meridian
Meridian·kreis der *(Astron.)* meridian circle
Meringe [me'rɪŋə] **die; ~, ~n** meringue
Merino [me'ri:no] **der; ~s, ~s a)** *(Schaf)* merino [sheep]; **b)** *(Stoff)* merino
Merino-: ~schaf das merino [sheep]; **~wolle die** merino wool
Meriten [me'ri:tn̩] *Pl. (geh. veralt.)* merits
merkantil [mɛrkan'ti:l] *Adj. (geh.)* mercantile
Merkantilismus der; ~ *(hist.)* mercantilism *no art.*
merkantilistisch *Adj. (hist.)* mercantilist
merkbar 1. *Adj.* **a)** perceptible; noticeable; *(deutlich)* noticeable; **b)** *(leicht zu behalten)* **eine gut** *od.* **leicht ~e Nummer** an easily remembered number; **leicht/schwer ~sein** be easy/difficult to remember. **2.** *adv.* perceptibly; noticeably; *(deutlich)* noticeably
Merk-: ~blatt leaflet; *(mit Anweisungen)* instruction leaflet; **~buch das** notebook
merken ['mɛrkn̩] **1.** *tr. V.* notice; **deutlich zu ~ sein** be plain to see; be obvious; **er hat [davon] nichts gemerkt** he didn't notice anything [of that]; **davon merkt man nicht viel** it's hardly noticeable; **an seinem Benehmen merkt man, daß ...** you can tell by his behaviour that ...; **das merkt doch jeder/keiner** everybody/nobody will notice; **jmdn. etw. ~ lassen** let sb. see sth.; **du merkst aber auch alles!** *(ugs. iron.)* how very observant of you!; **merkst du was?** *(ugs.)* have you noticed something?. **2.** *refl. V.* **sich** *(Dat.)* **etw. ~:** remember sth.; **hast du dir die Adresse gemerkt?** have you made a mental note of the address?; **diesen Mann muß man sich** *(Dat.)* **~:** this is a man to take note of; **ich werd' mir's** *od.* **werd's mir ~** *(ugs.)* I won't forget that; I'll remember that; **merk dir das** just remember that
Merk-: ~heft das notebook; **~hilfe die** mnemonic; memory aid
merklich 1. *Adj.* perceptible; noticeable; *(deutlich)* noticeable. **2.** *adv.* perceptibly; noticeably; *(deutlich)* noticeably
Merkmal das; ~s, ~e feature; characteristic; **besondere ~e** distinguishing features *or* marks
Merk-: ~satz der mnemonic sentence/phrase; mnemonic; **~spruch der a)** pithy maxim *or* saying; **b)** *(~hilfe)* mnemonic verse/sentence/phrase mnemonic
[1]**Merkur** [mɛr'ku:ɐ̯] **der; ~s** *(Astron.)*, [2]**Merkur (der)** *(Myth.)* Mercury
merkwürdig 1. *Adj.* strange; odd; peculiar. **2.** *adv.* strangely; oddly; peculiarly
merkwürdiger·weise *Adv.* strangely *or* oddly *or* curiously enough
Merkwürdigkeit die; ~, ~en a) *o. Pl.* strangeness; oddness; peculiarity; **b)** *Pl. (Erscheinungen)* curiosities *pl.*
Merk-: ~zeichen das mark; marker; **~zettel der** note; *(Liste)* list
Merowinger der; ~s, ~ *(hist.)* Merovingian
merzerisieren [mɛrtsəri'zi:rən] *tr. V. (Textilind.)* mercerize
Mesalliance [meza'li̯ã:s] **die; ~, ~n** *(geh.)* mésalliance
meschugge [me'ʃʊgə] *Adj.; nicht attrib. (salopp)* barmy *(Brit. sl.)*; nuts *pred. (sl.)*; off one's rocker *pred. (sl.)*
Meskalin [mɛska'li:n] **das; ~s** mescaline
Mesmerismus [mɛsmə'rɪsmʊs] **der; ~:** *Mesmer's theory of biomagnetic effects*
Mesner ['mɛsnɐ] **der; ~s, ~** *(kath. Kirche)* sexton
Mesolithikum [mezo'li:tikʊm] **das; ~s** *(Geol.)* mesolithic period
mesolithisch *Adj. (Geol.)* mesolithic
Mesopotamien [mezopo'ta:mi̯ən] **(das); ~s** Mesopotamia
Mesozoikum [mezo'tso:ikʊm] **das; ~s** *(Geol.)* Mesozoic era
mesozoisch *Adj. (Geol.)* Mesozoic
Meß·band das; *Pl.* **Meßbänder** measuring tape
meßbar ['mɛsba:ɐ̯] *Adj.* measurable; **schwer ~:** difficult to measure
Meß-: ~becher der measuring jug; **~bild das** *(Kartographie)* photogrammetric photograph; **~buch das** missal; mass book; **~diener der** *(kath. Kirche)* server
[1]**Messe** ['mɛsə] **die; ~, ~n** *(Gottesdienst, Musik)* mass; **die ~ halten** *od.* *(geh.)* **zelebrieren** say *or* celebrate mass; **für jmdn. eine ~ lesen** say a mass for sb.
[2]**Messe die; ~, ~n a)** *(Ausstellung)* [trade] fair; **auf der ~:** at the [trade] fair; **b)** *(landsch.: Jahrmarkt, Volksfest)* fair
[3]**Messe die; ~, ~n** *(Seew., Milit.)* mess; *(Raum)* mess-room
Messe-: ~besucher der visitor to a/the [trade] fair; **~gelände das** site of a/the [trade] fair; *(mit festen ~hallen)* exhibition centre; **~halle die** exhibition hall
messen 1. *unr. tr. V.* **a)** measure; **[jmdm.] den** *od.* **jmds. Blutdruck/Puls ~:** take sb.'s blood pressure/pulse; **jmds. Temperatur ~:** take sb.'s temperature; **die Zeit eines Sprinters ~:** time a sprinter; **am Morgen wurden schon 20° gemessen** the temperature was already 20° in the morning; **etw. nach Litern/Metern ~:** measure sth. in litres/metres; *s. auch* **Fieber; b)** *(beurteilen)* judge **(nach** by); **etw. an etw.** *(Dat.)* **~:** judge sth. by sth.; **jmdn. an jmdm. ~:** judge sb. by comparison with sb.; compare sb. with sb.; **ge~ an** (+ *Dat.*) having regard to; **c)** *(geh.)* **jmdn. mit den Augen** *od.* **Blicken ~:** look sb. up and down. **2.** *unr. itr. V.* measure; **er mißt 1,85 m** he's 1.85 m [tall]; **genau ~:** make an exact measurement/exact measurements. **3.** *unr. refl. V. (geh.)* compete **(mit** with); **sich mit jmdm./etw. [in etw.** *(Dat.)***] [nicht] ~ können** [not] be as good as sb./sth. [in sth.]
Messer das; ~s, ~ a) knife; *(Hack~)* chopper; *(Rasier~)* [cut-throat] razor; **mit ~ und Gabel essen** eat with a knife and fork; **jmdm. das ~ an die Kehle setzen** *(fig. ugs.)* hold sb. at gunpoint; **auf des ~s Schneide stehen** *(fig.)* hang in the balance; be balanced on a knife-edge; **es steht auf des ~s Schneide, ob ...:** it's touch and go whether ...; **jmdn. ans ~ liefern** *(fig. ugs.)* inform on sb.; **bis aufs ~** *(fig. ugs.)* ‹*fight etc.*› to the bitter end; **jmdm. ins [offene] ~ laufen** *(fig. ugs.)* play right into sb.'s hands; **da geht mir das ~ in der Tasche auf** *(fig. ugs.)* I see red; **b)** *(ugs.: Skalpell)* **jmdn. unter dem ~ haben** have sb. under the knife *(coll.)*; **unters ~ müssen** have to go under the knife *(coll.)*; **c)** *(Technik)* cutter; *(Klinge)* blade
messer-, Messer-: ~bänkchen das *(individual eater's)* knife-rest; **~griff der, ~heft das** knife-handle; handle of a/the knife; **~held der** *(abwertend)* thug with a knife; **~klinge die** knife-blade; blade of a/the knife; **~rücken der** back of a/the knife; **~scharf 1.** *Adj.* razor-sharp; *(fig.)* trenchant ‹*criticism*›; incisive ‹*logic*›; razor-sharp ‹*wit, intellect*›; **2.** *adv. (fig. ugs.)* ‹*think*› with penetrating insight; ‹*argue*› incisively; **~schmied der** *maker of saws, knives, and other cutting tools;* **~spitze die a)** point of a/the knife; **b)** *(Mengenangabe)* **eine ~spitze** just a trace; **eine ~spitze Salz** a large pinch of salt; **~stecher der** knifeman; **~stecherei** [-ʃtɛçə'rai̯] **die; ~, ~en** knife-fight; fight with knives; **~stich der** knife-thrust; *(Wunde)* knife-wound; stab wound; **~werfer der; ~s, ~:** knife-thrower
Messe-: ~stadt die town well known for its trade fairs; **die ~stadt Leipzig** Leipzig with its trade fairs; **~stand der** stand [at a/the trade fair]
Meß-: ~fühler der *(Technik)* sensor; **~gerät das** measuring device *or* instrument; *(Zähler)* meter; **~glas das** measuring glass; graduated measure; **~gewand das** chasuble
messianisch [mɛ'si̯a:nɪʃ] *Adj.* Messianic
Messianismus der; ~: Messianism *no art.*
Messias [mɛ'si:as] **der; ~:** Messiah
Messing ['mɛsɪŋ] **das; ~s** brass; **mit ~ beschlagen sein** have brass fittings *pl.*
messingen *Adj.; nicht präd.* brass
Messing·waren *Pl.* brassware *sing.*
Meß-: ~instrument das measuring instrument; **~latte die** surveyor's wooden rod *or* staff; **~opfer das** *(kath. Kirche)* sacrifice of the mass; **~stab der** measuring-rod; **~technik die** technology of measurement; **~tisch der** plane table; **~tisch·blatt das** large-scale map *(1:25,000)*; **~uhr die** dial flow-meter
Messung die; ~, ~en *(das Messen, Meßergebnis)* measurement; *(das Ablesen, Ableseergebnis)* reading
Meß-: ~wein der *(kath. Kirche)* Communion wine; altar wine; **~wert der** measured value; *(Ableseergebnis)* reading; **~zylinder der** measuring cylinder
Mestize [mɛs'ti:tsə] **der; ~n, ~n** mestizo
Met [me:t] **der; ~[e]s** mead
Metabolismus [metabo'lɪsmʊs] **der** *(Physiol.)* metabolism
Metall [me'tal] **das; ~s, ~e** metal
Metall-: ~arbeiter der metalworker; **~bearbeitung die;** *o. Pl.* metalworking
metallen 1. *Adj.* **a)** *nicht präd. (aus Metall)* metal; **b)** *(geh.: metallisch)* metallic. **2.** *adv. (geh.)* **ihr Haar glänzte/die Becken klirrten ~:** her hair gleamed/the cymbals sounded metallically
Metaller der; ~s, ~, Metallerin die; ~, ~nen *(ugs.)* metalworker
Metall·geld das; *o. Pl.* metal money; specie *(as tech. term)*
metall·haltig *Adj.* metalliferous
metallic [me'talɪk] *indekl. Adj.* metallic [grey/blue/*etc.*]
Metallic·lackierung die metallic finish
Metall·industrie die metal-processing and metal-working industries *pl.*
metallisch 1. *Adj.* metallic; metal *attrib.*, metallic ‹*conductor, coating*›. **2.** *adv.* metallically
metallisieren *tr. V. (Technik)* metallize
Metall-: ~kunde die; *o. Pl.* [physical] metallurgy *no art.*; **~säge die** hack-saw; **~über·zug der** metal *or* metallic coating
Metallurg [meta'lʊrk] **der; ~en, ~en, Metallurge der; ~n, ~n, Metallurgin die; ~, ~nen** metallurgist
Metallurgie [metalʊr'gi:] **die; ~:** [extractive] metallurgy *no art.*
metallurgisch *Adj.* metallurgical
metall·verarbeitend *Adj.* **~e Industrie** metalworking industry
Metall·waren *Pl.* metalware *sing.*
Metamorphose [metamɔr'fo:zə] **die; ~, ~n** metamorphosis
Metapher [me'tafɐ] **die; ~, ~n** *(Stilk.)* metaphor; **Gebrauch von ~n** use of metaphor
Metaphorik [meta'fo:rɪk] **die; ~** *(Stilk.)* **a)** *(Gebrauch von Metaphern)* use of meta-

phor; **b)** *(Metaphern)* imagery; metaphors *pl.*
metaphorisch *(Stilk.)* **1.** *Adj.* metaphorical. **2.** *adv.* metaphorically
Meta-, Meta-: **~physik die; ~; ~en a)** *o. Pl.* metaphysics *sing., no art.*; **b)** *(darstellendes Werk)* metaphysical work; **~physiker der** metaphysicist; **~physisch 1.** *Adj.* metaphysical; **2.** *adv.* metaphysically; **~physisch denken** think in metaphysical terms; **~sprache die** *(Sprachw., Math.)* metalanguage; **~stase** [~'sta:zə] **die; ~, ~n** *(Med.)* metastasis
Meteor [mete'o:ɐ̯] **der; ~s, ~e** *(Astron.)* meteor
Meteorit [meteo'ri:t] **der; ~en** *od.* **~s, ~e[n]** *(Astron.)* meteorite
Meteorologe [meteoro'lo:gə] **der; ~n, ~n** meteorologist; *(im Fernsehen)* weatherman
Meteorologie die; ~: meteorology *no art.*
Meteorologin die; ~, ~nen meteorologist; *(im Fernsehen)* weather lady
meteorologisch 1. *Adj.* meteorological. **2.** *adv.* meteorologically
Meter ['me:tɐ] **der** *od.* **das; ~s, ~:** metre; **drei ~ hoch/breit/tief/lang** three metres high/wide/deep/long; **[ungefähr] in 100 ~ Höhe/Entfernung** at a height/distance of [about] 100 metres; **nach ~n** by the metre; **auf den letzten ~n** in the last few metres; *s. auch* **laufend 1 c**
meter-, Meter-: **~dick** *Adj.* a metre thick *postpos.*; *(sehr dick)* metres thick *postpos.*; **~hoch** *Adj.* a metre high *postpos.*; *(sehr hoch)* metres high *postpos.*; ⟨*snow*⟩ a metre/metres deep; **der Schnee lag ~hoch** the snow was a metre/metres deep; **~lang** *Adj.* a metre long *postpos.*; *(sehr lang)* metres long *postpos.*; **~maß das** tape-measure; *(Stab)* [metre] rule; **~ware die** fabric/material *etc.* sold by the metre; **etw. als ~ware kaufen/verkaufen** buy/sell sth. by the metre; **~weise** *Adv.* by the metre; **ich habe den Stoff gleich ~weise gekauft** I bought yards of the material straight away; **~weit 1.** *Adj.* *(in der Länge)* a metre long *postpos.*; *(sehr lang)* metres long *postpos.*; *(in der Breite)* a metre wide *postpos.*; *(sehr breit)* metres wide *postpos.*; **2.** *adv.* **das Ziel ~weit verfehlen** be yards off [the] target; **einen Baumstamm ~weit schleudern** hurl a tree-trunk several yards
Methan [me'ta:n] **das; ~s** methane
Methan·gas das methane gas
Methanol [meta'no:l] **das; ~s** *(Chemie)* methanol
Methode [me'to:də] **die; ~, ~n** method; **~ haben** be quite deliberate
Methoden·lehre die *s.* **Methodologie**
Methodik [me'to:dɪk] **die; ~, ~en** methodology; **~ zeigen** be methodical
methodisch 1. *Adj.* methodological; *(nach einer Methode vorgehend)* methodical. **2.** *adv.* methodologically; *(nach einer Methode)* methodically; **~ vorgehen** proceed methodically
Methodist [meto'dɪst] **der; ~en, ~en** Methodist
Methodisten·kirche die Methodist church
Methodistin die; ~, ~nen Methodist
methodistisch *Adj.* Methodist
Methodologie [metodolo'gi:] **die; ~, ~n** methodology
methodologisch *Adj.* methodological
Methusalem [me'tu:zalɛm] **der; ~s, ~s** Methuselah; **[so] alt wie ~ sein** be as old as Methuselah; **als ~:** when a very old man
Methyl·alkohol der methyl alcohol
Methylen [mety'le:n] **das; ~s** *(Chemie)* methylene
Metier [me'tie:] **das; ~s, ~s** profession; **sein ~ beherrschen, sich auf sein ~ verstehen** know one's job; **Langstreckenlauf war sein ~:** long-distance running was his métier
Metonymie [metony'mi:] **die; ~, ~n** *(Rhet., Stilk.)* metonymy
Metren *s.* **Metrum**
Metrik ['me:trɪk] **die; ~, ~en a)** *(Verslehre)* metrics; **b)** *(Musik)* study of rhythm and tempo *or* of metre
metrisch 1. *Adj.* **a)** *(Verslehre, Musik)* metrical; **b)** *(auf den Meter bezogen)* metric. **2.** *adv.* metrically
Metro ['me:tro] **die; ~, ~s** Metro
Metronom [metro'no:m] **das; ~s, ~e** *(Musik)* metronome
Metropole [metro'po:lə] **die; ~, ~n** *(größte Stadt)* metropolis; *(Zentrum für etw.)* capital; metropolis
-metropole die capital; metropolis; **die deutsche Bier~:** the German beer capital; **die Schwarzwald~:** the chief city of the Black Forest
Metropolit [metropo'li:t] **der; ~en, ~en** *(kath. u. orthodoxe Kirche)* metropolitan
Metrum ['me:trʊm] **das; ~s, Metren** *(Verslehre, Musik)* metre
Mett [mɛt] **das; ~[e]s** *(landsch.)* minced meat, mince *(pork)*
Mettage [mɛ'ta:ʒə] **die; ~, ~n** *(Zeitungsw.)* page make-up
Mette ['mɛtə] **die; ~, ~n** *(kath. u. ev. Kirche)* midnight mass; *(am frühen Morgen)* early [morning] mass
Metteur [mɛ'tø:ɐ̯] **der; ~s, ~e, Metteurin die; ~, ~nen** *(Zeitungsw.)* make-up arranger
Mett·wurst die *soft smoked sausage made of minced pork and beef*
Metze ['mɛtsə] **die; ~, ~n** *(veralt.)* strumpet *(arch.)*; whore
Metzelei [mɛtsə'lai] **die; ~, ~en** *(abwertend)* slaughter; butchery
metzeln *tr. V. s.* **niedermetzeln**
Metzger ['mɛtsgɐ] **der; ~s, ~** *(bes. westmd., südd., schweiz.)* butcher; *(im Schlachthof)* slaughterman; *s. auch* **Bäcker**
Metzger- *s.* **Fleischer-**
Metzgerei die; ~, ~en *(bes. westmd., südd., schweiz.)* butcher's [shop]
Meuchel- ['mɔyçl̩-]: **~mord der** *(abwertend)* [cowardly/treacherous] murder; **~mörder der** *(abwertend)* [cowardly/treacherous] murderer
meucheln *(geh. abwertend) tr. V.* murder [in a cowardly/treacherous manner]; assassinate ⟨*king, ruler, etc.*⟩
meuchlerisch *(abwertend)* **1.** *Adj.* cowardly; *(heimtückisch)* treacherous. **2.** *adv.* in a cowardly/treacherous manner
meuchlings ['mɔyçlɪŋs] *Adv. (geh. abwertend)* treacherously
Meute ['mɔytə] **die; ~, ~n a)** *(Jägerspr.)* pack; **b)** *(ugs. abwertend: Menschengruppe)* mob
Meuterei [mɔytə'rai] **die; ~, ~en** mutiny; *(fig.)* revolt; mutiny
Meuterer ['mɔytərɐ] **der; ~s, ~:** mutineer; *(fig.)* rebel
meutern *itr. V.* **a)** mutiny **(gegen** against); ⟨*prisoners*⟩ riot; **b)** *(ugs.: Unwillen äußern)* moan **(gegen** about)
Mexikaner [mɛksi'ka:nɐ] **der; ~s, ~, Mexikanerin die; ~, ~nen** Mexican
mexikanisch *Adj.* Mexican
Mexiko ['mɛxiko] **(das); ~s** Mexico
MEZ *Abk.* **mitteleuropäische Zeit** CET
Mezzo·sopran ['mɛtso-] *(Musik)* mezzo-soprano
Mfg. *Abk.* **Mitfahrgelegenheit**
MfS das; ~ *Abk. (DDR)* **Ministerium für Staatssicherheit**
mg *Abk.* **Milligramm** mg
MG [ɛm'ge:] **das; ~s, ~s** *Abk.* **Maschinengewehr**
mhd. *Abk.* **mittelhochdeutsch** MHG
MHz *Abk. (Physik)* **Megahertz** MHz
Mi. *Abk.* **Mittwoch** Wed.
Mia. *Abk.* **Milliarde[n]** bn.
miau [mi'au] *Interj.* miaow
miauen *itr. V.* miaow
mich [mɪç] **1.** *Akk. des Personalpron.* **ich** me. **2.** *Akk. des Reflexivpron. der 1. Pers.* myself; **Was tust du im Badezimmer? – Ich wasche ~:** What are you doing in the bathroom? – I'm washing [myself]; **ich möchte ~ entschuldigen** I'd like to apologize
Michael ['mɪçae:l] **(der)** Michael
Michaeli[s] (das); ~, Michael[i]stag der Michaelmas
Michel ['mɪçl̩] **der; ~s, ~** *in* **der deutsche ~:** *proverbial figure representing the blinkered, simple-minded German, uninterested in politics and the world at large*
Michigan·see [mɪʃɪgən-] **der** Lake Michigan
mick[e]rig ['mɪk(ə)rɪç] *Adj. (ugs.)* miserable; measly *(sl.)*; miserable, paltry, *(sl.)* measly ⟨*amount*⟩; puny ⟨*person*⟩; puny, stunted ⟨*plant, tree*⟩
Mickymaus ['mɪki-] **die; ~:** Mickey Mouse *no art.*
midi ['mi:di] *Adj.; nicht attr. (Mode)* **~ tragen/gehen** wear a midi[-skirt/dress/coat]
Midlife·krise ['mɪtlaif-] **die** midlife crisis
mied [mi:t] *1. u. 3. Pers. Sg. Prät. v.* **meiden**
Mieder ['mi:dɐ] **das; ~s, ~ a)** *(Korsage)* girdle; **b)** *(Leibchen)* bodice
Mieder-: **~hose die** pantie-girdle; **~waren** *Pl.* corsetry *sing.*
Mief [mi:f] **der; ~[e]s** *(salopp abwertend)* fug *(coll.)*; **der ~ der Kleinstadt** *(fig.)* the claustrophobic small-town atmosphere
miefen *itr. V. (ugs. abwertend)* pong *(coll.)*; stink
Miene ['mi:nə] **die; ~, ~n** expression; face; **mit unbewegter ~:** with an impassive expression; impassively; **keine ~ verziehen** not turn a hair; **er schluckte die Medizin, ohne eine ~ zu verziehen** he swallowed the medicine without turning a hair; **~ machen, etw. zu tun** make as if to do sth.; **gute ~ zum bösen Spiel machen** grin and bear it
Mienen·spiel das facial expressions *pl.*
mies [mi:s] *(ugs.)* **1.** *Adj. (abwertend)* terrible *(coll.)*; lousy *(sl.)*; rotten *(sl.)*; lousy *(sl.)*, foul ⟨*mood*⟩. **2.** *adv.* **a)** *(abwertend: schlecht)* terribly badly *(coll.)*; lousily *(sl.)*; rottenly *(sl.)*; **das ist aber ~ gearbeitet** the workmanship on this is terrible *(coll.) or* lousy *(sl.) or* rotten *(sl.)*; **b)** *(unwohl)* **ihm geht es ~:** he's in a terrible state *(coll.)*
Miese ['mi:zə] *Pl.; adj. Dekl. (salopp)* **2 000 ~ auf dem Konto haben** be 2,000 marks in the red at the bank; **in den ~n sein** be in the red; *(beim Kartenspiel)* be down on points
Miese·peter der; ~s, ~ *(ugs. abwertend)* misery-guts *(coll.)*
miesepet[e]rig *Adj. (ugs. abwertend)* grumpy
mies-, Mies-: **~|machen** *tr. V. (ugs. abwertend)* **a)** *(schlechtmachen)* **jmdn./etw. ~machen** run sb./sth. down; **b)** *(die Freude nehmen an)* **jmdm. den Urlaub ~machen** spoil sb.'s holiday; **jmdm. die Wohnung/Arbeit ~machen** spoil sb.'s enjoyment of his/her flat/job; **~macher der** *(ugs. abwertend)* carping critic; *(Spielverderber)* kill-joy; **~muschel die** [common] mussel
Miet·ausfall der loss of rent
¹Miete ['mi:tə] **die; ~, ~n a)** rent; *(für ein Auto, Boot)* hire charge; *(für Fernsehgeräte usw.)* rental; **das ist schon die halbe ~** *(fig. ugs.)* I'm/you're *etc.* half-way there; **b)** *o. Pl. (das Mieten)* renting; **zur ~ wohnen** live in rented accommodation; rent a house/flat *(Brit.) or (Amer.)* apartment/room/rooms; **bei jmdm. zur ~ wohnen** lodge with sb.
²Miete die; ~, ~n *(Landw.)* pit
Miet·einnahmen *Pl.* income *sing.* from rents
mieten *tr. V.* **a)** rent; *(für kürzere Zeit)* hire; **b)** *(veralt.: in Dienst nehmen)* hire ⟨*servant*⟩

Mieter ['mi:tɐ] **der; ~s, ~:** tenant
Miet·erhöhung die rent increase
Mieterin die; ~, ~nen tenant
Mieter·schutz der protection of tenants; tenants' protection
miet·frei *Adj., adv.* rent-free
Miet·kauf der *(Wirtsch.)* ≈ hire purchase *(Brit.) or (Amer.)* installment plan *(with option to buy outright or terminate the agreement at a specified date)*
Mietling ['mi:tlɪŋ] **der; ~s, ~e** *(veralt. abwertend)* hireling
Miet-: ~partei die tenant; **~preis der** rent; *(für ein Auto, Boot)* hire charge; *(für Fernsehgeräte usw.)* rental; **~recht das;** *o. Pl.* law of landlord and tenant
Miets-: ~haus das block of rented flats *(Brit.) or (Amer.)* apartments; **~kaserne die** *(abwertend)* tenement block
Miet-: ~verhältnis das *(Amtsspr.)* tenancy; **~vertrag der** tenancy agreement; **~wagen der** hire-car; **~wohnung die** rented flat *(Brit.) or (Amer.)* apartment; **~wucher der** charging of exorbitant rents; **~zahlung die: mit seiner ~zahlung im Rückstand sein** be behind with the rent; **~zins der;** *Pl.* **~e** *(südd., österr., schweiz., Amtsspr.)* rent; **~zu·schuß der** assistance with the rent
Mieze ['mi:tsə] **die; ~, ~n a)** *(fam.: Katze)* puss; pussy *(child lang.)*; **b)** *(salopp: Mädchen)* chick *(sl.)*; *(als Anrede)* sweetie
Mieze·katze die *(fam.)* puss; pussy-cat *(child lang.)*
Migräne [mi'grɛ:nə] **die; ~, ~n** migraine
Migräne·anfall der attack of migraine
Mikado [mi'ka:do] **das; ~s** spillikins *sing.*; jack-straws *sing.*
Mikro ['mi:kro] **das; ~s, ~s** *(ugs.)* mike *(coll.)*
mikro-, Mikro- micro-
Mikrobe [mi'kro:bə] **die; ~, ~n** microbe
Mikro-: ~elektronik die microelectronics *sing., no art.*; **~fiche** [~fi:ʃ] **das** *od.* **der; ~s, ~s** microfiche; **~film der** microfilm; **~klima das** microclimate; **~kosmos der** *(Philos.)* microcosm; **~meter der** *od.* **das** micron
Mikronesien [mikro'ne:ziən] **(das); ~s** Micronesia
mikro-, Mikro-: ~organismus der *(Biol.)* micro-organism; **~phon** [--'-] **das; ~s, ~e** microphone; **~prozessor** [~pro'tsɛsɔr] **der; ~s, ~en** [...'so:rən] microprocessor; **~skop** [~'sko:p] **das; ~s, ~e** microscope; **~skopie** [~sko'pi:] **die; ~:** microscopy *no art.*; **~skopisch 1.** *Adj.* microscopic; **2.** *adv.* microscopically; **etw. ~skopisch untersuchen** examine sth. under the microscope; **~wellen** *Pl.* microwaves; **~wellen·herd der** microwave oven
Milan ['mi:lan] **der; ~s, ~e** *(Zool.)* kite
Milbe ['mɪlbə] **die; ~, ~n** mite; *(Zecke)* tick
Milch [mɪlç] **die; ~ a)** milk; **~ geben** give *or* yield milk; **aussehen wie ~ und Blut** have a lilies-and-roses complexion; **das Land, wo ~ und Honig fließt** *(bibl.)* the land flowing with milk and honey; **b)** *(Fischsamen)* milt; soft roe
Milch-: ~bar die milk bar; **~bart der** *(abwertend)* callow youth; **~becher der** milk mug; **~brötchen das** milk roll; **~drüse die** mammary gland; **~eiweiß das** *(Biol.)* milk protein; **~flasche die a)** *(für Säuglinge)* feeding-bottle; baby's bottle; **b)** *(Flasche für Milch)* milk-bottle; **~frau die** *(ugs.)* dairywoman; **~gebiß das** milk-teeth *pl.*; **~geschäft das** dairy; **~gesicht das** *(abwertend)* callow youth; **~glas das a)** *o. Pl.* milk glass; *(aufgerauht)* frosted glass; **b)** *(Trinkglas)* milk glass; **~händler der** dairyman
milchig 1. *Adj.* milky. **2.** *adv.* **~ weiß** milky-white; **die ~-trübe Färbung des Wassers** the milky cloudiness of the water

Milch-: ~kaffee der coffee with plenty of milk; **~kännchen das** milk-jug; **~kanne die** milk-can; *(zum Transportieren von ~)* [milk-]churn; **~kuh die** dairy *or* milk *or* milch cow; **~mädchen das** dairymaid; **~mädchen·rechnung die** *(ugs.)* naïve miscalculation; **~mann der** *(ugs.)* milkman; **~mix·getränk das** milk shake
Milchner ['mɪlçnɐ] **der; ~s, ~** *(Zool.)* milter
Milch-: ~pumpe die breast-pump; **~reis der** rice pudding; **~säure die** *(Chemie)* lactic acid; **~schokolade die** milk chocolate; **~schorf der** milk crust; crusta lactea *(Med.)*; **~straße die** Milky Way; Galaxy; *(System)* Galaxy; **~straßen·system das** *(Astron.)* galaxy; **~suppe die** milk soup; **~vieh das** dairy cattle; **~wirtschaft die** dairying *no art.*; **~zahn der** milk-tooth; **~zucker der** *(Chemie)* lactose
mild [mɪlt], **milde 1.** *Adj.* **a)** *(gütig)* lenient ⟨*judge, judgement*⟩; benevolent ⟨*ruler*⟩; mild, lenient, light ⟨*punishment*⟩; mild ⟨*words, accusation*⟩; mild, gentle ⟨*reproach*⟩; gentle ⟨*smile, voice*⟩; **jmdn. ~ stimmen** induce sb. to take a lenient attitude; **b)** *(nicht rauh)* mild ⟨*climate, air, winter, etc.*⟩; **c)** *(gedämpft)* soft ⟨*light, glow*⟩; **d)** *(nicht scharf)* mild ⟨*spice, coffee, tobacco, cheese, etc.*⟩; smooth ⟨*brandy*⟩; **~ schmecken** be mild/smooth; **e)** *(schonend)* mild ⟨*soap, shampoo, detergent*⟩; **f)** *nicht präd. (veralt.: mildtätig)* charitable; **eine ~e Gabe** alms *pl.* **2.** *adv.* **a)** *(gütig)* leniently; ⟨*smile, say*⟩ gently; **b)** *(nicht rauh)* **der Wind wehte/die Sonne schien ~:** the wind blew gently/a gentle sun shone down; **c)** *(sanft)* **~ schimmern/leuchten** shimmer softly/shine gently; **d)** *(gelinde)* mildly; **~ ausgedrückt** to put it mildly; putting it mildly
Milde die; ~ a) *(Gnade, Güte)* leniency; **[jmdm. gegenüber] ~ walten lassen** be lenient [with sb.]; **väterliche/christliche ~:** fatherly/Christian kindness; **b)** *(des Klimas usw.)* mildness; **c)** *(milder Geschmack) (von Tabak, Gewürzen usw.)* mildness; *(von Weinbrand)* smoothness; **d)** *(Gedämpftheit)* softness; **e)** *(veralt.: Wohltätigkeit)* charity
mildern 1. *tr. V.* **a)** *(herabmindern)* moderate ⟨*criticism, judgement*⟩; mitigate ⟨*punishment*⟩; **~de Umstände** mitigating circumstances; **b)** *(dämpfen)* moderate ⟨*language*⟩; soothe ⟨*anger*⟩; lessen ⟨*agitation*⟩; **c)** *(abschwächen)* reduce ⟨*intensity, strength, effect*⟩; modify ⟨*impression*⟩; ease, soothe, relieve ⟨*pain*⟩; alleviate ⟨*poverty, need*⟩; ease ⟨*sorrow*⟩. **2.** *refl. V.* **a)** *(geringer werden)* ⟨*anger, rage, agitation*⟩ abate; **b)** *(abschwächen)* ⟨*effect*⟩ be reduced; ⟨*impression*⟩ be modified; **c)** *(wärmer werden)* ⟨*weather*⟩ become milder
Milderung die; ~ a) *(eines Tadels, Urteils)* moderation; *(einer Strafe)* mitigation; **b)** *(Linderung) (von Schmerz)* easing; soothing; relief; *(von Armut, Not)* alleviation
Milderungs·grund der mitigating circumstance
mild·tätig 1. *Adj.* charitable; **für ~tätige Zwecke sammeln** collect for charity. **2.** *adv.* **~ wirken** perform charitable acts
Mild·tätigkeit die; *o. Pl.* charity
Milieu [mi'liø:] **das; ~s, ~s a)** *(soziales Umfeld)* milieu; environment; *(fig.: Prostitution usw.)* world of pimps and prostitutes; **das ~ der Berliner Kneipen** the world of Berlin pubs *(Brit.) or (Amer.)* bars; **er stammt aus kleinbürgerlichem ~:** his background is petit bourgeois; **b)** *(Biol.: Lebensraum)* environment
milieu-, Milieu-: ~geschädigt *Adj. (Psych.)* maladjusted *(as a result of adverse environmental influences)*; **~schilderung die** description of the physical and social environment; **~studie die** study of an environment; **~theorie die** *(Psych.)* environmentalism *no art.*

militant [mili'tant] *Adj.* militant
Militanz die; ~: militancy
¹Militär [mili'tɛ:ɐ̯] **das; ~s a)** armed forces *pl.*; military; **beim ~ sein/vom ~ entlassen werden** be in/be discharged from the forces; **zum ~ müssen** have to join the forces; **zum ~ einberufen werden** be called up; **b)** *(Soldaten)* soldiers *pl.*; army; **~ gegen jmdn. einsetzen** use the army against sb.
²Militär der; ~s, ~s [high-ranking military] officer
Militär-: ~akademie die military academy; **~arzt der** medical officer; **~attaché der** military attaché; **~basis die** military base; **~block der** military [alliance-]bloc; **~dienst der** military service; **seinen ~dienst ableisten** do one's military *or* national service; **~diktatur die** military dictatorship; **~fahrzeug das** military vehicle; **~flug·platz der** military airfield; **~flugzeug das** military aircraft; **~geistliche der** army chaplain; **~gericht das** military court; court martial; **vor ein ~gericht gestellt werden** be brought before *or* tried by a military court; be court martialled; **~gerichtsbarkeit die** military jurisdiction *no art.*; **~hilfe die** military aid *no art.*; **~hubschrauber der** military helicopter
Militaria [mili'ta:ria] *Pl.* military objects; militaria
militärisch 1. *Adj.* military; **jmdm. ~e Ehren erweisen** award *or* give sb. military honours; **mit allen ~en Ehren** with full military honours. **2.** *adv.* **gegen jmdn. ~ vorgehen** take military action against sb.; **jmdn. ~ grüßen** salute sb.; **~ strammstehen** stand to attention
militarisieren [militari'zi:rən] *tr. V.* militarize
Militarisierung die; ~: militarization
Militarismus der; ~ *(abwertend)* militarism
Militarist der; ~en, ~en *(abwertend)* militarist
militaristisch *Adj. (abwertend)* militarist; militaristic
Militär-: ~junta die military junta; **~kapelle die** *(Musik)* military band; **~marsch der** military march; **~musik die** military music; **~parade die** military parade; **~polizei die** military police; **~putsch der** military putsch; **~regierung die** military government; **~seelsorge die** pastoral care of military personnel; **in der ~seelsorge tätig sein** look after the spiritual welfare of military personnel; **~streife die** military patrol; **~stütz·punkt der** military base; **~wesen das;** *o. Pl.* military affairs *pl., no art.*; **~wissenschaft die** military science
Military ['mɪlɪtərɪ] **die; ~, ~s** *(Reiten)* three-day event
Militär·zeit die time in the forces *or* services
Miliz [mi'li:ts] **die; ~, ~en** militia; *(Polizei)* police
Milizionär [militsio'nɛ:ɐ̯] **der; ~s, ~e a)** militiaman; **b)** *(Polizist)* policeman
milk [mɪlk], **milkst, milkt** *(veralt.) Imperativ Sg., 2. u. 3. Pers. Sg. Präsens v.* **melken**
Mill. *Abk.* **Million** m.
Mille ['mɪlə] **die; ~, ~** *(salopp)* grand *(sl.)*; thousand marks/pounds *etc.*; **zwei ~:** two grand *(sl.)*
Millennium [mɪ'lɛniʊm] **das; ~s, Millennien** millennium
milli- ['mɪli-], **Milli-** milli-
Milliardär [miliar'dɛ:ɐ̯] **der; ~s, ~e, Milliardärin die; ~, ~nen** multi-millionaire *(possessing at least a thousand million marks etc.)*; billionaire *(Amer.)*; *s. auch* **Millionär**
Milliarde [mɪ'liardə] **die; ~, ~n** thousand million; billion; **mehrere ~n Mark/Einwohner** several thousand million *or* several billion marks/inhabitants; *s. auch* **Million**

Milliarden-: ~**höhe die** *in* **in** ~**höhe** of the order of a thousand million *or* a billion; ~**kredit der** credit of the order of a thousand million *or* a billion; *s. auch* **millionen-, Millionen-**
milliardst... *Ordinalz.* thousand millionth; billionth; *s. auch* **hundertst...**
milliardstel *Bruchz.* thousand millionth; billionth; *s. auch* **hundertstel**
Milliardstel das, *schweiz.* **der; ~s, ~:** part in a billion *or* thousand million; *s. auch* **Hundertstel**
Milli-: ~**bar das** *(Met.)* millibar; ~**gramm das** milligram; ~**liter der** *od.* **das** millilitre
Milli·meter der *od.* **das** millimetre
Millimeter-: ~**arbeit die;** *o. Pl. (ugs.) (am Steuer)* delicate piece of manœuvring; *(bei Ballspielen)* [neat] piece of precision play; ~**papier das** [graph] paper ruled in millimetre squares
Million [mɪ'li̯o:n] **die; ~, ~en a)** million; **eine ~ Menschen war** *od.* **waren ...:** a million people were ...; **zwei ~en [Einwohner]** two million [inhabitants]; **b)** *Pl. (unbestimmte Anzahl od. Summe)* millions; **~en von Menschen** millions of people; **in die ~en gehen** run into millions
Millionär [mɪli̯o'nɛ:ɐ̯] **der; ~s, ~e, Millionärin die; ~, ~nen** millionaire
millionen-, Millionen-: ~**auf·lage die** *(Buchw.)* **dieses Buch erschien in ~auflage** *od.* **erlebte eine ~auflage** [over] a million copies of this book were printed; ~**auftrag der** contract worth a million/worth millions; ~**fach 1.** *Adj.* millionfold ‹*increase etc.*›; **in ~fachen Tests** in a million tests; **~fache Zustimmung finden** meet with the approval of millions of people; **es kam zu ~fachen Protesten** there were millions of protests; **2.** *adv.* a million times; ~**geschäft das** deal worth a million/worth millions; ~**gewinn der a)** *(Ertrag)* profit of a million/of millions; **~gewinne** profits running into millions; **b)** *(Lotteriegewinn)* prize of a million/of millions; ~**heer das** millions *pl.;* ~**höhe die** *in* **in ~höhe** of the order of a million; ~**kredit der** credit of the order of a million; ~**mal** *Adv.* a million times; ~**schaden der** damage *no pl., no indef. art.* running into millions; ~**schwer** *Adj. (ugs.)* worth millions *pred.;* ~**stadt die** town with over a million inhabitants; ~**vermögen das** fortune of millions
millionst... *Ordinalz.* millionth; *s. auch* **hundertst...**
million[s]tel *Bruchz.* millionth; *s. auch* **hundertstel**
Million[s]tel das *od. (schweiz.)* **der; ~s, ~:** millionth; *(Teilmenge)* part in a million; ppm
Milz [mɪlts] **die; ~** *(Anat.)* spleen
Milz·brand der *(Tiermed.)* anthrax
Mime ['mi:mə] **der; ~n, ~n** *(geh.)* Thespian
mimen 1. *tr. V.* **a)** *(ugs. abwertend)* put on a show of ‹*admiration, efficiency*›; **Trauer/Besorgnis ~:** act sad/concerned *(coll.);* **den Kranken/Unschuldigen ~:** pretend to be ill/act the innocent; **den starken Mann ~:** act tough; **b)** *(darstellen)* play; act; **den Tell ~:** play Tell. **2.** *itr. V. (ugs. abwertend)* **auf Millionär/krank** *usw.* **~:** pretend to be a millionaire/to be ill *etc.*
Mimesis ['mi:mezɪs] **die; ~, Mimesen** *(Liter., Philos.)* mimesis; imitation
Mimik ['mi:mɪk] **die; ~:** gestures and facial expressions *pl.*
Mimikry ['mɪmikri] **die; ~** *(Zool.)* mimicry; *(fig.)* camouflage
mimisch 1. *Adj.; nicht präd.* mimic; **seine ~e Ausdruckskraft** the expressive power of his gestures and facial movements; **eine ~e Begabung** a gift for mimic expression. **2.** *adv.* ‹*show*› by means of gestures and facial expressions; **~ begabt sein** have a gift for mimic expression
Mimose [mi'mo:zə] **die; ~, ~n a)** mimosa; *(volkst.: Akazie)* silver wattle; **b)** *(empfindsamer Mensch)* over-sensitive person; **die reinste ~ sein** be extraordinarily sensitive
mimosenhaft 1. *Adj.* over-sensitive. **2.** *adv.* over-sensitively
Min. *Abk.* **Minute[n]** min.
Minarett [mina'rɛt] **das; ~s, ~e** *od.* **~s** minaret
mind. *Abk.* **mindestens**
minder ['mɪndɐ] *Adv. (geh.)* less; **[nicht] ~ angenehm sein** be [no] less pleasant; *s. auch* **mehr**
minder... *Adj.; nicht präd.* inferior ‹*goods, brand*›; **von ~er Bedeutung/Qualität sein** be of less importance/inferior *or* lower quality
minder-; Minder-: ~**begabt** *Adj.* less gifted *or* able; ~**begütert** *Adj.* less well-off; ~**bemittelt** *Adj.* without much money *postpos., not pred.;* **~bemittelt sein** not have much money; **er ist doch geistig ~bemittelt** *(fig. salopp abwertend)* he isn't all that bright *(coll.);* ~**bemittelte** *Pl.* needy persons; ~**einnahme die** decrease in revenue; *(geringere Einnahme, als kalkuliert)* shortfall in revenue
Minderheit die; ~, ~en minority
Minderheiten·recht das right of a/the minority
Minderheits·regierung die minority government
minder-, Minder-: ~**jährig** *Adj.* *(Rechtsw.)* ‹*child etc.*› who is/was a minor *or* under age; **~jährig sein** be a minor *or* under age; ~**jährige der/die;** *adj. Dekl.* *(Rechtsw.)* minor; person under age; ~**jährigkeit die; ~** *(Rechtsw.)* minority; **bis zum Ende der ~jährigkeit** until he/she comes/came of age
mindern *(geh.)* **1.** *tr. V.* reduce ‹*income, price, number of staff, tension, etc.*›; impair ‹*performance, abilities*›; diminish, reduce ‹*value, quality, dignity, pleasure, influence*›; detract from ‹*reputation*›. **2.** *refl. V.* diminish; ‹*vehemence*› lessen
Minderung die; ~, ~en *s.* **mindern 1:** reduction *(Gen.* in); impairment *(Gen.* of); diminution *(Gen.* of); detraction *(Gen.* from)
minder·wertig *Adj. (abwertend)* inferior, low-quality ‹*goods, material*›; low-quality, low-grade ‹*meat*›; *(fig.)* inferior; **ein moralisch ~wertiger Mensch** *(abwertend)* a person of questionable character
Minder·wertigkeit die; *o. Pl. s.* **minderwertig:** inferiority; low quality; low grade; *(fig.)* inferiority
Minderwertigkeits-: ~**gefühl das** *(Psych.)* feeling of inferiority; ~**komplex der** *(Psych.)* inferiority complex
Minder·zahl die; *o. Pl.* minority
mindest... ['mɪndəst...] *Adj.; nicht präd.* slightest; least; **ohne die ~e Angst** without the slightest *or* least trace of fear; **ich habe nicht die ~e Ahnung** I haven't the slightest idea; **das ist das ~e, was du tun kannst** it is the least you can do; **sie versteht nicht das ~e vom Kochen** she doesn't know the slightest *or* first thing about cooking; **nicht im ~en** not in the least; **zum ~en** at least
Mindest-: ~**alter das** minimum age; ~**anforderung die** minimum requirement; ~**betrag der** minimum amount
mindestens ['mɪndəstn̩s] *Adv.* at least
Mindest-: ~**gebot das** reserve price; ~**geschwindigkeit die** minimum speed; ~**größe die** minimum size; ~**haltbarkeits·datum das** best-before date; ~**lohn der** minimum wage; ~**maß das** minimum **(an +** *Dat.,* **von** of); ~**preis der** minimum [legal] price; ~**strafe die** *(Rechtsw.)* minimum penalty; ~**urlaub der** minimum holiday entitlement; ~**zahl die** minimum
Mine ['mi:nə] **die; ~, ~n a)** *(Erzbergwerk)* mine; **b)** *(Sprengkörper)* mine; **auf eine ~ laufen** strike a mine; **c)** *(Bleistift~)* lead; *(Kugelschreiber~, Filzschreiber~)* refill
Minen-: ~**feld das** minefield; ~**leger der** *(Milit.)* minelayer; ~**such·boot das** *(Milit.)* minesweeper; ~**such·gerät das** *(Milit.)* mine-detector; ~**werfer der** *(Milit. Hist.)* trench-mortar
Mineral [mine'ra:l] **das; ~s, ~e** *od.* **Mineralien** mineral
Mineral-: ~**bad das** spa; ~**brunnen der** *s.* **~quelle;** ~**dünger der** inorganic fertilizer
Mineraloge [mɪnera'lo:gə] **der; ~n, ~n** mineralogist
Mineralogie die; ~: mineralogy *no art.*
mineralogisch *Adj.; nicht präd.* mineralogical
Mineral·öl das mineral oil
Mineralöl-: ~**gesellschaft die** oil company; ~**industrie die** oil industry; ~**steuer die** tax on oil
Mineral-: ~**quelle die** mineral spring; ~**salz das,** ~**stoff der** mineral salt; ~**wasser das** mineral water
mini ['mɪni] *Adj.; nicht attr. (Mode)* **~ tragen/gehen** wear a mini *(coll.)*
Mini das; ~s, ~s *(Mode)* mini *(coll.);* **im ~:** in a mini *(coll.);* **diese Kleider sind alle in ~:** all these dresses are mini-length *or (coll.)* minis *pl.*
mini-, Mini- mini-
Miniatur [mini̯a'tu:ɐ̯] **die; ~, ~en** miniature
Miniatur-: ~**aus·gabe die** *(Buchw.)* abridged edition; ~**maler der** miniaturist; ~**malerei die** miniature painting
Mini·golf das minigolf; crazy golf
minimal [mini'ma:l] **1.** *Adj.* minimal; marginal ‹*advantage, lead*›; very slight ‹*benefit, profit*›. **2.** *adv.* minimally; **sie unterscheiden sich nur ~:** the differences between them are minimal
Minimal-: ~**forderung die** minimum demand; ~**gewicht das** minimum weight; ~**wert der** minimum value
minimieren *tr. V. (bes. Math.)* minimize
Minimierung die; ~, ~en *(bes. Math.)* minimization
Minimum ['mi:nimʊm] **das; ~s, Minima** minimum **(an +** *Dat.* of); **ein ~ an Vertrauen** a certain minimum degree of trust; **etw. unter dem ~ verkaufen** sell sth. below the minimum [legal] price
Mini-: ~**rock der** miniskirt; ~**spion der** miniaturized listening *or (coll.)* bugging device
Minister [mi'nɪstɐ] **der; ~s, ~:** minister **(für** for); *(eines britischen Hauptministeriums)* Secretary of State **(für** for); *(eines amerikanischen Hauptministeriums)* Secretary **(für** of)
Minister-: ~**amt das** ministerial office; ~**ebene die** *in* **auf ~ebene** at ministerial level
Ministerial-: ~**beamte der** ministry official; ~**direktor der** head of a ministry department; ~**dirigent der** head of a section within a ministry department
Ministeriale [minɪste'ri̯a:lə] **der/die;** *adj. Dekl. s.* **Ministerialbeamte**
Ministerial·rat der *s.* **Ministerialdirigent**
ministeriell [minɪste'ri̯ɛl] **1.** *Adj.* ministerial. **2.** *adv.* by the minister
Ministerin die; ~, ~nen *s.* **Minister**
Ministerium [minɪs'te:ri̯ʊm] **das; ~s, Ministerien** Ministry; Department *(Amer.)*
Minister-: ~**präsident der a)** *(eines deutschen Bundeslandes)* minister-president; prime minister *(Brit.);* governor *(Amer.);* **b)** *(Premierminister)* Prime Minister; ~**rat der** Council of Ministers; ~**sessel der** *(ugs.)* ministerial post
ministrabel [minɪs'tra:bl̩] *Adj.* capable of holding ministerial office *pred.*
Ministrant [minɪs'trant] **der; ~en, ~en** *(kath. Kirche)* server

ministrieren *itr. V. (kath. Kirche)* serve [at the altar]; act as server

Minna ['mɪna] **die; ~, ~s** *(ugs. veralt.)* maid; **jmdn. zur ~ machen** *(ugs.)* tear sb. off a strip *(Brit. sl.)*; bawl out *(coll.)*; **eine grüne ~** *(ugs.)* a Black Maria; a patrol wagon *(Amer.)*

Minne ['mɪnə] **die; ~** *(MA.)* courtly love

Minne-: dienst der *(MA.)* knight's homage to his lady; **~sang der** *(Literaturw.)* Minnesong; **~sänger, ~singer der** *(MA.)* Minnesinger

Minorität [minori'tɛ:t] **die; ~, ~en** *s.* **Minderheit**

Minuend [mi'nu̯ɛnt] **der; ~en, ~en** minuend

minus ['mi:nʊs] **1.** *Konj. (Math.)* minus. **2.** *Adv.* **a)** *(bes. Math.)* minus; **~ fünf Grad, fünf Grad ~:** minus five degrees; five degrees below [zero]; **b)** *(Elektrot.)* negative. **3.** *Präp. mit Gen. (Kaufmannsspr.)* less; minus

Minus das; ~ a) *(Fehlbetrag)* deficit; *(auf einem Konto)* overdraft; **~ machen** make a loss; **im ~ sein** be in debit; be in the red; **b)** *(Nachteil)* minus; drawback; *(im Beruf)* disadvantage

Minus·betrag der deficit

Minuskel [mi'nʊskḷ] **die; ~, ~n** *(Druckw.)* minuscule

Minus-: ~pol der *(Physik)* negative pole; *(einer Batterie)* negative terminal; **~punkt der a)** minus *or* penalty point; **b)** *(Nachteil)* disadvantage; **~zeichen das** minus sign

Minute [mi'nu:tə] **die; ~, ~n a)** minute; **6 ~n nach/vor zwei** six minutes to/past two; **es ist neun Uhr [und] sieben ~n** it is seven minutes past nine *or* nine seven; **~ um ~ verging** *od.* **verstrich** minutes went by *or* passed; **b)** *(Moment)* minute; moment; **hast du ein paar ~n Zeit für mich?** can you spare me a few minutes *or* moments?; **in letzter ~:** at the last minute *or* moment; **auf die ~ pünktlich sein** *od.* **kommen** be punctual to the minute

minuten·lang 1. *Adj.; nicht präd.* ⟨*applause, silence, etc.*⟩ lasting [for] several minutes; **sein ~langes Schweigen** his silence, which lasted for several minutes. **2.** *adv.* for several minutes

Minuten·zeiger der minute-hand

-minütig *Adj.* **ein fünf~er Heulton** a wail lasting five minutes; **eine fünfzehn~e Verspätung** a fifteen-minute delay; a delay of fifteen minutes

minütlich [mi'ny:tlɪç] **1.** *Adj.* **in ~en Abständen** at intervals of a minute. **2.** *adv.* every minute

minuziös [minu'tsi̯ø:s] *(geh.)* **1.** *Adj.* minutely *or* meticulously precise *or* detailed ⟨*account, description*⟩; minute ⟨*detail*⟩; ⟨*manœuvre*⟩ requiring minute precision. **2.** *adv.* meticulously

Minze ['mɪntsə] **die; ~, ~n** mint

Mio. *Abk.* **Million[en]** m.

mir [mi:ɐ̯] **1. a)** *Dat. Sg. des Personalpron.* **ich** to me; *(nach Präpositionen)* me; **gib es ~:** give it to me; give me it; **gib ~ das Buch** give me the book; **Freunde von ~:** friends of mine; **gehen wir zu ~:** let's got to my place; **~ nichts, dir nichts** *(ugs.)* just like that; without so much as a 'by your leave'; **von ~ aus** as far as I'm concerned; **Kann ich das Radio abstellen? – Von ~ aus** Can I turn the radio off? – As far as I'm concerned you can; **b)** *(Dativus ethicus)* **geht ~ nicht an meinen Schreibtisch!** keep away from my desk!; **und grüß ~ alle Verwandten!** and give my regards to all the relatives; **du bist ~ vielleicht einer!** *(ugs.)* a fine one you are!; **wie du ~, so ich dir** tit for tat; *(drohend)* I'll get my own back. **2.** *Dat. des Reflexivpron. der 1. Pers. Sg.* myself; **ich habe ~ deine Vorschläge genau überlegt** I have given careful thought to your suggestions; **ich habe ~ gedacht, daß ...:** I thought that ...; **ich will ~ ein neues Kleid kaufen** I want to buy myself a new dress; **ich nehme ~ noch von dem Braten** I'll help myself to some more roast

Mirabelle [mira'bɛlə] **die; ~, ~n** mirabelle

Mirakel [mi'ra:kḷ] **das; ~s, ~** *(geh. veralt.)* miracle

Misanthrop [mizan'tro:p] **der; ~en, ~en** *(geh.)* misanthrope

Misch-: ~batterie die mixer tap; mixing faucet *(Amer.)*; **~blut das** *(geh.) s.* **Mischling a; ~brot das** bread made from wheat and rye flour; **~ehe die** mixed marriage

mischen ['mɪʃn̩] **1.** *tr. V.* mix; **etw. in etw.** *(Akk.)* **~:** put sth. into sth.; **Wasser und Wein ~:** mix water with wine; **[sich** *(Dat.)***] Tees/Tabake ~:** blend [one's own] teas/tobaccos; **die Karten ~:** shuffle the cards. **2.** *refl. V.* **a)** *(sich ver~)* mix **(mit** with); ⟨*smell, scent*⟩ blend **(mit** with); **in meine Freude mischte sich Angst** my joy was mingled with fear; **b)** *(sich ein~)* **sich in etw.** *(Akk.)* **~:** interfere *or* meddle in sth.; **sich in das Gespräch ~:** butt into the conversation; **c)** *(sich begeben)* **sich unters Publikum** *usw.* **~:** mingle with the audience *etc.* **3.** *itr. V.* **a)** *(Kartenspiel)* shuffle; **wer muß ~?** whose shuffle is it?; **b)** *(Film, Rundf., Ferns.)* mix; *s. auch* **gemischt**

Mischer der; ~s, ~ *(Bauw.)* [cement-]mixer

Misch-: ~farbe die non-primary colour; **~form die** mixture; *(Kunstform)* fusion; **~futter das** mixed feed; **~gewebe das** mixture; **~kultur die a)** *(Landw.)* mixed cultivation; **b)** *(Soziol.)* mixed culture

Mischling ['mɪʃlɪŋ] **der; ~s, ~e a)** half-caste; half-breed; **b)** *(Biol.)* hybrid

Mischmasch ['mɪʃmaʃ] **der; ~[e]s, ~e** *(ugs., meist abwertend)* hotchpotch; mishmash; *(Essen)* concoction

Misch·maschine die *(Bauw.)* cement-mixer

Mischpoke [mɪʃ'po:kə] **die; ~** *(salopp abwertend)* **a)** *(Verwandtschaft)* tribe *(derog.)*; **b)** *(Gesellschaft)* mob *(sl.)*; shower *(Brit. sl.)*

Misch-: ~pult das *(Film, Rundf., Ferns.)* mixing desk *or* console; **~sprache die** hybrid language; **~trommel die** mixing drum

Mischung die; ~, ~en a) *(Gemisch, auch fig.)* mixture; *(Tee~, Kaffee~, Tabak~)* blend; *(Pralinen~)* assortment; **b)** *(das Mischen)* mixing; *(von Tee, Kaffee, Tabak)* blending

Mischungs·verhältnis das proportion in the mixture

Misch·wald der mixed [deciduous and coniferous] forest

miserabel [mizə'ra:bḷ] *(ugs.)* **1.** *Adj.* **a)** *(schlecht)* dreadful *(coll.)*, atrocious ⟨*film, wine, food*⟩; pathetic, miserable ⟨*achievement*⟩; miserable, dreadful *(coll.)*, atrocious ⟨*weather*⟩; **b)** *(elend)* miserable; wretched; **mir ist ~ zumute, ich fühle mich ~:** I feel dreadful; **c)** *(niederträchtig)* abominable ⟨*behaviour*⟩. **2.** *adv.* **a)** *(schlecht)* dreadfully *(coll.)*; atrociously; ⟨*sleep*⟩ dreadfully badly *(coll.)*; **~ bezahlt werden** be very badly *or* poorly paid; **b)** *(elend)* **ihm geht es gesundheitlich ~:** he's in a bad way; **c)** *(niederträchtig)* **sich ~ benehmen** *od.* **verhalten** behave abominably

Misere [mi'ze:rə] **die; ~, ~n** *(geh.)* wretched *or* dreadful state; *(Elend)* misery; *(Not)* distress; **seine finanzielle ~:** his wretched *or* dreadful financial state

Miserere [mize're:rə] **das; ~s** *(bibl.)* miserere

Mispel ['mɪspḷ] **die; ~, ~n** medlar

miß [mɪs] *Imperativ Sg. v.* **messen**

Miß, Miss [mɪs] **die; ~, Misses** ['mɪsɪz] Miss

miß·achten, miß·achten *tr. V.* **a)** *(ignorieren)* disregard; ignore; **b)** *(geringschätzen)* disdain; be contemptuous of; **sich mißachtet fühlen** feel scorned

Miß·achtung die a) *(Nichtbeachtung)* disregard (+ *Gen.* of, for); **die ~ der Vorschriften/meines Rates** disregarding *or* ignoring the regulations/my advice; **b)** *(Verachtung)* disdain, contempt (+ *Gen.* for)

miß·behagen[1] *itr. V. (geh.)* **das mißbehagt ihr** she is not happy about it

Miß·behagen das [feeling of] unease; uncomfortable feeling; **bei dem Gedanken daran befiel sie ein tiefes ~:** she did not at all like the thought of it

Miß·bildung die deformity

miß·billigen *tr. V.* disapprove of

Miß·billigung die disapproval

Miß·brauch der a) *(das Mißbrauchen)* abuse; misuse; *(falsche Anwendung)* misuse; *(von Feuerlöscher, Notbremse)* improper use; **mit seiner Stellung/Macht ~ treiben** abuse *or* misuse one's position/power; **unter ~ seines Amtes** by misusing his position; **b)** *(übermäßiger Gebrauch)* misuse; **c)** *(geh.: Vergewaltigung)* rape

miß·brauchen *tr. V.* **a)** abuse; misuse; abuse ⟨*trust*⟩; **jmdn. für** *od.* **zu etw. ~:** use sb. for sth.; **b)** *(übermäßig gebrauchen)* misuse ⟨*drugs, medicines*⟩; **c)** *(geh.: vergewaltigen)* rape

mißbräuchlich [-brɔyçlɪç] **1.** *Adj.* **~e Verwendung/Anwendung** misuse. **2.** *adv.* **etw. ~ verwenden/handhaben** misuse sth.

miß·deuten *tr. V.* misinterpret

Miß·deutung die misinterpretation

missen *tr. V. (geh.)* **a)** *(entbehren)* do *or* go without; do without ⟨*person*⟩; **jmdn./etw. nicht ~ können/mögen** be unable to do without/not want to be without sb./sth.; **b)** *(selten) s.* **vermissen 1**

Miß·erfolg der failure

Miß·ernte die crop failure

Misse·tat ['mɪsə-] **die** *(geh. veralt.)* misdeed

Misse·täter der, Misse·täterin die *(geh. veralt.)* malefactor

miß·fallen *unr. itr. V.* **etw. mißfällt jmdm.** sb. dislikes *or* does not like sth.; **es mißfiel mir, wie unfreundlich sie ...:** I disliked *or* did not like the unkind way she ...

Mißfallen das; ~s displeasure **(über** + *Akk.* at); *(Mißbilligung)* disapproval **(über** + *Akk.* of); **~ erregen** arouse displeasure/disapproval; **jmds. ~ erregen** incur sb.'s displeasure/disapproval

Mißfallens·äußerung die expression of displeasure/disapproval

miß·fällig *(veralt.)* **1.** *Adj.* disapproving. **2.** *adv.* disapprovingly

miß·gebildet *Adj.* deformed

Miß·geburt die *(Med.)* monster; monstrosity; **diese ~ von [einem] Krämer!** *(fig. abwertend)* that misbegotten scoundrel of a shopkeeper

miß·gelaunt *(geh.)* **1.** *Adj.* ill-humoured. **2.** *adv.* ill-humouredly

Miß·geschick das *(ärgerlicher Vorfall)* mishap; *(Pech)* bad luck; *(Unglück)* misfortune; **jmdm. passiert** *od.* **widerfährt ein ~:** sb. has a mishap/a piece *or* stroke of bad luck/a misfortune; **vom ~ verfolgt sein** be dogged by bad luck/misfortune

Mißgestalt die *(geh.)* misshapen figure

miß·gestaltet *Adj.* misshapen; deformed ⟨*person, child*⟩

miß·gestimmt 1. *Adj.* *(geh.)* ill-humoured; **~ sein** be in a bad mood. **2.** *adv.* ill-humouredly

miß·glücken *itr. V.; mit sein* fail; be unsuccessful; **der Kuchen/Plan ist mir mißglückt** the cake I made turned out a failure/my plan failed *or* was a failure; **ein mißglückter Versuch** a failed *or* unsuccessful attempt

miß·gönnen *tr. V.* **jmdm. etw. ~:** begrudge sb. sth.; **er mißgönnte ihr, daß sie ...:** he begrudged the fact that she ...

---

[1] *mißbehagt, mißzubehagen*

Miß·griff der error of judgement; **einen ~ tun** *od.* **machen** make an error of judgement
Miß·gunst die [envy and] resentment (**gegenüber** of); *(fig.: des Schicksals)* malevolence
miß·günstig 1. *Adj.* resentful; *(fig.)* malevolent ‹*fate*›. **2.** *adv.* resentfully; *(fig.)* malevolently
miß·handeln *tr. V.* maltreat; ill-treat; **mißhandelte Frauen/Kinder** battered wives/children
Miß·handlung die maltreatment; ill-treatment; **~en** maltreatment *sing.*; ill-treatment *sing.*
Miß·helligkeiten *Pl. (geh.)* differences
missingsch ['mɪsɪŋʃ] *Adv.* **~ sprechen** speak Missingsch
Missingsch das; ~: Missingsch *(Hamburg dialect made up of High German and some Low German elements)*
Mission [mɪ'si̯o:n] **die; ~, ~en a)** *(geh.: Auftrag)* mission; **in geheimer ~:** on a secret mission; **b)** *(geh.: Personengruppe)* mission; *(Delegation)* delegation; **c)** *o. Pl. (Rel.)* mission; **in der [äußeren/inneren] ~ tätig sein** do missionary work [abroad/in one's own country]; **d)** *(geh.: diplomatische Vertretung)* mission
Missionar [mɪsi̯o'na:ɐ̯], *(österr.)* **Missionär** [mɪsi̯o'nɛ:ɐ̯] **der; ~s, ~e, Missionarin die; ~, ~nen** missionary
missionarisch 1. *Adj.* missionary. **2.** *adv.* **~ tätig sein** do missionary work
Missionar·stellung die *(ugs.)* missionary position
missionieren 1. *itr. V.* do missionary work. **2.** *tr. V.* convert by missionary work; *(fig.)* convert to one's own ideas
Missionierung die; ~: die ~ eines Landes/eines Volkes missionary work in a country/among a people; *(als Ergebnis)* the conversion of a country/people [by missionary work]
Missions-: ~chef der *(Politik)* head of a/the mission; **~gesellschaft die** missionary society; **~station die** mission station; **~wissenschaft die;** *o. Pl.* missiology *no art.*; study of the Christian mission
Miß·klang der discord; dissonance; *(fig.)* discord; **mit einem ~ enden** *(fig.)* end on a note of discord; **es gab einige Mißklänge** *(fig.)* there was a certain amount of discord
Miß·kredit der *in* **jmdn./etw. in ~ bringen** bring sb./sth. into discredit; bring discredit on sb./sth.; **bei jmdm. in ~ geraten** get a bad name with sb.
mißlang *1. u. 3. Pers. Sg. Prät. v.* **mißlingen**
miß·launig *Adj. (geh.) s.* **mißgelaunt**
mißlich *Adj. (geh.)* awkward, difficult ‹*situation*›; difficult ‹*conditions*›; unfortunate ‹*consequences, incident*›; **es steht ~ um die [Finanzkraft der] Firma** the firm is not doing very well [financially]
Mißlichkeit die; ~, ~en *(geh.) (mißliche Situation)* awkward *or* difficult situation; *(mißlicher Vorfall)* unfortunate incident
mißliebig ['mɪsli:bɪç] *Adj.* unpopular; **~e Ausländer** unwanted foreigners; **sich ~ machen** make oneself persona non grata (**bei** with)
mißlingen [mɪs'lɪŋən] *unr. itr. V.; mit sein* fail; be unsuccessful; be a failure; **ein mißlungener Kuchen** an unsuccessful attempt at a cake; **ein mißlungener Versuch** a failed *or* unsuccessful attempt
Mißlingen das; ~s failure
mißlungen [mɪs'lʊŋən] *2. Part. v.* **mißlingen**
Miß·mut der ill humour *no indef. art.*; **mit leichtem ~:** somewhat in a bad temper; **jmds. ~** *(Akk.)* **erregen** put sb. in a bad mood
miß·mutig 1. *Adj.* bad-tempered; sullen ‹*face*›; **warum bist du heute so ~?** why are you in such a bad mood today?. **2.** *adv.* bad-temperedly

miß·raten *unr. itr. V.; mit sein* ‹*cake, photo, etc.*› turn out badly; **gänzlich ~:** be a complete failure; **das Bild/der Kuchen ist ihr ~/nicht ~:** her picture/cake turned out badly/well; **ein ~es Kind** a child who has turned out badly
Miß·stand der: die vorhandenen Mißstände the serious shortcomings that exist; **das ist ein ~:** it is deplorable; **Mißstände in der Verwaltung** serious irregularities in the administration; **soziale Mißstände** social evils; **einen ~ beseitigen** put an end to a deplorable state of affairs
Miß·stimmung die *(gedrückte Stimmung)* ill humour *no indef. art.*; *(gereizte Stimmung)* discord *no indef. art.*
mißt *2. u. 3. Pers. Sg. Präsens v.* **messen**
Miß·ton der discordant note; *(fig.)* note of discord; discordant note; **mit einem ~ enden** *(fig.)* end on a note of discord
mißtönend, mißtönig 1. *Adj.* discordant. **2.** *adv.* discordantly
miß·trauen *itr. V.* **jmdm./einer Sache ~:** mistrust *or* distrust sb./sth.; **sich** *(Dat.)* **selbst ~:** have no confidence in oneself
Mißtrauen das; ~s mistrust, distrust (**gegen** of); **voll[er] ~:** extremely mistrustful *or* distrustful (**gegen** of); **~ gegen jmdn./etw. haben, jmdm./einer Sache ~ entgegenbringen** mistrust *or* distrust sb./sth.
Mißtrauens-: ~antrag der motion of no confidence; **~votum das** vote of no confidence (**gegen[über]** in)
mißtrauisch ['mɪstrau̯ɪʃ] **1.** *Adj.* mistrustful; distrustful; *(argwöhnisch)* suspicious. **2.** *adv.* mistrustfully; distrustfully; *(argwöhnisch)* suspiciously
Miß·vergnügen das *(geh.) (Ärger)* annoyance; *(Unzufriedenheit)* discontentment; **jmdm. ~ bereiten** make sb. annoyed/discontented
miß·vergnügt *(geh.)* **1.** *Adj. (verärgert)* annoyed; *(unzufrieden)* discontented; *(verdrießlich)* ill-humoured. **2.** *adv. s. Adj.*: in an annoyed way; discontentedly; ill-humouredly
Miß·verhältnis das disparity; *(an Größe)* disproportion
miß·verständlich 1. *Adj.* unclear; ‹*formulation, concept, etc.*› that could be misunderstood; **~ sein** be liable to be misunderstood. **2.** *adv.* ‹*express oneself, describe*› in a way that could be misunderstood
Miß·verständnis das a) misunderstanding; **b)** *(Meinungsverschiedenheit)* misunderstanding; disagreement
miß·verstehen[1] *unr. tr. V.* misunderstand
Miß·wahl die *contest for the title of 'Miss Europe', 'Miss World' etc.*
Miß·weisung die *(Physik)* declination
Miß·wirtschaft die mismanagement
Mist [mɪst] **der; ~[e]s a)** dung; *(Dünger)* manure; *(mit Stroh usw. gemischt)* muck; **das ist nicht auf ihrem ~ gewachsen** *(fig. ugs.)* that didn't come out of her own head; **b)** *(~haufen)* dung/manure/muck heap; **c)** *(ugs. abwertend) (Schund)* rubbish, junk, trash *all no indef. art.*; *(Unsinn)* rubbish, nonsense, *(sl.)* rot *all no indef. art.*; *(lästige, dumme Angelegenheit)* nonsense; **mach deinen ~ doch alleine!** bloody *(Brit. sl.) or* damn well do it yourself!; **~ bauen** make a mess of things; mess things up; **mach bloß keinen ~!** just don't do anything stupid; **so ein ~!** what a damned *or* blasted nuisance!; damn *or* blast it!
Mist·beet das hotbed; forcing-bed
Mistel ['mɪstl̩] **die; ~, ~n** mistletoe
Mistel·zweig der piece of mistletoe
misten 1. *tr. V.* **a)** *(düngen)* manure; **b)** *s.* **ausmisten. 2.** *itr. V. (Landw.)* dung

[1] *ich mißverstehe, mißverstanden, mißzuverstehen*

Mist-: ~fink der *(derb)* dirty *or (coll.)* mucky so-and-so; **~forke die** *(nordd.)*, **~gabel die** dung-fork; **~haufen der** dung/manure/muck heap
mistig *(salopp)* **1.** *Adj.* rotten *(sl.)*. **2.** *adv.* in a rotten way *(sl.)*
Mist·käfer der dung-beetle
Mistral [mɪs'tra:l] **der; ~s** mistral
Mist-: ~stück das *(derb)* lousy good-for-nothing bastard *(sl.)*; *(Frau)* lousy good-for-nothing bitch *(sl.)*; **~vieh das** *(derb)* **a)** *(Tier)* bloody *(Brit. sl.) or* damn animal; **dieses ~vieh von Katze** that bloody *(Brit. sl.) or* damn cat; **b)** *s.* **~stück; ~wagen der** dung-cart; **~wetter das** *(salopp)* lousy weather *(sl.)*; **bei so einem ~wetter** in lousy weather like this *(sl.)*
Miszellen [mɪs'tsɛlən] *Pl. (geh.)* miscellany *sing.*
mit [mɪt] **1.** *Präp. mit Dat.* **a)** *(Gemeinsamkeit, Beteiligung)* with; **~ jdm. spielen/essen/streiten** play/eat/quarrel with sb.; **ein Fest ~ Damen** a celebration at which ladies are/were present; **Verkehrsunfälle ~ Kindern** traffic accidents involving children; **b)** *(Zugehörigkeit)* with; **ein Haus ~ Garten** a house with a garden; **Herr Müller ~ Frau** Herr Müller and his wife; **c)** *(einschließlich)* with; including; **ein Zimmer ~ Frühstück** a room with breakfast included; **~ mir waren ...:** including me *or* myself there were ...; **~ mir nicht!** *(ugs.)* count me out! *(coll.)*; **d)** *(Inhalt)* **ein Sack ~ Kartoffeln/Glas ~ Marmelade** a sack of potatoes/pot of jam; **e)** *(Begleitumstände)* with; **etw. ~ Absicht tun/~ Nachdruck fordern** do sth. deliberately/demand sth. forcefully; **~ 50 [km/h] fahren** drive at 50 [k.p.h]; **~ dem Auftrag, etw. zu tun** with the task of doing sth.; **f)** *(Hilfsmittel)* with; **~ Maschine geschrieben sein** be typed; **~ der Bahn/dem Auto fahren** go by train/car; **~ der Fähre/„Hamburg"** on the ferry/the 'Hamburg'; **g)** *(allgemeiner Bezug)* with; **~ der Arbeit ging es recht langsam voran** the work went very slowly; **~ Zustimmung seiner Eltern** with the consent of his parents; **~ einer Tätigkeit beginnen/aufhören** take up/give up an occupation; **was ist ~ ihm?** *(ugs.)* what's up with him? *(coll.)*; **raus/fort ~ dir!** out/off you go!; **h)** *(zeitlich)* **~ Einbruch der Dunkelheit/Nacht** when darkness/night falls/fell; **~ dem Einsetzen des Nachtfrostes** when we/they *etc.* start/started to get frosts at night; **~ 20 [Jahren]** at [the age of] twenty; **~ dem heutigen Tag bist du volljährig** today you have reached your majority; **~ der Zeit/den Jahren** in time/as the years go/went by; **i)** *(gleichlaufende Bewegung)* with; **~ dem Strom/Wind** with the tide/wind. **2.** *Adv.* **a)** *(auch)* too; as well; **~ dabeisein** be there too; *s. auch* **Partie f; b)** *(neben anderen)* also; too; as well; **es lag ~ an ihm** it was partly his doing; **das mußt du ~ berücksichtigen** you must also take that into account; you must take that into account too *or* as well; **c)** *(mit Sup.) (ugs.)* **dieses ist ~ das wichtigste der Bücher** this is one of the most important of the books; **seine Arbeit war ~ am besten** his work was among the best; **~ der Beste/beste** one of the best; **d)** *(vorübergehende Beteiligung)* **er ist bereit, heute ~ zu helfen** he's willing to help [just for] today; **ihr könntet ruhig einmal ~ anfassen** it wouldn't hurt you to lend a hand just for once; **e)** *s. auch* **damit 1 c; womit b**
Mit·angeklagte der/die co-defendant; *(mit geringerer Strafandrohung)* defendant to a lesser charge
Mit·arbeit die; *o. Pl.* **a)** *(das Tätigsein)* collaboration (**bei, an** + *Dat.* on); **die ~ in der Praxis ihres Mannes** working in her husband's practice; **unter ~** *(Dat.)* **von** in collaboration with; **b)** *(Mithilfe)* assistance (**bei, in** + *Dat.* in); **seine zwanzigjährige ~**

in der Organisation his twenty years of service to the organization; **unter ~ von** with the assistance of; **c)** *(Beteiligung)* participation (**in** + *Dat.* in)

mit|arbeiten *itr. V.* **a)** *(mithelfen)* **bei einem Projekt/an einem Buch ~:** collaborate on a project/book; **im elterlichen Geschäft ~:** work in one's parents' shop; **ich arbeite bei einem Projekt mit, das ...:** I'm working [with others] on a project that ...; **b)** *(sich beteiligen)* participate (**in** + *Dat.* in); **im Unterricht besser ~:** take a more active part in lessons; **c)** *(ugs.: auch arbeiten)* **seine Frau arbeitet mit** his wife works too

Mit·arbeiter der a) *(Betriebsangehörige[r])* employee; **b)** *(bei einem Projekt, an einem Buch)* collaborator; **ein freier ~:** a free lance; a free-lance worker; **ein freier/ständiger ~ bei einer Zeitung** a free-lance contributor to a newspaper/a writer on the permanent staff of a newspaper

Mitarbeiter·stab der staff; **zu jmds. engstem ~ gehören** be one of sb.'s closest assistants

Mit·begründer der co-founder

mit|bekommen *unr. tr. V.* **a) etw. ~:** be given *or* get sth. to take with one; *(fig.)* inherit sth.; **etw. bei der Heirat ~:** be given sth. on marriage; **b)** *(wahrnehmen)* be aware of; *(durch Hören, Sehen)* hear/see; **es war so laut, daß ich nur die Hälfte mitbekam** it was so noisy that I only caught half of it; **hast du das ~?** *(ugs.)* did you know?; **c)** *(miterleben)* **etw. ~:** manage to hear/see sth.; **etwas von etw. ~:** hear/see something of sth.; **nicht viel/nichts von etw. ~:** not be able to hear/see much/anything of sth.; **d)** *(verstehen)* **ich war so müde, daß ich nicht viel ~ habe** I was so tired that I did not grasp very much; **ich habe gar nicht ~, wie er das meinte** I did not realize at all how he meant it

mit|benutzen, *(bes. südd.)* **mit|benützen** *tr. V.* share; have the use of

Mit·benutzung, *(südd.)* **Mit·benützung die** use

Mit·besitz der share [of the ownership]; **an etw.** *(Dat.)* **[einen] ~ haben** have a share in sth.

Mit·besitzer der joint owner; co-owner

mit|bestimmen 1. *itr. V.* have a say (**in** + *Dat.* in); **mehr ~ können** *od* **dürfen** have a greater say. **2.** *tr. V.* have an influence on; **etw. maßgeblich ~:** have a determining influence on

Mit·bestimmung die; *o. Pl.* participation (**bei** in); *(der Arbeitnehmer)* co-determination; **betriebliche ~, ~ am Arbeitsplatz** involvement of employees in management decisions

Mit·bestimmungs-: ~gesetz das law of co-determination; **~recht das** right of co-determination

Mit·bewerber der competitor; **ich hatte nur einen ~ für** *od.* **um diese Stelle** there was only one other applicant for the job [besides me]; **alle ~ hatten bessere Qualifikationen** all the other applicants had better qualifications; **seine ~:** the other competitors/applicants

Mit·bewohner der other occupant; **seine ~:** his fellow occupants; the other occupants

mit|bringen *unr. tr. V.* **a) etw. ~:** bring sth. with one; **etw. aus der Stadt/dem Urlaub/von dem Markt/der Reise ~:** bring sth. back from town/holiday/the market/one's trip; **jmdm./sich etw. ~:** bring sth. with one for sb./bring sth. back for oneself; **Gäste ~:** bring guests home; **eine Grippe/großen Hunger ~** *(fig.)* come back with influenza/feeling very hungry; **b)** *(einbringen)* have, possess ⟨*ability, gift, etc.*⟩ (**für** for); **genügend Zeit ~:** come with enough time at one's disposal

Mitbringsel [-brɪŋzl] **das; ~s, ~:** [small] present; *(Andenken)* [small] souvenir

Mit·bürger der fellow citizen; **ältere ~** *(Amtsspr.)* senior citizens

mit|denken *unr. itr. V.* follow [the argument/explanation/what is being said *etc.*]; **ein Schüler, der mitdenkt** a pupil who follows the lesson; **die Fähigkeit zum Mitdenken** the ability to think for oneself

mit|dürfen *unr. itr. V. (ugs.) (mitkommen dürfen)* be allowed to come along *or* too; *(mitgehen, mitfahren dürfen)* be allowed to go along *or* too

Mit·eigentum das *s.* **Mitbesitz**

Mit·eigentümer der *s.* **Mitbesitzer**

mit·einander *Adv.* **a)** with each other *or* one another; **~ sprechen/kämpfen** talk to each other *or* one another/fight with each other *or* one another; **b)** *(gemeinsam)* together; **~ gegen jmdn. kämpfen** fight together against sb.; **alle ~:** all together; **ihr seid Gauner, alle ~!** you are all a pack of rogues!; your'e all rogues, the lot of you!

Mit·einander das; ~[s] living and working together *no art.*; **im ~:** by mutual cooperation

mit|empfinden 1. *unr. tr. V.* **jmds. Schmerz/Leid ~:** know the pain/sorrow sb. is/was feeling. **2.** *unr. itr. V.* **mit jmdm. ~:** sympathize with sb.

Mit·empfinden das sympathy

Mit·erbe der, Mit·erbin die *(Rechtsw.)* joint heir; co-heir

mit|erleben *tr. V.* **a)** *(dabeisein bei)* witness ⟨*events etc.*⟩; **sie hat das Unglück miterlebt** she was involved in the accident; **eine Premiere ~:** be present at a première; **b)** *(mitmachen)* be alive during

mit|essen 1. *unr. tr. V.* eat ⟨*skin etc.*⟩ as well; **bei dem Apfel habe ich einen Wurm mitgegessen** I've swallowed a grub along with the apple. **2.** *unr. itr. V.* **jmdn. einladen mitzuessen** invite sb. to eat with one *or* have a meal; **bei jmdm. ~:** eat *or* have a meal with sb.

Mit·esser der a) blackhead; **b)** *(ugs. scherzh.: zusätzlicher Esser)* **einen [zusätzlichen] ~ haben** have one more to dinner/lunch/*etc.*

mit|fahren *unr. itr. V.; mit sein* **bei jmdm. [im Auto] ~:** go with sb. [in his/her car]; *(auf einer Reise)* travel with sb. [in his/her car]; *(mitgenommen werden)* get *or* have a lift with sb. [in his/her car]; **jmdn. ~ lassen** let sb. go; *(jmdn. mitnehmen)* give sb. a lift

Mit·fahrer der fellow passenger; *(vom Fahrer aus gesehen)* passenger

Mitfahrer·zentrale die *office for putting those wanting lifts in touch with those who can offer them*

Mitfahr·gelegenheit die lift

mit|fühlen *tr., itr. V. s.* **mitempfinden**

mit·fühlend 1. *Adj.* sympathetic. **2.** *adv.* sympathetically

mit|führen *tr. V.* **a)** *(Amtsspr.: bei sich tragen)* **etw. ~:** carry sth. [with one]; **führen Sie zollpflichtige Waren mit?** have you anything to declare?; **b)** *(transportieren)* ⟨*river, stream*⟩ carry along

mit|geben *unr. tr. V.* **jmdm. etw. ~:** give sb. sth. to take with him/her; **er gab mir einen Brief an seine Eltern mit** he gave me a letter for *or* to give to his parents; **ich werde Ihnen eine Begleitung ~:** I'll get somebody to accompany you; **jmdm. eine gute Erziehung/Ausbildung ~geben** *(fig.)* provide sb. with a good training/education

Mit·gefangene der/die fellow prisoner

Mit·gefühl das; *o. Pl.* sympathy

mit|gehen *unr. itr. V.; mit sein* **a)** *(mitkommen)* go too; **mit jmdm. ~:** go with sb.; **sie ist bis zur Bushaltestelle mitgegangen** she went with him/her *etc.* to the bus-stop; **etw. ~ lassen** *(fig. ugs.)* walk off with sth. *(coll.)*; pinch sth. *(sl.)*; **b)** *(sich mitreißen lassen)* **begeistert/enthusiastisch ~:** respond enthusiastically (**bei, mit** to); **c)** *(weggerissen werden)* be carried away

mit·genommen *Adj.* **1.** *s.* **mitnehmen. 2.** *(beschädigt)* worn-out ⟨*furniture, carpet*⟩; **~ sein/aussehen** ⟨*book etc.*⟩ be/look to be in a sorry state; *(fig.)* ⟨*person*⟩ be/look worn out

Mit·gift die; ~, ~en *(veralt.)* dowry

Mitgift·jäger der *(veralt. abwertend)* dowry-hunter

Mit·glied das member (+ *Gen.*, **in** + *Dat.* of); **~ im Finanzausschuß sein** be a member of *or* sit on the finance committee; **„Zutritt nur für ~er"** 'members only'

Mitglieder-: ~liste die list of members; **~versammlung die** general meeting; **~zahl die** number of members; membership

Mitglieds-: ~ausweis der membership card; **~beitrag der** membership subscription

Mitgliedschaft die; ~: membership (+ *Gen.*, **in** + *Dat.*) of

Mitglied[s]·staat der member state *or* country

mit|haben *unr. tr. V. (ugs.)* **etw./jmdn. ~:** have got sth./sb. with one

mit|halten *unr. itr. V.* **a)** *(Schritt halten)* keep up (**bei** in, **mit** with); **keiner konnte [mit ihm] ~** *(in einer Diskussion, auf einem Fachgebiet usw.)* nobody could touch him; **b)** *(beim Essen, Trinken)* eat/drink one's share

mit|helfen *unr. itr. V.* help (**bei, in** + *Dat.* with); **ein bißchen ~:** lend a hand for a bit; **bei dem Bau der Garage ~:** help to build the garage

Mit·helfer der *(abwertend)* accomplice

Mit·herausgeber der joint editor; co-editor; *(Verlag)* co-publisher

Mit·hilfe die; *o. Pl.* help; assistance

mit·hin *Adv.* therefore

mit|hören 1. *tr. V.* listen to; *(zufällig)* overhear ⟨*conversation, argument, etc.*⟩; *(abhören)* listen in on. **2.** *itr. V.* listen; *(zufällig)* overhear; **fürchten, daß mitgehört wird** be afraid that somebody is listening in; *s. auch* **Feind**

Mit·inhaber der joint owner; co-owner; *(einer Firma, eines Restaurants auch)* joint proprietor

mit|kämpfen *itr. V.* take part in the fighting

Mit·kämpfer der comrade-in-arms; *(Sport)* team-mate

mit|klingen *unr. itr. V.: s.* **mitschwingen**

mit|kommen *unr. itr. V.; mit sein* **a)** come too; **kommst du mit?** are you coming [with me/us]?; **ich kann nicht ~:** I can't come; **bis zur Tür ~:** come with sb. to the door; **b)** *(Schritt halten)* keep up; **in der Schule/im Unterricht gut/schlecht ~:** get on well/badly at school/with one's lessons; **da komme ich nicht mehr mit!** *(fig. ugs.)* I can't understand it at all

mit|können *unr. itr. V. (ugs.)* **er kann ~:** he can come too; *(darf mitgehen, mitfahren)* he can go too

mit|kriegen *tr. V. (ugs.) s.* **mitbekommen**

mit|laufen 1. *unr. itr. V.; mit sein* **a) mit jmdm. ~:** run with sb.; **b)** *(Sport)* **beim 100-m-Lauf** *usw.* **~:** run in the 100 m. *etc.*; **c) ein Tonband ~ lassen** have a tape recorder running; **d)** *(ugs.: nebenbei erledigt werden)* **die Reparaturen müssen nebenher ~:** the repairs have to be fitted in along with everything else *or* as we go along. **2.** *unr. tr. V.; mit sein* **ein Rennen ~:** run in a race

Mit·läufer der *(abwertend)* [mere] supporter; *(Schmarotzer)* hanger-on

Mit·laut der consonant

Mit·leid das pity, compassion (**mit** for); *(Mitgefühl)* sympathy (**mit** for); **mit jmdm. ~ haben** *od.* **empfinden** feel pity *or* compassion/have *or* feel sympathy for sb.

Mit·leidenschaft die **in jmdn./etw. in ~ ziehen** affect sb./sth.
mitleid·erregend *Adj.* pitiful
mit·leidig 1. *Adj.* compassionate; *(mitfühlend)* sympathetic. **2.** *adv.* compassionately; *(mitfühlend)* sympathetically; *(iron.)* pityingly
mitleid[s]-: ~los 1. *Adj.* pitiless; *(herzlos)* unfeeling; **2.** *adv.* without pity; *(herzlos)* unfeelingly; **~voll 1.** *Adj.* compassionate; **2.** *adv.* compassionately
mit|lesen *unr. tr. V.* **a)** *(zur Kenntnis nehmen)* **etw. ~:** read sth. *(as well as sth. else)*; **b)** *(zugleich lesen)* **etw. [mit jmdm.] ~:** read sth. at the same time as sb.; **mein Gegenüber las meine Zeitung mit** the person opposite me was also reading my newspaper
mit|machen 1. *tr. V.* **a)** *(teilnehmen an)* go on ⟨*trip*⟩; join in ⟨*joke*⟩; follow ⟨*fashion*⟩; fight in ⟨*war*⟩; do ⟨*course, seminar*⟩; **b)** *(ugs.: billigen)* **das mache ich nicht mit** I can't go along with it; **ich mache das nicht länger mit!** I'm not standing for it any longer; **c)** *(ugs.: zusätzlich erledigen)* **jmds. Arbeit ~:** do sb.'s work as well as one's own; **d)** *(ugs.: erleiden)* **zwei Weltkriege/viele Bombenangriffe mitgemacht haben** have been through two world wars/many bomb attacks; **er hat viel mitgemacht** he has been through a great deal. **2.** *itr. V.* **a)** *(sich beteiligen)* join in; **bei einem Wettbewerb/einer Aktion ~:** take part in a competition/take part in *or* join in a campaign; **willst du ~?** do you want to join in?; **da[bei] mache ich nicht mit** I'm not joining in; you can count me out *(coll.)*; **b)** *(ugs.: funktionieren)* **meine Beine machen nicht mehr mit** my legs are giving up on me *(coll.)*; **mein Herz/Kreislauf macht nicht mit** my heart/circulation can't take it
Mit·mensch der fellow man; fellow human being; **urteile nicht so hart über deine ~en** don't be so harsh in your judgements of other people
mit·menschlich *Adj.; nicht präd.* human, interpersonal ⟨*relations, relationsships*⟩; interpersonal ⟨*contacts, communication*⟩
mit|mischen *itr. V. (ugs.)* **a)** *(sich einmischen)* interfere (**bei** in); *(sich beteiligen)* get involved (**bei** in); **b)** *(Sportjargon) (mit vollem Einsatz kämpfen)* give everything one's got; *(dem Gegner Paroli bieten)* give as good as one gets
mit|müssen *unr. itr. V. (mitkommen müssen)* have [got] to come with sb.; *(mitgehen, -fahren müssen)* have [got] to go with sb.
Mitnahme die; ~ *(Amtsspr.)* **die ~ von Taschen in das Museum ist nicht erlaubt** it is forbidden *or* visitors are not allowed to take bags into the museum; **die Diebe verschwanden unter ~ des gesamten Schmucks** the thieves vanished with all the jewelry *or* vanished, taking all the jewelry with them
Mitnahme·preis der *(Kaufmannsspr.)* take-away price
mit|nehmen *unr. tr. V.* **a) jmdn. ~:** take sb. with one; **etw. ~:** take sth. with one; *(verhüll.: stehlen)* walk off with sth. *(coll.)*; *(kaufen)* take sth.; **etw. wieder ~:** take sth. away [with one] again; **das Frachtschiff nimmt auch Passagiere mit** the cargo ship also carries passengers; **Essen/Getränke zum Mitnehmen** food/drinks to take away *or* *(Amer.)* to go; **könntest du einen Brief für mich ~?** could you take a letter for me?; **jmdn. im Auto ~:** give sb. a lift [in one's car]; **b)** *(ugs.: streifen)* **der LKW hat die Hecke mitgenommen** the truck *or* *(Brit.)* lorry took the hedge with it; **c)** *(ugs.: wahrnehmen)* do *(coll.)* ⟨*sights etc.*⟩; **auch Soho ~:** take in Soho as well; **sie nimmt alles mit, was sich ihr bietet** she makes the most of everything life has to offer her; **d)** *(in Mitleidenschaft ziehen)* **jmdn. ~:** take it out of sb.; **von etw. mitgenommen sein** be worn out by sth.; *(traurig gemacht)* be grieved by sth.; **e)** *(lernen)* **etw. aus einem Vortrag/einer Predigt ~:** get sth. out of *or* from a lecture/sermon
Mitnehm·preis der *s.* **Mitnahmepreis**
mitnichten *Adv. (veralt.)* in no way; not at all; by no means; **er gehorchte ~:** he wouldn't obey at all
Mitra ['mi'tra] **die; ~, Mitren** *(kath. Kirche)* mitre
mit|rauchen 1. *tr. V.* **eine [Zigarette] ~:** have a cigarette with sb. **2.** *itr. V.* inhale other people's tobacco-smoke
mit|rechnen 1. *itr. V.* work the sum out at the same time; **ich habe bei deiner Addition mitgerechnet** I did the addition at the same time as you. **2.** *tr. V.* **etw. ~:** include sth. [in the calculation]
mit|reden *itr. V.* **a)** *(Sinnvolles beisteuern)* join in the conversation; **die einzige Kunstart, bei der sie ~ kann** the only art form she knows enough about to hold a conversation; **b)** *(mitbestimmen)* have a say
mit|reisen *itr. V.* **[mit jmdm.] ~:** travel with sb.
Mit·reisende der/die fellow passenger; **einer der ~n** one of the other passengers
mit|reißen *unr. tr. V.* **a)** *(wegreißen)* ⟨*avalanche, flood*⟩ sweep away; **der Abstürzende hat die ganze Seilschaft mitgerissen** the falling climber dragged the whole of the roped party down with him; **b)** *(begeistern)* **die Begeisterung/seine Rede hat alle Zuhörer mitgerissen** the audience was carried away with enthusiasm/by his speech; **nicht gerade ~d** not exactly thrilling; **sein ~des Spiel** his exciting playing; **die ~de Musik** the rousing music
mitsammen [mɪt'zamən] *Adv. (österr.)* together
mit·samt *Präp. mit Dat.* together with; **die ganze Familie ~ Hund und Katze** the whole family, complete with cat and dog
mit|schicken *tr. V.* **ich schicke dir [im Brief] sein Foto mit** I'll send you his photo [with the letter]; **jmdm. einen Führer ~:** send a guide [along] with sb.
mit|schleifen *tr. V. (auch fig. ugs.)* **jmdn./etw. ~:** drag sb./sth. along
mit|schleppen *tr. V. (ugs.)* **a)** *(tragen)* **etw. ~:** lug *or (sl.)* cart sth. with one; **b)** *s.* **mitschleifen**
mit|schneiden *unr. tr. V. (Rundf., Ferns.)* record [live]
Mit·schnitt der *(Rundf., Ferns.)* [live] recording
mit|schreiben 1. *unr. tr. V.* **etw. ~:** take sth. down. **2.** *unr. itr. V.* write *or* take down what is/was said; *(in Vorlesungen usw.)* take notes
Mit·schuld die share of the blame *or* responsibility (**an** + *Dat.* for); *(an Verbrechen)* complicity (**an** + *Dat.* in)
mit·schuldig *Adj.* **an etw.** *(Dat.)* **~ sein/werden** be/become partly to blame *or* partly responsible for sth.; *(an Verbrechen)* be/become guilty of complicity in sth.; **sich ~ machen** put oneself in the position of being partly to blame *or* partly responsible for sth.; *(an Verbrechen)* become guilty of complicity as a result of one's own actions
Mit·schuldige der/die one who is/was partly to blame *or* partly responsible (**an** + *Dat.* for); *(an Verbrechen)* accomplice (**an** + *Dat.* in)
Mit·schüler der, Mit·schülerin die schoolfellow
mit|schwingen *unr. itr. V.* **in seinen Worten/seiner Stimme schwang Triumph/Freude mit** there was a note of triumph/joy in his words/voice
mit|sein *unr. itr. V.; mit sein; Zusammenschreibung nur im Inf. und Part. (ugs.)* **er ist beim letzten Ausflug nicht mitgewesen** he didn't come [with us] on our last trip; **waren eure Kinder im Urlaub mit?** did your children go on holiday with you?; **warst du auch mit im Konzert?** were you at the concert too?
mit|singen 1. *unr. tr. V.* join in ⟨*song etc.*⟩. **2.** *unr. itr. V.* join in [the singing]; sing along; **im Chor mitsingen** be a member of the choir
mit|sollen *itr. V. (ugs.)* **soll der Koffer auch mit?** is this case to go too?; **wenn ich mitsoll, mußt du es nur sagen** just say if you want me to go with you
mit|spielen *itr. V.* **a)** *(sich beteiligen)* join in the game; **wenn das Wetter mitspielt** *(fig.)* if the weather is kind; **b)** *(mitwirken)* **in einem Film/bei einem Theaterstück ~:** be *or* act in a film/play; **in einem Orchester/in** *od.* **bei einem Fußballverein ~:** play in an orchestra/for a football club; **c)** *(sich auswirken)* play a part (**bei** in); **viele Gründe haben bei der Entscheidung mitgespielt** there were many reasons for this decision; **d)** *(zusetzen)* **jmdm. übel** *od.* **böse ~:** ⟨*authorities*⟩ treat sb. badly; ⟨*opponent*⟩ give sb. a rough time
Mit·spieler der, Mit·spielerin die player; *(in derselben Mannschaft)* team-mate; **seine ~:** *(Sport)* his team-mates; *(bei Kartenspielen usw.)* the other players
Mit·sprache die say; **ein Recht auf ~:** the right to a share in decisions
Mitsprache·recht das; *o. Pl.* **ein/kein ~ bei etw. haben** have a say/no say in sth.; **ein ~ bekommen** gain the right to a share in decisions
mit|sprechen 1. *unr. tr. V. (gemeinsam sprechen)* join in [saying]. **2.** *unr. itr. V.: s.* **mitreden**
Mit·streiter der *(geh.)* comrade-in-arms; **er fand viele ~** *(fig.)* he found many people who were willing to join his campaign
Mitt·achtziger der man in his mid-eighties
mittag ['mɪta:k] *Adv.* **heute/morgen/gestern ~:** at midday *or* lunch-time today/tomorrow/yesterday; **Montag ~:** at midday on Monday; Monday at midday; Monday lunch-time; **seit Montag ~:** since Monday midday; **was gibt es heute ~ zu essen?** what's for lunch today?
[1]**Mittag der; ~s, ~e a)** midday *no art.*; **gegen ~:** around midday *or* noon; **jeden/diesen ~:** every day at lunch-time/at lunch-time today; **über ~:** at midday *or* lunch-time; **zu ~ essen** have lunch; **was essen wir zu ~?** what is there for lunch?; **was gibt's zu ~?** what's for lunch?; **b)** *o. Pl. (ugs.: Mittagspause)* lunch-hour; lunch-break; **~ machen** *(ugs.)* take one's lunch-hour *or* lunch-break; **c)** *(dichter. veralt.: Süden)* south
[2]**Mittag das; ~s** *(ugs.)* lunch; **~ essen** have lunch
Mittag-: ~brot das *(landsch.)*, **~essen das** lunch; midday meal; **beim ~essen sitzen** be having [one's] lunch *or* one's midday meal; **nach dem ~essen** after lunch
mittäglich ['mɪtɛ:klɪç] **1.** *Adj.; nicht präd.* midday; lunch-time ⟨*invitation*⟩. **2.** *adv.* at midday *or* lunch-time; **es war ~ heiß auf der Straße** the street was baking in the noonday heat
mittags ['mɪta:ks] *Adv.* at midday *or* lunch-time; **bis ~:** until midday *or* lunch-time; **12 Uhr ~:** 12 noon; 12 o'clock midday; **Dienstag ~** *od.* **dienstags ~:** Tuesday lunch-time; **von morgens bis ~:** in the morning until midday
Mittags-: ~glut die, ~hitze die midday *or* noonday heat; heat of midday; **~linie die** *(Astron.)* meridian; **~mahl das** *(geh.)* luncheon; **~pause die** lunch-hour; lunch-break; **~pause haben** have one's lunch-hour *or* lunch-break; **nach der ~pause** after lunch; **in der ~pause sein** *(ugs.)* have gone to lunch; **~ruhe die** period of quiet after

lunch; ~**ruhe halten** have one's after-lunch rest; ~**schlaf der** after-lunch sleep; **[seinen] ~schlaf halten** have an after-lunch sleep; ~**schläfchen das** *(ugs.)* after-lunch nap; **[s]ein ~schläfchen halten** have an after-lunch nap; ~**sonne die** midday *or* noonday sun; ~**sonne haben** get the midday sun; ~**stunde die** midday; **um die ~stunde** at midday; ~**tisch der a)** lunch-table; **der ~tisch ist gedeckt** the table is laid for lunch; **am ~tisch sitzen** be sitting at the table having lunch; **b)** *(veralt.: im Restaurant)* lunch; midday meal; **einen ~tisch für Studenten anbieten** do student lunches; ~**zeit die a)** *o. Pl. (Zeit gegen 12 Uhr)* lunch-time *no art.*; midday *no art.*; **in der ~zeit** at lunch-time; **um die ~zeit** at lunch-time; around midday; **b)** *(~pause)* lunch-hour; lunch-break

Mịt·täter der accomplice

Mịt·täterschaft die complicity; **jmdn. der ~ *(Gen.)* bei etw. anklagen** accuse sb. of complicity in sth.

Mịtt·dreißiger der man in his mid-thirties

Mitte ['mɪtə] **die; ~, ~n a)** *(Teil)* middle; *(Punkt)* middle; centre; *(eines Kreises, einer Kugel, Stadt)* centre; **bis zur ~ gekommen sein** *(beim Lesen)* be half-way through; **wir nahmen sie in die ~:** we had her between us; **eine Politik der ~** *(fig.)* a middle-of-the-road policy; **die goldene ~** *(fig.)* the golden mean; **ab durch die ~!** *(fig. ugs.)* off you go; **b)** *(Zeitpunkt)* middle; **~ des Monats/Jahres** in the middle of the month/year; **~ Februar** in mid-February; in the middle of February; **er ist ~ [der] Dreißig** he's in his mid-thirties; **c)** *(Politik) (Gruppierung)* centre; **eine Partei der ~:** a centrist party; **d)** *(Kreis von Menschen)* **wir haben sie wieder in unserer ~ begrüßt** we welcomed her back into our midst *or* amongst us; **der Tod hat ihn aus unserer ~ gerissen** *(geh.)* death has taken him from our midst; **e)** *(veralt.: Taille)* middle; waist

mịt|teilen 1. *tr. V.* **jmdm. etw. ~:** tell sb. sth.; *(informieren)* inform sb. of *or* about sth.; communicate sth. to sb. *(formal)*; *(amtlich)* notify *or* inform sb. of sth.; **er teilte mit, daß ...:** he announced that ...; **teile ihr die schlechte Nachricht schonend mit** break the news to her gently. **2.** *refl. V. (geh.)* **a)** *(sich anvertrauen)* **sich jmdm. ~:** confide in sb.; **b)** *(sich übertragen auf)* **sich jmdm. ~:** communicate itself to sb.

mịtteilsam *Adj.* communicative; *(gesprächig)* talkative

Mịtteilsamkeit die; ~: communicativeness; *(Gesprächigkeit)* talkativeness

Mịt·teilung die communication; *(Bekanntgabe)* announcement; **jmdm. eine vertrauliche ~ machen** give sb. confidential information; **ich muß dir eine traurige ~ machen** I have some sad news for you; **zweckdienliche ~en** useful information *sing.*

Mitteilungs·bedürfnis das need to talk [to others]

Mittel ['mɪtl] **das; ~s, ~ a)** means *sing.*; *(Methode)* way; method; *(Werbe~, Propaganda~, zur Verkehrskontrolle)* device (+ *Gen.* for); **mit allen ~n versuchen, etw. zu tun** try by every means to do sth.; **kein ~ unversucht lassen** try every means; **zum letzten *od.* äußersten ~ greifen, und das Kind in ein Erziehungsheim bringen** as a last resort put the child in a community home; **[nur] ~ zum Zweck sein** be [just] a means to an end; **~ und Wege suchen/finden** look for/find ways and means; **b)** *(Arznei)* **ein ~ gegen Grippe/Husten/Schuppen** *usw.* a remedy *or* cure for influenza/coughs *pl.*/dandruff *sing. etc.*; **ein ~ gegen Schmerzen** a pain-reliever; **ein ~ zum Einreiben** a cream/ointment *etc.* to be rubbed in; *s. auch* **schmerzstillend; c)** *(Substanz)* **ein ~ gegen Ungeziefer/Insekten** a pesticide/an insect repellent; **ein ~ zur Reinigung von Teppichböden/zum Entfernen von Flecken** a cleaning agent for carpets/a stain-remover; **d)** *Pl. (Geld~)* funds; [financial] resources; *(Privat~)* means; resources; **mit *od.* aus öffentlichen ~n** from public funds; **von seinen bescheidenen ~n** with his modest means; **meine ~sind erschöpft** my funds are exhausted; **etw. aus eigenen ~n bezahlen** pay for sth. out of one's own resources; **e)** *(Durchschnittswert)* average; **im ~:** on [the] average; **das arithmetische/geometrische ~** *(Math.)* the arithmetic/geometric mean

mịttel-, Mịttel-: ~**achse die** central axis; ~**alter das;** *o. Pl.* Middle Ages *pl.*; **das finstere ~alter** the Dark Ages *pl.*; **das sind Zustände wie im ~alter** *(ugs.)* it's positively medieval; ~**alterlich** *Adj.* medieval; ~**amerika (das)** Central America [and the West Indies]

mịttelbar 1. *Adj.* indirect. **2.** *adv.* indirectly

mịttel-, Mịttel-: ~**bau der a)** *(Gebäudeteil)* central *or* main part [of a/the building]; **b)** *o. Pl. (Hochschulw.)* non-professorial teaching staff; ~**deck das** *(Schiffbau)* middle deck; ~**deutsch** *Adj.* **a)** *(Geogr.)* of central Germany *postpos., not pred.*; **b)** *(Sprachw.)* middle German; **c)** *(Politik veralt.)* East German; ~**deutschland (das) a)** *(Geogr.)* central Germany; **b)** *(Politik veralt.)* East Germany; ~**ding das;** *o. Pl.* **ein ~ding sein** be something in between; **ein ~ding zwischen Moped und Fahrrad** something between a moped and a bicycle; ~**europa (das)** Central Europe; ~**europäer der** Central European; ~**europäisch** *Adj.* Central European; ~**fein 1.** *Adj.* medium-fine ⟨*thread*⟩; medium-grade ⟨*peas, sandpaper*⟩; medium-ground ⟨*coffee*⟩; ⟨*paper*⟩ containing 40–50% mechanical wood; **2.** *adv.* **~fein gemahlen** medium ground; ~**feld das a)** *(Fußball: Spielfeldteil, Spieler)* midfield; **b)** *(Sport: im Wettbewerb)* **im ~feld sein** be in the pack; *(in der Tabelle)* be in mid-table; ~**feld·spieler der** *(Fußball)* midfield player; ~**finger der** middle finger; ~**fristig** [-frɪstɪç] *(Finanzw.)* **1.** *Adj.* medium-term ⟨*solution, financial planning*⟩; **2.** *adv.* **[etw.] ~fristig planen** plan [sth.] on a medium-term basis; ~**fuß der** *(Anat., Zool.)* metatarsus; ~**gang der** *(eines Eisenbahnwagens, Schiffes)* central gangway; *(einer Kirche, eines Flugzeugs)* central *or* centre aisle; ~**gebirge das** low-mountain region; low mountains *pl.*; ~**gewicht das** *(Schwerathletik)* **a)** *o. Pl.* middleweight; *s. auch* **Fliegengewicht; b)** *(Sportler) s.* ~**gewichtler;** ~**gewichtler** [-gəvɪçtlɐ] **der; ~s, ~:** middleweight; ~**groß** *Adj.* medium-sized; ⟨*person*⟩ of medium height; ~**hand die** *(Anat.)* metacarpus; ~**hand·knochen der** *(Anat.)* metacarpal [bone]; ~**hochdeutsch** *Adj.* Middle High German; ~**hoch·deutsch das** Middle High German; ~**klasse die a)** *(Güteklasse)* middle range; *(Größenklasse)* middle [size-]range; **ein Wagen der ~klasse** a car in the middle range/a medium-sized car; **b)** *(~schicht)* middle class; ~**klasse·wagen der** car in the middle range; *(hinsichtlich der Größe)* medium-sized car; ~**kreis der** *(Ballspiele)* centre circle; ~**latein das** medieval Latin; ~**lateinisch** *Adj.* medieval Latin; ~**linie die** centre line; *(Fußball)* half-way line; ~**los** *Adj.* without means *postpos.*; penniless; *(arm)* poor; *(verarmt)* impoverished; **~los dastehen** be left without means; ~**losigkeit die** lack of means; *(Armut)* poverty; ~**maß das: gutes ~maß sein** be a good average; **das gesunde ~maß** the happy medium; ~**mäßig** *(oft abwertend)* **1.** *Adj.* mediocre; indifferent; indifferent ⟨*weather*⟩; **2.** *adv.* indifferently; ~**mäßigkeit die** *(oft abwertend)* mediocrity; ~**meer das** Mediterranean [Sea]; ~**meerisch** *Adj.* Mediterranean

Mịttelmeer-: ~**länder** *Pl.* Mediterranean countries; ~**raum der** Mediterranean [area]

mịttel-, Mịttel-: ~**ohr das** *(Anat.)* middle ear; ~**ohr·entzündung die** *(Med.)* inflammation of the middle ear; ~**prächtig** *(ugs. scherzh.)* **1.** *Adj.* **[nur] ~prächtig** not particularly marvellous; **2.** *adv.* **Wie geht's? – ~prächtig** How are you? – Fair to middling *(coll.)*; ~**punkt der a)** *(Geom.)* centre; *(einer Strecke)* midpoint; **b)** *(Mensch/Sache im Zentrum)* centre *or* focus of attention; **ein kultureller ~punkt** a cultural centre; **im ~punkt stehen** be the centre *or* focus of attention; **im ~punkt der Diskussion stehen** be the main topic of the discussion; **etw. in den ~punkt [seiner Rede] stellen** focus on sth. [in one's speech]; ~**punkt·schule die** *school centrally situated in a wide rural catchment area*

mịttels *Präp. mit Gen. (Papierdt.)* by means of

mịttel-, Mịttel-: ~**scheitel der** centre parting; ~**schicht die** *(Soziol.) s.* ~**klasse b;** ~**schiff das** *(Archit.)* nave; ~**schule die a)** *s.* **Realschule; b)** *(österr. veralt., schweiz.)* secondary school; high school *(Amer.)*; ~**schul·lehrer der a)** *s.* **Realschullehrer; b)** *(österr. veralt., schweiz.)* secondary school *or (Amer.)* high school teacher; ~**schwer** *Adj.* ⟨*climb, problem, etc.*⟩ of medium *or* moderate difficulty; moderately difficult ⟨*climb, problem, etc.*⟩; moderately heavy ⟨*suitcase etc.*⟩

Mịttels-: ~**mann der** *Pl.* **~männer** *od.* **~leute,** ~**person die** intermediary; go-between

mịttel-, Mịttel-: ~**stadt die** medium-sized town; ~**stand der;** *o. Pl.* middle class; ~**ständisch** *Adj.* middle-class; medium-sized ⟨*firm*⟩ *(in private ownership)*; ~**ständler** [-ʃtɛntlɐ] **der; ~s, ~** *(ugs.)* middle-class person; member of the middle class; ~**stein·zeit die** mesolithic period; ~**stellung die** intermediate *or* midway position; **etw. nimmt eine ~stellung zwischen A und B ein** sth. is intermediate between A and B; ~**stimme die** *(Musik)* middle part *or* voice

Mịttel·strecke die a) medium haul *or* distance; **auf ~n** over medium distances; **b)** *(Sport)* middle distance; **auf [den] ~n** in middle-distance running

Mịttelstrecken-: ~**flug der** medium-haul flight; ~**lauf der** *(Sport)* middle-distance race; *(Disziplin)* middle-distance running *no art.*; ~**läufer der** *(Sport)* middle-distance runner; ~**rakete die** medium-range missile

Mịttel-: ~**streifen der** central reservation; median strip *(Amer.)*; ~**stufe die** *(Schulw.)* middle school; ~**stürmer der** *(Sport)* centre-forward; ~**teil der** *od.* **das** middle section; *(eines Buches)* middle [part]; ~**weg der** middle course; **der goldene ~weg** the happy medium; ~**welle die** *(Physik, Rundf.)* medium wave; **auf *od.* über ~welle** on [the] medium wave; ~**wert der** mean [value]; ~**wort das** participle

mịtten *Adv.* **~ an/auf etw.** *(Akk. od. Dat.)* in the middle of sth.; **der Teller brach ~ durch** the plate broke in half; **~ in etw.** *(Akk./Dat.)* into/in the middle of sth.; **~ durch die Stadt** right through the town; **~ durch die Menge** through the middle of the crowd; **~ aus etw.** from the middle of sth.; **~ darin** *s.* **mittendrin; ~ unter uns** *(Dat.)* in our midst; **der Schuß traf ihn ~ ins Herz** the shot hit him right in the heart; **~ in der Luft/im Pazifik** in mid-air/mid-Pacific; **~ in der Aufregung** in the midst of the excitement

mịtten-: ~**drịn** *Adv.* **a)** *(zwischen anderen)* [right] in the middle; **b)** *(gerade dabei)* **~drin sein, etw. zu tun** be [right] in the middle of doing sth.; ~**dụrch** *Adv.* [right]

through the middle; sie schnitt den Kuchen ~durch she cut the cake in half *or* into two equal pieces; ~mang *Adv. (nordd., berlin.)* [right] in/into the middle of it/them

Mitter·nacht ['mɪtɐ-] die; *o. Pl.* midnight *no art.*

mitter·nächtlich *Adj.; nicht präd.* midnight; zu ~er Stunde at midnight; at the midnight hour *(literary)*

Mitternachts-: ~sonne die midnight sun; ~stunde die midnight hour; zur/bis zur ~stunde at/by around midnight

Mitt·fünfziger der man in his mid-fifties

mittig *(Technik)* 1. *Adj.* aligned. 2. *adv.* ⟨*arranged*⟩ in line; ⟨*divided*⟩ centrally

mittler... ['mɪtlər...] *Adj.; nicht präd.* a) *(zwischen anderen befindlich)* middle; der/die/das ~e the middle one; die ~e Reife *(Schulw.) standard of achievement for school-leaving certificate at a Realschule or for entry to the sixth form in a Gymnasium; s. auch* Osten c; b) *(einen Mittelwert darstellend)* average ⟨*temperature*⟩; moderate ⟨*speed*⟩; medium-sized ⟨*company, town*⟩; medium ⟨*quality, size*⟩; ein Mann ~en Alters a middle-aged man

Mittler ['mɪtlɐ] der; ~s, ~: mediator

Mittler·amt das role of mediator

Mittlerin die; ~, ~nen mediator

Mittler·rolle die mediating role

mittler·weile ['mɪtlɐ'vailə] *Adv.* a) *(seitdem, allmählich)* since then; *(bis jetzt)* by now; b) *(unterdessen)* in the mean time

mit|tragen *unr. tr. V.* bear part of, share ⟨*responsibility, cost*⟩; take part of, share ⟨*blame*⟩; give one's support to ⟨*aims, proposal*⟩

mit|trinken 1. *unr. tr. V.* etw. ~: drink sth. with me/us *etc.*; trinkst du einen mit? are you going to have a drink with me/us *etc.?* 2. *unr. itr. V.* mit jmdm. ~: have a drink with sb.

mitt-, Mitt-: ~schiffs *Adv. (Seemannsspr.)* amidships; ~sechziger der man in his mid-sixties; ~siebziger der man in his mid-seventies; ~sommer der midsummer; ~sommernacht die midsummer's night; *(Nacht der Sommersonnenwende)* Midsummer Night

mit|tun *unr. itr. V. (landsch.)* join in

Mitt·vierziger der man in his mid-forties

Mittwoch ['mɪtvɔx] der; ~[e]s, ~e Wednesday; *s. auch* Dienstag; Dienstag-

mittwochs *Adv.* on Wednesday[s]; *s. auch* dienstags

mit·unter *Adv.* now and then; from time to time; sometimes

mit·verantwortlich *Adj.* partly responsible *pred.*; *(beide/alle zusammen)* jointly responsible *pred.*

Mit·verantwortung die share of the responsibility; die ~ übernehmen take one's share of the responsibility

mit|verdienen *itr. V.* go out to work as well; der ältere Sohn verdient jetzt mit the eldest son is earning now too

Mit·verfasser der co-author; joint author

Mit·verschulden das: ihn trifft ein ~ an seinem Unfall he was partly to blame for his accident

mit|versichern *tr. V.* include in one's insurance

Mit·welt die fellow men *pl.*; die ~: sb.'s fellow men

mit·wirken *itr. V.* a) *(tätig sein)* an etw. *(Dat.)*/bei etw. ~: collaborate on/be involved in sth.; an der Aufklärung eines Verbrechens ~: help to solve a crime; ohne jmds. Mitwirken without sb.'s help *or* assistance; b) *(mitspielen)* in einem Orchester/Theaterstück ~wirken play in an orchestra/act *or* appear in a play; c) *(eine Bedeutung haben)* [bei etw.] ~: play a role [in sth.]

Mitwirkende der/die *adj. Dekl. (an einer Sendung)* participant; *(in einer Show)* performer; *(in einem Theaterstück)* actor; die ~n *(in einem Theaterstück)* the cast *sing.*

Mit·wirkung die; *o. Pl.* jmds. ~ an etw. *(Dat.)*/bei etw. sb.'s collaboration on/involvement in sth.; unter ~ vieler Fachwissenschaftler in collaboration with many experts; die Veranstaltung findet unter ~ bekannter Künstler statt some famous artists are taking part in the event

Mit·wisser der; ~s ~, **Mit·wisserin** die; ~, ~nen: ~ einer Sache *(Gen.)* sein know about sth.; *(einer Straftat)* be an accessory to sth.; er hatte zu viele ~: there were too many people who knew about what he'd done; zum ~ gemacht werden be told about it; *(bei einer Straftat)* be made an accessory

Mitwisserschaft die; ~: knowledge of the matter/crime; seine ~ leugnen deny all knowledge [of the matter]

mit|wollen *unr. itr. V. (ugs.) (mitkommen wollen)* want to come with sb.; *(mitgehen, mitfahren wollen)* want to go with sb.

mit|zählen 1. *itr. V.* a) count; die Sonntage zählen bei den Urlaubstagen nicht mit Sundays don't count as holidays; b) *(gelten)* ⟨*objection*⟩ be valid; ⟨*factor*⟩ be relevant. 2. *tr. V.* count in; include

mit|ziehen *unr. itr. V.; mit sein* a) *(mitgehen)* go with him/them *etc.*; mit der Kapelle ~: march along with the band; mit dem Zirkus ~: travel round with the circus; b) *(ugs.: mitmachen)* go along with it; *(bei einer Klage, Initiative)* give it one's backing; c) *(Sport)* go with him/her *etc.*

Mix·becher ['mɪks-] der [cocktail-]shaker

Mixed [mɪkst] das; ~[s], ~[s] *(Sport)* mixed doubles

Mixed Pickles [- 'pɪkl̩s] *Pl.* mixed pickles

mixen ['mɪksn̩] *tr. V. (auch Rundf., Ferns., Film)* mix; sich *(Dat.)* einen Drink ~: fix oneself a drink; etw. unter etw. *(Akk.)* ~ *(Kochk.)* mix sth. into sth.

Mixer der; ~s, ~ a) *(Bar~)* barman; bartender *(Amer.)*; b) *(Gerät)* blender and liquidizer

Mix·getränk das mixed drink; cocktail

Mixtur [mɪks'tu:ɐ̯] die; ~, ~en a) *(Pharm., fig.)* mixture; b) *(Musik)* mixture [stop]

mm *Abk.* Millimeter mm.

Mnemo·technik [mnemo-] die *(Psych.)* mnemonics *sing., no art.*

Mo. *Abk.* Montag Mon.

Mob [mɔp] der; ~s *(abwertend)* mob

Möbel ['mø:bl̩] das; ~s, ~ a) *Pl.* furniture *sing., no indef. art.*; b) piece of furniture

Möbel-: ~geschäft das furniture shop; ~haus das furniture store; ~industrie die furniture industry; ~lager das furniture warehouse; *(zur Einlagerung)* furniture repository; ~packer der removal man; ~politur die furniture polish; ~schreiner der *s.* Möbeltischler; ~spedition die furniture-removal firm; ~stück das piece of furniture; ~tischler der cabinet-maker; ~wagen der furniture van; removal van

mobil [mo'bi:l] *Adj.* a) *(auch Milit.)* mobile; *(einsatzbereit)* mobilized; ~ machen mobilize; rope in *(coll.)* ⟨*person*⟩; b) *(ugs.) (lebendig)* lively; *(rüstig)* sprightly; c) *(Rechtsw., Wirtsch.)* movable ⟨*property*⟩; floating ⟨*capital*⟩

Mobile ['mo:bilə] das; ~s, ~s mobile

Mobiliar [mobi'li̯a:ɐ̯] das; ~s furnishings *pl.*

Mobilisation [mobiliza'tsi̯o:n] die; ~, ~en *(Milit., Politik)* mobilization

mobilisieren *tr. V.* a) *(Milit., fig.)* mobilize; die Massen ~ *(fig.)* stir the masses into action; b) *(aktivieren)* activate ⟨*circulation etc.*⟩; summon up ⟨*energy etc.*⟩; c) *(Wirtsch.)* make ⟨*capital*⟩ available; realize ⟨*capital*⟩

Mobilisierung die; ~, ~en a) *(Milit., fig.)* mobilization; b) *(Aktivierung) (des Kreislaufs)* activation; *(von Energie)* summoning up; c) *(Wirtsch.: von Kapital)* realization

Mobilität [mobili'tɛ:t] die; ~ *(Soziol.)* mobility; geistige ~ *(fig.)* mental agility

Mobilmachung die; ~, ~en mobilization; die allgemeine ~ ausrufen order a general mobilization

Mobil·telefon das cellular phone

möbl. *Abk.* möbliert furn.

möblieren *tr. V.* furnish; ein möbliertes Zimmer a furnished room; möbliert wohnen live in furnished accommodation; ein möblierter Herr *(ugs. veralt.)* a lodger

Möblierung die; ~, ~en a) *o. Pl. (das Möblieren)* furnishing; b) *(Einrichtung)* furnishings and furniture (+ *Gen.* in)

Moçambique [mosam'bi:k] (das); ~s *s.* Mosambik

Mocca ['mɔka] *s.* Mokka

mochte ['mɔxtə] *1. u. 3. Pers. Sg. Prät. v.* mögen

möchte ['mœçtə] *1. u. 3. Pers. Sg. Konjunktiv II v.* mögen

Möchte·gern-: ~dichter/~casanova/~politiker would-be poet/Casanova/politician

modal [mo'da:l] *Adj. (Sprachw.)* modal

Modalität [modali'tɛ:t] die; ~, ~en a) *(geh.) (Bedingung)* provision; condition; *(Umstand)* circumstance; b) *(Sprachw., Philos.)* modality

Modal-: ~satz der *(Sprachw.)* modal sentence/phrase; ~verb das *(Sprachw.)* modal verb

Modder ['mɔdɐ] der; ~s *(nordd. ugs.)* mud

modd[e]rig ['mɔd(ə)rɪç] *Adj. (nordd. ugs.)* muddy

Mode ['mo:də] die; ~, ~n a) fashion; die ~ verlangt, daß ...: fashion dictates that ...; jede ~ mitmachen follow fashion's every whim; mit der ~ gehen follow the fashion; etw. ist [in] ~: sth. is in *or* the fashion; [ganz] groß in ~ *od.* große ~ sein be all the rage *or* very fashionable; nach der neuesten ~: in the latest style; in ~/aus der ~ kommen come into/go out of fashion; neue ~n *(abwertend)* new-fangled ideas; was sind denn das für neue ~n? *(ugs.)* what do you think you're/does he think he's *etc.* doing?; b) *Pl. (~kleidung)* fashions

mode-, Mode-: ~artikel der a) *(modisches Zubehör)* [fashion] accessory; b) *(vielgekaufter Artikel)* fashionable novelty; in thing; ~arzt der *(ugs.)* fashionable doctor; ~ausdruck der vogue word; 'in' expression *(coll.)*; ~beruf der fashionable occupation; ~bewußt 1. *Adj.* fashion-conscious; 2. *adv.* fashionably; ~branche die fashion *or (Brit. coll.)* rag trade; ~designer der, ~designerin die fashion designer; ~farbe die fashionable colour; ~geschäft das fashion store; *(kleiner)* boutique; ~haus das a) fashion house; b) *(Geschäft)* fashion store; ~journal das fashion magazine; ~krankheit die fashionable disease *or* complaint

Modell [mo'dɛl] das; ~s, ~e *(auch fig.)* model; *(Technik: Entwurf)* [design] model; pattern; *(in Originalgröße)* mock-up; jmdm. ~ sitzen *od.* stehen model *or* sit for sb.

Modell-: ~bauer der model-maker; ~charakter der: etw. hat ~charakter sth. can act as a model; etw. hat ~character für etw. sth. acts as *or* provides a model for sth.; ~eisen·bahn die model railway

Modelleur [modɛ'lø:ɐ̯] der; ~s, ~e modeller

Modell-: ~fall der a) model; perfect example; b) *(klassisches Beispiel)* textbook case; ~flugzeug das model aircraft

modellhaft *Adj.* exemplary; model *attrib.*; pilot ⟨*scheme*⟩; etw. hat ~en Charakter sth. can act as a model

modellieren 1. *tr. V.* a) model, mould ⟨*figures, objects*⟩; mould ⟨*clay, wax*⟩; jmdn./etw. in Ton ~: model sb./sth. in clay; etw. nach etw. ~ *(fig.)* model sth. on sth.; b) *(gestalten)* design ⟨*clothes*⟩; c) *(Wissensch.)*

model ⟨*processes*⟩. **2.** *itr. V.* model *(esp. in clay or wax)*

Modellier·masse die modelling material *(esp. clay or wax)*

Modell-: ~kleid das model dress; **~pflege die** *(Kfz-W.)* improving the specification; **~projekt das** pilot scheme; **~reihe die** *(Wirtsch.)* range [of models]; **~versuch der** pilot scheme; **~zeichnung die** drawing [of a model/mock-up]

modeln ['mo:dl̩n] *tr. V.* **etw. nach dem Vorbild von etw. ~:** model sth. on sth.

Moden-: ~schau die fashion show *or* parade; **~zeit·schrift die** *s.* **Modezeitschrift**

Mode-: ~püppchen das, ~puppe die fashion-crazy bird *(Brit. sl.) or (Amer. coll.)* dame

Moder ['mo:dɐ] **der; ~s a)** mould; *(~geruch)* mustiness; *(Verwesung, auch fig.)* decay; **es riecht nach ~:** there is a musty smell; **b)** *s.* **Modder**

moderat [mode'ra:t] *Adj.* moderate

Moderation [modera'tsi̯o:n] **die; ~, ~en** *(Rundf., Ferns.)* presentation; **die ~ haben** be the presenter

Moderator [mode'ra:tɔr] **der; ~s, ~en** [-'to:rən], **Moderatorin die; ~, ~nen** *(Rundf., Ferns.)* presenter

moderieren [mode'ri:rən] **1.** *tr. V. (Rundf., Ferns.)* present ⟨*programme*⟩. **2.** *itr. V.* be the presenter

moderig *Adj.* musty

¹modern ['mo:dɐn] *itr. V.; auch mit sein* go mouldy; *(verwesen)* decay; **~de Gebeine** mouldering skeletons

²modern [mo'dɛrn] **1.** *Adj.* modern; *(modisch)* fashionable. **2.** *adv.* in a modern manner *or* style; *(modisch)* fashionably; *(aufgeschlossen)* progressively; **~ denken** have modern/progressive ideas; **~ eingestellt** *od.* **denkend** with modern/progressive ideas *postpos., not pred.*

Moderne die; ~ a) die ~, das Zeitalter der ~: the modern age; modern times; **b)** *(Kunstrichtung)* **die ~:** modern arts *pl.*; **typisch für die ~:** typical of modern writing/painting/music *etc.*

modernisieren 1. *tr. V.* modernize; *(modisch gestalten)* bring ⟨*clothes*⟩ in line with the current fashion. **2.** *itr. V.* introduce modern methods

Modernisierung die; ~, ~en modernization

Modernismus der; ~, Modernismen a) *o. Pl.* modernism; **b)** *(Stilelement)* modernism; modernistic element

modernistisch *(abwertend)* **1.** *Adj.* modernistic. **2.** *adv.* in a modernistic style *or* manner

Modernität die; ~: modernity

Mode-: ~sache die *in* **[eine] ~sache sein** be a [passing] fashion; **~salon der** [smart] fashion boutique; **~schau die** *s.* **Modenschau; ~schmuck der** costume jewellery; **~schöpfer der** couturier; **~schöpferin die** couturière; **~schriftsteller der** fashionable author; **~tanz der** dance [briefly] in vogue; **~torheit die** crazy fashion; **~trend der** fashion trend; **~wort das;** *Pl.* **~wörter** vogue-word; 'in' expression *(coll.)*; **~zar der** *(ugs.)* fashion mogul; **~zeichner der** *(veralt.)*, **~zeichnerin die** *(veralt.)* dress-designer; **~zeit·schrift die** fashion magazine

Modi *s.* **Modus**

Modifikation [modifika'tsi̯o:n] **die; ~, ~en** modification

modifizierbar *Adj.* modifiable

modifizieren [modifi'tsi:rən] *tr. V. (geh.)* modify

Modifizierung die; ~, ~en *(geh.)* modification

modisch ['mo:dɪʃ] **1.** *Adj.* fashionable; trendy *(coll. derog.)*. **2.** *adv.* fashionably; trendily *(coll. derog.)*

Modistin [mo'dɪstɪn] **die; ~, ~nen** milliner

¹Modul ['mo:dʊl] **der; ~s, ~n** *(Math.)* modulus

²Modul [mo'du:l] **das; ~s, ~e** *(DV, Elektronik)* module

Modulation [modula'tsi̯o:n] *(auch Musik, Technik)* **die; ~, ~en** modulation

modulieren *tr., itr. V. (auch Musik, Technik)* modulate

Modus ['mɔdʊs] **der; ~, Modi a)** *(geh.)* procedure (+ *Gen.* for); method; **nach diesem ~:** by this method; **b)** *(Sprachw.)* mood

Modus vivendi [- vi'vɛndi] **der; ~ ~, Modi ~** *(geh.)* modus vivendi

Mofa ['mo:fa] **das; ~s, ~s** [low-powered] moped

Mofa·fahrer der moped rider

Mogelei die; ~, ~en *(ugs.)* cheating *no pl.*

mogeln *(ugs.)* **1.** *itr. V.* cheat; *(lügen)* fib; **beim Kartenspiel/bei der Klassenarbeit ~:** cheat at cards/in the class test. **2.** *tr. V.* **etw. in etw.** *(Akk.)* **~:** slip sth. into sth. **3.** *refl. V.* **sich in/zwischen etw.** *(Akk.)* **~** ⟨*error*⟩ slip into/in among sth.

Mogel·packung die *(abwertend)* deceptive packaging

mögen ['mø:gn̩] **1.** *unr. Modalverb; 2. Part.* **~: a)** *(wollen)* want to; **das hätte ich sehen ~:** I would have liked to see that; **sie mochte nicht länger bleiben** she didn't want to stay any longer; **b)** *(geh.: sollen)* **das mag genügen** that should be *or* ought to be enough; **bitte ihn** *od.* **sag ihm, er möge kommen** *(veralt.)* ask/tell him to come; **c)** *(geh.: Wunschform)* **möge er bald kommen!** I do hope he'll come soon!; **möge es so bleiben!** may it stay like that; **das möge der Himmel verhüten!** Heaven forbid!; **d)** *(Vermutung, Möglichkeit)* **sie mag/mochte vierzig sein** she must be/must have been [about] forty; **wie alt sie wohl sein mag?** I wonder how old she is; **Meier, Müller, Koch – und wie sie alle heißen ~:** Meier, Müller, Koch and [the rest,] whatever they're called; **wie viele Personen ~ das sein?** how many people would you say there are?; **was mag sie damit gemeint haben?** what can she have meant by that?; **[das] mag sein** maybe; **es mag sein, daß ...:** it may be *or* it is possible that ...; **e)** *(geh.: Einräumung)* **er mag tun, was er will** no matter what he does; **es mag kommen, was will** come what may; **mag er nur warten** let him wait; he can wait; **wer er auch sein mag** whoever he may be; **wie dem auch sein mag** be that as it may; **mag das Wetter auch noch so schlecht sein, ...:** however bad the weather may be, ...; *s. auch* **hingehen d; f)** *Konjunktiv II + Inf. (den Wunsch haben)* **ich/sie möchte gern wissen ...:** I would *or* should/she would like to know ...; **ich möchte ihn [gerne] sprechen** I should like to speak to him; **möchten Sie etwas essen/trinken?** would you like something to eat/drink?; **ich möchte nicht stören, aber ...:** I don't want to interrupt, but ...; **ich möchte zu gerne wissen** I'd love to know ...; **ich möchte sagen, ...** *(in zögernder Aussage)* I'd say ...; **man möchte meinen, er sei der Chef** one would [really] think he was the boss. **2.** *unr. tr. V.* **[gern] ~:** like; **sie mag keine Rosen** she does not like roses; **er mag mich nicht** he does not like me; **sie mag ihn sehr [gern]** she likes him very much; *(hat ihn sehr gern)* she is very fond of him; **sie ~ sich** they're fond of one another; **möchten Sie ein Glas Wein?** would you like a glass of wine?; **ich mag lieber/am liebsten Bier** I like beer better/best [of all]; **ich möchte lieber Tee** I would prefer tea *or* rather have tea; **ich möchte nicht, daß er heute kommt** I would not like him to come today. **3.** *unr. itr. V.* **a)** *(es wollen)* like to; **ich mag nicht** I don't want to; **magst du?** do you want to?; *(bei einem Angebot)* would you like one/some?; **magst du noch?** do you want any more?; **ich möchte schon, aber ...:** I should like to, but ...; **b)** *(fahren, gehen usw. wollen)* **ich möchte nach Hause/in die Stadt/auf die Schaukel** I want *or* I'd like to go home/into town/on the swing; **er möchte zu Herrn A** he would like to see Mr A

Mogler ['mo:glɐ] **der; ~s, ~, Moglerin die; ~, ~nen** *(ugs.)* cheat

möglich ['mø:klɪç] *Adj.* possible; **es war ihm nicht ~ [zu kommen]** he was unable [to come]; it was not possible for him [to come]; **sobald/so gut es mir ~ ist** as soon/as well as I can; **das ist schon eher ~:** that is more likely [to be possible]; **[jmdm.] etw. ~ machen** ⟨*thing*⟩ make sth. possible [for sb.]; ⟨*person*⟩ arrange sth. [for sb.]; **das** *od.* **alles Mögliche tun** do everything possible; do one's utmost; **dort kann man alles ~e kaufen** *(ugs.)* you can get all sorts of things there; **sie hatte alles ~e zu kritisieren** she criticized everything; **alle ~en Entschuldigungen** *(ugs.)* every excuse you can think of; **alle ~en Leute** *(ugs.)* all sorts of people; **das ist gut/leicht/durchaus ~:** that is very/wholly/entirely possible; **bei ihm ist alles ~:** he is capable of anything; **man sollte es nicht für ~ halten** one would not believe it possible; **[das ist doch] nicht ~!** impossible!; I don't believe it!; **ist das ~!** [that's] incredible!; whatever next!

möglicherweise *Adv.* possibly; **~ hat er Glück/Glück gehabt** he may be/may have been lucky; **wir werden ~ versetzt** we may [possibly] be transferred; **~ hast du es nur geträumt** it's possible that you just dreamt it

Möglichkeit die; ~, ~en a) *(möglicher Weg)* possibility; *(Methode)* way; **nach ~:** if possible; **b)** *o. Pl. (Möglichsein)* possibility; **es besteht die ~, daß ...:** there is a chance *or* possibility that ...; **es besteht die ~, eine Zusatzversicherung abzuschließen** it is possible to arrange additional insurance; **ist es die** *od.* **ist [denn] das die ~!** *(ugs.)* well, I'll be damned! *(coll.)*; whatever next!; **c)** *(Gelegenheit)* opportunity; chance; **die ~ haben, etw. zu tun** have an opportunity of doing sth. *or* to do sth.; **d)** *Pl. (Mittel)* [*esp.* financial] means *or* resources; **künstlerische ~en** artistic resources *or* potential *sing.*

Möglichkeits·form die *(Sprachw.)* subjunctive

möglichst 1. *Adv.* **a)** *(so weit wie möglich)* as much *or* far as possible; **sich ~ zurückhalten** restrain oneself as far as possible; **b)** *(wenn möglich)* if [at all] possible; **macht ~ keinen Lärm** don't make any noise if you can possibly help it; **c)** *(so ... wie möglich)* **~ groß/schnell/oft** as big/fast/often as possible; **mit ~ großer Sorgfalt** with the greatest possible care. **2.** *adj.* **in sein ~es tun** do one's utmost; do everything possible

Mogul ['mo:gʊl] **der; ~s, ~n** *(hist.)* Mogul

Mohair [mo'hɛ:ɐ̯] **der; ~s** mohair

Mohammed ['mo:hamɛt] **(der)** Muhammad

Mohammedaner der; ~s, ~, Mohammedanerin, die; ~, ~nen Muslim; Muhammadan

mohammedanisch 1. *Adj.* Muslim, Muhammadan. **2.** *adv.* **~ geprägt** imbued with Muslim *or* Muhammadan characteristics *postpos.*

Mohikaner [mohi'ka:nɐ] **der; ~s, ~:** Mohican; **der letzte ~, der Letzte der ~** *(ugs. scherzh.)* the last one; the last survivor *(joc.)*

Mohn [mo:n] **der; ~s a)** *(Pflanze)* poppy; **b)** *(Samen)* poppy seed; *(auf Brot, Kuchen)* poppy seeds *pl.*

Mohn-: ~blume die poppy; **~brötchen das** poppy-seed roll; **~feld das** field of poppies; **~kuchen der** poppy-seed cake

Mohr [mo:ɐ̯] **der; ~en, ~en** *(veralt.)* Moor; **schwarz wie ein ~:** as black as the ace of spades; **der ~ hat seine Schuldigkeit getan,**

der ~ kann gehen *(fig.)* when one has served one's purpose one is simply discarded

Möhre ['mø:rə] die; ~, ~n carrot

Mohren·kopf der a) chocolate marshmallow; b) *(Gebäck) small cream-filled spherical sponge cake covered with chocolate*

Möhren·saft der carrot juice

Mohren·wäsche die [attempt at] whitewashing *(fig.)*

Mohr·rübe die carrot

Moiré [moa're:] der; ~s, ~s moiré

mokant [mo'kant] *(geh.)* 1. *Adj.* mocking. 2. *adv.* mockingly

Mokassin [moka'si:n] der; ~s, ~s moccasin

Mokick ['mo:kɪk] das; ~s, ~s light motor cycle *(with kick-starter)*

mokieren [mo'ki:rən] *refl. V. (geh.)* sich über etw. *(Akk.)* ~: mock *or* scoff at sth.; sich über jmdn. ~: mock sb.

Mokka ['mɔka] der; ~s a) *(Bohnen)* mocha [coffee]; b) *(Getränk)* strong black coffee

Mokka-: ~löffel der [small] coffee-spoon; ~tasse die small coffee-cup

Mol [mo:l] das; ~s, ~e *(Chemie)* mole

Molar [mo'la:ɐ̯] der; ~s, ~en, **Molar·zahn** der molar

Molch [mɔlç] der; ~[e]s, ~e newt

¹Moldau ['mɔldau̯] die; ~: [river] Vltava

²Moldau die; ~ *(Sowjetrepublik)* Moldavia

Mole ['mo:lə] die; ~, ~n [harbour] mole

Molekül [mole'ky:l] das; ~s, ~e *(Chemie)* molecule

molekular [moleku'la:ɐ̯] *Adj.* molecular

Molekular-: molecular

Molesten [mo'lɛstn̩] *Pl. (veralt.)* minor ailments

molk [mɔlk] *1. u. 3. Pers. Sg. Prät. v.* melken

Molke die; ~: whey

Molkerei die; ~, ~en dairy

Molkerei-: ~butter die dairy butter; ~genossenschaft die co-operative dairy; ~produkt das dairy product

Moll [mɔl] das; ~ *(Musik)* minor [key]; in ~ enden finish in a minor key

Moll-: ~akkord der *(Musik)* minor chord; ~drei·klang der minor triad

Molle die; ~, ~n *(berlin.)* [glass of] beer; eine ~ zischen have a jar *(coll.)*

Mollen·friedhof der *(berlin. scherzh.)* beer-belly *(coll.)*

Molli ['mɔli] der; ~s, ~s *(salopp)* Molotov cocktail

mollig ['mɔlɪç] 1. *Adj.* a) *(rundlich)* plump; b) *(warm)* cosy; snug; ein ~er Wintermantel a warm and cosy winter coat. 2. *adv.* cosily; snugly; ~ warm warm and cosy

Moll-: ~ton·art die *(Musik)* minor key; ~ton·leiter die *(Musik)* minor scale

Molluske [mɔ'lʊskə] die; ~, ~n *(Biol.)* mollusc

Moloch ['mo:lɔx] der; ~s, ~e *(geh.)* Moloch; voracious giant

Molotow·cocktail ['mɔlotɔf-] der Molotov cocktail

Molybdän [molʏp'dɛ:n] das; ~s *(Chemie)* molybdenum

¹Moment [mo'mɛnt] der; ~[e]s, ~e moment; einen ~ zögern hesitate [for] a moment; einen ~ bitte! just a moment, please!; ~ [mal]! [hey!] just a moment!; wait a mo! *(coll.)*; im nächsten/gleichen ~: the next/at the same moment; jeden ~ *(ugs.)* [at] any moment; im ~: at the moment; *s. auch* licht a

²Moment das; ~[e]s, ~e a) *(Umstand)* factor, element (für in); das auslösende ~ für etw. sein be the trigger for sth.; b) *(Physik)* moment

momentan [momɛn'ta:n] 1. *Adj.* a) *nicht präd.* present; current; b) *(vorübergehend)* temporary; *(flüchtig)* momentary; eine ~e Besserung a short-lived improvement. 2. *adv.* a) at the moment; at present; b) *(vorübergehend)* temporarily; *(flüchtig)* momentarily; for a moment

Moment·aufnahme die *(Fot.)* snapshot

Monaco ['mo:nako] (das); ~s Monaco

Monade [mo'na:də] die; ~, ~n *(Philos.)* monad

Monarch [mo'narç] der; ~en, ~en monarch

Monarchie die; ~, ~n monarchy

Monarchin die; ~, ~nen monarch

monarchisch 1. *Adj.* monarchical. 2. *adv.* monarchically; ~ regiert ruled by a monarch/monarchs

Monarchismus der; ~: monarchism *no art.*

Monarchist der; ~en, ~en, **Monarchistin** die; ~, ~nen monarchist

monarchistisch 1. *Adj.* monarchist ‹*party, group*›; monarchistic ‹*tendency, views*›. 2. *adv.* monarchistically

Monat ['mo:nat] der; ~s, ~e month; letzten ~: last month; im ~ April in the month of April; am 10. dieses ~s on the tenth [of this month]; Ihr Schreiben vom 22. dieses ~s your letter of the 22nd [inst.]; sie ist im vierten ~ [schwanger] she is four months pregnant; er war drei ~e [lang] hier he was here for three months; er ist seit drei ~en hier he has been here for three months; was verdienst du im ~? how much do you earn per month?; ich bezahle 250 DM im ~: I pay 250 marks a month *or* per month; *s. auch* hinaus

monatelang 1. *Adj.; nicht präd.* lasting for months *postpos., not pred.*; die ~en Verhandlungen the negotiations, which lasted for several months; nach ~er Krankheit after months of illness; mit ~er Verspätung months late. 2. *adv.* for months [on end]

-monatig a) *(... Monate alt)* ...-month-old; ein achtmonatiges Kind an eight-month-old baby; b) *(... Monate dauernd)* ... month's/ months'; ...-month; eine viermonatige Kur a four-month course of treatment; mit dreimonatiger Verspätung three months late

monatlich 1. *Adj.* monthly. 2. *adv.* monthly; every month; *(im Monat)* per month; etw. ~ überweisen pay sth. monthly; sich ~ treffen meet every month

-monatlich 1. *Adj.* ...-monthly; acht~/ drei~: eight-monthly/three-monthly. 2. *adv.* every ... months

Monats-: ~ab·rechnung die monthly accounts *pl.*; *(Abrechnungsblatt)* monthly [statement of] account; ~anfang der, ~beginn der beginning of the month; zu/am ~anfang *od.* ~beginn at the beginning of the month; ~beitrag der monthly subscription; ~binde die sanitary towel *(Brit.)*; sanitary napkin *(Amer.)*; ~blutung die [monthly] period; ~einkommen das monthly income; ~ende das end of the month; ~erste der first [day] of the month; ~frist *o. Art.; o. Pl.* in *od.* innerhalb *od.* binnen ~frist within [a period of] a *or* one month; nach ~frist after [a period of] a *or* one month; vor ~frist in less than a month; within [a period of] a *or* one month; *(vor einem Monat)* a month ago; ~gehalt das month's salary; vier ~gehälter four months' salary *sing.*; ein dreizehntes ~gehalt an extra month's salary; ein ~gehalt von 3000 DM a monthly salary of 3,000 marks; ~hälfte die half of the month; ~karte die monthly season-ticket; ~letzte der last day of the month; ~lohn der month's wages; vier ~löhne four months' wages *pl.*; ein ~lohn von 2000 DM a monthly wage of 2,000 marks; ~miete die month's rent; zwei ~mieten two months' rent; eine ~miete von 1000 DM a monthly rent of 1,000 marks; ~mitte die middle of the month; ~rate die monthly instalment; ~wechsel der *(veralt.)* monthly allowance *(esp. for a student)*

monat[s]weise *Adv.* by the month

Mönch [mœnç] der; ~[e]s, ~e monk

mönchisch *Adj.* monkish; of a monk *postpos., not pred.*

Mönchs-: ~kloster das monastery; ~kutte die monk's habit *or* cowl; ~latein das monkish Latin; dog-Latin *(derog.)*; ~leben das monastic life; life of a monk; ~orden der monastic order

Mönch[s]tum das; ~s a) monasticism; b) *(das Mönchsein)* monkhood

Mönchs·zelle die monk's cell

Mond [mo:nt] der; ~[e]s, ~e a) moon; den ~ anbellen *(fig. ugs.)* talk to a brick wall; ich könnte *od.* möchte ihn auf den *od.* zum ~ schießen *(salopp)* I wish he'd get lost *(sl.)*; auf *od.* hinter dem ~ leben *(fig. ugs.)* be a bit behind the times *or* not quite with it *(coll.)*; lebst du auf dem ~? *(ugs.)* where have you been?; wir leben auch nicht hinter dem ~ *(ugs.)* we're not fuddy-duddies *(sl.)*; we do have some idea of what's going on; in den ~ gucken *(fig. ugs.)* be left empty-handed *or* *(coll.)* out in the cold; etw. in den ~ schreiben *(ugs.)* write sth. off; nach dem ~ gehen *(ugs.)* ‹*clock, watch*› be hopelessly wrong; b) *(dichter. veralt.)* month; viele ~e waren ins Land gegangen many moons had passed

Mondamin ⓦⓩ [monda'mi:n] das; ~s *(a proprietary brand of)* cornflour

mondän [mɔn'dɛ:n] 1. *Adj.* [highly] fashionable; smart; die ~e Welt the smart set. 2. *adv.* fashionably; in a fashionable style

mond-, Mond-: ~auf·gang der moonrise; ~auto das *(Raumf.)* moon buggy; ~bahn die orbit of a satellite; *(des Erdmondes)* lunar orbit; ~beschienen *Adj.* moonlit

Monden·schein der; *o. Pl. (dichter.)* moonlight

Mondes·finsternis die *(österr.) s.* Mondfinsternis

mond-, Mond-: fähre die *(Raumf.)* lunar module; ~finsternis die *(Astron.)* lunar eclipse; eclipse of the moon; ~flug der lunar expedition; ~gebirge das lunar mountain range *or* mountains *pl.*; ~gesicht das moon-face; ~gestein das moon rock; ~hell *Adj. (geh.)* moonlit; ~jahr das lunar year; ~kalb das *(salopp)* dim-wit *(coll.)*; dope *(coll.)*; ~krater der lunar crater; ~lande·fähre die *(Raumf.)* lunar module; ~landschaft die *(auch fig.)* lunar landscape; ~landung die moon landing; ~licht das; *o. Pl.* moonlight; ~los *Adj.* moonless; ~ober·fläche die lunar surface; ~phase die moon's phase; ~preis der *(Wirtsch. Jargon)* artificially high price *(from which the actual asking price is 'reduced')*; *(Wucherpreis)* exorbitant price; ~rakete die moon rocket; ~schein der; *o. Pl.* moonlight; der kann mir mal im ~schein begegnen *(salopp)* he can get lost *(sl.)*; ~sichel die crescent moon; ~sonde die lunar probe; ~stein der moonstone; ~süchtig *Adj.* sleep-walking *attrib. (esp. by moonlight)*; ~süchtig sein be a sleep-walker; ~süchtigkeit die sleep-walking *(esp. by moonlight)*; ~umkreisung die orbiting of the moon; ~umlauf·bahn die lunar orbit; ~untergang der moonset; ~wechsel der change of the moon

Monegasse [mone'gasə] der; ~n, ~n Monégasque

monegassisch *Adj.* Monégasque

monetär [mone'tɛ:ɐ̯] 1. *Adj.; nicht präd.* monetary. 2. *adv.* on a monetary basis

Monetarismus [moneta'rɪsmʊs] der; ~ *(Wirtsch.)* monetarism *no art.*

Moneten [mo'ne:tn̩] *Pl. (ugs.)* cash *sing.*; dough *sing. (sl.)*

Mongole [mɔŋ'go:lə] der; ~n, ~n a) Mongol; b) *(Bewohner der Mongolei)* Mongolian

Mongolei [mɔŋgo'lai̯] die; ~: Mongolia; in der Inneren/Äußeren ~: in Inner/Outer Mongolia

Mongolen-: ~falte die *(Anthrop.)* Mongolian fold; ~fleck der *(Anthrop.)* Mongolian spot

mongolid [mɔŋgo'li:t] *Adj. (Anthrop.)* Mongoloid

Mongolide der/die; *adj. Dekl. (Anthrop.)* Mongoloid

mongolisch *Adj.* Mongolian

Mongolismus der; ~ *(Med.)* mongolism *no art.*

mongoloid *Adj. (Med.)* mongoloid

Mongoloide der/die; *adj. Dekl. (Med.)* Mongoloid

monieren [mo'ni:rən] *tr. V.* criticize; *(beanstanden)* find fault with

Monismus [mo'nɪsmʊs] **der;** ~ *(Philos.)* monism *no art.*

Monitor ['mo:nitɔr] **der;** ~s, ~en [-'to:rən] *(Ferns., Technik, Physik)* monitor

mono ['mo:no] *Adv. (ugs.)* ‹*hear, play, etc.*› in mono *(coll.)*

mono-, Mono-: mono-

monochrom [mono'kro:m] *Adj. (Malerei, Fot.)* monochrome; monochromatic ‹*light*›

monocolor [monoko'lo:ɐ̯] *Adj. (österr. Politik)* one-party

monogam [mono'ga:m] **1.** *Adj.* monogamous. **2.** *adv.* monogamously

Monogamie die; ~: monogamy

Mono·gramm das; ~s, ~e monogram

Monographie [monogra'fi:] **die;** ~, ~n monograph

Monokel [mo'nɔkl̩] **das;** ~s, ~: monocle

Mono·kultur die *(Landw.)* monoculture

Monolith [mono'li:t] **der;** ~s *od.* ~en, ~en monolith

Monolog [mono'lo:k] **der;** ~s, ~e monologue; **einen ~ halten** hold a monologue

monologisch 1. *Adj.* monologic[al]; ‹*form*› of a monologue; ‹*statement*› in the form of a monologue. **2.** *adv.* in monologue

monologisieren *itr. V.* talk in monologue

monoman [mono'ma:n] *(Psych.)* **1.** *Adj.* monomaniacal. **2.** *adv.* monomaniacally

Monomanie [monoma'ni:] **die;** ~, ~n *(Psych.)* monomania

Monophthong [mono'ftɔŋ] **der;** ~s, ~e *(Sprachw.)* monophthong

Monopol [mono'po:l] **das;** ~s, ~e monopoly **(auf +** *Akk.*, **für** in, of)

monopolisieren *tr. V.* monopolize

Monopolisierung die; ~, ~en monopolization

Monopolist der; ~en, ~en, **Monopolistin die;** ~, ~nen monopolist

monopol-, Monopol-: ~kapital das; *o. Pl.* monopoly capital; **~kapitalismus der;** *o. Pl.* monopoly capitalism; **~kapitalistisch 1.** *Adj.* monopoly-capitalist; **2.** *adv.* ‹*structured, organized*› on the principles of monopoly capitalism; **~stellung die** [position of] monopoly

Monopoly ⓦ [mo'no:poli] **das;** ~: Monopoly **(P)** *(game)*

Monotheismus [monote'ɪsmʊs] **der;** ~ *(Rel.)* monotheism

monotheistisch *(Rel.)* **1.** *Adj.* monotheistic. **2.** *adv.* monotheistically

monoton [mono'to:n] **1.** *Adj.* monotonous. **2.** *adv.* monotonously

Monotonie die; ~, ~n monotony

Monotype ⓦ ['mɔnotaip] **die;** ~, ~s *(Druckw.)* Monotype **(P)** [composing-machine]

Mon·oxid *(fachspr.)*, **Mon·oxyd das** *(Chemie)* monoxide

Mono·zelle die *(Elektrot.)* [single-cell] battery

Monster ['mɔnstɐ] **das;** ~s, ~: monster; *(häßlich)* [hideous] brute

Monster- mammoth; *(sehr lange dauernd)* marathon

Monster-: ~film der a) *(ugs.)* mammoth [screen] epic; block-buster *(sl.)*; **b)** *(Film mit Monstern)* horror film [with a monster/monsters]; **~prozeß der** marathon trial; **~veranstaltung die** giant spectacular; *(sehr lange dauernd)* marathon [event]

Monstranz [mɔn'strants] **die;** ~, ~en *(kath. Kirche)* monstrance

Monstren *s.* **Monstrum**

monströs [mɔn'strø:s] *(geh.)* **1.** *Adj.* **a)** *(auch fig.)* monstrous; [huge and] hideous; **b)** *(gigantisch)* massive, overpowering ‹*building, monument*›. **2.** *adv.* monstrously

Monstrosität [mɔnstrozi'tɛ:t] **die;** ~, ~en monstrosity; *(fig.: monströse Tat)* monstrous action; atrocity

Monstrum ['mɔnstrʊm] **das;** ~s, **Monstren a)** *(auch fig.: Mensch)* monster; **b)** *(Ungetüm)* hulking great thing *(coll.)*; **das/ein ~ von ...:** the/a giant [of a] ...

Monsun [mɔn'zu:n] **der;** ~s, ~e *(Geogr.)* monsoon

Monsun-: ~regen der *(Geog.)* monsoon rains *pl.*; **~wald der** *(Geog.)* monsoon forest

Montag ['mo:nta:k] **der** Monday; *s. auch* **blau; Dienstag; Dienstag-**

Montag- Monday; *s. auch* **Dienstag-**

Montage [mɔn'ta:ʒə] **die;** ~, ~n **a)** *(Bauw., Technik) (Zusammenbau)* assembly; *(Einbau)* installation; *(Aufstellen)* erection; *(Anbringen)* fitting **(an +** *Akk. od. Dat.* to); mounting **(auf +** *Akk. od. Dat.* on); **auf ~:** *(ugs.)* away on a job; **b)** *(Film, bild. Kunst, Literaturw.)* montage; **c)** *(Druckw.)* make-up

Montage-: ~band das assembly line; **~halle die** assembly shop

montags *Adv.* on Monday[s]; *s. auch* **dienstags**

Montags·wagen der *(ugs.)* Friday car

Montan-: ~industrie die coal and steel industry; **~union die** European Coal and Steel Community

Monteur [mɔn'tø:ɐ̯] **der;** ~s, ~e mechanic; *(Installateur)* fitter; *(Elektro~)* electrician

Monteur·anzug der [mechanic's] overalls *pl.*

montieren [mɔn'ti:rən] *tr. V.* **a)** *(zusammenbauen)* assemble **(aus** from); erect ‹*building*›; **b)** *(anbringen)* fit **(an +** *Akk. od. Dat.* to; **auf +** *Akk. od. Dat.* on); *(einbauen)* install **(in +** *Akk.* in); *(befestigen)* fix **(an +** *Akk. od. Dat.* to); **eine Lampe an die** *od.* **der Decke ~:** put up *or* fix a light on the ceiling; **eine Antenne auf das** *od.* **dem Dach ~:** put up *or* mount an aerial on the roof; **c)** *(Film, bild. Kunst)* put together; *(Druckw.)* make up

Montierer der; ~s, ~, **Montiererin die;** ~, ~nen assembly worker

Montur [mɔn'tu:ɐ̯] **die;** ~, ~en **a)** *(ugs.)* outfit *(coll.)*; gear *no pl. (coll.)*; **b)** *(veralt.: Uniform)* uniform

Monument [monu'mɛnt] **das;** ~[e]s, ~e *(auch fig.)* monument

monumental 1. *Adj. (auch fig.)* monumental; *(massiv)* massive. **2.** *adv.* in a monumental style; *(überdimensional)* on a monumental scale

Monumental-: monumental

Moor [mo:ɐ̯] **das;** ~[e]s, ~e bog; *(Bruch)* marsh; *(Flach~)* fen; *(Hoch~)* high moor

Moor-: ~bad das mud-bath; **~boden der** bog soil; *(Torfboden)* peaty soil

moorig *Adj.* boggy

Moor-: ~kultur die bogland/fenland [reclamation and] cultivation; **~leiche die** [well-preserved] body found in a bog

Moos [mo:s] **das;** ~es, ~e **a)** moss; **~ ansetzen** gather moss; *(fig. ugs.)* become old hat *(coll.)*; **b)** *o. Pl. (salopp)* cash; dough *(sl.)*; **c)** *Pl. auch:* **Möser** *(südd., österr., schweiz.)* bog; *(Bruch)* marsh

moos-: ~bedeckt, ~bewachsen *Adj.* moss-covered; **~grün** *Adj.* moss-green

moosig *Adj.* **a)** mossy; *(moosbedeckt)* moss-covered; **b)** *(südd., österr., schweiz.: sumpfig)* marshy

Moos-: ~rose die, ~röschen das moss-rose

Mop der; ~s, ~s mop

Moped ['mo:pɛt] **das;** ~s, ~s moped

Moped·fahrer der moped-rider

Moppel ['mɔpl̩] **der;** ~s, ~ *(fam. scherzh.)* podge *(coll.)*

moppen ['mɔpn̩] *tr., itr. V.* mop; mop the floor in ‹*room*›

Mops [mɔps] **der;** ~es, **Möpse** ['mœpsə] **a)** *(Hund)* pug [dog]; **b)** *(salopp: dicke Person)* podge *(coll.)*; fatty *(derog.)*; **c)** *Pl. (salopp: Geld)* bread *(sl.)*; lolly *(Brit. sl.)*; **die paar Möpse** such a piffling sum *(coll.)*; such peanuts *(sl.)*

mopsen 1. *tr. V. (fam.)* pinch *(sl.)*. **2.** *refl. V. (ugs.)* be bored

mops·fidel *Adj. (ugs.)* very jolly *or* cheerful

mopsig *Adj. (ugs.)* **a)** podgy; tubby; **b) sich ~ machen, ~ werden** get fresh

Moral [mo'ra:l] **die;** ~ **a)** *(Norm)* morality; **gegen die ~ verstoßen** offend against morality *or* the code of conduct; **die herrschende ~:** [currently] accepted standards *pl.*; **b)** *(Sittlichkeit)* morals *pl.*; **keine ~ haben** have no sense of morals; **[eine] doppelte ~:** double standards *pl.*; **[jmdm.] ~ predigen** *(abwertend)* moralize [to sb.]; **c)** *(Selbstvertrauen)* morale; **die ~ ist gut/schlecht** morale is high/low; **d)** *(Lehre)* moral; **e)** *(Philos.)* ethics *sing.*

Moral-: ~apostel der *(abwertend)* upholder of moral standards; **~begriff der** [personal] moral code; sense of morals

Moralin das; ~s *(abwertend, scherzh.)* [hypocritical] moral indignation; *(rechthaberisch)* [priggish] self-righteousness

moralin·sauer *(abwertend, scherzh.)* **1.** *Adj.* [priggishly] indignant; *(rechthaberisch)* [priggishly] self-righteous; holier-than-thou *(coll.)*. **2.** *adv.* with [priggish] indignation

moralisch [mo'ra:lɪʃ] **1.** *Adj.* **a)** *nicht präd.* moral; **das war [für ihn] eine ~e Ohrfeige** that was a slap in the face [for him]; **[s]einen Moralischen haben** *(ugs.) (Gewissensbisse haben)* have a fit of remorse; *(niedergeschlagen sein)* be down in the dumps *(coll.)* *(as the result of a failure)*; **b)** *(sittlich einwandfrei)* moral; morally upright; *(tugendhaft)* virtuous; **c)** *(diszipliniert)* **eine gute ~e Verfassung** good morale; **~er Zusammenbruch** breakdown of *or* in morale. **2.** *adv.* **a)** morally; **ein ~ hochstehender Mensch** a person of unimpeachable morals *or* high moral standing; **b)** *(tugendhaft)* morally; virtuously; **jmdm. ~ kommen** *(ugs.)* adopt a high moral tone with sb.

moralisieren *itr. V. (geh.)* moralize

Moralismus der; ~ **a)** *(Moralität)* sense of morality; **b)** *(abwertend: das Moralisieren)* moralizing

Moralist der; ~en, ~en, **Moralistin die;** ~, ~nen moralist

moralistisch 1. *Adj.* moralistic. **2.** *adv.* moralistically; from a moralistic viewpoint

Moralität die; ~, ~en **a)** *o. Pl. (geh.)* morality; **b)** *(Literaturw.)* morality [play]

Moral-: ~kodex der moral code; **~philosophie die** moral philosophy; **~prediger der** *(abwertend)* moralizing prig; **~predigt die** *(abwertend)* [moralizing] lecture; homily; **[jmdm.] eine ~predigt halten** deliver a homily [to sb.]; **~theologie die** moral theology *no art.*; **~vor·stellung die** ideas *pl.* on *or* attitude to morality

Moräne [mo'rɛ:nə] **die;** ~, ~n *(Geol.)* moraine

Morast [mo'rast] **der;** ~[e]s, ~e *od.* **Moräste** [mo'rɛstə] **a)** bog; swamp; **b)** *o. Pl. (Schlamm)* mud; *(auch fig.)* mire; **im ~ versinken** sink into the mire

morastig *Adj.* muddy

Moratorium [mora'to:riʊm] **das;** ~s, **Moratorien** *(Wirtsch., Politik)* moratorium **(für** on)

morbid [mɔr'bi:t] *Adj. (geh.) (kränklich)* sickly; *(todgeweiht)* deathly pale; *(fig.)* moribund, degenerate ‹*society, institution, etc.*›
Morbidität [mɔrbidi'tɛ:t] **die;** ~ **a)** *(geh.)* sickliness; *(fig.)* moribund *or* degenerate state; **b)** *(Med.)* morbidity
Morchel ['mɔrçl] **die;** ~, ~**n** morel
Mord [mɔrt] **der;** ~**[e]s,** ~**e** murder (**an** + *Dat.* of); *(durch ein Attentat)* assassination; **einen** ~ **begehen** commit murder; **einen** ~ **an jmdm. begehen** murder sb.; **ein versuchter** ~: an attempted murder; **wegen** ~**es angeklagt/verurteilt** accused of *or* charged with murder/condemned for murder; *(in Schlagzeilen)* ~ **aus Eifersucht** jealousy killing; ~ **an Außenminister** foreign minister murdered/assassinated; **dann gibt es** ~ **und Totschlag** *(fig. ugs.)* all hell is/will be let loose; **das ist [glatter** *od.* **der reinste]** ~ *(fig. ugs.)* it's sheer murder; *(unverantwortlich)* it's sheer lunacy
Mord-: ~**an·klage die** charge of murder; **unter** ~**anklage stehen** be charged with murder; ~**an·schlag der** attempted murder (**auf** + *Akk.* of); *(Attentat)* assassination attempt (**auf** + *Akk.* on); **einen** ~**anschlag auf jmdn. verüben** make an attempt on sb.'s life; **einem** ~**anschlag zum Opfer fallen** be murdered/assassinated; ~**brenner der** *(veralt.)* murdering fire-raiser; ~**bube der** *(veralt.)* murdering thug; ~**drohung die** murder threat
morden *tr., itr. V.* murder; **das sinnlose Morden** the senseless killing
Mörder ['mœrdɐ] **der;** ~**s,** ~: murderer *(esp. Law)*; killer; *(politischer* ~*)* assassin; **vierfacher** ~ **sein** have committed four murders
Mörder-: ~**bande die** gang of murderers *or* killers; ~**grube die** *s.* **Herz b;** ~**hand** *in* **durch** *od.* **von** ~**hand sterben** *(geh.)* die at the hand of a murderer
Mörderin die; ~, ~**nen** murderer; murderess; *(politische* ~*)* assassin
mörderisch 1. *Adj.* **a)** *(ugs.: furchtbar, mächtig)* murderous; fiendish ‹*cold*›; dreadful *(coll.)* ‹*crowd, clamour, weather, storm*›; cutthroat ‹*competition*›; **b)** *(todbringend)* murderous. **2.** *adv.* **a)** *(ugs.)* dreadfully *(coll.)*; frightfully *(coll.)*; ~ **fluchen/toben** curse/rage like blazes *(sl.)*; **b)** *(todbringend)* murderously
mord-, Mord-: ~**fall der** murder case; **der** ~**fall Dr. Crippen** [the case of] the Dr Crippen murders; ~**gierig** *Adj.* intent on murder *postpos.*; *(blutgierig)* bloodthirsty; ~**instrument das a)** murder weapon; **b)** *(fig. scherzh.)* murderous[-looking] weapon *or* device
Mordio ['mɔrdio] *s.* **Zeter**
Mord-: ~**kommission die** murder *or* *(Amer.)* homicide squad; ~**prozeß der** murder trial; ~**sache die** murder case; **die** ~**sache Müller** the Müller murder [case]
mords-, Mords- *(ugs.)* terrific *(coll.)*; tremendous *(coll.)*
mords-, Mords-: ~**arbeit die;** *o. Pl. (ugs.)* **eine** ~**arbeit** a hell of a job *(coll.)*; **sich** *(Dat.)* **eine** ~**arbeit machen** take a tremendous amount of trouble *(coll.)* (**mit** over); ~**ding das** *(ugs.)* whopper *(coll.)*; ~**dusel der** *(ugs.) s.* ~**glück;** ~**gaudi die** *(bayr., österr. ugs.) s.* ~**spaß;** ~**geschrei das** *(ugs.)* terrific hubbub *(coll.)*; *(Lärm)* frightful racket *(coll.)*; *(furchtbares Theater)* terrible fuss *(coll.)* (**um** over); ~**glück das** *(ugs.)* **ein** ~**glück** incredible luck *(coll.)*; **ein** ~**glück haben** be incredibly lucky *(coll.)*; ~**hunger der** *(ugs.)* terrific hunger *(coll.)*; **einen** ~**hunger haben** be ravenous *or* famished; ~**kerl der** *(ugs.)* **a)** *(Riese)* enormous chap *(coll.)*; huge guy *(sl.)*; **b)** *(tüchtiger Kerl)* really good sort *(coll.)*; great guy *(Amer.)*; *(Kamerad)* real pal *(coll.)*; ~**krach der** *(ugs.)* **a)** terrible din *or* racket *(coll.)*; **b)** *(Streit)* terrific row *(coll.)*; ~**mäßig** *(ugs.)* **1.** *Adj.; nicht präd.* terrific *(coll.)*; tremendous *(coll.)*; *(entsetzlich)* terrible *(coll.)*; infernal *(coll.)* ‹*din, racket*›; ~**mäßiges Glück** incredible luck *(coll.)*; **2.** *adv.* tremendously *(coll.)*; incredibly *(coll.)*; *(entsetzlich)* terribly *(coll.)*; ~**schreck,** ~**schrecken der** *(ugs.)* hell of a fright *(coll.)*; terrible fright *(coll.)*; ~**spaß der** *(ugs.)* **ein** ~**spaß** tremendous fun *(coll.)*; **einen** ~**spaß haben** have a whale of a time *(coll.)*; ~**stimmung die** *(ugs.)* terrific atmosphere *(coll.)*; ~**wut die** *(ugs.)* towering rage; **eine** ~**wut [im Bauch] haben** be fuming with rage
Mord-: ~**tat die** *(geh.)* murder; ~**verdacht der** suspicion of murder; ~**versuch der** attempted murder; *(Attentat)* assassination attempt; ~**waffe die** murder weapon
Mores ['mo:re:s] *Pl. in* **jmdn.** ~ **lehren** *(ugs.)* tell sb. what's what *or* where he/she gets off *(coll.)*; **dich werde ich** ~ **lehren!** I'll give you a piece of my mind!
morganatisch [mɔrga'na:tɪʃ] *Adj. in* ~**e Ehe** *(hist.)* morganatic marriage
morgen ['mɔrgn̩] *Adv.* **a)** tomorrow; ~ **früh/mittag/abend** tomorrow morning/lunchtime/evening; ~ **in einer Woche/in vierzehn Tagen** tomorrow week/fortnight; a week/fortnight tomorrow; ~ **um diese** *od.* **die gleiche Zeit** this time tomorrow; **bis** ~! until tomorrow!; see you tomorrow!; ~ **ist auch [noch] ein Tag** tomorrow is another day; ~, ~, **nur nicht heute, sagen alle faulen Leute** *(Spr.)* ≈ never put off till tomorrow what you can do today; **die Mode/Technik von** ~ *(fig.)* tomorrow's fashions *pl.*/technology; **b)** *(am Morgen)* **heute/gestern** ~: this/yesterday morning; **[am] Sonntag** ~: on Sunday morning
[1]**Morgen das; das** ~: the future
[2]**Morgen der;** ~**s,** ~ **a)** morning; **am** ~, *(geh.)* **des** ~**s** in the morning; **am folgenden** *od.* **nächsten** ~: next *or* the following morning; **früh am** ~, **am frühen** ~: early in the morning; **am** ~ **seiner Abreise** on the morning of his departure; **eines [schönen]** ~**s** one [fine] morning; **bis in den [frühen]** ~ **feiern/arbeiten** celebrate/work until the early hours; **gegen** ~: towards morning; ~ **für** ~: every single morning; morning after morning; **es wird** ~: day *or* dawn is breaking; **sie gingen erst, als es bereits** ~ **wurde** they didn't go until it was already becoming daylight; **den ganzen** ~: all morning; **guten** ~! good morning!; ~! *(ugs.)* morning! *(coll.)*; **[jmdm.] guten** ~ **sagen** *od.* **wünschen** say good morning [to sb.]; wish [sb.] good morning; *(grüßen)* say hello [to sb.]; **schön** *od.* **frisch wie der junge** ~ *(scherzh.)* fresh as a daisy; **b)** *(fig. geh.)* **der** ~ **des Lebens** the springtide of life *(literary)*; **der** ~ **der Freiheit/eines neuen Zeitalters** the dawn of liberty/of a new age; **c)** *o. Pl. (geh. veralt.)* east; **gen** ~: towards the east; **d)** *(veralt.: Feldmaß)* ≈ acre; **fünf** ~ **Land** five acres of land
Morgen-: ~**andacht die** morning service; ~**aus·gabe die** morning edition; ~**dämmerung die** dawn; daybreak; **in der** ~**dämmerung** at daybreak
morgendlich *Adj.; nicht präd.* morning; **die** ~**e Kühle/Stille** the cool/peace of [early] morning; **der** ~**e Sturm aufs Badezimmer** *(scherzh.)* the fight for the bathroom every morning
morgen-, Morgen-: ~**frühe die** early morning; ~**gabe die** *(hist.) husband's present to wife on morning after wedding night;* ~**gebet das** morning prayer; ~**grauen das** daybreak; **im** *od.* **beim** ~**grauen** in the first light of day; ~**gymnastik die** morning exercises *pl.*; daily dozen *(coll.)*; ~**kaffee der a)** *(Mahlzeit)* light breakfast with coffee; **b)** *(Kaffee)* breakfast coffee; ~**land das** *(veralt.)* **das** ~**land** the East; the Orient; ~**ländisch** *(veralt.)* **1.** *Adj.* oriental; eastern; **2.** *adv.* in an oriental style *or* fashion; ~**licht das;** *o. Pl.* morning light; **beim ersten** ~**licht** in the first light of day; ~**luft die** morning air; ~**luft wittern** *(fig. scherzh.)* see one's chance; ~**mantel der** dressing-gown; ~**muffel der** *(ugs.)* **ein** ~**muffel sein** be grumpy in the mornings; ~**nebel der** morning fog; *(weniger dicht)* morning mist; ~**post die** morning post; ~**rock der** dressing-gown; ~**rot das,** ~**röte die** *(geh.)* rosy dawn; *(tiefer)* red dawn; *(fig.)* dawn
morgens *Adv.* in the morning; *(jeden Morgen)* every morning; ~ **um 7 Uhr, um 7 Uhr** ~: at 7 in the morning/every morning; **Dienstag** *od.* **dienstags** ~: on Tuesday morning[s]; **von** ~ **bis abends** all day long; from morning to evening
Morgen-: ~**sonne die** morning sun; ~**sonne haben** get the morning sun; ~**spaziergang der** *(esp. early)* morning walk; ~**stern der a)** morning star; **b)** *(hist.)* spiked mace; *(mit Kette)* nail-studed flail; ~**stunde die** hour of the morning; **die frühen** ~**stunden** the early *or* small hours [of the morning]; ~**stunde hat Gold im Munde** *(Spr.)* the early bird catches the worm *(prov.)*; ~**zeitung die** morning paper
morgig *Adj.; nicht präd.* tomorrow's; **der** ~**e Tag** tomorrow
moribund [mori'bʊnt] *Adj. (Med., auch fig.)* moribund
Moritat ['mo:rita:t] **die;** ~, ~**en** *(usually gruesome)* street ballad
Moritz ['mo:rɪts] *in* **wie sich der kleine** ~ **das vorstellt** *(ugs. scherzh.)* as some Simple Simon might imagine it
Mormone [mɔr'mo:nə] **der;** ~**n,** ~**n, Mormonin die;** ~, ~**nen** Mormon
Morph [mɔrf] **das;** ~**s,** ~**e** *(Sprachw.)* morph
Morphem [mɔr'fe:m] **das;** ~**s,** ~**e** *(Sprachw.)* morpheme
Morpheus ['mɔrfɔys] **(der)** *(Myth.)* Morpheus
Morphin [mɔr'fi:n] **das;** ~**s** *(Chemie, Med.) s.* **Morphium**
Morphinismus der; ~ *(Med.)* morphinism *no art.*; morphine addiction *no art.*
Morphinist der; ~**en,** ~**en, Morphinistin die;** ~, ~**nen** morphine addict
Morphium ['mɔrfi̯ʊm] **das;** ~**s** morphine
Morphium·sucht die; *o. Pl.*: *s.* **Morphinismus**
morphium·süchtig *Adj.* addicted to morphine *pred.*
Morphologie [mɔrfolo'gi:] **die;** ~ *(Biol., Sprachw.)* morphology
morphologisch *(Biol., Sprachw.)* **1.** *Adj.* morphological. **2.** *adv.* morphologically
morsch [mɔrʃ] *Adj. (auch fig.)* rotten; brittle ‹*bones*›; crumbling ‹*rock, masonry*›
Morse-: ~**alphabet das** Morse code *or* alphabet; ~**apparat der** Morse telegraph
morsen ['mɔrzn̩] **1.** *itr. V.* send a message/messages in Morse. **2.** *tr. V.* send ‹*signal, message*› in Morse
Mörser ['mœrzɐ] **der;** ~**s,** ~ *(auch Milit.)* mortar
Morse·zeichen das Morse symbol
Mortadella [mɔrta'dɛla] **die;** ~, ~**s** mortadella
Mortalität [mɔrtali'tɛ:t] **die;** ~: mortality [rate]
Mörtel ['mœrtl̩] **der;** ~**s** mortar
Mosaik [moza'i:k] **das;** ~**s,** ~**en** *od.* ~**e** *(auch fig.)* mosaic; **mit** ~**en ausgelegt** covered in mosaics
Mosaik-: ~**[fuß]boden der** mosaic floor; ~**stein der** tessera; *(fig.)* piece of a jigsaw
mosaisch [mo'za:ɪʃ] *(Rel.)* **1.** *Adj.* Mosaic ‹*Law*›; Jewish ‹*faith*›. **2.** *adv.* in the Jewish faith
Mosambik [mozam'bi:k] **(das);** ~**s** Mozambique

Moschee [mɔ'ʃe:] die; ~, ~n mosque
Moschus ['mɔʃʊs] der; ~: musk
Moschus·ochse der musk-ox
Mose ['mo:zə] (der); ~[s] (Rel.) Moses; die fünf Bücher ~: the Pentateuch
Möse ['mø:zə] die; ~, ~n (vulg.) cunt (coarse)
Mosel ['mo:zl̩] die; ~: Moselle
Mosel der; ~s, ~, **Mosel·wein** der Moselle [wine]
Möser ['mø:zɐ] s. Moos c
mosern ['mo:zɐn] itr. V. (ugs.) gripe (coll.) (über + Akk. about); du findest aber auch an allem etwas zu ~: you always manage to find something to complain about (coll.)
¹Moses der; ~, ~ (Seemannsspr.) ship's boy
²Moses (der) Moses; die fünf Bücher Mosis (Rel.) the Pentateuch
Moskau ['mɔskau] (das); ~s Moscow
Moskauer 1. indekl. Adj. Moscow attrib. 2. der; ~s, ~: Muscovite; s. auch Kölner
Moskauerin die; ~, ~en Muscovite
Moskito [mɔs'ki:to] der; ~s, ~s mosquito
Moskito·netz das mosquito-net
Moskowiter [mɔsko'vi:tɐ] der; ~s, ~ (veralt.) Muscovite
moskowitisch [mɔsko'vi:tɪʃ] Adj. (veralt.) Muscovite
Moslem ['mɔslɛm] der; ~s, ~s Muslim
moslemisch 1. Adj. Muslim; Islamic ⟨Republic⟩. 2. adv. on Muslim principles; ~ erzogen brought up in the Muslim faith
Moslime [mɔs'li:mə] die; ~, ~n Muslim woman/girl
Most [mɔst] der; ~[e]s, ~e a) (südd.: junger Wein) new wine; b) (Weinbasis) must; c) (südd.: Obstsaft) [cloudy fermented] fruit-juice; d) (südd., schweiz., österr.: Obstwein) fruit-wine; (Apfel~) [rough] cider
Most·apfel der [sour] cider apple
Mostert ['mɔstɐt] der; ~s (nordwestd.), **Mostrich** ['mɔstrɪç] der; ~s (nordostd.) mustard
Motel ['mo:tl̩] das; ~s, ~s motel
Motette [mo'tɛtə] die; ~, ~n (Musik) motet
Motion [mo'tsio:n] die; ~, ~en a) (schweiz.) motion (Gen. by); b) (Sprachw.) change of form determined by gender
Motiv [mo'ti:f] das; ~s, ~e a) motive; das ~ einer Tat the motive for an action; b) (Literaturw., Musik usw.: Thema) motif; theme; (bild. Kunst: Gegenstand) subject
Motivation [motiva'tsio:n] die; ~, ~en (Psych., Päd.) motivation
Motiv·forschung die motivation research
motivieren tr. V. (geh.) a) (begründen) give a [sufficient] reason for; eine Entscheidung/sein Verhalten ~: account for a decision/one's behaviour; b) (anregen) motivate
Motivierung die; ~, ~en (geh.) motivation
Moto-Cross [moto'krɔs] das; ~, ~e a) o. Pl. (Sport) [das] ~: moto-cross no pl.; b) (Veranstaltung) moto-cross event or meeting
Motodrom [moto'dro:m] das; ~s, ~e autodrome; speedway (Amer.)
Motor ['mo:tɔr] der; ~s, ~en (Verbrennungs~) engine; (Elektro~) motor; (fig.) driving force (Gen. behind)
Motor-: ~block der (Kfz-W.) engine block; cylinder block; ~boot das motor boat; (im Gegensatz zum Segelboot) power boat
Motoren-: ~geräusch das sound of the engine/engines; ~lärm der engine noise
Motor-: ~fahrzeug das motor vehicle; ~flug der [powered] flying (as a sport); ~haube die (Kfz-W.) bonnet (Brit.); hood (Amer.)
-motorig adj. -engined; ein~/zwei~: single-engined/twin-engined
Motorik [mo'to:rɪk] die; ~ a) (bes. Med.) motor functions pl.; b) (Lehre) study of motor functions
Motoriker der; ~s, ~ (Psych.) motor-minded [psychological] type
motorisch Adj. a) (Psych.) motor attrib.; b) (Kfz-W.) with regard to the engine postpos., not pred.
motorisieren 1. tr. V. motorize; (mit Maschinen ausrüsten) mechanize; ein Boot ~: fit a boat with an engine; motorisierte Besucher visitors with cars; sind Sie motorisiert? (ugs.) have you got any wheels? (coll.). 2. refl. V. get a car/motor cycle; get oneself wheels (coll.)
Motorisierung die; ~: s. motorisieren 1: motorization; mechanization
Motor-: ~jacht die motor yacht; ~leistung die (Kfz-W.) engine performance; (PS) power output; ~öl das (Kfz-W.) engine oil; ~rad das motor cycle
Motorrad-: ~brille die motor-cycling goggles; ~fahrer der motor-cyclist; ~rennen das motor-cycle race; (Sport) motor-cycle racing; ~sport motor-cycling
Motor-: ~raum der (Kfz-W.) engine compartment; ~roller der motor scooter; ~säge die power saw; ~schaden der engine trouble no indef. art.; (Panne) mechanical breakdown; ~schiff das motor ship or vessel; ~schlitten der motor rized sledge; ~sport der motor sport no art.; ~wäsche die engine wash-down
Motte ['mɔtə] die; ~, ~n a) moth; von etw. angezogen werden wie die ~en vom Licht be attracted by sth. as moths to the light; [ach,] du kriegst die ~n! (ugs.) my godfathers!; die ~n haben (salopp veralt.) have TB; b) (salopp veralt.: Mädchen) chick (sl.); flotte od. tolle ~: smasher (sl.); kesse ~: saucy or pert little miss (coll.)
motten-, Motten-: ~echt, ~fest Adj. moth-proof; ~fraß der moth [damage]; ~kiste die a) (veralt.) moth-proof chest; b) (fig.) Filme/Geschichten/Gags aus der ~kiste ancient films/stories/gags; ~kugel die moth-ball; ~pulver das moth-powder; ~zerfressen Adj. moth-eaten
Motto ['mɔto] das; ~s, ~s motto; (Schlagwort) slogan; der Kirchentag stand unter dem ~: ... the motto of the church assembly was ...; nach dem ~: ... leben live according to the maxim: ...
motzen ['mɔtsn̩] itr. V. (ugs.) grouch (coll.), bellyache (sl.) (über + Akk. about); was hast du schon wieder zu ~? what are you bellyaching about now? (sl.)
motzig (ugs.) 1. Adj. grouchy (coll.); grumpy. 2. adv. grouchily (coll.); grumpily
Mousse [mʊs] die; ~, ~s (Kochk.) mousse
moussieren [mʊ'si:rən] itr. V. sparkle; (als Eigenschaft) be sparkling; ~der Wein sparkling wine
Möwe ['mø:və] die; ~, ~n gull
Mozart·zopf ['mo:tsart-] der bag wig
MP ['ɛm'pi:] die; ~, ~s Abk. a) Maschinenpistole sub-machine-gun; b) Militärpolizei MPs pl.; military police pl.
Mrd. Abk. Milliarde bn.
m.s., MS Abk. multiple Sklerose MS
Ms., MS Abk. Manuskript MS
MS Abk. Motorschiff MV; MS (Amer.)
MTA [ɛmte:'|a:] die; ~, ~[s] Abk. medizinisch-technische Assistentin medical-laboratory assistant
mtl. Abk. monatlich mthly.
Mücke ['mʏkə] die; ~, ~n a) midge; gnat; (größer) mosquito; aus einer ~ einen Elefanten machen (ugs.) make a mountain out of a molehill; die ~ machen (salopp) push off (sl.); b) Pl. (salopp: Geld) bread (sl.); lolly (Brit. sl.)
Muckefuck ['mʊkəfʊk] der; ~s (ugs.) coffee substitute
mucken ['mʊkn̩] itr. V. (ugs.) grumble; mutter; ohne zu ~: without a murmur
Mucken Pl. (ugs.) whims; (Eigenarten) little ways or peculiarities; (Launen) moods; [seine] ~ haben ⟨person⟩ have one's little ways/one's moods; ⟨car, machine⟩ be a little unpredictable or temperamental; jmdm. seine ~ austreiben sort sb. out (coll.)
Mücken·stich der midge/mosquito bite
Mucker der; ~s, ~ (ugs. abwertend) yes-man
Muckertum das (ugs. abwertend) being no art. a yes-man (coll.)
Mucks [mʊks] der; ~es, ~e (ugs.) murmur [of protest]; slight[est] sound; keinen ~ sagen od. von sich geben not utter a [single] word or sound; die Kinder gaben keinen ~ von sich there was not the slightest sound/murmur out of the children
mucksen refl. V. (ugs.) a) (meist negativ) make a sound; (sich rühren) stir; budge; sie wagten nicht, sich zu ~: they didn't dare to budge [an inch]/make a sound; b) (aufbegehren) object; make noises (coll.)
Muckser der; ~s, ~ (ugs.) s. Mucks
mucks·mäuschen·still (ugs.) 1. Adj.; nicht attr. utterly silent; ⟨person⟩ as quiet as a mouse postpos.; es wurde ~: you could have heard a pin drop. 2. adv. in total silence; without making a sound
Mud[d] [mʊt] der; ~s (nordd.) mud
müde ['my:də] 1. Adj. tired; (ermattet) weary; (schläfrig) sleepy; mit ~n Schritten with weary steps; ich war zum Umfallen ~: I was out on my feet; Bier macht ~: beer makes you feel sleepy; sich ~ laufen/weinen tire oneself out with walking/crying; ein ~s Lächeln (auch fig.) a weary smile; jmdn./etw. od. jmds./einer Sache ~ sein (geh.) be tired of sb./sth.; jmds./einer Sache (Gen.) ~ werden (geh.) tire or grow tired of sb./sth.; nicht ~ werden, etw. zu tun never tire of doing sth.; (bei unangenehmer Tätigkeit) never stop doing sth.; s. auch ¹Mark. 2. adv. wearily; (schläfrig) sleepily
-müde adj. tired of ...; amts~/kino~/stadt~: tired of [holding] office/[going to] the cinema/city life postpos.
Müdigkeit die; ~: tiredness; ~/eine tiefe ~ kam über ihn he began to feel tired/a great weariness come over him; von ~ übermannt werden be overcome by fatigue; ich könnte vor ~ umfallen I'm so tired I can hardly stand; [nur] keine ~ vorschützen! (ugs.) it's no use saying you're tired!
-müdigkeit die weariness of ...; Zivilisations~: weariness of civilized living; culture fatigue; Kriegs~: war-weariness
Müesli ['my:ɛsli] das; ~s (schweiz.) s. Müsli
¹Muff [mʊf] der; ~[e]s (nordd.) musty smell; (Gestank) fug
²Muff der; ~[e]s, ~e muff
Muffe die; ~, ~n a) (Technik) sleeve; (Verbindungsstück) sleeve [coupling]; b) (fig.) jmdm. geht die ~ (salopp) sb. is shaking in his shoes; ~ haben (salopp) be in a funk (sl.) (vor + Dat. about)
Muffel ['mʊfl̩] der; ~s, ~ (ugs.) a) sourpuss (coll.); grouch (coll.); b) (desinteressierter Mensch) was ... betrifft, ist er ein [richtiger] ~: as far as ... is concerned he's just not interested
-muffel der; ~s, ~ (ugs.) person indifferent to ..
muffelig (ugs.) 1. Adj. grumpy; surly; du bist aber ~ heute! you 'are in a bad mood today! 2. adv. grumpily
¹muffeln (ugs.) 1. itr. V. be grumpy or in a huff. 2. tr., itr. V. mutter [grumpily]; grunt
²muffeln itr. V. (südd., österr.: muffig riechen) smell musty
Muffen·sausen das (salopp) ~ haben/kriegen be/get in a funk (sl.) (vor + Dat. about)
¹muffig Adj. (modrig riechend) musty; (stickig; auch fig.) stuffy
²muffig (ugs.) s. muffelig
Muffigkeit die; ~ (ugs.) grumpiness; surliness
Mufflon ['mʊflɔn] der; ~s, ~s (Zool.) mouflon

Mufti ['mʊfti] **der; ~s, ~s** mufti

Mugel ['mu:gl] **der; ~s, ~[n]** *(österr.)* hillock; *(auf der Skipiste)* mogul

muh [mu:] *Interj. (Kinderspr.)* moo

Müh [my:] *s.* Mühe

Mühe ['my:ə] **die; ~, ~n** trouble; **alle ~ haben, etw. zu tun** be hard put to do sth.; **mit jmdm./etw. seine ~ haben** have a lot of trouble *or* a hard time with sb./sth.; **die ~ hat sich gelohnt** it was worth the trouble *or* effort; **keine ~ scheuen** spare no pains *or* effort; **sich** *(Dat.)* **viel ~ machen** go to *or* take a lot of trouble **(mit** over); **machen Sie sich [bitte] keine ~!** *(tun Sie es nicht)* [please] don't put yourself out!; [please] don't bother!; **wenn es dir keine ~ macht, ...:** if it's no trouble *or* bother, ...; **es hat viel ~ gekostet** it took much time and effort; **die ~ kannst du dir sparen** you can save yourself the trouble; **sich** *(Dat.)* **~ geben[, etw. zu tun]** make an effort *or* take pains [to do sth.]; **sich** *(Dat.)* **mit jmdm./etw. ~ geben** take [great] pains *or* trouble over sb./sth.; **wenn du dir mehr ~ geben würdest** if you would take more trouble/try harder; **gib dir doch etwas ~!** do make some sort of an effort!; **gib dir keine ~!** you needn't bother; **mit Müh und Not** with great difficulty; only just; **der** *(Gen.) od.* **die ~ wert sein** be worth the trouble *or* worth it; **wäre es der ~ wert, nach X zu fahren?** would it be worth [while] going to X?

mühelos 1. *Adj.* effortless. **2.** *adv.* effortlessly; without the slightest difficulty

Mühelosigkeit die; ~: effortlessness

muhen *itr. V.* moo

mühen *refl. V. (geh.)* strive; **sich mit etw. ~:** take pains over sth.; **sosehr er sich auch mühte** hard though he tried

mühe·voll *Adj.* laborious; painstaking ⟨*work*⟩; **ein ~er Weg** an arduous path

Mühewaltung [-valtʊŋ] **die; ~** *(Papierdt.)* efforts *pl.*; *(im Brief)* **für Ihre ~ dankend** thanking you for your trouble

Muh·kuh die *(Kinderspr.)* moo-cow *(child lang.)*

Mühl·bach der mill-stream

Mühle ['my:lə] **die; ~, ~n a)** mill; **in die ~ der Justiz geraten** *(fig.)* become enmeshed in the wheels *or* machinery of justice; **das ist Wasser auf seine ~** *(ugs.)* it's [all] grist to his mill; it just confirms what he has always thought; *s. auch* **Gott; b)** *(Kaffee~)* [coffee-] grinder; **c)** *(Spiel) o. Art., o. Pl.* nine men's morris; **d)** *(Figur beim ~spiel)* mill; **e)** *(ugs. abwertend) (Auto, Motorrad)* heap *(coll.)*; *(Auto, Flugzeug)* crate *(coll.)*; *(Fahrrad)* rattletrap; boneshaker

Mühle·spiel das nine men's morris

Mühl-: ~rad das mill-wheel; **~stein der** millstone

Muhme ['mu:mə] **die; ~, ~n** *(veralt.)* aunt

Mühsal ['my:za:l] **die; ~, ~e** *(geh.)* tribulation; *(Strapaze)* hardship; *(Arbeit)* toil *no pl.*

mühsam 1. *Adj.* laborious; **ein ~es Lächeln** a forced smile. **2.** *adv.* laboriously; *(schwierig)* with difficulty; **~ verdientes Geld** hard-earned money

müh·selig *(geh.)* **1.** *Adj.* laborious; arduous ⟨*journey, life*⟩; **... alle, die ihr ~ und beladen seid** *(bibl.)* ... all ye that labour and are heavy laden. **2.** *adv.* with [great] difficulty

Müh·seligkeit die *(geh.)* laboriousness; *(einer Reise, des Lebens)* arduousness

Mulatte [mu'latə] **der; ~n, ~n, Mulattin die; ~, ~nen** mulatto

Mulde ['mʊldə] **die; ~, ~n a)** hollow; **b)** *(Trog)* trough

Muli ['mu:li] **das; ~s, ~s** mule

[1]Mull [mʊl] **der; ~[e]s** *(Stoff)* mull; *(Verband~)* gauze

[2]Mull der; ~[e]s, ~e *(nordd.: Humus)* mull

Müll [myl] **der; ~s a)** refuse; rubbish; garbage *(Amer.)*; trash *(Amer.)*; *(Industrie~)* [industrial] waste; **etw. in den ~ werfen** throw sth. in the dustbin *(Brit.) or (Amer.)* garbage can; **„~ abladen verboten"** 'no dumping'; 'no tipping' *(Brit.)*; **b)** *(alte Sachen)* rubbish; junk

Müll-: ~abfuhr die a) refuse *or (Amer.)* garbage collection; **b)** *(Unternehmen)* refuse *or (Amer.)* garbage collection [service]; **~ablade·platz der** [refuse] dump *or (Brit.)* tip; **~auto das** *s.* **~wagen; ~beutel der** dustbin *(Brit.) or (Amer.)* garbage can liner

Mull·binde die gauze bandage

Müll-: ~deponie die *(Amtsspr.)* refuse disposal site; **~eimer der** rubbish *or* waste bin; **~entsorgung die** refuse disposal

Müller ['mylɐ] **der; ~s, ~:** miller

Müller·bursche der *(veralt.)* miller's lad

Müllerin die; ~, ~nen *(veralt.)* miller's wife

Müll-: ~fahrer der dust-cart *(Brit.) or (Amer.)* garbage truck driver; **~halde die** refuse dump; **~haufen der** heap of rubbish *or (Amer.)* garbage; **~kippe die** *s.* **Müllabladeplatz; ~mann der;** *Pl.* **~männer** *(ugs.)* dustman *(Brit.)*; garbage man *(Amer.)*; **~sack der** refuse bag; **~schippe die** dustpan; **~schlucker der** rubbish *or (Amer.)* garbage chute; **~tonne die** dustbin *(Brit.)*; garbage *or* trash can *(Amer.)*; **~tüte die** bin bag; **~verbrennung die** refuse *or (Amer.)* garbage incineration; **~verbrennungs·anlage die** refuse *or (Amer.)* garbage incinerator; **~verwertung die** refuse *or (Amer.)* garbage recycling; **~wagen der** dust-cart *(Brit.)*; garbage truck *(Amer.)*; **~werker der** *(Berufsbez.)* refuse *or (Amer.)* garbage operative

Mull·windel die muslin nappy *(Brit.) or (Amer.)* diaper

mulmig ['mʊlmɪç] *Adj.* **a)** *(ugs.: bedenklich)* ticklish; tricky; *(unbehaglich)* uncomfortable; **als es ~ wurde** when things began to look nasty; **b)** *(ugs.: übel) (im Magen)* queasy; *(unbehaglich)* uneasy; **ein ~es Gefühl haben** feel queasy/uneasy; **mir war ganz ~ zumute** I felt quite weak at the knees; **c)** *(faulig)* rotten

Multi ['mʊlti] **der; ~s, ~s** *(ugs.)* multinational

multi-, Multi-: multi⟨*lateral, -lingual, -millionaire, -national*⟩

Multi·halle die multi-purpose hall

multi·medial 1. *Adj.* multi-media *attrib.*; **~medialer Unterricht** teaching with multi-media material. **2.** *adv.* on a multi-media basis

Multimedia- [-'me:dia]: **~-Show die** multi-media presentation; **~system das** *(Päd.)* multi-media method

multipel [mʊl'ti:pl] *Adj.; nicht präd. (bes. Fachspr.)* multiple; **multiple Sklerose** *(Med.)* multiple sclerosis

Multiple-choice-Verfahren ['mʌltɪpl'tʃɔɪs-] **das** *(Psych., Päd.)* multiple-choice method; **Prüfungen nach dem ~:** examinations using multiple-choice tests

Multiplikand [mʊltipli'kant] **der; ~en, ~en** *(Math.)* multiplicand

Multiplikation [mʊltiplika'tsio:n] **die; ~, ~en** *(Math.)* multiplication

Multiplikator [mʊltipli'ka:tɔr] **der; ~s, ~en** [-'to:rən] **a)** *(Math.)* muliplier; **b)** *(fig.)* disseminator *(of information, opinions)*

multiplizieren [mʊltipli'tsi:rən] **1.** *tr. V. (Math., fig.)* multiply **(mit** by). **2.** *refl. V. (fig.)* multiply [several times]

Mumie ['mu:miə] **die; ~, ~n** mummy

mumienhaft 1. *Adj.* mummy-like. **2.** *adv* like a mummy; as though mummified

Mumifikation [mumifika'tsio:n] **die; ~, ~en** mummification

mumifizieren [mumifi'tsi:rən] *tr. V.* mummify

Mumifizierung die; ~, ~en mummification

Mumm [mʊm] **der; ~s** *(ugs.) (Mut)* guts *pl. (coll.)*; spunk *(coll.)*; *(Tatkraft)* drive; zap *(sl.)*; *(Kraft)* muscle-power; *s. auch* **Knochen a**

Mummel·greis ['mʊml-] **der** *(ugs. abwertend)* old dodderer; doddery old man

Mümmel·mann ['myml-] **der;** *Pl.* **~männer** *(fam. scherzh.)* hare

[1]mummeln *tr., refl. V. (fam.)* **jmdn./sich in eine Decke ~:** wrap sb./oneself [up] snugly in a blanket

[2]mummeln *(nordd.)*, **mümmeln** *tr., itr. V. (fam.) (kauen)* chew; *(knabbern)* nibble

Mummenschanz ['mʊmənʃants] **der; ~es** *(veralt.)* **a)** *(Fest)* fancy-dress party *or* ball; **b)** *(Verkleidung)* fancy dress

Mumpf [mʊmpf] **der; ~s** *(schweiz.)* mumps *sing.*

Mumpitz ['mʊmpɪts] **der; ~es** *(ugs. abwertend)* rubbish; tripe *(sl.)*

Mumps [mʊmps] **der** *od.* **die; ~:** mumps *sing.*

München ['mʏnçn] **(das); ~s** Munich

Münch[e]ner ['mʏnçnɐ] **1.** *indekl. Adj.* Munich *attrib.* **2. der; ~s, ~:** inhabitant/native of Munich; *s. auch* **Kölner**

Münch[e]nerin die; ~, ~nen inhabitant/native of Munich

Mund [mʊnt] **der; ~[e]s, Münder** ['mʏndɐ] mouth; **seinen/den ~ verziehen** make a face; **seinen/den ~ spitzen** purse one's lips; **vor Staunen blieb ihm der ~ offenstehen** he gaped in astonishment; **er küßte ihren ~** *od.* **küßte sie auf den ~:** he kissed her on the lips; **den Finger auf den ~ legen** put one's finger to one's lips; **von ~ zu ~ beatmet werden** be given mouth-to-mouth resuscitation *or* the kiss of life; **aus dem ~ riechen** have bad breath; **mit vollem ~ sprechen** speak with one's mouth full; **etw. aus jmds. ~ hören** hear *or* have sth. from sb.'s [own] lips; **sein ~ steht nicht** *od.* **nie still** *(ugs.)* he never stops talking; **den ~ nicht aufbekommen** *od.* **aufkriegen** *(fig. ugs.)* not open one's mouth; have nothing to say for oneself; **den ~ aufmachen/nicht aufmachen** *(fig. ugs.)* say something/not say anything; **den ~ voll nehmen** *(fig. ugs.)* talk big *(coll.)*; **nimm doch den ~ nicht so voll!** don't be such a bighead!; **~ und Augen** *od.* **Nase aufreißen** *od.* **aufsperren** *(ugs.)* gape in astonishment; **einen großen ~ haben** *(fig. ugs.)* talk big *(coll.)*; **den** *od.* **seinen ~ halten** *(ugs.) (schweigen)* shut up *(coll.)*; *(nichts sagen)* not say anything; *(nichts verraten)* keep quiet **(über** + *Akk.* about); **jmdm. den ~ verbieten** silence sb.; **jmdm. den ~ [ganz] wäßrig machen** *(ugs.)* [really] make sb.'s mouth water; **er/sie ist nicht auf den ~ gefallen** *(fig. ugs.)* he's/she's never at a loss for words; **... ist in aller ~e** everybody's talking about ...; **etw./ein Wort in den ~ nehmen** utter sth./use a word; **jmdm. nach dem ~ reden** echo what sb. says; *(schmeichelnd)* butter sb. up; tell sb. what he/she wants to hear; **jmdm. über den ~ fahren** *(ugs.)* cut sb. short; **von ~ zu ~ gehen** be passed on from mouth to mouth; **sich** *(Dat.)* **etw. vom ~e absparen** scrimp and save for sth.; *s. auch* **[2]berufen a; fusselig; Hand f; stopfen 1 b; verbrennen 2 b**

Mund·art die dialect

Mundart-: ~dichter der dialect author; *(Lyriker)* dialect poet; **~dichtung die a)** *o. Pl.* dialect literature; **b)** *(Werk)* work [written] in dialect; **~forschung die;** *o. Pl.* dialectology; dialect research

mundartlich 1. *Adj.* dialectal ⟨*forms, expressions, words*⟩; ⟨*texts, poems, etc.*⟩ in dialect. **2.** *adv.* in dialect; **stark ~ gefärbt** strongly coloured by dialect

Mundart-: ~sprecher der dialect speaker; **~wörter·buch das** dialect dictionary

Mund·dusche die water pick

Mündel ['mʏndl] **das;** ~s, ~: ward
mündel·sicher *(Bankw.)* **1.** *Adj.* gilt-edged; trustee *attrib. (Amer.).* **2.** *adv.* in gilt-edged *or (Amer.)* trustee securities
munden *itr. V. (geh.)* taste good; **es mundete ihm nicht** he did not enjoy it; he did not like the taste of it; **das wird dir** ~: this will tickle your palate
münden ['mʏndn̩] *itr. V.; mit sein* ⟨*river*⟩ flow (**in** + *Akk.* into); ⟨*corridor, street, road*⟩ lead (**in** + *Akk. od. Dat.*, **auf** + *Akk. od. Dat.* into); **in eine/einer Frage** *usw.* ~ *(fig.)* ⟨*discussion*⟩ lead to a question *etc.*
mund-, Mund-: ~**falte die** line at the corner of the mouth; ~**faul** *(ugs.)* **1.** *Adj.* uncommunicative; **2.** *adv.* uncommunicatively; ~**fäule die** *(Med.)* ulcerative stomatitis; ~**gerecht 1.** *Adj.* bite-sized; *(fig.)* easily digestible ⟨*information*⟩; **2.** *adv.* ⟨*serve*⟩ in bite-sized pieces; ⟨*divided*⟩ into small mouthfuls; *(fig.)* in an easily digestible form; ~**geruch der** bad breath *no indef. art.;* ~**harmonika die** mouth-organ; ~**höhle die** oral cavity
mündig *Adj.* **a)** of age *pred.;* **drei** ~**e Töchter** three daughters who are of age; ~ **werden** come of age; **jmdn. für** ~ **erklären** declare sb. of age; **b)** *(urteilsfähig)* responsible adult *attrib.;* ~ **werden** become capable of mature judgement
mündig|sprechen *unr. tr. V.* declare of age
Mündig·sprechung die; ~, ~**en: jmds.** ~: the declaration that sb. is/was of age
mündlich 1. *Adj.* oral; ~**e Zusage** verbal agreement; ~**e Verhandlung** *(Rechtsw.)* hearing. **2.** *adv.* orally; ⟨*agree*⟩ verbally; **alles weitere** ~**!** *(im Brief)* I'll tell you the rest when we meet
Mund-: ~**öffnung die** *(Zool.)* oral aperture; ~**partie die** lower part of one's face; ~**pflege die** oral hygiene; ~**raub der** petty theft [of food/consumables]; ~**schenk** [~ʃɛŋk] **der;** ~**en,** ~**en** *(hist.)* cupbearer; ~**schutz der a)** *(Med.)* face-mask; **b)** *(Boxen)* gum-shield
M-und-S-Reifen ['ɛm ʊnt 'ɛs-] **der** snow tyre
mund-, Mund-: ~**stellung die** position of the mouth; ~**stück das a)** *(bei Instrumenten, Pfeifen usw.)* mouthpiece; **b)** *(bei Zigaretten)* tip; **c)** *(beim Zaumzeug)* bit; ~**tot** *Adj.* in **jmdn./eine Organisation** ~ **machen** silence sb./an organization; ~**tuch das;** *Pl.* ~**tücher** *(geh. veralt.)* [table-]napkin
Mündung die; ~, ~**en a)** mouth; *(größer)* estuary; **b)** *(bei Straßen)* end; **c)** *(bei Feuerwaffen)* muzzle
Mündungs·feuer das muzzle flash
Mund-: ~**verkehr der** oral sex; ~**voll der;** ~, ~: mouthful; ~**vorrat der** *(veralt.)* victuals *pl.;* ~**wasser das;** *Pl.* ~**wässer** mouthwash; ~**werk das;** *o. Pl. (ugs.)* **ein flinkes** ~**werk haben** talk nineteen to the dozen *(Brit.);* **ein loses** ~**werk [haben]** [have] a loose tongue; ~**winkel der** corner of one's mouth; ~**-zu-**~**-Beatmung die** mouth-to-mouth resuscitation; kiss of life; ~**-zu-Nase-Beatmung die** mouth-to-nose resuscitation
Munition [muni'tsi̯o:n] **die;** ~ *(auch fig.)* ammunition; **seine** ~ **verschossen haben** *(auch fig.)* have run out of ammunition
Munitions-: ~**depot das** ammunition dump; ~**fabrik die** munitions factory; ~**lager das** ammunition dump
Munkelei die; ~, ~**en** *(ugs.)* **a)** rumour-mongering; **b)** *(Gerücht[e])* rumour[s]
munkeln ['mʊŋkl̩n] *tr., itr. V. (ugs.)* **man munkelt so allerlei, es wird so allerlei gemunkelt** there are all kinds of rumours [flying about]; **es wird gemunkelt** *od.* **man munkelt, daß ...:** there is a rumour that ...
Münster ['mʏnstɐ] **das;** ~s, ~: minster; *(Dom)* cathedral; **das Straßburger** ~: Strasbourg Cathedral

munter ['mʊntɐ] **1.** *Adj.* **a)** cheerful; merry; *(lebhaft)* lively ⟨*eyes, game*⟩; ~ **werden** cheer up; liven up; **[gesund und]** ~ **sein** be as fit as a fiddle; ⟨*elderly person*⟩ be hale and hearty; **b)** *(wach)* awake; ~ **werden** wake up; come round *(joc.);* **jmdn.** ~ **machen** wake sb. up. **2.** *adv.* **a)** merrily; cheerfully; **b)** *(unbekümmert)* gaily; cheerfully
Munterkeit die; ~: cheerfulness; gaiety
Münz-: ~**anstalt die** mint; ~**automat der** slot-machine; *(Telefon)* payphone; pay station *(Amer.)*
Münze ['mʏntsə] **die;** ~, ~**n a)** coin; **klingende** *od.* **bare** ~ *(geh.)* cash; **etw. für bare** ~ **nehmen** *(fig.)* take sth. literally; **jmdm. [etw.] in** *od.* **mit gleicher** ~ **heimzahlen** pay sb. back in the same coin [for sth.]; **b)** *(Münzanstalt)* mint
Münz·einwurf der [coin] slot
münzen *tr. V.* coin; **auf jmdn./etw. gemünzt sein** *(fig.)* ⟨*remark etc.*⟩ be aimed at sb./sth.
Münzen·sammlung die coin collection
Münz-: ~**fälscher der** counterfeiter [of coins]; ~**fälschung die** counterfeiting [of coins]; ~**fern·sprecher der** coin-box telephone; payphone; pay station *(Amer.);* ~**fuß der** standard [for content] of coinage; ~**gewicht das** standard weight *(of a coin);* ~**hoheit die** coining prerogative *(of the State);* ~**kunde die** numismatics *sing.;* ~**recht das;** *o. Pl.* **a)** *s.* ~**hoheit; b)** *(~gesetze)* coinage laws *pl.;* ~**sammlung die** coin collection; ~**tank·stelle die** coin-in-the-slot petrol *(Brit.) or (Amer.)* gas station; ~**wechsler der** change machine; ~**wesen das;** *o. Pl.* coinage [system]; ~**zähler der** [slot-]meter
Muräne [mu'rɛ:nə] **die** moray eel
mürb [mʏrp] *(südd., österr.),* **mürbe** ['mʏrbə] *Adj.* **a)** crumbly ⟨*biscuit, cake, etc.*⟩; tender ⟨*meat*⟩; soft ⟨*fruit*⟩; mealy ⟨*apple*⟩; **das Fleisch** ~ **machen** tenderize the meat; **b)** *(brüchig)* crumbling; *(morsch)* rotten; ⟨*leather*⟩ worn soft; ~ **werden/sein** *(fig.: zermürbt)* get/be worn out; **jmdn.** ~ **machen** *(fig.)* wear sb. down
Mürbe·teig, *(südd., österr.)* **Mürb·teig der** short pastry
Murks [mʊrks] **der;** ~**es** *(salopp abwertend)* botch; mess; **das ist doch** ~**!** this is a right botch-up!; ~ **machen** make a botch *or* mess [of it]
murksen *itr. V. (salopp abwertend)* mess about (**an** + *Dat.* with); **bei einer Arbeit** ~: make a botch *or* mess of a job
Murmel ['mʊrml̩] **die;** ~, ~**n** marble; ~**n spielen** play [with] marbles
[1]**murmeln** *tr., itr. V.* **a)** mumble; mutter; *(sehr leise)* murmur; **etw. vor sich hin** ~: mutter *or* mumble/murmur sth. to oneself; **b)** *(dichter.)* ⟨*stream, fountain*⟩ murmur
[2]**murmeln** *itr. V. (Murmeln spielen)* play [with] marbles
Murmel·tier das marmot; *s. auch* **schlafen 1 a**
murren ['mʊrən] *itr. V.* grumble (**über** + *Akk.* about); **was hast du nun schon wieder zu** ~**?** what are you grumbling about now?; **ohne zu** ~: without a murmur
mürrisch ['mʏrɪʃ] **1.** *Adj.* grumpy; *(wortkarg)* surly; surly, sullen ⟨*expression*⟩. **2.** *adv.* grumpily; *(wortkarg)* sullenly
Mus [mu:s] **das** *od.* **der;** ~**es,** ~**e** purée; **zu** ~ **kochen** cook to a pulp; **jmdn./etw. zu** ~ **machen** *od.* **schlagen** *(salopp)* beat sb./sth. to a pulp
Muschel ['mʊʃl̩] **die;** ~, ~**n a)** mussel; **b)** *(Schale)* [mussel-]shell; **c)** *(am Telefon)* *(Hör~)* ear-piece; *(Sprech~)* mouthpiece; **d)** *(Ohr~)* [outer] ear
Muschel-: ~**bank die** mussel-bed; ~**kalk der** *(Geol.)* Muschelkalk
Muschi ['mʊʃi] **die;** ~, ~**s a)** *(Kinderspr.: Katze)* pussy[-cat]; **b)** *(salopp: Vulva)* pussy *(coarse)*

Muschkote [mʊʃ'ko:tə] **der;** ~**n,** ~**n** *(Soldatenspr. veralt., abwertend)* common soldier; squaddy *(Brit. sl.)*
Muse ['mu:zə] **die;** ~, ~**n** muse; **die leichte** ~: light [musical] entertainment; **von der** ~ **geküßt werden** *(scherzh.)* get some inspiration
museal [muze'a:l] *(geh.)* **1.** *Adj.* **a)** museum *attrib.;* of the museum *postpos.;* **b)** *(wie ein Museum, wie im Museum)* museum-like ⟨*building, appearance*⟩. **2.** *adv.* like a museum; in the style of a museum
Museen *s.* **Museum**
Muselman ['mu:zl̩man] **der;** ~**en,** ~**en, Muselmanin die;** ~, ~**nen, Musel·mann der;** *Pl.* ~**männer** *(veralt., noch scherzh.)* Muslim
Musen-: ~**almanach der** *(hist.) 18th/19th century annual anthology of mainly unpublished poetry;* ~**sohn der** *(veralt., noch scherzh.)* son of the Muses; ~**tempel der** *(veralt., noch scherzh.)* temple of the Muses
Museum [mu'ze:ʊm] **das;** ~s, **Museen** museum; **ins** ~ **gehen** go to a/the museum
museums-, Museums-: ~**aufseher der** museum attendant; ~**führer der** museum guide; ~**reif** *Adj. (ugs. iron.)* fit for a museum *postpos.;* **das ist wirklich** ~**reif** it's a real museum piece *or* positively antiquated; ~**stück das** *(auch fig. ugs. iron.)* museum piece; ~**wärter der** museum attendant; ~**wert der** *in* ~**wert haben** *(ugs.)* be a valuable museum piece; *(abwertend)* be positively antiquated *or* a museum piece
Musical ['mju:zɪkl] **das;** ~s, ~s musical
Music·box ['mju:zɪk-] **die;** ~, ~**en** *s.* **Musikbox**
Musik [mu'zi:k] **die;** ~, ~**en a)** *o. Pl.* music; **einen Text in** ~ **setzen** set a text to music; **die** ~ **lieben** like music; ~ **im Blut haben** have music in one's blood; ~ **in jmds. Ohren** *(Dat.)* **sein** *(fig. ugs.)* be music to sb.'s ears; **dahinter** *od.* **darin sitzt** *od.* **steckt** ~ *(fig. ugs.)* there is real power in it; **b)** *(Werk) Pl.:* ~**en** piece [of music]; *(Partitur)* score (**zu** for); **die** ~ **zu diesem Stück** the [incidental] music for this play; **c)** *(ugs.: Kapelle)* band; **d)** *(Gastr.) s.* **Handkäse**
Musikalien [muzi'ka:li̯ən] *Pl.* sheet music *sing.*
Musikalien·handlung die music shop
musikalisch [muzi'ka:lɪʃ] **1.** *Adj.* musical; **die** ~**e Leitung haben** be the musical director; *(als Dirigent)* be the conductor; ~**e Leitung: ...:** conducted by ... **2.** *adv.* musically; **er ist** ~ **veranlagt** he is musical
Musikalität [muzikali'tɛ:t] **die;** ~: musicality
Musikant [muzi'kant] **der;** ~**en,** ~**en** musician
Musikanten·knochen der funny-bone
musikantisch *(ugs.)* **1.** *Adj.* full of brio *postpos.;* with a swing to it *postpos.* **2.** *adv.* with brio
Musik-: ~**automat der a)** *(Spieluhr o. ä.)* mechanical instrument; **b)** *s.* ~**box;** ~**box die** juke-box; ~**direktor der** musical director; ~**drama das** music drama
Musiker der; ~s, ~, **Musikerin die;** ~, ~**nen** musician; **die Musiker stimmten ihre Instrumente** the players were tuning their instruments
musik-, Musik-: ~**erziehung die** *o. Pl.* musical education; ~**fest·spiele** *Pl.* music festival *sing.;* ~**freund der** music-lover; ~**geschichte die** history of music; **in die** ~**geschichte eingehen** find a place in musical history; ~**geschichtlich,** ~**historisch 1.** *Adj.* musico-historical; **2.** *adv.* in terms of the history of music; from the point of view of musical history; ~**hochschule die** academy *or* college of music; ~**instrument das** musical instrument; ~**kapelle die** band; ~**korps das** military band *(forming a separate unit);* ~**kritik die**

a) *o. Pl.* music criticism; **b)** *(Artikel)* music review; **~kritiker der** music critic; **~leben das** *o. Pl.* musical life; **~lehre die a)** *o. Pl.* musical theory *no art.*; **b)** *(Buch)* manual of musical theory; music textbook; **~lehrer der, ~lehrerin die** music-teacher; **~lexikon das** musical encyclopaedia; encyclopaedia of music; **~pädagogik die** [theory of] music-teaching; **~saal der a)** *(in der Schule)* music-room; **b)** *(Konzertsaal)* concert-hall; **~schule die** school of music; **~stück das** piece of music; **ein ~stück Chopins/von Chopin** a piece by Chopin; **~stunde die** music-lesson; **~theater das** *o. Pl.* music theatre *(where text and production are as important as the music)*; **~theorie die** *o. Pl.* **a)** *(theoretische Erfassung)* theory of music; **b)** *(Lehrfach)* musical theory *no art.*; **~therapie die** music therapy; **~truhe die** radiogram *(in a large cabinet)*; **~unterricht der a)** *o. Pl. (das Unterrichten)* music-teaching; **b)** *(Stunde)* music-lesson; *(Stunden)* music-lessons *pl.*; **c)** *(als Schulfach)* music; *s. auch* **Englischunterricht**

Musikus ['mu:zikʊs] **der;** ~, **Musizi** ['mu:zit͜si] *od.* **Musikusse** *(scherzh.)* musician

Musik-: ~verlag der music-publishers *pl.*; music-publishing house; **~werk das** musical work; composition; **~wissenschaft die** *o. Pl.* musicology; **~wissenschaftler der** musicologist

musisch 1. *Adj.* artistic ‹*talent, person, family, etc.*›; ‹*talent*› for the arts; ‹*education*› in the arts; **die ~en Fächer** art and music; **ein ~es Gymnasium:** *a* **Gymnasium** *specializing in teaching art and music.* **2.** *adv.* artistically; **~ veranlagt sein** have an artistic disposition

musizieren [muzi't͜si:rən] *itr. V.* play music; *(bes. unter Laien)* make music; **früher wurde viel mehr musiziert** there used to be a lot more music-making

Muskat [mʊs'ka:t] **der;** ~[e]s, ~e nutmeg

Muskateller [mʊska'tɛlɐ] **der;** ~s, ~: muscatel [wine]

Muskat·nuß die nutmeg

Muskel ['mʊskl̩] **der;** ~s, ~n muscle; **der hat vielleicht ~n!** *(ugs.)* he has quite some muscles *(coll.)*; he's really muscular; **~n bekommen** develop muscles; **seine ~n spielen lassen** flex one's muscles

Muskel-: ~atrophie die *(Med.)* muscular atrophy; **~faser die** muscle fibre; **~kater der** stiff muscles *pl.*; **~kater haben** be stiff and aching; **~kater in den Waden haben** have stiff calves; be stiff in one's calves; **~kraft die** muscle-power; **~krampf der** cramp; **~krämpfe/einen ~krampf bekommen** get cramp; **~mann der;** *Pl.* **~männer** *(ugs.)* muscleman; **~paket das** *(ugs.)* **a)** *(Muskeln)* bulging muscles *pl.* **b)** *s.* **~mann; ~protz der** *(ugs.)* muscleman; Tarzan *(joc.)*; **~riß der** torn muscle; **~schwund der** *(Med.)* muscular atrophy; **~zerrung die** *(Med.)* pulled muscle; **sich** *(Dat.)* **eine ~zerrung zuziehen** pull a muscle

Muskete [mʊs'ke:tə] **die;** ~, ~n *(hist.)* musket

Musketier [mʊske'ti:ɐ̯] **der;** ~s, ~e *(hist.)* musketeer

Muskulatur [mʊskula'tu:ɐ̯] **die;** ~, ~en musculature; muscular system

muskulös [mʊsku'lø:s] *Adj.* muscular

Müsli ['my:sli] **das;** ~s, ~s muesli

Muslim ['mʊslɪm] *s.* **Moslem**

muß [mʊs] *1. u. 3. Pers. Sg. Präsens v.* **müssen**

Muß das; ~: necessity; must *(coll.)*; **es ist kein ~:** it's not essential

Muß-Bestimmung die absolute *or* fixed rule

Muße ['mu:sə] **die;** ~: leisure; **dazu fehlt mir die ~:** I have no time to spare for it; **etw. in** *od.* **mit ~ tun** do sth. at one's leisure; take one's time over sth.

Muß·ehe die *(ugs.)* shotgun marriage

Musselin [mʊsə'li:n] **der;** ~s, ~e muslin

müssen ['mʏsn̩] **1.** *unr. Modalverb; 2. Part.* ~ **a)** *(gezwungen, verpflichtet, notwendig sein)* have to; **er muß es tun** he must do it; he has to *or (coll.)* has got to do it; **er muß es nicht tun** he does not have to do it; he has not got to do it *(coll.)*; **er mußte es tun** *od.* **hat es tun ~:** he had to do it; **du mußtest nicht kommen** you did not have to come; **muß er es tun?** must he do it?; does he have to *or (coll.)* has he got to do it?; **irgendwann muß es ja doch mal gemacht werden** after all, it's got to be done some time; **wir werden zurückkommen ~:** we shall have to come back; **heiraten ~** *(ugs.)* have to get married; **muß das jetzt sein?** does it have to be now?; **muß das sein?** it is really necessary?; *(Ärger über jmds. Verhalten ausdrückend)* do you have to?; **es muß nicht sein** it is not essential; **es muß ja nicht stimmen** it is not necessarily true; **so mußte es ja kommen** it was inevitable that it should come to this; it had to happen; **warum muß das ausgerechnet mir passieren?** why does it have to happen to me, of all people? **das muß man gesehen haben!** you mustn't miss ist!; it's not to be missed!; *(iron.)* it's a sight not to be missed!; **wir ~ Ihnen leider mitteilen, daß ...:** we regret to have to inform you that ...; **das muß man sich** *(Dat.)* **mal vorstellen!** just imagine!; **das muß 1968 gewesen sein** it must have been in 1968; **er muß gleich hier sein** he will be here *or* he is bound to be here at any moment; **b)** *2. Konjunktiv.* + *Inf.* **es müßte doch möglich sein** it ought to be possible; **das müßtest du eigentlich schon wissen** you really ought to *or* should know that by now; **so müßte es immer sein** it ought to be like this all the time; this is how it should always be; **reich müßte man sein!** how nice it would be to be rich!; all one needs is [plenty of] money!; **man müßte nochmals zwanzig sein** oh to be twenty again!; **c)** *verneint (nordd.: dürfen)* **du mußt nicht alles glauben, was er sagt** you must not believe everything he says. **2.** *unr. itr. V.* **a)** *(irgendwohin gehen müssen)* have to go; **ich muß zur Arbeit/nach Hause** I have to *or* must go to work/go home; **der Brief muß zur Post** the letter needs posting *or* taking to the post; **muß der Antrag heute zum Amt?** does the application have to be taken to the office today?; **ich muß mal** *(fam.)* I've got to *or* need to spend a penny *(Brit. coll.) or (Amer. coll.)* go to the john; **b)** *(gezwungen, verpflichtet sein)* **muß er?** does he have to?; has he got to? *(coll.)*; **er muß nicht** he doesn't have to *or (coll.)* hasn't got to; **kein Mensch muß ~:** nobody 'has to do 'anything; **c)** *(ugs.: an der Reihe sein)* **heute muß Peter** it's Peter's turn today

Muße·stunde die free hour; hour of leisure

müßig ['my:sɪç] **1.** *Adj.* **a)** idle ‹*person*›; ‹*hours, weeks, life*› of leisure; **b)** *(zwecklos)* pointless. **2.** *adv.* idly

Müßig-: ~gang der *o. Pl.* leisure; *(Untätigkeit)* idleness; **~gang ist aller Laster Anfang** *(Spr.)* the devil finds work for idle hands; **~gänger der** idler; **~gänger** *Pl.* people with time on their hands

Müßigkeit die; ~ *(geh.)* **a)** idleness; **b)** *(Zwecklosigkeit)* pointlessness

mußte ['mʊstə] *1. u. 3. Pers. Sg. Prät. v.* **müssen**

Mustang ['mʊstaŋ] **der;** ~s, ~s mustang

Muster ['mʊstɐ] **das;** ~s, ~ **a)** *(Vorlage)* pattern; **nach einem ~ stricken** knit from a pattern; **das ausgefüllte Formular dient als ~ für den Antragsteller** the form that is filled in is intended as a specimen for the applicant to follow; **nach diesem ~ arbeiten** *(fig.)* operate on these lines *or* on this model; **b)** *(Vorbild)* model **(an** + *Dat.* of); **er ist ein ~ an Fleiß** he is a model of industry; **er ist ein ~ von einem Ehemann** *(ugs.)* he is a model husband; **c)** *(Verzierung)* pattern; **~ entwerfen** produce designs; **in welchem ~ strickst du die Jacke?** which stitch are you using to knit the jacket?; **d)** *(Warenprobe)* sample; **unverkäufliches ~:** sample not for sale; *(veralt.: auf einer Warensendung)* **~ ohne Wert** sample with no commercial value

muster-, Muster-: ~beispiel das perfect example; *(Vorbild)* model; **ein ~beispiel dafür sein, wie ...:** be a perfect example of how ...; **~betrieb der** model enterprise; *(Fabrik)* model factory; **~buch das a)** *(Kunstwiss.: Motivsammlung)* pattern-book; **b)** *(mit Proben)* book of samples; pattern-book; **~ehe die** perfect *or* ideal marriage; **~exemplar das a)** *(oft iron.: Vorbild)* perfect specimen; **ein ~ von [einem] Sohn** a model son; **b)** *(Probeexemplar)* specimen copy; **~gültig 1.** *Adj.* exemplary; perfect, impeccable ‹*order*›; **2.** *adv.* in an exemplary fashion

musterhaft 1. *Adj.* exemplary; perfect, impeccable ‹*order, condition*›; model ‹*pupil*›. **2.** *adv.* in an exemplary fashion; **~ geführt** perfectly *or* impeccably run

Muster-: ~haus das show house; **~knabe der** *(oft abwertend)* model child; **~koffer der** case of samples; **~ländle** [~lɛndlə] **das,** ~s *(scherzh.) Baden-Württemberg, the 'model state' of the FRG*

mustern *tr. V.* **a)** *(betrachten)* eye; *(gründlich)* scrutinize; *(Milit.: inspizieren)* inspect ‹*troops*›; **jmdn. von Kopf bis Fuß** *od.* **von oben bis unten ~:** look sb. up and down; **b)** *(Milit.: ärztlich untersuchen)* **einen Wehrpflichtigen/den Jahrgang 1962 ~:** give somebody liable for military service his medical/give those born in 1962 their medicals

Muster-: ~prozeß der test case; **~schüler der, ~schülerin die** model pupil; **~sendung die** consignment of samples

Musterung die; ~, ~en **a)** *(das Betrachten)* scrutiny; *(Milit.: Inspektion)* inspection; **b)** *(Milit.: von Wehrpflichtigen)* medical examination; medical; **c)** *(Verzierung)* pattern

Musterungs·bescheid der summons to attend one's medical examination

Mut [mu:t] **der;** ~[e]s **a)** courage; **es gehört viel ~ dazu** it takes a lot of courage [to do it]; **allen** *od.* **all seinen ~ zusammennehmen** take one's courage in both hands; screw up one's courage; **sich** *(Dat.)* **~ antrinken** give oneself Dutch courage; **mit dem ~ der Verzweiflung** with courage born of desperation; **jmdm. ~ zusprechen** [try to] bolster up sb.'s courage; **sich gegenseitig ~ machen** keep each other's spirits up; **das gab** *od.* **machte ihr neuen ~:** that gave her new heart; **den ~ [nicht] sinken lassen** *od.* **verlieren** [not] lose heart; **[neuen] ~ fassen** take [new] heart; **nur ~!** don't lose heart!; *(trau dich)* be brave!; **b)** *(veralt.) in* **guten** *od.* **frohen ~es sein** be in good spirits; **mit frischem ~:** full of cheer *(dated)*; with a cheerful countenance *(formal)*

Mutation [muta't͜sio:n] **die;** ~, ~en *(Biol.)* mutation

Mütchen ['my:tçən] *in* **sein ~ [an jmdm.] kühlen** *(ugs. [scherzh.])* vent one's wrath [on sb.]

mutieren *itr. V. (Biol.)* mutate

mutig 1. *Adj.* brave; courageous, brave ‹*words, decision, speech*›; **dem Mutigen gehört die Welt** fortune favours the brave. **2.** *adv.* bravely; courageously

mut·los *Adj. (niedergeschlagen)* dejected; despondent; *(entmutigt)* disheartened; dispirited

Mut·losigkeit die; ~: dejection; despondency

mutmaßen ['mu:tma:sn̩] *tr., itr. V.* conjecture; ~, **daß ...**: suppose *or* surmise that ...; **darüber ist schon viel gemutmaßt worden** there has been much conjecture *or* speculation about that

mutmaßlich 1. *Adj.; nicht präd.* supposed; presumed; suspected ⟨*terrorist etc.*⟩. **2.** *adv.* *(geh.)* **es wird sich ~ noch verschlechtern** it is presumed it will get worse; **sie sind ~ ertrunken** they are presumed drowned

Mutmaßung die; ~, ~**en** conjecture

Mut·probe die test of courage

Muttchen ['mʊtçən] **das;** ~**s**, ~: *(ugs.)* **a)** *(Koseform)* mama; **b) [altes]** ~: little old lady; **c)** *(abwertend: biedere Frau)* good little housewife; *(mütterlicher Typ)* matronly sort *(coll.)*; motherly soul

[1]**Mutter** ['mʊtɐ] **die;** ~, **Mütter** ['mʏtɐ] **a)** mother; **sie wird ~** *(ist schwanger)* she is expecting a baby; **eine werdende ~**: an expectant mother; **eine ~ von drei Kindern** a mother of three; ~ **sein** be a mother; **grüßen Sie Ihre Frau ~!** remember me to your mother; **wie bei ~n** just like at home; ⟨*food*⟩ like mother makes/used to make; **die ~ Gottes** *(kath. Rel.)* the Mother of God; ~ **Erde/Natur** *(dichter.)* Mother Earth/Nature; **bei ~ Grün schlafen** *(ugs.)* sleep out in the open; **die ~ der Kompanie** *(Soldatenspr.)* the company sergeant-major; **b)** *(Wirtsch.:~gesellschaft)* parent company

[2]**Mutter die;** ~, ~**n** *(Schrauben~)* nut

Mütter·beratungs·stelle die advisory centre for [pregnant or nursing] mothers

Mutter-: ~**bindung die** *(Psych.)* attachment to the/one's mother; ~**boden der** topsoil; ~**brust die** mother's breast

Mütterchen ['mʏtɐçən] **das;** ~**s**, ~ **a)** *(Koseform)* mummy *(Brit. coll.)*; mommy *(Amer. coll.)*; **b) [altes]** ~: little old lady; **c)** *in* ~ **Rußland** Mother Russia

Mutter-: ~**erde die** *s.* ~**boden**; ~**freuden** *Pl.; in* ~ **entgegensehen** *(geh.)* be expecting a child

Mütter·genesungs·heim das convalescent home for mothers

Mutter-: ~**gesellschaft die** *(Wirtsch.)* parent company; ~**glück das** joys *pl.* of motherhood; ~**gottes** [--'--] **die** *(kath. Rel.)* mother of God; *(Bild)* Madonna

Mütter·heim das [residential] home for [unmarried] mothers and their children

Mutter-: ~**herz das** mother's heart; *(scherzh. Anrede)* mother [dear]; ~**instinkt der** maternal instinct; ~**komplex der** *(Psych.)* **a)** *(~bindung)* mother fixation; **b)** *(~instinkt)* [excessive] maternal instinct; mothering instinct; ~**korn das;** *Pl.* ~**korne** *(Bot.)* ergot; ~**kreuz das** *(ns.)* *medal awarded to prolific mothers (in the Nazi period)*; ~**kuchen der** *(Med.)* placenta; ~**land das** *Pl.* ~**länder a)** *(Kolonialstaat)* mother country; **b)** *(Heimat)* original home; motherland; ~**leib der** womb; *(Zool.)* uterus

mütterlich 1. *Adj.* **a)** *nicht präd. (von der Mutter)* his/her *etc.* mother's; *(verallgemeinernd)* the mother's; *(einer Mutter)* maternal ⟨*line, love, instincts, etc.*⟩; **die ~en Pflichten** the duties of a mother; **b)** *(fürsorglich)* motherly ⟨*woman, care*⟩. **2.** *adv.* in a motherly way

mütterlicher·seits *Adv.* on the/his/her *etc.* mother's side; **sein Großvater ~**: his maternal grandfather; his grandfather on his mother's side

Mütterlichkeit die; ~: motherliness; *(mütterliche Gefühle)* motherly feeling

mutter-, Mutter-: ~**liebe die** motherly love *no art.*; ~**los** *Adj.* motherless; ~**mal das;** *Pl.* ~**male** birthmark; ~**milch die** mother's milk; **etw. mit der ~milch einsaugen** *(fig.)* imbibe sth. with one's mother's milk; ~**mord der** matricide; ~**mund der** neck of the womb; cervix

Mütter·paß der *document carried by pregnant woman which gives details of her medical history, blood group, etc.*

Mutter-: ~**pflicht die** duty as a mother; maternal duty; ~**schaf das** mother ewe

Mutterschaft die; ~: motherhood

Mutterschafts-: ~**geld das** maternity benefit; ~**urlaub der** maternity leave

mutter-, Mutter-: ~**schiff das** mother ship; *(im Weltraum)* parent ship; ~**schutz der a)** *(Rechtsw.) laws pl. protecting working pregnant women and mothers of new-born babies;* **b)** *(ugs.: Urlaub)* maternity leave; ~**schwein das** mother sow; ~**seelen·allein** *Adj.; nicht attr.* all alone; all on my *etc.* own; ~**söhnchen das** *(abwertend)* mummy's *or (Amer.)* mama's boy; ~**sprache die** native language; mother tongue; ~**sprachler** [~ʃpra:xlɐ] **der;** ~**s**, ~ *(Sprachw.)* native speaker; ~**stelle die;** ~: **bei/an jmdm. ~stelle vertreten** take the place of a mother to sb.

Mütter·sterblichkeit die childbirth mortality

Mutter-: ~**stute die** dam; ~**tag der;** *o. Pl.* Mother's Day *no def. art.*; ~**tier das a)** *(Tier, das Junge hat)* mother [animal]; dam; **b)** *(Zuchttier)* brood animal; ~**witz der** *o. Pl.* **a)** *(Humor)* natural wit; **b)** *(Schläue)* native cunning

Mutti ['mʊti] **die;** ~, ~**s** mummy *(Brit. coll.)*; mum *(Brit. coll.)*; mommy *(Amer. coll.)*; mom *(Amer. coll.)*

mut-, Mut-: ~**wille der;** *o. Pl.* wilfulness; *(Übermut)* devilment; **aus [bloßem] ~n** from [sheer] devilment; ~**willig 1.** *Adj.* wilful; wanton ⟨*destruction*⟩; *(übermütig)* high-spirited; **2.** *adv.* wilfully; wantonly; *(aus Übermut)* from devilment; ~**willigkeit die;** ~: *s.* **Mutwille**

Mützchen das; ~**s**, ~**s** little cap

Mütze ['mʏtsə] **die;** ~, ~**n** cap; **etwas** *od.* **eins auf die ~ kriegen** *(fig. ugs.)* get told off; get a telling off; **eine ~ voll Schlaf** *(ugs.)* a nap; forty winks *pl.*

Mützen·schirm der peak of the/one's cap

MW *Abk.* **a)** *(Rundf.)* **Mittelwelle** MW; **b)** *(Physik)* **Megawatt** MW

Mw.-St., MwSt. *Abk.* **Mehrwertsteuer** VAT

mykenisch [my'ke:nɪʃ] *Adj.* Mycenaean

Mykologie [mykolo'gi:] **die;** ~: mycology *no art.*

Mykose [my'ko:zə] **die;** ~, ~**n** mycosis

Myom [my'o:m] **das;** ~**s**, ~**e** *(Med.)* myoma

Myriade [my'ri̯a:də] **die;** ~, ~**n** *(geh.)* myriad

Myrrhe ['myrə] **die;** ~, ~**n** myrrh

Myrte ['myrtə] **die;** ~, ~**n** myrtle

Myrten·kranz der myrtle wreath

Mysterien·spiel das miracle play

mysteriös [myste'ri̯ø:s] **1.** *Adj.* mysterious. **2.** *adv.* mysteriously

Mysterium [mys'te:ri̯ʊm] **das;** ~**s**, **Mysterien** mystery

Mystifikation [mystifika'tsi̯o:n] **die;** ~, ~**en** shrouding *no indef. art.* in mystery

mystifizieren [mystifi'tsi:rən] *tr. V.* shroud in mystery; *(unklar machen)* obfuscate

Mystifizierung die; ~, ~**en** *s.* **Mystifikation**

Mystik ['mystɪk] **die;** ~: mysticism

Mystiker der; ~**s**, ~, **Mystikerin die;** ~, ~**nen** mystic

mystisch 1. *Adj.* mystical. **2.** *adv.* mystically

Mystizismus [mysti'tsɪsmʊs] **der;** ~: mysticism

mythisch ['my:tɪʃ] *Adj.* **a)** mythical; ⟨*heroes, traditions*⟩ of myth [and legend], of mythology; **b)** *(legendär)* legendary

Mythologie [mytolo'gi:] **die;** ~, ~**n** mythology

mythologisch *Adj.* mythological

mythologisieren *tr. V.* mythologize

Mythos ['my:tɔs] **der;** ~, **Mythen a)** *(Sage, auch fig.: Unwahrheit)* myth; **b)** *(glorifizierte Person od. Sache)* legend

N

n, N [ɛn] **das;** ~, ~: n/N; *s. auch* **a, A**

N *Abk.* **Nord[en]** N

'n *s.* **ein; einen**

na [na] *Interj. (ugs.)* **a)** *(als Frage, Anrede, Aufforderung)* well; **na, wie geht's?** well, how are you?; **na, du?** oh, it's you?; **na los!** come on then!; **na, wird's bald?/wo bleibst du denn?** come on, aren't you ready yet?/what's happened to you?; **na und?** *(wennschon)* so what?; **b)** *(beschwichtigend)* **na, na, na!** now, now, come along; **c)** *([zögernd] zustimmend)* **na schön!, na gut!** oh, OK *(coll.)*; well, all right; **na ja, wenn du meinst** well [all right], if you think so; **na, dann bis später** right, see you later then; **d)** *(bekräftigend)* **na und ob!** and how! *(coll.)*; I'll say! *(coll.)*; **na, der wird schauen!** gosh, he'll get a surprise!; **na und wie!** and how! *(coll.)*; **na eben!** exactly!; **na dann!** oh, in 'that case!; **na endlich!** at last!; **e)** *(triumphierend)* **Na also! Ich hatte doch recht!** There you are! I was right!; **f)** *(zweifelnd, besorgt)* **na, wenn das mal gutgeht** *od.* **klappt** well, let's hope it'll be OK *(coll.)*; **na, wenn das dein Vater merkt!** oh dear, what if your father notices?; **g)** *(ablehnend)* **na, ich danke** you can keep it; **h)** *(unsicher)* **na, ich weiß nicht** hmm, I'm not sure; *(staunend)* **na so [et]was!** well I never!; **i)** *(konsterniert)* **na, was soll das denn?** now what's all this about?; **j)** *(drohend)* **na warte!** just [you] wait!; *(auf einen nicht Anwesenden bezogen)* just let him wait!

Nabe ['na:bə] **die;** ~, ~**n** hub

Nabel ['na:bl̩] **der;** ~**s**, ~: navel; **der ~ der Welt** *(geh.)* the hub of the universe

Nabel-: ~**binde die** umbilical bandage; ~**bruch der** *(Med.)* umbilical hernia; ~**schau die** *(salopp)* ~**schau halten** bare one's soul; **das Buch ist nichts als eine egozentrische ~schau** the book is nothing but a self-indulgent ego-trip *(coll.)*; ~**schnur die** *Pl.* ~**schnüre** umbilical cord

nach [na:x] **1.** *Präp. mit Dat.* **a)** *(räumlich)* to; ~ **Rom fahren** travel to Rome; **ist das der Zug ~ Köln?** is that the train for Cologne *or* the Cologne train?; **ja, der Zug fährt ~ Köln** yes, this train goes to Cologne; ~ **Hause gehen** go home; ~ **... abreisen** leave for ...; **sich ~ vorn/hinten beugen** bend forwards/backwards; **stell den Schrank weiter ~ hinten** put the cupboard further back; **komm ganz ~ vorn** come right to the front; ~ **links/rechts** to the left/right; ~ **der Seite** to the side; ~ **allen Richtungen** in all directions; ~ **Osten [zu]** eastwards; [towards the] east; ~ **... zu** towards ...; ~ **außen/innen** outwards/inwards; **ich bringe den Abfall ~ draußen** I am taking the rubbish outside; **ein Zimmer ~ der Straße** a room looking out on to *or* facing the street; **b)** *(zeitlich)* after; ~ **fünf Minuten** after five minutes; five minutes later; **zehn [Minuten] ~ zwei** ten [minutes] past two; **wird man noch ~ 100 Jahren daran denken?** will anyone remember it in a hundred years' time?; **1500 Jahre ~ Christi Geburt** *od. (bes. DDR)* ~ **unserer Zeitrechnung** in AD 1500; **vier Wochen ~ Erhalt der Rechnung** four weeks after receipt of *or* after receiving the invoice; **gleich ~ Erhalt der Rechnung** immediately upon *or* after receiving the invoice; **c)** *(mit bestimmten Verben, bezeichnet das Ziel der Handlung)* for; **greifen/streben/schicken ~:** grasp/strive/send for; **d)** *(bezeichnet [räumliche und zeitliche] Reihenfolge)* after; ~ **Ihnen/dir!** after you; **die Post kommt ~ dem Rathaus** the post office is after *or* past the town hall; ~ **„für" steht der Akkusativ** after 'für' one has the accusative; 'für' takes the accusative; **der Bundestagspräsident kommt ~ dem Bundespräsidenten** *(im gesellschaftlichen Rang)* the president of the Federal Parliament is lower in rank than the Federal President; *s. auch* **ander... b; e)** *(gemäß)* according to; *(in Übereinstimmung mit)* in accordance with; ~ **meiner Ansicht** *od.* **Meinung, meiner Ansicht** *od.* **Meinung ~:** in my view *or* opinion; ~ **menschlichem Ermessen** as far as anyone can judge; **aller Wahrscheinlichkeit ~:** in all probability; ~ **Lage der Dinge wird es kaum möglich sein** as matters stand it will hardly be possible; **je** *od.* **ganz ~ Wunsch** just as you/they *etc.* wish; however you/they *etc.* like; **Variationen ~ einem Thema von Händel** variations on a theme of Handel; **[frei] ~ Goethe** [freely] adapted from Goethe; ~ **einer Vorlage zeichnen** draw from an original; **eine Suppe ~ Art des Hauses** *(Kochk.)* a soup à la maison; ~ **rheinischer Art** *(Kochk.)* in the Rhenish style; ~ **altem Brauch** in accordance with *or* by ancient custom; ~ **der neuesten Mode gekleidet** dressed in [accordance with] the latest fashion; ~ **etw. schmecken/riechen** taste/smell of sth.; **seinem Wesen ~:** by nature; **sie kommt eher ~ dem Vater** *(ugs.)* she takes more after her father; ~ **dem [zu urteilen], was er gesagt hat** going *or* judging by what he said; from what he said; **jmdn. nur dem Namen ~ kennen** know sb. by name only; ~ **jmdm. genannt werden** be named after sb.; **Dienst ~ Vorschrift** work to rule; **dem Gesetz ~:** in accordance with the law; by law; ~ **Paragraph 5, Artikel 4** in accordance with *or* under paragraph 5, clause 4; **der Größe ~/~ dem Gewicht** according to *or* by size/weight; ~ **Stunden/Umsatz bezahlt werden** be paid by the hour/according to turnover; **15 Schillinge sind etwa 2 DM ~ unserem Geld** 15 schillings are about 2 marks in our money. **2.** *Adv.* **a)** *(räumlich)* **[alle] mir ~!** [everybody] follow me!; **b)** *(zeitlich)* ~ **und ~:** little by little; gradually; ~ **wie vor** still; as always

nach|äffen [-ɛfn̩] *tr. V. (abwertend)* mimic

Nachäfferei die; ~ *(abwertend)* mimicry; mimicking

nach|ahmen [-a:mən] *tr. V.* **a)** *(kopieren)* imitate; **b)** *(nacheifern)* emulate

nachahmens·wert *Adj.* worthy of imitation *postpos.*; exemplary; **nicht ~:** not to be imitated *postpos.*

Nachahmer der; ~s, ~, **Nachahmerin die;** ~, ~nen imitator

Nachahmung die; ~, ~en **a)** imitation; **b)** *(das Nacheifern)* emulation

Nachahmungs·trieb der *(Verhaltensf., Psych.)* imitative instinct

nach|arbeiten 1. *tr. V.* **a)** *(nachholen)* **eine Stunde ~:** work an extra hour to make up; **sie muß die versäumten Stunden ~:** she has to make up for the hours she missed; **b)** *(überarbeiten)* go over, finish off ‹*workpiece*›; *(retuschieren)* retouch ‹*picture*›; **c)** *(nachbilden)* copy (+ *Dat.* from). **2.** *itr. V.* do extra work to make up

Nachbar ['naxba:ɐ̯] **der;** ~n *od. selten* ~s, ~n neighbour; **Herr ~:** neighbour; **die lieben ~n** *(iron.)* the nice people next door *(iron.)*; ~s **Hund** the neighbours'/neighbour's dog; **mein ~ im Kino** the man [sitting] next to me in the cinema

Nachbar-: ~dorf das neighbouring village; **~haus das** house next door; **unser ~haus** the house next door to us

Nachbarin die; ~, ~nen neighbour; **meine ~ im Kino** the woman [sitting] next to me in the cinema

Nachbar·land das; *Pl.* **...länder** neighbouring country; **unser westliches ~:** our western neighbour

nachbarlich 1. *Adj.* **a)** *nicht präd. (dem Nachbarn/den Nachbarn gehörend)* neighbour's/neighbours'; *(benachbart)* neighbouring; next-door; **b)** *(unter Nachbarn üblich)* neighbourly; **in gutem ~em Einvernehmen leben** be good neighbours. **2.** *adv. (freundschaftlich)* in a neighbourly way

Nachbarschaft die; ~ **a)** *(die Nachbarn)* **die [ganze] ~:** all the neighbours *pl.*; the whole neighbourhood; **es hat sich in der ganzen ~ herumgesprochen** everybody in the neighbourhood has heard about it; **b)** *(Beziehungen)* **gute ~:** good neighbourliness; **wir halten** *od.* **pflegen eine gute ~:** we try to be good neighbours; **c)** *(Gegend)* neighbourhood; *(Nähe)* vicinity

nachbarschaftlich 1. *Adj.* neighbourly. **2.** *adv. s.* **nachbarlich 2**

Nachbarschafts-: ~haus das *(Sozialwesen)* neighbourhood [social] centre; **~hilfe die a)** *(gegenseitige Hilfe)* neighbourly help; **mit ~hilfe gebaut** built with the assistance of the neighbours; **b)** *(Sozialwesen)* neighbourhood social welfare organization *(run by independent welfare organizations)*

Nachbars-: ~familie die family next door; **~frau die** woman next door

Nachbar-: ~tisch der next *or* neighbouring table; **~wissenschaft die** allied *or* related science

Nach·beben das aftershock

nach|behandeln *tr. V.* **a)** *(nochmals behandeln)* treat again; **b)** *(nach ärztlicher Behandlung)* **jmdn./etw. ~:** give sb./sth. follow-up treatment

Nach·behandlung die follow-up treatment; after-care

nach|bekommen *unr. tr. V.* **a)** *(mehr bekommen)* **[noch] etw. ~:** have some more of sth.; *(bei Tisch)* have seconds of sth.; **b)** *(mehr kaufen können)* get more of

nach|bereiten *tr. V. (bes. Päd.)* **a)** *(analysieren)* assess the effectiveness of ‹*lesson*›; **b)** *(vertiefen)* go over [again] *(in order to internalize the material)*

Nachbereitung die; ~, ~en *(bes. Päd.)* **a)** *(Analyse)* assessment; **b)** *(Vertiefung)* further study *(for internalization)*

nach|bessern *tr. V.* repair; make good, put right ‹*defects*›

nach|bestellen *tr. V.* **[noch] etw. ~:** order more of sth.; ‹*shop*› order further stock of sth., reorder sth.; **die Teile des Geschirrs ~:** order more [parts] of the service

Nach·bestellung die; ~, ~en further order (+ *Gen.* for); *(vom Händler aufgegeben)* repeat order (+ *Gen.* for)

nach|beten *tr. V. (ugs. abwertend)* repeat parrot-fashion; regurgitate

nach|bezahlen *s.* **nachzahlen**

nach|bilden *tr. V.* reproduce, copy (+ *Dat.* from); **einem ägyptischen Original nachgebildet sein** be a reproduction *or* copy of an Egyptian original

Nach·bildung die a) *o. Pl. (das Nachbilden)* copying; **b)** *(Gegenstand)* copy; replica

nach|bleiben *unr. tr. V.; mit sein (landsch.)* be left *(from an injury etc.)*; **wenn da bloß nichts nachbleibt!** let's hope there's no lasting damage *or* after-effects

nach|blicken *tr. V. (geh.)* **jmdm./einer Sache ~:** look *or* gaze after sb./sth.

Nach·blutung die secondary haemorrhage

nach|bringen *unr. tr. V.* bring along ‹*sth. left behind*›; **sie hat ihm den Schirm nachgebracht** she brought the umbrella he left behind

nach·christlich *Adj.; nicht präd.* **im ersten ~en Jahrhundert** in the first century AD

nach|datieren *tr. V.* backdate

nach·dem *Konj.* **a)** *(zeitlich)* after; **ich ging erst, ~ ich mich vergewissert hatte** I only left when I had made sure; I did not leave until I had made sure; ~ **ich das Buch gelesen hatte** after *or* when I had read the book; **b)** *(südd.: kausal)* since; **c)** *s.* [1]**je 3 b**

nach|denken *unr. itr. V.* think (**über** + *Akk.* about); *(lange u. erwägend)* reflect (**über** + *Akk.* on); **darüber darf man gar nicht ~!** it doesn't bear thinking about; **denk mal [gut** *od.* **scharf] nach** have a [good] think; think carefully; **er dachte darüber nach, wie er sich entscheiden sollte** he considered how he should decide; **ohne nachzudenken** without stopping to think

Nach·denken das thought; **Zeit zum ~:** time to think; **nach langem ~:** after thinking about it for a long time; after mature consideration *(formal)*; **in tiefes ~ versunken** sunk in thought

nachdenklich 1. *Adj.* thoughtful; pensive; **jmdn. [sehr] ~ machen** *od.* **stimmen** [really] make sb. think; give sb. [much] cause for thought. **2.** *adv.* thoughtfully; pensively

Nach·dichtung die adaptation/re-creation *(in another language)*

nach|drängen *itr. V.; mit sein (nach vorn schieben)* push forwards; *(von hinten)* push from behind; **einige liefen auf das Spielfeld, andere drängten nach** some ran on to the pitch and others crowded after them

Nach·druck der; *Pl.* ~e **a)** *o. Pl.* **mit ~:** emphatically; **etw. mit ~/mit größtem ~ fordern** demand sth. vigorously *or* forcefully/with the utmost vigour; **seinen Worten ~ verleihen** give one's words emphasis; **auf etw.** *(Akk.)* **[besonderen] ~ legen** place [particular] emphasis on sth.; stress sth. [particularly]; **b)** *(Druckw.)* reprint; *(beim Copyrightvermerk)* ~ **[, auch auszugsweise,] verboten** not to be reproduced [in part or in whole]

nach|drucken *tr. V.* reprint ‹*book*›; print more ‹*invoices, letterheads, etc.*›

nachdrücklich 1. *Adj.; nicht präd.* emphatic ‹*warning, confirmation, advice*›; insistent ‹*demand*›; urgent ‹*request, appeal*›. **2.** *adv.* emphatically; **ich muß Sie ~ bitten, zu ...:** I must urgently request you to ...; **etw. ~ verlangen** demand sth. vigorously; ~ **darauf hinweisen, daß ...:** emphasize that ...:

Nachdrücklichkeit die; ~ *s.* **nachdrücklich:** emphatic nature; insistent nature; urgency

nach|dunkeln *itr. V.; mit sein* get darker

Nach·durst der morning-after thirst

nach|eifern *itr. V.* **jmdm. ~:** emulate sb.

nach|eilen *itr. V.; mit sein* **jmdm. ~:** hurry after sb.

nach·einander *Adv.* **a)** *(räumlich, zeitlich)* one after the other; **kurz/unmittelbar ~:** one shortly/immediately after the other; **fünfmal/drei Tage ~:** five times/three days in a row; **b)** *in Verbindung mit best. Verben* ~ **sehen** keep an eye on each other; **sich ~ richten** coordinate with one another; **sich ~ sehnen** long for one another

nach|empfinden *unr. tr. V.* **a)** *(nachfühlen)* empathize with ‹*feeling*›; share ‹*delight, sorrow*›; **ich kann [dir] deinen Ärger gut ~:** I can well understand *or* appreciate your feeling of anger; **b)** *(nachmachen)* re-create ⟨*expression, atmosphere, event*⟩; take ⟨*work of art*⟩ as a model; **einer Sache** *(Dat.)* **nachempfunden sein** take its inspiration from sth.; be modelled on sth.

Nachen ['naxn̩] **der; ~s, ~:** *(dichter.)* shallop

nach|erzählen *tr. V.* retell

Nach·erzählung die retelling [of a story]; *(Schulw.)* reproduction

Nachfahr [-fa:ɐ̯] **der; ~en** *od. selten* **~s, ~en, Nachfahre der; ~n, ~n** *(geh.)* descendant; *(fig.: Nachfolger)* successor

nach|fahren *unr. itr. V.; mit sein* follow [on]; **jmdm. ~:** follow sb.

nach|fassen 1. *itr. V.* **a)** *(noch einmal zufassen)* change one's grip **(an** + *Dat.* on); *(beim Fangen des Balls)* make a second attempt to gather the ball; **b)** *(ugs.: nachfragen)* ask a supplementary question; **c)** *(bes. Soldatenspr.)* **[noch einmal** *od.* **noch mal] ~:** have seconds. **2.** *tr. V. (bes. Soldatenspr.)* have seconds of ⟨*soup etc.*⟩

Nach·feier die belated celebration

nach|feiern 1. *tr. V.* celebrate ⟨*birthday, Christmas*⟩ at a later date. **2.** *itr. V.* have a belated celebration

Nach·folge die succession; **die ~ B.s regeln** settle who is to be B's successor; **jmds. ~ antreten** succeed sb.; **die ~ Christi** the discipleship of Christ

nach|folgen *itr. V.; mit sein* follow; **jmdm./einer Sache ~:** follow sb./sth.; **jmdm. im Amt ~:** succeed sb. in office

nach·folgend *Adj.; nicht präd.* following; subsequent ⟨*chapter, issue*⟩; **im ~en** below; in the text that follows

Nachfolge·organisation die successor organization (*Gen.* to)

Nachfolger der; ~s, ~, Nachfolgerin die; ~, ~nen successor

Nachfolge·staat der succession *or* successor state

nach|fordern *tr. V.* **[noch] 500 DM ~:** demand an additional 500 marks

Nach·forderung die additional demand (*Gen.*, **von** for)

nach|forschen *itr. V.* make inquiries; investigate [the matter]; **~, ob .../wer .../welcher ...:** try to find out *or* investigate whether .../who .../which ...; **einer Sache** *(Dat.)* **~** *(geh.)* investigate a matter

Nach·forschung die investigation; inquiry; **~en [nach etw.] anstellen** make inquiries [into sth.]; **die ~en, wohin ...:** the inquiries as to where ...

Nach·frage die a) *(Kaufmannsspr.)* demand **(nach** for); **es herrscht keine ~ mehr danach** there is no longer any demand for it; *s. auch* **Angebot; b)** *(veralt.: Frage)* inquiry; question; **danke der [gütigen] ~/für die [gütige] ~** *(meist scherzh.)* how kind of you to inquire

nach|fragen *itr. V.* ask; inquire; **bei jmdm. ~:** ask sb.; **ob ich mal ~ soll?** should I ask about it *or* make inquiries?; **um etw. ~:** ask for *or* request sth.

Nach·frist die *(Rechtsw.) additional time given for performance of a contract*

nach|fühlen *tr. V.* empathize with; **jmdm. seine Wut ~:** understand sb.'s anger; **das kann ich dir ~!** I know how you feel!

nach|füllen *tr. V.* refill ⟨*glass, vessel, etc.*⟩; *(wenn nicht leer)* fill up; top up; **jmdm. das Glas** *od.* **jmds. Glas ~:** refill/fill up sb.'s glass; **Salz/Wein ~:** put [some] more salt/wine in

Nach·gang *in* **im ~** *(Amtsspr.)* subsequently

nach|geben 1. *unr. itr. V.* **a)** give way; *(aus Schwäche)* give in; **jmdm. zuviel ~:** give in to sb. *or* let sb. have his/her way too often; **seiner Verzweiflung/Müdigkeit ~:** give in to one's despair/tiredness; **b)** *(sich dehnen)* stretch; **das Material gibt ein wenig nach** there is some give in the material; **c)** *(Bankw., Wirtsch.: sinken)* ⟨*prices, currency*⟩ weaken. **2.** *unr. tr. V.* **a)** *(mehr geben)* **jmdm. [etwas] Fleisch/Suppe** *usw.* **~:** give sb. [some] more meat/soup *etc.*; **b)** *in* **jmdm. nichts/nicht viel** *od.* **wenig ~:** be sb.'s equal/almost sb.'s equal **(an** + *Dat.* in)

nach·geboren *Adj.* **a)** posthumous ⟨*son, daughter*⟩; **b)** *(viel jünger)* much younger; born much later *postpos.*

Nach·gebühr die excess postage

Nach·geburt die a) *(Vorgang)* expulsion of the afterbirth; **b)** *(Gewebe)* afterbirth

nach|gehen *unr. itr. V.; mit sein* **a)** *(folgen)* **jmdm./einer Sache ~:** follow sb./sth.; **gehen Sie der Musik nach** follow the sound of the music; **einer Sache/einer Frage/einem Problem** *usw.* **~** *(fig.)* look into a matter/question/problem *etc.*; **b)** *(nicht aus dem Kopf gehen)* **jmdm. ~:** remain on sb.'s mind; occupy sb.'s thoughts; **c) seinen Geschäften** *od.* **Beschäftigungen/seinem Tagewerk ~:** go about one's business/daily work; **seinen Interessen/seinem Studium ~:** pursue one's interests/one's studies; **einem Beruf ~:** practise a profession; **d)** ⟨*clock, watch*⟩ be slow; **[um] eine Stunde ~:** be an hour slow; **eine Stunde am Tag ~:** lose an hour a day

nach·gelassen 1. *2. Part. v.* **nachlassen. 2.** *Adj.; nicht präd.* unpublished *(at the author's/composer's death)*; **die ~en Schriften des Autors** the unpublished writings left by the author

nach·gemacht 1. *2. Part. v.* **nachmachen. 2.** *Adj.* imitation ⟨*leather, gold*⟩; **~ aussehen** look like an imitation

nach·geordnet *Adj. (Amtsspr.)* inferior ⟨*authority*⟩; ⟨*person*⟩ subordinate

nach·gerade *Adv.* **a)** *(allmählich)* in time; by and by; **b)** *(geradezu)* positively; **das ist ~ eine Unverschämtheit** it's an absolute cheek

nach|geraten *unr. itr. V.; mit sein* **jmdm. ~:** take after sb.

Nach·geschmack der after-taste; **einen üblen** *od.* **unguten ~ hinterlassen** *(fig.)* leave a nasty taste in the mouth

nach·gewiesener·maßen *Adv.* as has been proved

nach·giebig [-gi:bɪç] *Adj.* **a)** *(nicht streng)* indulgent; yielding; **seinen Kindern gegenüber zu ~ sein** be too indulgent to *or (coll.)* soft with one's children; **b)** *(weich)* soft; yielding

Nachgiebigkeit die; ~: a) *(gütige Art)* indulgence; **b)** *(Weichheit)* softness

nach|gießen 1. *unr. tr. V.* pour [in] some more; **darf ich Ihnen [noch] Wein ~?** may I top up your wine? **2.** *unr. itr. V. (die Gläser nachfüllen)* top up the drinks; **jmdm. ~:** pour sb. some more; top sb. up *(coll.)*

nach|grübeln *itr. V.* ponder **(über** + *Akk.* over)

nach|gucken *(ugs.) s.* **nachsehen 1 a, b, c, 2 a, b**

nach|haken *itr. V.* **a)** *(ugs.: noch einmal fragen)* raise another question; **an einem Punkt muß ich ~:** I must come back on one point; **b)** *(ugs.: nachgehen)* make further inquiries; **c)** *(Fußball)* tackle from behind

Nach·hall der; ~[e]s, ~e reverberation; *(fig. geh.: Nachwirkung)* reverberations *pl.*; *(in der Literatur o. ä.)* lingering echo

nach|hallen *itr. V.* reverberate; **seine Schritte hallten in dem leeren Haus nach** his footsteps echoed in the empty house

Nachhall·zeit die *(Physik)* reverberation period

nach·haltig 1. *Adj.* lasting; **jmdm. einen ~en Schreck versetzen** give sb. a fright that he/she will not forget [for a long time]. **2.** *adv. (auf längere Zeit)* for a long time; *(nachdrücklich)* persistently; **jmdn. ~ prägen** have a lasting effect on sb.; **~ geschädigt werden** sustain lasting damage

nach|hängen *unr. itr. V.* **a)** *(in Gedanken)* dwell on; **seinen Gedanken ~:** lose oneself in one's thoughts; give oneself up to one's thoughts; **b)** *(anhaften)* **jmdm. ~:** stick to sb.; **c)** *(ugs.: in der Schule zurück sein)* lag behind

Nach·hause·weg der way home

nach|helfen *unr. itr. V.* help; **jmdm. ~:** help sb. along; lend sb. a hand; **der Schönheit ~:** improve on Mother Nature; **dem Glück ~:** assist one's chances

nach·her [*auch:* '--] *Adv.* **a)** afterwards; *(später)* later [on]; **bis ~!** see you later!; **ich kann mich erst ~ darum kümmern** I can't deal with it until after that *or* later; **b)** *(ugs.: womöglich)* then perhaps; *(sonst)* otherwise; **erzählen Sie die Geschichte nicht weiter, ~ ist sie nicht wahr** don't tell this story to anyone – it might turn out to be untrue

Nach·hilfe die coaching

Nachhilfe-: ~lehrer der coach; **~schüler der: mein ~schüler** the boy I am coaching; **sie hat drei ~schüler** she is coaching three boys; **~stunde die** private lesson; **~unterricht der** coaching

nach·hinein *in* **im ~** *(nachträglich)* afterwards; later; *(zurückblickend)* with hindsight; **im ~ ist man immer klüger** one is always wiser after the event

Nach·hol·bedarf der need to catch up; **ein ~ an etw.** *(Dat.)* a need to make up for the shortage of sth.

nach|holen *tr. V.* **a)** *(nachträglich erledigen)* catch up on ⟨*work, sleep*⟩; make up for ⟨*working hours missed*⟩; **er hat viel/einiges nachzuholen** he has a lot of/some catching up to do; **den Schulabschluß ~:** take one's final school examination as a mature student; **ich habe ihr nicht gratuliert – ich muß es morgen ~:** I didn't congratulate her – I shall have to do it tomorrow instead; **b)** *(zu sich holen)* fetch; **seine Familie ~:** bring one's family to join one

Nach·hut die; ~, ~en *(Milit.; auch fig.)* rearguard

Nach·impfung die booster injection

nach|jagen *itr. V.; mit sein* **jmdm./einer Sache ~:** chase after sb./sth.; **dem Erfolg/Geld ~** *(fig.)* devote oneself to the pursuit of success/money

Nach·klang der reverberation

nach|klingen *unr. itr. V.; mit sein* go on sounding; **in jmdm. ~** *(fig. geh.)* linger on in sb.'s mind; stay with sb.

Nachkomme der; ~n, ~n descendant; *(eines Tieres)* offspring; **ohne ~n sterben** die without issue

nach|kommen *unr. itr. V.; mit sein* **a)** follow [later]; come [on] later; **seine Familie wird [später] ~:** his family will join him later; **da kann noch etwas ~** *(ugs.)* something could still turn up; **die ~den Autos/Truppen** the cars/troops following behind; **b) seinen Pflichten ~:** fulfil one's duties; **seinen Verpflichtungen ~:** meet one's commitments; **einem Wunsch/Befehl/einer Bitte ~:** comply with a wish/an order/grant a request; **c)** *(Schritt halten können)* be able to keep up; **ich komme mit dem Abtrocknen nicht nach** I can't dry [the dishes] fast enough

Nachkommenschaft die; ~: descendants *pl.*; *(eines Tieres)* offspring

Nachkömmling [-kœmlɪŋ] **der; ~s, ~e** much younger child *(than the rest)*; afterthought *(joc.)*; **Christoph, unser ~:** Christoph, much the youngest child in our family

Nach·kriegs-: ~generation die post-war generation; **~zeit die** post-war period; **in der [ersten] ~zeit** [immediately] after the war

Nach·kur die [period of] convalescence *(after a health cure)*

nach|laden *unr. itr. V.* reload

Nach·laß der; Nachlasses, Nachlasse *od.*

Nachlässe **a)** estate; *(hinterlassene Gegenstände)* personal effects *pl. (left by the deceased);* **literarischer/künstlerischer ~:** unpublished/unexhibited works *pl. (left by a writer/an artist);* **aus dem ~ veröffentlichen** publish posthumously; **b)** *(Kaufmannsspr.: Rabatt)* discount; reduction; **ein hoher ~:** a high discount *or* big reduction

nach|lassen 1. *unr. itr. V.* **a)** *(schwächer/weniger werden)* let up; ⟨*rain, wind*⟩ ease, let up; ⟨*storm, heat*⟩ abate, die down; ⟨*anger*⟩ subside, die down; ⟨*pain, stress, pressure*⟩ ease, lessen; ⟨*noise*⟩ lessen; ⟨*fever*⟩ go down; ⟨*speed, demand*⟩ decrease, drop; ⟨*effect*⟩ wear off; ⟨*interest, enthusiasm, strength, courage*⟩ flag, wane; ⟨*resistance*⟩ weaken; *(schlechter werden)* ⟨*health, hearing, memory*⟩ get worse, deteriorate; ⟨*reactions*⟩ become slower; ⟨*performance*⟩ deteriorate, fall off; ⟨*business*⟩ drop off, fall off; **meine Augen haben stark nachgelassen** my eyesight has deteriorated considerably; **b)** *(landsch.: aufhören)* **mit etw. nicht ~:** keep on with sth.; **du sollst damit jetzt ~!** stop that at once!; *s. auch* **Schreck. 2.** *unr. tr. V.* **a)** *(Kaufmannsspr.)* give *or* allow a discount of; **man hat mir 30% des Preises nachgelassen** they gave me 30% off [the price] *or* a discount of 30%; **b)** *(erlassen)* **jmdm. seine Schulden ~:** let sb. off his/her debts; **c)** *(lockern)* slacken ⟨*rope*⟩

Nachlaß·gericht das *(Rechtsw.)* ≈ probate court

nach·lässig 1. *Adj.* **a)** *(unordentlich)* careless; untidy ⟨*dress*⟩; negligent ⟨*staff*⟩; lax, casual ⟨*behaviour, way of talking*⟩; **b)** *(unbeteiligt)* indifferent; apathetic. **2.** *adv.* **a)** *(unordentlich)* carelessly; untidily ⟨*dressed*⟩; **b)** *(unbeteiligt)* indifferently; apathetically

nachlässigerweise *Adv.* carelessly

Nach·lässigkeit die; ~, ~en a) *s.* **nachlässig 1a:** carelessness; untidiness; negligence; laxness; casualness; **b)** *(Fehler)* careless mistake; **die kleinste ~:** the slightest mistake

Nachlaß-: ~pfleger der *(Rechtsw.)* administrator [of an/the estate] *(appointed by the court until the estate is settled);* **~verwalter der** *(Rechtsw.)* executor

Nach·lauf der *(Kfz-W.)* castor angle

nach|laufen *unr. itr. V.; mit sein* **jmdm./einer Sache ~:** run *or* chase after sb./sth.; **einem Mädchen ~** *(ugs.)* chase a girl; **einer Illusion** *(Dat.)* **~** *(fig.)* chase after *or* pursue an illusion; **diese Kleider laufen sich nach** *(fig. ugs.)* these dresses are everywhere

nach|legen *tr., itr. V.* **[Holz/Kohlen] ~:** put some more wood/coal on

Nach·lese die a) gleaning; *(Ertrag)* gleanings *pl.;* **b)** *(geh.: Auswahl)* further selection

nach|lesen *unr. tr. V.* look up; *(überprüfen)* check; **in den Statistiken ist nachzulesen, daß ...:** the statistics show that ...

nach|liefern *tr. V. (später liefern)* supply later; *(zusätzlich liefern)* supply additionally; **der Rest wird nächste Woche nachgeliefert** the rest of the delivery will follow next week

Nach·lieferung die a) *o. Pl. (das Nachliefern)* [subsequent] delivery; **b)** *(Ware)* further consignment

nach|lösen 1. *tr. V.* **eine Fahrkarte ~:** buy a ticket [on the train/tram *(Brit.) or (Amer.)* streetcar]. **2.** *itr. V.* pay the excess [fare]; *(für die 1. Klasse)* pay the extra [fare]

nachm. *Abk.* **nachmittags** p.m.

nach|machen *tr. V.* **a)** *(auch tun)* copy; *(imitieren)* imitate; do an impersonation of ⟨*politician etc.*⟩; *(genauso herstellen)* reproduce ⟨*period furniture etc.*⟩; forge ⟨*signature*⟩; forge, counterfeit ⟨*money*⟩; **jmdm. alles ~:** copy everything sb. does; **das soll mir einer ~!** follow that!; **das macht ihm so schnell keiner nach** nobody is going to equal that in a hurry; *s. auch* **nachgemacht; b)** *(ugs.: später machen)* do later; take ⟨*exam*⟩ later; **Hausaufgaben ~:** catch up on one's homework

nach|malen *tr. V.* go over [with fresh paint]

nach·malig *Adj.; nicht präd. (veralt.)* future; **X, der ~e US-Präsident** X, who was to become President of the USA

nach|messen 1. *unr. tr. V.* check the measurements of; check ⟨*distance, length, etc.*⟩. **2.** *itr. V.* check the measurements

Nach·mieter der next tenant; **einen ~ stellen** find a tenant to take over the lease

nach·mittag *Adv.* **heute/morgen/gestern ~:** this/tomorrow/yesterday afternoon; **[am] Sonntag ~:** on Sunday afternoon

Nach·mittag der a) afternoon; **zwei ~e in der Woche arbeiten** work two afternoons a week; **den ganzen ~:** all afternoon; **am ~,** *(geh.)* **des ~s** in the afternoon; *(heute)* this afternoon; **am frühen/späten ~:** early/late in the afternoon; **am selben ~:** the same afternoon; **am ~ des 8. März** on the afternoon of 8 March; **an einem sonnigen ~ im Juli** one sunny afternoon in July; **b)** *(Veranstaltung)* social afternoon

nachmittäglich [-mɪtɛ:klɪç] *Adj.; nicht präd.* afternoon ⟨*walk, nap*⟩

nach·mittags *Adv.* in the afternoon; *(heute)* this afternoon; **dienstags** *od.* **Dienstag ~:** on Tuesday afternoons; **um vier Uhr ~:** at four in the afternoon; at 4 p.m.

Nach·mittags-: ~kaffee der afternoon coffee [and cakes]; **~vor·stellung die** afternoon performance; [afternoon] matinée

Nachnahme die; ~, ~n a) **per ~:** cash on delivery; COD; **b)** *(Sendung)* COD parcel

Nachnahme-: ~gebühr die *(Postw.)* cash on delivery fee; **~sendung die** *(Postw.)* COD parcel

Nach·name der surname; **wie heißt du mit ~n?** what is your surname?

nach|nutzen *tr. V. (DDR)* take over ⟨*sb. else's innovation/method*⟩; make use of ⟨*sb. else's experience*⟩

nach|plappern *tr. V. (oft abwertend)* repeat parrot-fashion; **jmdm. alles ~:** repeat everything sb. says

Nach·porto das excess postage

nach|prägen *tr. V.* **a)** mint more, re-mint ⟨*coins, medals*⟩; **[noch] 100 Stück wurden nachgeprägt** another 100 copies were minted; **b)** *(fälschen)* forge; counterfeit

Nach·prägung die a) *o. Pl. (Vorgang)* reminting; **b)** *(Münze)* copy; *(Fälschung)* forgery; counterfeit [coin]

nachprüfbar *Adj.* verifiable

Nachprüfbarkeit die; ~: verifiability

nach|prüfen 1. *tr. V.* **a)** check ⟨*document, statement, weight, alibi*⟩; verify ⟨*correctness*⟩; **b)** *(später prüfen)* examine ⟨*candidate*⟩ later; *(bei der Fahrprüfung)* test ⟨*learner driver*⟩ later. **2.** *itr. V.* check

Nach·prüfung die a) checking; **b)** *(spätere Prüfung)* postponed examination

nach|rechnen 1. *tr. V.* check ⟨*figures*⟩. **2.** *itr. V.* **a)** *(zur Kontrolle)* check [the figures]; **b)** *(zurückverfolgen)* [think back and] work it out

Nach·rede die: üble ~: malicious gossip; *(Rechtsw.)* defamation [of character]

nach|reden *tr. V.* **a)** *(wiederholen)* repeat; **b)** *s.* **nachsagen b**

nach|reichen *tr. V.* hand in subsequently

nach|reifen *itr. V.; mit sein* ripen further *(after picking)*

nach|reisen *itr. V.; mit sein* **jmdm. ~:** travel after sb.; *(losfahren)* set off after sb.

nach|rennen *unr. itr. V.: s.* **nachlaufen**

Nachricht ['na:xrɪçt] **die; ~, ~en a)** *(Mitteilung)* news *no pl.;* **das ist eine gute ~:** that is [a piece of] good news; **gute/schlechte ~en** good/bad news; **eine ~ hinterlassen** leave a message; **ich habe keine ~ von ihm** *(Brief usw.)* I haven't heard *or* had any word from him; **wir warten auf ~** *od.* **sind noch ohne ~** *(Bestätigung)* we are waiting to hear *or* have not heard yet; **jmdm. ~ geben** inform sb.; **b)** *Pl. (Ferns., Rundf.)* news *sing.;* **~en hören** listen to the news; **Sie hören ~en** here is the news; **das kam in den ~en** it was on the news

Nachrichten-: ~agentur die news agency; **~dienst der a)** *(Geheimdienst)* intelligence service; **b)** *s.* **~agentur; ~magazin das** news magazine; **~satellit der** communications satellite; **~sendung die** news broadcast; **~sperre die** news embargo *or* blackout; **~sprecher der, ~sprecherin die** news-reader; **~technik die** telecommunications [technology] *no art.;* **~übermittlung die** news transmission *no art.*

nach|rücken *itr. V.; mit sein (aufrücken)* move up; **[auf den Posten] ~:** be promoted [to the post]; take over [the post]; **dem Feind ~** *(Mil.)* move up behind the enemy

Nach·ruf der; ~[e]s, ~e obituary **(auf +** *Akk.* of)

nach|rufen *unr. tr., itr. V.* **jmdm. [etw.] ~:** call [sth.] after sb.

Nach·ruhm der; ~[e]s posthumous reputation

nach|rühmen *tr. V.* **jmdm. etw. ~:** credit sb. with sth.; **ihm rühmt man nach, daß er ...:** he is famous for the fact that he ...

nach|rüsten 1. *itr. V.* counter-arm. **2.** *tr. V. (Technik: zusätzlich ausstatten)* **mit etw. ~:** equip additionally with sth.; upgrade ⟨*television, hi-fi, etc.*⟩ with sth.

Nach·rüstung die; ~: a) *(Waffen)* counter-arming; **b)** *(Technik)* [additional] equipment; *(von Stereoanlagen usw.)* upgrading

Nachrüstungs·beschluß der *(Politik)* decision to counter-arm

nach|sagen *tr. V.* **a)** *(wiederholen)* repeat; **sag mir folgendes nach** repeat the following after me; **b)** *(über jmdn. sagen)* **jmdm. Schlechtes ~:** speak ill of sb.; **man sagt ihm nach, er verstehe etwas davon** he is said to know something about it; **du darfst dir nicht ~ lassen, daß ...:** you mustn't let it be said of you that ...; **wir wollen uns doch nichts ~ lassen!** we don't want anything said against us; we don't want to get a bad reputation

Nach·saison die late season

nach|salzen *unr. (auch regelm.) tr., itr. V.* **[etw.] ~:** put more salt in/on [sth.]

Nach·satz der a) *(letzte Bemerkung)* postscript; *(gesprochen)* final remark; **b)** *(Sprachw.)* postponed clause

Nach·schau *in:* **~ halten** *(geh.)* investigate; look into it

nach|schauen *(bes. südd., österr., schweiz.) s.* **nachsehen 1a, b, c, 2a, b**

nach|schenken *tr., itr. V.* top up one's/sb.'s glass; **jmdm. [Wein] ~:** top up sb.'s glass [with wine]

nach|schicken *tr. V.* **a)** *(durch die Post o.ä.)* forward; send on; **b)** *(folgen lassen)* **jmdn. jmdn. ~:** send sb. after sb.

Nach·schlag der a) *(ugs.: zusätzliche Portion)* second helping; seconds *pl.;* **b)** *(Musik: verzierender Ton)* grace note *(after another note); (Abschluß eines Trillers)* two-note termination *(of a trill)*

nach|schlagen 1. *unr. tr. V.* look up ⟨*word, reference, text*⟩; *(ugs.)* consult, look at ⟨*dictionary, book*⟩; **schlag mal nach, was X heißt** look up to see what X means. **2.** *unr. itr. V.* **a) im Lexikon/Wörterbuch ~:** consult the encyclopaedia/dictionary; **b)** *mit sein (geh.: ähnlich werden)* **jmdm. ~:** take after sb.

Nachschlage·werk das work of reference

nach|schleichen *unr. itr. V.; mit sein* **jmdm. ~:** creep *or* steal after sb.

[1]nach|schleifen *unr. tr. V.* resharpen ⟨*knife, blade*⟩; repolish ⟨*lens*⟩

²**nach|schleifen** *tr. V. (ugs.)* drag [along] behind one/it
Nach·schlüssel der duplicate key
nach|schmeißen *unr. tr. V. (ugs.)* **a)** *(billig o. ä. geben)* give away; **man bekommt sie nachgeschmissen** you get them for next to nothing; **sie haben ihm das Abitur nachgeschmissen** his school-leaving exam was handed to him on a plate *(coll.)*; **b)** *s.* **nachwerfen a**
Nach·schrift die a) notes *pl.* (+ *Gen.* on); **b)** *(Postskriptum)* postscript (+ *Gen.* to)
Nach·schub der *(Milit.)* **a)** supply (**an** + *Dat.* of); *(fig.)* [provision of] further *or* fresh supplies *pl.* (**an** + *Dat.* of); **der ~ ist schlecht organisiert** the supply services *or* supplies are badly organized; **b)** *(~material)* supplies *pl.* (**an** + *Dat.* of); *(fig.)* further supplies *pl.*
Nachschub·weg der *(Milit.)* supply line
Nach·schuß der a) *(Wirtsch.)* contribution in excess of one's original share; further call; **b)** *(Ballspiele)* shot on the rebound
nach|schütten *tr. V.* put on more ‹*coal, coke, etc.*›; pour in more ‹*water*›
nach|schwatzen, *(bes. südd., österr.)* **nach|schwätzen** *tr. V. (abwertend)* repeat [parrot-fashion]
nach|sehen 1. *unr. itr. V.* **a)** *(hintersehen)* **jmdm./einer Sache ~:** look *or* gaze after sb./sth.; **b)** *(kontrollieren)* check *or* have a look [to see]; **~, wer da ist** go and see *or* have a look who's there; **c)** *(nachschlagen)* look it up; have a look. **2.** *unr. tr. V.* **a)** *(nachlesen)* look up ‹*word, passage*›; **b)** *(überprüfen)* check [over]; look over; **c)** *(nicht verübeln)* overlook, let pass ‹*remark*›; **jmdm. etw./zuviel ~:** let sb. get away with sth./too much
Nach·sehen das *in* **das ~ haben** not get a look-in; *(nichts abbekommen)* be left with nothing; **jmdm. bleibt das ~:** sb. does not get a look-in; *(bekommt nichts ab)* sb. is left with nothing
nach|senden *unr. od. regelm. tr. V.: s.* **nachschicken**
Nach·sendung die *(Postw.)* forwarding
nach|setzen *itr. V.* **jmdm./einem Tier ~:** pursue sb./an animal
Nach·sicht die leniency; forbearance; **mit jmdm. ~ haben** *od.* **üben** be lenient with sb.; make allowances for sb.; **ich muß um ~ bitten, daß ich so spät komme** please forgive me *or* I must apologize for coming so late; **keine ~ kennen** make no allowances; *(bei Strafen)* show no mercy
nachsichtig 1. *Adj.* lenient, forbearing (**gegen, mit** towards); *(verständnisvoll)* understanding. **2.** *adv.* leniently; *(verständnisvoll)* understandingly
Nachsichtigkeit die; ~: leniency; forbearance
nachsichts·voll *s.* **nachsichtig**
Nach·silbe die *(Sprachw.)* suffix
nach|sinnen *unr. itr. V. (geh.)* ponder; **einer Sache** *(Dat.)* **~:** think back to sth.
nach|sitzen *unr. itr. V.* be in detention; **[eine Stunde] ~ müssen** have [an hour's] detention
Nach·sommer der Indian summer
Nach·sorge die; *o. Pl. (Med.)* aftercare *no indef. art.*
Nach·spann der *(Film, Ferns.)* [final] credits *pl.*
Nach·speise die dessert; sweet
Nach·spiel das a) die Sache wird noch ein ~ haben! this affair will have repercussions; **ein gerichtliches ~ haben** result in court proceedings; **b)** *(Theater o. ä.)* epilogue; *(Musik)* postlude; **c)** *(beim Geschlechtsverkehr)* afterplay
nach|spielen 1. *tr. V.* **a)** *(Kartenspiel)* **den Buben** *usw.* **~:** follow up with the jack *etc.*; **b)** *(auch spielen)* **er hat es mir vorgespielt, ich mußte es ~:** he played it over to me, and I then had to play it myself; **c)** *(nachahmen)* imitate, mimic ‹*person*›; re-enact ‹*scene*›; **d)** *(anderswo aufführen)* take up, put on ‹*new play etc.*›. **2.** *itr. V. (Ballspiele, bes. Fußball)* **[einige Minuten] ~:** play [a few minutes of] time added on; **der Schiedsrichter läßt ~:** the referee has added on time [for stoppages]
nach|spionieren *itr. V.* **jmdm. ~:** spy on sb.
nach|sprechen *unr. tr. V.* **[jmdm.] etw. ~:** repeat sth. [after sb.]
nach|spülen 1. *tr. V.* re-wash; wash again; *(mit klarem Wasser)* rinse. **2.** *itr. V.* **a)** *(ausspülen)* give it/them a rinse; **mit viel Wasser ~:** rinse out with plenty of water; **b)** *(ugs.: trinken)* **mit einem Bierchen ~:** have a beer as a chaser *(coll.) or* to wash it down
nach|spüren *itr. V.* **jmdm./einer Bande ~:** track down sb./a gang; **einer Sache** *(Dat.)* **~** *(fig.)* follow up *or* investigate sth.
nächst [nɛːçst] *Präp. mit Dat. (geh.)* next to
nächst... 1. *Sup. zu* **nahe. 2.** *Adj.* **a) der ~e Weg zum Bahnhof** the shortest way to the station; **in ~er Nähe** very near; **b)** *nicht präd. (unmittelbar danach)* next; **die ~e Straße links** the next street on the left; **beim ~en Bäcker** at the next baker's we come to; *s. auch* **best... b; c)** *nicht präd. (zeitlich)* next; **am ~en Tag** the next day; **am ~en ersten** on the first of next month; **bei ~er Gelegenheit** at the next opportunity; **in ~er Zukunft** in the very near future; **in den ~en Tagen/Jahren** in the next few days/years; **beim ~en Mal, das ~e Mal** the next time; **der ~e bitte!** next [one], please; **wer kommt als ~er dran?** whose turn is it next?; **als ~es räume ich den Speicher auf** the next thing I do *or* my next job will be to tidy the loft
nächst·beste *Adj. s.* **erstbeste**
Nächst·beste der/die/das; *adj. Dekl.* the first one [to turn up]; **das ~, was ich finde** the first thing I find
Nächste der; ~n, ~n *(geh.)* neighbour; **jeder ist sich selbst der ~:** one has to look after one's own interests
nach|stehen *unr. itr. V.* **jmdm. an etw.** *(Dat.)* **nicht ~:** be sb.'s match in sth.; **jmdm./einer Sache in nichts ~:** be in no way inferior to sb./sth.
nach·stehend 1. *Adj.* following. **2.** *adv.* below
nach|steigen *unr. itr. V.; mit sein (ugs.)* **einem Mädchen ~:** try to get off with *(Brit. coll.) or (Amer. coll.)* make it with a girl
nach|stellen 1. *tr. V.* **a)** *(Sprachw.)* **A wird B** *(Dat.)* **nachgestellt** A is placed after B; **nachgestellte Präposition** postpositive preposition; **nachgestellter Satz** postponed clause; **b)** *(zurückstellen)* put back ‹*clock, watch*›; **c)** *(neu/genauer einstellen)* [re]adjust; take up the adjustment on ‹*brakes, clutch*›; **d)** *(darstellen)* portray; represent. **2.** *itr. V. (geh.)* **einem Tier/einem Flüchtling ~:** hunt an animal/hunt *or* pursue a fugitive; **Hühnern** *usw.* **~** ‹*dog*› chase chickens *etc.*; **einem Mädchen ~** *(ugs.)* chase a girl
Nach·stellung die a) *(Sprachw.)* postposition; **b)** *Pl. (Verfolgung)* pursuit *sing.*; *(ugs.: Umwerbung)* advances
Nächsten·liebe die charity [to one's neighbour]; brotherly love
nächstens ['nɛːçstn̩s] *Adv.* **a)** *(demnächst)* shortly; in the near future; **passen Sie ~ besser auf!** be more careful next time; **b)** *(ugs.: wenn es so weitergeht)* if it goes on like this
nächst-: ~folgend *Adj.; nicht präd.* next; **~gelegen** *Adj.; nicht präd.* nearest; **~höher** *Adj.; nicht präd.* next higher; **die ~höhere Klasse** the next class [up]; **~jährig** *Adj.; nicht präd.* next year's; **~liegend** *Adj.; nicht präd.* first, immediate ‹*problem*›; [most] obvious ‹*explanation etc.*›; **das Nächstliegende** the [most] obvious thing; **~möglich** *Adj.; nicht präd.* earliest possible
nach|stoßen *unr. itr. V.* **a)** *mit sein (Milit.: vordringen)* move up *or* advance [behind them]; **b)** *(im Gespräch)* follow up [with another thrust]
nach|suchen *itr. V.* **a)** *(geh.: bitten)* **um etw. ~:** request sth.; *(bes. schriftlich)* apply for sth.; **b)** *(intensiv suchen)* search
nacht [naxt] *Adv.* **gestern/morgen/Dienstag ~:** last night/tomorrow night/on Tuesday night; **heute ~:** tonight; *(letzte Nacht)* last night
Nacht die; ~, Nächte ['nɛçtə] night; **es wird/ist ~:** it is getting dark/it is dark; night is falling/has fallen; **die ~ brach herein** night fell; **bei ~, in der ~,** *(geh.)* **des ~s** at night[-time]; **eines ~s** one night; **~ für ~:** night after night; **letzte ~:** last night; **die halbe ~:** half the night; **die ganze ~ [hindurch]** all night long; **diese ~:** tonight; **mitten in der ~:** in the middle of the night; **bis tief in die ~ hinein, bis spät in der ~:** until late at night; *(bis in die Morgenstunden)* into the small hours; **in der ~ vom 12. auf den 13. Mai** on the night of 12 May; **in der ~ auf Montag** on Sunday night; **über ~ bleiben** stay overnight; **über ~ berühmt werden** *(fig.)* become famous overnight; **zu[r] ~ essen** *(südd., österr.)* have one's evening meal; **gute ~!** good night!; **[na,] dann gute ~!** *(iron.)* [well,] that's that; **die ~ zum Tage machen, sich** *(Dat.)* **die ~ um die Ohren schlagen** *(ugs.)* stay up all night; **bei ~ und Nebel** under cover of darkness; *(heimlich)* furtively; like a thief in the night; **~ der langen Messer** *(salopp)* night of the long knives; **die ~ des Wahnsinns/Krieges/der Tyrannei** *(dichter.)* the dark night of madness/war/tyranny; *s. auch* **häßlich 1 a; heilig b; schwarz 1 a**
nacht·aktiv *Adj. (Zool.)* nocturnal
nach|tanken *tr., itr. V.* fill up; ‹*aircraft*› refuel; **20 Liter ~:** put in another 20 litres
nacht-, Nacht-: ~arbeit die; *o. Pl.* night work *no art.*; **~aufnahme die** night photograph *or* shot; **~bar die** night-spot *(coll.)*; **~blau** *Adj. (geh., dichter.)* midnight blue; **~blind** *Adj.* night-blind; **~blindheit die** night-blindness; **~creme die** night cream; **~dienst der** night duty; **~dienst haben** be on night duty; ‹*chemist's shop*› be open late
Nach·teil der disadvantage; **der ~, allein zu reisen** the disadvantage *or* drawback of travelling alone; **aus etw. entsteht** *od.* **erwächst jmdm. ein ~:** sth. puts sb. at a disadvantage; **im ~ sein, sich im ~ befinden** be at a disadvantage; **ich hatte nur ~e davon** I had nothing but disadvantages as a result; **der Prozeß ging zu seinem ~ aus** the trial went against him; **sich zu seinem ~ verändern** change for the worse; **jmdm. zum ~ gereichen, zu jmds. ~ gereichen** *(geh.)* be to sb.'s detriment
nachteilig 1. *Adj.* detrimental; harmful; **über sie ist nichts Nachteiliges bekannt** nothing to her disadvantage is known about her. **2.** *adv.* detrimentally; harmfully; **sich ~ auswirken** have a detrimental *or* harmful effect
nächte·lang 1. *Adj.; nicht präd.* lasting several nights *postpos.*; *(ganze Nächte dauernd)* all-night. **2.** *adv.* night after night
nachten ['naxtn̩] *itr. V. (unpers.) (schweiz., sonst dichter.)* **es nachtet** night *or* darkness is falling
Nacht-: ~essen das *(bes. südd., schweiz.)* evening meal; supper; *(formell)* dinner; **~eule die** *(ugs. scherzh.)* night-owl *(coll.)*; **~falter der** moth; **~flug der** night flight; **~frost der** night frost; **~gebet das** bedtime prayer; **~geschirr das** chamber-pot; **~gespenst das** [nocturnal] ghost; **~gewand das** *(geh.)* night-dress; **~hemd das** night-shirt; **~himmel der;** *o. Pl.* night sky

Nachtigall ['naxtɪgal] **die;** ~, **~en** nightingale; ~, **ich hör' dir trapsen** *(salopp)* I can see which way the wind blows *or* what he/she's after

Nachtigallen·schlag der song of the nightingale

nächtigen ['nɛçtɪgn̩] *(österr., sonst geh.)* spend the night

Nach·tisch der; *o. Pl.* dessert; sweet; **zum** *od.* **als ~:** as a *or* for dessert; **was gibt's zum ~?** what's for pudding *or (coll.)* afters?

Nacht-: ~kästchen das *(südd., österr.)* bedside table; **~klub der** night-club; **~lager das a)** *(geh.: Schlafstätte)* resting-place for the night; **b)** *(Biwak)* bivouac; **~leben das** night-life

nächtlich ['nɛçtlɪç] *Adj.; nicht präd.* nocturnal; night ‹*sky*›; ‹*darkness, stillness*› of the night; **durch den ~en Wald gehen** go through the dark woods [at night-time]; **~e Ruhestörung** *(Rechtsspr.) causing a disturbance at night*

Nacht-: ~lokal das night-spot *(coll.)*; **~luft die** night air; **~mahl das** *(österr., auch südd.)* evening meal; supper; *(formell)* dinner; **~mahr** [~maːɐ̯] **der a)** *(Gespenst)* [nocturnal] ghost *or* spectre; **b)** *(Alptraum)* nightmare; **~mensch der** night-owl *(coll.)*; **~mütze die** nightcap; **~portier der** night porter; **~quartier das** accommodation *no indef. art.* for the night

Nachtrag [-traːk] **der; ~[e]s, Nachträge** [-trɛːgə] appendix; *(als weiteres Buch/Heft)* supplement

nach|tragen *unr. tr. V.* **a)** *(hinterhertragen)* **jmdm. etw. ~:** follow sb. carrying sth.; **b)** *(schriftlich ergänzen)* insert, add; *(noch sagen)* add; **nachzutragen wäre noch, daß ...:** I should add that ...; it should be added that ...; **c)** *(übelnehmen)* **jmdm. etw. ~:** hold sth. against sb.

nach·tragend *Adj.* unforgiving; *(rachsüchtig)* vindictive; **ich bin nicht ~:** I don't bear grudges

nachträglich [-trɛːklɪç] **1.** *Adj.; nicht präd.* later; subsequent ‹*apology*›; *(verspätet)* belated ‹*greetings, apology*›; *(zusätzlich)* additional; **eine ~e Gratifikation** a retrospective bonus. **2.** *adv.* afterwards; subsequently; *(verspätet)* belatedly; **~ feiern** have a belated celebration

Nachtrags·haushalt der supplementary budget

nach|trauern *itr. V.* **jmdm./einer Sache ~:** bemoan *or* lament the passing of sb./sth.; *(sich sehnen nach)* pine for sb./sth.

Nacht·ruhe die night's sleep; **angenehme ~!** sleep well!; **er wünschte ihnen eine angenehme ~:** he [said he] hoped they would sleep well

nachts *Adv.* at night; **Montag** *od.* **montags ~:** on Monday nights; **um 3 Uhr ~, ~ um 3 [Uhr]** at 3 o'clock in the morning

nacht-, Nacht-: ~schatten·gewächs das *(Bot.)* plant of the Solanaceae family; **~schattengewächse** Solanaceae; **~schicht die** night-shift; **~schicht haben** be on night-shift; work nights; **~schlafend** *Adj. in* **bei/zu ~schlafender Zeit** *od.* **Stunde** *(ugs.)* at a time when all good people are in their beds; **~schwärmer der** *(scherzh.)* nocturnal reveller; **~schwarz** *Adj. (geh.)* jet-black; **~schwester die** night nurse; **~speicher·ofen der** night storage heater; **~strom der** off-peak electricity; **~stuhl der** commode

nachts·über *Adv.* overnight; during the night

Nacht-: ~tarif der night rate; *(für Strom)* off-peak rate; **~tisch der** bedside table; **~tisch·lampe die** bedside light; **~topf der** chamber-pot; **auf den ~topf gehen** use the chamber-pot; **~tresor der** night safe

nach|tun *unr. tr. V. (ugs.)* copy; **es jmdm. ~:** copy sb.

Nacht-und-Nebel-Aktion die hush-hush [*esp.* night-time] operation

nacht-, Nacht-: ~vorstellung die late-night show; **~wache die a)** *(Wachdienst)* night-watch; *(im Krankenhaus)* night-duty; *(eines Soldaten)* night guard-duty; **bei einem Kranken ~wache halten** sit up [at night] with a sick person; **b)** *(Person)* night-guard; *(für Fabrik, Büro o. ä.)* night-watchman; **~wächter der a)** night-watchman; **b)** *(salopp: Dummkopf)* dim-wit *(coll.)*; thickhead *(coll.)*; **~wächter·staat der** laissez-faire state providing for security only; **~wandeln** *itr. V.; auch mit sein* sleepwalk; **~wanderung die** nocturnal ramble; **~wandler** [-vandlɐ] **der; ~s, ~, ~wandlerin die; ~, ~nen** sleep-walker; somnambulist *(formal)*; **~wandlerisch** *Adj. in* **mit ~wandlerischer Sicherheit** with the sureness of a sleepwalker; with instinctive sureness; **~zeit die** *in* **zu später** *od.* **vorgerückter ~zeit:** at a late hour [of the night]; **~zeug das** *(ugs.)* overnight things *pl. (coll.)*; **~zug der** night train; **~zu·schlag der** night-work supplement

nach|untersuchen *tr. V.* **jmdn./etw. ~:** give sb. a follow-up examination/check sth.

Nach·untersuchung die follow-up examination; check-up

Nach·versicherung die a) *(Rentenversicherung)* retrospective state pension contributions *pl. (for previously uninsured employee)*; **b)** *(von Sachwerten o. ä.)* additional insurance cover

nachvollziehbar *Adj.* comprehensible; **leicht/schwer ~:** easy/difficult to comprehend; **das ist für mich nicht ~:** I find this impossible to understand *or* comprehend

nach|vollziehen *unr. tr. V.* reconstruct ‹*train of thought*›; *(begreifen)* comprehend

nach|wachsen *unr. itr. V.; mit sein* **[wieder] ~:** grow again

Nach·wahl die *(Politik)* postponed election; *(nach dem Tod o. ä. eines Abgeordneten)* by-election

Nach·wehen *Pl. (Med.)* afterpains; *(fig. geh.)* unpleasant after-effects

nach|weinen *itr. V.* **jmdm./einer Sache ~:** bemoan the loss of sb./sth.; **einer Sache** *(Dat.)* **nicht ~:** have no regrets about sth.; *s. auch* **Träne**

Nachweis [-vais] **der; ~es, ~e** proof *no indef. art.* (*Gen.,* **über** + *Akk.* of); *(Zeugnis)* certificate (**über** + *Akk.* of); **den ~ für etw. erbringen** *od.* **führen** produce *or* furnish proof of sth.; **als** *od.* **zum ~:** as proof; **es gelang ihm der ~, daß ...:** he managed to prove that ...

nachweisbar 1. *Adj.* demonstrable ‹*fact, truth, error, defect, guilt*›; provable ‹*fact, guilt*›; detectable ‹*substance, chemical*›; **die Siedlung ist bis ins 7. Jahrhundert ~:** the settlement can be shown to have existed up to the 7th century. **2.** *adv.* demonstrably

nach|weisen *unr. tr. V.* **a)** prove; **jmdm. einen Fehler/Diebstahl ~:** prove sb. made a mistake/committed a theft; **man konnte ihm nichts ~:** they could not prove anything against him; **im Körper wurden Spuren des Giftes nachgewiesen** traces of the poison were detected in the body; **b)** *(Amtsspr.) (vermitteln)* arrange ‹*hotel room*›; *(informieren über)* provide information on ‹*hotel room, job*›

nachweislich 1. *Adj.; nicht präd.* demonstrable; **eine ~e Falschmeldung** a demonstrably wrong report. **2.** *adv.* demonstrably; as can be proved

Nach·welt die; *o. Pl.* posterity *no art.*; future generations *pl., no art.*

nach|werfen *unr. tr. V.* **a) jmdm. etw. ~:** throw sth. after sb.; **jmdm. einen wütenden Blick ~** *(fig.)* cast a furious glance in sb.'s direction; **eine Münze ~:** put in another coin; **b)** *s.* **nachschmeißen a**

nach|winken *itr. V.* **jmdm./einer Sache ~:** wave after sb./sth.

nach|wirken *itr. V.* have a lasting effect (**bei** on); ‹*medicine*› continue to have an effect; ‹*literary work*› continue to have an influence

Nach·wirkung die after-effect; *(fig.: Einfluß)* influence

nach|wollen *itr. V. (ugs.)* **jmdm. ~:** want to follow sb.

Nach·wort das; *Pl.* **~worte** afterword, postface (**zu** to)

Nach·wuchs der; *o. Pl* **a)** *(fam.: Kind[er])* offspring; **sie erwartet ~:** she's expecting [a baby]; **b)** *(junge Kräfte)* new blood; *(für eine Branche usw.)* new recruits *pl.*; *(in der Ausbildung)* trainees *pl.*; **der musikalische ~:** the rising generation of musicians

Nachwuchs-: ~autor der up-and-coming author; **~kraft die** new recruit; *(in der Ausbildung)* trainee; **~kräfte** junior staff; **~mangel der** lack of new blood *or* new recruits; **~sorgen** *Pl.* recruitment problems; **~spieler der** *(Sport)* up-and-coming player

nach|zahlen *tr., itr. V.* **a)** pay later; pay ‹*salary*› in arrears; **1 000 DM Steuern ~:** pay 1,000 marks back tax; **b)** *(zusätzlich zahlen)* **25 DM ~:** pay another 25 marks

nach|zählen *tr., itr. V.* [re]count; check

Nach·zahlung die additional payment; *(spätere Zahlung)* deferred payment; *(Steuerzahlung)* back tax

nach|zeichnen *tr. V.* copy ‹*picture*›; draw ‹*tree, horse*›; *(mit Pauspapier o. ä.)* trace ‹*picture, tree, horse*›; *(fig.: schildern)* portray

Nach·zeitigkeit die; ~: *(Sprachw.)* future sense of the subordinate clause

nach|ziehen 1. *unr. itr. V.* **a)** *(ugs.: ebenso handeln)* do likewise; follow suit; **b)** *mit sein (hinterhergehen)* **jmdm./einer Sache ~:** follow sb./sth.; **c)** *mit sein (nachträglich übersiedeln)* **jmdm. ~:** [go to] join sb. **2.** *unr. tr. V.* **a)** *(hinter sich herziehen)* drag ‹*foot, leg*›; **b)** *(verstärkend)* retrace, go over ‹*line*›; pencil ‹*eyebrows*›; **die Lippen ~:** put on more lipstick; **c)** *(festziehen)* tighten [up] ‹*nut, bolt*›

Nach·zug der *(Eisenb.)* relief train

Nachzügler [-tsyːklɐ] **der** straggler; *(spät Ankommender)* latecomer

Nackedei ['nakədai] **der; ~s, ~s a)** *(fam. scherzh.: Kind)* **[kleiner] ~:** naked little thing *or* monkey; little bare-bum *(Brit. coll.)*; **b)** *(ugs. scherzh.: Person)* person in the buff; *(im Bild, Film usw.)* nude

Nacken ['nakn̩] **der; ~s, ~:** back *or* nape of the neck; *(Hals)* neck; **den Hut in den ~ schieben** push one's hat right back; **den Kopf in den ~ werfen** throw one's head right back; **das Haar fiel ihm bis in den ~:** his hair hung down the back of his neck; **die Arme im ~ verschränken** fold one's arms behind one's neck; **den ~ steifhalten** *(fig. ugs.)* keep one's chin up; **jmdm. im ~ sitzen** *(fig.)* be breathing down sb.'s neck; **die Furcht/Angst sitzt ihm im ~:** he is gripped by fear

nackend *(veralt., noch landsch.) s.* **nackt a**

Nacken-: ~haar das hair on the back of one's neck; neck hair; **~rolle die** bolster; **~schutz der** neck-guard

nackert ['nakɐt] *(südd., österr. ugs.)*, **nackig** *(bes. md.) s.* **nackt a**

nackt [nakt] *Adj.* **a)** *(unbekleidet)* naked; bare ‹*feet, legs, arms, skin, fists*›; **mit ~em Oberkörper** stripped to the waist; **~ und bloß** completely naked; **sich ~ ausziehen** strip naked; strip off completely; **~ baden** bathe in the nude; **b)** *(kahl)* bald ‹*head*›; hairless ‹*chin*›; featherless ‹*bird*›; bare ‹*rocks, island, tree, branch, walls, bulb*›; **auf dem ~en Boden schlafen** sleep on the bare floor; **c)** *(unverhüllt)* stark ‹*poverty, misery, horror*›; naked ‹*greed*›; plain ‹*fact, words*›; plain, unvarnished ‹*truth*›; **~e Angst** sheer *or* stark terror; **d)** bare ⟨*existence*⟩; **das ~e Leben retten** barely manage to escape with one's life; save one's skin [and nothing more]

Nackt-: ~arsch der *(salopp scherzh.)* bare-bum *(Brit. coll.)*; bare-bottom; **~baden das; ~s** nude bathing; **~bade·strand der** nudist beach

Nackte der/die; *adj. Dekl.* naked man/woman; *(im Bild, Film usw.)* nude; **die ~n am Strand** the naked people *or* people in the nude on the beach

Nackt-: ~foto das nude photo; **~frosch der** *(fam. scherzh.)* **[kleiner] ~frosch** naked little thing *or* monkey; litte bare-bum *(Brit. coll.)*

Nacktheit die; ~: nakedness; nudity; *(fig.: der Landschaft usw.)* bareness

Nackt-: ~kultur die; *o. Pl. (ugs.)* nudism *no art.*; **~samer** [-za:mɐ] **der; ~s, ~:** *(Bot.)* gymnosperm; **~tänzerin die** nude dancer

Nadel ['na:dl̩] **die; ~, ~n** needle; *(Steck~, Hut~, Haar~)* pin; *(Häkel~)* hook; *(für Tonabnehmer)* stylus; **etw. mit heißer/mit der heißen ~ nähen** *(fig. ugs.)* sew sth. in a great hurry; **an der ~ hängen** *(fig. ugs.)* be on the needle *(sl.)*; **man konnte eine ~ fallen hören** you could have heard a pin drop

nadel-, Nadel-: ~baum der conifer; coniferous tree; **~drucker der** *(DV)* dot matrix printer; **~förmig** *Adj.* needle-shaped; needle-like ⟨*point etc.*⟩; **~geld das** *(veralt.)* pin money *no indef. art.*; **~holz das;** *Pl.* **~hölzer a)** softwood; pine-wood; **b)** *(Baum)* conifer; **~kissen das** pincushion

nadeln *itr. V.* ⟨*tree*⟩ shed its needles

Nadel-: ~öhr das eye of a/the needle; **~spitze die** point of a/the needle; **~stärke die** needle size; size of needle; **~stich der a)** *(Stich)* needle-prick; *(einer Stecknadel usw.)* pinprick; *(fig.: Bosheit)* barbed *or (coll.)* snide remark; **jmdm. ~stiche versetzen** aim barbed *or (coll.)* snide remarks at sb.; **b)** *(Nähstich)* stitch; **~streifen der** pin-stripe; **~streifen·anzug der** pinstripe suit; **~wald der** coniferous forest

Nadir [na'di:ɐ̯] **der; ~s** *(Astron.)* nadir

Nagel ['na:gl̩] **der; ~s, Nägel** ['nɛ:gl̩] **a)** nail; *(Med.: für Bruchstellen)* pin; **b)** *(fig.)* **ein ~ zu jmds. Sarg sein** *(salopp)* be a nail in sb.'s coffin; **den ~ auf den Kopf treffen** *(ugs.)* hit the nail on the head *(coll.)*; **Nägel mit Köpfen machen** *(ugs.)* do things properly; make a real job of it; **den Sport** *usw.* **/den Beruf an den ~ hängen** *(ugs.)* give up sport *etc.*/*(coll.)* chuck in one's job; **seine Boxhandschuhe an den ~ hängen** *(ugs.)* hang up one's boxing-gloves; **c)** *(Finger~, Zehen~)* nail; **das brennt mir auf** *od.* **unter den Nägeln** *(fig. ugs.)* it's so urgent I just have to get on with it *or* it just won't wait; **sich** *(Dat.)* **etw. unter den ~ reißen** *(fig. salopp)* make off with sth.; *s. auch* ³**Schwarze b**

nagel-, Nagel-: ~bett das nail-bed; **~brett das** bed of nails; **~bürste die** nail-brush; **~feile die** nail-file; **~fest** *s.* **niet- und nagelfest**; **~haut die** cuticle; **~haut·entferner der; ~s, ~:** cuticle-remover

Nägel·kauen das; ~s nail-biting *no art.*

Nagel-: ~kopf der nail-head; **~lack der** nail varnish *(Brit.)*; nail polish; **~lack·entferner der; ~s, ~:** nail-varnish *(Brit.) or* nail polish remover

nageln *tr. V.* nail (**an** + *Akk.* to, **auf** + *Akk.* on); *(Med.)* pin ⟨*bone, leg, etc.*⟩; **aus Brettern Kisten ~:** nail planks together to make crates

nagel-, Nagel-: ~neu *Adj. (ugs.)* brand-new; **~pflege die** care of the nails; nail-care; **~probe die** *(fig.)* acid test (**auf** + *Akk.* of); **die ~probe machen** try the acid test; **~reiniger der** nail-cleaner; **~schere die** nail-scissors *pl.*; **~schuh der** hobnailed boot; **~zange die** nail-clippers *pl.*

nagen ['na:gn̩] **1.** *itr. V.* gnaw; **an etw.** *(Dat.)* **~:** gnaw [at] sth.; **an der Unterlippe ~:** chew one's lower lip; **an jmdm. ~** *(fig.)* prey on sb.; **an jmds. Gesundheit ~** *(fig.)* undermine sb.'s health. **2.** *tr. V.* gnaw off; **ein Loch ins Holz ~:** gnaw a hole in the wood. **3.** *refl. V.* **sich durch etw. ~:** gnaw through sth.

nagend *Adj.* gnawing ⟨*pain, hunger, fear*⟩; nagging ⟨*pain, doubts, uncertainty, etc.*⟩

Nage·tier das rodent

nah [na:] *s.* **nahe**

Näh·arbeit die [piece of] sewing; **~en** sewing jobs; sewing *sing.*

Nah-: ~aufnahme die *(Fot.)* close-up [photograph]; **~bereich der a)** *(Fot.)* foreground; **b)** *(nähere Umgebung)* [immediate] surrounding area; locality; *(Fernspr.)* local area

nahe ['na:ə] **1.** *Adj.* **näher** ['nɛ:ɐ], **nächst...** [nɛ:çst...] **a)** *(räumlich)* near *pred.*; close *pred.*; nearby *attrib.*; **es ist ganz ~ bis zum Bahnhof** it's not far to the station; **ich bin dir in Gedanken ~** *(geh.)* I am close to you *or* with you in my thoughts; **in der näheren Umgebung** in the neighbourhood; around here/there; **in der nächsten Umgebung von Köln** in the immediate neighbourhood of Cologne; *s. auch* **Osten c; b)** *(zeitlich)* imminent; near *pred.*; **in ~r Zukunft** in the near future; **Weihnachten ist/die Ferien sind ~:** Christmas is/the holidays are nearly here; **die Rettung ist ~:** help is imminent *or* at hand; **das ~ Wochenende** the fast approaching weekend; **c)** *(eng)* close ⟨*relationship, relative, friend*⟩; **seine nähere/nächste Verwandtschaft** his close/closest relatives *pl.* **2.** *adv.* **näher, am nächsten a)** *(räumlich)* **~ an** (+ *Dat./Akk.*), **~ bei** close to; **~ gelegen** nearby; **komm mir nicht zu ~!** don't come too close!; keep your distance!; **~ beieinander** close together; **von ~m** from close up; at close quarters; **aus** *od.* **von nah und fern** *(geh.)* from near and far; **jmdm. zu ~ treten** *(fig.)* offend sb.; **b)** *(zeitlich)* **~ an Mittag** nearly midday; **~ an die achtzig** *(ugs.)* pushing eighty *(coll.)*; **~ bevorstehen** be in the offing; be fast approaching; **~ daran sein, etw. zu tun** be on the point of doing sth.; **c)** *(eng)* closely; **~ befreundet sein** be close friends; *s. auch* **näher. 3.** *Präp. mit Dat. (geh.)* near; close to; **den Tränen/dem Wahnsinn ~ sein** be on the brink of tears/on the verge of madness; **dem Tode ~ sein** be close to death

Nähe ['nɛ:ə] **die; ~: a)** closeness; proximity; *(Nachbarschaft)* vicinity; **in der ~ der Stadt** near the town; **in nächster** *od.* **unmittelbarer ~ des Sees** right next to the lake; **in meiner ~:** near me; *(um mich herum)* around me; *(in der Nachbarschaft)* in my neighbourhood; near where I live; **ich traue mich nicht in seine ~:** I dare not go anywhere near him; **seine ~ stört mich** having him around puts me off; **jmds. ~ suchen** seek sb.'s company; **menschliche Wärme und ~ spüren** feel the warmth of human friendship around one; **er wohnt in der ~/ganz in der ~:** he lives in the vicinity *or* nearby/very near; **irgendwo hier/dort [ganz] in der ~:** somewhere [very] near here/there; **bleibt in der ~!** stay nearby; don't go too far away; **etw. aus der ~ betrachten** take a closer look at sth.; **aus der ~ betrachtet** *(auch fig.)* viewed more closely; **in unmittelbare ~ rücken** ⟨*events*⟩ become imminent; **die zeitliche ~ zu den Ereignissen erlaubt noch keine distanzierte Analyse** the closeness *or* recentness of the events does not yet permit a detached analysis; *s. auch* **greifbar 1 a**

nahe-: ~bei *Adv.* nearby; close by; **~|bringen** *unr. tr. V.* **jmdm. die moderne Kunst** *usw.* **~bringen** make modern art *etc.* accessible to sb.; *(lebendig machen)* bring modern art *etc.* to life for sb.; **das brachte sie einander ~:** that brought them closer together; *s. auch* **näher 3 a**; **~|gehen** *unr. itr. V.; mit sein* **jmdm. ~gehen** affect sb. deeply

Nah·einstellung die *(Fot.)* close focusing

nahe-: ~|kommen *unr. itr. V.; mit sein* **einer Sache** *(Dat.)* **~kommen** come close to sth.; ⟨*amount*⟩ approximate to sth.; **jmdm./sich [menschlich] ~kommen** get to know sb./one another well; **~|legen** *tr. V.* suggest; give rise to ⟨*suspicion, supposition, thought*⟩; **jmdm. etw. ~legen** suggest sth. to sb.; **jmdm. den Rücktritt ~legen, jmdm. ~legen, zurückzutreten** put it to sb. that he/she should resign; **~|liegen** *unr. itr. V.* ⟨*thought*⟩ suggest itself; ⟨*suspicion, question*⟩ arise; **~liegend** *Adj.* ⟨*question, idea*⟩ which [immediately] suggests itself; natural ⟨*suspicion*⟩; obvious ⟨*reason, solution*⟩; **das Naheliegende** the obvious thing [to do]

nahen *(geh.)* **1.** *refl. V.; mit sein (veralt.: sich nähern)* approach; draw near *or (arch.)* nigh; **sich jmdm. ~:** approach sb. **2.** *itr. V.; mit sein* draw near; **sein/ihr Ende nahte** the end was near; **eine ~de Katastrophe** imminent disaster

nähen 1. *itr. V.* sew; *(Kleider machen)* make clothes; **an einem Mantel ~:** work on [the sewing of] a coat. **2.** *tr. V.* **a)** sew ⟨*seam, hem*⟩; *(mit der Maschine)* machine ⟨*seam, hem*⟩; *(herstellen)* make ⟨*dress, coat, curtains, etc.*⟩; **etw. an** *od.* **auf etw.** *(Akk.)* **~:** sew sth. on to sth.; **b)** *(Med.)* stitch ⟨*wound etc.*⟩; **der Patient mußte genäht werden** *(ugs.)* the patient had to have stitches; *s. auch* **doppelt 2 a**

näher 1. *Komp. zu* **nahe. 2.** *Adj.; nicht präd.* **a)** *(kürzer)* shorter ⟨*way, road*⟩; **b)** *(genauer)* further, more precise ⟨*information*⟩; closer ⟨*investigation, inspection*⟩; **die ~en Umstände** the precise circumstances; **bei ~em Hinsehen** on closer examination; **wissen Sie Näheres [darüber]?** do you know any more [about it]?; do you know any details?; **Näheres hierzu siehe unten** for further information on this see below; **des ~en** *(geh.)* in detail. **3.** *adv.* **a) bitte treten Sie ~!** please come in/nearer/this way; **es bringt uns unserem Ziel nicht ~:** it does not bring us any closer to our goal; **b)** *(genauer)* more closely; *(im einzelnen)* in [more] detail; **etw. ~ ansehen** have a closer look at sth.; examine sth. more closely; **~ auf etw.** *(Akk.)* **eingehen, sich ~ mit etw. befassen** go into sth. in [more] detail; **jmdn./etw. ~ kennenlernen** get to know sb./sth. better; **ich kenne ihn nicht ~:** I don't know him well; **allmählich kommen wir der Sache ~:** we're gradually getting to the point

näher|bringen *unr. tr. V.* **jmdm. etw. ~:** make sth. more real *or* more accessible to sb.

Nah·erholungs·gebiet das nearby recreational area

Näherin die; ~, ~nen needlewoman; *(hist.)* seamstress

näher-: ~|kommen *unr. itr. V.; mit sein* **jmdm. [menschlich] ~kommen** get on closer terms with sb.; **sich** *(Dat.)*/*(geh.)* **einander ~kommen** become closer; **~|liegen** *unr. itr. V.* be more obvious; **was liegt da näher, als ...:** what can be more obvious *or* natural than ...

nähern 1. *refl. V.* **a)** *(herankommen)* approach; **die Tiere näherten sich bis auf wenige Meter** the animals came up to within a few metres; **sich jmdm./einer Sache** *(Dat.)* **~:** approach sb./sth.; draw nearer to sb./sth.; **sich dem Ende ~** ⟨*stay, summer*⟩ near its end, draw to an end; **sich dem Ziel der Reise ~:** near one's destination; **b)** *(Kontakt aufnehmen)* **sich jmdm. ~:** approach sb.; **c)** *(sich angleichen)* **sich einem Ideal ~:** come close to an ideal; approximate to an ideal. **2.** *tr. V. (heranbringen)* **etw. einer Sache** *(Dat.)* **~:** bring sth. closer to sth.

näher|stehen *unr. itr. V.* **jmdm./sich** *od.* *(geh.)* **einander ~:** be closer to sb./one another
Näherung die; ~, ~en approximation
Näherungs·wert der *(Math.)* approximate value
nahe-: ~|stehen *unr. itr. V.* **jmdm. ~stehen** be on close *or* intimate terms with sb.; **einer Partei ~stehen** sympathize with a party; **~stehend** *Adj.* **die ihm Nahestehenden** those close to him; **eine der Witwe ~stehende Cousine** a cousin who is/was on close terms with the widow; **~zu** *Adv. (mit Adjektiven)* almost; nearly; wellnigh ‹*impossible, superhuman*›; all but ‹*exhausted, impossible*›; *(mit Zahlenangabe)* close on
Näh-: ~faden der sewing thread; **~garn das** [sewing] cotton
Nah·kampf der a) *(Milit.)* close combat; **b)** *(Boxen)* infighting
Näh-: ~kästchen das a) *s.* **~kasten; b) aus dem ~kästchen plaudern** *(ugs. scherzh.)* tell all; *(als Kenner, Fachmann)* tell the inside story; **~kasten der** sewing-box; workbox; **~korb der** sewing-basket
nahm [na:m] *1. u. 3. Pers. Sg. Prät. v.* **nehmen**
Näh-: ~maschine die sewing-machine; **~nadel die** sewing-needle
Nah·ost *o. Art.* the Middle East
nah·östlich *Adj.* Middle Eastern
Nähr-: ~boden der culture medium; *(fig.)* breeding-ground; **~creme die** skin food
nähren ['nɛ:rən] **1.** *tr. V.* **a)** *(ernähren)* feed ‹*animal, child*› **(mit** on); **gut/schlecht genährt** well-fed/underfed; **b)** *(geh.: entstehen lassen)* nurture ‹*hope, suspicion, hatred*›; cherish ‹*desire, hope*›; foster ‹*plan, hatred*›; **c)** *(geh.: Lebensunterhalt geben)* provide a [good] living for; **dieser Beruf nährt seinen Mann** you can make a good living in this job. **2.** *itr. V. (nahrhaft sein)* be nourishing. **3.** *refl. V. (geh.)* **sich von etw. ~:** live on sth.; ‹*animal*› feed on sth.
nahrhaft *Adj.* nourishing; nutritious; **ein ~es Essen** *od. (geh.)* **Mahl** a square meal
Nähr-: ~lösung die a) fluid culture medium; **b)** *(für Hydrokultur, künstliche Ernährung)* nutrient solution; **~salze** *Pl.* nutrient salts; **~stoffe** *Pl.* nutrients
Nahrung ['na:rʊŋ] **die; ~:** food; **flüssige/feste ~:** liquids *pl.*/solids *pl.*; **die ~ verweigern** refuse food; **geistige ~** *(fig.)* intellectual nourishment; **dem Verdacht/den Gerüchten** *usw.* **~ geben** *od.* **bieten** *(fig.)* help to nurture *or* foster the suspicion/the rumours *etc.*; **es gab seinem Zorn neue ~** *(fig.)* it gave fresh fuel to his anger; it rekindled his anger
Nahrungs-: ~aufnahme die intake of food; **die ~aufnahme verweigern** refuse food; **~mittel das** food [item]; **~mittel** *Pl.* foodstuffs; **~mittel·chemie die** food chemistry *no art.*; **~mittel·industrie die** food *or* foodstuffs industry; **~quelle die** source of food; **~suche die** search for food; **auf ~suche gehen** search for food; *(jagen)* hunt for food
Nähr·wert der nutritional value; **keinen [sittlichen** *od.* **geistigen] ~ haben** *(fig. salopp)* be completely and utterly pointless
Näh·seide die sewing silk
Naht [na:t] **die; ~, Nähte** ['nɛ:tə] **a)** seam; **aus den** *od.* **allen Nähten platzen** *(fig. ugs.)* ‹*person, fig.: institution etc.*› be bursting at the seams; **b)** *(Med., Anat.)* suture
Näh·tisch der sewing-table
naht·los 1. *Adj.* seamless; *(fig.)* perfectly smooth ‹*transition*›. **2.** *adv.* **Studium und Beruf gehen nicht ~ ineinander über** there is not a perfectly smooth transition from study to work
Naht·stelle die a) *(Schweißnaht)* seam; **b)** *(Berührungsstelle)* point of contact, interface **(von** between); *(Grenzlinie)* borderline

Nah-: ~verkehr der local traffic; **nur im ~verkehr eingesetzt werden** be used only for local services; **~verkehrs·mittel das** form of local transport; **~verkehrs·zug der** local train
Näh·zeug das sewing things *pl.*
Nah·ziel das short-term *or* immediate aim
naiv [na'i:f] **1.** *Adj.* naïve; ingenuous ‹*look; child*›; unaffected ‹*pleasure*›; **ein ~er Zugang zur Musik** an unsophisticated approach to music; **die Naive/den Naiven spielen** act naïve. **2.** *adv.* naïvely; **sich ~ an etw.** *(Dat.)* **freuen** take an unaffected pleasure in sth.
Naive die; *adj. Dekl. (Theater)* ingénue
Naivität [naivi'tɛ:t] **die; ~:** naïvety; *(eines Blickes, Kindes)* ingenuousness; *(von Vergnügen)* unaffectedness
Naivling der; ~s, ~e *(ugs. abwertend)* [naïve] simpleton
Name ['na:mə] **der; ~ns, ~n,** *(seltener)* **Namen** ['na:mən] **der; ~s, ~:** name; **wie ist der ~ dieser Tiere/Leute?** what are these animals/people called?; **die Dinge/das Unrecht beim ~n nennen** call a spade a spade/acknowledge injustice as such; **[gestatten,] mein ~ ist Maier** [allow me to introduce myself,] my name is Maier; **wie war gleich Ihr ~?** what was your name again?; **ich kenne ihn/es nur dem ~n nach** I know him/it only by name; **der Hund hört auf den ~n Fifi** the dog answers to the name of Fifi; **unter jmds. ~n** *(Dat.)* under sb.'s name; **das Konto läuft auf meinen ~n/das Auto ist auf meinen ~n gemeldet** the account is in/the car is registered in my name; **ein Mann mit ~n Emil** a man by the name of Emil; **er rief mich bei** *od.* **mit meinem ~n** he called me by my name; **in jmds./einer Sache ~n, im ~n von jmdm./etw.** on behalf of sb./sth.; **im eigenen ~n handeln** act on one's own account; **im ~n des Volkes/Gesetzes** *(Rechtsspr.)* in the name of the people/the law; **in Gottes ~n!** *(ugs.)* for God's sake; **sich** *(Dat.)* **einen ~n machen** make a name for oneself; *s. auch* **daher b; Hase a; hergeben a; Kind a**
namen-, Namen-: ~forschung die; *o. Pl.: s.* **~kunde; ~gebung die; ~, ~en** *(allgemein)* giving of names; *(in einem bes. Fall)* choice of name; **~gedächtnis das** memory for names; **~kunde die;** *o. Pl.* onomastics *sing., no art.*; **~liste die** list of names; **~los 1.** *Adj.* **a)** nameless; *(unbekannt)* unknown; anonymous ‹*author, poet*›; **b)** *(geh.: unbeschreiblich)* unspeakable, indescribable ‹*misery*›; inexpressible ‹*joy*›; **2.** *adv. (geh.)* unspeakably; unutterably; **~register das** *s.* **~liste**
namens 1. *Adv.* by the name of; called. **2.** *Präp. mit Gen. (Amtsspr.)* on behalf of
Namens-: ~änderung die change of name; **~gebung die; ~, ~en** *s.* **Namengebung; ~nennung die** mention of a name/of names; *(Nennung des eigenen Namens)* giving of one's name; **~patron der** patron saint; **~schild das a)** *(an Türen usw.)* name-plate; **b)** *(zum Anstecken)* name-badge; **~tag der** name-day; **sie hat am ... ~tag** it is her name-day on the ...; **~vetter der** namesake; **~zug der a)** *(Unterschrift)* signature; **b)** *(veralt.: Monogramm)* monogram
namentlich ['na:məntlɪç] **1.** *Adj.* by name *postpos.*; **eine ~e Liste** a list of names; **eine ~e Abstimmung** a roll-call vote. **2.** *Adv.* **a)** *(mit Namen)* by name; **jmdn. ~ nennen** mention sb. by name; name sb.; **b)** *(besonders)* particularly; especially
namhaft 1. *Adj.* **a)** *nicht präd. (berühmt)* noted; of note *postpos.*; **b)** *(ansehnlich)* noteworthy ‹*sum, difference*›; notable ‹*contribution, opportunity*›; **c)** *in* **jmdn./etw. ~ machen** *(Papierdt.)* name sb./sth. **2.** *adv. (beträchtlich)* considerably

Namibia [na'mi:bia] **(das); ~s** Namibia
Namibier der; ~s, ~, Namibierin die; ~, ~nen Namibian
nämlich ['nɛ:mlɪç] **1.** *Adv.* **a) er kann nicht kommen, er ist ~ krank** he cannot come, as he is ill; he can't come – he's ill[, you see] *(coll.)*; **b)** *(und zwar)* namely; *(als Füllwort)* **das war ~ ganz anders** it was quite different in fact *or* actually. **2.** *Adj. nicht präd. (geh. veralt.)* same; *(steigernd)* selfsame
nannte ['nantə] *1. u. 3. Pers. Sg. Prät. v.* **nennen**
nanu [na'nu:] *Interj.* **~, was machst du denn hier?** hello, what are you doing here?; **~, wo ist denn der ganze Käse geblieben?** that's funny, what's happened to all that cheese?; **~, Sie gehen schon?** what, you're going already?
Napalm ['na:palm] **das; ~s** napalm
Napalm·bombe die napalm bomb
Napf [napf] **der; ~[e]s, Näpfe** ['nɛpfə] bowl *(esp. for animal's food)*
Napf·kuchen der gugelhupf; ring cake
Naphthalin [nafta'li:n] **das; ~s** naphthalene
Nappa ['napa] **das; ~[s] ~s, Nappa·leder das** nappa [leather]
Narbe ['narbə] **die; ~, ~n a)** scar; **von dieser Verletzung werden ~n zurückbleiben** this wound will leave scars; **tiefe ~n bei jmdm. hinterlassen** *(fig.)* leave sb. deeply scarred; **b)** *(Bot.)* stigma
Narben-: ~bildung die scar formation; **~leder das** *(Gerberei)* grained leather; **~seite die** *(Gerberei)* hair *or* grain side
narbig *Adj.* scarred; *(von Pocken o. ä.)* pitted; pock-marked
Narbung die; ~, ~en *(Gerberei)* grain[ing]
Narkose [nar'ko:zə] **die; ~, ~n** *(Med.)* narcosis; **mit** *od.* **in/ohne ~:** under anaesthesia/without an anaesthetic; **dem Patienten eine ~ geben** give the patient a general anaesthetic; **aus der ~ aufwachen** come round from the anaesthetic; **jmdn. aus der ~ holen** awaken sb. from the anaesthetic
Narkose-: ~arzt der anaesthetist; **~gewehr das** tranquillizer gun; **~mittel das** anaesthetic
Narkotikum [nar'ko:tikʊm] **das; ~s, Narkotika** *(Med.)* narcotic
narkotisch 1. *Adj. (Med., auch fig.)* narcotic; overpowering ‹*scent*›. **2.** *adv.* **auf jmdn. ~ wirken** have a narcotic effect on sb.
narkotisieren *tr. V. (Med.)* anaesthetize ‹*patient*›; put ‹*patient*› under a general anaesthetic
Narr [nar] **der; ~en, ~en** fool; *(Hof~)* jester; fool; *(Fastnachts~)* carnival jester *or* reveller; **sich zum ~en machen** let oneself be fooled; **jmdn. zum ~en haben** *od.* **halten** play tricks on sb.; *(täuschen)* pull the wool over sb.'s eyes; **einen ~en an jmdm. gefressen haben** *(ugs.)* be dotty about sb. *(coll.)*
narren ['narən] *tr. V. (geh.)* **jmdn. ~:** make a fool of sb.; *(täuschen)* deceive sb.
narren-, Narren-: ~freiheit die freedom to do as one pleases; **jmdm. ~freiheit gewähren** let sb. do as he/she pleases; **~hände** *Pl. in* **~hände beschmieren Tisch und Wände** *(Spr.)* little vandals scribble on everything; **~kappe die** *(hist.)* jester's cap and bells; **~possen** *Pl. (geh. veralt.)* tomfoolery *sing.*; **~sicher** *(ugs.)* **1.** *Adj.* foolproof; **2.** *adv.* in a foolproof way; **~zepter das** jester's sceptre *or* bauble
Narretei [narə'tai] **die; ~, ~en** *(geh.)* **a)** *(Scherz)* prank; **~en** fooling about *sing.*; **b)** *(Torheit)* folly; stupidity
Narrheit die; ~, ~en a) *o. Pl. (Art)* foolishness; **b)** *(Handlung)* foolish prank
Närrin ['nɛrɪn] **die; ~, ~nen** fool; **liebe ~nen und Narren!** my dear she-asses and jackasses! *(form of address used by speakers at carnival time)*
narrisch *(südd.) s.* **närrisch 1 a, b, 2 a, b**

närrisch ['nɛrɪʃ] 1. *Adj.* a) *(verrückt)* crazy; *(wirr im Kopf)* scatter-brained; dotty *(coll.)*; **[ein] ~es Zeug reden** talk gibberish; **halb/ganz ~ [vor Glück]** be almost/quite beside oneself [with joy]; **auf etw.** *(Akk.)* *od.* **nach etw. ganz ~ sein** be mad keen on sth. *(sl.)*; b) *(ugs.: sehr viel, groß)* terrific *(coll.)*; **ein ~es Geld** a fantastic amount of money *(coll.)*; c) *nicht präd. (karnevalistisch)* carnival-crazy ⟨*season*⟩; **das ~e Treiben [beim Karneval** *od.* **Fasching]** the mad *or* crazy carnival antics *pl.* 2. *adv.* a) *(verrückt)* crazily; **sich ~ benehmen** carry on like a madman/madwoman; act crazy; b) *(ugs. sehr)* terrifically *(coll.)*; **~ verliebt sein** be madly in love *(coll.)*

Narziß [nar'tsɪs] **der;** ~ *od.* **Narzisses, Narzisse** Narcissus

Narzisse [nar'tsɪsə] **die;** ~, **~n** narcissus; **gelbe ~:** daffodil

Narzißmus der; ~: *(Psych.)* narcissism

narzißtisch *Adj.* *(Psych.)* narcissistic

nasal [na'za:l] 1. *Adj.* nasal. 2. *adv.* nasally

Nasal der; ~s, ~e *(Sprachw.)* nasal

nasalieren *tr. V.* *(Sprachw.)* nasalize

Nasal·laut der *(Sprachw.)* nasal

naschen ['naʃn̩] 1. *itr. V.* a) *(Süßes essen)* eat sweet things; *(Bonbons essen)* eat sweets *(Brit.)* *or (Amer.)* candy; **[so] gern ~:** have [such] a sweet tooth; b) *(heimlich essen)* have a nibble; **er hat vom Pudding genascht** he's been at the pudding. 2. *tr. V.* a) *(essen)* eat ⟨*sweets, chocolate, etc.*⟩; b) *(heimlich essen)* **er/sie hat Milch genascht** he/she has been at the milk

Näschen ['nɛ:sçən] **das;** ~s, ~: little nose

Nascherei die; ~, **~en** a) *o. Pl.* [continually] eating sweet things; **hör auf mit der ~!** don't keep eating sweet things all the time!; b) *(Süßigkeit)* **~en** sweets

naschhaft *Adj.* fond of sweet things *postpos.*; sweet-toothed; **[so] ~ sein** have [such] a sweet tooth

Naschhaftigkeit die; ~: fondness for sweet things; **ihre ~ kostet viel Geld** her sweet tooth comes expensive

Nasch-: **~katze die** *(fam.)* compulsive nibbler; *(Süßigkeiten naschend)* compulsive sweet- *(Brit.)* *or (Amer.)* candy-eater; **~sucht die** *o. Pl.* addiction to sweet things; **~werk das;** *o. Pl. (veralt.)* sweet titbits

Nase ['na:zə] **die;** ~, **~n** a) nose; **mir blutet die ~:** my nose is bleeding; I've got a nosebleed; **mir läuft die ~, meine ~ läuft** I've got a runny nose; b) *(fig.)* **direkt vor deiner ~** *(ugs.)* right under your nose; **der Bus ist mir vor der ~ weggefahren** *(ugs.)* I missed the bus by a whisker; **jmdm. die Tür vor der ~ zuschlagen** *(ugs.)* shut the door in sb.'s face; **jmdm. etw. vor der ~ wegschnappen** *(ugs.)* snatch sth. from under sb.'s nose; **man hat ihm einen jungen Manager vor die ~ gesetzt** *(ugs.)* they have appointed a young manager over his head; **die ~ voll haben** *(ugs.)* have had enough; **von jmdm./etw. die ~ [gestrichen] voll haben** *(ugs.)* be sick [to death] of sb./sth.; **seine ~ in etw./alles stecken** *(ugs.)* stick one's nose into sth./everything *(coll.)*; **nicht weiter sehen als seine ~** *(ugs.)* see no further than the end of one's nose; **ihm paßt** *od.* **gefällt deine ~ nicht** *(ugs.)* he doesn't like your face; **sich** *(Dat.)* **die ~ begießen** *(ugs.)* have a drink or two; **die** *od.* **seine ~ in die Bücher stecken** *(ugs.)* get down to one's studies; **jmdm. eine lange ~ machen** *od.* **eine ~ drehen** *(ugs.)* cock a snook at sb.; **immer der ~ nach** *(ugs.)* just follow your nose; **faß dich an die eigene ~!** *(ugs.)* you're a fine one to talk!; **jmdn. an der ~ herumführen** *(ugs.)* pull the wool over sb.'s eyes; **auf der ~ liegen** *(ugs.)* be laid up; **auf die ~ fallen** *(ugs.)* come a cropper *(sl.)*; **jmdm. etw. auf die ~ binden** *(ugs.)* let sb. in on sth.; **jmdm. auf der ~ herumtanzen** *(ugs.)* play sb. up; **jmdm. eins** *od.* **was auf die ~ geben** *(ugs.)* put sb. in his/her place; **jmdm. etw. aus der ~ ziehen** *(ugs.)* worm sth. out of sb.; **das sticht mir schon lange in die ~** *(ugs.)* I've had my eye on that for a long time; **jmdn. mit der ~ auf etw.** *(Akk.)* **stoßen** *(ugs.)* spell sth. out to sb.; **pro ~** *(ugs.)* per head; **jmdm. unter die ~ reiben, daß ...** *(ugs.)* rub it in that ...; **das brauchst du mir nicht unter die ~ zu reiben** *(ugs.)* you don't have to rub my nose in it; *s. auch* **Mund; rümpfen;** c) *(Geruchssinn, Gespür)* nose; **eine gute ~ für etw. haben** have a good nose for sth.; *(etw. intuitiv wissen)* have a sixth sense for sth.; d) *(geh.: Bug)* bow; *(eines Flugzeugs)* nose; e) *(Felsvorsprung)* spur; e) *(ugs.: Farbtropfen)* run

nase·lang *s.* **nasenlang**

näseln ['nɛ:zl̩n] *itr. V.* talk through one's nose

näselnd 1. *Adj.* nasal. 2. *adv.* nasally; **~ sprechen** speak in a nasal tone

nasen-, Nasen-: **~bär der** coati; **~bein das** nasal bone; **~bluten das;** ~s bleeding from the nose; **~bluten haben/bekommen** have/get a nosebleed; **~flügel der** side of the nose; *(einschl. ~loch)* nostril; **~höhle die** *(Anat.)* nasal cavity; **~lang** *in* **alle ~lang** constantly; all the time; **~länge die: mit einer ~länge** *(Pferdesport)*, **um eine ~länge** *(fig.)* by a head; **er war mir um eine ~länge voraus** he was fractionally ahead of me; **~loch das** nostril; **~ring der** nosering; **~rücken der** ridge of the/one's nose; **~scheide·wand die** nasal septum; **~schleim der** nasal mucus; **~schleim·haut die** nasal mucous membrane; **~spitze die** tip of the/one's nose; **nicht weiter sehen, als die ~spitze reicht** *(fig. ugs.)* not be able to see further than the end of one's nose; **jmdm. etw. an der ~spitze ansehen** *(fig. ugs.)* tell sth. by sb.'s face; **~spray der** *od.* **das** nasal spray; **~stüber der** swat on the nose; **~tropfen** *Pl.* nosedrops; **~wurzel die** root of the nose

nase-, Nase-: **~rümpfen das: mit ~rümpfen** with a look of disgust *or* disdain; **dafür hat sie nur ein ~rümpfen übrig** she only turns up her nose at that; **~rümpfend** 1. *Adj.* disapproving; 2. *adv.* disdainfully; **~weis** 1. *Adj.* precocious; pert ⟨*remark, reply*⟩; **sei nicht so ~weis!** don't be such a little know-all!; 2. *adv.* precociously; **~weis der;** ~es, ~e *(fam.)* [little] know-all; [little] clever Dick *(coll.)*

nas-, Nas-: **~führen** *tr. V.* lead up the garden path; **sich genasführt fühlen** feel one has been led up the garden path; **~horn das** rhinoceros; **~lang** *s.* **nasenlang**

-nasig *adj.* -nosed

naß [nas] **nasser** *od.* **nässer** ['nɛsɐ], **nassest...** *od.* **nässest...** ['nɛsəst...] 1. *Adj.* a) wet; **~ machen** make wet; sprinkle ⟨*washing*⟩; **sich/das Bett ~ machen** wet oneself/one's bed; **mit nassen Augen** with tears in one's eyes; **durch und durch** *od.* **bis auf die Haut ~:** wet through; soaked to the skin; **wie ein nasser Sack** *(ugs.)* as limp as a wet sack; **ein nasses Grab** *(dichter.)* a watery grave; **mach dich bloß nicht ~!** *(fig. salopp)* don't overdo it! *(iron.)*; **jmdn. ~ machen** *(Sportjargon)* trounce sb.; beat sb. hollow *(coll.)*; b) **für ~** *(bes. berlin. u. ostmd.)* for free; for nothing. 2. *adv.* **sich ~ rasieren** have a wet shave; *(immer)* use a razor and shaving cream

Naß das; Nasses *(dichter. od. scherzh.)* a) *(Wasser)* water; *(Regen)* wetness *(esp. joc.)*; **hinein ins kühle ~!** in[to the water] we go!; b) *(Getränk)* **das edle** *od.* **kostbare ~:** the precious liquid

Nassauer ['nasauɐ] **der;** ~s, ~ *(ugs., abwertend)* sponger; *(Schnorrer)* scrounger *(coll.)*

nassauern *(ugs. abwertend)* 1. *tr. V.* **etw. bei jmdm. ~:** scrounge sth. from sb. *(coll.)*. 2. *itr. V.* scrounge *(coll.)*

Nässe ['nɛsə] **die;** ~: wetness; *(an Wänden usw.)* dampness; **bei ~:** in the wet; in wet weather; **„vor ~ schützen"** 'protect from damp'

nässen 1. *itr. V.* ⟨*wound, eczema*⟩ suppurate. 2. *tr. V.* *(geh.)* make wet; wet ⟨*bed, feet, etc.*⟩

naß-, Naß-: **~forsch** 1. *Adj.* brash. 2. *adv.* brashly; **~geschwitzt** *Adj.* soaked in sweat *postpos.*; **~kalt** *Adj.* cold and wet; raw; **~rasur die** wet shaving *no art.*; **zur ~rasur braucht man ...:** for a wet shave one needs ...; **~wäsche die** *washing not dried by the laundry*; wet washing

Nas·tuch das *(schweiz.)* handkerchief

Nation [na'tsio:n] **die;** ~, **~en** nation; **die Vereinten ~en** the United Nations *sing.*; **der Liebling der ~ sein** *(ugs.)* be a national hero

national [natsio'na:l] 1. *Adj.* a) national; **~e und internationale Märkte** domestic and international markets; **Nationale Front** *(DDR)* National Front; b) *(patriotisch)* nationalist. 2. *adv.* a) *(innerstaatlich)* at a national level; nationally; b) *(patriotisch)* ⟨*think, feel*⟩ nationalistically

national-, National-: **~bewußt** *Adj.* nationally conscious; **~bewußt sein** be conscious of one's nationality; have a sense of national identity; **~bewußt·sein das** [sense of] national consciousness; sense of national identity; **~charakter der** national character; **~china (das)** *(veralt.)* Nationalist China

Nationale das; ~s, ~ *(österr.)* a) personal details *or* particulars *pl.*; b) *(Fragebogen)* form *or* questionnaire asking for personal details

National-: **~elf die** *(Fußball)* national team *or* side; **~epos das** national epic; **~farben** *Pl.* national colours; **~feier·tag der** national holiday; **~flagge die** national flag; **~gefühl das** national feeling; feeling for one's country; **~gericht das** national dish; **~getränk das** national drink; **~held der** national hero; **~hymne die** national anthem

nationalisieren *tr. V.* nationalize

Nationalisierung die; ~, **~en** nationalization

Nationalismus der; ~: nationalism *usu. no art.*

Nationalist der; ~en, ~en, **Nationalistin die;** ~, **~nen** nationalist

nationalistisch 1. *Adj.* nationalist; nationalistic. 2. *adv.* nationalistically

Nationalität [natsionali'tɛ:t] **die;** ~, **~en** nationality; **welcher ~ sind Sie?** what nationality are you?

Nationalitäten-: **~frage die** problem of different nationalities within one state; **~staat der** multinational state

national-, National-: **~literatur die** national literature; **~mannschaft die** national team; **~ökonomie die** political economy *no art.*; **~park der** national park; **~preis der** *(DDR) annual award for achievement in science, technology, and the arts*; **~rat der** a) *(österr., schweiz.)* National Council; b) *(Mitglied)* member of the National Council; c) *(DDR) highest governing body of the 'Nationale Front'*; **~sozialismus der** National Socialism; **~sozialist der** National Socialist; **~sozialistisch** 1. *Adj.* National Socialist; 2. *adv.* **eindeutig ~sozialistisch geprägt sein** bear all the marks of National Socialism; **~spieler der** *(Sport)* national player; international; **~sprache die** national language; **~staat der** nation-state; **~staatlich** *Adj.* **~staatliche Bestrebungen** efforts towards the creation of a nation-state; **~staatliches Denken** thinking in nationalistic terms; **~stolz der** national pride; **~straße die** *(schweiz.)* national highway; **~tracht die** national costume; **~versammlung die** National Assembly

NATO, Nato ['na:to] **die; ~:** NATO; Nato *no art.*
nato·grün *Adj.* dark olive green
NATO-Staat der NATO state *or* country
Natrium ['na:triʊm] **das; ~s** *(Chemie)* sodium
Natron ['na:trɔn] **das; ~s [doppeltkohlensaures] ~:** sodium bicarbonate; bicarbonate of soda; bicarb *(coll.)*; **[kohlensaures] ~:** sodium carbonate; soda
Natron·lauge die caustic soda [solution]
Natter ['natɐ] **die; ~, ~n** colubrid; **eine ~ am Busen nähren** *(fig. geh.)* nurture a viper in one's bosom *(literary)*
Nattern·gezücht das *(veralt. abwertend)* nest of vipers
Natur [na'tu:ɐ̯] **die; ~, ~en a)** *o. Pl.* nature *no art.*; **die Wunder der Natur** the wonders of nature; **wider die ~:** unnatural; **zurück zur ~:** back to nature; **die unberührte ~:** unspoilt nature; **die freie ~:** [the] open countryside; **Tiere in freier ~ sehen** see animals in the wild; **nach der ~ zeichnen/malen** draw/paint from nature; **b)** *(Art, Eigentümlichkeit)* nature; **eine gesunde/eiserne/labile ~ haben** *(ugs.)* have a healthy/cast-iron/delicate constitution; **das widerspricht ihrer ~:** it is not in her nature; **jmdm. gegen** *od.* **wider die ~ gehen** go against sb.'s nature; **jmdm. zur zweiten ~ werden** become second nature to sb.; **die Verletzung war nur leichter ~:** the injury was only slight; **in der ~ der Sache/der Dinge liegen** be in the nature of things; **c)** *(Mensch)* sort *or* type of person; sort *(coll.)*; type *(coll.)*; **d)** *o. Pl.* *(natürlicher Zustand)* **Möbel in Kiefer ~:** natural pine furniture; **sie ist von ~ aus blond/ein gutmütiger Mensch** she is naturally fair/good-natured; **Hat sie eine Dauerwelle? – Nein, das ist alles ~:** Is her hair permed? – No, it's naturally curly
Natural·abgaben *Pl.* taxes [paid] in kind
Naturalien [natu'ra:li̯ən] *Pl.* natural produce *sing.* *(used as payment)*; **in ~** *(Dat.)* **bezahlen** pay in kind
Naturalien·kabinett das *(veralt.)* natural-history collection
naturalisieren *tr. V.* *(auch Biol.)* naturalize; **sich ~:** become naturalized
Naturalisierung die; ~, ~en *(auch Biol.)* naturalization
Naturalismus der; ~: naturalism
Naturalist der; ~en, ~en, Naturalistin die; ~, ~nen naturalist
naturalistisch 1. *Adj.* **a)** naturalistic; **b)** *(den Naturalismus betreffend)* naturalist. **2.** *adv.* **a)** ⟨*paint, describe*⟩ naturalistically; **b)** *(den Naturalismus betreffend)* naturalistically; ⟨*influenced*⟩ by naturalism
Natural-: ~lohn der wages *pl.* [paid] in kind; **~wirtschaft die** barter economy
natur-, Natur-: ~apostel der *(iron.)* back-to-nature freak *(sl.)*; **~belassen** *Adj.* natural ⟨*oils, foods, etc.*⟩; **~beobachtung die** observation of nature; **~beschreibung die** description of nature; **~blond** *Adj.* naturally fair *or* blond; **~bursche der** child of nature; **~darm der** natural [animal] intestine *(used as sausage-casing)*; **~denkmal das** natural monument; **~dünger der** natural fertilizer
nature [na'ty:ɐ̯] *indekl. Adj.* *(Gastr.)* ⟨*steak, escalope, etc.*⟩ au naturel
Naturell das; ~s, ~e disposition; temperament; **das widerspricht seinem ~:** it's not in his nature
natur-, Natur-: ~ereignis das natural phenomenon; *(Versicherungsw.)* act of God; **~erscheinung die** natural phenomenon; **~erzeugnis das** *s.* **~produkt**; **~farbe die a)** natural colour; **b)** *(Farbstoff)* natural dye; **~farben** *Adj.* natural-coloured ⟨*leather, wool, wood, etc.*⟩; **~faser die** natural fibre; **~film der** nature film; **~forscher der** naturalist; **~forschung die** natural-history research; **~freund der** nature-lover; **~gegeben** *Adj.* natural and inevitable ⟨*state of affairs*⟩; **etw. als ~gegeben ansehen** regard sth. as part of the natural order [of things]; **~gemäß 1.** *Adv.* naturally; **2.** *adj.* **a)** natural; ⟨*forest management*⟩ in keeping with the natural environment; **~geschichte die;** *o. Pl.* **a)** natural history; **b)** *(veralt.)* *s.* **~kunde**; **~geschichtlich 1.** *Adj.; nicht präd.* natural history; ⟨*teaching*⟩ of natural history; **die ~geschichtliche Entwicklung des Menschen** the natural history of mankind; **2.** *adv.* from the point of view of natural history; **~gesetz das** law of nature; **~getreu 1.** *Adj.;* lifelike ⟨*portrait, imitation*⟩; faithful ⟨*reproduction*⟩; **2.** *adv.* ⟨*draw*⟩ true to life; ⟨*reproduce*⟩ faithfully; **etw. ~getreu darstellen** portray sth. in a true-to-life way; **~gewalt die** force of nature; **~gottheit die** *(Rel.)* nature-deity; **~haft** *Adj.* *(geh.)* natural; **~heil·kunde die** naturopathy *no art.*; **~heil·verfahren das** naturopathic treatment; **~katastrophe die** natural disaster; **~kind das** child of nature; **~kraft die** force of nature; **~krause die** naturally frizzy hair *no indef. art.*; **~kunde die;** *o. Pl.* *(veralt.)* nature study *no art.*; **~kundlich** *Adj.; nicht präd.* natural-history ⟨*museum, field trip, etc.*⟩; **~landschaft die** natural *or* unspoilt landscape; **~lehr·pfad der** nature trail
natürlich [na'ty:ɐ̯lɪç] **1.** *Adj.* natural; **eines ~en Todes sterben** die a natural death; die of natural causes; **ein Bild in ~er Größe** a life-size portrait; **das ist die ~ste Sache der Welt** it is the most natural thing in the world; *s. auch* **Person. 2.** *adv.* ⟨*laugh, behave*⟩ naturally. **3.** *Adv.* **a)** *(selbstverständlich, wie erwartet)* naturally; of course; **b)** *(zwar)* of course; **er wird natürlich zustimmen, aber ...:** of course he is bound to agree, but ...
natürlicher·weise *Adv.* naturally; of course
Natürlichkeit die; ~: naturalness
natur-, Natur-: ~locken *Pl.* natural curls; **~nah[e]** *Adj.* ⟨*life, existence*⟩ close to nature; **~notwendigkeit die** objective necessity; **~park der** ≈ national park; **~philosophie die** philosophy of nature; **~produkt das** natural product; **~produkte** natural produce *sing.*; **~recht das;** *o. Pl.* natural law; **~rein** *Adj.* pure ⟨*honey, jam, fruit, juice, etc.*⟩; ⟨*wine*⟩ free of additives; **~religion die** nature religion; **~schauspiel das** natural spectacle; **~schönheit die** site of natural beauty; **~schutz der** [nature] conservation; **unter ~schutz** *(Dat.)* **stehen** be protected by law; be a protected species/variety/area *etc.*; **etw. unter ~schutz** *(Akk.)* **stellen** protect sth. by law; **~schutz·gebiet das** nature reserve; **~seide die** real *or* natural silk; **~stein der** natural stone; **~stoff der** natural substance; **~talent das** [great] natural talent *or* gift; *(begabter Mensch)* naturally talented *or* gifted person; **ein ~talent sein** have a [great] natural gift *or* talent; **~ton der** *(Musik)* natural note; **~trieb der** *(veralt.)* [natural] instinct; **~trüb** *Adj.* unfiltered, naturally cloudy ⟨*fruit juice*⟩; **~verbunden** *Adj.* ⟨*person*⟩ in tune with nature; **~volk das** primitive people; **~widrig** *Adj.* unnatural; against nature *postpos.*; **~wissenschaft die** natural science *no art.*; **die ~wissenschaften** the [natural] sciences; **~wissenschaftler der** [natural] scientist; **~wissenschaftlich 1.** *Adj.* scientific; **2.** *adv.* scientifically; **~wüchsig** *(Philos.)* **1.** *Adj.* natural; organic; **2.** *adv.* naturally; organically; **~wunder das** miracle *or* wonder of nature
'nauf [nauf] *(südd.)* *s.* **hinauf**
'naus [naus] *(südd.)* *s.* **hinaus**
Nautik ['nautɪk] **die; ~ a)** nautical science *no art.*; **b)** *(Navigation)* navigation *no art.*
nautisch ['nautɪʃ] *Adj.* *(Seew.)* naval ⟨*officer*⟩; navigational ⟨*instrument, calculation*⟩
Navel·orange ['na:vl̩-] **die** navel orange
Navigation [naviga'tsi̯o:n] **die; ~** *(Seew., Flugw.)* navigation *no art.*
Navigations-: ~fehler der *(Seew., Flugw.)* navigational error; **~instrument das** *(Seew., Flugw.)* navigational instrument; **~karte die** *(Seew., Flugw.)* navigational chart; **~offizier der** *(Seew., Flugw.)* navigating officer
Navigator [naviga'tɔr] **der; ~s, ~en** *(Seew., Flugw.)* navigator
navigieren *tr., itr. V.* navigate
Nazarener [natsa're:nɐ] **der; ~s, ~:** Nazarene
Nazareth ['na:tsarɛt] **(das); -s** Nazareth
Nazi ['na:tsi] **der; ~s, ~s** Nazi
Nazi·deutschland das Nazi Germany
Nazismus der; ~: Nazi[i]sm *no art.*
nazistisch *Adj.* Nazi
Nazi-: ~vergangenheit die Nazi past; **~zeit die** Nazi period
NB, N.B. *Abk.* **notabene** NB
n. Br. *Abk.* **nördliche[r] Breite; 60° n. Br.** lat. 60°N
n. Chr. *Abk.* **nach Christus** AD
NDR der; ~: *Abk.* **Norddeutscher Rundfunk** North German Radio
ne [nə] *(ugs.)* *s.* **nicht c**
'ne [nə] *(ugs.)* *s.* **eine**
Neandertaler [ne'andɐta:lɐ] **der; ~s, ~** *(Anthrop.)* Neanderthal man; **[die] Neandertaler lebten in ...:** Neanderthal man *sing.* lived in ...
Neapel [ne'a:pl̩] **(das); ~s** Naples
Neapolitaner [neapoli'ta:nɐ] **der; ~s, ~ a)** Neapolitan; **b)** *(österr.: Gebäck)* wafer biscuit with chocolate cream filling
nebbich ['nɛbɪç] *Interj.* *(salopp)* so what?
Nebel ['ne:bl̩] **der; ~s, ~ a)** fog; *(weniger dicht)* mist; **bei ~:** in fog/mist; when it is foggy/misty; **im ~ der Vergessenheit versinken** *(fig.)* sink into the mists *pl.* of oblivion; **ein ~ von Tabakrauch** a thick haze of tobacco smoke; **ausfallen wegen ~[s]** *(ugs. scherzh.)* be cancelled; *s. auch* **Nacht; b)** *(Astron.)* nebula
Nebel-: ~bank die; *Pl.:* **~bänke** *(über dem Meer)* fog-bank; *(über dem Land)* large patch of fog; **~bildung die** formation of fog; **stellenweise ~bildung** local mist or fog patches; **~feld das** mist/fog patch; patch of mist/fog
nebelhaft *Adj.* hazy ⟨*idea, recollection, etc.*⟩; **das liegt in ~er Ferne** that's in the distant future
Nebel·horn das *Pl.:* **~hörner** fog-horn
nebelig *s.* **neblig**
Nebel-: ~kammer die *(Atomphysik)* cloud chamber; **~krähe die** hooded crow
nebeln 1. *itr. V.* *(unpers.)* *(geh.)* **es nebelt** it is foggy; *(weniger dicht)* it is misty; **es begann zu ~:** it began to grow foggy/misty. **2.** *tr. V.* spray ⟨*pesticide, insecticide*⟩
nebel-, Nebel-: ~schein·werfer der fog-lamp; **~schleier der** *(geh. dichter.)* veil of mist; **~schluß·leuchte die** rear fog lamp; **~schwaden** *Pl.* swathes of mist; **~verhangen** *Adj.* *(geh.)* shrouded in mist *postpos.*; **~wand die** wall of fog; **~werfer der** *(Milit.)* six-barrelled rocket mortar; nebelwerfer
neben ['ne:bn̩] **1.** *Präp. mit Dat.* **a)** *(Lage)* next to; beside; **sie fuhren ~ dem Zug her** they kept pace with the train; **dicht ~ jmdm./etw. sitzen** sit close *or* right beside sb./sth.; **er duldet keinen Konkurrenten ~ sich** *(fig.)* he brooks no competition; **ihr sollt keine anderen Götter ~ mir haben!** *(bibl.)* thou shalt have no other gods before me; **b)** *(außer)* apart from; aside from

(Amer.); **wir brauchen ~ Schere und Papier auch Leim** as well as scissors and paper we need glue. **2.** *Präp. mit Akk.* **a)** *(Richtung)* next to; beside; **sich dicht ~ jmdn./etw. setzen** sit down close *or* right beside sb./sth.; **b)** *(verglichen mit)* beside; compared to *or* with

neben-, Neben-: ~absicht die secondary aim; **~akzent der** *(Phon.)* secondary accent *or* stress; **~amtlich 1.** *Adj.* ⟨*activity*⟩ relating to a secondary office/occupation; **2.** *adv.* **etw. ~ amtlich machen** do sth. as a secondary office/occupation

neben·an *Adv.* next door; **die Kinder von ~** *(ugs.)* the children from next door; **nach ~ gehen** go next door

Neben-: ~an·schluß der extension; **~arbeit die a)** second job; **b)** *(unwichtige Arbeit)* less important job; **~arbeiten** less important work *sing. or* jobs; **~arm der** branch; **~aus·gabe die** additional expense; **[eventuelle] ~ausgaben** incidental expenses; **~aus·gang der** side exit; **~bedeutung die** secondary meaning

neben·bei *Adv.* **a)** ⟨*work*⟩ on the side, as a sideline; *(zusätzlich)* as well; in addition; **sie versorgt ihren Haushalt und hilft ~ im Geschäft** she looks after the house and helps in the shop as well; **für Geologie interessiert er sich nur ~**: his interest in geology is only secondary; **b)** *(beiläufig)* ⟨*remark*⟩ incidentally, by the way; ⟨*ask*⟩ by the way; ⟨*inform*⟩ by the by; ⟨*mention*⟩ in passing; **~ gesagt** *od.* **bemerkt** incidentally; by the way; **dies nur ~**: that is only by the way

neben-, Neben-: ~bemerkung die incidental remark; **~beruf der** second job; sideline; **er ist im ~beruf Fotograf** he has a second job *or* sideline as a photographer; **~beruflich 1.** *Adj.* **eine ~berufliche Tätigkeit** a second job; **er mußte ~berufliche Tätigkeiten annehmen** he had to take on extra work *sing. or* jobs; **2.** *adv.* on the side; **er arbeitet ~beruflich als Übersetzer** he translates as a sideline; **~beschäftigung die** second job; sideline; **seine zahlreichen ~beschäftigungen** his many sidelines; **~buhler der; ~buhlerin die** rival; **~effekt der** side-effect

neben·ein·ander *Adv.* **a)** next to one another *or* each other; ⟨*be sitting, standing*⟩ next to one another, side by side; *(fig.: zusammen)* ⟨*live, exist*⟩ side by side; **~ wohnen** live next door to one another *or* each other; **sich zu zweit ~ aufstellen** line up two abreast; **b)** *(gleichzeitig)* together

Nebeneinander das; ~s juxtaposition

nebeneinander·her *Adv.* alongside each other *or* one another; ⟨*walk*⟩ side by side

nebeneinander-: ~|legen *tr. V.* lay *or* place ⟨*objects*⟩ next to each other *or* side by side; **~|schalten** *tr. V.* connect *or* wire ⟨*devices, lamps, etc.*⟩ in parallel; **~|setzen** *tr. V.* put *or* place ⟨*persons, objects*⟩ next to each other *or* one another; **~|sitzen** *unr. itr. V.* sit next to each other *or* one another; **~|stellen** *tr. V.* put *or* place ⟨*tables, chairs, etc.*⟩ next to each other

Neben-: ~ein·gang der side entrance; **~einkünfte** *Pl.* additional *or* supplementary income *sing.*; **~einnahme die: ~einnahme[n]** additional *or* supplementary income; **~erwerb der** second job; secondary occupation; **~erwerbs·betrieb der** *(Landw.) smallholding, market stall, etc. run to supplement a person's main income;* **~fach das** subsidiary subject; minor *(Amer.)*; **etw. im ~fach studieren** study sth. as a subsidiary subject; minor in sth. *(Amer.)*; **~fluß der** tributary; **~form die** variant; **~frage die** side issue; secondary issue; **~frau die** concubine; **~gebäude das a)** annexe; outbuilding; **b)** *(Nachbargebäude)* adjacent *or* neighbouring building; **~geordnet** *Adj. (Sprachw.)* co-ordinate ⟨*clause*⟩; **~geräusch das** background noise; **~geräusche** *(Funkw., Fernspr.)* interference *sing.*; noise *sing.*; *(bei Tonband, Plattenspieler)* [background] noise *sing.*; **~gleis das** *(Eisenb.)* siding; **jmdn. auf ein ~gleis [ab]schieben** *(fig.)* put sb. out of harm's way; **~handlung die** sub-plot; **~haus das** house next door; neighbouring house

neben·her *Adv. s.* **nebenbei**

nebenher-: ~|fahren *unr. itr. V.; mit sein* drive alongside; *(mit dem Rad, Motorrad)* ride alongside; **~|gehen** *unr. itr. V.; mit sein* walk alongside; **~|laufen** *unr. itr. V.; mit sein* **a)** run alongside; **b)** *(zugleich ablaufen)* proceed at the same time

neben·hin *Adv.* ⟨*ask*⟩ by the way; ⟨*mention, say*⟩ in passing

neben-, Neben-: ~höhle die *(Anat.)* paranasal sinus; **~kläger der, ~klägerin die** *(Rechtsw.)* accessory prosecutor; **~kosten** *Pl.* **a)** additional costs; **b)** *(bei Mieten)* heating, lighting, and services; **~kriegs·schau·platz der** secondary theatre of war; *(fig.)* secondary area of conflict; **~linie die a)** *(Eisenb.) s.* **~strecke**; **b)** *(Genealogie)* collateral branch; **~mann der;** *Pl.:* **~männer** *od.* **~leute** neighbour; **sein ~mann** the person sitting/standing/walking next to him; his neighbour; **~niere die** *(Anat.)* adrenal *or* suprarenal gland; **~nieren·rinde die** *(Anat.)* adrenal *or* suprarenal cortex; **~ordnend** *Adj.; nicht präd. (Sprachw.)* co-ordinating ⟨*conjunction*⟩; **~produkt das** *(auch fig.)* by-product; **~raum der** next *or* adjoining room; room next door; *(kleiner, unwichtiger)* side-room; **~rolle die** supporting role; **eine ~rolle [in etw. (Dat.)] spielen** *(fig.)* play a secondary *or* minor role [in sth.]; **~sache die** minor *or* inessential matter; **~sachen** inessentials; minor *or* inessential matters; **das ist ~sache** *(ugs.)* that's beside the point; **~sächlich** *Adj.* of minor importance *postpos.*; unimportant; minor, trivial ⟨*detail*⟩; **etw. als ~sächlich abtun** reject sth. as irrelevant *or* beside the point; **sich über ~sächliche Dinge aufregen** get worked up about trivial things *or* matters; **~sächlichkeit die; ~, ~en a)** *o. Pl.* unimportance; *(fehlender Bezug zur Sache)* irrelevance; **b)** *(Unwichtiges)* matter of minor importance; unimportant matter; *(nicht zur Sache Gehörendes)* irrelevancy; **~satz der** *(Sprachw.) s.* **Gliedsatz**; **~stehend** *Adj.; nicht präd.* accompanying ⟨*text, illustration, table, etc.*⟩; *(auf der Seite gegenüber)* ⟨*text, illustration, table, etc.*⟩ opposite; **~stelle die a)** extension; **b)** *(Filiale)* branch; **~straße die** side street; *(außerhalb der Stadt)* minor road; **~strecke die a)** *(Eisenb.)* branch *or* local line; **b)** *(Entlastungsstraße)* minor road running parallel to the main road; **~tätigkeit die** second job; sideline; **~tisch der** next *or* neighbouring table; **~tür die a)** side door; **b)** *(benachbarte Tür)* next *or* neighbouring door; **~verdienst der** additional earnings *pl. or* income; **~winkel der** *(Geom.)* adjacent angle; **~wirkung die** side-effect; **~zimmer das** next room; **sie gingen in ein ~zimmer** they went into an adjoining room; **~zweck der** secondary aim

neblig *Adj.* foggy; *(weniger dicht)* misty

nebst [ne:pst] *Präp. mit Dat. (veralt.)* together with; plus; *(zusätzlich zu)* in addition to

nebst·bei *(österr.) s.* **nebenbei**

nebst·dem *(schweiz.) s.* **außerdem**

nebulos [nebu'lo:s], **nebulös** [nebu'lø:s] *(geh.)* **1.** *Adj.* nebulous ⟨*idea, concept*⟩; obscure, vague ⟨*hint*⟩. **2.** *adv.* ⟨*talk, hint*⟩ vaguely

Necessaire [nesɛ'sɛ:ɐ̯] **das; ~s, ~s a)** sponge-bag *(Brit.)*; toilet bag *(Amer.)*; **b)** *(Behälter für Nähzeug)* sewing-bag

necken ['nɛkn̩] *tr. V.* tease; **jmdn. mit jmdm./etw. ~**: tease sb. about sb./sth.; **sich ~**: tease each other *or* one another; *s. auch* **lieben**

Neckerei die; ~: teasing

neckisch 1. *Adj.* **a)** teasing; *(verspielt)* playful; *(schelmisch)* mischievous; **b)** *(keß)* jaunty, saucy ⟨*cap*⟩; saucy, provocative ⟨*dress, blouse, etc.*⟩. **2.** *adv.* ⟨*smile, say*⟩ saucily, cheekily

nee [ne:] *(ugs.)* no; nope *(Amer. coll.)*

Neer [ne:ɐ̯] **die; ~, ~en** *(nordd.)* eddy

Neffe ['nɛfə] **der; ~n, ~n** nephew

neg. *Abk.:* **negativ** neg.

Negation [nega'tsi̯o:n] **die; ~, ~en** negation

negativ ['ne:gati:f] **1.** *Adj.* negative; **~e Zahlen** *(Math.)* negative *or* minus numbers. **2.** *adv.* ⟨*answer*⟩ in the negative; **einen Antrag ~ bescheiden** reject an application; **einer Sache** *(Dat.)* **~ gegenüberstehen** take a negative view of a matter; **etw. ~ beeinflussen** have a negative influence on sth.; **etw. ~ bewerten** judge sth. unfavourably; **sich ~ äußern** comment negatively (zu on); **der Test/die Testbohrung verlief ~**: the test proved unsuccessful/the test well yielded nothing; **~ geladen** *(Physik)* negatively charged

Negativ das; ~s, ~e *(Fot.)* negative

Negativ-: ~beispiel das negative example; **das ~beispiel Stalin** the negative example of Stalin; **~bilanz die** generally negative picture; *(Ergebnis)* generally negative outcome; **~bild das** *(Fot.)* negative image; **~film der** negative film

Negativität [negativi'tɛ:t] **die; ~**: negativity; negativeness

Negativum ['ne:gativʊm] **das; ~s, Negativa** *(Faktor)* negative factor; *(Eigenschaft)* negative characteristic

neger *(österr. ugs.) in:* **~ sein** be broke *(coll.)*

Neger ['ne:gɐ] **der; ~s, ~ a)** Negro ; **b)** *(Fernsehen: schwarze Tafel)* gobo; nigger; *(Texttafel)* cue card

Negerin die; ~, ~nen Negress

Neger-: ~krause die *(ugs. veralt.)* frizzy hair *no art.*; **~kuß der** *s.* **Mohrenkopf a**

Negerlein das; ~s, ~: little Negro

Neger·sklave der Negro slave

negieren *tr. V.* **a)** deny ⟨*fact, assertion, guilt, etc.*⟩; **b)** *(ablehnen)* reject ⟨*opinion, suggestion*⟩; **c)** *(Sprachw.)* negate

Negligé, *(schweiz.:)* **Négligé** [negli'ʒe:] **das; ~s, ~s** négligé; negligee

negrid [ne'gri:t] *Adj. (Anthrop.)* Negrid

negroid [negro'i:t] *Adj. (Anthrop.)* Negroid

nehmen ['ne:mən] *unr. tr. V.* **a)** *(ergreifen, an sich bringen, an~, als Beispiel ~)* take; **etw. in die Hand/unter den Arm ~**: take sth. in one's hand/take *or* put sth. under one's arm; **etw. an sich** *(Akk.)* **~**: pick sth. up; *(und aufbewahren)* take charge of sth.; **sich** *(Dat.)* **etw. ~**: take sth.; *(sich bedienen)* help oneself to sth.; **sich** *(Dat.)* **einen Mann/eine Frau ~**: take a husband/wife; **woher ~ und nicht stehlen?** *(scherzh.)* where on earth am I going to get hold of that/them *etc.?*; **zu sich ~**: take in ⟨*orphan*⟩; **sie nahm ihren Vater zu sich** she had her father come and live with her; **Gott hat ihn zu sich genommen** *(geh.)* God has taken him unto Himself ; **auf sich** *(Akk.)* **~**: take on ⟨*responsibility, burden*⟩; take ⟨*blame*⟩; **es auf sich** *(Akk.)* **~, etw. zu tun** take on the responsibility of doing sth.; **die Dinge ~, wie sie kommen** take things as they come; **jmdn. ~, wie er ist** take sb. as he is; **nimm doch mal den Fall, daß man dir einen Vertrag anböte** let's assume [that] they offered you a contract; **b)** *(wegnehmen)* **jmdm./einer Sache etw. ~**: deprive sb./sth. of sth.; **jmdm. die Sicht/den Ausblick ~**: block sb.'s view; **jmdm. den Glauben/alle Illusionen ~** *(fig.)* deprive *or* rob sb. of his/her belief/all his/her illusions; **die Angst/die Sorgen von jmdm. ~**:

relieve sb. of his/her fear/worries; **es sich** *(Dat.)* **nicht ~ lassen, etw. zu tun** not let anything stop one from doing sth.; **das nimmt der Sache den ganzen Reiz** it takes all the fun out of it ; **c)** *(benutzen)* use ⟨*ingredients, washing-powder, wool, brush, knitting-needles, etc.*⟩; **man nehme ...** *(in Rezepten)* take ...; **den Zug/das Auto/ein Taxi** *usw.* **~:** take the train/the car/a taxi *etc.;* **[sich** *(Dat.)***] einen Anwalt/Privatlehrer** *usw.* **~:** get a lawyer/private tutor *etc.;* **d)** *(aussuchen)* take; **ich nehme die Pastete/die broschierte Ausgabe** I'll have the pâté/the paperback; **e)** *(in Anspruch nehmen)* take ⟨*lessons, holiday, etc.*⟩; **einen Tag frei ~:** take a day off; **f)** *(verlangen)* charge; **was ~ Sie dafür?** what *or* how much do you charge for it?; **g)** *(einnehmen, essen)* take ⟨*medicines, tablets, etc.*⟩; **etwas [Richtiges] zu sich ~:** have something [decent] to eat; **sie nimmt die Pille** she's taking *or* she's on the pill *(coll.);* **das Frühstück/einen Imbiß ~** *(geh.)* take breakfast/a snack; **den Kaffee ~** *(geh.)* have [one's] coffee; **h)** *(auffassen)* take **(als** as); **etw. ernst/leicht ~:** take sth. seriously/lightly; **jmdn. ernst ~:** take sb. seriously; **gleichgültig/je nachdem, wie man's nimmt** *(ugs.)* however you look at it/depending on how you look at it; **jmdn. nicht für voll ~** *(ugs.)* not take sb. seriously; **i)** *(behandeln)* treat ⟨*person*⟩; **wissen, wie man jmdn. zu ~ hat** know how to treat sb.; **j)** *(überwinden, militärisch einnehmen)* take ⟨*obstacle, bend, incline, village, bridgehead, etc.*⟩; *(fig.)* take ⟨*woman*⟩; **k)** *(aufnehmen)* **etw. auf Videokassette/Band ~:** record sth. on video cassette/record *or* tape sth.; **l)** *(Sport)* take ⟨*ball, punch*⟩; **einen Spieler hart ~:** foul a player blatantly

Nehrung ['ne:rʊŋ] **die; ~, ~en** sand-bar

Neid [nait] **der; ~[e]s** envy; jealousy; **aus ~:** out of envy; **von ~ erfüllt [sein]** [be] filled with envy; **vor ~ platzen** *(ugs.)* die of envy *(coll.);* **gelb** *od.* **grün vor ~ werden, vor ~ erblassen** turn *or* go green with envy; **das muß der ~ ihr lassen** *(ugs.)* you've got to give her that; you've got to say that much for her; **das ist der ~ der Besitzlosen** *(ugs.)* that's just sour grapes; **nur kein ~!** don't be envious

neiden *tr. V. (geh.)* **jmdm. etw. ~:** envy sb. [for] sth.

Neider der; ~s, ~: envious person; **seine ~:** those who are/were envious of him; **erfolgreiche Leute haben immer viele ~:** successful people are always much *or* greatly envied

neid·erfüllt *Adj.* filled with *or* full of envy *postpos.*

Neid·hammel der *(salopp abwertend)* envious sod *(sl.)*

neidisch 1. *Adj.* envious; **auf jmdn./etw. ~ sein** be envious of sb./sth. **2.** *adv.* enviously

neid-: ~los 1. *Adj.* ungrudging ⟨*admiration*⟩; ⟨*joy*⟩ without envy; **2.** *adv.* ⟨*acknowledge, admire*⟩ without envy; **~voll 1.** *Adj.* envious ⟨*glance*⟩; ⟨*person*⟩ filled with *or* full of envy; ⟨*admiration*⟩ mixed with envy; **2.** *adv.* ⟨*watch*⟩ full of envy

Neige ['naigə] **die; ~** *(geh.)* dregs *pl.;* lees *pl.;* **ein Glas bis zur ~ leeren** drain a glass to the dregs; **etw. bis zur ~ auskosten** *(fig.)* enjoy sth. to the full; **etw. bis zur bitteren ~ durchstehen** *(fig.)* see sth. through to the bitter end; **zur ~ gehen** *(aufgebraucht sein)* ⟨*money, supplies, etc.*⟩ run low; *(zu Ende gehen)* ⟨*year, day, holiday*⟩ draw to its close

neigen 1. *tr. V.* tip, tilt ⟨*bottle, glass, barrel, etc.*⟩; incline ⟨*head, upper part of body*⟩; **den Kopf zum Gruß ~:** incline one's head in greeting. **2.** *refl. V.* **a)** ⟨*person*⟩ lean, bend; ⟨*ship*⟩ heel over, list; ⟨*scales*⟩ tip; ⟨*sun*⟩ sink; ⟨*branches*⟩ bow down; **sich nach vorne/zur Seite ~:** bend *or* lean over *or* forward/lean to one side; **b)** *(schräg abfallen)* ⟨*meadows*⟩ slope down; **eine geneigte Fläche** a sloping surface; **c)** *(geh.: zu Ende gehen)* ⟨*day, year, holiday*⟩ draw to its close. **3.** *itr. V.* **a) zu Erkältungen/Krankheiten ~:** be susceptible *or* prone to colds/illnesses; **zur** *od.* **zu Korpulenz/Schwermut ~:** have a tendency to put on weight/tend to be melancholy; **ein zum** *od.* **zu Jähzorn ~der Mensch** a person who is prone to violent outbursts of temper; **b)** *(tendieren)* tend; **zu der Ansicht** *od.* **der Auffassung ~, daß ...:** tend towards the view or opinion that ...; *s. auch* **geneigt 2**

Neigung die; ~, ~en a) *o. Pl. (des Kopfes)* nod; **b)** *o. Pl. (Geneigtsein)* inclination; *(eines Geländes)* slope; **die Straße weist eine leichte ~ auf** the street has a slight incline *or* gradient; **c)** *(Vorliebe)* inclination; **seine politischen/künstlerischen ~en** his political/artistic leanings; **eine ~ für etw.** a penchant *or* fondness for sth.; **d)** *o. Pl. (Anfälligsein)* tendency; **eine ~ zur Korpulenz/zum Faulsein haben** have a tendency to put on weight/to be lazy; **e)** *o. Pl. (Lust)* inclination; **f)** *(Liebe)* affection; fondness; liking; **jmds. ~ gewinnen/erwidern** win/return sb.'s affection

Neigungs-: ~ehe die love-match; **~messer der** clinometer; inclinometer; **~winkel der** angle of inclination

nein [nain] *Partikel* no; **~ danke** no, thank you; **sie kann nicht ~ sagen** she can't say no; **da sage ich nicht ~:** I wouldn't say no; **man muß auch ~ sagen können** one must be able to say no; **~, nicht!** no, don't!; **~, so was!** well I never!; **~ und abermals ~!** no, and that's final!; **aber ~!** good heavens no!; **du gehst doch jetzt noch nicht, ~?** you're not going now, are you?; **das wird dir doch nicht zu viel, ~?** that's not too much for you, is it?; **~, daß ich das noch erleben durfte!** simply wonderful, that I should live to see this!; **~, wie schön Sie das gesagt haben!** gosh, you really put that beautifully! *(coll.)*

Nein das; ~[s], ~[s] no; **bei seinem ~ bleiben** stick by one's refusal; **mit ~ stimmen** vote no

'nein *(südd.) s.* **hinein**

Nein-: ~sager der; ~s, ~ *(abwertend)* person who always says no *or* who says no to everything; **~stimme die** no-vote; vote against

Nekrolog [nekro'lo:k] **der; ~[e]s, ~e** *(geh.)* obituary; necrology *(rare)*

Nekrophilie [nekrofi'li:] **die; ~:** necrophilia *no art.*

Nektar ['nektar] **der; ~s, ~e a)** *(Bot., Myth.)* nectar; **b)** *(Getränk) drink made from crushed fruit, sugar, and water*

Nektarine [nekta'ri:nə] **die; ~, ~n** nectarine

Nelke ['nɛlkə] **die; ~, ~n a)** pink; *(Dianthus caryophyllus)* carnation; **b)** *(Gewürz)* clove

Nelken·öl das oil of cloves

Nelson ['nɛlzɔn] **der; ~[s], ~s** *(Ringen)* nelson

Nemesis ['ne:mezɪs] **die; ~:** nemesis

'nen [nən] *s.* **einen**

nennbar *Adj.* specifiable ⟨*change, problem*⟩; nameable ⟨*feeling*⟩; **nicht ~:** unspecifiable/unnameable

Nenn·betrag der *s.* **Nennwert**

nennen ['nɛnən] **1.** *unr. tr. V.* **a)** call; **jmdn. nach jmdm. ~:** call *or* name sb. after sb.; **sie nannten das Kind Günther** they called *or* named the child Günther; **jmdn. beim Vornamen ~:** call sb. by his/her first *or* Christian name; **jmdn. einen Lügner ~:** call sb. a liar; **wenn du es so ~ willst** if you want to call it that; **das nenne ich Mut/eine Überraschung** that's what I call courage/well, that 'is a surprise; **Max Müller, genannt „der weiße Würger"** Max Müller, known as the 'White Strangler'; **b)** *(mitteilen)* give ⟨*name, date of birth address, reason, price, etc.*⟩; **jmdm. ein gutes Hotel/einen Arzt ~:** give sb. the name of a good hotel/a doctor; **c)** *(anführen)* give, cite ⟨*example*⟩; *(erwähnen)* mention ⟨*person, name*⟩; **das oben Genannte** the item[s] mentioned above; **die im folgenden genannten Punkte** the points mentioned below. **2.** *unr. refl. V.* ⟨*person, thing*⟩ be called; **er nennt sich Maler/Dichter** *usw. (behauptet Maler/Dichter usw. zu sein)* he calls himself a painter/poet *etc.;* **und so was nennt sich nun ein Freund/tolerant** *(ugs.)* and he/she has the nerve to call himself/herself a friend/tolerant; **und das nennt sich ein gutes Hotel** and that's supposed to be a good hotel

nennens·wert *Adj.* considerable ⟨*influence, changes, delays, damage*⟩; **kaum ~e Veränderungen** changes scarcely worth mentioning; **es ist nichts Nennenswertes passiert** nothing worth mentioning *or* nothing of note has happened

Nenner der; ~s, ~ *(Math.)* denominator; **der gemeinsame ~:** the common denominator; **etw. auf einen [gemeinsamen] ~ bringen** *(fig.)* reduce sth. to a common denominator

Nenn-: ~fall der *s.* **Nominativ; ~form die** *s.* **Infinitiv; ~leistung die** *(Technik)* rated output; *(Elektrot.)* rated power; *(eines Motors)* rated horsepower; **~onkel der** uncle only in name; **er ist nicht mein richtiger Onkel, sondern nur ein ~onkel** he's not my real uncle, I just call him that; **~tante die** aunt only in name; *s. auch* **~onkel**

Nennung die; ~, ~en a) *s.* **nennen 1 b, c:** giving; citing; mentioning; **b)** *(Sport)* entry **(zu, für** for)

Nenn-: ~wert der *(Wirtsch.)* nominal *or* face value; *(von Aktien)* par *or* nominal *or* face value; **~wort das** *s.* **Substantiv**

neo-, Neo-: neo-

Neolithikum [neo'li:tikʊm] **das; ~s** *(Archäol.)* neolithic period

Neologismus [neolo'gɪsmʊs] **der; ~, Neologismen** *(Sprachw.)* neologism

Neon ['ne:ɔn] **das; ~s** *(Chemie)* neon

Neon-: ~licht das neon light; **~reklame die** neon sign; **~röhre die** neon tube; [neon] strip light

Nepal ['ne:pal] **(das); ~s** Nepal

Nepalese [nepa'le:zə] **der; ~n, ~n** Nepali; Nepalese

Nepotismus [nepo'tɪsmʊs] **der; ~:** nepotism *no art.*

Nepp [nɛp] **der; ~s** *(ugs. abwertend)* daylight robbery *no art.;* rip-off *(sl.)*

neppen *tr. V. (ugs. abwertend)* rook; rip ⟨*tourist, customer, etc.*⟩ off *(sl.)*

Nepper der; ~s, ~ *(ugs. abwertend)* shark; rip-off merchant *(sl.)*

Nepp·lokal das *(ugs. abwertend)* clip-joint *(sl.)*

[1]Neptun [nɛp'tu:n] **der; ~s** *(Astron.),* **[2]Neptun (der); ~s** *(Myth.)* Neptune

Nerv [nɛrf] **der; ~s, ~en a)** nerve; **an den ~ der Sache rühren** *(fig.)* get to the heart of the matter; **das Buch trifft den ~ der Zeit** *(fig.)* the book taps the pulse of the age; **den ~ haben, etw. zu tun** *(fig. ugs.)* have the nerve to do sth.; **jmdm. den ~ töten** *(fig. ugs.)* drive sb. up the wall *(coll.);* **b)** *Pl. (nervliche Konstitution)* nerves; **gute/schwache ~en haben** have strong/bad nerves; **meine ~en halten das nicht aus** my nerves won't stand it; **die ~en [dazu] haben, etw. zu tun** have the nerve to do sth.; **die ~en bewahren** *od.* **behalten** keep calm; **die ~en verlieren** lose control [of oneself]; lose one's cool *(sl.);* **ich bin mit den ~en fertig** *od.* **am Ende** my nerves cannot take any more; **du hast vielleicht ~en!** *(ugs.)* you've got a nerve!; **~en haben wie Drahtseile** *od.* **Stricke** *(ugs.)* have nerves of steel; **jmdm. auf die ~en gehen** *od.* **fallen** get on sb.'s nerves; **c)** *(in Blättern, Insektenflügeln)* vein; nerve

nerven *(salopp)* **1.** *tr. V.* **jmdn. ~:** get on sb.'s nerves. **2.** *itr. V.* be wearing on the nerves

nerven-, Nerven-: ~an·spannung die

nervous strain; nervous tension *no indef. art.;* **~arzt der** neurologist; **~aufreibend** *Adj.* nerve-racking; **~belastung die** strain on the nerves; **~beruhigend** *Adj.* sedative ⟨*effect, drug*⟩; **~beruhigend wirken** have a calming effect on the nerves; ⟨*drug*⟩ act as a sedative/tranquillizer; **~beruhigungs·mittel das** sedative; *(gegen Depressionen, Angstzustände)* tranquillizer; **~bündel das a)** *(ugs.)* bundle of nerves *(coll.)*; **b)** *(Anat.)* bundle of nerve fibres; **~entzündung die** *(Med.)* neuritis; **~faser die** *(Anat.)* nerve-fibre; **~gas das** nerve gas; **~gift das** neurotoxin; **~heil·anstalt die** *(veralt.)* mental *or* psychiatric hospital; **~kitzel der** *(ugs.)* kick *(coll.)*; **~klinik die a)** clinic for nervous diseases; **b)** *(ugs.)* mental *or* psychiatric hospital; **~kostüm das** *(ugs. scherzh.)* nerves *pl.*; **ein schwaches ~kostüm haben** have bad nerves; **~kraft die** nervous strength; **~krank** *Adj.* **a)** ⟨*person*⟩ suffering from a nervous disease *or* disorder; **b)** *(psychisch krank)* mentally ill; **~kranke der/die a)** person suffering from a nervous disease or disorder; **b)** *(psychisch Kranke)* mentally ill person; **~kranke sind ...:** the mentally ill are ...; **~krankheit die a)** nervous disease *or* disorder; **b)** *(psychische Krankheit)* mental illness; **~krieg der** *(ugs.)* war of nerves; **~leiden das** nervous complaint *or* disorder; **~nahrung die: ~nahrung sein** be good for the *or* one's nerves; **~probe die** mental trial; **~sache die** *in* **das ist reine ~sache** *(ugs.)* it's a matter *or* question of nerves; **~säge die** *(salopp)* pain in the neck *(coll.)*; **~schmerz der** *(Med.)* neuralgia; **~schock der** nervous *or* psychic shock; **~schwach** *Adj.* ⟨*person*⟩ with bad nerves *not pred.*; neurasthenic ⟨*person*⟩ *(Med.)*; **~schwäche die a)** neurasthenia *(Med.)*; **b)** *(psychische Schwäche)* bad nerves *pl.*; **~stärkend** *Adj.* nerve-strengthening; **ein ~stärkendes Mittel** a nerve-tonic; **~strang der** *s.* **~bündel b; ~system das** *(Anat.)* nervous system; **~zelle die** *(Anat.)* nerve cell; **~zusammen·bruch der** nervous breakdown

nervig *Adj. (auch fig.)* sinewy

nervlich 1. *Adj.* nervous ⟨*strain*⟩; **eine ~e Belastung für jmdn. sein** be a strain on sb.'s nerves. **2.** *adv.* **dieser ständigen Spannung war er ~ nicht gewachsen** his nerves were not up to this constant tension

nervös [nɛr'vø:s] **1.** *Adj.* **a)** nervy, jittery ⟨*person*⟩; nervous ⟨*haste, movement*⟩; **~ sein** be jittery *(coll.) or* on edge; **das macht mich ganz ~:** it really gets on my nerves; *(das beunruhigt mich)* it makes me really nervous; **b)** *(Med.)* nervous ⟨*twitch, gastric disorder, etc.*⟩. **2.** *adv.* **a)** nervously; **b)** *(Med.)* **~ bedingt sein** be caused by nerves

Nervosität [nɛrvozi'tɛ:t] **die; ~** nervousness; **voller ~:** nervously

nerv·tötend *Adj.* nerve-racking ⟨*wait*⟩; nerve-shattering ⟨*sound, noise*⟩; soul-destroying ⟨*activity, work*⟩

Nerz [nɛrts] **der; ~es, ~e** mink

Nerz·mantel der mink coat

[1]**Nessel** ['nɛsl̩] **die; ~, ~n** nettle; **sich in die ~n setzen** *(fig. ugs.)* get [oneself] into hot water *(coll.)*

[2]**Nessel der; ~s, ~** *(Stoff)* coarse, untreated cotton cloth

Nessel-: ~fieber das nettle-rash accompanied by fever; **~sucht die;** *o. Pl.* nettle-rash; hives

Nest [nɛst] **das; ~[e]s, ~er a)** nest; **sich** *(Dat.)* **gemeinsam ein ~ einrichten** *(fig.)* set up home together; **das eigene** *od.* **sein eigenes ~ beschmutzen** *(fig.)* foul one's own nest; **er hat sich ins warme** *od.* **gemachte ~ gesetzt** *(fig. ugs.)* he had his future made for him; **b)** *(fam.: Bett)* bed; **raus aus dem ~!** show a leg! *(sl.)*; **c)** *(ugs. abwertend: kleiner Ort)* little place; **ein winziges ~:** a tiny little place; **ein gottverlassenes/armseliges ~:** a God-forsaken/miserable hole; **d)** *(Schlupfwinkel)* hide-out; den; **e)** *(Haartracht)* plaited bun

Nest-: ~bau der; *o. Pl.* nest-building *no art.*; **~beschmutzer der; ~s, ~** *(abwertend)* person who is/was guilty of fouling his/her own nest

nesteln ['nɛstl̩n] *itr. V.* fiddle, *(ungeschickt)* fumble **(an +** *Dat.* with)

nest-, Nest-: ~flüchter der; ~s, ~ *(Zool.)* *(bird)* precocial *or* nidifugous bird; *(animal)* precocial animal; **~häkchen das** *(fam.)* [spoilt] baby of the family; **~hocker der** *(Zool.)* nidicolous bird/animal; **~warm** *Adj.* ⟨*eggs*⟩ warm from the nest; **~wärme die** warmth of a [happy] family upbringing *or* of [happy] family life

nett [nɛt] **1.** *Adj.* **a)** nice; *(freundlich)* nice; kind; **sei so ~ und hilf mir!** would you be so good *or* kind as to help me?; **sie war so nett, uns einen Kaffee anzubieten** she very kindly offered us a coffee; **das war [nicht] ~ von dir** that was[n't very] nice of you; **~, daß du anrufst** it's nice *or* kind of you to ring; **etwas Nettes erleben/sagen** have a pleasant experience/say something nice; **b)** *(hübsch)* pretty ⟨*girl, town, dress, etc.*⟩; nice, pleasant ⟨*pub, house, town, etc.*⟩; **c)** *nicht präd. (ugs.: beträchtlich)* nice little *(coll.)* ⟨*profit, extra earnings, income*⟩; **sie hat eine ganz ~e Oberweite** she's very well endowed *(coll.)*; **eine ~e Summe/eine ~e Stange Geld** a tidy sum *(coll.)*; **d)** *(ugs. iron.: unerfreulich)* nice *(coll.)* ⟨*affair*⟩; nice *(coll.)*, fine ⟨*state of affairs, mess*⟩; **das sind ja ~e Aussichten** that's a nice *or* charming prospect *(coll.)*; **das kann ja ~ werden!** that'll be fun *(coll.)*. **2.** *adv. (angenehm)* nicely; *(freundlich)* nicely; kindly; **sich ~ mit jmdm. unterhalten** have a pleasant conversation with sb.; **hier sitzt man sehr ~:** it's very nice *or* pleasant sitting here

netter·weise *Adv. (ugs.)* kindly; **würden Sie mir ~ diesen Platz überlassen?** would you be so kind as to let me have your seat?

Nettigkeit die; ~, ~en a) *o. Pl.* kindness; goodness; **b)** *(Äußerung)* **jmdm. ein paar ~en sagen** say a few nice *or* kind things to sb.; *(iron.)* say a few choice words to sb.

netto ['nɛto] *Adv.* ⟨*weigh, earn, etc.*⟩ net

Netto-: ~einkommen das net income; **~ertrag der** net return; **~gehalt das** net salary; **~gewicht das** net weight; **~preis der** net price; **~raum·zahl die** net register tonnage; **~register·tonne die** *(Seew.)* net register ton; **~sozial·produkt das** *(Wirtsch.)* net national product

Netz [nɛts] **das; ~es, ~e a)** *(auch Fischer~, Tennis~, Ballspiele)* net; *(Haar~)* [hair-]net; *(Einkaufs~)* string bag; *(Gepäck~)* [luggage-]rack; *(Sicherheits~)* safety net; **sich in einem ~ von Lügen verstricken** *(fig.)* become entangled in a web of lies; **jmdm. ins ~ gehen** *(fig.)* fall into sb.'s trap; **jmdm. durchs ~ gehen** *(fig.)* slip through sb.'s net; **seine ~e überall auswerfen** *(fig.)* put out feelers in all directions; **ans ~ gehen** *(Tennis)* go to the net; **b)** *(Spinnen~)* web; **c)** *(Verteiler~, Verkehrs~, System von Einrichtungen)* network; *(für Strom, Wasser, Gas)* mains *pl.*; **ans ~ gehen** ⟨*power station*⟩ go on stream; **das soziale ~:** the social security system; **d)** *(Math.)* net

netz-, Netz-: ~an·schluß der mains connection; **~artig** *Adj.* netlike ⟨*material, pattern, etc.*⟩; **~auge das** *(Zool.)* compound eye; **~ball der** *(Tennis, Volleyball)* net ball

netzen *tr. V. (geh.)* moisten ⟨*soil, plant, one's lips*⟩; wet ⟨*hair, cheeks*⟩

Netz-: ~frequenz die *(Elektrot.)* mains frequency; **~gerät das** *(Elektrot.)* power pack; **~gewölbe das** *(Kunstwiss.)* net vault; **~haut die** *(Anat.)* retina

Netzhaut~: ~ab·lösung die *(Med.)* detachment of the retina; retinal detachment; **~entzündung die** *(Med.)* retinitis

Netz-: ~hemd das string vest; **~karte die** area season ticket; *(Eisenb.)* unlimited travel ticket; **~magen der** *(Zool.)* reticulum; honeycomb stomach; **~roller der** *(Tennis)* net-cord [stroke]; **~spannung die** *(Elektrot.)* mains voltage; **~stecker der** mains plug; **~strumpf der** net stocking; **~werk das** *(auch Elektrot.)* network

neu [nɔy] **1.** *Adj.* **a)** new; **ein ganz ~es Fahrrad** a brand new bicycle; **die Neue Welt** the New World; **das Neue Testament** the New Testament; **die ~este Mode/die ~esten Schlager/der ~este Witz** the latest fashion/hits/joke; **die ~e Literatur/Physik** modern literature/physics; **die ~esten Nachrichten/Ereignisse** the latest news/most recent events; **viel Glück im ~en Jahr** best wishes for the New Year; Happy New Year; **er brachte eine ~e Flasche** he fetched another bottle; **das sieht aus wie ~:** that looks like new *or* as good as new; **das ist mir ~:** that is news to me; **ich bin ~ in dieser Gegend/in diesem Beruf** I am new to this area/job; **das Neue daran ist ...:** what's new about it is ...; **den Reiz des Neuen haben** have novelty value; **das Neueste auf dem Markt** the latest thing on the market; **der/die Neue** the new man/woman/boy/girl; **etw./nichts Neues wissen/berichten** know/report something/nothing new; **was gibt es Neues?** what's new?; **weißt du schon das Neueste?** *(ugs.)* have you heard the latest?; **etw. Neues unternehmen/anfangen** do/start something new *or* different; **eine ~e Flasche aufmachen** open another bottle; **eine ~e Seite/Zeile beginnen** start a new *or* fresh page/line; **aufs ~e** anew; afresh; again; **auf ein ~es!** let's try again!; **von ~em** all over again; *(noch einmal)* [once] again; **von ~em beginnen** start *or* begin all over again; make a fresh start; **seit ~estem werden dort keine Kreditkarten mehr akzeptiert** just recently they've started refusing to accept credit cards; **in ~erer/~ester Zeit** quite/just *or* very recently; **das ist ~eren Datums** that is of a more recent date; **die ~en** *od.* **~eren Sprachen** modern languages; **b)** *nicht präd. (kürzlich geerntet)* new ⟨*wine, potatoes*⟩; **c)** *(sauber)* clean ⟨*shirt, socks, underwear, etc.*⟩. **2.** *adv.* **a) ~ tapeziert/gespritzt/gestrichen/möbliert** repapered/resprayed/repainted/refurnished; **einen Sessel ~ beziehen** re-cover an armchair; **ein Geschäft ~ eröffnen** reopen a shop; **sich ~ einkleiden/einrichten** provide oneself with a new set of clothes/refurnish one's home; **noch einmal ~ beginnen** start again from scratch; **sich ~ formieren** ⟨*party, organization, etc.*⟩ reform; **b)** *(gerade erst)* **diese Ware ist ~ eingetroffen** this item has just come in *or* arrived; **das Geschäft ist ~ eröffnet** the shop has only just been opened; **~ erschienene Bücher** newly published books; books that have just come out *or* appeared; **3 000 Wörter sind ~ hinzugekommen** 3,000 new words have been added

neu-, Neu-: ~an·fertigung die a) making; *(serienweise)* manufacture; **b)** *(Angefertigtes)* **eine ~anfertigung sein** be new; **~ankömmling der** new arrival; **~an·schaffung die a) die ~anschaffung von Produktionsanlagen** the acquisition of new production plant; **~anschaffungen machen** buy new items; **b)** *(Artikel, Gegenstand)* new acquisition; **~apostolisch** *Adj. (christl. Rel.)* New Apostolic; **die Neuapostolische Gemeinde** the New Apostolic Church

neu·artig *Adj.* new; **ein ~er Staubsauger** a new type of vacuum cleaner; **das Neuartige an diesem Gerät** the novel feature of this device

Neuartigkeit die; ~: novelty

Neu-: ~auf·lage die reprint [with alterations]; *(mit umfangreichen Veränderungen)* new edition; **eine ~auflage des vorjährigen Endspiels** *(fig.)* a repeat of last years's final; **~aus·gabe die** new edition

Neu·bau der; *Pl.* **Neubauten a)** new house/ building; **b)** *(Wiedererrichtung)* rebuilding

Neubau-: ~viertel das new district; **~wohnung die** flat *(Brit.) or (Amer.)* apartment in a new block/house; new flat *(Brit.) or (Amer.)* apartment

neu-, Neu-: ~bearbeitet *Adj.* [newly] revised ⟨*edition*⟩; newly adapted ⟨*version*⟩; **~bearbeitung die a)** *(eines Buches, Textes)* revision; *(eines Theaterstücks)* adaptation; **b)** *(neue Fassung)* new version; **~bedeutung die** *(Sprachw.)* new meaning; **~beginn der** new beginning; **~besetzung die: die ~besetzung einer Stelle** the refilling of a post; **eine ~besetzung ihrer Rolle wurde notwendig** it became necessary to cast someone else in her part; **~bildung die a) die ~bildung der Regierung/des Kabinetts** the formation of a new government/ cabinet; **b)** *(von Gewebe)* regeneration; *(neu Gebildetes)* new growth; **die ~bildung von Geschwülsten** the growth of new tumours; *(wiederholt)* the regrowth of tumours; **c)** *(eines Wortes)* coining; *(neues Wort)* neologism; **~bürger der** new citizen

Neu-Delhi [nɔy'de:li] **(das); ~s** New Delhi

neu-, Neu-: ~deutsch *Adj. (meist abwertend)* modern West German ⟨*society*⟩; typical West German ⟨*arrogance, smugness, customs*⟩; **~druck der** reprint [with corrections]; **~ein·stellung die: eine ~einstellung vornehmen** take on a new employee; *(von Angestellten)* make a new appointment; **~einstellungen notwendig machen** make it necessary to take on new staff; **~einstudierung die** *(Theater)* new production

Neu·england (das) New England

neu·englisch *Adj.* modern English

Neu-: ~entdeckung die a) *(auch fig.)* new discovery; **b)** *(Wiederentdeckung)* rediscovery; **~entwicklung die a) die ~entwicklung von Heilmitteln/Maschinen** the development of new medicines/machines; **b)** *(neu Entwickeltes)* new development

neuerdings ['nɔyɐ'dɪŋs] *Adv.* **a)** recently; **Fahrkarten gibt es ~ nur noch am Automaten** as of a short while ago one can only get tickets from a machine; **~ kann man direkt dorthin fliegen** it has recently become possible to fly there direct; **er trägt ~ eine Perücke** he has recently started wearing a wig; **b)** *(südd., österr., schweiz.: erneut)* again

Neuerer der; ~s, ~ a) innovator; **b)** *(DDR) research worker contributing to technical and scientific advance*

neuerlich 1. *Adj.; nicht präd.* further. **2.** *adv.* again

neu-, Neu-: ~eröffnet *Adj.; präd. getrennt geschrieben* **a)** newly-opened; **b)** *(wiedereröffnet)* reopened; **~eröffnung die a)** opening; **b)** *(Wiedereröffnung)* reopening; **~erscheinung die** new publication; *(Schallplatte)* new release

Neuerung die; ~, ~en innovation

Neu·erwerbung die a) die ~ von Büchern/ Möbeln *usw.* the acquisition of new books/ furniture *etc.*; **b)** *(Gegenstand)* new acquisition; **c)** *(Sport)* new signing

neuestens ['nɔyəstn̩s] *Adv. s.* **neuerdings a**

Neu·fassung die revised version; *(eines Films)* remake

Neu·fund·land (das); ~s Newfoundland

Neufundländer der; ~s, ~ *(Hunderasse)* Newfoundland [dog]

neu-, Neu-: ~geboren *Adj.* newborn; **sich wie ~geboren fühlen** feel a new man/ woman; **~geborene das;** *adj. Dekl.* newborn child; **~geburt die** *(geh.)* rebirth; **~gestaltung die** *(einer Gemeinschaft, Gesellschaft)* reorganization; reshaping; *(der Politik, eines Programms)* reshaping; *(einer Titelseite, einer Einrichtung)* redesigning; *(eines Stadtviertels, einer Parkanlage)* replanning; **~gewürz das;** *o. Pl. (österr.)* allspice; pimento

Neu·gier, Neugierde [-gi:ɐ̯də] **die; ~:** curiosity; *(Wißbegierde)* inquisitiveness; **aus [reiner] ~:** out of [sheer] curiosity; **vor ~ platzen** be bursting with curiosity

neu·gierig 1. *Adj.* curious; inquisitive; prying *(derog.)*, nosy *(coll. derog.)* ⟨*person*⟩; **sei nicht so ~!** don't be so inquisitive *or (coll. derog.)* nosy!; **da bin ich aber ~!** *(iron.)* I'll believe it when I see it; I can hardly wait! *(iron.)*; **auf etw.** *(Akk.)* **~ sein** be curious about sth.; **viele Neugierige** many inquisitive people *or* spectators; **ich bin ~, was er dazu sagt** I'm curious to know what he'll say about it; **ich bin ~, ob er kommt** I wonder whether he'll come; **er war ~ [zu hören], was passiert war** he was curious to know what had happened. **2.** *adv.* ⟨*ask*⟩ inquisitively; ⟨*peer*⟩ nosily *(coll. derog.)*; **jmdn. ~ mustern** eye sb. curiously; **~ lehnten die Nachbarn aus dem Fenster** the neighbours leaned out of the window full of curiosity

neu-, Neu-: ~gliederung die reorganization; restructuring; **~gotik die** Gothic Revival; **~gotisch** *Adj.* neo-Gothic; **~gründung die a) die ~gründung eines Vereins/einer Partei/Universität** *usw.* the founding *or* establishment of a new club/party/university *etc.*; **b)** *(neu Gegründetes)* **eine ~gründung sein** have recently been founded *or* established; **c)** *(erneute Gründung)* refoundation; re-establishment

Neu·guinea (das) New Guinea

Neuheit die; ~, ~en a) *o. Pl.* novelty; **den Reiz der ~ haben** have novelty value; **b)** *(Neues)* new product/gadget/article *etc.*

neu·hoch·deutsch *adj.* New High German

Neu·hoch·deutsch das New High German

Neuigkeit die; ~, ~en piece of news; **~en** news *sing.*

Neu·inszenierung die *(Theater)* new production

Neu·jahr das New Year's Day; **~ feiern** celebrate New Year; *s. auch* **prosit**

Neujahrs-: ~abend der New Year's Eve; **~an·sprache die** New Year address; **~fest das** New Year's Day; *(Feier)* New Year celebration; **das jüdische/chinesische ~fest** the Jewish/Chinese New Year; **das ~fest begehen** celebrate New Year; **~gruß der** New Year greetings *pl.*; **~karte die** New Year card; **~konzert das** New Year concert; **~nacht die** New Year's night; **~tag der** New Year's Day

neu, Neu-: ~land das; *o. Pl.* **a)** newly reclaimed *or* new land; **b)** *(unerforschtes Land)* new *or* virgin territory; **wissenschaftliches/medizinisches ~land betreten** *(fig.)* break new ground in science/medicine; **~latein das** New Latin; Neo-Latin; **~lateinisch** *Adj.* Neo-Latin

neulich *Adv.* recently; the other day; **~ morgens/abends** the other morning/evening; **der Mann von ~, der in unserem Zugabteil saß** *(ugs.)* the man who was sitting in our compartment on the train the other day

Neuling ['nɔylɪŋ] **der; ~s, ~e** newcomer **(in** + *Dat.* to); new man/woman/girl/boy; *(auf einem Gebiet)* novice

neu·modisch *(abwertend)* **1.** *Adj.* newfangled *(derog.)*. **2.** *adv.* ⟨*dress*⟩ in a newfangled way

Neu·mond der new moon; **heute ist/haben wir ~:** there's a new moon today; **zwei Tage nach ~:** two days after the new moon

neun [nɔyn] *Kardinalz.* nine; **alle ~[e]** *(Kegeln)* a floorer; *s. auch* **acht**

Neun die; ~, ~en nine; **ach, du grüne ~e** *(ugs.)* oh, my goodness!; good grief!; *s. auch* **[1]Acht a, b, d, e, g**

neun-, Neun- *(s. auch* **acht-, Acht-**): **~eck das** nonagon; **~eckig** *Adj.* nonagonal; *s. auch* **achteckig; ~einhalb** *Bruchz.* nine and a half

Neuner der; ~s, ~ *(ugs.)* nine *s. auch* **[1]Acht a, b, e; Achter d**

neunerlei *Gattungsz.; indekl.* **a)** *attr.* nine kinds *or* sorts of; nine different ⟨*sorts, kinds, sizes, possibilities*⟩; **b)** *subst.* nine [different] things

Neuner·probe die *(Math.)* casting out nines [check]

neun-, Neun- *(s. auch* **acht-, Acht-**): **~fach** *Vervielfältigungsz.* ninefold; *s. auch* **achtfach; ~fache das; ~n: das ~fache von 4 ist 36** nine fours are *or* nine times four makes thirty-six; *s. auch* **Achtfache; ~hundert** *Kardinalz.* nine hundred; **~jährig** *Adj. (9 Jahre alt)* nine-year-old *attrib.*; *(9 Jahre dauernd)* nine-year *attrib.*; *s. auch* **achtjährig; ~köpfig** *Adj.* nine-headed ⟨*monster*⟩; ⟨*family, committee*⟩ of nine; **~mal** *Adv.* nine times; *s. auch* **achtmal; ~mal·gescheit, ~mal·klug** *(spöttisch)* **1.** *Adj.* smart-aleck *attrib. (coll.)*; **du bist immer so ~malgescheit** *od.* **~malklug** you're such a smart aleck *(coll.)*; **ein Neunmalgescheiter** *od.* **Neunmalkluger** a smart aleck *(coll.)*; **2.** *adv.* in a smart-aleck way *(coll.)*; **~schwänzig** [-ʃvɛnt͜sɪç] *Adj. in* **~schwänzige Katze** *(Seemannsspr.)* cat-o'-nine-tails; **~stellig** *Adj.* nine-figure *attrib.*; *s. auch* **achtstellig; ~stöckig** *Adj.* nine-storey *attrib.*; *s. auch* **achtstöckig; ~stündig** *Adj.* nine-hour *attrib.*; lasting nine hours *postpos., not pred.*; *s. auch* **achtstündig**

neunt [nɔynt] *in* **wir waren zu ~:** there were nine of us; *s. auch* **[2]acht**

neunt... *Ordinalz.* ninth; *s. auch* **acht...**

neun- *(s. auch* **acht-, Acht-**): **~tägig** *Adj. (9 Tage alt)* nine-day-old *attrib.*; *(9 Tage dauernd)* nine-day-long *attrib.*; *s. auch* **achttägig; ~tausend** *Kardinalz.* nine thousand

Neuntel das *(schweiz. meist* **der**); **~s, ~:** ninth

neuntens *Adv.* ninthly

Neun·töter der *(Zool.)* red-backed shrike

neun·zehn *Kardinalz.* nineteen; *s. auch* **achtzehn**

neunzehnt... *Ordinalz.* nineteenth; *s. auch* **acht...**

neunzig ['nɔynt͜sɪç] *Kardinalz.* ninety; *s. auch* **achtzig**

Neunzig die; ~, ~en ninety; *s. auch* **Achtzig**

neunzig-, Neunzig-: *s. auch* **achtzig-; Achtzig-**

neunziger *indekl. Adj.; nicht präd.* **die ~ Jahre** the nineties; *s. auch* **achtziger**

neunzigst... ['nɔynt͜sɪçst...] *Ordinalz.* ninetieth; *s. auch* **acht..., achtzigst...**

Neu-: ~ordnung die reorganization; **~orientierung die** reorientation; **~philologe der** modern linguist; **~philologie die** modern languages [and literature] *sing.; no art.*; **~prägung die a)** *(Münzk.)* new minting; **die ~prägung von Münzen** the minting of new coins; **b)** *(Sprachw.)* new coinage; neologism; **die ~prägung von Wörtern/Wendungen** *usw.* the coining of new words/expressions *etc.*

Neuralgie [nɔyral'gi:] **die; ~, ~n** *(Med.)* neuralgia

neuralgisch 1. *Adj.* **a)** *(Med.)* neuralgic; **b)** *(empfindlich)* **das ist mein ~er Punkt** it's a sore *or* touchy point with me. **2.** *adv. (empfindlich)* ⟨*react*⟩ touchily

neu-, Neu-: ~reg[e]lung die a); *o. Pl.* **die ~regelung der Arbeitszeit/der Zulassung zu den Universitäten** *usw.* the revision of regulations governing working hours/admission to university *etc.*; **b)** *(Bestimmung)* new regulation; **~reich** *(abwertend) Adj.*

nouveau riche; **Familie Neureich** *(ugs.)* the typical nouveau riche family; **~reiche der/die** nouveau riche; **die ~reichen** the nouveaux riches; the new rich
Neuritis [nɔy'ri:tɪs] **die; ~, Neuritiden** *(Med.)* neuritis
Neuro·chirurgie die; ~ *(Med.)* neurosurgery
Neurologe der; ~n, ~n neurologist
Neurologie die; ~ a) neurology; **b)** *(Abteilung)* neurology department; *(Station)* neurology ward; *(ugs.: Klinik)* neurology clinic
Neurologin die; ~, ~nen neurologist
neurologisch *Adj.* neurological
Neuron ['nɔyrɔn] **das; ~s, ~e** *od.* **~en** *(Anat.)* neuron
Neurose [nɔy'ro:zə] **die; ~, ~n** *(Med., Psych.)* neurosis
Neurotiker [nɔy'ro:tikɐ] **der; ~s, ~, Neurotikerin die; ~, ~nen** *(Med., Psych., auch ugs.)* neurotic
neurotisch *Adj. (Med., Psych., auch ugs.)* neurotic
Neu-: ~satz der *(Druckw.)* new setting; **~schnee der** fresh snow
Neu·see·land (das); ~s New Zealand
Neuseeländer der; ~s, ~: New Zealander
Neuseeländerin die; ~, ~nen New Zealander; New Zealand lady/woman/girl; *s. auch* **-in**
neuseeländisch *Adj.* New Zealand
neu-, Neu-: ~silber das German silver; nickel silver; **~sprachler** [~ʃpra:xlɐ] **der; ~s, ~:** modern linguist; **~sprachlich** *Adj.* modern languages *attrib.* ‹*teaching*›; **der ~sprachliche Zweig** *(Schulw.)* the modern languages side; **ein ~sprachliches Gymnasium** a grammar school with emphasis on modern languages
neustens ['nɔystn̩s] *s.* **neuerdings a**
Neutestamentler [-testamɛntlɐ] **der; ~s, ~:** New Testament scholar
neutestamentlich *Adj.* New Testament *attrib.*
neutral [nɔy'tra:l] **1.** *Adj.* **a)** *(auch Völkerr., Phys., Chem.)* neutral; **b)** *(Sprachw.)* neuter. **2.** *adv.* **sich ~ verhalten** remain neutral; **ich kann das nicht ~ entscheiden/beurteilen** I cannot give an impartial decision/judgement
-neutral *adj.* **kosten~/erfolgs~:** not affecting costs/profits *postpos., not pred.*; **geschmacks~/geruchs~:** neutral-tasting/ neutral-smelling
Neutralisation [nɔytraliza'tsio:n] **die; ~, ~en** *(auch Chemie)* neutralization
neutralisieren *tr. V. (auch Völkerr., Chem., Elektrot.)* neutralize; *(Rennsport)* stop ‹*race*›
Neutralisierung die; ~, ~en *(auch Völkerr., Chem., Elektrot.)* neutralization; *(Rennsport)* stopping
Neutralität [nɔytrali'tɛ:t] **die; ~, ~en** *(auch Völkerr., Chem., Elektrot.)* neutrality
Neutralitäts-: ~abkommen das *(Völkerr.)* treaty of neutrality; **~verletzung die** *(Völkerr.)* violation of neutrality
Neutron ['nɔytrɔn] **das; ~s, ~en** [-'tro:nən] *(Kernphysik)* neutron
Neutronen-: ~bombe die neutron bomb; **~waffe die** neutron weapon; **~zahl die** *(Kernphysik)* neutron number
Neutrum ['nɔytrʊm] **das; ~s, Neutra** *(österr. nur so) od.* **Neutren a)** *(Sprachw.)* neuter; **b)** *(abwertend: Mensch ohne erotische Ausstrahlung)* sexless individual
neu-, Neu-: ~vermählt *Adj. (geh.)* newly wed *or* married; **die Neuvermählten** the newly-weds; **~wagen der** new car; **~wahl** new election; **die ~wahl des Bundespräsidenten** the election of a new Federal President; **~wahlen ansetzen/ausschreiben** call new elections; **~wert der a)** value when new; original value; *(Versicherungsw.)* replacement value; **b)** *(marx.: neu geschaffener Wert)* new value; **~wertig** *Adj.* as new; **~wertiger Kühlschrank für 150 DM zu verkaufen** for sale, refrigerator, as new – 150 DM; **~wort das;** *Pl.* **~wörter** *(Sprachw.)* new word; neologism; **~zeit die;** *o. Pl. (Zeit nach 1500)* modern era *or* age; *(Gegenwart)* modern times *pl.*; modern age; **~zeitlich 1.** *Adj.* modern; since the Middle Ages *postpos., not pred.*; *(modern)* modern ‹*device, equipment, methods, etc.*›; **2.** *adv. (modern)* ‹*equip, fit*› with all modern conveniences; **~zu·gang der** *(im Krankenhaus)* new admission; *(im Gefängnis)* new inmate; *(bei Militär, bei einer Firma, einem Verein)* new recruit; *(Buch für eine Bibliothek)* new accession; **~zulassung die** *(Amtsspr.)* **a) die ~zulassung von Kraftfahrzeugen** the registration of new vehicles; **b)** *(Fahrzeug)* new registration
Nexus ['nɛksʊs] **der, ~, ~:** nexus
Niagara·fall [nia'ga:ra-] **der, Niagarafälle** *Pl.* Niagara Falls
Nibelungen·treue ['ni:bəlʊŋən-] **die; ~** *(oft abwertend)* unquestioning loyalty [unto death]
Nicaragua [nika'ra:gu̯a] **(das); ~s** Nicaragua
Nicaraguaner der; ~s, ~, Nicaraguanerin die; ~, ~nen Nicaraguan; *s. auch* **-in**
nicaraguanisch *Adj.* Nicaraguan
nicht [nɪçt] *Adv.* **a)** not; **sie raucht ~** *(im Moment)* she is not smoking; *(gewöhnlich)* she does not *or* doesn't smoke; **alle klatschten, nur sie ~:** they all applauded except for her; **Wer hat das getan? – Sie ~!** Who did that? – It wasn't her; **Gehst du hin? – Nein, ich gehe ~!** Are you going? – No, I'm not; **Ich mag ihn ~. – Ich auch ~:** I don't like him. – Neither do I; **ich kann das ~ mehr** *od.* **länger sehen** I can't stand the sight of it any more *or* longer; **~ einmal** *od. (ugs.)* **mal** not even; **~ mehr als** no more than; **~ ihn kenne ich, sondern sie** I don't know him, but I know her; **~ einer** not one; **~ daß ich nicht wollte, ich habe bloß keine Zeit** [it's] not that I don't want to, I just don't have the time; **das ist wirklich/absolut/gewiß/gar ~ schlimm!** it's not as bad as all that!; **b)** *(Bitte, Verbot o. ä. ausdrückend)* **~!** [no,] don't!; **„~ hinauslehnen!"** *(im Zug)* 'do not lean out of the window'; **bitte ~!** please don't!; **~ doch!** not at all!; *(bitte aufhören)* stop that!; **~ doch, ärgere dich doch ~!** come, come *or* come on, there's no need to get so worked up; **nur das ~!** anything but that!; **ärgere dich doch ~, das ist die Sache gar ~ wert** don't get so angry, it just isn't worth it; **c)** *(Zustimmung erwartend)* **er ist dein Bruder, ~?** he's your brother, isn't he?; **du magst das, ~ [wahr]?** you like that, don't you?; **kommst du [etwa] ~?** aren't you coming[, then]?; **willst du ~ mitkommen?** won't you come too?; **ist es ~ herrlich hier?** isn't it glorious here?; **d)** *(verwundert)* **was du ~ sagst!** you don't say!; **was ich mir ~ alles bieten lassen muß!** the things I have to put up with!; **e)** *([bedingte] Anerkennung ausdrückend)* **~ übel!** not bad!; **sie ist ~ dumm!** she's not stupid
nicht-, Nicht-: non-; **~beteiligung/~demokratisch/~akademiker** non-participation/ non-democratic/non-graduate
nicht-, Nicht-: ~achtung die a) *in* **jmdn. mit ~achtung strafen** punish sb. by ignoring him/her; send sb. to Coventry; **b)** *(Geringschätzung)* lack of regard *or* respect; **~achtung des Gerichts** contempt of court; **~amtlich** *Adj.; nicht präd.* unofficial; **~anerkennung die** non-recognition; **~angriffs·pakt der** non-aggression pact; **~beachtung die** non-observance; **~beachtung einer roten Ampel** failure to observe a red light; **~befolgung die: ~befolgung der Anweisungen/eines Befehls** failure to follow the instructions/to obey an order; **~befolgung der Bestimmungen/Vorschriften** non-compliance *or* failure to comply with the instructions/regulations; **~berufstätig** *Adj.; nicht präd.* non-employed ‹*housewives*›
Nichte die; ~, ~n niece
nicht-, Nicht-: ~ehelich *(bes. Rechtsspr.)* **1.** *Adj.* illegitimate ‹*child, birth*›; **aus ~ehelichen Beziehungen geborene Kinder** children born out of wedlock; **2.** *adv.* ‹*born*› out of wedlock; **~einhaltung die** non-compliance, failure to comply (*Gen.* with); non-observance; **~ein·mischung die** *(Politik)* non-intervention; non-interference; **~eisen·metall das** non-ferrous metal; **~erfüllung die** non-fulfilment; **~erscheinen das; ~s** non-appearance; failure to appear; **~fach·mann der** non-expert; layman; **~flektierbar** *Adj.; nicht präd. (Sprachw.)* non-inflected; **~gefallen das** *in* **bei ~gefallen** *(Kaufmannsspr.)* if not satisfied
nichtig *Adj.* **a)** *(geh.: wertlos, belanglos)* vain ‹*things, pleasures, etc.*›; paltry ‹*desire*›; trivial ‹*reason*›; petty ‹*quarrel*›; idle ‹*chatter, thoughts*›; empty ‹*pretext*›; **b)** *(Rechtsspr.: ungültig)* invalid, void ‹*contract, will, marriage, etc.*›; **für ~ erklären** *(Rechtsspr.)* declare ‹*contract, will, etc.*› invalid *or* void; annul ‹*marriage*›; *s. auch* **null**
Nichtigkeit die; ~, ~en a) *o. Pl. (geh.) s.* **nichtig a:** vanity; paltriness; pettiness, triviality; idleness; emptiness; **b)** *(geh.: belanglose Sache)* trifle; **c)** *o. Pl. (Rechtsspr.)* invalidity; voidness; *(einer Ehe)* nullity
Nichtigkeits·klage die *(Rechtsw.)* nullity suit
nicht-, Nicht-: ~in·anspruch·nahme die *(Amtsspr.)* failure to take advantage; **~kapitalistisch** *Adj.* non-capitalist ‹*country, state*›; **~leitend** *Adj. (Physik)* non-conducting; **~leiter der** *(Physik)* non-conductor; **~metall das** non-metal; **~mitglied das** non-member; **~öffentlich** *Adj.* not open to the public *pred.*; closed, private ‹*meeting*›; **die ~öffentliche Beweisaufnahme** the hearing of the evidence in camera; **~organisiert** *Adj.; nicht präd.* non-unionized ‹*employee, colleague, etc.*›; **~raucher der** non-smoker; **ich bin ~raucher** I don't smoke; I'm a non-smoker; **„~raucher"** 'no smoking'; **~raucher·abteil das** non-smoking *or* no-smoking compartment; **~rostend** *Adj.* non-rusting ‹*blade*›; stainless ‹*steel*›
nichts [nɪçts] *Indefinitpron.* nothing; **er sieht ~:** he sees nothing; he doesn't see anything; **hast du ~ gegessen?** haven't you eaten anything?; **ich möchte ~:** I don't want anything; **das ist ~ für mich** it's not for me; it isn't my cup of tea *(coll.)*; **für ~ und wieder ~** *(ugs.)* for nothing at all; **sich in ~ von jmdm./etw. unterscheiden** be no different from sb./sth.; **~ zu machen!** *(ugs.)* nothing doing *(coll.)*; **er ist durch ~ zu überzeugen** nothing will convince him; **von mir bekommst du ~ mehr** you'll get nothing more from me; you won't get anything more from me; **ich will ~ mehr davon hören** I don't want to hear any more about it; **die Ärzte konnten ~ mehr für ihn tun** the doctors could do nothing more *or* could not do any more for him; **~ anderes** nothing else; **jetzt interessiert er sich für ~ anderes mehr** he's now no longer interested in anything else; **haben Sie ~ anderes als Hamburger?** haven't you got anything else besides hamburgers?; **~ als** nothing but; **das/er ist zu ~ zu gebrauchen** it's/he's no use; it's/he's useless; **das war wohl ~** *(salopp)* that wasn't exactly brilliant; **wir wissen ~ Näheres/Genaues** we don't know any more/any details; **~ wie ins Bett/weg!** quick into bed/let's go!;

~ **wie hinterher!** put your skates on, after him/her/them! *(sl.)*; ~ **weiter** nothing else; **von ~ kommt ~**: you don't get anything without effort; ~ **da!** *(ugs.)* nothing doing! *(coll.)*; **wie ~**: in a trice *or* flash; **die Angelegenheit ist ~ weniger als schön** it's not at all a nice business; *s. auch* **danken 2 a**

Nichts das; ~, ~**e a)** *o. Pl. (Philos.: das Nicht-Sein)* nothingness *no art.*; **b)** *o. Pl. (leerer Raum)* void; **er war wie aus dem ~ aufgetaucht** he appeared from nowhere; **c)** *o. Pl. (wenig von etw.)* **er hat die Fabrik aus dem ~ aufgebaut** he built the factory up from nothing; **vor dem ~ stehen** be left with nothing; be faced with ruin; **ein ~ von einem Bikini** *usw.* **[sein]** [be] a scrap of a bikini *etc.*; **d)** *(abwertend: Mensch)* nobody; nonentity

nichts·ahnend *Adj.* unsuspecting

Nicht-: ~**schwimmer der** non-swimmer; **er war ~schwimmer** he could not swim; ~**schwimmer·becken das** non-swimmers' *or* learners' pool

nichts-: ~**desto·minder**, ~**desto·trotz** *(ugs. scherzh.)*, ~**desto·weniger** *Adv.* nevertheless; none the less

Nicht-: ~**sein das** *(Philos.)* non-existence *no art.*; non-being *no art.*; ~**seßhafte der/die**; *adj. Dekl. (Amtsspr.)* person of no fixed abode *(Admin. Lang.)*

nichts-, Nichts-: ~**könner der** *(abwertend)* incompetent; bungler; ~**nutz der**; ~**es**, ~**e** *(veralt. abwertend)* good-for-nothing; **mein ~nutz von Bruder** my good-for-nothing [of a] brother; ~**nutzig** *Adj. (veralt. abwertend)* good-for-nothing *attrib.*; worthless ⟨*existence*⟩; ~**sagend 1.** *Adj.* meaningless, empty ⟨*talk, phrases, etc.*⟩; *(fig.: ausdruckslos)* vacant ⟨*smile*⟩; expressionless ⟨*face*⟩; **ein ~sagender Typ** a nonentity; **2.** *adv.* meaninglessly ⟨*formulated*⟩; ⟨*smile*⟩ vacantly; ~**tuer** [~tu:ɐ] **der**; ~**s**, ~ *(abwertend)* layabout; loafer; **die reichen ~tuer** the idle rich; ~**tuerei** [---'-] **die**; ~ *(abwertend)* idle loafing; ~**tun das a)** *(Untätigkeit)* inactivity; doing nothing *no art.*; **b)** *(Müßiggang)* idleness *no art.*; lazing about *no art.*; **das süße ~tun** being gloriously idle; ~**würdig** *(geh. abwertend)* **1.** *Adj.* worthless, despicable ⟨*person*⟩; base, unworthy, despicable ⟨*deed*⟩; **Nichtswürdiger!** worthless *or* despicable wretch!; **2.** *adv.* ⟨*betray, deceive*⟩ basely; ⟨*act*⟩ unworthily; ~**würdigkeit die**; *o. Pl. (geh. veralt.) s.* ~**würdig**: worthlessness; despicableness; baseness; unworthiness

nicht-, Nicht-: ~**tänzer der**, ~**tänzerin die** non-dancer; **ich bin ~tänzer[in]** I don't dance; ~**zielend** *Adj. (Sprachw.)* intransitive; ~**zustande·kommen das** *(eines Vertrags)* non-conclusion; **das ~zustandekommen der Konferenz** the failure of the conference to take place; ~**zutreffende das**: ~**zutreffendes streichen** delete as applicable

[1]**Nickel** ['nɪkl] **das**; ~**s** nickel

[2]**Nickel der**; ~**s**, ~ *(ugs. veralt.: Münze)* 10-pfennig piece

Nickel-: ~**brille die** metal-rimmed glasses *or* spectacles; ~**legierung die** nickel alloy

nicken ['nɪkn̩] **1.** *itr. V.* **a)** nod; **befriedigt/zustimmend ~**: nod one's satisfaction/agreement; **mit dem Kopf ~**: nod one's head; **b)** *(fam.: schlafen)* doze; snooze *(coll.)*. **2.** *tr. V. (geh.: nickend ausdrücken)* nod; **Zustimmung/Beifall ~**: nod one's agreement/approval

Nickerchen das; ~**s**, ~ *(fam.)* nap; snooze *(coll.)*; **ein ~ halten** *od.* **machen** take *or* have forty winks *or* a nap

Nicki ['nɪki] **der**; ~**[s]**, ~**s** velour pullover *or* sweater

Nicotin *s.* **Nikotin**

nie [ni:] *Adv.* never; **mich besucht ~ jemand** nobody ever visits me; **fast ~**: hardly ever; ~ **mehr!** never again!; **[einmal und] ~ wieder** [only once and] never again; ~ **und nimmer!** never!; ~ **im Leben!** not on your life!; **das werde ich ~ im Leben vergessen** I shall never forget it as long as I live

nieder ['ni:dɐ] **1.** *Adj.*; *nicht präd.* **a)** *(von minderem Rang)* lower ⟨*class, intelligence*⟩; petty, minor ⟨*official*⟩; lowly ⟨*family, origins, birth*⟩; menial ⟨*task*⟩; **das ~e Volk** the common people; **der ~e Klerus/Adel** the lower clergy/aristocracy; **b)** *(bes. südd.) s.* **niedrig a**; **c)** *(Biol.: nicht hoch entwickelt)* lower ⟨*plant, animal, organism*⟩; *s. auch* **Jagd a. 2.** *Adv. (hinunter)* down; **die Waffen ~!** lay down your arms!; ~ **mit dem Militarismus!** down with militarism!

nieder-, Nieder-: ~**|beugen** *(geh.)* **1.** *tr. V.* bend ⟨*knee*⟩ downwards; bow ⟨*head*⟩; **2.** *refl. V.* bend down; ~**|brennen 1.** *unr. itr. V.*; *mit sein (herunterbrennen)* ⟨*fire*⟩ burn low; ⟨*building*⟩ burn down; **2.** *unr. tr. V.* burn down ⟨*building, village, etc.*⟩; ~**|brüllen** *tr. V. (ugs.)* **jmdn. ~brüllen** shout sb. down; ~**deutsch** *Adj.* Low German ⟨*dialect*⟩; North German ⟨*custom, farmhouse, landscape*⟩; ~**|donnern** *itr. V.*; *mit sein* ⟨*avalanche*⟩ thunder down; ⟨*roof*⟩ come crashing down; ~**druck der**; *Pl.* ~**drücke** *(Technik)* low pressure; ~**|drücken** *tr. V.* **a)** *(herunterdrücken)* press down; press *or* push down, *(formal)* depress ⟨*handle, lever*⟩; **b)** *(bedrücken)* depress; ⟨*memory*⟩ weigh on, oppress ⟨*person*⟩; *s. auch* ~**gedrückt**; ~**|fallen** *unr. itr. V.*; *mit sein (geh.)* ⟨*snow*⟩ fall; **vor jmdm. ~fallen** fall down [on one's knees] before sb.; ~**frequenz die** *(Physik)* low frequency; ~**gang der a)** *o. Pl. (Verfall)* fall; decline; **b)** *(Seemannsspr.: Treppe)* companion-way; companion-ladder; ~**gedrückt 1.** *2. Part. v.* ~**drücken**; **2.** *Adj.* depressed; dejected; ~**|gehen** *unr. itr. V.*; *mit sein* **a)** *(landen)* ⟨*plane, spacecraft, balloonist*⟩ come down; ⟨*parachutist*⟩ drop; ⟨*birds, flock*⟩ land; **b)** *(fallen)* ⟨*rain, satellite, avalanche*⟩ come down; ⟨*meteor*⟩ come to earth; **c)** *(Boxen: zu Boden fallen)* go down; **d)** *(sich senken)* ⟨*theatre curtain*⟩ fall; **e)** *(untergehen)* ⟨*sun, moon*⟩ go down; ⟨*epoch*⟩ decline; ~**geschlagen 1.** *2. Part. v.* ~**schlagen**; **2.** *Adj.* despondent; dejected; ~**geschlagenheit die**; ~: despondency; dejection; ~**|halten** *unr. tr. V.* **a)** *(unterdrükken)* oppress ⟨*nation, people, class*⟩; keep ⟨*nation, people, class*⟩ in subjection; keep ⟨*person*⟩ down; **b)** *(kontrollieren)* keep down ⟨*resistance*⟩; **c)** *(unten halten)* hold down; ~**|holen** *tr. V.* haul down, lower ⟨*sail, flag*⟩; ~**|kämpfen** *tr. V.* **a)** *(besiegen)* overcome ⟨*enemy, opponent*⟩; **b)** *(zurückhalten)* suppress ⟨*rage, excitement*⟩; fight back ⟨*tears*⟩; fight ⟨*tiredness*⟩; ~**|knien** *itr. V. (auch mit sein), refl. V.* kneel down; *(unterwürfig, demütig)* go down on one's knees; ~**|knüppeln** *tr. V.* **jmdn. ~knüppeln** beat *or* club sb. to the ground with a truncheon; ~**|kommen** *unr. itr. V.*; *mit sein (geh. veralt.)* be delivered (**mit** of); give birth (**mit** to); ~**kunft** [~kʊnft] **die**; ~, ~**künfte** [~kʏnftə] *(geh. veralt.)* confinement; ~**lage die a)** *(das Besiegtwerden)* defeat; **eine ~lage einstecken müssen** suffer a defeat; **jmdm. eine ~lage beibringen** inflict a defeat on sb.; **b)** *(Zweiggeschäft)* branch; *(Lager)* warehouse; depot

Nieder·lande *Pl.*: **die ~**: the Netherlands

Niederländer der; ~**s**, ~: Dutchman; Netherlander; **die ~**: the Dutch

Niederländerin die; ~, ~**nen** Dutchwoman; Netherlander; *s. auch* **-in**

niederländisch *Adj.* Dutch; Netherlands *attrib.* ⟨*government, embassy, etc.*⟩; **das Niederländische** Dutch

nieder-, Nieder-: ~**|lassen 1.** *unr. refl. V.* **a)** *(ein Geschäft, eine Praxis eröffnen)* set up *or* establish oneself in business; ⟨*doctor, lawyer*⟩ set up a practice *or* in practice; **sich als Fotograf ~lassen** set up as a photographer; ~**gelassene Ärzte** *registered doctors/specialists having their own independent practices;* **b)** *(seinen Wohnsitz nehmen)* settle; **c)** *(geh.: sich setzen)* sit down; seat oneself; ⟨*bird*⟩ settle, alight; **2.** *unr. tr. V.* lower ⟨*theatre curtain, blind, etc.*⟩; ~**lassung die**; ~, ~**en a)** *o. Pl. s.* ~**lassen a**: setting up in business; setting up of a practice *or* in practice; **b)** *(Ort)* settlement; **c)** *(Wirtsch.: Zweigstelle)* branch; ~**|legen** *tr. V.* **a)** *(geh.: hinlegen)* lay *or* put *or* set down; lay ⟨*wreath*⟩; **die Waffen ~legen** lay down one's arms; **b)** *(nicht weitermachen)* lay down, resign [from] ⟨*office*⟩; relinquish ⟨*command*⟩; discontinue ⟨*course of treatment*⟩; **das Mandat ~legen** ⟨*member of parliament*⟩ resign one's seat; ⟨*lawyer*⟩ give up the brief; *s. auch* **Arbeit a**; **c)** *(geh.: aufschreiben)* set down; ~**legung die**; ~, ~**en a)** *(geh.: eines Kranzes)* laying; **b)** *(eines Amtes)* resignation (+ *Gen.* from); *(eines Kommandos)* relinquishing; **die ~legung der Arbeit** stopping work; **c)** *(geh.: Niederschrift)* setting down; ~**|machen** *tr. V. (ugs.)* butcher; ~**|mähen** *tr. V.* mow down ⟨*prisoners, soldiers, etc.*⟩; ~**|metzeln** *tr. V.* butcher

Nieder·österreich (das) Lower Austria

nieder-: ~**|prasseln** *itr. V.*; *mit sein* ⟨*rain, hail*⟩ beat down; ⟨*blows, rebukes, questions, etc.*⟩ rain down; ~**|reißen** *unr. tr. V.* **a)** *(abreißen)* pull down ⟨*building, wall*⟩; **b)** *(zu Boden reißen)* **jmdn. ~reißen** knock sb. over; ~**rheinisch** *Adj.* in the Lower Rhine valley *postpos.*

Nieder·sachse der; ~**n**, ~**n** inhabitant of Lower Saxony; *(von Geburt)* native of Lower Saxony; *s. auch* **Kölner 2**

Nieder·sachsen (das) Lower Saxony

nieder-, Nieder-: ~**|schießen 1.** *unr. tr. V.* gun down; **der Niedergeschossene** the victim of the shooting; **2.** *unr. itr. V.*; *mit sein (herabfliegen)* ⟨*bird*⟩ stoop, swoop down; ⟨*aircraft*⟩ hurtle down; ~**schlag der a)** *(Met.)* precipitation; **es sind zeitweise ~schläge, teils Regen, teils Schnee, zu erwarten** occasional showers can be expected, some falling as snow; **b)** *(Boxen)* knockdown; **c)** *(Ausdruck)* expression; **[seinen] ~schlag in etw.** *(Dat.)* **finden** find expression in sth.; **d)** *(Chemie)* precipitate; **e) radioaktiver ~schlag** [radioactive] fall-out; ~**|schlagen 1.** *unr. tr. V.* **a)** *(zu Boden schlagen)* **jmdn. ~schlagen** knock sb. down; **b)** *(umschlagen)* turn down ⟨*hat-brim, collar*⟩; **c)** *(beenden)* suppress, put down ⟨*revolt, uprising, etc.*⟩; put an end to ⟨*strike*⟩; **d)** *(senken)* lower ⟨*eyes, eyelids*⟩; **den Blick ~schlagen** lower one's eyes; **e)** *(Rechtsspr.: einstellen)* abandon ⟨*proceedings*⟩; dismiss ⟨*claim*⟩; **ein Verfahren ~schlagen** dismiss a case; **f)** *(Rechtsspr.: erlassen)* waive ⟨*costs*⟩; remit ⟨*punishment*⟩; *s. auch* **niedergeschlagen**; **2.** *unr. refl. V.* **a) sich in etw.** *(Dat.)* ~**schlagen** ⟨*experience, emotion*⟩ find expression in sth.; ⟨*performance, hard work*⟩ be reflected in sth.; **b)** ⟨*steam*⟩ condense; ~**schlags·arm** *Adj.* ⟨*climate, area, period*⟩ with low precipitation *not pred.*; ~**schlags·frei** *Adj.* ⟨*period*⟩ without [any] precipitation *not pred.*; **die Aussichten: heiter bis wolkig und ~schlagsfrei** the outlook: dry with variable amounts of cloud; ~**schlagung die a)** *(einer Revolte, eines Aufstands)* suppression; putting down; **b)** *(Rechtsspr.) s.* ~**schlagen 1 e, f**: abandonment; dismissal; waiving; remission; ~**|schmettern** *tr. V.* **a)** *(~schlagen)* **jmdn. ~schmettern** send sb. crashing to the ground/floor; **b)** *(erschüttern)* ⟨*bad news*⟩ shatter; ⟨*rejection, result*⟩ devastate; ~**schmetternd** *Adj.* shattering ⟨*experience, news*⟩; devastating ⟨*result, review*⟩; ~**|schreiben** *unr. tr. V.* write down; write

⟨*essay, novel*⟩; ~|**schreien** *unr. tr. V.* **jmdn. ~schreien** shout sb. down; **~schrift die a)** *(das Schreiben)* writing down; **etw. zur ~schrift erklären** *(Rechtsspr.)* dictate a statement on sth.; **b)** *(Schriftstück)* document; *(Protokoll)* minutes *pl.*; ~|**setzen 1.** *refl. V.* sit down; **2.** *tr. V.* put *or* set down; ~|**sinken** *unr. itr. V.; mit sein* sink down; **ohnmächtig ~sinken** sink unconscious to the ground/floor; **~spannung die** *(Elektrot.)* low voltage *or* tension; ~|**stechen** *unr. tr. V.* stab; *(erstechen)* stab to death; ~|**stimmen** *tr. V.* vote ⟨*proposal, person, etc.*⟩ down; ~|**stoßen 1.** *unr. tr. V. (geh.: zu Boden stoßen)* **jmdn. ~stoßen** knock sb. down; **2.** *unr. itr. V.; mit sein* ⟨*hawk, etc.*⟩ stoop, swoop down; ⟨*aircraft*⟩ hurtle down; ~|**strecken** *(geh.)* **1.** *tr. V.* **jmdn. ~strecken** knock sb. down; *(mit einem Schuß)* shoot sb. down; **einen Tiger/Hirsch ~strecken** bring down a tiger/stag; **2.** *refl. V. (sich hinlegen)* lie down; **auf das** *od.* **dem Sofa ~gestreckt** stretched out on the sofa; ~|**stürzen** *itr. V.; mit sein (geh.)* **a)** *(zu Boden fallen)* fall down; **ohnmächtig ~stürzen** fall unconscious to the ground/floor; **b)** *(herabfallen)* ⟨*rocks*⟩ fall; ⟨*avalanche*⟩ sweep down; **~tourig** [~tu:rɪç] *(Technik)* **1.** *Adj.* **im ~tourigen Bereich** at low revs *(coll.)*; **2.** *adv.* at low revs *(coll.)*; **~tracht die;** ~ *(geh.)* malice; *(als Charaktereigenschaft)* vileness; despicableness; **etw. aus ~tracht tun** do sth. out of malice; **~trächtig 1.** *Adj.* malicious ⟨*person, slander, lie, etc.*⟩; *(verachtenswert)* vile, despicable ⟨*person*⟩; base, vile ⟨*misrepresentation, slander, lie*⟩; **2.** *adv.* ⟨*betray, lie, treat*⟩ in a vile *or* despicable way; ⟨*smile*⟩ maliciously; **~trächtigkeit die;** ~, **~en a)** *o. Pl. s.* **~trächtig 1:** maliciousness; vileness; despicableness; baseness; **b)** *(gemeine Handlung)* vile *or* despicable act; ~|**trampeln** *tr. V. (ugs.)*, ~|**treten** *unr. tr. V.* tread ⟨*grass, flowers, carpet-pile, etc.*⟩; *(fig.)* trample ⟨*person*⟩ underfoot

Niederung die; ~, **~en** low-lying area; *(an Flußläufen, Küsten)* flats *pl.*; *(Tal)* valley; **sumpfige ~en** marshes; **die ~en des [alltäglichen] Lebens** *(fig.)* the lowly spheres of everyday life

nieder-, Nieder-: ~|**walzen** *tr. V.* flatten; **jmdn. mit Argumenten ~walzen** *(fig.)* overwhelm sb. with arguments; ~|**werfen 1.** *unr. tr. V.* **a)** *(geh.: besiegen)* overcome, defeat ⟨*enemy, rebels, etc.*⟩; **b)** *(geh.: beenden) s.* **~schlagen 1c; c)** *(geh.: schwächen)* ⟨*illness, fever*⟩ lay ⟨*person*⟩ low; **d)** *(geh.: erschüttern)* ⟨*bad news*⟩ shake ⟨*person*⟩ profoundly; **der Tod seiner Frau hat ihn ~geworfen** he took the death of his wife very badly; **2.** *unr. refl. V.* throw oneself down; **sich vor jmdm. ~werfen** prostrate oneself before sb.; **~werfung die;** ~, **~en** *(geh.) (von Feinden, Aufständischen)* overthrow; defeat; *(einer Revolte, eines Aufstands)* suppression; putting down; **~wild das** *(Jägerspr.) smaller game animals, e.g. roe-deer, hare, fox, badger*; ~|**zwingen** *unr. tr. V. (geh.)* force ⟨*opponent*⟩ to the ground *or* down; *(fig.)* suppress ⟨*anger, excitement*⟩

niedlich ['ni:tlɪç] **1.** *Adj.* sweet; cute *(Amer. coll.)*; sweet little *attrib.*; dear little *attrib.* **2.** *adv.* ⟨*dance, nibble*⟩ sweetly, prettily; ⟨*babble, play*⟩ sweetly, cutely *(Amer. coll.)*; **auf dem Foto guckt die Kleine so ~:** in the photo the little girl has such a sweet expression

niedrig 1. *Adj.* **a)** *(von geringer Höhe)* low; short ⟨*grass*⟩; **b)** *(von geringem Rang)* lowly ⟨*origins, birth*⟩; low ⟨*rank, status, intellectual level*⟩; **c)** *(sittlich tiefstehend)* base ⟨*instinct, desire, emotion, person*⟩; vile ⟨*motive*⟩; **von ~er Gesinnung** low-minded. **2.** *adv.* ⟨*hang, fly*⟩ low

Niedrigkeit die; ~, **~en a)** *o. Pl. (geringe Höhe)* lowness; **b)** *o. Pl. (niedrige Gesinnung)* baseness; **c)** *(gemeine Tat)* base deed

Niedrig-: **~lohn der** low wages *pl.*; **~lohnland das** country with a low-wage economy; **etw. im ~lohnland Taiwan produzieren** produce sth. in Taiwan, with its low wages *or* low-wage economy; **~preis der** low price; **~wasser das;** *o. Pl.* **a)** *(von Seen/Flüssen)* **bei ~wasser** when the [level of the] lake/river is low; **b)** *(bei Ebbe)* low tide; low water; **bei ~wasser** at low tide *or* low water

niemals ['ni:ma:ls] *Adv.* never

niemand ['ni:mant] *Indefinitpron.* nobody; no one; **~ war im Büro** there was nobody *or* no one in the office; there wasn't anybody *or* any one in the office; **wir haben ~[en] gesehen** we saw nobody *or* no one; we didn't see anybody *or* any one; **~ anders** *od.* **anderer** nobody *or* no one else; **es kann ~ anders** *od.* **anderer als du gewesen sein** it can't have been anybody *or* any one [else] but you; **das war ~ anders als der Kaiser** it was none other than the emperor himself; **er hat mit ~[em] von uns reden wollen** he didn't want to talk to any of us; **das darfst du ~[em] sagen!** you mustn't tell anybody that!; **~ Bekanntes** nobody I know/he knows *etc.*; *(keine prominenten Leute)* nobody famous; **laß ~ Fremdes herein** don't let anybody *or* anyone in you don't know; don't let any strangers in; **er ist ~[e]s Feind** he has no enemies; **ein Niemand sein** be a nobody

Niemands·land das; *o. Pl.* **a)** *(auch fig.)* no man's land; **b)** *(unerforschtes Gebiet, auch fig.)* unknown *or* unexplored territory

Niere ['ni:rə] **die;** ~, **~n** kidney; **künstliche ~:** kidney machine; artificial kidney; **jmdm. an die ~n gehen** *(fig. ugs.)* get to sb. *(coll.)*

nieren, Nieren-: **~becken·entzündung die** pyelitis; **~entzündung die** nephritis; **~förmig** *Adj.* kidney-shaped; **~kolik die** renal colic; **~leiden das** kidney disease; **~stein der** kidney stone; renal calculus *(Med.)*; **~tisch der** kidney-shaped table

nieseln ['ni:zl̩n] *unpers. V.* drizzle

Niesel-: **~priem der** *(veralt. scherzh.)* misery[-guts] *(coll.)*; **~regen der** drizzle

niesen ['ni:zn̩] *itr. V.* sneeze

Nies-: **~pulver das** sneezing-powder; **~reiz der** urge to sneeze

Nieß·brauch ['ni:sbraux] **der;** *o. Pl. (Rechtsw.)* usufruct

Nies·wurz die *(Bot.)* hellebore

Niet [ni:t] **der,** *(auch:)* **das;** **~[e]s, ~e** *(fachspr.) s.* [2]**Niete**

[1]**Niete** ['ni:tə] **die;** ~, **~n a)** *(Los)* blank; **eine ~ ziehen** draw a blank; **b)** *(ugs.: Mensch)* dead loss *(coll.)* **(in + Dat.** at)

[2]**Niete die;** ~, **~n** rivet

nieten ['ni:tn̩] *tr. V.* rivet

Nieten·hose die [pair of] studded jeans

niet- und nagelfest *in* **[alles] was nicht ~ ~ ~ ist** *(ugs.)* [everything] that's not nailed *or* screwed down

nigel·nagel·neu *Adj. (schweiz. ugs.)* brand-new

[1]**Niger** ['ni:gɐ] **(das);** **~s** *(Staat)* Niger

[2]**Niger der;** **~[s]** *(Fluß)* Niger

Nigeria [ni'ge:ri̯a] **(das);** **~s** Nigeria

Nigerianer der; **~s,** ~, **Nigerianerin die;** ~, **~nen** Nigerian; *s. auch* **-in**

nigerianisch *Adj.* Nigerian

Nigger ['nɪgɐ] **der;** **~s,** ~ *(abwertend, oft als Schimpfwort)* nigger *(derog.)*

Nihilismus [nihi'lɪsmʊs] **der;** **~:** nihilism

Nihilist der; **~en, ~en** nihilist

nihilistisch *Adj.* nihilistic

[1]**Nikolaus** ['nɪkolaus] **der;** ~, **~e a)** *o. Art.* St Nicholas; **b)** *(Tag)* St Nicholas' Day

[2]**Nikolaus (der)** *(hist. Name)* Nicholas

Nikolaus·tag der St Nicholas' Day

Nikotin [niko'ti:n] **das;** **~s** nicotine

nikotin-, Nikotin-: **~arm** *Adj.* low-nicotine *attrib.*; low in nicotine *pred.*; **~frei** *Adj.* nicotine-free; **~gehalt der** nicotine content; **~haltig** *Adj.* containing nicotine *postpos., not. pred.*; **~haltig sein** contain nicotine; **~vergiftung die** nicotine poisoning

Nil [ni:l] **der;** **~[s]** Nile

Nil·pferd das hippopotamus; hippo *(coll.)*

Nimbus ['nɪmbʊs] **der;** ~, **~se a)** *o. Pl. (geh.: Ruhm)* aura; **sein ~ als großer Dichter** his reputation as a great poet; **b)** *(Kunstwiss.)* nimbus

nimm [nɪm] *Imperativ Sg. v.* **nehmen**

nimmer ['nɪmɐ] *Adv.* **a)** *(geh. veralt.: niemals)* never; **b)** *(südd., österr.)* never again; **das kann ich ~ aushalten** I can't endure it any longer; *s. auch* **nie**

Nimmerleinstag ['nɪmɐlainsta:k] *in* **am ~** *(ugs. scherzh.)* never; **etw. auf den** *od.* **bis zum ~ verschieben** *(ugs. scherzh.)* put sth. off indefinitely

nimmer-, Nimmer-: **~mehr** *Adv.* **a)** *(veralt.: nie)* never; **b)** *(südd., österr.: nie wieder)* never again; **~müde** *(geh.)* **1.** *Adj.* tireless, untiring ⟨*helper, worker, etc.*⟩; **in ~müder Arbeit** working tirelessly *or* untiringly; **2.** *adv.* tirelessy; untiringly; **~satt** *Adj.; nicht präd. (fam.)* insatiable; **~satt der;** ~ *od.* **~[e]s, ~e** *(fam.)* gannet *(sl.)*; **~wieder·sehen** *in* **auf ~wiedersehen verschwinden** *(ugs., oft scherzh.)* vanish never to be seen again

Nimrod ['nɪmrɔt] **der;** **~s, ~e** *(geh., oft scherzh.)* Nimrod

Nippel ['nɪpl̩] **der;** **~s,** ~ **a)** *(Technik; ugs.: Brustwarze)* nipple; **b)** *(am Wasserball)* valve

nippen ['nɪpn̩] *itr. V. (trinken)* sip; take a sip/sips; *(essen)* nibble **(von** at); **vom Wein ~:** sip [at] the wine; take a sip/sips of the wine; **am Glas ~:** sip from *or* take a sip/sips from the glass

Nippes ['nɪpəs], **Nipp·sachen** *Pl.* [porcelain] knick-knacks; small [porcelain] ornaments

Nipp·tide die neap tide

nirgend-: **~her** *Adv. s.* **nirgendwoher;** **~hin** *Adv. s.* **nirgendwohin**

nirgends ['nɪrgn̩ts] *Adv.* nowhere; **er war ~ zu finden** he was nowhere *or* wasn't anywhere to be found; **ich fühle mich ~ so wohl wie hier** there is nowhere *or* isn't anywhere I feel as happy as here; **sonst ~:** nowhere else; **er hält es ~ lange aus** he doesn't stay anywhere for long

nirgend-: **~wo** *Adv. s.* **nirgends;** **~woher** *Adv.* from nowhere; **sie konnten die Medikamente ~woher bekommen** they couldn't get the medicines from anywhere; **~wohin** *Adv.* **der Weg führt ~wohin** the path doesn't go anywhere; **wir gehen ~wohin** we're not going anywhere

Nirwana [nɪr'va:na] **das;** **~[s]** nirvana

Nische ['ni:ʃə] **die;** ~, **~n a)** *(Einbuchtung)* niche; **b)** *(Erweiterung eines Raumes)* recess

Niß [nɪs] **die;** ~, **Nisse** *(veralt.)*, **Nisse** ['nɪsə] **die;** ~, **~n** nit

nisten ['nɪstn̩] *itr. V.* nest; **eine tiefe Traurigkeit nistete in ihrem Herzen** *(fig. geh.)* a deep sadness dwelt in her heart

Nist-: **~kasten der** nest-box; nesting-box; **~platz der** nesting-site; **~zeit die** nesting time *or* season

Nitrat [ni'tra:t] **das;** **~[e]s, ~e** *(Chemie)* nitrate

Nitrid [ni'tri:t] **das;** **~s, ~e** *(Chemie)* nitride

nitrieren *tr. V.* **a)** *(Chemie)* nitrate; **b)** *(Technik)* nitride ⟨*steel*⟩

Nitrit [ni'tri:t] **das;** **~s, ~e** *(Chemie)* nitrite

Nitro·glyzerin [ni:tro-] **das;** *o. Pl.* nitroglycerine

Niveau [ni'vo:] **das;** **~s, ~s a)** level; **auf dem geistigen ~ eines Fünfjährigen stehen** have the mental age of a five-year-old; **über-**

haupt kein ~ haben ‹*programme, article, etc.*› be totally undistinguished, lack any distinction whatever; **eine Zeitung mit ~:** a quality newspaper; **er hat wenig ~:** he is not very cultured *or* knowledgeable; **der Unterricht dieses Lehrers hat ein sehr hohes ~:** this teacher's lessons are intellectually very demanding; **b)** *(Qualitäts~)* standard

niveau-, Niveau-: ~los *Adj.* intellectually undemanding ‹*lesson*›; mediocre ‹*performance, programme, exhibition*›; [intellectually] dull ‹*person*›; **~unterschied der** *s.* **Niveau a, b:** difference in level/standard; **~voll** *Adj. (bes. DDR)* intellectually demanding ‹*lecture*›; cultured and intelligent ‹*person*›; ‹*entertainment, programme*› of quality *postpos., not pred.*; [high-]quality ‹*goods*›

nivellieren [nivɛ'li:rən] *tr. V.* **a)** *(ausgleichen)* level *or* even out ‹*difference*›; *(nach unten)* level down; **b)** *(Vermessungsw.)* level

Nivellier·instrument das; ~[e]s, ~en [surveyor's] level

Nivellierung die; ~, ~en levelling out; evening out; *(nach unten)* levelling down

nix [nɪks] *Indefinitpron. (ugs.) s.* **nichts**

Nix der; ~es, ~e *(germ. Myth.)* nix; *(mit Fischschwanz)* merman

Nixe die; ~, ~n *(germ. Myth.)* nixie; *(mit Fischschwanz)* mermaid

Nizza ['nɪtsa] **(das);** ~s Nice

N. N. *Abk.* **nomen nescio** n. n.; *(vorläufig unbekannt)* A. N. Other

NN *Abk.* **Normalnull[punkt]; unter/über NN** below/above sea level

NNO *Abk.* **Nordnordost[en]** NNE

NNW *Abk.* **Nordnordwest[en]** NNW

NO *Abk.* **Nordost[en]** NE

nobel ['no:bl̩] **1.** *Adj.* **a)** *(geh.: edel)* noble; noble[-minded] ‹*person*›; **b)** *(oft spött.: luxuriös)* elegant, *(coll.)* posh ‹*boutique, house, hotel*›; fine ‹*cigar*›; **~, ~!** very posh *(coll.)*; **~ geht die Welt zugrunde** *(iron.)* one has to make a splash even if it's the last one *(coll.)*; **c)** *(ugs.: freigebig)* lavish, generous ‹*tip, present*›; generous ‹*person*›. **2.** *adv.* **a)** *(geh.: edel)* nobly; **b)** *(oft spött.: luxuriös)* ‹*dress, live, eat*› in the grand style

Nobel-: ~marke luxury brand; **~hotel/~restaurant/~boutique** posh hotel/restaurant/boutique *(coll.)*; **~herberge/~kutsche** *(salopp)* posh *or* swish hotel/car *(coll.)*

Nobel- [no'bɛl-]: **~preis der** Nobel prize; **~preis·träger der** Nobel prize-winner

Noblesse [no'blɛsə] **die;** ~ *(geh.)* **a)** *(edle Art)* nobility; noble-mindedness; **b)** *(Eleganz)* elegance

noch [nɔx] **1.** *Adv.* **a)** *([wie] bisher, derzeit)* still; **~ nicht** not yet; **~ regnet es nicht** it's not raining yet; it hasn't started raining yet; **sie sind immer ~ nicht da** they're still not here; **ich sehe ihn kaum ~:** I hardly ever see him any more; **ich habe ~ nie Pizza gegessen** I've never eaten a pizza before; **ich bleibe ~ ein Weilchen** I'll stay a little bit longer; **~ nach Jahren** even years later; **er hat [bis jetzt] ~ immer/nie gewonnen** he's won every time up until now/never won yet; **b)** *(als Rest einer Menge)* **ich habe [nur] ~ zehn Mark** I've [only] ten marks left; **es dauert ~ fünf Minuten** it'll be another five minutes; **Beuteltiere gibt es ~/nur ~ in Australien** marsupials still exist/now only exist in Australia; **es sind ~ 10 km bis zur Grenze** it's another 10 km. to the border; **es fehlt [mir/dir** *usw.*] **~ eine Mark** I/you *etc.* need another mark; **c)** *(bevor etw. anderes geschieht)* just; **ich will ~ [schnell] duschen** I just want to have a [quick] shower; **ich mache das [jetzt/dann] ~ fertig** I'll just get this finished; **d)** *(irgendwann einmal)* some time; one day; **du wirst ihn [schon] ~ kennenlernen** you'll get to know him yet; **er wird ~ anrufen/kommen** he will still call/come; **e)** *(womöglich)* if you're/he's *etc.* not careful; **du kommst ~ zu spät!** you'll be late if you're not careful; **er endet ~ im Gefängnis** he'll land up in prison if he doesn't watch out *or* isn't careful; **f)** *(drückt eine geringe zeitliche Distanz aus)* only; **gestern habe ich ihn ~ gesehen/ ~ mit ihm gesprochen** I saw him only yesterday/I was speaking to him only yesterday; **~ Ende des 19. Jahrhunderts** as late as the end of the 19th century; **sie war eben** *od.* **gerade ~ hier** she was here only a moment ago; **es ist ~ keine Woche her, daß ...:** it was less than a week ago that ...; **g)** *(nicht später als)* **das muß ~ diese Woche/vor Monatsende geschehen** that's got to happen this week/by the end of the month; **~ am selben Abend** the [very] same evening; **~ ehe er antworten konnte, legte sie auf** even before he could reply she hung up; **er wurde ~ am Unfallort operiert** he was operated on at the scene of the accident; **h)** *(drückt aus, daß etw. unwiederholbar ist)* **ich habe Großvater ~ gekannt** I'm old enough to have known grandfather; **daß er das ~ erleben durfte!** and to think that he lived long enough to experience that!; **i)** *(drückt aus, daß sich etw. im Rahmen hält)* **das lasse ich mir gerade ~ gefallen** I'll put up with it; **Er hat ~ Glück gehabt. Es hätte weit schlimmer kommen können** He was lucky. It could have been much worse; **das ist [im Vergleich] ~ billig** that's [still] cheap in comparison; **es ist immer ~ teuer genug** it's still expensive enough; **der Koffer geht ~ zu** the case will still close; **das geht ~:** that's [still] all right *or (coll.)* OK; **das ist ~ lange kein Grund** that still isn't any sort of reason; **wenn er sich [wenigstens] ~ entschuldigt hätte** if he had apologized at least; **das ist ja ~ [ein]mal gutgegangen** *(ugs.)* it was just about all right; **j)** *(außerdem, zusätzlich)* **wer war ~ da?** who else was there?; **er hat [auch/außerdem] ~ ein Fahrrad** he has a bicycle as well; **~ etwas Kaffee?** [would you like] some more coffee?; **wenn man alt ist und [dann auch] ~ allein** when you're old and [also] on your own; **hinzu kommt ~, daß ...:** on top of that there's the fact that ...; **~ ein/zwei Bier, bitte!** another beer/two more beers, please!; **und ~ eins** *od.* **etwas** and another thing; **ich habe das ~ einmal/~ einige Male gemacht** I did it again/several times more; **da möchte ich ~ einmal/einige Male hin** *(ugs.)* I'd like to go there again; **~ einmal so lang** as long again; **Spanien? Und ~ dazu im Juli?** Spain, and in July too?; **er ist frech und ~ dazu dumm** *od.* **dumm dazu** he's cheeky and stupid with it; **und es schneite ~ dazu** *od.* **auch ~:** and what's more, it was snowing; **Geld/Kleider** *usw.* **~ und ~** *od. (ugs. scherzh.)* **~ und nöcher** heaps and heaps of money/clothes *etc. (coll.)*; **k)** *(bei Vergleichen)* **er ist ~ größer [als Karl]** he is even taller [than Karl]; **das ist ~ viel wichtiger** that's far *or* much more important still; **er will ~ mehr haben** he wants even *or* still more; **das ist ~ besser** that's even better *or* better still; **es war ~ anders** it was different again; **darüber hat er sich ~ mehr gefreut** he was even more pleased about that; **jeder ~ so dumme Mensch versteht das** anyone, however stupid, can understand that; **und wenn er auch ~ so bittet** however much he pleads; **du kannst ~ so sehr bitten** you can plead as much as you like; **l)** *(nach etw. Vergessenem fragend)* **wie heißt/hieß sie [doch] ~?** [now] what's/what was her name again? **2.** *Partikel* **das ist ~ Qualität!** that's what I call quality; **auf ihn kann man sich wenigstens ~ verlassen** one can rely on 'him at least; **du wirst es ~ bereuen!** you'll regret it!; **der wird sich ~ wundern** *(ugs.)* he's in for a surprise; **das dauert ~ keine zehn Minuten** it won't even take ten minutes; **er kann ~ nicht einmal lesen** he can't even read; **~ in der größten Hitze trägt er seinen Pullover** however hot it is he still wears his pullover. **3.** *Konj. (und auch nicht)* nor; **weder ... noch** neither ... nor; **weder er ~ die Mutter ~ der Vater** neither he nor his mother nor his father; **er hat keine Verwandten** *od.* **nicht Verwandte ~ Freunde** he has no relatives or friends

nochmalig ['nɔxma:lɪç] *Adj.; nicht präd.* further

noch·mals *Adv.* again; *(einige Minuten später)* after another few minutes; **~: wo waren Sie zwischen ...?** once again: where were you between ...?

Nocken ['nɔkn̩] **der;** ~s, ~ *(Technik)* cam

Nocken·welle die *(Technik)* camshaft

Nockerl ['nɔkɐl] **das;** ~s, ~n *(österr., bayr. Kochk.)* [semolina] dumpling; **Salzburger ~n** Salzburg dumpling soufflé *sing.*

NOK [ɛnlo:'ka:] **das;** ~[s] *Abk.* **Nationales Olympisches Komitee** NOC

nölen ['nø:lən] *itr. V. (bes. nordd. abwertend)* **a)** *(trödeln)* dawdle; **b)** *(sprechen)* speak in a slow drawl

Nom. *Abk.* **Nominativ** Nom.

Nomade [no'ma:də] **der;** ~n, ~n nomad

nomadenhaft *Adj. (auch fig.)* nomadic

Nomadentum das; ~s *(Völkerk.)* nomadism

Nomadin die; ~, ~nen nomad

nomadisieren *itr. V.* lead a nomadic existence; **~de Stämme** nomadic tribes

Nomen ['no:mən] **das;** ~s, **Nomina a)** *(Substantiv)* noun; substantive; **b)** *(deklinierbares Wort)* declinable word *(including nouns, adjectives, and numerals)*

nomen est omen ['no:mən 'ɛst 'o:mən] *(geh.)* true to his/its *etc.* name

Nomenklatur [nomɛnkla'tu:ɐ̯] **die;** ~, ~en *(Wissensch.)* nomenclature

Nomina *s.* **Nomen**

nominal [nomi'na:l] *Adj. (Sprachw., Wirtsch.)* nominal

Nominal-: ~einkommen das *(Wirtsch.)* nominal income; **~lohn der** *(Wirtsch.)* nominal wages *pl.*; **~stil der;** *o. Pl. (Sprachw.)* style in which there is a preponderance of nominal constructions; **~wert der** *(Wirtsch.) s.* **Nennwert**

Nominativ ['no:minati:f] **der;** ~s, ~e *(Sprachw.)* nominative [case]; *(Wort im ~)* nominative [form]; **im ~ stehen** be in the nominative [case]

nominell [nomi'nɛl] **1.** *Adj.; nicht präd.* nominal ‹*member, leader*›; ‹*Christian*› in name only. **2.** *adv.* **er ist nur ~ Präsident** he is President in name only; **~ ist er nur Berater des Präsidenten** nominally he is just an adviser to the President

nominieren [nomi'ni:rən] *tr. V.* **a)** *(zur Wahl vorschlagen)* nominate; **b)** *(Sport: aufstellen)* name ‹*player, team*›

Nominierung die; ~, ~en **a)** *(für eine Wahl)* nomination; **b)** *(Sport: Aufstellung)* selection

Nonchalance [nõʃa'lã:s] **die;** ~: nonchalance

nonchalant [nõʃa'lã:] **1.** *Adj.* nonchalant. **2.** *adv.* nonchalantly

None ['no:nə] **die;** ~, ~n **a)** *(kath. Kirche)* nones; **b)** *(Musik)* ninth

Nonius ['no:ni̯ʊs] **der;** ~, **Nonien** [...i̯ən] *(Technik)* vernier

Nonkonformismus [nɔnkɔnfɔr'mɪsmʊs] **der;** ~: nonconformism

nonkonformistisch 1. *Adj.* nonconformist; unconventional ‹*dress*›. **2.** *adv.* ‹*think, behave, argue, etc.*› in an unconventional way

Nonne ['nɔnə] **die;** ~, ~n **a)** nun; **b)** *(Zool.)* nun [moth]

Nonnen-: ~kloster das convent; nunnery; **~schule die** *(ugs.)* convent school

Non·plus·ultra [nɔnplʊs'ʊltra] **das;** ~ *(geh., oft scherzh.)* ultimate (**an** + *Dat.* in);

non plus-ultra; **das/ein ~ an Handlichkeit** *usw.* the ultimate in handiness *etc.*
Nonsens ['nɔnzɛns] **der; ~[es]** nonsense
nonstop [nɔn'stɔp] *adv.* non-stop
Nonstop-: ~flug der non-stop flight; **~kino das** 24-hour cinema
Noppe ['nɔpə] **die; ~, ~n a)** *(in einem Faden, Gewebe)* knop; nub; **b)** *(auf einer Oberfläche)* bump; *(auf einem Tischtennisschläger)* pimple
[1]**Nord** [nɔrt] *o. Art.; o. Pl.* **a)** *(Seemannsspr., Met.: Richtung)* north; **nach ~:** northwards; **aus** *od.* **von ~:** from the north; **b)** *(nördliches Gebiet, Politik)* North; **~ und Süd** North and South; **aus ~ und Süd** from the North and [from] the South; **zwischen ~ und Süd** between [the] North and [the] South; **c)** *einem Subst. nachgestellt (nördlicher Teil, nördliche Lage)* **Autobahnkreuz Köln-~:** motorway intersection Cologne North; **Europa ~** *(Milit.)* Northern Europe
[2]**Nord der; ~[e]s, ~e** *(Seemannsspr.)* northerly; *(dichter.)* north wind
nord-, Nord-: ~afrika (das) North Africa; **~amerika (das)** North America; **~amerikaner der** North American; **~amerikanisch** *Adj.* North American; **~atlantik·pakt der** North Atlantic alliance; **~deutsch 1.** *Adj.* North German; **2.** *adv.* **etw. ~deutsch aussprechen** pronounce sth. with a North German accent; **~deutschland (das)** North Germany
norden *tr. V.* **etw. ~:** orient sth. to the north
Norden der; ~s a) *(Richtung)* north; **im ~:** in the north; **aus dem** *od.* **von ~:** from the north; **nach ~:** northwards; **die Grenze nach ~:** the northern border; **gegen** *od.* *(geh.)* **gen ~:** northwards; **b)** *(Gegend)* northern part; **aus dem ~:** from the north; **c)** *(Geogr.)* North; **der hohe/höchste ~:** the far North
nord-, Nord-: ~england (das) the North of England; **~europa (das)** Northern Europe; **~europäisch** *Adj.* Northern European; **~flanke die** *(Milit., Geogr.)* northern flank; *(Met.)* northern edge; **~hang der** northern slope; **~insel die** North Island; **~irland (das)** Northern Ireland
nordisch *Adj. (auch Völkerk.)* Nordic; **~e Kombination** *(Skisport)* Nordic combined
Nordistik [nɔr'dɪstɪk] **die; ~:** Scandinavian Studies *pl., no art.*
Nord-: ~kap das North Cape; **~korea (das)** North Korea; **~küste die** north *or* northern coast; **~länder der; ~s, ~:** native/inhabitant of [a country of] the North *(esp. Scandinavia)*
nördlich ['nœrtlɪç] **1.** *Adj.* **a)** *(im Norden gelegen)* northern; **15° ~er Breite** 15 degrees north; **das ~e Frankreich** northern France; **der ~ste Punkt** the most northerly point; *s. auch* **Eismeer; Polarkreis; Wendekreis a; b)** *(nach, aus dem Norden)* northerly; **c)** *(aus dem Norden kommend, für den Norden typisch)* Northern. **2.** *adv.* northwards; **~ von ...:** [to the] north of ...; **sehr [weit] ~ sein** be a long way north. **3.** *Präp. mit Gen.* [to the] north of
nord-, Nord-: ~licht ['--] **das a)** northern lights *pl.;* aurora borealis; **ein ~licht/~lichter** the northern lights; **b)** *(scherzh.)* Northerner; [1]**~nord·ost** *o. Art.; o. Pl. (Seemannsspr., Met.)* north-north-east; *s. auch* [1]**Nord a;** [2]**~nord·ost der** *(Seemannsspr.)* north-north-easter[ly]; **~nord·osten der** north-north-east; *s. auch* **Norden a;** [1]**~nord·west** *o. Art.; o. Pl. (Seemannsspr., Met.)* north-north-west; *s. auch* [1]**Nord a;** [2]**~nord·west der** *(Seemannsspr.)* north-north-wester[ly]; **~nord·westen der** north-north-west; *s. auch* **Norden a;** [1]**~ost** *o. Art.; o. Pl. (Seemannsspr., Met.)* north-east; **nach ~ost** north-eastwards; **aus** *od.* **von ~ost** from the north-east; [2]**~ost der** *(Seemannsspr.)* north-easter[ly]; *(dichter.)* north-east[erly] wind; **~osten der a)** *(Richtung, Gegend)* north-east; *s. auch* **Norden a; ~östlich 1.** *Adj.* **a)** *(im ~osten gelegen)* north-eastern; *s. auch* **nördlich 1 a; b)** *(nach ~osten gerichtet, aus ~osten kommend)* north-easterly; **2.** *adv.* north-eastwards; **~östlich von ...:** [to the] north-east of ...; *s. auch* **nördlich 2; 3.** *Präp. mit Gen.* [to the] north-east of; **~-Ostsee-Kanal der** Kiel Canal; **~ost·wind der** north-east[erly] wind; **~pol** ['--] **der a)** North Pole; **b)** *(eines Magneten)* north pole
Nordpolar-: ~gebiet das North Polar Region; **~meer das** Arctic Ocean
Nord-: ~pol·expedition die expedition to the North Pole; **~rand der** northern edge
Nord·rhein-Westfalen (das) North Rhine-Westphalia
Nord·see die; *o. Pl.* North Sea
nord-, Nord-: ~seite ['---] **die** northern side; *(eines Gebäudes, Geländes)* north side; **~stern** ['--] **der;** *o. Pl.* North Star; Polaris; **~-Süd-Dialog der** *(Politik)* North-South dialogue; **~-Süd-Gefälle das** *(Politik)* North-South gap; **~südlich 1.** *Adj.* **in ~südlicher Richtung** from north to south; **2.** *adv.* **~südlich verlaufen** run from north to south; **~wand** ['--] **die** *(Felswand)* north face; **~wärts** ['--] *Adv.* **a)** *(nach Norden)* northwards; **b)** *(im Norden)* to the north; [1]**~west** *o. Art.* **a)** *(Seemannsspr., Met.)* north-west; **nach ~west** north-westwards; **aus** *od.* **von ~west** from the north-west; **b)** *einem Subst. nachgestellt* **Autobahnkreuz Frankfurt-~west** motorway intersection Frankfurt North-West; [2]**~west der** *(Seemannsspr.)* north-wester[ly]; *(dichter.)* north-west[erly] wind; **~westen der a)** *(Richtung, Gegend)* north-west; *s. auch* **Norden a; ~westlich 1.** *Adj.* **a)** *(im ~westen gelegen)* north-western; *s. auch* **nördlich 1 a; b)** *(nach ~westen gerichtet, aus ~westen kommend)* north-westerly; **2.** *adv.* *(nach ~westen)* north-westwards; **~westlich von ...:** [to the] north-west of ...; *s. auch* **nördlich 2; 3.** *Präp. mit Gen.* [to the] north-west of; **~west·wind der** north-west[erly] wind; **~wind** ['--] **der** north *or* northerly wind
Nörgelei die; ~, ~en *(abwertend)* **a)** *o. Pl. (das Nörgeln)* moaning; grumbling; *(das Kritteln)* carping; **b)** *(Äußerung)* moan; grumble; **deine ewigen ~en** your constant moaning *sing. or* grumbling *sing.*
nörgelig *Adj. (abwertend)* moaning *attrib.;* grumbling *attrib.;* grumbly *(coll.);* **ein ~er Kerl** a moaner *or* grumbler; **müde und ~:** tired and niggly
nörgeln ['nœrgl̩n] *itr. V. (abwertend)* moan, grumble **(an +** *Dat.* about); *(kritteln)* carp **(an +** *Dat.* about)
Nörgler der; ~s, ~, Nörglerin die; ~, ~nen *(abwertend)* moaner; grumbler; *(Krittler)* carper; fault-finder
nörglerisch *(abwertend) Adj.* moaning *attrib.;* grumbling *attrib.;* grumbly *(coll.);* *(krittelig)* carping *attrib.*
nörglig *s.* **nörgelig**
Norm [nɔrm] **die; ~, ~en a)** norm; **zur ~ werden/als ~ gelten** become the norm/count as the norm; **b)** *(geforderte Arbeitsleistung)* quota; target; **die ~ erfüllen** fulfil one's/its quota; meet *or* achieve one's/its target; **c)** *(Sport)* qualifying standard; **d)** *(technische, industrielle ~)* standard; standard specifications *pl.;* **der ~ entsprechen** conform to the standard; **e)** *(DDR: Richtwert für die Produktion)* norm; **f)** *(Buchw.)* signature *(at foot of page)*
normal [nɔr'ma:l] **1.** *Adj.* **a)** normal; **du bist doch nicht ~!** *(ugs.)* there must be something wrong with you!; **b)** *(ugs.: gewöhnlich)* ordinary. **2.** *adv.* **a)** normally; **b)** *(ugs.: gewöhnlich)* in the normal *or* ordinary way; **c)** *(ugs.: normalerweise)* normally; usually
Normal das; ~s *(ugs.)* ≈ two star *(Brit.);* regular *(Amer.);* **für 50 Mark ~, bitte!** 50 marks' worth of two-star, please!
Normal·benzin das ≈ two-star petrol *(Brit.);* regular *(Amer.)*
Normale die; ~[n], ~n *(Math.)* normal
normalerweise *Adv.* normally; usually
Normal-: ~fall der normal case; **im ~fall** normally, usually; **~form die a)** *(Math.)* standard *or* normal form; **b)** *(Sport)* usual form; **~gewicht das** normal weight
normalisieren 1. *tr. V.* normalize. **2.** *refl. V.* return to normal
Normalisierung die; ~, ~en normalization
Normalität [nɔrmali'tɛ:t] **die; ~:** normality *no def. art.*
Normal-: ~maß das a) *(normales Maß)* normal size; *(normales Niveau)* normal level; **~maße haben** be [of] a normal size; **b)** *(Meßwesen)* standard measure; **~null das** *(Geodäsie)* national datum level; **~spur die** *(Eisenb.)* standard gauge; **~ton der a)** *(Akustik)* reference tone; **b)** *(Musik)* standard pitch; **~uhr die a)** *(genau gehende Uhr)* regulator; **b)** *(öffentliche Uhr)* public clock; **~verbraucher der a)** ordinary *or* average consumer; **b)** *(ugs.: Durchschnittsmensch)* average punter *(coll.);* **Otto ~verbraucher** *(scherzh.)* the average punter *(coll.);* **~zeit die** standard time; **~zu·stand der a)** normal state; **im ~zustand** in its/his normal state; **b)** *s.* **Normzustand**
Normandie [nɔrman'di:] **die; ~:** Normandy; **in/aus der ~:** in/from Normandy
Normanne [nɔr'manə] **der; ~n ~n** Norman
normannisch *Adj.* Norman
normativ [nɔrma'ti:f] *Adj.* normative
Norm·blatt das list of standard specifications
normen *tr. V.* standardize
Normen-: ~aus·schuß der standards committee; **~kontroll·verfahren das** *(Rechtsw.)* *suit brought before the FRG constitutional court relating to the constitutionality of a law*
Norm·erhöhung die raising of production targets
normieren *tr. V.* standardize
Normierung die; ~, ~en, Normung die; ~, ~en standardization
Norm·zustand der *(Physik, Technik)* standard state
Norne ['nɔrnə] **die; ~, ~n** *(nord. Myth.)* Norn
Norwegen ['nɔrve:gn̩] **(das); ~s** Norway
Norweger der; ~s, ~, Norwegerin die; ~, ~nen Norwegian; *s. auch* **-in**
Norweger·muster das *(Handarb.)* ≈ Fair Isle design
norwegisch *Adj.* Norwegian; *s. auch* **deutsch; Deutsch;** [2]**Deutsche**
Nostalgie [nɔstal'gi:] **die; ~:** nostalgia
nostalgisch 1. *Adj.* nostalgic. **2.** *adv.* nostalgically; **~ gestimmt** in a nostalgic mood
not [no:t] *in* **~ tun** *od.* **sein** *(geh., landsch.)* be necessary
Not die; ~, Nöte ['nø:tə] **a)** *(Bedrohung, Gefahr)* **in seiner ~:** at that perilous juncture; **jmdm. in der Stunde der ~ helfen** help sb. in his/her hour of need; **in höchster** *od.* **äußerster ~:** in extremis; **Rettung in** *od.* **aus höchster ~:** rescue from extreme difficulties; **in ~ sein** be in desperate straits; **~ bricht Eisen** desperation gives you strength; **~ lehrt beten** adversity teaches you to pray; **in ~ und Tod** *(geh.)* through thick and thin; **b)** *o. Pl.* *(Mangel, Armut)* need; poverty [and hardship]; **~ leiden** suffer poverty *or* want [and hardship]; **etw. aus ~ tun** do sth. from sheer need; **in ~ geraten/sein** encounter hard times/be suffering want [and deprivation]; **in diesem Land herrscht große ~:** there is great poverty and hardship in this country; **er kennt keine ~:** he's doing all right for

himself; ~ **macht erfinderisch** necessity is the mother of invention *(prov.)*; ~ **kennt kein Gebot** [when] needs must; **in der ~ frißt der Teufel Fliegen** beggars can't be choosers *(prov.)*; **c)** *o. Pl. (Verzweiflung)* anguish; distress; **d)** *(Sorge, Mühe)* trouble; **in** skin of one's teeth; **e)** *o. Pl. (veralt.: Notwen-* ~ **haben, etw. zu tun** have great difficulty in doing sth.; **seine [liebe] ~ mit jmdm./etw. haben** have a lot of trouble *or* a lot of problems with sb./sth.; **mit knapper ~:** by the skin of one's teeth; **f)** *o. Pl. (veralt.: Notwendigkeit)* necessity; **ohne ~** *(geh.)* without pressing cause; **zur ~:** if need be; if necessary; **wenn ~ am Mann ist** when the need arises; **aus der ~ eine Tugend machen** make a virtue of necessity

Notabeln [no'ta:bl̩n] *Pl. (hist.)* Notables

notabene [nota'be:nə] *Adv. (geh. veralt.)* nota bene *(arch. literary)*; please note

Not-: ~abitur das *early* **Abitur** *taken in wartime by students about to be conscripted;* **~anker der** *(Seew., auch fig.)* sheet anchor

Notar [no'ta:ɐ̯] **der; ~s, ~e** notary

Notariat [notar'i̯a:t] **das; ~[e]s, ~e a)** *(Amt)* notaryship; **b)** *(Kanzlei)* notary's office

notariell [nota'ri̯ɛl] **1.** *Adj.* notarial. **2.** *adv.* ~ **beglaubigt** attested by a notary

Notarin die; ~, ~nen notary

Not-: ~arzt der doctor on [emergency] call; emergency doctor; **~arzt·wagen der** doctor's car for emergency calls

Notation [nota'tsi̯o:n] **die; ~, ~en** *(Musik, Schach)* notation

Not-: ~aufnahme die *(Gesundheitswesen)* casualty department; casualty *no art.*; **~aus·gabe die** *(Zeitungsw.)* emergency edition; **~aus·gang der** emergency exit; **~behelf der** makeshift; **~beleuchtung die** emergency lighting *no indef. art.*; **~bremse die** emergency brake; **die ~bremse ziehen** pull the emergency brake; pull the communication cord *(Brit. Railw.)*; *(Sportjargon)* bring the attacker down; **~brücke die** temporary bridge; **~dienst der** *s.* **Bereitschaftsdienst**

Notdurft [-dʊrft] **die; ~ a)** *(geh.)* **seine [große/kleine] ~ verrichten** relieve oneself; **b)** *(geh. veralt.: das Nötige)* need; **mehr als seine knappe ~ verdienen** earn more than one needs to buy the bare necessities of life

not·dürftig 1. *Adj.* meagre ⟨*payment, pension*⟩; rough and ready, makeshift ⟨*shelter, repair*⟩; scanty ⟨*cover, clothing*⟩. **2.** *adv.* scantily ⟨*clothed*⟩; **etw. ~ reparieren** repair sth. in a rough and ready *or* makeshift way; **sich ~ verständigen** manage to communicate after a fashion

Note ['no:tə] **die; ~, ~n a)** *(Zeichen)* note; **eine ganze/halbe ~:** a crotchet/quaver *(Brit.)*; a whole note/half note *(Amer.)*; **etw. in ~n setzen** *(veralt.)* set sth. to music; **b)** *Pl. (Text)* music *sing.*; **nach/ohne ~n spielen** play from/without music; **c)** *(Schul~)* mark; **d)** *(Eislauf, Turnen)* score; **e)** *(Dipl.)* note; **f)** *o. Pl. (Flair)* touch; **einer Sache eine persönliche ~ geben** give sth. a personal touch; **g)** *(Bank~)* note

Noten-: ~aus·tausch der *(Dipl.)* exchange of notes; **~bank die** bank of issue; **~blatt das** sheet of music; **~druck der;** *o. Pl.* **a)** *(Druck von Banknoten)* printing of [bank]notes; **b)** *(Druck von Musikalien)* music-printing; printing of music; **c)** *(Leistungsdruck)* pressure to achieve high marks; **~durch·schnitt der** average mark; **~heft das a)** *(Publikation)* book of music; **b)** *(Heft mit ~papier)* manuscript book; **~linie die** *(Musik)* line [of the staff]; **~papier das** music-paper; **~pult das** music-rest; music-stand; **~schlüssel der** clef; **~schrift die** [musical] notation; **~ständer der** music-stand

not-, Not-: ~fall der a) *(Gefahr)* emergency; **im ~fall** in an emergency; **für den ~fall** in case of emergency; **in** *od.* **bei ~fällen** in emergencies; **b)** *(Schwierigkeiten)* case of need; **im ~fall** if need be; **für den ~fall habe ich immer einen Reservekanister im Kofferraum** I always have a spare can of petrol *(Brit.) or (Amer.)* gasoline in the boot *(Brit.) or (Amer.)* trunk, just in case; **~falls** *Adv.* if need be; if necessary; **~gedrungen** *Adv.* of necessity; **ich habe ~gedrungen eine neue gekauft** I had no choice but to *or* I was forced to buy a new one; **~geld das** *(Finanzw.)* necessity money; emergency money; **~gemeinschaft die a)** *(Interessengemeinschaft)* emergency action organization; **b)** *(durch gemeinsame Notlage Verbundene)* union born of necessity; **~groschen der** nest-egg; **die 500 DM lege ich als ~groschen zurück** I'll put that 500 marks away for a rainy day; **~hilfe die** *(Rechtsw.)* assistance in an emergency *(as required by law)*; **in ~hilfe schießen** shoot in defence of a third person

notieren [no'ti:rən] **1.** *tr. V.* **a)** **[sich** *(Dat.)*] **etw. ~:** note sth. down; make a note of sth.; **die Polizei hat den Fahrer notiert** the police took [down] the driver's particulars; **jmdn. für etw. ~:** put sb.'s name down for sth.; ~ **Sie bitte: ...:** please note that down: ...; **ein Musikstück ~:** write a piece of music down [in musical notation]; **b)** *(Börsenw., Wirtsch.)* quote **(mit** at). **2.** *itr. V. (Börsenw., Wirtsch.)* be quoted **(mit** at); **die meisten Rohstoffe ~ unverändert** most commodity prices are unchanged

Notierung die; ~, ~en a) *s.* **Notation; b)** *(Börsenw., Wirtsch.)* quotation; *(Preis)* quoted [price] **(für** of); *(von Devisen)* rate **(für** for)

nötig ['nø:tɪç] **1.** *Adj.* necessary; **dafür** *od.* **dazu fehlt mir die ~e Geduld/das ~e Geld** I don't have the patience/money necessary *or* needed for that; **es ist nicht ~, daß du dabei bist** there's no need for you to be there; you don't have to be there; **etw./jmdn. ~ haben** need sth./sb.; **Hilfe dringend ~ haben** be in urgent need of help; need help urgently; **es ~ haben, etw. zu tun** need to do sth.; **er hat es manchmal ~, daß man ihn zurechtweist** he sometimes needs reprimanding; **das habe ich nicht ~** *(das lasse ich mir nicht gefallen)* I won't have that; **sich zu entschuldigen, hat er natürlich nicht ~** *(iron.)* of course he does not feel the need to apologize; **du hast/er hat** *usw.* **es gerade ~** *(ugs.)* you're/he's a fine one to talk *(coll.)*; **das wäre [doch] nicht ~ gewesen!** *(ugs.)* you shouldn't have!; **das Nötige veranlassen** do all that is necessary; **das Nötigste** the bare essentials *pl.* **2.** *adv.* **er braucht ~ Hilfe** he is in urgent need of *or* urgently needs help; **was er am ~sten braucht, ist ...:** what he most urgently needs is ...; **ich muß ~ aufs Klo** *(ugs.)* I'm dying to go to the loo *(Brit. coll.) or (Amer. coll.)* the john

nötigen 1. *tr. V.* **a)** *(zwingen)* compel; force; *(Rechtsspr.)* intimidate; coerce; **jmdn. zur Unterschrift ~:** compel *or* force sb. to sign; **sich genötigt sehen, etw. zu tun** feel compelled to do sth.; **b)** *(geh.: auffordern)* press; urge; **laß dich nicht [lange] ~:** don't wait to be asked. **2.** *itr. V. (geh.)* **zur Wachsamkeit/zu einer vorsichtigen Fahrweise ~:** compel one to be vigilant/drive carefully

nötigenfalls *Adv.* if necessary; if need be

Nötigung die; ~, ~en a) *(bes. Rechtsspr.)* intimidation; coercion; **b)** *o. Pl. (geh.: Notwendigkeit)* necessity; **c)** *(geh.: das Nötigen)* urging

Notiz [no'ti:ts] **die; ~, ~en a)** note; **sich** *(Dat.)* **eine ~ machen** make a note; **b)** *(Zeitungs~)* **eine [kurze] ~:** a brief report; **c)** *in* **von jmdm./etw. [keine] ~ nehmen** take [no] notice of sb./sth.; **d)** *(Börsenw.) s.* **Notierung b**

Notiz-: ~block der; *Pl.* **~blocks,** *schweiz.:* **~blöcke** notepad; **~buch das** notebook; **~zettel der** note; **etw. als ~zettel benutzen** use sth. to write a note/notes on

not-, Not-: ~lage die serious difficulties *pl.*; **jmds. ~lage ausnutzen** exploit sb.'s plight; **~lager das** makeshift bed; **~landen**[1] **1.** *itr. V.; mit sein* do an emergency landing; **2.** *tr. V.* **er konnte/mußte die Maschine ~landen** he was able to do/had to do an emergency landing; **~landung die** emergency landing; **~leidend** *Adj.* needy; impoverished; *(fig.)* ailing ⟨*industry*⟩; *(Finanzw.)* ⟨*loan*⟩ in default; unsecured ⟨*credit*⟩; **die Notleidenden** the [poor and] needy; **~lösung die** stopgap; **~lüge die** evasive lie; *(aus Rücksichtnahme)* white lie; **um der Bestrafung zu entgehen, griff er zu einer ~lüge** he resorted to a lie to avoid punishment; **~maßnahme die** emergency measure; **~opfer das** *(Steuerw.)* emergency levy

notorisch [no'to:rɪʃ] **1.** *Adj.* notorious. **2.** *adv.* notoriously; ~ **lügen** be a notorious liar

not-, Not-: ~pfennig der *s.* **Notgroschen; ~ruf der a)** *(Hilferuf)* emergency call; *(eines Schiffes)* Mayday call; distress call; **b)** *(Nummer)* emergency number; **c)** *(eines Tieres)* alarm call; **~ruf·nummer die** emergency number; **~ruf·säule die** emergency telephone *(mounted in a piller)*; **~schlachten**[2] *tr., itr. V.* slaughter ⟨*sick or injured animal*⟩; **~schlachtung die** slaughtering *(of sick or injured animal)*; **~schrei der a)** *(geh. veralt.)* cry of distress; **b)** *s.* **Notruf c; ~situation die** emergency; **~sitz der** extra seat; *(ausklappbar)* tip-up seat; fold-away seat; **~stand der a)** *(Krise, Übelstand)* crisis; **b)** *(Staatsrecht)* state of emergency; **den ~stand erklären** *od.* **verkünden** *od.* **ausrufen** declare a state of emergency; **äußerer ~stand** threat of attack; **innerer/ziviler ~stand** internal/civil emergency; **c)** *(bes. Rechtsw.)* necessity; **rechtfertigender ~stand** *necessity which justifies a normally illegal act;* **~stands·gebiet das a)** *(auch fig.)* disaster area; **b)** *(Wirtsch.)* depressed area; **~stands·gesetz das** emergency law; **~stands·gesetzgebung die** emergency legislation; **~taufe die** emergency baptism *(by a layman)*; **~unterkunft die** emergency accommodation *no pl., no indef. art.*; **~unterkünfte** emergency accommodation *sing.*; **~verband der** emergency dressing; **~verordnung die** emergency decree; **~vorrat der** emergency supply; **~wassern**[3] *itr. V.; mit sein, tr. V.* ditch; **~wehr die** *(Rechtsw.)* self-defence; **in** *od.* **aus ~wehr** in self-defence

not·wendig 1. *Adj.* **a)** necessary; **es ist ~, daß wir etwas tun** we must do something; **das Notwendigste** the bare essentials *pl.*; **b)** *(zwangsläufig)* necessary; *(unvermeidlich)* inevitable; *s. auch* **Übel. 2.** *adv.* **a)** *s.* **nötig 2; b)** *(zwangsläufig, unbedingt)* necessarily

notwendiger·weise *Adv.* necessarily

Notwendigkeit die; ~, ~en necessity

not-, Not-: ~zeichen das distress signal; **~zeit die** time of emergency; *(Zeit des Mangels)* time of need; **~zucht die** *(Rechtsw. veralt.)* rape; **~zucht [an jmdm.] begehen** *od.* **verüben** commit rape [on sb.]; **~züchtigen**[4] *tr. V. (Rechtsw. veralt.)* rape; **~zucht·verbrechen das** *(Rechtsw. veralt.)* rape

Nougat ['nu:gat] **der;** *auch* **das; ~s** nougat

Nov. *Abk.* **November** Nov.

[1] *ich notlande, notgelandet, notzulanden*
[2] *ich notschlachte, notgeschlachtet, notzuschlachten*
[3] *ich notwassere, notgewassert, notzuwassern*
[4] *ich notzüchtige, genotzüchtigt, notzuzüchtigen*

Nova *s.* **Novum**
Novelle [no'vɛlə] **die;** ~, ~**n a)** *(Literaturw.)* novella; **b)** *(Gesetzes~)* amendment
novellieren *tr. V. (Politik, Rechtsw.)* amend
Novellierung die; ~, ~**en** *(Politik, Rechtsw.)* amendment
novellistisch 1. *Adj.* **die ~e Literatur** literature in novella form; the novella; **das ~e Werk Kellers** Keller's novellas. **2.** *adv.* **etw. ~ gestalten/bearbeiten** put sth. into/treat sth. in novella form
November [no'vɛmbɐ] **der;** ~**[s],** ~: November; *s. auch* **April**
novemberlich 1. *Adj.* Novemberish. **2.** *adv.* ~ **unfreundlich/trüb sein** be as dreary/grey as in November
Novität [novi'tɛ:t] **die;** ~, ~**en a)** novelty; *(neue Erfindung)* innovation; *(neue Schallplatte)* new release; *(neues Buch)* new publication; **b)** *(veralt.: Nachricht)* piece of news; ~**en** news *sing.*
Novize [no'vi:tsə] **der;** ~**n,** ~**n, Novize die;** ~, ~**n** novice
Noviziat [novi'tsia:t] **das;** ~**[e]s,** ~**e** noviciate
Novizin die; ~, ~**nen** novice
Novum ['no:vʊm] **das;** ~**s, Nova** novelty; *(neue Erfindung)* innovation; **ein ~ in der Geschichte der Partei** an unprecedented event in the history of the party
NPD [ɛnpe:'de:] **die;** ~ *Abk.* **Nationaldemokratische Partei Deutschlands** National Democratic Party of Germany
Nr. *Abk.* **Nummer** No
NRW *Abk.* **Nordrhein-Westfalen**
NSDAP [ɛnɛsde:a:'pe:] **die;** ~ *Abk.* **Nationalsozialistische Deutsche Arbeiterpartei** National Socialist German Workers' Party
N. T. *Abk.* **Neues Testament** NT
nu [nu:] *Adv. (bes. nordd.) s.* **nun**
Nu der *in* **im Nu, in einem Nu** in no time
Nuance ['nỹã:sə] **die;** ~, ~**n a)** *(Unterschied, Feinheit)* nuance; **b)** *(Grad)* shade; **[um] eine ~ dunkler/schneller** a shade darker/faster
nuancenreich 1. *Adj.* full of nuances *postpos.;* finely *or* subtly nuanced. **2.** *adv.* with subtlety of nuance
nuancieren *tr., itr. V.* **etw. ~:** give sth. subtle nuances; **farblich stärker ~:** give more definite nuances of colour
nuanciert 1. *Adj.* finely *or* subtly nuanced. **2.** *adv.* **[sehr] ~:** with [great] subtlety of nuance
'nüber ['ny:bɐ] *Adv. (südd.) s.* **hinüber**
nüchtern ['nʏçtɐn] **1.** *Adj.* **a)** *(nicht betrunken)* sober; **mit ~em Kopf** with a clear head; **wieder ~ werden** sober up; **b)** *(mit leerem Magen)* **der Patient muß ~ sein** the patient's stomach must be empty; **auf ~en Magen rauchen** smoke on an empty stomach; **das war ein Schreck auf ~en Magen** *(scherzh.)* that's just what I needed at that time of the morning *(iron.);* **c)** *(realistisch)* sober; sober, matter-of-fact ‹*account, assessment, question, etc.*›; bare ‹*figures*›; **d)** *(schmucklos, streng)* austere; bare ‹*room*›; unadorned, bare ‹*walls*›; *(ungeschminkt)* bare, plain ‹*fact*›; **e)** *(bes. nordostd.: ungewürzt, ungesalzen)* bland; *(fade)* insipid. **2.** *adv.* **a)** *(realistisch)* soberly; **wir sollten einmal ganz ~ darüber sprechen** we ought to have a down-to-earth talk about this sometime; **b)** *(schmucklos, streng)* austerely
Nüchternheit die; ~ **a)** sobriety; **b)** *(Realitätsbezogenheit)* sobriety; soberness; **c)** *(Schmucklosigkeit)* austerity
Nuckel ['nʊkl̩] **der;** ~**s,** ~ *(ugs.) s.* **Schnuller**
nuckeln *(ugs.)* **1.** *itr. V.* suck **(an +** *Dat.* at); **am Daumen/Schnuller ~:** suck one's thumb/a *or* one's dummy. **2.** *tr. V.* suck
Nuckel·pinne die *(salopp)* old banger *(Brit. coll.) or (sl.)* crate
Nudel ['nu:dl̩] **die;** ~, ~**n a)** piece of spaghetti/vermicelli/tortellini *etc.; (als Suppeneinlage)* noodle; ~**n** *(Teigwaren)* pasta *sing.; (als Suppeneinlage, Reis~n)* noodles; **Spaghetti und andere ~n** spaghetti and other types of pasta; **b)** *(ugs.)* **eine dicke ~:** a fatty *(coll.);* **eine giftige ~:** a nasty piece of work *(coll.);* **eine komische ~:** a real character
Nudel-: ~brett das board *(for rolling out pasta dough);* pastry board; **~holz das** rolling-pin
nudeln *tr. V.* cram ‹*geese*›; *(fig. ugs.)* stuff
Nudel-: ~salat der pasta salad; **~suppe die** soup with noodles; **~teig der** pasta dough
Nudismus [nu'dɪsmʊs] **der;** ~: nudism *no art.;* naturism *no art.*
Nudist [nu'dɪst] **der;** ~**en,** ~**en, Nudistin die;** ~, ~**nen** nudist; naturist
Nugat *s.* **Nougat**
nuklear [nukle'a:ɐ̯] **1.** *Adj.* nuclear. **2.** *adv.* ~ **angetrieben** nuclear-powered; ~ **bewaffnet** possessing nuclear weapons *postpos.*
Nuklear-: ~krieg der nuclear war; **~macht die** nuclear power; **~medizin die** nuclear medicine *no art.;* **~physik die** nuclear physics *sing., no art.;* **~waffe die** nuclear weapon
Nukleus ['nu:kleʊs] **der;** ~, **Nuklei** [...ei] *(Biol., Anat., Sprachw.)* nucleus
null [nʊl] **1.** *Kardinalz.* nought; **~ Komma sechs** [nought] point six; **sieben, ~, ~, sechs, ~, vier** *(Fernspr.)* seven double-O, six O four *(Brit.);* seven zero zero, six zero four (Amer.); **~ Grad Celsius** nought *or* zero degrees Celsius; **bei ~ Fehlern** if there are no mistakes; **fünf zu ~ Tore** five goals to nil; **fünf zu ~:** five–nil; **das Spiel endete ~ zu ~:** the game was a goalless draw; **fünfzehn ~** *(Tennis)* fifteen-love; **gegen ~ Uhr** around twelve midnight; **es ist ~ Uhr dreißig** it is twelve-thirty a.m.; **elf Uhr, ~ Minuten und fünfzehn Sekunden** eleven, no minutes, and fifteen seconds; **etw. für ~ und nichtig erklären** declare sth. null and void. **2.** *indekl. Adj. (ugs.)* **~ Ahnung/Interesse** no idea/interest at all; **auf etw.** *(Akk.)* **~ Bock haben** not fancy sth. at all
¹Null die; ~, ~**en a)** *(Ziffer)* nought; zero; **in ~ Komma nichts** *(ugs.)* in less than no time; **gleich ~ sein** *(fig.)* be practically zero; *s. auch* **Nummer; Stunde; b)** *o. Pl., o. Art. (Marke)* zero; **auf ~ stehen** ‹*indicator, needle, etc.*› be at zero; **fünf Grad unter/über ~:** five degrees below/above zero *or* freezing; **die Augen auf ~ gestellt haben** *(salopp)* have snuffed it *(sl.);* **jmdn. auf ~ bringen** *(salopp)* destroy sb. *(fig.);* **c)** *(abwertend) (Versager)* failure; dead loss *(coll.); (unbedeutender Mensch)* nonentity
²Null der *(auch:* **das);** ~**[s],** ~**s** *(Skat)* null; **~ Hand** null from hand
Null- zero
null·acht·fünfzehn, null·acht·fuffzehn *(ugs. abwertend)* **1.** *indekl. Adj.; nicht attr.* run-of-the-mill; **das Essen war eher ~:** the meal really wasn't anything to write home about. **2.** *adv.* **~ gekleidet/eingerichtet** dressed/furnished in a run-of-the-mill way
Null·acht·fünfzehn-, Null·acht·fuffzehn- *(ugs. abwertend)* run-of-the-mill
Null-: ~-Bock-Generation die *(ugs.)* switched-off generation; **~diät die** absolute diet
Nulleiter ['nʊlaitɐ] **der;** ~**s,** ~ *(Elektrot.)* neutral conductor
Null-: ~leiter der *s.* **Nulleiter; ~lösung die** *s.* **Nullösung; ~menge die** *(Math.)* empty set; **~meridian der** *(Geogr.)* Greenwich meridian; **~nummer die** *free first issue (of magazine etc.)*
Nullösung ['nʊløzʊŋ] **die** *(Politik)* zero option
Null ouvert [nʊlǀu've:ɐ̯] **der;** *(auch:)* **das;** ~**[s],** ~**s** *(Skat)* open null
Null-: ~punkt der zero; **die Temperatur ist auf den ~punkt abgesunken** the temperature has dropped to zero *or* to freezing-point; **die Stimmung war auf dem ~punkt angelangt** *od.* **hatte den ~punkt erreicht** *(fig.)* we/they were in very low spirits; **~spiel das** *(Skat)* null; **beim ~spiel** when playing null *or* a null game; **~tarif der: die Rentner haben ~tarif im Nahverkehr/Schwimmbad** *usw.* pensioners can use local public transport/the swimming-pool *etc.* free of charge; **zum ~tarif** free of charge; **zum ~tarif einkaufen/fernsehen** *(scherzh.)* go shoplifting/watch television without a licence; **~wachstum das** zero growth
Nulpe ['nʊlpə] **die;** ~, ~**n** *(ugs. abwertend)* drip *(coll.)*
Numerale [nʊmə'ra:lə] **das;** ~**s, Numeralien** *od.* **Numeralia** *(Sprachw.) s.* numeral
Numeri *s.* **Numerus**
numerieren [nʊmə'ri:rən] *tr. V.* number
Numerierung die; ~, ~**en** numbering
numerisch [nu'me:rɪʃ] **1.** *Adj.* numerical. **2.** *adv.* numerically; **~ überlegen sein** be superior in numbers
Numero ['nʊməro] *o. Art.; o. Pl.; in Verbindung mit einer Zahl (veralt.)* number
Numerus ['nʊmərʊs] **der;** ~, **Numeri a)** *(Sprachw.)* number; **b)** *(Math.)* antilogarithm; antilog *(coll.)*
Numerus clausus [~ 'klauzʊs] **der;** ~ ~: *fixed number of students admissible to a university to study a particular subject;* numerus clausus
Numismatik [numɪs'ma:tɪk] **die;** ~: numismatics *sing., no art.*
Nummer ['nʊmɐ] **die;** ~, ~**n a)** number; **ein Wagen mit [einer] Münchner ~:** a car with a Munich registration; **ich bin unter der ~ 24 26 79 zu erreichen** I can be reached on 24 26 79; **bloß eine ~ sein** *(fig.)* be just a *or* nothing but a number; **[die] ~ eins** [the] number one; **Thema ~ eins sein** be the number-one topic of conversation; **ich muß auf ~ Null** *(ugs. verhüll.)* I must go to the loo *(Brit. coll.) or (Amer. coll.)* the john; **er sitzt auf ~ Sicher** *(ugs.)* he's doing time *(coll.);* **auf ~ Sicher gehen** *(ugs.)* play safe; not take any chances; **bei jmdm. eine gute** *od.* **große** *od.* **dicke ~ haben** *(ugs.)* be well in with sb. *(coll.);* **b)** *(Ausgabe)* number; issue; **c)** *(Größe)* size; **diese Sache ist eine ~/ein paar ~n zu groß für dich** *(ugs.)* this business is in a different league from anything you could cope with; **d)** *(Darbietung)* turn; **e)** *(ugs.: Musikstück)* number; **f)** *(ugs.: Person)* character; **er ist eine ~ [für sich]** he is a real character *or* quite a character; **er ist eine große ~ im Verkaufen** he's quite a *or (sl.)* some salesman; **g)** *(derb: Koitus)* screw *(coarse)*
Nummern-: ~konto das *(Bankw.)* numbered account; **~oper die** *(Musik)* number opera; **~scheibe die** dial; **~-schild das a)** *(eines Fahrzeugs)* number-plate; license plate *(Amer.);* **b)** *(an Häusern, Straßen)* number; **~schlüssel der** *(DV)* numerical code
nun [nu:n] **1.** *Adv.* now; **von ~ an** from now on; **~, wo sie krank ist** now [that] she's ill; **~ erst, erst ~:** only now; **gestern ist er ~ endlich wiedergekommen** he finally came back yesterday. **2.** *Partikel* now; **so wichtig ist es ~ auch wieder nicht** it's not all 'that important; **~ ist es in der Tat zutreffend, daß ...:** now it is indeed quite correct that ...; **und bei dem Lärm soll man ~ schlafen können!** and people are supposed to sleep with that noise going on; **und so was nennt sich ~ Diplomübersetzer** and he calls himself a qualified translator; **das hast du ~ davon!** it serves you right!; **hat sich das ~ gelohnt?** was it really worth it?; **~ gib schon her!** now hand it over!; **~ mach dir deswegen mal keine Sorgen!** now don't you worry; **kommst du ~ mit oder nicht?** now are you coming or

not?; **er muß es tun, ob er ~ will oder nicht** he has to do it, whether he wants to or not; **so ist das ~ [einmal/mal]** that's just the way it is *or* things are; **er braucht ~ einmal viel Schlaf** he happens to need a lot of sleep; **~ gut** *od.* **schön** [well,] all right; **~, ~!** now, come on; **ja ~!** oh, well!; **~?** well?; **Das Brett ist etwas zu lang – Nun, das läßt sich ändern** The board is a bit too long – Well, that can be altered; **~ ja ...:** well, yes ...; **~ denn!** *(also gut)* well, all right!; *(also los)* well then; **3.** *Konj. (veralt. geh.)* now that

nun·mehr *Adv. (geh.)* **a)** now; **er ist ~ seit zehn Jahren Kanzler** he has been Chancellor now for ten years; **seine ~ 80jährige Mutter** his mother, [who is] now 80 years old; **b)** *(von ~ an)* from now on; henceforth

'nunter ['nʊntɐ] *Adv. (südd.) s.* **hinunter**

Nuntius ['nʊntsiʊs] **der; ~, Nuntien** nuncio; *s. auch* **apostolisch**

nur [nuːɐ̯] **1.** *Adv.* **a)** *(nicht mehr als)* only; just; **ich habe ~ eine Stunde Zeit/zehn Mark** I only have an hour/ten marks; **ich habe es für ~ fünf Mark gekauft** I bought it for just five marks; **er hat ~ einen einzigen Fehler gemacht** he made just a single mistake; **um eines ~ möchte ich dich bitten** I'd ask just one thing of you; **er tat es ~ ungern** he did it only reluctantly; **das ist ~ recht und billig** it is only right and proper; **ohne auch ~ zu lächeln** without so much as smiling; **eine ~ mittelmäßige Leistung** only a mediocre performance; **b)** *(ausschließlich)* only; **~ er darf das** only he is allowed to do that; **alle durften mitfahren, ~ ich nicht** everyone was allowed to go, all except me; **er will dir doch ~ helfen!** he only wants to help you; **~ darauf will ich mich beschränken** I want to restrict myself to just this; **ich frage mich ~, warum** I just want to know why; **er tut das mit Absicht, ~ um dich zu provozieren** he does it deliberately, just to provoke you; **nicht ~ ..., sondern auch ...:** not only ..., but also ...; **ich tue es nicht nur wegen des Geldes, sondern auch, weil ...:** I'm not doing it just for the money, but also because ...; **nicht ~, daß ...:** it's not just that ...; **[alles,] ~ das nicht** anything but that; **~ gut, daß ...:** it's a good thing that ...; **~ schade, daß ...:** it's just a pity that ...; **ich male ~ so zum Spaß** I paint just for fun; **Warum fragst du? – Ach, ~ so** Why do you ask? – Oh, no particular reason; **das hat er ~ so gesagt[, ohne sich dabei etwas zu denken]** he just said it without thinking; **~ daß ...:** except that ...; **das weiß ich ~ zu gut** I know that only too well; **das ist ~ zu wahr!** it's only too true! **2.** *Partikel* **a)** *(in Wünschen)* **wenn das ~ gut geht!** let's [just] hope it goes well; **daß ihm ~ nichts zustößt!** let's [just] hope nothing happens to him; **wenn er ~ käme/hier wäre** if only he would come/he were here; **b)** *(ermunternd, tadelnd)* **sag ihm ~ deine Meinung** just tell him what you think; **~ keine Hemmungen!** don't be inhibited!; **Laß ~! Ich schaffe das schon allein** Don't bother! I can do it by myself; **wehr dich ~!** stand up for yourself!; **~ her damit!** hand it over!; **~ weiter!** keep going; **~ zu!** go ahead; **sieh ~, was du gemacht hast!** just look what you've done; **c)** *(warnend)* **laß dich ~ nicht erwischen** just don't let me/him/her/them catch you; **er soll es ~ wagen** just let him try; **glaub ~ nicht, daß ich das nicht merke** don't think I don't notice; **~ vorsichtig/langsam** just be careful/take it easy; **~ Geduld** just be patient; **~ nicht!** don't, for goodness' sake!; **d)** *(fragend)* just; **wie soll ich ihm das ~ erklären?** just how am I supposed to explain it to him?; **was sollen wir ~ tun?** what on earth are we going to do?; **was hat er ~?** whatever's the matter with him?; **wie kann ich das ~ wiedergutmachen?** however can I make amends?; **e)** *(verallgemeinernd)* just; **er lief, so schnell er ~ konnte** he ran just as fast as he could; **alles, was man sich ~ vorstellen kann** everything one could imagine; **f)** *(sogar)* only; just; **davon werden die Schmerzen ~ [noch] schlimmer** that only *or* just makes the pain [even] worse; **g) es wimmelte ~ so von Insekten** it was just teeming with insects; **er schlug auf den Tisch, daß es ~ so krachte** he crashed his fist [down] on the table. **3.** *Konj.* but; **ich kann dir das Buch leihen, ~ nicht heute** I can lend you the book, but *or* only not today; **das Wetter ist schön, nur noch etwas kalt** the weather is fine, though still somewhat cold

Nur·haus·frau die full-time housewife; **sie ist ~:** she is only *or* just a housewife

Nürnberg ['nʏrnbɛrk] **(das);** **~s** Nuremberg

Nürnberger *Adj.; nicht präd.* Nuremberg *attrib.*; **bei ihm hilft nur der ~ Trichter** you really have to drum things into him; *s. auch* **Kölner**

nuscheln ['nʊʃl̩n] *tr., itr. V. (ugs.)* mumble

Nuß [nʊs] **die; ~, Nüsse** ['nʏsə] **a)** nut; **eine taube ~** *(fig.)* a useless article *or* item *(coll.)*; **eine harte ~ [für jmdn.]** *(fig.)* a hard *or* tough nut [for sb. to crack]; **b)** *(salopp abwertend: Mensch)* so-and-so *(coll.)*; **c)** *(Kochk.: Fleischstück)* eye; **d)** *(Technik)* socket; **e)** *in* **jmdm. eins** *od.* **eine auf/vor die ~ geben** *(ugs.)* belt sb. [one] in the head/face *(coll.)*

Nuß·baum der a) walnut-tree; **b)** *o. Pl. (Holz)* walnut

nuß·braun *Adj.* nut-brown

Nüßchen ['nʏsçən] **das; ~s, ~ a)** little nut; **b)** *(Kochk.)* eye

Nuß-: ~kern der [nut] kernel; **~knacker der** nutcrackers *pl.*; **~schale die** nutshell; *(fig.: Boot)* cockle-shell; **das Boot wurde wie eine ~schale umhergeworfen** the boat was tossed about like a cork; **~schokolade die** nut chocolate

Nüster ['nʏstɐ] **die; ~, ~n** nostril

Nut [nuːt] **die; ~, ~en, Nute** ['nuːtə] **die; ~, ~n** *(Technik)* groove

nuten *(Technik)* **1.** *tr. V.* groove. **2.** *itr. V.* cut grooves

¹Nutria ['nuːtria] **die; ~, ~s** *(Tier)* coypu

²Nutria der; ~s, ~s *(Pelz)* nutria [fur]; coypu fur

Nutsche ['nuːtʃə] **die; ~, ~n** *(Technik)* vacuum filter

Nutte ['nʊtə] **die; ~, ~n** *(derb abwertend)* tart *(sl.)*; pro *(Brit. coll.)*; hooker *(Amer. sl.)*

nutz [nʊts] *(südd., österr.) s.* **nütze**

Nutz *in* **jmdm. zu** *od.* **zu jmds. ~ und Frommen [dienen]** *(veralt.)* [be] for the benefit of sb.

nutz-, Nutz-: ~an·wendung die a) practical application; **b)** *(praktische Lehre)* moral; practical lesson; **~bar** *Adj.* usable; exploitable, utilizable ⟨*mineral resources, invention*⟩; cultivatable ⟨*land, soil*⟩; **etw. praktisch ~bar machen** turn sth. to practical use; **landwirtschaftlich ~bar** usable for agriculture *postpos.*; **die Sonnenenergie ~bar machen** harness solar energy **(für** for)

Nutzbarkeit die; ~: usability; *(von Bodenschätzen)* exploitability; utilizability

Nutzbarmachung [-maxʊŋ] **die; ~, ~en** utilization; *(von Bodenschätzen)* exploitation; utilization; *(von Forschungsergebnissen)* application

nutz·bringend 1. *Adj. (nützlich)* useful; *(gewinnbringend)* profitable. **2.** *adv.* profitably; **die Reserven so ~ wie möglich einsetzen** use the reserves to maximum advantage

nütze ['nʏtsə] *in* **zu etw. ~ sein** be good for sth.; **[jmdm.] zu nichts ~ sein** be no use *or* good [to sb.]; **du bist zu gar nichts ~:** you're totally useless; **wozu ist das ~?** what's the good of that?

Nutz·effekt der a) useful effect; **b)** *(Technik) s.* **Wirkungsgrad**

nutzen ['nʊtsn̩] **1.** *tr. V.* **a)** use; exploit, utilize ⟨*natural resources*⟩; cultivate ⟨*land, soil*⟩; use, harness ⟨*energy source*⟩; exploit ⟨*advantage*⟩; **eine Fläche landwirtschaftlich ~:** use an area for agriculture; **eine Erfindung industriell ~:** give an invention an industrial application; **b)** *(be~, aus~)* use; make use of; **wir müssen das herrliche Wetter ~:** we must take advantage of the marvellous weather; **eine Gelegenheit ~, etw. zu tun** take [advantage of] an opportunity to do sth.; **seine Chance ~:** take one's chance; **~ wir die Zeit!** let's make the most of the time. **2.** *itr. V. s.* **nützen 1**

Nutzen der; ~s a) benefit; **der ~ des Kanals für die Schiffahrt** the usefulness *or* benefits *pl.* of the canal to shipping; **die Maßnahme hat großen/wenig/keinen ~:** the measure is very useful/of little/no use; **den ~ [von etw.] haben** benefit *or* gain [from sth.]; **~ aus etw. ziehen** benefit from sth.; exploit sth.; **er hätte dem Land großen ~ gebracht** he would have been of great service to the country; **ich habe das Buch mit großem ~ gelesen** I profited greatly from reading the book; **[jmdm.] von ~ sein** be of use [to sb.]; **b)** *(Profit)* profit; **etw. mit ~ verkaufen** sell sth. at a profit

nützen ['nʏtsn̩] **1.** *itr. V.* be of use (+ *Dat.* to); **nichts ~:** be useless *or* no use; **seine Bitten nützten nichts** his pleas were to no avail *or* were in vain; **jmdm. sehr ~:** be very useful *or* of great use to sb.; **wem soll das ~?** who is supposed to gain from that?; **was hat ihm das genützt?** what good did it do him?; **wozu nützt das alles jetzt noch?** what's the point of all that now?; **es würde nichts/wenig ~:** it wouldn't be any/much use *or* wouldn't do any/much good; **dein Leugnen nützt jetzt auch nichts mehr** and it's no use your denying it any longer; **da nützt alles nichts** there's nothing to be done; **es nützt alles nichts, wir müssen jetzt anfangen** *(ugs.)* it's no good, we've got to start now. **2.** *tr. V. s.* **nutzen 1**

Nutzer der; ~s, ~ *(Amtsspr.)* user

Nutz-: ~fahrzeug das *(Lastwagen, Lieferwagen usw.)* commercial vehicle; goods vehicle; *(Bus, Straßenbahn usw.)* public-service vehicle; **~fläche die a)** *(von Gebäuden)* usable floor space; **b)** *(Landw.)* **landwirtschaftliche ~flächen** land *sing.* available for agriculture; **~garten der** kitchen garden; **~holz das** timber; **~land das;** *o. Pl.: s.* **~fläche b; ~last die** *(Kfz-W.)* maximum permitted load; **~leistung die** *(Technik)* effective *or* useful output *or* power

nützlich ['nʏtslɪç] **1.** *Adj.* useful; **jmdm. ~ sein** be useful *or* of use to sb.; **kann ich Ihnen ~ sein?** can I do anything for you?; **sich ~ machen** make oneself useful; *s. auch* **angenehm 1. 2.** *adv.* usefully

Nützlichkeit die; ~: usefulness

Nützlichkeits·denken das utilitarian thinking

nutzlos 1. *Adj.* useless; *(vergeblich)* futile; vain *attrib.*; in vain *pred.*; **es wäre ~, das zu tun** it would be useless *or* pointless *or* futile doing that; **all sein Flehen war ~:** all his pleading was in vain *or* of no avail. **2.** *adv.* uselessly; *(vergeblich)* futilely; in vain; **er hat das Geld ~ vergeudet** he squandered the money on useless items

Nutz·losigkeit die; ~: uselessness; *(Vergeblichkeit)* futility; vainness

nutznießen [-niːsn̩] *itr. V. (geh.)* **von etw. ~:** benefit *or* profit from sth.

Nutznießer der; ~s, ~, Nutznießerin die; ~, ~nen a) beneficiary; **b)** *(Rechtsw.)* usufructuary

Nutz·pflanze die economically useful plant

Nutz·tier das economically useful animal

Nutzung die; ~, ~en use; *(des Landes, des Bodens)* cultivation; *(von Bodenschätzen)* exploitation; utilization; *(einer Energiequelle)* use; harnessing; **die wirtschaftliche/**

landwirtschaftliche ~ einer Fläche the use of an area for financial benefit/for agriculture; **jmdm. etw. zur ~ überlassen** give sb. the use of sth.

Nutzungs·recht das *(Rechtsw.)* right of use; **das ~ an etw.** *(Dat.)* the right to use sth.

NVA *Abk.* **Nationale Volksarmee** *(DDR)* National People's Army

NW *Abk.* **Nordwest[en]** NW

Nylon Ⓦⓩ ['nailɔn] **das; ~s** nylon

Nylon·strumpf der nylon stocking

Nymphe ['nʏmfə] **die; ~, ~n** *(Myth., Zool.)* nymph

nymphoman [nʏmfo'ma:n] *Adj.* *(Psych.)* nymphomaniac; **~ sein** be a nymphomaniac

Nymphomanie die; ~: *(Psych.)* nymphomania *no art.*

Nymphomanin die; ~, ~nen *(Psych.)* nymphomaniac

nymphomanisch *Adj.* *(Psych.)* *s.* **nymphoman**

O

o, O [o:] **das; ~,** *(ugs.:)* **~s, ~,** *(ugs.:)* **~s** o/O; *s. auch* **a, A**

o [o:] *Interj.* **oh;** *s. auch* **oh**

O *Abk.* **Ost[en]** E

ö, Ö [ø:] **das; ~,** *(ugs.:)* **~s, ~,** *(ugs.:)* **~s** o/O umlaut; *s. auch* **a, A**

o. ä. *Abk.* **oder ähnlich[es]** or similar

ÖAMTC *Abk.* **Österreichischer Automobil-, Motorrad- und Touring Club** Austrian Automobile, Motor-cycle, and Touring Club

Oase [o'a:zə] **die; ~, ~n** *(auch fig.)* oasis

[1]**ob** [ɔp] *Konj.* **a)** whether; **ob du ihn anrufst?** would you give him a ring?; **ob wir es schaffen?** will we manage it?; **ob ich doch lieber zu Hause bleibe?** hadn't I better stay at home?; **ob ... oder ...:** whether ... or ...; **ob er will oder nicht** whether he wants to or not; **ob arm, ob reich** whether rich or poor; **b)** *(veralt.)* *in* **ob ... auch** *od.* **gleich** even though; **c)** *in* **und ob!** of course!; you bet! *(coll.)*; **Hast du keinen Hunger mehr? – Und ob!** Don't you want any more? – You bet I do! *(coll.)*; *s. auch* **als**

[2]**ob** *Präp.* **a)** *mit Gen., selten Dativ (veralt. geh.: wegen)* on account of; **b)** *mit Dativ (schweiz., veralt.: über)* above

o. B. *Abk.* **ohne Befund**

OB *Abk.* **Oberbürgermeister**

Obacht ['o:baxt] **die; ~** *(bes. südd.)* caution; **~, da kommt ein Auto!** watch out! *or* look out! *or* careful!, there's a car coming; **~ auf jmdn./etw. geben** look after *or* take care of sb./sth.; *(aufmerksam sein)* pay attention to sb./sth.; **~ geben, daß ...** take care that ...

ÖBB *Abk.* **Österreichische Bundesbahnen** Austrian Federal Railways

Obdach ['ɔpdax] **das; ~[e]s** *(geh.)* shelter; **kein ~ haben** be without shelter

obdach·los *Adj.* homeless; **~ werden** be made homeless

Obdachlose der/die; *adj. Dekl.* homeless person/man/woman; **die ~n** the homeless

Obdachlosen·asyl das, Obdachlosen·heim das hostel for the homeless

Obdachlosigkeit die; ~: homelessness

Obduktion [ɔpduk'tsio:n] **die; ~, ~en** *(Med., Rechtsw.)* post-mortem [examination]; autopsy

Obduktions·befund der *(Med., Rechtsw.)* findings *pl. or* results *pl.* of a/the post-mortem [examination] *or* autopsy

obduzieren [ɔpdu'tsi:rən] **1.** *tr. V.* carry out *or* perform a/the post-mortem [examination] *or* autopsy on. **2.** *itr. V.* carry out *or* perform a post-mortem examination *or* autopsy

O-Beine *Pl.* bandy legs; bow-legs

O-beinig *Adj.* bandy-legged; bow-legged

Obelisk [obe'lɪsk] **der; ~en, ~en** obelisk

oben ['o:bn̩] *Adv.* **a)** *(an hoch/höher gelegenem Ort)* **hier/dort ~:** up here/there; **[hoch] ~ am Himmel** [high] up in the sky; **~ bleiben** stay up; **weiter ~:** further up; **nach ~:** upwards; **der Weg nach ~:** the way up; **warme Luft steigt nach ~:** warm air rises; **das Auto blieb mit den Rädern nach ~ liegen** the car came to rest upside down; **~ auf dem Dach** up on the roof; **Wo ist er? – Da ~.** Where is he? Up there; **[im Bett] ~ schlafen** sleep in the upper bunk; **von ~:** from above; **von ~ herab** *(fig.)* condescendingly; **b)** *(im Gebäude)* upstairs; **du bleibst heute besser ~** *(in der Wohnung)* you had better stay at home today; **nach ~:** upstairs; **ich komme gerade von ~:** I have just come down; **der Aufzug fährt nach ~/kommt von ~:** the lift *(Brit.) or (Amer.)* elevator is going up/coming down; **hier ~:** up here; **c)** *(am oberen Ende, zum oberen Ende hin)* at the top; **~ im Schrank** at the top of the cupboard; **ein ~ offener Zylinder** a cylinder open at the top; **nach ~ [hin]** towards the top; **weiter ~ [im Tal/am Berg]** further *or* higher up [the valley/mountain]; **von ~:** from the top; **~ links/rechts** at the top on the left/right; **~ rechts in der Ecke** in the top right-hand corner; **~ [rechts] auf der Seite** on the top [right] of the page; **~ [links/rechts]** *(in Bildunterschriften)* above [left/right]; **auf Seite 25 ~:** at the top of page 25; **die fünfte Zeile von ~:** the fifth line from the top; the fifth line down; **~ auf dem Bücherschrank** up on top of the bookcase; **der Weisheitszahn ~ links** the upper left wisdom tooth; **nach ~ kommen** *(an die Oberfläche)* come up; **Fett schwimmt ~:** fat floats on the top *or* the surface; *(fig.)* there are always some people who do all right; **„~"** 'this side up'; **wo** *od.* **was ist [bei dem Bild] ~:** which is the right way up [on the picture]?; which is the top [of the picture]?; **bis ~ hin** *(ugs.)* up to the top; **bis ~ hin voll sein** *(ugs.)* be full to the top; **der Keller steht bis ~ hin unter Wasser** *(ugs.)* the cellar is full up with water; **von ~ bis unten** from top to bottom; **er musterte sie von ~ bis unten** he looked her up and down; **er ist ~ nicht ganz richtig** *(ugs.)* he's not quite right in the head *(coll.) or* up top *(coll.)*; **~ ohne** topless; **hier wird ~ ohne bedient** there are topless waitresses here; **~ herum** *(im Bereich der Brust)* round the top; **es steht mir bis hier ~** *(ugs.)* I'm fed up to the back teeth with it *(coll.)*; **~ an der Tafel** at the head of the table; **er saß weiter ~ als ich** *(fig.)* he sat further up the table than me; **d)** *(an der Oberseite)* on top; **e)** *(in einer Hierarchie, Rangfolge)* at the top; **weit/ganz ~:** near the top/right at the top; **der Befehl kam von ~:** the order came from above; **etw. nach ~ weitergeben** pass sth. on up; **die da ~** *(ugs.)* the high-ups *(coll.)*; **der Weg nach ~:** the road to the top; **er wollte nach ~:** he wanted to get to *or* make it to the top; **sich ~ halten** stay at the top; **die Band ist jetzt ganz ~:** the group is now riding high [in the charts]; **f)** *([weiter] vorn im Text)* above; **der ~ schon erwähnte Fall** the case [already] referred to above; **g)** *(im Norden)* up north; **hier/dort ~:** up here/there [in the north]; **~ in Dänemark/im Norden** up in Denmark/up [in the] north; **weiter ~:** further up [north]

oben-: ~an *Adv.* at the top; **diese Frage steht für mich immer ~an** this question will always have top priority for me; **~auf** *Adv.* **a)** *(zuoberst)* on [the] top; **b)** *(guter Dinge)* on top of the world; **c)** *(gesund)* fit and well; **~drauf** *Adv.* *(ugs.)* on top; **~drein** *Adv.* *(ugs.)* on top of that; **~drüber** *Adv.* *(ugs.)* above it/them; *(darauf)* on it/them; **~erwähnt, ~genannt** ['----] *Adj.; nicht präd.* above-mentioned; mentioned above *postpos.*; **von den Obengenannten ...:** of the above mentioned ...; **~hinaus** *in* **~hinaus wollen** *(ugs.)* be aiming at big things; **~stehend** ['----] *Adj.* above-mentioned; **das Obenstehende** the above

ober... ['o:bɐ] *Adj.* **a)** upper *attrib.*; top *attrib.*; *(ganz oben liegend)* top *attrib.*; **die ~e rechte Ecke** the top right-hand corner; **am ~en Ende der Tafel/der Straße** at the top [end] of the table/street; **das Oberste zuunterst kehren** turn everything upside down; **das ~ste Stockwerk/die ~ste Stufe** the top[most] storey/step; **b)** *(der Quelle näher gelegen)* upper; **c)** *(in der Rangfolge o. ä.)* higher ⟨*authority*⟩; upper ⟨*[social] class, storey, floor*⟩; **die ~en Klassen der Schule** the senior classes *or* forms of the school; **das ~ste Gericht des Landes** the highest court in the land; **der Oberste Sowjet** the Supreme Soviet; **das Oberste Gericht** *(DDR)* the Supreme Court; *s. auch* **Obere; zehntausend**

Ober der; ~s, ~ a) waiter; **Herr ~!** waiter!; **b)** *(Spielkarte)* ≈ queen

ober-, Ober-: ~arm der upper arm; **~arzt der** *(Vertreter des Chefarztes)* assistant medical director; *(Leiter einer Spezialabteilung)* consultant; **~auf·seher der** senior supervisor; **~auf·sicht die** overall supervision; **die ~aufsicht über etw.** *(Akk.)* **haben** have overall supervisory responsibility for sth.; **~bau der;** *Pl.* **~bauten a)** *(eines Gebäudes)* superstructure; **b)** *(Straßenbau)* pavement; **c)** *(Eisenb.)* permanent way; superstructure and road-bed; **~bauch der** *(Anat.)* upper abdomen; **~bayern (das)** Upper Bavaria; **~befehl der** *(Milit.)* supreme command *no art.*; **den ~befehl über etw.** *(Akk.)* **haben** be in supreme command of sth.; **~befehlshaber der** *(Milit.)* supreme commander; commander-in-chief; **~begriff der** generic term; **~bekleidung die** outer clothing; **~bett das** duvet *(Brit.)*; continental quilt *(Brit.)*; stuffed quilt *(Amer.)*; **~bürger·meister der** mayor; *(von bestimmten englischen/schottischen Großstädten)* Lord Mayor/Provost; **~deck der** upper deck; *(eines Busses)* upper *or* top deck; **~deutsch 1.** *Adj.* Upper German; **2.** *adv.* **etw. ~deutsch aussprechen** pronounce sth. with an Upper German accent

Obere der; *adj. Dekl.* **a)** *(geh.)* **die ~n [des Landes]** those in high places [in the country]; **seine ~n** his superiors; **b)** *(eines Klosters o. ä.)* superior

ober-, Ober-: ~faul *Adj.* *(ugs.)* very fishy *(coll.)*; **~feldwebel der** *(beim Heer)* staff sergeant *(Brit.)*; sergeant first class *(Amer.)*; platoon sergeant *(Amer.)*; *(bei der Luftwaffe)* flight sergeant *(Brit.)*; master sergeant *(Amer.)*; **~fläche die** surface; *(Flächeninhalt)* surface area; **an die ~fläche kommen** come to the surface; surface; **wieder an die ~fläche kommen** resurface; **die Diskussion blieb zu sehr an der ~fläche** *(fig.)* the discussion remained far too superficial; **~flächen·struktur die** *(auch Sprachw.)* surface structure

oberflächlich 1. *Adj.* superficial; **eine ~e Düngung des Bodens kann ...:** top-dressing the soil can ...; **eine erste, ~ Berechnung/Schätzung** a first, rough calculation/estimate. **2.** *adv.* superficially; **etw. nur ~ kennen** have only a superficial knowledge of sth.; **etw. ~ lesen** read sth. cursorily; **er arbeitet zu ~** he is too superficial in the way he works

Oberflächlichkeit die; ~: superficiality

ober-, Ober-: ~förster der *(veralt.) senior forestry official;* **~gärig** [~gɛ:rɪç] *Adj.* top-fermented ⟨*beer*⟩; top-fermenting ⟨*yeast*⟩; **~gefreite der** *(beim Heer)* lance-corporal *(Brit.);* private first class *(Amer.); (bei der Luftwaffe)* leading aircraftman *(Brit.);* airman first class *(Amer.); (bei der Marine)* able rating *(Brit.);* seaman *(Amer.);* **~geschoß das** upper storey; **das Haus hat zwei ~geschosse** the house has three storeys; **er wohnt im fünften ~geschoß** he lives on the fifth floor *(Brit.) or (Amer.)* the sixth floor; **~grenze die** upper limit

ober·halb 1. *Adv.* above; **weiter ~:** further up; **~ von** above. **2.** *Präp. mit Gen.* above

Ober-: ~hand die *in* **die ~hand [über jmdn./etw.] haben** have the upper hand [over sb./sth.]; **die ~hand [über jmdn./etw.] gewinnen/bekommen** gain *or* get the upper hand [over sb./sth.]; **~haupt das** head; *(einer Verschwörung)* leader; **~haus das** *(Parl.)* upper house *or* chamber; *(in Großbritannien)* House of Lords; Upper House; **~hemd das** shirt; **~herrschaft die** *o. Pl.* sovereignty; supreme power; **~hirte der** *(geh.)* spiritual leader *or* head; **~hoheit die;** *o. Pl.* sovereignty; supreme power

Oberin die; ~, ~nen a) *(christliche Kirche)* Mother Superior; **b)** *s.* **Oberschwester**

ober-, Ober-: ~inspektor der senior inspector; *(bei der Polizei)* detective chief inspector; **~irdisch 1.** *Adj.* surface *attrib.* ⟨*pipes, cables*⟩; ⟨*pipes, cables*⟩ laid above ground; **~irdische Lagerung** above-ground storage; storage above ground; **~irdische Pflanzenteile** parts of a/the plant above the ground; **2.** *adv.* **die U-Bahn fährt hier ~irdisch** the underground [system] runs above ground here; **~italien (das)** Northern Italy; **~kante die** top edge; **es steht mir bis ~kante Unterlippe** *(salopp)* I'm sick to death of it *(coll.);* **kellner der** head waiter; **~kiefer der** upper jaw; **~kirchen·rat der a)** *(Gremium) highest administrative body of some evangelical Land churches;* **b)** *(Person) member of an ~kirchenrat a;* **~klasse die a)** *(Soziol.)* upper class; **b)** *(Schulw.)* senior class *or* form; **c)** *(bei Autos)* luxury class; **ein Wagen der ~klasse** a large luxury car; **~kommandierende der/die;** *adj. Dekl. (Milit.)* supreme commander; commander-in-chief; **~kommando das** supreme command **(über +** *Akk.* of); **jmds. ~kommando** *(Dat.)* **unterstehen** be under the supreme command of sb.; **~körper der** upper part of the body; **mit nacktem ~körper** stripped to the waist; **den ~körper frei machen** strip to the waist; **~land das** *o. Pl.* uplands *pl.;* **das Berner ~land** the Bernese Oberland; **~landes·gericht das** Higher Regional Court; ≈ *high court and court of appeal of a Land;* **~länge die** ascender; **~lastig** *Adj. (Seemannsspr.)* top-heavy; **~lauf der** upper reaches *pl.;* **~leder das** upper; **~lehrer der** *(DDR) honorary title for teacher; (fig.)* schoolmaster; **~lehrerhaft** *Adj. (abwertend)* schoolmasterish; **~leitung die a)** *(elektrische Leitung)* overhead cable; **b)** *(Kontrolle)* overall control; **~leitungs·bus der** trolley bus *(Brit.);* **~leutnant der** *(beim Heer)* lieutenant *(Brit.);* first lieutenant *(Amer.); (bei der Luftwaffe)* flying officer *(Brit.);* first lieutenant *(Amer.);* **~leutnant zur See** sub-lieutenant *(Brit.);* lieutenant junior grade *(Amer.);* **~licht das a)** *o. Pl.* light from above; **b)** *Pl.:* **~lichter** *(Deckenlampe)* ceiling light; overhead light; **c)** *Pl.:* **~lichter** *od. selten* **~lichte** high window; *(über einer Tür)* fanlight; *(Klappfenster)* transom; **~lid das** upper [eye] lid; **~liga die** *(Sport)* **a)** second division; **b)** *(DDR)* first division; **~lippe die** upper lip; **~lippen·bart der** moustache; **~maat der** *(Marine)* petty officer; **~material das: „~material Leder"** 'leather uppers'; **~österreich (das)** Upper Austria; **~post·direktion die** *regional postal administration;* **~prima die** *(Schulw. veralt.)* top form *(of a Gymnasium);* ≈ upper sixth [form] *(Brit.);* **~primaner der** *(Schulw. veralt.)* pupil in the top form *(of a Gymnasium);* **~regierungs·rat der** *senior civil servant;* **~rheinisch** *Adj.* in the Upper Rhine valley *postpos.;* **Oberrheinische Tiefebene** Upper Rhine valley

Obers ['o:bɐs] **das; ~** *(österr.) s.* **Sahne**

ober-, Ober-: ~schenkel der thigh; **~schenkel·hals·bruch der** *(Med.)* fracture of the neck of the femur; **~schicht die** *(Soziol.)* upper class; **der ~schicht angehören** be a member of the upper classes *pl.;* **~schlesien (das)** Upper Silesia; **~schule die a)** secondary school; **b)** *(DDR)* unified comprehensive school; **[allgemeinbildende] polytechnische ~schule** *unified comprehensive school for children aged 7–17;* **erweiterte ~schule** *unified comprehensive school providing a further two years' preparation for university entrance qualification;* **~schul·rat der** local education officer; **~schwester die** senior nursing officer; *(Stationsschwester)* ward sister; matron; **~seite die** top[side]; upper side; *(eines Stoffes)* right side; **~sekunda die** *(Schulw. veralt.)* seventh year *(of a Gymnasium);* **~sekundaner der** *(Schulw. veralt.)* pupil in the seventh year *(of a Gymnasium);* **~seminar das** *(Hochschulw.)* graduate class

oberst... *s.* **ober...**

Oberst der; ~en *od.* **~s, ~en** *od.* **~e** *(beim Heer)* colonel; *(bei der Luftwaffe)* group captain *(Brit.);* colonel *(Amer.)*

Ober-: ~staats·anwalt der *senior public prosecutor (at a regional court);* **~stadt die** upper part of the town; upper town; **~stadt·direktor der** chief executive [of a/the town council]; **~steiger der** *(Bergbau)* under-manager; **~stimme die** *(Musik)* treble; *(Sopran)* soprano; *(Diskant)* descant

Oberst·leutnant der *(beim Heer)* lieutenant-colonel; *(bei der Luftwaffe)* wing commander; lieutenant-colonel *(Amer.)*

Ober-: ~stübchen das *s.* **richtig 1 b; ~studien·direktor der a)** headmaster *(Brit.);* principal; **b)** *(DDR) highest honorary title for a teacher;* **~studien·rat der a)** senior teacher; **b)** *(DDR) honorary title for a teacher;* **~stufe die** *(Schulw.)* upper school; **~teil das** *od.* **der** top [part]; *(eines Bikinis, Anzugs, Kleids usw.)* top [half]; **~tertia die** *(Schulw. veralt.)* fifth year *(of a Gymnasium);* **~tertianer der** *(Schulw. veralt.)* pupil in the fifth year *(of a Gymnasium);* **~ton der;** *meist Pl. (Musik, Physik)* overtone

Ober-: ~wasser das; *o. Pl.* headwater; *(fig.)* **~wasser haben** feel in a strong position; **~wasser bekommen/kriegen** have one's hand strengthened; **~weite die** bust measurement; **sie hat ~weite 91** she has a 36-inch bust; **eine beachtliche ~weite haben** *(ugs.)* be well-endowed *(joc.)*

Ob·frau die *s.* **Obmännin**

ob·gleich *Konj. s.* **obwohl**

Ob·hut die; ~: *(geh.)* care; **jmdn./etw. in seine ~ nehmen** take sb./sth. into one's care; **jmdn./etw. jmds. ~** *(Dat.)* **anvertrauen** entrust sb./sth. to sb.'s care; **unter jmds. ~** *(Dat.)* **stehen** be in sb.'s care

obig ['o:bɪç] *Adj.; nicht präd.* above; **die ~e Tabelle** the above table; the table above

Objekt [ɔp'jɛkt] **das; ~s, ~e a)** *(auch Sprachw., Kunstwiss.)* object; *(Fot., bei einem Experiment)* subject; **b)** *(Kaufmannsspr.: Immobilie)* property; **c)** *(bes. DDR: Projekt)* project; **d)** *(österr. Amtsspr.: Gebäude)* building; **e)** *(DDR: staatliche Einrichtung) (Fabrik)* factory; *(Gaststätte, Verkaufsstelle)* establishment

objektiv [ɔpjɛk'ti:f] **1.** *Adj.* objective; real, actual ⟨*cause, danger*⟩. **2.** *adv.* objectively; **er hat uns ~ geschadet** he did in fact do us harm

Objektiv das; ~s, ~e a) *(Optik)* objective; **b)** *(Fot.)* lens

objektivieren *tr. V.* objectify; objectivize

Objektivismus der; ~ *(Philos.)* objectivism *no def. art.*

Objektivität [ɔpjɛktivi'tɛ:t] **die; ~:** objectivity

Objekt-: ~satz der *(Sprachw.)* object clause; **~schutz der** *(Amtsspr.)* protection of property; **für etw. ~schutz beantragen** apply to have sth. protected; **~träger der** *(Optik)* [specimen-]slide

Oblate [o'bla:tə] **die; ~, ~n** wafer

Ob·leute *Pl. s.* **Obmann**

ob|liegen, ob·liegen *unr. itr. V. (geh.)* **etw. liegt jmdm. ob** *od.* **obliegt jmdm.** sth. is sb.'s responsibility

Obliegenheit die; ~, ~en *(geh.)* duty; **seine dienstlichen ~en erfüllen** carry out one's duties; **zu jmds. ~en gehören** be one of sb.'s duties

obligat [obli'ga:t] *Adj.* **a)** *(geh.) s.* **obligatorisch 1 a; b)** *(iron.: unvermeidlich)* obligatory; **c)** *(Musik)* obbligato

Obligation [obliga'tsio:n] **die; ~, ~en** *(Wirtsch.)* bond; debenture

obligatorisch [obliga'to:rɪʃ] **1.** *Adj.* **a)** obligatory; compulsory ⟨*subject, lecture, etc.*⟩; necessary ⟨*qualification*⟩; **b)** *s.* **obligat b. 2.** *adv.* obligatorily; compulsorily

Obligatorium [obliga'to:riʊm] **das; ~s, Obligatorien** *(schweiz.) (Verpflichtung)* compulsory duty; *(Beitrag)* compulsory contribution

Obligo ['o:bligo] **das; ~s, ~s** *(Wirtsch.)* liability; **ohne ~:** without recourse

Ob·mann der; ~[e]s, Obmänner *od.* **Obleute, Obmännin** ['ɔpmɛnɪn] **die; ~, ~nen** *(bes. österr.)* chairman; *(einer Delegation)* head; *(einer Gruppe)* representative

Oboe [o'bo:ə] **die; ~, ~n** oboe

Oboist [obo'ɪst] **der; ~en, ~en** oboist; oboe-player

Obolus ['o:bolʊs] **der; ~, ~** *od.* **~se** *(geh. scherzh.)* small sum; *(Spende)* small contribution

Obrigkeit ['o:brɪçkait] **die; ~, ~en** authorities *pl.*

obrigkeitlich *Adj.; nicht präd.* **a)** official ⟨*decree, approval, etc.*⟩; **b)** *(autoritär)* authoritarian

Obrigkeits-: ~denken das *(abwertend)* attitude of obedience to authority; **~staat der** authoritarian state

Obrist [o'brɪst] **der; ~en, ~en** *(veralt., noch abwertend)* colonel

ob·schon *Konj. (geh.)* although; though

Observanz [ɔpzɛr'vants] **die; ~, ~en a)** kind; type; **b)** *(Rel.)* observance

Observation [ɔpzɛrva'tsio:n] **die; ~, ~en a)** *(Überwachung)* surveillance *no pl.;* **~en** surveillance operations; **b)** *(wissenschaftlich)* observation

Observatorium [ɔpzɛrva'to:riʊm] **das; ~s, Observatorien** observatory

observieren *tr. V.* **a) jmdn./etw. ~:** keep sb./sth. under surveillance; **b)** *(wissenschaftlich)* observe; **einen Patienten ~:** keep a patient under observation

Obsession [ɔpzɛ'sio:n] **die; ~, ~en** *(Psych., geh.)* obsession

ob·siegen, *auch:* **obǀsiegen** *itr. V. (geh. veralt.)* be victorious
obskur [ɔps'ku:ɐ̯] *Adj. (geh.)* **a)** *(unbekannt, unklar)* obscure; **b)** *(dubios)* dubious
Obskurantismus [ɔpskuran'tɪsmʊs] **der;** ~ *(geh.)* obscurantism
obsolet [ɔpzo'le:t] *Adj. (geh.)* obsolete
Obst [o:pst] **das,** ~**[e]s** fruit
Obst-: ~**anbau,** ~**bau der;** *o. Pl.* fruit-growing; ~**anbau betreiben** grow fruit; ~**baum der** fruit-tree; ~**garten der** orchard; ~**händler der** fruiterer
obstinat [ɔpsti'na:t] *(geh.)* **1.** *Adj.* obstinate. **2.** *adv.* obstinately
Obst·kuchen der fruit flan
Obstler ['o:pstlɐ] **der;** ~**s,** ~ *(bes. südd.)* fruit brandy
Obst·messer das fruit-knife
Obstruktion [ɔpstrʊk'tsjo:n] **die;** ~, ~**en** *(auch Parl., Med.)* obstruction; *(Pol.: durch Dauerreden)* filibustering
Obstruktions·politik die *(Parl.)* policy of obstruction; *(durch Dauerreden)* filibustering policy
Obst-: ~**saft der** fruit juice; ~**salat der** fruit salad; ~**tag der** day for eating only fruit; ~**torte die** fruit flan; ~**wasser das** fruit brandy; ~**wein der** fruit wine
obszön [ɔps'tsø:n] **1.** *Adj.* obscene. **2.** *adv.* obscenely
Obszönität [ɔpstsøni'tɛ:t] **die;** ~, ~**en** obscenity
O·bus der trolley bus *(Brit.)*
obǀwalten, ob·walten *itr. V. (geh. veralt.)* prevail
ob·wohl 1. *Konj.* although; though. **2.** *Adv. (ugs.)* although
ob·zwar *Konj. (geh.)* ~ **[daß]** although
Occasion *(österr., schweiz.) s.* **Okkasion**
och [ɔx] *Interj. (ugs.)* oh
Ochs [ɔks] **der;** ~**en,** ~**en** *(südd., österr., schweiz., ugs.),* **Ochse** ['ɔksə] **der;** ~**n,** ~**n a)** ox; bullock; ~ **am Spieß** roast ox; **du sollst dem** ~**n, der da drischt, nicht das Maul verbinden** you shouldn't be too strict with those who have to work hard; *s. auch* **dastehen a; b)** *(salopp)* numskull *(coll.)*; **ich** ~**!** what a numskull I am!
ochsen *tr., itr. V. s.* **büffeln**
Ochsen-: ~**brust die** *(Kochk.)* brisket of beef; ~**frosch der** bullfrog; ~**gespann das a)** team *or* span of oxen; **b)** *(Wagen)* ox-cart; ~**maul·salat der** *(Kochk.)* ox-cheek salad; ~**schwanz·suppe die** *(Kochk.)* oxtail soup; ~**tour die** *(ugs. scherzh.)* **a)** long, hard climb; **b)** *(Schinderei)* hard slog; ~**ziemer der** [bull's] pizzle; ~**zunge die** *(Kochk.)* ox-tongue
Öchsle·grad der degree Öchsle
ocker ['ɔkɐ] *Adj.; nicht attr.* ochre
Ocker das; ~**s,** ~**:** ochre
ocker-: ~**braun** *Adj.* ochre-brown; ~**gelb** *Adj.* ochre-yellow
öd [ø:t] *(geh.) s.* **öde**
od. *Abk.* **oder**
Ode ['o:də] **die;** ~, ~**n** ode (**an** + *Akk.* to, **auf** + *Akk.* on)
öde ['ø:də] *Adj.* **a)** *(verlassen)* deserted ⟨*beach, village, house, street, etc.*⟩; *(unbewohnt)* desolate ⟨*area, landscape*⟩; **b)** *(unfruchtbar)* barren; **c)** *(langweilig)* tedious; dreary; dreary ⟨*life, time*⟩; barren, tedious, dreary ⟨*existence*⟩
Öde die; ~, ~**n a)** *o. Pl. s.* **öde a–c:** desertedness; desolateness; barrenness; **b)** *(öde Gegend)* wasteland; waste; **c)** *(Langeweile)* tediousness; dreariness
Odem ['o:dəm] **der;** ~**s** *(dichter. veralt.)* breath
Ödem [ø'de:m] **das;** ~**s,** ~**e** *(Med.)* oedema
oder ['o:dɐ] *Konj.* **a)** or; ~ **auch** or; ~ **aber** or else; *s. auch* **entweder; b)** *(in Fragen)* **du kommst doch mit,** ~**?** you will come, won't you?; **er ist doch hier,** ~**?** he is here, isn't he? *(zweifelnd)* he is here – or isn't he?; **das ist doch erlaubt,** ~ **[nicht** *od.* **etwa nicht]?** that is allowed, isn't it?; **das ist doch nicht erlaubt,** ~ **[doch** *od.* **etwa doch]?** that isn't allowed, is it?; **das hört sich gut an,** ~**?** it sounds good, don't you think *or* agree?
Odermennig ['o:dɐmɛnɪç] **der;** ~**[e]s,** ~**e** *(Bot.)* agrimony
Oder-Neiße-[Friedens]grenze *(DDR),* **Oder-Neiße-Linie die** Oder-Neisse Line
Ödipus·komplex ['ø:dipʊs-] **der** *(Psych.)* Oedipus complex
Odium ['o:dium] **das;** ~**s** *(geh.)* odium
Öd·land das; *Pl.:* **Ödländer** uncultivated land *(and land exploited for raw materials, e.g. gravel pits);* **Ödländer** uncultivated land *sing. or* areas
Ödnis die; ~**:** *(geh.) s.* **Öde**
Odyssee [ody'se:] **die;** ~, ~**n** odyssey; **Homers** ~**:** Homer's Odyssey
Odysseus [o'dysɔʏs] **(der);** ~**:** Odysseus
Œuvre ['ø:vrə] **das;** ~, ~**s** *(geh.)* œuvre
OEZ *Abk.* **osteuropäische Zeit** EET
Öfchen ['ø:fçən] **das;** ~**s,** ~**:** small stove *etc.; s.* **Ofen a–d**
Ofen ['o:fn̩] **der;** ~**s, Öfen a)** heater; *(Kohle~)* stove; *(Öl~, Petroleum~)* stove; heater; *(elektrischer ~)* heater; fire; **wenn sie uns erwischen, ist der** ~ **aus** *(ugs.)* if they catch us, it's all over; **jetzt ist bei mir der** ~ **aus** *(ugs.: jetzt habe ich aber genug)* that does it!; **b)** *(Back~)* oven; **c)** *(Industrie~)* furnace; *(Brenn~, Trocken~)* kiln; **d)** *(landsch.: Herd)* cooker; **e)** *in* **heißer** ~ *(salopp)* fast set of wheels *(coll.)*
ofen-, Ofen-: ~**bank die** bench round a/the stove; ~**frisch** *Adj.* oven-fresh; freshly baked; ~**heizung die;** *o. Pl.* heating *no art.* by stoves; **das Haus hat** ~**heizung** the house is heated by stoves; ~**klappe die a)** damper; **b)** *(~tür)* stove door; ~**rohr das** [stove] flue; ~**schirm der** fire-screen; ~**setzer der** *(der Öfen baut)* stove-builder; *(der Öfen instand setzt)* stove-fitter; ~**warm** *Adj.* oven-hot
offen ['ɔfn̩] **1.** *Adj.* **a)** open; **mit** ~**em Mund/** ~**en Augen** with one's mouth/eyes open; **der Knopf/Schlitz/Schuh ist** ~**:** the button is/one's flies/shoe-laces are undone; **ein** ~**es Hemd** a shirt with the collar unfastened; **sie trägt ihr Haar** ~**:** she wears her hair loose; **ein** ~**es Haus führen** *od.* **haben** keep open house; **eine** ~**e Anstalt** an open prison; ~ **haben** *od.* **sein** be open; **ein** ~**er Umschlag** an unsealed envelope; **ein** ~**er Brief** an open letter; **Tag der** ~**en Tür** open day; ~**e Beine** ulcerated legs; **die Tür ist** ~ *(nicht abgeschlossen)* the door is unlocked; **mit** ~**en Karten spielen** play with the cards face up on the table; *(fig.)* put one's cards on the table; ~**es Licht/Feuer** a naked light/an open fire; **eine** ~**e Bauweise** an open layout; **das** ~**e Meer, die** ~**e See** the open sea; ~**es Gelände** open terrain; **die Jagd ist** ~**:** it's open season; **Beifall auf** ~**er Szene** spontaneous applause; **unter** ~**em Himmel** in the open; ~**e Türen einrennen** *(fig.)* fight a battle that's/battles that are already won; **bei ihm rennst du** ~**e Türen ein** *(fig.)* you're preaching to the converted with him; **mit** ~**en Augen** *od.* **Sinnen durch die Welt** *od.* **durchs Leben gehen** go about/go through life with one's eyes open; **mit** ~**en Augen in sein Verderben/Unglück rennen** be heading for disaster with one's eyes open; **ein** ~**es Geheimnis** an open secret; **für neue Ideen** *od.* **gegenüber neuen Ideen** ~ **sein** be receptive *or* open to new ideas; *s. auch* **Arm a; Handelsgesellschaft; Karte g; Ohr b; Straße a; Strecke b; Visier a; b)** *(lose)* loose ⟨*sugar, flour, oats, etc.*⟩; ~**er Wein** wine on tap *or* draught; **ein Glas von dem** ~**en Rotwein** a glass of the draught red wine; **c)** *(frei)* vacant ⟨*job, post*⟩; ~**e Stellen** vacancies; *(als Rubrik)* 'Situations Vacant'; **lassen Sie die Zeile** ~**:** leave the line blank; **d)** *(ungewiß, ungeklärt)* open, unsettled ⟨*question*⟩; uncertain ⟨*result*⟩; **den Ausgang des Spiels ist noch völlig** ~**:** the result of the match is still wide open; **wann es stattfindet, ist immer noch** ~**:** it's not yet been decided when it will take place; **e)** *(noch nicht bezahlt)* outstanding ⟨*bill*⟩; **der** ~**e Betrag** the amount outstanding; **f)** *(freimütig, aufrichtig)* frank [and open] ⟨*person*⟩; frank, candid ⟨*look, opinion, reply*⟩; open, frank ⟨*confession, manner*⟩; frank ⟨*talk*⟩; honest ⟨*character, face*⟩; ~ **zu jmdm. sein** be open *or* frank with sb.; **g)** *nicht präd. (unverhohlen)* open ⟨*threat, mutiny, hostility, opponent, etc.*⟩; **in** ~**em Kampf** in an open fight; **h)** *(Sprachw.)* open ⟨*vowel, syllable*⟩. **2.** *adv.* **a)** *(frei zugänglich, sichtbar, unverhohlen)* openly; *s. auch* **zutage; b)** *(freimütig, aufrichtig)* openly; frankly; ~ **gesagt** frankly; to be frank *or* honest; ~ **gestanden** to tell you the truth; **darf ich** ~ **reden?** can I be frank?; can I speak frankly?; **c)** *(Sprachw.)*; **das e** ~ **aussprechen** pronounce 'e' as an open vowel
offen·bar 1. *Adj.* obvious; **seine Absicht war allen** ~**:** his intention was obvious *or* apparent to all. **2.** *adv.* **a)** *(offensichtlich)* obviously; clearly; **b)** *(anscheinend)* evidently
offenbaren *(geh.)* **1.** *tr. V.* reveal. **2.** *refl. V.* **a)** *(sich erweisen)* **sich als etw.** ~**:** ⟨*person*⟩ show *or* reveal oneself to be sth.; **seine Worte offenbarten sich als Lüge** his words were revealed as a lie *or* to be a lie; **b)** *(sich mitteilen)* **sich jmdm.** ~**:** confide in sb.
Offenbarung die; ~, ~**en a)** revelation; **b)** *(Rel.)* revelation; **die** ~ **[des Johannes]** [the Book of] Revelations
Offenbarungs·eid der *(Rechtsw.)* oath of disclosure
offen-: ~**ǀbleiben** *unr. itr. V.; mit sein* **a)** remain *or* stay open; **der Mund blieb ihm vor Staunen** ~**:** his mouth hung open in astonishment; **b)** *(ungeklärt bleiben)* remain open; ⟨*decision*⟩ be left open; **c)** *(unerfüllt bleiben)* ⟨*wish*⟩ remain unsatisfied; ~**ǀhalten** *unr. tr. V.* **etw.** ~**halten** keep sth. open
Offen·heit die; ~**:** *s.* **offen f:** frankness [and openness]; candidness; candour; openness; honesty; ~ **gegenüber den Problemen anderer zeigen** be responsive to other people's problems
offen-, Offen-: ~**herzig 1.** *Adj.* **a)** frank, candid ⟨*conversation, remark*⟩; frank and open ⟨*person*⟩; **b)** *(iron.: dekolletiert)* revealing, low-cut ⟨*dress*⟩; **2.** *adv.* frankly; openly; ~**herzigkeit die;** ~**:** frankness; candidness; candour; ~**kundig 1.** *Adj.* obvious, evident (**für** to); obvious, patent, manifest ⟨*lie, betrayal, misuse*⟩; ~**kundig werden** become apparent; **2.** *adv.* obviously; clearly; ~**ǀlassen** *unr. tr. V.* **etw.** ~**lassen** leave sth. open; ~**lassen, ob ...:** leave it open whether ...; ~**ǀlegen** *tr. V.* reveal; *(bekanntgeben)* disclose; ~**sichtlich 1.** *Adj.* obvious; evident; **2.** *adv.* obviously, evidently; *(anscheinend)* evidently
offensiv [ɔfən'zi:f] **1.** *Adj.* **a)** offensive; aggressive ⟨*marketing strategy*⟩; **b)** *(Sport)* attacking. **2.** *adv.* **a)** offensively; ⟨*speak, argue, behave*⟩ aggressively; **b)** *(Sport)* ~ **spielen** play an attacking game
Offensive die; ~, ~**n** *(auch Sport)* offensive; **in der** ~**:** on the offensive; **die** ~ **ergreifen, in die** ~ **gehen** go on to the offensive
Offensiv-: ~**krieg der** offensive war; ~**spiel das** *(Sport)* attacking game
offenǀstehen *unr. itr. V.* **a)** be open; **der Mund stand ihm vor Staunen offen** his mouth hung open in astonishment; **b)** *(zur Benutzung freigegeben sein)* be open (+ *Dat.* to); **c)** *s.* **freistehen a; d)** *(unbezahlt sein)* be outstanding; ~**stehende Rechnungen** outstanding bills
öffentlich ['œfn̩tlɪç] **1.** *Adj.* public; state *at-*

trib., [state-] maintained ⟨*school*⟩; **alle Teilnehmer am ~en Straßenverkehr** all road-users; **etw. in ~er Sitzung beraten** debate sth. in open session; **die ~e Ordnung/Sicherheit** public order/security; **Erregung ~en Ärgernisses** *(Rechtsw.)* creating a public nuisance; **~es Ärgernis erregen** create a public nuisance; **die ~e Meinung** public opinion; **das ~e Recht** *(Rechtsw.)* public law; **Anstalt des ~en Rechts** institution incorporated under public law; **Körperschaft des ~en Rechts** public corporation; **der ~e Dienst** the civil service; **die Ausgaben der ~en Hand** public spending *sing.*; **von der ~en Hand finanziert** financed out of public funds; **die ~en Hände** local authorities and the state; **ein ~es Haus** *(veralt. verhüll.)* a house of ill-repute; **ein ~es Geheimnis** an open secret; **eine Persönlichkeit des ~en Lebens** a public figure. **2.** *adv.* **a)** publicly; ⟨*perform, appear*⟩ in public; **~ tagen** meet in open session; **~ auftreten** appear in public; **etw. ~ versteigern** sell sth. by public auction; **b)** *(vom Staat usw.)* publicly ⟨*funded etc.*⟩

Öffentlichkeit die; ~: a) public; **unter Ausschluß der ~:** in private *or* secret; *(Rechtsw.)* in camera; **etw. an die ~ bringen** bring sth. to public attention; make sth. public; **mit etw. an die ~ gehen** make sth. public; **vor die ~ treten** appear in public; **in aller ~:** [quite openly] in public; *s. auch* [1]**Flucht b; b)** *(das Öffentlichsein)* **das Prinzip der ~ in der Rechtsprechung** the principle that justice be administered in open court; **die ~ einer Versammlung herstellen** throw a meeting open to the public

Öffentlichkeits·arbeit die; *o. Pl.* public relations work *no art.*

öffentlich-rechtlich *Adj.* under public law *postpos., not pred.*; **~es Fernsehen** state-owned television; **~e Körperschaften** bodies incorporated under public law

offerieren [ɔfəˈriːrən] *tr. V. (bes. Kaufmannsspr.)* offer

Offerte [ɔˈfɛrtə] **die; ~, ~n** *(Kaufmannsspr.)* offer

Offizial·verteidiger [ɔfiˈtsi̯aːl-] **der** *(Rechtsw.) s.* **Pflichtverteidiger**

offiziell [ɔfiˈtsi̯ɛl] **1.** *Adj.* **a)** official; **b)** *(förmlich)* formal. **2.** *adv.* **a)** officially; **b)** *(förmlich)* **bei der Feier ging es furchtbar ~ zu** the celebration was terribly formal

Offizier [ɔfiˈtsiːɐ̯] **der; ~s, ~e a)** officer; **~ werden** become an officer; gain a commission; **b)** *(Schach)* piece *(other than a pawn)*

Offiziers-: ~an·wärter der officer cadet; **~kasino das** officers' mess; **~korps das** officer corps; **~lauf·bahn die** officer's career; **~messe die** *(Seemannsspr.)* wardroom; **~rang der** officer's rank

Offizin [ɔfiˈtsiːn] **die; ~, ~en a)** *(Pharm.)* dispensary; **b)** *(veralt.: Apotheke)* chemist's [shop] *(Brit.)*; drugstore *(Amer.)*; **c)** *(veralt.: Druckerei)* printing works *sing. or pl.*

offiziös [ɔfiˈtsi̯øːs] **1.** *Adj.* semi-official. **2.** *adv.* semi-officially; **wie ~ verlautet wurde** according to semi-official sources

Offizium [ɔˈfiːtsi̯ʊm] **das; ~s, Offizien** *(kath. Kirche)* **a)** *s.* **Chorgebet; b)** *(hist.)* **das Heilige ~:** the Holy Office

öffnen [ˈœfnən] **1.** *tr. (auch itr.) V.* open; turn on ⟨*tap*⟩; undo ⟨*coat, blouse, button, zip*⟩; **die Grenzen ~:** open [up] the borders; **die Bank ist** *od.* **hat über Mittag geöffnet** the bank is open at lunch-time; **der Zoo wird um 9 Uhr geöffnet** the zoo opens at 9 a.m.; **sich** *(Dat.)* **die Pulsadern ~:** slash one's wrists; **„hier ~"** 'open here'; **jmdm. den Blick für etw. ~:** open sb.'s eyes to sth.; **mit geöffnetem Mund atmen** breathe with one's mouth open *or* through one's mouth; **eine Leiche ~:** carry out a post-mortem *or* an autopsy on a body; *s. auch* **Auge. 2.** *itr. V.* **a)** [**jmdm.**] **~:** open the door [to sb.]; **wenn es klingelt, mußt du ~:** if there's a ring at the door, you must go and answer it; **b)** *(geöffnet werden)* ⟨*shop, bank, etc.*⟩ open; **c)** *(sich ~)* ⟨*door*⟩ open. **3.** *refl. V.* **a)** open; **die Erde öffnete sich** the ground opened up; **b)** *(sich erweitern)* ⟨*valley, lane, forest, etc.*⟩ open out (**auf** + *Akk.*, **zu** on to); ⟨*view*⟩ open up; **c)** *(sich aufschließen)* **sich einer Sache** *(Dat.)* **~:** become receptive to sth.; **d)** *(sich ergeben)* ⟨*opportunity, etc.*⟩ open up; **e)** *(seine Verschlossenheit aufgeben)* open up (+ *Dat.* to); **f)** *(offen sein)* ⟨*plain, clearing, etc.*⟩ open up; **sich nach Süden/Norden ~** ⟨*room etc.*⟩ be open to the south/north

Öffner der; ~s, ~: opener

Öffnung die; ~, ~en a) *(offene Stelle)* opening; *(Fot., Optik)* aperture; **b)** *o. Pl. (das Öffnen)* opening; **die ~ der Grenzen** the opening [up] of the borders; **eine ~ der Leiche** a post-mortem on the body; **c)** *o. Pl. (das Aufgeschlossensein)* openness (**für** to); **eine ~ nach links anstreben** *(Pol.)* strive to open the party up to left-wing ideas

Öffnungs·zeit die ~zeiten *pl. (eines Geschäfts, einer Bank)* opening times; hours of business; *(eines Museums, Zoos usw.)* opening times

Offsetdruck [ˈɔfsɛt-] **der a)** *o. Pl.* offset printing; **b)** *(Produkt)* offset print

O-förmig *Adj.* circular

oft [ɔft] *Adv.* **öfter** [ˈœftɐ]; *(selten)* **öftest** [ˈœftəst] often; **wie ~ fährt der Bus?** how often does the bus go *or* run?; **wie oft soll ich dir noch sagen, daß ...?** how many [more] times do I have to tell you that ...?

öfter [ˈœftɐ] *Adv.* now and then; [every] once in a while; **des ~en** *(geh.)* on many occasions

öfters [ˈœftɐs] *Adv. (österr. ugs.) s.* **öfter**

oftmals *Adv.* often; frequently

o. g. *Abk.* **oben genannt**

o. G. *Abk.* **ohne Gewähr**

OG *Abk.* **Obergeschoß**

ÖGB *Abk.* **Österreichischer Gewerkschaftsbund** Austrian Trade Union Federation

ogottogott [ˈogɔtogɔt] *Interj.* goodness me; oh dear, oh dear

oh [oː] *Interj.* oh

Oheim [ˈoːhaim] **der; ~s, ~e** *(veralt.)* uncle

OHG *Abk.* **Offene Handelsgesellschaft** general partnership

oh, là, là [olaˈla] *Interj.* ooh-la-la

Ohm [oːm] **das; ~[s], ~:** *(Physik)* ohm

ohmsch [oːmʃ] *Adj. (Physik)* **das Ohmsche Gesetz** Ohm's Law; **der ~e Widerstand** ohmic resistance

ohne [ˈoːnə] **1.** *Präp. mit Akk.* without; **~ mich!** [you can] count me out!; **der Versuch blieb ~ Erfolg** the attempt was unsuccessful; **sie ist ~ Jacke gekommen** she came without a jacket; **~ Appetit sein** have no appetite; **ein Mann ~ jeglichen Humor** a man totally lacking in humour *or* without any sense of humour; **b)** *(mit Auslassung des Akkusativs)* **ich rauche nur ~:** I only smoke untipped *or* filterless cigarettes; **wir baden am liebsten ~:** we prefer to bathe in the nude; **wenn du keinen Zucker hast, trinke ich den Tee auch ~:** if you haven't got any sugar, I can have my tea without; **du brauchst ein Visum, ~ lassen sie dich nicht einreisen** you need a visa, they won't let you in without one; **er/sie ist [gar] nicht [so] ~** *(ugs.)* he's/she's quite something; **der Vorschlag ist [gar] nicht [so] ~** *(ugs.)* it's not such a bad *or* daft suggestion; *s. auch* **oben c; c) ~ weiteres** *(leicht, einfach)* easily; *(ohne Einwand)* readily; **das würde ich nicht so ~ weiteres glauben** I wouldn't believe it just like that; **die Genehmigung kriegst du ~ weiteres** you won't have any problem *or* difficulty getting approval; **das traue ich ihm ~ weiteres zu** I can quite *or* easily believe he's capable of that; **d)** excluding; **~ mich sind es 10 Teilnehmer** there are ten participants excluding *or* not counting *or* not including me. **2.** *Konj.* **er nahm Platz, ~ daß er gefragt hätte** he sat down without asking; **~ zu zögern** without hesitating; without hesitation

ohne-: ~dies *Adv. (geh.)* in any case; **die, die ~dies schon [am meisten] Geld haben** those who already have [the most] money in any case; **~einander** *Adv.* without each other; **~gleichen** *Adj.; attr. nachgestellt* unparalleled; **ein Skandal/eine Frechheit ~gleichen** an unprecedented scandal/impertinence; **das ist ein Unsinn ~gleichen** I've never heard such nonsense; **~hin** *Adv.* anyway; **er war ~hin schon überlastet** he was already overburdened as it was; **das hat ~hin keinen Zweck** there is really no point in it

Ohnmacht [ˈoːnmaxt] **die; ~, ~en a)** faint; swoon *(literary)*; **in ~ fallen** *od. (geh.)* **sinken** faint *or* pass out/swoon; **sich einer ~ nahe fühlen** feel faint; **aus der** *od.* **seiner ~ erwachen** come to; **von** *od.* **aus einer ~ in die andere fallen** *(ugs. scherzh.)* constantly be having fits *(coll.)*; **b)** *(Machtlosigkeit)* powerlessness; impotence

ohnmächtig 1. *Adj.* **a)** unconscious; **~ werden** faint; pass out; **~ sein** have fainted *or* passed out; be in a dead faint; **~ zusammenbrechen** collapse unconscious; **halb ~:** half fainting; **b)** *(machtlos)* powerless; impotent; impotent, helpless ⟨*fury, rage*⟩; helpless ⟨*bitterness, despair*⟩. **2.** *adv.* impotently; **~ zusehen** watch powerless *or* helplessly

Ohnmachts·anfall der fainting fit

oho [oˈhoː] **1.** *Interj.* oho; *(protestierend)* oh no. **2.** *s.* **klein 1 a**

Ohr [oːɐ̯] **das; ~[e]s, ~en a)** ear; **auf dem linken ~ taub sein** be deaf in one's left ear; **jmdm. etw. ins ~ flüstern** whisper sth. in sb.'s ear; **gute/schlechte ~en haben** have good/poor hearing *sing.*; **er hört nur auf einem ~:** he only has one good ear; **ein geschultes ~:** a trained ear; **mit den ~en wackeln** wiggle one's/its ears; **das war nicht für deine/fremde ~en [bestimmt]** that wasn't for your/everbody's ears; **ich habe seine Worte/die Melodie noch im ~:** his words are still ringing in my ears/the tune is still going around my head; **die Melodie geht einem gleich/leicht ins ~:** the tune is very catchy; **b)** *(fig.)* **wo hast du bloß deine ~en?** *(ugs.)*, **du sitzt wohl auf den** *od.* **deinen ~en!** *(ugs.)* are you deaf or something? *(coll.)*; **wasch dir mal die ~en!** *(ugs.)* get your ears seen to! *(coll.)*; **die ~en aufmachen** *od.* **aufsperren** *(ugs.)* pin back one's ears; **tauben ~en predigen** *(geh.)* preach to deaf ears; **ich bin ganz ~:** I'm all ears; **mir klingen die ~en** my ears are burning; **die Wände haben ~en** the walls have ears; **ein offenes ~ für jmdn./etw. haben** be ready to listen to sb./be open to *or* ready to listen to sth.; **jmdm. sein ~ leihen** lend sb. one's ear[s]; **bei jmdm. ein offenes ~ finden** *(geh.)* find a sympathetic *or* ready listener in sb.; **[vor jmdm./etw.] die ~en verschließen** *(geh.)* close one's ears to sb./sth.; **die ~en spitzen** *(ugs.)* prick up one's ears; **spitz mal die ~en!** *(ugs.)* pin back your ears *(coll.)*; **jmdm. die ~en langziehen** *(ugs.)* take sb. by the ear and give him/her a good talking-to *(coll.)*; **halt die ~en steif!** *(ugs.)* keep smiling!; **die ~en hängen lassen** *(ugs.)* lose heart; get downhearted; **sich** *(Dat.)* **[fast] die ~en brechen** *(salopp scherzh.)* bite off [almost] more than one can chew; **auf dem** *od.* **diesem ~ hört er schlecht/nicht** *(ugs.)* he doesn't want to hear anything about that; **sich aufs ~ legen** *od. (ugs.)* **hauen** get one's head down *(coll.)*; **noch feucht/nicht [ganz] trocken hinter den ~en sein** *(ugs.)* be still wet behind the ears; **schreib dir das mal hinter die ~en!** *(ugs.)* just you remember that!; **eine** *od.* **eins/ein**

paar hinter die ~en kriegen *(ugs.)* get a thick ear; **jmdm. [mit etw.] in den ~en liegen** *(ugs.)* pester sb. the whole time [with sth.]; **mit den ~en schlackern** *(ugs.)* be staggered; **da kannst du/kann man nur mit den ~en schlackern** it's just staggering; **bis über beide ~en verliebt [in jmdn.]** *(ugs.)* head over heels in love [with sb.]; **bis über beide** *od.* **die ~en in etw. stecken** *(ugs.)* be up to one's ears in sth. *(coll.)*; **jmdn. übers ~ hauen** *(ugs.)* take sb. for a ride *(sl.)*; put one over on sb. *(coll.)*; **viel** *od.* **eine Menge um die ~en haben** *(ugs.)* have a lot on one's plate *(coll.)*; **jmdm. etw. um die ~en hauen** *od.* **schlagen** *(ugs.)* throw sth. back at sb.; **jmdm. um die ~en fliegen** *(ugs.)* blow up in sb.'s face; **von einem ~ zum anderen strahlen** *(ugs.)* grin from ear to ear; **etw. kommt jmdm. zu den ~en heraus** *(ugs.)* sb. has got sth. coming out of his/her ears; **zum einen ~ rein- und zum anderen wieder rausgehen** *(ugs.)* go in one ear and out the other *(coll.)*; *s. auch* **Durchzug a; faustdick 2; Fell a; Floh a; Mann a; Nacht**

Öhr [ø:ɐ̯] **das, ~[e]s, ~e** eye

ohren-, Ohren-: ~arzt der otologist; ear specialist; **~beichte die** *(kath. Rel.)* auricular confession; **~betäubend 1.** *Adj.* ear-splitting; deafening; deafening ‹*applause*›; **2.** *adv.* deafeningly; **~betäubend lärmen** make a deafening noise; **~klappe die** ear-flap; **~leiden das** ear complaint; **~sausen das** ringing in the *or* one's ears; tinnitus *(Med.)*; **~schmalz das** ear-wax; **~schmaus der** *(ugs.)* **ein ~schmaus sein** be a joy to hear; **~schmerz der** earache; **~schmerzen haben** have [an] earache *sing.*; **~schützer der** ear-muff; **~sessel der** wing-chair; **~zeuge der; ich wurde ~zeuge des Gesprächs** I heard the conversation myself

ọhr-, Ọhr-: ~feige die box on the ears; **~feigen bekommen** *od.* *(ugs.)* **einstecken** get one's ears boxed; **jmdm. eine ~feige geben** *od.* *(ugs.)* **verpassen** box sb.'s ears; give sb. a box on the ears; **~feigen** [-faign̩] *tr. V.* **jmdn. ~feigen** box sb.'s ears; **ich könnte mich [selbst] ~feigen!** *(ugs.)* I could kick myself!; **~feigen·gesicht das** *(salopp abwertend)* **er hat ein richtiges ~feigengesicht** he's got the sort of face you'd like to clout; **~klipp** [~klɪp] **der; ~s, ~s** ear-clip; **~läppchen das** ear-lobe; **~muschel die** external ear; auricle; **~ring der** ear-ring; **~stecker der** ear-stud; **~wurm der a)** earwig; **b)** *(ugs.: Melodie)* catchy tune; **ein ~wurm sein** be really catchy

o. J. *Abk.* **ohne Jahr** n.d.

oje [o'je:] *Interj.* *(veralt.)*, **ojemine** [o'je:mine], **ojerum** [o'je:rʊm] *Interj.* *(veralt.)* oh dear; dear me

Okarina [oka'ri:na] **die; ~; ~s** *od.* **Okarinen** ocarina

okay [o'ke] *(ugs.)* *Interj., Adj., adv.* OK *(coll.)*; okay *(coll.)*; **das geht ~:** that's OK *or* okay

Okay das; ~[s], ~s *(ugs.)* OK *(coll.)*; okay *(coll.)*

Okkasion [ɔka'zi̯o:n] **die; ~, ~en** *(veralt.)* opportunity

okkult [ɔ'kʊlt] *Adj.* occult

Okkultịsmus der; ~: occultism *no art.*

Okkupation [ɔkupa'tsi̯o:n] **die; ~, ~en** *(abwertend)* occupation

Okkupant [ɔku'pant] **der; ~en, ~en** *(abwertend)* occupier

okkupieren *tr. V.* **a)** *(abwertend)* occupy; **b)** *(sich aneignen)* **jmds. Stuhl ~:** occupy sb.'s chair

öko-, Öko- [øko-]: eco-

Ökologe [øko'lo:gə] **der; ~n, ~n** ecologist

Ökologie die; ~: ecology

Ökologin die; ~, ~nen ecologist

ökologisch 1. *Adj.* ecological. **2.** *adv.* ecologically

Ökonom [øko'no:m] **der; ~en, ~en** economist

Ökonomie die; ~, ~n a) economics *sing.*; **politische ~:** political economy; **b)** *(Wirtschaft, Wirtschaftlichkeit)* economy

Ökonomik die; ~: a) economics *pl.*; **b)** *(DDR)* economy

Ökonomin die; ~, ~nen economist

ökonomisch 1. *Adj.* **a)** economic; **eine ~e Abhandlung** a treatise on economics; **b)** *(sparsam)* economical. **2.** *adv.* economically

Ökopax ['økopaks] *o. Art.*: *alliance of the ecological and peace movements*

Öko·system das ecosystem

Okt. *Abk.* **Oktober** Oct.

Ökotrophologie [økotrofolo'gi:] **die; ~:** home economics *sing., no art.*

Oktaeder [ɔkta'|e:dɐ] **das; ~s, ~** *(Math.)* octahedron

Oktan·zahl [ɔk'ta:n-] **die** octane rating *or* number

Oktav [ɔk'ta:f] **das; ~s** octavo

Oktav-: ~band der; *Pl.* **~bände** octavo volume; **~heft das** octavo notebook

Oktave [ɔk'ta:və] **die; ~, ~n** octave

Oktett [ɔk'tɛt] **das; ~[e]s, ~e** octet

Oktober [ɔk'to:bɐ] **der; ~[s], ~:** October; *s. auch* **April**

Oktober-: ~fest das Munich October festival; **~revolution die;** *o. Pl.* *(hist.)* October Revolution; **die Große Sozialistische ~revolution** *(DDR)* the Great Socialist October Revolution

oktroyieren [ɔktroa'ji:rən] *tr. V.* *(geh.)* impose; force; **jmdm. etw. ~:** impose *or* force sth. on sb.

Okular [oku'la:ɐ̯] **das; ~s, ~e** eyepiece

okulieren *tr. V.* *(Gartenbau)* bud

Ökumene [øku'me:nə] **die; ~** *(christl. Rel.)* **a)** ecumenical Christianity; **b)** *(Bewegung)* ecumenical movement

ökumenisch 1. *Adj.* *(christl. Rel.)* ecumenical; **Ökumenischer Rat der Kirchen** World Council of Churches. **2.** *adv.* ecumenically

Okzident ['ɔktsidɛnt] **der; ~s** *(veralt., geh.)* Occident

Öl [ø:l] **das; ~[e]s, ~e** oil; **auf Öl stoßen** strike oil; **in Öl malen** paint in oils; **eine Landschaft in Öl** a landscape in oils; **Öl auf die Wogen gießen** *(fig.)* pour oil on troubled waters; **Öl ins Feuer gießen** *(fig.)* add fuel to the flames; **das ging ihm runter wie Öl** *(fig. ugs.)* he lapped it up

Öl-: ~baum der olive-tree; **~berg der** Mount of Olives; **~bild das** oil-painting; **~bohrung die** drilling *no art.* for oil; **eine ~bohrung/~bohrungen durchführen** drill for oil; **~druck der;** *Pl.* **~drücke** *(Technik)* oil pressure; **~druck·bremse die** hydraulic brake

Oldtimer ['oʊldtaɪmə] **der; ~s, ~:** vintage car; *(vor 1905 gebaut)* veteran car

Oleander [ole'andɐ] **der; ~s, ~:** *(Bot.)* oleander

ölen *tr. V.* oil; oil, lubricate ‹*shaft, engine, etc.*›; **wie geölt** *(fig. ugs.)* like clockwork; *s. auch* **Blitz a**

öl-, Öl-: ~exportierend *Adj.*; *nicht präd.* oil-exporting; **~farbe die a)** oil-based paint; **b)** *(zum Malen)* oil-paint; **mit ~farben malen** paint in oils; **~feld das** oilfield; **~film der** film of oil

OLG *Abk.* **Oberlandesgericht**

öl-, Öl-: ~gemälde das oil-painting; **~götze der** *in* **wie ein ~götze/wie die ~götzen** *(ugs.)* like a zombie/zombies; **~hahn der** *in* **den ~hahn zudrehen** *(fig.)* stop the supply of oil; **~haltig** *Adj.* containing oil *postpos., not pred.*; oil-bearing ‹*rock, shale, etc.*›; **~heizung die** oil-fired heating *no indef. art.*

ölig 1. *Adj.* *(auch fig. abwertend)* oily. **2.** *adv.* **a) ~ glänzen** have an oily sheen; **b)** *(fig. abwertend)* in an oily way

Oligarchie [oligar'çi:] **die; ~, ~n** oligarchy

oliv [o'li:f] *Adj.* olive[-green]

Oliv das; ~s, ~ *od.* **~s** olive[-green]

Olive [o'li:və] **die; ~, ~n** olive

Oliven-: ~baum der olive-tree; **~öl das** olive oil

oliv·grün *Adj.* olive-green

Öl-: ~kanister der oilcan; **~jacke die** oilskin jacket; **~kanne die** oilcan; **~krise die** oil crisis; **~kuchen der** *o. Pl.* *(Landw.)* oilcake

oll [ɔl] *Adj.* *(ugs., bes. nordd.)* old; **je ~er, je doller** *(ugs. scherzh.)* the older they get, the more they want to live it up

Öl·lampe die oil-lamp

[1]Olle der; *adj. Dekl.* *(ugs., bes. nordd.)* **a)** *(alter Mann)* old boy *(coll.)*; **b)** *(Vater, Ehemann)* old man *(coll.)*; **meine ~n** my old man and old lady *(coll.)*; **c)** *(Chef)* old man *(sl.)*; boss *(coll.)*

[2]Olle die; *adj. Dekl.* *(ugs., bes. nordd.)* **a)** *(alte Frau)* old dear *(coll.)*; **b)** *(Mutter, Ehefrau)* old lady *(coll.)*; **c)** *(Chefin)* boss *(coll.)*

Öl-: ~leitung die oil pipe; *(größer)* oil pipeline; **~malerei die** oil painting *no art.*; **~meß·stab der** *(bes. Kfz-W.)* dipstick; **~mühle die** oil-mill; **~multi der** oil multinational; **~ofen der** oil heater; **~papier das** oiled paper; **~pest die** oil pollution *no indef. art.*; **~preis der** oil price; **~pumpe die** oil-pump; **~quelle die** oil-well; **~raffinerie die** oil-refinery; **~sardine die** sardine in oil; **eine Dose ~n** a tin of sardines; **~scheich der** *(ugs.)* oil sheikh; **~schiefer der** oil-shale; **~schinken der** *(ugs. abwertend)* large pretentious oil-painting; **~spur die** trail of oil; **~stand der** oil-level; **~tank der** oil-tank; **~tanker der** oil-tanker; **~teppich der** oil-slick

Ölung die; ~, ~en oiling; lubrication; **Letzte Ölung** *(kath. u. orthodoxe Kirche)* extreme unction

Öl-: ~wanne die *(bes. Kfz-W.)* sump; **~wechsel der** *(bes. Kfz-W.)* oil-change

Olymp [o'lʏmp] **der; ~s a)** Mount Olympus; **b)** *(ugs. scherzh.: im Theater)* **der ~:** the gods *pl.*; **auf dem ~:** [up] in the gods

[1]Olympia [o'lʏmpi̯a] *(das)*; **~s** *(Geogr.)* Olympia

[2]Olympia das; ~[s] *s.* **Olympiade a)**

Olympiade [olʏm'pi̯a:də] **die; ~, ~n a)** Olympic Games *pl.*; Olympics *pl.*; **die ~ 1980** the 1980 Olympic Games *or* Olympics; **b)** *(bes. DDR: Wettbewerb)* Olympiad; **c)** *(Zeitraum)* Olympiad

olympia-, Olympia-: ~dorf das Olympic village; **~mannschaft die** Olympic team *or* squad; **~sieger der, ~siegerin die; ~, ~nen** Olympic champion; **~stadion das** Olympic stadium; **~teilnehmer der** Olympic competitor; **~verdächtig** *Adj.* *(ugs.)* Olympic-standard; **~verdächtig sein** be of Olympic standard

Olympier [o'lʏmpi̯ɐ] **der; ~s, ~:** *(geh. veralt.)* Olympian

Olympionike [olʏmpi̯o'ni:kə] **der; ~n, ~n, Olympionikin die; ~, ~nen** *(geh.)* **a)** *(Sieger[in])* Olympic champion; **b)** *(Teilnehmer[in])* Olympic competitor

olympisch *Adj.* **a)** Olympic; **die Olympischen Spiele** the Olympic Games; the Olympics; **b)** *nicht präd.* *(zum Olymp gehörend, auch fig. geh.)* Olympian

Öl-: ~zeug das oilskins *pl.*; **~zweig der** olive-branch

Oma ['o:ma] **die; ~, ~s** *(fam.)* gran[ny] *(coll./child lang.)*; grandma *(coll./child lang.)*

Ombudsmann ['ɔmbʊts-] **der; ~[e]s, Ombudsmänner** *od.* **Ombudsleute** ombudsman

Omega ['o:mega] **das; ~[s], ~s** omega

Omelett das; ~[e]s, ~e *od.* **~s,** *(österr., schweiz.)* **Omelette** [ɔm(ə)'lɛt] **die; ~, ~n** *(Kochk.)* omelette

Omen ['o:mən] **das; ~s, ~** *od.* **Omina** ['o:mina] omen

Omi ['o:mi] **die;** ~, ~s *(fam.)* granny *(coll./child lang.)*
Omikron ['o:mikrɔn] **das;** ~[s], ~s omicron
ominös [omi'nø:s] **1.** *Adj.* **a)** ominous; **b)** *(bedenklich, zweifelhaft)* sinister; *(berüchtigt)* unsavoury. **2.** *adv.* ominously
Omnibus ['ɔmnibʊs] **der;** ~ses, ~se omnibus *(formal); (Privat- und Reisebus auch)* coach
Ọmnibus- *s.* **Bus-**
omnipotent [ɔmnipo'tɛnt] *Adj. (geh.)* omnipotent
Omnipotenz [ɔmnipo'tɛnts] **die;** ~: *(geh.)* omnipotence
Onanie [ona'ni:] **die;** ~: onanism *no art.*; masturbation *no art.*
onanieren *itr. V.* masturbate
Ondit [õ'di:] **das;** ~[s], ~s *(geh.)* on dit; rumour
ondulieren [ɔndu'li:rən] *tr. V. (veralt.)* crimp; wave
[1]**Onkel** ['ɔŋkl̩] **der;** ~s, ~ *od. (ugs.)* ~s **a)** uncle; **b)** *(Kinderspr.: Mann)* **der ~ dort** that man there; **sag dem ~ guten Tag!** say hello to the nice man; **der ~ Doktor** the nice doctor; **b)** *(ugs. abwertend)* bloke *(Brit. coll.)*; guy *(sl.)*
[2]**Ọnkel der;** ~s, ~s *in* **großer** *od.* **dicker ~:** big toe; **über den großen ~ gehen** walk pigeon-toed
Ọnkel·ehe die *(ugs.) cohabitation of a widow with a man who (in order to retain benefits due to her from the first marriage) is not married to her*
ọnkel·haft 1. *Adj.* avuncular. **2.** *adv.* in an avuncular manner
ONO *Abk.* **Ostnordost[en]** ENE
onomato·poetisch *(Sprachw.) Adj.* onomatopoeic; onomatopoetic
ontisch ['ɔntɪʃ] *(Philos.)* **1.** *Adj.* ontic. **2.** *adv.* ontically
Onto·genese [ɔnto-] **die** *(Biol.)* ontogeny; ontogenesis
onto·genetisch *(Biol.)* **1.** *Adj.* ontogenetic. **2.** *adv.* ontogenetically
onto·logisch *(Philos.)* **1.** *Adv.* ontological. **2.** *adv.* ontologically
Onyx ['o:nyks] **der;** ~[e]s, ~e *(Mineral., Med.)* onyx
o. O. *Abk.* **ohne Ort** n.p.
OP [o:'pe:] **der;** ~[s], ~[s] *Abk.* **Operationssaal**
Op. *Abk.* **Opus** op.
Opa ['o:pa] **der;** ~s, ~s *(fam.)* grandad *(coll./child lang.)*; grandpa *(coll./child lang.)*
opak [o'pa:k] *Adj.* opaque
Opal [o'pa:l] **der;** ~s, ~e opal
opalisieren *itr. V.* opalesce; **~d** opalescent
Op-art ['ɔpla:ɐ̯t] **die;** ~: op art
OPEC ['o:pɛk] **die;** ~ *Abk.* OPEC
Oper ['o:pɐ] **die;** ~, ~n opera; *(Institution, Ensemble)* Opera; *(Opernhaus)* Opera; opera-house; **in die ~ gehen** go to the opera; **an die/zur ~ gehen** *(als Sänger)* become an opera-singer; **quatsch keine ~n!** *(salopp)* don't talk rot! *(sl.)*
Opera *s.* **Opus**
Operateur [opəra'tø:ɐ̯] **der;** ~s, ~e **a)** *(Arzt)* [operating] surgeon; **b)** *(Filmvorführer)* projectionist
Operation [opəra'tsio:n] **die;** ~, ~en operation; **~ gelungen, Patient tot** *(ugs.)* [it was] a brilliant idea, but it hasn't done the trick *(coll.)*
operationalisieren [opəratsionali'zi:rən] *tr. V. (Wissensch., Päd.)* operationalize
Operations-: ~basis die *(bes. Milit.)* base of operations; **~gebiet das** *(Milit., auch fig.)* area of operations; **~narbe die** operation scar; **~saal der** operating-theatre *(Brit.) or* -room; **~schwester die** theatre sister *(Brit.)*; operating-room nurse *(Amer.)*; **~tisch der** operating-table
operativ [opəra'ti:f] **1.** *Adj.; nicht präd.* **a)** *(Med.)* operative; **b)** *(Milit.)* operational. **2.** *adv.* **a)** *(Med.)* by operative surgery; **etw. ~ entfernen** operate to remove sth.; **b)** *(Milit.)* operationally
Operator [opə'ra:tɔr] **der;** ~s, ~[s], **Operatorin die;** ~, ~nen *(DV)* [computer] operator
Operette [opə'rɛtə] **die;** ~, ~n operetta
operettenhaft 1. *Adj.* reminiscent of operetta *postpos.* **2.** *adv.* in a way reminiscent of operetta
Operetten·staat der *(abwertend)* little tin-pot state *(derog.)*
operieren 1. *tr. V.* operate on ⟨*patient*⟩; **jmdn. am Magen ~:** operate on sb.'s stomach; **sich ~ lassen** have an operation. **2.** *itr. V.* operate; **vorsichtig ~** *(vorgehen)* proceed carefully
Opern-: ~arie die [operatic] aria; **~bühne die** opera-house; **~führer der** opera guide; **~glas das** opera-glass[es *pl.*]; **~haus das** opera-house; **~sänger der, ~sängerin die** opera-singer
Opfer ['ɔpfɐ] **das;** ~s, ~ **a)** *(Verzicht)* sacrifice; **ein ~ [für etw.] bringen** make a sacrifice [for sth.]; **kein ~ scheuen** consider no sacrifice too great; **unter großen ~n** by making great sacrifices; **manches ~ auf sich** *(Akk.)* **nehmen** make quite a few sacrifices; **b)** *(Geschädigter)* victim; **das Haus wurde ein ~ der Flammen** *(geh.)* the house fell victim to the flames; **jmdm./einer Sache zum ~ fallen** fall victim to sb./sth.; be the victim of sb./sth.; **c)** *(~gabe)* sacrifice; **jmdm./einer Sache etw. zum ~ bringen** sacrifice sth. to sb./sth.
opfer-, Ọpfer-: ~bereit *Adj.* ⟨*person*⟩ who is ready *or* willing to make sacrifices; **~bereitschaft die** readiness *or* willingness to make sacrifices; **~gabe die** [sacrificial] offering; **~gang der a)** *(kath. Kirche)* offertory procession; **b)** *(geh.)* **seinen ~gang antreten** sacrifice oneself; **~lamm das** sacrificial lamb; **wie ein ~lamm** *(fig. ugs.)* like a lamb to the slaughter; **~mut der** *(geh.)* readiness *or* willingness to make sacrifices
opfern 1. *tr. V.* **a)** *(darbringen)* sacrifice; make a sacrifice of; offer up ⟨*fruit, produce, etc.*⟩; **b)** *(fig.: hingeben)* sacrifice, give up ⟨*time, holiday, money, life*⟩. **2.** *itr. V.* **[den Göttern] ~:** offer sacrifice [to the gods]. **3.** *refl. V.* **a) sich für jmdn./etw. ~:** sacrifice oneself for sb./sth.; **b)** *(ugs. scherzh.)* be the martyr; **wer opfert sich denn und ißt den Nachtisch auf?** who's going to volunteer to finish off the dessert?
Ọpfer-: ~stock der; *Pl.* **~stöcke** offertory box; **~tier das** sacrificial animal; **~tod der** *(geh.)* **den ~tod sterben** sacrifice one's life
Ọpferung die; ~, ~en **a)** sacrifice; **b)** *(kath. Kirche)* offertory
Ọpfer·wille der *s.* **Opfermut**
ọpfer·willig *Adj. s.* **opferbereit**
Opiat [o'pia:t] **das;** ~[e]s, ~e opiate
Opium ['o:piʊm] **das;** ~s *(auch fig.)* opium
Ọpium-: ~höhle die *(ugs.)* opium den; **~krieg der** *(hist.)* Opium War; **~raucher der** opium-smoker; **~rausch der** opium dream; **~sucht die** opium addiction
Opossum [o'pɔsʊm] **das;** ~s, ~s opossum
Opponent [ɔpo'nɛnt] **der;** ~en, ~en, **Opponentin die;** ~, ~nen opponent
opponieren *itr. V.* take the opposite side; **gegen jmdn./etw. ~:** oppose sb./sth.
opportun [ɔpɔr'tu:n] *Adj. (geh.)* appropriate; *(günstig)* advantageous
Opportunismus der; ~: opportunism
Opportunist der; ~en, ~en, **Opportunistin die;** ~, ~nen opportunist
opportunistisch 1. *Adj.* opportunist; opportunistic. **2.** *adv.* opportunistically; **~ handeln** be opportunistic; *(im Einzelfall)* act in an opportunistic fashion
Opportunität [ɔpɔrtuni'tɛ:t] **die;** ~, ~en *(geh.)* appropriateness
Opportunitäts·prinzip das *(Rechtsw.) principle that the public prosecutor has the power to decide whether or not to institute proceedings*
Opposition [ɔpozi'tsio:n] **die;** ~, ~en *(auch Politik, Sprachw., Astron., Schach, Fechten)* opposition; **etw. aus [reiner** *od.* **lauter] ~ tun** do sth. just to be contrary; **~ gegen jmdn./etw. machen** *(ugs.)* oppose sb./sth.; **in die ~ gehen** *(Politik)* go into opposition; **Jupiter und Mars stehen in ~:** Jupiter and Mars are in opposition
oppositionell [ɔpozitsio'nɛl] **1.** *Adj.* oppositional *attrib.* ⟨*group, movement, circle, etc.*⟩; ⟨*newspaper, writer, artist, etc.*⟩ opposed to the government; ⟨*feelings*⟩ of opposition; ⟨*attempts*⟩ at opposition; opposing ⟨*trend, tendency*⟩; **~es Verhalten** opposition; **die seit 1982 ~e SPD** the SPD, in opposition since 1982. **2.** *adv.* **~ eingestellt sein** hold opposing views
Oppositionelle der/die; *adj. Dekl.* member of the opposition; *(Regimekritiker)* dissident
Oppositions-: ~führer der opposition leader; *(in Großbritannien)* Leader of the Opposition; **~partei die** opposition party
Optativ ['ɔptati:f] **der;** ~s, ~e *(Sprachw.)* optative
optieren [ɔp'ti:rən] *itr. V.* **a)** *(Völkerr.)* opt; **für Polen ~:** opt for Polish citizenship; **b)** *(Rechtsw.)* **auf etw.** *(Akk.)* **~:** take an option on sth.
Optik die; ~, ~en **a)** *o. Pl. (Wissenschaft)* optics *sing., no art.*; **b)** *(Fot. ugs.) (Linse)* lens; *(Linsen)* optics *pl.*; lens system; **das ist eine Frage der ~** *(fig.)* it depends on your point of view; **c)** *o. Pl. (Erscheinungsbild)* appearance; **der ~ wegen** for visual effect
Ọptiker der; ~s, ~, **Ọptikerin die;** ~, ~nen optician
Ọptima *s.* **Optimum**
optimal [ɔpti'ma:l] **1.** *Adj.* optimal; optimum *attrib.* **2.** *adv.* **jmdn. ~ beraten** give sb. the best possible advice; **ein Problem ~ lösen** find the optimal *or* optimum solution to a problem
optimieren *tr. V.* optimize
Optimierung die; ~, ~en optimization
Optimismus der; ~: optimism
Optimist der; ~en, ~en, **Optimistin die;** ~, ~nen optimist; **~ sein** be an optimist
optimistisch 1. *Adj.* optimistic. **2.** *adv.* optimistically
Optimum ['ɔptimʊm] **das;** ~s, **Ọptima** *(auch Biol.)* optimum
Option [ɔp'tsio:n] **die;** ~, ~en **a)** *(Völkerr.)* opting; **b)** *(Rechtsw.)* option **(auf + Akk.** on)
optisch 1. *Adj.* optical; visual ⟨*impression*⟩; **eine ~e Täuschung** an optical illusion; **aus ~en Gründen** for [the sake of] optical *or* visual effect; *(fig.)* for [the sake of] effect. **2.** *adv.* optically; visually ⟨*impressive, successful, effective*⟩; **~ wahrnehmbar sein** be perceivable with the eye
opulent [opu'lɛnt] **1.** *Adj.* **a)** sumptuous ⟨*meal, banquet, etc.*⟩; **b)** *(aufwendig [gestaltet])* opulent; lavish ⟨*theatrical production*⟩. **2.** *adv.* opulently ⟨*dressed*⟩; **~ essen** eat a sumptuous meal
Opus ['o:pʊs] **das;** ~, **Opera** ['o:para] opus; *(Gesamtwerk)* œuvre
Orakel [o'ra:kl̩] **das;** ~s, ~ *(auch fig.)* oracle; **in ~n reden** *od.* **sprechen** *(fig.)* talk *or* speak in riddles
orakel·haft *Adj.* oracular
orakeln 1. *tr. V.* **~, daß ...:** make mysterious prophecies that ... **2.** *itr. V.* make mysterious prophecies
oral [o'ra:l] **1.** *Adj.* oral. **2.** *adv.* orally; **~ verkehren** have oral intercourse *or* sex
orange [o'rã:ʒ(ə)] *indekl. Adj.* orange
[1]**Orange das;** ~s, ~ *od. (ugs.)* ~s orange
[2]**Orange die;** ~, ~n *(bes. südd., österr., schweiz.: Apfelsine)* orange

Orangeade [orã'ʒa:də] **die;** ~, ~**n** orangeade
Orangeat [orã'ʒa:t] **das;** ~**s**, ~**e** candied orange-peel
orange·farben, orange·farbig *Adj.* orange[-coloured]
orangen [o'rã:ʒn̩] *Adj.* orange
orangen-, Orangen-: ~**baum** orange-tree; ~**farben,** ~**farbig** *Adj. s.* **orangefarben;** ~**marmelade die** orange marmalade; ~**saft der** orange-juice; ~**schale die** orange-peel *no pl.*
Orangerie [orãʒə'ri:] **die;** ~, ~**n** orangery
Orang-Utan ['o:raŋ'|u:tan] **der;** ~**s**, ~**s** orang-utan
Oranien [o'ra:ni̯ən] **(das);** ~**s** Orange; **Wilhelm von** ~: William of Orange
Oranier der; ~**s**, ~: member of the House of Orange
Oratorium [ora'to:ri̯ʊm] **das;** ~**s, Oratorien** oratorio
Orchester [ɔr'kɛstɐ] **das;** ~**s**, ~: orchestra; *(~graben)* orchestra [pit]
Orchester-: ~**begleitung die** orchestral accompaniment; ~**graben der** orchestra pit; ~**musiker der** orchestral musician
orchestral [ɔrkɛs'tra:l] **1.** *Adj.* orchestral. **2.** *adv.* ~ **begleitet** accompanied by an orchestra
orchestrieren *tr. V. (Musik, auch fig.)* orchestrate
Orchestrierung die; ~, ~**en** *(Musik, auch fig.)* orchestration
Orchidee [ɔrçi'de:(ə)] **die;** ~, ~**n** orchid
Orden ['ɔrdn̩] **der;** ~**s**, ~ **a)** *(Gemeinschaft)* order; **in einen** ~ **eintreten, einem** ~ **beitreten** join an order; become a member of an order; **b)** *(Ehrenzeichen)* decoration; *(Milit.)* decoration; *(in runder Form)* medal; **jmdm. einen** ~ **[für etw.] verleihen** decorate sb. [for sth.]; **ihm wurde der** ~ **pour le Mérite verliehen** he was given the Ordre pour le Mérite; **einen** ~ **bekommen** receive a decoration/medal
orden·geschmückt *Adj.* bemedalled and beribboned
Ordens-: ~**band das;** *Pl.* ~**bänder** ribbon; ~**bruder der** brother [of an/the order]; monk; ~**regel die** rule [of an/the order]; ~**schwester die** sister [of an/the order]; nun; ~**tracht die** habit [of an/the order]; ~**verleihung die** awarding of a/the decoration; **die jährliche** ~**verleihung** the annual award of decorations
ordentlich ['ɔrdn̩tlɪç] **1.** *Adj.* **a)** *(ordnungsliebend)* [neat and] tidy; *(methodisch)* orderly; **b)** *(geordnet)* [neat and] tidy ⟨*room, house, desk, etc.*⟩; neat ⟨*handwriting, clothes*⟩; **c)** *(anständig)* respectable; proper ⟨*manners*⟩; **etwas Ordentliches lernen** learn a proper trade; **d)** *nicht präd. (planmäßig)* regular, ordinary ⟨*meeting*⟩; ~**es Mitglied** full member; ~**es Gericht** court exercising civil and criminal jurisdiction; *s. auch* **Professor a; e)** *(ugs.: richtig)* proper; real; **etwas Ordentliches essen** have some proper food; **eine** ~**e Tracht Prügel** a real good hiding *(coll.)*; **f)** *(ugs.: tüchtig)* **ein** ~**es Stück Kuchen** a nice big piece of cake; **ein** ~**es Stück Arbeit/Weg** a fair old bit of work *(coll.)* /a fair old way *(coll.)*; **die haben ja** ~**e Preise** their prices are steep *(coll.)*; **g)** *(ugs.: recht gut)* decent ⟨*wine, flat, marks, etc.*⟩; **ganz** ~: pretty good. **2.** *adv.* *(geordnet)* tidily; neatly; ⟨*write*⟩ neatly; ~ **aufgeräumt** neatly tidied; **b)** *(anständig)* properly; **c)** *(ugs.: gehörig)* ~ **feiern** have a real good celebration *(coll.)*; ~ **einen heben** *(ugs.)* have a fair few drinks *(coll.)*; **greift** ~ **zu!** tuck in!; **sich** ~ **ausschlafen** have a really good sleep; **letzte Nacht hat es** ~ **geschneit** it really snowed last night; **es jmdm.** ~ **geben** give sb. a piece of one's mind; **d)** *(ugs.: recht gut)* ⟨*ski, speak, etc.*⟩ really well; **ganz** ~ **verdienen** earn a pretty good wage
Ordentlichkeit die; ~: [neatness and] tidiness; *(der Schrift, Kleidung)* neatness; *(methodische Veranlagung)* orderliness
Order ['ɔrdɐ] **die;** ~, ~**s** *od.* ~**n a)** *(Befehl)* order; ~ **haben, etw. zu tun** have orders to do sth.; **sich an seine** ~ **halten** obey one's orders; **b)** *Pl.* ~**s** *(Kaufmannsspr.: Auftrag)* order; **einer Firma eine** ~ **erteilen** place an order with a firm
ordern *tr., itr. V. (Kaufmannsspr.)* order
Order·papier das *(Bankw.)* instrument made out to order *(and transferable by endorsement)*
Ordinal·zahl die ordinal [number]
ordinär [ɔrdi'nɛ:ɐ̯] **1.** *Adj.* **a)** *(abwertend)* vulgar; common; vulgar ⟨*joke, song, expression, language*⟩; cheap and obtrusive ⟨*perfume*⟩; **b)** *nicht präd. (alltäglich)* ordinary. **2.** *adv.* vulgarly; in a vulgar manner
Ordinariat [ɔrdina'ri̯a:t] **das;** ~**[e]s**, ~**e a)** *(kath. Kirche)* ordinariate; **b)** *(Hochschulw.)* chair
Ordinarius [ɔrdi'na:ri̯ʊs] **der;** ~, **Ordinarien a)** *(Professor)* [full] professor *(holding a chair)* **(für** of); **b)** *(kath. Kirche)* ordinary
Ordinate [ɔrdi'na:tə] **die;** ~, ~**n** *(Math.)* ordinate
Ordinaten·achse die *(Math.)* axis of ordinates
Ordination [ɔrdina'tsi̯o:n] **die;** ~, ~**en a)** *(ev., kath. Kirche)* ordination; **b)** *(Med.: Verordnung)* prescription; **c)** *(Med. veralt.: Sprechstunde)* surgery
ordinieren *tr. V.* **a)** *(ev., kath. Kirche)* ordain; **b)** *(Med.)* prescribe
ordnen ['ɔrdnən] **1.** *tr. V.* **a)** arrange; *(systematisieren)* arrange, organize ⟨*ideas, thoughts, material, etc.*⟩; **b)** *(regeln)* regulate ⟨*traffic*⟩; **sein Leben/seine Finanzen** ~: straighten out one's life/put one's finances in order; **seine Angelegenheiten** ~: settle one's affairs; *s. auch* **geordnet. 2.** *refl. V.* form up; **ihre Gedanken ordneten sich** *(fig.)* her thoughts became more collected
Ordner der; ~**s**, ~ **a)** *(Hefter)* file; **b)** *(Aufsichtsperson)* steward; *(bei Demonstrationen)* marshal; steward
Ordnung die; ~, ~**en a)** *o. Pl. (ordentlicher Zustand)* order; tidiness; ~ **halten** keep things tidy; **durch sie kam etwas mehr** ~ **ins Haus** she made the house a little tidier; ~ **in die Papiere bringen** put the papers into order; **hier herrscht** ~: everything is neat and tidy here; **hier herrscht ja eine schöne** ~! *(iron.)* a nice mess we've got here!; **der** ~ **halber** *od.* **wegen** *(weil es sich so gehört)* for the sake of form; ~ **schaffen, für** ~ **sorgen** sort things out; **sehr auf** ~ **halten** set great store by tidiness; ~ **ist das halbe Leben** *(Spr.)* muddle makes trouble; **etw. in** ~ **bringen** sort sth. out; **in** ~ **kommen** sort itself out; **in** ~ **sein** *(ugs.)* be OK *(coll.) or* all right; **ist dein Paß in** ~**?** is your passport in order?; **das Fleisch ist nicht ganz in** ~: the meat has started to go bad; **hier ist etw. nicht in** ~: there's something wrong here; **mit ihr ist etwas nicht in** ~, **sie ist nicht in** ~ *(ugs.)* there's something wrong *or* the matter with her; **jetzt bin ich wieder in** ~ *(ugs.)* I'm better *or* all right now; **sie ist in** ~ *(ugs.: ist nett, verläßlich o. ä.)* she's OK *(coll.)*; **alles [ist] in schönster** *od.* **bester** ~: everything's [just] fine; [things] couldn't be better; **[das] geht [schon] in** ~ *(ugs.)* that'll be OK *(coll.) or* all right; **ich finde es nicht in** ~, **daß ...:** I don't think it's right that ...; **sie scheint es ganz in [der]** ~ **zu finden, wenn ...:** she doesn't seem to mind at all if ...; **in** ~**!** *(ugs.)* OK! *(coll.)*; all right!; **b)** *o. Pl. (geregelter Ablauf)* routine; **hier muß alles seine** ~ **haben** we/they *etc.* like to keep to a routine here; **c)** *o. Pl. (System von Normen)* order; **die** ~ **einer Gemeinschaft** the rules *pl.* of a community; *s. auch* **öffentlich 1; d)** *o. Pl. (Disziplin)* order; **hier/da herrscht** ~: we have some discipline here/they have some discipline there; **sich an** ~ **gewöhnen** get used to discipline; ~ **halten** ⟨*teacher etc.*⟩ keep order; **sehr auf** ~ **halten** be a great disciplinarian; **e)** *o. Pl. (System)* order; *(Struktur)* structure; **f)** *(Formation)* formation; **g)** *(Biol.)* order; **h)** *o. Pl. (Rang)* **eine Straße zweiter** ~: a second-class road; **ein Stern vierter** ~: a fourth-magnitude star; **ein Reinfall/Fehlschlag** *usw.* **erster** ~ *(fig. ugs.)* a disaster/failure *etc.* of the first order *or* water; **i)** *o. Pl. (Math.)* order; **j)** *(Mengenlehre)* ordered set; **k)** *o. Pl. (Gesellschafts~)* order
ordnungs-, Ordnungs-: ~**amt das** *[offices of] municipal authority responsible for registering residents, regulating public events such as demonstrations and galas, supervising trading standards, and licensing street traders, street musicians, etc.*; ~**gemäß 1.** *Adj.* ⟨*conduct etc.*⟩ in accordance with the regulations; **alles ging seinen** ~**gemäßen Gang** everything took its proper course; **2.** *adv.* in accordance with the regulations; ~**halber** *Adv.* as a matter of form; ~**hüter der** *(scherzh.)* custodian of the law *(joc.)*; ~**liebe die** liking for neatness and tidiness; ~**liebend** *Adj.* ⟨*person*⟩ who likes to see things neat and tidy; ~**ruf der** call to order; **jmdm. einen** ~**ruf erteilen** call sb. to order; ~**sinn der** liking for neatness and tidiness; ~**strafe die** *(Rechtsw.)* penalty for contempt of court; ~**widrig** *(Rechtsw.)* **1.** *Adj.* ⟨*actions, behaviour, etc.*⟩ contravening the regulations; illegal ⟨*parking*⟩; ~**widriges Verhalten im Verkehr** an infringement of traffic regulations; **2.** *adv.* ~**widrig parken** park illegally; ~**widrig handeln** act in contravention of the regulations; contravene *or* infringe the regulations; ~**widrigkeit die** *(Rechtsw.)* infringement of the regulations; ~**zahl die** ordinal [number]; *(Physik)* atomic number
Ordonnanz [ɔrdɔ'nants] **die;** ~, ~**en** *(Milit.)* orderly
Ordonnanz·offizier der *(Milit.)* aide[-de-camp]
Oregano [o're:gano] **der;** ~: oregano
ORF [o:|ɛr'ɛf] **der;** ~ *Abk.* **Österreichischer Rundfunk** Austrian Radio
Organ [ɔr'ga:n] **das;** ~**s**, ~**e a)** *(Anat., Biol.)* organ; **ein/kein** ~ **für etw. haben** *(fig.)* have a feeling/no feeling for sth.; **b)** *(ugs.: Stimme)* voice; **er hat ein furchtbar lautes** ~: his voice is awfully loud; **c)** *(Zeitung)* organ *(formal)*; **d)** *(Institution)* organ; *(Mensch)* agent; **die Polizei ist nur ausführendes** ~: the police act only as an executive agency; **staatliche** ~**e** organs of state; **bewaffnete** ~**e der DDR** armed defensive forces of the GDR
Organ·bank die; *Pl.* ~**banken** *(Med.)* organ bank
Organdy [ɔr'gandi] **der;** ~**s** organdy
Organ·empfänger der *(Med.)* organ recipient; recipient of an/the organ
Organisation [ɔrganɪza'tsi̯o:n] **die;** ~, ~**en** organization
Organisations-: ~**büro das** organizational headquarters *sing. or pl.*; ~**grad der** level of *(trade union etc.)* membership; **gewerkschaftlicher** ~**grad** degree of unionization; ~**talent das a)** *(Fähigkeit)* talent for organization; **b)** *(Mensch)* person with a talent for organization; **ein [ausgesprochenes]** ~**talent sein** have a [marked] talent for organization
Organisator [ɔrgani'za:tɔr] **der;** ~**s**, ~**en** [-'to:rən] organizer
organisatorisch 1. *Adj.* organizational. **2.** *adv.* organizationally; ~ **begabt sein** have a talent for organization
organisch 1. *Adj.* **a)** *(auch Chemie)* organic; ~**e Chemie** organic chemistry; **b)** *(Med.)* organic; physical. **2.** *adv.* **a)** organ-

ically; **sich ~ in etw.** *(Akk.)* **einfügen** form an organic part of sth.; **b)** *(Med.)* organically; physically

organisierbar *Adj.* organizable; **etw. ist ~:** sth. can be organized

organisieren 1. *tr. V.* **a)** *(vorbereiten, aufbauen)* organize; **b)** *(ugs.: beschaffen)* get [hold of]. **2.** *itr. V.* **gut ~ können** be a good organizer. **3.** *refl. V.* organize (**zu** into); **er will sich ~:** he wants to join the union *etc.*

organisiert *Adj.* organized ⟨*system etc.*⟩; **gewerkschaftlich ~e Arbeiter** unionized workers; **sind Sie politisch/gewerkschaftlich ~?** are you a member of a political party/trade union?

Organismus der; Organismen organism

Organist der; ~en, ~en, Organistin die; ~, ~nen organist; *s. auch* **-in**

Organ-: ~spender der organ donor; **~transplantation die, ~verpflanzung die** organ transplantation

Organza [ɔr'gantsa] **der; ~s** organza

Orgasmus [ɔr'gasmʊs] **der; ~, Orgasmen** orgasm

orgastisch *Adj.* orgastic; orgasmic

Orgel ['ɔrgl̩] **die; ~, ~n** organ; **~ spielen** play the organ

Orgel-: ~bauer der organ-builder; **~konzert das** organ concerto; *(Solo)* organ recital; **~musik die** organ music

orgeln *itr. V.* **a)** *(Drehorgel spielen)* grind the organ; **b)** *(ugs.: tönen)* ⟨*barrel-organ, song*⟩ grind on; **c)** *(Jägerspr.: schreien)* bell

Orgel-: ~pfeife die organ-pipe; **[dastehen] wie die ~pfeifen** *(scherzh.)* [stand in a row] from the tallest to the shortest; **~punkt der** *(Musik)* pedal *or* organ point; **~werk das** work for the organ

orgiastisch 1. *Adj.* orgiastic. **2.** *adv.* orgiastically

Orgie ['ɔrgiə] **die; ~, ~n** *(auch fig.)* orgy; **eine ~ feiern** have an orgy

Orient ['o:riɛnt] **der; ~s a)** *(Vorder- u. Mittelasien)* Middle East and south-western Asia *(including Afghanistan and Nepal);* **der Vordere ~:** the Middle East; **b)** *(veralt.: Osten)* Orient

Orientale [oriɛn'ta:lə] **der; ~n, ~n** *s.* **Orient a:** *man from the Middle East [or south-western Asia]*

Orientalin die; ~, ~nen *s.* **Orient a:** *woman from the Middle East [or south-western Asia]: s. auch* **-in**

orientalisch *Adj.* oriental

Orientalist der; ~en, ~en, Orientalistin die; ~, ~nen orientalist; *s. auch* **-in**

Orientalistik die; ~: [Middle Eastern and] oriental studies

orientieren 1. *refl. V.* **a)** *(sich zurechtfinden)* get one's bearings; **ich muß mich zuerst ~, wo ich eigentlich bin** first I must get my bearings [and find out where I am]; **sich an etw.** *(Dat.)* **/nach einer Karte ~:** get one's bearings by sth./using a map; **b)** *(sich unterrichten)* **sich über etw.** *(Akk.)* **~:** inform oneself about sth.; **c)** *(sich ausrichten)* **sich an etw.** *(Dat.)* **~:** be oriented towards sth.; ⟨*policy, advertising*⟩ be geared towards sth.; **politisch links/rechts orientiert sein** lean towards the left/right politically; **sich an bestimmten Leitbildern ~:** follow certain models; **d)** *(DDR: hinlenken)* **sich auf jmdn./etw. ~:** concentrate [one's attention] on sb./sth.; **sich auf etw.** *(Akk.)* **~** ⟨*factory*⟩ go over to sth. **2.** *tr. V.* **a)** *(unterrichten)* inform (**über + *Akk.*** about); **die Gespräche haben nur ~den Charakter** the talks are only for the purposes of exchanging information; **b)** *(ausrichten)* **sein Ziel nach etw. ~:** base one's aims on sth.; **gewerkschaftlich orientierte Interessen** interests centred on the trade unions; **c)** *(DDR: hinlenken, hinweisen)* **jmdn. auf etw.** *(Akk.)* **~:** direct sb.'s attention to sth.; **alle Kräfte auf eine Politik des Friedens ~:** concentrate every effort on a policy of promoting peace. **3.** *itr. V.* **a)** *(unterrichten)* **über etw.** *(Akk.)* **~:** report on sth.; **b)** *(DDR)* **auf etw.** *(Akk.)* **~** concentrate [one's/its attention] on sth.

-orientiert *adj.* orientated towards ...

Orientierung die; ~ a) *(Orientierungssinn, -möglichkeit)* **hier ist die ~ schwer** it's difficult to get your bearings here; **die ~ verlieren** lose one's bearings; **b)** *(Unterrichtung)* **zu Ihrer ~:** for your information; **die ~ der Bevölkerung** informing the population (**über + *Akk.*** about); **c)** *(das Sichausrichten)* orientation (**auf + *Akk.*** towards, **an + *Dat.*** according to); **d)** *(DDR: Hinwendung)* **die ~ auf etw.** *(Akk.)* concentration on sth.; **jmdm. die ~ auf etw.** *(Akk.)* **geben** direct sb.'s attention to sth.

orientierungs-, Orientierungs-: ~hilfe die aid to orientation; **als ~hilfe legen wir Ihnen eine Karte bei** we enclose a map to help you find your way; **~los** *Adj. (auch fig.)* disoriented; **~los umherirren** wander around in a state of disorientation; **~punkt der** landmark by which one can/could find one's bearings; *(fig.)* point of reference; **~sinn der** sense of direction; **~stufe die** *(Schulw.) s.* **Förderstufe**

Orient- ['o:riɛnt-]: **~tabak der** Oriental tobacco; **~teppich der** oriental carpet; *(Läufer)* oriental rug

orig. *Abk.* **original** genuine

Origano [o'ri:gano] **der; ~:** oregano

original [origi'na:l] **1.** *Adj.* original; *(echt)* genuine; authentic. **2.** *adv.* **~ indische Seide** genuine Indian silk; **etw. ~ übertragen** broadcast sth. live

Original das; ~s, ~e a) *(Urschrift o. ä.)* original; **b)** *(eigenwilliger Mensch)* character

original-, Original-: ~aus·gabe die original *or* first edition; **~fassung die** original version; **in der spanischen ~fassung** in the original Spanish version; **~getreu 1.** *Adj.* faithful *or* true [to the original] *postpos.;* **2.** *adv.* in a manner faithful *or* true to the original

Originalität [originali'tɛ:t] **die; ~ a)** *(Echtheit)* genuineness; authenticity; **b)** *(Einmaligkeit)* originality

Original-: ~titel der original-language title; **~ton der: Reportageausschnitte im ~ton von 1936** excerpts from news reports with the original 1936 soundtrack; **„~ton DDR-Fernsehen"** 'GDR television commentary'

originär [origi'nɛ:ɐ̯] *Adj.; adv.* original

originell [origi'nɛl] **1.** *Adj. (ursprünglich)* original; *(neu)* novel; *(ugs.: witzig)* witty, funny, comical ⟨*story*⟩; comical, funny ⟨*costume*⟩; **ein ~er Kopf sein** have an original mind. **2.** *adv. (ursprünglich)* ⟨*write, argue*⟩ with originality; *(ugs.: witzig)* ⟨*write, argue*⟩ wittily

Orkan [ɔr'ka:n] **der; ~[e]s, ~e** hurricane; *(fig.)* thunderous storm; **der Sturm schwoll zum ~ an** the storm rose to hurricane force

orkan·artig *Adj.* ⟨*winds, gusts*⟩ of almost hurricane force; **~er Beifall** *(fig.)* thunderous applause

Orkney·inseln ['ɔ:knɪ-] *Pl.* Orkney Islands; Orkneys

Orkus ['ɔrkʊs] **der; ~** *(geh.)* Orcus; Hades

Ornament [ɔrna'mɛnt] **das; ~[e]s, ~e** *(Kunstw.)* ornament

ornamental [ɔrnamɛn'ta:l] *(Kunstw.) Adj.* ornamental; decorative

Ornat [ɔr'na:t] **der; ~[e]s, ~e** *(eines Priesters)* vestments *pl.; (eines Hochschullehrers)* academic dress; *(eines Richters)* official robes *pl.;* **in vollem ~** *(ugs. scherzh.)* dressed [up] to the nines

Ornithologe [ɔrnito'lo:gə] **der; ~n, ~n** ornithologist

Ornithologie die; ~: ornithology *no art.*

Ornithologin die; ~, ~nen ornithologist

ornithologisch *Adj.* ornithological

¹Ort [ɔrt] **der; ~[e]s, ~e a)** *(Platz)* place; **an öffentlichen ~en** in public places; **etw. an seinem ~ lassen** leave sth. where it is/was; **ein ~ des Schreckens/der Stille** a place of terror/quiet; **~ der Handlung: ...:** the scene of the action is ...; **an den ~ des Verbrechens zurückkehren** return to the scene of the crime; **an ~ und Stelle** there and then; **an ~ und Stelle sein/ankommen** *(an der gewünschten Stelle)* be/arrive there; **höheren ~[e]s** higher up; **am angegebenen ~** *(Schrift- u. Druckw.)* in the same work; **der gewisse** *od.* **stille** *od.* **bewußte ~** *(ugs. verhüll.)* the smallest room *(coll. euphem.); s. auch* **Örtchen; b)** *(~schaft) (Dorf)* village; *(Stadt)* town; **am ~ wohnen** live in the village/town; **von ~ zu ~:** from place to place; **das beste Hotel am ~:** the best hotel in the place

²Ort *in* **vor ~:** on the spot; *(Bergmannsspr.)* at the [coal-]face

Örtchen ['œrtçən] **das; ~s, ~** *(ugs. verhüll.)* **das ~:** the smallest room *(coll. euphem.);* **aufs ~ müssen** have to pay a visit *(coll. euphem.)*

orten *tr. V. (bes. Flugw., Seew.)* find the position of

orthodox [ɔrto'dɔks] *Adj.* **a)** *(Rel.)* orthodox; **die ~en Kirchen** the Orthodox Churches; **b)** *(starr)* rigid; **c)** *(strenggläubig)* strict; **d)** *(fig.: traditionell)* orthodox

Orthodoxie [ɔrtodɔ'ksi:] **die; ~** *(Rel.)* orthodoxy

Orthographie die; ~; ~n orthography

orthographisch 1. *Adj.* orthographic; **~e Fehler** spelling mistakes. **2.** *adv.* orthographically; **~ richtig schreiben** spell correctly

Orthopäde [ɔrto'pɛ:də] **der; ~n, ~n** orthopaedist; orthopaedic specialist

Orthopädie [ɔrtopɛ'di:] **die; ~, ~n a)** *o. Pl.* orthopaedics *sing., no art.;* **Facharzt für ~:** *s.* **Orthopäde; b)** *(ugs.: Abteilung)* orthopaedic department; **auf/in der ~ liegen** be a patient in the orthopaedic department

Orthopädin die; ~, ~nen *s.* **Orthopäde**

orthopädisch 1. *Adj.* orthopaedic. **2.** *adv.* orthopaedically

örtlich ['œrtlɪç] **1.** *Adj.* **a)** *(Med.)* local ⟨*anaesthetic etc.*⟩; **b)** *(begrenzt)* local. **2.** *adv.* **a)** *(Med.)* locally; **~ betäubt werden** be given a local anaesthetic; **b)** *(begrenzt)* **~ begrenzte Kampfhandlungen** [limited] local encounters; **~ verschieden sein** vary from place to place

Örtlichkeit die; ~, ~en a) *(Gebiet)* locality; **sich mit den ~en vertraut machen** get to know the area; **b)** *(Stelle)* place; **c)** *s.* **Örtchen**

orts-, Orts-: ~an·gabe die indication of place; **~ansässig** *Adj.* local; **seine Familie ist schon lange ~ansässig** his family has lived locally for a long time; **die ~ansässigen** the local residents; **~aus·gang der** end of the village/town; **~bestimmung die** *(Geogr.)* determination of the latitude and longitude of a place

Ortschaft die; ~, ~en *(Dorf)* village; *(Stadt)* town; **geschlossene ~:** built-up area

orts-, Orts-: ~ein·gang der entrance to the village/town; **~fremd** *Adj.* **a)** *(nicht ~ansässig)* **~fremde Personen** visitors to the village/town; **die ~fremden Besucher** visitors from outside the village/town; **b)** *(nicht ~kundig)* **~fremd sein** be a stranger [to the village/town]; **Ortsfremde** *Pl.* strangers [to the village/town]; **~gebunden** *Adj.* tied to the locality *postpos.;* **~gespräch das** *(Fernspr.)* local call; **~gruppe die** local branch; **~kenntnis die** knowledge of the place; **[gute] ~kenntnisse haben** know the place [well]; **~kranken·kasse die** compulsory medical *or* health insurance scheme *(organized at district level);* **~kundig** *Adj.* **ein ~kundiger Führer** a guide who knows the place well; **ein Ortskundiger**

someone who knows the place well; **~name der** place-name; **~netz das a)** *(Fernspr.)* local exchange network; **b)** *(Energiewirtsch.)* local distribution network; **~netz·kennzahl die** *(Fernspr.)* dialling code; area code *(Amer.)*; **~schild das** place-name sign; **~sinn der** sense of direction; **~tarif der** local rate; **~teil der** area [of the village/town]; **~üblich** *Adj.* local ‹*customs, practices*›; **die ~übliche Miete** the rents *pl.* here/there; **~verkehr der a)** *(Straßenverkehr)* local traffic; **b)** *(Post)* local postal service; **c)** *(Telefon)* local telephone service; **~wechsel der** change of locality; **ein ~wechsel wird dir guttun** a change of environment will do you good; **~zeit die** local time; **~zu·lage die, ~zu·schlag der** *salary weighting allowance for employees in the public services*

Ortung die; ~, ~en *(bes. Flugw., Seew.)* **die ~ von feindlichen Schiffen/Flugzeugen** finding the position of enemy ships/aircraft

Öse ['ø:zə] **die; ~, ~n** eye; *(an Schuh, Stiefel)* eyelet

osmanisch [ɔs'ma:nɪʃ] *Adj. (hist.)* **das Osmanische Reich** the Ottoman Empire

Osmose [ɔs'mo:zə] **die; ~, ~n** *(chem., Bot.)* osmosis

OSO *Abk.* **Ostsüdost[en]** ESE

[1]**Ost** [ɔst] *o. Art.; o. Pl.* **a)** *(bes. Seemannsspr., Met.)* east; *s. auch* **Osten a**; **b)** *(Gebiet)* East; **in ~ und West** in the East and [in] the West; **aus ~ und West** from East and West; **c)** *(Politik)* East; **~ und West** the East and the West; **zwischen ~ und West** between [the] East and [the] West; **d)** *einem Substantiv nachgestellt* East; **Berlin (Ost)** East Berlin

[2]**Ost der; ~[e]s, ~e** *(Seemannsspr.)* easterly; *(dichter.)* east wind

[3]**Ost** *o. Art.; o. Pl. (ugs.: ~geld)* **in ~ bezahlen** pay in East German marks; **zehn Mark ~:** ten East German marks

ost-, Ost-: ~afrika (das) East Africa; **~asien (das)** East *or* Eastern Asia; **~asiatisch** *Adj.* East Asian

Ost-Berlin, Ost·berlin (das) East Berlin

Ost·berliner 1. der East Berliner. **2.** *Adj.; nicht präd.* East Berlin

ost-, Ost-: ~besuch der *(ugs.)* visitor/visitors from East Germany; **~block der;** *o. Pl.* Eastern bloc; **~block·staat der** Eastern-bloc state; **~deutsch 1.** *Adj.* **a)** Eastern German; **b)** *(politisch)* East German; **2.** *adv.* in an Eastern German manner; **~deutsche der/die a)** *(Politik)* East German; **b)** *(Geogr.)* Eastern German; **~deutschland (das) a)** *(Politik)* East Germany; **b)** *(Geogr.)* Eastern Germany; **~elbisch** *Adj.* from east of the Elbe *postpos.* *(usu. referring to the conservative landowners in 19th-century Prussia)*

Osten der; ~s a) *(Richtung)* east; **nach ~:** eastwards; **aus** *od.* **von ~:** from the east; *s. auch* **Norden a**; **b)** *(Gegend)* eastern part; **aus dem ~:** from the east; **c)** *(Geogr.)* **der ~:** the East; **der Ferne ~:** the Far East; **der Mittlere ~:** south-western Asia *(including Afghanistan and Nepal)*; **der Nahe ~:** the Middle East; **d)** *(Politik)* **der ~** *(der Ostblock)* the East; *(die DDR)* the East; East Germany

Ost·ende [ɔst'|ɛndə] **(das); ~s** Ostend

ostentativ [ɔstɛnta'ti:f] *(geh.)* **1.** *Adj.* pointed ‹*absence, silence*›; overt ‹*hostility*›; exaggerated ‹*heartiness*›; studied ‹*calm, casualness*›; ostentatious ‹*gesture*›. **2.** *adv.* pointedly; ‹*embrace*› ostentatiously

Oster-: ~ei das Easter egg; **~feier·tag der** *in* **über die ~feiertage** over Easter; on Easter Sunday and [Easter] Monday; **der erste/zweite ~feiertag** Easter Sunday/Monday; **~fest das** Easter [holiday]; **~glocke die** daffodil; **~hase der** Easter hare *(said to bring children their Easter Eggs)*; **~insel die** Easter Island; **~kerze die** *(kath. Rel.)* paschal *or* Easter candle; **~lamm das** Paschal lamb

österlich ['ø:stɐlɪç] **1.** *Adj.* Easter *attrib.* **2.** *adv.* **~ geschmückt** decorated for Easter

Oster-: ~marsch der Easter march *(against war and nuclear weapons)*; **~montag der** Easter Monday *no. def. art.*; *s. auch* **Dienstag**

Ostern ['o:stɐn] **das; ~, ~:** Easter; **Frohe** *od.* **Fröhliche ~:** Happy Easter!; **diese/letzte/nächste ~:** this/last/next Easter; **zu** *od.* *(bes. südd.)* **an ~:** at Easter; **[zu/über] ~ Besuch bekommen** have people to stay at/over Easter; **zu ~ einen Kuchen backen** bake a cake for Easter; **wenn ~ und Pfingsten** *od.* **Weihnachten zusammenfallen** *od.* **auf einen Tag fallen** *(ugs.)* not this side of doomsday *(coll.)*

Österreich ['ø:stəraiç] **(das); ~s** Austria; **~-Ungarn** *(hist.)* Austria-Hungary

Österreicher der; ~s, ~, Österreicherin die; ~, ~nen Austrian; **er/sie ist Österreicher/Österreicherin** he/she is Austrian; *s. auch* **-in**

österreichisch *Adj.* Austrian; **das Österreichische** what is Austrian; *(Sprache)* Austrian German; **~-ungarisch** *(hist.)* Austro-Hungarian; *s. auch* **deutsch; Deutsch**

Oster-: ~sonntag der Easter Sunday *no def. art.*; *s. auch* **Dienstag**; **~spiel das** Easter play; **~woche die** week before Easter; **~zeit die: in der ~zeit** at Easter time

ost-, Ost-: ~europa (das) Eastern Europe; **~europäisch** *Adj.* East[ern] European; **~europäische Zeit** Eastern European Time; **~flanke die** *(Milit., Geogr.)* eastern flank; *(Met.)* eastern edge

Ost·friesische Inseln *Pl.* East Frisian Islands

Ost·friesland (das); ~s East Friesland; Ostfriesland

Ost-: ~gebiet das a) *(Osten)* eastern part; **b)** *Pl. former German territories east of the Oder-Neisse line*; **~geld das;** *o. Pl. (ugs.)* East German money; **~germanisch** *Adj.* East Germanic; **~gote der** Ostrogoth; **~hang der** eastern slope; **~jude der** East[ern] European Jew; **~kirche die** Eastern Church; **~kolonisation die** *(hist.) German colonization of Eastern Europe in the Middle Ages*; **~küste die** east[ern] coast

Ostler ['ɔstlɐ] **der; ~s, ~, Ostlerin die; ~, ~en** *(ugs.)* East German

östlich ['œstlɪç] **1.** *Adj.* **a)** *(im Osten)* eastern; **15 Grad ~er Länge** 15 degrees east [longitude]; **~st** easternmost; **das ~e Ufer** the east bank; **der ~ste Punkt** the most easterly point; **b)** *(nach, aus dem Osten)* easterly; **c)** *(aus dem Osten kommend, für den Osten typisch)* Eastern; **d)** *(politisch)* Eastern; ‹*delegates, spies, etc.*› from the East; ‹*infiltration*› by the East; ‹*influence, policies*› of the East. **2.** *adv.* eastwards; **~ von ...:** [to the] east of ... **3.** *Präp. mit Gen.* [to the] east of

ost-, Ost-: [1]**~mark die** *(ugs.)* East German mark; [2]**~mark die;** *o. Pl. (hist.)* East March; [1]**~nord·ost** [--'-] *o. Art.; o. Pl. (Seemannsspr., Met.)* east-north-east; *s. auch* [1]**Nord a**; [2]**~nord·ost** [--'-] **der** *(Seemannsspr.)* east-north-easter[ly]; **~nord·osten** [--'--] **der** east-north-east; *s. auch* **Norden a**; **~politik die** Ostpolitik *(West German policy towards Eastern Europe, and towards East Germany in particular)*; **~preuße der** East Prussian; **~preußen (das)** East Prussia; **~preußisch** *Adj.* East Prussian

Östrogen [œstro'ge:n] **das; ~s, ~e** *(Physiol.)* oestrogen

Ost·see die; *o. Pl.* Baltic [Sea]

Ostsee- Baltic

ost-, Ost-: ~seite die eastern side; [1]**~süd·ost** [--'-] *o. Art.; o. Pl. (Seemannsspr., Met.)* east-south-east; *s. auch* [1]**Nord a**; [2]**~süd·ost** [--'-] **der** *(Seemannsspr.)* east-south-easter[ly]; **~süd·osten** [--'--] **der** east-south-east; *s. auch* **Norden a**; **~teil der** eastern part; **~verträge** *Pl. (Politik)* treaties with the Eastern bloc; **~wärts** *Adv.* **a)** *(nach Osten)* eastwards; **b)** *(im Osten)* to the east; **~-West-Dialog der** *(Politik)* East-West dialogue; **~-West-Konflikt der** *(Politik)* East-West conflict; **~westlich 1.** *Adj.* east-west *attrib.*; from east to west *postpos.*; **2.** *adv.* east-west; [from] east to west; **~wind der** east[erly] wind; **~zone die a)** *(veralt.: sowjetische Besatzungszone)* Eastern zone; **b)** *(hist., noch abwertend: DDR)* **die ~zone** the East

Oszillation [ɔstsɪla'tsio:n] **die; ~, ~en** *(Physik, auch fig.)* oscillation

oszillieren [ɔstsɪ'li:rən] *itr. V. (Physik, auch fig.)* oscillate

Oszillograph der; ~en, ~en *(Physik)* oscillograph

O-Ton *der s.* **Originalton**

[1]**Otter** ['ɔtɐ] **der; ~s, ~** *(Fisch~)* otter

[2]**Otter die; ~, ~n** *(Viper)* adder; viper

Ottern·gezücht das *(veralt. abwertend)* brood of vipers

Otto ['ɔto] **der; ~s, ~s** *(salopp)* whopper *(sl.)*; *s. auch* **flott; Normalverbraucher**

Ottomane [ɔto'ma:nə] **die; ~, ~n** *(veralt.)* ottoman

Otto·motor der Otto engine

Ottone [ɔ'to:nə] **der; ~n, ~n** *(hist.)* Ottonian *(Saxon emperor, esp. Otto I, II, or III)*

ÖTV [ø:te:'fau] **die; ~** *Abk.* **Gewerkschaft öffentliche Dienste, Transport und Verkehr** union of transport and public-service workers

Output ['autpʊt] **der** *od.* **das; ~s, ~s** output

Ouvertüre [uvɛr'ty:rə] **die; ~, ~n** *(auch fig.)* overture (+ *Gen.* to)

oval [o'va:l] *Adj.* oval

Oval das; ~s, ~e oval

Ovation [ova'tsio:n] **die; ~, ~en** ovation; **jmdm. ~en darbringen** give sb. an ovation

Overall ['oʊvərɔ:l] **der; ~s, ~s** overalls *pl.*

Ovid [o'vi:t] **(der)** Ovid

ÖVP [ø:fau'pe:] **die; ~** *Abk.* **Österreichische Volkspartei** Austrian People's Party

Ovulation [ovula'tsio:n] **die; ~, ~en** *(Zool., Physiol.)* ovulation

Ovulations·hemmer der; ~s, ~ *(Med.)* anovulant

Oxid, Oxid- *(Chemie) s.* **Oxyd, Oxyd-**

Oxyd [ɔ'ksy:t] **das; ~[e]s, ~e** *(Chemie)* oxide

Oxydation [ɔksyda'tsio:n] **die; ~, ~en** *(Chemie, Physik)* oxidation

oxydieren 1. *itr. V.; auch mit sein (Chemie, Physik)* oxidize. **2.** *tr. V. (Chemie)* oxidize

Ozean ['o:tsea:n] **der; ~s, ~e** *(auch fig.)* ocean

Ozean·dampfer der ocean-going steamer; *(für Passagiere)* ocean liner

Ozeanien [otse'a:niən] **(das); ~s** Oceania

ozeanisch *Adj.* oceanic; *(Ozeanien betreffend)* Oceanic

Ozeanographie [otseanogra'fi:] **die; ~:** oceanography *no art.*

Ozelot ['o:tselɔt] **der; ~s, ~e** *od.* **~s a)** *(Tier, Fell)* ocelot; **b)** *(Kleidungsstück)* ocelot coat/jacket *etc.*

Ozon [o'tso:n] **der** *od.* **das; ~s** ozone; **lieber warmer Mief als kalter ~!** *(ugs. scherzh.)* I'd rather be breathing a warm fug than cold fresh air

Ozon-: ~gürtel der ozone layer; **~loch das** *(ugs.)* hole in the ozone layer

P

p, P [pe] **das; ~, ~:** p/P; *s. auch* **a, A**
Pa [pa] **der; ~s, ~s** *(fam. veralt.)* dad *(coll.)*
p. A. *Abk. (österr.)* **per Adresse** c/o
paar [pa:ɐ̯] *indekl. Indefinitpron.* **ein ~ ...:** a few ...; *(zwei od. drei)* a couple of ...; a few ...; **ein ~ hundert Bücher** *usw.* a few hundred/a couple of hundred books *etc.*; **ein ~ waren dagegen** a few [people]/a couple [of people] were against [it]; **in ein ~ Tagen** in a few/a couple of days[' time]; **ein ~ Male** a few times/a couple of times; **deine ~ Mark** the few marks/couple of marks you've got; **die ~ Male, die ich dort war** the few times I've been there; **alle ~ Minuten** every few minutes/every couple of minutes; **du kriegst gleich ein ~ [gelangt]** *(ugs.)* I'll stick one on you *(coll.)*; *s. auch* **Zeile a**
Paar das; ~[e]s, ~e a) pair; *(Mann und Frau, Tanz~)* couple; **sich in** *od.* **zu ~en aufstellen** line up in pairs; **b)** *(Tiere, Dinge)* pair; **ein ~ Würstchen** two sausages; a couple of sausages; **ein ~ Schuhe** a pair of shoes; **zwei ~ Socken** two pairs of socks; **ein ~ Hosen** *(ugs.)* a pair of trousers
paaren 1. *refl. V.* **a)** *(sich begatten)* ⟨*animals*⟩ mate; ⟨*people*⟩ couple, copulate; **b)** *(sich verbinden)* **sich mit etw. ~:** be combined with sth. **2.** *tr. V.* **a)** *(kreuzen)* mate; **b)** *(zusammenstellen)* pair; **c)** *(verbinden)* combine **(mit** with**)**
Paarhufer der; ~s, ~ *(Zool.)* even-toed ungulate *(Zool.)*; cloven-hoofed animal
paarig *(bes. Biol., Anat.)* **1.** *Adj.* paired *attrib.*; **~ sein** occur in pairs. **2.** *adv.* **~ angeordnet** arranged in pairs *postpos.*
paar-, Paar-: ~lauf der, ~laufen das pair-skating; pairs *pl.*; **~mal** *Adv.* **ein ~mal** a few times; *(zwei- oder dreimal)* a couple of *or* a few times; **die ~mal** the few times; **~reim der** *(Verslehre)* rhyming couplets *pl.*
Paarung die; ~, ~en a) *(Zool.)* mating; **b)** *(das Zusammenstellen)* pairing; **die ~ der Mannschaften für das Endturnier** deciding which teams will/would play each other in the finals; **c)** *(das Verbinden)* combination
Paarungs-: ~verhalten das *(Zool.)* mating behaviour; **~zeit die** *(Zool.)* mating-season
paar·weise 1. *Adv.* in pairs. **2.** *adj.* ⟨*arrangement etc.*⟩ in pairs
Paar·zeher der; ~s, ~ *(Zool.) s.* **Paarhufer**
Pacht [paxt] **die; ~, ~en a)** *(Nutzung)* **etw. in ~ nehmen** lease sth.; take sth. on lease; **etw. in ~ haben** have sth. on lease; **etw. in ~ geben** lease sth.; let sth. on lease; **b)** *(Vertrag)* lease; **c)** *(Miete)* rent
Pacht·brief der lease
pachten *tr. V.* lease; take a lease on; **jmdn./etw. [für sich] gepachtet haben** *(fig. ugs.)* have got a monopoly on sb./sth. *(coll.)*
Pächter ['pɛçtɐ] **der; ~s, ~, Pächterin die; ~, ~nen** leaseholder; lessee; *(eines Hofes)* tenant
Pacht·geld das rent
Pachtung die; ~, ~en leasing
Pacht-: ~vertrag der lease; **~zins der** rent
¹Pack [pak] **der; ~[e]s, ~e** *od.* **Päcke** ['pɛkə] pile; *(zusammengeschnürt)* bundle; *(Packung)* pack; *(Kartenspiel)* pack *(Brit.)*; deck *(Amer.)*
²Pack das; ~[e]s *(ugs. abwertend)* rabble; riff-raff; **~ schlägt sich, ~ verträgt sich** *(ugs.)* rabble *or* riff-raff like that are at each other's throats one minute and the best of friends [again] the next
Päckchen ['pɛkçən] **das; ~s, ~ a)** *(kleines Paket)* package; small parcel; *(Bündel)* packet; bundle; *(Postw.)* small parcel *(below a specified weight)*; **sein ~ zu tragen haben** *(fig. ugs.)* have one's troubles; **b)** *s.* **Packung a**
Pack·eis das pack-ice
packeln ['pakl̩n] *itr. V. (österr. abwertend)* make *or* do a deal/deals
packen 1. *tr. V.* **a)** pack; **etw. in einen Koffer/ein Paket ~:** pack *or* put sth. in[to] a suitcase/put sth. in[to] a parcel; **etw. aus etw. ~:** unpack sth. from sth.; **sich/jmdn. ins Bett ~** *(ugs.)* go to bed/put sb. to bed; **der Bus war gepackt voll** *(fig. ugs.)* the bus was jam-packed *(coll.)*; **b)** *(fassen)* grab [hold of]; seize; **jmdn. am** *od.* **beim Kragen ~:** grab [hold of] *or* seize sb. by the collar; **eine Windbö packte das Auto** a gust of wind caught the car; *s. auch* **Ehre; c)** *(überkommen)* **Furcht/Angst** *usw.* **packte ihn/er wurde von Furcht/Angst** *usw.* **gepackt** he was seized with fear *etc.*; **es hat ihn gepackt** *(ugs.)* he's got it bad *(coll.)*; **d)** *(fesseln)* enthral; ⟨*thriller, crime story, etc.*⟩ grip; **ein ~des Rennen** a thrilling race; **e)** *(ugs.: schaffen)* **ein Examen ~:** manage to get through an exam *(coll.)*; **es ~:** make a go of it; **~ wir's noch?** are we going to make it?; **einen Gegner ~** *(Sportjargon: besiegen)* get the better of an opponent; **f)** *(ugs.: begreifen)* get *(coll.)*; **g)** *(salopp: weggehen)* **~ wir's?** shall we push off? *(sl.)*. **2.** *itr. V. (Koffer usw. ~)* pack. **3.** *refl. V. (ugs. veralt.)* beat it *(sl.)*; clear off *(coll.)*
Packen der; ~s, ~: pile; *(von Büchern, Zeitungen)* pile; stack; *(zusammengeschnürt)* bundle; *(von Geldscheinen)* wad
Packer der; ~s, ~ packer; *(Möbel~)* [packer and] removal man *(Brit.) or (Amer.)* moving man
Packerei die; ~, ~en a) *o. Pl. (ugs. abwertend)* packing and unpacking; **b)** *(eines Betriebs)* packing department
Packerin die; ~, ~nen packer
Pack-: ~esel der *(ugs.)* pack-donkey; *(fig.)* pack-horse; **~papier das** [stout] wrapping-paper; **~pferd das** pack-horse; **~tisch der** packing-table
Packung die; ~, ~en a) packet; pack *(esp. Amer.)*; **eine ~ Zigaretten** a packet *or (Amer.)* pack of cigarettes; **eine ~ Pralinen** a box of chocolates; **b)** *(Med., Kosmetik)* pack; **c)** *(Technik)* packing
Pack-: ~wagen der a) luggage-van *(Brit.)*; baggage car *(Amer.)*; **b)** *(hist.: Fuhrwerk)* baggage-wagon; **~zettel der** packing-slip
Pädagoge [pɛda'go:gə] **der; ~n, ~n a)** *(Erzieher, Lehrer)* teacher; **b)** *(Wissenschaftler)* educationalist; educational theorist
Pädagogik die; ~: [theory and methodology of] education
Pädagogin die; ~, ~nen *s.* **Pädagoge**
pädagogisch 1. *Adj.* **a)** *(erzieherisch)* educational; **seine ~en Fähigkeiten** his teaching ability *sing.*; **b)** *(die Pädagogik betreffend)* ⟨*lecture, dissertation, etc.*⟩ on education; **Pädagogische Hochschule** College of Education; **eine ~e Ausbildung** a training in education. **2.** *adv.* **a)** *(erzieherisch)* educationally ⟨*sound, wrong*⟩; **~ wirken** have an educational effect; **b)** *(die Pädagogik betreffend)* **~ nicht auf dem neuesten Stand sein** not be up with the latest developments in educational theory [and methodology]
pädagogisieren *tr. V. (oft abwertend)* **etw. ~:** look at sth. through the eyes of an educational theorist
Paddel ['padl̩] **das; ~s, ~:** paddle
Paddel·boot das canoe
paddeln *itr. V.; mit sein; ohne Richtungsangabe auch mit haben* **a)** *(Paddelboot fahren)* paddle; canoe; *(als Sport)* canoe; **b)** *(ugs.: schlecht schwimmen)* dog-paddle
Paddel·sport der canoeing *no art.*
Paddler der; ~s, ~, Paddlerin die; ~, ~nen canoeist
Päderast [pede'rast] **der; ~en, ~en** pederast
Päderastie [pɛderas'ti:] **die; ~:** pederasty *no art.*
Pädiater [pɛ'di̯a:tɐ] **der; ~s, ~** *(Med.)* paediatrician
Pädiatrie [pɛdi̯a'tri:] **die; ~** *(Med.)* paediatrics *sing., no art.*
pädiatrisch *Adj. (Med.)* paediatric
paff [paf] *Interj.* bang
paffen 1. *tr. V.* puff at ⟨*pipe etc.*⟩; puff out ⟨*smoke*⟩; **vierzig Zigaretten am Tag ~:** puff one's way through forty cigarettes a day. **2.** *itr. V.* puff away; **er pafft nur** he's just puffing at it
Page ['pa:ʒə] **der; ~n, ~n a)** *(Hotel~)* page; bellboy; **b)** *(hist.)* page
Pagen·kopf der page-boy cut *or* style
paginieren [pagi'ni:rən] *tr. V. (Schrift- und Buchw.)* paginate
Pagode [pa'go:də] **die; ~, ~n a)** *(Gebäude)* pagoda; **b)** *(österr., sonst veralt.: Figur)* mandarin
pah [pa:] *Interj.* bah; huh *(Amer.)*
Paillette [pai̯'jɛtə] **die; ~, ~n** *(Mode)* paillette; sequin; spangle
Pak [pak] **die; ~, ~** *od.* **~s** *(Milit.)* **a)** *(Panzerabwehrkanone)* anti-tank gun; **b)** *o. Pl. (Artillerie)* anti-tank force
Paket [pa'ke:t] **das; ~[e]s, ~e a)** pile; *(zusammengeschnürt)* bundle; *(Eingepacktes, Post~, Schachtel)* parcel; *(Packung)* packet; pack *(esp. Amer.)*; **b)** *(fig.: Gesamtheit)* package
Paket-: ~annahme die a) *o. Pl.* acceptance of parcels; **b)** *(Stelle)* parcels office; *(Schalter)* parcels counter; **~aus·gabe die a)** *o. Pl.* issue of parcels; **b)** *s.* **~annahme b; ~boot das** *(veralt.)* packet[-boat]; **~karte die** parcel dispatch form; **~post die a)** *(Beförderung)* parcel post; **b)** *(Fahrzeug)* parcel *or* post-office delivery van; **~schalter der** parcels counter; **~sendung die** parcel
Pakistan ['pa:kɪsta:n] **(das); ~s** Pakistan
Pakistaner der; ~s, ~, Pakistanerin die; ~, ~nen, Pakistani [pakɪs'ta:ni] **der; ~[s], ~[s]/die; ~, ~[s]** Pakistani
pakistanisch *Adj.* Pakistani
Pakt [pakt] **der; ~[e]s, ~e** pact; **einen ~ [ab]schließen** make *or* conclude a pact
paktieren *itr. V. (oft abwertend)* make *or* do a deal/deals **(mit** with**)**
Paladin [pala'di:n] **der; ~s, ~e a)** *(Myth.)* paladin; **b)** *(Gefolgsmann)* henchman
Palais [pa'lɛ:] **das; ~** [...ɛ:(s)], **~** [...ɛ:s] palace
Paläolithikum [palɛo'li:tikʊm] **das; ~s** Palaeolithic
Paläontologie [palɛontolo'gi:] **die; ~:** palaeontology *no art.*
Paläozän [palɛo'tsɛ:n] **das; ~s** *(Geol.)* Palaeocene
Paläozoikum [palɛo'tso:ikʊm] **das; ~s** palaeozoic era
Palast [pa'last] **der; ~[e]s, Paläste** [pa'lɛstə] palace
palast·artig *Adj.* palatial
Palästina [palɛ'sti:na] **(das); ~s** Palestine
Palästinenser der; ~s, ~, Palästinenserin die; ~, ~nen Palestinian
palästinensisch *Adj.* Palestinian
Palast·revolution die *(Politik, auch fig.)* palace revolution
Palatschinke [pala'tʃɪŋkə] **die; ~, ~n** *(österr.)* pancake with sweet filling
Palaver [pa'la:vɐ] **das; ~s, ~** *(ugs. abwertend)* palaver; **ein ~ abhalten** palaver
palavern *itr. V. (ugs. abwertend)* palaver
Paletot ['paləto] **der; ~s, ~s** *(man's double-breasted)* overcoat *[with high velvet collar]*

Palette [pa'lɛtə] **die; ~, ~n a)** *(Malerei)* palette; **b)** *(bes. Werbespr.: Vielfalt)* diverse range; **die ganze ~:** the whole range; **c)** *(Technik, Wirtsch.: Untersatz)* pallet

paletti *Adj. in* **alles ~** *(ugs.)* everything's OK *(coll.) or* all right

Palimpsest [palɪm'psɛst] **der** *od.* **das; ~[e]s, ~e** palimpsest

Palindrom [palɪn'dro:m] **das; ~s, ~e** palindrome

Palisade [pali'za:də] **die; ~, ~n a)** *(Pfahl)* pale; stake; **b)** *(Anlage)* palisade

Palisander [pali'zandɐ] **der; ~s, ~, Palisander·holz das** *(Dalbergia nigra)* Brazilian rosewood; *(Dalbergia latifolia)* blackwood

Palme ['palmə] **die; ~, ~n** palm[-tree]; **jmdn. auf die ~ bringen** *(ugs.)* ⟨*person*⟩ rile sb. *(coll.)*; ⟨*situation*⟩ make sb. wild; **auf die ~ gehen** *(ugs.)* go off the deep end *(coll.)*; **die ~ [des Sieges]** *(fig. geh.)* the palm [of victory]

Palmen-: *s.* **Palm-**

Palm-: ~kätzchen das [willow] catkin; **~öl das** palm-oil; **~sonntag** [auch: -'--] **der** *(christl. Kirche)* Palm Sunday; *s. auch* **Dienstag; ~wedel der** palm frond; **~zweig der a)** palm branch; **b)** *(christl. Kirche)* palm; **~wein der** palm wine

Pamp [pamp] **der; ~s** *(nordd., ostd.)* mush

Pampa ['pampa] **die; ~, ~s** pampa *usu. in pl.*; **[mitten] in der ~** *(Jugendspr.)* out in the wilds *(coll.)*

Pampe ['pampə] **die; ~** *(bes. nordd. u. md.)* **a)** *(Matsch)* mud; mire; **b)** *(Brei)* mush

Pampelmuse ['pamp|mu:zə] **die; ~, ~n** grapefruit

Pampf [pampf] **der; ~s** *(südd.)* mush

Pamphlet [pam'fle:t] **das; ~[e]s, ~e** *(Streitschrift)* polemical pamphlet; *(Schmähschrift)* defamatory pamphlet

pampig 1. *Adj.* **a)** *(ugs. abwertend: frech)* insolent; **b)** *(bes. nordd., ostd.: breiig)* mushy. **2.** *adv. (ugs. abwertend: frech)* insolently

Pamps *s.* **Pamp**

pan-, Pan- [pan-]: *in Zus.* pan-

Panade [pa'na:də] **die; ~, ~n** *(Kochk.)* breadcrumb coating

[1]**Panama** ['panama] **(das)** Panama

[2]**Panama der; ~s, ~s a)** *(Textilind.)* Panama fabric; **b)** *(Hut)* panama [hat]

Panamaer der; ~s, ~, Panamaerin die; ~, ~nen Panamanian

panamaisch *Adj.* Panamanian

Panama·kanal der; *o. Pl.* Panama Canal

Panda ['panda] **der; ~s, ~s** panda

Pandekten [pan'dɛktn̩] *Pl.* pandects; *(fig.)* jurisprudence *sing.*

Pandschab [pan'dʒa:p] **das; ~s** Punjab

Paneel [pa'ne:l] **das; ~s, ~e a)** *(einzelnes Feld)* panel; **b)** *(Täfelung)* panelling

paneelieren *tr. V.* panel

Pan·flöte die pan-pipes *pl.*

pan·germanisch *Adj.* pan-German

pan·hellenisch *Adj.* pan-Hellenic

[1]**Panier** [pa'ni:ɐ] **das; ~s, ~e** *(veralt.)* banner; *(Motto)* motto

[2]**Panier die; ~** *(österr. Kochk.) s.* **Panade**

panieren *tr. V. (Kochk.)* **etw. ~:** bread sth.; coat sth. with breadcrumbs

Panier·mehl das breadcrumbs *pl.*

Panik ['pa:nɪk] **die; ~, ~en** panic; **[eine] ~ brach aus** panic broke out; **jmdn. in ~** *(Akk.)* **versetzen** throw sb. into a state of panic; **von ~ ergriffen** panic-stricken; **nur keine ~!** don't panic!

Panik-: ~mache die; *o. Pl. (abwertend)* panic-mongering; **~macher der** *(abwertend)* panic-monger

panisch 1. *Adj.* panic *attrib.* ⟨*fear, terror*⟩; panic-stricken ⟨*voice, flight*⟩; **~e Angst vor etw.** *(Dat.)* **haben** have a panic fear of sth. **2.** *adv.* **sich ~ vor etw.** *(Dat.)* **fürchten** have a panic fear of sth.

Panje·wagen ['panjə-] **der** *small wooden cart drawn by a horse (in Eastern Europe)*

Pankreas ['pankreas] **das; ~, Pankreaten** *(Anat.)* pancreas

Panne ['panə] **die; ~, ~n a)** *(Auto~)* breakdown; *(Reifen~)* puncture; flat [tyre]; **ich hatte eine ~** *(mit dem Auto)* my car broke down/my car *or* I had a puncture; *(mit dem Fahrrad)* I had some trouble with my bicycle/my bicycle *or* I had a puncture; **b)** *(Betriebsstörung)* breakdown; **c)** *(Mißgeschick)* slip-up; mishap; **mit unserem Urlaub haben wir eine ganz schöne ~ erlebt** our holiday this year was a real disaster; **bei der Organisation gab es viele ~n** there were many organizational hitches

Pannen·dienst der breakdown service

Panoptikum [pa'nɔptikʊm] **das; ~s, Panoptiken a)** *(Kuriositätenkabinett)* collection of curios; **b)** *(Wachsfiguren)* waxworks *sing. or pl.*

Panorama [pano'ra:ma] **das; ~s, Panoramen** panorama

Panorama-: ~aufnahme die panorama; **~bus der** coach with panoramic windows; **~scheibe die** panoramic window; *(an Autos)* wraparound windscreen; **~spiegel der** *(Kfz-W.)* panoramic mirror

panschen ['panʃn̩] **1.** *tr. V. (ugs. abwertend)* water down; adulterate; **Whisky mit Wasser ~:** adulterate whisky with water. **2.** *itr. V.* **a)** *(ugs. abwertend: mischen)* water down *or* adulterate the wine/beer *etc.*; **b)** *(ugs.: planschen)* splash about

Panscher der; ~s, ~ *(ugs.)* adulterator

Panscherei die; ~, ~en a) *(ugs. abwertend: das Mischen)* watering-down; adulteration; **b)** *(ugs.: das Planschen)* splashing [about]

Pansen ['panzn̩] **der; ~s, ~ a)** *(Magen der Wiederkäuer)* rumen; **b)** *(nordd.: Magen)* stomach; belly

Pan·theismus der; *o. Pl.* pantheism *no art.*

pan·theistisch *Adj.* pantheistic

Panther der; ~s, ~: panther

Pantine [pan'ti:nə] **die; ~, ~n** *(nordd.)* clog; *s. auch* **Latschen**

Pantoffel [pan'tɔfl̩] **der; ~s, ~n a)** backless slipper; **b)** *(mit Absatz)* mule; **c)** *(fig.)* **unterm ~ stehen** *(ugs.)* be henpecked

Pantoffel-: ~held der *(ugs. abwertend)* henpecked husband; **~kino das** *(ugs.)* telly *(coll.)*; **~tierchen das** *(Biol.)* slipper animalcule

Panto·graph [panto-] **der; ~en, ~en** pantograph

Pantolette [panto'lɛtə] **die; ~, ~en** backless slipper

[1]**Pantomime** [panto'mi:mə] **die; ~, ~n** mime

[2]**Pantomime der; ~n, ~n** mime

Panto·mimik die mime

panto·mimisch 1. *Adj.* ⟨*presentation, depiction*⟩ in mime. **2.** *adv.* **etw. ~ darstellen/zeigen** present/show sth. in mime; mime sth.

pantschen *usw.* ['pantʃn̩] *s.* **panschen** *usw.*

Panzer ['pantsɐ] **der; ~s, ~ a)** *(Milit.)* tank; **die schwedischen ~:** the Swedish tanks *or* armour *sing.*; **b)** *(Zool.)* armour *no indef. art.*; *(von Schildkröten, Krebsen)* shell; **c)** *(hist.: Rüstung)* armour *no indef. art.*; **ein ~:** a suit of armour; **ein ~ der Gleichgültigkeit** *(fig.)* a defensive barrier of indifference; **d)** *(Panzerung)* armour-plating *or* -plate *no indef. art.*; *(eines Reaktors)* shielding

Panzer-: ~ab·wehr die *(Milit.)* **a)** *(Verteidigung)* anti-tank defence; **b)** *(Truppe)* anti-tank force; **~abwehr·kanone die** *(Milit.)* anti-tank gun; **~abwehr·rakete die** *(Milit.)* anti-tank rocket; **~division die** *(Milit.)* tank division; armoured division; **~faust die** *(Milit.)* anti-tank rocket launcher; bazooka; **~glas das** bullet-proof glass; **~grenadier der** *(Milit.)* soldier in the armoured infantry; **~hemd das** *(hist.)* coat of [chain-]mail; **~kette die** tank-track; **~kreuzer der** *(Marine hist.)* armoured cruiser; **„~kreuzer Potemkin"** 'The Battleship Potemkin'; **~mine die** anti-tank mine

panzern 1. *tr. V.* armour[-plate]. **2.** *refl. V. (hist.)* put on one's armour

Panzer-: ~platte die armour-plate; **~schlacht die** *(Milit.)* tank battle; **~schrank der** safe; **~späh·wagen der** *(Milit.)* armoured scout car; **~sperre die** *(Milit.)* anti-tank obstacle; **~truppe die** *(Milit.)* tank force

Panzer·wagen der *(Milit.)* **a)** *s.* **Panzer a; b)** *(Waggon)* armoured wagon

Papa ['papa, *geh., veralt.* pa'pa:] **der; ~s, ~** *(ugs.)* daddy *(coll.)*; **der Herr Papa** [-'-] your/my/his *etc.* [dear] father

Papagallo [papa'galo] **der; ~[s], ~s** *od.* **Papagalli** Latin Romeo

Papagei [papa'gai] **der; ~en** *od.* **~s, ~e[n]** parrot; **alles wie ein ~ nachplappern** repeat everything parrot-fashion

Papageien·krankheit die; *o. Pl. (Med.)* parrot-disease; psittacosis *no art.*

Paper ['peɪpə] **das; ~s, ~s** paper

Paperback ['peɪpəbæk] **das; ~s, ~s** paperback

Papeterie [papɛtə'ri:] **die; ~, ~n** *(schweiz.)* stationer's

Papi ['papi] **der; ~s, ~s** *(ugs.)* daddy *(coll.)*

Papier [pa'pi:ɐ] **das; ~s, ~e a)** paper; **ein Blatt/Fetzen/eine Rolle ~:** a sheet/scrap/roll of paper; **[nur] auf dem ~** *(fig.)* [only] on paper; **etw. aufs ~ werfen** *(fig. geh.)* jot sth. down; **etw. zu ~ bringen** get *or* put sth. down on paper; **~ ist geduldig** *(Spr.)* what's written down in black and white isn't necessarily true; **b)** *Pl. (Ausweis[e])* [identity] papers; **dann können Sie sich Ihre ~e holen** *(ugs.)* then you might as well collect your cards on the way out; **c)** *(Finanzw.: Wert~)* security

Papier-: ~blume die paper flower; **~deutsch das** *(abwertend)* officialese

papieren 1. *Adj.* **a)** *nicht präd. (aus Papier)* paper; **b)** *(fig.)* wooden ⟨*style etc.*⟩; **c)** *(wie Papier)* papery. **2.** *adv. (fig.)* ⟨*speak*⟩ woodenly; ⟨*write*⟩ in a wooden style

Papier-: ~fabrik die paper-mill; **~fähnchen das** paper pennant; **~fetzen der** scrap of [torn] paper; **~format das** paper size; **~geld das** paper money; **~geschäft das** stationer's; **~hand·tuch das** paper towel; **~korb der** waste-paper basket; *(öffentlicher)* litter bin; **~kram der** *(ugs. abwertend)* [tedious] paperwork; **~krieg der** *(ugs. abwertend)* tedious form-filling; *(Korrespondenz)* tiresome exchange of letters

Papiermaché [papiema'ʃe] **das; ~s, ~s** papier mâché

papier-, Papier-: ~mühle die a) *(Maschine)* [paper-pulp] beater; **b)** *(Fabrik)* paper-mill; **~rolle die** roll of paper; *(in Registrierkassen)* paper roll; **~schere die** paper-scissors *pl.*; **~schlange die** [paper] streamer; **~schnitzel der** *od.* **das** bit *or* scrap of paper; **~serviette die** paper serviette *or* napkin; **~taschen·tuch das** paper handkerchief; **~tiger der** paper tiger; **~verarbeitend** *Adj.; nicht präd.* paper-processing; **~währung die** paper currency; **~waren** *Pl.* stationery *sing.*; **~waren·handlung die** stationer's

Papist [pa'pɪst] **der; ~en, ~en** *(abwertend)* papist

papistisch *Adj. (abwertend)* papist

papp [pap] *in* **ich kann nicht mehr ~ sagen** *(ugs.)* I'm full to bursting-point *(coll.)*

Papp der; ~s, ~s *(bes. südd.)* mush

Papp-: ~band der; *Pl.* **~bände** book bound in boards; **~becher der** paper cup; **~deckel der** cardboard; **ein ~deckel** a piece of cardboard

Pappe ['papə] **die; ~, ~n a)** *(Karton)* cardboard; **eine ~:** a piece of cardboard; **b)**

(ugs.: Brei) mush; **er ist nicht von** *od.* **aus ~** *(ugs.)* he's not to be trifled with; **5000 Mark sind nicht von** *od.* **aus ~** *(ugs.)* 5,000 marks isn't chicken-feed *(coll.)*

Pappel ['papl̩] **die;** ~, ~n poplar

Pappel·allee **die** avenue of poplars

päppeln ['pɛpl̩n] *tr. V.* feed up; **eine Industrie ~** *(fig. ugs.)* featherbed an industry

pappen *(ugs.)* **1.** *tr. V.* stick **(an, auf +** *Akk.* on). **2.** *itr. V. (haftenbleiben)* stick **(an +** *Dat.* to); *(klebrig sein)* be sticky

Pappen-: **~deckel der** *(bes. südd.) s.* **Pappdeckel; ~heimer** [~haimɐ] *in* **ich kenne meine/wir kennen unsere ~heimer** *(ugs.)* I/we know them well *(coll.)*; **~stiel** *in* **das ist kein ~stiel** *(ugs.)* it's not chicken-feed *(coll.)*; **etw. für einen ~stiel kaufen/kriegen** *(ugs.)* buy/get sth. for a song *or* for next to nothing

papperlapapp [papɐla'pap] *Interj.* rubbish

pappig *Adj.* **a)** sticky; **b)** doughy ⟨*bread etc.*⟩; **c)** *(breiig)* mushy

Papp-: **~kamerad der** *(ugs., auch fig.)* cardboard figure; **~karton der** cardboard box; **~maché** [~ma'ʃe:] **das;** ~s, ~s papier mâché; **~nase die** false nose *(made of cardboard)*; **~schnee der** sticky snow; **~teller der** paper *or* cardboard plate

Paprika ['paprika] **der;** ~s, ~[s] **a)** pepper; **b)** *o. Pl. (Gewürz)* paprika

Paprika-: **~schnitzel das** cutlet with paprika sauce; **~schote die** pepper; **gefüllte ~schoten** stuffed peppers

Paps [paps] **der;** ~ *(ugs.)* dad *(coll.)*

Papst [pa:pst] **der;** ~[e]s, **Päpste** ['pɛ:pstə] pope; *(fig. iron.)* high priest

-papst *(fig. iron.)* **der** high priest of ...

päpstlich ['pɛ:pstlɪç] *Adj.* papal; *(fig. abwertend)* pontifical; **~er Gesandter** nuncio; **nicht ~er sein als der Papst** *(fig.)* not be a stickler for the regulations

Papsttum das; ~s papacy

Papua-Neu·guinea ['pa:pu̯a-] **(das);** ~s Papua New Guinea

Papyrus [pa'pʏ:rʊs] **der;** ~, **Papyri** papyrus

Papyrus·rolle die papyrus scroll

para-, Para- ['pa:ra] para-

Parabel [pa'ra:bl̩] **die;** ~, ~n **a)** *(bes. Literaturw.)* parable; **b)** *(Math.)* parabola

parabolisch [para'bo:lɪʃ] *Adj.* parabolic

Parabol·spiegel der *(Technik)* parabolic mirror

Parade [pa'ra:də] **die;** ~, ~n **a)** *(Milit.)* parade; **eine ~ abnehmen** take the salute at a parade; **b)** *(Ballspiele)* save; **jmdm. in die ~ fahren** *(fig. ugs.)* cut sb. short; **c)** *(Fechten)* parry; **d)** *(Pferdesport)* **ganze ~:** halt; **halbe ~:** half-halt; **in ~** *(Dat.)* **stehen** halt

Parade-: **~bei·spiel das** perfect example; **~bett das** *(veralt.)* large imposing bed

Paradeiser [para'daizɐ] **der;** ~s, ~ *(österr.)* tomato

Parade-: **~kissen das** *(veralt.)* decorative pillow; **~marsch der** *(Milit.)* marching in parade-step; *(Stechschritt)* goose-stepping; **~pferd das a)** *(Pferd)* parade-horse; **b)** *(ugs.: Musterexemplar)* show-piece; *(Person)* star; **~platz der** *(hist.)* parade-ground; **~schritt der** *(Milit.)* parade-step; *(Stechschritt)* goose-step; **~stück das** show-piece; **~uniform die** *(Milit.)* full-dress uniform

paradieren *itr. V. (Milit.)* parade

Paradies [para'di:s] **das;** ~es, ~e *(auch fig.)* paradise; **die Vertreibung aus dem ~:** the expulsion from paradise; **das ~ auf Erden** heaven on earth

paradiesisch 1. *Adj.* **a)** *(Rel.)* paradisical; **b)** *(herrlich)* heavenly; magnificent ⟨*view*⟩. **2.** *adv. (herrlich)* **~ ruhig gelegen** in a wonderfully peaceful situation; **dort ist es ~ schön** it's beautiful there, a real paradise

Paradies·vogel der bird of paradise; *(fig.)* strange and beautiful creature

Paradigma [para'dɪgma] **das;** ~s, **Paradigmen** *od.* **Paradigmata** *(bes. Sprachw.)* paradigm

paradigmatisch *(bes. Sprachw.)* **1.** *Adj.* paradigmatic. **2.** *adv.* paradigmatically

paradox [para'dɔks] *Adj.* **a)** paradoxical; **b)** *(ugs.: merkwürdig)* odd; strange

Paradox das; ~es, ~e *(bes. Philos., Rhet.)* paradox

paradoxer·weise *Adv.* **a)** paradoxically; **b)** *(ugs.: merkwürdigerweise)* strangely *or* oddly enough

Paradoxie [paradɔ'ksi:] **die;** ~, ~n **a)** paradox; **b)** *(Eigenschaft)* paradoxicalness

Paradoxon [pa'ra:dɔksɔn] **das;** ~s, **Paradoxa** *(Philos., Rhet.)* paradox

Paraffin [para'fi:n] **das;** ~s, ~e *(Chemie)* paraffin; *(für Kerzen)* paraffin wax

Paragraph [para'gra:f] **der;** ~en, ~en section; *(im Vertrag)* clause

Paragraphen-: **~dickicht das, ~gestrüpp das** *(abwertend)* jungle of regulations; **~hengst der** *(salopp abwertend)* lawyer; **~reiter der** *(abwertend)* **a)** *(Jurist)* lawyer; **b)** *(Pedant)* stickler for the rules

Paraguay ['paragvai̯] **(das);** ~s Paraguay

Paraguayer der; ~s, ~: Paraguayan

paraguayisch *Adj.* Paraguayan

Parallaxe [para'laksə] **die;** ~, ~n *(Physik, Astron.)* parallax

parallel [para'le:l] **1.** *Adj. (auch fig.)* parallel. **2.** *adv.* **~ verlaufen** *(auch fig.)* run parallel **(mit, zu** to); **~ zu etw.** *(fig.)* in parallel with sth.

Parallele die; ~, ~n **a)** *(Math.)* parallel [line]; **eine ~ zu etw. ziehen** draw a line parallel to sth.; **b)** *(fig.)* parallel; **jmdn./etw. mit jmdm./etw. in ~ setzen** *od.* **stellen** draw a parallel between sb./sth. and sb./sth.

Parallel·fall der parallel case

Parallelität [paraleli'tɛ:t] **die;** ~, ~en *(auch Math.)* parallelism

Parallel·klasse die *(Schulw.)* parallel class

Parallelogramm [paralelo'gram] **das;** ~s, ~e *(Math.)* parallelogram

Parallel-: **~schaltung die** *(Elektrot.)* parallel connection; **~schwung der** *(Skisport)* parallel swing; **~straße die** street running parallel **(von** to); **~ton·art die** *(Musik)* relative key

Paralyse [para'lʏ:zə] **die;** ~, ~n *(Med., fig.)* paralysis

paralysieren *tr. V. (Med., fig.)* paralyse

Paralytiker der; ~s, ~, **Paralytikerin die;** ~, ~nen paralytic

paralytisch *Adj. (Med.)* paralytic

Parameter [pa'ra:metɐ] **der;** ~s, ~ **a)** *(Wirtsch., Technik, Math.)* parameter; *(beim Kegelschnitt)* principal parameter

para·militärisch 1. *Adj.* paramilitary. **2.** *adv.* ⟨*operate, be organized*⟩ along paramilitary lines

Paranoia [para'nɔy̯a] **die;** ~ *(Med.)* paranoia

paranoid [parano'i:t] *Adj. (Med.)* paranoid

Paranoiker [para'no:ikɐ] **der;** ~s, ~ *(Med.)* paranoiac

paranoisch *Adj. (Med.)* paranoiac

Para·nuß die Brazil-nut

Paraphe [pa'ra:fə] **die;** ~, ~n **a)** *(geh.: Namenszug)* signature; **b)** *(Dipl.)* initials *pl.*

paraphieren *tr. V. (Dipl.)* initial

Paraphierung die; ~, ~en initialling

Para·phrase die *(Sprachw., Musik)* paraphrase

paraphrasieren *tr. V.* **a)** *(Sprachw.)* paraphrase; **b)** *(Musik)* compose a paraphrase on

Para·psychologie die parapsychology *no art.*

Parasit [para'zi:t] **der;** ~en, ~en *(Biol., fig. abwertend)* parasite

parasitär [parazi'tɛ:ɐ̯], **parasitisch** *(Biol., fig. abwertend)* **1.** *Adj.* parasitic. **2.** *adv.* parasitically; **~ leben** *(Biol.)* be parasitic; *(fig.)* be a parasite

Parasol [para'zo:l] **der;** ~s, ~e *od.* ~s, **Parasol·pilz der** parasol mushroom

Parasympathikus [parazʏm'pa:tikʊs] **der;** ~ *(Anat., Physiol.)* parasympathetic nervous system

parat [pa'ra:t] *Adj.* ready; **eine Ausrede/Antwort ~ haben** be ready with an excuse/answer; **ich habe kein passendes Beispiel ~:** I can't think of a suitable example

Para·typhus der *(Med.)* paratyphoid [fever]

Paravent [para'vã:] **der** *od.* **das;** ~s, ~s *(österr., sonst veralt.)* screen

Pärchen ['pɛ:ɐ̯çən] **das;** ~s, ~: pair; *(Liebespaar)* couple

pärchen·weise *Adv.* in pairs

Parcours [par'ku:ɐ̯] **der;** ~ [...ɐ̯(s)], ~ [...ɐ̯s] *(Pferdesport)* course

Pardon [par'dõ] **der** *od.* **das;** ~s pardon; **jmdn. um ~ bitten** *(veralt.)* ask sb.'s pardon; **jmdm. ~ gewähren** *(veralt.)* pardon sb.; **kein[en] ~ kennen** be completely ruthless; **~!** I beg your pardon

Parenthese [parɛn'te:zə] **die;** ~, ~n *(Sprachw.)* **a)** *(Satzteil)* parenthesis; **b)** *(Klammern o. ä.)* parenthesis; parentheses *pl.*; **in ~:** in parenthesis

par excellence [parɛksɛ'lã:s] *Adj.; nachgestellt* par exellence; **ein Gentleman ~:** an outstanding example of a gentleman

Parforce- [par'fɔrs-]: **~jagd die** *(Jagdw. veralt.)* hunt with horses and hounds; *(Art des Jagens)* riding to hounds; **~ritt der** *(geh.)* feat of concentrated effort

Parfum [par'fœ̃:], **Parfüm** [par'fy:m] **das;** ~s, ~s perfume; scent

Parfümerie [parfymə'ri:] **die;** ~, ~en perfumery

Parfüm-: **~fläschchen das, ~flasche die** perfume- *or* scent-bottle

parfümieren *tr. V.* perfume; scent; **sich [viel zu stark] ~:** put [too much] perfume *or* scent on

Parfüm-: **~wolke die** cloud of perfume *or* scent; **~zerstäuber der** perfume-spray; perfume-atomizer

pari ['pa:ri] **a)** *in* **zu/über/unter ~** *(Börsenw.)* at/above/below par; **b)** *in* **die/ihre Chancen stehen ~:** the odds are even/they have the same *or* an equal chance

Paria ['pa:ri̯a] **der;** ~s, ~s *(auch fig.)* pariah

[1]parieren [pa'ri:rən] *itr. V. (ugs.)* do what one is told; **jmdm. ~:** do what sb. tells one; **aufs Wort ~:** jump to it *(coll.)*

[2]parieren *tr. V.* **a)** *(Fechten, Boxen, fig.)* parry; **b)** *(Fußball)* save ⟨*shot*⟩; parry ⟨*attack*⟩; **c)** *(Pferdesport)* hold ⟨*horse*⟩ at half-halt; *(zum Stehen bringen)* halt

Pari·kurs der *(Wirtsch.)* par value; *(bei Devisen)* par rate of exchange

Pariser [pa'ri:zɐ] **1.** *indekl. Adj.* Parisian; Paris *attrib.*; **die ~ Metro** the Paris Metro; **2. der;** ~s, ~ **a)** *(Einwohner)* Parisian; **b)** *(ugs.: Kondom)* French letter *(coll.)*

Pariserin die; ~, ~nen Parisian

pariserisch *Adj.* Parisian

Parität [pari'tɛ:t] **die;** ~, ~en **a)** *(Gleichheit)* parity; equality; **b)** *(Wirtsch.)* parity

paritätisch 1. *Adj.* equal; **~e Mitbestimmung** co-determination based on equal representation. **2.** *adv.* equally; **Ausschüsse müssen ~ besetzt werden** there must be equal representation on committees

Park [park] **der;** ~s, ~s park; *(Schloß~ usw.)* grounds *pl.*

Parka der; ~s, ~s parka

Park-: **~an·lage die** park; *(bei Schlössern usw.)* grounds *pl.*; **~bahn die** *(Raumf.)* parking orbit; **~bank die;** *Pl.* **~bänke** park bench

parken 1. *tr. V.* park. **2.** *itr. V.* **a)** park; **„Parken verboten!"** 'No Parking'; **b)** *(stehen)* be parked; **ein ~des Auto** a parked car

Parkett [par'kɛt] **das;** ~[e]s, ~e **a)** *(Bodenbelag)* parquet floor; **~ legen** lay parquet flooring; **sich auf jedem ~ bewegen können** *(fig.)* be able to move in any circles; **b)** *(Theater)* [front] stalls *pl.*; parquet *(Amer.)*; **das ~ applaudierte** there was applause from the stalls; **c)** *in* **etw. aufs ~ legen** *(ugs.)* dance sth.; *s. auch* **Sohle a**

Parkett·[fuß]boden der parquet floor; **~ haben** have parquet flooring

parkettieren *tr. V.* lay parquet flooring; parquet

Parkett·platz der seat in the [front] stalls

Park-: ~gebühr die parking-fee; **~haus das** multi-storey car-park

parkieren *(schweiz.) s.* **parken**

Parkinsonsche Krankheit ['parkɪnzɔnʃə '--] **die** Parkinson's disease

Park-: ~kralle die wheel-clamp; **~landschaft die** parkland; **~leuchte die, ~licht das** parking-light; **~lücke die** parking-space; **~platz der a)** car-park; parking lot *(Amer.)*; **b)** *(für ein einzelnes Fahrzeug)* parking-space; place to park; **~scheibe die** parking-disc; **~schein der** car-park ticket; **~uhr die** parking-meter; **~verbot das** ban on parking; **hier ist ~verbot** you are not allowed to park here; **im ~verbot stehen** be parked illegally; **aus dem ~verbot wegfahren** move one's car from where it is/was parked illegally; **~verbots·schild das** no-parking sign

Parlament [parla'mɛnt] **das; ~[e]s, ~e** parliament; *(eines bestimmten Landes)* Parliament *no def. art.*

Parlamentär [parlamɛn'tɛːɐ̯] **der; ~s, ~e** peace negotiator

Parlamentarier [parlamɛn'taːri̯ɐ] **der; ~s, ~, Parlamentarierin die; ~, ~nen** member of parliament; *(in Großbritannien)* Member of Parliament; MP; *(in den Vereinigten Staaten)* Congressman/Congresswoman; **die Bonner ~:** the members of the Bonn Parliament; **die dem Europarat angehörenden ~:** the MPs *or* deputies in the Council of Europe

parlamentarisch 1. *Adj.; nicht präd.* parliamentary; **~er Staatssekretär [im Bundesministerium für ...]** parliamentary secretary [to the Federal Ministry of ...]. **2.** *adv.* **etw. ~ diskutieren** discuss sth. in parliament

Parlamentarismus der; ~: parliamentarianism *no art.*; parliamentary system

Parlaments-: ~aus·schuß der parliamentary committee; **~ferien** *Pl.* [parliamentary] recess *sing.*; **~gebäude das** parliament building[s *pl.*]; **die ~gebäude** *(in London)* the Houses of Parliament; **~mitglied das** member of parliament; *(in Großbritannien)* Member of Parliament; MP; *(in den Vereinigten Staaten)* member of Congress; **~reform die** parliamentary reform; **~sitzung die** sitting [of parliament]; **~wahl die** parliamentary election

parlieren [par'liːrən] *itr. V. (geh.; oft iron.)* make conversation; *(plaudern)* chat **(über + Akk.** about); *(reden)* talk ⟨*French etc.*⟩

Parmesan [parme'zaːn] **der; ~[s]** Parmesan

Parnaß [par'nas] **der; ~** *od.* **Parnasses** *(dichter.)* Parnassus *no def. art. (poet.)*

Parodie [paro'diː] **die; ~, ~n** parody; **eine ~ auf etw./jmdn.** a parody of sth./take-off of sb.

parodieren *tr. V.* parody ⟨*literary work, manner*⟩; take off ⟨*person*⟩; satirize ⟨*event*⟩

Parodist der; ~en, ~en parodist

parodistisch *Adj.* parodistic; ⟨*ability*⟩ as a parodist

Parodontose [parodɔn'toːzə] **die; ~, ~n** periodontosis *no art. (Dent.)*; receding gums *pl., no art.*

Parole [pa'roːlə] **die; ~, ~n a)** *(Wahlspruch)* motto; *(Schlagwort)* slogan; **b)** *(bes. Milit.: Kennwort)* password; **c)** *(Gerücht)* rumour

Paroli [pa'roːli] *in:* **jmdm./einer Sache ~ bieten** give sb. as good as one gets/pit oneself against sth.

Part [part] **der; ~s, ~s** *od.* **~e a)** *(Musik: Stimme, Partie)* part; **b)** *(Theater, Film: Rolle)* part; role; **einen/den [entscheidenden] ~ in** *od.* **bei etw.** *(Dat.)* **spielen** *(auch fig.)* play a/the [crucial] part *or* role in sth.

Parte ['partə] **die; ~, ~n** *(österr.: Todesanzeige)* death announcement

Partei [par'tai] **die; ~, ~en a)** *(Politik)* party; **in** *od.* **bei der ~ sein** be a party member; **die ~ wechseln** change parties; **b)** *(Rechtsw.)* party; **c)** *(Gruppe, Mannschaft)* side; **es mit beiden ~en halten** run with the hare and hunt with the hounds *(fig.)*; **~ sein** be an interested party; **jmds.** *od.* **für jmdn./für etw. ~ ergreifen** *od.* **nehmen** side with sb./take a stand for sth.; **gegen jmdn./etw. ~ nehmen** *od.* **ergreifen** side against sb./take a stand against sth.; **über den ~en stehen** be impartial; **d)** *(Miets~)* tenant; *(mehrere Personen)* tenants *pl.*

partei-, Partei-: ~ab·zeichen das party badge; **~aktiv das** *(DDR) team of party members with particular tasks*; **~amtlich** *Adj.* official party ⟨*regulations etc.*⟩; **~apparat der** party machine *or* organization; **~bonze der** *(abwertend)* party bigwig *(coll.)*; **~buch das** party membership book; **das falsche/richtige ~buch haben** belong to the wrong/right party; **~chef der** party leader; **~chinesisch das** *(ugs. scherzh.)* party gobbledegook; **~disziplin die** party discipline

Parteien-: ~landschaft die party political scene *or* set-up; **~verkehr der** *(österr.)* „**~verkehr von 9 bis 14 Uhr**" 'open to the public from 9 till 2'

partei-, Partei-: ~freund der fellow party member; party colleague; **~führer der** party leader; **~führung die** party leadership; **der ~führung angehören** be one of the party leaders *pl. or* executive; **~gänger der** *(oft abwertend)* [loyal] party supporter; **Mussolini und seine ~gänger** Mussolini and his party faithful; **~genosse der** *(hist.: Mitglied der NSDAP)* party member; *(einer Arbeiterpartei)* **~genosse X** Comrade X; **~hoch·schule die** *(DDR) college in Berlin for training SED leaders*; **~intern 1.** *Adj.; nicht präd.* internal [party] ⟨*conflict, matters, material, etc.*⟩; **2.** *adv.* within the party

parteiisch 1. *Adj.* biased. **2.** *adv.* in a biased manner

Partei-: ~lehr·jahr das *(DDR) year's course of ideological training (for SED members and others)*; **~leitung die** *s.* **~führung**

parteilich 1. *Adj.* **a)** *nicht präd. (eine Partei betreffend)* party ⟨*matter, work, principles, etc.*⟩; **b)** *(parteiisch)* biased ⟨*judgement, view, etc.*⟩; **c)** *(DDR: der Parteilinie folgend)* in accordance with the party line *postpos.* **2.** *adv.* **a)** *(von der Partei)* by the party; **b)** *(parteiisch)* in a biased manner; **c)** *(der Parteilinie folgend)* ⟨*think, behave, act*⟩ in accordance with the party line

Parteilichkeit die; ~: a) *(Linientreue)* adherence to the party line; **b)** *(einseitige Parteinahme)* bias, partiality **(für** towards)

partei-, Partei-: ~linie die party line; **~los** *Adj. (Politik)* independent ⟨*MP*⟩; **er ist ~los** he is not attached to *or* aligned with any party; **~lose der/die;** *adj. Dekl. (Politik)* independent; person not attached to a party; **~losigkeit die; ~:** *(Politik)* independence; **~mit·glied das** party member; **~nahme die; ~, ~n** partisanship; taking sides *no art.*; **~organ das a)** party representative; *(Gruppe)* group of persons representing a party; **b)** *(Zeitung)* party organ; **~politik die** party politics *sing.*; **~politisch 1.** *Adj.* party political; **2.** *adv.* from a party political point of view; **~programm das** party manifesto *or* programme; **~tag der** party conference *or (Amer.)* convention

Parteiung die; ~, ~en ⟨*political, religious*⟩ group

Partei-: ~verfahren das *proceedings instituted by the party against a member*; **~vorsitzende der/die** party leader; **~vorstand der** party executive; **~zugehörigkeit die** party membership

parterre [par'tɛr] *Adv.* on the ground *or (Amer.)* first floor

Parterre [par'tɛr] **das; ~s, ~s a)** *(Erdgeschoß)* ground floor; first floor *(Amer.)*; **im ~:** on the ground *or (Amer.)* first floor; **b)** *(Theater veralt.)* stalls *pl. (Brit.)*; parterre *(Amer.)*; parquet *(Amer.)*

Parterre·wohnung die ground-floor flat *(Brit.)*; first-floor apartment *(Amer.)*

Partie [par'tiː] **die; ~, ~n a)** *(Teil)* part; **b)** *(Spiel, Sport: Runde)* game; *(Golf)* round; **eine ~ Schach spielen** play a game of chess; **c)** *(Musik)* part; **d)** *(Ehepartner)* **eine gute ~ [für jmdn.] sein** be a good match [for sb.]; **sie hat eine gute/glänzende ~ gemacht** she has married well/extremely well; **e)** *(veralt.: Ausflug)* **eine ~ aufs Land machen** go on or for an outing *or* a trip into the country; **f) mit von der ~ sein** join in; *(bei einer Reise usw.)* go along too; **da bin ich mit von der ~!** count me in!; **g)** *(Kaufmannsspr.)* batch; **h)** *(österr.: Gruppe von Arbeitern)* gang

Partie·führer der *(österr.: Vorarbeiter)* foreman

partiell [par'tsi̯ɛl] **1.** *Adj.* partial. **2.** *adv.* partially

¹Partikel [par'tiːk]] **die; ~, ~n** *(Sprachw.)* particle

²Partikel das; ~s, ~ *od.* **die; ~, ~n** *(bes. Physik, Chemie, Technik)* particle

partikular [partiku'laːɐ̯], **partikulär** [partiku'lɛːɐ̯] *Adj. (geh.)* minority *attrib.* ⟨*interest, viewpoint*⟩

Partikularismus der; ~ *(meist abwertend)* particularism *no art.*

partikularistisch *Adj. (meist abwertend)* particularistic

Partisan [parti'zaːn] **der; ~s** *od.* **~en, ~en** guerrilla; *(gegen Besatzungstruppen im Krieg)* partisan

Partisanen·krieg der guerilla war; *(Kriegführung)* guerilla warfare

Partisanin die; ~, ~nen *s.* **Partisan**

Partita [par'tiːta] **die; ~, Partiten** *(Musik)* partita

Partitur [parti'tuːɐ̯] **die; ~, ~en** *(Musik)* score

Partizip [parti'tsiːp] **das; ~s, ~ien** [-'tsiːpi̯ən] *(Sprachw.)* participle; **das 1. ~** *od.* **~ Präsens/das 2. ~** *od.* **~ Perfekt** the present/past participle

Partizipation [partitsipa'tsi̯oːn] **die; ~, ~en** participation **(an + Dat.** in)

Partizipations·geschäft das *(Wirtsch.)* joint venture

Partizipial- *(Sprachw.)* participial

partizipieren *itr. V.* **an etw.** *(Dat.)* **~:** have a share in sth.

Partner ['partnɐ] **der; ~s, ~, Partnerin die; ~, ~nen** partner; *(Bündnis~)* ally; *(im Film/Theater)* co-star

Partner·look der co-ordinated fashion *(in which man and woman wear matching clothes)*; **~ tragen** wear matching his-and-hers outfits

Partnerschaft die; ~, ~en partnership

partnerschaftlich 1. *Adj.* ⟨*co-operation etc.*⟩ on a partnership basis; **wir haben ein ~es Verhältnis** ours is a relationship between equal partners; **sein Führungsstil ist [sehr] ~:** his style of leadership involves treating people [very much] as equal partners. **2.** *adv.* in a spirit of partnership; *(als Partnerschaft)* as a partnership; **sich jmdm. gegenüber** *od.* **zu jmdm. ~ verhalten** treat sb. as an equal [partner]

Partner-: ~stadt die twin town *(Brit.)*; sister city *or* town *(Amer.)*; **~tausch der** partner-swapping *(coll.)*; **~wahl die** choice of mate *or* partner

partout [par'tu:] *Adv. (ugs.)* at all costs; **er will es ~ nicht einsehen** but he absolutely refuses to see it

Party ['pa:ɐti] **die; ~, ~s** *od.* **Parties** party; **eine ~ [zu ihrem bestandenen Examen/zu seinem Geburtstag] geben** give a party [to celebrate her passing the exam/for his birthday]; **auf** *od.* **bei ~s** at parties; **auf eine** *od.* **zu einer ~ gehen** go to a party

Party-: ~keller der *basement room equipped for parties;* **~löwe der** *(iron.)* [male] party-goer *(who is the centre of attraction);* social lion

Parvenü, *(österr.:)* **Parvenu** [parve'ny:] **der; ~s, ~s** *(geh.)* parvenu

Parze ['partsə] **die; ~, ~n** *(röm. Myth.)* **die drei ~n** the Three Fates

Parzelle [par'tsɛlə] **die; ~, ~n** [small] plot [of land]

parzellieren *tr. V.* divide into [small] plots

Pasch [paʃ] **der; ~[e]s, ~e** *u.* **Päsche a)** *(beim Würfelspiel)* **einen ~ werfen** *(bei zwei Würfeln)* throw doubles *pl.; (bei drei Würfeln)* throw triplets; **b)** *(beim Domino)* double

Pascha ['paʃa] **der; ~s, ~s a)** *(hist.)* pasha; **b)** *(fig. abwertend)* male chauvinist; **den ~ spielen** act the lord and master

Paspel ['paspl̩] **die; ~, ~n** *od.* **der; ~s, ~:** piping *no pl.*

paspelieren *tr. V.* pipe ⟨*pocket, collar, hem, seam*⟩

Paß [pas] **der; Passes, Pässe** ['pɛsə] **a)** *(Reise~)* passport; **der diplomatischen Vertretung die Pässe zustellen** break off diplomatic relations; **b)** *(Gebirgs~)* pass; **c)** *(Ballspiele)* pass

passabel [pa'sa:bl̩] **1.** *Adj.* reasonable; tolerable; fair ⟨*report*⟩*;* presentable ⟨*appearance*⟩. **2.** *adv.* reasonably *or* tolerably well

Passage [pa'sa:ʒə] **die; ~, ~n a)** *(Ladenstraße)* [shopping] arcade; **b)** *(Abschnitt) (im Text)* passage; *(im Film)* sequence; *(beim Eistanz, bei Turnübungen)* routine; *(Musik)* [virtuoso] passage; **c)** *(Stelle zum Passieren, Schiffs~, Reiten)* passage

Passagier [pasa'ʒi:ɐ] **der; ~s, ~e** passenger; **~e der Lufthansa nach London** Lufthansa passengers [bound] for London; **blinder ~:** stowaway

Passagier-: ~dampfer der passenger steamer; **~flugzeug das** passenger aircraft; **~liste die** passenger list; **~schiff das** passenger ship

Passah ['pasa] **das; ~s** *(jüd. Rel.)* Passover

Passah·fest das *(jüd. Rel.)* Feast of the Passover

Paß·amt das passport office

Passant [pa'sant] **der; ~en, ~en, Passantin die; ~, ~nen a)** *(Fußgänger[in])* passer-by; **b)** *(schweiz.: Durchreisende[r])* traveller [passing through]

Passat [pa'sa:t] **der; ~[e]s, ~e, Passat·wind der** trade wind

Paß·bild das passport photograph

Passe ['pasə] **die; ~, ~n** *(Schneiderei)* yoke

passé [pa'se:] *Adj.; nicht attr. (ugs.) (überholt)* passé; out of date; *(vorüber)* over [and done with]; **er ist als Politiker ~:** as a politician he has had his day

Pässe ['pɛsə] *s.* **Paß**

passen 1. *itr. V.* **a)** *(die richtige Größe/Form haben)* fit; **etw. paßt [jmdm.] gut/nicht** sth. fits [sb.] well/does not fit [sb.]; **etw. paßt [nicht] in/auf/unter etw.** *(Akk.)* **/zwischen zwei Sachen** sth. fits/does not fit into/on [to]/underneath sth./between two things; **der Schlüssel paßt nicht ins Schloß** the key does not fit the lock; **das Buch paßt nicht in den Karton** the book won't go in the box; **ein Kleidungsstück ~d machen** make an article of clothing fit; **b)** *(geeignet sein)* be suitable, be appropriate **(auf +** *Akk.,* **zu** for); *(harmonieren)* ⟨*colour etc.*⟩ match; **dieses Bild paßt besser in die Diele** this picture goes better in the hall; **zu etw./jmdm. ~:** go well with sth./be well suited to sb.; **zueinander ~** ⟨*things*⟩ go well together; ⟨*two people*⟩ be suited to each other; **das** *od.* **dieses Benehmen paßt zu ihm/paßt nicht zu ihm** *(ugs.)* that's just like him *(coll.)*/that's not like him; **diese Beschreibung paßt [genau] auf sie/[absolut] nicht auf sie** this description fits her [exactly]/does not fit her [at all]; **sie paßt nicht hierher/nach X** she does not fit in here/in X; **nicht in die Welt ~:** be unsuited to this life; **sie paßt nicht zu uns** *od.* **in unseren Kreis** she is out of place in our circle; *s. auch* **Faust; Konzept; Kram; passend; c)** *(genehm sein)* **jmdm. ~** ⟨*time*⟩ be convenient for sb., suit sb.; **jmdm. paßt etw. nicht** sth. is inconvenient for sb.; *(jmd. mag etw. nicht)* sb. does not like sth.; **das könnte dir so ~!** *(ugs.)* you'd just love that, wouldn't you?; **d)** *(Kartenspiel)* pass; **bei dieser Frage muß ich ~** *(fig.)* I'll have to pass on that question; **e)** *(österr.: warten, lauern)* wait **(auf +** *Akk.* for). **2.** *tr.* **a)** *(auch itr.) V. (Ballspiele)* pass ⟨*ball*⟩; **b)** *(paßgerecht einfügen)* **etw. in etw.** *(Akk.)* **~:** fit sth. into sth. **3.** *refl. V. (ugs.: sich schicken)* be proper *or (coll.)* done; **das/es paßt sich einfach nicht** it simply isn't done *or* the done thing *(coll.)*

passend *Adj.* **a)** *(geeignet)* suitable ⟨*dress, present, etc.*⟩; appropriate, right ⟨*words, expression*⟩; right ⟨*moment*⟩; **bei einer ~en Gelegenheit** at an opportune moment; **haben Sie es ~?** *(ugs.)* have you got the right money?; **b)** *(harmonierend)* matching ⟨*shoes etc.*⟩; **die zum Kleid ~en Schuhe** the shoes to go with *or* match the dress

Passepartout [paspar'tu] **das;** *(schweiz.:)* **der; ~s, ~s a)** *(Umrahmung)* mount; **b)** *(bes. schweiz.) s.* **Hauptschlüssel**

paß-, Paß-: ~form die fit; **eine gute ~form haben** be a good fit; **~foto das** *s.* **~bild; ~gang der** amble; **im ~gang gehen** amble; **~genau, ~gerecht** *Adj.* that fits/fit exactly *or* perfectly *postpos., not pred.;* **die Schuhe sind ~genau** *od.* **~gerecht** the shoes fit exactly *or* are a perfect fit

passierbar *Adj.* passable ⟨*road*⟩; navigable ⟨*river*⟩; negotiable ⟨*path*⟩

passieren 1. *tr. V.* **a)** pass; **die Grenze ~:** cross the border; **eine Brücke/einen Tunnel ~:** pass over a bridge/through a tunnel; **die Zensur ~** *(fig.)* be passed by the censor; get past the censor; *s. auch* **Revue d; b)** pass through a sieve; strain ⟨*curd cheese etc.*⟩. **2.** *itr. V.; mit sein* happen; ⟨*murder, event*⟩ take place; **es ist ein Unglück/etwas Schreckliches passiert** there has been an accident/something dreadful has happened; **gib es ihm sofort zurück, sonst passiert was!** give it back to him straight away, or there'll be trouble!; **jmdm. ist etwas/nichts passiert** something/nothing happened to sb.; *(jmd. ist verletzt/nicht verletzt)* sb. was/was not hurt; **mir ist eine Panne/ein Versehen passiert** I [have] had a breakdown/made a mistake; **das kann doch jedem mal ~!** that can happen to anybody!

Passier-: ~schein der pass; permit; **~schlag der** *(Tennis)* passing shot

Passion [pa'sio:n] **die; ~, ~en a)** passion; **b)** *o. Pl. (christl. Rel., Kunst, Musik)* Passion

passioniert *Adj.; nicht präd.* ardent, passionate ⟨*collector, card-player, huntsman*⟩

Passions-: ~spiel das Passion play; **~zeit die** *(christl. Rel.)* Passiontide

passiv ['pasi:f] **1.** *Adj.* passive; non-active ⟨*member*⟩; **~e Handelsbilanz** balance of trade deficit; **das ~e Wahlrecht** eligibility [for political office]; **das ~e Wahlrecht haben** be eligible to stand as a candidate; *s. auch* **Bestechung. 2.** *adv.* passively; **sich [bei** *od.* **in etw.** *(Dat.)***] ~ verhalten** take a passive stance [in sth.]; take no active part [in sth.]

Passiv das; ~s, ~e *(Sprachw.)* passive; **im ~ stehen** be in the passive

Passiva [pa'si:va] *Pl. (Wirtsch.)* liabilities

Passiv·bildung die *(Sprachw.)* formation of the passive

Passiven *s.* **Passiva**

passivisch *(Sprachw.)* **1.** *Adj.* passive. **2.** *adv.* passively; in the passive form

Passivität [pasivi'tɛ:t] **die; ~:** passivity

Passiv-: ~posten der *(Kaufmannsspr.)* liability; **~saldo der** *(Kaufmannsspr.)* debit balance; **~seite die** *(Kaufmannsspr.)* liabilities side

Paß-: ~kontrolle die a) *(das Kontrollieren)* passport inspection *or* check; **b)** *(Stelle)* passport control; **~stelle die** *s.* **~amt; ~straße die** [mountain] pass road

Passung die; ~, ~en *(Technik)* fit; tolerance [for mating parts]

Passus ['pasʊs] **der; ~, ~** [pa'su:s] passage

Paß·zwang der obligation to carry a passport

Paste ['pastə] **die; ~, ~n** *(auch Pharm.)* paste

Pastell [pas'tɛl] **das; ~[e]s, ~e a)** *(Farbton)* pastel shade; **b)** *o. Pl. (Maltechnik)* pastel *no art.;* **in ~:** in pastel; **c)** *(Bild)* pastel [drawing]

pastell-, Pastell-: ~farbe die pastel colour; **~farben** *Adj.* pastel-coloured; **~malerei die** pastel drawing; **~ton der** pastel shade

Pastetchen das; ~s, ~: [small] vol-au-vent; *(Hülle)* [small] vol-au-vent case

Pastete [pas'te:tə] **die; ~, ~n a)** *(gefüllte ~)* vol-au-vent; *(Hülle)* vol-au-vent case; **b)** *(in einer Schüssel o.ä. gegart)* pâté; *(in einer Hülle aus Teig gebacken)* pie

pasteurisieren [pastøri'zi:rən] *tr. V.* pasteurize

Pasteurisierung die; ~, ~en pasteurization

Pastille [pas'tɪlə] **die; ~, ~n** pastille

Pastinake [pasti'na:kə] **die; ~, ~n** parsnip

Past·milch die *(schweiz.)* pasteurized milk

Pastor ['pastɔr] **der; ~s, ~en** pastor; *s. auch* **Pfarrer**

pastoral [pasto'ra:l] *Adj.* **a)** *(seelsorgerlich)* pastoral; **b)** *(salbungsvoll)* unctuous; **c)** *(idyllisch)* pastoral ⟨*literature*⟩

Pastorale das; ~s, ~s *od.* **die; ~, ~n a)** *(Musik)* pastorale; **b)** *(Literaturw., Kunst)* pastoral

Pastorin die; ~, ~nen pastor

Pate ['pa:tə] **der; ~n, ~n a)** *(Taufzeuge)* godparent; *(Patenonkel; in der Mafia)* godfather; *(Patin)* godmother; *(DDR)* sponsor *(responsible for the child's socialist upbringing);* **bei jmdm. ~ stehen** act as *or* be godfather/godmother to sb.; *(DDR: bei der Namengebung)* act as sponsor to sb.; **bei etw. ~ stehen** *(fig.)* be [the influence/influences] behind sth.; *(als Vorbild dienen)* act as the model for sth.; **b)** *(veralt.: Patenkind)* godchild

Patene [pa'te:nə] **die; ~, ~n** *(christl. Kirche)* paten

Paten-: ~kind das godchild; *(DDR)* sponsored child; **~onkel der** godfather; *(DDR)* [male] sponsor

Patenschaft die; ~, ~en *(christl. Rel.)* godparenthood; *(DDR, fig.)* sponsorship **(für, über +** *Akk.* of)

Paten-: ~sohn der godson; *(DDR)* sponsored boy; **~stadt die** twin town *(Brit.);* sister city *or* town *(Amer.)*

patent [pa'tɛnt] *(ugs.)* **1.** *Adj.* **a)** *(tüchtig)* capable; **ein ~er Kerl** a great guy *(sl.);* **b)** *(zweckmäßig)* ingenious ⟨*device, method, idea*⟩; clever ⟨*slogan etc.*⟩. **2.** *adv.* ingeniously; cleverly; neatly ⟨*solved*⟩

Patent das; ~[e]s, ~e a) *(Schutz)* patent; **ein ~ auf etw.** *(Akk.)* **haben** have a patent for sth.; **etw. zum** *od.* **als ~ anmelden, auf** *od.* **für etw. ein ~ anmelden** apply for a patent for sth.; **„als ~ angemeldet"** 'patent pending'; 'patent applied for'; **b)** *(Erfindung)* [patented] invention; *(fig.: Konstruktion/ Verfahren)* [patent] design/method; **c)** *(Ernennungsurkunde)* certificate [of appointment]; *(eines Kapitäns)* master's certificate; *(eines Offiziers)* commission

Patent-: **~amt das** Patent Office; **~an·meldung die** patent application

Paten·tante die *s.* **Patin**

patent-, Patent-: **~anwalt der** patent agent *or (Amer.)* attorney; **~fähig** *Adj.* patentable; **~gesetz das** Patents Act

patentieren *tr. V.* patent; **jmdm. etw. ~:** grant sb. a patent for sth.; **sich** *(Dat.)* **eine Erfindung ~ lassen** have an invention patented

Patent-: **~inhaber der** patentee; **~lösung die** patent remedy **(für, zu** for)

Paten·tochter die god-daughter; *(DDR)* sponsored girl

Patent-: **~recht das a)** *(Rechtsnormen)* patent law *no art.*; **b)** *(berechtigter Anspruch)* patent rights *pl.*; **~register das** *(österr., schweiz.) s.* **~rolle; ~rezept das** patent remedy **(gegen, für** for); **kein ~rezept dafür haben, wie man etw. tut** have no magic recipe for doing sth.; **~rolle die** ≈ Register of Patents *(Brit.)*; **~schrift die** patent specification; **~schutz der** patent protection

Pater ['pa:tɐ] **der; ~s, ~** *od.* **Patres** ['pa:tre:s] *(kath. Kirche)* Father

[1]**Paternoster** [pa:tɐ'nɔstɐ] **der; ~s, ~** *(Aufzug)* paternoster [lift]

[2]**Paternoster das; ~s, ~** *(Gebet)* Lord's Prayer

pathetisch [pa'te:tɪʃ] **1.** *Adj.* emotional, impassioned ⟨*speech, manner*⟩; melodramatic ⟨*gesture*⟩; emotive ⟨*style*⟩; pompous ⟨*voice*⟩. **2.** *adv.* emotionally; with much emotion; *(dramatisch)* [melo]dramatically

Pathologe [pato'lo:gə] **der; ~n, ~n** pathologist

Pathologie [patolo'gi:] **die; ~, ~n a)** *o. Pl. (Gebiet)* pathology *no art.*; **b)** *(Abteilung/ Institut)* pathology department/institute

Pathologin die; ~, ~nen pathologist

pathologisch 1. *(Med.; auch fig.) Adj.* pathological. **2.** *adv.* pathologically

Pathos ['pa:tɔs] **das; ~** emotionalism; **ein unechtes/hohles ~:** false/empty pathos; **eine Rede voller ~:** a speech full of emotion; **etw. mit ~ vortragen** recite sth. with much feeling

Patience [pa'siã:s] **die; ~, ~n** [game of] patience; **~n/eine ~ legen** play patience/a game of patience

Patient [pa'tsiɛnt] **der; ~en, ~en, Patientin die; ~, ~nen** patient; **~ von** *od.* **bei Dr. X sein** be a patient of Dr X

Patin die; ~, ~nen *(Taufzeugin)* godmother; *(DDR)* sponsor *(responsible for the child's socialist upbringing)*

Patina ['pa:tina] **die; ~:** patina; **~ ansetzen** become covered with a patina; *(fig.)* begin to show its age; become dated

patinieren *tr. V.* patinate

Patisserie [patɪsə'ri:] **die; ~, ~n** *(schweiz.)* patisserie

Patres *s.* **Pater**

Patriarch [patri'arç] **der; ~en, ~en** patriarch

patriarchalisch 1. *Adj.* patriarchal; *(fig.: autoritär)* authoritarian. **2.** *adv.* in a patriarchal *or (fig.)* authoritarian manner

Patriarchat das; ~[e]s, ~e a) *(Gesellschaftsordnung)* patriarchy; **b)** *(kath. u. orthodoxe Kirche)* patriarchate

Patriot [patri'o:t] **der; ~en, ~en, Patriotin die; ~, ~nen** patriot

patriotisch 1. *Adj.* patriotic. **2.** *adv.* patriotically; **~ erzogen werden** be brought up to be a patriot

Patriotismus der; ~: patriotism *usu. no def. art.*

Patrize [pa'tri:tsə] **die; ~, ~n** *(Druckw.)* steel punch *or* die

Patriziat [patri'tsia:t] **das; ~[e], ~e** *(hist.)* patriciate

Patrizier [pa'tri:tsiɐ] **der; ~s, ~** *(hist.)* patrician

Patron [pa'tro:n] **der; ~s, ~e a)** *(Schutzheiliger)* patron saint; **b)** *(Stifter einer Kirche)* patron; founder; **c)** *(ugs. abwertend: Kerl)* type *(coll.)*; **ein übler ~:** a nasty piece of work *(coll.)*; **d)** *(hist.: Schutzherr; veralt.: Gönner)* patron

Patronage [patro'na:ʒə] **die; ~, ~n** favouritism *no art.*; *(im Staatsapparat)* patronage *no art.*

Patronat [patro'na:t] **das; ~[e]s, ~e a)** *(hist.: Würde, Amt)* patronate; **b)** *(Schirmherrschaft; Kirchenrecht: Rechtstellung)* patronage

Patrone [pa'tro:nə] **die; ~, ~n a)** *(für das Gewehr, den Füller)* cartridge; *(für die Kleinbildkamera)* cassette; **b)** *(Textilind.)* point paper plan; draft

Patronen-: **~gurt der, ~gürtel der** cartridge-belt; *(über der Schulter getragen)* bandoleer; **~hülse die** cartridge-case; **~tasche die** cartridge-pouch

Patronin die; ~, ~nen a) *(Schutzheilige)* patron saint; **b)** *(veralt.: Gönnerin)* patroness

Patrouille [pa'trʊljə] **die; ~, ~n** patrol

Patrouillen-: **~boot das** patrol boat; **~gang der** patrol

patrouillieren [patrʊl'ji:rən] *itr. V.; auch mit sein* be on patrol; **durch die Straßen ~:** patrol the streets

patsch [patʃ] *Interj.* splat; slap; *(auf Wasser usw.)* splash

Patsche die; ~, ~n a) *(ugs.) s.* **Klemme b; b)** *(ugs.: Hand)* paw *(coll.)*; **kleine ~n** *(eines Kindes)* little hands; **c)** *(Feuer~)* fire-beater

patschen *itr. V. (ugs.)* **a)** *(klatschen)* slap; **sich** *(Dat.)* **auf die Schenkel ~:** slap one's thighs; **das Kind patschte in die Hände** the child clapped its hands; **b)** *mit sein (~d gehen/fallen)* splash; **über die Fliesen ~** *(mit nassen Stiefeln usw.)* go flip-flop over the tiles; *(unbeholfen)* lollop over the tiles; **durch die Pfützen ~:** splash *or* go splashing through the puddles; **c)** *(~des Geräusch hervorbringen)* ⟨*slush, wet shoes*⟩ squelch

patsch-, Patsch-: **~hand die; ~händchen das** *(fam.)* [little] hand; handy-pandy *(child lang.)*; **~naß** *Adj. (ugs.)* sopping wet; **~naß geschwitzt** soaked in sweat

patt [pat] *(Schach)* **~ sein** be stalemated

Patt das; ~s, ~s *(Schach; auch fig.)* stalemate; **mit einem ~ enden** *od.* **ausgehen** end in stalemate

Patte die; ~, ~n [pocket] flap

Patt·situation die [position of] stalemate

patzen ['patsn̩] *itr. V.* **a)** *(ugs.: Fehler machen)* slip up *(coll.)*; boob *(sl.)*; **der Pianist hat ziemlich/erheblich gepatzt** the pianist came rather/well and truly unstuck *(coll.)*; **b)** *(österr.: klecksen)* make a blot/blots

Patzer der; ~s, ~ *(ugs.)* slip *(coll.)*; boob *(sl.)*; **ein dicker ~:** a real howler *(coll.)*

patzig *(ugs. abwertend)* **1.** *Adj.* snotty *(coll.)*; *(frech)* cheeky. **2.** *adv.* snottily *(coll.)*; *(frech)* cheekily

Paukant [pau'kant] **der; ~en, ~en** *(Studentenspr.)* duellist

Pauke ['paukə] **die; ~, ~n** kettledrum; **~n** *(im Orchester)* timpani; **die ~ schlagen** beat the drum/drums; **auf die ~ hauen** *(ugs.) (feiern)* paint the town red *(sl.)*; *(großtun)* blow one's own trumpet; *(sich lautstark äußern)* come right out with it; **mit ~n und Trompeten durchfallen** *(ugs.)* ⟨*candidate*⟩ fail resoundingly; ⟨*broadcast, film, etc.*⟩ be a resounding failure; **jmdn. mit ~n und Trompeten empfangen** *(fig.)* give sb. the red-carpet treatment

pauken 1. *tr. V. (ugs.)* swot up *(Brit. sl.)*, bone up on *(Amer. coll.)* ⟨*facts, figures, etc.*⟩; **Latein/Mathe ~:** swot up one's Latin/maths. **2.** *itr. V.* **a)** *(ugs.: lernen)* swot *(Brit. sl.)*; *(fürs Examen)* cram *(coll.)*; **b)** *(Musik) (in einer Band o. ä.)* play the big drum[s]; *(im Orchester)* play the timpani; **c)** *(Studentenspr.)* duel

Pauken-: **~schlag der a)** drum-beat; **Haydns Sinfonie mit dem ~schlag** Haydn's Surprise Symphony; **b)** *(fig. Eklat)* sensation; bombshell; **~schlegel der** drumstick

Pauker der; ~s, ~ a) *(Musik) (im Orchester)* timpanist; *(in einer Band o. ä.)* big-drum player; **b)** *(Schülerspr.: Lehrer)* teacher; teach *(school sl.)*

Paukerei die; ~: *(ugs. abwertend)* swotting *(Brit. sl.)*; boning up *(Amer. coll.)*; *(fürs Examen)* cramming

Paukist der; ~en, ~en *s.* **Pauker a**

Paulus ['paulʊs] **(der); Paulus'** Paul

Pauperismus [paupə'rɪsmʊs] **der; ~** *(Soziol.)* pauperism *usu. no art.*

Paus·backen *Pl. (fam.)* chubby cheeks

pausbäckig ['pausbɛkɪç] *Adj.* chubby-cheeked; chubby-faced; chubby ⟨*face*⟩

pauschal [pau'ʃa:l] **1.** *Adj.* **a)** *(rund gerechnet)* all-inclusive ⟨*price, settlement*⟩; **eine ~e Summe/Bezahlung** a lump sum/payment; **b)** *(verallgemeinernd)* sweeping ⟨*judgement, criticism, statement*⟩; indiscriminate ⟨*prejudice*⟩; wholesale ⟨*discrimination*⟩. **2.** *adv.* **a)** *(alles zusammengenommen)* ⟨*cost*⟩ overall, all in all; ⟨*pay*⟩ in a lump sum; **das Angebot gilt ~ für 10 Tage** the offer covers all costs *or* is inclusive for 10 days; **eine Frage ~ beantworten** answer a question in general terms; **b)** *(ohne zu differenzieren)* wholesale

Pauschale die; ~, ~n *od.* **das; ~s, Pauschalien** [-'ʃa:liən] flat-rate payment; *(Pauschalsumme)* lump sum; **monatliche ~:** flat monthly rate

Pauschal·gebühr die flat-rate [charge]

Pauschal-: **~preis der** *(Einheitspreis)* flat rate; *(Inklusivpreis)* inclusive *or* all-in price; **~reise die** package holiday; *(mit mehreren Reisezielen)* package tour; **~summe die** lump sum; **~urteil das** *(abwertend)* sweeping judgement *or* statement

Pausch·betrag ['pauʃ-] **der** lump sum

[1]**Pause** ['pauzə] **die; ~, ~n a)** *(Unterbrechung)* break; *(Ruhe~)* rest; *(Theater)* interval *(Brit.)*; intermission *(Amer.)*; *(Kino)* intermission; *(Sport)* half-time interval; **kleine/große ~:** *(Schule)* short/[long] break; *(Theater)* short/main interval *(Brit.) or (Amer.)* intermission; **in** *od.* **während der ~** *(Schule)* in *or* during break; *(Theater)* in *or* during the interval *(Brit.) or (Amer.)* intermission; *(Sport)* at half-time; **wann haben wir [große] ~?** *(Schule)* when is [the long] break?; **es klingelt zur ~** *(Schule)* the bell is ringing for break; **[eine] ~ machen** take *or* have a break; *(zum Ausruhen)* have a rest; **wir machen kurz/eine Viertelstunde ~:** we'll take a short break/a quarter of an hour's break; **eine ~ einlegen** *od.* **einschieben** have a rest; **mach mal ~!** take a break!; **b)** *(in der Unterhaltung o. ä.)* pause; *(verlegenes Schweigen)* silence; **c)** *(Musik)* rest; **eine ganze/halbe ~:** a semibreve/minim rest; a whole [note]/half [note] rest *(Amer.)*

[2]**Pause die; ~, ~n** *(Kopie)* tracing; *(Licht~)* Photostat *(Brit.* **P)**

pausen *tr. V.* trace; *(eine Lichtpause machen)* Photostat *(Brit.* **P)**

Pausen-: **~brot das** sandwich *(eaten during break)*; **~füller der** *(ugs.)* interval material *no art.*; **~hof der** school yard

pausen·los 1. *Adj.; nicht präd.:* incessant ⟨*noise, moaning, questioning*⟩; continous, uninterrupted ⟨*work, operation*⟩. **2.** *adv.* incessantly; ceaselessly; ⟨*work*⟩ non-stop

Pausen·zeichen das a) *(Musik)* rest; **b)** *(Rundfunk, Ferns.)* interval signal

pausieren *itr. V.* **a)** *(innehalten)* pause; **b)** *(aussetzen)* have *or* take a rest; **acht Wochen ~ müssen** *(Sport)* ⟨*player*⟩ be out of the game for eight weeks

Paus·papier das *(durchsichtig)* tracing paper; *(Kohlepapier)* carbon paper

Pavian ['pa:via:n] **der; ~s, ~e** baboon

Pavillon ['pavɪljɔn] **der; ~s, ~s** *(Archit.)* pavilion; *(einer Schule o. ä.)* annexe

Pazifik [pa'tsi:fɪk] **der; ~s** Pacific

pazifisch *Adj.* Pacific ⟨*area*⟩; **der Pazifische Ozean** the Pacific Ocean

Pazifismus der; ~: pacifism *no art.*

Pazifist der; ~en, ~en, Pazifistin die; ~, ~nen pacifist

pazifistisch 1. *Adj.* pacifist. **2.** *adv.* in a pacifist way

PDS [pe:de:'ɛs] **die; ~** *Abk.* **Partei des Demokratischen Sozialismus** Party of Democratic Socialism

Pech [pɛç] **das; ~[e]s, ~e a)** pitch; **schwarz wie ~ sein** be pitch-black; ⟨*hair*⟩ be jet-black; **zusammenhalten wie ~ und Schwefel** *(ugs.)* be inseparable; ⟨*friends*⟩ be as thick as thieves *(coll.)*; **b)** *o. Pl. (Mißgeschick)* bad luck; **großes/unerhörtes ~:** rotten *(sl.)*/ *(coll.)* terrible luck; **bei** *od.* **mit etw./ mit jmdm. ~ haben** have bad luck with sth./ sb.; be unlucky with sth./sb.; **im Leben/in der Liebe/bei den Frauen/beim Examen ~ haben** have no luck in life/in love/with women/in the exam; **~ gehabt!** *(ugs.)* tough luck! *(coll.)*; **dein ~, wenn du nicht aufpaßt** *(ugs.)* that's just your hard luck *(coll.)* if you don't pay attention; **sein ~!** *(ugs.)* that's his look-out; **~ für dich** *(ugs.)* that's just too bad *(coll.)*; **vom ~ verfolgt sein** be dogged by bad luck

pech-, Pech-: ~blende die *(Mineral.)* pitchblende; **~[raben]schwarz** *Adj. (ugs.)* pitch-black ⟨*night, darkness, coffee*⟩; jet-black ⟨*eyes*⟩; raven[-black] ⟨*hair*⟩; **~strähne die** run of bad luck; **~vogel der** unlucky devil *(coll.)*; *(Opfer vieler Unfälle)* walking disaster area *(coll.)*

Pedal [pe'da:l] **das; ~s, ~e** pedal; *(bei der Orgel)* pedals *pl.*; **mit/ohne ~ spielen** *(beim Klavier)* use/not use pedal; **[kräftig] in die ~e treten** *(beim Fahrrad)* pedal [really] hard

pedant *(österr.)* *s.* **pedantisch**

Pedant [pe'dant] **der; ~en, ~en, Pedantin, die; ~, ~nen** pedant

Pedanterie [pedantə'ri:] **die; ~, ~n** pedantry; **seine ~n** his pedantic ways

pedantisch 1. *Adj.* pedantic. **2.** *adv.* pedantically

Peddig·rohr ['pɛdɪç-] **das;** *o. Pl.* rattan [cane]

Pedell [pe'dɛl] **der; ~s, ~e,** *(österr. meist:)* **~en, ~en** *(veralt.)* caretaker *(Brit.)*; janitor *(esp. Amer.)*

Pediküre [pedi'ky:rə] **die; ~, ~n a)** *o. Pl.*; *s.* **Fußpflege; b)** *(Berufsbez.)* chiropodist

pediküren *tr. V.* pedicure ⟨*feet, nails*⟩

Pegel ['pe:gl̩] **der; ~s, ~ a)** *(Gerät)* water-level indicator; *(für die Gezeiten am Meer)* tide-gauge; **b)** *(Wasserstand)* water-level; *(Technik, Physik; auch fig.)* level *(of noise, alcohol consumption, etc.)*

Pegel·stand der water-level

Peil·antenne die *(Funkw., Seew.)* direction-finding antenna

peilen ['pailən] **1.** *tr. V.* **a)** take a bearing on ⟨*transmitter, fixed point*⟩; *s. auch* **Daumen; Lage c; b)** *(Wassertiefe messen)* sound ⟨*depth*⟩; take soundings in ⟨*bay etc.*⟩. **2.** *itr. V.* **a)** take one's bearings; get a fix; **b)** *(Wassertiefe messen)* take a sounding/soundings; **c)** *(ugs.: spähen)* peek

Peilung die; ~, ~en *(Seew.)* **a)** *(das Peilen)* taking a bearing; *(des eigenen Standorts)* plotting one's position; *(Resultat)* fix; bearing; **b)** *(der Wassertiefe)* sounding

Pein [pain] **die; ~** *(geh.)* torment; **körperliche/seelische ~:** physical/mental anguish; **jmdm. [viel** *od.* **große] ~ bereiten** cause sb. [much] anguish

peinigen ['painɪgn̩] *tr. V. (geh.)* torment; *(foltern)* torture; **von Durst/Kälte gepeinigt werden** suffer agonies from thirst/cold; **von Schmerzen gepeinigt werden** be tormented by *or* racked with pain; *s. auch* **Blut**

Peiniger der; ~s, ~: *(geh.)* tormentor; *(Folterer)* torturer

Peinigung die; ~, ~en *(geh.)* torment; *(Folterung)* torture

peinlich 1. *Adj.* **a)** embarrassing; awkward ⟨*question, position, pause*⟩; **es ist mir sehr ~:** I feel very bad *(coll.)* or embarrassed about it; **es ist mir sehr ~, Ihnen das mitteilen zu müssen** I feel terrible about having to tell you this *(coll.)*; **es ist mir sehr ~, aber ich wollte Sie fragen, ...:** I don't know quite how to put this, but I wanted to ask you ...; **b)** *nicht präd. (äußerst genau)* meticulous; scrupulous; **er hielt sich mit ~ster Genauigkeit an diese Vorschrift** he was most punctilious in observing this regulation; **c)** *nicht präd. (Rechtsspr. veralt.)* **das ~e Gericht** the criminal *or* penal court; **ein ~es Verhör** an interrogation under torture. **2.** *adv.* **a)** unpleasantly ⟨*surprised*⟩; **[von etw.] ~ berührt** *od.* **betroffen sein** be painfully embarrassed [by sth.]; **b)** *(überaus [genau])* scrupulously; meticulously; **er vermied es ~[st], dieses heikle Thema zu berühren** he took [the utmost] pains to avoid touching on this delicate subject; **~ genau registriert** listed down to the last detail

Peinlichkeit die; ~, ~en a) *o. Pl.* embarrassment; **die ~ der Situation** the awkwardness of the situation; **b)** *o. Pl. (Genauigkeit)* scrupulousness; meticulousness; **c)** *(peinliche Situation)* embarrassing situation; *(heikle Situation)* awkward situation; *(Fehler)* embarrassing blunder

peinsam *Adj. (meist scherzh.)* *s.* **peinlich 1 a**

pein·voll *Adj. (geh.)* painful; agonizing ⟨*uncertainty*⟩; ⟨*period*⟩ full of anguish

Peitsche ['paitʃə] **die; ~, ~n** whip; **er knallte mit der ~:** he cracked the whip; *s. auch* **Zuckerbrot**

peitschen 1. *tr. V.* whip; *(fig.)* ⟨*storm, waves, rain*⟩ lash. **2.** *itr. V.*; *mit sein* ⟨*rain*⟩ lash **(an, gegen** + *Akk.* against, **in** + *Akk.* into); ⟨*shot*⟩ ring out

Peitschen-: ~hieb der lash [of the whip]; **wie ein ~hieb** like a whiplash; **~knall der** crack of the whip; **~lampe die** street lamp *(hanging over the street from a curved standard)*; **~stiel der** whip handle; whipstock

pejorativ [pejora'ti:f] *(Sprachw.)* **1.** *Adj.* pejorative. **2.** *adv.* perjoratively

Pekinese [peki'ne:zə] **der; ~n, ~n** Pekinese

Peking·mensch ['pe:kɪŋ-] **der;** *o. Pl.* Peking Man

Pektin [pɛk'ti:n] **das; ~, ~e** *(Biol.)* pectin

pekuniär [pɛku'niɛ:ɐ̯] **1.** *Adj.*; *nicht präd.* pecuniary; financial. **2.** *adv.* financially

Pelerine [pelə'ri:nə] **die; ~, ~n** cape

Pelikan ['pe:lika:n] **der; ~s, ~e** pelican

Pelle ['pɛlə] **die; ~, ~n** *(bes. nordd.)* skin; *(abgeschält)* peel; **Kartoffeln in** *od.* **mit der ~ kochen** boil potatoes in their skins; **sie hocken sich** *(Dat.)* **[dauernd] auf der ~** *(salopp)* they never leave each other alone; **jmdm. nicht von der ~ gehen** *(salopp)* refuse to leave sb. alone *or* in peace; *s. auch* **rücken 2 a; sitzen a**

pellen *(bes. nordd.)* **1.** *tr. V.* peel ⟨*potato, egg, etc.*⟩; **sie pellte sich/das Kind aus dem warmen Winterzeug** *(fig.)* she peeled off her/the child's warm winter things; *s. auch* **Ei a. 2.** *refl. V.* ⟨*person, skin*⟩ peel

Pell·kartoffel die potato boiled in its skin

Pelz [pɛlts] **der; ~es, ~e a)** fur; coat; *(des toten Tieres)* skin; pelt; **einen weichen ~ haben** have a soft coat; have soft fur; **einem Tier den ~ abziehen** skin an animal; **b)** *o. Pl. (gegerbt; als Material)* fur; **aus ~:** made of fur; **mit ~ gefüttert** fur-lined; **c)** fur; *(~mantel)* fur coat; *(~jacke)* fur jacket; **d)** *(ugs.: Haut)* **sich** *(Dat.)* **die Sonne auf den ~ brennen** *od.* **scheinen lassen** soak up the sun; **jmdm./einem Tier eins auf den ~ brennen** take a pot-shot at sb./an animal; *s. auch* **Laus; rücken 2 a; sitzen a**

pelz-, Pelz-: ~besatz der fur trimming; **~besetzt** *Adj.* fur-trimmed; **~futter das** fur lining; **~gefüttert** *Adj.* fur-lined; **~händler der** furrier; **~hand·schuh der** fur glove; *(pelzgefüttert)* fur-lined glove

pelzig *Adj.* **a)** *(wie Pelz, mit Flaum)* furry; downy ⟨*peach*⟩; **b)** *(bes. westd.: mehlig)* mealy ⟨*apple*⟩; *(holzig)* woody ⟨*radish*⟩; **c)** *(belegt)* furred, coated ⟨*tongue, mouth*⟩

Pelz-: ~imitation die imitation fur; **~jacke die** fur jacket; **~kragen der** fur collar; **~mantel der** fur coat; **~mütze die** fur hat; **~stiefel der** fur boot; *(pelzgefüttert)* fur-lined boot; **~tier das** animal prized for its fur; **~tier·farm die** fur-farm; **~tier·jäger der** fur-hunter; trapper; **~tier·zucht die** fur farming *no def. art.*; **~waren** *Pl.* furs; fur goods; **~werk das** *o. Pl.* fur

Pendant [pã'dã:] **das; ~s, ~s** *(Gegenstück)* counterpart **(zu** of); *(ein Stück von einem Paar)* companion piece **(zu** of); *(Entsprechung)* equivalent **(zu** of)

Pendel ['pɛndl̩] **das; ~s, ~:** pendulum

pendeln *itr. V.* **a)** *(hin u. her schwingen)* swing [to and fro] **(an** + *Dat.* by); *(mit weniger Bewegung)* dangle; **b)** *mit sein (hin- u. herfahren)* **zwischen X und Y ~** ⟨*bus, ferry, etc.*⟩ operate a shuttle service between X and Y; ⟨*person*⟩ commute between X and Y; **c)** *(Boxen)* weave

Pendel-: ~tür die swing-door; **~uhr die** pendulum clock; **~verkehr der a)** *(Berufsverkehr)* commuter traffic; **b)** *(mit Pendelzug o. ä.)* shuttle service; **~zug der** shuttle[-service] train

Pendler der; ~s, ~, Pendlerin die; ~, ~nen commuter

Penes *s.* **Penis**

penetrant [pene'trant] *(abwertend)* **1.** *Adj.* **a)** *(durchdringend)* penetrating, pungent ⟨*smell, taste*⟩; overpowering ⟨*stink, perfume*⟩; **b)** *(aufdringlich)* pushing, *(coll.)* pushy ⟨*person*⟩; overbearing ⟨*tone, manner*⟩; aggressive, pointed ⟨*question*⟩. **2.** *adv.* **a)** *(durchdringend)* overpoweringly; **es riecht/schmeckt ~ nach ...:** there is an overpowering smell/an overpowering *or* pungent taste of ...; **b)** *(aufdringlich)* overbearingly; in an overbearing manner

Penetranz [pene'trants] **die; ~ a)** *(von Geruch, Geschmack)* overpowering nature; **b)** *(Aufdringlichkeit)* overbearing nature

Penetration [penetra'tsio:n] **die; ~, ~en a)** *(Technik)* penetration; *(Wirtsch.)* penetration [of the market]; **b)** *(Med.)* perforation

penetrieren *tr. V. (geh.)* penetrate

peng [pɛŋ] *Interj.* bang

penibel [pe'ni:bl̩] **1.** *Adj.* over-meticulous ⟨*person*⟩; *(pedantisch)* pedantic; **penible Kleinarbeit** painstakingly detailed work. **2.** *adv.* painstakingly; over-meticulously ⟨*dressed*⟩

Penicillin *s.* **Penizillin**

Penis ['pe:nɪs] **der; ~, ~se** *od.* **Penes** ['pe:ne:s] penis

Penis·neid der *(Psych.)* penis envy

Penizillin [penitsɪ'li:n] **das; ~s, ~e** penicillin

Pennäler [pɛ'nɛ:lɐ] **der; ~s, ~s** *(ugs.)* [secondary] schoolboy

Pennälerin die; ~, ~nen *(ugs.)* [secondary] schoolgirl

Penn·bruder der *(ugs. abwertend)* tramp *(Brit.)*; hobo *(Amer.)*

Penne ['pɛnə] **die; ~, ~n a)** *(Schülerspr.: Schule)* [secondary] school; swot-shop *(Brit. sl.)*; **b)** *(ugs. abwertend: Nachtquartier)* doss-house *(Brit. sl.)*; flop-house *(sl.)*

pennen *itr. V. (salopp)* **a)** *(schlafen)* kip *(sl.)*; **auf einer Bank ~:** doss down on a bench *(sl.)*; **b)** *(fig.: nicht aufpassen)* be half asleep; **du hast im Unterricht wohl mal wieder gepennt?** *(fig.)* I suppose you were dreaming again during the lesson?; **c)** *(koitieren)* **mit jmdm. ~:** sleep with sb.

Penner der; ~s, ~, Pennerin die; ~, ~nen *(salopp abwertend)* **a)** *(Stadtstreicher)* tramp *(Brit.)*; hobo *(Amer.)*; **b)** *(jmd., der viel schläft)* sleepyhead

Pensa, Pensen *s.* **Pensum**

Pension [pã'zio:n] **die; ~, ~en a)** *o. Pl. (Ruhestand)* **[vorzeitig] in ~ gehen** retire [early]; **in ~ sein** be retired *or* in retirement; **einen Beamten in ~** *(Akk.)* **schicken** retire a civil servant; **b)** *(Ruhegehalt)* [retirement] pension; **c)** *(Haus für [Ferien]gäste)* guest-house; *(auf dem Kontinent)* pension; **d)** *o. Pl. (Unterkunft u. Verpflegung)* board; **[die] halbe/volle ~:** half/full board; **bei jmdm. in ~ sein** board with sb.

Pensionär [pãzio'nɛ:ɐ̯] **der; ~s, ~e, Pensionärin die; ~, ~nen a)** *(Beamter in Ruhestand)* retired civil servant; *(ugs.: Rentner)* [old-age] pensioner; **~ sein** be retired *or* in retirement; **b)** *(schweiz., sonst veralt.: Bewohner einer Pension)* boarder; [paying] guest

Pensionat [pãzio'na:t] **das; ~[e]s, ~e** *(veralt.)* boarding-school *(esp. for girls)*

pensionieren *tr. V.* pension off; retire; **sich [vorzeitig] ~ lassen** retire [early]; take [early] retirement

Pensionierung die; ~, ~en retirement; **bis zur ~:** up to [his, her, *etc.*] retirement

Pensionist, der; ~en, ~en, Pensionistin die; ~, ~nen *(südd., österr., schweiz.)* *s.* **Pensionär a**

pensions-, Pensions-: ~alter das retirement age; **~an·spruch der** pension entitlement; **~ansprüche** pension rights; **~berechtigt** *Adj.* entitled to a pension *postpos.*; **~berechtigung die** *o. Pl.* pension entitlement; **~gast der** patron [of a/the guest-house]; **~kasse die** *(Versicherungsw.)* [staff] pension fund; **~reif** *Adj. (ugs.)* ripe for retirement *pred.*; **~rückstellungen** *Pl. (Wirtsch.)* pension reserves

Pensum ['pɛnzʊm] **das; ~s, Pensen** *od.* **Pensa a)** *(Arbeit)* amount of work; work quota; **sein tägliches ~ [an Arbeit] erledigen** do one's daily stint [of work]; **b)** *(Päd. veralt.: Lehrstoff)* syllabus

Pentagon [pɛnta'go:n] **das; ~s, ~e a)** *(Geom.)* pentagon; **b)** *o. Pl. (amerikan. Verteidigungsministerium)* Pentagon

Penta-: ~gramm das pentagram; **~meter** [-'---] **der** *(Verslehre)* pentameter

Pentatonik [pɛnta'to:nɪk] **die; ~:** *(Musik)* pentatonic scale

Pent·haus ['pɛnt-] **das, Penthouse** ['pɛnthaʊs] **das; ~, ~s** penthouse

Penunse [pe'nʊnzə], **Penunze** [pe'nʊntsə] **die; ~, ~n** *(ugs.)* **~[n]** cash; dough *(sl.)*

Pep [pɛp] **der; ~[s]** *(ugs.)* pep *(sl.)*; zip; **~ haben** be dynamic *or* full of zip

Peperoni [pepe'ro:ni] **die; ~, ~:** chilli

Pepita [pe'pi:ta] **der** *od.* **das; ~s, ~s** shepherd's check

Pepsin [pɛ'psi:n] **das; ~s, ~e** *(Med.)* pepsin

per [pɛr] *Präp. mit Akk.* **a)** *(mittels)* by; **~ Post** by post; **~ Adresse X** care of X; c/o X; *s. auch* **Anhalter; du; Eilbote; Einschreiben; Nachnahme; b)** *(Kaufmannsspr.: [bis] zum)* by; *(am)* on; **~ Jahresende** by the end of the year; **~ sofort** immediately; as of now; **c)** *(Kaufmannsspr.: pro)* per; **etw. ~ Kilo/Stück verkaufen** sell sth. by the kilo/by the piece *or* separately

per definitionem [- defini'tsio:nɛm] *Adv. (geh.)* by definition

perennierend [perɛ'ni:rənt] *Adj. (Biol., Geogr., fig.)* perennial

Perf. *Abk.* **Perfekt** perf.

perfekt [pɛr'fɛkt] **1.** *Adj.* **a)** *(hervorragend)* outstanding; first-rate; *(vollkommen)* perfect ‹*crime, host*›; faultless ‹*English, French, etc.*›; **eine ~e Sekretärin** a fully accomplished secretary; **b)** *nicht attr. (ugs.: endgültig, abgeschlossen)* finalized; concluded; **~ sein/werden** ‹*contract, deal*› be concluded *or* finalized; ‹*scandal, defeat*› be complete; **~ machen** finalize ‹*contract, date, booking, deal*›; complete ‹*disaster*›. **2.** *adv.* **a)** *(hervorragend)* outstandingly well; *(vollkommen)* ‹*fit, work, etc.*› perfectly; **~ beherrschen** have a complete mastery of ‹*language, material*›; play ‹*game*› with complete mastery; **er spricht ~ Englisch** he speaks faultless *or* perfect English; **b)** *(ugs.: vollständig)* good and proper *(coll.)*; **er hat sich ~ blamiert** he made a complete fool of himself

Perfekt ['pɛrfɛkt] **das; ~s, ~e** *(Sprachw.)* perfect [tense]

Perfektion [pɛrfɛk'tsio:n] **die; ~:** perfection; **handwerkliche/technische ~:** mastery of a craft/technical mastery; **etw. mit [großer] ~ ausführen/spielen** do/play sth. to perfection; do/play sth. with great mastery; **Reitkunst in höchster** *od.* **absoluter ~:** the art of riding at its most perfect

perfektionieren *tr. V.* perfect

Perfektionismus der; ~: perfectionism

Perfektionist der; ~en, ~en, Perfektionistin die; ~, ~nen perfectionist

perfektionistisch 1. *Adj.* perfectionist ‹*standards etc.*›. **2.** *adv.* in a perfectionist manner

perfektiv ['pɛrfɛkti:f] *Adj. (Sprachw.)* perfective

perfid [pɛr'fi:t], **perfide** *(geh.)* **1.** *Adj.* perfidious. **2.** *adv.* perfidiously

Perfidie [pɛrfi'di:] **die; ~, ~n** *(geh.)* perfidy

Perforation [pɛrfora'tsio:n] **die; ~, ~en** *(Technik, Med.)* perforation

perforieren *tr. V. (Technik, Med.)* perforate

Pergament [pɛrga'mɛnt] **das; ~[e]s, ~e** parchment; *(bes. für Bucheinbände)* vellum

Pergament·band der vellum-bound volume

pergamenten *Adj.* **a)** parchment; vellum ‹*binding*›; vellum-bound ‹*book*›; **b)** *(wie aus Pergament)* ‹*skin, face*› like parchment

Pergament·papier das grease-proof paper

Pergola ['pɛrgola] **die; ~, Pergolen** pergola

Periode [pe'rio:də] **die; ~, ~n a)** *(auch Chemie, Physik, Technik, Astron., Met., Sprachw., Musik)* period; *(Geol.)* era; **sie hat ihre ~ nicht bekommen** she didn't get *or* have her period; **b)** *(Math.)* repetend; period; **3,3 ~:** 3.3 recurring

Perioden·system das *(Chemie)* periodic system; *(graphische Darstellung)* periodic table

Periodikum [pe'rio:dikʊm] **das; ~s, Periodika** *meist Pl.* periodical

periodisch 1. *Adj.* **a)** *(regelmäßig)* regular; ‹*meeting, statement of account*› at regular intervals; *(Chemie)* periodic ‹*system*›; **eine ~e Dezimalzahl** *(Math.)* a recurring decimal; **b)** *(zeitweilig)* sporadic ‹*moods etc.*›. **2.** *adv.* **a)** *(regelmäßig)* regularly; at regular intervals; **b)** *(zeitweilig)* periodically; from time to time

peripher [peri'fe:ɐ̯] **1.** *Adj. (auch Anat., fig.)* peripheral; **~e Stadtteile** districts on the outskirts of the town. **2.** *adv. (auch Anat., fig.)* peripherally; **die Siedlung liegt ~:** the estate is on the outskirts; **ein Thema nur ~ behandeln** just touch on a subject

Peripherie [perife'ri:] **die; ~, ~n a)** periphery; *(einer Stadt)* outskirts *pl.*; fringe; *(Geom.: Begrenzungslinie)* circumference; **die ~ des Körpers** the peripheral areas of the body; **b)** *(Datenverarb.: periphere Geräte)* peripherals *pl.*

Periskop [peri'sko:p] **das; ~s, ~e** periscope

Peristaltik [peri'staltɪk] **die; ~** *(Physiol.)* peristalsis

perkutan [pɛrku'ta:n] *(Med.) Adj.* percutaneous

Perle ['pɛrlə] **die; ~, ~n a)** *(auch fig.)* pearl; **~n vor die Säue werfen** *(fig. ugs.)* cast pearls before swine; *s. auch* **Krone a; b)** *(aus Holz, Glas o.ä.)* bead; *(Tröpfchen)* drop; *(Bläschen beim Sekt usw.)* bubble; **c)** *(ugs. scherzh.: Hausgehilfin)* [invaluable] home help

perlen *itr. V.* **a)** *auch mit sein* **auf etw.** *(Dat.)* **~:** form pearls on sth.; ‹*dew*› form droplets on sth.; **der Schweiß perlte ihm auf der Stirn** beads of perspiration stood out on his brow; **b)** *mit sein* **von etw. ~:** ‹*dew, sweat*› trickle *or* drip from sth.; **Tränen perlten über ihre Wangen** tears trickled *or* rolled down her cheeks; **c)** *(Bläschen bilden)* ‹*champagne etc.*› sparkle, bubble; **d)** *(melodisch ertönen)* ‹*laughter, music*› ripple

perlen-, Perlen-: ~bestickt *Adj.* embroidered *or* decorated with pearls *postpos.*; **~fischer der** pearl-fisher; **~fischerei die** pearl-fishing; **~kette die** string of pearls; pearl necklace; *(mit Holzperlen usw.)* string of beads; bead necklace; **~kollier das** pearl necklace; **~schnur die** string of pearls; *(mit Holzperlen usw.)* string of beads; **~stickerei die** pearl embroidery; *(mit Holzperlen usw.)* bead embroidery; **~taucher der** pearl-diver

perl-, Perl-: ~garn das pearl cotton; **~grau** *Adj.* pearl-grey; **~huhn das** guinea-fowl; **~muschel die** pearl-oyster; **~muster das** moss-stitch; **~mutt** [~mʊt] **das; ~s, ~mutter die; ~** *od.* **das; ~s** mother-of-pearl; **~muttern** *Adj.* mother-of-pearl; *(fig.: wie Perlmutter)* like mother-of-pearl *postpos.*

Perlon Ⓦⓩ **das; ~s** ≈ nylon

Perlon·strumpf der ≈ nylon stocking

Perl-: ~schrift die; *o. Pl.* elite; **~wein der** sparkling wine; **~zwiebel die** pearl *or* cocktail onion

permanent [pɛrma'nɛnt] **1.** *Adj.* permanent ‹*institution, deficit, crisis*›; constant ‹*danger, threat, squabble*›. **2.** *adv.* constantly

Permanenz [pɛrma'nɛnts] **die; ~** permanence; **in ~:** permanently; **in ~ tagen** sit continuously; be in permanent session

permissiv [pɛrmɪ'si:f] *(Soziol., Psych.) Adj.* permissive

per pedes *Adv. (ugs.)* on Shank's pony

Perpendikel [pɛrpɛn'di:kl̩] **der** *od.* **das; ~s, ~ a)** *(veralt.: einer Uhr)* pendulum; **b)** *(Schiffbau)* perpendicular

perpetuieren [pɛrpetu'i:rən] *tr. V. (geh.)* perpetuate

Perpetuum mobile [pɛr'pɛ:tuʊm 'mo:bilə] **das; ~ ~, ~ ~[s]** *od.* **Perpetua mobilia a)** *(utopische Maschine)* perpetual-motion machine; **b)** *(Musik)* perpetuum mobile

perplex [pɛr'plɛks] *(ugs.)* **1.** *Adj. (verblüfft)* baffled, puzzled (**über** + *Akk.* by); *(verwirrt)* bewildered. **2.** *adv.* **~ dreinschauen** look baffled/bewildered

per saldo [-'saldo] *(Kaufmannsspr.)* net; *(fig.: im Endeffekt)* on balance; **~ ~ rund 4 Millionen Verlust/Gewinn** a net loss/gain of about four million

Perron [pɛ'rõ:] **der; ~s, ~s** *(österr., schweiz.)* platform

Persenning [pɛr'zɛnɪŋ] **die; ~, ~e[n]** *od.* **~s a)** *(bes. Seemannsspr.: Bezug)* tarpaulin; **b)** *o. Pl. (Textilind.: Segeltuch)* [waterproof] canvas

Perser ['pɛrzɐ] **der; ~s, ~ a)** Persian; **b)** *s.* **Perserteppich**

Perserin die; ~, ~nen Persian

Perser-: ~katze die Persian [cat]; **~teppich der** Persian carpet; *(kleiner)* Persian rug

Persianer [pɛr'zia:nɐ] **der; ~s, ~:** Persian lamb; *(~mantel)* Persian lamb coat

Persianer·mantel der Persian lamb coat

Persien ['pɛrziən] **(das); ~s** Persia

Persiflage [pɛrzi'fla:ʒə] **die; ~, ~n** [gentle] mocking *no indef. art.;* **eine ~ auf jmdn./etw.** a [gentle] satire of sb./sth.

persiflieren *tr. V.* satirize

Persil·schein [pɛr'zi:l-] **der** *(ugs. scherzh.)* certificate of blamelessness

persisch *Adj.* Persian; *s. auch* **deutsch; Deutsch; ²Deutsche**

Person [pɛr'zo:n] **die; ~, ~en a)** person; **eine männliche/weibliche ~:** a male/female; **~en** *(als Gruppe)* people; **die Familie besteht aus fünf ~en** it is a family of five; **~en sind bei dem Brand nicht umgekommen** there was no loss of life in the fire; **pro ~:** per person; **seine** *od.* **die eigene ~ zu wichtig nehmen** take oneself too seriously; **deine ~/die ~ des Kanzlers soll nicht erwähnt werden** you are/the Chancellor is not to be mentioned in person; **ich für meine ~ ...:** I for my part ...; **sich in der ~ irren** get the wrong person; **der Minister in [eigener] ~:** the minister in person; **sie ist die Güte/Geduld in ~:** she is kindness/patience personified *or* itself; **Politiker und Lyriker in einer ~ sein** be a politician and a lyric poet rolled into one; **Fragen zur ~:** questions to sb. on his/her identity; **Angaben zur ~ machen** give one's personal details; **jmdn. zur ~ vernehmen** *od.* **befragen** *(Rechtsw.)* examine *or* question sb. concerning his/her identity; **eine natürliche/juristische ~** *(Rechtsw.)* a natural/juristic person; *s. auch* **Ansehen b; b)** *(in der Dichtung, im Film)* character; **die ~en der Handlung** the characters [in the action]; *(im Theater)* the dramatis personae; **komische** *od.* **lustige ~** *(Literaturw.)* [stock] comic figure; **c)** *(emotional: Frau)* female *(derog./joc.);* **d)** *o. Pl. (Sprachw.)* person; **in der dritten ~ Singular/Plural** in the third person singular/plural

Personal [pɛrzo'na:l] **das; ~s a)** *(in einem Betrieb o.ä.)* staff; *(hinsichtlich der Verwaltung)* personnel; **ungenügend/ausreichend mit ~ versehen** inadequately/adequately staffed; **das fliegende ~:** the flight personnel; the aircrews *pl.;* **b)** *(im Haushalt)* servants *pl.;* [domestic] staff *pl.*

Personal-: ~ab·bau der reduction in staff; *(in mehreren Abteilungen/Betrieben)* staff cuts *pl.;* **~ab·teilung die** personnel department; **~akte die** personal file *or* dossier; **~angaben** *Pl.* personal details *or* particulars; **~ausweis der** identity card; **~bedarf der** staffing requirements *pl.;* **~bestand der** number of staff *or* employees (+ *Gen.* in); **~büro das** personnel office; **~chef der** personnel manager; **~einsparung die** saving in staff

Personalien [pɛrzo'na:li̯ən] *Pl.* personal details *or* particulars; **die ~ angeben** give one's [personal] particulars

personalisieren *tr. V.* personalize; reduce ‹*quarrel, relations, etc.*› to a personal level

Personal-: ~kosten *Pl. (Wirtsch., Verwaltung)* staff costs; **~mangel der** staff shortage; **~planung die** *(bes. Wirtsch.)* personnel planning; **~politik die** staff *or* personnel policy; *(bei der Einstellung von ~)* staffing policy; **~pronomen das** *(Sprachw.)* personal pronoun; **~rat der a)** *(Ausschuß)* staff council *(for civil servants);* **b)** *(einzelnes Mitglied)* staff council representative; **~union die a)** *(im Staatsrecht)* personal union; **b)** *(Vereinigung von Ämtern)* combination of the functions **(zwischen +** *Dat.* of)

Persönchen [pɛr'zø:nçən] **das; ~s, ~:** little lady

personell [pɛrzo'nɛl] **1.** *Adj.; nicht präd.* staff ‹*changes, difficulties*›; ‹*savings*› in staff; ‹*questions, decisions*› regarding staff *or* personnel. **2.** *adv.* with regard to staff *or* personnel

Personen-: ~auf·zug der passenger lift *(Brit.) or (Amer.)* elevator; **~beförderung die** *(Verkehrsw.)* passenger transport *no art.;* **~beförderung mit der Bahn** carrying passengers by rail; **~beschreibung die** personal description; **~gedächtnis das** memory for faces; **~gesellschaft die** *(Wirtsch.)* general partnership; **~kraftwagen der** *(bes. Amtsspr.)* private car *or (Amer.)* automobile; **~kreis der** group [of people]; **~kult der** *(abwertend)* personality cult; **~name der** personal name; **~register das** index of names; **~schaden der** *(Versicherungsw.)* physical *or* personal injury; **bei dem Unfall entstand kein ~schaden** nobody was injured in the accident; **Unfälle mit ~schaden** accidents in which injuries are/were sustained; **~stands·register das** register of births, marriages, and deaths; **~verkehr der** *(Verkehrsw.)* passenger transport *no art.;* **~verzeichnis das a)** *(~register)* index of names; **b)** *(im Drama)* list of characters; **~waage die** scales *pl.;* **~wagen der a)** *(Auto)* [private] car; automobile *(Amer.); (im Unterschied zum Lastwagen)* passenger car *or (Amer.)* automobile; **b)** *(bei Zügen)* passenger coach; **~zug der** slow *or* stopping train; *(im Unterschied zum Güterzug)* passenger train

Personifikation [pɛrzonifika'tsi̯o:n] **die; ~, ~en** personification

personifizieren [pɛrzonifi'tsi:rən] *tr. V.* personify; **das personifizierte schlechte Gewissen** the very picture *or* personification of a guilty conscience

Personifizierung die; ~, ~en personification

persönlich [pɛr'zø:nlıç] **1.** *Adj.* personal; **er findet für jeden ein ~es Wort** he has a friendly word for everyone; **etw. steht jmdm. zur ~en Verfügung** sth. is available to sb. for his/her own *or* personal use; **eine ~e Bemerkung** an observation from one's personal point of view; **eine ~e Frage/Bemerkung** *(zur anderen Person)* a personal question/observation; **~ werden** get personal; **~es Fürwort** *(Sprachw.)* personal pronoun. **2.** *adv.* personally; *(auf Briefen)* 'private [and confidential]'; **sich um alles ~ kümmern** see to everything personally *or* oneself; **~ erscheinen/gehen/kommen** appear/go/come in person; **nimm doch nicht gleich alles [so] ~!** don't take everything so personally!

Persönlichkeit die; ~, ~en a) *o. Pl. (Wesensart)* personality; **b)** *(Mensch)* person of character; **eine/keine ~ sein** have a strong personality/lack personality; **c)** *(herausragende Person)* personality; **~en des öffentlichen Lebens** public figures

Persönlichkeits-: ~recht das *(Rechtsw.)* right to live one's own life; **~spaltung die** *(Psych.)* split personality; **~wahl die** *(Politik)* **a)** *electoral system in which votes are cast for a candidate rather than a party;* **b)** *(Wahl mit starken Persönlichkeiten)* personality contest; **diese Wahl war eine reine ~wahl** this election was fought purely on the basis of personalities

Perspektiv [pɛrspɛk'ti:f] **das; ~s, ~e** [handheld] telescope

Perspektive [pɛrspɛk'ti:və] **die; ~, ~n** *(Optik, bild. Kunst, auch fig.)* perspective; *(Blickwinkel)* angle; viewpoint; *(Zukunftsaussicht)* prospect; **aus soziologischer ~/aus der ~ des Soziologen** *(fig.)* from a sociological viewpoint/the viewpoint of a sociologist; **aus dieser ~ [gesehen]** *(fig.)* [seen] from this point of view; **eine neue ~ gewinnen** *(fig.)* gain a new perspective *or* aspect

perspektivisch 1. *Adj.* ‹*drawing etc.*› in perspective; ‹*effect, narrowing, etc.*› of perspective; **~e Verkürzung** foreshortening. **2.** *adv.* in perspective; **~ verkürzen** foreshorten

Peru [pe'ru:] **(das); ~s** Peru

Peruaner [pe'rua:nɐ] **der; ~s, ~, Peruanerin die; ~, ~nen** Peruvian

peruanisch *Adj.* Peruvian

Perücke [pɛ'rʏkə] **die; ~, ~n** wig

pervers [pɛr'vɛrs] *(abwertend)* **1.** *Adj.* **a)** *(bes. in sexueller Hinsicht)* perverted; *(fig.: gegen jede Vernunft)* perverse; **ein ~er Mensch** a pervert; **b)** *(ugs.: empörend, schändlich)* outrageous; scandalous. **2.** *adv.* in a perverted manner; **~ veranlagt sein** be of a perverted disposition

Perversion [pɛrvɛr'zi̯o:n] **die; ~, ~en** perversion

Perversität [pɛrvɛrzi'tɛ:t] **die; ~, ~en a)** *o. Pl. (Eigenschaft)* perversion; **b)** *(Handlung)* perversity; *(sexuell)* perverted act

pervertieren [pɛrvɛr'ti:rən] **1.** *tr. V.* pervert; *(verderben)* corrupt. **2.** *itr. V.; mit sein* become perverted **(zu** into)

perzentuell [pɛrtsɛn'tu̯ɛl] *(österr.) s.* **prozentual**

Perzeption [pɛrtsɛp'tsi̯o:n] **die; ~, ~en** *(Philos., Psych., Physiol.)* perception

perzeptiv [pɛrtsɛp'ti:f] *(Philos., Psych., Physiol.) Adj.* perceptive

pesen ['pe:zn̩] *itr. V.; mit sein (ugs.)* dash; *(mit Fahrzeug)* race

Pessar [pɛ'sa:ɐ̯] **das; ~s, ~e** pessary

Pessimismus [pɛsi'mısmʊs] **der; ~:** pessimism

Pessimist der; ~en, ~en, Pessimistin die; ~, ~nen pessimist

pessimistisch 1. *Adj.* pessimistic. **2.** *adv.* pessimistically; **etw. ~ sehen** *od.* **betrachten** take a pessimistic view of sth.; **sich zu etw. ~ äußern** express a pessimistic view on sth.

Pest [pɛst] **die; ~:** plague; *(fig.: Mensch, Ungeziefer)* pest; menace; **ich hasse ihn/es wie die ~** *(ugs.)* I hate his guts/can't stand it *(coll.);* **wie die ~ stinken** *(salopp)* stink to high heaven *(coll.)*

Pest-: ~beule die [pestilential] bubo; **~gestank der** *(abwertend)* foul stench; **~hauch der** *(geh.)* miasma

Pestilenz [pɛsti'lɛnts] **die; ~, ~en** *(veralt.)* pestilence *(arch.);* plague *(lit. or fig.)*

Pestizid [pɛsti'tsi:t] **das; ~s, ~e** pesticide

Pest·kranke der/die person stricken with the plague

¹Peter ['pe:tɐ] **(der)** Peter

²Peter der; ~s, ~: *(ugs.)* fellow; **ein vergeßlicher/dummer ~:** a forgetful/silly old thing *(coll.);* **Schwarzer ~** *(Kartenspiel)* ≈ old maid *(with a black cat card instead of an old maid);* **jmdm. den Schwarzen ~ zuschieben** *od.* **zuspielen** *(fig.)* pass the buck to sb. *(coll.)*

Petersilie [pete'zi:li̯ə] **die; ~:** parsley; **ihm ist die ~ verhagelt** *(ugs.)* he's down in the dumps

Peters·kirche die: die ~: St Peter's

Peter·wagen der *(ugs.)* [police] patrol car; panda car *(Brit.)*

Petition [peti'tsi̯o:n] **die; ~, ~en** *(Amtsspr.)* petition

Petitions-: ~aus·schuß der petitions committee *(in W. German parliaments);* **~recht das** right of petition

Petrarca [pe'trarka] **(der)** Petrarch

Petri Heil ['pe:tri-] *(Gruß der Angler)* good fishing!; make a good catch!

Petri·jünger der *(ugs. scherzh.)* angling buff *(coll.)*

Petro- ['petro:-]: **~chemie die a)** *(Wissenschaft)* petrochemistry; **b)** *(Erdölindustrie)* petrochemicals industry; **~dollar der;** *meist Pl. (Wirtsch.)* petrodollar

Petrol [pe'tro:l] **das; ~s** *(schweiz.),* **Petroleum** [pe'tro:leʊm] **das; ~s a)** paraffin *(Brit.);* kerosene *(Amer.);* **b)** *(veralt.) s.* **Erdöl**

Petroleum-: ~kocher der paraffin *(Brit.) or (Amer.)* kerosene stove; **~lampe die** paraffin *(Brit.) or (Amer.)* kerosene lamp

Petrus ['pe:trʊs] **(der); Petrus** *od.* **Petri a)** *(christl. Rel.: Apostel)* St Peter; **b)** *(Patron*

des Wetters) the clerk of the weather; **wenn ~ mitspielt** if [the clerk of] the weather doesn't let us down

Petschaft ['pɛtʃaft] **das; ~s, ~e** seal; *(zur Beglaubigung od. als Unterschrift)* signet

Petticoat ['pɛtɪkoʊt] **der; ~s, ~s** [stiffened] petticoat

Petting ['pɛtɪŋ] **das; ~[s], ~s** petting; **[mit jmdm.] ~ machen** have a petting session [with sb.]

Petunie [pe'tu:ni̯ə] **die; ~, ~n** *(Bot.)* petunia

Petze die; ~, ~n *(Schülerspr. abwertend)* tell-tale; sneak *(Brit. school sl.)*

petzen *(Schülerspr.)* **1.** *itr. V.* tell tales; sneak *(Brit. school sl.).* **2.** *tr. V.* **~, daß ...:** tell teacher/sb.'s parents that ...

Petzer der; ~s, ~ *(Schülerspr. abwertend)* tell-tale; sneak *(Brit. school sl.);* tattle-tale *(Amer. school sl.)*

Petz·liese die *(Schülerspr. abwertend)* [girl who is a] tell-tale

peu à peu [pøa'pø] *Adv.* bit by bit

Pf *Abk.* **Pfennig**

Pfad [pfa:t] **der; ~[e]s, ~e** path; **krumme ~e** *od.* **auf krummen ~en wandeln** *(fig. geh.)* deviate from the straight and narrow; **vom ~ der Tugend abweichen** *(fig. geh.)* stray from the path of virtue; *s. auch* **austreten 1 b**

Pfad-: ~finder der Scout; **er ist bei den ~n** he is in the Scouts; **~finderin die; ~, ~nen** Guide *(Brit.);* girl scout *(Amer.);* **sie ist bei den ~nen** she is in the Guides *(Brit.)* or *(Amer.)* girl scouts

Pfaffe ['pfafə] **der; ~n, ~n** *(abwertend)* cleric; Holy Joe *(derog.)*

pfäffisch ['pfɛfɪʃ] *Adj. (abwertend)* priestly; *(frömmelnd)* sanctimonious

Pfahl [pfa:l] **der; ~[e]s, Pfähle** ['pfɛ:lə] post; stake; *(Bauw.: Stütze für Gebäude)* pile; **[jmdm.] ein ~ im Fleisch[e] sein** be a thorn in sb.'s flesh

Pfahl-: ~bau der; ~[e]s, ~bauten pile-dwelling; **~bürger der a)** *(im Mittelalter) person living outside the town walls but retaining citizen's rights;* **b)** *(abwertend veralt.) s.* **Spießbürger; ~dorf das** pile-village

pfählen ['pfɛ:lən] *tr. V.* **a)** *(Landw.)* stake ⟨*trees etc.*⟩; **b)** *(hist.: hinrichten)* impale

Pfahl-: ~werk das pilework; piling; **~wurzel die** *(Bot.)* tap-root

Pfalz [pfalts] **die; ~, ~en a)** *o. Pl. (Gebiet)* **die ~:** the Palatinate; **b)** *(hist.: Palast)* [imperial *or* royal] palace

Pfälzer ['pfɛltsɐ] **1. der; ~s, ~: a)** *(Person)* inhabitant/native of the Palatinate; **b)** *(Wein)* wine from the Palatinate. **2.** *indekl. attr. Adj.* ⟨*wine etc.*⟩ from the Palatinate

Pfalz·graf der *(hist.)* Count Palatine

Pfand [pfant] **das; ~[e]s, Pfänder** ['pfɛndɐ] **a)** security; pledge *(esp. fig.);* **etw. auf ~ leihen** lend sth. against a security; **etw. als** *od.* **in ~ nehmen/etw. als** *od.* **zum** *od.* **in ~ geben** take/give sth. as [a] security; **ich gebe** *od.* **setze meine Ehre/mein Leben dafür zum ~, daß ...** *(fig. geh.)* I pledge my honour/stake my life on it that ...; **als ~ seiner Liebe** *(geh.)* as a token of his love; **b)** *(für leere Flaschen usw.)* deposit **(auf +** *Dat.* on); **[ein] ~ für etw. bezahlen** pay a deposit on sth.; **kostet die Flasche ~?** is there a deposit on the bottle?; **c)** *(beim Pfänderspiel)* forfeit

pfändbar *Adj.* distrainable *(Law)* ⟨*goods, chattels*⟩; attachable *(Law)* ⟨*wages etc.*⟩

Pfand·brief der *(Wirtsch., Bankw.)* mortgage bond

pfänden ['pfɛndn̩] *tr. (auch itr.) V.* impound, seize [under distress] *(Law)* ⟨*goods, chattels*⟩; attach ⟨*wages etc.*⟩ *(Law);* **bei ihm wurde gepfändet, er ist gepfändet worden** the bailiffs have been on to him; execution was levied against him *(Law.)*

Pfänder *s.* **Pfand**

Pfänder·spiel das [game of] forfeits

Pfand-: ~flasche die returnable bottle *(on which a deposit is payable);* **~haus das** *(veralt.),* **~leihe die** pawnshop; pawnbroker's; **etw. auf die** *od.* **in die** *od.* **zur ~leihe bringen** take sth. to the pawnbroker's; **~leiher der** pawnbroker; **~recht das** *(Rechtsw.)* [right of] lien **(an +** *Dat.* on, upon); **~schein der** pawn ticket

Pfändung die; ~, ~en seizure; distraint *(Law); (von Geldsummen, Vermögensrechten)* attachment *(Law);* **der Gerichtsvollzieher kam zur ~:** the bailiff came to seize *or* impound possessions

Pfändungs·verfügung die *(Rechtsw.)* garnishee *or* attachment order *(Law)*

Pfand·verkauf der sale of property put up as security; distress sale *(Law)*

Pfanne ['pfanə] **die; ~, ~n a)** *(zum Braten, Backen)* [frying-]pan; **sich** *(Dat.)* **ein paar Eier in die ~ schlagen** fry [up] some eggs; **jmdn. in die ~ hauen** *(ugs.) (kritisieren)* take sb. to pieces; *(ruinieren)* land sb. in trouble; *(vernichtend schlagen)* beat sb. hollow *(coll.);* **b)** *(hist.: Zünd~)* [priming] pan; **etw. auf der ~ haben** *(ugs. fig.)* have sth. at the ready; **c)** *(Geogr.: Senke)* pan; *(Salz~)* salt-pan; **d)** *(Hüttenw.)* [foundry] ladle; **e)** *(Bett~)* bed-pan; **f)** *(Bauw.: Dach~)* pantile; **g)** *(Anat.: Gelenk~)* socket

Pfannen·gericht das *(Kochk.)* fried dish

Pfann·kuchen der a) *(bes. südd.: Eierkuchen)* pancake; **b)** *(Berliner ~)* doughnut; **aufgehen wie ein ~** *(ugs.)* turn into a real dumpling

Pfarr-: ~amt das a) parish office; **b)** *(Stellung)* pastorate; **~bezirk der** parish

Pfarre ['pfarə] **die; ~, ~n** *(veralt.),* **Pfarrei** [pfa'rai̯] **die; ~, ~en a)** *(Bezirk)* parish; **b)** *(Dienststelle)* parish office; **c)** *s.* **Pfarrhaus**

Pfarrer ['pfarɐ] **der; ~s, ~** *(katholisch)* parish priest; *(evangelisch)* pastor; *(anglikanisch)* vicar; *(von Freikirchen)* minister; *(Militär~)* chaplain; padre; *(in der Anschrift)* **Herrn ~ Meyer** [the] Revd. Meyer; **Frau ~ Meyer** *(Pfarrerin)* [the] Revd. Meyer; *(Pfarrersfrau)* Mrs Meyer

Pfarrerin die; ~, ~nen [woman] pastor; *(in Freikirchen)* [woman] minister; **Frau ~ Schmidt** Pastor *or* [the] Revd. Schmidt

Pfarrers·frau die pastor's wife; *(in Freikirchen)* minister's wife; *(anglikanisch)* vicar's wife

Pfarr-: ~haus das vicarage; *(katholisch)* presbytery; *(in Schottland)* manse; **~kirche die** parish church

Pfau [pfau̯] **der; ~[e]s, ~en** *(österr. auch:)* **~en, ~e** peacock; **er ist ein [eitler] ~** *(fig.)* he is as vain as a peacock

Pfauen-: ~auge das peacock butterfly; *(Nachtpfauenauge)* peacock moth; **~feder die** peacock feather

Pfd. *Abk.* **Pfund** lb.

Pfeffer ['pfɛfɐ] **der; ~s, ~ a)** pepper; **roter ~:** cayenne [pepper]; red pepper; **spanischer ~:** paprika; **hingehen** *od.* **bleiben, wo der ~ wächst** *(ugs.)* go to hell *(coll.);* get lost *(sl.); s. auch* **Hase a; Hintern; b)** *(Textilw.)* **~ und Salz** pepper-and-salt; **c)** *(ugs.: Schwung)* punch *(coll.);* zap *(sl.);* **dahinter steckt ~:** it's got plenty of zap *(sl.) or (coll.)* zing

Pfeffer-: ~fresser der *(Zool.)* toucan; **~gurke die** pickled gherkin; **~korn das** peppercorn; **~kuchen der** ≈ gingerbread

Pfefferminz ['pfɛfɐmɪnts] *o. Art., indekl.* peppermint

Pfefferminz·bonbon der *od.* **das** peppermint [sweet]

Pfeffer·minze die; *o. Pl.* peppermint [plant]

Pfefferminz-: ~likör der peppermint liqueur; **~plätzchen das** peppermint drop; *(weich)* peppermint cream; **~tee der** peppermint tea

Pfeffer·mühle die pepper-mill

pfeffern *tr. V.* **a)** *(würzen)* season with pepper; **stark gepfeffert** very peppery; **b)** *(ugs.: werfen)* chuck *(coll.); (mit Wucht)* fling; hurl; **jmdm. eine ~** *(salopp)* sock *or* biff sb. one *(sl.);* **eine gepfeffert kriegen** *(salopp)* get a clout *or (sl.)* biff; *s. auch* **gepfeffert**

Pfeffer-: ~nuß die [small round] ginger-bread biscuit; **~steak das** steak au poivre; pepper steak; **~strauch der** pepper plant; **~streuer der** pepper-pot; **~-und-Salz-Muster das** pepper-and-salt pattern

pfeffrig ['pfɛfrɪç] *Adj.* peppery

Pfeifchen ['pfai̯fçən] **das; ~, ~** *(fam.: Tabakpfeife)* pipe

Pfeife ['pfai̯fə] **die; ~, ~n a)** *(Tabak~)* pipe; **~ rauchen** smoke a pipe; be a pipe-smoker; **eine ~ rauchen** smoke *or* have a pipe; **b)** *(Musikinstrument)* pipe; *(aus Zinn)* penny whistle; tin whistle; *(der Militärkapelle)* fife; *(Triller~, an einer Maschine usw.)* whistle; *(Orgel~)* [organ-]pipe; **nach jmds. ~ tanzen** *(fig.)* dance to sb.'s tune; **c)** *(salopp abwertend: Versager)* wash-out *(coll.)*

pfeifen 1. *unr. itr. V.* **a)** whistle; ⟨*bird*⟩ sing; pipe; ⟨*mouse*⟩ squeak; **dreimal kurz ~:** give three short whistles; **er pfiff vor Bewunderung** he gave a whistle of admiration; he whistled in admiration; **sie pfiff [nach] ihrem Hund/einem Taxi** she whistled her dog/for a taxi; **von den Rängen wurde laut gepfiffen und gebuht** there were loud catcalls and boos from the auditorium; **etwas** *od.* **es pfiff in der Leitung** there was a whistle *or* a whistling noise on the telephone line; **seine Lungen ~/es pfeift in seiner Brust** he wheezes in his lungs/chest; **~der Atem** wheezing [breath]; *s. auch* **Loch a; b)** *mit sein* **die Kugeln pfiffen ihm um die Ohren** the bullets whistled around him; **c)** *(auf einer Trillerpfeife o. ä.)* ⟨*policeman, referee, etc.*⟩ blow one's whistle; *(Sport: als Schiedsrichter fungieren)* act as referee; **er pfeift beim Endspiel** he is refereeing the final; **d)** *(salopp)* **auf jmdn./etw. ~:** not give a damn about sb./sth.; **ich pfeife auf dein Geld** you can keep your money *(coll.);* **e)** *(salopp: geständig sein)* squeal *(sl.).* **2.** *unr. tr. V.* **a)** whistle ⟨*tune etc.*⟩; ⟨*bird*⟩ pipe, sing ⟨*song*⟩; *(auf einer Pfeife)* pipe, play ⟨*tune etc.*⟩; *(auf einer Trillerpfeife o. ä.)* blow ⟨*signal etc.*⟩ on one's whistle; **einen Elfmeter ~** *(Sport)* blow [the whistle] for a penalty; **sich** *(Dat.)* **eins ~** *(ugs.)* whistle [nonchalantly] to oneself; *(fig.: sich nichts daraus machen)* shrug one's shoulders; **ich pfeif' dir was** *(salopp spött.)* go and get knotted *(sl.);* **b)** *(Sport: als Schiedsrichter leiten)* referee ⟨*match*⟩; **c)** *(salopp: verraten)* let out ⟨*secret*⟩; **wer hat dir das gepfiffen?** who let on to you about that? *(sl.);* **d)** *(salopp: trinken)* **einen ~:** knock one back *(sl.)*

Pfeifen-: ~deckel der [pipe-]bowl lid; **~deckel!** *(ugs.)* no way! *(coll.);* **~kopf der** pipe-bowl; **~raucher der** pipe-smoker; **~reiniger der** pipe-cleaner; **~ständer der** pipe-rack; **~stopfer der** tobacco-stopper; **~tabak der** pipe tobacco; **~werk das** *(Musik)* [organ-]pipes *pl.;* pipework

Pfeifer der; ~s, ~ a) *(Musik) (bes. hist.)* piper; *(in einer Militärkapelle)* fife-player; **b)** *(jmd., der pfeift)* whistler

Pfeiferei die; ~, ~en *(abwertend)* whistling

Pfeif-: ~kessel der whistling kettle; **~konzert das** chorus of catcalls; **~ton der;** *Pl.* **~töne** whistling sound

Pfeil [pfail] **der; ~[e]s, ~e** arrow; *(Wurf~)* dart; **~ und Bogen** bow and arrow; **wie ein ~ davonschießen** be off like a shot *or* like lightning; **schnell wie ein ~:** as quick as lightning; **alle [seine] ~e verschossen haben** *(fig.)* have run out of arguments; *s. auch* **Amor**

Pfeiler der; ~s, ~: *(Bauw., Bergbau; auch fig.)* pillar; *(Brücken~)* pier

pfeil, Pfeil-: ~flügel der *(Flugzeugtechnik)* swept-back wing; **~förmig 1.** *Adj.* arrow-shaped; sagittate ⟨*leaf*⟩; **2.** *adv.* **~ angeord-**

net arranged in the shape of an arrow *postpos.;* **~gerade 1.** *Adj.* [as] straight as an arrow *postpos.;* dead straight; **2.** *adv.* [as] straight as an arrow; **~gift das** arrow-poison; **~richtung die: in ~richtung** in the direction of the arrow; **~schnell 1.** *Adj.* lightning-swift; **2.** *adv.* like a shot; **~spitze die** arrowhead

Pfennig ['pfɛnɪç] **der; ~s, ~e** pfennig; **es kostet 20 ~:** it costs 20 pfennig[s]; **hast du ein paar einzelne ~e?** have you any single pfennig pieces?; **eine Briefmarke zu 60 ~:** a 60-pfennig stamp; **er hat keinen ~ [Geld]** he hasn't a penny *or (Amer.)* cent; **es ist keinen ~ wert** *(ugs.)* it isn't worth a penny *or (Amer.)* a [red] cent; **bis auf den letzten ~:** down to the last penny *or (Amer.)* cent; **auf den ~ genau** correct to the last penny *or (Amer.)* cent; **auf den ~ sehen** *(ugs.)* watch *or* count every penny *or (Amer.)* cent; **nicht für fünf ~ Anstand/Verstand/Geschmack/Humor** *usw.* **haben** *(ugs.)* have not an ounce of respectability/common sense/have no taste/sense of humour whatsoever; **das interessiert mich nicht für fünf ~** *(ugs.)* that doesn't interest me in the slightest; **wer den ~ nicht ehrt, ist des Talers nicht wert** *(Spr.)* take care of the pennies and the pounds will look after themselves *(prov.); s. auch* **Heller; [2]Mark a; umdrehen 1**

pfennig-, Pfennig-: ~ab·satz der stiletto heel; **~betrag der** amount of less than a mark; *(kleiner Betrag)* tiny amount; **~fuchser** [-fʊksɐ] **der; ~s, ~** *(ugs.)* penny-pincher; **~groß** *Adj.* ≈ the size of a 1p piece *(Brit.) or (Amer.)* a cent *postpos.*

Pferch [pfɛrç] **der; ~[e]s, ~e** pen

pferchen *tr. V.* cram; pack

Pferd [pfe:ɐt] **das; ~[e]s, ~e a)** horse; **zu ~[e]** on horseback; **aufs/vom ~ steigen** mount/dismount; **zu ~:** by horse; on horseback; **das hält ja kein ~ aus** *(ugs.)* that's more than flesh and blood can stand; **ich denk', mich tritt ein ~** *(salopp)* I'm absolutely flabbergasted; **man hat schon ~e kotzen sehen** *(salopp)* [you never know,] anything can happen; **immer sachte mit den jungen ~en** *(fig. ugs.)* not so fast! *(coll.);* **er ist das beste ~ im Stall** *(ugs.)* he is their/our number one man; **wie ein ~ arbeiten** *(ugs.)* work like a Trojan; **keine zehn ~e bringen mich dahin/dazu, es zu tun** *(ugs.)* wild horses would not drag me there/make me do it; **ihm gehen die ~e durch** *(ugs.)* he flies off the handle *(coll.);* **auf das falsche ~ setzen** *(fig.)* back the wrong horse; **die ~e scheu machen** *(ugs.)* put people off; **das ~ am** *od.* **beim Schwanze aufzäumen** *(ugs.)* put the cart before the horse; **mit ihr kann man ~e stehlen** *(ugs.)* she's game for anything; *s. auch* **trojanisch; b)** *(Turngerät)* horse; **c)** *(Schachfigur)* knight

Pferdchen das; ~s, ~ a) *(kleines Pferd)* little horse; **b)** *(salopp: Prostituierte)* tart *(sl.);* hooker *(Amer. sl.) (working for a pimp)*

Pferde-: ~anhänger der *s.* **~transportwagen; ~apfel der** *(ugs.)* piece of horse dung; **~äpfel** horse-droppings; horse-dung; **~bremse die** *(Zool.)* horse-fly; **~decke die** horse-blanket; **~fleisch das** horse-meat; **~fuhrwerk das** horse and cart; **~fuhrwerke** horse-drawn carts; **~fuß der a)** *(fig.: Mangel, Nachteil)* snag; drawback; **b)** *(eines ~s)* horse's foot; *(des Teufels)* cloven hoof; **~gebiß das a)** *(fig. ugs.)* **er hat ein ~gebiß** he has teeth *pl.* like a horse; **b)** *(eines ~s)* horse's teeth *pl.;* **~gesicht das** *(ugs.)* horsy face; **er hat ein ~gesicht** he has a face like a horse; **~händler der** horse-dealer; **~knecht der** *(veralt.)* groom; **~kopf der** horse's head; **~koppel die** paddock; **~länge die** length; **mit zwei ~längen Vorsprung siegen** win by two lengths **(vor +** *Dat.* from); **~mist der** horse-manure; **~pfleger der** groom; **~rasse die** breed of horse; **~renn·bahn die** racecourse; **~rennen das** horse-race; *(Sportart)* horse-racing; **beim ~rennen sein** be at the races *pl.;* **~schlachter, ~schlächter der** *(bes. nordd.)* horse-butcher; **~schlitten der** horse[-drawn] sleigh; **~schwanz der** horse's tail; *(fig.: Frisur)* pony-tail; **~sport der** equestrian sport *no art.; (~rennen)* horse-racing *no art.;* **~stall der** stable; **~stärke die** horse-power; **~transport·wagen der** horse-box; **~wagen der** *(für Güter)* cart; *(für Personen)* carriage; *(der amerikanischen Pioniere usw.)* wagon; **~wirt der** *(Berufsbez.)* fully qualified groom *(with veterinary training);* **~zucht die** horse-breeding *no art.*

pfiff [pfɪf] *1. u. 3. Pers. Sg. Prät. v.* **pfeifen**

Pfiff der; ~[e]s, ~e a) whistle; **b)** *(ugs.: besonderer Reiz)* style; **mit ~:** stylish; with style; *(adverbiell)* stylishly; ⟨*cook*⟩ with flair; **der letzte** *od.* **richtige ~:** the finishing touch; that extra something; **c)** *(ugs.) s.* **Dreh a**

Pfifferling ['pfɪfɐlɪŋ] **der; ~s, ~e** chanterelle; **keinen** *od.* **nicht einen ~ wert sein** *(ugs.)* be not worth a bean *(sl.)*

pfiffig 1. *Adj.* smart; bright, clever ⟨*idea*⟩; artful, knowing ⟨*smile, expression*⟩. **2.** *adv.* artfully; cleverly; **jmdn. ~ ansehen/anlächeln** look/smile knowingly *or* artfully at sb.

Pfiffikus ['pfɪfikʊs] **der; ~[ses], ~se** *(ugs.)* smart lad

Pfingsten ['pfɪŋstn̩] **das; ~, ~:** Whitsun; **zu** *od. (bes. südd.)* **an ~:** at Whitsun; **habt ihr schöne ~ gehabt?** did you have a nice Whitsun?; *s. auch* **Ostern**

Pfingst-: ~feier·tag der: über die ~feiertage over Whitsun; **an den ~feiertagen** on Whit Sunday and Whit Monday; **der erste/zweite ~feiertag** Whit Sunday/Monday; **~fest das** Whitsun [holiday]; *(Rel.)* Whitsun festival

pfingstlich 1. *Adj.* Whitsuntide *attrib.; (Rel.)* pentecostal ⟨*miracle*⟩. **2.** *adv.* **~ geschmückt** decorated for Whitsun *postpos.*

Pfingst-: ~montag der Whit Monday *no def. art.;* **~ochse der** *in* **er sah aus/hatte sich herausgeputzt wie ein ~ochse** *(ugs.)* he looked like/was dressed up like a dog's dinner *(coll.);* **~rose die** peony; **~sonntag der** Whit Sunday *no def. art.;* **~woche die** week before Whitsun

Pfirsich ['pfɪrzɪç] **der; ~s, ~e** peach

Pfirsich-: ~baum der peach-tree; **~blüte die** peach-blossom; **~haut die a)** peach-skin; **b)** *(fig.: Gesichtshaut)* peaches-and-cream complexion

Pflänzchen ['pflɛntsçən] **das; ~s, ~ a)** little plant; **b)** *(fig.: Mensch)* **ein [zartes] ~:** a delicate creature

Pflanze ['pflantsə] **die; ~, ~n a)** plant; **b)** *(ugs.: Mensch)* **du bist mir vielleicht eine ~!** you're a right one! *(coll.);* **eine echte Berliner ~** *(veralt.)* a genuine Berlin type

pflanzen 1. *tr. V.* plant **(in +** *Akk.* in); *(fig.)* plant, stick ⟨*flag*⟩. **2.** *refl. V. (ugs.)* plant oneself

pflanzen-, Pflanzen-: ~farb·stoff der a) *(pflanzlicher Farbstoff)* vegetable dye; **b)** *(Bot.: Pigment)* plant *or* vegetable pigment; **~fett das** vegetable fat; **~fressend** *Adj.; nicht präd.* herbivorous; **~fresser der** herbivore; **~kunde die** botany *no def. art.;* **~öl das** vegetable oil; **~reich das;** *o. Pl.* plant kingdom; **~schutz·mittel das** [crop] pesticide; *(für den Garten)* garden pesticide; **~welt die** flora

Pflanzer der; ~s, ~: planter; plantation-owner

Pflanz-: ~gut das; *o. Pl.* seed stock; **~holz das** dibble; **~kartoffel die** seed potato

pflanzlich *Adj.* plant *attrib.* ⟨*life, motif*⟩; vegetable ⟨*dye, fat*⟩; *(vegetarisch)* vegetarian

Pflänzling ['pflɛntslɪŋ] **der; ~s, ~e** seedling

Pflanzung die; ~, ~en a) plantation; **b)** *o. Pl. (das Pflanzen)* planting

Pflaster ['pflastɐ] **das; ~s, ~ a)** *(Straßen~)* road surface; *(auf dem Gehsteig)* pavement; **~ treten** *(ugs.)* trail through the streets; **b)** *(ugs.: Ort)* **ein teures/gefährliches** *od.* **heißes ~:** an expensive/dangerous place *or* spot to be; **mir wird das ~ hier zu heiß** this place is getting too hot for me; **c)** *(Wund~)* sticking-plaster

Pflaster·maler der pavement artist

pflastern *tr. (auch itr.) V.* surface ⟨*road, path*⟩; *(mit Kopfsteinpflaster, Steinplatten)* pave ⟨*street, path*⟩; *s. auch* **Vorsatz**

Pflaster·stein der paving-stone; *(Kopfstein)* cobble-stone

Pflaume ['pflaumə] **die; ~, ~n a)** plum; **getrocknete ~n** [dried] prunes; **b)** *(ugs. abwertend: Versager)* dead loss *(coll.); (Feigling)* baby; **c)** *(derb: Vulva)* pussy *(vulg.)*

pflaumen-, Pflaumen-: ~baum der plum-tree; **~kuchen der** plum flan; **~mus das** plum purée; **~saft der** plum juice; **~schnaps der** plum brandy; **~weich** *Adj. (ugs. abwertend)* weak-kneed; spineless

Pflege ['pfle:gə] **die; ~:** care; *(Maschinen~, Fahrzeug~)* maintenance; *(fig.: von Beziehungen, Kunst, Sprache)* cultivation; fostering; **die ~ des Körpers** personal hygiene; **die Blumen brauchen viel/kaum ~:** the flowers need a lot of/hardly any attention; **jmdn./etw. in ~** *(Akk.)* **nehmen** look after sb./sth.; **jmdm. etw.** *od.* **etw. bei jmdm. in ~** *(Akk.)* **geben** give sb. sth. to look after; entrust sth. to sb.'s care; **ein Kind in ~** *(Akk.)* **nehmen** look after a child; *(als Pflegeeltern)* foster a child; **jmdm. ein Kind** *od.* **ein Kind bei jmdm. in ~** *(Akk.)* **geben** give sb. a child to look after; *(bei Pflegeeltern)* have a child fostered by sb.; **bei jmdm. in ~** *(Dat.)* **sein** be looked after by sb.

pflege-, Pflege-: ~bedürftig *Adj.* needing care *or* attention *postpos.;* ⟨*person*⟩ in need of care; **~bedürftig sein** need looking after; need attention; **~eltern** *Pl.* foster-parents; **~fall der** person in [permanent] need of nursing; **ein ~fall sein/zum ~fall werden** be/become in [permanent] need of nursing; **~heim das** nursing home *(esp. Brit.);* **~kind das** foster-child; **~leicht** *Adj.* easy-care *attrib.* ⟨*textiles, flooring*⟩; minimum-care *attrib.* ⟨*plant, pan*⟩; **~leicht sein** require little attention *or* care; ⟨*cloth, clothing*⟩ be made of easy-care material; **~mutter die** foster-mother

pflegen 1. *tr. V.* look after; care for; care for, nurse ⟨*sick person*⟩; care for, take care of ⟨*skin, teeth, floor*⟩; look after, maintain ⟨*bicycle, car, machine*⟩; look after, tend ⟨*garden, plants*⟩; cultivate ⟨*relations, arts, interests*⟩; foster ⟨*contacts, co-operation*⟩; keep up, pursue ⟨*hobby*⟩; **jmdn./ein Tier gesund ~:** nurse sb./an animal back to health; **Kontakt/den Umgang mit jmdm. ~:** keep in touch with/associate with sb. **2.** *itr. V.; mit Inf.* **+ zu etw. zu tun ~:** be in the habit of doing sth.; usually do sth.; **..., wie er zu sagen pflegt/pflegte ...,** as he is wont to say/as he used to say; **er pflegte jeden Morgen um sieben Uhr aufzustehen** he used to get up every morning at seven. **3.** *refl. V.* take care of oneself; *(gesundheitlich)* look after oneself; **sie sollte sich mehr ~:** she should take more care of herself. **4.** *regelm. (veralt. auch unr.) itr. V. (geh.)* **einer Sache** *(Gen.)* **~:** indulge in sth.; **der Ruhe ~:** rest; take one's ease; *s. auch* **gepflegt**

Pfleger der; ~s, ~ a) *(Kranken~)* [male] nurse; **b)** *(Tier~)* keeper

Pflegerin die; ~, ~nen a) *(Kranken~)* nurse; **b)** *(Tier~)* keeper

pflegerisch *Adj.* nursing *attrib.*

Pflege-: ~satz der hospital [daily] rate;

charge for a hospital bed [per day]; **~sohn der** foster-son; **~tochter die** foster-daughter; **~vater der** foster-father; **~versicherung die** [long-term] care insurance

pfleglich **1.** *Adj.* careful. **2.** *adv.* with care

Pflegling ['pfle:klɪŋ] **der; ~s, ~e** charge; *(Pflegekind)* foster-child; **unsere ~e** the children/animals in our care

Pflegschaft die; ~, ~en *(Rechtsw.) (durch Pflegeeltern)* foster-care; *(eines Vermögens)* trusteeship

Pflicht [pflɪçt] **die; ~, ~en a)** duty; **seine alltäglichen [kleinen] ~en** his everyday chores; **die ~ ruft** duty calls; **~ sein** be obligatory; **es ist seine [(*salopp*) verdammte *od.* verfluchte] ~ und Schuldigkeit** [damn it all,] it's his bounden duty; **jmdn. in die ~ nehmen** *(geh.)* make sb. discharge his/her duties; **b)** *(Sport)* compulsory exercises *pl.*

pflicht-, Pflicht-: ~bewußt 1. *Adj.* conscientious; **~bewußt sein** have a sense of duty; **2.** *adv.* conscientiously; with a sense of duty; **~bewußt·sein das** sense of duty; **~eifer der** zeal; **~eifrig 1.** *Adj.* zealous; **2.** *adv.* zealously; full of zeal; **~erfüllung die;** *o. Pl.* performance of one's duty; **in treuer/gewissenhafter ~erfüllung** faithfully/conscientiously following the path of duty; **~exemplar das** *(Verlagsw.)* deposit copy; **~fach das** compulsory subject; **es ist ~fach** it is a compulsory subject; **~gefühl das;** *o. Pl.* sense of duty; **aus [bloßem] ~gefühl** [simply] from a sense of duty; **~gemäß 1.** *Adj.* in accordance with one's duty *postpos.*; **2.** *adv.* in accordance with one's duty; **ich teile Ihnen ~gemäß mit, daß ...:** it is my duty to inform you that ...

-pflichtig *Adj.* subject to ...; **beitrags~e Beschäftigung** occupation entailing the payment of insurance contributions; *s. auch* **abgabenpflichtig; zuschlagspflichtig**

pflicht-, Pflicht-: ~lektüre die required reading; *(Schulw.)* set books *pl.*; **zur ~lektüre gehören, ~lektüre sein** be required reading; *(in der Schule)* be a set book/be set books; **~schuldig 1.** *Adj.* dutiful; *(höflich)* polite; **2.** *adv.* dutifully; *(höflich)* politely; **~teil der** *od.* **das** *(Rechtsw.) portion of an estate that must go to the closest relation regardless of testator's dispositions;* legitimate portion; **jmdn. auf den** *od.* **das ~teil setzen** leave sb. nothing but the legal minimum; **~übung die a)** *(Sport)* compulsory exercise; **b)** *(fig.)* ritual exercise; *(Buch, Film usw.)* obligatory effort; **~um·tausch der** compulsory exchange of currency; **~vergessen 1.** *Adj.* neglectful of one's duty *postpos.*; negligent ⟨*behaviour*⟩; **2.** *adv.* negligently; **~verletzung die** breach of duty; **~versichert** *Adj.* compulsorily insured; **~versicherung die** compulsory insurance; **~verteidiger der** *(Rechtsw.) defense counsel appointed by the court;* assigned counsel; **~widrig** *Adj., adv.* in breach of one's duty *postpos.*

Pflock [pflɔk] **der; ~[e]s, Pflöcke** ['pflœkə] peg; *(für Tiere)* stake

pflog [pflo:k] *(veralt.) 1. u. 3. Pers. Sg. Prät. v.* **pflegen 4**

pflücken ['pflʏkn̩] *tr. V.* pick ⟨*flowers, fruit, hops*⟩; **Kirschen in einen Korb ~:** pick cherries and put them in a basket

Pflücker der; ~s, ~, Pflückerin die; ~, ~nen picker

Pflück·maschine die [mechanical] picker

Pflug [pflu:k] **der; ~[e]s, Pflüge** ['pfly:gə] plough; **Land unter den ~ nehmen** *(geh.)* put land to the plough

pflügen ['pfly:gn̩] *tr., itr. V.* plough; *(fig. geh.)* ⟨*ship*⟩ plough or carve a way through ⟨*waves, sea*⟩

Pflug·schar die ploughshare

Pforte ['pfɔrtə] **die; ~, ~n a)** *(Tor)* gate; *(Tür)* door; *(Eingang)* entrance; **seine ~n öffnen/schließen** *(fig. geh.)* open/close its doors; **Pforzheim, die ~ zum Schwarzwald** *(fig.)* Pforzheim, the gateway to the Black Forest; **b)** *(Geogr.)* **die Westfälische ~:** the Minden Gap; the Porta Westfalica; **die Burgundische ~:** the Belfort Gap

Pförtner ['pfœrtnɐ] **der; ~s, ~ a)** porter; *(eines Wohnblocks, Büros)* door-keeper; *(am Tor)* gatekeeper; **b)** *(Anat.)* pylorus

Pförtner·haus das gatehouse; porter's lodge

Pförtnerin die; ~, ~nen *s.* **Pförtner a**

Pförtner·loge die porter's lodge

Pfosten ['pfɔstn̩] **der; ~s, ~ a)** post; *(Tür~)* jamb; **b)** *(Sport: Tor~)* [goal-]post

Pfosten·schuß der *(Ballspiele)* shot hitting the [goal-]post

Pfötchen ['pfø:tçən] **das; ~s, ~:** [little] paw; **~ geben** hold out a paw; **[gib] ~!** [give us a] paw!

Pfote ['pfo:tə] **die; ~, ~n a)** paw; **die ~ geben** hold out a paw; **[gib die] ~!** [give us a] paw!; **b)** *(ugs.: Hand)* paw *(coll.)*; mitt *(sl.)*; **sich** *(Dat.)* **die ~n verbrennen** *(fig.)* burn one's fingers *(fig.)*; **seine ~n in etw.** *(Dat.)***/überall [drin] haben** *(fig. salopp)* have a hand in sth./everything; be mixed up in sth./everything; **c)** *(salopp abwertend: Schrift) s.* **Klaue d**

Pfriem [pfri:m] **der; ~[e]s, ~e** awl

Pfropf [pfrɔpf] **der; ~[e]s, ~e** blockage; *(in der Vene)* clot; **ein ~ aus Haaren** a plug *or (Brit. coll.)* wodge of hair

[1]**pfropfen** *tr. V. (ugs.)* cram; stuff; **gepfropft voll** crammed [full]; packed

[2]**pfropfen** *tr. V. (Gartenbau)* graft ⟨*scion*⟩ **(auf +** *Akk.* **on)**; improve ⟨*tree, vine*⟩ by grafting

Pfropfen der *(für Flaschen)* stopper; *(Korken)* cork; *(für Fässer)* bung

Pfröpfling ['pfrœpflɪŋ] **der; ~s, ~e** scion

Pfropf-: ~messer das grafting-knife; **~reis das** scion

Pfründe ['pfrʏndə] **die; ~, ~n a)** *(kath. Kirche)* living; benefice; **auf einer ~ sitzen** hold a living; **b)** *(fig.)* sinecure

Pfuhl [pfu:l] **der; ~[e]s, Pfühle** ['pfy:lə] muddy pool; *(fig.)* murky waters *pl.*; **ein ~ der Sünde** *od.* **Sittenlosigkeit** *(fig.)* a sink of iniquity

pfui [pfʊi] *Interj.* **a)** *(Ekel ausdrückend)* ugh; yuck *(sl.)*; *(zu Kindern, Hunden)* [ugh,] you mucky pup; *(hör auf)* stop that; **~ Teufel** *od.* **Deibel** *od.* **Spinne!** *(ugs.)* ugh *or (sl.)* yuck, how disgusting!; **das ist ~:** that's yucky *(sl.) or* disgusting; **b)** *(Mißbilligung, Empörung ausdrückend)* ugh; really; *(Ruf)* boo; **~, schäm dich!** shame on you!; **~ rufen** boo

Pfui·ruf der boo

Pfund [pfʊnt] **das; ~[e]s, ~e** *(bei Maßangaben ungebeugt)* **a)** *(Gewicht)* pound *(= 500 grams in German-speaking countries)*; **zwei ~ Kartoffeln** two pounds of potatoes; **überflüssige ~e loswerden** ⟨*person*⟩ get rid of unwanted pounds; **b)** *(Währungseinheit)* pound; **100 ~:** £100; one hundred pounds; **wieviel ist das in ~ [Sterling]?** how much is that in pounds [sterling]?; **mit seinem ~[e] wuchern** *(geh.)* make the most of one's capabilities

pfundig *(ugs.)* **1.** *Adj.* great *(coll.)*; fantastic *(coll.)*. **2.** *adv.* fantastically *(coll.)*

Pfunds-: ~kerl der *(ugs.)* great bloke *(Brit. coll.)*; great guy *(sl.)*; **~stimmung die** *(ugs.)* terrific atmosphere *(coll.)*

pfund·weise *Adv.* by the pound; **die könnte ich ~ essen** I could eat pounds of them

Pfund·zeichen das pound sign

Pfusch [pfʊʃ] **der; ~[e]s a)** *o. Art. (ugs. abwertend)* a botch-up; **[großen] ~ machen** botch it [in a big way]; **b)** *(österr.: Schwarzarbeit)* work done on the side *(and not declared for tax); (nach Feierabend)* moonlighting *(coll.)*; **etw. im ~ machen** do sth. on the side

Pfusch·arbeit die; *o. Pl. (ugs. abwertend)* botch; botched-up job

pfuschen *itr. V.* **a)** *(ugs. abwertend)* botch it; do a botched-up job; **b)** *(österr.: schwarzarbeiten)* do work on the side *(not declared for tax); (nach Feierabend)* moonlight *(coll.)*

Pfuscher der; ~s, ~ a) *(ugs. abwertend)* botcher; bungler; **b)** *(österr.: Schwarzarbeiter)* person doing work on the side; *(nach Feierabend)* moonlighter *(coll.)*

Pfuscherei die; ~, ~en botching *no pl.*; *(Pfuscharbeit)* botched-up job

Pfütze ['pfʏtsə] **die; ~, ~n** puddle

PH [pe:'ha:] **die; ~, ~s** *Abk.* **Pädagogische Hochschule**

Phalanx ['fa:laŋks] **die; ~, Phalangen** *(hist., fig.)* phalanx

phallisch ['falɪʃ] *(geh.)* **1.** *Adj.* phallic. **2.** *adv.* like a phallus

Phallus ['falʊs] **der; ~, Phalli** *od.* **Phallen,** *(auch:)* **~se** *(geh.)* phallus

Phallus-: ~kult der phallic cult; **~symbol das** phallic symbol

Phänomen [fɛno'me:n] **das; ~s, ~e** phenomenon; **er ist ein ~** *(ugs.)* he is phenomenal

phänomenal [fɛnome'na:l] **1.** *Adj.* phenomenal. **2.** *adv.* phenomenally

Phänomenologie die *(Philos.)* phenomenology

Phantasie [fanta'zi:] **die; ~, ~n a)** *o. Pl.* imagination; **mit [viel]/ohne [jede] ~:** [very] imaginatively *or* with [a lot of] imagination/[very] unimaginatively *or* without [any] imagination; **eine schmutzige ~ haben** have a dirty mind; **b)** *meist Pl. (Produkt der ~)* fantasy

phantasie·los 1. *Adj.* unimaginative; **2.** *adv.* unimaginatively

Phantasielosigkeit die; ~: lack of imagination; *(Eintönigkeit)* dullness

phantasieren 1. *itr. V.* **a)** indulge in fantasies, fantasize **(von** about); **phantasierst du, oder sagst du die Wahrheit?** are you making it up or telling the truth?; **b)** *(Med.: irrereden)* talk deliriously. **2.** *tr. V.* **was phantasierst du da?** what's all that nonsense?

phantasie·voll 1. *Adj.* imaginative. **2.** *adv.* imaginatively

Phantasie·vor·stellung die figment of the imagination

Phantast [fan'tast] **der; ~en, ~en** dreamer; starry-eyed idealist

Phantasterei die; ~, ~en fantasy; *(Wunschtraum)* pipe-dream

phantastisch 1. *Adj.* **a)** fantastic; ⟨*idea*⟩ divorced from reality; **eine ~e Erzählung** a tale of fantasy; **b)** *(ugs.: großartig)* fantastic *(coll.)*; terrific *(coll.)*. **2.** *adv. (ugs.)* fantastically *(coll.)*; **~ tanzen/kochen** *(ugs.)* dance/cook fantastically *(coll.) or* incredibly well

Phantom [fan'to:m] **das; ~s, ~e** phantom; illusion; **einem ~ nachjagen** *(fig.)* chase [after] an illusion *or* a shadow

Phantom-: ~bild das a) *(Kriminalistik)* Identikit [picture] **(P)**; *(aus Fotos)* photofit picture; **b)** *(Fot.)* see-through *or* cut-away picture; **~schmerz der** phantom limb [pain]

Pharao ['fa:rao] **der; ~s, ~nen** [fara'o:nən] Pharaoh

Pharisäer [fari'zɛ:ɐ] **der; ~s, ~** *(auch fig.)* Pharisee

pharisäerhaft *(geh.) Adj.* holier-than-thou

Pharisäertum das; ~s *(geh.)* Pharisaism; hypocrisy

Pharma-: ~berater der *s.* **~referent; ~industrie die** pharmaceutical industry

Pharmakologe [farmako'lo:gə] **der; ~n, ~n** pharmacologist

Pharmakologie [farmakolo'gi:] **die; ~:** pharmacology *no art.*

Pharmakologin die; ~, ~nen pharmacologist

pharmakologisch 1. *Adj.* pharmacological. 2. *adv.* pharmacologically; ~ **ausgebildet** trained in pharmacology *postpos.*
Pharma·referent der pharmaceutical representative
Pharmazeut [farma'tsɔyt] **der;** ~**en,** ~**en** pharmacist
Pharmazeutik [farma'tsɔytɪk] **die;** ~ *s.* **Pharmazie**
Pharmazeutin die; ~, ~**nen** pharmacist
pharmazeutisch 1. *Adj.* pharmaceutical. 2. *adv.* pharmaceutically; ~ **ausgebildet** with pharmaceutical training *postpos.*
Pharmazie [farma'tsi:] **die;** ~: pharmaceutics *sing., no art.;* pharmaceutical chemistry *no art.*
Phase ['fa:zə] **die;** ~, ~**n** phase
Phasen·verschiebung die *(Physik)* phase difference
-phasig *Adj.* -phase
Phenacetin [fenatse'ti:n] **das;** ~**s** *(Pharm.)* phenacetin
Philanthrop [filan'tro:p] **der;** ~**en,** ~**en** *(geh.)* philanthropist
philanthropisch *(geh.)* 1. *Adj.* philanthropic. 2. *adv.* philanthropically
Philatelie [filate'li:] **die;** ~: philately *no art.*
Philatelist der; ~**en,** ~**en** philatelist
Philharmonie [fɪlharmo'ni:] **die;** ~, ~**n a)** *(Orchester)* philharmonic [orchestra]; **b)** *(Gebäude, Saal)* philharmonic hall
Philharmoniker [fɪlhar'mo:nikɐ] **der;** ~**s,** ~: member of a/the philharmonic orchestra; **die Wiener** ~: the Vienna Philharmonic Orchestra
philharmonisch *Adj.* philharmonic
Philipp ['fi:lɪp] **(der)** Philip
Philippika [fi'lɪpika] **die;** ~, **Philippiken** *(geh.)* philippic; diatribe
Philippinen [fili'pi:nən] *Pl.* Philippines
Philister [fi'lɪstɐ] **der;** ~**s,** ~ *(geh.)* Philistine
philister·haft, philiströs *(geh.)* 1. *Adj.* Philistine. 2. *adv.* in a Philistine manner
Philologe [filo'lo:gə] **der;** ~**n,** ~**n** teacher/student of language and literature; philologist *(Amer.)*
Philologie die; ~, ~**n** study of language and literature; philology *no art. (Amer.)*
Philologin die; ~, ~**nen** *s.* **Philologe**
philologisch 1. *Adj.* literary and linguistic; philological *(Amer.).* 2. *adv.* from a literary and linguistic viewpoint; philologically *(Amer.)*
Philo·semit der [keen] supporter of the Jewish/Israeli cause
Philosoph [filo'zo:f] **der;** ~**en,** ~**en** philosopher
Philosophie die; ~, ~**n** philosophy
philosophieren *itr. (auch tr.) V.* philosophize
Philosophin die; ~, ~**nen** philosopher
philosophisch 1. *Adj.* philosophical; ‹*dictionary, principles*› of philosophy; ~**e Fakultät** *(Hochschulw.)* ≈ arts faculty. 2. *adv.* philosophically
Phiole ['fio:lə] **die;** ~, ~**n** pear-shaped flask *(with long neck)*
Phlegma ['flɛgma] **das;** ~**s** *od. (österr. meist:)* ~: phlegmatic disposition; *(Trägheit)* lethargy; *(Apathie)* apathy
Phlegmatiker [flɛ'gma:tikɐ] **der;** ~**s,** ~: phlegmatic person; *(träger Mensch)* lethargic person
phlegmatisch 1. *Adj.* phlegmatic; *(träge)* lethargic; *(apathisch)* apathetic. 2. *adv. s.* 1: phlegmatically; lethargically; apathetically
Phobie [fo'bi:] **die;** ~, ~**n** *(Psych.)* phobia
Phon [fo:n] **das;** ~**s,** ~**s** phon; **50** ~: 50 phons
Phonem [fo'ne:m] **das;** ~**s,** ~**e** *(Sprachw.)* phoneme
Phonetik [fo'ne:tɪk] **die;** ~: phonetics *sing.*
phonetisch 1. *Adj.* phonetic. 2. *adv.* phonetically
Phönix ['fø:nɪks] **der;** ~**[es],** ~**e** phoenix; **wie ein** ~ **aus der Asche** like a phoenix from the ashes
Phönizier [fø'ni:tsiɐ] **der;** ~**s,** ~ *(hist.)* Phoenician
Phono- ['fo:no-] phono ‹*socket, input*›; ~**geschäft/**~**abteilung** audio and record store/department
Phono·gerät das record-player
Phono·graph der *(veralt.)* [cylinder] phonograph
Phono·koffer der portable record-player
Phonologie die; ~ *(Sprachw.)* phonology
phonologisch *(Sprachw.)* 1. *Adj.* phonological. 2. *adv.* phonologically
Phono·typistin [-ty'pɪstɪn] **die;** ~, ~**nen** audio typist
phon·stark *Adj.* loud; noisy; high-volume ‹*reproduction*›
Phon·zahl die phon count; ≈ decibel level
Phosphat [fɔs'fa:t] **das;** ~**[e]s,** ~**e** *(Chemie)* phosphate
Phosphor ['fɔsfɔr] **der;** ~**s** phosphorus
Phosphor·bombe die phosphorus [incendiary] bomb
Phosphoreszenz [fɔsforɛs'tsɛnts] **die;** ~: phosphorescence
phosphoreszieren *itr. V.* phosphoresce; be phosphorescent; ~**d** phosphorescent
phosphor·haltig *Adj.* containing phosphorus *postpos., not pred.;* **stark** ~: with a high phosphorus content; **[stark]** ~ **sein** contain [a high level of] phophorus
Phosphor·säure die phosphoric acid
Photo ['fo:to] **das;** ~**s,** ~**s** *s.* **Foto**
photo-, Photo- *s. auch* **foto-, Foto-**
Photo-: ~**chemie die** photochemistry *no art.;* ~**element das** *(Elektrot.)* photoelement; photovoltaic cell; ~**metrie die;** ~ *(Physik)* photometry *no art.*
Photon ['fo:tɔn] **das;** ~**s,** ~**en** [fo'to:nən] *(Physik)* photon
Photo-: ~**synthese die** photosynthesis; ~**zelle die** photo[-electric] cell
Phrase ['fra:zə] **die;** ~, ~**n a)** *(abwertend)* [empty] phrase; cliché; **leere** ~**n** empty phrases; waffle *sing.;* ~**n dreschen** *(ugs.)* spout clichés; dole out catch-phrases; **b)** *(Musik, Sprachw.)* phrase
phrasen-, Phrasen-: ~**drescher der;** ~**s,** ~ *(ugs. abwertend)* phrase-monger; cliché-monger; ~**drescherei** [~drɛʃə'rai] **die;** ~, ~**en** *(ugs. abwertend)* phrase-mongering; cliché-mongering; ~**haft** *(abwertend)* 1. *Adj.* empty; trite; *(voller Klischees)* cliché-ridden; 2. *adv.* in an empty *or* trite manner
Phraseologie [frazeolo'gi:] **die;** ~, ~**n** *(Sprachw.)* idiomatic usage *no art.; (Buch)* dictionary of idioms
phraseologisch *(Sprachw.) Adj.* idiomatic; phrasal ‹*unit*›; ~**es Wörterbuch** dictionary of idioms
phrasieren *itr., tr. V. (Musik)* phrase
Phrasierung die; ~, ~**en** *(Musik)* phrasing
pH-Wert [pe:'ha:-] **der** *(Chemie)* pH[-value]
Physik [fy'zi:k] **die;** ~: physics *sing., no art.;* **ein Lehrbuch der** ~: a physics textbook
physikalisch [fyzi'ka:lɪʃ] 1. *Adj.* physics *attrib.* ‹*experiment, formula, research, institute*›; physical ‹*map, chemistry, therapy, process*›; ~**e Gesetze** laws of physics; physical laws. 2. *adv.* in terms of physics
Physiker der; ~**s,** ~, **Physikerin die;** ~, ~**nen** physicist
Physik·saal der *(Schulw.)* physics laboratory
Physikum ['fy:zikʊm] **das;** ~**s, Physika** *(Hochschulw.) examination ending the preclinical stage*
Physiognomie [fyziogno'mi:] **die;** ~, ~**n** physiognomy
Physiologe [fyzio'lo:gə] **der;** ~**n,** ~**n** physiologist
Physiologie [fyziolo'gi:] **die;** ~: physiology
Physiologin die; ~, ~**nen** physiologist
physiologisch 1. *Adj.* physiological. 2. *adv.* physiologically
Physio·therapie [fyzio-] **die** physiotherapy
physisch 1. *Adj.* physical. 2. *adv.* physically
Pi [pi:] **das;** ~**[s],** ~**s** pi
Pianist [pia'nɪst] **der;** ~**en,** ~**en, Pianistin die;** ~, ~**nen** pianist
Piano ['pia:no] **das;** ~**s,** ~**s** piano
Pianoforte [piano'fɔrtə] **das;** ~, ~**s** *(veralt.)* pianoforte *(formal/arch.)*
picheln ['pɪçl̩n] *(ugs.)* 1. *itr. V.* booze *(coll.).* 2. *tr. V.* **einen** ~ **gehen** go out for a jar *(Brit. coll.)*
Pickel ['pɪkl̩] **der;** ~**s,** ~ **a)** *(auf der Haut)* pimple; **b)** *(Spitzhacke)* pickaxe; *(Eis~)* ice-axe
Pickel·haube die spiked helmet
pickelig *Adj.* pimply; ~ **[im Gesicht] sein** have a spotty *or* pimply face
picken ['pɪkn̩] 1. *itr. V.* peck (**nach** at; **an** + *Akk.,* **gegen** on, against). 2. *tr. V.* **a)** ‹*bird*› peck; *(ugs.)* ‹*person*› pick; *(aufheben)* pick up; **b)** *(österr. ugs.: kleben)* stick
picklig *s.* **pickelig**
Picknick ['pɪknɪk] **das;** ~**s,** ~**e** *od.* ~**s** picnic; ~ **machen** *od.* **halten** have a picnic
picknicken *itr. V.* picnic
picobello ['pi:ko'bɛlo] *(ugs.)* 1. *indekl. Adj.* super-duper *(sl.); (makellos)* immaculate. 2. *adv.* immaculately; ~ **in Ordnung** in immaculate order; spick and span
Piefke ['pi:fkə] **der;** ~**s,** ~**[s] a)** *(bes. nordd. abwertend)* bumptious lout; **b)** *(österr. abwertend: Deutscher)* bloody *(Brit. sl.) or* damn German
pieken *s.* **piken**
piek·fein ['pi:k'fain] *(ugs.)* 1. *Adj.* posh *(coll.).* 2. *adv.* poshly *(coll.);* ~ **angezogen** wearing posh clothes *(coll.);* dressed to the nines
piep [pi:p] *Interj.* ~, ~! cheep, cheep!; **nicht** ~ **sagen** *(ugs.)* not say a word; **er kann nicht mehr** ~ **sagen** *(ugs.)* he's been silenced
Piep der; ~**s,** ~**e** *(ugs.)* **a)** *(Ton)* peep; **keinen** ~ **[davon] sagen** not say a thing [about it]; **b)** *in* **einen [kleinen]** ~ **haben** have a [bit of a] screw loose *(coll.)*
piepe ['pi:pə], **piep·egal** *Adj. in* **[jmdm.]** ~ **sein** *(ugs.)* not matter at all [to sb.]; **es ist mir** ~ *(ugs.)* I don't give a damn
piepen *itr. V. (ugs.)* squeak; ‹*small bird*› cheep; chirp; ‹*paging device*› bleep; **bei dir piept's wohl!** *(salopp)* you must be off your rocker *(sl.);* **zum Piepen sein** *(ugs.)* be a hoot *or* a scream *(coll.)*
Piepen *Pl. (salopp: Geld)* dough *sing. (sl.);* **50** ~: 50 marks/francs *etc.*
Piep-: ~**hahn der** *(Kinderspr.)* willy *(sl.);* ~**matz der** *(Kinderspr.)* dicky-bird *(coll.)*
pieps [pi:ps] *s.* **piep**
Pieps der; ~**es,** ~**e** *(ugs.) s.* **Piep a**
piepsen *(ugs.)* 1. *itr. V. s.* **piepen.** 2. *itr., tr. V. (mit hoher Stimme sprechen)* pipe; *(aufgeregt)* squeal
Piepser der; ~**s,** ~ *(ugs.)* **a)** *(Piepsen)* chirp; tweet; **b)** *(kleiner Empfänger)* bleeper
piepsig *Adj. (ugs.)* squeaky
Pier [pi:ɐ̯] **der;** ~**s,** ~**e** *od.* ~**s** *od. (Seemannsspr.)* **die;** ~, ~**s** jetty
piesacken ['pi:zakn̩] *tr. V. (ugs.)* pester; **hör endlich auf, mich damit zu** ~! stop pestering me about that!
pieseln ['pi:zl̩n] *itr. (auch tr.) V. (salopp) s.* **pinkeln**
Pietät [pie'tɛ:t] **die;** ~, ~**en a)** *o. Pl.* respect; *(Ehrfurcht)* reverence; **b)** *(Bestattungsinstitut)* [firm of] funeral directors *or (Amer.)* morticians
pietät-, Pietät-: ~**los** 1. *Adj.* irreverent; *(gefühllos)* unfeeling; *(respektlos)* disrespectful; lacking in respect *postpos.;* 2. *adv.* irreverently; ~**losigkeit die;** ~, ~**en** irreverence; *(Gefühllosigkeit)* lack of feeling;

(Respektlosigkeit) lack of respect; *(Handlung)* act of irreverence; **~voll 1.** *Adj.* respectful; *(ehrfurchtsvoll)* reverent; **2.** *adv.* respectfully; *(ehrfurchtsvoll)* reverently
Pietismus [pie'tɪsmʊs] **der;** ~: pietism *no art.*
Pietist der; ~en, ~en, Pietistin die; ~, **~nen** pietist
pietistisch 1. *Adj.* pietistic. **2.** *adv.* in a pietistic manner
piff, paff ['pɪf 'paf] *Interj. (Kinderspr.)* bang, bang
Pigment [pɪ'gmɛnt] **das; ~[e]s, ~e** pigment
Pigmentation [pɪgmɛnta'tsio:n] **die; ~, ~en** pigmentation
Pigment·fleck der pigmentation mark
[1]Pik [pi:k] **der** *in* **einen ~ auf jmdn. haben** *(ugs.)* have it in for sb.
[2]Pik das; ~[s], ~[s], *österr. auch* **die; ~, ~** *(Kartenspiel)* **a)** *o. Art., o. Pl. (Farbe)* spades *pl.*; **von ~ habe ich nur noch die Sieben** the only spade I have left is the seven; **~ ziehen/ausspielen** draw/play spades; **b)** *(Karte)* spade
pikant [pi'kant] **1.** *Adj.* **a)** piquant; *(würzig)* spicy; well-seasoned; *(appetitanregend)* appetizing; **ich möchte lieber etwas Pikantes** I'd rather have something savoury; **b)** *(fig.: witzig)* piquant; ironical; **c)** *(verhüll.: schlüpfrig)* racy ‹*joke, story*›; titillating ‹*pictures*›. **2.** *adv.* spicily; **etw. ~ zubereiten** season sth. well; **~ gewürzt** piquantly *or* appetizingly seasoned
Pikanterie [pikantə'ri:] **die; ~, ~n a)** *o. Pl. (fig.)* piquancy; *(Witzigkeit)* irony; **b)** *(verhüll.: schlüpfrige Geschichte)* racy story
pikanter·weise *Adv. (geh.)* ironically [enough]
Pik-: ~as das ace of spades; **~bube der** jack of spades; **~dame die** queen of spades
Pike ['pi:kə] **die; ~, ~n** pike; **etw. von der ~ auf [er]lernen** learn sth. by working one's way up from the bottom
Pikee [pi'ke:] **der;** *österr. auch* **das; ~s, ~s** *(Textilw.)* piqué
piken *tr., itr. V. (ugs.)* prick; **etw. in etw.** *(Akk.)* **~:** poke sth. into sth.; **jmdm. eine Nadel in den Arm ~:** poke a needle into sb.'s arm
pikieren *tr. V. (Gartenbau)* prick out ‹*seedlings*›
pikiert [pi'ki:ɐt] **1.** *Adj.* piqued; nettled; **ein ~es Gesicht machen** look aggrieved. **2.** *adv.* ‹*reply, say*› in an aggrieved tone *or* voice
[1]Pikkolo ['pɪkolo] **der; ~s, ~s** [trainee] waiter
[2]Pikkolo das; ~s, ~s *(Flöte)* piccolo
[3]Pikkolo die; ~, ~[s] *(Fläschchen)* miniature bottle of champagne *(for one person)*
Pikkolo·flöte die piccolo
Pik·könig der king of spades
piksen ['pi:ksn] *tr., itr. V. (ugs.) s.* **piken**
Pik·sieben die *(Kartenspiel)* seven of spades; **dastehen wie ~** *(ugs.)* stand there looking stupid
Pilger ['pɪlgɐ] **der; ~s, ~:** pilgrim
-pilger der: Mekka~/Rom~: pilgrim on his/her way to Rome/Mecca
Pilger·fahrt die pilgrimage
Pilgerin die; ~, ~nen pilgrim
pilgern *itr. V.* **a)** *(auch fig.)* go on *or* make a pilgrimage; **b)** *(ugs.: gehen)* traipse *(coll.)*
Pilgerschaft die; ~, ~en pilgrimage
Pilger-: ~stab der pilgrim's staff; **~väter** *Pl. (hist.)* Pilgrim Fathers
Pille ['pɪlə] **die; ~, ~n** pill; **sie nimmt schon seit Jahren die ~:** she's been on the pill for years *(coll.)*; **eine bittere ~ [für jmdn.] sein** *(fig.)* be a bitter pill [for sb.] to swallow; **jmdm. die bittere ~ versüßen** *od.* **verzuckern** *(fig.)* sugar the pill for sb.; *(es jmdm. erleichtern)* make it easier for sb.
Pillen-: ~dreher der a) *(Käfer)* scarab [beetle]; **b)** *(ugs. scherzh.: Apotheker)* pill-peddler *(coll.)*; **~knick der** decline in the birth rate [due to the pill]
Pilot [pi'lo:t] **der; ~en, ~en, Pilotin die; ~, ~nen a)** pilot; **b)** *(Motorsport)* [racing] driver
Pilot-: ~projekt das pilot project; **~studie die** pilot study
Pils [pɪls] **das; ~, ~:** Pils; Pils[e]ner [beer]
Pilz [pɪlts] **der; ~es, ~e a)** fungus; *(Speise~, auch fig.)* mushroom; **eßbare, giftige und ungenießbare ~e** mushrooms, poisonous and inedible fungi; **in die ~e gehen** *(ugs.)* go mushrooming; **wie ~e aus dem Boden** *od.* **der Erde schießen** be springing up like mushrooms; **b)** *o. Pl. (ugs.: ~infektion)* fungus [infection]
pilz-, Pilz-: ~förmig *Adj.* mushroom-shaped; **~krankheit die a)** *(Mykose)* mycosis; **b)** *(bei Pflanzen)* fungus [disease]; **~kultur die** fungus culture; **~kunde die** mycology
Pilzling ['pɪltslɪŋ] **der; ~s, ~e** *(österr.) s.* **Steinpilz**
Pilz·vergiftung die fungus poisoning *no art.*; *(durch verdorbene Pilze)* mushroom poisoning *no art.*
Piment [pi'mɛnt] **der** *od.* **das; ~[e]s, ~e** pimento; allspice
Pimmel ['pɪml̩] **der; ~s, ~** *(salopp)* willy *(sl.)*
pimpern ['pɪmpɐn] *(salopp)* **1.** *itr. V.* have it off *(sl.)*. **2.** *tr. V.* have it off with *(sl.)*
Pimpf [pɪmpf] **der; ~[e]s, ~e a)** *(ugs.: Junge)* kid *(coll.)*; **b)** *(ns.) member of the* **Jungvolk**
pingelig ['pɪŋəlɪç] *(ugs.)* **1.** finicky; pernickety *(coll.)*; *(wählerisch)* fussy; choosy *(coll.)*. **2.** *adv.* in a pernickety way *(coll.)*; *(pedantisch)* pedantically
Pingpong ['pɪŋpɔŋ] **das; ~s** *(ugs.)* ping-pong
Pinguin ['pɪŋgui:n] **der; ~s, ~e** penguin
Pinie ['pi:niə] **die; ~, ~n** [stone- *or* umbrella] pine
Pinke ['pɪŋkə] **die; ~** *(ugs. veralt.)* dough *(sl.)*; lolly *(Brit. sl.)*
Pinkel ['pɪŋkl̩] **der; ~s, ~** *(ugs. abwertend)* **ein [feiner] ~:** a stuck-up prig
pinkeln *itr. (auch tr.) V. (salopp)* **a)** pee *(coll.)*; ‹*esp. child*› wee *(sl.)*; **~ [gehen]** [go and] have a pee *(coll.)*; **b)** *(unpers.: regnen)* **es pinkelt** it's spitting
Pinkel·pause die *(ugs.)* stop for a pee *(coll.)*; rest stop *(Amer.)*
Pinke·pinke *s.* **Pinke**
pink·farben ['pɪŋk-] *Adj.* pink
Pinne ['pɪnə] **die; ~, ~n** *(Seemannsspr.)* tiller
pinnen *tr. V. (ugs.)* pin **(auf, an +** *Akk.* on)
Pinn·wand die pin-board
Pinscher ['pɪnʃɐ] **der; ~s, ~ a)** pinscher; **b)** *(ugs. abwertend: Mensch)* pip-squeak *(sl.)*
Pinsel ['pɪnzl̩] **der; ~s, ~ a)** brush; *(Mal~)* paintbrush; **mit leichtem/kühnem ~:** with light/bold brush-strokes; **b)** *(ugs. abwertend: Dummkopf)* nitwit *(coll.)*; idiot *(coll.)*
Pinsel·führung die brushwork *no indef. art.*
pinseln *tr. V.* **a)** *(ugs.: anstreichen)* paint ‹*room, house, etc.*›; **b)** *(malen)* paint ‹*landscape, picture*›; daub ‹*slogans*›; **c)** *(ugs.: schreiben)* write ‹*letters, homework*› in one's best writing; **d)** *(streichen)* brush [on] ‹*paint*›, put on ‹*paint*› with a brush; apply ‹*liquid*› [with a brush] **(auf +** *Akk.* to); **e)** *(Med.: ein~)* paint ‹*wound, gums, throat, etc.*›
Pinsel·strich der a) brush-stroke; **b)** *(Pinselführung)* brushwork *no indef. art.*
Pinte ['pɪntə] **die; ~, ~n a)** *(ugs.) s.* **Kneipe a; b)** *(hist.: Hohlmaß) [former] measure of capacity for liquids*
Pin-up-Girl [pɪn'ap-] **das; ~s, ~s** pin-up girl
Pinzette [pɪn'tsɛtə] **die; ~, ~n** tweezers *pl.*; **chirurgische ~:** surgical forceps *pl.*
Pionier [pio'ni:ɐ] **der; ~s, ~e a)** *(Milit.)* sapper; engineer; **b)** *(fig.: Wegbereiter)* pioneer; **c)** *(bes. DDR: Mitglied einer Jugendorganisation)* **[Junger] ~:** [Young] Pioneer
Pionier-: ~arbeit die; *o. Pl.* **a)** pioneering work; **b)** *(bes. DDR)* work with the [Young] Pioneers; **~truppe die** *(Milit.)* corps of engineers
Pipapo [pipa'po:] **das; ~s** *(salopp)* **das ganze ~:** all the frills; **mit allem ~:** with all the frills
Pipeline ['paiplain] **die; ~, ~s** pipeline
Pipette [pi'pɛtə] **die; ~, ~n** *(Chemie)* pipette
Pipi [pi'pi:] **das; ~s** *(Kindersspr.)* **~ machen** do wee-wees *(sl.)*; **~ müssen** have to do wee-wees *or* have a wee *(sl.)*
Pipifax ['pipifaks] **der; ~** *(salopp)* piffling trifles *pl. (sl.)*
Piranha [pi'ranja] **der; ~[s], ~s** piranha
Pirat [pi'ra:t] **der; ~en, ~en** pirate
Piraten-: ~schiff das pirate ship; **~sender der** pirate radio station
Piraterie [piratə'ri:] **die; ~, ~n** piracy *no art.*
Pirol [pi'ro:l] **der; ~s, ~e** oriole
Pirouette [pi'ruɛtə] **die; ~, ~n** pirouette
Pirsch [pɪrʃ] **die; ~** *(Jägerspr.)* [deer-]stalking; **auf die ~ gehen** go [deer-]stalking
pirschen 1. *itr. V.* **a)** *(Jägerspr.)* stalk; go stalking; **auf Rehwild** *(Akk.)* **~:** stalk roe-deer; **b)** *(ugs.: schleichen)* creep [silently]; steal. **2.** *refl. V. (ugs.)* creep [silently]; steal
Pisse ['pɪsə] **die; ~** *(derb)* piss *(coarse)*
pissen *itr. (auch tr.) V. (derb)* **a)** piss *(coarse)*; **ich muß ~ [gehen]** I must have a piss; **b)** *(unpers.: regnen)* piss down *(sl.)*
Pissoir [pɪ'soa:ɐ] **das; ~s, ~e** *od.* **~s** [public] urinal
Piß·pott der *(salopp)* piss-pot *(coarse)*
Pistazie [pɪs'ta:tsiə] **die; ~, ~n** pistachio
Piste ['pɪstə] **die; ~, ~n a)** *(Skisport)* piste; ski-run; *(Renn~)* course; **b)** *(Rennstrecke)* track; **c)** *(Flugw.)* runway; **auf der ~ aufsetzen** touch down; **d)** *(Straße)* dirt road
Pistole [pɪs'to:lə] **die; ~, ~n** pistol; **wie aus der ~ geschossen** like a shot *or* a flash; **jmdm. die ~ auf die Brust setzen** *(fig.)* hold a pistol to sb.'s head
Pistolen-: ~schuß der pistol-shot; **~tasche die** holster
pitsch·naß ['pɪtʃ'nas] *Adj. (ugs.)* dripping wet; wet through
pittoresk [pɪto'rɛsk] *(geh.)* **1.** *Adj.* picturesque. **2.** *adv.* picturesquely
Pizza ['pɪtsa] **die; ~, ~s** *od.* **Pizzen** pizza
Pizza·bäcker der pizza cook
Pizzeria [pɪtse'ri:a] **die; ~, ~s** *od.* **Pizzerien** pizzeria
Pkw, PKW ['pe:ka:ve:] **der; ~[s], ~[s]** [private] car; automobile *(Amer.)*
placieren [pla'tsi:rən] *s.* **plazieren**
placken ['plakn̩] *refl. V. (ugs.)* slave away
Plackerei die; ~, ~en *(ugs.)* drudgery *no indef. art.*; [hard] grind
pladdern ['pladɐn] *itr. V. (unpers.)* **es pladdert** *(nordd.)* it's pouring [down]
plädieren [plɛ'di:rən] *itr. V.* *(Rechtsw.)* plead **(auf +** *Akk.*, **für** for); *(das Plädoyer halten)* ‹*counsel*› make one's final speech, sum up; *(fig.)* argue **(für** for, in favour of); **auf Freispruch/auf schuldig ~:** plead for acquittal/for a verdict of guilty; **er plädiert dafür, daß ...:** he argues *or* advocates that ...
Plädoyer [plɛdoa'je:] **das; ~s, ~s** *(Rechtsw.)* final speech, summing up *(for the defence/prosecution)*; *(fig.)* plea; **sein ~ halten** make one's final speech; sum up
Plafond [pla'fõ:] **der; ~s, ~s** *(südd., österr., auch fig.)* ceiling
Plage ['pla:gə] **die; ~, ~n a)** [cursed *or (coll.)* pestilential] nuisance; **das macht ihm das Leben zur ~:** it makes his life a misery; **die ägyptischen ~n** *(bibl.)* the plagues of Egypt; **b)** *(ugs.: Mühe)* bother; trouble; **seine ~ mit jmdm./etw. haben** find sb./sth. a real handful

Plage·geist der *(fam.)* pest

plagen 1. *tr. V.* **a)** torment; plague; **Zweifel ~ ihn** he is plagued *or* beset with doubts; **von Kopfschmerzen/Träumen geplagt** plagued with headaches/dreams; **er ist ein geplagter Mensch** he has a hard time of it; **b)** *(ugs.: bedrängen)* harass; *(mit Bitten, Fragen)* pester. **2.** *refl. V.* **a)** *(sich abmühen)* slave away; **sie mußte sich ~, um die Arbeit zu bewältigen** she had to struggle to get through all the work; **b)** *(leiden)* **sich mit etw. ~:** be troubled *or* bothered by sth.

Plagiat [pla'gia:t] **das; ~[e]s, ~e** plagiarism *no art.*; **ein [eindeutiges] ~:** a [clear] case of plagiarism

Plagiator [pla'gia:tɔr] **der; ~s, ~en** *(geh.)* plagiarist

plagiieren [plagi'i:rən] *tr. (auch itr.) V.* *(geh.)* plagiarize

Plaid [ple:t] **das** *od.* **der; ~s, ~s a)** *(Decke)* tartan [travelling] rug *(Brit.) or (Amer.)* lap robe; **b)** *(Tuch)* plaid

Plakat [pla'ka:t] **das; ~[e]s, ~e** poster; *(zum Tragen)* placard; **„~e ankleben verboten"** 'post no bills'

plakatieren 1. *tr. V.* announce by poster. **2.** *itr. V.* put up posters

plakativ [plaka'ti:f] **1.** *Adj.* bold and simple, eye-catching ⟨*design, representation*⟩; bold ⟨*colours*⟩. **2.** *adv.* eye-catchingly; in a bold and simple style

Plakat-: ~kunst die; *o. Pl.* poster art *no art.*; **~maler der** poster artist; **~wand die** [poster] hoarding; billboard

Plakette [pla'kɛtə] **die; ~, ~n a)** *(Schildchen)* badge; *(Scheibe)* disc; **b)** *(an einem Gebäude)* plaque

plan [pla:n] *(Technik) Adj.* flat; plane ⟨*surface*⟩; **~ liegen** lie flat

¹Plan der; ~[e]s, Pläne ['plɛ:nə] **a)** plan; **nach ~ verlaufen** go according to plan; **auf dem ~ stehen** be on the agenda; be planned; **wir sind im ~** *(Zeit~)* we are on schedule; **b)** *(Karte)* map; plan; *(Stadt~)* [street] plan

²Plan der *in* **auf den ~ treten, auf dem ~ erscheinen** *(geh.)* appear on the scene; **auf den ~ rufen** *(geh.)* bring ⟨*person*⟩ on to the scene; bring ⟨*opponent*⟩ into the arena; arouse ⟨*curiosity*⟩

Plan-: ~auf·gabe die, ~auf·lage die *(DDR)* planned [production] target *(laid down in the five-year plan)*

Plane die; ~, ~n tarpaulin

planen *tr., itr. V.* plan

Planer der; ~s, ~: planner

Plan·erfüllung die *(bes. DDR)* attainment of the planned [production] target

planerisch *Adj.; nicht präd.* planning ⟨*measures, genius, ability*⟩; **eine ~e Meisterleistung** a masterpiece of planning

Pläne·schmieden das planning; making plans

Planet [pla'ne:t] **der; ~en, ~en** planet

Planetarium [plane'ta:ri̯ʊm] **das; ~s, Planetarien** planetarium

Planeten-: ~bahn die planetary orbit; **~system das** planetary system

Planetoid der; ~en, ~en asteroid, planetoid

planieren *tr. V.* level; grade *(as tech. term)*

Planier·raupe die bulldozer

Plan·jahr das *(bes. DDR)* planning year

Planke ['plaŋkə] **die; ~, ~n a)** plank; board; **b)** *(Zaun)* [close-boarded] wooden fence

Plänkelei die; ~, ~en *s.* **Geplänkel a**

plänkeln ['plɛŋkl̩n] *itr. V.* have a rough-and-tumble; fight playfully

Plankton ['plaŋktɔn] **das; ~s** *(Biol.)* plankton

plan-, Plan-: ~los 1. *Adj.* aimless; *(ohne System)* unsystematic; **2.** *adv. s.* **1:** aimlessly; unsystematically; **~losigkeit die; ~:** aimlessness; *(Mangel an System)* lack of system; **~mäßig 1.** *Adj.* **a)** regular, scheduled ⟨*service, steamer*⟩; **~mäßige Ankunft/Abfahrt** scheduled time of arrival/departure; **b)** *(systematisch)* systematic; **2.** *adv.* **a)** *(wie geplant)* according to plan; as planned; *(pünktlich)* on schedule; **b)** *(systematisch)* systematically; **~mäßigkeit die; ~:** methodicalness; *(Vorgehen)* systematic procedure; **~quadrat das** grid square

Plansch·becken ['planʃ-] **das** paddling-pool

planschen *itr. V.* splash [about]

Plan-: ~soll das planned [production] target; **~spiel das** simulation; *(Kriegsspiel)* war game; **~stelle die** established post

Plantage [plan'ta:ʒə] **die; ~, ~n** plantation

Planung die; ~, ~en a) *(das Planen)* planning; **in** *(Dat.)* **~ sein** be planned; **bei der ~:** at the planning stage; **b)** *(Plan)* plan

Planungs·stadium das planning stage; **im ~:** at the planning stage

plan-, Plan-: ~voll 1. *Adj.* methodical; systematic; **2.** methodically; systematically; **~wagen der** covered wagon; **~wirtschaft die** planned economy

Plapperei die; ~, ~en *(ugs. abwertend)* chatter

Plapper·maul das *(ugs. abwertend)* chatterbox

plappern ['plapɐn] *(ugs.)* **1.** *itr. V.* **a)** *(schwätzen)* chatter; **b)** *(ausplaudern)* blab. **2.** *tr. V.* babble ⟨*nonsense*⟩

plärren ['plɛrən] **1.** *tr. V.* bawl [out] ⟨*song*⟩; ⟨*radio etc.*⟩ blare out. **2.** *itr. V.* **a)** bawl; yell; ⟨*radio etc.*⟩ blare; **b)** *(ugs.: weinen)* wail; *(sehr laut)* howl

Pläsier [plɛ'zi:ɐ̯] **das; ~s, ~e** *(veralt.)* pleasure (**an** + *Dat.* in); **laß ihm doch sein ~:** let him have his fun

Plasma ['plasma] **das; ~s, Plasmen** *(Med., Physik)* plasma; *(Proto~)* protoplasm

Plast [plast] **der; ~[e]s, ~e** *(DDR)* plastic

Plaste ['plastə] **die; ~, ~n** *(DDR ugs.)* plastic

¹Plastik ['plastɪk] **die; ~, ~en a)** *(Werk, Kunst)* sculpture; **b)** *(Med.)* plastic surgery operation; **jmdm. eine ~ machen** perform plastic surgery on sb.

²Plastik das; ~s *(ugs.)* plastic

Plastik-: ~beutel der plastic bag; **~bombe die** plastic bomb; **~folie die** plastic film; **~geld das** *(ugs.)* plastic money *(coll.)*; **~tüte die** plastic bag

Plastilin [plasti'li:n] **das; ~s** ≈ Plasticine P

plastisch 1. *Adj.* **a)** *(knetbar)* plastic; workable; **b)** *nicht präd.* *(bildhauerisch)* sculptural; ⟨*ability*⟩ as a sculptor; **c)** *(dreidimensional)* three-dimensional ⟨*effect, formation, vision*⟩; sculptural ⟨*decoration*⟩; **d)** *(fig.: anschaulich)* vivid ⟨*description, picture*⟩; **e)** *(Med.)* plastic ⟨*surgery, surgeon*⟩. **2.** *adv.* **a)** *(bildhauerisch)* sculpturally; **etw. ~ ausarbeiten** *od.* **gestalten** sculpture sth.; **b)** *(dreidimensional)* three-dimensionally; **c)** *(fig.: anschaulich)* vividly; **sich** *(Dat.)* **etw. ~ vorstellen können** have a clear picture of sth. [in one's mind]

Plastizität [plastitsi'tɛ:t] **die; ~ a)** plasticity; **b)** *(fig.: Anschaulichkeit)* vividness; *(von Prosa usw.)* graphic quality; *(eines Bildes)* three-dimensional quality

Platane [pla'ta:nə] **die; ~, ~n** plane-tree

Plateau [pla'to:] **das; ~s, ~s** plateau

Plateau·sohle die platform sole

Platin ['pla:ti:n] **das; ~s** platinum

platin·blond *Adj.* platinum blonde

Platitüde [plati'ty:də] **die; ~, ~n** *(geh.)* platitude

Platon ['pla:tɔn] **(der)** Plato

platonisch [pla'to:nɪʃ] **1.** *Adj.* **a)** Platonic ⟨*philosophy, state*⟩; **b)** *(nicht sinnlich)* platonic ⟨*love, relationship*⟩. **2.** *adv.* platonically

platsch [platʃ] *Interj.* splash

platschen *itr. V.* **a)** splash; **b)** *mit sein (~d schlagen)* splash (**an** + *Akk.*, **gegen** against); **c)** *(planschen)* splash about

plätschern ['plɛtʃɐn] *itr. V.* **a)** splash; ⟨*rain*⟩ patter; ⟨*stream*⟩ burble; *(fig.)* **~de Unterhaltung** casual *or* desultory conversation; **b)** *(planschen)* splash about; **c)** *mit sein* ⟨*stream*⟩ burble along

platsch·naß *Adj. (ugs.) s.* **klatschnaß**

platt [plat] **1.** *Adj.* **a)** *(flach)* flat; **sich** *(Dat.)* **die Nase ~ drücken** flatten one's nose; **ein Platter** *(ugs.)* a flat *(coll.)*; a flat tyre; *(mit Loch)* a puncture; **das ~e Land** *(ugs.)* the countryside; the rural areas *pl.*; **sie ist ~ wie ein [Bügel]brett** *(salopp)* she is flat-chested; **b)** *(geistlos)* dull, vapid ⟨*conversation, book*⟩; vacuous, feeble ⟨*poem, joke*⟩; shallow, empty ⟨*materialism, argument, imitation*⟩; **c)** *nicht präd. (ausgesprochen)* downright ⟨*lie, swindle, slander*⟩; sheer ⟨*cynicism*⟩; absolute ⟨*matter of course*⟩; **d)** *nicht attr. (ugs., bes. nordd.: erstaunt)* dumbfounded; flabbergasted. **2.** *adv.* **a)** *(flach)* **sich ~ legen** lie down flat; **b)** *(geistlos)* feebly. **3.** *Adv.* **~ sprechen** talk Low German dialect

Platt das; ~[s] a) [local] Low German dialect; *(allgemein: Niederdeutsch)* Low German; **b)** *(ugs.: Dialekt)* patois

Plätt·brett das *(nordd., md.) s.* **Bügelbrett**

Plättchen ['plɛtçən] **das; ~s, ~:** small plate *or* disc

platt·deutsch *Adj.: s.* **niederdeutsch**

Platte die; ~, ~n a) *(Stein~)* slab; *(Metall~)* plate; sheet; *(Mikroskopie usw.: Glas~)* slide; *(Elektronik)* board; *(Paneel)* panel; *(Span~, Hartfaser~ usw.)* board; *(Styropor~ usw.)* sheet; *(Tisch~)* [table-]top; *(Grab~)* [memorial] slab; *(photographische ~)* [photographic] plate; *(Druck~)* [pressure] plate; *(Kachel, Fliese)* tile; *(zum Pflastern)* flagstone; paving-stone; **etw./jmdn. auf die ~ bannen** *(scherzh.)* immortalize sb./sth. [in a photograph] *(joc.)*; **b)** *(Koch~)* hotplate; **c)** *(Schall~)* [gramophone] record; **eine ~ mit Gitarrenmusik** a record of guitar music; **etw. auf ~** *(Akk.)* **aufnehmen** make a record of sth.; **die ~ kenne ich [schon]** *(fig. ugs.)* I've heard that one before; **leg [doch endlich mal] 'ne neue/andere ~ auf!** *(fig. ugs.)* can't you talk about sth. else for a change?; **immer dieselbe ~!** *(fig. ugs.)* always the same old tune; **d)** *(Teller)* plate; *(zum Servieren, aus Metall)* dish; **e)** *(Speise)* dish; **kalte ~:** selection of cold meats [and cheese]; **f)** *(ugs.: Glatze)* bald pate; **g)** *(Gaumen~)* [dental] plate; **h) die ~ putzen** *(salopp)* make oneself scarce *(coll.)*; **~ machen** *(salopp)* doss *or* kip down *(Brit. sl.)*; bed down; **i)** *(österr. ugs.: Bande)* gang

Plätte ['plɛtə] **die; ~, ~n** *(österr.)* flat-bottomed barge *(with pointed prow)*

Plätt·eisen ['plɛt-] **das** *(nordd., md.)* iron; *(hist.)* flat-iron

plätten *tr., itr. V. (nordd., md.)* iron

Platten-: ~album das record album; **~cover das** record sleeve; **~firma die** record company; **~hülle die** record sleeve; **~sammlung die** record collection

Platten·see der; *o. Pl. (Geogr.)* Lake Balaton

Platten-: ~spieler der *(als Baustein)* record deck; *(komplettes Gerät)* record-player; **~teller der** turntable; **~wechsler der** record-changer

platter·dings *Adv. (ugs.)* absolutely

platt, Platt-: ~fisch der flat-fish; **~form die a)** platform; **b)** *(fig.: Basis)* basic programme; *(Wahlplattform)* platform; [election] programme; **eine gemeinsame ~form** common ground; *(bei Wahlen)* a common platform; **~fuß der a)** flat foot; **b)** *(ugs.: Reifenpanne)* flat *(coll.)*; flat tyre; **~füßig** *Adj.* flat-footed

Plattheit die; ~, ~en a) *o. Pl.* flatness; **b)** *o. Pl. (fig.)* dullness; **c)** *(Platitüde)* platitude

Plätt·wäsche die *(nordd., md.)* laundry to be ironed; ironing

Platz [plats] **der; ~es, Plätze** ['plɛtsə] **a)** *(freie Fläche)* space; area; *(Bau~, Ausstellungsgelände usw.)* site; *(umbaute Fläche)* square; **ein freier ~:** an open space; **b)** *(Park~)* car park; [parking] lot *(Amer.)*; *(Camping~)* [camp]site; [camp]ground *(Amer.)*; *(Schrott~, Lager~)* yard; **c)** *(Sport~) (ganze Anlage)* ground; *(Spielfeld)* field; *(Tennis~, Volleyball~ usw.)* court; *(Golf~)* course; **der ~ ist nicht bespielbar** the ground is not playable; **einen Spieler vom ~ stellen/tragen** send/carry a player off [the field]; **auf eigenem/gegnerischem ~ spielen** play at home/away; **d)** *(Stelle)* place; spot; *(Position)* location; position; *(wo jmd., etw. hingehört)* place; **ein ~ an der Sonne** *(fig.)* a place in the sun; **auf die Plätze, fertig, los!** on your marks, get set, go!; **sich** *(Dat.)* **einen festen ~ in der Literatur erobern** become firmly established in literature; **am** *od.* **an seinem ~:** in its/his place; **nicht** *od.* **fehl am ~[e] sein** *(fig.)* be out of place; be inappropriate; **am ~[e] sein** *(fig.)* be appropriate; be called for; **e)** *(Sitz~)* seat; *(am Tisch, Steh~ usw.; fig.: im Kurs, Krankenhaus, Kindergarten usw.)* place; **der Bus/Saal hat 60 Plätze** the bus/hall will take 60 *or* has room for 60; **erster/zweiter ~** *(im Kino usw.)* seat at the front/back; **~ nehmen** sit down; **nehmen Sie ~!** take a seat; **~ behalten** *(geh.)* remain seated; **f)** *(bes. Sport: Plazierung)* place; **auf ~ drei** *od.* **dem dritten ~:** in third place; **den dritten ~ belegen** come third; **der Song ist auf ~ eins/neun der Hitparade** the song is number one/nine in the hit parade; **g)** *(Ort)* place; locality; **am ~:** in the town/village; **das größte Hotel am ~:** the largest hotel in the place; **die Bedeutung des ~es Frankfurt** *(bes. Wirtsch.)* the importance of Frankfurt as a location; **h)** *o. Pl. (Raum)* space; room; **im Kofferraum ist kein ~ mehr** there is no room left in the boot *(Brit.) or (Amer.)* trunk; **er/es hat [noch] ~/keinen ~:** there is enough space *or* room [left] for him/it/no room for him/it; **es nimmt viel ~ weg** it takes up a lot of space; **drei Familien/500 Autos** *(Dat.)* **~ bieten** have room for three families/500 cars; **der Saal bietet ~** *od.* **hat ~ für 3000 Personen** the hall takes *or* holds 3,000 people; **im Viktoriasee hätte ganz Irland ~:** the whole of Ireland could fit into Lake Victoria; **[jmdm./einer Sache] ~ machen** make room [for sb./sth.]; **macht doch mal ein bißchen ~:** clear a bit of space; *(aufrücken)* move up a bit; **einem neuen System ~ machen** give way to a new system; **~ da!** make way!; out of the way!; **~ greifen** *(fig.)* spread

Platz-: ~angst die a) *(volkst.: Klaustrophobie)* claustrophobia; **b)** *(Med.)* agoraphobia; **~anweiser der; ~s, ~:** usher; **~anweiserin die; ~, ~nen** usherette

Plätzchen ['plɛtsçən] **das; ~s, ~ a)** little place *or* spot; *(kleiner Raum)* little space; **b)** *(Keks)* biscuit *(Brit.)*; cookie *(Amer.)*; *(Schokoladen~)* [chocolate] pastille

platzen *itr. V.; mit sein* **a)** burst; *(explodieren)* explode; **dem Boxer war eine Augenbraue geplatzt** one of the boxer's eyebrows had split open; **vor Wut/Spannung** *(Dat.)* **~** *(fig.)* be bursting with rage/excitement; **er ist vor Lachen fast geplatzt** he nearly died with laughter; *s. auch* **Neid; b)** *(ugs.: scheitern)* fall through; **geplatzt sein** ⟨*concert, meeting, performance, holiday, engagement*⟩ be off; **der Wechsel ist geplatzt** the bill has bounced *(sl.)*; **etw. ~ lassen** put the kibosh on sth. *(sl.)*; **der Betrug platzte** *(ugs.)* the plot collapsed; **einen Spionagering/eine Bande ~ lassen** bust a spy ring/a gang *(coll.)*; **c)** *(ugs.: hinein~)* **in eine Versammlung ~:** burst into a meeting

platz, Platz-: ~hirsch der a) *(Jägerspr.)* dominant stag; *(fig. ugs.: beherrschende Figur)* boss-type *(coll.)*; **er ist hier der ~hirsch** he's the big noise around here *(sl.)*; **~karte die** reserved-seat ticket; **sich** *(Dat.)* **eine ~karte bestellen** reserve a seat; **~konzert das** open-air concert *(by a military or brass band)*; **~mangel der** lack of space; **~miete die a)** *(auf Märkten, Messen usw.)* pitch rent; **b)** *(Theater)* [cost of a] season ticket *(for a particular seat)*; **c)** *(Sport)* ground hire charge; *(Tennis)* court hire charge; court fees *pl.*; **~patrone die** blank [cartridge]; **~raubend** *Adj.* wasting space *postpos., not pred.*; bulky; **~raubend sein** take up a lot of space; **~regen der** downpour; cloudburst; **~sparend 1.** *Adj.* space-saving; **möglichst ~sparend** saving as much space as possible *postpos., not pred.*; **2.** *adv.* economically; in a space-saving manner; **~verweis der** *(Sport)* sending-off; **einen ~verweis gegen jmdn. verhängen** order sb. off the field; **~vor·teil der;** *o. Pl. (Sport)* home advantage; **~wart der** *(Sport)* groundsman; **~wunde die** lacerated wound

Plauderei die; ~, ~en chat

Plauderer der; ~s, ~, Plauderin die; ~, ~nen talker; conversationalist

plaudern ['plaudɐn] *itr. V.* **a)** chat **(über +** *Akk.*, **von** about); **nett ~:** have a nice chat; **b)** *(etw. aus~)* let on *(sl.)*; **er plaudert** he doesn't keep his mouth shut *(sl.)*

Plauder·ton der conversational *or* chatty tone; **im ~:** in a conversational tone

Plausch [plauʃ] **der; ~[e]s, ~e** *(bes. südd., österr.)* cosy chat

plauschen *itr. V. (bes. südd., österr.)* chat; **miteinander ~:** have a chat

plausibel [plau'zi:bl] **1.** *Adj.* plausible; **jmdm. etw. ~ machen** make sth. seem convincing to sb. **2.** *adv.* plausibly

Plauze ['plautsə] **die; ~, ~n** *(salopp, bes. ostmd.)* **a)** *(Lunge)* lung; **b)** *(Bauch)* belly; **auf der ~ liegen** *(fig.)* be laid up

Play·back ['pleɪbæk] **das; ~s, ~s** *(Tontechnik)* **a)** *(Aufnahme)* pre-recorded version; recording; *(Begleitung)* [pre-recorded] backing; **b)** *(Verfahren) (beim Fernsehen)* miming to a recording; *(bei Schallplatten)* double-tracking

Play·boy ['pleɪbɔɪ] **der** playboy

Plazenta [pla'tsɛnta] **die; ~, ~s** *od.* **Plazenten** *(Med.)* placenta

Plazet ['pla:tsɛt] **das; ~s, ~s** *(geh.)* approval

plazieren [pla'tsi:rən] **1.** *tr. V.* **a)** place; position ⟨*loudspeakers*⟩; **Polizisten an den Ausgängen ~:** post policemen by the exits; **b)** *(Sport: gezielt werfen, schlagen usw.)* place ⟨*shot, ball*⟩; *(Boxen, Fechten)* land ⟨*blow, hit*⟩; **ein plazierter Schuß** a well-aimed shot; **c)** *(Wirtsch.: unterbringen, anlegen)* place ⟨*money*⟩. **2.** *refl. V.* **a)** *(sich setzen)* place *or* seat oneself **(auf +** *Akk. od. Dat.* on); *(sich stellen)* take up position **(an +** *Akk. od. Dat.* at, by); **b)** *(Sport)* be placed; **er konnte sich nicht ~:** he was unplaced

Plazierung die; ~, ~en a) *(das Plazieren)* placing; *(auf Sitzplätze)* seating; *(das Aufstellen)* positioning; *(von Polizisten usw.)* posting; **b)** *(Sport)* placing; place; **eine gute ~/gute ~en erreichen** be well placed

Plebejer [ple'be:jɐ] **der; ~s, ~ a)** *(hist.)* plebeian; **b)** *(abwertend)* common type

plebejisch 1. *Adj.* **a)** *(hist.)* plebeian; **b)** *(abwertend)* common. **2.** *adv. (abwertend)* in a common manner

Plebiszit [plebɪs'tsi:t] **das; ~[e]s, ~e** plebiscite

plebiszitär [plebɪstsi'tɛ:ɐ] **1.** *Adj.* plebiscitary; ⟨*decision, legislation, election*⟩ by plebiscite. **2.** *adv.* by plebiscite

[1]Plebs [plɛps] **die; ~** *(hist.)* plebs *pl. (of ancient Rome)*

[2]Plebs der; ~es *od. österr.:* **die; ~** *(abwertend)* **der ~:** common herd; the masses *pl.*

pleite ['plaitə] *(ugs.)* *in* **~ sein** ⟨*person*⟩ be broke *(coll.)*; ⟨*company*⟩ have gone bust *(coll.)*; **~ gehen** go bust *(coll.)*

Pleite die; ~, ~n *(ugs.)* **a)** *(Bankrott)* bankruptcy *no def. art.*; **vor der ~ stehen** be faced with bankruptcy; **~ machen** *od.* **gehen** go bust *(coll.)*; **b)** *(Mißerfolg)* flop *(sl.)*; washout *(sl.)*

Pleite·geier der *(ugs.)* spectre of bankruptcy; **den ~ vertreiben** chase the wolf from the door

Plejaden [ple'ja:dn̩] *Pl. (Astron.)* Pleiades

Plektron ['plɛktrɔn], **Plektrum** ['plɛktrʊm] **das; ~s, Plektren** plectrum

plempern ['plɛmpɐn] *(ugs.)* **1.** *tr. V.* sprinkle; spatter. **2.** *itr. V.* potter

plemplem [plɛm'plɛm] *in* **~ sein** *(ugs.)* be nuts *(sl.) or* cuckoo *(sl.)*; **ich bin doch nicht ~:** I'm not crazy

Plenar- [ple'na:ɐ̯-]: **~saal der** plenary chamber; **~sitzung die** plenary session

Plenum ['ple:nʊm] **das; ~s** *(Versammlung)* plenary meeting; *(Sitzung)* plenary session

Pleonasmus [pleo'nasmʊs] **der; ~, Pleonasmen** *(Stilk.)* pleonasm

pleonastisch [pleo'nastɪʃ] *(Stilk.)* **1.** *Adj.* pleonastic. **2.** *adv.* pleonastically

Pleuel·stange ['plɔyəl-] **die** *(Technik)* connecting-rod

Plexi·glas ⓦⓩ ['plɛksigla:s] **das;** *o. Pl.* ≈ Perspex **(P)**

plieren ['pli:rən] *itr. V. (nordd.)* squint

plinkern ['plɪŋkɐn] *itr. V. (nordd.)* blink

Plissee [plɪ'se:] **das; ~s, ~s a)** *(Falten)* accordion pleats *pl.*; **b)** *(Stoff)* accordion-pleated material

Plissee·rock der accordion-pleated skirt

plissieren *tr. V.* pleat

PLO [pe:ɛl'o:] **die; ~** *Abk.* **Palästinensische Befreiungsorganisation** PLO

Plombe ['plɔmbə] **die; ~, ~n a)** *(Siegel)* [lead] seal; **b)** *(veralt.: Zahnfüllung)* filling

plombieren *tr. V.* **a)** *(versiegeln)* seal; **b)** *(veralt.)* fill ⟨*tooth*⟩

Plombierung die; ~, ~en a) *(Versiegelung)* sealing; **b)** *(veralt.: das Füllen)* filling

Plörre ['plœrə] **die; ~, ~n** *(nordd. abwertend)* dish-water *(coll.)*

Plot [plɔt] **der; ~s, ~s** *(Literaturw.)* plot

plötzlich ['plœtslɪç] **1.** *Adj.* sudden. **2.** *adv.* suddenly; **~ aufragen** rise up abruptly; **..., aber etwas** *od.* **ein bißchen ~** *(salopp)* ..., and jump to it; ..., and make it snappy *(coll.)*

Plötzlichkeit die; ~: suddenness

Pluder·hose ['plu:dɐ-] **die** pantaloons *pl.*; *(orientalischer Art)* Turkish trousers *pl.*; *(hist.)* slops *pl.*

Plumeau [ply'mo:] **das; ~s, ~s** duvet

plump [plʊmp] **1.** *Adj.* **a)** *(dick)* plump; podgy; massive ⟨*stone, lump*⟩; *(unförmig)* ungainly, clumsy ⟨*shape*⟩; *(rundlich)* bulbous; **b)** *(schwerfällig)* awkward, clumsy ⟨*movements, style*⟩; **c)** *(abwertend: dreist)* crude, blatant ⟨*lie, deception, trick*⟩; *(leicht durchschaubar)* blatantly obvious; *(unbeholfen)* clumsy ⟨*excuse, advances*⟩; crude ⟨*joke, forgery*⟩; **~e Vertraulichkeit** embarrassing over-familiarity. **2.** *adv.* **a)** *(schwerfällig)* clumsily; awkwardly; **b)** *(abwertend: dreist)* in a blatantly obvious manner; **~ gefälscht** crudely *or* clumsily forged

Plumpheit die; ~, ~en a) *o. Pl. (Dicke)* plumpness; podginess; *(Unförmigkeit)* ungainliness; clumsiness; *(Rundlichkeit)* bulbousness; **b)** *o. Pl. (Schwerfälligkeit)* clumsiness; awkwardness; *(eines dicken Menschen)* ponderousness; **c)** *o. Pl. (abwertend: Dreistigkeit)* blatant nature; *(primitive Art)* crudity; clumsiness

plumps *Interj.* bump; thud; *(ins Wasser)* splash; **~ machen** go bump

Plumps der; ~es, ~e *(ugs.)* bump; thud; *(ins Wasser)* splash

plumpsen a) *itr. V.* fall with a bump; thud; *(ins Wasser)* splash; **b)** *unpers.* **es plumpste** there was a thud *or* bump; *(ins Wasser)* there was a splash

Plumps·klo[sett] das *(ugs.)* earth-closet
plump-vertraulich 1. *Adj.* over-familiar; *(bei Männern)* hail-fellow-well-met. **2.** *adv.* with excessive familiarity
Plunder ['plʊndɐ] **der; ~s** *(ugs. abwertend)* junk; rubbish
Plünderei die; ~, ~en *s.* **Plünderung**
Plünderer der; ~s, ~: looter
plündern ['plʏndɐn] *itr., tr. V.* **a)** loot; plunder, pillage ‹*town*›; **b)** *(scherzh.: [fast] leeren)* raid ‹*larder, fridge, account*›; ‹*bird, animal*› strip ‹*tree, border*›
Plünderung die; ~, ~en looting; *(einer Stadt)* plundering; **~en** cases of looting/plundering
Plünnen *Pl. (bes. nordd. ugs.: Kleider)* gear *sing. (coll.)*
Plural ['plu:ra:l] **der; ~s, ~e a)** *o. Pl.* plural; **Atlanten ist [der] ~ von** *od.* **zu Atlas** 'Atlanten' is the plural of 'Atlas'; **b)** *(Wort)* word in the plural; plural form; **im ~ stehen** be [in the] plural
Pluraletantum [plurale'tantʊm] **das; ~s, Pluraliatantum** [pluralia'tantʊm] plural-only noun
pluralisch *(Sprachw.)* **1.** *Adj.* plural ‹*form, ending*›; ‹*word, clause*› in the plural. **2.** *adv.* in the plural
Pluralismus der; ~: pluralism
pluralistisch 1. *Adj.* pluralistic. **2.** *adv.* pluralistically; along pluralistic lines
plus [plʊs] **1.** *Konj. (Math.)* plus. **2.** *Adv.* **a)** *(bes. Math.)* plus; **b)** *(Elektrot.)* positive. **3.** *Präp. mit Dat. (Kaufmannsspr.)* plus
Plus das; ~ a) *(Überschuß)* surplus; *(auf einem Konto)* credit balance; **~ machen** make a profit; **im ~ sein** be in credit; **b)** *(Vorteil)* advantage; [extra] asset; **das ist ein ~ für dich** it's a point in your favour
Plüsch [ply:ʃ] **der; ~[e]s, ~e** plush
Plüsch-: ~sessel der plush chair; **~sofa das** plush sofa; **~tier das** cuddly toy
Plus-: ~pol der *(Physik)* positive pole; *(einer Batterie)* positive terminal; **~punkt der a)** [plus] point; **b)** *s.* **Plus b**
Plusquam·perfekt ['plʊskvampɛrfɛkt] **das** pluperfect [tense]
plustern ['plu:stɐn] **1.** *tr. V.* ruffle [up] ‹*feathers*›. **2.** *refl. V.* ‹*bird*› ruffle [up] its feathers
Plus·zeichen das plus sign
[1]**Pluto** ['plu:to] **der; ~** *(Astron.)*, [2]**Pluto (der)** *(Myth.)* Pluto
Plutokrat [pluto'kra:t] **der; ~en, ~en** *(geh. abwertend)* plutocrat
Plutokratie [plutokra'ti:] **die; ~, ~n** *(geh. abwertend)* plutocracy
Plutonium [plu'to:niʊm] **das; ~s** *(Physik)* plutonium
PLZ *Abk.* **Postleitzahl**
Pneu [pnɔy] **der; ~s, ~s** *(bes. österr., schweiz.)* tyre
[1]**Pneumatik** [pnɔy'ma:tɪk] **die; ~, ~en a)** *o. Pl.* pneumatics *sing., no art.*; **b)** *(Anlage)* pneumatic system
[2]**Pneumatik der; ~s, ~s,** *(österr.:)* **die; ~, ~en** *(österr., schweiz., veralt.)* tyre
pneumatisch *(Technik)* **1.** *Adj.* pneumatic. **2.** *adv.* pneumatically
Po [po:] **der; ~s, ~s** *(ugs.)* bottom
Pöbel ['pø:bl̩] **der; ~s** *(abwertend)* rabble
pöbelhaft *(abwertend)* **1.** *Adj.* loutish; uncouth. **2.** *adv.* in a loutish manner
Pöbel·herrschaft die mob rule
pöbeln *itr. V.* make rude *or* coarse remarks
pochen ['pɔxn̩] *itr. V.* **a)** *(meist geh.: klopfen)* knock **(gegen** at, on); *(kräftig)* rap; thump; **an die Tür ~:** knock at *or* on the door; **es pocht** somebody is knocking at *or* on the door; **b)** *(geh.: sich berufen)* **auf etw.** *(Akk.)* **~:** insist on sth.; **c)** *(geh.: pulsieren)* ‹*heart*› pound, thump; ‹*blood*› pound, throb
pochieren [pɔ'ʃi:rən] *tr. V. (Kochk.)* poach
Pocke ['pɔkə] **die; ~, ~n** pock
Pocken *Pl.* smallpox *sing.*
pocken-, Pocken-: ~narbe die pockmark; **~narbig** *Adj.* pock-marked; **~schutz·impfung die** smallpox vaccination
pockig *Adj.* pock-marked ‹*face, surface*›; pimpled ‹*leather*›
Podest [po'dɛst] **das** *od.* **der; ~[e]s, ~e a)** rostrum; **b)** *(bes. nordd.: Treppenabsatz)* landing
Podex der; ~[es], ~e *(fam.)* bottom; behind
Podium ['po:diʊm] **das; ~s, Podien a)** *(Plattform)* platform; *(Bühne)* stage; **b)** *(trittartige Erhöhung)* rostrum; podium
Podiums·diskussion die, Podiums·gespräch das panel discussion
Po·ebene die; *o. Pl. (Geogr.)* plain of the River Po
Poem [po'e:m] **das; ~s, ~e** *(veralt.)* poem
Poesie [poe'zi:] **die; ~, ~n a)** *o. Pl.* poetry; **ein Abend voller ~:** an evening full of magic; **b)** *(Gedicht)* poem
Poesie·album das autograph album *(with verses or sayings contributed by friends)*
Poet [po'e:t] **der; ~en, ~en** *(veralt.)* poet; bard *(literary)*
Poetik [po'e:tɪk] **die; ~, ~en a)** poetics *sing.*; **b)** *(Lehrbuch)* treatise on poetry
poetisch 1. *Adj.* poetic[al]. **2.** *adv.* poetically
pofen ['po:fn̩] *itr. V. (nordd. salopp)* kip *(Brit. sl.)*; snooze *(coll.)*
Pogrom [po'gro:m] **das** *od.* **der; ~s, ~e** pogrom
Pogrom-: ~hetze die hate campaign *(leading up to a pogrom)*; **~stimmung die** bloodthirsty mood
Pointe ['poɛ̃:tə] **die; ~, ~n** *(eines Witzes)* punch line; *(einer Geschichte)* point; *(eines Sketches)* curtain line; **die ~ verderben** spoil the effect of the story/joke; **eine überraschende ~:** a surprising twist
pointiert [poɛ̃'ti:ɐt] **1.** *Adj.* pointed ‹*remark*›. **2.** *adv.* pointedly
Pokal [po'ka:l] **der; ~s, ~e a)** *(Trinkgefäß)* goblet; **b)** *(Siegestrophäe, ~wettbewerb)* cup
Pokal-: ~sieger der *(Sport)* cup-winners *pl.*; **~spiel das** *(Sport)* cup-tie; **~wettbewerb der** *(Sport)* cup competition
Pökel-: ~fleisch das salt meat; **~hering der** salt herring
pökeln ['pø:kl̩n] *tr. V.* salt
Poker ['po:kɐ] **das** *od.* **der; ~s** poker; *(fig.)* manoeuvrings *pl.*
Poker-: ~gesicht das poker-face; **ein ~gesicht machen** put on a poker-faced expression; **~miene die** poker-face
pokern *itr. V.* **a)** *(Poker spielen)* play poker; **b)** *(fig.)* **um etw. ~:** bid for sth.
Pol [po:l] **der; ~s, ~e** pole; **der ruhende ~** *(fig.)* the calming influence
Polack [po'lak] **der; ~en, ~en, Polacke der; ~n, ~n** *(ugs. abwertend)* [dirty *(derog.)*] Pole
polar [po'la:ɐ] *Adj.* **a)** polar; **b)** *(gegensätzlich)* diametrically opposed; **~e Gegensätze** complete *or* polar opposites
Polar-: ~eis das polar ice; **~expedition die** polar expedition; **~front die** *(Met.)* polar front; **~fuchs der** Arctic fox
Polarisation [polariza'tsio:n] **die; ~, ~en** polarization
polarisieren 1. *tr. V. (Chemie, Physik)* polarize. **2.** *refl. V. (in Gegensätzen hervortreten)* become polarized
Polarisierung die; ~, ~en *(auch Chemie, Physik)* polarization
Polarität die; ~, ~en *(auch Geogr., Astron., Physik)* polarity
Polar-: ~kreis der polar circle; **nördlicher/südlicher ~kreis** Arctic/Antarctic Circle; **~licht das;** *Pl.* **~lichter** aurora; polar lights *pl.*
Polaroid·kamera Ⓦⓩ [polaro'i:t-] **die** Polaroid camera **(P)**
Polar-: ~station die polar [research] station; **~stern der** polar star; pole-star; **~zone die** frigid zone; polar region
Polder der; ~s, ~: polder
Pole der; ~n, ~n Pole
Polemik [po'le:mɪk] **die; ~, ~en** polemic; **ein Pamphlet voller ~:** a pamphlet full of polemics
polemisch 1. *Adj.* polemic[al]. **2.** *adv.* polemically
polemisieren *itr. V.* polemize
polen *tr. V. (Physik, Elektrot.)* connect; **auf diesem Sektor sind Paris und Bonn nicht gleich gepolt** *(fig.)* in this area Paris and Bonn hold different views
Polen (das); ~s Poland; **noch ist ~ nicht verloren** *(fig.)* all is not [yet] lost; **da/dann ist ~ offen** *(fig.)* all hell is/will be let loose
Polente [po'lɛntə] **die; ~** *(salopp)* cops *pl. (coll.)*
Police [po'li:sə] **die; ~, ~n** *(Versicherungsw.)* policy
Polier [po'li:ɐ] **der; ~s, ~e** [site] foreman
polieren *tr. V.* polish; *(fig.)* polish up; **jmdm. die Fresse ~** *(derb)* smash sb.'s face in
Polier-: ~mittel das polish; **~tuch das;** *Pl.* **~tücher** polishing-cloth
-polig ['po:lɪç] *adj.* **ein~/drei~/mehr~:** single-/three-/multi-pin
Poli·klinik die out-patients' department *or* clinic
Polin die; ~, ~nen Pole; *s. auch* **-in**
Polio ['po:lio] **die; ~:** polio
Polit- political; **~blatt** politically oriented publication
Polit·büro das politburo
Politesse [poli'tɛsə] **die; ~, ~n** [woman] traffic warden
Politik [poli'ti:k] **die; ~, ~en a)** *o. Pl.* politics *sing., no art.*; **eine gemeinsame/neue ~:** a common/new policy; **b)** *(eine spezielle ~)* policy; **eine ~ der kleinen Schritte** a gradualist policy; **c)** *(Taktik)* tactics *pl.*
-politik die ... policy; **die unterschiedliche Schul~ der einzelnen Länder** the different education policies of the different States
Politika *s.* **Politikum**
Politiker [po'li:tikɐ] **der; ~s, ~, Politikerin die; ~, ~nen** politician
Politikum [po'li:tikʊm] **das; ~s, Politika** political issue; *(Ereignis)* political event
Politik·wissenschaft die political science *no art.*
politisch 1. *Adj.* **a)** political; **b)** *(klug u. berechnend)* politic. **2.** *adv.* **a)** politically; **b)** *(klug u. berechnend)* politicly; judiciously
-politisch *adj., adv.* concerning ... policy
Politische der/die; *adj. Dekl. (ugs.)* political prisoner
politisieren 1. *itr. V.* talk politics; politicize; **es wurde viel politisiert** there was a great deal of political discussion. **2.** *tr. V.* **a)** *(politisch aktivieren)* make politically active; **b)** *(politisch behandeln)* politicize
Politisierung die; ~: politicization
Politologe [polito'lo:gə] **der; ~n, ~n** political scientist
Politologie die; ~: political science *no art.*
Politologin die; ~, ~nen political scientist
politologisch *Adj.* ‹*analysis*› in terms of political science; ‹*sense*› of political science; **~es Studium** political studies *pl.*
Politur [poli'tu:ɐ] **die; ~, ~en** polish
Polizei [poli'tsai] **die; ~, ~en a)** police *pl.*; **er ist** *od.* **arbeitet bei der ~:** he is in the police force; **b)** *o. Pl. (Dienststelle)* police station
Polizei-: ~apparat der police force; **~auf·gebot das** police contingent; **trotz überdurchschnittlichen ~aufgebots** despite the larger than average police presence; **~auto das** police car; **~beamte der** police officer; **~behörde die** police authority; **~chef der** chief of police; chief constable *(Brit.)*; **~direktion die** police authority;

~**ein·satz der** police operation; ~**eskorte die** police escort; ~**funk der** police radio; ~**gewahrsam der** [police] custody; ~**gewalt die a)** *(Machtbefugnis)* police powers *pl.;* **b)** *o. Pl. (ausgeübte Gewalt)* use of force by the police; ~**gewerkschaft die** police trade union; ~**griff der** [police] arm hold *or* lock; **er wurde im ~griff abgeführt** he was frog-marched away; ~**haupt·wacht·meister der** ≈ [police] superintendent; ~**hund der** police dog; ~**knüppel der** [policeman's] truncheon; ~**kommissar,** *(südd., österr., schweiz.)* ~**kommissär der** ≈ [police] superintendent; ~**kontrolle die** police check; *(Kontrollpunkt)* police check-point; ~**kräfte** *Pl.* police *pl.*

polizeilich 1. *Adj., nicht präd.* police; **~e Meldepflicht** obligation to register with the police. **2.** *adv.* by the police; **~ verboten** prohibited by order of the police

polizei-, Polizei-: ~**methoden** *Pl. (abwertend)* **das sind ja ~methoden!** that is sheer brutality *sing.;* ~**präsident der** chief of police; chief constable *(Brit.);* ~**präsidium das** police headquarters *sing. or pl.;* ~**revier das a)** *(~dienststelle)* police station; **sich auf dem ~revier melden** report to the police; **b)** *(Bezirk)* police district; ~**schutz der** police protection; ~**sirene die** [police-car] siren; ~**spitzel der** police informer; ~**staat der** police state; ~**streife die** police patrol; ~**stunde die** closing time; **die ~stunde verlängern** extend the opening hours *pl.;* **die ~stunde aufheben** waive the restrictions on opening hours *pl.;* ~**verordnung die** police regulation; ~**wache die** police station; ~**widrig 1.** *Adj.* against police regulations *postpos.;* illegal; **2.** *adv.* against police regulations; illegally

Polizist [poli'tsɪst] **der; ~en, ~en** policeman

Polizistin die; ~, ~nen policewoman

Polka ['pɔlka] **die; ~, ~s** polka

Pollen ['pɔlən] **der; ~s, ~** *(Bot.)* pollen

Poller der; ~s, ~: bollard

Pollution [pɔlu'tsio:n] **die; ~, ~en** *(Med.)* [nocturnal] emission

polnisch ['pɔlnɪʃ] *Adj.* Polish; **eine ~e Wirtschaft** *(ugs. abwertend)* a shambles; *s. auch* **deutsch; Deutsch; ²Deutsche**

Polo ['po:lo] **das; ~s** polo

Polo·hemd das short-sleeved shirt

Polonaise, Polonäse [polo'nɛ:zə] **die; ~, ~n** polonaise

Polster ['pɔlstɐ] **das** *od. (österr.)* **der; ~s, ~** *od. (österr.)* **Pölster** ['pœlstɐ] **a)** *(Polsterung)* upholstery *no pl., no indef. art.;* **b)** *(Schulter~)* [shoulder-]pad; **c)** *(Rücklage)* reserves *pl.;* **d)** *(Bot.)* cushion; **e)** *(österr.: Kissen)* cushion; *(Kopfkissen)* pillow

Pölsterchen das; ~s, ~: bulge of fat

Polsterer der; ~s, ~: upholsterer

Polster-: ~**garnitur die** suite; ~**möbel** *Pl.* upholstered furniture *sing.*

polstern *tr. V.* upholster ⟨*furniture*⟩; pad ⟨*door*⟩; **sie ist gut gepolstert** *(fig. ugs. scherzh.)* she is well-upholstered *(joc.);* **finanziell gut gepolstert sein** *(fig. ugs. scherzh.)* be comfortably off

Polster-: ~**sessel der** [upholstered] armchair; easy chair; ~**stuhl der** upholstered chair; ~**tür die** padded door

Polsterung die; ~, ~en a) *(Polster)* upholstery *no pl.; no indef. art.;* **b)** *(das Polstern)* upholstering

Polter·abend der *party on the eve of a wedding (at which crockery is smashed to bring good luck)*

Polter·geist der poltergeist

poltern ['pɔltɐn] **1.** *itr. V.* **a)** *(lärmen)* crash *or* thump about; **es poltert** there is a bang *or* crash; **ein ~der Lärm** a din *or* racket; **b)** *mit sein (sich laut bewegen)* **der Karren polterte über das Pflaster** the cart clattered over the cobble-stones; **er kam ins Zimmer gepoltert** he came clumping into the room; **c)** *(schimpfen)* rant [and rave]; **d)** *(ugs.: Polterabend feiern)* hold a **Polterabend. 2.** *tr. V.* **„Ruhe!" polterte er** 'Be quiet!' he bawled

poly-, Poly- [poly-] poly-

poly-, Poly-: ~**eder** [~'|e:dɐ] **das; ~s, ~** *(Geom.)* polyhedron; ~**ester** [~'|ɛstɐ] **der; ~s, ~** *(Chemie)* polyester; ~**gam** [~'ga:m] **1.** *Adj.* polygamous; **2.** *adv.* polygamously; ~**gamie** [~ga'mi:] **die; ~:** polygamy; ~**glott** [~'glɔt] *Adj.* polyglot

Polynesien [poly'ne:ziən] **(das); ~s** Polynesia

polynesisch *Adj.* Polynesian

Polyp [po'ly:p] **der; ~en, ~en a)** *(Zool., Med.)* polyp; **b)** *(salopp: Polizist)* cop *(sl.);* copper *(Brit. sl.);* **c)** *(veralt.: Krake)* octopus

poly-, Poly-: ~**phonie** [~fo'ni:] **die; ~** *(Musik)* polyphony; ~**technik die;** *o. Pl. (DDR),* ~**technikum das** polytechnic; ~**technisch 1.** *Adj.* polytechnic; **2.** *adv.* **er war ~technisch ausgebildet** he had a polytechnic training

Pomade [po'ma:də] **die; ~, ~n** pomade; hair-cream

pomadig 1. *Adj.* **a)** pomaded; greased down; *(fig.)* over-slick; **b)** *(bes. nordd.: blasiert)* blasé; **c)** *(ugs.: langsam)* sluggish. **2.** *adv.* **a)** *(bes. nordd.: blasiert)* in a blasé way; **b)** *(ugs.: langsam)* sluggishly

Pomeranze [pomə'rantsə] **die; ~, ~n** Seville *or* sour *or* bitter orange

Pommer der; ~n, ~n Pomeranian

Pommern (das); ~s Pomerania

Pommes frites [pɔm'frit] *Pl.* chips *pl. (Brit.);* French fries *pl. (Amer.)*

Pomp [pɔmp] **der; ~[e]s** pomp

Pompeji [pɔm'pe:ji] **(das); ~s** Pompeii

pomphaft, pompös [pɔm'pø:s] **1.** *Adj.* grandiose; ostentatious. **2.** *adv.* grandiosely; ostentatiously

Poncho ['pɔntʃo] **der; ~s, ~s** poncho

Pond [pɔnt] **das; ~s, ~** *(Physik)* gram-force

Pontifikal- [pɔntifi'ka:l-]: ~**amt das,** ~**messe die** *(kath. Kirche)* Pontifical Mass

Pontifikat [pɔntifi'ka:t] **das** *od.* **der; ~[e]s, ~e** *(kath. Kirche)* pontificate

Pontius ['pɔntsiʊs] *in* **von ~ zu Pilatus laufen** *(ugs.)* rush from pillar to post

Ponton [põ'tõ:] **der; ~s, ~s** pontoon

¹Pony ['pɔni] **das; ~s, ~s** pony

²Pony der; ~s, ~s *(Frisur)* fringe

Pony·frisur die [hair-style with a] fringe

Pool [pu:l] **der; ~s, ~s** *(Wirtsch.)* pool

Pool·billard das pool

Pop [pɔp] **der; ~[s]** pop

Popanz der; ~es, ~e a) *(abwertend)* bogey; bugbear; *(willenloser Mensch)* puppet; **b)** *(veralt.: Schreckgestalt)* scarecrow

Pop-art ['pɔp|a:ɐt] **die; ~:** pop art

Popcorn ['pɔpkɔrn] **das; ~s** popcorn

Pope der; ~n, ~n *(abwertend)* cleric

Popel ['po:pl̩] **der; ~s, ~** *(ugs.)* **a)** bogy *(sl.);* **b)** *(abwertend: Mensch)* nobody

popelig *(ugs. abwertend)* **1.** *Adj.* crummy *(coll.);* lousy *(sl.);* *(durchschnittlich)* second-rate. **2.** *adv.* crummily *(sl.)*

Popelin [popə'li:n] **der; ~s, ~e, Popeline der; ~s, ~** *od.* **die; ~, ~:** poplin

Popeline·mantel der poplin coat

popeln *itr. V. (ugs.)* **[in der Nase] ~:** pick one's nose

Pop-: ~**farbe die** brilliant colour; ~**festival das** pop festival; ~**gruppe die** pop group; ~**konzert das** pop concert

poplig *s.* **popelig**

Pop·musik die pop music

Popo [po'po:] **der; ~s, ~s** *(fam.)* bottom

Popo·scheitel der *(ugs. scherzh.)* straight middle *or* centre parting

Popper ['pɔpɐ] **der; ~s, ~:** *fashion-conscious, apolitical young person*

poppig ['pɔpɪç] **1.** *Adj.* trendy. **2.** *adv.* trendily

Pop·star der pop star

populär [popu'lɛ:ɐ̯] **1.** *Adj.* popular **(bei** with); **in ~em Deutsch** in German which is comprehensible to the layman. **2.** *adv.* popularly; **etw. ~ ausdrücken** express sth. in layman's language

popularisieren *tr. V.* popularize

Popularisierung die; ~, ~en popularization

Popularität die; ~: popularity

populär·wissenschaftlich 1. *Adj.* popular science *attrib.;* **zu ~ sein** be too much on the popular-science level. **2.** *adv.* in a popular scientific way

Population die; ~, ~en population

Populismus der; ~: populism *no art.*

Populist der; ~en, ~en populist

Pore ['po:rə] **die; ~, ~n** pore

poren·tief *(Werbespr.)* **1.** *Adj.* deep-down. **2.** *adv.* pore-deep

porig *Adj.* porous

Porno ['pɔrno] **der; ~s, ~s** *(ugs.)* **a)** *(~graphie)* porn[o] *(coll.);* **b)** *(~film, ~heft usw.)* porn[o] film/magazine *etc.*

porno-, Porno-: ~**film der** *(ugs.)* porn[o] film *(coll.);* ~**graphie** [~-'-] **die; ~, ~n** pornography; ~**graphisch** [~'--] **1.** *Adj.* pornographic; **2.** *adv.* pornographically

porös [po'rø:s] porous

Porosität [porozi'tɛ:t] **die; ~:** porousness

Porphyr ['pɔrfy:ɐ̯] **der; ~, ~e** [pɔr'fy:rə] *(Geol.)* porphyry

Porree ['pɔre] **der; ~s, ~s** leek; **ich mag ~:** I like leeks

Portal [pɔr'ta:l] **das; ~s, ~e** portal

Portefeuille [pɔrt(ə)'fø:j] **das; ~s, ~s** *(geh. veralt.)* wallet

Portemonnaie [pɔrtmɔ'ne:] **das; ~s, ~s** purse

Porti *Pl. s.* **Porto**

Portier [pɔr'tie:] **der; ~s, ~s,** *österr.:* [pɔr'ti:ɐ̯] **der; ~s, ~e 1.** *(Pförtner)* porter. **2.** *(veralt.: Hausmeister)* caretaker; **stiller ~** *(bes. berlin.)* list of tenants' names

portieren *tr. V. (schweiz.)* put up; nominate

Portier[s]·loge die porter's lodge

Portiers·frau die a) *(woman)* porter; **b)** *(Frau des Portiers)* porter's wife

Portion [pɔr'tsio:n] **die; ~, ~en a)** *(beim Essen)* portion; helping; **eine halbe ~** *(fig. ugs. spött.)* a feeble little titch *(coll.);* **eine ~ Eis** one ice-cream; **eine zweite ~:** a second helping; **b)** *(ugs.: Anteil)* amount; **eine große ~ Geduld** a fair amount of patience

portionieren *tr. V.* divide into portions

portions·weise *Adv.* in portions

Porto ['pɔrto] **das; ~s, ~s** *od.* **Porti** postage **(für** on, for); **„~ zahlt Empfänger"** 'postage will be paid by licensee'

porto-, Porto-: ~**frei** *Adj.* post-free; ~**kasse die** *(Wirtsch.)* cash-box *(for postal expenses);* ~**pflichtig** *Adj.* liable *or* subject to postage *postpos.*

Portrait, Porträt [pɔr'trɛ:] **das; ~s, ~s** portrait; **jmdm. ~ sitzen** sit for sb. [for a portrait]

Porträt·aufnahme die portrait [photograph]

porträtieren [pɔrtrɛ'ti:rən] *tr. V.* paint a portrait of/take a portrait [photograph] of; *(fig.)* portray

Porträtist der; ~en, ~en portrait-painter/-photographer; portraitist

Portugal ['pɔrtugal] **(das); ~s** Portugal

Portugiese [pɔrtu'gi:zə] **der; ~n, ~n, Portugiesin die; ~, ~nen** Portuguese; *s. auch* **-in**

portugiesisch *Adj.* Portuguese; *s. auch* **deutsch; Deutsch; ²Deutsche**

Portwein ['pɔrtvain] **der** port

Porzellan [pɔrtsɛ'la:n] **das; ~s, ~e a)** *o. Pl.* porcelain; china; **~ zerschlagen** *(fig. ugs.)* cause a lot of harm *or* trouble; **b)** *(Gegenstand aus ~)* piece of porcelain *or* china

Porzellan-: ~**erde die** china clay; kaolin;

~geschirr das china [crockery]; **~laden der** china shop; *s. auch* **Elefant**

pos. *Abk.* **positiv** pos.

Posaune [po'zaunə] **die; ~, ~n** trombone

posaunen 1. *itr. V. (musizieren)* play the trombone. **2.** *tr. V. (ugs. abwertend)* **a)** *(hinaus~)* **etw. in die** *od.* **alle Welt ~:** tell the whole world about sth.; **b)** *(laut sprechen)* bellow; bawl

Posaunen-: ~chor der brass ensemble; **~engel der a)** *(Kunst)* angel with a trumpet; **b)** *(ugs. scherzh.)* chubby-cheeks *sing.*

Posaunist der; ~en, ~en trombonist

Pose ['po:zə] **die; ~, ~n** pose

Posemuckel [po:zə'mʊkl̩] *o. Art.; ~s (salopp abwertend)* the back of beyond

posieren *itr. V.* pose

Position [pozi'tsio:n] **die; ~, ~en a)** position; **in gesicherter ~ sein** have a secure position; **b)** *(Wirtsch.: einzelner Posten)* item

Positions-: ~lampe die, ~licht das *(Seew., Flugw.)* navigation light; **~wechsel der** change of position *or* attitude

positiv ['po:ziti:f] **1.** *Adj.* positive; **~e Zahlen** *(Math.)* positive *or* plus numbers; **ist es schon ~, daß ...?** *(ugs.)* is it definite *or* certain that ...? **2.** *adv.* positively; **einen Antrag ~ bescheiden** accept an application; **einer Sache** *(Dat.)* **~ gegenüberstehen** take a positive view of a matter; **etw. ~ beeinflussen** have a positive influence on sth.; **etw. ~ bewerten** judge sth. favourably; **der Test verlief ~:** the test proved successful; **ich weiß das ~** *(ugs.)* I know that for certain *or* for sure; **sich ~ verändern** change for the better

[1]**Positiv der; ~s, ~e** *(Sprachw.)* positive

[2]**Positiv das; ~s, ~e a)** *(Fot.)* positive; **b)** *(kleine Orgel)* positive organ

Positiva *s.* **Positivum**

Positivismus der; ~: positivism *no art.*

positivistisch *Adj.* positivist[ic]

Positivum ['po:ziti:vʊm] **das; ~s, Positiva** *(geh.)* positive aspect

Positron ['po:zitrɔn] **das; ~s, -tronen** *(Physik)* positron

Positur [pozi'tu:ɐ̯] **die; ~, ~en a)** pose; posture; **sich in ~ setzen** *od.* **stellen** *od.* **werfen** *(ugs. leicht spött.)* strike a pose; take up a posture; **b)** *(Sport)* stance; **in ~ gehen/sein** take up/have taken up one's stance

Posse ['pɔsə] **die; ~, ~n** farce

Possen der; ~s, ~ *(veralt.)* **a)** *Pl.* pranks; tricks; **~ reißen** play tricks; **b) jmdm. einen ~ spielen** play a prank *or* trick on sb.

Possen·reißer der clown; buffoon

possessiv ['pɔsɛsi:f] *Adj. (Sprachw.)* possessive

Possessiv das; ~s, ~e, Possessiv·pronomen das, Possessivum [pɔsɛ'si:vʊm] **das; ~s, Possessiva** *(Sprachw.)* possessive pronoun

possierlich [pɔ'si:ɐ̯lɪç] **1.** *Adj.* sweet; cute *(Amer.).* **2.** *adv.* sweetly; cutely *(Amer.)*

Post [pɔst] **die; ~, ~en a)** post *(Brit.)*; mail; **er ist** *od.* **arbeitet bei der ~:** he works for the Post Office; **etw. mit der** *od.* **per ~ schicken** send sth. by post *or* mail; **ist ~ für mich da?** is there any post *or* mail for me?; **sonntags kommt** *od.* **gibt es keine ~:** there is no post *or* delivery on Sundays; **mit gleicher ~:** by the same post; **mit getrennter ~:** under separate cover; **auf [die] ~ warten** *(ugs.)* wait for [the] post; *s. auch* **ab 2 b; b)** *(~amt)* post office; **auf die** *od.* **zur ~ gehen** go to the post office; **c)** *(veralt.: ~kutsche)* mail[-coach]; **d)** *(~bus)* post[-office] bus; **e)** *(veralt.: Botschaft)* news *sing.*

Post·abholer der caller *(for mail)*

postalisch [pɔs'ta:lɪʃ] *Adj.; nicht präd.* postal; **auf ~em Wege** by post

Postament [pɔsta'mɛnt] **das; ~[e]s, ~e** pedestal

Post-: ~amt das post office; **~an·schrift die** postal address; **~an·weisung die a)** *(Geldsendung) remittance paid in at a post office and delivered to the addressee by a postman;* **b)** *(Formular)* postal remittance form; **~auto das** post-office *or* mail van; **~beamte der** post-office official; **~bote der** *(ugs.)* postman *(Brit.)*; mailman *(Amer.)*; **~bus der** post[-office] bus

Pöstchen ['pœstçən] **das; ~s, ~** *(abwertend)* little job *or* number *(coll.)*

Post·dienst der a) *o. Pl.* post office; **ein Beamter im ~:** a post-office official; **b)** *o. Pl. (die Post)* postal service; **c)** *(Service der Post)* postal service

Posten ['pɔstn̩] **der; ~s, ~ a)** *(bes. Milit.: Wach~)* post; **auf dem ~ sein** *(ugs.) (in guter körperlicher Verfassung sein)* be in good form; *(wachsam sein)* be on one's guard; **sich nicht [ganz] auf dem ~ fühlen** *(ugs.)* be a bit under the weather *(coll.)*; **auf verlorenem ~ stehen** *od.* **kämpfen** be fighting a losing battle; **b)** *(bes. Milit.: Wachmann)* sentry; guard; **~ stehen** *od. (Soldatenspr.:)* **schieben** stand guard *or* sentry; **c)** *(Anstellung)* post; position; job; **d)** *(Funktion)* position; **e)** *(bes. Kaufmannsspr.: Rechnungs~)* item; **f)** *(bes. Kaufmannsspr.: Waren~)* quantity

Posten-: ~dienst der *(bes. Milit.)* guard duty; **~jäger der** *(salopp)* careerist

Poster ['po:stɐ] **das** *od.* **der; ~s, ~[s]** poster

post-, Post-: ~fach das a) *(im ~amt)* post-office *or* PO box; **b)** *(im Büro, Hotel o. ä.)* pigeon-hole; **~flugzeug das** mail plane; **~frisch** *Adj. (Philat.)* in mint condition *postpos.*; **~gebühr die** [postal] charge *or* rate; **~geheimnis das** secrecy of the post; **~gewerkschaft die** post-office workers' union; **~giro·amt das** post-office giro office; ≈ national giro[bank] centre *(Brit.)*; **~giro·konto das** post-office giro account; ≈ national giro[bank] account *(Brit.)*; **~horn das** post-horn

posthum [pɔst'hu:m] *s.* **postum**

postieren *tr. V.* **a)** *(aufstellen)* post; station; **sich ~:** station *or* position oneself; **b)** *(stellen)* position

Postille [pɔs'tɪlə] **die; ~, ~n** *(spött. abwertend) (Zeitschrift)* mag *(coll.)*; *(Zeitung)* rag *(derog.)*

Postillion [pɔstɪl'jo:n] **der; ~s, ~e** *(veralt.)* mail-coach driver

Postillon d'amour [pɔstijõda'mu:r] **der; ~ ~, ~s ~** *(scherzh.)* go-between

post-, Post-: ~karte die postcard; **~karten·größe die** postcard size; **in ~kartengröße** postcard-sized; **~kasten der** *(bes. nordd.)* post-box; mail box *(Amer.)*; pillar box *(Brit.)*; **~kunde der** post-office user; **~kutsche die** mail-coach; **~lagernd** *Adj., adv.* poste restante; general delivery *(Amer.)*; **~leit·zahl die** postcode; postal code; Zip code *(Amer.)*; **~meister der** *(hist.)* postmaster; **~minister der** Postmaster General; **~paket das** parcel; **per ~paket** [by] parcel post; **~sache die;** *o. Pl. (Amtsspr.)* item of post-office mail; **~schalter der** post-office counter; **~scheck der** post-office giro cheque; ≈ national giro[bank] cheque *(Brit.)*; **~scheck·amt das** *(veralt.) s.* **~giroamt; ~scheck·konto das** *(veralt.) s.* **~girokonto; ~sendung die** postal item

Post·skriptum [-'skrɪptʊm] **das; ~s, Post·skripta** postscript

Post-: ~spar·buch das post-office savings book *(Brit.)*; **~spar·kasse die** post-office savings bank *(Brit.)*; **~stelle die a)** *(kleines ~amt)* sub-post office; **b)** *(in einem Betrieb)* post-room; **~stempel der a)** *(Gerät)* stamp [for cancelling mail]; **b)** *(Abdruck)* postmark

Postulat [pɔstu'la:t] **das; ~[e]s, ~e a)** *(Forderung)* demand; **b)** *(Gebot)* decree

postulieren *tr. V.* **a)** *(fordern)* postulate; demand; **b)** *(behaupten)* assert

postum [pɔs'tu:m] **1.** *Adj.; nicht präd.* posthumous. **2.** *adv.* posthumously

post-, Post-: ~wagen der *(Eisenb.)* mail van *(Brit.)*; mail car *(Amer.)*; **~weg der: auf dem ~weg** by post *or* mail; **~wendend** *Adv.* by return [of post]; *(fig.)* immediately; **~wert·zeichen das** *(Amtsspr.)* postage stamp; **~wesen das;** *o. Pl.* postal operations *pl.*; **~wurf·sendung die** direct-mail item; **~zug der** mail train; **~zu·stellung die** postal delivery *no def. art.*

Pot [pɔt] **das; ~s** *(Drogenjargon)* pot *(sl.)*

potemkinsch [po'tɛmki:nʃ] *Adj.; in* **Potemkinsche Dörfer** façade *sing.*; sham *sing.*

potent [po'tɛnt] *Adj.* **a)** *(zeugungsfähig)* potent; **b)** *(finanzstark)* [financially] strong; **c)** *(fähig)* capable; able

Potentat [potɛn'ta:t] **der; ~en, ~en** *(abwertend)* potentate

Potential [potɛn'tsia:l] **das; ~s, ~e a)** *(Mittel, Möglichkeit)* potential; **das ~ an Energie/Aggression** energy resources *pl.*/aggressive capacity; **b)** *(Physik)* potential

potentiell [potɛn'tsiɛl] **1.** *Adj.* potential. **2.** *adv.* potentially

Potenz [po'tɛnts] **die; ~, ~en a)** *o. Pl.* potency; **b)** *(Stärke)* power; **c)** *(Math.)* power; **mit ~en rechnen** do calculations involving powers; **eine Zahl in die sechste ~ erheben** raise a number to the power [of] six; **das ist Blödsinn in [höchster] ~** *(fig.)* that is complete *or* utter nonsense; **d)** *(Med.: Grad der Verdünnung)* potency

Potenz·angst die impotence anxiety

potenzieren 1. *tr. V.* **a)** *(verstärken)* increase; **b)** *(Math.)* **mit 5 ~:** raise to the power [of] 5; **mit diesem Rechner kann man auch ~:** you can calculate *or* work out powers on this calculator. **2.** *refl. V. (sich steigern)* increase

potenz·steigernd *Adj.* potency *attrib.*; to increase potency *postpos.*

Potpourri ['pɔtpʊri] **das; ~s, ~s** *od. österr.:* **die; ~, ~s** *(auch fig.)* pot-pourri, medley **(aus, von** of)

Pott [pɔt] **der; ~[e]s, Pötte** ['pœtə] *(ugs., bes. nordd.)* **a)** *(Topf)* pot; **b)** *(Nachttopf)* chamber-pot; po *(coll.)*; potty *(coll.)*; **zu ~[e] kommen** *(fig.)* get to the point; **c)** *(Schiff)* tub *(derog./joc.)*

pott-, Pott-: ~asche die potash; **~häßlich** *(ugs.) Adj.* dead ugly *(coll.)*; ⟨*person, face*⟩ [as] ugly as sin *(coll.)*; **~wal der** physeterid *(Zool.)*; *(Spermwal)* sperm whale

potz·tausend *Interj. (veralt.)* **a)** *(überrascht)* upon my soul *(dated)*; **b)** *(unwillig)* damn it [all]

poussieren [pʊ'si:rən] **1.** *itr. V. (ugs. veralt.: flirten)* flirt. **2.** *tr. V. (veralt.: umwerben)* curry favour with

power ['po:vɐ] *Adj. (veralt.)* miserable; **eine ~e Gegend** a poor area

Powidl ['pɔvidl̩] **der; ~s** *(österr.) s.* **Pflaumenmus**

PR *Abk.* **Public Relations** PR

Prä [prɛ:] **das; ~s: [das] ~ haben** have priority

Präambel [prɛ'ambl̩] **die; ~, ~n** preamble

Pracht [praxt] **die; ~:** splendour; magnificence; **eine [wahre] ~ sein** *(ugs.)* be [really] marvellous *or (coll.)* great; **in voller ~:** in all its/their splendour

Pracht-: ~aus·gabe die de luxe edition; **~bau der;** *Pl.* **~bauten** splendid *or* magnificent building; **~exemplar das** *(ugs.)* magnificent specimen; beauty

prächtig ['prɛçtɪç] **1.** *Adj.* **a)** *(prunkvoll)* splendid; magnificent; **b)** *(großartig)* splendid; marvellous; **ein ~er Muskelriß** *(iron.)* a terrific example of a torn muscle *(coll.).* **2.** *adv.* **a)** *(prunkvoll)* splendidly; magnificently; **b)** *(großartig)* splendidly; marvellously

pracht-, Pracht-: ~kerl der *(ugs.)* great chap *or (Brit. coll.)* bloke *or (sl.)* guy; **ein ~kerl [von einem Kind]** a great kid *(sl.)*;

~straße die boulevard; **~stück das** *(ugs.)* magnificent specimen; beauty; **ein ~stück von [einem] Karpfen** a beautiful specimen of a carp; **sie/er ist ein ~stück** *(Kind)* she/he is a really splendid girl/boy; *(Frau)* she is a magnificent *or* splendid woman; *(Mann)* he is a great chap *or (Brit. coll.)* bloke *or (sl.)* guy; **~voll** *Adj., adv. s.* **prächtig; ~weib das** *(ugs.)* magnificent *or* splendid woman; *(gutaussehend)* gorgeous female *(coll.)*
Prädestination [prɛdestina'tsi̯o:n] **die; ~:** predestination
prädestinieren *tr. V.* predestine
prädestiniert *Adj.* predestined; **etw. ist für ein Ziel ~:** sth. is just right for a purpose; **er ist für diese Rolle einfach ~:** he is just the man for this part
Prädikat [prɛdi'ka:t] **das; ~[e]s, ~e a)** *(Auszeichnung)* rating; **das ~ „gut"** the rating of 'good'; **Qualitätswein mit ~:** *wine made from selected grapes of specified maturity;* **b)** *(Sprachw.)* predicate
prädikativ [prɛdika'ti:f] *(Sprachw.)* **1.** *Adj.* predicative. **2.** *adv.* predicatively
Prädikativ das; ~s, ~e *s.* **Prädikatsnomen**
Prädikativ·satz der *(Sprachw.)* predicate *or* predicative clause
Prädikats·nomen das *(Sprachw.)* predicate nominative *or* complement
prä·disponieren *tr. V. (Med.)* predispose **(für to)**
Präferenz [prɛfe'rɛnts] **die; ~, ~en** preference
Präferenz-: ~liste die priority list; **~stellung die** *(Wirtsch.)* privileged status
Präfix [prɛ'fɪks] **das; ~es, ~e** *(Sprachw.)* prefix
Prag [pra:k] **(das); ~s** Prague
Präge die; ~, ~n mint
Präge-: ~druck der; *o. Pl.* embossing; **~form die** *(Münzwesen)* coining die
prägen ['prɛ:gn̩] *tr. V.* **a)** emboss ⟨*metal, paper, leather*⟩; **b)** *(herstellen)* mint, strike ⟨*coin*⟩; **c)** *(auf~) (vertieft)* impress; *(erhaben)* emboss; **d)** *(fig.: beeinflussen)* shape; mould; **Tempo und Wagemut ~ seinen Stil** his style is characterized by speed and daring; **eine männlich geprägte Arbeitswelt** a male-oriented work environment; **e)** *(fig.: erfinden)* coin ⟨*word, expression, concept*⟩
Präge-: ~stempel der *(Druckw.)* die; **~stock der** *(Druckw.)* punch
Pragmatik [pra'gma:tɪk] **die; ~ a)** pragmatism; **b)** *(Sprachw.)* pragmatics *sing., no art.*
Pragmatiker der; ~s, ~: pragmatist
pragmatisch 1. *Adj.* pragmatic. **2.** *adv.* pragmatically
Pragmatismus der; ~: pragmatism
prägnant [prɛ'gnant] **1.** *Adj.* concise; succinct. **2.** *adv.* concisely; succinctly
Prägnanz [prɛ'gnants] **die; ~:** conciseness; succinctness
Prägung die; ~, ~en a) *(von Papier, Leder, Metall)* embossing; *(von Münzen)* minting; striking; **b)** *(auf Metall, Papier) (vertieft)* impression; *(erhaben)* embossing; **c)** *(Eigenart)* character; **d)** *(eines sprachlichen Ausdrucks)* coining; **e)** *(geprägter Ausdruck)* coinage
prä·historisch *Adj.* prehistoric
prahlen ['pra:lən] *itr. V.* boast, brag **(mit** about)
Prahler der; ~s, ~: boaster; braggart
Prahlerei die; ~, ~en *(abwertend)* boasting; bragging; **~en** boasts
Prahlerin die; ~, ~nen boaster; braggart
Prahl·hans der; ~es, Prahlhänse [-hɛnzə] *(ugs.)* show-off
Prahm [pra:m] **der; ~[e]s, ~e** *od.* **Prähme** ['prɛ:mə] pra[a]m
Präjudiz [prɛju'di:ts] **das; ~es, ~e** *(Rechtsw., Politik)* precedent
präjudizieren *tr. V. (Rechtsw., Politik)* prejudge

Praktik ['praktɪk] **die; ~, ~en** practice
Praktika *s.* **Praktikum**
praktikabel [prakti'ka:bl̩] *Adj.* practicable; practical
Praktikant [prakti'kant] **der; ~en, ~en, Praktikantin die; ~, ~nen a)** *(in einem Betrieb)* student trainee; trainee student; **b)** *(an der Hochschule)* physics/chemistry student *(doing a period of practical training)*
Praktiker der; ~s, ~ a) practical person; **b)** *(ugs.: praktischer Arzt)* general practitioner; GP
Praktikum ['praktikʊm] **das; ~s, Praktika** period of practical instruction *or* training
praktisch ['praktɪʃ] **1.** *Adj.* **a)** *(auf die Praxis bezogen)* practical; **~es Jahr** year of practical training; **~er Arzt** general practitioner; **b)** *(wirklich)* practical ⟨*result, problem, matter, etc.*⟩; concrete ⟨*example*⟩; **c)** *(nützlich)* practical ⟨*furniture, clothes, etc.*⟩; useful ⟨*present*⟩; **d)** *(geschickt, realistisch)* practical; **er hat einen ~en Verstand** he is practically minded. **2.** *adv.* **a)** *(auf die Praxis bezogen)* in practice; **~ experimentieren/arbeiten** do practical experiments/work; **b)** *(wirklich)* in practice; **c)** *(nützlich)* practically; **d)** *(geschickt, realistisch)* practically; **~ veranlagt** practically minded; practical; **e)** *(ugs.: so gut wie)* practically; virtually
praktizieren [prakti'tsi:rən] **1.** *tr. V.* **a)** *(anwenden)* practise; **~de Katholiken** practising Catholics; **b)** *(ugs.: irgendwohin bringen)* conjure; **jmdm. etw. in die Tasche/ins Essen ~:** slip sth. into sb.'s pocket/food. **2.** *itr. V. (als Arzt)* practise
Prälat [prɛ'la:t] **der; ~en, ~en** *(Kirche)* prelate
Präliminarien [prɛlimi'na:ri̯ən] *Pl.* preliminaries
Praline [pra'li:nə] **die; ~, ~n, Praliné, Pralinee** *(österr., schweiz., sonst veralt.)* [prali'ne:] **das; ~s, ~s** [filled] chocolate
prall [pral] **1.** *Adj.* **a)** *(fest und straff)* hard ⟨*ball*⟩; firm ⟨*tomato, grape*⟩; bulging ⟨*sack, wallet, bag*⟩; big strong *attrib.* ⟨*thighs, muscles, calves*⟩; well-rounded ⟨*buttocks*⟩; full, well-rounded ⟨*breasts*⟩; full, swollen ⟨*udder*⟩; full, chubby ⟨*cheeks*⟩; taut, full ⟨*sail*⟩; firm ⟨*pillow, bed*⟩; *(fig.)* intense ⟨*life*⟩; vivid ⟨*picture*⟩; full, rich ⟨*laughter*⟩; fully inflated ⟨*balloon*⟩; **b)** *(intensiv)* blazing ⟨*sun*⟩; strong ⟨*light*⟩. **2.** *adv.* **a)** *(fest und straff)* fully ⟨*inflated*⟩; **ein ~ gestopfter Rucksack** a rucksack filled to bursting; **eine ~ gefüllte Brieftasche** a wallet bulging with banknotes; **b)** *(intensiv)* **die Sonne scheint ~:** the sun is blazing [down]
prallen *itr. V.* **a)** *mit sein (hart auftreffen)* crash **(gegen/auf/an** + *Akk.* into); collide **(gegen/auf/an** + *Akk.* with); **der Ball prallte an den Pfosten** the ball hit the post; **b)** *(scheinen)* blaze
prall·voll *Adj. (ugs.)* ⟨*suitcase, rucksack*⟩ full to bursting; packed ⟨*room*⟩; bulging ⟨*wallet*⟩; very full ⟨*diary*⟩
Präludium [prɛ'lu:di̯ʊm] **das; ~s, Präludien** [...i̯ən] prelude
Prämie ['prɛ:mi̯ə] **die; ~, ~n a)** *(Leistungs~; Wirtschaft: ~ zum Grundlohn)* bonus; *(Belohnung)* reward; *(Spar~, Versicherungs~)* premium; **b)** *(einer Lotterie)* [extra] prize
prämien-, Prämien-: ~begünstigt 1. *Adj.* ≈ premium[-account] *attrib.*; **~begünstigtes Bausparen** ≈ saving with a building society premium account; **2.** *adv.* **~begünstigt sparen** ≈ save with a premium account; **~los das** ≈ Premium [Savings] Bond *(Brit.)*; **~sparen das; ~s** ≈ Premium Bond saving *(Brit.)*
prämieren [prɛ'mi:rən], **prämiieren** [prɛmi'i:rən] *tr. V.* award a prize to ⟨*person, film*⟩; give an award for ⟨*best essay etc.*⟩
Prämierung, Prämiierung die; ~, ~en a) *(Auszeichnung)* **er/der Film wurde zur ~ vorgeschlagen** it was proposed that he should be given a prize/that a prize should be given for the film; **b)** *(Preisverleihung)* **die ~ der besten Schüler/Filme** the presentation of prizes to the best pupils/for the best films
Prämisse [prɛ'mɪsə] **die; ~, ~n a)** *(auch Philos.)* premiss; **unter der ~, daß ...:** on the premiss that ...
pränatal [prɛna'ta:l] *Adj. (Med.)* pre-natal
prangen ['praŋən] *itr. V.* **a)** be prominently displayed; **auf dem Sofa prangte ein großes Kissen** a large cushion was placed eye-catchingly on the sofa; **b)** *(geh.: auffallen)* be resplendent; **Sterne ~ am Himmel** stars are glittering in the sky
Pranger der; ~s, ~ *(hist.)* pillory; **jmdn./etw. an den ~ stellen** *(fig.)* pillory sb./sth.
Pranke ['praŋkə] **die; ~, ~n a)** *(Pfote)* paw; **b)** *(salopp: große Hand)* paw *(coll.)*
Präparat [prɛpa'ra:t] **das; ~[e]s, ~e a)** *(Mittel, Substanz)* preparation; **b)** *(Biol., Med.: präpariertes Objekt)* specimen
Präparation [prɛpara'tsi̯o:n] **die; ~, ~en** preparation
präparieren 1. *tr. V.* **a)** *(Biol., Med.: konservieren)* preserve; **b)** *(Biol., Anat.: zerlegen)* dissect; **c)** *(vorbereitend bearbeiten, geh.: vorbereiten)* prepare. **2.** *refl. V. (geh.: sich vorbereiten)* prepare oneself
Präposition [prɛpozi'tsi̯o:n] **die; ~, ~en** *(Sprachw.)* preposition
präpositional [prɛpozitsi̯o'na:l] *Adj. (Sprachw.)* prepositional
Präpositional- *(Sprachw.)* prepositional
präpotent [prɛpo'tɛnt] *Adj. (österr.)* officiously impertinent
Prärie [prɛ'ri:] **die; ~, ~n** prairie
Prärie·wolf der prairie wolf; coyote
Präsens ['prɛ:zɛns] **das; ~, Präsentia** [prɛ'zɛntsi̯a] *od.* **Präsenzien** [prɛ'zɛntsi̯ən] *(Sprachw.)* present [tense]
präsent [prɛ'zɛnt] *Adj.* present; **Forderungen/Fragen ~ haben** have one's demands/questions ready; **ich habe den Vorfall** *od.* **der Vorfall ist mir im Augenblick nicht ~:** I do not recall the incident at the moment
Präsent das; ~[e]s, ~e *(geh.)* present; **jmdm. ein ~ machen** give sb. a present
präsentabel [prɛzɛn'ta:bl̩] *(veralt.)* presentable
Präsentation [prɛzɛnta'tsi̯o:n] **die; ~, ~en a)** *(Vorstellung)* presentation; **b)** *(Wirtsch.)* presentment
präsentieren 1. *tr. V.* **a)** *(anbieten; überreichen)* offer; **b)** *(vorlegen)* present; **jmdm. die Rechnung [für etw.] ~:** present sb. with the bill [for sth.]; **c)** *(Milit.)* **präsentiert das Gewehr!** present arms! **2.** *refl. V. (sich zeigen)* present oneself; appear. **3.** *itr. V. (Milit.)* present arms
Präsentier·teller der: auf dem ~ sitzen *(ugs. abwertend)* be on show *or* display
Präsent·korb der gift hamper
Präsenz [prɛ'zɛnts] **die; ~:** presence
Präsenz-: ~bibliothek die reference library; **~liste die** [attendance] register; **~pflicht die** duty to attend
Präser ['prɛzɐ] **der, ~s, ~** *(salopp),* **Präservativ** [prɛzɛrva'ti:f] **das; ~s, ~e** condom
Präses ['prɛ:zɛs] **der; ~, Präsides** ['prɛ:zide:s] **a)** *(kath. Kirche)* chairman; **b)** *(ev. Kirche)* president *(of a synod)*
Präsident [prɛzi'dɛnt] **der; ~en, ~en** president
Präsidenten·wahl die presidential election
Präsidentin die; ~, ~nen president
Präsidentschaft die; ~, ~en presidency
Präsidentschafts·kandidat der candidate for the presidency
präsidial [prɛzi'di̯a:l] *Adj. (Politik)* presidential
Präsidial·demokratie die presidential democracy
Präsidien *Pl. s.* **Präsidium**

präsidieren 1. *itr. V.* preside. 2. *tr. V.* *(schweiz.)* **einen Verein** *usw.* ~: be president of a society *etc.*
Präsidium [prɛ'zi:diʊm] **das; ~s, Präsidien** a) *(Führungsgruppe)* committee; **im ~ sitzen** be on the committee; b) *(Vorsitz)* chairmanship; c) *(Polizei~)* police headquarters *sing.* *or pl.*
prasseln ['prasl̩n] *itr. V.* ‹*rain, hail*› pelt down; ‹*shots*› clatter; ‹*fire*› crackle; **Kies prasselte gegen das Auto** gravel rattled against the car; **~der Beifall** thunderous applause
prassen ['prasn̩] *itr. V.* live extravagantly; *(schlemmen)* feast
Prasser der; ~s, ~: spendthrift; extravagant person; *(Schlemmer)* glutton
Prasserei die; ~, ~en a) extravagant living *no pl.*; b) *(das Schlemmen)* gluttony *no pl.*; *(Gelage)* feasting *no pl.*
präsumtiv [prɛzʊm'ti:f] *Adj.* a) prospective; b) *(Rechtsw.)* presumptive
Prätendent [prɛtɛn'dɛnt] **der; ~en, ~en** pretender
prätentiös [prɛtɛn'tsiø:s] *Adj.* pretentious
Präteritum [prɛ'te:ritʊm] **das; ~s, Präterita** *(Sprachw.)* preterite [tense]
Pratze ['pratsə] **die; ~, ~n** *(bes. südd.)* *s.* **Pranke**
präventiv [prɛvɛn'ti:f] 1. *Adj.* preventive. 2. *adv.* preventively; **~ vorgehen** take preventive measures
Präventiv-: ~krieg der preventive war; **~maßnahme die** preventive measure
Praxis ['praksɪs] **die; ~, Praxen** a) *o. Pl. (im Unterschied zur Theorie)* practice *no art.*; **in der ~:** in practice; **etw. in die ~ umsetzen** put sth. into practice; **Beispiele aus der ~:** practical examples; **er ist ein Mann der ~:** he is a practical man; b) *o. Pl. (Erfahrung)* [practical] experience; c) *(eines Arztes, Anwalts, Psychologen, Therapeuten usw.)* practice; d) *(~räume) (eines Arztes)* surgery *(Brit.)*; office *(Amer.)*; *(eines Anwalts, Psychologen, Therapeuten usw.)* office; e) *(Handhabung)* procedure
praxis-: ~bezogen 1. *Adj.* practical ‹*experience, training*›; ‹*project*› based on practical work; 2. *adv.* practically; **~nah, ~orientiert** 1. *Adj.* practical; 2. *adv.* practically
Präzedenz·fall [prɛtse'dɛnts-] **der** precedent
präzis *(österr.)*, **präzise** [prɛ'tsi:zə] 1. *Adj.* precise ‹*definition, answer*›; specific ‹*wishes, suspicion*›. 2. *adv.* precisely
präzisieren *tr. V.* make more precise; state more precisely; **ein Angebot näher ~:** give more precise details of an offer; **seine Wünsche ~:** specify one's wishes
Präzision [prɛtsi'zio:n] **die; ~:** precision
Präzisions-: ~arbeit die precision work; *(genau nach Zeitplan)* precise timing; **~instrument das** precision instrument; **~uhr die** precision [stop-]watch/clock
predigen ['pre:dɪgn̩] 1. *itr. V. (Predigt halten)* deliver *or* give a/the sermon; **gegen etw. ~:** preach against sth. 2. *tr. V.* a) *(verkündigen)* preach; b) *(ugs.: auffordern zu)* preach; c) *(ugs.: belehrend sagen)* **wie oft habe ich dir das schon gepredigt!** how often have I told you that!
Prediger der; ~s, ~, Predigerin die; ~, ~nen preacher; **ein Prediger in der Wüste** *(fig.)* a voice [crying] in the wilderness
Predigt ['pre:dɪçt] **die; ~, ~en** a) sermon; **eine ~ halten** deliver *or* give a sermon; b) *(ugs.: Ermahnung)* lecture; **jmdm. eine ~ halten** lecture sb.; **ich bin deine endlosen ~en leid** I am tired of your endless lecturing
Predigt·text der text *(for a sermon)*
Preis [prais] **der; ~es, ~e** a) *(Kauf~)* price **(für** of); **das hat seinen ~:** it costs money; *(fig.)* there is a price to be paid for it; **im ~ steigen** rise in price; **jeden ~ für etw. zahlen** pay any price for sth.; **jmdm. einen guten ~ machen** give sb. a good price; **nach dem ~ fragen** ask the price; **eine Ware unter[m] ~ verkaufen** sell an article at a reduced *or* cut price; **etw. zum halben ~ erwerben** buy sth. at half-price; **hoch/gut im ~ stehen** fetch a high/good price; **diese Ausstellung möchte ich um jeden ~ besuchen** *(fig.)* I should like to go to this exhibition at all costs; **diese Einladung möchte ich um keinen ~ annehmen** *(fig.)* I wouldn't accept this invitation at any price; b) *(Belohnung)* prize; **einen ~ auf jmds. Kopf aussetzen** put a price on sb.'s head; **der Große ~ von Frankreich** *(Rennsport)* the French Grand Prix; **der ~ der Nationen** *(Reitsport)* Prix des Nations; c) *(geh.: Lob)* praise; **ein Gedicht zum ~e der Natur** a poem in praise of nature
-preis der price of ...
preis-, Preis-: ~ab·schlag der *(Kaufmannsspr.)* *s.* **~nachlaß; ~ab·sprache die** *(Wirtsch.)* price-fixing agreement; **~änderung die** price change *or* variation; **~an·gabe die** *(displayed or listed)* price; **~anstieg der** rise *or* increase in prices; **~auf·gabe die** [prize] competition; **eine ~aufgabe lösen** solve a puzzle *(in a prize competition)*; **~auf·schlag der** *(Kaufmannsspr.)* additional *or* extra charge; **~auf·trieb der** *(Wirtsch.)* rise *or* increase in prices; **~aus·schreiben das** [prize] competition; **~aus·zeichnung die** labelling with a price/prices; **~bewegung die** movement of prices; **~bewußt** 1. *Adj.* price-conscious; 2. *adv.* price-consciously; **~bewußt tanken** be conscious of petrol *(Brit.) or (Amer.)* gasoline prices [when filling up]; **~bindung die** *(Wirtsch.)* price-fixing; **~bindung der zweiten Hand** resale price maintenance; **~boxer der** *(ugs. veralt.)* prize-fighter; **~brecher der** cut-price operator; **~ein·bruch der** *(Wirtsch.)* [massive] drop in prices
Preisel·beere ['praizl̩be:rə] **die** cowberry; cranberry *(Gastr.)*
Preis·empfehlung die *(Kaufmannsspr.)* recommended price
preisen *unr. tr. V. (geh.)* praise; **man pries ihn als den besten Kenner auf diesem Gebiet** he was acclaimed as the leading authority in this field; **sich glücklich ~ [können]** [be able to] count *or* consider oneself lucky
Preis-: ~entwicklung die price trend; **~erhöhung die** price increase *or* rise
-preis·erhöhung die increase in the price of ...
preis-, Preis-: ~ermäßigung die price reduction; **~explosion die** snowballing prices *pl.*; **~frage die** a) *(bei einem ~ausschreiben)* [prize] question; *(fig.)* big question; sixty-four thousand dollar question; b) *(Geldfrage)* question of price; **~gabe die** *(geh.)* a) *(Verzicht)* abandonment; b) *(von Geheimnissen)* revelation; giving away; **~|geben** *unr. tr. V. (geh.)* a) *(ausliefern)* **jmdn. einer Sache** *(Dat.)* **~geben** expose sb. to *or* leave sb. to be the victim of sth.; **die Bauten waren dem Verfall ~gegeben** the buildings were left to fall into ruin; b) *(aufgeben)* relinquish ‹*ideal, independence*›; surrender ‹*territory*›; c) *(verraten)* betray; give away; **~gebunden** *Adj. (Wirtsch.)* subject to price maintenance *postpos.*; **~gefälle das** difference *or* variation in prices; **~gefüge das** *(Wirtsch.)* price structure; **~gekrönt** *Adj.* prize- *or* award-winning; **er/sein Werk ist ~gekrönt** he has been given/his work has won a prize *or* an award; **~gericht das** jury; panel of judges; **~gestaltung die** pricing; **~grenze die** price limit; **obere/untere ~grenze** ceiling *or* maximum/floor *or* minimum price; **~günstig** 1. *Adj.* ‹*goods*› available at unusually low prices; ‹*purchases*› at favourable prices; inexpensive ‹*holiday*›; **das ~günstigste Angebot** the best bargain *or* value; **das ist [sehr] ~günstig** that is [very] good value; 2. *adv.* **etw. ~günstig herstellen/verkaufen/bekommen** produce/sell/get sth. at a low price; **hier kann man ~günstig einkaufen** their prices are very reasonable here; **~index der** *(Wirtsch.)* price index; **~klasse die** price range; **~kontrolle die** price control; **~lage die** price range; **in jeder ~lage** at prices to suit every pocket; **~lawine die** *(ugs.)* snowballing prices *pl.*
preislich *Adj.; nicht präd.* price; in price *postpos.*; **in ~er Hinsicht** as regards price
preis-, Preis-: ~nachlaß der price reduction; discount; **mit erheblichem ~nachlaß** at a greatly reduced price; **~niveau das** *(Wirtsch.)* price level; **~politik die** policy on prices; **~rätsel das** [prize] competition; **~richter der** judge; **~schießen das** shooting competition *or* contest; **~schild das** price-tag; **~schlager der** *(ugs.)* bargain [offer]; **~schlager der Saison** best bargain of the season; **~schraube die;** *o. Pl.* *(Wirtschaftsjargon)* **an·der ~schraube drehen** put [one's] prices up; **~schwankung die** price fluctuation; **~senkung die** price reduction *or* cut; **~skat der** skat competition; **~steigerung die** rise *or* increase in prices; **~steigerungs·rate die** *(Wirtsch.)* rate of increase in prices; **~stopp der** price freeze; **~sturz der** sharp drop *or* fall in prices; **~träger der, ~trägerin die** prizewinner; **~treiber der** *(abwertend)* person who/company which forces prices up; **dieses Reiseunternehmen gilt als ~treiber** this tour operator is known for forcing prices up; **~treiberei die** *(abwertend)* forcing up of prices; **~vergleich der** price comparison; **~vergleiche anstellen** compare prices; **~verleihung die** presentation [of prizes/awards]; award ceremony; **~vor·teil der** price benefit; **~wert** 1. *Adj.* good value *pred.*; **ein ~wertes Angebot** a bargain [offer]; **haben Sie ~wertere Schuhe?** do you have any shoes which are less expensive?; 2. *adv.* **sie hat ~wert eingekauft** she bought things at reasonable prices; **dort kann man ~wert einkaufen** you get good value for money there; **hier kann man ~wert essen** you can eat at a reasonable price here; **~würdig** *Adj. (geh.)* praiseworthy
prekär [pre'kɛ:ɐ̯] *Adj.* precarious
Prell-: ~ball der *(Sport) game similar to volleyball*; **~bock der** *(Eisenb.)* buffer
prellen ['prɛlən] 1. *tr. V.* a) *(betrügen)* cheat **(um** out of); **die Zeche ~:** avoid paying the bill; b) *(verletzen)* bash; bruise; c) *(Ballsport)* bounce. 2. *refl. V. (sich verletzen)* bruise oneself; **ich habe mich an der Schulter geprellt** I have bruised *or* bashed my shoulder
Prellung die; ~, ~en bruise
Premier [prə'mie:] **der; ~s, ~s** premier
Premiere [prə'mie:rə] **die; ~, ~n** opening night; first night; *(Uraufführung)* première; *(fig.)* first appearance; **das Stück hat morgen ~:** the play has its opening night/première tomorrow
Premieren-: ~abend der opening night; first night; *(eines neuen Stückes)* première; **~publikum das** audience at a/the première/opening *or* first night
Premier- [prə'mie:-]: **~minister der, ~ministerin die** prime minister
Presbyter ['prɛsbytɐ] **der; ~s, ~** *(ev. Kirche)* presbyter; elder
Presbyterianer [prɛsbyte'ria:nɐ] **der; ~s, ~:** Presbyterian
presbyterianisch *Adj.* Presbyterian
preschen ['prɛʃn̩] *itr. V.; mit sein* tear; **sie kam ins Zimmer geprescht** she came dashing into the room
Presse ['prɛsə] **die; ~, ~n** a) *(zum Zusammenpressen)* press; b) *(zum Auspressen) (von Obst, Knoblauch)* press; *(von Zitronen)*

squeezer; **c)** *o. Pl. (Zeitungen, ~kritik)* press; **d)** *(Druckw. veralt.: Druckmaschine)* press; **e)** *(ugs., abwertend: Schule)* crammer

Presse-: ~agentur die press agency; news agency; **~amt das** press office; **~ausweis der** press card; **~ball der** *celebrity dance held by a national or provincial journalists' association;* **~bericht der** press report; **~chef der** [chief] press officer; **~dienst der** regular press release; **~empfang der** press reception; **~erklärung die** press statement; **~fotograf der** press photographer; **~freiheit die** freedom of the press; **~gesetz das** press law; **~kampagne die** press campaign; **~karte die** press ticket; **~kommentar der** press commentary; **~konferenz die** press conference; **~konzentration die** concentration of the press; **~meldung die** press report

pressen *tr. V.* **a)** *(zusammendrücken)* press; **b)** *(auspressen)* press ⟨*fruit, garlic*⟩; squeeze ⟨*lemon*⟩; **c)** *(drücken)* press; **Kleider in einen Koffer ~:** squash *or* squeeze clothes into a suitcase; **jmdm. die Hand auf den Mund ~:** press one's hand over sb.'s mouth; **mit gepreßter Stimme** *(fig.)* in a strained voice; **d)** *(herstellen)* press ⟨*record*⟩; mould ⟨*plastic object*⟩; **e)** *(zwingen)* force; **f)** *(veralt.: unterdrücken)* oppress

Presse-: ~notiz die news item; **etw. in einer kurzen ~notiz erwähnen** give sth. a mention in the press; **~organ das** *(Zeitung)* newspaper; *(Zeitschrift)* journal; magazine; **die ~organe** the press; **~recht das** press legislation; **~referent der** press officer; **~sprecher der** spokesman; press officer; **~stelle die** press office; **~stimmen** *Pl.* press commentaries *or* reviews; **~tribüne die** press-box; **auf der ~tribüne** in the press-box; **~vertreter der** representative of the press; **~zentrum das** press centre

Preß-: ~glas das; *Pl.* **~gläser** pressed glass; **~holz das** compressed wood

pressieren *itr. V. (bes. südd.)* ⟨*matter*⟩ be urgent; **er ist sehr pressiert/mir pressiert's sehr** he is/I am in a great hurry

Pression [prɛ'si̯o:n] **die; ~, ~en** pressure

Preß-: ~kohle die compressed coal *no pl.;* **~kopf der;** *o. Pl.* brawn; head cheese *(Amer.);* **~luft die;** *o. Pl.* compressed air

Preß·luft-: ~bohrer der pneumatic drill; **~hammer der** *(Bauw.)* pneumatic *or* air hammer

Pressung die; ~, ~en *(das Pressen)* pressure; *(das Gepreßtwerden)* compression

Preß·wehe die *(Med.)* contraction *(in second stage of labour)*

Prestige [prɛs'ti:ʒə] **das; ~s** prestige

Prestige-: ~denken das desire to establish one's prestige; **~frage die** question *or* matter of prestige; **~verlust der** loss of prestige

Pretiosen [pre'tsi̯o:zn̩] *Pl.* valuables

Preuße ['prɔysə] **der; ~n, ~n** Prussian; **so schnell schießen die ~n nicht** *(fig.)* these things take time

Preußen (das); ~s Prussia

Preußentum das; ~s a) *(preußische Wesensart)* Prussian character; **b)** *(Volkszugehörigkeit)* Prussianness; **c)** *(die Preußen)* Prussian people *pl.;* Prussians *pl.*

preußisch ['prɔysɪʃ] *Adj.* Prussian; *s. auch* **deutsch; Deutsch; ²Deutsche**

preußisch·blau *Adj.*, **Preußisch·blau das** Prussian blue

preziös [pre'tsi̯ø:s] *Adj. (geh.)* precious

Pricke ['prɪkə] **die; ~, ~n** *(Seew.)* perch

prickelig *Adj.* tingling

prickeln ['prɪkl̩n] *itr. V.* **a)** *(kribbeln, kitzeln)* tingle; **es prickelte ihm in den Fingerspitzen** his fingertips were tingling; **b)** *(perlen)* sparkle; **c)** *(reizen)* **eine ~de Spannung** a tingling atmosphere; **der ~de Reiz des Unbekannten** the thrill of the unknown

pricklig *Adj. s.* **prickelig**

Priel [pri:l] **der; ~[e]s, ~e** narrow channel *(in mud-flats)*

Priem [pri:m] **der; ~[e]s, ~e a)** *(Kautabak)* chewing-tobacco; **~ kauen** chew tobacco; **b)** *(Stück Kautabak)* quid [of tobacco]

priemen *itr. V.* chew tobacco

pries [pri:s] *1. u. 3. Pers. Sg. Prät. v.* **preisen**

Priester ['pri:stɐ] **der; ~s, ~:** priest

Priester·amt das priesthood

Priesterin die; ~, ~nen priestess

priesterlich *Adj.* priestly ⟨*function*⟩; clerical ⟨*robe, collar*⟩; priest's ⟨*blessing*⟩

Priester·rock der cassock

Priesterschaft die; ~: priests *pl.*

Priester·seminar das seminary

Priestertum das; ~s priesthood

Priester·weihe die ordination [to the priesthood]

prima ['pri:ma] **1.** *indekl. Adj.* **a)** *(ugs.)* great *(coll.);* fantastic *(coll.);* **b)** *nicht präd. (Kaufmannsspr. veralt.)* first-class; top-quality. **2.** *adv. (ugs.)* ⟨*taste*⟩ great *(coll.),* fantastic *(coll.);* ⟨*sleep*⟩ fantastically *(coll.) or* really well; **es geht mir ~:** I feel great *(coll.);* **es lief alles ~:** everything went really well; **das finde ich ~:** that's fantastic *or* great *(coll.);* **das hast du ~ gemacht** well done indeed

Prima die; ~, Primen *(Schulw.)* **a)** *(veralt.)* eighth and ninth years *(of a Gymnasium);* **b)** *(österr.)* first year *(of a Gymnasium)*

Prima-: ~ballerina die *(Theater)* prima ballerina; **~donna** [~'dɔna] **die; ~, Primadonnen** prima donna

Primaner [pri'ma:nɐ] **der; ~s, ~** *(Schulw.)* **a)** *(veralt.)* pupil in the eighth and ninth years *(of a Gymnasium);* **wie ein ~** *(fig.)* like a schoolboy; **b)** *(österr.)* pupil in the first year *(of a Gymnasium)*

primanerhaft 1. *Adj.* schoolboyish/schoolgirlish. **2.** *adv.* like a schoolboy/schoolgirl

Primanerin die; ~, ~nen *s.* **Primaner**

primär [pri'mɛ:ɐ̯] **1.** *Adj.* primary. **2.** *adv.* primarily

Primar·lehrer [pri'ma:ɐ̯-] **der** *(schweiz.)* primary school teacher

Primär·literatur die primary literature

Primar-: ~schule die *(schweiz.)* primary school; **~stufe die** primary stage *(of education)*

Primas ['pri:mas] **der; ~, ~se** *od.* **Primaten a)** *(kath. Kirche)* primate; **b)** *Pl. nur* **~se** *(Geiger)* leading fiddle-player

¹Primat [pri'ma:t] **der** *od.* **das; ~[e]s, ~e a)** *(Vorrang)* primacy, priority **(vor** + *Dat.,* **über** + *Akk.* over); **b)** *(kath. Kirche)* primacy

²Primat der; ~en, ~en *(Zool.)* primate

Prime ['pri:mə] **die; ~, ~n** *(Musik)* **a)** *(Einklang)* unison; **b)** *(Ton)* keynote; tone

Primel ['pri:ml̩] **die; ~, ~n** primula; primrose; *(Schlüsselblume)* cowslip; **eingehen wie eine ~** *(salopp)* go completely to pot *(coll.)*

Primi *Pl. s.* **Primus**

primitiv [primi'ti:f] **1.** *Adj.* **a)** *(einfach, schlicht)* simple; crude *(derog.);* **die ~sten Regeln des Anstands** the most basic rules of behaviour; **b)** *(oft abwertend: dürftig)* primitive; **c)** *(abwertend: niveaulos, ungebildet)* primitive ⟨*person, behaviour*⟩; crude ⟨*expression, view, idea, speech*⟩; **d)** *(urtümlich, ursprünglich, naiv)* primitive. **2.** *adv.* **a)** *(einfach, schlicht)* in a simple manner; crudely *(derog.);* **b)** *(oft abwertend: dürftig)* primitively; **c)** *(abwertend: niveaulos, ungebildet)* ⟨*argue*⟩ primitively; ⟨*talk*⟩ crudely; **d)** *(urtümlich)* primitively

Primitivität [primitivi'tɛ:t] **die; ~:** *s.* **primitiv 1b–d:** primitiveness; crudeness

Primitivling der; ~s, ~e *(abwertend)* peasant *(fig.)*

Primus ['pri:mʊs] **der; ~, Primi** *od.* **~se** *(veralt.)* top of the class

Prim·zahl die *(Math.)* prime [number]

Printe ['prɪntə] **die; ~, ~n** *kind of oblong sweet spiced cake*

Prinz [prɪnts] **der; ~en, ~en** prince

Prinzessin die; ~, ~nen princess

Prinz·gemahl der prince consort

Prinzip [prɪn'tsi:p] **das; ~s, ~ien** [-'tsi:pi̯ən] principle; **aus ~:** on principle; **er hat es aus ~ getan** he did it as a matter of principle; **im ~:** in principle; **ein Mensch von** *od.* **mit ~ien sein** be a man/woman of principle

Prinzipal [prɪntsi'pa:l] **der; ~s, ~e** *(veralt.)* **a)** *(eines Theaters)* [theatre] manager; *(einer Theatergruppe)* leader; **b)** *(Leiter eines Privatbetriebs)* proprietor; *(Lehrherr)* master

prinzipiell [prɪntsi'pi̯ɛl] **1.** *Adj.; nicht präd.* in principle *postpos., not pred.;* ⟨*rejection*⟩ on principle; **eine ~e Frage/Frage von ~er Bedeutung** a question of principle/of fundamental importance. **2.** *adv.* **a)** *(im Prinzip)* in principle; **b)** *(aus Prinzip)* on principle; as a matter of principle

prinzipien-, Prinzipien-: ~los *Adj.* unprincipled; **~losigkeit die; ~:** lack of principles; **~reiter der** *(abwertend)* person who sticks rigidly to his/her principles; **~reiterei die** *(abwertend)* rigid adherence to principles

prinzlich *Adj.; nicht präd.* prince's

Prinz·regent der Prince Regent

Prior ['pri:ɔr] **der; ~s, ~en** [pri'o:rən] *(kath. Kirche)* prior

Priorin die; ~, ~nen *(kath. Kirche)* prioress

Priorität [priori'tɛ:t] **die; ~, ~en a)** *o. Pl. (Vorrang)* priority; precedence; **~ vor etw.** *(Dat.)* **haben** have *or* take precedence over sth.; **b)** *Pl. (Rangfolge)* priorities; **~en setzen** establish priorities; **die richtigen ~en setzen** get one's priorities right

Prise ['pri:zə] **die; ~, ~n a)** pinch; **eine ~ Salz** a pinch of salt; **eine ~ Sarkasmus/Ironie** *(fig.)* a hint *or* touch of sarcasm/irony; **b)** *(Seew.)* prize; **eine ~ machen** take a prize

Prisma ['prɪsma] **das; ~s, Prismen** *(Math., Optik)* prism

prismatisch [prɪs'ma:tɪʃ] **1.** *Adj.* prismatic. **2.** *adv.* prismatically

Prismen *s.* **Prisma**

Pritsche ['prɪtʃə] **die; ~, ~n a)** *(Liegestatt)* plank bed; **b)** *(Ladefläche)* platform; **c)** *(Narren~)* slapstick

Pritschen·wagen der platform truck

privat [pri:va:t] **1.** *Adj.* private; personal ⟨*opinion, happiness, etc.*⟩; **eine Feier im ~en Kreis** a celebration restricted to one's intimate circle; **an/von Privat** to/from private individuals *pl.* **2.** *adv.* privately; **~ ist er ganz anders** he's completely different in private; **jmdn. ~ sprechen** speak to sb. in private *or* privately; **der Patient liegt ~:** the patient is in a/the private ward

Privat-: ~adresse die private *or* home address; **~an·gelegenheit die** private affair *or* matter; **das ist seine ~angelegenheit** that's his own business *or* his own private affair; **~audienz die** private audience; **~besitz der** private property; **das Gemälde befindet sich im ~besitz** the painting is privately owned *or* in private ownership; **~detektiv der** private detective *or* investigator; **~dozent der** *lecturer who is not a member of the salaried university staff;* **~druck der;** *Pl.* **~drucke** privately published edition; **als ~druck erscheinen** be published privately; **~eigentum das** private property; **das ~eigentum an den Produktionsmitteln** private ownership of the means of production; **~fernsehen das** privately operated television; ≈ commercial television; **~gelehrte der/die** *(veralt.)* scholar [working] on his/her own account; **~gespräch das** private conversation; *(Telefongespräch)* private call

Privatier [priva'ti̯e:] **der; ~s, ~s** *(veralt.)* man of private *or* independent means

privatim [pri'va:tɪm] *adv. (geh.)* privately

Privat-: ~initiative die private initiative; **~interesse das** private interest

privatisieren 1. *tr. V. (Wirtsch.)* privatize; transfer into private ownership. **2.** *itr. V. (geh.: als Privatier leben)* live on a private income

Privatisierung die; ~, ~en *(Wirtsch.)* privatization; transfer into private ownership

privat-, Privat-: ~klage die *(Rechtsw.)* private action *or* prosecution; **~kläger der** *(Rechtsw.)* plaintiff [in a/the private action]; **~klinik die** private clinic *or* hospital; **~leben das;** *o. Pl.* private life; **sich ins ~leben zurückziehen** return to private life; **~lehrer der** private tutor; **~mann der;** *Pl.* **~leute** *s.* **~person; ~patient der** private patient; **~person die** private individual; **als ~person auftreten** appear in a private capacity; **~quartier das** private accommodation *no pl.*; **zahlreiche ~quartiere** plentiful private accommodation *sing.*; **~recht das;** *o. Pl. (Rechtsw.)* private *or* civil law; **~rechtlich** *(Rechtsw.)* **1.** *Adj.* civil-law *attrib.*; under private *or* civil law *postpos.*; **2.** *adv.* in private *or* civil law; **~sache die** *s.* **~angelegenheit; ~sammlung die** private collection; **~schule die** private school; *(Eliteschule in Großbritannien)* public school; **~sekretär der, ~sekretärin** private secretary **(von,** *Gen.* to); **~sphäre die** privacy; *(~leben)* private life; **~station die** private ward; **~stunde die** private lesson; **~unternehmen das** private concern *or* enterprise; **~unterricht der** private tuition; private lessons *pl.*; **~vergnügen das** *(ugs.)* **eine Dienstreise ist kein ~vergnügen** you don't go on business trips for your own enjoyment; **das ist doch mein ~vergnügen** that's my own business *or* affair; **~vermögen das** private fortune; **~vermögen/kein ~vermögen haben** have a/no private fortune; **~versichert** *Adj.* privately insured; covered by private insurance *postpos.*; **~versicherung die** private insurance; **in einer ~versicherung sein** be privately insured; be in a private insurance scheme; **~weg der** private way; **~wirtschaft die** private sector; **~wirtschaftlich 1.** *Adj.* private-sector *attrib.*; ⟨*enterprise, company, firm*⟩ in the private sector; **auf ~wirtschaftlicher Basis** on a private-enterprise basis; **2.** *adv.* **~wirtschaftlich orientiert/gesehen** orientated towards/from the point of view of the private sector; **~wirtschaftlich geführt** run as a private enterprise; **~wohnung die** private flat *(Brit.) or (Amer.)* apartment

Privileg [privi'le:k] **das; ~[e]s, ~ien** [-'le:gi̯ən] privilege

privilegieren *tr. V.* grant privileges to

privilegiert *Adj.* privileged

pro [pro:] *Präp. mit Akk.* per; **~ Jahr/Monat** per year *or* annum/month; **~ Person** per person; **~ Kopf** per head; **~ Stück** each; apiece; **~ Nase** *(ugs.)* each; a head

Pro das *in* **[das] ~ und [das] Kontra** the pros and cons *pl.*

pro-: pro-; **~westlich/~kommunistisch** pro-western/pro-communist

Proband [pro'bant] **der; ~en, ~en a)** *(Psych., Med.: Testperson)* subject; **b)** *(Strafentlassener)* offender on probation

probat [pro'ba:t] *Adj.* tried and tested; *(wirksam)* effective

Probe ['pro:bə] **die; ~, ~n a)** *(Prüfung)* test; **die ~ aufs Exempel machen** put it to the test; **auf ~ sein** be on probation; **ein Beamter/eine Ehe auf ~:** a probationary civil servant/a trial marriage; **jmdn./etw. auf die ~ stellen** put sb./sth. to the test; **jmds. Geduld/Liebe/Freundschaft auf eine harte ~ stellen** sorely try *or* test sb.'s patience/sorely test sb.'s love/friendship; **jmdn. auf ~ einstellen** employ sb. on a trial basis; **b)** *(Muster, Teststück)* sample; **eine ~ seines Könnens zeigen** *od.* **geben** *(fig.)* show what one can do; **c)** *(Theater~, Orchester~)* rehearsal

probe-, Probe-: ~ab·zug der *(Druckw., Fot.)* proof; **~alarm der** practice alarm; *(Feueralarm)* fire-drill *or* -practice; **~aufnahme die a)** test take; **b)** *(bei der Auswahl von Filmschauspielern)* screen test; **mit jmdm. ~aufnahmen machen** screen-test sb.; **~bohrung die** test drilling *no indef. art., no pl.*; **~bohrungen/eine ~bohrung durchführen** drill test wells/a test well; **~druck der;** *Pl.* **~drucke** *(Druckw.)* proof; **~exemplar das** specimen copy; **~|fahren** *meist nur im Inf. u. 2. Part. gebr.; unr. tr. V.* test-drive ⟨*car*⟩; test ⟨*boat*⟩ out on the water; **~fahrt die** trial run; *(vor dem Kauf, nach einer Reparatur)* test drive; **eine ~fahrt machen** go for a trial run/test drive *or* test run; **hast du mit deinem neuen Boot schon eine ~fahrt gemacht?** have you tried out your new boat yet?; **~flug der** test flight; **~halber** *adv.* as a test; **jmdn. ~halber beschäftigen** employ sb. on a trial basis; **~jahr das** probationary year; **~lauf der** *(Technik)* test run

proben *tr., itr. V.* rehearse

Proben·arbeit die rehearsals *pl.* **(zu** for)

probe-, Probe-: ~nummer die specimen copy; **~weise 1.** *Adv.* ⟨*employ*⟩ on a trial basis; **den Motor ~weise laufen lassen** test[-run] the engine; **2.** *adj.; nicht präd.* trial; **~zeit die a)** probationary *or* trial period; **b)** *(schweiz. Rechtsspr.: Bewährungsfrist)* period of probation; **eine ~zeit von drei Jahren** three years' probation

probieren 1. *tr. V.* **a)** *(versuchen)* try; have a go *or* try at; **~, ob der Schlüssel paßt** try the key to see whether it fits; **b)** *(kosten)* taste; try; sample; **c)** *(aus~)* try out; *(an~)* try on ⟨*clothes, shoes*⟩; **d)** *(Theaterjargon: proben)* rehearse. **2.** *itr. V.* **a)** *(versuchen)* try; have a go *or* try; **Probieren geht über Studieren** the proof of the pudding is in the eating *(prov.)*; **b)** *(kosten)* have a taste; **willst du ~?** do you want a taste?; **probier mal!** have a taste!; try some!; **c)** *(Theaterjargon)* rehearse

Problem [pro'ble:m] **das; ~s, ~e** problem; **vor einem ~ stehen** be faced *or* confronted with a problem

Problem- problem; **ihr Kind war eine ~geburt** she had a difficult time with the birth of her child

Problematik [proble'ma:tɪk] **die; ~** *(Schwierigkeit)* problematic nature; *(Probleme)* problems *pl.*

problematisch *Adj.* problematic[al]

problematisieren *tr. V.* **etw. ~:** expound the problems of sth.

problem-, Problem-: ~bewußtsein das awareness of the problem/problems **(für** of); **~film der** serious film; **~kind das** problem child; **~los 1.** *Adj.* problem-free; **2.** *adv.* without any problems; **~stellung die** way of looking at *or* posing a problem/problems; *(zu erörterndes Thema)* problem; **~stück das** problem play

Produkt [pro'dʊkt] **das; ~[e]s, ~e** *(auch Math., fig.)* product; **~e der Landwirtschaft** agricultural produce *sing. or* products; **das ~ aus fünf mal zwei** the product of five times two

Produkten-: ~börse die *(Wirtsch.) s.* **Warenbörse; ~handel der** *(Kaufmannsspr.)* trade in agricultural commodities

Produktion [prodʊk'tsi̯o:n] **die; ~, ~en** production; **die ~ steigern/stoppen** increase/stop production

Produktions-: ~ab·lauf der production process; **~ab·teilung die** production department; **~an·lage die;** *meist Pl.* production unit; **~anlagen** production plant *sing.*; **~aus·fall der** loss of production; **~brigade die** *(DDR)* production brigade; **~genossenschaft die** *(DDR)* co-operative; **eine landwirtschaftliche ~genossenschaft** a collective farm; **~güter** *Pl. (Wirtsch.)* producer goods; **~kosten** *Pl.* production costs; **~leistung die** output; **~leiter der** production manager; **~mittel** *Pl. (marx.)* means of production; **~prozeß der** production process; **~verfahren das** production process; **~verhältnisse** *Pl. (marx.)* relations of production; **~weise die** production methods *pl.*; **~ziffern** *Pl.* production figures; **~zweig der** branch of production

produktiv [prodʊk'ti:f] **1.** productive; prolific ⟨*writer, artist, etc.*⟩. **2.** *adv.* ⟨*work, co-operate*⟩ productively

Produktivität [prodʊktivi'tɛ:t] **die; ~:** productivity

Produktiv·kraft die *(marx.)* productive force; force of production

Produzent [produ'tsɛnt] **der; ~en, ~en, Produzentin die; ~, ~nen** producer

produzieren 1. *tr. V.* **a)** *auch itr. (herstellen)* produce; **b)** *(ugs.: hervorbringen)* make ⟨*bow, noise*⟩; come up with ⟨*excuse, report*⟩. **2.** *refl. V. (ugs.: großtun)* show off

Prof. *Abk.* **Professor** Prof.

profan [pro'fa:n] **1.** *Adj.* **a)** *nicht präd. (weltlich)* profane; secular; secular ⟨*building*⟩; **b)** *(alltäglich)* mundane. **2.** *adv. (alltäglich)* mundanely; in a mundane way

Profan·bau der; *Pl.* **~bauten** *(Archit., Kunstwiss.)* secular building

profanieren *tr. V. (geh.)* **a)** *(entweihen)* profane; **b)** *(säkularisieren)* secularize

Profession [profɛ'si̯o:n] **die; ~, ~en** *(österr., sonst veralt.)* occupation; *(akademische, wissenschaftliche, medizinische ~)* profession; *(handwerkliche ~)* trade

Professionalismus [profɛsi̯ona'lɪsmʊs] **der; ~:** professionalism

professionell [profɛsi̯o'nɛl] **1.** *Adj.* professional. **2.** *adv.* professionally

Professor [pro'fɛsɔr] **der; ~s, ~en** [-'so:rən] **a)** *(Hochschul~)* professor; **ordentlicher ~:** [full] professor *(holding a chair)*; **außerordentlicher ~:** extraordinary professor *(not holding a chair)*; **außerplanmäßiger ~:** supernumerary professor; *s. auch* **zerstreut 1; b)** *(österr., sonst veralt.: Gymnasial~)* [grammar school] teacher; **Herr ~!** sir!

-professor der a) professor of ⟨*history, mathematics, etc.*⟩; **b)** *(österr., sonst veralt.: -lehrer)* ⟨*history, mathematics, etc.*⟩ teacher *(at a Gymnasium)*

professoral [profɛso'ra:l] *(auch abwertend) Adj.* professorial

Professorenschaft die; ~: professoriate

Professorin [profɛ'so:rɪn] **die; ~, ~nen a)** *(Hochschul~)* professor; *s. auch* **-in; b)** *(österr.: Studienrätin)* mistress

Professur [profɛ'su:ɐ̯] **die; ~, ~en** professorship, chair **(für** in)

Profi der; ~s, ~s *(ugs.)* pro *(coll.)*

Profi·fußball der; *o. Pl.* professional football

profihaft 1. *Adj.* professional. **2.** *adv.* professionally

Profil [pro'fi:l] **das; ~s, ~e a)** *(Seitenansicht)* profile; **im ~:** in profile; **b)** *(von Reifen, Schuhsohlen)* tread; **c)** *(ausgeprägte Eigenart)* image; **kein ~ haben** *od.* **besitzen** lack a distinctive image; **d)** *(Geol.)* profile

Profi·lager das *(Sportjargon)* **ins ~ überwechseln** turn professional

profilieren 1. *refl. V.* make one's name *or* mark; *(sich unterscheiden)* give oneself a clearer image. **2.** *tr. V.* profile ⟨*moulding, frame, etc.*⟩; put a tread on ⟨*tyre, shoe*⟩

profiliert *Adj.* **a)** *(markant, bedeutend)* prominent; **b) eine grob ~e Gummisohle** a rubber sole with a heavy tread

Profilierung die; ~, ~en a) *s.* **Profil a; b)** *(Unterscheidung)* image; **die politische ~ einer Gruppe** the political complexion of a group

profil-, Profil-: ~los *Adj.* ⟨*politican, writer*⟩ lacking any distinctive image; **~neurose die** neurosis about one's image; **~sohle die** treaded sole; **~stahl der** *(Technik)* sectional steel; **~träger der** *(Technik)* sectional beam

Profi-: ~spieler der professional player; **~sport der** professional sport

Profit [pro'fi:t] **der; ~[e]s, ~e** profit; **etw. mit ~ verkaufen** sell sth. at a profit; **aus etw. ~ ziehen** *od.* **herausschlagen** turn sth. to one's profit *or* advantage; **~ machen** make a profit; **mit/ohne ~ arbeiten** run/not run at a profit

profitabel [profi'ta:bl̩] **1.** *Adj.* profitable. **2.** *adv.* profitably

profit-, Profit-: ~bringend *s.* **profitabel; ~gier die** *(abwertend)* greed for profit; **~gierig** *Adj. (abwertend)* greedy for profit *postpos.;* profit-seeking

profitieren 1. *itr. V.* profit **(von, bei** *by*); *(fig.)* profit, gain **(von, bei, an** + *Dat.* from, by); **ich kann dabei nur ~:** I can't lose. **2.** *tr. V.* **er hat bei diesem Geschäft nichts/wenig profitiert** he did not make a profit/much of a profit on the deal

Profit-: ~jäger der profiteer; **~maximierung die** the maximization of profits; **~rate die** *(Wirtsch., marx.)* rate of profit; **~streben das** *(abwertend)* profit-seeking

pro forma [pro: 'fɔrma] *Adv.* **a)** *(der Form halber)* as a matter of form; **b)** *(zum Schein)* for the sake of appearances

profund [pro'fʊnt] *Adj. (geh.)* profound; deep

Prognose [pro'gno:zə] **die; ~, ~n** *(auch Med.)* prognosis; *(Wetter~, Wirtschafts~)* forecast; **eine ~ stellen** make a prognosis/give *or* make a forecast

prognostizieren [prognɔsti'tsi:rən] *tr. V. (geh.)* forecast; predict

Programm [pro'gram] **das; ~s, ~e a)** programme; program *(Amer., Computing); (Theater~ auch)* bill; *(bei Pferderennen)* card; *(Verlags~)* list; *(Ferns.: Sender)* channel; **das ~ für die kommende Woche** *(Ferns., Rundfunk)* the programmes *pl.* for the coming week; **etw. paßt jmdm. nicht ins** *od.* **in sein ~:** sth. doesn't fit in with sb.'s plans; **nach ~** *(fig.)* according to plan; **auf jmds./dem ~ stehen** *(fig.)* be on sb.'s/the programme *or* agenda; **auf dem ~ stehen** *(bei einer Sitzung, Versammlung)* be on the agenda; **b)** *(Kaufmannsspr.: Sortiment)* range

-programm das programme; program *(Amer., Computing);* **Besuchs~:** programme of visits

Programm·änderung die change of programme

Programmatik [progra'ma:tɪk] **die; ~, ~en** *(Politik)* [political] objectives *pl.*

programmatisch 1. *Adj.* programmatic ⟨*speech, statement*⟩; **die ~en Ziele/Absichten der Regierung** the aims of the government's programme. **2.** *adv.* **die ~ festgelegten Ziele der Partei** the aims laid down in the party's programme

programm-, Programm-: ~direktor der *(Ferns.)* director of programmes; **~folge die** *(Ferns.)* order of programmes; *(einer Show)* order of acts; running order; **~gemäß 1.** *Adj.* **die ~gemäße Abfolge der Darbietungen** the order of acts as stated in the programme; **2.** *adv.* according to programme *or* plan; **~gestaltung die** programme planning; **~heft das** programme; **~hinweis der** programme announcement

programmieren *tr. V.* **a)** *(DV)* program; **b)** *(auf etw. festlegen)* programme; condition; **auf Erfolg programmiert sein** be geared to achieving success; **c)** *(nach einem Programm ansetzen)* schedule

Programmierer der; ~s, ~, Programmiererin die; ~, ~nen *(DV)* programmer

Programmier·sprache die *(DV)* programming language

Programmierung die; ~, ~en *s.* **programmieren a–c:** programming; conditioning; scheduling

Programm·punkt der item on the programme; *(bei einer Sitzung)* item on the agenda

Programmusik die programme music

Programm-: ~vor·schau die *(im Fernsehen)* preview [of the week's/evening's *etc.* viewing]; *(im Kino)* trailers *pl.;* **~zeitschrift die** the radio and television magazine; **~zettel der** programme

Progression [progrɛ'sio:n] **die; ~, ~en** *(Steuerw.)* progressive tax system; **in die ~ kommen** move into a higher tax bracket

progressiv [progrɛ'si:f] **1.** *Adj.* progressive. **2.** *adv.* progressively; **er schreibt sehr ~:** he's a very progressive writer; **sie erziehen ihre Kinder sehr ~:** they are giving their children a very modern upbringing

Progressiv·steuer die *(Steuerw.)* progressive tax

Prohibition [prohibi'tsio:n] **die; ~:** prohibition

Projekt [pro'jɛkt] **das; ~[e]s, ~e** project

Projekt·gruppe die project team *or* group

projektieren *tr. V. (entwerfen)* draw up the plans for; plan; *(planen)* project; plan

Projektil [projɛk'ti:l] **das; ~s, ~e** projectile

Projektion [projɛk'tsio:n] **die; ~, ~en** *(Optik, Math., Geogr., Psych.)* projection

Projektions-: ~apparat der projector; **~ebene die** *(Math.)* plane of projection; **~wand die** projection screen

Projekt·leiter der project leader

Projektor [pro'jɛktɔr] **der; ~s, ~en** [-'to:rən] projector

Projekt·planung die project planning

projizieren [proji'tsi:rən] *tr. V. (Optik, Math., Psych.)* project

Proklamation [proklama'tsio:n] **die; ~, ~en** proclamation

proklamieren *tr. V.* proclaim

Pro-Kopf- per head *or* capita *postpos.*

Prokrustes·bett [pro'krʊstɛs-] **das;** *o. Pl. (geh.)* Procrustean bed

Prokura [pro'ku:ra] **die; ~, Prokuren** *(Kaufmannsspr.)* [full] power of attorney; procuration *(formal)*

Prokurist [proku'rɪst] **der; ~en, ~en, Prokuristin die; ~, ~nen** ≈ authorized signatory; **~ bei einer Firma sein** ≈ have [full] signing powers in a firm

Prolet [pro'le:t] **der; ~en, ~en a)** *(abwertend: ungebildeter Mensch)* peasant; boor; **b)** *(ugs. veralt.: Proletarier)* prole *(coll.)*

Proletariat [proleta'ria:t] **das; ~[e]s** proletariat

Proletarier [prole'ta:riɐ] **der; ~s, ~:** proletarian

proletarisch 1. *Adj.* proletarian. **2.** *adv.* ⟨*think, behave*⟩ like a proletarian

proletarisieren *tr. V.* proletarianize

proletenhaft *(abwertend)* **1.** *Adj.* boorish. **2.** *adv.* boorishly

Prolog [pro'lo:k] **der; ~[e]s, ~e** *(auch Radsport)* prologue

Prolongation [prolɔŋga'tsio:n] **die; ~, ~en a)** *(Wirtsch.)* renewal; **b)** *(bes. österr.)* prolonging; *(eines Vertrages)* extension

prolongieren *tr. V.* **a)** *(Wirtsch.: stunden)* renew; **b)** *(bes. österr.: verlängern)* extend ⟨*contract, engagement*⟩

Promenade [promə'na:də] **die; ~, ~n** promenade

Promenaden-: ~deck das promenade deck; **~konzert das** promenade concert; **~mischung die** *(scherzh.)* mongrel

promenieren *itr. V.; auch mit sein (geh.)* promenade

prometheisch [prome'te:ɪʃ] *(geh.)* **1.** *Adj.* Promethean. **2.** *adv.* like Prometheus

Promille [pro'mɪlə] **das; ~s, ~ a)** *(Tausendstel)* **ein Blutalkoholgehalt von zwei ~:** a blood alcohol level of two parts per thousand; **bei 0,4/unter einem ~ liegen** be 0.4/less than one in a *or* per thousand; **b)** *(ugs.: Blutalkohol)* alcohol level; **Ich fahre! Du hast zuviel ~:** I'll drive. You're over the limit; **er fährt nur ohne ~:** he never drinks and drives

Promille·grenze die legal [alcohol] limit

prominent [promi'nɛnt] *Adj.* prominent

Prominente der/die; *adj. Dekl.* prominent figure

Prominenz [promi'nɛnts] **die; ~:** prominent figures *pl.; (das Prominentsein)* prominence; **er gehört zur politischen ~** he is a prominent political figure

Promiskuität [promiskui'tɛ:t] **die; ~:** promiscuity

[1]Promotion [promo'tsio:n] **die; ~, ~en a)** *(Erlangung der Doktorwürde)* gaining of a/one's doctorate; **er schloß sein Studium mit der ~ ab** he completed his studies by gaining *or* obtaining his doctorate; **jmds. ~ [zum Doktor der Philosophie] feiern** celebrate the award of a doctorate *or* Ph.D. to sb.; **b)** *(österr.: offizielle Feier)* [doctoral] degree ceremony; **seine ~ zum Doktor der Philosophie** his Ph.D. ceremony

[2]Promotion [prə'moʊʃən] **die; ~** *(Wirtsch.)* promotion; **für etw. ~ machen** promote sth.

promovieren [promo'vi:rən] **1.** *itr. V.* **a)** *(die Doktorwürde erlangen)* gain *or* obtain a/one's doctorate; **b)** *(eine Dissertation schreiben)* do a doctorate **(über** + *Akk.* on). **2.** *tr. V.* confer a doctorate *or* the degree of doctor on

prompt [prɔmpt] **1.** *Adj.* prompt. **2.** *adv.* **a)** *(umgehend)* promptly; **b)** *(ugs., meist iron.: wie erwartet)* [and] sure enough; **er ist auf den Trick ~ hereingefallen** and sure enough he fell for the trick; **„Gleich fällt er", dachte ich, und ~ fiel er** 'He's going to fall,' I thought and sure enough he did; **er wird ~ in die Falle hineinlaufen** as sure as fate he'll fall into the trap

Promptheit die; ~: promptness

Pronomen [pro'no:mən] **das; ~s, ~** *od.* **Pronomina** [pro'no:mina] *(Sprachw.)* pronoun

pronominal [pronomi'na:l] *(Sprachw.)* **1.** *Adj.* pronominal. **2.** *adv.* pronominally

Pronominal- *(Sprachw.)* pronominal

prononciert [pronõ'si:ɐ̯t] *(geh.)* **1.** *Adj.* pronounced, definite, decided ⟨*opinion, views*⟩; staunch, determined ⟨*supporter, advocate, etc.*⟩. **2.** *adv. (entschieden)* clearly; **sich ~ über etw.** *(Akk.)* **äußern** express a definite opinion on sth.

Propädeutik [propɛ'dɔytɪk] **die; ~, ~en** *(Wissensch.)* **a)** *o. Pl.* preparatory instruction *no indef. art.;* **die philosophische ~:** philosophical propaedeutics *pl.;* **b)** *(Lehrbuch)* introductory textbook **(zu** on)

propädeutisch *Adj. (Wissensch.)* propaedeutic

Propaganda [propa'ganda] **die; ~: a)** *(auch fig. ugs.)* propaganda; **b)** *(Reklame)* publicity

Propaganda-: ~apparat der propaganda machine; **~feld·zug der** propaganda campaign; **~minister der** minister of propaganda; **~sender der** *(abwertend) (Rundf.)* propaganda station; *(Ferns.)* propaganda channel

Propagandist der; ~en, ~en, Propagandistin die; ~, ~nen a) propagandist; **b)** *(Wirtsch.: Werbefachmann/-frau)* demonstrator; *(Vertreter)* representative

propagandistisch 1. *Adj.* propagandist; propaganda *attrib.* ⟨*purposes, measures, success, effort*⟩. **2.** *adv.* ⟨*use, distort, etc.*⟩ for propaganda purposes

propagieren *tr. V. (geh.)* propagate ⟨*idea, view, belief, etc.*⟩; **ein vereinigtes Europa ~:** propagate the idea of a united Europe

Propan [pro'pa:n] **das**, ~s, **Propan·gas das**; *o. Pl.* propane
Propeller [pro'pɛlɐ] **der**; ~s, ~ **a)** propeller; airscrew; prop *(coll.)*; **b)** *(Seew.: Schiffsschraube)* propeller; screw
Propeller-: ~**an·trieb der** propeller drive; **mit ~antrieb** propeller-driven; ~**flug·zeug das** propeller-driven aircraft
proper ['prɔpɐ] **1.** *Adj.* **a)** *(adrett)* smart; **b)** *(ordentlich und sauber)* neat and tidy; **c)** *(sorgfältig, genau)* meticulous. **2.** *adv.* **a)** *(ordentlich und sauber)* neatly and tidily; **b)** *(sorgfältig, genau)* meticulously
Prophet [pro'fe:t] **der**; ~en, ~en prophet; **ich bin doch kein ~!** *(ugs.)* I can't see into the future!; **der ~ gilt nichts in seinem Vaterland[e]** *(Spr.)* a prophet is without honour in his own country; *s. auch* **Bart a; Berg a**
Prophetin die; ~, ~nen prophetess
prophetisch 1. *Adj.* prophetic. **2.** *adv.* prophetically
prophezeien [profe'tsaiən] *tr. V.* prophesy (*Dat.* for); predict ⟨*result, weather*⟩; **das kann ich dir ~!** I can promise you that!
Prophezeiung die; ~, ~en *s.* **prophezeien**: prophecy; prediction
prophylaktisch [profy'laktɪʃ] *(Med.)* **1.** *Adj.* prophylactic. **2.** *adv.* prophylactically; as a prophylactic measure
Prophylaxe [profy'laksə] **die**; ~, ~n *(Med.)* prophylaxis
Proportion [propɔr'tsio:n] **die**; ~, ~en *(auch Math., Musik)* proportion
proportional [propɔrtsio'na:l] *(auch Math.)* **1.** *Adj.* proportional; **umgekehrt ~ zu ...**: in inverse proportion to ...; *(Math. auch)* inversely proportional to ... **2.** *adv.* proportionally; in proportion; ~ **[zu** *od.* **mit] einer Sache** *(Dat.)* in proportion to sth.
proportioniert [propɔrtsio'ni:ɐt] *Adj.* proportioned
Proporz [pro'pɔrts] **der**; ~es, ~e *(Politik)* proportional representation *no art.*; **Ämter im** *od.* **nach dem ~ besetzen** fill posts in proportion to the number of votes received
Proporz·wahl die *(bes. österr. u. schweiz.) s.* **Verhältniswahl**
Proppen ['prɔpn̩] **der**; ~s, ~: **a)** *(nordd.) s.* **Pfropfen**; **b)** *(ugs.: Kind)* podge *(coll.)*
proppen·voll *(ugs.) Adj.* jam-packed *(coll.)*
Propst [pro:pst] **der**; ~[e]s, **Pröpste** ['prø:pstə] *(kath., ev. Kirche)* provost
Pro·rektor der *(Hochschulw.)* ≈ pro-vice-chancellor
Prosa ['pro:za] **die**; ~: prose
prosaisch 1. *Adj.* **a)** *(geh., oft abwertend: nüchtern)* prosaic; plain ⟨*building*⟩; **b)** *(veralt.: in Prosa abgefaßt)* prose *attrib.* **2.** *adv.* *(geh., oft abwertend)* prosaically
Prosaist der; ~en, ~en, **Prosaistin die**; ~, ~nen prose-writer
Proselyt [proze'ly:t] **der**; ~en, ~en proselyte; ~**en machen** *(geh. abwertend)* proselytize
Pro·seminar das *(Hochschulw.)* introductory seminar course *(for students in their first and second year)*
prosit ['pro:zɪt] *Interj.* your [very good] health; ~ **Neujahr!** happy New Year!
Prosit das; ~s, ~s toast; **ein ~ dem Geburtstagskind!** here's to the birthday boy/girl!
Prosodie [prozo'di:] **die**; ~, ~n *(Verslehre)* prosody
Prospekt [pro'spɛkt] **der** *od.* *(bes. österr.)* **das** ~[e]s, ~e **a)** *(Werbeschrift)* brochure; *(Werbezettel)* leaflet; *(Verlags~)* illustrated catalogue; *(nur mit Neuerscheinungen)* seasonal list; **b)** *(Theater: Bühnenbild)* backdrop; backcloth; **c)** *(bild. Kunst: Ansicht)* perspective view; **d)** *(Wirtsch.)* prospectus
prospektiv [prospɛk'ti:f] *Adj.*; *nicht präd.* prospective
prosperieren [prospe'ri:rən] *itr. V.* *(geh.)* prosper; ⟨*art, science*⟩ prosper, flourish
Prosperität [prosperi'tɛ:t] **die**; ~ *(geh.)* prosperity
prost [pro:st] *Interj.* *(ugs.)* cheers *(Brit. coll.)*; **na denn** *od.* **dann ~!** *(ugs. iron.)* that's brilliant! *(coll. iron.)*; *s. auch* **Mahlzeit**
Prost das; ~[e]s, ~e *(ugs.) s.* **Prosit**
Prostata ['prɔstata] **die**; ~, **Prostatae** ['prɔstatɛ] *(Anat.)* prostate [gland]
prosten *itr. V.* say cheers *(Brit. coll.)*
Prösterchen ['prø:stɛçən] *Interj.* *(fam.)* cheers *(Brit. coll.)*
prostituieren [prostitu'i:rən] **1.** *tr. V.* *(geh.)* prostitute. **2.** *refl. V.* *(auch fig., geh.)* prostitute oneself; **sich als Künstler ~** *(fig. geh.)* prostitute one's artistic talent
Prostituierte die/der; *adj. Dekl.* prostitute
Prostitution [prostitu'tsio:n] **die**; ~ *(auch fig. geh.)* prostitution *no art.*
Proszenium [pro'stse:nium] **das**; ~s, **Proszenien** *(Theater)* proscenium
Protagonist [protago'nɪst] **der**; ~en, ~en, **Protagonistin die**; ~, ~nen *(geh.)* protagonist
Protegé [prote'ʒe:] **der**; ~s, ~s *(geh.)* protégé
protegieren [prote'ʒi:rən] *tr. V.* *(geh.)* sponsor; patronize ⟨*artist, composer, etc.*⟩
Protein [prote'i:n] **das**; ~s, ~e *(Biochemie)* protein
Protektion [protɛk'tsio:n] **die**; ~, ~en *(geh.)* patronage *no indef. art.*
Protektionismus der; ~ *(Wirtsch.)* protectionism *no art.*
Protektorat [protɛkto'ra:t] **das**; ~[e]s, ~e **a)** *(geh.: Schirmherrschaft)* patronage; **b)** *(Völkerr.: Schutzherrschaft, Schutzgebiet)* protectorate
Protest [pro'tɛst] **der**; ~[e]s, ~e **a)** protest; **[bei jmdm.] ~ gegen jmdn./etw. erheben** *od.* **einlegen** make a protest [to sb.] against sb./sth.; **etw. aus ~ tun** do sth. as a *or* in protest; **unter [lautem] ~**: protesting [loudly]; **b)** *(Finanzw.)* protest; **der Wechsel ist zu ~ gegangen** the bill has been protested; **c)** *(DDR Rechtsw.)* protest
Protest·aktion die protest campaign
Protestant [protɛs'tant] **der**; ~en, ~en, **Protestantin die**; ~, ~nen Protestant
protestantisch 1. *Adj.* Protestant. **2.** *adv.* **[streng] ~ erzogen sein** have had a [strict] Protestant upbringing
Protestantismus der; ~: Protestantism *no art.*
Protest-: ~**bewegung die** protest movement; ~**demonstration die** protest demonstration
protestieren 1. *itr. V.* protest, make a protest (**gegen** against, about). **2.** *tr. V.* *(Finanzw.)* protest
Protest-: ~**kundgebung die** protest rally; ~**marsch der** protest march; ~**note die** *(Dipl.)* protest note; ~**ruf der** shout of protest; ~**sänger der** protest singer; ~**song der** protest song; ~**streik der** protest strike; ~**sturm der** storm of protest; ~**versammlung die** protest meeting; ~**welle die** wave of protest
Prothese [pro'te:zə] **die**; ~, ~n **a)** artificial limb; prosthesis *(Med.)*; **b)** *(Zahn~)* set of dentures; dentures *pl.*; prosthesis *(Med.)*
Protokoll [proto'kɔl] **das**; ~s, ~e **a)** *(wörtlich mitgeschrieben)* transcript; *(Ergebnis~)* minutes *pl.*; *(bei Gericht)* record; records *pl.*; *(einer Verhandlung auf diplomatischer Ebene)* protocol; **[das] ~ führen** make a transcript [of the proceedings]; *(bei einer Sitzung Notizen machen)* take *or* keep the minutes; **etw. zu ~ geben/zu ~ geben, daß ...**: make a statement about sth./to the effect that ...; **zu ~ nehmen** take down ⟨*statement etc.*⟩; *(bei Gericht)* enter ⟨*objection, statement*⟩ in the record; **b)** *(diplomatisches Zeremoniell)* protocol; **c)** *(Strafzettel)* ticket
Protokollant [protokɔ'lant] **der**; ~en, ~en, **Protokollantin die**; ~, ~nen transcript writer; *(eines Ergebnisprotokolls)* keeper of the minutes; *(bei Gericht)* court reporter
protokollarisch [protokɔ'la:rɪʃ] **1.** *Adj.* **a)** *nicht präd.* *(in Form, auf Grund eines Protokolls)* on record *postpos.*; *(bei einer Sitzung)* minuted; **b)** *(das diplomatische Zeremoniell betreffend)* **die ~en Vorschriften** the rules of protocol. **2.** *adv.* **a)** *(in Form, auf Grund eines Protokolls)* **etw. ~ niederschreiben** *(bei einer Sitzung)* take sth. down in the minutes; *(bei Gericht)* enter sth. in the *or* place sth. on record; **b)** *(das diplomatische Zeremoniell betreffend)* from the point of view of protocol
Protokoll-: ~**chef der** Chief of Protocol; ~**führer der** *s.* **Protokollant**
protokollieren 1. *tr. V.* take down; minute, take the minutes of ⟨*meeting*⟩; minute, record in the minutes ⟨*remark*⟩. **2.** *itr. V.* *(bei einer Sitzung)* take *or* keep the minutes; *(bei Gericht)* keep the record; *(bei polizeilicher Vernehmung)* keep a record
Proton ['pro:tɔn] **das**; ~s, ~en [-'to:nən] *(Physik)* proton
Proto·plasma [proto'plasma] **das**; *o. Pl.* *(Biol.)* protoplasm
Proto·typ ['pro:toty:p] **der a)** *(geh.: Inbegriff)* archetype; epitome; **b)** *(Urform, erste Ausführung, Motorsport)* prototype
Protozoon [proto'tso:ɔn] **das**; ~s, ...**zoen** *(Biol.)* protozoan
Protz [prɔts] **der**; ~en *od.* ~es, ~en *(ugs.)* **a)** *(Angeber)* swank[pot] *(coll.)*; show-off; **b)** *(Prunk)* swank *(coll.)*; show
-protz der *(ugs.)* **Bildungs~/Sex[ual]~** *usw.* swank[pot] *(coll.)* when it comes to education/sex *etc.*; **Muskel~**: muscleman
protzen *itr. V.* *(ugs.)* swank *(coll.)*; show off; **mit etw. ~**: show sth. off
Protzerei die; ~, ~en *(ugs.)* **a)** *o. Pl.* *(das Protzen)* swanking *(coll.)*; showing off; **b)** *(protzige Äußerung)* swanky remark *(coll.)*
protzig *(ugs. abwertend)* **1.** *Adj.* swanky *(coll.)*; showy. **2.** *adv.* swankily *(coll.)*
Provenienz [prove'niɛnts] **die**; ~, ~en *(geh.)* provenance
provenzalisch [provɛn'tsa:lɪʃ] *Adj.* Provençal
Proviant [pro'viant] **der**; ~s, ~e provisions *pl.*; ~ **[für die Reise] mitnehmen** take some food for the journey
Provinz [pro'vɪnts] **die**; ~, ~en **a)** *(Verwaltungsbezirk)* province; **b)** *o. Pl.* *(oft abwertend: kulturell rückständige Gegend)* **aus der ~ kommen/in der ~ leben** come from/live in the provinces *pl.*; **finsterste** *od.* **hinterste ~ sein** be terribly provincial
Provinz-: ~**bewohner der** *(oft abwertend)* provincial; ~**blatt das** *(abwertend)* provincial [news]paper; local rag *(derog.)*
Provinzialismus [provɪntsia'lɪsmʊs] **der**; ~, **Provinzialismen a)** *(Sprachw.)* provincialism; **b)** *o. Pl.* *(abwertend)* provincialism
provinziell [provɪn'tsiɛl] *(meist abwertend)* **1.** *Adj.* provincial; parochial ⟨*views*⟩. **2.** *adv.* provincially
Provinzler [pro'vɪntslɐ] **der**; ~s, ~ *(ugs. abwertend)* [narrow-minded] provincial
Provinz-: ~**nest das** *(ugs. abwertend)* [tiny] provincial backwater; ~**stadt die** provincial town
Provision [provi'zio:n] **die**; ~, ~en *(Kaufmannsspr.)* commission; **auf** *od.* **gegen ~ arbeiten** work on a commission basis
provisorisch [provi'zo:rɪʃ] **1.** *Adj.* temporary ⟨*accommodation, filling, bridge, etc.*⟩; provisional ⟨*status, capital, etc.*⟩; provisional, caretaker *attrib.* ⟨*government*⟩; provisional, temporary ⟨*measure, regulation, etc.*⟩; **bei uns ist alles noch sehr ~**: everything's still very makeshift in our house/flat *etc.* **2.** *adv.* temporarily; **etw. ~ reparieren** do *or* effect a temporary repair on sth.
Provisorium [provi'zo:rium] **das**; ~s, **Provisorien** *(geh.)* temporary measure

provokant [provo'kant] *(geh.) s.* **provokativ**
Provokateur [provoka'tø:ɐ] **der; ~s, ~e** agent provocateur; agitator
Provokation [provoka'tsi̯o:n] **die; ~, ~en** provocation
provokativ [provoka'ti:f], **provokatorisch** [provoka'to:rɪʃ] *(geh.)* **1.** *Adj.* provocative. **2.** *adv.* provocatively
provozieren [provo'tsi:rən] **1.** *tr. V.* **a)** *(herausfordern)* provoke; **b)** *(auslösen)* provoke; cause ⟨*accident, fight*⟩. **2.** *itr. V.* be provocative; **zum Nachdenken [über etw.** *(Akk.)*] **~:** provoke people into thinking [about sth.]
Prozedur [protse'du:ɐ] **die; ~, ~en** *(auch DV)* procedure
Prozent [pro'tsɛnt] **das; ~[e]s, ~e a)** *nach Zahlenangaben Pl. ungebeugt (Hundertstel)* per cent *sing.*; **fünf ~:** five per cent; **ich bin mir zu 90 ~ sicher** I'm 90 per cent certain; **der Plan wurde zu 90 ~ erfüllt** 90 per cent of the plan was fulfilled; **etw. in ~en ausdrücken** express sth. as a percentage; **60 ~ Alkohol enthalten** contain 60 per cent alcohol by volume; be 105 per cent proof; **b)** *Pl. (ugs.: Gewinnanteil)* share *sing.* of the profits; *(Rabatt)* discount *sing.*; **auf etw.** *(Akk.)* **~e bekommen** get a discount on sth.
-prozentig *adj.* -per-cent
Prozent-: ~punkt der percentage point; **~rechnung die** percentage calculation; **~satz der** percentage; **zu einem beträchtlichen ~satz** be to a considerable extent
prozentual [protsɛn'tu̯a:l] **1.** *Adj.; nicht präd.* percentage; **der ~e Anteil der Autobesitzer an der Bevölkerung** the percentage of car-owners in the population. **2.** *adv.* **~ am Gewinn beteiligt sein** have a percentage share in the profits
Prozeß [pro'tsɛs] **der; Prozesses, Prozesse a)** trial; *(Fall)* [court] case; **jmdm. den ~ machen** take sb. to court; **es wurde ihm wegen der Ermordung von X der ~ gemacht** he stood trial charged with the murder of X; **der ~ Meyer gegen Schulze** the case of Meyer versus Schulze; **einen ~ gewinnen/verlieren** win/lose a case *or* lawsuit; *s. auch* **anstrengen 2 c; führen 1 c; b)** *(Entwicklung, Ablauf)* process; **c)** *(fig.)* **mit jmdm./etw. kurzen ~ machen** *(ugs.)* make short work of sb./sth.; **jetzt wird kurzer ~ gemacht** *(ugs.)* we're going to sort this out once and for all
prozeß-, Prozeß-: ~bevollmächtigte der/die *(Rechtsspr.)* person with power of attorney in legal proceedings; **~führend** *Adj. (Rechtsspr.)* **die ~führenden Parteien** the litigants; **~gegner der** *(Rechtsspr.)* opposing party
prozessieren *itr. V.* go to court; **mit jmdm. um etw.** *od.* **wegen etw. ~:** be engaged in a court action *or* lawsuit with sb. about sth.; **gegen jmdn. ~:** bring an action *or* a lawsuit against sb.; *(seit längerer Zeit)* be engaged in an action *or* a lawsuit against sb.
Prozession [protsɛ'si̯o:n] **die; ~, ~en** procession
Prozeß·kosten *Pl.* legal costs
Prozessor [pro'tsɛsɔr] **der; ~s, ~en** [-'so:rən] *(DV)* [central] processor
Prozeß-: ~ordnung die *(Rechtsw.)* code of procedure; **~rechner der** *(DV)* process-control computer; **~recht das;** *o. Pl. (Rechtsw.)* procedural law; **~vollmacht die** *(Rechtsw.)* power of attorney in legal proceedings; **~wärme die** *(Kerntechnik)* process heat
prüde ['pry:də] *(abwertend)* **1.** *Adj.* prudish. **2.** prudishly; **~ erzogen worden sein** have had a prudish upbringing
Prüderie [pry:də'ri:] **die; ~** *(abwertend)* prudery; prudishness
prüfen ['pry:fn̩] *tr. V.* **a)** *auch itr.* test ⟨*pupil*⟩ **(in +** *Dat.* in); *(beim Examen)* examine ⟨*pupil, student, etc.*⟩ **(in +** *Dat.* in); **ein geprüfter Elektrotechniker** a qualified electrician; **mündlich/schriftlich geprüft werden** have an oral/a written test/examination; **Latein/Anatomie ~:** be the examiner for Latin/Anatomy; **jmds. Kenntnisse ~:** test sb.'s knowledge; **b)** *(untersuchen)* examine **(auf +** *Akk.* for); check, examine ⟨*device, machine, calculation*⟩ **(auf +** *Akk.* for); investigate, look into ⟨*complaint*⟩; *(testen)* test **(auf +** *Akk.* for); test, inspect ⟨*goods, materials, food*⟩; test, check ⟨*temperature*⟩; **einen Fall nochmals ~:** re-examine a case; **c)** *(kontrollieren)* check ⟨*papers, passport, application, calculation, information, correctness, etc.*⟩; audit, check, examine ⟨*accounts, books*⟩; **d)** *(vor einer Entscheidung)* check ⟨*price*⟩; examine ⟨*offer*⟩; consider ⟨*application*⟩; **drum prüfe, wer sich ewig bindet** *(Spr.)* marry in haste, repent at leisure *(prov.)*; **e)** *(forschend ansehen)* scrutinize; **jmdn. ~d** *od.* **mit ~den Blicken ansehen** scrutinize sb.; **f)** *(geh.: großen Belastungen aussetzen)* try; **sie ist vom Leben schwer geprüft worden** her life has been a hard trial; **g)** *(Sport: stark fordern)* test. **3.** *refl. V.* search one's heart
Prüfer der; ~s, ~, Prüferin die; ~, ~nen a) tester; inspector; *(Buch~)* auditor; **b)** *(im Examen)* examiner
Prüf·gerät das *(Technik)* piece of test equipment; test instrument
Prüfling ['pry:flɪŋ] **der; ~s, ~e** examinee; [examination] candidate
Prüf-: ~stand der *(Technik)* test bed; test stand; **auf dem ~stand** *(fig.)* under the microscope *(fig.)*; **~stein der** touchstone **(für** for, of); measure **(für** of); **~stück das** test-piece; [test] specimen
Prüfung die; ~, ~en a) *(Examen)* examination; exam *(coll.)*; **eine ~ machen** *od.* **ablegen** take *or* do an examination; **b)** *(das [Über]prüfen) s.* **prüfen b–d:** examination; investigation; inspection; *(Kontrolle)* check; *(das Kontrollieren)* checking *no indef. art.*; *(Test)* test; *(das Testen)* testing *no indef. art.*; **klinische ~en** clinical trials; **nach/bei ~ Ihrer Beschwerde** after/on examining *or* investigating your complaint; **nach nochmaliger ~ Ihres Antrags** on reconsidering your application; **c)** *(geh.: schicksalhafte Belastung)* trial
Prüfungs-: ~angst die examination phobia; *(im Einzelfall)* examination nerves *pl.*; **~arbeit die** examination; exam *(coll.)*; **~auf·gabe die** problem set in an/the examination; **~aus·schuß der** board of examiners; **~ergebnis das** examination result; **~kandidat der** [examination] candidate; **~ordnung die** examination regulations *pl.*; **~termin der** date of an/the examination; **~unterlagen** *Pl.* documents required on entering for an/the examination
Prüf·verfahren das test procedure
Prügel ['pry:gl̩] **der; ~s, ~ a)** *(Knüppel)* stick; cudgel; **b)** *Pl. (Schläge)* beating *sing.*; *(als Strafe für Kinder)* hiding *(coll.)*; **~ bekommen** *od.* **beziehen** get a hiding *(coll.) or* beating
Prügelei die; ~, ~en *(ugs.)* punch-up *(coll.)*; fight
Prügel·knabe der whipping-boy
prügeln 1. *tr. (auch itr.) V.* beat; **mußt du immer gleich ~?** do you have to resort to beatings straight away? **2.** *refl. V.* **sich ~:** fight; **sich mit jmdm. [um etw.] ~:** fight sb. [over *or* for sth.]
Prügel-: ~strafe die corporal punishment *no art.*; **~szene die a)** *(im Film, Theaterstück)* fight scene; **b)** *(Prügelei)* fight
Prunk [prʊŋk] **der; ~[e]s** splendour; magnificence; *(einer Ausstattung, eines Saales usw. auch)* sumptuousness; *(eines Gebäudes, einer Architektur usw.)* magnificence; grandeur; *(einer Zeremonie)* splendour; pageantry; **~ entfalten** put on a display of splendour
Prunk·bau der; *Pl.* **~bauten** magnificent building
prunken *itr. V.* **a)** be resplendent; **~d** magnificent; **b)** *(prahlen, sich hervortun)* show off; **mit etw. ~:** flaunt *or* make a great show of sth.
prunk-, Prunk-: ~stück das showpiece; **~süchtig** *Adj.* ⟨*person*⟩ with a passion for splendour [and grandeur]; **~voll 1.** *Adj.* magnificent; splendid; **2.** *adv.* magnificently; splendidly; magnificently, splendidly, sumptuously ⟨*furnished, decorated*⟩
prusten ['pru:stn̩] *itr. V. (ugs.) (schnauben)* snort; *(keuchen)* puff and blow; **vor Lachen ~:** snort with laughter
PS [pe:'ǀɛs] **das; ~, ~:** *Abk.* **a) Pferdestärke** h.p.; **b) Postskript[um]** PS
Psalm [psalm] **der; ~s, ~en** psalm
Psalmist der; ~en, ~en *(Rel.)* psalmist
Psalter ['psaltɐ] **der; ~s, ~ a)** *(Musik)* psaltery; **b)** *(Rel.)* psalter
PSchA *Abk.* **Postscheckamt**
pscht [pʃt] *s.* **pst**
pseudo-, Pseudo- [psɔydo-] *(abwertend)* pseudo-
Pseudonym [psɔydo'ny:m] **das; ~s, ~e** pseudonym; *(eines Schriftstellers)* pseudonym; nom de plume; pen-name
pst [pst] *Interj.* sh; hush
Psyche ['psy:çə] **die; ~, ~n a)** psyche; **b)** *(österr.: Frisiertoilette)* dressing-table
psychedelisch [psyçe'de:lɪʃ] **1.** *Adj.* psychedelic. **2.** *adv.* psychedelically
Psychiater [psy'çi̯a:tɐ] **der; ~s, ~:** psychiatrist
Psychiatrie [psyçi̯a'tri:] **die; ~, ~n a)** *o. Pl.* psychiatry *no art.*; **b)** *(ugs.) (Abteilung)* psychiatric department; *(Klinik)* psychiatric clinic
psychiatrisch 1. *Adj.; nicht präd.* psychiatric. **2.** *adv.* **jmdn. ~ untersuchen/behandeln** give sb. a psychiatric examination/psychiatric treatment
psychisch 1. *Adj.* psychological; psychological, mental ⟨*strain, disturbance, process*⟩; mental ⟨*illness*⟩. **2.** *adv.* psychologically; **~ gesund/krank sein** be mentally fit/ill; **ein ~ bedingtes Leiden** an illness of psychological origin
psycho-, Psycho- [psy:ço-]: **~analyse die** psychoanalysis *no art.*; **~analytiker der** psychoanalyst; **~analytisch 1.** *Adj.* psychoanalytical; **2.** *adv.* psychoanalytically; **~diagnostik die** psychodiagnostics *sing., no art.*; **~drama das a)** *(Literaturw.)* psychological drama; **b)** *(Psych.)* psychodrama; **~gen** [~'ge:n] *(Med., Psych.) Adj.* psychogenic; **~gramm das** *(Psych.)* psychograph; **~krimi** ['----] **der** *(ugs.)* psychological thriller; **~loge** [~'lo:gə] **der; ~n, ~n** psychologist; **~logie** [~lo'gi:] **die; ~:** psychology; **~login die** psychologist; **~logisch 1.** *Adj.* **a)** psychological; **b)** *(ugs.: psychologisch geschickt)* **das war nicht sehr ~logisch von dir** that wasn't very good psychology on your part; **2.** *adv.* psychologically; **~logisch geschult** trained in psychology; **~logisieren** *itr. (auch tr.) V. (abwertend)* psychologize; **~path** [~'pa:t] **der; ~en, ~en, ~pathin die; ~, ~nen** psychopath; **~pathie** [~pa'ti:] **die; ~, ~n** psychopathy *no art.*; **~pathisch 1.** *Adj.* psychopathic; **2.** *adv.* psychopathically; **~pathologie die** psychopathology *no art.*; **~pharmakon** [~'farmakɔn] **das; ~s, ~pharmaka** psychotropic drug
Psychose [psy'ço:zə] **die; ~, ~n** psychosis
psycho-, Psycho-: ~somatisch *(Med.)* **1.** *Adj.* psychosomatic; **2.** *adv.* **~somatisch bedingt** of psychosomatic origin *postpos.*; **~terror** ['----] **der** psychological intimidation; **~therapeut der** psychotherapist; **~therapeutisch 1.** *Adj.* psychotherapeutic; **2.** *adv.* **jmdn. ~therapeutisch behandeln** give sb. psychotherapeutic treatment;

~therapie die psychotherapy *no art.*; **~thriller** ['----] **der** psychological thriller
Psychotiker [psy'ço:tikɐ] **der**; **~s, ~, Psychotikerin die**; **~, ~nen** psychotic
psychotisch *Adj.* psychotic
PTA [pe:te:'|a:] **die**; **~, ~[s]** *Abk.* **pharmazeutisch-technische Assistentin** pharmaceutical-laboratory assistent
ptolemäisch [ptole'mɛ:ɪʃ] *Adj.*; *nicht präd.* Ptolemaic
Ptolemäus [ptole'mɛ:ʊs] **(der)** Ptolemy
PTT *Abk.* **Schweizerische Post-, Telefon- und Telegrafenbetriebe** *Swiss postal, telephone, and telegraph services*
pubertär [pubɛr'tɛ:ɐ̯] **1.** *Adj.* pubertal; **sein Benehmen ist typisch ~:** his behaviour is typical for the age of puberty. **2.** *adv.* **~ bedingt** caused by puberty *postpos.*
Pubertät [pubɛr'tɛ:t] **die**; **~:** puberty; **in die ~ kommen** reach puberty
pubertieren *itr. V.* reach puberty; **~d** pubescent
Publicity [pʌ'blɪsɪtɪ] **die**; **~:** publicity
publicity·scheu *Adj.* publicity-shunning *attrib.*; **~ sein** shun publicity
Public Relations ['pʌblɪk rɪ'leɪʃənz] *Pl.* public relations
publik [pu'bli:k] *Adj. in* **~ sein/werden** be/become public knowledge; **die Sache ist längst ~:** that's long been common knowledge; **etw. ~ machen** make sth. public
Publikation [publika'tsio:n] **die**; **~, ~en** publication
Publikum ['pu:blikʊm] **das**; **~s a)** *(Zuschauer, Zuhörer)* audience; *(bei Sportveranstaltungen)* crowd; **b)** *(Kreis von Interessierten)* public; *(eines Schriftstellers)* readership; **c)** *(Besucher)* clientele
publikums-, Publikums-: ~erfolg der success with the public; **~liebling der** idol of the public; **~verkehr der**; *o. Pl.* **„heute kein ~verkehr!"** 'closed to the public [today]'; **~wirksam** *Adj.* with public appeal *postpos., not pred.*; punchy ⟨*headline*⟩; ⟨*headline*⟩ with a strong appeal; effective, compelling ⟨*broadcast*⟩; **~wirksam sein** have public appeal
publizieren [publi'tsi:rən] *tr. (auch itr.) V.* publish; **in verschiedenen Fachzeitschriften ~:** have articles *or* work published in various journals
Publizist der; **~en, ~en** commentator on politics and current affairs; publicist
Publizistik die; **~:** mass communications *pl., no art.*; *(Journalismus)* journalism *no art.*
Publizistin die; **~, ~nen** *s.* **Publizist**
publizistisch 1. *Adj.* **seine ~e Aktivität** his journalistic activities *pl.*; **die Reise war ein ~er Mißerfolg** the trip failed to get the media's attention. **2.** *adv.* **etw. ~ verbreiten** disseminate sth. via the media; **~ tätig sein** work in mass communications/as a journalist
Publizität [publitsi'tɛ:t] **die**; **~:** publicity
Puck [pʊk] **der**; **~s, ~s** *(Eishockey)* puck
puckern ['pʊkɐn] *itr. V. (ugs.)* throb
Pudding ['pʊdɪŋ] **der**; **~s, ~e** *od.* **~s** *thick, usually flavoured, milk-based dessert*; ≈ blancmange; *s. auch* **hauen 2 c**
Pudding·pulver das ≈ blancmange powder
Pudel ['pu:dl̩] **der**; **~s, ~ a)** *(Hund)* poodle; **das war also des ~s Kern** *(fig.)* so 'that's what was behind it; **wie ein begossener ~ dastehen** *(ugs.)* stand there crestfallen; *(nach einer Zurechtweisung)* stand there sheepishly; **b)** *(ugs.: beim Kegeln)* miss; **einen ~ werfen** *od.* **schießen** miss
pudel-, Pudel-: ~mütze die bobble *or* pom-pom hat; **~naß** *Adj. (ugs.)* drenched; soaked to the skin; **~wohl** *Adv. (ugs.)* **sich ~wohl fühlen** feel on top of the world
Puder ['pu:dɐ] **der**; **~s, ~:** powder
Puder·dose die powder compact
pudern *tr. V.* powder; **sich** *(Dat.)* **die Nase ~:** powder one's nose
Puder-: ~quaste die powder-puff; **~zucker der** icing sugar *(Brit.)*; confectioners' sugar *(Amer.)*
Puertoricaner [puɛrtori'ka:nɐ] **der**; **~s, ~, Puertoricanerin die**; **~, ~nen** Puerto Rican; *s. auch* **-in**
puertoricanisch *Adj.* Puerto Rican
puff [pʊf] *Interj.* bang
¹Puff der; **~[e]s, Püffe** ['pʏfə] *(ugs.)* **a)** *(Stoß)* thump; *(leichter/kräftiger Stoß mit dem Ellenbogen)* nudge/dig; **einen ~** *od.* **einige Püffe vertragen [können]** *(fig.)* be able to take a few knocks; **b)** *(Knall)* bang
²Puff der *od.* **das**; **~s, ~s** *(salopp: Bordell)* knocking-shop *(Brit. sl.)*; brothel
³Puff der; **~[e]s, ~e** *od.* **~s a)** *(Wäsche~)* linen-basket; **b)** *(Sitzkissen)* pouffe; **c)** *(veralt.: Bausch)* puff
Puff·ärmel der puff *or* puffed sleeve
puffen *(ugs.)* **1.** *tr. (auch itr.) V.* **a)** *(stoßen)* thump; *(mit dem Ellenbogen)* nudge; dig; **~ und schubsen** push and shove; **b)** *(irgendwohin befördern)* push; shove; *(mit dem Ellenbogen)* elbow; **jmdn. zur Seite ~:** push *or* shove/elbow sb. aside. **2.** *itr. V.* ⟨*locomotive*⟩ puff
Puffer der; **~s, ~ a)** *(Vorrichtung)* buffer; **b)** *s.* **Kartoffel~**
Puffer-: ~staat der buffer state; **~zone die** buffer zone
Puff-: ~mutter die *(salopp)* madam; **~reis der** puffed rice
puh [pu:] *Interj.* ugh; *(erleichtert)* phew
pulen ['pu:lən] *(nordd. ugs.)* **1.** *itr. V.* pick **(an +** *Dat.* at); **[sich** *(Dat.)***] in der Nase ~:** pick one's nose. **2.** *tr. V.* pick **(aus** out of); **etw. von etw. ~:** pick sth. off sth.
Pulk [pʊlk] **der**; **~[e]s, ~s** *od.* **~e a)** *(Milit.: Verband)* group; **b)** *(Menge)* crowd; *(Sport: Hauptfeld)* pack; bunch
Pulle ['pʊlə] **die**; **~, ~n** *(salopp)* bottle; **volle ~** *(fig. salopp)* flat out
pullen 1. *itr. V. (Seemannsspr.)* row. **2.** *itr. V. (Pferdesport)* pull
pullern ['pʊlɐn] *itr. V. (fam., bes. ostmd.)* pee *(coll.)*
Pulli ['pʊli] **der**; **~s, ~s** *(ugs.)*, **Pullover** [pʊ'lo:vɐ] **der**; **~s, ~:** pullover; sweater
Pullunder [pʊ'lʊndɐ] **der**; **~s, ~:** slipover
Puls [pʊls] **der**; **~es, ~e a)** pulse; **jmds. ~ fühlen/messen** feel/take sb.'s pulse; **b)** *(Elektrot., Nachrichtent.)* pulse
Puls·ader die artery; **sich** *(Dat.)* **die ~n aufschneiden** slash one's wrists
pulsen *itr. V. (auch fig.)* pulse
pulsieren *itr. V. (auch fig.)* pulsate; ⟨*blood*⟩ pulse
Puls-: ~schlag der *(auch fig.)* pulse; *(einzelner ~schlag)* beat; **~wärmer der** wristlet; **~zahl die** *(Med.)* pulse rate
Pult [pʊlt] **das**; **~[e]s, ~e a)** desk; *(Lese~)* lectern; desk; **b)** *(Schalt~)* control desk; console
Pulver ['pʊlfɐ] **das**; **~s, ~ a)** powder; **b)** *(Schieß~)* [gun]powder; **das ~ hat er [auch] nicht [gerade] erfunden** *(ugs.)* he'll never set the world *or (Brit.)* the Thames on fire; **sein ~ verschossen haben** *(fig. ugs.)* have shot one's bolt; **c)** *(salopp: Geld)* dough *(sl.)*
Pülverchen ['pʏlfɐçən] **das**; **~s, ~** *(spött.)* [medicinal] powder
Pulver-: ~dampf der gun-smoke; **~faß das** barrel of gunpowder; *(kleiner)* powder-keg; **auf einem** *od.* **dem ~faß sitzen** *(fig.)* be sitting on a powder-keg *or* on top of a volcano; **~form die** *in* **in ~form** in powder form
pulverisieren *tr. V.* pulverize; powder
Pulver-: ~kaffee der instant coffee; **~kammer die a)** *(Schiffbau)* powder-magazine; **b)** *(Milit. veralt.)* chamber
pulvern *tr. V.* **zuviel Geld in die Rüstung ~:** throw money away on arms
Pulver·schnee der powder snow
Puma ['pu:ma] **der**; **~s, ~s** puma
Pummel ['pʊml̩] **der**; **~s, ~** *(ugs.)*, **Pummelchen das**; **~s, ~** *(ugs.)* podge
pumm[e]lig ['pʊm(ə)lɪç] *Adj. (ugs.)* chubby
Pump [pʊmp] **der**; **~s** *(salopp)* **auf ~:** on tick *(coll.)*
Pumpe ['pʊmpə] **die**; **~, ~n a)** pump; **b)** *(salopp: Herz)* ticker *(joc.)*
pumpen *tr., itr. V.* **a)** *(auch fig.)* pump; **b)** *(salopp: verleihen)* lend; **jmdm. etw. ~:** lend sb. sth.; **c)** *(entleihen)* borrow; **sich** *(Dat.)* **[bei** *od.* **von jmdm] etw. ~:** borrow sth. from *or (coll.)* off sb.
Pumpen·schwengel der pump-handle
pumpern ['pʊmpɐn] *itr. V. (südd., österr. ugs.)* thump; ⟨*heart*⟩ thump, pound; ⟨*heavy artillery*⟩ thud
Pumper·nickel der pumpernickel
Pump·hose die harem trousers *pl.*; *(veralt.: Knickerbocker)* knickerbockers *pl.*
Pumps [pœmps] **der**; **~, ~:** court shoe
Pump·station die pumping-station
Punier ['pu:niɐ̯] **der**; **~s, ~, Punierin die**; **~, ~nen** Phoenician
punisch *Adj.* Punic
Punk [paŋk] **der**; **~[s], ~s** punk
Punker ['paŋkɐ] **der**; **~s, ~ a)** *(Musiker)* punk rocker; **b)** *(Anhänger)* punk
Punk·rock der; *o. Pl.* punk rock
Punkt [pʊŋkt] **der**; **~[e]s, ~e a)** *(Tupfen)* dot; *(größer)* spot; **ein Stoff mit blauen ~en** a fabric with blue spots; **das ist [nicht] der springende ~** *(fig.)* that's [not] the point; **ein dunkler ~ [in jmds. Vergangenheit]** a dark chapter [in sb.'s past]; **b)** *(Satzzeichen)* full stop; period; **drei ~e bedeuten eine Auslassung im Zitat** three dots mean an omission in the quotation; **einen ~ machen** *od.* **setzen** put a full stop; **nun mach [aber] mal einen ~!** *(fig. ugs.)* come off it! *(coll.)*; **ohne ~ und Komma reden** *(ugs.)* talk nineteen to the dozen *(Brit.)*; rabbit *(Brit. coll.) or* talk on and on; **c)** *(I-Punkt)* dot; **den ~ auf dem i vergessen** forget to dot the i; **etw. auf den ~ genau wissen** know sth. quite precisely; *s. auch* **i, I**; **d)** *(Stelle)* point; **an einem ~ sein, wo ...** *(fig.)* have reached the point *or* stage where ...; **ein schwacher/wunder/neuralgischer ~** *(fig.)* a weak/sore/vulnerable *or* sensitive point; **die Unterhaltung war/die Verhandlungen waren an einem toten ~ angelangt** the conversation had come to a dead stop/the talks had reached deadlock *or* an impasse; **ein starker Kaffee half ihm über den toten ~ hinweg** a strong coffee helped him to get his second wind; **nachmittags um zwei Uhr habe ich meinen toten ~:** I'm at my lowest ebb at two o'clock in the afternoon; **e)** *(Gegenstand, Thema, Abschnitt)* point; *(einer Tagesordnung)* item; point; **in diesem/über diesen ~:** on this point; **sich in allen ~en einig sein** agree on all points; **~ für ~:** point by point; **etw. auf den ~ bringen** sum sth. up; put sth. in a nutshell; **jmdn. in allen ~en der Anklage freisprechen** acquit sb. on all counts; **f)** *(Bewertungs~)* point; *(bei einer Prüfung)* mark; **nach ~en siegen** win on points; **~e sammeln** *(fig.)* score points **(bei** with); **g)** *(Musik)* dot; **h)** *(Math.)* point; **i)** *(Zeit~)* point; **jetzt ist der ~ gekommen, wo ich ...:** the moment *or* time has now arrived when I ...; **~ 12 Uhr** at 12 o'clock on the dot; **j)** *nach Zahlenangaben ungebeugt (Druckw.)* point
Pünktchen ['pʏŋktçən] **das**; **~s, ~:** little dot *or* spot; **rote ~:** little red dots *or* spots
punkten *itr. V. (bes. Boxen)* pick up points; score [points]
punkt-, Punkt-: ~feuer das *(Milit.)* precision fire; **~förmig** *Adj.* **eine ~förmige Lichtquelle** a point source of light; **~gewinn der** *(Sport, bes. Ballspiele)* **sie blieben im Turnier ohne ~gewinn** they failed to win any points in the competition; **~gleich**

Adj. (Sport) level on points *pred.*; **~gleich stehen** be level on points; **die ~gleichen Teams** the teams on equal points; **~gleichheit die** *(Sport)* **bei ~gleichheit** if the same number of points have been scored

punktieren *tr. V.* **a)** *(mit Punkten darstellen)* dot; **b)** *(Med.)* puncture; **c)** *(Musik)* **eine Rolle ~:** transpose individual notes in a vocal part; **d)** *auch itr. (Musik: verlängern)* dot ⟨*note*⟩

Punktion [pʊŋk'tsi̯o:n] **die; ~, ~en** *(Med.)* puncture

pünktlich ['pʏŋktlɪç] **1.** *Adj.* **a)** punctual; **er ist immer ~:** he's always punctual *or* on time; **der Zug ist ~/nicht ~:** the train is on time/is late; **b)** *(veralt.: gewissenhaft genau)* meticulous. **2.** *adv.* **a)** punctually; on time; **das Konzert beginnt ~ um 20 Uhr** the concert will begin at 8 o'clock sharp; **~ auf die Minute** punctually to the minute; **b)** *(veralt.: gewissenhaft, genau)* meticulously

Pünktlichkeit die; ~: punctuality

punkt-, Punkt-: ~nieder·lage die *(Sport)* defeat on points; points defeat; **~richter der** *(Sport)* judge; **~schweißen** *tr., itr. V.; nur Inf. u. 2. Part. gebr.* spot weld; **~sieg der** *(Sport)* win on points; points win; **~spiel das** *(Mannschaftssport)* league game

punktuell [pʊŋk'tu̯ɛl] **1.** *Adj.* isolated ⟨*interventions, checks, approaches, initiatives, etc.*⟩; **einige ~e Verbesserungen** improvements in a few matters of detail. **2.** *adv.* **sich mit einem Thema nur ~ befassen** deal only with certain *or* particular points relating to a topic; **Kontrollen wurden nur ~ durchgeführt** only spot checks were carried out

Punktum *Interj. (veralt.) in* **[und damit] ~:** and that's that; and that's final *or* flat

Punkt-: ~wertung die points system; **~zahl die** score; number of points; *(beim Eiskunstlauf)* score; [number of] marks

Punsch [pʊnʃ] **der; ~[e]s, ~e** *od.* **Pünsche** ['pʏnʃə] punch

Punze ['pʊntsə] **die; ~, ~n a)** *(Werkzeug)* punch; *(zum Gravieren)* burin; **b)** *(Gütezeichen)* hallmark

Pupille [pu'pɪlə] **die; ~, ~n** pupil

Püppchen ['pʏpçən] **das; ~s, ~ a)** *([kleine] Puppe)* little doll *or (child lang.)* dolly; **b)** *(Kosewort)* pet; *(niedliches Mädchen)* little sweetie *(coll.)*; *(hübsches, aber nichtssagendes Mädchen)* dolly-bird *(Brit. sl.)*

Puppe ['pʊpə] **die; ~, ~n a)** doll[y]; **b)** *(Marionette)* puppet; marionette; *(fig.)* puppet; **die ~n tanzen lassen** *(fig. ugs.)* pull the strings; *(es hoch hergehen lassen)* paint the town red *(sl.)*; **c)** *(salopp: Mädchen)* bird *(sl.)*; *(als Anrede)* sweetie *(coll.)*; **d)** *(Zool.)* pupa; **e)** *(ostmd.: aus Getreidegarben)* stook; shock; **f)** *in* **bis in die ~n** *(ugs.)* till all hours

Puppen-: ~doktor der *(ugs.)* doll-repairer; **etw. zum ~doktor bringen** take sth. to the dolls' hospital; **~gesicht das** baby-doll face; **~haus das** doll's house; dollhouse *(Amer.)*; **~spiel das a)** puppet theatre; **b)** *(Stück)* puppet show; **~spieler der** puppeteer; **~stube die** doll's house; dollhouse *(Amer.)*; **~theater das** puppet theatre; **~wagen der** doll's pram

puppig *(ugs.) Adj.* **a)** *s.* **niedlich**; **b)** *(kinderleicht)* dead easy

pur [pu:ɐ̯] *Adj.* **a)** *(rein)* pure; **b)** *(unvermischt)* neat; straight; **bitte einen Whisky ~!** a neat whisky, please; **c)** *(bloß)* sheer; pure; **das ist ~er Wahnsinn** that's sheer *or* pure *or* absolute madness

Püree [py're:] **das; ~s, ~s a)** purée; **b)** *s.* **Kartoffelbrei**

pürieren [py'ri:rən] *(Kochk.) tr. V.* purée ⟨*potatoes, apples, etc.*⟩; *(zerstampfen)* mash

Purismus der; ~ *(Sprachw., Kunstw.)* purism

Purist der; ~en, ~en, Puristin die; ~, ~nen purist

puristisch 1. *Adj.* purist; puristic. **2.** *adv.* puristically

Puritaner [puri'ta:nɐ] **der; ~s, ~ a)** Puritan; **b)** *(fig.)* puritan

puritanisch *Adj.* **a)** Puritan; **b)** *(fig.)* puritanical

Puritanismus der; ~: Puritanism *no art.*

Purpur ['pʊrpʊr] **der; ~s a)** *(Farbton)* crimson; **b)** *(Gewand)* purple

purpur-, Purpur-: ~farben, ~farbig *Adj.* crimson; **~mantel der** crimson *or* purple robe

purpurn, purpur·rot *Adj.* crimson

Purzel·baum der *(ugs.)* somersault; **einen ~ machen** *od.* **schlagen** do *or* turn a somersault

purzeln ['pʊrtsl̩n] *itr. V.; mit sein (fam.)* tumble; **auf dem Eis ~:** fall over on the ice

Puschen ['pu:ʃn̩] **der; ~s, ~** *(nordd.)* slipper

pushen ['pʊʃn̩] **1.** *tr. V.* **a)** *(Drogenjargon)* push; **b)** *(Journalistenjargon)* push. **2.** *itr. V. (Drogenjargon)* be a pusher

Pusher der; ~s, ~ *(Drogenjargon)* pusher

pusselig *Adj. (ugs., bes. nordd.)* **a)** *(Geduld fordernd)* fiddly *(coll.)* ⟨*work, task*⟩; **b)** *(übergenau)* pernickety *(coll.)*; *(umständlich)* fussy

pusseln ['pʊsl̩n] *itr. V. (ugs.)* potter about; mess about (**an** + *Dat.* with)

Pußta ['pʊsta] **die; ~, Pußten** puszta; *steppe-land in Hungary*

Puste ['pu:stə] **die; ~** *(salopp)* puff; breath; **ganz aus der** *od.* **außer ~ sein** be out of puff; be puffed [out]; *s. auch* **ausgehen 1 b**

Puste-: ~blume die *(ugs.)* dandelion clock; **~kuchen** *in* **[ja** *od.* **aber] ~kuchen** *(ugs.) (es ist/war nicht der Fall)* not a bit of it!; *(es hat nicht geklappt)* nothing doing!

Pustel ['pʊstl̩] **die; ~, ~n** pimple; spot; pustule *(Med.)*

pusten *(ugs.)* **1.** *itr. V.* **a)** *(blasen)* ⟨*person, wind*⟩ blow; **es pustet draußen ganz schön** *(ugs.)* there's a fair old wind blowing out there *(coll.)*; **~ müssen** *(ugs.: bei einer Verkehrskontrolle)* have to blow into the bag; **b)** *(keuchen)* puff [and pant *or* blow]. **2.** *tr. V. (blasen)* blow; **jmdm. was** *od.* **eins ~** *(salopp)* tell sb. where to get off *(coll.)*

Puste·rohr das *(ugs.)* pea-shooter

putativ [puta'ti:f] *Adj. (Rechtsspr.)* putative

Putativ·notwehr die *(Rechtsw.)* **in ~ handeln** act in the mistaken belief that one is being attacked

Pute ['pu:tə] **die; ~, ~n a)** *(Truthenne)* turkey hen; *(als Braten)* turkey; **b)** *(salopp abwertend: Mädchen, Frau)* **eine dumme/extravagante ~:** a silly goose *or* creature/an extravagant creature; **eine eingebildete ~:** a stuck-up little madam

Puter der; ~s, ~: turkeycock; *(als Braten)* turkey

puter·rot *Adj.* scarlet; bright red

Putsch [pʊtʃ] **der; ~[e]s, ~e** putsch; coup [d'état]

putschen *itr. V.* organize a putsch *or* coup

Putschist der; ~en, ~en putschist; rebel

Putsch·versuch der attempted putsch *or* coup

Pütt [pʏt] **der; ~s, ~e** *od.* **~s** *(rhein., westfäl. Bergmannsspr.)* pit; mine; **auf dem ~ sein** work in the mine

Putte ['pʊtə] **die; ~, ~n** *(Kunstwiss.)* putto

Putz [pʊts] **der; ~es a)** *(Baumaterial)* plaster; *(für Außenmauern)* rendering; *(Rauh~)* roughcast; **eine Wand mit ~ bewerfen** *od.* **verkleiden** plaster/render/roughcast a wall; **die Rohre liegen über ~:** the pipes are exposed; **auf den ~ hauen** *(fig. salopp) (angeben)* boast; brag; *(ausgelassen feiern)* have a rave-up *(Brit. sl.)*; **b)** *(salopp: Streit)* row *(coll.)*; **wenn er spät nach Hause kommt, kriegt er ~ mit seiner Frau** when he gets home late, his wife starts rowing with him; **~ machen** *(salopp)* cause aggro *(Brit. sl.)*; **c)** *(veralt.: Kleidung)* finery

putzen *tr. V.* **a)** *(blank reiben)* polish; clean; **Schuhe/die Fenster ~:** polish *or* clean one's shoes/clean the windows; **den Teller blank ~** *(fig.)* clear one's plate; *s. auch* **Klinke a**; **b)** *(säubern)* clean; groom ⟨*horse*⟩; **[sich** *(Dat.)***] die Zähne/die Nase ~:** clean *or* brush one's teeth/blow one's nose; **er putzte seinem Kind die Nase** he wiped his child's nose; **sich ~** ⟨*cat*⟩ wash itself; ⟨*bird*⟩ preen itself; **c)** *auch itr. (bes. rhein., südd., schweiz.: saubermachen)* clean ⟨*room, shop, etc.*⟩; **~ gehen** work as a cleaner *or (Brit.)* char[woman]; **d)** *(zum Essen, Kochen vorbereiten)* wash and prepare ⟨*vegetables*⟩; **e)** *(Sportjargon: besiegen)* beat; **f)** *(beschneiden)* trim ⟨*wick, lamp, candle*⟩; **g)** *(österr.: chemisch reinigen)* [dry-]clean; **etw. ~ lassen** take sth. to the [dry-]cleaners; **h)** *(veralt.: schmücken)* dress ⟨*person*⟩ up; decorate ⟨*Christmas tree etc.*⟩; **sich ~:** dress [oneself] up; **i)** *auch itr. (veralt.: zieren)* decorate; adorn; **deine Schleife putzt aber ungemein!** your ribbon makes you look really pretty!

Putzerei die; ~, ~en a) *o. Pl. (ugs. abwertend: das Putzen)* [obsessive] cleaning; **b)** *(österr.: Reinigungsanstalt)* dry cleaner's

Putz-: ~fimmel der; *o. Pl. (ugs. abwertend)* mania for cleaning; **~frau die** cleaner; char[lady] *(Brit.)*

putzig *(ugs.)* **1.** *Adj.* **a)** *(entzückend)* sweet; cute *(Amer.)*; *(possierlich)* funny; comical; **b)** *(seltsam)* funny; peculiar. **2.** *adv.* **a)** *(entzückend)* sweetly; cutely *(Amer.)*; *(possierlich)* comically; **b)** *(seltsam)* peculiarly

putz-, Putz-: ~lappen der [cleaning-]rag; cloth; **~macherin die; ~, ~nen** milliner; **~mittel das** cleaning agent; **~munter** *(ugs.)* **1.** *Adj.* chirpy *(coll.)*; perky; **~munter sein** be as bright as a button; **2.** *adv.* chirpily *(coll.)*; perkily; **~tuch das;** *Pl.* **~tücher** cloth; *(Lappen)* [cleaning-]rag; **~wolle die** cotton waste

puzzeln ['pazl̩n] *itr. V.* do jigsaw puzzles/a jigsaw [puzzle]

Puzzle ['pazl̩] **das; ~s, ~s, Puzzle·spiel das** jigsaw [puzzle]

PVC [pe:fau̯'tse:] **das; ~[s]** *Abk.* **Polyvinylchlorid** PVC

Pygmäe [pʏ'gmɛ:ə] **der; ~n, ~n** pygmy

pygmäenhaft *Adj.* pygmy-like

Pyjama [pʏ'dʒa:ma] **der** *(österr., schweiz. auch:* **das); ~s, ~s** pyjamas *pl.*

Pyjama·hose die pyjama trousers *pl.*

Pykniker ['pʏknikɐ] **der; ~s, ~** *(Med., Anthrop.)* stocky person; pyknic *as tech. term*

pyknisch *Adj. (Med., Anthrop.)* stocky; pyknic *as tech. term*

Pylon [pʏ'lo:n] **der; ~en, ~en, Pylone die; ~, ~n a)** *(Tempeleingang)* pylon; **b)** *(bei Brücken)* [suspension-bridge] tower; **c)** *(Straßenmarkierung)* traffic cone

Pyramide [pyra'mi:də] **die; ~, ~n** pyramid

pyramiden·förmig *Adj.* pyramidal; pyramid-shaped

Pyrenäen [pyre'nɛ:ən] *Pl.* Pyrenees

Pyrenäen·halb·insel die Iberian Peninsula

pyro-, Pyro- [pyro-]: **~mane** [~'ma:nə] **der; ~n, ~n** *(Med., Psych.)* pyromaniac; **~manie die;** *o. Pl. (Med., Psych.)* pyromania; **~manin die; ~, ~nen** *s.* **~mane**; **~techniker der** fireworks expert; pyrotechnist

Pyrrhus·sieg ['pʏrʊs-] **der** *(geh.)* Pyrrhic victory

pythagoräisch [pytago'rɛ:ɪʃ] *s.* **pythagoreisch**

Pythagoras [pʏ'ta:goras] **(der)** Pythagoras

pythagoreisch [pytago're:ɪʃ] *Adj.; nicht präd.* Pythagorean; **der ~e Lehrsatz** *(Geom.)* Pythagoras' theorem

Python ['pʏ:tɔn] **der; ~s, ~s** *od.* **~en** [pʏ'to:nən], **Python·schlange die** python

Q

q, Q [ku:] **das; ~, ~** q, Q; **das Gütezeichen Q** *(DDR)* the grade A marking; *s. auch* **a, A**
qm *Abk.* **Quadratmeter** sq. m.
qua [kva] *(geh.)* **1.** *Präp., meist mit ungebeugtem Substantiv* **a)** *auch mit Gen. (mittels)* by means of; **b)** *(gemäß)* in accordance with; *(kraft)* by virtue of; **~ Herkunft** by virtue of its/their *etc.* origins. **2.** *Konj. (als)* **~ Beamter** [in his function] as an official
quabbelig ['kvabəlɪç], **quabblig** *Adj. (nordd.)* jelly-like ⟨*frog-spawn*⟩; *(weich und dick)* flabby, podgy ⟨*face*⟩
quackeln ['kvakl̩n] *(bes. nordd. ugs.)* **1.** *itr. V.* chatter; *(dauernd)* natter on *(Brit. coll.)*. **2.** *tr. V.* **dummes Zeug ~:** talk drivel
Quacksalber ['kvakzalbɐ] **der; ~s, ~** *(abwertend)* quack [doctor]
Quacksalberei die; ~, ~en *(abwertend)* quackery
Quaddel ['kvadl̩] **die; ~, ~n** [irritating] spot
Quader ['kva:dɐ] **der; ~s, ~** *od. (österr.:)* **~n** **a)** *(Steinblock)* ashlar block; [rectangular] block of stone; **b)** *(Geom.)* rectangular parallelepiped; cuboid
Quader·stein der *s.* **Quader a**
Quadrant [kva'drant] **der; ~en, ~en** *(Geom., Geogr. Astron., Math.)* quadrant
[1]**Quadrat** [kva'dra:t] **das; ~[e]s, ~e** **a)** *(Geom.)* square; **6 cm im ~:** 6 cm. square; **b)** *(Math.: zweite Potenz)* square; **eine Zahl ins ~ erheben** square a number; **drei im** *od.* **zum ~:** three squared; **Pech/Glück im ~** *(ugs.)* terrible [bad] luck/terrific luck *(coll.)*; **c)** *(bebaute Fläche)* block [of houses]; **ums ~ gehen** walk round the block
[2]**Quadrat das; ~[e]s, ~en** *(Druckw.)* quadrat
quadrat-, Quadrat- square ⟨*kilometre etc.*⟩
quadratisch *Adj.* **a)** square; **b)** *(Math.)* quadratic
Quadrat-: ~latschen der *(salopp)* **a)** *(Schuh)* dirty great shoe *(sl.)*; **b)** *(Pl.: Füße)* dirty great feet *(sl.)*; **~meter der** *od.* **das** square metre; **unsere Wohnung hat 92 ~meter** our flat *(Brit.)* or *(Amer.)* apartment has 92 square metres of floor space; **~schädel der a)** *(ugs.: Kopf)* dirty great nut *(sl.)*; **b)** *(ugs. abwertend: sturer Mensch)* mule; pig-headed type
Quadratur [kvadra'tu:ɐ̯] **die; ~, ~en** *(Math., Astron.)* quadrature; **die ~ des Zirkels** *(geh.)* the achievement of the impossible
Quadrat-: ~wurzel die *(Math.)* square root **(aus** of); **~zahl die** square number
quadrieren *(Math.)* **1.** *tr. V.* square. **2.** *itr. V.* square numbers
Quadriga [kva'dri:ga] **die; ~, Quadrigen** quadriga
Quadrille [ka'drɪljə] **die; ~, ~n** *(Tanz, Musik)* quadrille
Quadrillion [kvadrɪ'li̯o:n] **die; ~, ~en** quadrillion *(Brit.)*; septillion *(esp. Amer.)*
quadro-, Quadro- ['kva:dro-] quadraphonic ⟨*system, effect, sound, etc.*⟩
quadro·phon *(Akustik)* **1.** quadraphonic. **2.** *adv.* in quad[raphony]
Quadro·phonie die; ~ *(Akustik)* quadraphony
Quai [ke] **der** *od.* **das; ~s, ~s** *(schweiz.)* **a)** *s.* **Kai; b)** *(Uferstraße)* embankment [road]
quak *Interj.* **~!** *(von Enten)* quack!; *(von Fröschen)* croak!
quaken ['kva:kn̩] *itr. V.* ⟨*duck*⟩ quack; ⟨*frog*⟩ croak; *(fig. abwertend)* ⟨*person, radio*⟩ squawk
quäken ['kvɛ:kn̩] **1.** *tr. V.* squawk; bawl out ⟨*song*⟩. **2.** *itr. V.* **a)** *(unangenehm tönen)* ⟨*voice*⟩ squawk; *(kreischen)* screech; ⟨*radio*⟩ blare; **b)** *(klagen)* ⟨*child*⟩ whine, whinge
Quäker ['kvɛ:kɐ] **der; ~s, ~, Quäkerin die; ~, ~nen** Quaker
Qual [kva:l] **die; ~, ~en a)** *o. Pl.* torment; agony *no indef. art.*; **[für jmdn.] eine ~/eine einzige ~ sein** be agony *or* torment/one long torment for sb.; **er macht uns** *(Dat.)* **das Leben/den Aufenthalt zur ~:** he's making our lives *pl.*/our stay a misery; **er hat die ~ der Wahl** *(scherzh.)* he is spoilt for choice; **b)** *meist Pl. (Schmerzen)* agony; **~en** pain *sing.*; agony *sing.*; *(seelisch)* torment *sing.*; **jmds. ~en lindern** ease sb.'s pain *or* suffering; **jmdn. von seinen ~en erlösen** put sb. out of his/her agony; **unter [schlimmsten] ~en sterben** die in [the most terrible] agony; **jmdm. [große] ~en bereiten** cause sb. [great] pain; torment sb.; **er konnte sein letztes Werk nur unter ~en vollenden** he could only complete his last work in great pain *or* suffering
quälen ['kvɛ:lən] **1.** *tr. V.* **a)** *(körperlich, seelisch)* torment ⟨*person, animal*⟩; maltreat, be cruel to ⟨*animal*⟩; *(foltern)* torture; **~de Schmerzen** agonizing *or* excruciating pain *sing.*; **ihn quälte der Gedanke[, daß ...]** he was tormented by the thought [that ...]; **~de Ungewißheit** agonizing uncertainty; **b)** *(plagen)* ⟨*cough etc.*⟩ plague; *(belästigen)* pester; *s. auch* **gequält. 2.** *refl. V.* **a)** *(leiden)* suffer; **sich sehr ~:** suffer greatly; suffer agonies; **b)** *(sich abmühen)* struggle; **sich durch ein Buch ~:** struggle through a book
Quälerei die; ~, ~en a) torment; *(Folter)* torture; *(Grausamkeit)* cruelty; **Tierversuche sind [eine] reine ~:** animal experiments are simply cruel; **b)** *(das Belästigen)* pestering; **c)** *o. Pl. (ugs.: große Anstrengung)* **das Treppensteigen ist eine ~ für ihn** climbing stairs is a terrible struggle for him
quälerisch *(geh.) Adj.* agonizing
Quäl·geist der; *Pl.* **~er** *(fam.)* pest
Qualifikation [kvalifika'tsi̯o:n] **die; ~, ~en a)** *s.* **Qualifizierung a; b)** *(Befähigung)* capability; **c)** *(Sport)* qualification; *(Wettkampf zur ~)* qualifier; qualifying round; **sie schafften die ~ für die Endrunde** they managed to qualify for the final round
Qualifikations-: ~runde die *(Sport)* qualifying round; **~spiel das** *(Sport)* qualifier, qualifying match **(zu, für** for)
qualifizieren [kvalifi'tsi:rən] **1.** *refl. V.* **a)** *(sich bilden)* gain qualifications; **sich für einen Posten/zum Facharbeiter ~:** gain the qualifications needed for a post/to be a skilled worker; **b)** *(Sport)* qualify. **2.** *tr. V.* **a)** *(bes. DDR) (ausbilden)* **jmdn. [zu etw.] ~:** train sb. [to be sth.]; *(weiterbilden)* give sb. further training [for sth.]; **b)** *(befähigen)* qualify; **seine Berufserfahrung qualifiziert ihn zum** *od.* **als Abteilungsleiter** his experience gives him the necessary qualifications for the post of departmental manager
qualifiziert 1. *2. Part. v.* **qualifizieren. 2.** *Adj.* **a)** ⟨*work, post*⟩ requiring particular qualifications; **b)** *(sachkundig)* competent; skilled ⟨*work*⟩; **c) ~e Mitbestimmung** *(Wirtsch.)* full participation by employees in decision-making; **~e Straftat** *(Rechtsw.)* aggravated offence; *s. auch* **Mehrheit. 3.** *adv. (sachkundig)* competently
Qualifizierung die; ~, ~en a) *(Ausbildung)* training; *(erworbene Qualifikation)* qualifications *pl.*; **b)** *(bes. DDR: Weiterbildung)* further training
Qualität [kvali'tɛ:t] **die; ~, ~en a)** quality; **Waren guter/schlechter/erster ~:** goods of high/low/prime quality; **~ kaufen** buy quality goods; **b)** *(Textilw.)* material *no pl.*; **schwere ~en** heavy fabrics; **c)** *(Schach)* **die ~ gewinnen** win the exchange
qualitativ [kvalita'ti:f] **1.** *Adj.* qualitative; ⟨*difference, change*⟩ in quality. **2.** *adv.* with regard to quality; **~ gut** good-quality; of good quality *postpos.*; **~ besser werden** improve in quality
qualitäts-, Qualitäts-: ~arbeit die high-quality workmanship; **~bewußt** *Adj.* quality-conscious; **~erzeugnis das** quality product; **~kontrolle die** quality control; **~unterschied der** difference in quality; **~ware die ~ware[n]** quality goods *pl.*; **~wein der** [high-]quality wine *(from a recognized growing area, and made with a permitted type of grape)*
Qualle ['kvalə] **die; ~, ~n** jellyfish; **~n** jellyfish
quallig *Adj. s.* **quabbelig**
Qualm [kvalm] **der; ~[e]s a)** [thick] smoke; *(~wolken)* clouds of [thick] smoke; **b)** *(bes. nordd.: Dampf)* steam
qualmen 1. *itr. V.* **a)** give off clouds of [thick] smoke; **aus dem Kamin qualmt es** clouds of [thick] smoke are coming from the fireplace; **~de Schornsteine** chimneys belching [thick] smoke; **b)** *(ugs.: rauchen)* puff away. **2.** *tr. V. (ugs.: rauchen)* puff away at ⟨*cigarette etc.*⟩
qualmig *Adj. (ugs.)* thick with smoke *postpos.*; smoke-filled
qual·voll 1. *Adj.* agonizing; **einen ~en Tod sterben** die in great pain. **2.** *adv.* agonizingly; **~ sterben** die in great pain
Quant [kvant] **das; ~s, ~en** *(Physik)* quantum
quanteln ['kvantl̩n] *tr. V. (Physik)* quantize
[1]**Quanten** *s.* **Quant, Quantum**
[2]**Quanten** *Pl. (salopp)* dirty great feet *(sl.)*
Quanten-: ~mechanik die *(Physik)* quantum mechanics *sing., no art.*; **~sprung der** *(Physik, fig.)* quantum leap; **~theorie die** *(Physik)* quantum theory *no art.*
quantifizierbar *Adj.* quantifiable
quantifizieren [kvantifi'tsi:rən] quantify
Quantität [kvanti'tɛ:t] **die; ~, ~en** quantity; *(Zahl)* number
quantitativ [kvantita'ti:f] **1.** *Adj.* quantitative. **2.** *adv.* quantitatively
Quantum ['kvantʊm] **das; ~s, Quanten** quota **(an +** *Dat.* of); *(Dosis)* dose; **mein tägliches ~ Kaffee** my daily quota *or (joc.)* dose of coffee; **ein gehöriges ~ Glück** *(fig.)* a good helping *or* big slice of luck
Quappe ['kvapə] **die; ~, ~n a)** *(Fisch)* burbot; **b)** *(Kaul~)* tadpole
Quarantäne [karan'tɛ:nə] **die; ~, ~n** quarantine; **über jmdn./etw. ~ verhängen** put sb./sth. under quarantine; **unter ~ stellen** put into quarantine; **unter ~ stehen** be in quarantine
Quarantäne·station die isolation ward
Quargel ['kvargl̩] **der** *od.* **das; ~s, ~** *(österr.) soft, smelly sour-milk cheese*
[1]**Quark** [kvark] **der; ~s a)** quark; [sour skim milk] curd cheese; **b)** *(ugs. abwertend: Quatsch)* twaddle; piffle *(sl.)*; **so ein ~!** what a load of rubbish!; **sich über jeden ~ aufregen** make a fuss about every tiny *or (sl.)* piffling detail; **seine Nase in jeden ~ stecken** poke one's nose in everywhere
[2]**Quark** [kwɔ:k] **das; ~s, ~s** *(Physik)* quark
Quark·speise die quark dish
[1]**Quart** [kvart] **die; ~, ~en a)** *(Musik) s.* **Quarte; b)** *(Fechten)* quart
[2]**Quart das; ~s, ~e a)** *(hist.: Hohlmaß) (in Preußen)* quart; *(in Bayern)* ≈ half-pint; **b)** *o. Pl. (Buchw.)* quarto
Quarta ['kvarta] **die; ~, Quarten** *(Schulw.)* **a)** *(veralt.)* third year *(of a Gymnasium)*; **b)** *(österr.)* fourth year *(of a Gymnasium)*
Quartal [kvar'ta:l] **das; ~s, ~e** quarter [of the year]; **in diesem/im nächsten ~:** this quarter/next quarter

quartal[s]-, Quartal[s]-: ~ende das end of a/the quarter; **~säufer der** *(ugs.)* periodic boozer *(coll.)*; **~weise** *Adv.* quarterly
Quartaner [kvar'ta:nɐ] **der; ~s, ~, Quartanerin die; ~, ~nen** *(Schulw.)* **a)** *(veralt.)* pupil in the third year *(of a Gymnasium)*; **b)** *(österr.)* pupil in the fourth year *(of a Gymnasium)*
Quartär [kvar'tɛ:ɐ̯] **das; ~s** *(Geol.)* Quaternary [Period]
Quart·band der; *Pl.* **~bände** quarto volume
Quarte die; ~, ~n *(Musik)* fourth
Quarten *s.* **¹Quart, Quarta, Quarte**
Quartett [kvar'tɛt] **das; ~[e]s, ~e a)** quartet; **ein kriminelles ~:** a quartet of criminals; [a gang of] four criminals; **b)** *o. Pl. (Spiel) card-game in which one tries to get sets of four;* ≈ Happy Families; **c)** *(Spielkarten)* pack *(Brit.) or (Amer.)* deck of cards for *Quartett; (Satz von vier Spielkarten)* set of four *Quartett* cards; **d)** *(Verslehre)* quatrain
Quart·format das *(Buchw.)* quarto
Quartier [kvar'ti:ɐ̯] **das; ~s, ~e a)** *(Unterkunft)* accommodation *no indef. art.*; accommodations *pl. (Amer.)*; place to stay; *(Mil.)* quarters *pl.*; **die ~e der Truppen/der Athleten** the troops'/athletes' quarters; **ein billiges ~:** somewhere cheap to stay; **bei jmdm. ~ beziehen** put up *or* move in with sb.; **in einer Schule in ~ liegen** *(Milit. veralt.)* be quartered *or* billeted in a school; **b)** *(bes. schweiz., österr.: Stadtviertel)* quarter; district
Quartier·macher der *(Milit. veralt.)* billeting officer
Quart·sext·akkord der *(Musik)* six-four chord
Quarz [kva:ɐ̯ts] **der; ~es, ~e a)** *(Mineral)* quartz; **b)** *(~kristall)* quartz crystal
quarz·gesteuert *Adj.* quartz ⟨*clock, watch*⟩; crystal-controlled ⟨*transmitter*⟩
Quarz·glas das; *o. Pl.* quartz glass
Quarzit [kvar'tsi:t] **der; ~s, ~e** *(Geol., Mineral.)* quartzite
Quarz-: ~kristall der quartz crystal; **~lampe die** quartz lamp; **~steuerung die** *(Elektrot.)* [quartz-]crystal control; **~uhr die** quartz clock; *(Armbanduhr)* quartz watch
Quasar [kva'za:ɐ̯] **der; ~s, ~e** *(Astron.)* quasar
quasi ['kva:zi] *Adv.* **[so] ~:** more or less; *(so gut wie)* as good as; *(fast)* almost
quasi-, Quasi- quasi-⟨*military, religious, philosopher*⟩; *(fast)* semi-⟨*automatic, official*⟩
Quasselei die; ~, ~en *(ugs.)* [constant] prattling *or* jabbering
quasseln ['kvasl̩n] *(ugs.)* **1.** *itr. V.* chatter; rabbit on *(Brit. sl.)* **(von** about). **2.** *tr. V.* spout, babble ⟨*nonsense*⟩; **hör nicht auf sein Quasseln** don't listen to his blather *or* waffle
Quassel·strippe die a) *(ugs. scherzh.: Telefon)* blower *(Brit. coll.)*; **b)** *(ugs. abwertend: Schwätzer)* chatterbox
Quaste die; ~, ~n a) *(Troddel; auch fig.)* tassel; **b)** *(nordd.) s.* **Quast a**
Quästur [kvɛs'tu:ɐ̯] **die; ~, ~en** *(bes. Hochschulw.)* bursar's office
Quatsch [kvatʃ] **der; ~[e]s a)** *(ugs. abwertend: dumme Äußerung)* rubbish; **~ mit Soße** *(salopp)* absolute rubbish; stuff and nonsense *(coll.)*; **so ein ~!** what rubbish!; **b)** *(ugs. abwertend: dumme Handlung)* nonsense; *(ugs.: Unfug)* messing about; **laß den ~:** stop that nonsense; stop messing about; **mach keinen ~:** don't do anything stupid; **c)** *(ugs.: Jux)* lark *(coll.)*; **die Kinder haben nur ~ gemacht** the children were just larking about *(coll.) or* fooling around; **das habe ich aus ~ gesagt** I said it for a laugh; **d)** *(ugs.: wertloser Gegenstand)* trashy thing; *(wertloses Zeug)* trash *no indef. art.*
quatschen 1. *itr. V.* **a)** *(ugs.: dumm reden)* rabbit on *(Brit. coll.)*; blather; *(viel reden)* chatter; natter *(Brit. coll.)*; **im Unterricht ~:** chatter in class; **b)** *(ugs.: klatschen)* gossip; **es wird so viel gequatscht** there is so much gossip; **c)** *(ugs.: klatschen, berichten)* blab; open one's mouth; **d)** *(ugs.: sich unterhalten)* [have a] chat *or (coll.)* natter **(mit** with); *(ugs.: reden)* talk **(mit** to); **laß ihn erst mal ~:** let him say his bit *(coll.)*; **e)** *(landsch.: ein klatschendes Geräusch verursachen)* squelch. **2.** *tr. V.* **a)** *(ugs.: äußern)* spout ⟨*nonsense, rubbish*⟩; **was hast du da wieder gequatscht?** what sort of rubbish have you been talking?; **b)** *(salopp)* **jmdn. dämlich ~:** talk sb.'s head off
Quatsch·kopf der *(salopp)* stupid chatterbox; *(Schwätzer, Schwafler)* windbag
quatsch·naß *Adj. (ugs.)* sopping wet
Queck·silber ['kvɛk-] **das** mercury; *(fig.)* quicksilver; **~ im Leib** *od.* **im Hintern haben** *(fig. ugs.)* have ants in one's pants *(sl.)*
quecksilber-, Quecksilber-: ~haltig *Adj.* containing mercury *postpos., not pred.*; **~haltig sein** contain mercury; **~säule die** [column of] mercury; **~vergiftung die** mercury poisoning
queck·silbrig *Adj.* **a)** silvery; **b)** *(fig.: unruhig)* fidgety
Quell [kvɛl] **der; ~[e]s, ~e** *(geh.)* spring; *(fig.: Ursprung)* source; fount *(poet.)*
Quell·bewölkung die *(Met.)* cumulus clouds *pl.*
Quelle ['kvɛlə] **die; ~, ~n a)** spring; *(eines Baches, eines Flusses)* source; **b)** *(fig.)* source; **die ~ der Weisheit** the fount of wisdom *(poet.)*; **eine Mitteilung aus zuverlässiger ~:** a piece of information from a reliable source; **an der ~ sitzen** *(ugs.) (für Informationen)* have access to inside information; *(für günstigen Erwerb)* be at the source of supply
¹quellen *unr. itr. V.; mit sein* **a)** *(hervordringen)* ⟨*liquid*⟩ gush, stream; *(aus der Erde)* well up; ⟨*smoke*⟩ billow; ⟨*crowd*⟩ stream, pour; *(fig.)* ⟨*tears*⟩ well up; **b)** *(sich wölben)* bulge; **die Augen quollen ihm [fast] aus dem Kopf** his eyes nearly popped out [of his head]; **c)** *(sich ausdehnen)* swell [up]
²quellen *tr. V. (~ lassen)* soak ⟨*peas, beans*⟩; steep ⟨*barley*⟩
Quellen-: ~an·gabe die reference; **~forschung die** source research; **~nachweis der** *s.* **~angabe; ~sammlung die** collection of source materials; **~steuer die** *(Finanzw.)* tax deducted at source; **~studium das** study of [the] sources; **~verzeichnis das** list of references
Quell-: ~fluß der *(Geogr.)* headstream; **~gebiet das** *(Geogr.)* headwater region; **~wasser das;** *Pl.* **~wasser** spring water
Quengelei die; ~ *(ugs.)* nagging; pestering
quengelig *(ugs.)* **1.** *Adj.* whining; fretful; **~ werden** start whining *or (coll.)* grizzling. **2.** *adv.* in a whining voice; fretfully
quengeln ['kvɛŋl̩n] *itr. (auch tr.) V. (ugs.)* **a)** *(weinen)* ⟨*baby*⟩ whimper, *(coll.)* grizzle; **b)** *(drängen)* nag; **c)** *(nörgeln)* carp
Quentchen ['kvɛntçən] **das; ~s, ~** *(veralt.)* scrap; **ein ~ Salz** a pinch of salt; **kein ~:** not an iota; **ein ~ Glück** *(fig. geh.)* a little bit of luck; **dieses ~ Hoffnung** *(fig. geh.)* this glimmer of hope
quer [kve:ɐ̯] *Adv.* sideways; crosswise; *(schräg)* diagonally; at an angle; **~ zu etw.** at an angle to sth.; *(rechtwinklig)* at right angles to sth.; **der Wagen steht ~ auf der** *od.* **zur Fahrbahn** the car is standing sideways across the road; **das Blatt/den Stoff ~ legen** lay the sheet/material crosswise; **die Streifen verlaufen ~:** the stripes are diagonal/ *(horizontal)* horizontal; **~ auf dem Bett liegen** lie across the bed; **~ durch/über** (+ *Akk.*) straight through/across; **~ über die Straße gehen** go straight across the road; *(schräg)* cross the road at an angle; **~ durch Amerika fahren** travel right across America; **~ durch die Parteien** *(fig.)* across all party boundaries
quer-, Quer-: ~achse die transverse axis; **~balken der a)** cross-beam; *(kleiner)* cross-piece; **b)** *(Musik)* stroke; **~beet** *Adv. ugs. (~feldein)* across country; *(ohne Ziel)* at random; *(fig.: überall)* everywhere and anywhere; **~denker der** lateral thinker; **~durch** [-'-] *Adv.* straight through [the middle of] it/them
Quere die *in* **jmdm./sich in die ~ kommen** *od.* **geraten** *(jmdm./sich begegnen)* bump into sb./one another *(coll.)*; **jmdm. in die ~ kommen** *od.* **geraten** *(fig.: jmdn. behindern)* get in sb.'s way *(coll.)*; **jmdm./einem Auto/einem Flugzeug in die ~ geraten** cross sb.'s path/the path of a car/an aircraft
Querele [kve're:lə] **die; ~, ~n;** *meist Pl. (geh.)* squabble, wrangle **(um** about, over)
queren *tr. V. (geh.)* cross
quer·feld·ein *Adv.* across country
Querfeldein-: ~lauf der *(Wettbewerb)* cross-country [race]; *(Sportart)* cross-country running; **~rennen das** *(Wettbewerb)* cross-country [cycle] race; *(Sportart)* cyclo-cross *no def. art.*
quer-, Quer-: ~flöte die transverse flute; **~format das** landscape format; *(Bild/Buch)* picture/book in landscape format; **~gestreift** *Adj.* diagonally striped; *(horizontal)* horizontally striped; **~kopf der** *(ugs.)* awkward cuss *(coll.)*; *(komischer Kauz)* oddball *(coll.)*; **~köpfig** *Adj.* awkward; perverse; **~lage die** *(Med.)* transverse presentation; **~latte die** horizontal slat; *(Fuß-, Handball)* crossbar; **~|legen** *refl. V. (ugs.)* make difficulties; *(hartnäckig)* dig in one's heels; **~paß der** *(Fuß-, Handball)* crossfield pass; cross; lateral pass *(Amer.)*; **~richtung die** transverse direction; **in [der] ~richtung** transversely; crosswise; *(schräg)* diagonally; **~ruder das** *(Flugw.)* aileron; **~|schießen** *unr. itr. V. (ugs.)* put a spanner in the works *(coll.)*; **~schiff das** *(Archit.)* transept; **~schläger der** *(Geschoß)* deflected shot; ricochet; **~schnitt der a)** cross-section; **im ~schnitt** in cross-section; **b)** *(Auswahl)* selection **(durch** from); **ein repräsentativer ~schnitt der Wähler** a representative cross-section of voters; **~schnitt[s]·gelähmt** *Adj. (Med.)* paraplegic; **~schnitt[s]·gelähmte der/die** *(Med.)* paraplegic; **~schnitt[s]·lähmung die;** *o. Pl. (Med.)* paraplegia *no indef. art.*; paraplegic condition; **~schuß der** *(ugs.)* spanner in the works *(coll.)*; **~schüsse gegen jmds. Politik** attempts at obstructing sb.'s policies; **~straße die** *(Abzweigung)* turning; *(Nebenstraße)* side-street; **die zweite ~straße links** the second turning on the left; **~streifen der** diagonal stripe; *(horizontal)* horizontal stripe; **~summe die** *(Math.)* sum of the digits **(von, aus** of); **eine Zahl, deren ~summe 19 ergibt** a number the sum of whose digits is 19; **~treiber der** *(ugs. abwertend)* trouble-maker
Querulant [kveru'lant] **der; ~en, ~en, Querulantin die; ~, ~nen** *(abwertend)* malcontent
Quer-: ~verbindung die connection, link **(zu** with); *(Verkehrsw.)* cross-country route; *(direkte Verbindung)* direct connection; **~verweis der** *(Buchw.)* cross-reference
¹Quetsche ['kvɛtʃə] **die; ~, ~n** *(bes. südd., westmd.) s.* **Zwetsche**
²Quetsche die; ~, ~n a) *(bes. nordd.)* potato-crusher; **b)** *(ugs. abwertend: Ort, Betrieb)* miserable hole
quetschen 1. *tr. V.* **a)** crush ⟨*person, limb, thorax*⟩; **sich** *(Dat.)* **den Arm/die Hand ~:** get one's arm/hand caught; **sich** *(Dat.)* **den Finger/die Zehe ~:** pinch one's finger/toe;

b) *(drücken, pressen)* squeeze, squash (**gegen, an** + *Akk.* against, **in** + *Akk.* into); *(bes. nordd.: auspressen)* squeeze ⟨*juice*⟩ (**aus** out of); **ein paar Zeilen an den Rand ~** *(ugs.)* squeeze a few lines into the margin; **c)** *(bes. nordd.: zerdrücken)* mash ⟨*potatoes*⟩. **2.** *refl. V.* **sich in/durch etw.** *(Akk.)* **~:** squeeze [one's way] into/through sth.
Quetsch-: ~kartoffeln *Pl. (bes. berlin.)* mashed potatoes; **~kommode die** *(salopp scherzh.: Akkordeon)* squeeze-box *(sl.)*
Quetschung die; ~, ~en bruise; contusion *(Med.)*
Quetsch·wunde die *(Med.)* contusion
Queue [kø:] **das** *od. (österr.)* **der; ~s, ~s** cue
quick [kvɪk] *(bes. nordd.)* **1.** *Adj.* lively. **2.** *adv.* in a lively way; animatedly
quick·lebendig 1. *Adj.* [very] lively; active; *(bes. im Alter)* sprightly; spry; vivacious ⟨*personality*⟩; frisky ⟨*small animal*⟩; **~ sein** be full of [the joys of] life; be bright as a button; ⟨*child*⟩ be full of beans *(coll.)*. **2.** *adv.* bright as a button; ⟨*talk*⟩ animatedly
quiek[s]en ['kvi:k(s)n̩] **1.** *itr. V.* squeak; ⟨*piglet, fig.: person*⟩ squeal (**vor** with); **zum Quiek[s]en sein** be a hoot *(coll.)*. **2.** *tr. V.* squawk
Quietismus [kvie'tɪsmʊs] **der; ~:** quietism *no def. art.*
quietschen ['kvi:tʃn̩] *itr. V.* ⟨*thing*⟩ squeak; ⟨*brakes, tyres, crane*⟩ squeal, screech; *(ugs.)* ⟨*person*⟩ squeal, shriek (**vor** + *Dat.* with)
quietsch-, Quietsch-: ~fidel *(ugs.)* **1.** *Adj.* [really] chirpy *(coll.) or (esp. Amer.)* chipper; *(gesund und munter)* bright-eyed and bushy-tailed *pred. (coll.)*; **2.** *adv.* [really] chirpy *(coll.)*; **~lebendig** *(ugs.) Adj.* bright-eyed and bushy-tailed *pred. (coll.)*; *(sehr aktiv)* full of beans *pred. (coll.)*; *(hellwach)* wide awake; **~ton der** *(ugs.)* screeching noise; *(bes. durch Reibung)* squeal; **~vergnügt** *(ugs.)* **1.** *Adj.* [really] chirpy *(coll.) or (esp. Amer.)* chipper; **2.** *adv.* as happily *or (coll.)* chirpily as could be
Quinta ['kvɪnta] **die; ~, Quinten** *(Schulw.)* **a)** *(veralt.)* second year *(of a Gymnasium)*; **b)** *(österr.)* fifth year *(of a Gymnasium)*
Quintaner [kvɪn'ta:nɐ] **der; ~s, ~, Quintanerin die; ~, ~nen** *(Schulw.)* **a)** *(veralt.)* pupil in the second year *(of a Gymnasium)*; **b)** *(österr.)* pupil in the fifth year *(of a Gymnasium)*
Quinte ['kvɪntə] **die; ~, ~n** *(Musik)* fifth
Quinten·zirkel der *(Musik)* circle of fifths
Quint·essenz die *(geh.)* substance; *(wesentlicher Punkt)* essential point; *(Schlußfolgerung)* conclusion; **als ~ bleibt festzuhalten, daß ...:** the essential point *or* conclusion to be drawn is that ...
Quintett [kvɪn'tɛt] **das; ~[e]s, ~e** *(Musik)* quintet
Quint·sext·akkord der *(Musik)* six-five chord
Quirl [kvɪrl] **der; ~[e]s, ~e a)** *(Küchengerät) long-handled blender with a star-shaped head;* **b)** *(Mensch)* live wire
quirlen 1. *tr. V.* ≈ whisk. **2.** *itr. V.* swirl [about]
quirlig *Adj.* lively; *(flink)* nimble
quitt [kvɪt] *Adj.; nicht attr. (ugs.)* quits; **mit jmdm. ~ sein** be quits with sb.; *(mit jmdm. gebrochen haben)* be finished with sb.; **damit sind wir ~:** that makes us quits
Quitte ['kvɪtə] **die; ~, ~n** quince
quitte[n]·gelb *Adj.* pale greenish-yellow
quittieren *tr. V.* **a)** *auch itr. (bescheinigen)* acknowledge, confirm ⟨*receipt, condition*⟩; receipt, give a receipt for ⟨*sum, invoice*⟩; **würden Sie bitte auf der Rückseite der Rechnung ~?** could you please receipt the bill on the back?; **b)** *(reagieren auf)* **etw. mit etw. ~:** react *or* respond to sth. with sth.; **ein Urteil mit Pfiffen ~:** greet a decision with catcalls; **c) den Dienst ~** *(veralt.)* resign one's position; ⟨*officer*⟩ resign one's commission

Quittung die; ~, ~en a) receipt (**für, über** + *Akk.* for); **b)** *(fig.)* come-uppance *(coll.)*; deserts *pl.*; **nun hast du die ~ für deine Faulheit** you've got what you deserve for being lazy
Quittungs·block der; *Pl.* **~s** receipt pad
Quivive [ki'vi:f] **das** *in* **auf dem ~ sein** *(ugs.)* be on the alert *or (coll.)* watch it
Quiz [kvɪs] **das; ~, ~:** quiz
Quiz·sendung die quiz programme
quoll [kvɔl] *1. u. 3. Pers. Sg. Prät. v.* **quellen**
Quorum ['kvo:rʊm] **das; ~s** *(bes. Politik)* quorum
Quote ['kvo:tə] **die; ~, ~n** *(Anteil)* proportion; *(Zahl)* number
Quoten·regelung die *requirement that women should be adequately represented*
Quotient [kvo'tsi̯ɛnt] **der; ~en, ~en** *(Math.)* quotient (**aus** of)
quotieren *tr., itr. V. (Börsenw.)* quote

R

r, R [ɛr] **das; ~, ~:** r, R; **er rollt das R** he rolls his r's; *s. auch* **a, A**
R *Abk. (Physik)* **Reaumur** Réaum.
Rabatt [ra'bat] **der; ~[e]s, ~e** discount; **~ gewähren** give a discount
Rabatte [ra'batə] **die; ~, ~n** border
rabattieren *tr. V. (Kaufmannsspr.)* **[jmdm.] einen Auftrag mit 30 Prozent ~:** give [sb.] a discount of 30 per cent on an order
Rabatt·marke die trading stamp
Rabatz [ra'bats] **der; ~es** *(ugs.)* **a)** *(Lärm)* racket; din; **b)** *(Protest)* **~ machen** kick up a fuss, *(coll.)* raise a stink (**bei** with)
Rabauke [ra'baukə] **der; ~n, ~n** *(ugs.)* roughneck *(coll.)*; *(Rowdy)* hooligan
Rabbi ['rabi] **der; ~[s], ~nen** [ra'bi:nən] *od.* **~s a)** *(Titel)* Rabbi; **b)** *(Person)* rabbi
Rabbinat das rabbinate
Rabbiner [ra'bi:nɐ] **der; ~s, ~:** rabbi
rabbinisch *Adj.* rabbinical
Rabe ['ra:bə] **der; ~n, ~n** raven; **ein weißer ~** *(fig.)* a great rarity; **schwarz wie ein ~/wie die ~n** *(ugs.)* as black as pitch; *(schmutzig)* as black as soot; **stehlen** *od. (salopp)* **klauen wie ein ~/wie die ~n** *(ugs.)* pinch everything one can lay one's hands on *(coll.)*
raben-, Raben-: ~aas das *(salopp abwertend)* beast; wretch; **~eltern** *Pl. (abwertend)* uncaring [brutes of] parents; **~krähe die** carrion crow; **~mutter die** *(abwertend)* uncaring [brute of a] mother; **~schwarz** *Adj.* **a)** jet-black; raven-black ⟨*beard, hair*⟩; coal-black ⟨*man, woman*⟩; pitch-black ⟨*night*⟩; **b)** *(unheilvoll)* black ⟨*thoughts, soul, day*⟩; disastrous ⟨*day, year*⟩
rabiat [ra'bi̯a:t] **1.** *Adj.* **a)** *(gewalttätig)* violent; brutal; savage ⟨*kick*⟩; ruthless ⟨*methods*⟩; **b)** *(wütend)* furious; blistering, savage ⟨*attack*⟩; rabid ⟨*opponent*⟩. **2.** *adv.* **a)** *(gewalttätig)* violently; brutally; **b)** *(wütend)* furiously
Rabulist [rabu'lɪst] **der; ~en, ~en** *(geh.)* sophist; quibbler

Rabulistik die; ~ *(geh.)* sophistry
rabulistisch *(geh.)* **1.** *Adj.* sophistical. **2.** *adv.* sophistically
Rache ['raxə] **die; ~:** revenge; **[an jmdm.] ~ nehmen** take revenge [on sb.]; **~ üben** take revenge; wreak vengeance *(literary)*; **aus ~:** in revenge; **~ ist süß** *od. (ugs. scherzh.)* **Blutwurst** revenge is sweet; **das ist die ~ des kleinen Mannes** *(ugs., oft scherzh.)* that's how ordinary mortals get their own back [on the powers that be] *(coll.)*; **die ~ ist mein** *(bibl.)* vengeance is mine
Rache-: ~akt der *(geh.)* act of revenge, reprisal (*Gen.* by, on the part of); **~durst der** *(geh.)* thirst for revenge *or (literary)* vengeance; **~engel der** avenging angel; **~gefühl das** desire *no pl.* for revenge
Rachen ['raxn̩] **der; ~s, ~ a)** *(Schlund)* pharynx *(Anat.)*; **jmdm. den ~ pinseln** paint sb.'s throat; **b)** *(Maul)* mouth; maw *(literary)*; *(fig.)* jaws *pl.*; **jmdm. den ~ stopfen** *(salopp)* shut sb. up *(coll.)*; **jmdm. etwas in den ~ werfen** *od.* **schmeißen** *(salopp)* give sb. sth. to keep him/her happy
rächen ['rɛçn̩] **1.** *tr. V.* avenge ⟨*person, crime*⟩; take revenge for ⟨*insult, crime*⟩; **jmds. Mord an jmdm. ~:** take revenge on sb. for sb.'s murder. **2.** *refl. V.* **a)** take one's revenge; **sich an jmdm. [für etw.] ~:** take one's revenge on sb. [for sth.]; get even with sb. [for sth.]; **b)** *(sich übel auswirken)* ⟨*mistake[s], bad behaviour*⟩ take its/their toll; **dein Leichtsinn wird sich noch ~/es wird sich noch ~, daß du das tust** you will have to pay [the penalty] for your recklessness/for doing that
Rachen-: ~höhle die *(Anat.)* pharyngeal cavity; **~mandel die** *(Anat.)* [pharyngeal] tonsil
Rache·plan der plan for revenge
Rächer der; ~s, ~, Rächerin die; ~, ~nen *(geh.)* avenger
Rache·schwur der *(geh.)* oath of revenge
Rach·gier die lust for revenge
rach·gierig *(geh.) s.* **rachsüchtig**
Rachitis [ra'xi:tɪs] **die; ~** *(Med.)* rickets *sing.*
rachitisch *Adj.* with rickets *postpos., not pred.*; rachitic *(Med.)*
Rach·sucht die; *o. Pl. (geh.)* lust for revenge
rach·süchtig *(geh.)* **1.** *Adj.* vengeful; **~ sein** ⟨*person*⟩ be out for revenge. **2.** *adv.* vengefully; seeking to exact revenge
Racker der; ~s, ~ *(fam.)* rogue; rascal
rackern ['rakɐn] *itr. V. (ugs.)* drudge; toil
Racket ['rɛkət] **das; ~s, ~s** *(Tennis)* racket
Raclette ['raklɛt] **die; ~, ~s** *od.* **das; ~s, ~s** *(Kochk.)* raclette
[1]Rad [ra:t] **das; ~es, Räder** ['rɛ:dɐ] **a)** wheel; *(Zahn~)* gear; *(kleines Zahn~)* cog; *(einer Uhr)* [toothed] wheel; *(für Riemen)* pulley; **das ~ der Zeit/der Geschichte läßt sich nicht anhalten** *(fig.)* the march of time/of history cannot be halted; **fünftes** *od.* **das fünfte ~ am Wagen sein** *(fig. ugs.)* be superfluous; *(die Harmonie stören)* be in the way; **er kam unter die Räder des Lkws** he was run over by the lorry *(Brit.) or* truck; **unter die Räder kommen** *(fig. ugs.)* fall into bad ways; *(total verkommen)* go to the dogs *(coll.)*; **nur** *od.* **bloß ein ~ im Getriebe sein** be just a small cog in the machine; **b)** *(Fahr~)* bicycle; bike *(coll.)*; **mit dem ~ fahren** go by bicycle *or (coll.)* bike; *s. auch* **radfahren; c)** *(Turnen)* cart-wheel; **ein ~ schlagen** *od.* **ausführen** do *or* perform a cart-wheel; *s. auch* **radschlagen; d)** *(hist.: Foltergerät)* wheel; **jmdn. aufs ~ flechten** break sb. on the wheel; **e)** *(bei Vögeln: Schwanzfedern)* fan; **ein ~ schlagen** ⟨*peacock*⟩ fan out its tail
[2]Rad das; ~[s], ~ *(Physik)* rad
Rad·achse die *(Technik)* axle
Radar [ra'da:ɐ̯] **der** *od.* **das; ~s** *(Technik)* radar

Radar: ~an·lage die radar installation; **~astronomie die** radar astronomy *no art.*; **~falle die** *(ugs.)* [radar] speed trap; **~gerät das** radar [system]; **~geräte** radar [equipment] *sing.*; **~kontrolle die** *(Verkehrsw.)* [radar] speed check; **~schirm der** radar screen

Radau [ra'dau] **der; ~s** *(ugs.)* row *(coll.)*; racket

Radau·bruder der *(ugs. abwertend)* rowdy

Rad·aufhängung die *(Kfz-W.)* suspension

Rädchen ['rɛ:tçən] **das; ~s, ~ a)** [little] wheel; *(Zahnrad)* [small] cog; *s. auch* **Rad a; b)** *(Fahrrad)* [little] bicycle *or (coll.)* bike; **c)** *(für Schnittmuster)* tracing wheel; *(für Gebäckteig)* pastry-wheel

Rad·dampfer der paddle-steamer

radebrechen 1. *tr. V.* **Französisch/Deutsch** *usw.* **~:** speak broken French/German *etc.* **2.** *itr. V.* speak pidgin

radeln ['ra:dl̩n] *itr. (auch tr.) V.; mit sein (ugs., bes. südd.)* cycle; **irgendwohin ~:** go somewhere by bike *(coll.)*; bike it somewhere *(coll.)*; **50 km ~:** cycle 50 km

Rädels·führer ['rɛ:dls-] **der** *(abwertend)* ringleader

-räderig *s.* **-rädrig**

rädern ['rɛ:dɐn] *tr. V.* **jmdn. ~** *(hist.)* break sb. on the wheel; *s. auch* **gerädert**

Räder·werk das *(Mechanik)* mechanism; works *pl.*; *(Räder)* wheels *pl.*; *(Zahnräder)* gears *pl.*; cogs *pl.*; **das ~ der Justiz** *(fig.)* the wheels *pl. or* machinery of justice

rad-, Rad-: ~|fahren *unr. itr. V. (Zusammenschreibung nur im Inf. u. 2. Part.); mit sein* **a)** cycle; ride a bicycle *or (coll.)* bike; **er fährt gern Rad** he likes cycling; **b)** *(ugs. abwertend: unterwürfig sein)* suck up to people *(sl.)*; **~fahrer der, ~fahrerin die a)** cyclist; **b)** *(ugs. abwertend: Schmeichler)* toady; crawler *(coll.)*; **~fahr·weg der** cycle-path *or* -track

Radi ['ra:di] **der; ~s, ~** *(bayr., österr. ugs.)* [large white] radish

radial [ra'dia:l] **1.** *Adj.* radial. **2.** *adv.* radially; **~ verlaufend** radiating

Radiator [ra'dia:tɔr] **der; ~s, ~en** [-'to:rən] [central-heating] radiator

Radicchio [ra'dɪkio] **der; ~s** radicchio

Radien *s.* **Radius**

radieren [ra'di:rən] *tr. (auch itr.) V.* **a)** *(tilgen)* erase; **b)** *(Graphik)* etch

Radierer der; ~s, ~ a) *(ugs.) s.* **Radiergummi; b)** *(Künstler)* etcher

Radier-: ~gummi der rubber [eraser]; **~kunst die;** *o. Pl.* etching; **~nadel die** *(Graphik)* [dry-point] etching-needle

Radierung die; ~, ~en *(Graphik)* etching

Radieschen [ra'di:sçən] **das; ~s, ~:** radish; **sich** *(Dat.)* **die ~ von unten betrachten** *(salopp)* be pushing up the daisies *(sl.)*

radikal [radi'ka:l] **1.** *Adj.* radical; drastic ⟨*measure, method, cure*⟩; *(rücksichtslos)* ruthless ⟨*measure, method, hardness*⟩; **ein ~er Bruch mit der Vergangenheit** a complete break with the past. **2.** *adv.* radically; *(rücksichtslos)* ruthlessly; *(vollständig)* ⟨*abolish, eradicate*⟩ totally, completely; **~ gegen jmdn. vorgehen** adopt drastic *or* ruthless methods against sb.; **~ [links/rechts] denken/eingestellt sein** have radical [left-wing/right-wing] views

Radikal das; ~s, ~e a) *(Chemie)* [free] radical; **b)** *(Math., Sprachw.)* radical

Radikale der/die; *adj. Dekl.* radical

Radikalen·erlaß der *decree excluding members of extremist organizations from civil-service employment*

radikalisieren 1. *tr. V.* make [more] radical. **2.** *refl. V.* become more radical **(durch** owing to, as a result of**)**

Radikalisierung die; ~, ~en radicalization; *(das Radikalwerden)* growing radicalism, trend to radicalism (*Gen.* among)

Radikalismus der; ~, Radikalismen radicalism; *(Haltung)* radical attitude; *(Unnachgiebigkeit)* rigid attitude

Radikalität [radikali'tɛ:t] **die; ~:** radicalness; radical nature; *(Härte)* ruthlessness; *(Vollständigkeit)* completeness

Radikal·kur die *(auch fig.)* drastic remedy **(gegen** for**)**

Radio ['ra:dio] **das** *(südd., schweiz. auch:* **der); ~s, ~s** radio; **sie haben nicht einmal ~:** they don't even have a radio; **im ~:** on the radio; **~ hören** listen to the radio

radio-, Radio-: ~aktiv 1. *Adj.* radioactive; **2.** *adv.* radioactively; **~aktiv verseucht** contaminated by radioactivity *postpos.*; **~aktivität die;** *o. Pl.* radioactivity; **~apparat** ['-----] **der** radio set; **~astronomie die** radio astronomy *no art.*; **~biologie die** *s.* **Strahlenbiologie; ~gerät** ['----] **das** radio set; **~isotop das** *(Physik)* radioisotope; **~loge** [~'lo:gə] **der; ~n, ~n** radiologist; **~logie die; ~:** radiology *no art.*; **~login die; ~, ~nen** radiologist; **~musik** ['----] **die** music on the radio; **~sender** ['----] **der** radio station; **~therapie die;** *o. Pl. (Med.)* radiotherapy; **~wecker** ['----] **der** radio alarm clock; **~welle** ['----] **die** *(Technik, Physik)* radio wave

Radium ['ra:diʊm] **das; ~s** radium

Radius ['ra:diʊs] **der; ~, Radien** ['ra:diən] *(Math.)* radius

Rad-: ~kappe die hub-cap; **~kranz der** *(Technik)* **a)** *(beim Fahrrad)* wheel rim; **b)** *(beim Zahnrad)* toothed rim; **~lager das** wheel bearing

Radler der; ~s, ~ a) cyclist; **b)** *(bes. südd.: Getränk)* shandy

Radler·hose die cycle shorts *pl.*

Radlerin die; ~, ~nen cyclist

Rad·nabe die [wheel] hub

Radon ['ra:dɔn] **das; ~s** *(Chemie)* radon

Rad-: ~renn·bahn die cycle-racing track; *(Stadion)* velodrome; **~rennen das** cycle race; *(Sport)* cycle-racing; **~rennfahrer der** racing cyclist

-rädrig [-rɛ:drɪç] *Adj.* -wheeled; **drei/vier~:** three-/four-wheeled

rad-, Rad-: ~|schlagen *unr. itr. V. (Zusschr. nur im Inf. u. 2. Part.)* do a cartwheel; *(mehrmals)* do cart-wheels; **~sport der** cycling *no def. art.*; **~stand der** wheelbase; **~tour die** bicycle ride; *(länger)* cycling tour; **eine ~tour machen** go for a bicycle ride/on a cycling tour; **~wanderung die** cycling tour; **~wechsel der** wheel-change; **~weg der** cycle-path *or* -track

RAF [ɛrla:'lɛf] **die; ~:** *Abk.* **Rote-Armee-Fraktion** Red Army Faction

raffen ['rafn̩] *tr. V.* **a)** *(an sich reißen)* snatch; grab; rake in *(coll.)* ⟨*money*⟩; *(abwertend: in seinen Besitz bringen)* **etw. [an sich] ~:** seize sth.; *(eilig)* snatch *or* grab sth.; **b)** *(zusammenhalten)* gather ⟨*material, curtain*⟩; **c)** *(gekürzt wiedergeben)* condense ⟨*text*⟩; *(kürzen)* shorten ⟨*text, play, film*⟩

Raff·gier die rapacity; acquisitive greed

raff·gierig 1. *Adj.* greedy. **2.** *adv.* greedily

Raffinement [rafinə'mã:] **das; ~s, ~s** *(geh.)* **a)** *(Feinheit)* refinement; **b)** *o. Pl. s.* **Raffinesse a**

Raffinerie [rafinə'ri:] **die; ~, ~n** refinery

Raffinesse [rafi'nɛsə] **die; ~, ~n a)** *o. Pl. (Schlauheit)* guile; ingenuity; **b)** *meist Pl. (Finesse)* refinement

raffinieren [rafi'ni:rən] *tr. V. (bes. Chemie, Geol.)* refine

raffiniert 1. *Adj.* **a)** ingenious ⟨*plan, design*⟩; *(verfeinert)* refined, subtle ⟨*colour, scheme, effect*⟩; sophisticated ⟨*dish, cut (of clothes)*⟩; **b)** *(gerissen)* cunning, artful ⟨*person, trick*⟩. **2.** *adv.* **a)** ingeniously; cleverly; *(verfeinert)* with great refinement/sophistication; **eine ~ geschnittene Bluse** a blouse with a sophisticated cut; **b)** *(gerissen)* cunningly; artfully

Raffiniertheit die; ~ a) *(Klugheit)* ingenuity; *(Verfeinerung)* refinement; sophistication; *(der Kleidung)* stylishness; *(von Speisen)* subtle flavour; **b)** *(Gerissenheit)* cunning; artfulness

Raffke ['rafkə] **der; ~s, ~s** *(ugs. abwertend)* money-grubber

Rage ['ra:ʒə] **die; ~** *(ugs.)* fury; rage; **in [blinder] ~:** in a [blind] fury; **in ~ sein** be livid *(Brit. coll.) or* furious; **jmdn. in ~ bringen** make sb. hopping mad *(coll.) or* absolutely furious; **in ~ kommen** *od.* **geraten** fly into a rage; **immer mehr in ~ kommen** become more and more furious

ragen ['ra:gn̩] *itr. V.* **a)** *(vertikal)* rise [up]; ⟨*mountains*⟩ tower up; **aus dem Wasser ~:** stick *or* jut right out of the water; **in die Höhe** *od.* **in den Himmel ~:** tower *or* soar into the sky; **er ragte aus der Menge** he towered above the rest of the crowd; **b)** *(horizontal)* project, stick out **(in +** *Akk.* into; **über +** *Akk.* over**)**

Raglan·ärmel ['raglan-] **der** raglan sleeve

Ragout [ra'gu:] **das; ~s, ~s** *(Kochk.)* ragout

Ragoût fin [ragu'fɛ̃] **das; ~ ~, ~s ~s** *(Kochk.)* gourmet ragout *(in a scallop shell, in puff pastry, or au gratin)*

Ragtime ['rægtaɪm] **der; ~** *(Musik)* **a)** *(Stil, Musik)* ragtime *no art.*; **b)** *(Musikstück)* rag

Rah[e] ['ra:(ə)] **die; ~, Rahen** *(Seemannsspr.)* yard

Rahm [ra:m] **der; ~[e]s** *(bes. südd., österr., schweiz.)* cream; *s. auch* **abschöpfen**

[1]rahmen *tr. V.* frame

[2]rahmen *(bes. südd., österr., schweiz.) tr. V.* skim ⟨*milk*⟩

Rahmen der; ~s, ~ a) frame; *(Kfz-W.: Fahrgestell)* chassis; **b)** *(fig.: Bereich, Literaturw.: ~erzählung)* framework; *(szenischer Hintergrund)* setting; *(Zusammenhang)* context; *(Grenzen)* bounds *pl.*; limits *pl.*; **in großem/bescheidenem ~ feiern** celebrate on a grand/modest scale; **aus dem ~ fallen** be out of place; stick out; ⟨*behaviour*⟩ be unsuited to the occasion; **im ~ einer Sache** *(Gen.) (in den Grenzen)* within the bounds of sth.; *(im Zusammenhang)* within the context of sth.; *(im Verlauf)* in the course of sth.; **im ~ des Möglichen** within the bounds of possibility; **im ~ der Wiener Festwochen** as part of the Vienna Festival; **im ~ bleiben** stay within reasonable bounds; ⟨*person*⟩ not overdo it, not go too far; ⟨*prices*⟩ not be too high; **den ~ sprengen** be out of proportion; **den ~ einer Sache** *(Gen.)* **sprengen** go beyond the scope of sth.

Rahmen-: ~abkommen das basic agreement; **~antenne die** *(Funkw.)* frame aerial *or (Amer.)* antenna; **~bedingung die** prevailing condition *or* circumstance; *(Soziol.)* structural condition; **~erzählung die** *(Literaturw.)* framework story; **~gesetz das** *(Rechtsw.) law providing framework for more specific legislation;* **~gesetze** *Pl.* outline legislation *sing.*; **~handlung die** *(Literaturw.)* framework plot; sub-plot *(framing the main plot)*; **~programm das** supporting programme; **~richt·linie die;** *meist Pl.* overall guideline

rahmig *Adj. (bes. südd., österr., schweiz.)* creamy

Rahm-: ~käse der cream cheese; **~soße die** *(bes. südd., österr., schweiz.)* cream sauce

Rah·segel das *(Seemannsspr.)* square sail

Rain [rain] **der; ~[e]s, ~e a)** *(geh.: Ackergrenze)* margin of a/the field; **b)** *(südd., schweiz.: Abhang)* slope

räkeln ['rɛ:kl̩n] *s.* **rekeln**

Rakete [ra'ke:tə] **die; ~, ~n** rocket; *(Milit.: gelenkte ~)* missile

raketen-, Raketen-: ~ab·schuß·basis die missile [launching] base; **~an·trieb der** rocket propulsion; **~basis die** *s.* **~abschußbasis; ~flug·zeug das** rocket plane;

~getrieben *Adj.* rocket-propelled; **~schlitten der** *(Technik)* rocket sled; **~start·rampe die** rocket launching pad; **~stufe die** *(Technik)* rocket stage; **~träger der** missile-carrier; **~trieb·werk das** *(Technik)* rocket engine; **~werfer der** *(Milit.)* rocket-launcher

Raki ['ra:ki] **der; ~[s], ~s** raki

Ralle ['ralə] **die; ~, ~n** *(Zool.)* rail

Rallye ['rali] **die; ~, ~s** *od. schweiz.* **das; ~s, ~s** *(Motorsport)* rally; **die ~ Monte Carlo** the Monte Carlo Rally; **eine ~ fahren** take part in a rally

rạmm-, Rạmm-: ~bär der *(Bauw.)* [pile-driver] ram; **~bock der a)** *(hist.)* battering-ram; **b)** *s.* **~bär; c)** *s.* **Ramme; ~dösig** *(salopp) Adj.* **a)** *(benommen)* dizzy; **b)** *(dumm)* dopey *(sl.)*

Ramme ['ramə] **die; ~, ~n** *(Bauw.) (Pfahl~)* pile-driver; *(für Erde, Steine)* rammer

rammeln ['ramḷn] **1.** *itr. V.* **a)** *(Jägerspr.)* mate; **b)** *(derb: koitieren)* have a screw *(vulg.)*. **2.** *tr. V.* **a)** *(Jägerspr.)* serve; mount; **b)** *(derb: koitieren mit)* screw *(vulg.)*

rạmmen 1. *tr. V.* ram; **etw. in etw.** *(Akk.)* **~:** ram *or* jam sth. into sth. **2.** *itr. V.* *(stoßen)* ram, crash **(gegen, auf +** *Akk.* **into)**

Rạmmler der; ~s, ~ *(Jägerspr.)* buck [rabbit]

Rampe ['rampə] **die; ~, ~n a)** *(waagrechte Fläche)* [loading] platform; **b)** *(schiefe Fläche)* ramp; *(Auffahrt)* [sloping] drive; *(Bergsteigen)* sloping slab of rock; **c)** *s.* **Startrampe; d)** *(Theater)* apron; forestage; **an** *od.* **vor die ~ treten** come to the front of the stage; **[nicht] über die ~ kommen** *(Theaterjargon)* [not] come across

Rạmpen·licht das; ~[e]s, ~er *(Theater)* **a)** *o. Pl. (Licht)* [light *sing.* from the] footlights *pl.*; **im ~ [der Öffentlichkeit] stehen** be in the limelight; **b)** *(Lichtquelle)* footlight

ramponieren [rampo'ni:rən] *tr. V. (ugs.)* batter; **ramponiert** battered, knocked-about ‹*furniture, phone-box*›; run-down, down-at-heel ‹*dwelling, room*›; shabby ‹*suit*›; dented ‹*confidence*›

¹Ramsch [ramʃ] **der; ~[e]s, ~e** *(ugs. abwertend)* **a)** *(Ware)* trashy goods *pl.*; **b)** *(Kram)* junk

²Rạmsch der; ~[e]s, ~e *(Kartenspiel)* ramsch

rạmschen *tr., auch itr. V. (ugs.)* grab; **[Sachen] beim Schlußverkauf ~:** get masses of things cheap in a sale/the sales

Rạmsch-: ~laden der *(ugs. abwertend)* shop selling trashy goods; **~ware die** *(ugs. abwertend)* trashy goods *pl.*

ran [ran] *Adv. (ugs.)* **a)** *s.* **heran; b)** *(fang an)* off you go; get going; *(fangen wir an)* let's go; **los, ~ an die Arbeit!** come on, get down to work!; **c)** *(greif[t] an)* go at him/them!; *(beim Boxen)* let him/them have it!; *s. auch* **rangehen; ranhalten; rankommen** *usw.*

Ranch [rɛntʃ] **die; ~, ~[e]s** ranch

Rancher ['rɛntʃɐ] **der; ~s, ~[s]** rancher

Rand [rant] **der; ~[e]s, Ränder** ['rɛndɐ] **a)** edge; *(Einfassung)* border; *(Hut~)* brim; *(Brillen~, Gefäß~, Krater~)* rim; *(eines Abgrunds)* brink; *(auf einem Schriftstück)* margin; *(Weg~)* verge; *(Stadt~)* edge; outskirts *pl.*; **voll bis zum ~:** full to the brim; **etwas an den ~ schreiben** write sth. in the margin; *(fig.)* **etw. am ~e erwähnen** mention sth. in passing; **am ~e liegen** ‹*problem etc.*› be of marginal importance; **außer ~ und Band geraten/sein** *(ugs.)* go/be wild **(vor** with); *(rasen)* go/be berserk **(vor** with); **das versteht sich am ~e** it goes without saying; **am ~e der Pleite sein** be on the verge of bankruptcy; **jmdn. an den ~ des Wahnsinns/Ruins bringen** bring sb. to the verge *or* brink of insanity/ruin; **mit etw. [nicht] zu ~e kommen** *(ugs.)* [not] be able to cope with sth.; **mit jmdm. [nicht] zu ~e kommen** *(ugs.)* [not] get on with sb.; *s. auch* **Grab; b)** *(Schmutz~)* mark; *(rund)* ring; *(in der Wanne)* tide-mark *(coll.)*; **dunkle Ränder unter den/um die Augen haben** have dark lines under/dark rings round one's eyes; **c)** *(salopp: Mund)* gob *(sl.)*; trap *(sl.)*

Randale [ran'da:lə] **die** *(salopp)* riot; **~ machen/beginnen** riot/start to riot

randalieren *itr. V.* riot; rampage; *(Radau machen)* create an uproar; **~de Halbstarke** young hooligans on the rampage

Randalierer der; ~s, ~: hooligan

Rạnd·bemerkung die marginal note *or* comment; *(mündlich)* incidental remark; aside

Rande ['randə] **die; ~, ~n** *(schweiz.)* beetroot

Rändel ['rɛndl] **das; ~s, ~** *(Mech.)* knurl

rändeln *tr. V. (Mech.)* knurl; mill ‹*coins*›

Rạ̈nder *s.* **Rand**

rạnd-, Rạnd-: ~erscheinung die peripheral phenomenon; **~figur die** minor figure; *(Nebenrolle)* minor part; **~gebiet das** outlying district; *(Grenzgebiet)* frontier area *or* district; **die ~gebiete einer Stadt** the outskirts of a town; **ein ~gebiet der Medizin** a fringe area of medicine; **~gruppe die** *(Soziol.)* fringe *or* marginal group; **~los** *Adj.* rimless ‹*spectacles*›; brimless ‹*hat*›; ‹*paper*› with no margin; **~notiz die** marginal note; **~problem das** secondary problem; **~ständig** *Adj. (Soziol.)* marginal; **~stein der** kerb; **~streifen der** verge; *(auf Autobahnen)* hard shoulder

rạnd·voll 1. *Adj.* ‹*glass etc.*› full to the brim **(mit** with); brim-full ‹*glass, cup, bowl*› **(mit** of); **~ mit Notizen** crammed full of notes. **2.** *adv.* **~ gefüllt** jam-packed *(coll.)*; chock-full; *(mit Flüssigkeit)* full to the brim

Rạnd·zone die outlying area; *(einer Stadt)* outskirts *pl.*; *(fig.)* fringe area

rang [raŋ] *1. u. 3. Pers. Sg. Prät. v.* **ringen**

Rạng der; ~[e]s, Ränge ['rɛŋə] **a)** *(Stellung, Stufe)* rank; *(in der Gesellschaft)* status; *(in bezug auf Bedeutung, Qualität)* standing; **im ~ eines Generals stehen** hold the rank of general; **jmdm. den ~ streitig machen** try to step [up] into sb.'s shoes; **jmdm./einer Sache den ~ ablaufen** leave sb./sth. far behind; **alles, was ~ und Namen hat** everybody who is anybody; **ein Physiker von ~:** an eminent physicist; **einen außerordentlichen künstlerischen ~ haben** be of exceptional artistic importance; **ersten ~es** of the greatest significance; *(qualitätsmäßig)* of the first order; **b)** *(im Theater)* circle; **erster ~:** dress circle; **zweiter ~:** upper circle; **dritter ~:** gallery; **die Zuschauer auf den Rängen** the audience in the circle [and gallery] seats; **vor überfüllten/fast leeren Rängen spielen** play to a packed/a nearly empty house; **c)** *(Sport) s.* **Platz f; d)** *(Gewinnklasse in Lotterien)* prize category

Rạng-: ~ab·zeichen das insignia [of rank]; **~älteste der/die;** *adj. Dekl.* senior officer *(holding a particular rank)*

Range ['raŋə] **die; ~, ~n** *(bes. md.)* [young] tearaway; **freche** *od.* **kesse ~n** cheeky brats

rạn|gehen *unr. itr. V. (ugs.)* **a)** *s.* **herangehen; b)** *(erotisch)* **bei den Mädchen ~:** be a fast worker with the girls *(coll.)*

Rangelei die; ~, ~en *(ugs.) s.* **Gerangel**

rangeln ['raŋḷn] *itr. V. (ugs.)* wrestle; struggle; *(kämpfen)* ‹*children*› scrap; **um etw. ~:** scramble *or* tussle for sth.; *(fig.: argumentieren)* wrangle over sth.

Rạng-: ~folge die order of precedence; *(finanziell)* order of merit; **~höchste der/die;** *adj. Dekl.* most senior person; *(Tier)* dominant animal

Rangier·bahn·hof der marshalling yard

rangieren [raŋ'ʒi:rən] **1.** *tr. V.* shunt ‹*trucks, coaches*›; switch ‹*cars*› *(Amer.)*. **2.** *itr. V.* be placed; **an letzter Stelle/auf Platz zwei ~:** be placed last/second; **hinter/vor jmdm. ~** *(bei der Arbeit usw.)* be junior/senior to sb.

Rangierer der; ~s, ~: shunter *(Brit.)*; switchman *(Amer.)*

Rangier-: ~lok die *(ugs.)*, **~lokomotive die** shunting *or (Amer.)* switch engine

rạng-, Rạng-: ~liste die a) *(Sport)* ranking list; **Nummer eins der internationalen ~liste** number one in the world rankings; **b)** *(von Offizieren, Beamten)* army/navy/civil-service list; **~mäßig 1.** *Adj.* according to rank *postpos.*; ‹*equality etc.*› with regard to rank; **~mäßige Unterschiede** differences of rank; **2.** *adv.* according to *or* with regard to rank; **~ordnung die** order of precedence; *(Verhaltensf.)* pecking order; **der ~ordnung nach unter/über jmdm. stehen** be below/above sb. in the pecking order *or* hierarchy; **~unterschied der** difference in [social] status; *(Milit.)* difference in rank

rạn|halten *unr. refl. V. (ugs.)* get a move on *(coll.)*; *(bei der Arbeit)* get stuck in *(coll.)*

rạnk *Adj. (geh.)* lissom; **~ und schlank** lithe and lissom

Ranke ['raŋkə] **die; ~, ~n** *(Bot.)* tendril

Ränke ['rɛŋkə] *Pl. (geh. veralt.)* intrigues; **~ schmieden** *(geh.)* scheme; hatch plots

rạnken 1. *refl. V.* climb, grow **(an +** *Dat.* up, **über +** *Akk.* over); **sich um etw. ~:** entwine itself around sth.; *(fig. geh.)* ‹*legends, mysteries*› be woven around sth. **2.** *itr. V.* **a)** *mit sein s.* **ranken 1; b)** *(Ranken treiben)* put out tendrils

Rạnken-: ~gewächs das creeper; **~werk das;** *o. Pl.* **a)** *(verschlungene Ranken)* mass of entwined tendrils; **b)** *(Verzierung)* plant arabesques *pl.*

Rạ̈nke-: ~schmied der *(veralt.)* intriguer; schemer; **~spiel das** *(veralt.)* intrigues *pl.*

rạn-: ~|klotzen *itr. V. (salopp)* get stuck in *(coll.)*; pull one's finger out *(sl.)*; *(auf Dauer)* keep hard at it; **~|kommen** *unr. itr. V.; mit sein (ugs.) s.* **herankommen a, c; ~|können** *unr. itr. V. (ugs.)* **an etw.** *(Akk.)* **nicht ~können** be unable to get at sth.; **ich kann nicht ~:** I can't get at it/them

Ranküne [raŋ'ky:nə] **die; ~** *(geh. veralt.)* [sense of] rancour; acrimony

rạn-: ~|lassen *unr. tr. V.* **a)** *(ugs.: herankommen lassen)* **jmdn. ~lassen** let sb. get up close; *(salopp: sexuell)* **sie läßt ihn nicht ~:** she won't let him do it *(coll.)*; **sie läßt jeden ~:** she's anybody's; **jmdn. an etw.** *(Akk.)* **nicht ~lassen** not let sb. anywhere near sth.; **b)** *(ugs.: tätig werden lassen)* **jmdn. an etw.** *(Akk.)* **~lassen** let sb. have a go at sth.; **laß mich mal ~!** let me have a go!; **~|machen** *refl. V. (ugs.) s.* **heranmachen a, b; ~|müssen** *unr. itr. V. (ugs.: arbeiten müssen)* have to get stuck in *(coll.)*

rann [ran] *1. u. 3. Pers. Sg. Prät. v.* **rinnen**

rannte ['rantə] *1. u. 3. Pers. Sg. Prät. v.* **rennen**

rạn-: ~|schmeißen *unr. refl. V.* **sich an jmdn. ~schmeißen** *(ugs.)* throw oneself at sb.; **~|wollen** *unr. itr. V. (ugs.)* want to get down to work; **an etw.** *(Akk.)* **nicht ~wollen** not feel like getting on with sth.

Ranzen ['rantsṇ] **der; ~s, ~ a)** *(Schul~)* satchel; *(veralt.: Rucksack)* rucksack; **b)** *(salopp: Bauch)* [fat] belly

rạnzig *Adj.* rancid

rapid [ra'pi:t] *(südd., österr., schweiz.),* **rapide 1.** *Adj.* rapid. **2.** *adv.* rapidly

Rappe ['rapə] **der; ~n, ~n** black horse

Rappel ['rapḷ] **der; ~s, ~** *(ugs.)* crazy turn *(coll.)*; **du hast wohl einen ~?** are you crazy?

rạppelig *Adj. (ugs.)* nervy; **das macht mich ganz ~:** it really irritates me

rạppeln *itr. V.* **a)** *(ugs.: klappern, rütteln)* rattle **(an +** *Dat.* at); ‹*alarm, telephone*› jangle; **es rappelt an der Tür** there's a rattling at the door; **bei ihm rappelt's** *(salopp)* he's got one of his crazy turns *(coll.)*; **b)** *mit sein (ugs.: sich fortbewegen)* clatter [along]; **c)** *(österr. ugs.: verrückt sein)* be a bit crackers *(Brit. coll.)*

Rappen der; **~s, ~:** [Swiss] centime
rapplig *Adj. s.* rappelig
Rappen·spalter der; **~s, ~** *(schweiz. ugs.)* penny-pincher
Rapport [ra'pɔrt] **der;** **~s, ~e a)** *(veralt.)* report; **jmdm. ~ erstatten** report to sb.; **sich zum ~ melden** report; **jmdn. zum ~ bestellen** ask sb. to give a report; **b)** *(Psych.)* rapport
Raps [raps] **der;** **~es** *(Bot., Landwirtsch.)* rape
Raps·öl das rape-oil
Rapunzel [ra'pʊntsl̩] **die;** **~, ~n a)** *o. Pl.* *(Märchengestalt)* Rapunzel; **b)** *s.* **Feldsalat**
rar [ra:ɐ̯] *Adj.* *(knapp)* scarce; *(selten vorkommend; begehrt)* rare ‹*case, opportunity, stamp, etc.*›; **sich ~ machen** *(ugs.)* not be around much *(coll.)*; *(selten erscheinen)* make only rare appearances; **sie machten sich ~, als wir ihre Hilfe brauchten** they made themselves scarce when we needed their help; **du hast dich in letzter Zeit bei uns ~ gemacht** we haven't seen much of you at our place recently
Rarität [rari'tɛ:t] **die;** **~, ~en** rarity
Raritäten-: **~kabinett das** *room housing a display of rare specimens;* **~sammlung die** collection of rare specimens
rasant [ra'zant] **1.** *Adj.* **a)** *(ugs.)* *(sehr schnell)* tremendously fast *(coll.)*‹*car, horse, runner, etc.*›; tremendous *(coll.)*, lightning *attrib.* ‹*speed, acceleration*›; meteoric, lightning *attrib.* ‹*development, progress, growth*›; hairy *(coll.)* ‹*driving*›; *(schnittig)* racy ‹*car, styling*›; **in ~em Tempo, in ~er Fahrt** at a terrific speed *(coll.)*; **b)** *(ugs.)* *(schwungvoll)* dynamic, lively ‹*show*›; action-packed, exciting ‹*film, story*›; *(fabelhaft)* terrific *(coll.)* ‹*film, show, dress, song, etc.*›; *(rassig)* classy *(sl.)* ‹*woman*›; dashing ‹*style, dress*›; **eine ~e Kür laufen** skate an exciting programme; **c)** *(Ballistik: flach)* flat ‹*trajectory*›. **2.** *adv.* **a)** *(ugs.)* *(sehr schnell)* at terrific speed *(coll.)*; ‹*increase*› by leaps and bounds; **~ beschleunigen** ‹*car*› have terrific acceleration *(coll.)*; ‹*car, driver*› accelerate like a mad thing *(coll.)*; **~ gestylt** *od.* **geschnitten** *(schnittig)* racily styled; with racy lines; **b)** *(ugs.)* *(schwungvoll)* dashingly; *(rassig)* stylishly; **c)** *(Ballistik: flach)* **~ verlaufen** ‹*trajectory*› be flat
Rasanz [ra'zants] **die;** **~ a)** *(ugs.: Schnelligkeit)* terrific speed *(coll.)*; **die ~ der Beschleunigung** the terrific [rate of] acceleration *(coll.)*; **b)** *(ugs.: Dynamik)* verve; excitement
rasch [raʃ] **1.** *Adj.* quick; quick, rapid ‹*step, progress, decision, action*›; speedy, swift ‹*end, action, decision, progress*›; fast, quick ‹*service, work, pace, tempo, progress*›; **ein ~es Tempo** a fast pace; *(eines Fahrzeugs)* a high speed; **in ~er Folge** in rapid *or* swift succession. **2.** *adv.* quickly; ‹*drive, act*› quickly, fast; ‹*decide, end, proceed*› swiftly, rapidly; **das geht mir zu ~:** that's too quick for me; **notieren Sie das ~!** make a quick note of that
rascheln ['raʃl̩n] *itr. V.* rustle; **die Maus raschelte** the mouse made a rustling noise; **es raschelte im Stroh** there was a rustling in the straw; **mit der Zeitung ~:** rustle the newspaper
rasen ['ra:zn̩] *itr. V.* **a)** *mit sein (ugs.: eilen)* dash *or* rush [along]; *(fahren)* tear *or* race along; *(fig.)* ‹*pulse*› race; **gegen einen Baum ~:** crash [at full speed] into a tree; **ein Auto kam um die Ecke gerast** a car came tearing *or* racing round the corner; **die Zeit raste** *(fig.)* the time simply flew past; **b)** *(toben)* ‹*person*› rage; *(wie wahnsinnig)* rave; *(fig.)* ‹*storm, sea, war*› rage; **[vor Begeisterung] ~:** go wild [with enthusiasm]
Rasen der; **~s, ~:** grass *no indef. art.*; *(gepflegte ~fläche)* lawn; *(eines Spielfeldes usw., Grassode)* turf; **in unserem Garten ist hauptsächlich ~:** our garden is mainly grass *or* lawn; **ihn deckt der kühle** *od.* **grüne ~** *(geh. verhüll.)* he has been laid to rest; **er mußte den ~ verlassen** *(Sportjargon)* he was sent off [the field *or (coll.)* park]
rasend 1. *Adj.* **a)** *(sehr schnell)* **in ~er Fahrt, mit ~er Geschwindigkeit** at breakneck speed; **b)** *(tobend)* raging; *(wie wahnsinnig)* raving; *(verrückt)* mad; **[vor Wut** *usw.***] ~ werden** be beside oneself [with rage *etc.*]; **die Schmerzen machen mich ~:** the pain is driving me mad; **c)** *(heftig)* violent ‹*jealousy, rage*›; violent, excruciating ‹*pain*›; tumultuous ‹*applause*›; **~e Kopfschmerzen haben** have a splitting headache. **2.** *adv.* *(ugs.)* incredibly *(coll.)* ‹*fast, funny, expensive*›; madly *(coll.)* ‹*in love*›; insanely ‹*jealous*›; **ich täte es ~ gern** I'd really love to do it
Rasen-: **~fläche die** lawn; *(kleiner)* patch of grass; **~mäher** [~mɛ:ɐ] **der;** **~s, ~:** lawn-mower; **~platz a)** *s.* **~fläche; b)** *(Fußball usw.)* pitch; *(Tennis)* grass court; **~schere die** grass-shears *pl.*; **~sprenger der;** **~s, ~:** lawn-sprinkler; **~stück das** area of lawn
Raser der; **~s, ~** *(ugs. abwertend)* speedmerchant *(coll.)*; *(rücksichtslos)* road hog
Raserei die; **~, ~en a)** *(ugs.: schnelles Fahren)* tearing along *no art.*; **b)** *o. Pl.* *(das Toben)* [insane] frenzy; *(Wut)* rage; **jmdn. zur ~ bringen** drive sb. mad *or* to distraction
Rasier-: **~apparat der** [safety] razor; *(elektrisch)* electric shaver *or* razor; **~creme die** shaving-cream
rasieren [ra'zi:rən] *tr. V.* **a)** shave; **sich ~:** shave; **sich naß/trocken/elektrisch ~:** have a wet/dry shave/use an electric shaver; **sich** *(Dat.)***/jmdm. die Beine** *usw.* **~:** shave one's/sb.'s legs; *(ab~)* **sich** *(Dat.)* **/jmdm. die Haare/den Bart ~:** shave off one's/sb.'s hair/beard; **b)** *(zerstören)* raze to the ground
Rasierer der; **~s, ~** *(ugs.)* [electric] shaver
Rasier-: **~klinge die** razor-blade; **~messer das** cutthroat razor; **~pinsel der** shaving-brush; **~schaum der a)** *(in der Sprühdose)* shaving-foam; **b)** *(der ~seife)* shaving-lather; **~seife die** shaving-soap; **~wasser das** *(nach der Rasur)* aftershave; *(vor der Rasur)* pre-shave lotion; **~zeug das** shaving things *pl.*
Räson [rɛ'zɔŋ] **die** *in* **zur ~ kommen,** *(veralt.)* **~ annehmen** come to one's senses; **jmdn. zur ~ bringen** make sb. see reason
räsonieren [rɛzo'ni:rən] *itr. V.* *(veralt. abwertend)* **a)** *(sich wortreich äußern)* reason [at length]; expatiate; **b)** *(nörgeln)* grumble **(über** + *Akk.* about)
Raspel ['raspl̩] **die;** **~, ~n a)** *(grobe Feile)* rasp; **b)** *(Küchengerät)* grater
raspeln *tr. V.* **a)** *auch itr.* *(mit einer Feile)* rasp; **an etw.** *(Dat.)* **~:** work away at sth. with a rasp; **b)** *(Kochk.)* grate
raß [ra:s], **räß** [rɛ:s] *(südd., österr., schweiz.)* highly-seasoned; hot ‹*curry, goulash*›
Rasse ['rasə] **die;** **~, ~n a)** *(Biol.)* breed; **ein Pferd von edler ~:** a horse of noble pedigree; **b)** *(Anthrop.: Menschen~)* race; **c) ~ haben** *od.* **sein** *(ugs.)* be terrific *(coll.)*; *(Temperament haben)* have plenty of spirit *or* mettle; **von** *od.* **mit ~** *(ugs.)* terrific *(coll.)*; *(temperamentvoll)* [high-]spirited
Rasse·hund der pedigree dog
Rassel ['rasl̩] **die;** **~, ~n a)** *(Musikinstrument)* rattle, *esp.* maraca; **b)** *(Spielzeug)* rattle
Rassel·bande die *(ugs. scherzh.)* [gang of] little rascals *pl.*
rasseln *itr. V.* **a)** rattle; **mit seinen Ketten/seinem Schlüsselbund ~:** rattle one's chains/jangle one's bunch of keys; **der Wecker rasselt** the alarm goes off with a jangling sound; **~d atmen** *(fig.)* breathe stertorously; **seine Lunge rasselt** *(fig.)* he has a rattle in his lung; *s. auch* **Säbel; b)** *mit sein (sich ~d fortbewegen)* clatter; **gegen einen Baum ~** *(ugs.)* go smash into a tree *(coll.)*; **c)** *mit sein (salopp: durchfallen)* **durch eine Prüfung ~:** come unstuck in *or (Amer.)* flunk an exam *(coll.)*
Rassen-: **~diskriminierung die** racial discrimination *no art.*; **~frage die;** *o. Pl.* **die ~frage** the race issue *or* question; **~gesetze** *Pl.* race laws; **~haß der** racial hatred *no art.*; **~konflikt der** racial conflict; **~krawall der** race riot; **~problem das** racial problem; **das ~problem** the race problem; **~schranke die** racial barrier; **~trennung die;** *o. Pl.* racial segregation *no art.*; **~unruhen** *Pl.* racial unrest; **~vor·urteil das** racial prejudice
Rasse·pferd das thoroughbred [horse]
rasse·rein *Adj. s.* **reinrassig**
rassig *Adj.* spirited, mettlesome ‹*horse*›; spirited, vivacious ‹*woman*›; sporty ‹*car*›; tangy ‹*wine, perfume*›; *(markant)* striking ‹*face, features, beauty*›
rassisch 1. *Adj.* racial; **aus ~en Gründen** for reasons of race. **2.** *adv.* racially
Rassismus der; **~:** racism; racialism
Rassist der; **~en, ~en, Rassistin die;** **~, ~nen** racist; racialist
rassistisch 1. *Adj.* racist; racialist. **2.** *adv.* racialistically; **~ begründet** for racialist reasons *postpos.*; ‹*policy*› based on race; **~ gefärbt** with a racialist slant
Rast [rast] **die;** **~, ~en** rest; **~ machen** stop for a break; **ohne ~ und Ruh** *(geh.)* without respite
Raste die; **~, ~n** *(Technik)* notch
rasten *itr. V.* rest; take a rest *or* break; **eine Stunde ~:** have an hour's rest; **wer rastet, der rostet** *(Spr.)* if you don't keep at it, you get rusty; *s. auch* **ruhen d**
Raster der; **~s, ~ a)** *(Druckw.)* *(Platte, Linien)* screen; **b)** *(fig.)* [conceptual] framework; set pattern
Raster-: **~ätzung die** *(Druckw.)* half-tone engraving; **~fahndung die** *(Kriminologie)* *pinpointing of suspects by means of computer analysis of data on many people*
rastern *tr. V.* screen; *(Ferns.)* scan
Raster·punkt der *(Druckw.)* half-tone dot
Rasterung die; **~, ~en a)** *o. Pl.* *(das Rastern)* screening; *(Ferns.)* scanning; **b)** *(Struktur)* screen
rast-, Rast-: **~haus das** roadside café; *(mit Hotelbetrieb)* roadside hotel; motel; *(an der Autobahn)* motorway restaurant; **~hof der** [motorway] motel [and service area]; **~los 1.** *Adj.* restless ‹*person, spirit*›; restless, unsettled ‹*life*›; *(ununterbrochen)* unremitting, ceaseless ‹*work, search*›; *(unermüdlich)* tireless, unflagging ‹*work, enthusiasm*›; **2.** *adv. s. Adj.:* restlessly; unremittingly; ceaselessly; tirelessly; unflaggingly; **~losigkeit die;** **~:** restlessness; **~platz der a)** place to rest; **b)** *(an Autobahnen)* parking place *(with benches and WCs)*; picnic area; **~stätte die** service area
Rasur [ra'zu:ɐ̯] **die;** **~, ~en a)** *(das Rasieren)* shave; **nach der ~:** after shaving; **b)** *(ausradierte Stelle)* erasure
Rat [ra:t] **der;** **~[e]s, Räte** ['rɛ:tə] **a)** *o. Pl.* *(Empfehlung)* advice; **ein ~:** a piece *or* word of advice; **gib mir einen ~, was ich tun soll!** please tell me what I should do; **ich gab ihm den ~ zu ...:** I advised him to ...; **jmds. ~ einholen, sich** *(Dat.)* **bei jmdm. ~ holen** take advice from sb.; **bei jmdm. ~ suchen** seek sb.'s advice; **da ist guter ~ teuer** I/we *etc.* hardly know which way to turn; **jmdm. mit ~ und Tat zur Seite stehen** *od.* **beistehen** stand by sb. with moral and practical support; **mit sich zu ~[e] gehen** give the matter a lot of thought; **jmdn./etw. zu ~[e] ziehen** consult sb./sth.; **b)** *o. Pl.* *(Ausweg)* way out; solution; **[sich** *(Dat.)***] keinen ~ wissen** not know what to do; **ich wußte [mir] keinen ~ mehr** I was at my wit's end *or* com-

pletely at a loss; **weiß jemand ~?** has anybody any ideas?; **c)** *(Gremium)* council; *(Sowjet)* soviet; **der ~ der Stadt** the town council; **~ für Gegenseitige Wirtschaftshilfe** Council for Mutual Economic Aid; COMECON; **d)** *(Ratsmitglied)* councillor; council member; **e)** *o. Pl. (Titel)* Councillor

rät [rɛ:t] *3. Pers. Sg. Präsens v.* **raten**

Rate ['ra:tə] **die, ~, ~n a)** *(Teilbetrag)* instalment; **etw. auf ~n kaufen** buy sth. by instalments *or (Brit.)* on hire purchase *or (Amer.)* on the installment plan; **b)** *(Statistik: Verhältnis)* rate

Räte·demokratie die government by soviets *no art.*; sovietism *no art.*

raten 1. *unr. itr. V.* **a)** *(einen Rat, Ratschläge geben)* **jmdm. ~:** advise sb.; **laß dir von einem Freund ~:** take the advice of a friend; **er läßt sich von niemandem ~:** he won't listen to anybody; **wem nicht zu ~ ist, dem ist [auch] nicht zu helfen** *(Spr.)* you can't help some people – they just won't listen; ≈ you can take a horse to the water, but you can't make him drink *(prov.)*; **sich** *(Dat.)* **nicht zu ~ wissen** be quite at a loss; **wozu rätst du mir?** what do you advise me to do?; **ich würde zu diesem Bewerber ~:** my advice would be to choose this applicant; **b)** *(schätzen)* guess; **richtig/falsch ~:** guess right/wrong; **dreimal darfst du ~** *(ugs. iron.)* I'll give you three guesses. **2.** *tr. V.* **a)** *(an~)* **jmdm. ~, etw. zu tun** advise sb. to do sth.; **was rätst du mir?** what do you advise [me to do]?; **laß dir das ge~ sein!** you better had [do that]!; *(tu das nicht)* don't you dare do that!; **das möchte ich dir auch ge~ haben!** I should hope so!; **b)** *(er~)* guess

Raten-: ~kauf der purchase by instalments *or (Amer.)* on the installment plan; **~zahlung die a)** payment by instalments; **b)** *(das Zahlen des Teilbetrags)* hire-purchase *(Brit.) or (Amer.)* installment plan payment; **die dritte ~zahlung ist fällig** the third instalment is due

Räte·republik die *(hist.)* soviet republic

Rate·spiel das guessing-game

Rat-: ~geber der adviser; *(Buch)* guide; **~geberin die; ~, ~nen** adviser; **~haus das** town hall; **jmdn. ins ~haus wählen** elect sb. to the town council; **die FDP ist wieder ins ~haus eingezogen** the FDP is again represented on the town council; **~haus·saal der** town hall council-chamber

Ratifikation [ratifika'tsi̯o:n] **die; ~, ~en** ratification

ratifizieren [ratifi'tsi:rən] *tr. V.* ratify

Ratifizierung die; ~, ~en ratification

Rätin ['rɛ:tɪn] **die; ~, ~nen** councillor

Ratio ['ra:tsi̯o] **die; ~** *(geh.)* [pure] reason *no art.*; rational logic *no art.*

Ration [ra'tsi̯o:n] **die; ~, ~en** ration; **jmdn. auf halbe/doppelte ~ setzen** *(ugs.)* put sb. on half/double rations; *s. auch* **eisern 1 d**

rational [ratsi̯o'na:l] **1.** *Adj.* rational; **~e Zahlen** rational numbers. **2.** *adv.* rationally

rationalisieren *tr., itr. V.* rationalize

Rationalisierung die; ~, ~en rationalization; **~en** rationalization measures

Rationalisierungs·maßnahme die rationalization measure

Rationalismus der; ~: rationalism *no art.*

Rationalist der; ~en, ~en rationalist

rationalistisch 1. *Adj.* rationalistic; rationalist ‹*principles*›; **das ~e Zeitalter** the age of reason. **2.** *adv.* rationalistically

Rationalität [ratsi̯onali'tɛ:t] **die; ~:** rationality

rationell [ratsi̯o'nɛl] **1.** *Adj.* efficient; *(wirtschaftlich)* economic. **2.** *adv.* efficiently; *(wirtschaftlich, kräftesparend)* economically

rationieren *tr. V.* ration

Rationierung die; ~, ~en rationing *no indef. art.*; **~en vornehmen** introduce rationing [measures]

rat·los 1. *Adj.* baffled; at a loss *pred.*; helpless ‹*look*›; **einer Sache** *(Dat.)* **~ gegenüberstehen** not know what to do about sth. **2.** *adv.* helplessly; in a baffled way

Rat·losigkeit die; ~: perplexity; helplessness; **in meiner ~:** not knowing what to do

Rätoromanisch [rɛtoro'ma:nɪʃ] **das** Rhaeto-Romanic; Rhaeto-Romance

ratsam ['ra:tza:m] *Adj.; nicht attr.* advisable; *(weise)* prudent

ratsch [ratʃ] *Interj.* zip; *(beim Zerreißen)* rip; **es machte ~:** there was a ripping sound; *s. auch* **ritsch**

Ratsche ['ra:tʃə] *(bes. südd., österr.)*, **Rätsche** ['rɛ:tʃə] *(südd.)* **die; ~, ~n a)** *(Geräuschinstrument)* [football fan's] rattle; **b)** *(Technik: Sperre)* ratchet

¹ratschen *(ugs.)* **1.** *itr. V. (Geräusch erzeugen)* rip. **2.** *refl. V. (landsch.: kratzen)* scratch oneself

²ratschen *(bes. südd., österr.)*, **rätschen** *(südd.) itr. V.* **a)** *(Ratsche drehen)* swing a/one's rattle; *(fig.)* make a rasping noise; **b)** *(ugs.: schwatzen)* gossip

Rat-: ~schlag der [piece of] advice; *(Hinweis)* tip; **auf meinen ~schlag hin** acting on my advice; **~schläge** advice/tips; **kluge ~schläge** *(iron.)* brilliant advice *sing. (iron.)*; **~schluß der** *(geh.)* counsel *(formal)*; **nach Gottes unerforschlichem ~schluß** in accordance with the unfathomable will of God

Rätsel ['rɛ:tsl̩] **das; ~s, ~ a)** *(Denkaufgabe)* riddle; *(Bilder~, Kreuzwort~ usw.)* puzzle; **das ist des ~s Lösung** *(fig.)* [so] that is the explanation; **jmdm. ~/ein ~ aufgeben** ask *or* set sb. riddles/a riddle; *(fig.: vor Probleme stellen)* puzzle *or* baffle sb.; **b)** *(Geheimnis)* mystery; enigma; **jmdm.** *od.* **für jmdn. ein ~ sein/bleiben** be/remain a mystery to sb.; **vor einem ~ stehen** be baffled

Rätsel·ecke die *(ugs.)* puzzle corner *(in a magazine/newspaper)*

rätselhaft 1. *Adj.* mysterious; *(unergründlich)* enigmatic ‹*smile, expression, person*›; baffling ‹*problem*›; **es blieb/es ist [mir] ~, warum ...:** it remained/is a mystery [to me] why .... **2.** *adv.* mysteriously; *(unergründlich)* enigmatically

Rätselhaftigkeit die; ~: enigmatic nature; mysteriousness

Rätsel·heft das puzzle magazine

rätseln *itr. V.* puzzle, rack one's brains **(über + Akk.** over); **~, wer .../ob ...:** try to work out who .../whether ...

Rätsel·raten das a) *s.* **Rätsel a:** solving puzzles/riddles *no art.*; **b)** *(das Rätseln)* puzzling; *(Raten)* guessing; **das ~, wer sein Nachfolger werden soll** the guessing-game as to who is to be his successor

rätsel·voll 1. *Adj.* mysterious; enigmatic ‹*person*›. **2.** *adv.* mysteriously; ‹*smile*› enigmatically

Rats-: ~herr der [town/city] councillor; **~keller der** [restaurant in the] town-hall cellar; **~stube die** *(veralt.)* [town hall] council-chamber

Rattan ['ratan] **das; ~s** rattan [cane]

Ratte ['ratə] **die; ~, ~n** *(auch fig.)* rat; **die ~n verlassen das sinkende Schiff** the rats are leaving the sinking ship

Ratten-: ~bekämpfung die rat control; **~fänger der a)** rat-catcher; **der ~fänger von Hameln** *(Lit.)* the Pied Piper of Hamelin; **b)** *(abwertend: Volksverführer)* pied piper; **~gift das** rat poison; **~schwanz der a)** *(fig.: große Anzahl)* **ein ~schwanz von Änderungen/Gerüchten** a whole welter *or* string of changes/rumours; **b)** *(scherzh.: Zopf)* pigtail; **c)** *(Schwanz der Ratte)* rat's tail

rattern ['ratɐn] *itr. V.* **a)** *(knattern)* clatter; ‹*sewing-machine, machine-gun*› chatter; ‹*engine*› rattle; **b)** *mit sein (sich ~d fortbewegen)* clatter [along]

Ratz [rats] **der; ~es, ~e a)** *(südd., österr., schweiz.)* rat; **b)** *(volkst.: Siebenschläfer)* [edible] dormouse; **schlafen wie ein ~:** sleep like a log

ratze·kahl *Adv. (ugs.)* totally; completely

ratzen *itr. V. (ugs.)* [have a] kip *(Brit. sl.)*

Raub [raup] **der; ~[e]s a)** robbery; *(Entführung)* kidnapping; **jmdn. wegen ~es anklagen/verurteilen** accuse/convict sb. of robbery *or (jur.)* larceny [from the person]; **der ~ der Sabinerinnen** *(Myth.)* the rape of the Sabine women; **b)** *(Beute)* [robber's] loot; stolen goods *pl.*; **ein ~ der Flammen werden** *(geh.)* be consumed by the flames *(literary)*

Raub-: ~bau der; *o. Pl.* over-exploitation **(an + Dat.** of); *(beim Fischfang)* overfishing; *(beim Bergbau)* overworking; **~bau an etw.** *(Dat.)* **treiben** over-exploit sth.; **~bau mit seiner Gesundheit treiben** *(fig.)* ruin one's health by overdoing things; **~bau an seinen Kräften** *(fig.)* overtaxing one's strength; **~druck der;** *Pl.* **~drucke** pirated edition

rauben 1. *tr. V.* steal; kidnap ‹*person*›; **jmdm. etw. ~:** rob sb. of sth.; *(geh.: wegnehmen)* deprive sb. of sth.; **jmdm. den Atem/die Sprache ~:** take sb.'s breath away/render sb. speechless; **er hat ihr die Unschuld geraubt** *(veralt.)* he deprived her of her virginity; he deflowered her *(dated)*. **2.** *itr. V.* rob; *(plündern)* plunder

Räuber ['rɔybɐ] **der; ~s, ~ a)** robber; *(Entführer)* kidnapper; *(fig. scherzh.)* rascal; **~ und Gendarm** cops and robbers; **anscheinend bin ich unter die ~ gefallen** *(ugs.)* it seems I'm being fleeced *(coll.)*; **b)** *(Zool.: Tier)* predator

Räuber-: ~bande die *(veralt.)* band of robbers; **~geschichte die a)** story about robbers; **b)** *(ugs.: erlogene Geschichte)* tall story; **~haupt·mann der** *(veralt.)* robber chief; **~höhle die** *(veralt.)* robber's den; **hier sieht es aus wie in einer ~höhle** it's a frightful mess in here *(coll.)*

räuberisch 1. *Adj.* **a)** rapacious, predatory ‹*gang, horde, etc.*›; **~e Erpressung** *(Rechtsw.)* extortion by means of force or under threat of force; **b)** *(Zool.)* predatory ‹*animal, fish, etc.*›. **2.** *adv. (Zool.)* **~ lebend** living as a predator/as predators; predatory

räubern *itr. V.* go robbing; *(plündern)* loot

Räuber-: ~pistole die *(ugs. scherzh.)* tall story; **~zivil das** *(ugs. scherzh.)* scruffy clothes *pl.*

raub-, Raub-: ~fisch der predatory fish; **~gier die** rapacity; **~gierig** *Adj.* rapacious; **~katze die** wild cat; **~mord der** *(Rechtsw.)* murder **(an + Dat.** of) in the course of a robbery *or* with robbery as motive; **~mörder der** robber and murderer; **~ritter der** *(hist.)* robber baron; **~tier das** predator; beast of prey; **~tier·käfig der** predators' cage; *(für Löwen und Tiger)* lions' and tigers' cage; **~über·fall der** robbery **(auf + Akk.** of); *(von einer Bande auf eine Bank o. ä.)* raid **(auf + Akk.** on); **~vogel der** bird of prey; **~wild das** *(Jägerspr.)* predators *pl. (hunted as game)*; **~zug der** plundering raid

Rauch [raux] **der; ~[e]s** smoke; **kein ~ ohne Flammen** *(Spr.)* there's no smoke without fire *(prov.)*; **in ~ [und Flammen] aufgehen** go up in smoke *or* flames; **sich in ~ auflösen, in ~ aufgehen** *(fig.)* go up in smoke

Rauch-: ~ab·zug der smoke outlet; *(Rohr, Schacht)* flue; **~bombe die** smoke-bomb

rauchen 1. *itr. V.* smoke; **es rauchte in der Küche** there was smoke in the kitchen; **sonst raucht es!** *(ugs.)* or there'll be trouble. **2.** *tr. (auch itr.) V.* smoke ‹*cigarette, pipe, etc.*›; **~ Sie?** do you smoke?; **eine ~:** have a smoke; **stark** *od.* **viel ~:** be a heavy smoker; **„Rauchen verboten"** 'No smoking'

Rauch·entwicklung die build-up of smoke

Raucher der; ~s, ~ a) smoker; b) o. Art. (~abteil) smoker; smoking-compartment; möchten Sie ~ oder Nichtraucher [fliegen]? would you like smoking or no smoking?
Räucher·aal der smoked eel
Raucher-: ~ab·teil das smoking-compartment; smoker; ~bein das (Med.) narrowing of the arteries of the leg as a result of heavy smoking
Räucher·hering der smoked herring
Raucher·husten der smoker's cough
Raucherin die; ~, ~nen smoker
Räucher-: ~kammer die smokehouse; ~lachs der smoked salmon
Raucher·lunge die (volkst.) smoker's lung
räuchern ['rɔyçn̩] 1. tr. V. smoke ⟨meat, fish⟩. 2. itr. V. burn incense/joss-sticks etc.
Räucher-: ~schinken der smoked ham; ~speck der smoked [streaky] bacon; ~stäbchen das joss-stick
rauch-, Rauch-: ~fahne die plume of smoke; ~fang der a) (~abzug) chimney hood; b) (österr.: Schornstein) chimney; ~fang·kehrer der (österr.) chimney-sweep; ~farben, ~farbig Adj. smoke-coloured; smoke-grey; ~faß das (kath. Kirche) censer; ~gas das flue gas; ~gasentschwefelung die flue gas desulphurization; ~geschwängert Adj. smoke-filled; die Luft war ~geschwängert the air was heavy with smoke; ~geschwärzt Adj. smoke-blackened; ~glas das; o. Pl. smoked glass
rauchig Adj. smoky; husky ⟨voice⟩
rauch-, Rauch-: ~los Adj. smokeless; ~melder der smoke-detector; ~pilz der mushroom cloud; ~salon der smoking-room; ~säule die column or pillar of smoke; ~schwaden der cloud of smoke; ~signal das smoke signal; ~tisch der smoker's table; ~verbot das ban on smoking; aus Sicherheitsgründen herrscht ~verbot smoking is prohibited for safety reasons; ~vergiftung die poisoning no art. by smoke inhalation; ~verzehrer der; ~s, ~: air cleaner [and freshener]; ~ware die; ~, ~n a) Pl. (Tabak) tobacco products; b) (Kürschnerei) fur; ~wolke die cloud of smoke; ~zeichen das smoke signal
Räude ['rɔydə] die; ~, ~n mange no art.
räudig Adj. mangy; ein ~es Schaf (fig.) a bad apple (fig.); du ~er Hund! (derb) you dirty rat! (sl.)
rauf [rauf] Adv. (ugs.) up; ~ mit euch! up you go!; s. auch herauf; hinauf
rauf- (ugs.) up; ~brüllen/~klettern shout/climb
Raufbold [-bɔlt] der; ~[e]s, ~e (veralt.) ruffian
rauf|bringen unr. tr. V. (ugs.) (her) bring up; (hin) take up
Raufe die; ~, ~n hay-rack
raufen 1. itr., refl. V. fight; [sich] wegen od. um etw. ~: fight [each other] over sth. 2. tr. V. pull up ⟨weeds, plants, etc.⟩; pull ⟨flax⟩; sich (Dat.) die Haare/den Bart ~: tear one's hair/at one's beard
Rauferei die; ~, ~en fight
rauf|gehen unr. itr. V.; mit sein (ugs.) go up
Rauf·handel der; ~s, Raufhändel (veralt.) brawl; fight
rauf-: ~|holen tr. V. (ugs.) fetch or bring up; ~|kommen unr. itr. V.; mit sein (ugs.) come up
rauf·lustig Adj. (veralt.) pugnacious; er ist ein ~er Bursche he is always spoiling for a fight
rauh [rau] 1. Adj. a) (nicht glatt) rough; in einer ~en Schale steckt oft ein weicher Kern (Spr.) behind a rough exterior there often beats a heart of gold; b) (nicht mild) harsh, raw ⟨climate, winter⟩; raw ⟨wind⟩; c) (unwirtlich) bleak, inhospitable ⟨region, mountains, etc.⟩; rough ⟨weather⟩; d) (kratzig) husky, hoarse ⟨voice⟩; e) (entzündet) sore ⟨throat⟩; f) (grob, nicht feinfühlig) rough; harsh ⟨words, tone⟩; er ist ~, aber herzlich he is a rough diamond; g) (Ballspiele) rough ⟨play⟩; h) (ugs.) in ~en Mengen in huge or vast quantities. 2. adv. a) (kratzig) ⟨speak etc.⟩ huskily, hoarsely; b) (grob, nicht feinfühlig) roughly; c) (Ballspiele) roughly; ~ spielen play rough
rauh-, Rauh-: ~bauz [~bauts] der; ~es, ~e (ugs.) s. ~bein; ~bauzig Adj. (ugs.) s. ~beinig; ~bein das (ugs.) rough diamond; ~beinig Adj. (ugs.) gruff; rough and ready
Rauheit die; ~, ~en s. rauh a–d: roughness; harshness; rawness; bleakness; inhospitableness; huskiness; hoarseness
Rauh-: ~faser·tapete die woodchip wallpaper; ~frost der rime; ~haar·dackel der wire-haired dachshund; ~putz der roughcast; ~reif der hoar-frost
raum [raum] Adj. (Seemannsspr.) a) (weit) open ⟨sea⟩; b) (von hinten) quartering, following ⟨sea, current, wind⟩
Raum der; ~[e]s, Räume ['rɔymə] a) (Wohn~, Nutz~) room; im ~ stehen (fig.) be in the air; ⟨threat⟩ be hanging in the air; etw. im ~ stehen lassen (fig.) leave sth. hanging in the air; eine Anschuldigung im ~ stehen lassen leave an accusation unanswered; b) (nicht fest eingegrenztes Gebiet) expanse; ~ und Zeit (Philos.) space and time; c) o. Pl. (Platz) room; space; 5 m ~: a space of 5 m; auf engstem ~ leben live in a very confined space; einen zu breiten ~ einnehmen (fig.) be given too much attention; d) o. Pl. (Welt~) space no art.; e) (Gebiet) area; region; im ~ Hamburg in the Hamburg area or region; f) (Wirkungsfeld) sphere; g) (Math.) space
Raum-: ~akustik die (Physik) room acoustics sing., no art.; ~an·gabe die (Sprachw.) adverbial expression of place; ~an·zug der spacesuit; ~ausstatter der a) (Beruf) interior decorator; b) (Geschäft) [firm of] interior decorators pl.; ~bild das (Optik) stereoscopic picture; 3-D picture; ~deckung die (Ballspiele) zonal defence
räumen ['rɔymən] 1. tr. V. a) (entfernen) clear [away]; clear ⟨snow⟩; Minen ~: clear mines; (auf See) sweep or clear mines; etw. vom Tisch ~: clear sth. off the table; etw. aus dem Weg ~: clear sth. out [of] the way; b) (an einen Ort) clear; move; seine Sachen auf die Seite ~: clear or move one's things to one side; etw. in Schubfächer (Akk.) ~: put sth. away in drawers; c) (frei machen) clear ⟨street, building, warehouse, stocks, etc.⟩; d) (verlassen) vacate ⟨hotel room⟩; vacate, clear ⟨hall, cinema, etc.⟩; vacate, move out of ⟨house, flat⟩; evacuate, vacate ⟨military position, area⟩; e) (durch die Polizei usw. frei machen) clear ⟨room, hall, street, etc.⟩. 2. itr. V. clear up
Raum~: ~ersparnis die saving of space; ~fähre die space shuttle; ~fahrer der astronaut; (Kosmonaut) cosmonaut; ~fahrt die a) o. Pl. space flight; space travel; b) (~flug) space flight
Raumfahrt-: ~behörde die space agency; ~medizin die space medicine no art.; ~technik die space technology no art.
Raum·fahrzeug das spacecraft
Räum·fahrzeug das bulldozer; (für Schnee) snow-plough
raum-, Raum-: ~flug der space flight; ~forschung die; o. Pl. space research no art.; ~gestalter der interior designer; ~gleiter der; ~s, ~ (Raumf.) space shuttle; ~greifend Adj. (Sport) long ⟨pass, stride, etc.⟩; ~in·halt der (Math.) volume; ~kapsel die space capsule; ~klang der stereophonic sound
räumlich 1. Adj. a) (den Raum betreffend) spatial; aus ~en Gründen for reasons of space; wir sind ~ sehr beschränkt we are cramped for space; ~e Nähe physical proximity; b) (dreidimensional) three-dimensional; stereophonic ⟨sound⟩; stereoscopic ⟨vision⟩; ~ wirken have a three-dimensional effect; ~es Vorstellungsvermögen ability to visualize things in three dimensions. 2. adv. a) spatially; in zeitlich und ~ enger Nachbarschaft in close temporal and spatial proximity; b) (dreidimensional) three-dimensionally
Räumlichkeit die; ~, ~en a) Pl. rooms; uns (Dat.) fehlen die ~en we don't have enough space; die ~en des Museums the museum's premises; b) o. Pl. (räumliche Wirkung) three-dimensionality
raum-, Raum-: ~maß das measure of capacity; ~meter der od. das cubic metre (of stacked wood, logs); ~not die shortage or lack of space (Gen. in); ~ordnung die (Amtsspr.) regional planning; ~ordnungs·plan der (Amtsspr.) regional development plan; ~pfleger der cleaner; ~pflegerin die cleaning lady; cleaner; ~schiff das spaceship; ~sonde die space probe; ~sparend Adj. s. platzsparend; ~station die space station; ~teiler der room divider; ~transporter der space shuttle
Räumung die; ~, ~en a) clearing; b) (einer Wohnung, eines Hotelzimmers) vacation; vacating; c) (wegen Gefahr) evacuation; d) (von Vorräten, eines Geschäfts) clearance
Räumungs-: ~klage die (Rechtsw.) action for eviction; ~klage erheben ≈ apply for an eviction order; ~verkauf der (Kaufmannsspr.) clearance sale
raunen ['raunən] tr., itr. V. (geh.) whisper; ein Raunen ging durch die Reihen a murmur went through the ranks
raunzen ['rauntsn̩] itr. V. (bes. südd., österr.) grumble; grouse (coll.)
Raupe ['raupə] die; ~, ~n a) (Larve) caterpillar; b) s. Planier~; c) s. Raupenkette
Raupen-: ~fahrzeug das Caterpillar vehicle; Caterpillar (P); ~kette die Caterpillar track; ~schlepper der Caterpillar tractor
raus [raus] Adv. (ugs.) out; ~ mit euch! out you go!; Nazis ~! Nazis out!; s. auch heraus; hinaus
Rausch [rauʃ] der; ~[e]s, Räusche ['rɔyʃə] a) (durch Alkohol) state of drunkenness; sich (Dat.) einen ~ antrinken get drunk; einen [leichten/schweren] ~ haben be [slightly/very] drunk; seinen ~ ausschlafen sleep off the effects of drink; sleep it off (coll.); etw. im ~ tun do sth. while drunk; b) (durch Drogen) drugged state; einen ~ haben be drugged; be high (coll.) [on drugs]; etw. im ~ tun do sth. while drugged; c) (starkes Gefühl) transport; der ~ des Erfolgs/Sieges the exhilaration or intoxication of success/victory; ein wilder/blinder ~: a wild/blind frenzy; der ~ der Geschwindigkeit the exhilaration or thrill of speed
rausch·arm 1. Adj. low-noise. 2. adv. with a low noise-level
Rausche·bart der (scherzh.) a) full beard; b) (Mann) bearded [old] gentleman
rauschen itr. V. a) ⟨water, wind, torrent⟩ rush; ⟨trees, leaves⟩ rustle; ⟨skirt, curtains, silk⟩ swish; ⟨waterfall, strong wind⟩ roar; ⟨rain⟩ pour down; ich hörte das Wasser ~: I heard the sound of rushing water; es rauscht im Radio there's a hiss coming from the radio; das Rauschen der Brandung/des Meeres the roar of the surf/sea; ~der Beifall (fig.) resounding applause; ~de Feste (fig.) glittering parties; b) mit sein (sich bewegen) ⟨water, river, etc.⟩ rush; ⟨bird, bullet, etc.⟩ whoosh; der Ball rauschte ins Tor (Sport ugs.) the ball slammed into the back of the net; sie rauschte aus dem Zimmer she swept out of the room
Rausch·gift das drug; narcotic; ~ nehmen take drugs; be on drugs

rausch·gift-, Rausch·gift-: ~handel der drug-trafficking; **~händler der** drug-trafficker; **~süchtig** *Adj.* drug-addicted; addicted to drugs *postpos.;* **sie war ~süchtig** she was addicted to drugs *or* a drug addict; **~süchtige Jugendliche** young drug addicts; **~süchtige der/die;** *adj. Dekl.* drug addict; **~tote der/die** person who dies/died as a result of drug abuse; **im vergangenen Jahr gab es 400 ~tote** last year 400 people died as a result of drug abuse

Rausch·gold das Dutch metal

Rauschgold·engel der angel *(made of Dutch metal)*

rausch·haft *Adj.* ecstatic

Rausch·mittel das *s.* **Rauschgift**

raus-: ~|dürfen *unr. itr. V. (ugs.) s.* **heraus-, hinausdürfen; ~|ekeln** *tr. V. (ugs.) s.* **hinausekeln; ~|fahren** *unr. tr. V.; mit sein (ugs.) s.* **heraus-, hinausfahren; ~|feuern** *tr. V. (ugs.)* chuck out *(coll.);* **~|fliegen** *unr. itr. V.; mit sein (ugs.) s.* **heraus-, hinausfliegen; ~|gehen** *unr. itr. V.; mit sein (ugs.) s.* **heraus-, hinausgehen; ~|kommen** *unr. itr. V.; mit sein (ugs.) s.* **heraus-, hinauskommen; ~|können** *unr. itr. V. (ugs.)* be able to go/come out; *(sich befreien können)* be able to get out; **~|kriegen** *tr. V. (ugs.)* get out **(aus** of); **ich habe das Rätsel/die Aufgabe nicht ~gekriegt** I couldn't do the puzzle/exercise; **~|müssen** *unr. itr. V. (ugs.)* have got to go/come out; **wir müssen aus unserer Wohnung ~:** we have got to get out of our flat *(Brit.) or (Amer.)* apartment; **~|nehmen** *unr. tr. V. (ugs.) s.* **heraus-, hinausnehmen; ~|pauken** *tr. V. (ugs.)* **jmdn. ~pauken** get sb. off the hook *(sl.)*

räuspern ['rɔyspɐn] *refl. V.* clear one's throat

raus-, Raus-: ~|schmeißen *unr. tr. V. (ugs.)* chuck *(coll.) or* sling *(coll.)* ⟨*objects*⟩ out *or* away; give ⟨*employee*⟩ the push *(coll.) or* sack *(coll.) or* boot *(sl.);* chuck *(coll.) or* throw ⟨*customer, drunk, tenant*⟩ out **(aus** of); **das ist ~geschmissenes Geld** that's money down the drain *(coll.);* **~schmeißer der;** **~s, ~** *(ugs.)* **a)** *(Person)* chucker-out *(coll.);* bouncer *(coll.);* **b)** *(Tanz)* last dance; **~schmiß der** *(ugs.) s.* **~schmeißen:** chucking out *(coll.);* slinging out *(coll.);* sacking *(coll.);* chucking out *(coll.);* throwing out; **nach dem ~schmiß des Angetrunkenen ...:** after the drunk had been chucked out; **nach unserem ~schmiß aus der Wohnung** after we were chucked *(coll.) or* thrown out of our flat; **~|sollen** *itr. V. (ugs.)* **der Zahn/Blinddarm soll ~:** the tooth/appendix is to come out; **wir sollen zum Jahresende aus unserer Wohnung ~:** we're to be out of our flat by the end of the year; **~|wollen** *unr. itr. V. (ugs.)* want to go/come out; **ich will ~!** I want to get out!

Raute ['rautə] **die; ~, ~n a)** *(Pflanze)* rue; **b)** *(Geom.)* rhombus

rauten·förmig *Adj.* rhombic; diamond-shaped

rautiert [rau'tiːɐ̯t] *Adj.* squared ⟨*paper*⟩

Ravioli [ra'vi̯oːli] *Pl. (Kochk.)* ravioli *sing.*

Rayon [rɛ'jõː] **der; ~s, ~s** *od. (österr.)* **~e a)** *(Warenhausabteilung)* department; **b)** *(österr., schweiz.: Bezirk)* district

Rayons·inspektor der *(österr. schweiz.)* district inspector

Razzia ['ratsi̯a] **die; ~, Razzien** raid; **in dieser Kneipe führte die Polizei oft Razzien durch** the police has often raided this bar

Re das; ~s, ~s *(Skat)* redouble

Reagens das; ~, Reagenzien [rea'gɛntsi̯ən], **Reagenz** [rea'gɛnts] **das; ~es, ~ien** *(Chemie)* reagent

Reagenz-: ~glas das test-tube; **~papier das** test paper

reagieren *itr. V.* **a)** react **(auf +** *Akk.* to); **b)** *(Chemie)* react; **miteinander ~:** react together

Reaktanz [reak'tants] **die; ~, ~en** *(Elektrot.)* reactance

Reaktion [reak'tsi̯oːn] **die; ~, ~en** *(auch Politik abwertend, Chemie)* reaction **(auf +** *Akk.* to)

reaktionär [reaktsi̯o'nɛːr] *Adj. (Politik abwertend)* reactionary

Reaktionär der; ~s, ~e, Reaktionärin die; ~, ~nen *(Politik abwertend)* reactionary

reaktions-, Reaktions-: ~fähig *Adj.* **a)** capable of reacting *postpos.;* **durch den Alkoholgenuß war er nicht mehr voll ~fähig** his alcohol intake had impaired his reactions; **b)** *(Chemie)* reactive; **~fähigkeit die;** *o. Pl.* **a)** ability to react; **jmds. ~fähigkeit überprüfen** test sb.'s reactions; **b)** *(Chemie)* reactivity; **~geschwindigkeit die** *(Chemie)* reaction rate; **~schnell 1.** *Adj.* ⟨*person*⟩ with quick reactions; **~schnell sein** have quick reactions; **durch sein ~schnelles Abbremsen** through his quick reaction in braking; **2.** *adv.* **sie schrieb ~schnell die Autonummer auf** she reacted quickly and wrote down the car's number; **~schnelligkeit die** speed of reaction; **~vermögen das** *s.* **~fähigkeit; ~wärme die** *(Chemie)* heat of reaction; **~weg der** reaction distance; **~zeit die** *(Physiol.)* reaction time

reaktiv [reak'tiːf] **1.** *Adj.* reactive. **2.** *adv.* reactively

reaktivieren *tr. V.* **a)** *(wieder anstellen)* recall [to duty]; **b)** *(wieder in Gebrauch nehmen)* bring ⟨*vehicle, machine, etc.*⟩ back into service; *(fig.)* brush *or* polish up ⟨*knowledge, skill, etc.*⟩; **c)** *(Chemie)* reactivate ⟨*catalyst, serum*⟩

Reaktivierung die a) *(Wiedereinstellung)* recalling [to duty]; **b)** *(Wiederinbetriebnahme)* **die ~ einer Sache** *(Gen.)* **beschließen** decide to bring sth. back into service; **c)** *(Chemie)* reactivation

Reaktor [re'aktɔr] **der; ~s, ~en** [-'toːrən] reactor

real [re'aːl] **1.** *Adj.* **a)** real; **b)** *(wirklichkeitsbezogen)* realistic. **2.** *adv.* **a)** actually; **b)** *(wirklichkeitsbezogen)* realistically; **c)** *(Wirtsch.)* in real terms

Real-: ~einkommen das real income; **~enzyklopädie die** *(veralt.) s.* **~lexikon**

Realien [re'aːli̯ən] *Pl.* **a)** *(Tatsachen)* realities *pl.;* facts *pl.;* **b)** *(veralt.: Naturwissenschaften)* natural sciences

Real·injurie die *(Rechtsw.)* assault and battery

Realisation [realiza'tsi̯oːn] **die; ~, ~en a)** *s.* **realisieren a:** realization; implementation; **b)** *(Film, Ferns.)* production

realisierbar *Adj. s.* **realisieren a, c:** realizable; implementable; sellable

Realisierbarkeit die; ~: practicability; feasibility

realisieren [reali'ziːrən] *tr. V.* **a)** *(geh.: verwirklichen)* realize ⟨*plan, idea, proposals, aim, project, wish*⟩; implement ⟨*plan, programme, decision*⟩; **b)** *(geh.: verstehen)* realize; **c)** *(Wirtsch.)* realize ⟨*profit, assets, etc.*⟩; sell ⟨*property*⟩

Realisierung die; ~, ~en *s.* **realisieren a, c:** realization; implementation; selling

Realismus der; ~, Realismen realism

Realist der; ~en, ~en realist

Realistik die; ~: realism

Realistin die; ~, ~nen realist

realistisch 1. *Adj.* realistic. **2.** *adv.* realistically

Realität die; ~, ~en a) reality; **b)** *Pl. (österr.) s.* **Immobilien**

Realitäten-: ~händler der, ~vermittler der *(österr.)* estate agent *(Brit.);* real estate agent *(Amer.)*

realitäts-, Realitäts-: ~bezogen *Adj., adv. s.* **~nah; ~fern 1.** *Adj.* unrealistic; **2.** *adv.* unrealistically; **~nah 1.** *Adj.* realistic; **2.** *adv.* realistically; **~sinn der;** *o. Pl.* sense of reality

realiter [re'aːlitɐ] *Adv. (geh.)* in reality

Real-: ~kanzlei die *(österr.)* estate agency *(Brit.);* real estate office *(Amer.);* **~katalog der** *(Bibliothekswesen)* subject catalogue; **~konkurrenz die** *(Rechtsw.)* accumulation of offences *(dealt with at the same trial);* **~lexikon das** specialist encyclopaedia; **~lohn der** *(Wirtsch.)* real wages *pl.;* **~politik die** realpolitik; practical politics *sing.;* **~politiker der** practical politician; **~schule die** ≈ secondary modern school *(Brit. Hist.);* **~schüler der** ≈ secondary modern school pupil *(Brit. Hist.);* **~schul·lehrer der** ≈ secondary modern school teacher *(Brit. Hist.)*

Reanimation die *(Med.)* resuscitation

reanimieren *tr. V. (Med.)* resuscitate

Reaumur ['reːomyːɐ̯] Réaumur; *s. auch* **Grad c**

Rebbe ['rɛbə] **der; ~[s], ~s** *(jidd.) s.* **Rabbi**

Rebe ['reːbə] **die; ~, ~n a)** *(Wein~)* vine shoot; **b)** *(geh.: Weinstock)* [grape] vine

Rebell [re'bɛl] **der; ~en, ~en** rebel; *(Aufständischer)* rebel; insurgent

rebellieren *itr. V.* rebel **(gegen** against)

Rebellin die; ~, ~nen *s.* **Rebell**

Rebellion [rebɛ'li̯oːn] **die; ~, ~en** rebellion; *(Aufstand)* rebellion; insurrection

rebellisch 1. *Adj.* rebellious. **2.** *adv.* rebelliously

Reben·saft der; *o. Pl. (geh.)* juice of the grape

Reb-: ~huhn das partridge; **~laus die** phylloxera; **~sorte die** type of grape; **~stock der** vine

Rechaud [re'ʃoː] **der** *od.* **das; ~s, ~s a)** *(Gastr.)* food/tea/coffee warmer; réchaud; **b)** *(südd., österr., schweiz.)* gas cooker

rechen ['rɛçn̩] *tr. V. (bes. südd.)* rake

Rechen der; ~s, ~ a) *(bes. südd.: Harke)* rake; **b)** *(Gitter an Gewässern)* grating

Rechen-: ~an·lage die computer; **~art die** type of arithmetical operation; **~aufgabe die** arithmetical problem; **~automat der** calculator; **~brett das** abacus; **~buch das** *(veralt.)* arithmetic book; **~exempel das: das ist doch ein ganz einfaches ~exempel** that's a matter of simple arithmetic; **~fehler der** arithmetical error; **~heft das** arithmetic book; **~künstler der** mathematical genius *or* wizard; **~lehrer der** *(veralt.)* arithmetic teacher; **~maschine die** calculator; **~operation die** arithmetical operation; **~papier das** arithmetic paper

Rechenschaft die; ~: account; **jmdm. über etw.** *(Akk.)* **~ geben** *od.* **ablegen** account to sb. for sth.; **von jmdm. ~ über etw.** *(Akk.)* **verlangen** demand an explanation *or* account from sb. about sth.; **jmdm. über etw.** *(Akk.)* **~ schuldig sein** *od.* **schulden** have to account to sb. for sth.; **ich bin Ihnen keine ~ schuldig** I am not answerable to you; I owe you no explanation; **jmdn. für etw. zur ~ ziehen** call *or* bring sb. to account for sth.

Rechenschafts-: ~bericht der report; **~legung die** report; **zur öffentlichen ~legung verpflichtet sein** be obliged to render public account

Rechen-: ~schieber der, ~stab der slide-rule; **~stunde die** arithmetic lesson; **~unterricht der** teaching of arithmetic; *(Fach)* arithmetic *no art.;* **~zentrum das** computer centre

Recherche [re'ʃɛrʃə] **die; ~, ~n** *(geh.)* investigation; enquiry; **~n über jmdn./etw. anstellen** make investigations *or* enquiries about sb./into sth.

recherchieren *(geh.)* **1.** *itr. V.* investigate; make investigations *or* enquiries. **2.** *tr. V.* investigate

rechnen ['rɛçnən] **1.** *tr. V.* **a) eine Aufgabe ~:** work out a problem; **b)** *(veranschlagen)* reckon; estimate; **wir ~ pro Person drei Fla-**

schen Bier we are reckoning on three bottles of beer per person; **wir müssen zwei Stunden ~:** we must reckon on two hours; **alles in allem gerechnet** all in all; altogether; **gut/rund gerechnet** at a generous/rough estimate; **das ist zu hoch/niedrig gerechnet** that's an over-/underestimate; **c)** *(berücksichtigen)* take into account; **ich rechne es mir zur Ehre** *(geh.)* I consider it *or* count it an honour; **d)** *(einbeziehen)* count; **jmdn. zu seinen Freunden ~:** count sb. among *or* as one of one's friends; **jmdn. zu den Fachleuten ~:** rate sb. as an expert. **2.** *itr. V.* **a)** *(addieren)* do *or* make a calculation/calculations; **an einer Aufgabe/auf der Tafel ~:** do *or* make calculations on a problem/the blackboard; **der Lehrer rechnet mit den Kindern** the teacher is doing arithmetic with the children; **gut/schlecht ~ können** be good/bad at figures *or* arithmetic; **b)** *(zählen)* reckon; **vom 1. April an gerechnet** reckoning from 1 April; **in Schillingen/nach Lichtjahren ~:** reckon in shillings/light years; **c)** *(ugs.: berechnen)* calculate; estimate; **das ist zuviel gerechnet** that's too high an estimate; **er ist ein klug ~der Kopf** he is a shrewdly calculating person; **d)** *(wirtschaften)* budget carefully; **mit jeder Mark** *od.* **jedem Pfennig ~ müssen** have to count *or* watch every penny; **e)** *(sich verlassen)* **auf jmdn./etw.** *od.* **mit jmdm./etw. ~:** reckon *or* count on sb./sth.; **f)** *(etw. einkalkulieren)* **mit etw. ~:** reckon with sth.; **mit einer Antwort ~:** expect an answer; **wir haben mit mehr Besuchern gerechnet** we reckoned on *or* expected more visitors; **man muß mit allem/mit dem Schlimmsten ~:** one has to be prepared for anything/for the worst. **3.** *refl. V. (sich rentieren)* **das rechnet sich nicht** it doesn't pay

Rechnen das; ~s arithmetic

Rechner der; ~s, ~ **a)** *(Mensch)* **ein guter/schlechter ~ sein** be good/bad at figures *or* arithmetic; **ein nüchterner ~ sein** *(fig.)* be shrewdly calculating; **b)** *(Gerät)* calculator; *(Computer)* computer

Rechnerei die; ~, ~en *(ugs.)* **a)** *o. Pl. (das Rechnen)* **das war eine komplizierte ~:** that was a complicated piece of figure-work; **dazu war eine ewige ~ nötig** it involved [some] endless calculations; **b)** *(Rechnung)* calculation

rechner·gesteuert *Adj. (Elektronik)* computer-controlled

rechnerisch 1. *Adj.* arithmetical; ‹*value*› in figures; **die ~e Ermittlung des Schadens** calculating the damage in figures. **2.** *adv.* ‹*determine*› by calculation, mathematically; **diese Ergebnisse sind ~ falsch** the figure-work in these results is wrong

rechner·unterstützt *Adj.* computer-aided

Rechnung die; ~, ~en **a)** *(Aus~)* calculation; **[jmdm.] eine ~ aufmachen** work it out [for sb.]; **seine ~ geht [nicht] auf** *(fig.)* his plans [do not] work out; **b)** *(schriftliche Kosten~)* bill; invoice *(Commerc.)*; **eine hohe/niedrige ~:** a large/small bill; **eine ~ über 500 Mark** a bill for 500 marks; **die ~ beträgt** *od.* **macht ...:** the bill is for ...; **die ~ ist überfällig** the account is overdue; **etw. [mit] auf die ~ setzen** put sth. on *or* add sth. to the bill; **das geht auf meine ~:** I'm paying for that; **diese Runde** *od.* **Lage geht auf meine ~:** this round's on me; this is my round; **etw. auf ~ bestellen/kaufen** order/buy sth. on account; **er hatte aber die ~ ohne den Wirt gemacht** *(fig.)* there was one thing he hadn't reckoned with; **[mit jmdm.] eine [alte] ~ begleichen** *(fig.)* settle a[n old] score [with sb.]; **auf seine** *od.* *(schweiz.)* **die ~ kommen** get one's money's worth; **auf eigene ~:** on one's own account; *(auf eigenes Risiko)* at one's own risk; **[jmdm.] etw. in ~ stellen** charge [sb.] for sth.; **c)** *(Be~, Überlegung)* calculation; **nach meiner ~:** according to my calculations; **einer Sache** *(Dat.)* **~ tragen, etw. in ~ stellen** *od.* **setzen** take sth. into account; *s. auch* **begleichen**

Rechnungs-: **~art die** type of calculation; **~betrag der** amount of a/the bill/invoice; **~block der** receipt pad; **~buch das a)** accounts book *or* ledger; **b)** *(schweiz.) s.* **Rechenbuch**; **~einheit die** *(Geldw.)* unit of account; **~fehler der** *(schweiz.) s.* **Rechenfehler**; **~führung die** *s.* **Buchführung**; **~hof der** audit office; **~jahr das** financial *or* fiscal year; **~prüfer der** auditor; **~prüfung die** *(Wirtsch., Politik)* audit; **~wesen das;** *o. Pl. (Wirtsch.)* accountancy *no art.*

recht [rɛçt] **1.** *Adj.* **a)** *(geeignet)* right; **b)** *(richtig)* right; **ganz ~!** quite right!; **das ist ~, so ist es ~,** *(ugs.)* **~ so** that's fine; **bin ich hier ~?** am I in the right place?; **c)** *(gesetzmäßig, anständig)* right; proper; **was dem einen ~ ist, ist dem anderen billig** *(Spr.)* what's sauce for the goose is sauce for the gander *(prov.)*; **~ und billig** right and proper; **alles, was ~ ist** *(das kann man nicht leugnen)* you've got to give him/it *etc.* his/its *etc.* due; *(das geht zu weit)* there is a limit; **d)** *(wunschgemäß)* **jmdm. ~ sein** be all right with sb.; **es war ihr nicht ~, daß ...:** she was not pleased that ...; **wenn es dir ~ ist** if it's all right with you; **e)** *(wirklich, echt)* real; **keine ~e Lust haben, etw. zu tun** not particularly *or* really feel like doing sth.; **f)** *(ziemlich)* **er hat sich ~e Mühe gegeben** he made quite an effort; **er ist noch ein ~es Kind** *(veralt.)* he is still a child. **2.** *adv.* **a)** *(geeignet)* **du kommst gerade ~, um zu ...:** you are just in time *or* you've come just at the right time to ...; **du kommst mir gerade ~** *(auch iron.)* you're just the person I needed; **b)** *(richtig)* correctly; **wenn ich es mir ~ überlege, dann ...:** if I really stop and think about it; **verstehen Sie mich bitte ~:** please don't misunderstand me; **habe ich ~ gehört?** did I hear right *or* correctly?; **ich denke, ich höre nicht ~** *(ugs.)* I think I must be hearing things; **gehe ich ~ in der Annahme, daß ...?** am I right in assuming that ...?; **c)** *(gesetzmäßig, anständig)* **~ handeln/leben** act/live properly; **tue ~ und scheue niemand** *(Spr.)* do what's right and fear no one; *s. auch* **Recht d; geschehen c; d)** *(wunschgemäß)* **man kann ihm nichts ~ machen** there's no pleasing him; **man kann es nicht allen ~ machen** you can't please everyone; **e)** *(wirklich, echt)* really; rightly; **er kann sich nicht ~ entscheiden** he cannot really *or* rightly decide; **die Wunde will nicht ~ heilen** the wound is not healing properly; *s. auch* **erst 2; f)** *(ziemlich)* quite; rather; **„~ herzliche Grüße, Dein Peter"** 'best wishes, Peter'

recht... *Adj.* **a)** right; right[-hand] ‹*edge*›; **die ~e Spur** the right-hand lane; **~er Hand, zur ~en Hand, auf der ~en Seite** on the right-hand side; **auf der ~en Seite gehen** walk on the right; **der ~e Außenstürmer/Verteidiger** *(Ballspiele)* the outside right/the right back; **b)** *(außen, sichtbar)* right ‹*side*›; **~e Maschen** *(Handarb.)* knit stitches; **eine ~e Masche stricken** knit one; **c)** *(in der Politik)* right-wing; rightist *(derog.)*; **der ~e Flügel einer Partei** the right wing of a party; **d)** *(Geom.)* **ein ~er Winkel** a right angle

Recht das; ~[e]s, ~e **a)** *(Rechtsordnung)* law; **das ~ brechen/beugen** break/bend the law; **~ sprechen** administer the law; administer justice; **von ~s wegen** by law; *(ugs.: eigentlich)* by rights; **gegen ~ und Gesetz verstoßen** infringe *or* violate the law; **b)** *(Rechtsanspruch)* right; **das ~ haben, etw. zu tun** have the right to do sth.; **das ~ des Stärkeren** the law of the jungle; **das ist sein gutes ~:** that is his right; **alle ~e vorbehalten** all rights reserved; **mit welchem ~ hat er das getan?** by what right did he do that?; **gleiche ~e, gleiche Pflichten** *(Spr.)* equal rights mean equal obligations; **sein ~ fordern** *od.* **verlangen** demand one's rights; **der Körper verlangt sein ~:** the body demands its due; **zu seinem ~ kommen** *(fig.)* be given due attention; **auf sein ~ pochen** insist *or* stand on one's rights; **c)** *o. Pl. (Berechtigung)* right **(auf +** *Akk.* to); **gleiches ~ für alle!** equal rights for all!; **das ~ war auf seiner Seite** he had right on his side; **etw. mit [gutem] ~ tun** be [quite] right to do sth.; **das Gericht hat für ~ erkannt, daß ...:** the court has decided *or* has reached the verdict that ...; **im ~ sein** be in the right; **zu ~:** rightly; with justification; **d) recht haben** be right; **recht behalten** be proved right; **jmdm. recht geben** concede *or* admit that sb. is right; **e)** *Pl. (veralt.: Jura)* jurisprudence; **Doktor beider ~e** Doctor of Laws

[1]**Rechte der/die;** *adj. Dekl.* right-winger; rightist *(derog.)*; **die ~n** the right *sing.*

[2]**Rechte die;** *adj. Dekl.* **a)** *(Hand)* right hand; **seine ~ einsetzen** *(Boxen)* use one's right; **zur ~n des Königs** on *or* to the right of the king; **jmdm. zur ~n** to the right of sb.; **zur ~n** on the right; **b)** *(Politik)* right

Recht·eck das rectangle

recht·eckig *Adj.* rectangular

Rechte·hand·regel die *(Physik)* right-hand rule

rechten *itr. V. (geh.)* argue; dispute

rechtens *Adv. (von Rechts wegen)* legally; by law; *(zu od. mit Recht)* rightly

Rechtens *in* **~ sein** be legal

rechter·seits *Adv.* on the right[-hand side]

recht·fertigen 1. *tr. V.* justify; **sein Handeln ist durch nichts zu ~:** nothing can justify his behaviour; **etw. vor jmdm. ~:** justify sth. to sb.; **er hat sich bemüht, das in ihn gesetzte Vertrauen zu ~:** he tried to live up to the trust placed in him. **2.** *refl. V.* justify oneself **(vor +** *Dat.* to)

Recht·fertigung die justification; **er konnte nichts zu seiner ~ vorbringen** he could not say anything to justify himself

Rechtfertigungs·grund der justification

recht-, Recht-: **~gläubig** *Adj.* orthodox; **~gläubigkeit die** orthodoxy; **~haber der;** ~s, ~ *(abwertend)* self-opinionated person; **er ist ein ~haber** he's self-opinionated; he always thinks he's right; **~haberei die;** ~ *(abwertend)* self-opinionatedness; **~haberisch** *(abwertend)* **1.** *Adj.* self-opinionated; **2.** *adv.* in a self-opinionated manner

rechtlich 1. *Adj.* **a)** legal; **b)** *(veralt.: rechtschaffen)* upright; honest. **2.** *adv.* **a)** legally; **~ nicht zulässig** not permissible in law; illegal; **etw. ~ verankern** establish sth. in law; **b)** *(veralt.: rechtschaffen)* uprightly; honestly; **ein ~ denkender Mensch** an honest-minded person

Rechtlichkeit die; ~: *s.* **Rechtmäßigkeit**

recht·los *Adj.* without rights *postpos.*; **jmdn. ~ machen** deprive sb. of his/her *etc.* rights; **die ~e Stellung der Sklaven** the slaves' position without rights

Rechtlosigkeit die; ~: lack of rights

rechtmäßig 1. *Adj.* lawful; rightful; legitimate ‹*claim*›. **2.** *adv.* lawfully; rightfully; **das steht ihm ~ zu** that is his by right *or* rightfully his; **etw. ~ beanspruchen** have a legal *or* rightful claim to sth.

Rechtmäßigkeit die; ~: legality; lawfulness; *(eines Anspruchs)* legitimacy

rechts 1. *Adv.* **a)** *(auf der rechten Seite)* on the right; *(Theater)* stage left; **die zweite Straße ~:** the second street *or* turning on the right; **~ von jmdm./etw.** on sb.'s right *or* the right of sb./on *or* to the right of sth.; **von ~ kommen** come from the right; **nach ~ gehen/sich nach ~ wenden** go/turn to the right; **sich ~ halten** keep to the right; **sich ~ einordnen** move *or* get into the right-hand lane; *s. auch* **links a; b)** *(Politik)* on the right wing; ~ **stehen** *od.* **sein** be right-wing *or* on the right; ~ **eingestellt sein** have right-wing leanings; **weit ~ stehen** be on the far right; **c)** *(ugs.: ~händig)* right-handed; **alles mit ~ machen** do everything right-handed *or* with the right hand; **d)** *(Handarb.)* **ein glatt ~ gestrickter Pullover** a pullover in stocking stitch; *s. auch* **links 1 d; e)** *(~seitig)* on the right [side]; **etw. von ~ bügeln** iron sth. on the right side; **nach ~ wenden** turn 〈*dress, skirt, etc.*〉 right side out. **2.** *Präp. mit Gen.* ~ **des Rheins/der Straße** on the right side *or* bank of the Rhine/on the right-hand side of the road *or* to the right of the road

Rẹchts-: ~abbieger der *(Verkehrsw.)* motorist/cyclist/car *etc.* turning right; **die ~abbieger** the traffic *sing.* turning right; *s. auch* **Linksabbieger; ~abbieger·spur die** *(Verkehrsw.)* right-turn lane; **~ab·teilung die** legal department; **~abweichler der** *(Politik)* right deviationist; **~an·gelegenheit die** legal matter; **~an·spruch der** legal right *or* entitlement; **einen ~anspruch auf etw.** *(Akk.)* **haben** have a legal right to *or* be legally entitled to sth.; **~anwalt der, ~anwältin die** lawyer; solicitor *(Brit.)*; attorney *(Amer.)*; *(vor Gericht)* barrister *(Brit.)*; attorney[-at-law] *(Amer.)*; advocate *(Scot.)*; **sich** *(Dat.)* **einen ~anwalt nehmen** get a lawyer *or (Amer.)* an attorney

Rẹchtsanwalts-: ~büro das, ~kanzlei die *s.* **Anwaltsbüro**

rẹchts-, Rẹchts-: ~auf·fassung die *(Rechtsw.)* conception of legality; **~auf·sicht die** *state supervision of the legality of administrative acts;* **~auskunft die** piece of legal advice; **~auskünfte** legal advice *sing.*; **~ausleger der** *(Boxen)* southpaw *(coll.)*; **~außen** *Adv.* **a)** *(Ballspiele)* 〈*run, break through*〉 down the right wing; **nach ~außen spielen** play the ball out to the right wing; **b)** *(Politik ugs.)* 〈*move, drift*〉 to the extreme right; **ganz ~außen stehen** be on the extreme right [wing]; **~außen der; ~, ~ a)** *(Ballspiele)* right wing; outside right; **b)** *(Politik ugs.)* extreme right-winger; **~beistand der** legal adviser; **~beratung die** legal advice; **~beugung die** *(Rechtsw.)* perversion of justice *or* the law; **~bewußt·sein das** sense of [what is] right and wrong; **~brecher der; ~s, ~:** law-breaker

rẹcht-, Rẹcht-: ~schaffen 1. *Adj.* honest; upright; honest, decent 〈*work*〉; **2.** *adv.* **a)** *(ehrlich, redlich)* honestly; uprightly; **~schaffen leben** live an honest[, decent] life; **b)** *(intensivierend)* really 〈*tired, full, etc.*〉; **~schaffenheit die; ~:** honesty, uprightness; **~schreib[e]·buch das** spelling-book; speller; *(Wörterbuch)* spelling dictionary; **~schreiben** *itr. V.; nur im Inf. gebr.* spell; **sie ist im Rechtschreiben schwach** she's poor at spelling; **~schreibfehler der** spelling mistake; **~schreibung die** orthography; **~schreib·wörter·buch das** spelling dictionary

rẹchts-, Rẹchts-: ~drall der a) pull to the right; **der Wagen hatte einen ~drall** the car was pulling to the right; **der Tennisspieler gab dem Ball einen ~drall** the tennis player swerved the ball to the right; **b)** *(Waffent.)* right-handed twist; **c)** *(Politik ugs.)* tendency to the right; right-wing tendency; **~drehend** *Adj.* **a)** *(bes. Technik)* right-hand 〈*thread*〉; **b)** *(Chemie, Physik)* dextrorotatory; **~drehung die** *(Chemie, Physik)* dextrorotation; **~empfinden das** sense of [what is] right and wrong; **~extremismus der** *(Politik)* right-wing extremism; **~extremist der** *(Politik)* right-wing extremist; **~fähig** *Adj. (Rechtsw.)* having legal capacity *postpos., not pred.*; **~fähigkeit die;** *o. Pl.* legal capacity; **~fall der** *(Rechtsw.)* legal case; court case; **~findung die;** *o. Pl. (Rechtsw.)* legal finding; **~frage die** *(Rechtsw.)* legal question *or* issue; **~gängig** *Adj. s.* **rechtsdrehend a; ~gefühl das;** *o. Pl.* sense of [what is] right and wrong; **~gelehrte der/die** jurist; **~gerichtet** *Adj. (Politik)* right-wing orientated; **~geschäft das** legal transaction; **~geschichte die** legal history; **~gewinde das** *(Technik)* right-hand thread; **~grund der** *(Rechtsw.)* cause in law; **~grund·satz der** *(Rechtsw.)* legal principle; **~gültig** *(Rechtsw.)* **1.** *Adj.* legally valid; **2.** *adv.* **etw. ~gültig abschließen** conclude sth. in legally valid form; **~gut das** *(Rechtsw.)* object/interest protected by law; **~handel der;** *Pl.* **~händel** *(geh.)* lawsuit; court case; **~händer** [~hɛndɐ] **der; ~s, ~, ~händerin die; ~, ~nen** right-hander; **~händer[in] sein** be right-handed; **~händig 1.** *Adj.* right-handed; **2.** *adv.* right-handed; with one's right hand; **~händigkeit die** right-handedness; **~handlung die** *(Rechtsw.)* legal act; **~hängigkeit die; ~** *(Rechtsw.)* pendency; **~herum** *Adv.* [round] to the right; **etw. ~herum drehen** turn sth. clockwise *or* [round] to the right; **~hilfe die;** *o. Pl. (Rechtsw.)* [official] assistance between courts; **~kraft die;** *o. Pl. (Rechtsw.)* legal force; **einer Sache** *(Dat.)* **~kraft verleihen** make sth. law; give legal effect to sth.; **~kräfte** *Pl. (Politik)* right-wing forces; **~kräftig** *(Rechtsw.)* **1.** *Adj.* final [and absolute] 〈*decision, verdict, etc.*〉; **~kräftig sein/werden** 〈*contract, agreement*〉 be in/come into force; **2.** *adv.* **jmdn. ~kräftig verurteilen** pass a final sentence on sb.; **die Ehe wurde ~kräftig geschieden** the divorce became absolute; **~kundig** *Adj.* versed in the law *postpos.*; **~kurve die** right-hand bend; **~lage die** *(Rechtsw.)* legal situation; **~lastig** *Adj.* **a)** 〈*ship*〉 listing to the right; 〈*car*〉 down at the right, leaning to the right; **b)** *(Politik ugs.)* rightist; **~läufig** *Adj. (bes. Technik)* running from left to right; **~lehre die** *s.* **~wissenschaft; ~liberal** *Adj.* right-wing liberal; **~liberale der/die** right-wing liberal; **~miß·brauch der** *(Rechtsw.)* abuse of a/one's right; **~mittel das** *(Rechtsw.)* appeal; **es ist kein ~mittel zulässig** there is no right of appeal; **~mittel einlegen** lodge an appeal; appeal; **~mittelbelehrung die** *(Rechtsw.)* information *no pl., no indef. art.* on one's right to appeal; **~nach·folge die a)** *(Rechtsw.)* succession [to rights and obligations]; **b)** *(Staatensukzession)* succession; **~norm die** *(Rechtsw.)* legal norm; **~ordnung die** legal system; **~partei die** *(Politik)* right-wing party; **~pflege die** *(Rechtsw.)* administration of justice; **~pfleger der** *official with certain administrative and judicial powers;* **~philosophie die** philosophy of law

Rẹchtsprechung die; ~, ~en administration of justice; *(eines Gerichts)* jurisdiction

rẹchts-, Rẹchts-: ~radikal *(Politik)* **1.** *Adj.* radical right-wing; **2.** *adv.* **eine ~radikal orientierte Gruppe** a group with a radical right-wing orientation; **~radikale der/die** right-wing radical; **~radikalismus der** right-wing radicalism; **~rheinisch 1.** *Adj.; nicht präd.* on *or* to the right of the Rhine *postpos.*; **auf der ~rheinischen Seite** on the right side of the Rhine; **2.** *adv.* on *or* to the right of the Rhine; **~ruck der** *(Politik ugs.)* shift to the right; **~rum** *Adv. (ugs.) s.* **~herum; ~sache die** *(Rechtsw.)* legal matter; *(Streitsache)* case; **~schutz der** *(Rechtsw.)* legal protection; **~schutzversicherung die** insurance for legal costs; **~seitig 1.** *Adj.* 〈*paralysis*〉 of the right side; **die ~seitige Uferbefestigung** the reinforcement of the right bank; **2.** *adv.* on the right [side]; **~seitig gelähmt sein** be paralysed on *or* down the *or* one's right side; **~sicherheit die;** *o. Pl. (Rechtsw.)* certainty of the law; **~sprache die** *(Sprachw.)* legal terminology; **~spruch der** judgement; **~staat der** [constitutional] state founded on the rule of law; **~staatlich 1.** *Adj.* founded on the rule of law *postpos.*; **2.** *adv.* **~staatlich orientiert** oriented towards maintaining and promoting the rule of law *postpos.*; **~staatlich einwandfrei** legally correct; **~staatlichkeit die; ~:** rule of law; **~stehend** *Adj. (Politik)* right-wing; **~steuerung die** right-hand drive; **~streit der** lawsuit; **~titel der** *(Rechtsw.)* legal title; **~um** *Adv. (bes. Milit.)* to the right; **~um kehrt!** to the right about turn!; **~um machen** do a right turn; **~unsicherheit die;** *o. Pl. (Rechtsw.)* uncertainty regarding the law; **~verbindlich** *Adj. (Rechtsw.)* legally binding; **~verdreher der; ~s, ~ a)** *(abwertend)* person who twists the law; shyster *(Amer. sl.)*; **b)** *(ugs. scherzh.: ~anwalt)* legal eagle *(coll.)*; **~verkehr der** driving *no art.* on the right; **in Frankreich ist ~verkehr** they drive on the right in France; **~verletzung die** *(Rechtsw.)* infringement *or* violation of the law; **~verordnung die** *(Rechtsw.)* statutory instrument; **~vertreter der** *(Rechtsw.)* legal representative; **~weg der** *(Rechtsw.)* recourse to legal action *or* the courts *or* the law; **den ~weg beschreiten** *(geh.)* take legal proceedings *or* action; go to the courts *or* to court; **unter Ausschluß des ~wegs** without the possibility of recourse to legal action *or* the courts *or* the law; **~wesen das;** *o. Pl.* legal system; **~widrig 1.** *Adj.* unlawful; illegal; **2.** *adv.* unlawfully; illegally; **~widrigkeit die a)** *o. Pl.* unlawfulness; illegality; **b)** *(Handlung)* unlawful act; **~wirksam** *Adj. s.* **~gültig; ~wissenschaft die** jurisprudence; **Professor für ~wissenschaft** Professor of Law

recht-: ~wink[e]lig *Adj.* right-angled; **~zeitig 1.** *Adj. (früh genug)* timely; *(pünktlich)* punctual; **wir bitten um ~zeitige Lieferung** please deliver in good time; **2.** *adv. (früh genug)* in time; *(pünktlich)* on time; **~zeitig zu/zum/zur** in [good] time for; **sagen Sie mir bitte ~zeitig Bescheid** please let me know in good time; **~zeitig zu Bett gehen** go to bed early

Reck [rɛk] **das; ~[e]s, ~e** *od.* **~s** horizontal bar; high bar

Recke ['rɛkə] **der; ~n, ~n** *(geh.)* warrior

rẹcken 1. *tr. V.* **a)** stretch; **den Hals/Kopf ~:** crane one's neck; **die Faust ~:** raise one's fist; **b)** *(bes. nordd.: in Form ziehen)* **etw ~:** pull sth. back into shape. **2.** *refl. V.* stretch oneself; **sich ~ und strecken** have a good stretch

Rẹck-: ~stange die horizontal *or* high bar; **~turnen das** horizontal-bar exercises *pl.*

Recorder [re'kɔrdɐ] **der; ~s, ~:** recorder

Recycling [ri'saiklɪŋ] **das; ~s** recycling

Redakteur [redak'tø:ɐ̯] **der; ~s, ~e, Redakteurin die; ~, ~nen** editor; **~ für Politik/Wirtschaft** political/economics editor; **~ vom Dienst** duty editor

Redaktion [redak'tsi̯o:n] **die; ~, ~en a)** *(Redakteure)* editorial staff; **b)** *(Büro)* editorial department *or* office/offices *pl.*; **c)** *(Fach~)* editorial department; **d)** *o. Pl. (das Redigieren)* editing; **bei der ~ des Textes** when the text is/was being edited

redaktionell [redaktsi̯o'nɛl] **1.** *Adj.* editorial; **die ~e Verantwortung tragen** be responsible for the editing. **2.** *adv.* editorially; **etw. ~ bearbeiten** edit sth.

Redaktio̲ns·schluß der time of going to press; **nach ~:** after going to press

Redaktor [re'daktɔr] **der; ~s, ~en** [-'to:rən] *(bes. schweiz.)* editor

Rede ['re:də] **die; ~, ~n a)** speech; *(Ansprache)* address; speech; **eine ~ halten** give *or* make a speech; **die ~ des Betriebsleiters** the manager's speech; *s. auch* **schwingen; b)** *o. Pl. (Vortrag)* rhetoric; **die Kunst/Gabe der**

~: the art/gift of rhetoric; **etw. in freier ~ vortragen** make a speech *or* speak about sth. without notes; **c)** *(Äußerung, Ansicht)* **~ und Gegenrede** dialogue; **„...", das war seine stehende** *od.* **ständige ~:** '...' was one of his favourite sayings; **der langen ~ kurzer Sinn ist, daß ...:** the long and the short of it is that ...; **das war schon immer meine ~** *(ugs.)* that is what I've always said; **lockere/kluge ~n** loose/clever talk *sing.*; **dumme ~n führen** talk nonsense; **die ~ auf ein anderes Thema bringen** turn the conversation to another subject; **von jmdm./etw. ist die ~:** there is some talk about sb./sth.; **es ist die ~ davon, daß ...:** it is being said *or* people are saying that ...; **davon kann keine ~ sein** it's out of the question; **nicht der ~ wert sein** be not worth mentioning; **jmdm. ~ und Antwort stehen** give a full explanation [of one's actions] to sb.; **jmdn. zur ~ stellen** make someone explain himself/herself; **die in ~ stehende Person/der in ~ stehende Fall** *(Papierdt.)* the person/case in question; **d)** *(Gerücht)* **es geht die ~, daß ...** *(geh.)* there is a rumour *or* it is rumoured that ...; **e)** *(Sprachw.)* **[direkte** *od.* **wörtliche/indirekte] ~:** [direct/indirect] speech; **gebundene/ungebundene ~:** verse/prose

rede-, Rede-: ~duell das duel of words; **~figur die** *(Rhet., Stilk.)* figure of speech; **~fluß der** *(abwertend)* flow of words; **~freiheit die;** *o. Pl.* freedom of speech; **~gewandt** *Adj.* eloquent; **~gewandtheit die** eloquence; **~kunst die** rhetoric

reden 1. *tr. V.* **a)** *(sagen)* say; speak; **kein Wort ~:** not say *or* speak a word; **b)** *(sprechen)* talk; **Unsinn/viel ~:** talk nonsense/ *(coll.)* a lot; **es wird immer viel geredet** there is always a lot of talk *(coll.)*; **es kann dir doch egal sein, was über dich geredet wird** it should not matter to you what people say about you; **etw. zu ~ haben** have sth. to talk about; **c) jmdn. besoffen ~** *(salopp)* drive sb. round the bend with one's nattering *(Brit. coll.)* *or* chattering. **2.** *itr. V.* **a)** *(sprechen)* talk; speak; **viel/wenig ~:** talk a lot *(coll.)*/not talk much; **er redete vor sich hin** he was talking to himself; **darüber ließe sich ~:** that's a possibility; **b)** *(sich äußern, eine Rede halten)* speak; **er läßt mich nicht zu Ende ~:** he doesn't let me finish what I'm saying; **wer redet heute abend?** who is to speak this evening?; **gut ~ können** be a good speaker; *s. auch* **gut 2 b; c)** *(sich unterhalten)* talk; **mit jmdm./über jmdn. ~:** talk to/about sb.; **darüber wird noch zu ~ sein** we shall have to come back to that; **miteinander ~:** have a talk [with one another]; **mit ihm kann man nicht ~:** you just can't talk to him; **sie ~ nicht mehr miteinander** they are no longer on speaking terms; **so lasse ich nicht mit mir ~:** I won't be spoken to like that; **~ wir nicht mehr darüber!** let's not talk about it any more; **was gibt es da groß zu ~?** so what?; **nicht zu ~ von ...:** not to mention ...; **mit sich ~ lassen** *(bei Geschäften)* be open to offers; *(bei Meinungsverschiedenheiten)* be willing to discuss the matter; **von sich ~ machen** make a name for oneself. **3.** *refl. V.* **sich heiser/in Wut ~:** talk oneself hoarse/into a rage

Redens·art die a) expression; *(Sprichwort)* saying; **b)** *Pl. (Phrase)* empty *or* meaningless words; **allgemeine ~en** empty generalizations; **jmdn. mit ~en abspeisen** put sb. off with [fine] words

Reden·schreiber der speech-writer

Rederei die; ~, **~en a)** *o. Pl.* talking; talk; **b)** *(Pl.: Gerücht)* **die ~en über seine Vergangenheit** the gossip *sing.* about his past

Rede-: ~schwall der *(abwertend)* torrent of words; **~strom der** *s.* **~fluß; ~verbot das** ban on speaking; **~verbot haben/erhalten** be banned from speaking; **~weise die** manner of speaking; **~wendung die a)** *(Sprachw.)* idiom; idiomatic expression; **b)** *(Floskel)* expression; phrase; **~zeit die: die ~zeit auf zehn Minuten begrenzen** restrict speakers to ten minutes; **er mußte aufhören, seine ~zeit war abgelaufen** he had to stop speaking because he had run out of time

redigieren [redi'gi:rən] *tr. V.* edit

redlich 1. *Adj.* **a)** *(rechtschaffen, aufrichtig)* honest; honest, upright ⟨*person*⟩; **b)** *(intensivierend)* real ⟨*effort*⟩. **2.** *adv.* **a)** *(rechtschaffen, aufrichtig)* honestly; **sich ~ durchs Leben schlagen** make an honest living; **bleibe im Lande und nähre dich ~** *(Spr.)* stay here where you can earn a decent living; **b)** *(intensivierend)* really

Redlichkeit die; ~: honesty

Redner der; ~s, ~ **a)** *(Vortragender)* speaker; **b)** *(Rhetoriker)* orator; **er ist kein ~:** he is no orator; he is not a good speaker

Redner·bühne die [speaker's] platform *or* rostrum

Rednerin die; ~, **~nen** *s.* **Redner**

rednerisch 1. *Adj.* oratorical; **eine ~e Glanzleistung** a masterpiece of oratory. **2.** *adv.* oratorically

Redner-: ~liste die list of speakers; **~pult das** lectern

Redoute [re'du:tə] **die;** ~, **~n a)** *(veralt.: Festsaal)* ballroom; **b)** *(österr.) s.* **Maskenball**

red·selig *Adj.* talkative

Red·seligkeit die talkativeness

Reduktion [redʊk'tsio:n] **die;** ~, **~en** reduction

redundant [redʊn'dant] *Adj. (Sprachw., Kommunikationsf.)* redundant

Redundanz [redʊn'dants] **die;** ~, **~en** *(Sprachw., Kommunikationsf.)* redundancy

reduzieren [redu'tsi:rən] **1.** *tr. V. (auch Chemie, Physik)* reduce (**auf** + *Akk.* to). **2.** *refl. V.* decrease; diminish

Reduzierung die; ~, **~en** *s.* **Reduktion**

Reede ['re:də] **die;** ~, **~n** *(Seew.)* roads *pl.*; roadstead; **das Schiff liegt auf der ~:** the ship is [lying] in the roads

Reeder der; ~s, ~: shipowner

Reederei die; ~, **~en** shipping firm *or* company

Reederei·flagge die house flag

Reederin die; ~, **~nen** *s.* **Reeder**

reell [re'ɛl] **1.** *Adj.* **a)** *(anständig)* honest, straight ⟨*person, deal, etc.*⟩; sound, solid ⟨*business, firm, etc.*⟩; straight ⟨*offer*⟩; **b)** *(wirklich)* real; **c)** *(ugs.: den Erwartungen entsprechend)* decent; realistic ⟨*price*⟩; **ein ~es Mittagessen** a solid *or* decent lunch. **2.** *adv.* **a)** *(anständig)* honestly; **b)** *(wirklich)* actually; really; **c)** *(ugs.: den Erwartungen entsprechend)* **der Wirt hat ~ eingeschenkt** the landlord poured [out] a decent measure/decent measures

Reep [re:p] **das;** ~[e]s, ~e *(Seemannsspr.)* rope

Reet [re:t] **das;** ~s *(nordd.)* reeds *pl.*

Reet·dach das thatched roof *(with reeds)*

reet·gedeckt *adj.* thatched

REFA ['re:fa] *Abk.* **Reichsausschuß für Arbeitszeitermittlung** (*heute:* **Verband für Arbeitsstudien)** work study organization

REFA-Fachmann der work-study expert

Refektorium [refɛk'to:riʊm] **das;** ~s, **Refektorien** refectory

Referat [refe'ra:t] **das;** ~[e]s, **~e a)** *(umfangreichere Abhandlung)* paper; **ein ~ halten** give *or* present a paper; **b)** *(kurzer schriftlicher Bericht)* report (+ *Gen.* on); **c)** *(Abteilung, Fachgebiet)* department

Referendar [referɛn'da:ɐ̯] **der;** ~s, **~e, Referendarin die;** ~, **~nen** *candidate for a higher civil-service post who has passed the first state examination and is undergoing in-service training*

Referendum [refe'rɛndʊm] **das;** ~s, **Referenden** *od.* **Referenda** referendum

Referent [refe'rɛnt] **der;** ~en, **~en a)** *(Vortragender)* person presenting a/the paper; *(Redner)* speaker; **b)** *(Gutachter)* examiner; **c)** *(Sachbearbeiter)* expert (**für** on); *(eines Ministers)* adviser (**für** on)

Referentin die; ~, **~nen** *s.* **Referent**

Referenz [refe'rɛnts] **die;** ~, **~en a)** *(Empfehlung)* reference; **b)** *(Person, Stelle)* referee; **jmdn. als ~ angeben** give sb.'s name *or* give sb. as a reference

referieren [refe'ri:rən] **1.** *itr. V.* **über etw.** *(Akk.)* **~:** give *or* present a paper on sth.; *(zusammenfassend)* give a report on sth. **2.** *tr. V.* **etw. ~:** give *or* present a paper on sth.; *(zusammenfassend)* give a report on sth.

¹Reff [rɛf] **das;** ~s, ~s *(Seemannsspr.)* reef

²Reff das; ~[e]s, ~e *(ugs. abwertend)* old hag

reffen *tr. (auch itr.) V. (Seemannsspr.)* reef ⟨*sail*⟩; **wir müssen ~:** we must reef sail

Refinanzierung die *(Geldw.)* procurement of funds to provide credit

reflektieren [reflɛk'ti:rən] **1.** *tr. V. (zurückstrahlen)* reflect. **2.** *itr. V.* **a)** *(nachdenken)* reflect, ponder (**über** + *Akk.* [up]on); **b)** *(ugs.: streben nach)* **auf etw.** *(Akk.)* **~:** have [got] one's eye on sth. **3.** *tr. V. (nachdenken über)* reflect [up]on; ponder

reflektiert 1. *Adj.* reflective. **2.** *adv.* reflectively; in a reflective manner

Reflektor [re'flɛktɔr] **der;** ~s, **~en** [-'to:rən] reflector

reflektorisch *Adj. (Physiol.)* reflex *attrib.*

Reflex [re'flɛks] **der;** ~es, **~e a)** *(Physiol.)* reflex; **b)** *(Licht~)* reflection

Reflex-: ~bewegung die reflex movement; **~handlung die** reflex action

Reflexion [reflɛ'ksio:n] **die;** ~, **~en** reflection

Reflexions·winkel der *(Physik)* angle of reflection

reflexiv [reflɛ'ksi:f] **1.** *Adj.* **a)** *(Sprachw.)* reflexive; **b)** *(geh.: reflektiert)* reflective. **2.** *adv.* **a)** *(Sprachw.)* reflexively; **b)** *(geh.: reflektiert)* through reflection

Reflexiv das; ~s, **~e, Reflexiv·pronomen das** *(Sprachw.)* reflexive pronoun

Reform [re'fɔrm] **die;** ~, **~en** reform

Reformation die *o. Pl. (hist.)* Reformation

Reformations·fest das Reformation Day

Reformator [refɔr'ma:tɔr] **der;** ~s, **~en** [-ma'to:rən] **a)** reformer; **b)** *(hist.)* Reformer

reformatorisch *Adj.* reformational; reformatory, reformative ⟨*zeal, attempts*⟩

reform-, Reform-: ~bedürftig *Adj.* in need of reform *postpos.*; **~bestrebungen** *Pl.* efforts towards reform; **~bewegung die** reform movement

Reformer der; ~s, ~, **Reformerin die;** ~, **~nen** reformer

reformerisch *Adj.* reforming *attrib.* ⟨*government*⟩; ⟨*idea, policy, party, etc.*⟩ of reform; ⟨*efforts*⟩ towards reform

reform·freudig *Adj.* ⟨*person*⟩ eager for reform

Reform·haus das health-food shop

reformieren *tr. V.* reform; **die reformierte Kirche** the Reformed Church

Reformierte der/die; *adj. Dekl.* member of the Reformed Church

Reformismus der; ~ *(bes. Politik)* reformism

Reformist der; ~en, **~en, Reformistin die;** ~, **~nen** *(bes. Politik)* reformist

reformistisch *Adj. (Politik)* reformist

Reform-: ~kost die health food; **~kurs der** policy of reform; **auf ~kurs** *(Akk.)* **gehen** embark on a policy of reform; **~politik die** policy of reform

Refrain [rə'frɛ̃:] **der;** ~s, ~s *(eines Lieds)* chorus; refrain; *(eines Gedichts)* refrain

Refraktor [re'fraktɔr] **der;** ~s, **~en** [-'to:rən] *(Astron.)* refractor

Refugium [re'fu:giʊm] **das;** ~s, **Refugien** *(geh.)* refuge

¹Regal [re'ga:l] **das;** ~s, ~e [set *sing.* of]

shelves *pl.;* **ein Buch aus dem ~ nehmen/ins ~ zurückstellen** take a book from/put a book back on the shelf

[2]**Regal das; ~s, ~e** *(Musik)* regal

[3]**Regal das; ~s, ~ien** [...li̯ən] *(hist.)* [royal] prerogative

Regal·brett das shelf

Regatta [re'gata] **die; ~, Regatten** *(Sport)* regatta

Reg.-Bez. *Abk.* **Regierungsbezirk**

rege ['re:gə] **1.** *Adj.* **a)** *(betriebsam)* busy ⟨*traffic*⟩; brisk ⟨*demand, trade, business, etc.*⟩; **[ein] ~s Treiben** bustling activity; hustle and bustle; **~ Beteiligung** *od.* **Teilnahme** good participation *or* attendance; **~r Briefwechsel** lively correspondence; **b)** *(lebhaft)* lively; lively, animated ⟨*discussion, conversation*⟩; keen ⟨*interest*⟩; **geistig noch sehr ~ sein** be still mentally alert *or* active; **eine ~ Phantasie** a lively *or* vivid imagination. **2.** *adv.* **a)** *(betriebsam)* actively; **~ an etw.** *(Akk.)* **teilnehmen** take an active part in sth.; **b)** *(lebhaft)* actively; **für sein Alter bewegt er sich noch sehr ~:** he is still very active for his age; **~ plaudern** chat animatedly

Regel ['re:gl̩] **die; ~, ~n a)** *(Vorschrift)* rule; **die ~n eines Spiels/der Rechtschreibung** the rules of a game/of spelling; **die ~n des Anstands** the rules of decency; **die ~n des Verkehrs** traffic regulations; **nach allen ~n der Kunst** *(fig.)* well and truly; **b)** *o. Pl. (Gewohnheit)* rule; custom; **die ~ sein** be the rule; **das ist bei ihm die ~:** that is his rule *or* custom; **sich** *(Dat.)* **etw. zur ~ machen** make a habit *or* rule of sth.; **[bei jmdm.] zur ~ werden** become a rule *or* habit [with sb.]; **in der** *od.* **aller ~:** as a rule; **c)** *(Menstruation)* period; **die** *od.* **ihre ~ haben/bekommen** have a *or* her period; **sie hat mit 13 ihre ~ bekommen** her periods started when she was 13

regelbar *Adj.* adjustable

regel-, Regel-: ~fall der rule; **im ~fall** as a rule; **~los 1.** *Adj.* disorderly; *(ungeregelt)* irregular; **ein ~loses Durcheinander** a confused muddle; **sie stürmten in ~loser Flucht davon** they fled pell-mell; **2.** *adv.* in a disorderly manner; *(ungeregelt)* irregularly; **~losigkeit die; ~, ~en** disorderliness; irregularity; **~mäßig 1.** *Adj.* regular; **2.** *adv.* regularly; **sie schreibt ~mäßig** she has even *or* regular handwriting; **~mäßigkeit die** regularity

regeln 1. *tr. V.* **a)** *(festsetzen, einrichten)* settle ⟨*matter, question, etc.*⟩; put ⟨*finances, affairs, etc.*⟩ in order; **etw. durch Gesetz ~:** regulate sth. by law; **wir haben die Sache so geregelt, daß ...:** we've arranged things so that ...; **er wird die Sache schon ~** *od. (nordd. ugs.)* **geregelt kriegen** he will see to it; **kriegst du das geregelt?** *(nordd. ugs.)* can you manage it/that?; **b)** *(einstellen, regulieren)* regulate; *(steuern)* control. **2.** *refl. V.* take care of itself; **die Sache hat sich [von selbst] geregelt** the matter has sorted itself out *or* resolved itself

regel-, Regel-: ~recht 1. *Adj.; nicht präd.* **a)** *(ugs.: richtiggehend)* proper *(coll.);* real; real ⟨*shock*⟩; real, absolute ⟨*scandal*⟩; complete, utter ⟨*flop, disaster*⟩; real, downright ⟨*impertinence, insult*⟩; **eine ~rechte Schlägerei** a regular fight *or* brawl *(coll.);* **ich hatte ~rechte Angst** I was really afraid; **b)** *(ordnungsgemäß)* proper; **2.** *adv. (ugs.: richtiggehend)* really; **ich habe mich ~recht mit ihm angefreundet** I became quite friendly with him; **jmdn. ~recht hinauswerfen** throw sb. out good and proper *(coll.);* **~studien·zeit die** *(Hochschulw.) period within which a course must be completed;* **~technik die;** *o. Pl.* control engineering

Regelung die; ~, ~en a) *o. Pl. s.* **regeln 1 a, b:** settlement; putting in order; regulation; control; **b)** *(Vorschrift)* regulation

Regelungs·technik die; *o. Pl.* control engineering

regel·widrig 1. *Adj.* that is against the rules *postpos.; (gegen die Vorschriften)* that is against the regulations *postpos.; (Ballspiele)* improperly taken ⟨*penalty kick, throw-in, etc.*⟩; **~ sein** be against the rules/regulations; **~es Verhalten im Verkehr** breaking traffic regulations. **2.** *adv.* **sich [im Verkehr] ~ verhalten** break [traffic] regulations; **den Stürmer ~ attackieren** *(Ballspiele)* foul the forward

Regel·widrigkeit die breach of the rules/regulations

regen ['re:gn̩] **1.** *tr. V. (geh.)* move. **2.** *refl. V.* **a)** *(sich bewegen)* move; **kein Lüftchen/kein Blatt regte sich** not a breath of air/not a leaf stirred; **b)** *(geh.: sich bemerkbar machen)* ⟨*hope, doubt, desire, conscience*⟩ stir

Regen der; ~s, ~ a) rain; **bei strömendem ~:** in pouring rain; **bei ~ wird in der Halle gespielt** if it's raining the match will be played inside; **es wird ~ geben** it will rain; it is going to rain; **es sieht nach ~ aus** it looks like rain; **auf ~ folgt Sonnenschein** *(Spr.)* good times always follow bad; **ein warmer ~** *(fig.)* a windfall; **vom** *od.* **aus dem ~ in die Traufe kommen** *(fig.)* jump out of the frying-pan into the fire; **jmdn. im ~ stehen lassen** *od.* **in den ~ stellen** *(fig. ugs.)* leave sb. in the lurch; **b)** *(fig.)* shower; **ein ~ von Schimpfwörtern ging auf ihn nieder** curses rained down upon him

regen·arm *Adj.* ⟨*period, region, etc.*⟩ with little rain[fall], with low rainfall; **der letzte Sommer war so ~, daß ...:** there was so little rain last summer that ...

Regen·bogen der rainbow

regen·bogen-, Regen·bogen-: ~farben, ~farbig *Adj.* rainbow-coloured; **~haut die** *(Anat.)* iris; **~presse die** *(abwertend)* gossip magazines *pl.;* **~trikot das** *(Radsport)* rainbow jersey

regen-, Regen-: ~cape das rain cape; **~dach das** rain-canopy; **~dicht** *Adj.* rainproof

Regeneration die a) regeneration; **b)** *(Technik: Rückgewinnung)* reclamation

regenerations·fähig *Adj. (Biol., Med.)* capable of regeneration *postpos.*

Regenerator der *(Technik)* regenerator

regenerieren [regene'ri:rən] **1.** *refl. V. (Biol., Med.)* regenerate. **2.** *tr. V.* **a)** *(erneuern)* regenerate; **sich ~** ⟨*person*⟩ recuperate; ⟨*group, organization, etc.*⟩ regenerate itself; **b)** *(Technik: wiedergewinnen)* reclaim

regen-, Regen-: ~fall der fall of rain; **heftige/anhaltende ~fälle** heavy rains *or* heavy [falls *pl.* of] rain *sing.*/continuous rain *sing.;* **~frei** *Adj.* without rain *postpos.;* rainless; **~guß der** downpour; **~haut die** [light] plastic mackintosh *or (coll.)* mac; **~macher der** rain-maker; rain-doctor; **~mantel der** raincoat; mackintosh; mac *(coll.);* **~naß** *Adj.* that is/are wet from the rain *postpos., not pred.;* **~naß sein** be wet from the rain; **~pfeifer der** *(Zool.)* plover; **~pfütze die** [rain] puddle; **~reich** *Adj.* ⟨*period, region, etc.*⟩ with high rainfall; **der letzte Frühling war so ~reich, daß ...:** there was so much rain last spring that ...; **~rinne die** gutter; **~schauer der** shower [of rain]; rain-shower; **~schirm der** umbrella

Regent [re'gɛnt] **der; ~en, ~en a)** *(Herrscher)* ruler; *(Monarch)* monarch; **b)** *(Stellvertreter)* regent

Regen·tag der rainy day

Regentin die; ~, ~nen *s.* **Regent**

Regen·tonne die water-butt

Regentschaft die; ~, ~en regency

Regen-: ~um·hang der rain cape; **~wald der** *(Geogr.)* rain forest; **~wasser das;** *o. Pl.* rainwater; **~wetter das;** *o. Pl.* rainy *or* wet weather; **er macht ein Gesicht wie drei Tage ~wetter** *(ugs.)* he looks as miserable as sin; **~wolke die** rain cloud; **~wurm der** earthworm; **~zeit die** rainy season

Reggae ['rɛgeɪ] **der; ~[s]** reggae

Regie [re'ʒi:] **die; ~ a)** *(Theater, Film, Ferns., Rundf.)* direction; **die ~ bei etw. haben** *od.* **führen** direct sth.; **unter der ~ von ...:** directed by ...; **b)** *(Leitung, Verwaltung)* management; **etw. in eigene ~ bekommen** *od.* **nehmen** take over control of sth.; **unter staatlicher ~:** under state control; **etw. in eigener ~ tun** *(ugs.)* do sth. oneself

Regie-: ~an·weisung die stage direction; **~assistent der** assistant director; **~fehler der** *(fig. scherzh.)* slip-up

regieren [re'gi:rən] **1.** *itr. V.* rule, reign, rule **(über +** *Akk.* over); ⟨*monarch*⟩ reign, rule **(über +** *Akk.* over); ⟨*party, administration*⟩ govern; *(fig.)* ⟨*peace, corruption, terror, etc.*⟩ reign; **der Regierende Bürgermeister von Berlin** the Governing Mayor of Berlin. **2.** *tr. V.* **a)** rule; govern; ⟨*monarch*⟩ reign over, rule; **ein demokratisch regierter Staat** a democratically governed state; **b)** *(Sprachw.)* govern, take ⟨*case*⟩

Regierung die; ~, ~en a) *(o. Pl.: Herrschaft)* rule; *(eines Monarchen)* reign; **die ~ übernehmen** *od.* **antreten** take over; come to power; **b)** *(eines Staates)* government

regierungs-, Regierungs-: ~an·tritt der: bei ~antritt der Sozialisten when the Socialists come/came to power; *(nach der Wahl auch)* when the Socialists take/took office; **~bank die** government bench; **~beamte der** government official; **~bezirk der** *largest administrative division of a Land;* **~bildung die** formation of a/the government; **mit der ~bildung betraut werden** be asked to form a government; **~chef der** head of government; **~erklärung die** government statement; *(in Großbritannien)* Queen's/King's Speech; **~feindlich** *Adj.* anti-government; **~form die** form of government; **~freundlich** *Adj.* pro-government; **~gebäude das** government building; **~gewalt die** government power *no art.;* **~kreise** *Pl.* government circles; **~krise die** government crisis; **~partei die** ruling *or* governing party; party in power; **~präsident der** *head of a Regierungsbezirk;* **~rat der a)** *(Amtstitel)* senior civil servant; **b)** *(schweiz.: Kantonsregierung)* canton government; **~sitz der** seat of government; **~sprecher der** government spokesman; **~sprecherin die** government spokeswoman; **~treu** *Adj.* loyal to the government *postpos.;* **~truppe die** government troops *pl.;* **~um·bildung die** government reshuffle; **~vor·lage die** government bill; **~wechsel der** change of government; **~zeit die** rule; *(eines Monarchen)* reign; *(einer Regierung, eines Regierungschefs)* period *or* term of office; **nach 12jähriger ~zeit** after 12 years in power *or* in office

Regie·stuhl der director's chair

Regime [re'ʒi:m] **das; ~s, ~** [re'ʒi:mə] *(abwertend)* regime

Regime-: ~gegner der opponent of a/the regime; **~kritiker der** critic of a/the regime; dissident

Regiment [regi'mɛnt] **das; ~[e]s, ~e** *od.* **~er a)** *Pl.* **~e** *(Herrschaft)* rule; **das ~ antreten/an sich reißen** come to/seize power; **das ~ führen** *(fig.)* give the orders; **ein strenges/straffes ~ führen** *(fig.)* be strict/run a tight ship *(coll.);* **b)** *Pl.* **~er** *(Milit.)* regiment

Regiments·kommandeur der regimental commander

Region [re'gi̯o:n] **die; ~, ~en a)** region; **b)** *(geh.: Bereich, Sphäre)* sphere; **in höheren ~en schweben** have one's head in the clouds

regional [regi̯o'na:l] **1.** *Adj.* regional. **2.** *adv.* regionally; **~ verschieden sein** differ from region to region

Regional·aus·gabe die regional edition

Regionalismus der; ~: regionalism *no art.*
Regional-: **~liga die** regional league; **~programm das** regional programme
Regisseur [reʒɪ'sø:ɐ̯] **der**; ~s, ~e, **Regisseurin die**; ~, ~nen *(Theater, Film)* director; *(Ferns., Rundf.)* director; producer
Register [re'gɪstɐ] **das**; ~s, ~ **a)** index; **b)** *(Daumen~)* thumb index; **c)** *(amtliche Liste)* register; **d)** *(Musik) (bei Instrumenten)* register; *(Orgel~)* stop; *(Tonbereich)* register; **alle ~ ziehen** *(fig.)* pull out all the stops; **e)** *(hist.: Urkundensammlung)* file; **f)** *(Druckw.)* register; **~ halten** be in register
Register·tonne die register tonne
Registrator [regɪs'tra:tɔr] **der**; ~s, ~en [-stra'to:rən] *(veralt.)* registrar
Registratur [regɪstra'tu:ɐ̯] **die**; ~, ~en **a)** *(das Registrieren)* registration; **b)** *(Büro)* filing-room; **c)** *(Schrank, Regal)* filing cabinet; **d)** *(Musik: Orgel~)* stop-mechanism
registrieren [regɪs'tri:rən] *tr. V.* **a)** *(eintragen, verzeichnen)* register; **b)** *(aufzeichnen)* register; **c)** *(bemerken)* note; register; **d)** *(feststellen)* note; **alle Zeitungen registrierten den Fall** all the papers mentioned the case; **es wurde sehr wohl registriert, daß er häufig unpünktlich war** it did not pass unnoticed that he often arrived late
Registrier·kasse die cash register
Registrierung die; ~, ~en **a)** *(Eintragung, Aufzeichnung)* registration; **b)** *(Feststellung)* **sich auf die ~ der Tatsachen beschränken** restrict oneself/itself to noting the facts
Reglement [reglə'mã:, *schweiz.*: reglə'mɛnt] **das**; ~s, ~s *od. (schweiz.)* ~e rules *pl.*
reglementieren *tr. V.* regulate; regiment ‹*people, life*›
Reglementierung die; ~, ~en regulation; *(Bevormundung)* regimentation
Regler der; ~s, ~ *(Technik)* regulator; *(Kybernetik)* control
Reglette [re'glɛtə] **die**; ~, ~n *(Druckw.)* lead; reglet
reg·los *Adj. s.* **regungslos**
Reglosigkeit die; ~ *s.* **Regungslosigkeit**
regnen ['re:gnən] **1.** *itr., tr. V. (unpers.)* rain; **es regnet** it is raining; **es regnet/regnete jeden Tag** it rains/rained every day; *s. auch* **Strom a. 2.** *itr. V.; mit sein (fig.)* rain down; **es regnete Steine** *(fig.)* stones rained down; **es regnete Briefe/Anfragen** *usw. (fig.)* there was a flood *or* deluge of letters/enquiries *etc.*
Regner der; ~s, ~: sprinkler
regnerisch *Adj.* rainy; **~-trüb** dull and rainy *or* wet
regredieren [regre'di:rən] *itr. V. (Psych.)* regress
Regreß [re'grɛs] **der**; **Regresses, Regresse a)** *(Rechtsw.)* recourse; **~ auf jmdn. nehmen** have recourse against sb.; **b)** *(Philos.)* regress
Regreß-: **~an·spruch der** *(Rechtsw.)* right to compensation; **~forderung die** *(Rechtsw.)* demand *or* claim for compensation; **~forderungen stellen** demand *or* claim compensation
Regression [regrɛ'sio:n] **die**; ~, ~en **a)** **wirtschaftliche ~**: economic recession; **b)** *(Psych., Geol., Statistik, Biol.)* regression
regressiv [regrɛ'si:f] *Adj. (Psych., Geol., Statistik, Biol.)* regressive
regreß·pflichtig *Adj.* liable for compensation *postpos.*
regsam *Adj. (geh.)* lively; active; **geistig ~ sein** have a lively *or* active mind
Regsamkeit die; ~ *(geh.)* liveliness; activeness
regulär [regu'lɛ:ɐ̯] *Adj.* **a)** *(vorschriftsmäßig)* in accordance with the regulations *postpos.*; *(richtig, gesetzlich)* proper; regular ‹*troops*›; normal, regular ‹*working hours*›; **die ~e Spielzeit** *(Sport)* normal time; **b)** *(normal, üblich)* normal; regular ‹*flight*›; **c)** *(ugs.: regelrecht)* proper *(coll.)*; regular *(coll.)*

Regularität [regulari'tɛ:t] **die**; ~, ~en *(auch Sprachw.)* regularity
Regulation [regula'tsio:n] **die**; ~, ~en **a)** *s.* **Regulierung**; **b)** *(Biol., Med.)* regulation
Regulativ [regula'ti:f] **das**; ~s, ~e **a)** *(regulierendes Element)* regulative; regulator; **Angebot und Nachfrage sind ~e des Marktes** supply and demand have a regulating effect on the market; **b)** *(regelnde Vorschrift)* regulation
Regulator [regu'la:tɔr] **der**; ~s, ~en [-la'to:rən] **a)** *(regulierende Kraft, Technik)* regulator; **b)** *(veralt.: Pendeluhr)* pendulum clock
regulierbar *Adj.* regulable; adjustable ‹*backrest*›
regulieren [regu'li:rən] **1.** *tr. V.* regulate; *(einstellen)* adjust; regulate; set ‹*clock, watch*›; **automatisch regulierte Türen** automatically controlled doors. **2.** *refl. V.* regulate itself; **sich selbst ~d** self-regulating
Regulierung die; ~, ~en *s.* **regulieren**: regulation; adjustment; setting
Regung die; ~, ~en *(geh.)* **a)** *(Bewegung)* movement; **b)** *(Gefühl)* stirring; **seine erste ~ war Unmut** his first emotion was displeasure; **sie folgte einer ~ ihres Herzens** she followed the promptings of her heart; **c)** *(Bestrebung)* striving
regungs·los *Adj.* motionless
Regungslosigkeit die; ~: motionlessness; **in voller ~ verharren** stay completely motionless
Reh [re:] **das**; ~[e]s, ~e roe-deer
Rehabilitand der; ~en, ~en *(Med.)* person undergoing rehabilitation
Rehabilitation die; ~, ~en rehabilitation
Rehabilitations·zentrum das rehabilitation centre
rehabilitieren *tr. V.* rehabilitate
Rehabilitierung die rehabilitation
reh-, Reh-: **~bock der** roebuck; **~braten der** *(Kochk.)* roast venison; **~braun** *Adj.* light reddish brown; **~keule die** *(Kochk.)* haunch of venison; **~kitz das** fawn *or* kid [of a/the roe-deer]; **~rücken der** *(Kochk.)* saddle of venison; **~wild das** *(Jägerspr.)* roe-deer *pl.*
Reibach ['raibax] **der**; ~s *(ugs.)* profits *pl.*; **einen [kräftigen] ~ machen** make a killing *(coll.)*
Reib·ahle die *(Technik)* reamer
Reibe ['raibə] **die**; ~, ~n grater
Reib·eisen das grater; **rauh wie ein ~**: as rough as sandpaper; **eine Stimme wie ein ~**: a voice like a rasp
Reibe-: **~kuchen der** *(Kochk.) grated raw potatoes fried into a pancake;* **~laut der** *(Sprachw.)* fricative
reiben 1. *unr. tr. V.* **a)** rub; **jmdm./sich die Backen ~**: rub sb.'s/one's cheeks; **das Pferd rieb sich an der Mauer** the horse rubbed itself against the wall; **etw. sauber ~**: rub sth. clean; **etw. blank ~**: rub sth. until it shines; **einen Fleck aus einem Kleid ~**: rub a mark off a dress; **sich** *(Dat.)* **den Schlaf aus den Augen ~**: rub the sleep from one's eyes; **sich** *(Dat.)* **die Haut/die Hand wund ~**: chafe one's skin/hand; **b)** *(zerkleinern)* grate. **2.** *unr. itr. V.* **a)** rub; **mit einem Tuch über die Schuhe ~**: rub one's/sb.'s shoes with a cloth; **b)** *(scheuern)* ‹*collar, shoes, etc.*› rub **(an** + *Dat.* on). **3.** *unr. refl. V.* **sich an einem Problem ~**: come up against a problem; **sich mit jmdm. ~**: be at loggerheads with sb.; **sich [aneinander] ~**: rub each other up the wrong way
Reiberei die; ~, ~en friction *no pl.*; **er hatte ständig ~en mit seinen Eltern** there was constant friction between him and his parents
Reib·fläche die striking surface *(of matchbox)*
Reibung die; ~, ~en **a)** *(das Reiben)* rubbing; **b)** *s.* **Reiberei**; **c)** *(Physik)* friction
reibungs-, Reibungs-: **~elektrizität die** *(Physik)* frictional electricity; **~fläche die** *(fig.)* source of friction; **~los 1.** *Adj.* smooth; **2.** *adv.* smoothly; **~wärme die** *(Physik)* frictional heat; **~wider·stand der** *(Physik)* frictional resistance
reich [raiç] **1.** *Adj.* **a)** *(vermögend)* rich; **~ heiraten** marry [into] money; **b)** *(prächtig)* costly ‹*goods, gifts*›; rich ‹*décor, ornamentation, finery, furnishings*›; **c)** *(üppig)* rich; rich, abundant ‹*harvest*›; lavish, sumptuous ‹*meal*›; abundant ‹*mineral resources*›; productive ‹*oil-well*›; **~ an etw.** *(Dat.)* **sein** be rich in sth.; **in ~em Maße** *(geh.)* in abundance; **d)** *(vielfältig)* rich ‹*collection, possibilities, field of activity*›; wide, large, extensive ‹*selection, choice*›; wide ‹*knowledge, experience*›; full ‹*life*›. **2.** *adv.* richly
-reich rich in ...; **variations~/kontrast~**: rich in variation/contrast; **wasser~ sein** have abundant water
Reich das; ~[e]s, ~e **a)** empire; *(König~)* kingdom; realm; **das [Deutsche] ~** *(hist.)* the German Reich *or* Empire; **das Russische ~** *(hist.)* the Russian Empire; **das Dritte ~** *(hist.)* the Third Reich; **b)** *(fig.)* realm; **ins ~ der Fabel gehören** belong to the realm[s] of fantasy; **das ~ der Pflanzen/Tiere** the plant/animal kingdom; **Dein ~ komme** *(bibl.)* thy Kingdom come
Reiche der/die; *adj. Dekl.* rich man/woman; **die ~n** the rich
reichen 1. *itr. V.* **a)** *(aus~)* be enough; **das Geld reicht nicht** I/we *etc.* haven't got enough money; **der Stoff reicht für ein** *od.* **zu einem Kostüm** there's enough material to make a suit; **das Brot muß noch bis Montag ~**: the bread must last till Monday; **die Farbe hat gerade gereicht** there was just enough paint; **das Seil reicht nicht** the rope's not long enough; **jetzt reicht's mir aber!** now I've had enough!; **danke, es reicht** that's enough, thank you; *s. auch* **langen**; **b)** *(sich erstrecken)* reach; ‹*forest, fields, etc.*› extend; **bis zu etw. ~**: extend as far as sth.; **er reicht mit dem Kopf bis zur Decke** his head touches the ceiling; **bis zum Horizont ~**: extend *or* stretch to the horizon; **sein Einfluß reicht sehr weit** his influence extends a long way; **soweit das Auge reicht** *(geh.)* as far as the eye can see; **jmdm. bis an die Schultern ~**: come up to sb.'s shoulder; **an die Grenze des Pathologischen ~**: verge on the pathological; **c) mit dem Geld/Brot** *usw.* **[nicht] ~**: [not] have enough money/bread *etc.*; **damit müssen wir ~**: we'll have to make it last. **2.** *tr. V.* **a)** *(geh.: entgegenhalten)* hand; *(herüber~, hinüber~)* pass; hand; **jmdm. die Hand ~**: hold out one's hand to sb.; **das Abendmahl ~**: administer *or* give Communion; **sich** *(Dat.)* **die Hand ~**: shake hands; **jmdm. Feuer ~**: give sb. a light; **b)** *(servieren)* serve ‹*food, drink*›
reich-, Reich-: **~geschmückt** *Adj.* *(präd. getrennt geschrieben)* richly decorated; richly adorned ‹*façade, building*›; **~haltig** *Adj.* extensive; wide, large, extensive ‹*range, selection*›; varied ‹*programme*›; substantial ‹*meal*›; **~haltigkeit die**; ~: extensiveness; *(eines Programms)* varied content; *(einer Mahlzeit)* substantialness; **die ~haltigkeit des Materials** the wealth of material
reichlich 1. *Adj.* large; substantial; ample ‹*space, time, reward*›; plenty of ‹*time, space*›; good ‹*hour, year*›; generous ‹*tip*›; **~e Niederschläge** heavy rain/hail/snow; **der Mantel ist ein bißchen ~** *(ugs.)* the coat is a bit on the large side. **2.** *adv.* amply; **~ Trinkgeld geben** tip generously; **Fleisch ist noch ~ vorhanden** there is still plenty of meat left; **~ Zeit/Platz/Gelegenheit haben** have plenty of *or* ample time/room/opportunity; **das ist ~ gerechnet** that's a generous estimate; **~ spenden** give *or* donate gener-

ously; ~ **zu leben haben** live well. **3.** *Adv.* **a)** *(mehr als)* over; more than; **nach ~ einer Stunde** a good hour later; ~ **vier Wochen** a good month; ~ **5000 Mark** a good 5,000 marks; **b)** *(ugs.: ziemlich, sehr)* ~ **frech/teuer/spät** a bit too cheeky/dear/late

reichs-, Reichs-: **~acht die** *(hist.)* imperial ban; **~adel der** *(hist.)* nobility of the Empire; **~adler der** *(hist.)* Imperial Eagle; **~apfel der** *(hist.)* imperial orb; **~arbeits·dienst der** *(ns.)* Reich Labour Service; **~bahn die;** *o. Pl.* **a)** *(DDR)* **Deutsche ~bahn** [East German] State Railway; **b)** *(hist.)* German National Railway; **c) die schwedische/japanische ~bahn** the Swedish/Japanese National Railway; **~bank die a)** *(hist.)* German National Bank; **b) die schwedische/japanische ~bank** the National Bank of Sweden/Japan; **~deutsch** *Adj.* within the German Reich *postpos.;* **~deutsche der/die** German citizen living within the German Reich; **~grenze die** frontier of the Empire; **~insignien** *Pl. (hist.)* imperial insignia *pl.;* **~kanzler der a)** *(1871–1918)* Imperial Chancellor; **b)** *(Weimarer Republik)* Chancellor of the Republic; **c)** *(Drittes Reich)* Reich Chancellor; **~mark die** *(hist.)* Reichsmark; **~präsident der** *(hist.)* President of Germany; **~regierung die** government of a/the nation *(under a monarch);* **~stadt die** *(hist.)* free city *or* town of the [Holy Roman] Empire; **~stände** *Pl. (hist.)* estates of the Empire; **~tag der a)** *(in Schweden)* Riksdag; [Swedish] Diet; *(in Finnland)* Parliament; *(in Japan)* [Imperial *or* Japanese] Diet; **b)** *(hist.: bis 1806)* Imperial Diet; Diet of the Holy Roman Empire; **c)** *o. Pl. (1871–1945 in Deutschland)* Reichstag; **~tags·brand der;** *o. Pl. (hist.)* Reichstag Fire; **~unmittel·bar** *Adj. (hist.)* subordinate directly to the Kaiser *or* Emperor *postpos.;* **~verweser der** *(hist.)* Regent of the Empire; **~wehr die;** *o. Pl. (hist.)* German *or* Imperial Army *(1919–35);* Reichswehr

Reichtum der; ~s, Reichtümer ['raiçty:mɐ] **a)** *o. Pl. (Vermögen, Besitz)* wealth **(an** + *Dat.* of); **sein seelischer/innerer ~** *(fig.)* the richness of his spirit/inner life; **b)** *Pl. (Vermögenswerte)* riches; **die Reichtümer der Erde** the riches of the earth; **damit kann man keine Reichtümer erwerben** one cannot get rich that way; **c)** *o. Pl. (Reichhaltigkeit)* wealth **(an** + *Dat.* of); **der ~ an Singvögeln** the abundance of song-birds; **der ~ seiner Kompositionen** the richness of his compositions

reich·verziert *Adj. (präd. getrennt geschrieben)* highly ornate

Reich·weite die a) reach; *(eines Geschützes, Senders, Flugzeugs)* range ; **sich außer ~ halten** keep out of reach/range; **in ~ sein/kommen** be/come within reach/range; **Geschütze mit großer ~:** long-range guns; **b)** *(Physik: Strahlungsweite)* range

reif [raif] *Adj.* **a)** *(voll entwickelt)* ripe ⟨*fruit, grain, cheese*⟩; mature ⟨*brandy, cheese*⟩; **das Geschwür ist ~:** the boil has come to a head; **~ für etw. sein** *(ugs.)* be ready for sth.; **er ist ~ fürs Irrenhaus** *(ugs.)* he belongs in the loony bin *(sl.);* **er brauchte nur die ~e Frucht zu pflücken** *(fig.)* it just fell into his lap; **b)** *(erwachsen, erfahren)* mature; **in [den] ~eren Jahren, im ~eren Alter** in one's mature years; **die ~eren Jahrgänge** those of mature age; **c)** *(ausgewogen, durchdacht)* mature; **eine ~e Leistung** *(ugs.)* a solid achievement; **~ für die** *od.* **zur Veröffentlichung sein** be ready for publication; **die Zeit ist noch nicht ~:** the time is not yet ripe

-reif ready for ...; **kino-/test-/olympia~:** ready for the cinema/for testing/for the Olympics; **aufführungs~:** ready to be performed

[1]Reif der; ~[e]s hoar-frost

[2]Reif der; ~[e]s, ~e *(geh.) (Fingerring)* ring; *(Arm~)* bracelet; *(Diadem)* circlet

Reife die; ~ a) *(das Reifsein)* ripeness; *(das Reifen)* ripening; **während der ~:** during ripening; **zur ~ kommen** ripen; **b)** *(von Menschen)* maturity; **Zeugnis der ~:** Abitur certificate; **c)** *(von Gedanken, Produkten)* maturity; **mittlere ~** *(Schulw.)* school-leaving certificate usually taken after the fifth year of secondary school

Reife·grad der degree of ripeness

[1]reifen 1. *itr. V.* **a)** *mit sein (reif werden)* ⟨*fruit, cereal, cheese*⟩ ripen; ⟨*ovum, embryo, cheese*⟩ mature; **b)** *mit sein (geh.: älter, reifer werden)* mature **(zu** into); **diese Erfahrungen haben ihn [zum Manne] ~ lassen** *(geh.)* these experiences made a man of him; **ein gereifter Mann** *(geh.)* a mature man; **c)** *mit sein* ⟨*idea, plan, decision*⟩ mature; ⟨*resistance*⟩ develop, grow; **zur Gewißheit ~** *(geh.)* grow *or* harden into certainty. **2.** *tr. V. (geh.)* ripen ⟨*fruit, cereal*⟩; mature ⟨*person*⟩

[2]reifen *itr. V.* **es hat gereift** there is/was a hoar-frost

Reifen der; ~s, ~ a) *(Metallband, Sportgerät)* hoop; **b)** *(Gummi~)* tyre; **c)** *(Schmuckstück) (Fingerring)* ring; *(Arm~)* bracelet; *(Diadem)* circlet

Reifen-: **~druck der** tyre pressure; **~panne die** flat tyre; puncture; **~profil das** [tyre] tread; **~schaden der** tyre defect; faulty tyre; **~wechsel der** tyre change

Reife-: **~prüfung die** *school-leaving examination for university entrance qualification;* **~zeugnis das** Abitur certificate

Reif·glätte die ice on the roads

reiflich 1. *Adj.* [very] careful; **bei/nach ~er Überlegung** on mature consideration/after [very] careful consideration. **2.** *adv.* [very] carefully; **über etw.** *(Akk.)* **~ nachdenken** give [very] careful thought *or* consideration to sth.; consider sth. [very] carefully

Reif·rock der *(hist.)* hooped skirt

Reifung die; ~ *s.* **[1]reifen 1:** ripening; maturing; maturation

Reifungs·prozeß der *s.* **[1]reifen 1:** process of ripening *or* maturing; *(eines Menschen)* stage of becoming mature

Reigen ['raign̩] **der; ~s, ~ a)** round dance; **den ~ eröffnen/anführen** lead off [in the round dance]; **b)** *(fig.)* **den ~ eröffnen** start off; **den ~ der Gratulanten eröffnen** be the first to offer congratulations; **den ~ schließen** close; finish off; **ein bunter ~ von Melodien** a medley of tunes

Reihe ['raiə] **die; ~, ~n a)** row; **Geräte in ~ schalten** *(Elektrot.)* connect pieces of equipment in series; **in ~n** *(Dat.)* **antreten** line up; *(Milit.)* fall in; **sich in fünf ~n aufstellen** line up in five rows; form five lines; **die ~n der älteren Generation lichten sich** *(fig.)* the ranks of the older generation are thinning out; **in Reih und Glied** *(Milit.)* in rank and file; **aus der ~ tanzen** *(fig. ugs.)* be different; **nicht in der ~ sein** *(fig. ugs.)* be feeling below par; **etw. in die ~ bringen** *(fig. ugs.)* put sth. straight *or* in order; **[wieder] in die ~ kommen** *(fig. ugs.)* get [back] on one's feet; **b)** *o. Pl. (Reihenfolge)* series; **die ~ ist an ihm/ihr** *usw.*, **er/sie** *usw.* **ist an der ~:** it's his/her *etc.* turn; **wer ist an der ~?** *(ugs.)* whose turn is it?; **Punkt drei der Tagesordnung ist jetzt an der ~:** we now come to the third item on the agenda; **du kommst jetzt an die ~** *(ugs.)* it's your turn now; **der ~ nach, nach der ~:** in turn; one after the other; **c)** *(größere Anzahl)* number; **eine ganze ~ Frauen** a whole lot of women *(coll.);* **d)** *(Gruppe)* ranks *pl.;* **die ~n schließen** close ranks; **aus den eigenen ~n** from one's/its own ranks; **e)** *(bes. Fußball)* **aus der zweiten ~ schießen** take a long shot/long shots [at goal]; **f)** *(Math.)* series; **g)** *(Schach)* rank; **h)** *(Musik)* series

[1]reihen *(geh.)* **1.** *tr. V. (auf~)* string; thread; **Perlen auf eine Schnur ~:** string pearls [on a thread]; **um etw. gereiht sein** be ranged around sth.; **Zahl an Zahl ~:** string numbers together. **2.** *refl. V. (sich an~, ein~)* follow; **sich um jmdn. ~:** gather round sb.

[2]reihen *tr. V. (heften)* tack; baste

Reihen der; ~s, ~ *(veralt.) s.* **Reigen**

reihen-, Reihen-: **~dorf das** *s.* **Straßendorf; ~folge die** order; **die ~folge einhalten** keep in order *or* sequence; **in kurzer ~folge** in quick succession; **~haus das** terraced house; **~schaltung die** *(Elektrot.)* series connection; **~untersuchung die** *(Med.)* mass screening; **~weise** *Adv.* **a)** *(ugs.: in großer Zahl)* by the dozen; **b)** *(in Reihen)* in rows *or* lines

Reiher der; ~s, ~: heron

Reiher·feder die heron feather

reihern *itr. V. (salopp)* puke *(coarse)*

Reih·garn das tacking *or* basting thread

reih·um *Adv.* **etw. ~ gehen lassen** pass sth. round; **die Flasche ging ~:** the bottle went *or* was passed round; **etw. ~ tun** do sth. in turn

Reihung die; ~, ~en *s.* **[1]reihen 1:** stringing; threading; ranging

Reim [raim] **der; ~[e]s, ~e** rhyme; **einen ~ auf ein Wort suchen** try to find something to rhyme with a word; **sich** *(Dat.)* **keinen ~ auf etw.** *(Akk.)* **machen [können]** *(fig.)* not [be able] to see rhyme or reason in sth.

reimen 1. *itr. V.* make up rhymes. **2.** *tr. V.* rhyme; **ein Wort auf ein anderes ~:** rhyme one word with another; **eine gereimte Fabel** a fable in rhyme. **3.** *refl. V.* rhyme **(auf** + *Akk.* with); **das reimt sich nicht** *(fig.)* that makes no sense

Reimerei die; ~, ~en *(abwertend)* **eine ~:** a piece of doggerel; **~en** doggerel *sing.*

Reime·schmied der *(abwertend)* rhymester

reim-, Reim-: **~lexikon das** rhyming dictionary; **~los** *Adj.* unrhymed; rhymeless; **~paar das** *(Verslehre)* rhyming couplet

Reimport der *(Wirtsch.)* reimport

Reim-: **~wort das** rhyme word; **~wörter·buch das** rhyming dictionary

[1]rein [rain] *(ugs.)* **~ mit dir!** in you go/come!

[2]rein 1. *Adj.* **a)** *(unvermischt)* pure; **~es Hochdeutsch sprechen** speak faultless *or* perfect German; **b)** *(nichts anderes als)* pure; sheer; **etw. aus ~em Trotz tun** do sth. out of sheer *or* pure contrariness; **~e Theorie/Mathematik** pure theory/mathematics; **die ~e Wahrheit sagen** tell the plain *or* unvarnished truth; **c)** *(ohne Ausnahme)* **es war ~e Männersache** it was exclusively a men's affair; **eine ~e Arbeitergegend** a purely *or* entirely working-class district; **d)** *(ugs.: intensivierend)* pure; sheer; **das ist der ~ste Quatsch** that's pure *or* sheer *or* absolute nonsense; **Sie sind der ~ste Dichter** you are a real poet; **dein Zimmer ist der ~ste Saustall** *(derb)* your room is a real pigsty; **e)** *(meist geh.: frisch, sauber)* clean; fresh ⟨*clothes, sheet of paper, etc.*⟩; pure, clean ⟨*water, air*⟩; clear, fresh ⟨*complexion*⟩; **ein ~es Gewissen haben** *(fig.)* have a clear conscience; **~ klingen** make *or* have a pure sound; **etw. ins ~e schreiben** make a fair copy of sth.; **etw. ins ~e bringen** clear sth. up; put sth. straight; **mit jmdm./etw. ins ~e kommen** get things straightened out with sb./get sth. sorted *or* straightened out; **mit sich [selbst] ins ~e kommen** sort things out in one's own mind; **mit etw. im ~en sein** have got sth. sorted out; **mit jmdm. im ~en sein** have got things straightened out with sb. **2.** *Adv.* **a)** *(ausschließlich)* purely; **b)** *(vor allem, besonders)* purely; **~ zufällig/unmöglich** purely *or* quite by chance/quite impossible; **~ zeitlich** purely from the point of view of time; **c)** *(ugs.: intensivierend)* **~ gar nichts** absolutely nothing

rein-: ~|beißen *unr. itr. V. (ugs.)* take a bite; **in etw.** *(Akk.)* **~beißen** take a bite of sth.; **zum Reinbeißen sein** *od.* **aussehen** *(ugs.)* ‹*cake etc.*› look tempting; *(fig.)* ‹*girl*› look good enough to eat; **~|dürfen** *unr. itr. V.* be allowed in

Reineclaude [rɛ:nə'klo:də] *s.* **Reneklode**

Reineke ['rainəkə] **der; ~s, ~s** Reynard *no art.*; **Meister ~, ~ Fuchs** Reynard the Fox

Reine·mache·frau die cleaning lady; cleaner

Reine·machen das; ~s *(bes. nordd.)* cleaning session; **beim ~ sein** be doing the cleaning; **eine Frau kommt zum ~**: a woman comes to do the cleaning

rein-, Rein-: ~erbig *Adj. (Biol.)* homozygous; **~erlös der, ~ertrag der** net profits *pl. or* proceeds *pl.*

Reinette [rɛ'nɛtə] *s.* **Renette**

reine·weg *Adv. (ugs.)* really; *(ganz u. gar)* absolutely; **das ist ~ zum Verzweifeln** it's enough to drive you to despair

Rein·fall der *(ugs.)* let-down; **das Stück war ein böser ~**: the play was a complete flop *(coll.)*; **mit unserem letzten Auto haben wir einen großen ~ erlebt** our last car was a complete disaster

rein|fallen *unr. itr. V.; mit sein (ugs.) s.* **hereinfallen a, hineinfallen**

Reinfektion die *(Med.)* reinfection

rein|gehen *unr. itr. V.; mit sein (ugs.) s.* **hineingehen**

Reingeschmeckte [-gəʃmɛktə] **der/die;** *adj. Dekl. (scherzh.)* outsider

Rein-: ~gewicht das net weight; **~gewinn der** net profit

Rein·haltung die: die ~ der Seen/der Luft keeping the lakes/air clean *or* pure; **die ~ der Sprache** keeping the language pure

rein|hauen *unr. tr. V. (salopp)* **a)** *(schlagen)* bash; **in die Tasten ~**: pound *or* thump the keys; **Kokain haut viel mehr rein** *(fig.)* cocaine gives you much more of a kick *(coll.)*; **jmdm. eine ~**: thump sb. [one] *(coll.)*; **b)** *(essen)* tuck in *(coll.)*

Reinheit die; ~ a) *(Klarheit)* purity; **b)** *(Sauberkeit)* cleanness; *(des Wassers, der Luft)* purity; *(der Haut)* clearness

Reinheits-: ~gebot das beer purity regulations *pl.*; **~grad der** degree of purity

reinigen ['rainɪgn] *tr. V.* clean; clean, cleanse ‹*wound, skin*›; purify ‹*effluents, air, water, etc.*›; **Kleider [chemisch] ~ lassen** have clothes [dry-]cleaned; **das Gewitter hat die Luft gereinigt** the storm has cleared the air; **ein ~des Gewitter** *(fig.)* an argument that clears the air; **die Atmosphäre ~** *(fig.)* clear the air

Reinigung die; ~, ~en a) *s.* **reinigen:** cleaning; cleansing; purification; dry-cleaning; **b)** *(Betrieb)* [dry-]cleaner's

Reinigungs-: ~creme die cleansing cream; **~milch die** cleansing milk; **~mittel das** cleaning agent; *(für die Haut)* cleanser; cleansing product

Reinkarnation die; ~, ~en reincarnation

rein-, Rein-: ~|knien *refl. V. (ugs.) s.* **hineinknien**; **~|kommen** *unr. itr. V.; mit sein (ugs.) s.* **herein-, hineinkommen**; **~|können** *unr. itr. V.* be able to go/come in; **~|kriechen** *unr. itr. V.; mit sein (ugs.)* crawl in; **in etw.** *(Akk.)* **~kriechen** crawl into sth.; **jmdm. hinten ~kriechen** *(derb)* lick sb.'s arse *(coarse)*; **~|kriegen** *tr. V. (ugs.) s.* **hereinbekommen; hineinbekommen**; **~kultur die a)** *(Landw.)* monoculture; **b)** *(Biol.)* pure culture; **Kitsch/Konservatismus in ~kultur** *(fig.)* pure *or* unadulterated kitsch/pure *or* sheer Conservatism; **~|legen** *tr. V. (ugs.) s.* **hereinlegen**; **~leinen** *Adj.* pure linen

reinlich 1. *Adj.* **a)** *(reinlichkeitsliebend)* cleanly; **b)** *(sauber)* clean; neat ‹*dress*›; **c)** *(gründlich)* clear[-cut] ‹*division, distinction, etc.*›. **2.** *adv.* **a)** *(sauber)* cleanly; neatly ‹*dressed, folded*›; **b)** *(gründlich)* clearly

Reinlichkeit die; ~ *s.* **reinlich:** cleanliness; neatness; clearness

rein-, Rein-: ~mache·frau die *s.* **Reinemachefrau**; **~|müssen** *unr. itr. V.* have to go/come in; **~rassig** *Adj.* pure-bred, thoroughbred ‹*animal*›; **~rassigkeit die** purity of breeding; **~|reißen** *unr. tr. V. (ugs.)* **jmdn. ~reißen** drag sb. in *(fig.)*; **~|reiten** *unr. tr. V. (ugs.)* **jmdn. ~reiten** drag sb. in *(fig.)*; **~|riechen** *unr. itr. V. (ugs.)* **in die Exportabteilung ~riechen** get a taste of work in the export department; **~|schauen** *itr. V. (ugs.)* look in; **~schiff (das)** *(Seemannsspr.) in* **~schiff machen** clean the decks [thoroughly]; **~|schlagen** *unr. tr. V.* **a)** *(ugs.)* knock in; **etw. in etw.** *(Akk.)* **~schlagen** knock sth. into sth.; **b) jmdm. eine ~schlagen** *(salopp)* thump sb. [one] *(coll.)*; **~schrift die** fair copy; **~schriftlich** *Adj.* **eine ~schriftliche Fassung** a fair copy; **~seiden** *Adj.* pure silk; **~|sollen** *itr. V.* be supposed to go/come in; **~|stecken** *itr. V.* put in; **~|steigern** *refl. V. (ugs.)* work oneself up; become worked up; **~|treten** *(ugs.)* **1.** *unr. itr. V.; mit sein (hineintreten)* **in etw.** *(Akk.)* **~treten** step in[to] sth.; **2.** *unr. tr., itr. V.* **jmdm.** *od.* **jmdn. hinten ~treten** kick sb. up the backside; **~|waschen** *(ugs.)* **1.** *unr. tr. V.* **jmdn.** *od.* **jmds. Namen ~waschen** clear sb.; clear sb.'s name; **sein Gewissen ~waschen** appease one's conscience; **2.** *unr. refl. V.* clear oneself *or* one's name; **~weg** *Adv. s.* **reineweg**; **[1]~wollen** *Adj.* pure wool; **[2]~|wollen** *unr. itr. V. (ugs.)* want to come/go in; **seltsam, daß so viele Leute ins Kino ~wollten** it's odd that so many people wanted to get into the cinema; **~|würgen** *tr. V.* **a)** *(ugs.)* **sich** *(Dat.)* **~würgen** force ‹*food, medicine, etc.*› down; **etw. in sich** *(Akk.)* **~würgen** force sth. down; **b) jmdm. eine** *od.* **eins ~würgen** come down on sb. like a ton of bricks *(coll.)*; **er hat einen reingewürgt gekriegt** he/she/they *etc.* came down on him like a ton of bricks *(coll.)*

[1]Reis [rais] **der; ~es** rice

[2]Reis das; ~es, ~er a) *(geh.: Zweig)* twig; **~er** *(Reisig)* brushwood *sing.*; **b)** *(geh.: Sproß)* shoot; **c)** *(Propf~)* scion

Reis-: ~auf·lauf der *(Kochk.)* baked rice dish; *(süß) baked pudding of rice with layers of fruit etc.*; **~bauer der** rice-grower; **~brei der** rice pudding

Reise ['raizə] **die; ~, ~n a)** journey; *(kürzere Fahrt, Geschäfts~)* trip; *(Ausflug)* outing; excursion; trip; *(Schiffs~)* voyage; *(ins Weltall)* voyage; flight; *(im Flugzeug)* flight; *(Kreuzfahrt)* cruise; *(Überfahrt)* crossing; **eine ~ mit dem Auto/der Eisenbahn** a journey by car/train; a car/train journey; **eine ~ zur See** a sea voyage; *(Kreuzfahrt)* a cruise; **eine dienstliche ~**: a business trip; **eine ~ um die Welt** a journey round the world; **auf meinen ~n** on my travels; **eine ~ machen** make a journey/go on a trip/an outing; **auf ~n sein** travel; *(nicht zu Hause sein)* be away; **viel auf ~n sein** *od.* **gehen** travel a lot; do a lot of travelling; **jeden Sommer gehen wir auf die ~** *od.* **auf ~n** we travel every summer; **auf der ~ gab's viel zu sehen** there was a lot to see during *or* on the journey/trip; **wohin soll diesmal die ~ gehen?** where will you/shall we go this time?; **glückliche** *od.* **gute ~!** have a good journey; **wenn einer eine ~ tut, dann kann er was erzählen** *(Spr.)* travelling is always eventful; **die** *od.* **seine letzte ~ antreten** *(geh. verhüll.)* go to meet one's Maker; **b)** *(Drogenjargon)* trip *(coll.)*

-reise die ... journey/trip; **Schweiz~/Afrika~**: journey/trip to Switzerland/Africa; **Bus~**: bus trip *or* journey

reise-, Reise-: ~an·denken das souvenir; **~apotheke die** [traveller's] first aid kit; **~bedarf der** travel requisites *pl.*; **~begleiter der** *(~gefährte)* travelling companion; *(~leiter)* courier; *(für Kinder)* chaperon; **~bekanntschaft die** acquaintance made on a/the journey; **ich habe eine interessante ~bekanntschaft gemacht** I met somebody interesting on the journey; **~bericht der** *(privat)* account of one's journey; *(offiziell)* report of one's journey; *(Buch)* travel book; *(Film)* travelogue; travel film; *(Artikel)* travel story; **~beschreibung die** account of a journey/one's travels; *(Buch)* travel book; **~büro das** travel agent's; travel agency; **~bus der** coach; **~decke die** travelling rug; **~fähig** *Adj.* **~fähig sein** be able to travel; **ein ~fähiger Patient** a patient able to travel; **~fertig** *Adj.* **~fertig sein** be ready to leave; **~fieber das** *(ugs.)* nervous excitement about the journey; **~fieber haben** be nervous and excited about the journey; **~führer der a)** *(~leiter)* courier; **b)** *(Buch)* guidebook; **~führerin die** courier; **~geld das a)** *(Geld für die Reise)* money for the journey; **b)** *s.* **~spesen**; **~gepäck das** luggage *(Brit.)*; baggage *(Amer.)*; *(am Flughafen)* baggage; **~gepäck·versicherung die** luggage/baggage insurance; **~geschwindigkeit die** average speed for a/the journey; **~gesellschaft die a)** *(~gruppe)* party of tourists; **eine deutsche ~gesellschaft** a party of German tourists; **b)** *(ugs.: ~veranstalter)* travel firm; tour operator; **~gruppe die** *s.* **~gesellschaft a**; **~kasse die** holiday fund; **~koffer der** suitcase; **~kosten** *Pl.* travel expenses; **~kosten·abrechnung die** travel expenses claim; **~krankheit die** travel sickness *no pl.*; **~land das;** *Pl.:* **~länder: ein beliebtes/teures ~land sein** be a popular country with/an expensive country for tourists; **Spanien ist ~land Nr. 1 für die Deutschen** Spain is the most popular holiday destination for the Germans; **~leiter der, ~leiterin die** courier; **~leitung die a)** *(das Leiten)* **er hat die ~leitung übernommen** he has taken on the job of courier; **~leitung durch erfahrene Mitarbeiter** only experienced couriers are used; **b)** *(Person)* courier/couriers; **~lektüre die** reading matter for the journey; **etw. als ~lektüre kaufen** buy sth. to read on the journey; **~lustig** *Adj.* **~lustig sein** *(häufig Reisen unternehmend)* be a keen traveller; *(zum Reisen aufgelegt sein)* be keen to travel

reisen *itr. V.; mit sein* **a)** travel; **viel gereist sein** be well-travelled; **er reist für einige Tage nach Paris** he's going to Paris for a few days; **in Unterwäsche/Hundefutter** *usw.* **~** *(ugs.)* travel in underwear/dog food *etc.*; **b)** *(ab~)* leave; set off

Reisende der/die; *adj. Dekl.* **a)** traveller; *(Fahrgast)* passenger; **b)** *(Vertreter)* [travelling] sales representative; [commercial] traveller

Reise-: ~necessaire das sponge-bag *(Brit.)*; toiletries bag *(Amer.)*; **~paß der** passport; **~pläne** *Pl.* travel plans; **~prospekt der** travel brochure; **~route die** route; **~ruf der** SOS message for travellers; **~scheck der a)** traveller's cheque; **b)** *(DDR) coupon of entitlement to a holiday at a specified place*; **~schreib·maschine die** portable typewriter; **~spesen** *Pl.* travelling expenses; **~tag der a)** *(Abreisetag)* departure day; **b) am dritten ~tag erreichten sie Athen** on the third day after setting out they reached Athens; **~tasche die** hold-all; **~verkehr der** holiday traffic; *(zwischen der Bundesrepublik Deutschland und der DDR)* transit traffic; **~wecker der** travel alarm; **~welle die** surge of holiday traffic; **~wetter das** weather for travelling; **das ist ideales/kein ~wetter** that's ideal/no weather for travelling; **~wetter·bericht der** holiday weather forecast; **~zeit die a)** *(Zeit der An-, Abreise)* travelling time; **b)** *(günstige Zeit)* time to travel; **c)** *(Urlaubszeit)* holiday time *or* season; **~ziel das** destination; **unser ~ziel für diesen Sommer ist Mallorca** we're going on holiday to Mallorca this summer; **Paris ist ein beliebtes ~ziel** Paris is a popular holiday destination; **~zug der** *(Eisenb.)* holiday train

Reis·feld das paddy-field

Reisig das; ~s brushwood

Reisig-: ~besen der besom; **~bündel das** bundle of brushwood

Reis-: ~korn das grain of rice; **~mehl das** rice-flour; **~papier das** rice paper

reiß-, Reiß-: ~ahle die scriber; **~aus der** *in* **~aus nehmen** *(ugs.)* scram *(sl.)*; scarper *(Brit. sl.)*; **~brett das** drawing-board; **~brett·stift der** *s.* **~zwecke**

reißen ['raisn̩] **1.** *unr. tr. V.* **a)** *(zer~)* tear; *(in Stücke)* tear up; **ein Loch in die Hose ~:** tear *or* rip a hole in one's trousers; **b)** *(ab~, weg~)* tear; **eine Pflanze aus dem Boden ~:** tear a plant out of the ground; **jmdm. etw. aus den Händen/Armen ~:** snatch *or* tear sth. from sb.'s hands/arms; **der Sturm riß die Ziegel von den Dächern** the gale ripped *or* tore the tiles off the roofs; **sich** *(Dat.)* **die Kleider vom Leibe ~:** tear one's clothes off; **jmdn. aus seinen Gedanken ~** *(fig.)* awaken sb. rudely from his/her thoughts; **etw. aus dem Zusammenhang ~:** take sth. out of context; **c)** *(ziehen an)* pull; *(heftig)* yank *(coll.)*; **d)** *(werfen, ziehen)* **eine Welle riß ihn zu Boden** a wave knocked him to the ground; **er riß den Wagen zur Seite** he wrenched the [steering-]wheel over; **jmdn. in die Tiefe ~:** drag sb. down into the depths; **der Fluß hat die Brücke mit sich gerissen** the river swept *or* carried the bridge away; **das Boot wurde in den Strudel gerissen** the boat was sucked into the whirlpool; **er riß sie in seine Arme** he pulled her into his arms; **[innerlich] hin und her gerissen sein** *od.* **werden** *(fig.)* be torn [two ways]; **von Zweifeln hin und her gerissen werden** *(fig.)* be torn by doubt; **e)** *(töten)* ⟨*wolf, lion, etc.*⟩ kill, take ⟨*prey*⟩; **f)** *(sich einer Sache bemächtigen)* **an sich ~:** seize ⟨*object, power, control, advantage, etc.*⟩; **er will immer das Gespräch an sich ~:** he always wants to monopolize the conversation; **g)** *(ugs.: machen)* crack ⟨*joke*⟩; make ⟨*remark*⟩; **h)** *(Leichtathletik)* **die Latte/eine Hürde ~:** knock the bar down/knock a hurdle over; **i)** *unpers. (schmerzen)* **es reißt mich in den Waden** my calves are aching; **j)** *(veralt.: zeichnen)* draw; **k)** *in* **jmdm. eine ~** *(österr. salopp)* stick one on sb. *(sl.)*. **2.** *unr. itr. V.* **a)** *mit sein* ⟨*paper, fabric*⟩ tear, rip; ⟨*rope, thread*⟩ break, snap; ⟨*film*⟩ break; ⟨*muscle*⟩ tear; **wenn alle Stricke** *od.* **Stränge ~** *(fig.)* if all else fails; **b)** *(ziehen)* **an etw.** *(Dat.)* **~:** pull at sth.; **der Hund riß an der Leine** the dog strained at the leash; **c)** *(Leichtathletik)* bring the bar down/knock the hurdle over; **d)** *(Schwerathletik)* snatch. **3.** *unr. refl. V.* **a)** *(sich los~)* tear oneself/itself **(aus, von** from); **sich aus seinen Träumen ~:** jerk oneself out of one's reveries; **b)** *(ugs.: sich bemühen um)* **ich reiße mich nicht um diese Arbeit** I'm not all that keen on this work *(coll.)*; **sie ~ sich um die Eintrittskarten** they are scrambling to *or* fighting each other to get tickets; **sie ~ sich alle darum, mitzuspielen** they are all after the chance to play; **c)** *(sich verletzen)* scratch oneself; **d)** *(sich beibringen)* **sich eine Wunde ~:** cut oneself

Reißen das; ~s *(ugs.)* **ich habe ein ~ in allen Gliedern** all my limbs are aching; **das ~ haben** have got rheumatism

reißend *Adj.* rapacious ⟨*animal*⟩; stabbing ⟨*pain*⟩; **~en Absatz finden** sell like hot cakes; **ein ~er Fluß** a raging torrent

Reißer der; ~s, ~ a) *(ugs., oft abwertend)* thriller; **b)** *(ugs.: Verkaufserfolg)* big seller

reißerisch *(abwertend)* **1.** *Adj.* sensational; lurid ⟨*headline*⟩; garish, lurid ⟨*colour*⟩. **2.** *adv.* sensationally

reiß-, Reiß-: ~feder die ruling pen; **~fest** *Adj.* unbreakable; non-tear ⟨*fabric*⟩; **~festigkeit die** breaking strength; **~leine die** *(Flugw.)* rip-cord; **~nadel die** scriber; **~nagel der** *s.* **~zwecke**; **~schiene die** T-square; **~stift der** *s.* **~zwecke**

Reis·stroh das rice grass

Reiß-: ~verschluß der zip [fastener]; **den ~verschluß an etw.** *(Dat.)* **aufmachen/zumachen** undo/do up the zip on sth.; unzip/zip up sth.; **jmdm. den ~verschluß aufmachen** undo sb.'s zip; **~wolf der** shredder; *(Textilw.)* devil; **~wolle die** shoddy; **~zahn der** *(Zool.)* carnassial [tooth]; **~zeug das** drawing instruments *pl.*; **~zwecke die** drawing-pin *(Brit.)*; thumbtack *(Amer.)*

Reis-: ~tafel die *(Kochk.)* rijsttafel; **~wein der** rice wine

Reit·bahn die riding arena

reiten ['raitn̩] **1.** *unr. itr. V.; meist mit sein* ride; **auf etw.** *(Dat.)* **~:** ride [on] sth.; **im Schritt/Trab/Galopp ~:** ride at a walk/trot/gallop. **2.** *unr. tr. V.; auch mit sein* **a)** ride; **Schritt/Trab/Galopp ~:** ride at a walk/trot/gallop; **ein Pferd müde ~:** ride a horse until it is tired; **ein Turnier/einen Wettbewerb ~:** ride in a tournament/competition; **ein scharfes Tempo ~:** ride at a furious pace; **ich habe mir die Knie steif geritten** I rode until my knees were stiff; **was reitet denn den?** *(fig. ugs.)* what's eating him? *(coll.)*; **b)** *(begatten)* ride; mount. **3.** *unr. refl. V.* **im Regen reitet es sich schwerer** riding is more difficult in the rain

Reiten das; ~s riding *no art.*

Reiter der; ~s, ~ a) rider; **ich bin kein guter ~:** I'm not a good rider *or* horseman; *s. auch* **apokalyptisch; b)** *(Milit.: Absperrung)* barrier; **spanischer ~:** barbed-wire barricade; **c)** *(österr.: Heu~)* rickstand; **d)** *(an der Waage)* rider; **e)** *(Kartei~)* tab

Reiterei die; ~, ~en a) *(Kavallerie)* cavalry; **b)** *o. Pl. (ugs.: das Reiten)* riding *no art.*

Reiterin die; ~, ~nen rider; **sie ist eine gute ~:** she is a good rider *or* horsewoman

Reiter·regiment das *(Milit.)* cavalry regiment

Reiters·mann der; *Pl.* **~männer** *od.* **~leute** *(veralt.)* horseman

Reiter·stand·bild das equestrian statue

Reit-: ~gerte die riding whip; **~hose die** riding breeches *pl.*; **~knecht der** *(veralt.)* groom; **~kunst die** riding skills *pl.*; equestrian skills *pl.*; **~peitsche die** riding whip; **~pferd das** saddle-horse; **~schule die** riding school; **~sitz der a)** *(auf Pferd)* **im ~sitz auf etw.** *(Dat.)* **sitzen** sit astride sth.; **b)** *(Turnen)* straddle seat; **~sport der** [horse-]riding; **~stall der** riding stable; **~stiefel der** riding boot; **~stunde die** riding lesson; **~tier das** mount; **das ist ein ~tier** this animal is used for riding; **~turnier das** riding event; **~weg der** bridle-path; bridleway

Reiz [raits] **der; ~es, ~e a)** *(Physiol.)* stimulus; **b)** *(Anziehungskraft)* attraction; appeal *no pl.*; *(des Verbotenen, Fremdartigen, der Ferne usw.)* lure; **etw. übt einen großen ~ auf jmdn. aus** sth. holds *or* has great attraction *or* appeal for sb.; **in dieser Aufgabe liegt für mich ein besonderer ~:** this task has a particular attraction *or* appeal for me; **ich kann dieser Sache** *(Dat.)* **keinen ~ abgewinnen** this has no appeal for me; **die neue Aufgabe hat gewiß ihre ~e** the new job certainly has its attractions; **an ~ verlieren** lose some of its attraction *or* appeal; **c)** *(Zauber)* charm; **weibliche ~e** female charms; **sie ließ alle ihre ~e spielen** she used all her charms

reizbar *Adj.* **a)** *(leicht zu verärgern)* irritable; **leicht ~ sein** be very irritable; **b)** *(empfindlich)* sensitive

Reizbarkeit die; ~ a) *(Erregbarkeit)* irritability; **b)** *(Empfindlichkeit)* sensitivity

reizen 1. *tr. V.* **a)** annoy; tease ⟨*animal*⟩; *(herausfordern, provozieren)* provoke; *(zum Zorn treiben)* anger; **jmds. Zorn ~, jmdn. zum Zorn ~:** provoke sb. to anger; **jmdn. bis aufs Blut ~:** make sb.'s blood boil; *s. auch* **gereizt; b)** *(anziehen)* attract; **jmds. Verlangen ~:** rouse sb.'s desire; **c)** *(Physiol.)* irritate; **seine Nerven waren zu sehr gereizt** his nerves were too much on edge; **d)** *(Interesse erregen bei)* **jmdn. ~:** attract sb.; appeal to sb.; **jmds. Haß/Widerspruch ~:** arouse sb.'s hatred/make sb. want to contradict; **es würde mich sehr ~, das zu tun** I'd love to do that; **das Angebot reizt mich** I find the offer tempting; **e)** *(Kartenspiele)* bid. **2.** *itr. V.* **a)** *(Physiol.)* irritate; **der Qualm reizt zum Husten** the smoke makes you cough; **b)** *(anregen)* **das reizt zum Lachen** it makes people laugh; **eine solche Ansicht reizt zum Widerspruch** such an opinion invites contradiction; **c)** *(Kartenspiele)* bid; **hoch ~** *(fig.)* play for high stakes

reizend 1. *Adj.* charming; delightful, lovely ⟨*child*⟩; **das ist ja ~** *(iron.)* [that's] charming! *(iron.)*. **2.** *adv.* charmingly; **wir haben uns ~ unterhalten** we had a delightful chat

Reiz-: ~gas das irritant gas; **~husten der** *(Med.)* dry cough

Reizker ['raitskɐ] **der; ~s, ~** *(Bot.) Lactarius*; **Echter ~:** saffron milk cap

reiz-, Reiz-: ~klima das *(Med., Met.)* bracing climate; **~los 1.** *Adj.* unattractive ⟨*person, face, task, etc.*⟩; ⟨*landscape, scenery*⟩ lacking in charm; bland ⟨*food, diet*⟩; **2.** *adv.* unattractively; **~losigkeit die; ~** *s.* **~los:** unattractiveness; lack of charm; blandness; **~mittel das** *(Med.)* stimulant; **~schwelle die** *(Med., Psych.)* stimulus threshold; absolute threshold; **~stoff der** irritant; **~thema das** emotive issue; **~über·flutung die; ~, ~en** *(Psych.)* overstimulation

Reizung die; ~, ~en a) *o. Pl.* annoyance; *(Herausforderung)* provocation; *(eines Tieres)* teasing; **b)** *(Physiol., Med.)* irritation

reiz-, Reiz-: ~voll 1. *Adj.* **a)** *(hübsch)* charming; delightful; **b)** *(interessant)* attractive; **das ist wenig ~voll für ihn** it doesn't appeal to him much; **es wäre ~voll, mit ihm darüber zu sprechen** it would be interesting to talk to him about it; **die Aussicht ist nicht gerade ~voll** the prospect isn't exactly enticing. **2.** *adv. (hübsch)* charmingly; delightfully; **~wäsche die** *(ugs.)* sexy underwear; **~wort das a)** *(Emotionen hervorrufend)* emotive word; **b)** *(Psych.)* stimulus word

Rekapitulation die *(auch Biol.)* recapitulation

rekapitulieren *tr. V.* recapitulate

rekeln ['re:kl̩n] *refl. V. (ugs.)* stretch; **sich in der Sonne/im Liegestuhl ~:** stretch out in the sun/in the deck-chair

Reklamation [reklama'tsio:n] **die; ~, ~en** complaint **(wegen** about); **spätere ~[en] ausgeschlossen!** money cannot be refunded after purchase

Reklame [re'kla:mə] **die; ~, ~n a)** *o. Pl. (Werbung)* advertising *no indef. art.*; *(Ergebnis)* publicity *no indef. art.*; **schlechte ~:** poor advertising/publicity; **~ für jmdn./etw. machen** promote sb./advertise *or* promote sth.; **b)** *(ugs.: Werbemittel)* advert *(Brit. coll.)*; ad *(coll.)*; advertisement; *(im Fernsehen, Radio auch)* commercial; **nichts als ~:** nothing but adverts/commercials; **die BBC bringt keine ~:** there are no adverts *etc.*/commercials on BBC

Reklame-: ~rummel der *(ugs. abwertend)* [publicity] ballyhoo, hype *(sl.)* **(um** surrounding); **~schild das** advertising sign; **~trommel die** *in* **für jmdn./etw. die ~trommel rühren** *(ugs.)* promote sb./advertise *or*

promote sth. in a big way; **~zettel der** advertising leaflet

reklamieren 1. *itr. V. (sich beschweren)* complain; make a complaint. **2.** *tr. V.* **a)** *(beanstanden)* complain about, make a complaint about (**bei** to, **wegen** on account of); **reklamierte Güter** goods about which there has been a complaint; **b)** *(beanspruchen)* claim; **jmdn. für sich ~:** monopolize sb.; **etw. für sich ~:** claim sth. for oneself

rekognoszieren [rekɔgnɔs'tsi:rən] *tr. V. (österr., schweiz., Milit.)* reconnoitre

Rekommandation [rekɔmanda'tsio:n] **die; ~, ~en a)** *(österr.)* recommendation; **b)** *(österr. Postw.)* registered letter

rekommandieren *tr. V. (österr. Postw.)* register

rekonstruierbar *Adj.* reconstructible; **leicht/schwer ~ sein** be easy/difficult to reconstruct

rekonstruieren *tr. V.* **a)** reconstruct; **b)** *(DDR: modernisieren)* modernize; renovate ⟨*building*⟩

Rekonstruktion die a) reconstruction; **b)** *(DDR: Modernisierung)* modernization/renovation

Rekonvaleszent [rekɔnvalɛs'tsɛnt] **der; ~en, ~en, Rekonvaleszentin die; ~, ~nen** convalescent

Rekonvaleszenz [rekɔnvalɛs'tsɛnts] **die** *(Med.)* convalescence *no art.*

Rekord [re'kɔrt] **der; ~[e]s, ~e** record; **einen ~ aufstellen/innehaben** set up/hold a record

Rekord- record ⟨*harvest, temperature, fee*⟩

Rekord-: ~besuch der record number of visitors; **~halter der, ~inhaber der** record-holder; **~lauf der** record-breaking run; **~leistung die** record

Rekordler [re'kɔrtlɐ] **der; ~s, ~, Rekordlerin die; ~, ~nen** record-holder

Rekord-: ~marke die record; **~versuch der** attempt at a/the record; **~zeit die** record time

Rekrut [re'kru:t] **der; ~en, ~en** *(Milit.)* recruit

rekrutieren 1. *refl. V.* **sich aus einem bestimmten Kreis ~:** be drawn from a particular sphere; **sich aus Beamten/Selbständigen ~:** consist *or* be composed of civil servants/self-employed people; **2.** *tr. V. (Milit. veralt., auch fig.)* recruit (**aus** from)

Rekrutierung die; ~, ~en recruitment; recruiting

Rekta *s.* **Rektum**

rektal [rɛk'ta:l] *(Med.)* **1.** *Adj.* rectal. **2.** *adv.* rectally

Rektion [rɛk'tsi̯o:n] **die; ~, ~en** *(Grammatik)* **die ~ einer Präposition** the case governed by a preposition; **nur bei einigen Präpositionen schwankt die ~:** only a few prepositions can take more than one case

Rektor ['rɛktɔr] **der; ~s, ~en** [-'to:rən] **a)** *(Schulleiter)* head[master]; **b)** *(Universitäts~)* Rector; ≈ Vice-Chancellor *(Brit.)*; *(einer Fachhochschule)* principal

Rektorat [rɛkto'ra:t] **das; ~[e]s, ~e a)** *(Amt, Amtszeit)* headship; *(an der Universität)* Rectorship; ≈ Vice-Chancellorship *(Brit.)*; **b)** *(Amtszimmer)* head[master]'s room *or* office; *(an der Universität)* Rector's office; ≈ Vice-Chancellor's office *(Brit.)*

Rektorin die; ~, ~nen a) *(Schulleiterin)* head[mistress]; **b)** *s.* **Rektor b**

Rektoskop [rɛkto'sko:p] **das; ~s, ~e** *(Med.)* proctoscope; rectoscope

Rektoskopie [rɛktosko'pi:] **die; ~, ~n** *(Med.)* proctoscopy

Rektum ['rɛktʊm] **das; ~s, Rekta** ['rɛkta] *(Anat.)* rectum

rekultivieren *tr. V. (Landw.)* recultivate

rekurrieren [rekʊ'ri:rən] *itr. V.* **a)** *(geh.: Bezug nehmen)* **auf etw.** *(Akk.)* **~:** refer back to sth.; **b)** *(österr. Rechtsspr.)* **gegen etw. ~:** appeal against sth.

Rekurs der a) *(geh.: Bezug)* reference (**auf** + *Akk.* to); **auf etw.** *(Akk.)* **~ nehmen** refer back to sth.; **b)** *(Rechtsspr.)* appeal; **~ einlegen** lodge an appeal

Relais [rə'lɛ:] **das; ~** [rə'lɛ:(s)], **~** [rə'lɛ:s] *(Elektrot.)* relay

Relais-: ~schaltung die *(Elektrot.)* relay circuit; **~station die** *(Elektrot.)* relay station

Relation [rela'tsi̯o:n] **die; ~, ~en** *(auch Math.)* relation; **in einer/keiner ~ zu etw. stehen** bear a/no relation to sth.

relativ [rela'ti:f] **1.** *Adj.* relative; *s. auch* **Mehrheit; Gehör. 2.** *adv.* **a)** *(ziemlich)* relatively; **b)** *(vergleichsweise)* **~ zu** relative to

relativieren *tr. V.* relativize

Relativierung die; ~, ~en relativization

Relativismus der; ~ *(Philos.)* relativism

relativistisch *Adj. (auch Philos., Physik)* relativistic

Relativität [relativi'tɛ:t] **die; ~, ~en** relativity

Relativitäts·theorie die; *o. Pl. (Physik)* theory of relativity

Relativ-: ~pronomen das *(Sprachw.)* relative pronoun; **~satz der** *(Sprachw.)* relative clause

Relaxans [re'laksans] **das; ~, Relaxantien** *(Med.)* relaxant

relaxed [ri'lɛkst] *(salopp) Adj.; nicht attr.* laid-back *(coll.)*

Relegation [relega'tsi̯o:n] **die; ~, ~en** expulsion

relegieren [rele'gi:rən] *tr. V.* expel

relevant [rele'vant] *Adj.* relevant (**für** to)

Relevanz die; ~: relevance (**für** to)

Relief [re'li̯ɛf] **das; ~s, ~s** *od.* **~e** *(bild. Kunst; Geogr.)* relief

relief-, Relief-: ~artig 1. *Adj.* raised in relief *postpos.*; **2.** *adv.* **~artig erhoben** raised in relief *postpos.*; **~druck der a)** *o. Pl. (Verfahren)* relief printing; **b)** *(Erzeugnis)* relief print; **~karte die** relief map

Religion [reli'gi̯o:n] **die; ~, ~en a)** *(auch fig.)* religion; **b)** *o. Pl.; o. Art. (Unterrichtsfach)* religious instruction *or* education; RI; RE

religions-, Religions-: ~aus·übung die practice of religion; **freie ~ausübung** freedom to practise one's religion; **~bekenntnis die** religion; denomination; [religious] confession; **~freiheit die;** *o. Pl.* religious freedom; **~friede der** religious peace; **~gemeinschaft die** denomination; **~geschichte die** history of religion; **~krieg der** religious war; **~lehre die;** *o. Pl. s.* **Religion b; ~lehrer der** religious instruction *or* education teacher; RI *or* RE teacher; **~los** *Adj.* **a)** ⟨*person*⟩ who has no religious beliefs; **ich bin ~los** I'm not religious; **b)** *(gottlos)* irreligious; **~philosophie die;** *o. Pl.* philosophy of religion; **~stifter der** founder of a/the religion; **~streit der** religious dispute; **~stunde die** religious instruction *or* education lesson; RI *or* RE lesson; **~unterricht der** *s.* **Religion b;** *s. auch* **Englischunterricht; ~wissenschaft die;** *o. Pl.* religious studies *pl., no art.*; **vergleichende ~wissenschaft** comparative religion; **~wissenschaftler der** religious scholar; **~zugehörigkeit die** religion; religious confession; **~zwang der;** *o. Pl. compulsion to belong to a particular denomination*

religiös [reli'gi̯ø:s] **1.** *Adj.* religious. **2.** *adv.* in a religious manner; **religiös erzogen werden** have *or* receive a religious upbringing; **~ leben** live a religious life

Religiosität [religi̯ozi'tɛ:t] **die; ~:** religiousness

Relikt [re'lɪkt] **das; ~[e], ~e a)** *(auch Sprachw.)* relic; **b)** *(Biol.)* relict; relic

Reling ['re:lɪŋ] **die; ~, ~s** *od.* **~e** *(Seew.)* [deck-]rail

Reliquie [re'li:kvi̯ə] **die; ~, ~n** *(Rel., bes. kath. Kirche)* relic

Reliquien·schrein der reliquary

Rembours·geschäft [rã'bu:ɐ̯-] **das** *(Finanzw.)* documentary credit trading; **ein ~:** a documentary credit transaction

Remigrant [rɛmi'grant] **der; ~en, ~en, Remigrantin die; ~, ~nen** returning emigrant; *(nach der Rückkehr)* returned emigrant; **türkische ~en** returning/returned Turkish emigrants

remilitarisieren *tr. V.* remilitarize

Remilitarisierung die remilitarization

Reminiszenz [reminɪs'tsɛnts] **die; ~, ~en** *(geh.)* reminiscence (**an** + *Akk.* of)

remis [rə'mi:] *(bes. Schach) indekl. Adj.; nicht attr.* drawn; **~ enden/ausgehen** end in a draw; **sie trennten sich ~:** they held each other to a draw; **~ spielen** draw

Remis das; ~ [rə'mi:(s)], **~** [rə'mi:s] *od.* **~en** *(bes. Schach)* draw; **~ anbieten** offer a draw

Remise [re'mi:zə] **die; ~, ~n a)** *(veralt.)* coach-house; *(Geräteschuppen)* shed; **b)** *(Schach) s.* **Remis**

Remission die a) *(Buchw.)* return; **b)** *(Med.)* remission

Remittende [remɪ'tɛndə] **die; ~, ~n** *(Buchw.)* return

Remittent [remɪ'tɛnt] **der; ~en, ~en** *(Finanzw.)* payee

remittieren [remɪ'ti:rən] **1.** *tr. V. (Buchw.)* return. **2.** *itr. V. (Med.)* remit

Remmidemmi [rɛmi'dɛmi] **das; ~** *(ugs.)* row *(coll.)*; racket; **~ machen** make a row *(coll.) or* racket

Remoulade [remu'la:də] **die; ~, ~n, Remouladen·soße die** remoulade

Rempelei die; ~, ~en *(ugs.)* pushing and shoving; jostling; *(Sport)* pushing; **hören Sie doch mit der ~ auf!** stop pushing and shoving!

rempeln ['rɛmpl̩n] *(ugs.)* push; shove; jostle; *(Sport)* push

Rempler der; ~s, ~ *(ugs.)* **jmdm. einen ~ geben** push against sb.

Remuneration [remunera'tsi̯o:n] **die; ~, ~en** *(österr., sonst veralt.)* compensation

Ren [rɛn] **das; ~s, ~s** *od.* **~e** reindeer

Renaissance [rənɛ'sã:s] **die; ~, ~n a)** *o. Pl.* Renaissance; **b)** *(Wiederaufleben)* revival; **eine ~ erleben** enjoy a renaissance

Renaissance·musik die Renaissance music

Rendezvous [rãde'vu:] **das; ~** [...'vu:(s)], **~** ['rãde'vu:s] rendezvous

Rendezvous·manöver das *(Raumf.)* rendezvous manœuvre

Rendite [rɛn'di:tə] **die; ~, ~n** *(Wirtsch.)* [annual] yield *or* return

Rendite·objekt das investment property

Renegat [rene'ga:t] **der, ~en, ~en** *(abwertend)* renegade

Renegatentum das; ~s *(abwertend)* apostasy; **jmdm. ~ vorwerfen** accuse sb. of being a renegade

Reneklode [re:nə'klo:də] **die; ~, ~n** greengage

Renette [re'nɛtə] **die; ~, ~n** rennet

renitent [reni'tɛnt] **1.** *Adj.* refractory. **2.** *adv.* refractorily

Renitenz [reni'tɛnts] **die; ~** refractoriness

Renn-: ~auto das racing car; **~bahn die** *(Sport)* race-track; *(für Pferde)* racecourse; race-track; **~boot das** *(Motorboot)* powerboat; *(Segelboot)* racing yacht; *(Ruderboot)* racing shell

rennen ['rɛnən] **1.** *unr. itr. V.; mit sein* **a)** run; **um die Wette ~:** have a race; race each other; **wütend aus dem Zimmer ~:** storm out of the room; **in sein Verderben/den Tod ~** *(fig.)* rush headlong to one's doom/hasten to one's death; **meine Uhr rennt wieder** *(fig. ugs.)* my watch is fast again; **b)** *(ugs. abwertend: hingehen)* run [off]; **dauernd ins Kino/zur Polizei ~:** be always going to the cinema/running to the police; **c)** *(stoßen an)* **an/gegen jmdn./etw. ~:** run *or* bang into sb./sth.; **mit dem Kopf an** *od.* **gegen etw.** *(Akk.)* **~:** bang one's head against *or* on sth. **2.** *unr. tr. V.* **a)** *(sich zuziehen)* **sich** *(Dat.)* **an etw.** *(Dat.)* **ein Loch in den Kopf/ins Knie ~:** run *or* bang into sth. and hurt one's head/knee; **b)** *(ugs.: stoßen)* **jmdm. etw. in das Bein/die Rippen ~:** run sth. into sb.'s leg/ribs

Rẹnnen das; ~s, ~ running; *(Pferde~, Auto~)* racing; *(einzelner Wettbewerb)* race; **zum ~ gehen** *(Pferde~)* go to the races; *(Auto~)* go to the racing; **gut im ~ liegen** be well placed; *(fig.)* be one of the front runners; **das ~ ist gelaufen** the race is over *or* has been run; *(fig.)* it's all over; **ein totes ~:** *(Sport)* a dead heat; **das ~ machen** *(ugs.)* win; **das ~ aufgeben** give up

Rẹnner der; ~s, ~ a) *(ugs.: Verkaufserfolg)* big seller; **b)** *(Pferd)* racer

Rennerei die; ~, ~en *(ugs.)* running around; **du glaubst nicht, was das für eine ~ war** you wouldn't believe how much running *or* chasing around it involved; **die ~ mit den Weihnachtsgeschenken** running around getting the Christmas presents; **das Schlimmste ist die ewige ~ zum Klo** the worst thing is having to run to the loo *(Brit. coll.) or (Amer. coll.)* john all the time

Rẹnn-: ~fahrer der racing driver; *(Radsport)* racing cyclist; *(Motorradsport)* racing motor-cyclist; **~jacht die** racing yacht; **~leitung die a)** *o. Pl. (das Leiten)* race organization; **b)** *(Personen)* race organizers *pl.*; **~pferd das** racehorse; **~platz der** *s.* **~bahn; ~rad das** racing cycle; **~sport der** racing *no art.*; **~stall der a)** racing stable; *(die Pferde allein)* string; **b)** *(Mannschaft)* team; **~strecke die** *(~bahn)* race-track; *(Distanz)* race distance; **~wagen der** racing car

Renommee [renɔ'me:] **das; ~s, ~s** *(geh.)* reputation

renommieren [renɔ'mi:rən] *itr. V.* show off; **mit etw. ~:** brag about sth.; **mit seinem Titel/Wissen ~:** flaunt one's title/show off *or* flaunt one's knowledge

Renommier-: ~stück das: das ~stück des Museums the museum's showpiece [exhibit]; **ihr ~stück, das dreireihige Perlen hat** her finest piece of jewelry with its three rows of pearls; **~sucht die** *(abwertend)* urge to show off

renommiert *Adj.* renowned (**wegen** for)

renovieren [reno'vi:rən] *tr. V.* renovate; redecorate ‹*room, flat*›

Renovierung die; ~, ~en renovation; *(eines Zimmers, einer Wohnung)* redecoration

rentabel [rɛn'ta:bl̩] **1.** *Adj.* profitable; **~ sein** be profitable; ‹*equipment, machinery*› pay its way. **2.** *adv.* profitably

Rentabilität [rɛntabili'tɛ:t] **die; ~** *(bes. Wirtsch.)* profitability; *(von Geräten usw.)* cost-effectiveness

Rentabilitäts·prüfung die *(Wirtsch.)* profitability analysis

Rente ['rɛntə] **die; ~, ~n a)** pension; **auf** *od.* **in ~ gehen** *(ugs.)* retire; **auf** *od.* **in ~ sein** *(ugs.)* be retired; **jmdn. auf ~ setzen** *(ugs.)* pension sb. off; **b)** *(Kapitalertrag)* annuity

rẹnten-, Rẹnten-: ~alter das pensionable age *no art.*; **im ~alter sein** *od.* **stehen** be of pensionable age; **~anpassung die** index-linking of pensions *(to the average national wage)*; **~an·spruch der** pension entitlement; **~berechtigt** *Adj.* entitled to a pension *postpos.*; **~empfänger der** pensioner; **~erhöhung die** pension increase; **~markt der** *(Börsenw.)* fixed securities market; **~papier das** *(Finanzw.)* fixed interest security; **~pflichtig** *Adj.* responsible for providing a pension *postpos.*; **~versicherung die a)** *(Versicherung)* pension scheme; **eine private ~versicherung abschließen** join a private pension scheme; **b)** *(Behörde) state pension authority*

¹Rẹn·tier das reindeer

²Rentier [rɛn'tje:] **der; ~s, ~s a)** *(veralt.: mit Vermögen)* man with a private income; **b)** *(selten: Rentner)* pensioner

rentieren [rɛn'ti:rən] *refl. V.* be profitable; ‹*equipment, machinery*› pay its way; ‹*effort, visit, etc.*› be worth while; **eine Geschirrspülmaschine rentiert sich für uns nicht** it's not worth our having *or* not worth our while to have a dishwasher

Rentner ['rɛntnɐ] **der; ~s, ~, Rẹntnerin die; ~, ~nen** pensioner

Reorganisation die reorganization

reorganisieren *tr. V.* reorganize

Reorganisierung die reorganization

reparabel [repa'ra:bl̩] *Adj.* repairable; **nicht mehr ~ sein** be no longer repairable; be beyond repair; **die Ehe ist nicht mehr ~** *(fig.)* the marriage has failed irretrievably

Reparationen [repara'tsi̯o:nən] *Pl. (Politik)* reparations; **~ leisten** *od.* **zahlen** make *or* pay reparations

Reparations·zahlung die reparation payment

Reparatur [repara'tu:ɐ̯] **die; ~, ~en** repair (**an** + *Dat.* to); **in ~ sein** be being repaired; **etw. in ~ geben** take sth. in to have it repaired

reparatur-, Reparatur-: ~anfällig *Adj.* prone to break down *postpos.*; **~arbeit die** repair work; **~en** repair work *sing.*; repairs; **~bedürftig** *Adj.* ‹*device, appliance, vehicle, etc.*› [which is] in need of repair; **~bedürftig sein** be in need of repair; need repairing; **~kosten** *Pl.* repair costs; **die ~kosten für das Auto** the cost of repairing the car; **~werkstatt die** repair [work]shop; *(für Autos)* garage

reparieren [repa'ri:rən] *tr. V.* repair; mend; *(bei komplexeren Geräten, größeren Schäden)* repair; **einen Fehler ~** *(fig.)* put right an error

repatriieren [repatri'i:rən] *tr. V. (Politik, Rechtsw.)* **a)** *(wieder einbürgern)* **jmdn. ~:** restore sb.'s citizenship; **b)** *(wieder heimführen)* repatriate

Repatriierung die; ~, ~en a) *(Wiedereinbürgerung)* **jmds. ~** the restoration of sb.'s citizenship; **b)** *(Heimführung)* repatriation

Repertoire [repɛr'to̯a:ɐ̯] **das; ~s, ~s** *(auch fig.)* repertoire

Repertoire·stück das stock play

Repertorium [repɛr'to:ri̯ʊm] **das; ~s, Repertorien** reference work

repetieren [repe'ti:rən] *tr. V.* **a)** *(einüben)* learn by repetition; **b)** *(veralt.: wiederholen)* repeat ‹*year*›

Repetier-: ~gewehr das repeating rifle; repeater; **~uhr die** repeating watch; repeater

Repetitor [repe'ti:tɔr] **der; ~s, ~en** [-ti'to:rən] **a)** *(für Studenten) private tutor who coaches (esp. law) students for examinations;* **b)** *(Musik)* répétiteur

Replik [re'pli:k] **die; ~, ~en a)** *(geh.: Erwiderung)* reply; rejoinder; **b)** *(Rechtsw.)* reply; replication; **c)** *(Kunst)* replica

Replikat [repli'ka:t] **das; ~[e]s, ~e** *(Kunst)* replica

Report [re'pɔrt] **der; ~[e]s, ~e a)** *(Bericht)* report; **b)** *(Finanzw.)* premium

Reportage [repɔr'ta:ʒə] **die; ~, ~n** report

Reporter [re'pɔrtɐ] **der; ~s, ~, Repọrterin die; ~, ~nen** reporter; *s. auch* **-in**

repräsentabel [reprɛzɛn'ta:bl̩] **1.** *Adj.* imposing. **2.** *adv.* imposingly

Repräsentant [reprɛzɛn'tant] **der; ~en, ~en** representative

Repräsentạnten·haus das House of Representatives

Repräsentạntin die; ~, ~nen representative; *s. auch* **-in**

Repräsentanz [reprɛzɛn'tants] **die; ~, ~en a)** *o. Pl. (Interessenvertretung)* representation; **b)** *(Wirtsch.)* branch

Repräsentation die; ~, ~en a) *(bes. Politik)* representation; **b)** *o. Pl. (das Typischsein)* representativeness; **c)** *(Vertretung in der Öffentlichkeit)* **die Rolle des Präsidenten besteht vorwiegend in der ~:** the role of the President is primarily that of official figure-head; **die wichtigste Pflicht einer Diplomatenfrau ist die ~:** the most important duty of a diplomat's wife is attending official and social functions; **d)** *(aufwendiger Lebensstil)* **etw. dient nur der ~:** sth. is for prestige purposes only

repräsentativ [reprɛzɛnta'ti:f] **1.** *Adj.* **a)** *(auch Politik)* representative; **für etw. ~ sein** be representative of sth.; **b)** *(ansehnlich)* imposing; *(mit hohem Prestigewert)* prestigious; **eine ~e Erscheinung** a man/woman of distinguished *or* imposing appearance. **2.** *adv.* **a)** *(bes. Politik)* representatively; **ein ~ strukturiertes politisches System** a political system with a representative structure; **b)** *(luxuriös)* imposingly

Repräsentativ·umfrage die *(Statistik)* representative survey

repräsentieren [reprɛzɛn'ti:rən] **1.** *tr. V.* represent. **2.** *itr. V. (Repräsentation betreiben)* attend official and social functions

Repressalie [reprɛ'sa:li̯ə] **die; ~, ~n** repressive measure; *(Vergeltungsmaßnahme)* reprisal; **~n anwenden** *od.* **ergreifen** resort to repressive measures/take reprisals

Repression [reprɛ'si̯o:n] **die; ~, ~en** repression

repressions·frei 1. *Adj.* free of repression *postpos.* **2.** *adv.* **~ erzogen werden** have an upbringing that is/was free of repression

repressiv [reprɛ'si:f] **1.** *Adj.* repressive. **2.** *adv.* repressively

Reprint [re'prɪnt] **der; ~s, ~s** *(Buchw.)* reprint

Reprise die a) *(Theater)* revival; *(Film)* rerun; **b)** *(einer Schallplatte)* re-issue; **c)** *(Musik)* reprise; **d)** *(Börsenw.)* recovery

reprivatisieren *tr. V. (Wirtsch., Politik)* reprivatize

Reprivatisierung die *(Wirtsch., Politik)* reprivatization

Repro ['re:pro] **die; ~, ~s** *(Druckw.)* repro

Reproduktion die reproduction

Reproduktions-: ~bedingung die; *meist Pl. (polit. Ökonomie)* condition of reproduction *usu. pl.*; **~kamera die** *(Druckw.)* process camera; **~kosten** *Pl. (Wirtsch.)* reproduction costs; **~prozeß der** *(polit. Ökonomie)* reproduction process; **~verfahren das** *(Druckw.)* reproduction process

reproduzieren *tr. V. (auch Druckw., polit. Ökonomie)* reproduce

Repro-: ~graphie [~gra'fi:] **die; ~, ~n** *(Druckw.)* **a)** *(Verfahren)* reprography *no art.*; **b)** *(Erzeugnis)* reproduction; **~technik** ['----] **die** reproduction technology *no art.*

Reps [rɛps] *Pl. (ugs.)* Republicans

Reptil [rɛp'ti:l] **das; ~s, ~ien** [rɛp'ti:li̯ən] reptile

Reptilien·fonds der *(Politik)* slush fund

Republik [repu'bli:k] **die; ~, ~en** republic

Republikaner [republi'ka:nɐ] **der; ~s, ~ a)** republican; **b)** *(Angehöriger der republikanischen Partei)* Republican

republikanisch 1. *Adj.* **a)** republican; **b)** *(eine ~e Partei betreffend)* Republican. **2.** *adv.* **a) ein ~ aufgebauter Staat** a state with a republican structure; **b) ~ wählen** vote Republican

Republik-: ~flucht die *(DDR veralt.)* illegal emigration; **~flüchtling der** *(DDR veralt.)* illegal emigrant

Repulsions·motor [repʊl'zi̯o:ns-] **der** *(Technik)* repulsion motor

repulsiv [repʊl'zi:f] *Adj. (Physik)* repulsive

Repunze [re'pʊntsə] **die; ~, ~n** hallmark

Reputation [reputa'tsi̯o:n] **die; ~, ~en** reputation; standing

reputierlich *Adj. (veralt.)* upright; decent
Requiem ['re:kviɛm] **das;** ~, ~s requiem
requirieren [rekvi'ri:rən] *tr. V. (veralt.)* requisition
Requisit [rekvi'zi:t] **das;** ~[e]s, ~en **a)** *(Theater)* prop *(coll.)*; property; **b)** *(fig.)* requisite
Requisiten·kammer die *(Theater)* prop store *or* room *(coll.)*; property store *or* room
Requisiteur [rekvizi'tø:ɐ̯] **der;** ~s, ~e *(Theater)* prop-man *(coll.)*; property man
Requisition die; ~, ~en *(veralt.)* requisition
resch [rɛʃ] *(bayr., österr.) Adj.* **a)** *(knusprig)* crusty ‹*rolls, bread*›; crisp ‹*fried potatoes, batter*›; **b)** *(ugs.: lebhaft)* vivacious
Reseda [re'ze:da] **die;** ~, ~s, **Resede die;** ~, ~n Reseda; *(Garten~)* mignonette
Reservat [rezɛr'va:t] **das;** ~[e]s, ~e **a)** *(Tier~)* reserve; **b)** *(für Volksstämme)* reservation
Reserve [re'zɛrvə] **die;** ~, ~n **a)** *(Vorrat)* reserve **(an** + *Dat.* **of)**; **etw. in ~ haben** have sth. in reserve; **etw. in ~ halten** keep *or* hold sth. in reserve; *s. auch* **eisern 1 d; still 1 f; b)** *(Milit.)* reserves *pl.*; **Offizier der ~:** reserve officer; **c)** *(Sport)* reserves *pl.*; **d)** *o. Pl. (Zurückhaltung)* reserve; **jmdn. aus der ~ [heraus]locken** *(ugs.)* bring sb. out of his/her shell; **e)** *(Bedenken)* reservation
Reserve-: ~bank die *Pl.* **~bänke** *(Sport)* substitutes' bench; **~fonds der** *(Wirtsch.)* reserve [fund]; **~kanister der** spare [petrol *(Brit.) or (Amer.)* gasoline] can; **~mann der;** *Pl.* **~männer** *od.* **~leute** replacement; *(Sport)* substitute; reserve; **~offizier der** reserve officer; **~rad das** spare wheel; **~reifen der** spare tyre; **~spieler der** *(Sport)* substitute; reserve; **~tank der** reserve [fuel] tank; **~truppe die** *(Milit.)* reserve troops *pl.*; **~übung die** *(Milit.)* reservists' exercise
reservieren *tr. V.* reserve
reserviert 1. *Adj.* reserved. **2.** *adv.* in a reserved way
Reserviertheit die; ~: reserve
Reservierung die; ~, ~en reservation
Reservist der; ~en, ~en *(Milit.)* reservist; *(Sportjargon)* substitute; reserve
Reservisten·übung die *(Milit.)* reservists' exercise
Reservoir [rezɛr'vo̯a:ɐ̯] **das;** ~s, ~e *(auch fig.)* reservoir **(an** + *Dat.* **of)**
Residenz [rezi'dɛnts] **die;** ~, ~en **a)** *(Wohnsitz)* residence; **b)** *(Hauptstadt)* [royal] capital
Residenz-: ~pflicht die a) *(von Beamten)* obligation to live within a reasonable distance of one's place of work; **b)** *(ev. u. kath. Kirche)* obligation [on a clergyman] to live in the accommodation provided with the post; **~stadt die** *s.* **Residenz b**
residieren [rezi'di:rən] *itr. V.* reside
Resignation [rezɪgna'tsi̯o:n] **die;** ~, ~en resignation; **in ~ versinken** become resigned
resignativ [rezɪgna'ti:f] *Adj.* ‹*mood, atmosphere*› of resignation
resignieren [rezɪ'gni:rən] *itr. V.* give up
resigniert 1. *Adj.* resigned. **2.** *adv.* resignedly
Resistance [rezis'tã:s] **die;** ~ *(hist.)* Resistance
resistent [rezɪs'tɛnt] *Adj. (Biol., Med.)* resistant **(gegen** to**)**
Resistenz [rezɪs'tɛnts] **die;** ~, ~en *(auch Biol., Med.)* resistance **(gegen** to**)**
resolut [rezo'lu:t] **1.** *Adj.* resolute. **2.** *adv.* resolutely
Resolutheit die; ~: resoluteness
Resolution [rezolu'tsi̯o:n] **die;** ~, ~en resolution
Resonanz [rezo'nants] **die;** ~, ~en **a)** *(Physik, Musik)* resonance; **b)** *(Reaktion)* response **(auf** + *Akk.* to**)**; **~/keine ~ finden, auf ~/auf keine ~ stoßen** meet with a/no response
Resonanz-: ~boden der *(Musik)* sounding-board; sound-board; **~körper der** *(Musik)* sound-box
Resopal Ⓦⓩ [rezo'pa:l] **das;** ~s ≈ melamine
resorbieren [rezɔr'bi:rən] *tr. V. (Biol., Med.)* absorb
Resorption [rezɔrp'tsi̯o:n] **die;** ~, ~en *(Biol., Med.)* absorption
resozialisierbar *Adj. (bes. Rechtsspr.)* able to be reintegrated into society *postpos.*
resozialisieren *tr. V. (bes. Rechtsspr.)* reintegrate into society
Resozialisierung die; ~, ~en *(bes. Rechtsspr.)* reintegration into society
Respekt [re'spɛkt] **der;** ~[e]s **a)** *(Achtung)* respect; **~ vor jmdm./etw. haben** have respect for sb./sth.; **jmdm. ~ einflößen** *od.* **abnötigen** command sb.'s respect; **bei allem ~:** with all due respect **(vor** + *Dat.* to**)**; **allen ~!, ~, ~!** good for you!; well done!; **b)** *(Furcht)* **jmdm. ~ einflößen** intimidate sb.; **vor jmdm./etw. [größten] ~ haben** be [much] in awe of sb./sth.; **sich** *(Dat.)* **den nötigen ~ verschaffen** command proper respect; **c)** *(Schrift- u. Buchw., Kunstwiss.)* margin
respektabel [respɛk'ta:bl̩] **1.** *Adj.* respectable. **2.** *adv.* respectably
respekt·einflößend *Adj.* impressive; fearsome ‹*claws, teeth*›
respektieren *tr. V.* **a)** respect; **b)** *(Finanzw.)* honour ‹*bill of exchange etc.*›
respektierlich *Adj. (veralt.)* respectable
respektive [rɛspɛk'ti:və] *Konj. (geh.)* **a)** *(oder)* or; **b)** *(oder vielmehr)* or rather; *(oder genauer gesagt)* or more precisely; **c)** *(und im anderen Fall)* **grün ~ blau** green and blue respectively
respekt·los 1. *Adj.* disrespectful. **2.** *adv.* disrespectfully
Respektlosigkeit die; ~, ~en **a)** *o. Pl. (Haltung)* disrespectfulness; lack of respect; **b)** *(Äußerung)* disrespectful remark; *(Handlung)* impertinence
Respekts·person die person who commands/commanded respect
respekt·voll 1. *Adj.* respectful. **2.** *adv.* respectfully
Respiration [respira'tsi̯o:n] **die;** ~ *(Med.)* respiration
Respirator [rɛspi'ra:tɔr] **der;** ~s, ~en [-ra'to:rən] *(Med.)* respirator
respirieren [rɛspi'ri:rən] *itr. V. (Med.)* respire
Ressentiment [rɛsãti'mã:] **das;** ~s, ~s **a)** *(geh.: Abneigung)* antipathy **(gegen** towards**)**; **b)** *(Psych.)* resentment
Ressort [rɛ'so:ɐ̯] **das;** ~s, ~s area of responsibility; *(Abteilung)* department; **in jmds. ~ fallen** come within sb.'s area of responsibility; **das Abwaschen ist mein ~** *(scherzh.)* the washing-up is my department
Ressort-: ~chef der, ~leiter, der head of department; **~minister der** departmental minister
Ressource [rɛ'sʊrsə] **die;** ~, ~n **a)** resource; **b)** *Pl. (Ersparnisse)* resources
Rest [rɛst] **der;** ~[e]s, ~e **a)** rest; *(~betrag)* rest; balance; **~e** *(historische ~e, Ruinen, Leiche)* remains; *(einer Kultur)* relics; **jmdm./einer Sache den ~ geben** *(ugs.)* finish sb./sth. off; **das ist der ~ von meinem Vermögen** this is all that's left of my fortune; **ein ~ von Farbe/Leim/Käse/Wein ist noch da** there's still a little bit of paint/glue/cheese/a little bit *or* a drop of wine left; **bis auf einen ~ ist es alles verbraucht** it's all been used up apart from a little bit; **der letzte ~** the last bit; **ein trauriger ~ von Käse/Kuchen** a few pathetic scraps *pl.* of cheese/cake; **morgen gibt es ~e** tomorrow we're having left-overs; **~ machen** *(nordd.)* finish up what's left; **machen Sie doch ~ mit dem Fleisch** *(nordd.)* do finish up the meat; **das ist der ~ vom Schützenfest** *(ugs.)* that's all there is left; **hast du den letzten ~ von Verstand verloren?** have you lost all the sense you had left?; **der ~ ist Schweigen** *(man schweigt besser darüber)* the less said, the better; *(das Weitere ist unbekannt)* the rest is a mystery; **b)** *(Endstück)* remnant; **c)** *(Math.)* remainder; **20 durch 6 ist 3, ~ 2** 20 divided by 6 is 3 with *or* and 2 left over
Rest-: ~alkohol der residual alcohol; **~auf·lage die** remaindered stock
Restaurant [rɛsto'rã:] **das;** ~s, ~s restaurant
Restauration [restaura'tsi̯o:n] **die;** ~, ~en **a)** *(auch Politik)* restoration; **b)** *(hist.)* Restoration; **c)** *(österr., sonst veralt.)* restaurant
Restaurations-: ~arbeit die restoration work; **~arbeiten** restoration work *sing.*; **~betrieb der** restaurant; **~zeit die** restoration; *(hist.)* Restoration
restaurativ [restaura'ti:f] **1.** *Adj.* **a)** *(Geschichte, Politik)* ‹*efforts*› to restore the old order; ‹*phase, time*› in which the old order is/was restored; ‹*policies*› aimed at restoring the old order; **b)** *(das Restaurieren betreffend)* restorative; **eine ~e Meisterleistung** a masterpiece of restoration. **2.** *adv. (das Restaurieren betreffend)* **etw. ~ aufarbeiten** restore sth.; **etw. ~ retten** save sth. by restoration
Restaurator [restau'ra:tɔr] **der;** ~s, ~en [-ra'to:rən], **Restauratorin die;** ~, ~nen restorer
restaurieren [restau'ri:rən] **1.** *tr. V.* restore. **2.** *refl. V. (ugs. scherzh.: sein Äußeres herrichten)* make oneself presentable
Restaurierung die; ~, ~en restoration
Rest-: ~bestand der remaining stock; *(an Büchern)* remaindered stock; **~betrag der** balance; amount *or* sum remaining
Reste-: ~essen das *(fam.)* left-overs *pl.*; **~verkauf der** remnants sale; **~verwertung die** making use of left-overs
restituieren [restitu'i:rən] *tr. V. (bes. Rechtsw.)* **a)** *(aufheben)* set aside ‹*judgement, decision*›; **b)** *(erstatten)* **etw. ~:** make restitution for sth.
Restitution [restitu'tsi̯o:n] **die;** ~, ~en **a)** *(bes. Rechtsw.: Wiederherstellung)* restitution; **b)** *(Rechtsw.: Aufhebung)* setting aside; **c)** *(Biol.)* regeneration
Restitutions·klage die *(Rechtsw.)* action for a retrial
restlich *Adj.; nicht präd.* remaining; **die ~en** the rest
rest·los 1. *Adj.; nicht präd.* complete; total. **2.** *adv.* completely; totally; **~ verzweifelt sein** be in complete *or* total despair; **alles ~ aufessen** eat every last morsel; **~ ausverkauft sein** be completely sold out
Rest·posten der *(Kaufmannsspr.)* remaining stock *no indef. art.*
Restriktion [restrɪk'tsi̯o:n] **die;** ~, ~en *(auch Sprachw.)* restriction
restriktiv [restrɪk'ti:f] **1.** *Adj. (auch Sprachw.)* restrictive. **2.** *adv.* restrictively; **sich ~ auf etw.** *(Akk.)* **auswirken** have a restrictive effect on sth.
restringieren [restrɪŋ'gi:rən] *tr. V. (Sprachw.)* **restringierter Kode** restricted code
Rest-: ~strafe die remainder of a/the/one's sentence; **~summe die** amount remaining; *(von Geld)* balance; **~zahlung die** payment of the balance; **eine ~zahlung von 500 Mark leisten** pay off the balance of 500 marks
Resultante [rezʊl'tantə] **die;** ~, ~n *(Physik)* resultant
Resultat [rezʊl'ta:t] **das;** ~[e]s, ~e result; **zum ~ kommen, daß ...:** come to the conclusion that ...
resultieren [rezʊl'ti:rən] *itr. V.* result **(aus** from**)**; **daraus resultiert, daß ...:** the result *or* upshot of this is that ...

Resultierende die; ~n, ~n *(Physik)* resultant
Resümee [rezy'me:] **das; ~s, ~s** résumé
resümieren [rezy'mi:rən] **1.** *tr. V.* **etw. ~:** summarize sth.; give a résumé of sth. **2.** *itr. V.* sum up
retardieren [retar'di:rən] *tr. V.* retard; **~des Moment** *(Literaturw.)* retardation
retirieren [reti'ri:rən] *itr. V. (Milit.)* retreat; *(geh.: sich zurückziehen)* retire
Retorte [re'tɔrtə] **die; ~, ~n** *(Chemie)* retort; **aus der ~** *(ugs., oft abwertend)* artificial; **ein Baby aus der ~:** a test-tube baby
Retorten·baby das *(ugs.)* test-tube baby
retour [re'tu:ɐ̯] *Adv. (bes. südd., österr., schweiz.)* back; **~ laufen** walk back; **Sie bekommen 1,50 DM ~:** you get 1.50 marks back
Retour-: ~fahr·karte die *(österr.)* return ticket; **~gang der** *(österr.)* reverse gear; **~kutsche die** *(ugs.)* tit-for-tat response
retournieren [retʊr'ni:rən] **1.** *tr. V.* return. **2.** *itr. V. (Sport, bes. Tennis)* make a return; return the ball
retrograd [retro'gra:t] *Adj. (Med.)* **~e Amnesie** retroactive *or* retrograde amnesia
Retrospektive [retrospɛk'ti:və] **die; ~, ~n a)** *(Rückblick)* retrospective view; **in der ~** in retrospect; **b)** *(Ausstellung)* retrospective
retten ['rɛtn̩] **1.** *tr. V.* save; *(vor Gefahr)* save; rescue; *(befreien)* rescue; **jmdm. das Leben ~:** save sb.'s life; **jmdn. aus der Gefahr ~:** save sb. from danger; **jmdn. vor jmdm./etw. ~:** save sb. from sb./sth.; **jmdm. kommt die ~de Idee** sb. sees the perfect answer; **das ~de Ufer erreichen** reach the safety of the shore; **versuchen zu ~, was zu ~ ist** try to save what can be saved; **ist er noch zu ~?** *(ugs. fig.)* has he gone [completely] round the bend? *(coll.)*; **das alte Haus/der Patient ist nicht mehr zu ~:** the old house is past saving/the patient is beyond help; **nicht mehr zu ~ sein** *(ugs.)* be a hopeless case; **seine Habe über den Krieg ~:** manage to keep one's possessions through the war. **2.** *refl. V. (fliehen)* escape **(aus** from); **sich vor etw.** *(Dat.)* **~:** escape [from] sth.; **sich ans Ufer ~:** manage to reach the bank; **der Pilot rettete sich mit dem Schleudersitz** the pilot saved himself by using the ejector-seat; **rette sich, wer kann!** [it's] every man for himself!; **sich vor jmdm./etw. nicht [mehr]** *od.* **kaum [noch] ~ können** be besieged by sb./be swamped with sth.; **sich ins Ziel ~** *(Sport)* just hold on to cross the line first. **3.** *itr. V. (Ballspiele)* save
Retter der; ~s, ~, Retterin die; ~, ~nen rescuer; *(eines Landes, einer Bewegung o. ä.)* saviour; **der/ein ~ in der Not** the/a helper in my/our *etc.* hour of need; **Christ der ~:** Christ the Saviour
Rettich ['rɛtɪç] **der; ~s, ~e** radish
Rettung die a) rescue; *(Rel., eines Landes usw.)* salvation; *(vor Zerstörung)* saving; **jmdm. ~ bringen** rescue *or* save sb.; **die ~ kam in der letzten Minute** rescue came at the last moment *or* the eleventh hour; **er verdankt dem Medikament seine ~:** he owes his life to the medicine; **er dachte nur an seine eigene ~:** he thought only of saving himself *or* saving his own skin; **auf ~ warten/hoffen** wait for rescue/hope to be rescued; **für jmdn/etw. gibt es keine ~:** sb. is beyond help/sth. is past saving; **es war jmds. ~, daß ...:** sb. was saved by the fact that ...; **das war meine letzte ~:** that was my last hope [of salvation]; *(es hat mich schließlich gerettet)* that was my salvation; **b)** *(österr.: ~sdienst)* ambulance service; **c)** *(österr.: ~swagen)* ambulance
rettungs-, Rettungs-: ~aktion die rescue operation; **~anker der** sheet-anchor; **~boje die** *(Seew.)* lifebuoy; **~boot das** lifeboat; **~dienst der** ambulance service; *(Bergwacht, Seerettungsdienst, bei Katastrophen)* rescue service; **~flugzeug das** rescue aircraft *or* plane; **~gürtel der** lifebelt; **~hubschrauber der** rescue helicopter; **~insel die** *(Seew.)* [inflatable] life-raft; **~kommando das** rescue team; **~los 1.** *Adj.* hopeless; inevitable ‹*disaster*›; **2.** *adv.* hopelessly; **~mannschaft die** rescue team; **~medaille die** life-saving medal; **~ring der a)** lifebelt; **b)** *(ugs.: Fettwulst)* spare tyre *(coll.)*; **~schuß der** *in* **finaler ~schuß** fatal shot fired to save lives; **~schwimmen das** life-saving *no art.*; **~schwimmer der, ~schwimmerin die** life-saver; *(am Strand, im Schwimmbad)* life-guard; **~trupp der** rescue team; **~versuch der** rescue attempt; **~wagen der** ambulance; *(der Bergwacht, bei Katastrophen)* rescue vehicle; **~weste die** *(Seew.)* life-jacket
Retusche [re'tʊʃə] **die; ~, ~n** *(bes. Fot., Druckw.)* retouching; *(Stelle)* retouch; **eine ~/~n vornehmen** retouch
Retuscheur [retʊ'ʃø:ɐ̯] **der; ~s, ~e** *(bes. Fot., Druckw.)* retoucher
retuschieren *tr. V. (bes. Fot., Druckw.)* retouch; *(fig.)* gloss over ‹*statement, remark*›
Reue ['rɔyə] **die; ~:** remorse **(über +** *Akk.* for); *(Rel.)* repentance; *s. auch* **tätig**
Reue·gefühl das *(geh.)* feeling of remorse; **~ überkam sie** she was overcome by [feelings of] remorse
reuen *tr. V. (meist geh.)* **etw. reut jmdn.** sb. regrets sth.; **das Geld reut mich** I regret having spent the money
reue·voll *(geh.) s.* **reumütig**
Reu·geld das *(Rechtsw., Wirtsch., Pferderennen)* forfeit
reuig *(geh.) s.* **reumütig**
reu·mütig 1. *Adj.; nicht präd.* remorseful; repentant, penitent ‹*sinner*›. **2.** *adv.* remorsefully; **~ gestand er seine Sünden** repentantly *or* penitently he confessed his sins; **du wirst ~ zurückkehren** you'll be back, saying you're sorry
Reuse [:rɔyzə] **die; ~, ~n** fish-trap
reüssieren [relʏ'si:rən] *itr. V.* be successful; succeed; achieve success
Revalvation [revalva'tsio:n] **die; ~, ~en** *(Wirtsch.)* revaluation
Revanche [re'vã:ʃ(ə)] **die; ~, ~n** revenge; *(Sport: Rückkampf, ~spiel)* return match/fight/game; **jmdm. ~ geben** give sb. his/her revenge; **~ nehmen** *od.* **üben** get one's revenge; **~ fordern** *(Sport, Spiel)* demand a return match/fight/game
Revanche-: ~kampf der *(Sport)* return fight; **~partie die** *(bes. Schach)* return match; **~politik die** revanchist policy
revanchieren *refl. V.* **a)** get one's revenge, *(coll.)* get one's own back **(bei** on); **b)** *(ugs.: sich erkenntlich zeigen)* **sich bei jmdm. für eine Einladung/seine Gastfreundschaft ~:** return sb.'s invitation/repay sb.'s hospitality; **ich werde mich für eure Hilfe beim Umzug ~:** I'll return your favour of helping me move
Revanchismus der; ~ *(Politik)* revanchism *usu. no art.*
Revanchist der; ~en, ~en *(Politik)* revanchist
revanchistisch *Adj. (Politik)* revanchist
Revenue [rəvə'ny:] **die; ~, ~n** *(Wirtsch.)* revenue
Reverenz [reve'rɛnts] **die; ~, ~en a)** *(Hochachtung)* esteem, respect **(vor +** *Dat.* for); **jmdm. seine ~ erweisen** pay sb. one's respects; **b)** *(Verbeugung)* bow; **seine ~ vor jmdm. machen** bow to sb.
[1]Revers [rə've:ɐ̯] **das** *od. (österr.)* **der; ~** [rə'vɛ:ɐ̯(s)], **~** [rə'vɛ:ɐ̯s] lapel
[2]Revers [re'vɛrs] **der; ~es, ~e** *(Münzk.)* reverse
[3]Revers [re'vɛrs] **der; ~es, ~e** *(Rechtsw.)* [written] undertaking
reversibel [revɛr'zi:bl] *Adj. (Technik, Med.)* reversible
reversieren *itr. V. (österr.)* reverse
Reversion [revɛr'zio:n] **die; ~, ~en** *(Biol., Psych.)* reversion
revidieren [revi'di:rən] *tr. V.* **a)** *(abändern)* revise; amend ‹*law, contract*›; **b)** *(kontrollieren)* check; *(Buchf.)* audit ‹*accounts, books*›
Revier [re'vi:ɐ̯] **das; ~s, ~e a)** *(Aufgabenbereich)* province; **der Weinkeller ist mein ~** *(scherzh.)* the wine cellar is my province *or* preserve; **b)** *(Zool.)* territory; **c)** *(Polizei~) (Dienststelle)* [police] station; *(Bereich)* district; *(des einzelnen Polizisten)* beat; **d)** *(Forst~)* district; **e)** *(Jagd~)* preserve; shoot; **f)** *(Bergbau)* coalfield; **das ~:** the Ruhr/Saar coalfields *pl.*; **g)** *(Milit. veralt.: Unterkunft)* barracks *sing. or pl.*; **h)** *(Milit. veralt.: Kranken~)* sick-bay
Revier-: ~förster der forest warden; forester; **~stube die** *(Milit. veralt.)* sick-bay
Revirement [revirə'mã:] **das; ~s, ~s** reshuffle
Revision [revi'zio:n] **die; ~, ~en a)** *(das Ändern)* revision; *(eines Gesetzes, Vertrags)* amendment; **b)** *(Rechtsw.)* appeal [on a point/points of law]; **~ einlegen, in die ~ gehen** lodge an appeal [on a point/points of law]; **c)** *(Kontrolle)* inspection; *(Buchf.)* audit; **d)** *(Druckw.)* revision of the page proofs; **~ lesen** read the page proofs
Revisionismus der; ~ *(Politik)* revisionism *usu. no art.*
Revisionist der; ~en, ~en *(Politik)* revisionist
revisionistisch *Adj. (Politik)* revisionist
Revisions-: ~bogen der *(Druckw.)* final page proof; **~gericht das** *(Rechtsw.)* court of appeal [dealing with points of law]; **~verfahren das** *(Rechtsw.)* appeal proceedings *pl.* [on a point/points of law]; **~verhandlung die** *(Rechtsw.)* hearing of an/the appeal [on a point/points of law]
Revisor [re'vi:zɔr] **der; ~s, ~en** [revi'zo:rən] **a)** *(Buchf.)* auditor; **b)** *(Druckw.)* reader of the page proofs
Revolte [re'vɔltə] **die; ~, ~n** revolt
revoltieren *itr. V.* revolt, rebel **(gegen** against); *(fig.)* ‹*stomach*› rebel
Revolution [revolu'tsio:n] **die; ~, ~en a)** *(auch fig.)* revolution; **b)** *(Skat)* revolution
revolutionär [revolutsio'nɛ:ɐ̯] **1.** *Adj.* revolutionary. **2.** *adv.* in a revolutionary way
Revolutionär der; ~s, ~e, Revolutionärin die; ~, ~nen revolutionary
revolutionieren *tr. V.* revolutionize; **eine ~de Entdeckung** a revolutionary discovery
Revolutions-: ~rat der *(Politik)* revolutionary council; **~regierung die** revolutionary government; **~tribunal das** *(hist.)* Revolutionary Tribunal
Revoluzzer [revo'lʊtsɐ] **der; ~s, ~** *(abwertend)* phoney revolutionary
Revoluzzertum das; ~s *(abwertend)* phoney revolutionary fervour
Revolver [re'vɔlvɐ] **der; ~s, ~ a)** revolver; **b)** *(Technik)* turret
Revolver-: ~blatt das *(abwertend)* scandal rag; **~held der** *(abwertend)* gun-slinger; **~kopf der** *(Technik)* turret; **~lauf der** revolver barrel; **~presse die** *(abwertend)* yellow press; scandal rags *pl.*; **~schnauze die** *(ugs. abwertend)* **a)** *(Mundwerk)* big trap *(sl.) or* mouth; **b)** *(Mensch)* loud-mouth; **~tasche die** holster
Revue [re'vʏ] **die; ~, ~n a)** *(Theater)* revue; **b)** *(Truppe)* revue company; **c)** *(Zeitschrift)* review; **d)** *(Milit.)* review; **etw. ~ passieren lassen** *(fig.)* review sth.; **er ließ seine Freunde ~ passieren** *(fig.)* he brought back to mind *or* he recalled his friends
Revue·theater das revue theatre
Rezensent [retsɛn'zɛnt] **der; ~en, ~en, Rezensentin die; ~, ~nen** reviewer

rezensieren [retsɛn'zi:rən] **1.** *tr. V.* review. **2.** *itr. V.* write reviews
Rezension [retsɛn'zio:n] **die; ~, ~en** review
Rezensions·exemplar das review copy
rezent [re'tsɛnt] *Adj. (Geol.)* Recent
Rezept [re'tsɛpt] **das; ~[e]s, ~e a)** *(Med.)* prescription; *(fig.)* remedy **(gegen** for); **nur auf ~:** only on prescription; **b)** *(Anleitung)* recipe; *(fig.)* formula
Rezept·block der; *Pl.* **-blocks** prescription pad
rezept·frei 1. *Adj.* **~e Mittel** medicines obtainable without a prescription. **2.** *adv.* **etw. ~ verkaufen/erhalten** sell/obtain sth. without a prescription *or* over the counter
rezeptieren *tr. (auch itr.) V.* prescribe
Rezeption [retsɛp'tsio:n] **die; ~, ~en a)** *(im Hotel)* reception *no art.;* **b)** *(Aufnahme)* reception
rezeptiv [retsɛp'ti:f] *Adj.* receptive **(für** to)
rezept·pflichtig *Adj.* ⟨*medicine, drug, etc.*⟩ obtainable only on prescription; **nicht ~ sein** be obtainable without a prescription *or* over the counter
Rezeptur [retsɛp'tu:ɐ̯] **die; ~, ~en a)** *(das Rezeptieren)* prescription; **b)** *(für Nahrungsmittel)* recipe *(Gen.* for); *(für Arzneimittel, Farbe, Baustoff)* formula
Rezession [retsɛ'sio:n] **die; ~, ~en** *(Wirtsch.)* recession
rezessiv [retsɛ'si:f] *(Biol.)* **1.** *Adj.* recessive. **2.** *adv.* recessively
rezipieren [retsi'pi:rən] *tr. V.* receive; *(übernehmen)* adapt
reziprok [retsi'pro:k] *(bes. Math., Sprachw.) Adj.* reciprocal
Rezitation [retsita'tsio:n] **die; ~, ~en** recitation
Rezitations·abend der [evening] recitation; *(mit Rezitation von Gedichten)* [evening] poetry-reading; poetry evening
Rezitativ [retsita'ti:f] **das; ~s, ~e** *(Musik)* recitative
rezitieren [retsi'ti:rən] *tr. (auch itr.) V.* recite; **er rezitierte aus seinem Roman** he gave a reading *or* he read from his novel; **er rezitiert gern** he enjoys giving recitations
R-Gespräch ['ɛr-] **das** *(Fernspr.)* reverse-charge call *(Brit.);* collect call *(Amer.)*
RGW [ɛrge:we:] **der; ~** *Abk.* **Rat für Gegenseitige Wirtschaftshilfe** COMECON
rh [ɛr'ha:] *Abk. (Med.)* **Rhesusfaktor negativ** Rh negative
Rh [ɛr'ha:] *Abk. (Med.)* **Rhesusfaktor positiv** Rh positive
¹Rhabarber [ra'barbɐ] **der; ~s** rhubarb
²Rhabarber das; ~s *(ugs.)* **sie murmelten „~, ~":** they mumbled 'rhubarb, rhubarb' *(coll.)*
Rhapsode [ra'pso:də] **der; ~n, ~n** *(Musik, Literaturw.)* rhapsodist; rhapsode; *(fig.)* rhapsodic composer
Rhapsodie [rapso'di:] **die; ~, ~n** *(Musik, Literaturw.)* rhapsody
rhapsodisch *Adj.* rhapsodic
Rhein [rain] **der; ~[e]s** Rhine
Rhein·fall der Rhine Falls
rheinisch *Adj.* Rhenish; **eine ~e Spezialität** a speciality of the Rhine region
Rhein·land das; ~[e]s Rhineland
Rhein·länder der; ~s, ~ *(auch Tanz)* Rhinelander
Rheinland-Pfalz *o. Art.* the Rhineland-Palatinate
rheinland-pfälzisch *Adj.* ⟨*capital, citizen, etc.*⟩ of the Rhineland-Palatinate
Rhein·wein der Rhine wine; Rhenish [wine]; *(Weißwein auch)* hock
Rhesus- ['re:zʊs]: **~affe der** rhesus monkey; **~faktor der;** *o. Pl. (Med.)* rhesus factor; Rh factor
Rhetorik [re'to:rɪk] **die; ~, ~en** rhetoric
Rhetoriker der; ~s, ~ rhetorician
rhetorisch 1. *Adj.* rhetorical; **eine ~e Frage** a rhetorical question. **2.** *adv.* rhetorically
Rheuma ['rɔyma] **das; ~s** *(ugs.)* rheumatism; rheumatics *pl. (coll.)*
Rheuma-: ~decke die thermal blanket; **~mittel das** *(ugs.)* rheumatism pills *pl.*/cream *etc.;* **~wäsche die;** *o. Pl.* thermal underwear
Rheumatiker [rɔy'ma:tikɐ] **der; ~s, ~** *(Med.)* rheumatic; rheumatism sufferer
rheumatisch *(Med.)* **1.** *Adj.* rheumatic. **2.** *adv.* rheumatically
Rheumatismus [rɔyma'tɪsmʊs] **der; ~, Rheumatismen** *(Med.)* rheumatism
Rhinozeros [ri'no:tserɔs] **das; ~[ses], ~se a)** *(Nashorn)* rhinoceros; rhino *(coll.);* **b)** *(ugs.: Trottel)* nitwit *(coll.);* fat-head *(coll.)*
Rhizom [ri'tso:m] **das; ~s, ~e** *(Bot.)* rhizome
Rhododendron [rodo'dɛndrɔn] **der** *od.* **das; ~s, Rhododendren** rhododendron
Rhodos ['ro:dɔs] **(das); ~** Rhodes
Rhomben *s.* **Rhombus**
rhombisch *Adj. (bes. Math.)* rhombic
Rhomboid [rɔmbo'i:t] **das; ~[e]s, ~e** *(Math.)* rhomboid
Rhombus ['rɔmbʊs] **der; ~, Rhomben** ['rɔmbn̩] rhombus
Rhythmen *s.* **Rhythmus**
Rhythmik ['rʏtmɪk] **die; ~ a)** *(auch Musik)* rhythm; **b)** *(Päd.)* rhythmics *sing., no art.*
Rhythmiker der; ~s, ~ rhythmist
rhythmisch 1. *Adj.* rhythmical; rhythmic; **~e Instrumente** rhythm instruments; **~e Gymnastik** rhythmic gymnastics *sing.* **2.** *adv.* rhythmically
Rhythmus ['rʏtmʊs] **der; ~, Rhythmen** ['rʏtmən] *(auch fig.)* rhythm; **aus dem ~ kommen** lose the rhythm
Rhythmus-: ~gitarre die rhythm guitar; **~gruppe die** rhythm section; **~instrument das** rhythm instrument
RIAS, Rias ['ri:as] **der; ~** *Abk.* **Rundfunk im amerikanischen Sektor [Berlin]** RIAS; Radio in the American Sector [of Berlin]
ribbeln ['rɪbl̩n] *tr. V. (landsch.)* rub
Ribisel ['ri:bi:zl̩] **die; ~, ~[n]** *(österr.) s.* **Johannisbeere**
Richt-: ~antenne die directional aerial *or (Amer.)* antenna; **~baum der** *tree used for topping-out ceremony;* **~beil das** *(hist.)* executioner's axe; **~blei das** *(Bauw.)* plumb[-bob]; **~block der** [execution] block
richten ['rɪçtn̩] **1.** *tr. V.* **a)** *(lenken)* direct ⟨*gaze*⟩ **(auf +** *Akk.* at, towards); turn ⟨*eyes, gaze*⟩ **(auf +** *Akk.* towards); point ⟨*torch, telescope, gun*⟩ **(auf +** *Akk.* at); aim, train ⟨*gun, missile, telescope, searchlight*⟩ **(auf +** *Akk.* on); *(fig.)* direct ⟨*activity, attention*⟩ **(auf +** *Akk.* towards); **etw. nach jmdm./etw. ~:** arrange sth. to suit sb./sth.; **die Augen gen Himmel ~:** look heavenwards; **die Waffe gegen sich selbst ~:** turn the weapon on oneself; **das Schiff/den Kurs eines Schiffes nach Norden ~:** steer the ship on/steer a northerly course; **b)** *(zukommen lassen)* address ⟨*letter, remarks, words*⟩ **(an +** *Akk.* to); direct, level ⟨*criticism*⟩ **(an +** *Akk.* at); send ⟨*letter of thanks, message of greeting*⟩ **(an +** *Akk.* to); **eine Bitte/Frage an jmdn. ~:** put a request/question to sb.; **ein Gesuch an jmdn. ~:** petition sb.; **eine Mahnung an jmdn. ~:** give sb. a warning; **das Wort an jmdn. ~** *(geh.)* address sb.; **c)** *(gerade~)* straighten; set ⟨*fracture*⟩; **d)** *(einstellen)* aim ⟨*cannon, missile*⟩; direct ⟨*aerial*⟩; **e)** *(aburteilen)* judge; *(verurteilen)* condemn; **f)** *(bes. südd., österr., schweiz.: instand setzen, in Ordnung bringen)* fix; repair ⟨*shoes*⟩; *(einrichten)* arrange; fix; **[sich** *(Dat.)***] die Haare/den Schlips ~:** do one's hair/adjust *or* straighten one's tie; **es wird sich schon alles ~:** everything will sort itself out; **das läßt sich schon ~:** it can be arranged; **g)** *(bes. südd., österr., schweiz.: vorbereiten)* get ready; prepare; make ⟨*bed, nest*⟩; get ⟨*food, meal*⟩; **den Tisch/das Zimmer ~:** lay *or* set the table/get the room ready; **[jmdm.] ein Bad ~:** run a bath [for sb.]; **h)** *(geh. veralt.: hin~)* execute; **sich selbst ~:** die by one's own hand; *s. auch* **zugrunde a. 2.** *refl. V.* **a)** *(sich hinwenden)* **sich auf jmdn./etw. ~** *(auch fig.)* be directed towards sb./sth.; **ihre Augen richteten sich auf mich** her gaze was turned towards me; **b)** *(sich wenden)* **sich an jmdn./etw. ~** ⟨*person*⟩ turn on sb./sth.; ⟨*appeal, explanation*⟩ be directed at sb./sth.; **c)** *(kritisieren, schädigen)* **sich gegen jmdn./etw. ~** ⟨*person*⟩ criticize sb./sth.; ⟨*criticism, accusations, etc.*⟩ be aimed *or* levelled *or* directed at sb./sth.; **diese Lehre richtet sich gegen den Staat** this doctrine is directed against the state; **d)** *(sich orientieren)* **sich nach jmdm./jmds. Wünschen ~:** fit in with sb./sb.'s wishes; **sich nach jmds. Anweisungen ~:** comply with sb.'s instructions; **sich nach den Vorschriften ~:** keep to *or* follow the rules; **sich nach den Wünschen seiner Kunden ~:** be guided by one's customers' wishes; **e)** *(abhängen)* **sich nach jmdm./etw. ~:** depend on sb./sth.; **f)** *(Milit.)* **richt't euch!** right dress! **3.** *itr. V. (urteilen)* judge; pass judgement; **über jmdn. ~:** judge sb.; pass judgement on sb.; *(zu Gericht sitzen)* sit in judgement over sb.
Richter der; ~s, ~ judge; **die ~** *(Richterschaft)* the judiciary *sing.;* **sich zum ~ über jmdn./etw. aufwerfen** presume to pass judgement *or* sit in judgement on sb./sth.; **jmdn. vor den ~ bringen** take sb. to court; **der himmlische/höchste ~:** the Heavenly/Supreme Judge; **vor dem höchsten ~ stehen** stand before the Judgement Seat *or* the Throne of Judgement
Richter·amt das; *o. Pl.* office of judge
Richterin die; ~, ~nen judge
richterlich 1. *Adj.; nicht präd.* judicial. **2.** *adv.* ⟨*examined, approved, etc.*⟩ by a judge
Richterschaft die; ~, ~en judiciary
Richter-: ~spruch der judge's verdict; *(Verkündigung der Strafe)* sentence; **~stuhl der;** *o. Pl.* bench; **der ~stuhl Gottes** the Judgement Seat; the Throne of Judgement
Richt-: ~fest das topping-out ceremony; **~funk der** *(Funkw.)* directional radio; **~geschwindigkeit die** *(Verkehrsw.)* recommended maximum speed
richtig 1. *Adj.* **a)** right; *(zutreffend)* right; correct; correct ⟨*realization*⟩; accurate ⟨*prophecy, premonition*⟩; **sehr ~!** quite right!; **bin ich hier ~ bei Schulzes?** is this the Schulzes' home?; **die ~e Haltung von Katzen** the right way to keep cats; **ich halte es für das ~ste, wenn du mitkommst** I think the best thing would be for you to come [too]; **das ist genau das ~e für mich** that's just right for me; **b)** *(ordentlich)* proper; **ein ~er Mann/Fachmann** a real man/expert; **er ist ~** *(ugs.)* he's OK *(coll.) or* all right; **nicht ganz ~ [im Kopf** *od. (ugs.)* **im Oberstübchen] sein** be not quite right in the head *(coll.) or* not quite all there *(coll.);* **c)** *(wirklich, echt)* real; *(regelrecht)* real; proper *(coll.);* **du bist ein ~er Esel** you're a right *or* proper idiot *(coll.).* **2.** *adv.* **a)** right; correctly; **sehe ich das ~?** *(fig.)* am I right?; **habe ich ~ gehört?** *(fig.)* do my ears deceive me?; **~ sitzen** *od.* **passen** ⟨*clothes*⟩ fit properly; **meine Uhr geht ~:** my watch is right; **das Radio funktioniert nicht mehr ~:** the radio doesn't work properly anymore; **etw. ~ anpacken** tackle sth. the right way; **~ wählen** make the right choice; **du kommst [mir] gerade ~!** you've come at just the right moment; *(ugs. iron.)* nothing doing!; **b)** *(ordentlich)* properly; **~ ausschlafen/frühstücken** have a good sleep/breakfast; **c)** *(richtiggehend)* really; **d)** *(in der Tat)* yes; **ja ~!** yes, that's right!; **das habe ich doch ~ wieder versäumt** sure enough, I've missed it again
¹Richtige der/die; *adj. Dekl.* right man/

woman/person; **sie sucht noch den ~n** she's still looking for Mr Right; **an die ~/den ~n geraten** *(iron.)* choose the wrong person to try it on with *(Brit. coll.)*; **du bist mir der ~!** *(ugs.)* you're a right one!

[2]**Richtige der**; *adj. Dekl.* **drei/sechs ~ im Lotto** three/six right in the lottery

[3]**Richtige das**; *adj. Dekl.* right thing; **das ~ sein** be right; **hast du was ~s gegessen?** have you eaten properly?; have you had a proper meal?; **nichts ~s gefunden haben** not have found anything suitable; **nichts ~s gelernt haben** have had no proper education

richtig·gehend 1. *Adj.; nicht präd.* **a)** accurate ⟨*clock, watch*⟩; **b)** *(regelrecht)* real; proper *(coll.)*. 2. *adv. (regelrecht)* really

Richtigkeit die; ~: correctness; *(einer Ahnung, Prophetie)* accuracy; **die ~ einer Abschrift bescheinigen** certify a copy as [being] accurate; **etw. hat seine ~, mit etw. hat es seine ~**: sth. is right; **das wird schon seine ~ haben** I'm sure it's all right *or (coll.)* OK

richtig-, Richtig-: **~|liegen** *unr. itr. V. (ugs.)* **mit etw. ~liegen** get it right with sth.; **ich habe ~gelegen** I was right; **~|stellen** *tr. V.* correct; **~stellung die** correction

Richt-: **~kranz der** *wreath used in the topping-out ceremony;* **~linie die** guideline; **~mikrophon das** directional microphone; **~platz der** place of execution; **~preis der** recommended price; **unverbindlicher ~preis** manufacturer's recommended price; **~scheit das** *(Bauw.)* straight-edge; **~schnur die**; *Pl.* **~schnuren a)** *(fig.)* guiding principle; **b)** *(Bauw.)* line; **~schwert das** *(hist.)* executioner's sword; **~spruch der a)** *(beim Richtfest) verse address at the topping-out ceremony;* **b)** *(veralt.: Urteilsspruch)* judgement; *(Verkündigung der Strafe)* sentence; **~stätte die** *(geh.) s.* **Richtplatz**; **~strahler der** *(Funkt.)* directional aerial *or (Amer.)* antenna

Richtung die; ~, ~en **a)** direction; **die ~ ändern** *od.* **wechseln** change direction; **in ~ Osten** in an easterly direction; eastwards; *(auf der Autobahn)* on the eastbound carriageway; **in ~ Ulm** in the direction of Ulm; **nach/aus allen ~en** in/from all directions; **der Zug/die Autobahn ~ Ulm** the train to Ulm/the motorway in the direction of Ulm; **eine ~ einschlagen** head in a direction; **eine andere ~ einschlagen** change direction; ⟨*ship, aircraft*⟩ change course; **~ auf den Wald nehmen, die ~ zum** *od.* **nach dem Wald einschlagen** head in the direction of the wood; **[in] ~** *(Akk.)* **Bad verschwinden** *(ugs.)* disappear in the direction of the bathroom *(coll.)*; **aus welcher ~ kam der Schuß?** from what direction did the shot come?; **wir gehen in diese ~**: we're going this way *or* in this direction; **ihre Gedanken nahmen eine andere ~** *(fig.)* her thoughts took a different turn; **ein erster Schritt in ~ auf die Integration** *(fig.)* a first step towards *or* in the direction of integration; **der Pullover lag nicht so ganz in meiner ~** *od.* **war nicht so ganz meine ~** *(fig.)* the pullover wasn't quite [to] my taste; **er hat Angst, sich in irgendeine ~ festzulegen** *(fig.)* he's afraid to commit himself in any way; **der erste Versuch in dieser ~** *(fig.)* the first experiment of this kind; **die ~ stimmt** *(fig. ugs.)* it's/he's *etc.* on the right lines; **ich hätte jetzt Lust auf Fisch oder irgend etwas in dieser ~**: I could just fancy some fish or something in that line; **b)** *(fig.: Tendenz)* movement; trend; *(die Vertreter einer ~) (in der Kunst, Literatur)* movement; *(in einer Partei)* faction; *(Denk~, Lehrmeinung)* school of thought; **die ganze ~ seiner Äußerungen** the whole tendency *or* drift of his remarks

richtung·gebend *s.* **richtungsweisend**

richtungs-, Richtungs-: **~änderung die** change in *or* of direction; *(eines Schiffs, Flugzeugs)* change of course; **die politische ~änderung XYs** *(fig.)* XY's change of political course; **~gewerkschaft die** *trade union linked to one party, ideology, etc.*; **~kämpfe** *Pl.* factional struggles; **~los** 1. *Adj.* lacking [a sense of] direction *postpos.*; **~los sein** lack [a sense of] direction; 2. *adv.* aimlessly; **~losigkeit die**; *o. Pl.* lack of [a sense of] direction

richtung·weisend 1. *Adj.* ⟨*idea, resolution, paper, speech*⟩ that points the way ahead; *(in der Mode)* trend-setting; **für jmdn./etw. ~ sein** point the way ahead for sb./sth. 2. *adv.* **sie hat sich zu diesem Thema ~ geäußert** she set out ideas on this subject which point the way ahead; **Kunststoffe haben die heutige Technik ~ beeinflußt** plastics have had a determining influence on the direction in which today's technology has developed

Richt·waage die spirit-level

Ricke ['rɪkə] **die**; ~, ~n *(Jägerspr.)* doe *(of roe-deer)*

rieb [ri:p] *1. u. 3. Pers. Sg. Prät. v.* **reiben**

riechen ['ri:çn̩] 1. *unr. tr. V.* **a)** smell; **ich rieche Tabak gern** I like the smell of tobacco; **ich rieche Gas** I [can] smell gas; **jmdn./etw. nicht ~ können** *(fig. salopp)* not be able to stand sb./sth.; **b)** *(wittern)* ⟨*dog etc.*⟩ scent, pick up the scent of ⟨*animal*⟩; **er roch die Gefahr sofort** *(fig.)* he scented *or* sensed danger immediately; **ich konnte ja nicht ~, daß ...** *(fig.)* [I'm not psychic,] I couldn't know that ... 2. *unr. itr. V.* **a)** *(Gerüche wahrnehmen)* smell; **Hunde können sehr gut ~**: dogs have a very good sense of smell; **an jmdm./etw. ~**: smell sb./sth.; **laß mich mal [daran] ~**: let me have a sniff; **b)** *(einen Geruch haben)* smell **(nach** of); **gut/schlecht ~**: smell good/bad; **diese Blumen ~ nicht** these flowers have no smell *or* scent; **hier riecht es verbrannt/nach Krankenhaus** there is a burnt/hospital smell *or* smell of burning/hospital here; **er roch aus dem Mund** he had bad breath; his breath smelt; **das riecht nach Betrug** *(fig.)* that smells *or* smacks of deceit

Riecher der; ~s, ~ *(salopp)* **a)** *(Nase)* conk *(sl.)*; **b)** *(fig.: Gespür)* nose; **einen guten ~ für etw. haben** have a sixth sense for sth.

Riech-: **~fläschchen das** smelling-bottle; **~kolben der** *(salopp scherzh.)* conk *(sl.)*; **~organ das** olfactory organ; **~salz das** smelling-salts *pl.*

[1]**Ried** [ri:t] **das**; ~[e]s, ~e **a)** *o. Pl. (Schilf)* reeds *pl.*; **b)** *(Gebiet)* reedy marsh

[2]**Ried die**; ~, ~en, **Riede die**; ~, ~n *(österr.)* [patch of] vineyard

Ried·gras das *(Bot.)* sedge

rief [ri:f] *1. u. 3. Pers. Sg. Prät. v.* **rufen**

Riefe die; ~, ~n groove

Riege ['ri:gə] **die**; ~, ~n *(Turnen)* squad; *(fig.)* team

Riegel ['ri:gl̩] **der**; ~s, ~: **a)** *(an der Tür usw.)* bolt; **einer Sache** *(Dat.)* **einen ~ vorschieben** *(fig.)* put a stop to sth.; *(etw. verhindern)* not let sth. happen; **b) ein ~ Schokolade** a bar of chocolate; **c)** *(bes. Fußball: Abwehr)* packed defence; **d)** *(Milit.)* [defensive] wall; **e)** *(Schneiderei) (Lasche)* loop; *(an Jacke, Mantel usw.)* half-belt

Riegel·haus das *(schweiz.)* half-timbered house

Riemchen das; ~s, ~: [small] strap *or* belt

Riemen ['ri:mən] **der**; ~s, ~ **a)** *(Gurt)* strap; *(Treib~, Gürtel)* belt; **sich am ~ reißen** *(ugs.)* pull oneself together; get a grip on oneself; **den ~ enger schnallen** *(fig. ugs.)* tighten one's belt; **b)** *(Schnürsenkel)* leather shoe-lace; **c)** *(derb: Penis)* prick *(coarse)*; **d)** *(Ruder)* [long] oar; **sich [kräftig] in die ~ legen** *(auch fig.)* put one's back into it

Riemen-: **~an·trieb der** belt drive; **~scheibe die** belt pulley

Ries [ri:s] **das**; ~es, ~e *(bei Maßangaben ungebeugt)* two reams

Riese ['ri:zə] **der**; ~n, ~n **a)** giant; **ein ~ von einem Menschen** a giant of a man/woman; *s. auch* **abgebrochen 2 b**; **b)** *(salopp: Tausender [Banknote])* thousand-mark/dollar *etc.* note; **das kostet drei ~n** that costs three grand [in marks *etc.*] *(sl.)*

-riese der giant; **Automobil~**: giant car manufacturer; **Chemie~**: giant chemical firm; **Branchen~**: giant of the industry

Riesel·feld das *(Landw.)* field irrigated with sewage

rieseln ['ri:zl̩n] *itr. V.; mit Richtungsangabe mit sein;* **a)** *(rinnen)* trickle; **b)** *(fallen)* ⟨*sand, lime*⟩ trickle [down]; ⟨*snow*⟩ fall gently *or* lightly; **der Kalk rieselte von den Wänden** lime was crumbling off the walls

Riesen- giant ⟨*building, tree, salamander, tortoise, etc.*⟩; enormous ⟨*task, selection, profit, sum, portion*⟩; tremendous *(coll.)* ⟨*effort, rejoicing, success, hit*⟩; *(abwertend: schrecklich)* terrific *(coll.)*, terrible *(coll.)* ⟨*stupidity, mess, scandal, fuss*⟩; **ich habe einen ~hunger** I am tremendously *or* terribly hungry *(coll.)*; **ein ~rindvieh** *(ugs.)* an almighty idiot *(sl.)*; **ein ~spaß** *(ugs.)* tremendous *or* terrific fun *(coll.)*

riesen-, Riesen-: **~baby das** *(ugs.)* **a)** oversize baby *(joc.)*; **b)** *(abwertend) s.* **Elefantenküken**; **~bock·wurst die** giant bockwurst; **~groß** *Adj.* enormous; huge; gigantic; terrific *(coll.)* ⟨*surprise*⟩; **eine ~große Dummheit** something terribly stupid *(coll.)*; **~haft** *Adj.* enormous; huge; gigantic; **~rad das** big wheel; Ferris wheel; **~rad fahren** go on the big wheel *or* Ferris wheel; **~saurier der** giant dinosaur; **~schlange die** boa; **~schritt der** giant stride; **~slalom der** *(Skisport)* giant slalom; **~stern der** *(Astron.)* giant [star]; **~wuchs der** *(Biol.)* gigantism

riesig 1. *Adj.* **a)** *(sehr groß)* enormous; huge; gigantic; vast ⟨*country*⟩; tremendous ⟨*joy, enthusiasm, effort, progress, strength*⟩; terrific *(coll.)*, terrible *(coll.)* ⟨*hunger, thirst*⟩; **~e Ausmaße haben** be of enormous size; **ein ~er Spaß** terrific *or* tremendous fun *(coll.)*; **b)** *(ugs.: großartig)* fabulous *(coll.)*, tremendous *(coll.)* ⟨*party, film, etc.*⟩. 2. *adv. (ugs.)* tremendously *(coll.)*; terribly *(coll.)*

Riesin die; ~, ~nen giantess

Riesling ['ri:slɪŋ] **der**; ~s, ~e Riesling

riet [ri:t] *1. u. 3. Pers. Sg. Prät. v.* **raten**

[1]**Riff** [rɪf] **das**; ~[e]s, ~e reef

[2]**Riff der**; ~s, ~s *(Jazz)* riff

Riffel ['rɪfl̩] **die**; ~, ~n **a)** corrugation; *(Vertiefung)* groove; *(in einer Säule)* flute; *(Erhöhung)* rib; **b)** *(Textilw.) (Maschine)* ripple [machine]; *(Kamm)* ripple

riffeln *tr. V.* **a)** rib ⟨*glass*⟩; ripple ⟨*lake*⟩; *s. auch* **geriffelt**; **b)** *(Textilw.)* ripple ⟨*flax*⟩

Rififi ['rɪfifi] **das**; ~s *(ugs.)* master-crime

Rigg [rɪk] **das**; ~s, ~s *(Seemannsspr.)* rig

rigid [ri'gi:t], **rigide** 1. *Adj. (geh., Med.)* rigid. 2. *adv. (geh.)* rigidly

Rigidität [rigidi'tɛ:t] **die**; ~ *(geh., Med.)* rigidity

Rigorismus [rigo'rɪsmʊs] **der**; ~ *(geh.)* rigorism

rigoros [rigo'ro:s] 1. *Adj.* rigorous. 2. *adv.* rigorously; **etw. ~ ablehnen** reject sth. categorically

Rigorosität die; ~ *(geh.)* rigorousness

Rigorosum [rigo'ro:zʊm] **das**; ~s, **Rigorosa** *od. bes. österr.* **Rigorosen** *(Hochschulw.)* oral part of the doctoral examination

Rikscha ['rɪkʃa] **die**; ~, ~s rickshaw

Rille ['rɪlə] **die**; ~, ~n groove; *(in einer Säule)* flute

Rind [rɪnt] **das**; ~[e]s, ~er **a)** cow; *(Stier)* bull; **~er** cattle *pl.*; **20 ~er** twenty head of cattle; **ein gemästetes ~**: a fattened ox; **Hackfleisch/ein Steak vom ~**: minced *or (Amer.)* ground beef/a beef steak; **b)** *(ugs.: ~fleisch)* beef; **c)** *(Zool.)* bovine

Rinde die; ~, ~n **a)** *(Baum~)* bark; **b)** *(Brot~)* crust; *(Käse~)* rind; **c)** *(Hirn~)* cortex

Rinder-: **~braten der** *(gebraten)* roast beef *no indef. art.*; *(roh)* roasting beef *no indef. art.*; **ein ~braten** a joint of roast beef; *(roh)* a joint of [roasting] beef; **~bremse die** horse-fly; **~brust die** brisket of beef; **~filet das** fillet of beef; **~herde die** herd of [beef] cattle; **~leber die** ox liver; **~lende die** loin of beef; **~pest die** rinderpest; cattle-plague; **~talg der** *(zum Kochen)* beef suet; *(für Salbe usw.)* beef tallow; **~zucht die** cattle-breeding *or* -rearing *no art.*

Rind-: **~fleisch das** beef; **~fleisch·brühe die** beef broth; **~fleisch·supppe die** beef soup

rinds-, Rinds-: **~braten der** *(bes. südd., österr.)* s. **Rinderbraten**; **~fett das** *(südd., österr.)* clarified butter; **~leber die** *(bes. südd., österr.)* s. **Rinderleber**; **~leder das** cowhide; oxhide; **~ledern** *Adj.*; *nicht präd.* cowhide; oxhide; **~lende die** *(bes. südd., österr.)* s. **Rinderlende**

Rind·vieh das; *Pl.* **Rindviecher a)** *o. Pl.* cattle *pl.*; **20 Stück ~**: twenty head of cattle; **b)** *(ugs. abwertend)* ass; [stupid] fool; **ich ~!** what an idiot I am! *(coll.)*

Ring [rɪŋ] **der**; **~[e]s, ~e a)** ring; **die ~e tauschen** *od.* **wechseln** *(geh.)* exchange rings; **an den ~en turnen** perform *or* exercise on the rings; **10 ~e schießen** shoot *or* score a ten; **einen ~ bilden** ⟨*spectators etc.*⟩ form a ring *or* circle; ⟨*stones, road*⟩ form a ring; **b)** *(~straße)* ring road; **den ~ fahren** take the ring road; **c)** *(Box~)* ring; **~ frei zur zweiten Runde** seconds out for the second round; **d)** *(Vereinigung)* **ein ~ für Theaterbesuche** a theatre-going circle; **ein ~ von Händlern** a ring of dealers; **e)** *(Wurf~)* hoop

Ring-: **~bahn die** circle line; **~buch das** ring binder

Ringel ['rɪŋl̩] **der**; **~s, ~**: [small] ring; **die ~ ihrer Haare** the ringlets in her hair

Ringel·blume die marigold

ringelig *Adj.* curly; ⟨*hair*⟩ in ringlets

Ringel·locke die ringlet

ringeln 1. *tr. V.* curl; coil ⟨*tail*⟩; *s. auch* **geringelt. 2.** *refl. V.* curl

Ringel-: **~natter die** ring-snake; **~piez** [-pi:ts] **der**; **~[es], ~e** *(ugs. scherzh.)* **~piez [mit Anfassen]** hop *(coll.)*; hoedown *(Amer.)*; **~reigen, ~reihen der** ring-a-ring-o'-roses; **~reigen tanzen** *od.* **spielen** play ring-a-ring-o'-roses; **~schwanz der** curly tail; **~söckchen das, ~socke die** [horizontally] striped sock; **~spiel das** *(österr.)* merry-go-round; **~taube die** wood-pigeon; ring-dove; **~wurm der** *(Zool.)* annelid

ringen 1. *unr. tr. V. (Sport, fig.)* wrestle; *(fig.: kämpfen)* struggle, fight (**um** for); **gegen jmdn.** *od.* **mit jmdm. ~** *(Sport)* wrestle with sb.; *(fig.)* **mit den Tränen ~**: fight back one's tears; **die Ärzte ~ um sein Leben** the doctors are struggling *or* fighting to save his life; **nach Atem** *od.* **Luft ~**: struggle for breath; **nach** *od.* **um Fassung ~**: fight to maintain one's composure; **er rang nach Worten** *od.* **um Worte** he struggled to find the right words; **ich habe lange mit mir gerungen, ob ...**: I had a long struggle with my conscience to decide whether ... **2.** *unr. tr. V.* **a)** *(bes. Sport)* **den Gegner zu Boden ~**: bring one's opponent down; **b)** *(gewaltsam reißen)* **jmdm. etw. aus den Händen/der Hand ~**: wrest sth. from sb.'s hands/hand; **c)** *in* **die Hände ~**: wring one's hands. **3.** *unr. refl. V. (geh.)* **ein Seufzer rang sich aus ihrer Brust** a sigh forced its way up from deep within her

Ringen das; **~s** *(Sport)* wrestling *no art.*

Ringer der; **~s, ~**: wrestler

ring-, Ring-: **~fahndung die** intensive man-hunt [over a wide area]; **~finger der** ring-finger; **~förmig 1.** *Adj.* in the shape of a ring *postpos.*; circular; annular ⟨*eclipse*⟩; **~förmige Verbindungen** *(Chem.)* ring *or* cyclic compounds; **2.** *adv.* ⟨*arrange*⟩ in a ring *or* circle; ⟨*spread out*⟩ in rings *or* circles; **die Straße verläuft ~förmig um die ganze Stadt** the road rings the whole town; **~kampf der a)** [stand-up] fight; **b)** *(Sport) (Wettbewerb)* wrestling bout; *(Sportart)* s. **Ringen**; **~kämpfer der** wrestler

Ringlein das; **~s, ~**: [little] ring

Ringlotte [rɪŋ'glɔtə] **die**; **~, ~n** *(bes. österr.)* greengage

Ring-: **~mauer die** ring-wall; **~muskel der** *(Anat.)* sphincter; **~richter der** *(Boxen)* referee

rings [rɪŋs] *Adv.* all around; **sich ~ im Kreise umsehen** look all around one; **~ von Bergen umgeben** completely surrounded by mountains

Ring·schlüssel der ring spanner

rings·herum *Adv.* all around [it/them *etc.*]; *s. auch* **rings**

Ring·straße die ring road; *(um den Stadtkern)* inner ring road

rings-: **~um, ~umher** *Adv.* all around; *s. auch* **rings**

Ring-: **~tennis das** deck tennis; **~wall der** *(Archäol.)* ring-wall

Rinne ['rɪnə] **die**; **~, ~n** channel; *(Dach~, Rinnstein)* gutter; *(tiefer)* gully; *(Abfluß)* drainpipe; *(Rille)* groove; *(im Meeresboden)* trench

rinnen *unr. itr. V.* **a)** *mit sein* run; **das Geld rinnt ihm durch die Finger** money just slips through his fingers; **b)** *(südd.: undicht sein)* leak

Rinnsal ['rɪnza:l] **das**; **~[e]s, ~e** *(geh.)* rivulet; **ein ~ von Blut/Öl** a trickle of blood/oil

Rinn·stein der gutter; **jmdn. aus dem ~ auflesen** *(fig.)* pick sb. out of the gutter; **im ~ enden** *od.* **landen** *(fig.)* end up in the gutter

Riposte [ri'pɔstə] **die**; **~, ~n** *(Fechten)* riposte

Rippchen das; **~s, ~** *(Kochk. südd.)* rib [of pork]

Rippe ['rɪpə] **die**; **~, ~n a)** *(Anat., Bot., Technik, Textilw., Bautechnik, fig.)* rib; *(Technik: Kühl~)* fin; **sie hat nichts auf den ~n** *(ugs.)* she is only skin and bone; **bei ihm kann man die ~n zählen** *(ugs.)* you can see his ribs sticking out; **daß er was auf die ~n kriegt** *(ugs.)* to put some flesh on his bones; **ich kann es mir nicht aus den ~n schneiden** *(ugs.)* I can't just produce it out of thin air; **b)** *(einer Zitrusfrucht)* segment; *(einer Tafel Schokolade)* strip

Rippen-: **~bogen der** *(Anat.)* costal arch; **~bruch der** *(Med.)* rib fracture; **~fell das** *(Anat.)* costal pleura; **~fell·entzündung die** *(Med.)* pleurisy *no indef. art.*; **~speer der** *od.* **das**; **~[e]s** *o. Pl.* **[Kasseler] ~speer** cured rib of pork; **~stoß der** dig in the ribs; *(sanfter, auch fig.)* nudge; **~stück das** *(Kochk.)* piece of rib

Ripp·samt der corduroy

Rips [rɪps] **der**; **~es, ~e** *(Textilw.)* rep[p]

Risiko ['ri:ziko] **das**; **~s, Risiken** *od.* **~s** *od. österr.* **Risken** risk; **das ~ eingehen, daß etw. geschieht** run the risk of sth. happening; **ein/kein ~ eingehen** take a risk/not take any risks; **die Sache ist mit einem gewissen ~ verbunden** there is a certain amount of risk involved [in it]; **auf eigenes/dein/mein ~**: at one's/your/my own risk

risiko-, Risiko-: **~faktor der** risk factor; **der ~faktor Alkohol** the risk factor represented by alcohol; **~frei** *s.* **~los**; **~freudig 1.** *Adj.* risky ⟨*driving*⟩; ⟨*player, speculator*⟩ who likes taking risks; **er ist sehr ~freudig** he likes playing with fire *or* taking [a lot of] risks; **2.** *adv.* **er fährt/spielt sehr ~freudig** he likes to take [a lot of] risks when he drives/plays; **~geburt die** *(Med.)* difficult *or* complicated birth; **~los 1.** *Adj.* safe; without risk *postpos.*; **2.** *adv.* safely; without taking risks; **~reich** *Adj.* very risky; **~schwangerschaft die** pregnancy involving some risk

riskant [rɪs'kant] **1.** *Adj.* risky. **2.** *adv.* riskily; **er fährt zu ~**: he takes too many risks [in his driving]

riskieren [rɪs'ki:rən] *tr. V.* risk; venture ⟨*smile, remark*⟩; run the risk of ⟨*accident, thrashing, etc.*⟩; *(gefährden)* put ⟨*reputation, job*⟩ at risk; risk ⟨*life, reputation*⟩; **etwas/nichts ~**: take a risk/not take any risks; **einen verstohlenen Blick ~**: steal a furtive glance

Rispe ['rɪspə] **die**; **~, ~n** *(Bot.)* panicle

riß [rɪs] *1. u. 3. Pers. Sg. Prät. v.* **reißen**

Riß [rɪs] **der**; **Risses, Risse a)** *(im Stoff, Papier, Gewebe)* tear; *(im Tonband)* break; **die Hose hat einen ~/du hast einen ~ in der Hose** the trousers/your trousers are torn *or* have a tear; **einen ~ bekommen** tear; **b)** *(Spalt, Sprung)* crack; *(fig.: Kluft)* rift; split; **einen ~ bekommen** become cracked; *(fig.)* ⟨*friendship*⟩ begin to break up; **c)** *(Zeichnung)* plan; *(Entwurf)* sketch

rissig *Adj.* cracked; chapped ⟨*lips*⟩

Rist [rɪst] **der**; **~es, ~e** *(des Fußes)* instep; *(der Hand)* back [of the hand]

Rist·griff der *(Turnen)* overgrasp

rite ['ri:tə] *Adv. (Hochschulw.)* **~ bestehen** get a pass *(in one's doctoral examination)*; **mit „~" bewertet werden** be given a pass

Riten *s.* **Ritus**

ritsch *Interj.* rip; zip; **~, ratsch** rip, rip

ritt *1. u. 3. Pers. Sg. Prät. v.* **reiten**

Ritt der; **~[e]s, ~e** ride; **einen weiten/scharfen ~ machen** go for a long/hard ride; **auf einen** *od.* **in einem ~** *(ugs.)* in one go *(coll.)*

Rittberger ['rɪtbɛrgɐ] **der**; **~s, ~** *(Sport)* loop jump; **einen ~ springen** do a loop jump

Ritter der; **~s, ~ a)** knight; **jmdn. zum ~ schlagen** *(hist.)* knight sb.; dub sb. [a] knight; **fahrender ~** *(hist.)* knight errant; **~ ohne Furcht und Tadel** chevalier sans peur et sans reproche; *(fig. geh., oft scherzh.)* knight in shining armour; **b)** *(Adelstitel) (als Teil eines Namens)* Ritter; *(Ordens~)* Knight; **c)** *in* **arme ~** *(Kochk.)* French toast

Ritter-: **~burg die** knight's castle; **~dichtung die** *(Literaturwiss.)* knightly poetry; **~gut das** *(hist.)* ≈ manor; feudal estate; **~kreuz das** *(ns.)* Knight's Cross

ritterlich 1. *Adj.* **a)** chivalrous; **b)** *(zum Rittertum gehörend)* knightly ⟨*life, culture, virtues, ideals*⟩. **2.** *adv.* chivalrously

Ritterlichkeit die; **~**: chivalrousness; chivalry

Ritter-: **~orden der** order of knights; knightly order; **~roman der** romance of chivalry; knightly romance

Ritterschaft die; **~** *(hist.)* knighthood

Ritter-: **~schlag der** *(hist.)* knightly accolade; **den ~schlag empfangen** be knighted; be dubbed [a] knight; **~sporn der** *(Bot.)* larkspur; *(Garten~sporn)* delphinium; **~stand der** *(hist.)* knighthood; **jmdn. in den ~stand aufnehmen** make sb. a knight

Rittertum das; **~s** *(hist.)* knighthood

Ritterzeit die; *o. Pl.* days *pl.* of the knights; *(Zeit der Ritterlichkeit)* Age of Chivalry

rittlings ['rɪtlɪŋs] *Adv.* astride; **~ auf einem Stuhl sitzen** sit astride a chair

Ritt·meister der *(Milit. hist.)* cavalry captain

Ritual [ri'tu̯a:l] **das**; **~s, ~e** *od.* **Ritualien** [-li̯ən] *(Rel., fig.)* ritual

ritualisieren *tr. V. (geh.)* ritualize

Ritual·mord der ritual murder

rituell [ri'tu̯ɛl] *(Rel., fig.)* **1.** *Adj.* ritual. **2.** *adv.* ritually

Ritus ['ri:tʊs] **der**; **~, Riten** *(Rel., fig.)* rite

Ritz [rɪts] **der**; **~es, ~e a)** *(Kratzer)* scratch; **b)** *s.* **Ritze**

Ritze die; **~, ~n** crack; [narrow] gap; **durch**

eine ~ spähen peer through a crack *or* slit; **auf der ~ schlafen** *(ugs. scherzh.)* sleep on the join *(of a pair of [twin] beds)*

Ritzel ['rɪtsl̩] **das; ~s, ~** *(Technik)* pinion

ritzen *tr. V.* **a)** scratch; *(tiefer)* cut; **sich** *(Dat.)* **das Kinn ~:** scratch/cut one's chin; **b)** *(einritzen)* carve ⟨*name etc.*⟩ **(in +** *Akk.* in); *(in eine Metallplatte)* engrave ⟨*drawing etc.*⟩

Rivale [ri'va:lə] **der; ~n, ~n, Rivalin die; ~, ~nen** rival

rivalisieren *itr. V.* **mit jmdm. um etw. ~:** compete with sb. for sth.; **~de Gruppen** rival groups

Rivalität [rivali'tɛ:t] **die; ~, ~en** rivalry *no indef. art.*

Riviera [ri'vie:ra] **die; ~:** Riviera

Rizinus ['ri:tsinʊs] **der; ~, ~** *od.* **~se a)** *(Pflanze)* castor-oil plant; **b)** *(~öl)* castor oil

Roastbeef ['ro:stbi:f] **das; ~s, ~s a)** *(roh)* sirloin *(Brit.)*; **b)** *(gebraten)* roast [sirloin *(Brit.)* of] beef

Robbe ['rɔbə] **die; ~, ~n** seal

robben *itr. V.; meist. mit Richtungsangabe nur. mit sein* crawl

Robben-: ~fang der sealing; seal-hunting; **~schlag der** seal cull

Robe ['ro:bə] **die; ~, ~n a)** robe; *(schwarz)* gown; **b)** *(Abendkleid)* evening gown

Robinie [ro'bi:niə] **die; ~, ~n** *(Bot.)* robinia; false acacia

Robinsonade [robɪnzo'na:də] **die; ~, ~n** *(Roman/Abenteuer)* Robinson-Crusoe style novel/adventure

roboten ['rɔbɔtn̩] *itr. V. (ugs.)* slave [away]

Roboter ['rɔbɔtɐ] **der; ~s, ~:** robot

robust [ro'bʊst] *Adj.* robust

Robustheit die; ~: robustness; *(Gesundheit)* robust constitution

roch [rɔx] *1. u. 3. Pers. Sg. Prät. v.* **riechen**

Rochade [rɔ'xa:də] **die; ~, ~n** *(Schach)* castling; **kleine/große ~:** short/long castling; **die ~ ausführen** castle

röcheln ['rœçl̩n] *itr. V.* breathe stertorously; ⟨*dying person*⟩ give the death-rattle

Rochen ['rɔxn̩] **der; ~s, ~** *(Zool.)* ray

rochieren [rɔ'xi:rən] *itr. V.* **a)** *(Schach)* castle; **b)** *mit Richtungsangabe mit sein (Sport)* change over; switch positions

[1]**Rock** [rɔk] **der; ~[e]s, Röcke** ['rœkə] **a)** skirt; *(Schotten~)* kilt; **hinter jedem ~ hersein** *od.* **herlaufen** *(ugs.)* be after *or* chase every bit of skirt *(sl.)*; **b)** *(landsch.: Jacke)* jacket; **der grüne ~ [des Försters]** the [forester's] green coat; **den bunten ~ anziehen/ausziehen** *(fig. veralt.)* go for a soldier *(arch.)*/leave the army; **des Königs ~ tragen** *(fig. veralt.)* be a soldier of the King; **der letzte ~ hat keine Taschen** *(fig.)* you can't take it with you

[2]**Rock der; ~[s]** *(Musik)* rock [music]

Rock and Roll ['rɔk ɛnt 'rɔl] **der; ~ ~ ~[s], ~ ~ ~[s]** rock and roll *no pl.*

Rock·auf·schlag der [jacket] lapel; **am ~:** in one's lapel

Röckchen ['rœkçən] **das; ~s, ~:** little skirt; *(kurz)* short skirt

rocken *itr. V.* rock

Rocker der; ~s, ~: rocker

rockig *Adj.* rock ⟨*music*⟩; rock-like ⟨*jazz etc.*⟩

Rock·musik die rock music

Rock-: ~oper die rock opera; **~schoß der** coat-tail; *s. auch* **~zipfel; ~zipfel der** *in* **an jmds.** *od.* **jmdm. am ~zipfel hängen** cling *or* hang on to sb.; *(fig.: unselbständig sein)* lean on *or* be dependent on sb.; **jmdn. [gerade noch] am ~zipfel erwischen** just [manage to] catch sb.; *s. auch* [1]**Rock a**

Rodel ['ro:dl̩] **der; ~s, ~** *(südd.) s.* **Rodelschlitten**

Rodel·bahn die toboggan-run; *(bei sportlichen Veranstaltungen)* luge-run

rodeln ['ro:dl̩n] *itr. V.; meist. mit Richtungsangabe nur. mit sein* sledge; toboggan; *(als Sport)* luge

Rodeln das; ~s sledging *no art.*; tobogganing *no art.*; *(Sport)* luge

Rodel·schlitten der sledge; toboggan; *(bei sportlichen Veranstaltungen)* luge

roden ['ro:dn̩] **1.** *tr. V.* **a)** clear ⟨*wood, land*⟩; *(ausgraben)* grub up ⟨*tree*⟩; **b)** *(ernten)* lift ⟨*potatoes etc.*⟩. **2.** *itr. V.* clear the land

Rodeo [ro'de:o] **das** *od.* **der; ~s, ~s** rodeo

Rodler ['ro:dlɐ] **der; ~s, ~, Rodlerin die; ~, ~nen** tobogganer; *(bei sportlichen Veranstaltungen)* luger

Rodung die; ~, ~en a) *(das Roden)* clearing; clearance; *(das Ausgraben)* grubbing up; **b)** *(gerodete Fläche)* clearance

Rogen ['ro:gn̩] **der; ~s, ~:** roe

Roggen ['rɔgn̩] **der; ~s** rye

Roggen-: ~brot das rye bread; **ein ~brot** a loaf of rye bread; **~brötchen das** rye-bread roll

Rogner ['ro:gnɐ] **der; ~s, ~:** spawner

roh [ro:] **1.** *Adj.* **a)** raw ⟨*food*⟩; unboiled ⟨*milk*⟩; raw, uncooked ⟨*ham*⟩; **jmdn./etw. wie ein ~es Ei behandeln** handle sb./sth. with kid gloves; **b)** *(nicht bearbeitet)* rough, unfinished ⟨*wood*⟩; rough, uncut ⟨*diamond*⟩; rough-hewn, undressed ⟨*stone*⟩; crude ⟨*ore, metal*⟩; unbleached ⟨*cloth*⟩; untreated ⟨*skin*⟩; raw ⟨*silk, sugar*⟩; **c)** *(ungenau)* rough; **d)** *(brutal)* brutish ⟨*person, treatment, etc.*⟩; *(grausam)* callous ⟨*person, treatment*⟩; *(grob)* coarse, uncouth ⟨*manners, words, joke*⟩; brute *attrib.* ⟨*force*⟩. **2.** *adv.* **a)** *(ungenau)* roughly; **~ zusammengeschlagen** crudely knocked together; **b)** *(brutal)* brutishly; *(grausam)* callously; *(grob)* coarsely; in an uncouth manner

Roh-: ~bau der shell [of a/the building]; **das Haus ist im ~bau fertig** the shell of the house is complete; **~diamant der** rough *or* uncut diamond; **~eisen das** pig-iron

Roheit ['ro:hait] **die; ~, ~en a)** *o. Pl. (Brutalität)* brutishness; *(Grausamkeit)* callousness; *(Grobheit)* coarseness; uncouthness; **b)** *(Handlung)* brutish/callous deed; *(Äußerung)* callous remark

Roh-: ~ertrag der *(Wirtsch.)* gross return; **~erz das** crude ore; **~erzeugnis das** *s.* **~produkt; ~fassung die** unfinished version; **~kost die** raw fruit and vegetables *pl.*

Rohköstler ['ro:kœstlɐ] **der; ~s, ~, Rohköstlerin die; ~, ~nen** *person who eats raw fruit and vegetables only*

Rohling ['ro:lɪŋ] **der; ~s, ~e a)** *(abwertend: Mensch)* brute; beast; **b)** *(Technik)* blank

Roh-: ~material das raw material; **~öl das** crude oil; **~produkt das** natural product [requiring further treatment]; *(Rohstoff)* raw material

Rohr [ro:ɐ̯] **das; ~[e]s, ~e a)** *(Leitungs~)* pipe; *(als Bauteil)* tube; *(Geschütz~)* barrel; **das Schiff feuerte aus allen ~en** the ship fired with all its guns; **b)** *o. Pl. (Röhricht)* reeds *pl.*; **c)** *o. Pl. (Schilf usw. als Werkstoff)* reed; *(Bambus, Zucker~ usw.)* cane; **ein aus ~ geflochtener Korb/Stuhl** a reed basket/chair; **ein Korb/Stuhl aus ~** *(aus Peddigrohr)* a cane basket/chair; **spanisches ~:** rattan cane; **d)** *(Schilf-, Riedhalm)* reed; **e)** *(südd., österr.: Backofen)* oven

Rohr-: ~ammer die *(Zool.)* reed bunting; **~blatt das** reed, **~bruch der** burst pipe

Röhrchen ['rø:ɐ̯çən] **das; ~s, ~:** small pipe; *(Behälter)* small tube; *(Reagenzglas)* test-tube; **ins ~ blasen** take the breathalyser test

Rohrdommel [-dɔməl] **die** *(Zool.)* bittern

Röhre ['rø:rə] **die; ~, ~n a)** *(Rohr)* tube; *(Leitungs~)* pipe; *(Tunnel~)* bore; *(Jägerspr.: Gang eines Baus)* gallery; *s. auch* **kommunizieren a; b)** *(Leuchtstoff~)* [fluorescent] tube; *(Elektronen~)* valve *(Brit.)*; tube *(Amer.)*; *(ugs.: Bild~)* [picture] tube; **vor der ~ sitzen** sit in front of the box *(coll.)*; **c)** *(Behälter)* **eine ~ [mit] Tabletten** a tube of pills; **d)** *(eines Ofens)* oven; **in die ~ sehen** *od.* **gucken** *(fig. ugs.)* be left out [in the cold]

röhren *itr. V.* ⟨*stag etc.*⟩ bell; *(fig.)* roar

röhren-, Röhren-: ~förmig *Adj.* tubular; **~hose die** drainpipe trousers; **~knochen der** long bone; **~pilz der** boletus

Rohr-: ~flöte die reed-pipe; *(Panflöte)* pan-pipes *pl.*; **~geflecht das** woven cane

Röhricht ['rø:rɪçt] **das; ~s, ~e** reeds *pl.*

Rohr-: ~kolben der reed-mace; cat's-tail; **~krepierer der; ~s, ~:** barrel burst; **~leger der; ~s, ~:** pipe-layer; **~leitung die** pipe; *(über längere Entfernung)* pipeline

Röhrling ['rø:ɐ̯lɪŋ] **der; ~s, ~e** boletus

Rohr-: ~post die pneumatic dispatch; **etw. mit ~post befördern** convey sth. by pneumatic tube; **~sänger der** *(Zool.)* reed-warbler; **~spatz der** *in* **schimpfen wie ein ~spatz** *(ugs.)* really create *(coll.)*; **~stock der** cane [walking-stick]; **~zange die** foot-print; **~zucker der** cane-sugar

Roh·seide die raw silk

roh·seiden *Adj.* raw-silk *attrib.*

Roh·stoff der raw material

Rohstoff-: ~mangel der; *o. Pl.* lack of raw materials; **~preis der** raw material price; **~reserven** *Pl.* reserves of raw materials

Roh-: ~übersetzung die rough translation; **~zucker der** raw *or* unrefined sugar; **~zu·stand der** raw state; **im ~zustand** in a raw state; *(von Gütern)* in an unfinished state; *(von einem Schriftstück usw.)* in a rough draft

Rokoko ['rɔkoko] **das; ~[s]** rococo; *(Zeit)* rococo period

Rokoko·möbel das rococo furniture

Rolladen ['rɔla:dn̩] **der; ~s, Rolläden** ['rɔlɛ:dn̩] [roller] shutter

Roll·bahn die *(Flugw.)* taxiway

Röllchen ['rœlçən] **das; ~s, ~ a)** *(Spule)* little reel *or* spool; **b)** *(etwas Zusammengerolltes)* little roll; **c)** *(Walze)* little roller; **d)** *s.* **Rolle d**

Rolle ['rɔlə] **die; ~, ~n a)** *(Spule)* reel; spool; **eine ~ Film** a spool of film; *(Schmalfilm)* a reel of film; **b)** *(zylindrischer [Hohl]körper; Zusammengerolltes)* roll; *(zum Verschicken von Plakaten o. ä.)* [cardboard] tube; *(von Papier zum Drucken)* reel; *(Schrift~)* scroll; **eine ~ Bindfaden/Drops/Markstücke/Kekse** a reel of string/tube of fruit drops/roll of one-mark pieces/[round] packet of biscuits; **c)** *(Walze)* roller; *(Teig~)* rolling-pin; **d)** *(Rad)* [small] wheel; *(an Möbeln usw.)* castor; *(für Gardine, Schiebetür usw.)* runner; *(mit einer Rille für ein Seil o. ä.)* pulley; **e)** *(Turnen, Kunstflug)* roll; **eine ~ [vorwärts/rückwärts] machen** do a [forward/backward] roll; **f)** *(Theater, Film usw., fig.)* role; part; *(Soziol.)* role; **sich in die ~ eines anderen versetzen** put oneself in sb. else's position; **[bei jmdm./einer Sache] eine entscheidende/überragende ~ spielen** be of crucial/overriding importance [to sb./for sth.]; **es spielt keine ~:** it is of no importance; *(es macht nichts aus)* it doesn't matter; *(es gehört nicht zur Sache)* it is irrelevant; **Geld spielt [bei ihm] keine ~:** money is no object [for him]; **solche Erwägungen dürfen dabei keine ~ spielen** such considerations must not be allowed to enter into it *or* influence things; **aus der ~ fallen** forget oneself; **g)** *(Radsport)* roller *(on a pacing motor cycle)*; *(fig. ugs.)* **von der ~ kommen** get left behind; lose ground

rollen 1. *tr. V.* **a)** roll; *(im Rollstuhl)* wheel; **die Augen ~:** roll one's eyes; **das R ~:** roll one's r's; **sich** *(Dat.)* **eine Zigarette ~:** roll oneself a cigarette; **b)** *(auf~, zusammen~, ein~)* roll up ⟨*blanket, carpet, map, etc.*⟩; **jmdn./etw./sich in eine Decke ~:** roll sb./sth./oneself up in a blanket; **c)** *(aus~)* roll out ⟨*dough*⟩. **2.** *itr. V.* **a)** *mit sein* ⟨*ball, wheel, etc.*⟩ roll; ⟨*vehicle*⟩ move; ⟨*aircraft*⟩ taxi; **mit den Augen ~:** roll one's eyes; **ins Rollen kommen** start to move; get under way *(lit. or fig.)*; *(unbeabsichtigt)* start to move; **es werden Köpfe ~** *(fig.)* heads will roll; **etw. ins Rollen bringen** set sth. in motion; get sth. going *(lit. or fig.)*; *(unbeabsichtigt)* set sth. moving; **b)** *(Seemannsspr.: schlingern [und stampfen])* ‹*ship*› roll [and pitch]; **c)** *(donnern) mit Richtungsangabe mit sein* ‹*thunder, guns, echo*› rumble. **3.** *refl. V.* **a)** *(sich ein~)* ‹*paper, carpet*› curl [up]; **b)** *(sich wälzen)* roll; **er rollte sich in die Rückenlage** he rolled over on to his back

rollen-, Rollen-: ~fach das *(Theater)* type of role; **das ~fach der Naiven** the ingénue type of role; **~förmig** *Adj.* cylindrical; **~konflikt der** *(Soziol.)* role conflict; **~lager das** *(Technik)* roller bearing; **~spiel das** *(Sozialpsych.)* role-playing *no pl., no art.*; role-play *no pl., no art.*; **~tausch der** exchange of roles; *(bei entgegengesetzten Rollen)* role reversal; **~verhalten das** role[-specific] behaviour; **~verteilung die** *(Sozialpsych.)* allocation of roles

Roller der; ~s, ~ a) scooter; **~ fahren** ride a/one's scooter; **b)** *(Fußball)* half-hit shot along the ground; **c)** *(Deo~)* roll-on [container]

rollern *itr. V.; meist, mit Richtungsangabe nur, mit sein* ride a/one's scooter

Roll-: ~feld das [operational] airfield; landing-field; **~film der** roll film; **~geld das** *(Eisenb.)* parcel freight [charge] *(for delivery to and collection from station or depot)*; **~gut das** *(Eisenb.)* freight *(delivered to and collected from station or depot)*; **~kommando das** party of bully-boys; **~kragen der** polo-neck; **~kragen·pullover der** polo-neck[ed] sweater; **~kur die** *(Med.) treatment in which the patient takes medicine and then lies in different positions;* **~laden der** *s.* **Rolladen; ~mops der** rollmops

Rollo ['rɔlo] **das; ~s, ~s** [roller] blind

Roll-: ~schinken der rolled smoked ham; **~schuh der** roller-skate; **~schuh laufen** roller-skate

Rollschuh-: ~bahn die roller-skating rink; **~laufen das** roller-skating *no art.*; **~läufer der** roller-skater

Roll-: ~splitt der loose chippings *pl.*; **~sprung der** *(Leichtathletik)* Western roll; **~stuhl der** wheelchair; **~stuhl·fahrer der** person in a wheelchair; **~treppe die** escalator

[1]Rom [ro:m] *(das)*; **~s** Rome; **viele Wege führen nach ~** *(Spr.)* there is more than one way to skin a cat *(prov.)*; **Zustände wie im alten ~** *(fig.)* everything in chaos; **~ ist auch nicht an einem Tag erbaut worden** *(Spr.)* Rome wasn't built in a day *(prov.)*

[2]Rom [rɔm] **der; ~s, ~a** European gypsy

Roman [ro'ma:n] **der; ~s, ~e** novel; **einen ganzen/langen ~ erzählen** *(fig.)* tell a very long story *or (derog.)* a long rigmarole; **erzähl keine ~e** *(fig.)* don't tell stories; *(faß dich kürzer)* we don't want any long rigmaroles

Romancier [romã'si̯e:] **der; ~s, ~s** novelist

Romane [ro'ma:nə] **der; ~n, ~n** speaker of a Romance language; Latin

Roman-: ~figur die character from *or* in a novel; **eine ~figur bei Dickens** a character from *or* in a Dickens novel; **~form die** novel form; **in ~form** in the form of a novel; **~heft das** [paper-covered] novelette

Romani ['romani] **das; ~s** *(Sprachw.)* Romany

Romanik [ro'ma:nɪk] **die; ~:** Romanesque; *(Zeit)* Romanesque period

Romanin die; ~, ~nen *s.* **Romane;** *s. auch* **-in**

romanisch 1. *Adj.* **a)** Romance ‹*language, literature*›; Latin ‹*people, country, charm*›; ‹*Department*› of Romance Studies; **b)** *(Kunstwiss.: der Romanik)* Romanesque. **2.** *adv.* ‹*build*› in a Romanesque style

romanisieren *tr. V.* **a)** *(romanisch machen)* give ‹*town etc.*› a Latin character; **b)** *(hist.: römisch machen)* romanize ‹*country etc.*›

Romanist der; ~en, ~en Romance scholar; Romanist; *(Student)* student of Romance languages and literature

Romanistik [roma'nɪstɪk] **die; ~:** Romance studies *pl., no art.*; *(Sprache und Literatur)* Romance languages and literature *no art.*

Romanistin die; ~, ~nen *s.* **Romanist**

romanistisch *Adj.; nicht präd.* Romance ‹*studies*›; ‹*periodical*› for Romance studies

Romantik [ro'mantɪk] **die; ~ a)** *(romantischer Charakter)* romanticism; romantic nature; **die ~ des Zigeunerlebens/der Straße** the romance of gypsy life/of the road; **b)** *(Literaturw., Musik usw.) (Bewegung)* Romanticism *no art.*; Romantic movement; *(Epoche)* Romantic period; **die jüngere/ältere ~:** the younger/older Romantics *pl.*

Romantiker der; ~s, ~, Romantikerin die; ~, ~nen a) *(Kunstwiss.)* Romantic; **b)** *(romantischer Mensch)* romantic

romantisch 1. *Adj.* **a)** romantic; **b)** *(Literaturw., Musik usw.)* Romantic. **2.** *adv.* romantically; **~ veranlagt sein** have a romantic disposition

romantisieren *tr. V.* romanticize

Roman·werk das a) *(Roman)* novel; **b)** *(Romane eines Autors)* novels *pl.*

Romanze [ro'mantsə] **die; ~, ~n** *(Literaturw., Musik, fig.)* romance

Römer ['rø:mɐ] **der; ~s, ~ a)** *(Person)* Roman; **die [alten] ~:** the [ancient] Romans; **b)** *(Weinglas)* rummer

Römer·brief der Epistle to the Romans

Römerin die; ~, ~nen Roman; *s. auch* **-in**

Römer·topf Ⓦⓩ **der** oval earthenware cooking pot; ≈ cooking brick

römisch 1. *Adj.* Roman. **2.** *adv.* **das ~ besetzte Gallien** the part of Gaul occupied by the Romans

römisch-katholisch 1. *Adj.* Roman Catholic. **2.** *adv.* **~ getauft** baptized into the Roman Catholic church

röm.-kath. *Abk.* **römisch-katholisch** RC

Rommé ['rɔme] **das; ~s, ~s** *(Kartenspiele)* rummy *no art.*

Rondeau [rõ'do] **das; ~s, ~s a)** *(Literaturw.)* rondeau; **b)** *(österr.: Beet, Platz) s.* **Rondell a, b**

Rondell [rɔn'dɛl] **das; ~s, ~e a)** *(Beet)* circular flower-bed; **b)** *(Platz)* circus; **c)** *(österr.: Weg)* circular path; **d)** *(Archit.: Turm)* round tower

Rondo ['rɔndo] **das; ~s, ~s a)** *(Literaturw.)* rondeau; **b)** *(Musik)* rondo

röntgen ['rœntgn̩] *tr. V.* X-ray; **sich** *(Akk.)*/**sich** *(Dat.)* **den Magen ~ lassen** have an X-ray/have one's stomach X-rayed

Röntgen-: ~aufnahme die, ~bild das X-ray [image/photograph *or* picture]; **~gerät das** X-ray apparatus

röntgenisieren *tr. V. (österr.) s.* **röntgen**

Röntgenologe [rœntgeno'lo:gə] **der; ~n, ~n** radiologist

Röntgenologie die; ~: radiology *no art.*

Röntgenologin die; ~, ~nen radiologist

Röntgen-: ~schirm der X-ray screen; **~strahlen** *Pl.* X-rays; **~therapie die** X-ray treatment *no indef. art.*; **eine ~therapie** a course of X-ray treatment; **~untersuchung die** X-ray examination

Roquefort ['rɔkfo:ɐ̯] **der; ~s, ~s** Roquefort

Ro-Ro-Schiff [ro'ro:-] **das** ro-ro *or* roll-on roll-off ship

rosa ['ro:za] **1.** *indekl. Adj.* pink; *s. auch* **Brille. 2.** *adv.* pink

Rosa das; ~s, ~ *od.* **~s** pink

rosa-: ~farben, ~farbig *Adj.* pink; **~rot** *Adj.* [deep] pink; *(fig.)* rosy; *s. auch* **Brille**

rösch [rø:ʃ] *Adj. (südd.)* crisp

Röschen ['rø:sçən] **das; ~s, ~ a)** *(kleine Rose)* [little] rose; **b)** *(Blumenkohl~)* [cauliflower] floweret; *(Rosenkohl~)* [Brussels] sprout

Rose ['ro:zə] **die; ~, ~n a)** rose; **sie sind nicht [gerade] auf ~n gebettet** their life is no bed of roses; **keine ~ ohne Dornen** *(Sprichw.)* no rose without a thorn; **b)** *(Fenster~)* rose-window; **c)** *(Jägerspr.)* burr

rosé [ro'ze:] **1.** *indekl. Adj.* pale pink. **2.** *adv.* pale pink

[1]Rosé das; ~s, ~ *od.* **~s** pale pink

[2]Rosé der; ~s, ~s rosé [wine]

rosen-, Rosen-: ~beet das rose-bed; **~blatt das** rose-petal; *(Laubblatt)* rose-leaf; **~blüte die a)** rose[-bloom]; **b)** *o. Pl. (das Blühen)* flowering period for roses; **die ~blüte hat begonnen** the roses have started to flower *or* bloom; **~duft der** scent of roses; **~garten der** rose-garden; **~gewächs das** *(Bot.)* rose; rosaceous plant; **die ~gewächse** the Rosaceae; **~holz das** rosewood; **~kohl der;** *o. Pl.* [Brussels] sprouts *pl.*; **~kranz der** *(kath. Kirche)* rosary; **einen ~kranz beten** say a rosary; **~montag der** the day before Shrove Tuesday; **~montags·zug der** *carnival procession on the day before Shrove Tuesday;* **~öl das** attar of roses; **~quarz der** rose quartz; **~rot** *Adj.* deep pink; **~stock der** rose-tree; standard rose; **~strauß der** bunch *or* bouquet of roses; **~wasser das** *o. Pl.* rose-water; **~züchter der** rose-grower

Rosette [ro'zɛtə] **die; ~, ~n a)** *(Archit.)* rose-window; **b)** *(Verzierung, Bot.)* rosette

Rosé·wein der rosé wine

rosig 1. *Adj.* **a)** rosy ‹*face, complexion, etc.*›; pink ‹*piglet etc.*›; **~ und gesund aussehen** be glowing with health; **b)** *(fig.)* rosy; optimistic ‹*mood*›; **etw. in den ~sten Farben schildern** paint sth. in the most glowing colours. **2.** *adv.* **ihm geht es nicht gerade ~:** things aren't too good with him

Rosine [ro'zi:nə] **die; ~, ~n** raisin; *(Korinthe)* currant; **[große] ~n im Kopf haben** *(fig. ugs.)* have big ideas; **sich** *(Dat.)* **die ~n herauspicken** *od.* **aus dem Kuchen picken** *(fig. ugs.)* take the pick of the bunch [for oneself]

Rosinen-: ~brot *das* currant bread; *(Laib)* currant loaf; **~kuchen der** currant cake

Rosmarin ['ro:smari:n] **der; ~s** rosemary

Roß [rɔs] **das; Rosses, Rosse** *od.* **Rösser** ['rœsɐ] **a)** *(geh.; südd., österr., schweiz. noch Normalspr.)* horse; steed *(poet./joc.)*; **hoch zu ~:** on horseback; *(scherzh.)* on one's [trusty] steed *(joc.)*; **auf dem** *od.* **seinem hohen ~ sitzen** be on one's high horse; **von seinem** *od.* **vom hohen ~ herunterkommen** *od.* **-steigen** get down off one's high horse; **~ und Reiter nennen** name names; **b)** *Pl.* **Rösser** *(ugs.: Trottel)* fool; idiot

Roß- *s. auch* **Pferde-**

Rössel ['rœsl̩] **das; ~s, ~ a)** *(landsch.)* small horse; **b)** *(Schach)* knight

Rössel·sprung der *puzzle in which certain syllables make up a phrase or saying when taken in a sequence of knight's moves in a squared diagram*

Roß-: ~haar das horsehair; **~kastanie die** horse-chestnut; **~kur die** *(ugs.)* drastic cure *or* remedy; **~täuscher der** *(abwertend)* con man *(coll.)*; **~täuscherei die** *(abwertend)* confidence *or (coll.)* con trick

[1]Rost [rɔst] **der; ~[e]s, ~e a)** *(Gitter)* grating; grid; *(eines Ofens, einer Feuerstelle)* grate; *(Brat~)* grill; *(im Freien)* barbecue; **vom ~** *(Gastr.)* fresh from the grill; **auf dem ~ gegrillte Steaks** grilled steaks; *(im Freien)* barbecued steaks; **b)** *(Bett~)* base; frame

[2]Rost der; -[e]s *(auch Bot.)* rust; **~ ansetzen** begin to rust; go rusty

rost-, Rost-: ~beständig *Adj.* rust-resistant; *(absolut)* rust-proof; **~bildung die** rust-formation; rusting; **~braten der** grilled steak; *(österr.: Entrecote)* entrecôte; rib steak; **~brat·wurst die** grilled sausage; **~braun** *Adj.* reddish-brown; russet; auburn ‹*hair*›

Röst·brot ['rœst-, 'rø:st-] **das** toast
Röste ['rø:stə] **die; ~, ~n** *(Hüttenw.)* roasting furnace
rọsten *itr. V.; auch mit sein* rust; *(auch fig.)* get rusty; **alte Liebe rostet nicht** *(scherzh.)* old habits die hard
rösten ['rœstn̩, 'rø:stn̩] *tr. V.* **a)** roast ‹*coffee, malt, chestnuts, etc.*›; toast ‹*bread*›; **sich [in der Sonne] ~ lassen** roast oneself in the sun; **b)** *(bes. südd., österr., schweiz.: braten)* roast ‹*meat*›; *(auf dem Grill)* grill ‹*meat*›; *(in der Pfanne)* fry ‹*meat, fish, egg, potatoes, etc.*›; *(in der heißen Asche/Glut)* bake ‹*potatoes*›; **c)** *(Hüttenw.)* roast, calcine ‹*ore*›
Rọ̈ster der; ~s, ~ a) *(Toaster)* toaster; **b)** *(österr.) (Zwetschgenmus)* plum purée; *(Holunderbeerenmus)* elderberry purée
Rösterei die; ~, ~en [coffee-/etc.] roasting establishment
rọst-, Rọst-: ~farben, ~farbig *Adj.* rust-coloured; russet; **~fleck der a)** rust stain; **b)** *(rostige Stelle)* rust spot; *(größer)* patch of rust; **~fraß der** rusting process; rusting *no art.*; **~frei** *Adj.* **a)** *(nicht rostend)* stainless ‹*steel*›; **b)** *(ohne Rost)* rust-free
Rösti ['rø:sti] **die; ~** *(schweiz. Kochk.)* thinly sliced fried potatoes *pl.*
rọstig *Adj.* rusty
Rọ̈st·kartoffeln *Pl.* fried potatoes
rọst-, Rọst-: ~laube die *(ugs.)* picturesque old rust-heap; **~rot** *Adj.* rust-coloured; russet; **~schutz der a)** protection *no art.* against rust; rust protection *no art.*; **b)** *(Mittel)* rust-proofing agent; **~schutzfarbe die** anti-rust paint; **~schutz·mittel das** *s.* **~schutz b**; **~stelle die** patch of rust; *(kleiner)* rust spot
rot [ro:t] **1.** *Adj.* red; **ein Roter** *(ugs.: Wein)* a red [wine]; **ein Roter/eine Rote** *(ugs.) (Mensch mit roten Haaren)* a redhead; *(Sozialist)* a red *(coll.)*; a leftie *(coll.)*; **der Rote Platz** Red Square; **die Rote Armee** *(hist.)* the Red Army; **das Rote Meer** the Red Sea; **das Rote Kreuz** the Red Cross; **der Rote Halbmond/Löwe/Davidstern/die Rote Sonne** the Red Crescent/Lion/Star of David/Sun; **~ werden** turn red; ‹*person*› go red; blush; ‹*traffic-light*› change to red; **er bekam einen ~en Kopf** he went red in the face; he blushed; **heute ~, morgen tot** *(Spr.)* here today, gone tomorrow; **lieber ~ als tot** *(ugs.)* better red than dead; *s. auch* **Faden a; Zahl. 2.** *adv.* red; **~ gepunktet** with red dots *postpos., not pred.*; **etw. ~ schreiben/anstreichen** write/mark sth. in red; **[im Gesicht] ~ anlaufen** go red in the face
Rọt das; ~s, ~ *od.* **~s a)** red; *(Schminke)* rouge; **die Ampel zeigt ~:** the traffic-lights are red; **bei ~ über die Kreuzung fahren** cross the junction on the red; **b)** *(Spielkartenfarbe)* hearts *pl.*; *s. auch* **²Pik**
Rotarier [ro'ta:ri̯ɐ] **der; ~s, ~:** Rotarian
Rotarmist ['ro:tarmɪst] **der; ~en, ~en** *(hist.)* Red Army soldier
Rotation [rota'tsi̯o:n] **die; ~, ~en** rotation
Rotatiọns-: ~achse die axis [of rotation]; **~druck der;** *o. Pl.* rotary printing *no art.*; **~fläche die** *(Math.)* surface of revolution; **~körper der** *(Math.)* solid of revolution; **~maschine die** *(Druckw.)* rotary press
rọt-, Rọt-: ~auge das *(Zool.)* roach; **~backig, ~bäckig** *Adj.* rosy-cheeked ‹*child, girl*›; ruddy-cheeked ‹*old man, farmer, etc.*›; **~barsch der** rose-fish; **~bart der** *(ugs.)* red-beard; red-bearded type *(coll.)*; **~blond** *Adj.* sandy ‹*hair*›; sandy-haired ‹*person*›; **~braun** *Adj.* reddish-brown; russet; **~buche die** [European] beech; **~dorn der** [pink] hawthorn
Röte ['rø:tə] **die; ~, ~n a)** *o. Pl.* red[ness]; **eine ~ stieg ihm ins Gesicht** his face reddened; he blushed; **b)** *(Bot.)* madder
Rötel ['rø:tl̩] **der; ~s, ~:** red chalk
Röteln ['rø:tl̩n] *Pl.* **[die] ~:** German measles *sing.*
rọ̈ten 1. *tr. V.* redden; make red; **Scham rötete ihr Gesicht** her face went red with embarrassment. **2.** *refl. V.* go *or* turn red
rọt-, Rọt-: ~fuchs der a) *(Tier, Pelz)* red fox; **b)** *(Pferd)* chestnut; *(heller)* sorrel; **c)** *(ugs.: Rothaariger)* redhead; **~gardist der, ~gardistin die** Red Guard; **~gesichtig** *Adj.* red-faced; *(gesund, mit roten Backen)* ruddy-cheeked; **~geweint** *Adj.* ‹*eyes*› red from crying; **~glühend** *Adj.* red-hot; **~glut die** red heat; **~gold das** red gold; **~grün** *Adj. (Politik)* ‹*coalition*› of Greens and Socialists; red-green ‹*coalition*›; **~grün·blindheit** [-'---] **die** *(Med.)* [red-green] colour-blindness; daltonism; **~guß der** red brass; **~haarig** *Adj.* red-haired; **eine Rothaarige/ein Rothaariger** a redhead; **~haut die** *(ugs. scherzh.)* redskin; **~hirsch der** red deer
rotieren [ro'ti:rən] *itr. V.* **a)** rotate; **b)** *(ugs.: hektisch sein)* flap *(coll.)*; get into a flap *(coll.)*; **er ist am Rotieren** he is in a flap *(coll.)*
Rọt-: ~käppchen (das) Little Red Riding Hood; **~kehlchen das; ~s, ~:** robin [redbreast]; **~kohl der,** *(bes. südd., österr.)* **~kraut das** red cabbage; **~kreuzschwester die** Red Cross nurse; **~lauf der** *(Tiermed.)* swine erysipelas
rötlich ['rø:tlɪç] *Adj.* reddish
rötlich·braun *Adj.* reddish-brown
rọt-, Rọt-: ~licht das; *o. Pl.* red light; **bei ~licht** under a red light; **~liegende das; ~n** *(Geol.)* Rothliegende; **~nasig** *Adj.* red-nosed
Rotor ['ro:tɔr] **der; ~s, ~en** [ro'to:rən] *(Technik)* rotor
rọt-, Rọt-: ~schwanz der, ~schwänzchen das redstart; **~|sehen** *unr. itr. V. (ugs.)* see red; **~stichig** [~ʃtɪçɪç] *Adj. (Fot.)* with a red cast *postpos., not pred.*; **~stichig sein** have a red cast; **~stift der** red pencil; *(Kugelschreiber)* red ballpoint; **dem ~stift zum Opfer fallen** *(aufgegeben werden)* be scrapped; *(gestrichen werden)* be deleted; **den ~stift ansetzen** *(fig.)* make economies; **~tanne die** common *or* Norway spruce
Rotte ['rɔtə] **die; ~, ~n a)** gang; mob; **b)** *(Milit.)* pair [operating together]; **c)** *(Jägerspr.) (von Wildschweinen)* herd; *(von Wölfen)* pack; **d)** *(Eisenb.)* gang
rọtten *tr. V. (Textilw.)* ret ‹*flax, hemp*›
Rọtten·führer der *(Eisenb.)* foreman
Rottweiler ['rɔtvai̯lɐ] **der; ~s, ~** *(Hunderasse)* Rottweiler
Rotunde [ro'tʊndə] **die; ~, ~n** *(Archit.)* rotunda
Rọ̈tung die; ~, ~en reddening
rọt·wangig [-vaŋɪç] *Adj. (geh.) s.* **rotbackig**
Rọt·wein der red wine
Rọtwein-: ~glas das glass for red wine; **~fleck der** red wine stain
Rọtwelsch das; ~[s] thieves' cant *or* argot
Rọt-: ~wild das *(Jägerspr.)* red deer; **~wurst die** blood sausage
Rotz [rɔts] **der; ~es** *(salopp)* **a)** snot *(sl.)*; **frech wie ~** *(salopp)* cheeky as anything; **~ und Wasser heulen** *(salopp)* cry one's eyes out; **der ganze ~** *(salopp)* the whole bloody *(Brit. sl.) or (coll.)* damn lot; **b)** *(Tiermed.)* glanders *pl.*
Rọtz·bengel der *(derb abwertend)* snotty brat *(sl.)*
rọtzen *(derb)* **1.** *itr. V.* **a)** blow one's nose loudly; **b)** *(Schleim in den Mund ziehen)* sniff back one's snot *(sl.)*; **c)** *(ausspucken)* gob *(coarse)*. **2.** *tr. V.* spit
Rọtz·fahne die *(derb)* snot-rag *(sl.)*
rọtz·frẹch *(salopp)* **1.** *Adj.* insolent; snotty *(sl.)*; **ein ~er Bengel** a snotty little brat *(sl.)*. **2.** *adv.* insolently; snottily *(sl.)*
rọtzig 1. *Adj.* **a)** *(derb)* snotty *(sl.)* ‹*nose, handkerchief, child*›; **b)** *(salopp: frech)* insolent; snotty *(sl.)*. **2.** *adv. (salopp abwertend)* insolently; snottily *(sl.)*
Rọtz·nase die a) *(derb)* snotty nose *(sl.)*; **b)** *(salopp abwertend: Bengel)* snotty little brat *(sl.)*
rotznäsig [-nɛ:zɪç] *(derb abwertend)* **1.** *Adj.* **a)** snotty-nosed *(sl.)*; **b)** *(ungezogen)* snotty *(sl.)*. **2.** *adv.* snottily *(sl.)*
Rouge [ru:ʒ] **das; ~s, ~s** rouge
Roulade [ru:la:də] **die; ~, ~n** *(Kochk.)* [beef/veal/pork] olive
Rouleau [ru'lo:] **das; ~s, ~s** [roller] blind
Roulett [ru'lɛt] **das; ~[e]s, ~e, Roulette** [ru'lɛtə] **das; ~s, ~s** roulette
Route ['ru:tə] **die; ~, ~n** route
Routine [ru'ti:nə] **die; ~ a)** *(Erfahrung)* experience; *(Übung)* practice; *(Fertigkeit)* proficiency; expertise; **b)** *(gewohnheitsmäßiger Ablauf)* routine *no def. art.*; **in ~ erstarrt sein** have got into a rut
routịne-, Routịne-: ~angelegenheit die routine matter; **~mäßig 1.** *Adj.* routine; **2.** *adv.* as a matter of routine; **~sache die** *s.* **~angelegenheit**; **~untersuchung die** routine examination
Routinier [ruti'ni̯e:] **der; ~s, ~s** experienced man; *(Experte)* expert
routiniert [ruti'ni:ɐ̯t] **1.** *Adj. (gewandt)* expert; skilled; *(erfahren)* experienced; **ihr Auftreten ist mir zu ~:** her manner is too slick for my taste. **2.** *adv.* expertly; skilfully
Rowdy ['raudi] **der; ~s, ~s** *(abwertend)* hooligan
Rọwdytum das; ~s *(abwertend)* hooliganism
Royalist [rọaja'lɪst] **der; ~en, ~en** royalist
royalịstisch 1. *Adj.* royalist. **2.** *adv.* along royalist lines; **~ eingestellt sein** have royalist ideas
Ruanda ['rụanda] **(das); ~s** Rwanda
rubbeln ['rʊbl̩n] *tr., itr. V. (bes. nordd.)* rub [vigorously]
Rübe ['ry:bə] **die; ~, ~n a)** turnip; *(Zucker~)* [sugar-]beet; **rote ~:** beetroot; **gelbe ~** *(südd.)* carrot; **b)** *(salopp: Kopf)* nut *(sl.)*; **eins auf die ~ kriegen** get a bonk *or* bash on the nut *(sl.)*; **~ runter** *od.* **ab!** off with his/her head!
Rubel ['ru:bl̩] **der; ~s, ~:** rouble; **der ~ rollt** *(fig. ugs.)* the money keeps rolling in
Rụ̈ben-: ~kraut das; *o. Pl. (westdt.)* [sugar-beet] syrup; **~zucker der** beet sugar
rüber ['rʏ:bɐ] *Adv. (ugs.)* over
rụ̈ber-: ~|dürfen *unr. itr. V.* be allowed over; **über etw.** *(Akk.)* **~dürfen** be allowed to cross sth.; **~|gehen** *unr. itr. V.; mit sein* go over; **bei Rot ~gehen** cross over when the lights are red; **~|kommen** *unr. itr. V.; mit sein* **a)** come over; **komm doch einen Moment ~:** come over here a moment; **b)** *(~können)* manage to get over/across; **über die Straße/die Mauer nicht ~kommen** be unable to cross the road/get over the wall; **c)** *(salopp: verstanden werden)* come across; **~|können** *unr. itr. V.* be able to get over *or* across; **über etw.** *(Akk.)* **~können** be able to cross sth.; **~|müssen** *unr. itr. V.* have to get over *or* across; **über etw.** *(Akk.)* **~müssen** have to cross sth.; **er muß wieder ~ nach Amerika** he has to go back to America; **~|schicken** *tr. V.* send over; **~|sollen** *itr. V.* be supposed to go over; **soll der Schrank auch ~?** is the cupboard to go over there too?; **~|steigen** *unr. itr. V.; mit sein* **[über etw.** *(Akk.)***] ~steigen** climb over [sth.]; **~|wollen** *unr. itr. V.* want to get over *or* across; **über etw.** *(Akk.)* **~wollen** want to cross sth.; **[in den Westen/Osten] ~wollen** want to cross over to the West/East
Rübezahl ['ry:bətsa:l] **(der); ~s** Rübezahl *(spirit of the Sudeten Mountains)*
Rubikon ['ru:bikɔn] **der; ~s** *(hist.)* *in:* **den ~ überschreiten** *(geh.)* cross the Rubicon
Rubin [ru'bi:n] **der; ~s, ~e** ruby
rubịn·rot *Adj.* ruby[-red]
Rüb- ['ry:p-]: **~kohl der** *(schweiz.)* kohlrabi; **~öl das** rape-oil

Rubrik [ru'bri:k] **die;** ~, ~**en** *(Spalte)* column; *(Zeitungs~)* column; section; *(fig.: Kategorie)* category; **unter der ~ ...:** under the heading [of] ...; *(in der Zeitung usw.)* in the ... section

Rüb·samen der oilseed rape

Ruch [ru:x] **der;** ~[e]s [bad] reputation; **im ~ der Korruption stehen** have the reputation of being corrupt

ruch·bar *Adj. in* ~ **werden** *(geh.)* become known

ruch·los *(geh.)* **1.** *Adj.* dastardly; heinous ‹*crime*›. **2.** *adv.* in a dastardly fashion

Ruchlosigkeit die; ~: dastardliness

Ruck [rʊk] **der;** ~[e]s, ~e jerk; **ein ~ nach links** *(Politik)* a sudden swing to the left; **in einem ~** *(fig. ugs.)* in one go; **sich** *(Dat.)* **einen ~ geben** *(fig.)* pull oneself together

Rück·antwort die reply; **um ~ wird gebeten** please reply

ruck·artig 1. *Adj.* jerky. **2.** *adv. (mit einem Ruck)* with a jerk

rück-, Rück-: ~besinnung die recollection **(auf** + *Akk.* of); **eine ~besinnung auf bewährte Tugenden** a return to traditional virtues; **~bezüglich** *(Sprachw.)* **1.** *Adj.* reflexive; **2.** *adv.* reflexively; **~bildung die a)** *(Biol.)* atrophy; **b)** *(Med.)* regression; **c)** *(Sprachw.)* back-formation; **~blende die** flashback; **~blick der** look back **(auf** + *Akk.* at); retrospective view **(auf** + *Akk.* of); **im ~blick** in retrospect; **~blickend 1.** *Adj.* retrospective; **2.** *adv.* retrospectively; in retrospect; **~datieren** *tr. V.; nur im Inf. u. 2. Part.* backdate

ruckeln ['rʊkl̩n] *itr. V. (bes. nordd., mitteld.)* give a slight jolt

rucken 1. *itr. V.* jerk; give a jerk; ‹*car*› jolt; give a jolt; **2.** *tr. V.* jerk

rücken ['rʏkn̩] **1.** *tr. V.* move; **den Tisch an die Wand ~:** move *or* push the table against the wall; **es ließ sich nicht von der Stelle ~:** it was impossible to shift it; **etw. in ein völlig neues Licht ~** *(fig.)* show sth. in a completely new light. **2.** *itr. V.* **a)** *mit sein* move; **der Zeiger rückte auf 12** the hand moved up to 12; **mit seinem Stuhl näher an den Tisch ~:** move one's chair closer to the table; **jmdm. auf den Balg** *od.* **Pelz** *od.* **die Pelle ~** *(ugs.)* squeeze right up to sb; **die Polizei ist mir auf die Pelle** *od.* **den Pelz gerückt** *(fig.)* the police are breathing down my neck; **kannst du ein bißchen ~?** could you move up/over a bit?; **mit dem König ein Feld nach vorn ~** *(Schach)* move the king forwards one square; **ins Feld/ins Manöver ~** *(Milit.)* move into the field/go on manœuvres; **in weite Ferne ~** *(fig.)* recede into the distance; ‹*project*› become an increasingly remote possibility; **b) an etw.** *(Dat.)* **~** *(ziehen)* pull at sth.; *(schieben)* push at sth.; **an seiner Krawatte/Brille ~:** adjust one's tie/glasses; **hört auf, mit den Stühlen zu ~:** stop shifting your chairs

Rücken der; ~s, ~: **a)** back; **ein Stück vom ~** *(Rindfleisch)* a piece of chine; *(Hammel, Reh)* a piece of saddle; **auf dem ~ liegen** lie on one's back; **legen Sie sich bitte auf den ~!** please lie [down] on your back; **jmdm. die Hände auf den ~ binden** tie sb.'s hands behind his/her back; **~ gegen** *od.* **an ~ stehen** stand back to back; **es lief mir [heiß und kalt] über den ~:** [hot and cold] shivers ran down my spine; **die Sonne/den Wind im ~ haben** have the sun/wind behind one; **verlängerter ~** *(scherzh.)* backside; posterior *(joc.)*; **jmdm. den ~ zuwenden** turn one's back on sb.; **jmdm./einer Sache den ~ kehren** *(fig.)* turn one's back on sb./sth.; give sb./sth. up; **jmdm. den ~ stärken** *od.* **steifen** *(fig.)* give sb. moral support; **den ~ frei haben** *(fig.)* be free of any obligations; not be tied [down]; **sich** *(Dat.)* **den ~ freihalten** *(fig.)* not commit oneself; not enter into any obligations; **jmdm. den ~ freihalten** *od.* **decken** *(fig.)* ensure sb. is not troubled with other problems; **hinter jmds. ~** *(Dat.) (fig.)* behind sb.'s back; **im ~** *(fig.)* behind one; **er hat die Gewerkschaft im ~** *(fig.)* he has the backing of the union; **jmdm. in den ~ fallen** *(fig.)* stab sb. in the back; **mit dem ~ an der** *od.* **zur Wand** *(fig.)* with one's back to the wall; **mit dem ~ zur Wand stehen** *(fig.)* have one's back to the wall; **b)** *(Rückseite)* back; *(Buch~)* spine; *(der Nase)* bridge; *(des Berges)* ridge; **c)** *o. Pl. s.* **~schwimmen**

rücken-, Rücken-: ~aus·schnitt der back neckline; **mit tiefem ~ausschnitt** with a low[-cut] back; **~deckung die a)** *(bes. Mittel)* rear cover; **b)** *(Unterstützung)* backing; **jmdm. ~deckung geben** give sb. one's backing; **~flosse die** dorsal fin; **~frei** *Adj.* backless ‹*dress*›; **~lage die** supine position; **in [der] ~lage** on one's back; **~lehne die** [chair/seat] back; **~mark das** *(Anat.)* spinal marrow *or* cord

Rücken·mark[s]-: ~entzündung die *(Med.)* myelitis *no indef. art.*; **~erweichung die** *(Med.)* myelomalacia *no indef. art.*; **~punktion die** *(Med.)* spinal puncture

Rücken-: ~muskulatur die back *or* *(Anat.)* dorsal muscles *pl.*; **~schild das** *(Bürow.)* spine label; **~schmerzen** *Pl.* backache *sing.*; **~schwimmen das** backstroke; **~stärkung die** [moral] support

Rück·entwicklung die *s.* **Rückbildung a, b**

Rücken-: ~wind der tail *or* following wind; **~wind haben** have a tail *or* following wind; *(fig.)* be making good progress; **mit ~wind spielen** play with the wind behind one; **~wirbel der** *(Anat.)* dorsal vertebra

rück-, Rück-: ~erinnerung die recollection; reminiscence; **~|erstatten** *tr. V.; nur im Inf. u. 2. Part.* repay; **jmdm. die Reisekosten ~erstatten** repay *or* reimburse sb. his/her travelling expenses; **~erstattung die** repayment; reimbursement; *(von Steuern)* rebate; **~fahr·karte die; ~fahr·schein der** return [ticket]; **~fahr·scheinwerfer der** *(Kfz-W.)* reversing light; **~fahrt die** return journey; **auf der ~fahrt** on the return journey *or* way back; **~fall der a)** *(Med., auch fig.)* relapse; **einen ~fall bekommen** *od.* **erleiden** have *or* suffer a relapse; **ein ~ in alte Gewohnheiten/in die Barbarei** *usw.* *(fig.)* a relapse into *or* return to old habits/ to barbarism *etc.*; **b)** *(Rechtsspr.)* **Diebstahl/ Einbruch im ~fall** subsequent *or* second offence of theft/burglary; **~fällig** *Adj.* **a)** *(Med., auch fig.)* relapsed ‹*patient, alcoholic, etc.*›; **[wieder] ~fällig werden** have a relapse; ‹*alcoholic etc.*› go back to one's old ways; **b)** *(Rechtsspr.)*; **~fällig werden** commit a second offence; **~fall·täter der** *(Rechtsspr.)* recidivist; subsequent *or* second offender; **~flug der** return flight; **~fluß der** reflux; return flow; **~frage die** query; **nach telefonischer ~frage** after checking up on the telephone; **~|fragen** *itr. V.; nur im Inf. u. 2. Part.* query it; **bei jmdm. ~fragen** raise a query with sb.; check with sb.; **~front die** back; rear; **~führung die** return; *(in die Heimat)* repatriation; **~gabe die a)** return; **gegen ~gabe der Eintrittskarte** upon returning the [entrance] ticket; **b)** *(Ballspiele)* back pass; **~gaberecht das** right of return; **~gang der** drop, fall (+ *Gen.* in); *(qualitätsmäßig)* decline (+ *Gen.* in); **ein ~gang an Besuchern/Geburten** *usw.* a decrease in the number of visitors/births *etc.*

-rückgang der decrease in ...; **Preis-/Produktions~:** drop in price/fall in output

rück-, Rück-: ~gängig *Adj.* **a) ~gängig machen** cancel ‹*agreement, decision, etc.*›; break off ‹*engagement*›; **einen Kauf ~gängig machen** return what one has bought; **es läßt sich nicht mehr ~gängig machen** what's done cannot be undone; **b)** *(im ~gang begriffen)* on the decline *postpos.*; **~gebildet** *Adj.* **a)** *(Biol.)* atrophied; **b)** *(Sprachw.)* produced by back-formation; **~gewinnung die** recovery **(aus** from); **die ~gewinnung von Rohstoffen aus Müll** the recovery *or* reclaiming of raw materials from waste products; **der Partei ist die ~gewinnung des Rathauses nicht gelungen** the party did not succeed in regaining control of the town council; **~grat das** spine; *(bes. fig.)* backbone; **~grat haben/kein ~grat haben** have guts *(coll.)*/be spineless; **~grat zeigen** show [real] guts *(coll.) or* fight; **jmdm. das ~grat brechen** *(fig.)* break sb.'s resistance; **~grat[s]·verkrümmung die** *(Med.)* spinal curvature; **~griff der a)** recourse; **es bleibt immer noch der ~griff auf unsere Reserven** we can always have recourse to our reserves; **b)** *(das Wiederaufgreifen)* return **(auf** + *Akk.* to); **~halt der a)** support; backing; **er hat an seinen Freunden einen festen ~halt** he gets firm support *or* backing from his friends; **b)** *in* **ohne ~halt** without reservation; unreservedly; **~halt·los 1.** *Adj.* unreserved, unqualified ‹*criticism, support*›; complete, absolute ‹*frankness*›; ‹*fight*› with no holds barred; **2.** *adv.* unreservedly; without reservation; ‹*trust*› completely, absolutely; ‹*confess*› with complete frankness; ‹*fight*› with total commitment; **~hand die** *(Sport, bes. Tennis)* backhand; **einen Ball mit [der] ~hand schlagen/ annehmen** hit/take the ball on one's backhand; **~kauf der** repurchase; *(einer Versicherung)* surrender; **~verkaufs·recht das** *(Rechtsw.)* right of repurchase

Rückkehr ['rʏkke:ɐ̯] **die;** ~: return; **jmdn. zur ~ [nach Litauen] bewegen** persuade sb. to return [to Lithuania]

Rückkehrer der; ~s, ~: home-comer; **~ aus dem Urlaub** people returning from holiday

rückkoppeln *tr. V.; nur im Inf. u. 2. Part.* *(Elektrot.)* feed back; **A mit B ~** *(fig.)* [re-]create links between A and B

Rück·kopp[e]lung die *(Elektrot.)* feedback; *(fig.)* [re-]creation of links

Rückkunft [-kʊnft] **die;** ~ *(geh.)* return

rück-, Rück-: ~lage die a) *(Spargeld)* savings *pl.*; **eine kleine ~lage haben** have a small sum saved up; have a small nest-egg; **b)** *(Wirtsch.: Reserve)* reserves *pl.*; *(Sozialw.)* credit reserve; **~lauf der a)** *(~fluß)* return flow; **b)** *(~transport)* return; **c)** *(bei Maschinen)* return travel; *(beim Tonbandgerät)* rewind; **~läufig 1.** *Adj.* **a)** *(sinkend)* decreasing ‹*number*›; declining ‹*economic growth etc.*›; falling ‹*rate, production, etc.*›; **~e Entwicklung** downward trend; decline; **b)** *(rückwärts verlaufend)* reverse ‹*process, dictionary*›; reverse, retrograde ‹*motion*›; **~läufiges Wachstum** reversal of growth; **2.** *adv.* in reverse order; **~licht das** rear- *or* tail-light

rücklings *Adv.* **a)** *(auf dem Rücken)* on one's back; **b)** *(mit dem Rücken nach vorn)* facing backwards

Rück-: ~marsch der march back; *(~zug)* retreat; **sich auf dem ~marsch befinden** ‹*troops, tanks*› be returning from the front/ be retreating; **~nahme** [~na:mə] **die** taking back; *(einer Behauptung, einer Anordnung, einer Klage usw.)* withdrawal; *(eines Verbotes)* cancellation; **die ~nahme von etw. verweigern** refuse to take sth. back; **~paß der** *(Sport)* back pass; **~porto das** return postage; **~prall der** rebound; *(eines Geschosses)* ricochet; **~reise die** return journey; **~ruf der a)** *(Fernspr.)* return call; **ich erwarte deinen ~ruf** I shall wait for you to phone back; **b)** *(das Zurückbeordern)* recall

Ruck·sack der rucksack; *(Touren~)* backpack

Rucksack·tourist der back-packer

rück-, Rück-: ~schau die review (**auf** + *Akk.* of); **~schau halten** look back; **~schau auf etw.** *(Akk.)* **halten** pass sth. in review; review sth.; **~schlag der a)** set-back; **in seinem Leben gab es immer wieder ~schläge** throughout his life he suffered repeated set-backs; **b)** *(Tennis, Tischtennis usw.)* return; **~schlag·ventil das** *(Technik)* non-return valve; check-valve; **~schluß der** conclusion (**auf** + *Akk.* about); **aus etw. ~schlüsse auf etw.** *(Akk.)* **ziehen** draw conclusions from sth. about sth.; **~schritt der** retrograde step; **das ist kein Fortschritt, sondern ein ~schritt** that's not a forward, but a backward step; **~schrittlich 1.** *Adj.* reactionary; retrograde ‹*development*›; **2.** *adv.* **~schrittlich eingestellt sein** have reactionary ideas; **~schwung der** *(Turnen)* backward swing; **~seite die** back; *(eines Gebäudes usw.)* back; rear; *(einer Münze usw.)* reverse; *(des Mondes)* far side; **siehe ~seite** see over[leaf]; **auf der ~seite eines Tiefs** *(Met.)* in the rear of *or* behind a depression; **~seitig 1.** *Adj.; nicht präd.* rear, back ‹*entrance*›; ‹*explanation etc.*› overleaf; **2.** *adv.* **~seitig gelegen** situated at the back *or* rear; **~sendung die** return; **~sicht die a)** *o. Pl.* consideration; **mit ~sicht auf etw.** *(Akk.)* taking sth. into consideration; in view of sth.; **~sicht auf jmdn. nehmen** show consideration for *or* towards sb.; *(Verständnis haben)* make allowances for sb.; **ohne ~sicht auf etw.** *(Akk.)* with no regard for *or* regardless of sth.; **ohne ~sicht auf Verluste** *(ugs.)* regardless; **keine ~sicht kennen** show no consideration; *(unbarmherzig sein)* be ruthless; **b)** *(Erwägung, Grund)* **~en** considerations; **aus finanziellen ~en** for financial reasons; **c)** *o. Pl. (Sicht nach hinten)* rear view; **~sicht·nahme die; ~:** consideration; **unter ~sichtnahme** *(Dat.)* **auf etw.** *(Akk.)* taking sth. into consideration/making allowances for sth.; **gegenseitige ~sichtnahme ist notwendig** it is essential that people show mutual consideration

rücksichts-, Rücksichts-: ~los 1. *Adj.* **a)** inconsiderate; thoughtless; **ein ~loser Autofahrer** an inconsiderate driver; *(verantwortungslos)* a reckless driver; **b)** *(schonungslos)* ruthless; **ein ~loser Kampf** a bitter struggle; a fight with no holds barred; **2.** *adv.* **a)** inconsiderately; thoughtlessly; *(verantwortungslos)* recklessly; **sich ~los durch die Menge schieben** shove one's way through the crowd regardless of anyone else; **b)** *(schonungslos)* ruthlessly; **jmdm. ~los die Wahrheit sagen** tell sb. the truth regardless of his/her feelings; **~losigkeit die; ~, ~en a)** lack of consideration; thoughtlessness; *(Verantwortungslosigkeit)* recklessness; **so eine ~losigkeit!** how inconsiderate *or* thoughtless!; **b)** *(Schonungslosigkeit)* ruthlessness; **~voll** *Adj.* considerate; thoughtful; **2.** *adv.* considerately; thoughtfully

rück-, Rück-: ~sitz der back seat; **auf dem ~sitz/den ~sitzen** in the back; in *or* on the back seat/seats; **~spiegel der** rear-view mirror; **~spiel das** *(Sport)* second *or* return leg; **~sprache die** consultation; **[mit jmdm.] ~sprache nehmen** *od.* **halten** *(Papierdt.)* consult [sb.]; **~stand der a)** *(Übriggebliebenes, Rest)* residue; **radioaktive ~stände** traces of radioactivity; **b)** *(offener Rechnungsbetrag)* **~stände/ein ~stand** arrears *pl.*; **~stände eintreiben** collect outstanding debts; **ein ~stand in der Miete** rent arrears *pl.*; **c)** *(Zurückbleiben hinter dem gesetzten Ziel, Soll usw.)* backlog; *(bes. Sport: hinter dem Gegner)* deficit; **[mit den Zahlungen/mit der Arbeit** *usw.*] **im ~stand sein/in ~stand** *(Akk.)* **geraten** be/get behind [with one's payments/work *etc.*]; **seinen/einen ~stand aufholen** *(bei der Arbeit)* make up *or* catch up one's/a backlog; *(bei einem Spiel/Rennen/(fig.) bei der Rüstung usw.)* make up the deficit; close the gap; **die Mannschaft lag mit 0:3 im ~stand** *(Sport)* the team was trailing by three to nil; **mit 38 Hundertstel Sekunden ~stand auf den zweiten Platz kommen** *(Sport)* take second place .38 of a second behind; **~ständig** *Adj.* **a)** *(unterentwickelt)* underdeveloped; backward; **b)** *(überholt)* outdated; antiquated; **~ständig sein** be behind the times; **c)** *(schon länger fällig)* outstanding ‹*payment, amount*›; ‹*wages*› still owing; **~ständige Steuern** tax arrears; **~ständigkeit die; ~ a)** backwardness; **b)** *(Überholtheit)* outdated nature; *(Ansichten)* old-fashioned *or* antiquated ideas *pl.*; **~stau der** *(von Wasser)* backing up; backwater; *(von Fahrzeugen)* tailback; **~stellung die a)** *(das Zurückstellen)* postponement (**um** by); **eine ~stellung vom Wehrdienst** a temporary exemption from military service; **b)** *(Wirtsch.)* reserve [fund]; **~stoß der** *(Physik)* reaction; *(einer Feuerwaffe)* recoil; **~strahler der** reflector; **~stufung die** downgrading; **~taste die** backspacer; backspace key; **~tausch der: beim ~tausch [von Devisen]** when changing currency back; **~tritt der a)** *(von einem Amt)* resignation (**von** from); *(von einer Kandidatur, von einem Vertrag usw.)* withdrawal (**von** from); **b)** *s.* **~trittbremse; ~tritt·bremse die** back-pedal brake

Rücktritts-: ~drohung die threat to resign; **~erklärung die** announcement of one's intention to resign; **~gesuch das** offer of resignation; **sein ~gesuch einreichen** hand in *or* tender one's resignation; **~recht das** right to withdraw [from a contract]

rück-, Rück-: ~|übersetzen *tr. V.; nur im Inf. u. 2. Part.* translate back; **~übersetzung die** back-translation; **~|vergüten** *tr. V.; nur im Inf. u. 2. Part.* refund; **~vergütung die** refund; **~versicherer der a)** *(ugs. abwertend)* cagey type *(coll.) (who does nothing without covering himself/herself)*; **b)** *(Versicherungsgesellschaft)* reinsurer; **~|versichern** *refl. V.; nur im Inf. u. 2. Part.* **a)** cover oneself [two ways]; hedge one's bets; **b)** *(Versicherungsw.)* reinsure; **~versicherung die a)** [double] insurance; *(Schutz)* safeguard; protection; **b)** *(Versicherungsw.)* reinsurance; **~wand die** back wall; *(eines Regals usw.)* back; **~wanderer der** repatriate

rückwärtig [-vɛrtɪç] **1.** *Adj.* **a)** back; rear; **die ~e Seite** the back *or* rear; **auf den ~en Verkehr achten** keep an eye on the traffic behind [one]; **b)** *(Milit.)* rearward ‹*lines of communication*›. **2.** *adv.* **die ~ gelegene Tür** the door at the back

rückwärts [-vɛrts] *Adv.* **a)** backwards; **ein Blick [nach] ~:** a look back; a backward look; **ein Salto/eine Rolle ~:** a back somersault/backward roll; **~ fahren** reverse; **~ einparken** reverse *or* back into a parking-space; **b)** *(südd., österr.: hinten)* behind; **[etwas] weiter ~:** [a little] further back; **~ einsteigen!** enter at the rear [of the vehicle]; **sich nach ~ fallen lassen/lehnen** fall/lean back

rückwärts-, Rückwärts-: ~bewegung die backward movement; **~drehung die** turn backwards; **durch ~drehung einer Sache** *(Gen.)* by turning sth. back; **~gang der** *(Kfz-W.)* reverse [gear]; **im ~gang** in reverse; **den ~gang einlegen** *(auch fig.)* go into reverse; **~|gehen** *unr. itr. V.; mit sein* go down; *(unpers.: schlechter werden)* get worse; **es ist mit dem Umsatz immer mehr rückwärtsgegangen** the turnover has gone down and down; **~gewandt** *Adj.* **a)** turned backwards *postpos.*; **b)** *(fig.: rückblickend)* backward-looking

Rückweg der return journey; **auf dem ~:** on the way back; **den ~ antreten, sich auf den ~ machen** set off *or* start on one's way back; **jmdm. den ~ abschneiden** cut off sb.'s line of retreat

ruck·weise 1. *Adv. (mit einem Ruck)* with a jerk; *(mit mehreren)* in a series of jerks. **2.** *adj.* jerky

rück-, Rück-: ~wendung die reorientation; **~wirkend 1.** *Adj.* retrospective; backdated ‹*pay increase*›; **2.** retrospectively; **~wirkend vom** *od.* **zum 1. April in Kraft treten** take effect [retrospectively] as from 1 April; **die Gehaltserhöhung erfolgt ~wirkend vom 1. Januar** the rise *(Brit.) or (Amer.)* raise is *or* has been backdated to 1 January; **~wirkung die a)** *(zeitlich)* retrospective force; **mit ~wirkung vom ...:** [retrospectively] as from ...; **b)** *(Auswirkung)* repercussion (**auf** + *Akk.* on); **~zahlbar** *Adj.* repayable; **~zahlung die** repayment; **~zahlungs·bedingungen** *Pl.* repayment terms; **~zieher der; ~s, ~ a)** *(Fußball)* overhead kick; **b)** *(fig. ugs.) (von Behauptungen, Forderungen usw.)* climb-down; *(von einem Vorhaben)* backing out *no art.*; **einen ~zieher machen** climb down/back out; *(salopp: Coitus interruptus)* pull out *(coll.)*

ruck, zuck [rʊk 'tsʊk] *Interj.* in no time; **~, ~ gehen** only take a moment *or* second

Rück·zug der retreat; **auf dem ~ sein** be retreating; **jmdn. zum ~ zwingen** force sb. to retreat

Rückzugs-: ~gebiet das reserve *(for native inhabitants/wild animals)*; **~gefecht das** *(Milit., fig.)* rearguard action

rüde ['ry:də] **1.** *Adj.* uncouth; coarse ‹*language*›. **2.** *adv.* in an uncouth manner

Rüde der; ~n, ~n a) *(Hund)* [male] dog; *(Fuchs/Wolf)* [male] fox/wolf; **unser Hund ist ein ~:** our dog is a male; **b)** *(Jägerspr.: Hetzhund)* hound; hunting dog

Rudel ['ru:dl̩] **das; ~s, ~** *(von Hirschen, Gemsen)* herd; *(von Wölfen, Hunden)* pack; *(fig.: von Menschen)* horde

Ruder ['ru:dɐ] **das; ~s, ~ a)** *(Riemen)* oar; **sich in die ~ legen** *(kräftig rudern)* row strongly *or* vigorously; *(fig. ugs.: etw. in Angriff nehmen)* put one's back into it; **b)** *(Steuer~)* rudder; *(Steuerrad)* helm; **am ~ sein/bleiben** *(fig.)* be/stay at the helm; **das ~ fest in der Hand haben** *(fig.)* be firmly in control; **das ~ herumwerfen** *(fig.)* change course *or* tack; **ans ~ kommen** *(fig.)* take the helm; ‹party, leader› come to power; **aus dem ~ laufen** *(auch fig.)* go off course; **c)** *(eines Flugzeugs) (Höhen~)* elevator; *(Quer~)* aileron; *(Seiten~)* rudder

Ruder-: ~bank die; *Pl.* **~bänke** thwart; *(einer Galeere)* oarsman's bench; **~blatt das a)** *(eines Steuerruders)* rudder [blade]; **b)** *(eines Riemens)* blade; **~boot das** rowboat; rowing-boat *(Brit.)*

Ruderer der; ~s, ~: oarsman; rower

Ruder-: ~gänger der; ~s, ~, ~gast der *(Seemannsspr.)* helmsman; **~haus das** *(Seemannsspr.)* wheel-house

-ruderig *Adj.* -oared

Ruderin die; ~, ~nen oarswoman; rower

rudern 1. *itr. V.* **a)** *meist, mit Richtungsangabe nur, mit sein* row; **b)** *(fig.)* **mit den Armen ~:** swing one's arms [about]; **c)** *mit sein* ‹*water-fowl*› paddle. **2.** *tr. V.* row ‹*boat, person, object*›

Ruder-: ~pinne die tiller; **~regatta die** rowing regatta; **~sport der** rowing *no art.*

Rudiment [rudi'mɛnt] **das; ~[e]s, ~e a)** *(Biol., geh.)* vestige; **b)** *Pl. (veralt.: Grundbegriffe)* rudiments

rudimentär [rudimɛn'tɛ:ɐ̯] *(Biol., geh.)* **1.** *Adj.* rudimentary. **2.** *adv.* in a rudimentary form

Ruf [ru:f] **der; ~[e]s, ~e a)** call; *(Schrei)* shout; cry; *(Tierlaut)* call; **b)** *o. Pl. (fig.:*

Aufforderung, Forderung) call (**nach** for); **der ~ zu den Waffen** *(geh.)* the call to arms; **dem ~ des Herzens/Gewissens/der Natur folgen** *od.* **gehorchen** follow one's heart/listen to the voice of conscience/nature; **der ~ nach der Todesstrafe** the call for the death penalty; **c)** *(Berufung)* **sie bekam einen ~ an die Universität Bremen** *od.* **nach Bremen** she was offered a chair *or* professorship at Bremen University; **d)** *o. Pl. (Papierdt.: Telefonnummer)* telephone [number]; **~ 33700** tel. [no.] 33700; **e)** *(Leumund)* reputation; **eine Firma von ~:** a firm of repute *or* with a good reputation; **ein Mann von gutem/schlechtem ~:** a man with a good/bad reputation; **jmdn./etw. in schlechten ~ bringen** give sb./sth. a bad name; **besser als sein ~ sein** be not as bad as one/it is made out to be; **ist der ~ erst ruiniert, lebt es sich ganz ungeniert** *(Spr.)* you needn't worry if you've no reputation to lose

Rufe ['ru:fə], **Rüfe** ['ry:fə] **die; ~, ~n** *(schweiz.)* landslide

rufen 1. *unr. itr. V.* **a)** call (**nach** for); *(schreien)* shout (**nach** for); ⟨*animal*⟩ call; **hast du sein Rufen nicht gehört?** didn't you hear him calling?; **jmdm. ~** *(südwestd., schweiz.)* call to sb.; **Mutter/der Gong ruft zum Essen** mother is calling [out] that lunch/dinner is ready/the gong is sounding for lunch/dinner; **die Glocke ruft zum Gottesdienst/Gebet** the bell is calling to worship/prayer; **die Pflicht/die Arbeit ruft** *(fig.)* duty calls; **b)** *(schweiz.: hervorrufen)* **einer Sache** *(Dat.)* **~:** cause sth.; give rise to sth. **2.** *unr. tr. V.* **a) etw. ~:** call sth.; *(schreien)* shout sth.; *(unpers.)* **aus dem Zimmer rief es: „Herein!"** from inside the room a voice called 'come in!'; **b)** *(herbei-)* **jmdn. ~:** call sb.; **jmdn. zu Hilfe ~:** call to sb. to help; **dringende Geschäfte riefen ihn nach München** *(fig.)* he was called to Munich on urgent business; **jmdm./sich** *(Dat.)* **etw. ins Gedächtnis** *od.* **in Erinnerung ~:** remind sb. of sth./recall sth.; **[jmdm.] wie gerufen kommen** *(ugs.)* come at just the right moment; **du kommst/der Wind kommt mir wie gerufen** you're just the person I wanted/the wind is just what I wanted; **c)** *(telefonisch)* call; **jmdn. [unter der Nummer 347106] ~:** call *or* ring sb. [on 347106]; **~ Sie 888666** ring 888666; *(über Funk)* **Teddybär ruft Zeppelin** Teddy Bear calling Zeppelin; **d)** *(nennen)* **jmdn./***(südwestd., schweiz.:)* **jmdm. etw. ~:** call sb. sth.; **e)** *(geh., veralt.: anreden)* **jmdn. bei** *od.* **mit seinem Namen ~:** address sb. by name. **3.** *refl. V.* **sich heiser ~:** call until one is hoarse; *(schreien)* shout oneself hoarse

Rufer der; ~s, ~: person calling; **ein ~ in der Wüste** *(fig. geh.)* a voice [crying] in the wilderness

Rüffel ['rʏfl] **der; ~s, ~** *(ugs.)* ticking-off *(coll.)*

rüffeln *tr. V. (ugs.)* **jmdn. ~:** tick sb. off *(coll.)*

Ruf-: ~mord der character assassination; **~mord·kampagne die** smear campaign; **~name der** first name *(by which one is generally known)*; **~nummer die** telephone number; **~säule die** emergency telephone *(mounted in a pillar)*; **~weite die: in/außer ~weite sein** be within/beyond hailing distance; **~zeichen das a)** *o. Pl. (Fernspr.)* ringing tone; **b)** *(österr.: Ausrufezeichen)* exclamation mark

Rugby ['rakbi] **das; ~[s]** rugby [football]

Rüge ['ry:gə] **die; ~, ~n** reprimand; **jmdm. eine ~ wegen etw.** *(Gen.)* **erteilen** reprimand sb. for sth.; **eine ~ erhalten** be reprimanded

rügen *tr. V.* reprimand ⟨*person*⟩ (**wegen** for); *(mit Nachdruck kritisieren)* censure ⟨*carelessness etc.*⟩; **Mängel ~:** complain about faults *or* defects

Ruhe ['ru:ə] **die; ~ a)** *(Stille)* silence; **im Saal herrschte absolute ~:** there was dead silence *or* a complete hush in the hall; **endlich war im Klassenzimmer ~ eingetreten** at last the classroom had become quiet; **die nächtliche ~ stören** disturb the nocturnal peace; **~ [bitte]!** quiet *or* silence [please]!; **[einen Moment] um ~ bitten** ask for [a moment's] silence; **jmdn. um ~ bitten** ask sb. to be quiet; **~ geben/halten** be/keep quiet; **jmdn. zur ~ ermahnen** tell sb. to be quiet; **b)** *(Ungestörtheit)* peace; **in ~ [und Frieden]** in peace [and quiet]; **vor jmdm. ~ haben** not be bothered by sb.; **ich möchte mal meine ~ haben** I should like [to have] some peace [and quiet]; **er braucht ~ bei seiner Arbeit** he needs peace and quiet *or* must not be disturbed while he is working; **die [öffentliche] ~ wiederherstellen** restore [law and] order; **für ~ und Ordnung sorgen** uphold *or* preserve law and order; **jmdn. in ~ lassen** leave sb. in peace; **laß mich in ~!** leave me alone!; **jmdn. mit etw. in ~ lassen** stop bothering sb. with sth.; **jmdn. nicht zur ~ kommen lassen** give sb. no peace; **keine ~ geben** not stop pestering; *(nicht nachgeben)* not give up; *(weiter protestieren)* go on protesting; **hier hast du fünf Mark, aber nun gib auch ~!** here's five marks, but now stop bothering me/us; **c)** *(Unbewegtheit)* rest; **zur ~ kommen** come to rest; ⟨*weel*⟩ stop turning; **die ~ vor dem Sturm** the calm before the storm; **d)** *(Erholung, das Sichausruhen)* rest *no def. art.*; **der ~ pflegen** *(geh.)* take it *or* things easy; seek repose *(literary)*; **angenehme ~** *(geh.)* sleep well; **sich zur ~ begeben** *(geh.)* retire [to bed]; **die ewige ~** *(geh.)* eternal rest; **jmdn. zur letzten ~ betten** *(geh.)* lay sb. to rest; **e)** *(Ruhestand)* **sich zur ~ setzen** take one's retirement; retire (**in** + *Dat.* to); **f)** *(Gelassenheit)* calm[ness]; composure; **er ist die ~ selbst** *(ugs.)* he is calmness itself; **[die] ~ bewahren/die ~ verlieren** keep calm/lose one's composure; keep/lose one's cool *(coll.)*; **sich aus der ~ bringen lassen** let oneself get worked up; *(ängstlich werden)* let oneself get rattled *(sl.)*; **in [aller] ~:** [really] calmly; **lesen Sie sich die Prüfungsaufgaben in [aller] ~ durch** read through the examination questions calmly and in your own time; **ich muß mir das in [aller] ~ überlegen** I must have a quiet think about it; **jmdm. keine ~ lassen** not give sb. any peace; **der Gedanke läßt ihm keine ~ mehr** he can't stop thinking about it; **die ~ weghaben** *(ugs.)* be completely unflappable *(coll.)*; **~ ist die erste Bürgerpflicht** *(veralt.)* orderly behaviour is the first duty of the citizen; *(scherzh.)* the main thing is to keep calm; **immer mit der ~!** *(nur keine Panik)* don't panic!; *(nichts überstürzen)* one thing at a time; no need to rush

ruhe-, Ruhe-: ~bank die; *Pl.* **~bänke** bench; **~bedürfnis das;** *o. Pl.* need of rest; **~bedürftig** *Adj.* in need of rest *postpos.*; **~gehalt das** [retirement] pension; **~geld das** [old-age] pension; **~genuß der** *(österr. Amtsspr.)* [retirement] pension; **~kissen das** cushion; *(Kopfkissen)* pillow; *s. auch* **Gewissen; ~lage die a)** *(Körperlage)* [fully] relaxed position; **b)** *(eines beweglichen Gegenstands)* neutral position; *(unbeweglich)* immobile position; **~los 1.** *Adj.* restless; **2.** *adv.* restlessly; **~losigkeit die; ~:** restlessness

ruhen *itr. V.* **a)** *(aus~)* rest; **hier läßt es sich gut ~:** it's very restful here; **nach dem Essen sollst du ~ oder tausend Schritte tun** *(Spr.)* after a meal one should take either a rest or a good walk; **b)** *(geh.: schlafen)* sleep; **ich wünsche gut** *od.* **wohl zu ~:** I hope you sleep well; **c) im Grabe ~:** lie in one's grave; **in fremder Erde ~:** be buried in foreign soil; **„Ruhe sanft** *od.* **in Frieden!"** 'Rest in Peace'; **„Hier ruht in Gott ..."** 'Here lies ...'; **d)** *(stillstehen)* ⟨*work, business*⟩ have stopped; ⟨*production, firm*⟩ be at a standstill; ⟨*field*⟩ rest; ⟨*employment, insurance*⟩ be suspended; **der Verkehr ruht fast völlig** there is hardly any traffic; **die Waffen ~:** there is a cease-fire; **ihre Hände ~ nie** her hands are never still; **nicht ~ [und rasten]** *od.* **nicht ~ noch rasten** *od.* **weder ~ noch rasten, bis ...:** not rest until ...; **e)** *(liegen)* rest; **der Braten muß zehn Minuten ~:** the roast must be left to stand for ten minutes; **in sich** *(Dat.)* **[selbst] ~:** be a well-balanced [and harmonious] person

ruhend *Adj.; nicht präd. (unbeweglich)* stationary; *(liegend)* reclining ⟨*Venus etc.*⟩; **~er Verkehr** parked vehicles *pl.*

ruhen|lassen *unr. tr. V.; 2. Part. meist* **~:** let ⟨*matter etc.*⟩ rest; leave ⟨*problem etc.*⟩ [on one side]; *(vorläufig)* shelve ⟨*matter etc.*⟩

ruhe-, Ruhe-: ~pause die break; **eine ~pause einlegen** take a break; **~punkt der** resting-point; *(in einer Entwicklung)* restful *or* quiet point; **~stand der;** *o. Pl.* retirement; **in den ~stand gehen/versetzt werden** go into retirement/be retired; **er ist im ~stand/Lehrer im ~stand** he is retired/a retired teacher; **seine Versetzung in den ~stand** his retirement; **~ständler der, ~ständlerin die** retired person; **~statt die; ~, ~stätten, ~stätte die** *(fig. geh.)* [last] resting-place; **~störend** *Adj.* **~störender Lärm** disturbance of the peace; **~störung die** disturbance; *(Rechtsw.)* disturbance of the peace; **jmdn. wegen ~störung anzeigen** report sb. [to the police] for disturbing the peace; **~strom der** *(Elektrot.)* closed-circuit current; **~tag der a)** *(einer Gaststätte)* closing day; **[wir haben] dienstags** *od.* **Dienstag ~tag** [we are] closed on Tuesdays; **b)** *(arbeitsfreier Tag)* day of rest; **~zeit die** rest period; time of rest; *(für Bäume usw.)* dormant period *or* season

ruhig ['ru:ɪç] **1.** *Adj.* **a)** *(still, leise)* quiet; **seid doch mal ~!** do be quiet!; **um diese Angelegenheit/diesen Politiker ist es sehr ~ geworden** one does not hear much about this matter/politician any more; **b)** *(friedlich, ungestört)* peaceful ⟨*times, life, scene, valley, etc.*⟩; quiet ⟨*talk, reflection, life*⟩; **wir suchten uns ein ~es Plätzchen** we looked for a quiet *or* peaceful spot; **überleg es dir mal in einer ~en Stunde** think about it when you have a quiet moment; **er hat keine ~e Minute** he doesn't have a moment's peace; **ein ~er Job** *od.* **Posten** *(ugs.)* a cushy job *or* number *(coll.)*; **einen ~en Verlauf nehmen** go smoothly; be uneventful; **c)** *(unbewegt)* calm ⟨*sea, weather*⟩; still ⟨*air*⟩; *(fig.)* peaceful ⟨*melody*⟩; quiet ⟨*pattern*⟩; *(gleichmäßig)* steady ⟨*breathing, hand, flame, steps*⟩; smooth ⟨*flight, crossing*⟩; **d)** *(gelassen)* calm ⟨*voice etc.*⟩; quiet, calm ⟨*person*⟩; **er gab sich Mühe, ~ zu bleiben** he made an effort to keep calm *or (coll.)* keep his cool; **~en Gewissens** with an easy *or* a clear conscience; **sei ganz ~:** you needn't worry; **[nur immer] ~ Blut!** *(ugs.)* keep your hair on! *(sl.)*. **2.** *adv.* **a)** *(still, leise)* quietly; **wir wohnen sehr ~:** we live in a very quiet area; **sich ~ verhalten** keep quiet; **b)** *(friedlich, ohne Störungen)* ⟨*sleep*⟩ peacefully; ⟨*go off*⟩ smoothly, peacefully; *(ohne Zwischenfälle)* uneventfully; ⟨*work, think*⟩ in peace; **hier geht es sehr ~ zu** it is very peaceful here; **ich kann nicht ~ schlafen** I can't sleep properly; **c)** *(unbewegt)* ⟨*sit, lie, stand*⟩ still; *(gleichmäßig)* ⟨*burn, breathe*⟩ steadily; ⟨*run, fly*⟩ smoothly; **d)** *(gelassen)* ⟨*speak, watch, sit*⟩ calmly; **sie sahen ~ zu, wie das Kind geschlagen wurde** they watched unmoved as the child was beaten. **3.** *Adv.* by all means; **du kannst ~ mitkommen** by all means come along; you're welcome to come along; **streichle ihn ~ mal** go ahead and stroke him; **man kann ihm das ~ ganz direkt sagen** there's no harm in telling him to his face;

du kannst es mir ~ glauben/sagen it's OK, you can take my word for it/you can tell me; **du könntest dich ~ entschuldigen/ihm ~ etwas helfen** it wouldn't hurt you to apologize/to help him a bit; **lach mich ~ aus** all right *or* go ahead, laugh at me[, I don't care]; **soll er ~ meckern** *(ugs.)* let him moan[, I don't care]

ruhig|stellen *tr. V.* **a)** immobilize ‹*limb etc.*›; **b)** *(fig. verhüll.)* calm ‹*patient*›

Ruhm [ru:m] **der; ~[e]s** fame; **diese Erfindung begründete seinen ~:** this invention made him famous *or* made his name; **sich mit ~ bedecken** *(geh.)* cover oneself with glory; **er hat sich nicht [gerade] mit ~ bekleckert** *(ugs. iron.)* he didn't exactly cover himself with glory *or* distinguish himself; **der zweifelhafte ~ dieser Erfindung** *(fig.)* the dubious reputation of this invention

rühmen ['ry:mən] **1.** *tr. V.* praise. **2.** *refl. V.* **sich einer Sache** *(Gen.)* **~:** boast about sth.; **wenige dürfen sich ~, ihn gesehen zu haben** only a few can claim to have seen him

rühmens·wert *Adj.* laudable; praiseworthy

Ruhmes·blatt das: das war kein ~ für ihn/die Bundesrepublik it did not reflect any credit on him/the Federal Republic; it did him/the Federal Republic no credit

rühmlich *Adj.* laudable, praiseworthy ‹*behaviour, action, etc.*›; notable ‹*exception*›; **er hat kein ~es Ende genommen** he came to a discreditable end

ruhm·los 1. *Adj.* inglorious. **2.** *adv.* ingloriously

ruhm·reich 1. *Adj.* glorious ‹*victory, history*›; celebrated ‹*general, army, victory*›. **2.** *adv.* **~ kämpfen** fight with great glory; **~ siegen** win a famous *or* glorious victory

Ruhr [ru:ɐ̯] **die; ~, ~en** dysentery *no art.*

Rühr·ei das scrambled egg[s *pl.*]

rühren ['ry:rən] **1.** *tr. V.* **a)** *(um~)* stir ‹*sauce, dough, etc.*›; *(ein~)* stir ‹*egg, powder, etc.*› ‹**an, in** + *Akk.* into›; **b)** *(bewegen)* move ‹*limb, fingers, etc.*›; **ich konnte die Glieder nicht mehr ~:** I could no longer move; *s. auch* **Finger b; c)** *(erweichen)* move; touch; **jmdn. zu Tränen ~:** move sb. to tears; **es rührte ihn überhaupt nicht, daß ...:** it didn't bother him at all that ...; *s. auch* **gerührt; rührend; d)** *(geh. veralt.)* **die Trommel/die Leier ~:** beat the drum/play the lyre. **2.** *itr. V.* **a)** *(um~)* stir; **im Kaffee** *od.* **in der Kaffeetasse ~:** stir one's coffee; **b)** *(Milit.)* stand at ease; **c)** *(geh.: her~)* **das rührt daher, daß ...:** that stems from the fact that ...; **d)** *(geh.: vorsichtig anfassen)* **an etw.** *(Akk.)* **~:** touch sth.; *(fig.: im Gespräch berühren)* touch on sth.; **wir wollen nicht [mehr] daran ~:** let's not go into that [any further]. **3.** *refl. V.* **a)** *(sich bewegen)* move; **er rührte sich nicht von der Stelle** he did not budge *or* stir; **niemand rührte sich** nobody moved *or* stirred; *(fig.: unternahm etwas)* nobody did anything; **kein Blatt/kein Lüftchen rührte sich** not a leaf stirred/there was not a breath of wind; **es rührte sich nichts** there was no sign of movement; *(nichts geschah)* nothing happened; **er hat sich seit zwei Monaten nicht gerührt** *(ugs.: nicht geschrieben)* he has given no sign of life for two months; **b)** *(Milit.)* **rührt euch!** at ease!

Rühren das; ~s a) stirring *no art.*; **beim ~ des Teigs** when stirring the dough; **b) ein menschliches ~ verspüren** *(scherzh.)* feel the call of nature

rührend 1. *Adj.* touching; **er sorgt in ~er Weise für seine Eltern** it is touching how he looks after his parents; **das ist ~ von Ihnen** that is terribly sweet *or* kind of you *(coll.)*; **das ist ja ~!** *(auch iron.)* that's really charming! **2.** *adv.* touchingly; **er sorgt ~ für sie** it is touching the way he looks after her/them

Ruhr·gebiet das; *o. Pl.* Ruhr [district]

rührig 1. *Adj.* active; *(mit Unternehmungsgeist)* enterprising; go-ahead; *(emsig)* busy; industrious. **2.** *adv.* actively; *(mit Unternehmungsgeist)* enterprisingly; *(emsig)* busily; industriously

Rührigkeit die; ~: active nature; *(Unternehmungsgeist)* enterprise

rühr-, Rühr-: ~löffel der mixing-spoon; **~mich·nicht·an das; ~, ~** *(Bot.)* touch-me-not; *s. auch* **Kräutchen; ~selig 1.** *Adj.* **a)** emotional ‹*person*›; **b)** *(allzu gefühlvoll)* over-sentimental ‹*manner, mood, etc.*›; maudlin, *(coll.)* tear-jerking ‹*play, song, etc.*›; **2.** *adv.* in an over-sentimental manner; **der Film endete ~selig** the film had a tear-jerking *or* weepy ending *(coll.)*; **~seligkeit die;** *o. Pl.* sentimentality; **~stück das** *(Literaturw.)* sentimental drama; melodrama; **~teig der** [cake-]mixture

Rührung die; ~: emotion; **von tiefer ~ ergriffen** deeply moved

Ruin [ru'i:n] **der; ~s** ruin; **jmdn. an den Rand des ~s bringen** bring sb. to the brink of ruin; **du bist noch mein ~** *(ugs.)* you'll be the ruin *or* end of me

Ruine die; ~, ~n ruin

Ruinen·feld das [expanse *sing.* of] ruins *pl.*

ruinieren *tr. V.* ruin; **sich finanziell ~:** ruin oneself [financially]; **du ruinierst meine Nerven** you are turning me into a nervous wreck; *s. auch* **Ruf e**

ruinös [rui'nø:s] *Adj.* ruinous

Ruländer ['ru:lɛndɐ] **der; ~s, ~:** Ruländer [grape/wine]

rülpsen ['rʏlpsn̩] *itr. V. (ugs.)* belch

Rülpser der; ~s, ~ *(ugs.)* belch

rum [rʊm] *Adv. (ugs.) s.* **herum**

Rum [rʊm] **der; ~s, ~s** rum

Rumäne [ru'mɛ:nə] **der; ~n, ~n** Romanian

Rumänien (das); ~s Romania

Rumänin die; ~, ~nen Romanian

rumänisch 1. *Adj.* Romanian. **2.** *adv.* Romanian; *s. auch* **deutsch; Deutsch; ²Deutsche**

Rumba ['rʊmba] **die; ~, ~s** *od.* **der; ~s, ~s** rumba

rum-: ~|ballern *itr. V. (ugs.)* blast away; **~|brüllen** *itr. V. (ugs.) s.* **herumbrüllen; ~|fliegen** *(ugs.)* **1.** *unr. itr. V.; mit sein* **a)** *s.* **herumfliegen 1 a; b)** *(herumliegen)* lie about *or* around; **im Zimmer ~fliegen** litter the room; **2.** *unr. tr. V. s.* **herumfliegen 2; ~|fummeln** *itr. V. (ugs.) s.* **herumfummeln; ~|gammeln** *itr. V. (ugs.) s.* **gammeln b; ~|hampeln** *itr. V. (ugs.)* hop *or* jig about; **~|hängen** *unr. itr. V. (ugs.)* **a)** *(sich ziellos aufhalten/untätig od. arbeitslos sein)* hang about *or* around; **b)** *s.* **herumhängen a; ~|kriegen** *tr. V. (ugs.) s.* **herumkriegen; ~|labern** *itr. V. (salopp abwertend)* natter *(Brit. coll.) or* chatter away *(coll.)*; rabbit on *(Brit. sl.)*; **~|laufen** *unr. itr. V.; mit sein (ugs.) s.* **herumlaufen; ~|liegen** *unr. itr. V. (ugs.) s.* **herumliegen; ~|lungern** *itr. V. (salopp) s.* **herumlungern; ~|machen** *itr. V. (salopp)* **a)** *s.* **herummachen; b)** *s.* **herumfummeln a; c)** *(sich [sexuell] einlassen)* play around; *(koitieren)* do it *(sl.)*; *(schmusen)* neck *(sl.)*

Rummel ['rʊml̩] **der; ~s** *(ugs.)* **a)** *(laute Betriebsamkeit)* commotion; *(Aufhebens)* fuss, to-do (**um** about); **der ganze ~:** the whole business; **b)** *(bes. nordd.: Jahrmarkt)* fair; **auf den ~ gehen** go to the fair

Rummel·platz der *(bes. nordd.)* fairground

Rummy ['rœmi] **das; ~s, ~s** *(österr.) s.* **Rommé**

rumoren [ru'mo:rən] *itr. V. (ugs.)* **a)** *(rumpeln)* make a noise; *(poltern)* ‹*person*› bang about; **es rumorte in seinem Bauch** *(fig.)* his stomach rumbled; **b)** *(aufbegehren)* protest; stage a protest/protests

Rumpel·kammer die *(ugs.)* box-room *(Brit.)*; junk-room

rumpeln ['rʊmpl̩n] *itr. V. (ugs.)* **a)** *(poltern)* bump and bang about; **es rumpelte** *unpers.* there was banging and bumping; *(im Magen)* there was a rumble *or* rumbling; **b)** *mit sein (sich rumpelnd fortbewegen)* rumble; bump and bang

Rumpelstilzchen ['rʊmpl̩ʃtɪltsçən] **(das); ~s** Rumpelstiltskin *no art.*

Rumpf [rʊmpf] **der; ~[e]s, Rümpfe** ['rʏmpfə] **a)** *(bei Lebewesen)* trunk [of the body]; **den ~ drehen/beugen** turn one's body/bend from the hips; **b)** *(beim Schiff)* hull; **c)** *(beim Flugzeug)* fuselage

Rumpf·beuge die *(Gymnastik)* trunk-bend; bend from the hips; **~ rückwärts** arch

rümpfen ['rʏmpfn̩] *tr. V.* **die Nase [bei etw.] ~:** wrinkle one's nose at sth.; **über jmdn./etw. die Nase rümpfen** *(fig.)* look down one's nose at sb./turn up one's nose at sth.

Rumpsteak ['rʊmp-ste:k] **das; ~s, ~s** rump steak

rums [rʊms] *Interj. (Geräusch)* bump; *(lauter, heller)* bang; *(beim Zusammenstoß)* crash

rumsen *itr. V. (ugs.)* **a)** *unpers.* **es rumst** there's a bump *or* bang; *(wiederholt)* there's bumping and banging; *(laut, beim Zusammenstoß)* there's a crash; **b)** *mit sein (auftreffen)* **gegen etw. ~:** bang into sth.

rum-: ~|sitzen *unr. itr. V. (ugs.) s.* **herumsitzen; ~|stehen** *unr. itr. V. (ugs.) s.* **herumstehen; ~|toben** *itr. V. (ugs.)* **a)** *auch mit sein* ‹*child*› charge *or* romp [noisily] about; ‹*students etc.*› rag; **b)** *(wüten)* rant and rave

Rum·topf der *fruits preserved in rum and sugar*

rum|treiben *unr. refl. V. (ugs.) s.* **herumtreiben**

Rum·verschnitt der rum blend *(with other spirits)*

rum|ziehen *unr. tr., itr. V. (ugs.) s.* **herumziehen**

Run [rʌn] **der; ~s, ~s** [big] rush; **ein [starker] ~ auf etw.** *(Akk.)* a [big] run on sth.

rund [rʊnt] **1.** *Adj.* **a)** *(kreis~)* round; **~e Augen machen** *(ugs.)* ‹*child*› gaze wide-eyed; **ein Gespräch am ~en Tisch** *(fig.)* a round-table conference; **b)** *(dicklich)* plump ‹*arms etc.*›; chubby ‹*cheeks*›; fat ‹*stomach*›; **er ist dick und ~ geworden** he has become rather rotund *or* stout; **c)** *(ugs.: ganz)* round ‹*dozen, number, etc.*›; **~e drei Jahre** three years or as near as makes no difference; **d)** *(abgerundet)* full, rounded ‹*tone, sound, flavour*›; **eine ~e Sache** a nice piece of work. **2.** *adv.* **~ laufen** *(Kfz-W.)* ‹*engine*› run smoothly; *s. auch* **rundgehen. 3.** *Adv.* **a)** *(ugs.: etwa)* about; approximately; **b) ~ um jmdn./etw.** [all] around sb./sth.; **eine Sendung ~ um das Kind** a broadcast on all aspects of childhood; *s. auch* **Uhr**

Rund das; ~[e]s, ~e *(geh.)* **a)** *(runde Form)* round; *(Mond usw.)* orb *(literary)*; **b)** *(runde Fläche)* circle

Rund-: ~bau der; *Pl.* **~bauten** circular building; rotunda; **~blick der** panorama; view in all directions; **~bogen der** *(Kunstwiss., Archit.)* round arch; **~brief der** circular [letter]

Runde ['rʊndə] **die; ~, ~n a)** *(Sport: runde Strecke)* lap; **die schnellste ~ fahren** do the fastest lap; **seine ~n ziehen** *od.* **drehen** do one's laps; **b)** *(Sport: Durchgang, Partie; Boxen: Abschnitt)* round; **eine ~ Golf/Skat** a round of golf/skat; **über die ~n kommen** *(fig. ugs.)* get by; manage; **c)** *(Personenkreis)* circle; *(Gesellschaft)* company; **in fröhlicher ~ beisammensitzen** sit together in a happy circle *or* group; **d)** *(Umkreis)* **in der ~:** round about; **in die ~ blicken** look all around one; **e)** *(Rundgang)* round; *(Spaziergang)* walk; **eine ~ durch die Kneipen machen** go on a pub crawl *(Brit. coll.)*; go bar-hopping *(Amer.)*; **die ~ machen** *(ugs.)* ‹*drink, rumour*› go the rounds *pl.*; circulate; **f) eine ~ Bier schmeißen** *(ugs.)* buy *or* stand a round of beer; die ~ geht auf mich/auf den Wirt this round is on me/on the house

runden 1. *tr. V.* a) *(rund machen)* round; b) *(fig.: abrunden)* round off, fill out ‹*picture, impression*›. 2. *refl. V.* become round

Runden·rekord der *(Motorsport)* lap record

rund-, Rund-: ~erneuern *tr. V. (Kfz-W.)* remould; retread; ~erneuerte Reifen remoulds; retreads; ~erneuerung die *(Kfz-W.)* remoulding; retreading; ~fahrt die *(auch Sport)* tour (durch of); eine ~fahrt durch Amsterdam a circular tour of *or* a trip round Amsterdam; eine ~fahrt machen go on a [circular] tour; ~flug der [short] circular flight; circuit; ~frage die survey *(using a questionnaire)*; questionnaire

Rund·funk der a) radio; *(das Senden)* radio broadcasting *no art.*; im ~: on the radio; ~ hören listen to the radio; b) *(Einrichtung, Gebäude)* radio station; der Westdeutsche ~: West German Radio; sie ist *od.* arbeitet beim ~: she works in radio

Rundfunk-: ~ansager der *(veralt.) s.* ~sprecher; ~anstalt die broadcasting corporation; *(Sender)* radio station; ~empfang der radio reception *no indef. art.*; ~empfänger der radio receiver; ~gebühren *Pl.* radio licence fees; ~gerät das radio set; ~hörer der [radio] listener; ~programm das a) *(Sendefolge)* [schedule *sing.* of] radio programmes *pl.*; b) *(Programmheft)* radio programme guide; ~redakteur der radio producer; ~reporter der radio reporter; ~sender der radio station; *(technische Anlage)* radio transmitter; ~sendung die radio programme; ~sprecher der radio announcer; ~station die radio station; ~techniker der radio engineer; ~teilnehmer der radio licence holder; *(Hörer)* radio listener; ~übertragung die radio broadcast

rund-, Rund-: ~gang der a) *(des Wachmanns, Chefarztes usw.)* round (durch of); einen ~gang durch die Stadt machen go for a walk round the town; b) *(Umgang)* gallery; ~|gehen *unr. itr. V.; mit sein* a) *unpers. (ugs.)* es geht rund *(es ist viel Betrieb)* it's all go *(coll.)*; *(es geht flott zu)* things are going with a swing; b) *(herumgereicht werden)* be passed round; *(fig.)* ‹*story, rumours*› go *or* do the rounds; er ließ die Flasche ~gehen he passed the bottle round; ~heraus *Adv.* straight out; ‹*say, ask*› bluntly; ‹*refuse*› flatly; ~herum *Adv.* a) *(ringsum)* all around; *(darum herum)* all round it; ~herum an der Wand all round the walls; b) *(völlig)* completely; *(fig.)* entirely ‹*satisfied, practical*›; ~kurs der *(bes. Motor-, Fahrradsport)* circuit

rundlich *Adj.* a) *(fast rund)* roundish; b) *(mollig)* plump; chubby

rund-, Rund-: ~reise die [circular] tour (durch of); eine ~reise [mit dem Bus/Auto] durch den Schwarzwald machen tour the Black Forest [by coach/car]; ~schädel der *(Anthrop.)* round *or (as tech. term)* brachycephalic skull; ~schau die a) *(geh.) s.* ~blick; b) *(in Zeitungstiteln)* review; ~schlag der *(Boxen, Faustball, Eishockey)* swing; *(fig.)* [general] broadside; ~schreiben das *s.* ~brief; ~sicht die *s.* ~blick; ~spruch der; *o. Pl. (schweiz.) s.* Rundfunk; ~strecke die circuit; ~strick·nadel die circular-knitting needle; ~stück das *(nordd.)* [oval] roll; ~um *Adv. s.* ~herum

Rundung die; ~, ~en curve; *(hervortretend)* bulge

rund·weg *Adv.* ‹*refuse, deny*› flatly, point-blank

Rund·weg der circular path *or* walk

Rune ['ru:nə] die; ~, ~n rune

Runen-: ~schrift die runic alphabet; ~stein der rune stone; ~zeichen das runic character

Runge ['rʊŋə] die; ~, ~n [load-retaining] stanchion

Runkel·rübe ['rʊŋkḷry:bə] die mangel-wurzel

runter ['rʊntɐ] *Adv. (ugs.)* ~ [da, das ist mein Platz]! get off [there, that's my seat]; ~ mit den Klamotten off with your clothes; get those clothes off; ~ mit den Füßen take your feet [down] off the table; Kopf ~! head/heads down; *s. auch* herunter; hinunter

runter-: ~|bringen *unr. tr. V. s.* herunterbringen; ~|dürfen *unr. itr. V. (ugs.)* be allowed to come down; *(hinausgehen dürfen)* be allowed out; ~|fallen *unr. itr. V.; mit sein (ugs.)* fall down; *(von der Leiter usw.)* fall off; die Leiter/von der Leiter ~fallen fall off the ladder; die Kreide fiel ihm ~: he dropped the chalk; ~|gehen *unr. itr. V.; mit sein (ugs.)* a) *(nach unten gehen)* go down; b) *(niedriger werden)* ‹*price, temperature, pressure, etc.*› go down, drop; c) *(die Höhe senken)* go down (auf + *Akk.* to); *(langsamer fahren)* slow down (auf + *Akk.* to); wir müssen mit den Preisen ~gehen we must reduce our prices; *s. auch* heruntergehen d, e; hinuntergehen; ~|hauen *unr. tr. V.* jmdm. eine/ein paar ~hauen *(salopp)* give sb. a clip/a couple of clips round the ear; ~|holen *tr. V. (ugs.)* a) fetch down; *s. auch* herunterholen b; b) sich/jmdm. einen ~holen *(vulg.)* jerk off *(coarse) or (Brit. coarse)* wank/jerk *(coarse) or (Brit. coarse)* wank sb. off; ~|kommen *unr. itr. V.; mit sein (ugs.)* come down; *s. auch* herunterkommen b, c; ~|können *unr. itr. V. (ugs.) s.* herunterkönnen; ~|kriegen *tr. V. (ugs.)* a) get down; etw. ~kriegen [können] manage to get sth. down; b) *(wegbekommen)* get off ‹*dirt, sth. sticky*›; ~|lassen *unr. tr. V. (ugs.) s.* herunterlassen; hinunterlassen; ~|machen *tr. V. (salopp) s.* heruntermachen; ~|müssen *unr. itr. V. (ugs.)* have to go/come down; ich muß von der Autobahn ~ *(fig.)* I'll have to get off the motorway; ~|reißen *unr. tr. V. (ugs.) s.* herunterreißen; ~|rutschen *itr. V.; mit sein (ugs.) s.* herunterrutschen; *s. auch* Buckel a; ~|spülen *tr. V. (ugs.) s.* hinunterspülen

Runzel ['rʊntsḷ] die; ~, ~n wrinkle

runzelig *Adj.* wrinkled

runzeln 1. *tr. V.* die Stirn/die Brauen ~: wrinkle one's brow/knit one's brows; *(ärgerlich)* frown; mit gerunzelter Stirn with wrinkled brow; *(ärgerlich)* frowning. 2. *refl. V.* wrinkle

runzlig *Adj. s.* runzelig

Rüpel ['ry:pḷ] der; ~s, ~ *(abwertend)* lout

Rüpelei die; ~, ~en *(abwertend)* a) *o. Pl. (Benehmen)* loutishness; loutish behaviour; b) *(Handlung)* piece of coarseness; noch so eine ~ von dir, und wir gehen nach Hause any more of that coarseness from you and we're going home; ~en coarseness *sing.*

rüpelhaft *(abwertend)* 1. *Adj.* loutish. 2. *adv.* in a loutish manner

rupfen ['rʊpfn̩] *tr. V.* a) pluck ‹*goose, hen, etc.*›; *s. auch* Hühnchen; b) *(abreißen)* pull up ‹*weeds, grass*›; pull off ‹*leaves etc.*›; c) *(ugs.: übervorteilen)* fleece ‹*person*› [of his/her money]

Rupfen der; ~s hessian

Rupie ['ru:pi̯ə] die; ~, ~n rupee

ruppig ['rʊpɪç] 1. *Adj. (abwertend)* gruff ‹*person, behaviour*›; sharp ‹*tone*›; er war ~ zu ihr he was short with her; he snapped at her. 2. *adv. (abwertend)* gruffly; ~ spielen play rough *or* a rough game

Ruppigkeit die; ~, ~en *(abwertend)* a) *o. Pl. (Benehmen)* gruffness; b) *(Handlung)* piece of uncouthness; ~en rough *or* uncouth behaviour *sing.*

Ruprecht *s.* Knecht b

Rüsche ['ry:ʃə] die; ~, ~n ruche; frill

Ruß [ru:s] der; ~es soot

Russe ['rʊsə] der; ~n, ~n Russian; der ~ *(ugs.)* Russians *pl.*; *(die russische Regierung)* the Russians *pl.*

Rüssel ['rʏsḷ] der; ~s, ~ a) *(des Elefanten)* trunk; *(des Schweins)* snout; *(bei Insekten u. ä.)* proboscis; b) *(salopp: Nase)* conk *(sl.)*

Rüssel·tier das proboscidean

rußen 1. *itr. V.* give off sooty smoke. 2. *tr. V. (schwärzen)* blacken with soot

Russen·bluse die, **Russen·kittel** der Russian blouse

Ruß·fleck der soot mark

ruß·geschwärzt *Adj.* blackened with soot *postpos.*

rußig *Adj.* sooty

Russin die; ~, ~nen Russian; *s. auch* -in

russisch 1. *Adj.* Russian; ~es Roulett Russian roulette; *s. auch* Ei a. 2. *adv.* a) ~ verwaltet/besetzt administered/occupied by Russia; b) *(auf ~)* in Russian; *s. auch* deutsch; ²Deutsche

Russisch das; ~[s] Russian; *s. auch* Deutsch

Russisch Brot das; ~ ~[e]s alphabet biscuits *pl. (Brit.) or (Amer.)* cookies

Russisch·grün das Russian green

Ruß·land (das); ~s Russia

rüsten ['rʏstn̩] 1. *itr. V. (sich bewaffnen)* arm; zum Krieg ~: arm for war. 2. *itr., refl. V. (geh.: sich bereit machen, auch fig.)* get ready; prepare; sich zur Reise ~: get ready *or* prepare oneself for the journey

Rüster ['ry:stɐ] die; ~, ~n a) *s.* Ulme; b) *s.* Rüsternholz

Rüstern·holz das elmwood

rüstig 1. *Adj.* a) *(leistungsfähig)* sprightly; active; er ist noch ~: he is still hale and hearty; b) *(geh.: kraftvoll)* strong. 2. *adv. (geh.: kraftvoll)* strongly; ~ ausschreiten stride out vigorously

rustikal [rʊsti'ka:l] 1. *Adj.* country-style ‹*food, inn, clothes, etc.*›; farmhouse *attrib.* ‹*food*›; rustic ‹*pattern*›; rustic, farmhouse *attrib.* ‹*furniture*›; *(als Nachahmung)* rustic-style ‹*furniture etc.*›; ein Schrank aus Eiche ~: a rustic-style oak cupboard. 2. *adv.* in [a] country style; ~ essen eat farmhouse *or* country-style food; ‹*furnish*› in a rustic *or* farmhouse style

Rüst-: ~kammer die *(hist.)* armoury; ~tag der *(jüd. Rel.)* day of preparation

Rüstung die; ~, ~en a) *(Bewaffnung)* armament *no art.*; *(Waffen)* arms *pl.*; weapons *pl.*; b) *(hist.: Schutzbekleidung)* suit of armour; in voller ~: in full armour

Rüstungs-: ~auftrag der arms order; ~aus·gaben *Pl.* arms expenditure *sing.*; ~begrenzung die arms limitation; ~betrieb der, ~fabrik die armaments factory; ~haus·halt der armaments *or* arms budget; ~industrie die armaments *or* arms industry; ~kontrolle die arms control; ~politik die arms policy; ~produktion die arms production *no art.*; ~stopp der arms freeze; ~wett·lauf der arms race

Rüst-: ~zeit die a) *(ev. Kirche)* period of reflection; retreat; b) *(Arbeitswiss.)* set-up time; ~zeug das a) *(Wissen)* requisite know-how; b) *(Ausrüstung)* equipment [for the job *or* task]

Rute ['ru:tə] die; ~, ~n a) *(Stock)* switch; *(Birken~, Angel~, Wünschel~)* rod; *(zum Züchtigen)* cane; *(Bündel)* birch; b) *(veralt.: Längenmaß)* rod; perch; c) *(Jägerspr.: männliches Glied)* penis; *(derb: menschlicher Penis)* prick *(vulg.)*; d) *(Jägerspr.: Schwanz)* tail

Ruten-: ~bündel das a) bundle of [birch] rods; b) *(altröm.: Faszes)* fasces *pl.*; ~gänger der; ~s, ~: dowser; diviner

Ruthenium [ru'te:ni̯ʊm] das; ~s *(Chemie)* ruthenium

Rutsch [rʊtʃ] der; ~[e]s, ~e a) *(das Rutschen)* slide; in einem *od.* auf einen ~ *(fig.*

ugs.) in one go; **b)** *(Erdmasse)* landslide; **c)** *(ugs.: Ausflug)* trip; jaunt; **guten ~ [ins neue Jahr]!** happy New Year!
Rutsch·bahn die slide; *(auf dem Rummelplatz)* helter-skelter
Rutsche die; ~, ~n chute
rutschen *itr. V.; mit sein* **a)** slide; ‹*clutch, carpet*› slip; *(aus~)* ‹*person*› slip; ‹*car etc.*› skid; *(nach unten)* slip [down]; **rutsch mal zur Seite!** *(ugs.)* move up a bit *(coll.)*; **ins Rutschen kommen** ‹*person*› [start to] slip; ‹*car etc.*› go into a skid; **auf seinem Platz hin und her ~:** slide *or* shift about on one's seat; **von/aus etw. ~:** slip *or* slide off/out of sth.; **die Brille/der Rock rutscht** the glasses keep/skirt keeps slipping [down]; **das trockene Brot rutscht schlecht/will nicht ~** *(ugs.)* the dry bread doesn't go down easily/won't go down; **b)** *(ugs.: kurz verreisen)* slip off
rutsch·fest *Adj.* **a)** *(strapazierfähig)* hard-wearing; **b)** *(nicht rutschig)* anti-skid ‹*tyre*›; skid-proof ‹*road surface*›; non-slip ‹*mat, material*›
Rutsch·gefahr die the danger of skidding
rutschig *Adj.* slippery
Rutsch·partie die *(ugs.)* succession of slides; *(im Auto)* succession of skids
rütteln ['rʏtl̩n] **1.** *tr. V.* **a)** shake; **jmdn. aus dem Schlaf** *od.* **wach ~:** shake sb. out of his/her sleep; **jmdn. am Arm/an der Schulter ~:** shake sb. by the arm/shoulder; **b)** *(Bauw.)* vibrate ‹*concrete etc.*›. **2.** *itr. V.* **a)** shake; **an der Tür/den Fenstern ~:** shake the door/windows; *(so daß es klappert)* rattle at the door/windows; ‹*wind*› make the door/windows rattle; **an den Fundamenten von etw. ~** *(fig.)* rock *or* shake the foundations of sth.; **daran ist nicht** *od.* **gibt es nichts zu ~** *(fig.)* there's nothing you can do about that; **b)** *(sich ruckartig hin u. her bewegen)* shake about; ‹*engine*› hunt; run unevenly
Rüttler ['rʏtlɐ] **der; ~s, ~** *(Bauw.)* vibrator

S

s, S [ɛs] **das; ~, ~:** s, S; *s. auch* **a, A**
s *Abk.* **Sekunde** sec.; s.
S *Abk.* **a) Süden** S.; **b)** *(österr.)* **Schilling** Sch.
s. *Abk.* **siehe**
S. *Abk.* Seite p.
s. a. *Abk.* **siehe auch**
Sa. *Abk.* **Samstag** Sat.
SA [ɛs'|a:] **die; ~** *(ns.) Abk.* **Sturmabteilung** SA
Saal [za:l] **der; ~[e]s, Säle** ['zɛ:lə] **a)** hall; *(Ball~)* ballroom; *(für Konzerte)* **der große/kleine ~:** the large/small auditorium; **b)** *(Publikum)* audience
Saal-: ~ordner der steward; **~schlacht die** [violent] brawl, rough-house *(between rival political factions)*
Saar·land ['za:ɐ̯lant] **das; ~[e]s** Saarland; Saar *(esp. Hist.)*
Saar·länder [-lɛndɐ] **der; ~s, ~, Saarländerin die; ~, ~nen** Saarlander
saar·ländisch *Adj.* Saarland *attrib.* ‹*government, population, etc.*›; Saar *attrib.* ‹*industry, miners, etc.*›; ‹*history*› of the Saar
Saat [za:t] **die; ~, ~en a)** *(Getreide usw.)* [young] crops *pl.*; *(fachspr.: Pflanzgut)* seedlings *pl.*; young plants *pl.*; **die ~ des Bösen ist aufgegangen** *(fig. geh.)* the seeds of evil have borne fruit; **b)** *o. Pl. (das Säen)* sowing; **mit der ~ beginnen** start sowing; **c)** *(Samenkörner)* seed[s *pl.*]
Saat-: ~gut das; *o. Pl.* seed[s *pl.*]; **~kartoffel die** seed-potato; **~korn das a)** *o. Pl. (zum Aussäen)* seed-corn; **b)** *(Samenkorn)* grain; **~krähe die** rook
Sabbat ['zabat] **der; ~s, ~e** sabbath; **es ist ~:** it is the sabbath
Sabbat·jahr das *(jüd. Rel.)* sabbatical year
Sabbel ['zabl] **der; ~s, ~** *(nordd. abwertend)* **a)** *(Mund)* gob *(sl.)*; **halt den ~:** shut your trap *(sl.)*; **b)** *o. Pl. s.* **Sabber**
sabbeln *(nordd.)* **1.** *itr. V.* **a)** *(abwertend: sprechen)* natter *(Brit. coll.) or* chatter [on]; rabbit on *(Brit. sl.)*; **b)** *s.* **sabbern 1 a. 2.** *tr. V. (abwertend)* jabber ‹*nonsense, rubbish*›
Sabber ['zabɐ] **der; ~s** *(ugs.)* slobber; *(eines Kindes)* dribble
sabbern 1. *itr. V.* **a)** ‹*dog, person*› slaver, slobber; ‹*baby*› dribble; **b)** *(abwertend) s.* **sabbeln 1 a. 2.** *tr. V. (abwertend) s.* **sabbeln 2**
Säbel ['zɛ:bl̩] **der; ~s, ~:** sabre; **mit dem ~ rasseln** *(fig. abwertend)* rattle the sabre
Säbel-: ~beine *Pl. (ugs. scherzh.)* bandy *or* bow legs; **~fechten das** *(Fechten)* sabre fencing *no art.*; **Weltmeister im ~fechten** world champion at sabre; world sabre champion; **~gerassel das** *(abwertend)* sabre-rattling
säbeln *tr. V. (ugs.)* hack, saw ‹*bread etc.*›
Säbel·rasseln das; ~s *(abwertend)* sabre-rattling
säbel·rasselnd *Adj.; nicht präd. (abwertend)* sabre-rattling
Sabotage [zabo'ta:ʒə] **die; ~, ~n** sabotage *no art.*; **Versuch der ~:** attempted sabotage
Sabotage·akt der act of sabotage
Saboteur [zabo'tø:ɐ̯] **der; ~s, ~e, Saboteurin die; ~, ~nen** saboteur
sabotieren *tr. V.* sabotage; disobey ‹*order*›
Saccharin [zaxa'ri:n] **das; ~s** saccharin
sach-, ~Sach-: ~bearbeiter der person responsible **(für** for); *(Experte)* specialist, expert **(für** on); **~bereich der** area; field; **der ~bereich Öffentlichkeitsarbeit** the field of public relations; all matters *pl.* concerning public relations; **~beschädigung die** *(Rechtsw.)* wilful damage to property; **~bezogen 1.** *Adj.* relevant; pertinent ‹*remark*›; **2.** *adv.* to the point; **~bezüge** *Pl.* payment *sing.* in kind; **~buch das** [popular] non-fiction *or* informative book; **~bücher lesen** read non-fiction *sing.*; **~dienlich** *Adj. (Papierdt.)* useful; helpful
Sache ['zaxə] **die; ~, ~n a)** *Pl.* things; **scharfe ~n trinken** drink the hard stuff *(coll.)*; **bewegliche/unbewegliche ~n** *(Rechtsspr., Wirtsch.)* movable/fixed assets; *(Rechtsw.: Eigentum)* movables *or* chattels/immovables *or* real estate *sing.*; **b)** *(Angelegenheit)* matter; business *(esp. derog.)*; **das ist eine andere ~/eine ~ für sich** that's a different/a separate matter; **eine ernste/schlimme/heikle/faule ~:** a serious/a bad/an awkward/a shady business; **es ist beschlossene ~[, daß ...]** it's [all] arranged *or* settled [that ...]; **es ist die einfachste ~ [von] der Welt** it's the simplest thing in the world; **das ist meine/seine ~:** that's my business/his own affair; **das ist so eine ~:** it's a bit tricky; **das ist nicht jedermanns ~:** it's not everyone's cup of tea; **du hast dir die ~ sehr leicht gemacht** you made it *or* things *pl.* very easy for yourself; **so kommen wir der ~ näher** we are getting warmer *or* coming to the point; **~n gibt's[, die gibt's gar nicht]!** *(ugs.)* would you believe *or* credit it!; **mach ~n!** you don't say!; **was sind denn das für ~n!** *(ugs.)* what's all this then!; what's going on!; **von dir hört man ja nette ~n!** *(iron.)* I've heard some things about you!; **[mit jmdm.] gemeinsame ~ machen** join forces [with sb.]; **sagen/jmdm. sagen, was ~ ist** *(ugs.)* come out with it/come clean with sb. *(coll.)*; *(die Dinge beim Namen nennen)* say/tell sb. what's what; *(sagen, worum es geht)* say/tell sb. what gives *(coll.)*; *(bestimmen)* say/tell sb. what goes *(coll.)*; **[sich** *(Dat.)*] **seiner ~ sicher** *od.* **gewiß sein** be sure one is right; **bei der ~ sein/bleiben** concentrate/keep one's mind on it; *(im Gespräch usw.)* stick to the point; **nicht bei der ~ sein** let one's mind wander; **zur ~ kommen** come to the point; **das tut nichts zur ~:** that's irrelevant; that's got nothing to do with it; **c)** *(Rechts~)* case; **die Verhandlung in ~n Maier gegen Schulze** the hearing in the case of Maier versus Schulze; **Fragen/Angaben zur ~:** questions/statements about the case; **d)** *o. Pl. (Anliegen)* cause; **es dient der großen ~:** it's in a good cause; **e)** *Pl. (ugs.: Stundenkilometer)* **100 ~n** 100 kilometres per hour; **wieviel ~n hat er drauf gehabt?** how fast was he going?
Sach·ein·lage die *(Wirtsch.)* investment in kind
Sächelchen ['zɛçlçən] **das; ~s, ~:** [little] thing
Sachen·recht das; *o. Pl. (Rechtsw.)* law of property
Sacher·torte ['zaxɐ-] **die** *rich iced chocolate cake*; Sachertorte
sach-, Sach-: ~frage die question about the matter/issue itself *(as opposed to personalities, methods, etc.)*; **~gebiet das** subject [area]; field; **das ~gebiet Ornithologie** the field of ornithology; **~gemäß, ~gerecht 1.** *Adj.* proper; correct; **2.** *adv.* properly; correctly; **~katalog der** *(Buchw.)* subject catalogue; **~kenner der** expert; **~kenntnis die** expertise; knowledge of the subject; **von keiner ~kenntnis getrübt** *(scherzh.)* without having the faintest idea [what it's all about]; **~kunde die a)** *s.* **~kenntnis; b)** ≈ general subjects *pl.*; **~kundig 1.** *Adj.* with a knowledge of the subject *postpos.*, *not pred.*; **sich ~kundig machen** acquaint oneself with the subject; **2.** *adv.* expertly; **~lage die;** *o. Pl.* situation; **~leistung die;** *meist Pl. (Amtsspr., Versicherungsw.)* benefit in kind
sachlich 1. *Adj.* **a)** *(objektiv)* objective; *(nüchtern)* functional ‹*building, style, etc.*›; matter-of-fact, down-to-earth ‹*letter etc.*›; **b)** *nicht präd. (sachbezogen)* factual ‹*error*›; actual, material ‹*difference*›; material ‹*consideration*›; **aus ~en Gründen** for practical reasons. **2.** *adv.* *(objektiv)* objectively; ‹*state*› as a matter of fact; *(nüchtern)* ‹*furnished*› in a functional style; ‹*written*› in a matter-of-fact way; **b)** *(sachbezogen)* factually ‹*wrong*›; actually ‹*justified*›
sächlich ['zɛçlɪç] *Adj. (Sprachw.)* neuter
Sachlichkeit die; ~: objectivity; *(Nüchternheit)* functionalism; **Neue ~** *(Kunstwiss.)* new objectivity
Sach-: ~mangel der; *meist Pl. (Rechtsw.)* material defect; **~register das** [subject] index; **~schaden der** damage [to property] *no indef. art.*; **ein ~schaden von 30 000 Mark** damage amounting to 30,000 marks
Sachse ['zaksə] **der; ~n, ~n** Saxon
sächseln ['zɛksl̩n] *itr. V.* **er sächselt** he speaks in Saxon dialect
Sachsen (das); ~s Saxony
Sachsen-Anhalt (das); ~s Saxony-Anhalt
sächsisch ['zɛksɪʃ] **1.** *Adj.* Saxon; ‹*capital, economy, etc.*› of Saxony. **2.** *adv.* ‹*speak, write*› in Saxon dialect; *s. auch* **badisch**
Sach·spende die gift *or* contribution in kind

sacht [zaxt] **1.** *Adj.* **a)** *(behutsam)* gentle; *(langsam)* smooth ⟨*take-off*⟩; gentle, gradual ⟨*acceleration*⟩; **b)** *(leise)* quiet. **2.** *adv.* **a)** gently; **b)** *(leise)* quietly

sachte 1. *s.* **sacht. 2.** *adv.* *(ugs.)* **a)** *(Beschwichtigung)* **~[, ~]** take it easy; *(nicht so hastig)* not so fast; **b) so [ganz] ~** *(allmählich)* gradually

sach-, Sach-: ~verhalt der; ~[e]s, ~e facts *pl.* [of the matter]; **~versicherung die** *(Versicherungsw.)* property insurance; **~verstand der** expertise; grasp of the subject; **~verständig 1.** *Adj.* expert ⟨*opinion etc.*⟩; knowledgeable ⟨*person*⟩; **2.** *adv.* expertly; knowledgeably; **~verständige der/die;** *adj. Dekl.* expert; **~verständigen·aus·schuß der** committee of experts; **~verständigen·gutachten das** expert's report; *(von mehreren)* experts' report; **~walter** [~valtɐ] **der; ~s, ~, ~walterln die; ~, ~nen a)** *(geh.: Fürsprecher)* champion; **b)** *(Rechtsw.: Interessenvertreter der Gläubiger)* trustee in bankruptcy; **~wert der a)** *o. Pl.* intrinsic *or* real value; **b)** *(Wertobjekt)* material asset; **~wissen das** specialist knowledge; **~wörter·buch das** specialist *or* subject dictionary; **ein ~wörterbuch der Literatur** a dictionary of literature; **~zwang der** [factual *or* material] constraint

Sack [zak] **der; ~[e]s, Säcke** ['zɛkə] **a)** *(Behältnis)* sack; *(aus Papier, Kunststoff)* bag; **ein ~ Zement** a bag of cement; **drei Säcke [voll] Kartoffeln** three sacks of potatoes; **einen ~ voll ...** *(fig.)* a [whole] load *or* mass of ... *(coll.)*; **den ~ schlägt man, den Esel meint man** *(Spr.)* he/she is being used as a scapegoat; **jmdn. im ~ haben** *(salopp)* have got round sb.; **etw. im ~ haben** *(salopp)* have sth. in the bag *(coll.)*; **jmdn. in den ~ stecken** *(ugs.)* put sb. in the shade; **mit ~ und Pack** with bag and baggage; *s. auch* **naß 1 a; schlafen 1 a; b)** *(Hautfalte)* **Säcke unter den Augen haben** have bags under one's eyes; **c)** *(derb: Hoden~)* balls *pl.* *(coarse)*; **d)** *(derb abwertend: Mensch)* sod *(Brit. sl.)*; **e)** *(bes. südd., österr., schweiz.)* *(Hosentasche)* [trouser-]pocket; *(Geldbeutel)* purse

Sack·bahn·hof der *s.* **Kopfbahnhof**

Säckchen ['zɛkçən] **das; ~s, ~:** small sack; bag

Säckel ['zɛkl] **der; ~s, ~** *(bes. südd., österr.)* **a)** *(veralt.: Geldbeutel)* money-bag; purse; **b)** *(Hosentasche)* [trouser-]pocket; **c)** *s.* **Sack d**

sacken *itr. V.; mit sein* ⟨*person*⟩ slump; ⟨*ship etc.*⟩ sink; ⟨*plane*⟩ drop rapidly, plummet; **er sackte in die Knie** his knees gave way

säcke·weise *Adv. s.* **sackweise b**

sack-, Sack-: ~gasse die cul-de-sac; *(fig.)* impasse; **~hüpfen das; ~s** sack race; **beim ~hüpfen** in the sack race; **~kleid das** sack; **~leinen das, ~lein·wand die** sacking; **~pfeife die** bagpipes *pl.*; **~tuch das a)** *Pl.* **~tuche** *s.* **~leinen; b)** *Pl.* **~tücher** *(südd., österr., schweiz.)* handkerchief; **~weise** *Adv.* **a)** *(in Säcken)* in sacks; **b)** *(massenhaft)* loads *or* masses of *(coll.)*

Sadismus [za'dɪsmʊs] **der; ~, Sadismen a)** *o. Pl.* *(Veranlagung; abwertend: Quälerei)* sadism *no art.*; **b)** *(Handlung)* act of sadism

Sadist der; ~en, ~en, Sadistin die; ~, ~nen sadist

sadistisch 1. *Adj.* sadistic. **2.** *adv.* sadistically; **~ veranlagt sein** have sadistic tendencies

Sado·masochismus [zadomazɔ'xɪsmʊs] **der** *(Med.)* sado-masochism *no art.*

sado·masochistisch *(Med.)* **1.** *Adj.* sadomasochistic. **2.** *adv.* sado-masochistically; **~ veranlagt sein** have sado-masochistic tendencies

säen ['zɛ:ən] *tr. (auch itr.) V. (auch fig.)* sow; **dünn** *od.* **nicht gerade dicht gesät sein** *(fig.)* be thin on the ground

Safari [za'fa:ri] **die; ~, ~s** safari

Safe [seɪf] **der** *od.* **das; ~s, ~s a)** safe; **b)** *(Schließfach)* safe-deposit box

Saffian ['zafi̯an] **der; ~s, Saffian·leder das** morocco [leather]

Safran ['zafran] **der; ~s, ~e** saffron

Saft [zaft] **der; ~[e]s, Säfte** ['zɛftə] **a)** juice; **jmdn. im eigenen ~ schmoren lassen** *(fig. ugs.)* let sb. stew in his/her own juice; **b)** *(in Pflanzen)* sap; **Blut ist ein ganz besonderer ~:** blood is thicker than water *(fig.)*; **ohne ~ und Kraft** *(abwertend)* weak and lifeless; *(adv.)* without any zest; **c)** *(salopp: Elektrizität)* juice *(sl.)*; **d)** *(veralt.: Körperflüssigkeit)* fluid; **e)** *(österr.: Soße)* gravy

saft·grün *Adj.* lush green

Saft·heini der *(ugs.)* right twit *(Brit. sl.)*; jerk *(sl.)*

saftig 1. *Adj.* **a)** *(voll Saft)* juicy; sappy ⟨*stem*⟩; lush ⟨*meadow, green*⟩; *(fig.: lebensvoll)* lusty; **b)** *(ugs.: stark, intensiv)* hefty ⟨*slap, blow*⟩; good ⟨*thrashing*⟩; steep *(coll.)* ⟨*prices, bill*⟩; terrific, big ⟨*surprise, punch-up*⟩; crude, coarse ⟨*joke, song, etc.*⟩; strongly-worded ⟨*letter etc.*⟩; strong, juicy ⟨*curse*⟩. **2.** *adv.* **a) eine ~ grüne Wiese** a lush green meadow; **b)** *(ugs.: kräftig)* ⟨*curse, hit out*⟩ well and truly, good and proper

Saftigkeit die; ~, ~en a) *o. Pl.* juiciness; **die ~ der Wiesen** the lushness of the meadows; **b)** *(Äußerung)* crude remark

saft-, Saft-: ~kur die juice diet; **~laden der;** *Pl.* **~läden** *(salopp abwertend)* lousy outfit *(sl.)*; **~los** *Adj.* **a)** juiceless; **~los sein** have *or* contain no juice; **b)** *(fig.)* feeble, anodyne ⟨*language*⟩; **~- und kraftlos** feeble; wishy-washy; *(adv.)* without any zest; **~presse die** juice extractor; **~sack der** *(derb abwertend)* bastard *(coll.)*; **~tag der** juice[-diet] day

Saga ['za(:)ga] **die; ~, ~s** *(Literaturw.)* saga

Sage ['za:gə] **die; ~, ~n** legend; *(bes. nordische)* saga; *(fig.: Gerücht)* rumour

Säge ['zɛ:gə] **die; ~, ~n a)** saw; **b)** *(bayr., österr.: ~werk)* sawmill

Säge-: ~blatt das saw-blade; **~bock der** saw-horse; **~fisch der** sawfish; **~mehl das** sawdust; **~mühle die** sawmill

sagen 1. *tr. V.* **a)** *(äußern, behaupten)* say; **so etwas sagt man nicht** it's not done to say things like that; **das kann man nicht [so ohne weiteres] ~:** you can't really say *or* tell; **das kann jeder ~:** anybody can claim that; it's easy to talk; **das ist nicht zu viel gesagt** that's not overstating the case *or* no exaggeration; **man sagt [von ihm** *od.* **über ihn], daß ...:** it is said [of him] that ...; **das sagst du so einfach!** that's easy to say *or* easily said; **da soll noch einer ~** *od.* **da sage noch einer, daß ...:** never let it be said that ...; **na, wer sagt's denn!** *(ugs.)* there you are[, I knew it]!; **sag das nicht!** *(ugs.)* don't [just] assume that; not necessarily; **das ist nicht gesagt** it's not necessarily the case; it's by no means certain; **dann will ich nichts gesagt haben** in that case forget I said anything; **was ich noch ~ wollte** [oh] by the way; before I forget; **unter uns gesagt** between you and me; **das oben Gesagte** what has been said above; the above remarks *pl.*; *(in einem Vortrag)* the foregoing [remarks]; **das mußte einmal gesagt werden** it had to be said; **wie gesagt** as I've said *or* mentioned; **das ist leichter gesagt als getan** that's easier said than done; **das kann man wohl ~, das kann man** *od.* **kannst du laut ~** *(ugs.)* you can say 'that again; **gesagt, getan** no sooner said than done; **das kostet Tausende, [ach,] was sage ich, Millionen!** it costs thousands, what am I talking about, millions!; **~ wir einmal** *od.* *(ugs.)* **mal** let's say; **wir treffen uns, ~ wir, um 10 vor 8** let's meet at, say, ten to eight; **sage und schreibe** *(ugs.)* believe it or not; would you believe; **um nicht zu ~:** not to say; **sag bloß, du hast es vergessen!** *(ugs.)* don't say you've forgotten it!; **b)** *(meinen)* say; **was ~ Sie dazu?** what do you think about that?; **was soll man dazu noch ~?** *(ugs.)* what 'can one say; **was sagst du nun?** *(ugs.)* now what do you say?; what do you say to that?; **c)** *(mitteilen)* **jmdm. etw. ~:** say sth. to sb.; *(zur Information)* tell sb. sth.; **[jmdm.] seinen Namen/seine Gründe ~:** give [sb.] one's name/reasons; **[jmdm.] die Wahrheit ~:** tell [sb.] the truth; **sag mal/~ Sie [mal], gibt es ...?** tell me, is there ...?; **ich habe mir ~ lassen, daß ...:** I've been told that ...; **das sag' ich dir** *(ugs.)* I'm telling *or* warning you; **ich hab's [dir] ja gleich gesagt!** *(ugs.)* I told you so!; *(habe dich gewarnt)* I warned you!; **ich will dir mal was ~:** let me tell you something; **laß dir das gesagt sein** *(ugs.)* make a note of *or* remember what I'm saying; **das sag' ich [deinen Eltern** *usw.*] *(Kinderspr.)* I'll tell on you [to your parents *etc.*]; **wem ~ Sie das!** *(ugs.)* you don't need to tell me [that]!; **das brauchst du mir nicht zu ~** *(ugs.)* you don't need to tell me that; I know that only too well; **was Sie nicht ~!** *(ugs., oft iron.)* you don't say!; **das kann ich dir ~!** *(ugs.)* you can be sure of that *or* bank on that; **wenn ich es [dir] sage!** *(ugs.)* I promise [you]; **jmdm. Grobheiten ~:** speak rudely to sb.; **und dann muß ich mir von ihm auch noch ~ lassen, daß ...:** and then I have to put up with him telling me that ...; **er läßt sich** *(Dat.)* **nichts ~:** he won't be told; you can't tell him anything; **d)** *(nennen)* **zu jmdm./etw. X ~:** call sb./sth. X; **du kannst du zu mir ~:** you can call me 'du' *or* say 'du' to me; **e)** *(formulieren, ausdrücken)* say; **das hast du gut gesagt** you put that well; that was well said; **so kann man es auch ~:** you could put it like that; **etw. in aller Deutlichkeit ~:** make sth. perfectly clear; **das sagt er nur so** he doesn't mean it; **es ist nicht zu ~, wie ...:** no words can express *or* say *or* there is no expressing how ...; **du sagst es!** very true!; **willst du damit ~, daß ...?** are you trying to say *or* do you mean [to say] that ...?; **das wollte ich damit nicht ~:** I didn't mean that; **will ~:** or rather; that is to say; **f)** *(bedeuten)* mean; **damit ist viel/wenig/nichts gesagt** that's saying a lot/not saying much/that doesn't mean anything; **das will** *od.* **hat nichts zu ~:** that doesn't mean anything; that isn't important; **hat das etwas zu ~?** does that mean anything?; **g)** *(anordnen, befehlen)* tell; **du hast mir gar nichts zu ~:** you've no right to order me about; **von ihm lasse ich mir nichts ~:** I'm not taking any orders from him; **sich** *(Dat.)* **etw. nicht zweimal ~ lassen** *(ugs.)* not need to be told *or* asked twice; **das lass'/ließ ich mir nicht zweimal ~:** I'd love to/I jumped at it; **etwas/nichts zu ~ haben** ⟨*person*⟩ have a/no say; *(zuständig/nicht zuständig sein)* be in authority/have no authority. **2.** *refl. V.* **a) sich** *(Dat.)* **etw. ~:** say sth. to oneself; **das hättest du dir damals schon ~ können** you should have realized [that] then; **b) das sagt sich so einfach** *(ugs.)* that's easy to say *or* easily said. **3.** *itr. V.* **wie sagt man [da]?** what does one say?; what's the [right] word?; *(Aufforderung an ein Kind)* what do you say [now]?; **wenn ich so ~ darf** if I may put it this way; *(bei einem etwas gewagten Ausdruck)* if you will pardon the expression; **sag bloß!** *(ugs.)* you don't say!

sägen ['zɛ:gn̩] **1.** *itr. V.* **a)** saw; *(fig.: auf einer Geige usw.)* saw away; **an jmds. Stuhl ~** *(fig.)* try to undermine sb.'s position; **b)** *(ugs. scherzh.: schnarchen)* snore loudly. **2.** *tr. V.* saw; *(zersägen)* saw up ⟨*tree etc.*⟩

Sagen-: ~buch das book of legends; **~gestalt die** legendary figure

sagenhaft 1. *Adj.* **a)** *(ugs.)* incredible *(coll.)* ⟨*wealth, mess, memory, etc.*⟩; fabulous *(coll.)* ⟨*party, wealth*⟩; **b)** *(der Sage angehörend)* legendary. **2.** *adv.* incredibly *(coll.)*

sagen·umwoben *Adj. (geh.)*⟨*castle, place*⟩ steeped in legend; ⟨*historical figure*⟩ at the centre of many legends

Sagen·welt die; *o. Pl.* legendary world

Säge-: ~späne *Pl.* wood shavings; **~werk das** sawmill; **~zahn der** sawtooth

Sago ['za:go] **der** *od.* **das; ~s** sago

sah [za:] *1. u. 3. Pers. Sg. Prät. v.* **sehen**

Sahel·zone ['za:hɛl- *od.* za'he:l-] **die;** *o. Pl.* Sahel

Sahne ['za:nə] **die; ~:** cream

Sahne-: ~bonbon der *od.* **das** cream toffee; **~eis das** cream ice; **~quark der** creamy quark; quark with a high fat content; **~torte die** cream cake *or* gateau

sahnig *Adj.* creamy

Saison [zɛ'zõ:] **die; ~, ~s** season; **während/außerhalb der ~:** during the season/out of season *or* in the off-season; **~ haben** have one's busy time *or* season; ⟨*hotel*⟩ be open for the season; *(ugs.: sehr gefragt sein)* ⟨*goods*⟩ be much in demand

saisonal [zɛzo'na:l] **1.** *Adj.* seasonal. **2.** *adv.* ⟨*fluctuate*⟩ according to the season

saison-, Saison-: ~arbeit die seasonal work; **~arbeiter der** seasonal worker; **~aus·verkauf der** end-of-season sale; **~bedingt 1.** *Adj.* seasonal; **2.** *adv.* due to seasonal influences; **~zu·schlag der** seasonal supplement

Saite ['zaitə] **die; ~, ~n** *(Musik, Sport)* string; **das/sie brachte in mir eine verwandte ~ zum Klingen** *(fig.)* it/she struck a responsive chord in me; **andere** *od.* **strengere ~n aufziehen** *(fig.)* take stronger measures; get tough *(coll.)*

Saiten-: ~halter der *(Musik) (an der Geige)* tailpiece; *(an der Laute, Gitarre)* stringholder; **~instrument das** stringed instrument; **~spiel das** *(geh.)* string playing; *(Musik)* string music

-saitig [-zaitɪç] -string[ed]

Sakko ['zako] **der** *od.* **das; ~s, ~s** jacket

sakral [za'kra:l] *Adj.* religious; **~e Gewänder** priest's vestments; **~e Gesänge** sacred songs *or* chants

Sakral·bau der; *Pl.* **~bauten** *(Archit., Kunstwiss.)* religious building

Sakrament [zakra'mɛnt] **das; ~[e]s, ~e a)** *(christl., bes. kath. Kirche)* sacrament; **b) ~ [noch mal]!** for Heaven's sake

sakramental [zakramɛn'ta:l] *Adj.* sacramental

Sakramentalien [zakramɛn'ta:liən] *Pl. (kath. Rel.)* sacramentals

Sakrileg [zakri'le:k] **das; ~s, ~e** act of sacrilege; **ist es ein ~?** is it sacrilege?

Sakristan [zakrɪs'ta:n] **der; ~s, ~e** sacristan

Sakristei [zakrɪs'tai] **die; ~, ~en** sacristy

sakrosankt [zakro'zaŋkt] *Adj.* sacrosanct

säkular [zɛku'la:ɐ] *Adj.* **a)** *(geh.: weltlich; auch Astron., Geol.)* secular; **b)** *(geh.: herausragend)* outstanding

säkularisieren *tr. V.* secularize ⟨*property, art, etc.*⟩; deconsecrate ⟨*church*⟩

Salamander [zala'mandɐ] **der; ~s, ~:** salamander; **einen** *od.* **den ~ reiben** *(Studentenspr.) scrape one's glass three times on the table, empty it, and after brief drumming put it down with a bang (as a mark of honour)*

Salami [za'la:mi] **die; ~, ~[s]** salami

Salami·taktik die step-by-step policy

Salär [za'lɛ:ɐ] **das; ~s, ~e** *(bes. schweiz., auch südd., österr., sonst veralt.)* salary

Salat [za'la:t] **der; ~[e]s, ~e a)** salad; **b)** *o. Pl.* **[grüner] ~:** lettuce; **ein Kopf ~:** a [head of] lettuce; **c)** *o. Pl. (ugs.: Wirrwarr)* muddle; mess; **jetzt haben wir den ~!** *(ugs. iron.)* now we're in a right mess

Salat-: ~besteck das salad-servers *pl.*, **~blatt das** lettuce-leaf; **~gurke die** cucumber; **~kartoffel die** *potato suitable for potato salad;* **~kopf der** lettuce; **~öl das** salad-oil; **~schüssel die** salad-bowl; **~soße die** salad-dressing

salbadern [zal'ba:dɐn] *tr. V. (ugs. abwertend)* waffle [pretentiously]

Salbe ['zalbə] **die; ~, ~n** ointment; *(gegen Muskelkater usw.)* embrocation

Salbei ['zalbai] **der** *od.* **die; ~:** sage

salben *tr. V.* **a)** *(einreiben)* put ointment on ⟨*part of body*⟩; **b)** *(kath. Kirche)* anoint ⟨*sick or dying person, (Hist.) king, emperor, etc.*⟩; *(hist.)* **jmdn. zum Kaiser ~:** anoint sb. emperor

Salbung die; ~, ~en *(Weihung)* anointing; *(kath. Kirche)* unction; **die letzte ~:** extreme unction

salbungs·voll *(abwertend)* **1.** *Adj.* unctuous. **2.** *adv.* unctuously

saldieren [zal'di:rən] **1.** *tr. V.* **a)** *(Buchf., Finanzw.)* balance ⟨*credit and debit sides*⟩; **einen Gewinn ~:** produce a profit balance; **b)** *(österr.: quittieren)* confirm payment of; give a receipt for. **2.** *itr. V.* **a)** *(Buchf., Finanzw.)* balance the books; **b)** *(österr.: quittieren)* confirm payment

Saldo ['zaldo] **der; ~s, ~s** *od.* **Saldi** *od.* **Salden** *(Buchf., Finanzw.)* balance; **im ~ sein/bleiben** be/remain in debt

Saldo-: ~übertrag der, ~vortrag der *(Buchf.)* balance brought forward

Säle *s.* **Saal**

Salicylsäure *(chem. fachspr.) s.* **Salizylsäure**

Salier ['za:liɐ] **der; ~s, ~** *(hist.)* Salian

Saline [za'li:nə] **die; ~, ~n** salt-works *sing. or pl.*

Salizyl·säure [zali'tsy:l-] **die** *(Chemie)* salicylic acid

Salm [zalm] **der; ~[e]s, ~e** *(bes. rhein.)* salmon

Salmiak [zal'miak] **der** *od.* **das; ~:** sal ammoniac

Salmiak-: ~geist der [liquid] ammonia; ammonia water; **~pastille die** sal ammoniac pastille

Salmonelle [zalmo'nɛlə] **die; ~, ~n;** *meist Pl.* salmonella *sing.*

Salomon ['za:lomɔn] **(der)** Solomon

Salomonen [zalo'mo:nən] *Pl.* Solomon Islands

salomonisch *(geh.)* **1.** *Adj.* Solomon-like; **ein ~es Urteil** a judgment of Solomon. **2.** *adv.* with the wisdom of Solomon

Salon [za'lõ:] **der; ~s, ~s a)** *(Raum)* drawing-room; salon; **b)** *(Geschäft)* [hair- *etc.*] salon; **c)** *(veralt.: Zirkel)* [literary] salon; **d)** *(Ausstellung)* Salon

salon-, Salon-: ~fähig 1. *Adj.* socially acceptable; *(nach einem Bad o. ä.)* **ich bin noch nicht ~fähig** I am not yet presentable; **2.** *adv.* in a socially acceptable manner; properly ⟨*dressed*⟩; **~kommunist der** *(iron.)* parlour communist; **~löwe der** *(abwertend)* society man; **~musik die** salon music; **~wagen der** Pullman car *or* coach

salopp [za'lɔp] **1.** *Adj.* casual ⟨*clothes*⟩; free and easy, informal ⟨*behaviour, household, etc.*⟩; very colloquial, slangy ⟨*saying, expression, etc.*⟩. **2.** *adv.* ⟨*dress*⟩ casually; informally; **~ reden** use slangy *or* [very] colloquial language

Salpeter [zal'pe:tɐ] **der; ~s** saltpetre

Salpeter·säure die nitric acid

salpetrig *Adj.* **~e Säure** nitrous acid

Salto ['zalto] **der; ~s, ~s** *od.* **Salti a)** somersault; *(beim Turnen auch)* salto; **ein ~ vorwärts/rückwärts** a forward/backward somersault; **einen ~ springen** do *or* turn a somersault; **b)** *(Fliegerspr.) s.* **Looping**

Salto mortale [~ mɔr'ta:lə] **der; ~ ~, ~ ~** *od.* **Salti mortali** salto mortale

Salut [za'lu:t] **der; ~[e]s, ~e** *(Milit.)* salute; **~ schießen** fire a salute; **21 Schuß ~ abgeben** fire a twenty-one-gun salute

salutieren *itr. V. (bes. Milit.)* salute; **vor jmdm. ~:** salute sb.

Salut·schuß der; *meist Pl. (Milit.)* gun salute; **sieben Salutschüsse** a seven-gun salute

Salvadorianer [zalvado'ria:nɐ] **der; ~s, ~:** Salvadoran

Salve ['zalvə] **die; ~, ~n** *(Milit.)* salvo; *(aus Gewehren)* volley; **eine ~ des Beifalls/von Gelächter** *(fig.)* a burst of applause/laughter

Salz [zalts] **das; ~es, ~e** salt; **das ~ der Ironie** *(fig.)* the spice of irony; **~ auf die** *od.* **in die Wunde streuen** *(fig.)* rub salt into the wound; **jmdm. nicht das ~ in der Suppe gönnen** *(ugs.)* begrudge sb. everything

salz-, Salz-: ~arm 1. *Adj.* low in salt *postpos.*; low-salt; **2.** *adv.* **~arm kochen** use little salt in cooking; **~arm essen** eat food containing little salt; **~berg·werk das** salt-mine; **~brezel die** [salted] pretzel

salzen *tr. V.* salt; **die Suppe ist stark/zu wenig/kaum gesalzen** the soup has a lot of/too little/hardly any salt in it

salz-, Salz-: ~fäßchen das a) salt-cellar; **b)** *(ugs. scherzh.: beim Menschen)* hollow between the collar-bones; **~fleisch das** *s.* **Pökelfleisch; ~haltig** *Adj.* containing salt *postpos., not pred.;* salty; **sehr ~haltig sein** have a high salt content; **~hering der** salted herring

salzig *Adj.* salty

salz-, Salz-: ~kartoffel die; *meist Pl.* boiled potato; **~korn das;** *Pl.* **~körner** grain of salt; **~lake die** brine; **~lecke die** *(Jägerspr.)* salt-lick; **~los 1.** *Adj.* salt-free; *(nicht gesalzen)* unsalted; **2.** *adv.* ⟨*cook*⟩ without any salt; **~los essen** eat unsalted food; **~lösung die** saline solution; **~mandel die** salted almond; **~napf der** salt-cellar; **~säule die** pillar of salt; **zur ~säule erstarren** *(fig.)* be rooted to the spot *or* turned to stone; **~säure die;** *o. Pl. (Chemie)* hydrochloric acid; **~see der** salt lake; *(ausgetrocknet)* salt flats *pl.;* **~sieder der; ~s, ~** *(veralt.)* salt-maker; **~sole die** brine; **~stange die** salt stick; **~streuer der; ~s, ~:** salt-sprinkler; salt-shaker *(Amer.);* **~wasser das;** *Pl.* **~wässer a)** *o. Pl. (zum Kochen)* salted water; **b)** *(Meerwasser)* salt water; **c)** *(Lake)* brine; **~werk das** salt-works *sing. or pl.;* **~wüste die** salt desert

SA-Mann [ɛs'|a:-] **der;** *Pl.* **SA-Männer** *od.* **SA-Leute** *(ns.)* SA man; storm-trooper

Sä·mann der; *Pl.* **Sämänner** *(dichter.)* sower

Samariter [zama'ri:tɐ] **der; ~s, ~ a) [barmherziger] ~:** good Samaritan; **bei jmdm. ~ spielen** play *or* act the good Samaritan to sb.; **b)** *(schweiz.) s.* **Sanitäter**

Samariter·dienst der selfless act [of kindness]

Sä·maschine die seeder, *(esp.)* seed-drill

Samba ['zamba] **der; ~s, ~s** *od.* **die; ~, ~s** samba

Sambesi [zam'be:zi] **der; ~[s]** Zambezi

Sambia ['zambia] **(das); ~s** Zambia

Sambier ['zambiɐ] **der; ~s, ~, Sambierin die; ~, ~nen** Zambian

[1]Same ['za:mə] **der; ~n, ~n** *s.* **Lappe**

[2]Same der; ~ns, ~n *(geh.)* seed

Samen ['za:mən] **der; ~s, ~ a)** *(~korn)* seed; **b)** *o. Pl. (~körner)* seed[s. *pl.*]; **c)** *o. Pl. (Sperma)* sperm; semen

Samen-: ~an·lage die *(Bot.)* ovule; **~bank die;** *Pl.* **~banken** *(Med., Tiermed.)* sperm bank; **~erguß der** ejaculation; **~faden der** *s.* **Spermium; ~flüssigkeit die** seminal fluid; **~handlung die** seed merchant's [shop *or (Amer.)* store]; **~kapsel die** seed capsule; **~korn das;** *Pl.* **~körner** seed; **~leiter der** *(Anat.)* sperm[atic] duct; **~strang der** *(Anat.)* spermatic cord; **~zelle die** sperm cell

Sämereien [zɛ:mə'raiən] *Pl.* seeds

sämig ['zɛ:mɪç] *Adj.* thick ⟨*sauce, soup, etc.*⟩; viscous ⟨*liquid*⟩

Sämisch·leder das chamois leather

Sämling ['zɛ:mlɪŋ] **der; ~s, ~e** seedling

Sammel-: ~album das [collector's] album;

~auftrag der *(Postw.)* multiple *or* combined transfer; **~band der;** *Pl.* **~bände** anthology (**über** + *Akk.* of); **~becken das** collecting basin; reservoir; *(fig.)* gathering-point *or* -place; **~bestellung die** joint order; **~bezeichnung die** *(Sprachw.)* collective term; **~büchse die** collecting-box; **~fahr·schein der** group ticket; **~konto das** *(Buchf.)* collation account; **~lager das** assembly *or* transit camp; **~mappe die** folder; file

sammeln ['zam|n] **1.** *tr. (auch itr.) V.* **a)** collect; gather ‹*honey, firewood, fig.: material, experiences, impressions, etc.*›; gather, pick ‹*berries, herbs, mushrooms, etc.*›; **Kräfte ~:** summon up one's strength; **die gesammelten Werke Tolstois** Tolstoy's collected works; **b)** *(zusammenkommen lassen)* gather ‹*people*› [together]; assemble ‹*people*›; cause ‹*light rays*› to converge. **2.** *refl. V.* **a)** *(sich versammeln)* gather [together]; ‹*light rays*› converge; **sich um jmdn./etw. ~:** gather round sb./sth.; **b)** *(sich konzentrieren)* collect oneself; gather oneself together

Sạmmel-: ~platz der *(für Gegenstände)* collection *or* collecting point; *(für Menschen)* assembly point; **~punkt der a)** *(~platz)* assembly point; **b)** *(Brennpunkt)* focal point; **~stelle die** *s.* **~platz**

Sammelsurium [zaml'zu:ri̯ʊm] **das; ~s,** Sammelsurien *(abwertend)* hotchpotch; **ein ~ von alten Gläsern und Flaschen** a jumble of old glasses and bottles

Sạmmel-: ~tasse die [collector's] ornamental cup and saucer; **~transport der** *(von Menschen, Vieh)* mass transport; *(von Gütern)* bulk shipment; **~visum das** collective *or* group visa; **~wut die** collecting mania

Sammet ['zamət] **der; ~s, ~e** *(schweiz., sonst veralt.) s.* **Samt**

Sammler ['zamlɐ] **der; ~s, ~ a)** collector; *(von Pilzen, Kräutern, Beeren usw.)* gatherer; picker; **b)** *(Technik: Akkumulator)* accumulator; storage battery

Sạmmler·fleiß der keenness *or* dedication to collecting; **mit ~:** with the dedication of a true collector

Sạmmlerin die; ~, ~nen *s.* **Sammler a**

Sạmmler-: ~objekt das, ~stück das collector's item; **~wert der** value to collectors; **~wert haben** be of value to collectors

Sạmmlung die; ~, ~en a) collection; **b)** **[innere] ~:** composure

Sạmmlungs·bewegung die movement combining disparate elements; all-embracing movement

Samoa·inseln [za'mo:a-] *Pl.* **die ~** *(als Ganzes)* Samoa *sing.*; *(als einzelne Inseln)* the Samoan Islands

Samoaner [zamo'a:nɐ] **der; ~s, ~, Samoanerin die; ~, ~nen** Samoan

samoanisch *Adj.* Samoan

Samowar [zamo'va:ɐ̯] **der; ~s, ~e** samovar

Samstag ['zamsta:k] **der; ~[e]s, ~e** Saturday; **langer ~:** Saturday on which the shops stay open late; *s. auch* **Dienstag; Dienstag-**

samstägig ['zamstɛ:gɪç] *Adj.; nicht präd.* on Saturday *postpos.*

sạmstäglich 1. *Adj.; nicht präd.* [regular] Saturday. **2.** *adv.* on Saturdays

sạmstags *Adv.* on Saturdays

samt [zamt] **1.** *Präp. mit Dat.* together with. **2.** *Adv.* **~ und sonders** one and all; without exception

Sạmt der; ~[e]s, ~e velvet; **eine Haut wie ~:** a velvety skin; **in ~ und Seide** *(veralt.)* in all one's finery

sạmt·artig 1. *Adj.* velvety. **2.** *adv.* ‹*soft etc.*› as velvet

Sạmt·band das; *Pl.* **~bänder** velvet ribbon; *(breit)* velvet band

sạmten *Adj.; nicht präd.* **a)** *(aus Samt)* velvet; **b)** *(wie Samt)* velvety

Sạmt·hand·schuh der velvet glove; **jmdn. mit ~en anfassen** *(fig.)* handle sb. with kid gloves

sạmtig *Adj.* velvety

Sạmt·kleid das velvet dress

sämtlich ['zɛmtlɪç] *Indefinitpron. u. unbest. Zahlwort* **a)** *attr.* all the; **die Kleidung ~er Gefangener** *od.* **Gefangenen** all the prisoners' clothes; **Goethes ~e Werke** the complete works of Goethe; **b)** *alleinstehend* all

Sạmt·pfötchen das velvety paw; **wie auf ~ gehen** tread softly

sạmt·weich *Adj.* velvety[-soft]; soft as velvet *postpos.*

Sanatorium [zana'to:ri̯ʊm] **das; ~s, Sanatorien** sanatorium

Sand [zant] **der; ~[e]s, ~e** *od.* **Sände** ['zɛndə] **a)** *o. Pl.* sand; **... gibt es wie ~ am Meer** *(ugs.)* there are countless ...; ... are pretty thick on the ground *(coll.)*; **da ist ~ im Getriebe** *(fig. ugs.)* there's something gumming up the works *(coll.)*; **jmdm. ~ ins Getriebe streuen** *(fig. ugs.)* put a spanner in sb.'s works; **jmdm. ~ in die Augen streuen** *(fig.)* pull the wool over sb.'s eyes; **da habe ich auf ~ gebaut** *(fig.)* I was on shaky ground; **im ~[e] verlaufen** *(fig. ugs.)* come to nothing; **etw. [total] in den ~ setzen** *(fig. ugs.)* make a [complete] mess of sth.; **b)** *Pl.* **~e** *(bes. Geol.: ~art)* [type of] sand; **c)** *(Seemannsspr.)* sands *pl.*; sandbank; **auf [einen] ~ geraten** *od.* **laufen** run aground on a sandbank

Sandale [zan'da:lə] **die; ~, ~n** sandal

Sandalette [zanda'lɛtə] **die; ~, ~n** [high-heeled] sandal

Sạnd-: ~bahn·rennen das *(Motorradsport)* speedway racing; **~bank die;** *Pl.* **~bänke** sandbank; **~boden der** sandy soil; **~burg die** sand-castle; **~dorn der;** *Pl.* **~dorne** *(Bot.)* hippophaë; **[Echter] ~dorn** sea buckthorn

Sandel- ['zand|-]: **~holz das** sandalwood; **~öl das;** *o. Pl.* sandalwood oil

sạnd-, Sạnd-: ~farben, ~farbig *Adj.* sand-coloured; **~förmchen** [-fœrmçən] **das; ~s, ~:** sand mould; **~haufen der** pile of sand; **~hose die** sand-spout

sạndig *Adj.* sandy

Sandinist [zandi'nɪst] **der; ~en, ~en, Sandinistin die; ~, ~nen** Sandinista

Sạnd-: ~kasten der a) [child's] sand-pit; sand-box *(Amer.)*; **b)** *(Milit.)* sand-table; **~kasten·spiel das** *(Milit.)* sand-table exercise; **~korn das;** *Pl.* **~körner** grain of sand; **~kuchen der** Madeira cake; **~mann der, ~männchen das;** *o. Pl.* sandman; **~papier das** sandpaper; **~sack der a)** sandbag; **b)** *(Boxen)* punching-bag; **~stein der a)** *o. Pl.* sandstone; **b)** *(als Baustein)* sandstone block; **~strahlen** *tr. V. (Technik)* sand-blast; **~strahl·gebläse das** *(Technik)* sand-blaster; **~strand der** sandy beach; **~sturm der** sandstorm

sandte ['zantə] *1. u. 3. Pers. Sg. Prät. v.* **senden**

Sạnd·uhr die sand-glass

Sandwich ['zɛntvɪtʃ] **der** *od.* **das; ~s, ~[e]s** sandwich

Sạndwich·bau·weise die; *o. Pl.* sandwich construction

Sạnd·wüste die [sandy] desert

sanforisieren Ⓦ [zanfori'zi:rən] *tr. V.* Sanforize (P)

sanft [zanft] **1.** *Adj.* gentle; *(leise, nicht intensiv)* soft ‹*music, colour, light*›; *(friedlich)* peaceful; **kommen Sie mir bloß nicht auf die ~e [Tour]** *(ugs.)* it's no use trying to soft-soap me; **es auf die ~e Tour versuchen** *(ugs.)* try the gentle *or* diplomatic approach; *(bei Bitten)* try wheedling *or* cajolery. **2.** *adv.* gently; *(leise)* ‹*speak, play*› softly; *(friedlich)* peacefully; **ruhe ~** *(auf Grabsteinen)* rest in peace; **es regnete ~:** a gentle rain was falling

Sänfte ['zɛnftə] **die; ~, ~n** litter; *(geschlossen)* sedan-chair

Sạnftheit die; ~: gentleness; *(von Klängen, Licht, Farben)* softness

Sạnft·mut die; ~: gentleness; **mit ~:** gently; *(nachsichtig)* leniently

sạnftmütig [-my:tɪç] **1.** *Adj.* gentle; docile ‹*horse*›. **2.** *adv.* gently

Sạnftmütigkeit die; ~: gentleness; *(Fügsamkeit)* docility

sang [zaŋ] *1. u. 3. Pers. Sg. Prät. v.* **singen**

Sạng der; ~[e]s *(veralt.)* song; singing; **mit ~ und Klang** singing and playing [music]; **er ist mit ~ und Klang durchs Examen gefallen** *(ugs. iron.)* he failed the exam in style *(iron.)*

Sänger ['zɛŋɐ] **der; ~s, ~ a)** *(Singender)* singer; *(Vogel)* songbird; **darüber schweigt des ~s Höflichkeit** let's draw a veil over that; **b)** *(veralt.: Dichter)* bard; **ein fahrender** *od.* **wandernder ~** *(hist.)* a wandering minstrel

Sạ̈nger-: ~bund der choral union; **~fest das** choral *or* choir festival

Sạ̈ngerin die; ~, ~nen singer; *s. auch* **-in**

Sạ̈nger·knabe der *s.* **²Wiener**

Sạnges·bruder der *(geh., veralt.)* fellow choir-member

sạng·los *Adv. in* **sang- und klanglos** *(ugs.)* *(ohne viel Aufhebens)* simply; without any ado *or* fuss; *(unbemerkt)* unnoticed

Sanguiniker [zaŋ'gui:nikɐ] **der; ~s, ~, Sanguinikerin die; ~, ~nen** sanguine person

sanguinisch 1. *Adj.* sanguine. **2.** *adv.* sanguinely; **~ veranlagt sein** have a sanguine disposition

sanieren [za'ni:rən] **1.** *tr. V.* **a)** *(umgestalten)* redevelop ‹*area*›; rehabilitate ‹*building*›; *(renovieren)* renovate [and improve] ‹*flat etc.*›; **b)** *(Wirtsch.)* restore ‹*firm*› to profitability; *(rehabilitieren)* put ‹*firm*› back on its feet; rehabilitate ‹*agriculture, coal mining, etc.*›; **c)** *(Med.: heilen)* heal ‹*wound, ulcer, etc.*›; clear up the infection in, treat ‹*tooth etc.*›. **2.** *refl. V.* ‹*company etc.*› restore itself to profitability, get back on its feet again; ‹*person*› get oneself out of the red

Sanierung die; ~, ~en a) *s.* **sanieren a:** redevelopment; rehabilitation; renovation; **b)** *(Wirtsch.)* restoration to profitability; **c)** *(Med.: Heilung)* healing; *(Behandlung)* treatment

Sanierungs-: ~gebiet das redevelopment area; **~maßnahme die;** *meist Pl.* **a)** *(bei einem Stadtteil usw.)* redevelopment measure; **b)** *(Wirtsch.)* [financial] rehabilitation measure

sanitär [zani'tɛ:ɐ̯] *Adj.; nicht präd.* sanitary; **~e Anlagen** sanitary installations

Sanitär-: ~bereich der [field of] sanitation; **~installation die a)** *o. Pl. (das Einbauen)* fitting of sanitation *no indef. art.*; **b)** *(Anlage)* sanitary installation

Sanität [zani'tɛ:t] **die; ~, ~en** *(schweiz., österr.)* **a)** *o. Pl. (Milit.)* medical service; **b)** *(ugs.: Sanitätswagen)* ambulance

Sanitäter [zani'tɛ:tɐ] **der; ~s, ~ a)** *(Krankenpfleger)* first-aid man; *(im Krankenwagen)* ambulance man; **b)** *(Soldat)* medical orderly

Sanitäts-: ~auto das *(ugs.)* ambulance; **~dienst der a)** *o. Pl.* first-aid duty; *(im Krankenwagen)* ambulance duty; **b)** *(Milit.)* medical service *or* corps; **~kasten der** *(bes. Milit.)* first-aid box *or* kit; **~offizier der** *(Milit.)* medical officer; **~truppe die** *(Milit.)* medical corps; **~wache die** first-aid post; **~wagen der** ambulance; **~wesen das;** *o. Pl. (bes. Milit.)* medical service

sank [zaŋk] *1. u. 3. Pers. Sg. Prät. v.* **sinken**

Sanktion [zaŋk'tsi̯o:n] **die; ~, ~en a)** *(geh., Rechtsspr.: Billigung)* approval; sanction;

b) *meist Pl. (Völkerr., Soziol.)* sanction; *(geh.: Bestrafung)* punitive measure *or* sanction; **c)** *(Rechtsw.) (Gesetzesklausel)* penalty [clause]; sanction

sanktionieren *tr. V.* sanction

Sanktionierung die; ~, ~en sanctioning *no indef. art.*

Sankt-Lorenz-Strom [zaŋkt'lo:rɛnts-ʃtro:m] **der;** *o. Pl.* St Lawrence [river]

Sankt-Nimmerleins-Tag [zaŋkt'nɪmɐ-lains-] **der;** *o. Pl.: s.* **Nimmerleinstag**

sann [zan] *1. u. 3. Pers. Sg. Prät. v.* **sinnen**

Sansibar ['zanziba:ɐ̯] **(das); ~s** Zanzibar

Sanskrit ['zanskrɪt] **das; ~s** Sanskrit

Saphir ['za:fɪr] **der; ~s, ~e** sapphire

sapperlot [zapɐ'lo:t] *Interj. (veralt.)* upon my soul *(dated)*

sapphisch ['zapfɪʃ] **1.** *Adj.* **a)** Sapphic; **~e Strophe** sapphic verse *or* stanza; **b)** *(geh.: lesbisch)* sapphic; lesbian. **2.** *adv.* **a)** *(wie Sappho)* in the style of Sappho; **b)** *(geh.)* **~ veranlagt** with sapphic *or* lesbian tendencies

Sarabande [zara'bandə] **die; ~, ~n** *(Musik)* saraband

Sarde ['zardə] **der; ~n, ~n** Sardinian

Sardelle [zar'dɛlə] **die; ~, ~n** anchovy

Sardellen·paste die anchovy paste

Sardin die; ~, ~nen Sardinian

Sardine [zar'di:nə] **die; ~, ~n** sardine

Sardinen·büchse die tin of sardines; *(leer)* sardine-tin; **das Schiff war eine schwimmende ~** *(fig.)* they were packed like sardines on the ship

Sardinien [zar'di:ni̯ən] **(das); ~s** Sardinia

sardisch *Adj.* Sardinian

sardonisch [zar'do:nɪʃ] *(geh.)* **1.** *Adj.* sardonic. **2.** *adv.* sardonically

Sarg [zark] **der; ~[e]s, Särge** ['zɛrgə] coffin; *s. auch* **Nagel b**

Sarg-: -deckel der coffin lid; **~nagel der** *(Nagel, ugs. scherzh.: Zigarette)* coffin-nail *(lit., or fig. sl.)*; **~träger der** pallbearer

Sari ['za:ri] **der; ~[s], ~s** sari

Sarkasmus [zar'kasmʊs] **a)** *o. Pl. (Spott)* sarcasm; **b)** *(Äußerung)* sarcastic remark

sarkastisch 1. *Adj.* sarcastic. **2.** *adv.* sarcastically

Sarkophag [zarko'fa:k] **der; ~s, ~e** sarcophagus

saß [za:s] *1. u. 3. Pers. Sg. Prät. v.* **sitzen**

Satan ['za:tan] **der; ~s, ~e a)** *o. Pl. (bibl.)* Satan *no def. art.*; *s. auch* **Teufel; b)** *(ugs. abwertend: Mensch)* fiend

satanisch 1. *Adj.* satanic; fiendish. **2.** *adv.* satanically

Satans·braten der *(ugs.)* devil

Satellit [zatɛ'li:t] **der; ~en, ~en** *(Raumf., Astron., auch fig.)* satellite

Satelliten-: ~bild das *s.* **~foto; ~fernsehen das** satellite television; **~foto das** *(bes. Met.)* satellite picture; **~staat der** *(abwertend)* satellite [state]; **~übertragung die** *(Ferns.)* satellite transmission

Satin [za'tɛ̃:] **der; ~s, ~s** satin

Satire [za'ti:rə] **die; ~, ~n** satire

Satiriker der; ~s, ~ a) satirist; **b)** *(Spötter)* lampooner; mocker

satirisch 1. *Adj.* **a)** satirical; **b)** *(spöttisch)* mocking ‹*remarks*›. **2.** *adv.* **a)** satirically; with a satirical touch; **b)** *(spöttisch)* mockingly; in a satirical vein

Satisfaktion [zatɪsfak'tsi̯o:n] **die; ~, ~en** *(geh. od. Studentspr. veralt.)* satisfaction

satisfaktions·fähig *Adj. (veralt.)* able to give/demand satisfaction [in a duel] *pred.*

satt [zat] **1.** *Adj.* **a)** full [up] *pred.*; well-fed; **~ sein** be full [up]; have had enough [to eat]; **~ werden** have enough [to eat]; eat one's fill; **von so einem Salat werde ich nicht ~:** a salad like that is not enough for me *or* to fill me up; **sich ~ essen/trinken** eat/drink as much as one wants; eat/drink one's fill; **etw. macht ~:** sth. is filling; **ich kann mich an ihr/an der Akropolis nicht ~ sehen** *(fig.)* I can't take my eyes off her/I can gaze endlessly at the Acropolis; **b)** *(selbstgefällig)* smug, self-satisfied ‹*person, smile, expression, etc.*›; **c) jmdn./etw. ~ haben** *(ugs.)* be fed up with sb./sth. *(coll.)*; **ich habe es ~, allein zu fahren** I'm fed up with travelling alone *(coll.)*; **etw. ~ bekommen** *od.* **kriegen** *(ugs.)* get fed up with sth.; **d)** *(intensiv)* rich, deep ‹*colour*›; rich, pure ‹*sound*›; **e)** *(ugs.: beeindruckend)* tremendous *(coll.)* ‹*price*›; **ein ~er Schuß** a super shot *(coll.)*; **~e 100 000 Mark** a cool 100,000 marks *(coll.)*; **~e 180 km/h** an impressive 180 k.p.h. **2.** *adv.* **a)** *(selbstgefällig)* smugly; complacently; **b)** *(reichlich)* **nicht ~ zu essen haben** not have enough to eat; **Hummer ~:** as much lobster as one can eat; **Tennis ~** *(fig.)* as much tennis as one could possibly want; **c)** *(schweiz.: straff)* tightly

satt·blau *Adj.* deep blue

Sattel ['zatl̩] **der; ~s, Sättel** ['zɛtl̩] **a)** saddle; **ohne ~ reiten** ride bareback; **jmdm. in den ~ helfen, jmdn. in den ~ heben** help sb. into the saddle; *(fig.: fördern)* give sb. a leg up; *(fig.: an die Macht bringen)* put sb. in the driving-seat; **jmdn. aus dem ~ heben** unseat sb.; *(fig.: jmdm. die Macht nehmen)* depose sb.; remove sb. from office; **fest im ~ sitzen** *(fig.)* be firmly in the saddle; **in allen Sätteln gerecht sein** *(fig.)* be able to turn one's hand to anything; **b)** *(Berg~)* saddle; col; **c)** *(Schneidern: Passe)* yoke; **d)** *(bei Saiteninstrumenten)* nut; **e)** *(Turnen: beim Seitpferd)* saddle

sattel-, Sattel-: ~dach das gable *or* saddle roof; **~decke die** saddle-cloth; **~fest** *Adj.* experienced; **in etw.** *(Dat.)* **~fest sein** be au fait with sth.; be well up in sth.; **weniger ~feste Kandidaten** candidates less sure of their facts; **~gurt der** girth

satteln 1. *tr. V.* saddle. **2.** *itr. V.* saddle the/one's horse

Sattel-: ~nase die saddle nose; **~punkt der** *(Math.)* saddle point; **~schlepper der** tractor [unit]; *(mit Anhänger)* articulated lorry *(Brit.)*; semi[-trailer] *(Amer.)*; **~tasche die** *(am Pferd, Fahrrad)* saddle-bag; **~zeug das** saddle equipment; saddlery; **~zug der** articulated vehicle

Sattheit die; ~ a) repleteness *no def. art.*; **die ~ der Konsumgesellschaft** the satiety of the consumer society; **b)** *(Selbstgefälligkeit)* smugness; complacency; **c)** *(Intensität)* richness; fullness

sättigen ['zɛtɪgn̩] **1.** *itr. V.* be filling. **2.** *tr. V.* **a)** *(ausfüllen)* saturate ‹*market, colour*›; **b)** *(erfüllen)* **gesättigt sein von etw.** be filled with *or* full of sth.; **c)** *(geh.: satt machen)* fill ‹*sb.*›; satisfy ‹*sb., fig.: curiosity, ambition, etc.*›. **3.** *refl. V.* **sich mit** *od.* **an etw.** *(Dat.)* **~** *(geh.)* satisfy one's appetite with sth.

sättigend *Adj.* filling

Sättigung die; ~, ~en a) *(bes. Chemie, Physik)* saturation; **b)** *(das Sattsein)* repleteness *no def. art.*; *(das Sättigen)* satisfying; **die ~ der Hungernden** the feeding of the starving

Sättigungs-: ~grad der *(Wirtsch.)* [degree of] saturation; **~punkt der** *(Chemie)* saturation point

Sattler ['zatlɐ] **der; ~s, ~:** saddler; *(allgemein: Hersteller von Lederwaren)* leatherworker

Sattlerei die; ~, ~en a) *o. Pl. (Handwerk)* saddlery; **b)** *(Werkstatt)* saddler's workshop

sattsam *Adv.* ad nauseam; **~ bekannt** only too well known; notorious

saturiert [zatu'ri:ɐ̯t] *Adj. (geh.)* **a)** *(zufriedengestellt)* satisfied; **b)** *(abwertend: selbstgefällig)* **~e Wohlstandsbürger** sated and self-satisfied members of the affluent society

¹Saturn [za'tʊrn] **der; ~s** *(Astron.)*, **²Saturn (der)** *(Myth.)* Saturn *no def. art.*

Satyr ['za:tʏr] **der; ~s** *od.* **~n, ~n** satyr

Satyr·spiel das satyric drama

Satz [zats] **der; ~es, Sätze** ['zɛtsə] **a)** *(sprachliche Einheit)* sentence; *(Teil~)* clause; **in** *od.* **mit einem ~:** in one sentence; briefly; **b)** *(Teil eines Musikwerks)* movement; *(Periode)* period; **c)** *(Musik: Kompositionsweise)* [method of] composition; **der vierstimmige/kontrapunktische ~:** four-part/contrapuntal writing; **d)** *(Sport) (Tennis, Volleyball)* set; *(Tischtennis, Badminton)* game; **e)** *(Sprung)* leap; jump; **einen ~ über etw.** *(Akk.)* **machen** *od.* **tun** jump *or* leap across sth.; **er war mit einem ~ an der Tür** in one bound he was at the door; **in** *od.* **mit wenigen Sätzen** in a few strides; **f)** *(Amtsspr.: Tarif)* rate; **g)** *(Set)* set; **ein ~ Reifen** a set of tyres; **h)** *(Boden~)* sediment; *(von Kaffee)* grounds *pl.*; **i)** *o. Pl. (Druckw.: das Setzen)* setting; *(Gesetztes)* type matter; **mit dem ~ beginnen** start setting; **das Manuskript ist in ~/geht in [den] ~:** the manuscript is being set/is being sent for setting; **j)** *(DV)* record

Satz-: ~an·weisung die *(Druckw.)* setting instructions *pl.*; **~aus·sage die** *(Sprachw.)* predicate; **~ball der** *(Tennis, Volleyball)* set point; *(Tischtennis, Badminton)* game point; **~bau der;** *o. Pl.* sentence construction; **~bau·plan der** *(Sprachw.)* sentence pattern

Sätzchen ['zɛtsçən] **das; ~s, ~ a)** *(Sprung)* little jump; **b)** *(Äußerung)* little sentence

satz-, Satz-: ~ergänzung die *(Sprachw.)* complement; **~fehler der** *(Druckw.)* literal; printer's error; **~fertig** *Adj.* *(Druckw.)* ready for setting *postpos.*; **~gefüge das** *(Sprachw.)* complex sentence; **~gegen·stand der** *(Sprachw.)* subject [of a/the sentence]; **~glied das** *(Sprachw.)* component part [of a/the sentence]; **~konstruktion die** *(Sprachw.)* sentence construktion; **~lehre die a)** *(Sprachw.)* syntax *no art.*; **b)** *(Musik)* composition theory *no art.*; **~rechner der** *(Druckw.)* composer; **~reif** *Adj. (Druckw.)* ready for setting *postpos.*; **~spiegel der** *(Druckw.)* type area; **~technisch** *(Druckw.)* **1.** *Adj.* **aus ~technischen Gründen** for reasons of setting; **2.** *adv.* **~technisch gesehen** from the typographic point of view; **~teil der** *(Sprachw.) s.* **~glied**

Satzung ['zatsʊŋ] **die; ~, ~en** articles of association *pl.*; statutes *pl.*

satzungs-: ~gemäß *Adj., adv.* in accordance with the articles of association *or* the statutes; **~widrig** *Adj., adv.* contrary to the articles of association *or* the statutes

satz-, Satz-: ~weise *Adv.* sentence by sentence; **~wertig** *Adj. (Sprachw.)* forming a clause *postpos.*; **~wertiger Infinitiv/~wertiges Partizip** infinitive/participial clause; **~zeichen das** *(Sprachw.)* punctuation mark; **~zusammen·hang der** *(Sprachw.)* sentence correlation *or* interrelation

Sau [zau̯] **die; ~, Säue** ['zɔy̯ə] **a)** *(weibliches Schwein)* sow; **b)** *(bes. südd.: Schwein)* pig; **jmdn. zur ~ machen** *(derb)* tear a strip off sb. *(sl.)*; **wie eine gesengte Sau fahren** *(derb)* drive like a madman; **unter aller ~** *(derb abwertend)* bloody awful *(Brit. sl.)*; the pits *(sl.)*; **keine ~** *(derb)* not a bloody *(Brit. sl.) or (coll.)* damn soul; **c)** *(derb abwertend: schmutziger Mensch) (Mann)* dirty pig; *(Frau)* dirty cow *(sl.)*; **d)** *(derb abwertend: gemeiner Mensch)* swine

-sau die *(derb)* ... pig *or* swine; pig *or* swine of a/an ...

sau-, Sau- *(salopp)* bloody ... *(Brit. sl.)*; damn ... *(coll.)*; *(sehr schlecht)* lousy ... *(sl.)*; **~dreckig/~schwer** bloody *(Brit. sl.) or (coll.)* damn filthy/difficult

Sau-: ~arbeit die *(salopp)* bloody awful job *(Brit. sl.)*; hell of a job *(coll.)*; **~bande die** *(salopp)* wretched swine *(derog.) pl.*;

(mehr scherzh.) bunch of good-for-nothings *(sl.)*
sauber ['zaubɐ] **1.** *Adj.* **a)** clean; **~e Flüsse/Wälder** unpolluted rivers/forests; **das Kind ist ~:** the child is toilet-trained; **ein Glas ~ ausspülen** rinse [out] a glass; **der ~e Bildschirm** *(fig.)* the unpolluted TV screen; **mein Tor bleibt ~** *(fig. Fußball)* I'll keep a clean sheet; **b)** *(sorgfältig)* neat ‹*handwriting, division, work, etc.*›; **c)** *(fehlerlos)* perfect, faultless ‹*accent, technique, etc.*›; **d)** *(anständig)* upstanding ‹*attitude, person*›; upright ‹*young man*›; unsullied ‹*character*›; **er ist ~** *(ugs.)* he is straight; *(hat nichts Kriminelles gemacht)* he has a clean record; **~ bleiben** keep one's hands clean *(coll.)*; **nicht [ganz] ~ sein** *(ugs.)* be a bit shady *or* dodgy *(coll.)*; **also dann alles Gute, und bleib ~!** *(ugs. scherzh.)* all the best, and be good!; **e)** *(gerecht)* fair ‹*solution, description*›; equitable ‹*solution, plan*›; **f)** *nicht präd. (iron.: unanständig)* nice, fine *(iron.)*; *s. auch* **Früchtchen; g)** *(ugs., bes. südd., österr., schweiz.: beachtlich)* fantastic *(coll.)*; **ein ~es Sümmchen** a tidy little sum *(coll.)*; **h)** *(südd., österr., schweiz.: schmuck)* smart ‹*girl etc.*›. **2.** *adv.* **a)** *(sorgfältig)* neatly ‹*written, dressed, mended, etc.*›; **b)** *(fehlerlos)* **[sehr] ~:** [quite] perfectly *or* faultlessly; **c)** *(anständig)* conscientiously; **d)** *(gerecht)* ‹*judge etc.*› fairly; **e)** *(iron.: unanständig)* nicely *(iron.)*; **das hast du ~ hingekriegt** a nice *or* fine job you made of that
sauber|halten *unr. tr. V.* **a)** keep ‹*room, floor, etc.*› clean; **b)** *(freihalten)* **von bestimmten Personen ~:** keep ‹*room, district, etc.*› clear of certain people
Sauberkeit die; ~ a) cleanness; *(bes. der Person)* cleanliness; **ihre Wohnung blitzt vor ~:** her flat *(Brit.) or (Amer.)* apartment is sparkling clean; **b)** *(Sorgfältigkeit)* neatness; **c)** *(Anständigkeit)* uprightness
Sauberkeits·fimmel der *(ugs. abwertend)* mania for cleanliness; **einen ~ haben** have a thing about cleanliness *(coll.)*
säuberlich ['zɔybɐlɪç] **1.** *Adj.* neat. **2.** *adv.* neatly; **fein ~ geordnet/verpackt** *usw.* neatly arranged/packed *etc.*
sauber|machen 1. *tr. V.* clean. **2.** *itr. V.* clean; do the cleaning; **bei jmdm. ~:** clean for sb.
Sauber·mann der; *Pl.* **-männer** *(iron.)* decent and upright fellow; nice guy *(sl.)*; *(Moralapostel)* upholder of moral standards
säubern ['zɔybɐn] *tr. V.* **a)** *(saubermachen)* clean; **die Schuhe vom Lehm ~:** clean the mud off the shoes; **eine Wunde ~:** cleanse a wound; **das Wasser von Schadstoffen ~:** cleanse the water of pollutants; purify the water; **b)** *(befreien)* clear, rid **(von** of); purge ‹*party, government, etc.*› **(von** of); **Bibliotheken von verbotenen Büchern ~:** rid libraries of banned books
Säuberung die; ~, ~en a) *(das Saubermachen)* cleaning; **b)** *(Entfernung)* purging; **einer ~ zum Opfer fallen** be the victim of a purge
Säuberungs·aktion die purge; clean-up operation
sau·blöd[e] *(salopp abwertend)* **1.** *Adj.* bloody silly *or* stupid. **2.** *adv.* in an bloody silly *or* stupid manner *(sl.)*; **frag doch nicht so ~:** don't ask such bloody silly *or* stupid questions *(sl.)*
Sauce *s.* **Soße a**
Saucier [zo'sie:] **der; ~s, ~s** sauce chef
Sauciere [zo'siɛ:rə] **die; ~, ~n** sauce-boat
Saudi [zaudi] **der; ~s, ~s, Saudi·araber der** Saudi
Saudi-Arabien (das); ~s Saudi Arabia
saudiarabisch, saudisch *Adj.* Saudi Arabian; Saudi
sau·dumm *s.* **saublöd**
sauer ['zauɐ] **1.** *Adj.* **a)** sour; sour, tart ‹*fruit*›; sharp-tasting ‹*bread, coffee, etc.*›; pickled ‹*herring, gherkin, etc.*›; acid[ic] ‹*wine, vinegar*›; **saure Drops** acid drops *(Brit.)*; **saure Nieren** *(Kochk.) dish of sliced kidneys with lemon-flavored sauce;* **saurer Regen** acid rain; *s. auch* **Apfel a; Bier; b)** *nicht attr. (ugs.: verärgert)* cross, annoyed **(auf + Akk.** with); *(verdrossen)* sour; **c)** *(bes. Landw.)* acidic; **d)** *(Chemie)* acid[ic]; **e)** *(mühselig)* hard; difficult; **gib ihm Saures!** *(ugs.)* let him have it! *(coll.)*. **2.** *adv.* **a)** *(in, mit Essig)* in vinegar; **b)** *(ugs.: verärgert)* crossly; **~ [auf jmdn./etw.] reagieren** get annoyed *or* cross [with sb./sth.]; **c)** *(Chemie)* **~ reagieren** react acidically; **d)** *(mühsam)* with difficulty; **~ erspartes/verdientes Geld** hard-saved/hard-earned money; **jmdn. ~ ankommen** be hard for sb. to take *or* accept; **e) ~ aufstoßen** belch *(with acid taste)*; **das wird ihm noch einmal ~ aufstoßen** *(fig. ugs.)* he will live to regret that
Sauer-: ~ampfer [~ampfɐ] **der** sorrel; **~braten der** *braised beef marinated in vinegar and herbs;* sauerbraten *(Amer.)*; **~brunnen der a)** *(Quelle)* mineral spring containing carbon dioxide; **b)** *(Wasser)* mineral water containing carbon dioxide
Sauerei die; ~, ~en *(salopp abwertend)* **a)** *(Unflätigkeit)* obscenity; **~en erzählen** tell filthy stories **b)** *(Gemeinheit)* bloody *(Brit. sl.) or (coll.)* damn scandal *(sl.)*
Sauer-: ~kirsche die sour cherry; **~klee der** wood sorrel; **~kohl der** *o. Pl. (bes. nordd.)*; **~kraut das** *o. Pl.* sauerkraut; pickled cabbage
säuerlich 1. *Adj.* **a) [leicht] ~:** slightly sour; slightly sharp ‹*sauce*›; slightly sour *or* tart ‹*fruit*›; **ein leicht ~er Riesling** a Riesling with a touch of acidity; **b)** *(verdorben)* sourish; slightly sour; **c)** *(mißvergnügt)* sourish; slightly sour. **2.** *adv. (mißvergnügt)* somewhat sourly
Säuerling der; ~s, ~e a) *(Mineralwasser) s.* **Sauerbrunnen b; b)** *(ugs.: Wein)* acidy wine
Sauer·milch die sour milk
säuern ['zɔyɐn] **1.** *tr. V.* **a)** *(gären lassen)* leaven ‹*bread, dough, etc.*›; pickle ‹*cabbage, cucumber, etc.*›; **b)** *(Kochk.: würzen)* give zest *or* piquancy to. **2.** *itr. V.; auch mit sein (gären)* turn sour; **der Kohl säuert in Fässern** the cabbage is pickling in vats
Sauer-: ~rahm der sour cream; **~rahm·butter die** butter made from sour cream
Sauer·stoff der; *o. Pl.* oxygen
sauerstoff-, Sauerstoff-: ~apparat der oxygen apparatus; **~arm** *Adj.* low in oxygen *postpos.*; **~flasche die** oxygen cylinder; **~gerät das** oxygen apparatus; **~haltig** *Adj.* containing oxygen *postpos., not pred.*; **~haltig sein** contain oxygen; **~mangel der;** *o. Pl.* lack of oxygen; **~mangel im Blut/Zellgewebe** oxygen deficiency in the blood/cell tissue; **~maske die** oxygen mask; **~zelt das** *(Med.)* oxygen tent; **~zufuhr die** oxygen supply
Sauer·teig der leaven
sauer·töpfisch [-tœpfɪʃ] *Adj. (ugs.: abwertend)* sour ‹*expression, look, etc.*›; sour-faced ‹*person*›
Säuerung die; ~, ~en *(von Brot, Teig)* leavening; *(von Kohl, Kraut usw.)* pickling
Saufbold [-bɔlt] **der; ~[e]s, ~e** *(veralt. abwertend)* drunkard; boozer *(coll.)*
Sauf·bruder der *(salopp, oft abwertend)* boozing companion *(coll.)*
saufen ['zaufn̩] **1.** *unr. itr. V.* **a)** drink; **b)** *(salopp) (trinken)* drink; swig *(coll.)*; *(Alkohol trinken)* drink; booze *(coll.)*; **~ wie ein Loch** drink like a fish; **c)** *(salopp: alkoholabhängig sein)* drink. **2.** *unr. tr. V.* **a)** drink; **b)** *(salopp: trinken)* drink; **er hat so viel [Schnaps] gesoffen, daß ...:** he knocked back so much booze that ... *(coll.)*; **einen ~ gehen** go for a drink. **3.** *unr. refl. V. (salopp)* **sich dumm/zu Tode ~:** drink oneself stupid/to death; **sich arm ~:** drink one's last penny away; **sich** *(Dat.)* **die Jacke** *od.* **Hucke voll ~:** get tanked up *(sl.)*;
Säufer ['zɔyfɐ] **der; ~s, ~** *(salopp, oft abwertend)* boozer *(coll.)*; piss artist *(sl.)*
Sauferei die; ~, ~en *(salopp)* **a)** *(Gelage)* booze-up *(coll.)*; **b)** *o. Pl. (das Saufen)* boozing *no def. art. (coll.)*
Säuferin die; ~, ~nen *(salopp, oft abwertend)* boozer *(coll.)*; drunkard
Säufer-: ~leber die *(ugs.)* hobnail[ed] liver; **~nase die** *(ugs.)* drinker's nose; **~wahn der** *(Med. veralt.)* delirium tremens
Sauf-: ~gelage das *(salopp)* booze-up *(coll.)*; **~kumpan der** *(salopp)* boozing companion *(coll.)*
Sau·fraß der *(salopp abwertend)* pigswill *(coll.)*; rubbish
säufst [zɔyfst] *2. Pers. Sg. Präsens v.* **saufen**
säuft [zɔyft] *3. Pers. Sg. Präsens v.* **saufen**
saugen ['zaugn̩] **1.** *tr. V.* **a)** *auch unr. (aufnehmen)* suck; *s. auch* **Finger b; b)** *auch itr. (mit dem Staubsauger)* vacuum; hoover *(coll.)*; **c)** *(entfernen)* suck up. **2.** *regelm. (auch unr.) itr. V.* **an etw.** *(Dat.)* **~:** suck [at] sth.; **an einer Pfeife/Zigarette ~:** draw on a pipe/cigarette. **3.** *unr. (auch regelm.) refl. V.* **a)** *(eindringen)* soak **(in + Akk.** into); **b)** *(aufnehmen)* **sich voll etw. ~:** become soaked with sth.
säugen ['zɔygn̩] *tr. V.* suckle
Sauger der; ~s, ~ a) *(auf Flaschen)* teat; **b)** *(Saugheber)* siphon; **c)** *s.* **Schnuller**
Säuger ['zɔygɐ] **der; ~s, ~, Säuge·tier das** *(Zool.)* mammal
saug-, Saug-: ~fähig *Adj.* absorbent; **~fähigkeit die** *o. Pl.* absorbency; **~glocke die** *(Med.)* suction cup; *(zur Geburtshilfe)* vacuum extractor; venteuse; **~heber der** siphon; **~kraft die** suction [strength]
Säugling ['zɔyklɪŋ] **der; ~s, ~e** baby; infant
Säuglings-: ~alter das; *o. Pl.* infancy; babyhood; **im ~alter** in *or* during infancy; **~heim das** home for babies; **~pflege die** baby care; **~schwester die** infant *or* baby nurse; **~station die** baby ward; **~sterblichkeit die** infant mortality
Saug-: ~napf der *(Zool.)* sucker; **~organ das** *(Biol.)* suctorial organ; **~reflex der** sucking reflex; **~rüssel der** *(Zool.)* proboscis; **~wurm der** *(Zool.)* trematode
Sau-: ~hatz die *(Jägerspr.)* [wild] boar hunt; **~haufen der** *(salopp abwertend)* bunch of layabouts *(sl.)*; **~hund der** *(derb abwertend)* bastard *(coll.)*; bloody *(Brit. sl.) or (coll.)* damn swine
säuisch ['zɔyɪʃ] *(salopp)* **1.** *Adj.* **a)** *(abwertend: unanständig)* obscene ‹*phone call*›; filthy, obscene ‹*book, joke, behaviour*›; **b)** *(stark, groß)* hellish *(coll.)*. **2.** *adv. (sehr)* hellishly *(coll.)*; **~ viel Glück haben** have a hell of a lot of luck *(coll.)*
sau-, Sau-: ~kalt *Adj. (salopp)* bloody cold *(Brit. sl.)*; damn cold *(coll.)*; **~kälte die** *(salopp)* bloody cold *(Brit. sl.) or (coll.)* damn cold weather; **das ist eine ~kälte** it's bloody *(Brit. sl.) or (coll.)* damn cold *or* freezing; **~kerl der** *(salopp abwertend)* bastard *(coll.)*; **~laden der** *(salopp abwertend)* dump *(coll.)*
Säule ['zɔylə] **die; ~, ~n a)** column; *(nur als Stütze, auch fig.)* pillar; **b)** *(Zapf~)* [petrol *(Brit.) or (Amer.)* gasoline] pump
Säulen-: ~bau der; *Pl.* **~bauten** building with columns; **~fuß der** base [of a/the column/pillar]; **~gang der** colonnade; **~halle die** columned hall; **~heilige der** stylite; **er ist ja kein ~heiliger** *(fig.)* he's no plaster saint; **~kaktus der** cereus; **~ordnung die** *(Archit.)* order [of columns]; **die dorische ~ordnung** the Doric order; **~portal das** *(Archit.)* columned doorway
Saum [zaum] **der; ~[e]s, Säume** ['zɔymə] hem; *(fig. geh.)* edge

Sau·magen der *(Kochk.)* stuffed pig's stomach
sau·mäßig *(salopp)* **1.** *Adj.* **a)** *(sehr groß)* **das ist eine ~e Arbeit/Hitze** that's a hell of a job/temperature *(coll.)*; **~es Glück haben** be damned lucky *(coll.)*; **b)** *(abwertend: schlecht)* lousy *(sl.)*. **2.** *adv.* **a)** *(sehr)* damned *(coll.)*; **~ viel verdienen** earn a hell of a lot *(coll.)*; **es tat ~ weh** it hurt like hell; **b)** *(abwertend: sehr schlecht)* lousily *(sl.)*
[1]**säumen** ['zɔymən] *tr. V.* hem; *(fig. geh.)* line
[2]**säumen** *itr. V. (geh.: zögern)* tarry *(literary)*
säumig *(geh.) Adj.* tardy; dilatory
Säumigkeit die; ~ *(geh.)* tardiness; dilatoriness
Säumnis ['zɔymnɪs] **die;** ~, **~se** *od.* **das;** ~ses, ~se *(geh.)* **a)** delay; **b)** *(Unterlassung)* omission; failing
saum-, Saum-: **~pfad der** mule-track; **~selig** *(geh.)* **1.** *Adj.* dilatory; slow; **2.** *adv.* in a dilatory manner; slowly; **~seligkeit die** *(geh.)* dilatoriness; slowness
Saum·tier das pack animal
Sauna ['zauna] **die;** ~, **~s** *od.* **Saunen** sauna
Sauna·bad das sauna
saunieren [zau'ni:rən] *itr. V.* have *or* take a sauna
Säure ['zɔyrə] **die;** ~, **~n a)** *o. Pl. (von Früchten)* sourness; tartness; *(von Wein, Essig)* acidity; *(von Soßen)* sharpness; **b)** *(Chemie)* acid
säure-, Säure-: **~arm** *Adj.* low in acid *postpos.*; **~beständig,** *Adj.* acid-resistant; **~fest** *Adj.* acid-proof; **~frei** *Adj.* acid-free; **~gehalt der** acid content
Saure·gurken·zeit die *(ugs.)* slack *or* dead season; *(in den Medien)* silly season *(Brit.)*
säure·haltig *Adj.* acid[ic]
Saurier ['zaurie] **der;** ~s, ~: large prehistoric reptile
Saus [zaus] *in* **in ~ und Braus leben** live the high life
Sause die; ~, **~n** *(ugs. veralt.)* **a)** *(Gelage)* booze-up *(coll.)*; **b)** *(Zug durch die Kneipen)* pub crawl *(Brit. coll.)*; **eine ~ machen** go on a pub crawl *(Brit. coll.)*; go bar-hopping *(Amer.)*
säuseln ['zɔyzl̩n] **1.** *itr. V. (rascheln)* ‹*leaves, branches, etc.*› rustle; ‹*wind*› murmur. **2.** *tr. V. (iron.: sagen)* whisper
sausen *itr. V.* **a)** *(Geräusch machen)* ‹*wind*› whistle; ‹*storm*› roar; ‹*head, ears*› buzz; ‹*propeller, engine, etc.*› whirr, **das Blut sauste ihm in den Ohren** blood was pounding in his ears; **b)** *mit sein (hinfahren, -gehen)* ‹*person*› rush; ‹*vehicle*› roar; **er sauste mit dem Fahrrad um die Ecke** he sped round the corner on his bike; **durchs Examen ~** *(fig.)* fail one's exam; **c)** *mit sein* ‹*whip, bullet, etc.*› whistle; **d) einen ~ lassen** *(salopp)* blow off *(sl.)*
sausen|lassen *unr. tr. V. (salopp)* **a) ein Konzert ~:** give a concert a miss; **eine Einladung ~:** not take up an invitation; **eine Stellung/ein Geschäft ~:** let a job/a business deal go; **ein Vorhaben ~:** not bother to follow up a plan; **b)** *(sich trennen von)* drop ‹*boy-friend, girl-friend, etc.*›
Sauser der; ~s, ~ *(bes. südwestd., österr., schweiz.)* new wine
Sause-: **~schritt der** *in* **im ~** *(ugs.)* at breakneck speed; **~wind der a)** *(Kinderspr.)* wind; **b)** *(ugs.: Mensch)* live wire
sau-, Sau-: **~stall der a)** pigsty; **b)** *(fig. salopp abwertend)* hole *(coll.)*; dump *(coll.)*; **~wetter das** *(salopp abwertend)* lousy weather *(sl.)*; **~wohl** *Adj.*; *in* **sich ~wohl fühlen** *(salopp)* feel bloody *(Brit. sl.) or (coll.)* damn good *or* great; **~wut die** *(salopp)* **eine ~wut [auf jmdn.] haben** be bloody *(Brit. sl.) or (coll.)* damn mad [with sb.]
Savanne [za'vanə] **die;** ~, **~n** savannah
Savoyen [za'vɔyən] **(das);** ~s Savoy

Saxophon [zakso'fo:n] **das;** ~s, **~e** saxophone
Saxophonist der; ~en, **~en** saxophonist
S-Bahn ['ɛs-] **die** city and suburban railway; S-bahn
S-Bahn-: **~hof der, ~-Station die** S-bahn station; **~-Zug der** city and suburban train; S-bahn train
SBB *Abk.* **Schweizerische Bundesbahn** Swiss Federal Railways
SB- [ɛs'be:-]: **~-Laden der** self-service shop; **~-Tank·stelle die** self-service petrol *(Brit.) or (Amer.)* gasoline station
SBZ [ɛsbe:'tsɛt] **die;** ~ *Abk.* **Sowjetische Besatzungszone** Soviet occupied zone
Scampi ['skampi] *Pl.* scampi
Scanner ['skænə] **der;** ~s, ~ *(Med., graph. Technik)* scanner
Scene [si:n] **die;** ~, **~s** *(salopp)* scene
sch [ʃ] *Interj.* **a)** *(ruhig)* sh[h]; hush; **b)** *(weg da)* shoo
Schabe ['ʃa:bə] **die;** ~, **~n a)** cockroach; **b)** *(südd., schweiz.: Motte)* moth
Schabe·fleisch das minced beef
Schab·eisen das scraper
schaben **1.** *tr. V.* **a)** *(schälen)* scrape ‹*carrots, potatoes, etc.*›; *(glätten)* shave ‹*leather, hide, etc.*›; plane ‹*wood, surface, etc.*›; **sich** *(Dat.)* **den Bart ~** *(ugs. scherzh.)* have a shave; shave; **b)** *(scheuern)* rub; **c)** *(entfernen)* scrape. **2.** *itr. V.* scrape; **an/auf etw.** *(Dat.)* **~:** scrape against sth./scrape sth.
Schaber der; ~s, ~: scraper
Schabernack ['ʃa:bɐnak] **der;** ~[e]s, **~e a)** *(Streich)* prank; **jmdm. einen ~ spielen, mit jmdm. seinen ~ treiben** play a prank on sb.; **b)** *o. Pl. (Scherz, Spaß)* **aus ~ etw. tun** do sth. for a joke; **c)** *(scherzh.: Kind)* monkey; rascal
schäbig ['ʃɛ:bɪç] **1.** *Adj.* **a)** *(abgenutzt)* shabby; **b)** *(jämmerlich, gering)* pathetic; miserable; **~e Gehälter** paltry wages; **c)** *(gemein)* shabby; mean; **d)** *(geizig)* stingy. **2.** *adv.* **a)** *(abgenutzt)* shabbily; **b)** *(jämmerlich)* miserably; **~ bezahlen** pay poorly; **c)** *(gemein)* meanly
Schäbigkeit die; ~ shabbiness; *(des Gehalts)* paltriness; *(Geiz)* stinginess
Schablone [ʃa'blo:nə] **die;** ~, **~n a)** pattern; **b)** *(fig., meist abwertend)* **in ~n denken/sprechen** *od.* **reden** think in stereotypes/speak in clichés; **nach ~ arbeiten** work according to a set pattern *or* routine
schablonen-, Schablonen-: **~denken das** stereotyped way of thinking; **~druck der a)** *(Vervielfältigungsverfahren)* stencil printing; **b)** *(Siebdruck)* screen-printing; **~haft** **1.** *Adj.* stereotyped ‹*thinking*›; clichéd ‹*remark, expression, etc.*›; **2.** *adv.* ‹*speak*› in a clichéd manner; ‹*think, act, argue, etc.*› in a stereotyped manner
Schab·messer das a) *(Schabeisen)* scraper; scraping-knife; **b)** *(zur Holzbearbeitung)* spokeshave
Schabracke [ʃa'brakə] **die;** ~, **~n a)** *(Pferdedecke)* caparison; **b)** *(an Fenstern)* pelmet
Schabsel ['ʃa:psl] **das;** ~s, ~: shavings *pl.*
Schab·technik die mezzotint technique
Schach [ʃax] **das;** ~s, **~s a)** *o. Pl. (Spiel)* chess; **b)** *(Schachspiel: Stellung)* check; **~ [dem König]!** check; **[dem gegnerischen König/dem Gegner] ~ bieten** check the opponent's king/the opponent; **der Turm/der Gegner bietet ~:** the rook/the opponent gives check; **ewiges ~:** perpetual check; **im ~:** in check; **jmdn./etw. in ~ halten** *(ugs. fig.)* keep sb./sth. in check; *s. auch* **matt 1f**
Schach-: **~auf·gabe die** chess problem; **~brett das** chessboard; **~brett·muster das** chequer-board pattern; *(auf Stoff)* chequered pattern; **~ecke die** *(ugs.)* chess column
Schacher ['ʃaxɐ] **der;** ~s *(abwertend)* haggling **(um** over); *(bes. Politik)* horse-trading **(um** about)

Schächer ['ʃɛçɐ] **der;** ~s, ~ *(bibl.)* thief
schachern *itr. V.* haggle **(um** over)
schach-, Schach-: **~figur die** chess piece; chessman; **~matt** *Adj.* **a)** *(Schachspiel)* **~matt!** checkmate; **~matt sein** be checkmated; **jmdn. ~matt setzen** *(Schachspiel)* checkmate sb.; *(fig.: ausschalten)* render sb. powerless; **b)** *(erschöpft)* exhausted; **~partie die** game of chess; **~spiel das a)** *o. Pl. (Spiel)* chess; **b)** *o. Pl. (das Spielen)* chess-playing; **c)** *(Partie)* game of chess; **d)** *(Brett und Figuren)* chess set; **~spieler der** chess-player
Schacht [ʃaxt] **der;** ~[e]s, **Schächte** ['ʃɛçtə] shaft
Schachtel ['ʃaxtl] **die;** ~, **~n a)** box; **eine ~ Zigaretten** a packet *or (Amer.)* pack of cigarettes; **eine ~ Pralinen/Streichhölzer** a box of chocolates/matches; **b)** *in* **alte ~** *(salopp abwertend)* old bag *(sl.)*
Schächtelchen ['ʃɛçtl̩çən] **das;** ~s, ~: [little] box
Schachtel-: **~halm der** *(Bot.)* horsetail; **~satz der** *(Sprachw.)* involved sentence
schächten ['ʃɛçtn̩] *tr., itr. V.* slaughter according to Jewish rites
Schach-: **~turnier das** chess tournament; **~zug der a)** *(Schachspiel)* move [in chess]; **b)** *(fig.)* move
schade ['ʃa:də] *Adj.; nicht attr.* **[ach, wie] ~!** [what a] pity *or* shame; **es/das ist [sehr] ~!** it's/that's a [terrible] pity *or* shame; **[es ist zu] ~, daß ...:** it's a [real] pity *or* shame that ...; **nur ~** *od.* **~ nur, daß ...:** it's just a pity *or* shame that ...; **[es ist] ~ um jmdn./etw.** it's a pity *or* shame about sb./sth.; **~ drum!** what a pity *or* shame; **um die Vase ist es nicht weiter ~:** it doesn't matter about the vase; the vase is no great loss; **für jmdn./für** *od.* **zu etw. zu ~ sein** be too good for sb./sth.; **sich** *(Dat.)* **zu ~ für** *od.* **zu etw./für jmdn. sein** consider oneself too good for sth./sb.
Schade *in* **es soll dein ~ nicht sein** *(veralt.)* it will not be to your disadvantage
Schädel ['ʃɛ:dl] **der;** ~s, **~ a)** head; *(Skelett)* skull; **jmdm. eins auf** *od.* **über den ~ geben** *(ugs.)* hit *or* knock sb. over the head; **mir brummt der ~** *(ugs.)* my head is throbbing; **einen dicken** *od.* **harten ~ haben** *(fig.)* be stubborn *or* pigheaded; **sich** *(Dat.)* **[an etw.** *(Dat.)***] den ~ einrennen** *(fig.)* beat *or* run one's head against a brick wall [with sth.]; **b)** *(fig.: Verstand)* **streng deinen ~ mal an!** tax your brains a bit; **es geht** *od.* **will nicht in seinen ~ [hinein], daß ...** *(ugs.)* he can't get it into his head that ...
Schädel-: **~basis·bruch der** *(Med.)* basal skull fracture; **~bruch der** *(Med.)* skull fracture; **~decke die** *(Anat.)* skull-cap; calvaria; **~lage die** *(Med.)* cephalic *or* head presentation; **~naht die** *(Anat.)* suture
schaden *itr. V.* **jmdm./einer Sache ~:** damage *or* harm sb./sth.; **Rauchen schadet Ihrer Gesundheit/Ihnen** smoking damages your health/is bad for you; **jmds. Ansehen [sehr] ~:** do [great] damage to sb.'s reputation; **das würde dir nichts ~** *(ugs.)* that wouldn't hurt you *or* do you any harm; **das schadet nichts** *(ugs.) (ist nicht schlimm)* that doesn't matter; *(ist ganz gut)* that won't do any harm; **es kann nichts ~, wenn ...** *(ugs.)* it would do no harm if ...
Schaden der; ~s, **Schäden** ['ʃɛ:dn̩] **a)** *(Beschädigung)* damage *no pl., no indef. art.*; **ein kleiner/großer ~:** little/major damage; **jmdm. [einen] ~ zufügen** harm sb.; **~ leiden** *(geh.)* suffer; **wer den ~ hat, braucht für den Spott nicht zu sorgen** *(Spr.)* the laugh is always on the loser; **aus ~ wird man klug** *(Spr.)* once bitten, twice shy *(prov.)*; **er hat an seiner Gesundheit ~ genommen** *(geh.)* his health has suffered; **b)** *(Nachteil)* disadvantage; **es ist dein eigener** *od.* **zu deinem ei-**

genen ~: it is to your own disadvantage; **es soll Ihr ~ nicht sein** it will not be to your disadvantage; **zu ~ kommen** suffer; be adversely affected; **c)** *(Defekt)* damage *no pl., no indef. art.;* **das Haus weist einige Schäden auf** the house has some defects; **d)** *(Verletzung)* injury; **zu ~ kommen** be hurt *or* injured

schaden-, Schaden-: ~ersatz der *(Rechtsw.)* damages *pl.; (Versicherungsw.)* **~ersatz leisten** pay damages/compensation; **jmdn. auf ~ersatz verklagen** sue sb. for damages/compensation; **~ersatz·anspruch der, ~ersatz·forderung die** *(Rechtsw.)* claim for damages; *(Versicherungsw.)* claim for compensation; **~freude die** *o. Pl.* malicious pleasure; **..., sagte er voller ~freude** ... he said gloatingly; **~froh 1.** *Adj.* gloating; **~froh sein** gloat; **2.** *adv.* with malicious pleasure

Schadens·fall der *(Rechtsw., Versicherungsw.)* case of damage; *(Verlust)* case of loss; **im ~:** in the event of damage/loss

schadhaft ['ʃa:thaft] *Adj.* defective

Schadhaftigkeit die; ~: defectiveness

schädigen ['ʃɛ:dɪgn̩] *tr. V.* damage ⟨*health, reputation, interests*⟩; harm, hurt ⟨*person*⟩; cause losses to ⟨*firm, industry, etc.*⟩; **er hat den Betrieb um mehrere tausend Mark geschädigt** he caused losses of several thousand marks to the firm; **jmdn. gesundheitlich ~:** damage sb.'s health

Schädigung die; ~, ~en damage *no pl., no indef. art.* (*Gen.* to); **materielle/gesundheitliche ~en** financial losses/damage to one's/your *etc.* health

schädlich ['ʃɛ:tlɪç] *Adj.* harmful; **~ für die Gesundheit** damaging *or* injurious to the health; **~e Folgen/Wirkungen/Einflüsse** damaging or detrimental consequences/effects/influences

Schädlichkeit die; ~: harmfulness

Schädling ['ʃɛ:tlɪŋ] **der; ~s, ~e** pest

Schädlings-: ~bekämpfer der pest control expert; **~bekämpfung die** pest control; **~bekämpfungs·mittel das** pesticide

schadlos *Adj.* **in sich an jmdm./etw. ~ halten** take advantage of sb./sth.

Schad·stoff der harmful chemical

schadstoff·arm *Adj. (bes. Kfz-W.)* low in harmful substances *postpos.;* clean-exhaust ⟨*vehicle*⟩; *(mit Katalysator)* ⟨*vehicle*⟩ with exhaust emission control

Schaf [ʃa:f] **das; ~[e]s, ~e a)** sheep; *s. auch* **Bock a; schwarz b; b)** *(ugs.: Dummkopf)* twit *(Brit. sl.);* idiot *(coll.)*

Schaf·bock der ram

Schäfchen ['ʃɛ:fçən] **das; ~s, ~ a)** [little] sheep; *(Lamm)* lamb; **sein[e] ~ ins trockene bringen** *(ugs.)* take care of number one *(coll.);* **sein[e] ~ im trockenen haben** *(ugs.)* have taken care of number one *(coll.);* **~ zählen** *(zum Einschlafen)* count sheep; **b)** *Pl. (ugs.: Schutzbefohlene)* flock *sing. or pl.;* **c)** *(fam.: einfältiger Mensch)* silly thing

Schäfchen·wolke die fleecy cloud

Schäfer der; ~s, ~: shepherd

Schäfer·dichtung die *(Literaturw.)* pastoral *or* bucolic poetry

Schäferei die; ~, ~en a) *o. Pl.* **[die] ~:** sheep-farming; sheep-rearing; **b)** *(Betrieb)* sheep-farm

Schäfer·hund der a) *(Rasse)* Alsatian *(Brit.);* German shepherd; **ein deutscher ~:** an Alsatian *(Brit.);* a German shepherd; **b)** *(Hirtenhund)* sheep-dog

Schäferin die; ~, ~nen shepherdess

Schäfer-: ~spiel das *(Literaturw.)* pastoral [play]; **~stündchen das** lovers' tryst

Schaf·fell das sheepskin

schaffen ['ʃafn̩] **1.** *unr. tr. V.* **a)** *(schöpferisch gestalten)* create; **der ~de Mensch** creative man; **für jmdn./etw.** *od.* **zu jmdm./etw. wie geschaffen sein** be made *or* perfect for sb./sth.; **b)** *auch regelm. (herstellen)* create ⟨*conditions, jobs, situation, etc.*⟩; make ⟨*room, space, fortune*⟩; **klare Verhältnisse ~:** clear things up; straighten things out; *s. auch* **Abhilfe; Ordnung a. 2.** *tr. V.* **a)** *(bewältigen)* **etw. ~:** manage to do sth.; **viel ~:** manage to do a great deal; **eine Arbeit ~:** get a job done; **wenn wir uns beeilen, ~ wir es vielleicht noch** we might still make it if we hurry; **das schafft er nie** he'll never manage it; **das hätten wir geschafft, das wäre geschafft** there, that's done; **er hat die Prüfung nicht geschafft** *(ugs.)* he didn't pass the exam; **b)** *(ugs.: erschöpfen)* wear out; **die Hitze/Arbeit hat mich geschafft** the heat/work took it out of me; **c)** *(befördern)* **etw. aus etw./in etw.** *(Akk.)* **~:** get sth. out of/into sth.; **die Kisten auf den Speicher/in den Keller ~:** take the boxes to the attic/cellar. **3.** *itr. V.* **a)** *(südd.: arbeiten)* work; **b) sich** *(Dat.)* **zu ~ machen** *(an etw. hantieren)* busy oneself; *(Tätigkeit vortäuschen)* fiddle *or* tinker about; **was machst du dir an meinem Schreibtisch zu ~?** what are you doing at my desk?; **mit ihm will ich nichts zu ~ haben** I don't want to have anything to do with him; **was habe ich mit dieser Angelegenheit zu ~?** what does this matter have to do with me?; **jmdm. zu ~ machen** cause sb. trouble

Schaffen das; ~s work; **im Zenit seines ~s** at the peak of his creative work

Schaffens~: ~drang der; *o. Pl.* energy; **~freude die** *o. Pl.* enthusiasm [for one's work]; *(eines Künstlers)* pleasure in creating things; **~kraft die** *o. Pl.* energy for work; *(eines Künstlers)* creativity; creative power

Schaffer der; ~s, ~ *(bes. südd.)* hard worker

Schafferei die; ~ *(bes. südd.)* hard work

Schaf·fleisch das mutton

Schaffner ['ʃafnɐ] **der; ~s, ~** *(im Bus)* conductor; *(im Zug)* guard *(Brit.);* conductor *(Amer.); (der Fahrausweise verkauft/kontrolliert)* inspector

Schaffnerin die; ~, ~nen *(im Bus)* conductress *(Brit.); (im Zug)* guard *(Brit.);* conductress *(Amer.); (die Fahrausweise verkauft/kontrolliert)* inspector

schaffner·los *Adj. (Verkehrsw.)* ⟨*bus, tram, etc.*⟩ without a conductor; ⟨*train*⟩ without a guard *(Brit.) or (Amer.)* conductor/an inspector *postpos.*

Schaffung die; ~: creation

Schaf-: ~garbe die yarrow; **~herde die** flock of sheep; **~hirt der** shepherd; **~kälte die** *spell of cold weather frequently occurring in mid-June;* **~kopf** *s.* **Schafskopf**

Schäflein ['ʃɛ:flain] **das; ~s, ~** *s.* **Schäfchen a, b**

Schafott [ʃa'fɔt] **das; ~[e]s, ~e** scaffold

Schaf·schur die sheep-shearing

Schafs-: ~käse der sheep's milk cheese; **~kopf der a)** *o. Pl. (Kartenspiel)* sheep's head; **b)** *(ugs.: Trottel)* dope *(coll.);* idiot *(coll.);* **~pelz der** sheepskin

Schaf·stall der sheep-fold

Schaft [ʃaft] **der; ~[e]s, Schäfte** ['ʃɛftə] **a)** *(Griff; auch Archit.)* shaft; *(eines Messers, Beils, Meißels)* handle; *(eines Gewehrs usw.)* stock; **b)** *(eines Baumes, einer Feder)* shaft; **c)** *(am Schuh)* upper; **d)** *(am Stiefel)* leg; **e)** *(Bot.)* stem; stalk

Schaft·stiefel der high boot

Schaf-: ~wolle die sheep's wool; **~zucht die a)** *(das Züchten)* sheep-breeding *no art.;* **b)** *(Betrieb)* sheep-farm

Schah [ʃa:] **der; ~s, ~s** Shah

Schakal [ʃa'ka:l] **der; ~s, ~e** jackal

Schäker ['ʃɛ:kɐ] **der; ~s, ~** *(veralt.)* **a)** *(Witzbold)* joker; **b)** *(jmd., der flirtet)* flirt

schäkern *itr. V. (veralt.)* **a)** *(spaßen)* fool about; **b)** *(flirten)* flirt

schal [ʃa:l] *Adj.* stale ⟨*drink, taste, smell, joke*⟩; empty ⟨*words, feeling*⟩

Schal der; ~s, ~s *od.* **~e a)** *(Halstuch)* scarf; **b)** *(Vorhang~)* curtain

Schälchen ['ʃɛ:lçən] **das; ~s, ~:** small bowl *or* dish

Schale ['ʃa:lə] **die; ~, ~n a)** *(Obst~)* skin; *(abgeschälte ~)* peel *no pl.;* **Kartoffeln in der ~** *(Kochk.)* jacket potatoes; **b)** *(Nuß~, Eier~)* shell; **c)** *(tieferes Gefäß)* bowl; *(flaches Gefäß)* dish; *(Waag~)* pan; scale; *(Sekt~)* champagne-glass; **d)** *in* **[groß] in ~ sein** *(ugs.)* be dressed up to the nines; **sich in ~ werfen** *od.* **schmeißen** *(ugs.)* get dressed [up] to the nines; **e)** *(Zool.)* shell; **f)** *(bes. österr.: Tasse)* [shallow] cup; **g)** *(des BH)* cup

schälen ['ʃɛ:lən] **1.** *tr. V.* peel ⟨*fruit, vegetable*⟩; shell ⟨*egg, nut, pea*⟩; skin ⟨*tomato, almond*⟩; **einen Baumstamm ~:** remove the bark from a tree-trunk; **den Knochen aus einem Schinken ~:** bone a ham; **etw. aus der Verpackung ~** *(fig.)* get sth. out of its wrappings; **sich aus den Kleidern ~** *(fig.)* get oneself out of one's clothes. **2.** *refl. V.* **a)** *(sich ~ lassen)* peel; **Tomaten/Eier ~ sich leichter** tomatoes/eggs can be skinned/shelled more easily; **b)** ⟨*person, skin, nose, etc.*⟩ peel; **du schälst dich am Rücken/auf der Nase/im Gesicht** your back/nose/face is peeling

Schalen-: ~obst das nuts *pl.;* **~sitz der** bucket seat; **~tier das** shell animal; **~wild das** *(Jägerspr.)* hoofed game

Schalheit die; ~ *s.* **schal:** staleness; emptiness

Schalk [ʃalk] **der; ~[e]s, ~e** *od.* **Schälke** ['ʃɛlkə] rogue; prankster; **jmdm. sitzt der ~/jmd. hat den ~ im Nacken** *(fig.)* sb. is really roguish *or* mischievous; **jmdm. schaut der ~ aus den Augen** *(fig.)* sb. has a roguish *or* mischievous look in his eye

schalkhaft *(geh.)* **1.** *Adj.* roguish; mischievous. **2.** *adv.* roguishly; mischievously

Schal·kragen der shawl collar

Schalks·narr der *(veralt.)* **a)** *(Hofnarr)* jester; fool; **b)** *(Schalk)* rogue; prankster; wag

Schall [ʃal] **der; ~[e]s, ~e** *od.* **Schälle** ['ʃɛlə] **a)** *(Klang)* sound; **mit lautem ~:** loudly; **leerer ~ sein** be meaningless *or* irrelevant; **~ und Rauch sein** not mean anything; **Name ist ~ und Rauch** names mean nothing; **b)** *o. Pl. (Physik)* sound *no art.*

schall-, Schall-: ~dämmend *Adj.* sound-deadening; sound-absorbing; **~dämmung die** sound insulation; **~dämpfer der a)** *(am Auto, für Feuerwaffen)* silencer; **b)** *(Musik)* mute; **~dicht** *Adj.* sound-proof

Schallehre die; *o. Pl.* acoustics *sing., no art.*

schallen *regelm. (auch unr.) itr. V.* ring out; *(nachhallen)* resound; echo; **eine ~de Ohrfeige** a resounding slap; **~des Gelächter** ringing laughter; **~d lachen** roar with laughter

Schall-: ~geschwindigkeit die speed *or* velocity of sound; **~lehre** *s.* **Schallehre; ~loch** *s.* **Schalloch; ~mauer die** sound *or* sonic barrier

Schalloch das a) *(Musik)* sound-hole; **b)** *(an einem Turm usw.)* belfry window

Schall·platte die record

Schallplatten-: *s.* **Platten-**

schall-, Schall-: ~quelle die sound-source; **~schluckend** *Adj.* sound-absorbent; sound-deadening; **~trichter der** *(am Grammophon)* horn; *(am Blasinstrument)* bell; **~welle die** *(Physik)* sound-wave; **~wort das** *Pl.* **~wörter** *(Sprachw.)* onomatopoeic word

Schalmei [ʃal'mai] **die; ~, ~en** shawm

Schalotte [ʃa'lɔtə] **die; ~, ~n** shallot

schalt [ʃalt] *1. u. 3. Pers. Sg. Prät. v.* **schelten**

Schalt·anlage die *(Elektrot.)* switch-gear

schalten ['ʃaltn̩] **1.** *tr. V.* **a)** switch; **ein Gerät auf „aus" ~**: turn an appliance to 'off'; **b)** *(Elektrot.: verbinden)* connect; **in Reihe/parallel ~**: connect in series/in parallel. **2.** *itr. V.* **a)** *(Schalter betätigen)* switch, turn (**auf** + *Akk.* to); **du mußt zweimal ~**: you have to operate the switch twice; **er schaltet immer gleich auf stur** *(fig. ugs.)* he immediately digs his heels in *(fig.)*; **b)** ‹*machine*› switch (**auf** + *Akk.* to); ‹*traffic light*› change (**auf** + *Akk.* to); **c)** *(im Auto)* change [gear]; **in den 4. Gang ~**: change into fourth gear; **d)** *(geh.: verfahren)* act; **er kann mit dem Geld frei ~**: he can do as he pleases with the money; he has a free hand with the money; **~ und walten** manage one's affairs; **sie kann ~ und walten, wie sie will** she can manage things as she pleases; **e)** *(ugs.: begreifen)* twig *(coll.)*; catch on *(coll.)*. **3.** *refl. V. (sich ~ lassen)* **das Gerät schaltet sich leicht/schwer** the switch on this device is easy/difficult to operate; **der Wagen schaltet sich schlecht** it's difficult to change gear in this car

Schalter ['ʃaltɐ] **der; ~s, ~ a)** *(Strom~)* switch; **b)** *(Post~, Bank~, Fahrkarten~ usw.)* counter; *(mit Fenster auch)* window

Schalter-: ~beamte der counter clerk; *(im Bahnhof)* ticket clerk; **~halle die** hall; *(im Bahnhof)* booking-hall *(Brit.)*; ticket office; **~raum der** counter-room; *(im Bahnhof)* ticket office; **~schluß der** closing-time; **~stunden** *Pl.* business hours; hours of business

Schalt-: ~getriebe das *(Kfz-W.)* [manual] gearbox; **~hebel der a)** *(am Schalter)* switch; **an den ~hebeln der Macht sitzen** *(fig.)* hold the reins of power; **b)** *(im Auto)* gear-lever; gear-shift *(Amer.)*; **~jahr das** leap year; **alle ~jahre [ein]mal** *(ugs.)* once in a blue moon; **~knüppel der** [floor-mounted] gear-lever; **~kreis der** *(Elektrot.)* circuit; **~pause die** *(Rundfunk)* pause [in transmission]; **~plan der** *(Elektrot.)* wiring *or* circuit diagram; **~pult das** control desk; *(kleiner)* control panel; **~satz der** *(Sprachw.)* parenthetic clause; **~stelle die** control centre; **~tafel die** *(Elektrot.)* control panel; **~tag der** leap-day

Schaltung die; ~, ~en a) *(Rundfunk: Verbindung)* link-up; **b)** *(Gang~)* manual gear change; **c)** *(Elektrot.)* circuit; wiring system; **d)** *s.* **Schaltplan**

Schalt·zentrale die *(Technik)* control centre

Schaluppe [ʃa'lʊpə] **die; ~, ~n** *(Frachtschiff)* sloop

Scham [ʃa:m] **die; ~ a)** shame; **ohne/ohne jede ~**: unashamedly/without the slightest shame; **ich hätte vor ~ in den Boden versinken können** I could have sunk through the floor with embarrassment *or* shame; **aus/vor ~ erröten** blush with shame; **nur keine falsche ~**: no need for any false modesty; **b)** *(geh. verhüll.: ~gegend)* private parts *pl.*

Schamane [ʃa'ma:nə] **der; ~n, ~n** *(Völkerk.)* shaman

Scham·bein das *(Anat.)* pubic bone

schämen ['ʃɛmən] *refl. V.* be ashamed; **sich einer Sache** *(Gen.)* *od.* **für etw.** *od.* **wegen etw. ~**: be ashamed of sth.; **sich für jmdn. ~**: be ashamed for sb.; **du solltest dich [was** *(ugs.)*] **~!** you [really] should be ashamed of yourself; **schäm dich** shame on you

Scham-: ~gefühl das; *o. Pl.* sense of shame; **~haar das;** *o. Pl.* pubic hair

schamhaft 1. *Adj.* bashful ‹*person, look, etc.*›; modest ‹*clothing*›. **2.** *adv.* ‹*look, smile, etc.*› bashfully; ‹*dress, behave*› modestly

Schamhaftigkeit die; ~: modesty

scham-, Scham-: ~lippe die *(Anat.)* labium; **innere/äußere ~lippen** labia minora/majora; **~los 1.** *Adj.* **a)** *(skrupellos, dreist)* shameless; barefaced, shameless ‹*lie, slander*›; **b)** *(unanständig)* indecent ‹*gesture, remark, dress, etc.*›; shameless ‹*person*›; **2.** *adv.* **a)** *(skrupellos, dreist)* shamelessly; **b)** *(unanständig)* indecently; **~losigkeit die; ~, ~en** *(Skrupellosigkeit, Dreistigkeit)* shamelessness; *(Unanständigkeit)* indecency; shamelessness; **ich kann solche ~losigkeiten nicht dulden** I cannot tolerate such shameless behaviour *sing.*

Schamotte·stein [ʃa'mɔtə-] **der** fire-brick

Schampon ['ʃampɔn] *s.* **Shampoo**

schamponieren *tr. V.* shampoo

Schampus ['ʃampʊs] **der; ~** *(ugs.)* bubbly *(coll.)*; champers *sing. (Brit. coll.)*

scham·rot *Adj.* red with shame *postpos.*; **~ werden** blush with shame

Scham·röte die: ihm stieg die ~ ins Gesicht he blushed with shame

schandbar *s.* **schändlich**

Schande ['ʃandə] **die; ~**: disgrace; shame; **es ist eine [wahre] ~**: it is a[n absolute] disgrace; **es wäre doch eine ~, das wegzuwerfen** it would be a shame to throw it away; **zu meiner ~ muß ich sagen, daß ...**: it must be said to my shame that ...; **~ über dich!** shame on you!; **jmdm./einer Sache [keine] ~ machen** [not] disgrace sb./sth.; bring [no] disgrace *or* shame on sb./sth.; **etw. gereicht jmdm. zur ~** *(geh.)* sth. is a disgrace to sb.

schänden ['ʃɛndn̩] *tr. V.* **a)** dishonour, discredit ‹*name, reputation, etc.*›; **b)** *(beschädigen)* defile ‹*memorial, work of art, etc.*›; desecrate, defile ‹*holy place, grave, relic*›; violate ‹*corpse*›; **c)** *(veralt.: vergewaltigen)* violate; *s. auch* **Arbeit a**

Schand·fleck der blot; **ein ~ in der Landschaft sein** be a blot on the landscape; **er war schon immer der ~ [in] unserer Familie** he always 'was the disgrace of our family

schändlich 1. *Adj.* **a)** *(verwerflich)* shameful; disgraceful; **b)** *(ugs.: scheußlich)* disgraceful; dreadful *(coll.)*, terrible *(coll.)* ‹*weather*›. **2.** *adv.* **a)** *(verwerflich)* shamefully; disgracefully; **b)** *(ugs.: überaus)* dreadfully *(coll.)*, terribly *(coll.)*

Schändlichkeit die; ~, ~en a) *o. Pl. (Eigenschaft)* shamefulness; disgracefulness; **b)** *(Handlung)* shameful action

Schand-: ~mal das a) *(hist.)* brand; **b)** *(geh.: Schandfleck)* blemish; **~tat die** disgraceful *or* abominable deed; **zu jeder ~tat** *od.* **zu allen ~taten bereit sein** *(ugs. scherzh.)* be game for anything

Schändung die; ~, ~en a) *s.* **schänden a, b:** dishonouring; discrediting; desecration; defilement; **b)** *(veralt.: Vergewaltigung)* violation

Schanker ['ʃaŋkɐ] **der; ~s, ~** *(Med.)* chancre; **harter/weicher ~**: hard/soft chancre

Schank-: ~erlaubnis die licence [to sell alcohol]; **~tisch der** bar; **~wirtschaft die** public house *(Brit.)*; bar *(Amer.)*

Schanze ['ʃantsə] **die; ~, ~n a)** *(Milit. veralt.)* entrenchment; fieldwork; **b)** *(Sprung~)* [ski-]jump

Schanzen·rekord der *(Skispringen)* ski-jump record

Schar [ʃa:ɐ̯] **die; ~, ~en** crowd; horde; *(von Vögeln)* flock; **in [großen** *od.* **hellen] ~en** in swarms *or* droves

Scharade [ʃa'ra:də] **die; ~, ~n** charade

Schäre ['ʃɛ:rə] **die; ~, ~n** skerry

scharen 1. *refl. V. (sich zusammenfinden)* gather. **2.** *tr. V.* **die Kinder/Klasse um sich ~**: gather the children/class around one[self]

Schären·küste die skerry coast

scharen·weise *Adv.* in swarms *or* hordes

scharf [ʃarf]; **schärfer** ['ʃɛrfɐ], **schärfst...** ['ʃɛrfst...] **1.** *Adj.* **a)** sharp; **b)** *(stark gewürzt, brennend, stechend)* hot; strong ‹*drink, vinegar, etc.*›; caustic ‹*chemical*›; pungent, acrid ‹*smell*›; **c)** *(durchdringend)* shrill; *(hell)* harsh; *(kalt)* biting ‹*cold, wind, air, etc.*›; sharp ‹*frost*›; **d)** *(deutlich wahrnehmend)* keen; sharp; **e)** *(stark)* strong ‹*spectacles*›; powerful ‹*lens, microscope, telescope, etc.*›; **f)** *(deutlich hervortretend)* sharp ‹*contours, features, nose, photograph*›; **g)** *(schonungslos)* tough, fierce ‹*resistance, competition, etc.*›; sharp ‹*criticism, remark, words, etc.*›; strong, fierce ‹*opponent, protest, etc.*›; severe, harsh ‹*sentence, law, measure, etc.*›; strict, tough ‹*examiner, teacher*›; tough, rigorous ‹*inquiry, interrogation*›; bitter, fierce ‹*fighting, argument, etc.*›; fierce ‹*dog*›; **eine ~e Zunge haben** have a sharp tongue; **jmdn./etw. in ~er Form kritisieren** criticize sb./sth. in strong terms; **h)** *(schnell)* fast; hard ‹*ride, gallop, etc.*›; **ein ~es Tempo fahren** drive at quite a speed; **i)** *(explosiv)* live; *(Ballspiele)* powerful ‹*shot*›; **~e Schüsse abgeben** fire live bullets; **j)** *(Sprachw.)* pronounced; clear; **das ~e S** *(bes. österr.)* the German letter 'ß'; **k)** *(ugs.: großartig)* great *(coll.)*; **l)** *(ugs. empörend)* outrageous; **m)** *(ugs.: geil)* sexy ‹*girl, clothes, pictures, etc.*›; randy ‹*fellow, thoughts, etc.*›; **n)** *in* **~ auf jmdn./etw. sein** *(ugs.)* really fancy sb. *(coll.)*/be really keen on sth. **2.** *adv.* **a) ~ würzen/abschmecken** season/flavour highly; **~ riechen** smell pungent *or* strong; **b)** *(durchdringend)* shrilly; *(hell)* harshly; *(kalt)* bitingly; **c)** *(deutlich wahrnehmend)* ‹*listen, watch, etc.*› closely, intently; ‹*think, consider, etc.*› hard; **~ aufpassen** pay close attention; **d)** *(deutlich hervortretend)* sharply; **einen Sender ~ einstellen** tune in a radio station properly; **etw. ~ umreißen** *(fig.)* outline sth. clearly *or* precisely; **e)** *(schonungslos)* ‹*attack, criticize, etc.*› sharply, strongly; ‹*contradict, oppose, etc.*› strongly, fiercely; ‹*examine, investigate, etc.*› rigorously; ‹*watch, observe, etc.*› closely; ‹*fight, quarrel, etc.*› fiercely, bitterly; **~ durchgreifen** take vigorous *or* strong action; **f)** *(schnell)* fast; **~ bremsen** brake hard *or* sharply; **das Auto fuhr ~ rechts heran** the car pulled up well over to the right; **g) das Gewehr ist ~ geladen** the rifle is loaded with live ammunition; **~ schießen** shoot with live ammunition; **den Ball ~ ins Netz schießen** hammer the ball into the net *(coll.)*; **h)** *(akzentuiert)* clearly; **i)** *(ugs.: großartig)* splendidly

Scharf·blick der; *o. Pl.* perspicacity

Schärfe ['ʃɛrfə] **die; ~, ~n a)** *o. Pl. (von Messer usw.)* sharpness; **b)** *o. Pl. (von Geschmack)* hotness; *(von Chemikalien)* causticity; *(von Geruch)* pungency; **c)** *o. Pl. (Intensität)* shrillness; *(von Licht, Farbe usw.)* harshness; *(des Windes)* bitterness; *(des Frostes)* sharpness; **d)** *o. Pl. (Empfindlichkeit, analytische Fähigkeit)* sharpness; keenness; **e)** *o. Pl. (Klarheit)* clarity; sharpness; **f)** *o. Pl. (Härte) s.* **scharf 1 g:** toughness; ferocity; sharpness; strength; severity; harshness; strictness; rigour; bitterness; **g)** *(Heftigkeit)* harshness; **h)** *o. Pl. (Ballspiele)* power

schärfen 1. *tr. V. (auch fig.)* sharpen. **2.** *refl. V.* become sharper *or* keener

Schärfen·tiefe die *(Fot.)* depth of focus

schärfer *s.* **scharf**

scharf-, Scharf-: ~kantig *Adj.* sharp-edged; **~|machen** *tr. V. (ugs.)* stir up; **einen Hund ~machen** urge a dog on; **~macher der** *(ugs.)* rabble-rouser; **~macherei** [~maxə'rai] **die; ~, ~en** *(ugs.)* rabble-rousing; **~richter der** hangman; executioner; **~schütze der** *(Milit.)* marksman; *(auch fig. Ballspiele)* sharpshooter; **~sichtig** [~zɪçtɪç] **1.** *Adj.* sharp-sighted; perspicacious; **2.** *adv.* with sharp-sightedness; **~sinn der** *o. Pl.* astuteness; acumen; **~sinnig 1.** *Adj.* astute; **2.** *adv.* astutely

schärfst... *s.* **scharf**

Schärfung die; ~, ~en sharpening

scharfzüngig [-tsʏŋɪç] **1.** *Adj.* sharp-tongued. **2.** *adv.* sharply; in a sharp-tongued manner

Scharlach ['ʃarlax] **der; ~s** *(Med.)* scarlet fever
scharlach·rot *Adj.* scarlet
Scharlatan ['ʃarlatan] **der; ~s, ~e** *(abwertend)* charlatan
Scharlatanerie die; ~, ~n a) *o. Pl.* charlatanism; **b)** *(einzelne Handlung)* charlatanry
Scharmützel [ʃar'mytsl] **das; ~s, ~** *(Milit.)* skirmish
Scharnier [ʃar'ni:ɐ] **das; ~s, ~e** hinge
Schärpe ['ʃɛrpə] **die; ~, ~n** sash
scharren ['ʃarən] **1.** *itr. V.* **a)** *(schaben, schleifen)* scrape; **die Pferde ~ ungeduldig** the horses are pawing at the ground impatiently; **der Hund scharrte an der Tür** the dog scratched *or* pawed at the door; **mit den Füßen ~:** scrape one's feet; **b)** *(wühlen)* scratch. **2.** *tr. V.* **a)** scrape ‹*fallen leaves, twigs, sand, dirt*›; **b)** *(herstellen)* scrape, scratch out ‹*hole, hollow, etc.*›
Scharte ['ʃartə] **die; ~, ~n a)** nick; **eine ~ auswetzen** *(fig.)* make good a/the mistake; **b)** *(Gebirgs~)* wind gap; **c)** *(Schieß~)* crenel
Scharteke [ʃar'te:kə] **die; ~, ~n** *(abwertend)* **a)** *(Buch)* trashy old tome; **b)** *(Frau)* [old] hag; [old] bag *(sl.)*
schartig *Adj.* nicked; jagged
Schaschlik ['ʃaʃlɪk] **der** *od.* **das; ~s, ~s** *(Kochk.)* shashlik
schassen ['ʃasn] *tr. V. (ugs.)* throw *or (coll.)* chuck out
Schatten ['ʃatn] **der; ~s, ~ a)** shadow; **nur noch ein ~ seiner selbst sein** *(fig.)* be only a shadow of one's former self; **einen** *od.* **seinen ~ auf etw.** *(Akk.)* **werfen** *(fig. geh.)* cast a *or* its shadow over sth.; **das große Ereignis wirft schon seine ~ voraus** *(fig.)* the big event is already making itself felt; **jmd./man kann nicht über seinen [eigenen] ~ springen** a leopard cannot change its spots *(prov.)*; **b)** *o. Pl. (schattige Stelle)* shade; **40° im ~:** 40° in the shade; **das Tal lag im ~:** the valley lay in shadow; **in jmds. ~ stehen** *(fig.)* be in sb.'s shadow; **jmdn./etw. in den ~ stellen** *(fig.)* put sb./sth. in the shade; **c)** *(dunkle Stelle, auch fig.)* shadow; **nicht der ~ eines Verdachts** not a shadow of suspicion; **d)** *(Gestalt)* shadow; **e) das Reich der ~** *(Myth.)* the realm of shades; **f)** *(Beobachter)* shadow
Schatten-: ~bild das a) *(Schatten)* shadow; **b)** *(Schattenriß)* silhouette; **~boxen das** shadow-boxing; **~dasein das** *in* **ein ~dasein fristen** lead a shadowy existence; **aus dem** *od.* **seinem ~dasein heraustreten** emerge from its/one's shadowy existence
schattenhaft *Adj.* shadowy; **etw. ist nur ~ zu erkennen** sth. is only vaguely recognizable
schatten-, Schatten-: ~kabinett das *(Politik)* shadow cabinet; **~los** *Adj.* shadeless; without shade *postpos.*; **~morelle** [~morɛlə] **die; ~, ~n** morello cherry; **~reich das** *(Myth.)* realm of shades; **~riß der** silhouette; **~seite die a)** shady side; **die ~seiten des Lebens kennenlernen** *(fig.)* get to know the dark side of life; **b)** *(Kehrseite)* disadvantage; negative aspect; **~spender der** *(geh.)* source of shade; **~spiel das a)** *o. Pl. (Theater)* shadow theatre; **b)** *(Stück)* shadow-play; shadow show; **c)** *(Kinderspiel)* **~spiele machen** make shadow-pictures; **~wirtschaft die** ≈ black economy [and social security scrounging]
schattieren *tr. V.* shade
Schattierung die; ~, ~en a) shading; **b)** *(Variante, Nuance)* shade; **aller ideologischen/religiösen ~en** of every ideological/religious shade *or (Amer.)* stripe
schattig *Adj.* shady
Schatt·seite die *(österr., schweiz.) s.* **Schattenseite**
Schatulle [ʃa'tʊlə] **die; ~, ~n** casket
Schatz [ʃats] **der; ~es, Schätze** ['ʃɛtsə] **a)** treasure *no indef. art.*; **ein ~ von Erinnerungen/Erfahrungen** *(fig.)* a wealth of memories/experience; **b)** *Pl. (Bodenschätze)* natural resources; **c)** *(ugs.: Anrede)* love *(coll.)*; darling; **d)** *(ugs.: hilfsbereiter Mensch)* treasure *(coll.)*; **sei ein ~ und räum schnell auf** be a dear and clear up quickly
Schätzchen ['ʃɛtsçən] **das; ~s, ~:** darling
schätzen ['ʃɛtsn] **1.** *tr. V.* **a)** *(ein~, bewerten)* estimate; **wie alt schätzt du ihn?** how old do you think he is?; **sich glücklich ~:** deem oneself lucky; **grob geschätzt** at a rough estimate; **ein Haus/einen Gebrauchtwagen ~:** value a house/a second-hand car; **b)** *(ugs.: annehmen)* reckon; think; **c)** *(würdigen, hochachten)* **jmdn. ~:** hold sb. in high regard *or* esteem; **ein geschätzter Künstler** a highly regarded artist; **etw. zu ~ wissen** appreciate sth.; **ich weiß es zu ~, daß ...:** I appreciate the fact that ... **2.** *itr. V.* guess; **schätz mal** guess; have a guess
schätzen|lernen *tr. V.* come to appreciate *or* value
Schatz-: ~kammer die *(hist.)* treasure-chamber; **~kanzler der** Chancellor of the Exchequer *(Brit.)*; **~meister der** treasurer
Schätzung die; ~, ~en estimate; *(eines Gebäudes, Grundstückwerts usw.)* valuation; **nach grober/vorsichtiger ~:** at a rough/cautious estimate; **nach meiner ~:** according to my reckoning
schätzungs·weise *Adv.* roughly; approximately
Schätz·wert der estimated value
Schau [ʃau] **die; ~, ~en a)** *(Ausstellung)* exhibition; **b)** *(Vorführung)* show; **es war eine reine ~:** it was all show; **die** *od.* **eine ~ sein** *(Jugendspr.)* be really something; be something else *(coll.)*; **eine ~ machen** *od.* **abziehen** *(ugs.) (sich in Szene setzen)* put on a show; *(sich aufspielen)* show off; *(sich lautstark ereifern)* make a scene *or* fuss; **jmdm. die ~ stehlen** steal the show from sb.; **c)** *in* **zur ~ stellen** *(ausstellen)* exhibit; display; *(offen zeigen)* display; **seine Gefühle zur ~ tragen** make a show of one's emotions; **d)** *(geh.: Betrachtung)* vision; **e)** *(geh.: Blickwinkel)* perspective
Schau-: ~bild das a) *(Diagramm)* chart; **b)** *(Nachbildung)* diagram; **~bude die** show booth; **~bühne die** *(veralt.)* theatre
Schauder ['ʃaudɐ] **der; ~s, ~** *(vor Kälte, Angst)* shiver; *(vor Angst)* shudder; **mir lief ein ~ den Rücken hinunter** a shiver/shudder ran down my spine
schauderbar *(ugs. scherzh.) s.* **schauderhaft**
schauder·erregend *Adj.* terrifying; horrifying
schauderhaft 1. *Adj.* **a)** *(fürchterlich)* terrible; dreadful; awful; **b)** *(schaudererregend)* ghastly; terrible; horrifying. **2.** *adv.* **a)** *(fürchterlich)* terribly; dreadfully; **b)** *(überaus)* terribly *(coll.)*; dreadfully *(coll.)*
schaudern *itr. V.* **a)** *(vor Kälte)* shiver; **b)** *(vor Angst)* shudder; **c)** *unpers.* **es schauderte ihn [vor Kälte]** he shivered [with cold]; **bei dem Gedanken schauderte [es] ihn** he shuddered at the thought
schauen 1. *itr. V. (bes. südd., österr., schweiz.)* **a)** *(sehen)* look; **jmdm./einander [fest] in die Augen ~:** look [straight] into sb.'s/each other's eyes; **auf jmdn./etw. ~:** look at sb./sth.; *(fig.)* look to sb./sth.; **um sich ~:** look around [one]; **zu tief in den Becher** *od.* **ins Glas geschaut haben** have had a drop too much [to drink]; have had one too many; **b)** *(dreinblicken)* look; **der hat vielleicht geschaut, als er uns sah** his eyes opened wide when he saw us; **seine Augen schauten vergnügt/spöttisch** amusement/mockery showed in his eyes; **c) schau, schau!** well, well; what do you know; **da schau her!** *(Verwunderung ausdrückend)* well, well; how about that?; *(Empörung ausdrückend)* well, what about 'that?; **da schau her, was du ...:** just look what you ...; **schau [mal], ich finde, du solltest ...:** look, I think you should ...; **d)** *(sich kümmern um)* **nach jmdm./etw. ~:** take *or* have a look at sb./sth.; **die Nachbarn haben nach den Blumen geschaut** the neighbours looked after the flowers; **e)** *(achtgeben)* **auf etw.** *(Akk.)* **~:** set store by sth.; **er schaut darauf, daß alle pünktlich sind** he sets store by everybody being punctual; **f)** *(ugs.: sich bemühen)* **schau, daß du ...:** see *or* mind that you ...; **g)** *(nachsehen)* have a look. **2.** *tr. V.* **a)** *(sich ansehen)* **Fernsehen ~:** watch television; **schauen Sie, was ich gefunden habe** look what I've found; **b)** *(geh.: erfassen)* behold
Schauer der; ~s, ~ a) *(Met.)* shower; **b)** *(geh.) s.* **Schauder**
schauer·artig *(Met.) Adj.* **~e Regenfälle** showers; **~e Schneefälle** snow showers
Schauer·geschichte die horror story
schauerlich 1. *Adj.* **a)** *(schauererregend)* horrifying; ghastly; **b)** *(ugs.: fürchterlich)* terrible *(coll.)*; dreadful *(coll.)*. **2. a)** *(ugs.: fürchterlich)* dreadfully *(coll.)*, terribly *(coll.)*; **ein ~ gemusterter Teppich** a hideously patterned carpet; **b)** *(überaus)* terribly *(coll.)*; dreadfully *(coll.)*
Schauer·roman der Gothic novel
Schaufel ['ʃaufl] **die; ~, ~n a)** shovel; *(für Mehl usw.)* scoop; *(Kehr~)* dustpan; *(vom Schaufelrad, Mühlrad)* paddle; **zwei ~n Erde** two shovelfuls of soil; **b)** *(Jägerspr.: vom Geweih)* palm
schaufeln ['ʃaufln] *tr. V.* shovel; dig ‹*hole, grave, trench, etc.*›
Schaufel-: ~rad das paddle-wheel; **~rad·dampfer der** paddle-steamer; **~rad·bagger der** bucket excavator
Schau·fenster das shop-window
Schaufenster~: ~aus·lage die window display; **~bummel der** window-shopping expedition; **einen ~bummel machen** go window-shopping; **~puppe die** mannequin
Schau-: ~flug der air display; *(von einem Flugzeug)* aerobatics demonstration; **~geschäft das;** *o. Pl.* show business *no art.*; **~kampf der** *(Boxen)* exhibition fight; **~kasten der** display case; show-case
Schaukel ['ʃaukl] **die; ~, ~n a)** swing; **b)** *(bes. südd.: Wippe)* see-saw
schaukeln 1. *itr. V.* **a)** swing; *(im Schaukelstuhl)* rock; **auf einem Stuhl ~:** rock one's chair backwards and forwards; **b)** *(sich hin und her bewegen)* sway [to and fro]; *(sich auf und ab bewegen)* ‹*ship, boat*› pitch and toss; ‹*vehicle*› bump [up and down]; **c)** *(unpers.)* **auf der Überfahrt/in dem klapprigen Bus hat es ganz schön geschaukelt** the boat pitched and tossed quite a bit during the crossing/it was a pretty bumpy ride in the rickety bus. **2.** *tr. V.* **a)** rock; **ein Kind auf den Knien ~:** dandle a child on one's knee; **b)** *(ugs.: fahren)* take; **jmdn. durch die Gegend ~:** drive sb. round the area; **c)** *(ugs.: bewerkstelligen)* manage; **wir werden die Sache schon ~:** we'll manage it somehow
Schaukel-: ~pferd das rocking-horse; **~stuhl der** rocking-chair
schau-, Schau-: ~laufen das *(Eislauf)* exhibition skating *no art.*; **~lustig** *Adj.* curious; **~lustige der/die;** *adj. Dekl.* curious onlooker
Schaum [ʃaum] **der; ~s, Schäume** ['ʃɔymə] **a)** foam; *(von Seife usw.)* lather; *(von Getränken, Suppen usw.)* froth; **etw. zu ~ schlagen** *(Kochk.)* beat sth. until frothy; **den ~ von etw. abschöpfen** *(Kochk.)* skim sth.; **~ schlagen** *(fig. ugs.)* talk big; **b)** *(Geifer)* foam; froth; **~ vor dem Mund haben** *(auch fig.)* foam *or* froth at the mouth
Schaum·bad das a) *(Badezusatz)* bubble bath; **b)** *(Wannenbad)* bubble *or* foam bath

schäumen ['ʃɔymən] **1.** *itr. V.* **a)** *(Schaum bilden)* foam; froth; ⟨*soap etc.*⟩ lather; ⟨*beer, fizzy drink, etc.*⟩ froth [up]; **b)** *(mit Wasser)* produce lather; **stark/schwach ~:** produce a large amount of/little lather; **eine stark ~de Zahnpasta** a very frothy toothpaste; **c)** *(wütend sein)* fume; **vor Wut ~:** fume with anger. **2.** *tr. V. (Technik)* foam ⟨*plastics, concrete, etc.*⟩; **geschäumter Kunststoff** foamed plastic

Schaum-: ~gebäck das meringues *pl.*; **~gummi der** foam rubber

schaumig *Adj.* frothy ⟨*drink, dessert, etc.*⟩; sudsy, lathery ⟨*water*⟩; **Butter und Zucker ~ rühren** beat butter and sugar until fluffy

Schaum-: ~krone die a) *(auf Wellen)* white crest; **b)** *(auf Bier)* head [of froth]; **~schläger der a)** *(abwertend)* boaster; **b)** *s.* **Schneebesen; ~schlägerei die;** *o. Pl. (abwertend)* boasting; **~stoff der** [plastic] foam; **~wein der** sparkling wine

Schau-: ~platz der scene; **direkt vom ~platz berichten** give an on-the-spot report; **~prozeß der** show trial

schaurig ['ʃaurɪç] **1.** *Adj.* **a)** *(furchtbar)* dreadful; frightful; *(unheimlich)* eerie; **eine ~e Geschichte** a blood-curdling story; **b)** *(ugs.: gräßlich, geschmacklos)* hideous; dreadful *(coll.)*. **2.** *adv.* **a)** *(fürchterlich)* dreadfully; *(unheimlich)* eerily; **b)** *(ugs.: gräßlich, geschmacklos)* hideously; horribly *(coll.)*; **c)** *(ugs.: überaus)* dreadfully *(coll.)*

schau-, Schau-: ~spiel das a) *o. Pl. (Drama)* drama *no art.*; **b)** *(ernstes Stück)* play; **c)** *(geh.: Anblick)* spectacle; **~spieler der** *(auch fig.)* actor; **~spielerei die a)** *(Beruf)* acting *no art.*; **b)** *(fig. ugs.: das Sichverstellen)* play-acting; **~spielerin die** *(auch fig.)* actress; **~spielerisch 1.** *Adj.; nicht präd.* acting ⟨*career*⟩; **eine großartige ~spielerische Leistung** a great piece of acting; **eine ~spielerische Begabung** a gift of *or* talent for acting. **2.** *adv.* **etw. ~spielerisch darstellen** act sth.; **sie ist ~spielerisch begabt** she has acting talent

schauspielern *itr. V. (ugs.)* **a)** *(als Schauspieler)* act; **b)** *(fig.)* play-act

Schauspiel-: ~führer der theatre-goer's guide; **~haus das** theatre; playhouse; **~kunst die;** *o. Pl.* dramatic art

Schausteller [-ʃtɛlɐ] **der; ~s, ~:** showman

Schau-: ~tafel die illustrated chart; **~turnen das** gymnastic display

Scheck [ʃɛk] **der; ~s, ~s** cheque

Scheck·buch das *(veralt.)* cheque-book

¹Schecke ['ʃɛkə] **der; ~n, ~n** *(Pferd)* piebald; *(Rind)* mottled bull

²Schecke die; ~, ~n *(Pferd)* piebald; *(Rind)* mottled cow

Scheckheft das cheque-book

scheckig *Adj.* **a)** *s.* **gescheckt; b)** *(voller Flecken)* blotchy ⟨*face, skin, etc.*⟩; **sich ~ lachen** *(ugs.)* laugh oneself silly

Scheck·karte die cheque card

scheel [ʃe:l] *(ugs.)* **1.** *Adj.* disapproving; *(mißtrauisch)* suspicious; *(neidisch)* envious; jealous. **2.** *adv.* disapprovingly; *(mißtrauisch)* suspiciously; *(neidisch)* enviously; jealously

Scheffel ['ʃɛfl̩] **der; ~s, ~:** bushel; *s. auch* **Licht**

scheffeln *tr. V. (ugs.)* rake in *(coll.)* ⟨*money, profits, etc.*⟩; pile up, accumulate ⟨*medals, awards, etc.*⟩

scheffel·weise *Adv. (ugs.)* by the sackful; in large quantities; **~ Geld haben/verdienen** have/earn stacks of money *(coll.)*

Scheibchen ['ʃaipçən] **das; ~s, ~** *(von Fleisch, Brot usw.)* [small] slice; *(aus Kunststoff, Metall usw.)* [small] disc

Scheibe ['ʃaibə] **die; ~, ~n a)** *(flacher, runder Gegenstand)* disc; *(Sportjargon: Puck)* puck; *(Schieß~)* target; *(Wähl~)* dial; **b)** *(abgeschnittene ~)* slice; **etw. in ~n schneiden** slice sth. up; cut sth. [up] into slices; **sich** *(Dat.)* **von jmdm./etw. eine ~ abschneiden können** *(fig.)* be able to learn a thing or two from sb./sth.; **... in ~n** slices of *or* sliced ...; **c)** *(Glas~)* pane [of glass]; *(Fenster~)* [window-] pane; *(Windschutz~)* windscreen *(Brit.)*; windshield *(Amer.)*; *(Spiegel~)* glass; **die ~n des Wagens herunterdrehen** wind down the car windows; **d)** *(ugs.: Schallplatte)* disc; record

Scheiben-: ~bremse die *(Kfz-W.)* disc brake; **~gardine die** net curtain; **~honig der a)** comb honey; **b)** *s.* **~kleister; ~kleister der** *(ugs. verhüll.)* **~kleister!** blast [it]! *(coll.)*; damn it! *(coll.)*; **so ein ~kleister!** what a blasted nuisance *or* mess!; **~schießen das** *(Milit., Sport)* target-shooting; **~wasch·anlage die** *(Kfz-W.)* windscreen washer system *or* unit; **~wischer der** windscreen-wiper

Scheich [ʃaiç] **der; ~[e]s, ~s** *od.* **~e a)** sheikh; **b)** *(ugs.: Freund)* guy *(sl.)*; bloke *(Brit. sl.)*

Scheichtum das; ~s, Scheichtümer [-ty:mɐ] sheikhdom

Scheide ['ʃaidə] **die; ~, ~n a)** *(Waffen~)* sheath; *(des Schwerts, Säbels)* scabbard; sheath; **b)** *(Anat.)* vagina

scheiden 1. *unr. tr. V.* **a)** dissolve ⟨*marriage*⟩; divorce ⟨*married couple*⟩; **eine geschiedene Frau** a divorced woman; a divorcée; **sich [von jmdm.] ~ lassen** get divorced *or* get a divorce [from sb.]; **sie läßt sich nicht [von ihm] ~:** she won't give him a divorce; **ich bin [schuldig/unschuldig] geschieden** I am divorced [and I was the guilty/innocent party]; **b)** *(geh.: trennen)* divide; separate; **von dem Moment an waren wir geschiedene Leute** from that moment on, we went our separate ways; **wir sind geschiedene Leute!** you and I must part; **c)** *(geh.: unterscheiden)* distinguish; **d)** *(bes. Chemie)* separate; extract. **2.** *unr. itr. V.; mit sein (geh.)* **a)** *(auseinandergehen)* part; **b)** *(sich entfernen)* depart; leave; **von jmdm. ~:** part from sb.; **aus dem Dienst/Amt ~:** retire from service/one's post *or* office; **aus dem Leben ~:** depart this life. **3.** *unr. refl. V. (sich unterscheiden)* diverge; differ; *s. auch* **Geist d**

Scheide·weg der *in* **am** *od.* **an einem ~ stehen** face a crucial decision

Scheidung die; ~, ~en a) *(Ehe~)* divorce; **die ~ einreichen** file [a petition] for divorce; **die ~ aussprechen** grant the divorce; **in ~ leben** be in the process of getting a divorce; **b)** *(Unterscheidung)* distinction

Scheidungs-: ~grund der grounds *pl.* for divorce; **sie war der ~grund** they got divorced because of her; **~klage die** petition for divorce; **~urkunde die** divorce certificate

Schein [ʃain] **der; ~[e]s, ~e a)** *o. Pl. (Licht~)* light; **der ~ des brennenden Hauses/der sinkenden Sonne** the glow of the burning house/setting sun; **b)** *o. Pl. (An~)* appearances *pl., no art.*; *(Täuschung)* pretence; **den ~ wahren** keep up appearances; **der ~ spricht gegen ihn** appearances are against him; **der ~ trügt** appearances are deceptive; **~ und Wirklichkeit** *od.* **Sein** appearances and reality; **etw. nur zum ~ tun** [only] pretend to do sth.; make a show of doing sth.; **c)** *(Bescheinigung)* receipt; *(vom Arzt)* doctor's certificate; *(Hochschulw.)* certificate; **d)** *(Geld~)* note

Schein·argument das spurious argument

scheinbar 1. *Adj. (nicht wirklich)* apparent; seeming. **2.** *adv.* **a)** *(nicht wirklich)* seemingly; **b)** *(ugs.) s.* **anscheinend**

Schein·blüte die a) *(Bot.)* composite flower; **b)** *(fig.)* illusory boom

scheinen *unr. itr. V.* **a)** *(Helligkeit ausstrahlen)* shine; **b)** *(den Eindruck erwecken)* seem; appear; **es scheint, daß .../als ob ...:** it appears that .../as if ...; **mir scheint, [daß] ...:** it seems *or* appears to me that ...; **wie es scheint ...:** apparently; **er kommt scheint's nicht mehr** *(ugs.)* it doesn't look as though he's coming now; **sie schienen es zufrieden zu sein** *(veralt.)* they seemed to be satisfied *or* happy with it

schein-, Schein-: ~gefecht das *(auch fig.)* mock fight *or* battle; **~heilig 1.** *Adj. (heuchlerisch)* hypocritical; *(Nichtwissen vortäuschend)* innocent; **2.** *adv. (heuchlerisch)* hypocritically; *(Nichtwissen vortäuschend)* innocently; **~heiligkeit die** hypocrisy; **~schwangerschaft die** *(Med.)* false pregnancy; **~tod der** *(Med.)* apparent death; **~tot** *Adj.* **a)** *(Med.)* apparently *or* seemingly dead; **b)** *(salopp: alt)* with one foot in the grave *postpos.*; **~tot sein** have one foot in the grave; **~welt die** illusory *or* unreal world; **~werfer der** floodlight; *(am Auto)* headlight; *(im Theater, Museum usw.)* spotlight; *(Suchscheinwerfer)* searchlight; **~werfer·licht das** floodlight; *(des Autos)* headlights *pl.*; *(im Theater, Museum usw.)* spotlight [beam]; *(des Suchscheinwerfers)* searchlight [beam]; **im ~werferlicht [der Öffentlichkeit] stehen** be in the [public] spotlight

Scheiß [ʃais] **der; ~** *(salopp)* shit *no indef. art. (coarse)*; crap *no indef. art. (coarse)*; **so ein ~!** oh, shit! *(coarse)*; **~ machen** *(Fehler machen)* make a bloody mess *(Brit. sl.)*; *(unklug handeln)* act in a bloody silly way *(Brit. sl.)*

scheiß-, Scheiß- *(derb)* bloody *(Brit. sl.)*

Scheiß·dreck der *(derb)* **a)** *(Kot)* shit *(coarse)*; crap *(coarse)*; **b)** *(Blödsinn, Minderwertiges)* shit *no indef. art. (coarse)*; crap *no indef. art. (coarse)*; *(Angelegenheiten)* bloody *(Brit.) or* damned business *(sl.)*; **red keinen ~!** don't talk carp! *(coarse)*; **das geht dich einen ~ an** that's none of your bloody business *(Brit. sl.)*; **einen ~ werde ich tun** like hell I will *(coll.)*

Scheiße ['ʃaisə] **die; ~** *(derb) (auch fig.)* shit *(coarse)*; crap *(coarse)*; **[bis zum Hals] in der ~ sitzen** *od.* **stecken** *(fig.)* be in the shit *(coarse)*; be up shit creek *(coarse)*; **der Film ist große ~** *(fig.)* the film is a load of shit *or* crap *(coarse)*; **verdammte/schöne ~!** shit *(coarse)*; bloody hell *(Brit. sl.)*

scheiß·egal *Adj.; nicht attr.* **in ~ sein** not matter a damn *(sl.)*; **das ist mir ~:** I don't give a damn *(sl.) or (coarse)* shit; **das kann dir doch ~ sein** you needn't give a damn *(sl.) or (coarse)* shit about that

scheißen *unr. itr. V. (derb)* **a)** *(den Darm entleeren)* [have *or (Amer.)* take a] shit *(coarse)*; crap *(coarse)*; have a crap *(coarse)*; **in die Hose ~:** shit one's pants *(coarse)*; **auf jmdn./etw. ~** *(fig.)* not give a shit *(coarse) or (sl.)* damn about sb./sth.; **wir ~ auf ihn/drauf** *(fig.)* to hell with him/with it/that *(coll.)*; **b) [einen] ~** *(eine Blähung entweichen lassen)* fart *(coarse)*

Scheißer der; ~s, ~ a) *(derb)* bastard *(coll.)*; shithead *(coarse)*; **b)** *(salopp: unbedeutender Mensch)* arse- *(Brit.) or (Amer.)* ass-hole *(coarse)*; **c)** *(fam.: Kosewort)* monkey

scheiß-, Scheiß-: ~freundlich *Adj., adv. (derb)* as nice as pie; **~haufen der** *(derb)* pile of shit *(coarse)*; **~haus das** *(derb)* bog *(sl.)*; shithouse *(coarse)*; **~kerl der** *(derb)* bastard *(coll.)*; **~vornehm** *Adj. (derb)* bloody *(Brit. sl.) or (coll.)* damn posh

Scheit [ʃait] **der; ~[e]s, ~e** *od.* **~er** *s.* **Holzscheit**

Scheitel ['ʃaitl̩] **der; ~s, ~ a)** parting; *(geh.: Haar)* hair; **einen ~ ziehen** make a parting; **b)** *(oberste Stelle)* top of one's head; **vom ~ bis zur Sohle** from head to toe; **c)** *(höchster Punkt)* vertex; **d)** *(Math.: bei Winkel)* apex; vertex; **e)** *(Math.: bei Kurve)* vertex

scheiteln *tr. V.* part ⟨*hair*⟩

Scheitel-: ~punkt der vertex; **~winkel der** *(Math.)* vertically opposite angle

Scheiter·haufen der: auf dem ~ sterben/verbrannt werden die/be burned at the stake; einen ~ für die Hexe errichten build a pile of wood on which the witch is to be burnt

scheitern ['ʃaitɐn] *itr. V.; mit sein* fail; ⟨*talks, marriage*⟩ break down; ⟨*plan, project*⟩ fail, fall through; **an jmdn./etw. ~:** fall through *or* fail because of sb./sth.; **die Partei scheiterte an der Fünfprozentklausel** the party was defeated by the five-per-cent clause; **jmds. Pläne zum Scheitern bringen** thwart *or* frustrate sb.'s plans; **zum Scheitern verurteilt sein** be doomed to failure; **eine gescheiterte Existenz sein** be a failure

Schekel ['ʃe:kl̩] **der;** ~s, ~: shekel

Schelde ['ʃɛldə] **die;** ~: Schelde [tributary]

Schelf [ʃɛlf] **der** *od.* **das;** ~s, ~e *(Geogr.)* continental shelf

Schellack ['ʃɛlak] **der;** ~s, ~e shellac

Schelle ['ʃɛlə] **die;** ~, ~n **a)** bell; **b)** *Pl.; o. Art. (Spielkartenfarbe)* bell; *s. auch* **²Pik**

schellen *itr. V. (westd.)* ring; **an der Tür dreimal ~:** ring the [door] bell three times; **nach jmdm. ~:** ring for sb.; **es schellt** the bell is ringing

Schellen-: ~**baum der** Turkish crescent; pavillon chinois; ~**kranz der** tambourine *(without drumskin)*; ~**trommel die** tambourine

Schell·fisch der cod

Schell·kraut das: [großes] ~: [greater] celandine

Schelm [ʃɛlm] **der;** ~[e]s, ~e rascal; rogue

Schelmen-: ~**roman der** *(Literaturw.)* picaresque novel; ~**streich der,** ~ **stück das** roguish prank

Schelmerei die; ~, ~en **a)** *o. Pl. (Eigenschaft)* roguishness; roguery; **b)** roguish prank

schelmisch 1. *Adj.* roguish; mischievous. **2.** *adv.* roguishly; mischievously

Schelte ['ʃɛltə] **die;** ~, ~n *(geh.)* scolding; ~ **bekommen** be given *or* get a scolding; **sei pünktlich, sonst gibt es ~:** be punctual, otherwise you'll get a scolding

schelten *(bes. südd., sonst geh.)* **1.** *unr. itr. V.* **auf** *od.* **über jmdn./etw. ~:** moan about sb./sth.; **[mit jmdm.] ~:** scold [sb.]. **2.** *unr. tr. V.* **a)** *(tadeln)* scold; **b)** *(geh.: nennen)* call

Schelt·wort das; *Pl.* ~**worte** *(geh.)* oath

Schema ['ʃe:ma] **das;** ~s, ~s *od.* ~ta *od.* **Schemen a)** *(Muster)* pattern; **sie läßt sich in kein ~ pressen** *(fig.)* she does not fit into any pattern *or* mould; *s. auch* **F; b)** *(Skizze)* diagram

schematisch 1. *Adj.* **a)** *(einem Schema folgend)* diagrammatic; **b)** *(mechanisch)* mechanical. **2.** *adv.* **a)** *(als Schema)* in diagram form; **b)** *(mechanisch)* mechanically

schematisieren *tr. V.* **a)** schematize; **etw. schematisiert darstellen** describe sth. by means of a simple formula; **b)** *(vereinfachen)* simplify

Schematisierung die; ~, ~en **a)** schematization; **b)** *(Vereinfachung)* simplification

Schemel ['ʃe:ml̩] **der;** ~s, ~ **a)** *(Hocker)* stool; **b)** *(südd.: Fußbank)* footstool

¹Schemen *s.* Schema

²Schemen ['ʃe:mən] **der** *od.* **das;** ~s, ~: shadowy figure

schemenhaft 1. *Adj.* shadowy. **2.** *adv.* **etw. ~ erkennen/sehen** make out/see only the outline *or* silhouette of sth.

Schenke ['ʃɛŋkə] **die;** ~, ~n pub *(Brit. coll.)*; bar *(Amer.)*; *(bes. auf dem Lande)* inn

Schenkel ['ʃɛŋkl̩] **der;** ~s, ~ **a)** *(Ober~)* thigh; **sich** *(Dat.)* **auf die ~ schlagen** slap one's thigh; **dem Pferd die ~ geben** press one's horse on; **b)** *(Math.)* side; **c)** *(von einer Zange, Schere)* shank; *(vom Zirkel)* leg

Schenkel-: ~**bruch der** *(Med.)* fracture of the femur; ~**druck der,** ~**hilfe die** *(Reiten)* knee pressure *no indef. art.*

schenken 1. *tr. V.* **a)** *(geben)* give; **jmdm. etw. [zum Geburtstag] ~:** give sb. sth. *or* sth. to sb. [as a birthday present *or* for his/her birthday]; **etw. geschenkt bekommen** be given sth. [as a present]; **sich gegenseitig etw. ~:** give each other presents; exchange presents; **den Rest des Geldes schenke ich dir** you can keep the rest of the money; **ich möchte nichts geschenkt haben** I don't want any presents; *(bevorzugt werden)* I don't want to be given special *or* preferential treatment; **das möchte ich nicht geschenkt haben, das wäre mir geschenkt zu teuer** *(ugs.)* I wouldn't want that if it was given to me; **das ist ja geschenkt!** *(ugs.)* it's a gift!; **geschenkt ist geschenkt** a gift is a gift; **sie schenkte ihm fünf Kinder** *(fig. geh.)* she bore him five children; *s. auch* **Gaul; b)** *(verleihen)* give; **c)** *(ugs.: erlassen)* **jmdm./sich etw. ~:** spare sb./oneself sth.; **ihr ist im Leben nichts geschenkt worden** she has never had it easy in life; **d) jmdm./einer Sache Beachtung/Aufmerksamkeit ~:** give sb./sth. one's attention; **jmdm. das Leben ~:** spare sb.'s life; **einem Kind das Leben ~** *(geh.)* give birth to a child; **e)** *(geh. veralt.: eingießen)* pour. **2.** *refl. V. (ugs.: erlassen)* **sich** *(Dat.)* **etw. ~:** give sth. a miss; **deine Ausreden kannst du dir ~:** you can save your excuses. **3.** *itr. V.* give presents *or* gifts

Schenker der; ~s, ~, **Schenkerin die;** ~, ~nen **a)** giver; **b)** *(Rechtsspr.)* donator

Schenkung die; ~, ~en *(Rechtsw.)* gift

scheppern ['ʃɛpɐn] *itr. V. (ugs.)* clank; ⟨*bell*⟩ clang; **es hat gescheppert** there was a clatter *or* clanking; *(beim Autounfall)* there was a smash *or* crash; *(es gab eine Ohrfeige)* he/she got a box on the ears

Scherbe ['ʃɛrbə] **die;** ~, ~n fragment; *(archäologischer Fund)* [pot]sherd; **die ~n zusammenkehren** sweep up the [broken] pieces; **die ~n des Tellers/Spiegels** the fragments *or* [broken] pieces of the plate/mirror; **beim Spülen hat es ~n gegeben** something got broken during the washing-up; **es gab ~n** *(fig.)* sparks flew; **in tausend ~n zerspringen** be smashed to smithereens; **die ~n ihrer Ehe** *(fig.)* the shattered remains of their marriage; **~n bringen Glück** *(Spr.)* break a thing, mend your luck

Scherben-: ~**gericht das** ostracism *no art.*; **ein ~gericht über jmdn. veranstalten** *(fig.)* judge sb. with unnecessary harshness; ~**haufen der** pile of broken fragments *or* pieces; *(fig.)* shattered remains

Schere ['ʃe:rə] **die;** ~, ~n **a)** *(Werkzeug)* scissors *pl.*; **eine ~:** a pair of scissors; **b)** *(Zool.)* claw; **c)** *(Turnen)* scissors

¹scheren *unr. tr. V.* **a)** crop; *(von Haar befreien)* shear, clip ⟨*sheep*⟩; clip ⟨*dog, horse, etc.*⟩; **sich** *(Dat.)* **den Bart ~** *(veralt.)* trim one's beard; *(abrasieren)* shave one's beard; **b)** *(Textilind.)* shear; **c)** *(kürzen)* cut, mow ⟨*lawn*⟩; clip, trim ⟨*hedge, bush, etc.*⟩

²scheren *tr., refl. V.* **sich um jmdn./etw. nicht ~:** not care about sb./sth.; **es schert ihn [herzlich] wenig** *od.* **nicht im geringsten** he could not care less *or* in the least

³scheren *refl. V.* **scher' dich in dein Zimmer** go *or* get [off] to your room; **~ Sie sich an die Arbeit/in Ihr Büro** get to work/[off] to your office; **sich ins Bett ~:** get [off] to bed; *s. auch* **Henker b; Teufel**

Scheren-: ~**gitter das** [folding] grille; ~**griff der** *(Turnen)* scissors hold; ~**schlag der** *(Fußball)* scissors kick; ~**schleifer der** knife-grinder; ~**schnitt der** silhouette

Schererei die; ~, ~en *(ugs.)* trouble *no pl.*

Scherflein ['ʃɛrflain] **das;** ~s, ~ *(geh.)* mite; **[s]ein ~ [zu etw.] beitragen** *od.* **beisteuern** make one's/a little contribution [to sth.]

Scherge ['ʃɛrgə] **der;** ~n, ~n *(geh.)* henchman

Scher-: ~**messer das** [cutting] blade; ~**sprung der** *(bes. Turnen)* scissors jump

Scherung die; ~, ~en **a)** *(Math.)* shearing; **b)** *(Mechanik)* shear[ing]

Scherz [ʃɛrts] **der;** ~es, ~e joke; **seine ~e mit jmdm. treiben** play jokes on sb.; **er versteht keinen ~:** he can't take a joke; **mach keine ~e** you must be joking; **seine ~e über jmdn./etw. machen** make *or* crack jokes about sb./sth.; **etw. aus** *od.* **zum ~ sagen** say sth. as a joke *or* in jest; **... und solche** *od.* **ähnliche ~e** *(ugs.)* ... and what have you *(coll.)*; **~ beiseite** joking aside *or* apart; **[ganz] ohne ~** *(ugs.)* no kidding *(sl.)*

Scherz·artikel der joke article

scherzen *itr. V.* joke; **mit etw.** *od.* **über etw.** *(Akk.)* **~:** joke about sth.; **Sie belieben zu ~** *(geh., oft iron.)* you jest; **ich scherze nicht** I'm not joking; **mit jmdm./etw. ist nicht zu ~:** sb./sth. is not to be trifled with

Scherz-: ~**frage die** riddle; ~**gedicht das** humorous poem

scherzhaft 1. *Adj.* jocular; joking *attrib.* **2.** *adv.* jocularly; jokingly; **etw. ~ sagen/meinen** say/mean sth. as a joke *or* in fun

Scherzo ['skɛrtso] **das;** ~s, ~s *od.* **Scherzi** *(Musik)* scherzo

Scherz·wort das; *Pl.* ~**worte** joke; witticism

schesen ['ʃe:zn̩] *itr. V.; mit sein (bes. nordd.)* rush

scheu [ʃɔy] **1.** *Adj. (schüchtern)* shy; timid ⟨*animal*⟩; *(ehrfürchtig)* awed; **~ machen** frighten ⟨*animal*⟩; *s. auch* **Pferd. 2.** *adv.* **a)** *(schüchtern)* shyly; **b)** *(von Tieren)* timidly

Scheu die; ~ **a)** *(Schüchternheit)* shyness; *(Ehrfurcht)* awe; **voller ~ sein** be very shy *or* timid/be full of awe; **ohne jede ~:** without any inhibitions; **b)** *(von Tieren)* timidity

Scheuche ['ʃɔyçə] **die;** ~, ~n scarecrow

scheuchen *tr. V.* **a)** *(treiben)* shoo; drive; **b)** *(fig.)* force; **jmdn. zum Arzt/an die Arbeit ~:** make sb. go *or* urge sb. to go to the doctor/to work

scheuen 1. *tr. V. (meiden)* shrink from; shun ⟨*people, light, company, etc.*⟩; **weder Kosten noch Mühe ~:** spare neither expense nor effort; **Arbeit scheue ich nicht** I'm not afraid of work. **2.** *refl. V.* **sich vor etw.** *(Dat.)* **~:** be afraid of *or* shrink from sth. **3.** *itr. V.* ⟨*horse*⟩ shy **(vor +** *Dat.* at)

Scheuer die; ~, ~n *(bes. südd.)* barn

Scheuer-: ~**bürste die** scrubbing-brush; ~**lappen der** cleaning-cloth *(for wiping surfaces)*; ~**leiste die a)** *(Fußleiste)* skirting[-board] *(Brit.)*; baseboard *(Amer.)*; **b)** *(Seew.)* rubbing strake; ~**mittel das** scouring agent

scheuern 1. *tr., itr. V.* **a)** *(reinigen)* scour; scrub; **b)** *(reiben)* rub; chafe. **2.** *tr. V.* **a)** *(reiben an)* rub; **b) in jmdm. eine ~** *(ugs.)* give sb. a clout; clout sb.; **eine gescheuert kriegen** *(ugs.)* get a clout round the ears *(coll.)*. **3.** *refl. V. (reiben)* **sich** *(Akk.)* **wund ~:** rub oneself raw; chafe oneself; **sich** *(Dat.)* **das Knie [wund] ~:** rub one's knee raw; chafe one's knee

Scheuer-: ~**pulver das** scouring powder; ~**sand der** scouring sand; ~**tuch das;** *Pl.* ~**tücher** scouring cloth

Scheu·klappe die blinker; **~n haben** *od.* **tragen** wear blinkers; be blinkered *(also fig.)*

Scheune ['ʃɔynə] **die;** ~, ~n barn

Scheunen: ~**drescher der in wie ein ~drescher essen** *od.* **fressen** *(salopp)* eat like a horse *(coll.)*; ~**tor das** barn door; *s. auch* **dastehen a**

Scheusal ['ʃɔyza:l] **das;** ~s, ~e *od. (ugs.)* **Scheusäler** ['ʃɔyzɛ:lɐ] *(abwertend)* monster

scheußlich ['ʃɔyslɪç] **1.** *Adj.* **a)** dreadful; **b)** *(ugs.: äußerst unangenehm)* terrible *(coll.)*; dreadful *(coll.)*; dreadful *(coll.)*, ghastly *(coll.)* ⟨*weather, taste, smell*⟩. **2.** *adv.* **a)** dreadfully; **b)** *(ugs.: sehr)* terribly *(coll.)*; dreadfully *(coll.)*; **sich ~ erkälten** catch a dreadful cold *(coll.)*

Scheußlichkeit die; ~, ~en **a)** *o. Pl.* dreadfulness; **b)** *meist Pl.* *(etw. Scheußliches)* dreadful thing; *(Grausamkeit)* atrocity

Schi [ʃi:] *usw. s.* **Ski** *usw.*

Schicht [ʃɪçt] **die;** ~, ~en **a)** *(Lage)* layer; *(Geol.)* stratum; *(von Farbe)* coat; *(sehr dünn)* film; **b)** *(Gesellschafts~)* stratum; **breite ~en [der Bevölkerung]** broad sections of the population; **in allen ~en** at all levels of society; **die besitzenden ~en** the propertied classes; **c)** *(Abschnitt eines Arbeitstages, Arbeitsgruppe)* shift; **~ haben, auf ~ sein** be working one's shift; **er geht morgens zur ~:** he's on the morning shift; **~ arbeiten** work shifts; be on shift work

Schicht-: ~arbeit die; *o. Pl.* shift work; **~arbeiter der** shift worker

schichten *tr. V.* stack; **die Bretter zu einem Stapel ~:** stack the boards [up]

Schicht-: ~gestein das *(Geol.) s.* **Sedimentgestein; ~käse der** *low-fat quark containing a layer of higher-fat quark;* **~stufe die** *(Geol.)* cuesta

Schichtung die; ~, ~en stacking; *(Geol., Met., Soziol.)* stratification

schicht-, Schicht-: ~unterricht der teaching *no art.* in shifts; **~wechsel der** change of shifts; **~wechsel ist um 6** we/they *etc.* change shifts at 6; **~weise** *Adv.* **a)** in layers; layer by layer; *(bei Farben)* in coats; **b)** *(in Gruppen)* in shifts

schick [ʃɪk] **1.** *Adj.* **a)** stylish; stylish, chic ⟨*clothes, fashions*⟩; *(elegant)* smart ⟨*woman, girl, man*⟩; **b)** *(ugs.: großartig, toll)* great *(coll.)*; fantastic *(coll.)*. **2.** *adv.* **a)** stylishly; stylishly, smartly ⟨*furnished, decorated*⟩; **~ frisiert sein** have a fashionable hairstyle *or (coll.)* hair-do; **b)** *(ugs.: großartig, toll)* **abends sind wir ~ ausgegangen** we had a great evening out *(coll.)*

Schick der; ~[e]s **a)** style; *(von Frauenmode, Frau)* chic; style; **b)** *(oberd., niederd.)* **nun hat** *od.* **kriegt alles wieder seinen ~!** now everything's as it should be

schicken 1. *tr. V.* send; **jmdm. etw. ~, etw. an jmdn. ~:** send sth. to sb.; send sb. sth.; **jmdm. etw. ins Haus ~:** send sth. to sb.'s home; **jmdn. nach Hause/auf** *od.* **in die** *od.* **zur Schule/ins** *od.* **zu Bett/in den Krieg ~:** send sb. home/to school/to bed/to war; **jmdn. einkaufen** *od.* **zum Einkaufen ~:** send sb. to do the shopping. **2.** *itr. V. (rufen, holen lassen)* **nach jmdm. ~:** send for sb. **3.** *refl. V.* **a)** *(unpers. veralt.: sich ziemen)* be proper *or* fitting; **das schickt sich nicht für eine junge Dame** it does not befit *or* become a young lady; it is not proper for a young lady; **b)** *(geduldig ertragen)* **sich in etw.** *(Akk.)* **~:** resign *or* reconcile oneself to sth.

Schickeria [ʃɪkəˈri:a] **die;** ~ *(ugs.)* smart set

Schicki[micki] [ˈʃɪkɪ(ˈmɪkɪ)] **der;** ~s, ~s *(ugs.)* **a)** *(Mensch)* trendy *(coll.)*; **b)** *(Modisches)* trendy *(coll.)* goods *pl.*/clothes *pl.*/architecture *etc.*

schicklich *(veralt.)* **1.** *Adj.* proper; fitting; *(dezent)* seemly. **2.** *adv.* fittingly; *(dezent)* in a seemly way

Schicksal [ˈʃɪkza:l] **das;** ~s, ~e **a)** *(Geschick, Los)* fate; destiny; *(schweres Los)* fate; **ich habe manche schwere ~e miterlebt** I've witnessed many a hard fate; **[das ist] ~** *(ugs.)* it's just fate; **er hat ein schweres ~ gehabt** fate has been unkind to him; **b)** *o. Pl.* *(höhere Macht)* fate *no art.*; destiny *no art.*; **das ~ hat es mit ihm gut gemeint** fortune smiled on him; **~ spielen** play the role of fate *or* destiny

-schicksal das: ein Emigranten~/Flüchtlings~/Behinderten~: life *or* experiences as an emigré/a refugee/a handicapped person

schicksalhaft 1. *Adj.* fateful. **2.** *adv.* **~ bedingt/verbunden** determined/linked by fate; **sie sind ~ aufeinander angewiesen** their fates are inextricably linked

schicksals-, Schicksals-: ~drama das *(Literaturw.)* fate drama; **~frage die** crucial question; *(Angelegenheit)* fundamental issue; **~gefährte der** companion in misfortune; **die drei waren ~gefährten** the three shared the same fate; **~gemeinschaft die: sie bildeten** *od.* **waren eine ~gemeinschaft** they shared a common fate; **~genosse der** *s.* **~gefährte; ~glaube der** fatalism; **~göttin die** goddess of fate; **die ~göttinnen** the Fates; **~schlag der** stroke of fate; **~schwer** *Adj.* momentous ⟨*day, decision*⟩; **~tragödie die** *(Literaturw.) s.* **~drama**

Schickse [ˈʃɪksə] **die;** ~, ~n *(salopp abwertend)* floozie *(coll.)*

Schickung die; ~, ~en *(geh.)* stroke of fate

Schiebe-: ~dach das sliding roof; sunroof; **~fenster das** sliding window

schieben [ˈʃi:bn̩] **1.** *unr. tr. V.* **a)** push; push, wheel ⟨*bicycle, pram, shopping trolley*⟩; *(drängen)* push; shove; **die Lokomotive schob die Waggons auf ein Nebengleis** the locomotive shunted the wagons into a siding; **b)** *(stecken)* put; *(gleiten lassen)* slip; **den Riegel vor die Tür ~:** slip the bolt across; **den Ball ins Tor ~** *(Fußballjargon)* slip the ball into the net; **etw. von einem Tag auf den anderen ~** *(fig.)* keep putting sth. off from one day to the next; **c) etw. auf jmdn./etw. ~:** blame sb./sth. for sth.; **die Schuld/die Verantwortung auf jmdn. ~:** put the blame on sb. *or* lay the blame at sb.'s door/lay the responsibility at sb.'s door; **d)** *(salopp: handeln mit)* traffic in; push ⟨*drugs*⟩. **2.** *unr. refl. V.* **a)** *(sich zwängen)* **sich durch die Menge ~:** push one's way through the crowd; **b)** *(sich bewegen)* move; **ihr Rock schob sich nach oben** her skirt slid up; **sich an die Spitze ~** *(Sportjargon)* move up to the front. **3.** *unr. itr. V.* **a)** push; *(heftig)* push; shove; **b)** *mit sein (salopp: gehen)* mooch *(sl.)*; **c)** *(ugs.: mit etw. handeln)* **mit etw. ~:** traffic in sth.; **d)** *(Skat)* shove

Schieber der; ~s, ~ **a)** *(an einer Tür)* bolt; *(am Ofen)* damper; *(an Rohrleitungen)* sluice valve; **b)** *(ugs.: Schwarzhändler)* black marketeer; *(Drogen~)* pusher; *(Waffen~)* gun-runner; **c)** *(ugs.: Tanz)* one-step

Schieber·mütze die *s.* **Schlägermütze**

Schiebe-: ~tür die sliding door; **~wand die** sliding partition

Schieb-: ~lade die *s.* **Schublade; ~lehre die** *(Technik)* vernier [calliper] gauge

Schiebung die; ~, ~en *(ugs.)* **a)** *(betrügerisches Geschäft)* shady deal; **b)** *(o. Pl.: Begünstigung)* pulling strings; *(bei einer Wahl, einem Wettbewerb)* rigging; *(bei einem Wettlauf, -rennen)* fixing; **„[das ist ja] ~!" riefen die Zuschauer** the spectators shouted '[it's a] fix!'

schied [ʃi:t] *1. u. 3. Pers. Sg. Prät. v.* **scheiden**

schiedlich-friedlich *Adv.* amicably

Schieds-: ~gericht das a) *(Rechtsw.)* arbitration tribunal; **b)** *(Sport)* panel of judges; *(Fechten)* jury; **~kommission die** *(Rechtsw.) s.* **~gericht a; ~mann der;** *Pl.* **~leute** *od.* **~männer** arbitrator; **~richter der a)** *(Sport)* referee; *(Tennis, Tischtennis, Hockey, Kricket, Federball)* umpire; *(Eislauf, Ski, Schwimmen)* judge; **b)** *(Rechtsw.)* arbitrator; **~richter·ball der** *(Fußball)* drop ball; *(Basketball)* jump ball; *(Wasserball)* neutral throw; **~richterlich** *Adj.* **a)** *(Sport)* ⟨*decision, permission, etc.*⟩ of the referee/umpire; **b)** *(Rechtsw.)* **die ~richterliche Entscheidung** the decision of the arbitrator/arbitrators; **~richtern** *itr., tr. V.* *(Sport)* referee; *(Tennis, Tischtennis, Hockey, Kricket, Federball)* umpire; **~spruch der** *(Rechtsw.)* arbitration decision

schief [ʃi:f] **1.** *Adj.* **a)** *(schräg)* leaning ⟨*wall, fence, post*⟩; *(nicht parallel)* crooked; not straight *pred.*; crooked ⟨*nose*⟩; sloping, inclined ⟨*surface*⟩; worn[-down] ⟨*heels*⟩; *(fig.)* wry ⟨*smile, look*⟩; **eine ~e Schulter haben** have one shoulder higher than the other; **er hält den Kopf ~:** he holds his head to one side; **der Schiefe Turm von Pisa** the Leaning Tower of Pisa; **eine ~e Ebene** *(Math., Phys.)* an inclined plane; *s. auch* **Bahn a; Gesicht a; b)** *(fig.: verzerrt)* distorted ⟨*picture, presentation, view, impression*⟩; false ⟨*comparison*⟩. **2.** *adv.* **a)** *(schräg)* **der Baum ist ~ gewachsen** the tree has grown crooked *or* hasn't grown straight; **das Bild hängt/der Teppich liegt ~:** the picture/carpet is crooked; **der Tisch steht ~:** the table isn't level; **sich** *(Dat.)* **die Mütze ~ aufsetzen** put one's cap on at an angle; **jmdn. ~ ansehen** *(ugs.)* look at sb. askance; *s. auch* **Haussegen; b)** *(fig.: verzerrt)* **etw. ~ darstellen** give a distorted account of sth.

Schiefer [ˈʃi:fɐ] **der;** ~s **a)** *(Gestein)* slate; **b)** *(südd., österr.: Splitter)* splinter

schiefer-, Schiefer-: ~dach das slate roof; **~grau** *Adj.* slate-grey; **~tafel die** slate

schief-: ~|gehen *unr. itr. V.; mit sein (ugs.)* go wrong; **es wird schon ~gehen** *(iron.)* it'll all turn out OK *(coll.)*; **~gewickelt** *Adj.* **in ~gewickelt sein** *(ugs.)* be very much mistaken; **~|lachen** *refl. V. (ugs.)* kill oneself laughing *(coll.)*; laugh one's head off; **~|laufen 1.** *unr. tr. V. (ablaufen)* wear down ⟨*heels*⟩ on one side; **2.** *unr. itr. V.; mit sein (ugs.: ~gehen)* go wrong; **~|liegen** *unr. itr. V. (ugs.)* be on the wrong track; **~|treten** *unr. tr. V.* wear down ⟨*heels*⟩ on one side

schielen [ˈʃi:lən] *itr. V.* **a)** squint; have a squint; **leicht/stark ~:** have a slight/pronounced squint; **auf dem rechten Auge ~:** have a squint in one's right eye; **b)** *(ugs.: blicken)* look out of the corner of one's eye; **nach etw. ~:** steal a glance at sth.; *(fig.)* have one's eye on sth.; **c)** *(ugs.: spähen)* peep; **nach rechts und links ~:** glance right and left

schien [ʃi:n] *1. u. 3. Pers. Sg. Prät. v.* **scheinen**

Schien·bein das shinbone; **sich ans** *od.* **am ~ stoßen** bang one's shin; **jmdm.** *od.* **jmdn. vor das ~ treten** kick sb. on the shin

Schiene [ˈʃi:nə] **die;** ~, ~n **a)** rail; **~n legen** lay track; **aus den ~n springen** come off the rails; **b)** *(Gleit~)* runner; **in einer ~ laufen** move on a runner; **c)** *(Med.: Stütze)* splint; **d)** *(Reiß~)* T-square; **e)** *(schmale Leiste)* right-angle moulding; *(in Korbwaren)* rib; **f)** *(hist.: Teil der Rüstung)* splint

-schiene die: Nord~/Süd~/Rhein~: northern/southern/Rhine sector

schienen *tr. V.* **jmds. Arm/Bein ~:** put sb.'s arm/leg in a splint/splints; put a splint/splints on sb.'s arm/leg

Schienen-: ~bus der railbus; **~fahrzeug das** track vehicle; **~strang der** [railway] line *or* track; **~verkehr der** rail traffic

¹schier [ʃi:ɐ̯] *Adv. (veralt.: geradezu)* well-nigh; almost

²schier *Adj. (bes. nordd.)* pure; *(fig.)* sheer ⟨*malevolence, stupidity*⟩

Schierling [ˈʃi:ɐ̯lɪŋ] **der;** ~s, ~e hemlock

Schierlings·becher der cup of hemlock

Schieß-: ~befehl der order to shoot; **~bude die** shooting-gallery; **~buden·figur die** target [in a shooting-gallery]; **du siehst aus wie eine ~budenfigur** *(ugs.)* you look a real clown; **~eisen das** *(ugs.)* shooting-iron *(sl.)*

schießen [ˈʃi:sn̩] **1.** *unr. itr. V.* **a)** shoot; ⟨*pistol, rifle*⟩ shoot, fire; **auf jmdn./etw. ~:** shoot/fire at sb./sth.; **gut/schlecht ~** ⟨*person*⟩ be a good/bad shot; **es wurde aus dem Fenster geschossen** a shot/shots came from the window; **sie schoß ihm/sich ins Bein** she shot him/herself in the leg; **mit Schrot/einem Pfeil ~:** fire shot/shoot an arrow; **b)**

(Fußball) shoot; **der Stürmer schoß hoch über das Tor** the forward's shot went high over the goal; **c)** *mit sein (ugs.: schnellen)* shoot; **er schoß vom Stuhl in die Höhe** he shot up out of his chair; **ein Gedanke schoß ihr durch den Kopf** *(fig.)* a thought flashed through her mind; **zum Schießen sein** *(ugs.)* be a scream *(sl.)*; **d)** *mit sein (fließen, heraus~)* gush; *(spritzen)* spurt; **ich spürte, wie mir das Blut in den Kopf schoß** I felt the blood rush to my head; **aus dem Dachstuhl schossen Flammen** flames were shooting from the attic; **e)** *mit sein (schnell wachsen)* shoot up; *(fig.)* ⟨*building*⟩ spring up; **der Junge ist sehr in die Höhe geschossen** the boy has shot up a lot; **die Preise ~ in die Höhe** *(fig.)* prices are shooting up *or* rocketing; **f)** *(Drogenjargon)* fix. **2.** *unr. tr. V.* **a)** shoot; fire ⟨*bullet, missile, rocket*⟩; **jmdn./etw. in den Weltraum ~:** launch sb./sth. into space; **an der Schießbude einen Preis ~:** win a prize at the shooting-gallery; **jmdn. zum Krüppel ~:** shoot and maim sb.; **b)** *(Fußball)* score ⟨*goal*⟩; **den Ball ins Netz ~:** put the ball in the net; **er schoß seine Mannschaft in Führung** he scored the goal that put his team ahead; **das 3:2 ~:** make it 3–2; **c)** *(ugs.: fotografieren)* **einige Aufnahmen ~:** take a few snaps

schießen|lassen *unr. tr. V. (salopp)* drop; ditch *(sl.)*, drop ⟨*plan*⟩

Schießerei die; ~, ~en a) shooting *no indef. art., no pl.*; **b)** *(Schußwechsel)* gun-battle; **die ~ am Ende des Films** the shoot-out at the end of the film

Schieß-: ~gewehr das *(Kinderspr.)* rifle; **~hund der** *(Jägerspr., veralt.: Jagdhund)* gun dog; **aufpassen wie ein ~hund** *(ugs.)* be on one's toes; **~platz der** firing range; **~pulver das** gunpowder; **er hat das ~pulver [auch] nicht erfunden** *(ugs.)* he's not exactly a genius; **~scharte die** crenel; **~scheibe die** target; **~sport der** shooting *no art.*; **~stand der a)** shooting range; **b)** *s.* **~bude; ~übung die** target practice

Schiff [ʃɪf] **das; ~[e]s, ~e a)** ship; **mit dem** *od.* **per** *od.* **zu ~:** by ship *or* sea; **~ voraus!** ship ahead!; **das ~ der Wüste** *(fig.)* the ship of the desert; **b)** *(Archit.: Kirchen~) (Mittel~)* nave; *(Quer~)* transept; *(Seiten~)* aisle; **c)** *(Druckw.)* galley

Schiffahrt die; *o. Pl. (Schiffsverkehr)* shipping *no indef. art.*; *(Schiffahrtskunde)* navigation; **die ~ einstellen** suspend all shipping movements

Schiffahrts-: ~gesellschaft die shipping company; **~linie die** shipping route; **~straße die, ~weg der** [navigable] waterway

schiffbar *Adj.* navigable

Schiffbarmachung die; ~: seit der ~ dieses Flusses since this river was made navigable

schiff-, Schiff-: ~bau der; *o. Pl.* shipbuilding *no art.*; **~bauer der** shipbuilder; **~bruch der** *(veralt.)* shipwreck; **~bruch erleiden** ⟨*ship*⟩ be wrecked; ⟨*person*⟩ be shipwrecked; **[mit etw.] ~bruch erleiden** *(fig.)* fail [in sth.]; **~brüchig** *Adj.* shipwrecked; **~brüchige der/die;** *adj. Dekl.* shipwrecked man/woman; **die ~brüchigen** those shipwrecked

Schiffchen das; ~s, ~ a) *(Spielzeug)* [little] boat; **b)** *(ugs.: Kopfbedeckung)* forage cap; **c)** *(Weberei, Handarbeit, Nähen)* shuttle

schiffen *itr. V.* **a)** *mit sein (veralt.: mit dem Schiff fahren)* ship; travel by ship; **b)** *(derb: urinieren)* piss *(coarse)*; **c)** *(unpers. salopp: regnen)* **es schifft** it's pissing down *(sl.)*; it's chucking it down *(sl.)*

Schiffer der; ~s, ~: boatman; *(eines Lastkahns)* bargee; *(Kapitän)* skipper

Schiffer-: ~klavier das accordion; **~knoten der** seaman's knot; **~mütze die** [peaked] sailor's cap

Schiff-fahrt *Schreibung von* **Schiffahrt** *bei Silbentrennung*

Schiffs-: ~arzt der ship's doctor; **~ausrüster der; ~s, ~** ship's chandler; **~bau der;** *o. Pl. s.* **Schiffbau; ~bauch der** *(ugs.)* belly of a/the ship; **~brücke die** pontoon bridge

Schiff·schaukel die swing-boat; **~ fahren** go on a/the swing-boat

Schiffs-: ~eigner der shipowner; **~fahrt die** boat trip; *(länger)* cruise; **~führer der** *s.* **Schiffer; ~glocke die** ship's bell; **~junge der** ship's boy; **~ladung die** [ship's] cargo; **eine ganze ~ladung** an entire shipload; **~laterne die** *(Seemannsspr.)* ship's lantern; **~makler der** ship-broker; **~modell das** model ship; **~name der** ship's name; **~papiere** *Pl.* ship's papers; **~passage die** passage; **~reise die** voyage; *(Vergnügungsreise)* cruise; **~rumpf der** [ship's] hull; **~schraube die** ship's propeller *or* screw; **~taufe die** naming of a/the ship; **~verkehr der** shipping traffic; **auf dem Fluß war lebhafter** *od.* **reger ~verkehr** the river was busy with traffic; **~zimmermann der** ship's carpenter; **~zwieback der** hard tack; ship's biscuit

Schiit [ʃi'iːt] **der; ~en, ~en** Shiite

schiitisch *Adj.* Shiite

Schikane [ʃi'kaːnə] **die; ~, ~n a)** *(Bosheit)* harassment *no indef. art.*; **das ist eine ~:** that amounts to *or* is harassment; **aus reiner ~:** purely in order to harass him/her *etc.*; **Beschimpfungen und ~n** abuse and harassment; **b)** *in* **mit allen ~n** *(ugs.)* ⟨*kitchen, house*⟩ with all mod cons *(Brit. coll.)*; ⟨*car, bicycle, stereo*⟩ with all the extras; **c)** *(Motorsport)* chicane

schikanieren *tr. V.* **jmdn. ~:** harass sb.; mess sb. about *(coll.)*; **Rekruten/seine Ehefrau ~:** bully recruits/one's wife

schikanös [ʃika'nøːs] **1.** *Adj.* harassing ⟨*action, measure*⟩; bullying ⟨*husband, superior officer*⟩; **~e Behandlung** harassment/bullying. **2.** *adv.* **jmdn. ~ behandeln** harass sb.

[1]Schild [ʃɪlt] **der; ~[e]s, ~e a)** shield; **jmdn. auf den ~ [er]heben** *(geh.) (als Anführer)* make sb. one's leader; *(als Leitbild)* make sb. one's figurehead; **etw./nichts im ~e führen** be up to something/not be up to anything; **etwas gegen jmdn./etw. im ~e führen** be plotting sth. against sb./sth.; **b)** *(Wappen~)* shield; escutcheon; **c)** *s.* **Schirm c**

[2]Schild das; ~[e]s, ~er *(Verkehrs~)* sign; *(Nummern~)* number-plate; *(Namens~)* nameplate; *(Plakat)* placard; *(an einer Mütze)* badge; *(auf Denkmälern, Gebäuden, Gräbern)* plaque; *(Etikett)* label

Schild-: ~bürger der *(abwertend)* ≈ wise man of Gotham; Gothamite; fool; **~bürger·streich der** *(abwertend)* act of monumental dim-wittedness; **~drüse die** *(Med.)* thyroid [gland]

Schilder-: ~brücke die *(Verkehrsw.)* sign gantry; **~haus das, ~häuschen das** sentry-box

schildern ['ʃɪldɐn] *tr. V.* describe; *(in einer Erzählung)* portray; describe; **die Greuel dieses Krieges sind kaum zu ~:** the atrocities committed in this war beggar description; *s. auch* **Farbe b**

Schilderung die; ~, ~en description; *(von Ereignissen)* account; description; *(in einer Erzählung)* portrayal; description

Schilder·wald der *(Verkehrsw. abwertend)* maze of traffic-signs

Schild-: ~knappe der *(hist.)* squire; shield-bearer; **~kröte die** tortoise; *(Seeschildkröte)* turtle; **~kröten·suppe die** turtle soup; **~laus die** scale insect; **~patt das; ~[e]s** tortoiseshell; **~wache die** *(veralt.)* sentry; **~wache stehen** stand sentry

Schilf [ʃɪlf] **das; ~[e]s, ~e a)** *(~rohr)* reed; **b)** *o. Pl. (Röhricht)* reeds *pl.*

Schilf-: ~dach das roof thatched with reeds; **~gras das, ~rohr das** *s.* **Schilf a; ~rohr·sänger der** sedge warbler

Schiller-: ~kragen der large open-necked collar; **~locke die a)** *(Gebäck)* cream horn; **b)** *(Räucherfisch)* strip of smoked fish *(esp. dogfish)*

schillern ['ʃɪlɐn] *itr. V.* shimmer; **in allen Regenbogenfarben ~:** shimmer with all the colours of the rainbow; **ein ~der Charakter** *(fig.)* an ambivalent character; **ein ~der Begriff** *(fig.)* a shifting concept

Schilling ['ʃɪlɪŋ] **der; ~s, ~e** schilling; **das kostet 30 ~:** that costs 30 schillings

Schillum ['ʃɪlʊm] **das; ~s, ~s** chillum

schilpen ['ʃɪlpn̩] *s.* **tschilpen**

schilt [ʃɪlt] *3. Pers. Sg. Präsens v.* **schelten**

Schimäre [ʃi'mɛːrə] **die; ~, ~n** chimera

schimärisch *Adj.* chimerical

Schimmel ['ʃɪml̩] **der; ~s, ~ a)** *o. Pl. (Belag)* mould; *(auf Leder, Papier)* mildew; **b)** *(Pferd)* white horse

schimmelig *Adj.* mouldy; mildewy ⟨*paper, leather*⟩; **~ werden** go mouldy/get covered with mildew

schimmeln *itr. V.; auch mit sein* go mouldy; ⟨*leather, paper*⟩ get covered with mildew

Schimmel·pilz der mould

Schimmer ['ʃɪmɐ] **der; ~s a)** *(Schein)* gleam; *(von Perlmutt)* lustre; shimmer; *(von Seide)* shimmer; sheen; *(von Haar)* sheen; *(von Kerzen)* [soft] glow; **b)** *(Anflug, Hauch)* glimmer; **noch einen ~ [von] Anstand haben** still have a scrap of decency; **keinen [blassen]** *od.* **nicht den leisesten ~ [von etw.] haben** *(ugs.)* not have the faintest *or* foggiest idea [about sth.] *(coll.)*

schimmern *itr. V.* **a)** *(matt glänzen)* gleam; ⟨*water, sea*⟩ glisten, shimmer; ⟨*teeth*⟩ glisten; ⟨*metal*⟩ glint, gleam; ⟨*silk, mother-of-pearl*⟩ shimmer; **der Stoff/die Seide schimmert rötlich** the material has a reddish tinge/the silk has a reddish sheen; **b)** *(durch~)* show (**durch** through)

schimmlig *s.* **schimmelig**

Schimpanse [ʃɪm'panzə] **der; ~n, ~n** chimpanzee

Schimpf der; ~[e]s *(geh.)* affront; **jmdm. einen ~ antun/zufügen** affront sb.; **mit ~ und Schande** in disgrace

Schimpfe die; ~ *(ugs.)* **~ bekommen** get an earful *(coll.)*

schimpfen 1. *itr. V.* **a)** carry on *(coll.)* (**auf, über +** *Akk.* about); *(meckern)* grumble, moan (**auf, über +** *Akk.* at); **b)** *(zurechtweisen)* **mit jmdm. ~:** tell sb. off; scold sb. **2.** *tr. V.* **a)** *(bes. md.: aus~)* **jmdn. ~:** tell sb. off; scold sb.; **b) jmdn. dumm/faul ~:** call sb. stupid/lazy. **3.** *refl. V. (spött.: vorgeben zu sein)* **sich Professor/Dichter ~:** call oneself a professor/poet

Schimpferei die; ~, ~en *(abwertend)* carrying on *(coll.)*; *(Meckerei)* grumbling; moaning; *(das Zurechtweisen)* telling off, scolding (**mit** of)

schimpflich *(geh.)* **1.** *Adj.* shameful, disgraceful ⟨*behaviour, treatment*⟩; dishonourable ⟨*occupation*⟩; *(entwürdigend)* humiliating ⟨*defeat, terms, etc.*⟩. **2.** *adv.* shamefully; disgracefully; *(entwürdigend)* humiliatingly

Schimpf-: ~name der [abusive] nickname; **jmdn. mit ~namen belegen** call sb. names; **~wort das** *(Beleidigung)* insult; *(derbes Wort)* swear-word

Schindel ['ʃɪndl̩] **die; ~, ~n** shingle

Schindel·dach das shingle roof

schinden ['ʃɪndn̩] **1.** *unr. tr. V.* **a)** maltreat; ill-treat; *(ausbeuten)* slave-drive; **jmdn./ein Tier zu Tode ~:** work sb./an animal to death; **b)** *(ugs.: herausschlagen)* **Zeilen ~:** pad as much as possible; fill up space with as little as possible; **[bei jmdm.] Eindruck ~:** make an impression [on sb.]; **Applaus ~ wollen** fish for applause; **Zeit ~:** play for time. **2.** *unr. refl. V. (ugs.: sich abplagen)* slave away; **sich mit einer Arbeit ~:** slave away at a job

Schinder der; ~s, ~ a) slave-driver; **b)** *(veralt.: Abdecker)* knacker *(Brit.)*

Schinderei die; ~, ~en a) ill-treatment *no pl.; (Ausbeutung)* slave-driving *no pl.;* **b)** *(Strapaze, Qual)* struggle; *(Arbeit)* toil

Schind-: ~luder das *in* **mit etw. ~luder treiben** *(ugs.) (ausbeuten)* take advantage of *or* abuse sth.; *(vergeuden)* squander sth.; **wir dürfen nicht länger mit der Natur ~luder treiben** we must stop this appalling waste of natural resources; **~mähre die** *(abwertend)* nag

Schinken ['ʃɪŋkn̩] **der; ~s, ~ a)** ham; **b)** *(ugs.) (Buch)* great tome; *(Gemälde)* enormous painting; *(Film, Theaterstück)* epic

Schinken-: ~brot das slice of bread and ham; *(zugeklappt)* ham sandwich; **~speck der** bacon

Schintoismus [ʃɪnto'ɪsmʊs] **der; ~:** Shintoism *no art.*

Schippe ['ʃɪpə] **die; ~, ~n a)** *(nordd., md.: Schaufel)* shovel; **~ und Eimer** bucket and spade; **~ und Handfeger** dustpan and brush; **jmdn. auf die ~ nehmen** *(fam.)* kid sb. *(sl.);* pull sb.'s leg; **dem Tod von der ~ springen** *(ugs.)* escape death by a hair's breadth; **b)** *(Kartenspiel) s.* **²Pik; c)** *(ugs.: Flunsch)* **eine ~ ziehen** *od.* **machen** pout

schippen *tr. V. (nordd., md.)* **a)** shovel; **b)** *(ausheben)* dig ‹*ditch, grave, etc.*›

Schipper der; ~s, ~ *(nordd.) s.* **Schiffer**

schippern *(ugs.)* **1.** *itr. V.; mit sein* cruise. **2.** *tr. V.* ship ‹*goods, materials*›; skipper ‹*ship*›

Schirm [ʃɪrm] **der; ~[e]s, ~e a)** umbrella; brolly *(Brit. coll.); (Sonnen~)* sunshade; parasol; **b)** *(Lampen~)* shade; **c)** *(Mützen~)* peak; **d)** *(gegen Licht)* eyeshade; *(Ofen~, Kamin~)* guard; *(Strahlen~)* shield; *(beim Schweißen o. ä.)* mask; visor; **e)** *(Bild~)* screen; **f)** *(Schutz)* shield

Schirm-: ~bild das *(Med.)* X-ray [picture]; **~bild·gerät das** *(Med.)* X-ray machine; **~herr der** patron; **~herrin die** patroness; **~herrschaft die** patronage; **die ~herrschaft über etw.** *(Akk.)* **übernehmen** become patron of sth.; **~mütze die** peaked cap; **~pilz der** parasol mushroom; **~ständer der** umbrella stand

Schirokko [ʃi'rɔko] **der; ~s, ~s** sirocco

Schisma ['ʃɪsma] **das; ~s, Schismen** *od.* **~ta** *(Kirche, Politik)* schism

schiß [ʃɪs] *1. u. 3. Pers. Sg. Prät. v.* **scheißen**

Schiß der; Schisses *(salopp: Angst)* **[vor etw.] ~ haben** be shit-scared [of sth.] *(coarse);* **~ kriegen** get the shits *(coarse)*

schizoid [ʃɪtso'i:t] *(Med.)* **1.** *Adj.* schizoid. **2.** *adv.* **~ veranlagt sein** have schizoid tendencies

schizophren [ʃɪtso'fre:n] *(Med., auch fig.)* **1.** *Adj.* schizophrenic. **2.** *adv.* schizophrenically

Schizophrenie die; ~, ~n *(Med., auch fig.)* schizophrenia

schlabberig *Adj. (ugs.)* **a)** *(locker fallend)* baggy ‹*clothes*›; loose, limp ‹*material*›; **b)** *(abwertend: wäßrig)* watery

schlabbern ['ʃlabɐn] **1.** *tr. V. (ugs.) (schlürfen)* ‹*person*› slurp; ‹*animal*› lap up. **2.** *itr. V.* **a)** *(abwertend)* slobber; **b)** *(schlenkern)* ‹*dress*› flap; ‹*trousers*› be baggy

schlabbrig *Adj. s.* **schlabberig**

Schlacht [ʃlaxt] **die; ~, ~en** battle; **die ~ bei** *od.* **von/um X** the battle of/for X; **in die ~ ziehen** go into battle; **sich eine ~ liefern** do battle; **sich eine erbitterte ~ liefern** *(fig.)* fight fiercely; **jmdm. eine ~ liefern** do battle with sb.; **eine ~ schlagen** fight a battle

Schlacht·bank die; *Pl.* **~bänke** slaughtering-block; **sich wie ein Lamm zur ~ führen lassen** *(geh.)* let oneself be led like a lamb to the slaughter

schlachten *tr. (auch itr.) V.* slaughter; kill ‹*rabbit, chicken, etc.*›; **sein Sparschwein ~** *(scherzh.)* raid one's piggy bank

Schlachtenbummler [-bʊmlɐ] **der** *(Sportjargon)* away supporter; **die englischen ~:** the visiting English supporters

Schlachter der; ~s, ~, Schlächter der; ~s, ~ *(nordd.)* butcher

Schlachterei die; ~, ~en, Schlächterei die; ~, ~en a) *(nordd.: Fleischerei)* butcher's [shop]; **b)** *(abwertend: Gemetzel)* slaughter; butchery *no indef. art.*

Schlacht-: ~feld das battlefield; **auf dem ~feld bleiben** *(veralt. verhüll.)* fall in battle; **das Zimmer sah wie ein ~feld aus** the room looked as if a bomb had hit it; **~fest das** *feast at which the meat of freshly slaughtered animals, esp. pork, is eaten;* **~haus das** slaughterhouse; **~hof der** slaughterhouse; abattoir; **~opfer das** *(Rel.)* animal sacrifice; **~ordnung die** *(Milit. hist.)* battle order; **~plan der** *(Milit.)* plan of battle; battle plan; *(fig.)* plan of action; **~platte die** *dish with assorted cooked meats, sausages, and sauerkraut;* **~reif** *Adj.* ready for slaughtering *postpos.;* **~roß das** *(veralt.)* war-horse; charger; **ein altes ~roß** *(fig. scherzh.)* an old war-horse; **~schiff das** *(Milit.)* battleship; **~tier das** animal kept for meat; *(kurz vor der Schlachtung)* animal for slaughter

Schlachtung die; ~, ~en slaughter[ing]

Schlachtvieh das animals *pl.* kept for meat; *(kurz vor der Schlachtung)* animals *pl.* for slaughter

Schlacke ['ʃlakə] **die; ~, ~n a)** cinders *pl.; (größere Stücke)* clinker; **b)** *Pl. (Physiol.: Ballaststoffe)* roughage *sing.;* **c)** *(Hochofen~)* slag; **d)** *(Geol.: Lava)* slag; clinker

schlackern ['ʃlakɐn] *itr. V. (nordd., westmd.)* **a)** *(schlenkern)* ‹*dress*› flap; ‹*bag*› dangle; ‹*trousers*› be baggy; **b)** *(wackeln, zittern)* shake; tremble; **mit den Armen ~:** flap one's arms about; *s. auch* **Ohr**

Schlack·wurst die *s.* **Zervelatwurst**

Schlaf [ʃla:f] **der; ~[e]s** sleep; **einen leichten/festen/gesunden ~ haben** be a light/heavy/good sleeper; **keinen ~ finden** *(geh.)* be unable to sleep; **jmdn. um den** *od.* **seinen ~ bringen** ‹*worry etc.*› give sb. sleepless nights/a sleepless night; ‹*noise*› stop sb. from sleeping; **jmdn. in den ~ singen/wiegen** sing/rock sb. to sleep; **jmdn. aus dem ~ reißen** wake sb. up with a start; **den ~ des Gerechten schlafen** *(scherzh.)* sleep the sleep of the just; **das kann** *od.* **mache ich im ~** *(fig.)* I can do that with my eyes closed *or* shut; **halb im ~:** half asleep

Schlaf-: ~an·zug der pyjamas *pl.;* **ein ~anzug** a pair of pyjamas; **~bedürfnis das** need for sleep

Schläfchen ['ʃlɛ:fçən] **das; ~s, ~:** nap; snooze *(coll.);* **ein ~ halten** have a nap *or (coll.)* snooze

Schlaf·couch die bed-settee; sofa-bed

Schläfe ['ʃlɛ:fə] **die; ~, ~n** temple; **er hat/bekommt graue ~n** his hair has gone/is going grey at the temples

schlafen 1. *unr. itr. V.* **a)** *(auch fig.)* sleep; **tief** *od.* **fest ~** *(zur Zeit)* be sound asleep; *(gewöhnlich)* sleep soundly; be a sound sleeper; **lange ~:** sleep for a long time; *(am Morgen)* sleep in; **~ gehen** go to bed; **sich ~ legen** lie down to sleep; *(ins Bett gehen)* go to bed; **im Hotel/bei Bekannten ~:** stay in a hotel/with friends; **schlaf gut!** sleep well!; **hast du gut ge~?** did you sleep well?; **schläft sie immer noch?** is she still asleep?; **er schläft noch halb** he's still half asleep; **darüber muß ich noch ~:** I'd like to sleep on it; **~ wie ein Murmeltier** *od.* **Bär** *od.* **Sack** *od.* **Stein** *(ugs.)* sleep like a log *or* top; **bei jmdm. ~:** sleep at sb.'s house/in sb.'s room *etc.;* **mit jmdm. ~** *(verhüll.)* sleep with sb. *(euphem.);* **b)** *(ugs.: nicht aufpassen)* be asleep. **2.** *unr. refl. V. (unpers.)* **auf dem Sofa schläft es sich gut** the sofa's good to sleep on

Schläfen·bein das *(Anat.)* temporal bone

Schlafen·gehen das; ~s going *no def. art.* to bed

Schlafens·zeit die bedtime

Schläfer ['ʃlɛ:fɐ] **der; ~s, ~, Schläferin die; ~, ~nen** sleeper

schlaff [ʃlaf] **1.** *Adj.* **a)** *(nicht straff, nicht fest)* slack ‹*cable, rope, sail*›; flaccid, limp ‹*penis*›; loose, slack ‹*skin*›; sagging ‹*breasts*›; flabby ‹*stomach, muscles*›; **die Fahne war ~:** the flag hung limply; **b)** *(schlapp, matt)* limp ‹*body, hand, handshake*›; shaky ‹*knees*›; feeble ‹*blow*›; **c)** *(abwertend: träge)* lethargic; **~e Nachfrage** *(fig.)* weak demand. **2.** *adv.* **a)** *(locker, nicht straff)* slackly; **das Segel hing ~:** the sail hung limply; **ihre Brüste hingen ~:** her breasts sagged; **b)** *(schlapp, matt)* limply; **er saß ~ herum** *(ugs.)* he sat around listlessly

Schlaffheit die; ~: limpness; *(der Haut)* looseness, slackness; *(des Bauches, der Muskeln)* flabbiness

Schlaf-: ~gast der overnight guest; **~gelegenheit die** place to sleep; **~gewohnheiten** *Pl.* sleeping habits

Schlafittchen [ʃla'fɪtçən] **das** *in* **jmdn. am** *od.* **beim ~ kriegen** *od.* **fassen** *(ugs.)* collar *or (sl.)* nab sb.

schlaf-, Schlaf-: ~krankheit die sleeping sickness; **~lied das** lullaby; **~los** *Adj.* sleepless ‹*night*›; **~los liegen** lie awake, unable to sleep; **~losigkeit die; ~:** sleeplessness; insomnia; **an ~losigkeit leiden** be an insomniac; suffer from insomnia; **~mittel das** sleep-inducing drug; soporific [drug]; **dieser Roman ist das reinste ~mittel** *(fig.)* this novel sends you [right off] to sleep; **~mütze die a)** *(ugs.)* sleepyhead; *(jmd., der unaufmerksam ist)* day-dreamer; **b)** *(veralt.: Nachtmütze)* nightcap; **~mützig** *Adj. (ugs.)* dozy *(coll.);* **~raum der** bedroom; *(in Heim o. ä.)* dormitory

schläfrig ['ʃlɛ:frɪç] **1.** *Adj.* sleepy; **~ sein/werden** ‹*person*› be/become sleepy *or* drowsy. **2.** *adv.* sleepily

Schläfrigkeit die; ~: sleepiness; drowsiness

Schlaf-: ~rock der *(veralt.)* nightgown; *s. auch* **Apfel a; ~saal der** dormitory; **~sack der** sleeping-bag

schläfst [ʃlɛ:fst] *2. Pers. Sg. Präsens v.* **schlafen**

Schlaf-: ~stadt die dormitory town; **~stelle die** place to sleep; *(Bett)* bed; **~störungen** *Pl. (Med.)* insomnia *sing.*

schläft [ʃlɛ:ft] *3. Pers. Sg. Präsens v.* **schlafen**

schlaf-, Schlaf-: ~tablette die sleeping-pill *or* -tablet; **~trunk der** nightcap; **~trunken 1.** *Adj. (geh.)* drowsy; **2.** *adv.* drowsily; [still] half asleep; **~wagen der** sleeping-car; sleeper; **~wandeln** *itr. V.; auch mit sein* sleep-walk; **~wandler der; ~s, ~, ~wandlerin die; ~, ~nen** sleepwalker; **~wandlerisch** *Adj.* somnambulistic; **mit ~wandlerischer Sicherheit** with the sureness of a sleepwalker; with instinctive sureness; **~zimmer das** bedroom; *(Einrichtung)* bedroom suite; **~zimmerblick der;** *o. Pl. (scherzh.)* bedroom eyes *pl.;* seductive eyes *pl.*

Schlag [ʃla:k] **der; ~[e]s, Schläge** ['ʃlɛ:gə] **a)** blow; *(Faust~)* punch; blow; *(Klaps)* slap; *(leichter)* pat; *(als Strafe für ein Kind)* smack; *(Peitschenhieb)* lash; *(Tennis~, Golf~)* stroke; shot; **ein ~ auf den Kopf/ins Genick** a blow on the head/neck; **Schläge kriegen** *(ugs.)* get *or* be given a thrashing *or* beating; **~ auf ~** *(fig.)* in quick *or* rapid succession; **alles ging ~ auf ~:** everything went quickly; **die Fragen/Nachrichten kamen ~ auf ~:** the questions/news came thick and fast; **ein ~ ins Gesicht sein** *(fig.)* be a slap in the face; **das war ein ~ ins Kontor** *(ugs.)* that was a real blow *(coll.)*; **ein ~ ins Wasser** a wash-out *(coll.)*; **einen ~ [weg]haben** *(salopp)* be round the bend *(coll.)*; be nuts *(sl.)*; **keinen ~ tun** *(ugs.)* not do a stroke [of work]; **jmdm. einen ~ versetzen** deal sb. a blow; *(fig.)* be a blow to sb.; **einen vernichtenden ~ gegen jmdn. führen** *(fig.)* deal sb. a crushing blow; **auf einen ~** *(ugs.)* at one go; all at once; **mit einem ~[e]** *(ugs.)* suddenly; all at once; **mit einem ~ berühmt werden** become famous overnight; **zum entscheidenden ~ ausholen** *(fig.)* prepare to deal the decisive blow; *s. auch* **Gürtellinie; b)** *(Auf~, Aufprall)* bang; *(dumpf)* thud; *(Klopfen)* knock; **c)** *o. Pl. (des Herzens, Pulses, der Wellen)* beating; *(eines Pendels)* swinging; **d)** *(einzelne rhythmische Bewegung) (Herz~, Puls~, Takt~)* beat; *(eines Pendels)* swing; *(Ruder~, Kolben~)* stroke; **e)** *o. Pl. (Töne) (einer Uhr)* striking; *(einer Glocke)* ringing; *(einer Trommel)* beating; *(eines Gongs)* clanging; **f)** *(einzelner Ton) (Stunden~)* stroke; *(Glocken~)* ring; *(Trommel~)* beat; *(Gong~)* clang; ~ *od. (österr., schweiz.)* **schlag acht Uhr** on the dot *or* stroke of eight; **g)** *o. Pl. (Vogelgesang)* song; **h)** *(Blitz~)* flash [of lightning]; **i)** *(Stromstoß)* shock; **j)** *(ugs.: ~anfall)* stroke; **jmdn. trifft** *od.* **rührt der ~** *(ugs.)* sb. is flabbergasted; **ich dachte, mich trifft** *od.* **rührt der ~** *(ugs.)* I was flabbergasted; you could have knocked me down with a feather; **wie vom ~ getroffen** *od.* **gerührt** *(ugs.)* as if thunderstruck; **k)** *(Schicksals~)* blow; **l)** *(Tauben~)* cote; **m)** *(ugs.: Portion)* helping; **[einen] ~ bei jmdm. haben** *(fig. ugs.)* be well in with sb. *(coll.)*; **n)** *o. Pl. (österr.: ~sahne)* whipped cream; **o)** *(Wagen~, Kutschen~)* door; **p)** *(Menschen~)* type; **ein Beamter vom alten ~**: a civil servant of the old school

schlag-, Schlag-: ~ab·tausch der exchange of blows; *(fig.)* clash; **~ader die** artery; **~anfall der** stroke; **einen ~anfall bekommen [haben]** have [had] a stroke; **~artig 1.** *Adj.; nicht präd.* very sudden; *(innerhalb kürzester Zeit geschehend)* instantaneous; **2.** *adv.* quite suddenly; *(innerhalb kürzester Zeit)* instantly; **~ball der a)** *o. Pl. (Ballspiel) ball game similar to rounders;* **b)** *(Ball) ball used in Schlagball;* **~baß der** *(Musik)* plucked bass; **~baum der** barrier; **~bohrer der, ~bohr·maschine die** percussion drill; hammer drill

schlagen 1. *unr. tr. V.* **a)** hit; beat; strike; *(mit der Faust)* punch; hit; *(mit der flachen Hand)* slap; *(mit der Peitsche)* lash; **ein Kind ~**: smack a child; *(aufs Hinterteil)* spank a child; **jmdn. bewußtlos/zu Boden ~**: beat sb. senseless/to the ground; *(mit einem Schlag)* knock sb. senseless/to the ground; **jmdn. zum Krüppel ~**: cripple sb. with a beating; **ich schlage dich zum Krüppel!** *(derb)* I'll beat you to a pulp *(coll.)*; **etw. in Stücke ~**: smash sth. to pieces; **die Hände vors Gesicht ~**: cover one's face with one's hands; **jmdm. einen Schirm auf den Kopf ~**: hit sb. over the head with an umbrella; **sie schlug ihm das Buch aus der Hand** she knocked the book out of his hand; **ein Loch ins Eis ~**: break *or* smash a hole in the ice; **er hat ihr ein Loch in den Kopf ge~**: he hit her and cut her head open; *s. auch* **grün a; b)** *(mit Richtungsangabe)* hit ⟨*ball*⟩; *(mit dem Fuß)* kick; **einen Nagel in etw.** *(Akk.)* **~**: knock a nail into sth.; **einen Pflock in den Boden ~**: knock a post into the ground; **die Eier in die Pfanne ~**: crack the eggs into the pan; **etw. durch ein Sieb ~**: press sth. through a sieve; **der Adler schlug die Fänge in seine Beute** the eagle sank its talons into its prey; **c)** *(rühren)* beat ⟨*mixture*⟩; whip ⟨*cream*⟩; *(mit einem Schneebesen)* whisk; **die Sahne steif ~**: beat the cream till stiff; **d)** *(läuten)* ⟨*clock*⟩ strike; ⟨*bell*⟩ ring; **die Uhr schlägt acht** the clock strikes eight; **eine geschlagene Stunde** *(ugs.)* a whole hour; **die Stunde der Rache/Wahrheit hat ge~** *(fig.)* the moment of revenge/truth has come; *s. auch* **dreizehn; Stunde a; e)** *(legen)* throw; **die Decke zur Seite ~**: throw aside the blanket; **ein Bein über das andere ~**: lay *or* put one leg over the other; cross one's legs; **f)** *(einwickeln)* wrap **(in +** *Akk.* in); **g)** *(besiegen, übertreffen)* beat; **jmdn. in etw.** *(Dat.)* **~**: beat sb. at sth.; **jmdn. um einige Meter ~**: beat sb. by a few metres; **eine Mannschaft [mit] 2:0 ~**: beat a team [by] 2–0; **sich geschlagen geben** admit defeat; **h)** *auch itr. (bes. Schach)* take ⟨*chessman*⟩; **i)** *(fällen)* fell ⟨*tree*⟩; **j)** *s.* **Alarm a; Bogen a; Falte a; Haken a; Krach c; Kreis a; Kreuz c; Lärm; [1]Rad c, e; k)** *(spielen)* beat ⟨*drum*⟩; *(geh.)* play ⟨*lute, zither, harp*⟩; **einen Wirbel auf der Trommel ~**: play a roll on the drum; **den Takt/Rhythmus ~**: beat time; **l)** *(hinzufügen)* annex ⟨*territory*⟩; **etw. in etw./auf etw.** *(Akk.)* **~**: add sth. to sth.; **m)** *(befestigen) (mit Nägeln)* nail; *(mit Reißzwecken)* pin; *(mit Krampen)* staple; **n)** *(prägen)* mint, strike ⟨*coin*⟩; strike ⟨*medal*⟩; **o)** *(geh.)* **ein geschlagener Mann** a broken man; **das Schicksal hat ihn schwer ge~**: fate has treated him cruelly; **Gott hat ihn mit Blindheit ge~**: God struck him blind. **2.** *unr. itr. V.* **a)** *(hauen)* **er schlug mit der Faust auf den Tisch/gegen die Tür** he beat the table/beat [on] the door with his fist; **jmdm. auf die Hand/ins Gesicht ~**: slap sb.'s hand/hit sb. in the face; **er hat nach mir ge~**: he hit *or* lashed out at me; **sie schlug wie wild um sich** she lashed *or* hit out wildly all round her; **b) mit den Flügeln ~** ⟨*bird*⟩ beat or flap its wings; **c)** *mit sein (prallen)* bang; **mit dem Kopf auf etw.** *(Akk.)***/gegen etw. ~**: bang one's head on/against sth.; **auf den Boden ~**: land with a thud on the floor; **die Wellen schlugen über den Deich** the waves broke over the dike; **d)** *mit sein (schädigen)* **jmdm. auf den Magen ~**: affect sb.'s stomach; **e)** *(pulsieren)* ⟨*heart, pulse*⟩ beat; *(heftig)* ⟨*heart*⟩ pound; ⟨*pulse*⟩ throb; **ihr schlug das Gewissen** *(fig.)* her conscience pricked her; **f)** *(läuten)* ⟨*clock*⟩ strike; ⟨*bell*⟩ ring; ⟨*funeral bell*⟩ toll; **g)** *auch mit sein (auftreffen)* **gegen/an etw.** *(Akk.)* **~** ⟨*rain, waves*⟩ beat against sth.; **das Segel schlug gegen den Mast** the sail flapped against the mast; **h)** *meist mit sein (einschlagen)* **in etw.** *(Akk.)* **~** ⟨*lightning, bullet, etc.*⟩ strike *or* hit sth.; **i)** *mit sein (ähnlich werden)* **nach dem Großvater/Onkel** *usw.* **~**: take after one's grandfather/uncle *etc.*; **j)** *(sich hin und her bewegen)* bang; ⟨*sail, flag*⟩ flap; **k)** *meist mit sein (sich irgendwohin bewegen)* ⟨*flames*⟩ shoot, leap; ⟨*smoke*⟩ billow; **l)** *mit sein (irgendwohin dringen)* **der Lärm schlug an mein Ohr** the noise reached my ears; **die Röte/das Blut schlug ihr ins Gesicht** the colour/blood rushed to her face; **m)** *(singen)* ⟨*nightingale, thrush, etc.*⟩ sing; **n)** *auch mit sein (gehören)* **in jmds. Fach/Gebiet/Branche ~**: be sb.'s line. **3.** *unr. refl. V.* **a)** *(sich prügeln)* fight; **sich mit jmdm. ~**: fight with sb.; **sich um etw. ~** *(auch fig.)* fight over sth.; **b)** *(ugs.: sich behaupten)* hold one's own; **sich gut** *od.* **wacker** *od.* **tapfer ~**: hold one's own well; put up a good showing; **c)** *(sich schädlich auswirken)* **sich/sich jmdm. auf das Gehirn/die Leber ~**: affect the/sb.'s brain/liver; **d)** *(veralt.: sich duellieren)* **sich mit jmdm. ~**: fight a duel with sb.; *s. auch* **Mensur a; e)** *(sich begeben)* make one's way; **sich ins Gebüsch/Kornfeld ~**: slip away into the bushes/corn

schlagend 1. *Adj.* cogent, compelling ⟨*argument, reason*⟩; cogent ⟨*comparison*⟩; conclusive ⟨*proof, evidence*⟩; *s. auch* **Verbindung j; [2]Wetter c. 2.** *adv.* ⟨*prove, disprove*⟩ conclusively; ⟨*formulate*⟩ cogently

Schlager der; ~s, ~ a) *(Lied)* pop song; *(Hit)* hit; **b)** *(Erfolg) (Buch)* best seller; *(Ware)* best-selling line; *(Film, Stück)* hit

Schläger ['ʃlɛ:gɐ] **der; ~s, ~ a)** *(abwertend: Raufbold)* tough; thug; **b)** *(Tennis~, Federball~, Squash~)* racket; *(Tischtennis~, Kricket~)* bat; *([Eis]hockey~, Polo~)* stick; *(Golf~)* club; **c)** *(Baseball, Schlagball: Spieler)* batter; **d)** *(Fechten: Waffe)* straight-edged sabre

Schlägerei die; ~, ~en brawl; fight

Schlager·musik die; *o. Pl.* popular music; pop music

Schläger·mütze die *large soft peaked cap*

Schlager-: ~sänger der pop singer; **~spiel das** *(Sportjargon)* big match; **~text der** pop [song] lyric; **~texter der** pop [song] lyricist

Schläger·typ der *(abwertend)* tough; thug

schlag-, Schlag-: ~fertig 1. *Adj.* quick-witted ⟨*reply*⟩; ⟨*person*⟩ who is quick at repartee; **er ist ~fertig** he is quick at repartee; **2.** *adv.* **~fertig antworten/parieren** give a quick-witted reply/riposte; **~fertigkeit die;** *o. Pl.* quickness at repartee; **~fluß der** *(veralt.) s.* **~anfall; ~instrument das** percussion instrument; **~kraft die;** *o. Pl.* **a)** *(Kraft zum Schlagen)* weight of punch; **b)** *(Milit.: Kampfkraft)* strike power; **c)** *(fig.: Wirkungskraft)* effectiveness; *(von Argumenten)* compellingness; *(von Beispielen)* convincingness; **~kräftig 1.** *Adj.* **a)** *(Milit.: über große Kampfkraft verfügend)* powerful; **b)** *(überzeugend)* compelling ⟨*argument*⟩; convincing ⟨*example*⟩; **c)** *(effektiv)* strong, effective ⟨*support, back-up, team*⟩; **2.** *adv. (überzeugend)* ⟨*argue*⟩ compellingly; **~licht das;** *Pl.* **~lichter** *(Kunst, Phot.)* shaft of light; **ein ~licht auf etw. werfen** highlight sth.; **~loch das** pothole; **~mann der;** *Pl.* **~männer** *(Rudern)* stroke; **~obers** [~|o:bɐs] **das;** ~ *(österr.)*, **~rahm der** *(bes. südd., österr., schweiz.) s.* **~sahne; ~ring der** knuckleduster; **~sahne die** whipping cream; *(geschlagen)* whipped cream; **~schatten der** [harsh] shadow; **~seite die;** *meist o. Art.* list; **[starke** *od.* **schwere] ~seite haben/bekommen** be listing [heavily] *or* have a [heavy] list/develop a [heavy] list; **~seite haben** *(ugs. scherzh.)* be rolling drunk; **~stock der** cudgel; *(für Polizei)* truncheon; **die Polizisten setzten ~stöcke ein** the police used their truncheons; **~werk das** striking mechanism; **~wetter** *Pl. (Bergbau)* firedamp *sing.*; **~wort das a)** *Pl. meist* **~worte** *(Parole)* slogan; catchphrase; **b)** *Pl. meist* **~worte** *(abwertend: Redensart)* cliché; **c)** *Pl.* **~wörter** *(Buchw.: Stichwort)* headword; **nach ~wörtern und Verfassern katalogisieren** catalogue by subject and author; **~wort·katalog der** *(Buchw.)* subject catalogue; **~zeile die** *(Zeitungsw.)* headline; **~zeilen machen** *(fig.)* make headlines; **~zeug das** drums *pl.*; *(Schlaginstrumente)* percussion instruments *pl.*; **~zeuger der; ~s, ~, ~zeugerin die** drummer; *(Perkusionist[in])* percussionist

schlaksig ['ʃla:ksɪç] *(ugs.)* **1.** *Adj.* gangling; lanky. **2.** *adv.* lankily

Schlamassel [ʃla'masl] **der** *od.* **das; ~s** *(ugs.)* mess; **da haben wir den ~!** a right *or* fine mess we're in now!

Schlamm [ʃlam] **der; ~[e]s, ~e** *od.* **Schlämme** ['ʃlɛmə] **a)** *(aufgeweichte Erde)* mud; **b)** *(Schlick)* sludge; silt

Schlamm·bad das *(Med.)* mud-bath

schlammig *Adj.* **a)** muddy; **b)** *(schlickig)* sludgy; muddy

Schlämm·kreide ['ʃlɛm-] **die** whiting

Schlamm·schlacht die *(fig.)* mud-slinging *no indef. art.*

Schlampe die; ~, ~n *(ugs. abwertend)* slut

schlampen *itr. V. (ugs. abwertend)* be sloppy; **bei etw. ~:** do sth. sloppily; **sie haben bei der Reparatur geschlampt** they made a sloppy job of the repair
Schlamperei die; ~, ~en *(ugs. abwertend)* **a)** *(Unordentlichkeit)* sloppiness; *(Nachlässigkeit)* slackness; **eine unerhörte ~!** an outrageous example of sloppiness/slackness; **b)** *o. Pl. (Unordnung)* mess
schlampert ['ʃlampɐt] *(österr.),* **schlampig** *(ugs. abwertend)* **1.** *Adj.* **a)** *(liederlich)* slovenly; **b)** *(nachlässig)* sloppy, slipshod ‹*work*›. **2.** *adv.* **a)** *(liederlich)* in a slovenly way; **b)** *(nachlässig)* sloppily; in a sloppy *or* slipshod way
Schlampigkeit die; ~, ~en *(ugs. abwertend)* **a)** *o. Pl. (Liederlichkeit)* slovenliness; **b)** *(Nachlässigkeit)* sloppiness
schlang [ʃlaŋ] *1. u. 3. Pers. Sg. Prät. v.* **schlingen**
Schlange die; ~, ~n a) snake; *s. auch* **Busen a; b)** *(Menschen~)* queue; line *(Amer.)*; **~ stehen** queue; stand in line *(Amer.)*; **c)** *(Auto~)* tailback *(Brit.)*; backup *(Amer.)*; **d)** *(abwertend: Frau)* viper
schlänge ['ʃlɛŋə] *1. u. 3. Pers. Sg. Konjunktiv II v.* **schlingen**
schlängeln ['ʃlɛŋl̩n] *refl. V.* **a)** ‹*snake*› wind [its way]; ‹*road*› wind, snake [its way]; **eine geschlängelte Linie** a wavy line; **b)** *(sich irgendwo hindurch bewegen)* wind one's way
Schlangen-: ~beschwörer der; ~s, ~: snake-charmer; **~biß der** snake-bite; **~brut die** *(geh. abwertend)* brood of vipers; **~fraß der** *(salopp abwertend)* muck *(coll.)*; **~gift das** snake venom *or* poison; **~haut die** snake's skin; **~leder das** snakeskin; **~linie die** wavy line; **er fuhr mit seinem Moped ~linien** he weaved along on his moped; **~mensch der** contortionist
schlank [ʃlaŋk] *Adj.* slim ‹*person*›; slim, slender ‹*build, figure*›; slender ‹*column, tree, limbs*›; **~ werden** get slimmer; slim down; **dieser Rock macht [dich] ~:** this skirt makes you look slim; **Joghurt macht ~:** yoghurt helps you slim; **sich ~ machen** *(fig.)* breathe in; *s. auch* **Linie a**
Schlankheit die; ~ *s.* **schlank:** slimness; slenderness
Schlankheits·kur die slimming diet; **eine ~ machen/beginnen** be/go on a slimming diet; *(in einer Klinik usw.)* have/start a course of slimming treatment
schlank·weg *Adv. (ugs.)* ‹*refuse*› flatly, point-blank; ‹*accept*› straight away; **jmdn. ~ einen Lügner nennen** come right out and call sb. a liar; **das ist alles ~ erfunden** that's all pure invention
schlankwüchsig [-vy:ksɪç] *Adj.* ‹*person*› of slender or slim build; slender ‹*tree*›
schlapp [ʃlap] **1.** *Adj.* **a)** worn out; tired out; *(wegen Schwüle)* listless; *(wegen Krankheit)* run-down; listless; **b)** *(ugs.: ohne Schwung)* wet *(sl.)*; feeble; **c)** slack ‹*rope, cable*›; loose, slack ‹*skin*›; flabby ‹*stomach, muscles*›. **2.** *adv. (schlaff)* slackly; **das Segel hing ~:** the sail hung limply
Schlappe die; ~, ~n setback; **eine [schwere] ~ einstecken [müssen]** *od.* **erleiden** suffer a [severe] setback
schlappen 1. *itr. V.* **a)** *(zu weit sein)* ‹*shoe*› be too wide; **b)** *mit sein (schlurfend gehen)* shuffle. **2.** *tr. V. (schlabbern)* lap [up]
Schlappen der; ~s, ~ *(ugs.)* slipper
Schlappheit die; ~: weariness; *(wegen Krankheit, Schwüle)* listlessness; *(ugs.: Schwunglosigkeit)* feebleness
schlapp-, Schlapp-: ~hut der slouch hat; **~|machen** *itr. V. (ugs.)* flag; *(zusammenbrechen)* flake out *(coll.)*; *(aufgeben)* give up; **~ohr das** lop ear; **~schwanz der** *(salopp abwertend)* weed; wet *(sl.)*
Schlaraffen·land [ʃla'rafn̩-] **das;** *o. Pl.* Cockaigne
schlau [ʃlau] **1.** *Adj.* **a)** shrewd; astute; *(gerissen)* wily; crafty; cunning; **sich** *(Dat.)* **ein ~es Leben machen** *(ugs.)* make life cushy for oneself *(coll.)*; **das war besonders ~ [von dir]** *(iron.)* that was very clever *or* bright [of you] *(iron.)*; **b)** *(ugs.: gescheit)* clever; bright; smart; **aus etw. nicht ~ werden** *(ugs.)* not be able to make head or tail of sth.; **aus jmdm. nicht ~ werden** *(ugs.)* not be able to make sb. out; *s. auch* **Buch a. 2.** *adv.* shrewdly; astutely; *(gerissen)* craftily; cunningly
Schlauberger ['ʃlaubɛrgɐ] **der; ~s, ~** *(ugs. scherzh.)* wily *or* crafty customer *(coll.)*
Schlauch [ʃlaux] **der; ~[e]s, Schläuche** ['ʃlɔyçə] **a)** hose; **das war ein [ganz schöner] ~!** *(fig. ugs.)* it was a [real] slog; **b)** *(Fahrrad~, Auto~)* tube; **c)** *(für Wein usw.)* skin; **d)** *(ugs.: schmaler Raum)* tunnel
Schlauch·boot das rubber dinghy; inflatable [dinghy]
schlauchen *(ugs.) tr. V.* **a)** *auch itr. (anstrengen)* **jmdn. ~:** take it out of sb.; **geschlaucht sein** be whacked *(Brit. coll.)*; be worn out; **b)** *(scharf herannehmen)* **jmdn. ~:** put sb. through the mill
schlauch·los *Adj.* tubeless ‹*tyre*›
Schläue ['ʃlɔyə] **die; ~:** shrewdness; astuteness; *(Gerissenheit)* wiliness; craftiness; cunning
Schlaufe ['ʃlaufə] **die; ~, ~n** *(zum Festhalten)* strap; *(Gürtel~, Verschluß)* loop
Schlau-: ~kopf der *(ugs.).* **~meier der** *(ugs. scherzh.) s.* **~berger**
Schlawiner [ʃla'vi:nɐ] **der; ~s, ~** *(ugs.)* trickster; *(scherzh.: Schlingel)* rogue; rascal
schlecht [ʃlɛçt] **1.** *Adj.* **a)** bad; poor, bad ‹*food, quality, style, harvest, health, circulation*›; poor ‹*salary, eater, appetite*›; poor-quality ‹*goods*›; bad, weak ‹*eyes*›; **nicht ~!** not bad!; **in Mathematik ~ sein** be bad at mathematics; **[ein] ~es Englisch sprechen** speak poor English; **~ für die Gesundheit sein** be bad for one's health; **das wäre nicht ~/das ~este** that wouldn't be a bad idea/a bad idea at all; **mit jmdm.** *od.* **um jmdn./mit etw. steht es ~:** sb./sth. is in a bad way; *(jmd./etw. hat schlechte Aussichten)* things look bad for sb./sth.; **b)** *(böse)* bad; wicked; **das Schlechte im Menschen/in der Welt** the evil in man/the world; **ich hatte nur Schlechtes über ihn gehört** I had heard only bad things about him; **sie ist nicht die Schlechteste** she's not too bad; *s. auch* **Eltern; c)** *nicht attr. (ungenießbar)* off; **die Milch/das Fleisch ist ~ geworden** the milk/meat has gone off; **d)** *(unwohl, elend)* **jmdm. ist [es] ~:** sb. feels ill *or* unwell *or* poorly; **in ~er Verfassung sein** be in a bad way; **da kann einem ja ~ werden!** *(fig. ugs.)* it's enough to make you ill. **2.** *adv.* **a)** badly; **er verdient ziemlich ~:** he is badly *or* poorly paid; **die Vorstellung war ~ besucht** the performance was poorly attended; **sie vertragen sich ~:** they don't get on well; **sie spricht ~ Englisch** she speaks poor English; **die Farben vertragen sich ~:** the colours don't go well together; **er sieht/hört ~:** his sight is poor/he has poor hearing; **sie waren nicht ~ beeindruckt** *(ugs.)* they weren't half impressed *(sl.)*; **die Geschäfte gehen im Moment ~:** business is bad at the moment; **über jmdn.** *od.* **von jmdm. ~ sprechen** speak ill of sb.; **b)** *(schwer)* **heute geht es ~:** today is difficult; **heute paßt es mir ~:** it's not very convenient for me today; **das läßt sich ~ machen** that's difficult to manage; **das kann ich ~ sagen** I can't really say; **das wird sich ~ vermeiden lassen** it can hardly be avoided; **das kann er sich** *(Dat.)* **als Pfarrer ~ leisten** *od.* **erlauben** [in his position] as a vicar he really cannot afford to do that; **c)** *in* **~ und recht, mehr ~ als recht** after a fashion; **sie hat sich ~ und recht durchs Leben geschlagen** she got by in life as best she could
schlecht-: ~beraten *Adj. (präd. getrennt geschrieben)* badly-advised; **~bezahlt** *Adj. (präd. getrennt geschrieben)* badly *or* poorly paid
schlechter·dings *Adv.* simply
schlecht-: ~|gehen *unr. itr. V.; unpers.; mit sein* **es geht ihr/mir ~:** she is/I am doing badly; things are going badly for her/me; *(gesundheitlich)* she is/I am ill *or* unwell *or* poorly; **wenn sie das herausfindet, geht's dir ~!** *(ugs.)* if she finds out, you'll be [in] for it; **~gelaunt** [~gəlaunt] *Adj. (präd. getrennt geschrieben)* ill-tempered; bad-tempered; **~hin** *Adv.* **a)** *einem Subst. nachgestellt* **er war der Romantiker ~hin** he was the quintessential Romantic *or* the epitome of the Romantic; **das Prinzip des Privateigentums ~hin anfechten** attack the very principle of private property; **b)** *(geradezu, ganz einfach)* quite simply
Schlechtigkeit die; ~, ~en a) *o. Pl.* badness; wickedness; **b)** *(böse Tat)* bad *or* wicked deed
schlecht-, Schlecht-: ~|machen *tr. V.* **jmdn. ~machen** run sb. down; disparage sb.; **~sitzend** *Adj.; nicht präd.* ill-fitting; **~weg** *Adv. s.* **~hin b; ~wetter·geld** [-'---] **das** bad-weather allowance *(paid to building workers to make up for work lost due to bad weather)*; **~wetter·periode** [-'-----] **die** *(Met.)* period of bad weather
schlecken ['ʃlɛkn̩] *(bes. südd., österr.)* **1.** *tr. V.* lap up. **2.** *itr. V.* **a) an etw.** *(Dat.)* **~:** lick sth.; **b)** *s.* **naschen 1 a**
Schleckerei die; ~, ~en *(bes. südd., österr.)* **a)** *o. Pl. (das Naschen) s.* **Nascherei; b)** *(Süßigkeit)* sweet
Schlegel ['ʃle:gl̩] **der; ~s, ~ a)** *(Werkzeug)* mallet; **b)** *(für Schlaginstrumente)* stick; **c)** *(südd., österr.) s.* **Keule c**
Schleh·dorn der; *Pl.* **~e** blackthorn; sloe
Schlehe ['ʃle:ə] **die; ~, ~n** sloe
Schleiche die; ~, ~n *(Zool.)* one of the Anguidae; **die ~n** the Anguidae
schleichen ['ʃlaiçn̩] **1.** *unr. itr. V.; mit sein* creep; *(heimlich)* creep; steal; sneak; ‹*cat*› slink, creep; *(langsam fahren)* crawl along; **die Zeit schlich** time crept by. **2.** *unr. refl. V.* creep; steal; sneak; ‹*cat*› slink, creep; **Mißtrauen schlich sich in ihr Herz** *(geh.)* distrust crept into her heart; **schleich dich!** *(ugs., bes. österr.)* get lost! *(sl.)*; buzz off! *(sl.)*
schleichend *Adj.* insidious ‹*disease*›; slow[-acting], insidious ‹*poison*›; creeping ‹*inflation*›; gradual ‹*crisis*›
Schleicher der; ~s, ~ *(abwertend)* toadying hypocrite
Schleich-: ~handel der black marketeering **(mit in)**; **im ~handel** on the black market; **~katze die** viverrid *(Zool.)*; **~weg der** secret path; **auf ~wegen, auf dem ~weg** *(fig.)* clandestinely; *(unrechtmäßig)* illicitly; by illicit means; **~werbung die** surreptitious advertising
Schleie ['ʃlaiə] **die; ~, ~n** *(Zool.)* tench
Schleier ['ʃlaiɐ] **der; ~s, ~ a)** *(durchsichtiges Gewebe)* veil; **den ~ nehmen** *(fig. geh.)* take the veil; **den ~ [des Geheimnisses] lüften** *(fig. geh.)* lift the veil of secrecy; **den ~ der Vergessenheit** *od.* **des Vergessens über etw.** *(Akk.)* **breiten** *(fig. geh.)* draw a veil over sth.; **b)** *(Nebel~, Dunst~)* veil of mist/smoke; **c)** *(Fot.: Farb~)* fog; **einen ~ haben** be fogged
schleier-, Schleier-: ~eule die barn owl; **~haft** *Adj.* **jmdm. [völlig** *od.* **vollkommen] ~haft sein/bleiben** be/remain a [total *or* complete] mystery to sb.; **~kraut das** *(Bot.)* baby's breath; **~schwanz der** *(Zool.)* fantail; **~tanz der** dance of the veils
Schleife ['ʃlaifə] **die; ~, ~n a)** bow; *(Fliege)* bow-tie; **b)** *(starke Biegung)* loop; *(eines Flusses)* loop; horseshoe bend; **c)** *(Kranz~)* [inscribed] ribbon *(attached to a wreath)*
[1]**schleifen** *unr. tr. V.* **a)** *(schärfen)* sharpen;

grind, sharpen 〈axe〉; b) (glätten) grind; cut 〈diamond, glass〉; (mit Sand-/Schmirgelpapier) sand; s. auch geschliffen; c) (bes. Soldatenspr.: drillen) jmdn. ~: drill sb. hard

²schleifen 1. tr. V. a) (auch fig.) drag; jmdn. ins Kino ~ (fig.) drag sb. along to the cinema (Brit.) or (Amer.) movie; b) (niederreißen) etw. ~: raze sth. [to the ground]. 2. itr. V.; auch mit sein drag; die Kette schleift am Schutzblech the chain scrapes the guard; die Kupplung ~ lassen (Kfz-W.) slip the clutch; etw. ~ lassen (fig.) let sth. slide; s. auch Zügel

Schleifer der; ~s, ~ a) grinder; (Diamanten~) cutter; b) (Soldatenspr.) slave-driver; c) (Musik) slur

Schleiferei die; ~, ~en a) s. ¹schleifen a, b: sharpening; grinding; cutting; sanding; b) (bes. Soldatenspr.: das Drillen) hard drilling; c) (Betrieb) grinding shop

Schleif-: ~lack·möbel das; meist Pl. matt-lacquered furniture; ~spur die dragmark; ~stein der grindstone; dasitzen wie ein Affe auf dem ~stein (ugs. scherzh.) sit crouched there looking a proper charlie (coll.)

Schleifung die; ~, ~en razing [to the ground]

Schleim [ʃlaim] der; ~[e]s, ~e a) mucus; (im Hals) phlegm; (von Schnecken, Aalen) slime; (Bot.) mucilage; b) (sämiger Brei) gruel

Schleim-: ~beutel der (Anat.) synovial bursa; mucous bursa; ~haut die mucous membrane

schleimig 1. Adj. a) slimy; (Physiol., Zool.) mucous; b) (abwertend: heuchlerisch) slimy. 2. adv. (abwertend) slimily

schleim-, Schleim-: ~lösend Adj. expectorant; ~pilz der slime mould or fungus; ~suppe die (Kochk.) gruel

schleißen ['ʃlaisn̩] regelm. (auch unr.) tr. V. a) strip 〈feathers〉; b) (bes. südd.: spalten) split 〈wood〉

Schlemihl [ʃle'mi:l] der; ~s, ~e a) (Pechvogel) unlucky devil; b) (ugs.: Schlitzohr) crafty devil

schlemmen ['ʃlɛmən] 1. itr. V. (prassen) have a feast. 2. tr. V. (verzehren) feast on

Schlemmer der; ~s, ~: gourmet

Schlemmerei die; ~, ~en (oft abwertend) a) o. Pl. (das Schlemmen) feasting; gormandizing (derog.); b) s. Schlemmermahl

Schlemmerin die; ~, ~nen s. Schlemmer

Schlemmer-: ~lokal das gourmet restaurant; ~mahl das gourmet meal

schlendern ['ʃlɛndɐn] itr. V.; mit sein stroll

Schlendrian ['ʃlɛndria:n] der; ~[e]s (ugs. abwertend) slackness

Schlenker ['ʃlɛŋkɐ] der; ~s, ~ (ugs.) a) (Bogen) swerve; einen ~ machen swerve; (fig.) dodge; b) (Umweg) detour

schlenkern 1. itr. V. a) swing; dangle; mit den Armen/mit den Beinen ~: swing or dangle one's arms/legs; b) 〈curtain, dress〉 flap; 〈car〉 swerve. 2. tr. V. swing, dangle 〈arms, legs〉

schlenzen ['ʃlɛntsn̩] tr. V. (Sport, bes. [Eis]hockey, Fußball) flick

Schlepp [ʃlɛp] der in ein Fahrzeug in ~ nehmen take a vehicle in tow

Schlepp-: ~bügel der (Skisport) T-bar; ~dampfer der (Seew.) [steam-driven] tug

Schleppe die; ~, ~n a) train; b) (Pferdesport, Jagdw.: künstliche Fährte) drag

schleppen 1. tr. V. a) (hinter sich herziehen) tow 〈vehicle, ship〉; b) (tragen) carry; lug; c) (ugs.: mitnehmen) drag; jmdn. vor den Richter ~: haul sb. up before the judge. 2. refl. V. a) drag or haul oneself; b) (sich hinziehen) 〈trial, negotiations, etc.〉 drag on; c) (bes. nordostd.: sich abmühen) ich mußte mich allein mit dem Kasten ~: I had to lug the box around by myself. 3. itr. V. (schleifen) drag

schleppend 1. Adj. a) (schwerfällig) shuffling, dragging 〈walk, steps〉; b) (gedehnt) dragging 〈speech〉; slow 〈song, melody〉; c) (nicht zügig) slow 〈service〉; er beklagte sich über die ~e Bearbeitung seines Antrags he complained about the delays in processing his application; die Unterhaltung wurde immer ~er the conversation dragged more and more. 2. adv. a) (schwerfällig) ~ gehen shuffle along; b) (gedehnt) 〈speak〉 in a dragging voice; 〈sing, play〉 slowly; c) (nicht zügig) die Unterhaltung kam nur ~ in Gang conversation was slow to get going; die Arbeiten gehen nur ~ voran the work is progressing slowly

Schlepper der; ~s, ~ a) (Schiff) tug; b) (Traktor) tractor; c) (ugs.: jmd., der Kunden zuführt) tout; d) (ugs.: Fluchthelfer) person who aids the entry of illegal immigrants or escape of illegal emigrants

Schlepperei die; ~, ~en (ugs. abwertend) lugging around

Schlepp-: ~kahn der dumb barge; ~lift der T-bar [lift]; ~netz das trawl[-net]; ~seil das s. ~tau; ~start der (Segelfliegen) aero-tow; ~tau das tow-line; row-rope; (aus Draht) tow-line; tow-cable; etw. ins ~tau nehmen take sth. in tow; in jmds. ~tau (fig.) in sb.'s wake; ~zug der (Schiffahrt) train of barges

Schlesien ['ʃle:zi̯ən] (das); ~s Silesia

Schlesier ['ʃle:zi̯ɐ] der; ~s, ~, **Schlesierin** die; ~, ~nen Silesian

schlesisch Adj. Silesian

Schleuder ['ʃlɔydɐ] die; ~, ~n a) sling; (mit Gummiband) catapult (Brit.); slingshot (Amer.); b) s. Wäsche~; c) s. Zentrifuge

Schleuder-: ~ball der a) o. Pl.; team game played with a Schleuderball b; b) (Ball) leather ball with a strap attached for throwing; ~honig der extracted honey

schleudern 1. tr. V. a) (werfen) hurl; fling; der Wagen wurde aus der Kurve geschleudert the car was sent skidding off the bend; jmdm. Beleidigungen ins Gesicht ~ (fig.) hurl insults at sb.; b) (rotieren lassen) centrifuge; spin 〈washing〉. 2. itr. V. a) mit sein (rutschen) skid; ins Schleudern geraten od. kommen go into a skid; (fig. ugs.) run into trouble; dein Argument hat ihn ins Schleudern gebracht (ugs.) your argument completely threw him (coll.); b) (rotieren) spin

Schleuder-: ~preis der (ugs.) knockdown price; ~sitz der ejector seat; ~ware die; Pl. selten (ugs.) cut-price item

schleunig ['ʃlɔynɪç] 1. Adj.; nicht präd. a) (unverzüglich) speedy; rapid; b) (eilig) hurried. 2. adv. a) (unverzüglich) rapidly; speedily; b) (eilig) hurriedly

schleunigst Adv. a) (auf der Stelle) at once; immediately; straight away; b) (eilends) hastily; with all haste

Schleuse ['ʃlɔyzə] die; ~, ~n a) sluice[-gate]; die ~n des Himmels öffneten sich (fig.) the heavens opened; b) (Schiffs~) lock; c) (Luft~) airlock

schleusen tr. V. a) ein Schiff ~: pass a ship through a/the lock; b) (geleiten) shepherd; c) (schmuggeln) smuggle 〈secrets〉; infiltrate 〈spy, agent, etc.〉 (in + Akk. into)

Schleusen-: ~kammer die lock chamber; ~tor das lock gate; ~wärter der lock-keeper

schlich [ʃlɪç] 1. u. 3. Pers. Sg. Prät. v. schleichen

Schlich der; ~[e]s, ~e trick; alle ~e kennen know all the tricks; jmdm. auf die ~e od. hinter jmds. ~e kommen get on to sb.

schlicht [ʃlɪçt] 1. Adj. a) simple; plain, simple 〈pattern, furniture〉; (geh.: glatt) smooth 〈hair〉; in ~en Verhältnissen leben live in modest circumstances; b) (unkompliziert) simple, unsophisticated 〈person, view, etc.〉; c) nicht präd. (bloß, rein) simple; pure; ein ~es Ja oder Nein a simple yes or no. 2. adv. simply; simply, plainly 〈dressed, furnished〉; wir haben ihn ~ Karl genannt we gave him the plain, straightforward name Karl; ~ und einfach (ugs.) quite or just simply; er hat es ~ und ergreifend vergessen (ugs. scherzh.) he just plain forgot

schlichten 1. tr. V. a) settle 〈argument, difference of opinion〉; settle 〈industrial dispute etc.〉 by mediation; b) (fachspr.) smooth 〈wood, metal〉; dress 〈stone, leather〉; size 〈warp threads〉. 2. itr. V. mediate (in + Dat. in, zwischen between); in einem Konflikt ~d eingreifen intervene as mediator in a dispute

Schlichter der; ~s, ~: mediator; (durch Schiedsspruch) arbitrator

Schlichtheit die; ~ s. schlicht a, b: simplicity; plainness; unsophisticatedness

Schlichtung die; ~, ~en settlement; (in einem Arbeitskampf usw.) mediation; (durch Schiedsspruch) arbitration

Schlichtungs-: ~aus·schuß der arbitration committee; ~verfahren das arbitration process

schlicht·weg Adv. er gab es ~ zu he simply admitted it; das ist ~ kriminell that's just plain criminal

Schlick [ʃlɪk] der; ~[e]s, ~e silt

schlief [ʃli:f] 1. u. 3. Pers. Sg. Prät. v. schlafen

Schliere ['ʃli:rə] die; ~, ~n (Technik, Optik, Geol.) schliere

Schließe ['ʃli:sə] die; ~, ~n clasp; (Schnalle) buckle

schließen 1. unr. tr. V. a) (zumachen) close; shut; put the top on 〈bottle〉; turn off 〈tap〉; fasten 〈belt, bracelet〉; do up 〈button, zip〉; close 〈street, route, electrical circuit〉; close off 〈pipe〉; (fig.) close 〈border〉; fill, close 〈gap〉; mit geschlossenen Beinen with one's legs together; die Augen für immer geschlossen haben (geh. verhüll.) have passed away; b) (unzugänglich machen) close, shut 〈shop, factory〉; (außer Betrieb setzen) close [down] 〈shop, school〉; close or shut [down] 〈factory〉; c) (ein~) etw./jmdn./sich in etw. (Akk.) ~: lock sth./sb./oneself in sth.; d) (beenden) close 〈meeting, proceedings, debate〉; end, conclude 〈letter, speech, lecture〉; die Rednerliste ist geschlossen the list of speakers is closed; e) (befestigen) etw. an etw. (Akk.) ~: connect sth. to sth.; (mit Schloß) lock sth. to sth.; f) (eingehen, vereinbaren) conclude 〈treaty, pact, cease-fire, agreement〉; reach 〈settlement, compromise〉; enter into 〈contract〉; wann wurde Ihre Ehe geschlossen? when did you get married?; Freundschaft/Bekanntschaft mit jmdm. ~: make friends with/get to know sb.; s. auch Frieden; g) (umfassen) jmdn. in die Arme ~: take sb. in one's arms; embrace sb.; etw. in seine Hand ~: clasp sth. in one's hand; etw. in sich ~ (fig.) contain sth.; h) (folgern) etw. aus etw. ~: infer or conclude sth. from sth.; aus etw. ~, daß ...: infer or conclude from sth. that ... 2. unr. itr. V. a) close; shut; der Schlüssel/das Schloß schließt schlecht the key won't turn properly/the lock doesn't work properly; b) 〈shop〉 close, shut; 〈stock exchange〉 close; (den Betrieb einstellen) 〈shop〉 close [down]; 〈factory〉 close or shut [down]; c) (enden) end; conclude; d) (urteilen) [aus etw.] auf etw. (Akk.) ~: infer or conclude sth. [from sth.]; die Symptome lassen auf Hepatitis ~: the symptoms indicate hepatitis; etw. läßt darauf ~, daß ...: sth. indicates or suggests that ...; vom Besonderen auf das Allgemeine ~: proceed from the particular to the general; von sich auf andere ~: judge others by one's own standards. 3. unr. refl. V. a) 〈door, window〉 close, shut; 〈wound, circle〉 close; 〈flower〉 close [up]; sich um etw. ~: close around sth.; s. auch geschlossen; b) (sich an~) an den Vortrag schloß sich

eine Diskussion the lecture was followed by a discussion
Schließer der; ~s, ~ a) *(Tür~)* doorkeeper; *(Vorrichtung)* [door-]closer; **b)** *(im Gefängnis)* warder
Schließ-: ~fach das locker; *(bei der Post)* post-office box; PO box; *(bei der Bank)* safe-deposit box; **~frucht die** *(Bot.)* indehiscent fruit; **~korb der** hamper
schließlich *Adv.* **a)** finally; in the end; *(bei Erwünschtem auch)* at last; **~ und endlich** *(ugs.)* in the end; finally; **b)** *(bei einer Aufzählung)* **..., und ~ ...:** ... and finally ...; **c)** *(immerhin, doch)* after all; **er ist ~ mein Freund** he is my friend, after all; **er hat ~ nur seine Pflicht getan** after all, he was only doing his duty
Schließ·muskel der *(Anat.)* sphincter
Schließung die; ~, ~en a) *(der Geschäfte, Büros usw.)* closing; shutting; *(Stillegung, Einstellung)* closure; closing; *(fig.: einer Grenze)* closing; **zur ~ seiner Haushaltslücke** to fill the gap in his budget; **b)** *(Beendigung)* **vor/nach ~ der Versammlung** before/after the meeting was closed; before/after the conclusion of the meeting; **die ~/einstweilige ~ der Debatte** the closure/adjournment of the debate; **c)** *s.* **schließen 1f:** conclusion; reaching; **die ~ einer Ehe** the solemnization of a marriage
schliff [ʃlɪf] *1. u. 3. Pers. Sg. Prät. v.* **schleifen**
Schliff der; ~[e]s, ~e a) *o. Pl. (das Schleifen)* cutting; *(von Messern, Sensen usw.)* sharpening; **b)** *(Art, wie etw. geschliffen wird)* cut; *(von Messern, Scheren, Schneiden)* edge; **c)** *o. Pl. (Lebensart)* refinement; polish; **d)** *o. Pl. (Vollkommenheit)* **einem Brief/Text** *usw.* **den letzten ~ geben** put the finishing touches *pl.* to a letter/text *etc.*; **der Mannschaft den letzten ~ geben** put the finishing touches *pl.* to the team's training
schlimm [ʃlɪm] **1.** *Adj.* **a)** *(schwerwiegend)* grave, serious ⟨*error, mistake, accusation, offence*⟩; bad, serious ⟨*error, mistake*⟩; **man hat ihm die ~sten Dinge nachgesagt** the most terrible things have been said about him; **das ist ~ für ihn** that's serious for him; **b)** *(übel)* bad; nasty, bad ⟨*experience*⟩; **das war eine ~e Geschichte für ihn** that was a nasty business for him; **im ~sten Fall muß ich ...:** if the worst comes to the worst I'll have to ...; **ist es ~, wenn wir erst morgen kommen?** does it matter if we don't come till tomorrow?; **[das ist alles] halb so ~:** it's not as bad as all that; **das ~ste ist, daß ...:** the worst thing is *or* the worst of it is that ...; **es wurde immer ~er** it got worse and worse; **es ist nichts Schlimmes** it's nothing serious; **wenn es nichts Schlimmeres ist!** if it's nothing worse than that!; **ist nicht ~!** [it] doesn't matter; **es gibt Schlimmeres** there are worse things; **c)** *(schlecht, böse)* wicked; *(ungezogen)* naughty ⟨*child*⟩; **er ist ein ganz Schlimmer** *(scherzh.)* he's really wicked; **d)** *(fam.: schmerzend, entzündet)* bad; sore; bad, nasty ⟨*wound*⟩. **2.** *adv. (übel, arg)* **~ d[a]ran sein** *(körperlich, geistig)* be in a bad way; *(in einer ~en Situation)* be in dire straits; **es steht ~ um jmdn.** things look bad *or* serious for sb.; **es hätte ~er ausgehen können** things could have turned out worse
schlimmsten·falls *Adv.* if the worst comes to the worst; **~ kriegt man eine Verwarnung** at worst you'll get a caution
Schlinge ['ʃlɪŋə] **die; ~, ~n a)** *(Schlaufe)* loop; *(für den gebrochenen Arm o. ä.)* sling; *(zum Aufhängen)* noose; **jmdm. die ~ um den Hals legen** put a noose round sb.'s neck; **die ~ zusammenziehen** *(fig.)* tighten the noose; *s. auch* **Kopf a**; **b)** *(Fanggerät)* snare; **~n legen** lay *or* set snares; **sich in der eigenen ~ fangen** *(fig.)* be hoist with one's own petard; **in jmds. ~ geraten** *(fig.)* fall into sb.'s trap
Schlingel ['ʃlɪŋl̩] **der; ~s, ~:** rascal; rogue
schlingen 1. *unr. tr. V.* **a)** *(winden)* **etw. um etw. ~:** loop sth. round sth.; *(und zusammenbinden)* tie sth. round sth.; **sich** *(Dat.)* **einen Schal um den Hals ~:** wrap a scarf round one's neck; **die Arme um jmdn./etw. ~:** wrap one's arms round sb./sth.; **b)** *(binden)* tie ⟨*knot*⟩; **etw. zu einem Knoten ~:** tie sth. up in a knot; **c)** *(flechten)* plait. **2.** *unr. refl. V. (sich winden)* **sich um etw. ~** ⟨*snake*⟩ wind *or* coil itself round sth.; ⟨*plant*⟩ wind *or* twine itself round sth. **3.** *unr. itr. V.* bolt one's food; wolf one's food [down]; **schling nicht so hastig!** don't bolt your food like that!
Schlinger·bewegung die *(Seew.)* rolling motion; **in ~en geraten** start to roll
schlingern ['ʃlɪŋɐn] *itr. V.; meist, mit Richtungsangabe nur, mit sein* ⟨*ship, boat*⟩ roll; ⟨*train, vehicle*⟩ lurch from side to side; **ins Schlingern geraten** *od.* **kommen** *(ugs.)* run into trouble
Schling·pflanze die creeper
Schlips [ʃlɪps] **der; ~es, ~e** tie; **jmdm. auf den ~ treten** *(fig. ugs.)* tread on sb.'s toes; **sich auf den ~ getreten fühlen** *(fig. ugs.)* feel *or* be put out; **mit ~ und Kragen** *(fig. ugs.)* wearing a collar and tie; with a collar and tie on
Schlitten ['ʃlɪtn̩] **der; ~s, ~ a)** sledge; sled; *(Pferde~)* sleigh; *(Rodel~)* toboggan; **~ fahren** go tobogganing; **die Kinder fuhren mit dem ~ den Hang hinunter** the children tobogganed down the slope; **mit jmdm. ~ fahren** *(fig. ugs.)* bawl sb. out *(coll.)*; **ich werde mit ihm ~ fahren** *(fig. ugs.)* I'm going to give him hell *(coll.)*; **b)** *(salopp: Auto)* car; motor *(Brit.)*; **ein alter ~:** an old banger *(Brit. sl.)*; a jalopy; **c)** *(Technik: Maschinenteil)* carriage
Schlitten-: ~fahrt die sleigh ride; **~hund der** sled dog
schlittern ['ʃlɪtɐn] *itr. V.* **a)** *auch mit sein (rutschen)* slide; **b)** *mit sein (ins Rutschen kommen)* slip; slide; ⟨*vehicle*⟩ skid; ⟨*wheel*⟩ slip; **c)** *mit sein (fig.)* **in die Pleite ~:** slide into bankruptcy; **in ein Abenteuer ~:** stumble into an adventure
Schlitt-: ~schuh der [ice-]skate; **~schuh laufen** *od.* **fahren** [ice-]skate; **~schuh·laufen das** [ice-]skating *no art.*; **~schuh·läufer der** [ice-]skater
Schlitz [ʃlɪts] **der; ~es, ~e a)** slit; *(Briefkasten~, Automaten~)* slot; **seine Augen wurden zu ~en** *(fig.)* his eyes narrowed to slits; **b)** *(Hosen~)* flies *pl.*; fly; *(Jacken~)* vent
Schlitz·auge das; *meist Pl.* slit eye
schlitzäugig [-ɔygɪç] *Adj.* slit-eyed
schlitzen *tr. V.* slit; *(auf~)* slit open
Schlitz·ohr das *(ugs.)* wily *or* crafty devil
schlitzohrig *(ugs.)* **1.** *Adj.* wily; crafty. **2.** *adv.* craftily
schloh·weiß ['ʃlo:'vais] *Adj.* snow-white ⟨*hair, head*⟩; **er ist ~:** he has snow-white hair
schloß [ʃlɔs] *1. u. 3. Pers. Sg. Prät. v.* **schließen**
Schloß das; Schlosses, Schlösser ['ʃlœsɐ] **a)** *(Tür~, Gewehr~)* lock; **die Tür fiel/fiel krachend ins ~:** the door clicked/slammed to *or* shut; **b)** *(Vorhänge~)* padlock; **hinter ~ und Riegel** *(ugs.)* behind bars; **c)** *(Verschluß)* clasp; **d)** *(Wohngebäude)* castle; *(Palast)* palace; *(Herrschaftshaus)* mansion; *(in Frankreich)* château
Schloß-: ~an·lage die a) castle buildings *pl.*; **b)** *Pl.*; *s.* **~park**; **~berg der** castle hill
Schlößchen ['ʃlœsçən] **das; ~s, ~** *s.* **Schloß d:** small castle *etc.*
Schloße ['ʃlo:sə] **die; ~, ~n;** *meist Pl. (bes. md.)* hailstone
Schlosser der; ~s, ~: metalworker; *(Maschinen~)* fitter; *(für Schlösser)* locksmith; *(Auto~)* mechanic
Schlosserei die; ~, ~en a) *(Werkstatt)* metalworking shop; *(für Schlösser)* locksmith's workshop; **b)** *o. Pl.*; *s.* **~handwerk**
Schlosser-: ~handwerk das; *o. Pl.*; *s.* **Schlosser:** metalworking; fitter's trade; locksmithery; mechanic's trade; **das ~handwerk lernen** train to be a metalworker/fitter/locksmith/mechanic; **~werkstatt die** *s.* **Schlosserei a**
Schloß-: ~garten der castle *etc.* gardens *pl.*; **~herr der** owner of a/the castle *etc.*; **~hof der** castle *etc.* courtyard; **~hund der** *in* **heulen wie ein ~hund** *(ugs.)* cry one's eyes out; **~kapelle die** castle *etc.* chapel; **~park der** castle *etc.* grounds *pl.*; **~ruine die** ruined castle *etc.*
Schlot [ʃlo:t] **der; ~[e]s, ~e** *od.* **Schlöte** ['ʃlø:tə] **a)** *(bes. md.: Schornstein)* chimney[-stack]; *(eines Schiffes)* funnel; **rauchen** *od.* **qualmen wie ein ~** *(ugs.)* smoke like a chimney; **b)** *(Geol.: Eruptionsschacht)* chimney; vent; **c)** *(ugs. abwertend: Nichtsnutz)* good-for-nothing
Schlot·baron der *(abwertend)* industrial baron *or* tycoon
schlotterig *s.* **schlottrig**
schlottern ['ʃlɔtɐn] *itr. V.* **a)** shake; tremble; **jmdm. ~ die Knie** sb.'s knees are shaking *or* trembling; **am ganzen Leibe ~:** shake *or* tremble all over; **b)** ⟨*clothes*⟩ hang loose
schlottrig *Adj.* **a)** trembling; shaking; **b)** baggy ⟨*clothes*⟩
Schlucht [ʃlʊxt] **die; ~, ~en** ravine; gorge
schluchzen ['ʃlʊxtsn̩] *itr. V.* sob; **unter** *od.* **mit Schluchzen** sobbing; **in heftiges Schluchzen ausbrechen** burst into heavy sobbing; **die ~den Klänge der Geigen** *(fig.)* the sobbing strains of the violins
Schluchzer der; ~s, ~: sob
Schluck [ʃlʊk] **der; ~[e]s, ~e** *od.* **Schlücke** ['ʃlʏkə] **a)** swallow; mouthful; *(großer ~)* gulp; *(kleiner ~)* sip; **einen tüchtigen ~ [Bier] trinken** take a good *or* long swig [of beer] *(coll.)*; **sein Glas mit** *od.* **in einem** *od.* **auf einen ~ leeren** empty one's glass in one go *or (coll.)* swig; **hast du einen ~ zu trinken für uns?** have you got a drop of something for us to drink?; **b)** *(ugs.: Getränk)* **ein guter ~:** a good drop [of stuff] *(coll.)*; *(Wein)* a pleasant little number *(coll.)*
Schluck·auf der; ~s hiccups *pl.*; hiccoughs *pl.*; **[den** *od.* **einen] ~ haben/bekommen** have/get [the] hiccups *or* hiccoughs
Schlückchen ['ʃʏkçən] **das; ~s, ~:** sip; **du nimmst doch noch ein ~?** you'll have another drop, won't you?; **ich geh' zu Peter auf ein ~:** I'm off to Peter's for a drink
schlucken 1. *tr. V.* **a)** *(auch fig. ugs.)* swallow; **etw. hastig ~:** gulp sth. down; **b)** *(ugs.: einatmen)* swallow ⟨*dust*⟩; breathe in ⟨*gas*⟩; **c)** *(ugs. abwertend: in seinen Besitz bringen)* swallow [up]; **d)** *(ugs.: verbrauchen)* swallow up; guzzle ⟨*petrol*⟩. **2.** *itr. V. (auch fig.)* swallow; **Beschwerden beim Schlucken haben** have difficulty swallowing; **an etw.** *(Dat.)* **zu ~ haben** *(fig. ugs.)* find sth. hard to come to terms with
Schlucken der; ~s *s.* **Schluckauf**
Schlucker der; ~s, ~: *in* **armer ~** *(ugs.)* poor devil *or (Brit. coll.)* blighter
Schluck·impfung die oral vaccination
schlucksen ['ʃlʊksn̩] *itr. V. (ugs.)* hiccup; hiccough
schluck·weise *Adv.* in sips
Schluderei die; ~, ~en *(ugs. abwertend)* **a)** *o. Pl.* sloppiness; slipshod work; **b)** *(Fall von Nachlässigkeit)* slipshod piece of work; botched job; **~en** slipshod work *sing.*; botching *sing.*
schluderig *s.* **schludrig**
schludern ['ʃlu:dɐn] *itr. V. (ugs. abwertend)* work sloppily; **bei etw. ~:** make a botched job of sth.; *(etw. oberflächlich bearbeiten)* skimp sth.; **es wird zuviel geschludert** too much work is being botched

schludrig *(ugs. abwertend)* **1.** *Adj.* **a)** *(nachlässig)* slipshod ‹*work, examination*›; botched ‹*job*›; slapdash ‹*person, work*›; **eine ~e Schrift** a messy scrawl; **b)** *(schlampig [aussehend])* scruffy. **2.** *adv.* **a)** *(nachlässig)* in a slipshod *or* slapdash way; **b)** *(schlampig [aussehend])* scruffily

Schludrigkeit die; ~, ~en *(ugs. abwertend)* **a)** *o. Pl.* sloppiness; *(eines Menschen)* slapdash ways *pl.*; *(der Kleidung)* scruffiness; **b)** *(Fall von Nachlässigkeit)* sloppiness; **diese ~en im Detail** this sloppiness when it comes to detail; this slipshod treatment of detail

schlug [ʃlu:k] *1. u. 3. Pers. Sg. Prät. v.* **schlagen**

Schlummer ['ʃlʊmɐ] **der; ~s** *(geh.)* slumber *(poet./rhet.)*; *(Nickerchen)* doze; **nach langem ~:** after a long slumber *(poet./rhet.)*

Schlummer·lied das *(geh.)* lullaby; cradle-song

schlummern *itr. V.* **a)** *(geh.: schlafen)* slumber *(poet./rhet.)*; *(dösen)* doze; **tief ~d** in a deep slumber; **b)** *(fig.: verborgen liegen)* **[in jmdm.] ~:** lie dormant [in sb.]; **~des Talent/~de Energie** latent talent/energy

Schlummer·rolle die bolster

Schlumpf [ʃlʊmpf] **der; ~s, Schlümpfe** ['ʃlʏmpfe] *(Comicfigur)* smurf

Schlund [ʃlʊnt] **der; ~[e]s, Schlünde** ['ʃlʏndə] **a)** *(Rachen)* [back of the] throat; pharynx *(Anat.)*; *(eines Tieres)* maw; **b)** *(geh.: gähnende Öffnung)* [gaping] mouth; *(Abgrund)* chasm; abyss

Schlunze ['ʃlʊntsə] **die; ~, ~n** *(salopp abwertend, bes. nordd.)* slut

schlüpfen ['ʃlʏpfn̩] *itr. V.; mit sein* slip; **in ein/aus einem Kleid** *usw.* **~:** slip into *or* slip on/slip out of *or* slip off a dress *etc.*; **[aus dem Ei] ~:** ‹*chick*› hatch out; **keiner kann aus seiner Haut ~** *(fig.)* nobody can completely change his/her identity

Schlüpfer der; ~s, ~ *(veralt.)* *(für Damen)* knickers *pl. (Brit.)*; panties *pl.*; *(für Herren)* [under]pants *pl. or* trunks *pl.*; **ein ~:** a pair of knickers/underpants

Schlupf·loch ['ʃlʊpf-] **das a)** *(Schlupfwinkel)* hiding-place; **b)** *(Durchschlupf)* hole; *(Lücke im Gesetz usw.)* loophole

schlüpfrig ['ʃlʏpfrɪç] *Adj.* **a)** *(feucht u. glatt)* slippery; **b)** *(abwertend: anstößig)* lewd

Schlüpfrigkeit die; ~, ~en a) *o. Pl. (feuchte Glätte)* slipperiness; **b)** *(Anstößigkeit)* lewdness

Schlupf-: ~wespe die ichneumon fly; **~winkel der** hiding-place; *(von Banditen, Flüchtlingen usw.)* hide-out

schlurfen ['ʃlʊrfn̩] *itr. V.; mit sein* shuffle; *(ohne Richtungsangabe)* shuffle along

schlürfen ['ʃlʏrfn̩] **1.** *tr. V. (geräuschvoll)* slurp [up] *(coll.)*; drink noisily; *(genußvoll)* savour; *(in kleinen Schlucken)* sip. **2.** *itr. V.* slurp *(coll.)*; drink noisily

Schluß [ʃlʊs] **der; Schlusses, Schlüsse** ['ʃlʏsə] **a)** *o. Pl. (Endzeitpunkt)* end; *(eines Vortrags o. ä.)* conclusion; *(Laden~)* closing time; *(Dienst~)* knocking-off time; **nach/gegen ~ der Aufführung** after/towards the end of the performance; **mit etw. ist ~:** sth. is at an end *or* over; *(ugs.: etw. ist ruiniert)* sth. has had it *(coll.)*; **mit ihm ist ~** *(ugs.)* it's all up with him; *(das Verhältnis ist beendet)* it's all over with him; *(seine Karriere ist beendet)* he's past it; **mit dem Rauchen/Trinken ist jetzt ~:** there's to be no more smoking/drinking; you must stop smoking/drinking; *(auf sich bezogen)* I've given up smoking/drinking; **jetzt ist aber ~ [damit]!** that's enough of that; **~ jetzt!, ~ damit!** stop it!; that'll do!; **~ für heute!** that's it *or* that'll do for today; **am** *od.* **zum ~:** at the end; *(schließlich)* in the end; finally; **am** *od.* **zum ~ des Jahres** at the end of the year; **zum ~ möchte ich noch darauf hinweisen, daß ...:** finally *or* in conclusion I should like to mention that ...; **kurz vor ~:** just before closing time; *(im Büro)* just before knocking-off time; **~ machen** *(ugs.)* stop; *(Feierabend machen)* knock off; *(seine Stellung aufgeben)* pack in one's job *(sl.)*; *(eine Freundschaft usw. lösen)* break it off; *(sich das Leben nehmen)* end it all *(coll.)*; **ich mache ~ für heute** I'm calling it a day; **ich muß jetzt ~ machen** *(am Telefon)* I'll have to go now; *(am Briefende)* I must stop now; **mit etw. ~ machen** stop sth.; **mit jmdm. ~ machen** finish with sb.; break it off with sb.; **b)** *(letzter Abschnitt)* end; *(eines Zuges)* back; *(eines Buchs, Schauspiels usw.)* ending; **c)** *(Folgerung)* conclusion **(auf +** *Akk.* regarding); *(Logik: Ableitung)* deduction; **Schlüsse aus etw. ziehen** draw conclusions from sth.; **ich werde meine Schlüsse daraus ziehen** I shall draw my own conclusions; **d)** *o. Pl. (Technik, Bauw.)* **einen guten ~ haben** ‹*piston*› form a good seal; ‹*door, window*› be a good fit; **e)** *(Reiten) o. Pl.* **diese Reiterin hat einen guten ~:** this rider keeps a good leg position; **mit den Knien ~ nehmen** grip with one's knees; **f)** *(Musik)* cadence

Schluß-: ~ab·stimmung die *(Parl.)* final vote; **~akkord der** *(Musik)* final chord; *(geh. fig.: Ausklang)* conclusion; finale; **~akte die** *(Dipl.)* final communiqué; **~bemerkung die** concluding remark; **~bilanz die** *(Kaufmannsspr.)* annual balance sheet; *(nach Abwicklung eines Unternehmens)* final balance [sheet]; **~drittel das** *(Eishockey)* third *or* final period

Schlüssel ['ʃlʏsl̩] **der; ~s, ~ a)** key; **der ~ zur Wohnung/Wohnungstür** the key of the flat *(Brit.) or (Amer.)* apartment/the front door key; **b)** *(Schrauben~)* spanner; **c)** *(Lösungsweg, Lösungsheft)* key; *(Kode)* code; cipher; **der ~ zum Erfolg** *(fig.)* the key to *or* secret of succes; **d)** *(Musik)* clef; **e)** *(Aufgliederungsschema)* scheme *or* pattern [of distribution]

schlüssel-, Schlüssel-: ~bart der bit [of a/the key]; **~anhänger der** key-fob; **~bein das** *(Anat.)* collar-bone; clavicle *(Anat.)*; **~blume die** cowslip; *(Primel)* primula; **~brett das** keyboard; **~bund der** *od.* **das** bunch of keys; **~erlebnis das** *(Psych.)* crucial experience; **~fertig** *Adj.* ready to move into *postpos.*; **~figur die** key figure; **~industrie die** *(Wirtsch.)* key industry; **~kind das** *(ugs.)* latchkey child; **~loch das** keyhole; **~position die** *s.* **~stellung**; **~ring der** key-ring; **~roman der** *(Literaturw.)* roman à clef; **~stellung die** key position; **~wort das;** *Pl.* **~wörter** keyword; *(für ein Kombinationsschloß, fig.: verschlüsseltes Wort)* code word

schluß-, Schluß-: ~endlich *Adv. (bes. schweiz.)* finally; *(immerhin)* after all; **~folgern** *tr. V.* conclude **(aus** from); **~folgerung die** conclusion, inference **(aus** from); **~formel die** conventional ending

schlüssig ['ʃlʏsɪç] **1.** *Adj.* **a)** conclusive ‹*proof, evidence*›; convincing, logical ‹*argument, conclusion, statement*›; **b) sich** *(Dat.)* **[darüber] ~ sein** have made up one's mind; **sich** *(Dat.)* **[darüber] ~ werden** make up one's mind. **2.** *adv.* conclusively

Schlüssigkeit die; ~: conclusiveness

Schluß-: ~kapitel das *(auch fig.)* final *or* closing chapter; **~läufer der** *(Leichtathletik)* last runner, anchor man *(in a relay team)*; **~leuchte die** *s.* **~licht**; **~licht das;** *Pl.* **~lichter a)** *(an Fahrzeugen)* tail- *or* rear-light; **b)** *(ugs.: letzter einer Kolonne)* **das ~licht machen** *od.* **bilden/sein** bring up the rear; **c)** *(ugs.: Letzter, Schlechtester)* **das ~licht der Bundesliga/Klasse sein** be bottom of the [national] league table/class; **~mann der;** *Pl.* **~männer** *(Ballspiele)* goalie *(coll.)*; **~pfiff der** *(Ballspiele)* final whistle; **~phase die** final phase; final stages *pl.*; **~punkt der a)** *(Satzzeichen)* full stop; **b)** *(Abschluß)* conclusion; *(einer Feier)* finale; **einen ~punkt unter etw.** *(Akk.)* **setzen** put an end to sth. once and for all; *(etw. beendet sein lassen)* declare sth. to be over and done with; **~runde die** *(Sport: eines Rennens)* final *or* last lap; *(Boxen, Ringen, fig.: des Wahlkampfes usw.)* final *or* last round; **~satz der a)** *(abschließender Satz)* last *or* concluding sentence; **b)** *(Musik)* last movement; finale; **c)** *(bes. Philos.)* conclusion; **~sprung der** *(Turnen)* jump with legs together; **~stein der** *(Archit.)* keystone; *(im Rippengewölbe)* boss; **~strich der** [bottom] line; **einen ~strich ziehen/unter etw.** *(Akk.)* **ziehen** *(fig.)* make a clean break/draw a line under sth.; **~verkauf der** [end-of-season] sale[s *pl.*]; **~wort das;** *Pl.* **~worte** final word[s]; **ein kurzes ~wort** a few closing remarks; **das ~wort haben** make the closing speech; *(in einer Debatte)* wind up

Schmach [ʃma:x] **die; ~** *(geh.)* ignominy; shame; *(Demütigung)* humiliation; **etw. als ~ empfinden** consider sth. a disgrace; regard sth. as ignominious; **jmdm. [eine] ~ antun** *od.* **bereiten** bring shame/humiliation upon sb.; **[mit] ~ und Schande** [in] deep disgrace

schmachten ['ʃmaxtn̩] *itr. V. (geh.)* **a)** *(leiden)* languish; **in der Hitze ~:** fade away in the heat; **jmdn./einen Liebhaber ~ lassen** leave sb. to suffer *or (coll.)* stew/let a lover pine away; **b)** *(spött.: sich sehnen)* **nach jmdm./etw. ~:** pine *or* yearn for sb./sth.

schmachtend *(spött.)* **1.** *Adj.* soulful *(coll.)* ‹*look, song*›; languishing ‹*tones*›; schmaltzy *(coll.)* ‹*song, music*›. **2.** *adv.* soulfully *(coll.)*

Schmacht·fetzen der *(salopp abwertend)* tear-jerker *(coll.)*

schmächtig *Adj.* slight; weedy *(coll. derog.)*; **einen ~en Körper haben** be of slight build

Schmacht·locke die *(ugs. spött.)* kiss-curl

schmach·voll *(geh.)* **1.** *Adj.* ignominious; *(erniedrigend)* humiliating. **2.** *adv.* ignominiously; *(erniedrigend)* humiliatingly; **~ untergehen** come to an ignominious end

schmackhaft ['ʃmakhaft] **1.** *Adj.* tasty; **jmdm. etw. ~ machen** *(fig. ugs.)* make sth. palatable to sb. **2.** *adv.* in a tasty way; **etw. ~ zubereiten** make sth. tasty

Schmäh der; ~s, ~[s] *(österr. ugs.)* **a)** [tall] story; *(Trick)* con *(coll.)*; **einen ~ führen** entertain; tell jokes; **b)** *(Sarkasmus)* sarcasm; **Wiener ~:** Viennese snide humour *(coll.)*

schmähen ['ʃmɛ:ən] *tr. V. (geh.)* revile

schmählich 1. *Adj.* shameful; *(verächtlich)* despicable. **2.** *adv.* shamefully; *(in verächtlicher Weise)* despicably

Schmäh-: ~rede die diatribe; **~schrift die** piece of invective; *(Pamphlet)* defamatory pamphlet

Schmähung die; ~, ~en diatribe; **~en** abuse *sing.*; invective *sing.*; **jmdn. mit ~en überschütten** heap invective *or* abuse on sb.

Schmäh·wort das; *Pl.* **~worte** term of abuse; **~e** abuse *sing.*

schmal [ʃma:l]; **schmaler** *od.* **schmäler** ['ʃmɛ:lɐ]; **schmalst...** *od.* **schmälst...: 1.** *Adj.* **a)** narrow; slim, slender ‹*hips, hands, figure, etc.*›; thin ‹*lips, face, nose, etc.*›; **ein ~er Band, ein ~es Büchlein** a slim volume; **~er werden** ‹*person, face*› get thinner; **b)** *(geh.: knapp, karg)* meagre ‹*income, profit, etc.*›; meagre, scanty ‹*food, selection*›; **mit ~em Geldbeutel** of restricted means. **2.** *adv.* **a) eine ~ geschnittene Hose** slim-fit trousers; **b)** *(geh.: knapp, karg)* meagrely

schmalbrüstig [-brʏstɪç] narrow-chested; *(fig.)* narrow ‹*cupboard, views, etc.*›

schmäler *s.* **schmal**

schmälern *tr. V.* diminish; reduce; restrict, curtail ‹*rights*›; *(herabsetzen)* belittle

Schmälerung die; ~, ~en reduction; *(Herabsetzung)* belittlement
Schmal-: ~film der 8 mm/16 mm cine film; **~filmer der** cine photographer *(using 16 mm or 8 mm camera)*; **~film·kamera die** 8 mm/16 mm cine camera; **~hans** *in* **bei ihnen ist ~hans Küchenmeister** *(ugs. veralt.)* they are on short commons; **~seite die** short side; *(eines Korridors usw.)* end; **~spur die** *(Eisenb.)* narrow gauge
Schmalspur- *(ugs.)* small-time *(coll.)* ⟨*politician, academic*⟩; *(dilettantisch)* lightweight ⟨*academic*⟩; amateur ⟨*engineer*⟩
Schmalspur·bahn die narrow-gauge railway
schmälst... *s.* **schmal**
schmal·wüchsig *Adj.* slender ⟨*person, tree, etc.*⟩; ⟨*person*⟩ of slender build
[1]**Schmalz** [ʃmalts] **das; ~es** *(Schweine~)* lard
[2]**Schmalz der; ~es** *(ugs. abwertend)* **a)** *(Sentimentalität)* schmaltz *(coll.)*; **mit viel ~**: with plenty of slushy *or* soppy sentimentality *(coll.)*; **b)** *(Lied o. ä.)* schmaltz *no indef. art. (coll.)*
Schmalz·brot das slice of bread and dripping
schmalzig *(abwertend)* **1.** *Adj.* schmaltzy *(coll.)*; slushy[-sentimental]. **2.** *adv.* with schmaltzy *(coll.) or* slushy sentimentality; **~ sprechen** talk in a slushy-sentimental way; ⟨*lover*⟩ talk in a lovey-dovey tone *(coll.)*
Schmalzler ['ʃmaltslɐ] **der; ~s** *(bayr.)* snuff *(containg a trace of animal fat)*
Schmankerl ['ʃmaŋkɐl] **das; ~s, ~n** *(bayr., österr.)* delicacy; *(fig.)* treat
schmarotzen [ʃma'rɔtsn̩] *itr. V.* **a)** *(abwertend)* sponge; free-load *(sl.)*; **bei jmdm. ~**: sponge on sb.; **b)** *(Biol.)* live as a parasite **(in/auf** + *Dat.* in/on); **~d** parasitic
Schmarotzer der; ~s, ~ a) *(abwertend)* sponger; free-loader *(sl.)*; **b)** *(Biol.)* parasite
Schmarotzer·pflanze die parasitic plant
Schmarotzertum das; ~s a) *(Biol.)* parasitism; **b)** *(abwertend)* sponging; free-loading *(sl.)*
Schmarren ['ʃmarən] **der; ~s, ~ a)** *(österr., auch südd.) pancake broken up with a fork after frying;* **b)** *(ugs. abwertend: Unsinn)* trash; rubbish; **das ist ein ~**: it's a load *(coll.)* of trash *or* rubbish; **c) einen ~** *(salopp: nichts)* not a thing; damn all *(sl.)*; *(adverbiell)* not at all; no way; **das geht dich einen ~ an** it's none of your damn business *(coll.)*
Schmatz [ʃmats] **der; ~es, ~e** *od.* **Schmätze** ['ʃmɛtsə] *(ugs.)* loud kiss; smacker *(sl.)*
schmatzen *itr. V.* smack one's lips; *(geräuschvoll essen)* eat/drink noisily; *(fig.)* ⟨*mud, wet ground*⟩ squelch; **sie küßten sich, daß es schmatzte** they gave one another a resounding kiss *or* a *(sl.)* real smacker
schmauchen ['ʃmauxn̩] **1.** *tr. V.* puff away at ⟨*pipe, cigar, etc.*⟩. **2.** *itr. V.* puff away
Schmaus [ʃmaus] **der; ~es, Schmäuse** ['ʃmɔyzə] *(veralt., noch scherzh.)* [good] spread *(coll.)*; *(reichhaltig)* feast; **ein köstlicher ~**: a delicious repast *(formal/joc.) or (coll.)* spread
schmausen *(veralt.)* **1.** *itr. V.* eat with relish; **vergnügt ~**: tuck in contentedly *(coll.)*. **2.** *tr. V.* eat ⟨*food*⟩ with relish
schmecken ['ʃmɛkn̩] **1.** *itr. V.* taste **(nach** of); **[gut] ~**: taste good; **das hat geschmeckt** that was good; *(war köstlich)* that was delicious; **nach nichts ~**: not taste of anything; be tasteless; **das schmeckt nach mehr** *(ugs.)* it tastes *or* it's moreish *(coll.)*; **schmeckt es [dir]?** are you enjoying it *or* your meal?; [how] do you like it?; **wenn man krank ist, schmeckt es einem oft nicht [richtig]** when you're ill you're often off your food; **bei dir schmeckt es mir immer ausgezeichnet** your meals are always delicious; **laßt es euch ~!** enjoy your food!; tuck in *(coll.)!*; **wie schmeckt dir die Ehe?** *(fig.)* how do you like married life?; **diese Kritik schmeckte ihm gar nicht** *(fig.)* this criticism was not at all to his liking. **2.** *tr. V.* taste; *(kosten)* sample; **die Rute zu ~ bekommen** *(fig.)* get a taste of the rod
Schmeichelei die; ~, ~en flattering remark; blandishment; **die ~en, die er ihr sagte** the flattering things he said to her
schmeichelhaft 1. *Adj.* flattering; complimentary ⟨*words, speech*⟩; **wenig ~**: not very flattering. **2.** *adv.* flatteringly
schmeicheln ['ʃmaiçl̩n] *itr. V.* **a) jmdm. ~**: flatter sb.; **er schmeichelte ihr, sie sei ...** *od.* **daß sie ... sei** he flattered her by saying she was ...; **etw. in ~dem Ton sagen** say sth. in honeyed tones; **es schmeichelt ihm, daß ...**: he finds it flattering that ...; **„Zwerg" ist noch geschmeichelt** 'dwarf' is putting it mildly; **b)** *(liebkosen)* be affectionate; **die Katze strich ~d um ihre Füße** the cat rubbed affectionately against her feet
Schmeichel·wort das; *Pl.* **~worte;** *meist Pl.* blandishment; **~e** honeyed words; flattery *sing.*
Schmeichler ['ʃmaiçlɐ] **der; ~s, ~, Schmeichlerin die; ~, ~nen** flatterer
schmeichlerisch 1. *Adj.* flattering; honeyed ⟨*words, tone*⟩; *(sich anbiedernd)* cajoling ⟨*words, tone, glance*⟩. **2.** *adv.* cajolingly; *(im ~en Ton)* in honeyed tones
schmeißen ['ʃmaisn̩] *(ugs.)* **1.** *unr. tr. V.* **a)** *(werfen)* chuck *(coll.)*; sling *(coll.)*; *(schleudern)* fling; hurl; **etw. nach jmdm. ~**: throw *or (coll.)* chuck sth. at sb.; **die Tür [ins Schloß] ~**: slam the door; **jmdn. aus dem Zimmer/der Schule ~**: chuck sb. out of the room/school *(coll.)*; **b)** *(abbrechen, aufgeben)* chuck in *(coll.)* ⟨*job, studies, etc.*⟩; **c)** *(spendieren)* stand ⟨*drink*⟩; **eine Lage** *od.* **Runde [Bier] ~**: get *or* stand a round [of beer]; **[für jmdn.] eine Party ~**: throw a party [for sb.] *(coll.)*; **d)** *(bewältigen)* handle; deal with; **wir werden den Laden schon ~**: we'll manage OK *(coll.)*; **e)** *(Theater-, Fernsehjargon: mißlingen lassen)* fluff *(sl.)* ⟨*scene, number*⟩; make a mess of ⟨*performance*⟩. **2.** *unr. refl. V.* **a)** *(sich werfen)* throw oneself; *(mit Wucht)* hurl oneself; **sich jmdm. an den Hals ~** ⟨*woman*⟩ throw oneself at sb.; *s. auch* **Schale d; b) sich in seinen Smoking/in ein festliches Kleid** *usw.* **~**: get togged up *(sl.)* in one's dinner-jacket/a party dress *etc.* **3.** *unr. itr. V.* **mit Steinen/Tomaten** *usw.* **[nach jmdm.] ~**: chuck stones/tomatoes *etc.* [at sb.] *(coll.)*; **mit Geld um sich ~** *(fig.)* throw one's money around; lash out *(coll.)*; **mit Geschenken um sich ~** *(fig.)* lash out *(coll.)* on masses of presents
Schmeiß·fliege die blowfly; *(blaue ~)* bluebottle
Schmelz der; ~es, ~e a) *(Glasur)* glaze; *(Email, Zahn~)* enamel; **b)** *(geh.: Lieblichkeit) (der Jugend)* bloom; *(von Farben)* lustre; soft gleam; *(Wohlklang)* mellifluousness
Schmelze die; ~, ~n a) *(das [Zer]schmelzen)* [process of] melting; **b)** *(Technik: verflüssigtes Material)* melt
schmelzen ['ʃmɛltsn̩] **1.** *unr. itr. V.; mit sein* **a)** melt; *(fig.)* ⟨*doubts, apprehension, etc.*⟩ dissolve, fade away; **sein Vermögen war geschmolzen** *(fig.)* his fortune had melted away; **b)** *(fig.: weich werden)* soften; **ihm schmolz das Herz** his heart melted. **2.** *unr. tr. V.* melt; smelt ⟨*ore*⟩; render ⟨*fat*⟩
schmelzend 1. *Adj.* melting ⟨*glance, tones*⟩; mellifluous, mellow ⟨*voice, tones, etc.*⟩. **2.** *adv.* **~ singen** sing in melting tones
Schmelz-: ~hütte die smelting works *sing. or pl.*; **~käse der** processed cheese; **~ofen der** *(Technik)* smelting furnace; **~punkt der** melting-point; **~tiegel der** crucible; melting-pot *(esp. fig.)*; **~wasser das;** *Pl.* **~wasser** melted snow and ice; melt-water *(Geol.)*
Schmerbauch ['ʃme:ɐ̯-] **der** *(ugs.)* **a)** *(dicker Bauch)* pot-belly; paunch; **b)** *(dickbäuchiger Mensch)* pot-belly
Schmerle ['ʃmɛrlə] **die; ~, ~n** *(Zool.)* loach
Schmerz [ʃmɛrts] **der; ~es, ~en a)** *(physisch)* pain; *(dumpf u. anhaltend)* ache; **wo haben Sie ~en?** where does it hurt?; **~en im Rücken/Arm** pain in one's back/arm; *(an verschiedenen Stellen)* pains in one's back/arm; **~en haben** be in pain; **etw. mit** *od.* **unter ~en tun** do sth. in pain *or* agony; **vor ~[en] weinen/sich vor ~en winden** cry with/writhe in pain *or* agony; **~, laß nach!** *(ugs. scherzh.)* oh no! it can't be!; that's the last straw!; **b)** *(psychisch)* pain; *(Kummer)* grief; **ein seelischer ~**: mental anguish *or* suffering; **jmdm. ~en bereiten** cause sb. pain/grief; **der ~ um jmdn.** grief for sb.; **tiefen ~ über etw.** *(Akk.)* **empfinden** be deeply grieved by sth.; **etw. mit ~en erkennen** realize sth. with a sense of grief; **jmdn./etw. mit ~en erwarten** wait for sb./sth. in an agony of impatience; **hast du sonst noch ~en?** *(ugs. spött.)* is there anything else you want?
schmerz·empfindlich *Adj.* sensitive to pain *pred.*; **~ sein** have a low pain threshold
Schmerz·empfindlichkeit die; ~: sensitivity to pain
schmerzen 1. *tr. V.* **jmdn. ~**: hurt sb.; *(Kummer bereiten)* grieve sb.; cause sb. sorrow; **es schmerzt mich, daß ...**: it grieves *or* pains me that ... **2.** *itr. V.* hurt; **seine Wunde schmerzt** his wound is hurting *or* painful; **heftig ~**: be intensely painful
Schmerzens-: ~geld das *(Rechtsspr.)* compensation *(for pain and suffering caused)*; exemplary damages *(Law)*; **~laut der** cry of pain; *(stöhnend)* moan; **~mann der** *(Kunstwiss.)* Ecce Homo; **~mutter die** *(Kunstwiss.)* Mater Dolorosa; **~schrei der** cry of pain; *(laut)* scream [of pain]
schmerz·frei *Adj.* free of pain *pred.*; painless ⟨*operation*⟩
Schmerz·grenze die *(fig.)* **jetzt/dann ist die ~ erreicht** this/that is the absolute limit
schmerzhaft *Adj.* painful; *(wund)* sore
schmerzlich 1. *Adj.* painful; distressing; **die ~e Gewißheit haben, daß ...**: be painfully aware that ...; **es ist mir eine ~e Pflicht, Ihnen mitteilen zu müssen, daß ...**: it is my painful duty to inform you that ... **2.** *adv.* painfully
schmerz-, Schmerz-: ~lindernd 1. *Adj.* pain-relieving; **~linderndes Mittel** pain-relieving drug; palliative; **2.** *adv.* **~lindernd wirken** relieve pain; **~los 1.** *Adj.* painless; **2.** *adv.* painlessly; *s. auch* **kurz 2c; ~schwelle die** *(Physiol.)* pain threshold; **~stillend 1.** *Adj.* pain-killing; analgesic *(Med.)*; **~stillendes Mittel** pain-killer; analgesic; **2.** *adv.* **~stillend wirken** have a pain-killing *or* analgesic effect; **~tablette die** pain-killing *or (Med.)* analgesic tablet; **~unempfindlich** *Adj.* insensitive to pain *pred.*; **~verzerrt** *Adj.* ⟨*face, smile*⟩ distorted *or* twisted with pain; **~voll 1.** *Adj.* **a)** *(physisch)* [very] painful; **b)** *(psychisch)* painful; distressing; **2.** *adv.* painfully
Schmetter·ball der *(Tennis usw.)* smash
Schmetterling der; ~s, ~e a) butterfly; *(Nachtfalter)* moth; **~e Europas** butterflies and moths of Europe; **b)** *o. Art. u. o. Pl. (Schwimmen)* butterfly
Schmetterlingsblütler [-bly:tlɐ] **der; ~s, ~**: papilionaceous plant
Schmetterlings·stil der; *o. Pl. (Schwimmen)* butterfly [stroke]
schmettern ['ʃmɛtɐn] **1.** *tr. V.* **a)** *(schleudern)* hurl **(an** + *Akk.* at, **gegen** against); **jmdn./etw. zu Boden ~**: send sb./sth. crashing to the ground; **die Tür ins Schloß ~**:

slam the door hard; **b)** *(laut spielen, singen usw.)* blare out ⟨*march, music*⟩; ⟨*person*⟩ sing lustily ⟨*song*⟩; bellow ⟨*order*⟩; **einen Tusch ~:** unleash a loud flourish; **c)** *(Tennis usw.)* smash ⟨*ball*⟩. **2.** *itr. V.* **a)** *mit sein (aufprallen)* crash; smash; **b)** *(schallen)* ⟨*trumpet, music, etc.*⟩ blare out; **ein ~der Klang** a blare

Schmetter·schlag der *(bes. Faustball, Volleyball)* smash

Schmied [ʃmi:t] **der; ~[e]s, ~e** blacksmith; *s. auch* **Glück b**

schmiedbar *Adj.* malleable

Schmiede die; ~, ~en smithy; forge

schmiede-, Schmiede-: ~arbeit die piece of wrought-iron work; **~arbeiten** [pieces *pl.* of] wrought-iron work *sing.*; **~eisen das** wrought iron; *(schmiedbares Eisen)* forgeable iron; **~eisern** *Adj.* wrought-iron; **~hammer der** drop-hammer; **~kunst die** blacksmith's craft

schmieden *tr. V. (auch fig.)* forge (**zu** into, **aus** from, out of); **Pläne/ein Komplott ~** *(fig.)* hatch plans/a plot; **Verse** *od.* **Reime ~** *(spött.)* concoct verses; **an eine Mauer** *usw.* **geschmiedet werden** ⟨*prisoner*⟩ be fettered to a wall *etc.*

schmiegen ['ʃmi:gn̩] **1.** *refl. V.* snuggle, nestle (**in** + *Akk.* in); **sich an jmdn. ~:** snuggle [close] up to sb.; **sie schmiegte sich eng an seine Seite** she pressed *or* nestled close to his side; **sich an etw.** *(Akk.)* **~** *(fig.)* ⟨*road*⟩ hug sth.; ⟨*village*⟩ cling to sth.; **sich an jmds. Körper ~** *(fig.)* ⟨*dress*⟩ hug sb.'s figure. **2.** *tr. V.* press (**an** + *Akk.* against)

schmiegsam *Adj.* supple ⟨*leather, material*⟩

Schmierage [ʃmi'ra:ʒə] **die; ~** *(ugs. scherzh.) s.* **Schmiererei a**

[1]**Schmiere die; ~, ~n a)** *(Schmierfett)* grease; **b)** *(schwieriger Schmutz)* greasy *or* slimy mess; **c)** *(ugs. abwertend: Provinztheater)* flea-pit *(sl.)* of a provincial theatre; *(veralt.: Wanderbühne)* troop of second-rate barnstormers

[2]**Schmiere die; ~:** *in* **[bei etw.] ~ stehen** *(ugs.)* act as look-out [while sth. takes place]; *(in der Schule)* keep cave *(Sch. sl.)* [while sth. is going on]

schmieren ['ʃmi:rən] **1.** *tr. V.* **a)** *(mit Schmiermitteln)* lubricate; *(mit Schmierfett)* grease; **[gehen** *od.* **laufen] wie geschmiert** *(ugs.)* [go] like clockwork *or* without a hitch; **b)** *(streichen, auftragen)* spread ⟨*butter, jam, etc.*⟩ (**auf** + *Akk.* on); **Salbe auf eine Wunde ~:** apply ointment to a wound; **sich** *(Dat.)* **Creme ins Gesicht/Pomade ins Haar ~:** rub cream into one's face/haircream into one's hair; **c)** *(mit Aufstrich)* **Brote/Schmalzbrote ~:** spread slices of bread/bread and dripping; **d)** *(abwertend: unsauber schreiben)* scrawl ⟨*essay, school work*⟩; *(schnell und nachlässig schreiben)* scribble, dash off ⟨*article, play, etc.*⟩; **Parolen an Wände** *usw.* **~:** scrawl *or* daub slogans on walls *etc.*; **e)** *(salopp: bestechen)* **jmdn. ~:** grease sb.'s palm; **f) jmdm. eine ~** *(salopp)* give sb. a clout *(coll.)*; **eine geschmiert kriegen** *(salopp)* get a clout *(coll.)*; **g)** *(Kartenspiel, bes. Skatjargon)* play ⟨*high-counting card*⟩ to a trick won by one's partner. **2.** *itr. V.* **a)** ⟨*oil, grease*⟩ lubricate; **b)** *(ugs. unsauber schreiben)* ⟨*person*⟩ scrawl, scribble; ⟨*pen, ink*⟩ smudge, make smudges

Schmieren-: ~komödiant der *(abwertend)* cheapjack play-actor; **~komödie die, ~theater das** *(abwertend)* shoddy farce

Schmiererei die; ~, ~en *(ugs. abwertend)* **a)** *o. Pl. (unsauberes Schreiben)* scrawling; scribbling; **eine einzige ~:** one long scrawl; *(Kleckserei)* nothing but a smudgy mess; **b)** *(unsauber Geschriebenes)* scrawl; scribble

Schmier-: ~fett das grease; **~film der a)** *(auf der Straße usw.)* greasy surface; **b)** *(Technik)* film of lubricant; **~fink der** *(ugs. abwertend)* **a)** *(im Schreiben)* messy writer; *(jmd., der Wände beschmiert)* graffiti-writer; *(jmd., der Diffamierendes schreibt)* muck-raker; **b)** *(Kind, das sich/etw. schmutzig macht)* mucky pup *(coll.)*; **~geld das** *(ugs. abwertend)* slush-money; **~heft das** rough-book

schmierig *Adj.* **a)** *(feucht-klebrig)* greasy ⟨*surface, clothes, hands, step, etc.*⟩; slimy ⟨*earth, surface*⟩; **b)** *(schmutzig)* mucky; *(dreckig)* filthy; **c)** *(abwertend: widerlich freundlich)* slimy, *(coll.)* smarmy ⟨*person*⟩; **d)** *(abwertend: zweideutig)* dirty, smutty ⟨*joke etc.*⟩

Schmier-: ~käse der *(bes. nordd.) s.* **Streichkäse; ~mittel das** lubricant; **~öl das** lubricating oil; **~papier das** scrap paper; **~seife die** soft soap

schmilzt [ʃmɪltst] *2. u. 3. Pers. Sg. Präsens v.* **schmelzen**

Schminke ['ʃmɪŋkə] **die; ~, ~n** make-up

schminken 1. *tr. V.* make up ⟨*face, eyes*⟩; **die Lippen ~:** put lipstick on; **der Bericht ist stark geschminkt** *(fig.)* the report has been given a very favourable slant. **2.** *refl. V.* make oneself up; put on make-up; **sich leicht/stark** *od.* **kräftig ~:** put on a little/a lot of make-up

Schmink-: ~stift der stick of make-up *or* greasepaint; **~tisch der** make-up table; **~topf der** make-up jar

Schmirgel ['ʃmɪrgl̩] **der; ~s** emery

schmirgeln ['ʃmɪrgln] *tr. V.* **a)** *(schleifen)* rub down; *(bes. mit Sandpapier)* sand; **b)** *(durch Schmirgeln entfernen)* remove ⟨*paint, rust*⟩ with emery-paper/sandpaper

Schmirgel·papier das emery-paper; *(Sandpapier)* sandpaper

schmiß [ʃmɪs] *1. u. 3. Pers. Sg. Prät. v.* **schmeißen**

Schmiß der; Schmisses, Schmisse a) *(Fechtwunde)* [sabre] cut; *(Narbe)* duelling scar; **b)** *o. Pl. (veralt.: Schwung, Elan)* punch; zip

schmissig *(veralt.)* **1.** *Adj.* rousing ⟨*march, song*⟩; zippy ⟨*couplets etc.*⟩. **2.** *adv.* rousingly; with a swing

Schmock [ʃmɔk] **der; ~[e]s, Schmöcke** ['ʃmœkə] *(abwertend: Schreiberling)* hack writer

Schmöker ['ʃmø:kɐ] **der; ~s, ~** *(ugs.)* lightweight adventure story/romance; **ein dicker ~:** a thick tome of light reading

schmökern *(ugs.)* **1.** *itr. V.* bury oneself in a book. **2.** *tr. V.* bury oneself in ⟨*book*⟩

schmollen ['ʃmɔlən] *itr. V.* sulk; ⟨*lips, mouth*⟩ pout; **mit jmdm. ~:** be in a huff and refuse to speak to sb.

Schmoll-: ~mund der pouting mouth; **einen ~mund machen** *od.* **ziehen** pout; **~winkel der** *in* **sich in den ~winkel zurückziehen** *(ugs.)* go off into a corner to sulk; get a fit of the sulks; **im ~winkel sitzen** *(ugs.)* have [a fit of] the sulks

schmolz [ʃmɔlts] *1. u. 3. Pers. Sg. Prät. v.* **schmelzen**

Schmonzes ['ʃmɔntsəs] **der; ~** *(ugs. abwertend)* idle chatter; silly talk

Schmonzette [ʃmɔn'tsɛtə] **die; ~, ~n** *(ugs. abwertend)* trashy play; *(Film)* trashy film

Schmor·braten der pot roast; braised beef

schmoren ['ʃmo:rən] **1.** *tr. V.* braise; **jmdn. [im eigenen Saft] ~ lassen** *(ugs.)* leave sb. to stew in his/her own juice. **2.** *itr. V.* **a)** *(garen)* braise; **b)** *(ugs.: schwitzen)* swelter; **in der Sonne ~:** roast in the sun

Schmor·fleisch das braising steak

Schmu [ʃmu:] **der; ~s** *(ugs.)* little game; **erzähl mir keinen ~!** don't tell me any stories *(coll.)*; **~ machen** cheat; work a fiddle *(sl.)*

schmuck [ʃmʊk] *(veralt.)* **1.** *Adj.* attractive; pretty; *(schick)* smart ⟨*clothes, house, ship, etc.*⟩. **2.** *adv.* attractively; smartly

Schmuck der; ~[e]s a) *(~stücke)* jewelry; jewellery *(esp. Brit.)*; **b)** *(~stück)* piece of jewelry/jewellery; **c)** *(Zierde)* decoration; **ornamentaler ~:** ornamentation; **die Stadt zeigte sich im ~ der Fahnen** *(geh.)* the town was decked with flags

schmücken ['ʃmʏkn̩] *tr. V.* decorate; embellish ⟨*writings, speech*⟩; **sie schmückten sich mit Blumenkränzen** they adorned themselves with garlands; **~de Beiwörter/Zusätze** embellishments

schmuck-, Schmuck-: ~kästchen das, ~kasten der jewelry *or (esp. Brit.)* jewellery box; **ihr Haus ist das reinste ~kästchen** her house is an absolute picture; **~los** *Adj.* plain; bare ⟨*room*⟩; **ein ~loses Grab** an undecorated grave

Schmucklosigkeit die; ~: plainness; *(eines Zimmers)* bareness

Schmuck-: ~sachen *Pl.* jewelry *sing.*; jewellery *sing. (esp. Brit.)*; **~stein der** attractive stone *(used in jewelry)*; gemstone; **~stück das** piece of jewelry *or (esp. Brit.)* jewellery; **ein ~stück/das ~stück seiner Sammlung** *(fig.)* one of the jewels/the jewel of his collection; **~waren** *Pl.* jewelry *sing.*; jewellery *sing. (esp. Brit.)*

Schmuddel der; ~s *(ugs. abwertend)* muck *(coll.)*; grime

schmuddelig *Adj. (ugs. abwertend)* grubby; mucky *(coll.)*; *(schmutzig u. unordentlich)* messy; grotty *(Brit. sl.)*

Schmuggel ['ʃmʊgl̩] **der; ~s** smuggling *no art.*; **~ treiben** smuggle

schmuggeln *tr. (auch itr.) V.* smuggle (**in** + *Akk.* into; **aus** out of); **jmdm. einen Zettel in die Handtasche ~** *(fig.)* smuggle a note into sb.'s handbag

Schmuggel·ware die smuggled goods *pl.*; contraband *no pl.*

Schmuggler der; ~s, ~, Schmugglerin die; ~, ~nen smuggler

schmunzeln ['ʃmʊntsl̩n] *itr. V.* **[vor sich** *(Akk.)* **hin] ~:** smile [quietly] to oneself; **ein Schmunzeln unterdrücken** suppress a smile

Schmus [ʃmu:s] **der; ~es** *(ugs.)* *(Angeberei)* big talk; *(Geschwafel)* waffle; *(Schmeicheleien)* soft soap; **so ein ~!** what a load of waffle/soft soap

Schmuse·katze die *(fam.)* cuddly sort *(coll.)*; *(kleines Mädchen)* cuddly little thing *(coll.)*; **eine ~ sein** be the cuddly sort *(coll.)*

schmusen ['ʃmu:zn̩] *itr. V. (ugs.)* **a)** *(zärtlich sein)* cuddle; ⟨*couple*⟩ kiss and cuddle; *(knutschen)* neck *(sl.)*; **mit jmdm. ~:** cuddle sb.; ⟨*lover*⟩ kiss and cuddle *or (sl.)* neck with sb.; **miteinander ~:** have a cuddle; ⟨*couple*⟩ have a kiss and a cuddle; **~de Pärchen** snogging *(Brit. sl.) or (sl.)* necking couples; **b)** *(abwertend: schmeicheln)* soft-soap

Schmuser der; ~s, ~ *(ugs.)* affectionate type; cuddly sort *(coll.)*; **er ist ein kleiner ~:** he's a cuddly little thing

Schmutz [ʃmʊts] **der; ~es a)** dirt; *(Schlamm)* mud; **der ~ von den Malern** the mess left by the painters; **etw. macht viel/keinen ~:** sth. makes a great deal of/leaves no mess; **durch den dicksten ~ laufen** walk through the worst bit of mud; **jmdn./etw. durch den ~ ziehen** *od.* **in den ~ treten** *(fig.)* drag sb./sth. through the mud *(fig.)*; **b)** *(abwertend: minderwertige, geschmacklose Literatur, Filme usw.)* filth; **~ und Schund** trash and filth; *s. auch* **bewerfen a**

schmutz·abweisend *Adj.* dirt-resistant

schmutzen *itr. V.* get dirty

Schmutz-: ~fänger der a) *(etw., das Schmutz anzieht)* dirt-trap; **b)** *(bei Fahrzeugen)* mud-flap; **~fink der; ~en** *od.* **~s, ~en** *(ugs.)* **a)** *(unsauberer Mensch)* [dirty] pig *(coll.)*; *(Kind)* dirty brat; **b)** *(unmoralischer Mensch)* depraved type *(coll.)*; **alter ~fink** dirty old man; **~fleck der** dirty mark (**in** + *Dat.* on); *(in der Landschaft usw.)* blot

schmutzig 1. *Adj.* **a)** *(unsauber)* dirty; *(un-*

gepflegt) dirty, slovenly ⟨*person, restaurant, etc.*⟩; **sich/sich** *(Dat.)* **die Finger ~ machen** get [oneself] dirty/get one's fingers dirty *or* grubby; *s. auch* **Finger a; b)** *(abwertend: unverschämt)* cocky ⟨*remarks*⟩; **ein ~es Lächeln** a smirk; **c)** *(abwertend: obszön)* smutty ⟨*joke, song, story*⟩; dirty ⟨*thoughts*⟩; **d)** *(abwertend: unlauter)* dirty ⟨*business, war*⟩; crooked, shady ⟨*practices, deal*⟩; **eine ~e Gesinnung** a devious cast of mind. **2.** *adv. (abwertend)* **~ grinsen** smirk

Schmutzigkeit die; ~: dirtiness

Schmutz-: ~titel der *(Druckw.)* half-title; **~wäsche die** dirty washing; **~wasser das;** *Pl.* **~wässer** dirty water; *(Abwasser)* sewage

Schnabel ['ʃnaːbl̩] **der; ~s, Schnäbel** ['ʃnɛːbl̩] **a)** beak; **b)** *(ugs.: Mund)* gob *(sl.)*; **reden, wie einem der ~ gewachsen ist** say just what one thinks; **c)** *(an einer Kanne)* spout; *(an einem Krug)* lip; **d)** *(hist.: an Schiffen)* prow; **e)** *(Musik: Mundstück)* mouthpiece

Schnabel·hieb der peck

schnäbeln ['ʃnɛːbl̩n] *itr. V.* **a)** ⟨*birds*⟩ bill; **b)** *(ugs. scherzh.: sich küssen)* bill and coo

Schnabel-: ~schuh der *(hist.)* pointed shoe *(often with turned-up toe)*; **~tier das** duck-billed platypus

schnabulieren [ʃnabu'liːrən] *tr., itr. V. (fam.)* eat with great enjoyment

Schnack [ʃnak] **der; ~[e]s, ~s** *od.* **Schnäcke** ['ʃnɛkə] *(nordd.)* **a)** *(Unterhaltung)* chat; **b)** *(abwertend: Gerede)* [idle] chatter; gossip; **c)** *(witziger Spruch)* witty saying; bon mot

schnackeln *itr. V. (ugs.)* **a)** *(bes. bayr.: schnalzen)* **mit der Zunge/den Fingern ~:** click one's tongue/snap one's fingers; **b)** *(unpers.)* **es hat geschnackelt** *(bes. südd.) (es ist geglückt)* it's come off; success [at last]!; *(jmd. hat begriffen)* it's clicked *(sl.)*; **bei den beiden hat's geschnackelt** those two have fallen for one another *(coll.)*

schnacken *itr. V. (nordd.)* chat; **platt ~:** talk in Low German dialect

Schnake ['ʃnaːkə] **die; ~, ~n a)** daddy-long-legs; crane-fly; **b)** *(bes. südd.: Stechmücke)* mosquito

Schnaken·stich der *(bes. südd.)* mosquito bite

Schnalle ['ʃnalə] **die; ~, ~n a)** *(Gürtel~)* buckle; **b)** *(österr.: Türklinke)* door-handle; **c)** *(salopp: weibliche Person)* cow *(sl. derog.)*; *(Prostituierte)* tart *(sl.)*

schnallen *tr. V.* **a)** *(mit einer Schnalle festziehen)* buckle ⟨*shoe, belt*⟩; fasten ⟨*strap*⟩; **den Gürtel/Riemen enger/weiter ~:** tighten/loosen one's belt/the strap; **b)** *(mit Riemen/Gurten befestigen)* strap **(auf +** *Akk.* on to); **c)** *(los~)* **etw. von etw. ~:** unstrap sth. from sth.; **d)** *(salopp: begreifen)* twig *(coll.)*

Schnallen·schuh der buckle-shoe

schnalzen *itr. V.* **[mit der Zunge/den Fingern] ~:** click one's tongue/snap one's fingers; **mit der Peitsche ~:** crack the whip

schnapp *Interj.* click; *(beim Zufallen eines Deckels o. ä.)* bang; *(beim Schneiden)* snip; **~ machen** go click/bang/snip

Schnäppchen ['ʃnɛpçən] **das; ~s, ~** *(ugs.)* bargain; **ein ~ machen** get a bargain

schnappen ['ʃnapn̩] **1.** *itr. V.* **a) nach jmdm./etw. ~** ⟨*animal*⟩ snap *or* take a snap at sb./sth.; **nach Luft ~** *(fig.)* gasp for breath *or* air; **b)** *mit sein (schnellen)* **[in die Höhe] ~:** spring up [with a snap]; **ins Schloß ~** ⟨*door*⟩ click shut; ⟨*bolt*⟩ snap home; **c)** *(leise knallen)* snap; ⟨*scissors*⟩ snip. **2.** *tr. V.* **a)** ⟨*dog, bird, etc.*⟩ snatch; **[sich** *(Dat.)***] jmdn./etw. ~** *(ugs.)* ⟨*person*⟩ grab sb./sth.; *(mit raschem Zugriff)* snatch sb./sth.; *s. auch* **Luft a; b)** *(ugs.: festnehmen)* catch, *(sl.)* nab ⟨*thief etc.*⟩

Schnapper der; ~s, ~ *(Türfalle)* latch

Schnapp-: ~messer das a) clasp-knife; **b)** *(Stichwaffe)* flick-knife; **~schloß das** spring lock; **~schuß der** snapshot

Schnaps [ʃnaps] **der; ~es, Schnäpse** ['ʃnɛpsə] **a)** spirit; *(Klarer)* schnapps; **zwei Schnäpse** two glasses of spirit/schnapps; **b)** *o. Pl. (Spirituosen)* spirits *pl.*

Schnaps·brennerei die distillery

Schnaps·bruder der *(ugs. abwertend)* boozer *(coll.)*

Schnäpschen ['ʃnɛpsçən] **das; ~s, ~** *(fam.)* small schnapps

Schnaps·drossel die *(scherzh.)* boozer *(coll.)*

schnäpseln ['ʃnɛpsl̩n] *itr. V. (ugs. scherzh.)* booze [the hard stuff] *(coll.)*

Schnaps-: ~flasche die spirits/schnapps bottle; **~glas das** schnapps glass; **~idee die** *(ugs.)* hare-brained idea; **~zahl die** *(scherzh.) number in which all the digits are the same*

schnarchen ['ʃnarçn̩] *itr. V.* snore

Schnarcher der; ~s, ~ *(ugs.)* **a)** *(Mensch)* snorer; **b)** *(Geräusch)* snore

schnarren ['ʃnarən] *itr. V.* ⟨*alarm clock, telephone, doorbell*⟩ buzz [shrilly]; **mit ~der Stimme** in a rasping voice

schnattern ['ʃnatɐn] *itr. V.* **a)** ⟨*goose etc.*⟩ cackle, gaggle; **b)** *(ugs.: eifrig schwatzen)* jabber [away]; chatter; **c)** *(bes. nordd.: zittern)* **er schnatterte vor Kälte** his teeth were chattering with the cold

schnauben ['ʃnaubn̩] *regelm. (auch unr.) itr. V.* **a)** ⟨*person, horse*⟩ snort ⟨**vor** with⟩; *(fig.)* ⟨*steam locomotive*⟩ puff, chuff; **heftig ~:** pant heavily; **wütend ~:** snort with fury; **b)** *(bes. südd.: atmen)* breathe

schnaufen ['ʃnaufn̩] *itr. V.* puff, pant **(vor** with); *(fig.)* ⟨*steam locomotive*⟩ puff, chuff

Schnaufer der; ~s, ~ *(ugs.)* breath; **einen ~ lang** for a second; **den letzten ~ tun** *(verhüll.)* breathe one's last

Schnauferl das; ~s, ~, (österr.:) ~n *(ugs. scherzh.)* venerable old vehicle; oldie *(coll.)*

Schnauz [ʃnauts] **der; ~es, Schnäuze** ['ʃnɔytsə] *(bes. schweiz.) s.* **Schnauzbart a**

Schnauz·bart der a) *(Bartform)* large moustache; mustachio *(arch.)*; *(an den Seiten herabhängend)* walrus moustache; **b)** *(ugs.: Bartträger)* heavily mustachioed fellow *(dated/literary)*

schnauz·bärtig *adj.* mustachioed *(dated/literary)*

Schnäuzchen ['ʃnɔytsçən] **das a)** *(von Tieren)* little nose; *(der Maus usw.)* little snout; **b)** *(von Menschen)* little mouth

Schnauze die; ~, ~n a) *(von Tieren)* muzzle; *(der Maus usw.)* snout; *(Maul)* mouth; **eine kalte ~:** a cold nose; **b)** *(derb: Mund, Mundwerk)* gob *(sl.)*; **jmdm. in die ~ hauen** smack sb. in the gob *(sl.)*; **die ~ voll haben** *(salopp)* be fed up to the back teeth *(coll.)*; **eine große ~ haben** shoot one's mouth off *(sl.)*; **eine freche/lose ~ haben** be a cheeky so-and-so *(coll.)*/have a loose tongue; **die ~ halten** keep one's trap shut *(sl.)*; **[halt die] ~!** shut your trap! *(sl.)*; **frei [nach] ~, nach ~** *(salopp)* as one thinks fit; as the mood takes one; *s. auch* **verbrennen 2b; c)** *(ugs.)* *s.* **Schnabel c; d)** *(ugs.: Vorderteil) (eines Flugzeugs)* nose; *(eines Fahrzeugs)* front

schnauzen *tr., itr. V. (ugs.)* bark; *(ärgerlich)* snap; snarl

Schnauzer der; ~s, ~ a) *(Hund)* schnauzer; **b)** *(ugs.) s.* **Schnauzbart a**

Schnecke ['ʃnɛkə] **die a)** *(Tier)* snail; *(Nackt~)* slug; **jmdn. [so] zur ~ machen** *(ugs.)* give sb. [such] a good carpeting *(coll.)*; **b)** *(ugs.: Gebäck)* Belgian bun; **c)** *meist Pl. (Frisur)* coiled plait *(over the ear)*; earphone; **d)** *(Anat.: im Ohr)* cochlea; **e)** *(bei Streichinstrumenten)* scroll; **f)** *(Kunstwiss.) s.* **Volute**

Schnecken-: ~frisur die earphones *pl.*; **~gewinde** *das (Technik)* worm; **~haus das** snail-shell; **~nudel die** *(bes. südd.) s.* **Schnecke b; ~post die** *(scherzh.) in* **mit der ~post** at a crawl; **~tempo das** *(ugs.)* snail's pace; **im ~tempo** at a snail's pace

Schnee [ʃneː] **der; ~s a)** snow; **in tiefem ~ liegen** lie under deep snow; **~ von gestern** *(ugs.)* things *pl.*/a thing of the past; ancient history *(fig.)*; **anno ~, im Jahre ~** *(österr.)* in the year dot *(coll.)*; **b)** *(Eier~)* beaten egg-white; **das Eiweiß zu ~ schlagen** beat the egg-white until stiff; **c)** *(Jargon: Kokain)* snow *(sl.)*

Schnee·ball der a) snowball; **b)** *(Strauch)* snowball-tree; guelder rose

Schneeball-: ~schlacht die snowball fight; **eine ~schlacht machen** have a snowball fight; **~system das a)** *(Form des Warenabsatzes)* pyramid selling *no art.*; **b)** *(Verbreitungsart)* cumulative [distribution] process; snowball; *(Fernspr.)* cascade system; *(von Briefen)* chain-letter system

schnee-, Schnee-: ~bedeckt *Adj.* snow-covered; **~besen der** whisk; **~blind** *Adj.* snow-blind; **~blindheit die** snow-blindness; **~brett das** [stretch of] wind-slab; **~brille die** snow-goggles *pl.*; **~decke die** blanket *or* covering of snow; **~fall der** snowfall; fall of snow; **dichter ~fall setzte ein** thick snow began to fall; **~flocke die** snowflake; **~fräse die** rotary [snow-]plough; **~frei** *Adj.* free of snow *postpos.*; **~gestöber das** snow flurry; **~glatt** *Adj.* slippery with [packed] snow *postpos.*; **~glätte die** [slippery surface due to] packed snow; **bei ~glätte** when the roads are slippery because of packed snow; **~glöckchen das** snowdrop; **~grenze die** snow-line; *(beweglich)* snow limit; **~hase der** snow hare; **~huhn das** snow-grouse; ptarmigan

schneeig *Adj.* snowy

schnee-, Schnee-: ~kette die snow-chain; **~könig der** *in* **sich freuen wie ein ~könig** *(ugs.)* be as pleased as Punch; **~landschaft die** snowy *or* snow-covered landscape; **~mann der** snowman; **~matsch der** slush; **~pflug der** *(auch Ski)* snow-plough; **~raupe die** snowmobile *(for preparing ski-runs)*; **~regen der** sleet; **~schauer der** snow-shower; **~schmelze die** melting of the snow; thaw; **~schuh der a)** *(veralt.)* ski; **b)** *(Lauffläche)* snow-shoe; **~sturm der** snowstorm; **~treiben das** driving snow; **~verhältnisse** *Pl.* snow conditions; **~verwehung die: ~verwehung[en]** snow-drifts *pl.*; **eine ~verwehung** a mass of snow-drifts; **~wächte die** cornice; **~wehe die** snow-drift; **~weiß** *Adj.* snow-white; as white as snow *postpos.*

Schneewittchen [-'vɪtçən] **das; ~s** Snow White

Schneid der; ~[e]s, *südd., österr.:* **die; ~** *(ugs.)* guts *pl. (coll.)*; **ihm fehlt der ~:** he hasn't got the guts [to do it]; **dazu gehört ~:** that takes some nerve; **jmdm. den** *od.* **die ~ abkaufen** take the fight out of sb.

Schneid·brenner der *(Technik)* cutting torch; oxy-acetylene cutter

Schneide ['ʃnaidə] **die; ~, ~n** [cutting] edge; *(Klinge)* blade; **eine doppelte ~ haben** be two-edged

schneiden 1. *unr. itr. V.* **a)** cut **(in +** *Akk.* into); **b)** *(Medizinerjargon: operieren)* operate; **c)** *(beim Fahren)* **bei Überholmanövern ~:** cut in after overtaking; **d)** *(Schmerz verursachen)* ⟨*wind, cold*⟩ be biting; **~d** biting ⟨*wind, cold, voice, sarcasm*⟩; **es schnitt ihm ins Herz** *(fig.)* it cut him to the quick. **2.** *unr. tr. V.* **a)** cut; cut, reap ⟨*corn etc.*⟩; cut, mow ⟨*grass*⟩; *(in Scheiben)* slice ⟨*bread, sausage, etc.*⟩; *(klein ~)* cut up, chop ⟨*wood, vegetables*⟩; *(zu~)* cut out ⟨*dress*⟩; *(stutzen)* prune ⟨*tree, bush*⟩; trim ⟨*beard*⟩; **Kräuter in die Suppe/Wurst unter die Kartoffeln ~:** cut up herbs/sausage and add them/it to the soup/potatoes; **sich** *(Dat.)* **von jmdm. die Haare ~ lassen** have one's hair cut by sb.; **hier ist ei-**

ne Luft zum Schneiden *(fig.)* there's a terrible fug in here *(coll.)*; **ein eng/weit/gut geschnittenes Kleid** a tight-fitting/loose-fitting/well-cut dress; **ein regelmäßig geschnittenes Gesicht** *(fig.)* a face with regular features; **b)** *(Medizinerjargon: auf~)* operate on ‹*patient*›; cut [open] ‹*tumour, ulcer, etc.*›; lance ‹*boil, abscess*›; **c)** *(Film, Rundf., Ferns.: cutten)* cut, edit ‹*film, tape*›; **d)** *(beim Fahren)* **eine Kurve ~:** cut a corner; **jmdn./einen anderen Wagen ~:** cut in on sb./another car; **e)** *(kreuzen)* ‹*line, railway, etc.*› intersect, cross; **die Linien/Straßen ~ sich** the lines/roads intersect; **f)** *(Tennis usw.)* slice, put spin on ‹*ball*›; *(Fußball)* curve ‹*ball, free kick*›; *(Billard)* put side on ‹*ball*›; **g) eine Grimasse ~:** grimace; **h)** *(ignorieren)* **jmdn. ~:** cut sb. dead; send sb. to Coventry *(Brit.)*. **3.** *refl. V.* **ich habe mir** *od.* **mich in den Finger geschnitten** I've cut my finger; **wenn du das meinst, hast du dich geschnitten** *(fig.)* it you think that, you've made a big mistake

Schneider der; ~s, ~ a) tailor; *(Damen~)* dressmaker; **frieren wie ein ~** *(ugs.)* be frozen stiff; **b)** *(ugs.: Schneidegerät)* cutter; *(für Scheiben)* slicer; **c)** *(Skat: 30 Punkte)* schneider; **[im] ~ sein** have less than 30 points; be schneidered; **~ ansagen** declare schneider; **aus dem ~ sein** have made schneider; *(fig. ugs.: eine schwierige Situation überwunden haben)* be in the clear; be clear of trouble; **d)** *(Tischtennis: unter 11 Punkte)* [score of] less than 11 points

Schneiderei die; ~, ~en a) tailor's shop; *(Damen~)* dressmaker's shop; **b)** *o. Pl.* *(das Schneidern)* tailoring; *(von Damenkleidern)* dressmaking

Schneiderin die; ~, ~nen tailor; *(Damen~)* dressmaker

Schneider-: ~kostüm das tailor-made *or* tailored suit; **~kreide die** tailor's chalk; French chalk; **~meister der** master tailor; *(für Damenkleider)* master dressmaker

schneidern 1. *tr. V.* make ‹*dress, clothes*›; make, tailor ‹*suit*›; **sie schneidert ihre Sachen selbst** she makes her own clothes. **2.** *itr. V.* make clothes/dresses; *(beruflich)* work as a tailor; *(als Schneiderin)* work as a dressmaker

Schneider-: ~puppe die tailor's dummy; *(eines Damenschneiders)* dressmaker's dummy; **~sitz der** cross-legged position; **im ~sitz** cross-legged

Schneide-: ~tisch der *(Film, Ferns.)* editing *or* cutting table; **~zahn der** incisor

schneidig 1. *Adj.* **a)** *(forsch, zackig)* dashing; *(waghalsig)* daring; bold; rousing, brisk ‹*music*›; **b)** *(flott, sportlich)* dashing ‹*appearance, fellow*›; trim ‹*figure*›. **2.** *adv.* briskly; **~ spielen** play in a rousing/lively manner

schneien ['ʃnaiən] **1.** *itr., tr. V.* *(unpers.)* **es schneit** it is snowing; **es schneit/schneite jeden Tag** it snows/snowed every day; **es schneit dicke Flocken** *od.* **in dicken Flocken** big flakes of snow are falling; **es schneit auf dem Bildschirm** *(fig.)* there's a snowstorm on the screen. **2.** *itr. V.*; *mit sein* *(fig.)* ‹*blossom, confetti, etc.*› rain down, fall like snow

Schneise ['ʃnaizə] **die; ~, ~n a)** *(Wald~)* aisle; *(als Feuerschutz)* firebreak; **b)** *(Flug~)* [air] corridor

schnell [ʃnɛl] **1.** *Adj.* quick ‹*journey, decision, service, etc.*›; fast ‹*car, skis, road, track, etc.*›; quick, rapid, swift ‹*progress*›; quick, swift ‹*movement, blow, action*›; **ein ~es Tempo** a high speed; a fast pace; **um ~e Erledigung der Angelegenheit bitten** request that the matter be handled speedily; **sie ist sehr ~ bei der Arbeit** she is a very quick worker; **~es Geld** *(ugs.)* money for jam *(coll.)*; **die** *od.* **eine ~e Mark machen** *(salopp)* make a fast buck *(sl.)*; **auf die ~e** *(ugs.)* in a trice; *(übereilt)* in [too much of] a hurry; in a rush; *(kurzfristig)* at short notice; quickly; **auf die ~e ein Bier/eins auf die ~e trinken** have a quick beer/a quick one. **2.** *adv.* quickly; ‹*drive, move, etc.*› fast, quickly; ‹*spread*› quickly, rapidly; *(bald)* soon ‹*sold, past, etc.*›; **nicht so ~!** not so fast!; **mach ~!** *(ugs.)* move it! *(coll.)*; **so ~ macht ihm das keiner nach** nobody is going to equal that in a hurry; **wie heißt er noch ~?** *(ugs.)* what's his name again?; **es ging ~er, als man dachte** it went quicker than expected; **das geht mir zu ~:** that's too quick for me

Schnell-: ~bahn die *(Verkehrsw.)* municipal railway; **~boot das** high-speed patrol boat; *(Torpedoschnellboot)* motor torpedo boat; PT boat *(Amer.)*; **~dienst der** express service

Schnelle die; ~, ~n a) *o. Pl.* *(Schnelligkeit)* rapidity; *(Tempo)* speed; **b)** *(Geog.: Strom~)* rapids *pl.*

schnellebig [-le:bɪç] *Adj.* **a)** *(Biol.: kurzlebig)* short-lived ‹*animal, insect*›; **b)** *(hektisch, betriebsam)* fast-moving ‹*age*›

schnellen 1. *itr. V.*; *mit sein* shoot (**aus** + *Dat.* out of; **in** + *Akk.* into); **in die Höhe ~:** ‹*person*› leap to one's feet *or* up; ‹*rocket, fig.: prices etc.*› shoot up. **2.** *tr. V.* send ‹*ball, stone, etc.*› flying; hurl ‹*ball, stone, etc.*›; whip ‹*fishing-line*›; **sich mit dem Trampolin in die Höhe ~:** leap high into the air on a/the trampoline

Schnell-: ~feuer das; *o. Pl.* *(Milit.)* rapid fire; **~feuer·gewehr das** semi-automatic rifle; **~gast·stätte die** fast-food restaurant; *(~imbiß)* snack-bar; **~gericht das** convenience food; *(in Lokalen)* quick snack; **~hefter der** loose-leaf binder; quick-release file

Schnelligkeit die; ~, ~en a) *(Tempo)* speed; **die ~, mit der sie arbeitet** the speed at which she works; **b)** *o. Pl.* *(das Schnellsein)* rapidity; speed

schnell-, Schnell-: ~imbiß der snack-bar; **~koch·platte die** high-speed ring; **~koch·topf der** pressure-cooker; **~kraft die;** *o. Pl.* springiness; **~kurs der** crash course; **~lebig** *s.* **schnellebig; ~paket das** *(Postw.)* express parcel; **~reinigung die** express cleaner's

schnellstens *Adv.* as quickly as possible; *(möglichst bald)* as soon as possible

schnellst·möglich 1. *Adj.* quickest possible; **auf ~e Erledigung der Arbeit drängen** press for the earliest possible completion of the work. **2.** *adv. s.* **schnellstens**

Schnell-: ~straße die expressway *(on which slow-moving vehicles are prohibited)*; **~verfahren das a)** *(bes. Technik)* high-speed process; **im ~verfahren** *(fig.)* at high speed; in a crash programme; **b)** *(Rechtsw.)* summary trial; summary proceedings *pl.*; **im ~verfahren** in summary proceedings; **~verkehr der** *(Kfz-W.)* fast-moving traffic; *(~verkehrsnetz)* express services *pl.*; **~zug der** express [train]; **~zug·zuschlag der** express train supplement

Schnepfe ['ʃnɛpfə] **die; ~, ~n a)** *(Vogel)* snipe; *(Wald~)* woodcock; **b)** *(salopp abwertend: weibliche Person)* **[blöde] ~:** [silly] cow *(sl. derog.)*; **c)** *(salopp abwertend: Prostituierte)* tart *(sl.)*

schnetzeln ['ʃnɛtsl̩n] *(bes. südd.)* cut ‹*meat*› into thin strips

schneuzen ['ʃnɔytsn̩] **1.** *tr. V.* **einem Kind die Nase ~:** blow a child's nose; **sich** *(Dat.)* **die Nase ~:** blow one's nose. **2.** *refl. V.* *(geh.)* blow one's nose

Schnick·schnack der *(ugs.; meist abwertend)* **a)** *(wertloses Zeug)* trinkets *pl.*; *(Zierat)* frills *pl.* *(fig.)*; **überflüssiger ~:** superfluous paraphernalia *sing.*; **b)** *(Geschwätz)* waffle; *(Unsinn)* drivel; **~!** rubbish!

schniefen ['ʃni:fn̩] *itr. V.* sniffle; *(bes. beim Weinen)* snivel

schniegeln ['ʃni:gl̩n] *refl. V.* spruce oneself up; *s. auch* **geschniegelt**

schnieke ['ʃni:kə] **1.** *Adj.* *(berlin.)* **a)** *(schick, elegant)* snazzy *(sl.)* ‹*clothes, fashion, etc.*›; **b)** *(großartig)* super *(Brit. coll.)*. **2.** *adv.* snazzily *(sl.)*

schnipp *Interj.* snip; **~, schnapp!** snip, snip

Schnippchen das; ~s trick; **jmdm. ein ~ schlagen** *(ugs.)* outsmart sb. *(coll.)*; put one over on sb. *(sl.)*; **dem Tod/Schicksal ein ~ schlagen** *(ugs.)* cheat death/fate

Schnippel der *od.* **das; ~s, ~** *(ugs.)* scrap; *(Papier~, Stoff~)* snippet; shred

Schnippelchen das; ~s, ~: tiny scrap; *(Papier~, Stoff~)* tiny snippet *or* shred

schnippeln *(ugs.)* **1.** *itr. V.* *(mit der Schere)* snip [away] (**an** + *Dat.* at); **an der Wurst ~** *(mit dem Messer)* cut little snippets of sausage. **2.** *tr. V.* **a)** *(ausschneiden)* snip [out]; **b)** *(zerkleinern)* shred ‹*vegetables*›; chop ‹*beans etc.*› [finely]

schnippen ['ʃnɪpn̩] **1.** *itr. V.* **a)** *(mit der Schere)* snip; **b)** *(mit den Fingern)* snap one's fingers (**nach** at); **mit Daumen und Mittelfinger ~:** snap one's thumb and middle finger together. **2.** *tr. V.* **a)** *(wegschleudern)* flick (**von** off, from); **die Asche von der Zigarette ~:** flick the ash off one's cigarette; **b)** *(herausschleudern)* tap ‹*cigarette, card, etc.*› (**aus** out of)

schnippisch *(abwertend)* **1.** *Adj.* pert ‹*reply, tone, etc.*›; *(anmaßend)* cocky ‹*girl, tone, expression*›. **2.** *adv.* pertly; *(anmaßend)* cockily

Schnipsel ['ʃnɪpsl̩] **der** *od.* **das; ~s, ~:** scrap; *(Papier~, Stoff~)* snippet; shred

schnipseln *s.* **schnippeln**

schnitt [ʃnɪt] *1. u. 3. Pers. Sg. Prät. v.* **schneiden**

Schnitt der; ~[e]s, ~e a) cut; *(Operations~)* incision; cut; **etw. mit einem [schnellen] ~ durchtrennen** divide sth. by cutting it [quickly]; **sich** *(Dat.)* **einen ~ beibringen** cut oneself; **b)** *(das Mähen) (von Gras)* mowing; cut; *(von Getreide)* harvest; **das Korn ist reif für den ~:** the corn is ready for reaping *or* harvesting; **einen** *od.* **seinen ~ [bei etw.] machen** *(fig. ugs.)* make a profit [from sth.]; **c)** *(Form von Kleidung, Haar, Edelsteinen usw.)* cut; **eine Wohnung mit gutem ~** *(fig.)* a well-planned flat *(Brit.) or (Amer.)* apartment; **ihr Profil hat einen klassischen ~** *(fig.)* she has a classical profile; **d)** *(Film, Ferns.)* editing; cutting; **ein harter/weicher ~:** editing with straight *or* sudden/gradual cuts; **~: Gisela Meyer** edited by *or* editor Gisela Meyer; **e)** *(~muster)* [dressmaking] pattern; **f)** *(Längs~, Quer~, Schräg~)* section; **etw. im ~ darstellen** show sth. in section; **g)** *(ugs.: Durch~)* average; **er fährt einen ~ von 200 km/h** he is driving at *or* doing an average [speed] of 125 m.p.h.; **im ~:** on average; **h)** *(Math.) s.* **golden 1c; i)** *(Geom.: ~fläche)* intersection; **j)** *(Ballspiele: Drall)* spin; **den Ball mit ~ spielen** *od.* **schlagen** put spin on the ball

Schnitt-: ~blume die cut flower; **~bohne die** French bean; **~brot das** cut *or* sliced bread

Schnittchen das; ~s, ~: canapé; [small] open sandwich

Schnitte die; ~, ~n a) *(bes. nordd.: Scheibe)* slice; **eine ~ [Brot]** a slice of bread; **eine [belegte] ~:** an open sandwich; **b)** *meist Pl.* *(österr.: Waffel)* wafer

Schnitter der; ~s, ~ *(veralt.)* reaper

schnitt-, Schnitt-: ~fest *Adj.* firm ‹*tomato, sausage, etc.*›; **~fläche die** cut surface; **die ~fläche des Käses** the cut end of the cheese; **~holz das** cut timber

schnittig 1. *Adj.* stylish, smart ‹*suit, appearance, etc.*›; *(sportlich)* racy ‹*car, yacht, etc.*›; *(stromlinienförmig)* streamlined ‹*car, bow, etc.*›. **2.** *adv.* stylishly; *(sportlich)* racily

schnitt-, Schnitt-: ~käse der cheese suitable for slicing; hard cheese; *(in Scheiben)* cheese slices *pl.*; **~lauch der** chives *pl.*; **~linie die** line of intersection; *(Linie, die eine andere kreuzt)* intersecting line; **~menge die** *(Math.)* **die ~menge** $A \cap B$ the intersection of the sets A and B; **~muster das a)** [dressmaking] pattern; **b)** *(ugs.) s.* **~musterbogen; ~muster·bogen der** pattern chart; **~punkt der** intersection; *(Geom.)* point of intersection; **~reif** *Adj.* ⟨*corn etc.*⟩ ready for reaping *or* harvesting; **~stelle die** *(DV)* interface; **~wunde die** cut; *(lang u. tief)* gash

Schnitz·arbeit die carving

Schnitzel ['ʃnɪtsl̩] **das; ~s, ~ a)** *(Fleisch)* [veal/pork] escalope; **b)** *(Stückchen) (von Papier)* scrap; snippet; *(von Holz)* shaving; *(von Früchten usw.)* sliver

Schnitzel·jagd die paper-chase

schnitzeln *tr. V.* chop up ⟨*vegetables etc.*⟩ [into small pieces]; shred ⟨*cabbage*⟩

schnitzen 1. *itr. V.* carve; **an etw.** *(Dat.)* **~:** carve away at sth. **2.** *tr. V.* carve

Schnitzer der; ~s, ~ a) *(Handwerker)* carver; **b)** *(ugs.: Fehler)* boob *(Brit. sl.)*; goof *(sl.)*; **sich** *(Dat.)* **einen groben ~ leisten** make an awful boob *(Brit. sl.) or (sl.)* goof; *(mit einer Bemerkung)* drop an awful clanger *(sl.)*

Schnitzerei die; ~, ~en a) *(Geschnitztes)* carving (*Gen.* by); **b)** *o. Pl. (das Schnitzen)* carving *no art.*

Schnitz-: ~messer das wood-carving knife; **~werk das** carving; *(mehrere Stücke)* carvings *pl.*

schnob [ʃno:p] *1. u. 3. Pers. Sg. Prät. v.* **schnauben**

schnöd [ʃnø:t] *Adj. (bes. südd., österr.) s.* **schnöde**

schnodderig ['ʃnɔdərɪç] *(ugs. abwertend)* **1.** *Adj.* brash; **ein ~es Mundwerk haben** have a big mouth. **2.** *adv.* brashly

Schnodderigkeit die; ~, ~en *(ugs.)* **a)** *o. Pl. (Art, Wesen)* brashness; **b)** *(Äußerung/ Handlung)* brash remark/action

schnoddrig *s.* **schnodderig**

schnöde *(geh. abwertend)* **1.** *Adj.* **a)** *(verachtenswert)* despicable; contemptible; base ⟨*cowardice*⟩; *s. auch* **Mammon; b)** *(gemein)* contemptuous, scornful ⟨*glance, reply, etc.*⟩; harsh ⟨*reprimand*⟩; **~r Undank** blatant ingratitude. **2.** *adv. (gemein)* contemptuously; ⟨*reprimand*⟩ harshly; ⟨*exploit, misuse*⟩ flagrantly, blatantly

Schnorchel ['ʃnɔrçl̩] **der; ~s, ~:** snorkel

Schnörkel ['ʃnœrkl̩] **der; ~s, ~:** scroll; curlicue; *(der Handschrift, in der Rede)* flourish

schnorren ['ʃnɔrən] *tr., itr. V. (ugs.)* scrounge *(coll.)*; **etw. bei** *od.* **von jmdm. ~:** scrounge *(coll.) or* cadge sth. off sb.

Schnorrer der; ~s, ~ *(ugs.)* scrounger *(coll.)*; sponger

Schnösel ['ʃnø:zl̩] **der; ~s, ~** *(ugs. abwertend)* young whippersnapper

schnöselig *(ugs. abwertend)* **1.** *Adj.* cheeky; insolent. **2.** *adv.* cheekily; insolently

Schnuckelchen ['ʃnʊkl̩çən] **das; ~s, ~** *(fam.)* sweetie[-pie] *(coll.)*; **mein kleines ~:** my little darling *or* pet

schnuckelig *Adj. (ugs.)* sweet; cute *(Amer. coll.)*

Schnüffelei die; ~, ~en *(ugs. abwertend)* **a)** *o. Pl. (dauerndes Schnüffeln)* [constant] snooping *(coll.)*; **b)** *(Vorfall von ~)* case of snooping *(coll.)*

schnüffeln ['ʃnʏfl̩n] **1.** *itr. V.* **a)** *(riechen)* sniff; **an etw.** *(Dat.)* **~:** sniff sth.; **b)** *(ugs. abwertend: heimlich suchen; spionieren)* snoop [about] *(coll.)*; **in etw.** *(Akk.)* **~:** pry into sth.; stick one's nose into sth. *(coll.)*; **in jmds. Papieren ~:** nose about in sb.'s papers; **c)** *(Drogenjargon: Dämpfe ~)* sniff [glue/paint *etc.*]; **d)** *(ugs.: die Nase hochziehen)* sniff. **2.** *tr. V. (Drogenjargon: zum Schnüffeln benutzen)* sniff ⟨*glue etc.*⟩

Schnüffler der; ~s, ~ a) *(ugs. abwertend)* Nosey Parker; *(Spion)* snooper *(coll.)*; **b)** *(Drogenjargon)* [glue-, paint-, *etc.*]sniffer

Schnuller ['ʃnʊlɐ] **der; ~s, ~:** dummy *(Brit.)*; pacifier *(Amer.)*

Schnulze ['ʃnʊltsə] **die; ~, ~n** *(ugs. abwertend) (Lied/Melodie)* slushy song/tune; *(Theaterstück, Film, Fernsehspiel)* tear-jerker *(coll.)*; slushy play; **etw. als ~ singen** sing sth. in a slushy version

schnupfen ['ʃnʊpfn̩] **1.** *itr. V.* **a)** *(Tabak ~)* take snuff; **b)** *(bei Tränen, Nasenschleim)* sniff. **2.** *tr. V.* take a sniff of ⟨*cocaine etc.*⟩; *(gewohnheitsmäßig)* sniff ⟨*cocaine etc.*⟩; **Tabak ~:** take snuff

Schnupfen der; ~s, ~: [head] cold; **[den** *od.* **einen] ~ haben** have a [head] cold; **sich** *(Dat.)* **den ~ holen** catch a [head] cold

Schnupfer der; ~s, ~: snuff-taker

Schnupf-: ~tabak der snuff; **~tabak[s]·dose die** snuff-box

schnuppe ['ʃnʊpə] *in* **~ sein** *(ugs.)* be neither here nor there; **das/er ist mir ~/mir völlig ~** *(ugs.)* I don't care/I couldn't care less about it/him *(coll.)*

schnuppern ['ʃnʊpɐn] **1.** *itr. V.* sniff; **an etw.** *(Dat.)* **~:** sniff sth.. **2.** *tr. V.* sniff; **Seeluft ~** *(fig.)* get some sea air

Schnur [ʃnu:ɐ̯] **die; ~, Schnüre** ['ʃny:rə] *od.* **Schnuren a)** *(Bindfaden)* piece of string; *(Kordel)* piece of cord; *(Zelt~)* guy[-rope]; *(für Marionette, Drachen usw.)* string; **eine ~ um ein Paket binden** tie string round a parcel; **Perlen auf eine ~ aufziehen** string pearls; **b)** *(Zierkordel)* piece of braid; **mit vielen Schnüren** with much braid[ing] *sing.*; **c)** *(ugs.: Kabel)* flex *(Brit.)*; lead; cord *(Amer.)*

Schnür·boden der a) *(Theater)* flies *pl.*; **b)** *(Schiffbau)* mould loft

Schnürchen das; ~s, ~: *in* **wie am ~ [gehen** *od.* **klappen]** *(ugs.)* [go] like clockwork *or* without a hitch; **ein Gedicht wie am ~ aufsagen** *(ugs.)* say a poem off pat

schnüren ['ʃny:rən] **1.** *tr. V.* **a)** tie ⟨*bundle, string, sb.'s hands, etc.*⟩; tie [up] ⟨*parcel, person*⟩; tie, lace up ⟨*shoe, corset, etc.*⟩; **etw. zu Bündeln/Paketen ~:** tie sth. up in bundles/ parcels; **etw. um/auf etw.** *(Akk.)* **~:** tie sth. round/[on] to sth.; **b) Angst schnürte ihm die Kehle/den Atem** *(fig.)* fear constricted his throat/almost stopped him from breathing. **2.** *refl. V. (sich hineindrücken)* **sich in das Fleisch** *usw.* **~:** cut into the flesh *etc.* **3.** *itr. V.* **a)** *(zu eng sein)* be too tight; pinch; **b)** *mit sein (Jägerspr.)* ⟨*fox, lynx, wolf*⟩ trot in a straight line; ⟨*fig.: person*⟩ trot

schnur·gerade, schnur·grade *(ugs.)* **1.** *Adj.* dead straight. **2.** *adv.* dead straight; **~ auf sein Ziel losgehen** *(fig.)* make straight for one's goal

Schnur·keramik die; *o. Pl. (Archäol.)* corded ware

Schnürl- ['ʃny:ɐ̯l-]: **~regen der** *(österr.)* persistent rain; **~samt der** *(österr.)* corduroy

Schnurr·bart der moustache

schnurr·bärtig *Adj.* with a moustache *postpos.*; **~ sein** have a moustache

Schnurre die; ~, ~n *(veralt.)* anecdote

schnurren ['ʃnʊrən] *itr. V.* ⟨*cat*⟩ purr; ⟨*machine*⟩ hum; ⟨*camera, spinning-wheel, etc.*⟩ whirr

Schnurr·haar das *(Zool.)* whiskers *pl.*

Schnür·riemen der a) strap; **b)** *s.* **Schnürsenkel**

schnurrig *Adj. (veralt.)* droll; comic; funny; comic ⟨*old man etc.*⟩

Schnür-: ~schuh der lace-up shoe; **~senkel** [~zɛŋkl̩] **der** *(bes. nordd.)* [shoe-]lace; *(für Stiefel)* bootlace; **sich** *(Dat.)* **die ~senkel binden** tie one's shoe-laces

schnur·springen *unr. itr. V.; nur im Inf. und 2. Partizip; mit sein (österr.)* skip

Schnür·stiefel der lace-up boot

schnur·stracks *Adv. (ugs.)* straight; **der Weg geht ~ geradeaus** the way goes straight ahead; **~ auf jmdn./etw. zugehen** make a bee-line for sb./sth.

Schnürung die; ~, ~en lacing; *(Schnürsenkel)* laces *pl.*

schnurz [ʃnʊrts] *Adj. (ugs.) in* **es ist [jmdm.] ~** *(salopp)* it doesn't matter a hoot [to sb.] *(sl.)*; **ihm ist jmd./etw./alles ~ [und piepe]** he doesn't give a damn *or* couldn't care less about sb./sth./anything *(coll.)*

Schnute ['ʃnu:tə] **die; ~, ~n** *(fam., bes. nordd.: Mund)* mouth; gob *(sl.)*; **eine ~ ziehen** *od.* **machen** make *or* pull a [sulky] face

schob [ʃo:p] *1. u. 3. Pers. Prät. v.* **schieben**

Schober ['ʃobɐ] **der; ~s, ~ a)** open-sided barn; **b)** *(Heuhaufen)* [hay-]stack; [hay-]rick

[1]Schock [ʃɔk] **das; ~[e]s, ~e** *(bei Maßangaben ungebeugt)* **a)** *(veralt.: 60 Stück)* **ein ~:** three score; five dozen; **7 bis 8 ~ Eier** 35–40 dozen eggs; **b)** *(ugs.: Menge)* [whole] load of *(coll.)*

[2]Schock der; ~[e]s, ~s *(auch Med.)* shock; **jmdm. einen [schweren/leichten] ~ versetzen** *od.* **geben** give sb. a [nasty/slight] shock *or* a [nasty/bit of a] fright; **unter ~ stehen** be in [a state of] shock; be suffering from shock

Schock·behandlung die shock treatment

schocken *tr. V. (ugs.: schockieren)* shock

Schocker der; ~s, ~ *(ugs.) (Roman/Film)* sensational book/film; shocker *(coll.)*; *(Mensch)* sensationalist

Schock·farbe die *(ugs.)* violent colour

schockieren *tr. V.* shock; **über etw.** *(Akk.)* **schockiert sein** be shocked at sth.

schock-, Schock-: ~therapie die *(auch fig.)* shock therapy *or* treatment; **~weise** *Adv.* **a)** *(in Schocks)* by the three score; five dozen at a time; **b)** *(ugs.: scharenweise)* in droves; **~wirkung die** shock effect; **unter ~wirkung stehen** be in a state of shock; be suffering from shock

schofel ['ʃo:fl̩], **schofelig** *(ugs. abwertend)* **1.** *Adj.* horrid *(coll.)*; beastly *(coll.)*; *(schändlich)* disgusting. **2.** *adv.* horridly

Schöffe ['ʃœfə] **der; ~n, ~n** lay judge *(acting together with another lay judge and a professional judge)*

Schöffen·gericht das *court presided over by a professional judge and two lay judges*

Schöffin die; ~, ~nen *s.* **Schöffe**

Schokolade [ʃoko'la:də] **die; ~, ~n a)** *(Süßigkeit)* chocolate; **b)** *(Getränk)* [drinking] chocolate

schokolade[n]-, Schokolade[n]-: ~braun *Adj.* chocolate[-brown]; **~eis das** chocolate ice-cream; **~farben** *Adj.* chocolate-coloured; chocolate ⟨*brown*⟩; **~guß der** chocolate icing

Schokoladen-: ~pudding der chocolate blancmange; **~raspel** *Pl.* chocolate flakes; grated chocolate *sing.*; **~seite die** *(ugs.)* best side; **~torte die** chocolate cake *or* gateau

Scholar [ʃo'la:ɐ̯] **der; ~en, ~en** *(hist.)* [itinerant] scholar

Scholastik [ʃo'lastɪk] **die; ~** *(Philosophie)* scholasticism

Scholastiker der; ~s, ~, Scholastikerin die; ~, ~nen scholastic

scholastisch *Adj.* scholastic

scholl [ʃɔl] *1. u. 3. Pers. Sg. Prät. v.* **schallen**

Scholle ['ʃɔlə] **die; ~, ~n a)** *(Erd~)* clod [of earth]; **b)** *(Eis~)* [ice-]floe; **c)** *(Fisch) (Goldbutt)* flounder, *esp.* plaice; **die ~n** the plaice; *(als Familie)* the Pleuronectidae; **d)** *o. Pl. (Erdboden, Acker)* soil; **die heimatliche ~** *(fig.)* one's native soil; **auf eigener ~ sitzen** have a farm of one's own; **e)** *(Geol.)* massif

Scholli ['ʃɔli] *in* **mein lieber ~!** *(ugs.)* my goodness!; good heavens!

Schöll·kraut ['ʃœl-] **das** *(Bot.)* celandine
schon [ʃo:n] **1.** *Adv.* **a)** *(bereits) (oft nicht übersetzt)* already; *(in Fragen)* yet; **er hat das ~ vergessen** he has already forgotten that; **hat Walter ~ angerufen?** has Walter telephoned yet?; **wollt ihr wirklich ~ gehen?** do you really mean to go already *or* so soon?; **er kommt ~ heute/ist ~ gestern gekommen** he's coming today/he came yesterday; **er ist ~ da/[an]gekommen** he is already here/has already arrived; **~ die Römer hatten gute Heizungen** even the Romans *or* the Romans already had good heating systems; **er ist ~ gestern angekommen** he arrived as early as yesterday; **ich bin ~ seit Mai/~ ein Jahr in Bremen** I've been here in Bremen since May/for a year; **wie lange bist du ~ hier?** how long have you been here?; **~ damals/jetzt** even at that time *or* in those days/even now; **~ [im Jahre] 1926** as early as 1926; back in 1926; **er war ~ immer faul** he always was lazy; **wie ~ gesagt ...**: as I have already said, ...; as I said before, ...; **gestern kam er, wie ~ so oft, zu spät zur Arbeit** yesterday he was late for work, as so often before *or* as has so often been the case; **b)** *(fast gleichzeitig)* there and then; **er schwang sich auf das Fahrrad, und ~ war er weg** he jumped on the bicycle and was away [in a flash]; **kaum hatte er sich umgedreht, ~ ging der Krach los** he had scarcely turned his back when the row broke out; **in dem selben Augenblick ~**: at that very *or* at the selfsame moment; *s. auch* **kaum e; c)** *(jetzt)* **~ [mal]** now; *(inzwischen)* meanwhile; **wir treffen uns dann gleich, ihr könnt ja ~ mal vorgehen** we'll meet up in a minute, you can be going on ahead [meanwhile]; **d)** *(selbst, sogar)* even; *(nur)* only; **~ ein Tropfen von dem Gift kann tödlich sein** even a small amount *or* a mere drop of this poison can be fatal; **das weiß normalerweise ~ ein Zwölfjähriger** even a child of twelve would usually know that; **~ zwei Bier reichen aus, um ihn völlig betrunken zu machen** it only takes two beers to get him completely drunk; **das bekommt man ~ für 150 Mark** you can get it for as little as 150 marks; **für so ein Essen muß man ~ 30 Mark hinlegen** you have to pay as much as 30 marks for a meal like that; **e)** *(ohne Ergänzung, ohne weiteren Zusatz)* on its own; **das ist auch so ~ genug** that's [already] enough as it is; **[allein] ~ der Gedanke daran ist schrecklich** the mere thought *or* just the thought of it is dreadful; **~ der Name ist bezeichnend** the very name is significant; **~ darum** *od.* **aus diesem Grund** for this reason alone. **2.** *Partikel* **a)** *(verstärkend)* really; *(gewiß)* certainly; **du wirst ~ sehen!** you'll see!; **ich kann mir ~ denken, was du willst** I can well imagine what you want; **wenn wir ~ eine neue Maschine kaufen müssen, dann aber eine ordentliche** if we have to get a new machine, let's get a decent one; **wenn du ~ so früh gehen mußt** if you really have to go so early; **b)** *(ugs. ungeduldig: endlich)* **nun sagen Sie [doch] ~!** come on, out with it; **nun komm ~!** come on!; hurry up!; **du hast meine Zigaretten geklaut, nun gib's ~ zu!** you've pinched my cigarettes, go on, admit it *(coll.)*; **und wenn ~!** so what; what if he/she/it does/did/was *etc.*; **c)** *(beruhigend: wahrscheinlich)* all right; **es wird ~ gehen** *od.* **werden** it'll work out all right [in the end]; **er wird sich ~ wieder erholen** he'll recover all right; he's sure to recover; **doch, doch, das wird ~ stimmen** yes, yes, that must be right; **d)** *(zustimmend, aber etwas einschränkend)* **~ gut** OK *(coll.)*; **ich glaube dir ~**: I believe you all right; fair enough, I believe you; **Lust hätte ich ~, nur keine Zeit** I'd certainly like to, but I've no time; **das ist ~ möglich, nur ...**: that is quite possible, only ...; **er hat ~ recht, aber ...** he's right enough, but ...; **e)** *(betont: andererseits)* **er ist nicht besonders intelligent, aber sein Bruder ~**: he's not particularly intelligent, but his brother is; **ob Willy kommt, weiß ich nicht, aber ich [komme] ~**: I don't know whether Willy's coming, but 'I'm coming *or* 'I am; **f)** *(einschränkend, abwertend)* **was weiß der ~!** what does 'he know [about it]!; **was ist** *od.* **bedeutet ~ Geld!** what does money matter?; what's the good of money [anyway]?; **wem nützt das ~?** what's the use of that [to anybody]?; **Ist was? – Nee, was soll ~ sein?** *(ugs.)* Is anything the matter? – No, should anything be [wrong]?; **was soll das ~ heißen?** what's 'that supposed to mean?
schön [ʃø:n] **1.** *Adj.* **a)** *(anziehend, reizvoll)* beautiful; handsome ⟨*youth, man*⟩; **das ~e Geschlecht** the fair sex; **die ~en Künste** the fine arts; **sie ist ~ von Gestalt** *(geh.)* she has a lovely figure; **das Schöne** beauty; *(~e Dinge)* beautiful things *pl.*; **~e Literatur** belles-lettres *pl.*; **~e Frau, was wünschen Sie?** *(scherzh.)* what is your wish, my pretty one?; **ich finde das Buch ~**: the book appeals to me; **bring mir etwas Schönes mit** bring me back something nice; **b)** *(angenehm, erfreulich)* pleasant, nice ⟨*day, holiday, dream, relaxation, etc.*⟩; fine ⟨*weather*⟩; *(nett)* nice; **das war eine ~e Zeit** those were wonderful days; **einen ~en Tod haben** die peacefully; **das war alles nicht ~ für sie** it was all rather unpleasant for her; **mach dir ein paar ~e Stunden** enjoy yourself for a few hours; **das ist ~ von dir** it's nice of you; **das ist ein ~er Zug an ihm** that is one of the good *or* nice things about him; **das Schöne daran/an ihm** the nice thing about it/him; **das ist zu ~, um wahr zu sein** that is too good to be true; **alles war in ~ster Ordnung** everything was in perfect order; **was hier vor sich geht, das ist nicht mehr ~** *(ugs.)* the goings-on here are beyond a joke; **c)** *(gut)* good ⟨*wine, beer, piece of work, etc.*⟩; **~ schmecken/riechen** *(nordd. ugs.)* taste/smell really good *or (esp. Amer. coll.)* real good; **d)** *(in Höflichkeitsformeln)* **~e Grüße** best wishes; **[ich soll Ihnen einen] ~en Gruß von meiner Mutter [bestellen]** my mother sends you her kind regards; **recht ~en Dank für ...**: thank you very much for ...; many thanks for ...; **e)** *(ugs.: einverstanden)* OK *(coll.)*; all right; **also ~**: right then; **~ und gut** *(ugs.)* all well and good; **das ist alles ~ und gut, aber ...** *(ugs.)* that's all very well but ...; **f)** *(iron.: leer)* **eine ~e Floskel** a splendid platitude; **~e Worte** fine[-sounding] words; *(schmeichlerisch)* honeyed words; **g)** *(ugs.: beträchtlich)* handsome, *(coll.)* tidy ⟨*sum, fortune, profit*⟩; considerable ⟨*quantity, distance*⟩; pretty good ⟨*pension*⟩; **das hat ein ganz ~es Gewicht** it's quite a weight; **ein ~es Alter erreichen** reach a fine old age; **einen ~en Schrecken davontragen** get a real *or* quite a fright; **eine ~e Leistung** no mean *or* quite an achievement; **h)** *(iron.: unerfreulich)* nice *(coll. iron.)*; **das sind ja ~e Aussichten!** this is a fine look-out *sing. (iron.)*; what a delightful prospect! *sing. (iron.)*; **eine ~e Bescherung** a nice *or* fine mess *(coll. iron.)*; **ein ~er Reinfall** a real disaster; **du machst [mir] ja ~e Geschichten!** you do get up to some fine tricks *(iron.)*. **2.** *adv.* **a)** *(anziehend, reizvoll)* beautifully; **der Wein ist ~ klar** the wine is beautifully clear; **sie ist ~ eingerichtet** she has a lovely home; **sich ~ zurechtmachen** make oneself look nice; **b)** *(angenehm, erfreulich)* nicely; **~ warm/weich/langsam** nice and warm/soft/slow; **wir haben es ~ hier** we're very well off here; **c)** *(gut, ausgezeichnet)* well; **das habt ihr ~ gemacht** you did that well *or* nicely; you made a good job of that; **d)** *(in Höflichkeitsformeln)* **bitte ~, können Sie mir sagen, ...**: excuse me, could you tell me ...; **grüß deine Mutter ~ von mir** give your mother my kind regards; **e)** *(iron.)* **wie es so ~ heißt, wie man so ~ sagt** as they say; **f)** *(ugs.: beträchtlich)* really; *(vor einem Adjektiv)* pretty; **ganz ~ arbeiten müssen** have to work jolly hard *(Brit. coll.)*; **[ganz] ~ dämlich** damned stupid; **er sitzt [ganz] ~ in der Tinte** he's well and truly in the soup *(sl.)*; **ganz ~ trinken/lügen** drink like a fish *(coll.)*/lie like anything *(coll.)*. **3.** *Partikel (ugs. verstärkend)* **~ der Reihe nach!** one after the other in a nice orderly line; **~ ruhig bleiben/~ langsam fahren** be nice and quiet/drive nice and slowly; **bleib ~ liegen!** lie there and be good; **paßt ~ auf!** pay careful attention; **jetzt gehst du ~ nach Hause** now go home like a good boy/girl; **sei ~ brav** be a good boy/girl
Schöne die; *adj. Dekl.* beauty; *(iron.: Frau)* member of the fair sex; **die ~n der Nacht** *(geh.)* the ladies of the night
schonen 1. *tr. V.* treat ⟨*clothes, books, furniture, etc.*⟩ with care; *(schützen)* protect ⟨*hands, furniture*⟩; *(nicht strapazieren)* spare ⟨*voice, eyes, etc.*⟩; conserve ⟨*strength*⟩; *(nachsichtig behandeln)* go easy on, spare ⟨*person*⟩; **jmdm. eine Nachricht ~d beibringen** break news gently to sb.; **eine ~de Behandlung** gentle treatment. **2.** *refl. V.* take care of oneself; *(sich nicht überanstrengen)* take things easy; **sich mehr ~**: take things easier; **er schont sich nicht, wenn es um seine Patienten geht** he doesn't spare himself when it comes to his patients
schönen *tr. V.* brighten ⟨*colour*⟩; clarify ⟨*wine*⟩; *(mit Gelatine)* fine ⟨*wine*⟩; touch up ⟨*picture*⟩; enhance ⟨*picture, figure*⟩; **[idealistisch] geschönt** *(fig.)* idealized; flattering
Schoner der; **~s, ~** *(Seemannsspr.)* schooner
Schön·färberei die; **~, ~en** embellishment; **frei von jeder** *od.* **ohne jede ~**: without any whitewashing
Schon-: **~frist die** period of grace; *(nach einer Operation)* period of convalescence; **~gang der a)** *(Kfz-W.)* high gear; *(Overdrive)* overdrive; **b)** *(bei Waschmaschinen)* programme for delicate fabrics
Schön·geist der aesthete
schön·geistig *Adj.* aesthetic; **die ~e Literatur** belletristic literature
Schönheit die; **~, ~en** beauty; **die ~en der Umgebung** the attractions of the area
Schönheits-: **~chirurgie die** cosmetic surgery *no art.*; **~farm die** health farm; **~fehler der** blemish; *(fig.)* minor defect; *(Nachteil)* slight drawback; **~ideal das** ideal of beauty; **~königin die** beauty queen; **~konkurrenz die** beauty contest; **~pflästerchen** [~pflɛstɐçən] **das** *(Kosmetik)* beauty spot; **~pflege die** beauty care *no art.*; **~reparatur die** cosmetic repair; *(in einem Haus/einer Wohnung)* redecorating *no pl.*; **~sinn der**; *o. Pl.* sense of beauty; aesthetic sense; **~wettbewerb der** beauty contest
Schon-: **~klima das** benign climate; **~kost die** light food; **auf ~kost gesetzt werden** be put on a light diet
schön|machen *(ugs.)* **1.** *tr. V.* smarten ⟨*person, thing*⟩ up; make ⟨*person, thing*⟩ look nice; do up ⟨*building*⟩. **2.** *refl. V.* smarten oneself up; make oneself look smart. **3.** *itr. V.* ⟨*dog*⟩ [sit up and] beg
Schon·platz der *(DDR) job given to someone temporarily incapacitated;* light job
schön-, Schön-: **~|reden** *itr. V. (abwertend)* turn on the smooth talk; sweet-talk *(Amer.)*; **das Schönreden** smooth talking; sweet talk *(Amer.)*; **~redner der** *(abwertend)* smooth *or (Amer.)* sweet talker; **~rednerei die**; **~, ~en** *(abwertend)* smooth *or (Amer.)* sweet talk *no pl.*; **~en** blandishments; **~|schreiben** *unr. itr. (auch tr.) V.* write neatly; *(Schönschrift schreiben)* do

calligraphy; **Schönschreiben** *(als Unterrichtsfach)* handwriting *no art.*; **~schreibheft das** writing-book; *(mit vorgedruckten Buchstaben)* copy-book; **~schrift die a)** *(Zierschrift)* calligraphy; *(sorgfältige Schrift)* neat handwriting; **etw. in ~schrift abschreiben** copy sth. out neatly *or* in one's best handwriting; **b)** *(ugs.: Reinschrift)* neat *or* clean copy; **~|tun** *unr. itr. V. (ugs.)* **jmdm. ~tun** soft-soap sb.; butter sb. up

Schonung die; ~, ~en a) *o. Pl. (Nachsicht)* consideration; *(nachsichtige Behandlung)* considerate treatment; *(nach Krankheit/Operation)* [period of] rest; *(von Gegenständen)* careful treatment; **sein Zustand/Magen verlangt ~:** his condition/his stomach needs careful treatment; **sie braucht noch ~:** she still needs to be treated considerately; *(muß sich selbst schonen)* she must still take things easy; **er kannte ihr gegenüber keine ~:** he knew no mercy towards her; he did not spare her; **b)** *(Jungwald)* [young] plantation

-schonung die ⟨*fir, spruce, etc.*⟩ plantation

schonungs-: ~bedürftig *Adj.* in need of rest *postpos.*; **~bedürftig sein** need to take things carefully *or* easy; **~los 1.** *Adj.* unsparing, ruthless ⟨*criticism etc.*⟩; blunt ⟨*frankness*⟩; **eine ~lose Aufklärung der Affäre** a rigorous elucidation of the affair; **2.** *adv.* unsparingly; ⟨*say*⟩ without mincing one's words

Schonungslosigkeit die; ~: ruthlessness; *(Strenge)* rigour

Schön·wetter·periode die spell of fine weather; fine spell

Schon·zeit die a) *(Jagdw.)* close season; **b)** *(Schonung)* period of rest; *(Erholungszeit)* period of convalescence; recovery period; *(fig.: Anfangszeit, in der man nachsichtig behandelt wird)* honeymoon period

Schopf [ʃɔpf] **der; ~[e]s, Schöpfe** ['ʃœpfə] **a)** *(Haar~)* shock of hair; **die Gelegenheit beim ~[e] fassen** *od.* **nehmen** *od.* **packen** *od.* **ergreifen** *(ugs.)* seize *or* grasp the opportunity with both hands; **b)** *(Jägerspr.: Kopffedern)* crest

¹schöpfen ['ʃœpfn̩] **1.** *tr. V.* **a)** scoop [up] ⟨*water, liquid*⟩; *(mit einer Kelle)* ladle ⟨*soup*⟩; **Wasser aus einem Brunnen ~:** draw water from a well; **Wasser aus dem Boot ~:** bale water out of the boat; **b)** *(geh.: einatmen)* draw, take ⟨*breath*⟩; **frische Luft ~:** take a breath of fresh air; **c)** *(geh.: für sich gewinnen)* draw ⟨*wisdom, strength, knowledge*⟩ **(aus** from); **neuen Mut/neue Hoffnung ~:** take fresh heart/find fresh hope; **Argwohn** *od.* **Vedacht ~:** become suspicious. **2.** *itr. V.* **aus der Phantasie/jahrelanger Erfahrung** *usw.* **~:** draw on one's imagination/on years of experience *etc.*

²schöpfen *tr. V. (veralt.: schaffen)* create; coin ⟨*word*⟩

¹Schöpfer der; ~s, ~: creator; *(Gott)* Creator

²Schöpfer der; ~s, ~ *(Kelle)* ladle

Schöpferin die; ~, ~nen creator

schöpferisch 1. *Adj.* creative; constructive ⟨*criticism*⟩; **der ~e Augenblick** the moment of inspiration; **eine ~e Pause** a pause for inspiration. **2.** *adv.* creatively; **~ tätig sein** be creative

Schöpferkraft die creative powers *pl.*; creativity

Schöpf-: ~kelle die, ~löffel der ladle

Schöpfung die; ~, ~en a) *o. Pl. (geh.: Erschaffung)* creation; *(Erfindung)* invention; **b)** *(geh.: ~ der Welt)* **die ~:** the Creation; *(von Gott Erschaffenes)* Creation; **c)** *(geh.: Kunstwerk, ~ der Mode usw.)* creation; *(Werk)* work

Schöpfungs-: ~geschichte die Creation story; **~tag der** day of the Creation

Schöppchen ['ʃœpçən] **das, ~s, ~:** small glass of wine/beer

Schoppen ['ʃɔpn̩] **der; ~s, ~ a)** [quarter-litre/half-litre] glass of wine/beer; **b)** *(veralt.: Hohlmaß)* **ein ~:** ≈ half a litre

Schoppen·wein der wine by the glass

Schöps [ʃœps] **der; ~es, ~e** *(österr.) s.* **Hammel a, b**

Schöpserne ['ʃœpsɐnə] **das;** *adj. Dekl.; o. Pl. (österr.)* mutton

schor [ʃoːɐ̯] *1. u. 3. Pers. Sg. Prät. v.* **scheren**

Schorf [ʃɔrf] **der; ~[e]s, ~e a)** *(Wund~)* scab; **b)** *(Pflanzenkrankheit)* scab *no art.*

schorfig *Adj.* scabby ⟨*wound*⟩

Schorle ['ʃɔrlə] **die; ~, ~n** wine with mineral water; ≈ spritzer; *(mit Apfelsaft)* apple juice with mineral water

Schorn·stein ['ʃɔrn-] **der** chimney; *(Schiffs~, Lokomotiv~)* funnel; **der ~ raucht** *(fig.)* things are ticking over nicely; business is good; **Geld in den ~ schreiben** *(fig. ugs.)* write off money

Schornstein·feger der; ~s, ~: chimney-sweep

schoß [ʃɔs] *1. u. 3. Pers. Sg. Prät. v.* **schießen**

Schoß [ʃoːs] **der; ~es, Schöße** ['ʃøːsə] **a)** lap; **ein Kind auf den ~ nehmen** take *or* sit a child on one's lap; **seine Frau saß bei ihm auf dem ~:** his wife sat on his knee; **die Hände in den ~ legen** *(fig.)* sit back and do nothing; **jmdm. in den ~ fallen** *(fig.)* just fall into sb.'s lap; **im ~ der Familie/der Kirche** *(fig.)* in the bosom of the family/of Mother Church; *s. auch* **Abraham b; Hand f; b)** *(geh.: Mutterleib)* womb; **im ~ der Erde** *(fig.)* in the bowels of the earth; **c)** *(geh.: Vulva)* pudenda *pl.*; **d)** *(Rock~)* [coat-]tail

Schoß·hund der, Schoß·hündchen das lap-dog

Schößling ['ʃœslɪŋ] **der; ~s, ~e a)** *(Trieb)* shoot; **b)** *(Ableger zum Pflanzen)* cutting

Schot [ʃoːt] **die; ~, ~en** *(Seew.)* sheet

Schote ['ʃoːtə] **die; ~, ~n a)** pod; siliqua *(as tech. term)*; **fünf ~n Paprika** five peppers; **b)** *(landsch.: Erbse)* **~n** peas

Schott [ʃɔt] **das; ~[e]s, ~en** *(Seemannsspr.)* bulkhead; **die ~en dicht machen** *(fig. ugs.)* shut all the doors and windows

Schotte ['ʃɔtə] **der; ~n, ~n** Scot; Scotsman; **er ist ~:** he's a Scot; he's Scottish; **die ~n** the Scots; the Scottish

Schotten der; ~s, ~ *(Textilw.)* tartan [material]

Schotten-: ~muster das tartan pattern; **~rock der** tartan skirt; *(Kilt)* kilt; **~witz der** Scottish joke *(concerning thriftiness)*

Schotter ['ʃɔtɐ] **der; ~s, ~ a)** *(für Straßen)* [road-]metal; gravel; *(für Schienen)* ballast; **b)** *(Geol.)* gravel; **c)** *o. Pl. (salopp: Geld)* dough *(sl.)*; lolly *(Brit. sl.)*

Schotter-: ~decke die [loose] gravel surface; **~straße die** road with [loose] gravel surface

Schottin die; ~, ~nen Scot; Scotswoman

schottisch 1. *Adj.* Scottish; Scots, Scottish ⟨*dialect, accent, voice, etc.*⟩; **~er Whisky** Scotch whisky. **2.** *adv.* ⟨*speak*⟩ with a Scots *or* Scottish accent

Schottland (das); ~s Scotland

schraffieren [ʃraˈfiːrən] *tr. V.* hatch; *(feiner)* shade ⟨*drawing*⟩

Schraffierung die; ~, ~en, Schraffur [ʃraˈfuːɐ̯] **die; ~, ~en** hatching *no indef. art.*; *(feiner)* shading *no indef. art.*

schräg [ʃrɛːk] **1.** *Adj.* **a)** diagonal ⟨*line, beam, cut, etc.*⟩; sloping ⟨*surface, roof, wall, side, etc.*⟩; slanting, slanted ⟨*writing, eyes, etc.*⟩; tilted ⟨*position of the head etc., axis*⟩; *(nicht genau diagonal)* oblique ⟨*line etc.*⟩; **ein ~er Blick** *(fig. ugs.)* a sideways *or* sidelong glance; **b)** *(ugs.: unseriös)* off-beat; weird ⟨*ideas*⟩; *(wild)* hot ⟨*music*⟩; **c)** *(ugs.: zweifelhaft)* shady, *(coll.)* dodgy ⟨*type, firm, etc.*⟩. **2.** *adv.* at an angle; *(diagonal)* diagonally; *(nicht genau diagonal)* obliquely; **den Kopf ~ halten** hold one's head to one side; tilt one's head; **~ stehende Augen** slanting eyes; **~ gegenüber** diagonally opposite; **~ links fahren/abbiegen** bear left; **die Sonnenstrahlen fallen ~ ein** the sun is slanting in; **er saß ~ vor/hinter mir** he was sitting in front of/behind me and to one side; **das Boot liegt ~:** the boat is listing *or* down at one side; **~ gedruckt** [printed] in italics *postpos.*; **jmdn. ~ angucken** *(fig. ugs.)* look askance at sb.

Schräge die; ~, ~n a) *(schräge Fläche)* sloping surface; *(Hang)* slope; **das Zimmer hat eine ~:** the room has a sloping wall; **b)** *(Neigung)* slope; *(Dach~)* pitch; slope; **eine ~ von 10°** a 10° slope *or* incline

Schräg-: ~heck das *(Kfz-W.) s.* **Fließheck; ~lage die** angle; *(eines Schiffes)* list; *(eines Kindes bei der Geburt)* oblique position *or* presentation; *(eines Flugzeugs)* bank; **etw. in ~lage bringen** tilt *or* slant sth.; **das Schiff hat ~lage** the ship is listing *or* is at an angle; **~streifen der** diagonal stripe; **~strich der** oblique stroke

schrak [ʃraːk] *1. u. 3. Pers. Sg. Prät. v.* **schrecken**

Schramme ['ʃramə] **die; ~, ~n** scratch

Schrammel·musik ['ʃraml̩-] **die** *Viennese popular music played on violins, guitar, and accordion;* Schrammeln ensemble music

Schrammeln *Pl. quartet playing violins, guitar, and accordion;* Schrammeln ensemble *sing.*

schrammen *tr. V.* scratch **(an +** *Dat.* on)

Schrank [ʃraŋk] **der; ~[e]s, Schränke** ['ʃrɛŋkə] **a)** cupboard; closet *(Amer.)*; *(Glas~; kleiner Wand~)* cabinet; *(Kleider~)* wardrobe; *(Bücher~)* bookcase; *(im Schwimmbad, am Arbeitsplatz usw.)* locker; **b)** *(ugs.: großer Mann)* **ein [ganz schöner] ~:** a hulking great fellow *(coll.)*

Schrank·bett das foldaway bed

Schränkchen ['ʃrɛŋkçən] **das; ~s, ~:** cabinet

Schranke ['ʃraŋkə] **die; ~, ~n a)** *(auch fig.)* barrier; **jmdn. in die ~ fordern** *(geh.)* throw down the gauntlet to sb.; **vor den ~n des Gerichts** before a/the court; **b)** *(fig.: Grenze)* limit; **er kennt keine ~n** he knows no limits *or* bounds; **die ~n der Konvention durchbrechen** break the bounds of convention; **jmdn. in die** *od.* **seine ~n [ver]weisen** *(geh.)* put sb. in his/her place

Schranken der; ~s, ~ *(österr.)* barrier

schrankenlos 1. *Adj.* boundless, unbounded ⟨*admiration, confidence, loyalty, etc.*⟩; unlimited, limitless ⟨*power, freedom, etc.*⟩; unbridled, untrammelled ⟨*individualism, despotism*⟩; unrestrained, unrestricted ⟨*exploitation*⟩; unrestrained ⟨*brutality*⟩; **sein Egoismus/seine Habgier war ~:** his egoism/greed knew no bounds. **2.** *adv.* boundlessly; ⟨*exploit*⟩ without restraint

Schranken·wärter der level-crossing *(Brit.) or (Amer.)* grade-crossing attendant; crossing-keeper

Schränker der; ~s, ~ *(ugs.) s.* **Geldschrankknacker**

schrank-, Schrank-: ~fach das [cupboard *or (Amer.)* closet] shelf; **~fertig** *Adj.* laundered; washed and ironed ⟨*laundry*⟩; **~koffer der** wardrobe trunk; **~tür die** cupboard door; *(eines Kleiderschranks)* wardrobe door; **~wand die** shelf *or* wall unit

Schranze ['ʃrantsə] **die; ~, ~n** *(abwertend)* sycophantic courtier; *(fig.)* lackey

Schrapnell [ʃrapˈnɛl] **das; ~s, ~e** *od.* **~s** *(Milit.)* shrapnel [shell]

Schrat [ʃraːt], **Schratt** [ʃrat] **der; ~[e]s, ~e** forest goblin

Schrat·segel das *(Seew.)* fore-and-aft sail

Schraub·deckel *der* screw-top

Schraube ['ʃraubə] **die; ~, ~n a)** *(Schlitz~)* screw; *(Sechskant~/Vierkant~)* bolt; **eine ~ ohne Ende** *(fig.)* a vicious *or* never-ending spiral; **bei ihm ist eine ~ locker** *od.* **los** *(fig. salopp)* he has [got] a screw loose *(coll.)*; **b)** *(Schiffs~)* propeller; screw; **c)** *(Turnen)* twist; *(Kunstspringen)* twist dive; **d)** *(Kunstflug)* vertical spin

schrauben 1. *tr. V.* **a)** *(befestigen)* screw **(an, auf +** *Akk.* on to); *(mit Sechskant-/Vierkantschrauben)* bolt **(an, auf +** *Akk.* [on] to); *(entfernen)* unscrew/unbolt **(von** from); **b)** *(drehen)* screw ‹*nut, hook, light-bulb, etc.*› **(auf +** *Akk.* on to; **in +** *Akk.* into); *(lösen)* unscrew ‹*cap etc.*› **(von** from); **den Deckel vom Marmeladenglas ~:** twist the top off the jam-jar; **c) etw. höher/niedriger ~:** screw sth. up/down; **die Preise/Erwartungen in die Höhe ~:** push prices up *or* make prices spiral/raise expectations. **2.** *refl. V.* **sich [in die Höhe] ~:** spiral upwards; *s. auch* **geschraubt**

Schrauben-: ~dreher der; ~s, ~ *(Technik)* screwdriver; **~mutter die;** *Pl.* **~muttern** nut; **~schlüssel der** spanner; **~zieher der; ~s, ~:** screwdriver

Schraub-: ~glas das screw-top jar; **~stock der** vice; **~verschluß der** screw-top; **~zwinge die** screw-clamp

Schreber- ['ʃre:bɐ-]: **~garten der** ≈ allotment *(cultivated primarily as a garden)*; **~gärtner der** ≈ allotment-holder

Schreck [ʃrɛk] **der; ~[e]s, ~e** fright; scare; *(Schock)* shock; **jmdm. einen ~ einjagen** give sb. a fright *or* scare/shock; **vor ~:** with fright; ‹*run away*› in one's fright; **ein freudiger ~:** a thrill of joy; **ein heftiger ~ packte ihn** he was seized by a sudden terror; **auf den ~ [hin] muß ich einen trinken** *(ugs. scherzh.)* I must have a drink to get over the shock; **der ~ fuhr ihm in die Knochen** *od.* **Glieder** the fright/shock went right through him; **der ~ saß ihm noch in den Knochen** *od.* **Gliedern** he still hadn't recovered from the fright/shock; **krieg keinen ~!** *(ugs.)* don't be [too] shocked; **ach du ~!** *(ugs.)* oh my God!; **[oh] ~, laß nach!** *(scherzh.)* God help us!; oh no, not that!

Schreck·bild das terrible *or* frightening sight; *(Vorstellung)* terrible vision

schrecken 1. *tr. V.* **a)** *(geh.)* frighten; scare; **b)** *(auf~)* startle **(aus** out of); make ‹*person*› jump; **du hast mich aus meinen Gedanken geschreckt** you startled me – I was thinking. **2.** *regelm. (auch unr.) itr. V.* start [up]; **aus dem Schlaf ~:** awake with a start; start from one's sleep

Schrecken der; ~s, ~ a) *(Schreck)* fright; scare; *(Entsetzen)* horror; *(große Angst)* terror; **jmdm. einen ~ einjagen** give sb. a fright *or* scare; **ein jäher ~ durchfuhr ihn** *(geh.)* he was seized by a sudden terror; **jmdn. voll[er] ~ ansehen** look at sb. with fear *or* terror in one's eyes; **Angst und ~ verbreiten** spread fear and terror; **jmdn. in Angst und ~ versetzen** terrify sb.; **zu meinem [großen] ~:** to my [great] horror; **mit dem [bloßen] ~ davonkommen** escape with no more than a scare *or* fright; **lieber ein Ende mit ~ als ein ~ ohne Ende** it's better to make a painful break than draw out the agony; **b)** *(Schrecklichkeit, Schrecknis)* horror; **ein Bild des ~s** a terrible *or* terrifying picture; **c)** *(fig.: gefürchtete Sache, Person)* **der ~ des Volkes/** *(scherzh.)* **der Schule** *usw.* the terror of the nation/*(joc.)* the school *etc.*

schrecken·erregend 1. *Adj.* terrifying. **2.** *adv.* terrifyingly

schreckens-, Schreckens-: ~bleich *Adj. (geh.)* pale with terror *postpos.*; as white as a sheet *postpos.*; **~herrschaft die** reign of terror; **~nachricht die** terrible piece of news; **die ~nachricht vom ...:** the terrible news of ...; **~tat die** terrible deed *or* act; atrocity

Schreck·gespenst das a) spectre; *(gegenwärtig)* nightmare; **das ~ Aids** the spectre of Aids; **b)** *(ugs. abwertend: häßlicher Mensch) (Frau)* hideous hag; *(Mann)* ugly brute

schreckhaft 1. *Adj.* **a)** *(leicht zu erschrecken)* easily scared; **b)** *(erschrocken)* frightened, scared ‹*movement, reaction*›. **2.** *adv.* ‹*react*› in a frightened *or* scared way; ‹*start, gaze*› in fright

Schreckhaftigkeit die; ~: easily scared nature; tendency to take fright

schrecklich 1. *Adj.* **a)** terrible; **er war ~ in seinem Zorn** *(geh.)* he was terrible in his wrath; **b)** *(ugs.: unerträglich)* terrible *(coll.)*; **es war mir ~, es zu tun** I felt terrible about doing it; **c)** *(ugs.: sehr groß)* **es hat ihm ~en Spaß gemacht** he found it terrific fun *(coll.)*. **2.** *adv.* **a)** terribly; horribly; **b)** *(ugs. abwertend: unerträglich)* terribly *(coll.)*; dreadfully *(coll.)*; **c)** *(ugs.: sehr, äußerst)* terribly *(coll.)*; **ich habe es ~ eilig** I'm in a terrible *or* terrific hurry *(coll.)*

Schrecknis das; ~ses, ~se *(geh.)* horror

Schreck-: ~schraube die *(ugs. abwertend)* battleaxe; **~schuß der** *(auch fig.)* warning shot; **~schuß·pistole die** blank [cartridge] gun *or* pistol; **~sekunde die** moment of terror/shock; *(Reaktionszeit)* reaction time; **eine ~sekunde lang** for one horrifying moment

Schrei [ʃrai] **der; ~[e]s, ~e** cry; *(lauter Ruf)* shout; *(durchdringend)* yell; *(gellend)* scream; *(kreischend)* shriek; *(des Hahns)* crow; **der ~ nach Gerechtigkeit** *(fig. geh.)* the cry for justice; **der letzte ~** *(fig. ugs.)* the latest thing; **nach dem letzten ~ gekleidet** *(fig. ugs.)* dressed in the latest style

Schreib-: ~arbeit die: an einer ~arbeit sitzen sit doing some writing; **~arbeiten** clerical work *sing.*; **~automat der** word processor; **~bedarf der** stationery; **~block der;** *Pl.* **~blocks** *od.* **~blöcke** writing-pad

Schreibe die; ~ *(ugs.: Schreibstil)* style [of writing]

schreiben ['ʃraibn̩] **1.** *unr. itr. V.* write; ‹*typewriter*› type; **orthographisch richtig ~:** spell correctly; **auf** *od.* **mit der Maschine ~:** type; **mit der Hand/mit dem Bleistift/mit Tinte ~:** write in longhand/in pencil/in ink; **hast du mal was zum Schreiben?** have you got anything to write with?; **der Bleistift schreibt weich/hart** the pencil is soft/hard *or* has a soft/hard lead; **die Feder schreibt zu breit** the nib is too broad; **er hat großes Talent zum Schreiben** he has great talent as a writer; **an einem Roman** *usw.* **~:** be writing a novel *etc.*; **jmdm.** *od.* **an jmdn. ~:** write to sb. **2.** *unr. tr. V.* **a)** write; **etw. mit der Hand/Maschine ~:** write sth. by hand *or* in longhand/type sth.; **wie schreibt man dieses Wort?** how is this word spelt?; **das Wort ist falsch/richtig/mit f geschrieben** the word is spelt wrongly *or* misspelt/spelt correctly/written *or* spelt with an f; **den Titel schreibt man groß** the title is written with capitals [at the beginning of each word]; **Noten ~:** write [out] music; **200 Anschläge pro Minute ~:** have a typing speed of 200 strokes *or* 40 words a minute; **wo steht das denn geschrieben?** *(fig.)* there's no law that says that, is there?; who says? *(coll.)*; **die geschriebene Sprache/das geschriebene Wort** the written language/word; **er schreibt einen guten Stil** he has a good style [of writing]; **eine Klausur/Klassenarbeit ~:** do an exam/a class test; **die Zeitungen ~ viel Unsinn** the newspapers print a lot of nonsense; **was schreibt denn die NZZ darüber?** what does the NZZ have to say about it?; **Karl hat geschrieben. – So, was schreibt er denn?** I've had a letter from Karl. – Oh, what does he say?; **ich werde es ihm sofort ~/ihm ~, daß ...:** I'll write and tell him at once/write and tell him that ...; **bitte ~ Sie mir den Betrag auf die Rechnung** please put the amount on my bill; **b)** *(veralt.)* **wir ~ heute den 21. September** today is 21 September; **man schreibt das Jahr 1925** the year is 1925; **den Wievielten ~ wir heute?** what is the date today *or* today's date?; **c)** *(erklären für)* **jmdn. gesund/krank ~:** certify sb. as fit/give sb. a doctor's certificate; **er wollte sich vom Arzt krank** *od.* **arbeitsunfähig ~ lassen** he wanted the doctor to give him a certificate. **3.** *unr. refl. V.* **a)** *(richtig geschrieben werden)* be spelt; **schreibst du dich mit ei oder mit ey?** is your name spelt with ei or ey?; **b) sich mit jmdm. ~** *(ugs.)* correspond with sb.; **c) sich** *(Dat.)* **die Finger wund ~:** write until one's fingers are weary

Schreiben das; ~s, ~ a) *o. Pl.* writing *no def. art.*; **b)** *(Brief)* letter; **mit ~ vom ...:** in a letter dated ...; **auf Ihr ~ vom ... teilen wir Ihnen mit, ...:** in reply to your letter of the ... we inform you ...

Schreiber der; ~s, ~ a) writer; *(Verfasser)* author; **er ist ein armseliger ~** *(abwertend)* he is a miserable hack [writer]; **b)** *(veralt.: Sekretär, Schriftführer)* secretary; clerk; **c)** *(ugs.: Schreibgerät)* **ich habe keinen ~ bei mir** I've got nothing to write with

Schreiberin die; ~, ~en writer; *(Verfasserin)* authoress

Schreiberling ['ʃraibɐlɪŋ] **der; ~s, ~e** *(abwertend)* hack [writer]; scribbler

schreib-, Schreib-: ~faul *Adj.* lazy about [letter-]writing *postpos.*; **ich bin [sehr] ~faul** I'm a poor correspondent *or* not much of a letter-writer; **~faulheit die** laziness about [letter-]writing; **~fehler der** spelling mistake; *(Versehen)* slip [of the pen]; **~gerät das** writing implement; **~heft das** *(usu. lined)* exercise-book; *(im Gegensatz zum Rechenheft)* writing-book; **~kraft die** clerical assistant; *([Steno]typistin)* [shorthand] typist; **~krampf der** writer's cramp; **einen ~krampf haben/bekommen** have/get writer's cramp; **~kundig** *Adj.* able to write *postpos.*; **~mappe die** writing-case; **~maschine die** typewriter; **etw. mit [der]** *od.* **auf der ~maschine schreiben** type sth.; **mit [der] ~maschine geschrieben** typewritten; typed; **sie kann gut ~maschine schreiben** she is a good typist; **~maschinen·papier das** typing paper; **~papier das** writing-paper; **~pult das** [writing-]desk; **~schrift die** cursive writing; *(gedruckt)* [cursive] script; **~stil der** written style; **~stube die a)** *(veralt.)* office *(for clerical staff)*; *(hist.)* scriptorium; **b)** *(Milit.)* orderly room; **~tafel die a)** *(hist.)* [writing-]tablet; **b)** *(für die Schule)* slate; **~tisch der** desk; **~tisch·täter der** mastermind behind the scenes; *(Beamter)* desk-bound director of operations; **~übung die** writing exercise

Schreibung die; ~, ~en spelling; **eine falsche ~:** a misspelling; an incorrect spelling

Schreib-: ~unter·lage die desk pad; **~verbot das** writing ban; **ihm wurde ~verbot erteilt** he was banned from writing; **~waren** *Pl.* stationery *sing.*; writing materials; **~waren·geschäft das** stationer's; stationery shop *or (Amer.)* store; **~weise die** spelling; **~zeug das** writing things *pl.*

schreien 1. *unr. itr. V.* ‹*person*› cry [out]; *(laut rufen/sprechen)* shout; *(durchdringend)* yell; *(gellend)* scream; ‹*baby*› yell, bawl; ‹*animal*› scream; ‹*owl, gull, etc.*› screech; ‹*cock*› crow; ‹*donkey*› bray; ‹*crow*› caw; ‹*cat*› howl; ‹*monkey*› shriek; **vor Lachen ~:** scream with laughter; **zum Schreien sein** *(ugs.)* be a scream *(sl.)*; **nach etw. ~:** yell for sth.; *(fig.)* cry out for sth.; *(fordern)* demand sth.; **die Kinder schrien nach der Mutter** the children were yelling *or* bawling for their mother. **2.** *unr. tr. V.* shout; **Hilfe ~:** shout for help. **3.** *unr. refl. V.* **sich heiser/müde ~:** shout *or* yell oneself hoarse/tire onself out with shouting *or* yelling

schreiend *(fig.)* **1.** *Adj.* **a)** *(grell)* garish ‹*colour, poster, etc.*›; loud ‹*pattern*›; **b)** *(empö-*

rend) glaring, flagrant ⟨*injustice, anomaly*⟩; blatant ⟨*wrong*⟩. **2.** *adv.* **a)** *(grell)* garishly; ~ **bunt** garishly coloured; **b)** *(empörend)* flagrantly; blatantly

Schreier der; ~s, ~: noisy person; bawler; **die größten ~:** the noisiest people; those who make/made the most noise

Schrei-: ~hals der *(ugs.)* **a)** *(Kind)* bawler; **b)** *(abwertend: Randalierer)* rowdy; **~krampf der** screaming fit

Schrein [ʃrain] **der; ~[e]s, ~e** *(geh.)* shrine

Schreiner der; ~s, ~ *(bes. südd.) s.* **Tischler**

Schreinerei die; ~, ~en *(bes. südd.) s.* **Tischlerei**

schreinern *(bes. südd.)* **1.** *itr. V.* do joinery; **er kann gut ~:** he is good at joinery *or* woodworking. **2.** *tr. V.* make ⟨*furniture etc.*⟩

schreiten [ˈʃraitn̩] *unr. itr. V.; mit sein (geh.)* **a)** walk; *(mit großen Schritten)* stride; *(marschieren)* march; **auf und ab ~:** pace up and down; **von Sieg zu Sieg ~** *(fig.)* march on from one victory to another; **b) zu etw. ~** *(fig.)* proceed to sth.; **zur Tat** *od.* **zum Werk ~:** go into action/get down to work

schrickt [ʃrɪkt] *3. Pers. Sg. Präsens v.* **schrecken**

schrie [ʃri:] *1. u. 3. Pers. Sg. Prät. v.* **schreien**

schrieb [ʃri:p] *1. u. 3. Pers. Sg. Prät. v.* **schreiben**

Schrieb der; ~[e]s, ~e *(ugs.)* missive *(coll.)*

Schrift [ʃrɪft] **die; ~, ~en a)** *(System)* script; *(Alphabet)* alphabet; **in kyrillischer/phonetischer ~:** in Cyrillic/phonetic script; in the Cyrillic/phonetic alphabet; **b)** *(Hand~)* [hand]writing; **er hat eine gute/unleserliche ~:** he has good/illegible handwriting; his writing is good/illegible; **c)** *(Druckw.: ~art)* [type-]face; **d)** *(Text)* text; *(wissenschaftliche Abhandlung)* paper; *(Werk)* work; *(Bitt~)* petition; **Karl Hubers [frühe/gesammelte] ~en** Karl Hubers [early/collected] writings; **die [Heilige] ~:** the Scriptures *pl.*; **e)** *Pl. (schweiz.: Ausweispapiere)* [identity] papers

schrift-, Schrift-: ~art die *(Druckw.)* [type-]face; **~bild das** *(bei Druckschrift)* [appearance of the] type; *(bei Handschrift)* [appearance of one's] writing; **~deutsch** *Adj.* **a)** written German; **b)** *s.* **hochdeutsch; ~deutsch das a)** written German; **das schweizerische ~deutsch** written Swiss German; **b)** *s.* **Hochdeutsch**

Schriften·verzeichnis das bibliography

Schrift-: ~form die; *o. Pl. (Rechtsspr.)* written form; **... bedarf der ~form** ... must be drawn up in writing [and signed] by the party in question; **~führer der** secretary; **~gelehrte der** scribe *(Bibl.)*; *(Islam)* mullah; **~grad der, ~größe die** *(Druckw.)* type-size; **~leiter der** *(veralt.)* editor; **~leitung die** *(veralt.)* **a)** *(Funktion)* editorship; **b)** *(Abteilung)* editorial department

schriftlich 1. *Adj.* written; **das Schriftliche** written work; *(ugs.: die ~e Prüfung)* the written exam; **ich habe [darüber] leider nichts Schriftliches** I'm afraid I haven't got anything in writing. **2.** *adv.* in writing; **soll ich es ~ machen?** should I put it in writing?; **jmdn. ~ einladen** send sb. a written invitation; **das lasse ich mir ~ geben** I'll get that in writing; **das kann ich dir ~ geben** *(fig. ugs.)* you can take that from me

schrift-, Schrift-: ~probe die a) *(einer Handschrift)* sample *or* specimen of [one's] handwriting; **b)** *(Druckw.)* type specimen; **~rolle die** scroll; **~satz der a)** *(Druckw.)* type matter; **b)** *(Rechtsw.: Erklärung)* written statement; **~setzer der** typesetter; **~sprache die** written language; **die deutsche ~sprache** written German; **~sprachlich 1.** *Adj.* used in the written language *postpos.*; **2.** *adv.* in the written language; **sich ~sprachlich ausdrücken** express oneself in language appropriate to a written style; **~steller der** writer; **die antiken ~steller** the authors of classical antiquity; **~stellerei die; ~:** writing *no def. art.*; **~stellerin die; ~, ~nen** writer; **~stellerisch 1.** *Adj.* literary ⟨*work, activity*⟩; ⟨*talent*⟩ as a writer; **die ~stellerische Tätigkeit** working as a writer; **2.** *adv.* **~stellerisch begabt/tätig sein** be talented as a writer/work as a writer; **~stellern** *itr. V.* work as a writer; do literary work; **~stück das** [official] document

Schrifttum das; ~s literature; **das ~ zu diesem Thema** the literature on this subject

Schrift-: ~verkehr der; *o. Pl.* correspondence; **mit jmdm. in regem ~verkehr stehen** have an active correspondence with sb.; **~wechsel der** correspondence; **~zeichen das** character; **~zug der a)** *Pl.* lettering *sing.*; *(Handschrift)* handwriting *sing.*; **b)** *(Namenszug)* lettering; *(als Firmenzeichen)* logo

schrill [ʃrɪl] **1.** *Adj.* **a)** shrill; *(fig.)* strident ⟨*propaganda, colours, etc.*⟩; **b)** *(Jugendspr.)* fab *(sl.)*. **2.** *adv.* shrilly

schrillen *itr. V.* shrill; sound shrilly

Schrippe [ˈʃrɪpə] **die; ~, ~n** *(bes. berlin.)* long [bread] roll

schritt [ʃrɪt] *1. u. 3. Pers. Sg. Prät. v.* **schreiten**

Schritt der; ~[e]s, ~e a) step; **mit großen/gemessenen ~en** with big/measured strides; **die ersten ~e machen** *(auch fig.)* take one's first steps; **er verlangsamte/beschleunigte seine ~e** he slowed/quickened his pace; **die Freude beflügelte meine ~e** *(geh.)* joy gave me wings; **einen ~ zur Seite/nach vorn machen** *od.* **tun** take a step sideways/forwards; **der Schnee knirschte unter unseren ~en** the snow crunched under our footsteps; **~ für ~, ~ um ~** *(auch fig.)* step by step; **den ersten ~ machen** *od.* **tun** *(fig.) (den Anfang machen)* take the first step; *(als erster handeln)* make the first move; **in einem zweiten ~** *(fig.)* as a second stage; **den zweiten ~ vor dem ersten machen** *od.* **tun** *(fig.)* put the cart before the horse; **der erste ~ zur Diktatur** *usw.* the first step on the road to dictatorship *etc.*; **auf ~ und Tritt** wherever one goes; at every step; **er folgte ihr auf ~ und Tritt** he followed her wherever she went; **b)** *Pl. (Geräusch)* footsteps; **c)** *(auch ungebeugt: Entfernung)* pace; **nur ein paar ~e von uns entfernt** only a few yards away from us; **in etwa 100 ~[en] Entfernung** at [a distance of] about 100 paces; **ein paar ~e gehen** take a little walk; **einen ~ weiter gehen** *(fig.)* go a step *or* stage further; **einen ~ zu weit gehen** *(fig.)* go too far; overstep the mark; **jmdn. einen großen** *od.* **guten ~ weiterbringen** *(fig.)* take sb. a lot further; **er ist der Konkurrenz immer ein paar ~e voraus** *(fig.)* he is always a few steps ahead of the competition; **sich** *(Dat.)* **jmdn. drei ~e vom Leibe halten** *(fig. ugs.)* keep sb. at arm's length; **d)** *(Gleich~)* **aus dem ~ kommen** *od.* **geraten** get out of step; **im ~ gehen** walk in step; **e)** *o. Pl. (des Pferdes)* walk; **im ~:** at a walk; **f)** *o. Pl. (Gangart)* walk; **jmdn. am ~ erkennen** recognize sb. by his/her walk *or* gait; **seinen ~ verlangsamen/beschleunigen** slow/quicken one's pace; **[mit jmdm./etw.] ~ halten** *(auch fig.)* keep up *or* keep pace [with sb./sth.]; **g)** *(~geschwindigkeit)* walking pace; **[im] ~ fahren** go at walking pace *or* a crawl; **„~ fahren"** 'dead slow'; **h)** *(fig.: Maßnahme)* step; measure; **~e unternehmen** *od.* **veranlassen** take steps; **i)** *(Teil der Hose, Genitalbereich)* crotch

Schrittempo das; ~s walking pace; **[im] ~ fahren** go at walking pace *or* a crawl

schritt-, Schritt-: ~geschwindigkeit die walking pace; **[mit] ~geschwindigkeit fahren** go at walking pace *or* a crawl; **~macher der** *(Sport, Med.; auch fig.)* pacemaker; **~tempo** *s.* **Schrittempo; ~weise 1.** *Adv.* step by step; gradually; **2.** *adj.; nicht präd.* step by step; gradual

schroff [ʃrɔf] **1.** *Adj.* **a)** precipitous, sheer ⟨*rock etc.*⟩; **b)** *(plötzlich)* sudden, abrupt ⟨*transition, change*⟩; *(kraß)* stark ⟨*contrast*⟩; **im ~en Widerspruch zu etw. stehen** be totally incompatible with sth.; **c)** *(barsch)* abrupt, curt ⟨*refusal, manner*⟩; brusque ⟨*manner, behaviour, tone*⟩. **2.** *adv.* **a)** ⟨*rise, drop*⟩ sheer; ⟨*fall away*⟩ precipitously; **b)** *(plötzlich, unvermittelt)* suddenly; abruptly; **c)** *(barsch)* curtly; ⟨*interrupt*⟩ abruptly; ⟨*treat*⟩ brusquely

Schroffheit die; ~, ~en a) *o. Pl.* precipitousness; **b)** *o. Pl. (Plötzlichkeit)* suddenness; abruptness; *(Kraßheit)* starkness; **c)** *o. Pl. (Barschheit)* curtness; abruptness; brusqueness; **mit ~:** curtly; **d) seine ~en** his curt *or* brusque behaviour *sing.*; *(Bemerkungen)* his curt remarks

schröpfen [ˈʃrœpfn̩] *tr. V.* **a)** *(ugs.)* fleece; **b)** *(Med.)* cup

Schrot [ʃro:t] **der** *od.* **das; ~[e]s, ~e a)** coarse meal; *(aus Getreide)* whole meal *(Brit.)*; whole grain; *(aus Malz)* grist; crushed malt; **b)** *(aus Blei)* shot; **einem Hasen eine Ladung ~ aufbrennen** pepper a hare with shot; **c)** *in* **ein Mann von echtem/bestem ~ und Korn** a man of sterling qualities; **ein Offizier/Kavalier** *usw.* **von altem ~ und Korn** an officer/a gentleman *etc.* of the old school

schroten *tr. V.* grind ⟨*grain etc.*⟩ [coarsely]; crush ⟨*malt*⟩ [coarsely]

Schrot-: ~flinte die shotgun; **~kugel die** pellet; **~ladung die** round of shot; small-shot charge

Schrott [ʃrɔt] **der; ~[e]s, ~e a)** scrap [-metal]; **das gehört auf den ~:** it belongs on the scrap-heap; **ein Auto zu ~ fahren** *(ugs.)* write a car off; **b)** *o. Pl. (salopp abwertend: minderwertiges Zeug)* rubbish; junk

schrott-, Schrott-: ~händler der scrap-dealer; scrap-merchant; **~haufen der** scrap-heap; *(ugs. fig.)* rusty heap; *(Unfallwagen)* heap of scrap; **~platz der** scrap-yard; **~reif** *Adj.* ready for the scrap-heap *postpos.*; fit for scrap *postpos.*; **ein Auto ~reif fahren** write a car off; **~wert der** scrap value

schrubben [ˈʃrʊbn̩] *tr. (auch itr.) V.* scrub

Schrubber der; ~s, ~: [long-handled] scrubbing-brush

Schrulle [ˈʃrʊlə] **die; ~, ~n a)** *(seltsame Idee)* cranky idea; *(Marotte)* quirk; **b)** *(ugs. abwertend: Frau)* **[alte] ~:** old crone

schrullen·haft, schrullig *Adj.* cranky ⟨*person, idea*⟩; zany *(coll.)* ⟨*story etc.*⟩

Schrulligkeit die; ~: crankiness; zaniness

schrumpelig *Adj. (ugs.)* wrinkly; wrinkled

schrumpeln [ˈʃrʊmpl̩n] *itr. V.; mit sein (ugs.)* ⟨*skin*⟩ go wrinkled; ⟨*apple etc.*⟩ shrivel

schrumpfen [ˈʃrʊmpfn̩] *itr. V.; mit sein* shrink; ⟨*metal, rock*⟩ contract; ⟨*apple etc.*⟩ shrivel; ⟨*skin*⟩ go wrinkled; *(abnehmen)* decrease; ⟨*supplies, capital, hopes*⟩ dwindle

Schrumpf-: ~kopf der *(Völkerk.)* shrunken head; **~leber die** cirrhotic liver; **eine ~leber haben/kriegen** have/get cirrhosis of the liver; **~niere die** cirrhotic kidney; **eine ~niere haben** have cirrhosis of the kidney

schrumplig *s.* **schrumpelig**

Schrunde [ˈʃrʊndə] **die; ~, ~n** crack; *(von Kälte)* chap

schrundig *Adj.* cracked, chapped ⟨*skin, hands, etc.*⟩

Schub [ʃu:p] **der; ~[e]s, Schübe** [ˈʃy:bə] **a)** *(Physik: ~kraft)* thrust; *(eines Kolbenmotors)* pulling power; **b)** *(Med.: Phase)* phase; stage; **c)** *(Gruppe, Anzahl)* batch; **~ auf** *od.* **um ~:** [in] one batch after another; **d)** *(bes. ostmd.: ~lade)* drawer

Schuber [ˈʃu:bɐ] **der; ~s, ~ a)** slip-case; **b)** *(österr.: Riegel)* bolt

Schub·fach das *s.* **Schublade**

Schub-: ~karre die, ~karren der wheelbarrow; **~kasten der** drawer; **~kraft die**

thrust; ~lade die drawer; *(fig.: Kategorie)* pigeon-hole; in der ~lade liegen *(fig.)* be ready for use

schubladisieren *tr. V. (schweiz.)* pigeon-hole

Schubs [ʃʊps] der; ~es, ~e *(ugs.)* shove; *(fig.: Ermunterung)* prod

Schub·schiff das push boat; pusher

schubsen *tr. (auch itr.) V. (ugs.)* push; shove

schub·weise 1. *Adv.* a) in batches; b) *(Med.)* in phases *or* stages. 2. *adj.; nicht präd.* a) in batches *postpos.;* b) *(Med.)* phased

schüchtern ['ʃʏçtṇ] 1. *Adj.* a) shy ⟨*person, smile, etc.*⟩; shy, timid ⟨*voice, knock, etc.*⟩; b) *(fig.: zaghaft)* tentative, cautious ⟨*attempt, beginnings, etc.*⟩; cautious ⟨*hope*⟩. 2. *adv.* a) shyly; ⟨*knock, ask, etc.*⟩ timidly; er schwieg ~: he was too shy to say anything; b) *(fig.: zaghaft)* tentatively; cautiously

Schüchternheit die; ~: shyness

Schuft [ʃʊft] der; ~[e]s, ~e *(abwertend)* scoundrel; swine

schuften *(ugs.)* 1. *itr. V.* slave *or* slog away; er schuftet für zwei he does the work of two [people]. 2. *refl. V.* sich müde/krank *usw.* ~: tire oneself out/make oneself ill *etc.* with [over]work; sich zu Tode ~: work oneself to death

Schufterei die; ~ *(ugs.)* slaving away *no indef. art.;* slog

schuftig 1. *Adj.* mean; despicable. 2. *adv.* meanly; despicably

Schuftigkeit die; ~, ~en a) *o. Pl.* meanness; b) *(schuftige Handlung)* mean *or* despicable thing

Schuh [ʃu:] der; ~[e]s, ~e a) shoe; *(hoher ~, Stiefel)* boot; umgekehrt wird ein ~ draus *(fig. ugs.)* the reverse *or* opposite is true; wo drückt der ~? *(fig. ugs.)* what's on your mind?; what's bugging you? *(sl.)*; wissen, wo jmdn. der ~ drückt *(fig. ugs.)* know where sb.'s problems lie; jmdm. etw. in die ~e schieben *(fig. ugs.)* pin the blame for sth. on sb.

Schuh-: ~anzieher der; ~s, ~: shoehorn; ~band das; *Pl.* ~bänder *(bes. südd.)* shoelace; ~bürste die shoe-brush

Schuhchen, Schühchen ['ʃy:çən] das; ~s, ~: [little] shoe; *(Stiefelchen)* bootee

Schuh-: ~creme die shoe-polish; ~größe die shoe size; welche ~größe hast du? what size shoe[s] do you take?; ~löffel der shoehorn; ~macher der; ~s, ~: shoemaker; *s. auch* Bäcker; ~macherei die; ~, ~en a) shoemaker's; b) *o. Pl. (Handwerk)* shoemaking *no art.;* ~nummer die shoe size; ~plattler [~platlɐ] der; ~s, ~: *folk dance in Tirol, Bavaria and Carinthia, involving the slapping of the thighs, knees, and shoe soles;* ~putzer der; ~s, ~: shoeblack; shoe-cleaner; *(Gerät)* shoe-cleaning machine; ~riemen der a) sandal-strap; b) *(bes. westmd.: Schnürsenkel)* shoe-lace; ~sohle die sole [of a/one's shoe]; sich *(Dat.)* etw. an den ~sohlen abgelaufen haben *(fig. ugs.)* have found sth. out ages ago; ~spanner der shoe-tree; ~werk das; *o. Pl.* footwear; shoes *pl.;* ~wichse die *(veralt.)* shoe-polish

Schuko·stecker Ⓦz ['ʃu:ko-] der two-pin earthed *(Brit.) or (Amer.)* grounded plug

Schul-: ~abgänger der; ~s, ~: school-leaver; ~ab·schluß der school-leaving qualification; ~alter das; *o. Pl.* school age; Kinder im ~alter children of school age; er kommt bald ins ~alter he will soon be of school age; ~amt das education authority; ~an·fang der a) *(Anfang des ~besuches)* first day at school; etw. zum ~anfang bekommen get sth. for starting school; b) *(Anfang des ~tages)* um 8 Uhr ist ~anfang school starts at 8 o'clock; ~an·fänger der child [just] starting school; ~arbeit die a) *s.* ~aufgabe; b) *(österr.: Klassenarbeit)* [written] class test; c) *o. Pl. (Praxis des Unterrichts)* schoolwork *no art.;* ~atlas der school atlas; ~auf·gabe die item of homework; ~aufgaben homework *sing.;* ~auf·satz der school essay; ~aus·flug der school outing; ~bank die; *Pl.* ~bänke [school] desk; die ~bank drücken *(ugs.)* go to *or* be at school; ~beginn der *s.* ~anfang; ~beispiel das textbook example (für of); ~besuch der school attendance; ~bildung die; *o. Pl.* [school] education; schooling; ~brot das sandwich *(eaten during break);* ~buch das school-book; ~bus der school bus

schuld *s.* Schuld b

Schuld [ʃʊlt] die; ~, ~en a) *o. Pl. (das Schuldigsein)* guilt; die Schwere einer ~: the seriousness *or* degree of guilt; er ist ohne [jede] ~: he is [entirely] guiltless *or* blameless; er ist sich *(Dat.)* keiner ~ bewußt he is not conscious of having done any wrong; ~ und Sühne crime and punishment; ... und vergib uns unsere ~ *(bibl.)* ... and forgive us our sins *or* trespasses; b) *o. Pl. (Verantwortlichkeit)* blame; es ist [nicht] seine ~: it is [not] his fault; ihn trifft keine ~: no blame attaches to him; er sucht die ~ immer zuerst bei anderen he always tries to blame others first; der Unfallgegner hat seine ~ anerkannt the other party admitted liability for the accident; er ist durch eigene ~ in diese Lage geraten it was his own fault that he got into this situation; jetzt hat er durch deine ~ seinen Zug verpaßt now he has missed his train because of you; [an etw. *(Dat.)*] schuld haben *od.* sein be to blame [for sth.]; er ist nicht schuld daran it is not his fault; he is not to blame [for this]; sie ist an allem ~: it's all her fault; c) *(Verpflichtung zur Rückzahlung)* debt; *(Hypothek)* mortgage; ich habe [bei der Bank] 5 000 Mark ~en I have debts of 5,000 marks [with the bank]; I owe [the bank] 5,000 marks; das Haus ist frei von ~en the house is unmortgaged *or* free of mortgage; in ~en geraten/sich in ~en stürzen get into debt/into serious debt; ich mache ungern ~en I don't like getting into debt *or* running up debts; er hat mehr ~en als Haare auf dem Kopf *(ugs.)* he is up to his eyes *or* ears in debt; d) *in* [tief] in jmds. ~ stehen *od.* sein *(geh.)* be [deeply] indebted to sb.

Schuld·bekenntnis das a) confession [of guilt]; b) *(Rechtsw.)* acknowledgement of indebtedness

schuld·bewußt 1. *Adj.* guilty ⟨*look, face, etc.*⟩. 2. *adv.* guiltily; jmdn. ~ ansehen give sb. a guilty look

schulden *tr. V.* owe ⟨*money, respect, explanation*⟩; was schulde ich Ihnen? how much do I owe you?

schulden-, Schulden-: ~berg der *(ugs.)* pile of debts; ~frei *Adj.* debt-free ⟨*person etc.*⟩; unmortgaged ⟨*house etc.*⟩; ich bin/das Haus ist ~frei I am free of debt/the house is free of mortgage; ~macher der *(ugs. abwertend)* [habitual] debtor

schuld-, Schuld-: ~frage die question of guilt; ~gefühl das feeling of guilt; guilty feeling; ~gefühle haben/bekommen feel/start to feel guilty; ~haft 1. *Adj.* culpable; 2. *adv.* culpably

Schul·dienst der; *o. Pl.* [school-]teaching *no art.;* in den ~ gehen go into teaching; im ~ tätig sein be in the teaching profession

schuldig *Adj.* a) *(Schuld tragend)* guilty; jmdn. ~ sprechen *od.* für ~ erklären find sb. guilty; er hat sich des Diebstahls ~ gemacht he has been guilty of *or* committed theft; er bekennt sich ~: he admits his guilt; er wurde/ist ~ geschieden *(veralt.)* he was the guilty party in the divorce; auf ~ plädieren ⟨*public prosecutor*⟩ ask for a verdict of guilty; das Gericht erkannte auf ~: the court returned a verdict of guilty; b) *(verantwortlich)* der [an dem Unfall] ~e Autofahrer the driver to blame *or* responsible [for the accident]; c) jmdm. etw. ~ sein/bleiben owe sb. sth.; was bin ich Ihnen ~? what *or* how much do I owe you?; jmdm. eine Erklärung/Dank *usw.* ~ sein owe sb. an explanation/a debt of gratitude *etc.;* dafür bin ich dir keine Rechenschaft ~: I don't have to account to you for that; den Beweis bist du mir immer noch ~: you have still not given *or* shown me any proof; das bin ich ihm/der Partei ~: I owe it to him/the party; das ist er seiner gesellschaftlichen Stellung ~: his social position requires it of him; jmdm. die Antwort/Erklärung ~ bleiben [still] owe sb. an answer/explanation; er blieb ihnen die Antwort nicht ~: he did not fail to give them an answer *or* leave them without an answer; d) *nicht präd. (gebührend)* due; proper; jmdm. den ~en Respekt erweisen show sb. due respect *or* the respect due to him/her

Schuldige der/die; *adj. Dekl.* guilty person; *(im Strafprozeß)* guilty party; der an dem Unfall ~: the person responsible for *or* to blame for the accident; einer muß ja der ~ sein 'someone must have done it

Schuldiger der; ~s, ~ *(bibl.)* wie wir vergeben unsern ~n as we forgive those who sin *or* trespass against us

Schuldigkeit die; ~, ~en duty; meine [verdammte] Pflicht und ~: my bounden duty; seine ~ getan haben *(fig.)* have served its/his purpose

Schuld·komplex der guilt complex

schuld·los *Adj.* innocent (an + *Dat.* of); er wurde/ist ~ geschieden he was the innocent party in the divorce

Schuldner der; ~s, ~, **Schuldnerin** die; ~, ~nen debtor

Schuld-: ~schein der IOU; promissory note *(Commerc.); (formell)* bond; ~spruch der verdict of guilty; ~turm der *(hist.)* debtors' prison; ~verschreibung die *(Wirtsch.)* debenture bond; ~zu·weisung die recrimination

Schule ['ʃu:lə] die; ~, ~n a) school; die ~ wechseln change schools; zur *od.* in die ~ gehen, die ~ besuchen go to school; zur *od.* in die ~ kommen come to school; *(als Schulanfänger)* start school; von der ~ abgehen leave school; auf *od.* in der ~: at school; er ist an der ~: he is a [school-]teacher; he teaches school *(Amer.);* er ist durch eine harte ~ gegangen *(fig.)* he has been through a hard school; aus der ~ plaudern *(fig.)* reveal [confidential] information; spill the beans *(sl.);* ~ machen *(fig.)* become the accepted thing; form a precedent; ein Diplomat *usw.* alter *od.* der alten ~: a diplomat *etc.* of the old school; b) *o. Pl. (Ausbildung)* training; [keine] ~ haben ⟨*dog, singer, etc.*⟩ [not] be trained; Hohe ~ *(Reiten)* haute école; c) *(Lehr-, Übungsbuch)* manual; handbook; eine ~ des Klavierspiels a piano tutor; eine ~ der Liebe a handbook of *or* guide to love

schulen *tr. V.* train; jmdn. politisch ~: give sb. a political schooling; er hat sich/seinen Stil an Adorno geschult he modelled himself/his style on Adorno; ein geschultes Auge a practised *or* expert eye

Schul-: ~englisch das school English; ~entlassene der/die; *adj. Dekl.* school-leaver *(Brit.);* school graduate *(Amer.)*

Schüler ['ʃy:lɐ] der; ~s, ~ a) pupil; *(Schuljunge)* schoolboy; ~ und Studenten schoolchildren and students; die ~ der Grundschule the primary school children *or* pupils; ein ehemaliger ~ [der Schule] a former pupil *or* an old boy [of the school]; er ist noch ~: he is still at school; als ~ bekomme ich ...: as I am [still] at school, I receive ...; b) *(fig.: eines Meisters)* pupil; *(Jünger)* disciple

schüler-, Schüler-: ~aus·tausch der school exchange; **~ausweis der** schoolchild's pass; **~brigade die** *(DDR)* work team of schoolchildren *(usu. working on a farm)*; **~haft 1.** *Adj. (wie ein Schuljunge)* schoolboyish; *(wie ein Schulmädchen)* schoolgirlish; **2.** *adv.* like a schoolboy/schoolgirl

Schülerin die; ~, ~nen pupil; schoolgirl; **eine ehemalige ~ [der Schule]** a former pupil *or* an old girl [of the school]

Schüler-: ~karte die schoolchild's season ticket; **~lotse der** *pupil trained to help other schoolchildren to cross the road;* **~mit·verwaltung die** pupil participation *no art.* in school administration

Schülerschaft die; ~, ~en pupils *pl.*

Schüler-: ~sprache die school slang; **~zeitung die** school magazine

schul-, Schul-: ~fach das school subject; **... ist ~fach ...** is taught in schools *or* is a school subject; **~ferien** *Pl.* school holidays *or (Amer.)* vacation *sing.*; **es sind noch ~ferien** the schools are still on holiday *or (Amer.)* vacation; **~fest das** school open day; **~frei** *Adj.* ⟨*day*⟩ off school; **morgen ist/haben wir ~frei** there is/we have no school tomorrow; **~frei bekommen** be let off school; **~freund der** school-friend; **~funk der** schools broadcasting *no art.*; *(Sendungen)* [radio] programmes *pl.* for schools; **~gebäude das** school [building]; **~gebrauch der: für den ~gebrauch** for school use; for use in schools; **~gegenstand der** *(österr.) s.* **~fach; ~gelände das** school grounds *pl. or* premises *pl.*; **~geld das** school fees *pl.*; **laß dir dein ~geld wiedergeben!** *(ugs.)* they can't have taught you a thing at school; **~grammatik die** grammar [book] for schools; **~haus das** schoolhouse; **~heft das** exercise book; **~hof der** school yard

schulisch 1. *Adj.; nicht präd.* ⟨*conflicts, problems, etc.*⟩ at school; school ⟨*work etc.*⟩; scholastic ⟨*questions etc.*⟩; **seine ~en Leistungen** [the standard of] his school work *sing.* **2.** *adv.* at school

schul-, Schul-: ~jahr das a) school year; **b)** *(Klasse)* year; **ein zehntes ~jahr** a tenth-year class; **~jugend die** schoolchildren *pl.*; **~junge der** schoolboy; **~kamerad der** *(veralt.)* schoolmate; **~kind das** schoolchild; **~klasse die** [school] class; **~landheim das** [school's] country hostel *(visited by school classes)*; **~lehrer der** schoolteacher; **~leiter der** headmaster; head teacher; **~leiterin die** headmistress; head teacher; **~leitung die a)** [school] headship; **b)** *(Person)* head teacher; *(Personen)* school management; **~lektüre die** school reading [material]; *(einzelner Text)* school text; **~mädchen das** schoolgirl; **~mann der;** *Pl.* **~männer** *(veralt.)* schoolteacher; **~mappe die** school-bag; **~medizin die;** *o. Pl.* orthodox *or* traditional medicine *no art.*; **~meister der a)** *(veralt., scherzh.)* schoolmaster; **b)** *(abwertend: Krittler)* schoolmasterly type; pedagogue; **~meistern** *(abwertend) tr. (auch itr.) V.* lecture; **er ~meistert gern** he likes lecturing people; **~musik die** music *no art.* in schools; **~orchester das** school orchestra; **~ordnung die** school rules *pl.*; **~pflicht die;** *o. Pl.* obligation to attend school; **die Einführung der [allgemeinen] ~pflicht** the introduction of compulsory school attendance [for all children]; **~pflichtig** *Adj.* required to attend school *postpos.*; **~pflichtig sein** have to attend school; **im ~pflichtigen Alter** of school age; **~praktikum das** teaching practice; **~ranzen der** [school] satchel; **~rat der** schools inspector; **~reif** *Adj.* ready for school *postpos.*; **~reife die** readiness for school; **~schiff das** training ship; **~schluß der;** *o. Pl.* end of school; **nach ~schluß** after school; **~schwänzer der** *(ugs.)* truant; **~speisung die** school meals *pl.*; **~sport der** sport *no art.* in schools; **~sprecher der** pupils' representative; ≈ head boy; **~sprecherin die** pupils' representative; ≈ head girl; **~stunde die** [school] period; lesson; **~system das** school system; **~tag der** school day; **der erste/letzte ~tag** the first/last day of school; **~tasche die** school-bag; *(Ranzen)* [school] satchel

Schulter [ˈʃʊltɐ] **die; ~, ~n** shoulder; **hängende ~n** drooping shoulders; *(als Merkmal)* round shoulders; **seine Frau reicht ihm gerade bis an die ~:** his wife only comes up to his shoulder; **er nahm das Kind auf die ~[n]** he lifted the child on to his shoulder[s]; **der Ringer zwang seinen Gegner auf die ~n** the wrestler forced his opponent on to his back; **~ an ~** *(auch fig.)* shoulder to shoulder; **mit den ~n** *od.* **die ~n zucken** shrug one's shoulders; **jmdn. über die ~ ansehen** *(fig.)* look down on sb.; look down one's nose at sb.; **jmdm. auf die ~ klopfen** pat sb. on the shoulder *or (fig.)* back; **sich** *(Dat.)* **selbst auf die ~ klopfen** *(fig.)* pat oneself on the back; **auf beiden ~n Wasser tragen** *(fig.)* have a foot in both camps; *s. auch* **kalt 1; leicht a**

schulter-, Schulter-: ~blatt das *(Anat.)* shoulder-blade; **~frei** *Adj.* off-the-shoulder ⟨*dress*⟩; **~halfter der** shoulder-holster; **~höhe die** shoulder height; **~klappe die** shoulder-strap; epaulette; **~lang** *Adj.* shoulder-length

schultern *tr. V.* shoulder; **das Gewehr ~:** shoulder arms; **etw. geschultert tragen** carry sth. on one's shoulder

Schulter-: ~riemen der shoulder-strap; *(Milit.)* shoulder-belt; **~schluß der** *(Solidarität)* solidarity; *(Zusammenarbeit)* collaboration; **~stand der** *(Turnen, Kunstfahren)* shoulder stand; **~stück das a)** *(~klappe)* shoulder-strap; epaulette; **b)** *(Stück Fleisch)* piece of shoulder

Schultheiß [ˈʃʊltai̯s] **der; ~en, ~en** *(hist.)* sheriff; *(im Dorf)* mayor

Schul·tüte die *cardboard cone of sweets given to a child on its first day at school*

Schulung die; ~, ~en training; *(Veranstaltung)* training course; **politische ~:** political schooling

Schulungs·kurs der training course

Schul-: ~unterricht der school lessons *pl., no art.*; **~weg der** way to school; **er hat einen ~weg von 10 km/Minuten** he lives 10 kilometres/minutes from his school; **~weisheit die** *(abwertend)* book-learning; **~wesen das;** *o. Pl.* school system

Schulze [ˈʃʊltsə] **der; ~n, ~n** *(hist.) s.* **Schultheiß**

Schul-: ~zeit die school-days *pl.*; **~zentrum das** school complex; **~zeugnis das** school report; **~zimmer das** schoolroom

Schummel [ˈʃʊml̩] **der; ~s** *(ugs.)* cheating *no indef. art.*

Schummelei die; ~, ~en *(ugs.) s.* **Mogelei**

schummeln *itr., tr., refl. V. (ugs.) s.* **mogeln**

schummerig [ˈʃʊmərɪç] **1.** *Adj.* dim ⟨*light etc.*⟩; dimly lit ⟨*room etc.*⟩. **2.** *adv.* dimly

Schummler der; ~s, ~, Schummlerin die; ~, ~nen *(ugs.)* cheat

schummrig *s.* **schummerig**

Schund der; ~[e]s *(abwertend)* trash

Schund-: ~literatur die *(abwertend)* trashy literature; **~roman der** *(abwertend)* trashy novel

schunkeln [ˈʃʊŋkl̩n] *itr. V.* rock to and fro together *(in time to music, with linked arms)*

schupfen [ˈʃʊpfn̩] *tr. V. (österr., schweiz., südd.)* **a)** *(stoßen)* give sb. a shove *or* push; **b)** *(werfen)* throw; chuck *(coll.)*

Schupfen der; ~s, ~ *(österr., südd.)* shed; *(Wetterdach)* [wooden] shelter

¹Schupo [ˈʃuːpo] **die; ~** *Abk.* **Schutzpolizei**

²Schupo der; ~s, ~s *(veralt. ugs.)* cop *(sl.)*

Schuppe [ˈʃʊpə] **die; ~, ~n a)** scale; **es fiel ihm wie ~n von den Augen** he had a sudden, blinding realization; the scales fell from his eyes; **b)** *Pl. (auf dem Kopf)* dandruff *sing.*; *(auf der Haut)* flaking skin *sing.*

schuppen 1. *tr. V.* scale ⟨*fish*⟩. **2.** *refl. V.* ⟨*skin*⟩ flake; ⟨*person*⟩ have flaking skin

Schuppen der; ~s, ~ a) shed; **b)** *(ugs. abwertend) (häßliches Gebäude)* dump *(coll.)*; *(kastenförmiger Bau)* box; **c)** *(ugs.: Lokal)* joint *(sl.)*

schuppen·artig 1. *Adj.* scale-like. **2.** *adv.* like scales

Schuppen·flechte die *(Med.)* psoriasis

schuppig *Adj.* **a)** scaly; **b)** *(mit Haut-, Kopfschuppen bedeckt)* flaky ⟨*skin*⟩; dandruffy ⟨*hair*⟩

Schur [ʃuːɐ̯] **die; ~, ~en a)** *(das Scheren)* shearing; **b)** *(Landw.: das Mähen, Schneiden)* cut

Schür·eisen das poker

schüren [ˈʃyːrən] *tr. V.* **a)** poke ⟨*fire*⟩; *(gründlich)* rake ⟨*fire, stove, etc.*⟩; **b)** *(fig.)* stir up ⟨*hatred, envy, etc.*⟩; fan the flames of ⟨*passion*⟩; **jmds. Hoffnung ~:** raise sb.'s hopes

schürfen [ˈʃʏrfn̩] **1.** *itr. V.* **a)** scrape; **b)** *(Bergbau)* dig [experimentally] **(nach** for); **nach Gold** *usw.* **~:** prospect for gold *etc.*; **tiefer ~** *(fig.)* dig deeper. **2.** *tr. V.* **a) sich** *(Dat.)* **das Knie** *usw.* **[wund/blutig] ~:** graze one's knee *etc.* [and make it sore/bleed]; **b)** *(Bergbau)* mine ⟨*ore etc.*⟩ open-cast *or (Amer.)* opencut. **3.** *refl. V.* graze oneself

Schürf·wunde die graze; abrasion

Schür·haken der poker *(with hooked end)*; *(für den Ofen)* rake

schurigeln [ˈʃuːriːgl̩n] *tr. V. (ugs. abwertend)* **jmdn. ~:** make life unpleasant for sb.; *(schikanieren)* bully sb.

Schurke [ˈʃʊrkə] **der; ~n, ~n** *(abwertend)* rogue; villain; **die Rolle des ~n** the part of the villain *or (coll.)* baddy

Schurkerei die; ~, ~en *(veralt. abwertend)* villainous deed

schurkisch *(veralt. abwertend)* **1.** *Adj.* villainous. **2.** *adv.* villainously

Schur·wolle die: [reine] ~: pure new wool

Schurz [ʃʊrts] **der; ~es, ~e a)** apron; **b)** *(Lenden~)* loincloth

Schürze [ˈʃʏrtsə] **die; ~, ~n** apron; *(Frauen~, Latz~)* pinafore; **jmdm. an der ~ hängen** *(fig.)* be tied to sb.'s apron-strings; **hinter jeder ~ hersein** *od.* **herlaufen** *(ugs.)* run *or* chase after anything in a skirt

schürzen *tr. V.* **a)** gather up; **b)** *(aufwerfen)* purse ⟨*lips, mouth*⟩; **c)** *(geh.: binden)* tie ⟨*knot*⟩; knot ⟨*thread etc.*⟩

Schürzen-: ~band *s.* **Schürzenzipfel; ~jäger der** *(ugs. abwertend)* skirt-chaser *(sl.)*; **~zipfel der** apron-string; **jmdm. am ~zipfel hängen** *(fig. ugs.)* be tied to sb.'s apron-strings

Schuß [ʃʊs] **der; Schusses, Schüsse** [ˈʃʏsə] *(bei Maßangaben ungebeugt)* **a)** shot **(auf +** *Akk.* at); **21 ~ Salut** a 21-gun salute; **zum ~ kommen** get a chance of a shot; get a shot in; **weit** *od.* **weitab vom ~** *(fig. ugs.) (in sicherer Entfernung)* well away from the action; at a safe distance; *(abseits)* far off the beaten track; **der ~ kann nach hinten losgehen** *(fig. ugs.)* it could backfire *or* turn out to be an own goal; **ein ~ ins Schwarze** *(fig.)* a bull's-eye; **ein ~ in den Ofen** *(fig.)* a complete waste of effort; **jmdm. einen ~ vor den Bug setzen** *od.* **geben** *(fig.)* fire a shot across sb.'s bows; **einen ~ haben** *(salopp)* be off one's rocker *(sl.)*; **b)** *(Menge Munition/Schießpulver)* round; **drei ~ Munition** three rounds of ammunition; **keinen ~ Pulver wert sein** *(fig. ugs.)* be worthless *or* not worth a thing; **c)** *(~wunde)* gunshot wound; **d)** *(mit einem Ball, Puck usw.)* shot **(auf +** *Akk.* at); **er ließ ihn nicht zum ~**

kommen he didn't let him get a shot in; **e)** *(kleine Menge)* dash; **ein ~ Whisky** a dash *or* shot of whisky; **Cola** *usw.* **mit ~:** Coke **(P)** *etc.* with something strong; brandy/rum *etc.* and Coke **(P)** *etc.*; **eine Weiße mit ~:** *a light top-fermented beer with a dash of fruit syrup, esp. raspberry-flavoured;* **f)** *(Drogenjargon)* shot; fix *(sl.)*; **jmdm./sich einen ~ setzen** give sb./oneself a fix; **der goldene ~:** the fatal shot; **g)** *(Skisport)* schuss; **~ fahren** schuss; **im ~ abfahren** schuss down; **in ~ kommen** *(fig.)* get speed up; **h)** *(ugs.)* **in in ~ sein/kommen** be in/get into [good] shape; **etw. in ~ bringen** *od.* **kriegen/halten/haben** get sth. into/keep sth. in/have got sth. in [good] shape; **i)** *(Weberei)* weft

schuß·bereit *Adj.* ready to shoot *postpos.*

Schussel ['ʃʊsl̩] **der; ~s, ~** *(ugs.)* scatter-brain; wool-gatherer

Schüssel ['ʃʏsl̩] **die; ~, ~n** bowl; *(flacher)* dish; **vor leeren ~n sitzen** *(fig.)* go hungry; have nothing to eat

schusselig *(ugs.)* **1.** *Adj.* scatter-brained; *(fahrig)* dithery. **2.** *adv.* in a scatter-brained way

Schusseligkeit die; ~ *(ugs.)* wool-gathering; muddle-headedness; *(schusselige Art)* scatter-brained way

schusseln *itr. V. (ugs.)* be scatter-brained; *(bei der Arbeit)* be careless; make careless *or* silly mistakes; **er hat mal wieder geschusselt** he's been wool-gathering again

Schusser der; ~s, ~ *(bes. südd.) s.* **Murmel**

schuß-, Schuß-: ~faden der *(Weberei)* weft thread; **~fahrt die a)** *(Ski)* schuss; **b)** *(fig.)* wild career; headlong rush; **~feld das** field of fire; **er hatte freies ~feld** he had a clear view of the target; *(Fußball usw.)* he had a clear shot [at goal]; **ins ~feld geraten** *(fig.)* come under fire; **~fest** *Adj.* bullet-proof

schußlig ['ʃʊslɪç] *s.* **schusselig**

Schuß-: ~linie die line of fire; **in die/jmds. ~linie geraten** *od.* **kommen** *(auch fig.)* come under fire/come under fire from sb.; **~verletzung die** gunshot wound; **~waffe die** weapon *(firing a projectile)*; *(Gewehr usw.)* firearm; **~waffen·gebrauch der** use of firearms; **~wechsel der** exchange of shots; **~wunde die** gunshot wound

Schuster ['ʃu:stɐ] **der; ~s, ~** *(ugs.)* shoemaker; *(Flick~)* shoe-repairer; cobbler *(dated)*; **auf ~s Rappen** *(scherzh.)* on Shanks's pony; **~, bleib bei deinem Leisten!** *(Spr.)* the cobbler should stick to his last *(prov.)*; don't meddle with things you don't understand; *s. auch* **Bäcker**

Schuster-: ~ahle die [shoemaker's] awl; **~draht der** waxed end; **~handwerk das;** *o. Pl.* shoemaking *no art.*

schustern *tr., itr. V. (veralt.)* cobble *(dated)*

Schuster-: ~palme die *(volkst.)* aspidistra; **~werkstatt die** shoemaker's workshop; *(für Schuhreparaturen)* shoe-repairer's workshop

Schute ['ʃu:tə] **die; ~, ~n a)** *(Wasserfahrzeug)* barge; lighter; **b)** *(Hut)* poke-bonnet

Schutt [ʃʊt] **der; ~[e]s a)** rubble; **„~ abladen verboten"** 'no tipping'; 'no dumping'; **in ~ und Asche liegen/sinken** *(geh.)* lie in ruins/be reduced to rubble; **b)** *(Geol.)* debris; detritus

Schutt·ablade·platz der rubbish dump *or (Brit.)* tip; garbage dump *(Amer.)*

Schütte ['ʃʏtə] **die; ~, ~n a)** *(Behälter)* [kitchen] drawer-container *(for flour etc.)*; **b)** *(Rutsche)* chute; **c)** *(landsch.: Bündel)* sheaf

Schüttel·frost der [violent] shivering fit; **~ haben** have violent shivers

schütteln ['ʃʏtl̩n] **1.** *tr. (auch itr.) V.* **a)** shake; **den Kopf [über etw.** *(Akk.)***]/die Faust [gegen jmdn.] ~:** shake one's head [over sth.]/one's fist [at sb.]; **jmdm. die Hand ~:** shake sb.'s hand; shake sb. by the hand; **das Fieber/die Angst/das Grauen schüttelte ihn** he was shivering *or* shaking with fever/fear/gripped with horror; **von Angst/Ekel geschüttelt sein/werden** be gripped with fear/filled with revulsion; **das von Katastrophen und Krieg geschüttelte Land** the country [that was] torn by catastrophe and war; **b)** *(unpers.)* **es schüttelte ihn [vor Kälte]** he was shaking [with *or* from cold]. **2.** *refl. V.* shake oneself/itself; **sich im Fieber/vor Lachen ~:** be racked with fever/shake with laughter; **ich könnte mich [vor Ekel] ~:** I feel utterly revolted. **3.** *itr. V.* **mit dem Kopf ~:** shake one's head

Schüttel·reim der *humorous rhyming couplet with two pairs of rhyming words having interchanging initial consonants*

schütten ['ʃʏtn̩] **1.** *tr. V.* **a)** pour ⟨*liquid, flour, grain, etc.*⟩; *(unabsichtlich)* spill ⟨*liquid, flour, etc.*⟩; tip ⟨*rubbish, coal, etc.*⟩; **jmdm./sich Wein über den Anzug ~:** spill wine on sb.'s/one's suit; **b) einen Eimer** *usw.* **voll Wasser** *usw. (Akk.)* **~** *(ugs.)* fill a bucket *etc.* with water *etc.* **2.** *itr. V. (unpers.) (ugs.: regnen)* pour [down]

schütter ['ʃʏtɐ] *Adj.* sparse; thin

Schütter der; ~s, ~: [coal-]hod

Schütt·gut das bulk goods *pl.*

Schutt-: ~halde die pile *or* heap of rubble; **~haufen der** pile of rubble; *(Abfallhaufen)* rubbish heap; **~platz der** [rubbish] dump *or (Brit.)* tip; garbage dump *(Amer.)*

Schutz [ʃʊts] **der; ~es, ~e a)** *o. Pl.* protection **(vor +** *Dat.*, **gegen** against); *(Feuer~)* cover; *(Zuflucht)* refuge; **im ~ der Dunkelheit/Nacht** under cover of darkness/night; **unter einem Baum ~ [vor dem Regen** *usw.***] suchen/finden** seek/find shelter *or* take refuge [from the rain *etc.*] under a tree; **jmdm. ~ gewähren** give *or* afford sb. protection; **jmdn. [vor jmdm.** *od.* **gegen jmdn./gegen etw.] in ~ nehmen** defend sb. *or* take sb.'s side [against sb./sth.]; *s. auch* **Trutz; b)** *(Vorrichtung)* guard

schutz-, Schutz-: ~an·strich der protective coating; **~bedürftig** *Adj.* in need of protection *postpos.*; **~befohlene der/die;** *adj. Dekl. (veralt.)* charge; **~behauptung die** *(bes. Rechtsw.)* attempt to justify one's behaviour; **~blech das** mudguard; **~brief der** *(Kfz-W.)* travel insurance; *(Dokument)* travel insurance certificate; **~brille die** [protective] goggles *pl.*; **~dach das** shelter; *(über der Haustür usw.)* canopy

Schütze ['ʃʏtsə] **der; ~n, ~n a)** marksman; **ein guter/schlechter ~:** a good/poor shot *or* marksman; **der ~ konnte ermittelt werden** it was possible to establish who fired the shot/shots; **b)** *(Fußball usw.: Tor~)* scorer; **c)** *(Mitglied eines Schützenvereins)* **er ist ~** *od.* **bei den ~n** he is a member of a/the shooting *or* rifle club; **d)** *(Milit.: einfacher Soldat)* private; **~ Arsch [im letzten** *od.* **dritten Glied]** *(derb)* the lowest of the low; **e)** *(DDR Milit.)* soldier in the motorized arm; **f)** *(Astrol., Astron.)* Sagittarius; **er/sie ist [ein] ~:** he/she is a Sagittarian

schützen 1. *tr. V.* protect **(vor +** *Dat.* from, **gegen** against); *(vor Regen, Wind usw.)* ⟨*roof, wall*⟩ shelter **(vor +** *Dat.* from); ⟨*coat*⟩ protect **(gegen** against); *(absichern)* protect **(vor +** *Dat.* from); safeguard ⟨*interest, property, etc.*⟩ **(vor +** *Dat.* from); **sich ~d vor jmdn./etw. stellen** stand protectively in front of sb./sth.; **ein geschützter Platz** a sheltered spot; **geschützte Arten/Tiere/Pflanzen** protected species/animals/plants; **etw. patentrechtlich/urheberrechtlich/als Warenzeichen ~ lassen** patent sth./copyright sth./register sth. as a trade-mark; **gesetzlich geschützt** registered [as a trademark]; **„vor Wärme/Kälte/Licht ~":** 'keep away from heat/cold/light'; **„vor Nässe ~":** 'keep dry'. **2.** *itr. V.* provide *or* give protection **(vor +** *Dat.* from, **gegen** against); *(vor Wind, Regen)* provide *or* give shelter **(vor +** *Dat.* from)

Schützen-: ~bruder der fellow-member of a/the shooting *or* rifle club; **~fest das** *shooting competition with fair*

Schutz·engel der guardian angel

Schützen-: ~graben der *(Milit.)* trench; **~haus das** [shooting *or* rifle club] clubhouse; **~hilfe die** *(ugs.)* support; **~könig der** shooting champion; champion marksman; **~panzer der** armoured personnel carrier; **~platz der** *fairground where the Schützenfest takes place;* **~stand der** *(Milit.)* firing-point *(in a foxhole)*; **~verein der** shooting *or* rifle club

Schutz-: ~film der protective film; **~gebiet das a)** [nature] reserve; **b)** *(hist.: Kolonie)* protectorate; **~gebühr die a)** token *or* nominal charge; **b)** *(verhüll.: erpreßte Zahlung)* protection money *no pl., no indef. art.*; **~gitter das** protective grid; **~gott der** tutelary *or* protective god; **~hafen der** port of refuge; **~haft die** preventive detention; **~heilige der/die** *(kath. Rel.)* patron saint; **~helm der** helmet; *(bei Renn-, Motorradfahrern)* crash-helmet; *(bei Bauarbeitern usw.)* safety helmet; **~herrschaft die** *(Völkerr.)* protectorate; **~hülle die** [protective] cover; *(für Dokumente usw.)* folder; *(~umschlag)* dust-jacket; **~hund der** guard-dog; **~hütte die a)** *(Unterstand)* shelter; **b)** *(Berghütte)* mountain hut; **~impfung die** vaccination; inoculation; **~kleidung die** protective clothing; **~kontakt der** *(Elektrot.)* earth contact; **~leute** *s.* **~mann**

Schützling ['ʃʏtslɪŋ] **der; ~s, ~e** protégé; *(Anvertrauter)* charge

schutz-, Schutz-: ~los *Adj.* defenceless; unprotected; **dem Gegner/Wind ~los ausgeliefert sein** be completely at the mercy of the enemy/the wind; **~mann der;** *Pl.* **~männer** *od.* **~leute** *(ugs. veralt.)* [police] constable; copper *(Brit. coll.)*; **~marke die: [eingetragene] ~marke** registered trademark; **~patron der** patron saint; **~polizei die** constabulary; police [force]; **~polizist der** *(veralt.)* police constable; **~raum der** shelter; **~schicht die** protective layer **(aus** of); *(flüssig aufgetragen)* protective coating; **~schild der** shield; *(der Polizei)* riot shield; **~suchend** *Adj.* seeking protection *postpos.*; **~truppe die a)** peace-keeping force; **b)** *(hist.: Kolonialtruppe)* colonial force *or* army; **~um·schlag der** dust-jacket; *(für Papiere)* cover; **~verband der** protective bandage *or* dressing; **~vorrichtung die** safety device; *(Geländer, Gitter usw.)* safety measure; **~wall der** protective wall; *(fig.)* [protective] barrier; **der antifaschistische ~wall** *(DDR Amtsspr.)* the Berlin Wall; **~weg der** *(österr.)* pedestrian crossing; **~zoll der** protective tariff

Schwa [ʃva:] **das; ~[s], ~[s]** *(Sprachw.)* schwa

schwabbelig ['ʃvabəlɪç] *Adj.* flabby ⟨*stomach, person, etc.*⟩; wobbly ⟨*jelly etc.*⟩

schwabbeln *itr. V. (ugs.)* wobble

schwabblig *s.* **schwabbelig**

Schwabe ['ʃva:bə] **der; ~n, ~n** Swabian

schwäbeln ['ʃvɛ:bl̩n] *itr. V.* **er schwäbelt** he speaks in Swabian dialect

Schwaben (das); ~s Swabia

Schwaben·streich der *(scherzh.)* piece of folly

Schwäbin ['ʃvɛ:bɪn] **die; ~, ~nen** Swabian

schwäbisch 1. *Adj.* Swabian; **die Schwäbische Alb** the Swabian Mountains *pl.* **2.** *adv.* in Swabian dialect; *(mit ~em Akzent)* with a Swabian accent; *s. auch* **badisch; deutsch; Deutsch**

schwach [ʃvax]; **schwächer** ['ʃvɛçɐ], **schwächst...** ['ʃvɛçst...] **1.** *Adj.* **a)** *(kraftlos)* weak; weak, delicate ⟨*child, woman*⟩; frail ⟨*invalid, old person*⟩; low-powered ⟨*engine,* *car, bulb, amplifier, etc.*⟩; weak, poor ⟨*eyesight, memory, etc.*⟩; poor ⟨*hearing*⟩; delicate ⟨*health, constitution*⟩; **die Birne/die Brille ist ziemlich ~**: the light-bulb is of rather a low wattage/the glasses are not very strong; **auf ~en Beinen stehen** *(fig.)* ⟨*theory, evidence, argument, etc.*⟩ be shaky; **~ werden** grow weak; *(fig.: schwanken)* weaken; waver; *(nachgeben)* give in; **mir wird [ganz] ~**: I feel [quite] faint; **in einem ~en Moment, in einer ~en Stunde** in a weak moment; **er hat einen ~en Willen/Charakter** he is weak-willed/lacks strength of character; **b)** *(nicht gut)* poor ⟨*pupil, player, runner, performance, result, effort, etc.*⟩; weak ⟨*candidate, argument, opponent, play, film, etc.*⟩; **sein schwächstes Buch/der schwächste Schüler** his worst book/the worst pupil; **er ist in Latein sehr ~**: he is very bad at Latin; **das ist aber ein ~es Bild!** *(fig. ugs.)* that's a poor show *(coll.)*; **die Party war ~** *(ugs.)* the party wasn't up to much *(coll.)*; **c)** *(gering, niedrig, klein)* poor, low ⟨*attendance etc.*⟩; sparse ⟨*population*⟩; slight ⟨*effect, resistance, gradient, etc.*⟩; light ⟨*wind, rain, current*⟩; faint ⟨*groan, voice, pressure, hope, smile, smell*⟩; weak, faint ⟨*pulse*⟩; lukewarm ⟨*applause, praise*⟩; faint, dim ⟨*light*⟩; pale ⟨*colour*⟩; low ⟨*fire, heat*⟩; **die zahlenmäßig schwächere Gruppe** the group which is/was smaller in number; **die Nachfrage/das Geschäft ist zur Zeit ~**: demand/business is slack at the moment; **das ist nur ein ~er Trost** that is only a slight consolation; *(ugs.: hilft nur wenig)* that is little consolation *or* cold comfort; **das Licht wird schwächer** the light is fading; **d)** *(wenig konzentriert)* weak ⟨*solution, acid, tea, coffee, beer, poison, etc.*⟩; **Sherry ist schwächer als Whisky** sherry is not as strong as whisky; **e)** *(Sprachw.)* weak ⟨*conjugation, verb, noun, etc.*⟩. **2.** *adv.* **a)** *(kraftlos)* weakly; **b)** *(nicht gut)* poorly; **sehr ~ argumentieren** offer very weak arguments; **c)** *(in geringem Maße)* poorly ⟨*attended, developed*⟩; sparsely ⟨*populated*⟩; slightly ⟨*poisonous, acid, alcoholic, sweetened, salted, inclined, etc.*⟩; ⟨*rain*⟩ slightly; ⟨*remember, glow, smile, groan*⟩ faintly; lightly ⟨*accented*⟩; ⟨*beat*⟩ weakly; **der Saal war nur ~ besetzt** there was only a small audience in the hall; **es war ~ windig** there was a light wind; **er wehrte sich nur ~**: he offered only faint resistance; **d)** *(Sprachw.)* **~ gebeugt/konjugiert** weak

schwạch-: ~besiedelt, ~bevölkert *Adj.; präd. getrennt geschrieben* sparsely populated

Schwạ̈che [ˈʃvɛçə] **die; ~, ~n a)** *(Kraftlosigkeit)* weakness; *(plötzlich auftretend)* [feeling of] faintness; **allgemeine ~**: general debility *(Med.)*; **b)** *(Mangel an Können)* weakness; **seine ~ in Mathematik** *usw.* his lack of ability in mathematics *etc.*; **c)** *(Mangel)* weakness; failing; **d)** *o. Pl. (Vorliebe)* weakness; **eine ~ für jmdn./etw. haben** have a soft spot for sb./a weakness for sth.

Schwạ̈che-: ~anfall der sudden feeling of faintness; **~gefühl das** feeling of faintness

schwạ̈chen *tr. V.* weaken

schwạ̈cher *s.* **schwach**

Schwạ̈che·zustand der [state of] weakness; weak condition

Schwạchheit die; ~, ~en a) *o. Pl.* weakness; **die ~ des Greises/des Alters** the frailty of the old man/of old age; **b)** *(Mangel, Fehler)* weakness; failing; **bilde dir nur keine ~en ein!** *(fig. ugs.)* don't kid yourself! *(sl.)*

Schwạch·kopf der *(salopp abwertend)* bonehead *(sl.)*; dimwit *(coll.)*

schwạ̈chlich *Adj.* weakly, delicate ⟨*person*⟩; frail ⟨*old person, constitution*⟩; delicate ⟨*nerves, stomach, constitution*⟩

Schwạ̈chlichkeit die; ~, ~en weakness; *(der Nerven, der Konstitution)* delicateness

Schwächling [ˈʃvɛçlɪŋ] **der; ~s, ~e** weakling

schwạch-, Schwạch-: ~punkt der weak point; **~sichtig** *Adj. (Med.)* weak-sighted; **~sichtigkeit die; ~**: dimness of sight; amblyopia; **~sinn der;** *o. Pl.* **a)** *(Med.)* mental deficiency; **b)** *(ugs. abwertend: Unsinn)* [idiotic *(coll.)*] rubbish *or* nonsense; **~sinnig 1.** *Adj.* **a)** *(Med.)* mentally deficient; **b)** *(ugs. abwertend: unsinnig)* idiotic *(coll.)*, nonsensical ⟨*measure, policy, etc.*⟩; rubbishy ⟨*film etc.*⟩; **2.** *adv. (ugs. abwertend)* idiotically *(coll.)*; stupidly

schwächst... *s.* **schwach**

Schwạch-: ~stelle die weak spot *or* point; **~strom der** *(Elektrot.)* current of low amperage; *(mit niedriger Spannung)* low-voltage current

Schwạchung die; ~, ~en weakening

Schwaden [ˈʃva:dn̩] **der; ~s, ~**: [thick] cloud

Schwadron [ʃvaˈdro:n] **die; ~, ~en** *(Milit. hist.)* squadron

Schwadroneur [ʃvadroˈnø:ɐ̯] **der; ~s, ~e** *(geh. abwertend)* windbag

schwadronieren *itr. V. (abwertend)* bluster; **von etw. ~**: sound off about sth. *(coll.)*

Schwafelei die; ~, ~en *(ugs. abwertend)* **a)** *o. Pl.* rabbiting on *(Brit. sl.)*; **b)** *(Bemerkung)* rubbishy remark; **~en** blether *sing.*

schwafeln [ˈʃva:fl̩n] *(ugs. abwertend)* **1.** *itr. V.* rabbit on *(Brit. sl.)*, waffle (**von** about). **2.** *tr. V.* blether ⟨*nonsense*⟩

Schwager [ˈʃva:gɐ] **der; ~s, Schwäger** [ˈʃvɛ:gɐ] **a)** brother-in-law; **b)** *(veralt.: Postkutscher)* mail-coach driver

Schwägerin [ˈʃvɛ:gərɪn] **die; ~, ~nen** sister-in-law

Schwalbe [ˈʃvalbə] **die; ~, ~n a)** swallow; **eine ~ macht noch keinen Sommer** *(Spr.)* one swallow does not make a summer *(prov.)*; **b)** *(ugs.: Papierflieger)* paper aeroplane

Schwạlben-: ~nest das a) swallow's nest; **b)** *(Seemannsspr.)* cockpit locker; **~schwanz der a)** swallow's tail; **b)** *(Schmetterling)* swallow-tail; **c)** *(scherzh. veralt.: Frack)* [swallow-]tails *pl.*; **d)** *(Tischlerei)* dovetail [joint]

Schwall [ʃval] **der; ~[e]s, ~e** torrent; flood; **ein ~ Wasser/***(fig.)* **von Lauten/Worten** a torrent of water/*(fig.)* sounds/words

schwạllen *tr., itr. V. (salopp) s.* **schwafeln**

schwamm [ʃvam] *1. u. 3. Pers. Sg. Prät. v.* **schwimmen**

Schwạmm der; ~[e]s, Schwämme [ˈʃvɛmə] **a)** sponge; **~ drüber!** *(ugs.)* [let's] forget it; **b)** *(südd., österr.: Pilz)* mushroom; **giftige Schwämme** poisonous fungi; **c)** *(Pilzbefall)* dry rot *no art.*

Schwammerl [ˈʃvamɐl] **das; ~s, ~[n]** *(bayr., österr.)* mushroom; *s. auch* **Pilz a**

schwạmmig 1. *Adj.* **a)** spongy; **b)** *(abwertend: aufgedunsen)* flabby, bloated ⟨*face, body, etc.*⟩; **c)** *(abwertend: unpräzise)* woolly ⟨*concept, manner of expression, etc.*⟩. **2.** *adv. (abwertend: unpräzise)* vaguely

Schwạmmigkeit die; ~ a) sponginess; **b)** *(abwertend: Aufgedunsenheit)* flabbiness; bloated appearence; **c)** *(abwertend: Vagheit)* woolliness

Schwan [ʃva:n] **der; ~[e]s, Schwäne** [ˈʃvɛ:nə] **a)** swan; **mein lieber ~!** *(ugs.) (staunend)* my goodness!; good heavens!; *(warnend)* for heaven's sake!; **b)** *(Sternbild)* **der ~**: Cygnus

schwand [ʃvant] *1. u. 3. Pers. Sg. Prät. v.* **schwinden**

schwạnen *itr. V. (ugs.)* **jmdm. schwant etw.** sb. senses sth.; **ihm schwante nichts Gutes** he had a sense of foreboding

Schwạnen-: ~gesang der *(geh.)* swansong; **~hals der a)** swan's neck; **b)** *(oft scherzh.: langer Hals)* swan-like neck; **c)** *(Technik)* swan-neck

schwang [ʃvaŋ] *1. u. 3. Pers. Sg. Prät. v.* **schwingen**

Schwạng der *in* **im ~[e] sein** be in vogue; ⟨*rumour*⟩ be going the rounds; **in ~ kommen** come into vogue; ⟨*rumour*⟩ come into circulation

schwanger [ˈʃvaŋɐ] *Adj.* pregnant (**von** by); **sie ist im vierten Monat ~**: she is in her fourth month [of pregnancy]; **mit etw. ~ gehen** *(fig.)* be big with sth. *(literary)*; *(mit etw. erfüllt sein)* be full of sth.; *(scherzh.)* be mulling over sth.

Schwạngere die; *adj. Dekl.* expectant mother; pregnant woman

schwängern [ˈʃvɛŋɐn] *tr. V.* make ⟨*woman*⟩ pregnant; **sich von jmdm. ~ lassen** get [oneself] pregnant by sb.; **von Duft geschwängert sein** *(fig. geh.)* ⟨*air*⟩ be heavy with scent

Schwạngerschaft die; ~, ~en pregnancy

Schwạngerschafts-: ~ab·bruch der termination of pregnancy; abortion; **~streifen der** stretch mark

schwạnk *Adj. in* **wie ein ~es Rohr im Wind** *(geh.)* like a swaying reed

Schwank [ʃvaŋk] **der; ~[e]s, Schwänke** [ˈʃvɛŋkə] **a)** *(Literaturw.: Erzählung)* comic tale; *(auf der Bühne)* farce; **b)** *(komische Episode)* comic event; **einen ~ aus seinem Leben erzählen** *(scherzh.)* tell the story of something funny that happened to one

schwạnken *itr. V. (mit Richtungsangabe mit sein)* **a)** sway; ⟨*boat*⟩ rock; *(heftiger)* roll; ⟨*compass-needle etc.*⟩ swing [to and fro]; ⟨*ground, floor*⟩ shake; **mit ~den Schritten** with wavering steps; **b)** *(fig.: unbeständig sein)* ⟨*prices, temperature, etc.*⟩ fluctuate; ⟨*number, usage, etc.*⟩ vary; **c)** *(fig.: unentschieden sein)* waver; *(zögern)* hesitate; **zwischen zwei Möglichkeiten ~**: be unable to decide between two possibilities; **er schwankt noch, ob ...**: he is still undecided [as to] whether ...; **~d werden, ins Schwanken kommen** *od.* **geraten** begin to waver *or* hesitate; become undecided; **jmdn. ~[d] machen** make sb. waver *or* uncertain

Schwạnkung die; ~, ~en variation; *(der Kurse usw.)* fluctuation

Schwanz [ʃvants] **der; ~es, Schwänze** [ˈʃvɛntsə] **a)** tail; **ein Tier am** *od.* **beim ~ fassen** catch an animal by the tail; **den ~ des Festzugs bilden** *(fig.)* bring up the rear of the procession; **kein ~** *(fig. salopp)* not a bloody *(Brit. sl.)* *or* *(coll.)* damn soul; **den ~ einziehen** *od.* **einklemmen** *od.* **einkneifen** *(fig. salopp)* draw in one's horns; **jmdm. auf den ~ treten** *(fig. salopp)* tread *or* step on sb.'s toes; **da beißt sich die Katze in den ~** *(fig.)* that is a circular argument; **b)** *(salopp: Penis)* prick *(coarse)*; cock *(coarse)*

Schwạ̈nzchen das; ~s, ~ a) [little] tail; **b)** *(fam.: Penis)* willy *(sl.)*

schwänzeln [ˈʃvɛntsl̩n] *itr. V.* **a)** wag its tail/their tails; **b)** *mit sein (~d laufen)* ⟨*dog etc.*⟩ run wagging its tail; **c)** *mit Richtungsangabe mit sein (ugs. iron.: tänzeln)* mince; trip; *(ugs. abwertend: herumscharwenzeln)* **vor jmdm. ~**: crawl to sb.

schwänzen [ˈʃvɛntsn̩] *tr., itr. V. (ugs.)* skip, cut ⟨*lesson etc.*⟩; **[die Schule] ~**: play truant *or* *(Amer.)* hookey; **den Dienst ~**: skive [off] *(Brit. sl.)*

schwạnz-, Schwạnz-: ~feder die tail-feather; **~flosse die** *(Zool., Flugw.)* tail-fin; *(des Wals)* tail flukes *pl.*; **~lastig** *Adj.* tail-heavy; **~lurch der** *(Zool.)* caudate; **~wedelnd** *Adj.* tail-wagging *attrib.*; wagging its tail/their tails *postpos.*; **~wirbel der** *(Anat., Zool.)* caudal vertebra

schwappen [ˈʃvapn̩] **1.** *itr. V.* **a) [hin und her] ~**: slosh [around]; **an die Bordwand ~**: splash *or* slap against the side of the boat; **b)** *mit Richtungsangabe mit sein* splash, slosh (**über** + *Akk.* over, **aus** out of). **2.** *tr. V.* slosh ⟨*water, beer, etc.*⟩ (**auf** + *Akk.* on)

Schwäre ['ʃvɛːrə] **die**; ~, ~**n** *(geh.)* [festering] ulcer
schwären *itr. V. (geh.)* fester; **eine** ~**de Wunde** *(auch fig.)* a festering wound *or (esp. fig.)* sore
Schwarm [ʃvarm] **der**; ~**[e]s, Schwärme** ['ʃvɛrmə] **a)** swarm; **ein ~ Krähen/Heringe** a flock of crows/shoal of herrings; **b)** *(fam.: Angebetete[r])* idol; heart-throb; **sie hat einen neuen** ~: she's got a new flame; **c)** *(Vorliebe)* **mein/sein** *usw.* ~ *(Tätigkeit)* my/his *etc.* passion; *(Gegenstand)* the apple of my/his *etc.* eye
schwärmen ['ʃvɛrmən] *itr. V.* **a)** *mit Richtungsangabe mit sein* swarm; **b)** *(begeistert sein)* **für jmdn./etw.** ~: be mad about *or* really keen on sb./sth.; **sie schwärmt für ihren Skilehrer** she has a crush on her skiing instructor *(sl.)*; **von etw.** ~: go into raptures about sth.; **ins Schwärmen geraten** go into raptures
Schwärmer der; ~**s**, ~ **a)** *(Phantast)* dreamer; *(Begeisterter)* [passionate] enthusiast; **b)** *(Zool.: Schmetterling)* hawk-moth; **c)** *(Feuerwerkskörper) firework emitting sparks and hopping short distances;* ≈ *jumping jack*
Schwärmerei die; ~, ~**en a)** *(Begeisterung)* [passionate *or* rapturous] enthusiasm; **eine ~ für jmdn./etw.** a passion for sb./sth.; **romantische** ~: romantic rapture *or* ecstasy; **b)** *(schwärmerische Worte)* **[überschwengliche]** ~**[en]** rapturous hyperbole; *(Beschreibung)* rapturous description **(von** of); **c)** *(Phantasterei)* fantasy
schwärmerisch 1. *Adj.* rapturous ⟨*enthusiasm, admiration, letter, etc.*⟩; effusive ⟨*person, language*⟩; *(begeistert)* wildly enthusiastic. **2.** *adv.* rapturously; ⟨*speak*⟩ effusively
Schwarm·geist der woolly-headed enthusiast; **b)** *(hist.)* adventist
Schwarte ['ʃvartə] **die**; ~, ~**n a)** *(Speck~)* rind; *(Haut~)* skin; **b)** *(ugs. abwertend: dickes Buch)* **[dicke]** ~: thick *or* weighty tome; **c)** *(salopp: menschliche Haut)* skin; hide *(joc.)*; **arbeiten, daß die ~ kracht** *(salopp)* work one's fingers to the bone; work until one drops; **d)** *(Jägerspr.: Tierhaut)* skin; hide; **e)** *(Brett mit Rinde)* slab
Schwarten·magen der *(Kochk.)* brawn
schwarz [ʃvarts]; **schwärzer** ['ʃvɛrtsɐ], **schwärzest...** ['ʃvɛrtsəst...] **1.** *Adj.* **a)** black; Black ⟨*person*⟩; filthy[-black] ⟨*hands, fingernails, etc.*⟩; ~ **wie die Nacht/wie Ebenholz** as black as pitch/jet-black; **mir wurde ~ vor den Augen** everything went black; **der Kaffee/Tee ist mir zu** ~: the coffee/tea is too strong for me; **der Kuchen ist schon ganz** ~: the cake is quite burnt; **b)** *(fig.)* **der ~e Erdteil** *od.* **Kontinent** the Dark Continent; **die ~e Rasse** the Blacks *pl.*; ~**e Blattern** *od.* **Pocken** smallpox *sing.*; **das ~e Schaf sein** be the black sheep; ~**e Liste** blacklist; ~**e Messe** Black Mass; ~**e Gedanken** black *or* dismal thoughts; **das habe ich ~ auf weiß** *(fig.)* I've got it in black and white *or* in writing; **das kann ich dir ~ auf weiß geben** *(fig.)* you can take that from me; **er kann warten, bis er ~ wird** *(ugs.)* he can wait till the cows come home *(coll.)*; ~ **werden** *(Skat ugs.)* lose every trick; get whitewashed *(coll.)*; ~ **von Menschen** *(fig.)* packed with people; **die Schwarze Kunst** *(fig.)* [the art of] printing; *(Magie)* the black art; *(Kartenspiel)* **Schwarzer Peter** ≈ old maid *(with a black cat card instead of an old maid)*; **aus ~ weiß machen [wollen]** *(ugs.)* [try to] argue that black is white; **er sieht/malt alles ~ in** ~: he is deeply pessimistic about everything/paints a black picture of everything; **der Schwarze Tod** *(geh.)* the Black Death; **das Schwarze Meer** the Black Sea; *s. auch* **Mann a**; **c)** *(illegal)* illicit, shady ⟨*deal, exchange, etc.*⟩; **eine ~e Kasse führen** run a separate account for underhand purposes; **der ~e Markt** the black market; **d)** *(ugs.: katholisch)* Catholic; **e)** *(ugs.: christdemokratisch)* Christian Democrat. **2.** *adv.* **a)** ⟨*write, underline, etc.*⟩ in black; ~ **gestreift/gemustert** with black stripes/a black pattern; **b)** *(illegal)* illegally; illicitly; **etw. ~ kaufen/verkaufen** buy/sell sth. illegally *or* on the black market; ~ **Straßenbahn fahren** go on the tram *(Brit.) or (Amer.)* streetcar without paying; **die Arbeiten lassen wir ~ machen** we're going to get the work done by a moonlighter *(coll.)*; **c)** *(ugs.: christdemokratisch)* ⟨*vote*⟩ Christian Democrat; ⟨*ruled*⟩ by the Christian Democrats
Schwarz das; ~**[es]**, ~: black; **in ~ gehen,** ~ **tragen** wear black
schwarz-, Schwarz-: ~**afrika (das)** Black Africa; ~**arbeit die**; *o. Pl.* work done on the side *(and not declared for tax)*; *(abends)* moonlighting *(coll.)*; ~**|arbeiten** *itr. V.* do work on the side *(not declared for tax)*; *(abends)* moonlight *(coll.)*; ~**arbeiter der** person who does work on the side; *(abends)* moonlighter *(coll.)*; ~**äugig** *Adj.* black-eyed; ~**bär der** black bear; ~**beere die** *(südd., österr.)* bilberry; ~**braun** *Adj.* blackish-brown; ~**brenner der** illicit distiller; moonshiner *(Amer.)*; ~**brot das** black bread; **ein [Laib] ~brot** a loaf of black bread; ~**bunt** *Adj. (Landw.)* black pied, Frisian ⟨*cattle*⟩; ~**drossel die** blackbird
[1]**Schwarze der**; *adj. Dekl.* **a)** *(Neger)* Black; *(Dunkelhaariger)* dark-haired man/boy; **b)** *(österr.: Kaffee)* black coffee; **c)** *(ugs.: Konservativer)* Conservative
[2]**Schwarze die**; *adj. Dekl.* **a)** *(Negerin)* Black [woman/girl]; *(Dunkelhaarige)* dark haired woman/girl; **b)** *(ugs.: Konservative)* Conservative
[3]**Schwarze das**; *adj. Dekl.* **a)** *(der Zielscheibe)* bull's eye; **ins ~ treffen** hit the bull's eye; *(fig.)* hit the nail on the head; **b) er gönnt ihr nicht das ~ unter den Nägeln** *(ugs.)* he begrudges her everything; **c) ihr kleines ~s** her plain black dress; her little black number *(coll.)*
Schwärze ['ʃvɛrtsə] **die**; ~, ~**n a)** *o. Pl. (Dunkelheit)* blackness; **b)** *(Farbstoff)* black [dye]
schwärzen *tr. V.* blacken; black out ⟨*words*⟩
schwarz-, Schwarz-: ~**|fahren** *unr. itr. V.; mit sein* travel without a ticket *or* without paying; dodge paying the fare; ~**fahrer der** fare-dodger; **er ist ~fahrer** he's a fare-dodger; ~**gerändert** *Adj.; präd. getrennt geschrieben* black-edged; edged in black *postpos.*; dark-rimmed ⟨*eyes*⟩; ~**haarig** *Adj.* black-haired; ~**handel der** black market **(mit** in); *(Tätigkeit)* black marketeering **(mit** in); ~**händler der** black marketeer; *(mit Eintrittskarten)* tout; ~**|hören** *itr. V. (Radio)* use a radio without [having] a licence; dodge paying one's radio licence fee; ~**hörer der** *(Radio)* radio user without a licence; radio licence dodger; ~**kittel der a)** *(scherzh.: Wildschwein)* wild boar; **b)** *(abwertend: Geistlicher)* [Catholic] priest
schwärzlich *Adj.* blackish
schwarz-, Schwarz-: ~**|malen** *itr., tr. V.* **etw. ~malen** paint a black *or* gloomy picture of sth.; **vielleicht male ich zu** ~: perhaps I'm painting too black a picture; ~**malerei die** pessimism; gloominess; **hör auf mit dieser ewigen ~malerei!** stop always painting things so black!; ~**markt der** black market; ~**markt·preis der** black-market price; ~**pulver das** black powder; ~**rot·golden** *Adj.* black, red, and gold; ~**|schlachten 1.** *itr. V.* slaughter animals illegally; **2.** *tr. V.* slaughter ⟨*animal*⟩ illegally; ~**|sehen** *unr. itr. V.* **a)** *(pessimistisch sein)* look on the black side; be pessimistic; **für jmdn./etw. ~sehen** be pessimistic about sb./sth.; **b)** *(Ferns.)* watch television without a licence; ~**seher der a)** *(ugs.)* pessimist; **b)** *(Ferns.)* [television] licence dodger; ~**sender der** pirate [radio] station; *(beim Amateurfunk)* pirate [radio] transmitter; ~**specht der** black woodpecker; ~**storch der** black stork
Schwärzung die; ~, ~**en** blackening
Schwarz·wald der; ~**[e]s** Black Forest
Schwarzwälder [-'vɛldɐ] **die**; ~, ~ *(Torte)* Black Forest gateau
schwarz·weiß *Adj.* black and white
schwarzweiß-, Schwarzweiß-: ~**aufnahme die** black and white photograph; ~**fernseher der,** ~**fernseh·gerät das** black and white television [set]; ~**film der** black and white film; ~**foto das** black and white photo; ~**|malen** *itr. V.* paint *or* put things in [crude] black-and-white terms; ~**malerei die: der Bericht ist eine einzige ~malerei** the report paints *or* puts things in [crude] black-and-white terms; ~**rot** *Adj.* black, white, and red; ~**zeichnung die** black-and-white drawing
Schwarz-: ~**wild das** *(Jägerspr.)* wild boars *pl.*; ~**wurzel die** black salsify
Schwatz [ʃvats] **der**; ~**es**, ~**e** *(fam.)* chat; natter *(coll.)*; **einen ~ halten** have a chat *or (coll.)* natter
Schwätzchen ['ʃvɛtsçən] **das**; ~**s**, ~ *(fam.)* [little] chat; [little] natter *(coll.)*; *s. auch* Schwatz
schwatzen, *(bes. südd.)* **schwätzen** ['ʃvɛtsn̩] **1.** *itr. V.* **a)** *(sich unterhalten)* chat; **schwatzt nicht über Politik** don't talk about politics; **b)** *(sich über belanglose Dinge auslassen)* chatter; natter *(coll.)*; **c)** *(etw. ausplaudern)* talk; blab; **d)** *(in der Schule)* talk. **2.** *tr. V.* say; talk ⟨*nonsense, rubbish*⟩
Schwätzer der; ~**s**, ~, **Schwätzerin die**; ~, ~**nen** *(abwertend)* chatterbox; *(geistloser Redner)* windbag; *(klatschhafter Mensch)* gossip
schwatzhaft *Adj. (abwertend)* talkative; garrulous; *(klatschhaft)* gossipy
Schwatzhaftigkeit die; ~: *(abwertend)* talkativeness; garrulousness; *(Klatschsucht)* gossipiness
Schwebe ['ʃveːbə] **die** *in* **in der ~ bleiben, sich in der ~ halten** keep one's balance; ⟨*balloon*⟩ float in the air, hover; **in der ~ sein/bleiben** *(fig.)* be/remain in the balance; **eine Frage in der ~ lassen** *(fig.)* leave a question open *or* undecided
Schwebe-: ~**bahn die** *(Seilbahn)* cableway; *(Hängebahn)* [overhead] monorail; *(Magnetschwebebahn)* levitation railway; ~**balken der** *(Turnen)* [balance] beam
schweben *itr. V.* **a)** ⟨*bird, balloon, etc.*⟩ hover; ⟨*cloud, balloon, mist*⟩ hang; *(im Wasser)* float; **ihr war, als ob sie schwebte** she felt as if she were standing on air; **in Gefahr** ~ *(fig.)* be in danger; **zwischen Leben und Tod** ~ *(fig.)* hover between life and death; **was mir vor Augen schwebt, ist ...** *(fig.)* what I have in mind is ...; **b)** *mit sein (durch die Luft)* float; *(herab~)* float [down]; *(mit dem Fahrstuhl)* glide; *(wie schwerelos gehen)* ⟨*dancer etc.*⟩ glide; **sich ~d fortbewegen** glide along; **c)** *(unentschieden sein)* be in the balance; **das Verfahren schwebt noch** the trial is still pending; **alle ~den Fragen/Probleme** all outstanding questions/problems
Schwebe·zustand der state of uncertainty
Schweb·stoff der matter in suspension; suspended matter
Schwede ['ʃveːdə] **der**; ~**n**, ~**n a)** Swede; **er ist** ~: he's a Swede; he's Swedish; **b)** *in* **[du] alter ~!** *(ugs.)* old mate *(coll.)*
Schweden ['ʃveːdn̩] **(das)**; ~**s** Sweden
Schweden-: ~**bombe die** Ⓦⓩ *(österr.) s.* **Mohrenkopf a**; ~**platte die** *(Gastr.)* smorgasbord; ~**punsch der** Swedish punch; arrack punch; ~**stahl der** Swedish steel

Schwedin die; ~, ~**nen** Swede; *s. auch* **-in; Schwede a**

schwedisch ['ʃve:dɪʃ] *Adj.* **a)** Swedish; *s. auch* **deutsch; Deutsch;** [2]**Deutsche; b)** *in* **hinter ~en Gardinen** *(ugs.)* behind bars *(coll.)*

Schwefel ['ʃve:fl] **der;** ~**s** sulphur

schwefel-, Schwefel-: ~blume, ~blüte die *(Chemie)* flowers of sulphur *pl.*; **~dioxyd das** *(Chemie)* sulphur dioxide; **~gelb** *Adj.* sulphur-yellow; **~haltig** *Adj.* containing sulphur *postpos., not pred.*; sulphurous ⟨*Quelle, Boden*⟩; **schwach ~haltig sein** have a low sulphur content; **~holz das** *(veralt.)* lucifer *(arch.)*; match

schwefelig *s.* **schweflig**

schwefeln *tr. V.* sulphurize

Schwefel-: ~säure die *(Chemie)* sulphuric acid; **~wasser·stoff der** *(Chemie)* hydrogen sulphide

schweflig *Adj.* sulphurous ⟨*acid*⟩

Schweif [ʃvaif] **der;** ~**[e]s,** ~**e** *(auch fig.: eines Kometen)* tail; *(eines Fuchses)* brush; *(fig.: von Anhängern, Fans o. ä.)* retinue

schweifen 1. *itr. V.; mit sein (geh.: umher~; auch fig.)* wander; roam. **2.** *tr. V. (formen)* curve

Schweif·säge die turning saw

Schweige-: ~geld das hush money; **er deckte die Geschäfte des Chefs und bekam dafür ~geld** he covered up his boss's deals and received a bribe to keep quiet; **~marsch der** silent [protest-]march; **~minute die** minute's silence

schweigen *unr. itr. V.* **a)** *(nicht sprechen)* remain *or* stay *or* keep silent; say nothing; **kannst du ~?** can you keep a secret?; **~ Sie!** be silent *or* quiet! hold your tongue!; **auf etw.** *(Akk.)* **od. zu etw. ~:** say nothing in reply to sth.; **ganz zu ~ von ...:** not to mention ...; let alone ...; **in ~der Andacht/Zustimmung** in silent worship/agreement; **die ~de Mehrheit** the silent majority; **b)** *(aufhören zu tönen usw.)* ⟨*music, noise, etc.*⟩ stop; **der Sender schwieg ab ein Uhr nachts** the radio station stopped broadcasting at 1 a.m.; **die Geschütze ~** *(geh.)* the guns are silent

Schweigen das; ~**s** silence; **das/sein ~ brechen** break the/one's silence; **..., da herrschte ~ im Lande od. Walde ...** [then] nobody said a word; **sich in ~ hüllen** maintain one's silence; **jmdn. zum ~ bringen** *(auch verhüll.)* silence sb.

Schweige·pflicht die *(eines Priesters)* obligation of secrecy; *(eines Arztes, Anwalts)* duty to maintain confidentiality

schweigsam *Adj.* silent; quiet; *(verschlossen)* taciturn; *(verschwiegen)* discreet

Schweigsamkeit die; ~: silence; quietness; *(Verschlossenheit)* taciturnity; *(Verschwiegenheit)* discretion

Schwein [ʃvain] **das;** ~**[e]s,** ~**e a)** pig; **Hackfleisch vom ~:** pork mince; **besoffen wie ein ~** *(derb)* pissed as a newt *(coarse)*; **wie ein ~ bluten** *(derb)* bleed like a stuck pig; **sich benehmen wie ein ~/die ~e** *(derb)* behave like a pig/like pigs; **haben wir mal zusammen ~e gehütet?** *(spött.)* since when have we been on such familiar terms?; **b)** *o. Pl. (Fleisch)* pork; **c)** *(salopp abwertend) (gemeiner Mensch)* swine; *(Schmutzfink)* dirty *or* mucky devil *(coll.)*; mucky pig *(coll.)*; **d)** *(salopp: Mensch)* **ein armes ~:** a poor devil; **kein ~ war da** there wasn't a bloody *(Brit. sl.) or (coll.)* damn soul there; **es macht kein ~ auf** nobody's opening the door; **e)** *(ugs.: Glück)* **[großes] ~ haben** have a [big] stroke of luck; *(davonkommen)* get away with it *(coll.)*; **hast du ein ~!** you're a lucky beggar!; **ich habe ~ gehabt** I was in luck

-schwein das *(derb abwertend)* pig; **Kapitalisten~/Kommunisten~:** capitalist pig/communist swine

Schweine- *(salopp)* **eine ~arbeit** a hell *(coll.) or (Brit. sl.)* sod of a job; **ein ~glück haben** be incredibly jammy *(Brit. coll.) or (coll.)* lucky; **heute ist wieder eine ~kälte** it's bloody *(Brit. sl.) or (coll.)* damn cold again today

Schweine-: ~bande die *(derb)* pack of so-and-sos *(coll.)*; *(stärker)* pack of bastards *(sl.)*; **~bauch der** *(Kochk.)* belly pork; **~braten der** *(Kochk.)* roast pork *no indef. art.*; **ein ~braten** a joint of pork; **~filet das** *(Kochk.)* fillet of pork; **~fleisch das** pork; **~fraß der** *(derb abwertend)* pigswill *(coll.)*; **~geld das;** *o. Pl. (salopp)* **ein ~geld kosten/verdienen** cost/earn a packet *(coll.) or* a fortune; **~hund der** *(derb abwertend)* bastard *(sl.)*; swine; **der innere ~hund** lack of willpower; **~koben der** *(Stall)* pigsty; pigpen *(Amer.)*; *(Verschlag)* pen *(in a sty)*; **~kotelett das** *(Kochk.)* pork chop; *(vom Nacken)* pork cutlet; **~lende die** *(Kochk.)* loin of pork; **~mast die** fattening of pigs; pig-fattening; **~pest die** swine fever

Schweinerei die; ~, ~**en** *(ugs. abwertend)* **a)** *(Schmutz)* mess; **so eine ~!** what a mess!; **b)** *(Gemeinheit)* mean *or* dirty trick; **es ist eine ~, daß das nicht erlaubt ist** it's disgusting that that's not allowed; **Er verdient mehr Geld als du? So eine ~!** He earns more money than you? Disgraceful!; **c)** *(Zote)* dirty *or* smutty joke; *(Handlung)* obscene act

schweinern *Adj.; nicht präd. (südd., österr.)* pork

Schweinerne das; *adj. Dekl. (südd., österr.)* pork

Schweine-: ~schmalz das lard; *(zum Streichen)* dripping; **~schnitzel das** *(Kochk.)* escalope of pork; **~stall der** *(auch fig.)* pigsty; pigpen *(Amer.)*; **ich halte es nicht länger aus in diesem ~stall** *(fig.)* I can't stand it any longer in this lousy joint *(sl.)*; **~steak das** pork steak; **~zucht die** pig-breeding *no art.*; **~zucht betreiben** breed pigs

Schwein·igel der *(ugs. abwertend)* **a)** *(Schmutzfink)* dirty *or* mucky devil *(coll.)*; mucky pig *(coll.)*; **b)** *(unanständiger Mensch)* dirty so-and-so *(coll.)*

Schweinigelei die; ~, ~**en** *(ugs. abwertend)* **a)** *o. Pl.* making *no art.* a [filthy] mess; *(Schmutz)* [filthy] mess; **b)** *(Zote)* dirty *or* smutty story

schweinigeln *itr. V. (ugs. abwertend)* **a)** *(Schmutz machen)* make a [filthy] mess; **b)** *(Zoten reißen)* tell dirty *or* smutty stories

schweinisch *(ugs. abwertend)* **1.** *Adj.* **a)** *(schmutzig)* filthy; **b)** *(unanständig)* dirty; smutty. **2.** *adv. (unanständig)* ⟨*behave*⟩ obscenely, disgustingly

schweins-, Schweins-: ~äuglein das piggy eye; **~braten der** *(Kochk., bes. südd., österr., schweiz.) s.* **Schweinebraten; ~galopp der im ~galopp** *(scherzh.)* at a gallop; **im ~galopp angerannt kommen** come charging up [at a gallop]; **~hachse die,** *(bes. südd.)* **~haxe die** *(Kochk.)* knuckle of pork; **~kopf der** *(Kochk.)* pig's head; **~leder das** pigskin; **~ledern** *Adj.* pigskin; **~stelze die** *(österr.) s.* **~hachse**

Schweiß [ʃvais] **der;** ~**es a)** sweat; *(höflicher: Transpiration)* perspiration; **in ~ kommen od. geraten** start to sweat; **mir brach der ~ aus** I broke out in a sweat; **ihm brach der kalte ~ aus** he came out in a cold sweat; **in ~ gebadet sein** be bathed in sweat; **etw. im ~e seines Angesichts tun** *(geh.)* do sth. in *or* by the sweat of one's brow; **das hat viel ~ gekostet** that was a real sweat *(coll.)*; **b)** *(Jägerspr.: Blut)* blood

schweiß-, Schweiß-: ~ausbruch der sweat; **einen ~ausbruch bekommen** start to sweat; **~band das;** *Pl.* **~bänder** sweatband; **~bedeckt** *Adj.* covered in *or* with sweat *postpos.*; **~brenner der** *(Technik)* welding torch; **~draht der** *(Technik)* filler wire; welding wire; **~drüse die** *(Anat.)* sweat gland

schweißen *tr., itr. V.* weld

Schweißer der; ~**s,** ~, **Schweißerin die;** ~, ~**nen** welder

schweiß-, Schweiß-: ~fleck der sweat stain; **~fuß der** sweaty foot; **~gebadet** *Adj.* bathed in sweat *postpos.*; **~geruch der** smell of sweat

schweißig *Adj.* sweaty

schweiß- Schweiß-: ~naht die *(Technik)* weld; **~naß** *Adj.* sweaty; damp with sweat *pred.*; **~perle die** bead of sweat; **~treibend** *Adj.* sudorific; diaphoretic; **Holzhacken ist eine ~treibende Arbeit** chopping wood makes you work up a sweat; **~tropfen der** drop of sweat; **~tuch das;** *Pl.* **~tücher** *(veralt.)* sudarium; **das ~tuch der Veronika** *(Bibl.)* the sudarium; the Veronica; Veronica's veil

Schweiz ['ʃvaits] **die;** ~: Switzerland *no art.*; **in die ~ reisen** travel to Switzerland; **aus der ~ stammen** come from Switzerland

Schweizer der; ~**s,** ~ **a)** *(Einwohner)* Swiss; **b)** *(Landw.: Melker)* dairyman; **c)** *(in der Schweizergarde)* Swiss Guard; **d)** *(~ Käse)* Swiss cheese

schweizer- Schweizer-: ~bürger der Swiss citizen; **~deutsch** *Adj.* Swiss German; *s. auch* **deutsch; Deutsch;** [2]**Deutsche; ~garde die** Swiss Guard

Schweizerin die; ~, ~**nen** Swiss; *s. auch* **-in**

schweizerisch *Adj.* Swiss

Schweizer Käse der Swiss cheese

Schweizer-: ~land das; *o. Pl.* Switzerland *no art.*; **~psalm der;** *o. Pl.* Swiss national anthem; **~volk das;** *o. Pl.* **das ~volk** the Swiss people

Schwel·brand der smouldering fire

schwelen ['ʃve:lən] **1.** *itr. V. (auch fig.)* smoulder. **2.** *tr. V. (Technik)* carbonize ⟨*coal, peat, etc.*⟩ at low temperature

schwelgen ['ʃvɛlgn̩] *itr. V.* **a)** *(essen u. trinken)* feast; **in etw.** *(Dat.)* **~:** feast on sth.; **b) in Erinnerungen/Gefühlen** *usw.* **~:** wallow in memories/emotions *etc.*; **in Farben ~** *(geh.)* revel in colours

schwelgerisch 1. *Adj.* epicurean ⟨*person*⟩; sumptuous, opulent ⟨*meal, grandeur*⟩; rapturous ⟨*look, expression*⟩; luxuriant ⟨*blossom*⟩. **2.** *adv.* rapturously; with rapturous pleasure

Schwelle ['ʃvɛlə] **die;** ~, ~**n a)** *(auch Physiol., Psych., fig.)* threshold; **ich werde keinen Fuß mehr über seine ~ setzen** *(fig. geh.)* I shall not set foot in his house/flat *etc.* again; **jmdn. von der ~ weisen** *(fig. geh.)* turn sb. from one's door; **sich an der ~ des Todes befinden** *(fig. geh.)* be at death's door; **b)** *(Eisenbahn~)* sleeper *(Brit.)*; [cross-]tie *(Amer.)*; **c)** *(Geogr.)* swell; **d)** *(Bauw.)* sill; sole plate; abutment piece *(Amer.)*

[1]**schwellen** *unr. itr. V.; mit sein* swell; ⟨*limb, face, cheek, etc.*⟩ swell [up], become swollen; ⟨*river*⟩ become swollen, rise; **~d** full ⟨*lips*⟩; ample ⟨*bosom*⟩; thick ⟨*cushion, carpet*⟩; bulging ⟨*wallet*⟩; **der Sturm schwoll zum Orkan** the storm rose to a hurricane force; *s. auch* **Kamm**

[2]**schwellen** *tr. V. (geh.)* belly, fill ⟨*sail, curtain*⟩; **der Stolz schwellte ihm die Brust** *(fig.)* his breast swelled with pride

Schwellen-: ~angst die; *o. Pl.* fear of entering a place; **~land das** *country at the stage of economic take-off*

Schweller der; ~**s,** ~ *(Musik)* swell

Schwell·körper *(Physiol.)* **der** corpus cavernosum

Schwellung die; ~, ~**en** *(Med.)* swelling

Schwemme ['ʃvɛmə] **die;** ~, ~**n a)** *(Wirtsch.)* glut **(an** + *Dat.* of**); b)** *(Kneipe)* bar; [basic] pub *(Brit. coll.)*; **c)** *(für Tiere)* watering-place; **d)** *(österr.: im Warenhaus)* bargain basement

-schwemme die glut; **Tomaten~/Milch~:** tomato/milk glut; **Lehrer~/Juristen~:** glut of teachers/lawyers
schwemmen *tr. V.* **a)** *(treiben)* wash; **an Land geschwemmt werden** be washed ashore; **b)** *(bes. österr.: spülen)* rinse
Schwemm-: ~land das; *o. Pl.* alluvial land; **~sand der** alluvial sand
Schwengel ['ʃvɛnl̩] **der; ~s, ~ a)** *(Glocken~)* clapper; **b)** *(Pumpen~)* handle; **c)** *(salopp: Penis)* tool *(sl.)*
Schwenk [ʃvɛŋk] **der; ~s, ~s a)** *(Drehung)* swing; **die Kolonne machte einen ~ nach rechts** the column swung *or* wheeled to the right; **die Partei macht einen ~ nach links** *(fig.)* the party is swinging *or* shifting to the left; **b)** *(Film, Ferns.)* pan; **die Kamera machte einen ~ auf den Helden** the camera panned to the hero
Schwenk·arm der swivel arm; swivelling arm
schwenkbar *Adj.* swivelling; **das Periskop ist ~:** the periscope can be swivelled round
schwenken 1. *tr. V.* **a)** *(schwingen)* swing; wave ⟨*flag, handkerchief*⟩; **b)** *(spülen)* rinse; **c)** *(drehen)* swing round; swivel; pan ⟨*camera*⟩; swing, traverse ⟨*gun*⟩; **d)** *(Kochk.)* toss. **2.** *itr. V.; mit sein* ⟨*marching column*⟩ swing, wheel; ⟨*camera*⟩ pan; ⟨*path, road, car*⟩ swing; **er schwenkte in den Hof** he turned into the courtyard; **rechts schwenkt!** *(Milit.)* right wheel!
Schwenker der; ~s, ~: balloon glass
Schwenk·kran der swing-jib crane
Schwenkung die; ~, ~en *s.* **Schwenk**
schwer [ʃveːɐ̯] **1.** *Adj.* **a)** heavy; heavy [-weight] ⟨*fabric*⟩; *(massiv)* solid ⟨*gold*⟩; **die Äste sind ~ von Früchten** the branches are heavy with fruit; **~es Geld kosten** *(fig. ugs.)* cost a packet *(coll.) or* a fortune; **mir wurden die Beine ~:** my legs grew heavy; **ihm wurde ~ ums Herz** *(geh.)* his heart grew heavy; **b)** *(bestimmtes Gewicht habend)* **2 Kilo ~ sein** weigh two kilos; **ein zwei Zentner ~er Sack** a two-centner sack; a sack weighing two centners; **wie ~ bist du?** how much do you weigh?; **eine mehrere Millionen ~e Frau** *(fig. ugs.)* a woman who's worth a few millions; **c)** *(anstrengend, mühevoll)* heavy ⟨*work*⟩; hard, tough ⟨*job*⟩; hard ⟨*day*⟩; difficult ⟨*birth*⟩; troubled ⟨*dream*⟩; **d)** *(schwierig)* difficult; hard; **es ~/nicht ~ haben** have it hard/easy; **sie hat es ~ mit ihrem Mann gehabt** she's had a hard time with her husband; **sich** *(Dat.)* **die Entscheidung ~ machen** find it hard to make a decision; find the decision a hard one; **Schweres durchmachen** go through hard times; **wir haben das Schwerste überstanden** we're over the worst; **e)** *(schlimm)* severe ⟨*shock, disappointment, strain, storm*⟩; serious, grave ⟨*wrong, injustice, error, illness, blow, reservation*⟩; serious ⟨*accident, injury*⟩; heavy ⟨*punishment, strain, loss, blow*⟩; grave ⟨*suspicion*⟩; **ein ~er Junge** *(ugs.)* a crook with a record *(coll.)*; **f)** *(~ verträglich)* heavy ⟨*food, wine*⟩; **g)** *(intensiv)* heavy ⟨*fragrance, perfume, etc.*⟩; **h)** *(anspruchsvoll)* heavy ⟨*book, music, etc.*⟩; **i)** *(Seemannsspr.)* heavy ⟨*sea, weather*⟩; **j)** *(schwül)* heavy; oppressive ⟨*air, atmosphere*⟩. **2.** *adv.* **a)** heavily ⟨*built, laden, armed*⟩; **~ wiegen** be heavy; **~tragen** be carrying sth. heavy [with difficulty]; **~ heben** lift heavy weights; **~ zu tragen haben** have a heavy load to carry; **daran hat er ~ zu tragen** *(fig.)* it is a hard cross for him to bear; **~ auf jmdm./etw. liegen** *od.* **lasten** *(auch fig.)* weigh heavily on sb./sth.; **das Essen lag mir ~ im Magen** *(fig.)* the food lay heavily on my stomach; **b)** *(anstrengend, mühevoll)* ⟨*work*⟩ hard; ⟨*breathe*⟩ heavily; **~ erkämpft sein** be hard won; **das habe ich mir ~ erkämpft** I gained it at great cost; **~ erkauft** dearly bought; bought at great cost *post-pos.*; **er lernt nur ~:** he is a slow learner; **~ hören** be hard of hearing; **c)** *(schwierig)* with difficulty; **ein ~ zu lesender Text** a text that is hard *or* difficult to read; **d)** *(sehr)* seriously ⟨*injured*⟩; greatly, deeply ⟨*disappointed*⟩; ⟨*punish*⟩ severely, heavily; **etw. ~ büßen** pay dearly for sth.; **~ aufpassen** *(ugs.)* take great care; **~ stürzen** fall heavily; have a heavy fall; **~ verunglücken** have a serious accident; **~ im Irrtum sein** *(ugs.)* be very much mistaken; **~ in Fahrt sein** *(ugs.)* be really worked up; **~ betroffen sein** be deeply affected; **~ beleidigt/betrunken sein** *(ugs.)* be deeply *or* very insulted/blind drunk; **sich ~ ärgern** *(ugs.)* get very annoyed; **sich ~ blamieren** *(ugs.)* make a proper fool of oneself; **das will ich ~ hoffen** *(ugs.)* I should jolly well think so *(Brit. coll.)*; **er ist ~ in Ordnung** *(ugs.)* he's a good bloke *(Brit. coll.) or (sl.)* guy; **wir haben ~ einen draufgemacht** *(ugs.)* we really painted the town red *(sl.)*; **e)** *(unverträglich)* **~ essen** eat heavy food; **sie kocht zu ~:** the food she cooks is too heavy
schwer-, Schwer-: ~arbeit die; *o. Pl.* heavy work; **~arbeiter der** worker engaged in heavy physical work; **~athlet der** weight-lifter/wrestler/boxer/judoka/shot-putter/discus-thrower; **~athletik die** weightlifting *no art.*/combat sports *no art.*/shot-putting *no art.*/discus-throwing *no art.*; **~behindert** *Adj.* severely handicapped; *(körperlich auch)* severely disabled; **~behinderte der/die** severely handicapped person; *(körperlich auch)* severely disabled person; **die ~behinderten** the severely handicapped/disabled; **~behinderten·ausweis der** disabled person's pass; **~beladen** *Adj.; präd. getrennt geschrieben* heavily laden *or* loaded ⟨*vehicle*⟩; heavily laden ⟨*person, animal*⟩; **~beschädigt** *Adj.* **a)** *präd. getrennt geschrieben* badly damaged; **b)** *(veralt.: schwerbehindert)* severely disabled; **~beschädigte der/die;** *adj. Dekl.* severely disabled person; **die ~beschädigten** the severely disabled; **~bewaffnet** *Adj.; präd. getrennt geschrieben* heavily armed; **~blütig** *Adj.* stolid; phlegmatic
Schwere die; ~: a) weight; **eine ~ in den Gliedern** a heaviness in one's limbs; **b)** *(Physik: Schwerkraft)* gravity; **c)** *s.* **schwer 1 e:** severity; seriousness; gravity; heaviness; **d)** *(Schwierigkeitsgrad)* difficulty; **e)** *(von Speisen, Parfums usw.)* heaviness
Schwere·feld das *(Geophysik)* gravitational field; field of gravity
schwere·los 1. *Adj.* weightless. **2.** *adv.* weightlessly
Schwerelosigkeit die; ~: weightlessness
Schwerenöter ['ʃveːrənøːtɐ] **der; ~s, ~** *(ugs. scherzh.)* lady-killer *(coll.)*
schwer-, Schwer-: ~erziehbar *Adj.; präd. getrennt geschrieben* difficult ⟨*child*⟩; **~|fallen** *unr. itr. V.; mit sein* **jmdm. fällt etw. ~:** sb. finds sth. difficult; **auch wenn's schwerfällt** whether you like it or not; **~fällig 1.** *Adj.* ponderous, slow-moving ⟨*animal*⟩; ponderous, heavy ⟨*movement, steps*⟩; *(auch geistig)* ponderous ⟨*person*⟩; *(fig.)* cumbersome ⟨*bureaucracy, procedure*⟩; ponderous ⟨*style, thinking*⟩; **2.** *adv.* ponderously; **~fällig denken/antworten** think/answer slowly and ponderously; **~fälligkeit die;** *o. Pl. s.* **~fällig:** ponderousness; heaviness; *(fig.)* cumbersomeness; ponderousness; **~gewicht das a)** *o. Pl.* heavyweight; **die Meisterschaften im ~gewicht** the heavyweight championships; **b)** *(Sportler)* heavyweight; **c)** *o. Pl. (Schwerpunkt)* main focus; emphasis; **sie studiert Russisch mit ~gewicht Sprachwissenschaft** she's studying Russian, specializing in linguistics; **d)** *(ugs. scherzh.: dicker Mensch)* heavyweight; **~gewichtig** *Adj.* heavyweight *attrib.*; **~gewichtler** ['gəvɪçtlɐ] **der; ~s, ~** *(Schwerathletik)* heavyweight; **~|halten** *unr. itr. V. (unpers.)* **es wird ~halten, das zu tun** it will be difficult to do it *or* that; **~hörig** *Adj.* hard of hearing *pred.*; **auf dem Ohr ist er ~hörig** *(fig.)* when it comes to that sort of thing, he doesn't want to know; **~hörige der/die;** *adj. Dekl.* person who is hard of hearing; **die ~n** the hard of hearing; **~hörigkeit die; ~:** hardness of hearing; **~industrie die** heavy industry; **~kraft die;** *o. Pl. (Physik, Astron.)* gravity; **~krank** *Adj.; präd. getrennt geschrieben* seriously ill; **~kranke der/die** seriously ill person; **die ~kranken** the seriously ill; **~kriegs·beschädigte der/die** severely war disabled person; **die ~kriegsbeschädigten** the severely war disabled
schwerlich *Adv.* hardly; **das wird dir ~ jemand glauben** it's hardly likely that anyone will believe you
schwer-, Schwer-: ~|machen *tr. V.* **jmdm./sich etw. ~machen** make sth. difficult for sb./oneself; **~metall das** heavy metal; **~mut die** melancholy; **~mütig 1.** *Adj.* melancholic; **2.** *adv.* melancholically; **er starrte ~ vor sich hin** he stared ahead full of melancholy; **~|nehmen** *unr. tr. V.* **etw. ~nehmen** take sth. seriously; **~öl das** heavy oil; **~punkt der** *(Physik)* centre of gravity; *(fig.)* main focus; *(Hauptgewicht)* main stress; **der ~punkt seiner Tätigkeit liegt in** *od.* **auf der Forschung** his activity centres on research; **den ~punkt auf etw.** *(Akk.)* **legen** *(fig.)* put the main stress on sth.; focus mainly on sth.; **~punkt·mäßig 1.** *Adj.; nicht präd.* selective ⟨*strike, action*⟩; **2.** *adv.* **im Lager und in der Packerei soll ~punktmäßig gestreikt werden** there are to be selective strikes in the warehouse and the packing department; **~punkt·programm das** programme of selective measures; **~reich** *Adj.; nicht präd. (ugs.)* immensely rich *(coll.)*
Schwerst-: ~arbeiter der worker engaged in very heavy work; **~behinderte der/die;** *adj. Dekl.* severely disabled person *(with a disablement of over 80%)*; *s. auch* **Schwerbehinderte**
Schwert [ʃveːɐ̯t] **das; ~[e]s, ~er a)** sword; **das ~ ziehen** *od.* **zücken** draw one's sword; **~er zu Pflugscharen** swords to ploughshares; *s. auch* **zweischneidig; b)** *(Schiffbau)* centreboard
schwert-, Schwert-: ~fisch der swordfish; **~leite** ['laitə] **die; ~, ~n** *(hist.)* accolade; dubbing ceremony; **~lilie die** iris; **~schlucker der** sword-swallower
schwer|tun *unr. refl. V. (ugs.)* **sich** *(Akk. od. Dat.)* **mit** *od.* **bei etw. ~:** have trouble with sth.; **sich** *(Akk. od. Dat.)* **mit jmdm. ~:** not get along with sb.
Schwert·wal der [großer] ~: killer whale; **[kleiner] ~:** false killer whale
schwer-, Schwer-: ~verbrecher der serious offender; **ich lasse mich nicht wie ein ~verbrecher behandeln** I won't be treated like a common criminal; **~verdaulich** *Adj.; präd. getrennt geschrieben (auch fig.)* hard to digest *pred.*; **~verletzt** *Adj.; präd. getrennt geschrieben* seriously injured; **~verletzte der/die** seriously injured person; serious casualty; **die ~verletzten** the seriously injured; **~verständlich** *Adj.; präd. getrennt geschrieben* scarcely comprehensible; **~verwundet** *Adj.; präd. getrennt geschrieben* seriously wounded; **~verwundete der/die** seriously wounded person; **die ~verwundeten** the seriously wounded; **~wiegend** *Adj.* serious, grave ⟨*reservation, consequence, objection, accusation, etc.*⟩; momentous ⟨*decision*⟩; serious ⟨*case, problem*⟩
Schwester ['ʃvɛstɐ] **die; ~, ~n a)** sister; **b)** *(Nonne)* nun; *(als Anrede)* Sister; **~ Petra**

Sister Petra; **c)** *(Kranken~)* nurse; *(als Anrede)* Nurse; *(zur Oberschwester)* Sister; **d)** *(ugs.: ~firma)* associate firm
Schwesterchen das, ~s, ~: little sister; **ein kleines ~:** a little sister
Schwester-: ~firma die associate firm *or* company; **~herz das** *(veralt., noch scherzh.)* dear sister; **hör mal, ~herz** listen, sister dear
schwesterlich 1. *Adj.* sisterly. **2.** *adv.* **~ handeln** act in a sisterly way
Schwester-: ~liebe die sisterly love; **~mord der** sororicide; **~mörder der, ~mörderin die** sororicide
Schwestern·helferin die nursing auxiliary; auxiliary nurse
Schwesternschaft die; ~: nurses *pl.*; nursing staff
Schwestern-: ~schülerin *die* probationer; **~wohn·heim das** nurses' home *or* hostel
Schwester-: ~partei die sister party; **~schiff das** sister ship
Schwib·bogen ['ʃvɪp-] **der** *(Archit.)* flying buttress
schwieg [ʃviːk] *1. u. 3. Pers. Prät. v.* **schweigen**
Schwieger-: ['ʃviːgɐ-] **~eltern** *Pl.* parents-in-law; **~mutter die** mother-in-law; **~sohn der** son-in-law; **~tochter die** daughter-in-law; **~vater der** father-in-law
Schwiele ['ʃviːlə] **die; ~, ~n** callus; **~n an den Händen** horny hands
schwielig *Adj.* callused; **~e Hände** horny hands
schwierig ['ʃviːrɪç] *Adj.* difficult
Schwierigkeit die; ~, ~en difficulty; **in ~en** *(Akk.)* **geraten** get into difficulties; **jmdm. ~en machen** make difficulties for sb.; **Latein macht ihm ~en** he has difficulty *or* trouble with Latin; **mach keine ~en!** don't make difficulties!; don't be difficult *or* awkward!; **~en bekommen** have problems *or* trouble; **jmdn./sich in ~en** *(Akk.)* **bringen** get sb./oneself into trouble; **ohne ~en** without difficulty
Schwierigkeits·grad der degree of difficulty; *(von Lehrmaterial usw.)* level of difficulty
Schwimm-: ~an·zug der swim-suit; *(für Taucher)* wet suit; **~bad das** swimming-baths *pl. (Brit.)*; swimming-pool; **~bagger der** dredger; **~becken das** swimming-pool; **~blase die** swim bladder; air bladder; **~dock das** floating dock
Schwimmeister der; ~s, ~: swimming-supervisor [and instructor]
schwimmen 1. *unr. itr. V.* **a)** *meist mit sein* swim; **~ gehen** go swimming; **b)** *meist mit sein (treiben, nicht untergehen)* float; **die Kinder ließen ihre Schiffchen ~:** the children sailed their boats; **koreanische Schiffe ~ auf allen Meeren** Korean ships sail on all the seas of the world; **c)** *(ugs.: unsicher sein)* be all at sea; **ins Schwimmen geraten** *od.* **kommen** start to flounder; **d)** *(überschwemmt sein)* be awash; **f)** *mit sein (triefen von)* **in etw.** *(Dat.)* **~:** be swimming in sth.; **im [eigenen] Blut ~:** be bathed in [one's own] blood; **in** *od.* **im Geld ~** *(fig.)* be rolling in money *or* in it *(coll.)*; **g)** *mit sein (ver~)* swim; **mir schwimmt es vor den Augen** everything is swimming in front of my eyes; **h)** *in* **~des Fett** *(Kochk.)* deep fat; **etw. in ~dem Fett braten** deep-fry sth.; fry sth. in deep fat. **2.** *unr. tr. V.; auch mit sein* swim; **einen neuen Rekord ~:** swim a new record time
Schwimmen das; ~: swimming *no art.*
Schwimmer der; ~s, ~: a) swimmer; **b)** *(der Angel, Technik)* float
Schwimmer·becken das swimmers' pool
Schwimmerin die; ~, ~nen swimmer
schwimm-, Schwimm-: ~fähig *Adj.* buoyant ⟨*material*⟩; amphibious ⟨*vehicle*⟩; **~flosse die** flipper; **~fuß der** webbed foot; **~gürtel der** swimming-belt; **~halle die** indoor swimming-pool; **bevor man in die ~halle kommt, muß man durch den Duschraum gehen** before entering the pool area, you have to go through the showers; **~haut die** web *(of bird's webbed foot)*; **~kran der** floating crane; **~lehrer der** swimming instructor; **~meister der** *s.* **Schwimmeister**; **~sport der** [competitive] swimming *no art.*; **~stadion das** swimming stadium; **~stil der** stroke; **~vogel der** web-footed bird; **~weste die** life-jacket
Schwindel ['ʃvɪndl̩] **der; ~s a)** *(Gleichgewichtsstörung)* dizziness; giddiness; vertigo; **b)** *(Anfall)* dizzy *or* giddy spell; attack of dizziness *or* giddiness *or* vertigo; **c)** *(abwertend) (Betrug)* swindle; fraud; *(Lüge)* lie; **das ist alles ~, was er sagt** what he says is all lies; **den ~ kenne ich** *(ugs.)* that's an old trick; I know that trick; **er fällt auf jeden ~ rein** he'll fall for any trick; **d)** *in der* **ganze ~** *(ugs. abwertend)* the whole lot *(coll.) or (sl.)* shoot
Schwindel·anfall der *s.* **Schwindel b**
Schwindelei die; ~, ~en *(ugs.)* **a)** *o. Pl.* fibbing; **b)** *(Lüge)* fib
schwindel-, Schwindel-: ~erregend vertiginous ⟨*height, speed, depths*⟩; *(fig.)* meteoric ⟨*career, success*⟩; **in ~erregender Höhe** at a dizzy height; **die Preise kletterten in ~erregende Höhe** *(fig.)* the prices rose sky high; **~frei** *Adj.* **~frei sein** have a head for heights; not suffer from vertigo; **~gefühl das** feeling of dizziness *or* giddiness *or* vertigo
schwindelig *s.* **schwindlig**
schwindeln 1. *itr. V.* **a)** *(sich drehen)* **mich** *od.* **mir schwindelt** I feel dizzy *or* giddy; **in ~der Höhe** at a dizzy height; **ein ~der Abgrund** a vertiginous drop; **b)** *(lügen)* tell fibs. **2.** *tr. V. (lügen)* **„...", schwindelte sie** '...,' she said, lying; **das ist alles geschwindelt** that's all lies. **3.** *refl. V.* **sich ins Kino/durch den Zoll ~:** trick *or (coll.)* wangle one's way in to the cinema/through the customs; **sich durchs Examen ~:** wangle one's way through the exam *(coll.)*
schwinden ['ʃvɪndn̩] *unr. itr. V.; mit sein* **a)** *(geh.: abnehmen)* fade; ⟨*sound*⟩ die away, fade; ⟨*supplies, money*⟩ run out, dwindle; ⟨*effect*⟩ wear off; ⟨*interest*⟩ fade, wane, fall off; ⟨*fear, mistrust*⟩ lessen, diminish; ⟨*powers, influence*⟩ wane, decline; ⟨*courage, strength*⟩ fail; ⟨*years, time*⟩ pass by; ⟨*snow, illusion*⟩ disappear; **ihm schwand der Mut** his courage failed him; **im Schwinden [begriffen] sein** ⟨*effect*⟩ be wearing off; ⟨*interest, powers, influence*⟩ be on the wane; **b)** *(fachspr.: Volumen verlieren)* shrink; ⟨*metal*⟩ contract, shrink
Schwindler der; ~s, ~ *(Lügner)* liar; *(Betrüger)* swindler; *(Hochstapler)* confidence trickster; con man *(coll.)*
schwindlig *Adj.* dizzy; giddy; **jmdm. wird es ~:** sb. gets dizzy *or* giddy; **da wird einem ja ~!** *(fig.)* it fairly makes your head spin
Schwind·sucht die *(veralt.)* consumption; tuberculosis; *s. auch* **galoppieren**
schwind·süchtig *Adj. (veralt.)* consumptive; tubercular
Schwinge ['ʃvɪŋə] **die; ~, ~n a)** *(geh.; auch fig.)* wing; **b)** *(bes. österr.: Korb)* shallow oval basket
schwingen 1. *unr. itr. V.* **a)** *mit sein (sich hin- u. herbewegen)* swing; **b)** *(vibrieren)* vibrate; **etw. zum Schwingen bringen** cause sth. to vibrate; **c)** *(Physik)* ⟨*wave*⟩ oscillate; **d)** *(geh.: anklingen)* **in ihren Worten schwang Kritik** her words had a tone of criticism; **e)** *(nachklingen)* linger; **f)** *mit sein (Skilaufen)* swing; **g)** *(schweiz.: ringen)* wrestle Swiss style *(with one's right hand on the belt of one's opponent's wrestling-suit and the left hand on his rolled-up right trouser-leg)*. **2.** *unr. tr. V.* **a)** *(hin- u. herbewegen)* swing; wave ⟨*flag, wand*⟩; *(fuchteln mit)* brandish ⟨*sword, axe, etc.*⟩; **eine Rede ~:** *(ugs.)* hold forth; **große Reden ~** *(ugs.)* talk big; *s. auch* **geschwungen 2; Tanzbein; b)** *(Landw.)* swingle ⟨*flax, hemp*⟩. **3.** *unr. refl. V.* **a)** *(sich schnell bewegen)* **sich über die Mauer ~:** swing oneself *or* vault over the wall; **sich aufs Pferd/Fahrrad ~:** swing oneself *or* leap on to one's horse/bicycle; **sich ins Auto/hinters Steuer ~** *(ugs.)* jump into one's car/get behind the wheel; **der Vogel schwang sich in die Luft** *(fig.)* the bird soared [up] into the air; **b)** *(geh.: in einem Bogen verlaufen)* arch
Schwinger der; ~s, ~ a) *(Boxen)* swing; **b)** *(schweiz.: Ringer)* [Swiss-style] wrestler; *see also* **schwingen 1 g**
Schwing-: ~kreis der *(Elektrot.)* oscillatory circuit; **~tür die** swing-door
Schwingung die; ~, ~en a) swinging; *(Vibration)* vibration; **etw. in ~ versetzen** set sth. swinging/vibrating; **b)** *(Physik)* oscillation
Schwingungs·zahl die *(Physik)* frequency of oscillation
Schwipp-: [ʃvɪp-] **~schwager der** *(ugs.)* husband's/wife's/brother's/sister's brother-in-law; **~schwägerin die** *(ugs.)* husband's/wife's/brother's/sister's sister-in-law
Schwips [ʃvɪps] **der; ~es, ~e** *(ugs.)* **einen [kleinen] ~ haben** be [a bit] tipsy *or (coll.)* merry
schwirren ['ʃvɪrən] *itr. V.* **a)** *(tönen)* ⟨*insect*⟩ buzz; ⟨*bowstring*⟩ twang; **b)** *mit sein* ⟨*arrow, bullet, etc.*⟩ whiz; ⟨*bird*⟩ whir; ⟨*insect*⟩ buzz; **allerlei schwirrte mir durch den Kopf** *(fig.)* all sorts of things buzzed through my head; **von den vielen Zahlen schwirrte mir der Kopf** *(fig.)* my head was buzzing *or* spinning from all the figures; **c)** *(erfüllt sein von)* **die Stadt schwirrt von Gerüchten** the town is buzzing with rumours
Schwitz·bad das sweat bath
Schwitze die; ~, ~n *(Kochk.)* roux
schwitzen 1. *itr. V.* **a)** *(auch fig.)* sweat; **ins Schwitzen kommen** *(auch fig.)* start to sweat; **b)** *(beschlagen)* steam up; **c)** *(Harz absondern)* sweat. **2.** *refl. V.* **sich bei der Arbeit klatschnaß ~:** get soaked with sweat from working; **sich halb tot ~** *(ugs.)* sweat like anything *(coll.)*. **3.** *tr. V. (Kochk.: in heißem Fett)* sweat
schwitzig *Adj. (ugs.)* sweaty
Schwitz-: ~kasten der; *o. Pl. (Ringen)* headlock; **jmdn. in den ~kasten nehmen** get sb. in a headlock; **~kur die** sweat cure
schwofen ['ʃvoːfn̩] *itr. V. (ugs.)* shake a leg *(coll.)*; **~ gehen** go and shake a leg
schwor [ʃvoːɐ̯] *1. u. 3. Pers. Sg. Prät. v.* **schwören**
schwören ['ʃvøːrən] **1.** *unr. itr., tr. V.* swear ⟨*fidelity, allegiance, friendship*⟩; swear, take ⟨*oath*⟩; **ich schwöre es[, so wahr mir Gott helfe]** I swear it[, so help me God]; **jmdm./sich etw. ~:** swear sth. to sb./oneself. **2.** *unr. itr. V.* swear an/the oath; **auf die Bibel/die Verfassung ~:** swear on the Bible/the Constitution; **ich könnte darauf ~** *(ugs.)* I could swear to it; **sie schwört auf ihren Kräutertee** she swears by her herbal tea
Schwuchtel ['ʃvʊxtl̩] **die; ~, ~n** *(salopp)* queen *(sl.)*
schwul [ʃvuːl] *Adj. (ugs.)* gay *(coll.)*
schwül [ʃvyːl] *Adj.* **a)** *(feuchtwarm)* sultry; close; **b)** *(beklemmend)* oppressive; **c)** *(sinnlich)* sensuous ⟨*perfume, fantasy, etc.*⟩; steamy ⟨*eroticism*⟩; sultry ⟨*look*⟩; seductive ⟨*lighting, music*⟩
Schwule der; *adj. Dekl. (ugs.)* gay *(coll.)*; *(abwertend)* queer *(sl.)*
Schwüle die; ~: sultriness
Schwulen-: ~bewegung die *(ugs.)* gay rights movement; **~lokal das** *(ugs.)* gay bar *(coll.)*

Schwulität [ʃvuli'tɛ:t] **die;** ~, ~**en** *(ugs.)* **in ~en kommen** *od.* **geraten** get into a fix *or* jam *(coll.)*; **jmdn./sich in ~en bringen** get sb./oneself into a fix *or* jam *(coll.)*

Schwulst [ʃvʊlst] **der;** ~[e]s *(abwertend)* bombast; pompousness; *(im Baustil)* over-ornateness; **dieser Film ist sentimentaler ~:** this film is full of sentimental affectation

schwülstig ['ʃvʏlstɪç] **1.** *Adj.* bombastic, pompous ‹*writing*›; bombastic, pompous, grandiloquent ‹*speech*›; over-ornate ‹*art, architecture*›. **2.** *adv.* bombastically; pompously; ‹*speak*› bombastically, pompously, grandiloquently

schwumm[e]rig ['ʃvʊmərɪç] *Adj.* *(ugs.)* **a)** *(unwohl)* queasy; funny *(coll.)*; **ihr wurde ~:** she started to feel queasy *or (coll.)* funny; **b)** *(bang)* jittery *(coll.)*; nervous; apprehensive; **mir wird schon ~:** I'm already starting to get the jitters *(coll.)*; I'm already getting butterflies [in my stomach]

Schwund [ʃvʊnt] **der;** ~[e]s **a)** decrease, drop (*Gen.* in); *(an Interesse)* waning; falling off; **einen ~ an Wählerstimmen befürchten** ‹*party*› fear a decline in its share of the vote; **b)** *(Kaufmannsspr.)* shrinkage; **c)** *(Technik: Ausschuß)* wastage; **d)** *(Med.)* atrophy; **e)** *(Rundfunkt., Funkt.)* fading

Schwung [ʃvʊŋ] **der;** ~[e]s, **Schwünge** ['ʃvʏŋə] **a)** *(Bewegung)* swing; **b)** *(Linie)* sweep; **der elegante ~ ihrer Brauen/ihrer Nase** the elegant arch of her eyebrows/curve of her nose; **mit kühnem ~ überspannt die Brücke das Tal** the bridge crosses the valley in a bold arc; **c)** *o. Pl. (Geschwindigkeit)* momentum; **~ holen** build *or* get up momentum; *(auf einer Schaukel usw.)* work up a swing; **~ in etw.** *(Akk.)* **bringen, etw. in ~ bringen** *(fig. ugs.)* get sth. going; **jmdn. in ~ bringen, jmdm. ~ geben** *(fig. ugs.)* put some life into sb.; get sb. going; **in ~ sein** *(fig. ugs.) (in guter Stimmung)* have livened up; *(wütend)* be worked up; *(gut laufen)* ‹*business, practice*› do a lively trade; *(gut vorankommen)* be getting on well; be right in the swing [of it]; **in ~ kommen** *(fig. ugs.) (in gute Stimmung kommen)* get going; liven up; *(wütend werden)* get worked up; *(gut vorankommen)* get right in the swing [of it]; ‹*business*› pick up; **jmdn./einen Betrieb in ~ haben** *od.* **halten** *(ugs.)* keep sb. on his/her toes/keep a firm doing a flourishing *or* good trade; **in die Sache kommt ~** *(ugs.)* things are picking up; **d)** *o. Pl. (Antrieb)* drive; energy; **e)** *o. Pl. (mitreißende Wirkung)* sparkle; vitality; **f)** *o. Pl. (ugs.: größere Menge)* stack *(coll.)*; *(von Menschen)* crowd; bunch *(sl.)*

schwung·haft 1. *Adj.* thriving; brisk, flourishing ‹*trade, business*›. **2.** *adv.* **die Aktien werden ~ gehandelt** there's a brisk *or* flourishing trade in the shares; **das Geschäft entwickelt sich ~:** business is booming

schwung-, Schwung-: ~kraft die *(Physik)* centrifugal force; **~los 1.** *Adj.* **a)** *(antriebsschwach)* lacking in energy *or* drive *postpos.*; listless; **b)** *(langweilig)* lack-lustre ‹*speech, performance, etc.*›; **2.** *adv.* ‹*sing, dance, etc.*› in a lack-lustre way; **~rad das** *(Technik)* flywheel; *(an einer Nähmaschine)* band wheel; **~voll a)** *(mitreißend)* lively; spirited; spirited ‹*words*›; lively, *(coll.)* snappy ‹*tune*›; **b)** *(kraftvoll)* vigorous; **ein ~er Handel** a roaring trade; **c)** *(elegant)* sweeping ‹*movement, gesture*›; bold ‹*handwriting, line, stroke*›; **2.** *adv.* **a)** *(mitreißend)* spiritedly; with verve; ‹*speak*› spiritedly; **b)** *(kraftvoll)* with great vigour

Schwur [ʃvu:ɐ̯] **der;** ~[e]s, **Schwüre** ['ʃvy:rə] **a)** *(Gelöbnis)* vow; **b)** *(Eid)* oath; **die Hand zum ~ erheben** raise one's hand to take the oath

Schwur·gericht das *court with a jury;* **vor das ~ kommen** be tried by a jury

Schwyzerdütsch ['ʃvi:tsədy:tʃ], **Schwyzertütsch** ['ʃvi:tsəty:tʃ] **das** *(schweiz.)* Swiss German

Science-fiction ['saɪəns'fɪkʃən] **die;** ~: science fiction

Scotch·terrier ['skɔtʃ-] **der** Scotch terrier

Scylla ['stsvla] *s.* **Szylla**

SDR [ɛsde:'ɛr] **der;** ~: *Abk.* **Süddeutscher Rundfunk** South German Radio

SDS [ɛsde:'ɛs] **der;** ~: *Abk.* **Sozialistischer Deutscher Studentenbund** Socialist German Students' Federation

Séance [ze'ã:s(ə)] **die;** ~, ~**n** seance

Seborrhö, Seborrhöe [zebo'rø:] **die;** ~, **Seborrhöen** *(Med.)* seborrhoea

sechs [zɛks] *Kardinalz.* six; *s. auch* **acht**

Sechs die; ~, ~**en** six; **eine ~ schreiben/bekommen** *(Schulw.)* get a 'fail' mark; *s. auch* [1]**Acht a, b, d, e, g; Zwei b**

sechs-, Sechs-: ~achtel·takt der six-eight time; **im ~achteltakt** in six-eight time; **~eck das** hexagon; **~eckig** *Adj.* hexagonal; *s. auch* **achteckig**

Sechser der; ~s, ~ **a)** *(ugs.) (Ziffer, beim Würfeln)* six; *(Bahn, Bus)* [number] six; *(im Lotto)* six winning numbers; **b)** *(berlin.: Fünfpfennigstück)* five-pfennig piece

sechserlei *Gattungsz.; indekl.* **a)** *attr.* six kinds *or* sorts of; six different ‹*sorts, kinds, sizes, possibilities*›; **b)** *subst.* six [different] things

Sechser·pack der, Sechser·packung die pack of six; *(bes. von Bier)* six-pack

sechs-, Sechs-: ~fach *Vervielfältigungsz.* sixfold; *s. auch* **achtfach; ~fache das;** *adj. Dekl.* **etw. um ein ~faches/um das ~fache erhöhen** increase sth. by a factor of six; *s. auch* **Achtfache; ~flach das;** ~[e]s, ~e, **~flächner** [~flɛçnɐ] **der** hexahedron; **~hundert** *Kardinalz.* six hundred; **~jährig** *Adj. (6 Jahre alt)* six-year-old *attrib.*; six years old *postpos.*; *(6 Jahre dauernd)* six-year *attrib.*; *s. auch* **achtjährig; ~kant·mutter die** hexagon nut; **~köpfig** *Adj.* six-headed ‹*monster*›; ‹*family, committee*› of six

Sechsling ['zɛkslɪŋ] **der;** ~s, ~e sextuplet

sechs-: ~mal *Adv.* six times; *s. auch* **achtmal; ~malig** *Adj.; nicht präd.* **nach ~maliger Wiederholung konnte er es auswendig** after repeating it six times, he knew it by heart; *s. auch* **achtmalig; ~seitig** *Adj.* six-sided; six-page *attrib.* ‹*letter, article*›; **~stellig** *Adj.* six-figure; *s. auch* **achtstellig; ~stöckig** *Adj.* six-storey *attrib.*; *s. auch* **achtstöckig**

sechst [zɛkst] **in wir waren zu ~:** there were six of us; *s. auch* [2]**acht**

sechst... *Ordinalz.* sixth; *s. auch* **acht...**

sechs-, Sechs-: ~tage·rennen das *(Radsport)* six-day race; **~tage·woche die** six-day week; **~tägig** *Adj. (6 Tage alt)* six-day-old *attrib.*; *(6 Tage dauernd)* six-day[-long] *attrib.*; *s. auch* **achttägig; ~tausend** *Kardinalz.* six thousand

Sechste der/die; *adj. Dekl.* sixth; *s. auch* **Achte**

sechs·teilig *Adj.* six-piece ‹*tool-set etc.*›; six-part ‹*serial*›; *s. auch* **achtteilig**

sechstel *Bruchz.* sixth

Sechstel das, *schweiz. meist* **der;** ~s, ~: sixth; *s. auch* **Achtel**

sechstens *Adv.* sixthly

Sechs-: ~tonner der; ~s, ~: six-tonner; **~und·sechzig das;** ~: sixty-six; **~zylinder·motor der** six-cylinder engine

sechzehn ['zɛçtse:n] *Kardinalz.* sixteen; *s. auch* **achtzehn**

sechzehn-, Sechzehn-: ~jährig *Adj. (16 Jahre alt)* sixteen-year-old *attrib.*; sixteen years old *pred.*; *(16 Jahre dauernd)* sixteen-year *attrib.*; *s. auch* **achtjährig; ~meter·raum der** *(Fußball)* penalty area; **~millimeter·film der** sixteen-millimetre film; 16-mm film

sechzehnt... *Ordinalz.* sixteenth

Sechzehntel das; ~s, ~ sixteenth

Sechzehntel·note die sixteenth note

sechzig ['zɛçtsɪç] *Kardinalz.* sixty; *s. auch* **achtzig**

sechziger *indekl. Adj.; nicht präd.* **die ~ Jahre** the sixties; **zwei ~ Briefmarken/Zigarren** two sixty-pfennig stamps/cigars; **eine ~ Glühbirne** a 60-watt bulb

[1]**Sechziger der;** ~s, ~ **a)** *(60jähriger)* sixty-year-old; sexagenarian; **b)** *(Bus, Bahn)* number sixty; **c)** *(Wein von 1960)* **der ~:** the '60 vintage

[2]**Sechziger die;** ~, ~ **a)** *(Briefmarke)* sixty-pfennig/schilling *etc.* stamp; **b)** *(Zigarre)* sixty-pfennig cigar; *(Glühbirne)* 60-watt bulb

[3]**Sechziger** *Pl.* sixties; **in den ~n sein** be in one's sixties

sechzig·jährig *Adj. (60 Jahre alt)* sixty-year-old *attrib.*; sixty years old *postpos.*; *(60 Jahre dauernd)* sixty-year *attrib.*

Sechzig·jährige der/die; *adj. Dekl.* sixty-year-old

sechzigst... ['zɛçtsɪçst] *Ordinalz.* sixtieth; *s. auch* **achtzigst...**

SED [ɛs|e:'de:] **die;** ~: *Abk.* **Sozialistische Einheitspartei Deutschlands** Socialist Unity Party of Germany

Sedativum [zeda'ti:vʊm] **das;** ~s, **Sedativa** *(Med.)* sedative

Sediment [zedi'mɛnt] **das;** ~[e]s, ~e *(Geol., Chemie, Med.)* sediment

Sediment·gestein das *(Geol.)* sedimentary rock

[1]**See** [ze:] **der;** ~s, ~n lake; **der Baikalsee** Lake Baikal

[2]**See die;** ~, ~n **a)** *o. Pl. (Meer)* sea; **an die ~ fahren** go to the seaside; **an der ~:** by the sea[side]; **auf ~:** at sea; **er ist auf ~:** he is away at sea; **auf ~ bleiben** *(geh. verhüll.)* be lost at sea; **auf hoher ~:** on the high seas; **in ~ gehen** *od.* **stechen** put to sea; **Leutnant/Kapitän zur ~** *(Marine)* sub-lieutenant/[naval] captain; **zur ~ fahren** be a seaman; **zur ~ gehen** *(ugs.)* go to sea; **b)** *o. Pl. (Seemannsspr.: ~gang)* **ruhige/rauhe** *od.* **grobe** *od.* **schwere ~:** calm/rough or heavy sea; **c)** *(Seemannsspr.: Woge)* sea

see-, See-: ~aal der; *o. Pl.* flake; **~adler der** sea eagle; white-tailed [sea] eagle; **~anemone die** sea anemone; **~bad das** seaside health resort; **~bär der a)** *(Zool.)* fur seal; **b)** *(fam.: ~mann)* sea dog *(coll.)*; **~beben das** seaquake; **~bestattung die** burial at sea; **~blockade die** naval blockade; **~bühne die** lake stage; **~-Elefant der** elephant seal; **~fahrend** *Adj.; nicht präd.* seafaring; **~fahrer der** *(veralt.)* seafarer; **Sindbad der ~fahrer** Sindbad the Sailor; **~fahrer·volk das** seafaring people; **~fahrt die a)** *o. Pl.* seafaring *no art.*; sea travel *no art.*; *(~fahrtskunde)* navigation; *s. auch* **christlich; b)** *(~reise)* voyage; *(Kreuzfahrt)* cruise; **~fahrt[s]·buch das** *(Seew.)* seaman's discharge book; **~fahrt[s]·schule die** merchant navy college; **~fest** *Adj.* **a)** *s.* **~tüchtig; b)** *(nicht leicht ~krank)* **~fest sein** not suffer from seasickness; not get seasick; **c)** *(gesichert, fest angebracht)* secured [for sea]; **~fisch der** sea fish; salt-water fish; **~fracht die** sea freight; **~funk der** maritime radio; **~gang der;** *o. Pl.* **leichter/starker** *od.* **hoher** *od.* **schwerer ~gang** light/heavy *or* rough sea; **bei leichtem/schwerem ~gang** with a calm/heavy sea; **~gefecht das** naval engagement; sea battle; naval battle; **~gestützt** *Adj. (Milit.)* sea-based; **~gras das** eel grass; *(als Polstermaterial)* sea grass; **~hafen der a)** *(Hafenanlagen)* harbour; **b)** *(Stadt)* seaport; **~handel der** maritime trade; **~hase der** *(Zool.)* lumpsucker; **~herrschaft die;** *o. Pl.* maritime supremacy; **~hund der a)** common seal; **b)**

o. Pl. (Pelz) seal[skin]; **~igel der** sea-urchin; **~jung·frau die** *(Myth.)* mermaid; **~karte die** sea chart; **~klar** *Adj. (Seemannsspr.)* ready to sail *pred.*; **~klima das** *(Geogr.)* maritime climate; **~krank** *Adj.* seasick; **~krankheit die;** *o. Pl.* seasickness; **~krieg der** naval war; *(Kriegsführung)* naval warfare; **~lachs der** pollack
Seelchen ['zeːlçən] **das; ~s, ~** *(spött.)* tender soul
Seele ['zeːlə] **die; ~, ~n a)** *(auch Rel., fig.)* soul; *(Psyche)* mind; **nun hat die liebe ~ Ruh** *(ugs.)* now he's *etc.* satisfied at last; **zwei ~n, ein Gedanke** two minds with but a single thought; **sich** *(Dat.)* **die ~ aus dem Leib schreien** *(ugs.)* shout/scream one's head off *(coll.)*; **jmdm. auf der ~ lasten** *od.* **liegen** *(geh.)* weigh on sb.['s mind]; **jmdm. aus der ~ sprechen** *od.* **reden** *(ugs.)* take the words out of sb.'s mouth; **aus tiefster** *od.* **ganzer ~:** with all one's heart; ⟨*thank*⟩ from the bottom of one's heart; ⟨*sing*⟩ with all one's heart and soul; **jmdn. in tiefster ~ kränken/enttäuschen** cut sb. to the quick/profoundly *or* deeply disappoint sb.; **das tut mir in der ~ weh** it hurts me deeply; **mit ganzer ~:** heart and soul; **sich** *(Dat.)* **etw. von der ~ reden** unburden oneself about sth.; **die ~ einer Sache** *od.* **von etw. sein** be the heart of sth.; **eine arme ~:** a poor soul; *s. auch* **aushauchen; Herz b; Leib a; Teufel; b)** *(Mensch)* soul; **eine ~ von Mensch** *od.* **von einem Menschen sein** be a good[-hearted] soul; **c)** *(Waffent.)* bore; **d)** *(Technik: eines Kabels usw.)* core
seelen-, Seelen-: ~amt das *(kath. Kirche)* requiem mass; **~arzt der** psychoanalyst; **~friede[n] der** peace of mind; **~heil das** *(christl. Rel.)* salvation of one's/sb.'s soul; **ich mache das, wenn dein ~heil davon abhängt** *(iron.)* I'll do it, if it's a matter of life and death *(joc.)*; **~hirt[e] der** *(veralt.)* pastor; **~leben das;** *o. Pl. (geh.)* inner life; **~los 1.** *Adj.* soulless; **2.** *adv.* soullessly; **~qual die** *(geh.)* mental anguish *or* torment *no pl.*; **~ruhe die** calmness; **in aller ~ruhe** calmly; **~ruhig 1.** *Adj.* calm; unruffled; **2.** *adv.* calmly; **~vergnügt 1.** *Adj.* cheerful; contented; **2.** *adv.* cheerfully; contentedly; **~verkäufer der** *(Seemannsspr. abwertend)* coffin-ship; **~verwandtschaft die unsere/ihre ~verwandtschaft** the fact that we/they are kindred spirits; **~voll 1.** *Adj.* soulful; **2.** *adv.* soulfully; **~wanderung die** *(bes. ind. Religionen)* transmigration of souls; **~zu·stand der** mental state; state of mind
seelisch 1. *Adj.* psychological ⟨*cause, damage, tension*⟩; mental ⟨*equilibrium, breakdown, illness, health*⟩; mental [and emotional] ⟨*state, strain, low [point]*⟩. **2.** *adv.* **~ bedingt sein** have psychological causes; **~ krank** mentally ill
See·löwe der sea-lion
Seel·sorge die; *o. Pl.* pastoral care
Seelsorger der; ~s, ~: pastoral worker; *(Geistlicher)* pastor
seelsorgerisch, seelsorg[er]lich 1. *Adj.* pastoral. **2.** *adv.* **eine Gemeinde ~ betreuen** provide pastoral care for a parish
See-: ~luft die *o. Pl.* sea air; **~macht die** maritime *or* naval power; sea power; **~mann der;** *Pl.* **~leute** seaman; sailor
seemännisch ['zeːmɛnɪʃ] *Adj.* nautical
Seemanns-: ~braut die sailor's lass; **~garn das;** *o. Pl.* seaman's yarn; **~garn spinnen** spin yarns; **~grab das;** *o. Pl.* **ein ~grab finden** *(geh.)* go to a watery grave; **~heim das** sailors' home; **~lied das** sailors' song; **~sprache die** seaman's language; nautical language; **~tod der;** *o. Pl.* **den ~tod finden** *od.* **sterben** be drowned [at sea]
See-: ~meile die nautical mile; **~mine die** naval mine

Seen-: ~gebiet das lakeland [region]; **~kunde die;** *o. Pl.* limnology *no art.*
See·not die; *o. Pl.* distress [at sea]; **jmdn. aus ~ retten** rescue sb. in distress; **in ~ geraten** get into difficulties *pl.*
Seen·platte ['zeːən-] **die** *(Geogr.)* lakeland area *(of glacial origin)*
see-, See-: ~pferd[chen] das sea-horse; **~räuber der** pirate; **~räuberei die;** *o. Pl.* piracy *no art.*; **~recht das;** *o. Pl.* maritime law; **~reise die** voyage; *(Kreuzfahrt)* cruise; **~rose die a)** *(Pflanze)* water-lily; **b)** *(Tier)* sea anemone; **~sack der** kitbag; **~sand der** sea sand; **~schiff das** sea-going ship; **~schiffahrt die** maritime shipping *no art.*; sea shipping *no art.*; **~schlacht die** sea battle; naval battle; **~schwalbe die** tern; **~stern der** starfish; **~streitkräfte** *Pl.* naval forces; **~stück das** *(Kunstwiss.)* seascape; *(mit Schiffen usw.)* marine; **~tang der** seaweed; **~tüchtig** *Adj.* seaworthy; **~ufer das** lake shore; shore of a/the lake; **~vogel der** sea-bird; **~wärts** *Adv.* seawards; **~weg der** sea route; **auf dem ~weg** by sea; **~wind der** onshore wind; **~zeichen das** sea-mark; navigation mark; **~zunge die** sole
Segel ['zeːgl̩] **das; ~s, ~:** sail; **mit vollen ~n** under full sail; *(fig.)* full speed ahead; **unter ~** *(Seemannsspr.)* under sail; **die ~ streichen** strike sail; *(fig.)* throw in the towel (**vor** + *Dat.* in the face of)
segel-, Segel-: ~boot das sailing-boat; **~fahrt die** sailing trip; sail; *(länger)* sailing voyage; **~fliegen** *itr. V.; nur im Inf.* **~fliegen lernen** learn to fly a glider *or* to be a glider pilot; **man kann heute nicht ~fliegen** one can't go gliding today; **~fliegen das;** *o. Pl.* gliding *no art.*; **~flieger der** glider pilot; **~flugzeug das** glider; **~jacht die** sailing-yacht; **~macher der** sail-maker
segeln 1. *itr. V.* **a)** *mit sein, ohne Richtungsangabe auch mit haben* sail; **~ gehen** go sailing; go for a sail; **b)** *mit sein (ugs.: fallen)* fall; go flying; **durch die Prüfung ~** *(fig.)* fail *or (Amer. coll.)* flunk the examination; **c)** *mit sein (schweben)* ⟨*cloud, bird, leaf*⟩ sail. **2.** *tr. V.; auch mit sein* sail in ⟨*regatta*⟩; **die Strecke in drei Stunden ~:** sail the course in three hours
Segel-: ~regatta die sailing regatta; **~schiff das** sailing ship; **~sport der** sailing *no art.*; **~tuch das** sailcloth
Segen ['zeːgn̩] **der; ~s, ~ a)** blessing; *(Gebet in der Messe)* benediction; **jmdm. den ~ erteilen** *od.* **spenden** ⟨*priest*⟩ pronounce the blessing on sb.; **über jmdn./etw. den ~ sprechen** bless sb./sth.; **[jmdm.] seinen ~ [zu etw.] geben** *(ugs.)* give [sb.] one's blessing [on sth.]; **meinen ~ hat er!** *(ugs.)* I have no objection [to his doing that]; *(iron.)* the best of luck to him!; **b)** *o. Pl. (Glück, Wohltat)* blessing; **ein wahrer ~:** a real blessing *or* boon; **darauf ruht kein ~** *(geh.)* no good will come of it; **etw. zum ~ der Menschheit nutzen** exploit sth. to the benefit of mankind; **c)** *o. Pl. (geh.: Ertrag)* yield; **der ganze ~** *(ugs.)* the whole lot *(coll.)*; **reichen ~ tragen** *(fig. geh.)* have rich rewards
segen·bringend 1. *Adj.* beneficent. **2.** *adv.* **sich auf etw.** *(Akk.)* **~ auswirken** have a beneficent effect on sth.
segens·reich *Adj.* **a)** prosperous ⟨*life, future*⟩; **b)** *s.* **segenbringend 1**
Segens·wunsch der a) *(Bitte)* blessing; **b)** *Pl. (geh.: Glückwünsche)* good wishes
Segler der; ~s, ~ a) *(Schiff)* sailing-ship *or* -vessel; **b)** *(Sportler)* yachtsman; **c)** *(Zool.)* swift
Seglerin die; ~, ~nen yachtswoman
Segment [zɛˈgmɛnt] **das; ~[e]s, ~e** segment
segmentieren *tr. V.* segment
segnen ['zeːgnən] *tr. V.* **a)** bless; **er hob ~d die Hände** he raised his hands in blessing; **b)** *(ausstatten mit)* **mit jmdm./etw. gesegnet** **sein** *(auch iron.)* be blessed with sb./sth.; **im gesegneten Alter von 88 Jahren** at the venerable age of 88 years; **gesegnetes Leibes sein** *(geh. veralt.)* be with child; **einen gesegneten Appetit/Schlaf haben** *(fam.)* have a healthy appetite/sleep like a log
Segnung die; ~, ~en a) *(Wirkung)* blessing; *(iron.)* dubious blessing; **b)** *(das Segnen)* blessing
seh·behindert *Adj.* partially sighted; visually handicapped; **stark ~ sein** have severely impaired vision
sehen ['zeːən] **1.** *unr. itr. V.* **a)** see; **schlecht/gut ~:** have bad *or* poor/good eyesight; **sehe ich recht?** am I seeing things?; **hast du ge~?** did you see?; **mal ~, wir wollen** *od.* **werden ~** *(ugs.)* we'll see; **siehste!** *(ugs.)*, **siehst du wohl!** there, you see!; **laß mal ~:** let me *or* let's see; let me *or* let's have a look; **siehe oben/unten/Seite 80** see above/below/page 80; **wie ich sehe, haben Sie zu tun** I see you're busy; **da kann man** *od.* *(ugs.)* **kannste mal ~, ...:** that just goes to show ...; **b)** *(hin~)* look; **auf etw.** *(Akk.)* **~:** look at sth.; **nach der Uhr ~:** look at one's watch; **jmdm. über die Schulter ~:** look over sb.'s shoulder; **sieh mal** *od.* **doch!** look!; **siehe da!** lo and behold!; **sieh einmal!** just look!; **alle Welt sieht auf Washington** *(fig.)* all eyes are turned on Washington; **in die Zukunft ~** *(fig.)* look into the future; **c)** *(zeigen, liegen)* **nach Süden/Norden ~:** face south/north; **d)** *(nach~)* have a look; see; **kannst du mal ~?** can you just have a look?; **nach der Post ~** see whether there is any post; **e) nach jmdm. ~** *(betreuen)* keep an eye on sb.; *(besuchen)* drop by to see sb.; *(nach~)* look in on sb.; **nach etw. ~** *(betreuen)* keep an eye on sth.; *(nach~)* take a look at sth.; **f)** *(suchen)* **nach jmdm./etw. ~:** look for sb./sth.; **g)** *(achten)* **auf Sauberkeit/Ordnung ~:** be particular about cleanliness/tidiness; **er sieht nur auf seinen Vorteil/aufs Geld** he's only out for himself/he's only concerned about the money; **darauf ~, daß die Bestimmungen eingehalten werden** make sure that the regulations are adhered to; **h)** *(zu~, sich bemühen)* see; **wir müssen ~, daß wir pünktlich sind** we must see [to it] that we're on time; **man muß ~, wo man bleibt** *(ugs.)* you've got to take what chances you get; **i)** *(hervorragen)* show; **das Boot sah nur ein Stück aus dem Wasser** only a part of the boat showed above the water. **2.** *unr. tr. V.* **a)** *(erblicken)* see; **jmdn./etw. [nicht] zu ~ bekommen** [not] get to see sb./sth.; **sich am Fenster ~ lassen** show oneself at the window; **siehst du meine Brille?** can you see my glasses?; **von ihm/davon ist nichts zu ~:** he/it is nowhere to be seen; **hier gibt es nichts/etwas zu ~:** there's nothing/something to see here; **ich habe ihn kommen [ge]~:** I saw him coming; **das sieht man** you can see that; **sieht man das?** does it show?; **den möchte ich ~, der das gern tut** I'd like to meet the person who 'does enjoy doing it; **wenn ich das schon sehe, wird mir übel** just looking at it makes me feel sick; I feel sick just looking at it; **hat man so was schon ge~!** did you ever see anything like it!; **er hat schon bessere Zeiten ge~:** he has seen better days; **ich habe ihn selten so fröhlich ge~:** I've rarely seen him so happy; **[überall] gern ge~ sein** be welcome [everywhere]; **jmdn. vom Sehen kennen** know sb. by sight; **etw. gern ~:** approve of sth.; **er sieht es nicht gern, wenn seine Frau raucht** he doesn't like his wife to smoke; **jmdn./etw. nicht mehr ~ können** *(fig. ugs.)* not be able to stand the sight of sb./sth. any more; **kein Blut ~ können** *(ugs.)* not be able to stand the sight of blood; **er kann sich in dieser Gegend nicht mehr ~ lassen** he can't show his face around here any more; **mit ihm kann sie sich ~ lassen** she needn't be

ashamed to be seen with him; **mit dieser Frisur kann ich mich nicht ~ lassen** I can't let people see me with my hair like this; **eine Leistung, die sich ~ läßt** an impressive *or* a considerable achievement; **du läßt dich ja überhaupt nicht mehr ~:** we never see anything of you any more; **b)** *(an~, betrachten)* watch ⟨*television, performance*⟩; look at ⟨*photograph, object*⟩; **hast du ihn gestern im Fernsehen ge~?** did you see him yesterday on television?; **c)** *(treffen)* see; **wann ~ wir uns?** when shall we see each other next?; **wir ~ uns morgen!** see you tomorrow!; **in letzter Zeit ~ wir Schulzes häufiger** we've seen more of the Schulzes [just] recently; **d)** *(sich vorstellen)* see; **er sah sich schon als neuen Chef** he already saw himself as the new boss *(coll.)*; **e)** *(feststellen, erkennen)* see; **ich möchte doch einmal ~, ob er es wagt** I'd just like to see whether he dares [to]; **das sieht man an der Farbe** you can tell by the colour; **er sieht nur seinen Vorteil** he's only out for himself; **ich sehe schon, ich komme zu spät** I see I've come too late; **wir sahen, daß wir nicht mehr helfen konnten** we saw that we could not help any more; **etw. in jmdm. ~:** see sth. in sb.; **das wollen wir [doch] erst mal ~!** we'll 'see about that; **man wird ~ [müssen]** we'll [just have to] see; **das sehe ich noch nicht** *(ugs.)* I can't see that happening; **da sieht man es [mal] wieder** it's the same old story; **f)** *(beurteilen)* see; **das sehe ich anders** I see it differently; **so sehe ich das nicht** that's not how I see it; **so darf man das nicht ~:** you mustn't look at it that way *or* like that; **das darfst du nicht so eng ~:** you mustn't take such a narrow view; **so ge~:** looked at that way *or* in that light; **dienstlich/menschlich/rechtlich ge~:** seen from a professional/human/legal point of view; **..., oder wie sehe ich das?** *(ugs.)* ..., am I right?; **ich werde ~, was ich für Sie tun kann** I'll see what I can do for you. **3.** *unr. refl. V.* **a) er kann sich nicht satt ~:** he can't see enough (**an** + *Dat.* of); **ich habe mich müde ge~:** I've seen more than enough; **b)** *(sich betrachten als)* **ich sehe mich getäuscht** I feel cheated; **sich genötigt/veranlaßt ~, ... zu ...:** feel compelled to ...; **sich in der Lage ~, ... zu ...:** feel able to ...; think one is able to ...; **ich sehe mich außerstande, Ihnen zu helfen** I do not feel able to help you

sehens-, Sehens-: ~wert, ~würdig *Adj.* worth seeing *postpos.*; **~würdigkeit die** sight; **die ~würdigkeiten [der Stadt] besichtigen** go sightseeing [in the town]; see the sights [of the town]

Seher der; ~s, ~: seer; prophet

Seher·blick der; *o. Pl.* prophetic *or* visionary powers *pl.*

Seherin die; ~, ~nen seer; prophetess

Seh-: ~fehler der sight defect; defect of vision; **~kraft die;** *o. Pl.* sight

Sehne ['ze:nə] **die; ~, ~n a)** *(Anat.)* tendon; sinew; **b)** *(Bogen~)* string; **c)** *(Geom.)* chord

sehnen *refl. V.* **sich nach jmdm./etw. ~:** long *or* yearn for sb./sth.; **sich [danach] ~, etw. zu tun** long *or* yearn to do sth.; **er sehnt sich nach Hause** he longs to go home; **~des Verlangen** *(geh.)* longing; yearning

Sehnen das; ~s *(geh.)* longing; yearning

Sehnen·scheiden·entzündung die *(Med.)* tendovaginitis *no indef. art.*

Seh·nerv der *(Anat.)* optic nerve

sehnig *Adj.* **a)** stringy ⟨*meat*⟩; **b)** *(kräftig)* sinewy ⟨*figure, legs, arms, etc.*⟩

sehnlich 1. *Adj.; nicht präd.* **das ist mein ~stes Verlangen/mein ~ster Wunsch** that's what I long for most/that's my dearest wish. **2.** *adv.* **etw. ~[st] herbeiwünschen** look forward longingly to sth.; **sich** *(Dat.)* **etw. ~st wünschen** long *or* yearn for sth.; **jmdn. ~st erwarten** look forward eagerly to sb. coming

Sehn·sucht die longing; yearning; **~ nach jmdm. haben** long *or* yearn to see sb.; **die ~ nach der Ferne** the longing for far-away parts

sehn·süchtig 1. *Adj.* longing *attrib.*, yearning *attrib.* ⟨*desire, look, gaze, etc.*⟩; ⟨*letter*⟩ full of longing *or* yearning; *(wehmütig verlangend)* wistful ⟨*gaze, sigh, etc.*⟩; **~es Verlangen** longing; yearning. **2.** *adv.* longingly; *(wehmütig verlangend)* wistfully; **jmdn./etw. ~ erwarten** look forward longingly to seeing sb./to sth.; long for sb. to come/for sth.

sehnsuchts·voll *(geh.)* **1.** *Adj.* longing *attrib.*, yearning *attrib.* ⟨*desire, look, gaze, etc.*⟩; ⟨*letter, lines, song*⟩ full of longing *or* yearning; *(wehmütig)* wistful ⟨*gaze, sigh, tremolo, etc.*⟩. **2.** *adv.* longingly; yearningly; *(wehmütig)* wistfully

sehr [ze:ɐ̯] *Adv.* **a)** *mit Adj. u. Adv.* very; **~ viel** a great deal; **ich bin ~ dafür/dagegen** I'm very much in favour/against [it]; **~ zu meiner Überraschung** [very] much to my surprise; **ich bin Ihnen ~ dankbar** I'm most grateful to you; **ich bin Ihnen ~ verbunden** I'm [very] much obliged to you; **jmdn. ~ gern haben** like sb. a lot *(coll.) or* a great deal; **er wäre ~ wohl imstande gewesen, es zu tun** he would perfectly well have been able to do it; **b)** *mit Verben* very much; greatly; **er hat ~ geweint** he cried a great deal *or (coll.)* a lot; **er hat sich darüber ~ geärgert** he was greatly *or* very annoyed about it; **das muß ich mir ~ überlegen** I'll have to give that a great deal of thought; I'll have to consider that very carefully; **du mußt dich ~ vorsehen** you must be very careful; **es regnet ~:** it's raining hard; **danke ~!** thank you *or* thanks [very much]; **bitte ~, Ihr Schnitzel!** here's your steak, sir/madam; **Danke ~! – Bitte ~!** Thank you – You're welcome; **er hat sich so ~ geärgert/gefreut, daß ...:** he was so annoyed/delighted that ...; **du glaubst nicht, wie ~ er sich gefreut hat** you wouldn't believe how delighted he was; **ja, ~!** yes, very much!; **nein, nicht ~!** no, not much!; **langweilst du dich? – Sehr sogar!** Are you bored? – Yes, very!; **zu ~:** too much; **Hat es ihr gefallen? – Nicht so ~!** Did she like it? – Not all that much!

Seh-: ~rohr das periscope; **~schärfe die** visual acuity; **~schwäche die** weak vision *or* sight *no indef. art.*; **~störung die** sight defect; visual defect; **~störungen** impaired vision *sing.*; **~test der** eye test; **~vermögen das;** *o. Pl.* sight

sei [zai] *1. u. 3. Pers. Sg. Präsens Konjunktiv u. Imperativ Sg. v.* **sein**

seibern ['zaibɐn] *itr. V.* dribble

seichen ['zaiçn̩] *itr. V. (bes. schwäb. salopp)* **a)** pee *(coll.)*; **ins Bett ~:** wet the bed; **b)** *(dummes Zeug reden)* talk drivel

seicht [zaiçt] **1.** *Adj.* shallow; *(fig.)* shallow; superficial. **2.** *adv. (fig.)* shallowly; superficially

Seichtheit die; ~ *(auch fig.)* shallowness

seid [zait] *2. Pers. Pl. Präsens u. Imperativ Pl. v.* **sein**

Seide ['zaidə] **die; ~, ~n** silk

Seidel ['zaidl̩] **das; ~s, ~** *(half-litre)* beer-mug

Seidel·bast der daphne

seiden 1. a) *nicht präd. (aus Seide)* silk; **b)** *(wie Seide)* silky. **2.** *adv.* silkily

seiden-, Seiden-: ~atlas der silk satin; **~bau der;** *o. Pl.* sericulture *no art.*; **~kleid das** silk dress; **~papier das** tissue paper; **~raupe die** silkworm; **~raupen·zucht die** sericulture *no art.*; **~spinner der** *(Zool.)* silk[worm] moth; **~straße die** *(hist.)* silk road; **~strumpf der** silk stocking; **~weich** *Adj.* silky-soft

seidig 1. *Adj.* silky. **2.** *adv.* silkily

Seiende ['zaiəndə] **das;** *adj. Dekl. (Philos.)* **das ~:** that which exists

Seife ['zaifə] **die; ~, ~n a)** soap; **b)** *(Geol.)* alluvial deposit; placer

Seifen-: ~blase die soap bubble; *(fig.)* bubble; **~blasen machen** blow bubbles; **~kisten·rennen das** soap-box race; **~lauge die** [soap]suds *pl.*; **~oper die** *(ugs.)* soap opera; **~pulver das** soap powder; **~schale die** soap-dish; **~schaum der;** *o. Pl.* lather; **~sieder der** *(veralt.)* soap-boiler

seifig *Adj.* soapy

seihen ['zaiən] *tr. V.* strain

Seil [zail] **das; ~s, ~e** rope; *(Draht~)* cable; **auf dem ~ tanzen** dance on the high wire; **in den ~en hängen** *(Boxen)* be on the ropes; *(fig. ugs.: müde sein)* be knackered *(Brit. sl.) or* shattered *(Brit. coll.) or (Amer. coll.)* tuckered

Seil·bahn die cableway

Seiler der; ~s, ~: rope-maker

Seilerei die; ~, ~en a) *o. Pl. (Herstellung)* rope-making *no art.*; **b)** *(Betrieb)* rope-maker's

seil·hüpfen *itr. V.; nur im Inf. u. im 2. Part.; mit sein s.* **seilspringen**

Seilschaft die; ~, ~en *(Bergsteigen)* rope; *(fig.)* followers *pl.*

seil-, Seil-: ~springen *unr. itr. V.; nur im Inf. u. im 2. Part.; mit sein* skip; **~tanz der** tightrope *or* high-wire act; **~tanzen** *itr. V.; nur im Inf. u. im 2. Part.* walk the tightrope *or* high wire; **~tänzer der, ~tänzerin die** tightrope-walker; **~winde die** cable winch

Seim [zaim] **der; ~[e]s, ~e** *(geh.)* glutinous *or* viscid mass; *(Honig~)* honey

seimig *Adj.* glutinous; viscid

[1]**sein** [zain] **1.** *unr. itr. V.* **a)** be; **wie ist der Wein?** how is the wine?; **wie ist das Wetter?** what is the weather like?; **wie wäre es mit einem Schnaps?** how about a schnaps?; **wie war das noch mit dem Scheck?** what was that again about a cheque?; **nun, wie ist es, gehst du mit oder nicht?** well, what about it? are you going too, or not?; **wie ist es mit dir, möchtest du ein Glas Glühwein?** how about you, would you like a glass of mulled wine?; **ist das kalt heute!** it's so cold today; **wie dem auch sei, sei es, wie es wolle** *(geh.)* be that as it may; **seien Sie bitte so freundlich und geben Sie mir ...:** [would you] be so kind as to give me ...; **das Buch ist meins** *od. (ugs.)* **mir** the book is mine; **die Sache ist die: ...:** it's like this: ...; **wenn ich du wäre ...:** if I were you ...; **das wären neun Mark** that will be nine marks; **hier wären wir** here we are; **das wär's** that's that; *(beim Einkaufen)* that's all; that's it *(coll.)*; **und das wäre?** and what might *or* would that be?; **er ist Schwede/Lehrer** he is Swedish *or* a Swede/a teacher; **was ist er [von Beruf]?** what does he do [for a living]?; **bist du es?** is that you?; **Karl war's** *(ist verantwortlich)* it was Karl [who did/said *etc.* it]; **keiner will es gewesen ~:** no one will admit it was him; **wer** *(ugs.) od.* **jemand ~:** be somebody; **nichts ~** *(ugs.)* be a nothing *or* a nonentity; **Everton ist Fußballmeister** Everton are football champions; **x sei 4** let x be 4; **b)** *(unpers.)* **mir ist kalt/besser** I am *or* feel cold/better; **mir ist schlecht** I feel sick; **ist dir etwas?** are you all right?; is something the matter?; **jmdm. ist, als [ob] ...:** sb. feels as if ...; *(jmd. hat den Eindruck [als])* sb. has a feeling that ...; **jmdm. ist nach etw.** *(ugs.)* sb. feels like *or* fancies sth.; **mir ist nicht nach Scherzen** *(ugs.)* I'm not in a mood for joking; **c)** *(ergeben)* be; make; **drei und vier ist** *od. (ugs.)* **sind sieben** three and four is *or* makes seven; **d)** *(unpers.) (bei Zeitangabe)* be; **es ist drei Uhr/Mai/Winter** it is three o'clock/May/winter; **e)** *(sich befinden)* be; **ist noch Bier im Haus?** is there any more beer in the house?; **morgen bin ich zu Hause** I shall be [at] home tomorrow; **wo warst du so lange?** where have you been all this time?; **bist du schon mal bei Eva gewesen?**

have you ever been to Eva's?; **f)** *(stammen)* be; come; **er ist aus Berlin** he is *or* comes from Berlin; **g)** *(stattfinden)* be; *(sich ereignen)* be; happen; **es war an einem Sonntag im April** it was on a Sunday in April; **muß das ~?** is that really necessary?; **es hat nicht sollen ~** *(veralt., geh.)* it was not meant to be; **was darf es ~?** *(im Geschäft)* what can I get you?; **das kann schon ~:** that may well be; **das kann doch nicht ~!** that's just not possible!; **wenn etwas ist, ruf mich an** *(ugs.)* if anything comes up, give me a ring; **war etwas während meiner Abwesenheit?** did anything happen during my absence?; **es sei!** so be it; **was ~ muß, muß ~:** what must be, must be; **sei's drum!** all right!; **sei es ..., sei es ...** *(geh.)* whether ... or ...; **h)** *(existieren)* be; exist; **er ist nicht mehr** *(verhüll.)* he is no longer with us; **ist was?** *(ugs.)* is anything wrong *or* the matter?; **sie taten, als ob nichts wäre** they acted as if nothing had happened; **das war einmal** that's all past now; **es war einmal ein Prinz** once upon a time there was a prince; **es ist keine Hoffnung mehr** there is no hope [left]; **was nicht ist, kann noch werden** things can always change; **wenn du nicht gewesen wärest** if it hadn't been for you. **2.** *Hilfsverb* **a)** *(... werden können)* **es ist niemand zu sehen** there's no one to be seen; **das war zu erwarten** that was to be expected; **die Schmerzen sind kaum zu ertragen** the pain is hardly bearable; **mit ihm ist zu reden** he's quite approachable; **es ist zu verkaufen** it is for sale; **b)** *(... werden müssen)* **das Bemalen der Wände ist zu unterlassen** painting on the walls is prohibited; **die Richtlinien sind strengstens zu beachten** the guidelines are to be strictly followed; **c)** *(zur Perfektumschreibung)* have; **er ist gestorben** he has died; **sie sind gerade mit dem Wagen in die Stadt** *(ugs.)* they've just driven off into town; **gestern bin ich gleich von der Arbeit nach Hause** *(ugs.)* I went straight home from work yesterday; **die Kinder sind spielen** *(ugs.)* the children have gone off to play; **d)** *(zur Bildung des Zustandspassivs)* be; **wir waren gerettet** we were saved

²sein *Possessivpron.* **a)** *(vor Substantiven) (bei Männern)* his; *(bei Mädchen)* her; *(bei Dingen, Abstrakta)* its; *(bei Tieren)* its; *(bei Männchen auch)* his; *(bei Weibchen auch)* her; *(bei Ländern)* its; her; *(bei Städten)* its; *(bei Schiffen)* her; its; *(nach man)* one's; his *(Amer.)*; **jeder hat ~e Sorgen** everyone has his *or (coll.)* their troubles; **er trinkt am Tag ~e acht Tassen Kaffee** *(ugs.)* he regularly drinks eight cups of coffee a day; **das hat ~e zwei Millionen gekostet** *(ugs.)* it cost a good two million; **wenn man sich** *(Dat.)* **~er eigenen Unzulänglichkeit bewußt ist** when you're aware of your own inadequacy; when one is aware of one's own inadequacy; **dem Willi ~ Hund** *(salopp)* Willi's dog; **b)** *o. Subst.* his; **endlich war sie ~** *(geh. veralt.)* at last she was his; **der/die/das ~e** *(geh.)* his; **die Seine** *(veralt.)* his wife; **die Seinen** *(geh.)* his family; **das Seine** *(Eigentum)* what is his; **er hat das Seine getan** *(was er konnte)* he has done what *or* all he could; *(sein Teil)* he has done his part *or (coll.)* bit; **jedem das Seine** to each his own; *(jeder nach seinem Geschmack)* each to his own; **den Seinen gibt's der Herr im Schlaf** some people have all the luck

³sein *Gen. der Personalpronomen* **er, es** *(dichter. veralt.) s.* **seiner**

Sein das; ~s *(Philos.)* being; *(Dasein)* existence; **~ und Schein** appearance and reality

seiner *(geh.)* **1.** *Gen. des Personalpronomens* **er: sich ~ erbarmen** have pity on him; **~ gedenken** remember him. **2.** *Gen. des Personalpronomens* **es: das Tier lag dort, bis sich jemand ~ annahm** the animal lay there until somebody came and looked after it

seiner-: ~seits *Adv.* for his part; *(von ihm)* on his part; **er ~seits wollte nichts davon wissen** he for his part wanted nothing to do with it; **er unternimmt auch ~seits nichts** he doesn't do anything himself either; **~zeit** *Adv.* **a)** *(damals)* at that time; in those days; **b)** *(österr. veralt.: später)* later; **~zeitig** *Adj.; nicht präd.* **der ~zeitige Präsident** the President at that time; the then President; **die ~zeitigen Verhältnisse** the conditions prevailing then *or* at that time

seines·gleichen *indekl. Pron.* **a)** *(nach er)* his own kind; people *pl.* like himself; **er verkehrt am liebsten mit ~:** he prefers to associate with his own kind; **der König hat mich wie ~ behandelt** the King treated me as an equal; **b)** *(nach man)* one's own kind; **c)** *(nach es)* **das Kind soll mit ~ spielen** the child should play with others its own age; **das sucht** *od.* **hat nicht ~:** it is without equal *or* is unequalled

seinet-: ~halben *(veralt.)*, **~wegen** *Adv.* **a)** *(wegen seiner)* because of him; on his account; **das Kind ist schon lange weg: die Mutter macht sich ~wegen Sorgen** the child's been gone for a long time: the mother is worried for him/her; **b)** *(ihm zuliebe, für ihn)* for his sake; for him; **c)** *(von ihm aus)* **er sagte, ~wegen sollten wir ruhig gehen** he said as far as he was concerned we could go; **~willen** *Adv.* **in um ~willen** for his sake; for him

seinige ['zainɪgə] *Possessivpron. (geh. veralt.)* **der/die/das ~:** his; **er hat das Seinige getan** *(was er konnte)* he had done what *or* all he could; *(sein Teil)* he has done his part; **die Seinige** his wife; **die Seinigen** his family

sein|lassen *unr. tr. V. (ugs.)* **a)** *(aufhören mit)* stop; **laß das sein!** stop it!; **lassen wir die Idee/das Ganze lieber sein** let's drop the idea/the whole thing; **b)** *(in Ruhe lassen)* **jmdn./etw. ~:** leave sb. alone *or (coll.)* be/leave sth. alone

seismisch 1. *Adj.* seismological; *(Erdbeben betreffend)* seismic. **2.** *adv.* seismologically

Seismo- [zaismo-]: **~gramm das** seismogram; **~graph der; ~en, ~en** seismograph; **~loge der; ~n, ~n** seismologist; **~logie die; ~:** seismology *no art.*; **~login die; ~, ~nen** seismologist

seit [zait] **1.** *Präp. mit Dat. (Zeitpunkt)* since; *(Zeitspanne)* for; **~ dem zweiten Weltkrieg/1955/dem Unfall** since the Second World War/1955/the accident; **~ Wochen/Jahren/einiger Zeit** for weeks/years/some time [past]; **ich bin ~ zwei Wochen hier** I've been here [for] two weeks; **er geht ~ vier Wochen zur Schule** he has been going to school for four weeks; **~ damals, ~ der Zeit** since then; **~ wann hast du ihn nicht mehr gesehen?** when was the last time you saw him?. **2.** *Konj.* since; **~ du hier wohnst** since you have been living here; **~ er das gehört hat** since he heard that

seit·dem 1. *Adv.* since then; **das Haus steht ~ leer** since then the house has stood empty. **2.** *Konj. s.* **seit 2**

Seite ['zaitə] **die; ~, ~n a)** side; **auf** *od.* **zu beiden ~n der Straße/des Tores** on both sides of the road/gate; **die hintere/vordere ~:** the back/front; **mit der ~ nach vorne** sideways [on]; **zur** *od.* **auf die ~ gehen** *od.* **treten** move aside *or* to one side; move out of the way; **zur ~!** make way!; **die ~n wechseln** *(Fußball)* change ends; **ein Auto auf die ~ winken** wave a car [over] to the side [of the road]; **jmdn. zur ~ nehmen** take sb. aside; **etw. zur ~ legen** *od.* **räumen** move *or* put sth. to one side *or* aside; **etw. auf die ~ schaffen** *(ugs.)* help oneself to sth.; **etw. auf die ~ legen** *(ugs.: sparen)* put sth. away *or* aside; **zur ~** *(Theater)* aside; **die eine/die andere ~ der Medaille** *(fig.)* the one/the other side of the coin; **alles** *od.* **jedes Ding hat seine zwei ~n** *(fig.)* there are two sides to everything; **ich schlafe auf der ~:** I sleep on my side; **er ist auf einer ~ gelähmt** he's paralysed down one side; **ich wünsche dir, daß du an seiner ~ glücklich wirst** *(geh.)* I hope you'll be happy with him; **halte dich an meiner ~:** stay beside me *or* by my side; **~ an ~:** side by side; **~ an ~ kämpfen** *(fig.)* stand shoulder to shoulder and fight; **jmdm. zur ~ stehen** stand by sb.; **jmdm. nicht von der ~ gehen** *od.* **weichen** not move from *or* leave sb.'s side; **setz dich an meine grüne ~!** *(scherzh.)* come and sit by me *or* by my side; **jmdn. von der ~ ansehen** look at sb. from the side; *(fig.)* look at sb. askance; **eine ~ Speck** a side of bacon; **b)** *(Richtung)* side; **von allen ~n** *(auch fig.)* from all sides; **nach allen ~n** in all directions; *(fig.)* on all sides; **c)** *(Buch~, Zeitungs~)* page; **die erste/letzte ~** *(eines Buchs)* the first/last page; *(einer Zeitung)* the front/back page; **d)** *(Eigenschaft, Aspekt)* side; **auf der einen ~, ... auf der anderen ~ ...:** on the one hand ... on the other hand ...; **von der ~ kenne ich ihn noch nicht** I haven't seen that side of him yet; **etw. ist jmds. schwache ~** *(ugs.)* sth. is not exactly sb.'s forte; *(ist jmds. Schwäche)* sb. has a weakness for sth.; **jmds. starke ~ sein** *(ugs.)* be sb.'s forte *or* strong point; **sich von der besten ~ zeigen** show one's best side; **e)** *(Partei)* side; **sich auf jmds. ~** *(Akk.)* **schlagen** take sb.'s side; **die ~n wechseln** *(fig.)* change sides; **auf jmds. ~ stehen** *od.* **sein** be on sb.'s side; **jmdn. auf seine ~ bringen** *od.* **ziehen** win sb. over; **auf/von seiten der Direktion** on/from the management side; **von anderer/offizieller ~ verlautete, daß ...:** it was learned from other/official sources that ...; **ich werde von meiner ~ aus nichts unternehmen** I for my part will not do anything; **f)** *(Familie)* side; **auf der väterlichen ~ stammt sie von ...:** on her father's side she descends from ...

seiten *in* **auf/von ~:** *s.* **Seite e**

seiten-, Seiten-: ~altar der side altar; **~ansicht die** side view; *(Aufriß)* side elevation; **~arm der** arm; branch; **~ausgang der** side exit; **~blick der** sidelong look; *(kurzer Blick)* sidelong glance; **~ein·gang der** side entrance; **~flügel der a)** *(eines Gebäudes)* wing; **b)** *(eines Flügelaltars)* side panel; **~gebäude das** annex; *(eines Bauernhofs o. ä.)* outbuilding; **~gewehr das** *(Milit.)* bayonet; **~halbierende die;** *adj. Dekl. (Math.)* median; **~hieb der a)** *(fig.)* side-swipe **(auf + Akk.** at); **b)** *(Fechten)* flank cut; **~lage die;** *o. Pl.* **in ~lage schlafen/schwimmen** sleep/swim on one's side; **den Verletzten in ~lage bringen** put the injured man on his side; **~lang 1.** *Adj.* ‹*letter*› that goes on for pages; **2.** *adv.* **so geht es ~lang weiter!** it goes on like that for pages; **~leit·werk das** *(Flugw.)* vertical tail; **~linie die a)** *(Geneal.)* offset; offshoot; **b)** *(Fußball, Rugby)* touch-line; *(Tennis, Hockey, Federball)* sideline; **~ruder das** *(Flugw.)* rudder

seitens *Präp. mit Gen. (Papierdt.)* on the part of; **~ der Arbeitgeber wird noch beraten** the employers are still discussing the matter

seiten-, Seiten-: ~schiff das [side] aisle; **~sprung der** infidelity; **einen ~sprung machen** have an affair; **~stechen das;** *o. Pl.* **~stechen haben/bekommen** have/get a stitch; **~straße die** side-street; **eine ~straße der Schillerstraße** a side-street off the Schillerstrasse; **~streifen der** verge; *(einer Autobahn)* hard shoulder; **„~streifen nicht befahrbar"** 'Soft Verges'; **~tal das** side valley; **~tasche die** side pocket; **~verkehrt** *Adj.* reversed; **~wand die** side wall; **~wechsel der** *(Ballspiele)* change of ends; **~wind der;** *o. Pl.* side wind; cross-wind; **~zahl die a)** page number; **b)** *(Anzahl der Seiten)* number of pages

seit·her *Adv.* since then; ~ **habe ich ihn nicht gesprochen** I haven't spoken to him since [then]
seitherig *Adj.; nicht präd.* **seine ~e Abwesenheit/Arbeit** his absence/work since then
-seitig *adj.* -page; **tausend~:** thousand-page *attrib.;* **ein mehrseitiger Brief/Bericht** a letter/report several pages long
seitlich 1. *Adj.* **der Eingang ist ~:** the entrance is at the side; **ein ~er Wind** a side wind; a cross-wind. **2.** *adv. (an der Seite)* at the side; *(von der Seite)* from the side; *(nach der Seite)* to the side; **~ von jmdm. stehen** stand to the side of sb.; **~ gegen etw. prallen** crash sideways into sth. **3.** *Präp. mit Gen.* beside; to the side of
seitlings ['zaitlɪŋs] *Adv. (veralt.)* **~ reiten** ride side-saddle; **~ schlafen/liegen/fallen** sleep/lie/fall on one's side
Seit·pferd das *(Turnen)* side horse; pommel horse
-seits *adv.* **französischer~:** from the French side; **ärztlicher~:** from the medical angle
seit·wärts 1. *Adv.* **a)** *(zur Seite)* sideways; **b)** *(an, auf der Seite)* to one side; **~ von etw.** to the side of sth. **2.** *Präp. mit Gen.* beside; to the side of
sek., Sek. *Abk.* **Sekunde** sec.
Sekante [ze'kantə] **die; ~, ~n** *(Math.)* secant
sekkant [zɛ'kant] *(österr., sonst veralt.)* **1.** *Adj.* tiresome. **2.** *adv.* tiresomely
sekkieren *tr. V. (österr., sonst veralt.)* annoy; *(bedrängen)* pester
Sekret [ze'kre:t] **das; ~[e]s, ~e** *(Med., Biol.)* secretion
Sekretär [zekre'tɛ:ɐ̯] **der; ~s, ~e a)** secretary; **b)** *(Beamter)* middle-ranking civil servant; **c)** *(Schreibschrank)* secretaire; secretary; bureau *(Brit.);* **d)** *(Zool.)* secretary-bird
Sekretariat [zekreta'ria:t] **das; ~[e]s, ~e** [secretary's/secretaries'] office
Sekretärin die; ~, ~nen secretary
Sekretion [zekre'tsio:n] **die; ~, ~en** *(Med., Biol.)* secretion
Sekt [zɛkt] **der; ~[e]s, ~e** high-quality sparkling wine; ≈ champagne
Sekte ['zɛktə] **die; ~, ~n** sect
Sekt·flasche die champagne-bottle
Sektierer der; ~s, ~, Sektiererin die; ~, ~nen sectarian; *(Politik: Abweichler)* deviationist
sektiererisch 1. *Adj.* sectarian; *(Politik)* deviationist. **2.** *adv.* in a sectarian way; *(Politik)* in a deviationist way
Sektierertum das; ~s sectarianism; *(Politik)* deviationism
Sektion [zɛk'tsio:n] **die; ~, ~en a)** *(Abteilung)* section; *(im Ministerium)* department; **b)** *(DDR: an Hochschulen)* department; **c)** *(Med.)* autopsy; post mortem [examination] (+ *Gen.* on)
Sektions·chef der *(österr.) head of a ministry department*
Sekt-: ~kellerei die champagne-producer's; *(Gebäude)* champagne cellars *pl.;* **~kühler der** champagne-cooler
Sektor ['zɛktɔr] **der; ~s, ~en** [-'to:rən] **a)** *(Fachgebiet)* field; sphere; **industrieller/wirtschaftlicher ~:** industrial/economic sector; **b)** *(Geom.; Besatzungszone)* sector
Sektoren·grenze die sector boundary
Sekunda [ze'kʊnda] **die; ~, Sekunden** *(Schulw.)* **a)** *(veralt.)* sixth and seventh years *(of a Gymnasium);* **b)** *(österr.)* second year *(of a Gymnasium)*
Sekundaner der; ~s, ~, Sekundanerin die; ~, ~nen *(Schulw.)* **a)** *(veralt.) (Ober~)* pupil in the seventh year *(of a Gymnasium); (Unter~)* pupil in the sixth year *(of a Gymnasium);* **b)** *(österr.)* pupil in the second year *(of a Gymnasium)*
Sekundant [zekʊn'dant] **der; ~en, ~en** second *(in a duel or match)*
sekundär [zekun'dɛ:ɐ̯] **1.** *Adj.* secondary. **2.** *adv.* secondarily
Sekundar·lehrer der *(schweiz.)* secondary-school teacher
Sekundär·literatur die secondary literature
Sekundar-: ~schule die *(schweiz.)* secondary school; **~stufe die** secondary stage *(of education)*
Sekunde [ze'kʊndə] **die; ~, ~n a)** *(auch Math., Musik)* second; **es ist auf die ~ 12 Uhr** it is twelve o'clock precisely; **meine Uhr geht auf die ~ genau** my watch keeps perfect time; **b)** *(ugs.: Augenblick)* second; moment
sekundenlang 1. *Adj.* momentary. **2.** *adv.* for a moment; momentarily
Sekunden-: ~schnelle die; *o. Pl.* **in ~schnelle** in a matter of seconds; *(blitzschnell)* in a flash; **~zeiger der** second hand
sekundieren *itr. V. (geh.)* **jmdm. [bei etw.] ~:** support sb., back sb. up [in sth.]; **jmdm. [bei einem Duell] ~:** act as sb.'s second [in a duel]
Sekurit Ⓦᶻ [zeku'ri:t] **das; ~s** [toughened] safety glass
selb... [zɛlp...] *s.* **derselbe**
selber ['zɛlbɐ] *indekl. Demonstrativpron. s.* **selbst 1**
Selber·machen das; ~s *(ugs.)* do-it-yourself *no art.;* **Möbel zum ~:** furniture to make oneself *or* for the do-it-yourselfer
selbig *Demonstrativpron. (veralt.)* [the] same; **am ~en Tag** that same *or* very day
selbst [zɛlpst] **1.** *indekl. Demonstrativpron.* **ich/du/er ~:** I myself/you yourself/he himself; **wir/ihr ~:** we ourselves/you yourselves; **sie ~:** she herself; *(Pl.)* they themselves; **Sie ~:** you yourself; *(Pl.)* you yourselves; **das Haus/der König ~:** the house itself/the king himself; **du hast es ~ gesagt** you said so yourself; *(betonter)* you yourself said so; **ich habe ihn nicht ~ gesprochen** I didn't speak to him myself; **sie backt/kocht ~:** she does the baking/cooking herself; **er denkt nur an sich ~:** he only thinks of himself; **Wie geht's dir? – Gut! Und ~?** *(ugs.)* How are you? – Fine! And how about you?; **von ~:** automatically; **etw. läuft ganz von ~:** sth. runs itself *or* requires no attention; **es versteht sich von ~:** it goes without saying; **die Ruhe/Bescheidenheit ~ sein** *(ugs.)* be calmness/modesty itself; **~ ist der Mann** you have to get on and do things for yourself. **2.** *adv.* even; **~ wenn er wollte** even if he wanted [to]
Selbst das; ~ *(geh.)* self; **das eigene ~:** one's own self
Selbst-: ~abholer der; ~s, ~ a) *(Kaufmannsspr.) buyer who collects the goods himself/herself;* **ein Möbelmarkt für ~abholer** a cash-and-carry furniture store; **b)** *(Postw.) person who collects his post himself;* **~abholer sein** collect the post oneself; **~achtung die** self-respect; self-esteem
selb·ständig 1. *Adj.* independent; **an ~es Arbeiten gewöhnt sein** be used to working on one's own *or* independently; **ein ~er Unternehmer** a self-employed business man; **sich ~ machen** set up on one's own; *(fig. scherzh.)* ⟨*pram, child, etc.*⟩ take off [on its/his/her own]. **2.** *adv.* independently; **~ arbeiten** work on one's own *or* independently; **~ denken** think for oneself
Selbständige der/die; *adj. Dekl.* self-employed [business] person
Selbständigkeit die; ~: independence
selbst-, Selbst-: ~anzeige die *(Rechtsw.)* self-denunciation; **~auf·opferung die** self-sacrifice *no art.;* **unter großer ~aufopferung** at the cost of considerable self-sacrifice; **~auslöser der** *(Fot.)* delayed-action shutter release; **~bedienung die** self-service *no art.;* **hier ist ~bedienung** it's self-service here; **~bedienungs·laden der** self-service shop; **~befriedigung die a)** masturbation *no art.;* **b)** *(fig.)* **er tut das aus reiner ~befriedigung** he only does it for self-gratification; **~behauptung die;** *o. Pl.* self-assertion *no art.;* **~beherrschung die** self-control *no art.;* **die ~beherrschung bewahren/verlieren** keep/lose one's self-control; **~beobachtung die** self-observation *no art.;* **~beschränkung die** self-restraint *no art.;* **in kluger ~beschränkung** wisely exercising self-restraint; **~besinnung die** *(geh.)* [inward] contemplation *no art.;* **~bestätigung die** *(Psych.)* self-affirmation *no art.;* **eine ~bestätigung** a boost to the ego; **~bestimmung die;** *o. Pl.* self-determination *no art.;* **~bestimmungs·recht das;** *o. Pl.* right of self-determination; **~beteiligung die** *(Versicherungsw.)* [personal] excess; **~betrug der** self-deception *no art.;* **~beweih·räucherung die** *(ugs.)* self-adulation *no art.;* **~bewußt 1.** *Adj.* **a)** self-confident; self-possessed; **b)** *(Philos.)* self-aware; **2.** *adv.* self-confidently; **~bewußt·sein das a)** self-confidence *no art.; (einer sozialen Schicht o. ä.)* self-assurance; **nationales ~bewußtsein** sense of national identity; **b)** *(Philos.)* self-awareness *no art.;* **~bildnis das** self-portrait; **~disziplin die;** *o. Pl.* self-discipline *no art.;* **~ein·schätzung die** self-assessment *no art.;* self-appraisal *no art.;* **~entfaltung die** blossoming of one's personality; **sie hatte keine Möglichkeit zur ~entfaltung** there was no opportunity for her to develop as an individual; **~entfremdung die** *(Soziol., Philos.)* self-alienation *no art.;* **~erfahrungs·gruppe die** *(Psych.)* sensitivity group; **~erhaltung die;** *o. Pl.* self-preservation *no art.;* **~erhaltungs·trieb der** instinct for self-preservation; survival instinct; **~erkenntnis die;** *o. Pl.* self-knowledge *no art.;* **~erkenntnis ist der erste Schritt zur Besserung** knowing your faults is the first step towards curing them; **~fahrer der a)** *person who drives a car himself/herself;* **Autovermietung an ~fahrer** self-drive car hire; **b)** *(Krankenfahrstuhl)* self-propelled wheelchair; **~findung die; ~:** self-discovery *no art.;* **~gebacken** *Adj.* home-made; home-baked; **~gebraut** *Adj.* home-brewed ⟨*beer*⟩; **~gedreht** *Adj.* **~gedrehte Zigaretten, Selbstgedrehte** [one's own] rolled cigarettes; **~gefällig** *(abwertend)* **1.** *Adj.* self-satisfied; smug; **2.** *adv.* smugly; in a self-satisfied way; **~gefälligkeit die;** *o. Pl.* self-satisfaction; smugness; **~gemacht** *Adj.* home-made ⟨*jam, liqueur, sausage, basket, etc.*⟩; self-made ⟨*dress, pullover, etc.*⟩; ⟨*dress, pullover, etc.*⟩ one has made oneself; **~genügsam 1.** *Adj.* modest [in one's demands]; **2.** *adv.* modestly; **~gerecht** *(abwertend)* **1.** *Adj.* self-righteous; **2.** *adv.* self-righteously; **~gespräch das** conversation with oneself; **~gespräche führen** talk to oneself; **~gestrickt** *Adj.* **a)** home-made; hand-knitted; **b)** *(fig. ugs.)* homespun ⟨*ideology etc.*⟩; **~haß der** self-hatred; **~herrlich 1.** *Adj.* high-handed; autocratic ⟨*ruler, decision*⟩; **2.** *adv.* high-handedly; in a high-handed manner; ⟨*decide, rule*⟩ autocratically; **~hilfe die;** *o. Pl.* self-help *no art.;* **Hilfe zur ~hilfe leisten** help people to help themselves; **~hilfe·gruppe die** self-help group; **~ironie die;** *o. Pl.* self-mockery; **~justiz die** self-administered justice; **~justiz üben** take the law into one's own hands; **~klebe·folie die** self-adhesive plastic sheeting; **~klebend** *Adj.* self-adhesive; **~kontrolle die** self-restraint; *(in den Medien)* self-regulation; **~kosten** *Pl. (Wirtsch.)* prime costs; **~kosten·preis der** *(Wirtsch.)* cost price; **zum [reinen] ~kostenpreis** at [no more than] cost; **etw. unter**

dem ~kostenpreis abgeben sell sth. below cost *or* at less than cost; **~kritik die;** *o. Pl.* self-criticism; **~kritisch 1.** *Adj.* self-critical; **2.** *adv.* self-critically; **~laut der** vowel; **~los 1.** *Adj.* selfless; **2.** *adv.* selflessly; unselfishly; **~mit·leid das** self-pity; **~mord der** suicide *no art.*; **~mord begehen** *od.* **verüben** commit suicide; **mit ~mord drohen** threaten [to commit] suicide; **~mord mit Messer und Gabel** *(ugs. scherzh.)* suicide by unhealthy eating; eating one's way to an early grave; **~mörder der** suicide; **~mörderisch** *Adj.* suicidal

selbstmord-, Selbstmord-: ~gedanken *Pl.* thoughts of suicide; **sich mit ~gedanken tragen** contemplate suicide; **~gefährdet** *Adj.* potentially suicidal; **~kandidat der** potential suicide; **~kommando das** suicide squad; **~versuch der** suicide attempt; **einen ~versuch unternehmen** attempt suicide

selbst-, Selbst-: ~porträt das self-portrait; **~redend** *Adv.* naturally; of course; **~schuß der;** *meist Pl.* automatic firing device; **~schutz der** self-protection *no art.*; **~sicher 1.** *Adj.* self-confident; **2.** *adv.* in a self-confident manner; full of self-confidence; **~sicherheit die;** *o. Pl.* self-confidence; **~studium das;** *o. Pl.* self-study; private study; **im ~studium** through self-study; by studying on one's own; **~sucht die;** *o. Pl.* selfishness; self-interest; **~süchtig 1.** *Adj.* selfish; **2.** *adv.* selfishly; **~tätig 1.** *Adj.* automatic; **2.** *adv.* automatically; **~täuschung die** self-deception; delusion; **~tötung die** *(Amtsspr.)* suicide; **~über·schätzung die** overestimation of one's abilities; **er leidet an ~überschätzung** *(ugs.)* he has an exaggerated opinion of himself; **~über·windung die** will-power *no indef. art.*; **das kostete mich viel ~überwindung** I really had to force myself to do it; **~verachtung die** self-contempt; **~verbrennung die** self-immolation *no art.* [by burning]; **~verdient** *Adj.* **~verdientes Geld** money one has earned oneself; **mein erstes ~verdientes Geld** the first money I earned myself; **~verfaßt** *Adj.* ⟨*poem, song*⟩ of one's own composition; **~vergessen** *(ugs.)* **1.** *Adj.*; *nicht präd.* oblivious of all around one *postpos.*; lost to the world *postpos.*; **2.** *adv.* obliviously; **~verlag der;** *o. Pl.* private publishing venture; **~verleugnung die** self-denial; **~vernichtung die** self-destruction; **~verschulden das** *(Amtsspr.)* **das war ~verschulden** it was his/their *etc.* own fault; **~verschuldet** *Adj.* **~verschuldete Unfälle** accidents for which people are themselves to blame; **deine Notlage ist ~verschuldet** you have brought your predicament on yourself; **~versorger der** self-sufficient person; *(im Urlaub)* self-caterer; **~verständlich 1.** *Adj.* natural; **es war für ihn ~verständlich** it was completely natural *or* a matter of course for him; **etw. für ~verständlich halten, etw. als ~verständlich betrachten** regard sth. as a matter of course; *(für gegeben hinnehmen)* take sth. for granted; **das ist doch ~verständlich** that goes without saying; **2.** *adv.* naturally; of course; **~verständlich nicht!** of course not!; **~verständlichkeit die** matter of course; **ein Badezimmer ist heute eine ~verständlichkeit** a bathroom is no longer considered a luxury; **etw. mit der größten ~verständlichkeit tun** do sth. as if it were the most natural thing in the world; **~verständnis das;** *o. Pl.* conception of oneself; **~verstümmelung die** self-mutilation; self-inflicted injury; **~verteidigung die** self-defence *no art.*; **~vertrauen das** self-confidence; **~verwaltung die** self-government *no art.*; **~verwirklichung die** self-realization *no art.*; **~wähl·ferndienst der** *(Postw.)* direct dialling; STD; **~wert·gefühl das;** *o. Pl. (Psych.)* [sense of] self-esteem; **~zerstörerisch** *Adj.* self-destructive; **~zerstörung die** self-destruction; **~zufrieden** *(oft abwertend)* **1.** *Adj.* self-satisfied; **2.** *adv.* in a self-satisfied manner; smugly; **~zweck der;** *o. Pl.* end in itself; **~zweck sein/zum ~zweck werden** be/become an end in itself

selchen ['zɛlçn̩] *tr. V. (bayr., österr.)* smoke ⟨*meat, ham, etc.*⟩

selektieren [zelɛk'ti:rən] **1.** *tr. V.* select; pick out. **2.** *itr. V.* make a choice; **~de Methoden** selective methods

Selektion die; ~, **~en** selection

selektiv 1. *Adj.* selective. **2.** *adv.* selectively; on a selective basis

Selen [ze'le:n] **das;** **~s** *(Chemie)* selenium

Selfmademan ['zɛlfme:tmɛn] **der;** **~s, Selfmademen** self-made man

selig ['ze:lɪç] **1.** *Adj.* **a)** *(Rel.)* blessed; **bis an sein ~es Ende** until his dying day; **Gott hab' ihn ~:** God rest his soul; *s. auch* **Angedenken; geben a; glauben b; b)** *(tot)* late [lamented]; **Schwester Modesta ~** *(veralt.)* Sister Modesta of blessed memory; **c)** *(kath. Kirche: seliggesprochen)* **die ~e Dorothea** the blessed Dorothy; **d)** *(glücklich)* blissful ⟨*idleness, slumber, etc.*⟩; blissfully happy ⟨*person*⟩; **~ [über etw. (Akk.)] sein** be overjoyed *or (coll.)* over the moon [about sth.]; **werde ~ mit deinem Geld!** *(ugs.)* you can keep *or (sl.)* stuff your money. **2.** *adv.* blissfully

Selige der/die; *adj. Dekl.* **a)** *o. Pl. (veralt., noch scherzh.)* **mein ~r/meine ~:** my late lamented *or* dear departed husband/wife; **b)** *Pl.* **die ~n** *(die Toten)* the blessed spirits [of the departed]; **die Gefilde der ~n** the Elysian fields; **c)** *(kath. Kirche: Seliggesprochene[r])* beatified person

Seligkeit die; ~, **~en a)** *o. Pl. (Rel.)* [state of] blessedness; beatitude; **die ewige ~:** eternal bliss; **von dieser Reise hängt doch nicht seine ~ ab** *(fig.)* he won't be heartbroken if he doesn't go on this trip; **b)** *(Glücksgefühl)* bliss *no pl.*; [blissful] happiness *no pl.*

selig-, Selig-: ~|preisen *unr. tr. V.* **a)** *(geh.)* consider ⟨*person, oneself*⟩ incredibly fortunate; **b)** *(religiös)* declare blessed; **~preisung die: die ~preisungen** *(bibl.)* the Beatitudes; **~|sprechen** *unr. tr. V. (kath. Kirche)* beatify; **~sprechung die;** ~, **~en** *(kath. Kirche)* beatification

Sellerie ['zɛləri] **der;** **~s,** **~[s]** *od.* **die;** ~, ~ *(Stauden~)* celeriac; *(Stangen~)* celery

selten ['zɛltn̩] **1.** *Adj.* rare; infrequent ⟨*visit, visitor*⟩; **in den ~sten Fällen** very rarely; **seine Besuche sind ~ geworden** his visits have become few and far between; **ein ~er Vogel** *(fig. ugs.)* an odd character; a queer fish *(coll.)*. **2.** *adv.* **a)** rarely; **wir sehen uns nur noch ~:** we seldom *or* hardly ever see each other now; **ein Sommer wie ~ einer** a summer such as is only too rare; **~ so gelacht!** that was a good laugh!; *(iron.: gar nicht komisch)* very funny[, I don't think]; **b)** *(sehr)* exceptionally; uncommonly

Seltenheit die; ~, **~en** rarity; **es ist eine ~, daß ...:** it is rare that ...

Seltenheits·wert der; **~[e]s** rarity value

Selters·wasser ['zɛltəs-] **das** seltzer [water]

seltsam 1. *Adj.* strange; peculiar; odd; **alt und ~ werden** become rather odd in one's old age. **2.** *adv.* strangely; peculiarly

seltsamerweise *Adv.* strangely enough

Seltsamkeit die; ~, **~en a)** *o. Pl. (Art)* strangeness; oddness; **b)** *(Ereignis, Merkmal)* peculiarity; oddity

Semantik [ze'mantɪk] **die;** ~ *(Sprachw.)* semantics *sing., no art.*

semantisch *(Sprachw.)* **1.** *Adj.* semantic. **2.** *adv.* semantically

Semasiologie [zemaziolo'gi:] **die;** ~ *(Sprachw.)* semasiology *no art.*

Semester [ze'mɛstɐ] **das;** **~s,** ~ **a)** semester; **er hat 14 ~ Jura studiert** he studied law for seven years; **Studenten des dritten ~s** students in their third semester; ≈ second-year students; **b)** *(ugs.: Student)* **ein höheres ~:** a senior student; **die ersten ~:** the first-year students; **ein älteres ~** *(fig. scherzh.)* a member of the older generation

Semesterferien *Pl.* [university] vacation *sing.*

semi-, Semi- [zemi-] semi-

Semi·finale das *(Sport)* semi-final

Semikolon [zemi'ko:lɔn] **das;** **~s, ~s** *od.* **Semikola** semicolon

Seminar [zemi'na:ɐ̯] **das;** **~s, ~e,** *österr., schweiz. auch* **~ien** [...i̯ən] **a)** *(Lehrveranstaltung)* seminar (**über** + *Akk.* on); **b)** *(Institut)* department; **das juristische ~/~ für Alte Geschichte** the Law Department/Department of Ancient History; **c)** *(Priester~)* seminary; **d)** *(für Referendare) course for student teachers prior to their second state examination*

Seminar·arbeit die seminar paper

Seminarist der; **~en, ~en** seminarist

Seminar·schein der certificate of attendance [at a seminar]

Semiotik [ze'mio:tɪk] **die;** ~ *(Philos., Sprachw.)* semiotics *sing., no art.*

Semit [ze'mi:t] **der;** **~en, ~en, Semitin die;** ~, **~nen** Semite

semitisch *Adj.* Semitic

Semmel ['zɛml̩] **die;** ~, **~n** *(bes. österr., bayr., ostmd.)* [bread] roll; **weggehen wie warme ~n** *(ugs.)* sell like hot cakes

semmel-, Semmel-: ~blond *Adj.* flaxen ⟨*hair*⟩; flaxen-haired ⟨*person*⟩; **~brösel der** *od. österr.*: **das;** *meist Pl.* breadcrumb; **~knödel der** *(bayr., österr.)* bread dumpling

sen. *Abk.* **senior** sen.

Senat [ze'na:t] **der;** **~[e]s, ~e a)** *(Hist., Politik, Hochschulw.)* senate; **der US-~:** the US Senate; **b)** *(an Gerichten)* panel of judges

Senator der; **~s, ~en, Senatorin die;** ~, **~nen** senator; **Herr ~ X** Senator X

Senats·aus·schuß der senate committee

Send·bote der *(veralt.)* envoy; *(fig.)* ambassador

Sende- ['zɛndə-]: **~anlage die** *(Elektrot.)* transmitter; **~bereich der** *(Rundf., Ferns.)* transmitting area; **~folge die** *(Rundf., Ferns.)* **a)** *(Reihenfolge)* sequence [of programmes]; **b)** *(einer Geschichte)* episode; **~gebiet das** *(Rundf., Ferns.) s.* **~bereich; ~mast der** transmitter mast

[1]**senden** *unr. (auch regelm.) tr. V. (geh.)* send; **jmdm. etw. ~:** send sb. sth.; **etw. an jmdn. ~:** send sth. to sb.; **wir ~ Ihnen die Waren ins Haus** we will despatch the goods to you at your home address

[2]**senden** *regelm. (schweiz. unr.) tr., itr. V.* broadcast ⟨*programme, play, etc.*⟩; transmit ⟨*concert, signals, Morse, etc.*⟩; **Hilferufe ~:** send out distress signals

Sende·pause die *(Rundf., Ferns.)* intermission

Sender der; **~s,** ~: [broadcasting] station; *(Anlage)* transmitter

Sende-: ~raum der *(Rundf., Ferns.)* [broadcasting] studio; **~reihe die** *(Rundf., Ferns.)* series [of programmes]

Sender·such·lauf der *(Rundf., Ferns.)* [automatic] station search

Sende-: ~saal der *(Rundf., Ferns.)* [broadcasting] studio; **~schluß der** *(Rundf., Ferns.)* close-down; end of broadcasting; **zum ~schluß noch ein Krimi** now as our last programme, a thriller; **~station die** *(Funk, Rundf., Ferns.)* broadcasting station; *(Anlage)* transmitter; **~zeit die** *(Rundf., Ferns.)* broadcasting time; **die ~zeit um zehn Minuten überschreiten** overrun by ten minutes;

~zentrale die *(Rundf., Ferns.)* main studio; **wir geben zurück in die ~zentrale** we return you to the studio
Sendschreiben das *(veralt.)* circular letter; *(des Papstes)* encyclical
Sendung die; ~, ~en a) consignment; **b)** *o. Pl. (geh.: Aufgabe)* mission; **c)** *(Rundf., Ferns.: Darbietung)* programme; broadcast; **d)** *(Rundfunkt., Ferns.: Ausstrahlung)* transmission; broadcast[ing]; **auf ~ sein** be on the air
Sendungs·bewußt·sein das sense of mission
Senegal ['ze:negal] **(das); ~s** *od.* **der; ~[s]: [der] ~:** Senegal
Senegalese [zenega'le:zə] **der; ~n, ~n, Senegalesin die; ~, ~nen** Senegalese
Seneschall ['ze:nəʃal] **der; ~s, ~e** *(hist.)* seneschal
Senf [zɛnf] **der; ~[e]s, ~e** mustard; **seinen ~ dazugeben** *(fig. ugs.)* get one's word in *or* have one's say
Senf-: ~gas das mustard gas; **~gurke die** *gherkin pickled with mustard seeds;* **~korn das** mustard seed; **~soße die** mustard sauce; **~topf der** mustard pot
Senge ['zɛŋə] *Pl. (ostmd. ugs.) s.* **Prügel b**
sengen 1. *tr. V.* singe. **2.** *itr. V.* **a)** *(brennen)* singe; **b)** *(heiß sein)* be scorching; **eine ~de Hitze** a scorching heat; **c) ~ und brennen** *(veralt.)* burn and pillage
senil [ze'ni:l] **1.** *Adj. (Med., auch abwertend)* senile. **2.** *adv.* in a senile manner
Senilität die; ~ *(Med., auch abwertend)* senility
senior ['ze:ni̯ɔr] *indekl. Adj.; nach Personennamen* senior
Senior der; ~s, ~en [ze'ni̯o:rən] **a)** *(Kaufmannsspr.)* senior partner; **b)** *(Sport)* senior [player]; **c)** *(Rentner)* senior citizen; **d)** *(Ältester)* oldest member; **e)** *(scherzh.: Vater)* old man *(coll.);* **f)** *(Werbesprache: älterer Mensch)* older person
Senior·chef der *(Kaufmannsspr.)* boss *(coll.) (in a family firm)*
Senioren-: ~heim das home for the elderly; **~mannschaft die** senior team; **~meister der** senior champion; *(Mannschaft)* senior champions
Seniorin [ze'ni̯o:rɪn] **die; ~, ~nen** *s.* **Senior a, b, d**
Senk·blei das *(Bauw.)* plumb[-bob]
Senke ['zɛŋkə] **die; ~, ~n** hollow
Senkel ['zɛŋkl̩] **der; ~s, ~ a)** *(Schnür~)* shoe-lace; **b) jmdn. in den ~ stellen** *(ugs.)* put sb. in his/her place
senken 1. *tr. V.* **a)** lower; *(Bergbau)* sink ⟨*shaft*⟩; lower ⟨*flag*⟩; drop ⟨*starting flag*⟩; **den Kopf ~:** bow one's head; **die Augen** *od.* **den Blick/die Stimme ~:** lower one's eyes *or* glance/voice; **mit gesenktem Blick** with [one's] eyes cast down; **b)** *(herabsetzen)* reduce ⟨*fever, pressure, prices, etc.*⟩; **c)** *(Technik)* countersink ⟨*hole*⟩. **2.** *refl. V.* ⟨*curtain, barrier, etc.*⟩ fall, come down; ⟨*ground, building, road*⟩ subside, sink; ⟨*water-level*⟩ fall, sink; ⟨*lift-cage*⟩ go down, descend; **sein Brustkorb hob und senkte sich** his chest rose and fell
senk-, Senk-: ~fuß der *(Anat.)* flat foot; **~grube die** *(Bauw.)* cesspit; **~kasten der** *(Technik)* caisson; **~lot das** *(Technik)* plumb[-bob]; **~recht 1.** *Adj.* vertical; **~rechte Linie** *(Geom.)* perpendicular line; perpendicular; **in ~rechter Stellung** in an upright position; **bleib** *od.* **halt dich ~recht!** *(ugs.)* stay upright *or (coll.)* on your two pins; **das ist das einzige Senkrechte** *(ugs.)* that's the only thing worth doing/eating/reading *etc.;* **2.** *adv.* vertically; **~recht aufeinander stehen** *(Geom.)* be perpendicular *or* at right angles to each other; **~recht von oben** from vertically above; **~rechte die a)** *(Geom.)* perpendicular; **b)** vertical line; vertical; upright; **~recht·starter der; ~s, ~ a)** *(Flugzeug)* vertical take-off aircraft; **b)** *(ugs.) (Aufsteiger)* whizz-kid *(coll.); (Sache)* instant success
Senkung die; ~, ~en a) *o. Pl.* lowering; **b)** *o. Pl. (Reduzierung)* reduction; lowering; **eine ~ des Preises um 5 %** a reduction of the price by 5 %; **c)** *(Geol.)* [case of] subsidence; **d)** *(Verslehre)* unstressed syllable
Senk·waage die hydrometer
Senne ['zɛnə] **die; ~, ~n** *(bayr., österr.)* Alpine pasture
Senner der; ~s, ~ *(bayr., österr.) Alpine herdsman and dairyman*
Sennerin die; ~, ~nen *(bayr., österr.) Alpine herdswoman and dairywoman*
Sennes·blätter ['zɛnəs-] *Pl.* senna leaves
Senn·hütte die *(bayr., österr.)* Alpine hut
Sensation [zɛnza'tsi̯o:n] **die; ~, ~en** sensation; *(Darbietung)* sensational performance; **~en sehen wollen** want to see something sensational *or* spectacular
sensationell 1. *Adj.* sensational. **2.** *adv.* in a sensational manner; sensationally; **eine ~ aufgemachte Story** a sensationalized story
Sensations-: ~gier die *(abwertend)* craving for sensation; **~meldung die** sensational report *or* piece of news; **~prozeß der** sensational trial
Sense ['zɛnzə] **die; ~, ~n a)** scythe; **b)** *(salopp)* **jetzt ist ~:** this really is [the end of] it *(coll.)*
Sensen·mann der; *o. Pl. (verhüll.)* Great Reaper
sensibel [zɛn'zi:bl̩] **1.** *Adj.* sensitive. **2.** *adv.* sensitively
sensibilisieren *tr. V.* **a)** *(geh.)* make ⟨*person*⟩ more sensitive **(für** to); **b)** *(Physiol.)* sensitize
Sensibilität die; ~: sensitivity
sensitiv [zɛnzi'ti:f] *Adj.* sensitive
Sensor ['zɛnzɔr] **der; ~s, ~en** [-'zo:rən] *(Technik)* **a)** sensor; **b)** *s.* **~taste**
sensorisch *Adj. (Physiol.)* sensory
Sensorium [zɛn'so:ri̯ʊm] **das; ~s, Sensorien** [...ri̯ən] *(Physiol.)* sensorium
Sensor·taste die *(Technik)* touch panel; touch pad *(Computing)*
Sensualismus der; ~ *(Philos.)* sensationalism
Sentenz [zɛn'tɛnts] **die; ~, ~en** aphorism; maxim
sentimental [zɛntimɛn'ta:l] **1.** *Adj.* sentimental. **2.** *adv.* sentimentally
Sentimentalität die; ~, ~en sentimentality; **das sind bloße/überflüssige ~en** that is mere/unnecessary sentimentality
separat [zepa'ra:t] **1.** *Adj.* separate; **~e Wohnung** self-contained flat *(Brit.) or (Amer.)* apartment. **2.** *adv.* separately; **er wohnt ~:** he has self-contained accommodation
Separat·friede[n] der separate peace [treaty]
Separatismus der; ~: separatism *no art.*
Separatist der; ~en, ~en, Separatistin die; ~, ~nen separatist
separatistisch *Adj.* separatist
Séparée [zepa're:] **das; ~s, ~s** private room
separieren *tr. V.* separate
Sepia ['ze:pi̯a] **die; ~, Sepien a)** *(Tier)* cuttlefish; **b)** *o. Pl. (Farbstoff)* sepia
Sepia·zeichnung die sepia drawing
Sepp[e]l·hose ['zɛpl̩-] **die** *(scherzh.)* lederhosen *pl.*
Sepsis ['zɛpsɪs] **die; ~, Sepsen** *(Med.)* sepsis
Sept. *Abk.* **September** Sept.
September [zɛp'tɛmbɐ] **der; ~[s], ~:** September; *s. auch* **April**
Septett [zɛp'tɛt] **das; ~[e]s, ~e** *(Musik)* septet
Septime [zɛp'ti:mə] **die; ~, ~n** *(Musik)* seventh
septisch *Adj. (Med.)* septic
Septuaginta [zɛptu̯a'gɪnta] **die; ~:** Septuagint
Sequenz [ze'kvɛnts] **die; ~, ~en** sequence
sequestrieren [zekvɛs'tri:rən] *tr. V. (Rechtsw.)* sequestrate; sequester
Serail [ze'ra:j] **das; ~s, ~s** seraglio
Seraph ['ze:raf] **der; ~s, ~e** *od.* **~im** *(Rel.)* seraph
Serbe ['zɛrbə] **der; ~n, ~n** Serb; Serbian; **~ sein** be a Serb *or* Serbian
Serbien ['zɛrbi̯ən] **(das); ~s** Serbia
Serbin die; ~, ~nen *s.* **Serbe**
serbisch *Adj.* Serbian; *s. auch* **deutsch; Deutsch; [2]Deutsche**
serbo·kroatisch [zɛrbokro'a:tɪʃ] *Adj.* Serbo-Croat; *s. auch* **deutsch; Deutsch; [2]Deutsche**
Serenade [zere'na:də] **die; ~, ~n** *(Musik)* serenade
Sergeant [zɛr'ʒant] **der; ~en, ~en** *od. (bei engl. Ausspr.:)* ['sɑ:dʒənt] **~s, ~s** *(Milit.)* sergeant
Serie ['ze:ri̯ə] **die; ~, ~n** series; **eine ~ Briefmarken** a set of stamps; **etw. in ~ herstellen** *od.* **fertigen** produce *or* manufacture sth. in series; **in ~ gehen** go into [series *or* full-scale] production
seriell *Adj. (Musik)* serial
serien-, Serien-: ~fertigung die series production; **~mäßig 1.** *Adj.* standard ⟨*product, model, etc.*⟩; *(immer eingebaut)* ⟨*feature, accessory*⟩ fitted as standard; **2.** *adv.* **a) ~mäßig gefertigt** *od.* **gebaut** produced in series; **b)** *(nicht als Sonderausstattung)* ⟨*fitted, supplied, etc.*⟩ as standard; **~mäßig mit etw. ausgerüstet sein** have sth. as a standard fitting; **~produktion die** series production; **~reif** *Adj.* ready for [series] production *postpos.;* production ⟨*version, model*⟩; **~weise** *Adv.* **a) ~weise gebaut** *od.* **hergestellt werden** be in series production; **b)** *(ugs.: in großer Zahl)* en masse; wholesale
Serigraphie [zerigra'fi:] **die; ~, ~n** serigraphy *no art.*
seriös [ze'ri̯ø:s] **1.** *Adj.* **a)** *(solide)* respectable ⟨*person, hotel, etc.*⟩; *(vertrauenswürdig)* reliable, trustworthy ⟨*firm, partner, etc.*⟩; **b)** *(ernstgemeint)* serious ⟨*offer, applicant, artist, etc.*⟩. **2.** *adv.* **a)** *(solide)* respectably; *(vertrauenswürdig)* in a trustworthy manner; **b)** *(ernstgemeint)* seriously
Seriosität [zeri̯ozi'tɛ:t] **die; ~** *(geh.)* **a)** *(Solidität)* respectability; *(Vertrauenswürdigkeit)* reliability; trustworthiness; *(eines Geschäftsmanns, einer Firma)* probity; **b)** *(Ernsthaftigkeit)* seriousness
Sermon [zɛr'mo:n] **der; ~s, ~e a)** *(veralt.: Predigt)* sermon; **b)** *(abwertend: langatmige Rede)* [long] lecture
serologisch *Adj.* serological
Serpentine [zɛrpɛn'ti:nə] **die; ~, ~n a)** *(Weg)* zigzag mountain road *(with numerous hairpin bends);* **b)** *(Kehre)* hairpin bend
Serum ['ze:rʊm] **das; ~s, Seren** *od.* **Sera** *(Med., Physiol.)* serum
[1]Service [zɛr'vi:s] **das; ~, ~:** [dinner *etc.*] service
[2]Service ['zø:ɐ̯vɪs] **der** *od.* **das; ~, ~s** ['zø:ɐ̯vɪsɪs] **a)** *o. Pl. (Bedienung, Kundendienst)* service; *(Kundendienstabteilung)* service department; **b)** *(Tennis: Aufschlag)* serve; service; **beim ~:** when serving
servieren [zɛr'vi:rən] **1.** *tr. V.* **a)** *(auftragen)* serve ⟨*food, drink*⟩; *(fig.)* serve up ⟨*information*⟩; deliver ⟨*line, punchline, etc.*⟩; **jmdm. etw. ~:** serve sb. sth.; **b)** *(Ballspiele)* **jmdm. den Ball ~:** feed/*(Tennis)* serve the ball to sb. **2.** *itr. V.* **a)** serve [at table]; **gleich wird serviert** dinner/lunch *etc.* is [about to be] served; **b)** *(Fußball)* pass; make a pass; *(Tennis)* serve
Serviererin die; ~, ~nen waitress
Servier-: ~tochter die *(schweiz.)* waitress; **~wagen der** [serving-]trolley
Serviette [zɛr'vi̯ɛtə] **die; ~, ~n** napkin; serviette *(Brit.)*

Serviẹtten·ring der napkin *or (Brit.)* serviette ring
servil [zɛr'vi:l] *(geh. abwertend)* **1.** *Adj.* obsequious; servile. **2.** *adv.* obsequiously; in a servile manner
Servilität die; ~ *(geh. abwertend)* servility; obsequiousness
Servo- ['zɛrvo-]: **~bremse die** servo [-assisted] brake; **~lenkung die** power [-assisted] steering *no indef. art.*
Servus ['zɛrvʊs] *Interj. (bes. südd., österr.) (beim Abschied)* goodbye; so long *(coll.); (zur Begrüßung)* hello
Sesam ['ze:zam] **der; ~s, ~s a)** *(Pflanze)* sesame; *(Samen)* sesame seeds *pl.;* **b)** **~, öffne dich!** open sesame!
Sesam·brötchen das sesame-seed roll
Sessel ['zɛsl] **der; ~s, ~ a)** easy chair; *(mit Armlehne)* armchair; **b)** *(österr.: Stuhl)* chair
Sẹssel-: ~lehne die chair-back; **~lift der** chair-lift
seßhaft ['zɛshaft] *Adj.* settled ⟨*tribe, way of life*⟩; **~ werden** settle [down]
Sẹßhaftigkeit die; ~: settled way of life
Session [zɛ'si̯o:n] **die; ~, ~en** *(bes. Parl.)* [parliamentary *etc.*] session
Set [zɛt] **das** *od.* **der; ~[s], ~s a)** *(Satz)* set, combination **(aus** of); **b)** *(Deckchen)* table- *or* place-mat; **c)** *(Sozialpsych.)* set
Sẹtter der; ~s, ~: setter
Sẹtz·ei das *(bes. nordostd.) s.* **Spiegelei**
setzen ['zɛtsn̩] **1.** *refl. V.* **a)** *(hin~)* sit [down]; **setz dich/setzt euch/setzen Sie sich** sit down; take a seat; **sich aufs Sofa/in den Sessel/in den Schatten** *usw.* **~:** sit on the sofa/in the chair/in the shade *etc.;* **sich zu jmdm. ~:** [go and] sit with sb.; join sb.; **setz dich zu uns** come and sit with us; **der Vogel setzte sich auf seine Schulter** the bird landed *or* alighted on his shoulder; **sich an den Tisch** *od.* **zu Tisch ~:** sit [down] at the table; **b)** *(sinken)* ⟨*coffee, solution, froth, etc.*⟩ settle; ⟨*sediment*⟩ sink to the bottom; **das Erdreich setzt sich** there is some settlement *or* subsidence; **c)** *(in präp. Verbindungen)* **sich mit jmdm. ins Einvernehmen ~:** come to an agreement with sb.; *s. auch* **Spitze d, e; Unrecht b; Verbindung h; Wehr; d)** *(dringen)* **der Staub/Geruch/Rauch setzt sich in die Kleider** the dust/smell/smoke gets into one's clothes. **2.** *tr. V.* **a)** *(plazieren)* put; **ein Kind jmdm. auf den Schoß ~:** put *or* sit a child on sb.'s lap; **ein Schiff auf Grund ~:** run a ship aground; **eine Figur/einen Stein ~:** move a piece/man; *s. auch* **Fuß a; b)** *(einpflanzen)* plant ⟨*tomatoes, potatoes, etc.*⟩; **c)** *(aufziehen)* hoist ⟨*flag etc.*⟩; set ⟨*sails, navigation lights*⟩; **d)** *(Druckw.)* set ⟨*manuscript etc.*⟩; **e)** *(schreiben)* put ⟨*name, address, comma, etc.*⟩; **seinen Namen unter etw.** *(Akk.)* **~:** put one's signature to sth.; sign sth.; **einen Punkt/ein Komma [falsch] ~:** put a full stop/comma [in the wrong place]; **f)** *(in präp. Verbindungen)* **jmdn. auf schmale Kost ~:** put sb. on short rations; **in/außer Betrieb ~:** start up/stop ⟨*machine etc.*⟩; put ⟨*lift etc.*⟩ into operation/take ⟨*lift etc.*⟩ out of service; *(ein-/ausschalten)* switch on/off; **jmdn. in Erstaunen ~** *(geh.)* astonish sb.; *s. auch* **Fuß b; Musik a; Stelle a; Szene a; Trab; Umlauf b; Werk a; Wort b; Zeitung; g)** *(aufstellen)* put up, build ⟨*stove*⟩; stack ⟨*logs, bricks*⟩; *s. auch* **Denkmal; h) sein Geld auf etw.** *(Akk.)* **~:** put one's money on sth.; **seine Hoffnungen auf jmdn. ~:** place one's hopes in sb.; *s. auch* **Vertrauen; i)** *(festlegen)* set ⟨*limit, deadline*⟩; **einer Sache** *(Dat.)* **Grenzen** *od.* **Schranken ~:** keep sth. within limits; **sich** *(Dat.)* **ein Ziel ~:** set oneself a goal; *s. auch* **Akzente; Ende; Priorität; Zeichen b; j)** *(ugs.)* **es setzt was** *od.* **Prügel** *od.* **Hiebe** he/she *etc.* gets a hiding *(coll.) or* thrashing; **k)** *(Jägerspr.: zur Welt bringen)* give birth to. **3.** *itr. V.* **a)** *meist mit sein (im Sprung)* leap, jump **(über +** *Akk.* over); **über einen Fluß ~** *(mit einer Fähre o. ä.)* cross a river; **b)** *(beim Wetten)* bet; **auf ein Pferd/auf Rot ~:** back a horse/put one's money on red; **c)** *(Jägerspr.: Junges, Junge zur Welt bringen)* give birth
Sẹtzer der; ~s, ~ *(Druckw.)* [type]setter
Setzerei die; ~, ~en *(Druckw.)* composing-room
Sẹtzerin die; ~, ~nen *s.* Setzer
Sẹtz-: ~fehler der *(Druckw.)* setting error; misprint; **~holz das** dibber; dibble; **~kasten der a)** *(Gartenbau)* seedling box; **b)** *(Druckw.)* [type-]case
Setzling ['zɛtslɪŋ] **der; ~s, ~e a)** *(Pflanze)* seedling; **b)** *(Fisch)* young fish; **~e** fry *pl.*
Sẹtz·maschine die *(Druckw.)* composing *or* typesetting machine
Seuche ['zɔyçə] **die; ~, ~n** epidemic; *(fig.)* scourge
seuchen-, Seuchen-: ~artig 1. *Adj.* epidemic-like; **2.** *adv.* ⟨*spread*⟩ like an epidemic; **~bekämpfung die** epidemic control *no art.;* **~gefahr die;** *o. Pl.* danger of an epidemic; **~herd der** source of the epidemic
seufzen ['zɔyftsn̩] *itr., tr. V.* sigh; **schwer/erleichtert ~:** give *or* heave a deep sigh/a sigh of relief
Seufzer der; ~s, ~: sigh; **seinen letzten ~ tun** *(verhüll.)* breathe one's last
Seufzer·brücke die Bridge of Sighs
Sevilla [ze'vɪlja] **(das); ~s** Seville
Sex [zɛks] **der; ~[es]** sex *no art.; (Anziehungskraft)* sex appeal; sexiness
Sẹx-: ~-Appeal [~ ə'pi:l] **der; ~s** sex appeal; **~bombe die** *(salopp)* sex-bomb *(coll.);* sexpot *(coll.);* **~boutique die** sex shop; **~film der** sex film
Sexịsmus der; ~: sexism *no art.*
sexịstisch 1. *Adj.* sexist. **2.** *adv.* ⟨*behave, think, etc.*⟩ in a sexist manner
Sẹx·muffel der *(scherzh.) person not interested in sex;* sexless wonder *(joc.)*
Sexologie die; ~: sexology *no art.*
Sẹx·shop der; ~s, ~s sex shop
Sexta ['zɛksta] **die; ~, Sẹxten** *(Schulw.)* **a)** *(veralt.)* first year *(of a Gymnasium);* **b)** *(österr.)* sixth year *(of a Gymnasium)*
Sextaner der; ~s, ~ *(Schulw.)* **a)** *(veralt.)* pupil in the first year *(of a Gymnasium);* **b)** *(österr.)* pupil in the sixth year *(of a Gymnasium)*
Sextaner·blase die *(ugs. scherzh.)* bladder of a five-year-old
Sextanerin die; ~, ~nen *s.* **Sextaner**
Sextant [zɛks'tant] **der; ~en, ~en** sextant
Sẹxte die; ~, ~n *(Musik)* sixth
Sextett [zɛks'tɛt] **das; ~[e]s, ~e** *(Musik)* sextet
Sexual- [zɛ'ksu̯a:l-]: **~erziehung die** sex education; **~ethik die;** *o. Pl.* sexual ethics *pl.;* **~hormon das** sex hormone
Sexualität [zɛksu̯ali'tɛ:t] **die; ~:** sexuality *no art.*
Sexual-: ~kunde die; *o. Pl. (Schulw.)* sex education *no art.;* **~leben das;** *o. Pl.* sex life; **~mord der** sex murder; **~mörder der** sex killer; **~objekt das** sex object; **~partner der** sexual partner; **~trieb der** sex[ual] drive *or* urge; **~verbrechen das** sex crime; **~verbrecher der** sex offender; **~wissenschaft die;** *o. Pl.* sexology *no art.*
sexuẹll 1. *Adj.* sexual. **2.** *adv.* sexually; **sich ~ befriedigen** get sexual satisfaction; *(masturbieren)* masturbate
Sexus ['zɛksu:s] **der; ~, ~** *(geh.)* sexuality *no art.*
sexy ['zɛksi] *(ugs.)* **1.** *indekl. Adj.* sexy. **2.** *adv.* sexily
Seychellen [ze'ʃɛlən] *Pl.* Seychelles
Sezession [zetsɛ'si̯o:n] **die; ~, ~en** secession
Sezessionịst der; ~en, ~en secessionist
sezessionịstisch *Adj.* secessionist
Sezessions·krieg der; *o. Pl.* [American] Civil War
sezieren [ze'tsi:rən] **1.** *tr. V.* dissect ⟨*corpse*⟩; *(fig.)* analyse ⟨*policy etc.*⟩; dissect ⟨*language etc.*⟩. **2.** *itr. V.* perform dissections/a dissection
Sezier·messer das dissecting-knife
SFB [ɛsɛf'be:] **der; ~** *Abk.* **Sender Freies Berlin** Radio Free Berlin
S-förmig ['ɛs-] *Adj.* S-shaped
sfr., *(schweiz. nur:)* **sFr.** *Abk.* **Schweizer Franken**
Sg. *Abk.* **Singular** sing.
SGB [ɛsge:'be:] **der; ~** *Abk.* **schweizerischer Gewerkschaftsbund** Swiss Trades Union Federation
Shampoo [ʃam'pu:], **Shampoon** [ʃam'po:n] **das; ~s, ~s** shampoo
shampoonieren [ʃampo'ni:rən] shampoo
Sheriff ['ʃɛrɪf] **der; ~s, ~s** sheriff
Shẹriff·stern der sheriff's star
Sherry ['ʃɛri] **der; ~s, ~s** sherry; *s. auch* **Bier**
Shetland- ['ʃɛtlənd-]: **~inseln** *Pl.* Shetland Islands; Shetlands; **~pony das** Shetland pony; **~wolle die** Shetland wool
Shop [ʃɔp] **der; ~s, ~s** shop
Shorts [ʃɔrts] *Pl.* shorts
Show [ʃoʊ] **die; ~, ~s** show; *s. auch* **Schau**
Show·master ['-ma:stə] **der; ~s, ~:** compère
Siam [zi:am] **(das); ~s** *(hist.)* Siam
Siamese [zia'me:zə] **der; ~n, ~n, Siamesin die; ~, ~nen** Siamese
siamesisch *Adj.* Siamese
Siam·katze die Siamese cat
Sibirien [zi'bi:ri̯ən] **(das); ~s** Siberia
sibịrisch *Adj.* Siberian; **~e Kälte** Arctic temperatures *pl.*
Sibylle [zi'bʏlə] **die; ~, ~n** sibyl; fortune-teller
sibyllinisch *(geh.)* **1.** *Adj.* sibylline, mysterious ⟨*words, expression*⟩. **2.** *adv.* in a sibylline manner; mysteriously
sich [zɪç] *Reflexivpron. der 3. Pers. Sg. und Pl. Akk. und Dat.* **1.** *Akk.* **a)** *(nach* **man** *od. Inf.)* oneself; *(3. Pers. Sg.)* himself/herself/itself; *(3. Pers. Pl.)* themselves; *(Höflichkeitsform Sg./Pl.)* yourself/yourselves; **er/sie hat ~ umgebracht** he killed himself/she killed herself; **sie versteckten ~:** they hid [themselves]; **b)** *(bei reflexiven Verben)* **~ freuen/wundern/schämen/täuschen** be pleased/surprised/ashamed/mistaken. **2.** *Dat.* **a)** *(nach* **man** *od. Inf.)* oneself; *(3. Pers. Sg.)* himself/herself/itself; *(3. Pers. Pl.)* themselves; *(Höflichkeitsform Sg./Pl.)* yourself/yourselves; **b)** *(bei reflexiven Verben)* **~ etw. einbilden** imagine sth.; **~ etw. erhoffen** hope for sth. [for oneself]; **sie hat ~ den Fuß verstaucht/verrenkt** she sprained/twisted her ankle. **3.** *nach Präp. (nach* **man** *od. Inf.)* oneself; *(3. Pers. Sg.)* himself/herself/itself; *(3. Pers. Pl.)* themselves; *(Höflichkeitsform Sg./Pl.)* yourself/yourselves; **die Schuld auf ~ nehmen** take the blame upon oneself; **das ist eine Sache für ~:** that is a separate question; **das hat nichts auf ~:** that is of no consequence; **das hat etwas/viel für ~:** there is something/a great deal in that; **das Ding an ~** *(Philos.)* the thing in itself; **von ~ aus** on one's own initiative; without being told to; *s. auch* **an 2b; für 1a; kommen q. 4.** *(in unpers. Ausdrucksweisen für man od. passivisch)* **auf dieser Straße fährt es ~ gut** this is a good road to drive on; **es läßt ~ nicht schneiden/öffnen** it cannot be cut/opened; it is impossible to cut/open it. **5.** *(einander)* one another; each other; **sie küßten ~:** they kissed [one another]; **sie sind ~ spinnefeind** they are at daggers drawn [with one another]; **sie sehen ~ ähnlich** they look alike

Sichel ['zɪçl̩] die; ~, ~n sickle

sichel·förmig 1. *Adj.* crescent- *or* sickle-shaped. 2. *adv.* in [the shape of] a crescent *postpos.*

sicher ['zɪçɐ] 1. *Adj.* a) *(ungefährdet)* safe ⟨*road, procedure, etc.*⟩; secure ⟨*job, investment, etc.*⟩; in ~em Abstand at a safe distance; vor jmdm./etw. ~ sein be safe from sb./sth.; ~ ist ~: it's better to be on the safe side; better safe than sorry; *s. auch* Nummer a; b) *(zuverlässig)* reliable ⟨*evidence, source*⟩; secure ⟨*income*⟩; certain, undeniable ⟨*proof*⟩; *(vertrauenswürdig)* reliable, sure ⟨*judgment, taste, etc.*⟩; eine ~e Hand a sure *or* steady hand; c) *(selbstbewußt)* [self-]assured, [self-]confident ⟨*person, manner*⟩; d) *(gewiß)* certain; sure; der ~e Sieg/Tod certain victory/death; er war sich *(Dat.)* seines Erfolges ~: he was confident of success; eine Strafe ist ihm ~: he is certain *or* sure to be punished; seiner *(Gen.)* selbst sehr ~ sein be very sure of oneself. 2. *adv.* a) *(ungefährdet)* safely; ~ die Straße überqueren cross the street in safety; Geld ~ aufbewahren keep money in a safe place; um ganz ~ zu gehen to be quite sure; b) *(zuverlässig, vertrauenswürdig)* reliably; ~ [Auto] fahren be a safe driver; [nicht mehr] ~ auf den Beinen stehen be [un]steady on one's legs; c) *(selbstbewußt)* [self-]confidently; ~ auftreten behave in a self-assured *or* self-confident manner. 3. *Adv.* certainly; *(plädierend)* surely; Kommst du? – Aber ~: Are you coming? – Certainly; Of course; du hast ~ schon gehört, daß ...: you are bound to *or* must have heard that ...; ~ kommt er bald he is sure to come soon

sicher|gehen *unr. itr. V.; mit sein* play safe; um sicherzugehen to be on the safe side

Sicherheit die; ~, ~en a) *o. Pl.* safety; *(der Öffentlichkeit)* security; die ~ der Arbeitsplätze job security; ein Gefühl der ~: a sense of security; in ~ sein be safe; jmdn./etw. in ~ [vor etw. *(Dat.)*] bringen save *or* rescue sb./sth. [from sth.]; sich vor etw. *(Dat.)* in ~ bringen escape from sth.; zur ~: to be on the safe side; for safety's sake; jmdn./sich in ~ wiegen lull sb./[allow oneself to] be lulled into a [false] sense of security; *s. auch* öffentlich 1; b) *o. Pl. (Gewißheit)* certainty; mit an ~ *(Akk.)* grenzender Wahrscheinlichkeit with almost complete certainty; almost certainly; mit ~! *(als Antwort)* certainly!; of course!; c) *(Wirtsch.: Bürgschaft)* security; d) *o. Pl. (Zuverlässigkeit, Vertrauenswürdigkeit)* reliability; soundness; e) *o. Pl. (Selbstbewußtsein)* [self-]confidence; [self-]assurance; ~ im Auftreten/Benehmen [self-]confidence of manner

sicherheits-, Sicherheits-: ~ab·stand der *(Verkehrsw.)* safe distance between vehicles; einen zu geringen ~abstand einhalten drive too close to the vehicle in front; ~beauftragte der/die security officer; ~bindung die *(Ski)* safety binding; ~glas das safety glass; ~gurt der a) *(im Auto, Flugzeug)* seat-belt; b) *(für Bauarbeiter, Segler)* safety harness; ~halber *Adv.* to be on the safe side; for safety's sake; ~kette die safety *or* door chain; ~maßnahme die safety measure; precaution; ~nadel die safety-pin; ~organe *Pl.* security service *sing. or* services *pl.*; ~rat der; *o. Pl.* Security Council; ~risiko das security risk; ~schloß das safety lock; ~ventil das *(Technik)* safety-valve; ~verschluß der safety-catch; ~vorkehrung die [safety] precaution; safety measure; ~vorschrift die safety regulation

sicherlich *Adv.* certainly; er wird es ~ tun he is certain *or* sure to do it

sichern 1. *tr. V.* a) make ⟨*door etc.*⟩ secure; *(garantieren)* safeguard ⟨*rights, peace*⟩; *(schützen)* protect ⟨*rights etc.*⟩; etw./sich gegen etw. *od.* vor etw. *(Dat.)* ~: protect sth./oneself against sth.; ein gesichertes Einkommen a secure *or* guaranteed income; eine Schußwaffe ~: put the safety-catch on a firearm; b) *(verschaffen; polizeilich ermitteln)* secure ⟨*ticket, clue, etc.*⟩; [sich *(Dat.)*] etw. ~: secure sth. 2. *itr. V. (Jägerspr.)* scent; test the wind

sicher|stellen *tr. V.* a) *(beschlagnahmen)* impound ⟨*goods, vehicle*⟩; seize ⟨*stolen goods*⟩; confiscate ⟨*licence etc.*⟩; b) *(gewährleisten)* guarantee ⟨*supply, freedom, etc.*⟩; c) *(beweisen)* establish [beyond doubt]

Sicher·stellung die a) *s.* sicherstellen a: impounding; seizure; confiscation; b) *(Gewährleistung)* guarantee

Sicherung die; ~, ~en a) *o. Pl. (das Sichern)* safeguarding (vor + *Dat.*, gegen from, against); *(das Schützen)* protection (vor + *Dat.*, gegen from, against); b) *(Elektrot.)* fuse; *s. auch* durchbrennen a; c) *(techn. Vorrichtung)* safety-catch; d) *(Schutz)* safeguard (gegen against)

Sicherungs-: ~kasten der fuse-box; ~verwahrung die *(Rechtsw.)* preventive detention

Sicht [zɪçt] die; ~, ~en a) *o. Pl.* (~weite) visibility *no art.*; *(Ausblick)* view (auf + *Akk.*, in + *Akk.* of); gute *od.* klare/schlechte ~: good/poor visibility; die ~ beträgt nur fünfzig Meter visibility is down to fifty metres; in ~ kommen come into sight; außer ~ sein be out of sight; Land in ~! land ahoy!; auf ~ fliegen fly by VFR; b) *o. Pl. (Kaufmannsspr.)* Wechsel auf ~: bill payable on demand *or* at sight; c) auf lange/kurze ~: in the long/short term; auf lange *od.* weite ~ planen plan on a long-term basis; d) *(Betrachtungsweise)* point of view; aus meiner ~/in der ~ des Historikers as I see it/as the historian sees it; in my/the historian's view

sichtbar 1. *Adj.* visible; *(fig.)* apparent ⟨*reason*⟩; für jedermann ~ sein be obvious *or* evident to everyone; sich *(Dat.)* ~e Mühe geben go to obvious *or* appreciable trouble; etw. ~ machen clarify sth. 2. *adv.* visibly; immer ~er zutage treten *(fig.)* become increasingly obvious *or* apparent

Sicht·blende die screen; *(Jalousie)* blind

sichten *tr. V.* a) *(erspähen)* sight; b) *(durchsehen)* sift [through]; *(prüfen)* examine

Sicht-: ~flug der contact *or* VFR flying; ~gerät das VDU; ~grenze die: die ~grenze liegt bei 30 Metern [maximum] visibility is 30 metres; ~karte die pass

sichtlich 1. *Adj.* obvious; evident. 2. *adv.* obviously; evidently; visibly ⟨*impressed*⟩

Sicht·linie die *(Verkehrsw.)* sight-line; bis zur ~ vorfahren drive up to a/the point where one can see what is coming

Sichtung die; ~, ~en a) *o. Pl.* sighting; b) *(das Durchsehen)* sifting; *(das Prüfen)* examination; inspection

Sicht-: ~verhältnisse *Pl.* visibility *sing.*; ~vermerk der visa; ~weite die visibility *no art.*; außer/in ~weite sein be out of/in sight; in ~weite kommen come into sight

sickern ['zɪkɐn] *itr. V.; mit sein* seep; *(spärlich fließen)* trickle; *(fig.)* ⟨*money*⟩ leak away

Sicker·wasser das; *o. Pl.* a) *(im Boden)* gravitational *or* drainage water; b) *(aus einem Damm o. ä.)* seepage *(from a dam etc.)*

sie [ziː] 1. *Personalpron.; 3. Pers. Sg. Nom. Fem. (bei weiblichen Personen und Tieren)* she; *(bei Dingen, Tieren)* it; *(bei Behörden)* they *pl.*; Wer hat es gemacht? – Sie war es/Sie Who did it? – It was her/She did; ich weiß mehr als ~: I know more than she does; I know more than her *(coll.)*; *s. auch* ¹ihr; ihrer a. 2. *Personalpron.; 3. Pers. Pl. Nom.* a) they; Wer hat es gemacht? – Sie waren es/Sie Who did it? – It was them/They did; ich weiß mehr als ~: I know more than they do; I know more than them *(coll.)*; *s. auch* ihnen; ihrer b; b) *(ugs.: man)* mir haben ~ mein Rad gestohlen somebody's stolen my bike; hier wollen ~ das neue Rathaus bauen here's where they are going to build the new town hall; den haben ~ verhaftet he's been arrested. 3. *Akk. des Personalpron.* sie 1 *(bei weiblichen Personen und Tieren)* her; *(bei Dingen und Tieren)* it; *(bei Behörden)* them *pl.* 4. *Akk. des Personalpron.* sie 2a them

¹Sie *Personalpron.* a) *Anrede an eine od. mehrere Personen* you; jmdn. mit ~ anreden address sb. as 'Sie'; use the polite form of address to sb.; kommen ~ her! come here!; b) *(veralt.: Anrede an eine Untergebene)* you

²Sie die; ~, ~s *(ugs.)* she

Sieb [ziːp] das; ~[e]s, ~e a) sieve; *(Kaffee~, Tee~)* strainer; *(für Sand, Kies usw.)* riddle; *(Technik: Filter)* filter; er hat ein Gedächtnis wie ein ~: he's got a memory like a sieve; b) *(Druckw.)* screen

Sieb·druck der; *Pl.* ~e a) *o. Pl. (Verfahren)* [silk-]screen printing *no art.*; b) *(Erzeugnis)* [silk-]screen print

¹sieben 1. *tr. V.* a) *(durch ~)* sieve ⟨*flour etc.*⟩; riddle ⟨*sand, gravel, etc.*⟩; b) *(auswählen)* screen ⟨*candidates, visitors, etc.*⟩. 2. *itr. V.* a) use a sieve/strainer/riddle; b) *(auswählen)* pick and choose; bei der Prüfung haben sie [schwer] gesiebt *(ugs.)* they weeded out [a lot of] people in the examination

²sieben *Kardinalz.* seven; die ~ fetten/mageren Jahre the seven years of plenty/lean years; die Sieben Freien Künste the liberal arts; *s. auch* acht

Sieben die; ~, ~en a) *(Ziffer)* seven; b) *(Spielkarte)* seven; c) *(ugs.: Bus-, Bahnlinie)* number seven; *s. auch* Acht a, g; böse 1b

sieben·armig *Adj.* seven-armed; ~er Leuchter *(jüd. Rel.)* seven-branched candelabrum; menorah

Sieben·bürgen (das); ~s Transylvania

Sieben·eck das heptagon

sieben·eckig *Adj.* heptagonal

Siebener der; ~s, ~ *(ugs.)* a) *(im Lotto usw.)* seven winning numbers *pl.*; b) *s.* Sieben a, b, c

siebenerlei *Gattungsz.; indekl.* a) *attr.* seven kinds *or* sorts of; seven different ⟨*sorts, kinds, sizes, possibilities*⟩; b) *subst.* seven [different] things

sieben-, Sieben-: ~fach *Vervielfältigungsz.* sevenfold; *s. auch* achtfach; ~fache das; *adj. Dekl.* das ~fache seven times as much; *s. auch* Achtfache; ~gestirn das; *o. Pl.* Pleiades *pl.*; ~hundert *Kardinalz.* seven hundred; ~jährig *Adj.* a) *(7 Jahre alt)* seven-year-old *attrib.*; seven years old *pred.*; b) *(7 Jahre dauernd)* seven-year *attrib.*; der Siebenjährige Krieg the Seven Years War; *s. auch* achtjährig; ~köpfig *Adj.* seven-headed ⟨*monster*⟩; ⟨*family, committee*⟩ of seven; ~mal *Adj.* seven times; *s. auch* achtmal; ~malig *Adj.; nicht präd.* nach ~maligem Versuch after the seventh attempt; *s. auch* achtmalig; ~meilenstiefel *Pl. (scherzh.)* seven-league boots; ~meilenstiefel anhaben *(ugs. scherzh.)* have got one's seven-league boots on; mit ~meilenstiefeln *(ugs. scherzh.)* with giant strides; ~meter der *(Hockey)* penalty [shot]; *(Hallenhandball)* penalty [throw]; ~monatskind das child born two months prematurely; ~sachen *Pl. (ugs.)* meine/deine *usw.* ~sachen my/your *etc.* belongings *or (coll.)* bits and pieces; ~schläfer der a) *(Tier)* dormouse; b) *(volkst.: Tag)* 27 June *(rain on which is supposed to foretell rain for seven weeks)*; ≈ St. Swithin's Day; ~seitig *Adj.* seven-sided ⟨*figure*⟩; seven-page ⟨*letter, article, etc.*⟩; ~stöckig *Adj.* seven-storey ⟨*building*⟩; *s. auch* achtstöckig

siebent *s.* siebt

siebent... *Ordinalz. s.* siebt...

sieben·tausend *Kardinalz.* seven thousand

Siebente der/die; *adj. Dekl. s.* **Siebte**
sieben·teilig *Adj.* seven-piece ‹*tool-set etc.*›; seven-part ‹*serial*›; *s. auch* **achtteilig**
siebentel ['zi:bn̩tl] *s.* **siebtel**
Siebentel das; ~s, ~ *s.* **Siebtel**
siebentens *Adv. s.* **siebtens**
sieben·zehn *(veralt., zur Verdeutlichung) s.* **siebzehn**
siebt [zi:pt] *in* **wir waren zu** ~: there were seven of us; *s. auch* **[2]acht**
siebt... [zi:pt...] *Ordinalz.* seventh; *s. auch* **acht...**
Siebte der/die; *adj. Dekl.* seventh; *s. auch* **Achte**
siebtel ['zi:ptl̩] *Bruchz.* seventh
Siebtel das *(schweiz. meist* **der); ~s, ~:** seventh
siebtens *Adv.* seventhly
sieb-, Sieb-: ~zehn *Kardinalz.* seventeen; **~zehn·jährig** *Adj. (17 Jahre alt)* seventeen-year-old *attrib.*; seventeen years old *postpos.*; *(17 Jahre dauernd)* seventeen-year *attrib.*; *s. auch* **achtjährig; ~zehnt...** *Ordinalz.* seventeenth; **~zehntel das** seventeenth; **~zehn·und·vier das;** ~: vingt-et-un
siebzig ['zi:ptsɪç] *Kardinalz.* seventy; *s. auch* **achtzig**
[1]Siebziger der; ~s, ~ a) *(70jähriger)* seventy-year-old; **b)** *(ugs.: Autobus usw.)* number seventy; **c)** *(Wein)* '70 vintage
[2]Siebziger die; ~, ~ *(ugs.)* **a)** *(Briefmarke)* seventy-pfennig/centimes *etc.* stamp; **b)** *(Zigarre)* seventy-pfennig cigar; **c)** *Pl. (ugs.: 70er Jahre)* seventies
siebzig·jährig *Adj. (70 Jahre alt)* seventy-year-old *attrib.*; seventy years old *pred.*; *(70 Jahre dauernd)* seventy-year *attrib.*; *s. auch* **achtjährig**
siebzigst... *Ordinalz.* seventieth
siech [zi:ç] *Adj. (geh.)* infirm; ailing
Siechtum das; ~s *(geh.)* [long] infirmity
siedeln ['zi:dl̩n] *itr. V.* settle
sieden ['zi:dn̩] **1.** *unr. od. regelm. itr. V.* (*bes. südd.; fachspr. nur:* **siedete, gesiedet**) boil. **2.** *unr. od. regelm. tr. V.* **a)** *(meist:* **sott, gesotten;** *bes. südd.)* boil; **b)** *(veralt.)* obtain ‹*salt, soap, etc.*› by boiling
siedend·heiß *Adj. (präd. getrennt geschrieben)* boiling hot
Siede-: ~punkt der *(Physik; auch fig.)* boiling-point; **auf den ~punkt steigen** *(fig.)* reach boiling point; **~wasser·reaktor der** *(Kerntechnik)* boiling-water reactor
Siedler der; ~s, ~, Siedlerin die; ~, ~nen settler
Siedlung die; ~, ~en a) *(Wohngebiet)* [housing] estate; **b)** *(Niederlassung)* settlement
Siedlungs·haus das house on an estate; estate house
Sieg [zi:k] **der; ~[e]s, ~e** victory, *(bes. Sport)* win (**über** + *Akk.* over); **auf ~ spielen** go for a win; **den ~ davontragen** *od.* **erringen** *(geh.)* be victorious; *(Sport)* be the winner/winners; **ein ~ der Vernunft** *(fig.)* a victory for common sense
Siegel ['zi:gl̩] **das; ~s, ~:** seal; *(von Behörden)* stamp; *(des Gerichtsvollziehers)* bailiff's seal; **unter dem ~ der Verschwiegenheit** *(fig.)* under the seal of secrecy
Siegel·lack der sealing-wax
siegeln *tr. V.* seal
Siegel·ring der signet-ring
siegen *itr. V.* win; **über jmdn. ~:** gain *or* win a victory over sb.; *(bes. Sport)* win against sb.; beat sb.; **mit 2:0 ~** *(Sport)* win 2–0 *or* by two goals to nil
Sieger der; ~s, ~: winner; *(Mannschaft)* winners *pl.*; *(einer Schlacht)* victor; **als ~ hervorgehen** emerge victorious (**aus** from); **zweiter ~ sein** *(Sportjargon)* be runner-up/runners-up
Sieger·ehrung die presentation ceremony; awards ceremony

Siegerin die; ~, ~nen *s.* **Sieger**
Sieger-: ~macht die victorious power; **~podest das** winners' rostrum; **~urkunde die** winner's certificate
sieges-, Sieges-: ~bewußt 1. *Adj.* confident of victory *postpos.*; *(erfolgssicher)* confident of success *postpos.*; **2.** *adv.* confident of victory; confidently; **~gewiß** *(geh.) s.* **~sicher; ~göttin die** *(Myth.)* goddess of victory; **~palme die** palm [of victory]; **die ~palme davontragen** *(fig.)* carry off the palm; **~säule die** victory column; **~sicher 1.** *Adj.* certain *or* confident of victory *pred.*; *(erfolgssicher)* certain *or* confident of success *pred.*; **2.** *adv.* confident of victory; ‹*say, smile*› confidently; **~trunken** *(geh.)* **1.** *Adj.* intoxicated *or* drunk with victory *pred.*; **2.** *adv.* intoxicated *or* drunk with victory; **~zug der** *(auch fig.)* triumphant progress
sieg-, Sieg-: ~gewohnt *Adj.* ‹*army*› accustomed to victory; ‹*team*› used to winning; **~los** *Adj.* without a victory *postpos.*; *(Sport)* without a win *postpos.*; **~reich** *Adj.* victorious; winning ‹*team*›; successful ‹*campaign*›; **nach einer ~reichen Schlacht** after winning a battle; **~treffer der** *(bes. Fußball)* winning goal
sieh [zi:], **siehe** *Imperativ Sg. v.* **sehen**
siehst [zi:st] *2. Pers. Sg. Präsens v.* **sehen**
sieht [zi:t] *3. Pers. Sg. Präsens v.* **sehen**
Siel [zi:l] **der** *od.* **das; ~[e]s, ~e** *(nordd.)* **a)** *(Deichschleuse)* dike sluice *or* floodgate; **b)** *(Abwasserkanal)* sewer
Siele die; ~, ~n *(veralt.)* breast harness; **in den ~n sterben** *(fig.)* die in harness
siena ['zi̯e:na] *indekl. Adj.* sienna
siezen ['zi:tsn̩] *tr. V.* call 'Sie' *(the polite form of address)*; **sich ~:** call each other 'Sie'; **sich mit jmdm. ~:** call sb. 'Sie'
Sigel ['zi:gl̩] **das; ~s, ~** *(Zeichen)* logogram; *(in der Stenographie)* grammalogue; *(Kürzel)* abbreviation
Signal [zɪ'gna:l] **das; ~s, ~e** signal; **das ~ zum Angriff geben** give the signal to attack; **~e setzen** *(fig.)* set a new direction; **das ~ steht auf „Halt"** the signal is at 'stop'
Signal-: ~an·lage die *(Verkehrsw.)* signals *pl.*; **~brücke die** *(Eisenb.)* [signal] gantry
Signalement [zɪgnalə'mɛnt] **das; ~s, ~e** *(schweiz.)* personal description *or* details *pl.*
Signal-: ~flagge die *(Seew.)* signal flag; **~horn das** horn; hooter *(Brit.)*
signalisieren *tr. V.* indicate ‹*danger, change, etc.*›; *(fig.: übermitteln)* signal ‹*message, warning, order*› (+ *Dat.* to)
Signal-: ~lampe die indicator light; **~mast der a)** *(Seew.)* signalling mast; **b)** *(Eisenb.)* signal post *or* mast; **~wirkung die** knock-on effect
Signatar·macht [zɪgna'ta:ɐ̯-] **die** *(Politik)* signatory power
Signatur [zɪgna'tu:ɐ̯] **die; ~, ~en a)** *(Namenszeichen)* initials *pl.*; *(Kürzel)* abbreviated signature; *(des Künstlers)* autograph; **b)** *(veralt.: Unterschrift)* signature; **c)** *(in einer Bibliothek)* shelf-mark; **d)** *(auf Landkarten)* [map] symbol
Signet [zɪn'je:] **das; ~s, ~s** *(Buchw.)* [publisher's] imprint
signieren 1. *tr. V.* sign; autograph ‹*one's own work*›. **2.** *itr. V.* sign *or* autograph one's work
signifikant [zɪgnifi'kant] *(geh.)* **1.** *Adj.* **a)** *(wesentlich)* significant; **b)** *(typisch)* characteristic, typical (**für** of). **2.** *adv.* significantly
Signifikanz die; ~ *(geh.)* significance
Sigrist ['zi:grɪst] **der; ~en, ~en** *(schweiz.)* sexton
Silbe ['zɪlbə] **die; ~, ~n** syllable; **etw. mit keiner ~ erwähnen** not say a word about sth.
Silben-: ~rätsel das *puzzle in which syllables must be combined to form words*; **~trennung die** word-division *(by syllables)*
Silber ['zɪlbɐ] **das; ~s a)** *(Edelmetall, Farbe)* silver; **b)** *(silbernes Gerät)* silver[ware]; **c)** *o. Art. (Sport: ~medaille)* silver [medal]; **sie hat schon zweimal olympisches ~ geholt** she has already won two Olympic silver medals
silber-, Silber-: ~ader die vein of silver; **~arbeit die** silverwork; *(Gegenstand)* piece of silverwork; **~auf·lage die** silver plating *no indef. art.*; **~barren der** silver bar *or* ingot; **~blech das** rolled silver; **~besteck das** silver cutlery; **~blick der;** *o. Pl. (ugs. scherzh.)* [slight] squint; **~blond** *Adj.* silver-blond; **~distel die** carline thistle; **~farben, ~farbig** *Adj.* silver; **~fischchen das** silver-fish; **~fuchs der** silver fox; **~führend** *Adj. s.* **~haltig; ~gehalt der** silver content; **~geld das;** *o. Pl.* silver; **~geschirr das** silver plate; silverware; **~grau** *Adj.* silver-grey; **~haar das** *(geh.)* silvery hair; **~haltig** *Adj.* silver-bearing; argentiferous; **~hoch·zeit die** silver wedding; **~kette die** silver necklace; **~legierung die** silver alloy
Silberling der; ~s, ~e *(veralt.)* piece of silver
Silber-: ~medaille die silver medal; **~mine die** silver mine; **~möwe die** herring-gull; **~münze die** silver coin
silbern 1. *Adj.* **a)** *nicht präd. (aus Silber)* silver; **b)** *(silberfarben)* silver; silvery ‹*moonlight, shade, gleam, etc.*›. **2.** *adv.* **a)** *(mit Silber)* ‹*ornament, coat, etc.*› with silver; **b)** ‹*shine, shimmer, etc.*› with a silvery lustre; **c)** *(wohltönend)* ‹*chime etc.*› with a silvery sound
silber-, ~Silber-: ~papier das silver paper; **~pappel die** white poplar; **~streif der, ~streifen der** silver line *or* strip; **ein ~streifen am Horizont** *(fig.)* a ray of hope on the horizon; **~weiß** *Adj.* silvery-white; **~zwiebel die** *s.* **Perlzwiebel**
-silbig *Adj.* -syllable
silbrig *Adj. (geh.)* silvery
Silhouette [zi'lu̯ɛtə] **die; ~, ~n a)** silhouette; **b)** *(Mode)* line; **mit** *od.* **in modischer ~:** with a fashionable line *or* shape
Silicat *(fachspr.) s.* **Silikat**
Silicium [zi'li:tsi̯ʊm] **das; ~s** silicon
Silicon *(fachspr.) s.* **Silikon**
Silikat [zili'ka:t] **das; ~[e]s, ~e** *(Chemie)* silicate
Silikon [zili'ko:n] **das; ~s, ~e** *(Chemie)* silicone
Silikose [zili'ko:zə] **die; ~, ~n** *(Med.)* silicosis
Silizium *s.* **Silicium**
Silo ['zi:lo] **der** *od.* **das; ~s, ~s** silo
Silur [zi'lu:ɐ̯] **das; ~s** *(Geol.)* Siluran
Silvaner [zɪl'va:nɐ] **der; ~s, ~:** silvaner [wine]
Silvester [zɪl'vɛstɐ] **der** *od.* **das; ~s, ~:** New Year's Eve; **~ feiern** see the New Year in
Silvester·nacht die the night of New Year's Eve
Simbabwe [zɪm'ba:bvə] **(das); ~s** Zimbabwe
Simili·stein ['zi:mili-] **der** *(bes. Mineralogie)* imitation stone
Simmer·ring Ⓦⓩ ['zɪmɐ-] **der** *(Technik)* ring-type oil seal
Simonie [zimo'ni:] **die; ~, ~n** *(kath. Kirche)* simony
simpel ['zɪmpl̩] **1.** *Adj.* **a)** *(einfach)* simple ‹*question, task*›; **b)** *(abwertend: beschränkt)* simple-minded ‹*person*›; simple ‹*mind*›; **c)** *(oft abwertend: schlicht)* basic ‹*toy, dress, etc.*›. **2.** *adv.* **a)** *(einfach)* simply; **b)** *(abwertend: beschränkt)* in a simple-minded manner; **c)** *(oft abwertend: schlicht)* simply; basically
Simpel der; ~s, ~ *(bes. südd. ugs.)* simpleton; fool; **ich ~:** fool that I am/was
Simplex ['zɪmplɛks] **das; ~, ~e** *od.* **Simplizia** [zɪm'pli:tsi̯a] *(Sprachw.)* simplex
simplifizieren *tr., itr. V.* over-simplify
Simplizität die; ~: simplicity

Sims [zɪms] **der** *od.* **das; ~es, ~e** ledge; sill; *(Kamin~)* mantelpiece
Simse ['zɪmzə] **die; ~, ~n** *(Bot.)* bulrush
Simson ['zɪmzɔn] **(der); ~s** Samson
Simulant [zimu'lant] **der; ~en, ~en, Simulantin die; ~, ~nen** malingerer
Simulator [zimu'la:tɔr] **der; ~s, ~en** [-'to:rən] *(Technik)* simulator
simulieren 1. *tr. V.* feign, sham ‹*illness, emotion, etc.*›; simulate ‹*situation, condition, etc.*›. **2.** *itr. V. (Krankheit vortäuschen)* feign illness; pretend to be ill; **er simuliert nur** he's just putting it on
simultan [zimʊl'ta:n] **1.** *Adj.* simultaneous. **2.** *adv.* simultaneously
Simultan-: ~dolmetschen das simultaneous interpreting *no art.*; **~dolmetscher der** simultaneous interpreter
Sinai·halb·insel ['zi:nai-] **die** Sinai Peninsula
sind [zɪnt] *1. u. 3. Pers. Pl. Präsens v.* **sein**
sine tempore ['zi:nə 'tɛmporə] *(Hochschulw.)* at the time stated
Sinfonie [zɪnfo'ni:] **die; ~, ~n** *(auch fig.)* symphony
Sinfonie-: ~konzert das symphony concert; **~orchester das** symphony orchestra
Sinfoniker *Pl. (Orchester)* symphony orchestra *sing.*
sinfonisch *(Musik)* **1.** *Adj.* symphonic. **2.** *adv.* symphonically
Singapur ['zɪŋgapu:ɐ̯] **(das); ~s** Singapore
Sing·drossel die song-thrush
singen ['zɪŋən] **1.** *unr. itr. V.* **a)** sing; **einen ~den Tonfall haben** have a lilting cadence; **b)** *(salopp: vor der Polizei aussagen)* squeal *(sl.)*; **jmdn. zum Singen bringen** make sb. talk; **c)** *(dichter. veralt.)* **von etw. ~** ‹*poet, poem*› sing of sth.. **2.** *unr. tr. V.* **a)** sing ‹*song, aria, contralto, tenor, etc.*›; **jmds. Lob/Ruhm ~** *(fig. geh.)* sing sb.'s praises; **das kannst du ~** *(fig. ugs.)* you can bet your life on that; **b) sich heiser/müde ~:** sing until one is hoarse/tired; **jmdn. in den Schlaf ~:** sing sb. to sleep
¹Single ['zɪŋl̩] **die; ~, ~s** *(Schallplatte)* single
²Single der; ~[s], ~s single person; **~s** single people *no art.*
³Single das; ~[s], ~[s] *(Badminton, Tennis)* singles *sing. or pl.*
Sing-: ~sang der; ~[e]s a) *(das Singen)* singsong; **b)** *(Melodie)* simple tune; **~spiel das** *(Musik)* Singspiel; **~stimme die** voice
Singular ['zɪŋgula:ɐ̯] **der; ~s, ~e a)** *o. Pl.* singular; **Sinto ist der ~ von** *od.* **zu Sinti** 'Sinto' is the singular of 'Sinti'; **b)** *(Wort)* word in the singular
singulär *(geh.)* **1.** *Adj.* **a)** rare; **b)** *(einzigartig)* unique; singular. **2.** *adv.* rarely
Singularetantum [zɪŋgulare'tantʊm] **das; ~s, Singulariatantum** singular-only noun
singularisch *(Sprachw.)* **1.** *Adj.* singular ‹*form, ending*›. **2.** *adv.* in the singular
Sing·vogel der songbird
sinken ['zɪŋkn̩] *unr. itr. V.; mit sein* **a)** ‹*ship, sun*› sink, go down; ‹*plane, balloon*› descend, go down; *(geh.)* ‹*leaves, snowflakes*› fall; **die ~de Sonne** the setting sun; **er ist tief gesunken** *(fig.)* he has sunk low; **er wäre am liebsten in den Boden gesunken** he wished the earth would [open and] swallow him up; **ins Bett/in einen Sessel ~** *(fig.)* fall into bed/sink into a chair; **in Ohnmacht ~** *(geh.)* swoon; fall into a faint; **in Schlaf ~** *(geh.)* sink into a sleep; **b)** *(nieder~)* fall; **jmdm. an die Brust ~:** fall upon sb.'s breast; **den Kopf ~ lassen** let one's head drop; **der Kopf sank ihm auf die Brust** his head dropped to his chest; **auf** *od.* *(geh.)* **in die Knie ~:** sink *or* fall to one's knees; **die Hände in den Schoß ~ lassen** let one's hands drop to one's lap; **c)** *(niedriger werden)* ‹*temperature, level*› fall, drop; **das Thermometer/Barometer sinkt** the temperature is falling/the barometer is going back; **d)** *(an Wert verlieren)* ‹*price, value*› fall, go down; **in jmds. Gunst/Achtung ~:** go down in sb.'s favour/estimation; **e)** *(nachlassen, abnehmen)* fall; go down; ‹*excitement, interest*› diminish, decline; **jmds. Mut/Vertrauen sinkt** sb. loses courage/confidence; **ihre gute Laune sank** her good mood gradually disappeared
Sinn [zɪn] **der; ~[e]s, ~e a)** sense; **den** *od.* **einen sechsten ~ [für etw.] haben** have a sixth sense [for sth.]; **seine fünf ~e nicht beisammenhaben** *(ugs.)* be not quite right in the head; **b)** *Pl. (geh.: Bewußtsein)* senses; mind *sing.*; **ihm schwanden die ~e** he lost consciousness; **nicht bei ~en sein** be out of one's senses *or* mind; **bist du noch bei ~en?** have you gone out of your mind?; have you taken leave of your senses?; **wie von ~en** as if he/she had gone out of his/her mind; **c)** *o. Pl. (Gefühl, Verständnis)* feeling; **einen ~ für Schönheit/Stil/Gerechtigkeit/Humor** *usw.* **haben** have a sense of beauty/style/justice/humour *etc.*; **er hatte wenig ~ für Familienfeste** he didn't care much for family parties; **d)** *o. Pl. (geh.: Gedanken, Denken)* mind; **er hat ganz in meinem ~ gehandelt** he acted correctly to my mind *or* my way of thinking; **das ist nach meinem ~:** I like that; I agree with that; **mir steht der ~ [nicht] danach/nach etw.** I [don't] feel like it/sth.; **sich** *(Dat.)* **etw. aus dem ~ schlagen** put [all thoughts of] sth. out of one's mind; **etw. im ~ haben** have sth. in mind; **jmdm. in den ~ kommen** come to sb.'s mind; **das will mir nicht in den ~** *(veralt.)* I simply can't understand it; **e)** *o. Pl. (geh.: Denkungsart)* mind; way of thinking; **f)** *o. Pl. (~gehalt, Bedeutung)* meaning; **im strengen/wörtlichen ~:** in the strict/literal sense; **jmds. Rede dem ~e nach wiedergeben** convey the gist of sb.'s speech; **g)** *(Ziel u. Zweck)* point; **der ~ des Lebens** the meaning of life; **ohne ~ sein** be pointless *or* meaningless; **ohne ~ und Verstand** without thinking [about it/them]; **h)** *Pl. (sexuelles Verlangen)* desire *sing.*; desires
Sinn·bild das symbol
sinn·bildlich 1. *Adj.* symbolic. **2.** *adv.* symbolically
sinnen *(geh.) unr. itr. V.* **a)** *(nachdenken)* think; ponder; **sie schaute ~d aus dem Fenster** she looked thoughtfully out of the window; **b)** *(planen)* **auf etw.** *(Akk.)* **~:** plan *or* plot sth.; **auf Rache ~:** be out for revenge
sinnen-, Sinnen-: ~freude die *(geh.)* joie de vivre; zest for life; **~froh** *(geh.) Adj.* sensuous; **~lust die;** *o. Pl.* sensuality; **~rausch der;** *o. Pl. (geh.)* [sensual] passion
sinn·entstellend 1. *Adj.* which distorts/distorted the meaning *postpos., not pred.* **2.** *adv.* ‹*translate, shorten*› so that the *or* its meaning is distorted
Sinnes-: ~art die disposition; **~eindruck der** sense impression; sensation; **~organ das** sense-organ; sensory organ; **~täuschung die** trick of the senses; **~wandel der** change of mind *or* heart
sinn-, Sinn-: ~fällig 1. *Adj.* obvious; visible ‹*expression*›; **2.** *adv.* **etw. ~fällig zum Ausdruck bringen** express sth. intelligibly *or* in an easily understood way; **~gebung** [~ge:bʊŋ] **die** *(geh.)* meaning; **~gedicht das** *(Literaturw.)* epigram; **~gehalt der** *s.* **Sinn f; ~gemäß 1.** *Adj.* **a) eine ~gemäße Übersetzung** a translation which conveys the general sense; **b)** *(folgerichtig)* logical; **2.** *adv.* **a)** *(inhaltlich)* **etw. ~gemäß übersetzen/wiedergeben** translate the general sense of sth./give the gist of sth.; **b)** *(folgerichtig)* logically
sinnieren *itr. V.* ponder **(über +** *Akk.* over); muse **(über +** *Akk.* [up]on)
sinnig *Adj. (meist spött. od. iron.)* clever; sensible *(iron.)*
sinnlich 1. *Adj.* **a)** sensory ‹*impression, perception, stimulus*›; **b)** *(sexuell)* sensual ‹*love, mouth*›; **~es Verlangen** sexual desire; **c)** *(sinnenfroh)* sensuous ‹*pleasure, passion*›. **2.** *adv.* **a)** ‹*perceive, understand*› through the senses; **die ~ wahrnehmbare Welt** the world perceived by the senses; **b)** *(sexuell)* sensually; **jmdn. ~ erregen** arouse sb. sexually
Sinnlichkeit die; ~ **a)** sensuality; **b)** *(sinnliche Wahrnehmbarkeit)* sensuousness
sinn·los 1. *Adj.* **a)** *(unsinnig)* senseless; **b)** *(zwecklos)* pointless; **c)** *(abwertend: übermäßig)* mad; wild. **2.** *adv.* **a)** *(unsinnig)* senselessly; **b)** *(zwecklos)* pointlessly; **c)** *(abwertend: übermäßig)* like mad; **~ betrunken** blind drunk; **sich ~ besaufen** *(salopp)* get completely plastered *(sl.)*
Sinnlosigkeit die *(Wesen, Art)* senselessness; **b)** *(Zwecklosigkeit)* pointlessness
sinn-, Sinn-: ~reich *Adj.* **a)** *(zweckmäßig)* useful; **b)** *(tiefsinnig)* profound; **~spruch der** saying; **~stiftung die: ~stiftung durch Kunst** the endowment of life with meaning through art; **~verwandt** *Adj. (Sprachw.)* synonymous ‹*words*›; **~verwandte Wörter** synonyms; **~voll 1.** *Adj.* **a)** *(vernünftig)* sensible; **b)** *(mit Sinn erfüllt, einen Sinn ergebend)* meaningful; **dieser Satz ist nur ~voll, wenn ...:** this sentence only makes sense if ...; **2.** *adv.* **a)** *(vernünftig)* sensibly; **b)** *(mit Sinn erfüllt, einen Sinn ergebend)* meaningfully; **~widrig** *Adj. (geh.)* nonsensical; **~zusammenhang der** context
Sinologe [zino'lo:gə] **der; ~n, ~n** sinologist; sinologue
Sinologie die; ~: sinology *no art.*
Sinologin die; ~, ~nen *s.* **Sinologe**
sinte·mal [zɪntə'ma:l] *Konj. (veralt., noch scherzh.)* because; since
Sinter ['zɪntɐ] **der; ~s, ~:** sinter
sintern *(Technik) tr., itr. V.* sinter
Sint·flut ['zɪnt-] **die** Flood; Deluge; **nach mir/uns die ~:** I/we don't care what happens after I've/we've gone
sintflut·artig 1. *Adj.* torrential. **2.** *adv.* in torrents
Sinto ['zɪnto] **der; ~, Sinti** Sinte
Sinus ['zi:nʊs] **der; ~, ~** *od.* **~se a)** *(Math.)* sine; **b)** *(Anat.)* sinus
Sinus·kurve die sine curve
Siphon ['zi:fõ] **der; ~s, ~s a)** siphon; **b)** *(Geruchsverschluß)* [anti-siphon] trap; **c)** *(österr.: Sodawasser)* soda[-water]
Sippe ['zɪpə] **die; ~, ~n a)** *(Völkerk.)* sib; **b)** *(meist scherzh. od. abwertend: Verwandtschaft)* clan; **c)** *(Biol.)* species
Sippen·haft die *punishment of other members of a family or group for the crimes of one member*
Sippschaft die; ~, ~en a) *(meist abwertend: Sippe)* clan; **b)** *(abwertend: Gesindel)* bunch *(coll.)*; crowd *(coll.)*
Sirene [zi're:nə] **die; ~, ~n a)** siren; **b)** *(Zool.)* sirenian
Sirenen·geheul das wail of a/the siren/of sirens
sirren ['zɪrən] *itr. V.* buzz
Sirtaki [zɪr'ta:ki] **der; ~, ~s** syrtos
Sirup ['zi:rʊp] **der; ~s, ~e** syrup; *(streichfähig auch)* treacle *(Brit.)*; molasses *sing. (Amer.)*
Sisal ['zi:zal] **der; ~s** sisal
sistieren [zɪs'ti:rən] *tr. V. (Rechtsw.)* detain
Sistierung die; ~, ~en *(Rechtsw.)* detention
Sisyphus·arbeit ['zi:zyfʊs-] **die** Sisyphean task; never-ending task
Sitte ['zɪtə] **die; ~, ~n a)** *(Brauch)* custom; tradition; **es ist in England [nicht] ~ ...:** it is [not] the custom in England ...; **die ~n und Gebräuche eines Volkes** the customs and traditions of a people; **nach alter ~:** in the traditional way *or* manner; **b)** *(moralische Norm)* common decency; **gegen die guten ~n verstoßen** offend [against] common decency; **c)** *Pl. (Benehmen)* manners; **das sind**

ja feine ~n! *(iron.)* that's a nice way to behave! *(iron.)*; **d)** *o. Pl. (ugs.: Sittenpolizei)* vice squad
sitten-, Sitten-: ~dezernat das vice squad; **~geschichte die** history of life and customs; **~lehre die** ethics *sing.*; moral philosophy; **~los 1.** *Adj.* immoral; **2.** *adv.* immorally; **~polizei die** *(volkst.)* vice squad; **~richter der** *(oft abwertend)* moralist; moralizer; **sich zum ~richter erheben** sit in moral judgement [over sb.]; **~streng** *Adj. (veralt.)* morally strict; puritanical; **~strolch der** *(Pressejargon)* [sexual] molester; **~verfall der** moral decline; decline in moral standards; **~widrig 1.** *Adj.* **a)** *(Rechtsw.)* illegal ‹*methods, advertising, etc.*›; **b)** *(unmoralisch)* immoral ‹*behaviour*›; **2.** *adv. s.* **1**: illegally; immorally
Sittich ['zɪtɪç] **der; ~s, ~e** parakeet
sittlich 1. *Adj.* moral; **ihm fehlt die ~e Reife** he is morally immature. **2.** *adv.* morally
Sittlichkeit die; *o. Pl.* morality; morals *pl.*
Sittlichkeits-: ~verbrechen das sexual crime; **~verbrecher der** sex offender
sittsam *(veralt.)* **1.** *Adj.* **a)** well-behaved ‹*child etc.*›; decorous ‹*behaviour*›; **b)** *(keusch)* demure. **2.** *adv.* **a)** in a well-behaved way; **b)** *(keusch)* demurely
Situation [zitu̯a'tsi̯o:n] **die; ~, ~en** situation
Situations·komik die comedy deriving from a/the situation
situiert *Adj.* **gut/schlechter ~ [sein]** [be] well off/worse off
Sitz [zɪts] **der; ~es, ~e a)** seat; **er hat sich einen Stein als ~ ausgesucht** he picked a rock to sit on; **b)** *(mit Stimmrecht)* seat; **~ und Stimme haben** have a seat and a vote; **c)** *(Regierungs~)* seat; *(Verwaltungs~)* headquarters *sing. or pl.*; *(einer Firma)* head office; headquarters *sing. or pl.*; **d)** *(sitzende Haltung)* sitting position; *(beim Reiten)* seat; **e)** *(von Kleidungsstücken)* fit; **f) auf einen ~** *(ugs.)* in *or* at one go
Sitz-: ~bad das sitz-bath; hip-bath; **~bade·wanne die** sitz-bath; hip-bath; **~bank die** bench; **~blockade die** sit-down blockade; **~ecke die** sitting area; *(Möbelstück)* corner seating unit
sitzen *unr. itr. V.; südd., österr., schweiz. mit sein* **a)** sit; **eine ~de Lebensweise** a sedentary life; **bleiben Sie bitte ~:** please don't get up; please remain seated; **er saß den ganzen Tag an der Schreibmaschine/in der Kneipe** he spent the whole day at the typewriter/in the pub *(Brit. coll.)*; **auf der Anklagebank ~:** be in the dock; **er sitzt noch bei Tisch** *od.* **beim Essen** he is still eating *or* having his meal; **ich habe stundenlang beim Friseur ~ müssen** I had to spend hours at the hairdresser's; **im Sattel ~:** be in the saddle; **er sitzt viel über den Büchern** he spends a lot of time sitting over his books; **auf etw.** *(Dat.)* **~** *(salopp: etw. nicht hergeben)* hang on to sth.; not let go of sth.; **jmdm. auf der Pelle** *od.* **dem Pelz ~** *(salopp)* keep bothering sb.; keep on at sb. *(coll.)*; **b)** *(sein)* be; **die Firma sitzt in Berlin** the firm is based in Berlin; **die Tür sitzt schief in den Angeln** the door is not hanging straight; **der Schreck sitzt ihr noch in den Gliedern** she is still suffering from the shock; **einen ~ haben** *(salopp)* have had one too many; **c)** *([gut] passen)* fit; **die Krawatte sitzt nicht** the tie isn't straight; **d)** *(ugs.: gut eingeübt sein)* **Lektionen so oft wiederholen, bis sie ~:** keep on repeating lessons till they stick *(coll.)*; **wir hatten so lange geübt, bis jede Schrittkombination wie im Schlafe saß** we had practised till we could do every step in our sleep; **e)** *(ugs.: wirksam treffen)* hit home; **f)** *(Mitglied sein)* be, sit (**in +** *Dat.* on); **g)** *(ugs.: eingesperrt sein)* be in prison *or (sl.)* inside
sitzen-, Sitzen-: ~|bleiben *unr. itr. V. (ugs.)* **a)** *(nicht versetzt werden)* stay down [a year]; have to repeat a year; **b)** *(abwertend: als Frau unverheiratet bleiben)* be left on the shelf; **c)** *(keinen Käufer finden)* **auf etw.** *(Dat.)* **~bleiben** be left *or (coll.)* stuck with sth.; **~bleiber der; ~s, ~** *(ugs. abwertend)* pupil repeating a year; pupil who has to repeat a year; **~|lassen** *unr. tr. V. (ugs.)* **a)** *(nicht heiraten)* jilt; **b)** *(im Stich lassen)* leave in the lurch; **er hat Frau und Kinder ~lassen** *od. (seltener:)* **~gelassen** he left his wife and children; **c) jmdn. ~lassen** *(vergeblich warten lassen)* stand sb. up *(coll.)*; *(warten lassen)* leave sb. waiting; **d)** *(hinnehmen)* **etw. nicht auf sich** *(Dat.)* **~lassen** not take sth.; not stand for sth.
Sitz-: ~fleisch das *(ugs. scherzh.)* **kein ~fleisch haben** not have the staying power; not be able to stick at it; *(nicht stillsitzen können)* not be able to sit still; **~gelegenheit die** seat; **~gruppe die** group of seats; **~kissen das** *(im Sessel, Sofa)* [seat] cushion; *(auf dem Fußboden)* [floor] cushion; **~ordnung die** seating plan *or* arrangement; **~platz der** seat; **~riese der** *(ugs. scherzh.) person who looks tall when sitting down;* **~stange die** perch; **~streik der** sit-down strike
Sitzung die; ~, ~en a) meeting; *(Parlaments~)* sitting; session; **b)** *(beim Zahnarzt)* visit; *(beim Psychotherapeuten)* session; *(ugs. scherzh.: Toilettenbesuch)* session; **c)** *(das Porträtsitzen)* sitting
Sitzungs-: ~bericht der minutes *pl.*; **~periode die** session; **~saal der** conference hall; *(eines Gerichts)* court-room; **~zimmer das** conference room
sixtinisch [zɪks'ti:nɪʃ] *Adj.* Sistine
Sizilianer [zitsi'li̯a:nɐ] **der; ~s, ~, Sizilianerin die; ~, ~nen** Sicilian; *s. auch* **-in**
sizilianisch [zitsi'li̯a:nɪʃ] *Adj.* Sicilian
Sizilien [zi'tsi:li̯ən] **(das); ~s** Sicily
Skagerrak·schlacht ['ska:gərak-] **die** *(hist.)* Battle of Jutland
Skala ['ska:la] **die; ~, Skalen a)** *(Maßeinteilung, Musik)* scale; **b)** *(Reihe)* range
Skalar der; ~s, ~s *(Math., Physik)* scalar
Skalde ['skaldə] **der; ~n, ~n** skald
Skalden·dichtung die skaldic poetry
Skalp [skalp] **der; ~s, ~e** scalp
Skalpell [skal'pɛl] **das; ~s, ~e** scalpel
skalpieren *tr. V.* scalp
Skandal [skan'da:l] **der; ~s, ~e a)** scandal; **b)** *(bes. nordd.: Lärm)* row *(coll.)*
Skandal-: ~geschichte die [piece of] scandal; **~nudel die** *(ugs.)* **sie ist eine ~nudel** she is always involved in some scandal or other
skandalös *Adj.* scandalous
skandieren [skan'di:rən] *tr. V.* **a)** chant; **b)** *(Verslehre)* scan
Skandinavien [skandi'na:vi̯ən] **(das); ~s** Scandinavia
Skandinavier [skandi'na:vi̯ɐ] **der; ~s, ~, Skandinavierin die; ~, ~nen** Scandinavian; *s. auch* **-in**
skandinavisch *Adj.* Scandinavian
Skarabäus [skara'bɛ:ʊs] **der; ~, Skarabäen** scarab
Skat [ska:t] **der; ~[e]s, ~e** *od.* **~s** skat; **~ dreschen** *od.* **klopfen** *(salopp)* play skat
Skat·blatt das skat pack *(Brit.) or (Amer.)* deck
skaten *itr. V. (ugs.)* play skat
Skat·spieler der skat-player
Skeet·schießen ['ski:t-] **das; ~s** *(Sport)* skeet [shooting] *no art.*
Skelett [ske'lɛt] **das; ~[e]s, ~e** skeleton; **er ist nur noch ein ~** *od.* **das reinste ~:** he is little more than a skeleton
Skelett·bauweise die *(Bauw.)* skeleton construction
Skepsis ['skɛpsɪs] **die; ~:** scepticism
Skeptiker der; ~s, ~: sceptic
skeptisch 1. *Adj.* sceptical. **2.** *adv.* sceptically
Skeptizismus der; ~: scepticism
Sketch [skɛtʃ] **der; ~[es], ~e[s]** *od.* **~s** sketch
Ski [ʃi:] **der; ~s, ~er** *od.* **~:** ski; **~ laufen** *od.* **fahren** ski; **er läuft** *od.* **fährt gut ~:** he is a good skier; **~ Heil!** ski heil!; good skiing!
Ski-: ~bindung die ski binding; **~bob der** ski-bob; **~fliegen das, ~flug der** ski flying *no art.*; **~haserl das; ~s, ~** *(südd., österr. scherzh.)* girl skier; **~lauf der, ~laufen das** skiing *no art.*; **~läufer der** skier; **~lehrer der** ski-instructor; **~lift der** ski-lift; **~springen das; ~s, ~:** ski-jumping *no art.*; **~springer der** ski-jumper; **~stiefel der** ski boot; **~stock der** skistick; ski pole; **~zirkus der** *(Sportjargon)* ski circus
Skizze ['skɪtsə] **die; ~, ~n a)** *(Zeichnung)* sketch; **b)** *(Konzept)* outline; **c)** *(kurze Aufzeichnung)* [brief] account
Skizzen·block der sketch-pad; sketch-block
skizzen·haft 1. *Adj.* rough ‹*drawing, outline*›. **2.** *adv.* roughly
skizzieren *tr. V.* **a)** *(zeichnen)* sketch; **b)** *(aufzeichnen)* outline; **c)** *(entwerfen)* draft
Sklave ['skla:və] **der; ~n, ~n** slave; **jmdn. zum ~n machen** make a slave of sb.; **er ist der ~ seiner Gewohnheiten** *(fig. abwertend)* he is a slave to habit
Sklaven-: ~arbeit die a) slavery *no art.*; work as slaves *no art.*; **b)** *(abwertend: schwere Arbeit)* drudgery *no art.*; **~halter der** slave-owner; **~halter·gesellschaft die;** *o. Pl. (bes. marx.)* slave-owning society; **~händler der** *(auch fig. abwertend)* slave-trader
Sklaverei die; ~ a) *(auch fig. abwertend)* slavery *no art.*; **b)** *(oft abwertend: harte Arbeit)* drudgery *no art.*
Sklavin die; ~, ~nen *s.* **Sklave;** *s. auch* **-in**
sklavisch ['skla:vɪʃ] *(abwertend)* **1.** *Adj.* slavish. **2.** *adv.* slavishly
Sklerose [skle'ro:zə] **die; ~, ~n** *(Med.)* sclerosis *no art.*
skontieren [skɔn'ti:rən] *tr. V. (Kaufmannsspr.)* **eine Rechnung ~:** allow a [cash] discount on a bill
Skonto ['skɔnto] **der** *od.* **das; ~s, ~s** *(Kaufmannsspr.)* [cash] discount; **bei Barzahlung binnen 10 Tagen gewähren wir 3 % ~ auf den Rechnungsbetrag** we allow a 3 % discount if payment is made in cash within ten days
Skooter ['sku:tɐ] **der; ~s, ~:** dodgem; bumper car
Skorbut [skɔr'bu:t] **der; ~[e]s** *(Med.)* scurvy *no art.*
Skorpion [skɔr'pi̯o:n] **der; ~s, ~e a)** *(Tier)* scorpion; **b)** *(Astrol.)* Scorpio; *s. auch* **Fisch**
Skribent [skri'bɛnt] **der; ~en, ~en** *(veralt. abwertend)* scribbler
Skript [skrɪpt] **das; ~[e]s, ~en** *od.* **~s** script; *(Manuskript)* manuscript
Skript·girl das *(Film)* script girl
Skriptum ['skrɪptʊm] **das; ~s, Skripten** *od.* **Skripta** *(österr., sonst veralt.)* manuscript
Skrotum ['skro:tʊm] **das; ~s, Skrota** *(Anat.)* scrotum
Skrupel ['skru:pl̩] **der; ~s, ~:** scruple; **~ haben** *od.* **kennen** have scruples
skrupel·los *(abwertend)* **1.** *Adj.* unscrupulous. **2.** *adv.* unscrupulously
Skrupellosigkeit die; ~ *(abwertend)* unscrupulousness
skrupulös [skrupu'lø:s] *(veralt.) Adj.* scrupulous
Skull [skʊl] **das; ~s, ~s** *(Seemannsspr., Rudersport)* scull
skullen *itr. V.; auch mit sein (Seemannsspr., Rudersport)* scull
Skulptur [skʊlp'tu:ɐ̯] **die; ~, ~en** sculpture
skurril [skʊ'ri:l] **1.** *Adj.* absurd; droll ‹*person*›. **2.** *adv.* absurdly
Skurrilität die; ~, ~en absurdity
S-Kurve ['ɛs-] **die** S-bend; double bend
Slalom ['sla:lɔm] **der; ~s, ~s** *(Ski-, Kanusport)* slalom; **im ~ fahren** *(fig.)* zigzag

Slang [slæŋ] **der; ~s a)** *(oft abwertend: Umgangssprache)* slang; **b)** *(Jargon)* jargon
S-Laut ['ɛs-] **der** *(stimmlos)* s-sound; *(stimmhaft)* z-sound
Slawe ['sla:və] **der; ~n, ~n, Slawin die; ~, ~nen** Slav; *s. auch* **-in**
slawisch *Adj.* Slav[ic]; Slavonic
Slawist der; ~en, ~en Slavicist; Slavist
Slawistik die; ~: Slavonic studies *pl., no art.*
Slibowitz ['sli:bovɪts] **der; ~[es], ~e** slivovitz
Slip [slɪp] **der; ~s, ~s** briefs *pl.*
Slipper der; ~s, ~[s] slip-on [shoe]
Slogan ['slo:gn̩] **der; ~s, ~s** slogan
Slowake [slo'va:kə] **der; ~n, ~n** Slovak
Slowakei die; ~: Slovakia *no art.*
Slowakin die; ~, ~nen Slovak
slowakisch *Adj.* Slovak; Slovakian
Slowene [slo've:nə] **der; ~n, ~n** Slovene; Slovenian
Slowenien (das); ~s Slovenia
Slowenin die; ~, ~nen Slovene; Slovenian
Slowenisch das; ~en Slovene; Slovenian; *s. auch* **Deutsch**
Slow·fox ['slo:fɔks] **der** slow foxtrot
Slum [slam] **der; ~s, ~s** slum
Smaragd [sma'rakt] **der; ~[e]s, ~e** emerald
Smaragd·eidechse die green lizard
smaragden *Adj.* emerald
smaragd·grün *Adj.* emerald green
smart [sma:ɐ̯t] *Adj.* smart
Smog [smɔk] **der; ~[s], ~s** smog
Smog·alarm der smog warning; **bei ~:** if there is a smog warning
Smoking ['smo:kɪŋ] **der; ~s, ~s** dinner-jacket *or (Amer.)* tuxedo and dark trousers
Smutje ['smʊtjə] **der; ~s, ~s** *(Seemannsspr.)* ship's cook
Snob [snɔp] **der; ~s, ~s** *(abwertend)* snob
Snobismus der; ~ *(abwertend)* snobbery; snobbishness
snobistisch *Adj. (abwertend)* snobbish
so [zo:] **1.** *Adv.* **a)** *meist betont (auf diese Weise; in, von dieser Art)* like this/that; this/that way; **schreibe den Brief so, wie ich es dir gesagt habe** write the letter as I told you; **er hat sich nicht so verhalten, wie allgemein erwartet wurde** he did not behave in the way that was generally expected; **so ist sie nun einmal** that's the way she is; **ist das [wirklich] so?** is that [really] true?; **wenn dem so ist** if that's the case; **sei doch nicht so** don't be like that; **ich will [mal] nicht so sein** I don't want to be awkward; **so ist das!** *(resigniert)* that's the way it goes!; that's how it goes!; **so ist es!** *(zustimmend)* that's correct *or* right!; **ach, so ist das!** *(erfassend)* oh, I 'see!; **recht so!, gut so!** right!; that's fine!; **mir ist so, als ob ...:** I have a feeling that ...; **so kann es einem gehen, wenn ...:** that's what can happen if ...; **und das kam so** and this is what happened; and it happened like this; **du mußt dich entscheiden, so oder so** you must make up your mind one way or the other; **so oder so gerät der Minister unter Druck** either way the minister will come under pressure; **weiter so!** carry on in the same way!; **b)** *(meist betont) (dermaßen)* so; **eine so große Frau** such a big woman; **er ist nicht so dumm, das zu tun** he is not so stupid as to do that; **er schlug die Tür zu, daß es nur so knallte** he slammed the door shut; **c)** *betont (überaus)* so; **d)** *meist betont (genauso)* as; **so gut ich konnte** as best I could; **so gut es geht** as best I/he *etc.* can; **er ist [nicht] so groß wie du** he is [not] as tall as you [are]; **ihr sollt alles so lassen, wie es ist** you are to leave everything the way it is; **so weiß wie Schnee** as white as snow; **e)** *meist betont (ugs.: solch[e])* such; **so ein Mann/so eine Frau/so ein Kind** such a man/woman/child; a man/woman/child like that; **ein so schönes Fest** such a lovely party; **so ein Pech/eine Frechheit!** what bad luck/a cheek!; **so ein Idiot!** what an idiot!; **hast du so etwas schon mal gesehen?** have you ever seen such a thing *or* anything like it?; **so etwas kann passieren** such things *pl.* can happen; **so etwas ist mir noch nie passiert** a thing like that has never *or* nothing like that has ever happened to me before; **so was von fett habe ich noch nie gesehen** I've never seen anyone so fat; **die Suppe war so was von ekelhaft** the soup was absolutely disgusting; **er ist so was von dämlich** he is so stupid; **so was von dämlich!** talk about stupidity! *(coll.)*; **ist sie nicht Kontoristin oder so was?** isn't she a clerk or something?; **[na** *od.* **nein** *od.* **also] so was!** *(überrascht/empört)* well, I never!; **so etwas Schönes** something as beautiful as that; such a beautiful thing; **und so was nennt** *od.* **schimpft sich Wissenschaft/Mutter** and they call that science/she calls herself a mother; **so einer/eine/eins** one like that; one of those; **mit so einer würde ich mich nicht einlassen** I wouldn't get mixed up with that sort of woman *or* a woman of that sort; **so einer** *od.* **jemand wie Schmidt** somebody like Schmidt; **Ein Grahambrötchen? – Nein, so eins** A granary roll? – No, one of those *or* one like that; **das ist so ein** *od.* **so'n kleiner Dicker** *(ugs.)* he's a little fat man; **so nennt man das also** so 'that's what it's called; **so einer bist du also!** so 'that's the sort of person you are!; **f)** *betont (eine Zäsur ausdrückend)* right; OK *(coll.)*; **so, und nun?** right, [and] now what?; **g)** *(ugs.: schätzungsweise)* about; **so** *od.* **so um die** *od.* **so an die** *od.* **so etwa** *od.* **so ungefähr 50 Mark** about 50 marks; **h)** *unbetont (bei Zitaten od. Quellenangaben)* **die Religion, so Marx, ist ...:** religion, according to Marx is ...; **„die Ausgaben", so der Minister, „...":** 'the expenditure', said the minister *or* the minister said, '...'; **i)** *unbetont (ugs.: und/oder ähnliches)* **Banker und so** bankers and people like that; **heißt sie nicht Karobowski oder so?** isn't her name Karobowski or something like that?; **ich spiele ein bißchen Tischtennis, Billard und so** I play a bit of table tennis, billiards and that sort of thing; **j)** *betont (erstaunt, zweifelnd)* **so?** really?; **so, so** *(meist iron.)* oh, I see; **k)** *betont (ohne Hilfsmittel)* **ich brauche keine Leiter, da komme ich auch so ran** *(ugs.)* I don't need a ladder, I can reach it [without one]; **geht es so, oder soll ich Ihnen eine Tüte geben?** can you manage, or shall I give you a bag?; **l)** *betont (ohne Zutaten)* just as it is; **einfach ~:** just as it is; **m)** *betont (ugs.: umsonst)* for nothing; **die können Sie so mitnehmen** you can take these – they're free. **2.** *Konj.* **a)** *(konsekutiv, in Verbindung mit „daß")* **so daß ...** *(damit)* so that ...; *(und deshalb)* and so ...; **er war krank, so daß er die Reise verschieben mußte** he was sick, [and] so he had to postpone the trip; **b)** *(konzessiv)* however; **so sehr ich ihn auch immer unterstützt habe, dieses Mal kann ich ihm nicht helfen** however much I have always supported him, this time I can't help him ; **so leid es mir tut, ich muß absagen** much as I regret it, I'll have to cry off; **c)** *(geh.: falls)* if; **so Gott will** God willing. **3.** *Partikel* **a)** just; **wie ich so ging, da sah ich ...:** I was just walking along, when I saw ...; **ich weiß nicht so recht, ob ich gehen soll** I'm not really sure if I should go; **Warum fragst du? – Ach, nur so** Why do you ask? – Oh, no particular reason; **ach, das hab' ich nur so gesagt** oh, I didn't mean anything by that; **das ist mir nur so rausgerutscht** *(ugs.)* it just slipped out; **wie ist der neue Chef denn so?** *(ugs.)* what's the new boss like, then? *(coll.)*; **b)** *(in Aufforderungssätzen verstärkend)* **so halt doch endlich deinen Mund!** just hold your tongue, will you!; **so komm doch** come on now; **so glaub mir doch** you must believe me
So. *Abk.* **Sonntag** Sun.
s. o. *Abk.* **siehe oben**
SO *Abk.* **Südost[en]** SE
sobald *Konj.* as soon as
Söckchen ['zœkçən] **das; ~s, ~ a)** [little] sock; **b)** *(Damen-, Kinderstrumpf)* [short] sock; ankle-sock
Socke ['zɔkə] **die; ~, ~n** sock; **sich auf die ~n machen** *(ugs.)* get going; **von den ~n sein** *(ugs.)* be flabbergasted
Sockel ['zɔkl̩] **der; ~s, ~ a)** *(einer Säule, Statue)* plinth; **b)** *(unterer Teil eines Hauses, Schrankes)* base; **c)** *(Elektrot.)* base
Sockel·betrag der *(Wirtsch.)* basic sum
Socken der; ~s, ~ *(südd., österr., schweiz.) s.* **Socke**
Socken·halter der [sock] suspender
Soda ['zo:da] **die; ~** *od.* **das; ~s** soda
so·dann *Adv.* **a)** *(danach)* then; thereupon; **b)** *(außerdem)* and furthermore
so daß *(österr. auch:* **sodaß)** *s.* **so 2 a**
Soda·wasser das; *Pl.* **Sodawässer** soda; soda-water
Sod·brennen das; ~s heartburn; pyrosis
Sodom ['zo:dɔm] **das; ~:** Sodom; **~ und Gomorrha** Sodom and Gomorrah
Sodomie die; ~: sodomy *no art.*
sodomitisch *Adj.* sodomitic[al]
so·eben *Adv.* just; **die Nachricht kam ~:** the news came just now
Sofa ['zo:fa] **das; ~s, ~s** sofa; settee
Sofa·kissen das [sofa] cushion; scatter cushion
so·fern *Konj.* provided [that]
soff [zɔf] *1. u. 3. Pers. Sg. Prät. v.* **saufen**
so·fort *Adv.* immediately; at once; **er war ~ tot** he died instantly; **komm ~ her!** come here this instant *or* at once!; **diese Regelung gilt ab ~:** this ruling has immediate effect *or* takes effect immediately; **Ingenieure ab ~ gesucht** engineers required, should be ready to start immediately; **ich bin ~ fertig** I'll be ready in a moment; *(mit einer Arbeit)* I'll be finished in a moment; **[ich] komme ~:** [I'm] just coming; *(Bedienung)* I'll be right with you
Sofort·bild·kamera die *(Fot.)* instant-picture camera
Sofort·hilfe die emergency relief *or* aid
sofortig *Adj. (unmittelbar)* immediate
Sofort·maß·nahme die immediate measure
Soft-Eis ['zɔft|ais] **das** soft ice-cream
Softie ['zɔfti] **der; ~s, ~s** *(ugs.)* softy
Software ['zɔftvɛ:ɐ̯] **die; ~, ~s** *(DV)* software
sog [zo:k] *1. u. 3. Pers. Sg. Prät. v.* **saugen**
Sog der; ~[e]s, ~e a) *(saugende Strömung)* suction; *(bei Schiffen)* wake; *(bei Fahr-, Flugzeugen)* slip-stream; *(von Wasser, auch fig.)* current; **b)** *(Meeresk.)* undertow
sog. *Abk.* **sogenannt**
so·gar *Adv.* even; **sie ist krank, ~ schwer krank** she is ill, in fact *or* indeed seriously ill
so·genannt *Adj. (oft spött.)* so-called
so·gleich *Adv.* immediately; at once
Sohle ['zo:lə] **die; ~, ~n a)** *(Schuh~)* sole; **eine kesse** *od.* **heiße ~ aufs Parkett legen** *(ugs.)* put up a good show on the dance-floor; **auf leisen ~n** softly; noiselessly; **b)** *(Fuß~)* sole [of the foot]; **auf** *od.* **mit nackten ~n** barefoot; with bare feet; **c)** *(Tal~)* bottom; *(eines Flusses)* bottom; bed; **d)** *(Bergmannsspr.)* level; *(Gruben~)* floor; **e)** *(Einlege~)* insole
sohlen *tr. V.* sole
Sohn [zo:n] **der; ~es, Söhne** ['zø:nə] **a)** *(männlicher Nachkomme)* son; **der ~ Gottes** the Son of God; **der verlorene ~:** the prodigal son; **b)** *o. Pl. (fam.: Anrede an einen Jüngeren)* son; boy
Söhnchen ['zø:nçən] **das; ~s, ~:** little son; little boy
Sohne·mann der; *o. Pl. (fam.)* son

soigniert [zoan'ji:ɐt] *Adj. (geh.)* soigné ⟨*man, appearance*⟩; soignée ⟨*woman*⟩
Soiree [zoa're:] **die;** ~, ~**n** *(geh.)* soirée
Soja- ['zo:ja-]: ~**bohne die** soy[a] bean; ~**soße die** soy[a] sauce
Sokrates ['zo:kratɛs] **(der); Sokrates'** Socrates
Sokratiker [zo'kra:tikɐ] **der;** ~**s,** ~: Socratic
sokratisch *Adj.* Socratic
Sol das; ~**s,** ~**e** *(Chemie)* sol
so·lang[e] *Konj.* so *or* as long as; ~ **du nicht alles aufgegessen hast** unless *or* until you have eaten everything up
solar [zo'la:ɐ] *Adj.* solar
Solar-: ~**batterie die** *(Elektrot.)* solar battery; ~**energie die** *(Physik)* solar energy
Solarium [zo'la:ri̯ʊm] **das;** ~**s, Solarien** [...i̯ən] solarium
Solar-: ~**kraftwerk das** *s.* **Sonnenkraftwerk;** ~**plexus** [~plɛksʊs] **der** *(Anat.)* solar plexus; ~**technik die** *(Energietechnik)* solar technology *no art.*; ~**zelle die** *(Physik, Elektrot.)* solar cell
Sol·bad das a) *(Kurort)* salt-water spa; **b)** *(Bad)* salt-water bath; brine-bath
solch [zɔlç] *Demonstrativpron.* **a)** *attr.* such; ~**e Leute** such people; people like that; **[ein]** ~**er Glaube** such a belief; **ich habe** ~**en Hunger** I am so hungry; **ich habe** ~**e Kopfschmerzen** I've got such a headache; **das macht** ~**en Spaß!** it's so much fun!; **b)** *selbständig* ~**e wie die** people like that; **sie ist keine** ~**e** she is not like that; **die Sache als** ~**e** the thing as such; **es gibt** ~**e und** ~**e** *(ugs.)* it takes all sorts *or* kinds [to make a world]; **Ärzte gibt es** ~**e und** ~**e** there are doctors and doctors; **c)** *ungebeugt (geh.: so [ein])* such; **bei** ~ **einem herrlichen Wetter** when the weather is so beautiful
solcher-: ~**art 1.** *indekl. Demonstrativpron.* such; **2.** *Adv.* thus; ~**gestalt** *Adv.* thus; in such a way
solcherlei *indekl. Adj.; s.* **derlei**
solcher·maßen *Adv.* in such a way; in this way; *(in solchem Grade)* to such an extent
Sold [zɔlt] **der;** ~**[e]s,** ~**e a)** *(veralt.)* pay; **in jmds.** ~ **stehen** be in the pay of sb. *or* sb.'s pay; **im** ~**e des Kaisers stehen** be in the service of the emperor; **b)** *s.* **Wehrsold**
Soldat [zɔl'da:t] **der;** ~**en,** ~**en** soldier; ~ **auf Zeit** soldier serving for a fixed period
Soldaten-: ~**fried·hof der** military *or* war cemetery; ~**sprache die** army *or* soldiers' slang
Soldatin die; ~, ~**nen** [female *or* woman] soldier; **sie ist** ~: she is a soldier
soldatisch 1. *Adj.* military ⟨*discipline, expression, etc.*⟩; soldierly ⟨*figure, virtue*⟩. **2.** *adv.* in a military *or* soldierly manner
Sold·buch das *(hist.)* [military] pay-book
Söldner ['zœldnɐ] **der;** ~**s,** ~: mercenary
Söldner-: ~**heer das** mercenary army; army of mercenaries; ~**truppe die** mercenary force; force of mercenaries
Sole ['zo:lə] **die;** ~, ~**n** salt water; brine
Sol·ei das pickled egg
solid [zo'li:t] *s.* **solide**
Solidar·gemeinschaft die mutually supportive group; *(die Gesellschaft)* caring society
solidarisch 1. *Adj.* ~**es Verhalten zeigen** show one's solidarity; **sich mit jmdm.** ~ **erklären** declare one's solidarity with sb. **2.** *adv.* ~ **handeln/sich** ~ **verhalten** act in/show solidarity
solidarisieren *refl. V.* show [one's] solidarity
Solidarität die; ~: solidarity
Solidaritäts·streik der solidarity strike
solide 1. *Adj.* **a)** *(massiv, gediegen)* solid ⟨*rock, wood, house*⟩; sturdy ⟨*shoes, shed, material, fabric*⟩; solid, sturdy ⟨*furniture*⟩; [good-]quality ⟨*goods*⟩; **b)** *(gut fundiert)* sound ⟨*work, workmanship, education, knowledge*⟩; solid ⟨*firm, business*⟩; **c)** *(anständig)* respectable ⟨*person, life, occupation, profession*⟩. **2.** *adv.* **a)** *(gediegen)* solidly ⟨*built*⟩; sturdily ⟨*made*⟩; **b)** *(gut fundiert)* soundly ⟨*educated, constructed*⟩; **c)** *(anständig)* ⟨*live*⟩ respectably, steadily
Solidität die; ~ *s.* **solide 1 a–c:** solidness; sturdiness; soundness; respectability
Solipsismus [zolɪ'psɪsmʊs] **der;** ~ *(Philos.)* solipsism *no art.*
Solist [zo'lɪst] **der;** ~**en,** ~**en** soloist
solistisch *Adj.* solo
Solitär [zoli'tɛ:ɐ] **der;** ~**s,** ~**e** solitaire
soll *1. u. 3. Pers. Sg. Präsens v.* **sollen**
Soll [zɔl] **das;** ~**[s],** ~**[s] a)** *(Kaufmannsspr., Bankw.: Schulden)* debit; ~ **und Haben** debit and credit; **im** ~: in debit; **b)** *(Kaufmannsspr.: linke Buchführungsseite)* debit side; **etw. im** ~ **verbuchen** enter sth. on the debit side; **c)** *(Wirtsch.: Arbeits~)* quota; **sein** ~ **erfüllen** *od.* **erreichen** achieve *or* meet one's target; **d)** *(Wirtsch.: Plan~)* quota; target
Soll-Bruch·stelle die *(Technik)* predetermined breaking-point
sollen 1. *unr. Modalverb; 2. Part.* ~ **a)** *(bei Aufforderung, Anweisung, Auftrag)* **er soll sofort kommen** he is to come immediately; **solltest du nicht bei ihm anrufen?** were you not supposed to ring him?; **was soll ich als nächstes tun?** what should I do next?; what do you want me to do next?; **du sollst Vater und Mutter ehren** *(bibl.)* honour thy father and thy mother; **du sollst das lassen!** stop that *or* it!; **soll ich dir mal erzählen, was mir gestern passiert ist?** shall I tell you what happened to me yesterday?; **du weißt, daß du das nicht tun sollst** you know that you shouldn't *or* are not supposed to do that; **sie sagte, daß das nicht mehr vorkommen soll** she said it wouldn't happen again; **[sagen Sie ihm,] er soll hereinkommen** tell him to come in; **der soll mir nur mal kommen, dem werde ich's schon zeigen!** *(ugs.)* just let him come and I'll show him what for! *(sl.)*; **und da soll man nicht böse werden/nicht lachen** and I'm not supposed to get angry/laugh; **ich soll dir schöne Grüße von Herrn Meier bestellen** Herr Meier asked me to give you *or* sends his best wishes; **b)** *(bei Wunsch, Absicht, Vorhaben)* **es soll ihm nützen** may it be of use to him; **du sollst dich hier wie zu Hause fühlen** I/we should like you to feel at home here; **niemand soll sagen, daß ich meine Pflicht vernachlässigt hätte** let no one say *or* no one shall say [that] I neglected my duty; **das soll dich doch nicht stören** don't let it bother you; ~ **wir heute ein wenig früher gehen?** should we leave a little earlier today?; **du sollst alles haben, was du brauchst** you shall have everything you require; **der Schal soll zum Mantel passen** the scarf is to *or* should match the coat; **er hat alles für sich behalten; soll er doch!** *(ugs. abwertend)* he has kept everything to himself; well, let him, if he wants to!; **das sollte ein Witz sein** that was meant to be a joke; **was soll denn das heißen?** what is that supposed to mean?; **wozu soll denn das gut sein?** what's the good of that?; **c)** *(bei Ratlosigkeit)* **was soll ich nur machen?** what am I to do?; **was soll nur aus ihm werden?** what is to become of him?; **er wußte nicht, wie er aus der Situation herauskommen sollte** he didn't know how to get out of the situation; **d)** *(Notwendigkeit ausdrückend)* **man soll so etwas nicht unterschätzen** it's not to be taken *or* it shouldn't be taken so lightly; **e)** *häufig im Konjunktiv II (Erwartung, Wünschenswertes ausdrückend)* **du solltest dich schämen** you ought to be ashamed of yourself; **das hättest du besser nicht tun** ~: it would have been better if you hadn't done that; **mit deiner Erkältung solltest du besser zu Hause bleiben** with your cold you had better stay at home; **wie sollte ich das wissen?** how was I to know that?; **f)** *(jmdm. beschieden sein)* **er sollte seine Heimat nicht wiedersehen** he was never to see his homeland again; **es hat nicht sein** ~ *od.* **nicht** ~ **sein** it was not to be; **es sollte ganz anders kommen, als man erwartet hatte** things were to turn out quite differently than expected; **g)** *im Konjunktiv II (eine Möglichkeit ausdrückend)* **sollte es regnen, [dann] bleiben wir zu Hause** if it should rain, we will stay at home; **sollte ich mich geirrt haben, tut es mir leid** if I have made *or* should I have made a mistake, I'm sorry; **wenn du ihn sehen solltest, sage ihm bitte ...:** if you should see him, please tell him ...; **ich versuche es, und sollte ich auch verlieren** *(geh.)* I'll try, even though I may lose; **h)** *im Präsens (sich für die Wahrheit nicht verbürgend)* **das Restaurant soll sehr teuer sein** the restaurant is supposed *or* said to be very expensive; **wir** ~ **eine Gehaltserhöhung bekommen** we are supposed to be getting a pay rise; **das soll vorkommen** things like that can happen; **i)** *im Konjunktiv II (Zweifel ausdrückend)* **sollte das sein Ernst sein?** is he really being serious?; **sollte das wirklich wahr sein?** is that really true?; **j)** *(können)* **mir soll es gleich sein** it's all the same to me; it doesn't matter to me; **man sollte glauben, daß ...:** you would think that ...; **so etwas soll es geben** it's not unheard of. **2.** *tr., itr. V.* **was soll das?** what's the idea?; **Was soll's? Ich kann ja doch nichts ändern** So what? I can't change anything anyway; **Soll ich? – Ja, du sollst!** Should I? – Yes, you should!; **was soll ich dort?** what would I do there?; **was soll der Unsinn?** what's all this nonsense about?; **warum soll ich das?** why am I to do that?; why should I do that?; **was man nicht alles soll/sollte!** the things one has to do!/is supposed to do!
Söller ['zœlɐ] **der;** ~**s,** ~ *(Archit.)* balcony
Soll-: ~**seite die** *(Kaufmansspr., Bankw.)* debit side; ~**zinsen** *Pl.* interest *sing.* on [one's] debit balance
Solmisation [zɔlmiza'tsi̯o:n] **die;** ~ *(Musik)* solmization
solo ['zo:lo] *indekl. Adj.; nicht attr.* **a)** *(bes. Musik: als Solist)* solo; **b)** *(ugs., oft scherzh.: ohne Begleitung)* on one's own *postpos.*
Solo ['zo:lo] **das;** ~**s,** ~**s** *od.* **Soli** ['zo:li] **a)** *(bes. Musik)* solo; **b)** *(bes. Fußballjargon)* solo run
Solo-: ~**gesang der** solo; ~**tänzer der,** ~**tänzerin die** soloist
Sol·quelle die salt-water *or* brine spring
solvent [zɔl'vɛnt] *Adj. (bes. Wirtsch.)* solvent
Solvenz [zɔl'vɛnts] **die;** ~, ~**en** *(bes. Wirtsch.)* solvency
Somalia [zo'ma:li̯a] **(das);** ~**s** Somalia
Somalier der; ~**s,** ~, **Somalierin die;** ~, ~**nen** Somali
somatisch [zo'ma:tɪʃ] *Adj. (Physiol.)* somatic
Sombrero [zɔm'bre:ro] **der;** ~**s,** ~**s** sombrero
so·mit [auch: '--] *Adv.* consequently; therefore; **... und somit kommen wir zu Punkt 3** ... and so *or* thus we come to number 3
Sommer ['zɔmɐ] **der;** ~**s,** ~: summer; *s. auch* **Frühling**
Sommer-: ~**abend der** summer['s] evening; ~**anfang der** beginning of summer; ~**an·zug der** summer suit; ~**fahr·plan der** summer timetable; ~**fell das** summer coat; ~**ferien** *Pl.* summer holidays; ~**frische die** *(veralt.)* **a)** *(Aufenthalt)* summer holiday; ~**frische machen** be on one's summer holiday; **b)** *(Ort)* summer [holiday] resort; ~**frischler der;** ~**s,** ~ *(veralt.)* summer holiday-maker; ~**gast der** summer

visitor *or* holiday-maker; **~getreide das** *(Landw.)* summer cereal *or* corn; **~halbjahr das** summer season; **~haus das** [summer] holiday house; **~kleid das** summer dress; **~kleidung die** summer clothes *pl. or* clothing

sommerlich 1. *Adj.* summer; summery ⟨*warmth, weather*⟩; summer's *attrib.* ⟨*day, evening*⟩; **draußen ist es schon ganz ~:** it is already quite summery outside. **2.** *adv.* **es war oft schon ~ warm** it was often as warm as summer; **sich ~ kleiden** wear summer clothes

Sommer-: ~loch das *(ugs.)* summer recess; **~mantel der** summer coat; **~mode die** summer fashions *pl.; (eines Modehauses)* summer collection; **~monat der** summer month; **~nacht die** summer['s] night; **~olympiade die** Summer Olympics *pl.;* **~pause die** summer break; *(im Parlament)* summer recess; **das Theater hat ~pause** the theatre is closed for the summer; **~reifen der** standard tyre; **~residenz die** summer residence

sommers *Adv.* in summer

sommer-, Sommer-: ~saison die summer season; **~schluß·verkauf der** summer sale/sales; **wann ist ~schlußverkauf?** when are the summer sales?; **~semester das** summer semester; **~sonnen·wende die** summer solstice; **~spiele** *Pl.* **a)** *(Theater)* summer festival *sing.;* **b)** *(Olympische ~spiele)* Summer Olympics; **~sprosse die** freckle; **~sprossig** *Adj.* freckled; **~tag der** summer['s] day; **~wetter das** summer weather; **~zeit die a)** *o. Pl. (Jahreszeit)* summer-time; **zur ~zeit** in summer-time; **b)** *(Uhrzeit)* summer time

Somnambulismus der; ~ *(Med.)* somnambulism *no art.*

son [zo:n] *Demonstrativpron. (salopp)* **~e nette Person/~ altes Haus** such a nice person/an old house; **~ Idiot!** what an idiot!

so·nach *Adv. (veralt.)* therefore; consequently

Sonate [zo'na:tə] **die; ~, ~n** *(Musik)* sonata

Sonatine die; ~, ~n *(Musik)* sonatina

Sonde ['zɔndə] **die; ~, ~n a)** *(Med.) (zur Untersuchung)* probe; *(zur Ernährung)* tube; **b)** *(Raum~)* [space] probe

sonder ['zɔndɐ] *Präp. mit Akk. (veralt.)* without; **~ Zahl** innumerable

Sonder-: ~ab·schreibung die *(Wirtsch., Steuerw.) (das Abschreiben)* special amortization; *(Betrag)* special depreciation provision; **~an·fertigung die** special design; **das Auto ist eine ~anfertigung** the car has been custom-built *or* specially made; **~angebot das** special offer; **etw. im ~angebot anbieten** have a special offer on sth.; **~aus·gabe die a)** special edition; **b)** *(Steuerw.: private Aufwendungen)* tax-deductible expenditure *(e.g. pensions, insurance contributions, interest payment);* **c)** *(Extraausgabe)* extra expense

sonderbar 1. *Adj.* strange; odd. **2.** *adv.* strangely; oddly

sonderbarer·weise *Adv.* strangely *or* oddly enough

Sonderbarkeit die; ~: strangeness; oddness

Sonder-: ~behandlung die a) special treatment; **b)** *(ns. verhüll.: Liquidierung)* liquidation; **~bewacher der** *(Sport)* marker; **er hat einen ~bewacher** a player has been specially assigned to mark him; **~botschafter der** ambassador extraordinary; **~druck der;** *Pl.* **~e** offprint; **~fahrt die** special excursion; **~fall der** special case; exception; **~genehmigung die** special permit

sonder·gleichen *Adv., nachgestellt* **eine Frechheit/Unverschämtheit ~:** the height of cheek/impudence; **mit einer Hartnäckigkeit ~:** with unparalleled obstinacy

Sonder-: ~kommando das special unit; **~konto das** special account

sonderlich 1. *Adj.* **a)** *(besonders groß, stark)* particular; [e]special; **b)** *(sonderbar)* strange; peculiar; odd. **2.** *adv.* **a)** *(besonders, sehr)* particularly; especially; **ihm geht es nicht ~:** he is not particularly *or (coll.)* all that well; **b)** *(sonderbar)* strangely

Sonderling der; ~s, ~e strange *or* odd person

Sonder-: ~marke die special issue [stamp]; **~maschine die** special plane *or* aircraft; **~meldung die** *(Rundf., Ferns.)* news flash; **~müll der** hazardous waste

[1]**sondern** *tr. V. (geh.)* separate **(von** from)

[2]**sondern** *Konj.* but; **nicht er hat es getan, ~ sie** 'he didn't do it, 'she did; **nicht nur ..., ~ [auch] ...:** not only ... but also ...; **Er ist kein Linguist. – Sondern?** He is not a linguist. – What is he then?; **es ist kein Original, ~ nur eine Reproduktion** it is not an original, but only a reproduction

Sonder-: ~nummer die special edition *or* issue; **~preis der** special *or* reduced price; **~reg[e]lung die** special ruling

sonders *s.* **samt 2**

Sonder-: ~schule die special school; **~stempel der** special postmark; **~urlaub der a)** *(Milit.)* special leave; **b)** *(zusätzlicher Urlaub)* special *or* extra holiday; **~wunsch der** special request *or* wish; **~ziehungs·rechte** *Pl. (Wirtsch.)* special drawing rights; **~zug der** special train

sondieren [zɔn'di:rən] *tr. V.* **a)** sound out; **das Terrain ~:** see *or* find out how the land lies; **b)** *(Med.)* probe

Sondierungs·gespräch das exploratory talks *pl.*

sone *s.* **son**

Sonett [zo'nɛt] **das; ~[e]s, ~e** sonnet

Song [sɔŋ] **der; ~s, ~s** song

Sonn·abend ['zɔn|a:bn̩t] **der** *(bes. nordd.)* Saturday; **an ~en und Sonntagen** on Saturdays and Sundays; **der verkaufsoffene** *od.* **lange ~:** Saturday on which the shops are open all day; *s. auch* **Dienstag; Dienstag-**

sonn·abends *Adv.* on Saturday[s]; *s. auch* **dienstags**

Sonne die; ~, ~n sun; *(Licht der ~)* sun[light]; **das Zimmer hat den ganzen Tag über ~:** the room gets sun[light] all day long

sonnen *refl. V.* sun oneself; **sich in etw.** *(Dat.)* **~** *(fig.)* bask in sth.

sonnen-, Sonnen-: ~anbeter der; ~s, ~ *(scherzh.)* sun-worshipper; **~auf·gang der** sunrise; **~bad das** sunbathing *no pl., no indef. art.;* **ein ~bad nehmen** sunbathe; **~baden** *itr. V.* sunbathe; **das Sonnenbaden** sunbathing *no art.;* **~bahn die** *(Astron.)* path of the sun; sun's path; **~bank die** sunbed; **~beschienen** *Adj. (geh.)* sunny; **~bestrahlung die: bestimmte Pflanzen dürfen keiner direkten ~bestrahlung ausgesetzt werden** certain plants are not supposed to be put in direct sunlight; **~blende die a)** *(Fot.)* lens-hood; **b)** *(im Auto)* sun visor; **~blume die** sunflower; **~blumen·kern der** sunflower seed; **~brand der** sunburn *no indef. art.;* **~bräune die** sun-tan; **~brille die** sun-glasses *pl.;* **~dach das** sun-canopy; **~deck das** sun-deck; **~durchflutet** *Adj. (geh.)* sunny; **~ein·strahlung die** *(Met.)* insolation; **~energie die** *(Physik)* solar energy; **~finsternis die** *(Astron.)* solar eclipse; eclipse of the sun; **~fleck der** *(Astron.)* sunspot; **~gebräunt** *Adj.* sun-tanned; **~geflecht das** *(Anat.)* solar plexus; **~gott der** *(Rel.)* sun-god; **~hut der** sun-hat; **~klar** *Adj. (ugs.)* crystal-clear; **die Sache ist ~klar, er ist der Dieb** he is the thief – it's as clear as daylight; **~kollektor der** *(Energietechnik)* solar collector; **~kraft·werk das** solar power station; **~licht das** sunlight; **~öl das** sun-tan oil; sun-oil; **~schein der a)** *o. Pl.* sunshine; **bei ~schein** in sunshine; **bei ~schein steigen die Temperaturen bis auf 24 °C** where the sun shines temperatures will rise to 24 °C; **b)** *(fam.: geliebtes Kind)* [little] ray of sunshine; **~schirm der** sunshade; *(zum Tragen)* parasol; sunshade; **~schutz·creme die** suntan lotion; **~segel das a)** *(Schutzdach)* awning; **b)** *(bei Raumflugkörpern)* solar sail; **~seite die** sunny side; **die ~seite des Lebens** *(fig.)* the bright side of life; **~stich der** *(Med.)* sunstroke *no indef. art.;* **du hast wohl einen ~stich** *(fig. salopp)* you must be mad; **~strahl der** ray of sun[shine]; **~system das** *(Astron.)* solar system; **~tag der a)** sunny day; day of sunshine; **b)** *(Astron.)* solar day; **~tau der** *(Bot.)* sundew; **~uhr die** sundial; **~unter·gang der** sunset; **~wende die** solstice; **~wind der** *(Astron.)* solar wind; **~zelle die** *(Physik, Elektrot.)* solar cell

sonnig *Adj.* **a)** sunny; *(fig.)* happy ⟨*youth, childhood, time*⟩; cheerful ⟨*sense of humour, ways*⟩; **b)** *(iron.: naiv)* naive

Sonn·tag der Sunday; *s. auch* **Dienstag; Dienstag-**

sonn·täglich 1. *Adj.* Sunday *attrib.* **2.** *adv.* **~ gekleidet sein** be dressed in one's Sunday best

sonntags *Adv.* on Sunday[s]; *s. auch* **dienstags**

Sonntags-: ~arbeit die; *o. Pl.* Sunday working *no art.;* **~aus·flug der** Sunday outing; **~aus·gabe die** Sunday issue *or* edition; **~bei·lage die** Sunday supplement; **~braten der** Sunday roast; **~dienst der** Sunday duty; **~fahrer der** *(abwertend)* Sunday driver; **~kind das a)** Sunday's child; **b)** *(Glückskind)* lucky person; **er ist ein ~kind** he was born lucky *or* under a lucky star; **~predigt die** Sunday sermon; **~reden** *Pl. (abwertend)* soap-box oratory *no pl., no art.;* **~schule die** Sunday school; **~staat der;** *o. Pl. (scherzh.)* Sunday best; **im ~staat** in one's Sunday best; **~zeitung die** Sunday [news]paper

Sonnwend·feier die midsummer/midwinter festival *or* celebrations *pl.*

Sonny·boy ['sʌnɪ-] **der; ~s, ~s** golden boy

sonor [zo'no:ɐ̯] *Adj.* sonorous

sonst [zɔnst] *Adv.* **a) der ~ so freundliche Mann ...:** the man, who is/was usually so friendly, ...; **er hat es wie ~ gemacht/besser als ~ gemacht** he did it as usual/better than usual; **alles war wie ~:** everything was [the same] as usual; **war das auch ~ so?** has it always been like that?; **~ war alles unverändert** otherwise nothing had changed; **wie geht's ~?** how are things otherwise?; **haben Sie ~ noch Fragen?** have you any other questions?; **kommt ~ noch jemand** *od.* **wer?** is anybody else coming?; **es wußte ~ niemand** nobody *or* no one else knew; **hat er ~ nichts erzählt?** [apart from that,] he didn't say anything else?; **er war ganz gut in Mathematik, aber ~?** he was quite good in mathematics, but apart from that?; **~ noch was?** *(ugs., auch iron.)* anything else?; **~ nichts, nichts ~:** nothing else; **und wer weiß wer ~ noch** and goodness knows who else; **[aber] ~ geht's dir gut** *od.* **~ tut dir nichts weh?** *(salopp iron.)* anything else [you'd want]? *(iron.);* **wer/was/wie/wo [denn] ~?** who/what/how/where else?; **b)** *(andernfalls)* otherwise; or

sonstig... *Adj.; nicht präd.* other; further; **sein ~es Verhalten war gut** his behaviour was otherwise good; **„Sonstiges"** 'miscellaneous'

sonst-: ~jemand *Indefinitpron. (ugs.)* somebody else; *(fragend, verneinend)* anybody else; **da könnte ja ~jemand kommen** anybody could *or* might come; **~was** *Indefinitpron. (ugs.)* anything else; **er hat ~was unternommen** he has tried all sorts of things; **man hätte annehmen können, die Kinder hätten ~was angestellt** you would have thought the children had done something terrible; **~wer** *Indefinitpron. (ugs.)* somebody else; *(fragend, verneinend)* anybody else; **er meint, er ist ~wer** he thinks he's really something *(coll.)*; he thinks he's the bee's knees *(coll.)*; **~wie** *Adv. (ugs.)* in some other way; *(fragend, verneinend)* in any other way; **~wo** *Adv. (ugs.)* somewhere else; *(fragend, verneinend)* anywhere else; **~woher** *Adv. (ugs.)* [from] somewhere else; *(fragend, verneinend)* [from] anywhere else; **~wohin** *Adv. (ugs.)* somewhere else; *(fragend, verneinend)* anywhere else

so · ọft *Konj.* whenever; **ich komme, ~ du es wünschst** I'll come as often as you wish

Soor [zo:ɐ̯] **der; ~[e]s, ~e** *(Med.)* thrush *no art.*

Sophismus [zo'fɪsmʊs] **der; ~, Sophismen** *(Philos.)* sophism

Sophisterei die; ~, ~en *(abwertend)* sophistry

Sophistik die; ~ *(Philos.)* sophistry

sophistisch 1. *Adj.* sophistic[al]. **2.** *adv.* sophistically

Sophokles ['zo:foklɛs] **der; Sophokles'** Sophocles

Sopran [zo'pra:n] **der; ~s, ~e** *(Musik)* **a)** *(Stimmlage)* soprano [voice]; **b)** *o. Pl. (im Chor)* sopranos *pl.*; **c)** *(Sängerin)* soprano

Sopranist der; ~en, ~en sopranist

Sopranistin die; ~, ~nen soprano

Sorbe ['zɔrbə] **der; ~n, ~n** Sorb

Sorbet ['zɔrbɛt] **der** *od.* **das; ~s, ~s** *(Gastr.)* sorbet

Sore ['zo:rə] **die; ~, ~n** *(Gaunerspr.)* loot

Sorge ['zɔrgə] **die; ~, ~n a)** *o. Pl. (Unruhe, Angst)* worry; **keine ~:** don't [you] worry; **[keine] ~ haben, daß ...:** [not] be worried that ...; **in ~ um jmdn./etw. sein** be worried about sb./sth.; **etw. erfüllt jmdn. mit ~:** sth. worries sb.; **b)** *(sorgenvoller Gedanke)* worry; **ich mache mir ~n um dich/um deine Gesundheit** I am worried about you/about your health; **mach dir darum** *od.* **darüber** *od.* **deswegen keine ~:** don't worry about that; **der hat ~n!** *(ugs. iron.)* and he thinks 'he's got problems *(coll. iron.)*; **lassen Sie das meine ~ sein** let 'me worry about that; **er ertränkte seine ~n im Alkohol** he drowned his sorrows in alcohol; **c)** *o. Pl. (Mühe, Fürsorge)* care; **die ~ für die Familie** caring for the family; **die ~ um das tägliche Brot** the worry of providing one's daily bread; **für etw./***(schweiz. auch:)* **einer Sache** *(Dat.)* **~ tragen** *(geh.)* take care of sth.; **ich werde dafür ~ tragen, daß ...:** I will see to it *or* make sure that ...; **das laß nur meine ~ sein** let that be 'my concern *or* responsibility

sọrgen 1. *refl. V.* worry, be worried (**um** about); **sie sorgt sich wegen jeder Kleinigkeit** she worries about every little detail. **2.** *itr. V.* **a) für jmdn./etw. ~:** take care of *or* look after sb./sth.; **für das Essen/Ruhe und Ordnung/gute Laune ~:** look after the food/make sure that law and order prevail/make sure that people are in a good mood; **für die Zukunft der Kinder ist gesorgt** the children's future is provided for; **b)** *(verblaßt: bewirken)* **für etw. ~:** cause sth.

sọrgen-, Sọrgen-: ~frei 1. *Adj.* carefree ⟨*person, future, existence, etc.*⟩; **2.** *adv.* **~frei leben** live in a carefree manner; **~kind das** *(auch fig.)* problem child; **~voll 1.** *Adj.* worried; anxious; **2.** *adv.* worriedly; anxiously

Sọrge-: ~pflicht die; *o. Pl.* **eine ~pflicht gegenüber seinen Kindern haben** have a duty to provide for one's children; **~recht das;** *o. Pl. (Rechtsw.)* custody (**für** of)

Sọrg · falt ['zɔrkfalt] **die; ~:** care; **große ~ auf etw.** *(Akk.)* **verwenden** *od.* **legen** take great *or* a great deal of care over sth.

sọrg · fältig 1. *Adj.* careful; **eine ~e Arbeit** a job/piece of work done with care. **2.** *adv.* carefully

Sọrgfältigkeit die; ~: carefulness

Sọrgfalts · pflicht die duty of care

sọrg · los 1. *Adj.* **a)** *(ohne Sorgfalt)* careless; **b)** *(unbekümmert)* carefree. **2.** *adv.* **~ mit etw. umgehen** treat sth. carelessly

Sọrglosigkeit die; ~ a) *(Mangel an Sorgfalt)* carelessness; **b)** *(Unbekümmertheit)* carefreeness

sọrgsam 1. *Adj.* careful. **2.** *adv.* carefully

Sorte ['zɔrtə] **die; ~, ~n a)** sort; type; kind; *(Marke)* brand; **bitte ein Pfund von der besten ~:** a pound of the best quality, please; **b)** *Pl. (Devisen)* foreign currency *sing.*

Sọrten · kurs der *(Bankw.)* exchange rate

sortieren *tr. V.* sort [out] ⟨*pictures, letters, washing, etc.*⟩; grade ⟨*goods etc.*⟩; *(fig.)* arrange ⟨*thoughts*⟩; **die Stücke werden nach der Größe sortiert** the pieces are sorted according to size

Sortier · maschine die sorter; sorting-machine

sortiert *Adj.* **a) ein gut/schlecht ~es Lager** a well-stocked/badly stocked warehouse; **dieses Geschäft ist sehr gut in französischen Rotweinen ~:** this shop has a good range of French red wines; **b)** *(erlesen)* selected

Sortiment [zɔrti'mɛnt] **das; ~[e]s, ~e a)** range (**an** + *Dat.* of); **b)** *(Buchhandel)* retail book trade

Sortimenter der; ~s, ~, Sortimenterin die; ~, ~nen retail bookseller; book retailer

Sortiments-: ~buch · handel der retail book trade; **~buch · handlung die** retail bookshop

SOS [ɛs/o:'/ɛs] **das; ~:** SOS; **~ funken** send *or* put out an SOS

so · sehr *Konj.* however much

so · so 1. *Interj.* **a)** *(ironisch, zweifelnd)* I see; **b)** *(gleichgültig)* oh yes?; really? **2.** *Adv. (ugs.)* so-so

SOS-Ruf [ɛs/o:'/ɛs-] **der** SOS [call]

Soße ['zo:sə] **die; ~, ~n a)** sauce; *(Braten~)* gravy; sauce; *(Salat~)* dressing; **b)** *(salopp abwertend: schmutzige Flüssigkeit)* muck *(coll.)*

Soßen-: ~löffel der gravy- *or* sauce-ladle; **~schüssel die** gravy- *or* sauce-boat

sott [zɔt] *1. u. 3. Pers. Sg. Prät. v.* **sieden**

Soubrette [zu'brɛtə] **die; ~, ~n** *(Musik, Theater)* soubrette

Soufflé [zu'fle:] **das; ~s, ~s** *(Gastr.)* soufflé

Souffleur [zu'flø:ɐ̯] **der; ~s, ~e** *(Theater)* prompter

Souffleur · kasten der prompt-box

Souffleuse [zu'flø:zə] **die; ~, ~n** prompter

soufflieren [zu'fli:rən] *tr. V.* prompt; **jmdm. etw. ~:** prompt sb. by whispering sth.

Soul · musik ['soʊl-] **die** soul music

so · und · so 1. *Adv.; vorangestellt* **~ groß/breit/lang** [of] such-and-such a size/width/length; **~ viel kosten** cost such-and-such; cost so-and-so much. **2.** *Adj.; nachgestellt* **Paragraph ~:** paragraph such-and-such *or* so-and-so; **Fanny ~:** Fanny something-or-other; **die Soundso** what's-her-name

Souper [zu'pe:] **das; ~s, ~s** *(geh.)* dinner[-party]

soupieren *itr. V. (geh.)* dine

Soutane [zu'ta:nə] **die; ~, ~n** soutane

Souterrain ['zu:tɛrɛ̃] **das; ~s, ~s** basement

Souvenir [zuvə'ni:ɐ̯] **das; ~s, ~s** souvenir

souverän [zuvə'rɛ:n] **1.** *Adj.* **a)** *(unabhängig)* sovereign; **b)** *(geh.: überlegen)* superior. **2.** *adv.* **die Lage ~ meistern** be in total command of the situation; **er siegte ganz ~:** he won in a very impressive way

Souverän der; ~s, ~e a) *(Herrscher, Fürst)* sovereign; **b)** *(schweiz.: die Stimmbürger)* electorate

Souveränität die; ~ sovereignty

so · viel 1. *Konj.* **a)** *(nach dem, was)* as *or* so far as; **~ mir bekannt ist** so far as I know; **~ ich sehe** as far as I can see; **b)** *(in wie großem Maße auch immer)* however much. **2.** *Indefinitpron.* **~ wie** *od.* **als** as much as; **das war ~ wie eine Zusage** that was tantamount to a commitment; **das ist ~ wie gar nichts** this is almost nothing; **nimm, ~ [wie] du willst** take as much as you like; **noch einmal ~:** the same again; **halb/doppelt ~:** half/twice as much; **~ für heute** *(ugs.)* that's all *or* enough for today

Sowchose ['zɔfço:zə] **die; ~, ~n** sovkhoz

so · weit 1. *Konj.* **a)** *(nach dem, was)* as *or* so far as; **~ mir bekannt ist** so far as I know; **~ ich sehe** as far as I can see; **b)** *(in dem Maße, wie)* [in] so far as; **~ ich dazu in der Lage bin, will ich gerne helfen** [in] so far as I am in a position to do so *or* am able to, I should like to help. **2.** *Adv.* by and large; on the whole; *(bis jetzt)* up to now; **~ wie** *od.* **als möglich** as far as possible; **~ sein** *(ugs.)* be ready; **es ist ~:** the time has come

so · wenig 1. *Konj.* however little. **2.** *Indefinitpron.* **~ wie** *od.* **als möglich** as little as possible; **ich kann es ~ wie du** I can't do it any more than you can

so · wie *Konj.* **a)** *(und auch)* as well as; **b)** *(sobald)* as soon as

so · wie · so *Adv.* anyway; **das ~!** *(ugs.)* that goes without saying!; of course!; **Herr Sowieso** Mr What's-his-name

Sowjet [zɔ'vjɛt] **der; ~s, ~s a)** *(Behörde)* soviet; **der Oberste ~:** the Supreme Soviet; **b)** *Pl. (Führung)* Soviets; Russians

Sowjet-: ~armee die; *o. Pl.* Soviet army; **~bürger der** Soviet citizen

sowjetisch *Adj.* Soviet

sowjetisieren *tr. V.* sovietize

Sowjet · mensch der Soviet citizen

Sowjetologie die; ~: sovietology *no art.*

Sowjet-: ~republik die a) *(Gliedstaat)* Soviet republic; **Union der Sozialistischen ~republiken** Union of Soviet Socialist Republics; **b)** *(hist.)* soviet republic; **~russe der** Soviet Russian; **~stern der** Soviet star; star of the Soviets; **~union die** Soviet Union; **~zone die** *(hist.)* Soviet zone

so · wohl *Konj.* **~ ... als** *od.* **wie [auch] ...:** both ... and ...; ... as well as ...

Sozi ['zo:tsi] **der; ~s, ~s** *(ugs., auch abwertend)* socialist

sozial [zo'tsi̯a:l] **1.** *Adj.* social; **die ~e Frage** *(hist.)* the social question; **~e Einrichtungen** public amenities; **ich habe heute meinen ~en Tag** *(ugs.)* I'm feeling charitable *or* generous today; **dieses Verhalten ist nicht sehr ~:** this behaviour is not very public-spirited; **~e Marktwirtschaft** social market economy. **2.** *adv.* socially; **~ denken** be socially minded; **~ handeln** act in a socially conscious *or* public-spirited way

sozial-, Sozial-: ~ab · bau der dismantling of the welfare state; **~ab · gaben** *Pl.* social welfare contributions; **~amt das** social welfare office; **~arbeit die;** *o. Pl.* social work; **~arbeiter der, ~arbeiterin die** social worker; **~beruf der** social services profession; **in ~berufen arbeiten** work for *or* in the social services; **~demokrat der** Social Democrat; **~demokratie die** social democracy *no art.*; **~demokratisch** *Adj.* social democratic; **Sozialdemokratische Partei [Deutschlands]** [German] Social Democratic Party; **~ethik die** social ethics *sing.*; **~fall der** hardship case; **~gericht das** social welfare court; **~geschichte die** social history; **~gesetz · gebung die** social welfare legislation; **~hilfe die** social welfare; **~hygiene die** community medicine; **~imperialismus der** social imperialism

Sozialisation die; ~ *(Soziol., Psych.)* socialization

sozialisieren *tr. V.* **a)** *(Wirtsch.: vergesellschaften)* nationalize; **b)** *(Soziol., Psych.:*

zum Gemeinschaftsleben befähigen) socialize
Sozialismus der; ~ socialism *no art.*
Sozialist der; ~en, ~en, Sozialistin die; ~, ~nen socialist
sozialistisch 1. *Adj.* socialist. **2. ~ regierte Länder** countries with socialist governments
sozial-, Sozial-: ~kritisch *Adj.* socially critical; critical of society *postpos.;* **~kunde die;** *o. Pl.* social studies *sing., no art.;* **~leistungen** *Pl.* social welfare benefits; **~liberal** *Adj.* **a)** *(sozial und liberal)* liberal socialist ‹*politician etc.*›; **b)** *(aus SPD und FDP)* liberal-social democrat ‹*coalition etc.*›; **~pädagogik die** social education *no art.;* **~partner der: die ~partner** employers and employees *or* trade unions; **~plan der** *written agreement between employer and works council which seeks to protect employees;* **~politik die** social policy; **~prestige das** social status; **~produkt das** *(Wirtsch.)* national product; **~psychologie die** social psychology *no art.;* **~rente die** state pension; **~rentner der** old-age pensioner; **~staat der** welfare state; **~struktur die** social structure; **~union die** unified social welfare system; *s. auch* **Währungsunion; ~versicherung die** social security; **~wissenschaft die** social science *no art.;* **die ~wissenschaften** the social sciences; **~wohnung die** ≈ council flat *(Brit.);* municipal housing unit *(Amer.)*
Sozietät [zotsie'tɛ:t] **die; ~, ~en a)** *(Soziol.)* society *no art.;* **b)** *(Verhaltensf.)* society; social unit; **c)** *(gemeinsame Praxis)* joint practice
sozio·kulturell *Adj.* sociocultural
Soziolekt [zotsio'lɛkt] **der; ~[e]s, ~e** *(Sprachw.)* sociolect; social dialect
Sozio·linguistik die sociolinguistics *sing.*
Soziologe [zotsio'lo:gə] **der; ~n, ~n** sociologist
Soziologie die; ~: sociology; **die ~ lehrt uns, daß ...:** sociology teaches us that ...
Soziologin die; ~, ~nen sociologist
soziologisch 1. *Adj.* sociological. **2.** *adv.* sociologically
sozio·ökonomisch *Adj.* socio-economic
Sozius ['zo:tsiʊs] **der; ~, ~se a)** *Pl. auch:* Sozii ['zo:tsii] *(Wirtsch.: Teilhaber)* partner; **b)** *(beim Motorrad)* pillion
Sozius·sitz der pillion
so·zu·sagen *Adv.* so to speak; as it were; **es geschah ~ offiziell** it took place officially, so to speak *or* as it were
Spachtel ['ʃpaxtl̩] **der; ~s, ~** *od.* **die; ~, ~n a)** *(für Kitt)* putty-knife; *(zum Abkratzen von Farbe)* paint-scraper; *(zum Malen)* palette-knife; spatula; **b)** *(~masse)* filler
Spachtel·masse die filler
spachteln *tr. V.* **a)** stop, fill ‹*hole, crack, etc.*›; smooth over ‹*wall, panel, surface, etc.*›; smooth ‹*filler, putty*› **(in +** *Akk.* into); apply ‹*paints*› with a palette-knife; **b)** *(ugs.: essen)* put away *(coll.)* ‹*food, meal*›
[1]**Spagat** [spa'ga:t] *der od.* **das; ~[e]s, ~e** splits *pl.;* **[einen] ~ machen** do the splits
[2]**Spagat der; ~[e]s, ~e** *(südd., österr.)* string
[1]**Spaghetti** [ʃpa'gɛti] *Pl.* spaghetti *sing.*
[2]**Spaghetti der; ~[s], ~s** *(salopp abwertend) s.* **Spaghettifresser**
Spaghetti-: ~fresser der *(salopp abwertend)* Eyetie *(sl. derog.);* wop *(sl. derog.);* **~träger der** *(Mode)* spaghetti strap
spähen ['ʃpɛ:ən] *itr. V.* peer; *(durch ein Loch, eine Ritze usw.)* peep
Späher der; ~s, ~ *(Milit.)* scout; *(Posten)* look-out; *(Spitzel)* informer
Späh·trupp der *(Milit.)* reconnaissance *or* scouting patrol *or* party
Spalett [ʃpa:lɛt] **das; ~[e]s, ~e** *(österr.)* [wooden] shutter
Spalier [ʃpa'li:ɐ̯] **das; ~s, ~e a)** trellis; *(für Obstbäume)* espalier; **b)** *(aus Menschen)* double line; *(Ehren~)* guard of honour; **~ stehen** line the route; ‹*soldiers*› form a guard of honour
Spalier·obst das a) *(Früchte)* espalier fruit; **b)** *(Pflanzen)* espalier
Spalt [ʃpalt] **der; ~[e]s, ~e** opening; *(im Fels)* fissure; crevice; *(zwischen Vorhängen)* chink; gap; *(langer Riß)* crack; **die Tür einen ~ [weit] öffnen** open the door a crack *or* slightly; **einen ~ [weit] offen sein** ‹*door*› be open a crack, be *or* stand slightly ajar
spalt-, Spalt-: ~bar *Adj. (Physik)* fissionable ‹*material, element, etc.*›; **~breit** *Adj.* narrow ‹*opening*›; **~breit der** crack
Spalte die; ~, ~n a) crack; *(Fels~)* crevice; cleft; *(Gletscher~)* crevasse; crack; **b)** *(Druckw.: Druck~)* column; **c)** *(derb: Scham-, Gesäßspalte)* crack *(coarse);* **d)** *(österr.: Scheibe)* slice
spalten 1. *unr. (auch regelm.) tr. V.* **a)** *(auch Physik, fig.)* split; **Holz ~:** chop wood; **b)** *(Chemie)* split; break down. **2.** *unr. (auch regelm.) refl. V.* **a)** *(auch Physik, fig.)* split; **b)** *(Chemie)* split; break down
-spaltig *adj. (Druckw.)* -column
Spalt-: ~pilz der a) *(Biol.)* bacterium; **b)** *(fig.)* divisive tendency; **~produkt das** *(Physik)* fission product
Spaltung die; ~, ~en a) *(auch fig.)* splitting; *(fig.: durch eine Grenze)* division; **b)** *(fig.: das Gespaltensein)* split (*Gen.* in; **zwischen +** *Dat.* between); *(durch eine Grenze)* division; **c)** *(Physik)* fission; splitting; **d)** *(Chemie)* splitting; breaking down
Span [ʃpa:n] **der; ~[e]s, Späne** ['ʃpɛ:nə] *(Hobel~)* shaving; *(Feil~)* filing *usu. in pl.; (beim Bohren)* boring *usu. in pl.; (beim Drehen)* turning *usu. in pl.; (zum Feueranzünden)* splint; **feine [Metall]späne** swarf *sing.;* **wo gehobelt wird, [da] fallen Späne** *(Spr.)* you cannot make an omelette without breaking eggs *(prov.)*
spänen ['ʃpɛ:nən] *tr. V. (Technik)* scour with steel wool
Span·ferkel das sucking pig
Spange ['ʃpaŋə] **die; ~, ~n** clasp; *(Haar~)* hair-slide *(Brit.);* barrette *(Amer.); (Arm~)* bracelet; bangle
Spangen·schuh der strap shoe
Spaniel ['ʃpa:niəl] **der; ~s, ~s** spaniel
Spanien ['ʃpa:niən] **(das); ~s** Spain
Spanier ['ʃpa:niɐ] **der; ~s, ~:** Spaniard; **die ~:** the Spanish *or* Spaniards; **seid ihr ~?** are you Spanish?; **stolz wie ein ~** *(scherzh.)* as proud as a peacock
spanisch 1. *Adj.* Spanish; **das kommt mir/dir** *usw.* **~ vor** *(ugs.)* that strikes me/you *etc.* as odd. **2.** *adv.* **sich ~ unterhalten** talk Spanish; *s. auch* **deutsch; Deutsch; Reiter a; Rohr c; Wand b**
Span·korb der chip basket; chip
spann [ʃpan] *1. u. 3. P. Sing. Prät. v.* **spinnen**
Spann der; ~[e]s, ~e instep
Spann·beton der *(Bauw.)* pre-stressed concrete
Spanne die; ~, ~n a) *(Zeit~)* span of time; **eine ~ von 12 Tagen/fünfzig Jahren** a period of twelve days/span *or* period of fifty years; **b)** *(veralt.: Längenmaß)* span; **c)** *(Handels~)* margin
spannen 1. *tr. V.* **a)** tighten, tauten ‹*violin string, violin bow, etc.*›; draw ‹*bow*›; tension ‹*spring, tennis net, drumhead, saw-blade*›; stretch ‹*fabric, shoe, etc.*›; draw *or* pull ‹*line*› tight *or* taut; tense, flex ‹*muscle*›; cock ‹*gun, camera shutter*›; **eine Kamera ~:** cock the shutter on a camera; **seine Nerven waren zum Zerreißen gespannt** *(fig.)* his nerves were stretched to breaking-point; **b)** *(befestigen)* put up ‹*washing-line*›; stretch ‹*net, wire, tarpaulin, etc.*› **(über +** *Akk.* over); **einen Bogen Papier in die Schreibmaschine ~:** insert *or* put a sheet of paper in the typewriter; **etw. in einen Schraubstock ~:** clamp sth. in a vice; **c)** *(schirren)* hitch up, harness **(vor, an +** *Akk.* to); **d)** *(bes. südd., österr.: merken)* notice; *s. auch* **Lage c. 2.** *refl. V.* **a)** become *or* go taut; ‹*muscles*› tense; **b)** *(geh.: sich wölben)* **sich über etw.** *(Akk.)* **~** ‹*bridge, rainbow*› span sth. **3.** *itr. V.* **a)** *(zu eng sein)* ‹*clothing*› be [too] tight; ‹*skin*› be taut; **b) auf jmdn./etw. ~** *(ugs.) (warten)* wait [impatiently] for sb./sth.; *(lauern)* lie in wait for sb./sth.
spannend 1. *Adj.* exciting; *(stärker)* thrilling; **mach's nicht so ~!** *(ugs.)* don't keep me/us in suspense. **2.** *adv.* excitingly; *(stärker)* thrillingly
spannen·lang *Adj. (veralt.)* a span tall/in length *postpos.*
Spanner der; ~s, ~ a) *(Schuh~)* shoe-tree; *(Stiefel~)* boot-tree; *(Hosen~)* [trouser-] hanger; *(Gardinen~)* curtain-stretcher; *(für Tennisschläger)* [racket-]press; **b)** *(Zool.)* geometer; **c)** *(ugs.: Voyeur)* peeping Tom
Spann·kraft die; *o. Pl.* vigour
Spannung die; ~, ~en a) *o. Pl.* excitement; *(Neugier)* suspense; tension; **jmdn. mit** *od.* **voll ~ erwarten** await sb. eagerly; **b)** *o. Pl. (eines Romans, Films usw.)* suspense; **c)** *(Zwistigkeit, Nervosität)* tension; **d)** *(das Straffsein)* tension; tautness; **e)** *(elektrische ~)* tension; *(Voltzahl)* voltage; **unter ~ stehen** be live; **f)** *(Mechanik)* stress
spannungs-, Spannungs-: ~gebiet das *(Politik)* area of tension; **~geladen** *Adj.* **a)** *(gespannt)* ‹*atmosphere etc.*› charged with tension; **b)** *(spannend)* ‹*novel, film, etc.*› full of suspense; **~messer der** *(Elektrot.)* voltmeter; **~verhältnis das** relationship of tension; **~zu·stand der a)** *(Psych.)* state of tension; **b)** *(Mechanik)* condition of stress
Spann·weite die a) *(Zool.: Flügel~)* [wing-]span; wing-spread; *(eines Flugzeugs)* [wing-]span; **b)** *(Bauw.)* span
Span-: ~platte die chipboard; **~schachtel die** small box made of thin strips of wood *(for storing jewellery, letters, etc.)*
Spant [ʃpant] **das** *od.* **der; ~[e]s, ~en** *(eines Schiffs)* rib; *(eines Flugzeugs)* frame; former
Spar-: ~brief der *(Bankw.)* savings certificate; **~buch das** *(Bankw.)* savings book; passbook; *(bei der Bank auch)* bank-book; **~büchse die** money-box; **~ein·lage die** *(Bankw.)* savings deposit
sparen ['ʃpa:rən] **1.** *tr. V.* save; *(zurücklegen)* save, put away ‹*money*›; **die Mühe/den Ärger hätten wir uns sparen können** we could have saved *or* spared ourselves the effort/trouble; **du kannst dir jedes Wort ~:** you can save your breath; **deine Ratschläge kannst du dir ~:** you can keep your advice. **2.** *itr. V.* **a)** *(Geld zurücklegen)* save; **für** *od.* **auf etw.** *(Akk.)* **~:** save up for sth.; **spare in der Zeit, so hast du in der Not** *(Spr.)* waste not, want not *(prov.);* **b)** *(sparsam wirtschaften)* economize **(mit** on); **er sparte nicht mit Lob** *(fig.)* he was unstinting *or* generous in his praise; **an etw.** *(Dat.)* **~** *(weniger nehmen)* be sparing with sth.; *(Billigeres nehmen)* economize on sth.; **am falschen Ort** *od.* **Ende ~:** make a false economy/false economies
Sparer der; ~s, ~, Sparerin die; ~, ~nen saver
Spar·flamme die; *o. Pl.* low flame *or* heat; **auf ~:** on a low flame *or* heat
Spargel ['ʃpargl̩] **der; ~s, ~,** *schweiz. auch* **die; ~, ~n** asparagus *no pl., no indef. art.;* **ein ~:** an asparagus stalk
Spargel-: ~creme·suppe die cream of asparagus soup; **~kraut das;** *o. Pl.* asparagus fern; **~spitze die** asparagus tip
Spar-: ~groschen der *(ugs.)* nest-egg; savings *pl.;* **~gut·haben das** credit balance *(in a savings account);* **ein ~guthaben von 500 Mark haben** have 500 marks in one's savings *or* deposit account; **~kasse die** savings bank; **~kassen·buch das** sav-

ings book; passbook; **~konto das** savings *or* deposit account
spärlich ['ʃpɛ:ɐ̯lɪç] **1.** *Adj.* sparse ⟨*vegetation, beard, growth*⟩; thin ⟨*hair, applause*⟩; scanty ⟨*left-overs, knowledge, news, evidence*⟩; scanty, skimpy ⟨*clothing*⟩; slack ⟨*demand*⟩; scattered ⟨*remains, remnants*⟩; poor ⟨*lighting, harvest, result, source*⟩; meagre ⟨*income, salary*⟩; meagre, frugal ⟨*food, meal*⟩. **2.** *adv.* sparsely, thinly ⟨*populated, covered*⟩; poorly ⟨*lit, attended*⟩; scantily, skimpily ⟨*dressed*⟩; **die Nachrichten kamen/die Geldmittel flossen nur ~:** news/money was only coming in in dribs and drabs
Spar- **~maßnahme die** economy measure; **~pfennig der** *(ugs.) s.* **~groschen; ~prämie die** savings premium; **~programm das a)** *(bes. Politik)* programme of economy measures; **b)** *(Technik)* economy programme
Sparren ['ʃparən] **der; ~s, ~ a)** *(Dach~)* rafter; **b)** *(Her.)* chevron; **c)** *(ugs.: Spleen)* daft idea; **er hat einen ~ [zuviel** *od.* **zuwenig im Kopf]** *(ugs.)* he has a screw loose *(coll.)*
Sparring ['ʃparɪŋ] **das; ~s** *(Boxen)* sparring *no art.*
Sparrings·partner der *(Boxen)* sparring partner
sparsam 1. *Adj.* **a)** thrifty ⟨*person*⟩; *(wirtschaftlich)* economical; **durch ~en Umgang mit dem Material** by being economical *or* sparing with the material; **durch ~es Wirtschaften** by economizing; **mit etw. ~ sein** be economical with sth.; **er ist mit Worten/Lob immer sehr ~** *(fig.)* he is a man of few words/he is very sparing in his praise; **b)** *(im Verbrauch)* economical; **c)** *(fig.: gering, wenig, klein)* sparse ⟨*detail, decoration, interior, etc.*⟩; economical ⟨*movement, manner of expression, etc.*⟩; **er machte von dieser Möglichkeit nur ~en Gebrauch** he made little use of this opportunity; **die Wirkung ist schon bei ~ster Dosierung groß** even the most sparing dose has a strong effect. **2.** *adv.* **a) ~ mit der Butter/dem Papier umgehen** use butter/paper sparingly; economize on butter/paper; **~ leben** live frugally; **~ mit seinen Kräften umgehen** conserve one's energy; **~ wirtschaften** economize; budget carefully; **b)** *(wirtschaftlich)* economically; **c)** *(fig.: in geringem Maße)* ⟨*use*⟩ sparingly; sparsely ⟨*decorated, furnished*⟩; **etw. ~ dosieren** use sth. in small doses
Sparsamkeit die; ~ a) thrift[iness]; **das ist ~ am falschen Platze** that's a false economy; **aus ~:** for the sake of economizing; **b)** *(Wirtschaftlichkeit)* economicalness; **c)** *(fig.: geringes Maß)* economy
Spar-: **~schwein das** piggy bank; **~strumpf der** stocking for keeping one's savings in
Spartakiade [ʃparta'ki̯a:də] **die; ~, ~n** Spartakiad
Spartakist [ʃparta'kɪst] **der; ~en, ~en** Spartacist; Spartakist
Spartaner [ʃpar'ta:nɐ] **der; ~s, ~** *(hist.)* Spartan
spartanisch 1. *Adj. (auch fig.).* Spartan. **2.** *adv.* **~ leben** lead a Spartan life
Sparte ['ʃpartə] **die; ~, ~n a)** *(Teilbereich)* area; branch; *(eines Geschäfts)* line [of business]; *(des Wissens)* branch; field; speciality; *(des Sports, der Kunst)* discipline; **b)** *(Rubrik)* section; *(Spalte)* column
Spar-: **~vertrag der** savings agreement; **~zins der;** *Pl.* **~en** interest *no pl.* on a savings account
spasmisch ['ʃpasmɪʃ] *(Med.)* **1.** *Adj.* spasmodic. **2.** *adv.* spasmodically
Spasmus ['ʃpasmʊs] **der; ~, Spasmen** *(Med.)* spasm
Spaß [ʃpa:s] **der; ~es, Späße** ['ʃpɛ:sə] **a)** *o. Pl. (Vergnügen)* fun; **wir hatten alle viel ~:** we all had a lot of fun *or* a really good time; we all really enjoyed ourselves; **~ an etw.** *(Dat.)* **haben** enjoy sth.; **verdirb ihm doch nicht seinen ~:** don't spoil his fun; **laß ihn doch, wenn er ~ dran hat!** let him, if it makes him happy; **meinetwegen, wenn du ~ daran hast** all right, if you want to; **~ an etw.** *(Dat.)* **finden** find sth. fun; **[jmdm.] ~/keinen ~ machen** be fun/no fun [for sb.]; **die Schule macht ihm großen/keinen/nicht viel ~:** he likes *or* enjoys school a great deal/doesn't like school/doesn't like school very much; **du machst mir [vielleicht] ~!** *(iron.)* you must be joking *or (sl.)* kidding; **sich** *(Dat.)* **einen ~ daraus machen, etw. zu tun** take great delight in doing sth.; **ein teurer ~** *(ugs.)* an expensive business; **was kostet der ~?** *(ugs.)* how much will that little lot cost? *(coll.)*; **viel ~!** have a good time!; *(iron.)* have fun!; **das ist kein ~!** it's no fun; **b)** *(Scherz)* joke; *(Streich)* prank; antic; **er macht nur ~:** he's only joking *or (sl.)* kidding; **~ beiseite!** joking aside *or* apart; **~ muß sein!** there's no harm in a joke; **da hört [für mich] der ~ auf** that's getting beyond a joke; **~/keinen ~ verstehen** be able/not be able to take a joke; have a/have no sense of humour; **in Gelddingen versteht er keinen ~:** he won't stand for any nonsense where money is concerned; **laß diese albernen Späße!** stop fooling around!; **er ist immer zu Späßen aufgelegt** he's always ready for a laugh; **im** *od.* **zum** *od.* **aus ~:** as a joke; for fun; **aus ~ an der Freude** *(scherzh.)* for the [sheer] fun of it; **sich** *(Dat.)* **einen ~ mit jmdm. machen** *od.* **erlauben** play a joke on sb.; **macht keine Späße!** surely you don't mean it; **aus [lauter] ~ und Tollerei** *(ugs.)* [just] for a laugh; just for the hell of it *(coll.)*; **das ist kein ~ mehr!** that's gone beyond a joke; **seine Späße mit jmdm. treiben** get a laugh at sb.'s expense
Späßchen ['ʃpɛ:sçən] **das; ~s, ~:** little joke
spaßen ['ʃpa:sn̩] *itr. V.* **a)** *(Spaß machen)* joke; kid *(coll.)*; **Sie ~ wohl!** you must be joking *or (coll.)* kidding; **b) er läßt nicht mit sich ~:** he won't stand for any nonsense; **mit ihm/damit ist nicht zu ~:** he/it is not to be trifled with; **mit so einer Entzündung ist nicht zu ~:** an inflammation like that shouldn't be shrugged off lightly
spaßes·halber *Adv.* for the fun of it; for fun
spaßhaft *Adj.* amusing; comical; funny
spaßig 1. *Adj.* funny; comical; amusing. **2.** *adv.* in an amusing way
Spaß-: **~macher der** joker; **~verderber der; ~s, ~:** spoil-sport; killjoy; wet blanket; **~vogel der** joker; **du bist vielleicht ein ~vogel!** you must be joking *or (coll.)* kidding
spastisch *(Med.)* **1.** *Adj.* spastic. **2.** *adv.* **~ gelähmt sein** suffer from spastic paralysis; **ein ~ Gelähmter** a spastic
Spat [ʃpa:t] **der; ~[e]s, ~e** *od.* **Späte** ['ʃpɛ:tə] *(Mineral)* spar
spät [ʃpɛ:t] **1.** *Adj.* late; belated ⟨*fame, repentance*⟩; **am ~en Abend** in the late evening; **bis in die ~e Nacht** until late into the night; **die Werke des ~en Goethe** Goethe's late works; **wie ~ ist es?** what time is it?; **bei der Party ist es ziemlich ~ geworden** the party went on until quite late; **er kam zu ~er Stunde** *(geh.)* he came at a late hour; **ein ~es Mädchen** *(scherzh.)* an old maid; **ein ~es Glück** happiness late in life. **2.** *adv.* late; **~ am Abend** late in the evening; **du kommst aber ~!** you're very late; **wenn ich jetzt nicht losfahre, komme ich zu ~:** if I don't leave now I'll be late; **wir sind eine Station zu ~ ausgestiegen** we got out one station too far down the line; **wir sind [schon ziemlich] ~ dran** *(ugs.)* we're late [enough already]; **so ~ am Tage** so late in the day; **er hat erst ~ angefangen zu studieren** he began studying late in life; *s. auch* **früh 2**
spät-, Spät-: **~abends** *Adv.* [-'--] late in the evening; in the late evening; **~aussiedler der** *person of German origin who emigrated from countries East of the Oder-Neisse border relatively late after 1945;* **~barock das** *od.* **der** *(Kunstwiss.)* late Baroque; **~dienst der** late duty; *(im Betrieb)* late shift; **~ dienst haben** be on late shift
Spatel ['ʃpa:tl̩] **der; ~s, ~ a)** spatula; **b)** *s.* **Spachtel a**
Spaten ['ʃpa:tn̩] **der; ~s, ~:** spade
Spaten·stich der cut of the spade; **das Foto zeigt den Oberbürgermeister beim ersten ~:** the photo shows the mayor digging the first turf
Spät·entwickler der late developer
später 1. *Adj.; nicht präd.* **a)** *(nachfolgend, kommend)* later ⟨*years, generations, etc.*⟩; **b)** *(zukünftig)* future ⟨*owner, wife, etc.*⟩. **2.** *Adv.* later; **er soll ~ [einmal] die Leitung der Firma übernehmen** he is to take over management of the firm at some future date; **was willst du denn ~ [einmal] werden?** what do you want to do when you grow up?; **jmdn. auf ~ vertrösten** put sb. off until later; **ich hebe es mir für ~ auf** I'll save it for later [on]; **[also dann] bis ~!** see you later!
später·hin *Adv. (geh.)* later [on]
spätestens *Adv.* at the latest; **~ gestern/[am] Freitag** yesterday/[by] Friday at the latest
Spät-: **~folge die** long-term consequence; *(Med.)* late sequela; **~geburt die** post-term birth; **~gotik die** *(Kunstwiss.)* late Gothic; **~heimkehrer der** late returnee *(from a prisoner-of-war camp)*; **~herbst der** late autumn *or (Amer.)* fall; **~lese die** late vintage; **~nach·mittag der** late afternoon; **~schaden der** long-term damage *no pl., no indef. art.*; **~schalter der** *counter that is open late;* **~schicht die** late shift; **~sommer der** late summer; **~vorstellung die** *(Film)* late showing; *(Theater)* late performance; **~werk das** late work
Spatz [ʃpats] **der; ~en, ~en a)** sparrow; **er ißt wie ein ~:** he eats like a bird; **besser ein ~ in der Hand als eine Taube auf dem Dach** *(Spr.)* a bird in the hand is worth two in the bush *(prov.)*; **die ~en pfeifen es von den** *od.* **allen Dächern** it's common knowledge; **b)** *(fam.: Liebling)* pet; **c)** *(fam.: kleines Kind)* mite; tot *(coll.)*
Spätzchen ['ʃpɛtsçən] **das; ~s, ~ a)** little sparrow; **b)** *s.* **Spatz b, c**
Spätzeit die end; **in der ~ der Renaissance** in the late Renaissance; **Dürers Bildnisse der ~:** Dürer's late portraits
Spatzen·[ge]hirn das *(salopp abwertend)* birdbrain *(coll.)*; **sie hat ein ~:** she's birdbrained *(coll.)*; she's a birdbrain *(coll.)*
Spätzle ['ʃpɛtslə] *Pl.* spaetzle; spätzle; *kind of noodles*
Spät-: **~zug der** late train; **~zünder der** *(ugs. scherzh.)* **ein ~zünder sein** be slow on the uptake; **~zündung die** *(Technik)* retarded ignition
spazieren [ʃpa'tsi:rən] *itr. V.; mit sein* **a)** stroll; **b)** *(veralt.: spazierengehen)* go for a walk *or* a stroll; **wir sind ~ gewesen** we went for a walk *or* a stroll
spazieren-: **~|fahren 1.** *unr. itr. V.; mit sein (im Auto)* go for a drive *or* ride *or* spin; *(im Bus usw., mit dem Fahrrad od. Motorrad)* go for a ride; *(mit einem Schiff)* go for a [boat-]trip; *(mit einem Ruderboot)* go for a row; *(mit einem Segelboot)* go for a sail. **2.** *tr. V.* **jmdn. ~fahren** *(im Auto)* take sb. for a drive *or* ride *or* spin; **ein Kind [im Kinderwagen] ~fahren** take a baby for a walk [in a pram]; **die Kinder mit dem Schlitten/im Boot ~fahren** take the children out on the sledge/on a boat-trip; **~|gehen** *unr. itr. V.; mit sein* go for a walk *or* stroll; **ein Stück ~gehen** go for a little walk *or* stroll; **hier kann man schön ~gehen** you can go for

pleasant walks here; **eine schöne Gegend zum Spazierengehen** a pleasant area for walks

Spazier-: ~fahrt die *(mit dem Auto)* drive; ride; spin; *(mit dem Bus usw., mit dem Fahrrad od. Motorrad)* ride; *(mit einem Schiff)* [boat-]trip; *(mit einem Ruderboot)* row; *(mit einem Segelboot)* sail; **~gang der** walk; stroll; **~gänger der; ~s, ~, ~gängerin die; ~, ~nen** person out for a walk *or* stroll; **~ritt der** ride; **~stock der;** *Pl.* **~stöcke** walking-stick; **~weg der** footpath

SPD [ɛspe:'de:] **die; ~** *Abk.* **Sozialdemokratische Partei Deutschlands** SPD

Specht [ʃpɛçt] **der; ~[e]s, ~e** woodpecker

Speck [ʃpɛk] **der; ~[e]s, ~e a)** bacon fat; *(Schinken~)* bacon; **durchwachsener ~:** streaky bacon; **fetter ~:** bacon fat; **ran an den ~!** *(ugs.)* get stuck in! *(coll.)*; get to it! *(coll.)*; **mit ~ fängt man Mäuse** *(Spr.)* if the bait is tempting enough, the fish will bite; **b)** *(von Walen, Robben)* blubber; **c)** *(ugs. scherzh.: Fettpolster)* fat; flab *(sl.)*; **er hat ganz schön ~ auf den Rippen** he's well padded

Speck·bauch der *(ugs.)* pot-belly; paunch

speckig *Adj.* greasy

Speck-: ~nacken der *(ugs.)* fat neck; **~scheibe die** rasher *or* slice of bacon; **~schwarte die** bacon rind; **~seite die** side of bacon; **~stein der** *(Mineral)* lard stone; soapstone; steatite

Spediteur [ʃpedi'tø:ɐ̯] **der; ~s, ~e a)** *(Vermittler)* forwarding agent; *(per Schiff)* shipping agent; *(per Flugzeug)* air freight agent; **b)** *(Beförderer)* carrier; haulier; haulage contractor; *(per Schiff)* carrier; *(Möbel~)* furniture-remover

Spedition [ʃpedi'tsio:n] **die; ~, ~en a)** *(Beförderung)* carriage; transport; **b)** *s.* **Speditionsfirma**

Speditions-: ~firma die forwarding agency; *(per Schiff)* shipping agency; *(Transportunternehmen)* haulage firm; firm of hauliers; *(per Schiff)* firm of carriers; *(Möbelspedition)* removal firm; **~kaufmann der** forwarding agent; shipping agent; *(für Möbelspedition)* furniture-remover

Speedway·rennen ['spi:dweɪ-] **das** *(Motorsport)* speedway racing; *(Veranstaltung)* speedway race

Speer [ʃpe:ɐ̯] **der; ~[e]s, ~e a)** spear; **b)** *(Sportgerät)* javelin

Speer-: ~spitze die a) *(auch fig.)* spearhead; **b)** *(des Sportgeräts)* tip of a/the javelin; **~werfen das; ~s** *s.* **~wurf a; ~werfer der** *(Sport)* javelin-thrower; **~wurf der a)** *o. Pl. (Disziplin)* javelin-throwing; **b)** *(Wurf)* javelin-throw

Speiche ['ʃpaiçə] **die; ~, ~n a)** spoke; **b)** *(Anat.)* radius

Speichel ['ʃpaiçl̩] **der; ~s** saliva; spittle

Speichel-: ~drüse die salivary gland; **~fluß der a)** salivation *no art.*; **b)** *(Med.: übermäßige Sekretion)* salivation *no art.*; ptyalism *no art.*

speicheln *itr. V.* salivate

Speicher ['ʃpaiçɐ] **der; ~s, ~ a)** storehouse; *(Lagerhaus)* warehouse; *(~becken)* reservoir; *(fig.)* store; **b)** *(südd.: Dachboden)* loft; attic; **auf dem ~:** in the loft *or* attic; **c)** *(Elektronik)* memory; store

Speicher·kapazität die storage capacity; *(DV)* memory *or* storage capacity

speichern *tr. V.* store

Speicherung die; ~, ~en storing; storage

speien ['ʃpaiən] *(geh.) unr. tr., itr. V.* **a)** *(spucken)* spit; spew [forth] ‹*lava, fire, etc.*›; belch ‹*smoke*›; spout ‹*water*›; **der Drache spie Feuer** the dragon breathed fire; **b)** *(erbrechen)* vomit

Speise ['ʃpaizə] **die; ~, ~n a)** *(Gericht)* dish; **~n und Getränke** food and drink; **„kalte/warme ~n"** 'cold/hot dishes'; **b)** *o. Pl. (geh.: Nahrung)* food; **c)** *(nordd.: süße Nachspeise)* dessert; sweet *(Brit.)*

Speise-: ~eis das ice-cream; **~fett das** edible fat; **~fisch der** food fish; **~gaststätte die** restaurant; **~kammer die** larder; pantry; **~karte die** menu; **~lokal das** restaurant

speisen 1. *itr. V. (geh.)* eat; *(dinieren)* dine; **haben Sie schon gespeist?** have you eaten yet?; **zu Mittag/Abend ~:** lunch *or* have lunch/dine *or* have dinner. **2.** *tr. V.* **a)** *(geh.: verzehren)* eat; *(dinieren)* dine on; **was wünschen Sie zu ~?** what do you wish to eat?; **b)** *(geh.) (ernähren, auch fig.)* feed; *(bewirten)* dine; **c)** *(Technik)* **etw. mit Strom/Wasser ~:** supply sth. with electricity/water; **ein von Batterien gespeister Elektromotor** an electric motor powered by batteries; **Strom in das öffentliche Netz ~:** feed electricity [in]to the national grid. **3.** *refl. V.* be fed **(aus, von** by)

Speisen-: ~auf·zug der dumb waiter; **~folge die** *(geh.)* menu

Speise-: ~öl das edible oil; **~plan der** menu *(for the week etc.)*; **~reste** *Pl.* leftovers; *(zwischen den Zähnen)* food particles; **~röhre die** *(Anat.)* gullet; oesophagus *(Anat.)*; **~saal der** dining-hall; *(im Hotel, in einer Villa usw.)* dining-room; *(auf Schiffen)* dining-saloon; dining-room; **~schrank der** food-cupboard; **~wagen der** dining-car; restaurant car *(Brit.)*; **~würze die** seasoning additive; **~zettel der** menu; **auf dem ~zettel des Eichhörnchens stehen auch Vogeleier** *(fig.)* the squirrel's diet also includes birds' eggs; **~zimmer das** dining-room

Speisung die; ~, ~en a) *(geh.)* feeding; **b)** *(Technik)* supplying

spei·übel *Adj.; nicht attr.* **mir ist ~:** I think I'm going to be violently sick

Spektabilität [ʃpɛktabili'tɛ:t] **die; ~, ~en** *(Hochschulw.) title of the dean of a university*; **an seine ~ den Dekan der ... Fakultät** to the Dean of the Faculty of ...

¹Spektakel [ʃpɛk'ta:kl̩] **der; ~s, ~** *(ugs.)* **a)** *(Lärm)* row *(coll.)*; rumpus *(coll.)*; racket; **b)** *(laute Auseinandersetzung, Theater)* fuss; **einen ~ machen** kick up *or* make a fuss

²Spektakel das; ~s, ~ a) *(veralt.)* spectacle; show; **b)** *(fig.)* spectacle

spektakulär [ʃpɛktaku'lɛ:ɐ̯] **1.** *Adj.* spectacular; *(sensationell)* sensational. **2.** *adv.* spectacularly; *(sensationell)* sensationally

Spektral-: ~analyse die *(Technik)* spectral analysis; **~farbe die** colour of the spectrum

Spektren *s.* **Spektrum**

Spektroskop [ʃpɛktro'sko:p] **das; ~s, ~e** *(Technik)* spectroscope

Spektrum ['ʃpɛktrʊm] **das; ~s, Spektren** *(auch fig.)* spectrum

Spekula *s.* **Spekulum**

Spekulant [ʃpeku'lant] **der; ~en, ~en** speculator

Spekulation [ʃpekula'tsio:n] **die; ~, ~en a)** *(Mutmaßung, Erwartung; auch Philos.)* speculation; **das sind alles nur ~en** that is all merely speculation *sing. or* conjecture *sing.*; **b)** *(Wirtsch.)* speculation **(mit** in); **die ~ mit Grundstücken** property speculation

Spekulations-: ~geschäft das *(Wirtsch.)* speculative deal; **~objekt das** object of speculative investment

Spekulatius [ʃpeku'la:tsiʊs] **der; ~, ~:** *spiced biscuit in the shape of a human or other figure, eaten at Christmas*

spekulativ [ʃpekula'ti:f] **1.** *Adj.* speculative. **2.** *adv.* speculatively

spekulieren [ʃpeku'li:rən] *itr. V.* **a)** *(ugs.)* **darauf ~, etw. tun zu können** count on being able to do sth.; **er spekuliert auf den Laden** he's counting on getting the shop; **b)** *(mutmaßen)* speculate; **c)** *(Wirtsch.)* speculate **(mit** in); *s. auch* **Baisse; Hausse**

Spekulum ['ʃpe:kulʊm] **das; ~s, Spekula** *(Med.)* speculum

Spelunke [ʃpe'lʊŋkə] **die; ~, ~n** *(ugs. abwertend)* dive *(coll.)*

Spelze ['ʃpɛltsə] **die; ~, ~n** *(des Getreidekorns)* husk; *(der Grasblüte)* glume

spelzig *Adj.* full of husks *postpos.*

spendabel [ʃpɛn'da:bl̩] *Adj.* generous; open-handed

Spende ['ʃpɛndə] **die; ~, ~n** donation; contribution; **eine kleine ~ bitte!** would you like to make a small donation?

spenden *tr., itr. V.* **a)** donate; give; contribute; **[etw.] fürs Rote Kreuz ~:** contribute [sth.] to *or* for the Red Cross; **Blut/eine Niere ~:** give blood/donate a kidney; **b)** *(fig. geh.)* give ‹*light*›; afford, give ‹*shade*›; give off ‹*heat*›; provide ‹*water*›; administer ‹*communion, baptism*›; give, bestow ‹*blessing*›; confer ‹*holy orders*›; **jmdm. Beifall/Trost ~:** give sb. applause/comfort; applaud/comfort sb.

Spenden-: ~aktion die campaign for donations; **~auf·ruf der** appeal for donations; **~konto das** donations account

Spender der; ~s, ~ a) donor; donator; contributor; *(Organ~, Blut~)* donor; **wer war der edle ~?** to whom am I indebted?; **b)** *(Behälter)* dispenser

Spenderin die; ~, ~nen *s.* **Spender a**

spendieren *tr. V. (ugs.)* get, buy ‹*drink, meal, etc.*›; stand ‹*round*›; **jmdm. ein Bier/eine Tafel Schokolade ~:** stand *or* get sb. a beer/buy *or* get sb. a bar of chocolate

Spendier·hosen *Pl.* in **die/seine ~ anhaben** be in a generous mood; be feeling generous

Spengler ['ʃpɛŋlɐ] **der; ~s, ~** *(südd., österr., schweiz.) s.* **Klempner**

Spenzer ['ʃpɛntsɐ] **der; ~s, ~ a)** *(Jacke)* spencer; **b)** *(Unterhemd)* tight-fitting short-sleeved vest

Sperber ['ʃpɛrbɐ] **der; ~s, ~:** sparrow-hawk

Sperenzchen [ʃpe'rɛntsçən] *Pl. (ugs.)* **~ machen** give trouble; **mach keine ~!** don't be difficult!

Sperling ['ʃpɛrlɪŋ] **der; ~s, ~e** sparrow; **besser ein ~ in der Hand als eine Taube auf dem Dach** *(Spr.)* a bird in the hand is worth two in the bush *(prov.)*

Sperma ['ʃpɛrma] **das; ~s, Spermen** *od.* **Spermata** sperm; semen

Spermium ['ʃpɛrmiʊm] **das; ~s, Spermien** *(Biol.)* spermatozoon; sperm

sperr·angel·weit *Adv. (ugs.)* **~ offen** *od.* **geöffnet** wide open

Sperr·bezirk der a) restricted *or* prohibited area; **b)** *(für Prostituierte) area in which prostitution is prohibited*; **c)** *(Gesundheitswesen)* infected area

Sperre die; ~, ~n a) *(Barriere)* barrier; *(Straßen~)* road-block; **b)** *(Milit.)* obstacle; *(Draht~)* entanglement; **c)** *(Eisenb.)* barrier; **d)** *(fig.: Verbot, auch Sport)* ban; *(Handels~)* embargo; *(Import~, Export~)* blockade; *(Nachrichten~)* [news] blackout; **e)** *(Psych.: Blockierung, Hemmung)* block; **f)** *(Technik)* locking device

sperren 1. *tr. V.* **a)** close ‹*road, tunnel, bridge, entrance, border, etc.*›; close off ‹*area*›; **etw. für jmdn./etw. ~:** close sth. to sb./sth.; **b)** *(blockieren)* block ‹*entrance, access, etc.*›; **c)** *(Technik)* lock ‹*mechanism etc.*›; **d) jmdm. das Gehalt/den Urlaub ~:** stop sb.'s salary/leave; **einem Soldaten den Ausgang ~:** confine a soldier to barracks; **e)** cut off, disconnect ‹*water, gas, electricity, etc.*›; **jmdm. den Strom/das Telefon ~:** cut off *or* disconnect sb.'s electricity/telephone; **f)** *(Bankw.)* stop ‹*cheque, overdraft facility*›; freeze ‹*bank account*›; **jmdm. das Konto ~:** freeze sb.'s account; **g)** *(ein~)* **ein Tier/jmdn. in etw.** *(Akk.)* **~:** shut *or* lock an animal/sb. in sth.; **jmdn. ins Gefängnis ~:**

put sb. in prison; lock sb. up [in prison]; **h)** *(Sport: behindern)* obstruct; **i)** *(Sport: von der Teilnahme ausschließen)* ban; **j)** *(Druckw.: spationieren)* print ⟨*word, text*⟩ with the letters spaced. **2.** *refl. V.* **sich [gegen etw.] ~:** balk *or* jib [at sth.]. **3.** *itr. V. (Sport)* obstruct; **Sperren ohne Ball** obstruction off the ball

Sperr-: ~feuer das *(Milit.)* barrage; **~frist die** *(auch Rechtsspr.)* waiting period; **~gebiet** *s.* **~bezirk; ~gürtel der** cordon; **~holz das** plywood

sperrig *Adj.* unwieldy

Sperr-: ~konto das *(Bankw.)* blocked account; **~minorität die** *(Wirtsch., Politik)* blocking minority; **~müll der** bulky refuse *(for which there is a separate collection service);* **morgen ist ~müll** *(ugs.)* they're collecting bulky refuse tomorrow; **~sitz der** *(im Kino)* seat in the back stalls; *(im Zirkus)* front seat; *(im Theater)* seat in the front stalls; **wir saßen ~sitz** we sat in the back stalls/front seats/front stalls; **~stunde die** closing time

Sperrung die; ~, ~en *s.* **sperren 1 a–f, i:** closing; closing off; blocking; locking; stopping; cutting off; disconnection; freezing; banning

Sperr·vermerk der restriction note *(regarding sale of property, withdrawal of investment, disclosure of information, etc.)*

Spesen ['ʃpe:zn̩] *Pl.* expenses; **auf ~:** on expenses; **~ machen** incur expenses; **außer ~ nichts gewesen** *(scherzh.)* [it was] a waste of time and effort

Spezerei [ʃpe:tsə'rai] **die; ~, ~en** *(veralt.)* spice

Spezi ['ʃpe:tsi] **der; ~s, ~[s] a)** *(südd., österr., schweiz. ugs.)* [bosom] pal *(coll.);* chum *(coll.);* **b)** *(ugs.: Getränk)* lemonade and cola

Spezial-: ~gebiet das special *or* specialist field; **~geschäft das** specialist shop

spezialisieren *refl. V.* specialize (**auf** + *Akk.* in)

Spezialist der; ~en, ~en, Spezialistin die; ~, ~nen specialist

Spezialität [ʃpetsiali'tɛ:t] **die; ~, ~en** speciality; specialty

Spezialitäten·restaurant das speciality restaurant

Spezial·slalom der *(Ski)* special slalom

speziell [ʃpe'tsiɛl] **1.** *Adj.* special; specific ⟨*question, problem, etc.*⟩; specialized ⟨*book, knowledge, etc.*⟩; **er ist mein ~er Freund** he's a special friend of mine; *(iron.)* we're the best of enemies *(joc.);* **auf dein Spezielles!** your very good health!. **2.** *Adv. (besonders, gerade)* especially; *(eigens)* specially; **~ du** you especially; you of all people

Spezies ['ʃpe:tsiɛs] **die; ~, ~:** species; **eine besondere ~ [von] Mensch** a special type of person

Spezifikation [ʃpetsifika'tsio:n] **die; ~, ~en** specification

Spezifikum [ʃpe'tsi:fikʊm] **das; ~s, Spezifika a)** *(Besonderheit)* specific characteristic; **b)** *(Pharm.)* specific

spezifisch 1. *Adj.* specific; characteristic ⟨*smell, style*⟩; **~es Gewicht/~e Wärme** *(Phys.)* specific gravity/heat. **2.** *adv.* specifically

spezifizieren *tr. V.* specify; *(einzeln aufführen)* itemize ⟨*bill, expenses, etc.*⟩

Spezifizierung die; ~, ~en specification; *(einer Rechnung, von Kosten)* itemization

Sphäre ['sfɛ:rə] **die; ~, ~n** *(auch fig.)* sphere; **in höheren ~n schweben** *(scherzh.)* have one's head in the clouds

Sphären·harmonie die *(Philos.)* harmony of the spheres

sphärisch *Adj.* **a)** spherical; **b)** *(fig.: himmlisch)* heavenly

Sphäroid [sfɛro'i:t] **das; ~[e]s, ~e** *(Geom.)* spheroid

¹Sphinx [sfɪŋks] **die** *od.* **der; ~, ~e** *od.* **Sphingen** ['sfɪŋən] *(Ägyptologie, Kunstwiss.)* sphinx; **die ~ von Gise** the Sphinx at Giza

²Sphinx die; ~, ~e *od.* **Sphingen** *(griech. Myth., Kunstwiss.)* Sphinx

Spick·aal der *(bes. nordd.)* smoked eel

spicken ['ʃpɪkn̩] **1.** *tr. V.* **a)** *(Kochk.)* lard; **jmdn. ~** *(fig. ugs.)* grease sb.'s palm; **b)** *(fig. ugs.: reichlich versehen)* **eine Rede mit Zitaten ~:** lard a speech with quotations; **das Diktat war mit Fehlern gespickt** the dictation was full of mistakes. **2.** *itr. V. (bes. südd. ugs.)* crib *(coll.)*

Spick-: ~nadel die larding-needle; **~zettel der** *(bes. südd. ugs.)* crib *(coll.); (fig.: eines Redners)* notes *pl.*

spie [ʃpi:] *1. u. 3. Pers. Sg. Prät. v.* **speien**

Spiegel ['ʃpi:gl̩] **der; ~s, ~ a)** mirror; **in den ~ sehen** *od.* **schauen** look in the mirror; **im ~ der Presse** *(fig.)* as mirrored *or* reflected in the press; **dieser Roman ist ein ~ unserer Zeit** *(fig.)* this novel is a reflection of our time; **jmdm. den ~ vorhalten** *(fig.)* hold the mirror up to sb.; **das kannst du dir hinter den ~ stecken!** *(fig. ugs.)* you'll do well to remember that!; **b)** *(Wasserstand, Blutzucker~, Alkohol~ usw.)* level; *(Wasseroberfläche)* surface; **c)** *(am Frack, Smoking)* [silk] lapel; **d)** *(am Kragen)* tab; **e)** *(Jägerspr., Zool.) (bei Rehen, Hirschen usw.)* [white] rump patch; *(bei Vögeln)* speculum; **f)** *(fig.: Übersicht)* breakdown

spiegel-, Spiegel-: ~bild das *(auch fig., Math.)* reflection; **~bildlich 1.** *Adj.* **eine ~bildliche Abbildung** a mirror image; **2.** *adv.* **~bildlich abgebildet** reproduced as a *or* in mirror image; **~blank** *Adj.* shining; **den Fußboden ~blank bohnern** polish the floor until it shines [like a mirror]; **~ei das** fried egg; **~fechterei die; ~, ~en: das ist ~fechterei/sind ~fechtereien** that's all a sham; **~glas das** mirror glass; **~glatt** *Adj.* like glass *postpos.;* as smooth as glass *postpos.;* **die Straße war ~glatt gefroren** the road was like a sheet of glass; **~karpfen der** mirror carp

spiegeln 1. *itr. V.* **a)** *(glänzen)* shine; gleam; **b)** *(als Spiegel wirken)* reflect the light; **nicht ~des Glas** non-reflective glass. **2.** *tr. V.* **a)** *(reflektieren)* reflect; mirror; **b)** *(Med.)* examine ⟨*body cavity*⟩ with a speculum. **3.** *refl. V. (auch fig.)* be mirrored *or* reflected; **in ihrem Gesicht spiegelte sich Freude** *(fig.)* her face shone with delight

Spiegel-: ~reflex·kamera die reflex camera; **~saal der** hall of mirrors; **~schrank der** wardrobe/cupboard/cabinet with mirror doors; **~schrift die** mirror writing; **~teleskop das** reflecting telescope; reflector

Spiegelung die; ~, ~en a) *(auch fig., Math.)* reflection; **b)** *(Med.)* speculum examination

spiegel·verkehrt 1. *Adj.* back-to-front ⟨*lettering*⟩; **eine ~e Abbildung** a mirror image. **2.** *adv.* **etw. ~ abbilden** reproduce sth. as a *or* in mirror image

Spiel [ʃpi:l] **das; ~[e]s, ~e a)** *(das Spielen, Spielerei)* play; **er treibt ein ~ mit ihr** he's playing games *pl.* with her; **für ihn ist alles nur ein ~:** everything's just a game to him; **paß auf, daß du das ~ nicht zu weit treibst** be careful that you don't push your luck too far; **das ist doch ein ~ mit dem Leben** that's risking your/his *etc.* life; **wie im ~:** as if it were child's play; **ein ~ mit dem Feuer** *(fig.)* playing with fire; **ein [merkwürdiges] ~ des Zufalls/Schicksals** a whim of chance/fate; **ein seltsames ~ der Natur** a freak of nature; **freies ~ haben** be able to do what one wants *or* as one pleases; **genug des grausamen ~s!** *(scherzh.)* enough is enough!; **b)** *(Glücks~; Gesellschafts~)* game; *(Wett~)* game; match; **ein ~ spielen/gewinnen** play/win a game; **einen Spieler aus dem ~ nehmen/ins ~ schicken** take a player off/send a player on; **dem ~ verfallen sein** be addicted to gambling *or* gaming; **sein Geld beim ~ verlieren** gamble one's money away; **machen Sie Ihr ~!** *(Roulette)* place your bets; faites vos jeux; **das ~ ist aus** the game is up; **gewonnenes ~ haben** be home and dry; **leichtes ~ [mit jmdm.] haben** have an easy job [with sb.]; **mit Frauen ihres Typs hat ein Casanova wie er leichtes ~:** women like her are easy game for a Casanova like him; **das ~ verloren geben** give the game up for lost; *(fig.)* throw in the towel *or* one's hand; **auf dem ~ stehen** be at stake; **etw. aufs ~ setzen** put sth. at stake; risk sth.; **ein falsches/doppeltes/unfaires ~ spielen** *od.* **treiben** play sb. false/double-cross sb./treat sb. unfairly; **jmdn./etw. aus dem ~ lassen** *(fig.)* leave sb./sth. out of it; **aus dem ~ bleiben** *(fig.)* ⟨*person*⟩ stay out of it; **jmdn./etw. ins ~ bringen** *(fig.)* bring sb./sth. into it; **ins ~ kommen** *(fig.)* ⟨*factor*⟩ come into play; ⟨*person, authorities, etc.*⟩ become involved; ⟨*matter, subject, etc.*⟩ come into it; **im ~ sein** *(fig.)* be involved; *s. auch* **Hand f; c)** *(Utensilien)* game; **ein ~ Karten** a pack of cards; **das ~ ist nicht mehr vollständig** there's something missing from the set; **ein ~ Stricknadeln/Saiten** *(fig.)* a set of knitting-needles/strings; **d)** *o. Pl. (eines Schauspielers)* performance; **e)** *(eines Musikers)* performance; playing; *s. auch* **klingend 2; f)** *(Sport: ~weise)* game; **g)** *(Schau~)* play; **h)** *(Technik: Bewegungsfreiheit)* [free] play; **i)** *o. Pl. (fig.: Bewegung)* play

Spiel-: ~alter das playing stage; **~anzug der** play-suit; rompers *pl.;* **~art die** variety; **~automat der** gaming-machine; *(Geschicklichkeitsspiel)* amusement machine; **~ball der a)** *(Sport) (Tennis)* game point; *(Volleyball)* match ball; **b)** *(Billard)* red [ball]; **c)** *(fig.)* plaything; **das Boot war ein ~ball der Wellen** the boat was at the mercy of *or* was tossed about by the waves; **sie ist der ~ball ihrer Leidenschaften** she allows herself to be torn hither and thither by her passions; **d)** *(Ball, mit dem gespielt wird)* match ball; **~bank die** casino; **~bein das** *(Sport)* free leg; *(Fußball)* striking leg; **~dose die** musical box *(Brit.);* music box *(Amer.)*

spielen 1. *itr. V.* **a)** play; **~ gehen** go off to play; **der Wind spielte mit ihrem Haar** *(fig.)* the wind played in her hair; **um die Meisterschaft ~:** play for the championship; **sie haben 1:0/unentschieden gespielt** the match ended 1–0/in a draw; **er spielt in der Abwehr/als Libero** he plays in defence/as sweeper; **auf der Gitarre ~:** play the guitar; **er kann vom Blatt/nach Noten ~:** he can sight-read/play from music; **vierhändig ~:** play a [piano] duet/[piano] duets; **sie spielt nur mit ihm/seinen Gefühlen** she's only playing a game with him/playing with his feelings; **du darfst nicht mit deinem Leben ~:** you mustn't gamble with *or* risk your life; **b)** *(um Geld)* play; **er begann zu trinken und zu ~:** he began to drink and to gamble; **um Geld ~:** play for money; **mit hohem Einsatz ~:** play for high stakes; **an einem Spielautomaten ~:** play a fruit machine/*(Geschicklichkeitsspiel)* an amusement machine; *s. auch* **Lotto; c)** *(als Schauspieler)* act; perform; **d)** *(sich abspielen)* **der Roman/Film spielt im 17. Jahrhundert/in Berlin** the novel/film is set in the 17th century/in Berlin; **e)** *(fig.: sich bewegen)* ⟨*wind, water, etc.*⟩ play; **ein Lächeln spielte um ihre Lippen** *(fig.)* a smile played on her lips; **seine Muskeln ~ lassen** flex one's muscles; **seinen Charme/seine Beziehungen ~ lassen** *(fig.)* bring one's charm/connections to bear; **seine Phantasie ~ lassen** use one's imagination; **f)** *(fig.: übergehen)* **das Blau spielt ins Violette** the blue is tinged with purple; **ein ins Bräunliche ~des Rot** a red with a brownish tinge. **2.** *tr. V.* **a)** play; **Räuber und Gendarm ~:** play cops and robbers; **Cowboy ~:** play at being a cowboy; **er spielt hervorragend Schach/Tennis** he's an excellent chess-/tennis-player; **Geige/Akkordeon/Gitarre** *usw.* **~:** play the violin/accordion/guitar *etc.*; **er spielt hervorragend Gitarre** he's an outstanding guitarist; **Trumpf/Pik/ein As ~:** play a trump/spades/an ace; **b)** *(aufführen, vorführen)* put on ⟨*play*⟩; show ⟨*film*⟩; perform ⟨*piece of music*⟩; play ⟨*record*⟩; **spiel doch mal die Beatles** put the Beatles on; **das Radio spielte Jazz** there was jazz on the radio; **was wird hier gespielt?** *(fig. ugs.)* what's going on here?; **c)** *(schauspielerisch darstellen)* play ⟨*role*⟩; **den Beleidigten/Unschuldigen ~** *(fig.)* act offended/play the innocent; **sie spielt gern die große Dame** *(fig.)* she likes playing *or* acting the grand lady; **[für jmdn.] den Chauffeur ~:** act as chauffeur for sb.; **[bei jmdm.] Babysitter ~** *(fig.)* be baby-sitter *or* do the baby-sitting [for sb.]; **sie reagierte mit gespielter Gleichgültigkeit** she reacted with feigned indifference; **sein Interesse war [nur] gespielt** he [only] pretended to be interested; his interest was [merely] feigned; **in gespieltem Ernst** with mock seriousness; **d)** *(Sport: werfen, treten, schlagen)* play; **einen Ball mit Rückhand/mit dem linken Fuß ~:** play a ball backhand/with the left foot; **den Ball ins Aus/vors Tor ~:** put the ball out/play the ball in towards the goal; **einen Ball mit dem Kopf ~:** head a ball. **3.** *refl. V.* **sich warm ~:** warm up; **sich hungrig/müde ~:** work up an appetite/tire oneself out playing

spielend 1. *Adj.; nicht präd.* **mit ~er Leichtigkeit** with consummate *or* effortless ease. **2.** *adv.* easily; **etw. ~ beherrschen** master sth. effortlessly; **~ leicht** without the slightest effort

Spieler der; ~s, ~ a) *(auch Sport, Musik)* player; **b)** *(Glücks~)* gambler; **c)** *(Schau~)* actor

Spielerei die; ~, ~en a) *o. Pl.* playing *no art.*; *(im Glücksspiel)* gambling *no art.*; *(das Herumspielen)* playing *or* fiddling about *or* around (**an** + *Dat.* with); **b)** *(müßiges Tun, Spiel)* **eine ~ mit Worten/Zahlen** playing [around] with words/numbers; **eine mathematische ~:** a mathematical game; **für ihn ist das nur eine ~:** he's just playing about; **c)** *(Kinderspiel, Leichtigkeit)* child's play *no art.*; **das ist keine ~:** it has to be taken seriously; **d)** *(Tand)* gadget; **technische ~en** technical gadgetry *sing.*

Spielerin die; ~, ~nen a) *s.* **Spieler a, b; b)** *(Schau~)* actress

spielerisch 1. *Adj.* **a)** playful; **mit ~er Leichtigkeit** with consummate *or* effortless ease; **b)** *nicht präd. (Sport)* **sein ~es Können** his skill as a player; **~e Elemente** playing skills; **eine ausgezeichnete ~e Leistung** an outstanding [playing] performance; **c)** *nicht präd. (Musik)* **~es Können** playing ability. **2.** *adv.* **a)** playfully; **seine Hände glitten ~ über die Tasten** his hands glided lightly and easily over the keys; **b)** *(Sport)* in playing terms; **c)** *(Musik)* in terms of performance

spiel-, Spiel-: ~feld das *(Fußball, Hockey, Rugby usw.)* field; pitch *(Brit.)*; *(Tennis, Squash, Federball, Volleyball usw.)* court; **~figur die** piece; **~film der** feature film; **~frei** *Adj.* **ein ~freier Tag** *(Theater)* a day when there is no performance/are no performances; *(Sport)* a day without a match; **~führer der** *(Sport)* [team] captain; **~gefährte der, ~gefährtin die** *(geh.)* playmate; playfellow; **~geld das** play *or* toy money; **~hölle die** *(ugs. abwertend)* gambling-den

Spieliothek [ʃpi:lio'te:k] **die; ~, ~en** games library

Spiel-: ~kamerad der playmate; playfellow; **~karte die** playing-card; **~kasino das** casino; **~leidenschaft die** passion for gambling; **~leiter der a)** *(im Fernsehen)* quiz-master; *(im Roulett)* tourneur; **b)** *s.* **Regisseur; ~macher der** *(Sportjargon)* key player; **~mann der** *Pl.* **~leute a)** *(hist.: fahrender Sänger)* minstrel; **b)** *(Mitglied eines ~mannszuges)* bandsman; **~manns·zug der** marching band; **~marke die** chip; jetton; **~minute die** *(Sport)* minute [of play]

Spielothek [ʃpi:lo'te:k] **die; ~, ~en** games library

Spiel-: ~phase die stage of the game; **~plan der a)** *(Theater)* programme; **das Stück steht noch bis nächsten Monat auf dem ~plan** the play will continue running until next month; **b)** *(eines Brettspiels)* board; **~platz der** playground; **~raum der a)** room to move *(fig.)*; scope; latitude; *(bei Ausgaben, Budget)* leeway; **b)** *(Technik)* clearance; **~regel die** *(auch fig.)* rule of the game; **gegen die ~regeln verstoßen** *(auch fig.)* break the rules; **~runde die** round [of the game]; **~saal der** gambling-room; **~sachen** *Pl.* toys; **~salon der** gaming-room; **~schuld die** gambling debt; **~stand der: beim ~stand 1:1** with the score at 1–1; **bei diesem ~stand muß Schwarz gewinnen** as the game stands, Black must win; **~stärke die: der FC Sachsenfurt demonstrierte seine ~stärke** FC Sachsenfurt demonstrated the strength of its play; **~stein der** piece; *(beim Damespiel, Schach)* piece; man; **~straße die** play street; **~tag der** day of play; **~teufel der: dem ~teufel verfallen** *od.* **vom ~teufel besessen sein** have been bitten by the gambling bug *(coll.)*; **~tisch der a)** games table; *(für Glücksspiele)* gaming-table; *(für Kartenspiele)* card-table; **b)** *(der Orgel)* console; **~trieb der** play instinct; **~uhr die a)** musical clock; **b)** musical box *(Brit.)*; music box *(Amer.)*; **~verderber der; ~s, ~, ~verderberin die; ~, ~nen** spoil-sport; **~verlauf der** *(Sport)* **der weitere ~verlauf** the rest of the game; **~waren** *Pl.* toys; **~waren·geschäft das** toyshop; **~wiese die** grass play area; *(fig.)* playground; **~zeit die a)** *(Theater: Saison)* season; **b)** *(Aufführungsdauer)* run; **c)** *(Sport)* playing time; **die normale ~zeit** normal time; **~zeug das a)** toy; *(fig.)* toy; plaything; **b)** *o. Pl. (~sachen, ~waren)* toys *pl.*; **~zeug·eisen·bahn die** [toy] train set; **~zimmer das** playroom; **~zug der** *(Sport, in einem Brettspiel)* move

Spieß [ʃpi:s] **der; ~es, ~e a)** *(Waffe)* spear; **den ~ umdrehen** *od.* **umkehren** *(ugs.)* turn the tables; **wie am ~ schreien** *od.* **brüllen** *(ugs.)* scream one's head off; scream blue murder *(sl.)*; **b)** *(Brat~)* spit; *(Schaschlik~)* skewer; *(Cocktail~)* cocktail stick; **ein am ~ gebratener Ochse** an ox roasted on the spit; a spit-roasted ox; **c)** *(Fleisch~)* kebab; **d)** *(Soldatenspr.: Kompaniefeldwebel)* [company] sergeant-major; **e)** *(Jägerspr.)* spike; pricket

spieß-, Spieß-: ~bürger der *(abwertend)* [petit] bourgeois; **~bürgerlich** *s.* **spießig; ~bürgertum das** *(abwertend)* **a)** [petit] bourgeois existence; *(spießiges Wesen)* [petit] bourgeois conformism; **b)** *(die Spießbürger)* [petite] bourgeoisie

Spießchen das; ~s, ~ a) *(Cocktailspieß)* cocktail stick; **b)** *(Schaschlikspieß)* skewer; **c)** *(Fleischspieß)* kebab

spießen *tr. V.* **a) die Fleischstücke werden auf einen Schaschlikspieß gespießt** the pieces of meat are pushed on to a skewer; **ein Stück Käse/eine Olive auf einen Cocktailspieß ~:** spear a piece of cheese/an olive with a cocktail stick; **etw. in etw.** *(Akk.)* **~:** stick sth. in sth.

Spießer der; ~s, ~ *(abwertend)* [petit] bourgeois

spießerhaft *s.* **spießig**

Spießertum das; ~s *(abwertend) s.* **Spießbürgertum**

Spieß·geselle der a) *(abwertend: Komplize)* accomplice; **b)** *(veralt.: Kumpan)* companion

spießig *(abwertend)* **1.** *Adj.* [petit] bourgeois; **~e Kleinbürgerlichkeit** petit bourgeois narrow-mindedness. **2.** *adv.* ⟨*think, behave, etc.*⟩ in a [petit] bourgeois way; **eine ~ eingerichtete Wohnung** a flat *(Brit.) or (Amer.)* apartment furnished in a typically petit bourgeois style

Spießigkeit die; ~ *(abwertend)* [petit] bourgeois narrow-mindedness; *(einer Wohnungseinrichtung)* [petit] bourgeois style

Spieß·rute die *in* **~n laufen** *(auch fig.)* run the gauntlet

Spike [ʃpaik] **der; ~s, ~s a)** spike; **b)** *Pl. (Schuhe)* spikes; **c)** *(eines Reifens)* stud; **d)** *Pl. (Reifen)* studded tyres

Spike[s]·reifen der studded tyre

spillerig ['ʃpɪlərɪç] *Adj. (bes. nordd.)* spindly, skinny ⟨*limbs*⟩; skinny ⟨*person*⟩

spinal [ʃpi'na:l] *(Anat.)* **1.** *Adj.* spinal; **~e Kinderlähmung** infantile paralysis; polio [myelitis]. **2.** *adv.* **~ gelähmt sein** suffer from spinal paralysis

Spinat [ʃpi'na:t] **der; ~[e]s, ~e** spinach

Spinat·wachtel die *(ugs. abwertend)* skinny old bag *(sl.)*

Spind [ʃpɪnt] **der** *od.* **das; ~[e]s, ~e** locker

Spindel ['ʃpɪndl̩] **die; ~, ~n a)** spindle; **b)** *(einer Treppe)* newel

spindel·dürr *Adj.* skinny ⟨*person*⟩; spindly, skinny ⟨*limbs, finger*⟩; **sie ist ~:** she's as thin as a rake

Spinett [ʃpi'nɛt] **das; ~[e]s, ~e** spinet

Spinnaker ['ʃpɪnakɐ] **der; ~s, ~** *(Seemannsspr.)* spinnaker

Spinne ['ʃpɪnə] **die; ~, ~n** spider

spinne·feind *Adj. (ugs.)* **jmdm. ~ sein** hate sb.'s guts *(coll.)*

spinnen ['ʃpɪnən] **1.** *unr. tr. V.* **a)** spin *(fig.)*; plot ⟨*intrigue*⟩; think up ⟨*idea*⟩; hatch ⟨*plot*⟩; **ein Lügengewebe/Netz von Intrigen ~:** weave a tissue of lies/a web of intrigue; **b)** *(ugs.: lügen)* make up; **das spinnst du!** you're making it up!. **2.** *unr. itr. V.* **a)** spin; **an einer Intrige ~:** plot an intrigue; **b)** *(ugs.: verrückt sein)* be crazy *or (sl.)* nuts *or (sl.)* crackers; **Ich soll bezahlen? Du spinnst wohl!** [What,] me pay? You must be joking *or (sl.)* kidding; **ich glaube, ich spinne!** I don't believe it!; **du spinnst wohl [,das zu tun]** you must be crazy [to do it]; **c)** *(ugs.: Unsinn reden)* talk rubbish; **d)** *(ugs.: lügen)* make it up

Spinnen-: ~gewebe das *s.* **Spinngewebe; ~netz das** spider's web

Spinner der; ~s, ~ a) *(Beruf)* spinner; **b)** *(ugs. abwertend)* nut-case *(sl.)*; idiot; **c)** *(Zool. veralt.)* silk-moth; **d)** *(Angeln)* spinner

Spinnerei die; ~, ~en a) *o. Pl.* spinning *no art.*; **b)** *(Werkstatt)* spinning mill; **c)** *(ugs. abwertend)* crazy idea

Spinnerin die; ~, ~nen a) *(Beruf)* spinner; **b)** *(ugs. abwertend)* nut-case *(sl.)*; idiot

spinnert ['ʃpɪnɐt] *Adj. (ugs., bes. südd.)* slightly potty *(sl.)*

Spinn·gewebe das cobweb

spinnig *Adj. (ugs.)* slightly potty *(sl.)*

Spinn-: ~rad das spinning-wheel; **~rocken der** distaff; **~webe die; ~, ~n** cobweb; **~wirtel der** whorl; wharve

spintisieren [ʃpɪnti'zi:rən] *itr. V. (ugs.)* get weird *or* crazy ideas *(coll.)*

Spintisiererei die; ~, ~en *(ugs.)* crazy fantasizing *no indef. art.*

Spion [ʃpi'o:n] **der; ~s, ~e a)** spy; **b)** *(Guckloch)* spyhole; **c)** *(Spiegel am Fenster)* telltale mirror

Spionage [ʃpio'na:ʒə] **die; ~:** spying; espionage; **~ treiben** spy; carry out espionage

Spionage-: ~**abwehr die a)** *(Tätigkeit)* counter-espionage; counter-intelligence; **b)** *(Dienst)* counter-espionage *or* counter-intelligence service; **er arbeitet in der ~abwehr** he works in counter-espionage *or* counter-intelligence; ~**fall der** spy *or* espionage case; ~**netz das** spy *or* espionage network; ~**ring der** spy ring

spionieren *itr. V.* **a)** spy **(gegen** against); **b)** *(fig. abwertend)* spy; snoop [about] *(coll.)*

Spioniererei die; ~, ~**en** *(fig. abwertend)* snooping [about] *no pl. (coll.)*

Spionin die; ~, ~**nen** spy

Spiral·bohrer der twist drill *or* bit

Spirale [ʃpiˈraːlə] **die;** ~, ~**n a)** *(auch Geom., fig.)* spiral; *(Heiz~)* coil; **b)** *(zur Empfängnisverhütung)* coil

Spiral·feder die coil spring

spiral·förmig 1. *Adj.* spiral[-shaped]. **2.** *adv.* spirally

spiralig 1. *Adj.* spiral. **2.** *adv.* spirally

Spiral·nebel der *(Astron.)* spiral nebula

Spirant [spiˈrant] **der;** ~**en,** ~**en** *(Sprachw.)* spirant

Spiritismus [ʃpiritɪsmʊs] **der;** ~: spiritualism; spiritism

Spiritist der; ~**en,** ~**en** spiritualist; spiritist

spiritistisch 1. *Adj.* spiritualist[ic]; spiritistic. **2.** *adv.* spiritualistically; spiritistically

Spiritual [ˈspɪrɪtjʊəl] **das** *od.* **der;** ~**s,** ~**s** [negro] spiritual

spiritualisieren *tr. V.* spiritualize

Spiritualismus [spiritu̯aˈlɪsmʊs] **der;** ~ *(Philos.)* spiritualism

spiritualistisch 1. *Adj.* spiritualist[ic]. **2.** *adv.* spiritualistically

Spiritualität [spiritu̯aliˈtɛːt] **die;** ~: spirituality

Spirituose [spiriˈtu̯oːzə] **die;** ~, ~**n** spirit *usu. in pl.*

Spiritus [ˈʃpiːritʊs] **der;** ~, ~**se** spirit; ethyl alcohol; **ein Organ in ~ konservieren** preserve an organ in alcohol; **mit ~ kochen** cook on a spirit stove

Spiritus·kocher der spirit stove

Spital [ʃpiˈtaːl] **das;** ~**s, Spitäler** [ʃpiˈtɛːlɐ] *(bes. österr., schweiz.)* hospital; *(veralt.: Altersheim)* old people's home; *(veralt.: Armenhaus)* almshouse

Spittel [ˈʃpɪtl̩] **das,** *(schweiz.:)* **der;** ~**s,** ~ *(bes. schweiz. ugs.)* hospital

spitz [ʃpɪts] **1.** *Adj.* **a)** *(nicht stumpf)* pointed ⟨*tower, arch, shoes, nose, beard, etc.*⟩; sharp ⟨*pencil, needle, stone, etc.*⟩; fine ⟨*pen nib*⟩; *(Geom.)* acute ⟨*angle*⟩; **b)** *(schrill)* shrill ⟨*cry etc.*⟩; **c)** *(ugs.: abgezehrt)* haggard; haggard, pinched ⟨*face*⟩; **d)** *(boshaft)* cutting ⟨*remark, etc.*⟩; ~ **werden** get spiteful; **e)** *(ugs.: geil)* randy; horny *(sl.)*; ~ **auf jmdn. sein** really fancy sb. **2.** *adv.* **a)** ~ **zulaufen** taper to a point; ~ **zulaufend** pointed; **b)** *(boshaft)* cuttingly

Spitz der; ~**es,** ~**e** *(Hund)* spitz

spitz-, Spitz-: ~**ahorn der** Norway maple; ~**bart der a)** goatee; pointed beard; **b)** *(Mann)* man with a/the goatee *or* pointed beard; ~**bauch der** pot-belly; ~|**bekommen** *unr. tr. V. (ugs.) s.* ~**kriegen;** ~**bogen der** pointed arch; ~**bogen·fenster das** lancet window; ~**bube der a)** *(veralt. abwertend: Gauner)* rogue; scoundrel; **b)** *(scherzh.: Schlingel)* rascal; scallywag; scamp; **c)** *(österr.: Plätzchen) sandwich of two or three biscuits stuck together with jam;* ~**büberei** [~byːbəˈrai] **die;** ~, ~**en a)** piece of roguery; **b)** *o. Pl.* roguery; ~**bübisch 1.** *Adj.* **a)** *(verschmitzt)* roguish; mischievous; **b)** *(veralt. abwertend: schurkisch)* villainous; **2.** *adv.* **a)** *(verschmitzt)* roguishly; mischievously; **b)** *(veralt. abwertend: schurkisch)* villainously

spitze *indekl. Adj. (ugs.) s.* **klasse**

Spitze die; ~, ~**n a)** *(Nadel~, Bleistift~ usw.)* point; *(Pfeil~, Horn~ usw.)* tip; **einer Sache** *(Dat.)* **die ~ nehmen** *od.* **abbrechen** *(fig.)* take the sting out of sth. *(fig.)*; **b)** *(Turm~, Baum~, Mast~ usw.)* top; *(eines Dreiecks, Kegels, einer Pyramide)* top; apex; vertex *(Math.)*; *(eines Berges)* summit; top; **ein auf der ~ stehendes Dreieck** an inverted triangle; **c)** *(Zigarren~, Haar~, Zweig~)* end; *(Schuh~)* toe; *(Finger~, Nasen~, Schwanz~, Flügel~, Spargel~)* tip; *(Lungen~)* apex; **die südliche ~ der Insel** the southern tip of the island; **d)** *(vorderes Ende)* front; **an der ~ des Zuges/der Kolonne marschieren** march at the head of the procession/column; **an der ~ liegen** *(Sport)* be in the lead *or* in front; **sich an die ~ [des Feldes] setzen** *(Sport)* go into *or* take the lead; **e)** *(führende Position)* top; **an der ~ [der Tabelle] stehen** *od.* **liegen** *(Sport)* be [at the] top [of the table]; **sich an die ~ [einer Bewegung] setzen** put oneself at the head [of a movement]; **die ~ halten/übernehmen** stay top/go to the top; **f)** *(einer Firma, Organisation usw.)* head; *(einer Hierarchie)* top; *(leitende Gruppe)* management; **an der ~ des Unternehmens/der Partei stehen** be at the head of the company/party; **die ~n der Gesellschaft/der Partei** the leading figures of society/in the party; **g)** *(Höchstwert)* maximum; peak; *(ugs.: Spitzenzeit)* peak period; **das Auto fährt 160 km ~:** the car has *or* does a top speed of 160 km. per hour; **wir wollen die Sache doch nicht auf die ~ treiben** we don't want to carry things too far; **h) [absolute/einsame] ~ sein** *(ugs.)* be [absolutely] great *(coll.)*; **i)** *(fig.: Angriff)* dig **(gegen** at); ~**n austeilen** make pointed remarks; **j)** *(Textilwesen)* lace; **k)** *(Sport: Sturm~)* striker; **l)** *(Zigaretten~, Zigarrenhalter)* [cigarette/cigar] holder; **m)** *(Wirtsch.: Überschuß)* surplus

Spitzel der; ~**s,** ~ *(abwertend)* informer; **ein ~ der Polizei** a police informer; a copper's nark *(Brit. sl.)*

Spitzel·dienste *Pl. (abwertend)* **für jmdn. ~ leisten** act as an informer for sb.; **für ~ bin ich mir zu schade** I couldn't stoop to acting as *or* being an informer

spitzeln *itr. V. (abwertend)* act as an informer

spitzen 1. *tr. V.* sharpen ⟨*pencil*⟩; purse ⟨*lips, mouth*⟩; **die Ohren ~** ⟨*dog*⟩ prick up its ears; *(fig.)* ⟨*person*⟩ prick up one's ears. **2.** *refl. V.* **sich auf etw.** *(Akk.)* ~ *(ugs.)* look forward [expectantly] to sth.; *(dringlich erhoffen)* have one's heart set on sth. **3.** *(landsch.: aufmerken)* prick up one's ears

Spitzen-: ~**bluse die** lace blouse; ~**deckchen das** lace mat; ~**erzeugnis das** top-quality product; ~**funktionär der** top official; ~**gehalt das** top-level salary; ~**geschwindigkeit die** top speed; ~**kandidat der** leading *or* top candidate; ~**klasse die a)** top class; **ein Hotel der ~klasse** a top-class hotel; **zur ~klasse gehören** be top-class; **b) ~klasse sein** *(ugs.)* be really great *(coll.)*; ~**können der** top-class talent; ~**kraft die** top-class *or* top-flight professional; ~**kragen der** lace collar; ~**leistung die** top-class performance; **eine ~leistung der Ingenieurskunst** a supreme achievement of engineering; ~**politiker der** top *or* leading politician; ~**position die a)** *(Sport)* leading position; **b)** *(leitende Position)* top position; ~**qualität die** top quality; **Erzeugnisse in ~qualität** top-quality products; ~**reiter der** top rider; *(fig.)* leader; *(Ware)* top *or* best seller; *(Mannschaft)* top team; ~**spiel das** *(Sport)* top match *or* game; ~**spieler der** top[-class] player; ~**sportler der** top sportsman; ~**stellung die** top position; ~**tanz der** dancing *no art.* on points *or* on [full] point; ~**technologie die** state-of-the-art technology; ~**wert der** peak; maximum [value]; ~**zeit die a)** peak time *or* period; **b)** *(Sport) (beste Zeit)* best time; *(sehr gute Zeit)* outstanding *or* excellent time

Spitzer der; ~**s,** ~: [pencil-]sharpener

spitz-, Spitz-: ~**findig 1.** *Adj.;* hair-splitting, over-subtle; quibbling ⟨*distinction*⟩; pettifogging ⟨*quibble*⟩; **jetzt wirst du [zu] ~ findig** now you're splitting hairs *or* being too subtle; **2.** *adv.* in an over-subtle way; **[zu] ~findig argumentieren** be over-subtle in one's arguments; split hairs; ~**findigkeit die;** ~, ~**en a)** *o. Pl.* over-subtlety; *(Haarspalterei)* hair-splitting; **b)** *(etwas Spitzfindiges)* nicety; *(Äußerung)* hair-splitting remark; ~**hacke die** pick; pickaxe

spitzig *Adj. (veralt.) s.* **spitz 1a–d, 2**

spitz-, Spitz-: ~**kehre die a)** *(Haarnadelkurve)* hairpin bend; **b)** *(Ski)* kick turn; ~|**kriegen** *tr. V. (ugs.)* tumble to *(coll.)*; get wise to *(sl.)*; **[es] ~ kriegen, daß ...:** tumble to *or* get wise to the fact that ...; ~**maus die a)** shrew; **b)** *(ugs. abwertend)* weasel-faced female *(derog.)*; ~**name der** nickname; ~**wegerich** [~veːgərɪç] **der** *(Bot.)* ribwort; ~**winklig 1.** *Adj.* acute-angled ⟨*triangle*⟩; **2.** *adv.* at an acute angle; ~**züngig 1.** *Adj.* sharp-tongued; **2.** *adv.* ⟨*reply*⟩ sharply

Spleen [ʃpliːn] **der;** ~**s,** ~**e** *od.* ~**s** strange *or* peculiar habit; eccentricity; **du hast ja einen ~!** there must be something the matter with you!; you must be dotty *(coll.)*; **die Lexikographen haben doch alle einen kleinen ~:** lexicographers are all a bit cracked *(coll.)*

spleenig *Adj.* eccentric; dotty *(coll.)*

spleißen [ˈʃplaisn̩] *(Seemannsspr.)* **1.** *unr. od. regelm. tr. V.* splice ⟨*rope*⟩. **2.** *unr. od. regelm. itr. V.* make a splice/splices

splendid [ʃplɛnˈdiːt] *(veralt.)* **1.** *Adj.* **a)** generous; **b)** *(kostbar)* sumptuous; magnificent. **2.** *adv.* **a)** generously; **b)** *(kostbar)* sumptuously; magnificently

Splint [ʃplɪnt] **der;** ~**[e]s,** ~**e** *(Technik)* split pin

Splint·holz das sapwood; alburnum

spliß [ʃplɪs] *1. u. 3. Pers. Sg. Prät. v.* **spleißen**

Splitt [ʃplɪt] **der;** ~**[e]s,** ~**e** [stone] chippings *pl.*; *(zum Streuen)* grit; *(in Beton)* aggregate

splitten *tr. V. (Wirtsch.)* **a)** split ⟨*shares*⟩; **b)** *(Politik)* **die Stimmen ~:** *give one's first vote to a particular candidate and one's second to a party other than that of the chosen candidate*

Splitter der; ~**s,** ~: splinter; *(Granat~, Bomben~)* splinter; fragment; **du siehst den ~ im fremden Auge, aber nicht den Balken im eigenen** *(geh.)* you can see a mote in another's eye but not the beam that is in your own

splitter-, Splitter-: ~**bombe die** fragmentation bomb; ~**bruch der** *(Med.)* comminuted fracture; ~**faser·nackt** *Adj. (ugs.)* absolutely stark naked; completely starkers *pred. (Brit. sl.)*; ~**frei** *Adj.* shatterproof; ~**gruppe die** splinter group

splitterig *Adj.* **a)** *(leicht splitternd)* ⟨*wood, plastic, etc.*⟩ that splinters easily; ~ **sein** splinter easily; **b)** *(voller Splitter)* splintery

splittern *itr. V.* **a)** *(Splitter bilden)* splinter; **b)** *mit sein (in Splitter zerbrechen)* ⟨*glass, windscreen, etc.*⟩ shatter

splitter·nackt *Adj. (ugs.)* stark naked; starkers *pred. (Brit. sl.)*

Splitter·partei die splinter party

Splitting [ˈʃplɪtɪŋ] **das;** ~**s,** ~**s a)** *o. Pl. (Steuerw.) taxation of husband and wife whereby each is taxed on half the total of their combined incomes;* **b)** *(Wirtsch.)* splitting; **c)** *(Politik) division of one's first and second votes between a particular candidate and a party other than that of the chosen candidate*

Splitting·system das *(Steuerw.) tax system in which husband and wife each pay income tax on half the total of their combined incomes*

splittrig *s.* **splitterig**
SPÖ [ɛspe:'ø:] **die;** ~: *Abk.:* **Sozialistische Partei Österreichs** Austrian Socialist Party
Spoiler ['ʃpɔylɐ] **der;** ~s, ~ *(Kfz-W.)* spoiler
Spökenkieker ['ʃpø:kn̩ki:kɐ] **der;** ~s, ~ **a)** *(nordd.: Hellseher)* clairvoyant; person who has second sight; **b)** *(ugs.: spintisierender Mensch)* crazy fantasist
Spökenkiekerei die; ~, ~en *(ugs.)* crazy fantasizing *no indef. art.*
Spondeus [ʃpɔn'de:ʊs] **der;** ~, **Spondeen** *(Verslehre)* spondee
sponsern ['ʃpɔnzɐn] *tr. V.* sponsor
Sponsor ['ʃpɔnzɐ] **der;** ~s, ~s *od.* ~en [-'zo:rən] sponsor
spontan [ʃpɔn'ta:n] **1.** *Adj.* spontaneous. **2.** *adv.* spontaneously
Spontaneität [ʃpɔntanei'tɛ:t] **die;** ~ *(auch Psych., Med.)* spontaneity
Sponti ['ʃpɔnti] **der;** ~s, ~s *(ugs.) member of an undogmatic leftist group*
sporadisch [ʃpo'ra:dɪʃ] **1.** *Adj.* sporadic. **2.** *adv.* sporadically
Spore ['ʃpo:rə] **die;** ~, ~n *(Biol.)* spore
Sporen *s.* **Spore, Sporn**
sporen-, Sporen-: ~**klirrend** *adv.* with a clatter of spurs; ~**pflanze die** *(Bot.)* cryptogam; ~**tierchen das** *(Zool.)* sporozoan
Sporn [ʃpɔrn] **der;** ~[e]s, ~e *od.* **Sporen** ['ʃpo:rən] **a)** *Pl.* **Sporen** *od. (Zool.)* ~e spur; **einem Pferd die Sporen geben** spur a horse; **sich die [ersten] Sporen verdienen** *(fig.)* win one's spurs; **b)** *Pl.* ~e *(hist.: am Schiff)* ram; **c)** *Pl.* ~e *(eines Flugzeugs)* tail-skid
spornen *tr. V.* spur ⟨*horse*⟩
sporn·streichs *Adv. (veralt.)* straight away
Sport [ʃpɔrt] **der;** ~[e]s **a)** sport; *(als Unterrichtsfach)* sport; physical education; PE; ~ **treiben** do sport; **beim** ~: while doing sport; **und hier noch eine Meldung vom** ~: and finally an item of sports news; **b)** *(~art)* sport; **c)** *(Hobby, Zeitvertreib)* hobby; pastime; **sich** *(Dat.)* **einen** ~ **aus etw. machen** get a kick *(coll.)* out of sth.
Sport-: ~**ab·zeichen das** sports badge; ~**angler der** club angler; ~**an·lage die** sports complex; ~**art die** [form of] sport; ~**artikel der** piece of sports equipment; ~**artikel** *Pl.* sports equipment *sing.;* ~**arzt der** sports doctor; ~**bericht der** sports report; ~**bericht·erstattung die** sports reporting; ~**boot das** sports boat; ~**coupé das** sports coupé; ~**dreß der** *s.* **Dreß a**
Sport-: ~**feld das** sports ground; *(Stadion)* sports stadium; ~**fest das** sports festival; *(einer Schule)* sports day; ~**fischen das** club fishing *no art. or* angling *no art.;* ~**flieger der** sports pilot; ~**flugzeug das** sports plane; ~**freund der a)** sports fan; **b)** *(Kamerad)* sporting friend; ~**funktionär der** sports official; ~**geist der;** *o. Pl.* sportsmanship; sporting spirit; ~**gerät das** piece of sports apparatus; ~**geräte** *(als Gesamtheit)* sports apparatus *sing.;* ~**hemd das** sports shirt; ~**hoch·schule die** college of physical education
sportiv [spɔr'ti:f] **1.** *Adj.* sporty. **2.** *adv.* sportily
Sport-: ~**journalist der** sports journalist; ~**kamerad der** sporting friend; ~**kleidung die** sportswear; sports clothes *pl.;* ~**lehrer der** sports instructor; *(in einer Schule)* PE *or* physical education teacher; games teacher
Sportler ['ʃpɔrtlɐ] **der;** ~s, ~: sportsman
Sportler·herz das athletic heart
Sportlerin die; ~, ~nen sportswoman
sportlich 1. *Adj.* **a)** sporting *attrib.* ⟨*success, performance, interests, etc.*⟩; ~**e Veranstaltungen** sports events; sporting events; **auf** ~**em Gebiet** in the field of sport; **b)** *(fair)* sportsmanlike; sporting; **c)** *(fig.: flott, rasant)* sporty ⟨*car, driving, etc.*⟩; **d)** *(zu sportlicher Leistung fähig)* sporty, athletic ⟨*person*⟩; **e)** *(jugendlich wirkend)* sporty, smart but casual ⟨*clothes*⟩; smart but practical ⟨*hair-style*⟩. **2.** *adv.* **a)** as far as sport is concerned; ~ **aktiv sein** be an active sportsman/sportswoman; **b)** *(fair)* sportingly; **c)** *(fig.: flott, rasant)* in a sporty manner
sportlich-elegant 1. *Adj.* casually elegant. **2.** *adv.* casually but elegantly ⟨*dressed*⟩
sport-, Sport-: ~**maschine die** sports plane; ~**medizin die** sports medicine *no art.;* ~**medizinisch** *Adj.* ~**medizinische Betreuung/Forschung** medical care of sportsmen/research into sports medicine; ~**nachrichten** *Pl.* sports news *sing.;* ~**platz der** sports field; *(einer Schule)* playing field/fields *pl.;* ~**presse die** sports press; ~**schuh der a)** sports shoe; **b)** *(sportlicher Schuh)* casual shoe; ~**sendung die** sports programme
Sports-: ~**freund der** sports enthusiast; **Hallo, ~freund! Wie geht's?** *(ugs.)* hello, mate *(coll.),* how are you?; ~**kanone die** *(ugs.)* sporting ace; ~**mann der;** *Pl.* ~**männer** *od.* ~**leute** sportsman
Sport-: ~**stadion das** [sports] stadium; ~**student der** sports student; ~**taucher der** skin-diver; ~**un·fall der** sporting *or* sports accident; ~**verband der** sports association; ~**verein der** sports club; ~**verletzung die** sports injury; ~**wagen der a)** *(Auto)* sports car; **b)** *(Kinderwagen)* push-chair *(Brit.);* stroller *(Amer.);* ~**wissenschaft die** sports science *no art.*
Spot [spɔt] **der;** ~s, ~s **a)** *(Werbe~)* commercial; advertisement; ad *(coll.);* **b)** *(Leuchte)* spotlight; spotlamp; **c)** *(Theat., Film, Fernsehen)* spot[light]
Spot·markt der *(Wirtsch.)* spot market
Spott [ʃpɔt] **der;** ~[e]s mockery; *(höhnischer)* ridicule; derision; ~ **und Hohn** scorn and derision; **jmdn./etw. dem** ~ **preisgeben** hold sb./sth. up to ridicule; **seinen** ~ **mit jmdm./etw. treiben** make fun of sb./sth.
spott-, Spott-: ~**bild das** travesty; mockery; *(eines Menschen)* caricature; ~**billig** *(ugs.)* **1.** *Adj.* dirt cheap; **2.** *adv.* **da kann man ~billig einkaufen** you can get *or* buy things dirt cheap there; ~**drossel die a)** mocking-thrush; **[Eigentliche]** ~**drossel** mocking-bird; **b)** *(fig.) s.* **Spötter**
Spöttelei die; ~, ~en **a)** *o. Pl.* [gentle] mocking; [gentle] mockery; **b)** *(spöttelnde Äußerung)* mocking remark
spötteln ['ʃpœtl̩n] *itr. V.* mock [gently]; poke *or* make [gentle] fun; **über jmdn./etw.** ~: mock sb./sth. gently; poke gentle fun at *or* make [gentle] fun of sb./sth.
spotten ['ʃpɔtn̩] *itr. V.* **a)** mock; poke *or* make fun; *(höhnischer)* ridicule; be derisive; **über jmdn./etw.** ~: mock sb./sth.; make fun of sb./sth.; *(höhnischer)* ridicule sb./sth.; be derisive about sb./sth.; **du hast gut/leicht** ~: it's easy *or* all very well for you to mock *or* laugh; **jmds./einer Sache** ~ *(geh.)* mock sb./sth.; **b)** *(fig.)* be contemptuous of; scorn; **er spottete der Gefahr** *(Gen.) (geh.)* he was contemptuous of *or* scorned the danger; **das spottet jeder Beschreibung** *(ugs.)* it defies *or* beggars description
Spötter ['ʃpœtɐ] **der;** ~s, ~: mocker
Spötterei die; ~, ~en **a)** *o. Pl.* mockery; mocking; making fun; **b)** *(spottende Äußerung)* mocking remark
Spott-: ~**geburt die** *(geh. abwertend)* monstrosity; ~**gedicht das** satirical poem, verse satire (**auf** + *Akk.* about); ~**geld das;** *o. Pl. (ugs.)* **etw. für** *od. (veralt.)* **um ein ~geld bekommen** get sth. dirt cheap
spöttisch ['ʃpœtɪʃ] **1.** *Adj.* mocking ⟨*smile, remark, speech, etc.*⟩; *(höhnischer)* derisive, ridiculing ⟨*remark, speech, etc.*⟩; **ein** ~**er Mensch** a person who likes poking fun. **2.** *adv.* mockingly; ~ **lächeln** give a mocking smile
Spott-: ~**lust die;** *o. Pl.* love of *or* delight in mockery *or* poking fun; ~**name der** [derisive] nickname; ~**preis der** *(ugs.)* ridiculously low price; **etw. für einen** *od.* **zu einem ~preis bekommen** get sth. dirt cheap *or* for a song
sprach [ʃpra:x] *1. u. 3. Pers. Sg. Prät. v.* **sprechen**
Sprach-: ~**barriere die** *(Soziol.)* language barrier; *(zwischen Gesellschaftsklassen)* linguistic barrier; ~**bau der** *(Sprachw.)* linguistic structure; ~**begabung die;** *o. Pl.* talent *or* gift for languages; ~**denkmal das** linguistic monument
Sprache ['ʃpra:xə] **die;** ~, ~n **a)** language; **in englischer** ~: in English; **die ~ der Jäger/Mediziner** the language of the hunt/of medicine; hunting/medical language; **ihm blieb die ~ weg** *(ugs.)* he was speechless; he was at a loss for words; **es verschlug** *od.* **raubte mir die** ~: it took my breath away; **hast du die ~ verloren?** *(ugs.)* haven't you got a tongue in your head?; **b)** *(Sprechweise)* way of speaking; speech; *(Stil)* style; **eine deutliche/unmißverständliche** ~ **[mit jmdm.] sprechen** speak bluntly [to sb.]; **c)** *(Rede)* **die ~ auf jmdn./etw. bringen** bring the conversation round to sb./sth.; **etw. zur ~ bringen** bring sth. up; raise sth.; **zur ~ kommen** be brought up *or* raised; come up; **mit der ~ herausrücken/herauswollen** come out/want to come out with it; **heraus mit der** ~! come on, out with it!
spräche ['ʃprɛ:çə] *1. u. 3. Pers. Sg. Konjunktiv II v.* **sprechen**
Sprachen-: ~**schule die** language school; ~**studium das** language studies *pl., no art.*
sprach-, Sprach-: ~**entwicklung die** development of a/the language; ~**erwerb der** *(Sprachw.)* language acquisition; ~**familie die** language family; family of languages; ~**fehler der** speech impediment *or* defect; ~**forscher der** linguistic researcher; ~**führer der** phrase-book; ~**gebrauch der** [linguistic] usage; **im ~gebrauch der Nazis** in Nazi usage *or* language; in the language of the Nazis; ~**gefühl das;** *o. Pl.* feeling for language; ~**genie das** linguistic genius; ~**geographie die** linguistic geography *no art.;* ~**geschichte die a)** history of a/the language; *(Teilgebiet der ~wissenschaft)* historical linguistics *sing., no art.;* **b)** *(Buch)* history of a/the language; ~**geschichtlich 1.** *Adj.* historical-linguistic ⟨*studies, dissertation, etc.*⟩; **2.** *adv.* from the point of view of historical linguistics; ~**gewaltig** *Adj.* powerfully eloquent; ~**grenze die** language boundary; ~**insel die** linguistic enclave *or* island; ~**kenntnisse** *Pl.* knowledge *sing.* of a language/languages; **seine französischen ~kenntnisse** his knowledge of French; ~**kompetenz die** linguistic competence; ~**kritik die** critique of language; ~**kultur die;** *o. Pl.* level of compliance with linguistic norms; ~**kundig** *Adj.* proficient in *or* conversant with the language *postpos.;* ~**kurs der** language course; ~**labor das** language laboratory *or (coll.)* lab; ~**lehre die a)** grammar; **b)** *(Buch)* grammar [book]
sprachlich 1. *Adj.* linguistic; ~**e Feinheiten** subtleties of language. **2.** *adv.* linguistically; **ein ~ hervorragender Aufsatz** an excellently written essay
sprach-, Sprach-: ~**los** *Adj.* **a)** *(überrascht)* speechless; dumbfounded; **b)** *(wortlos)* silent ⟨*protest*⟩; silent, tacit ⟨*agreement*⟩; ~**losigkeit die a)** *(Überraschtheit)* speechlessness; dumbfoundedness; **b)** *(Wortlosigkeit) (eines Protests)* silence; ~**mittler der** mediator between languages; ~**norm die** linguistic norm; ~**pflege die** language cultivation; ~**philosophie die** philosophy of language; ~**raum der** language area; ~**regelung die** instructions *pl.*

as to the wording to be used; **nach der offiziellen ~regelung ist er „aus gesundheitlichen Gründen" zurückgetreten** according to the official version *or* as the official version has it, he resigned 'for reasons of health'; **~rohr das** *(Repräsentant)* spokesman; *(Propagandist)* mouthpiece; **~schöpfer der** linguistic innovator; **~schöpferisch** *Adj.* linguistically innovative *or* creative; **~silbe die** word element; element of word-formation; **~spiel das** *(Sprachw.)* language game; **~spielerei die** game with words; **~störung die** *(Med., Psych.)* language disorder; *(Sprechstörung)* speech disorder; **~studium das** *s.* **Sprachenstudium; ~übung die** language exercise; linguistic exercise; **~unterricht der** language teaching *or* instruction; **~verwirrung die** linguistic confusion; **~wissenschaft die** linguistics *sing., no art.*; **~wissenschaftler der** linguist; **~wissenschaftlich 1.** *Adj.* linguistic; **eine ~wissenschaftliche Abhandlung** a linguistics dissertation; **2.** *adv.* linguistically; **~wissenschaftlich interessierte Laien** laymen interested in linguistics

sprang [ʃpraŋ] *1. u. 3. Pers. Sg. Prät. v.* **springen**

spränge [ˈʃprɛŋə] *1. u. 3. Pers. Sg. Konjunktiv II v.* **springen**

Spray [ʃpreː] **das** *od.* **der; ~s, ~s** spray

Spray·dose die aerosol [can]

sprayen *tr., itr. V.* spray

Sprech-: ~an·lage die intercom *(coll.)*; **~blase die** balloon *(coll.)*; **~bühne die** theatre staging plays only; **~chor der** chorus; **im ~chor rufen** shout in chorus; chant ⟨*slogan*⟩

sprechen [ˈʃprɛçn̩] **1.** *unr. itr. V.* speak (**über** + *Akk.* about; **von** about, of); *(sich unterhalten, sich besprechen auch)* talk (**über** + *Akk.*, **von** about); ⟨*parrot etc.*⟩ talk; **deutsch/flüsternd ~:** speak German/in a whisper *or* whispers; **er spricht wenig** he doesn't say *or* talk much; **Das war das Hörspiel „...". Es sprachen: ...:** That was the play for radio '...'. Taking part were: ...; **es spricht Pfarrer N.** the speaker is the Revd. N.; **für/gegen etw. ~:** speak in favour of/against sth.; **das Sprechen fiel ihr noch schwer** she still found it difficult to speak; **mit jmdm. ~:** speak *or* talk with *or* to sb.; **seit dem Streit ~ sie nicht mehr miteinander** since the quarrel they are no longer on speaking terms *or* haven't been speaking to each other; **ich muß mit dir ~:** I must talk *or* speak with you; **er spricht mit sich selbst** he talks to himself; **wie sprichst du mit mir?** who do you think you're talking to?; **so spricht man nicht mit seiner Mutter** that's no way to talk *or* speak to one's mother; **sie spricht nicht mit jedem** she doesn't speak *or* talk to just anybody; **mit wem spreche ich?** who is speaking please?; to whom am I speaking, please?; **~ Sie noch?** *(am Telefon)* are you still there?; **er spricht gerade** *(telefoniert)* he's on the phone *(coll.)*; **worüber habt ihr gesprochen?** what were you talking about?; **es wurde über alles mögliche gesprochen** we/they *etc.* talked about all sorts of things; **darüber spricht er nicht gern** he doesn't like talking about that; **gut/schlecht von jmdm.** *od.* **über jmdn. ~:** speak well/ill of sb.; **für jmdn. ~:** speak for sb.; speak on *or (Amer.)* in behalf of sb.; **ich kann nur für mich ~:** I can only speak for myself; **vor einer Hörerschaft/der Betriebsversammlung ~:** speak in front of an audience/speak to *or* address a meeting of the work-force; **zu einem** *od.* **über ein Thema ~:** speak on *or* about a subject; **frei ~:** extemporize; speak without notes; **~ Sie!/bitte ~!** *(am Telefon)* you're through [now]; go ahead, please; **sprich!** *(geh.)* speak! *(literary)*; **also sprach der Herr/Buddha/Zarathustra** *(dichter.)* thus spake the Lord/Buddha/Zarathustra *(Bibl./literary)*; **laß Blumen ~!** say it with flowers!; **sein Herz ~ lassen** follow the dictates of one's heart; **aus seinen Worten/seinem Blick sprach Haß/Neid/Angst** *usw.* his words/the look in his eyes expressed hatred/envy/fear *etc.*; **auf jmdn./etw. zu ~ kommen** get to talking about sb./sth.; **auf jmdn. schlecht/nicht gut zu ~ sein** be ill-disposed towards sb.; **für/gegen jmdn./etw. ~** *(in günstigem/ungünstigem Licht erscheinen lassen)* be a point in sb.'s/sth.'s favour/against sb./sth.; **es scheint alles dafür/dagegen zu ~, daß die Regierung im Amt bleiben wird** it seems there is every reason to believe that the government will/won't stay in power; **was spricht denn dafür/dagegen?** what is there to be said for/against it?; **für sich [selbst] ~** *(fig.)* speak for itself/themselves. **2.** *unr. tr. V.* **a)** speak ⟨*language, dialect*⟩; say ⟨*word, sentence*⟩; **~ Sie Französisch?** do you speak French?; **„Hier spricht man Deutsch"** 'German spoken'; 'we speak German'; **b)** *(rezitieren)* say, recite ⟨*poem, text*⟩; say ⟨*prayer*⟩; recite ⟨*spell*⟩; pronounce ⟨*blessing, oath*⟩; **ein Schlußwort ~:** give *or* make a concluding speech; *s. auch* **Recht a; Urteil; c) jmdn. ~:** speak to sb.; **Sie haben mich ~ wollen?** you wanted to see me *or* speak to me?; **ich bin heute für niemanden mehr zu ~:** I can't see anyone else today; **kann ich Sie mal einen Moment ~?** can I see you for a moment?; can I have a quick word?; **wir [beide] ~ uns noch!** you haven't heard the last of this; **d)** *(aus~)* pronounce ⟨*name, word, etc.*⟩; **sprich ...:** *(auszusprechen)* pronounced ...; *(das heißt)* that is to say ...; **e)** *(sagen)* say; **und Gott sprach: „Es werde Licht!"** and God said, 'Let there be light'; **die Wahrheit ~:** speak the truth; **was spricht denn die Uhr?** *(fig. scherzh.)* what's the time?

sprechend *Adj.* convincing ⟨*example, evidence*⟩; expressive ⟨*face, eyes*⟩; eloquent ⟨*facial expression, glance, portrayal*⟩; descriptive ⟨*name*⟩

Sprecher der; ~s, ~ a) spokesman; **b)** *(Ansager)* announcer; *(Nachrichten~)* newscaster; news-reader; **c)** *(Kommentator, Erzähler)* narrator; **d)** *(Sprachw.: Sprachteilhaber, Sprechender)* speaker

Sprecherin die; ~, ~nen a) spokeswoman; **b)** *s.* **Sprecher b, c, d**

sprech-, Sprech-: ~erziehung die speech training; elocution; **~faul** *Adj.* uncommunicative; reluctant to talk *pred.*; **~funk der** radio-telephone system; **~funk·gerät das** radio-telephone; *(Walkie-talkie)* walkie-talkie; **~gesang der** sprechgesang; **sein Vortrag war eine Art ~gesang** he delivered his speech in a kind of singsong; **~muschel die** mouthpiece; **~platte die** spoken-word record; **~rolle die** speaking part; **~silbe die** [phonological] syllable; **~stimme die** speaking voice; *(Mus.)* sprechstimme; **~stunde die** consultation hours *pl.*; *(eines Arztes)* surgery; consulting hours *pl.*; *(eines Rechtsanwalts usw.)* office hours *pl.*; **wann haben Sie ~stunde?** when are your consultation hours/when is your surgery *or* what are your surgery hours?; **zum Zahnarzt/zu einem Abgeordneten in die ~stunde gehen** go to the dentist's/MP's surgery; **~stunden·hilfe die** *(eines Arztes)* receptionist; *(eines Zahnarztes)* assistant; **~tag der** *day on which authorities' offices are open to the public;* **heute ist kein ~tag** we/they are not open today; **~übung die** elocution *or* speech exercise; *(zu therapeutischen Zwecken)* speech exercise; **~weise die** manner of speaking; **~werkzeuge** *Pl.* speech-organs; organs of speech; **~zeit die** visiting time; **~zelle die** telephone booth; **~zimmer das** consulting-room

Spree-Athen (das) *(scherzh.)* Berlin

Spreißel [ˈʃpraisl̩] **der,** *(österr.)* **das; ~s, ~ a)** *(bes. südd.: Splitter)* splinter; **b)** *(bes. österr.: Span)* splint

Spreiz·dübel der expanding anchor

Spreize [ˈʃpraitsə] **die; ~, ~n a)** *(Bauw.)* horizontal stay *or* brace; **b)** *(Turnen)* **in der ~ stehen** stand with one leg extended behind/forward/to the side

spreizen 1. *tr. V.* spread ⟨*fingers, toes, etc.*⟩; **die Flügel/den Schwanz ~** ⟨*bird*⟩ spread its wings/tail; **die Beine ~:** spread one's legs apart; open one's legs; **mit gespreizten Beinen stehen/sitzen** stand/sit with one's legs apart; **das rechte Bein vorwärts/seitwärts ~:** extend one's right leg in front/to the side. **2.** *refl. V. (geh.)* **a)** *(sich zieren)* **sie spreizte sich erst dagegen, dann stimmte sie zu** she made a fuss at first, [but] then agreed; **b)** *(sich aufspielen)* give oneself airs; put on airs; **sie spreizte sich vor ihren Bewunderern** she strutted about in front of her admirers

Spreiz-: ~fuß der *(Med.)* spread foot; **~hose die** ≈ Frejka pillow *(kind of romper incorporating a padded steel splint for keeping an infant's legs in the frog position)*

Spreng·bombe die high-explosive bomb

Sprengel [ˈʃprɛŋl̩] **der; ~s, ~ a)** *(Kirchen~)* parish; *(Diözese)* diocese; **b)** *(österr.)* administrative district

sprengen [ˈʃprɛŋən] **1.** *tr. V.* **a)** blow up; blast ⟨*rock*⟩; **etw. in die Luft ~:** blow sth. up; **b)** *(gewaltsam öffnen, aufbrechen)* force [open] ⟨*door*⟩; force ⟨*lock*⟩; break open ⟨*burial chamber etc.*⟩; burst, break ⟨*bonds, chains*⟩; *(fig.)* break up ⟨*meeting, demonstration*⟩; **Eis sprengt den Felsen** ice is breaking up the rock; **die Freude sprengte ihm fast die Brust** *(fig.)* his heart was bursting with joy; *s. auch* **²Bank b; Rahmen b; c)** *(be~)* water ⟨*flower-bed, lawn*⟩; sprinkle ⟨*street, washing*⟩ with water; *(verspritzen)* sprinkle; *(mit dem Schlauch)* spray. **2.** *itr. V.* **a) im Steinbruch wird wieder gesprengt** they're blasting again in the quarry; **b)** *mit sein (geh.)* ⟨*rider*⟩ thunder

Spreng-: ~kammer die blast *or* charge chamber; **~kapsel die** blasting cap; **~kommando das** demolition squad; **~kopf der** warhead; **~kraft die** explosive power; **~ladung die** explosive charge; **~meister der** *(im Steinbruch)* blaster; shot firer; *(bei Abbrucharbeiten)* demolition expert; **~satz der** explosive charge

Sprengsel [ˈʃprɛnzl̩] **der** *od.* **das; ~s, ~** *(ugs.) s.* **Sprenkel**

Spreng-: ~stoff der explosive; **~stoffanschlag der** bomb attack

Sprengung die; ~, ~en a) blowing-up; *(im Steinbruch)* blasting; **er drohte mit der ~ des Gebäudes** he threatened to blow up the building; **b)** *s.* **sprengen 1b:** forcing [open]; forcing; breaking open; bursting; breaking; *(fig.)* breaking up; **c)** *(das Besprengen)* sprinkling; *(mit dem Schlauch)* spraying

Spreng·wagen der watering-cart; [street-]sprinkler

Sprenkel [ˈʃprɛŋkl̩] **der; ~s, ~:** spot; dot; speckle

sprenkeln *tr. V.* **a)** *(mit Flecken versehen)* sprinkle spots of ⟨*colour*⟩; **b)** *(spritzen)* sprinkle ⟨*water*⟩

Spreu [ʃprɔy] **die; ~:** chaff; **die ~ vom Weizen trennen** *od. (geh.)* **sondern** *(fig.)* separate the wheat from the chaff

sprich [ʃprɪç] *Imperativ Sg. v.* **sprechen**

sprichst [ʃprɪçst] *2. Pers. Sg. Präsens v.* **sprechen**

spricht [ʃprɪçt] *3. Pers. Sg. Präsens v.* **sprechen**

Sprich·wort das; *Pl.* **Sprichwörter** proverb

sprich·wörtlich 1. *Adj.* **a)** proverbial; **b)** *(fig.: notorisch)* proverbial. **2.** *adv.* **a) ..., so heißt es ~:** ..., as the proverb has it; **b)** *(fig.: notorisch)* proverbially

sprießen [ˈʃpriːsn̩] *unr. itr. V.; mit sein* ⟨*leaf,*

bud⟩ shoot, sprout; ⟨*seedlings*⟩ come *or* spring up; ⟨*beard*⟩ sprout; *(fig.)* ⟨*mistrust, envy, etc.*⟩ well up; ⟨*club, organization, etc.*⟩ spring up

Spriet [ʃpri:t] **das; ~[e]s, ~e** *(Seemannsspr.)* sprit

Spriet·segel das *(Seemannsspr.)* spritsail

Spring·brunnen der fountain

springen [ˈʃprɪŋən] **1.** *unr. itr. V.* **a)** *mit sein* jump; *(mit Schwung)* leap; spring; jump; ⟨*frog, flea*⟩ hop, jump; **vom Fünfmeterbrett ~:** dive from the five-metre board; **mit Anlauf/aus dem Stand ~:** take a running/standing jump; **jmdm. an die Kehle ~:** leap at sb.'s throat; **auf die Beine** *od.* **Füße ~:** jump to one's feet; **b)** *meist mit sein (Sport)* jump; *(beim Stabhochsprung, beim Kasten, Pferd)* vault; *(beim Turm~, Kunst~)* dive; **c)** *mit sein (sich in Sprüngen fortbewegen)* bound; **wenn sie einen Wunsch hat, springt die ganze Familie** when she wants something the whole family jumps to it; **d)** *(ugs.) in* **eine Runde Bier ~ lassen** stand a round of beer; **er könnte ruhig mal was ~ lassen** he could easily fork out something just once in a while *(sl.)*; **e)** *mit sein (fig.: schnellen, hüpfen, fliegen)* ⟨*pointer, milometer, etc.*⟩ jump (**auf** + *Akk.* to); ⟨*traffic-lights*⟩ change (**auf** + *Akk.* to); ⟨*spark*⟩ leap; ⟨*ball*⟩ bounce; ⟨*cork*⟩ pop out (**aus** + *Dat.* of); ⟨*spring*⟩ jump out; **[von etw.] ~** ⟨*fan belt, bicycle-chain, button, tyre, etc.*⟩ come off [sth.]; **die Lokomotive ist aus dem Gleis gesprungen** the locomotive jumped the rails; **f)** *mit sein (zer~, zerbrechen, zerreißen)* ⟨*string, glass, porcelain, etc.*⟩ break; **g)** *mit sein (aufplatzen, bersten)* ⟨*seed-pod*⟩ burst [open]; **gesprungene Lippen** cracked *or* chapped lips; **h)** *mit sein (Risse, Sprünge bekommen)* crack; **i)** *mit sein (fig. geh.: spritzen, sprudeln)* ⟨*fountain, jet of water, blood, etc.*⟩ spurt; **j)** *mit sein (südd.: laufen)* run; *(eilen)* hurry. **2.** *unr. tr. V.; auch mit sein (Sport)* perform ⟨*somersault, twist dive, etc.*⟩; **5,20 m/einen neuen Rekord ~:** jump 5.20m/make a record jump

Springer der; ~s, ~ a) *(Weit~, Hoch~, Ski~)* jumper; *(Stabhoch~)* [pole-]vaulter; *(Kunst~, Turm~)* diver; *(Fallschirm~)* parachutist; **b)** *(Schachfigur)* knight; **c) junger ~** *(ugs.)* greenhorn; **d)** *(Arbeiter)* worker who is moved from job to job as required

Springerin die; ~, ~nen *s.* **Springer a, d**

spring-, Spring-: ~flut die spring tide; **~form die** spring form; **~ins·feld der; ~[e]s, ~e** *(scherzh.) (leichtsinniger junger Mensch)* [young] madcap; *(lebhaftes Kind)* lively little nipper *(Brit. sl.)*; **~kraut das** impatience; **~lebendig** *Adj.* extremely lively; full of beans *pred. (coll.)*; **er ist trotz seines hohen Alters noch ~lebendig** he is still extremely sprightly despite his age; **~maus die** jerboa; **~messer das** flick-knife; **~pferd das** jumper; **~quell der** *(dichter.)* fountain; **~reiten das** show-jumping *no art.*; **~rollo das** roller blind; **~seil das** skipping-rope *(Brit.)*; jump-rope *(Amer.)*; **~turnier das** *(Reiten)* show-jumping competition

Sprinkler [ˈʃprɪŋklɐ] **der; ~s, ~:** sprinkler

Sprint [ʃprɪnt] **der; ~s, ~s** *(auch Sport)* sprint; **die letzten 100 Meter im ~ zurücklegen** sprint the last 100 metres

sprinten *itr. (auch tr.) V.; meist, mit Richtungsangaben nur, mit sein (Sport; ugs.: schnell laufen)* sprint

Sprinter der; ~s, ~, Sprinterin die; ~, ~nen *(Sport)* sprinter

Sprint·strecke die sprint distance

Sprit [ʃprɪt] **der; ~[e]s, ~e a)** *(ugs.: Treibstoff)* gas *(Amer. coll.)*; juice *(sl.)*; petrol *(Brit.)*; **b)** *(ugs.: Schnaps)* shorts *pl.*; **c)** *(Äthylalkohol)* ethanol; ethyl alcohol

Spritze [ˈʃprɪtsə] **die; ~, ~n a)** *(zum Vernichten von Ungeziefer)* spray; *(Teig~, Torten~, Injektions~)* syringe; **b)** *(Injektion)* injection; jab *(coll.)*; **eine ~ bekommen** have an injection *or (coll.)* jab; **an der ~ hängen** *(salopp)* be on the needle *(sl.)*; **c)** *(Feuer~)* hose; *(Löschfahrzeug)* fire engine

spritzen [ˈʃprɪtsn̩] **1.** *tr. V.* **a)** *(versprühen)* spray; *(ver~)* splash ⟨*water, ink, etc.*⟩; spatter ⟨*ink etc.*⟩; *(in Form eines Strahls)* spray, squirt ⟨*water, foam, etc.*⟩; pipe ⟨*cream etc.*⟩; **b)** *(be~, besprühen)* water ⟨*lawn, tennis-court*⟩; water, spray ⟨*street, yard*⟩; spray ⟨*plants, crops, etc.*⟩; pump ⟨*concrete*⟩; *(mit Lack)* spray ⟨*car etc.*⟩; **jmdn. naß ~:** splash sb.; *(mit Wasserpistole, Schlauch)* spray sb.; **den Fußboden/die Wände naß ~:** splash/spray water over the floor/walls; **jmdn. ~** *(ugs.: naß~)* squirt sb.; **c)** *(injizieren)* inject ⟨*drug etc.*⟩; **d)** *(~d herstellen)* create ⟨*ice-rink*⟩ by spraying; pipe ⟨*cake-decoration etc.*⟩; produce ⟨*plastic article*⟩ by injection moulding; **e)** *(ugs.: einer Injektion unterziehen)* **jmdn./sich ~:** give sb. an injection/inject oneself; **er hat sich mit einer Überdosis Heroin zu Tode gespritzt** he gave himself a fatal shot of heroin; **jmdm. ein Schmerzmittel ~:** give sb. a pain-killing injection; **f)** *(verdünnen)* dilute ⟨*wine etc.*⟩ with soda-water/lemonade *etc.* **2.** *itr. V.* **a) die Kinder planschten und spritzten** the children splashed and threw water about; **in meinem Garten wird nicht gespritzt** chemical sprays aren't used in my garden; **b)** *mit Richtungsangabe mit sein* ⟨*hot fat*⟩ spit; ⟨*mud etc.*⟩ spatter, splash; ⟨*blood, water*⟩ spurt; **das Wasser spritzte ihm ins Gesicht** the water splashed up into his face; **c)** *mit sein (ugs.: rennen)* dash; *(diensteifrig)* dash *or* chase about; **d)** *(ugs.: sich Rauschgift injizieren)* shoot *(sl.)*; **e)** *(derb: ejakulieren)* come [off] *(coll.)*

Spritzen·haus das *(veralt.)* fire station

Spritzer der; ~s, ~ *(kleiner Tropfen)* splash; *(von Farbe)* splash; spot; *(Schuß)* dash; splash; **ein paar ~ Spülmittel** a few squirts of washing-up liquid

Spritz-: ~flasche die a) spray-bottle; **b)** *(Chemie)* wash-bottle; **~gebäck das** *biscuit[s]/small cake[s] made by squeezing the dough through a piping bag*; **~guß der;** *o. Pl.* injection moulding *no art.*

spritzig 1. *Adj.* **a)** sparkling ⟨*wine*⟩; tangy ⟨*fragrance, perfume*⟩; **b)** *(lebendig)* lively ⟨*show, music, article*⟩; sparkling ⟨*production, performance*⟩; racy ⟨*style*⟩; **c)** *(temperamentvoll)* nippy *(coll.)*; zippy ⟨*car, engine*⟩; **d)** *(flink)* agile, nimble ⟨*person*⟩. **2.** *adv.* sparklingly ⟨*produced, performed, etc.*⟩; racily ⟨*written*⟩; **die Mannschaft spielte sehr ~:** the team played with great speed and agility

Spritz-: ~lack der spray paint; **~pistole die** spray-gun; **~tour die** *(ugs.)* spin

spröd, spröde [ʃprø:t] *Adj.* **a)** brittle ⟨*glass, plastic, etc.*⟩; dry ⟨*hair, lips, etc.*⟩; *(rissig)* chapped ⟨*lips, skin*⟩; *(rauh)* rough ⟨*skin*⟩; **b)** *(fig.: rauh klingend)* harsh, rough ⟨*voice*⟩; **c)** *(fig.: schwer handhabbar)* unwieldy ⟨*subject, problem*⟩; refractory ⟨*material*⟩; **d)** *(fig.: abweisend)* aloof ⟨*person, manner, nature*⟩; **eine Landschaft von spröder Schönheit** a landscape of forbidding beauty

Sprödheit, Sprödigkeit die; ~ a) *s.* **spröde a:** brittleness; dryness; roughness; **b)** *(fig.: rauher Klang)* harshness; roughness; **c)** *s.* **spröde c:** unwieldiness; refractoriness; **d)** *(fig.: abweisendes Wesen)* aloofness

sproß [ʃprɔs] *1. u. 3. Pers. Sg. Prät. v.* **sprießen**

Sproß der; Sprosses, Sprosse *od.* **Sprossen a)** *Pl.* **Sprosse** *(Bot.)* shoot; **b)** *Pl.* **Sprosse** *(geh.: Nachkomme)* scion; **c)** *Pl.* **Sprossen** *(Jägerspr.) s.* **Sprosse c**

Sprosse die; ~, ~n a) *(auch fig.)* rung; **b)** *(eines Fensters)* glazing bar; sash bar; **c)** *(Jägerspr.)* point; tine

sprossen *itr. V.* ⟨*plant*⟩ shoot, put forth shoots

Sprossen-: ~fenster das window with glazing bars; **~kohl der** *(österr.) s.* **Rosenkohl**; **~wand die** wall bars *pl.*

Sprößling [ˈʃprœslɪŋ] **der; ~s, ~e** *(ugs. scherzh.)* offspring; **seine ~e** his offspring *pl.*

Sproß·vokal der *(Sprachw.)* svarabhakti

Sprotte [ˈʃprɔtə] **die; ~, ~n** sprat; **Kieler ~n** smoked [Kiel] sprats

Spruch [ʃprʊx] **der; ~[e]s, Sprüche** [ˈʃprʏçə] **a)** *(Wahl~)* motto; *(Sinn~)* maxim; adage; *(Aus~)* saying; aphorism; *(Zitat)* quotation; quote; *(Parole)* slogan; *(Bibel~)* quotation; saying; **b)** *Pl. (ugs. abwertend: Phrase)* **das sind doch alles nur Sprüche** that's just talk *or* empty words *pl.*; **Sprüche machen** *od.* **klopfen** talk big *(coll.)*; **c)** *(Gedicht, Lied)* medieval lyric poem; **das Buch der Sprüche** *od.* **die Sprüche Salomos** *(bibl.)* [the Book of] Proverbs; **d)** *(Richter~)* judgement; *(Schieds~)* ruling; *(Orakel~)* oracle

Spruch-: ~band das; *Pl.* **~bänder a)** banner; **b)** *(auf einem Bild)* banderol[e]; **~dichtung die** [medieval] didactic poetry

Sprüche·klopfer der; ~s, ~ *(ugs. abwertend)* big mouth *(coll.)*

Spruch·kammer die *(Rechtsw. hist.)* denazification court

Sprüchlein [ˈʃprʏçlain] **das; ~s, ~ a)** *(kleiner Spruch)* short maxim; **b)** *(vorgefertigter Text)* little piece

spruch·reif *Adj.* **das ist noch nicht ~:** that's not definite, so people mustn't start talking about it yet; **die Angelegenheit ist jetzt ~:** the matter can now be discussed/decided

Spruch·weisheit die wise saying

Sprudel [ˈʃpru:dl̩] **der; ~s, ~ a)** *(Selterwasser)* sparkling mineral water; **b)** *(österr.: Erfrischungsgetränk)* fizzy drink

sprudeln 1. *itr. V.* **a)** *mit sein* ⟨*spring, champagne, etc.*⟩ bubble (**aus** out of); **b)** *(beim Kochen)* bubble; **c)** *(beim Entweichen von Gas)* ⟨*lemonade, champagne, etc.*⟩ fizz, effervesce; **ein ~des Getränk** a fizzy drink; **d)** *(fig.: überschäumen)* ⟨*person*⟩ bubble [over] (**vor** + *Dat.* with); **ein ~des Temperament** a bubbly *or* an effervescent temperament. **2.** *tr. V. (österr.: quirlen)* whisk

Sprudel·wasser das; *Pl.* **-wässer** sparkling mineral water

Sprudler der; ~s, ~ *(österr.)* whisk

Sprüh·dose die aerosol [can]

sprühen [ˈʃpry:ən] **1.** *tr. V.* spray; **Wasser auf die Blätter ~:** spray the leaves with water; **ich sprühte mir etwas Spray aufs Haar** I put some spray on my hair; **seine Augen sprühten Feuer** *od.* **Funken/Haß** *(fig.)* his eyes flashed fire/hatred. **2.** *itr. V.* **a)** *mit Richtungsangabe mit sein* ⟨*sparks, spray*⟩ fly; ⟨*flames*⟩ spit; ⟨*waterfall*⟩ send out a fine spray; *(fig.)* ⟨*eyes*⟩ sparkle (**vor** + *Dat.* with); ⟨*intellect, wit*⟩ sparkle; **ein feiner Regen sprühte gegen die Scheibe** a fine rain drifted against the window pane; **aus seinen Augen sprühte Feuer/Zorn** *(fig.)* fire/anger flashed in his eyes; **~der Witz** sparkling wit; **ein ~des Temperament** a bubbly *or* effervescent temperament; **von Ideen/vor Witz** *(Dat.)* **~** *(fig.)* bubble [over] with ideas/sparkle with wit; **b)** *unpers. (regnen)* **es sprüht** it is drizzling

Sprüh-: ~flasche die spray-bottle; **~pflaster das** spray dressing; **~regen der** drizzle; fine rain

Sprung [ʃprʊŋ] **der; ~[e]s, Sprünge** [ˈʃprʏŋə] **a)** *(auch Sport)* jump; *(schwungvoll)* leap; *(Satz)* bound; *(Sprung über das Pferd)* vault; *(Wassersport)* dive; *(fig.)* leap; **zum ~ ansetzen** ⟨*tiger etc.*⟩ get ready to pounce; **sein Herz machte vor Freude einen ~** *(fig.)* his heart leapt for joy; **ein [großer] ~ nach vorn** *(fig.)* a [great] leap forward; **sie hat den ~ zum Film nicht geschafft** *(fig.)* she didn't manage to move into films; **ein qualitativer ~** *(Philos.)* a qualitative leap; **~ auf, marsch, marsch!** *(Milit.)* on your feet, quick march!; **ein ~ ins kalte Wasser** *(fig.)* jumping in at the deep end; **keine großen Sprünge machen können** *(fig. ugs.)* not be able to afford many luxuries; **auf einen ~** *(fig. ugs.)* for a few minutes; **auf dem ~[e] sein** *(fig. ugs.)* be in a rush; **b)** *(ugs.: kurze Entfernung)* stone's throw; *(mit dem Auto)* short drive; **c)** *(Riß)* crack; **einen ~ haben/bekommen** be cracked/crack; **einen ~ in der Schüssel haben** *(salopp)* be cracked *(coll.)*; **d)** *in* **jmdm. auf die Sprünge helfen** *(ugs.)* help sb. on his/her way; **jmds. Gedächtnis auf die Sprünge helfen** jog sb.'s memory; **jmdm. auf** *od.* **hinter die Sprünge kommen** *(fig. ugs.)* get on to sb.; **e)** *(Jägerspr.: Gruppe von Rehen)* herd; **f)** *(Geol.)* fault

sprung-, Sprung-: ~bein das a) take-off leg; **b)** *(Anat.)* ankle bone; **~bereit** *Adj.* ready to jump *pred.*; ‹cat› ready to pounce *pred.*; **~brett das** *(auch fig.)* springboard; **~deckel der** spring lid; **~feder die** [spiral] spring; **~gelenk das** *(Anat.)* ankle joint

sprunghaft 1. *Adj.* **a)** *(unstet)* erratic ‹*person, character, manner*›; **b)** *(unzusammenhängend)* disjointed ‹*conversation, thoughts*›; **c)** *(unvermittelt)* sudden; abrupt; **d)** *(ruckartig)* rapid ‹*change*›; sharp ‹*increase*›. **2.** *adv.*; *s.* **1 b–d:** disjointedly; suddenly; abruptly; rapidly; sharply

Sprunghaftigkeit die; ~: *s.* **sprunghaft 1 a, b:** erraticness; disjointedness

Sprung-: ~höhe die height; **~lauf der** *(Ski)* ski-jumping *no art.*; **~rahmen der** spring bed-frame; **~schanze die** *(Ski)* ski-jumping hill; **~seil das** skipping-rope *(Brit.)*; jump-rope *(Amer.)*; **~tuch das;** *Pl.* **~tücher** safety blanket; **~turm der** *(Sport)* diving-platform

Spucke die; ~: spit; **mir blieb die ~ weg** *(ugs.)* it took my breath away; I was speechless; *s. auch* **Geduld**

spucken ['ʃpʊkn̩] **1.** *itr. V.* **a)** spit; **in die Hände ~** *(fig.: an die Arbeit gehen)* go to work with a will; **b)** *(ugs.: erbrechen)* throw up *(coll.)*; be sick *(Brit.)*; **c) auf etw.** *(Akk.)* **~** *(salopp)* not give a damn about sth. **2.** *tr. V.* spit; spit [up], cough up ‹*blood, phlegm*›; spew out ‹*lava*›; **Feuer ~:** breathe fire; ‹*volcano*› belch fire; *s. auch* **²Ton d**

Spuck·napf der spittoon

Spuk [ʃpu:k] **der; ~[e]s, ~e a)** [ghostly *or* supernatural] manifestation; **b)** *(abwertend: schreckliches Geschehen)* horrific episode

spuken *itr. V.* **a)** *auch unpers.* **in dem Haus spukt ein Geist** this house is haunted by a ghost; **hier/in dem Haus spukt es** this place/the house is haunted; **gestern hat es wieder gespukt** there was another manifestation *or* haunting yesterday; **dieser Aberglaube spukt noch immer in den Köpfen vieler Menschen** *(fig.)* this superstition still lurks in many people's minds; **b)** *mit sein* **durch die Gänge ~:** walk *or* haunt the corridors

Spuk-: ~gestalt die ghostly figure; **~schloß das** haunted castle

Spül-: ~becken das a) sink; **b)** *(beim Zahnarzt usw.)* basin; **~bürste die** washing-up brush

Spule ['ʃpu:lə] **die; ~, ~n a)** spool; bobbin; *(für Tonband, Film)* spool; reel; **b)** *(Elektrot.)* coil

Spüle die; ~, ~n sink unit; *(Becken)* sink

spulen *tr., itr. V.* spool; *(am Tonbandgerät)* wind; **etw. auf etw.** *(Akk.)* **~:** wind sth. on to sth.

spülen ['ʃpy:lən] **1.** *tr. V.* **a)** rinse; bathe ‹*wound*›; **b)** *(landsch.: abwaschen)* wash up ‹*dishes, glasses, etc.*›; **Geschirr ~:** wash up; **c)** *(schwemmen)* wash. **2.** *itr. V.* **a)** *(beim WC)* flush [the toilet]; **b)** *(den Mund ausspülen)* rinse out [one's mouth]; **c)** *(landsch.) s.* **abwaschen 2**

Spül-: ~kasten der cistern; **~maschine die** dishwasher; **~mittel das** washing-up liquid; **~schwamm der** washing-up sponge; **~tuch das;** *Pl.* **~tücher** dish cloth

Spülung die, ~, ~en a) *(Med.)* irrigation; *(der Vagina)* douche; **b)** *(beim WC)* flush

Spül·wasser das; *Pl.* **~wässer a)** rinse water; **b)** *(Abwaschwasser)* dish-water

Spul·wurm der ascarid

Spund [ʃpʊnt] **der; ~[e]s, ~e/Spünde** ['ʃpyndə] **a)** *Pl.* **Spünde** *(Zapfen)* bung; **b)** *Pl.* **~e** *(ugs.)* **[junger** *od.* **grüner] ~:** young greenhorn *or* tiro

Spund-: ~loch das bung-hole; **~wand** *(Bauw.)* sheet-pile wall

Spur [ʃpu:ɐ] **die; ~, ~en a)** *(Abdruck im Boden)* track; *(Folge von Abdrücken)* tracks *pl.*; *(Blut~, Schleim~ usw.)* trail; **von dem Vermißten fehlt jede ~:** there is no trace of the missing person; **eine heiße ~** *(fig.)* a hot trail; **eine heiße ~ haben** *(fig.)* have a really good lead; **jmdm./einer Sache auf die ~ kommen** get on to the track of sb./sth.; **jmdm./einer Sache auf der ~ sein** be on the track *or* trail of sb./sth.; **b)** *(Anzeichen)* trace; *(eines Verbrechens)* clue *(Gen.* to); **die ~en des Krieges/häufigen Gebrauchs** the marks of war/frequent use; **c)** *(sehr kleine Menge; auch fig.)* trace; **da fehlt noch eine ~ Paprika** it needs just a touch of paprika; **er hat keine ~ [von] Ehrgefühl** he has not the slightest sense of honour; **von Reue/Mitgefühl keine ~/nicht die leisteste ~:** not a trace *or* sign/not the slightest trace *or* sign of penitence/sympathy; **keine** *od.* **nicht die ~** *(ugs.: als Antwort)* not in the slightest; **d)** *(Verkehrsw.: Fahr~)* lane; **die ~ wechseln** change lanes; **in** *od.* **auf der rechten/linken ~ fahren** drive in the right-hand/left-hand lane; **e)** *(Fahrlinie)* **[die] ~ halten** stay on its line; **aus der ~ kommen** be thrown off its line; **f)** *(Technik) s.* **~weite; g)** *(Elektrot., DV)* track

spürbar 1. *Adj.* noticeable; perceptible; distinct, perceptible ‹*improvement*›; evident ‹*relief, embarrassment*›. **2.** *adv.* noticeably; perceptibly; *(sichtlich)* clearly ‹*relieved, on edge*›; **die Temperatur ist ~ gesunken/gestiegen** there has been a noticeable drop/rise in temperature; **~ besser/schlechter werden** distinctly improve/deteriorate

Spur·breite die *s.* **~weite**

spuren 1. *itr. V. (ugs.)* toe the line *(coll.)*; do as one's told. **2.** *tr. V. (Ski)* prepare ‹*cross-country course*›

spüren [ʃpy:rən] **1.** *tr. V.* feel; *(instinktiv)* sense; *(merken)* notice; **nach der Anstrengung spürte ich alle Knochen** I could feel every bone in my body after the exertion; **ich spüre mein Kreuz/meinen Magen** I have a pain in my back/my stomach; **die Peitsche zu ~ bekommen** get a taste of the whip; **jmds. Haß zu ~ bekommen** suffer sb.'s hatred; **von Kameradschaft war nichts zu ~:** there wasn't a sign *or* trace of comradeship; **er ließ uns seine Verärgerung nicht ~:** he gave [us] no sign of his annoyance; **sie ließ ihn ~, daß sie ihn nicht mochte** she made it plain [to him] *or* let him see that she didn't like him. **2.** *itr. V. (Jägerspr.)* **[nach einem Tier] ~:** track [an animal]

Spuren-: ~element das; *meist Pl. (Biochemie)* trace element; **~sicherung die** *(Polizeiw.)* **a)** *(Vorgang)* collection of evidence; **b)** *(Abteilung)* scene-of-crime *or* forensic unit

Spür·hund der tracker dog; *(fig.: Spitzel)* bloodhound; snooper *(coll.)*

spur·los 1. *Adj.; nicht präd.* total, complete ‹*disappearance*›. **2.** *adv.* ‹*disappear*› completely *or* without trace; **an jmdm. ~ vorübergehen** leave sb. untouched; have no effect on sb.; **es ist nicht ~ an ihm vorübergegangen** it has not failed to leave its mark on him

Spür-: ~nase die *(ugs.)* **a)** *(Geruchssinn, fig.)* nose; **b)** *(Person)* bloodhound; snooper *(coll.)*; **~sinn der;** *o. Pl. (feiner Instinkt)* intuition

Spurt [ʃpʊrt] **der; ~[e]s, ~s** *od.* **~e a)** spurt; **b)** *o. Pl. (Sport.: ~vermögen)* turn of speed

spurten *itr. V.* **a)** *mit Richtungsangabe mit sein* spurt; **b)** *mit sein (ugs.: schnell laufen)* sprint

spurt·stark *Adj. (bes. Sport)* capable of putting on a strong spurt *or* of sprinting strongly *postpos.*; nippy *(coll.)* ‹*car*›

Spur-: ~wechsel der change of lane; **~weite die** *(Kfz-W.)* track; *(Eisenb.)* gauge

sputen ['ʃpu:tn̩] *refl. V. (veralt.)* make haste

Sputnik ['ʃpʊtnɪk] **der; ~s, ~s** sputnik

Squash [skvɔʃ] **das; ~:** *(Sport)* squash *no art.*

Squaw [skwɔ:] **die; ~, ~s** squaw

SR *Abk.* **Saarländischer Rundfunk** Saarland Radio

SRG *Abk.* **Schweizerische Radio- und Rundfunkgesellschaft** Swiss Broadcasting Company

Sri Lanka ['sri: 'laŋka] **(das); ~s** Sri Lanka

Srilanker der; ~s, ~, Srilankerin die; ~, ~nen Sri Lankan

srilankisch *Adj.* Sri Lankan

¹SS [ɛs'/ɛs-] *(ns.)* **die; ~** *Abk.* **Schutzstaffel** SS

²SS *Abk.* **Sommersemester**

SSD [ɛs/ɛs'de:] *(DDR)* **der; ~** *Abk.* **Staatssicherheitsdienst**

SS-Mann der; *Pl.* **-Männer** *od.* **-Leute** SS man

SSO *Abk.* **Südsüdost[en]** SSE

SSV *Abk.* **Sommerschlußverkauf**

SSW *Abk.* **Südsüdwest[en]** SSW

St. *Abk.* **a) Sankt** St.; **b) Stück**

s. t. *Abk.* **sine tempore**

Staat ['ʃta:t] **der; ~[e]s, ~en a)** state; **die ~en** *(die USA)* the States; **von ~s wegen** on the part of the [state] authorities; **beim ~ [angestellt] sein** be a civil servant *or* in the civil service; **s. auch Vater a; b)** *o. Pl. (ugs.: Festkleidung, Pracht)* finery; **in vollem ~:** in all one's finery; **damit ist kein ~ zu machen** *(fig.)* it's not up to much *(coll.)*; **mit diesem Mantel ist kein ~ mehr zu machen** *(fig. ugs.)* this coat is past it *(coll.)*; **c)** *(Zool.: Insekten~)* colony

staaten-, Staaten-: ~bildend *Adj.; nicht präd. (Zool.)* social ‹*insect*›; **~bund der** confederation; **~los** *Adj.* stateless; **~lose der/die;** *adj. Dekl.* stateless person *or* subject

staatlich 1. *Adj.* state *attrib.* ‹*sovereignty, institutions, authorities, control, etc.*›; ‹*power, unity, etc.*› of the state; state-owned ‹*factory etc.*›; **~e Mittel** government *or* public money *sing.* **2.** *adv.* by the state; **~ anerkannt/geprüft/gelenkt/finanziert** state-approved/-certified/-managed/-financed; **~ subventioniert werden** receive a state subsidy

staats-, Staats-: ~affäre die: eine ~affäre aus etw. machen *(ugs.)* make a song and dance about sth. *(coll.)*; **~akt der a)** *(Festakt)* state ceremony; **b)** *(Rechtsvorgang)* act of state; **~aktion die: eine ~aktion aus etw. machen** *(ugs.)* make a song and dance about sth. *(coll.)*; **~amateur der** *(Sport) state-sponsored, nominally amateur, sportsman*; **~amt das** public office; **~angehörige der/die** national; **~angehörigkeit die** nationality; **~anleihe die** government bond; **~anwalt der** public prosecutor; **~anwaltschaft die** public prosecutor's office; **~apparat der** state machine; **~aus·gaben** *Pl.* public expenditure *sing.*; **~bank die** national bank; **~beamte der** civil servant; **~begräbnis das** state funeral; **~besuch der** state visit; **~bürger der** citizen; **er ist deutscher ~bürger** he is a German citizen *or* national; *s. auch* **Uni-**

form; ~**bürger·kunde die** *(DDR) school subject involving ideological education of socialist citizens;* ≈ civics *sing. no art.*; ~**bürgerlich** *Adj.; nicht präd.* civil ‹*rights*›; civic ‹*duties, loyalty*›; ‹*education, attitude*› as a citizen; ~**bürgerschaft die** *s.* ~angehörigkeit; ~**chef der** head of state; ~**diener der** *(meist scherzh.)* public servant; ~**dienst der** civil service; ~**eigen** *Adj.* state-owned; ~**eigentum das** state property; ~**examen das** *final university examination;* ~**examen machen** ≈ take one's finals; ~**feind der** enemy of the state; ~**feindlich** *Adj.* anti-state; ‹*organization, attitude*› hostile to the state; ~**finanzen** *Pl.* public finances; ~**flagge die** state flag; *(Nationalflagge)* national flag; ~**form die** type of state; state system; ~**gebiet das** territory [of a/the state]; ~**gefährdend** *Adj.* subversive; anti-state; ~**gefährdung die** subversion [of the state]; ~**geheimnis das** *(auch fig.)* state secret; ~**geschäft das;** *meist Pl.* affair of state; ~**gewalt die** *o. Pl.* authority of the state; *(Exekutive)* executive power; ~**grenze die** state frontier *or* border; ~**haushalt der** national budget; ~**hoheit die** sovereignty; ~**hymne die** *(bes. DDR)* national anthem; ~**kanzlei die** *(BRD)* Minister-President's Office; *(Schweiz)* Cantonal Chancellory; ~**karosse die** state coach; *(fig. scherzh.)* prestige limo *(Amer. coll.) or* limousine; ~**kasse die a)** public purse ; **b)** *(Fiskus)* treasury; ~**kirche die** state *or* established church; ~**kosten** *Pl.* **auf ~kosten** at public expense; ~**kunst die;** *o. Pl. (geh.)* statemanship; statecraft; ~**macht die** power [of government]; ~**mann der;** *Pl.* **-männer** statesman; ~**männisch** [~mɛnɪʃ] **1.** *Adj.* statesmanlike ‹*wisdom, far-sightedness, etc.*›; ‹*abilities, skill*› of a statesman; **2.** *adv.* in a statesmanlike manner; ~**minister der** minister of state; *(Minister ohne Ressort)* minister without portfolio; *(BRD: Staatssekretär)* secretary of state; ~**ober·haupt das** head of state; ~**oper die** State Opera; ~**organ das** organ *or* instrument of state; ~**partei die** [totalitarian] government party; ~**politisch 1.** *Adj.* ‹*aims, tasks, etc.*› of national policy; **2.** *adv.* from the point of view of national policy; ~**polizei die** state police; ~**präsident der** [state] president; ~**prüfung die** state examination; ~**raison die,** ~**räson die** reasons *pl.* of State *no def. art.*; **aus [Gründen der] ~:** for reasons of state; ~**recht das;** *o. Pl.* constitutional law; ~**rechtler** [...rɛçtlɐ] **der** expert in constitutional law; ~**regierung die** national government; ~**religion die** state religion; ~**säckel der** *(scherzh.)* state coffers *pl.*; ~**schatz der** national *or* state reserves *pl.*; ~**schiff das** *(geh.)* ship of state; ~**schuld die;** *meist Pl.* national debt; ~**sekretär der** permanent secretary; ~**sicherheit die;** *o. Pl.* **a)** state security; **b)** *(DDR ugs.) s.* ~**sicherheitsdienst;** ~**sicherheits·dienst der** *(DDR)* State Security Service; ~**streich der** coup d'état; ~**theater das** state theatre; ~**trauer die** national mourning *no indef. art.*; ~**verbrechen das** crime against the state; ~**verschuldung die** national debt; ~**vertrag der** international treaty; *(zwischen Gliedstaaten)* inter-state treaty *or* agreement; **der Österreichische ~vertrag** the Austrian State Treaty; ~**wesen das** state [system]; ~**wohl das** welfare *or* good of the state

Stab [ʃta:p] **der;** ~[e]s, **Stäbe** ['ʃtɛ:bə] **a)** rod; *(länger, für ~hochsprung o. ä.)* pole; *(eines Käfigs, Gitters, Geländers)* bar; *(Staffel~; geh.: Taktstock)* baton; *(Bischofs~)* crosier; *(Hirten~)* crook; **den ~ über jmdn./etw. brechen** *(geh.)* condemn sb./sth. out of hand; **b)** *(Milit.)* staff; **c)** *(Team)* team

Stäbchen ['ʃtɛ:pçən] **das;** ~s, ~ **a)** *(kleiner Stab)* little rod; [small] stick; **b)** *(Eß~)* chopstick

Stabelle [ʃta'bɛlə] **die;** ~, ~n *(schweiz.)* stool

Stab-: ~**hoch·springen das** pole-vaulting *no art.*; ~**hoch·springer der** pole-vaulter; ~**hoch·sprung der a)** *o. Pl. (Disziplin)* pole-vaulting *no art.*; **im ~hochsprung** in the pole-vault; **b)** *(Sprung)* pole-vault

stabil [ʃta'bi:l] **1.** *Adj.* **a)** *(solide, kräftig)* sturdy ‹*chair, cupboard*›; solid, sturdy ‹*construction*›; robust, sound ‹*health, constitution*›; **b)** *(beständig, dauerhaft)* stable ‹*prices, government, economy, Chem.: solution, etc.*›. **2.** *adv.* ~ **gebaut** solidly built

Stabilisator [ʃtabili 'za:tɔr] **der;** ~s, ~en [-'to:rən] *(Technik, Chemie)* stabilizer; *(Kfz-W.)* anti-roll bar

stabilisieren 1. *tr. V.* stabilize. **2.** *refl. V.* **a)** stabilize; become more stable; **b)** ‹*health, circulation, etc.*› become stronger

Stabilisierung die; ~, ~en **a)** stabilization; **b)** *(Kräftigung)* strengthening

Stabilität [ʃtabili'tɛ:t] **die;** ~ **a)** *(einer Konstruktion)* sturdiness; *(von Gesundheit, Konstitution usw.)* robustness; soundness; **b)** *(das Beständigsein)* stability

Stab-: ~**lampe die** torch *(Brit.)*; flashlight *(Amer.)*; ~**magnet der** bar magnet; ~**reim der** *(Verslehre)* stave-rhyme; head rhyme

Stabs-: ~**arzt der** *(Milit.)* medical officer, MO *(with the rank of captain);* ~**feldwebel der** *(Milit.)* warrant-officer 2nd class; ~**offizier der** *(Milit.)* staff officer

Staccato [sta'ka:to] *s.* Stakkato

stach [ʃta:x] *1. u. 3. Pers. Sg. Prät. v.* **stechen**

Stachel ['ʃtaçl̩] **der;** ~s, ~n **a)** spine; *(Dorn)* thorn; **b)** *(Gift~)* sting; **c)** *(spitzes Metallstück)* spike; *(von ~draht)* barb; *s. auch* **löcken; d)** *(geh.: etw. Quälendes)* barb; **der ~ der Eifersucht** the torment of jealousy; **einer Sache** *(Dat.)* **den ~ nehmen** take the sting out of sth.; **ein ~ im Fleisch** a thorn in the flesh; **e)** *(etw. Stimulierendes)* **der ~ des Ehrgeizes** the spur of ambition

Stachel-: ~**beere die** gooseberry; ~**draht der** barbed wire; ~**häuter** [-hɔytɐ] **der;** ~s, ~ *(Zool.)* echinoderm

stachelig *Adj.* prickly

stacheln *itr. V.* prick; ‹*beard*› prickle

Stachel·schwein das porcupine

stachlig *s.* stachelig

Stadel [ʃta:dl̩] **der;** ~s, ~ *od. (schweiz.)* **Städel** *od. (österr.)* ~n *(südd., österr., schweiz.)* barn

Stadion ['ʃta:di̯ɔn] **das;** ~s, **Stadien** stadium

Stadium ['ʃta:di̯ʊm] **das;** ~s, **Stadien** stage

Stadt [ʃtat] **die;** ~, **Städte** ['ʃtɛ(:)tə] **a)** town; *(Groß~)* city; **die ~ Basel** the city of Basel; **in die ~ gehen** go into town; go downtown *(Amer.)*; ~ **und Land** town and country; **in ~ und Land** throughout the country; **b)** *(Verwaltung)* town council; *(in der Großstadt)* city council; city hall *no art. (Amer.)*; **bei der ~ [angestellt] sein/arbeiten** work for the council *or (Amer.)* for city hall

stadt-, Stadt-: ~**auswärts** *Adv.* out of town; ~**auto·bahn die** urban motorway *(Brit.) or (Amer.)* freeway; ~**bahn die** urban railway; ~**bekannt** *Adj.* well known in the town/city *postpos.*; known all over the town/city *postpos.*; *(berüchtigt)* notorious throughout the town/city *postpos.*; ~**bevölkerung die** urban population; *(einer bestimmten Stadt)* townspeople *pl.*; ~**bewohner der** town-/city-dweller; ~**bibliothek die** municipal library; ~**bild das** townscape; *(einer Großstadt)* cityscape; ~**bücherei die** municipal [lending] library; ~**bummel der** *(ugs.)* **einen ~bummel machen** take a stroll through the town/city centre

Städtchen ['ʃtɛ(:)tçən] **das;** ~s, ~: little town; **andere ~, andere Mädchen** move to a new town and you find a new girl

Stadt·chronik die history of the town/city

Städte·bau der; *o. Pl.* urban building *or* development *no art.*; *(Planung)* town planning *no art.*

städte·baulich 1. *Adj.; nicht präd.* ‹*development*› of urban building/town planning; town-planning ‹*measure*›. **2.** *adv.* from the point of view of town planning

stadt·einwärts *Adv.* into town; downtown *(Amer.)*

Städte·partnerschaft die twinning *(Brit.) or (Amer.)* sister-city arrangement *(between towns/cities)*

Städter der; ~s, ~, **Städterin die;** ~, ~nen **a)** town-dweller; *(Großstädter, -städterin)* city-dweller; **b)** *(Stadtmensch)* townie *(coll.)*

Stadt-: ~**flucht die** migration from the city; ~**führer der** town/city guidebook; ~**gas das** town gas; ~**gespräch das a)** *(Telefongespräch)* local call; **b)** *in* ~**gespräch sein** be the talk of the town; [1]~**guerilla die** urban guerilla group; [2]~**guerilla der** urban guerrilla; ~**halle die** civic *or* municipal hall; ~**haus das a)** *(Verwaltungsgebäude)* council office building; **b)** *(Wohnhaus)* town house

städtisch 1. *Adj.* **a)** *(kommunal)* municipal; **das Altersheim ist ~:** the old people's home is owned by the town/city; **b)** *(urban)* urban ‹*life, way of life, etc.*›; town ‹*clothes*›; ‹*manners, clothes*› of a town-dweller. **2.** *adv.* **a)** *(kommunal)* municipally; ~ **verwaltet** run by the town/city council; **b)** *(urban)* ~**/ausgesprochen ~ gekleidet** wearing town clothes/wearing clothes with a decidedly town style

Stadt-: ~**kämmerer der** town/city treasurer; ~**kasse die a)** *(Geldmittel)* municipal funds *pl., no art.*; **b)** *(Stelle)* town/city treasurer's office; ~**kern der** *s.* ~**mitte;** ~**kind das a)** town/city child; **b)** *(~mensch)* townie *(coll.)*; ~**kreis der** urban district; ~**landschaft die** townscape; urban landscape; ~**mauer die** town/city wall; ~**mensch der** townie *(coll.)*; ~**mission die** town/city mission; ~**mitte die** town centre; *(einer Großstadt)* city centre; downtown area *(Amer.)*; ~**park der** municipal park; ~**parlament das** city council; ~**plan der** [town/city] street plan *or* map; ~**planung die** town planning *no art.*; ~**rand der** outskirts *pl.* of the town/city; **am ~:** on the outskirts of the town/city; ~**rat der a)** town/city council; **b)** *(Mitglied)* town/city councillor; ~**recht das** town ordinances and privileges *pl.*; ~**recht erhalten** receive its town charter; ~**rund·fahrt die** sightseeing tour round a/the town/city; ~**sanierung die** town/city redevelopment; ~**schreiber der a)** *(hist.)* town clerk; **b)** *(Schriftsteller)* writer-in-residence *(living in a town/city and writing about it);* ~**staat der** city-state; ~**streicher der** town/city tramp; ~**teil der** district; part [of a/the town]; ~**theater das** municipal theatre; ~**tor das** town/city gate; ~**väter** *Pl. (ugs. scherzh.)* city fathers; ~**verkehr der** town/city traffic; ~**verordnete der/die;** *adj. Dekl.* town/city councillor; ~**verwaltung die** municipal authority; town/city council; ~**viertel das** district; ~**wappen das** town/city coat-of-arms; ~**werke** *Pl.* municipal *or* council services; ~**wohnung die** town/city flat *(Brit.) or (Amer.)* apartment; ~**zentrum das** town/city centre; downtown area *(Amer.)*

Stafette [ʃta'fɛtə] **die;** ~, ~n **a)** *(hist.: reitender Bote)* courier *(as one of a relay);* **b)** *(Gruppe von Kurieren)* relay; **c)** *(Formation als Begleitung)* formation of outriders

Staffage [ʃta'fa:ʒə] **die;** ~, ~n, **a)** *(Beiwerk)* accessories *pl.*; *(Dekoration)* decoration; **b)** *(bild. Kunst)* staffage

Staffel ['ʃtafl] **die; ~, ~n a)** *(Sport: Mannschaft)* team; *(für den ~lauf)* relay team; **b)** *(Sport: ~lauf)* relay race; **c)** *(Luftwaffe: Einheit)* flight; **d)** *(Formation von Schiffen, begleitenden Polizisten, usw.)* escort formation

Staffelei die; ~, ~en easel

Staffel-: ~lauf der *(Sport)* relay race; **~läufer der** *(Sport)* relay runner/skier

staffeln *tr. V.* **a)** *(aufstellen, formieren)* arrange in a stagger *or* in an echelon; **gestaffelte Abwehr** *(Fußball)* staggered defence [line-up]; **b)** *(einteilen, abstufen)* grade ‹*salaries, fees, prices*›; stagger ‹*times, arrivals, starting-places*›

Staffelung die; ~, ~en a) *(Anordnung)* staggered arrangement; **b)** *(Einteilung, Abstufung) (von Gebühren, Gehältern, Preisen)* grad[u]ation; *(von Vorgängen)* staggering

Stag [ʃta:k] **das; ~[e]s, ~e[n]** *(Seew.)* stay

Stagflation [ʃtakfla'tsio:n] **die; ~, ~en** *(Wirtsch.)* stagflation

Stagnation [ʃtagna'tsio:n] **die; ~, ~en** stagnation

stagnieren *itr. V.* stagnate

Stag·segel das *(Seew.)* staysail

stahl [ʃta:l] *1. u. 3. Pers. Sg. Prät. v.* **stehlen**

Stahl der; ~[e]s, Stähle ['ʃtɛ:lə] *od.* **~e a)** steel; **Nerven wie** *od.* **aus ~ haben** have nerves of steel; **b)** *(dichter.: Dolch, Schwert)* blade

stahl-, Stahl-: ~arbeiter der steelworker; **~bau der;** *Pl.* **~bauten a)** *o. Pl. (Bautechnik)* steel construction *no art.*; **b)** *(Gebäude)* steel-frame building; **~besen der** *(Musik)* wire brush; **~beton der** *(Bauw.)* reinforced concrete; ferroconcrete; **~beton·bau der;** *o. Pl.* reinforced concrete construction; **~blau** *Adj.* steel-blue; **~blech das** sheet steel

stählen *tr. V. (geh.)* toughen; harden

stählern *Adj.* **a)** *nicht präd. (aus Stahl)* steel; **b)** *(fig. geh.)* ‹*muscles, nerves*› of steel; ‹*will*› of iron

stahl-, Stahl-: ~grau *Adj.* steel-grey; **~hart** *Adj.* as hard as steel *postpos.*; **~helm der** *(Milit.)* steel helmet; **~kammer die** strong-room; **~kocher der** *(ugs.)* steelworker; **~mantel·geschoß das** *(Milit.)* steel-jacketed bullet; **~rohr das** steel tube; **~rohr·möbel das;** *meist Pl.* tubular steel furniture *no pl.*; **~roß das** *(ugs. scherzh.)* bike *(coll.)*; trusty steed *(coll. joc.)*; **~stich der** *(Graphik)* steel engraving; **~verarbeitend** *Adj.; nicht präd.* steel-processing; steel ‹*industry, firm*›; **~waren** *Pl.* steelware *sing.*; **~wolle die** steel wool

stak [ʃta:k] *1. u. 3. Pers. Sg. Prät. v.* **stecken**

Stake die; ~, ~n, Staken der; ~s, ~ *(nordd.)* pole

staken 1. *tr. V.* punt ‹*boat*›. **2.** *itr. V.; mit sein* punt

Staket [ʃta'ke:t] **das; ~[e]s, ~e a)** *(Lattenzaun)* paling [fence]; **b)** *(Latte)* pale

Stakete die; ~, ~n *(bes. österr.) s.* **Staket b**

Staketen·zaun der paling fence

Stakkato [ʃta'ka:to] **das; ~s, ~s** *od.* **Stakkati** *(Musik; auch fig.)* staccato

staksen ['ʃta:ksn̩] *itr. V.; mit sein (ugs.)* stalk; *(taumelnd)* teeter

staksig *(ugs.)* **1.** *Adj.* spindly, shaky-legged ‹*foal etc.*›; teetering ‹*steps*›; **einen ~en Gang haben** walk as though on stilts. **2.** *adv.* **~ gehen** walk as though on stilts; *(unsicher)* walk with teetering steps

Stalagmit [ʃtalak'mi:t] **der; ~s** *od.* **~en, ~e[n]** *(Geol.)* stalagmite

Stalaktit [ʃtalak'ti:t] **der; ~s** *od.* **~en, ~e[n]** *(Geol.)* stalactite

Stalinismus [stalinɪsmʊs] **der; ~:** Stalinism *no art.*

Stalinist der; ~en, ~en Stalinist

stalinistisch 1. *Adj.* Stalinist. **2.** *adv.* in a Stalinist way; along Stalinist lines

Stalin·orgel die *(Soldatenspr.)* multiple rocket launcher

Stall [ʃtal] **der; ~[e]s, Ställe** ['ʃtɛlə] **a)** *(Pferde~, Renn~)* stable; *(Kuh~)* cowshed; *(Hühner~)* [chicken-]coop; *(Schweine~)* [pig]sty; *(für Kaninchen, Kleintiere)* hutch; *(für Schafe)* pen; **aus einem guten/demselben ~ kommen** *(fig. ugs. scherzh.)* have a good/the same background; **ein ganzer ~ voll Kinder** *(ugs.)* a whole horde of kids *(coll.); s. auch* **Pferd a**; **b)** *(Sportjargon: Rennfahrermannschaft* [racing] team

Stallaterne die stable lamp

Stall·bursche der stable lad

Ställchen ['ʃtɛlçən] **das; ~s, ~** *s.* **Stall a:** little stable/cowshed/coop/sty/hutch/pen

Stall-: ~dung der *(von Kühen/Schweinen/Schafen)* cow/pig/sheep dung; *(von Pferden)* horse manure; **~hase der** *(ugs.)* domestic rabbit; **~knecht der** *(veralt.)* stable lad; *(für Kühe)* cowhand; **~laterne die** *s.* **Stallaterne; ~meister der** head groom; **~mist der** *s.* **~dung**

Stallung die; ~, ~en; *meist Pl. (Pferdestall)* stable; *(Kuhstall)* cow-shed; *(Schweinestall)* [pig]sty; **die ~en** the stables and other animal buildings

Stallwache die *(fig.)* caretakers *pl.*; **~ halten** keep an eye on things; hold the fort

Stamm [ʃtam] **der; ~[e]s, Stämme a)** *(Baum~)* trunk; **eine Hütte aus rohen Stämmen** a hut of rough-hewn boles; *s. auch* **Apfel a**; **b)** *(Volks~, Geschlecht)* tribe; **der ~ Davids** the house of David; **vom ~e Nimm sein** *(ugs. scherzh.)* be out for what one can get *(coll.)*; **c)** *o. Pl. (fester Bestand)* core; *(von Fachkräften, Personal)* permanent staff; **zum ~ gehören** be one of the regulars *(coll.)*; *(der Belegschaft einer Firma)* be a permanent member of staff; **ein [fester] ~ von Kunden/Gästen** a number of regular customers/patrons; **d)** *(Sprachw.)* stem; **e)** *(Biol.: Kategorie)* phylum; *(Mikrobiol.: Bakterien~; Tierzucht)* strain

Stamm-: ~aktie die *(Wirtsch.)* ordinary share; **~baum der** family tree; *(eines Tieres)* pedigree; *(Biol.)* phylogenetic tree; **~buch das a) jmdm. etw. ins ~buch schreiben** *(fig.)* make sb. take sth. to heart; **b)** *(Familien~buch)* family album *(recording births, marriages, deaths, etc.)*

stammeln ['ʃtamln̩] *tr., itr. V.* stammer

Stamm·eltern *Pl.* progenitors

stammen *itr. V.* come **(aus, von** from); *(datieren)* date **(aus, von** from); **aus einem alten Geschlecht ~:** be descended from an ancient lineage; **der Schmuck stammt von meiner Mutter** the jewellery used to belong to my mother; **der Satz/die Idee stammt nicht von ihm** the saying/idea isn't his

stammes-, Stammes-: ~fürst der tribal chieftain; **~geschichte die;** *o. Pl. (Biol.)* phylogenesis *no art.* **~geschichtlich 1.** *Adj.; nicht präd.* phylogenetic; **2.** *adv.* phylogenetically; **~häuptling der** tribal chief

stamm-, Stamm-: ~essen das set meal; **~form die;** *meist Pl. (Sprachw.)* principal part; **~gast der** *(im Lokal/Hotel)* regular customer/visitor; regular *(coll.)*; **~gericht das** set dish; **~halter der** *(oft scherzh.)* son and heir *(esp. joc.)*; **~haus das** original building; **~hirn das** *(Anat.) s.* **Hirnstamm; ~holz das** *(Forstw.)* round timber

stämmig ['ʃtɛmɪç] *Adj.* burly; sturdy ‹*arms, legs*›

stamm-, Stamm-: ~kapital das *(Wirtsch.)* authorized *or* registered capital; **~kneipe die** *(ugs.)* favourite *or* usual pub *(Brit. coll.) or (Amer.)* bar; **~kunde der** regular customer; **~land das;** *Pl.* **~länder** *od. (geh.)* **~e** ancestral homeland; *(fig.)* home territory; **~lokal das** favourite *or* usual restaurant/pub *(Brit.) or* bar *(Amer.)*/café; **dieses Café ist sein ~:** this café is his favourite haunt; **~personal das** permanent staff; **~platz der** *(auch fig.)* regular place; *(Sitz)* regular *or* usual seat; *(für Wohnwagen, Zelt usw.)* regular site; **~schloß das** ancestral castle; **~silbe die** *(Sprachw.)* stem syllable; **~sitz der a)** *(eines Adelsgeschlechts)* family seat; **b) der ~sitz der Firma ist [in] X** the firm's head office is in X; **~tafel die** genealogical table; **~tisch der a)** *(Tisch)* regulars' table *(coll.)*; **b)** *(~tischrunde)* group of regulars *(coll.)*; **c)** *(Treffen)* get-together with the regulars *(coll.)*; **~tisch·politik die;** *o. Pl. (abwertend)* bar-room politics *pl.*; **~tisch·runde die** group of regulars *(coll.)*; **~vater der** progenitor; **~vokal der** *(Sprachw.)* stem vowel; **~wähler der** committed *or* loyal voter ; **~würze die** *(Brauerei)* original wort; *(Gehalt)* original gravity

Stamperl ['ʃtampɐl] **das; ~s ~n** *(südd., österr. ugs.)* [small] schnaps glas; **trinken wir ein ~:** let's have a snifter *(sl.)*

stampfen ['ʃtampfn̩] **1.** *itr. V.* **a)** *(laut auftreten)* stamp; **mit den Füßen/dem Fuß/den Hufen ~:** stamp one's feet/foot/its hoofs; **b)** *mit sein (sich fortbewegen)* tramp; *(mit schweren Schritten)* trudge; **c)** *(mit wuchtigen Stößen sich bewegen)* ‹*machine, engine, etc.*› pound; **d)** *(Seemannsspr.)* ‹*ship*› pitch. **2.** *tr. V.* **a) mit den Füßen den Rhythmus ~:** tap the rhythm with one' s feet; **etw. aus dem Boden** *od.* **der Erde ~** *(fig.)* produce sth. out of thin air; **b)** *(fest~)* compress; *(rammen)* drive ‹*pile*› **(in + Akk.** into); **c)** *(zerkleinern)* mash ‹*potatoes*›; pulp ‹*fruit*›; crush ‹*sugar*›; pound ‹*millet, flour*›

Stampfer der; ~s, ~ a) *(für Erde usw.)* tamper; *(Stößel)* pestle; **b)** *(Küchengerät)* masher

Stampf·kartoffeln *Pl. (nordd.)* mashed potatoes

stand [ʃtant] *1. u. 3. Pers. Sg. Prät. v.* **stehen**

Stand der; ~[e]s, Stände ['ʃtɛndə] **a)** *o. Pl. (das Stehen)* standing position; **keinen guten/sicheren ~ haben** not have a good/secure footing; **aus dem ~** *(Sport)* from a standing position; **ein Sprung/Start aus dem ~:** a standing jump/start; **[bei jmdm.** *od.* **gegen jmdn.] einen schweren/keinen leichten ~ haben** *(fig.)* have a tough/not have an easy time [of it] [with sb.]; **etw. aus dem ~ [heraus] beantworten** *(ugs.)* answer sth. off the top of one's head *(coll.)*; **die neue Partei schaffte aus dem ~ [heraus] fast 7%** starting from scratch, the new party managed to get almost 7% [of the vote]; **b)** *(~ort)* position; **c)** *(Verkaufs~; Box für ein Pferd)* stall; *(Messe~, Informations~)* stand; *(Zeitungs~)* [newspaper] kiosk; *(Taxi~)* rank *(Brit.)*; stand; **d)** *o. Pl. (erreichte Stufe; Zustand)* state; **jmdn. in den ~ setzen, etw. zu tun** put sb. in a position *or* enable sb. to do sth.; **der heutige ~ der Technik** the state of technological development today; **etw. auf den neu[e]sten ~ [der Wissenschaft] bringen** bring sth. up to date *or* update sth. [in line with the latest scientific research]; **ich werde Sie über den ~ der Dinge informieren** I'll keep you informed about how things stand; **bei dem jetzigen ~ der Dinge** as things stand *or* are now; **e)** *(des Wassers, Flusses)* level; *(des Thermometers, Zählers, Barometers)* reading; *(der Kasse, Finanzen)* state; *(eines Himmelskörpers)* position; **den ~ des Thermometers ablesen** take the thermometer reading; **f)** *o. Pl. (Familien~)* status; **in den [heiligen] ~ der Ehe treten** *(geh., auch scherzh.)* enter the state of [holy] matrimony; **g)** *(Gesellschaftsschicht)* class; *(Berufs~)* trade; *(Ärzte, Rechtsanwälte)* [professional] group; **der geistliche ~:** the clergy; **Leute von ~:** persons of rank; **der dritte ~** *(hist.)* the third estate; **die Stände** *(hist.)* the estates; **h)** *(schweiz.: Kanton)* canton

Standard ['ʃtandart] **der; ~s, ~s** standard

Standard-: standard ‹*equipment, example,*

letter, form, solution, model, work, language⟩
standardisieren *tr. V.* standardize
Standardisierung die; ~, ~en standardization
Standard·situation die *(Sport)* set piece
Standarte [ʃtan'dartə] **die; ~, ~n a)** *(Feldzeichen, Fahne)* standard; **b)** *(ns.: Verband)* [SA/SS] unit; **c)** *s.* **Lunte b**
Stand-: ~bein das *(bes. Sport)* support leg; *(Fechten)* rear leg; *(Basketball)* pivot leg; *(Eislauf)* tracing leg; **~bild das** statue
Ständchen ['ʃtɛntçən] **das; ~s, ~:** serenade; **jmdm. ein ~ bringen** serenade sb.
Stände·ordnung die *(hist.)* system of estates
Stander ['ʃtandɐ] **der; ~s, ~:** pennant
Ständer ['ʃtɛndɐ] **der; ~s, ~ a)** *(Gestell, Vorrichtung)* stand; *(Kleider~)* coat-stand; *(Wäsche~)* clothes-horse; *(Kerzen~)* candle-holder; *(Pfeifen~, Platten~, Geschirr~)* rack; **b)** *(Elektrot.)* stator; **c)** *(salopp: erigierter Penis)* hard-on *(sl.)*
Stände·rat der *(schweiz.)* **a)** *o. Pl. (Vertretung)* upper chamber; **b)** *(Mitglied)* member of the upper chamber
Ständer·pilz der basidiomycete
standes-, Standes-: ~amt das registry office; **~amtlich 1.** *Adj.; nicht präd.* registry office ⟨*wedding, document*⟩; **2.** *adv.* **sich ~amtlich trauen lassen, ~amtlich heiraten** get married in a registry office; **~beamte der** registrar; **~bewußt** *Adj.* conscious of one's social standing *or* rank *postpos.*; **~bewußtsein das** consciousness of one's social standing *or* rank; **~dünkel der** *(abwertend)* snobbery; **~gemäß 1.** *Adj.* befitting sb.'s station *or* social standing *postpos.*; **~gemäß sein** befit sb.'s station *or* social standing; **2.** *adv.* as befits one's station *or* social standing; **~organisation die** professional association; **~person die** *(veralt.)* person of rank; **~schranke die;** *meist. Pl.* class barrier
Stände·staat der *(hist.)* corporative state
Standes·unterschied der difference of rank; class difference
Stände·wesen das; *o. Pl.* corporative system
stand-, Stand-: ~fest *Adj.* **a)** *(fest stehend)* steady; stable; strong ⟨*stalk, stem*⟩; **nicht mehr ganz ~fest sein** *(ugs. scherzh.)* be a bit wonky *(Brit. sl.) or* shaky on one's feet; **b)** *(standhaft)* steadfast; **~festigkeit die a)** stability; *(eines Gebäudes)* structural strength; **b)** *(Standhaftigkeit)* steadfastness; **~foto das** *(Film)* still; **~gas das** *(Kfz-W.)* idling speed; **~geld das** stall fee; **~gericht das** drumhead court martial; **~haft 1.** *Adj.* steadfast; **2.** *adv.* steadfastly; **~haftigkeit die; ~:** steadfastness; **~|halten** *unr. itr. V.* stand firm; **einer Sache** *(Dat.)* **~halten** withstand *or* stand up to sth.; **der Kritik ~halten** stand [up to] criticism; **einer näheren Überprüfung nicht ~halten** not stand [up to] *or* bear closer scrutiny
ständig 1. *Adj.; nicht präd.* **a)** *(andauernd)* constant ⟨*noise, worry, pressure, etc.*⟩; **mit jmdm. in ~er Feindschaft leben** live in a permanent state of enmity with sb.; **b)** *(fest)* permanent ⟨*residence, correspondent, staff, member, etc.*⟩; standing ⟨*committee*⟩; regular ⟨*income*⟩. **2.** *adv.* constantly; **mußt du sie ~ unterbrechen?** do you have to keep [on] interrupting her?; **sie kommt ~ zu spät/ist ~ krank** she's forever coming late/[being] ill; **Macht er das oft? – Ständig** Does he do that often? – All the time
ständisch 1. *Adj.* corporative; **eine ~e Gesellschaftsordnung** a social order based on privilege. **2.** *adv.* corporatively
stand-, Stand-: ~licht das; *Pl.* **~lichter** *(Kfz-W.) (Beleuchtung)* sidelights *pl.*; *(Leuchte, Lampe)* sidelight; **mit ~licht fahren** drive on sidelights; **~ort der;** *Pl.* **~orte a)** position; *(eines Betriebes o.ä.)* location; site; **von seinem ~ort aus konnte er nichts sehen** he couldn't see anything from where he was standing; **jmds. politischer ~ort** *(fig.)* sb.'s political stance *or* position; **b)** *(Milit.: Garnison)* garrison; base; **~ort·kommandant der** *(Milit.)* garrison commander; **~pauke die** *(ugs.)* dressing down; **jmdm. eine [gehörige] ~pauke halten** give sb. a [good] dressing down; **~punkt der** *(fig.)* point of view; viewpoint; **den ~punkt vertreten/auf dem ~punkt stehen/sich auf den ~punkt stellen, daß ...:** take the view that ...; **das ist doch kein ~punkt!** *(ugs.)* that's no attitude to take!; **~quartier das** base; **~rechtlich 1.** *Adj.; nicht präd.* summary ⟨*execution, shooting*⟩; **2.** *adv.* **jmdn. ~rechtlich erschießen** shoot sb. summarily; **~spur die** *(Verkehrsw.)* hard shoulder; **~uhr die** grandfather clock; **~vogel der** *(Zool.)* sedentary bird
Stange ['ʃtaŋə] **die; ~, ~n a)** *(aus Holz)* pole; *(aus Metall)* bar; *(dünner)* rod; *(Kleider~)* rail; *(Vogel~)* perch; **Kleider/Anzüge von der ~** *(ugs.)* off-the-peg-dresses/suits; **von der ~ kaufen** *(ugs.)* buy off the peg clothes; **jmdm. die ~ halten** *(ugs.)* stick up for sb. *(coll.)*; **jmdn. bei der ~ halten** *(ugs.)* keep sb. at it *(coll.)*; **bei der ~ bleiben** *(ugs.)* keep at it *(coll.)*; **eine ~ Zimt/Vanille/Lakritze** *usw.* a stick of cinnamon/vanilla/liquorice *etc.*; **eine ~ Zigaretten** *a carton containing ten packets of cigarettes;* **eine [schöne] ~ Geld** *(ugs.)* a small fortune *(coll.)*; **b)** *(bes. md.: zylindrisches Glas)* [straight] glass; **c)** *meist Pl. (Jägerspr.: Teil des Geweihs)* beam
Stangen-: ~bohne die runner bean; **~brot das** French bread; **ein französisches ~brot** a baguette; **~spargel der** asparagus spears *pl. or* stalks *pl.*
stank [ʃtaŋk] *1. u. 3. Pers. Sg. Prät. v.* **stinken**
Stänkerer der; ~s, ~ *(ugs. abwertend)* grouser *(coll.)*; stirrer
stänkern ['ʃtɛŋkɐn] *itr. V. (ugs. abwertend)* stir *(coll.)*; **gegen jmdn./etw. ~:** go on about sb./sth.
Stanniol [ʃta'nio:l] **das; ~s, ~e** tin foil; *(Silberpapier)* silver paper
Stanniol·papier das silver paper
stante pede ['stantə 'pe:də] *Adv. (ugs. scherzh.)* post-haste; lickety-split *(coll.)*
[1]**Stanze** ['ʃtantsə] **die; ~, ~n** *(Verslehre)* ottava rima *(with eleven-syllable lines)*
[2]**Stanze die; ~, ~n** press; *(Prägestempel)* die; *(zum Lochen)* punch
stanzen *tr. V.* press; *(prägen)* stamp; *(ausstanzen)* punch ⟨*holes, numbers, punch-cards, discs, etc.*⟩
Stapel ['ʃta:pl̩] **der; ~s, ~ a)** pile; **ein ~ Holz** a pile *or* stack of wood; **b)** *(Schiffbau)* stocks *pl.*; **vom ~ laufen** be launched; **vom ~ lassen** launch ⟨*ship*⟩; *(ugs. abwertend: von sich geben)* trot out *(coll. derog.)* ⟨*sayings, jokes, slogans, etc.*⟩
Stapel·lauf der launch[ing]
stapeln 1. *tr. V. (schichten)* pile up; stack; *(fig.: ansammeln)* accumulate. **2.** *refl. V.* pile up; *(gestapelt sein)* be piled up
stapel·weise *Adv.* **~ Briefe** piles *or* stacks of letters; **ich habe sie ~:** I have piles of them
Stapfe ['ʃtapfə] **die; ~, ~n, Stapfen der; ~s, ~:** footprint
stapfen *itr. V.; mit sein* tramp; **in jede Pfütze ~:** stamp in every puddle
[1]**Star** [ʃta:ɐ̯] **der; ~[e]s, ~e** *od. (schweiz.)* **~en** *(Vogel)* starling
[2]**Star der; ~s, ~s** *(berühmte Persönlichkeit)* star
[3]**Star der; ~[e]s, ~e: der graue ~:** cataract; **der grüne ~:** glaucoma; **er ist am ~ operiert worden** he has been operated on for cataract/glaucoma
Star-: star ⟨*conductor, guest singer, etc.*⟩; top ⟨*lawyer, model, agent*⟩
Star·allüren *Pl.* prima donna behaviour *sing.*; **~ zeigen/haben** put on the airs of a star
starb [ʃtarp] *1. u. 3. Pers. Sg. Prät. v.* **sterben**
Star·besetzung die all-star cast
Staren·kasten der starlings' nest-box
stark [ʃtark]; **stärker** ['ʃtɛrkɐ], **stärkst...** ['ʃtɛrkst...] **1.** *Adj.* **a)** strong ⟨*man, current, structure, team, drink, verb, pressure, wind, etc.*⟩; potent ⟨*drink, medicine, etc.*⟩; powerful ⟨*engine, lens, voice, etc.*⟩; *(ausgezeichnet)* excellent ⟨*runner, player, performance*⟩; **den ~en Mann markieren** *od.* **mimen** *(ugs.)* put on a strong-man act *(coll.)*; **sein stärkstes Werk/Theaterstück** his best work/play; **jetzt heißt es ~ bleiben** we must not yield now; **sich für jmdn./etw. ~ machen** *(ugs.)* throw one's weight behind sb./sth.; *s. auch* **Seite d; Stück c; Tobak; b)** *(dick)* thick; stout ⟨*rope, string*⟩; *(verhüll.: korpulent)* well-built *(euphem.)*; **Kleidung für stärkere Damen** clothes for the fuller figure; **eine 20 cm ~e Wand** a wall 20 cm thick; **c)** *(zahlenmäßig groß, umfangreich)* sizeable, large ⟨*army, police, presence, entourage*⟩; big ⟨*demand*⟩; **wir hoffen auf ~e Beteiligung** we hope a large number of people will take part; **eine 100 Mann ~e Truppe** a 100-strong unit; **das Kontingent ist 1400 Mann ~:** the contingent is 1,400 strong; **d)** *(heftig, intensiv)* heavy ⟨*rain, snow, traffic, smoke, heat, cold, drinker, smoker, demand, pressure*⟩; severe ⟨*heat, cold, frost, pain*⟩; strong ⟨*impression, influence, current, resistance, sign, dislike*⟩; grave ⟨*doubt, reservations*⟩; great ⟨*heat, hunger, thirst, exaggeration, interest*⟩; hearty ⟨*eater, appetite*⟩; loud ⟨*applause*⟩; **~es Fieber** high temperature; **unter ~er Anteilnahme der Bevölkerung** with large numbers of the population attending; **~er Widerhall** *(fig.)* a considerable response; **das ist [wirklich] ~** *(ugs.)* that [really] is a bit much! *(coll.)*; **e)** *(Jugendspr.: großartig)* great *(coll.)*; fantastic *(coll.)*. **2.** *adv.* **a)** *(sehr, überaus, intensiv) (mit Adj.)* very; heavily ⟨*indebted, stressed*⟩; greatly ⟨*increased, reduced, enlarged*⟩; strongly ⟨*emphasized, characterized*⟩; badly ⟨*damaged, worn, affected*⟩; thickly, densely ⟨*populated*⟩; *(mit Verb)* ⟨*rain, snow, drink, smoke, bleed*⟩ heavily; ⟨*exaggerate, impress*⟩ greatly; ⟨*enlarge, reduce, increase*⟩ considerably; ⟨*support, oppose, suspect*⟩ strongly; ⟨*remind*⟩ very much; **~ wirkend** with a powerful effect *postpos.*; **es erinnert ~ an ...:** it is very reminiscent of ...; **~ riechen/duften** have a strong smell/scent; **~ gewürzt** strongly seasoned; **es ist ~/zu ~ gesalzen** it is very/too salty; **~ erkältet sein** have a heavy *or* bad cold; **er geht ~ auf die Sechzig zu** *(ugs.)* he's pushing sixty *(coll.)*; **b)** *(Jugendspr.: großartig)* fantastically *(coll.)*; **c)** *(Sprachw.)* **~ flektieren** *od.* **flektiert werden** be a strong noun/verb
Stark·bier das strong beer
Stärke ['ʃtɛrkə] **die; ~, ~n a)** *o. Pl.* strength; *(eines Motors)* power; *(einer Glühbirne)* wattage; **eine Politik der ~:** power politics *sing.*; **b)** *(Dicke)* thickness; *(Technik)* gauge; **c)** *o. Pl. (zahlenmäßige Größe)* strength; size; **eine Truppe von 300 Mann ~:** a 300-strong unit; **d)** *(besondere Fähigkeit, Vorteil)* strength; **jmds. ~/nicht jmds. ~ sein** be sb.'s forte/not be sb.'s strong point; **e)** *(von Wind, Strömung, Eindruck, Einfluß, Nachfrage, Empfindung, Widerstand usw.)* strength; *(von Hitze, Kälte, Licht, Druck, Regenfall, Sturm, Schmerzen, Abneigung)* intensity; *(von Frost)* severity; *(von Lärm, Verkehr)* volume; *(von Appetit)* heartiness; **f)** *(organischer Stoff)* starch
stärke·haltig *Adj.* starchy
Stärke·mehl das cornflour *(Brit.)*; cornstarch *(Amer.)*

stärken 1. *tr. V.* **a)** *(kräftigen, festigen; auch fig.)* strengthen; boost ⟨*power, prestige*⟩; ⟨*drink, food, etc.*⟩ fortify ⟨*person*⟩; **die** *od.* **jmds. Gesundheit ~:** fortify *or* strengthen sb.'s constitution; **jmds. Selbstbewußtsein ~** *(fig.)* give sb.'s self-confidence a boost; **jmdn. in seinem Glauben~:** reinforce sb.'s faith; *s. auch* **Rücken a; b)** *(steif machen)* starch ⟨*washing etc.*⟩. **2.** *refl. V. (sich erfrischen)* fortify *or* refresh oneself; **nun stärkt euch erst mal** have something to give you strength. **3.** *itr. V.* **ein ~des Mittel** a tonic

stärker *s.* **stark**

Stärke·zucker der glucose

stärkst... *s.* **stark**

Stark-: ~strom der *(Elektrot.)* heavy current; *(mit hoher Spannung)* high-voltage current; **~strom·leitung die** *(Elektrot.)* power line; **~ton der** *(Sprachw.)* stress

Star·kult der *(abwertend)* star worship **(um** of)

Stärkung die; ~, ~en a) *o. Pl.* strengthening; **zur ~ trank er erst mal einen Whisky** he drank a whisky to fortify himself; **die ~ des Parlaments** the increase in the power *or* influence vested in parliament; **b)** *(Erfrischung)* refreshment

Stärkungs·mittel das tonic

Starlet[t] ['ʃtɑ:lɛt] **das; ~s, ~s** *(spött. abwertend)* starlet

starr [ʃtar] **1.** *Adj.* **a)** rigid; *(steif)* stiff **(vor +** *Dat.* with); fixed ⟨*expression, smile, stare*⟩; **~ vor Schreck** paralysed with terror; **b)** *(nicht abwandelbar)* inflexible, rigid ⟨*law, rule, principle*⟩; **c)** *(unnachgiebig)* inflexible, obdurate ⟨*person, attitude, etc.*⟩. **2.** *adv.* **a)** rigidly; *(steif)* stiffly; **jmdn. ~ ansehen/~ geradeaus schauen** look at sb./look straight in front of one with a fixed stare; **b)** *(unnachgiebig)* **~ bleibt er bei seiner Meinung** he sticks obdurately to his opinion

Starre die; ~: *s.* **Starrheit**

starren *itr. V.* **a)** *(starr blicken)* stare **(in +** *Akk.* into, **auf, an, gegen +** *Akk.* at); **jmdm. ins Gesicht ~:** stare sb. in the face; **b)** *(ganz bedeckt sein mit)* **vor/von Schmutz** *od.* **Dreck ~:** be filthy; be covered in filth; **vor Perlen und Diamanten/Gold und Geschmeiden ~:** be covered in *or* laden with pearls and diamonds/gold and precious stones; **vor Waffen ~:** be bristling with weapons

Starrheit die; ~: *s.* **starr 1: a)** rigidity; stiffness; fixity; **b)** inflexibility; rigidity; **c)** inflexibility; obduracy

starr-, Starr-: ~kopf der *(abwertend)* pig-headed person; **ein ~kopf sein** be pig-headed; **~köpfig** *Adj. (abwertend)* pig-headed; **~krampf der** *s.* **Wundstarrkrampf; ~sinn der;** *o. Pl.* pig-headedness; **~sinnig** *Adj. (abwertend)* pig-headed

Start [ʃtart] **der; ~[e]s, ~s a)** *(Sport; auch fig.)* start; **einen guten/schlechten/langsamen ~ haben** get off to *or* make a good/bad/slow start; **den ~ freigeben** give clearance to start; **das Zeichen zum ~ geben** give the starting signal; **b)** *(Sport: ~platz)* start; **an den ~ gehen/am ~ sein** *(fig.: teilnehmen)* start; **c)** *(Sport: Teilnahme)* participation; **sein ~ ist in Frage gestellt** it is uncertain whether he will start; **d)** *(eines Flugzeugs)* take-off; *(einer Rakete)* launch; **den ~ der Maschine freigeben** give the aircraft clearance for take-off; **zum** *od.* **an den ~ rollen** taxi to the runway for take-off

start-, Start-: ~automatik die *(Kfz-W.)* automatic choke; **~bahn die** [take-off] runway; **~bereit** *Adj.* ready to start *postpos.*; ⟨*aircraft*⟩ ready for take-off; *(zum Aufbruch bereit)* ready to set off *postpos.*; **~block der;** *Pl.* **~blöcke** *(Leichtathletik, Schwimmen)* starting-block

starten 1. *itr. V.; mit sein* **a)** start; ⟨*aircraft*⟩ take off; ⟨*rocket*⟩ blast off, be launched; **zu früh ~** *(Sport)* jump the start; **gut/schnell ~** *(Sport)* make a good/quick start; get away well/quickly; **b)** *(an einem Wettkampf teilnehmen)* compete; *(bei einem Rennen)* start **(bei, in +** *Dat.* in); **c)** *(den Motor anlassen)* start the engine; **d)** *(aufbrechen)* set off; set out; **in den Urlaub ~:** set off on holiday; **e)** *(beginnen)* start; begin. **2.** *tr. V.* start ⟨*race, campaign, tour, production, etc.*⟩; launch ⟨*missile, rocket, satellite, attack*⟩; start [up] ⟨*engine, machine, car*⟩

Starter der; ~s, ~ *(Sport, Kfz-W.)* starter

Starter·klappe die *(Kfz-W.)* choke flap

start-, Start-: ~erlaubnis die a) *(Sport)* authorization to compete; **b)** *(Flugw.)* clearance [for take-off]; **~geld das** *(Sport)* **a)** *(vom Teilnehmer bezahlt)* entry fee; **b)** *(vom Veranstalter bezahlt)* starting money; **~hilfe die a)** *(Unterstützung)* financial help, backing *(to get a project off the ground)*; **jmdm. [finanzielle] ~hilfe geben** help sb. [financially] to get started; **b) ich brauche ~hilfe** I need help to get my car started; **~hilfe·kabel das** jump leads *pl.*; **~kapital das** starting capital; **~klar** *Adj.* ready to start *postpos.*; ⟨*aircraft*⟩ clear or ready for take-off; **~kommando das** *(Sport)* starter's order[s]; **~linie die** *(Sport)* starting-line; **~loch das;** *meist Pl. (Leichtathletik)* **in die ~löcher gehen** get on one's marks; **in den ~löchern kauern/hocken** *(fig.)* be waiting in the wings; **~nummer die** *(Sport)* [start] number; **~platz der** *(Sport)* starting position; **~rampe die** *(Raumflug; auch fig.)* launching pad; **~schuß der** *(Sport)* **der ~schuß fiel** the starter's gun went off; **den ~schuß zum 100-m-Lauf geben** fire the gun for the start of the 100 metres; **vor dem ~schuß loslaufen** jump the gun; **den ~schuß zu** *od.* **für etw. geben** *(fig.)* give sth. the go-ahead *or* the green light

[1]Stasi ['ʃta:zi] **die; ~** *od.* **der; ~s** *(DDR ugs.) Abk.* **Staatssicherheit**

[2]Stasi der; ~s, ~s *(DDR ugs.)* state security man

Statement ['steɪtmənt] **das; ~s, ~s** statement

Statik ['ʃta:tɪk] **die; ~ a)** *(Physik)* statics *sing., no art.*; **b)** *(Bauw.)* static equilibrium; **c)** *(geh.: statischer Zustand)* stasis

Statiker der; ~s, ~: structural engineer [concerned with statics]

Station [ʃta'tsio:n] **die; ~, ~en a)** *(Haltestelle)* stop; **b)** *(Bahnhof, Sender, Forschungs~, Raum~)* station; **c)** *(Zwischen~, Aufenthalt)* stopover; **die ~en seiner Reise waren ...:** the places where he stopped [off] on his journey were ...; **~ machen** stop over *or* off; make a stopover; **d)** *(Kranken~)* ward; **auf ~ sein** ⟨*doctor*⟩ be on ward duty; **e)** *(einer Entwicklung, Karriere usw.)* stage

stationär [ʃtatsio'nɛ:ɐ̯] **1.** *Adj.* **a)** *(Med.)* ⟨*admission, examination, treatment*⟩ in hospital, as an in-patient; **ein ~er Patient** an in-patient; **b)** *(ortsfest)* permanently stationed ⟨*troops, units*⟩; **c)** *(Raumf.)* fixed ⟨*orbit*⟩; **ein ~er Satellit** a satellite in a fixed orbit. **2.** *adv.* **a)** *(Med.)* in hospital; **jmdn. ~ behandeln/aufnehmen** treat/admit sb. as an in-patient; **b)** *(ortsfest)* in one place

stationieren *tr. V.* station ⟨*troops*⟩; deploy ⟨*weapons, bombers, etc.*⟩

Stationierung die; ~, ~en stationing; *(von Waffen, Raketen usw.)* deployment

Stations-: ~arzt der ward doctor; **~schwester die** ward sister; **~taste die** *(Rundf.)* preset [tuning] button; preset; **~vorsteher der** *(Eisenb.)* station-master

statisch ['ʃta:tɪʃ] **1.** *Adj.* static; ⟨*laws*⟩ of statics; **~er Auftrieb** *(Physik)* static lift; **~e Berechnungen** *(Bauw.)* calculations relating to static equilibrium. **2.** *adv. (Bauw.)* with regard to static equilibrium

Statist [ʃta'tɪst] **der; ~en, ~en** *(Theater, Film)* extra; *(fig.)* bystander; supernumerary; **zum ~en degradiert werden** *(fig.)* be demoted to the role of a mere accessory

Statisten·rolle die *(Theater, Film)* walk-on part

Statistik [ʃta'tɪstɪk] **die; ~, ~en a)** *o. Pl. (Wissenschaft)* statistics *sing., no art.*; **b)** *(Zusammenstellung)* statistics *pl.*; **eine ~:** a set of statistics; **eine ~ über etw.** *(Akk.)* **erstellen** make a statistical study of sth.

statistisch 1. *Adj.* statistical; **~es Amt/~e Behörde** office of statistics. **2.** *adv.* statistically

Stativ [ʃta'ti:f] **das; ~s, ~e** tripod

statt [ʃtat] **1.** *Konj. s.* **anstatt 1. 2.** *Präp. mit Gen.* instead of; **~ dessen** instead [of this]

Statt die; ~ *(veralt., geh.)* abode *(arch.)*; **an jmds./einer Sache ~:** in sb.'s place/in place of sth.; instead of sb./sth.; *s.* **auch Eid; Kind a**

Stätte ['ʃtɛtə] **die; ~, ~n** *(geh.)* place; **eine heilige/historische ~:** a holy/historic site; **die ~ des Sieges/der Niederlage** the scene of the victory/defeat

statt-, Statt-: ~|finden *unr. itr. V.* take place; ⟨*process, development*⟩ occur; **~|geben** *unr. itr. V. (Amtsspr.)* **einer Sache** *(Dat.)* **~geben** accede to sth.; **einer Klage ~geben** uphold a complaint; **~|haben** *unr. itr. V. (veralt.) s.* **~finden; ~haft** *Adj.; nicht attr.* permissible; **~halter der** *(hist.)* governor; **~halterschaft die; ~** *(hist.)* governorship

stattlich 1. a) well-built; strapping ⟨*lad*⟩; *(beeindruckend)* imposing ⟨*figure, stature, building, etc.*⟩; fine ⟨*farm, estate*⟩; impressive ⟨*trousseau, collection*⟩; **ein ~er Mann/eine ~e Frau** a fine figure of a man/woman; **b)** *(beträchtlich)* considerable; sizeable ⟨*part*⟩; considerable, appreciable ⟨*sum, number*⟩; **~e 8 000 Mark** an impressive 8,000 marks; all of 8,000 marks *(coll.)*. **2.** *adv.* impressively; splendidly

Stattlichkeit die; ~: imposing nature; *(von Statur)* fine build *or* figure; **seine ~/die ~ seiner Erscheinung** his fine build *or* imposing stature

Statue ['ʃta:tu̯ə] **die; ~, ~n** statue

statuenhaft 1. *Adj.* statuesque. **2.** *adv.* like a statue; statuesquely

Statuette [ʃta'tu̯ɛtə] **die; ~, ~n** statuette

statuieren *tr. V. (geh.)* establish ⟨*principle, purpose*⟩; lay down ⟨*right, principle*⟩; *s. auch* **Exempel**

Statur [ʃta'tu:ɐ̯] **die; ~, ~en** build; **kräftig von ~** *od.* **von kräftiger ~ sein** have a powerful build; **seine große/kleine/imponierende ~:** his tall/small/imposing stature

Status ['ʃta:tʊs] **der; ~, ~** ['ʃta:tu:s] **a)** *(geh.: Stand, Zustand)* state; **b)** *([rechtliche] Stellung)* status

Status quo ['sta:tʊs kvo:] **der; ~ ~** *(geh.)* status quo

Status·symbol das status symbol

Statut [ʃta'tu:t] **das; ~[e]s, ~en** statute

Stau der; ~[e]s, ~s *od.* **~e a)** *(von Wasser, Blut usw.)* build-up; **b)** *(von Fahrzeugen)* tailback *(Brit.)*; backup *(Amer.)*; **3 km ~:** a tailback *(Brit.) or* backup *(Amer.) or* jam stretching for three kilometres; **im ~ stehen** sit *or* be stuck in a jam

Staub [ʃtaup] **der; ~[e]s** dust; **[im ganzen Haus] ~ wischen** dust [the whole house]; **[im Wohnzimmer] ~ saugen** vacuum *or (Brit. coll.)* hoover [the sitting-room]; **[viel] ~ aufwirbeln** *(fig. ugs.)* stir things up [quite a bit] *(coll.)*; cause [a lot of] aggro *(Brit. sl.)*; **sich aus dem ~[e] machen** *(fig. ugs.)* make oneself scarce *(coll.)*

Staub-: ~beutel der a) *(Bot.)* anther; **b)** *(eines Staubsaugers)* dust-bag; **~blatt das** *(Bot.)* stamen

Stäubchen ['ʃtɔypçən] **das; ~s, ~:** speck of dust

Stau·becken das reservoir

stauben *itr. V.* cause dust; ⟨*person*⟩ cause *or* raise dust; **es staubt sehr/mehr** there is a lot of dust/more dust; **er galoppierte davon,**

daß es nur so staubte he galloped off raising clouds of dust

stäuben ['ʃtɔybn̩] **1.** *tr. V.* **etw. auf/über etw.** *(Akk.)* ~: sprinkle sth. on/over sth.; **dem Baby Puder auf die Haut** ~: dust the baby's skin with powder. **2.** *itr. V.* **a)** *(zerstieben)* scatter; ‹*water*› form spray, spray out; ‹*sparks*› fly; **b)** *s.* **stauben**

Staub-: ~faden der *(Bot.)* filament; **~fänger der** *(abwertend)* dust-trap; **ein ~fänger sein** catch the dust; **~gefäß das** *(Bot.)* stamen

staubig *Adj.* dusty

staub-, Staub-: ~korn das; *Pl.* **~körner** speck *or* particle of dust; **~lappen der** duster; **~lunge die: eine ~lunge haben** have pneumoconiosis *(Med.)*; **~saugen 1.** *tr. V.* vacuum, *(Brit. coll.)* hoover ‹*room, carpet, etc.*›; **2.** *itr. V.* hoover *(Brit. coll.)*; **~sauger der** vacuum cleaner; Hoover *(Brit.* P); **~tuch das;** *Pl.* **~tücher** duster; **~wedel der** feather duster; **~wolke die** cloud of dust; **~zucker der** *(veralt., südd., österr.) s.* **Puderzucker**

stauchen ['ʃtauxn̩] *tr. V.* **a)** compress; *(Technik)* upset ‹*metal*›; **b)** *(stoßen)* thrust; jab ‹*stick, arms, etc.*›

Stau·damm der dam

Staude ['ʃtaudə] **die; ~, ~n a)** *(Bot.)* herbaceous perennial; **b)** *(bes. südd.: Strauch)* bush

Stauden·gewächs das *(Bot.)* herbaceous perennial

stauen ['ʃtauən] **1.** *tr. V.* **a)** dam [up] ‹*stream, river*›; staunch *or* stem flow of ‹*blood*›; **b)** *(Seemannsspr.: verladen)* stow. **2.** *refl. V.* ‹*water, blood, etc.*› accumulate, build up; ‹*people*› form a crowd; ‹*traffic*› form a tailback/tailbacks *(Brit.) or (Amer.)* backup/backups; *(fig.)* ‹*anger*› build up

Stauer der; ~s, ~: stevedore

Staufer ['ʃtaufɐ] **der; ~s, ~** *(hist.)* Hohenstaufen; **die ~:** the Hohenstaufen dynasty *sing.*

Stau·mauer die dam [wall]

staunen ['ʃtaunən] *itr. V.* be amazed *or* astonished (**über** + *Akk.* at); *(beeindruckt sein)* marvel (**über** + *Akk.* at); **er staunte nicht schlecht, als er das hörte/sah** *(ugs.)* he was flabbergasted when he heard it/saw it; **da staunst du, was?** *(ugs.)* quite a shock, isn't it?; shattered, eh? *(coll.)*; **da kann man nur [noch] ~:** one can only marvel *or* wonder at it; **~d** with *or* in amazement; **sie betrachtete ihn mit ~den Augen** she gazed at him wide-eyed with amazement; *s. auch* **Bauklotz; hören 2 c**

Staunen das; ~s amazement, astonishment (**über** + *Akk.* at); *(staunende Bewunderung)* wonderment; **jmdn. in ~ [ver]setzen** astonish *or* amaze sb.; **er kam aus dem ~ nicht mehr heraus** he couldn't get over it

Staupe ['ʃtaupə] **die; ~, ~n** distemper *no art.*

Stau-: ~see der reservoir; **~stufe die** barrage

Stauung die; ~, ~en a) *(eines Bachs, Flusses)* damming; *(des Blutes, Wassers)* stemming the flow; *(das Sichstauen)* build-up; **b)** *(Verkehrsstau)* tailback *(Brit.)*; backup *(Amer.)*; jam

Stau·werk das barrage

Std. *Abk.* **Stunde** hr.

Steak [ste:k] **das; ~s, ~s** steak

Stearin [ʃtea'ri:n] **das; ~s, ~e** stearin

Stech·apfel der *(Bot.)* thorn-apple; **[Gemeiner] ~:** jimson weed

stechen ['ʃtɛçn̩] **1.** *unr. itr. V.* **a)** ‹*thorn, thistle, spine, needle*› prick; ‹*wasp, bee*› sting; ‹*mosquito*› bite; ‹*fig.: sun*› be scorching; **das Insekt hat ihm ins Bein gestochen** the insect bit him in the leg; **sich** *(Dat.)* **in den Finger ~:** prick one's finger; **b)** *(hinein~)* **mit etw. in etw.** *(Akk.)* **~:** stick *or* jab sth. into sth.; **jmdm. mit einer Nadel in den Hintern ~:** jab a needle into sb.'s behind; **nach jmdm. ~:** stab at sb.; try to stab sb.; **c)** *(die Stechuhr betätigen) (bei Arbeitsbeginn)* clock on; *(bei Arbeitsende)* clock off; **d)** *(Kartenspiel)* ‹*suit*› be trumps; **e)** *(Sport)* jump-off; **f)** *s.* [2]**See a. 2.** *unr. tr. V.* **a)** *(mit dem Messer, Schwert)* stab; *(mit der Nadel, mit einem Dorn usw.)* prick; ‹*bee, wasp*› sting; ‹*mosquito*› bite; *(Fischereiw.: fangen)* spear ‹*eel, pike*›; *(ab~)* stick ‹*pig, calf*›; **sich an etw.** *(Dat.)* **~:** prick oneself on sth.; **sich in den Finger ~:** prick one's finger; **b)** *(hervorbringen)* make ‹*hole, pattern*›; **jmdm. Löcher in die Ohren ~:** pierce sb.'s ears; **c)** *(unpers.)* **es sticht mich in der Seite** I've got a stabbing pain in my side; **d)** *(herauslösen)* cut ‹*peat, turf, asparagus, etc.*›; pick ‹*lettuce, mushrooms*›; **e)** *(gravieren)* engrave ‹*design etc.*›; **f)** *(Kartenspiel)* take ‹*card*›

Stechen das; ~s, ~ *(Sport)* jump-off

stechend *Adj.* penetrating, pungent ‹*smell*›; penetrating ‹*glance, eyes*›

Stech-: ~fliege die stomoxyine fly; *(Wadenstecher)* stable-fly; **~ginster der** *(Bot.)* gorse; **~kahn der** punt; **~karte die** clocking-on card; **~mücke die** mosquito; gnat; **~palme die** holly; **~schritt der** *(Milit.)* goose-step; **im ~schritt marschieren** goose-step; **~uhr die** time clock; **~zirkel der** dividers *pl.*

steck-, Steck-: ~brief der description [of a/the wanted person]; *(Plakat)* 'wanted' poster; *(fig.: eines Menschen)* personal details *pl.*; *(fig.: eines Geräts)* [brief] specification; **~brieflich** *Adv.* **der ~brieflich Gesuchte** the wanted man; **der Mörder wird ~brieflich gesucht** descriptions/'wanted' posters of the murderer have been circulated; **~dose die** socket; power point

stecken ['ʃtɛkn̩] **1.** *tr. V.* **a)** put; **etw. in die Tasche ~:** put *or (coll.)* stick sth. in one's pocket; **steck dein Hemd in die Hose** tuck your shirt in[to your trousers]; **ein Kind ins Bett ~:** put a child to bed; **sein ganzes Vermögen in etw.** *(Akk.)* **~:** put *or* invest all one's money in sth.; **sich hinter etw. ~** *(ugs.)* set to work on sth. with a will; **b)** *(mit Nadeln)* pin ‹*hem, lining, etc.*›; pin [on] ‹*badge*›; pin up ‹*hair*›; **c)** *(pflanzen)* put in, plant ‹*potatoes, onions, beans*›; **d)** *(ugs.: mitteilen)* **etw. der Polizei** *usw.* **~:** tip the police *etc.* off about sth.; **es jmdm. ~** *(ugs.)* give sb. a piece of one's mind *(coll.)*. **2.** *regelm. (geh. auch unr.) itr. V.* be; **der Schlüssel steckt [im Schloß]** the key is in the lock; **voller Ideen ~:** be full of ideas; **wo hast du denn so lange gesteckt?** *(ugs.)* where did you get to *or* have you been all this time?; **wo steckt meine Brille?** *(ugs.)* where have my glasses got to *or* gone?; **er steckt in Schwierigkeiten** *(ugs.)* he's having problems; **in den Anfängen ~:** be in the early stages; **ein Abzeichen steckte an seinem Revers** a badge was pinned to his lapel; **hinter etw.** *(Dat.)* **~** *(fig. ugs.)* be behind sth.

Stecken der; ~s, ~ *(bes. südd.)* stick

stecken-, Stecken-: ~|bleiben *unr. itr. V.; mit sein* get stuck; *(fig.)* ‹*negotiations etc.*› get bogged down; **die Kugel ist in der Lunge steckengeblieben** the bullet lodged in the lung; **es blieb in den Anfängen ~** *(fig.)* it never got beyond the early stages; **das Wort blieb ihm vor Angst im Halse** *od.* **in der Kehle ~:** he was speechless with fear; **~|lassen 1.** *unr. tr. V.* **den Schlüssel [im Schloß] ~lassen** leave the key in the lock; **2.** *unr. itr. V.* **lassen Sie ~!** *(ugs.: lassen Sie mich bezahlen)* put your money away!; **~pferd das a)** *(Spielzeug)* hobby-horse; **b)** *(Liebhaberei)* hobby; **sein ~pferd reiten** go on about one's hobby-horse; *(sich seinem Hobby widmen)* pursue one's [favourite] hobby

Stecker der; ~s, ~: plug

Steck·kissen das papoose-carrier; carrynest

Steckling ['ʃtɛklɪŋ] **der; ~s, ~e** cutting

Steck-: ~nadel die pin; **es ist so still, man könnte eine ~nadel fallen hören** it's so quiet you could hear a pin drop; **jmdn./etw. suchen wie eine ~nadel** *(ugs.)* search high and low for sb./sth.; **eine ~nadel im Heuhaufen suchen** *(ugs.)* look for a needle in a haystack; **~nadel·kopf der** pinhead; **~rübe die** *(bes. nordd.)* swede; **~schloß das** safety lock *(inserted in main lock)*; **~schlüssel der** socket spanner; **~schuß der** *internal gunshot wound with bullet;* **er hat einen ~schuß in der Lunge** he has a bullet/pellet lodged in his lung; **~tuch das** dress handkerchief

Steg [ʃte:k] **der; ~[e]s, ~e a)** *(schmale Brücke)* [narrow] bridge; *(Fußgänger~)* foot-bridge; *(Laufbrett)* gangplank; *(Boots~)* landing-stage; **b)** *(veralt.: Pfad)* path; **c)** *(bei Saiteninstrumenten, Brillen)* bridge

Steg·reif der: aus dem ~: impromptu; **er hielt aus dem ~ eine kleine Rede** he gave a short speech extempore *or* off the cuff; **etw. aus dem ~ beantworten** answer sth. off the top of one's head *(coll.)*; **aus dem ~ spielen** improvise; ad-lib

Stegreif·rede die impromptu *or* extempore speech

Steh-: ~auf·männchen das tumbling figure; tumbler; **er/sie ist ein [richtiges] ~aufmännchen** *(fig. ugs.)* nothing gets him/her down *(coll.)*; **~bierhalle die** stand-up beer hall; **~empfang der** stand-up reception

stehen ['ʃte:ən] **1.** *unr. itr. V.; südd., österr., schweiz. mit sein* **a)** stand; **den ganzen Tag am Herd ~:** stand over the cooker all day; **er arbeitet ~d** *od.* **im Stehen** he works standing up; **sie steht zwischen ihnen** *(fig.)* she comes between them; **mit jmdm./etw. ~ und fallen** *(fig.)* stand or fall with sb./sth.; **das Haus steht noch** the house is still standing; **er steht ihm** *(salopp)* he's got a hard-on *(sl.)*; **b)** *(sich befinden)* be; ‹*upright object, building*› stand; **das Verb steht am Satzende** the verb comes at the end of the sentence; **wo steht dein Auto?** where is your car [parked]?; **sie haben dort einen Schrank ~:** they have a cupboard *or (Amer.)* closet [standing] there; **Schweißperlen standen auf seiner Stirn** beads of sweat stood out on his brow; **ich tue alles, was in meinen Kräften** *od.* **meiner Macht steht** I'll do everything in my power; **im Rentenalter ~:** be of pensionable age; **vor einer Entscheidung/dem Bankrott ~:** be faced with a decision/with bankruptcy; **c)** *(einen bestimmten Stand haben)* **auf etw.** *(Dat.)* **~** ‹*needle, hand*› point to sth.; **das Barometer steht hoch/tief/auf Regen** the barometer is reading high/low/indicating rain; **die Uhr steht auf 12** the clock shows 12; **die Ampel steht auf Rot** the traffic lights are [on] red; **es steht mir bis zum Hals[e]** *od.* **bis oben** *od.* **bis hier[hin]** I'm fed up to the back teeth with it *(sl.)*; I'm sick to death of it *(coll.)*; **der Wind steht günstig/nach Norden** *(Seemannsspr.)* the wind stands fair/is from the north; **das Spiel/es steht 1:1** *(Sport)* the score is one all; **wie steht es/ das Spiel?** *(Sport)* what's the score?; **die Chancen ~ fifty-fifty** the chances are fifty-fifty; **die Sache steht gut/schlecht** things are going well/badly; **[wie geht's,] wie steht's?** how are things?; **wie steht es mit deinen Finanzen/mit deiner Gesundheit?** how are your finances/how is your health?; **wie steht es mit deinen Ferien?** what is happening about your holidays?; **der Weizen steht gut** the wheat is growing well; **in Blüte ~:** be in bloom; **d)** *(einen bestimmten Kurs, Wert haben)* ‹*currency*› stand (**bei** at); **wie steht das Pfund?** what is the rate for the pound?; how is the pound doing? *(coll.)*; **der Schweizer Franken steht am besten** the Swiss franc is currently strongest; **die Aktie steht gut/schlecht** the share price is high/low; **e)** *(nicht in Bewegung sein)* be stationary; ⟨*machine etc.*⟩ be at a standstill; **meine Uhr steht** my watch has stopped; **ein ~der Zug** a stationary train; **etw./den Verkehr zum Stehen bringen** stop sth./bring traffic to a standstill; **zum Stehen kommen** come to a standstill; **f)** *(geschrieben, gedruckt sein)* be; **auf einer Liste ~:** be *or* appear on a list; **was steht in dem Brief?** what does it say in the letter?; **in der Zeitung steht, daß ...:** it says in the paper that ...; **das Zitat steht bei Schiller** the quotation is from Schiller; **g)** *(Sprachw.: gebraucht werden)* ⟨*subjunctive etc.*⟩ occur; be found; **mit dem Dativ ~:** be followed by *or* take the dative; **h) zu jmdm./etw. ~:** stand by sb./sth.; **wie stehst du dazu?** what's your view on this?; **hinter jmdm./etw. ~** *(jmdn. unterstützen)* be [right] behind sb./sth.; support sb./sth.; **i) jmdm. [gut] ~** ⟨*dress etc.*⟩ suit sb. [well]; **Lächeln steht dir gut** *(fig.)* it suits you *or* you look nice when you smile; **j)** *(sich verstehen)* **mit jmdm. gut/schlecht ~:** be on good/bad terms *or* get on well/badly with sb.; **k) das** *od.* **die Entscheidung steht [ganz] bei Ihnen** that's [entirely] up to you; it's for you to decide; **l) auf etw.** *(Akk.)* **steht Gefängnis** sth. is punishable by imprisonment; **m)** *(ugs.: fertig-, zusammengestellt sein)* ⟨*plan, speech, team, programme, etc.*⟩ be finalized; **n) für etw. ~** *(Gewähr bieten)* be a guarantee of sth.; *(stellvertretend)* stand for sth.; **o) auf etw.** *(Akk.)* **~** *(ugs., bes. Jugendspr.: mögen)* be into sth. *(coll.)*; **sie steht total auf ihn** she's nuts about him *(sl.)*; *s. auch* **Modell; Pate a; Posten b; Spalier b; Wache a. 2.** *unr. refl. V.; südd., österr., schweiz. mit sein (ugs.)* **a)** *(in bestimmten Verhältnissen leben)* **sich gut/schlecht/auf 3000 Mark monatlich ~:** be comfortably/badly off/on 3,000 marks a month; **b)** *(sich verstehen)* **sich gut/schlecht mit jmdm. ~:** be on good/bad terms *or* get on well/badly with sb. **3.** *tr. V. (Skisport, Eislauf)* **einen Sprung ~:** perform a jump without falling

stehen: ~|bleiben *unr. itr. V.; mit sein* **a)** *(anhalten)* stop; ⟨*traffic*⟩ come to a standstill; *(fig.)* ⟨*time*⟩ stand still; **~bleiben!** *(Milit.)* halt!; **wo sind wir ~geblieben?** *(fig.)* where had we got to?; where were we?; **das Kind ist in der Entwicklung ~geblieben** the child is a case of arrested development; **mir blieb das Herz fast ~:** my heart nearly stopped; **b)** *(unverändert gelassen werden)* stay; be left; *(zurückgelassen werden)* be left behind; *(der Zerstörung entgehen)* ⟨*building*⟩ be left standing; **~|lassen** *unr. tr. V.* **a)** *(belassen, nicht entfernen)* leave; **du kannst es nicht so ~lassen** you can't leave it as it is; **laß die Vase ~:** leave the vase where it is; **den Teig ca. eine Stunde ~lassen** leave the dough to stand for about an hour; **alles ~ und liegenlassen** drop everything; **sich** *(Dat.)* **einen Bart ~lassen** *(ugs.)* grow a beard; **b)** *(vergessen)* leave [behind]; **c)** *(sich abwenden von)* **jmdn. ~lassen** walk off and leave sb. standing there

Steher der; ~s, ~ a) *(Pferdesport)* stayer; **b)** *(Radsport)* motor-paced racer

Steher·rennen das *(Radsport)* motor-paced race

Steh-: ~geiger der café violinist; **~kneipe die** stand-up bar; **~konvent der** *(scherzh. fig.)* [stand-up] chat; **einen ~konvent halten** *od.* **machen** stand around chatting *or (Brit. coll.)* having a good natter; **~kragen der** stand-up collar; *(für Herrenhemden)* choker; *(mit Ecken)* wing collar; **~lampe die** standard lamp *(Brit.)*; floor lamp *(Amer.)*; **~leiter die** step-ladder

stehlen [ˈʃte:lən] **1.** *unr. tr., itr. V.* steal; **jmdm. etw. ~:** steal sth. from sb.; **jmdm. das Portemonnaie ~:** steal sb.'s purse; **jmdm. die Zeit ~** *(fig.)* take up *or* waste sb.'s time; *s. auch* **gestohlen 2; nehmen a. 2.** *unr. refl. V.* steal; creep

Steh-: ~platz der *(im Theater/Stadion)* standing place; *(im Bus)* space to stand; **40 ~plätze** standing-room for 40; **es gab nur noch ~plätze** there was standing-room only; **~pult das** high desk; **~vermögen das;** *o. Pl.* stamina; staying-power

Steiermark [ˈʃtaiɐmark] **die; ~:** Styria *no art.*

steif [ʃtaif] **1.** *Adj.* **a)** stiff; *(ugs.: erigiert)* erect ⟨*penis*⟩; **~ vor Kälte** stiff with cold; **~ gefroren** frozen stiff; **die Sahne ~ schlagen** beat the cream until stiff; **der Pudding ist noch nicht ~:** the blancmange has not set yet; **~ wie ein Stock** as stiff as a ramrod; **er kam uns mit ~en Schritten entgegen** he walked towards us stiffly; **b)** *(förmlich)* stiff, formal ⟨*person, greeting, style*⟩; formal ⟨*reception*⟩; **c)** *(Seemannsspr.: stark)* stiff ⟨*wind, breeze*⟩; **d)** *(ugs.: stark)* strong ⟨*coffee*⟩; stiff, strong ⟨*alcoholic drink*⟩. **2.** *adv.* **a)** stiffly; **bei ihnen geht es sehr ~ zu** things are very formal at their house; **b)** *(Seemannsspr.: stark)* **der Wind steht** *od.* **weht ~ aus Südost** there's a stiff wind blowing from the south-east; **c) ~ und fest behaupten/glauben, daß ...** *(ugs.)* swear blind/be completely convinced that ...

steif|halten *unr. tr. V. s.* **Nacken; Ohr b**

Steifheit die; ~: stiffness; *(Förmlichkeit)* formality; stiffness

Steif·leinen das buckram

Steig der; ~[e]s, ~e [mountain] path

Steig-: ~bügel der *(auch Anat.)* stirrup; **~bügel·halter der** *(abwertend)* backer; **die ~bügelhalter für Xs Karriere** those who advance/advanced X's career

Steige die; ~, ~n a) *(bes. südd., österr.: Steig)* [mountain] path; **b)** *(bes. nordd.: Treppe)* steps *pl.*; *(Leiter)* ladder; **c)** *(bes. südd., österr.: Lattenkiste)* open crate

Steig·eisen das *(in Schächten usw.)* step-iron; *(am Schuh anschnallbar)* climbing-iron; *(Bergsteigen)* crampon

steigen [ˈʃtaign̩] **1.** *unr. itr. V.; mit sein* **a)** ⟨*person, animal, aircraft, etc.*⟩ climb; ⟨*mist, smoke, sun, object*⟩ rise; ⟨*balloon*⟩ climb, rise; **Drachen ~ lassen** fly kites; **ins Tal/in den Keller ~:** climb *or* go down into the valley/go down into the cellar; **auf einen Turm/eine Leiter ~:** climb a tower/ladder; **auf die Leiter ~:** get on to the ladder; **aus dem Wasser/Auto/Bett/aus der Wanne ~:** get out of the water/out of the car/out of bed/out of the bath; **ins Wasser/ins Auto/in die Wanne/ins Bett ~:** get into the water/car/bath/into bed; **in den/aus dem Bus/Zug ~:** board *or* get on/get off *or* out of the bus/train; **ins/aus dem Flugzeug ~:** board/leave the aircraft; **aufs/vom Fahrrad ~:** get on [to]/off one's bicycle; **aufs Pferd/aus dem Sattel** *od.* **vom Pferd ~:** mount *or* get on [to]/get off one's horse; **auf die Bremse/aufs Gas ~** *(ugs.)* step on the brakes/the gas *(coll.)*; **in die Kleider ~** *(ugs.)* slip into one's clothes; **das Blut/eine Röte stieg ihm ins Gesicht** the blood rose into *or* rushed to his face/he blushed; **der Duft steigt mir in die Nase** the scent gets up my nose; *s. auch* **Kopf a; b)** *(ansteigen, zunehmen)* rise **(auf + Akk.** to, **um** by) ⟨*price, cost, salary, output*⟩ increase, rise; ⟨*debts, tension*⟩ increase, mount; ⟨*chances*⟩ improve; **~de Preise** rising prices; **~de Ansprüche** growing *or* increasing demands; **in jmds. Achtung ~** *(fig.)* go up *or* rise in sb.'s estimation; **c)** *(ugs.: stattfinden)* be on; **morgen soll ein Fest ~:** there's to be a party tomorrow; **d)** *(Reitsport: sich aufbäumen)* ⟨*horse*⟩ rear. **2.** *unr. tr. V.; mit sein* climb ⟨*stairs, steps*⟩

Steiger der; ~s, ~ *(Bergbau)* overman

steigern 1. *tr. V.* **a)** increase ⟨*speed, value, sales, consumption, etc.*⟩ **(auf + Akk.** to); step up ⟨*demands, production, etc.*⟩; raise ⟨*standards, requirements*⟩; *(verstärken)* intensify ⟨*fear, tension*⟩; heighten, intensify ⟨*effect*⟩; exacerbate ⟨*anger*⟩; **das Tempo ~:** step up the pace; **seine Leistung ~:** improve one's performance; **b)** *(Sprachw.)* compare ⟨*adjective*⟩. **2.** *refl. V.* **a)** ⟨*confusion, speed, profit, etc.*⟩ increase; ⟨*pain, excitement, tension*⟩ become more intense; ⟨*excitement, tension*⟩ mount; ⟨*hate, anger*⟩ grow, become more intense; ⟨*costs*⟩ escalate; ⟨*effect*⟩ be heightened *or* intensified; **der Sturm steigerte sich zum Orkan** the gale increased to hurricane strength; **sich** *od.* **seine Leistung[en] ~:** improve one's performance; **b)** *(hineinsteigern)* **sich [mehr und mehr] in Wut/Zorn/einen Erregungszustand ~:** work oneself up into [more and more of] a fury/rage/state [of excitement]

Steigerung die; ~, ~en a) increase (+ *Gen.* in); *(Verstärkung)* intensification; *(einer Wirkung)* heightening; *(des Zorns)* exacerbation; *(Verbesserung)* improvement (+ *Gen.* in); *(bes. Sport: Leistungs~)* improvement [in performance]; **~ der Produktion/des Absatzes** increase in production/in sales; **b)** *(Sprachw.)* comparison

Steigerungs-: ~form die *(Sprachw.)* comparative [form]; **~stufe die** *(Sprachw.)* degree of comparison

Steigung die; ~, ~en gradient; *(ansteigende Strecke)* gradient; climb; **in sanfter ~:** climbing gently

Steigungs·winkel der [angle of] gradient

steil [ʃtail] **1.** *Adj.* **a)** steep; upright, straight ⟨*handwriting, flame*⟩; meteoric ⟨*career*⟩; rapid ⟨*rise*⟩; **b)** *nicht präd. (Jugendspr. veralt.: beeindruckend)* fabulous *(coll.)*; super *(coll.)*; **c)** *(Ballspiele)* deep ⟨*pass, ball*⟩. **2.** *adv.* **a)** steeply; **sie saß ~ aufgerichtet** she sat bolt upright; **b)** *(Ballspiele)* **jmdn. ~ anspielen** play a deep ball to sb.; **er spielt [immer wieder] zu ~:** he's playing too many deep balls

Steil·hang der steep escarpment

Steilheit die; ~: steepness

Steil-: ~küste die *(Geogr.)* cliffs *pl.*; **~paß der** *(Fußball)* deep [forward] pass; **~ufer das** steep bank; **~wand die** rock wall; **~wand·fahrer der** wall-of-death rider; **~wand·zelt das** frame tent

Stein [ʃtain] **der; ~[e]s, ~e a)** *o. Pl.* stone; *(Fels)* rock; **ihr Gesicht war zu ~ geworden** *(fig.)* her face had hardened; **b)** *(losgelöstes Stück, Kern, Med., Edel~, Schmuck~)* stone; *(Kiesel~)* pebble; **der ~ der Weisen** *(geh.)* the philosophers' stone; **ein ~ des Anstoßes** *(geh.)* a bone of contention; **mir fällt ein ~ vom Herzen** that's a weight off my mind; **es friert ~ und Bein** *(ugs.)* it's freezing hard; **~ und Bein schwören** *(ugs.)* swear blind; **den ~ ins Rollen bringen** *(fig.)* set the ball rolling; **jmdm. [die** *od.* **alle] ~e aus dem Weg räumen** *(fig.)* smooth sb.'s path; make things easy for sb.; **jmdm. ~e in den Weg legen** *(fig.)* create obstacles *or* make things difficult for sb.; **eine Uhr mit 12 ~en** a 12-jewel watch; *s. auch* **Krone a; c)** *(Bau~)* [stone] block; *(Ziegel~)* brick; **keinen ~ auf dem anderen lassen** not leave one stone upon another; **d)** *(Spiel~)* piece; *(rund, flach)* counter; **bei jmdm. einen ~ im Brett haben** *(fig.)* be in sb.'s good books; **e)** *(Grab~)* gravestone

stein-, Stein-: ~adler der golden eagle; **~alt** *Adj.* aged; ancient; **~alt werden** live to a great age; **~axt die** *(hist.)* stone axe; **~bau der;** *Pl.* **~bauten** stone building; **~block der;** *Pl.* **~blöcke** block of stone; **~bock der a)** *(Tier)* ibex; **b)** *(Astrol.)* Capricorn; the Goat; *s. auch* **Fisch c; ~boden der** stone floor; **~brech** [~brɛç] **der; ~[e]s, ~e** *(Bot.)* saxifrage; **~bruch der** quarry; **~butt der** turbot

Steinchen das; ~s, ~: little stone; *(Kiesel~)* pebble

Stein·druck der; *Pl.* **~drucke a)** *o. Pl. (Verfahren)* lithography *no art.;* **b)** *(Graphik)* lithograph; **~eiche die** holm-oak
steinern *Adj.* **a)** *nicht präd.* stone ⟨*floor, bench, etc.*⟩; **b)** *(wie versteinert)* stony ⟨*face, features*⟩; **ein ~es Herz** a heart of stone
stein-, Stein-: ~erweichen das: zum ~erweichen so as to make your heart bleed; heart-rendingly; **~frucht die** *(Bot.)* stone-fruit; **~fuß·boden der** *s.* **~boden; ~garten der** rockery; rock-garden; **~gut das** earthenware; **~hart** *Adj.* rock-hard
steinig *Adj.* stony
steinigen *tr. V.* stone ⟨*person*⟩
stein-, Stein-: ~kauz der little owl; **~kohle die** [hard] coal; **~krug der** earthenware jug; **~marder der** stone marten; **~metz** [~mɛts] **der** stonemason; **~obst das** stone-fruit; **~pilz der** cep; **~reich** *Adj. (ugs.)* filthy rich; **~reich sein** be rolling [in money] *(coll.);* **~reich werden** make pots of money *(coll.);* **~salz das** rock-salt; **~schlag der** *(Fachspr.)* rock fall; **„Achtung ~schlag"** 'beware falling rocks'; **~schleuder die** catapult *(Brit.);* slingshot *(Amer.);* **~topf der** earthenware pot; **~wurf der: jmdn. mit ~würfen wegjagen** chase sb. away by throwing stones [at him/her]; **[nur] einen ~wurf weit [entfernt]** *(fig.)* [only] a stone's throw away; **~wüste die** rocky desert; *(fig.: leere Stadt)* waste land of stone and concrete; **~zeit die** Stone Age; *(fig.)* stone age; **~zeitlich** *Adj.* Stone-Age *attrib.; (fig.: völlig veraltet)* antediluvian *(coll.);* **~zeug das** stoneware
Steirer ['ʃtairɐ] **der; ~s, ~, Steierin die; ~, ~nen** Styrian
steirisch ['ʃtairɪʃ] *Adj.* Styrian
Steiß [ʃtais] **der; ~es, ~e a)** *(~bein)* coccyx; **b)** *(ugs.: Gesäß)* backside; behind *(coll.)*
Steiß-: ~bein das *(Anat.)* coccyx; **~lage die** *(Med.)* breech presentation
Stellage [ʃtɛ'la:ʒə] **die; ~, ~n** rack
Stell·dich·ein das; ~[s], ~[s] *(veralt.)* rendezvous; tryst *(arch./literary);* **sich** *(Dat.)* **ein ~ geben** *(fig.)* gather; assemble
Stelle ['ʃtɛlə] **die; ~, ~n a)** place; **eine schöne ~ zum Campen** a nice spot for camping; **an dieser ~ ereignete sich der Unfall** this is the spot where the accident happened; **die Truhe ließ sich nicht von der ~ rücken** the chest could not be shifted *or* would not budge; **sich nicht von der ~ rühren** not budge *or* move; **an jmds. ~ treten** take sb.'s place; **ich an deiner ~ würde das nicht machen** I wouldn't do it if I were you; **ich möchte nicht an deiner ~ sein** I shouldn't like to be in your place; **A an die ~ von B setzen** replace B with A; **an ~ +** *Gen.* instead of; **auf der ~:** immediately; **er war auf der ~ tot** he died instantly; **ich könnte auf der ~ einschlafen** I could go to sleep here and now; **auf der ~ treten** *(ugs.),* **nicht von der ~ kommen** *(fig.)* make no headway; not get anywhere; **zur ~ sein** be there *or* on the spot; **pünktlich zu ~ sein** arrive punctually; **Gefreiter Schulz meldet sich zur ~!** *(Milit.)* Lance-Corporal Schulz reporting; **b)** *(begrenzter Bereich)* patch; *(am Körper)* spot; **eine kahle ~:** a bare patch; *(am Kopf)* a bald patch; **seine empfindliche ~** *(fig.)* his sensitive *or* sore spot; **eine schwache ~ in der Argumentation** *(fig.)* a weak point in the argument; **c)** *(Passage)* passage; **an anderer ~:** elsewhere; in another passage; **d)** *(Punkt im Ablauf einer Rede usw.)* point; **an dieser/früherer ~:** at this point *or* here/earlier; **e)** *(Platz in einer Rangordnung, Reihenfolge)* place; **an achter ~ liegen** be in eighth place; **er steht an führender ~:** he has a leading position; **etw. kommt an vorderster** *od.* **oberster ~:** sth. has top priority; **an erster ~ geht es hier um ...:** here it is primarily a question of...; **f)** *(Math.)* figure; **die erste ~ hinter** *od.* **nach dem Komma** the first decimal place; **etw. bis auf zwei ~n hinter dem Komma ausrechnen** calculate sth. to two decimal places; **g)** *(Arbeits~)* job; *(formeller)* position; *(bes. als Beamter)* post; **eine halbe/ganze ~:** a half-time/full-time job; **ohne ~ sein** be unemployed; **eine freie ~:** a vacancy; **h)** *(Dienst~)* office; *(Behörde)* authority; **die zuständige ~:** the competent authority
stellen 1. *tr. V.* **a)** put; *(mit Sorgfalt, ordentlich)* place; *(aufrecht hin~)* stand; **die Stühle um den Tisch ~:** place *or* put the chairs round the table; **wie sollen wir die Möbel ~?** how should we position the furniture?; **man soll die Flaschen ~, nicht legen** one should stand the bottles [up], not lay them down; **jmdn. wieder auf die Füße ~** *(fig.)* put sb. back on his/her feet; **jmdn. vor eine Entscheidung ~** *(fig.)* confront sb. with a decision; **auf sich [selbst] gestellt sein** *(fig.)* be thrown back on one's own resources; **etw. in den Mittelpunkt der Diskussion ~** *(fig.)* make sth. the focus of discussion; **b)** *(ein~, regulieren)* set ⟨*points, clock, scales*⟩; set ⟨*clock*⟩ to the right time; **den Wecker auf 6 Uhr ~:** set the alarm for 6 o'clock; **den Schalter auf Null ~:** turn the switch to zero; set the switch at zero; **das Radio lauter/leiser ~:** turn the radio up/down; **die Heizung höher/niedriger ~:** turn the heating up/down; **c)** *(bereit~)* provide; produce ⟨*witness*⟩; **jmdm. etw. ~:** provide sb. with sth.; *s. auch* **Verfügung b; d) jmdn. besser ~:** ⟨*firm*⟩ improve sb.'s pay; **gut/schlecht/besser gestellt** comfortably/badly/better off; **e)** *(auf~)* set ⟨*trap*⟩; lay ⟨*net*⟩; **f) kalt ~:** put ⟨*food, drink*⟩ in a cold place; leave ⟨*champagne etc.*⟩ to chill; **warm ~:** put ⟨*plant*⟩ in a warm place; keep ⟨*food*⟩ warm *or* hot; **g)** *(fassen, festhalten)* catch ⟨*game*⟩; apprehend ⟨*criminal*⟩; **h)** *(aufrichten)* ⟨*dog, horse, etc.*⟩ prick up ⟨*ears*⟩; stick up ⟨*tail*⟩; **i)** *(erstellen)* prepare ⟨*horoscope, bill*⟩; make ⟨*diagnosis, prognosis*⟩; **j)** *verblaßt* put ⟨*question*⟩; set ⟨*task, essay, topic, condition*⟩; make ⟨*application, demand, request*⟩; **jmdm. eine Frage/Aufgabe ~:** ask sb. a question/set sb. a task; **jmdn. unter Aufsicht/etw. unter Denkmalschutz ~:** place sb. under supervision/sth. under a conservation order; **jmdn. vor Gericht/unter Anklage ~:** take sb. to court/charge sb.; **k)** *(bes. Theater, Film: arrangieren)* block in the moves for ⟨*scene*⟩; **das Foto wirkt gestellt** the photo looks posed. **2.** *refl. V.* **a)** place oneself; **sie stellte sich auf eine Leiter** she got on a ladder; **stell dich neben mich/ans Ende der Schlange/in die Reihe** come and stand by me/go to the back of the queue *(Brit.) or (Amer.)* line/get into line; **sich auf die Zehenspitzen ~:** stand on tiptoe; **ich stelle mich lieber** *(ugs.)* I'd rather stand; **sich gegen jmdn./etw. ~** *(fig.)* oppose sb./sth.; **sich hinter jmdn./etw. ~** *(fig.)* give sb./sth. one's backing; **sich vor jmdn. ~** *(fig.)* take sb.'s part; *(verteidigen)* defend sb.; *s. auch* **Standpunkt; b) sich schlafend/taub/tot** *usw.* **~:** feign sleep/deafness/death *etc.;* pretend to be asleep/deaf/dead *etc.; s. auch* **dumm 1 a; c)** *(sich ausliefern)* **sich [der Polizei] ~:** give oneself up [to the police]; **d)** *(nicht ausweichen)* **sich einem Herausforderer/der Presse ~:** face a challenger/the press; **sich einer Disskusion ~:** consent to take part in a discussion; **er stellte sich der Kamera** he made himself available for photographs; **e)** *(Stellung beziehen)* **sich positiv/negativ zu jmdm./etw. ~:** take a positive/negative view of sb./sth.; **sich mit jmdm. gut ~:** try to get on good terms with sb.
stellen-, Stellen-: ~angebot das offer of a job; *(Inserat)* job advertisement; **„~angebote"** 'situations vacant'; **~anzeige die** job advertisement; **~gesuch das** 'situation wanted' advertisement; **„~gesuche"** 'situations wanted'; **~markt der** job market; **~suche die** job-hunting *no art.;* search for a job; **auf ~suche sein** be looking for a job; be job-hunting; **~weise** *Adv.* in places; **~weise Nebel/Schauer** fog patches/scattered showers; **~wert der a)** *(Math.)* place value; **b)** *(fig.: Bedeutung)* standing; status
-stellig -figure ⟨*number, salary*⟩; -place ⟨*decimal*⟩
Stell-: ~macher der cartwright; **~platz der** space; *(auf einem Campingplatz)* pitch; site; **~probe die** *(Theater)* blocking rehearsal; **~schraube die** adjusting screw
Stellung die; ~, ~en a) position; **in gebückter/kniender ~:** in a bent/kneeling posture; **die ~ der Frau in der Gesellschaft** the position *or* standing of women in society; **in ~ gehen** *(Milit.)* take up [one's] position; **geh nur, ich halte in der Zwischenzeit die ~** *(fig.)* you can go while I hold the fort; **[zu/gegen etw.] ~ beziehen** *(fig.)* take a stand [on/against sth.]; **b)** *(Posten)* job; *(formeller)* position; *(bes. als Beamter)* post; **c)** *o. Pl. (Einstellung)* attitude **(zu** to, towards); **zu etw. ~ nehmen** express one's opinion *or* state one's view on sth.; **er hat zu dem Vorschlag offiziell ~ genommen** he made an official statement on the proposal
Stellungnahme die; ~, ~n opinion; *(kurze Äußerung)* statement; **eine ~ zu etw. abgeben** give one's opinion *or* views on sth.; *(sich kurz zu etw. äußern)* make a statement on sth.
stellungs-, Stellungs-: ~befehl der *(Milit.)* call-up papers *pl.;* draft card *(Amer.);* **~krieg der** positional warfare *no pl., no indef. art.;* **~los** *Adj.* unemployed; jobless; **~spiel das;** *o. Pl. (Fußball)* positioning; **~suche die** *s.* **Stellensuche; ~suchende der/die;** *adj. Dekl.* job-hunter; **~wechsel der** change of position; *(Wechsel der Arbeitsstelle)* change of job
stell-, Stell-: ~vertretend 1. *Adj.; nicht präd.* acting; *(von Amts wegen)* deputy ⟨*minister, director, etc.*⟩; **2.** *adv.* as a deputy; **~vertretend für jmdn.** deputizing for sb.; on sb.'s behalf; **~vertreter der** deputy; **jmdn. als seinen ~vertreter schicken** send sb. as one's representative; **der ~vertreter Christi** *(kath. Rel.)* the Vicar of Christ; **~vertreter·krieg der** proxy war; **~vertretung die** deputizing *no art.;* acting as deputy *no art.;* **die ~vertretung für jmdn.** *od.* **jmds. ~vertretung übernehmen** stand in *or* deputize for sb.; **~wand die** partition; **~werk das** *(Eisenb.)* signal-box *(Brit.);* switch-tower *(Amer.); (Anlage)* control gear for signals and points *(Brit.) or (Amer.)* switches
Stelze die; ~, ~n a) *meist Pl.* stilt; **b)** *(ugs.: Bein)* leg; **der hat vielleicht ~n!** what long skinny legs *or* spindle-shanks he's got!
stelzen *itr. V.; mit sein* strut; stalk
Stemm-: ~bogen der *(Skisport)* stem [turn]; **~eisen das** chisel
stemmen ['ʃtɛmən] **1.** *tr. V.* **a)** *(hoch~)* lift [above one's head]; *(Gewichtheben)* lift ⟨*weight*⟩; **b)** *(drücken)* brace ⟨*feet, knees*⟩ **(gegen** against); **die Arme in die Hüften/Seiten ~:** place one's arms akimbo; put one's hands on one's hips; **die Arme in die Hüften gestemmt** with arms akimbo; **c)** *(meißeln)* chisel ⟨*hole etc.*⟩. **2.** *refl. V.* **sich gegen etw. ~:** brace oneself against sth.; *(fig.: sich auflehnen)* resist sth.; **sich in die Höhe ~:** haul oneself to one's feet. **3.** *itr. V. (Skisport)* stem
Stempel ['ʃtɛmpl̩] **der; ~s, ~ a)** stamp; *(Post~)* postmark; **jmdm./einer Sache seinen** *od.* **den ~ aufdrücken** *(fig.)* leave one's mark on sb./sth.; **den ~ einer Person/Sache tragen** *(fig.)* bear the stamp *or* imprint of sb./sth.; **b)** *(Punze)* hallmark; **c)** *(Bot.: Teil der Blüte)* pistil; **d)** *(Technik) (zum Stanzen)* punch; *(zum Formen)* die; **e)** *(Bauw., Berg-*

bau: Stütze) prop; **f)** *(salopp: dicke Beine)* **[richtige] ~ haben** have legs like tree-trunks
Stempel-: ~farbe die stamp-pad ink; **~geld das;** *o. Pl. (ugs. veralt.)* dole [money] *(coll.)*; **~kissen das** stamp pad; ink-pad
stempeln 1. *tr. V.* **a)** stamp ⟨*passport, form*⟩; postmark ⟨*letter*⟩; cancel ⟨*postage stamp*⟩; **das Eingangsdatum auf die Briefe ~:** stamp the letters with the date of receipt; **b)** hallmark ⟨*gold, silver, ring, brooch, etc.*⟩; **c)** *(brandmarken)* **jmdn. zum Verbrecher ~:** brand sb. [as] a criminal. **2.** *itr. V. (ugs. veralt.)* be on the dole *(coll.)*; **~ gehen** be on the dole *(coll.)*; **er muß ~ gehen** he has to go on the dole
stempelpflichtig [-pflɪçtɪç] *Adj. (österr.) s.* **gebührenpflichtig**
Stempel·schneider der punch-cutter
Stengel [ˈʃtɛŋl] **der; ~s, ~:** stem; stalk
[1]**Steno** [ˈʃteːno] **die; ~;** *meist o. Art. (ugs.)* shorthand; **kannst du ~?** do you know shorthand?
[2]**Steno das; ~s, ~s** *(ugs.) s.* **Stenogramm**
steno-, Steno-: ~block [ˈ---] **der** *s.* **~grammblock; ~gramm das** shorthand text; **ein ~gramm aufnehmen** take a dictation in shorthand; **~gramm·block der;** *Pl.* **~blöcke** *od.* **~blocks** shorthand pad; **~graph der; ~en, ~en** stenographer; **~graphie die; ~, ~n** stenography *no art.*; shorthand *no art.*; **~graphie lernen/können** learn shorthand/be able to do shorthand; **~graphieren 1.** *itr. V.* do shorthand; **sie kann gut ~graphieren** her shorthand is good; **2.** *tr. V.* **etw. ~graphieren** take sth. down in shorthand; **~graphisch 1.** *Adj.; nicht präd.* **a)** shorthand *attrib.*; stenographic ⟨*symbols*⟩; **2.** *adv.* **~graphisch abgefaßte Notizen** shorthand notes; **~stift** [ˈ---] **der** shorthand pencil; **~typistin die** shorthand typist
Stentor·stimme [ˈʃtɛntɔr-] **die** stentorian voice; **mit ~:** in a stentorian voice
Stenz [ʃtɛnts] **der; ~es, ~e** *(ugs. abwertend)* dandy; fop
Step [ʃtɛp] **der; ~s, ~s** tap-dance
Stepp·decke die quilt
Steppe [ˈʃtɛpə] **die; ~, ~n** steppe
[1]**steppen** *tr. (auch itr.) V. (nähen)* backstitch; **eine gesteppte Jacke** a quilted jacket
[2]**steppen** *itr. V. (tanzen)* tap-dance
Steppen-: ~fuchs der corsac; **~wolf der** *s.* **Präriewolf**
Stepperei die; ~, ~en backstitching *no pl.*
Stepp-: ~futter das quilted lining; **~jacke die** quilted jacket
Steppke [ˈʃtɛpkə] **der; ~[s], ~s** *(ugs., bes. berlin.)* lad; nipper *(coll.)*
Stepp-: ~naht die backstitched seam; **~stich der** backstitch
Step-: ~tanz der tap-dance; **~tänzer der, ~tänzerin die** tap-dancer
Sterbe-: ~bett das death-bed; **auf dem ~bett liegen** be on one's death-bed; **~datum das** date of death; **~fall der** *s.* **Todesfall; ~geläut das** death-knell; **~glocke die** funeral bell; **~hilfe die** *s.* **Euthanasie**
sterben [ˈʃtɛrbn̩] **1.** *unr. itr. V.; mit sein* die; **eines sanften Todes ~** *(geh.)* die peacefully; **er starb als Christ** he died a Christian; **im Sterben liegen** lie dying; **und wenn sie nicht gestorben sind, dann leben sie noch heute** and they lived happily ever after; **davon stirbt man/stirbst du nicht gleich** *(ugs.)* it/they won't kill you; **zum Sterben langweilig/müde** deadly boring/dead tired; **er ist für mich gestorben** *(fig.)* he's finished *or* he doesn't exist as far as I'm concerned; **gestorben!** *(Film-, Fernsehjargon) (abgeschlossen)* [OK,] in the can!; *(abgebrochen)* cut!; **vor Angst/Scham/Neugier ~** *(ugs.)* die of fright/shame/be dying of curiosity. **2.** *unr. tr. V.; mit sein* **den Hungertod ~:** die of starvation; starve to death; **den Heldentod ~:** die a hero's death

sterbens-, Sterbens-: ~angst die terrible fear; **eine ~angst haben** be scared to death; be terribly afraid; be terrified; **~elend** *Adj.* wretched; **~krank** *Adj.* **a)** *s.* **~elend; b)** *(sehr krank)* mortally ill; **~langweilig** *Adj.* deadly boring; **~wort, ~wörtchen das** *in* **kein** *od.* **nicht ein ~wort** *od.* **~wörtchen** not a [single] word; **darüber haben wir kein ~wort** *od.* **~wörtchen gesagt** we didn't breathe a word [of it]
Sterbe-: ~sakramente *Pl. (kath. Kirche)* last rites; **~stunde die** *s.* **Todesstunde; ~urkunde die** death certificate; **~zimmer das: sein ~zimmer** the room in which he died
sterblich *Adj.* mortal; *s. auch* **Hülle a; Überrest**
Sterbliche der/die; *adj. Dekl.* **a)** *(dichter.)* mortal; **b) ein gewöhnlicher ~r** an ordinary mortal *or* person
Sterblichkeit die; ~: mortality
stereo [ˈʃteːreo] *Adv. (Akustik)* in stereo
Stereo das; ~s *(Akustik)* stereo
stereo-, Stereo- stereo-
stereo-, Stereo-: ~anlage die stereo [system]; **~aufnahme die** stereo recording; **~empfang der;** *o. Pl.* stereo reception; **~kamera die** stereocamera; stereoscopic camera; **~metrie** [~meˈtriː] **die; ~** *(Math.)* stereometry *no art.*; **~phon** [~ˈfoːn] *(Akustik)* **1.** *Adj.* stereophonic; **2.** *adv.* stereophonically; **~phonie** [~foˈniː] **die; ~** *(Akustik)* stereophony *no art.*; **~skop** [~ˈskoːp] **das; ~s, ~e** stereoscope; **~skopie** [~skoˈpiː] **die; ~:** stereoscopy *no art.*; **~skopisch** *Adj.* stereoscopic; **~ton der** stereo sound; **~typ** [---ˈ-] **1.** *Adj.* **a)** stereotyped ⟨*discussion, pattern, etc.*⟩; stereotyped, stock ⟨*question, reply, phrase, utterance*⟩; mechanical ⟨*smile*⟩; **b)** *(Druckw.)* stereotype; **2.** *adv.* **a)** in a stereotyped way; **b)** *(Druckw.)* in stereotype; **~typie** [~tyˈpiː] **die; ~ a)** *(Druckw.)* stereotyping *no art.*; **b)** *(Psychiatrie, Med.)* stereotypy
steril [ʃteˈriːl] **1.** *Adj. (auch fig. abwertend)* sterile; **etw. ~ machen** sterilize sth. **2.** *adv.* **a)** *(keimfrei)* **~ verpackt sein** be in a sterile pack/sterile packs; **etw. ~ auskochen** sterilize sth. by boiling; **b)** *(fig. abwertend: unschöpferisch, nüchtern)* sterilely
Sterilisation [ʃterilizaˈtsi̯oːn] **die; ~, ~en** sterilization
sterilisieren *tr. V.* sterilize
Sterilität [ʃteriliˈtɛːt] **die; ~** *(auch fig. abwertend)* sterility
Sterling [ˈstɛːlɪŋ] **der; ~s, ~e: 2 Pfund ~:** £2 sterling; **einen Betrag in Pfund ~ tauschen** change a sum into sterling
Sterling·silber das sterling silver
Stern [ʃtɛrn] **der; ~[e]s, ~e a)** star; **~e sehen** *(ugs.)* see stars; **unter fremden ~en** *(geh.)* in foreign parts; **nach den ~en greifen** *(geh.)* reach for the moon; **in den ~en stehen** *(fig.)* be in the lap of the gods; **unter einem guten** *od.* **günstigen/ungünstigen ~ stehen** *(geh.)* have an auspicious start/be ill-starred; **b)** *(Orden, Auszeichnung)* star; **ein Hotel mit fünf ~en** a five-star hotel; **c)** *(bei Pferden, Rindern)* blaze; **d)** *(Jägerspr.)* iris
Stern·bild das constellation
Sternchen das; ~s, ~ a) [little] star; **b)** *(als Verweis)* asterisk; **c)** *s.* **Starlet[t]**
Stern-: ~deuter [~dɔytɐ] **der; ~s, ~:** astrologer; **~deutung die;** *o. Pl.* astrology *no art.*
sternen-, Sternen-: ~banner das Star-spangled Banner, Stars and Stripes *pl.*; **~himmel der** *(geh.)* starry sky; **~klar** *Adj.* starlit, starry ⟨*sky, night*⟩; **~licht das;** *o. Pl. (geh.)* starlight; **~zelt das;** *o. Pl. (dichter.)* starry canopy
stern-, Stern-: ~fahrt die rally *(in which the participants converge from various starting-points)*; **eine ~fahrt nach X** a rally converging on X; **~förmig** *Adj.* star-shaped; stellate ⟨*leaf*⟩ *(Bot.)*; **~globus der** *(Astron.)* celestial globe; **~gucker der; ~s, ~** *(ugs. scherzh.: Astronom)* star-gazer; **~hagel·voll** *Adj. (salopp)* paralytic *(Brit. sl.)*; blotto *(sl.)*; **~haufen der** *(Astron.)* star cluster; **~hell** *Adj. (geh.)* starlit; starry; **~himmel der** starry sky; **~jahr das** sidereal year; **~karte die** *s.* **Himmelskarte; ~klar** *Adj.* starlit, starry ⟨*sky, night*⟩; **~kunde die;** *o. Pl.* astronomy *no art.*; **~kundig** *Adj.* **~kundig sein** have a knowledge of astronomy; **~los** *Adj.* starless; **~marsch der** [protest] march *(with marchers converging from various starting points)*; **~miere** [~miːrə] **die** *(Bot.)* starwort; **~schnuppe die; ~, ~n** shooting star; **~stunde die** *(geh.)* great moment; **seine ~stunde haben** have one's moment *or* hour of glory; **~tag der** *(Astron.)* sidereal day; **~warte die** observatory; **~zeichen das** *s.* **Tierkreiszeichen; ~zeit die** sidereal time
[1]**Sterz** [ʃtɛrts] **der; ~es, ~e** *(südd., österr.: Speise) (boiled or fried)* dumpling pieces *pl.*
[2]**Sterz der; ~es, ~e** *(Bürzel)* rump
stet [ʃteːt] *Adj. (geh.)* **a)** constant ⟨*goodwill, devotion, companion*⟩; steady ⟨*rhythm*⟩; **b)** *(ständig)* constant; continous
Stethoskop [ʃtetoˈskoːp] **das; ~s, ~e** *(Med.)* stethoscope
stetig [ˈʃteːtɪç] **1.** *Adj.* steady ⟨*growth, increase, decline*⟩; constant, continuous ⟨*movement, vibration*⟩. **2.** *adv.* ⟨*grow, increase, drop*⟩ steadily; ⟨*move, vibrate*⟩ constantly, continuously
Stetigkeit die; ~ *s.* **stetig:** steadiness; constancy; continuousness
stets [ʃteːts] *Adv.* always
[1]**Steuer** [ˈʃtɔyɐ] **das; ~s, ~** *(von Fahrzeugen)* [steering-]wheel; *(von Schiffen)* helm; **ins ~ greifen** grab the [steering-]wheel; **sich ans** *od.* **hinters ~ setzen** get behind the wheel; **das ~ herumreißen** pull the [steering-]wheel over hard; **das ~ übernehmen** take over the wheel *or* the driving; *(bei Schiffen, fig.)* take over the helm; **Trunkenheit am ~:** drunken driving; being drunk at the wheel; **das ~ fest in der Hand haben** *(fig.)* have one's hand firmly on the helm
[2]**Steuer die; ~, ~n a)** tax; **~n zahlen** *(Lohn-/Einkommensteuer)* pay tax; **etw. von der ~ absetzen** set sth. off against tax; **etw. mit einer ~ belegen** impose a tax on sth.; **b)** *o. Pl. (ugs.: Behörde)* tax authorities *pl.*
steuer-, Steuer-: ~aufkommen das *(Steuerw.)* tax revenue; **~bar** *Adj.* controllable; **~behörde die** tax authorities *pl.*; **~berater der** *(Steuerw.)* tax consultant *or* adviser; **~bescheid der** *(Steuerw.)* tax assessment; **~bevollmächtigte der/die;** *adj. Dekl. (Steuerw.)* tax consultant *or* adviser; **~bord das** *od. österr.* **der;** *o. Pl. (Seew., Flugw.)* starboard; **nach ~bord gehen** turn to starboard; **~bord[s]** *Adv. (Seew., Flugw.)* to starboard; **~erhöhung die** *(Steuerw.)* tax increase; **~erklärung die** *(Steuerw.)* tax return; **~ermäßigung die** *(Steuerw.)* tax relief; **~erstattung die** *(Steuerw.)* tax refund; **~fahnder der** tax investigator; **~fahndung die** *(Steuerw.)* tax investigation; **~flucht die** *(Steuerw.)* tax evasion *(by transferring capital out of the country or living abroad)*; **~frei** *Adj. (Steuerw.)* tax-free; free of tax *pred.*; **~freibetrag der** *(Steuerw.)* tax allowance; **~gelder** *Pl. (Steuerw.)* taxes; **~gerät das a)** *(Rundfunkt.)* receiver; **b)** *(Elektrot.)* control device *or* unit; **~gesetz das;** *meist Pl. (Steuerw.)* tax law; **~hinter·ziehung die** *(Steuerw.)* tax evasion; **~klasse die** *(Steuerw.)* tax category *(dependent on marital status [and number of children])*; **~knüppel der** control column; joystick *(coll.)*
steuerlich 1. *Adj.; nicht präd.* tax ⟨*advant-*

ages, benefits, etc.›. **2.** *adv.* ~ **absetzbar** tax-deductible

steuer-, Steuer-: ~**los** *Adj.* out of control; ~**mann der;** *Pl.* ~**leute** *od.* ~**männer a)** *(Seew. veralt.)* helmsman; steersman; **b)** *(Seew.) s.* **Bootsmann b; c)** *(Rudersport)* cox; **Vierer mit/ohne** ~**mann** coxed/coxless fours; **Einer mit** ~**mann** coxed single; **d)** *(Elektrot.)* controller; ~**marke die** revenue stamp; *(für Hunde)* licence disc; ~**moral die** tax-payer honesty; attitude to paying tax

steuern 1. *tr. V.* **a)** *(fahren)* steer; *(fliegen)* pilot, fly ‹*aircraft*›; fly ‹*course*›; **b)** *(Technik)* control; **c)** *(beeinflussen)* control, regulate ‹*process, activity, price, etc.*›; steer ‹*discussion etc.*›; influence ‹*opinion etc.*›. **2.** *itr. V.* **a)** *(im Fahrzeug)* be at the wheel; *(auf dem Schiff)* be at the helm; **b)** *mit sein (Kurs nehmen, ugs.: sich hinbewegen; auch fig.)* head; **c)** *(geh.: entgegenwirken)* **jmdm./einer Sache** ~: curb sb./remedy sth.

steuer-, Steuer-: ~**oase die** *(ugs.)* tax haven; ~**pflicht die;** *o. Pl. (Steuerw.)* liability to [pay] tax; ~**pflichtig** *Adj. (Steuerw.)* ‹*person*› liable to [pay] tax; taxable ‹*goods, assets, income, profits, etc.*›; ~**pflichtige der/die;** *adj. Dekl. (Steuerw.)* person liable to [pay] tax; ~**progression die** progressive taxation; ~**prüfer der** *s.* **Wirtschaftsprüfer;** ~**pult das** *(Elektrot.) s.* **Schaltpult;** ~**rad das a)** *s.* **Lenkrad; b)** *(Seew.)* [ship's] wheel; helm; ~**recht das** tax law; ~**rechtlich** *Adj. (Steuerw.)* under the tax laws *postpos.;* ~**ruder das** *(Seew.)* rudder; ~**satz der** *(Steuerw.)* tax rate; rate of tax; ~**schraube die** *in* **die** ~**schraube anziehen/überdrehen** *(ugs.)* squeeze the taxpayer/squeeze the taxpayer too hard *(coll.);* ~**schuld die** *(Steuerw.)* tax[es] owing *no indef. art.;* *(Verpflichtung)* tax liability; ~**senkung die** *(Steuerw.)* tax cut; reduction in taxation; ~**system das** *(Technik) s.* **Steuerung a;** ~**tabelle die** *(Steuerw.)* ≈ tax table

Steuerung die; ~, ~**en a)** *(System)* controls *pl.;* **die automatische** ~ *(Flugw.)* the automatic pilot; the autopilot; **b)** *o. Pl. s.* **steuern 1 a, c, d:** steering; piloting; flying; control; regulation; steering; influencing; **die** ~ **übernehmen** *(Flugw.)* take over the controls; **c)** *s.* **Steuergerät b**

Steuer-: ~**verkürzung die** *(Steuerw.)* tax evasion; ~**vorteil der** *(Steuerw.)* tax advantage; ~**zahler der;** ~**s,** ~: taxpayer

Steven [ˈʃteːvn̩] **der;** ~**s,** ~ *(Vorder~)* stem; *(Achter~)* stern-post

Steward [ˈstjuːɐt] **der;** ~**s,** ~**s** steward

Stewardeß [ˈstjuːɐdɛs] **die;** ~, **Stewardessen** stewardess

StGB *Abk.* **Strafgesetzbuch**

stibitzen [ʃtiˈbɪtsn̩] *tr. V. (fam.)* pinch *(sl.);* swipe *(sl.)*

stich [ʃtɪç] *Imper. Sg. v.* **stechen**

Stich der; ~**[e]s,** ~**e a)** *(mit einer Waffe)* stab; *(fig.: böse Bemerkung)* dig; gibe; **b)** *(Dornen~, Nadel~)* prick; *(von Wespe, Biene, Skorpion usw.)* sting; *(Mücken~ usw.)* bite; **c)** *(~wunde)* stab wound; **d)** *(beim Nähen)* stitch; **e)** *(Schmerz)* stabbing *or* shooting *or* sharp pain; **es gab mir einen** ~ **[ins Herz]** *(fig.)* I was cut to the quick; **f)** *(Kartenspiel)* trick; **g) jmdn. im** ~ **lassen** leave sb. in the lurch; **mein Gedächtnis hat mich im** ~ **gelassen** my memory has failed me; **etw. im** ~ **lassen** abandon sth.; ~ **halten** ‹*argument, alibi, etc.*› hold water; **h)** *(Fechten)* hit; **i)** *(bild. Kunst)* engraving; **j)** *o. Pl. (Farbschimmer)* tinge; **ein** ~ **ins Blaue** a tinge of blue; **sie hat einen** ~ **ins Ordinäre** *(fig.)* she is a touch vulgar; **k) einen [leichten]** ~ **haben** *(ugs.)* ‹*food, drink*› be off, have gone off; *(salopp)* ‹*person*› be nuts *(sl.);* be round the bend *(coll.);* **l)** *(Kochk. landsch.)* **ein** ~ **Butter** a knob of butter

Stichel der; ~**s,** ~: graver; burin

Stichelei die; ~, ~**en** *(ugs. abwertend)* **a)** *(Bemerkung)* dig; gibe; **b)** *o. Pl.* **hör auf mit deiner** ~: stop getting at me/him *etc. (coll.)*

sticheln *itr. V.* **a)** *(Anspielungen machen)* make snide remarks *(coll.)* **(gegen** about); **b)** *(nähen)* sew; *(sticken)* embroider

stich-, Stich-: ~**fest** *s.* **hiebfest;** ~**flamme die** tongue *or* jet of flame; ~**|halten** *(österr.) s.* **Stich g;** ~**haltig,** *(österr.)* ~**hältig 1.** *Adj.* sound, valid ‹*argument, reason*›; valid ‹*assertion, reply*›; conclusive ‹*evidence*›; **dieses Argument ist nicht** ~**haltig** this argument doesn't hold water; **2.** *adv.* **etw.** ~**haltig begründen** back sth. with sound *or* valid reasons; ~**haltigkeit,** *(österr.)* ~**hältigkeit die;** ~ *s.* ~**haltig:** soundness; validity; conclusiveness; ~**kampf der** *(Sport)* play-off **(um** for)

Stichling [ˈʃtɪçlɪŋ] **der;** ~**s,** ~**e** stickleback

Stich-: ~**probe die** [random] sample; *(bei Kontrollen)* spot check; ~**säge die** compass saw

stichst [ʃtɪçst] *2. Pers. Sg. Präsens v.* **stechen**

Stich·straße die cul-de-sac

sticht [ʃtɪçt] *3. Pers. Sg. Präsens v.* **stechen**

Stich-: ~**tag der** set date; *(letzter Termin)* deadline; ~**waffe die** stabbing weapon; ~**wahl die** final *or* deciding ballot; run-off; ~**wort das a)** *Pl.* ~**wörter** headword; *(in Registern)* entry; **b)** *Pl.* ~**worte** *(Theater)* cue; **c)** *Pl.* ~**worte** *(Äußerung)* cue **(zu** for); **d)** *Pl.* ~**worte** *(Gedächtnisstütze)* keyword; *(Notiz)* note; ~**wort·verzeichnis das** [subject] index; ~**wunde die** stab wound

Stick·arbeit die *(Handarb.)* piece of embroidery

sticken [ˈʃtɪkn̩] **1.** *itr. V.* do embroidery. **2.** *tr. V.* embroider

¹Sticker der; ~**s,** ~: embroiderer

²Sticker [ˈstɪkɐ] **der;** ~**s,** ~ *(Aufkleber)* sticker

Stickerei die; ~, ~**en** *(Handarb.)* **a)** *(Verzierung)* embroidery *no pl.;* embroidered pattern; ~**en** embroidery *sing.;* **b)** *(gestickte Arbeit)* piece of embroidery

Stickerin die; ~, ~**nen** embroiderer; embroideress

Stick·garn das embroidery thread

stickig *Adj.* stuffy; stale ‹*air*›

stick-, Stick-: ~**luft die** stale air; ~**muster das** *(Handarb.)* embroidery pattern; ~**rahmen der** embroidery frame; ~**stoff der** nitrogen; ~**stoff·haltig** *Adj.* nitrogenous; containing nitrogen *postpos.;* ~**stoffoxid das** *(Chem.)* nitrogen oxide

stieben [ˈʃtiːbn̩] *unr. (auch regelm.) itr. V. (geh., veralt.)* **a)** *auch mit sein (auseinanderwirbeln)* ‹*dust, snow*› be thrown up in a cloud; ‹*sparks*› fly; ‹*water*› spray; **sie rannten davon, daß es nur so stiebte** you couldn't see them for dust; **b)** *mit sein* **Schnee stiebt durch die Ritzen** snow blows through the cracks; **c)** *mit sein (davoneilen)* dash; **nach allen Seiten** ~: scatter in all directions

Stief·bruder [ˈʃtiːf-] **der** stepbrother; *(ugs.: Halbbruder)* half-brother

Stiefel [ˈʃtiːfl̩] **der;** ~**s,** ~ **a)** boot; **das sind zwei Paar** ~ *(fig.)* they are totally different things; **er kann einen [tüchtigen** *od.* **gehörigen]** ~ **vertragen** *(ugs.)* he can really put away the beer *(coll.);* **b) einen** ~ **zusammenreden/-schreiben** *(ugs. abwertend)* talk/write a lot of nonsense *or* a load of rubbish; **seinen** *od.* **den [alten]** ~ **weitermachen** *(ugs.)* carry on in the same old way

Stiefelette [ʃtiːfəˈlɛtə] **die;** ~, ~**n** ankle-boot

Stiefel·knecht der bootjack

stiefeln *itr. V.; mit sein (ugs.)* stride

Stiefel·schaft der boot-leg; leg of a/the boot

stief-, Stief-: ~**eltern** *Pl.* step-parents; ~**geschwister** *Pl.* **a)** stepbrother[s] and [step]sister[s]; *(ugs.: Halbgeschwister)* half-brother[s] and -sister[s]; ~**kind das** stepchild; *(fig.)* poor relation *(fig.);* **sie ist ein** ~**kind des Glücks** *(geh.)* she's always having bad luck; ~**mutter die** stepmother; ~**mütterchen das** *(Bot.)* pansy; ~**mütterlich 1.** *Adj.* poor, shabby ‹*treatment*›; **2.** *adv.* ~**mütterlich behandeln** treat ‹*person*› poorly *or* shabbily; neglect ‹*pet, flowers, doll, problem*›; ~**schwester** die stepsister; *(ugs.: Halbschwester)* half-sister; ~**sohn der** stepson; ~**tochter die** stepdaughter; ~**vater der** stepfather

stieg [ʃtiːk] *1. u. 3. Pers. Sg. Prät. v.* **steigen**

¹Stiege die; ~, ~**n a)** *(Holztreppe)* [wooden] staircase; [wooden] stairs *pl.;* **b)** *(südd., österr.: Treppe)* stairs *pl.;* steps *pl.;* **c)** *(Kiste für Gemüse, Obst)* [wooden] box; *(größer)* [wooden] crate

²Stiege die; ~, ~**n** *(nordd. veralt.)* score

Stiegen·haus das *(südd., österr.) s.* **Treppenhaus**

Stieglitz [ˈʃtiːglɪts] **der;** ~**es,** ~**e** goldfinch

stiehl [ʃtiːl] *Imp. Sg. v.* **stehlen**

stiehlst *2. Pers. Sg. Präsens v.* **stehlen**

stiehlt *3. Pers. Sg. Präsens v.* **stehlen**

stiekum [ˈʃtiːkʊm] *Adv. (ugs.)* secretly; on the quiet

Stiel [ʃtiːl] **der;** ~**[e]s,** ~**e a)** *(Griff)* handle; *(Besen~)* [broom-]stick; *(für Süßigkeiten)* stick; **ein Eis am** ~: an ice-lolly *(Brit.);* a Popsicle *(Amer.* **P)**; **b)** *(bei Gläsern)* stem; **c)** *(bei Blumen)* stem; stalk; *(an Obst, Obstblüten usw.)* stalk

Stiel-: ~**auge das** stalked eye; **er machte** *od.* **bekam** ~**augen** *(ugs. scherzh.) (erstaunt)* his eyes nearly popped out of his head; he stared goggle-eyed; *(begehrlich)* his eyes stood out on stalks; ~**kamm der** tail comb; ~**stich der** *(Handarb.)* stem stitch

stier 1. *Adj.* vacant. **2.** *adv.* vacantly

Stier [ʃtiːɐ̯] **der;** ~**[e]s,** ~**e a)** bull; **brüllen wie ein** ~: bellow like a bull; **den** ~ **bei den Hörnern fassen** *od.* **packen** take the bull by the horns; **b)** *(Astrol.)* Taurus; the Bull; **er/sie ist [ein]** ~: he/she is a Taurus *or* Taurean

stieren *itr. V.* stare [vacantly] **(auf** + *Akk.* at); **in die Luft** *od.* **vor sich hin** ~: stare [vacantly] into space

Stier-: ~**kampf der** bullfight; ~**kämpfer der** bullfighter; ~**nacken der** *(fig.)* bull-neck

Stiesel [ˈʃtiːzl̩] **der;** ~**s,** ~ *(ugs.: abwertend)* boor; churl

stieß [ʃtiːs] *1. u. 3. Pers. Sg. Prät. v.* **stoßen**

¹Stift [ʃtɪft] **der;** ~**[e]s,** ~**e a)** *(aus Metall)* pin; *(aus Holz)* peg; **b)** *(Blei~, Bunt~, Zeichen~)* pencil; *(Mal~)* crayon; *(Schreib~)* pen; **c)** *(ugs.: Lehrling)* apprentice

²Stift das; ~**[e]s,** ~**e a)** *(christl. Kirche: Institution)* foundation; **b)** *(österr.: Kloster)* monastery; **c)** *(Schule)* seminary; *(für Mädchen)* convent [school]; **d)** *(Altenheim)* home for elderly gentlewomen

stiften *tr. V.* **a)** found, establish ‹*monastery, hospital, prize, etc.*›; endow ‹*prize, professorship, scholarship*›; *(als Spende)* donate, give **(für** to); **b)** *(herbeiführen)* cause, create ‹*unrest, confusion, strife, etc.*›; bring about ‹*peace, order, etc.*›; arrange ‹*marriage*›

stiften|gehen *unr. itr. V.; mit sein (ugs.)* disappear; hop it *(sl.);* do a bunk *(sl.)*

Stifter der; ~**s,** ~: founder; *(Spender)* donor

Stifter·figur die *(bild. Kunst)* likeness of the founder/donor

Stifts-: ~**hütte die** *(jüd. Rel.)* tabernacle; ~**kirche die** collegiate church

Stiftung die; ~, ~**en a)** *(Rechtsspr.)* foundation; endowment; **b)** *(Anstalt)* foundation; **c)** *(Spende)* donation *(Gen.* by); **d)** *(o. Pl.: das Spenden)* donation *(Gen.,* **von** of)

Stift·zahn der *(Zahnmed.)* post crown

Stigma [ˈstɪgma] **das;** ~**s, Stigmen** *od.* ~**ta** *(auch fig., kath. Kirche)* stigma

Stigmatisation [stɪgmatiza'tsi̯o:n] **die;** ~, ~en stigmatization

stigmatisieren *tr. V.* stigmatize

Stigmen *s.* Stigma

Stil [ʃti:l] **der;** ~[e]s, ~e **a)** style; **einen flüssigen ~ schreiben** write in a flowing style; **das ist schlechter politischer ~:** that is bad form politically; **in dem ~ ging es weiter** *(ugs.)* it went on in that vein; **im großen** *od.* **in großem ~:** on a grand scale; **b) alten/neuen ~s** according to the old *or* Julian calendar/ new *or* Gregorian calendar

-stil der style of ...; **Schreib~:** style of writing

stil-, Stil-: ~bildend *Adj.* that influences *or* shapes style *postpos., not pred.;* **~bildend wirken** influence *or* shape style; **~blüte die** howler *(coll.);* **~bruch der** inconsistency of style; **~ebene die** style level; **~echt 1.** *Adj.* period *attrib.* ⟨*furniture*⟩; **2.** *adv.* true to style; **~element das** stylistic element

Stilett [ʃti'lɛt] **das;** ~s, ~e stiletto

Stil·gefühl das; *o. Pl.* sense of *or* feeling for style

stilisieren *tr. V.* stylize

Stilisierung die; ~, ~en stylization

Stilist der; ~en, ~en stylist

Stilistik die; ~, ~en **a)** *o. Pl. (Lehre)* stylistics *sing., no art.;* **b)** *(Buch)* book on stylistics

Stilistin die; ~, ~nen stylist

stilistisch 1. *Adj.* stylistic. **2.** *adv.* stylistically

Stil·kunde die *s.* **Stilistik a, b**

still [ʃtɪl] **1.** *Adj.* **a)** *(ruhig, leise)* quiet; *(ganz ohne Geräusche)* silent; still; quiet, peaceful ⟨*valley, area, etc.*⟩; **sei ~!** be quiet!; **im Saal wurde es ~:** the hall went quiet; **um ihn ist es ~ geworden** *(fig.)* you don't hear much about him any more; **in ~em Gedenken** in loving memory; **b)** *(reglos)* still; **~es [Mineral-/Tafel-]wasser** still [mineral/table] water; **c)** *(ohne Aufregung, Hektik)* quiet ⟨*day, life*⟩; quiet, calm ⟨*manner*⟩; **in einer ~en Stunde** in a quiet moment; **d)** *(nicht gesprächig)* quiet; *s. auch* **Wasser b; e)** *(wortlos)* silent ⟨*reproach, grief, etc.*⟩; **f)** *(heimlich)* secret; **im ~en** in secret; **~e Reserven** *(Wirtsch.)* secret *or* hidden reserves; *(ugs.)* [secret] savings; **g) der Stille Ozean** the Pacific [Ocean]. **2.** *adv.* **a)** *(ruhig, leise)* quietly; *(geräuschlos)* silently; **b)** *(zurückhaltend)* quietly; **c)** *(wortlos)* in silence

Still-BH der nursing bra

Stille die; ~ **a)** *(Ruhe)* quiet; *(Geräuschlosigkeit)* silence; stillness; **in der ~ der Nacht** in the still of the night; **tiefe ~:** deep silence; **gefräßige ~** *(scherzh.)* silence of people too busy eating to talk; **b)** *(Regungslosigkeit) (des Meeres)* calm[ness]; *(der Luft)* stillness; **c) in aller ~ heiraten** have a quiet wedding; **die Beerdigung fand in aller ~ statt** it was a quiet funeral

Stilleben das *(bild. Kunst)* still life

stillegen *tr. V.* close *or* shut down; close ⟨*railway line*⟩; lay up ⟨*ship, vehicle, fleet*⟩; **eine stillgelegte Bahn** a disused railway

Stillegung die; ~, ~en closure; shut-down; *(von Schiff, Fahrzeug, Flotte)* laying up; *(einer Eisenbahnstrecke)* closure

stillen 1. *tr. V.* **a) ein Kind ~:** breast-feed a baby; **ich muß das Baby jetzt ~:** I must feed the baby *or* give the baby a feed now; **b)** *(befriedigen)* satisfy ⟨*hunger, desire, curiosity*⟩; quench ⟨*thirst*⟩; still *(literary)* ⟨*hunger, thirst, desire*⟩; **c)** *(eindämmen)* stop ⟨*bleeding, tears, pain*⟩; stanch ⟨*blood*⟩. **2.** *itr. V.* breast-feed; **~de Mütter** nursing mothers

Still·halte·abkommen das *(Polit., Finanzw.)* moratorium; standstill agreement

still|halten *unr. itr. V.* **a)** *(sich nicht bewegen)* keep *or* stay still; **b)** *(nicht reagieren)* keep quiet

still-, Still-: ~leben das *s.* **Stilleben; ~|legen** *s.* **stillegen; ~legung die** *s.* **Stillegung**

stil·los 1. *Adj.* **a)** *(ohne Stil)* lacking *or* without any definite *or* recognizable style *postpos.;* **b)** *(gegen den Stil)* in bad *or* poor style *postpos.;* lacking in style *postpos.;* styleless; **Wein aus Biergläsern zu trinken ist ~:** drinking wine out of beer glasses shows a lack of style. **2.** *adv.* **a)** *(ohne Stil)* without any definite *or* recognizable style; **b)** *(gegen den Stil)* in bad *or* poor style; stylelessly

Stillosigkeit die; ~, ~en **a)** *o. Pl.* lack of any definite *or* recognizable style; **b)** *o. Pl. s.* **stillos b:** bad *or* poor style; lack of style; stylelessness; **c)** *(stilloses Verhalten)* [piece of] styleless behaviour

still-, Still-: ~schweigen das a) *(Schweigen)* silence; **mit ~schweigen** in silence; **b)** *(Diskretion)* **~schweigen bewahren** maintain silence; keep silent; **~schweigend 1.** *Adj.; nicht präd.* **a)** *(wortlos)* silent; **b)** *(ohne Abmachung)* tacit ⟨*assumption, agreement*⟩; **2.** *adv.* **a)** *(wortlos)* in silence; **b)** *(ohne Abmachung)* tacitly; **das Projekt wurde ~schweigend eingestellt** the project was quietly shelved; **~|sitzen** *unr. itr. V.* sit still; **~stand der;** *o. Pl.* standstill; **den Motor/die Entzündung/den Zug/den Verkehr zum ~stand bringen** stop the engine/inflammation/train/bring the traffic to a standstill; **die Blutung ist zum ~stand gekommen** the bleeding has stopped; **~|stehen** *unr. itr. V.* **a)** ⟨*factory, machine*⟩ be *or* stand idle; ⟨*traffic*⟩ be at a standstill; ⟨*heart etc.*⟩ stop; **ihr Mundwerk steht nie ~** *(ugs.)* she never stops talking; **die Zeit schien ~zustehen** time seemed to stand still; **b)** *(Milit.)* stand at *or* to attention; **~gestanden!** attention!

Stillung die; ~ *s.* **stillen 1 b, c:** satisfying; quenching; stilling *(literary);* stopping; stanching; relieving

still·vergnügt 1. *Adj.* inwardly contented. **2.** *adv.* ⟨*listen, smile, etc.*⟩ with inner contentment

Still·zeit die lactation period

stil-, Stil-: ~mittel das stylistic device; **~möbel** *Pl.* period furniture *sing.;* **~richtung die** style; **~voll 1.** *Adj.* stylish; **2.** *adv.* stylishly

stimm-, Stimm-: ~ab·gabe die voting *no art.;* **zur ~abgabe erscheinen** come to vote *or* to cast one's vote; **~band das;** *meist Pl.* vocal cord; **~berechtigt** *Adj.* entitled to vote *postpos.;* **~bruch der: er ist im ~bruch** his voice is breaking; **~bürger der** *(schweiz.)* voter; elector

Stimmchen das; ~s, ~: little *or* small voice

Stimme ['ʃtɪmə] **die;** ~, ~n **a)** voice; **die ~ des Blutes** *(fig.)* the call of the blood; **der ~ der Vernunft folgen** *(fig.)* listen to the voice of reason; **der ~ des Herzens/Gewissens folgen** *(fig. geh.)* follow [the dictates of] one's heart/conscience; **mit stockender ~:** in a faltering voice; **mit halber ~ singen** sing at half-power; **gut/nicht bei ~ sein** be in good/ bad voice; **b)** *(Meinung)* voice; **die ~n in der Presse waren kritisch** press opinion was critical; **c)** *(bei Wahlen, auch Stimmrecht)* vote

stimmen 1. *itr. V.* **a)** *(zutreffen)* be right *or* correct; **stimmt es, daß ...?** is it true that ...?; **das kann unmöglich ~:** that can't possibly be right; **stimmt's, oder hab' ich recht?** *(ugs. scherzh.)* am I not right?; **b)** *(in Ordnung sein)* ⟨*bill, invoice, etc.*⟩ be right *or* correct; **stimmt so** that's all right; keep the change; **hier stimmt etwas nicht** there's something wrong here; **bei ihm stimmt es** *od.* **etwas nicht** *(salopp)* there must be something wrong with him; **c)** *(seine Stimme geben)* vote; **mit Ja ~:** vote yes *or* in favour. **2.** *tr. V.* **a)** *(in eine Stimmung versetzen)* make; **das stimmt mich traurig** that makes me [feel] sad; **sentimental gestimmt sein** be feeling sentimental; **b)** *(Musik)* tune ⟨*instrument*⟩; **eine Gitarre höher/tiefer ~:** raise/lower the pitch of a guitar

Stimmen-: ~fang der; *o. Pl.* vote-catching *no art.;* **er ist auf ~fang** he is out to catch votes; **~gewinn der** gain in votes; **~gewirr das** babble of voices; **~gleichheit die** tied vote; tie; **bei ~gleichheit** in the event of a tied vote *or* a tie; **~kauf der** vote-buying *no art.;* buying votes *no art.;* **~mehrheit die** majority [of votes]

Stimm·enthaltung die abstention; **~ üben** abstain; **bei vier ~en angenommen** accepted with four abstentions

Stimmen·verlust der loss of votes; **~e erleiden** lose votes

Stimm·gabel die *(Musik)* tuning-fork

stimm·gewaltig 1. *Adj.* ⟨*singer etc.*⟩ with a strong *or* powerful voice; strong, powerful ⟨*bass, contralto, etc.*⟩. **2.** *adv.* ⟨*sing, speak*⟩ with *or* in a strong *or* powerful voice

stimmhaft *(Sprachw.)* **1.** *Adj.* voiced. **2.** *adv.* **~ gesprochen werden** be voiced

stimmig *Adj.* harmonious; **die Argumentation ist [in sich** *(Dat.)***] ~:** the argument is consistent

Stimm·lage die a) voice; **b)** *(Musik)* voice; register

stimmlich 1. *Adj.* vocal. **2.** *adv.* vocally

stimm-, Stimm-: ~los *(Sprachw.)* **1.** *Adj.* voiceless; unvoiced; **2.** *adv.* **~los ausgesprochen werden** not be voiced; **~recht das** right to vote; **~um·fang der** vocal range

Stimmung die; ~, ~en **a)** mood; **er ist in gereizter ~:** he is in a very touchy mood; **in ~ sein** be in a good mood; **in ~ kommen** get in the mood; liven up; **jmdn. in ~ bringen** liven sb. up; **jmdm. die ~ verderben** spoil sb.'s [good] mood; **nicht in der [rechten] ~ sein, etw. zu tun** not be in the [right] mood to do sth.; **~en unterworfen sein** be moody; **für gute ~ sorgen** ensure a good atmosphere; **b)** *(Atmosphäre)* atmosphere; **c)** *(öffentliche Meinung)* opinion; **~ für/gegen jmdn./etw. machen** stir up [public] opinion in favour of/against sb./sth.; **d)** *(Musik)* pitch

stimmungs-, Stimmungs-: ~barometer das *in* **das ~barometer steht auf Null** *(ugs.)* the mood is bleak; **~bild das: ein ~bild von dem Ball geben** report on the atmosphere at the ball; **~kanone die** *(ugs. scherzh.)* entertainer who is always the life and soul of the party; **~um·schwung der** change of mood; **~voll 1.** *Adj.* atmospheric; **2.** *adv.* ⟨*describe, light*⟩ atmospherically; ⟨*sing, recite*⟩ with great feeling

Stimm-: ~vieh das *(abwertend)* **für ihn sind die Wähler doch nur ~vieh** he sees voters as nothing more than a means of getting to power; **~zettel der** ballot-paper

Stimulans ['sti:mulans] **das;** ~, **Stimulanzien** *od.* **Stimulantia** [stimu'lantsi̯a] *(auch fig.)* stimulant

Stimuli *s.* **Stimulus**

stimulieren *tr. V.* stimulate

Stimulus ['sti:mulʊs] **der;** ~, **Stimuli** *(Psych., fig.)* stimulus **(für** to)

stink-, Stink- *(salopp)* stinking *(sl.)* ⟨*drunk, mood*⟩; terribly *(coll.)* ⟨*bourgeois, posh*⟩

Stink·bombe die stink-bomb

stinken ['ʃtɪŋkn̩] *unr. itr. V.* **a)** *(abwertend)* stink; pong *(coll.);* **nach etw. ~:** stink *or* reek of sth.; **es stinkt nach Chemikalien/ faulen Eiern** there's a stink *or* reek *or* stench of chemicals/bad eggs; **nach Geld ~** *(fig. ugs.)* be stinking rich *(sl.);* **vor Faulheit/Selbstgerechtigkeit ~** *(fig. ugs.)* be bone idle *(coll.)*/appallingly self-righteous; **b)** *(ugs.: Schlechtes vermuten lassen)* **die Sache/es stinkt** it smells; it's fishy *(coll.);* **c)** *(salopp: mißfallen)* **die Hausarbeit stinkt mir** I'm fed up to the back teeth with housework *(sl.);* **mir stinkt's** I'm fed up to the back teeth *(sl.)*

stink·faul *Adj.* *(salopp abwertend)* bone idle *(coll.)*

stịnkig *Adj. (salopp abwertend)* **a)** *(stinkend)* stinking; smelly; **b)** *(widerwärtig)* vile *(coll.)*, stinking *(sl.)*⟨*mood*⟩; **du bist heute so ~** *(fig.)* you're in such a vile *or* stinking mood today

stịnk-, Stịnk-: ~lạngweilig *(ugs.)* **1.** *Adj.* deadly boring; **2.** *adv.* in a deadly boring way; **~morchel die** *(Bot.)* stink-horn; **~normal** *(salopp)* **1.** *Adj.* dead *(coll.) or* boringly ordinary; **2.** *adv.* in a dead ordinary way *(coll.)*; **~reich** *Adj. (salopp)* stinking rich *(sl.)*; **~tier das** skunk; **~vornehm** *Adj. (salopp)* terribly posh *(coll.)*; **~wut die** *(salopp)* towering rage; **eine ~wut [auf jmdn.] haben** be livid *(Brit. coll.) or* furious [with sb.]

Stint [ʃtɪnt] **der; ~[e]s, ~e a)** *(Fisch)* smelt; **b)** *(nordd.: Junge)* boy; lad

Stipendiat [ʃtipɛn'dia:t] **der; ~en, ~en** person receiving a scholarship/grant

Stipendium [ʃtipɛndịʊm] **das; ~s, Stipẹndien** *(als Auszeichnung)* scholarship; *(als finanzielle Unterstützung)* grant

Stịppe die; ~, ~n *(bes. nordd.)* [thick] gruvy

stịppen ['ʃtɪpn̩] *tr. V. (bes. nordd.)* dunk

Stịpp·visite die *(ugs.)* flying visit

stipulieren [stipu'li:rən] *tr. V.* establish; lay down; *(als Bedingung)* stipulate

stirb [ʃtɪrp] *Imp. Sg. v.* **sterben**

stịrbst *2. Pers. Sg. Präsens v.* **sterben**

stịrbt *3. Pers. Sg. Präsens v.* **sterben**

Stirn ['ʃtɪrn] **die; ~, ~en** forehead; brow; **sich** *(Dat.)* **die Haare aus der ~ kämmen** comb one's hair from one's forehead; **jmdm./einer Sache die ~ bieten** *(fig.)* stand *or* face up to sb./sth.; **die ~ haben, etw. zu tun** *(fig.)* have the nerve *or* gall to do sth.; **jmdm. an** *od.* **auf der ~ geschrieben stehen** *(geh.)* be written in *or* all over sb.'s face

Stịrn-: ~band das; *Pl.* **~bänder** headband; **~bein das** *(Anat.)* frontal bone

Stịrne die; ~, ~n *s.* **Stirn**

Stịrn-: ~falte die wrinkle [on one's forehead]; **~höhle die** *(Anat.)* frontal sinus; **~höhlen·vereiterung die** suppurative *or* purulent frontal sinusitis; **~locke die** quiff *(Brit.)*; cow-lick; **~rad das** *(Technik)* spur wheel; spur gear; **~runzeln das; ~s** frown; **mit ~runzeln** with a frown; **~seite die** front [side]

stob [ʃto:p] *1. u. 3. Pers. Sg. Prät. v.* **stieben**

stöbern [ʃtø:bɐn] *itr. V. (ugs.)* rummage

stochern ['ʃtɔxɐn] *itr. V.* poke; **sich** *(Dat.)* **in den Zähnen ~:** pick one's teeth; **mit dem Feuerhaken im Feuer ~:** poke the fire; **im Essen ~:** pick at one's food

[1]Stock [ʃtɔk] **der; ~[e]s, Stöcke** ['ʃtœkə] **a)** *(Ast, Spazier~)* stick; *(Zeige~)* pointer; stick; *(Takt~)* baton; **steif wie ein ~:** as stiff as a poker; **den ~ gebrauchen/zu spüren bekommen** use/get the stick *or* cane; **am ~ gehen** walk with a stick; *(ugs.: erschöpft sein)* be whacked *(Brit. coll.) or* dead-beat; *(ugs.: finanzielle Schwierigkeiten haben)* be [completely] broke *(coll.)*; **b)** *(Ski~)* pole; stick; **c)** *(Pflanze) (Rosen~)* [rose-]bush; *(Reb~)* vine; **d)** *(Eishockey, Hockey, Rollhockey)* stick; **e)** *(veralt.: Baumstumpf)* stump [and roots]; **über ~ und Stein** over hedge and ditch

[2]Stọck der; ~[e]s, ~ *(Etage)* floor; storey; **das Haus hat vier ~:** the house is four storeys high; **in welchem ~?** on which floor?; **im fünften ~:** on the fifth *(Brit.) or (Amer.)* sixth floor

stọck-: ~besoffen *Adj. (derb)* pissed as a newt/as newts *pred. (coarse)*; blind drunk; **~blịnd** *Adj. (ugs.)* as blind as a bat *pred. (coll.)*; totally blind

Stöckchen ['ʃtœkçən] **das; ~s, ~:** little stick

stọck·dụnkel *Adj. (ugs.)* pitch-dark

Stọ̈ckel·ab·satz der high *or* stiletto heel

stöckeln ['ʃtœkl̩n] *itr. V.; mit sein (ugs.)* totter [on high heels]

Stọ̈ckel·schuh der high- *or* stiletto-heeled shoe; **~e** high heels; high- *or* stiletto-heeled shoes

stọcken *itr. V.* **a)** *(aussetzen, stillstehen)* **ihm stockte das Herz/der Puls** his heart/pulse missed *or* skipped a beat; **ihm stockte der Atem** he caught his breath; **das Blut stockte ihm in den Adern** *(fig.)* the blood froze in his veins; **b)** *(unterbrochen sein)* ⟨*traffic*⟩ be held up, come to a halt; ⟨*conversation, production*⟩ stop; ⟨*business*⟩ slacken *or* drop off; ⟨*journey*⟩ be interrupted; **die Antwort kam ~d** he/she gave a hesitant reply; **ins Stocken geraten** ⟨*traffic*⟩ be held up, come to a halt; ⟨*conversation, production*⟩ stop; ⟨*talks, negotiations, etc.*⟩ grind to a halt; **c)** *(innehalten)* falter; **er sprach ein wenig ~d** he faltered a little; **d)** *auch mit sein (bes. südd., österr., schweiz.: gerinnen)* ⟨*milk*⟩ curdle

stọck-, Stọck-: ~ente die mallard; **~fịnster** *Adj. (ugs.)* pitch-dark; **~fisch der a)** stockfish; **b)** *(ugs. abwertend: Mensch)* boring *or* dull old stick; **~fleck der** mildew *or* mould spot; **~fleckig** *Adj.* mildewed; mouldy

stọckig *Adj.* **a)** *(muffig)* musty ⟨*clothes, smell, etc.*⟩; **b)** *(stockfleckig)* mildewed; mouldy

-stöckig ['ʃtœkɪç] -storey *attr.*; -storeyed

stọck-, Stọck-: ~konservativ *Adj. (ugs.)* arch-conservative; **~nüchtern** *Adj. (ugs.)* stone-cold sober; **~sauer** *Adj.; nicht attr. (salopp)* pissed off *(Brit. sl.)* **(auf +** *Akk.* with); **~schirm der** walking-length umbrella; **~schnupfen der** heavy cold; **~steif** *(ugs.)* **1.** *Adj.* extremely stiff ⟨*gait*⟩; **2.** *adv.* extremely stiffly; as stiff as a poker; **~taub** *Adj. (ugs.)* stone-deaf; as deaf as a post

Stọckung die; ~, ~en a) *(Unterbrechung)* hold-up **(+** *Gen.* in); **b)** *(des Pulses, der Atmung)* stoppage

Stọckwerk das floor; storey; **im dritten ~:** on the third *(Brit.) or (Amer.)* fourth floor; **ein Haus mit fünf ~en** a five-storey[ed] house

Stoff [ʃtɔf] **der; ~[e]s, ~e a)** *(für Textilien)* material; fabric; **b)** *(Materie)* substance; **c)** *o. Pl. (Philos.)* matter; **d)** *(Thema)* subject[-matter]; **~ für einen Roman sammeln** collect material for a novel; **einen ~ in der Schule durchnehmen** do a subject at school; **e)** *(Gesprächsthema)* topic; **viel ~ zum Nachdenken** much food for thought; **f)** *o. Pl. (salopp: Alkohol)* booze *(coll.)*; **g)** *o. Pl. (salopp: Rauschgift)* stuff *(sl.)*; dope *(sl.)*

Stọff·druck der; *o. Pl.* textile printing

Stoffel ['ʃtɔfl̩] **der; ~s, ~** *(ugs. abwertend)* boor; churl

stọffelig *Adj. (ugs. abwertend)* boorish; churlish

stọfflich *Adj.; nicht präd.* **a)** *(materiell)* material; **b)** *(thematisch)* thematic ⟨*effect etc.*⟩; **die ~e Fülle des Buches** the richness *or* breadth of the book's subject-matter

Stọfflichkeit die; ~: materiality

Stọff-: ~muster das a) *(Zeichnung)* pattern; **b)** *(kleines Stück)* swatch; sample of material; **~puppe die** rag doll; **~rest der** remnant; **~wechsel der;** *o. Pl.* metabolism; **~wechsel·krankheit die** metabolic disease; **~wechsel·produkt das** product of metabolism

stöhnen ['ʃtø:nən] *itr. V.* moan; *(vor Schmerz)* groan

Stoiker ['ʃto:ikɐ] **der; ~s, ~** *(Philos.)* Stoic; *(fig.)* stoic

stoisch 1. *Adj. (Philos.)* Stoic; *(fig.)* stoic. **2.** *adv.* stoically

Stoizịsmus der; ~ *(Philos.)* Stoicism *no art.*; *(fig.)* stoicism

Stola ['ʃto:la] **die; ~, Stolen a)** shawl; *(Pelz~)* stole; **b)** *(bes. kath. Kirche)* stole

Stọlle die; ~, ~n *(bes. nordd.)* stollen

Stollen ['ʃtɔlən] **der; ~s, ~ a)** *(Kuchen)* Stollen; **b)** *(unterirdischer Gang)* gallery; tunnel; **c)** *(Bergbau)* gallery; **d)** *(bei Sportschuhen)* stud; **e)** *(beim Hufeisen)* calk; **f)** *(Verslehre)* stollen *(in Meistergesang)*

stolpern ['ʃtɔlpɐn] *itr. V.; mit sein* **a)** stumble; trip; **ins Stolpern kommen** stumble; trip; *(fig.)* lose one's thread; **über jmdn. ~** *(fig. ugs.)* bump *or* run into sb.; **ich bin über dieses Wort/diesen Satz gestolpert** *(fig.)* I was puzzled by that word/sentence; **b)** *(fig.: straucheln)* come to grief, *(coll.)* come unstuck **(über +** *Akk.* over)

Stọlper·stein der stumbling-block; **jmdm. ~e in den Weg legen** put obstacles in sb.'s way

stolz [ʃtɔlts] **1.** *Adj.* **a)** proud **(auf +** *Akk.* of); **b)** *(überheblich)* proud[-hearted]; **warum so ~?** don't you know me any more?; **c)** *(imposant)* proud ⟨*building, castle, ship, etc.*⟩; **d)** *(ugs.: beträchtlich)* steep *(coll.)*, hefty *(coll.)* ⟨*price*⟩; tidy *(coll.)* ⟨*sum*⟩; **~ wie ein Spanier** as proud as can be; **~ wie ein Pfau** as proud as a peacock. **2.** *adv.* proudly

Stọlz der; ~es a) pride; **sie setzte ihren ganzen ~ daran** she made it a point of pride; **b)** *(Freude über etw.)* pride **(auf +** *Akk.* in); **die Rosen sind sein ganzer ~:** his roses are his pride and joy

stọlzgeschwellt [-gəʃvɛlt] *Adj.* **mit ~er Brust** his/her breast swelling with pride

stolzieren *itr. V.; mit sein* strut

stop [stɔp] *Interj.* stop; *(Verkehrsw.)* halt

Stọp der; ~s, ~s *s.* **Stoppball**

Stọpf·ei das darning-egg

stopfen ['ʃtɔpfn̩] **1.** *tr. V.* **a)** darn ⟨*socks, coat, etc., hole*⟩; **b)** *(hineintun)* stuff; **jmdm./sich etwas in den Mund ~:** stuff sth. into sb.'s/one's mouth; **die ganze Familie ins Auto ~** *(ugs.)* cram the whole family into the car; **c)** *(füllen)* stuff ⟨*cushion, quilt, etc.*⟩; fill ⟨*pipe*⟩; **der Saal war gestopft voll** *(fig. südd.)* the hall was cram-full; **d)** *(ausfüllen, verschließen)* plug, stop [up] ⟨*hole, leak*⟩; **jmdm. das Maul ~** *(salopp)* shut sb. up; **er hat fünf hungrige Mäuler zu ~** *(fig. ugs.)* he has five hungry mouths to feed; **e)** *(mästen)* stuff, cram ⟨*poultry*⟩. **2.** *itr. V.* **a)** *(den Stuhlgang hemmen)* cause constipation; **b)** *(ugs.: sehr sättigen)* be very filling

Stọpfen der; ~s, ~ *(bes. westmd.)* stopper; *(Korken)* cork

Stọpf-: ~garn das darning-cotton *or* -thread; **~nadel die** darning-needle

Stọpp der; ~s, ~s a) *(das Anhalten)* stop; **ohne ~:** without stopping; **die Fahrer mußten zum ~ an die Boxen** the drivers had to make a pit-stop; **b)** *(Einstellung)* freeze *(Gen.* on)

Stọpp·ball der *(Badminton, [Tisch]tennis)* drop-shot

[1]Stọppel ['ʃtɔpl̩] **die; ~, ~n;** *meist Pl. (auch Bart~)* stubble *no pl.*

[2]Stọppel der; ~s, ~[n] *(österr.)* stopper; *(Korken)* cork

Stọppel-: ~bart der *(ugs.)* stubble; **~feld das** stubble-field

stọppelig *Adj.* stubbly

stọppen 1. *tr. V.* **a)** stop; **den Ball ~** *(Fußball)* trap *or* stop the ball; **er war nicht mehr zu ~** *(fig.)* there was no stopping him; **b)** time ⟨*athlete, run*⟩; **ich habe 11 Sekunden/103 km/h gestoppt** I made the time 11 seconds/the speed 103 k.p.h. **2.** *itr. V.* stop; **der Angriff stoppte** *(fig.)* the attack got no further *or* fizzled out

Stọpper der; ~s, ~ *(Fußball)* centre-half; stopper

Stọpp·licht das; *Pl.* **~er** stop-light

stọpplig *Adj. s.* **stoppelig**

Stọpp-: ~schild das stop sign; **~signal das** stop signal; signal to stop; **~straße die** side-road; road with a stop sign/stop signs; **~uhr die** stop-watch

Stöpsel ['ʃtœpsl̩] **der; ~s, ~ a)** plug; *(einer*

Karaffe usw.) stopper; **b)** *(Elektrot.)* [jack-] plug

stöpseln *(Fernspr.)* **1.** *tr. V.* **jmdm. eine Verbindung ~:** put sb. through (**nach** to). **2.** *itr. V.* operate the plugs

Stör [ʃtø:ɐ̯] **der; ~s, ~e** sturgeon

stör·an·fällig *Adj.* susceptible to faults *postpos.;* liable to break down *postpos.; (fig.)* liable to break down *postpos.*

Storch [ʃtɔrç] **der; ~[e]s, Störche** ['ʃtœrçə] stork; **wie ein ~ im Salat gehen** walk clumsily and stiff-leggedly; **da brat' mir einer einen ~** *(ugs.)* well, I'll be damned *(coll.)*

Storchen·nest das stork's nest

Storch·schnabel der a) *(Pflanze)* crane's-bill; **b)** *(Zeichenhilfe)* pantograph

Store [ʃto:ɐ̯] **der; ~s, ~s** net curtain

stören 1. *tr. V.* **a)** *(behindern)* disturb; disrupt ‹*court proceedings, lecture, church service, etc.*›; **bitte lassen Sie sich nicht ~:** please don't let me disturb you; **jmdn. in seiner Ordnung ~:** upset sb.'s routine; **b)** *(stark beeinträchtigen)* disturb ‹*relation, security, law and order, peaceful atmosphere, etc.*›; interfere with ‹*transmitter, reception*›; *(absichtlich)* jam ‹*transmitter*›; **ein gutes Verhältnis ~:** spoil a good relationship; **hier ist der Empfang oft gestört** there is often interference [with reception] here; **c)** *(mißfallen)* bother; **das stört mich nicht** I don't mind; that doesn't bother me; **das stört mich an ihr** that's what I don't like about her; **stört es Sie, wenn ich das Fenster aufmache?** do you mind *or* will it bother you if I open the window? **2.** *itr. V.* **a) darf ich reinkommen, oder störe ich?** may I come in, or am I disturbing you?; **entschuldigen Sie bitte, daß** *od.* **wenn ich störe** I'm sorry to bother you; **bitte nicht ~!** [please] do not disturb; **wenn ich störe, müßt ihr es mir sagen!** if I'm in the way, you must tell me; **sein Verhalten/seine Anwesenheit empfinde ich als ~d** I find his behaviour/presence irritating *or* annoying; **der Lärm machte sich sehr störend bemerkbar** the noise was very intrusive; **b)** *(als Mangel empfunden werden)* spoil the effect; **c)** *(Unruhe stiften)* make *or* cause trouble. **3.** *refl. V.* **sich an jmdm./etw. ~:** take exception to sb./sth.

Störenfried ['ʃtø:rənfri:t] **der; ~[e]s, ~e** *(abwertend)* trouble-maker

Störer der; ~s, ~: trouble-maker

Stör-: ~faktor der disruptive factor *or* influence; **~fall der** *(Technik)* fault

stornieren *tr. V.* **a)** *(Finanzw., Kaufmannsspr.)* reverse ‹*wrong entry*›; **b)** *(Kaufmannsspr.)* cancel ‹*order, contract*›

Storno ['ʃtɔrno] **der** *od.* **das; ~s, Storni** *(Finanzw., Kaufmannsspr.)* reversal

störrisch ['ʃtœrɪʃ] **1.** *Adj.* stubborn; obstinate; refractory ‹*child, horse*›; unmanageable ‹*hair*›; **~ wie ein Esel** as stubborn as a mule. **2.** *adv.* stubbornly; obstinately

Stör·sender der jammer

Störung die; ~, ~en a) disturbance; *(einer Gerichtsverhandlung, Vorlesung, eines Gottesdienstes)* disruption; **bitte entschuldigen Sie die ~, aber ...:** I'm sorry to bother you, but ...; **b)** *(Beeinträchtigung)* disturbance; disruption; **eine technische ~:** a technical fault; **eine nervöse ~:** a nervous disorder; **atmosphärische ~** *(Met.)* atmospheric disturbance; *(Rundf.)* atmospherics *pl.*

Story ['stɔrɪ] **die; ~, ~s** *od.* **Stories** story

Stoß [ʃto:s] **der; ~es, Stöße** ['ʃtø:sə] **a)** *(mit der Faust)* punch; *(mit dem Fuß)* kick; *(mit dem Kopf, den Hörnern)* butt; *(mit dem Ellbogen)* dig; **jmdm. einen kleinen ~ mit dem Ellenbogen geben** nudge sb.; give sb. a nudge; **die Fahrgäste spürten einen leichten ~:** the passengers felt a slight bump; **jmdm. einen ~ versetzen** *(fig.)* give sb. a jolt; **b)** *(mit einer Waffe) (Stich)* thrust; *(Schlag)* blow; **c)** *(beim Schwimmen, Rudern)* stroke; **d)** *(Stapel)* pile; stack; **e)** *(beim Kugelstoßen)* put; throw; **f)** *(stoßartige Bewegung)* thrust; *(Atem~)* gasp; **g)** *(Erd~)* tremor; **h)** *(Technik)* joint; **i)** *(Jägerspr.)* tail [feathers]

Stoß-: ~band das; *Pl.* **~bänder** edging tape; **~dämpfer der** *(Kfz-W.)* shock absorber

Stößel ['ʃtø:sl̩] **der; ~s, ~:** pestle

stoß·empfindlich *Adj.* sensitive to shock *postpos.;* **meine Uhr ist nicht ~:** my watch is shock-proof

stoßen 1. *unr. tr. V.* **a)** *auch itr. (mit der Faust)* punch; *(mit dem Fuß)* kick; *(mit dem Kopf, den Hörnern)* butt; *(mit dem Ellbogen)* dig; **jmdn.** *od.* **jmdm. in die Seite ~:** dig sb. in the ribs; *(leicht)* nudge sb. in the ribs; **b)** *(hineintreiben)* plunge, thrust ‹*dagger, knife*›; push ‹*stick, pole*›; **jmdm. ein Messer in die Rippen ~:** plunge *or* thrust a knife into sb.'s ribs; **c)** *(stoßend hervorbringen)* knock, bang ‹*hole*›; **d)** *(schleudern)* push; **den Ball mit dem Kopf ~:** head the ball; **die Kugel ~:** *(beim Kugelstoßen)* put the shot; *(beim Billard)* strike the ball; **jmdn. von der Leiter/aus dem Zug ~:** push sb. off the ladder/out of the train; **man muß ihn immer erst darauf ~** *(fig.)* he always has to have things pointed out to him; **e)** *(zer~)* pound ‹*sugar, cinnamon, pepper*›; **f)** *(ugs.: hinweisen)* **jmdm. etw. ~:** hammer sth. home to sb.; hammer sth. into sb.'s head. **2.** *unr. itr. V.* **a)** *mit sein (auftreffen)* bump (**gegen** into); **mit dem Kopf gegen etw. ~:** bump one's head on sth.; **b)** *mit sein (begegnen)* **auf jmdn. ~:** bump *or* run into sb.; **c)** *mit sein (entdecken)* **auf etw.** *(Akk.)* **~:** come upon *or* across sth.; **auf Erdöl ~:** strike oil; **auf Ablehnung ~** *(fig.)* meet with disapproval; **d)** *mit sein* **zu jmdm. ~** *(jmdn. treffen)* meet up with sb.; *(sich jmdm. anschließen)* join sb.; **e)** *mit sein (zuführen)* **auf etw.** *(Akk.)* **~:** ‹*path, road*› lead [in]to sth.; **f)** *(grenzen)* **an etw.** *(Akk.)* **~** ‹*room, property, etc.*› be [right] next to sth.; **g)** *mit sein (Jägerspr.)* **auf etw.** *(Akk.)* **~** ‹*bird*› swoop down on sth.; **h)** *(veralt.: blasen)* **in die Trompete/ins Horn** *usw.* **~:** blow *or* sound the trumpet/horn *etc.* **3.** *unr. refl. V.* bump *or* knock oneself; **ich habe mich am Kopf gestoßen** I bumped *or* banged my head; **sich** *(Dat.)* **den Kopf blutig ~:** bang one's head and cut it; **sich an etw.** *(Dat.)* **~** *(fig.)* object to *or* take exception to sth.

stoß-, Stoß-: ~fest *Adj.* shock-proof ‹*watch, container, etc.*›; hard-wearing ‹*fabric, wallpaper, etc.*›; **~gebet das** quick prayer; **~kraft die a)** force of the impact; **b)** *o. Pl. (vorwärtsdrängende Kraft)* force and momentum; *(Milit.)* strike power; *(Sport)* striking power; **~seufzer der** heartfelt groan; **~stange die** bumper

stößt [ʃtø:st] *3. Pers. Sg. Präsens v.* **stoßen**

stoß-, Stoß-: ~trupp der *(Milit.)* unit of shock troops; **~verkehr der;** *o. Pl.* rush-hour traffic; **~waffe die** thrust weapon; **~weise** *Adv.* **a)** *(ruckartig)* spasmodically; ‹*breathe*› spasmodically, jerkily; **b)** *(in Stapeln)* by the pile; in piles; **~zahn der** tusk

Stotterer der; ~s, ~: stutterer; stammerer

stottern ['ʃtɔtɐn] **1.** *itr. V.* stutter; stammer; **sie stottert stark** she has a strong *or* bad stutter *or* stammer; **ins Stottern kommen** *od.* **geraten** start stuttering *or* stammering; **der Motor stottert** *(fig.)* the engine is spluttering. **2.** *tr. V.* stutter [out]; stammer [out]

Stövchen ['ʃtø:fçən] **das; ~s, ~:** [teapot *etc.*] warmer

StPo *Abk.* **Strafprozeßordnung**

Str. *Abk.* **Straße** St./Rd.

StR. *Abk.* **Studienrat**

stracks [ʃtraks] *Adv.* **a)** *(direkt)* straight; **b)** *(sofort)* straight away

Stradivari [stradi'va:ri] **die; ~, ~[s]** Stradivarius

straf-, Straf-: ~an·drohung die threat of punishment; **~anstalt die** penal institution; prison; **~antrag der a)** *(des Klägers)* action; legal proceedings *pl.;* **~antrag stellen** bring an action; institute legal proceedings; **b)** *(des Staatsanwalts)* petition for a penalty *or* sentence; **~anzeige die** reporting of an offence; **[eine] ~anzeige erstatten** report an offence; **~arbeit die** imposition *(Brit.);* **~auf·schub der** *(Rechtsw.)* **[bedingter] ~ aufschub** [conditional] deferral of sentence; **~aussetzung die** suspension of sentence; **~bank die;** *Pl.* **~bänke** *(Eishockey, Handball)* penalty bench; **~bar** *Adj.* punishable; **das ist ~bar** that is a punishable offence; **sich ~bar machen** make oneself liable to prosecution

Strafe ['ʃtra:fə] **die; ~, ~n** punishment; *(Rechtsspr.)* penalty; *(Freiheits~)* sentence; *(Geld~)* fine; **auf dieses Delikt steht eine hohe ~:** this offence carries a heavy penalty; **sie empfand die Arbeit als ~:** she found the work a real drag *or (coll.)* bind; **das ist bei ~ verboten/steht unter ~:** it is a punishable offence; **etw. unter ~ stellen** make sth. punishable; **die ~ folgt auf dem Fuße** punishment is swift to follow; **~ muß sein!** discipline is necessary; you'll/he'll *etc.* have to be punished; **das ist die ~ [dafür]** that's what you get; **das ist ja eine ~ Gottes!** it's a real pain [in the neck]; **es ist eine ~, mit ihm arbeiten zu müssen** it's a pain having to work with him; **zur ~:** as a punishment

strafen *tr. V.* punish; **ein ~der Blick** a reproachful look; **jmdn. ~d ansehen** give sb. a reproachful look; **jmdn. mit Verachtung ~:** treat sb. with contempt as a punishment; **er ist gestraft genug** *(fig.)* he has been punished enough; **Gott strafe mich, wenn ich lüge!** *(veralt.)* may God strike me down if I am lying; **mit ihm/dieser Arbeit sind wir gestraft** he/this work is a real pain; **das Schicksal hat ihn schwer gestraft** fate has been hard on him; *s. auch* **Lüge**

Straf-: ~entlassene der/die; *adj. Dekl.* ex-convict; ex-prisoner; **~erlaß der** *(Rechtsw.)* remission [of a/the sentence]; **bedingter ~erlaß** conditional remission; **~expedition die** punitive expedition

straff [ʃtraf] **1.** *Adj.* **a)** *(fest, gespannt)* tight, taut ‹*rope, lines, etc.*›; firm ‹*breasts, skin*›; erect ‹*posture, figure*›; tight ‹*rein[s]*›; **b)** *(energisch)* tight ‹*organization, planning, etc.*›; strict ‹*discipline, leadership, etc.*›. **2.** *adv.* **a)** *(fest, gespannt)* **die Saiten sind ~ gespannt** the strings are tight; **[zu] ~ sitzen** ‹*clothes*› be [too] tight; **die Jacke ~ über die Schultern ziehen** pull one's jacket tightly round one's shoulders; **er zog die Zügel ~ an** he pulled the reins tight; **~ zurückgekämmtes Haar** hair combed back tightly; **b)** *(energisch)* tightly, strictly ‹*organized, planned, etc.*›

straf·fällig *Adj.* **~ werden** commit a criminal offence; **die Zahl der Straffälligen** the number of offenders; **~e Jugendliche** young offenders

straffen 1. *tr. V.* **a)** *(spannen)* tighten; **diese Creme strafft die Haut** this cream firms the skin; **sich** *(Dat.)* **das Gesicht ~ lassen** have a face-lift; **den Körper ~:** straighten oneself; draw oneself up; **b)** *(raffen)* tighten up ‹*text, procedure, organization, etc.*›. **2.** *refl. V.* ‹*person*› straighten oneself, draw oneself up; ‹*rope etc.*› tighten; ‹*body, back*› stiffen; ‹*posture, bearing*› straighten

straf-, Straf-: ~frei *Adj.* **jmdn. für ~frei erklären** declare sb. exempt from punishment; **~frei ausgehen** go unpunished; get off [scot-]free *(coll.);* **~freiheit die;** *o. Pl.* exemption from punishment; **~gefangene der/die** prisoner; **~gericht das** *(fig.)* judgement; **ein ~gericht des Himmels** divine judgement; **ein grausames ~gericht abhalten** mete out cruel judgement; **~gesetz das** criminal *or* penal law; **~gesetz·buch**

das criminal *or* penal code; **~justiz die** criminal *or* penal justice; **~kammer die** *(Rechtsw.)* criminal division *(of a district court)*; **~kolonie die** penal colony; **~kompanie die** punishment battalion; **~lager das** penal camp
sträflich [ˈʃtrɛːflɪç] **1.** *Adj.* criminal. **2.** *adv.* criminally
Sträfling [ˈʃtrɛːflɪŋ] **der; ~s, ~e** prisoner
Sträflings·kleidung die prison clothing; prison clothes *pl.*
straf-, Straf-: ~los *Adj.* unpunished; **~mandat das** [parking, speeding, *etc.*] ticket; **~maß das** sentence; **~minute die a)** *(bes. Eishockey, Handball)* minute of penalty time; **die drei ~minuten** the three-minute penalty *sing.*; **b)** *(Rennsport, Springreiten, Biathlon, usw.)* penalty minute; **~mündig** *Adj. (Rechtsw.)* of the age of criminal responsibility *postpos.*; **er ist noch nicht ~mündig** he is under the age of criminal responsibility; **~porto das** surcharge; **~predigt die** *(ugs.)* lecture; **jmdm. eine ~predigt halten** lecture sb.; **~prozeß der** criminal proceedings *pl.*; **~prozeß·ordnung die** *(Rechtsw.)* code of criminal procedure; **~punkt der** *(Sport)* penalty point; **~raum der** *(bes. Fußball)* penalty area; **~recht das** criminal law; **~rechtlich 1.** *Adj.* criminal *attrib.* ⟨*case, investigation, responsibility*⟩; **~rechtliche Fragen/Probleme** questions/problems of criminal law; **im ~rechtlichen Sinne** according to criminal law; **2.** *adv.* under criminal law; **etw. ~rechtlich verfolgen** prosecute sth.; **~register das** criminal records *pl.*; **~richter der** *(Rechtsw.)* criminal judge; **~sache die** criminal case; **~stoß der** *(Fußball) s.* **Elfmeter**; **~tat die** criminal offence; **~täter der** offender; **~verbüßung die** serving [of] one's sentence; **~verfahren das** criminal proceedings *pl.*; **~verfolgung die** *(Rechtsw.)* [criminal] prosecution; **~|versetzen** *tr. V. nur im Inf. u. Part. gebr.* transfer for disciplinary reasons; **~versetzung die** disciplinary transfer; **~verteidiger der** defence lawyer *or* counsel; **~vollzug der** penal system; **~würdig** *Adj. (Rechtsw.)* punishable; **~zettel der** *(ugs.)* [parking-, speeding-, *etc.*] ticket
Strahl [ʃtraːl] **der; ~[e]s, ~en a)** *(Licht, fig.)* ray; *(von Scheinwerfern, Taschenlampen)* beam; **ein ~ fiel durch den Türspalt** a shaft of light came through the crack of the door; **b)** *(Flüssigkeit)* jet; **ein dünner ~ Wasser** a thin trickle of water; **c)** *(Math., Phys.)* ray
Strahl·an·trieb der *(Technik)* jet propulsion
strahlen *itr. V.* **a)** shine; **ein ~d heller Morgen** a gloriously bright morning; **bei ~dem Wetter/Sonnenschein** in glorious sunny weather/in glorious sunshine; **eine ~de Schönheit/Stimme** *(fig.)* a radiant beauty/marvellously pure voice; **~d weiß** sparkling white; **b)** *(glänzen)* sparkle; **c)** *(lächeln)* beam (**vor** + *Dat.* with); **er strahlte über das ganze Gesicht** *od. (ugs.)* **über beide Backen** he was beaming all over his face; **d)** *(Physik)* radiate; emit rays
strahlen-, Strahlen-: ~behandlung die *(Med.)* radiotherapy *no art.*; **~belastung die** radioactive contamination; **~biologie die** radiobiology *no art.*; **~bündel das** *(Optik, Math.)* pencil of rays; **~förmig 1.** *Adj.* radial; **2.** *adv.* radially; **~pilz der;** *meist Pl. (Biol.)* ray fungus; **~schutz der** radiation protection; **~therapie die** *(Med.)* radiotherapy *no art.*; **~tierchen das** radiolarian; **~unfall der** radiation accident
Strahler der; ~s, ~ a) radiator; **b)** *(Heiz~)* radiant heater
strahlig 1. *Adj.* radial. **2.** *adv.* radially
Strahl·triebwerk das jet engine
Strahlung die; ~, ~en radiation
Strahlungs-: ~energie die *(Physik)* radiant energy; **~gürtel der** *(Physik)* radiation belt; **~intensität die** *(Physik)* intensity of radiation
Strähne [ˈʃtrɛːnə] **die; ~, ~n a)** *(Haare)* strand; **eine graue ~:** a grey streak; **b)** *(fig.: Zeitspanne)* streak
strähnig 1. *Adj.* straggly ⟨*hair*⟩. **2.** *adv.* in strands
stramm [ʃtram] **1.** *Adj.* **a)** *(straff)* tight, taut ⟨*rope, line, etc.*⟩; tight ⟨*clothes*⟩; **b)** *(kräftig)* strapping ⟨*girl, boy*⟩; sturdy ⟨*legs, body*⟩; *s. auch* **Max**; **c)** *(gerade)* upright, erect ⟨*posture, etc.*⟩; **eine ~e Haltung einnehmen** stand to attention; **d)** *(energisch)* strict ⟨*discipline*⟩; strict, staunch ⟨*Marxist, Catholic, etc.*⟩; brisk ⟨*step*⟩. **2.** *adv.* **a)** *(straff)* tightly; **die Hose saß ziemlich ~:** the trousers were rather tight; **der Gurt soll ~ am Körper anliegen** the belt is supposed to be tight; **b)** *(kräftig)* sturdily ⟨*built*⟩; **c)** *(energisch)* ⟨*bring up*⟩ strictly; strictly, staunchly ⟨*Marxist, Catholic, etc.*⟩; ⟨*hold out*⟩ resolutely; **d)** *(ugs.: zügig)* ⟨*work*⟩ hard; ⟨*walk, march*⟩ briskly; ⟨*drive*⟩ fast, hard
stramm|stehen *unr. itr. V.* stand to *or* at attention
Strampel·höschen das, Strampel·hose die rompers *pl.*; romper suit; playsuit
strampeln [ˈʃtrampl̩n] *itr. V.* **a)** ⟨*baby*⟩ kick [his/her feet] [and wave his/her arms about]; **b)** *mit sein (ugs.: mit dem Rad)* pedal; **c)** *(ugs.: sich sehr anstrengen)* sweat; struggle
Strampler der; ~s, ~: *s.* **Strampelhöschen**
Strand [ʃtrant] **der; ~[e]s, Strände** [ˈʃtrɛndə] beach; *(geh. veralt.: Flußufer)* bank; strand; *(geh. veralt.: Seeufer)* shore; strand; **am ~:** on the beach; **an den ~ gehen** go to the beach; **auf ~ laufen** ⟨*ship*⟩ run aground; **ein Schiff auf ~ setzen** beach a ship
Strand-: ~bad das bathing beach *(on river, lake)*; **~burg die** sand den *(built as a windbreak)*; **~café das** beach café; **~distel die** sea holly
stranden *itr. V.; mit sein* **a)** *(festsitzen)* ⟨*ship*⟩ run aground; *(fig.)* be stranded; **b)** *(geh.: scheitern)* fail
Strand-: ~gut das; *o. Pl.* flotsam and jetsam; **~haubitze die** *in voll od.* **blau wie eine ~haubitze sein** *(ugs.)* be dead drunk; **~hotel das** beach hotel; **~kleid das** beach dress; **~korb der** basket chair; **~leben das** beach life; **~promenade die** promenade; **~räuber der** wrecker; **~segeln das** *(Sport)* sand-yachting
Strang [ʃtraŋ] **der; ~[e]s, Stränge** [ˈʃtrɛŋə] **a)** *(Seil)* rope; **jmdn. zum Tod durch den ~ verurteilen** *(geh.)* sentence sb. to be hanged; **b)** *(von Wolle, Garn usw.)* hank; skein; **c)** *(Nerven~, Muskel~, Sehnen~)* cord; *(der DNS)* strand; **d)** *(Leine)* trace; **über die Stränge schlagen** *(ugs.)* kick over the traces; *s. auch* **reißen 2a; ziehen 2a**
strangulieren [ʃtraŋguˈliːrən] *tr. V.* strangle
Strapaze [ʃtraˈpaːtsə] **die; ~, ~n** strain *no pl.*; **sich von den ~n erholen** recover from the strain *sing.*
strapaz·fähig *Adj. (österr.) s.* **strapazierfähig**
strapazieren 1. *tr. V.* be a strain on ⟨*person, nerves*⟩; **die tägliche Rasur strapaziert die Haut** shaving daily is hard on the skin; **die Reise würde ihn zu sehr ~:** the journey would be too much [of a strain] for him; **jmds. Geduld ~** *(fig.)* tax sb.'s patience; **wir haben unsere Wanderschuhe/Wintermäntel stark strapaziert** we gave our walking-shoes/winter coats a great deal of hard wear; **diese Ausrede ist schon zu oft strapaziert worden** *(fig.)* this excuse has been flogged to death. **2.** *refl. V.* strain *or* tax oneself
strapazier·fähig *Adj.* hard-wearing ⟨*clothes, shoes*⟩; hard-wearing, durable ⟨*material*⟩; sturdy ⟨*book*⟩
Strapazier·fähigkeit die; *o. Pl. s.* **strapazierfähig:** hard-wearingness; durability; sturdiness
strapaziös [ʃtrapaˈtsiøːs] *Adj.* wearing
Straps [ʃtraps] **der; ~es, ~e** suspender
Straß [ʃtras] **der; ~** *od.* **Strasses, Strasse a)** *o. Pl. (Glasfluß)* paste; **b)** *(Nachbildung aus ~)* paste gem
Straßburg [ˈʃtraːsbʊrk] **(das); ~s** Strasbourg
Sträßchen [ˈʃtrɛːsçən] **das; ~s, ~:** little *or* narrow street
Straße [ˈʃtraːsə] **die; ~, ~n a)** *(in Ortschaften)* street; road; *(außerhalb)* road; *(fig. abwertend: Pöbel)* mob; rabble; **auf offener ~:** in [the middle of] the street; **man traut sich abends kaum noch auf die ~:** you hardly dare go out in the evenings any more; **Verkauf über die ~:** take-away sales *pl.*; *(von alkoholischen Getränken)* off-licence sales *pl.*; **Jugendliche von der ~ holen** get young people off the streets; **der Mann auf der ~** *(fig.)* the man in the street; **mit jugendlichen Arbeitslosen/Prostituierten kann man hier die ~n pflastern** *(ugs.)* the place is full of young unemployed people/prostitutes *(coll.)*; **jmdn. auf die ~ setzen** *od.* **werfen** *(ugs.) (aus einer Stellung)* sack sb. *(coll.)*; give sb. the sack *(coll.)*; *(aus einer Wohnung)* turn sb. out on to the street; **auf der ~ liegen** *od.* **sitzen** *od.* **stehen** *(ugs.) (arbeitslos sein)* be out of work; *(ohne Wohnung sein)* be on the streets; **auf die ~ gehen** *(ugs.) (demonstrieren)* take to the streets; *(der Prostitution nachgehen)* go on *or* walk the streets; **jmdn. auf die ~ schicken** *(ugs.)* send sb. out on the streets; **sich [nicht] dem Druck der ~ beugen** [not] bow to mob rule; **b)** *(Meerenge)* strait[s *pl.*]; **die ~ von Gibraltar/Hormus** the Straits of Gibraltar/Strait of Hormuz
Straßen-: ~anzug der lounge suit *(Brit.)*; business suit *(Amer.)*; **~bahn die** tram *(Brit.)*; streetcar *(Amer.)*; **~bahner der; ~s, ~, ~bahnerin die; ~, ~nen** *(ugs.)* tramway employee *(Brit.)*
Straßen·bahn-: ~fahrer der a) *(Führer)* tram driver *(Brit.)*; **b)** *(Benutzer)* tram passenger *(Brit.)*; **~halte·stelle die** tram stop *(Brit.)*; **~linie die** tram route *(Brit.)*; **die ~linie 24** the number 24 tram *(Brit.)*; **~schaffner der** tram conductor *(Brit.)*; **~schiene die** tramline *(Brit.)*; **~wagen der** tram[car] *(Brit.)*
Straßen-: ~bau der; *o. Pl.* road building *no art.*; road construction *no art.*; **~bekanntschaft die: sie ist nur eine ~bekanntschaft** she is just someone I talk to when I meet her in the street; **~beleuchtung die** street lighting; **~benutzungs·gebühr die** *s.* **Maut**; **~bild das** street scene; **mehr und mehr gehörten Uniformen wieder zum ~bild** uniforms were increasingly seen in the streets again; **~café das** pavement café; street café; **~decke die** road surface; **~dorf das** street village; **~ecke die** street corner; **~fahrer der** *(Rennsport)* road racer; **~feger der a)** *(bes. nordd.)* road-sweeper; **b)** *(ugs. scherzh.: spannende Fernsehsendung)* programme/series which pulls a huge audience; **~fest das** street party; **~glätte die** slippery road surface; **~graben der** ditch [at the side of the road]; **~händler der** street trader; **~junge der** *(abwertend)* street urchin; **~kampf der a)** street fight; street battle; **b)** *o. Pl. (Taktik, Strategie)* streetfighting; **~kämpfer der** streetfighter; **~karte die** road-map; **~kehrer der; ~s, ~** *(bes. südd.) s.* **~feger a**; **~kreuzer der** *(ugs. veralt.)* limousine; **~kreuzung die** crossroads *sing.*; **~lage die** road-holding *no indef. art.*; **eine gute ~lage haben** have good road-holding; hold the road well; **~lärm der** street noise;

~**laterne die** street lamp; ~**mädchen das** *(abwertend)* street-walker; ~**musikant der** street musician; busker; ~**name der** street-name; name of a/the street; ~**netz das** road network; ~**rand der** roadside; side of the road; ~**raub der** street robbery; *(gewalttätig)* mugging; ~**räuber der** street robber; *(gewalttätig)* mugger; ~**reinigung die** street-cleaning; ~**rennen das** *(Rennsport)* road race; ~**sammlung die** street collection; ~**schild das** street-name sign; ~**schlacht die** street battle; ~**schmutz der** *(auf der Straße)* dirt in the street/streets; *(von der Straße)* dirt from the street/streets; ~**schuh der** walking-shoe; ~**seite die** side of the street/road; *(eines Gebäudes)* street side; **das Fenster ging zur ~seite** the window looked out on [to] the street/road; ~**sperre die** road-block; ~**sperrung die** closing [off] of a/the street/road; ~**staub der** dust of the street/road; ~**theater das a)** *o. Pl. (Institution)* street theatre; **b)** *(Ensemble)* street theatre group; ~**tunnel der** road tunnel; ~**über·führung die** *(für Fußgänger)* footbridge; *(für Fahrzeuge)* road bridge; ~**unter·führung die** *(für Fußgänger)* subway; *(für Fahrzeuge)* underpass; ~**verhältnisse** *Pl.* road conditions; ~**verkauf der a)** *(auf der Straße)* street trading; **b)** *(über die Straße)* take-away sales *pl.*; *(von alkoholischen Getränken)* off-licence sales *pl.*; ~**verkäufer der** street vendor; ~**verkehr der** traffic; **im ~verkehr** in traffic; ~**verkehrs·ordnung die** road traffic act; ~**zoll der** *s.* **Maut**; ~**zug der** street; ~**zu·stand der** road conditions *pl.*

Stratege [ʃtraˈteːgə] **der; ~n, ~n** strategist

Strategie [ʃtrateˈgiː] **die; ~, ~n** strategy

strategisch 1. *Adj.* strategic. **2.** *adv.* strategically

Strato·sphäre [ʃtrato-] **die** stratosphere

Stratus [ˈʃtraːtʊs] **der; ~, Strati** *(Met.)* stratus

Stratus·wolke die stratus cloud

sträuben [ˈʃtrɔybn̩] **1.** *tr. V.* ruffle [up] ⟨*feathers*⟩; bristle ⟨*fur, hair*⟩. **2.** *refl. V.* ⟨*hair, fur*⟩ bristle, stand on end; ⟨*feathers*⟩ become ruffled; **bei dieser Nachricht sträubten sich mir die Haare** the news made my hair stand on end; **b)** *(sich widersetzen)* resist; **sich ~, etw. zu tun** resist doing sth.; **sie hat sich mit Händen und Füßen gegen die Versetzung gesträubt** she resisted the transfer with all her might; **die Feder sträubt sich, das zu schildern** *(fig. geh.)* one hesitates *or* is reluctant to put it on paper

Strauch [ʃtraux] **der; ~[e]s, Sträucher** [ˈʃtrɔyçɐ] shrub

Strauch·dieb der *(veralt. abwertend)* footpad *(hist.)*; **wie ein ~ aussehen** *(ugs.)* look like a tramp

straucheln [ˈʃtrauxl̩n] *itr. V.; mit sein (geh.)* **a)** *(stolpern)* stumble; **sein Fuß strauchelte** *(geh.)* he stumbled; **b)** *(scheitern)* fail; **c)** *(straffällig werden)* go astray

Strauch·werk das shrubbery; bushes *pl.*

[1]**Strauß** [ʃtraus] **der; ~es, Sträuße** [ˈʃtrɔysə] bunch of flowers; *(bes. als Geschenk, zu offiziellem Anlaß)* bouquet [of flowers]; *(von kleinen Blumen)* posy

[2]**Strauß der; ~es, ~e** *(Vogel)* ostrich; **wie der Vogel ~:** like an ostrich

[3]**Strauß der; ~es, Sträuße** *(veralt.)* **a)** *(Kampf)* battle; **b)** *(Streit)* quarrel; **ich habe einen ~ mit dir auszufechten** I have a bone to pick with you

Sträußchen [ˈʃtrɔysçən] **das; ~s, ~:** posy

Straußen-: ~ei das ostrich egg; ~**feder die** ostrich feather *or* plume

Strauß·wirtschaft die *(bes. südd.) [temporarily opened] bar selling new wine when a bundle of twigs is displayed*

Strebe [ˈʃtreːbə] **die; ~, ~n** brace; strut

Strebe-: ~balken der shore; prop; ~**bogen der** *(Archit.)* flying buttress

streben *itr. V.* **a)** *mit sein (hinwollen)* make one's way briskly; **er strebte zur Tür** he made briskly for the door; **die Pflanzen ~ zum Licht** the plants reach up towards the light; **die Partei strebt an die Macht** the party is reaching out for power; **b)** *(trachten)* strive **(nach** for); **danach ~, etw. zu tun** strive to do sth.; **das Streben nach Vollkommenheit** [the] striving for perfection; **c)** *(abwertend)* ⟨*pupil*⟩ swot *(Brit. sl.)*; cram

Strebe·pfeiler der *(Archit.)* buttress

Streber der; ~s, ~ *(abwertend)* over-ambitious *or* pushing *or (coll.)* pushy person; *(in der Schule)* swot *(Brit. sl.)*; cram

streberhaft, streberisch *(abwertend) Adj.* over-ambitious; pushing; pushy *(coll.)*; **ein ~er Schüler** a swot *(Brit. sl.)*; grind *(Amer. sl.)*

Streberin die; ~, ~nen *s.* **Streber**

Strebe·werk das *(Archit.)* [system *sing.* of] buttresses *pl.*

strebsam *Adj.* ambitious and industrious

Strebsamkeit die; ~: ambition and industriousness

Streck·bett das *(Med.)* orthopaedic bed

Strecke [ˈʃtrɛkə] **die; ~, ~n a)** *(Weg~)* distance; **über weite ~n sah man kein einziges Dorf** for long distances there was not a single village to be seen; **das Land war über weite ~n überschwemmt** large parts of the countryside were flooded; **auf der ~ bleiben** *(ugs.)* fall by the wayside; **b)** *(Abschnitt, Route)* route; *(Eisenbahn~)* line; **er fliegt diese ~ oft** he often flies this route; **der Zug hielt auf freier** *od.* **offener ~:** the train stopped between stations; **c)** *(Sport)* distance; **viele Zuschauer waren an der ~:** there were a lot of spectators lining the route/track; **die Läufer gehen auf die ~:** the runners are setting off; **d)** *(Geom.)* line segment; **e)** *(Bergbau)* gallery; **f)** *(Jägerspr.)* bag; kill; **ein Tier zur ~ bringen** bag *or* kill an animal; **jmdn. zur ~ bringen** *(fig.)* hunt sb. down

strecken 1. *tr. V.* **a)** *(gerade machen)* stretch ⟨*arms, legs*⟩; **ein gebrochenes Bein ~:** straighten a broken leg; **b)** *(dehnen)* stretch [out] ⟨*arms, legs, etc.*⟩; **den Hals ~:** crane one's neck; **c)** *(lehnen)* stick *(coll.)*; **den Kopf aus dem Fenster ~:** stick one's head out of the window *(coll.)*; **d)** *(größer, länger, breiter machen)* stretch; hammer/roll out ⟨*metal*⟩; **e)** *(verdünnen)* thin down; **f)** *(rationieren)* eke out ⟨*provisions, fuel, etc.*⟩. **2.** *refl. V.* stretch out

strecken-, Strecken-: ~ab·schnitt der section; ~**arbeiter der** platelayer; track worker; ~**begehung die** track inspection; ~**führung die** routing; *(Strecke)* route; ~**netz das** route network; *(Eisenbahnw.)* rail network; ~**wärter der** track inspector; ~**weise** *Adv.* in places; *(fig.: zeitweise)* at times; **das Buch war ~weise langweilig** the book was boring in parts

Strecker der; ~s, ~ *(Anat.)* extensor

Streck-: ~muskel der *(Anat.)* extensor [muscle]; ~**verband der** *(Med.)* extension *or* traction bandage

Streich [ʃtraiç] **der; ~[e]s, ~e a)** *(geh.: Hieb)* blow; **jmdm. einen ~ versetzen** strike sb.; **auf einen ~** *(veralt.)* at one blow; *(fig.)* at one fell swoop; at one go; **b)** *(Schabernack)* trick; prank; **jmdm. einen ~ spielen** play a trick on sb.; **mein Gedächtnis hat mir wieder einen ~ gespielt** my memory has been playing tricks on me again

Streichel·einheiten *Pl. (ugs.)* share *sing.* of kindness and affection; *(bei Mitarbeitern)* share *sing.* of encouragement and appreciation

streicheln [ˈʃtraiçl̩n] *tr. (auch itr.) V.* stroke; *(liebkosen)* stroke; caress; **einem Hund über den Rücken ~:** stroke a dog's back; **er streichelte ihr übers Haar** he stroked her hair

streichen 1. *unr. tr. V.* **a)** stroke; **die Geige ~** *(geh.)* play the violin; *s. auch* **gestrichen 2, 3; b)** *(an~)* paint; **eine Wand grün/beige** *usw.* **~:** paint a wall green/beige *etc.*; **„frisch gestrichen"** 'wet paint'; **c)** *(wegstreifen)* sweep ⟨*crumbs etc.*⟩; **sich** *(Dat.)* **das Haar aus der Stirn ~:** push *or* smooth the hair back from one's forehead; **d)** *(drücken)* **Kitt in die Fugen ~:** press putty into the joints; **Tomaten durch ein Sieb ~:** rub *or* press tomatoes through a sieve; **e)** *(auftragen)* spread ⟨*butter, jam, ointment, etc.*⟩; **f)** *(be~)* **ein Brötchen [mit Butter]/mit Honig ~:** butter a roll/spread honey on a roll; **g)** *(aus~, tilgen)* delete; cross out; cancel ⟨*train, flight*⟩; **jmdn. von der Liste ~:** cross sb. off the list; **Nichtzutreffendes bitte ~!** please delete as appropriate *or* applicable; **etw. aus seinem Gedächtnis** *od.* **seiner Erinnerung ~:** erase sth. from one's memory *or* mind; **einen Auftrag/Zuschuß ~:** cancel an order/a subsidy; **h)** *(Rudern)* **die Riemen ~:** back water; **i)** *(Seemannsspr. veralt.)* strike ⟨*sail*⟩; *s. auch* **Flagge; Segel. 2.** *unr. itr. V.* **a)** stroke; **jmdm. durch die Haare/über den Kopf ~:** run one's fingers through sb.'s hair/stroke sb.'s head; **er strich sich** *(Dat.)* **nachdenklich über den Bart** he stroked his beard thoughtfully; **mit der Hand über die Tischdecke ~:** smooth the tablecloth with one's hand; **b)** *(an~)* paint; **c)** *mit sein (umhergehen)* wander; **d)** *(Geol.)* ⟨*stratum*⟩ strike; *(Geogr.)* ⟨*mountain range*⟩ stretch; **e)** *mit sein (bes. Jägerspr.)* ⟨*bird*⟩ wing

Streicher der; ~s, ~ *(Musik)* string-player; **die ~:** the strings

streich·fähig *Adj.* easy to spread *pred.*

Streich·holz das match; *(als Spielzeug)* matchstick; **eine Schachtel Streichhölzer** a box of matches

Streichholz-: ~briefchen das book of matches; ~**spiel das** game with matchsticks

Streich-: ~instrument das string[ed] instrument; ~**käse der** cheese spread; ~**orchester das** string orchestra; ~**quartett das** string quartet; ~**trio das** string trio

Streichung die; ~, ~en a) *(Tilgung)* deletion; *(Kürzung)* cutting *no indef. art.*; **~en vornehmen** make deletions/cuts; **b)** *(gestrichene Stelle)* deletion; *(Kürzung)* cut

Streich·wurst die [soft] sausage for spreading; ≈ meat spread

Streif [ʃtraif] **der; ~[e]s, ~e** *(geh.)* strip; *(Licht~)* shaft

Streif·band das; *Pl.* **~bänder** wrapper

Streife die; ~, ~n a) *(Personen)* patrol; **b)** *(Streifengang)* patrol; **auf ~ gehen/sein** go/be on patrol

streifen 1. *tr. V.* **a)** *(leicht berühren)* touch; brush [against]; ⟨*shot*⟩ graze; **jmdn. am Arm/an der Schulter ~:** touch sb. on the arm *or* brush against sb.'s arm/touch sb. on the shoulder; **mit dem Wagen das Garagentor ~:** scrape the garage door with the car; **ein Windhauch streifte ihre Wangen** *(geh.)* she felt a breath of wind on her cheeks; **jmdn. mit einem Blick ~** *(fig.)* glance fleetingly at sb.; **b)** *(kurz behandeln)* touch [up]on ⟨*problem, subject, etc.*⟩; **c) den Ring auf den/vom Finger ~:** slip the ring on/off one's finger; **die Ärmel nach oben ~:** pull/push up one's sleeves; **die Butter vom Messer ~:** wipe the butter off the knife; **sich** *(Dat.)* **die Kapuze/den Pullover über den Kopf ~:** pull the hood/slip the pullover over one's head; **sich die Strümpfe von den Beinen ~:** slip one's stockings off; **die Blätter von den Zweigen ~:** strip the leaves from the twigs; strip the twigs of leaves. **2.** *itr. V. mit sein* roam; **durch die Wälder ~:** roam the forests

Streifen der; ~s, ~ a) *(Linie)* stripe; *(auf der Fahrbahn)* line; **ein heller ~ am Horizont** a streak of light on the horizon; **graue**

~ im Haar haben have grey streaks in one's hair; **b)** *(Stück, Abschnitt)* strip; *(Speck~)* rasher; *(Tresse)* braid; **c)** *(ugs.: Film)* film

Streifen-: ~beamte der policeman on patrol duty; **~dienst der** patrol duty; **~gang der** patrol; **~muster das** striped pattern; **ein Hemd mit ~muster** a striped shirt; **~wagen der** patrol car

streifig *Adj.* streaky

Streif-: ~licht das; *Pl.* ~er streak of light; **ein ~licht auf etw.** *(Akk.)* **werfen** *(fig.)* highlight sth.; **~schuß der** grazing shot; *(Wunde)* graze; **~zug der** expedition; *(fig.)* expedition; journey; *(eines Tieres)* prowl

Streik [ʃtraik] **der;** ~[e]s, ~s strike; **in den ~ treten** come out *or* go on strike; **den ~ ausrufen** call a strike; **jmdn. zum ~ aufrufen** call sb. out on strike; **mit ~ drohen** threaten to strike; threaten strike action; *s. auch* **wild 1 b**

Streik-: ~auf·ruf der strike call; **~brecher der** strike-breaker; blackleg *(derog.)*; scab *(derog.)*; **~drohung die** strike threat; threat of strike action

streiken *itr. V.* **a)** strike; be on strike; *(in den Streik treten)* come out *or* go on strike; strike; **b)** *(ugs.: nicht mitmachen)* go on strike; **c)** *(ugs.: nicht funktionieren)* pack up *(coll.)*; **der Kühlschrank streikt** the fridge has packed up *(coll.)*

Streikende der/die; *adj. Dekl.* striker

Streik-: ~front die strike; **an der ~front** in the strike/strikes; **~geld das** strike pay; **~kasse die** strike fund; **~leitung die** strike leadership; strike leaders *pl.*; **~posten der** picket; **~posten beziehen** picket; stand on the picket-line; **vor einer Fabrik ~posten stehen** picket a factory; **~recht das** right to strike

Streit [ʃtrait] **der;** ~[e]s **a)** quarrel; argument; *(Zank)* squabble; quarrel; *(Auseinandersetzung)* dispute; argument; **~ anfangen** start a quarrel *or* an argument; **sie sind im ~ auseinandergegangen** they parted in disharmony; **er sucht immer ~:** he is always looking for an argument *or* a quarrel; **die beiden haben oft ~:** those two are always arguing *or* quarrelling *or* fighting; **ein ~ der Meinungen** a clash of opinions; **mit jmdm. ~ bekommen** get into an argument *or* a quarrel with sb.; **er hat ihn im ~ erschlagen** he beat him to death during a quarrel; **miteinander in ~ leben** be always at loggerheads with each other; **ein ~ um des Kaisers Bart** an argument over nothing; **b)** *(veralt.: Kampf)* battle

Streit·axt die battleaxe

streit·bar *Adj. (geh.)* **a)** pugnacious; **b)** *(veralt.: tapfer)* brave; valiant

streiten 1. *unr. itr., refl. V.* quarrel; argue; *(sich zanken)* squabble; quarrel; *(sich auseinandersetzen)* argue; have an argument; **die Erben stritten [sich] um den Nachlaß** the heirs argued *or* fought over *or* disputed the estate; **darüber läßt sich ~:** one can argue about that; that's a debatable point; **die ~den Parteien in einem Prozeß** the litigants in a lawsuit; **die Streitenden** the quarrellers. **2.** *unr. itr. V. (geh.: kämpfen)* fight

Streiter der; ~s, ~ *(geh.: Kämpfer)* fighter **(für** for, **gegen** against); champion **(für** of)

Streiterei die; ~, ~en arguing *no pl., no indef. art.*; *(Gezänk)* quarrelling *no pl.*; **bei ihnen gibt es immer ~en** they are always quarrelling

Streiterin die; ~, ~nen *s.* **Streiter**

Streit-: ~fall der *(Rechtsw.)* case; *(Kontroverse)* dispute; conflict; **das ist ein ~fall** that is a disputed point; **im ~fall** in [the] case of dispute *or* conflict; **~frage die** disputed question *or* issue; **~gespräch das** debate; disputation; **~hahn der;** *meist Pl. (ugs., oft scherzh.)* quarreller; squabbler; *(fig.: Kampfhahn)* fighter; brawler; **~hammel der** *(fam.)* quarreller

streitig *Adj.* **a)** disputed ⟨*question, issue*⟩; **jmdm. jmdn./etw. ~ machen** dispute sb.'s right to sb./sth.; **b)** *(Rechtsw.)* disputed

Streitigkeit die; ~, ~en *meist Pl.* **a)** quarrel; argument; **b)** *(Streitfall)* dispute

streit-, Streit-: ~kräfte *Pl.* armed forces; **~macht die;** *o. Pl. (veralt.)* forces *pl.*; **~punkt der** contentious issue; **~roß das** *(veralt.) s.* **Schlachtroß; ~sache die a)** dispute; **b)** *(Rechtsw.) s.* **Rechtsstreit; ~schrift die** polemical treatise; **~sucht die** quarrelsomeness; **~süchtig** *Adj.* quarrelsome; **~wagen der** chariot; **~wert der** amount in dispute

streng [ʃtrɛŋ] **1.** *Adj.* **a)** *(hart)* strict ⟨*teacher, parents, upbringing, principle*⟩; severe ⟨*punishment*⟩; stringent, strict ⟨*rule, regulation, etc.*⟩; stringent ⟨*measure*⟩; rigorous ⟨*examination, check, test, etc.*⟩; stern ⟨*reprimand, look*⟩; **b)** *nicht präd. (strikt)* strict ⟨*order, punctuality, diet, instruction, Catholic*⟩; absolute ⟨*discretion*⟩; complete ⟨*rest*⟩; **~ gegen sich selbst sein** be strict with oneself; **im ~en Sinne** in the strict sense; **c)** *nicht präd. (schnörkellos)* austere, severe ⟨*cut, collar, style, etc.*⟩; severe ⟨*hairstyle*⟩; **der ~e Aufbau eines Romans** the tight structure of a novel; **d)** *(herb)* severe ⟨*face, features, etc.*⟩; **e)** *(durchdringend)* pungent, sharp ⟨*taste, smell*⟩; **er riecht etwas ~:** he smells a bit strong; **f)** *(rauh)* severe ⟨*winter*⟩; sharp, severe ⟨*frost*⟩. **2.** *adv.* **a)** *(hart)* ⟨*mark, judge, etc.*⟩ strictly, severely; ⟨*punish*⟩ severely; ⟨*look, reprimand*⟩ sternly; **~ durchgreifen** take rigorous action; **b)** *(strikt)* strictly; **~ verboten** strictly prohibited; **c)** *(schnörkellos)* **sie trug ein ~ geschnittenes Kostüm** she wore a severe suit; **d)** *(durchdringend)* ⟨*smell*⟩ strongly

Strenge die; ~ **a)** *s.* **streng a:** strictness; severity; stringency; rigour; sternness; **jmdn. mit äußerster ~ bestrafen** punish sb. extremely severely; **b)** *(Striktheit)* strictness; **c)** *(von [Gesichts]zügen)* severity; **d)** *(von Geruch, Geschmack)* pungency; sharpness; **ein Geruch von beißender ~:** a bitingly pungent smell; **e)** *s.* **streng f.:** severity; sharpness; **f)** *(Schnörkellosigkeit)* austerity; severity

streng-, Streng-: ~genommen *adv.* strictly speaking; **~gläubig** *Adj.* strict; **~gläubigkeit die** strict beliefs *pl.*

strengstens [ˈʃtrɛŋstn̩s] *Adv.* [most] strictly

Streptokokkus [ʃtrɛptoˈkɔkʊs] **der;** ~, **Streptokokken** streptococcus

Strese·mann der *formal suit with dark jacket, grey waistcoat, and striped trousers*

Streß [ʃtrɛs] **der; Stresses, Stresse** stress; **im ~ sein** be under stress

stressen *(ugs.)* **1.** *tr. V.* **jmdn. ~:** put sb. under stress; **vollkommen gestreßt sein** be under an enormous amount of stress; **die gestreßten Großstädter** the stressed city-dwellers. **2.** *itr. V.* be stressful

stressig *Adj. (ugs.)* stressful

Streß·situation die stress situation

Stretch [ʃtrɛtʃ] **der;** ~[e]s, ~es stretch fabric *or* material

Streu [ʃtrɔy] **die;** ~, ~en straw

Streu·büchse die shaker; *(für Zucker)* shaker; castor; *(für Mehl)* dredger

streuen 1. *tr. V.* **a)** spread ⟨*manure, sand, grit*⟩; sprinkle ⟨*salt, herbs, etc.*⟩; strew, scatter ⟨*flowers*⟩; *(fig.)* spread ⟨*rumour*⟩; **den Vögeln Futter ~:** scatter food for the birds; **weit gestreut** *(fig.)* scattered *or* spread over a wide area; **b)** *(auch itr.) (mit Streugut)* **die Straßen [mit Sand/Salz] ~:** grit/salt the roads; put grit/salt down on the roads; **[den Weg] ~:** put grit/salt *etc.* down [on the path]. **2.** *itr. V.* **a)** *(beim Schießen)* scatter; **b)** *(bes. Physik)* ⟨*particles, ions, etc.*⟩ scatter; **c)** *(Med.)* spread

Streu-: ~fahr·zeug das gritter; gritting-lorry; **~gut das** *o. Pl.* grit/salt *(for icy roads etc.)*

streunen *itr. V.; meist mit sein (oft abwertend)* wander *or* roam about *or* around; **~de Katzen/Hunde** stray cats/dogs; **durch die Straßen/Felder ~:** roam *or* wander the streets/across the fields

Streuner der; ~s, ~ *(abwertend)* tramp

Streu-: ~salz das salt *(for icy roads etc.)*; **~sand der a)** grit *(for icy roads etc.)*; **b)** *(veralt.: zum Trocknen)* sand

Streusel der *od.* **das;** ~s, ~ *crumble [topping] made of butter, sugar, flour;* streusel

Streusel·kuchen der streusel cake

Streuung die; ~, ~en **a)** *(Verbreitung)* dissemination; **b)** *(Ballistik)* scattering; **c)** *(Med.)* generalization; metastasis *(Med.)*

Streu·zucker der granulated sugar

strich [ʃtrɪç] *1. u. 3. Pers. Sg. Prät. v.* **streichen**

Strich der; ~[e]s, ~e **a)** *(Linie)* line; *(in einer Zeichnung)* stroke; line; *(Gedanken~)* dash; *(Schräg~)* diagonal; slash; *(Binde~, Trennungs~)* hyphen; *(Markierung)* mark; **beim Lesen ~e an den Rand machen** sideline passages when reading; **etw. mit groben** *od.* **in großen ~en zeichnen** *od. (fig.)* **umreißen** sketch sth. in broad strokes *(lit. or fig.)*; **er ist nur noch ein ~ [in der Landschaft]** *(ugs.)* he's as thin as a rake; **keinen ~ tun** *od.* **machen** *od.* **arbeiten** not do a stroke *or* a thing; **jmdm. einen ~ durch die Rechnung/durch etw.** *(Akk.)* **machen** *(ugs.)* mess up *or* wreck sb.'s plans/mess up sb.'s plans for sth.; **dem werden wir einen ~ durch die Rechnung machen!** we'll put a stop to his little game; **einen ~ unter etw.** *(Akk.)* **machen** *od.* **ziehen** put sth. behind one; make a [clean] break with sth.; **unter dem ~:** at the end of the day; all things considered; **unter dem ~ sein** *(ugs.)* not be up to scratch; be below par; **b)** *(Winkeleinheit)* point; **c)** *o. Pl.* **der ~** *(salopp) (Prostitution)* [street] prostitution; street-walking; *(Gegend)* the street-walkers' patch; the red-light district; **auf den ~ gehen** walk the streets; **d)** *(streichende Bewegung)* stroke; **e)** *o. Pl. (Pinselführung)* strokes *pl.*; **van Goghs kräftiger ~:** van Gogh's powerful brush-strokes *pl. or* brush; **f)** *(Streichung)* deletion; **g)** *o. Pl. (Bogen~)* bowing *no indef. art.*; **h)** *o. Pl. (Haar~, Fell~)* lie; *(eines Teppichs)* pile; *(von Samt o. ä.)* nap; **gegen den/mit dem ~ bürsten** brush ⟨*hair, fur*⟩ the wrong/right way; brush ⟨*carpet*⟩ against/with the pile; brush ⟨*velvet*⟩ against/with the nap; **jmdm. gegen den ~ gehen** *(ugs.)* go against the grain [with sb.]; **nach ~ und Faden** *(ugs.)* good and proper *(coll.)*; well and truly; **jmdn. nach ~ und Faden belügen** *(ugs.)* lie through one's teeth to sb.; **i)** *(bes. Jägerspr.) (Flug)* flight; *(Schwarm)* flock

Strich·ätzung die *(Druckw.)* line block *or* plate

Strichelchen das; ~s, ~: little line; *(dünn)* fine line

stricheln [ˈʃtrɪçl̩n] *tr. V.* **a)** *(zeichnen)* sketch in [with short lines]; **eine gestrichelte Linie** a broken line; **b)** *(schraffieren)* hatch

Strich-: ~junge der *(salopp)* [young] male prostitute; **~kode der** bar code

strichlieren *(österr.) s.* **stricheln**

strich-, Strich-: ~mädchen das *(salopp)* street-walker; hooker *(Amer. sl.)*; **~männchen das** matchstick man; **~punkt der** semicolon; **~vogel der** *(Zool.)* flocking bird; **~weise** *(bes. Met.)* **1.** *Adv.* ⟨*rain etc.*⟩ in places; **2.** *adj.; nicht präd.* in places *postpos.*; local; **~zeichnung die** line-drawing

[1]Strick [ʃtrɪk] **der;** ~[e]s, ~e **a)** cord; *(Seil)* rope; **jmdm. aus etw. einen ~ drehen** *(fig.)* use sth. against sb.; **da kann ich mir ja gleich einen ~ nehmen** *od.* **kaufen!** I might as well end it all now; *s. auch* **reißen 2 a; ziehen 2 a; b)** *(fam.: Schlingel)* rascal

[2]Strick das; ~[e]s *(bes. Mode)* knitted material; **in lässigem ~:** knitted in casual style

Strick-: ~arbeit die [piece of] knitting; **~bündchen das** knitted welt

stricken *tr., itr. V.* knit; **an etw.** *(Dat.)* **~:** be knitting sth.; **eine sauber gestrickte Story** *(fig.)* a neatly constructed story

Strickerei die; ~, ~en a) *o. Pl. (Tätigkeit)* knitting; **b)** *(Produkt)* piece of knitting

Strickerin die; ~, ~en knitter

Strick-: ~jacke die cardigan; **~kleid das** knitted dress; **~leiter die** rope-ladder; **~maschine die** knitting-machine; **~mode die** knitwear fashion; **~muster das** knitting-pattern; *(fig.)* formula; **~nadel die** knitting-needle; **~waren** *Pl.* knitwear *sing.*; **~zeug das** knitting

Striegel ['ʃtri:gl̩] **der; ~s, ~:** curry-comb

striegeln *tr. V.* groom ⟨*horse*⟩; **gestriegelt und gebügelt** *(fig.)* all spruced up

Strieme ['ʃtri:mə] **die; ~, ~n, Striemen der; ~s, ~:** weal

Striezel ['ʃtri:tsl̩] **der; ~s, ~** *(bes. ostd.)* long plaited bun

strikt [ʃtrɪkt] **1.** *Adj.* strict; exact ⟨*opposite*⟩. **2.** *adv.* strictly; **ich bin ~ dagegen** I am totally opposed to it

stringent [ʃtrɪŋ'gɛnt] *(geh.)* **1.** *Adj.* compelling ⟨*conclusion, reasoning, proof, argument*⟩. **2.** *adv.* ⟨*prove, deduce*⟩ by compelling logic; ⟨*prove, argue*⟩ compellingly

Stringenz [ʃtrɪŋ'gɛnts] **die; ~** *(geh.)* compelling nature

Strip [ʃtrɪp] **der; ~s, ~s a)** *(Striptease)* strip[tease]; **b)** *(Pflaster)* strip [of sticking-plaster]

Strippe ['ʃtrɪpə] **die; ~, ~n** *(ugs.)* string; **an der ~ hängen** *(fig.)* be on the phone *(coll.)*; *(dauernd)* hog the phone *(coll.)*; **jmdn. an der ~ haben** *(fig.)* have sb. on the phone *(coll.) or* line; **jmdn. an die ~ kriegen** *(fig.)* get sb. on the phone *(coll.)*; **sich an die ~ hängen** *(fig.)* get on the phone *(coll.)*

strippen *itr. V. (ugs.)* do strip-tease; strip

Stripperin die; ~, ~nen *(ugs.)* stripper

Striptease ['ʃtrɪpti:s] **der** *od.* **das; ~:** striptease

Striptease·tänzerin die strip-tease dancer

stritt [ʃtrɪt] *1. u. 3. Pers. Sg. Prät. v.* **streiten**

strittig *Adj.* contentious ⟨*point, problem*⟩; disputed ⟨*territory*⟩; ⟨*question*⟩ in dispute, at issue; **~ ist nur, ob ...:** the only point at issue is whether ...

Strizzi ['ʃtrɪtsi] **der; ~s, ~s** *(bes. südd., österr.)* **a)** *(Zuhälter)* pimp; **b)** *(Strolch)* rascal

Stroh [ʃtro:] **das; ~[e]s** straw; **mit ~ gedeckt** ⟨*roof, cottage*⟩ thatched with straw; **es brannte wie ~:** it went up like dry tinder; **~ im Kopf haben** *(ugs.)* have sawdust between one's ears *(coll.)*

stroh-, Stroh-: ~ballen der bale of straw; straw bale; **~blond** *Adj.* flaxen-haired ⟨*person*⟩; straw-coloured, flaxen ⟨*hair*⟩; **~blume die a)** *(Immortelle)* immortelle; everlasting [flower]; **b)** *(Korbblütler)* strawflower; **~dach das** roof thatched with straw; **~dumm** *Adj. (ugs.)* witless *(coll.)*; thick-headed; **~feuer das: wie ein ~feuer aufflammen** flare up briefly; **das war nur ein ~feuer** *(fig.)* it was just a flash in the pan; **~gedeckt** *Adj.* ⟨*roof, house*⟩ thatched with straw; **~gelb** *Adj.* straw-coloured; flaxen ⟨*hair*⟩; **~halm der** straw; **sich [wie ein Ertrinkender] an einen ~halm klammern** *(fig.)* grasp at a straw [like a drowning man]; **der letzte ~halm** *(fig.)* the last ray of hope; **nach einem/jedem ~halm greifen** *(fig.)* clutch at a/any straw; **~hut der** straw hat

strohig *Adj.* strawy; **eine ~e Apfelsine** a dried-up orange; **~ sein/werden/schmecken** be/become/taste like straw

stroh-, Stroh-: ~kopf der *(ugs. abwertend)* thickhead; **~mann der;** *Pl.* **~männer** *(fig.)* front man; **~puppe die** straw doll; **~sack der** palliasse; **[ach du] heiliger ~sack!** *(ugs.)* jeepers creepers! *(coll.)*; goodness gracious [me]!; **~witwe die** *(ugs. scherzh.)* grass widow; **~witwer der** *(ugs. scherzh.)* grass widower

Strolch [ʃtrɔlç] **der; ~[e]s, ~e a)** *(veralt.)* ruffian; **b)** *(fam. scherzh.: Junge)* rascal

strolchen *itr. V.; mit sein* roam *or* wander [aimlessly] about; **durch die Straßen ~:** roam the streets

Strom [ʃtro:m] **der; ~[e]s, Ströme** ['ʃtrø:mə] **a)** river; *(von Blut, Schweiß, Wasser, fig.: Erinnerungen, Menschen, Autos usw.)* stream; *(große Menge)* torrent; *(fig.: von Tränen)* flood; **ein reißender ~:** a raging torrent; **in Strömen regnen** *od. (ugs.)* **gießen** pour with rain; **in Strömen fließen** *(fig.)* flow freely; **das Blut floß in Strömen** *(fig.)* there was heavy bloodshed; **b)** *(Strömung)* current; **mit dem/gegen den ~ schwimmen** *(fig.)* swim with/against the tide *(fig.)*; **c)** *(Elektrizität)* current; *(~versorgung)* electricity; **das Kabel führt** *od.* **steht unter ~:** the cable is live; **jmdm. den ~ sperren** *od.* **abstellen** cut off sb.'s electricity supply; **mit ~ betrieben sein** run on electricity; be electric; **der ~ ist ausgefallen** there has been a power failure

strom-, Strom-: ~ab *Adv.* downstream; **~abnehmer** ['----] **der** *(Technik)* current-collector; **~abwärts** *Adv.* downstream; **~auf[wärts]** *Adv.* upstream; **~aus·fall** ['---] **der** power failure

strömen ['ʃtrø:mən] *itr. V.; mit sein* stream; *(intensiv)* pour; *(fließen)* flow; **~der Regen** pouring rain

Stromer der; ~s, ~ *(ugs.)* vagabond; roamer

stromern *itr. V.; mit Richtungsangabe mit sein (ugs.)* roam *or* wander around; **durch die Gegend/Stadt ~:** roam *or* wander around the place/through the town

strom-, Strom-: ~führend *Adj.* live; **~kreis der** [electric] circuit; **~leitung die** power line *or* cable; **~linien·form die** streamlined shape; streamlining *no indef. art.*; **~linien·förmig** *Adj.* streamlined; **~netz das** electricity supply; mains [network]; **~rechnung die** electricity bill; **~schlag der** electric shock; **~schnelle die** rapids *pl.*; **~stärke die** current strength; **~stoß der** electric shock

Strömung die; ~, ~en a) current; *(Met.)* airstream; **b)** *(fig.) (Bewegung)* movement; *(Tendenz)* trend

Strom-: ~verbrauch der electricity consumption; **~verbraucher der** *(Technik)* current-consuming device; **~versorgung die** electricity *or* power supply; **~zähler der** electricity meter

Strontium ['ʃtrɔntsiʊm] **das; ~s** strontium

Strophe ['ʃtro:fə] **die; ~, ~n** verse; *(einer Ode)* strophe

Strophen·form die a) verse form; **b)** *(strophische Form)* strophic form

-strophig *adj.* **drei~ sein** have three verses; **ein mehr~es/drei~es Lied** a song with several verses/a three-verse song

strophisch 1. *Adj.* strophic. **2.** *adv.* **~ gestaltet/gebaut** in strophic form

strotzen ['ʃtrɔtsn̩] *itr. V.* **von** *od.* **vor etw.** *(Dat.)* **~:** be full of sth.; **von** *od.* **vor Kraft/Gesundheit ~:** be bursting with strength/health

strubbelig ['ʃtrʊb(ə)lɪç] *Adj.* tousled; **du bist ja so ~!** your hair is in such a mess

Strubbel·kopf der *(ugs.)* **a)** mop *or* shock of [tousled] hair; **b)** *(Mensch)* tousle-head

strubblig *s.* **strubbelig**

Strudel ['ʃtru:dl̩] **der; ~s, ~ a)** whirlpool; *(kleiner)* eddy; **der ~ der Ereignisse** *(fig.)* the whirl of events; **b)** *(bes. südd., österr.: Gebäck)* strudel

strudeln *itr. V.* ⟨*water*⟩ eddy, swirl

Struktur [ʃtrʊk'tu:ɐ̯] **die; ~, ~en a)** structure; **b)** *(von Stoffen usw.)* texture

Strukturalismus [ʃtrʊktura'lɪsmʊs] **der; ~:** structuralism *no art.*

strukturalistisch 1. *Adj.* structuralist. **2.** *adv.* structuralistically

Struktur·analyse die structural analysis

strukturell [ʃtrʊktu'rɛl] **1.** *Adj.* structural. **2.** *adv.* structurally

Struktur·formel die *(Chemie)* structural formula

strukturieren *tr. V.* structure; **neu ~:** restructure

Strukturierung die; ~, ~en a) *o. Pl.* structuring; organization; **b)** *(Struktur)* structure

struktur-, Struktur-: ~politik die economic development policy; structural policy; **~schwach** *Adj. (Wirtsch.)* economically underdeveloped; **~wandel der** structural change

Strumpf [ʃtrʊmpf] **der; ~[e]s, Strümpfe** ['ʃtrʏmpfə] stocking; *(Socke, Knie~)* sock; **lange Strümpfe** stockings; **auf Strümpfen** in stockinged feet/in one's socks

Strumpf·band das; *Pl.* **~bänder** garter; *(Straps)* suspender *(Brit.)*; garter *(Amer.)*

Strümpfchen ['ʃtrʏmpfçən] **das; ~s, ~:** little stocking; *(Socke, Kniestrumpf)* little sock

Strumpf-: ~halter der suspender *(Brit.)*; garter *(Amer.)*; **~hose die** tights *pl. (Brit.)*; pantyhose *(esp. Amer.)*; **eine ~hose** a pair of tights *(Brit.)*; **~maske die** stocking mask

Strunk [ʃtrʊŋk] **der; ~[e]s, Strünke** ['ʃtrʏŋkə] stem; stalk; *(Baum~)* stump

struppig ['ʃtrʊpɪç] *Adj.* shaggy ⟨*coat, dog, beard*⟩; tangled, tousled ⟨*hair*⟩

Struwwel·peter ['ʃtrʊvl̩-] **der** tousle-head

Strychnin [ʃtrʏç'ni:n] **das; ~s** strychnine

Stübchen ['ʃty:pçən] **das; ~s, ~:** [little] room

Stube ['ʃtu:bə] **die; ~, ~n a)** *(veralt.: Wohnraum)* [living-]room; parlour *(dated)*; **in der ~ hocken** *(ugs.)* sit around indoors; **die gute ~:** the front room *or (dated)* parlour; **immer rein in die gute ~!** *(ugs.)* come on in!; **b)** *(Milit.)* [barrack-]room

stuben-, Stuben-: ~älteste der/die; *adj. Dekl. (Milit.)* senior man/woman in a/the barrack-room; **~arrest der** *(ugs.)* detention *(in one's room)*; **[zwei Tage] ~arrest bekommen** be kept in [for two days]; **~fliege die** [common] house-fly; **~hocker der** *(ugs. abwertend)* stay-at-home; **~hockerei die; ~** *(ugs. abwertend)* sticking *(coll.) or* sitting around indoors *no art.*; **~kamerad der** room-mate; **~rein** *Adj.* **a)** house-trained; **b)** *(scherzh.: nicht zotig)* clean ⟨*joke etc.*⟩; **~wagen der** bassinet; wicker cot

Stuck [ʃtʊk] **der; ~[e]s** stucco

Stück [ʃtʏk] **das; ~[e]s, Stücke a)** piece; *(kleines)* bit; *(Teil, Abschnitt)* part; **ein ~ Kuchen** a piece *or* slice of cake; **ein ~ Zucker/Seife** a piece *or* lump of sugar/ a piece *or* bar of soap; **ein ~ [Weg** *od. (geh.)* **Weges]** a little [way]; a short distance; **ein ~ spazierengehen** go for a little walk; **ein [gutes] ~ weiterkommen** get a [good] bit further; **ein ~ Autobahn** a section *or* stretch of motorway *(Brit.) or (Amer.)* freeway; **jmdn. wie ein ~ Dreck/Mist behandeln** *(ugs. abwertend)* treat sb. like dirt; **ein ~ Heimat** a bit of home; **ein gewaltiges/hartes ~ Arbeit** a really big/tough job; **ein ~ Hoffnung/Wahrheit** a ray of hope/a grain of truth; **alles in ~e schlagen** smash everything [to pieces]; **es ist nur ein ~ Papier** it's only a scrap of paper; **sich für jmdn. in ~e reißen lassen** *(ugs.)* do anything for sb.; **im** *od.* **am ~:** unsliced ⟨*sausage, cheese, etc.*⟩; **aus einem ~ gemeißelt** carved from the solid; **in einem ~** *(ugs.)* ⟨*talk, rain*⟩ non-stop; **b)** *(Einzel~)* item; article; *(Exemplar)* specimen; *(Möbel~)* piece [of furniture]; **zwanzig ~ Vieh** twenty head of cattle; **ich nehme 5 ~/5 ~ von den Rosen** I'll take five [of them]/five of the roses; **30 Pfennig das ~, das ~ 30**

Pfennig thirty pfennigs each; ~ **für** ~: piece by piece; *(eins nach dem andern)* one by one; **das gute** ~ *(oft iron.)* the precious thing; **große** ~**e auf jmdn. halten** *(ugs.)* think the world of sb.; **Vater, unser bestes** ~ *(scherzh.)* father, our pride and joy; *s. auch* **frei 1 q; c) das ist [ja] ein starkes** *od.* **tolles** ~ *(ugs.)* that's a bit much *or* a bit thick *(coll.)*; **da hast du dir aber ein [tolles]** ~ **geleistet** you've [really] gone too far there; **das ist ja ein** ~ **aus dem Tollhaus!** that's [a piece of] pure lunacy; **d)** *(salopp abwertend: Person)* **ein faules/freches** ~: a lazy/cheeky thing *or* devil; **ein dummes** *od.* **blödes** ~: a stupid thing; **e)** *(Bühnen~)* play; **f)** *(Musik~)* piece

Stückchen das; ~s, ~: [little] piece; bit; **es ist bloß noch ein kleines** ~: it's only another few yards

Stuck·decke die stucco[ed] ceiling

stückeln 1. *tr. V.* put together ⟨*sleeve, curtain*⟩ with patches. **2.** *itr. V.* sew on patches

Stücke·schreiber der playwright

stück-, Stück-: ~**gut das** [individually] packaged goods *pl.*; ~**lohn der** *(Wirtsch.)* piece-work pay; *(Akkordsatz)* piece-rate; ~**preis der** unit price; ~**weise** *Adv.* piece by piece; *(einzeln)* ⟨*sell*⟩ separately; ~**werk das:** ~**werk sein/bleiben** be/remain incomplete; ⟨*book, work of art*⟩ remain a torso; **unsere Korrekturen sind nur** ~**werk, wir müssen das ganze Buch neu bearbeiten** our corrections are only half-measures, we must revise the whole book; ~**zahl die** *(Wirtsch.)* number of units; **in hohen** ~**zahlen produzieren** manufacture in large numbers; **eine** ~**zahl von 300** an output of 300 units

Student [ʃtu'dɛnt] **der;** ~en, ~en **a)** student; **b)** *(österr.: Schüler)* [secondary-school] pupil

Studenten-: ~**ausweis der** student card; ~**bewegung die** student movement; ~**bude die** *(ugs.)* student's room; ~**heim das** student hostel; students' [hall of] residence; ~**lokal das** students' [favourite] haunt; ~**parlament das:** students' assembly

Studentenschaft die; ~, ~en student body; **die verfaßte** ~ *(Hochschulw.)* the students' assembly

Studenten·verbindung die society; *(für Männer)* fraternity *(Amer.)*; *(für Frauen)* sorority *(Amer.)*

Studentin die; ~, ~nen *s.* **Student;** *s. auch* **-in**

studentisch *Adj.; nicht präd.* student

Studie ['ʃtu:diə] **die;** ~, ~n study

studien-, Studien-: ~**assessor der** *graduate teacher who has recently passed the second State Examination;* ≈ probationary teacher; ~**aufenthalt der** study visit **(in +** *Dat.* to); ~**bewerber der** *applicant for a place in higher education;* ~**direktor der a)** *(Bundesrepublik Deutschland)* deputy headmaster; **b)** *(DDR) honorary title conferred on a secondary-school teacher;* ~**fach das** subject [of study]; ~**freund der,** ~**freundin die** university/college friend; ~**gang der** course of study; ~**gebühr die** tuition fee; ~**halber** *Adv.* for study purposes; ~**kolleg das** *(Hochschulw.)* preparatory course *(esp. for foreign students)*; ~**platz der** university/college place; ~**rat der,** ~**rätin die a)** *(Bundesrepublik Deutschland) established graduate secondary-school teacher (Brit.); graduate high-school teacher with tenure (Amer.)*; **b)** *(DDR) honorary title conferred on a teacher;* ~**referendar der** probationary graduate teacher; ~**reise die** study trip; ~**zeit die a)** *(Zeit als Student)* time as a student; student days *pl.*; **b)** *(Dauer)* period of study

studieren [ʃtu'di:rən] **1.** *itr. V.* study; **er studiert in Berlin** he is studying *or* at university in Berlin; **er studiert noch** he is still a student. **2.** *tr. V.* study

Studierende der/die; *adj. Dekl.* student

Studier·stube die *(veralt., scherzh.)* study

studiert *Adj. (ugs.)* ⟨*person*⟩ who has been to university; ⟨*painter etc.*⟩ with an academic training

Studierte der/die; *adj. Dekl. (ugs.)* person with a university education

Studio ['ʃtu:dio] **das;** ~s, ~s **a)** studio; **b)** *(Einzimmerwohnung)* [one-room] flatlet *(Brit.)*; studio flat *(Brit.)*; studio apartment *(Amer.)*

Studio·bühne die studio theatre

Studiosus [ʃtu'dio:zʊs] **der;** ~, **Studiosi** *(veralt., scherzh.)* student

Studium ['ʃtu:diʊm] **das;** ~s, **Studien a)** *o. Pl.* study; *(Studiengang)* course of study; **zum** ~ **der Medizin zugelassen werden** get a place to study medicine; **das** ~ **mit dem Staatsexamen abschließen** complete one's studies *or* course [of study] with the State Examination; **neben dem** ~ **arbeitet sie als Kellnerin** she works as a waitress while she is studying; **während seines** ~**s** *(als er Student war)* in his student days; **b)** *(Erforschung)* study; **Studien über etw.** *(Akk.)* **betreiben** carry out studies into sth.; **c)** *o. Pl. (genaues Lesen)* study; **beim** ~ **der Akten** while studying the files

Studium generale das; ~ ~: general studies course

Stufe ['ʃtu:fə] **die;** ~, ~n **a)** step; *(einer Treppe)* stair; *(Gelände~)* terrace; **„Achtung** *od.* **Vorsicht,** ~**!"** 'mind the step'; **b)** *(Raketen~, Geol., fig.: Stadium)* stage; *(Niveau)* level; *(Steigerungs~, Grad)* degree; *(Rang)* grade; **eine** ~ **der Entwicklung** a stage of development; **auf einer hohen** ~ **stehen** be of a high standard; **auf der gleichen** ~ **stehen [wie ...]** be of the same standard [as ...]; have the same status [as ...]; *(gleichwertig sein)* be equivalent [to ...]; **jmdn./etw. mit jmdm./etw. auf eine** *od.* **auf die gleiche** ~ **stellen** equate sb./sth. with sb./sth.; **zwei Dinge auf die gleiche** ~ **stellen** equate two things; **sich mit jmdm./etw. auf eine** *od.* **auf die gleiche** ~ **stellen** put oneself on a level with sb./sth.; **c)** *(Technik) (Funktions~)* mark; position; *(Geschwindigkeits~)* speed; *(Heiz~)* heat-setting; **Gas:** ~ **III** gas mark III; **d)** *(Musik)* degree; **die erste** ~ **der Tonleiter** the first step on the scale

stufen *tr. V.* **a)** step; terrace ⟨*slope*⟩; **b)** *(ab~)* grade ⟨*salaries*⟩; graduate ⟨*prices*⟩

stufen-, Stufen-: ~**barren der** *(Turnen)* asymmetric bars *pl.*; ~**heck das** *(Kfz-W.)* booted rear; ~**leiter die** *(fig.)* hierarchy; ladder *(fig.)*; ~**los 1.** *Adj.* continuously variable; **2.** *adv.* ~**los verstellbar** continuously adjustable; ~**plan der** phased plan; ~**pyramide die** *(Kunstwiss.)* step pyramid; ~**weise 1.** *Adv.* in stages *or* phases; **2.** *adj.; nicht präd.* phased

stufig 1. *Adj.* layered ⟨*hair [style]*⟩; terraced ⟨*terrain*⟩. **2.** *adv.* ~ **geschnittenes Haar** layered hair; hair cut in layers; ~ **gegliedertes Gelände** terraced terrain

-stufig *adj.* -step; *(fig.)* -stage ⟨*development, rocket, filter, etc*⟩; -phase ⟨*plan*⟩

Stuhl [ʃtu:l] **der;** ~[e]s, **Stühle** ['ʃty:lə] **a)** chair; **b)** *(fig.)* **sein** ~ **wackelt** his position is threatened *or* no longer secure; **der Minister klebt an seinem** ~ *(ugs.)* the minister is not to be shifted [from office]; **jmdm. den** ~ **vor die Tür setzen** kick sb. out; show sb. the door; **[fast] vom** ~ **fallen** *(ugs.)* [nearly] have a fit *(coll.)*; **jmdn. vom** ~ **reißen** *od.* **jagen/hauen** *(ugs.)* get sb. excited/take sb.'s breath away; **das hat mich fast** *od.* **bald vom** ~ **gehauen** *(ugs.)* you could have knocked me down with a feather; **sich zwischen zwei Stühle setzen/zwischen zwei Stühlen sitzen** fall/have fallen between two stools; *s. auch* **elektrisch 1; c)** *(kath. Kirche)* see; **der** ~ **Petri** the Holy See *or* See of Rome; *s. auch* **apostolisch b; heilig a; d)** *(Med.)* stool; **e)** *s.* **Stuhlgang a**

Stuhl·bein das chair-leg

Stühlchen ['ʃty:lçən] **das;** ~s, ~: little chair

Stuhl-: ~**gang der;** *o. Pl.* **a)** bowel movement[s]; **b)** *(Kot)* stool; ~**lehne die a)** *(Rückenlehne)* chair-back; **b)** *(Armlehne)* chair-arm; ~**verstopfung die** constipation

Stuka ['ʃtu:ka] **der;** ~s, ~s *(Milit.)* dive-bomber; *(Ju 87)* stuka

Stukkateur [ʃtʊka'tø:ɐ̯] **der;** ~s, ~e [stucco] plasterer

Stulle ['ʃtʊlə] **die;** ~, ~n *(nordostd.)* slice of bread; *(Butter~)* piece of bread and butter; *(belegt)* sandwich

Stulpe ['ʃtʊlpə] **die;** ~, ~n *(am Ärmel)* turned-up cuff; *(am Stiefel)* bucket-top

stülpen ['ʃtʏlpn̩] *tr. V.* **etw. auf** *od.* **über etw.** *(Akk.)* ~: pull/put sth. on to *or* over sth.; **die Taschen nach außen** ~: turn the/one's pockets inside out

Stulpen·stiefel der bucket-top boot

stumm [ʃtʊm] *Adj.* dumb ⟨*person*⟩; *(schweigsam)* silent ⟨*person, reproach, greeting, prayer, etc.*⟩; *(wortlos)* wordless ⟨*greeting, complaint, prayer, gesture, dialogue*⟩; mute ⟨*glance, gesture*⟩; *(Theater)* non-speaking ⟨*part, character*⟩; ~ **vor Schreck** speechless with fear; **sie sahen sich** ~ **an** they looked at one another without speaking *or* in silence; **ein** ~**er Konsonant/Vokal** *(Sprachw.)* a silent *or* mute consonant/vowel; **das** ~**e h** the silent h; the h mute; ~**er Diener** *(Kleiderständer)* valet; *(Serviertisch)* dumb waiter

Stumme der/die; *adj. Dekl.* mute; **die** ~**n** the dumb

Stummel ['ʃtʊml̩] **der;** ~s, ~: stump; *(Bleistift~)* stub; *(Zigaretten~/Zigarren~)* [cigarette-/cigar-]butt

Stummel·schwanz der stumpy tail

Stumm·film der silent film

Stummheit die dumbness; *(Schweigsamkeit)* silence

Stumpen ['ʃtʊmpn̩] **der;** ~s, ~: stumpy cigar

Stümper ['ʃtʏmpɐ] **der;** ~s, ~ *(abwertend)* botcher; bungler

Stümperei die; ~, ~en *(abwertend)* **a)** *o. Pl.* botching; incompetence; **b)** *(Ergebnis)* botched job; piece of incompetence

stümperhaft *(abwertend)* **1.** *Adj.* incompetent; botched ⟨*job*⟩; *(laienhaft)* amateurish ⟨*attempt, drawing*⟩. **2.** *adv.* incompetently; *(laienhaft)* amateurishly

stümpern *itr. V. (abwertend)* work incompetently; *(pfuschen)* bungle

stumpf [ʃtʊmpf] **1.** *Adj.* **a)** blunt ⟨*pin, needle, knife, etc.*⟩; snub ⟨*nose*⟩; flat-topped ⟨*tower*⟩; *(Math.)* truncated ⟨*cone, pyramid*⟩; obtuse ⟨*angle*⟩; **b)** *(glanzlos, matt)* dull ⟨*paint, hair, metal, colour, etc.*⟩; *(rauh)* rough ⟨*stone, wood*⟩; **c)** *(Verslehre)* masculine ⟨*rhyme*⟩; **d)** *(abgestumpft, teilnahmslos)* impassive, lifeless ⟨*person, glance*⟩; impassive, apathetic ⟨*indifference, resignation*⟩; dulled ⟨*senses*⟩; blank ⟨*look, despair*⟩; **e)** *(Med.)* contused ⟨*wound*⟩. **2.** *adv. (abgestumpft)* ⟨*sit, stare*⟩ impassively

Stumpf der; ~[e]s, **Stümpfe** ['ʃtʏmpfə] stump; **etw. mit** ~ **und Stiel ausrotten/vernichten** eradicate/destroy sth. root and branch

Stümpfchen ['ʃtʏmpfçən] **das;** ~s, ~: [little] stump

Stumpfheit die; ~ **a)** bluntness; **b)** *(Abgestumpftheit)* impassiveness; apathy; *(des Blickes)* lifelessness; blankness; *(der Sinne)* dullness

stumpf-, Stumpf-: ~**sinn der;** *o. Pl.* **a)** apathy; **b)** *(Monotonie)* monotony; tedium; ~**sinnig 1.** *Adj.* **a)** apathetic; vacant ⟨*look*⟩; **b)** *(monoton)* tedious; dreary; soul-destroying ‹*job, work*›. **2.** *adv.* **a)** apathetically; ‹*stare*› vacantly; **b)** *(monoton)* tediously; monotonously; **~winklig** *Adj.* obtuse-angled ‹*triangle, intersection*›

Stund [ʃtʊnt] *s.* **Stunde b**

Stündchen ['ʃtʏntçən] **das; ~s, ~** *(fam.)* **[für** *od.* **auf] ein ~:** for an hour or so; **jmds. letztes ~ ist gekommen** *od.* **hat geschlagen** sb.'s last hour has come

Stunde ['ʃtʊndə] **die; ~, ~n a)** hour; **eine ~ Aufenthalt/Pause** an hour's stop/break; a stop/break of an hour; **drei ~n zu Fuß/mit dem Auto** three hours' walk/drive; **120 km in der ~ fahren** do 120 kilometres per hour; **20 Mark [für] die** *od.* **in der** *od.* **pro ~ bekommen** get 20 marks an hour *or* per hour; **jede ~:** once an hour; **nach Stunden bezahlt werden** be paid by the hour; **zur vollen ~:** on the hour; **alle halbe ~:** every half hour; **~ um ~, ~n und ~n** [for] hours; [for] hour after hour; **jmds. letzte ~ hat geschlagen** *od.* **ist gekommen** sb.'s last hour has come; **wissen, was die ~ geschlagen hat** *(fig.)* know how things [really] stand; *(wissen, was einem bevorsteht)* know what's in store *or* what one is in for; **die Männer und Frauen der ersten ~** *(einer Partei o. ä.)* the founder members; **b)** *(geh.) (Zeitpunkt)* hour; *(Zeit)* time; *(Augenblick)* moment; **in ~n der Not/Gefahr** in times of need/danger; **in einer stillen ~:** in a quiet moment; **zu früher/vorgerückter** *od.* **später ~:** at an early/a late hour; **zur ~:** at the present time; **die Gunst der ~ nutzen** make hay while the sun shines *(fig.)*; strike while the iron is hot *(fig.)*; **seine [große] ~ war gekommen** his big moment had come; **die ~ der Wahrheit** the moment of truth; **die ~ Null** [the time of] the new beginning *(esp. in Germany after World War II)*; **von Stund an** *(geh. veralt.)* thenceforth *(arch.)*; *s. auch* **blau; Gebot e; c)** *(Unterrichts~)* lesson; **in der dritten ~:** in the third period; **eine freie ~:** a free period

stünde ['ʃtʏndə] *1. u. 3. Pers. Sg. Konjunktiv II v.* **stehen**

stunden *tr. V.* **jmdm. einen Betrag/eine Rate** *usw.* **~:** give sb. [extra] time to pay *or* allow sb. to defer payment of a sum/an instalment *etc.*; **können Sie mir den Rest bis morgen ~?** will you give me until tomorrow to pay you the rest?

stunden-, Stunden-: ~buch das *(Hist., Kunstwiss.)* book of hours; **~gebet das** *(kath. Kirche) prayer said at the canonical hours;* **~geschwindigkeit die: bei/mit einer ~geschwindigkeit von 60 km** at a speed of 60 k.p.h.; **~glas das** *(veralt.)* hourglass; **~hotel das** sleazy hotel *(which lets rooms by the hour)*; **~kilometer der** *(ugs.)* kilometre per hour; k.p.h.; **er fuhr 120 ~kilometer** he was driving at *or* doing 120 k.p.h.; **~lang 1.** *Adj.; nicht präd.* lasting hours *postpos.*; **das ~lange Warten/Stehen** the hours of waiting/standing; **2.** *adv.* for hours; **~lohn der** hourly wage; **sie bekommt 12 Mark ~lohn** she gets paid 12 marks an hour *or* per hour; **~plan der** timetable; **~schlag der** stroke [of the clock]; **mit dem ~schlag** on the stroke of the hour; **~weise 1.** *Adv.* for an hour or two [at a time]; **er wird ~weise bezahlt** he is paid by the hour; **2.** *adj.; nicht präd.* ‹*hiring, payment*› by the hour; **~zahl die** number of hours; *(von Unterrichtsstunden)* number of lessons; **~zeiger der** hour-hand

-stündig *adj.* -hour

Stündlein das; ~s, ~ *s.* **Stündchen**

-stündlich *adj.* -hourly; **zwei~/halb~:** two-hourly/half-hourly; *adv.* every two hours/half an hour

stündlich 1. *Adj.* hourly. **2.** *adv.* **a)** hourly; once an hour; **sich ~ verändern** change from hour to hour *or* from one hour to the next; **b)** *(jeden Augenblick)* at any moment; **etw. ~ erwarten** expect sth. hourly

Stundung die; ~, ~en deferment of payment

Stunk [ʃtʊŋk] **der; ~s** *(ugs.)* trouble; **~ machen/anfangen** cause/start trouble

stupid[e] [ʃtu'pi:də] *(abwertend)* **1.** *Adj.* **a)** moronic, empty-headed ‹*person*›; moronic, vacuous ‹*expression*›; **b)** *(monoton)* soul-destroying. **2.** *adv.* moronically

Stupidität [ʃtupidi'tɛ:t] **die; ~** *(abwertend)* **a)** moronic stupidity *or* vacuity; **b)** *(Monotonie)* deadly monotony *or* tedium

Stups [ʃtʊps] **der; ~es, ~e** *(ugs.)* push; shove; *(leicht)* nudge

stupsen *tr. V. (ugs.)* push; shove; *(leicht)* nudge

Stups·nase die snub nose

stur *(ugs.)* **1.** *Adj.* **a)** *(abwertend) (eigensinnig, unnachgiebig)* obstinate; pig-headed; obstinate, dogged ‹*insistence*›; *(phlegmatisch)* stolid; dour; **ein ~er Bock** a pig-headed so-and-so *(coll.)*; **du ~er Bock!** you're as obstinate as a mule!; **~ wie ein Panzer** stubborn as a mule; **auf ~ schalten** dig one's heels in; **sich ~ stellen, ~ bleiben** not give in; **b)** *(unbeirrbar)* dogged; persistent; **~es Geradeausgehen** just keeping straight on; **c)** *(abwertend: stumpfsinnig)* tedious; **~es Auswendiglernen** soul-destroying *or* mechanical learning by rote. **2.** *adv.* **a)** *(abwertend: eigensinnig, unnachgiebig)* obstinately; **b)** *(unbeirrbar)* doggedly; **sie las/redete ~ weiter** she carried on reading/kept on talking regardless; **c)** *(abwertend: stumpfsinnig)* tediously; ‹*learn, copy*› mechanically

stürbe ['ʃtʏrbə] *1. u. 3. Pers. Sg. Konjunktiv II v.* **sterben**

Sturheit die; ~ *(ugs. abwertend)* **a)** *(Eigensinnigkeit, Unnachgiebigkeit)* obstinacy; pig-headedness; *(phlegmatisches Wesen)* stolidity; dourness; **b)** *(Stumpfsinnigkeit)* deadly monotony

Sturm [-] **der; ~[e]s, Stürme** ['ʃtʏrmə] **a)** storm; *(heftiger Wind)* gale; **bei** *od.* **in ~ und Regen** in the wind and rain; **ein ~ im Wasserglas** a storm in a teacup; **das Barometer steht auf ~** *(fig.)* there's a storm brewing; **ein ~ der Begeisterung/des Protests** tumultuous *or* tempestuous applause/a storm of protest; **~ und Drang** *(Literaturw.)* Storm and Stress; *s. auch* **Ruhe c; b)** *(Milit.: Angriff)* assault **(auf + Akk.** on); **der ~ auf die Bastille** *(hist.)* the storming of the Bastille; **etw. im ~ erobern** *od.* **nehmen** *(auch fig.)* take sth. by storm; **gegen etw. ~ laufen** *(fig.)* be up in arms against sth.; **~ klingeln** ring the [door]bell like mad; lean on the [door]bell; **c)** *(Sport: die Stürmer)* forward line; **im ~ spielen** play up front; **d)** *o. Pl. (österr.: Most) s.* **Federweiße**

Sturm-: ~ab·teilung die *(ns.) armed and uniformed branch of the NSDAP;* SA; **~an·griff der** *(Milit.)* assault **(auf + Akk.** on); **~bock der** *(hist.)* battering-ram

stürmen ['ʃtʏrmən] **1.** *itr. V.* **a)** *unpers.* **es stürmt [heftig]** it's blowing a gale; **b)** *mit sein (rennen)* rush; *(verärgert)* storm; **zum Ausgang ~:** make a rush for the exit; **c)** *(Sport: als Stürmer spielen)* play up front *or* as a striker; **d)** *(Sport, Milit.: angreifen)* attack. **2.** *tr. V. (Milit.)* storm ‹*town, position, etc.*›; *(fig.)* besiege ‹*booking-office, shop, etc.*›; **den Saal ~:** force one's way into the hall

Stürmer ['ʃtʏrmɐ] **der; ~s, ~ a)** *(Sport)* striker; forward; **b) ~ und Dränger** *(Literaturw.)* Storm and Stress writer; **die ~ und Dränger in der Partei** *(fig.)* the radical faction in the party

sturm-, Sturm-: ~flut die storm tide; **~frei** *Adj. (scherzh.)* **eine ~freie Bude haben** have a place where one can do as one likes [without interference/objections]; **~gepäck das** *(Milit.)* combat pack; **~gepeitscht** *Adj. (geh.)* ‹*forest, trees*› bending before the storm; storm-tossed ‹*sea*›

stürmisch ['ʃtʏrmɪʃ] **1.** *Adj.* **a)** stormy; *(fig.)* tempestuous, turbulent ‹*days, life, times, years*›; **b)** *(ungestüm)* tempestuous ‹*nature, outburst, welcome*›; tumultuous ‹*applause, welcome, reception*›; wild ‹*enthusiasm*›; passionate ‹*lover, embrace, temperament*›; vehement ‹*protest*›; **~es Gelächter** gales of laughter; **er näherte sich mit ~en Schritten** he approached with impetuous steps; **nicht so ~!** calm down!; take it easy!; **c)** *(rasant)* meteoric ‹*development, growth*›; lightning, breakneck ‹*speed*›. **2.** *adv.* **a)** ‹*protest*› vehemently; ‹*embrace*› impetuously, passionately; ‹*demand*› clamorously; ‹*applaud*› wildly; **jmdn. ~ begrüßen/empfangen** give sb. a tumultuous welcome/reception; **b)** *(rasant)* at a tremendous rate *or* speed; at lightning speed

sturm-, Sturm-: ~laterne die storm-lantern *(Brit.)*; hurricane-lamp; **~lauf der: im ~lauf** at the double; **~leiter die** *(Milit. hist.)* scaling-ladder; **~möwe die** sea-mew; common gull; **~reif** *Adj. (Milit. hist.)* ready to be stormed *postpos.*; **die Stadt ~reif schießen** soften the town up with a bombardment [preparatory to the assault]; **~schaden der** gale *or* storm damage *no pl., no indef. art.*; **~schritt der: im ~schritt** at the double; **~segel das** storm-sail; **~tief das** *(Met.)* deep low

Sturm-und-Drang-Zeit die; *o. Pl. (Literaturw.)* Storm and Stress period; **in meiner ~** *(fig. scherzh.)* [in the days] when I was sowing my wild oats

Sturm-: ~vogel der *(Zool.)* petrel; **~warnung die** *(Seew.)* gale warning; **~wind der** *(dichter., geh.)* tempest *(literary)*

Sturz [ʃtʊrts] **der; -es, Stürze** ['ʃtʏrtsə] **a)** fall **(aus, von** from); *(Unfall)* accident; **ein ~ in die Tiefe** a plunge into the depths; **bei einem ~ vom Pferd** falling off a horse; **b)** *(fig.: von Preis, Temperatur usw.)* [sharp] fall, drop (*Gen.* in); **c)** *(Verlust des Amtes, der Macht)* fall; *(Absetzung)* overthrow; *(Amtsenthebung)* removal from office; **d)** *(Kfz-W.)* camber; **e)** *Pl. auch* **~e** *(Fenster~, Tür~)* lintel

Sturz·bach der [mountain] torrent; *(fig.: von Fragen usw.)* torrent

stürzen ['ʃtʏrtsn̩] **1.** *itr. V.; mit sein* **a)** fall **(aus, von** from); *(in die Tiefe)* plunge; plummet; *(fig.)* ‹*temperature, exchange rate, etc.*› drop [sharply]; ‹*prices*› tumble; ‹*government*› fall, collapse; **beim Rollschuhlaufen/auf dem Eis ~:** have a fall while roller-skating/on the ice; **mit dem Pferd/Fahrrad ~:** come off one's horse/bicycle; **b)** *(laufen)* rush; dash; **er stürzte ins Zimmer** he burst into the room; **jmdm. in die Arme ~:** hurl *or* fling oneself into sb.'s arms; **c)** *(fließen)* stream; pour; **d)** *(geh.: steil abfallen)* plunge. **2.** *refl. V.* **sich auf jmdn./etw. ~** *(auch fig.)* pounce on sb./sth.; **sich in etw.** *(Akk.)* **~:** throw oneself *or* plunge into sth.; **sich in die Arbeit ~:** throw oneself into one's work; **sich ins Vergnügen ~:** abandon oneself to pleasure. **3.** *tr. V.* **a)** throw; *(mit Wucht)* hurl; **sich aus dem Fenster/von der Brücke ~:** hurl oneself *or* leap out of the window/off the bridge; **sich in die Tiefe ~:** plunge into the depths; **jmdn. ins Verderben/Unglück ~:** plunge sb. into ruin/misfortune; **b)** *(umdrehen)* upturn, turn upside-down ‹*mould, pot, box, glass, cup*›; turn out ‹*pudding, cake, etc.*›; **„[bitte] nicht ~"** 'this way up'; **c)** *(des Amtes entheben)* oust ‹*person*› [from office]; *(gewaltsam)* overthrow, topple ‹*leader, government*›

Sturz-: ~flug der *(Flugw.)* [nose-]dive; **im ~flug** in a [nose-]dive; **~geburt die** *(Med.)* precipitate delivery; **~helm der** crash-helmet; **~kampf·flugzeug das** dive-bomber; **~regen der** torrential downpour; **~see die, ~welle die** breaking wave; [heavy] sea; *(am Strand usw.)* breaker

Stuß [ʃtʊs] **der; Stusses** *(ugs. abwertend)* rubbish; twaddle *(coll.)*

Stute ['ʃtu:tə] **die; ~, ~n** mare; *(Esel~)* she-ass

Stuten der; ~s, ~ *(nordd.)* currant bread; fruit loaf

Stut[en]-: ~fohlen das, ~füllen das filly

Stütz der; ~es, ~e *(Geräteturnen)* support

Stütze die; ~, ~n a) *(auch fig.)* support; *(für die Wäscheleine)* prop; **~n für Kopf, Arme und Füße** head-, arm-, and foot-rests; **an jmdm. eine ~ haben** *(fig.)* get support *or* help from sb.; **er ist die ~ der Familie** *(fig.)* he is he mainstay of the family; **die ~n der Gesellschaft** *(fig.)* the pillars of society; **b)** *(salopp: Arbeitslosengeld)* dole *(coll.)*; **von der ~ leben** live on the dole *(Brit. coll.)*

[1]**stutzen** ['ʃtʊtsn̩] *itr. V.* stop short

[2]**stutzen** *tr. V.* trim; dock ‹*tail*›; clip ‹*ear, hedge, wing*›; prune ‹*tree, bush*›

Stutzen der; ~s, ~ a) *(Gewehr)* carbine; **b)** *(Technik: Rohrstück)* pipe-end; spout; *(zum Einfüllen)* filler pipe; **c)** *(Kniestrumpf)* [knee-]sock *(without a foot)*; *(Fußball)* [football]sock

stützen ['ʃtʏtsn̩] **1.** *tr. V.* **a)** support; *(mit Pfosten o.ä.)* prop up; *(aufstützen)* rest ‹*head, hands, arms, etc.*› **(auf** + *Akk.* on); **die Hände in die Seiten/den Kopf in die Hände gestützt** hands on hips/head in hands; **wo sind die Beweise, auf die Sie Ihre Anschuldigungen ~?** where is the evidence to support your accusations *or* on which your accusations are based?; **b)** *(Wirtsch.)* support ‹*currency, exchange rate, price*›; *(DDR: niedrig halten)* peg ‹*prices*›. **2.** *refl. V.* **sich auf jmdn./etw. ~:** lean *or* support oneself on sb./sth.; **sich auf Fakten** *(Akk.)* **~** *(fig.)* ‹*theory, statement etc.*› be based on facts; **er kann sich auf keinerlei Fakten ~:** he has no facts to support his case

Stutzer der; ~s, ~ *(veralt. abwertend)* dandy; fop

stutzerhaft 1. *Adj.* dandyish. **2.** *adv.* like a dandy

Stutz·flügel der *(Musik)* baby grand [piano]

Stütz·gewebe das *(Anat., Biol.)* stroma

stutzig *Adj.* **~ werden** begin to wonder; get suspicious; **jmdn. ~ machen** make sb. wonder; make sb. suspicious

Stütz-: ~korsett das [support] corset; **~mauer die** supporting wall; **~pfeiler der** [supporting] pillar; **~punkt der** *(bes. Milit.)* base; **~rad das** stabilizer *(for bicycle)*; **~strumpf der** support stocking

Stützung die; ~, ~en a) support; **zur ~ seiner Behauptung sagte er ...:** in support of his statement, he said ...; **b)** *(Wirtsch.)* *(von Währung, Kursen)* support; *(DDR: von Preisen)* pegging

Stützungs·kauf der *(Wirtsch.)* support purchase

Stütz·verband der *(Med.)* support bandage

StVO [ɛste vau'o:] **die; ~** *Abk.* **Straßenverkehrsordnung**

stylen ['stailən] *tr. V.* *(ugs.)* style ‹*car etc.*›; do up ‹*person*›; **ein hervorragend gestyltes Modell** a model with outstanding lines

Styling ['stailɪŋ] **das; ~s, ~s** styling

Styropor Ⓦⓩ [ʃtyro'po:ɐ̯] **das; ~s** polystyrene [foam]

Styx [ʃtʏks] **der; ~** *(griech. Myth.)* Styx

s.u. *Abk.* **siehe unten** see below

SU *Abk.* **Sowjetunion**

Suada ['zu̯a:da] **die; ~, Suaden** *(geh. abwertend)* harangue; diatribe

Suaheli [zu̯a'he:li] **das; ~[s]** Swahili; *s. auch* **Deutsch**

subaltern [zʊp|al'tɛrn] *(geh.)* **1.** *Adj.* **a)** *(untergeordnet)* subordinate; **b)** *(abwertend)* *(unselbständig)* unoriginal ‹*mind, literature*›; *(unterwürfig)* servile. **2.** *adv.* *(abwertend: unterwürfig)* in a servile manner

Subbotnik [zʊ'bɔtnɪk] **der; ~[s], ~s** *(DDR)* *voluntary work (usually on a Saturday) done without payment*

Sub·dominante ['zʊp-] **die** *(Musik)* subdominant; *(Dreiklang)* subdominant chord

Subjekt [zʊp'jɛkt] **das; ~[e]s, ~e a)** subject; **b)** *(abwertend: Mensch)* creature; type *(coll.)*

subjektiv [zʊpjɛk'ti:f] **1.** *Adj.* subjective. **2.** *adv.* subjectively

subjektivieren *tr. V.* *(geh.)* subjectivize

Subjektivismus der; ~: subjectivism

Subjektivität [zʊpjɛktivi'tɛ:t] **die; ~:** subjectivity

Subjekt·satz der *(Sprachw.)* subject clause

Sub-: ~kontinent der *(Geogr.)* subcontinent; **~kultur die** *(Soziol.)* subculture

subkutan [zʊpku'ta:n] *(Anat., Med.)* **1.** *Adj.* subcutaneous. **2.** *adv.* subcutaneously

sublim [zu'bli:m] *(geh.)* **1.** *Adj.* subtle; *(erhaben)* sublime. **2.** *adv.* subtly

Sublimation [zublima'tsi̯o:n] **die; ~, ~en** *(Chemie)* sublimation

sublimieren *tr., itr. V.* sublimate

Sublimierung die; ~, ~en sublimation

Sublimität [zublimi'tɛ:t] **die; ~** *(geh.)* subtlety

submarin *Adj.* submarine

Subordination die *(bes. Logik)* subordination **(unter** + *Akk.* to)

subsidiär [zʊpzi'di̯ɛ:ɐ̯] *(bes. Rechtsw.)* **1.** *Adj.* **a)** *(unterstützend)* supplementary ‹*measures*›; **b)** *(als Behelf dienend)* provisional ‹*law etc.*›. **2.** *adv.* **a) ~ tätig werden** play a supporting role; **b)** *(behelfsmäßig)* on a provisional basis

Subsidiarität [zʊpzidi̯ari'tɛ:t] **die; ~** *(Politik, Soziol.)* subsidiarity *no art.*

Subskribent [zʊpskri'bɛnt] **der, Subskribentin die** *(Buchw.)* subscriber

subskribieren [zʊpskri'bi:rən] *(Buchw.)* **1.** *tr. V.* subscribe to. **2.** *itr. V.* take out a subscription

Subskription [zʊpskrɪp'tsi̯o:] **die; ~, ~en** *(Buchw.)* subscription

Subskriptions·preis der *(Buchw.)* subscription price

substantiell [zʊpstan'tsi̯ɛl] *(geh.)* **1.** *Adj.* substantial. **2.** *adv.* substantially

Substantiv ['zʊpstanti:f] **das; ~s, ~e** *(Sprachw.)* noun

substantivieren *tr. V.* *(Sprachw.)* nominalize

substantivisch *(Sprachw.)* **1.** *Adj.* nominal. **2.** *adv.* **~ gebraucht** used as nouns/a noun; nominalized

Substanz [zʊp'stants] **die; ~, ~en a)** *(auch fig.)* substance; **b)** *(Grundbestand)* **die ~:** the reserves *pl.*; **etw. geht an die ~** *(fig. ugs.)* *(seelisch, nervlich)* sth. gets you down; *(körperlich)* sth. takes it out of you; **von der ~ zehren** live off one's reserves *or* capital

substituieren [zʊpstitu'i:rən] *tr. V.* *(geh., fachspr.)* replace

Substitut [zʊpsti'tu:t] **der; ~en, ~en** assistant manager

Substitution [zʊpstitu'tsi̯o:n] **die; ~, ~en** *(geh., fachspr.)* replacement

Substrat [zʊp'stra:t] **das; ~[e]s, ~e** *(geh., fachspr.)* substratum

subsumieren [zʊpzu'mi:rən] *tr. V.* *(geh.)* subsume **(unter** + *Dat. od. Akk.* under)

subtil [zʊp'ti:l] *(geh.)* **1.** *Adj.* subtle. **2.** *adv.* subtly

Subtilität [zʊptili'tɛ:t] **die; ~, ~en** *(geh.)* subtlety

Subtrahend [zʊptra'hɛnt] **der; ~en, ~en** *(Math.)* subtrahend

subtrahieren *tr., itr. V.* *(Math.)* subtract

Subtraktion [zʊptrak'tsi̯o:n] **die; ~, ~en** *(Math.)* subtraction

Sub·tropen *Pl.* *(Geogr.)* subtropics

sub·tropisch *Adj.* subtropical

Subvention [zʊpvɛn'tsi̯o:n] **die; ~, ~en** *(Wirtsch.)* subsidy

subventionieren *tr. V.* *(Wirtsch.)* subsidize

Sub·version die *(Politik)* subversion

subversiv [zʊpvɛr'zi:f] *(Politik)* **1.** *Adj.* subversive. **2.** *adv.* subversively

Such-: ~aktion die search [operation]; **~anzeige die a)** missing-person report; **b)** *(in der Zeitung)* 'lost' advertisement; **~bild das** *s.* **Vexierbild**

Suche ['zu:xə] **die; ~, ~n** search **(nach** for); **auf der ~ [nach jmdm./etw.] sein** be looking/ *(intensiver)* searching [for sb./sth.]; **sich [nach jmdm./etw.] auf die ~ machen, [nach jmdm/etw.] auf die ~ gehen** start searching *or* start a search [for sb./sth.]

suchen 1. *tr. V.* **a)** look for; *(intensiver)* search for; **gesucht wird der 54jährige XY** a search is going on for the 54-year-old XY; **„Kellner/Leerzimmer gesucht“** 'waiter/unfurnished room wanted'; **„Gesucht: Jesse James“** 'Wanted: Jesse James'; **die beiden haben sich gesucht und gefunden** *(ugs.)* those two were made for each other; **solche Menschen/jemanden wie ihn kann man ~** *(ugs.)* you don't come across people like that/someone like him every day; **seinesgleichen ~:** be without equal *or* unequalled; **b)** *(bedacht sein auf, sich wünschen)* seek ‹*protection, advice, company, warmth, etc.*›; look for ‹*adventure*›; **Kontakt** *od.* **Anschluß ~:** try to get to know people; **Streit ~:** seek a quarrel; **was sucht er denn hier?** what does he want here?; **er hat hier nichts zu ~** *(ugs.)* he has no business [to be] here; **an meinem Schreibtisch hat sie nichts zu ~** *(ugs.)* she's got no right *or* business to be at my desk; **c)** *(geh.: trachten)* **~, etw. zu tun** seek *or* endeavour to do sth. **2.** *itr. V.* search; **ich habe überall gesucht** I've looked everywhere; **nach jmdm./etw. ~:** look/search for sb./sth.; **da kannst du lange ~!** *(ugs.)* you're wasting your time looking for that; **sich ~d umsehen** look around; **such, such!** *(an einen Hund)* seek, seek!; **wer sucht, der findet** he who seeks shall find; seek, and ye shall find *(Bibl.)*; **Suchen spielen** *(landsch.)* play hide-and-seek

Sucher der; ~s, ~ *(Fot.)* viewfinder

Sucherei die; ~, ~en *(ugs., oft abwertend)* [endless] searching *no pl.*

Such-: ~hund der tracker dog; **~meldung die** announcement about a missing or wanted person; **~schein·werfer der** searchlight

Sucht [zʊxt] **die; ~, Süchte** [zʏçtə] *od.* **~en a)** addiction **(nach** to); **[bei jmdm.] zur ~ werden** *(auch fig.)* become addictive [in sb.'s case]; **b)** *Pl.* **Süchte** *(übermäßiges Verlangen)* craving, obsessive desire **(nach** for); **ihre krankhafte ~, immer alles besser zu wissen** her pathological obsession with knowing better all the time

süchtig ['zʏçtɪç] *Adj.* **a)** addicted; **~ machen** *(auch fig.)* be addictive; **~ [nach etw.] sein** *(auch fig.)* be an addict *or* addicted [to sth.]; **b)** *(versessen, begierig)* obsessive; **nach etw. ~ sein** be obsessed with sth.

-süchtig a) ‹*drug-, heroin-, morphine-, etc.*› addicted; **alkohol~ sein** be an alcoholic; **b)** *(fig.)* addicted to ‹*television*›; obsessed with ‹*death*›; craving for ‹*liberation, love, home, sex*›

Süchtige der/die; *adj. Dekl.*, **Suchtkranke der/die** addict

Sud [zu:t] **der; ~[e]s, ~e a)** stock; **b)** *(Extrakt)* decoction

[1]**Süd** [zy:t] *o. Art.; o. Pl.* **a)** *(Seemannsspr., Met.: Richtung)* **nach ~:** southwards; to the south; **aus** *od.* **von ~:** from the south; **b)** *(südliches Gebiet, Politik)* South; *s. auch* [1]**Nord b; c)** *einem Subst. nachgestellt* **Autobahnausfahrt Frankfurt-~:** Frankfurt South motorway *(Brit.) or (Amer.)* freeway exit; **Europa ~** *(Milit.)* Southern Europe

[2]**Süd der; ~[e]s, ~e** *(Seemannsspr., dichter.)* southerly

süd-, Süd-: ~afrika (das) South Africa; **~afrikanisch** *Adj.* South African; **~amerika (das)** South America; **~amerikaner der** South American; **~amerikanisch** *Adj.* South American

Sudan [zu'da:n] **(das); ~s** *od.* **der; ~s** Sudan

Sudanese der; ~n, ~n Sudanese

süd·deutsch *Adj.* South German; *s. auch* **norddeutsch**

Süd·deutschland (das) South Germany

Sudelei die; ~, ~en *(ugs. abwertend)* **a)** *(das Sudeln)* making *no art.* a [disgusting] mess; **b)** *(gesudelte Arbeit)* **[eine] ~ sein** be a [disgusting] mess

sudeln ['zu:dl̩n] *itr. V. (ugs. abwertend)* make a [disgusting] mess; *(pfuschen)* make a mess of it; botch it

Süden der; ~s a) *(Richtung)* south; *s. auch* **Norden a; b)** *(Gegend)* southern part; **aus dem ~:** from the south; **c)** *(Geogr.)* South; **der tiefe/tiefste ~:** the far South

Süd·england (das) Southern England; the South of England

Sudeten [zu'de:tn̩] *Pl.* **die ~:** the Sudeten [Mountains]

Sudeten·deutsche der/die Sudeten German

Sudeten·land das; ~[e]s Sudetenland

süd-, Süd-: ~europa (das) Southern Europe; **~europäisch** *Adj.* Southern European; **~flanke die** *(Met., Milit.)* southern flank; *(Geogr.: eines Gebirges)* southern escarpment; **~frucht die** tropical [or subtropical] fruit; **~hang der** southern slope

Sud·haus das mashhouse

Süd-: ~insel die South Island; **~korea (das)** South Korea; **~küste die** south coast

Südländer ['zy:tlɛndɐ] **der; ~s, ~:** Southern European; Mediterranean type

südländisch *Adj.* Southern [European]; Mediterranean; Latin ⟨*temperament*⟩; **~ aussehen** have Latin looks; look like a Southern European

südlich 1. *Adj.* **a)** *(im Süden gelegen)* southern; *s. auch* **Eismeer; nördlich 1 a; Polarkreis; Wendekreis a; b)** *(nach Süden gerichtet, von Süden kommend)* southerly; **c)** *(aus dem Süden kommend, für den Süden typisch)* Southern. **2.** *adv.* southwards; *s. auch* **nördlich 2. 3.** *Präp. mit Gen.* [to the] south of

süd-, Süd-: ~licht ['--] **das;** *Pl.* **~lichter a)** *(Polarlicht)* southern lights *pl.*; *(einzelne Erscheinung)* display of the southern lights; **b)** *(iron.: Mensch aus Süddeutschland)* South German type; [1]**~ost** *o. Art.; o. Pl. (Seemannsspr., Met.)* south-east; *s. auch* [1]**Nord a;** [1]**Nordost;** [2]**~ost der** *(Seemannsspr.)* southeaster[ly]; south-easter[ly] [wind]; **~osten der** south-east; **der ~osten [Englands]** the South-East [of England]; *s. auch* **Norden; ~östlich 1.** *Adj.* south-eastern; south-easterly ⟨*direction, wind, course*⟩; **2.** *adv.* **~östlich [von X] liegen** be to the south-east [of X]; **3.** *Präp. mit Gen.* [to the] south-east of; **~ost·wind der** south-east[erly] wind; **~pol** ['--] **der a)** South Pole; **b)** *(eines Magneten)* south pole

Süd·polar-: ~gebiet das Antarctic [Region]; **~meer das; ~[e]s** Antarctic Ocean

süd-, Süd-: ~pol·expedition ['-------] **die** expedition to the South Pole; **~rand** ['--] **der** southern edge; **~see** ['--] **die; ~: die ~:** the South Seas *pl.*; **~see·insel** ['----] **die** South Sea island; **~seite** ['---] **die** south side; **~staaten** ['---] *Pl.* southern States; [1]**~süd·ost** *o. Art.; o. Pl. (Seemannsspr., Met.)* south-south-east; *s. auch* [1]**Nord a;** [2]**~süd·ost der;** *Pl. selten (Seemannsspr.)* south-south-easterly; **~süd·osten der** south-south-east; *s. auch* **Norden a;** [1]**~süd·west** *o. Art.; o. Pl. (Seemannsspr., Met.)* south-south-west[erly]; *s. auch* [1]**Nord a;** [2]**~süd·west der,** *Pl. selten (Seemannsspr.)* south-south-westerly; **~süd·westen der** south-south-west; *s. auch* **Norden a; ~tirol** ['---] **(das)** South Tirol; **~wand** ['--] **die** south face; **~wärts** ['--] *Adv.* southwards; **~wein** ['--] **der** dessert wine; [1]**~west** *o. Art.; o. Pl.* south-west; *s. auch* [1]**Nord a;** [1]**Nordwest;** [2]**~west der;** *Pl. selten (Seemannsspr.)* southwester[ly]; *(dichter.)* south-west[erly] wind; **~west·afrika (das)** South-West Africa; **~westen der** south-west; **der ~westen [Deutschlands]** the South-West [of Germany]; *s. auch* **Norden a; ~wester der; ~s, ~:** sou'wester; **~west·funk der** South West German Radio; **~westlich 1.** *Adj.* south-western; south-westerly ⟨*direction, course, wind*⟩; **2.** *adv.* **~ [von X] liegen** be to the south-west [of X]; **3.** *Präp. mit Gen.* [to the] south-west of; **~west·wind der** south-west[erly] wind; **~wind** ['--] **der** south *or* southerly wind

Sues·kanal ['zu:ɛs-] **der; ~s** Suez Canal

Suff [zʊf] **der; ~[e]s** *(salopp)* **a) im ~:** while under the influence *(coll.)*; **b)** *(Trunksucht)* boozing *(coll.)*; **dem ~ verfallen sein/sich dem ~ ergeben** be/become a victim of the demon drink; be on/take to the bottle *(coll.)*

süffeln ['zyfl̩n] *tr., itr. V. (ugs.)* tipple *(coll.)*

süffig *Adj. (ugs.)* [very] drinkable; **dieser Wein ist sehr ~:** this wine goes down very well

Süffisance [zyfi'zã:s] **die; ~** *s.* **Süffisanz**

süffisant [zyfi'zant] *(geh. abwertend)* **1.** *Adj.* smug. **2.** *adv.* smugly

Süffisanz [syfi'zants] **die; ~** *(geh. abwertend)* smugness

Suffix [zʊ'fɪks] **das; ~es, ~e** *(Sprachw.)* suffix

Suffragette [zʊfra'gɛtə] **die; ~, ~n** *(hist.)* suffragette; *(veralt. abwertend: Frauenrechtlerin)* campaigner for women's rights

suggerieren [zʊge'ri:rən] *tr. V.* **a)** *(geh., Psych.)* suggest; **jmdm. etw. ~:** suggest sth. to sb.; put sth. into sb.'s mind; **b)** *(geh.: den Eindruck erwecken)* suggest; give the *or* an impression of; **das mußte ~, daß ...:** this was bound to give the impression that ...

Suggestion [zʊgɛs'ti̯o:n] **die; ~, ~en a)** *(geh., Psych.)* suggestion; **b)** *o. Pl. (geh.: suggestive Wirkung)* suggestive effect *or* power

suggestiv [zʊgɛs'ti:f] *(geh., Psych.)* **1.** *Adj.* suggestive. **2.** *adv.* suggestively

Suggestiv·frage die leading question

Suhle ['zu:lə] **die; ~, ~n** muddy pool

suhlen *refl. V.* wallow

Sühne ['zy:nə] **die; ~, ~n** *(geh.)* atonement; expiation; **~ [für etw.] leisten** make atonement *or* atone [for sth.]

sühnen 1. *tr., itr. V. (abbüßen)* **[für] etw. ~:** atone for *or* pay the penalty for sth. **2.** *tr. V. (bestrafen)* punish ⟨*wrongdoing*⟩

Sühne-: ~opfer das *(Rel.)* expiatory sacrifice; **~termin der** *(Rechtsw.)* conciliation hearing

Sühn·opfer das *s.* **Sühneopfer**

Suite ['svi:t(ə)] **die; ~, ~n** suite

Suizid [zui'tsi:t] **der** *od.* **das; ~[e]s, ~e** *(bes. Med., Psych.)* suicide

Sujet [zy'ʒe] **das; ~s, ~s** *(bes. Literaturw., bild. Kunst)* subject

Sukkade [zʊ'ka:də] **die; ~, ~n** candied peel

Sukkulente [zʊku'lɛntə] **die; ~, ~n** *(Bot.)* succulent

sukzessiv [zʊktsɛ'si:f] **1.** *Adj.* gradual. **2.** *adv.* gradually

sukzessive *Adv.* gradually

Sulfat [zʊl'fa:t] **das; ~[e]s, ~e** *(Chemie)* sulphate

Sulfid [zʊl'fi:t] **das; ~[e]s, ~e** *(Chemie)* sulphide

Sulfit [zʊl'fi:t] **das; ~s, ~e** *(Chemie)* sulphite

Sulfonamid [sʊlfona'mi:t] **das; ~[e]s, ~e** *(Pharm.)* sulphonamide

Sulky ['zʊlki] **das; ~s, ~s** *(Pferdesport)* sulky

Sultan ['zʊlta:n] **der; ~s, ~e** sultan

Sultanat [zʊlta'na:t] **das; ~[e]s, ~e** sultanate

Sultanine [sʊlta'ni:nə] **die; ~, ~n** sultana

Sülze ['zʏltsə] **die; ~, ~n a)** diced meat/fish in aspic; *(vom Schweinskopf)* brawn; **b)** *(Aspik)* aspic

sülzen ['zʏltsn̩] *tr., itr. V. (salopp) s.* **quatschen 1 a, 2**

Sülz·kotelett das boned pork chop in aspic

Sumerer [zu'me:rɐ] **der; ~s, ~:** Sumerian

summ [zʊm] *Interj.* buzz

summa cum laude ['zʊma kʊm 'laudə] *Adv. (Hochschulw.)* with the utmost distinction; *highest of four grades of successful doctoral examination*

Summand [zʊ'mant] **der; ~en, ~en** *(Math.)* summand

summarisch [zʊ'ma:rɪʃ] *(geh.)* **1.** *Adj.* summary; brief ⟨*summary*⟩; **ein ~es Verfahren** *(Rechtsw.)* summary proceedings *pl.* **2.** *adv.* summarily; briefly

summa summarum ['zʊma zʊ'ma:rʊm] *Adv.* in all; altogether

Sümmchen ['zʏmçən] **das; ~s, ~** *(ugs.)* **ein hübsches** *od.* **nettes ~:** a tidy little sum *(coll.)*

Summe ['zʊmə] **die; ~, ~n** sum

summen 1. *itr. V.* hum; *(lauter, heller)* buzz; **es summt** there's a hum/buzzing. **2.** *tr., auch itr. V.* hum ⟨*tune, song, etc.*⟩

Summer der; ~s, ~: buzzer

summieren *refl. V.* add up **(auf +** *Akk.* to); *(anwachsen)* ⟨*number*⟩ grow, increase **(auf +** *Akk.* to)

Summ·ton der buzzing [tone]; *(leiser)* hum

Sumpf [zʊmpf] **der; ~[e]s, Sümpfe** ['zʏmpfə] marsh; *(bes. in den Tropen)* swamp; *(fig.)* morass; quagmire; **im ~ steckenbleiben** be stuck in the mire

Sumpf·dotter·blume die marsh marigold

sumpfen *itr. V. (salopp)* make whoopee *(coll.) or* live it up into the small hours

Sumpf-: ~fieber das malaria; **~gas das** marsh gas; **~gebiet das** marsh[land]; *(bes. in den Tropen)* swamp[land]; **~huhn das** crake

sumpfig *Adj.* marshy

Sumpf·pflanze die marsh plant

Sums [zʊms] **der; ~es** *(ugs.)* **viel ~ um etw. machen** make a lot of fuss about sth.

Sund [zʊnt] **der; ~[e]s, ~e** *(Geogr.)* sound

Sünde ['zʏndə] **die; ~, ~n** sin; *(fig.)* misdeed; transgression; **in ~ leben** *(veralt.)* live in sin; **faul wie die ~:** bone idle; **eine ~ wert sein** *(scherzh.)* be worth a little transgression; ⟨*food*⟩ be naughty but nice; **es ist eine ~ [und Schande]** it's a crying shame

Sünden-: ~babel das sink of iniquity; **~bekenntnis das** confession of one's sins; **~bock der** *(ugs.)* scapegoat; **~fall der** *(christl. Rel.)* Fall of Man; *(fig.)* fall from grace; **~geld das: ein ~geld** *(ugs.)* a small fortune; **~pfuhl der** *(abwertend)* sink of iniquity; **~register das** *(ugs. scherzh.)* catalogue of misdeeds

Sünder der; ~s, ~, Sünderin die; ~, ~nen sinner

Sünd·flut die; *o. Pl. s.* **Sintflut**

sündhaft 1. *Adj.* **a)** sinful; **b)** *(ugs.)* **ein ~er Preis/~es Geld** an outrageous price/amount of money. **2.** *adv.* **a)** sinfully; **b)** *(ugs.: sehr)* outrageously ⟨*expensive*⟩; stunningly ⟨*beautiful*⟩; **~ faul** bone idle

Sündhaftigkeit die; ~: sinfulness

sündig 1. *Adj.* sinful; *(lasterhaft)* wicked. **2.** *adv.* sinfully

sündigen *itr. V.* sin; *(scherzh.: viel essen)* indulge oneself [sinfully]; **gegen die Natur ~** *(fig.)* offend against nature

Sunnit [zʊ'ni:t] **der; ~en, ~en** Sunnite

sunnitisch *Adj.* Sunnite

super *(salopp)* **1.** *indekl. Adj.* super *(coll.)*; fantastic *(coll.)*; **~ aussehen/ sich ~ fühlen**

look/feel great *(coll.)*. **2.** *adv.* fantastically *(coll.)*
Super ['zu:pɐ] **das;** ~s, ~: four star *(Brit.)*; premium *(Amer.)*; *s. auch* **Normal**
super- ultra-‹*long, high, fast, modern, masculine, etc.*›; **~geheim** top secret; **~günstig** extra cheap
Super- super-‹*hero, figure, car, group, etc.*›; terrific *(coll.)*, tremendous *(coll.)* ‹*success, offer, chance, idea, etc.*›
Super-8-Film der super 8 film
superb [zu'pɛrp], **süperb** [zy'pɛrp] *(geh.)* **1.** *Adj.* superb. **2.** *adv.* superbly
Super·benzin das four-star petrol *(Brit.)*; premium *(Amer.)*
Super·ding das; *Pl.* **~er** *(salopp)* terrific thing *(coll.)*
Superintendent [zupɐlɪntɛn'dɛnt] **der;** ~en, ~en *(ev. Kirche)* dean
Superiorität [zuperi̯orit'tɛ:t] **die;** ~ *(geh.)* **a)** superiority (**über** + *Akk.* in relation to); **b)** *(Vormachtstellung)* supremacy (**über** + *Akk.* over)
super·klug *(iron.)* **1.** *Adj.* extra clever; smart-aleck *(coll. derog.)*. **2.** *adv.* in a smart-aleck way *(coll. derog.)*
Superlativ ['zu:pɐlati:f] **der;** ~s, ~e *(Sprachw.)* superlative
superlativisch *Adj. (Sprachw.)* superlative
super-, Super-: ~mann der; *Pl.* **~männer** *(ugs.)* superman; **~markt der** supermarket; **~modern 1.** *Adj.* ultra-modern; **2.** *adv.* ‹*furnished, dressed*› in ultra-modern style; **~schlau** *Adj. (iron.) s.* **~klug; ~schnell** *(ugs.)* **1.** *Adj.* ultra-fast; **2.** *adv.* at tremendous speed; **~star der** superstar
Süppchen ['zʏpçən] **das;** ~s, ~: soup; **sein ~ am Feuer anderer kochen** *(ugs.)* use others for one's own ends
Suppe ['zʊpə] **die;** ~; ~**n** soup; **jmdm. die ~ versalzen** *(ugs.)* put a spoke in sb.'s wheel; put a spanner in sb.'s works; **jmdm. in die ~ spucken** *(salopp)* mess things up for sb.; *s. auch* **auslöffeln a; einbrocken**
Suppen-: ~ein·lage die *rice, noodles, dumplings, etc. put into a clear soup;* **~fleisch das** beef for making soup; **~grün das** green vegetables for making soup *(comprising parsley, carrots, celery, and leeks)*; **~huhn das** boiling fowl; **~kasper der** *(ugs.)* poor *or* finicky eater; **~kelle die** soup-ladle; **~knochen der** soup bone; **~löffel der** soup-spoon; **~nudel die;** *meist Pl.* noodle *(for use in soup)*; **~schüssel die** soup-tureen; **~tasse die** soup-bowl *(with handles)*; **~teller der** soup-plate; **~terrine die** soup-tureen; **~würfel der** stock cube
suppig *Adj.* watery; thin
Supplement [zʊple'mɛnt] **das;** ~[e]s, ~e supplement
Suppositorium [zʊpozi'to:ri̯ʊm] **das;** ~s, **Suppositorien** *(Pharm.)* suppository
Supremat [zupre'ma:t] **der** *od.* **das;** ~[e]s, ~e supreme authority
Sure ['zu:rə] **die;** ~, ~**n** sura
Surf·brett ['sə:f-] **das** surf-board
surfen ['sə:fn̩] *itr. V.* surf
Surfer ['sə:fɐ] **der;** ~s, ~: surfer
Sur·realismus [zʊrea'lɪsmʊs] **der;** ~: surrealism *no art.*
Sur·realist der surrealist
surrealistisch 1. *Adj.* surrealist ‹*movement, painting, literature*›; surrealistic ‹*image, story, scene*›. **2.** *adv.* surrealistically; ‹*paint*› in a surrealistic style; ‹*influenced*› by surrealism
surren ['zʊrən] *itr. V.* **a)** *(summen)* hum; ‹*camera, fan*› whirr; **es surrt** there's a hum/whirr; **b)** *mit sein (schwirren)* whirr
Surrogat [zʊro'ga:t] **das;** ~[e]s, ~e *(geh.)* surrogate
suspekt [zʊs'pɛkt] **1.** *Adj.* suspicious; **jmdm. ~ sein** seem suspicious to sb.; arouse sb.'s suspicions. **2.** *adv.* suspiciously
suspendieren [zʊspɛn'di:rən] *tr. V.* suspend; *(entlassen)* dismiss; **jmdn. vom Dienst/von seinem Amt ~:** suspend/dismiss sb. from his/her post
Suspendierung, Suspension [zʊspɛn'zi̯o:n] **die;** ~, ~**en** suspension; *(Entlassung)* dismissal
Suspensorium [zʊspɛn'zo:ri̯ʊm] **das;** ~s, **Suspensorien** *(Med.)* suspensory [bandage]
süß [zy:s] **1.** *Adj.* sweet; *(geh.: lieblich klingend)* melodious; sweet; *(fig.: übertrieben freundlich)* sweet, sugary ‹*smile, words*›; **er ißt gern Süßes** he likes sweet things; he has a sweet tooth; **na, mein Süßer/meine Süße?** well, sweetheart? **2.** *adv.* sweetly; **~ duften** give off a sweet scent; **den Salat ~ anmachen** sweeten the salad-dressing; **träum ~!** sweet dreams!; **das hast du ~ gemalt** *(fam.)* you've painted this enchantingly
Süße die; ~: sweetness
süßen 1. *tr. V.* sweeten. **2.** *itr. V.* sweeten things; **mit Saccharin ~:** use saccharine as a sweetener
Süß·holz das; *o. Pl.* liquorice [plant]; **~ raspeln** *(fig. ugs.)* ooze charm
Süßholz·raspler der; ~s, ~ *(ugs.)* smoothie *(coll.)*
Süßigkeit die; ~, ~**en a)** *meist Pl. (Bonbon usw.)* sweet *(Brit.)*; candy *(Amer.)*; **~en** sweets *(Brit.)*; candy *sing. (Amer.)*; *(als Ware)* confectionery *sing.*; **b)** *o. Pl. (fig. geh.: Süße)* sweetness
Süß·kirsche die sweet cherry
süßlich 1. *Adj.* **a)** [slightly] sweet; on the sweet side *pred.*; **ein widerlich ~er Geruch/Geschmack** an unpleasantly sickly *or* cloying smell/taste; **b)** *(abwertend) (sentimental)* sickly mawkish ‹*film*›; *(heuchlerisch freundlich)* sugary ‹*smile etc.*›; smarmy *(coll.)* ‹*expression, manners*›; honeyed ‹*words*›. **2.** *adv. (abwertend)* ‹*write, paint*› mawkishly *or* in a sickly-sentimental style; ‹*smile*› smarmily *(coll.)*
süß-, Süß-: ~most der unfermented fruit juice; **~rahm·butter die** sweet cream butter; **~-sauer 1.** *Adj.* sweet-and-sour; *(fig.)* wry ‹*smile, face*›; **etw. gern ~-sauer essen** like eating sth. with a sweet-and-sour sauce; **2.** *adv.* **a) etw. ~-sauer zubereiten** give sth. a sweet-and-sour flavour; **b)** *(fig.)* ‹*smile*› wryly; **~speise die** sweet; dessert; **~stoff der** sweetener; **~waren** *Pl.* confectionery *sing.*; candy *sing. (Amer.)*; **~wasser das;** *Pl.* **~wasser** fresh water: **~wasser·fisch der** freshwater fish; **~wein der** sweet wine
Sutane *s.* **Soutane**
Sütterlin·schrift ['zʏtɐli:n-] **die;** *o. Pl.* Sütterlin script
SV ['ɛsfau̯] **der;** ~ *Abk.* **Sportverein** SC
SVP [ɛsfau̯'pe:] **die;** ~ *Abk.* **Schweizer Volkspartei**
svw. *Abk.* **soviel wie**
SW *Abk.* **Südwest[en]** SW
Swahili [sva'hi:li] *s.* **Suaheli**
Swastika ['svastika] **die;** ~, **Swastiken** swastika
Sweatshirt ['swɛt-ʃə:t] **das;** ~s, ~s sweatshirt
SWF [ɛsve:'ɛf] **der;** ~: *Abk.* **Südwestfunk**
Swimmingpool, Swimming-pool ['svɪmɪŋpu:l] **der;** ~s, ~s [swimming-]pool
Swing [svɪŋ] **der;** ~[s] **a)** *(Musik)* swing *no art.*; **b)** *(Wirtsch.)* swing
swingen *itr. V.* **a)** *(Musik)* ‹*player*› swing [it]; ‹*music*› have a swing [to it]; **b)** *(tanzen)* swing
Syllogismus [zylo'gɪsmʊs] **der;** ~s, **Syllogismen** *(Philos.)* syllogism
Sylphe ['zʏlfə] **der;** ~n, ~n sylph
Symbiose [zʏm'bi̯o:zə] **die;** ~, ~n *(Biol., fig.)* symbiosis (**zwischen** + *Dat.* of); **eine ~ eingehen** *(fig.)* form a symbiotic relationship
symbiotisch *Adj. (Biol., fig.)* symbiotic
Symbol [zʏm'bo:l] **das;** ~s, ~e symbol
symbolhaft 1. *Adj.* symbolic (**für** of). **2.** *adv.* symbolically
Symbolik [zʏm'bo:lɪk] **die;** ~: symbolism
symbolisch 1. *Adj.* symbolic. **2.** *adv.* symbolically
symbolisieren 1. *tr. V.* symbolize. **2.** *refl. V.* be symbolized (**in** + *Dat.* by)
Symbolismus der; ~: symbolism; *(Kunstrichtung)* Symbolism *no art.*
Symbolist der; ~en, ~en Symbolist
symbolistisch *Adj.* Symbolist
Symbol·sprache die *(DV)* assembly language
Symmetrie [zʏme'tri:] **die;** ~, ~**n** symmetry
Symmetrie·achse die axis of symmetry
symmetrisch 1. *Adj.* symmetrical. **2.** *adv.* symmetrically
Sympathie [zʏmpa'ti:] **die;** ~, ~**n** sympathy; **~ für jmdn. haben** sympathize with *or* have sympathy with sb.; **sich** *(Dat.)* **jmds./alle ~n verscherzen** forfeit sb.'s/everybody's sympathy; **bei aller ~:** with the best will in the world
Sympathie·streik der sympathy strike; **in ~ [mit jmdm.] treten** strike in sympathy [with sb.]
Sympathikus der; ~ *(Anat., Physiol.)* sympathetic nervous system
Sympathisant [zʏmpati'zant] **der;** ~en, ~en, **Sympathisantin die;** ~, ~**nen** sympathizer (*Gen.* with)
sympathisch 1. *Adj.* **a)** congenial, likeable ‹*person, manner*›; appealing, agreeable ‹*voice, appearance, material*›; **jmdm. ~ sein** appeal to sb.; **er war mir gleich ~:** I took to him at once; I took an immediate liking to him; **b)** *(Anat., Physiol.)* sympathetic ‹*nerve, nervous system, etc.*›. **2.** *adv.* in a likeable *or* appealing way; *(angenehm)* agreeably
sympathisieren *itr. V.* sympathize (**mit** with); **mit einer Partei ~:** be sympathetic towards a party
Symphonie [zʏmfo'ni:] *usw. s.* **Sinfonie** *usw.*
Symposion [zʏm'po:zi̯ɔn], **Symposium** [zʏm'po:zi̯ʊm] **das;** ~s, **Symposien** symposium (**über** + Akk., **zu** on)
Symptom [zʏmp'to:m] **das;** ~s, ~e *(Med., geh.)* symptom (*Gen.*, **für, von** of)
Symptomatik [zʏmpto'ma:tɪk] **die;** ~ *(Med., geh.)* symptoms *pl.*; symptom complex
symptomatisch *(Med., geh.)* **1.** *Adj.* symptomatic (**für** of). **2.** *adv.* symptomatically
Synagoge [zyna'go:gə] **die;** ~, ~**n** synagogue
Synästhesie [zynɛste'zi:] **die;** ~, ~**n** *(Med., Literaturw.)* synaesthesia
synchron [zʏn'kro:n] **1.** *Adj.* **a)** synchronous; **b)** *(Sprachw.)* synchronic. **2.** *adv.* **a)** synchronously; **b)** *(Sprachw.)* synchronically
Synchronisation [zʏnkronizə'tsi̯o:n] **die;** ~, ~**en** *s.* **Synchronisierung**
synchronisch *Adj. (Sprachw.)* synchronic
synchronisieren *tr. V.* **a)** *(Film)* dub ‹*film*›; **b)** *(Technik, fig.)* synchronize ‹*watches, operations, etc.*›; fit synchromesh to ‹*gearbox*›; **alle Gänge sind synchronisiert** *(Kfz-W.)* there is synchromesh on all gears; **synchronisiertes Getriebe** synchromesh gearbox
Synchronisierung die; ~, ~**en a)** *(Film)* dubbing; **b)** *(Technik, fig.)* synchronization; *(Kfz-W.)* fitting of synchromesh (*Gen.* to)
Synchron·schwimmen das *(Sport)* synchronized swimming
Synchron·sprecher der dubbing actor
Synchrotron ['zʏnkrotro:n] **das;** ~s, ~e *od.* ~s *(Kernphysik)* synchrotron
Syndikalismus [zʏndika'lɪsmʊs] **der;** ~: syndicalism *no art.*

syndikalistisch *Adj.* syndicalist
Syndikat [zyndi'ka:t] **das; ~[e]s, ~e** *(bes. Wirtsch.)* syndicate
Syndikus ['zyndikʊs] **der; ~s, ~e** *od.* **Syndizi** ['zyndit͡si] *(Rechtsspr.)* legal adviser; *(Rechtsanwalt einer Firma)* company lawyer *or (Amer.)* attorney
Syndrom [zyn'dro:m] **das; ~s, ~e** *(Med.)* syndrome
Synkope die; ~, ~n a) [zyn'ko:pə]; *(Musik)* syncopation; **b)** ['zynkope] *(Sprachw.)* syncope
synkopieren [zynko'pi:rən] *tr. V. (Musik, Sprachw.)* syncopate
synkopisch *Adj. (Musik)* syncopated
Synodale [zyno'da:lə] **der/die;** *adj. Dekl.* synod member
Synode [zy'no:də] **die; ~, ~n** *(ev., kath. Kirche)* synod
synonym [zyno'ny:m] *(Sprachw.)* **1.** *Adj.* synonymous. **2.** *adv.* synonymously
Synonym [zyno'ny:m] **das; ~s, ~e** *(Sprachw.)* synonym
Synonomie [zynony'mi:] **die; ~, ~n** *(Sprachw.)* synonymity
Synonym·wörterbuch das dictionary of synonyms
Synopse [zyn'ɔpsə], **Synopsis** ['zy:nɔpsɪs] **die; ~, Synopsen a)** textual comparison; **b)** *(bibl.)* comparative parallel text of the Synoptic Gospels; **c)** *(geh.: Zusammenschau)* overall view; survey
Synoptiker der; ~s, ~ *meist Pl.* synoptist
syntaktisch [zyn'taktɪʃ] *(Sprachw.)* **1.** *Adj.* syntactic. **2.** *adv.* syntactically
Syntax ['zyntaks] **die; ~, ~en** *(Sprachw.)* syntax
Synthese [zyn'te:zə] **die; ~, ~n** synthesis (*Gen.*, **von, aus** of)
Synthesizer ['sɪntəsaizɐ] **der; ~s, ~** *(Musik)* synthesizer
Synthetik [zyn'te:tɪk] **das; ~s** *(ugs.)* synthetic material
synthetisch 1. *Adj.* synthetic. **2.** *adv.* synthetically
Syphilis ['zy:filɪs] **die; ~** *(Med.)* syphilis
Syrakus [zyra'ku:s] **(das); Syrakus'** Syracuse
Syrer ['zy:rɐ] **der; ~s, ~, Syrerin die; ~, ~nen** Syrian
Syrien ['zy:riən] **(das); ~s** Syria
syrisch ['zy:rɪʃ] *Adj.* Syrian
System [zys'te:m] **das; ~, ~e** system; **~ in etw.** *(Akk.)* **bringen** introduce some system into sth.; get sth. into some sort of order; **~ haben** be methodical; have system; **hinter etw.** *(Dat.)* **steckt ~:** there's method in sth.
System-: ~analyse die systems analysis; **~analytiker der** systems analyst
Systematik [zyste'ma:tɪk] **die; ~, ~en a)** systematics *sing.*; **b)** *(Biol.)* taxonomy
systematisch [zyste'ma:tɪʃ] **1.** *Adj.* systematic. **2.** *adv.* systematically
systematisieren *tr. V.* systematize
system-, System-: ~immanent 1. *Adj.* part of the system *pred.*; **~immanente Faktoren** factors inherent in the system; **2.** *adv.* in a manner inherent in the system; **~kritiker der** critic of the system; **~los 1.** *Adj.* unsystematic; **2.** *adv.* unsystematically; **~veränderung die** change in the system; **~wette die** betting based on an agreed system of permutations; **~zwang der** pressure imposed by the system
Systole ['zystole] **die; ~, ~n** *(Med.)* systole
Szenario [st͡se'na:ri̯o] **das; ~s, ~s, Szenarium** [st͡se'na:ri̯ʊm] **das; ~s, Szenarien** *(Theater, Film)* scenario
Szene ['st͡se:nə] **die; ~, ~n a)** scene; **hinter der ~:** backstage; behind the scenes; **er erhielt Beifall auf offener ~:** he was applauded during the scene; **die ~ beherrschen** *(fig.)* dominate the scene; **ein Theaterstück in ~ setzen** stage a play; **sich in ~ setzen** *(fig.)* put oneself in the limelight; **b)** *(Auseinandersetzung)* scene; **[jmdm.] eine ~ machen** make a scene [in front of sb.]; **c)** *(ugs.: bestimmtes Milieu)* scene *(coll.)*
-szene *(ugs.)* scene *(coll.)*; **die Terror[isten]~/Literatur~:** the terrorist/literary scene
Szenen-: ~applaus der applause during the scene; spontaneous burst of applause; **~folge die** sequence of scenes; **~wechsel der** *(Theater)* scene-change
Szenerie [st͡senə'ri:] **die; ~, ~n a)** *(Bühnendekoration)* set (*Gen.* for); **b)** *(Schauplatz)* scene; *(eines Romans)* setting
szenisch *Adj.* dramatic; **~e Gestaltung/Effekte** staging/stage effects
Szepter ['st͡sɛptɐ] **das; ~s, ~** *s.* **Zepter**
Szientismus [st͡siɛn'tɪsmʊs] **der; ~:** *(Fachspr.)* scientism *no art.*
Szilla ['st͡sɪla] **die; ~, Szillen** *(Bot.)* scilla
Szylla ['st͡sʏla] *in* **zwischen ~ und Charybdis** *(geh.)* between Scylla and Charybdis

T

t, T [te:] **das; ~, ~,** *(ugs.)* **~s, ~s** t/T; *s. auch* **a, A**
t *Abk.* **Tonne** t
Tab. *Abk.* **Tabelle**
Tabak ['ta(:)bak] **der; ~s, ~e** tobacco
Tabak·monopol das *(Wirtsch.)* tobacco monopoly
Tabaks-: ~beutel der tobacco-pouch; **~dose die** tobacco-tin; **~pfeife die** [tobacco-]pipe
Tabak-: ~steuer die duty *or* tax on tobacco; **~trafik** [-'---] **die** *(österr.)* tobacconist['s] [shop]; **~waren** *Pl.* tobacco *sing.*
Tabatiere [taba'ti̯e:rə] **die; ~, ~n a)** *(veralt.)* snuff-box; **b)** *(österr.) s.* **Tabaksdose; c)** *(österr.) s.* **Zigarettenetui**
tabellarisch [tabɛ'la:rɪʃ] **1.** *Adj.* tabular; **ein ~er Lebenslauf** a curriculum vitae in tabular form. **2.** *adv.* in tabular form
Tabelle [ta'bɛlə] **die; ~, ~n a)** *(Übersicht)* table; **b)** *(Sport)* [league/championship] table; **die ~ anführen** be at the top of the [league/championship] table
Tabellen-: ~führer der *(Sport)* top team/player in the [league/championship] table; **~führer sein** be top of the table; **~platz der** *(Sport)* position *or* place in the [league/championship] table; **~stand der** *(Sport)* state of the [league/championship] table
tabellieren *tr. V. (Fachspr.)* tabulate
Tabernakel [tabɛr'na:kl̩] **das** *od.* **der; ~s, ~** *(kath. Kirche, Archit.)* tabernacle
Tableau [ta'blo:] **das; ~s, ~s** *(bes. Literaturw.)* tableau
Tablett [ta'blɛt] **das; ~[e]s, ~s** *od.* **~e** tray; **jmdm. etw. auf einem silbernen ~ servieren** *(fig.)* hand sth. to sb. on a silver platter
Tablette die; ~, ~n tablet
tabletten-, Tabletten-: ~form die tablet form; **~röhrchen das** tablet tube; **~süchtig** *Adj.* addicted to pills *postpos.*
tabu [ta'bu:] *Adj.* taboo
Tabu das; ~s, ~s taboo
tabuieren, tabuisieren *tr. V. (geh.)* **etw. ~:** taboo sth.; make sth. taboo
tabula rasa ['ta:bula 'ra:za] *in* **~ ~ machen** make a clean sweep
Tabulatur [tabula'tu:ɐ̯] **die; ~, ~en** *(Musik)* tablature
Taburett [tabu'rɛt] **das; ~[e]s, ~e** *(schweiz., sonst veralt.)* tabouret
Tabu·wort das *(Sprachw., Psych.)* taboo word
Tacheles ['taxələs] *in* **[mit jmdm.] ~ reden** *(ugs.)* do some straight talking [to sb.]
tachinieren [taxi'ni:rən] *itr. V. (österr. ugs.)* loaf [about]
Tachinierer der; ~s, ~ *(österr. ugs.)* slacker *(coll.)*; loafer
Tachismus [ta'ʃɪsmʊs] **der; ~** *(Kunstwiss.)* tachism *no art.*
Tacho ['taxo] **der; ~s, ~s** *(ugs.)* speedo *(coll.)*
Tacho·meter der *od.* **das** speedometer
Tacho·nadel die speedometer needle
Tacho·stand der *(ugs.: Kilometerstand)* mileometer *or* odometer reading
Tadel ['ta:dl̩] **der; ~s, ~ a)** censure; **jmdm. einen ~ erteilen** give sb. a rebuke; rebuke sb.; **ihn trifft kein ~:** he is not to blame; **öffentlicher ~** *(DDR Rechtsw.)* public censure; **b)** *(im Klassenbuch)* black mark; **c)** *(geh.: Mangel, Makel)* blemish; flaw; **ohne ~:** perfect, flawless ⟨*figure, copy, etc.*⟩; impeccable ⟨*dress, appearance, etc.*⟩; irreproachable ⟨*life, character, person, etc.*⟩
tadel·los 1. *Adj.* **a)** *(makellos)* impeccable; immaculate ⟨*hair, clothing, suit, etc.*⟩; perfect ⟨*condition, teeth, pronunciation, German, etc.*⟩; **b)** *(ugs.: sehr gut)* excellent; **c)** ['--'-] *(ugs.: als Ausruf der Zustimmung)* splendid *(coll.)*. **2.** *adv.* **a)** *(makellos)* ⟨*dress*⟩ impeccably, immaculately; ⟨*fit, speak, etc.*⟩ perfectly; ⟨*live, behave, etc.*⟩ irreproachably; **b)** *(ugs.: sehr gut)* **hier wird man ~ bedient** the service is excellent here
tadeln *tr. V.* **jmdn. [für sein Verhalten** *od.* **wegen seines Verhaltens] ~:** rebuke sb. [for his/her behaviour]; **jmds. Arbeit ~:** criticize sb.'s work; **er hatte an ihr/ihrer Handlungsweise etw. zu ~:** he found some fault with her/the way she behaved; **~de Worte/~der Blick** reproachful words/look
tadelns·wert *Adj.* reprehensible
Tadels·antrag der *(Parl.)* censure motion
Tafel ['ta:fl̩] **die; ~, ~n a)** *(Schiefer~)* slate; *(Wand~)* blackboard; **b)** *(plattenförmiges Stück)* slab; **eine ~ Schokolade** a bar of chocolate; **c)** *(Gedenk~)* plaque; **d)** *(geh.: festlicher Tisch)* table; **die ~ aufheben** *(fig.)* rise from the table; **e)** *(Druckw.)* plate
Tafel-: ~apfel der *(Kaufmannsspr.)* dessert apple; **~auf·satz der** centre-piece; **~berg der** *(Geol.)* mesa; **~besteck das** cutlery *or (Amer.)* flatware service; **~bild das** *(bild. Kunst)* panel painting
Täfelchen ['tɛ:fl̩çən] **das; ~s, ~:** *s.* **Tafel b:** [small] slab; [small] bar
tafel-, Tafel-: ~fertig *Adj. (Kochk.)* ready to serve *postpos.*; *(noch zu erwärmen)* ready to heat and serve *postpos.*; **~fertige Gerichte** ready-to-serve/ready-to-heat-and-serve dishes; **~freuden** *Pl. (geh.)* culinary delights; **~lappen der** blackboard cloth; **~musik die** musical entertainment *(provided at a banquet, festive dinner, etc.)*
tafeln *itr. V. (geh.)* feast
täfeln ['tɛ:fl̩n] *tr. V.* panel
Tafel-: ~obst das [dessert] fruit; **~runde die** *(geh.)* gathering [round a table]; **die ~runde des Königs Artus** King Arthur's Round Table; **~salz das** table salt; **~spitz der** *(österr.)* boiled fillet of beef
Täfelung die; ~, ~en a) *(das Täfeln)* panelling; **b)** *(Paneel)* [wooden] panelling
Tafel-: ~wasser das; *Pl.* **~wässer** [bottled] mineral water; **~wein der** table wine

Taft [taft] **der; ~[e]s, ~e** taffeta

Tag [ta:k] **der; ~[e]s, ~e a)** day; **es wird/ist ~:** it's getting/it is light; **solange es noch ~ ist** while it's still light; **der ~ bricht an** *od.* **graut** *od.* **erwacht/neigt sich** *(geh.)* the day breaks/draws to an end *or* a close; **die ~e nehmen ab/zu** the days are getting shorter/longer; **am ~[e]** during the day[time]; **am hellichten ~:** in broad daylight; **bei ~[e] reisen/ankommen** travel during the day/arrive while it's light; **[drei Stunden] vor ~** *(geh.)* [three hours] before daylight; **er redet viel, wenn der ~ lang ist** *(ugs.)* you can't put any trust in what he says; **sie sind wie ~ und Nacht** they are as different as chalk and cheese; **man soll den ~ nicht vor dem Abend loben** *(Spr.)* don't count your chickens before they're hatched *(prov.)*; **es ist noch nicht aller ~e Abend** we haven't yet seen the end of the matter; **guten ~!** hello; *(bei Vorstellung)* how do you do?; *(nachmittags auch)* good afternoon; **jmdm. einen guten ~ wünschen** wish sb. good day; **~!** *(ugs.)* hello; hi *(Amer. coll.)*; *(nachmittags auch)* afternoon; **bei jmdm. guten ~ sagen** *(ugs.)* pop in to sb. to say 'hello' *(coll.)*; **etw. an den ~ legen** display sth.; **etw. an den ~ bringen** *od. (geh.)* **ziehen** bring sth. to light; reveal sth.; **an den ~ kommen** come to light; **unter ~s** *(landsch.)* during the day [time]; **über/unter ~[e]** *(Bergmannsspr.)* above ground/underground; **b)** *(Zeitraum von 24 Stunden)* day; **~ und Stunde des Treffens stehen fest** the date and time of the meeting are fixed; **welchen ~ haben wir heute?** *(Wochentag)* what day is it today? what's today?; *(Datum)* what date is it today?; **heute in/vor drei ~en** three days from today/three days ago today; **den ~ über** during the day; **einen ~ um den anderen** every other day; **jmdm. den ~ stehlen** waste sb.'s time; **an diesem ~:** on this day; **dreimal am ~:** three times a day; **früh/spät am ~[e]** early/late in the day; **am ~e vorher** on the previous day; the day before; **auf den ~ [genau]** on the [very] day; **~ für ~:** every [single] day; **von ~ zu ~:** day by day; **in den nächsten ~en** in the next few days; **der ~ X** the great day; **am folgenden ~:** the next day; **heute ist sein [großer] ~:** it's his big day today; **er hatte heute einen schlechten ~:** today was one of his bad days; **sich** *(Dat.)* **einen schönen/faulen ~ machen** *(ugs.)* have a nice/lazy day; **den lieben langen ~:** all day long; **der ~ des Herrn** *(christl. Rel.)* the Lord's Day; **~ der offenen Tür** open day; **der Brief muß/kann jeden ~ ankommen** the letter will surely/can arrive any day now; **eines ~es** one day; some day; **eines schönen ~es** one of these days; **dieser ~e werde ich ...:** in the next few days, I will ...; **dieser ~e kam ein Mann ...:** the other day *or* recently, a man came ...; **von einem ~ auf den anderen** from one day to the next; overnight; **jmdn. von einem ~ auf den anderen vertrösten** put sb. off from day to day; **in den ~ hinein leben** live from day to day; **den ~ über** during the day; **c)** *(Ehren~, Gedenk~)* **~ der deutschen Einheit** *(Bundesrepublik Deutschland)* Day of German Unity; **~ der Republik** *(DDR veralt.)* Republic Day; **d)** *Pl. ([Lebens]zeit)* days; **sie hat schon bessere ~e gesehen** she has seen better days; **seine ~e sind gezählt** his days are numbered; **bis in unsere ~e** until our day; **auf meine/deine** *usw.* **alten ~e** in my/your *etc.* old age; **e)** *Pl. (ugs.: verhüll.: Menstruation)* period *sing.*; **wenn sie ihre ~e hat** when it's her time of the month

tag-, Tag-: ~aktiv *Adj. (Zool.)* diurnal; **~aus** *Adv.* **~aus, tagein** day in, day out; day after day; **~dienst der** day duty; **~dienst haben** be on day duty

Tage-: ~bau der; *Pl.* **~e** *(Bergbau)* **a)** *o. Pl. (Bergbau über Tage)* opencast mining *no art.*; **b)** *(Anlage)* opencast mine; **~blatt das a)** *(veralt.: Tageszeitung)* daily [news]paper; **b)** *(in Namen)* **das Offenburger ~blatt** the Offenburg Daily News; **~buch das** diary; **[über etw.** *(Akk.)***] ~buch führen** keep a diary [about sth.]; **~buch·auf·zeichnung die** diary entry; **~dieb der** *(abwertend)* idler; lazy-bones *sing.*; **~geld das a)** *(Verpflegungsbetrag)* daily [expense] allowance; **b)** *Pl. (Diäten)* daily [parliamentary] allowance *sing.*; **c)** *(Tagesvergütung)* daily compensation

tag·ein *Adv. s.* tagaus

tage-, Tage-: ~lang 1. *Adj.; nicht präd.* lasting for days *postpos.*; **das ~lange Warten** the days of waiting; **nach ~langem Regen** after days of rain; **2.** *adv.* for days [on end]; **~lohn der** daily *or* day's wage[s]; **im ~lohn arbeiten** be paid by the day; **~löhner** [~lø:nɐ] **der; ~s, ~:** day-labourer

tagen *itr. V.* **a)** *(konferieren)* meet; **das Gericht/Parlament tagt** the court/parliament is in session; **über etw.** *(Akk.)* **~:** confer about *or* meet to discuss sth.; **bis in den frühen Morgen hinein ~** *(fig.)* celebrate until the early hours; **b)** *(geh.: dämmern)* **es tagt** day is breaking *or* dawning

Tage·reise die day's journey; **nach Passau sind es zehn ~n** it's a ten-day journey to Passau

Tages-: ~ab·lauf der day; daily routine; **~an·bruch der** daybreak; dawn; **~arbeit die** day's work; **~aus·flug der** day's outing; **~aus·zug der** *(Bankw.)* daily statement of account transactions; **~bedarf der** daily requirement; **~befehl der** *(Milit.)* order of the day; **~creme die** *(Kosmetik)* day cream; **~decke die** bedspread; **~dessert das** dessert *or (Brit.)* sweet of the day; **~einnahme die** day's takings *pl.*; **~ereignis das** event of the day; **~fahrt die** day trip; day excursion; **~gespräch das** topic of the day; **~karte die a)** *(Gastron.)* menu of the day; **b)** *(Fahr-, Eintrittskarte)* day ticket; **~kasse die a)** box-office *(open during the day)*; **b)** *(~einnahme)* day's takings *pl.*; **~kilometer·zähler der** trip mileage recorder; **~kurs der** *(Börsenw.)* current rate of exchange; **~lauf der** daily routine; **~licht das;** *o. Pl.* daylight; **bei ~licht** in [the] daylight; **das ~licht scheuen** *(fig.)* shun the light of day; **etw. ans ~licht bringen** *od.* **ziehen** *(fig.)* bring sth. to light; **ans ~licht kommen** *(fig.)* come to light; **~losung die** day's password; **~marsch der a)** *(Fußmarsch)* day's hike; **b)** *(Strecke eines ~marsches)* day's march; **drei ~märsche entfernt** three days' march away; **~menü das** set menu of the day; **~mutter die;** *Pl.* **~mütter** child-minder; **~ordnung die** agenda; **einen Punkt auf die ~ordnung setzen/von der ~ordnung absetzen** place an item on the agenda/delete an item from the agenda; **an der ~ordnung sein** *(fig.)* be the order of the day; **zur ~ordnung übergehen** *(fig.)* proceed as if nothing had happened; **~ordnungs·punkt der** item on the agenda; **~politik die;** *o. Pl.* day-to-day politics *sing.*; **~preis der** *(Wirtsch.)* current price; **~presse die;** *o. Pl.* daily press; **~ration die** daily ration; **~raum der** day-room; **~satz der a)** *(Rechtsw.: Geldstrafe) unit, based on net daily income etc., used to calculate a fine;* **b)** *(Unterbringungskosten)* daily rate; **~suppe die** soup of the day; **~tour die** *s.* **~fahrt; ~wanderung die** day's hike; **~wanderungen** one-day hikes; **~zeit die** time of day; **um diese ~zeit** at this time; **jmdm. die ~zeit [ent]bieten** *(veralt.)* give sb. the time of day; **zu jeder ~- und Nachtzeit** at any time of the day or night; **~zeitung die** daily newspaper; daily

Tagetes [ta'ge:tɛs] **die; ~, ~:** tagetes

tage·weise *Adv.* on some days

Tage·werk das; *o. Pl. (veralt. geh.)* day's labour

Tag·falter der *(Zool.)* butterfly

tag·hell 1. *Adj.; nicht attr.* **a)** *(durch Tageslicht)* [day]light; **b)** *(wie am Tag)* bright as daylight *postpos.* **2.** *adv.* **etw. ist ~ erleuchtet** sth. is very brightly lit [up]

-tägig [-tɛ:gɪç] **a)** *(... Tage alt)* **ein sechstägiges Küken** a six-day-old chick; **b)** *(... Tage dauernd)* **nach dreitägiger Vorbereitung** after three days' preparation; **mit dreitägiger Verspätung** three days late

täglich ['tɛ:klɪç] **1.** *Adj.; nicht präd.* daily. **2.** *adv.* every day; **zweimal ~:** twice a day; **~ zwei Stunden** for two hours a day; **~ drei Tabletten einnehmen** take three tablets daily

Tag·pfauen·auge das *(Zool.)* peacock butterfly

tags *Adv.* **a)** by day; in the daytime; **b) ~ zuvor/davor** the day before; **~ darauf** the next *or* following day; the day after

Tag·schicht die day shift; **~ haben** be on [the] day shift; **in ~ arbeiten** work a day shift

tags·über *Adv.* during the day

tag·täglich *(intensivierend)* **1.** *Adj.* day-to-day; daily. **2.** *adv.* every single day

Tag-: ~träumer der day-dreamer; **~und·nacht·gleiche die; ~, ~n** equinox

Tagung die; ~, ~en conference

Tagungs-: ~ort der; *Pl.* **~orte** venue [for a/the conference]; **~teilnehmer der** participant in a/the conference

Taifun [tai'fu:n] **der; ~s, ~e** typhoon

Taiga die; ~: taiga

Taille ['taljə] **die; ~, ~n** waist; **in der ~:** at the waist

Taillen·weite die waist measurement

Tailleur [ta'jø:ɐ] **das; ~s, ~s** *(schweiz.)* tailored suit/coat *(fitted at the waist)*

taillieren [ta'ji:rən] *tr. V.* fit [at the waist]; **ein tailliertes Kostüm** a suit with the jacket fitted at the waist

Taiwan ['taivan] **(das); ~s** Taiwan

Taiwaner der; ~s, ~, Taiwanerin die; ~, ~nen Taiwanese

Takelage [takə'la:ʒə] **die; ~, ~n** *(Seew.)* masts and rigging

takeln ['ta:kl̩n] *tr. V. (Seemannsspr.)* rig

Takelung die; ~, ~en *(Seemannsspr.)* rig

Takt [takt] **der; ~[e]s, ~e a)** *(Musik)* time; *(Einheit)* bar; measure *(Amer.)*; **im ~ bleiben** stay in time; **den ~ [ein]halten** keep in time; **den ~ angeben/schlagen/wechseln** give the beat/beat time/change the time *or* beat; **aus dem ~ kommen** lose the beat; **sich nicht aus dem ~ bringen lassen** not lose the beat; **mit ihm muß ich mal ein paar ~e reden** *(fig. ugs.)* I need to have a serious talk with him; **b)** *o. Pl. (rhythmischer Bewegungsablauf)* rhythm; **im/gegen den ~:** in/out of rhythm; **im ~ bleiben** keep the rhythm; **aus dem ~ kommen** lose the rhythm; **c)** *o. Pl. (Feingefühl)* tact; **etw. aus ~ tun** do sth. out of tact[fulness]; **d)** *(Verslehre)* foot

takt·fest *(Musik)* **1.** *Adj.* **ein nicht ganz ~er Pianist** a pianist who has some difficulty keeping time; **~ sein** keep good time. **2.** *adv.* in time

Takt·gefühl das; *o. Pl.* sense of tact; **etw. mit großem ~ tun** do sth. with great delicacy

taktieren *itr. V.* proceed tactically; **vorsichtig/klug ~:** use caution/clever tactics

Taktik ['taktɪk] **die; ~, ~en: [eine] ~:** tactics *pl.*; **die ~ der verbrannten Erde** *(Milit.)* scorched-earth tactics

Taktiker der; ~s, ~: tactician

taktisch 1. *Adj.* tactical. **2.** *adv.* tactically; **~ klug vorgehen** use clever *or* good tactics

takt·los 1. *Adj.* tactless. **2.** *adv.* tactlessly

Taktlosigkeit die; ~, ~en a) *o. Pl. (taktlose Art)* tactlessness; **b)** *(taktlose Handlung)* piece of tactlessness; **derartige ~en** such tactlessness *sing.*

Takt-: ~stock der baton; **den ~stock schwingen** *(scherzh.)* wield the baton; **~strich der** *(Musik)* bar[-line]

takt·voll 1. *Adj.* tactful. **2.** *adv.* tactfully

Takt·wechsel der *(Musik)* change of time

Tal [ta:l] **das; ~[e]s, Täler** ['tɛ:lɐ] valley; **das Vieh zu ~ treiben** drive the cattle down into the valley

tal·abwärts *Adv.* down the valley

Talar [ta'la:ɐ̯] **der; ~s, ~e** robe

tal·aufwärts *Adv.* up the valley

Tal·brücke die bridge across a/the valley

Tälchen ['tɛ:lçən] **das; ~s, ~:** [little] valley

Talent [ta'lɛnt] **das; ~[e]s, ~e a)** *(Befähigung)* talent **(zu, für** for); **~ für Sprachen haben** have a gift for languages; **sie hat das ~, immer das richtige Wort zu finden** she has a gift for always finding the right word; **b)** *(Mensch)* talented person; **junge ~e fördern** promote young talent

talentiert [talɛn'ti:ɐ̯t] *Adj.* talented

Talent·suche die search for talent; **zur ~ in die Provinz kommen** come in search of talent in the provinces

Taler ['ta:lɐ] **der; ~s, ~** *(hist.)* thaler

Tal·fahrt die a) *(Schiffahrt)* passage downstream; **b)** *(Fahrt abwärts)* drive down into the valley; *(mit dem Lift)* descent into the valley; *(mit Skiern)* skiing down into the valley; *(fig.)* fall; plunge; **die Wirtschaft befindet sich auf einer ~** *(fig.)* the economy is on the decline

Talg [talk] **der; ~[e]s, ~e a)** *(Speisefett)* suet; *(zur Herstellung von Seife, Kerzen usw.)* tallow; **b)** *(Haut~)* sebum

Talg-: ~drüse die sebaceous gland; **~licht das;** *Pl.* **~er** tallow candle

Talisman ['ta:lɪsman] **der; ~s, ~e** talisman

Talk [talk] **der; ~[e]s** talc

Talk-Show ['tɔ:kʃoʊ] **die** *(Ferns.)* talk show; chat show

Talmi ['talmi] **das; ~s a)** *(wertloser Schmuck)* imitation *or* cheap jewellery; *(fig.)* tinsel; **b)** *(vergoldete Legierung)* pinchbeck

Talmi·glanz der glitter

Talmud ['talmu:t] **der; ~[e]s, ~e** Talmud

Talschaft die; ~, ~en *(schweiz., westösterr.)* valley people *pl. or* inhabitants *pl.*

Tal-: ~sohle die valley floor *or* bottom; *(fig.)* depression; **die Wirtschaft befindet sich auf** *od.* **in einer ~sohle** the economy is going through a depression; **~sperre die** dam *(with associated reservoir and power-station);* **~station die** valley station

Tamarinde [tama'rɪndə] **die; ~, ~n** tamarind

Tamariske [tama'rɪskə] **die; ~, ~n** tamarisk

Tambour ['tambu:ɐ̯] **der; ~s, ~e** *od. (schweiz.)* **~en** *(veralt.)* drummer

Tambour·major der drum major

Tamburin [tambu'ri:n] **das; ~s, ~e** tambourine

Tampon ['tampɔn] **der; ~s, ~s a)** *(Med.: Wattebausch)* tampon; plug; **b)** *(Menstruations~)* tampon

tamponieren *tr. V. (Med.)* plug

Tamtam [tam'tam] **das; ~s, ~s a)** *(Musikinstrument)* tam-tam; **b)** *o. Pl. (ugs. abwertend: großer Aufwand)* **[großes] ~:** [a big] fuss; **~ machen** make a fuss

Tand [tant] **der; ~[e]s** trumpery

Tändelei die; ~, ~en a) *(Spielerei)* dalliance; **b)** *(Liebelei)* flirtation

tändeln ['tɛndḷn] *itr. V.* **a)** *(spielen)* dally; **b)** *(schäkern)* flirt

Tandem ['tandɛm] **das; ~s, ~s** tandem; *(fig.)* pair; **als ~ arbeiten** work in tandem

Tang [taŋ] **der; ~[e]s, ~e** seaweed

Tanga ['taŋga] **der; ~s, ~s** tanga

Tangens ['taŋgɛns] **der; ~, ~** *(Math.)* tangent

Tangente [taŋ'gɛntə] **die; ~, ~n a)** *(Math.)* tangent; **b)** *(Straße)* ring road; bypass

tangential [taŋgɛn'tsi̯a:l] *(Math.)* **1.** *Adj.* tangential. **2.** *adv.* tangentially

Tanger ['taŋɐ] **(das); ~s** Tangier

tangieren [taŋ'gi:rən] *tr. V.* **a)** affect; **b)** *(Math.)* be tangent to

Tango ['taŋgo] **der; ~s, ~s** tango

Tank [taŋk] **der; ~s, ~s,** *(seltener)* **~e** tank

tanken *tr., itr. V.* fill up; **Benzin/Öl ~:** fill up with petrol *(Brit.) or (Amer.)* gasoline/oil; **er tankte dreißig Liter [Super]** he put in thirty litres [of four-star]; **hast du schon getankt?** have you already put petrol *(Brit.) or (Amer.)* gasoline in?; **frische Luft/Sonne ~** *(fig.)* get one's fill of fresh air/sun; **er hat aber reichlich getankt** *(fig. salopp)* he really got tanked up *(sl.)*

Tanker der; ~s, ~: tanker

Tanker·flotte die fleet of tankers

Tank-: ~fahr·zeug das tanker; **~füllung die a)** *(das Füllen)* filling of the tank; **b) eine ~füllung reicht für ...:** one full tank is enough for ...; **~lager das** tank farm; **~säule die** petrol-pump *(Brit.);* gasoline pump *(Amer.);* **~stelle die** petrol station *(Brit.);* gas station *(Amer.);* **freie ~stelle** unbranded petrol/gas station; **~wagen der** tanker; **~wart** [~vart] **der; ~s, ~e** petrol-pump attendant *(Brit.)*

Tann [tan] **der; ~[e]s, ~e** *(dichter.)* [pine] forest

Tanne ['tanə] **die; ~, ~n a)** fir[-tree]; **schlank wie eine ~:** slender as a reed; **b)** *(Holz)* fir

Tannen-: ~baum der a) *(ugs.: Tanne a)* fir-tree; **b)** *(Weihnachtsbaum)* Christmas tree; **~grün das;** *o. Pl.* fir sprigs *pl.;* **~holz das** fir; **~nadel die** fir-needle; **~wald der** fir forest; **~zapfen der** fir-cone; **~zweig der** fir branch

Tansania [tan'za:ni̯a] **(das); ~s** Tanzania

Tansanier [tan'za:ni̯ɐ] **der; ~s, ~, Tansanierin die; ~, ~nen** Tanzanian

Tantalus·qualen ['tantalʊs-] *Pl.* **~ leiden** suffer agonizing frustration *sing.*

Tantchen das; ~s, ~: auntie *(coll.)*

Tante ['tantə] **die; ~, ~n a)** aunt; **b)** *(Kindersp.: Frau)* lady; **c)** *(ugs.: Frau)* woman

Tante-Emma-Laden der [small] corner shop

tantenhaft 1. *Adj.* old-maidish; *(belehrend)* nannyish. **2.** *adv.* like an old maid; *(belehrend)* nannyishly

Tantieme [tã'ti̯e:mə] **die; ~, ~n a)** *(Gewinnbeteiligung)* percentage of the profits; **b)** *(von Künstlern)* royalty

Tanz [tants] **der; ~es, Tänze** ['tɛntsə] **a)** dance; **jmdn. zum ~ auffordern** ask sb. to dance *or* for a dance; **ein ~ auf dem Vulkan** *(fig.)* sitting on a powder-keg; **der ~ ums Goldene Kalb** *(fig.)* worship of the golden calf; **b)** *o. Pl. (~veranstaltung)* dance; **heute Abend ist ~:** there is dancing this evening; **zum ~ gehen** go dancing; **ein ~ in den Mai/Frühling** a dance to mark the beginning of May/Spring; **c)** *(Zank, Auftritt)* song and dance *(fig. coll.)*

Tanz-: ~abend der evening dance; **~bar die** night-spot *(coll.)* with dancing; **~bär der** dancing bear; **~bein das** *in* **das ~bein schwingen** *(ugs. scherzh.)* shake a leg *(coll.);* **~boden der** dance-floor; **~café das** coffee-house with dancing

Tänzchen ['tɛntsçən] **das; ~s, ~:** [little] dance; **ein ~ wagen** take a turn around the floor

Tanz·diele die *(veralt.)* dance-hall

tänzeln ['tɛntsḷn] *itr. V.* **a)** prance; **jmdm. mit ~den Schritten entgegenkommen** skip towards sb.; **b)** *mit sein* **sie tänzelte ins Zimmer** she skipped into the room

tanzen 1. *itr. V.* **a)** dance; **~ gehen** go dancing; **auf dem Seil ~:** walk the tightrope; **das Schiff tanzt auf den Wellen** the ship is bobbing up and down on the waves; **sich heiß/müde ~:** dance until one is hot/tired; **b)** *mit sein (sich ~d fortbewegen)* dance; skip. **2.** *tr. V.* **Walzer/Tango ~:** dance a waltz/tango; waltz/tango

Tänzer ['tɛntsɐ] **der; ~s, ~ a)** dancer; **b)** *(Tanzpartner)* dancing-partner; **c)** *(Balletttänzer)* ballet-dancer

Tanzerei die; ~, ~en a) *(ugs.)* [small] dancing-party; **b)** *(oft abwertend: dauerndes Tanzen)* [continual] dancing *no pl.*

Tänzerin die; ~, ~nen *s.* **Tänzer**

tänzerisch 1. *Adj.* dance-like ‹*movement, rhythm, step*›; **~e Begabung** talent for dancing. **2.** *adv.* **~ begabt sein** have a talent for dancing; **~ ausgebildet sein** be trained as a dancer; **eine ~ hervorragende Leistung** an outstanding achievement in dance

Tanz-: ~fläche die dance-floor; **~gruppe die** dance group; **~kapelle die** dance band; **~kurs der** dancing-class; **~lehrer der** dancing-teacher; **~lokal das** café/restaurant with dancing; **~musik die** dance music; **~orchester das** dance band; **~partner der** dancing-partner; **~platte die** record of dance music; **~platz der** [open-air] dance-floor; **~saal der** dance-hall; *(in hotel, castle, etc.)* ballroom; **~schritt der** dance-step; **~schuh der** dance- *or* dancing-shoe; **~schule die** dancing-school; school of dancing; **~sport der** ballroom *or* competition dancing *no art.;* **~stunde die a)** *(~kurs)* dancing-class; **~stunde nehmen, in die ~stunde gehen** take dancing lessons; go to dancing-class; **b)** *(einzelne Stunde)* dancing lesson; **~tee der** tea dance; thé dansant; **~turnier das** dancing competition; **~veranstaltung die** dance; **~vergnügen das** dance

Taoismus [tao'ɪsmʊs] **der; ~:** Taoism *no art.*

Tapet das *in* **aufs ~ kommen** *(ugs.)* be brought up; come up [for discussion]; **etw. aufs ~ bringen** *(ugs.)* bring sth. up; broach sth.

Tapete [ta'pe:tə] **die; ~, ~n** wallpaper; **die ~n wechseln** *(ugs.)* have a change of scene

Tapeten-: ~rolle die roll of wallpaper; **~tür die** concealed door; **~wechsel der** *(ugs.)* change of scene

tapezieren [tape'tsi:rən] *tr. V.* [wall]paper

Tapezierer der; ~s, ~: paper-hanger

Tapezier-: ~nagel der tack; **~tisch der** pasteboard; paper-hanger's bench

tapfer ['tapfɐ] **1.** *Adj.* brave; courageous; brave ‹*child*›; **~en Widerstand leisten** resist bravely. **2.** *adv.* **a)** bravely; courageously; *(von Kindern)* bravely; **sich ~ halten** be brave; **b)** *(kräftig)* ‹*eat, drink*› heartily; **~ zulangen** have *or* take a big helping

Tapferkeit die; ~: courage; bravery

Tapioka [ta'pi̯o:ka] **die; ~:** tapioca

Tapir ['ta:pi:ɐ̯] **der; ~s, ~e** *(Zool.)* tapir

Tapisserie [tapɪsə'ri:] **die; ~, ~n** tapestry

tapp [tap] *Interj.* patter; **~, ~!** pitter patter!

tappen *itr. V.* **a)** *mit sein* patter; **in eine Falle ~** *(fig.)* stumble into a trap; **b)** *(tastend greifen)* grope **(nach** for)

täppisch ['tɛpɪʃ] **1.** *Adj.* awkward; clumsy. **2.** *adv.* awkwardly; clumsily

Taps [taps] **der; ~es, ~e** *(ugs. abwertend)* clumsy oaf

tapsig *(ugs.)* **1.** *Adj.* awkward; clumsy. **2.** *adv.* awkwardly; clumsily

Tarantel [ta'rantḷ] **die; ~, ~n** *(Zool.)* tarantula; **er sprang wie von der ~ gestochen auf** he jumped up as if something had bitten him

Tarantella [taran'tɛla] **die; ~, ~s** *od.* **Tarantellen** *(Musik)* tarantella

Tarif [ta'ri:f] **der; ~s, ~e a)** *(Preis, Gebühr)* charge; *(Post~, Wasser~)* rate; *(Verkehrs~)* fares *pl.;* *(Zoll~)* tariff; **b)** *(~verzeichnis)* list of charges/rates/fares; tariff; **der Fahrpreis beträgt laut ~ 1,20 DM** the fare is fixed at DM 1.20; **c)** *(Lohn~)* [wage] rate; *(Gehalts~)* [salary] scale; **weit über/unter ~ verdienen** earn well above/far below the agreed rate

Tarif-: ~autonomie die free collective bargaining *no art.;* **~gruppe die** *(Lohngruppe)* wage group; *(Gehaltsgruppe)* salary group; **~kommission die** wages commission

tariflich 1. *Adj.; nicht präd.* wage ⟨*demand, dispute, etc.*⟩. **2.** *adv.* **Löhne und Gehälter sind ~ festgelegt** there are fixed rates for wages and salaries; **die Arbeitszeit ist ~ geregelt** the number of working hours is fixed [by collective agreement]

tarif-, Tarif-: ~lohn der wage under the collective agreement; **~los** *Adj.* **es herrscht ein ~loser Zustand** no wage agreement is in force; **~partner der: die ~partner** union and management; employers and employees; **wegen der Unnachgiebigkeit des ~partners** because of the inflexibility of management/the union; **~verhandlung die** pay negotiations *pl.*; **~vertrag der** pay agreement

tarnen ['tarnən] **1.** *tr., itr. V.* camouflage; **seine Aufregung ~** *(fig.)* disguise one's excitement. **2.** *refl. V.* camouflage oneself; *(fig.)* disguise oneself

Tarn-: ~farbe die camouflage [colour]; **etw. mit ~farbe bemalen** paint sth. with camouflage paint; **~kappe die** *(Myth.)* magic hat *(making the wearer invisible)*

Tarnung die; ~, ~en *(auch fig.)* camouflage; **zur ~ dienen** serve as camouflage

Tarock [ta'rɔk] **das** *(österr. nur so) od.* **der** taroc

Tartan·bahn ['tartan-] **die** Tartan track **(P)**

Täschchen ['tɛʃçən] **das; ~s, ~:** *s.* **Tasche:** [little] bag/pocket

Tasche ['taʃə] **die; ~, ~n a)** bag; **b)** *(in Kleidung, Koffer, Rucksack usw.)* pocket; **c)** *(fig.)* **jmdm. die ~n leeren** *(ugs.)* fleece sb.; **sich** *(Dat.)* **die eigenen ~n füllen** *(ugs.)* line one's own pockets *or* purse; **jmdm. auf der ~ liegen** *(ugs.)* live off sb.; **etw. aus eigener** *od.* **der eigenen ~ bezahlen** pay for sth. out of one's own pocket; **jmdm. etw. aus der ~ ziehen** *(ugs.)* wangle money out of sb. *(coll.)*; **[für etw.] tief in die ~ greifen [müssen]** *(ugs.)* [have to] dig deep in *or* into one's pocket [for sth.]; **etw. in die eigene ~ stecken** *(ugs.)* pocket sth.; put sth. in one's own pocket; **in die eigene ~ arbeiten** *od.* **wirtschaften** *(ugs.)* line one's own pocket[s]; **jmdn. in die ~ stecken** *(ugs.)* put sb. in the shade; **sich** *(Dat.)* **in die eigene ~ lügen** *(ugs.)* fool oneself; **etw. in der ~ haben** *(ugs.)* have sth. in one's pocket

Taschen-: ~buch das paperback; **~buch·ausgabe die** paperback edition; **~dieb der** pickpocket; **~fahr·plan der** pocket timetable; **~format das** pocket size; **ein Wörterbuch im ~format** a pocket-size dictionary; **~geld das** pocket-money; **~kalender der** pocket calendar; **~krebs der** edible crab; **~lampe die** [pocket] torch *(Brit.) or (Amer.)* flashlight; **~messer das** pocket-knife; penknife; **~rechner der** pocket calculator; **~schirm der** telescopic umbrella; **~spiegel der** pocket mirror; **~spieler der** *(veralt.)* conjurer; **~spieler·trick der** *(abwertend)* trick; **~tuch das;** *Pl.* **~tücher** handkerchief; **~uhr die** pocket-watch; **~wörter·buch das** pocket dictionary

Täßchen ['tɛsçən] **das; ~s, ~:** [small] cup

Tasse ['tasə] **die; ~, ~n a)** cup; **eine ~ Tee** a cup of tea; **trübe ~** *(ugs. abwertend)* drip *(coll.)*; **komm, du trübe ~!** come on, don't be such a drip *(coll.)*; **b)** *(~ mit Untertasse)* cup and saucer; **nicht alle ~n im Schrank haben** *(ugs.)* not be right in the head *(coll.)*

Tastatur [tasta'tu:ɐ̯] **die; ~, ~en** keyboard

Taste ['tastə] **die; ~, ~n a)** *(eines Musikinstruments, einer Schreibmaschine)* key; **[mächtig] in die ~n greifen** start to play with great gusto; **b)** *(Fuß~)* pedal [key]; **c)** *(am Telefon, Radio, Fernsehgerät, Taschenrechner usw.)* button

Tast·empfindung die sense of touch

tasten 1. *itr. V. (fühlend suchen)* grope, feel (**nach** for); **~de Versuche/Fragen** *(fig.)* tentative attempts/questions. **2.** *refl. V. (sich tastend bewegen)* grope *or* feel one's way. **3.** *tr. V.* **a)** *(über eine Tastatur eingeben)* key in; **b)** *(tastend feststellen)* feel

Tasten-: ~druck der; *o. Pl.* touch of a/the button; **auf ~druck** at the touch of a/the button; **~instrument das** keyboard instrument; **~telefon das** push-button telephone

Taster der; ~s, ~ a) *(Technik: Maschine)* keyboard; **b)** *(Fachspr.: Mensch)* keyboard operator; **c)** *(Druck~)* button

Tast·sinn der; *o. Pl.* sense of touch

tat [ta:t] *1. u. 3. Pers. Sg. Prät. v.* **tun**

Tat die; ~, ~en a) *(Handlung)* act; *(das Tun)* action; **ein Mann der ~:** a man of action; **jmdm. mit Wort und ~ beistehen** stand by sb. in word and deed; **etw. durch ~en beweisen** prove sth. by one's actions; **zur ~ schreiten** proceed to action; **die gute Absicht/den guten Willen für die ~ nehmen** take the will for the deed; **jmdn. auf frischer ~ ertappen** catch sb. red-handed *or* in the act; **etw. in die ~ umsetzen** put sth. into action *or* effect; **das ist die ~ eines Wahnsinnigen** that is the action of a madman; **eine verbrecherische ~:** a crime; a criminal act; **eine gute ~ vollbringen** do a good deed; **ein Buch über Leben und ~en des ...:** a book on the life and exploits of ...; **zu seiner ~ stehen** stand by one's action; **b) in der ~** *(verstärkend)* actually; *(zustimmend)* indeed

¹Tatar [ta'ta:ɐ̯] **der; ~en, ~en** Tartar

²Tatar das; ~[s], Tatar·beefsteak das steak tartare

tatarisch *Adj.* Tartar

tatauieren [tatau'i:rən] *(Völkerk.) s.* **tätowieren**

Tat-: ~bestand der a) facts *pl.* [of the matter *or* case]; **einen ~bestand feststellen** establish the facts [of a matter *or* case]; **b)** *(Rechtsw.)* elements *pl.* of an offence; **der ~bestand der vorsätzlichen Tötung** the offence of premeditated murder; **~einheit die;** *o. Pl. (Rechtsw.)* concomitance of offences; **Mord in ~einheit mit Raub** murder [in concomitance] with robbery

taten-, Taten-: ~drang der desire *or* thirst for action; **trotz seines hohen Alters war er noch voller ~drang** in spite of his old age he was still full of energy; **~durst der** *(geh.)* thirst for action; **er brennt vor ~durst** he is thirsting for action; **~durstig** *Adj. (geh.)* thirsty *or* eager for action *postpos.*; **~los 1.** *Adj.* idle; **2.** *adv.* idly; **einer Sache** *(Dat.)* **~los zusehen** watch sth. without taking any action

Täter ['tɛ:tɐ] **der; ~s, ~:** culprit; **wer ist der ~?** who did it?; **der ~ hat sich der Polizei gestellt** the person who committed the crime gave himself/herself up to the police; **nach dem ~ fahnden** search *or* look for the person responsible [for the crime]; **die Polizei hat die ~ noch nicht gefunden** the police have not yet found those responsible [for the crime]

Täterin die; ~, ~nen *s.* **Täter**

Täter·kreis der group of people involved in a/the crime; *(bei mehreren Verbrechen)* group of offenders

Täterschaft die; ~ a) seine ~ ist erwiesen his responsibility for the crime has been proved; **b)** *(schweiz.: Täter)* culprit/culprits

Tat-: ~form die *(Sprachw.) s.* **¹Aktiv; ~her·gang der** [course *sing.* of] events *pl.*

tätig ['tɛ:tɪç] *Adj.* **a) ~ sein** work; **der in unserer Firma ~e Ingenieur** the engineer who works for our firm; **~ werden** *(bes. Amtsspr.)* take action; **~e Reue** *(Rechtsw.) remorse for one's crime, accompanied by action to avert its effects;* **b)** *(rührig, aktiv)* active; **~e Nächstenliebe** charity [to one's neighbour]; brotherly love; **ein ~er Vulkan** an active vulcano

tätigen ['tɛ:tɪgn̩] *tr. V. (Kaufmannsspr., Papierdt.)* transact ⟨*business, deal, etc.*⟩; **Einkäufe ~:** effect purchases; **Anrufe ~:** put through [telephone] calls

Tätigkeit die; ~, ~en a) activity; *(Arbeit)* job; **eine fieberhafte ~:** a frenzy of activity; **das gehört zu den ~en einer Hausfrau** that is part of a housewife's work *sing.*; **eine ~ ausüben** do work; do a job; **seine ~ aufnehmen** start work; **nach zweijähriger ~:** after two years' work; **b)** *o. Pl. (das In-Betrieb-Sein)* operation; **in ~ treten** come into operation

Tätigkeits-: ~bereich der sphere *or* field of activity; **~bericht der** progress report; **~form die** *(Sprachw.) s.* **¹Aktiv; ~merkmal das** key activity; **~wort das** *(Sprachw.) s.* **Verb**

Tat·kraft die energy; drive

tat·kräftig 1. *Adj.* energetic, active ⟨*person*⟩; active ⟨*help, support*⟩. **2.** *adv.* energetically; actively

tätlich ['tɛ:tlɪç] **1.** *Adj.* physical ⟨*clash, attack, resistance, etc.*⟩; **gegen jmdn. ~ werden** become violent towards sb. **2.** *adv.* physically; **jmdn. ~ angreifen** attack sb. physically; assault sb.

Tätlichkeit die; ~, ~en act of violence; **es kam zu ~en** violence occurred

Tat-: ~mensch der man/woman of action; **~motiv das** motive [for a/the crime]; **~ort der;** *Pl.* **~e** scene of a/the crime

tätowieren [tɛto'vi:rən] *tr. V.* tattoo; **sich** *(Dat.)* **etw. ~ lassen** have oneself tattooed with sth.

Tätowierung die; ~, ~en a) tattoo; **b)** *(das Tätowieren)* tattooing

Tat·sache die fact; **es ist [eine] ~, daß ...:** it's a fact that ...; **~!** *(ugs.)* it's true; it's a fact; **~?** *(ugs.)* really?; is that true?; **den ~n entsprechen** be true; **nackte ~n** hard facts; *(scherzh.)* naked bodies; **den ~n ins Auge sehen** face facts; **vollendete ~n schaffen** create a fait accompli; **jmdn. vor die vollendete ~** *od.* **vollendete ~n stellen** present sb. with a fait accompli; *s. auch* **Vorspiegelung**

Tatsachen-: ~bericht der factual report; **~material das** facts *pl.*

tatsächlich ['ta:tzɛçlɪç] **1.** *Adj.* actual; real; **der ~e Grund** the real reason. **2.** *adv.* actually; really; **ist das ~ wahr?** is that really true?; **~?** really?; **ich habe mich ~ geirrt** I was indeed mistaken; **Er hat es geschafft. – Tatsächlich!** He made it. – So he did!

tätscheln ['tɛtʃl̩n] *tr. V.* pat

tatschen ['tatʃn̩] *itr. V. (ugs. abwertend)* **an/auf etw.** *(Akk.)* **~:** paw sth.

Tattergreis ['tatɐ-] **der** *(ugs. abwertend)* doddery old man

Tatterich ['tatərɪç] **der; ~s** *(ugs.)* **einen ~ kriegen** get shaking hands; **er hat einen ~:** his hands are shaking

tatterig, tattrig *Adj. (ugs.)* shaky ⟨*hands, movements, etc.*⟩; doddery ⟨*person*⟩

tatütata [ta'ty:ta'ta:] *Interj.* pah-paw-pah-paw; **mit „Tatütata" und Blaulicht** with siren wailing and blue light flashing

tat·verdächtig *Adj.* suspected; **[dringend] ~ sein** be under [strong] suspicion

Tat·waffe die weapon [used in the crime]

Tatze ['tatsə] **die; ~, ~n** *(auch fig. ugs.)* paw

Tat·zeit die: [zur] ~: [at the] time of the crime

¹Tau [tau] **der; ~[e]s** dew; **vor ~ und Tag** *(dichter.)* before dawn of day

²Tau das; ~[e]s, ~e *(Seil)* rope

taub [taup] *Adj.* **a)** deaf; **~ werden** go deaf; **er war ~ gegen** *od.* **für alle Bitten** *(fig.)* he was deaf to all requests; **auf diesem Ohr ist er ~** *(ugs. scherzh.)* he's deaf to that sort of thing; **b)** *(wie abgestorben)* numb; **c)** *(leer, unbefruchtet usw.)* empty ⟨*nut*⟩; unfruitful ⟨*ear of corn*⟩; unfertilized ⟨*bird's egg*⟩; dead ⟨*rock*⟩

taub·blind *Adj.* deaf and blind

Täubchen ['tɔypçən] **das; ~s, ~:** [little] pigeon; *(Turtel~)* [little] dove; **mein ~** *(fig.)* my little dove

¹Taube die; ~, ~n pigeon; *(Turtel~; auch Politik fig.)* dove

²Taube der/die; *adj. Dekl.* deaf person; deaf man/woman; **die ~n** the deaf

tauben·blau *Adj.* greyish-blue

Tauben·ei das pigeon['s] egg

taubenei·groß *Adj.* as big as *or* the size of a golf ball *postpos.;* **~e Stücke** pieces as big as *or* the size of golf balls

Tauben·schlag der pigeon-loft; *(für Turteltauben)* dovecot; **hier geht es zu wie in einem** *od.* **im ~** *(ugs.)* it's like Piccadilly Circus here *(Brit. coll.);* it's like being in the middle of Times Square *(Amer.)*

Tauber der; ~s, ~, Täuberich ['tɔybərɪç] **der; ~s, ~e** cock pigeon

Taubheit die; ~: deafness

taub-, Taub-: ~nessel die dead nettle; **~stumm** *Adj.* deaf and dumb; **~stumme der/die;** *adj. Dekl.* deaf mute; **~stummen·sprache die** deaf-and-dumb language

tauchen 1. *itr. V.* **a)** *auch mit sein* dive (**nach** for); **früher habe ich viel getaucht** I used to do a lot of skin-diving *or* underwater swimming; **er kann zwei Minuten [lang] ~:** he can stay under water for two minutes; **er ist 3 Meter tief getaucht** he dived down three metres; **die Sonne tauchte unter den Horizont** *(fig.)* the sun disappeared *or* sank below the horizon; **b)** *mit sein (ein~)* dive; *(auf~)* rise; emerge; **er tauchte ins Dunkel des Gartens** *(fig.)* he plunged into the darkness of the garden. **2.** *tr. V.* **a)** *(ein~)* dip; **der Raum war in Licht getaucht** *(geh.)* the room was bathed in light; **die Landschaft war in Dunkelheit getaucht** *(geh.)* the countryside was shrouded in darkness; **b)** *(unter~)* duck

Tauch·ente die scaup [duck]

Taucher der; ~s, ~: diver; *(mit Flossen und Atemgerät)* skin-diver

Taucher-: ~an·zug der diving-suit; **~aus·rüstung die** diving equipment; **~brille die** diving-goggles *pl.;* **~glocke die** diving-bell

Taucherin die; ~, ~nen *s.* **Taucher**

Tauch-: ~gerät das diving equipment *no pl., no indef. art.;* **~maske die** diving-mask; **~sieder der; ~s, ~:** portable immersion heater; **~sport der** skin-diving *no art.;* **~station die: auf ~station gehen** *(auf dem U-Boot)* go to one's diving station; *(fig. ugs.)* go to ground; **~tiefe die** diving depth

tauen 1. *itr. V.* **a)** *(unpers.)* **es taut** it's thawing; **b)** *mit sein (schmelzen)* melt. **2.** *tr. V.* melt; thaw

Tauf·becken das font

Taufe die; ~, ~n a) *o. Pl. (christl. Rel.: Sakrament)* baptism; **b)** *(christl. Rel.: Zeremonie)* christening; baptism; **jmdn. über die ~ halten** *od. (veralt.)* **aus der ~ heben** be [a] godparent to sb.; **etw. aus der ~ heben** *(fig. ugs.)* launch sth.

taufen *tr. V.* **a)** *(die Taufe vollziehen an)* baptize; **katholisch getauft sein** be baptized a Catholic; **b)** *(einen Namen geben)* christen ⟨*child, ship, animal, etc.*⟩; **ein Kind auf den Namen Peter ~:** christen a child Peter; **er wurde nach seinem Großvater [Hermann] getauft** he was named [Hermann] after *or (Amer.)* for his grandfather

Tauf-: ~kapelle die baptistery; **~kleid das** christening robe *or* gown

Täufling ['tɔyflɪŋ] **der; ~s, ~e** child to be baptized; *(Erwachsener)* person to be baptized

Tauf-: ~name der Christian name; **~pate der** godparent; *(männlicher ~pate)* godfather; **~patin die** godmother; **~register das** register of baptisms; baptismal register

tau·frisch a) *(feucht vom Tau)* dew-covered; dewy; **b)** *(ganz frisch)* fresh; **sie ist auch nicht mehr ganz ~** *(fig.)* she's not exactly a spring chicken any more

Tauf-: ~schein der certificate of baptism; baptismal certificate; **~stein der** font

taugen ['taugn̩] *itr. V.* **nichts/wenig** *od.* **nicht viel/etwas ~:** be no/not much/some good *or* use; **zu** *od.* **für etw. ~** ⟨*person*⟩ be suited to sth.; ⟨*thing*⟩ be suitable for sth.; **zu einem** *od.* **zum Lehrer ~** ⟨*person*⟩ make a good teacher; **dazu ~, etw. zu tun** be good at doing sth.; **nicht wissen, was etw. wirklich taugt** not know how useful sth. really is

Taugenichts der; ~[es], ~e *(veralt. abwertend)* good-for-nothing

tauglich *Adj.* **a)** *(geeignet, brauchbar)* **[nicht] ~:** [un]suitable; **der Arzt hat ihn für ~ erklärt, ein Auto zu führen** the doctor has pronounced him fit to drive a car; **b)** *(für Militärdienst)* fit [for service]

Taumel der; ~s a) *(Schwindel, Benommenheit)* [feeling of] dizziness *or* giddiness; **ein ~ überkam ihn** he was overcome by a feeling of dizziness *or* giddiness; **b)** *(Begeisterung, Rausch)* frenzy; fever; **ein ~ der Begeisterung/Leidenschaft** a fever of excitement/passion; **ein ~ des Entzückens/Glücks** a transport of delight/happiness

taumelig 1. *Adj.* dizzy; giddy; **ihm war/wurde ~ vor Glück** he was transported with happiness/went into transports of happiness. **2.** *adv.* **~ gehen** reel *or* stagger

taumeln ['tauml̩n] *itr. V.* **a)** *auch mit sein (wanken)* reel, sway (**vor** + *Dat.* with); **das Flugzeug begann zu ~:** the aircraft began to roll; **b)** *mit sein (sich ~d bewegen)* stagger; **in den Abgrund/ins Unglück ~:** tumble into the abyss/plunge into disaster

tau·naß *Adj.* wet with dew *postpos.*

Tau·punkt der *(Physik)* dew-point

Tausch der; ~[e]s, ~e exchange; **ein guter/schlechter ~:** a good/bad deal; **im ~ gegen** *od.* **für etw.** in exchange for sth.; **etw. durch ~ erwerben** acquire sth. through an exchange; **etw. zum ~ anbieten** offer to exchange sth. for sth.; **etw. im ~ erhalten** receive sth. in exchange

tauschen 1. *tr. V.* exchange (**gegen** for); **Briefmarken/Münzen ~:** exchange *or* swap stamps/coins; **sie tauschten die Partner/Pferde/Plätze** they changed *or* swapped partners/horses/places; **wollen wir ~:** shall we swap *(coll.);* **Küsse ~** *(geh.)* kiss; **einen Händedruck ~:** shake hands. **2.** *itr. V.* **mit den Rollen/Plätzen/Partnern ~:** change *or* swap roles/places/partners; **mit jmdm. ~** *(fig.)* change *or* swap places with sb.

täuschen ['tɔyʃn̩] **1.** *tr. V.* deceive; **ich sah mich in meinen Erwartungen getäuscht** I was disappointed in my expectations; **der Schüler versuchte zu ~:** the pupil tried to cheat; **der Schein täuscht uns oft** appearances are often deceiving; **wenn mich nicht alles täuscht** unless I'm completely mistaken. **2.** *itr. V.* **a)** *(irreführen)* be deceptive; **b)** *(bes. Sport: ablenken)* make a feint. **3.** *refl. V.* be wrong *or* mistaken (**in** + *Dat.* about); **ich habe mich in ihm getäuscht** I was wrong about him; he disappointed me; **da täuschst du dich aber [gewaltig]** but that's where you're [very much] mistaken

täuschend 1. *Adj.* remarkable, striking ⟨*similarity, imitation*⟩. **2.** *adv.* remarkably; **jmdm. ~ ähnlich sehen** look remarkably like sb.

Täuscher der; ~s, ~: swindler

Tausch-: ~geschäft das exchange [deal]; **ein gutes ~geschäft machen** make a good deal in an/the exchange; **~gesellschaft die** *(Soziol.)* barter society; **~handel der a)** bartering; **~handel treiben** barter; **b)** *(Wirtsch.)* trade by barter; **~objekt das** object of barter[ing]

Täuschung die; ~, ~en a) *(das Täuschen)* deception; **auf eine ~ hereinfallen** be deceived; **b)** *(Selbst~)* delusion; illusion; **einer ~ unterliegen** be under an illusion; **er gibt sich der ~ hin, daß ...:** he mistakenly believes that ...; **optische ~:** optical illusion

Täuschungs-: ~absicht die intent to deceive; **~manöver das** ploy

tausend ['tauznt] *Kardinalz.* **a)** a *or* one thousand; **einige/mehrere ~ Zuschauer** a few/several thousand spectators; **~ und aber ~ Ameisen** thousands and thousands of ants; *s. auch* **acht; b)** *(ugs.: sehr viele)* thousands of; **noch ~ Sachen zu erledigen haben** still have thousands of *or* a thousand things to do; **~ Dank/Küsse** a thousand thanks/kisses

¹Tausend das; ~s, ~e *od.* **~ a)** *nicht in Verbindung mit Kardinalzahlen; Pl.:* **~** *(Einheit von tausend Stück)* thousand; **ein volles/halbes ~:** a full/half a thousand; a thousand/five hundred; **vom ~:** per thousand; **b)** *Pl. (eine unbestimmte große Zahl)* thousands; **~e Zuschauer** thousands of spectators; **die Kosten gehen in die ~e** *(ugs.)* the costs run into thousands; **die Tiere starben zu ~en** the animals died in [their] thousands

²Tausend die; ~, ~en thousand

tausend·ein[s] *Kardinalz.* a *or* one thousand and one

Tausender der; ~s, ~ a) *(ugs.) (Tausendmarkschein usw.)* thousand-mark/-dollar *etc.* note; *(Betrag)* thousand marks/dollars *etc.;* **b)** *(Math.)* thousand

tausenderlei *Gattungsz.; indekl. (ugs.)* **a)** *(von verschiedener Art)* a thousand and one different ⟨*answers, kinds, etc.*⟩; **b)** *(viele)* a thousand and one; *s. auch* **hunderterlei**

tausendfach *Vervielfältigungsz.* thousandfold; *(ugs.: sehr häufig)* a thousand and one times; **die ~e Menge** a thousand times the amount; **~en Dank** a thousand thanks; *s. auch* **achtfach**

Tausendfüßer ['tauzntfy:sɐ], **Tausendfüßler der; ~s, ~:** millipede

Tausend·gülden·kraut das *(Bot.)* centaury

Tausend·jahr·feier die millenary; millennial; *(Festlichkeit auch)* millenary *or* millennial celebrations *pl.; s. auch* **Hundertjahrfeier**

tausend·jährig *Adj.; nicht präd.* **a)** *(tausend Jahre alt)* [one-]thousand-year-old; **b)** *(tausend Jahre dauernd)* thousand-year[-long]; **~es Reich** *(ns.)* thousand-year Reich; **Tausendjähriges Reich** *(Theol.)* millennium

tausendköpfig *Adj.; nicht präd.* thousand-strong; *(fig.)* thousands strong *postpos.*

Tausend·künstler der *(ugs. scherzh.)* jack of all trades

tausend·mal *Adv.* a thousand times; **ich bitte [dich] ~ um Entschuldigung** *(ugs.)* a thousand pardons *or* apologies; *s. auch* **achtmal**

Tausend·mark·schein der thousand-mark note

Tausendsas[s]a ['tauzntsasa] **der; ~s, ~[s]** jack of all trades

Tausendschönchen [-ʃø:nçən] **das; ~s, ~:** daisy

tausendst... *Ordinalz.* thousandth; *s. auch* **acht...**

tausendstel ['tauzntstl] *Bruchz.* thousandth; *s. auch* **achtel**

Tausendstel das *(schweiz. meist* **der***);* **~s, ~:** thousandth

Tausendstel·sekunde die; ~, ~n thousandth of a second

tausend·und·ein[s] *Kardinalz. s.* **tausendein[s]**

Tautologie [tautolo'gi:] **die; ~, ~n** *(Rhet., Stilk.)* tautology

tautologisch *Adj. (Rhet., Stilk.)* tautological; tautologous

Tau-: ~tropfen der dew-drop; **~wasser das;** *Pl.* **~:** meltwater; **~werk das;** *o. Pl.* **a)**

(Material) rope; **b)** *(auf einem Schiff)* rigging; **~wetter das** *(auch fig.)* thaw; **gestern war bei uns ~wetter** yesterday we had a thaw; **~ziehen das; ~s** *(auch fig.)* tug-of-war
Taverne [ta'vɛrnə] **die; ~, ~n** taverna
Taxa·meter [taxa-] **der** [taxi]meter
Taxator [ta'ksa:tɔr] **der; ~s, ~en** [taksa'to:rən] *(Wirtsch.)* valuer
Taxe ['taksə] **die; ~, ~n a)** taxi; **b)** *(Gebühr)* charge; **c)** *(taxierter Preis)* valuation
Taxi ['taksi] **das; ~s, ~s** taxi; **mit dem ~:** by taxi *or* in a taxi; **~ fahren** drive a taxi; *(als Fahrgast)* go by taxi
taxieren *tr. V.* **a)** *(ugs.: schätzen)* estimate **(auf + *Akk.*** at); **er hat falsch taxiert** his estimate is wrong; **etw. zu hoch/niedrig ~:** overestimate/underestimate sth.; **b)** *(den Wert ermitteln von)* value **(auf + *Akk.*** at); **etw. zu hoch/niedrig ~:** overvalue/undervalue sth.; **c)** *(ugs.: mustern, prüfen)* size up *(coll.)*; **d)** *(einschätzen)* assess
Taxi-: ~fahrer der taxi-driver; **~fahrt die** taxi ride; **~stand der** taxi-rank *(Brit.)*; taxi-stand
Taxus ['taksʊs] **der; ~, ~:** yew[-tree]
Tb, Tbc [te:'be:, te:be:'tse:] **die; ~** *Abk.* **Tuberkulose** TB
Tb-krank [te:'be:-] *Adj.* suffering from TB *postpos.*; **~e Patienten** patients with TB
Tb-Kranke [te:'be:-] **der/die;** *adj. Dekl.* TB patient; patient with TB
Teak [ti:k] **das; ~s, Teak·holz das** teak
Team [ti:m] **das; ~s, ~s** team
Team·chef der *(Sport)* team manager
Teamwork ['ti:mwɔ:k] **das; ~s** team-work
Tea-Room ['ti:ru:m] **der; ~s, ~s** *(schweiz.)* tea-room *(without alcoholic drinks)*
Technik ['tɛçnɪk] **die; ~, ~en a)** *o. Pl.* technology; *(Studienfach)* engineering *no art.*; **auf dem neuesten Stand der ~:** incorporating the latest technical advances; **im Zeitalter der ~ leben** live in the technological age *or* age of technology; **b)** *o. Pl. (technische Ausrüstung)* equipment; machinery; **c)** *(Arbeitsweise, Verfahren)* technique; **d)** *o. Pl. (eines Gerätes)* workings *pl.*
Techniker der; ~s, ~, Technikerin die; ~, ~nen a) technical expert; **b)** *(im Sport, in der Kunst)* technician
Technikum ['tɛçnikʊm] **das; ~s, Technika** *od.* **Techniken** technical college
technisch ['tɛçnɪʃ] **1.** *Adj.* technical; technological ⟨*progress, age*⟩; **ein ~er Fehler** a technical fault. **2.** *adv.* technically; ⟨*interested*⟩ in technology; technologically ⟨*advanced*⟩; **~ begabt sein** have a technical flair
technisieren [tɛçni'zi:rən] *tr. V.* mechanize
Technisierung die; ~, ~en mechanization
Technokrat [tɛçno'kra:t] **der; ~en, ~en** technocrat
Technokratie [tɛçnokra'ti:] **die; ~:** technocracy
Technokratin die; ~, ~nen technocrat
technokratisch *Adj.* technocratic
Technologie [tɛçnolo'gi:] **die; ~, ~n** technology
Technologie·park der science park
technologisch 1. *Adj.* technological. **2.** *adv.* technologically
Techtelmechtel [tɛçtl'mɛçtl] **das; ~s, ~:** affair
Teckel ['tɛkl] **der; ~s, ~** dachshund
Teddy·bär ['tɛdi-] **der** teddy bear
Tedeum [te'de:ʊm] **das; ~s, ~s** Te Deum
TEE [te:le:'le:] **der; ~[s], ~[s]** *Abk.* **Trans-Europ-Express** TEE
Tee [te:] **der; ~s,** *(Sorten:)* **~s** tea; **der ~ muß noch ziehen** the tea must stand *or* brew a while; **einen ~ machen** make some tea; **einen ~ geben** *(geh.)* give a tea-party; **einen im ~ haben** *(fig. ugs.)* be tipsy; have had one over the eight *(sl.)*; **abwarten und ~ trinken** *(fig. ugs.)* just wait and see
Tee-: ~beutel der tea-bag; **~butter die** *(österr.) s.* **Markenbutter; ~-Ei das** tea-ball; tea-egg; **~gebäck das** [tea] biscuits *pl. (Brit.) or (Amer.)* cookies *pl.*; **~glas das;** *Pl.* **~gläser** tea-glass; **~kanne die** teapot; **~kessel der a)** tea-kettle; **b)** *(Spiel) game in which homonymous words must be guessed*; **~küche die** [small] kitchen; **~licht das;** *Pl.* **~er** *od.* **~e** tea-warmer; **~löffel der** teaspoon
Teen [ti:n] **der; ~s, ~s, Teenager** ['ti:neɪdʒə] **der; ~s, ~:** teenager
Tee-: ~pause die tea-break; **~pflücker der, ~pflückerin die** tea-picker
Teer [te:ɐ̯] **der; ~[e]s,** *(Arten:)* **~e** tar
Teer·decke die tar surface
teeren *tr. V.* tar; **jmdn. ~ und federn** tar and feather sb.
teer-, Teer-: ~farb·stoff der aniline dye; **~faß das** tar barrel; **~haltig** *Adj.* containing tar *postpos., not pred.*
Tee·rose die tea-rose
Teer·pappe die bituminous roofing-felt
Tee-: ~service das tea-service; tea-set; **~sieb das** tea-strainer; **~strauch der** tea-plant; **~stube die** tea-room; **~tasse die** teacup; **~trinker der** tea-drinker; **~wagen der** tea-trolley; **~wasser das** water for the tea; *s. auch* **Kaffeewasser; ~wurst die** *soft German smoked sausage for spreading*; ≈ meat-spread
Teich [taiç] **der; ~[e]s, ~e** pond; **der große ~** *(ugs. scherzh.: das Meer)* the [herring-]pond *(joc.)*
Teig [taik] **der; ~[e]s, ~e** dough; *(Kuchen~, Biskuit~)* pastry; *(Pfannkuchen~, Waffel~)* batter; *(in Rezepten auch)* mixture; **~ für Fleischklößchen** meat-ball mixture; **den ~ gehen lassen** let the dough rise
teigig *Adj.* **a)** *(wie Teig)* doughy; **b)** *(blaß u. schwammig)* pasty ⟨*face, skin, complexion*⟩
Teig-: ~rolle die a) *(Rolle aus Teig)* roll of dough; **b)** *(Nudelholz)* rolling-pin; **~waren** *Pl.* pasta *sing.*
Teil [tail] **a) der; ~[e]s, ~e** *(etw. von einem Ganzen)* part; **weite ~e des Landes** wide areas of the country; **ein [großer** *od.* **guter] ~ der Presse/Bevölkerung** a [large] section of the press/population; **ich habe das Buch zum größten ~ gelesen** I have read most of the book; **zum ~:** partly; **es waren zum ~ schöne Exemplare** some of them were beautiful specimens; **fünfter ~:** fifth; **den größten ~ des Weges hat er zu Fuß zurückgelegt** he walked most of the way; **ein gut ~ Glück/Mut** a lot of *or* a good bit of luck/courage *(coll.)*; **b) der** *od.* **das; ~[e]s, ~e** *(Anteil)* share; **sein[en] ~ [schon noch] bekommen** *od.* **kriegen** get one's comeuppance *(coll.)*; **sein[en] ~ weghaben** *(ugs.)* have [already] had one's due; *(die verdiente Strafe bekommen haben)* have got what was coming to one; **sich** *(Dat.)* **sein ~ denken** have one's own thoughts on the matter; **ich für mein ~ ...:** for my part, I ...; **c) der** *od.* **das; ~[e]s, ~e** *(Beitrag)* share; **ich will gerne mein[en] ~ dazu beisteuern** I should like to do my share *or* bit; **sein[en] ~ geben** *od.* **[zu etw.] tun** do one's share *or* bit [towards sth.]; **d) der; ~[e]s, ~e** *(beteiligte Person[en]; Rechtsw.: Partei)* party; **e) das; ~[e]s, ~e** *(Einzel~)* part; **~e des Motors** [component] parts of the engine; **etw. in seine ~e zerlegen** take sth. apart *or* to pieces
Teil-: ~ansicht die partial view; **~aspekt der: nur ein ~aspekt des Problems** only one aspect of the problem
teil·bar *Adj.* divisible **(durch** by)
Teilbarkeit die; ~: divisibility
Teil-: ~bereich der *(eines Fachs)* branch; *(einer Organisation)* section; **~betrag der** instalment; *(einer Rechnung)* item
Teilchen das; ~s, ~ a) *(kleines Stück)* [small] part; **b)** *(Partikel)* particle; **c)** *(bes. nordd.: Gebäckstück)* tart
Teilchen·beschleuniger der; ~s, ~ *(Kerntechnik)* particle accelerator
teilen 1. *tr. V.* **a)** *(zerlegen, trennen)* divide [up]; **b)** *(dividieren)* divide **(durch** by); **c)** *(auf~)* share **(unter + *Dat.*** among); **d)** *(teilweise überlassen, gemeinsam nutzen, teilhaben an)* share; **e)** *(in zwei Teile ~)* divide; **das Schiff teilt die Wellen** *(geh.)* the ship cuts through the waves; *s. auch* **Leid a. 2.** *refl. V.* **a) sich** *(Dat.)* **etw. [mit jmdm.] ~:** share sth. [with sb.]; **sich** *(Dat.)* **[mit jmdm.] in etw.** *(Akk.)* **~** *(geh.)* share sth. [with sb.]; **b)** *(auseinandergehen)* **der Vorhang teilt sich** the curtain opens; **der Weg teilt sich** the road forks; **geteilter Meinung sein** have different views *or* opinions. **3.** *itr. V.* share
Teiler der; ~s, ~ *(Math.)* factor
Teil-: ~erfolg der partial success; **~gebiet das** branch; **~habe die** participation **(an + *Dat.*** in)
teil|haben *unr. itr. V.* share **(an + *Dat.*** in)
Teilhaber der; ~s, ~: partner; **stiller ~:** sleeping partner
Teilhaberschaft die; ~, ~en participation, *(Anteil)* share **(an + *Dat.*** in)
teilhaftig [-'haftɪç] *Adj.* **in einer Sache** *(Gen.)* **~ werden/sein** *(geh. veralt.)* be blessed with sth.; **eines Anblicks ~ werden** be privy to a sight
Teil·kasko·versicherung die *insurance giving limited cover*
teil·möbliert 1. *Adj.* partially furnished. **2.** *adv.* **~ wohnen** live in partly furnished accommodation
Teilnahme ['tailna:mə] **die; ~, ~n a)** *(das Mitmachen)* participation **(an + *Dat.*** in); **~ an einem Kurs** attendance at a course; **b)** *(Interesse)* interest **(an + *Dat.*** in); **c)** *(geh.: Mitgefühl)* sympathy
teilnahme·berechtigt *Adj.* eligible **(bei** for)
Teilnahme·berechtigung die eligibility
teilnahms·los *Adj. (gleichgültig)* indifferent; *(apathisch)* apathetic
Teilnahmslosigkeit die *(Gleichgültigkeit)* indifference; *(Apathie)* apathy
teilnahms·voll 1. *Adj.* compassionate. **2.** *adv.* compassionately; **jmdn. ~ ansehen** look at sb. with compassion
teil|nehmen ['tailne:mən] *unr. itr. V.* **a)** *(dabei sein bei)* **[an etw. (*Dat.*)] ~:** attend [sth.]; **b)** *(beteiligt sein)* **[an etw. (*Dat.*)] ~:** take part [in sth.]; **am Krieg ~:** fight in the war; **an einem Wettkampf ~:** take part in *or* enter a competition; **c)** *(als Lernender)* **[an einem Lehrgang] ~:** attend [a course]; **am Unterricht ~:** attend lessons; **d)** *(Teilnahme zeigen)* **an jmds. Schmerz/Glück ~:** share sb.'s pain/happiness
teilnehmend *s.* **teilnahmsvoll**
Teilnehmer der; ~s, ~ a) participant *(Gen.,* **an + *Dat.*** in); *(bei Wettbewerb auch)* competitor, contestant **(an + *Dat.*** in); **b)** *(Fernspr.)* subscriber; **der ~ meldet sich nicht** there is no reply
Teilnehmerin die; ~, ~nen *s.* **Teilnehmer**
Teilnehmer·zahl die the number of participants; *(Sport)* number of competitors
teils [tails] *Adv.* partly; **~ ... ~ ...:** partly ... partly ...; **Kostüme, ~ mit Seitenschlitzen** costumes, some with side slits; **Wie hat es dir gestern gefallen? – Teils, ~** *(ugs.)* How did you like it yesterday? – So so
Teil-: ~strecke die *(einer Straße)* stretch; *(einer Buslinie usw.)* stage; *(Rennsport)* stage; **~strich der** graduation line; **~stück das** piece; part
Teilung die; ~, ~en division
teil·weise 1. *Adv.* partly; **~ gut** good in parts. **2.** *adj.* partial
Teil-: ~zahlung die instalment; **etw. auf ~zahlung kaufen** buy sth. on hire-purchase *(Brit.) or (Amer.)* on installment plan; **~zeit·arbeit die** part-time work *no indef. art.*; *(Stelle)* part-time job; **~zeit·be-**

schäftigung die part-time employment *or* work *no indef. art.; (Stelle)* part-time job

Teint [tɛ̃:] **der; ~s, ~s** complexion

Tektonik [tɛk'to:nɪk] **die;** ~ *(Geol.)* tectonics *sing., no art.*

tektonisch *Adj.* tectonic

tele-, Tele- ['te:le-] tele-

Tele·brief der fax message

Tele·fax das fax

Telefon ['te:lefo:n, *auch* tele'fo:n] **das; ~s, ~e** telephone; phone *(coll.)*; **ans ~ gehen** answer the [tele]phone; **jmdn. ans ~ rufen** call sb. to the [tele]phone; **am ~ verlangt werden** be wanted on the [tele]phone; **am ~ hängen** *(ugs.)* be on the [tele]phone; **sich ans ~ hängen** *(ugs.)* get on the phone *(coll.)*

Telefon-: ~an·ruf der [tele]phone call; **~an·schluß der** telephone; line; **~apparat der** telephone

Telefonat [telefo'na:t] **das; ~[e]s, ~e** telephone call

Telefon-: ~buch das [tele]phone book *or* directory; **~gebühr die** telephone charge; **~gespräch das** telephone conversation; **~häuschen das** *s.* **~zelle; ~hörer der** telephone receiver

telefonieren [telefo'ni:rən] *itr. V.* make a [tele]phone call; **mit jmdm. ~:** talk to sb. [on the telephone]; **nach einem Taxi ~:** [tele]phone a taxi; **du telefonierst zu viel** you're on the phone too much; you're making too many [tele]phone calls; **nach Hause ~:** phone home; **nach England ~:** make a [tele]phone call to England; **lange [mit jmdm.] ~:** be on the telephone [to sb.] for a long time; **er telefoniert gerade** he is on the phone at the moment; **bei jmdm. ~:** use sb.'s [tele]phone

telefonisch 1. *Adj.* telephone; **die ~e Zeitansage** the speaking clock *(Brit. coll.)*; the telephone time service; **~e Bestellung** telephone order; order by telephone. **2.** *adv.* by telephone; **jmdm. etw. ~ mitteilen** inform sb. of sth. over the *or* by telephone; **ich bin ~ zu erreichen** *od.* **erreichbar** I can be contacted by telephone; **er hat sich ~ entschuldigt** he telephoned to apologize

Telefonist [telefo'nɪst] **der; ~en, ~en, Telefonistin die; ~, ~nen** telephonist; *(in einer Firma)* switchboard operator

Telefon-: ~leitung die telephone line; **~nummer die** [tele]phone number; **~rechnung die** [tele]phone bill; **~seelsorge die** pastoral advice service; **die ~seelsorge** ≈ the Samaritans *(Brit.)*; **~überwachung die** telephone surveillance; **~verbindung die** telephone line; **~verzeichnis das** telephone list; **~zelle die** [tele]phone-booth *or (Brit.)* -box; call-box *(Brit.)*; **~zentrale die** telephone exchange

tele·gen [tele'ge:n] *Adj.* telegenic

Telegraf [tele'gra:f] **der; ~en, ~en** telegraph

Telegrafen-: ~amt das telegraph office; **~mast der** telegraph-pole

Telegrafie die; ~: telegraphy *no art.*

telegrafieren [telegra'fi:rən] *itr., tr. V.* telegraph; **jmdm. ~:** send a telegram to sb.; **nach Berlin ~:** send a telegram to Berlin

telegrafisch 1. *Adj.* telegraphic; **eine ~e Mitteilung** a message by telegraph *or* telegram. **2.** *adv.* by telegraph *or* telegram; **~ überwiesenes Geld** money sent by telegram *or* cable

Telegramm das telegram

Telegrammstil der; *o. Pl.* telegram style; telegraphese [style]; **im ~:** in telegraphese

Telegraph, Telegraphie *usw. s.* **Telegraf, Telegrafie** *usw.*

Telekinese [teleki'ne:zə] **die;** ~ *(Parapsych.)* telekinesis *no art.*

Tele·kolleg das ≈ Open University *(Brit.)*

Tele·objektiv das *(Fot.)* telephoto lens

Teleologie [teleolo'gi:] **die;** ~ *(Philos.)* teleology *no art.*

teleo·logisch [teleo'lo:gɪʃ] **1.** *Adj.* teleological. **2.** *adv.* teleologically

Telepathie [telepa'ti:] **die;** ~: telepathy *no art.*

telepathisch 1. *Adj.* telepathic; **auf ~em Weg** by telepathic means. **2.** *adv.* telepathically

Telephon, telephonieren *usw. s.* **Telefon, telefonieren** *usw.*

tele·scheu *Adj.* camera-shy

Tele·skop [tele'sko:p] **das; ~s, ~e** telescope

Teleskop·antenne die telescopic aerial *or (Amer.)* antenna

Tele·spiel das video game

Tele·vision [televi'zio:n] **die;** ~: television *no art.*

Telex ['te:lɛks] **das; ~, ~[e]** telex

telexen *itr. V.* telex

Teller ['tɛlɐ] **der; ~s, ~ a)** plate; **ein ~ Suppe** a plate of soup; **b)** *(beim Skistock)* basket

Teller-: ~eisen das *(Jagdw.)* steel jaw trap; **~fleisch das** *(bes. österr.) pieces of boiled beef or pork served in soup;* **~gericht das** *(Gastr.)* one-course meal; **~mine die** Teller mine; anti-tank mine; **~rand der** rim; edge of a/the plate; **über den eigenen ~rand** *(fig.)* beyond one's own nose; **~wäscher der** dishwasher; **vom ~wäscher zum Millionär [werden]** [go] from rags to riches

Tellur [tɛ'lu:ɐ] **das; ~s** *(Chemie)* tellurium

Tempel ['tɛmpl] **der; ~s, ~:** temple

Tempel-: ~herr der *(hist.)* Templar; **~orden der** *(hist.)* Order of the Knights Templars; **~ritter der** *(hist.)* Templar; **~schändung die** desecration of a/the temple

Tempera- ['tɛmpəra-]: **~farbe die** tempera colour; distemper; **~malerei die a)** *o. Pl. (Maltechnik)* tempera painting *no art.*; painting *no art.* in distemper; **b)** *(Bild)* tempera painting

Temperament [tɛmpəra'mɛnt] **das; ~[e]s, ~e a)** *(Wesensart)* temperament; **die vier ~e** the four humours; **eine Sache des ~s** a matter *or* question of temperament; **b)** *o. Pl. (Schwung, Lebhaftigkeit)* **eine Frau mit ~:** a lively *or* vivacious woman; a woman with spirit; **[viel] ~ haben** be [very] lively; have [plenty of] spirit; **sie hat kein/wenig ~:** she is not a lively/not a very lively person; **sein ~ reißt alle mit** his vivacity infects everyone; c) *o. Pl. (Erregbarkeit)* **das ~ geht oft mit mir durch** I often lose my temper; **sein ~ zügeln** control one's temper

temperament·los *Adj.* spiritless; lifeless

Temperaments-: ~aus·bruch der temperamental outburst; **~sache die** *in* **etw./das ist ~sache** sth./that is a matter *or* question of temperament

temperament·voll *Adj.* spirited ‹*person, speech, dance, etc.*›; lively ‹*start etc.*›; nippy *(coll.)* ‹*car*›

Temperatur [tɛmpəra'tu:ɐ] **die; ~, ~en a)** *(Wärmezustand)* temperature; **die richtige ~ haben** be [at] the right temperature; **b)** *(Körper~)* temperature; **[erhöhte] ~ haben** have *or* be running a temperature; **jmds. ~ messen** take sb.'s temperature

Temperatur-: ~anstieg der rise in temperature; **~regler der** thermostat; **~rück·gang der** drop *or* fall in temperature; **~schwankung die** fluctuation in temperature; **~sturz der** [sudden] fall *or* drop in temperature; **~unterschied der** difference in temperature

temperieren [tɛmpə'ri:rən] *tr. V.* bring to the right temperature; **das Zimmer angenehm/richtig ~:** bring the room to a pleasant/the right temperature; **das Wasser ist gut temperiert** the water is [at] the right temperature; **ein schlecht temperierter Wein** a wine at the wrong temperature

Templer ['tɛmplɐ] **der; ~s, ~** *(hist.)* Templar

¹Tempo ['tɛmpo] **das; ~s, ~s** *od.* **Tempi a)** *Pl.* **~s** speed; **das ~ erhöhen** speed up; accelerate; **in** *od.* **mit hohem ~:** at high speed; **hier gilt ~ 100** there is a 100 k.p.h. speed limit here; **der hat ein ~ drauf!** *(ugs.)* he's going at quite a *or (Brit. coll.)* at a fair old speed!; **~ [~]!** *(ugs.)*, **macht mal ein bißchen ~** *(ugs.)* get a move on; **b)** *(Musik)* tempo; time; **c)** *(Fechten)* period; *(Hieb)* stop cut; *(Stoß)* stop thrust *or* point

²Tempo Ⓦⓩ **das; ~s, ~s** *(ugs.)* tissue

Tempo·limit das *(Verkehrsw.)* speed limit

Tempora *s.* **Tempus**

temporal [tɛmpo'ra:l] *(Sprachw.)* temporal

Temporal·satz der *(Sprachw.)* temporal clause

temporär [tɛmpo'rɛ:ɐ] *(geh.)* **1.** *Adj.* temporary. **2.** *adv.* temporarily

Tempo·taschen·tuch das *(ugs.)* paper tissue *or* handkerchief

Tempus ['tɛmpʊs] **das; ~, Tempora** ['tɛmpora] *(Sprachw.) s.* **Zeitform**

Tendenz [tɛn'dɛnts] **die; ~, ~en a)** trend; **es herrscht die ~/die ~ geht dahin, ... zu ...:** there is a tendency to ...; the trend is to ...; **die Preise haben eine steigende/fallende ~:** prices are rising/falling; **b)** *(Hang, Neigung)* tendency; **die ~ haben, etw. zu tun** have a tendency to do sth.; **seine Ansichten haben eine ~ zum Dogmatismus** his attitudes tend towards dogmatism; **c)** *(oft abwertend: Darstellungsweise)* slant; bias

tendenziell [tɛndɛn'tsiɛl] **1.** *Adj.* **der ~e Fall der Profitrate** the [general] trend towards a drop in profit margins. **2.** *adv.* **~ scheint sich eine Verschärfung dieser Krise abzuzeichnen** the trend seems to indicate a deepening of the crisis; **eine ~ faschistische Haltung** an attitude tending towards fascism

tendenziös [...'tsiø:s] *Adj.* tendentious

Tendenz·wende die change in a/the trend *or* in direction

Tender ['tɛndɐ] **der; ~s, ~** *(Eisenb., Seew.)* tender

tendieren [tɛn'di:rən] *itr. V.* tend **(zu** towards); **er tendiert zu solchen Auffassungen** he tends to [hold] such opinions; **nach links/rechts ~:** tend to[wards] the left/right; **der nach links ~de Flügel dieser Partei** the branch of the party with left-wing leanings

Teneriffa [tene'rɪfa] **(das); ~s** Tenerife

Tenne ['tɛnə] **die; ~, ~n** threshing-floor *(in barn)*

Tennis ['tɛnɪs] **das; ~:** tennis *no art.*

Tennis-: ~arm der *(Med.)* tennis elbow; **~ball der** tennis-ball; **~platz der** tennis-court; **~schläger der** tennis-racket; **~schuh der** tennis-shoe; **~spiel das a)** *o. Pl. (Tennis)* tennis *no art.*; **b)** *(Einzelspiel)* game of tennis; **~spielen das; ~s** tennis *no art.*; **~spieler der** tennis-player

¹Tenor [te'no:ɐ] **der; ~s, Tenöre** [te'nø:rə], *(österr. auch:)* **~e** *(Musik)* **a)** *(Stimmlage, Sänger)* tenor; **den ~ singen** sing tenor *or* the tenor part; **b)** *o. Pl. (im Chor)* tenors *pl.*; tenor voices *pl.*

²Tenor ['te:nɔr] **der; ~s** tenor

Tenor·schlüssel der *(Musik)* tenor clef

Tentakel [tɛn'ta:kl] **der** *od.* **das; ~s, ~** *(Zool., Bot.)* tentacle

Tenü, Tenue [tə'ny] **das; ~s, ~s** *(schweiz.)* style of dress

Teppich ['tɛpɪç] **der; ~s, ~e** carpet; *(kleiner)* rug; **auf dem ~ bleiben** *(fig. ugs.)* keep one's feet on the ground; **etw. unter den ~ kehren** *(fig. ugs.)* sweep sth. under the carpet

Teppich-: ~boden der fitted carpet; **~fliese die** carpet tile; **~kehrer der** carpet-sweeper; **~klopfer der** carpet-beater; **~stange die** *frame for beating carpets*

Term [tɛrm] **der; ~s, ~e** *(Math., Logik, Physik)* term

Termin [tɛr'mi:n] **der; ~s, ~e a)** *(festgelegter Zeitpunkt)* date; *(Anmeldung)* appointment; *(Verabredung)* engagement; **der letz-**

te *od.* **äußerste ~ für die Zahlung** the deadline *or* final date for payment; **sich** *(Dat.)* **einen ~ geben lassen** make an appointment; **b)** *(Rechtsw.)* hearing; **heute ist ~ in Sachen ...:** the ... case comes on today
Terminal ['tø:ɐ̯minəl] **das;** ~s, ~s terminal
termin-, Termin-: ~gebunden *Adj.* scheduled; **~gebunden sein** have a deadline; **~gemäß 1.** *Adj.* on time *postpos.;* **~gemäße Fertigstellung** completion on time *or* schedule; **2.** *adv.* on time; on schedule; **~gemäß beginnen** start punctually; **~geschäft das** *(Börsenw.)* forward transaction *or* operation
Termini *s.* Terminus
terminieren [tɛrmi'ni:rən] *tr. V.* **a)** *(befristen)* limit the duration of (**auf** + *Akk.* to); **b)** *(zeitlich festlegen)* **eine Veranstaltung** *usw.* ~: set *or* fix a date for an event *etc.*
Terminierung die; ~, ~en scheduling
Termini technici *s.* **Terminus technicus**
Termin·kalender der appointments book; *(für gesellschaftliche Termine)* engagements diary; **den ~ einhalten** *(fig.)* keep to the schedule
terminlich 1. *Adj.; nicht präd.* **~e Schwierigkeiten/Grenzen** difficulties/limits with regard to schedule; **~e Gründe** reasons of schedule. **2.** *adv.* **es läßt sich ~ vereinbaren** it fits in with the/our/their *etc.* schedule
Terminologie [tɛrminolo'gi:] **die;** ~, ~n terminology
terminologisch [tɛrmino'lo:gɪʃ] *Adj.; nicht präd.* terminological
Terminus ['tɛrminʊs] **der;** ~, **Termini** term
Terminus technicus [- 'tɛçnikʊs] **der;** ~ ~, **Termini technici** [...nitsi] technical term
Termite [tɛr'mi:tə] **die;** ~, ~n termite
Termiten·hügel der termite hill
Terpentin [tɛrpɛn'ti:n] **das,** *(österr. meist:)* **der;** ~s **a)** *(Harz)* turpentine; **b)** *(ugs.: Terpentinöl)* turps *sing. (coll.)*
Terpentin·öl das oil of turpentine
Terrain [tɛ'rɛ̃:] **das;** ~s, ~s **a)** *(Gelände)* terrain; **~ verlieren** lose ground; **es ist für ihn ein unbekanntes ~** *(fig.)* it is unknown territory to him; **das ~ sondieren** *(fig. geh.)* sound out the situation; **b)** *(Baugelände)* building land
Terrakotta [tɛra'kɔta] **die;** ~, **Terrakotten, Terrakotte die;** ~, ~n terracotta
Terrarium [tɛ'ra:riʊm] **das;** ~s, **Terrarien** terrarium
Terrasse [tɛ'rasə] **die;** ~, ~n terrace
terrassen·förmig 1. *Adj.* terraced. **2.** *adv.* in terraces
Terrassen·haus das block of flats *(Brit.) or (Amer.)* apartments/house built in terraces on a slope
Terrazzo [tɛ'ratso] **der;** ~[s], **Terrazzi** terrazzo
terrestrisch [tɛ'rɛstrɪʃ] *Adj.* terrestrial
Terrier ['tɛriɐ] **der;** ~s, ~: terrier
Terrine [tɛ'ri:nə] **die;** ~, ~n tureen
territorial [tɛrito'ria:l] *Adj.* territorial
Territorial-: ~hoheit die; *o. Pl.* territorial sovereignty; **~staat der** *(hist.)* territorial state
Territorium [tɛri'to:riʊm] **das;** ~s, **Territorien a)** *(Gebiet, Land)* land; territory; **ein unbesiedeltes ~:** uninhabited land *or* territory; **ein riesiges ~:** a huge area *or* region; **b)** *(Hoheitsgebiet)* territory
Terror ['tɛrɔr] **der;** ~s **a)** terrorism *no art.;* **blutiger ~:** terror and bloodshed; **~ ausüben** use terror tactics; **b)** *(ugs.: Zank u. Streit)* trouble; **c)** *(ugs.: großes Aufheben)* big row *(coll.) or* fuss; **~ machen** raise hell *(coll.)*
Terror-: ~akt der act of terrorism; **~an·schlag der** terrorist attack
terrorisieren *tr. V.* **a)** *(durch Terror unterdrücken)* terrorize; **b)** *(ugs.: belästigen)* pester
Terrorismus der; ~: terrorism *no art.*
Terrorist der; ~en, ~en, **Terroristin die;** ~, ~nen terrorist
terroristisch *Adj.; nicht präd.* terrorist
Terror·welle die wave of terror
Tertia ['tɛrtsia] **die;** ~, **Tertien** *(Schulw.)* **a)** *(veralt.)* fourth and fifth year *(of a Gymnasium);* **b)** *(österr.)* third year *(of a Gymnasium)*
Tertianer [tɛr'tsia:nɐ] **der;** ~s, ~, **Tertianerin die;** ~, ~nen *(Schulw.)* **a)** *(veralt.)* *(Ober~)* pupil in the fifth year *(of a Gymnasium); (Unter~)* pupil in the forth year *(of a Gymnasium);* **b)** *(österr.)* pupil in the third year *(of a Gymnasium)*
tertiär [tɛr'tsiɛ:ɐ̯] *Adj. (Geol.)* Tertiary
Tertiär das; ~s *(Geol.)* Tertiary [Period]
Tertium comparationis ['tɛrtsiʊm kɔmpara'tsio:nɪs] **das;** ~ ~, **Tertia ~** *(geh.)* common element *(as a basis for comparison)*
Terz [tɛrts] **die;** ~, ~en **a)** *(Musik)* third; **b)** *(Fechten)* tierce
Terzett [tɛr'tsɛt] **das;** ~[e]s, ~e **a)** *(Musik)* trio; **[im] ~ singen** sing a trio; **b)** *(Verslehre)* triplet
Terzine [tɛr'tsi:nə] **die;** ~, ~n *(Verslehre)* terza rima
Tesa·film Ⓦᶻ ['te:za-] **der;** ~[e]s Sellotape *(Brit.)* **(P)**; Scotch tape *(Amer.)* **(P)**
Test [tɛst] **der;** ~[e]s, ~s *od.* ~e test
Testament [tɛsta'mɛnt] **das;** ~[e]s, ~e **a)** *(letzte Verfügung eines Erblassers)* will; **das ~ eröffnen** read the will; **ohne Hinterlassung eines ~s sterben** die intestate; **das politische ~** *(fig.)* the political legacy; **er kann sein ~ machen** *(fig. ugs.)* he is [in] for it *(coll.);* **b)** *(christl. Rel.)* Testament; **das Alte/Neue ~:** the Old/New Testament
testamentarisch [tɛstamɛn'ta:rɪʃ] **1.** *Adj.; nicht präd.* testamentary. **2.** *adv.* **etw. ~ bestimmen** *od.* **festlegen** *od.* **verfügen** write sth. in one's will
Testaments-: ~eröffnung die reading of a/the will; **~vollstrecker der** executor
Testat [tɛs'ta:t] **das;** ~[e]s, ~e **a)** certification; **b)** *(Hochschulw. veralt.: Vorlesungsnachweis)* certificate of attendance
Test·bild das *(Ferns.)* test card
testen *tr. V.* test (**auf** + *Akk.* for)
Test-: ~fall der test case; **~frage die** test question
testieren *tr. V. (Hochschulw. veralt.)* certify
Testosteron [tɛstoste'ro:n] **das;** ~s *(Physiol.)* testosterone
Test-: ~pilot der test pilot; **~verfahren das** test[ing] procedure
Tetanus ['te:tanʊs] **der;** ~ *(Med.)* tetanus *no art.*
Tetanus·schutz·impfung die tetanus vaccination
Tête-à-tête [tɛta'tɛ:t] **das;** ~s, ~s *(veralt., scherzh.)* tête-à-tête
Tetraeder [tetra'le:dɐ] **das;** ~s, ~ *(Geom.)* tetrahedron
Tetralogie [tetralo'gi:] **die;** ~, ~n tetralogy
teuer ['tɔyɐ] **1.** *Adj.* **a)** expensive; dear *usu. pred.;* **wie ~ war das?** how much did that cost?; **das ist mir zu ~:** that's too expensive *or* too much [for me]; **Kaffee soll wieder teurer werden** coffee is supposed to be going up again; **zu teuren Preisen** at high prices; **teures Geld** *(fig.)* good money; **das ist ihn ~ zu stehen gekommen** *(fig.)* that cost him dear; *s. auch* **Rat a; b)** *(veralt.: geschätzt)* dear; **teurer Freund!** [my] dear friend!; **[mein] Teuerster!** [my] dearest; *(von Mann zu Mann)* [my] dearest friend; *s. auch* **lieb 1 d. 2.** *adv.* expensively; dearly; **etw. ~ kaufen/verkaufen** pay a great deal for sth./sell sth. at a high price; **~ essen gehen** eat in an expensive restaurant/expensive restaurants; **sie haben ihren Sieg ~ erkauft** they paid a high price for their victory; **ein ~ erkaufter Sieg** a victory won at a high price; **diese Gemeinheit wird er [mir] ~ bezahlen!** I'll make him pay for that dirty trick!
Teuerung die; ~, ~en rise in prices
Teuerungs-: ~rate die rate of price increases; **~zu·schlag der** cost-of-living supplement
Teufel ['tɔyfl̩] **der;** ~s, ~: devil; **der ~:** the Devil; **wie der ~ fahren/reiten** drive/ride in daredevil fashion; **armer ~:** poor devil; **der ~ steckt im Detail** it's [always] the little things that cause all the problems; **der ~ ist los** all hell's let loose *(coll.);* **dich reitet wohl der ~!** what's got into you?; **ich weiß auch nicht, was für ein ~ mich da geritten hat** I don't know what got into me; **hol' dich/ihn** *usw.* **der ~!** *(salopp)* sod *(Brit. sl.) or (coll.)* damn you/him *etc.;* **hol's der ~!** *(salopp)* sod *(Brit. sl.) or (coll.)* damn it!; **der ~ soll dich/ihn/es** *usw.* **holen!** *(salopp)* sod *(Brit. sl.) or (coll.)* damn you/him/it *etc.;* **in ihn/dich** *usw.* **ist wohl der ~ gefahren** *(salopp) (er ist/du bist usw. frech)* what does he think he's/do you think you're *etc.* doing?; *(er ist/du bist usw. leichtsinnig)* he/you *etc.* must be mad; **~ auch!** *(salopp)* damn [it all]! *(coll.);* **das weiß der ~!** *(salopp)* God [only] knows; **weiß der ~, was/wie/wo ...** *(salopp)* God knows what/how/where ...; **hinter etw. hersein wie der ~ hinter der armen Seele** *(ugs.)* be greedy for sth.; **etw. fürchten/scheuen wie der ~ das Weihwasser** *(ugs.)* fear nothing more than sth./avoid sth. like the plague; **den ~ werde ich [tun]!** *(salopp)* like hell [I will]! *(coll.);* **mal bloß nicht den ~ an die Wand!** *(ugs.)* don't invite trouble/ *(stärker)* disaster by talking like that!; **des ~s sein** *(ugs.)* be mad; have taken leave of one's senses; **des ~s Gebetbuch** *od.* **Gesangbuch** *(scherzh.)* a pack *or (Amer.)* deck of cards; **in ~s Küche kommen** *(ugs.)* get into a hell of a mess *(coll.);* **jmdn. in ~s Küche bringen** *(ugs.)* put sb. in a hell of a mess *(coll.);* **warum mußt du den jetzt auf ~ komm raus überholen?** *(ugs.)* why are you so hell-bent on overtaking him now? *(coll.);* **vom ~ besessen sein** *(fig.) (verrückt, wahnsinnig)* be mad; *(wild, ungestüm)* be wild; **zum ~ gehen** *(ugs.: kaputtgehen)* be ruined; **scher dich** *od.* **geh zum ~!** *(salopp)* go to hell! *(coll.);* **er soll sich zum ~ scheren!** *(salopp)* he can go to hell *(coll.) or* blazes *(coll.);* **zum** *od.* **beim ~ sein** *(ugs.: kaputt sein)* have had it *(coll.);* be ruined; **jmdn./etw. zum ~ wünschen** *(salopp)* wish sb. in hell/curse sth.; **jmdn. zum ~ jagen** *od.* **schicken** *(salopp)* send sb. packing; **zum ~!** *(salopp)* damn it! *(coll.);* **zum ~ mit dir/damit!** *(salopp)* to hell with you/it! *(coll.);* **wer/wo** *usw.* **zum ~ ...** *(salopp)* who/where *etc.* the hell ... *(coll.);* **wenn man vom ~ spricht[, dann ist er nicht weit]** *(scherzh.)* speak *or* talk of the devil [and he will appear]
Teufelei die; ~, ~en **a)** *o. Pl.* devilry; **b)** *(Handlung)* piece of devilry; **diese ~en** this devilry *sing.*
Teufelin die; ~, ~nen *(abwertend)* she-devil
Teufels-: ~austreibung die *(Rel.)* casting-out of devils; exorcism; **~braten der** *(ugs.)* devil; **~kerl der** *(ugs.)* amazing fellow; **~kreis der** vicious circle; **~messe die** Black Mass; **~rochen der** *(Zool.)* devil ray; **~weib das** *(ugs.)* **a)** *(bewundernd)* **sie ist ein ~weib** she's some woman *(coll.);* **b)** *(abwertend)* she-devil; **~werk das** devil's work *no indef. art.;* **~zeug das** *(ugs.)* terrible stuff *(coll.)*
teuflisch 1. *Adj.* **a)** devilish, fiendish ⟨*plan, trick, etc.*⟩; fiendish, diabolical ⟨*laughter, pleasure, etc.*⟩; **das Teuflische an dieser Krankheit** the devilish *or* diabolical thing about this illnes; **b)** *(ugs.: groß, intensiv)* terrible *(coll.);* dreadful *(coll.).* **2.** *adv.* **a)** fiendishly; diabolically; **b)** *(ugs.)* terribly *(coll.);* dreadfully *(coll.)*
Teutone [tɔy'to:nə] **der;** ~n, ~n Teuton
teutonisch *(auch fig.)* **1.** *Adj.* Teutonic. **2.** *adv.* Teutonically; in a Teutonic way

Text [tɛkst] **der; ~[e]s, ~e a)** text; *(eines Gesetzes, auf einem Plakat)* wording; *(eines Theaterstücks)* script; *(einer Oper)* libretto; **ein Telegramm mit folgendem ~: ...:** a telegram which reads/read ...; **weiter im ~!** *(ugs.)* [let's] carry on!; **b)** *(eines Liedes, Chansons usw.)* words *pl.*; *(eines Schlagers)* words *pl.*; lyrics *pl.*; **c)** *(zu einer Abbildung)* caption

Text-: ~analyse die *(Sprachw.)* text analysis; *(Literaturw.)* textual analysis; **~aufgabe die** *(Schule)* problem; **~buch das** libretto; **~dichter der** librettist

texten 1. *tr. V.* write ‹*song, advertisement, etc*›. **2.** *itr. V.* ‹*composer*› write one's own words

Texter der; ~s, ~: writer; *(in der Werbung)* copy-writer

Text·erfassung die text capture

textil *Adj.* textile

textil-, Textil-: ~frei *(ugs. scherzh.) Adj.* nude; **~gewerbe das** textile trade *or* industry; **~handwerk das** textile trade

Textilien *Pl.* **a)** textiles; **b)** *(Fertigwaren)* textile goods

Textil-: ~industrie die textile industry; **~ingenieur der** textile engineer; **~strand der** *(ugs. scherzh.)* beach where there is no nude bathing; **~waren** *Pl.* textile goods

text-, Text-: ~kritik die textual criticism; **~kritisch** *Adj.* textual ‹*study, commentary*›; critical ‹*edition*›; **~linguistik die** text linguistics *sing., no art.*; **~sorte die** *(Sprachw.)* type of text; **~stelle die** passage [in a/the text]

Textur [tɛks'tu:ɐ̯] **die; ~, ~en** *(geh., Geol.)* texture

Text·verarbeitung die text processing; word processing

¹Thai [tai] **der; ~[s], ~[s]** Thai

²Thai das; ~s *(Sprache)* Thai

Thailand (das); ~s Thailand

Thailänder der; ~s, ~, Thailänderin die; ~, ~nen Thai

thailändisch *Adj.* Thai

Thalamus ['ta:lamʊs] **der; ~, Thalami** *(Anat.)* thalamus

Thälmann·pionier ['tɛ:l-] **der** *(DDR)* Thälmann Pioneer

Theater [te'a:tɐ] **das; ~s, ~ a)** theatre; **ins ~ gehen** got to the theatre; **im ~:** at the theatre; **zum ~ gehen** *(ugs.)* go into the theatre; tread the boards; **beim** *od.* **am ~ sein** be *or* work in the theatre; **das englische ~:** English theatre; **~ spielen** act; *(fig.)* play-act; pretend; put on an act; **b)** *o. Pl.* *(fig. ugs.)* fuss; **mach [mir] kein ~!** don't make a fuss; **das ist doch alles nur ~:** that's all just play-acting; **dieses ~ mache ich nicht mehr mit** I'm not having any more to do with this farce; **das war vielleicht ein ~[, bis ich mein Visum hatte]** what a performance *or (coll.)* palaver [it was, getting my visa]; **jetzt geht das ~ wieder los!** now we have to go through all 'that performance again

Theater-: ~abonnement das theatre subscription [ticket]; **~besuch der** visit to the theatre; **~besucher der** theatre-goer; **~ferien** *Pl.* theatre holidays; **~karte die** theatre ticket; **~kasse die** theatre box-office; **~kritiker der** theatre *or* drama critic; **~stück das** [stage] play; **~wissenschaft die** theatre studies *pl., no art.*; study of theatre arts

theatralisch [tea'tra:lɪʃ] *(auch fig.)* **1.** *Adj.* theatrical. **2.** *adv.* theatrically

Thebaner [te'ba:nɐ] **der; ~s, ~:** Theban

Theben ['te:bn̩] **(das); ~s** Thebes

Theismus [te'ɪsmʊs] **der; ~** *(Philos., Rel.)* theism *no art.*

Theist [te'ɪst] **der; ~en, ~en** *(Philos., Rel.)* theist

theistisch *(Philos., Rel.)* **1.** *Adj.* theistic. **2.** *adv.* theistically

Theke ['te:kə] **die; ~, ~n a)** *(Schanktisch)* bar; **b)** *(Ladentisch)* counter; **unter der ~** *(fig.)* under the counter

Thema ['te:ma] **das; ~s, Themen** *od.* **~ta a)** subject; topic; *(einer Abhandlung)* subject; theme; *(Leitgedanke)* theme; **das ist für uns kein ~:** that's not a matter for discussion [as far as we are concerned]; **das ~ wechseln** change the subject; **vom ~ abkommen** *od.* **abschweifen** wander off the subject *or* point; **beim ~ bleiben** stick to the subject *or* point; **das ~ verfehlen** go completely off the subject; **damit ist das ~ [für mich] erledigt** [as far as I'm concerned] that's the end of the matter; **lassen wir das ~!** let's drop the subject; *s. auch* **Nummer a; b)** *(Musik)* theme

Thematik [te'ma:tɪk] **die; ~, ~en** theme; *(Themenkreis)* themes *pl.*; *(Themenkomplex)* complex of themes

thematisch 1. *Adj. (auch Musik)* thematic; **etw. nach ~en Gesichtspunkten ordnen** arrange sth. according to subject. **2.** *adv.* *(auch Musik)* thematically; *(was das Thema betrifft)* as regards subject matter

thematisieren *tr. V.* take as a *or* one's/its theme

Themen *s.* **Thema**

Themen-: ~kreis der group of themes; **~stellung die** the presentation of a/the subject; *(Thema)* subject; **~wahl die** choice of subject

Themse ['tɛmzə] **die; ~:** Thames

Theologe [teo'lo:gə] **der; ~n, ~n** theologian

Theologie [teolo'gi:] **die; ~, ~n** theology *no art.*

Theologin die; ~, ~nen theologian

theologisch 1. *Adj.* theological. **2.** *adv.* theologically

Theorem [teo're:m] **das; ~s, ~e** theorem

Theoretiker [teo're:tikɐ] **der; ~s, ~:** theoretician; theorist

theoretisch [teo're:tɪʃ] **1.** *Adj.* theoretical. **2.** *adv.* theoretically

theoretisieren *itr. V. (geh.)* theorize

Theorie [teo'ri:] **die; ~, ~n** theory; **das ist graue ~:** that's just pure theory

Theosophie [teozo'fi:] **die; ~, ~n** theosophy *no art.*

theosophisch 1. *Adj.* theosophical. **2.** *adv.* theosophically

Therapeut [tera'pɔyt] **der; ~en, ~en** therapist; therapeutist

Therapeutik [tera'pɔytɪk] **die; ~** *(Med.)* therapeutics *no art.*

Therapeutikum das; ~s, Therapeutika *(Med.)* therapeutic agent

Therapeutin die; ~, ~nen therapist; therapeutist

therapeutisch 1. *Adj.* therapeutic. **2.** *adv.* therapeutically

Therapie [tera'pi:] **die; ~, ~n** therapy **(gegen** for); *(fig.)* remedy **(gegen** for); **eine ~ machen** *(ugs.)* undergo *or* have therapy *or* treatment

therapieren *tr V.* treat

Thermal-: ~bad das a) *(Ort)* thermal spa; **b)** *(Bad)* thermal bath; **~quelle die** thermal spring

Therme ['tɛrmə] **die; ~, ~n a)** *(Quelle)* thermal spring; **b)** *Pl. (Bäder)* baths; thermae

Thermik ['tɛrmɪk] **die; ~** *(Met.)* thermal

thermisch 1. *Adj.* thermal. **2.** *adv.* thermally

thermo-, Thermo- [tɛrmo-]: **~dynamik die** thermodynamics *sing., no art.*; **~dynamisch 1.** *Adj.* thermodynamic; **2.** *adv.* thermodynamically; **~meter das** (*österr. u. schweiz.* **der** *od.* **das)** thermometer

Thermos·flasche Ⓦⓩ ['tɛrmɔs-] **die** Thermos flask **(P)**; vacuum flask

Thermostat [tɛrmo'sta:t] **der; ~[e]s** *od.* **~en, ~e** *od.* **~en** thermostat

Thesaurus [te'zaurʊs] **der; ~, Thesauren** *od.* **Thesauri** thesaurus

These ['te:zə] **die; ~, ~n** thesis

Thing [tɪŋ] **das; ~[e]s, ~e** *(hist.)* thing

Thing·platz der *(hist.)* thingstead

Thomas ['to:mas] **der; ~, ~se** *in* **ungläubiger ~:** doubting Thomas

Thora [to'ra:] **die; ~** *(jüd. Rel.)* Torah

Thora·rolle die *(jüd. Rel.)* Torah [scroll]

Thriller ['θrɪlə] **der; ~s, ~:** thriller

Thrombose [trɔm'bo:zə] **die; ~, ~n** thrombosis

Thron [tro:n] **der; ~[e]s, ~e a)** throne; **sein ~ wackelt** *(fig.)* his position is becoming very shaky; **b)** *(ugs. scherzh.: Nachttopf)* pot *(coll.)*

Thron-: ~an·wärter der heir apparent; **~besteigung die** accession [to the throne]

thronen *itr. V.* sit enthroned; *(fig.: erhöht liegen)* tower

Thron-: ~folge die; *o. Pl.* succession [to the throne]; **die ~folge antreten** succeed [to the throne]; **~folger der; ~s, ~:** heir to the throne; **~rede die** King's/Queen's speech; **~saal der** throne room

Thuja ['tu:ja], *österr. auch:* **Thuje** ['tu:jə] **die; ~, Thujen** *(Bot.)* thuja

Thun·fisch ['tu:n-] **der** tuna

Thüringen ['ty:rɪŋən] **(das); ~s** Thuringia

Thüringer Wald der Thuringian Forest

thüringisch *Adj.* Thuringian; *s. auch* **badisch**

Thusnelda [tʊs'nɛlda] **die; ~** *(salopp abwertend)* bird *(sl.)*

Thymian ['ty:mia:n] **der; ~s, ~e** thyme

Thymus·drüse ['ty:mʊs-] **die** *(Anat.)* thymus [gland]

Tiara [ti'a:ra] **die; ~, Tiaren** tiara

Tibet ['ti:bɛt] **(das); ~s** Tibet

Tibetaner [tibe'ta:nɐ] **der; ~s, ~** *s.* **Tibeter**

tibetanisch *Adj. s.* **tibetisch**

Tibeter [ti'be:tɐ] **der; ~s, ~, Tibeterin die; ~, ~nen** Tibetan

tibetisch *Adj.* Tibetan; *s. auch* **deutsch; Deutsch; ²Deutsche**

Tic [tɪk] **der; ~s** *(Med.)* tic

Tick der; ~[e]s, ~s a) *(ugs.: Schrulle)* quirk; thing *(coll.)*; **du hast wohl einen kleinen ~:** you must be round the bend *(coll.)*; **b)** *(Med.)* tic; c) *(ugs.: Nuance)* tiny bit; shade

ticken 1. *itr. V.* tick; **du tickst wohl nicht richtig** *(salopp)* you must be off your rocker *(sl.)*. **2.** *tr. V. (salopp: erkennen, merken)* catch on to *(coll.)*

Ticker der; ~s, ~ *(bes. Pressejargon)* teleprinter; telex

Ticket ['tɪkət] **das; ~s, ~s** ticket

tick tack ['tɪk 'tak] *Interj.* tick-tock

Tide ['ti:də] **die; ~, ~n** *(nordd., bes. Seemannsspr.)* tide

Tiden·hub der tidal range

tief [ti:f] **1.** *Adj.* **a)** *(auch fig.)* deep; low ‹*neckline, bow*›; long ‹*fall*›; **eine fünf Meter ~e Grube** a pit five metres deep; **~es Einatmen** breathing in deeply; **b)** *(niedrig)* low ‹*table, chair, temperature, tide, level, cloud*›; **den Sattel/die Heizung etwas ~er stellen** lower the saddle/turn the heating down a bit; **c)** *(intensiv, stark)* deep; intense ‹*pain, suffering*›; utter ‹*misery*›; great ‹*need, want*›; **d)** *(weit im Innern gelegen)* **im ~en/~sten Afrika** in the depths of/in darkest Africa; **es freut mich aus ~stem Herzen/~ster Seele** I really am delighted; **in ~er/~ster Nacht** in the *or* at dead of night; **im ~en/~sten Winter** in the depths of winter; **im ~sten Mittelalter** in the depths of the middle Ages. **2.** *adv.* **a)** *(weit unten)* deep; **100 m ~ in/unter der Erde** 100 metres [down] under the earth; **er war ~ in Gedanken** he was deep in thought; **die Mütze saß ihm ~ in der Stirn** the cap was low over his forehead; **b)** *(weit nach unten)* ‹*dig, drill*› deep; ‹*fall, sink*› a long way; ‹*stoop, bow*› low; **~er graben/bohren** dig/drill deeper *or* more deeply; **ein ~ ausgeschnittenes Kleid** a low-cut dress; *s. auch* **¹Glas b; c)** *(in nur geringer Höhe)* ‹*fly, hover, etc.*› low; ~

liegen be at a lower level; **er wohnt einen Stock ~er** he lives one floor down; **d)** *(nach unten)* ‹*hang etc.*› low; **~er gehen** ‹*pilot*› go lower ; **einen Stock ~er gehen** go one floor down; **~ herabhängende Äste** low-hanging branches; **e)** *(weit innen)* deep; **~ in Afrika/im Dschungel** deep in Africa/in the jungle; **f)** *(weit nach innen)* deep; ‹*breathe, inhale*› deeply; **er sah ihr ~ in die Augen** he looked deep into her eyes; **~er ins All vorstoßen** push deeper into space; **bis ~ in die Nacht/in den Winter** *(fig.)* until deep *or* late into the night/well into winter; **das geht bei ihm nicht sehr ~** *(ugs.)* it doesn't go very deep with him; **g) er sprach ganz ~:** he spoke in a deep voice; **zu ~ gestimmt** tuned too low; **zu ~ singen** sing flat; **er spielt das Lied ~er/eine Terz ~er** he plays the song in a lower key *or* lower/a third lower; **h)** *(intensiv, stark)* ‹*feel etc.*› deeply; ‹*sleep*› deeply, soundly

Tief das; ~s, ~s *(Met.)* low; depression; *(fig.)* low

tief-, Tief-: ~bau der; *o. Pl.* civil engineering *no art. (at or below ground level)*; **~betrübt** *Adj. (präd. getrennt geschrieben)* deeply distressed *or* saddened; **~bewegt** *Adj. (präd. getrennt geschrieben)* deeply moved; **~blau** *Adj.* deep blue; **[1]~druck der;** *o. Pl. (Met.)* low pressure; **[2]~druck der;** *Pl.* **~drucke a)** *o. Pl.* intaglio *or* gravure [printing]; **b)** *(Erzeugnis)* intaglio *or* gravure [print]; **~druck·gebiet das** *(Met.)* area of low pressure; depression

Tiefe die; ~, ~n a) *(Ausdehnung, Entfernung nach unten)* depth; **eine ~ von 300 m** a depth of 300 metres; **in großen ~n** at great depths; **b)** *(weit unten, im Innern gelegener Bereich; auch fig.)* depths *pl.*; **in die ~ stürzen** plunge into the depths; **in der ~ ihres Herzens** *(fig.)* deep down in her heart; *s. auch* **Höhe h; c)** *(Ausdehnung nach hinten)* depth; **der Schrank hat eine ~ von 60 cm** the cupboard is 60 cm deep; **d)** *o. Pl. s.* **tief 1 c:** depth; intensity; greatness; **e)** *(von Tönen, Klängen, Stimmen)* deepness; **f)** *o. Pl. (fig.: Tiefgründigkeit)* depth; profundity; **g)** *Pl. (Akustik)* bass *sing.*; **h)** *(Geogr.: Meeres~)* deep

Tief·ebene die *(Georgr.)* lowland plain

tief·empfunden *Adj. (präd. getrennt geschrieben)*; **tiefer empfunden, am tiefsten empfunden** *od.* **tiefstempfunden** deep[ly]-felt; heartfelt ‹*thanks, sympathy*›

Tiefen-: ~gestein das *(Geol.)* plutonic rock; **~psychologie die** depth psychology *no art.*; **~schärfe die** *(Fot.) s.* **Schärfentiefe; ~wirkung die a)** deep action; **b)** *(optisch)* effect of depth

tief-, Tief-: ~ernst 1. *Adj.* deadly serious; **2.** *adv.* deadly seriously; **~flieger der** low-flying aircraft; **~flug der** low-altitude flight *no art.*; flying *no art.* at low altitude; **im ~flug** at low altitude; **~gang der** *(Schiffbau)* draught; *(fig.)* depth; **~garage die** underground car park; **~gefrieren** *unr. tr. V.* [deep-]freeze; **~gehend; tiefer gehend, am tiefsten gehend** *od.* **tiefstgehend, ~greifend; tiefer greifend, am tiefsten greifend** *od.* **tiefstgreifend 1.** *Adj.* profound; far-reaching; profound, deep ‹*crisis*›; far-reaching ‹*improvement*›; **2.** *adv.* profoundly; **~gründig** [~grʏndɪç] **1.** *Adj.* profound; **2.** *adv.* ‹*discuss, examine*› in depth; **~gründigkeit die; ~:** profundity; **~kühlen** *tr. V.* [deep-]freeze

Tief·kühl-: ~fach das freezer [compartment]; **~kost die** frozen food; **~truhe die** [chest] freezer *or* deep-freeze

tief-, Tief-: ~lader der low-loader; **~land das;** *Pl.* **~länder** *od.* **~lande** lowlands *pl.*; **~liegend** *Adj.; nicht präd.*; **tiefer liegend, am tiefsten liegend** *od.* **tiefstliegend** low-lying ‹*area*›; deep-set ‹*eyes*›; **~punkt der a)** *(fig.)* low [point]; **b)** *(Math.: Minimum)* minimum; **~religiös** *Adj.* deeply religious; **~schlaf der** deep sleep; **~schlag der** *(Boxen)* low punch; punch below the belt *(lit. or fig.)*; **~schürfend; tiefer schürfend, am tiefsten schürfend** *od.* **tiefstschürfend 1.** *Adj.* profound; **2.** *adv.* profoundly; **~schwarz** *Adj.* jet-black; **~see die** *(Geogr.)* deep sea; **~see·graben der** deep-sea trench; **~sinn der;** *o. Pl.* profundity; **~sinnig 1.** *Adj.* profound; **2.** *adv.* profoundly; **~stand der** *(auch fig.) (tiefer Stand)* low level; *(tiefster Stand)* lowest level; **~stapelei** [~ʃta:pə'lai] **die; ~:** understatement; *(aus Bescheidenheit)* modesty; **~stapeln** *itr. V.* understate the case; *(aus Bescheidenheit)* be modest; **~stehend** *Adj.; nicht präd.*; **tiefer stehend, am tiefsten stehend** *od.* **tiefststehend: die ~stehende Sonne** the sun low down on the horizon; **ein moralisch ~stehender Mensch** a person of little moral principle; **~strahler der** floodlight

Tiefst-: ~temperatur die minimum *or* lowest temperature; **~wert der** minimum *or* lowest value

tief-: ~traurig *Adj.* very *or* deeply sad; **~verschneit** *Adj. (präd. getrennt geschrieben)* covered in deep snow *postpos.*; deep in snow *postpos.*

Tiegel ['ti:gl̩] **der; ~s, ~** *(zum Kochen)* pan; *(Schmelz~)* crucible; *(Behälter)* pot

Tier [ti:ɐ̯] **das; ~[e]s, ~e** animal; *(in der Wohnung gehaltenes)* pet; **niedere/höhere ~e** lower/higher animals; **er ist ein ~** *(fig.)* he is an animal; **das ist das ~ im Menschen** that's the beast in man; **ein hohes** *od.* **großes ~** *(ugs.)* a big noise *(sl.) or* shot *(sl.)*

tier-, Tier-: ~art die animal species; species of animal; **~arzt der** veterinary surgeon; vet; **~ärztlich 1.** *Adj.; nicht präd.* veterinary; **2.** *adv.* by a veterinary surgeon/veterinary surgeons; **~asyl das** animal home

Tierchen das; ~s, ~: [little] animal; **was für ein possierliches ~!** what a funny little creature!; **jedem ~ sein Pläsierchen** *(ugs.)* each to his own; if that's what he/she wants

Tier-: ~fabel die animal fable; **~fänger der** animal-collector; **~freund der** animal-lover; **~garten der** zoo; zoological garden; **~geschichte die** animal story

tierhaft *Adj.* animal *attrib.* ‹*behaviour, warmth, etc.*›

Tier-: ~halter der animal-owner; **~halter sein** keep an animal/animals; **~haltung die;** *o. Pl.* keeping of animals; **~handlung die** pet shop; **~heil·kunde die** *s.* **~medizin; ~heim das** animal home

tierisch 1. *Adj.* **a)** animal *attrib.*; bestial, savage ‹*cruelty, crime*›; **b)** *(ugs.: unerträglich groß)* terrible *(coll.)*; **~er Ernst** deadly seriousness; **c)** *(Jugendspr.: sehr gut, sehr schön)* great *(coll.)*. **2.** *adv.* **a)** ‹*roar*› like an animal; savagely ‹*cruel*›; **b)** *(ugs.: unerträglich)* terribly *(coll.)*; deadly ‹*monotonous, serious*›; baking ‹*hot*›; perishing *(coll.)* ‹*cold*›; **c)** *(Jugendspr.: sehr)* really; **es hat ~ Spaß gemacht** it was great fun

tier-, Tier-: ~kind das baby animal; **~kreis der;** *o. Pl. (Astron., Astrol.)* zodiac; **~kreis·zeichen das** *(Astron., Astrol.)* sign of the zodiac; **er ist im ~kreiszeichen der Jungfrau geboren** he was born under [the sign of] Virgo; **~kunde die** zoology *no art.*; **~lieb** *Adj.* animal-loving *attrib.*; fond of animals *postpos.*; **~liebe die;** *o. Pl.* love of animals; **~liebend** *Adj. s.* **~lieb; ~medizin die;** *o. Pl.* veterinary medicine; **~park der** zoo; **~pfleger der** animal-keeper; **~quäler der; ~s, ~:** person who is cruel to animals; **ein ~quäler sein** be cruel to animals; **~quälerei** [---'-] **die** cruelty to animals; **das ist ~quälerei** *(fig. ugs. scherzh.)* that's cruelty to dumb animals *(joc.)*; **~reich das;** *o. Pl.* animal kingdom; **~schau die** menagerie; **~schutz·verein der** society for the prevention of cruelty to animals; animal protection society; **~versuch der** animal experiment; **~welt die** fauna; **~zucht die;** *o. Pl.* [animal] breeding *no art.*

Tiger ['ti:gɐ] **der; ~s, ~:** tiger

Tiger-: auge das tiger['s] eye; **~hai der** tiger shark

Tigerin die; ~, ~nen tigress

Tiger·katze die tiger-cat; margay

tigern *itr. V.; mit sein (ugs.)* walk; go

Tilde ['tɪldə] **die; ~, ~n** tilde

tilgen ['tɪlgn̩] *tr. V.* **a)** *(geh.)* delete ‹*word, letter, error*›; erase ‹*record, endorsement*›; *(fig.)* wipe out ‹*shame, guilt, traces*›; **b)** *(Wirtsch., Bankw.)* repay; pay off

Tilgung die; ~, ~en a) *(geh.) s.* **tilgen a:** deletion; erasure; wiping out; **b)** *(Wirtsch., Bankw.)* repayment

Till [tɪl] **(der)** *in* **~ Eulenspiegel** Till Eulenspiegel; *(fig.)* practical joker

Tilsiter ['tɪlzɪtɐ] **der; ~s, ~:** Tilsit [cheese]

Timbre ['tɛ̃:br(ə)] **das; ~s, ~s** timbre

timen ['taimən] *tr. V.* time

Timing ['taimɪŋ] **das; ~s, ~s** timing

tingeln ['tɪŋl̩n] *itr. V.* **a)** play the [small] clubs/theatres/pubs *etc.*; **b)** *mit sein* **er tingelte durch die Hamburger Clubs** he played the Hamburg clubs

Tingeltangel ['tɪŋl̩taŋl̩] **das** *od.* **der; ~s, ~** *(veralt. abwertend)* **a)** *(Lokal)* cheap night-club/dance-hall; honky-tonk *(coll.)*; **b)** *(Unterhaltung)* cheap night-club entertainment

Tinktur [tɪŋk'tu:ɐ̯] **die; ~, ~en** tincture

Tinnef ['tɪnɛf] **der; ~s** *(ugs. abwertend)* **a)** *(wertloses Zeug)* rubbish; junk; **b)** *(Unsinn)* rubbish; nonsense

Tinte ['tɪntə] **die; ~, ~n** ink; **das ist klar wie dicke ~** *(ugs.)* that's as clear as daylight; that's crystal-clear; **in der ~ sitzen** *(ugs.)* be in the soup *(coll.)*

tinten-, Tinten-: ~blau *Adj.* deep blue; **~faß das** ink-pot; *(eingelassen)* ink-well; **~fisch der** cuttlefish; *(Kalmar)* squid; *(Krake)* octopus; **~fleck der** ink stain; **~klecks der** ink blot; **~kleckser der** *(ugs. abwertend)* scribbler; **~stift der** *s.* **Kopierstift**

Tip [tɪp] **der; ~s, ~s a)** *(ugs.: Fingerzeig)* tip; *(an die Polizei)* tip-off; **b)** *(bei Toto, Lotto usw.)* [row of] numbers

Tippel·bruder ['tɪpl̩-] **der** *(fam.)* tramp

tippeln *itr. V.; mit sein (ugs.)* walk; **wir mußten nach Hause ~:** we had to foot it home

tippen ['tɪpn̩] **1.** *itr. V.* **a) an/gegen etw.** *(Akk.)* **~:** tap sth.; **an seine Mütze ~:** touch one's cap; **sich** *(Dat.)* **an die Stirn ~:** tap one's forehead; **aufs Gaspedal ~:** touch the accelerator; **daran ist nicht zu ~** *(ugs.)* there's no question about that; **b)** *(ugs.: maschineschreiben)* type; **c)** *(ugs.: vermuten)* reckon; **auf jmds. Sieg ~:** tip sb. to win; **darauf hätte ich nicht getippt** I hadn't reckoned with that; **du hast gut/richtig getippt** you were right; **d)** *(wetten)* do the pools/lottery *etc.*; **im Lotto ~:** do the lottery. **2.** *tr. V.* **a)** tap; **jmdn. auf die Schulter ~:** tap sb. on the shoulder; **b)** *(ugs.: mit der Maschine schreiben)* type; **c)** *(bei der Registrierkasse)* ring up; **d)** *(setzen auf)* choose; **sechs Richtige ~:** make six correct selections

Tipper der; ~s, ~: person who does the pools/lottery *etc.*

Tipp-: ~fehler der typing error *or* mistake; **~gemeinschaft die** poools/lottery *etc.* syndicate; **~schein der** [pools/lottery *etc.*] coupon

Tippse ['tɪpsə] **die; ~, ~n** *(ugs. abwertend)* typist

tipp, tapp *Interj.* pitter-patter; pit-a-pat

tipp·topp *(ugs.)* **1.** *Adj. (tadellos)* immaculate; *(erstklassig)* tip-top. **2.** *adv.* immaculately; **~ in Ordnung** in immaculate *or* tip-top order

Tipp·zettel der *(ugs.) s.* **Tippschein**
Tirade [ti'ra:də] **die; ~, ~n** *(geh. abwertend)* interminable speech; **sich in langen ~n ergehen** talk interminably
tirilieren [tiri'li:rən] *itr. V.* trill; warble
Tirol [ti'ro:l] **(das); ~s** [the] Tyrol
Tiroler der; ~s, ~, Tirolerin die; ~, ~nen Tyrolese; Tyrolean
Tisch [tɪʃ] **der; ~[e]s, ~e a)** table; *(Schreib~)* desk; **er zahlte bar auf den ~:** he paid cash down; **vor/nach ~:** before/after lunch/dinner/the meal *etc.*; **bei ~ sein** *od.* **sitzen** be at table; **zu ~ sein** be having one's lunch/dinner *etc.*; **zu ~ gehen** go to lunch/dinner *etc.*; **vom ~ aufstehen** get up from the table; ‹*child*› get down [from the table]; **bitte zu ~:** please take your places for lunch/dinner; **es wird gegessen, was auf den ~ kommt!** [you'll] eat what's put on the table!; **ein Gespräch am runden ~:** round-table talks *pl.*; **b)** *(fig.)* **am grünen ~, vom grünen ~ aus** merely academically; **reinen ~ machen** *(ugs.)* clear things up; sort things out; **reinen ~ mit etw. machen** *(ugs.)* clear sth. up; sort sth. out; **sich [mit jmdm.] an einen ~ setzen** get round the table [with sb.]; **auf den ~ hauen** *(ugs.)* take a hard line; **etw. auf den ~ legen** *(Angebot machen)* put sth. on the table; *(bezahlen)* lay sth. out; **jmdn. über den ~ ziehen** *(ugs.)* outmanœuvre sb.; **unter den ~ fallen** *(ugs.)* go by the board; **jmdn. unter den ~ trinken** *(ugs.)* drink sb. under the table; **die Füße** *od.* **Beine unter jmds. ~** *(Akk.)* **strecken** *(ugs.)* live under sb.'s roof and eat at sb.'s table; **vom ~ sein** *(ugs.)* be out of the way; ‹*subject, topic*› be closed; *s. auch* **fegen 1 b**
Tisch·bein das table-leg; leg of the table
Tischchen das; ~s, ~: [little] table
Tisch-: ~dame die dinner partner; **~decke die** table-cloth; **~feuerzeug das** table lighter; **~fußball der** table-football; **~gebet das** grace; **ein/das ~gebet sprechen** say grace; **~gespräch das** breakfast/lunch/dinner conversation; **~herr der** dinner partner; **~karte die** place card; **~lampe die** table-lamp
Tischlein·deck·dich das; ~: easy life; **was er sucht, ist so eine Art ~:** he's looking to get on the gravy train *(sl.)*
Tischler der; ~s, ~: joiner; *(bes. Kunst~)* cabinet-maker
Tischlerei die; ~, ~en a) *(Werkstatt)* joiner's/cabinet-maker's [workshop]; **b)** *o. Pl. (Handwerk)* joinery/cabinet-making
tischlern 1. *itr. V.* do woodwork. **2.** *tr. V.* make ‹*shelves, cupboard, etc.*›
Tisch-: ~manieren *Pl.* table manners; **~nachbar der** person next to one [at table]; **wer ist dein ~nachbar?** who is sitting next to you?; **~platte die** table-top; **~rede die** after-dinner speech; **~rücken das; ~s** table-turning *no art. or* -lifting *no art.*; **~tennis das** table tennis
Tisch·tennis-: ~platte die table-tennis table; **~schläger der** table-tennis bat
Tisch-: ~tuch das; *Pl.* **~tücher** table-cloth; **~vor·lage die** hand-out; **~wäsche die** table-linen; **~wein der** table wine; **~zeit die** lunch-time; **wir haben eine halbe Stunde ~zeit** we have half an hour for lunch
[1]**Titan** [ti'ta:n] **der; ~en, ~en** *(Myth., fig.)* Titan
[2]**Titan das; ~s** *(Chemie)* titanium
titanenhaft *Adj.* titanic
titanisch *Adj. (Myth., fig.)* titanic
Titel ['ti:tl̩] **der; ~s, ~ a)** title; **unter dem ~ „...“** under the title '...'; **b)** *(ugs.: Musikstück, Song usw.)* number
Titel-: ~an·wärter der *(Sport)* title contender; contender for the title; **~bild das a)** cover picture; **b)** *(Frontispiz)* frontispiece; **~blatt das** title-page
Titelei die; ~, ~en *(Buchw.)* prelims *pl.*
Titel-: ~geschichte die cover story *or* article; **~held der** eponymous hero; **~kampf der** *(Sport)* final; *(Boxen)* title fight; **~rolle die** title-role; **~schutz der;** *o. Pl. (Rechtsw.)* copyright *(in a title)*; **~seite die a)** *(einer Zeitung, Zeitschrift)* [front] cover; **b)** *(eines Buchs)* title-page; **~sucht die** mania for titles; **~träger der a)** titled person; person with a title; **b)** *(Sport)* title-holder; **~verteidiger der** *(Sport)* title-holder; *(Mannschaft)* title-holders *pl.*
Titoismus [tito:'ɪsmʊs] **der; ~** *(Politik)* Titoism *no art.*
Titte ['tɪtə] **die; ~, ~n** *(derb)* tit *(coarse)*
titulieren [titu'li:rən] *tr. V.* **a)** *(bezeichnen)* call; **jmdn. als** *od.* **mit „Flasche“ ~:** call sb. a dead loss *(coll.)*; **b)** *(veralt.: mit dem Titel anreden)* address; **jmdn. [als** *od.* **mit] Herr Doktor ~:** address sb. as Doctor
Titulierung die; ~, ~en a) *(Bezeichnung)* name; **gegen seine ~ als ... hatte er nichts einzuwenden** he had no objection to being called ...; **b)** *(veralt.: Anrede mit dem Titel, Nennung des Titels)* title
Tizian ['ti:tsia:n] **(der); ~s** Titian
tizianrot *Adj.* Titian [red]
tja [tja(:)] *Interj.* [yes] well; *(Resignation ausdrückend)* oh, well
Toast [to:st] **der; ~[e]s, ~e** *od.* **~s a)** *(getoastetes Brot)* toast; *(Scheibe ~)* piece of toast; **b)** *(Trinkspruch)* toast
Toast·brot das; *o. Pl.* [sliced white] bread for toasting
toasten *tr. V.* toast
Toaster der; ~s, ~: toaster
Tobak ['to:bak] **der; ~s** *in* **starker ~ sein** *(ugs.)* be a bit thick *(Brit. coll.) or (coll.)* much; *s. auch* **Anno**
Tobel ['to:bl̩] **der** *od.* **das** (*österr.* **das**)**; ~s, ~** *(Geogr., österr., schweiz., südd.)* ravine
toben ['to:bn̩] *itr. V.* **a)** go wild **(vor + Dat.** with); *(fig.)* ‹*storm, sea, battle*› rage; **wie ein Wilder** *od.* **Berserker ~:** go wild *or* berserk; **b)** *(tollen)* romp *or* charge about; **c)** *mit sein (laufen)* charge
Toberei die; ~: romping *or* charging about
tob-, Tob-: ~sucht die; *o. Pl.* frenzied *or* mad rage; [mad] frenzy; **~süchtig** *Adj.* frenzied; raving mad; **~suchts·anfall der** fit of frenzied *or* mad rage; **einen ~suchtsanfall bekommen** *od.* **erleiden** fly into a fit of frenzied rage *or* into a frenzy
Toccata [tɔ'ka:ta] *s.* **Tokkata**
Tochter ['tɔxtɐ] **die; ~, Töchter** ['tœçtɐ] **a)** daughter; **die ~ des Hauses** the daughter *or* young lady of the house; **Ihre Frau/Ihr Fräulein ~:** your daughter; **höhere ~:** young lady; **b)** *(schweiz.: Mädchen, Bedienstete)* girl; **c)** *(Wirtschaftsjargon)* subsidiary
Töchterchen ['tœçtɐçən] **das; ~s, ~:** little daughter; *(Kleinkind)* baby daughter
Tochter-: ~geschwulst die *(Med.)* secondary tumour; **~gesellschaft die** *(Wirtsch.)* subsidiary [company]
Tod [to:t] **der, ~[e]s, ~e** *(auch fig.)* death; **es wäre unser aller sicherer ~:** it would mean certain death for us all; **diese Krankheit führt zum ~:** this illness is fatal; **eines natürlichen/gewaltsamen ~es sterben** die a natural/violent death; **jmdn. zum ~e/zum ~ durch den Strang/zum ~ durch Erschießen verurteilen** sentence sb. to death/to death by hanging/to death by firing-squad; **~ durch Ersticken/Erfrieren** death by suffocation/freezing to death; **jmdm. den ~ wünschen** wish sb. dead; **bis in den ~:** till death; **das ist kein schöner ~:** that's not a pleasant way to die; **in den ~ gehen** go to one's death; **für jmdn./etw. in den ~ gehen** die for sb./sth.; **jmdn. vom ~[e] erretten** save sb.'s life; **sich zu ~e stürzen/trinken** fall to one's death/drink oneself to death; **zu ~e kommen, den ~ finden** die; lose one's life; **des ~es sein** *(veralt.)* be doomed; **jmdn./etw. auf den ~ nicht leiden/ausstehen können** *(ugs.)* not be able to stand or abide sb./sth.; **er haßte ihn auf den ~:** he utterly detested him; **sich zu ~e schämen/langweilen** be utterly ashamed/bored to death; **zu ~e betrübt** extremely distressed; **etw. zu ~e reiten** *(fig. ugs.)* flog sth. to death *(coll.)*; **tausend ~e sterben** *(ugs.)* die a thousand deaths; **sich** *(Dat.)* **den ~ holen** *(ugs.)* catch one's death [of cold]; **der Schwarze ~:** the Black Death; **der Weiße ~:** death in the snow; **~ und Teufel!** *(veralt.)* by the devil!; **weder ~ noch Teufel fürchten** fear nothing
tod-: ~bringend *Adj.* fatal ‹*illness, disease, etc.*›; deadly, lethal ‹*poison etc.*›; **~elend** *Adj.* utterly miserable; **~ernst 1.** *Adj.* deadly serious; **2.** *adv.* deadly seriously; **etw. ~ernst sagen** say sth. in deadly seriousness
todes-, Todes-: ~ahnung die presentiment *or* premonition of death; **~angst die a)** fear of death; **b)** *(große Angst)* extreme fear; **~ängste ausstehen** be scared to death; **~anzeige die a)** *(in einer Zeitung)* death notice; **„~anzeigen“** 'Deaths'; **b)** *(Karte) card announcing a person's death*; **~art die: eine schreckliche ~:** a terrible way to die; **~erklärung die** *(Rechtsw.)* declaration of death *(of missing person)*; **~fall der a)** death; *(in der Familie)* bereavement; **b)** *(Versicherungsw.)* **im ~fall** in [the] case *or* in the event of death; **~folge die;** *o. Pl. (Rechtsw.)* **Körperverletzung mit ~folge** physical injury resulting in death; **~furcht die** *(geh.)* fear of death; **~gefahr die** mortal danger; **~jahr das** year of death; **in seinem ~jahr** in the year of his death; **~kampf der** death throes *pl.*; **~kandidat der** *(Verurteilter)* condemned man/woman; *(Schwerkranker)* terminal case; **~mutig 1.** *Adj.* utterly fearless; **2.** *adv.* utterly fearlessly; **~nachricht die** news of his/her/their *etc.* death; **~not die** *(geh.)* mortal danger; **in ~not** *od.* **~nöten** in mortal danger; **~opfer das** death; fatality; **der Unfall forderte drei ~opfer** the accident claimed three lives; **~qual die** *(geh.)* [terrible] agony; **~schrei der** death cry; **~schuß der** fatal shot; **war die Abgabe eines ~schusses zulässig?** was it permissible to shoot to kill?; **~schütze der** person who fired the fatal shot; *(Attentäter)* assassin; killer; **~sehn·sucht die** longing to die; **~spirale die** *(Eis-, Rollkunstlauf)* death spiral; **~stoß der** death-blow; **jmdm./***(fig.)* **einer Sache den ~stoß geben** deal sb. the death-blow/the death-blow to sth.; **~strafe die** death penalty; **~streifen der** death strip; **~stunde die** hour of death; **~ursache die** cause of death; **~urteil das** death sentence; **~verachtung die** [utter] fearlessness in the face of death; **etw. mit ~verachtung essen/trinken** *(ugs.)* force sth. down [without showing one's distaste]; **~zelle die** death cell
tod-, Tod-: ~feind *Adj.; nicht attr.* **jmdm./sich** *od.* **einander ~feind sein** be sb.'s deadly enemy/be deadly enemies; **~feind der** deadly enemy; **~geweiht** *Adj. (geh.)* doomed [to die]; **~krank** *Adj.* critically ill
tödlich ['tø:tlɪç] **1.** *Adj.* **a)** fatal ‹*accident, illness, outcome, etc.*›; lethal, deadly ‹*poison, bite, shot, trap, etc.*›; lethal ‹*dose*›; deadly, mortal ‹*danger*›; **b)** *(sehr groß, ausgeprägt)* deadly ‹*hatred, seriousness, certainty, boredom*›. **2.** *adv.* **a)** fatally; **er ist ~ verunglückt/abgestürzt** he was killed in an accident/he fell to his death; **die Krankheit verläuft in der Regel ~:** the illness is usually fatal; **b)** *(sehr)* terribly *(coll.)*; **sich ~ langweilen** be bored stiff *or* to death *(coll.)*
tod-, Tod-: ~müde *Adj.* dead tired; **~schick** *(ugs.)* **1.** *Adj.* dead smart *(coll.)*; **2.** *adv.* dead smartly *(coll.)*; **~sicher** *(ugs.)* **1.** *Adj.* sure-fire *(coll.)* ‹*system, method, tip, etc.*›; **eine ~sichere Sache** a dead certainty *or (coll.)* cert; **2.** *adv.* for certain *or* sure;

~sterbens·krank *Adj. (ugs.)* critically ill; **~sünde die** *(auch fig.)* deadly *or* mortal sin; **~traurig 1.** *Adj.* extremely sad; **2.** *adv.* extremely sadly; with extreme sadness; **~unglücklich** *Adj. (ugs.)* extremely *or* desperately unhappy

Toffee ['tɔfi] **das; ~s, ~s** toffee

Toga ['to:ga] **die; ~, Togen** toga

Togo ['to:go] **(das); ~s** Togo

Togoer der; ~s, ~: Togolese

togoisch *Adj.* Togolese

Tohuwabohu ['to:huva'bo:hu] **das; ~s, ~s** chaos; **im ganzen Haus war ein großes ~:** the whole house was in total *or* utter chaos

Toilette [toa'lɛtə] **die; ~, ~n a)** toilet; lavatory; **auf die** *od.* **zur ~ gehen** go to the toilet *or* lavatory; **eine öffentliche ~:** a public lavatory *or* convenience; **b)** *o. Pl. (geh.: das Sichzurechtmachen)* toilet; **~ machen** make one's toilet; **c)** *(geh.: Aufzug)* dress; toilet *(arch.)*; **in großer ~:** in full dress

Toilette- *(österr.)*, **Toiletten-: ~artikel der** toiletry; **~becken das** lavatory *or* toilet bowl *or* pan; **~frau die, ~mann der** lavatory attendant; **~papier das** toilet paper; **~seife die** toilet soap; **~sitz der** lavatory *or* toilet seat

toi, toi, toi ['tɔy 'tɔy 'tɔy] *Interj.* **a)** *(gutes Gelingen!)* good luck!; **~ für deine Prüfung!** good luck in your exam! *(coll.)*; **b)** *(unberufen!)* touch wood!

Tokaier [to'kaiɐ] **der; ~s ~:** Tokay

Tokio ['to:kio] **(das); ~s** Tokyo

Tokioter [to'kio:tɐ] **1. der; ~s, ~:** Tokyoite. **2.** *Adj.; nicht präd.* Tokyo *attrib.*; *s. auch* **Kölner**

Tokkata [tɔ'ka:ta] **die; ~, Tokkaten** *(Musik)* toccata

tolerant [tole'rant] **1.** *Adj.* tolerant **(gegen** of). **2.** *adv.* tolerantly

Toleranz die; ~, ~en a) *o. Pl. (auch Med.)* tolerance; **b)** *(Technik)* tolerance

Toleranz·grenze die a) limit of tolerance; **b)** *(Med.)* tolerance level; **c)** *(Technik)* tolerance limit

tolerierbar *Adj.* tolerable

tolerieren [tole'ri:rən] *tr. V.* tolerate

toll [tɔl] **1.** *Adj.* **a)** *(ugs.) (großartig)* great *(coll.)*; fantastic *(coll.)*; *(erstaunlich)* amazing; *(heftig, groß)* enormous ‹*respect*›; terrific *(coll.)* ‹*noise, storm*›; **b)** *(wild, ausgelassen, übermütig)* wild; wild, mad ‹*tricks, antics*›; **die [drei] ~en Tage** the [last three] days of Fasching; **c)** *(ugs.: schlimm, übel)* terrible *(coll.)*; **d)** *(veralt.) s.* **verrückt 1 a; e)** *(veralt.: tollwütig)* rabid. **2.** *adv.* **a)** *(ugs.: großartig)* terrifically well *(coll.)*; **~ hast du das gemacht** you've made a great job of that *(coll.)*; **b)** *(ugs.: heftig, sehr)* ‹*rain, snow*› like billy-o *(coll.)*; **es regnet immer ~er** it's chucking it down harder and harder *(coll.)*; **c)** *(wild, ausgelassen, übermütig)* **bei dem Fest ging es ~ zu** it was a wild party; **d)** *(ugs.: schlimm, übel)* **treibt es nicht zu ~:** don't go too mad; **aber es kommt noch ~er** but that's not all

Tolle die; ~, ~n quiff

tollen *itr. V.* **a)** romp about; **b)** *mit sein* romp

Tollerei die; ~, ~en *(ugs.)* romping about

Toll·haus das *(veralt.)* lunatic asylum *(Hist.)*; **hier geht es ja zu wie in einem ~:** it's like a madhouse here

Tollheit die; ~, ~en *(veralt.) s.* **Verrücktheit**

toll-, Toll-: ~kirsche die Atropa; **Schwarze ~kirsche** deadly nightshade; belladonna; **~kühn 1.** *Adj.* daredevil *attrib.*; daring; **2.** *adv.* daringly; **~kühnheit die a)** *o. Pl.* daring; **b)** *(tollkühne Handlung)* daredevil *or* daring exploit; **~wut die** rabies *sing.*; **~wütig** *Adj.* rabid

Tolpatsch [tɔlpatʃ] **der; ~[e]s, ~e** *(ugs.)* clumsy *or* awkward creature

tolpatschig *(ugs.)* **1.** *Adj.* clumsy; awkward. **2.** *adv.* clumsily; awkwardly

Tölpel ['tœlpl̩] **der; ~s, ~ a)** *(abwertend; einfältiger Mensch)* fool; **b)** *(Zool.) (Gattung Sula)* booby; *(Gattung Morus)* gannet

tölpelhaft *(abwertend)* **1.** *Adj.* foolish. **2.** *adv.* foolishly

Tomahawk ['tɔmaha:k] **der; ~s, ~s** tomahawk

Tomate [to'ma:tə] **die; ~, ~n** tomato; **du hast wohl ~n auf den Augen!** *(salopp)* you must be blind!; **er wurde rot wie eine ~** *(ugs. scherzh.)* he turned *or* went as red as a beetroot; **du [bist vielleicht eine] treulose ~** *(ugs. scherzh.)* a fine friend you are

Tomaten- tomato ‹*juice, salad, sauce, soup, etc.*›

Tomaten·mark das tomato purée

tomaten·rot *Adj.* brilliant red

Tombola ['tɔmbola] **die; ~, ~s** *od.* **Tombolen** raffle

Tommy ['tɔmi] **der; ~s, ~s** *(ugs.: Engländer)* Tommy

Tomographie [tomogra'fi:] **die; ~** *(Med.)* tomography *no art.*

¹Ton [to:n] **der; ~[e]s, ~e** clay

²Ton der; ~[e]s, Töne ['tø:nə] **a)** *(auch Physik, Musik; beim Telefon)* tone; *(Klang)* note; **der ~ macht die Musik** *(fig. ugs.)* it's not what you say but the way that you say it; **den ~ angeben** *(Musik)* give the note; *(fig.) (in der Mode, Kunst usw.)* set the tone; *(in einer Gruppe o. ä.)* have the most *or* greatest say; **jmdn./etw. in den höchsten Tönen loben** praise sb./sth. to the skies; **b)** *(Film, Ferns. usw., ~wiedergabe)* sound; **~ ab!** turn over sound!; **~ läuft** sound running; **c)** *(Sprechweise, Umgangs~)* tone; **den richtigen ~ finden** strike the right note; **ich verbitte mir diesen ~!** I will not be spoken to like that!; **sich im ~ vergreifen** adopt the wrong tone; strike the wrong note; **einen unverschämten/frechen** *usw.* **~ anschlagen** adopt an impudent/a cheeky tone; **der gute ~:** good form; **das gehört zum guten ~:** it is considered good form; **hier gehört es zum guten ~, ... zu ...** *(iron.)* here it's the done thing to ... *(coll.)*; **d)** *(ugs.: Äußerung)* word; **ich möchte keinen ~ mehr hören** I don't want to hear another word; **er konnte keinen ~ herausbringen** he couldn't say a word; **hast du/hat der Mensch [da noch] Töne?** that's just unbelievable; **große Töne reden** *od.* **spucken** *(ugs.)* talk big; **e)** *(Farb~)* shade; tone; **~ in ~ gehalten** colour co-ordinated; **f)** *(Akzent)* stress; **g)** *(Sprachw.: ~höhe)* tone

Ton·abnehmer der; ~s, ~: pick-up

tonal [to'na:l] *(Musik) Adj.* tonal

Tonalität [tonali'tɛ:t] **die; ~** *(Musik)* tonality

ton-, Ton-: ~angebend *Adj.* predominant; **~angebend sein** *(in der Mode, Kunst usw.)* set the tone; *(in einer Gruppe o. ä.)* have the most *or* greatest say; **~arm der** pick-up arm; **~art die a)** *(Musik)* key; **b)** *(fig.)* tone; **eine andere/schärfere** *usw.* **~art anschlagen** take a stronger *or* tougher line; **~aufnahme die** [sound] recording; **~band das;** *Pl.* **~bänder a)** tape; **b)** *(ugs.: ~bandgerät)* tape recorder

Ton·band-: ~aufnahme die tape recording; **~gerät das** tape recorder; **~protokoll das** tape transcript

Ton-: ~blende die *(Rundf., Ferns.)* tone control; **~dichtung die** tone-poem

tonen *tr. V. (Fot.)* tone

tönen ['tø:nən] **1.** *itr. V.* **a)** *(geh.)* sound; ‹*bell*› sound, ring; *(schallen, widerhallen)* resound; **mit ~der Stimme** in a resounding voice; **~de Worte/Phrasen** empty words/phrases; **b)** *(ugs. abwertend)* boast. **2.** *tr. V. (färben)* tint

Ton·erde die *s.* **essigsauer**

tönern ['tø:nɐn] *Adj.; nicht präd.* clay; *s. auch* **Fuß c**

Ton-: ~fall der tone; *(Intonation)* intonation; **~film der** sound-film; talkie *(coll.)*; **~folge die** sequence of notes; **~frequenz die** *(Akustik)* sound frequency; audio frequency; **~gefäß das** earthen[ware] vessel; **~geschlecht das** *(Musik)* scale; **~höhe die** pitch

Toni *s.* **Tonus**

Tonic ['tɔnɪk] **das; ~[s], ~s** tonic [water]

¹Tonika *s.* **Tonikum**

²Tonika ['to:nika] **die; ~, Toniken** *(Musik)* tonic

Tonika-Do das; ~ *(Musik)* Tonika-Doh [method]

Tonikum ['to:nikʊm] **das; ~s, Tonika** tonic

Ton·ingenieur der sound engineer

tonisch *Adj. (Physiol.)* tonic

ton-, Ton-: ~kopf der head; **~kunst die;** *o. Pl. (geh.)* music; **~künstler der** *(geh.)* composer; **~lage die** *(Musik)* pitch; **~leiter die** *(Musik)* scale; **~los 1.** *Adj.* toneless; **2.** *adv.* tonelessly; **~meister der** sound engineer, recording engineer

Tonnage [tɔ'na:ʒə] **die; ~, ~n** *(Seew.)* tonnage

Tönnchen ['tœnçən] **das; ~s, ~** *(ugs.: dicker Mensch)* dumpling *(coll.)*

Tonne ['tɔnə] **die; ~, ~n a)** *(Behälter)* drum; *(Müll~)* bin; *(Regen~)* water-butt; **b)** *(Gewicht)* tonne; metric ton; **c)** *(ugs.: dicker Mensch)* fatty *(coll.)*; **d)** *(Seew.)* buoy

Tonnen·gewölbe das *(Archit.)* barrel *or* tunnel vault

tonnen·weise 1. *Adv.* by the tonne *or* metric ton; *(in großer Menge)* by the ton; **ich habe das Zeug ~:** I've got tons of the stuff *(coll.)*. **2.** *adj.* by the ton *postpos.*

Ton-: ~pfeife die clay pipe; **~setzer der** *(veralt.)* composer

Ton-: ~spur die sound-track; **~störung die** *(Rundf., Film, Ferns.)* sound interference; *(durch Geräteschaden usw.)* fault on sound; **~stufe die** *(Musik)* note

Tonsur [tɔn'zu:ɐ̯] **die; ~, ~en** tonsure

Ton-: ~system das *(Musik)* tone *or* tonic system; **~tafel die** clay tablet; **~tauben·schießen das** clay-pigeon shooting *no art.*; **~techniker der** *(Rundf., Ferns., Film)* sound technician; **~träger der** sound[-recording and] storage medium; **~umfang der** *(Musik)* register; range

Tönung die; ~, ~en a) *(das Tönen)* tinting; **b)** *(Farbton)* tint; shade

Tonus ['to:nʊs] **der; ~, Toni** *(Physiol.)* tone

Ton·ware die earthenware *no pl.*

Top [tɔp] **das; ~s, ~s** *(Mode)* top

top- ultra ‹*modern, topical*›

Top- top; outstanding ‹*location, performance, time*›

Topas [to'pa:s] **der; ~es, ~e** topaz

Topf [tɔpf] **der; ~es, Töpfe** ['tœpfə] **a)** pot; *(Braten~, Schmor~)* casserole; *(Stielkasserolle)* saucepan; **alles in einen ~ werfen** *(fig. ugs.)* lump everything together; **b)** *(zur Aufbewahrung)* pot; jar; **c)** *(Krug)* jug; **d)** *(Nacht~)* chamber pot; po *(coll.)*; *(für Kinder)* potty *(Brit. coll.)*; **e)** *(Blumen~)* [flower]pot; **f)** *(salopp: Toilette)* loo *(Brit. coll.)*; john *(Amer. coll.)*

Topf·blume die [flowering] pot plant

Töpfchen ['tœpfçən] **das; ~s, ~** *s.* **Topf a–d:** [small] pot/saucepan/jug *etc.*; *(Nachttopf)* po *(coll.)*; *(für Kinder)* potty *(Brit. coll.)*

Topfen der; ~s *(bayr., österr.) s.* **¹Quark a**

Töpfer ['tœpfɐ] **der; ~s, ~:** potter

Töpferei die; ~, ~en a) *o. Pl. (Handwerk)* pottery *no art.*; **b)** *(Werkstatt)* pottery; potter's workshop; **c)** *(Erzeugnis)* piece of pottery; **~en** pottery *sing.*

Töpferin die; ~, ~nen potter

töpfern 1. *itr. V.* do pottery. **2.** *tr. V.* make ‹*vase, jug, etc.*›; **getöpferte Teller** handmade pottery plates

Töpfer-: ~scheibe die potter's wheel; **~ware die** piece of pottery; **~waren** pottery *sing.*

Topf·gucker der; ~s, ~ *(scherzh.)* Nosy

Parker who looks into all the pots and saucepans to see what's cooking

top·fit *Adj.* in *or* on top form *postpos.* *(gesundheitlich)* in fine fettle; as fit as a fiddle; **jetzt ist der Wagen wieder ~:** the car is in perfect order again now

Topf-: **~kuchen der** *s.* **Napfkuchen; ~lappen der** oven cloth; **~pflanze die** pot plant; **~reiniger der** [pot-]scourer; scouring-pad

Topinambur [topinam'bu:ɐ̯] **der; ~s, ~s** *od.* **~e** *od.* **die; ~, ~en** Jerusalem artichoke

Topographie [topogra'fi:] **die; ~, ~n** *(Geogr.)* topography *no art.*

topographisch *(Geogr.)* **1.** *Adj.* topographic[al]. **2.** *adv.* topographically

Topologie [topolo'gi:] **die;** ~ *(Math.)* topology *no art.*

topologisch *(Math.) Adj.* topological

Topos ['tɔpɔs] **der; ~, Topoi** ['tɔpɔy] **a)** *(Literaturw.)* topos; **b)** *(geh.: Gemeinplatz)* commonplace

topp [tɔp] *Interj. (veralt.)* done! agreed!

Topp der; ~s, ~e[n] *od.* **~s** *(Seemannsspr.)* masthead; **das Schiff war über die ~en geflaggt** the ship was dressed overall

Topp·segel das *(Seew.)* topsail

Topspin ['tɔpspɪn] **der; ~s, ~s** *(bes. Golf, Tennis, Tischtennis)* top spin

¹Tor [to:ɐ̯] **das; ~[e]s, ~e a)** gate; *(einer Garage, Scheune)* door; *(fig.)* gateway; **vor den ~en der Stadt** just outside the town; *s. auch* **dastehen; b)** *(Ballspiele)* goal; **mit 3:2 ~en gewinnen** *od.* **siegen** win 3–2 *or* by three goals to two; **im ~ stehen** be in goal; **c)** *(Ski)* gate

²Tor der; ~en, ~en *(geh.: Narr)* fool

Tor-: **~aus das** *(Ballspiele)* **der Ball ging ins ~aus** the ball went over the by-line *or* went behind; **~bogen der** arch[way]

Torero [to're:ro] **der; ~[s], ~s** torero

Tores·schluß der *in* **kurz vor ~** *(ugs.)* at the last minute *or* the eleventh hour

Torf [tɔrf] **der; ~[e]s, ~e** peat

Torf-: **~ballen der** bale of peat; **~moor das** peat bog; **~mull der** [loose] garden peat; **~stecher der** peat-cutter

Torheit die; ~, ~en *(geh.)* **a)** *o. Pl.* foolishness; **b)** *(Handlung)* foolish act; **eine [große] ~ begehen** do something [extremely] foolish

Tor·hüter der *(Ballspiele)* goalkeeper

töricht ['tø:rɪçt] *(geh.)* **1.** *Adj.* foolish ⟨*behaviour, action, hope*⟩; stupid ⟨*person, question, smile, face*⟩. **2.** *adv.* ⟨*behave, act*⟩ foolishly; ⟨*smile, ask*⟩ stupidly

törichterweise *Adv. (geh.)* foolishly

Törin ['tø:rɪn] **die; ~, ~nen** fool

Tor·jäger der *(Ballspiele)* goal-scorer

torkeln ['tɔrkl̩n] *itr. V.; mit sein* stagger; reel

tor-, Tor-: **~linie die** *(Ballspiele)* [goal-]line; **~los** *Adj. (Ballspiele)* goalless; **~mann der;** *Pl.* **~männer** *od.* **~leute** *(Ballspiele)* goalkeeper

Törn [tœrn] **der; ~s, ~s** *(Seemannsspr.)* trip

Tornado [tɔr'na:do] **der; ~s, ~s** tornado

Tornister [tɔr'nɪstɐ] **der; ~s, ~ a)** knapsack; **b)** *(Schulranzen)* satchel

torpedieren [tɔrpe'di:rən] *tr. V. (Milit., fig.)* torpedo

Torpedierung die; ~, ~en *(Milit., fig.)* torpedoing

Torpedo [tɔr'pe:do] **der; ~s, ~s** torpedo

Torpedo·boot das torpedo-boat

Tor-: **~pfosten der** *(Ballspiele)* [goal-]post; **~raum der** *(Ballspiele)* goal area; **~schluß der** *s.* **Toresschluß; ~schlußpanik die** last-minute panic; *(Furcht, keinen Partner mehr zu finden)* fear of being left on the shelf; **~schlußpanik haben** *od.* **bekommen** *od.* **kriegen** panic at the last minute/be frightened of being left on the shelf; **~schuß der** *(Ballspiele)* shot [at goal]; **~schütze der** *(Ballspiele)* [goal-]scorer

Torsi *s.* **Torso**

Torsion [tɔr'zi̯o:n] **die; ~, ~en** *(Physik, Technik, Math.)* torsion

Torso ['tɔrzo] **der; ~s, ~s** *od.* **Torsi** *(Kunstwiss., auch fig. geh.)* torso

Tort [tɔrt] **der; ~[e]s** *(ugs. veralt.)* wrong; injury; **jmdm. einen ~ antun** do sb. wrong; **jmdm. etw. zum ~ tun** do sth. to spite sb.

Törtchen ['tœrtçən] **das; ~s, ~:** tartlet

Torte ['tɔrtə] **die; ~, ~n** *(Creme~, Sahne~)* gateau; *(Obst~)* [fruit] flan

Tortelett [tɔrtə'lɛt] **das; ~s, ~s, Tortelette die; ~, ~n** tartlet

Torten-: **~boden der** flan case; *(ohne Rand)* flan base; **~guß der** glaze; **~heber der** cake-slice; **~platte die** cake-plate; **~schaufel die** *s.* **~heber**

Tortur [tɔr'tu:ɐ̯] **die; ~, ~en a)** ordeal; **b)** *(veralt.: Folter)* torture

Tor-: **~verhältnis das** *(Ballspiele)* goal average; **~wächter der a)** gatekeeper; **b)** *(Ballspiele)* goalkeeper; **~wart der; ~[e]s, ~e** *(Ballspiele)* goalkeeper; **~weg der** gateway

tosen ['to:zn̩] *itr. V.; mit Richtungsangabe mit sein* ⟨*sea, surf*⟩ roar, rage; ⟨*storm*⟩ rage; ⟨*torrent, waterfall*⟩ roar, thunder; ⟨*wind*⟩ roar; **~der Lärm/Beifall** *(fig.)* thunderous noise/applause

Toskana [tɔs'ka:na] **die; ~:** Tuscany

tot [to:t] *Adj.* **a)** dead; **das Kind wurde ~ geboren** the baby was stillborn; **er war auf der Stelle ~:** he died instantly; **~ zusammenbrechen** collapse and die; **~ umfallen** drop dead; **ich will auf der Stelle ~ umfallen, wenn das nicht wahr ist** may I be struck down if it isn't true; **er ist [politisch] ein ~er Mann** *(fig.)* he is finished [as a politician]; **er ist ein ~er Mann** he is a dead man *or (coll.)* a goner; **halb ~ vor Angst/Schrecken** *usw.* *(ugs.)* paralysed with fear/shock; **den ~en Mann machen** *(ugs.)* float on one's back; **b)** *(abgestorben)* dead ⟨*tree, branch, leaves, etc.*⟩; **c)** *(fig.)* dull ⟨*colour*⟩; bleak ⟨*region etc.*⟩; dead ⟨*town, telephone line, socket, language*⟩; disused ⟨*railway line*⟩; extinct ⟨*volcano*⟩; dead, quiet ⟨*time, period*⟩; useless ⟨*knowledge*⟩; **ein ~er Flußarm** a backwater; *(Schleife)* an ox-bow lake; **das Tote Meer** the Dead Sea; *s. auch* **Briefkasten b; Hose b; Punkt d; Winkel a**

total [to'ta:l] **1.** *Adj.* total. **2.** *adv.* totally

Total·aus·verkauf der clearance sale

Totale die; ~, ~n *od. adj. Dekl.* complete view; *(Film)* long shot

Totalisator [totali'za:tɔr] **der; ~s, ~en** [-za'to:rən] totalizator; tote *(coll.)*

totalitär [totali'tɛ:ɐ̯] *(Politik)* **1.** *Adj.* totalitarian. **2.** *adv.* in a totalitarian way; ⟨*organized, run*⟩ along totalitarian lines

Totalitarismus [totalita'rɪsmʊs] **der;** ~ *(Politik)* totalitarianism *no art.*

totalitaristisch *s.* **totalitär**

Totalität [totalitɛ:t] **die; ~, ~en** *(geh.)* totality

Total-: **~operation die** *(Med.)* extirpation; *(Gynäkologie)* hysterectomy; **~schaden der** *(Versicherungsw.)* **an beiden Fahrzeugen entstand ~schaden** both vehicles were a write-off

tot-: **~|arbeiten** *refl. V. (ugs.)* work oneself to death; **~|ärgern** *refl. V. (ugs.)* get livid *(coll.)*; **ich könnte mich ~ärgern** I'm livid *(coll.) or* really furious

Tote ['to:tə] **der/die;** *adj. Dekl.* dead person; dead man/woman; **die ~n** the dead; **es gab zwei ~:** two people died *or* were killed; there were two fatalities; **wie ein ~r schlafen** sleep like a log; **na, bist du von den ~n auferstanden?** *(ugs. scherzh.)* oh, you're back in the land of the living, are you?; **die ~n soll man ruhen lassen** *(ugs.)* let the dead rest in peace

Totem ['to:tɛm] **das; ~s, ~s** *(Völkerk.)* totem

Totem·pfahl der totem-pole

töten ['tø:tn̩] *tr., itr. V.* kill; deaden ⟨*nerve etc.*⟩; **einen kranken Hund ~ lassen** have a sick dog put down; *s. auch* **Blick a; Nerv a**

toten-, Toten-: **~acker der** *(veralt.)* graveyard; **~ähnlich** *Adj.* deathlike ⟨*sleep*⟩; **~amt das** *(kath. Kirche) s.* **~messe; ~bahre die** bier; **~bett das** deathbed; **~blaß, ~bleich** *Adj.* deathly pale; pale as death *postpos.*; **~feier die** memorial service; **~glocke die** death-knell; **~gräber der a)** grave-digger; **b)** *(Zool.)* grave-digger; burying-beetle; **~hemd das** shroud; **~klage die a)** lamentation *or* bewailing of the dead; **b)** *(Literaturw.)* lament; dirge; **~kopf der a)** skull; **b)** *(als Symbol)* death's head; *(mit gekreuzten Knochen)* skull and cross-bones; **~kult der** *(Völkerk.)* cult of the dead; **~maske die** death-mask; **~messe die** *(kath. Kirche)* requiem [mass]; **~reich das** kingdom of the dead; **~schädel der** skull; **~schein der** death certificate; **~sonntag der** *(ev. Kirche) Sunday before Advent on which the dead are commemorated;* **~starre die** rigor mortis; **~still** *Adj.* deathly quiet *or* silent; **~stille die** deathly quiet *or* silence; **~tanz der** *(bild. Kunst)* Dance of Death; **~wache die** vigil by the body; **die ~wache halten** keep vigil by the body

tot-, Tot-: **~|fahren 1.** *unr. tr. V.* [run over and] kill; **2.** *unr. refl. V.* kill oneself; **~geboren** *Adj. (präd. getrennt geschrieben)* stillborn; **ein ~geborenes Kind sein** *(fig.)* ⟨*project*⟩ be stillborn, not get off the ground; **~geburt die a)** still birth; **b)** *(Kind)* still birth; stillborn baby; **ihr erstes Kind war eine ~geburt** her first child was stillborn; **~geglaubte der/die;** *adj. Dekl.* person believed dead; **~gesagte der/die;** *adj. Dekl.* person declared dead; **~|kriegen** *tr. V. (ugs.)* kill; kill, get rid of ⟨*insect pests, weeds, etc.*⟩; **er/dieser Mantel ist nicht ~zukriegen** *(fig.)* he's irrepressible/this coat just never wears out; **~|lachen** *refl. V. (ugs.)* kill oneself laughing; **zum Totlachen sein** be killing *(coll.)*; be killingly funny *(coll.)*; **~|laufen** *unr. refl. V. (ugs.)* ⟨*movement, trend, fashion*⟩ peter *or* die out; ⟨*talks, discussions*⟩ peter out; **~|machen** *tr. V. (ugs.)* kill

Toto ['to:to:] **das** *od.* **der; ~s, ~s a)** *(Pferde~)* tote *(sl.)*; **im ~:** on the tote; **b)** *(Fußball~)* [football] pools *pl.*; **[im] ~ spielen** do the pools

Toto-: **~gewinn der** win on the pools/*(sl.)* tote; **~schein der** pools coupon/*(sl.)* tote ticket

tot-, Tot-: **~|sagen** *tr. V.* declare ⟨*person*⟩ dead; **eine Partei** *usw.* **~sagen** *(fig.)* say a party *etc.* is dead *or* finished; **~|schießen** *unr. tr. V. (ugs.)* **jmdn. ~schießen** shoot sb. dead; **~schlag der** *(Rechtsw.)* manslaughter *no indef. art.*; **~|schlagen** *unr. tr. V.* beat to death; **und wenn du mich totschlägst** for the life of me; **eher/lieber lasse ich mich ~schlagen** *(ugs.)* I'd rather die *or* be dead; **die Zeit ~schlagen** kill time; **~schläger der a)** *(Mensch)* manslaughterer; **b)** *(Waffe)* cosh *(Brit. coll.)*; blackjack *(Amer.)*; **~|schweigen** *unr. tr. V.* hush up; **jmdn. ~schweigen** keep quiet about sb.; **~|stellen** *refl. V.* pretend to be dead; play dead; **~|treten** *unr. tr. V.* trample ⟨*person*⟩ to death; step on and kill ⟨*insect*⟩

Tötung die; ~, ~en killing; **fahrlässige ~** *(Rechtsspr.)* manslaughter by culpable negligence

Tötungs-: **~absicht die** *(Rechtsw.)* intent *or* intention to kill; **~versuch der** *(Rechtsw.)* attempted murder

Touch [tatʃ] **der; ~s, ~s** *(ugs.)* touch

Toupet [tu'pe:] **das; ~s, ~s** toupee

toupieren [tu'pi:rən] *tr. V.* backcomb

Tour [tu:ɐ̯] **die; ~, ~en a)** tour **(durch** of); *(Kletter~)* [climbing] trip; *(kürzere Fahrt, Ausflug)* trip; *(mit dem Auto)* drive; *(mit* *dem Fahrrad)* ride; *(Zech~)* pub-crawl *(Brit. coll.)*; **eine ~ machen** go on a tour/trip *or* outing; *(Zech~)* go on a pub-crawl *(Brit. coll.)*; bar-hop *(Amer.)*; **das ist 'ne ganz schöne ~** *(ugs.)* it's a fair *or (Brit. coll.)* fair old way; **b)** *(feste Strecke)* route; **die ~ Hamburg-Neapel** the run from Hamburg to Naples; **c)** *(Tournee)* tour; **auf ~ gehen** go on tour; **eine ~ durch Europa** a European tour; **d)** *(ugs.: Methode)* ploy; **die ~ zieht bei mir nicht** that [one] won't work with me; **etw. auf die sanfte/gemütliche ~ machen** get sth. by soft-soaping/take one's time doing sth.; **seine ~ kriegen/haben** *(ugs.)* get/be in one of one's moods; *s. auch* **krumm 1 b; e)** *(ugs.: Unternehmen)* plan; **jmdm. die ~ vermasseln** *(ugs.)* put paid to sb.'s [little] plans; **f)** *(Technik: Umdrehung)* revolution; rev *(coll.)*; **die Maschine kam schnell auf ~en** the machine/engine was soon running at full speed; **jmdn. auf ~en bringen** *(ugs.)* really get sb. going; *(jmdn. böse machen)* get sb. worked up; **auf vollen/höchsten ~en laufen** *(ugs.)* ⟨*production, preparations, work, etc.*⟩ be in full swing; **g)** *in* **in einer ~** *(ugs.)* the whole time

Touren-: ~ski der touring ski; **~wagen der** *(Motorsport)* touring car; **~zahl die** *(Technik)* number of revolutions *or (coll.)* revs

Tourismus [tu'rɪsmʊs] **der; ~:** tourism *no art.*

Tourist der; ~en, ~en tourist

Touristen·klasse die tourist class

Touristik die; ~: tourism *no art.*; tourist industry *or* business

Touristin die; ~, ~nen tourist

touristisch 1. *Adj.* tourist *attrib.* **2.** *adv.* **das Land ist ~ noch kaum erschlossen** the country is still scarcely developed as a tourist area

Tournedos [tʊrnə'do:] **das; ~** [tʊrnə'do:(s)], **~s** tournedos

Tournee [tʊr'ne:] **die; ~, ~s** *od.* **~n** [tʊr'ne:ən] tour; **auf ~ sein/gehen** be/go on tour

-tournee die ... tour; **auf Europa~/Deutschland~** on a European/German tour

Tower ['taʊə] **der; ~[s], ~s** *(Flugw.)* [control] tower

toxisch ['tɔksɪʃ] *Adj.* toxic

Trab [tra:p] **der; ~[e]s** trot; **im ~:** at a trot; **im ~ reiten** trot; **in [den] ~ fallen** drop into a trot; **sich in ~ setzen** *(ugs.)* get going; get a move on *(coll.)*; **jmdn. auf ~ bringen** *(ugs.)* make sb. get a move on; **jmdn. in ~ halten** *(ugs.)* keep sb. on the go *(coll.)*

Trabant [tra'bant] **der; ~en, ~en a)** *(Astron.)* satellite; **b)** *Pl. (fam. scherzh. veralt.: Kinder)* kids *(coll.)*

Trabanten·stadt die satellite town

traben *itr. V.; mit sein (auch ugs.: laufen)* trot

Traber der; ~s, ~: trotter

Trab·rennen das trotting; *(einzelne Veranstaltung)* trotting race

Tracht [traxt] **die; ~, ~en a)** *(Volks~)* traditional *or* national costume; *(Berufs~)* uniform; **die ~ der Nonnen** the nuns' dress *or* habit; **b)** *in* **eine ~ Prügel** a beating *or* thrashing; *(als Strafe für ein Kind)* a hiding; **c)** *(Imkerei)* yield

trachten *itr. V. (geh.)* strive **(nach** for, after); **all sein** *od.* **sein ganzes Trachten** all his striving *or* endeavours; *s. auch* **Leben a**

Trachten-: ~anzug der *suit in the style of a traditional or national costume;* **~fest das** *festival at which traditional or national costume is worn;* **~kapelle die** *band in traditional or national costume*

trächtig ['trɛçtɪç] pregnant

Trächtigkeit die; ~, ~en pregnancy

tradieren [tra'di:rən] *tr. V. (geh.)* hand down, pass on ⟨*ideas, customs, values, etc.*⟩

Tradition [tradi'tsi̯o:n] **die; ~, ~en** tradition; **~ sein/haben** be a tradition

Traditionalismus [traditsi̯ona'lɪsmʊs] **der; ~** *(geh.)* traditionalism *no art.*

Traditionalist der; ~en, ~en *(geh.)* traditionalist

traditionell [traditsi̯o'nɛl] **1.** *Adj.* traditional. **2.** *adv.* traditionally

traditions-: ~bewußt 1. *Adj.* tradition-conscious; conscious of tradition *postpos.*; **2.** *adv.* in a tradition-conscious way; **~reich** *Adj.* rich in tradition *postpos.*

traf [tra:f] *1. u. 3. Pers. Sg. Prät. v.* **treffen**

träfe ['trɛ:fə] *1. u. 3. Pers. Sg. Konjunktiv II v.* **treffen**

Trafik [tra'fɪk] **die; ~, ~en** *(österr.)* tobacconist's [shop]

Trafikant [trafi'kant] **der; ~en, ~en** *(österr.)* tobacconist

Trafo ['tra:fo] **der; ~s, ~s** transformer

träg [trɛ:k] *s.* **träge**

Trag·bahre die stretcher

tragbar *Adj.* **a)** portable; **b)** wearable ⟨*clothes*⟩; **c)** *(finanziell)* supportable ⟨*cost, debt, etc.*⟩; **d)** *(erträglich, tolerierbar)* bearable; tolerable; **er ist für die Partei nicht mehr ~:** the party can no longer tolerate him

Trage die; ~, ~n a) *(Bahre)* stretcher; **b)** *(Traggestell)* pannier

träge ['trɛ:gə] **1.** *Adj.* **a)** sluggish; *(geistig)* lethargic; **b)** *(Physik)* inert. **2.** *adv. s.* **träge 1:** sluggishly; lethargically

Trage·korb der pannier

tragen [tra:gn̩] **1.** *unr. tr. V.* **a)** carry; **das Auto wurde aus der Kurve getragen** *(fig.)* the car went off the bend; **b)** *(bringen)* take; **vom Wasser/Wind getragen** *(fig.)* carried by water/[the] wind; **c)** *(ertragen)* bear ⟨*fate, destiny*⟩; bear, endure ⟨*suffering*⟩; **d)** *(halten)* hold; **einen/den linken Arm in der Schlinge ~:** have one's arm/one's left arm in a sling; **e)** *(von unten stützen)* support; **die Schwimmweste trägt dich** the life-jacket will hold you up; **zum Tragen kommen** ⟨*advantage, improvement, quality*⟩ become noticeable; **ein solcher Boykott kann nur zum Tragen kommen, wenn ...:** such a boycott can be effective only if ...; *s. auch* **tragend 2 a–c; f)** *(belastbar sein durch)* be able to carry *or* take ⟨*weight*⟩; **der Ast trägt dich nicht** the branch won't take your weight; **g)** *(übernehmen, aufkommen für)* bear, carry ⟨*costs etc.*⟩; take ⟨*blame, responsibility, consequences*⟩; *(unterhalten, finanzieren)* support; maintain, support ⟨*school*⟩; **er trägt die Schuld** he is to blame; **die Versicherung trägt den Schaden** the insurance will pay for the damage; **die Organisation trägt sich selbst** the organisation is self-supporting; **h)** *(am Körper)* wear ⟨*clothes, wig, glasses, jewellery, etc.*⟩; have ⟨*false teeth, beard, etc.*⟩; **man trägt [wieder] Hüte** hats are in fashion [again]; **getragene Kleider** second-hand clothes; **i)** *(fig.: haben)* have ⟨*label etc.*⟩; have, bear ⟨*title*⟩; bear, carry ⟨*signature, inscription, seal*⟩; **j)** *(hervorbringen)* ⟨*tree*⟩ bear ⟨*fruit*⟩; ⟨*field*⟩ produce ⟨*crops*⟩; *(fig.)* yield ⟨*interest*⟩; **gut/wenig ~** ⟨*tree*⟩ produce a good/poor crop; ⟨*field*⟩ produce a good/poor yield; **k)** *(geh.: schwanger sein mit)* be carrying; *s. auch* **Bedenken b; getragen 2, 3; Sorge c. 2.** *unr. itr. V.* **a)** carry; **wir hatten schwer zu ~:** we were heavily laden; **schwer an etw.** *(Dat.)* **zu ~ haben** have difficulty carrying sth.; find sth. very heavy to carry; *(fig.)* find sth. hard to bear; **das Eis trägt noch nicht** the ice is not yet thick enough to skate/walk *etc.* on; **b)** *(am Körper)* **man trägt [wieder] kurz/lang** short/long skirts are in fashion [again]; **c) der Baum trägt gut** the tree produces a good crop; *(in diesem Sommer)* the tree has a lot of fruit on it ; **d)** *(trächtig sein)* be carrying young; **eine ~de Sau/Kuh** a pregnant sow/cow; **e)** *([weit] reichen)* ⟨*voice*⟩ carry; *s. auch* **tragend 2 d. 3.** *unr. refl. V.* **a) sich gut/schlecht** *usw.* ~ ⟨*load*⟩ be easy/difficult *or* hard *etc.* to carry; **zu zweit trägt sich der Korb besser** two can carry the basket more easily; **b) der Mantel/Stoff trägt sich angenehm** the coat/material is pleasant to wear; **c)** *in* **sich mit etw. ~:** be contemplating sth.; **er trägt sich mit dem Gedanken** *od.* **der Absicht, auszuwandern** he is contemplating [the idea of] emigrating; **d)** *(sich kleiden)* dress

tragend 1. *1. Part. von* **tragen. 2.** *Adj.* **a)** *(Stabilität gebend)* load-bearing; supporting ⟨*wall, column, function, etc.*⟩; **b)** *(fig.: grundlegend)* basic, main ⟨*idea, motif*⟩; **c)** *(fig.: wichtig, zentral)* leading, major ⟨*role, figure*⟩; **d)** *(weithin hörbar)* ⟨*voice*⟩ that carries [a long way]

Träger ['trɛ:gɐ] **der; ~s, ~ a)** porter; *(Sänften~, Sarg~)* bearer; **b)** *(Zeitungs~)* paper boy/girl; delivery boy/girl; **c)** *(Bauw.)* girder; [supporting] beam; **d)** *(an Kleidung)* strap; (Hosen~) braces *pl.*; **e)** *(Inhaber) (eines Amts)* holder; *(eines Namens, Titels)* bearer; *(eines Preises)* winner; **f)** *(fig.: Urheber, treibende Kraft)* moving force; **g)** *(fig.: Unterhalter)* **die Schule hat einen privaten ~:** the school is privately maintained; **~ der Arbeitslosenversicherung ist der Staat** unemployment insurance is financed *or* funded by the state; **h)** *(fig.: einer Substanz, eines Erregers usw.)* carrier; **i)** *(Flugzeug~)* carrier; **j)** *(jmd., der etw. als Kleidung, Schmuck usw. trägt)* wearer

Trägerin die; ~, ~nen *s.* **Träger a, b, e, f, g, h, j**

träger-, Träger-: ~kleid das pinafore dress; **~los** *Adj.* strapless; **~rakete die** carrier vehicle *or* rocket; **~rock der** skirt with straps

Trägerschaft die; ~, ~en *(einer Schule)* maintenance; **in freier ~ sein** be privately maintained

Trage-: ~tasche die carrier-bag; **~zeit die** gestation [period]

trag-, Trag-: ~fähig *Adj.* able to take a load *or* weight *postpos.*; **eine ~fähige Mehrheit** *(fig.)* a workable majority; **~fähigkeit die** load- *or* weight-bearing capacity; **~fläche die** wing; *(eines Boots)* hydrofoil; **~flächen·boot das** hydrofoil; **~flügel der** *s.* **~fläche; ~flügel·boot das** hydrofoil

Trägheit die; ~, ~en a) *o. Pl. s.* **träge 1 a:** sluggishness; lethargy; **b)** *(Physik)* inertia

Trägheits-: ~gesetz das *(Physik)* law of inertia; **~moment das** *(Physik)* moment of inertia

Tragik ['tra:gɪk] **die; ~** tragedy

Tragiker der; ~s, ~: tragedian

tragi-, Tragi- [tragi-]: **~komik die** tragicomedy; **~komisch 1.** *Adj.* tragicomic; **2.** *adv.* tragicomically; **~komödie die** tragicomedy

tragisch ['tra:gɪʃ] **1.** *Adj.* tragic; **das ist nicht [so] ~** *(ugs.)* it's not the end of the world *(coll.)*; **etw. ~ nehmen** take sth. to heart *(coll.)*. **2.** *adv.* tragically; **der Film/die Tour endete ~:** the film had a tragic ending/the trip ended in tragedy

Trag-: ~kraft *s.* **~fähigkeit; ~last die** load; **~luft·halle die** air hall

Tragöde [tra'gø:də] **der; ~n, ~n** tragedian

Tragödie [tra'gø:di̯ə] **die; ~, ~n** tragedy; **er macht immer gleich eine ~ daraus** *(ugs.)* he always acts as if it's the end of the world *(coll.)*

Tragödien·dichter der tragedian

Tragödin die; ~, ~nen tragedienne

Trag-: ~sessel der sedan[-chair]; **~weite die;** *o. Pl.* consequences *pl.*; **von großer ~weite sein** have far-reaching consequences; **ein Ereignis von großer/weltpolitischer ~:** an event of great consequence *or* moment/of moment in world politics; **~zeit die** gestation [period]

Trainer ['trɛ:nɐ] **der; ~s, ~ a)** coach;

trainer; *(eines Schwimmers, Tennisspielers)* coach; *(einer Fußballmannschaft)* manager; **b)** *(Pferdesport)* trainer
Trainer·bank die *(Sport)* trainer's bench
Trainerin die; ~, ~nen *s.* **Trainer**
trainieren 1. *tr. V.* **a)** train; coach; coach ⟨*swimmer, tennis-player*⟩; train ⟨*horse*⟩; manage ⟨*football team*⟩; exercise ⟨*muscles etc.*⟩; **sein Gedächtnis ~** *(fig.)* train one's memory; **darauf trainiert sein, etw. zu tun** be trained to do sth.; **jmdn./ein Tier darauf ~, etw. zu tun** train sb./an animal to do sth.; **ein trainierter Schwimmer/Radfahrer/Bergsteiger** *usw.* a swimmer/cyclist/mountaineer *etc.* [who is] in training; **ein trainierter Körper** a body made fit by training; **b)** *(üben, einüben)* practise ⟨*exercise, jump, etc.*⟩; **c)** *(zu Trainingszwecken ausüben)* **Fußball/Tennis ~**: do football/tennis training. **2.** *itr. V.* train; *(Motorsport)* practise; **mit jmdm. ~**: ⟨*trainer*⟩ coach sb.; ⟨*player*⟩ train with sb.
Training ['trɛ:nɪŋ] **das**; ~s, ~s *(Fitneß~, auch fig.: Ausbildung)* training *no indef. art.*; *(Motorsport, fig.)* practice; **Radfahren ist ein gutes ~**: cycling is a good form of training *or* exercise; **sich einem strengen ~ unterziehen** submit oneself to a rigorous training programme; **er hat sich beim ~ verletzt** he injured himself in training/practice; **geistiges ~** *(fig.)* mental exercises *pl.*; **er hat das ~ der Mannschaft übernommen** he has taken over the coaching of the team *or* as coach to the team; **im ~ sein/bleiben** be/keep in training; *s. auch* **autogen**
Trainings-: ~anzug der track suit; **~hose die** track-suit bottoms *pl.*; **~jacke die** track-suit top; **~lager das**; *Pl.* **~lager** training camp; **~rück·stand der** lack of training; **einen ~rückstand haben** be behind with one's training; **~runde die** *(Rennsport)* practice lap; **~schuh der** training-shoe; trainer
Trakehner [tra'ke:nɐ] **der**; ~s, ~ *(Pferd)* Trakehner
Trakt [trakt] **der**; ~[e]s, ~e section; *(Flügel)* wing
Traktat [trak'ta:t] **der** *od.* **das**; ~[e]s, ~e **a)** *(Abhandlung)* treatise; **b)** *(religiöse Flugschrift)* tract
Traktätchen [trak'tɛ:tçən] **das**; ~s, ~ *(abwertend)* tract
traktieren *tr. V.* **a)** set about ⟨*person, thing*⟩; **jmdn. mit Ohrfeigen/Faustschlägen ~**: slap sb. round the face/punch sb.; **b)** *(veralt.: bewirten)* ply (**mit** with)
Traktor ['traktɔr] **der**; ~s, ~en [-'to:rən] tractor
Traktorist der; ~en, ~en *(DDR)* tractor-driver
trällern ['trɛlɐn] *itr., tr. V.* warble
Tram [tra:m] **die**; ~, ~s *od. schweiz.* **das**; ~s, ~s *(bes. südd., schweiz.)*, **Tram·bahn die** *(südd.)* tram *(Brit.)*; streetcar *(Amer.)*
Traminer [tra'mi:nɐ] **der**; ~s, ~ **a)** *o. Pl.* *(Rebsorte)* Traminer [grape]; **b)** *(Weißwein)* Traminer [white wine]
Tramp [trɛmp] **der**; ~s, ~s tramp; hobo *(Amer.)*
Trampel der *od.* **das**; ~s, ~ *(ugs. abwertend)* clumsy clot *(Brit. sl.) or* oaf
trampeln 1. *itr. V.* **a)** *(aufstampfen)* **[mit den Füßen] ~**: stamp one's feet; **b)** *mit sein (abwertend: treten)* trample (**auf** + *Akk.* on). **2.** *tr. V.* trample
Trampel-: ~pfad der [beaten] path; **~tier das a)** *(Kamel)* Bactrian camel; **b)** *(salopp abwertend)* clumsy clot *(Brit. sl.) or* oaf
trampen ['trɛmpn̩] *itr. V. mit sein* hitch-hike
Tramper der; ~s, ~, **Tramperin die**; ~, ~nen hitch-hiker
Trampolin ['trampoli:n] **das**; ~s, ~e trampoline
Tramway ['tramve] **die**; ~, ~s *(österr.)* tram *(Brit.)*; streetcar *(Amer.)*

Tran [tra:n] **der**; ~[e]s **a)** *(vom Wal)* train-oil; *(von Fischen)* fish-oil; **b) im ~** *(ugs.)* befuddled; in a daze; *(durch Alkohol, Drogen)* stoned *(sl.)*
Trance ['trã:s(ə)] **die**; ~, ~n trance; **in ~**: in a trance; **in ~ fallen** go into a trance
Trance·zustand der trance
Tranche ['trã:ʃ(ə)] **die**; ~, ~n **a)** *(Kochk.)* thick slice; **b)** *(Wirtsch.)* tranche
Tränchen ['trɛ:nçən] **das**; ~s, ~: [little] tear
tranchieren *tr. V. (Kochk.)* carve
Tranchier·messer das carving-knife
Träne ['trɛ:nə] **die**; ~, ~n tear; **~ traten ihr in die Augen** tears came into her eyes; **seine ~n trocknen** dry one's eyes; wipe away one's tears; **ihr kommen leicht die ~n** she cries easily; **~n lachen** laugh till one cries *or* till the tears run down one's cheeks; **in ~n aufgelöst sein** be in floods of tears; **in ~n zerfließen** dissolve in tears; **mit einer ~ im Knopfloch** *(scherzh.)* wiping away a tear *(fig.)*; **jmdm./einer Sache keine ~ nachweinen** not shed any tears over sb./sth.
tränen *itr. V.* ⟨*eyes*⟩ water
Tränende Herz das; ~n ~ens, ~n ~en bleeding heart; lyre-flower
tränen-, Tränen-: ~drüse die *(Anat.)* tear-gland; **auf die ~drüsen drücken** *(fig.)* lay on the agony; **~erstickt** *Adj. (geh.)* **mit ~ ersticker Stimme** in a voice choked with tears; **~gas das** tear-gas; **~sack der** *(Anat.)* lachrymal sac; **~säcke [unter den Augen]** bags under the eyes; **~überströmt** *Adj.* tear-stained ⟨*face*⟩
Tran·funzel die *(ugs. abwertend)* **a)** *(trübe Lampe)* miserable lamp; **b)** *(langweiliger Mensch)* ponderous dim-wit *(coll.)*; *(langsamer Mensch)* slowcoach; slowpoke *(Amer.)*
tranig *Adj.* **a)** *(voller Tran)* ⟨*meat, fish*⟩ full of train-oil; **b)** *(wie Tran)* ⟨*taste*⟩ like *or* of train-oil; **c)** *(ugs. abwertend: langsam)* sluggish; slow
trank [traŋk] *1. u. 3. Pers. Sg. Prät. v.* **trinken**
Tränke ['trɛŋkə] **die**; ~, ~n watering-place; *(Gefäß)* drinking-trough
tränken *tr. V.* **a)** *(auch fig.)* water; **b)** *(sich vollsaugen lassen)* soak; **ein mit Hohn getränkter Brief** *(fig.)* a letter brimming with scorn
Tranquilizer ['træŋkwɪlaɪzə] **der**; ~s, ~ *(Pharm.)* tranquillizer
trans-, Trans- [trans-]: **~aktion die** transaction; **~alpin, ~alpinisch** *Adj.* transalpine; **~atlantisch** *Adj.* transatlantic; across the Atlantic *postpos.*; **~-Europ-Express der** Trans-Europe Express
Transfer [trans'fe:ɐ] **der**; ~s, ~s *(bes. Wirtsch., Sport)* transfer
transferieren *tr. V. (bes. Wirtsch., Sport)* transfer (**auf** + *Akk.*, **in** + *Akk.*, **zu** to)
Transfer·liste die *(Fußball)* transfer list
trans-, Trans-: ~formation die transformation; **~formations·grammatik die** *(Sprachw.)* transformational grammar; **~formator** [~fɔr'ma:tɔr] **der**; ~s, ~en [-'to:rən] transformer; **~formator·häuschen das** transformer station; **~formieren** *tr. V.* transform (**in** + *Akk.* into, **auf** + *Akk.* to); **~fusion die** *(Med.)* transfusion
Transistor [tran'zɪstɔr] **der**; ~s, ~en [-'to:rən] **a)** *(Elektronik)* transistor; **b)** *s.* **~radio**
Transistor·radio das transistor radio
[1]**Transit** [*auch:* '--] **der**; ~s, ~e transit
[2]**Transit** [tran'zi:t, *auch:* 'tranzɪt] **das**; ~s, ~s transit visa
Transit·handel der transit trade
transitiv ['tranziti:f] *(Sprachw.)* **1.** *Adj.* transitive. **2.** *adv.* transitively
Transit·verkehr der transit traffic
transkribieren [transkri'bi:rən] *tr. V. (Sprachw.)* transcribe
Transkription [transkrɪp'tsio:n] **die**; ~, ~en *(Sprachw.)* transcription

Trans-: ~literation [~lɪtera'tsio:n] **die**; ~, ~en *(Sprachw.)* transliteration; **~mission die** *(Technik)* transmission; **~missions-riemen der** transmission belt
transparent [transpa'rɛnt] *Adj.* **a)** transparent; *(Licht durchlassend)* translucent, diaphanous ⟨*curtain, fabric, etc.*⟩; **b)** *(fig.: verständlich)* intelligible
Transparent das; ~[e]s, ~e **a)** *(Spruchband)* banner; **b)** *(Bild)* transparency
Transparenz die; ~ **a)** transparency; *(von Gewebe, Porzellan usw.)* translucence; **b)** *(fig.: Verständlichkeit)* intelligibility
Transpiration [transpira'tsio:n] **die**; ~, ~en **a)** *(geh.)* perspiration; **b)** *(Bot.)* transpiration
transpirieren *itr. V. (bes. Med.)* perspire
trans-, Trans-: ~plantation [~planta'tsio:n] **die**; ~, ~en *(Med.)* transplant; *(von Haut)* graft; **~plantieren** [~plan'ti:rən] *tr. V. (Med.)* transplant ⟨*organ, tissue*⟩; graft ⟨*skin*⟩; **~ponieren** [~po'ni:rən] *tr. V. (Musik)* transpose
Transport [trans'pɔrt] **der**; ~[e]s, ~e **a)** *(Beförderung)* transportation; **beim** *od.* **auf dem ~**: during carriage; **b)** *(beförderte Lebewesen od. Sachen) (mit dem Zug)* trainload; *(mit mehreren Fahrzeugen)* convoy; *(Fracht)* consignment; shipment; **c)** *(Technik)* transport
transportabel [transpɔr'ta:bl̩] *Adj.* transportable; mobile ⟨*field kitchen*⟩; *(tragbar)* portable
Transport·behälter der container
Transporter der; ~s, ~ *(Flugzeug)* transport aircraft; *(Auto)* goods vehicle; *(Schiff)* cargo ship
Transporteur [...'tø:ɐ] **der**; ~s, ~e carrier
transportfähig *Adj.* moveable
Transport·flugzeug das transport aircraft
transportieren 1. *tr. V.* **a)** transport ⟨*goods, people*⟩; move ⟨*patient*⟩; *(fig.)* convey ⟨*feeling, information, knowledge*⟩; **b)** *(Technik: weiterschieben)* transport, wind on ⟨*film*⟩. **2.** *itr. V. (Technik)* ⟨*camera*⟩ wind on
Transport-: ~kosten *Pl.* carriage *sing.*; transport costs; **~mittel das** means *sing.* of transport; **~unter·nehmen das** haulage firm *or* contractor
Trans·uran das *meist Pl. (Chemie, Physik)* transuranic element
Tran·suse die *(ugs. abwertend) s.* **Tranfunzel b**
Transvestit [transvɛs'ti:t] **der**; ~en, ~en transvestite
transzendent [transtsɛn'dɛnt] *Adj.* **a)** *(Philos.)* transcendent; **b)** *(Math.)* transcendental
transzendental [transtsɛndɛn'ta:l] *Adj.* *(Philos.)* transcendental
Transzendental·philosophie die; *o. Pl.* transcendental philosophy *no art.*
Transzendenz [transtsɛn'dɛnts] **die**; ~ **a)** transcendency; transcendent nature; **b)** *(Philos.)* transcendence
transzendieren *tr. V. (geh.)* transcend
Trapez [tra'pe:ts] **das**; ~es, ~e **a)** *(Geom.)* trapezium *(Brit.)*; trapezoid *(Amer.)*; **b)** *(im Zirkus o. ä.)* trapeze
Trapez-: ~akt der trapeze act; **~künstler der** trapeze artist
Trapezoid [trapetso'i:t] **das**; ~[e]s, ~e *(Geom.)* trapezoid *(Brit.)*; trapezium *(Amer.)*
Trappe ['trapə] **die**; ~, ~n bustard
trappeln ['trapl̩n] *itr. V.*; *mit sein* patter [along]; ⟨*feet*⟩ patter; ⟨*hoofs*⟩ go clip-clop
Trapper ['trapɐ] **der**; ~s, ~: trapper
Trappist [tra'pɪst] **der**; ~en, ~en Trappist
Trappisten-: ~käse der Trappist cheese; **~orden der** order of Trappists
Trappistin die; ~, ~nen Trappistine
trapsen ['trapsn̩] *itr. V.*; *mit sein (ugs.)* tramp; clump; *s. auch* **Nachtigall**

trara [tra'ra:] *Interj.* tantara
Trara das; ~s *(ugs. abwertend)* razzmatazz *(coll.)*; **viel ~ um etw.** *(Akk.)* **machen** make a great song and dance about sth. *(coll.)*
Traß [tras] **der; Trasses, Trasse** *(Geol.)* trass
Trassant [tra'sant] **der; ~en, ~en** *(Finanzw.)* drawer
Trassat [tra'sa:t] **der; ~en, ~en** *(Finanzw.)* drawee
Trasse ['trasə] **die; ~, ~n a)** *(Verkehrsweg)* [marked-out] route *or* line; **b)** *(Damm)* [rail-way/road] embankment
trat [tra:t] *1. u. 3. Pers. Sg. Prät. v.* **treten**
Tratsch [tra:tʃ] **der; ~[e]s** *(ugs. abwertend)* gossip; tittle-tattle
tratschen *itr. V. (ugs. abwertend)* gossip; *(schwatzen)* chatter
Tratscherei die; ~, ~en *(ugs. abwertend)* gossiping
Tratte ['tratə] **die; ~, ~n** *(Finanzw.)* bill [of exchange]
Trau·altar der *in* **[mit jmdn.] vor den ~ treten** *(geh.)* enter into matrimony [with sb.]; **jmdn. zum ~ führen** *(geh. veralt.)* lead sb. to the altar
Träubchen ['trɔypçən] **das; ~s, ~:** little grape
Traube ['traubə] **die; ~, ~n a)** *(Beeren)* bunch; *(von Johannisbeeren o.ä.)* cluster; **b)** *(Wein~)* grape; **jmdm. sind die ~n zu sauer** *(fig.)* it's just sour grapes on sb.'s part; **c)** *(Menschenmenge)* bunch; cluster; **d)** *(Bot.: Blütenstand)* raceme
Trauben-: ~hyazinthe die grape hyacinth; **~lese die** grape harvest; **~saft der** grape-juice; **~zucker der** glucose
trauen ['trauən] **1.** *itr. V.* **jmdm./einer Sache ~:** trust sb./sth.; **ich traue dem Braten nicht** *(ugs.)* I think something's up *(coll.)*; it seems fishy to me *(coll.)*; **trau, schau, wem!** make sure you know who you're dealing with; mind you're not taken for a ride *(sl.)*; *s. auch* **Auge a. 2.** *refl. V.* dare; **sich** *(Akk., selten Dat.)* **~, etw. zu tun** dare [to] do sth.; **du traust dich ja nicht!** you haven't the courage *or* nerve; **sich irgendwohin ~:** dare [to] go somewhere; **ich traue mich nicht in seine Nähe** I daren't go near him. **3.** *tr. V. (verheiraten)* ⟨*vicar, registrar, etc.*⟩ marry; *s. auch* **kirchlich 1 b, 2; standesamtlich 2**
Trauer ['trauɐ] **die; ~ a)** grief **(über +** *Akk.* over); *(um einen Toten)* mourning **(um +** *Akk.* for); **~ haben, in ~ sein** be in mourning; **in stiller/tiefer ~ X** *(in Todesanzeigen)* [much loved and] sadly mourned by X; **b)** *(~zeit)* [period of] mourning; **c)** *(~kleidung)* mourning
Trauer-: ~akt der memorial ceremony; *(beim Begräbnis)* funeral ceremony; **~arbeit die;** *o. Pl. (Psychol.)* process of grieving; **~fall der** bereavement; **~feier die** memorial ceremony; *(beim Begräbnis)* funeral ceremony; **~flor der** mourning-band; black [crape] ribbon; **~gemeinde die** [congregation *sing.* of] mourners *pl.*; **~gottes·dienst der** funeral service; **~haus das** house of mourning; **~jahr das** year of mourning; **~karte die** [pre-printed] card of condolence; **~kleidung die** mourning clothes *pl.*; mourning; **~kloß der** *(ugs. scherzh.)* wet blanket; **~mantel der** *(Zool.)* Camberwell Beauty; mourning cloak [butterfly] *(Amer.)*; **~marsch der** *(Musik)* funeral march; **~miene die** *(ugs.)* long face
trauern *itr. V.* **a)** mourn; **um jmdn. ~:** mourn for sb.; **die ~den Hinterbliebenen** the bereaved; **b)** *(Trauer tragen)* be in mourning
Trauer-: ~rand der black border *or* edging; **~ränder unter den Nägeln haben** *(fig. scherzh.)* have black *or* grubby finger-nails; **~rede die** funeral oration; **~schleier der** black veil; mourning veil; **~spiel das** tragedy; *(fig. ugs.)* deplorable business; **es ist doch ein ~ spiel, daß ...:** it's quite pathetic that ...; **~weide die** weeping willow; **~zeit die** period of mourning; **~zug der** funeral procession
Traufe ['traufə] **die; ~, ~n** eaves *pl.*
träufeln ['trɔyfl̩n] *tr. V.* [let] trickle **(in +** *Akk.* into); drip ⟨*ear-drops etc.*⟩
traulich ['traulɪç] **1.** *Adj.* cosy; **in ~er Runde** in a friendly *or* an intimate circle. **2.** *adv.* cosily; *(vertraut)* intimately
Traulichkeit die; ~: cosiness; *(Vertrautheit)* intimacy; friendliness
Traum [traum] **der; ~[e]s, Träume** ['trɔymə] dream; **sie ist mir im ~ erschienen** she appeared to me in a dream; **wir denken nicht im ~ daran, hier wegzuziehen** we wouldn't dream of moving away from here; **nicht im ~ habe ich mit der Möglichkeit gerechnet, zu gewinnen** I didn't imagine in my wildest dreams that I could win; **Träume sind Schäume** *(Spr.)* dreams are but shadows; **Fliegen war schon immer sein ~:** he had always dreamed of flying; **der ~ ist ausgeträumt,** *(ugs.)* **aus [ist] der ~!** that's the end of 'that dream; 'that dream is over; *s. auch* **kühn b**
Traum- dream ⟨*house, hotel, job, etc.*⟩; ⟨*house, hotel, woman*⟩ of one's dreams; ideal, perfect ⟨*couple, job*⟩
Trauma ['trauma] **das; ~s, Traumen** *od.* **~ta** *(Psych., Med.)* trauma
traumatisch *(Psych., Med.)* **1.** *Adj.* traumatic. **2.** *adv.* traumatically
Traum-: ~bild das vision; *(Wunschbild)* dream; *(idealisiert)* ideal; **~deutung die** interpretation of dreams
Traumen *s.* **Trauma**
träumen ['trɔymən] **1.** *itr. V.* dream **(von** of, about); *(unaufmerksam sein)* [day-]dream; **[schlaf gut und] träum süß** [sleep well and] sweet dreams; **träum nicht!** pay attention; stop day-dreaming. **2.** *tr. V.* dream; **etwas Schreckliches/Schönes ~:** have a terrible/beautiful dream; **er träumte** *od. (geh.)* **ihm träumte, er sei ...:** he dreamt that he was ...; **das hast du doch nur geträumt!** you must have imagined that; **ich hätte mir nie ~ lassen, daß ...:** I should never have imagined it possible that ...; I never imagined that ...
Träumer der; ~s, ~: dreamer
Träumerei die; ~, ~en day-dream; reverie
Träumerin die; ~, ~nen dreamer
träumerisch 1. *Adj.* dreamy; *(sehnsüchtig)* wistful. **2.** *adv.* dreamily; *(sehnsüchtig)* wistfully
Traum·fabrik die dream-factory
traumhaft 1. *Adj.* **a)** dreamlike; **b)** *(ugs.: schön)* marvellous; fabulous *(coll.)*; **~es Glück haben** have a fantastic piece of luck *(coll.)*. **2.** *adv.* **a)** as if in a dream; **b)** *(ugs.: schön)* fabulously *(coll.)*; **eine ~ eingerichtete Wohnung** a superbly furnished flat
traum-, Traum-: ~tänzer der *(abwertend)* wooly-headed idealist; fantasizer; **~verloren 1.** *Adj.* dreamy; **2.** *adv.* in a dream; dreamily; **~wandlerisch** *Adj.* somnambulistic; **mit ~wandlerischer Sicherheit** with the sureness of a sleep-walker; with instinctive sureness; **~welt die** dream world
traurig ['traurɪç] **1.** *Adj.* **a)** sad; sad, sorrowful ⟨*eyes, expression*⟩; unhappy ⟨*childhood, youth*⟩; unhappy, painful ⟨*duty*⟩; **ein ~es Kapitel** *(fig.)* a sad story; **b)** *(kümmerlich)* sorry, pathetic ⟨*state etc.*⟩; miserable ⟨*result*⟩; pitiful, wretched ⟨*conditions*⟩; down-at-heel ⟨*area*⟩; **eine ~e Berühmtheit/Rolle** an unfortunate notoriety/role. **2.** *adv.* sadly
Traurigkeit die; ~: sadness; sorrow; **eine große/allgemeine ~:** a great/general feeling of sadness
Trau-: ~ring der wedding-ring; **~schein der** marriage certificate
traut *Adj.; nicht präd. (geh.)* **a)** *(heimelig)* cosy; secure; **das ~e Familienglück** happiness in the bosom of a/the family; **b)** *(vertraut)* familiar; close, intimate ⟨*friend, family circle*⟩
Traute ['trautə] **die; ~** *(ugs.)* guts *(coll.)*
Trauung die; ~, ~en wedding [ceremony]
Trau·zeuge der witness *(at wedding ceremony)*
Traveller·scheck ['trɛvəlɐʃɛk] **der** traveller's cheque
Traverse [tra'vɛrzə] **die; ~, ~n a)** *(Technik)* cross-beam; **b)** *(Fechten)* sideways movement to avoid opponent's attack
Travers·flöte [tra'vɛrs-] **die** transverse flute
Travestie [travɛs'ti:] **die; ~, ~n** travesty
Trebe ['tre:bə] **die** *in* **auf ~ sein** *(ugs.)* be a runaway
Trebegänger [-gɛŋɐ] **der; ~s, ~** *(ugs.)* runaway
Treber *Pl.* **a)** *(Brauereiwesen)* draff *sing.*; **b)** *(Weinbau)* marc *sing.*
Treck [trɛk] **der; ~s, ~s** train, column *(of refugees etc.)*
Trecker der; ~s, ~: tractor
[1]Treff das; ~s, ~s *(Spielkartenfarbe)* clubs *pl.*; *s. auch* **[2]Pik**
[2]Treff [trɛf] **der; ~s, ~s** *(ugs.)* **a)** *(Treffen)* rendezvous; *(bes. von mehreren Personen)* get-together *(coll.)*; **b)** *(Ort)* meeting-place
treffen 1. *unr. tr. V.* **a)** *(erreichen [und verletzen/schädigen])* hit; ⟨*punch, blow, object*⟩ strike; **jmdn. am Kopf/ins Gesicht ~:** hit *or* strike sb. on the head/in the face; **von einer Kugel tödlich getroffen** fatally wounded by a bullet; **vom Blitz getroffen** struck by lightning; **er fühlte sich von den Vorwürfen nicht getroffen** he did not consider that the reproaches applied to him; **ihn trifft keine Schuld** he is in no way to blame; **b)** *(erraten)* hit on; hit ⟨*right tone*⟩; **du hast genau das Richtige getroffen** you've hit on just the right thing; *(das stimmt haargenau)* you've got it exactly right; **getroffen!** you've got it!; **mit dem Geschenk hast du seinen Geschmack getroffen/nicht getroffen** that present is just the sort of thing he likes/not the sort of thing he likes; **auf dem Foto ist er gut getroffen** the photo is a good likeness of him; that's a good photo of him; **c)** *(erschüttern)* affect [deeply]; *(verletzen)* hurt; **jmdn. tief** *od.* **schwer ~:** affect sb. deeply; **es hat ihn in seinem Stolz getroffen** it hurt his pride; **d)** *(schaden)* hit; damage; **warum muß es immer mich ~?** why does it always have to be me [who is affected *or* gets it]?; **e)** *(begegnen)* meet; **jmdn. zum Mittagessen ~:** meet sb. for lunch; **ich traf ihn zufällig auf der Straße** I happened to run into him in the street; **ihre Blicke trafen sich** *(fig.)* their eyes met; **f)** *(vorfinden)* come upon, find ⟨*anomalies etc.*⟩; **es gut/schlecht ~:** be *or* strike lucky/be unlucky; **g)** *(als Funktionsverb)* make ⟨*arrangements, choice, preparations, decision, etc.*⟩; **eine Vereinbarung** *od.* **Absprache ~:** conclude an agreement. **2.** *unr. itr. V.* **a)** ⟨*person, shot, etc.*⟩ hit the target; **nicht ~:** miss [the target]; **ins Schwarze ~:** score a bull's eye; **b)** *mit sein* **auf etw.** *(Akk.)* **~:** come upon sth.; **auf Widerstand/Ablehnung/Schwierigkeiten ~:** meet with *or* encounter resistance/rejection/difficulties; **auf jmdn./eine Mannschaft ~** *(Sport)* come up against sb./a team. **3.** *unr. refl. V.* **a) sich mit jmdm. ~:** meet sb.; **b)** *(unpers.)* **es trifft sich gut/schlecht** it is convenient/inconvenient
Treffen das; ~s, ~ a) meeting; **ein ~ alter Kameraden** a reunion of old comrades; **b)** *(Sport)* encounter; **ein faires/spannendes ~:** a fair/exciting contest; **c)** *(Milit. veralt.)* encounter; **etw. ins ~ führen** *(fig. geh.)* bring sth. into the attack
treffend 1. *Adj.* apt; apposite ⟨*remark*⟩; **ein ~es Urteil** an accurate assessment. **2.** *adv.* aptly; **kurz und ~ sagte er ...:** he said, short and to the point, ...

Trẹffer der; ~s, ~ **a)** *(Milit., Boxen, Fechten usw.)* hit; *(Schlag)* blow; *(Ballspiele)* goal; **schwere ~ an Kopf und Körper einstecken** *(Boxen)* take heavy blows *or* punches to the head and body; **er hatte auf zehn Schüsse acht ~:** of his ten shots eight were on target; **b)** *(Gewinn)* win; *(Los)* winner

trẹfflich *(geh.)* **1.** *Adj.* excellent; splendid ‹*person*›; first-rate ‹*scholar*›. **2.** *adv.* excellently; splendidly

trẹff-, Trẹff-: ~punkt der a) *(Stelle, Ort)* meeting-place; rendezvous; **b)** *(Geom.)* point of incidence; *(Schnittpunkt)* point of intersection; **~sicher 1.** *Adj.* with a sure aim *postpos., not pred.*; accurate ‹*marksman*›; *(fig.)* accurate ‹*language, mode of expression*›; unerring ‹*judgement*›; **2.** *adv.* *(auch fig.)* accurately; with unerring accuracy; **~sicherheit die;** *o. Pl. s.* **~sicher 1:** accuracy; sureness of aim; *(fig.)* accuracy; unerringness

Treib-: ~anker der *(Seew.)* sea anchor; **~ball der a)** *o. Pl. (Spiel)* [*informal*] *ball game played by two teams trying to throw the ball over the back line of the opposing team;* **b)** *(Badminton)* drive; **~eis das** drift-ice

treiben ['traibn̩] **1.** *unr. tr. V.* **a)** drive ‹*animals, people, leaves, etc.*›; *(Fußball)* dribble ‹*ball*›; **er ließ sich von der Strömung ~:** he let himself be carried along by the current; **die Arbeit trieb ihm den Schweiß auf die Stirn** the effort brought the sweat to his brow; **die Preise in die Höhe ~:** push *or* force up prices; **jmdn. in den Wahnsinn** *od.* **zur Raserei/zur Verzweiflung/in den Tod ~:** drive sb. mad/to despair/to his/her death; **b)** *(an~)* drive ‹*wheels etc.*›; **die ~de Kraft [des Ganzen] ist ...** the moving spirit [behind the whole affair] is ...; **jmdn. zur Eile ~:** make sb. hurry up; **c)** *(einschlagen)* drive ‹*nail, wedge, stake, etc.*› **(in +** *Akk.* into); **d)** *(durch Bohrung schaffen)* drive, cut ‹*tunnel, gallery*› **(in +** *Akk.* into; **durch** through); sink ‹*shaft*› **(in +** *Akk.* into); **e)** *(durchpressen)* force; press; **f)** *(sich beschäftigen mit)* go in for ‹*farming, cattle-breeding, etc.*›; study ‹*French etc.*›; carry on, pursue ‹*studies, trade, craft*›; **viel Sport ~:** do a lot of sport; go in for sport in a big way; **Handel ~:** trade; **Unfug ~:** get up to mischief; **Unsinn ~:** mess *or* fool about; **was treibt ihr denn hier?** *(ugs.)* what are you up to *or* doing here?; **was habt ihr den ganzen Tag getrieben?** *(ugs.)* what did you do with yourself *or* get up to all day?; *s. auch* **Aufwand b; Mißbrauch a; Scherz; Spionage; Spott; g)** *(ugs. abwertend: in Verbindung mit „es“:)* **es wüst/übel/toll ~:** lead a dissolute/bad life/live it up; **es zu toll ~:** overdo it; take things too far; **er hat es zu weit getrieben** he overstepped the mark; he went too far; **es [mit jmdm.] ~** *(ugs. verhüll.: koitieren)* have it off [with sb.] *(sl.)*; **h)** *(formen)* beat ‹*metal, object*›; chase ‹*silver, gold*›; **i)** *(Gartenbau)* force ‹*plants*›; **j)** *(aufgehen lassen)* cause ‹*dough*› to rise. **2.** *unr. itr. V.* **a)** *meist, mit Richtungsangabe nur, mit sein* drift; **die Dinge ~ lassen** *(fig.)* let things take their course; **sich ~ lassen** *(fig.)* drift; go with the tide; **b)** *(ugs.) (harntreibend sein)* get the bladder going; *(schweißtreibend sein)* make you sweat; **ein ~des Mittel** a diuretic/sudorific; **c)** *(ausschlagen)* ‹*tree, plant*› sprout

Treiben das; ~s, ~ **a)** *o. Pl. (Durcheinander)* bustle; **in der Fußgängerzone herrscht ein lebhaftes ~:** the pedestrian precinct is full of bustling activity; *s. auch* **närrisch 1 c; b)** *o. Pl. (Tun)* activities *pl.*; doings *pl.*; *(Machenschaften)* wheelings and dealings *pl.*; **c)** *(Jägerspr.) s.* **Treibjagd**

Treiber der; ~s, ~ *(Jägerspr.)* beater

Treib-: ~gas das a) *(für Motoren)* liquefied petroleum gas; LPG; **b)** *(in Spraydosen)* propellant; **~gut das** flotsam; **~haus das** hothouse; **~haus·effekt der** greenhouse effect; **~haus·luft die;** *o. Pl.* hothouse atmosphere; *(im Freien)* sultry atmosphere; **~holz das;** *o. Pl.* driftwood; **~jagd die** *(Jägerspr.)* battue; shoot *(in which game is sent up by beaters)*; **eine ~jagd auf kritische Journalisten** *(fig.)* a witch-hunt against critical jounalists; **~mittel das a)** *(Kochk.)* raising agent; **b)** *(Chemie: für feste Stoffe)* foaming agent; **c)** *s.* **~gas b; ~riemen der** *(Technik)* drive belt; **~sand der** quicksand; **~satz der** *(Technik)* [solid] rocket propulsion element; **~schlag der** *(Badminton, Golf, Tennis, Tischtennis)* drive; **~stoff der** fuel

treideln ['traidl̩n] *tr. V. (veralt.)* tow ‹*barge*› upstream

treife ['traifə] *Adj.* trefa; not kosher *pred.*

Trema ['tre:ma] **das;** ~s, ~s *od.* ~ta *(Sprachw.)* diaeresis

tremolieren *itr. V. (Musik)* play/sing with a tremolo

Tremolo ['tre:molo] **das;** ~s, ~s *od.* **Tremoli** *(Musik)* tremolo

Trenchcoat ['trɛntʃkoʊt] **der;** ~[s], ~s trench coat

Trend [trɛnt] **der;** ~s, ~s trend **(zu +** *Dat.* towards); *(Mode)* vogue; **im ~ liegen** be in vogue

Trend·setter der; ~s, ~ *(bes. Werbejargon)* trend-setter *(Gen.* in)

trennbar *Adj.* **a)** *(nicht fest zusammengesetzt)* separable ‹*verb, prefix*›; **b)** *(sich trennen lassend)* **dieses Wort ist [nicht] ~:** this word can[not] be split *or* divided

trennen ['trɛnən] **1.** *tr. V.* **a)** separate **(von** from); *(abschneiden)* cut off; sever ‹*head, arm*›; **der Krieg hatte die Familie getrennt** the war had split up the family; **das Kind von der Mutter ~:** take the child away from the mother; **das Futter aus der Jacke ~:** cut the lining out of the jacket; **nur noch wenige Tage ~ uns von den Ferien** the holidays are only a few days away; **b)** *(auf~)* unpick ‹*dress, seam*›; **c)** *(teilen)* divide ‹*word, parts of a room etc., fig.: people*›; **ein Zaun trennte die Grundstücke** a fence divided the plots from one another; a fence formed the boundary between the plots; **uns ~ Welten** *(fig.)* we are worlds apart; **„st“ darf nicht getrennt werden** 'st' cannot be split *or* divided; **d)** *(beim Telefon)* **wir wurden getrennt** we were cut off; **e)** *(zerlegen)* separate ‹*mixture*›; **f)** *(auseinanderhalten)* differentiate *or* distinguish between; make a distinction between ‹*terms*›; **die Arbeit von der Freizeit ~:** keep work separate from leisure. **2.** *itr. V. (Rundf., Funkw.)* **gut** *od.* **scharf ~** ‹*radio*› have good selectivity. **3.** *refl. V.* **a)** *(voneinander weggehen)* part [company]; *(fig.)* **die Mannschaften trennten sich 0:0** the game ended in a goalless draw; the two teams drew 0:0; **die Firma hat sich von ihm getrennt** the company has dispensed with his services; **b)** *(eine Partnerschaft auflösen)* ‹*couple, partners*› split up; **sich in Güte ~:** part on good terms; **sie hat sich von ihrem Mann getrennt** she has left her husband; *s. auch* **getrennt; c)** *(hergeben)* **sich von etw. ~:** part with sth.

Trenn-: ~schärfe die; *o. Pl. (Rundf., Funkw.)* selectivity; **~scheibe die** glass partition

Trennung die; ~, ~en **a)** *(von Menschen)* separation **(von** from); **in ~ leben** have separated; **die ~ von Tisch und Bett** separation from bed and board; separation without divorce; **b)** *(von Gegenständen)* parting; **die ~ von allem irdischen Besitz** parting with all one's worldly goods; **c)** *(von Wörtern)* division; **d)** *(von Begriffen)* distinction **(von** between)

Trennungs-: ~linie die *(auch fig.)* dividing line; **~schmerz der;** *o. Pl.* pain of separation; **~strich der a)** hyphen; **b)** *(fig.)* **einen ~strich ziehen** *od.* **machen** make a [clear] distinction; draw a [clear] line; **er zog einen ~strich zwischen sich und seiner Vergangenheit** he made a clean break with the past

Trenn·wand die partition

Trense ['trɛnzə] **die;** ~, ~n **a)** *(Gebiß)* snaffle-bit; **b)** *(Zaumzeug)* snaffle

trepp- [trɛp'-]: **~ab** *Adv.* down the stairs; **~auf** *Adv.* up the stairs

Treppchen das; ~s, ~ **a)** small staircase; **b)** *(Sportjargon)* [winner's] rostrum

Treppe ['trɛpə] **die;** ~, ~n **a)** staircase; [flight *sing.* of] stairs *pl.*; *(im Freien, auf der Bühne)* [flight *sing.* of] steps *pl.*; **~n steigen** climb stairs; **eine ~ höher/tiefer** one floor *or* flight up/down; **die ~ hinauffallen** *(fig. ugs.)* rise in the world; **die ~ runtergefallen sein** *(fig. ugs. scherzh.)* have been to the sheep-shearer's *(joc.)*; **b)** *(in der Frisur)* step

Treppen-: ~ab·satz der half-landing; **~geländer das** banisters *pl.*; **~giebel der** *(Archit.)* stepped gable; **~haus das** stairwell; **das Licht im ~haus** the light on the staircase; **~steigen das;** ~s climbing stairs *no art.*; **~stufe die** stair; *(im Freien)* step; **~witz der: ein ~witz der [Welt]geschichte** one of history's cruel ironies

Tresen ['tre:zn̩] **der;** ~s, ~ *(bes. nordd.)* **a)** *(Theke)* bar; **b)** *(Ladentisch)* counter

Tresor [tre'zo:ɐ̯] **der;** ~s, ~e **a)** safe; **b)** *(~raum)* strong-room

Tresse ['trɛsə] **die;** ~, ~n; *meist Pl.* [strip of] braid; *(Rangabzeichen)* stripe

Trester ['trɛstɐ] *Pl. (Landw.)* **a)** *(von Trauben)* marc; **b)** *(von Äpfeln o. ä.)* pomace

Trester·brannt·wein der marc

Tret-: ~boot das pedalo; **~eimer der** pedal bin

treten ['tre:tn̩] **1.** *unr. itr. V.* **a)** *mit sein (einen Schritt, Schritte machen)* step **(in +** *Akk.* into, **auf +** *Akk.* on to); **ins Zimmer/in einen Laden ~:** enter the room/a shop; **ans Fenster ~:** go to the window; **zur Seite ~:** step *or* move aside; **von einem Fuß auf den anderen ~:** shift from one foot to the other; **der Schweiß ist ihm auf die Stirn getreten** *(fig.)* the sweat came to his brow; **der Fluß ist über die Ufer getreten** *(fig.)* the river has overflowed its banks; *s. auch* **Stelle a; b)** *(seinen Fuß setzen)* **auf etw.** *(Akk.)* **~** *(absichtlich)* tread on sth.; *(unabsichtlich; meist mit sein)* step *or* tread on sth.; **jmdm. auf den Fuß ~:** step/tread on sb.'s foot *or* toes; **auf das Gas[pedal]/die Bremse ~:** step on the accelerator/the brake; **kräftig in die Pedale ~:** pedal hard; **c)** *mit sein (verblaßt in Verbindungen mit Substantiven)* **in jmds. Dienste ~:** enter sb.'s service; **in Kontakt** *od.* **Verbindung ~:** get in touch; **in den Ruhestand ~:** go into retirement; *s. auch* **Aktion c; Ehestand; Hungerstreik; Streik; d)** *(ausschlagen)* kick; **jmdm. an** *od.* **gegen das Schienbein ~:** kick sb. on the shin; **gegen die Tür ~:** kick the door. **2.** *unr. tr. V.* **a)** *(Tritt versetzen)* kick ‹*person, ball, etc.*›; **jmdn. in den Bauch ~:** kick sb. in the stomach; **eine Ecke ~** *(Fußball)* take a corner; **man muß ihn immer ~, damit er etwas tut** *(fig.)* you always have to give him a kick to make him do anything; **b)** *(trampeln)* trample, tread ‹*path*›; **sich** *(Dat.)* **einen Dorn in den Fuß ~:** get a thorn in one's foot; **sich** *(Dat.)* **den Lehm von den Schuhen ~:** stamp the mud off one's shoes; **c)** *(mit dem Fuß niederdrücken)* step on ‹*brake, pedal*›; operate ‹*bellows, clutch*›; **die Pedale ~:** pedal; **d)** *(bei Geflügel: begatten)* tread; mate with

Treter der; ~s, ~ *(ugs., oft abwertend)* casual shoe; casual

Tret-: ~mine die anti-personnel mine; **~mühle die** *(fig. ugs. abwertend)* treadmill; **in die ~mühle zurückkehren** return to the daily grind *(coll.)*; **~roller der** pedalscooter

treu [trɔy] **1.** *Adj.* **a)** *(beständig)* faithful, loyal ‹*friend, dog, customer, servant, etc.*›; faithful ‹*husband, wife*›; loyal ‹*ally, subject*›; *(unbeirrt)* staunch, loyal ‹*supporter*›; **jmdm. ~ sein/bleiben** be/remain true to sb.; **eine ~e Seele** a faithful *or* devoted soul; **jmdm. ~e Dienste leisten** serve sb. faithfully; **b) sich selbst** *(Dat.)***/seinem Glauben ~ bleiben** be true to oneself/one's faith; **seinen Grundsätzen ~ bleiben** stick to one's principles; **das Glück/der Erfolg ist ihm ~ geblieben** his luck has held out/success keeps coming his way; *s. auch* **Hand f; c)** *(ugs.: ~herzig)* ingenuous, trusting ‹*eyes, look*›. **2.** *adv.* **a)** *(beständig)* faithfully; loyally; **jmdm. ~ ergeben sein** *(veralt., sonst scherzh.)* be utterly devoted to sb.; **b)** *(ugs.: ~herzig)* trustingly; **alles ~ und brav tun** do everything unquestioningly

Treu *s.* **Treue a**

treu-, Treu-: ~bruch der a) landesverräterischer ~bruch *(DDR Rechtsw.)* state treason; **b)** *(hist.: Bruch der Lehnstreue)* felony *(Law Hist.)*; **~deutsch** *(ugs., meist abwertend) Adj.* typically German; **~doof** *(ugs. abwertend)* **1.** *Adj.* gormlessly naïve *(coll.)*; gormless *(coll.)*; **2.** *adv.* gormlessly *(coll.)* and naïvely

Treue die; ~ a) loyalty; *(von [Ehe]partnern)* fidelity; **jmdm. ~ schwören** swear to be true *or* faithful to sb.; **jmdm. die ~ halten** keep faith with sb.; be loyal to sb.; **meiner Treu!** *(veralt.)* upon my word! *(dated)*; **Treu und Glauben** *(Rechtsw.)* equity; **auf Treu und Glauben** *(ugs.)* in good faith; **b)** *(Genauigkeit)* accuracy

Treue·gelöbnis das pledge of loyalty; *(von Ehepartnern)* pledge of fidelity

Treu·eid der oath of allegiance; *(hist.: im Lehnswesen)* oath of fealty

Treue-: ~pflicht die *(Rechtsw.)* loyalty to one's employer; *(des Arbeitgebers)* loyalty to one's employee; **~prämie die** long-service bonus

treu·ergeben *Adj. (präd. getrennt geschrieben) (veralt.)* devoted

Treue·schwur der oath of loyalty *or* allegiance

treu-, Treu-: ~hand die; *o. Pl. (Rechtsw.)* trusteeship; **~händer** [~hɛndɐ] **der; ~s, ~** *(Rechtsw.)* trustee; **~händerisch 1.** *Adj.* fiduciary; **~händerische Übertragung** assignment on trust. **2.** *adv.* on trust; **etw. ~händerisch verwalten** hold sth. in trust; **~herzig 1.** *Adj.* ingenuous; *(naiv)* naïve; *(unschuldig)* innocent; **2.** *adv.* ingenuously; *(naiv)* naïvely; *(unschuldig)* innocently; **~herzigkeit die; ~:** ingenuousness; *(Naivität)* naivety; *(Unschuld)* innocence

treulich *(veralt.)* **1.** *Adj.* faithful. **2.** *adv.* faithfully

treu-, Treu-: ~los 1. *Adj.* disloyal, faithless ‹*friend, person*›; unfaithful ‹*husband, wife, lover*›; **2.** *adv.* faithlessly; **~losigkeit die; ~:** disloyalty; faithlessness; *(von [Ehe]partnern)* infidelity; **~sorgend** *Adj.; nicht präd.* devoted

Trevira Ⓦ [tre'vi:ra] **das; ~:** Trevira **(P)**

Triangel ['tri:aŋl] **der;** *österr.* **das; ~s, ~** *(Mus.)* triangle

Trias ['tri:as] **die; ~, ~ a)** *o. Pl. (Geol.)* Triassic; Trias; **b)** *(geh.)* trio; trinity

Trias·formation die; *o. Pl. (Geol.)* Triassic system

Tribun [tri'bu:n] **der; ~s** *od.* **~en, ~e[n]** *(hist.)* tribune

Tribunal [tribu'na:l] **das; ~s, ~e a)** tribunal; **b)** *(im antiken Rom)* tribune *(for the municipal authorities in the Forum Romanum)*

Tribüne [tri'by:nə] **die; ~, ~n** [grand]stand

Tribut [tri'bu:t] **der; ~[e]s, ~e a)** *(hist.)* tribute *no indef. art.*; **b)** *(fig.)* due; **jmdm./einer Leistung ~ zollen** pay sb. his/her due/give an achievement its due; **einen hohen ~ [an Menschenleben] fordern** take a heavy toll [of human lives]

Trichine [trɪ'çi:nə] **die; ~, ~n** trichina

trichinös [trɪçi'nø:s] *Adj.* trichinous

Trichter ['trɪçtɐ] **der; ~s, ~ a)** funnel; **auf den [richtigen] ~ kommen** *(fig. ugs.)* get the message *(coll.)*; *s. auch* **Nürnberger; b)** *(Granat~, Bomben~, Geogr.)* crater

Trick [trɪk] **der; ~s, ~s** trick; *(fig.: List)* ploy; **technische ~s** cunning techniques; **den ~ heraushaben** have got the knack

trick-, Trick-: ~betrüger der confidence trickster; **~film der** animated cartoon [film]; **~kiste die** *(ugs.)* repertoire of tricks/ploys; bag of tricks; **in die ~kiste greifen** dip into one's bag of tricks; **~reich 1.** *Adj.* wily; **2.** *adv.* artfully; ‹*play*› trickily; **~reich geschlagene Bälle** cunningly hit shots

tricksen ['trɪksn̩] *(ugs., bes. Sportjargon)* **1.** *itr. V.* use tricks; work a fiddle *(sl.)*; ‹*footballer*› play trickily. **2.** *tr. V.* fiddle *(sl.)*

Trick·ski·laufen das acrobatic *or (Amer. sl.)* hot-dog skiing *no art.*

Tricktrack ['trɪktrak] **das; ~s, ~s** tric-trac

trieb [tri:p] *1. u. 3. Pers. Sg. Prät. v.* **treiben**

Trieb der; ~[e]s, ~e a) *(innerer Antrieb)* impulse; *(Drang)* urge; *(Verlangen)* [compulsive] desire; **b)** *(Sproß)* shoot; **c)** *(Technik: Übertragung)* transmission; drive

trieb-, Trieb-: ~befriedigung die [*esp.* sexual] gratification; **~feder die** mainspring; *(fig.)* driving *or* motivating force; *(Beweggrund)* motive (+ *Gen.* behind); **~haft 1.** *Adj.* compulsive ‹*need, behaviour, action, etc.*›; carnal ‹*sensuality*›; **ein ~hafter Mensch** a person ruled by his/her [physical] impulses; **2.** *adv.* compulsively; **~handlung die** compulsive act; *(bei Tieren)* instinctive act; **~kraft die** *(bes. Soziol.)* driving *or* motivating force; **~stoff der** *(schweiz.) s.* **Treibstoff; ~täter der, ~verbrecher der** *offender committing a crime in gratifying a compulsive desire; (Sexualtäter)* sexual offender; **~wagen der** *(Eisenb.)* railcar; **~werk das** engine

Trief·auge das watery eye; *(eitrig)* bleary *or (Med.)* blear eye

triefen ['tri:fn̩] *unr. od. regelm. itr. V.* **a)** *mit sein (fließen) (in Tropfen)* drip; *(in kleinen Rinnsalen)* trickle; **b)** *(naß sein)* be dripping wet; ‹*nose*› run; **~d naß** dripping wet; *(durchnäßt)* wet through; **von** *od.* **vor Fett/Nässe ~:** be dripping with fat/be dripping wet; **von** *od.* **vor Edelmut ~** *(fig. iron.)* be oozing with nobility

Trief·nase die runny nose

triezen ['tri:tsn̩] *tr. V. (ugs.)* torment; *(plagen)* pester; plague

triff [trɪf] *Imperativ Sg. v.* **treffen**

trifft *3. Pers. Sg. Präsens v.* **treffen**

Trift [trɪft] **die; ~, ~en a)** *(Strömung)* drift [current]; **b)** *(Weide)* common [*esp.* mountain] pasturage; **c)** *(Weg)* cattle-track

triften *tr. V.* raft ‹*tree-trunks*›

triftig 1. *Adj.* good ‹*reason, excuse*›; valid, convincing ‹*motive, argument*›. **2.** *adv.* convincingly

Triftigkeit die; ~: validity

Trigonometrie [trigonome'tri:] **die; ~:** trigonometry *no art.*

trigonometrisch *Adj.* trigonometric; **~er Punkt** triangulation point

¹Trikot [tri'ko] **der** *od.* **das; ~s, ~s** *(Stoff)* cotton jersey

²Trikot das; ~s, ~ *(ärmellos)* singlet; *(eines Tänzers)* leotard; *(eines Fußballspielers)* shirt; **das gelbe ~** *(Radsport)* the yellow jersey

Trikotage [triko'ta:ʒə] **die; ~, ~n;** *meist Pl.* [cotton] jersey garments *pl.*; *(Unterwäsche)* cotton [jersey] underwear

Triller ['trɪlɐ] **der; ~s, ~:** trill

trillern 1. *itr. V. (Musik)* trill; *(mit vielen Trillern singen)* ‹*bird, person*› warble. **2.** *tr. V.* warble ‹*song*›

Triller·pfeife die police/referee's whistle

Trillion [trɪ'lio:n] **die; ~, ~en** trillion *(Brit.)*; quadrillion *(Amer.)*

Trilogie [trilo'gi:] **die; ~, ~n** trilogy

Trimester [tri'mɛstɐ] **das; ~s, ~** *(Hochschulw.)* term

Trimm-dich-Pfad der keep-fit *or* trim trail

trimmen ['trɪmən] *tr. V.* **a)** *(durch Sport)* get ‹*person*› into shape; **trimm dich durch Sport** keep fit with sport; **b) etw. auf alt/„Western"** *usw.* **~:** do sth. up to look old/like the wild west *etc.*; **c)** *(durch Scheren)* clip ‹*dog*›; *(durch Bürsten)* groom ‹*dog*›; **d)** *(Seew., Flugw.)* trim ‹*ship, aircraft, cargo*›; stow ‹*barrels, bales, etc.*› properly; **Kohlen ~:** take on [a load of] coal

Trimm-: ~gerät das exerciser; **~trab der** jogging *no art.*

Trinität [trini'tɛ:t] **die; ~** *(christl. Rel.)* Trinity

Trinitatis [trini'ta:tɪs] **(das); ~, Trinitatis·fest das** Trinity Sunday *no art.*

trinkbar *Adj.* drinkable; **hast du was Trinkbares im Haus?** *(ugs.)* have you anything to drink in the house?

trinken ['trɪŋkn̩] **1.** *unr. itr. V.* drink; **in** *od.* **mit kleinen Schlucken/in großen Zügen ~:** drink in little sips/in big gulps; **laß mich mal [von dem Saft] ~:** let me have a drink [of the juice]; **jmdm. etw. zu ~ geben** give sb. sth. to drink; **was ~ Sie?** what are you drinking?; *(was möchten Sie ~?)* what would you like to drink?; **man merkte, daß er getrunken hatte** one could see that he had been drinking; **auf jmdn./etw. ~:** drink to sb./sth.; **ich trinke auf deine Gesundheit** I'll drink [to] your health; **das Trinken lassen** give up drink. **2.** *unr. tr. V.* drink; **einen Kaffee/ein Bier** *usw.* **~:** have a coffee/beer *etc.*; **ich trinke keinen Tropfen [Alkohol]** I don't drink; I don't touch alcohol; **einen Schluck Wasser ~:** have a drink of water; **einen ~:** have a drink; **einen ~ gehen** *(ugs.)* go for a drink. **3.** *refl. V.* **der Wein trinkt sich gut** the wine is pleasant to drink; **sich satt ~:** drink one's fill; **sich krank/zu Tode ~:** make oneself ill through drink/drink oneself to death

Trinker der; ~s, ~: alcoholic; **ein heimlicher/starker ~:** a secret/heavy drinker

Trinkerei die; ~, ~en drinking *no art.*

Trinker·heil·anstalt die drying-out clinic; detoxification centre

Trinkerin die; ~, ~nen *s.* **Trinker**

trink-, Trink-: ~fest *Adj.* **~fest sein** be able to hold one's drink; **ein ~fester Matrose** a sailor used to hard drinking; **~festigkeit die** ability to hold one's drink; **~freudig** *Adj.* fond of drinking *pred.*; **~gefäß das** drinking-vessel *(formal)*; **~gelage das** *(oft scherzh.)* drinking spree; **~geld das** tip; **wieviel ~geld gibst du ihm?** how much do you tip him?; how big a tip do you give him?; **~glas das;** *Pl.* **~gläser** [drinking-]glass; **~halle die a)** *(in einem Heilbad)* pump-room; **b)** *(Kiosk)* refreshment kiosk; *(größer)* refreshment stall; **~halm der** [drinking-]straw; **~lied das** *(veralt.)* drinking-song; **~milch die** low-fat pasteurized milk; **~spruch der** toast **(auf +** *Akk.* to); **einen ~spruch auf jmdn. ausbringen** propose a toast to sb.; **~wasser das;** *Pl.* **~wässer** drinking-water; **„kein ~wasser"** 'not for drinking'; **~wasser·aufbereitung die** purification of drinking-water

Trio ['tri:o] **das; ~s, ~s** *(Musik, fig.)* trio

Triole [tri'o:lə] **die; ~, ~n** *(Musik)* triplet

Trio·sonate die *(Musik)* trio sonata

Trip [trɪp] **der; ~s, ~s a)** *(ugs.: Ausflug)* trip; jaunt; *(untertreibend:)* **ein ~ in die Staaten** a little trip to the States; **b)** *(Drogenjargon: Rausch)* trip *(coll.)*; **auf dem ~ sein** be tripping *(coll.)*; **auf dem religiösen/anarchistischen** *usw.* **~ sein** *(fig. ugs.)* be going through a religious/anarchist *etc.* phase; **c)** *(Drogenjargon: Dosis)*; fix *(sl.)*; **~s werfen**

od. **schmeißen** pop LSD *(or other hallucinogen) (sl.)*

Tripel-: ~fuge triple ⟨*fugue, concerto, etc.*⟩; **~allianz** Triple Alliance

trippeln ['trɪpl̩n] *itr. V.; mit sein* trip; ⟨*child*⟩ patter; *(affektiert)* mince

Trippel·schritt der short, rapid step; *(affektiert)* mincing step

Tripper ['trɪpɐ] **der; ~s, ~:** gonorrhoea; **sich** *(Dat.)* **einen ~ holen** *(ugs.)* get a dose of the clap *(coarse)*

Triptik *s.* **Triptyk**

Triptychon ['trɪptyçɔn] **das; ~s, Triptychen** *od.* **Triptycha** *(Kunstwiss.)* triptych

Triptyk ['trɪptyk] **das; ~s, ~s** triptyque

trist [trɪst] *Adj.* dreary; dismal

Tristheit die; ~: dreariness

Tritons·horn ['tri:tɔns-] **das;** *Pl.* **~hörner** *(Zool.)* triton *or* trumpet shell

tritt [trɪt] *Imperativ Sg. u. 3. Pers. Sg. Präsens v.* **treten**

Tritt der; ~[e]s, ~e a) *(Aufsetzen des Fußes)* step; *(einmalig)* [foot]step; **mit festem ~:** with a firm step *or* tread; *s. auch* **Schritt a; b)** *(Gleichschritt)* **im ~ marschieren** march in step; **aus dem ~ geraten** *od.* **kommen** get out of step; **ohne ~, marsch!** break step!; **~ fassen** fall in step; *(fig.: sich fangen)* recover oneself; **c)** *(Fuß~)* kick; **jmdm. einen ~ versetzen** give sb. a kick; kick sb.; **einen ~ bekommen** *od.* **kriegen** *(fig. ugs.)* be given the push *(Brit. sl.)*; get kicked out; **d)** *(~brett)* step; **e)** *(Bergsteigen) (Halt für Füße)* foothold; *(im Eis)* step; **f)** *(Gestell)* small step-ladder; *(in der Bibliothek)* library steps *pl.*; **g)** *(Jägerspr.: Abdruck)* footprint

Tritt-: ~brett das step; *(an älterem Auto)* running-board; **~brett·fahrer der** *(fig. abwertend)* ≈ free rider *(Amer.)*; *person who profits from another's work;* **~leiter die** step-ladder

Triumph [tri'ʊmf] **der; ~[e]s, ~e** triumph; **~e/einen großen ~ feiern** have a series of triumphs/a great triumph *or* success; be hugely successful/a huge success; **im ~:** in triumph

triumphal [triʊm'fa:l] *Adj.* **a)** *(begeisternd)* triumphant ⟨*success etc.*⟩; **~ sein** be a triumph; **b)** *(mit Jubel)* triumphal ⟨*entry etc.*⟩; **jmdm. einen ~en Empfang bereiten** give sb. a hero's welcome

Triumphator [triʊm'fa:tɔr] **der; ~s, ~en** [-'to:rən] **a)** *(hist.)* triumphator; **b)** *(geh.: Sieger)* conquering hero

Triumph-: ~bogen der *(Archit.)* triumphal arch; **~geschrei das** triumphant cheering *no indef. art.*

triumphieren *itr. V.* **a)** *(Genugtuung empfinden)* exult; **~d** triumphant; exultant; **~d lachen** laugh triumphantly; **b)** *(siegen)* be triumphant *or* victorious; triumph *(lit. or fig.)* **(über + Akk.** over)

Triumph·zug der *(hist.)* triumph; **im ~** *(fig.)* in a triumphal procession

Triumvirat [triʊmvi'ra:t] **das; ~[e]s, ~e** *(hist.)* triumvirate

trivial [tri'vi̯a:l] **1.** *Adj.* **a)** *(platt)* banal; trite; *(unbedeutend)* trivial; **b)** *(alltäglich)* humdrum ⟨*life, career*⟩. **2.** *adv. (platt)* banally; ⟨*say etc.*⟩ tritely; ⟨*written*⟩ in a banal style

Trivialität die; ~, ~en a) *o. Pl. (Plattheit, Alltäglichkeit)* banality; triteness; **b)** *(platte Äußerung)* banality; *(Gemeinplatz)* commonplace [remark]

Trivial·roman der light [trashy] novel

Trochäus [trɔ'xɛ:ʊs] **der; ~, Trochäen** *(Verslehre)* trochee

trocken ['trɔkn̩] **1.** *Adj.* **a)** dry; **~en Auges** *(geh.)* dry-eyed; without shedding a tear; **etw. ~ bügeln/reinigen** dry-iron/dry-clean sth.; **sich ~ rasieren** use an electric razor; **noch ~ nach Hause kommen** get home without getting wet; **wieder auf dem Trock[e]nen sein** be on dry land *or* terra firma again; **auf dem trock[e]nen sitzen** *od.* **sein** *(ugs.)* be completely stuck *(coll.)*; *(pleite sein)* be skint *(Brit. sl.)*; **b)** *(ohne Zutat)* **~es** *od.* *(ugs.)* **~ Brot essen** eat dry bread; **c)** *(sachlich-langweilig)* dry, factual ⟨*account, report, treatise*⟩; bare ⟨*words, figures*⟩; dull, dry ⟨*person*⟩; **d)** *(unverblümt)* dry ⟨*humour, remark, etc.*⟩; **e)** *(dem Klang nach)* dry ⟨*laugh, cough, sound*⟩; sharp ⟨*crack*⟩; clear ⟨*acoustics*⟩; **f)** *(Sportjargon, bes. Boxen, Fußball)* sharp ⟨*blow*⟩; snappy ⟨*shot*⟩; **eine ~e Rechte** a straight right. **2.** *adv.* **a)** *(sachlich-langweilig)* ⟨*speak, write*⟩ drily, in a matter-of-fact way; **b)** *(unverblümt)* drily; **c)** *(dem Klang nach)* **das Gewehr knallte kurz und ~:** the rifle went off with a short, sharp report

Trocken-: ~beeren·aus·lese die *wine made from selected grapes left to dry on the vine at the end of the season;* **~blume die;** *meist Pl.* dried flower; **~boden der** attic drying-room; **~dock das** dry dock; **~eis das** dry ice; **~futter das** *(Landw.)* dry fodder; **~gebiet das** *(Geogr.)* arid region; **~gestell das** *(für Wäsche)* clothes-airer *or* -horse; **~haube die** [hood-type] hair-drier

Trockenheit die; ~, ~en a) *o. Pl. (auch fig.)* dryness; **b)** *(Dürreperiode)* drought

trocken-, Trocken-: ~kurs der dry-skiing course; **~|legen** *tr. V.* **a) ein Baby ~legen** change a baby's nappies *(Brit.) or (Amer.)* diapers; **b)** *(entwässern)* drain ⟨*marsh, pond, etc.*⟩; **~legung die; ~, ~en** draining; **~milch die** dried milk; **~rasierer der** *(ugs.)* **a)** *(Rasierapparat)* electric razor; **b)** *(Person)* user of an electric razor; **~|reiben** *unr. tr. V.* rub ⟨*hair, child, etc.*⟩ dry; wipe ⟨*crockery, window, etc.*⟩ dry; **~reinigung die** dry-cleaning; **~|schleudern** *tr. V.* spin-dry; **~schwimmen das** preparatory swimming exercises *pl.* [on land] *(for learners)*; **~|sitzen** *unr. itr. V.* *(ugs.)* have nothing to drink; **~spiritus der** solid fuel *(for camping-stove)*; **~übung die** preliminary [swimming/skiing] exercise; *(fig.)* dry run; **~zeit die** dry season

trocknen 1. *itr. V.; meist mit sein* dry. **2.** *tr. V.* dry; **die Kleider zum Trocknen aufhängen** hang up the clothes to dry

Trockner der; ~s, ~: drier; *(Trockengestell)* airer

Troddel ['trɔdl̩] **die; ~, ~n** tassel

Trödel ['trø:dl̩] **der; ~s** *(ugs., oft abwertend)* junk; *(für den Flohmarkt)* jumble

Trödelei die; ~, ~en *(ugs. abwertend)* dawdling *no pl.*

trödeln *itr. V.* **a)** *(ugs., oft abwertend)* dawdle **(mit** over); **b)** *mit sein (ugs.: schlendern)* saunter

Trödler der; ~s, ~, Trödlerin die; ~, ~nen a) *(ugs. abwertend)* dawdler; slowcoach; slowpoke *(Amer.)*; **b)** *(ugs.: Händler[in])* junk-dealer; **etw. beim ~ kaufen** buy sth. from *or* at the junk-shop

troff [trɔf] *1. u. 3. Pers. Sg. Prät. v.* **triefen**

trog [tro:k] *1. u. 3. Pers. Sg. Prät. v.* **trügen**

Trog der; ~[e]s, Tröge ['trø:gə] *(auch Geol.)* trough

Troika ['trɔyka] **die; ~, ~s** troika; *(fig.: Führungsgruppe)* triumvirate

Troja ['tro:ja] **(das); ~s** Troy

Trojaner der; ~s, ~: Trojan

trojanisch *Adj.* Trojan; **das Trojanische Pferd** *(Myth.; auch fig.)* the Trojan Horse

Troll [trɔl] **der; ~[e]s, ~e** *(Myth.)* troll

Troll·blume die globe-flower

trollen *(ugs.) refl. V.* push off *(coll.)*; **der Junge trollte sich in sein Zimmer** the boy took himself off to his room

Trolley·bus ['trɔli-] **der** *(bes. schweiz.)* trolleybus

Trollinger ['trɔlɪŋɐ] **der; ~s, ~:** Trollinger [grape/wine]

Trommel ['trɔml̩] **die; ~, ~n a)** *(Schlaginstrument)* drum; **die ~ für jmdn./etw. rühren** *(ugs.)* beat the drum for sb./sth.; **b)** *(Behälter; Kabel~, Seil~)* drum

Trommel-: ~bremse die *(Kfz-W.)* drum brake; **~fell das a)** *(bei Trommeln)* drumhead; **b)** *(im Ohr)* ear-drum; **~feuer das** *(Milit.; auch fig.)* [constant] barrage

trommeln 1. *itr. V.* **a)** beat the drum; *(als Beruf, Hobby usw.)* play the drums; **b)** *([auf etw.] schlagen, auftreffen)* drum **(auf + Akk.** on, **an + Akk.** against); **sie trommelte mit den Fäusten gegen die Tür** she hammered the door with her fists. **2.** *tr. V.* **a)** beat [out] ⟨*march, rhythm, etc.*⟩; **b) jmdn. aus dem Bett/Schlaf ~:** get sb. out of bed/wake sb. up by hammering on the door

Trommel-: ~revolver der revolver; **~schlag der** drum-beat; **~schlegel der, ~stock der** drumstick; **~wirbel der** drum-roll

Trommler der; ~s, ~, Trommlerin die; ~, ~nen drummer

Trompete [trɔm'pe:tə] **die; ~, ~n** trumpet; **[eine Melodie] auf der ~ blasen** play [a tune on] the trumpet

trompeten 1. *itr. V.* **a)** play the trumpet; *(fig.)* ⟨*elephant*⟩ trumpet; **b)** *(ugs. scherzh.: sich laut schneuzen)* blow one's nose like a fog-horn. **2.** *tr. V.* play ⟨*piece*⟩ on the trumpet; *(fig.)* proclaim ⟨*news etc.*⟩ loudly

Trompeten·stoß der blast on a/the trumpet

Trompeter der; ~s, ~, Trompeterin die; ~, ~nen trumpeter

Tropen *Pl.* tropics

Tropen- tropical

Tropen-: ~fieber das [falciparum] malaria *(Med.)*; **~helm der** sun-helmet; **~koller der** tropical madness; **~tauglichkeit die** fitness for service/travel in the tropics

¹Tropf [trɔpf] **der; ~[e]s, Tröpfe** ['trœpfə] *(abwertend)* twit *(Brit. sl.)*; moron *(coll.)*; **armer ~:** poor devil

²Tropf der; ~[e]s, ~e *(Med.)* drip; **am ~ hängen** be on a drip

Tröpfchen ['trœpfçən] **das; ~s, ~:** droplet; *(kleine Menge)* drop; *(scherzh.: Wein)* **ein wahrhaft edles ~:** a really fine vintage

Tröpfchen·infektion die *(Med.)* droplet infection

tröpfchen·weise *Adv.* in small drops

tröpfeln ['trœpfl̩n] **1.** *itr. V.* **a)** *mit sein* drip **(auf + Akk.** on to, **aus, von** from); **b)** *(unpers.) (ugs.: leicht regnen)* **es tröpfelt** it's spitting [with rain]. **2.** *tr. V.* let ⟨*sth.*⟩ drip **(in + Akk.** into, **auf + Akk.** on to)

tropfen 1. *itr. V.; mit Richtungsangabe mit sein* drip; ⟨*tears*⟩ fall; **seine Nase tropft** his nose is running; *(unpers.)* **es tropft [vom Dach** *usw.***]** water is *or* it's dripping from the roof *etc.*; **es tropft** *(es regnet)* it's spitting [with rain]. **2.** *tr. V.* let ⟨*sth.*⟩ drip **(in + Akk.** into, **auf + Akk.** on to); **jmdm. eine Tinktur auf die Wunde ~:** pour drops of a tincture into sb.'s wound

Tropfen der; ~s, ~ a) drop; **ein paar ~ Parfüm** a few drops of perfume; **es regnet dicke ~:** the rain is falling in large drops *or* spots; **die ersten ~ fallen** the first spots [of rain] are falling; **er hat keinen ~ [Alkohol] getrunken** he hasn't touched a drop; **steter ~ höhlt den Stein** *(Spr.)* constant dropping wears away the stone *(prov.)*; persistence gets there in the end; **ein ~ auf den heißen Stein sein** *(fig. ugs.)* be a drop in the ocean; **b) ein guter/edler ~:** a good/fine vintage

Tropfen·form die; *o. Pl.* tear shape; **in ~:** tear-shaped *attrib.*

tropfen·weise *Adv.* drop by drop; a drop at a time

tropf-, Tropf-: ~infusion die *(Med.)* intravenous drip; **~naß** *Adj.* dripping *or* soaking wet; **~stein·höhle die** limestone cave with stalactites and/or stalagmites

Trophäe [tro'fɛ:ə] **die; ~, ~n** *(hist., Jagd, Sport)* trophy

tropisch 1. *Adj.* tropical. **2.** *adv.* tropically ⟨*warm*⟩

Tropo·sphäre [tropo'sfɛ:rə] **die;** ~ *(Meteor.)* troposphere

Troß [trɔs] **der; Trosses, Trosse a)** *(Milit.)* baggage train; **b)** *(Gefolge)* retinue; *(fig.: Zug)* procession [of hangers-on]

Trosse ['trɔsə] **die;** ~, ~**n** hawser *(Naut.)*

Trost [tro:st] **der;** ~**[e]s** consolation; *(bes. geistlich)* comfort; **jmdm. ~ zusprechen** *od.* **spenden** comfort *or* console sb.; **jmdm. ein/kein ~ sein** be a/no comfort to sb.; **ein schwacher ~!** that's little *or* not much consolation; **in der Arbeit ~ suchen/finden** seek/find solace in work; **als ~:** as a consolation; **nicht [ganz** *od.* **recht] bei ~ sein** *(ugs.)* be out of one's mind; have taken leave of one's senses

trösten ['trø:stn̩] **1.** *tr. V.* comfort, console (**mit** with); **sie wollte sich nicht ~ lassen** she was not to be *or* refused to be comforted; she was inconsolable; ~**de Worte** words of comfort; comforting words; ~**d den Arm um jmdn. legen** put one's arm around sb. to comfort him/her; **etw. tröstet jmdn.** sth. is a comfort to sb.; **der Gedanke konnte ihn nicht ~:** the thought was no comfort to him. **2.** *refl. V.* console oneself; **sich damit ~, daß ...:** console oneself with the thought that ...; **sich mit einer anderen Frau ~:** find consolation with another woman

Tröster der; ~**s,** ~, **Trösterin die;** ~, ~**nen** comforter; *(fig.: Sache)* consolation

tröstlich *Adj.* comforting

trost-, Trost-: ~**los** *Adj.* **a)** *(ohne Trost)* hopeless; without hope *postpos.*; *(verzweifelt)* in despair *postpos.*; **mir war ~los zumute, ich fühlte mich ~los** I was in despair; **b)** *(deprimierend, öde)* miserable, dreary ‹*time, weather, area, food, etc.*›; hopeless ‹*situation*›; ~**losigkeit die;** ~ **a)** *(einer Person, der Lage usw.)* hopelessness; *(Verzweiflung)* despair; **b)** *(Öde)* dreariness; ~**pflaster das** *(scherzh.)* consolation; ~**preis der** consolation prize; ~**reich 1.** *Adj.* comforting; **2.** *adv.* comfortingly

Tröstung die; ~, ~**en** comfort *no indef. art.*; **mit den ~en der Kirche versehen sterben** die after having received the last rites

Trost·wort das; *Pl.* ~**e** word of comfort

Trott [trɔt] **der;** ~**[e]s,** ~**e a)** *(Gangart)* trot; **im ~ gehen** [go at a] trot; **b)** *(leicht abwertend: Ablauf)* routine; **in den alten ~ verfallen** fall back into the same old rut

Trottel der; ~**s,** ~ *(ugs. abwertend)* fool; wally *(sl.)*

trottelhaft *(ugs. abwertend)* **1.** *Adj.* bumbling ‹*idiot, person*›; oafish ‹*behaviour*›. **2.** *adv.* oafishly

trottelig *(ugs. abwertend)* **1.** *Adj.* doddery; gaga *pred.* *(sl.)* **2.** *adv.* in a feeble-minded *or* doddery way

Trotteligkeit die; ~ *(ugs. abwertend)* doddery state; feeble-mindedness

trotten *itr. V.; mit sein* trot [along]; *(freudlos)* trudge

Trottoir [trɔ'toa:ɐ̯] **das;** ~**s,** ~**e** *od.* ~**s** pavement

trotz [trɔts] *Präp. mit Gen., seltener mit Dat.* in spite of; despite; ~ **Frost[s] und Schnee[s]** despite the frost and snow; ~ **allem** *od.* **alledem** in spite of everything

Trotz der; ~**es** defiance; *(eines Pferdes)* disobedience; *(Oppositionsgeist)* cussedness *(coll.)*; contrariness; **jmdm./einer Sache zum ~:** in defiance of sb./sth.

Trotz·alter das difficult age

trotz·dem [*auch:* '-'-] **1.** *Adv.* nevertheless; **er tat es ~:** he did it all *or* just the same. **2.** [-'-] *Konj. (ugs.)* although; even though

trotzen *itr. V.* **a)** *(geh.: widerstehen)* **jmdm./einer Sache ~** *(auch fig.)* defy sb./sth.; **Gefahren/der Kälte ~:** brave dangers/the cold; **b)** *(trotzig sein)* be contrary

trotzig 1. *Adj.* defiant; *(widerspenstig)* contrary; bolshie *(coll.)*; difficult ‹*child*›. **2.** *adv.* defiantly

Trotzkismus [trɔts'kɪsmʊs] **der;** ~**:** Trotskyism *no art.*

Trotzkist der; ~**en,** ~**en** Trotskyist

Trotz-: ~**kopf der** bolshie [little] so-and-so *(coll.)*; ~**phase die** *(Psych.) s.* ~**alter**; ~**reaktion die** act of defiance

Troubadour ['tru:badu:ɐ̯] **der;** ~**s,** ~**e** *od.* ~**s** *(hist.)* troubadour; *(fig.: Schlagersänger)* songster

Trouble ['trʌbl̩] **der;** ~**s** *(ugs.)* trouble; ~ **haben wegen Drogen** be in trouble over drugs

trüb[e] ['try:b(ə)] **1.** *Adj.* **a)** *(nicht klar)* murky ‹*stream, water*›; cloudy ‹*liquid, wine, juice*›; *(schlammig)* muddy ‹*puddle*›; *(schmutzig)* dirty ‹*glass, window-pane*›; dull ‹*eyes*›; **im trüben fischen** *(ugs.)* fish in troubled waters; **b)** *(nicht hell)* dim ‹*light*›; dull, dismal ‹*day, weather*›; grey, overcast ‹*sky*›; dull, dingy ‹*red, yellow*›; **c)** *(gedrückt)* gloomy ‹*mood, voice, etc.*›; dreary ‹*time*›; *s. auch* **Tasse a; d)** *(unerfreulich)* unfortunate, bad ‹*experience etc.*›; *(zweifelhaft)* dubious ‹*sources*›. **2.** *adv.* **a)** *(nicht hell)* ‹*shine, light*› dimly; **b)** *(gedrückt)* ‹*smile, look*› gloomily; **c)** *(unerfreulich)* ~ **laufen** go badly

Trubel ['tru:bl̩] **der;** ~**s** [hustle and] bustle; **sie stürzten sich in den dicksten ~:** they plunged into the thick of the hurly-burly; **im ~ der Ereignisse** *(fig.)* in the excitement of the moment; in the rush of events

trüben 1. *tr. V.* **a)** make ‹*liquid*› cloudy; cloud ‹*liquid*›; *s. auch* **Wässerchen a; b)** *(beeinträchtigen)* dampen, cast a cloud over ‹*mood*›; mar ‹*relationship*›; cloud ‹*judgement*›; **jmds. Blick [für etw.] ~:** blind sb. [to sth.]. **2.** *refl. V.* **a)** ‹*liquid*› become cloudy; ‹*eyes*› become dull; ‹*sky*› darken; **b)** *(sich verschlechtern)* ‹*relationship*› deteriorate; ‹*awareness, memory, etc.*› become dulled *or* dim

Trübsal ['try:pza:l] **die;** ~, ~**e** *(geh.)* **a)** *(Leiden)* affliction; **b)** *o. Pl. (Kummer)* grief; ~ **blasen** *(ugs.)* mope (**wegen** over, about)

trüb-, Trüb-: ~**selig 1.** *Adj.* **a)** *(öde)* dreary, depressing ‹*place, area, colour*›; dismal ‹*house*›; **b)** *(traurig)* gloomy, melancholy ‹*thoughts, mood*›; gloomy, miserable ‹*face*›; **2.** *adv.* *(traurig)* gloomily; ~**seligkeit die;** ~ **a)** *(Ödheit)* dreariness; **b)** *(Traurigkeit)* gloom; ~**sinn der;** *o. Pl.* melancholy; gloom; ~**sinnig 1.** *Adj.* melancholy; gloomy; **2.** *adv.* gloomily

Trübung die; ~, ~**en a)** clouding; *(des Auges)* dimming; **b)** *(Beeinträchtigung)* deterioration; *(der Stimmung)* dampening

trudeln ['tru:dl̩n] *itr. V.* **a)** *mit sein (rollen)* roll; **auf die Erde ~:** flutter *or* twirl to the ground; **das Flugzeug geriet ins Trudeln** the plane went into a spin; **b)** *(bes. berlin.: würfeln)* play dice

Trüffel ['trʏfl̩] **die;** ~, ~**n** *od. (ugs.)* **der;** ~**s,** ~**:** truffle

Trüffel·leber·wurst die liver sausage with truffles

trug [tru:k] *1. u. 3. Pers. Prät. v.* **tragen**

Trug der; ~**[e]s** *(geh.)* deception (**um** over, concerning); *s. auch* **Lug**

Trug·bild das hallucination; illusion; *(Bild der Phantasie)* figment of the imagination

trüge ['try:gə] *1. u. 3. Pers. Sg. Konjunktiv II v.* **tragen**

trügen 1. *unr. tr. V.* deceive; **dieses Gefühl hatte uns getrogen** this feeling had been a delusion; **wenn mich nicht alles trügt** unless I am very much mistaken. **2.** *unr. itr. V.* be deceptive; ‹*feeling, deception*› be a delusion; *s. auch* **Schein b**

trügerisch 1. *Adj.* **a)** deceptive; false ‹*hope, sign, etc.*›; treacherous ‹*ice*›; **b)** *(veralt.: auf Betrug zielend)* deceitful; **in ~er Absicht** with intent to deceive. **2.** *adv.* **a)** deceptively; **b)** *(veralt.: auf Betrug zielend)* deceitfully

Trug·schluß der a) wrong conclusion; *(Irrtum)* fallacy; **b)** *(Musik)* false *or* deceptive cadence

Truhe ['tru:ə] **die;** ~, ~**n** chest

Trumm [trʊm] **das;** ~**[e]s, Trümmer** ['trʏmɐ] *(bes. südd., österr., schweiz.)* large lump; *(großes Exemplar)* whopper *(coll.)*; **ein ~ von ...:** a whopping great ... *(coll.)*

Trümmer ['trʏmɐ] *Pl. (eines Gebäudes)* rubble *sing.*; *(Ruinen)* ruins; *(eines Flugzeugs usw.)* wreckage *sing.*; *(kleinere Teile)* debris *sing.*; **die Stadt lag in ~n** the town lay in ruins; **eine Stadt in ~ legen** reduce a town to rubble; flatten a town [completely]; **er stand vor den ~n seines Lebens** *(fig.)* he contemplated the ruins of what had once been his life

Trümmer-: ~**feld das** expanse of rubble; ~**frau die** *(hist.) woman who cleared away rubble after World War II*; ~**grund·stück das** bomb-site; *(nach einem Erdbeben)* ruined site; ~**haufen der** pile *or* heap of rubble; **der ~haufen seiner Ehe** *(fig.)* the ruins *pl.* of what had been his marriage

Trumpf [trʊmpf] **der;** ~**[e]s, Trümpfe** ['trʏmpfə] *(auch fig.)* trump [card]; *(Farbe)* trumps *pl.*; **was ist ~?** what are trumps?; **lauter ~** *od.* **Trümpfe haben** have nothing but trumps; **seinen [letzten] ~ ausspielen** *(fig.)* play one's [last] trump card; **alle Trümpfe in der Hand haben** *(fig.)* hold all the [trump] cards; **seine besten Trümpfe aus der Hand geben** *(fig.)* throw away one's greatest advantages; **einen ~ in der Hinterhand haben** *(fig.)* have a card up one's sleeve; ~ **sein** *(fig.) (das Nötigste sein)* be what matters; be the order of the day; *(Mode sein)* be the in thing

trumpfen *itr. V.* play a trump

Trumpf·karte die *(auch fig.)* trump card

Trunk [trʊŋk] **der;** ~**[e]s, Trünke** ['trʏŋkə] *(geh.)* **a)** *(Getränk)* drink; beverage *(formal)*; **b)** *(das Trinken)* **er ist dem ~ verfallen** he is a victim of the demon drink; **sich dem ~ ergeben** take to drink

trunken *Adj. (geh.; auch fig.)* drunk, intoxicated (**von, vor** + *Dat.* with); **jmdn. ~ machen** make sb. drunk; *(fig.)* intoxicate sb.

Trunkenbold [-bɔlt] **der;** ~**[e]s,** ~**e** *(abwertend)* drunkard

Trunkenheit die; ~ **a)** drunkenness; **im Zustand der ~:** in a state of intoxication; in an intoxicated state; ~ **am Steuer** drunken driving; **b)** *(geh.: Begeisterung)* [state of] intoxication

Trunk·sucht die; *o. Pl.* alcoholism *no art.*

trunk·süchtig *Adj.* alcoholic; ~ **sein** be an alcoholic

Trupp [trʊp] **der;** ~**s,** ~**s** troop; *(von Arbeitern, Gefangenen)* gang; *(von Soldaten, Polizisten)* detachment; squad

Trüppchen ['trʏpçən] **das;** ~**s,** ~**:** [small] group; *(von Soldaten)* small detachment

Truppe die; ~, ~**n a)** *(Einheit der Streitkräfte)* unit; **nicht von der schnellen ~ sein** *(fig. ugs.)* not be exactly a fast worker; **b)** *Pl. (Soldaten)* troops; **c)** *o. Pl. (Streitkräfte)* [armed] forces *pl.*; *(Heer)* army; **die kämpfende ~:** the front-line *or* combat troops *pl.*; **der Dienst bei der ~:** military service; **d)** *(Gruppe von Schauspielern, Artisten)* troupe; company; *(von Sportlern)* squad; *(Mannschaft)* team

Truppen-: ~**ab·zug der** withdrawal of troops; troop withdrawal; ~**bewegung die;** *meist Pl.* troop movement; ~**gattung die** arm [of the service]; corps; ~**konzentration die** massing of troops; ~**parade die** military parade; ~**teil der** unit; ~**übungs·platz der** military training area

Trust [trast] **der;** ~**[e]s,** ~**e** *od.* ~**s** *(Wirtsch.)* trust

Trut- ['tru:t-]: ~**hahn der** turkey [cock]; *(als Braten)* turkey; ~**henne die** turkey [hen]

Trutz [trʊts] **der;** ~**es** *(veralt.)* resistance; **Schutz und ~:** protection and shelter

Trutz·burg die *(hist.) castle built to besiege an enemy castle*
trutzig *(veralt.)* **1.** *Adj.* massive, formidable ⟨*wall, building*⟩. **2.** *adv.* defiantly
Tschad [tʃat] **(der); ~s** Chad *no art.*
Tschador [tʃa'dɔr] **der; ~s, ~s** chador
Tschako ['tʃako] **der; ~s, ~s** *(hist.)* shako
tschau [tʃau̯] *(ugs.)* ciao *(coll.);* so long *(coll.)*
Tscheche ['tʃɛçə] **der; ~n, ~n** Czech
Tschechei die; ~ *(ugs. veralt.)* Czechoslovakia *no art.*
tschechisch 1. *Adj.* Czech. **2.** *adv.* **~ sprechend** Czech-speaking; *s. auch* **deutsch; Deutsch; ²Deutsche**
Tschechoslowakei [tʃɛçoslova'kai̯] **die; ~:** Czechoslovakia *no art.*
tschechoslowakisch *Adj.* Czechoslovak[ian]
Tschick [tʃɪk] **der; ~s, ~** *(österr. ugs.)* fag *(Brit. sl.); (Zigarettenstummel)* fag-end *(Brit. sl.)*
tschilpen ['tʃɪlpn̩] *itr. V.* chirp
Tschinelle [tʃi'nɛlə] **die; ~, ~n;** *meist Pl. (veralt., noch südd., österr.)* cymbal
tschingderassabum [tʃɪŋdərasa'bʊm] *Interj.* crash! crash! boom! boom! *(onomatopoeic for cymbals and drums)*
tschüs [tʃy:s] *(ugs.)* bye *(coll.);* so long *(coll.)*
Tsd. *Abk.* **Tausend**
Tsetse·fliege ['tse:tse-] **die** tsetse fly
T-Shirt ['ti:ʃɔ:t] **das; ~s, ~s** T-shirt
T-Träger der *(Bauw.)* T-girder
TU *Abk.* **technische Universität**
Tuba ['tu:ba] **die; ~, Tuben** tuba
Tube ['tu:bə] **die; ~, ~n** tube; **eine ~ Zahnpasta** a tube of toothpaste; **auf die ~ drücken** *(fig. ugs.)* step on it *(coll.);* put one's foot down
Tuberkel·bazillus [tu'bɛrkl̩-] **der** *(Med.)* tubercle bacillus
tuberkulös [tubɛrku'lø:s] *Adj. (Med.)* tubercular
Tuberkulose [tubɛrku'lo:zə] **die; ~, ~n** *(Med.)* tuberculosis *no art.*
Tuch [tu:x] **das; ~[e]s, Tücher** ['ty:çɐ] *od.* **~e a)** *Pl.* **Tücher** cloth; *(Geschirr~)* dish-cloth; *(Bade~)* [bath-]towel; *(Kopf~, Hals~)* – 1/scarf; **das rote ~ des Matadors** the matador's red cape; **ein rotes ~ für jmdn. sein** *(ugs.)* be like a red rag to a bull for sb.; make sb. see red; **b)** *Pl.* **~e** *(Gewebe)* cloth; **c)** *Pl.* **~e** *(Seemannsspr.) s.* **Segeltuch**
Tuchent ['tʊxn̩t] **die; ~, ~en** *(österr.)* feather bed
Tuch·fühlung die *(scherzh.)* physical contact; *(fig.: Kontakte)* [close] contact; **auf** *od.* **mit ~:** close together
Tüchlein das; ~s, ~: [little] handkerchief
tüchtig ['tʏçtɪç] **1.** *Adj.* **a)** efficient ⟨*secretary, assistant, worker, etc.*⟩; *(fähig)* capable, competent **(in + Dat.** at); **freie Bahn dem Tüchtigen!** let ability win through; **b)** *(von guter Qualität)* excellent ⟨*performance, piece of work, etc.*⟩; **~, ~!** *(auch iron.)* well done!; **c)** *nicht präd. (ugs.: beträchtlich)* sizeable ⟨*piece, portion*⟩; big ⟨*gulp*⟩; hearty ⟨*eater, appetite*⟩; **eine ~e Tracht Prügel** a good hiding *(coll.);* **ein ~er Schrecken** quite a fright. **2.** *adv.* **a)** efficiently; *(fähig)* competently; **~ arbeiten** work hard; **b)** *(ugs.: sehr)* really ⟨*cold, warm*⟩; ⟨*snow, rain*⟩ good and proper *(coll.);* ⟨*eat*⟩ heartily; **~ heizen** have the heating up good and high *(coll.)*
Tüchtigkeit die; ~ a) efficiency; *(Fähigkeit)* ability; competence; *(Fleiß)* industry; **b) körperliche ~:** physical fitness
Tücke ['tʏkə] **die; ~, ~n a)** *o. Pl. (Hinterhältigkeit)* deceit[fulness]; *(List)* guile; scheming *no indef. art.; (fig.: des Schicksals)* fickleness; **die ~ des Objekts** the perversity *or (coll.)* cussedness of inanimate objects; *s. auch* **List b; b)** *meist Pl. (hinterhältige Handlung)* wile; ruse; *(Betrug)* deception; **c)** *meist Pl. ([verborgene] Gefahr/Schwierigkeit)* [hidden] danger/difficulty; *(unberechenbare Eigenschaft)* vagary; **seine ~n haben** ⟨*engine, machine*⟩ be temperamental; have its vagaries; ⟨*mountain, river, course*⟩ be treacherous
tuckern ['tukɐn] *itr. V.; mit Richtungsangabe mit sein* chug
tückisch 1. *Adj.* **a)** *(hinterhältig)* wily; *(betrügerisch)* deceitful; **b)** *(gefährlich)* treacherous ⟨*bend, slope, spot, etc.*⟩; *(Gefahr signalisierend)* menacing ⟨*look, eyes*⟩. **2.** *adv.* **a)** *(hinterhältig)* craftily; **b)** *(Gefahr signalisierend)* menacingly
Tuff [tʊf] **der; ~s, ~e** *(Geol.)* **a)** tuff; **b)** *s.* **Sinter**
Tuff·stein der tuff
Tüftel·arbeit die *(ugs.)* fiddly job *(coll.)*
Tüftelei die; ~, ~en *(ugs.)* **a)** *o. Pl.* fiddling [about]; *(geistig)* racking one's brains; **b)** *(tüftelige Arbeit)* fiddly job *(coll.)*
Tüfteler der; ~s, ~ *s.* **Tüftler**
tüfteln ['tʏftl̩n] *itr. V. (ugs.)* fiddle **(an + Dat.** with); do finicky work **(an + Dat.** on); *(geistig)* rack one's brains, puzzle **(an + Dat.** over)
Tüftler der; ~s, ~ *(ugs.) person who likes finicky jobs/niggling problems; (jmd., der gern Rätselspiele macht)* puzzle freak *(coll.)*
Tugend ['tu:gn̩t] **die; ~, ~en** virtue; **auf dem Pfad der ~ wandeln** keep to the path of virtue *or* the straight and narrow
tugendhaft 1. *Adj.* virtuous. **2.** *adv.* virtuously; **~ leben** live a life of virtue
Tukan ['tu:kan] **der; ~s, ~e** toucan
Tüll [tʏl] **der; ~s, ~e** tulle
Tülle die; ~, ~n *(bes. nordd.)* spout
Tüll-: ~gardine die net curtain; **~spitze die** tulle lace
Tulpe ['tʊlpə] **die; ~, ~n a)** *(Pflanze)* tulip; **b)** *(Glas)* tulip glas
Tulpen-: ~baum der tulip-tree; **~zwiebel die** tulip-bulb
tumb [tʊmp] *(scherzh.) Adj.* guileless; naïve; **~er Tor** simple Simon
Tumbheit die; ~ *(scherzh.)* guilelessness; ingenuousness
tummeln ['tʊmln̩] *refl. V.* **a)** *(umhertollen)* romp [about]; *(im Wasser)* splash about; **b)** *(bes. westmd., österr., sich beeilen)* stir one's stumps *(coll.);* get a move on *(coll.)*
Tummel·platz der *(auch fig.)* playground; **ein ~ der Linksradikalen** *(fig.)* a happy hunting-ground for left-wing radicals
Tümmler ['tʏmlɐ] **der; ~s, ~ a)** *(Delphin)* bottle-nosed dolphin; **b)** *(Taube)* tumbler
Tumor ['tu:mɔr] **der; ~s, ~en** [tu'mo:rən], *ugs. auch* **~e** [tu'mo:rə] *(Med.)* tumour
Tümpel ['tʏmpl̩] **der; ~s, ~:** pond
Tumult [tu'mʊlt] **der; ~[e]s, ~e** tumult; commotion; *(Protest)* uproar; **schwere ~e** serious disturbances
tumultuarisch [tumʊl'tu̯a:rɪʃ] *Adj. (geh.)* turbulent; ⟨*scenes*⟩ of uproar
tun [tu:n] **1.** *unr. tr. V.* **a)** *(machen)* do; **er tat, wie ihm befohlen** he did as he was told; **ich habe anderes zu ~, als hier herumzusitzen** I can't sit around here [all day], I've other things to do; **er tut nichts als meckern** *(ugs.)* he does nothing but moan; **ich weiß nicht, was ich ~ soll** I don't know what to do; **so etwas tut man nicht** that is just not done; **so tu doch etwas!** well, do something [about it], then!; **er hat sein möglichstes getan** he did his [level] best; **du kannst ~ und lassen, was du willst** you can do just as you please; **was tust du hier/mit dem Messer?** what are you doing here/with that knife?; **dagegen kann man nichts ~:** there is nothing one can do about it; **es hat sich so ergeben, ohne daß ich etwas dazu getan hätte** it turned out that way without my having done anything [towards it]; **was ~?** what is to be done?; **was tut denn die tote Fliege in meiner Suppe?** what's that dead fly doing in my soup?; **man tut, was man kann** one does what one can; one tries one's best; **ich will sehen, was sich ~ läßt** I'll see what can be done; **was tut man nicht alles [...]!** the things I/you *etc.* do [...]!; **b)** *(erledigen)* do ⟨*work, duty, etc.*⟩; **er tut nichts** he doesn't do a thing; **ich muß noch etwas [für die Schule] ~:** I've still got some [school-]work to do; **tu's doch!** go on, do it!; **nach getaner Arbeit** when the work is/was done; **mit Geld/einer Entschuldigung** *usw.* **ist es nicht getan** money/an apology *etc.* is not enough; **es ~** *(ugs. verhüll.: koitieren)* do it *(sl.); s. auch* **Handschlag b; c) [etwas] zu ~ haben** have something to do ; **ich hatte dort zu ~/dort geschäftlich zu ~:** I had things/business to do there; **es mit jmdm./etw. zu ~ haben** be dealing with sb./sth.; **wir haben es mit einem gefährlichen Verbrecher zu ~:** we're up against a dangerous criminal; **er hat es mit dem Herzen zu ~** *(ugs.)* he's got heart trouble; **[es] mit jmdm. zu ~ bekommen** *od. (ugs.)* **kriegen** get into trouble with sb./sth.; **mit sich [selbst] zu ~ haben** have problems [of one's own]; **[etwas] mit etw./jmdm. zu ~ haben** be concerned with sth./have dealings with sb.; **er hat noch nie [etwas] mit der Polizei zu ~ gehabt** he has never been involved with the police; **mit etw. nichts zu ~ haben** have nothing to do with sth.; not be concerned with sth.; **er hat mit dem Mord nichts zu ~:** he had nothing to do with *or* was not involved in the murder; **mit Kunst hat das kaum etwas zu ~:** that has very little to do with art; **mit jmdm./etw. nichts zu ~ haben wollen** not want [to have] anything to do with sb./sth.; **es ist mir um dich/deine Gesundheit zu ~** *(geh.)* I'm concerned about you/your health; **d)** *nimmt die Aussage eines vorher gebrauchten Verbs auf* **ich riet ihm zu verschwinden, was er schleunigst tat** I advised him to disappear, which he did at the double *or* and he did so at the double; **es sollte am nächsten Tag regnen, und das tat es dann auch** it was expected to rain the next day, and it did [so]; **e)** *als Funktionsverb* make ⟨*remark, catch, etc.*⟩; take ⟨*step, jump*⟩; do ⟨*deed*⟩; **einen Blick aus dem Fenster ~:** glance out of the window; *(unpers.)* **plötzlich tat es einen furchtbaren Knall** suddenly there was a dreadful bang; **f)** *(bewirken)* work, perform ⟨*miracle*⟩; **seine Wirkung ~:** have its effect; **was tut's?, was tut das schon?** *(ugs.)* so what?; what does it matter?; **das tut nichts** it doesn't matter; *s. auch* **Sache b; g)** *(an~)* **jmdm. etw. ~:** do sth. to sb.; **jmdm. einen Gefallen ~:** do sb. a favour; **er tut dir nichts** he won't hurt *or* harm you; **der Hund tut nichts** the dog doesn't bite; **h) es ~** *(ugs.: genügen)* be good enough; **die Schuhe ~ es noch einen Winter** the shoes will do for another winter; **i)** *(ugs.: irgendwohin bringen)* put; **Salz an** *od.* **in die Suppe ~:** put salt in *or* add salt to the soup; **den Kleinen zur Oma ~:** take the little boy to granny *(coll.).* **2.** *unr. itr. V.* **a)** *(ugs.: funktionieren)* work; **die Kaffeemaschine tut nicht mehr** the coffee-machine has had it *(coll.);* **b) freundlich/geheimnisvoll ~:** pretend to be *or (coll.)* act friendly/act mysteriously; **vornehm ~:** act all genteel *(coll.);* **er tut [so], als ob** *od.* **als wenn** *od.* **wie wenn er nichts wüßte** he pretends not to know anything; **er tut nur so [als ob]** he's only pretending; **tu doch nicht so!** stop pretending!. **3.** *unr. refl. V. (unpers.) (geschehen)* **es hat sich einiges getan** quite a bit has happened; **es tut sich nichts** there's nothing happening. **4.** *Hilfsverb* **a)** *betonend (ugs.)* **rechnen tut er gut** he's good at arithmetic; **kennen tue ich sie nicht** I don't know her; *(in nicht korrektem Sprachgebrauch)* **ich tu' den Fleck einfach nicht wegkriegen** I simply can't get rid of the stain; **b)** *zur Umschreibung des Konjunktivs (ugs.)* **das täte**

mich interessieren/freuen I'd be interested in/pleased about that
Tun das; ~s action; activity; **unser nächtliches** ~: our nocturnal activities *pl.*; **jmds.** ~ **und Treiben** *(geh.)* [all] sb.'s doings
Tünche ['tʏnçə] **die;** ~, ~n **a)** *(Farbe)* distemper; wash; **[weiße]** ~: whitewash; **b)** *o. Pl., (abwertend: Oberfläche)* veneer *(fig.)*
tünchen *tr. (auch itr.) V.* distemper; **weiß** ~: whitewash
Tüncher der; ~s, ~ *(veralt.)* decorator
Tundra ['tʊndra] **die;** ~, **Tundren** tundra
Tunell [tu'nɛl] **das;** ~s, ~s *(südd., österr., schweiz.) s.* **Tunnel**
tunen ['tju:nən] *tr. V. (Kfz-W.)* tune
Tuner ['tju:nɐ] **der;** ~s, ~ **a)** *(Elektronik)* tuner; **b)** *(Kfz-W.)* tuner; tuning expert
Tunesien [tu'ne:zi̯ən] **(das);** ~s Tunisia
Tunesier der; ~s, ~: Tunisian
tunesisch *Adj.* Tunisian
Tu·nicht·gut der; ~ *od.* ~[e]s, ~e good-for-nothing; ne'er-do-well
Tunika ['tu:nika] **die;** ~, **Tuniken** tunic; *(hist.)* tunica; tunic
Tunke ['tʊŋkə] **die;** ~, ~n *(bes. ostmd.)* sauce; *(Bratensoße)* gravy
tunken *tr. V. (bes. ostmd.)* dip; dip, dunk ⟨*biscuit, piece of bread, etc.*⟩
tunlichst ['tu:nlɪçst] *Adv.* *(geh.)* **a)** *(möglichst)* as far as possible; **b)** *(unbedingt)* at all costs; **das hat in Zukunft** ~ **zu unterbleiben** this must not happen in future at any cost
Tunnel ['tʊnl̩] **der;** ~s, ~ *od.* ~s tunnel
tunnelieren *tr. V. (österr.)* tunnel through ⟨*mountain etc.*⟩
Tunte ['tʊntə] **die;** ~, ~n **a)** *(ugs. abwertend: Frau)* female; **b)** *(salopp, auch abwertend: Homosexueller)* queen *(sl.)*
tuntenhaft, tuntig 1. *Adj.* **a)** *(ugs. abwertend: tantenhaft)* prissy; **b)** *(salopp abwertend: feminin)* poofy *(Brit. coll.)*. **2.** *adv.; s.* **1: a)** prissily; **b)** poofily *(Brit. coll.)*
Tüpfelchen ['tʏpfl̩çən] **das;** ~s, ~: dot; **das** ~ **auf dem i** the final touch
tüpfeln *tr. V.* stipple; *(sprenkeln)* speckle
tupfen ['tʊpfn̩] *tr. V.* **a)** dab; **sich** *(Dat.)* **den Schweiß von der Stirn** ~: dab the sweat from one's brow; **etw. auf etw.** *(Akk.)* ~: dab sth. on to sth.; **b)** *(mit Tupfen versehen)* dot; **ein getupftes Kleid** a spotted dress
Tupfen der; ~s, ~: dot; *(größer)* spot
Tupfer der; ~s, ~ **a)** *(ugs.) s.* **Tupfen; b)** *(Med.)* swab
Tür [ty:ɐ̯] **die;** ~, ~en door; *(Garten~)* gate; **an die** ~ **gehen** *(öffnen)* [go and] answer the door; **in der** ~ **stehen** stand in the doorway; **den Kopf zur** ~ **hereinstecken** put one's head round the door; **mach die** ~ **von außen zu!** *(ugs.)* out with you!; out you go!; **jmdm. die** ~ **einlaufen** *od.* **einrennen** *(fig. ugs.)* keep badgering sb.; **jmdm. die** ~ **vor der Nase zuschlagen** *(fig.)* slam the door in sb.'s face; **einer Sache** *(Dat.)* ~ **und Tor öffnen** *(fig.)* open the door *or* way to sth.; **hinter verschlossenen** ~**en** behind closed doors; **mit der** ~ **ins Haus fallen** *(fig. ugs.)* blurt out what one is after; **vor verschlossener** ~ **stehen** be locked out; **zwischen** ~ **und Angel** *(fig. ugs.)* in passing; **[ach,] du kriegst die** ~ **nicht zu!** *(fig. ugs.)* Good Lord!; well I never!; **jmdm. die** ~ **weisen** *(fig. geh.)* show sb. the door; **vor die** ~ **gehen** go outside; **jmdn. vor die** ~ **setzen** *(fig. ugs.)* chuck *(coll.)* *or* throw sb. out; **vor seiner eigenen** ~ **kehren** *(fig. ugs.)* set one's own house in order; **Pfingsten steht/die Sommerferien stehen vor der** ~ *(fig.)* Whitsun is/the summer holidays are [just] coming up; **der Winter steht vor der** ~ *(fig.)* winter is just around the corner
Tür·angel die door-hinge
Turban ['tʊrba:n] **der;** ~s, ~e turban
Turbine [tʊr'bi:nə] **die;** ~, ~n *(Technik)* turbine
turbinen-, Turbinen-: ~**antrieb der** turbine propulsion; ~**flugzeug das** turbo-jet aircraft; ~**getrieben** *Adj.* turbine-propelled ⟨*ship, aircraft*⟩; turbine-driven ⟨*generator*⟩
Turbo- ['turbo-]: *(Technik)* turbo-
Turbo-Prop-Flugzeug das turbo-prop aircraft
turbulent [tʊrbu'lɛnt] **1.** *Adj. (auch Physik, Astron., Met.)* turbulent; *(allzu lebhaft)* chaotic. **2.** *adv. (auch Physik, Astron., Met.)* turbulently; *(allzu lebhaft)* chaotically; **bei uns/an den Devisenmärkten geht es** ~ **zu** things are chaotic [around] here/the exchange markets are in turmoil
Turbulenz [tʊrbu'lɛnts] **die;** ~, ~en *(auch Physik, Astron., Met.)* turbulence *no pl.*
Tür·drücker der; ~s, ~ **a)** doorknob; **b)** *(Türöffner)* [automatic] door-opener
Turf [tʊrf] *(Pferdesport Jargon)* turf
Tür·griff der door-handle
Türke ['tʏrkə] **der;** ~n, ~n **a)** Turk; **b)** *(ugs.)* **einen** ~**n bauen** tell a cock-and-bull story/cock-and-bull stories
Türkei die; ~: Turkey *no art.*
türken *tr. V. (ugs.)* fake ⟨*scene, letter, document, etc.*⟩; make up ⟨*story, report*⟩
Türken·bund·lilie die turk's-cap lily
türkis [tʏr'ki:s] *indekl. Adj.* turquoise
[1]**Türkis der;** ~es, ~e *(Mineral.)* turquoise
[2]**Türkis das;** ~ *(Farbe)* turquoise
türkisch *Adj.* Turkish; ~**er Honig** nougat; *s. auch* **deutsch; Deutsch;** [2]**Deutsche**
türkis·farben *Adj.* turquoise
Tür-: ~**klinke die** door-handle; ~**klopfer der** door-knocker
Turkologie [tʊrkolo'gi:] **die;** ~: Turkish studies *pl., no art.*
Turk-: ~**sprache die** Turkic language; ~**volk das** Turkic people
Turm [tʊrm] **der;** ~[e]s, **Türme** ['tʏrmə] **a)** tower; *(spitzer Kirch~)* spire; steeple; **b)** *(Schach)* rook; castle; **c)** *s.* **Sprung~; d)** *(hist.) s.* **Schuld~; Hunger~; e)** *(Milit.)* turret
Turmalin [tʊrma'li:n] **der;** ~s, ~e *(Mineral.)* tourmaline
Turm·bau der; *o. Pl.* building of a/the tower; **der** ~ **zu Babel** the building of the Tower of Babel
Türmchen ['tʏrmçən] **das;** ~s, ~: turret
[1]**türmen 1.** *tr. V. (stapeln)* stack up; *(häufen)* pile up. **2.** *refl. V.* be piled up; ⟨*clouds*⟩ gather
[2]**türmen** *itr. V.; mit sein (salopp)* scarper *(Brit. sl.)*; do a bunk *(Brit. sl.)*; beat it *(sl.)*; **aus dem Knast** ~: do a bunk from prison
Türmer der; ~s, ~ *(hist.)* tower-keeper
turm-, Turm-: ~**falke der** kestrel; ~**haube die** *(Archit.)* cupola; ~**hoch 1.** *Adj.* towering; **2.** *adv.* **sich** ~**hoch stapeln** be piled high; ~**hoch mit etw. beladen** piled high with sth.; ~**springen das;** *o. Pl.* high diving *no art.*; ~**uhr die** tower clock
Turn-: ~**an·zug der** leotard; ~**beutel der** PE bag
turnen ['tʊrnən] **1.** *itr. V.* **a)** *(Sport)* do gymnastics; *(Schulw.)* do gym *or* PE; **sie turnt gut** she's good at gymnastics *or* a good gymnast; *(Schulw.)* she's good at gym *or* PE; **er turnte am Reck/auf der Matte** he was doing *or* performing exercises *or* was working on the horizontal bar/the mat; **b)** *mit sein (ugs.: klettern)* clamber; **c)** *(ugs.: herumklettern)* clamber about. **2.** *tr. V. (Sport)* do, perform ⟨*exercise, routine*⟩
Turnen das; ~s gymnastics *sing., no art.*; *(Schulw.)* gym *no art.*; PE *no art.*
Turner der; ~s, ~, **Turnerin die;** ~, ~nen gymnast
turnerisch 1. *Adj.; nicht präd.* gymnastic. **2.** *adv.* gymnastically
Turn-: ~**fest das** gymnastics festival; ~**gerät das** gymnastics apparatus; ~**halle die** gymnasium; ~**hemd das** [gym] singlet; *(für Turnunterricht)* gym *or* PE vest; ~**hose die** *(mit langem Bein)* gym trousers *pl.*; *(mit kurzem Bein)* gym shorts *pl.*; *(für Turnunterricht)* gym *or* PE shorts *pl.*
Turnier [tʊr'ni:ɐ̯] **das;** ~s, ~e *(auch hist.)* tournament; *(Reit~)* show; *(Tanz~)* competition; **ein** ~ **reiten** ride in a tournament
Turnier-: ~**pferd das** show horse; ~**tanz der a)** *o. Pl. (Tanzsport)* competitive ballroom dancing; **b)** *(Tanz)* ballroom dance
Turn-: ~**lehrer der** gym *or* PE teacher; ~**schuh der** gym shoe; *(Trainingsschuh)* training shoe; trainer *(coll.)*; ~**schuh·generation die;** *o. Pl.* youth of the '80s; ~**stunde die** gym *or* PE lesson; ~**übung die** gymnastics exercise; ~**unterricht der** gym *or* PE *no art.*
Turnüre [tʊr'ny:rə] **die;** ~, ~n *(Mode, hist.)* bustle
Turnus ['tʊrnʊs] **der;** ~, ~se **a)** regular cycle; **in einem 4jährigen** ~ **stattfinden** take place on a four-year cycle; **er führt das Amt im** ~ **mit seinen Kollegen** he and his colleagues hold the office in rotation; **b)** *(österr.) s.* **Schicht c**
turnus-: ~**gemäß 1.** *Adj.* **die** ~**gemäße Ablösung des Vorsitzenden erfolgt im April** the chairmanship rotates in April; **2.** *adv.* **er wird den Vorsitz** ~**gemäß am ersten Januar übernehmen** it will be his turn to take over the chair on 1 January; ~**gemäß finden die Verhandlungen in X statt** it is the turn of X to host the negotiations; ~**mäßig 1.** *Adj.* regular ⟨*inspection, check, etc.*⟩; **2.** *adv.* on a regular cycle; ~**mäßig hat er morgen Nachtdienst** according to the rota he's on duty tomorrow night
Turn-: ~**verein der** gymnastics club; ~**zeug das** gym *or* PE kit
Tür-: ~**öffner der** door-opener; ~**öffnung die** doorway; ~**pfosten der** doorpost; door-jamb; ~**rahmen der** door-frame; ~**schild das** sign on a/the door; *(Namensschild)* name-plate; door-plate; ~**schloß das** door-lock; ~**schnalle die** *(österr.)* door-handle; ~**schwelle die** threshold; ~**spalt der** crack [of the door]; ~**sturz der** *(Bauw.)* lintel
turteln *itr. V.* **a)** *(scherzh.: zärtlich sein)* bill and coo; **b)** *(veralt.: gurren)* coo
Turtel·taube ['tʊrtl̩-] **die** turtle-dove; *(fig.)* love-bird
Tür·vorleger der doormat
Tusch [tʊʃ] **der;** ~[e]s, ~e fanfare
Tusche die; ~, ~n **a)** Indian *(Brit.)* *or* *(Amer.)* India ink; **b)** *(nordd., md.: Wasserfarbe)* water-colour; **c)** *(ugs.: Wimpern~)* mascara
Tuschelei die; ~, ~en **a)** *o. Pl. (das Tuscheln)* whispering; **b)** *(Äußerung)* whisper
tuscheln ['tʊʃl̩n] *itr., tr. V.* whisper
tuschen 1. *tr. V.* **a) etw.** ~: draw sth. in Indian *(Brit.)* *or* *(Amer.)* India ink/paint sth. in water-colours; **b) sich** *(Dat.)* **die Wimpern** ~: put one's mascara on. **2.** *itr. V.* paint in water-colours
Tusch-: ~**kasten der** *(nordd., md.)* box of water-colours; **die ist der reinste** ~**kasten** *(fig.)* she's got all her war-paint on *(coll. joc.)*; ~**zeichnung die** pen-and-ink drawing
Tussi ['tʊsi] **die;** ~, ~s *(salopp)* female *(derog.)*; *(Mädchen)* bird *(sl.)*; chick *(coll.)*
tut [tu:t] *Interj. (Kinderspr.)* beep; toot
Tütchen ['ty:tçən] **das;** ~s, ~: small bag
Tüte ['ty:tə] **die;** ~, ~n **a)** bag; ~**n kleben** *od.* **drehen** *(fig. ugs.)* be doing time; **das kommt nicht in die** ~! *(fig. ugs.)* not on your life! *(coll.)*; no way!; **b)** *(Eis~)* cone; cornet; **c)** *(ugs.: beim Alkoholtest)* bag; **in die** ~ **blasen müssen** be breathalysed; **d)** *(salopp: Person)* jerk *(sl.)*
tuten ['tu:tn̩] *itr. V.* hoot; ⟨*siren, fog-]horn*⟩ sound; **das Schiff tutet** the ship sounds its fog-horn/hooter; **er wählte die Nummer,**

und es tutete he dialled the number, and heard the ringing tone; **er tutete auf seiner Spielzeugtrompete** he tooted on his toy trumpet; *s. auch* **Ahnung c**

Tutor ['tu:tɔr] **der; ~s, ~en** [tu'to:rən] *(Päd.)* **a)** *senior student who helps beginners integrate into student life;* **b)** *(Mentor)* tutor

Tutorium [tu'to:ri̯ʊm] **das; ~, Tutorien** *(Päd.) seminar conducted by a postgraduate*

TÜV [tʏf] **der; ~** *Abk.* **Technischer Überwachungsverein** ≈ MOT *(Brit.);* **ein Auto durch** *od.* **über den TÜV bringen** ≈ get a car through its MOT

Tu·wort ['tu:-] **das;** *Pl.* **Tuwörter** doing word

Twen [tvɛn] **der; ~[s], ~s** twenty-to-thirty-year-old; **Mode für ~s** fashions for people in their 20s

[1]**Twist** [tvɪst] **der; ~[e]s, ~e** *(Faden)* twist

[2]**Twist der; ~s, ~s a)** *(Tanz)* twist; **~ tanzen** dance the twist; **b)** *(Tennis)* spin

twisten *itr. V.* twist; dance the twist

Tympanon ['tʏmpanɔn] **das; ~s, Tympana** *(Archit.)* tympanum

Typ [ty:p] **der; ~s, ~en a)** type; **sie ist genau mein ~** *(ugs.)* she's just my type; **dein ~ wird verlangt** *(salopp)* you're wanted; **dein ~ ist hier nicht gefragt** *(salopp)* we don't want your sort here; **er ist ein dunkler/blonder ~:** he's dark/fair; **die beiden sind ganz verschiedene ~en** they're very different sorts of people; **b)** *Gen. auch* **~en** *(ugs.: Mann)* bloke *(Brit. sl.);* guy *(sl.);* **c)** *(Technik: Modell) (Auto)* model; *(Flugzeug)* type; **d)** *(bes. Philos.)* type

Type ['ty:pə] **die; ~, ~n a)** *(Druck~, Schreibmaschinen~)* type; **b)** *(ugs.) (Person)* type; sort; character; *(seltsame Person)* odd type *or* sort *or* character; **eine seltsame/originelle ~:** an odd sort *or* character/an oddball; **c)** *(bes. österr.) s.* **Typ d; d)** *(Fachspr.: Mehl~)* grade

Typen-: ~hebel der type-bar; **~rad das** daisy wheel; **~rad·schreib·maschine die** daisy-wheel typewriter

Typhus ['ty:fʊs] **der; ~** typhoid [fever]

Typhus·epidemie die typhoid epidemic

typisch 1. *Adj.* typical (**für** of). **2.** *adv.* typically; **das ist ~ Mann/Frau** that's just typical of a man/woman; **~ Gisela!** typical Gisela!; that's Gisela all over!

Typographie [typogra'fi:] **die; ~, ~n** *(Druckw.)* typography

typographisch *(Druckw.)* **1.** *Adj.* typographical. **2.** *adv.* typographically

Typologie [typolo'gi:] **die, ~, ~n** *(bes. Psych.)* typology

typologisch *(bes. Psych.)* **1.** *Adj.* typological. **2.** *adv.* typologically

Typo·skript das; *Pl.* **~e** typescript

Typus ['ty:pʊs] **der; ~, Typen** *(auch Literaturw., bild. Kunst, Philos.)* type

Tyrann [ty'ran] **der; ~en, ~en** *(auch fig.)* tyrant

Tyrannei die; ~, ~en *(auch fig.)* tyranny

Tyrannen-: ~herrschaft die tyranny; tyrannical rule; **~mord der** tyrannicide

Tyrannis die; ~ *(hist.)* tyranny

tyrannisch 1. *Adj.* tyrannical. **2.** *adv.* tyrannically

tyrannisieren *tr. V.* tyrannize

tyrrhenisch [tʏ're:nɪʃ] *Adj.* **Tyrrhenisches Meer** Tyrrhenian Sea

U

u, U [u:] **das; ~, ~:** u, U; *s. auch* **a, A; X**

ü, Ü [y:] **das; ~, ~:** u umlaut; *s. auch* **a, A**

U *Abk.* **Umleitung**

u. *Abk.* **und**

u. a. *Abk.* **unter anderem**

u. ä. *Abk.* **und ähnliche[s]**

u. a. m. *Abk.* **und andere[s] mehr** etc.

u. *od.* **U. A. w. g.** *Abk.* **um Antwort wird gebeten** RSVP

UB [u'be:] *Abk.* **die; ~, ~s: Universitätsbibliothek**

U-Bahn die underground *(Brit.);* subway *(Amer.); (bes. in London)* tube

U-Bahnhof der, U-Bahn-Station die underground station *(Brit.);* subway station *(Amer.); (bes. in London)* tube station

übel ['y:bl̩] **1.** *Adj.* **a)** foul, nasty ⟨*smell, weather*⟩; bad, nasty ⟨*headache, cold, taste*⟩; nasty ⟨*situation, consequences*⟩; sorry ⟨*state, affair*⟩; foul, *(coll.)* filthy ⟨*mood*⟩; **nicht ~** *(ugs.)* not bad at all; **ein übles Ende nehmen** come to a bad end; **b)** *(unwohl)* **jmdm. ist/wird ~:** sb. feels sick; **es kann einem ~ werden, wenn man so was hört** hearing that sort of thing is enough to make you sick; **c)** *(verwerflich)* bad; wicked; nasty, dirty ⟨*trick*⟩; **ein übler Bursche** a bad sort *(coll.) or* lot; **in üble Gesellschaft geraten** fall in with a bad crowd. **2.** *adv.* **a) Wie geht's? – Danke, nicht ~:** How are things? – Not so bad, thanks; **nicht ~ Lust haben, etw. zu tun** have a good mind to do sth.; **etw. ~ aufnehmen** take sth. badly; **~ gelaunt sein** be in a bad mood; **er spielt nicht ~:** he plays pretty well; **b)** *(nachteilig, schlimm)* badly; **er ist ~ dran** he's in a bad way; **etw. ~ vermerken** take sth. amiss; **jmdn. ~ zurichten** give sb. a working over *(coll.);* **c)** *(verwerflich)* wickedly

Übel das; ~s, ~ a) *(Mißstand, Ärgernis)* evil; **zu allem ~:** on top of everything else; to make matters [even] worse; **ein notwendiges ~:** a necessary evil; **das kleinere ~:** the lesser evil; **das sind nur kleinere ~:** they are just minor annoyances *or* irritations; **b)** *(veralt.: Krankheit)* illness; malady; **c)** *(veralt.: das Böse)* evil *no art.;* **von** *od.* **vom ~ sein** be an evil

übel-: ~gelaunt 1. *Adj. (präd. getrennt geschrieben)* ill-humoured; ill-tempered; *s. auch* **übel 2 a; 2.** *adv.* ill-humouredly; ill-temperedly; **~gesinnt** *Adj. (präd. getrennt geschrieben)* ill-disposed

Übelkeit die; ~, ~en nausea; **von einer plötzlichen ~ befallen werden** have a sudden feeling of nausea

übel-, Übel-: ~launig 1. *Adj.* ill-humoured; ill-tempered; **2.** *adv.* ill-humouredly; ill-temperedly; **~|nehmen** *unr. tr. V.* **jmdm. etw. ~nehmen** hold sth. against sb.; take sth. amiss; **etw. ~nehmen** take offence at sth.; take sth. amiss; **nehmen Sie es [mir] bitte nicht ~, wenn ich ...:** please don't take it amiss *or* be offended if I ...; **~riechend** *Adj.; nicht präd.* foul-smelling; evil-smelling; **~stand der** evil; **~tat die** *(geh.)* evil *or* wicked deed; misdeed; **~täter der** wrongdoer; *(Verbrecher)* criminal; *(Verantwortlicher)* culprit; **~|wollen** *unr. itr. V.* **jmdm. ~wollen** wish sb. ill; **~wollend** malevolent ⟨*intentions*⟩

üben ['y:bn̩] **1.** *tr. V.* **a)** *(auch itr.)* practise; rehearse ⟨*scene, play*⟩; practise on ⟨*musical instrument*⟩; **b)** *(trainieren, schulen)* exercise ⟨*fingers*⟩; train ⟨*memory*⟩; **mit geübten Händen** with practised hands; **c)** *(geh.: bekunden, tun)* exercise ⟨*patience, restraint, etc.*⟩; commit ⟨*treason*⟩; take ⟨*revenge, retaliation*⟩; **Kritik an etw.** *(Dat.)* **~:** criticize sth. **2.** *refl. V.* **sich in etw.** *(Dat.)* **~:** practise sth.; **sich in Geduld/Zurückhaltung ~** *(geh.)* exercise patience/restraint

über ['y:bɐ] **1.** *Präp. mit Dat.* **a)** *(Lage, Standort)* over; above; *(in einer Rangfolge)* above; **das Bild hängt ~ dem Sofa** the picture hangs above the sofa; **~ jmdm. wohnen** live above sb.; **Nebel lag ~ der Wiese** fog hung over the meadow; **zehn Grad ~ Null/dem Gefrierpunkt** ten degrees above zero/freezing point; **sie trug eine Jacke ~ dem Kleid** she wore a jacket over her dress; **~ jmdm. stehen** *(fig.)* be above sb.; **b)** *(während)* during; **~ dem Lesen/der Arbeit einschlafen** fall asleep over one's book/magazine *etc.*/over one's work; **c)** *(infolge)* because of; as a result of; **~ der Aufregung vergaß ich, daß ...:** in all the excitement I forgot that ... **2.** *Präp. mit Akk.* **a)** *(Richtung)* over; *(quer hinüber)* across; **~ die Straße gehen** go across the road; cross the road; **~ Karlsruhe nach Stuttgart** via Karlsruhe to Stuttgart; **Tränen liefen ihr ~ die Wangen** tears ran down her cheeks; **ihr Rock reicht ~ die Knie** her skirt comes down to below the knee; **ein Wettlauf ~ eine Distanz von 5 000 Metern** a race over a distance of 5,000 metres; **er zog sich** *(Dat.)* **die Mütze ~ die Ohren** he pulled the cap down over his ears; **bis ~ die Knöchel im Schlamm versinken** sink up past one's ankles in mud; **es ist zwei Stunden ~ die Zeit** it should have happened two hours ago; *(er/sie/es hat schon zwei Stunden Verspätung)* he/she/it is two hours late; **Tennis/seine Tochter geht ihm ~ alles** tennis/his daughter means more to him than anything; **italienisches Essen geht ihm ~ alles** he loves Italian food more than anything else; **b)** *(während)* over; **~ Mittag** over lunchtime; **~ das Wochenende nach Hause fahren/zu Hause sein** go/be home for the weekend; **~ Wochen/Monate** for weeks/months; **~ Ostern/Weihnachten** over Easter/Christmas; **die ganze Zeit ~:** the whole time; **die Woche/den Sommer ~:** during the week/summer; **den ganzen Winter/Tag ~:** all winter/day long; **c)** *(betreffend)* about; **~ etw. reden/schreiben** talk/write about sth.; **ein Buch ~ die byzantinische Kunst** a book about *or* on Byzantine art; **ein Scheck/eine Rechnung ~ 1000 Mark** a cheque/bill for 1,000 marks; **d) Kinder ~ 10 Jahre** children over ten [years of age]; **e) Gewalt ~ jmdn. haben** have power over sb.; **Wellingtons Sieg ~ Napoleon** Wellington's victory over Napoleon; **f) das geht ~ meine Kraft** that's too much for me; **jmdm. ~ den Verstand gehen** be beyond sb.; **g) sie macht Fehler ~ Fehler** she makes mistake after mistake; **er hat Schulden ~ Schulden** he's up to his ears in debt; **h)** *(mittels, durch)* through ⟨*person*⟩; by ⟨*post, telex, etc.*⟩; over ⟨*radio, loudspeaker*⟩; **ich bin ~ die Autobahn gekommen** I came along the motorway; **etw. ~ alle Sender bringen/ausstrahlen** broadcast sth. on all stations; **i)** *(geh. veralt.: bei Verwünschungen)* on; **Schande/Fluch ~ ihn!** shame/a curse on him! **3.** *Adv.* **a)** *(mehr als)* over; **b) ~ und ~:** all over; **sie war ~ und ~ mit Schmutz bedeckt** she was covered all over in dirt. **4.** *Adj.; nicht attr. (ugs.)* **a)** *(überlegen)* **jmdm. ~ sein** have the edge on sb. *(coll.);* **b)** *(übrig)* left [over]; **c)** *(zuviel, lästig)* **das ist mir ~:** I'm fed up with it *(coll.)*

über·all [*od.* --'-] *Adv.* **a)** *(an allen Orten)* everywhere; **sie weiß ~ Bescheid** *(auf allen*

Gebieten) she knows about everything; **b)** *(bei jeder Gelegenheit)* always
überall-: ~her *Adv.* from all over the place; **~hin** *Adv.* everywhere
über·altert [y:bɐ'|altɐt] *Adj.* **a)** ⟨*population*⟩ containing a disproportionately high proportion of elderly people; **das Kabinett ist ~:** the cabinet has too many elderly members; **b)** *(überholt)* outdated; obsolete ⟨*machine, vehicle, etc.*⟩
Über·alterung die; ~, ~en a) increase in the proportion of elderly people/workers/members *etc.*; **b)** *s.* **überaltert b:** outdatedness; obsolescence
Über·angebot das surplus **(an** + *Dat.* of); *(Schwemme)* glut **(an** + *Dat.* of)
über·ängstlich 1. *Adj.* over-anxious. **2.** *adv.* over-anxiously
über·anstrengen *tr. V.* overtax ⟨*person, energy*⟩; strain ⟨*eyes, nerves, heart*⟩; **sich ~:** overstrain *or* over-exert oneself; **überanstreng dich nicht!** *(iron.)* don't strain yourself!
Über·anstrengung die over-exertion; **~ der Augen/des Herzens** strain on the eyes/heart; **vermeiden Sie jede ~ der** *od.* **Ihrer Augen** avoid straining your eyes
über·antworten *tr. V. (geh.)* **a)** *(anvertrauen)* **jmdn./etw. jmdm. ~:** entrust sb./sth. to sb.; **die Funde wurden dem Museum überantwortet** the finds were handed over to the museum; **b)** *(ausliefern)* **jmdn. dem Gericht ~:** hand sb. over to the courts
über·arbeiten 1. *tr. V.* rework; revise ⟨*text, edition*⟩. **2.** *refl. V.* overwork
Über·arbeitung die; ~, ~en a) reworking; *(von Text, Manuskript, Ausgabe usw.)* revision; *(überarbeitete Fassung)* revised version; **b)** *(Überanstrengung)* overwork
über·aus *Adv. (geh.)* extremely
über·backen *unr. tr. V.* **etw. mit Käse** *usw.* **~:** top sth. with cheese *etc.* and brown it lightly [under the grill/in a hot oven]; **ein mit Käse ~er Auflauf** a soufflé au gratin
Über·bau der; *Pl.* **~e** *(Philos., Soziol.)* superstructure
überbeanspruchen[1] *tr. V.* put too great a strain on ⟨*heart, circulation, etc.*⟩; strain ⟨*nerves*⟩; overstrain, overstress ⟨*material*⟩; overburden, overstretch ⟨*facilities, services*⟩; overload ⟨*machine*⟩; make excessive use of ⟨*right, privilege*⟩; overtax ⟨*person, body, strenght*⟩; *(mit Arbeit)* overwork ⟨*person*⟩; *(psychisch)* put too great a strain on ⟨*person*⟩
Über·beanspruchung die *s.* **überbeanspruchen:** straining; overstraining; overstressing; overburdening; overloading; excessive use; overtaxing, overworking; **die ~ des Herzens führt zu ...:** putting too great a strain on the heart leads to ...
über|behalten *unr. tr. V. (ugs.) s.* **übrigbehalten**
Über·bein das *(Med.)* ganglion
über|bekommen *unr. tr. V. (ugs.)* **a)** *(satt bekommen)* get fed up with *(sl.)*; **b) einen** *od.* **eins ~:** get a clout
überbelasten[2] *tr. V.* **a)** overload; **b)** *(zu stark in Anspruch nehmen)* overburden ⟨*person*⟩; place too much strain on ⟨*bodily organ*⟩
Über·belastung die a) overloading; **b)** *(zu starke Inanspruchnahme)* overburdening; **die ~ der Leber führt zu ...:** placing too much strain on the liver leads to ...
über·belegt *Adj.* overcrowded; over-subscribed ⟨*course*⟩
Über·belegung die overcrowding; **wegen der ~ des Kurses** because the course is/was over-subscribed

[1] *ich überbeanspruche, überbeansprucht, überzubeanspruchen*
[2] *ich überbelaste, überbelastet, überzubelasten*

überbelichten[1] *tr. V. (Fot.)* over-expose
Über·belichtung die *(Fot.)* over-exposure
Über·beschäftigung die; *o. Pl. (Wirtsch.)* over-employment
überbetonen[2] *tr. V.* overstress
Über·bevölkerung die; *o. Pl.* over-population
überbewerten[3] *tr. V.* overvalue; *(überschätzen)* overvalue; overrate; mark ⟨*pupil, piece of work, gymnast, skater, etc.*⟩ too high; **er warnte davor, diesen Faktor überzubewerten** he warned people not to attach too much significance to this factor
Über·bewertung die overvaluation; *(Überschätzung)* overvaluation; overrating
überbezahlen[4] *tr. V.* overpay
Über·bezahlung die overpayment
überbietbar *Adj.* **kaum noch ~ sein** take some beating; **das ist ein kaum ~es Beispiel für Intoleranz** as an example of intolerance that takes some beating
über·bieten *unr. tr. V.* **a)** outbid **(um** by); **b)** *(übertreffen)* surpass; outdo ⟨*rival*⟩; break ⟨*record*⟩ **(um** by); exceed ⟨*target*⟩ **(um** by); **das ist kaum noch zu ~:** that takes some beating
über|bleiben *unr. itr. V.; mit sein (ugs.) s.* **übrigbleiben**
Überbleibsel [-blaipsl] **das; ~s, ~:** remnant; *(einer Kultur)* relic
über|blenden *tr. V. (Rundf., Ferns., Film)* dissolve
Über·blick der a) view; **einen guten ~ über etw.** *(Akk.)* **haben** have a good view over sth.; **b)** *(Abriß)* survey; **c)** *o. Pl. (Einblick)* overall view *or* perspective; **den ~ über etw.** *(Akk.)* **verlieren** lose track of sth.; **einen ~ über etw.** *(Akk.)* **gewinnen/haben** gain/have an overview of sth.
über·blicken *tr. V. s.* **²übersehen a, b**
über·bordend *Adj.* exuberant
über|braten *unr. tr. V.* **jmdm. eins** *od.* **einen ~** *(ugs.)* belt sb. one
Über·breite die: Transport/Ladung mit ~: wide load; **~ haben** be over normal width
über·bringen *unr. tr. V.* deliver; convey ⟨*greetings, congratulations*⟩
Über·bringer der; ~s, ~: bearer
über·brücken *tr. V.* **a)** *(veralt.)* bridge ⟨*river, ravine, etc.*⟩; **b)** *(fig.)* bridge ⟨*gap, gulf*⟩; reconcile ⟨*difference*⟩; **um die finanzielle Notlage zu ~, mußte sie ...:** to tide herself over the financial crisis, she had to ...
Überbrückung die; ~, ~en *(fig.)* bridging; *(von Gegensätzen)* reconciliation; **zur ~ der finanziellen Notlage mußte sie ...:** to tide herself over the financial crisis, she had to ...
Überbrückungs-: ~hilfe die: jmdm. eine ~hilfe gewähren give sb. interim financial help; **~kredit der** *(Finanzw.)* bridging loan
über·dachen *tr. V.* roof over; **überdacht** covered ⟨*terrace, station platform, etc.*⟩
über·dauern *tr. V.* survive ⟨*war, separation, hardship*⟩
Über·decke die cover; *(auf einem Bett)* bedspread
¹über|decken *tr. V. (ugs.)* **jmdm. etw. ~:** cover sb. [up] with sth.
²über|decken *tr. V.* **a)** *(bedecken)* cover; **b)** *(verdecken)* cover up
über·dehnen *tr. V.* overstretch; strain ⟨*muscle*⟩
über·denken *unr. tr. V.* **etw. ~:** think sth. over
über·deutlich 1. *Adj.* unusually clear. **2.** *adv.* unusually clearly; with unusual clarity; **er hat mir ~ klargemacht, daß ...:** he made it only too plain to me that ...

[1] *ich überbelichte, überbelichtet, überzubelichten*
[2] *ich überbetone, überbetont, überzubetonen*
[3] *ich überbewerte, überbewertet, überzubewerten*
[4] *ich überbezahle, überbezahlt, überzubezahlen*

über·dies *Adv.* moreover; what is more
über·dimensional 1. *Adj.* inordinately large ⟨*spectacles, table, statue, etc.*⟩; inordinate ⟨*love, influence*⟩. **2.** *adv.* enormously ⟨*enlarged*⟩
überdosieren[1] *tr. V.* **ein Medikament ~:** give/take too large a dose/doses of a medicine
Über·dosis die overdose
über·drehen *tr. V.* **a)** overwind ⟨*watch*⟩; over-tighten ⟨*screw, nut*⟩; **b)** *(Technik)* overrev *(coll.)* ⟨*engine*⟩; **einen Wagen ~:** over-rev *(coll.)* the engine of a car
überdreht *Adj. (ugs.)* wound up; *(verrückt)* crazy
¹Über·druck der; *Pl.* **~drücke** excess pressure; **der Reifen hat ~:** the tyre is over-inflated
²Über·druck der; *Pl.* **~e** *(Philat.)* overprint
über·drucken *tr. V.* overprint
Überdruck·ventil das pressure-relief valve
Überdruß [-drʊs] **der; Überdrusses** surfeit **(an** + *Dat.* of); **etw. bis zum ~ tun** do sth. until one has wearied of it; **das habe ich schon bis zum ~ gehört!** I'm tired of hearing that
überdrüssig [-drʏsɪç] *Adj.* **jmds./einer Sache ~ sein/werden** be/grow tired of sb./sth.
über·durchschnittlich 1. *Adj.* above average. **2.** *adv.* **sie ist ~ begabt** she is more than averagely gifted *or* talented; **er verdient ~ gut** he earns more than the average
über·eck *Adv.* across a/the corner; **die Decke liegt ~ auf dem Tisch** the table-cloth lies diagonally on the table
Über·eifer der over-eagerness; *(zu große Emsigkeit)* over-zealousness
über·eifrig 1. *Adj.* over-eager; *(zu emsig)* over-zealous. **2.** *adv.* over-eagerly; *(zu emsig)* over-zealously
über·eignen *tr. V.* **jmdm. etw. ~:** transfer sth. *or* make sth. over to sb.
Über·eignung die transfer **(an** + *Akk.* to)
über·eilen *tr. V.* rush; **übereilt** over-hasty
über·einander *Adv.* **a)** *(räumlich)* one on top of the other; **sie wohnen ~:** they live one above the other; **b)** *(fig.: voneinander)* about each other; about one another
übereinander-: ~|legen *tr. V.* **Holzscheite** *usw.* **~legen** lay pieces of wood *etc.* one on top of the other; **~|liegen** *unr. itr. V.; südd., österr. schweiz. mit sein* lie one on top of the other; **ihre Wohnungen liegen ~:** their flats *(Brit.)* or *(Amer.)* apartments are situated over each other; **~|schichten** *tr. V.* **Bretter** *usw.* **~schichten** pile boards *etc.* one on top of the other; **~|schlagen** *unr. tr. V.* **die Enden des Tuches ~schlagen** fold the edges of the cloth over; **die Arme/Beine ~schlagen** fold one's arms/cross one's legs; **mit ~geschlagenen Armen** with [one's] arms folded; **~|stehen** *unr. itr. V.* stand one on top of the other; **~|stellen** *tr. V.* **Teller** *usw.* **~stellen** put plates *etc.* one on top of the other
überein|kommen *unr. itr. V.; mit sein* agree; come to an agreement
Überein·kommen das; ~s, ~, Übereinkunft [-'ainkʊnft] **die; ~, Übereinkünfte** agreement; **ein Übereinkommen** *od.* **eine Übereinkunft treffen/erzielen** enter into *or* make an agreement/reach [an] agreement
überein|stimmen *itr. V.* **a)** *(einer Meinung sein)* agree; **mit jmdm. in etw.** *(Dat.)* **~:** agree with sb. on sth.; **wir stimmen darin überein, daß ...:** we are in agreement that ...; **b)** *(sich gleichen)* ⟨*colours, styles*⟩ match; ⟨*figures, statements, reports, results*⟩ tally, agree; ⟨*views, opinions*⟩ coincide; *(Sprachw.: kongruieren)* agree

[1] *ich überdosiere, überdosiert, überzudosieren*

übereinstimmend **1.** *Adj.; nicht präd.* concurrent ⟨*views, opinions, statements, reports*⟩. **2.** *adv.* **sie stellten ~ fest, daß ...:** they agreed in stating that ...; **wir sind ~ der Meinung, daß ...:** we share the view that ...
Überein·stimmung die a) *(von Meinungen)* agreement **(in + *Dat.*** on); **b)** *(Einklang, Gleichheit, Sprachw.: Kongruenz)* agreement (*Gen.* between); **die ~ von *od.* zwischen Theorie und Praxis** the correspondence between theory and practice; **in ~ mit einem Vertrag stehen** be in accordance with a contract; **etw. mit etw. in ~ bringen** reconcile sth. with sth.
über·empfindlich 1. *Adj.* over-sensitive **(gegen** to); *(Med.)* hypersensitive **(gegen** to). **2.** *adv.* over-sensitively; *(Med.)* hypersensitively
Über·empfindlichkeit die over-sensitivity **(gegen** to); *(Med.)* hypersensitivity **(gegen** to)
übererfüllen[1] *tr. V.* overfulfil
Über·erfüllung die overfulfilment
[1]über|essen *unr. tr. V.* **sich *(Dat.)* Hamburger/Nougat ~:** eat too many hamburgers/ too much nougat
[2]über·essen *unr. refl. V.* **sich [an etw. *(Dat.)*] ~:** gorge oneself [on sth.]
[1]über|fahren 1. *unr. tr. V.* **jmdn. ~:** ferry *or* take sb. over. **2.** *unr. itr. V.; mit sein* cross over
[2]über·fahren *unr. tr. V.* **a)** run over; **b)** *(übersehen u. weiterfahren)* go through ⟨*red light, stop-signal, etc.*⟩; **c)** *(hinwegfahren über)* cross; go over ⟨*crossroads*⟩; **d)** *(ugs.: überrumpeln)* **jmdn. ~:** catch *or* take sb. unawares
Über·fahrt die crossing **(über + *Akk.*** of)
Über·fall der attack **(auf + *Akk.*** on); *(aus dem Hinterhalt)* ambush **(auf + *Akk.*** on); *(mit vorgehaltener Waffe)* hold-up; *(auf eine Bank o. ä.)* raid **(auf + *Akk.*** on); *(fig. ugs.)* surprise visit
über·fallen *unr. tr. V.* **a)** attack; raid ⟨*bank, enemy position, village, etc.*⟩; *(hinterrücks)* ambush; *(mit vorgehaltener Waffe)* hold up; *(fig.: besuchen)* descend on; **jmdn. mit Wünschen/Fragen ~** *(fig.)* bombard sb. with requests/questions; **b)** *(überkommen)* ⟨*tiredness, homesickness, fear*⟩ come over; **ein Schauder überfiel mich** a shiver ran through me
über·fällig *Adj.* overdue
Überfall·kommando, *(österr.)* **Überfalls·kommando das** flying squad
über·fischen *tr. V.* overfish
über·fliegen *unr. tr. V.* **a)** *(hinwegfliegen über)* fly over; overfly *(formal)*; **b)** *(flüchtig lesen)* skim [through]
über|fließen *unr. itr. V.; mit sein s.* **überlaufen a, b; sein Herz floß über** *(fig.)* his heart was full
über·flügeln *tr. V.* outshine; outstrip
Über·fluß der; *o. Pl.* abundance **(an +** *Dat.* of); *(Wohlstand)* affluence; **etw. im ~ haben** have sth. in abundance; **im ~ vorhanden sein** be in abundant *or* plentiful supply; **zu allem ~:** to cap *or* crown it all
Überfluß·gesellschaft die; *o. Pl.* affluent society
über·flüssig *Adj.* superfluous; unnecessary ⟨*purchase, words, work*⟩; *(zwecklos)* pointless; **~e Pfunde** *(ugs. scherzh.)* excess weight *sing.*; **~ zu erwähnen, daß ...:** needless to say, ...
überflüssiger·weise *Adv.* unnecessarily; *(sinnloserweise)* pointlessly
über·fluten *tr. V. (auch fig.)* flood
über·fordern *tr. V.* **jmdn. [mit etw.] ~:** overtax sb. [with sth.]; ask *or* demand too much of sb. [with sth.]; **mit diesem Posten ist er überfordert** this job is too much for him; he is not up to this job

[1] *ich übererfülle, übererfüllt, überzuerfüllen*

Über·forderung die a) eine [körperliche] ~ für jmdn. sein be too much for sb. [physically]; **eine intellektuelle ~ für jmdn. sein** ask *or* demand too much of sb. intellectually; **b)** *o. Pl. (das Überfordern)* overtaxing
über·frachten *tr. V.* overload; *(fig.)* overcharge
über·fragen *tr. V.* **da bin ich überfragt** I don't know the answer to that
über·fremden *tr. V.* **überfremdet werden/ sein** ⟨*language, culture, etc.*⟩ be swamped [by foreign influences]; ⟨*economy*⟩ be dominated [by foreign firms/capital]; ⟨*country*⟩ be dominated [by foreign influences]
Über·fremdung die; ~, ~en domination [by foreign influences]; **eine amerikanische ~ des Marktes** domination of the market by American capital
über·fressen *unr. refl. V.* overeat; **der Hund/** *(salopp)* **sie hat sich an Schokolade ~:** the dog gorged itself/she gorged herself on chocolate
über·frieren *unr. itr. V.; mit sein* freeze over; **~de Nässe** black ice
Über·fuhr die; ~, ~en *(österr.)* ferry
[1]über|führen *tr. V.* **a)** *(an einen anderen Ort bringen)* transfer; **der Tote wurde in seine Heimat übergeführt** the body of the dead man was brought back to his home town/ country; **b)** *(in einen anderen Zustand bringen)* convert; **etw. in die Praxis ~:** give sth. practical application
[2]über·führen *tr. V.* **a)** *s.* **[1]überführen a; b) jmdn. [eines Verbrechens] ~:** find sb. guilty [of a crime]; convict sb. [of a crime]; **c)** *s.* **[1]überführen b**
Über·führung die a) transfer; **die ~ des Toten in seine Heimat** bringing back the body of the dead man to his home town/country; **b)** *(eines Verdächtigen)* conviction; **c)** *(Brücke)* bridge; *(Hochstraße)* overpass; *(Fußgänger~)* [foot-]bridge
Über·fülle die superabundance; **die ~ des Angebots** the excessive amount on offer
über·füllt *Adj.* crammed full, chock-full **(von** with); *(mit Menschen)* overcrowded, packed **(von** with); over-subscribed ⟨*course*⟩
Über·füllung die; *o. Pl.* overcrowding; **„Wegen ~ geschlossen"** 'Full up'
Über·funktion die *(Med.)* hyperfunction
über·füttern *tr. V.* overfeed
Über·gabe die a) handing over **(an + *Akk.*** to); *(einer Straße, eines Gebäudes)* opening; *(von Macht)* handing over; transfer; **b)** *(Auslieferung an den Gegner)* surrender **(an + *Akk.*** to)
Über·gang der a) crossing; **b)** *(Stelle zum Überqueren)* crossing; *(Bahn~)* level crossing *(Brit.)*; grade crossing *(Amer.)*; *(Fußgängerbrücke)* foot-bridge; *(an der Grenze, eines Flusses)* crossing-point; **c)** *(Wechsel, Überleitung)* transition **(zu, auf + *Akk.*** to); **ohne ~:** without any transition
übergangs-, Übergangs-: ~bestimmung die interim regulation; **~erscheinung die** transitional phenomenon; **~los 1.** *Adj.; nicht präd.* without any transition *postpos.*; **2.** *adv.* without any transition; **~lösung die** interim *or* temporary solution; **~mantel der** coat for spring and autumn; **~stadium das** transitional stage; **~zeit die a)** transitional period; **b)** *(Frühling)* spring; *(Herbst)* autumn; *(Frühling und Herbst)* spring and autumn
Über·gardine die curtain
über·geben 1. *unr. tr. V.* **a)** hand over; pass ⟨*baton*⟩; **etw. den Flammen ~** *(fig. geh.)* consign sth. to the flames; **b)** *(übereignen)* transfer, make over (*Dat.* to); **c)** *(ausliefern)* surrender (*Dat.*, **an + *Akk.*** to); **d) eine Straße dem Verkehr ~:** open a road to traffic; **das neue Gemeindezentrum wurde seiner Bestimmung ~:** the new community centre was [officially] opened; **e)** *(abgeben, überlassen)* **er hat sein Amt ~:** he has handed over his position; **jmdm. etw. ~:** entrust sb. with sth.; **ich übergebe diese Angelegenheit meinem Anwalt** I am placing this matter in the hands of my lawyer. **2.** *unr. refl. V. (sich erbrechen)* vomit
[1]über|gehen *unr. itr. V.; mit sein* **a)** pass; **an jmdn./in jmds. Besitz ~:** become sb.'s property; *s. auch* **Fleisch a; b) zu etw. ~:** go over to sth.; **dazu ~, etw. zu tun** go over to doing sth.; **zu einem anderen Thema ~:** move on to another subject; **c) in etw.** *(Akk.)* **~** *(zu etw. werden)* turn into sth.; **in Gärung/Verwesung ~:** begin to ferment/ decompose; **ineinander ~** *(sich vermischen)* merge; **d) uns gingen die Augen über** we were overwhelmed by the sight; **e)** *(Seemannsspr.)* ⟨*wave*⟩ break over the side
[2]über·gehen *unr. tr. V.* **a)** *(nicht beachten)* ignore; *(nicht eingehen auf)* **etw. [mit Stillschweigen] ~:** pass sth. over in silence; **b)** *(auslassen, überspringen)* skip [over]; **c)** *(nicht berücksichtigen)* pass over; **jmdn. bei der Beförderung ~:** pass sb. over for promotion; **jmdn. im Testament ~:** leave sb. out of one's will
über·genau 1. *Adj.* over-meticulous. **2.** *adv.* over-meticulously
über·genug *Adv.* more than enough
über·geordnet 1. *s.* **überordnen. 2.** *Adj.* higher ⟨*authority, position, court*⟩; greater ⟨*significance*⟩; superordinate ⟨*concept*⟩; **einer Sache *(Dat.)* ~ sein** ⟨*authority, position, court*⟩ be higher than sth.
Über·gepäck das *(Flugw.)* excess baggage
Über·gewicht das a) excess weight; *(von Person)* overweight; **[5 kg] ~ haben** ⟨*person*⟩ be [5 kilos] overweight; **b)** *(fig.)* predominance; **das ~ [über jmdn./etw.] haben/gewinnen** be/become predominant [over sb./sth.]; **militärisches ~ haben/gewinnen** have/ achieve military superiority; **c) das ~ bekommen *od.* kriegen** *(ugs.)* ⟨*person*⟩ overbalance
über·gewichtig *Adj.* overweight
[1]über|gießen *unr. tr. V.* **jmdm. etw. ~:** pour sth. over sb.
[2]über·gießen *unr. tr. V.* **etw. mit Wasser/ Soße ~:** pour water/sauce over sth.; **sich mit etw. ~:** pour sth. over oneself; **von Licht übergossen sein** *(fig.)* be flooded with light
über·glücklich *Adj.* blissfully happy; *(hoch erfreut)* overjoyed
über·golden *tr. V.* gild; *(fig. dichter.)* ⟨*sun*⟩ bathe ⟨*countryside*⟩ in gold
über|greifen *unr. itr. V.* **a)** *(bes. beim Klavierspiel, Turnen)* cross one's hands over; **b)** *(sich ausdehnen)* **auf etw. *(Akk.)* ~:** spread to sth.; **auf *od.* in jmds. Machtbereich ~:** encroach on sb.'s area of authority
übergreifend *Adj.* predominant; *(allumfassend)* all-embracing
Über·griff der *(unrechtmäßiger Eingriff)* encroachment **(auf + *Akk.*** on); infringement **(auf + *Akk.*** of); *(Angriff)* attack **(auf + *Akk.*** on)
über·groß *Adj.* huge; enormous; overwhelming ⟨*majority*⟩
Über·größe die outsize; **Kleider/Schuhe** *usw.* **in ~n** outsize dresses/shoes *etc.*
über|haben *unr. tr. V. (ugs.)* **a)** *(übergezogen haben)* have ⟨*coat, jacket, etc.*⟩ on; be wearing ⟨*coat, jacket, etc.*⟩; **b)** *(satthaben)* be fed up with *(coll.)*; **c)** *(übrig haben)* **etw. ~:** have sth. left [over]
überhand|nehmen *unr. itr. V.* get out of hand; ⟨*attacks, muggings, etc.*⟩ increase alarmingly; ⟨*weeds*⟩ run riot
Über·hang der a) *(Überschuß)* surplus **(an + *Dat.*** of); **b)** *(Fels~, Archit.)* overhang
[1]über|hängen *unr. itr. V.; südd., österr., schweiz. mit sein* ⟨*part of building*⟩ overhang; ⟨*branch*⟩ hang over; ⟨*rock face*⟩ form an overhang
[2]über|hängen *tr. V.* **sich *(Dat.)* eine Jacke**

~: put a jacket round one's shoulders; **sich** *(Dat.)* **das Gewehr/die Tasche ~:** hang *or* sling the rifle/bag over one's shoulder

Überhang·mandat das *(Politik) seat won in addition to the number a party has gained through proportional representation*

über·hasten *tr. V.* rush; **überhastet handeln** act hastily *or* hurriedly

über·häufen *tr. V.* **jmdn. mit etw. ~:** heap *or* shower sth. on sb.; **jmdn. mit Ratschlägen/Vorwürfen ~:** bombard sb. with advice/pour reproaches on sb.

überhaupt 1. *Adv.* **a)** *(insgesamt, im allgemeinen)* in general; **soweit es ~ Zweck hat** as far as there's any point in it at all; **~ fühlte er sich jetzt wohler** he felt better all round; **er ist ~ selten zu Hause** he's not at home much at all; **b)** *(meist bei Verneinungen: gar)* **~ nicht** not at all; **das ist ~ nicht wahr** that's not true at all; **~ keine Zeit haben** have no time at all; not have any time at all; **das kommt ~ nicht in Frage** it's quite *or* completely out of the question; **~ nichts** nothing at all; nothing what[so]ever; **wenn ~:** if at all; **wenn ~, dann komme ich morgen** if I come at all, it will be tomorrow; **c)** *(überdies, außerdem)* besides; **d)** *(besonders)* particularly. **2.** *Partikel* anyway; **wer sind Sie ~?** who are you anyway?; **wer hat dir das ~ gesagt?** who told you that anyway?; **was willst du hier ~?** what ar you doing here anyway?; **wie konnte das ~ passieren?** how could it happen in the first place?; **das klingt verlockend, aber haben wir ~ Geld dafür?** that sounds tempting, but have we got the money for it?; **wissen Sie ~, mit wem Sie reden?** do you realize who you're talking to?

über·heben *unr. refl. V.* **a)** *s.* **verheben; b)** *(überheblich sein)* be arrogant

überheblich [-'he:plıç] **1.** *Adj.* arrogant; supercilious ⟨*grin*⟩. **2.** *adv.* arrogantly; ⟨*grin*⟩ superciliously

Überheblichkeit die; ~: arrogance

über·heizen *tr. V.* overheat

über·hitzen *tr. V. (auch fig.)* overheat

über·höhen *tr. V.* raise ⟨*dike, embankment, etc.*⟩; bank ⟨*track, curve*⟩

überhöht [y:bɐ'hø:t] *Adj. (zu hoch)* excessive

[1]**über|holen 1.** *tr., itr. V.* **jmdn. ~:** ferry sb. across. **2.** *itr. V. (Seemannsspr.)* keel over

[2]**über·holen 1.** *tr. V.* **a)** overtake *(esp. Brit.)*; pass *(esp. Amer.)*; **b)** *(übertreffen)* outstrip; **c)** *(wieder instand setzen)* overhaul. **2.** *itr. V.* overtake *(esp. Brit.)*; pass *(esp. Amer.)*

Überhol: ~manöver das overtaking *(esp. Brit.) or (esp. Amer.)* passing manœuvre; **~spur die** overtaking lane *(esp. Brit.)*; pass lane *(esp. Amer.)*

überholt *Adj. (veraltet)* outdated; **durch etw. ~ sein** have become outdated as a result of sth.

Überholung die; ~, ~en overhaul; **der Wagen muß zur ~ in die Werkstatt** the car has to go into the garage for an overhaul

Überhol-: ~verbot das prohibition of overtaking; „~" 'no overtaking' *(esp. Brit.)*; 'no passing' *(Amer.)*; **hier besteht ~verbot** overtaking is prohibited here; **~vorgang der** overtaking *no art.*; **während des ~vorgangs** while overtaking

über·hören *tr. V.* not hear; **das möchte ich überhört haben** I'll pretend I didn't hear that

Über-Ich das *(Psych.)* super-ego

über·irdisch 1. *Adj.* **a)** *(himmlisch)* celestial; heavenly; *(übernatürlich)* supernatural; ethereal ⟨*beauty*⟩; **b)** *(veralt.) s.* **oberirdisch 1. 2.** *adv.* **a)** *(himmlisch)* celestially; *(übernatürlich)* supernaturally; ethereally ⟨*beautiful*⟩; **b)** *(veralt.) s.* **oberirdisch 2**

über·kandidelt [-kandi:dlt] *Adj. (ugs.)* affected

Über·kapazität die; *meist Pl. (Wirtsch.)* over-capacity *no pl.*

über|kippen *itr. V.; mit sein* tip over

über·kleben *tr. V.* **die alten Plakate mit neuen ~:** stick new posters over the old ones; **wir überklebten die Anschrift** we stuck something over the address; we covered the address by sticking something over it

über·klettern *tr. V.* climb over

über|kochen *itr. V.; mit sein (auch fig. ugs.)* boil over

[1]**über|kommen** *unr. itr. V.; mit sein (Seemannsspr.)* ⟨*water*⟩ wash over the deck; ⟨*wave*⟩ break over the side

[2]**über·kommen** *unr. tr. V.* **Mitleid/Ekel/Furcht überkam mich** I was overcome by pity/revulsion/fear; **ein Gefühl der Verlassenheit überkam sie** a feeling of desolation came over her

[3]**überkommen** *Adj. (geh.)* traditional

über·kompensieren[1] *tr. V. (bes. Psych., Wirtsch.)* over-compensate for

über·kreuzen 1. *tr. V. s.* **kreuzen 1a. 2.** *refl. V.* cross; **sich ~de Linien** intersecting lines

über|kriegen *tr. V. (ugs.)* **jmdn./etw. ~:** get fed up with sb./sth. *(coll.)*

über·kronen *tr. V. (Zahnmed.)* crown

über·krusten *tr. V.* **das Salz hatte den Boden überkrustet** the ground was encrusted with salt *or* covered with a crust of salt; **von Dreck überkrustete Stiefel** boots caked with dirt

[1]**über·laden** *unr. tr. V. (auch fig.)* overload

[2]**überladen** *Adj.* over-ornate ⟨*façade, style, etc.*⟩; overcrowded ⟨*shop window*⟩

über·lagern *tr. V.* **a)** overlie; *(fig.)* combine with; **sich ~:** combine; **von Sedimentschichten überlagertes Gestein** rock with overlying sedimentary strata; **sich ~de Gesteinsschichten** superimposed rock strata; **b)** *(Physik)* ⟨*wave*⟩ interfere with; ⟨*force, field*⟩ be superimposed on; **sich ~** ⟨*waves*⟩ interfere; ⟨*forces, fields*⟩ be superimposed

Über·lagerung die a) superposition; *(fig.)* combination; **b)** *(Physik) (von Wellen)* interference; *(von Kräften, Feldern)* superposition

Überland- [*od.* --'-]: **~bus der** country bus; **~leitung die** transmission line

über·lang *Adj.* unusually long

Über·länge die: ~ haben be unusually long; **eine Ladung mit ~:** a long load; „**wegen ~ geänderte Anfangszeiten**" 'starting times changed due to the unusually long running-time of the film'

über·lappen *tr. V. (auch fig.)* overlap

[1]**über|lassen** *unr. tr. V. (ugs.)* **etw. ~:** leave sth. over

[2]**über·lassen 1.** *unr. tr. V.* **a)** *(geben)* **jmdm. etw. ~:** let sb. have sth.; **er hat mir sein Auto übers Wochenende ~:** he let me use his car over the weekend; **er hat es mir billig ~:** he let me have it cheap; **b) jmdn. jmds. Fürsorge ~:** leave sb. in sb.'s care; **sich** *(Dat.)* **selbst ~ sein** be left to one's own devices; **c) etw. jmdm. ~** *(etw. jmdn. entscheiden/tun lassen)* leave sth. to sb.; **das bleibt [ganz] dir ~:** that's [entirely] up to you; **überlaß das bitte mir** let that be my concern; let me worry about that; **jmdm. alle Arbeit ~:** leave sb. to do all the work; **etw. dem Zufall ~:** leave sth. to chance; **d) jmdn. seinem Kummer ~:** leave sb. to cope with his/her grief alone. **2.** *unr. refl. V.* **sich der Leidenschaft/dem Gefühl/den Träumen** *usw.* **~:** abandon oneself to one's passions/emotions/dreams *etc.*

über·lasten *tr. V.* overload; overburden, overstretch ⟨*facilities, authorities*⟩; put too great a strain on ⟨*heart, circulation, etc.*⟩; strain ⟨*nerves*⟩; overstress ⟨*structure, material*⟩; overtax ⟨*person*⟩; *(mit Arbeit)* overwork ⟨*person*⟩; *(psychisch)* put too great a strain on ⟨*person*⟩

Überlastung die; ~, ~en *s.* **überlasten:** overloading; overstretching; straining; overstressing; overtaxing; overworking; **die ständige ~ führte schließlich zu seinem Zusammenbruch** the continuous strain he was under led eventually to collapse

Über·lauf der *(auch DV)* overflow

[1]**über|laufen** *unr. itr. V.; mit sein* **a)** ⟨*liquid, container*⟩ overflow; **b)** *(auf die gegnerische Seite überwechseln)* defect; ⟨*partisan*⟩ go over to the other side; **zum Feind/zu den Rebellen ~:** go over *or* desert to the enemy/the rebels

[2]**über·laufen** *unr. tr. V.* **a)** *(befallen)* seize; **ein Frösteln/Schauer überlief mich, es überlief mich [eis]kalt** a cold shiver ran down my spine; **es überlief sie heiß** a hot flush came over her; **b)** *(Sport: hinauslaufen über)* run past; **c)** *(Sport: umspielen)* run through, beat ⟨*defence*⟩

[3]**überlaufen** *Adj.* overcrowded; over-subscribed ⟨*course, subject*⟩; **der Arzt ist sehr ~:** the doctor's list is very full

Über·läufer der *(auch fig.)* defector

Überlauf·rohr das overflow pipe

über·laut 1. *Adj.* too loud *pred.*; over-loud ⟨*voice, laugh*⟩; ⟨*engine*⟩ too noisy *pred.* **2.** *adv.* too loudly

über·leben 1. *tr., auch itr. V.* survive; **das überleb' ich nicht!** I'll never get over it!; **du wirst es schon** *od.* **wohl ~** *(iron.)* you'll survive; **jmdn. ~:** survive *or* outlive sb. **(um** by). **2.** *refl. V.* become outdated *or* outmoded; **sich überlebt haben** have become outdated; have had its day; **überlebt** outdated; out-of-date

Über·lebende der/die; *adj. Dekl.* survivor

Überlebens·chance die chance of survival

über·lebens·groß *Adj.* larger than lifesize

Überlebens·training das survival training; **ein ~training** a survival-training course

[1]**über|legen 1.** *tr. V.* **a) jmdm. etw. ~:** put sth. over sb.; **b)** *(ugs.: verhauen)* **jmdn. ~:** put sb. over one's knee. **2.** *refl. V.* lean over; ⟨*ship*⟩ list

[2]**über·legen 1.** *tr. V.* consider; think over *or* about; **etw. noch einmal ~:** reconsider sth.; **das muß gut überlegt werden** that needs some careful consideration *or* thought; **es wäre zu ~, ob ...:** one might consider whether ...; **es sich anders ~:** change one's mind; **wenn ich es mir recht überlege, ...:** now I come to think of it, ...; **das hättest du dir auch vorher ~ können** you could have thought about that *or* given that some thought before. **2.** *itr. V.* think; reflect; **überleg doch mal!** think about it!; **ohne zu ~** *(unbedacht)* without thinking; *(spontan)* without a moment's thought; **ohne lange zu ~:** without much reflection; **laß mich mal ~:** let me think; **lange hin und her ~:** agonize for ages; **ich habe hin und her überlegt** I've turned it over and over in my mind; **am Überlegen sein, ob ...:** be thinking over whether ...

[3]**überlegen 1.** *Adj.* **a)** superior; clear, convincing ⟨*win, victory*⟩; **jmdm. ~ sein** be superior to sb. **(an** + *Dat.* in); **zahlenmäßig ~ sein** be superior in numbers; **b)** *(herablassend)* supercilious; superior. **2.** *adv.* **a)** in a superior manner; ⟨*play*⟩ much the better: ⟨*win, argue*⟩ convincingly; **b)** *(herablassend)* superciliously; superiorly

Überlegenheit die; ~ superiority

überlegt [y:bɐ'le:kt] **1.** *Adj.* carefully considered. **2.** *adv.* in a carefully considered way

Überlegung die; ~, ~en a) *o. Pl.* thought; reflection; **nach reiflicher ~:** on careful consideration; **mit ~ handeln** act in a con-

[1] *ich überkompensiere, überkompensiert, überzukompensieren*

sidered way; **einer ~ wert sein** be worth considering; **b)** *(Gedanke)* idea; **~en** *(Gedankengang)* thoughts; reflections; **~en zu etw. anstellen** give one's thoughts on sth.

über|leiten *itr. V.* **zum nächsten/zu einem neuen Thema ~** ⟨*speaker*⟩ move on to the next topic; **in etw.** *(Akk.)* **~:** lead into sth.; **in eine andere Tonart ~** ⟨*player*⟩ change key

Über·leitung die transition; **eine ~ zum nächsten Thema suchen** look for a way of moving on to the next subject

über·lesen *unr. tr. V.* overlook; miss

über·liefern *tr. V.* hand down; **überlieferte Sitten/Formen** *usw.* traditional customs/forms *etc.;* **in alten Chroniken ist überliefert, daß ...:** it is recorded in ancient chronicles that ...

Über·lieferung die a) *(etw. Überliefertes)* tradition; **schriftliche ~en** written records; **b)** *(Brauch)* tradition; custom; **c)** *o. Pl. (das Überliefern)* handing down

überlisten *tr. V.* outwit

überm *Präp. + Art.* = **über dem**

Über·macht die; *o. Pl.* superior strength; *(zahlenmäßig)* superior numbers *pl.;* **in der ~ sein, die ~ haben** be superior in strength/numbers

über·mächtig 1. *Adj.* **a)** superior; **b)** *(nicht mehr bezähmbar)* overpowering ⟨*desire, hatred, urge, etc.*⟩. **2.** *adv.* **~ loderte das Feuer der Leidenschaft in ihnen** the fire of passion blazed uncontrollably in them; **es zog ihn ~ in die Ferne** he felt an overpowering desire to travel

über·malen *tr. V.* **etw. ~:** paint sth. over

über·mannen *tr. V.* overcome

Über·maß das; *o. Pl.* excessive amount, excess (**an** + *Dat.* of); **ein ~ an Arbeit** *od.* **Arbeit im ~ haben** have an excessive amount of work *or* more than enough work; **etw. im ~ produzieren** produce sth. in excess; produce an excess of sth.

über·mäßig 1. *Adj.* **a)** excessive; **b)** *(Musik)* **ein ~es Intervall** an augmented interval. **2.** *adv.* excessively; **~ viel essen** eat to excess *or* excessively; **nicht ~ attraktiv** not especially attractive; **man braucht sich nicht mal ~ zu beeilen** you don't even need to hurry overmuch

Über·mensch der superman

über·menschlich *Adj.* superhuman; **er hat Übermenschliches geleistet** he has achieved the almost impossible

über·mitteln *tr. V.* send; *(als Mittler weitergeben)* pass on, convey ⟨*greetings, regards, etc.*⟩

Übermitt[e]lung die sending

über·morgen *Adv.* the day after tomorrow

über·müde *Adj.* overtired; exhausted

über·müden *tr. V.* overtire; **übermüdet** overtired; exhausted

Übermüdung die; ~: overtiredness; exhaustion

Über·mut der high spirits *pl.;* **etw. aus [lauter]** *od.* **im ~ tun** do sth. out of [pure] high spirits; **~ tut selten gut** *(Spr.)* high spirits mustn't get out of hand

übermütig ['y:bɐmy:tɪç] **1.** *Adj.* high-spirited; in high spirits *pred.;* **in ~er Stimmung** high-spirited; in high spirits. **2.** *adv.* high-spiritedly

übern *Präp. + Art.* = **über den**

über·nächst... *Adj.; nicht präd.* **im ~en Jahr, ~es Jahr** the year after next; **~e Woche** the week after next; **am ~en Tag** two days later; the next day but one; **~en Montag** a week on Monday; Monday week; **er wohnt im ~en Haus** he lives in the next house but one *or* lives two doors away

über·nachten *itr. V.* stay overnight; **bei jmdm. ~:** stay *or* spend the night at sb.'s house/flat *(Brit.) or (Amer.)* apartment *etc.;* **im Hotel ~:** stay the night at the hotel; **im Freien ~:** sleep in the open air

übernächtigt [y:bɐ'nɛçtɪçt] *Adj.* ⟨*person*⟩ tired *or* worn out [through lack of sleep]; tired ⟨*face, look, etc.*⟩

Übernachtung die; ~, ~en overnight stay; **~ und Frühstück** bed and breakfast; **sechs ~en kosten ...:** six nights cost ...

Übernahme ['y:bɐna:mə] **die; ~, ~n a)** *o. Pl. (von Waren, einer Sendung)* taking delivery *no art.; (des Staffelstabs)* receiving *no indef. art.; (einer Idee, eines Themas, von Methoden)* adoption, taking over *no indef. art.; (einer Praxis, eines Geschäfts, der Macht)* takeover; *(von Wörtern, Ausdrücken)* borrowing (**von** from); **er erklärt sich zur ~ der Kosten/des Falles bereit** he says he is prepared to meet the cost himself/to take on the case; **b)** *(etw. Übernommenes)* borrowing; *(Sendung)* re-broadcast; *(Live-Sendung)* relay

über·natürlich *Adj.* supernatural

über·nehmen 1. *unr. tr. V.* **a)** take delivery of ⟨*goods, consignment*⟩; receive ⟨*relay baton*⟩; take over ⟨*power, practice, business, building, school class*⟩; take on ⟨*job, position, task, role, case, leadership*⟩; undertake to pay ⟨*costs*⟩; **es ~, etw. zu tun** take on the job of doing sth.; **das laß mich ~:** let me do that; *s. auch* **Befehl b; Bürgschaft a; Garantie a; Gewähr; Kommando b; ¹Steuer; Verantwortung a; Verpflichtung a; b)** *(bei sich einstellen)* take on ⟨*staff*⟩; **c)** *(Seemannsspr.: an Bord nehmen)* take on board; **d)** *(sich zu eigen machen)* adopt, take over ⟨*ideas, methods, subject, etc.*⟩ (**von** from); borrow ⟨*word, phrase*⟩ (**von** from); **eine Textstelle wörtlich ~:** use a passage verbatim; **das ZDF hat die Sendung vom britischen Fernsehen übernommen** the programme was retransmitted/*(als Live-Sendung)* relayed from British television by ZDF; **e)** *(österr. ugs.) s.* **übertölpeln. 2.** *unr. refl. V.* overdo things *or* it; **er hat sich beim Training übernommen** he overdid things *or* it [while] training; **sich mit etw. ~:** take on too much with sth.; **übernimm dich nur nicht** *(iron.)* don't strain yourself!

über|ordnen *tr. V.* **a) etw. einer Sache** *(Dat.)* **~:** give sth. precedence over sth.; **b) jmdn. jmdm. ~:** place sb. above sb.; *s. auch* **übergeordnet 2**

über·örtlich *(Amtsspr.)* **1.** *Adj.* regional. **2.** *adv.* regionally

über·parteilich 1. *Adj.* non-party *attrib.;* **ein ~es Komitee** an all-party committee; **das Amt des Bundespräsidenten ist ~:** the office of Federal President is *or* stands above party politics. **2.** *adv.* in a non-partisan way

über·pinseln *tr. V. (ugs.)* paint over

Über·produktion die *(Wirtsch., Med.)* over-production

über·prüfbar *Adj.* checkable; **die Angaben waren nicht ~:** the details could not be checked

über·prüfen *tr. V.* **a)** check (**auf** + *Akk.* for); check [over], inspect, examine ⟨*machine, device*⟩; check, inspect, examine ⟨*papers, luggage*⟩; review ⟨*issue, situation, results*⟩; *(Finanzw.)* examine, inspect ⟨*accounts, books*⟩; **b)** *(überdenken)* think over; consider; **etw. noch mal ~:** think sth. over again; reconsider sth.

Über·prüfung die a) *o. Pl. s.* **überprüfen a:** checking *no indef. art.* (**auf** + *Akk.* for); checking [over] *no indef. art.;* inspection; examination; **b)** *(Kontrolle)* check; *(des Ausweises, der Geschäftsbücher)* examination; inspection; *(einer Lage, Frage, der Ergebnisse)* review; **c)** *(das Überdenken)* consideration; **erneute ~:** reconsideration

über|quellen *unr. itr. V.; mit sein* **a)** spill over; **b)** *(zu voll sein)* be brimming; **die Tribüne quoll von Zuschauern über** *(fig.)* the stand was overflowing with spectators

über·queren *tr. V.* cross; *(schneiden)* cut across; cross

¹über|ragen *itr. V.* jut out; project

²über·ragen *tr. V.* **a)** *(hinausragen über)* **jmdn./etw. ~:** tower above sb./sth.; **jmdn. um Kopfeslänge ~:** be a head taller than sb.; **der Berg überragt die Ebene** the mountain towers over the plain; **b)** *(übertreffen)* **jmdn. an etw.** *(Dat.)* **~:** be head and shoulders above sb. in sth.

überragend 1. *Adj.* outstanding. **2.** *adv.* outstandingly

überraschen *tr. V.* surprise; ⟨*storm, earthquake*⟩ take by surprise; *(durch einen Angriff)* take by surprise; catch unawares; **jmdn. beim Rauchen/Stehlen ~:** catch sb. smoking/stealing; **jmdn. überrascht ansehen** look at sb. in surprise; **überrascht tun** pretend to be surprised; **lassen wir uns ~:** let's wait and see; **vom Gewitter/vom Regen überrascht werden** be caught in the thunderstorm/caught [out] in the rain

überraschend 1. *Adj.* surprising; surprise *attrib.* ⟨*attack, visit*⟩; *(unerwartet)* unexpected. **2.** *adv.* surprisingly; *(unerwartet)* unexpectedly; **die Nachricht kam ~:** the news came as a surprise

überraschender·weise *Adv.* surprisingly; *(unerwartet)* unexpectedly

Überraschung die; ~, ~en surprise; **zu meiner [großen] ~:** to my [great] surprise; **für eine ~ sorgen** cause a surprise; **jmdm. eine kleine ~ mitbringen** bring sb. a little something as a surprise

Überraschungs·moment das element of surprise

über·reden *tr. V.* persuade; **jmdn. ~, etw. zu tun** persuade sb. to do sth.; talk sb. into doing sth.; **jmdn. zum Mitmachen/zu einer Fahrt ~:** persuade sb. to take part/make a journey; talk sb. into taking part/making a journey; **ich habe mich zum Kauf eines neuen Autos ~ lassen** I was persuaded to buy *or* was talked into buying a new car

Überredung die; ~: persuasion

Überredungs·kunst die powers *pl.* of persuasion

über·regional 1. *Adj.* national ⟨*newspaper, radio station*⟩; **eine Angelegenheit von ~er Bedeutung** a matter of more than just regional importance; **~e Veranstaltungen** events involving several regions. **2.** *adv.* nationally; **~ bekannt werden** become known outside one's/its own region

über·reich 1. *Adj.* lavish ⟨*meal, decoration*⟩; abundant, very rich ⟨*harvest*⟩; **~ an Bodenschätzen sein** be very rich in mineral resources; **eine an Ereignissen ~e Zeit** an extremely eventful time; **in ~em Maß vorhanden sein** be there in great quantity. **2.** *adv.* **jmdn. ~ beschenken/belohnen** lavish gifts on sb./reward sb. lavishly; **~ verziert sein** be lavishly decorated

über·reichen *tr. V.* **[jmdm.] etw. ~:** present sth. [to sb.]

über·reichlich 1. *Adj.* over-ample; **etw. ist in ~er Fülle vorhanden** there is an over-abundance of sth. **2.** *adv.* over-amply

Überreichung die; ~: presentation

über·reif *Adj.* over-ripe

über·reizen 1. *tr. V.* **a)** overtax ⟨*person*⟩; overstrain ⟨*eyes, nerves, etc.*⟩; **[nervlich] überreizt** overwrought; **b)** *(bes. Skat)* overbid ⟨*hand*⟩. **2.** *refl. V. (bes. Skat)* overbid

Überreiztheit die; ~: *s.* **überreizen 1:** overtaxed/-strained/-wrought state

Über·reizung die *s.* **überreizen 1:** overtaxing; overstraining; **ein Zeichen nervöser ~:** a sign of nervous strain

über·rennen *unr. tr. V.* **a)** *(Milit.)* overrun; **b)** *(umrennen)* run down

über·repräsentiert *Adj.* over-represented

Über·rest der; *meist Pl.* remnant; **~e** *(eines Gebäudes)* remains; ruins; *(einer Mahlzeit)* left-overs; **die sterblichen ~e** *(geh. verhüll.)* the mortal remains

Überroll·bügel der roll-bar

über·rollen *tr. V.* **a)** *(Milit.)* overrun; *(fig.)*

overwhelm ‹person›; ‹fashion, craze› sweep through ‹country›; **b)** *(hinwegrollen über)* run down
über·rụmpeln *tr. V.* **jmdn. ~:** take sb. by surprise; *(bei einem Angriff)* catch sb. unawares; take sb. by surprise; **jmdn. mit etw. ~:** surprise sb. with sth.; take sb. by surprise with sth.
Überrụmp[e]lung die; ~, ~en surprise attack
über·rụnden *tr. V.* **a)** *(Sport)* lap; **b)** *(übertreffen)* outstrip
übers *Präp. + Art.* **a) = über das; b) ~ Jahr** one year later
übersät [y:bɐˈzɛ:t] *Adj.* **mit** *od.* **von etw. ~ sein** be covered with sth.; *(abwertend)* be strewn with sth.; **mit** *od.* **von Sternen ~:** star-studded; studded with stars *postpos.*
über·sạttigen *tr. V.* supersaturate ‹solution›; glut ‹market›; satiate ‹public›
Überschall-: ~flugzeug das supersonic aircraft; **~geschwindigkeit die** supersonic speed
über·schạtten *tr. V.* overshadow; cast its/their shadow over; *(fig.)* cast a shadow over
über·schạ̈tzen *tr. V.* overestimate; overrate ‹writer, performer, book, performance, talent, ability›
Über·schạ̈tzung die *s.* **überschätzen:** overestimation; overrating
überschaubar *Adj.* **eine ~e Menge/Zahl** a manageable quantity/number; **das sind ~e Größen** these are quantities one can grasp; **das Risiko ist nicht ~:** the risks cannot be calculated; **ein ~er Zeitraum/~es Gebiet** a reasonably short period/small area
über·schauen *tr. V. s.* **²übersehen a, b**
über|schäumen *itr. V.; mit sein* froth over; **~de Begeisterung** bubbling enthusiasm
über·schlafen *unr. tr. V.* sleep on ‹matter, problem, etc.›
Über·schlag der a) rough calculation *or* estimate; **b)** *(Turnen)* handspring; *(am Barren)* forward roll; **c)** *s.* **Looping**
¹über|schlagen 1. *unr. tr. V.* **die Beine ~:** cross one's legs; **mit übergeschlagenen Beinen** with [one's] legs crossed. **2.** *unr. itr. V.; mit sein* ‹wave› break; ‹spark› jump
²über·schlagen 1. *unr. tr. V.* **a)** *(auslassen)* skip ‹chapter, page, etc.›; **b)** *(ungefähr berechnen)* calculate *or* estimate roughly; make a rough calculation *or* estimate of. **2.** *unr. refl. V.* **a)** go head over heels; ‹car› turn over; **sich vor Höflichkeit ~** *(fig.)* fall over oneself to be polite *(coll.)*; **b)** ‹voice› crack; **c)** ‹events, reports, etc.› come thick and fast; **die Gedanken überschlugen sich in meinem Kopf** the thoughts raced round and round in my head
³überschlagen *Adj. (bes. md.)* lukewarm ‹liquid›; moderately warm ‹room›
überschlägig [-ʃlɛ:gɪç] **1.** *Adj.* [roughly] estimated; rough, approximate ‹estimate›. **2.** *adv.* ‹calculate, estimate› roughly, approximately
über|schnappen *itr. V.; mit sein* **a)** *(ugs.: den Verstand verlieren)* go crazy; go round the bend *(coll.)*; **b)** *(ugs.: sich überschlagen)* ‹voice› crack
über·schneiden *unr. refl. V.* ‹lines, rays› cross, intersect; *(fig.)* ‹problems, areas of responsibility, events, etc.› overlap
Überschneidung die; ~, ~en *s.* **überschneiden:** intersection; *(fig.)* overlapping
über·schreiben *unr. tr. V.* **a)** entitle; head ‹chapter, section›; **b)** *(übertragen)* **etw. jmdm.** *od.* **auf jmdn. ~:** transfer sth. to sb.; make sth. over to sb.
über·schreien *unr. tr. V.* shout down
über·schreiten *unr. itr. V.* **a)** cross; *(fig.)* pass; **Überschreiten der Gleise verboten!** do not cross the line!; **er hat die Siebzig überschritten** *(fig.)* he is past seventy; **b)** *(hinausgehen über)* exceed ‹authority, powers, budget, speed, limit, deadline, etc.›; **das überschreitet jedes Maß** that's going too far; **die Grenzen des Erlaubten ~:** go beyond what is permissible
Über·schrift die heading; *(in einer Zeitung)* headline; *(Titel)* title
Über·schuh der overshoe; galosh *usu. pl. (Brit.)*
über·schuldet *Adj.* heavily indebted ‹person, firm, country›; heavily mortgaged ‹house, property, etc.›; **hoffnungslos ~ sein** ‹person› be hopelessly in debt
Überschuldung die; ~, ~en heavy indebtedness
Über·schuß der surplus (**an +** *Dat.* of)
überschüssig [ˈy:bɐʃʏsɪç] *Adj.* surplus
¹über|schütten *tr. V. (ugs.)* spill
²über·schütten *tr. V.* cover; **jmdn./etw. mit Wasser ~:** throw water over sb./sth.; **jmdn. mit Vorwürfen/Lob/Ehrungen ~:** heap reproach/praise/honours on sb.; **jmdn. mit Fragen ~:** fire questions at sb.; **jmdn. mit Geschenken/Geld ~:** shower sb. with presents/lavish money on sb.
Überschwang der; ~[e]s exuberance; **im ~ der Begeisterung** in one's exuberant enthusiasm; **im ~ der Gefühle** out of sheer exuberance
über|schwappen *itr. V.; mit sein* ‹liquid, container› slop over
über·schwemmen *tr. V. (auch fig.)* flood; **von Touristen überschwemmt werden** *(fig.)* be flooded *or* swamped with tourists; **den Markt mit Waren ~** *(fig.)* flood *or* swamp the market/with goods
Überschwemmung die; ~, ~en flood; *(das Überschwemmen)* flooding *no pl.*; **zu ~en führen** lead to flooding *or* floods
Überschwemmungs-: ~gebiet das flood area; **~ gefahr die** the danger of flooding; **~ katastrophe die** disastrous floods *pl.*
über·schwenglich [-ʃvɛŋlɪç] **1.** *Adj.* effusive ‹words, manner, etc.›; wild ‹joy, enthusiasm›. **2.** *adv.* effusively
Überschwenglichkeit die; ~: effusiveness
Über·see *o. Art.* **aus** *od.* **von ~:** from overseas; **in ~ leben** live overseas; **nach ~ auswandern** emigrate overseas; **Exporte/Post nach ~:** overseas exports/mail; **Besitzungen in ~:** overseas possessions
Übersee-: ~dampfer der ocean-going steamer; **~gebiet das** overseas territory; **Britische ~gebiete** British territories overseas; **~hafen der** international port; **~handel der** overseas trade
überseeisch [ˈy:bɐze:ɪʃ] *Adj.; nicht präd.* overseas
Übersee-: ~kabel das transoceanic cable; **~koffer der** cabin trunk
übersehbar *Adj. (abschätzbar)* assessable; **der Schaden ist noch nicht ~:** the damage cannot yet be assessed
¹über|sehen *unr. refl. V. (ugs.)* **sich** *(Dat.)* **etw. ~:** get fed up *(coll.) or* tired of seeing sth.; **diese Tapete habe ich mir übergesehen** I'm fed up with the sight of this wallpaper
²über·sehen *unr. tr. V.* **a)** look out over; *(fig.)* survey ‹subject›; **man kann von hier die ganze Bucht ~:** you can look [right] out over the whole bay from here; **etw. gut** *od.* **leicht ~ können** have a good view of sth.; **b)** *(abschätzen)* assess ‹damage, situation, consequences, etc.›; **c)** *(nicht sehen)* overlook; miss; miss ‹turning, signpost›; **mit seinen roten Haaren ist er nicht zu ~:** you can't miss him with his red hair; **d)** *(ignorieren)* ignore
über·senden *unr. (auch regelm.) tr. V.* send; remit, send ‹money›; **die übersandten Waren sind fehlerhaft** the goods sent are faulty; **anbei übersende ich Ihnen ...:** please find enclosed ...
Über·sendung die sending; *(von Geld)* remittance; sending
übersetzbar *Adj.* translatable; **schwer/leicht ~ sein** be difficult/easy to translate
¹über|setzen 1. *tr. V.* ferry over. **2.** *itr. V.; auch mit sein* cross [over]
²über·setzen *tr., itr. V. (auch fig.)* translate; **etw. ins Deutsche/aus dem Deutschen ~:** translate sth. into/from German
Über·setzer der, Übersetzerin die; ~, ~nen translator; *s. auch* **-in**
übersetzt *Adj.* **a)** *(bes. schweiz.: überhöht)* excessive; **b)** *(Technik)* **hoch/niedrig ~ sein** have a high/low transmission ratio
Übersetzung die; ~, ~en a) translation; **b)** *(Technik)* transmission ratio
Übersetzungs-: ~büro das translation agency; **~fehler der** translation error
Über·sicht die a) *o. Pl.* overall view, overview (**über +** *Akk.* of); **die ~ [über etw.** *(Akk.)***] verlieren** lose track [of sth.]; **b)** *(Darstellung)* survey; *(Tabelle)* summary
über·sichtlich 1. *Adj.* clear; ‹crossroads› which allows a clear view. **2.** *adv.* clearly
Übersichtlichkeit die; ~: clarity; *(einer Kreuzung)* clear lay-out
Übersichts·karte die outline map
¹über|siedeln, ²über·siedeln *itr. V.; mit sein* move (**nach** to)
Über·sied[e]lung [*od.* --ˈ-(-)-] **die** move (**nach** to)
Über·siedler der *German native moving to the Federal Republic from East Germany*
über·sinnlich *Adj.* supersensory; *(übernatürlich)* supernatural
über·spannen *tr. V.* **a)** *(bespannen)* cover; **b)** *(zu stark spannen)* over-tension, overtighten ‹string, cable›; overdraw ‹bow›; over-tension ‹spring›; *s. auch* **Bogen c; c)** *(sich spannen über)* span ‹river, valley, etc.›
überspannt *Adj.* exaggerated ‹ideas, behaviour, gestures›; extreme ‹views›; inflated ‹demands, expectations›
über·spielen *tr. V.* **a)** *(hinweggehen über)* cover up; cover up, gloss over ‹mistake›; smooth over ‹difficult situation›; **b)** *(aufnehmen)* **[auf ein Tonband] ~:** transfer ‹record› to tape; put ‹record› on tape; **[auf ein anderes Tonband] ~:** transfer to another tape; **c)** *(Funkw., Ferns.)* transfer; **d)** *(Sport)* outplay; **die Abwehr ~:** beat the defence
über·spitzen *tr. V.* **etw. ~:** push *or* carry sth. too far; **überspitzt ausgedrückt, könnte man sagen, daß ...:** to exaggerate, one might say that ...
über·sprechen *unr. tr. V.* **etw. ~:** talk *or* speak over sth.
¹über|springen *unr. itr. V.; mit sein* **a)** ‹spark, fire› jump across; **seine Begeisterung sprang auf uns alle über** *(fig.)* his enthusiasm communicated itself to all of us; **b)** *(unvermittelt übergehen zu)* **auf etw.** *(Akk.)* **~:** switch abruptly to sth.
²über·springen *unr. tr. V.* **a)** jump ‹obstacle›; **b)** *(auslassen)* miss out; skip; **eine Klasse ~:** jump a class
über|sprudeln *itr. V.; mit sein (auch fig.)* bubble over (**von** with)
über·spülen *tr. V.* ‹water, waves› wash over; **bei Flut überspült** covered at high tide
über·staatlich *Adj.* supranational
¹über|stehen *unr. itr. V.; südd., österr., schweiz. mit sein* jut out; project
²über·stehen *unr. tr. V.* come through ‹danger, war, operation›; get over ‹illness›; withstand ‹heat, strain›; ‹boat› weather, ride out ‹storm›; *(überleben)* survive; **das Schlimmste ist jetzt überstanden** we're/they're *etc.* over the worst; the worst is over; **nach überstandener Gefahr** when the danger was over; **das hätten wir** *od.* **das wäre überstanden** that's 'that over with
über·steigen *unr. tr. V.* **a)** climb over; **b)** *(fig.: hinausgehen über)* exceed; **jmds. Fähigkeiten/Kräfte/Mittel ~:** be beyond sb.'s abilities/strength/means; **das übersteigt meinen Horizont** that's above my head

über·steigern *tr. V.* push up ⟨*demands, speed*⟩ too far *or* high; **ein übersteigertes Ehrgefühl** an exaggerated sense of honour
Über·steigerung die excessive increase; *(einer Forderung)* excessive pushing-up
über·stellen *tr. V.* transfer ⟨*convict*⟩; *(an Gericht, Polizei)* hand over (**an** + *Akk.* to)
über·steuern 1. *tr. V. (Elektrot.)* overdrive. **2.** *itr. V. (Kfz-W.)* ⟨*vehicle*⟩ oversteer
über·stimmen *tr. V.* outvote
über·strahlen *tr. V.* **a)** *(geh.)* light up; illuminate; **Freude überstrahlte sein Gesicht** *(fig.)* his face lit up with joy; **b)** *(fig.: in den Schatten stellen)* outshine
überstrapazieren[1] *tr. V.* overtax ⟨*person*⟩; overstrain ⟨*nerves*⟩; make excessive demands on ⟨*patience, willingness*⟩; treat ⟨*car*⟩ too roughly; **das Prinzip wird überstrapaziert** the principle is overworked
über·streichen *unr. tr. V.* paint over
über|streifen *tr. V.* **[sich** *(Dat.)***] etw. ~:** slip sth. on
[1]**über|strömen** *itr. V.; mit sein* **a)** *(über den Rand strömen)* overflow; **er strömt über vor Glück/Dankbarkeit** *(fig.)* he is brimming *or* bursting with happiness/gratitude; **b)** *(geh.: übergehen)* ⟨*mood, feeling, etc.*⟩ communicate itself, spread (**auf** + *Akk.* to)
[2]**über·strömen** *tr. V.* flood; **von Tränen/Blut überströmt [sein]** [be] streaming with tears/blood; **eine Welle des Glücks überströmte ihn** *(fig.)* a wave of happiness flooded over him
über|stülpen *tr. V.* pull on ⟨*hat etc.*⟩
Über·stunde die: er hat eine ~/drei ~n gearbeitet he did one hour's/three hours' overtime; **~n machen** *od.* **leisten** *od. (salopp)* **schieben** do overtime
Überstunden·zuschlag der overtime supplement; **der ~ beträgt 50%** overtime is paid at time and a half
über·stürzen 1. *tr. V.* rush; **nur nichts ~:** don't rush things; take it easy. **2.** *refl. V.* rush; *(rasch aufeinanderfolgen)* ⟨*events, news, etc.*⟩ come thick and fast; **sich bei etw. ~:** rush sth.
überstürzt 1. *Adj.* hurried ⟨*escape, departure*⟩; over-hasty ⟨*decision*⟩. **2.** *adv.* ⟨*decide, act*⟩ over-hastily; ⟨*depart*⟩ hurriedly
über·tariflich 1. *Adj.* **~e Bezahlung/Zulagen** payment/bonuses above agreed rates. **2.** *adv.* **jmdn. ~ bezahlen** pay sb. above agreed rates
über·teuert *Adj.* over-expensive
übertölpeln *tr. V.* dupe; con *(coll.)*
Übertölpelung die; ~, ~en duping; conning *(coll.)*
über·tönen *tr. V.* drown out
Über·topf der [decorative] outer pot
Übertrag ['y:bɐtra:k] **der; ~[e]s, Überträge** [-trɛ:gə] *(bes. Buchf.)* carry-over
über·tragbar *Adj.* transferable (**auf** + *Akk.* to); *(auf etw. anderes anwendbar)* applicable (**auf** + *Akk.* to); *(übersetzbar)* translatable; *(ansteckend)* communicable, infectious ⟨*disease*⟩
über·tragen 1. *unr. tr. V.* **a)** transfer (**auf** + *Akk.* to); transmit ⟨*power, torque, etc.*⟩ (**auf** + *Akk.* to); communicate ⟨*disease, illness*⟩ (**auf** + *Akk.* to); carry over ⟨*subtotal*⟩; *(auf etw. anderes anwenden)* apply (**auf** + *Akk.* to); *(übersetzen)* translate; render; **ein Stenogramm in Langschrift ~:** write a piece of shorthand out in longhand; *(mit der Schreibmaschine)* type out a piece of shorthand; **eine Erzählung in Verse ~:** put a story into verse; **etw. ins reine** *od.* **in die Reinschrift ~:** make a fair copy of sth.; **etw. in ein Heft ~:** copy sth. out into a book; **seine Begeisterung** *usw.* **auf jmdn. ~:** communicate one's enthusiasm *etc.* to sb.; **etw. vom** *od.* **aus dem Englischen ins Deutsche ~:** translate sth. from English into German; **in ~er Bedeutung, im ~en Sinne** in a transferred sense; **b)** *(senden)* broadcast ⟨*concert, event, match, etc.*⟩; *(im Fernsehen)* televise; **etw. direkt** *or* **live ~:** broadcast/televise sth. live; **etw. im Fernsehen ~:** televise sth.; **c)** *(geben)* **jmdm. Aufgaben/Pflichten** *usw.* **~:** hand over tasks/duties *etc.* to sb.; *(anvertrauen)* entrust sb. with tasks/duties *etc.*; **jmdm. ein Recht ~:** confer a right on sb.; **d)** *(Med.: zu lange nicht gebären)* **sie hat ihr Kind ~:** she had a post-term birth; **ein ~es Kind** a post-term infant. **2.** *refl. V.* **sich auf jmdn. ~** ⟨*disease, illness*⟩ be communicated *or* be passed on to sb.; *(fig.)* ⟨*enthusiasm, nervousness, etc.*⟩ communicate itself to sb.
Über·träger der *(Med.)* carrier
Übertragung die; ~, ~en a) *s.* **übertragen 1 a:** transference; transmission; communication; carrying over; application; translation; rendering; **die ~ einer Erzählung in Verse** putting a story into verse; **die ~ der Krankheit erfolgt über das Trinkwasser** the disease is spread through drinking-water; **b)** *(das Senden)* broadcasting; *(Programm, Sendung)* broadcast; *(im Fernsehen)* televising/television broadcast; **c)** *(von Aufgaben, Pflichten usw.)* entrusting; *(von Rechten)* conferral; **d)** *(Med.: eines Kindes)* post-term birth
Übertragungs·wagen der outside broadcast vehicle; OB vehicle
über·trainiert *Adj.* overtrained
über·treffen *unr. tr. V.* **a)** surpass, outdo (**an** + *Dat.* in); break ⟨*record*⟩; **jmdn. an Ausdauer ~:** be superior to sb. in stamina; **jmdn. an Fleiß/Intelligenz ~:** be more diligent/intelligent than sb.; **jmdn. in einem Fach/einem Sport ~:** be better than sb. at a subject/a sport; **in etw.** *(Dat.)* **nicht zu ~ sein** be unbeatable at sth.; **sich selbst ~:** excel oneself; **b)** *(übersteigen)* exceed; exceed, surpass ⟨*expectations*⟩
über·treiben *unr. tr. V.* **a)** *auch itr.* exaggerate; **b)** *(zu weit treiben)* overdo; take *or* carry too far; take *or* push ⟨*claim, demand*⟩ too far; **es mit etw. ~:** take *or* carry sth. too far; **man kann es auch ~:** you can take things *or* go too far
Übertreibung die; ~, ~en exaggeration; **er neigt zu ~en** he tends to exaggerate
[1]**über|treten** *unr. itr. V.; mit sein* **a)** *auch mit haben (Sport)* step over the line/step out of the circle; **b)** *(überwechseln)* change sides; **zu einer anderen Partei ~:** join another party; switch parties; **[von der KPD] zur SPD ~:** switch [from the KPD] to the SPD; **zum Katholizismus/Islam ~:** convert to Catholicism/Islam; **c)** *(gelangen)* **in etw.** *(Akk.)* **~:** enter sth.
[2]**über·treten** *unr. tr. V.* break, contravene ⟨*law*⟩; infringe, violate ⟨*regulation, prohibition*⟩
Übertretung die; ~, ~en a) *s.* [2]**übertreten:** breaking; contravention; infringement; violation; **b)** *(Vergehen)* misdemeanour
Übertretungs·fall der: im ~[e] *(Amtsspr.)* if the law is contravened; in the event of an infringement *or* a violation
übertrieben [-tri:bn] **1.** *2. Part. v.* **übertreiben. 2.** exaggerated; *(übermäßig)* excessive ⟨*care, thrift, etc.*⟩; **das finde ich reichlich ~:** I really think that's going too far. **3.** *adv.* excessively
Über·tritt der change of allegiance, switch (**zu** to); *(Rel.)* conversion (**zu** to)
über·trumpfen *tr. V.* **a)** *(Kartenspiel)* trump; **b)** *(übertreffen)* outdo
über·tünchen *tr. V.* cover with whitewash; *(fig.)* cover up
über·übermorgen *Adv.* in three days' time
übervölkern [-'fœlkɐn] *tr. V.* over-populate
Übervölkerung die; ~: over-population
über·voll *Adj.* overfull; overcrowded, packed ⟨*room, train, tram, etc.*⟩; packed ⟨*theatre, cinema*⟩
über·vorsichtig 1. *Adj.* over-cautious. **2.** *adv.* over-cautiously
über·vor·teilen *tr. V.* cheat
über·wachen *tr. V.* watch, keep under surveillance ⟨*suspect, agent, area, etc.*⟩; supervise ⟨*factory, workers, process*⟩; control ⟨*traffic*⟩; monitor ⟨*progress, production process, experiment, patient*⟩; **die Polizei überwacht sein Telefon** the police are monitoring his telephone calls; **er überwacht jeden ihrer Schritte** he watches her every move
über·wachsen *unr. tr. V.* overgrow
Überwachung die; ~, ~en *s.* **überwachen:** surveillance; supervision; controlling; monitoring
überwältigen [-'vɛltɪgn̩] *tr. V.* **a)** overpower; **b)** *(fig.)* ⟨*sleep, emotion, fear, etc.*⟩ overcome; ⟨*sight, impressions, beauty, etc.*⟩ overwhelm; **von Rührung überwältigt werden** be overcome with emotion
überwältigend 1. *Adj.* overwhelming ⟨*sight, impression, victory, majority, etc.*⟩; overpowering ⟨*smell*⟩; stunning ⟨*beauty*⟩; **das ist nicht [gerade] ~:** that isn't [exactly] anything to write home about *(coll.)*. **2.** *adv.* stunningly ⟨*beautiful*⟩; **das hat er ~ gespielt** he played that quite magnificently
über·wälzen *tr. V. (bes. Wirtsch.)* pass on ⟨*costs etc.*⟩ (**auf** + *Akk.* to); shift ⟨*burden, blame, responsibility*⟩ (**auf** + *Akk.* on to)
über|wechseln *itr. V.; mit sein* **a)** cross over (**auf** + *Akk.* to); **auf eine andere Spur ~:** change lanes; move to another lane; **b)** *(übertreten)* change sides; **ins feindliche Lager/zur anderen Partei ~:** go over to the enemy/the other party; **von der SPD zur KPD ~:** switch from the SPD to the KPD; **c)** *(mit etw. anderem beginnen)* **zu etw. ~:** change over to sth.; **zu einem anderen Thema ~:** turn to another topic; **aufs Gymnasium ~:** go on to grammar school
über·weisen *unr. tr. V.* **a)** transfer ⟨*money*⟩ (**an, auf** + *Akk.* to); **er bekommt sein Gehalt [auf sein Konto] überwiesen** his salary is paid into his account; **b)** *(zu einem anderen Arzt schicken)* refer (**an** + *Akk.* to); **jmdn. in die Klinik ~:** refer sb. to the clinic; **c)** *(zuleiten)* refer ⟨*proposal*⟩ (**an** + *Akk.* to); pass on ⟨*file, application*⟩ (**an** + *Akk.* to)
Über·weisung die a) *o. Pl.* transfer (**an, auf** + *Akk.* to); **b)** *(Summe)* remittance; **c)** *(eines Patienten)* referral (**an** + *Akk.* to); **d)** *s.* **Überweisungsschein**
Überweisungs-: ~auftrag der *(Bankw.)* [credit] transfer order; **~formular das** *(Bankw.)* [credit] transfer form; **~schein der** *(Med.)* certificate of referral
Über·weite die outsize; **Röcke in ~n** outsize skirts
[1]**über|werfen** *unr. tr. V.* throw on ⟨*clothes*⟩; **er warf dem Pferd eine Decke über** he threw a blanket over the horse
[2]**über·werfen** *unr. refl. V.* **sich mit jmdm. ~:** fall out with sb.; **sie haben sich überworfen** they have fallen out
über·wiegen 1. *unr. itr. V.* predominate; **es überwog die Einsicht, daß ...:** the recognition prevailed that ... **2.** *unr. tr. V.* ⟨*advantages, disadvantages, etc.*⟩ outweigh; ⟨*emotion, argument*⟩ prevail over
überwiegend 1. [*auch* --'--] *Adj.* overwhelming; **der ~e Teil der Bevölkerung** the majority of the population. **2.** *adv.* mainly
über·winden 1. *unr. tr. V.* **a)** overcome ⟨*resistance*⟩; overcome, surmount ⟨*difficulty, obstacle, gradient*⟩; conquer ⟨*capitalism, apartheid, etc.*⟩; overcome, get over ⟨*fear, inhibitions, disappointment, grief*⟩; get past ⟨*stage*⟩; **b)** *(aufgeben)* overcome ⟨*doubt, misgivings, reservations, suspicions*⟩; give up ⟨*way of thinking, point of view*⟩; **c)**

---
[1] *ich überstrapaziere, überstrapaziert, überzustrapazieren*

(geh.: besiegen) overcome; vanquish *(literary)*. **2.** *unr. refl. V.* overcome one's reluctance; **sich [dazu] ~, etw. zu tun** bring oneself to do sth.; **ich konnte mich nur schwer [dazu] ~, es zu tun** I could hardly bring myself to do it; **dazu konnte ich mich nicht ~**: I could not bring myself to do that

Über·windung die a) *s.* **überwinden 1a**: overcoming; surmounting; conquest; getting over/past; **b)** *(Besiegung)* overcoming; vanquishing *(literary)*; **c)** *(das Sichüberwinden)* **es war eine große ~ für ihn** it cost him a great effort; **das hat mich viel ~ gekostet** that was a real effort of will for me

über·wintern 1. *itr. V.* [over]winter; spend the winter. **2.** *tr. V.* overwinter ⟨*plant*⟩

über·wölben *tr. V.* arch over

über·wuchern *tr. V.* overgrow

Über·wurf der a) *(Umhang)* wrap; **b)** *(österr.) s.* **Zierdecke; c)** *(Ringen)* shoulder throw

Über·zahl die; *o. Pl.* majority; **in der ~ sein** be in the majority; ⟨*army, enemy*⟩ be superior in numbers

überzählig [-tsɛlɪç] *Adj.* surplus; spare; **einige Damen waren ~**: there were a few ladies too many

über·zeichnen *tr. V.* **a)** *(Börsenw.)* oversubscribe; **b)** *(zugespitzt darstellen)* overdraw ⟨*figure, character, etc.*⟩

Über·zeit die *(schweiz.)* overtime

überzeugen 1. *tr. V.* convince; *(umstimmen)* persuade; convince; **jmdn. von etw. ~**: convince/persuade sb. of sth. **2.** *itr. V.* be convincing. **3.** *refl. V.* convince *or* satisfy oneself; **sich persönlich** *od.* **mit eigenen Augen [von etw.] ~**: see [sth.] for oneself

überzeugend 1. *Adj.* convincing; convincing, persuasive ⟨*arguments, proof, words, speech*⟩. **2.** *adv.* convincingly; ⟨*argue, speak*⟩ convincingly, persuasively

überzeugt *Adj.* **a)** *nicht präd.* convinced; **b) von etw. ~ sein** *(etw. hoch einschätzen)* be convinced by sth.; **er ist sehr von sich [selbst] ~**: he's very sure of himself

Über·zeugung die a) *o. Pl.* convincing; *(das Umstimmen)* persuasion; **b)** *(feste Meinung)* conviction; **der festen ~ sein, daß ...**: be firmly convinced that ...; **zu der ~ kommen** *od.* **gelangen, daß ...**: become convinced that ...; **meiner ~ nach ...**: I am convinced that ...

Überzeugungs-: ~arbeit die propaganda work; **~kraft die;** *o. Pl.* power[s] of persuasion; persuasiveness; **mit ~kraft reden** speak persuasively; **~täter der** *(Rechtsspr.)* offender who has acted on grounds of conscience

[1]**über|ziehen** *unr. tr. V.* **a)** pull on ⟨*clothes*⟩; **b) jmdm. eins** *od.* **ein paar ~** *(ugs.)* give sb. a clout

[2]**über·ziehen 1.** *unr. tr. V.* **a) etw. mit etw. ~**: cover sth. with sth.; **die Torte mit Guß ~**: glaze the gateau; **die Betten frisch ~**: put clean sheets on the beds; change the sheets on the beds; **das Land mit Krieg ~** *(fig.)* spread war over the land; **b)** overdraw ⟨*account*⟩ **(um by); sie hat ihr Konto [um 300 Mark] überzogen** she is [300 marks] overdrawn; **seinen Urlaub ~**: take too much time off; **die Mittagspause um 10 Minuten ~**: take an extra ten minutes over lunch; **die vorgesehene Sendezeit [um drei Minuten] ~**: overrun the programme time [by three minutes]; **c)** *(übertreiben)* overdo ⟨*criticism etc.*⟩; **überzogene Leistungen/Erwartungen/Preiserhöhungen** *usw.* excessive payments/expectations/price increases *etc.* **2.** *unr. itr. V.* **a)** overdraw one's account; go overdrawn; **b)** *(bei einer Sendung, einem Vortrag)* overrun. **3.** *unr. refl. V.* ⟨*sky*⟩ cloud over, become overcast

Überzieher der; ~s, ~ a) *(veralt.: Herrenmantel)* [light] overcoat; **b)** *(salopp: Kondom)* johnny *(Brit. sl.)*; rubber *(sl.)*

Überziehungs·kredit der *(Finanzw.)* overdraft facility

überzüchtet [y:bɐˈtsʏçtət] *Adj.* overbred; over-sophisticated ⟨*engines, systems*⟩

über·zuckern *tr. V.* sugar

Überzug der a) *(Beschichtung)* coating; **b)** *(Bezug)* cover

üblich [ˈy:plɪç] *Adj.* usual; *(normal)* normal; *(gebräuchlich)* customary; **das ist hier so ~**: that's the accepted *or (coll.)* done thing here; **das ist nicht mehr ~**: that's no longer done *(coll.)*; **wie ~**: as usual; **sie gebrauchte die ~e Ausrede** she used the same old excuse

üblicher·weise *Adv.* usually; generally

U-Boot das submarine; sub *(coll.)*

übrig [ˈy:brɪç] *Adj.* remaining *attrib.*; *(ander...)* other; **alle ~en Gäste sind bereits gegangen** all the other guests have already gone; **das/alles ~e erzähle ich dir später** I'll tell you the rest/all the rest later; **die/alle ~en** the/all the rest *or* others; **im ~en** besides; **ein ~es tun** *(geh.)* do one last thing; **es ist etwas ~**: there is some left; **es ist noch Suppe ~**: there is some soup left [over]; **ich habe noch Geld ~**: I [still] have some money left; *(ich habe mehr Geld, als ich brauche)* I [still] have some money to spare; **hast du vielleicht eine Mark [für mich] ~?** can you spare me a mark?; **für jmdn./etw. wenig/nichts ~ haben** have little/no time for sb./sth. *(fig.)*

übrig-: ~|behalten *unr. tr. V.* have left over; **~|bleiben** *unr. itr. V.; mit sein* be left; remain; ⟨*food, drink*⟩ be left over; **ihm bleibt nichts [anderes** *od.* **weiter] ~, als zu ...**: he has no [other] choice but to ...; there is nothing he can do but to ...

übrigens [ˈy:brɪgn̩s] *Adv.* by the way; incidentally

übrig|lassen *unr. tr. V.* leave; leave ⟨*food, drink*⟩ over; **laßt mir etwas davon übrig** leave some of it for me; **zu wünschen ~**: leave something to be desired; **sehr** *od.* **viel/nichts zu wünschen ~**: leave much *or (coll.)* a lot/nothing to be desired

Übung [ˈy:bʊŋ] **die; ~, ~en a)** exercise; **b)** *o. Pl. (das Üben, Geübtsein)* practice; **das erfordert ~**: that takes practice; **das macht die ~, das ist alles nur ~**: it's [just] a question of practice; **etw. zur ~ tun** do sth. for practice; **außer ~ sein** be out of practice; **~/viel ~/keine ~ haben** have had some/a lot of *(coll.)*/no practice; **aus der ~ kommen** get out of practice; **in der ~ sein/bleiben** be/stay in practice; **~ macht den Meister** *(Spr.)* practice makes perfect *(prov.)*; **c)** *(Lehrveranstaltung)* class; seminar

übungs-, Übungs-: ~buch das book of exercises; *(Lehrbuch)* textbook with exercises; **~halber** *Adv.* for practice; **~munition die** *(Milit.)* blank ammunition; **~sache die: ~sache sein** be a matter of practice

UdSSR [u:de:|ɛs|ɛsˈ|ɛr] *Abk.* **die; ~: Union der Sozialistischen Sowjetrepubliken** USSR

UEFA [u:ˈe:fa:] *Abk.* **die; ~** *(Fußball)* UEFA

U-Eisen das channel iron

Ufer [ˈu:fɐ] **das; ~s, ~**: bank; *(des Meers)* shore; **ans ~ gespült werden** be washed ashore; **der Fluß trat über die ~**: the river burst its banks; **das sichere ~ erreichen** reach dry land; **das Haus liegt direkt am ~**: the house is right by the lake/river/sea

ufer-, Ufer-: ~befestigung die bank reinforcement; **~böschung die** [river/canal] embankment; **~los** *Adj.* limitless; boundless ⟨*love, indulgence, etc.*⟩; endless ⟨*discussions, talks, quarrel, subject*⟩; **ins ~lose gehen** ⟨*plans, ambitions, etc.*⟩ know no bounds; **~promenade die** riverside walk; *(am Meer)* promenade; **~straße die** riverside/lakeside road; *(am Meer)* coast road

uff [ʊf] *Interj.* oof; phew

UFO, Ufo [ˈu:fo] **das; ~[s], ~s** UFO

U-förmig *Adj.* U-shaped

UG *Abk.* **Untergeschoß**

Uganda [uˈganda] **(das); ~s** Uganda

Ugander [uˈgandɐ] **der; ~s, ~, Ugạnderin die; ~, ~nen** Ugandan; *s. auch* **-in**

ugandisch *Adj.* Ugandan

U-Haft die *s.* **Untersuchungshaft**

Uhr [u:ɐ̯] **die; ~, ~en a)** clock; *(Armband~, Taschen~)* watch; *(Wasser~, Gas~)* meter; *(an Meßinstrumenten)* dial; gauge; **auf die** *od.* **nach der ~ sehen** look at the time; **ein Arbeiter, der dauernd auf die ~ sieht** a worker who is always clock-watching; **nach meiner ~**: by *or* according to my clock/watch; **jmds. ~ ist abgelaufen** *(fig.)* the sands of time have run out for sb.; **wissen, was die ~ geschlagen hat** *(fig.)* know what's what; know how things stand; **rund um die ~** *(ugs.)* round the clock; **b)** *(bei Uhrzeitangaben)* **acht ~**: eight o'clock; **acht ~ dreißig** half past eight; 8.30 [eɪtˈθɜ:tɪ]; **wieviel ~ ist es?** what's the time?; what time is it?; **um wieviel ~ treffen wir uns?** [at] what time shall we meet?; when shall we meet?

Uhr·armband das watch-strap

Uhren·industrie die clock- and watch-making industry

Uhr-: ~glas das watch-glass; **~kette die** watch-chain; **~macher der** watchmaker/clockmaker; **~werk das** clock/watch mechanism; **~zeiger der** clock-/watch-hand; **~zeiger·sinn der: im ~zeigersinn** clockwise; **entgegen dem ~zeigersinn** anticlockwise; **~zeit die** time; **jmdn. nach der ~zeit fragen** ask sb. the time; **hast du [die] genaue ~zeit?** do you have the exact time?

Uhu [ˈu:hu] **der; ~s, ~s** eagle owl

Ukas [ˈu:kas] **der; ~ses, ~se** *(scherzh.)* edict

Ukraine [ukraˈi:nə] **die; ~**: Ukraine

Ukrainer der; ~s, ~, Ukrainerin die; ~, ~nen Ukrainian

ukrainisch *Adj.* Ukrainian; *s. auch* **deutsch**

UKW [u:ka:ˈve:] *o. Art.; Abk.* **Ultrakurzwelle** VHF

UKW-Sender der VHF station; ≈ FM station

Ulan [uˈla:n] **der; ~en, ~en** *(hist.)* uhlan

Ulk [ʊlk] **der; ~s, ~e** lark *(coll.)*; *(Streich)* trick; [practical] joke; **etw. aus ~ sagen/tun** say/do sth. for fun *or (coll.)* for a laugh

ulken *itr. V.* clown *or (coll.)* lark about; **über jmdn./etw. ~**: make fun of sb./sth.

ulkig *(ugs.)* **1.** *Adj.* funny. **2.** *adv.* in a funny way

Ulkus [ˈʊlkʊs] **das; ~, Ulzera** [ˈʊltsera] *(Med.)* ulcer

Ulme [ˈʊlmə] **die; ~, ~n** elm

Ultima ratio [ˈʊltima ˈra:tsio] **die; ~ ~** *(geh.)* last resort

ultimativ [ʊltimaˈti:f] **1.** *Adj.* ⟨*demand*⟩ made as an ultimatum; **~en Charakter haben** constitute an ultimatum. **2.** *adv.* **etw. ~ fordern** demand sth. in [the form of] an ultimatum; **jmdn. ~ auffordern, etw. zu tun** give sb. an ultimatum to do sth.

Ultimatum [ʊltiˈma:tʊm] **das; ~s, Ultimaten** ultimatum; **[jmdm.] ein ~ stellen** give *or* set [sb.] an ultimatum

Ultimo [ˈʊltimo] **der; ~s, ~s** last day of the month

Ultra [ˈʊltra] **der; ~s, ~s** extremist

Ultra·kurz·welle [ʊltraˈkʊrtsvɛlə] **die a)** *(Phys., Funkw., Rundf.)* ultra-short wave; **b)** *(Rundf.: Wellenbereich)* very high frequency; VHF

Ultrakurzwellen·sender der very high frequency station; VHF station; ≈ FM station

ultra-, Ultra-: ~marin *indekl. Adj.* ultramarine; **~marin das; ~s** ultramarine; **~montan** *Adj. (geh.)* ultramontane; **~schall** [ˈ---] **der** *(Physik, Med.)* ultrasound

Ultraschall~: ~behandlung die *(Med.)* ultrasound therapy *or* treatment; *(Technik)* ultrasound treatment; **~untersuchung die** *(Med.)* ultrasound examination

ultra·violett *Adj. (Physik)* ultraviolet
Ulzera *s.* **Ulkus**
um [ʊm] **1.** *Präp. mit Akk.* **a)** *(räumlich)* [a]round; **um etw. herum** [a]round sth.; **um das Haus gehen** walk round the house; **das Rad dreht sich um seine Achse** the wheel turns on its axle; **um die Ecke** round the corner; **um sich schlagen** lash *or* hit out; **er warf mit Steinen um sich** he threw stones around *or* about; *s. auch* **greifen 2 a**; **scharen 2**; **b)** *(zeitlich) (genau)* at; *(etwa)* around [about]; **der Unterricht beginnt um acht [Uhr]** lessons start at eight [o'clock]; **um den 20. August [herum]** around [about] 20 August; **um die Mittagszeit [herum]** around midday; **c) Tag um Tag/Stunde um Stunde** day after day/hour after hour; **Meter um Meter/Schritt um Schritt** metre by metre/step by step; **d)** *(bei Maß- u. Mengenangaben)* by; **die Temperatur stieg um 5 Grad** the temperature rose [by] five degrees; **um 3 cm zu lang sein** be 3 cm too long; **um nichts/einiges/vieles besser sein** be no/somewhat/a lot better; **e)** *(südd., österr.: bei Preisangaben)* for. **2.** *Adv.* around; about; **um [die] 10 Mark/50 Personen [herum]** around *or* about *or* round about ten marks/50 people. **3.** *Konj.* **a)** *(final)* **um ... zu** [in order] to; **um es gleich zu sagen, ich kann nicht lange bleiben** I'd better say straight away that I can't stay for long; **b)** *(konsekutiv)* **er ist groß genug/ist noch zu klein, um ... zu ...:** he is big enough/is still too young to ...; **sie heirateten, um sich schon nach einem Jahr wieder scheiden zu lassen** they got married, only to get divorced again after just one year; **c)** *(desto)* **je schneller der Wagen, um so größer die Gefahr** the faster the car, the greater the danger; **je länger ..., um so besser ...:** the longer ..., the better ...; **um so besser/schlimmer!** all the better/worse!; **um so mehr, als ...** *(zumal, da ...)* all the more so, as *or* since ...
um|ackern *tr. V.* plough over
um|adressieren *tr. V.* redirect
um|ändern *tr. V.* change; alter; revise ⟨*text, novel*⟩; alter ⟨*garment*⟩
um|arbeiten *tr. V.* alter ⟨*garment*⟩; revise, rework ⟨*text, novel, music*⟩; **einen Roman zu einem Drama/Drehbuch ~:** adapt a novel for the stage/screen
Umarbeitung die; ~, ~en *(eines Kleidungsstücks)* alteration; *(eines Romans, Textes, Musikstücks)* revision; reworking; *(zu einem Drehbuch, Drama o. ä.)* adaptation
umarmen *tr. V.* embrace; put one's arms around; *(an sich drücken)* hug; **sie umarmten sich** they embraced/hugged; **sei umarmt [von Deiner/Deinem ...]** *(als Briefschluß)* lots of love [from ...]
Umarmung die; ~, ~en *s.* **umarmen:** embrace; hug
Um·bau der; ~[e]s, ~ten a) rebuilding; reconstruction; *(kleinere Änderung)* alteration; *(zu etw. anderem)* conversion; *(fig.: eines Systems, einer Verwaltung)* reorganization; **„wegen ~[s] geschlossen"** 'closed for alterations'; **das Gebäude befindet sich im ~:** the building is being rebuilt/altered/converted; **b)** *(das Umgebaute) s.* **a:** reconstruction/altered building/conversion
¹um|bauen *tr., auch itr. V.* rebuild; reconstruct; *(leicht ändern)* alter; *(zu etw. anderem)* convert **(zu** into); *(fig.)* reorganize ⟨*system, administration, etc.*⟩; **das Bühnenbild ~:** change the set; **wir bauen um** we're rebuilding/making alterations
²um·bauen *tr. V.* surround; **umbauter Raum** interior space
um|behalten *unr. tr. V.* keep ⟨*apron, scarf, etc.*⟩ on
um|benennen *unr. tr. V.* change the name of, rename ⟨*street, square, etc.*⟩; **etw. in etw.** *(Akk.)* **~:** change the name of sth. to sth.; rename sth. sth.

um|beschreiben *unr. tr. V. (Geom.)* circumscribe
um|besetzen *tr., auch itr. V.* change ⟨*team*⟩; recast ⟨*role, play*⟩; re-allocate ⟨*post, position*⟩
um|bestellen *itr. V.* change the order
um|betten *tr. V.* **a) jmdn. ~:** move sb. to another bed; **b)** *(in ein anderes Grab legen)* move *or* transfer ⟨*body*⟩ to another grave
um|biegen 1. *unr. tr. V.* bend. **2.** *unr. itr. V.; mit sein* turn; ⟨*path*⟩ bend, turn
um|bilden *tr. V.* reorganize, reconstruct ⟨*department etc.*⟩; reshuffle ⟨*government, cabinet*⟩; **etw. zu etw. ~** *(Biol.)* develop sth. into sth.
um|binden *unr. tr. V.* put on ⟨*tie, apron, scarf, etc.*⟩
um|blasen *unr. tr. V.* blow over
um|blättern 1. *tr. V.* turn [over] ⟨*page*⟩. **2.** *itr. V.* turn the page/pages
um|blicken *refl. V.* **a)** look around; **sich nach allen Seiten ~:** look all around; **b)** *(zurückblicken)* [turn to] look back **(nach** at)
Umbra [ˈʊmbra] **die; ~** *(Farbe)* umber
um·branden *tr. V. (geh.)* surge around
um·brausen *tr. V.* roar around
¹um|brechen 1. *unr. tr. V.* **a)** bring down ⟨*telephone pole, tree, etc.*⟩; **b)** *(umpflügen)* break up, turn over ⟨*land*⟩; plough up ⟨*field*⟩. **2.** *unr. itr. V.; mit sein* collapse; fall down
²um·brechen *unr. tr. V. (Druckw.)* make up
um|bringen *unr. tr. V.* kill; **dieses Material ist nicht umzubringen** *(fig. ugs.)* this material is indestructible; **diese Packerei bringt mich fast um** *(fig. ugs.)* all this packing's nearly killing me *(coll.)*; **sich vor Höflichkeit ~** *(fig. ugs.)* fall over oneself to be polite *(coll.)*; **sich für jmdn. ~** *(fig. ugs.)* do everything for sb.
Um·bruch der a) radical change; *(Umwälzung)* upheaval; **im ~ sein** be in a state of flux; **b)** *o. Pl. (Druckw.)* make-up; *(Ergebnis)* page proofs *pl.*
um|buchen 1. *tr. V.* **a)** change ⟨*flight, journey route*⟩ **(auf +** *Akk.* to); **b)** *(Finanzw.)* transfer **(auf +** *Akk.* to). **2.** *itr. V.* change one's booking **(auf +** *Akk.* to)
Um·buchung die a) change of booking; **eine ~ Ihres Fluges ist jederzeit möglich** you can change your flight at any time; **b)** *(Finanzw.)* transfer **(auf +** *Akk.* to)
um|datieren *tr. V.* change the date of; redate ⟨*contract, letter, etc.*⟩
um|denken *unr. itr. V.* revise one's thinking; rethink; **ein Prozeß des Umdenkens** a process of rethinking
um|deuten *tr. V.* reinterpret; give a new interpretation to
um|dichten *tr. V.* adapt, recast ⟨*poem, song, etc.*⟩
um|disponieren *itr. V.* change one's arrangements; make new arrangements
um·drängen *tr. V.* crowd round; mob ⟨*actor, pop star, etc.*⟩
um|drehen 1. *tr. V.* turn round; turn over ⟨*coin, hand, etc.*⟩; turn ⟨*key*⟩; turn ⟨*pockets, bag, garment, sock, etc.*⟩ inside out; **jede Mark** *od.* **jeden Pfennig [dreimal] ~** *(ugs.)* watch every penny; **einen Spion ~** *(fig.)* turn a spy. **2.** *refl. V.* turn round; *(den Kopf wenden)* turn one's head; **sich nach jmdm. ~:** turn/turn one's head to look at sb.; **ein Mädchen, nach dem sich die Männer ~:** a girl who turns men's heads. **3.** *itr. V.; auch mit sein (ugs.: umkehren)* turn back; *(ugs.: wenden)* turn round
Um·drehung die turn; *(eines Motors usw.)* revolution; rev *(coll.)*; *(eines Planeten)* rotation
um·einander *Adv.* **sich ~ kümmern/sorgen** take care of/worry about each other *or* one another; **~ besorgt sein** be concerned about each other *or* one another; **sich ~ drehen** revolve around each other

um|erziehen *tr. V.* re-educate; **jmdn. zu etw. ~:** re-educate sb. to be *or* as sth.
¹um|fahren *unr. tr. V.* knock over *or* down
²um·fahren *unr. tr. V.* go round; make a detour round ⟨*obstruction, busy area*⟩; *(im Auto)* drive *or* go round; *(im Schiff)* sail *or* go round; *(auf einer Umgehungsstraße)* bypass ⟨*town, village, etc.*⟩
Umfahrungs·straße die *(österr., schweiz.) s.* **Umgehungsstraße**
Um·fall der *(ugs. abwertend)* about-face; U-turn
um|fallen *unr. itr. V.; mit sein* **a)** *(umstürzen)* fall over; **b)** *(zusammenbrechen)* collapse; **tot ~:** fall down dead; **~ wie die Fliegen** go down like flies; **ich falle vor Müdigkeit um** I'm just about ready to drop; **vor Hunger/Durst fast ~:** be faint with hunger/thirst; **vor Schreck fast ~:** nearly die with fright; nearly have a heart attack *(coll.)*; **c)** *(ugs. abwertend: seine Meinung ändern)* do an about-face; do a U-turn
Um·fang der a) circumference; *(eines Quadrats usw.)* perimeter; *(eines Baums, Menschen usw.)* girth; circumference; **er hat einen ganz schönen ~** *(scherzh.)* he has quite a girth; **b)** *(Größe)* size; **der Band hat einen ~ von 250 Seiten** the volume contains 250 pages *or* is 250 pages thick; **c)** *(Ausmaß)* extent; *(von Wissen)* range; extent; *(einer Stimme)* range; *(einer Arbeit, Untersuchung)* scope; **in vollem ~:** fully; completely; **in großem ~:** on a large scale
um·fangen *unr. tr. V. (geh.)* embrace; *(fig.)* ⟨*silence, warmth, etc.*⟩ envelop
umfänglich [ˈʊmfɛŋlɪç] *Adj.* extensive; ⟨*case, parcel, etc.*⟩ of considerable size; voluminous, extensive ⟨*correspondence*⟩
umfang·reich *Adj.* extensive; substantial ⟨*book*⟩
um·fassen *tr. V.* **a)** grasp; *(umarmen)* embrace; **jmds. Arme/Taille/Knie ~:** grasp *or* clasp sb. round the arms/waist/knees; **jmdn. umfaßt halten** hold sb. in one's arms *or* in an embrace; **b)** *(enthalten)* contain; *(einschließen)* include; take in; span, cover ⟨*period*⟩; **c)** *(umgeben)* enclose; surround; **d)** *(Milit.: umzingeln)* surround; encircle
umfassend 1. *Adj.* full ⟨*reply, information, survey, confession*⟩; extensive, wide, comprehensive ⟨*knowledge, powers*⟩; broad ⟨*education*⟩; extensive ⟨*preparations, measures*⟩. **2.** *adv.* ⟨*inform*⟩ fully
Um·fassung die enclosure
Um·feld das a) *(Psych., Soziol.)* milieu; **b)** *s.* **Umgebung a**
um·flechten *unr. tr. V.* put wicker round; **eine umflochtene Flasche** a wickered bottle; **eine mit Bast umflochtene Flasche** a raffia-covered bottle
¹um|fliegen *unr. itr. V.; mit sein (salopp)* go flying *(coll.)*
²um·fliegen *unr. tr. V.* fly round
um·fließen *unr. tr. V.* flow round
um|formen *tr. V.* **a)** reshape; remodel; recast, revise ⟨*poem, novel*⟩; transform ⟨*person*⟩; **b)** *(Elektrot.)* convert
Um·former der *(Elektrot.)* converter
Um·formung die a) *s.* **umformen a:** reshaping; remodelling; recasting; revision; transformation; **b)** *(Elektrot.)* conversion
Um·frage die survey; *(Politik)* opinion poll; **eine ~ machen** *od.* **veranstalten** carry out a survey/conduct an opinion poll
um·fried[ig]en *tr. V. (geh.) s.* **einfried[ig]en**
Umfried[ig]ung die; ~, ~en *(geh.) s.* **Einfried[ig]ung**
um|füllen *tr. V.* **etw. in etw.** *(Akk.)* **~:** transfer sth. into sth.; **der Kaffee muß umgefüllt werden** the coffee has to be put into another container
um|funktionieren *tr. V.* change the function of; **etw. zu etw. ~:** turn sth. into sth.
Um·gang der a) *o. Pl. (gesellschaftlicher*

Verkehr) contact; dealings *pl.*; **jmd. hat guten/schlechten ~:** sb. keeps good/bad company; **mit jmdm. ~ haben/pflegen** associate with sb.; **mit jmdm. keinen ~ haben** have nothing to do with sb.; **er ist kein ~ für dich!** he is not suitable *or* fit company for you; **b)** *o. Pl. (das Umgehen)* **den ~ mit Pferden lernen** learn how to handle horses; **im ~ mit Kindern erfahren sein** be experienced in dealing with children; **c)** *(bild. Kunst, Archit.)* gallery

umgänglich ['ʊmgɛŋlɪç] *Adj. (verträglich)* affable; friendly; *(gesellig)* sociable

umgangs-, Umgangs-: ~form die; *meist Pl.* **gute/schlechte/keine ~formen haben** have good/bad/no manners; **~sprache die** colloquial language; **die englische ~sprache** colloquial English; **~sprachlich 1.** *Adj.* colloquial; **2.** *adv.* colloquially

um·garnen *tr. V.* beguile

um·geben *unr. tr. V.* **a)** surround; ⟨*hedge, fence, wall, etc.*⟩ enclose; ⟨*darkness, mist, etc.*⟩ envelop; **b) etw. mit etw. ~:** surround sth. with sth.; *(einfrieden)* enclose sth. with sth.; **sich mit jmdm./etw. ~:** surround oneself with sb./sth.

Umgebung die; ~, ~en a) surroundings *pl.*; *(Nachbarschaft)* neighbourhood; *(eines Ortes)* surrounding area; **die nähere/weitere ~ Mannheims** the immediate/broader environs *pl.* of Mannheim; **Wiesbaden und ~:** Wiesbaden and the surrounding area; **b)** *(fig.)* milieu; **jmds. nähere ~:** those *pl.* close to sb.; **das Kind braucht seine vertraute ~:** the child needs familiar faces around it

Um·gegend die *(ugs.)* surrounding area; **die ~ der Stadt** the area surrounding the town

[1]**um|gehen** *unr. itr. V.; mit sein* **a)** *(im Umlauf sein)*⟨*list, rumour, etc.*⟩ go round, circulate; ⟨*illness, infection*⟩ go round; **Angst geht in der Bevölkerung um** fear is spreading in the population; **b)** *(spuken)* **hier geht ein Gespenst um** this place is haunted; **im Schloß geht ein Gespenst um** a ghost haunts this castle; the castle is haunted; **c)** *(behandeln)* **mit jmdm. freundlich/liebevoll** *usw.* **~:** treat sb. kindly/lovingly *etc.*; **mit etw. sorgfältig/nachlässig** *usw.* **~:** treat sth. carefully/carelessly *etc.*; **er versteht es, mit Kindern umzugehen** he knows how to handle children; **er kann mit Geld nicht ~:** he can't handle money; **mit Pinsel und Farbe ~ können** be able to use a brush and paint; **d)** *(verkehren)* **mit jmdm. ~:** associate with sb.; **e) mit dem Plan/Gedanken ~, etw. zu tun** think of doing sth.; **f)** *(bes. nordd.: einen Umweg machen)* make a detour

[2]**um·gehen** *unr. tr. V.* **a)** *(herumgehen, -fahren um)* go round; make a detour round ⟨*obstruction, busy area*⟩; *(auf einer Umgehungsstraße)* bypass ⟨*town, village, etc.*⟩; **b)** *(vermeiden)* avoid; avoid, get round ⟨*problem, difficulty*⟩; evade ⟨*question, issue*⟩; **c)** *(nicht befolgen)* get round, circumvent ⟨*law, restriction, etc.*⟩; evade ⟨*obligation, duty*⟩

umgehend 1. *Adj.; nicht präd.* immediate. **2.** *adv.* immediately

Umgehung die; ~, ~en a) durch ~ der Innenstadt by bypassing *or* avoiding the town centre; **b)** *s.* [2]**umgehen c:** circumvention; evasion; **das ließe sich nur unter ~ der Bestimmung durchführen** that could only be done by circumventing the regulations; **c)** *s.* **Umgehungsstraße**

Umgehungs·straße die bypass

umgekehrt 1. *Adj.* inverse ⟨*ratio, proportion*⟩; reverse ⟨*order*⟩; opposite ⟨*sign*⟩; **es verhält sich** *od.* **ist genau ~:** the very opposite *or* reverse is true *or* the case. **2.** *adv.* inversely ⟨*proportional*⟩; **vom Englischen ins Deutsche und ~ übersetzen** translate from English into German and vice versa; **~ wirst du kaum erwarten können, daß ...:** conversely you can hardly expect that ...

um|gestalten *tr. V.* reshape; remodel; redesign ⟨*square, park, room, etc.*⟩; rework ⟨*text, music, etc.*⟩; *(reorganisieren)* reorganize; *(verändern)* change; **der Garten wurde zu einem Park umgestaltet** the garden was turned into a park

um|gießen *unr. tr. V.* **a) etw. ~:** pour sth. into another container/into bottles *etc.*; **etw. in etw.** *(Akk.)* **~:** pour sth. into sth.; **b)** *(in eine andere Form gießen)* recast

um·glänzen *tr. V. (dichter.)* **etw. ~:** bathe sth. in light

um|graben *unr. tr. V.* dig over

um·grenzen *tr. V.* ⟨*wall, fence, etc.*⟩ surround, enclose; *(fig.)* define; delimit

Umgrenzung die; ~, ~en a) *s.* **umgrenzen:** surrounding; enclosing; *(fig.)* definition; delimitation; **b)** *(Grenzlinie)* boundary

um|gruppieren *tr. V.* rearrange

Um·gruppierung die rearrangement

um|gucken *refl. V. (ugs.) s.* **umsehen**

um|gürten *tr. V. (veralt.)* put on ⟨*belt*⟩; **[sich** *(Dat.)***] das Schwert ~:** gird on one's sword

um|haben *unr. tr. V.* **etw. ~:** have sth. on

um·halsen *tr. V.* embrace; **sie umhalsten sich** they embraced

Um·hang der cape

um|hängen *tr. V.* **a) etw. ~:** hang sth. somewhere else; **die Bilder müssen umgehängt werden** the pictures must be changed around; **b) jmdm./sich einen Mantel/eine Decke ~:** drape a coat/blanket round sb.'s/one's shoulders; **sich** *(Dat.)* **ein Gewehr ~:** sling a rifle from one's shoulder; **sich** *(Dat.)* **einen Fotoapparat ~:** hang *or* sling a camera round one's neck; **jmdm. eine Medaille ~:** hang a medal round sb.'s neck

Umhänge·tasche die shoulder-bag

um|hauen *unr. tr. V.* **a)** *(fällen)* fell; **b)** *(ugs.: niederwerfen)* knock down; floor; **diese Hitze haut einen glatt um** *(salopp)* this heat is enough to knock you over *(coll.)*; **schon ein Bier haut mich um** *(salopp)* just one beer's enough to put me under the table *(coll.)*; **es hat mich fast umgehauen, als ich davon hörte** *(salopp)* I was flabbergasted when I heard

um·hegen *tr. V. (geh.)* care lovingly for; **sie umhegt die Kinder mit mütterlicher Liebe** she looks after the children with maternal love

um·her *Adv.* around; **weit ~:** all around

umher-: *s.* **herum-**

umhin|können *unr. itr. V.* **sie konnte nicht/kaum umhin, das zu tun** she had no/scarcely had any choice but to do it; *(einem inneren Zwang folgend)* she couldn't help/could scarcely help but do it

um|hören *refl. V.* keep one's ears open; *(direkt fragen)* ask around; **ich werde mich danach bei** *od.* **unter meinen Kollegen ~:** I'll ask around my workmates *(Brit.) or (esp. Amer.)* fellow workers

um·hüllen *tr. V.* wrap; *(fig.)*⟨*mist, fog, etc.*⟩ shroud; **jmdn./etw. mit etw. ~:** wrap sb./sth. in sth.

um·jubeln *tr. V.* cheer

um·kämpfen *tr. V.* fight over ⟨*position, village, etc.*⟩; contest ⟨*victory*⟩; **ein heiß umkämpfter Sieg** a hotly contested victory

Umkehr ['ʊmkeːɐ̯] **die; ~** *(auch fig.)* turning back; **zur ~ gezwungen werden** be forced to turn back

umkehr·bar *Adj.* reversible

um|kehren 1. *itr. V.; mit sein* turn back; *(fig. geh.: sich wandeln)* change one's ways; **auf halbem Wege ~** *(fig.)* stop half-way. **2.** *tr. V.* **a)** turn upside down; turn over ⟨*sheet of paper*⟩; *(nach links drehen)* turn ⟨*garment etc.*⟩ inside out; *(nach rechts drehen)* turn ⟨*garment etc.*⟩ right side out; **das ganze Haus [nach etw.] ~** *(fig.)* turn the whole house upside down [looking for sth.]; **b)** *(ins Gegenteil verkehren)* reverse; invert ⟨*ratio, proportion*⟩; **c)** *(Musik)* invert; **d)** *(Logik)* convert ⟨*proposition*⟩. **3.** *refl. V.* be reversed; **der Magen kehrte sich ihm um** *(fig.)* his stomach turned over

Umkehr·film der *(Fot.)* reversal film

Umkehrung die a) reversal; **b)** *(Musik)* inversion; **c)** *(Logik)* conversion

um|kippen 1. *itr. V.; mit sein* **a)** fall over; ⟨*boat*⟩ capsize, turn over; ⟨*vehicle*⟩ overturn; **b)** *(ugs.: ohnmächtig werden)* keel over; **c)** *(ugs. abwertend) s.* **umfallen c; d)** *(ugs.: umschlagen)* ⟨*wine*⟩ go off; **e)** *(Ökologie)* ⟨*river, lake*⟩ reach the stage of biological collapse; **f)** *(ugs.: ins Gegenteil umschlagen)* ⟨*mood*⟩ turn; ⟨*voice*⟩ crack. **2.** *tr. V.* tip over; knock over ⟨*lamp, vase, glass, cup*⟩; capsize ⟨*boat*⟩; turn ⟨*boat*⟩ over; overturn ⟨*vehicle*⟩

um·klammern *tr. V.* clutch; clasp; **seine Hände umklammerten den Griff** his hands gripped *or* clasped the handle; **die Ringer/Boxer ~ sich** the wrestlers are locked together/the boxers are in a clinch; **etw./jmdn. fest umklammert halten** keep a firm grip on sth./clutch sb. tightly

Umklammerung die; ~, ~en clutch; clasp; *(mit den Händen)* clutch; grip; clasp; *(Umarmung)* firm embrace; *(Boxing)* clinch

um·klappbar *Adj.* fold-down ⟨*seat*⟩; **~ sein** fold down

um|klappen 1. *tr. V.* fold down. **2.** *itr. V.; mit sein (ugs.: ohnmächtig werden)* keel over

Umkleide·kabine die changing-cubicle

[1]**um|kleiden** *(geh.)* **1.** *refl. V.* change; change one's clothes. **2.** *tr. V.* **jmdn. ~:** change sb.; change sb.'s clothes

[2]**um·kleiden** *tr. V.* cover

Umkleide·raum der changing-room *(Brit.)*; *(im Theater)* green-room

um|knicken 1. *itr. V.; mit sein* **a) [mit dem Fuß] ~:** go over on one's ankle; **b)** ⟨*tree, stalk, blade of grass, etc.*⟩ bend; ⟨*branch*⟩ bend and snap; **umgeknickte Äste/Halme** snapped branches/bent straws. **2.** *tr. V.* **a)** *(falten)* fold ⟨*page, sheet of paper*⟩ over; **b)** *(abknicken)* bend over; break ⟨*flower, stalk*⟩

um|kommen *unr. itr. V.; mit sein* **a)** die; *(bei einem Unglück, durch Gewalt)* get killed; die; **ich komme um vor Hitze** *(fig. ugs.)* I'm dying in this heat *(coll.)*; **ich komme um vor Hunger/Durst** *(fig. ugs.)* I'm dying of hunger/thirst *(coll.)*; **vor Langeweile ~** *(fig. ugs.)* be bored to death *(coll.)*; die of boredom *(coll.)*; **b)** *(ungenießbar werden)* ⟨*food*⟩ go off

umkränzen [ʊm'krɛntsn̩] *tr. V.* garland; *(fig.: umgeben)* encircle

Um·kreis der a) *o. Pl.* surrounding area; **im ~ von 5 km** within a radius of 5 km.; **der ~ der Stadt** the city's environs *pl. or* immediate surroundings *pl.*; **im [näheren] ~ der Stadt** in the [immediate] vicinity of the town; **aus dem ~ des Vorsitzenden hört man, ...** *(fig.)* one learns from those close to the chairman ...; **b)** *(Geom.)* circumcircle

um·kreisen *tr. V.* circle; ⟨*spacecraft, satellite*⟩ orbit; ⟨*planet*⟩ revolve [a]round; **seine Gedanken umkreisten das Thema** *(fig.)* he kept turning the matter over in his mind

um|krempeln *tr. V.* **a)** *(aufkrempeln)* turn up ⟨*cuff*⟩; roll up ⟨*sleeve, trouser-leg*⟩; **b) das ganze Haus [nach etw.] ~** *(ugs.)* turn the whole house upside down [looking for sth.]; **c)** *(ugs.: von Grund auf ändern)* **etw. ~:** give sth. a shake-up; **jmdn. ~:** [completely] change sb.

um|laden *unr. tr. V.* transfer ⟨*goods etc.*⟩

Um·lage die: ~[n] share of the cost[s]; *(bei einer Wohnung)* share of the bill[s]; **die ~ beträgt 30 Mark pro Person** the cost is 30 marks per person

um·lagern *tr. V.* besiege

Um·land das; *o. Pl.* surrounding area; **das ~ von Köln** the area around Cologne

ụm|lassen *unr. tr. V. (ugs.)* leave ⟨*garment, watch, etc.*⟩ on
Ụm·lauf der a) rotation; **ein ~ [der Erde um die Sonne] dauert ein Jahr** one revolution [of the earth around the sun] takes a year; **b)** *o. Pl. (Zirkulation)* circulation; **in** *od.* **im ~ sein** ⟨*magazine, report, etc.*⟩ be circulating; ⟨*coin, banknote*⟩ be in circulation; **in ~ bringen** *od.* **setzen** circulate ⟨*report, magazine, etc.*⟩; circulate, put about, start ⟨*rumour*⟩; bring ⟨*coin, banknote*⟩ into circulation; **c)** *(Rundschreiben)* circular
Ụmlauf·bahn die *(Astron., Raumf.)* orbit; **etw. in eine ~ bringen** put sth. into orbit
[1]**ụm|laufen 1.** *unr. tr. V.* knock over. **2.** *unr. itr. V.; mit sein* **a)** *(rotieren)* rotate; revolve; ⟨*planet, satellite, etc.*⟩ orbit; **b) ~d** *(ringsherum verlaufend)* surrounding; **c)** *(kursieren, zirkulieren)* circulate
[2]**um·laufen** *unr. tr. V.* run around; ⟨*planet, satellite, etc.*⟩ orbit
Ụm·laut der *(Sprachw.)* umlaut
ụm|lauten *tr. V. (Sprachw.)* **ein umgelautetes a** an a umlaut; **das „a" wird hier umgelautet** the 'a' takes an umlaut in this case
ụm|legen *tr. V.* **a)** *(um einen Körperteil)* put on; **jmdm. etw. ~:** put sth. on sb.; **sich** *(Dat.)* **etw. ~:** put sth. on; **jmdm. eine Stola/Decke ~:** put a stole round sb.'s shoulders/put a blanket round sb.; **b)** *(auf den Boden, die Seite legen)* lay down; flatten ⟨*corn, stalks, etc.*⟩; *(fällen)* fell; **c)** *(umklappen)* fold down; turn down ⟨*collar*⟩; turn up ⟨*cuff*⟩; throw ⟨*lever*⟩; turn over ⟨*calendar-page*⟩; **d)** *(ugs.: zu Boden werfen)* floor, knock down ⟨*person*⟩; **e)** *(salopp: ermorden)* **jmdn. ~:** do sb. in *(sl.)*; bump sb. off *(sl.)*; **f)** *(verlegen)* transfer ⟨*patient, telephone call*⟩; **den Termin ~:** change the date (**auf +** *Akk.* to); **g)** *(anteilmäßig verteilen)* split, share ⟨*costs*⟩ (**auf +** *Akk.* between); **h)** *(derb: koitieren mit)* lay *(sl.)*
ụm|leiten divert; re-route; divert ⟨*river, stream*⟩
Ụm·leitung die diversion; re-routing; **die ~ fahren** take the diversion
ụm|lernen *itr. V.* **a)** *(beruflich)* retrain; **auf Feinmechaniker ~:** retrain as a precision engineer; **b)** *(seine Anschauungen ändern)* learn to think differently
ụmliegend *Adj.* surrounding ⟨*area, district*⟩; *(nahe)* nearby ⟨*building*⟩
Ụm·luft die; *o. Pl. (Technik)* recirculated air
um·mauern *tr. V.* surround with a wall; **ummauert** walled ⟨*garden, town*⟩
ụm|melden *tr. V.* **sich ~:** report a change of address; **ein Auto ~:** inform the authorities of a change of ownership of a car/*(am neuen Wohnort)* of the new address of a car's owner
ụm|modeln *tr. V. (ugs.)* change ⟨*house, flat*⟩ round; refashion, alter ⟨*jacket etc.*⟩
ụm|münzen *tr. V.* **etw. in etw.** *(Akk.)* **~:** convert sth. into sth.; **eine Niederlage in einen Sieg ~** *(fig.: umdeuten)* make a defeat out to be victory
um·nachtet *Adj. (geh.)* **[geistig] ~ sein** be [mentally] deranged
Umnạchtung die; ~, ~en *(geh.)* derangement; **im Zustand der ~, in geistiger ~:** in a state of mental derangement *or* insanity
um·nebeln *tr. V. (fig.)* cloud ⟨*senses, glance*⟩; befog ⟨*thoughts*⟩; **leicht umnebelt** slightly befuddled
ụm|organisieren *tr. V.* reorganize
ụm|packen 1. *itr. V.* repack. **2.** *tr. V.* repack; **seine Sachen aus der Reisetasche in einen Koffer ~:** take one's things out of the holdall and pack them into a suitcase
ụm|pflanzen *tr. V.* transplant
ụm|pflügen *tr. V.* plough up
ụm|polen *tr. V. (Elektrot.)* reverse the polarity/connections of; *(fig. ugs.: umwandeln)* convert ⟨*homosexual*⟩
ụm|quartieren *tr. V.* re-accommodate ⟨*person*⟩ (**in +** *Akk.* in); re-quarter, re-billet ⟨*troops*⟩ (**in +** *Akk.* in); move ⟨*patient*⟩
um|rahmen *tr. V.* frame ⟨*face etc.*⟩; **eine Feier mit Musik** *od.* **musikalisch ~** *(fig.)* begin and end a ceremony with music; give a ceremony a musical framework
Um|rahmung die; ~, ~en a) *(das Umrahmen)* bordering; **musikalische ~** *(fig.)* musical framework; music before and after; **b)** *(Umrahmendes)* border; *(fig.)* setting
um·rạnden *tr. V.* ring ⟨*letter, error, etc.*⟩; border ⟨*handkerchief, flower-bed, etc.*⟩
umrändert [ʊmˈrɛndɐt] *Adj.* **schwarz ~:** with a black border; **rot ~e Augen** red-rimmed eyes
Umrạndung die; ~, ~en a) bordering; **b)** *(Umrandendes)* border; surround
ụm|räumen 1. *tr. V.* rearrange. **2.** *itr. V.* rearrange things
ụm|rechnen *tr. V.* convert (**in +** *Akk.* into); **Waren im Wert von umgerechnet 300 Mark** goods worth the equivalent of 300 marks
Ụm·rechnung die conversion (**in +** *Akk.* into)
Ụmrechnungs·kurs der exchange rate
[1]**ụm|reißen** *unr. tr. V.* pull ⟨*mast, tree*⟩ down; knock ⟨*person*⟩ down; ⟨*wind*⟩ tear ⟨*tent etc.*⟩ down
[2]**um·reißen** *unr. tr. V.* outline; summarize ⟨*subject, problem, situation*⟩; **fest** *od.* **klar** *od.* **scharf umrissen** clearly defined ⟨*programme*⟩; clear-cut ⟨*ideas, views*⟩
ụm|rennen *unr. tr. V.* [run into and] knock down
um·rịngen *tr. V.* surround; *(in großer Zahl)* crowd round
Ụm·riß der *(auch fig.)* outline; **in Umrissen** in outline
ụm|rühren *tr. (auch itr.) V.* stir; **unter ständigem Umrühren** [while] stirring constantly
um·rụnden *tr. V.* go round ⟨*lake, town*⟩; *(Raumf.)* orbit; *(Seew.)* round ⟨*cape*⟩
ụm|rüsten 1. *tr. V.* **a)** *(Technik)* convert (**auf +** *Akk.* to, **zu** into); **b)** *(Milit.)* **eine Armee [auf Atomwaffen] ~:** re-equip an army [with nuclear weapons]. **2.** *itr. V.* re-equip; **auf etw.** *(Akk.)* **~:** change over to sth.
ums [ʊms] *Präp. + Art.* **a) = um das; b) ~ Leben kommen** lose one's life; **ein Jahr ~ andere** *(geh.)* one year after another; year after year
ụm|satteln *itr. V. (ugs.)* change jobs; ⟨*student*⟩ change courses; **[von etw.] auf etw.** *(Akk.)* **~:** switch [from sth.] to sth.
Ụm·satz der turnover; *(Verkauf)* sales *pl.* (**an +** *Dat.* of); **~ machen** *(ugs.)* make money; **1000 Mark ~ machen** turn over 1,000 marks
Ụmsatz-: ~beteiligung die share of the turnover; *(eines Verkäufers)* commission; **~steuer die** turnover *or (Amer.)* sales tax
[1]**ụm|säumen** *tr. V.* hem
[2]**um·säumen** *tr. V. (fig.)* surround
ụm|schalten 1. *tr. V. (auch fig.)* switch [over] (**auf +** *Akk.* to); move ⟨*lever*⟩. **2.** *itr. V.* **a)** *(auch fig.)* switch *or* change over (**auf +** *Akk.* to); **in den zweiten Gang ~:** change into second gear; **wir schalten jetzt ins Stadion um** now we're going over to the stadium; **b)** *(umgeschaltet werden)* **die Ampel schaltet [auf Grün] um** the traffic lights are changing [to green]
Ụmschalt·hebel der [change-over] lever
Ụm·schau die: [nach jmdm./etw.] ~ halten look round *or* out [for sb./sth.]; **„Politische ~"** 'Political Review'
ụm|schauen *refl. V. (bes. südd., österr., schweiz.) s.* **umsehen**
ụm|schichten 1. *tr. V.* **a)** restack; **b)** *(Wirtsch.)* restructure ⟨*investments*⟩; reinvest ⟨*capital*⟩. **2.** *refl. V. (Soziol.)* be restructured
ụm·schichtig 1. *Adv.* ⟨*work*⟩ in shifts; **wir müssen ~ essen gehen** we have to eat on a rota basis. **2.** *adj.* shift *attrib.* ⟨*work*⟩; ⟨*work*⟩ in shifts; ⟨*lunch-break*⟩ taken on a rota basis
Ụm·schichtung die *s.* **umschichten 1, 2:** restacking; *(Wirtsch.)* restructuring; reinvestment; *(Soziol.)* restructuring
um·schiffen *tr. V.* round ⟨*headland, cape*⟩; steer clear of ⟨*rocks, fig.: obstacle*⟩
Ụm·schlag der a) cover; **b)** *(Brief~)* envelope; **c)** *(Schutz~)* jacket; *(einer Broschüre, eines Heftes)* cover; **d)** *(Med.: Wickel)* compress; *(warm)* poultice; **e)** *(Hosen~)* turn-up; *(Ärmel~)* cuff; **f)** *(Veränderung)* [sudden] change (*Gen.* in); **g)** *(Wirtsch.: Güter~)* transfer; trans-shipment
Ụmschlag·bahnhof der transfer station
ụm|schlagen 1. *unr. tr. V.* **a)** *(umklappen)* turn up ⟨*sleeve, collar, trousers*⟩; turn over ⟨*page*⟩; **b)** *(umladen, verladen)* turn round, trans-ship ⟨*goods*⟩. **2.** *unr. itr. V.; mit sein* ⟨*weather, mood*⟩ change (**in +** *Akk.* into); ⟨*wind*⟩ veer [round]; ⟨*voice*⟩ break; ⟨*wine*⟩ go off; **ins Gegenteil ~:** change completely; become the opposite
Ụmschlage·tuch das; *Pl.* **~tücher** shawl
Ụmschlag-: ~hafen der port of trans-shipment; **~platz der** trans-shipment centre; **~tuch das** *s.* **Umschlagetuch**
um·schließen *unr. tr. V.* **a)** ⟨*river, wall*⟩ surround; ⟨*shell, husk, etc.*⟩ enclose; ⟨*hand, fingers, tentacles*⟩ clasp, hold; **er umschloß sie mit beiden Armen** he put both arms around her; **b)** *(einschließen, umzingeln)* surround, encircle ⟨*position, enemy*⟩; **c)** *(zum Inhalt haben)* embrace
um·schlịngen *unr. tr. V.* **a) jmdn./etw. [mit den Armen] ~:** put one's arms around sb./sth.; embrace sb./sth.; **sich umschlungen halten** hold one another in an embrace; **eng umschlungen** in a tight embrace *postpos.*; **b)** *(sich schlingen um)* twine [itself] round
Umschlịngung die; ~, ~en embrace; *(einer Boa o. ä.)* grip
Ụm·schluß der *(Rechtsw.)* limited freedom of association *(for prisoners awaiting trial)*
um·schmeicheln *tr. V.* heap flattery on; *(fig.)* caress ⟨*part of body*⟩
ụm|schmeißen *unr. tr. V. (ugs.) s.* **umwerfen a, b**
ụm|schnallen *tr. V.* **[sich** *(Dat.)***] ~:** buckle on ⟨*belt, sword*⟩; **jmdm./einem Tier etw. ~:** buckle *or* strap sth. on to sb./an animal
[1]**ụm|schreiben** *unr. tr. V.* **a)** rewrite; **b)** *(übertragen)* transfer ⟨*money, property*⟩ (**auf +** *Akk.* to); **c)** *(transkribieren)* transcribe
[2]**um·schreiben** *unr. tr. V.* **a)** *(in Worte fassen)* describe; *(definieren)* define ⟨*meaning, sb.'s task, etc.*⟩; *(paraphrasieren)* paraphrase ⟨*word, expression*⟩; **b)** *(Sprachw.)* construct (**mit** with); **das Perfekt wird mit „sein" umschrieben** the perfect is conjugated with 'sein'; **c)** *(mit einer Linie umgeben)* outline; *(andeuten)* indicate; **umschrieben** *(Med.)* localized ⟨*eczema etc.*⟩
Um·schreibung die a) description; *(Definition)* definition; *(Verhüllung)* circumlocution (*Gen.* for); **b)** *s.* [2]**umschreiben b:** construction; conjugation
Ụm·schrift die a) *(Sprachw.)* transcription; **b)** *(bes. Münzk.)* circumscription
ụm|schulden *tr. (auch itr.) V. (Finanzw.)* convert ⟨*loan*⟩; *(mit längerer Laufzeit)* reschedule ⟨*loan, debt*⟩
Ụmschuldung die; ~, ~en *(Finanzw.)* loan conversion; *(mit längerer Laufzeit)* extension of credit; rescheduling [of a/the loan/loans]
ụm|schulen 1. *tr. V.* **a) ein Kind [auf eine andere Schule] ~:** transfer a child [to another school]; **b)** *(beruflich)* retrain; **jmdn. auf** *od.* **zum Monteur ~:** retrain sb. as a fitter. **2.** *itr. V.* retrain (**auf +** *Akk.* as)
Ụmschulung die a) transfer [to another school]; **b)** *(beruflich)* retraining *no pl.* (**auf +** *Akk.* as)

ụm|schütten *tr. V.* **a)** pour [into another container]; decant ⟨*liquid*⟩; **b)** *(verschütten)* spill

um·schwạ̈rmen *tr. V.* **a)** swarm around; **von Moskitos umschwärmt werden** be besieged by mosquitoes; **b)** *(fig.)* flock around; **sie war sehr** *od.* **von vielen umschwärmt** she had many admirers

Ụm·schweif der circumlocution; **ohne ~e** without beating about the bush; **mach keine [langen] ~e!** get on with it!

ụm|schwenken *itr. V.; mit sein* **a)** ⟨*person, column*⟩ swing round; ⟨*wind*⟩ veer [round]; **b)** *(fig.)* do an about-face

um·schwịrren *tr. V.* buzz around

Ụm·schwung der a) complete change; *(in der Politik usw.)* U-turn; volte-face; **b)** *(Turnen)* circle

um·sẹgeln *tr. V.* sail round ⟨*world, island, etc.*⟩; circumnavigate ⟨*world*⟩; *(fig.)* negotiate ⟨*obstacle etc.*⟩

ụm|sehen *unr. refl. V.* **a)** look; **sich im Zimmer ~:** look [a]round the room; **sehen Sie sich ruhig um** *(im Geschäft usw.)* by all means have a look round; **du wirst dich noch ~!** *(ugs.)* you're in for a [nasty] shock; **sich nach etw. ~** *(fig.)* be looking *or* on the look-out for sth.; **b)** *(zurücksehen)* look round *or* back; **eine Frau, nach der sich alle Männer ~:** a woman who makes every man turn his head

ụm|sein *unr. itr. V. (Zusschr. nur im Inf. u. Part.) (ugs.)* ⟨*time*⟩ be up

ụmseitig 1. *Adj.* ⟨*text, illustration, etc.*⟩ overleaf. **2.** *adv.* overleaf

ụmsetz·bar *Adj. (fig.: umwandelbar)* convertible (**in + *Akk.*** into); **der Vorschlag ist kaum in die Praxis ~:** the suggestion can scarcely be translated into practice

ụm|setzen 1. *tr. V.* **a)** move; *(auf anderen Sitzplatz)* move to another seat/other seats; *(im Restaurant)* move to another table; *(auf anderen Posten, Arbeitsplatz usw.)* move, transfer (**in + *Akk.*** to); *(in andere Wohnung)* rehouse (**in + *Akk.*** in); *(umpflanzen)* transplant ⟨*bush etc.*⟩; *(in anderen Topf)* repot ⟨*plant*⟩; **b)** *(verwirklichen)* implement ⟨*plan*⟩; translate ⟨*plan, intention, etc.*⟩ into action *or* reality; realize ⟨*ideas*⟩; **Erlebnisse in Literatur ~:** give experiences literary form; *s. auch* **Praxis a; Tat a; c)** *(in Waren, Geld usw.)* spend, dispose of ⟨*money*⟩; **etw. in Geld/Bares ~:** turn sth. into money/cash; **Geld in Schnaps/Geschenke ~:** spend money on schnapps/presents; **d)** *(Wirtsch.)* turn over, have a turnover of ⟨*x marks etc.*⟩; sell ⟨*shares, goods*⟩. **2.** *refl. V.* **a)** *(den Sitzplatz wechseln)* move to another seat/other seats; change seats; *(den Tisch wechseln)* move to another table; change tables; **b)** *(sich verwandeln)* transform itself, *(Physik)* be converted (**in + *Akk.*** into)

Ụmsetzung die; ~, ~en a) *(auf einen anderen Posten)* transfer (**in + *Akk.*** to); *(in eine andere Wohnung)* rehousing (**in + *Akk.*** in); *(Umpflanzung)* transplant[ing]; *(in einen anderen Topf)* repotting; **durch die ~ des Schülers** by moving the pupil [to another seat/desk]; **b)** *(Verwirklichung)* realization; *(eines Plans)* implementation; *(Umformung)* transformation (**in + *Akk.*** into); *(bes. Technik, Physik)* conversion (**in + *Akk.*** into); **chemische ~en** chemical changes; **c)** *(Wirtsch.: Verkauf)* turnover; sale

Ụm·sicht die; *o. Pl.* circumspection; prudence

ụm·sichtig 1. *Adj.* circumspect; prudent. **2.** *adv.* circumspectly; prudently

ụm|siedeln 1. *tr. V.* resettle; **nach X umgesiedelt werden** be moved to X. **2.** *itr. V.; mit sein* move (**in + *Akk.*, nach** to); **in ein anderes Land ~:** settle in another country; emigrate

Ụm·siedler der resettled person; *(freiwillig)* resettler

Ụm·siedlung die resettlement; **seit meiner ~ aus der DDR in den Westen** since I moved to the West from the GDR

ụm|sinken *unr. itr. V.; mit sein* sink *or* fall to the ground

um·sọnst *Adv.* **a)** *(unentgeltlich)* free; for nothing; **für ~** *(ugs.)* free, gratis, and for nothing *(joc.)*; **~ sein** *(ugs.)* be free [of charge]; not cost anything; **das hast du nicht ~ getan!** *(ugs.)* you'll pay for that!; **b)** *(vergebens)* in vain; **c) nicht ~ hat er davor gewarnt** not for nothing did he warn of that

um·sọrgen *tr. V.* care for; look after

um·spạnnen *tr. V.* **a)** clasp ⟨*hand, wrist, ankle, etc.*⟩; put one's hands round ⟨*neck etc.*⟩; **b)** *(fig.: einschieben)* encompass ⟨*subjects, period*⟩; **alles ~d** all-embracing

Ụmspann·werk das *(Elektrot.)* transformer station

um·spiẹlen *tr. V.* **a)** ⟨*smile, light*⟩ play about; ⟨*waves*⟩ lap about *or* around; ⟨*skirt etc.*⟩ swirl about *or* around; **b)** *(Ballspiele)* go round ⟨*defender*⟩

ụm|springen *unr. itr. V.; mit sein* **a)** ⟨*wind*⟩ veer round (**auf + *Akk.*** to); ⟨*traffic-light, fig.: mood*⟩ change; **b)** *(ugs. abwertend)* **mit jmdm. grob/übel** *usw.* **~:** treat sb. roughly/badly *etc.*

ụm|spulen *tr. V.* rewind ⟨*tape, film*⟩

um·spụ̈len *tr. V.* wash round; **ein von den Wellen umspültes Riff** a reef washed by the waves

Ụm·stand der a) *(Gegebenheit)* circumstance; *(Tatsache)* fact; **die näheren Umstände** the particular circumstances; *(Einzelheiten)* the details; **ein glücklicher ~:** a lucky *or* happy chance; **den Umständen entsprechend** as one would expect [in *or* under the circumstances]; **den Umständen entsprechend gut** *(ugs.)* as well as can be expected [given the circumstances]; **das kommt unter gar keinen Umständen in Frage** there is no question of that under any circumstances; **unter allen Umständen** whatever happens; **unter Umständen** possibly; **in anderen Umständen sein** *(ugs.)* be expecting; be in the family way *(coll.)*; **b)** *(Aufwand)* business; hassle *(coll.)*; **macht keine [großen] Umstände** please don't go to any bother *or* trouble; **das macht gar keine Umstände** it's no bother *or* trouble at all

ụmstände·halber *Adv.* owing to circumstances; **„~ zu verkaufen"** 'forced to sell'; 'genuine reason for sale'

umständlich [ˈʊmʃtɛntlɪç] **1.** *Adj.* involved, elaborate ⟨*procedure, method, description, explanation, etc.*⟩; elaborate, laborious ⟨*preparation, check, etc.*⟩; awkward, difficult ⟨*journey, job*⟩; *(kompliziert)* involved; complicated; *(weitschweifig)* long-winded; *(Umstände machend)* awkward, *(coll.)* pernickety ⟨*person*⟩; **das ist mir zu ~:** that is too much trouble *or (coll.)* hassle [for me]; **es ist etwas ~, mit dem Auto dorthin zu kommen** getting there by car is rather awkward *or* rather a business. **2.** *adv.* in an involved *or* roundabout way; *(weitschweifig)* ⟨*explain etc.*⟩ at great length *or* in a long-winded way; **sie drückt sich manchmal etwas ~ aus** she is sometimes rather long-winded; **er verabschiedete/entschuldigte sich ~:** he made a meal of saying 'goodbye'/'sorry'; **warum einfach, wenn's auch ~ geht?** *(iron.)* why do things the easy way if you can make them difficult? *(iron.)*

Ụmstands-: ~an·gabe, ~bestimmung die *(Sprachw.)* adverbial qualification; **~ergänzung die** *(Sprachw.)* adverbial complement; **~für·wort das** *(Sprachw.)* pronominal adverb; **~kleid das** maternity dress; **~kleidung die** maternity wear; **~krämer der** *(ugs. abwertend)* fuss-pot *(coll.)*; **~moden** *Pl.* maternity styles; **~satz der** *(Sprachw.)* adverbial clause; **~wort das** *(Sprachw.)* adverb

um·stẹhen *unr. tr. V.* stand round; surround

ụmstehend 1. *Adj.; nicht präd.* **a)** standing round *postpos.*; **die ~en Personen, die Umstehenden** the bystanders; **b)** *(umseitig)* overleaf *postpos.* **2.** *adv.* overleaf

ụm|steigen *unr. itr. V.* **a)** change (**in + *Akk.*** [on] to); **nach Frankfurt ~:** change for Frankfurt; **b)** *(fig. ugs.)* change over, switch (**auf + *Akk.*** to)

[1]**ụm|stellen 1.** *tr. V.* **a)** *(anders stellen)* rearrange, change round ⟨*furniture, books, etc.*⟩; reorder ⟨*words etc.*⟩; transpose ⟨*two words*⟩; reshuffle ⟨*team*⟩; **b)** *(anders einstellen)* reset ⟨*lever, switch, points, clock*⟩; **c)** *(ändern)* change *or* switch over (**auf + *Akk.*** to). **2.** *refl. V.* adjust (**auf + *Akk.*** to); **er hat sich auf Rohkost umgestellt** he has changed his diet to raw fruit and vegetables. **3.** *itr. V.* switch over (**auf + *Akk.*** to)

[2]**um·stẹllen** *tr. V.* surround

Ụm·stellung die *s.* [1]**umstellen 1, 2: a)** rearrangement; reordering; transposition; redeployment; reshuffle; **b)** resetting; **c)** change-over, switch (**auf + *Akk.*** to); **d)** *(das Sichumstellen)* change; [re-]adjustment

ụm|stimmen *tr. V. (fig.: zu einer anderen Haltung bewegen)* win ⟨*person*⟩ round; **er ließ sich nicht ~:** he was not to be persuaded; he refused to change his mind

ụm|stoßen *unr. tr. V.* **a)** knock over; **b)** *(rückgängig machen)* reverse ⟨*judgement, decision*⟩; change ⟨*plan, decision*⟩; **c)** *(zunichte machen)* upset, wreck ⟨*plan, theory*⟩

umstrịtten *Adj.* disputed; controversial ⟨*bill, book, author, proposal, policy, etc.*⟩

ụm|strukturieren *tr. V.* restructure

ụm|stülpen *tr. V.* **a)** turn inside out; *(umkrempeln)* turn *or* roll up ⟨*trousers, sleeves, etc.*⟩; **b)** *(auskippen)* turn out, empty ⟨*purse, bag, etc.*⟩; **c)** *(umdrehen)* turn upside down; *(fig.)* turn on its head

Ụm·sturz der coup

ụm|stürzen 1. *tr. V.* overturn; knock over; *(fig.)* topple, overthrow ⟨*political system, government*⟩. **2.** *itr. V.* overturn; ⟨*wall, building, chimney*⟩ fall down

Umstürzler [ˈʊmʃtʏrt͜slɐ] **der; ~s, ~** *(abwertend)* subversive agent

ụmstürzlerisch *(abwertend)* **1.** *Adj.* subversive. **2.** *adv.* **sich ~ betätigen** engage in subversive activities

Ụmsturz·versuch der attempted coup

ụm|taufen *tr. V.* **jmdn./*(ugs.)* etw. ~:** rename sb./sth.; change sb.'s name/the name of sth. (**auf + *Akk.*** to)

Ụm·tausch der exchange; **beim ~:** when exchanging goods/changing money; **reduzierte Ware ist vom ~ ausgeschlossen** sale goods cannot be exchanged

ụm|tauschen *tr. V.* exchange ⟨*goods, article*⟩ (**gegen** for); change ⟨*dollars, pounds, etc.*⟩ (**in + *Akk.*** into)

ụm|topfen *tr. V.* repot ⟨*plant*⟩

um·tọsen *tr. V. (geh.)* surge around; **von etw. umtost** buffeted by sth.

Ụm|triebe *Pl. (abwertend)* [subversive] intrigues; subversion *sing.*

Ụm·trunk der communal drink

ụm|tun *unr. refl. V. (ugs.)* look [a]round; **sich nach etw. ~:** be on the look-out *or* looking for sth.

U̱-Musik die; *o. Pl.* light music

ụm|verteilen *tr. V.* redistribute

Ụm·verteilung die redistribution

ụm|wälzen *tr. V.* **a)** roll over; **~d** *(fig.)* revolutionary ⟨*ideas, effect*⟩; epoch-making ⟨*events*⟩; **b)** *(zirkulieren lassen)* circulate ⟨*water, air*⟩

Ụmwälz·pumpe die circulating pump

Ụmwälzung die; ~, ~en *(fig.)* revolution

ụm|wandeln 1. *tr. V.* convert ⟨*substance, building, etc.*⟩ (**in + *Akk.*** into); commute ⟨*sentence*⟩ (**in + *Akk.*** to); *(ändern)* change; alter; **er ist wie umgewandelt** he is a changed man. **2.** *refl. V.* be converted (**in** + *Akk.* into)

Um·wandlung die conversion (**in** + *Akk.* into); *(einer Strafe)* commutation (**in** + *Akk.* to); *(der Gesellschaft usw.)* transformation

um|wechseln *tr. V.* change ⟨*marks, note, etc.*⟩ (**in** + *Akk.* into)

Um·weg der detour; **auf einem ~ nach Hause fahren** go a long way round *or* make a detour to get home; **auf ~en** by a circuitous *or* roundabout route; *(fig.)* in a roundabout way; **auf dem ~ über** (+ *Akk.*) *(fig.)* [indirectly] via

Um·welt die a) environment; **b)** *(Menschen)* people *pl.* around sb.; **meine/deine/seine ~:** those *pl.* around me/you/him

umwelt-, Umwelt-: ~bedingt *Adj.* caused by the *or* one's environment *postpos.*; **~belastung die** environmental pollution *no indef. art.*; **~feindlich 1.** *Adj.* inimical to the environment *postpos.*; ecologically undesirable; **2.** *adv.* in an ecologically undesirable way; ⟨*drive, behave*⟩ without regard for the environment; **~forschung die;** *o. Pl.* **a)** *(Biol.)* ecology; **b)** *(Soziol.)* environmental studies *pl., no art. or* science *no art.*; **~freundlich 1.** *Adj.* environment-friendly; ecologically desirable; **2.** *adv.* in an ecologically desirable way; ⟨*act*⟩ with some regard for the environment; **~kriminalität die** environmental crime; **~politik die** ecological policy; **~schäden** *Pl.* environmental damage *sing.*; damage *sing.* to the environment; **~schädlich 1.** *Adj.* harmful to the environment *postpos.*; ecologically harmful; **2.** *adv.* in an ecologically harmful way; **~schutz der** environmental protection *no art.*; conservation of the environment; **~schützer der** environmentalist; conservationist; **~sünder der** *(ugs.)* deliberate polluter of the environment; **~verschmutzung die** pollution [of the environment]

um|wenden 1. *regelm. (auch unr.) tr. V.;* **a)** *(auf die andere Seite)* turn over ⟨*page, joint, etc.*⟩; **b)** *(in die andere Richtung)* turn round ⟨*vehicle, horse*⟩; **c)** *(von innen nach außen)* turn ⟨*garment*⟩ inside out. **2.** *unr. od. regelm. refl. V.* turn round

um·werben *unr. tr. V.* court; woo

um|werfen *unr. tr. V.* **a)** knock over; knock ⟨*person*⟩ down *or* over; *(fig. ugs.: aus der Fassung bringen)* bowl ⟨*person*⟩ over; stun ⟨*person*⟩; *(fig. ugs.: betrunken machen)* knock ⟨*person*⟩ out *(sl.)*; **das wirft selbst den stärksten Mann um!** it's more than even the strongest man can take; **b)** *(fig. ugs.; umstoßen)* knock ⟨*plan*⟩ on the head *(coll.)*; **c)** *(umlegen, umhängen)* throw *or* put sth. round sb.'s/one's shoulders

umwerfend *(ugs.)* **1.** *Adj.* fantastic *(coll.)*; stunning *(coll.)*. **2.** *adv.* fantastically [well] *(coll.)*; brilliantly; **~ komisch** hilariously funny; **~ schön** stunningly beautiful *(coll.)*

um·wickeln *tr. V.* wrap; bind; *(mit einem Verband)* bandage; **etw. mit Schnur/Draht ~:** wind string/wire round sth.

um|widmen *tr. V.* *(Verwaltung)* redesignate (**in** + *Akk.*, **zu** as)

Um·widmung die *(Verwaltung)* redesignation (**in** + *Akk.* as)

um·wittern *tr. V. (geh.)* **von Gefahren/einem Geheimnis umwittert sein** be beset *or* fraught with danger/shrouded in mystery

umwohnend *Adj.; nicht präd.* living in the neighbourhood *postpos.*

um·wölken [ʊmˈvœlkn̩] **1.** *refl. V. (geh.)* ⟨*sky*⟩ cloud over; *(fig.)* ⟨*brow, look*⟩ darken. **2.** *tr. V.* shroud; veil

um|wühlen *tr. V.* churn *or* plough up

um·zäunen *tr. V.* fence round *or* off

Umzäunung die; ~, ~en a) *(das Umzäunen)* fencing round *or* off; **b)** *(Zaun)* fence, fencing (*Gen.* round)

um|ziehen 1. *unr. itr. V.; mit sein* move (**an** + *Akk.*, **in** + *Akk.*, **nach** to). **2.** *unr. tr. V. (umkleiden)* **jmdn./sich ~:** change sb. *or* get sb. changed/change *or* get changed; **sich zum Essen ~:** change for dinner

um·zingeln [ʊmˈtsɪŋl̩n] *tr. V.* surround; encircle

Umzingelung die; ~: encirclement

Um·zug der a) move; *(von Möbeln)* removal; **jmdm. beim ~ helfen** help sb. move; help with the removal; **b)** *(Festzug)* procession; *(Demonstrationszug)* demonstration

Umzugs·kosten *Pl.* removal costs

UN [uːˈɛn] *Pl.* UN *sing.*

unabänderlich [ʊnlapˈlɛndɐlɪç] **1.** *Adj.* unalterable; irrevocable ⟨*decision*⟩; **sich in das Unabänderliche fügen** resign oneself to the inevitable. **2.** *adv.* irrevocably; **das steht ~ fest** that is absolutely certain

unabdingbar [ʊnlapˈdɪŋbaːɐ̯] *Adj.* **a)** *(geh.)* indispensable; **b)** *(Rechtsspr.)* inalienable

unabhängig 1. *Adj.* independent (**von** of); *(unbeeinflußt)* unaffected (**von** by); **sich ~ machen** go one's own way; ⟨*colony*⟩ become independent. **2.** *adv.* independently (**von** of); **~ voneinander** independently [of one another]; separately; **es kostet 20 Pfennig, ~ von der Gesprächsdauer** it costs 20 pfennigs irrespective *or* regardless of the length of the call; **~ davon, ob .../was .../wo ...** *usw.* irrespective *or* regardless of whether .../what .../where ... *etc.*

Unabhängigkeit die independence

Unabhängigkeits·erklärung die declaration of independence

unabkömmlich [ʊnlapˈkœmlɪç] *Adj.* indispensable; **sie ist im Moment ~:** she is otherwise engaged

unablässig [ˈʊnlaplɛsɪç] **1.** *Adj.* incessant; constant ⟨*repetition*⟩; unremitting ⟨*effort*⟩. **2.** *adv.* incessantly; constantly

unabsehbar 1. *Adj.* **a)** *(fig.)* incalculable, immeasurable ⟨*extent, damage, etc.*⟩; **in ~er Ferne** *(zeitlich)* in the unforeseeable future; **auf ~e Zeit** far into the future; **b)** *(noch nicht vorauszusehen)* unforeseeable ⟨*consequences*⟩. **2.** *adv.* **a)** incalculably; immeasurably; **b)** *(in einem noch nicht erkennbaren Ausmaß)* to an unforeseeable extent

unabsichtlich 1. *Adj.* unintentional. **2.** *adv.* unintentionally

unabweisbar 1. *Adj.* irrefutable; absolute ⟨*necessity*⟩. **2.** *adv.* irrefutably; undeniably

unabwendbar *Adj.* inevitable

unachtsam 1. *Adj.* **a)** inattentive; **einen Augenblick ~ sein** let one's attention wander for a moment; **b)** *(nicht sorgfältig)* careless. **2.** *adv. (ohne Sorgfalt)* carelessly

Unachtsamkeit die; ~ a) inattentiveness; **b)** *(mangelnde Sorgfalt)* carelessness

unähnlich *Adj.* dissimilar; **jmdm./einer Sache ~ sein** be unlike sb./sth.

unanfechtbar *Adj.* incontestable

unangebracht *Adj.* inappropriate; misplaced

unangefochten *Adj.* unchallenged ⟨*victor, leadership, etc.*⟩; *(unbestritten)* undisputed, unchallenged ⟨*assertion, thesis*⟩; *(Rechtsw.)* uncontested ⟨*verdict, will, etc.*⟩

unangemeldet *Adj.* **a)** *(unangekündigt)* unexpected ⟨*visit, guest*⟩; unauthorized ⟨*demonstration*⟩; **~ kommen** come unannounced; **~ zum Arzt gehen** go to the doctor without an appointment; **b)** *(nicht registriert)* unregistered ⟨*person, participant*⟩; unlicensed ⟨*television set, radio*⟩

unangemessen 1. *Adj.* unsuitable; inappropriate; unreasonable, disproportionate ⟨*demand, claim, sentence, etc.*⟩. **2.** *adv.* unsuitably; inappropriately; disproportionately ⟨*high, low*⟩; **er reagierte völlig ~:** his reaction was out of all proportion; *(unpassend)* his reaction was entirely inappropriate

unangenehm 1. *Adj.* unpleasant (+ *Dat.* for); *(peinlich)* embarrassing, awkward ⟨*question, situation*⟩; **es ist mir sehr ~, daß ich mich verspätet habe** I am most upset about being late; **die Frage war ihm sichtlich ~:** he clearly found the question embarrassing; **~ werden** ⟨*person*⟩ get *or* turn nasty. **2.** *adv.* unpleasantly; *(peinlich)* **die Frage schien ihn ~ zu berühren** the question appeared to embarrass him; **~ auffallen** make a bad impression

unangepaßt 1. *Adj.* nonconformist. **2.** *adv.* in a nonconformist way

unangetastet *Adj.* untouched

unangreifbar *Adj. (auch fig.)* unassailable; impregnable ⟨*fortress*⟩; *(unanfechtbar)* irrefutable ⟨*argument, thesis*⟩; incontestable ⟨*judgement etc.*⟩

unannehmbar *Adj.* unacceptable

Unannehmlichkeit die trouble; **mit/durch etw. ~en bekommen** get [a lot of *(coll.)*] trouble with sth./as a result of sth.; **~en auf sich** *(Akk.)* **nehmen** take on unpleasant business; **jmdm. ~en bereiten** cause sb. [a lot of *(coll.)*] problems *or* difficulties

unansehnlich *Adj.* unprepossessing; plain ⟨*girl*⟩

unanständig 1. *Adj.* **a)** improper; *(anstößig)* indecent ⟨*behaviour, remark*⟩; dirty ⟨*joke*⟩; rude ⟨*word, song*⟩; **b)** *(verwerflich)* immoral. **2.** *adv.* **a)** improperly; **~ kurze Röcke** indecently short skirts; **b)** *(verwerflich)* immorally; **c)** *(ugs.; unmäßig, allzu)* disgustingly ⟨*fat*⟩; indecently ⟨*often*⟩; **~ viel essen** eat a disgusting amount

Unanständigkeit die a) *o. Pl.* impropriety; indecency; *(Obszönität)* obscenity; **b)** *(anstößige Handlung)* impropriety; *(anstößige Äußerung)* obscenity; indecent remark; **c)** *o. Pl. (Verwerflichkeit)* immorality; **d)** *(verwerfliche Handlung)* immoral action

unantastbar *Adj.* inviolable

unappetitlich 1. *Adj.* unappetizing; *(fig.)* unsavoury ⟨*joke*⟩; unsavoury-looking ⟨*person*⟩; disgusting ⟨*wash-basin, nails, etc.*⟩. **2.** *adv.* unappetizingly

Unart die bad habit

unartig 1. *Adj.* naughty. **2.** *adv.* naughtily; ⟨*behave*⟩ badly

unartikuliert 1. *Adj.* inarticulate; *(fig.: nicht ausgedrückt)* unexpressed ⟨*feeling, thought, desire, etc.*⟩. **2.** *adv.* inarticulately

unästhetisch 1. *Adj.* unpleasant, unsavoury ⟨*sight etc.*⟩; ugly ⟨*building etc.*⟩; *(abstoßend)* disgusting. **2.** *adv.* in an unsavoury/a disgusting way

unaufdringlich 1. *Adj.* unassuming ⟨*person*⟩; *(fig.)* unobtrusive, discreet ⟨*music, décor, etc.*⟩; discreet ⟨*perfume, colour, elegance, etc.*⟩. **2.** *adv.* discreetly

unauffällig 1. *Adj.* inconspicuous; unobtrusive ⟨*scar, defect, skill, behaviour, surveillance, etc.*⟩; discreet ⟨*signal, elegance*⟩; **sie ist eine eher ~e Erscheinung** she is not at all striking. **2.** *adv.* inconspicuously; unobtrusively; ⟨*behave, follow, observe, disappear, leave*⟩ unobtrusively, discreetly

unauffindbar *Adj.* untraceable; **~ sein** *od.* **bleiben** be nowhere to be found

unaufgefordert *Adv.* without being asked; **~ eingesandte Manuskripte** unsolicited manuscripts

unaufgeklärt *Adj.* **a)** unresolved ⟨*misunderstanding*⟩; unsolved ⟨*crime, mystery*⟩; **b)** *(ignorant)* unenlightened ⟨*age, person*⟩; *(sexualkundlich)* ignorant of the facts of life *postpos.*

unaufhaltsam 1. *Adj.* inexorable. **2.** *adv.* inexorably

unaufhörlich 1. *Adj.; nicht präd.* constant; incessant; continuous ⟨*rain*⟩. **2.** *adv.* constantly; ⟨*rain, snow*⟩ continuously; **das Telefon klingelte ~:** the telephone was for ever ringing *or* never stopped ringing

unauflöslich *Adj.* irreconcilable ⟨*contradiction etc.*⟩; indissoluble ⟨*marriage, link*⟩

ụnaufmerksam 1. *Adj.* inattentive (**gegenüber** to); careless ‹*driver*›. **2.** *adv.* **sich seinen Gästen gegenüber ~ verhalten** not pay enough attention to one's guests
Ụnaufmerksamkeit die inattentiveness; *(Fahrlässigkeit)* carelessness
ụnaufrichtig *Adj.* insincere; **jmdm. gegenüber ~ sein** not be honest with sb.
Ụnaufrichtigkeit die a) *o. Pl.* insincerity; **b)** *(Handlung)* insincere action
unaufschiebbar *Adj.* **es war ~:** it could not be put off *or* postponed
unausbleiblich *Adj.* inevitable; unavoidable
unausdẹnkbar *Adj.* unimaginable
ụnausgefüllt *Adj.* uncompleted, blank ‹*form*›; *(fig.)* unfulfilled ‹*person*›; unfilled ‹*time*›; empty ‹*life*›
ụnausgeglichen *Adj.* **a)** *(emotional)* [emotionally] unstable ‹*person, behaviour*›; **b)** *(Wirtsch.)* ‹*balance of payments*› not in balance; unsettled ‹*account, debt*›; **c)** *(unausgewogen)* unbalanced ‹*report, relationship, etc.*›; unequal ‹*distribution*›; *(ungleichmäßig)* uneven, changeable ‹*climate*›
Ụnausgeglichenheit die a) *(eines Menschen)* instability; **b)** *(Wirtsch.)* imbalance; **c)** *(Unausgewogenheit)* imbalance; *(Ungleichmäßigkeit)* unevenness; inconsistency
ụnausgegoren *Adj. (abwertend)* immature
ụnausgeschlafen *Adj.* **[völlig] ~ sein/aussehen** have not had/look as though one has not had [anything like] enough sleep; **~ zur Schule kommen** come to school tired through lack of sleep
unauslọ̈schlich 1. *Adj. (geh.)* indelible ‹*impression*›; unforgettable ‹*experience*›. **2.** *adv.* indelibly
unaussprẹchlich 1. *Adj.* **a)** inexpressible; **b)** *(geh.: unbeschreiblich)* indescribable ‹*misery, joy*›; unutterable ‹*misery, sorrow*›. **2.** *adv. (geh.)* unutterably; indescribably; ‹*suffer, love*› beyond expression
unausstehlich 1. *Adj.* unbearable ‹*person, noise, smell, etc.*›; insufferable ‹*person*›; intolerable ‹*noise, smell*›. **2.** *adv.* unbearably; intolerably; insufferably ‹*stupid, curious*›
unausweichlich *Adj.* unavoidable; inevitable
unbändig ['ʊnbɛndɪç] **1.** *Adj.* **a)** boisterous ‹*person, horse, temperament*›; **b)** *(überaus groß/stark)* unbridled, unrestrained ‹*desire, longing, joy, merriment*›; unbridled, uncontrollable ‹*fury, hate, anger*›; ravenous ‹*hunger*›. **2.** *adv.* **a)** wildly; **b)** *(sehr, äußerst)* unrestrainedly; tremendously *(coll.)*; **~ jubeln** *od.* **jauchzen, sich ~ freuen** jump for joy
ụnbar 1. *Adj.*; *nicht präd.* cashless. **2.** *adv.* ‹*pay*› without using cash
ụnbarmherzig 1. *Adj. (auch fig.)* merciless; remorseless, unsparing ‹*severity*›; *(fig.)* very severe ‹*winter, cold*›; **jmdm. gegenüber** *od.* **gegen jmdn. ~ sein** show sb. no mercy. **2.** *adv.* mercilessly; without mercy
ụnbeabsichtigt 1. *Adj.* unintentional. **2.** *adv.* unintentionally
ụnbeachtet *Adj.* unnoticed; obscure ‹*existence*›; **~ leben** live in obscurity; **jmdn./etw. ~ lassen** not take any notice of sb./sth.
ụnbeanstandet 1. *Adj.* **etw. ~ lassen** let sth. pass; **~ bleiben** be allowed to pass. **2.** *adv.* without objection; **~ durch die Gütekontrolle gehen** be allowed to pass through quality control [without any problems]
ụnbeantwortet *Adj.* unanswered
ụnbearbeitet *Adj.* **a)** undealt with *pred.*; which has/have not been dealt with *postpos.*; **b)** *(roh)* untreated ‹*wood, leather, metal*›; *(unbestellt)* uncultivated ‹*land, field*›; *(nicht redigiert)* unedited ‹*manuscript*›; *(nicht verändert, adaptiert)* unchanged, unadapted ‹*play, version*›
ụnbebaut *Adj.* **a)** undeveloped ‹*site, land*›; **b)** *(unbestellt)* uncultivated ‹*land, area*›
ụnbedacht 1. *Adj.* rash; thoughtless. **2.** *adv.* rashly; thoughtlessly
ụnbedarft 1. *Adj. (ugs.)* **a)** inexpert; lay; **er ist literarisch [völlig/ziemlich] ~:** he has no/little idea about literature; **b)** *(naiv)* naïve; *(dümmlich)* gormless *(coll.)*. **2.** *adv.* naïvely; *(dümmlich)* gormlessly *(coll.)*
ụnbedeckt *Adj.* uncovered; bare; **mit ~em Kopf** bare-headed
ụnbedenklich 1. *Adj.* **a)** harmless, safe ‹*substance, drug*›; ‹*state of health, situation*› giving no cause for concern; unobjectionable ‹*joke, plan, reading matter*›; **es ist nicht ganz ~:** it is to some extent open to objection; **b)** *(hemmungslos, skrupellos)* unthinking; unconsidered. **2.** *adv.* without second thoughts
ụnbedeutend 1. *Adj.* insignificant; minor ‹*artist, poet*›; slight, minor ‹*improvement, change, error*›. **2.** *adv.* slightly
ụnbedingt 1. *Adj.* **a)** absolute ‹*trust, faith, reliability, secrecy, etc.*›; complete ‹*rest*›; **b)** *(Physiol.)* **~e Reflexe** unconditioned reflexes. **2.** *Adv.* absolutely; *(auf jeden Fall)* whatever happens; **etw. ~ tun müssen/wollen** really *or* absolutely have to/be absolutely determined to do sth.; **der Brief muß ~ heute noch weg** the letter really must be posted today; **ich brauche ~ neue Reifen** I need new tyres whatever happens; I really have to have new tyres; **nicht ~:** not necessarily; **nicht ~ nötig** not absolutely necessary; **~!** absolutely!; of course!
ụnbeeidigt *Adj. (Rechtsw.)* unsworn; **der Zeuge blieb ~:** the witness was not on *or* under oath
ụnbeeindruckt *Adj.* unimpressed
ụnbeeinflußt *Adj.* uninfluenced; **von jeder Propaganda ~:** not influenced by any propaganda *postpos.*
ụnbefahrbar *Adj.* **a)** *(für Landfahrzeuge)* impassable; **b)** *(für Wasserfahrzeuge)* unnavigable; not navigable *pred.*
ụnbefangen 1. *Adj.* **a)** *(ungehemmt)* uninhibited; natural, uninhibited ‹*behaviour*›; **er ist anderen gegenüber ganz ~:** he is perfectly natural with other people; **b)** *(unvoreingenommen)* impartial. **2.** *adv.* freely; without inhibition; ‹*behave*› naturally; **jmdm./einer Sache ~ gegenübertreten** approach sb./sth. with an open mind
Ụnbefangenheit die *s.* **unbefangen 1 a, b:** uninhibitedness; naturalness; impartiality
ụnbefleckt *Adj. (geh.)* undefiled; unsullied *(literary)*; **die Unbefleckte Empfängnis** *(christl. Rel.)* the Immaculate Conception
ụnbefriedigend *Adj.* unsatisfactory
ụnbefriedigt *Adj.* dissatisfied (**von** with); unsatisfied ‹*need, curiosity, desire, etc.*›; *(unausgefüllt)* unfulfilled (**von** by); *(sexuell)* [sexually] unsatisfied *or* frustrated
ụnbefristet 1. *Adj.* for an indefinite *or* unlimited period *postpos.*; indefinite ‹*strike*›; unlimited ‹*visa*›. **2.** *adv.* for an indefinite *or* unlimited period
ụnbefugt 1. *Adj.* unauthorized; **ein Unbefugter** an unauthorized person. **2.** *adv.* without authorization
ụnbegabt *Adj.* ungifted; untalented; **für Sprachen ~ sein** have no talent for languages
unbegreiflich 1. *Adj.* incomprehensible (+ *Dat.*, **für** to); incredible ‹*love, goodness, stupidity, carelessness, etc.*›; **auf ~e Weise** in a baffling *or* mysterious manner
unbegreiflicherweise *Adv.* inexplicably
ụnbegrenzt 1. *Adj.* unlimited; **ein zeitlich ~er Vertrag** a contract with no time limit; **Kosten in ~er Höhe** costs up to an unlimited amount. **2.** *adv.* ‹*stay, keep, etc.*› indefinitely; ‹*trust*› absolutely; **ich habe nicht ~ Zeit** I don't have unlimited time
ụnbegründet *Adj.* unfounded, groundless ‹*fear, accusation, suspicion*›
ụnbehaart *Adj.* hairless; bald ‹*head*›
Ụnbehagen das uneasiness, disquiet; *(Sorge)* concern (**an** + *Dat.* about); **etw. mit ~ feststellen/betrachten** note/watch sth. with concern; **ein leichtes körperliches ~:** a slight physical discomfort; **das bereitet mir ~:** it makes me feel uneasy
ụnbehaglich 1. *Adj.* uneasy, uncomfortable ‹*feeling, atmosphere*›; uncomfortable ‹*thought, room*›; **mir war ~ zumute** I was *or* felt uneasy; **er/es war mir ~:** he/it made me feel uneasy *or* uncomfortable. **2.** *adv.* uneasily; uncomfortably; **~ kühl** uncomfortably *or* unpleasantly cool
ụnbehauen *Adj.* unhewn
ụnbehelligt *Adj.* unmolested; *(ohne Störung)* ‹*read, work*› undisturbed, in peace; **er gelangte ~ von Journalisten in das Gebäude** he got into the building without being intercepted by journalists; **die Zollbeamten ließen uns ~ passieren** the customs let us through without stopping us
ụnbeherrscht 1. *Adj.* uncontrolled; intemperate, wild ‹*reaction, behaviour, remark*›; **er ist ~:** he has no self-control. **2.** *adv.* without any self-control
Ụnbeherrschtheit die; ~, ~en a) *o. Pl.* lack of self-control; **b)** *(Handlung)* uncontrolled fit; *(Äußerung)* wild outburst
ụnbehindert *Adj.* unhindered; unimpeded
ụnbeholfen 1. *Adj.* clumsy; awkward. **2.** *adv.* clumsily; awkwardly
unbeirrbar 1. *Adj.* unwavering. **2.** *adv.* unwaveringly; unswervingly
unbeirrt 1. *Adj.* unwavering. **2.** *adv.* without wavering
ụnbekannt 1. *Adj.* **a)** unknown; *(nicht vertraut)* unfamiliar; unidentified ‹*caller, donor, flying object*›; **das war mir bisher ~:** I didn't know that until now; **es ist mir nicht ~, daß ...:** I am not unaware that ...; **sie ist hier ~:** she is not known here; **~e Täter** unknown *or* unidentified culprits; **„Empfänger ~"** 'not known at this address'; **eine ~e Größe** *(Math.; auch scherzh.: Mensch)* an unknown quantity; **ich bin hier ~** *(ugs.)* I'm a stranger here; **[Straf]anzeige gegen Unbekannt** *(Rechtsw.)* charge against person or persons unknown; **b)** *(nicht vielen bekannt)* little known; obscure ‹*poet, painter, etc.*›. **2.** *adv.* **„Empfänger ~ verzogen"** 'moved'; 'address unknown'
[1]**Ụnbekannte der/die;** *adj. Dekl.* unknown *or* unidentified man/woman; *(Fremde[r])* stranger; **er ist [hier/dem Fernsehpublikum] kein ~er [mehr]** he is no stranger [here/to television viewers]; **der große ~** *(scherzh.)* the mystery man *or* person
[2]**Ụnbekannte die;** *adj. Dekl. (Math.; auch fig.)* unknown
ụnbekannter·weise *Adv.* **grüßen Sie ihn/sie ~ [von mir]** give him/her my regards, although we haven't met
ụnbekleidet *Adj.* without any clothes on *postpos.*; bare ‹*torso etc.*›; naked ‹*corpse*›
ụnbekümmert 1. *Adj. (unbeschwert)* carefree; *(ohne Bedenken, lässig)* casual; **sie ist [ziemlich] ~:** she doesn't worry [much]; she is [pretty] unconcerned; **um etw. ~ sein** be unconcerned about sth. **2.** *adv.* **a)** *(unbeschwert)* in a carefree way; without a care in the world; **~ leben** live a carefree life; **b)** *(ohne Bedenken)* without caring *or* worrying; **ganz** *od.* **völlig ~:** entirely unconcerned; without a second thought; **er raucht ~ weiter** he happily goes on smoking
Ụnbekümmertheit die; ~ a) carefree manner *or* attitude; carefreeness; **b)** *(Bedenkenlosigkeit)* lack of concern
ụnbelastet *Adj.* **a)** not under load *postpos.*; **im ~en Zustand** when not under load; **b)** *(von Sorgen, Problemen usw.)* free from care *or* worries *postpos.*; **von Sorgen ~:** free from worries; **c)** *(ohne Schuld)* **~ sein** have a clean record; **d)** *(schuldenfrei)* unmortgaged ‹*property, land*›

ụnbelebt *Adj.* **a)** inanimate 〈*nature*〉; *(anorganisch)* inorganic 〈*matter*〉; **b)** *(ohne Lebewesen)* uninhabited; deserted; empty 〈*streets*〉
ụnbeleckt *Adj. (salopp)* **von etw. ~ sein** not have a clue about sth. *(coll.)*; **sie sind von jeder Kultur ~:** they are complete savages
unbelehrbar *Adj.* incorrigible; not accessible to reason *postpos.*; **er ist ~:** he will not learn
ụnbeleuchtet *Adj.* unlit 〈*street, corridor, etc.*〉; 〈*vehicle*〉 without [any] lights
ụnbelichtet *Adj. (Fot.)* unexposed
ụnbeliebt *Adj.* unpopular (**bei** with)
Ụnbeliebtheit die unpopularity
ụnbemannt *Adj.* **a)** unmanned; **b)** *(scherzh.) (ohne Mann)* husbandless *(joc.)*; *(ohne Freund)* without a man *postpos.*
ụnbemerkt *Adj., adv.* unnoticed
ụnbemittelt *Adj.* penniless; impecunious; **nicht ganz ~:** not exactly penniless
unbenọmmen *Adj. in* **es ist/bleibt jmdm. ~, zu ...:** sb. is/remains free *or* at liberty to ...; **dieses Recht bleibt Ihnen ~:** this remains your right
unbenụtzbar *Adj.* unusable
ụnbenutzt *Adj.* unused
ụnbeobachtet *Adj.* unobserved; **in einem ~en Augenblick** *od.* **Moment** when no one is/was watching; **wenn er sich ~ fühlt** *od.* **glaubt** when he thinks no one is looking
ụnbequem 1. *Adj.* **a)** uncomfortable; **b)** *(lästig)* awkward, embarrassing 〈*question, opinion*〉; awkward, troublesome 〈*politician etc.*〉; unpleasant 〈*criticism, truth, etc.*〉; **er wurde ihnen ~:** he became a nuisance *or* an embarrassment to them. **2.** *adv.* uncomfortably
Ụnbequemlichkeit die a) *o. Pl.* lack of comfort; **b)** *o. Pl. (Lästigkeit)* awkwardness; **c)** *(etw., was unbequem ist)* discomfort
unberẹchenbar 1. *Adj.* unpredictable. **2.** *adv.* unpredictably
ụnberechtigt 1. *Adj.* **a)** *(ungerechtfertigt)* unjustified; **b)** *(unbefugt)* unauthorized. **2.** *adv.* **a)** *(unbefugt)* without authorization; **b)** *(ungerechtfertigt)* without justification; unjustifiably 〈*expensive etc.*〉
ụnberücksichtigt *Adj.* unconsidered; **etw. ~ lassen** leave sth. out of consideration; ignore sth.; **~ bleiben** not be considered; be ignored
[1]ụnberufen *Adj.* **in ~e Hände fallen** fall into the wrong hands
[2]unberufen *Interj.* **~ [toi, toi, toi]!** touch wood!; knock on wood! *(Amer.)*
Unberührbare der/die; *adj. Dekl. (Rel.)* untouchable
ụnberührt *Adj.* **a)** untouched; virgin 〈*snow, forest, wilderness*〉; **ein Stück ~er Natur** a stretch of unspoilt countryside; **b)** *(geh.: jungfräulich)* in the virgin state; **sie ist noch ~:** she is still a virgin; **c)** *(unbeeindruckt)* unmoved (**von** by); **die Nachricht ließ ihn ~:** he was unmoved by the news
Ụnberührtheit die; ~ a) *(natürlicher Zustand)* unspoilt state; **b)** *(geh.: Jungfräulichkeit)* virginity; **c)** *(das Unbeeindrucktsein)* lack of emotion; impassivity
ụnbeschadet 1. *Präp. mit Gen.* regardless of; notwithstanding. **2.** *Adj., nicht attr. (veralt.) s.* **unbeschädigt a, b**
ụnbeschädigt *Adj.* **a)** undamaged; **b)** *(veralt.: unverletzt)* unharmed
ụnbescheiden *Adj.* presumptuous; **wenn ich mir die ~e Frage/Bitte erlauben darf** if you don't mind my asking; **ist es sehr ~, wenn ich Sie bitte ...?** I hope you don't mind my asking you ...
ụnbescholten *Adj.* respectable; *(veralt.: keusch)* chaste 〈*girl*〉; **~ sein** *(Rechtsspr.)* have no [previous] convictions
Ụnbescholtenheit die; ~: *s.* **unbescholten:** respectability; chastity; absence of [previous] convictions
ụnbeschrankt *Adj.* 〈*crossing*〉 without gates, with no gates
unbeschränkt 1. *Adj.* unlimited; limitless 〈*possibilities, power*〉; *(hist.)* absolute 〈*ruler*〉; **die Teilnehmerzahl ist ~:** there is no limit on the number of participants. **2.** *adv.* **für etw. ~ haften** have unlimited liability for sth.
unbeschreiblich 1. *Adj.* indescribable; unimaginable 〈*fear, beauty*〉; 〈*fear, beauty*〉 beyond description. **2.** *adv.* indescribably 〈*beautiful*〉; unbelievably 〈*busy*〉; **~ viele Menschen** an incredible number of people; **sich ~ freuen** be overjoyed
ụnbeschrieben *Adj.* blank, empty 〈*piece of paper, page*〉; *s. auch* **Blatt b**
ụnbeschwert 1. *Adj.* carefree. **2.** *adv.* free from care; 〈*dance, play*〉 with a light heart
unbesehen 1. *Adj.* unquestioning 〈*acceptance*〉. **2.** *adv.* without hesitation; **das glaube ich ~:** I don't doubt it for a moment
unbesiegbar *Adj.* invincible
ụnbesiegt *Adj.* undefeated 〈*army*〉; unbeaten 〈*team, player*〉
ụnbesonnen 1. *Adj.* impulsive 〈*person, nature*〉; unthinking 〈*remark*〉; *(übereilt)* ill-considered, rash 〈*decision, action*〉. **2.** *adv.* 〈*act*〉 without thinking; *(übereilt)* rashly
ụnbesorgt *Adj.* unconcerned; **seien** *od.* **bleiben Sie ~!** don't [you] worry; you can set your mind at rest; **du darfst ~ nach Hause gehen** you can go home without worrying/with an easy mind
unbespielbar *Adj. (Sport)* unplayable 〈*pitch*〉
ụnbespielt *Adj.* blank 〈*tape, cassette*〉
ụnbeständig *Adj.* changeable, unsettled 〈*weather*〉; erratic, inconsistent 〈*performance, person, etc.*〉; inconstant, fickle 〈*lover etc.*〉; *(vergänglich)* transitory 〈*love, luck*〉
ụnbestätigt *Adj.* unconfirmed
unbestechlich *Adj.* **a)** incorruptible; **b)** *(fig.)* uncompromising 〈*critic*〉; incorruptible 〈*character*〉; unerring 〈*judgement*〉; unwavering 〈*honesty, love of truth*〉
unbestịmmbar *Adj.* unidentifiable 〈*plant, sound, colour, etc.*〉; indeterminable 〈*age, distance*〉; *(Bot., Zool.)* unclassifiable
ụnbestimmt 1. *Adj.* **a)** *(nicht festgelegt)* indefinite; indeterminate 〈*age, number*〉; *(ungewiß)* uncertain; **auf ~e Zeit** for an indefinite period; **b)** *(ungenau)* vague; **c)** *(Sprachw.)* indefinite 〈*article, pronoun*〉; non-finite 〈*verb form*〉. **2.** *adv. (ungenau)* vaguely
Ụnbestimmtheit die a) *(Ungenauigkeit)* vagueness; **b)** *(Ungewißheit)* uncertainty
unbestreitbar 1. *Adj.* indisputable; unquestionable. **2.** *adv.* indisputably; unquestionably
ụnbestritten 1. *Adj.* undisputed; **~ ist, daß ...:** it is undisputed that ...; there is no disputing that ... **2.** *adv.* indisputably
ụnbeteiligt 1. *Adj.* **a)** *(passiv, nicht mitwirkend)* uninvolved; **~e Passanten/Zuschauer** passers-by/onlookers who are/were not involved; **ein Unbeteiligter** someone who is/was not involved; an outsider; *(ein Unschuldiger)* an innocent party; **b)** *(gleichgültig)* indifferent; detached 〈*manner, expression*〉. **2.** *adv.* with a detached *or* indifferent air; **~ dabeistehen** stand by without taking any interest in the proceedings
ụnbetont *Adj.* unstressed
ụnbeträchtlich 1. *Adj.* insignificant; **nicht ~:** not inconsiderable. **2.** *adv.* insignificantly; slightly; **nicht ~:** not inconsiderably
ụnbeugsam *Adj.* uncompromising; tenacious; indomitable, unshakeable 〈*will, pride*〉; unwavering, resolute 〈*character*〉
ụnbewacht *Adj.* unsupervised 〈*pupils, prisoners, etc.*〉; unattended 〈*car-park*〉; **in einem ~en Moment** when no one is/was watching
ụnbewaffnet *Adj.* unarmed
ụnbewältigt *Adj.* unmastered, uncompleted 〈*task*〉; unresolved 〈*conflict, problem*〉; **unsere ~e Vergangenheit** the past with which we have not come to terms
ụnbeweglich *Adj.* **a)** *(bewegungslos)* motionless; still 〈*air, water*〉; fixed 〈*gaze, expression*〉; **~ sitzen/stehen** sit/stand motionless; **b)** *(starr)* immovable, fixed 〈*part, joint, etc.*〉; **~es Eigentum** real estate; **ein ~es Fest** an immovable feast; **c)** *(nicht mobil)* immobile; **d)** *(schwerfällig) (geistig)* ponderous; *(körperlich)* slow-moving; slow on one's feet *pred.*
ụnbewegt *Adj.* motionless; fixed 〈*expression*〉
ụnbeweibt *Adj. (ugs. scherzh.)* wifeless
ụnbewiesen *Adj.* unproved
unbewọhnbar *Adj.* uninhabitable; **ein Gebäude für ~ erklären** declare a building unfit for human habitation
ụnbewohnt *Adj.* uninhabited 〈*area*〉; unoccupied 〈*house, flat*〉
ụnbewußt 1. *Adj.* **a)** unconscious; **b)** *(ungewollt)* unconscious, unintentional 〈*distortion, exaggeration, etc.*〉. **2.** *adv.* **a)** unconsciously; **b)** *(ungewollt)* unconsciously; unintentionally
Ụnbewußte das; *adj. Dekl. (Psych.)* unconscious
unbezahlbar *Adj.* **a)** *(teuer)* prohibitive; *(zu teuer)* prohibitively expensive 〈*article*〉; **b)** *(kostbar)* priceless 〈*painting, china*〉; **meine Sekretärin ist einfach ~** *(ugs.)* my secretary is worth her weight in gold
ụnbezahlt *Adj.* unpaid; 〈*goods etc.*〉 not [yet] paid for
unbezähmbar *Adj.* uncontrollable; insatiable 〈*hunger, thirst, curiosity*〉
unbezwịnglich *Adj.* **a)** impregnable 〈*fortress*〉; invincible 〈*enemy, opponent*〉; **b)** *(fig.: unbezähmbar)* uncontrollable 〈*urge*〉; insatiable 〈*hunger, thirst, curiosity, desire*〉
Unbilden ['ʊnbɪldn̩] *Pl. (geh.)* rigours
Unbill ['ʊnbɪl] **die; ~** *(geh.) (Unrecht)* wrong; injustice; *(Beschwernis)* rigours *pl.*
ụnblutig 1. *Adj.* **a)** bloodless; **b)** *(Med.: nichtoperativ)* non-surgical. **2.** *adv.* **a)** without bloodshed; **b)** *(Med.: nichtoperativ)* without [the need for] surgery
ụnbot·mäßig 1. *Adj.* insubordinate; **~e Kritik** disrespectful criticism. **2.** *adv.* insubordinately
Ụnbot·mäßigkeit die insubordination
ụnbrauchbar *Adj.* unusable; *(untauglich)* useless 〈*method, person*〉; **~ machen** make 〈*machine*〉 unserviceable; put 〈*machine*〉 out of action; **er ist dafür ~:** he is no use for this
ụnbürokratisch 1. *Adj.* unbureaucratic; **auf möglichst ~e Weise** with as little red tape as possible. **2.** *adv.* unbureaucratically; without a great deal of red tape
ụnbuß·fertig *Adj.* impenitent; unrepentant
ụnchristlich 1. *Adj.* **a)** unchristian; **b) zu ~er Zeit** at an ungodly hour *(coll.)*. **2.** *adv.* in an unchristian way
und [ʊnt] *Konj.* **a)** *(nebenordnend)* and; *(folglich)* [and] so; **das deutsche ~ das französische Volk** the German and French peoples; **zwei ~ drei ist fünf** two and *or* plus three makes five; **es wollte ~ wollte nicht gelingen** it simply *or* just wouldn't work; **es gibt Konservative ~ Konservative** there are conservatives and conservatives; **hoch ~ höher** higher and higher; **~ die anderen/ich?** [and] what about the others/about me?; **~ warum?** why [is that]?; **der ~ der** so-and-so; **zu der ~ der Zeit** at such-and-such a time; **so ~ so ist es gewesen** it was like this; **~?** and?; well?; **ich ~ tanzen?** what, me dance?; **der ~ arbeiten/arm?** what, him work/poor?; *s. auch* **na a**; **[1]ob c**; **wie 1 c**; **b)** *(unterordnend) (konsekutiv)* **tu mir den Gefallen ~ komm mit** be so kind as to come too; **sei so gut ~ mach das Fenster zu** be so

good as to shut the window; **warum bist du auch so leichtsinnig ~ schließt dein Fahrrad nicht ab?** why are you so careless as to leave your bicycle unlocked?; **es fehlte nicht viel, ~ der Deich wäre gebrochen** it wouldn't have taken much to breach the dike; *(konzessiv)* **du mußt es tun, ~ fällt es dir noch so schwer** you must do it however difficult you may find it; *s. auch* **wenn c**

Ụndank der ingratitude; **nur ~ ernten** get no thanks; meet only with ingratitude; **~ ist der Welt Lohn** *(Spr.)* that's all the thanks you get

ụndankbar 1. *Adj.* **a)** ungrateful ‹*person, behaviour*›; **b)** *(wenig lohnend)* thankless ‹*task*›; unrewarding ‹*role, subject, job, etc.*›. **2.** *adv.* ungratefully

ụndatiert *Adj.* undated

undefinierbar *Adj.* **a)** indefinable; **b)** *(nicht bestimmbar)* unidentifiable; indeterminable ‹*feeling*›; indeterminate ‹*colour*›

undeklinierbar *Adj.* *(Sprachw.)* indeclinable

undẹnkbar *Adj.* unthinkable; inconceivable

undẹnklich *Adj.* *in* **vor ~er Zeit** *od.* **~en Zeiten** an eternity ago; **seit ~er Zeit** *od.* **~en Zeiten** since time immemorial

ụndeutlich 1. *Adj.* unclear; indistinct; *(ungenau)* vague ‹*idea, memory, etc.*›. **2.** *adv.* indistinctly; *(ungenau)* vaguely; **du schreibst zu ~:** you don't write clearly enough

ụndicht *Adj.* leaky; leaking; **~ werden** start to leak; develop a leak; **eine ~e Stelle** *(auch fig.)* a leak; **~e Fenster/Türen** windows/doors which do not fit tightly

ụndifferenziert 1. *Adj.* **a)** *(geh.)* indiscriminate ‹*criticism*›; ‹*criticism*› which fails to discriminate; over-generalized, simplistic ‹*account*›; **b)** *(Biol.)* undifferentiated. **2.** *adv.* *(geh.)* in an over-generalized *or* indiscriminate way

Ụnding das *in* **ein ~ sein** be preposterous *or* ridiculous

ụndiplomatisch 1. *Adj.* undiplomatic. **2.** *adv.* undiplomatically

ụndiszipliniert 1. *Adj.* undisciplined; ‹*pupils, class*› lacking in discipline. **2.** *adv.* in an undisciplined way

ụndogmatisch 1. *Adj.* undogmatic. **2.** *adv.* undogmatically

ụnduldsam 1. *Adj.* intolerant. **2.** *adv.* intolerantly

undurchdrịnglich *Adj.* **a)** impenetrable; pitch-dark ‹*night*›; **b)** *(undurchschaubar)* inscrutable ‹*person, expression, mask*›

undurchführbar *Adj.* impracticable

ụndurchlässig *Adj.* impermeable; *(wasserdicht)* watertight; waterproof; *(luftdicht)* airtight

-undurchlässig *adj.* **licht~/wasser~/luft~:** lightproof/waterproof/airtight

undurchschaubar *Adj.* inscrutable ‹*person, plan, etc.*›; unfathomable ‹*cause, etc.*›; **für jmdn. ~ sein** be baffling to sb.

ụndurchsichtig *Adj.* **a)** opaque ‹*glass*›; non-transparent ‹*fabric etc.*›; dense, impenetrable ‹*fog, mist*›; **b)** *(fig.)* unfathomable, inscrutable ‹*plan, intention, role*›; shady ‹*character, business*›

ụneben *Adj.* uneven; *(holprig)* bumpy ‹*road, track*›

Ụnebenheit die; ~, ~en a) *o. Pl.* unevenness; *(Holprigkeit)* bumpiness; **b)** *(unebene Stelle)* lumpy *or* uneven patch

ụnecht *Adj.* **a)** *(falsch, imitiert)* artificial ‹*fur, hair*›; false ‹*teeth*›; imitation ‹*jewellery, marble, etc.*›; *(gefälscht)* counterfeit ‹*notes*›; bogus, fake ‹*painting*›; **b)** *(gespielt, vorgetäuscht)* false, insincere ‹*friendliness, sympathy, smile, etc.*›; simulated ‹*enthusiasm, affection, etc.*›; **c)** *(Math.)* improper ‹*fraction*›

ụnehelich *Adj.* illegitimate ‹*child*›; unmarried ‹*mother*›; **~ geboren sein** be born out of wedlock

Ụnehre die; ~ *(geh.)* dishonour; **etw. macht jmdm. ~** *od.* **gereicht jmdm. zur ~:** sth. brings dishonour on sb.

ụnehrenhaft 1. *Adj.* dishonourable. **2.** *adv.* dishonourably; **er wurde ~ aus der Armee entlassen** *(Milit.)* he was given a dishonourable discharge from the army

ụnehrlich 1. *Adj.* dishonest; **ein ~es Spiel treiben** play a double game. **2.** *adv.* dishonestly; by dishonest means

Ụnehrlichkeit die a) *o. Pl.* dishonesty; **b)** *(Handlung)* dishonest action

ụneigennützig 1. *Adj.* unselfish; selfless. **2.** *adv.* unselfishly; selflessly; ‹*help*› from selfless motives

Ụneigennützigkeit die unselfishness; selflessness

ụneingeschränkt 1. *Adj.* unlimited ‹*freedom, power, etc.*›; absolute ‹*trust, authority*›; unreserved ‹*praise, admiration, recognition*›. **2.** *adv.* ‹*agree*› without reservation

ụneingeweiht *Adj.* uninitiated

ụneinig *Adj.* ‹*party*› divided by disagreement; **[sich** *(Dat.)***] ~ sein** disagree; be in disagreement; **ich bin [mir] mit ihm darin ~:** I disagree with him on that

Ụneinigkeit die disagreement **(in +** *Dat.* on)

uneinnehmbar *Adj.* impregnable

ụneins *Adj.*; *nicht attr.* **~ sein** be divided **(in +** *Dat.* on); ‹*persons, bodies*› be at variance *or* at cross purposes **(in +** *Dat.* over); **mit jmdm. ~ sein[, wie ...]** be unable to agree with sb. [how ...]; **er ist mit sich [selbst] ~:** he is undecided *or* cannot decide

ụnempfänglich *Adj.* unreceptive **(für** to)

ụnempfindlich *Adj.* **a)** insensitive **(gegen** to); **b)** *(nicht anfällig, immun)* immune **(gegen** to, against); **c)** *(strapazierfähig)* hard-wearing; *(pflegeleicht)* easy-care *attrib.*

unẹndlich 1. *Adj.* infinite, boundless ‹*space, sea, expanse, fig.: love, care, patience, etc.*›; *(zeitlich)* endless; never-ending; *(Math.)* infinite ‹*number etc.*›; **das Unendliche** the infinite *(Philos.)*; infinity *(Math.)*; **sich im Unendlichen schneiden** *(Math.)* meet at infinity; **auf ~ stellen** *(Fot.)* focus ‹*lens*› on infinity; **bis ins Unendliche** *(auch fig.)* endlessly. **2.** *adv.* infinitely ‹*lovable, sad*›; immeasurably ‹*happy*›; ‹*happy*› beyond measure; **~ langsam** with infinite slowness; **~ lang** endless; **~ groß/hoch** of infinite size/height *postpos.*; immensely *(coll.)* large/high; **sich ~ freuen** be tremendously pleased; **~ viele Menschen/Elemente** countless people/an infinite number of elements; **ein ~ ferner Punkt** *(Math.)* a point at an infinite distance; **~ klein** *(Math.)* infinitesimal

Unẹndlichkeit die; ~ a) infinity *no def. art.*; *(des Himmels/Ozeans)* infinite expanse; boundlessness; **b)** *(geh.: Ewigkeit)* eternity *no def. art.*

unentbehrlich *Adj.* indispensable (*Dat.*, **für** to)

unentgẹltlich [*od.* '----] **1.** *Adj.* free; **~ sein** be free of charge. **2.** *adv.* free of charge; ‹*work*› for nothing, without pay

unentrịnnbar *(geh.)* **1.** *Adj.* inescapable. **2.** *adv.* inescapably

ụnentschieden 1. *Adj.* **a)** unsettled ‹*case, matter*›; undecided ‹*question*›; **b)** *(Sport, Schach)* drawn ‹*game, match*›; **bei ~em Spielausgang** if the game ends in a draw; **der Spielstand ist ~:** the scores are level; **c)** *(unentschlossen)* indecisive ‹*person*›. **2.** *adv.* *(Sport, Schach)* **~ spielen** draw; **~ enden** end in a draw; **das Spiel steht 0:0 ~:** the game is a goalless draw [so far]

Ụnentschieden das; ~s, ~ *(Sport, Schach)* draw

ụnentschlossen *Adj.* **a)** undecided; **b)** *(entschlußunfähig)* indecisive

Ụnentschlossenheit die a) indecision *no def. art.*; **b)** *(Entschlußunfähigkeit)* indecisiveness

unentschụldbar 1. *Adj.* inexcusable. **2.** *adv.* inexcusably

ụnentschuldigt 1. *Adj.* without giving any reason *postpos., not pred.*; **~es Fernbleiben vom Unterricht/Arbeitsplatz** absence from school/work. **2.** *adv.* without giving any reason

ụnentwegt [*od.* --'-] **1.** *Adj.* **a)** *(beharrlich, ausdauernd)* persistent ‹*fighter, champion, efforts*›; **ein paar Unentwegte** a few stalwarts; **b)** *(unaufhörlich)* constant; incessant. **2.** *adv.* **a)** *(beharrlich)* persistently; **b)** *(unaufhörlich)* constantly; incessantly

unentwịrrbar 1. *Adj.* inextricable ‹*tangle*›; ‹*threads, tangle*› that cannot be unravelled; *(fig.)* irredeemable ‹*muddle, chaos*›. **2.** *adv.* inextricably

unerbịttlich 1. *Adj.* *(auch fig.)* inexorable; unsparing, unrelenting ‹*critic*›; relentless ‹*battle, struggle*›; implacable ‹*hate, enemy*›; **gegen jmdn. ~ sein** be completely unyielding towards sb. **2.** *adv.* *(auch fig.)* inexorably; relentlessly; **~ durchgreifen** take uncompromising action; **~ gegen jmdn./etw. vorgehen** take ruthless action against sb./sth.

ụnerfahren *Adj.* inexperienced

unerfịndlich *Adj.* *(geh.)* unfathomable; inexplicable; **es ist mir ~, warum/wie** *usw.* **...:** it is a mystery to me why/how *etc.* ...

unerfọrschlich *Adj.* *(geh.)* unfathomable; *s. auch* **Ratschluß**

ụnerfreulich 1. *Adj.* unpleasant; bad ‹*news*›; **[etwas] Unerfreuliches** something unpleasant; *(schlechte Nachricht)* bad news. **2.** *adv.* unpleasantly; **~ verlaufen** take a disagreeable course

unerfüllbar *Adj.* unrealizable

ụnergiebig *Adj.* *(auch fig.)* unproductive; *(fig.: nicht lohnend)* unrewarding ‹*work, subject*›

unergründlich *Adj.* unfathomable, inscrutable ‹*motive, mystery, etc.*›; inscrutable ‹*expression, smile*›

ụnerheblich 1. *Adj.* insignificant; **nicht ~:** not inconsiderable; **es ist ~, ob ...:** it is of no significance *or* importance whether ... **2.** *adv.* insignificantly; [very] slightly

unerhört 1. *Adj.* **a)** enormous, tremendous ‹*sum, quantity, etc.*›; incredible *(coll.)*, phenomenal ‹*speed, effort, performance, increase*›; incredible *(coll.)*, fantastic *(coll.)* ‹*splendour, luck*›; **b)** *(abwertend: empörend)* outrageous; scandalous. **2.** *adv.* **a)** *(überaus)* incredibly *(coll.)*; **~ viel arbeiten** do a fantastic *or* incredible amount of work *(coll.)*; **b)** *(abwertend: empörend)* outrageously

ụnerkannt 1. *Adj.* unrecognized; *(nicht identifiziert)* unidentified. **2.** *adv.* without being recognized/identified

unerklärlich *Adj.* inexplicable; **es ist mir ~, wie das geschehen konnte** I simply cannot understand how that could happen

unerläßlich [ʊnlɛɐ̯'lɛslɪç] *Adj.* indispensable; essential; **es ist ~, ... zu ...:** it is essential *or* imperative to ...

ụnerlaubt 1. *Adj.* ‹*entry, parking, absenteeism*› without permission; unauthorized ‹*parking, entry*›; *(illegal)* illegal ‹*act*›. **2.** *adv.* without authorization *or* permission; *(illegal)* illegally; **der Schule** *(Dat.)* **~ fernbleiben** play truant

ụnerledigt *Adj.* not dealt with *postpos.*; ‹*work*› not done; unanswered ‹*mail, letters*›; unprocessed ‹*application*›

unermẹßlich 1. *Adj.* *(geh.)* **a)** *(räumlich)* immeasurable ‹*expanse, distance*›; boundless ‹*spaces*›; **b)** *(mengen-, zahlenmäßig)* immeasurable, immense ‹*wealth, fortune*›; **ins ~e** beyond measure; **c)** *(überaus groß)* untold ‹*suffering, misery, damage*›; ines-

timable ‹*value, importance*›. **2.** *adv.* immeasurably; ‹*rich*› beyond measure; ~ **viel** an inestimable amount
unermüdlich 1. *Adj.* tireless, untiring (**bei**, **in** + *Dat.* in). **2.** *adv.* tirelessly
unernst *Adj.* frivolous
unerquicklich *(geh.) Adj.* unpleasant
unerreichbar 1. *Adj.* **a)** inaccessible; **in ~er Ferne** *od.* **Entfernung** so distant as to be beyond reach; **sie ist für ihn ~** *(fig.)* she is beyond his reach; **b)** *(nicht kontaktierbar)* unobtainable; **c)** *(fig.)* unattainable ‹*aim, ideal, accuracy, etc.*›. **2.** *adv.* **a)** *(räumlich)* inaccessibly; **b)** *(fig.)* unattainably
unerreicht *Adj.* unequalled ‹*record, achievement*›; ~ **bleiben** remain unequalled; ‹*goal*› not be attained
unersättlich *Adj.* insatiable
unerschlossen *Adj.* unexploited, undeveloped ‹*area*›; unexploited, untapped ‹*market, resources, deposits*›
unerschöpflich *Adj.* inexhaustible; **ihre Geduld war ~**: there was no end to her patience
unerschrocken 1. *Adj.* intrepid; fearless. **2.** *adv.* intrepidly; fearlessly
unerschütterlich 1. *Adj.* unshakeable; imperturbable ‹*calm, equanimity*›; tenacious ‹*fighter*›. **2.** *adv.* unshakeably
unerschwinglich 1. *Adj.* prohibitively expensive; prohibitive ‹*price*›; **für jmdn. ~ sein** be beyond sb.'s means. **2.** *adv.* prohibitively ‹*expensive, high*›
unersetzlich *Adj.* irreplaceable; irretrievable, irrecoverable ‹*loss*›; irreparable ‹*harm, damage, loss of person*›
unersprießlich *Adj.* *(geh.)* unprofitable; unproductive
unerträglich [*od.* '----] **1.** *Adj.* unbearable ‹*pain, heat, person, etc.*›; intolerable ‹*situation, conditions, moods, etc.*›; **er/es ist mir ~**: I find him/it unbearable; I cannot stand him/it. **2.** *adv.* unbearably
unerwähnt *Adj.* unmentioned; **völlig ~ bleiben** not be mentioned at all
unerwartet 1. *Adj.* unexpected; **es war** *od.* **kam für alle ~**: it came as a surprise to everybody; **etwas Unerwartetes** something unexpected. **2.** *adv.* unexpectedly
unerwidert *Adj.* unreturned ‹*visit*›; unrequited ‹*love*›; ~ **bleiben** ‹*greetings*› receive no response
unerwünscht *Adj.* unwanted; unwelcome ‹*interruption, visit, visitor*›; undesirable ‹*side-effects*›; **Sie sind hier ~**: you are not wanted *or* welcome here; **ein ~er Ausländer** an undesirable alien
unerzogen *Adj.* badly behaved
UNESCO [u'nɛsko] **die; ~**: UNESCO
unfähig *Adj.* **a)** ~ **sein, etw. zu tun** *(ständig)* be incapable of doing sth.; *(momentan)* be unable to do sth.; **er ist solch eines Verbrechens ~**: he is incapable of such a crime; **b)** *(abwertend: inkompetent)* incompetent
Unfähigkeit die a) inability; **b)** *(Inkompetenz)* incompetence
unfair 1. *Adj.* unfair (**gegen** to). **2.** *adv.* unfairly
Unfall der accident; **bei einem ~**: in an accident
unfall-, Unfall-: **~arzt der** casualty doctor; **zum ~arzt gehen** go to the doctor in the casualty department *or* casualty; **~flucht die** *(Rechtsspr.)* **wegen ~flucht** for failing to stop after [being involved in] an accident; **~flucht begehen** fail to stop after [being involved in] an accident; **~folge die** consequence *or* effect of an/the accident; **er starb an den ~folgen** he died as a result of the accident; **~frei 1.** *Adj.* accident-free; free from accidents *postpos.*; **2.** *adv.* without an accident; **~gefahr die** risk of accidents/an accident; accident risk; **~kranken·haus das** accident *or* casualty hospital; **~opfer das** accident victim; **~rente die** disability pension *(paid by an accident insurance)*; **~station die** accident *or* casualty department; **~stelle die** scene of an/the accident; **~tod der** accidental death; death in an accident; **~ursache die** cause of an/the accident; **~versicherung die** accident insurance; **~wagen der a)** *(Rettungswagen)* incident vehicle; *(Krankenwagen)* ambulance; **b)** *(beschädigter Wagen)* car [that has been] damaged in an/the accident
unfaßbar 1. *Adj.* incomprehensible; *(unglaublich)* incredible, unimaginable ‹*poverty, cruelty, etc.*›; **es ist mir ~, wie ...**: it is incomprehensible to me *or* I cannot understand how ... **2.** *adv.* incomprehensibly; incredibly, unimaginably ‹*cruel*›
unfehlbar *Adj.* infallible
Unfehlbarkeit die; ~: infallibility
unfein 1. *Adj.* ill-mannered, unrefined ‹*behaviour etc.*›; unrefined, coarse ‹*manner, word*›; bad ‹*manners*›; **das gilt als ~**: it's considered bad manners. **2.** *adv.* ‹*behave*› badly, in an ill-mannered way
unfertig *Adj.* **a)** unfinished ‹*manuscript, article, etc.*›; **b)** *(fig.: unreif)* immature
unfest *(Sprachw.)* **1.** *Adj.* separable. **2.** *adv.* ~ **zusammengesetzte Verben** separable [compound] verbs
Unflat ['ʊnfla:t] **der; ~[e]s** *(geh. veralt.)* filth
unflätig ['ʊnflɛ:tɪç] *(geh. abwertend)* **1.** *Adj.* coarse ‹*behaviour, manners, speech, etc.*›; obscene ‹*expression, word, curse*›; dirty ‹*song*›. **2.** *adv.* coarsely; obscenely
unflektiert *Adj.* *(Sprachw.)* uninflected
unflott *Adj.* **in nicht ~** *(ugs.)* not bad; *(modisch, schick)* quite with it *(coll.)*. **2.** *adv.* **nicht ~**: not at all badly; **sie tanzt nicht ~** *(ugs.)* she's a pretty useful dancer *(coll.)*
unförmig 1. *Adj.* shapeless ‹*lump, shadow, etc.*›; huge ‹*legs, hands, body*›; bulky, ungainly ‹*shape, shoes, etc.*›. **2.** *adv.* ~ **dick** fat and unshapely *or* bulky; ~ **angeschwollen** swollen and unsightly
unfrankiert *Adj.* unstamped
unfrei 1. *Adj.* **a)** not free *pred.*; subject, dependent ‹*people*›; ‹*life*› of bondage *or* without liberty; **die Bauern waren noch ~** *(hist.)* the peasants were still serfs; **sich etwas ~ fühlen** feel a bit tied *or* unable to act freely; **b)** *(gehemmt)* inhibited; **c)** *(keine Freiheit gewährend)* restrictive ‹*education, regime*›; **d)** *(Postw.)* unstamped. **2.** *adv.* *(gehemmt)* in an inhibited manner
Unfreie der/die; *adj. Dekl.* *(hist.)* serf
Unfreiheit die; *o. Pl.* slavery *no art.*; bondage *(esp. Hist./literary) no art.*; **ein Leben in ~**: a life of bondage *or* without freedom
unfreiwillig 1. *Adj.* involuntary; *(erzwungen)* enforced ‹*stay*›; *(nicht beabsichtigt)* unintended ‹*publicity, joke, humour*›. **2.** *adv.* involuntarily; without wanting to; *(unbeabsichtigt)* unintentionally
unfreundlich 1. *Adj.* **a)** unfriendly (**zu, gegen** to); unkind ‹*words, remark*›; **ein ~er Akt** *(Politik)* an unfriendly *or* a hostile act; **b)** *(fig.)* unpleasant ‹*area, climate, environment*›; unpleasant, inclement ‹*weather, summer*›; cheerless ‹*room*›. **2.** *adv.* in an unfriendly way
Unfreundlichkeit die a) *o. Pl.* unfriendliness; **sie behandelte ihn mit einer solchen ~, daß ...**: she treated him in such an unfriendly way that ...; **b)** *(Handlung)* unfriendly act; *(Äußerung)* unkind remark
Unfriede[n] der discord; **in ~ leben/auseinandergehen** live in a state of strife/part in hostility
unfrisiert *Adj.* ungroomed ‹*hair*›; **sie war ~**: she had not done her hair
unfruchtbar *Adj.* **a)** infertile ‹*soil, field, land*›; **meine Anregungen fielen auf ~en Boden** *(fig.)* my suggestions fell on stony ground; **b)** *(Biol.)* infertile; sterile; **ein Tier ~ machen** sterilize *or* neuter an animal; **die ~en Tage der Frau** the days of infertility; **c)** *(fig.)* unfruitful, unproductive ‹*discussion, comparison, etc.*›; infertile ‹*years, period*›; ‹*idea*› which does not lead anywhere
Unfruchtbarkeit die a) infertility; **b)** *(Biol.)* infertility; sterility; **c)** *(fig.)* unproductiveness
Unfug ['ʊnfu:k] **der; ~[e]s a)** [piece of] mischief; **allerlei ~ anstellen** get up to all kinds of mischief *or (coll.)* monkey business; **grober ~**: public nuisance; **was soll dieser ~?** what's this monkey business? *(coll.)*; **laß diesen ~!** stop monkeying about *(coll.)* *or* making a nuisance of yourself; **b)** *(Unsinn)* nonsense
Ungar ['ʊngar] **der; ~n, ~n, Ungarin die; ~, ~nen** Hungarian; *s. auch* **-in**
ungarisch 1. *Adj.* Hungarian. **2.** *adv.* in Hungarian; *s. auch* **deutsch; ²Deutsche**
Ungarisch das; ~[s] Hungarian; *s. auch* **Deutsch**
Ungarn (das); ~s Hungary
ungastlich 1. *Adj.* inhospitable. **2.** *adv.* inhospitably
ungeachtet *Präp. mit Gen.* *(geh.)* notwithstanding; despite
ungeahnt 1. *Adj.* unsuspected; *(stärker)* undreamt-of *attrib.* **2.** *adv.* unexpectedly
ungebärdig 1. *Adj.* unruly ‹*child, horse, etc.*›; wild ‹*temperament, mountain stream, etc.*›. **2.** *adv.* wildly
ungebeten 1. *Adj.* uninvited; *(nicht gern gesehen)* unwelcome. **2.** *adv.* uninvited
ungebeugt *Adj.* *(Sprachw.)* uninflected
ungebildet *Adj.* uneducated; **ein Ungebildeter** an uneducated person
ungeboren *Adj.* unborn
ungebräuchlich *Adj.* uncommon; rare; rarely used ‹*method, process*›
ungebraucht *Adj.* unused; mint ‹*stamp*›
ungebrochen *Adj.* **a)** *(Physik)* unrefracted ‹*rays, waves*›; **b)** *(fig.)* unbroken ‹*will, person*›; undiminished ‹*strength, courage*›
Ungebühr die; *o. Pl.* *(geh.)* impropriety; ~ **vor Gericht** *(Rechtsspr.)* contempt of court
ungebührlich *(geh.)* **1.** *Adj.* improper, unseemly ‹*behaviour*›; unreasonable ‹*demand*›. **2.** *adv.* ‹*behave*› improperly; unreasonably ‹*high, long, etc.*›
ungebunden 1. *Adj.* **a)** unbound ‹*book etc.*›; **b)** *(Literaturw.)* **in ~er Rede** in prose; **c)** *(frei von Bindungen)* independent; without ties *postpos.*; *(ohne Partner/Partnerin)* unattached. **2.** *adv.* ~ **leben** live an independent life *or* a life without ties
ungedeckt *Adj.* **a)** uncovered ‹*cheque, bill of exchange, etc.*›; unsecured ‹*bond*›; **b)** unlaid ‹*table*›; **c)** *(ungeschützt)* unprotected; **d)** *(Ballspiele)* unmarked ‹*player*›
Ungeduld die impatience
ungeduldig 1. *Adj.* impatient. **2.** *adv.* impatiently
ungeeignet *Adj.* unsuitable; *(für eine Aufgabe, Stellung)* unsuited (**für, zu** to, for)
ungefähr ['ʊngəfɛ:ɐ̯] **1.** *Adj.*; *nicht präd.* approximate; rough ‹*idea, outline*›. **2.** *Adv.* approximately; roughly; *(mit nachgestellter Zahl)* about; roughly; ~ **so** something like this; **so ~** *(ugs.)* more or less; **kannst du mir so ~ sagen, wie/wann** *usw.* **...?** can you give me some idea *or* a rough idea how/when *etc.* ...?; **wann wirst du ~ zurückkommen?** roughly *or* about when will you be back?; **wo ~ ...?** whereabouts ...?; **kannst du es ~ beschreiben?** can you give a rough description?; **ich kann es mir ~ vorstellen** I can imagine; **[wie] von ~**: [as if] by chance; **es kommt nicht von ~[, daß ...]** it's no accident [that ...]
ungefährdet *Adj.* safe; *(gesichert)* assured ‹*promotion etc.*›; ‹*play, swim, etc.*› in safety
ungefährlich 1. *Adj.* safe; harmless ‹*animal, person, illness, etc.*›; **nicht ~ sein** be not without danger. **2.** *adv.* safely
ungefällig 1. *Adj.* disobliging, churlish (ge-

genüber to). 2. *adv.* in a disobliging way; churlishly

ụngefärbt *Adj.* **a)** undyed ⟨*wool, hair*⟩; ⟨*food, drink*⟩ without colouring matter; **b)** *(fig.)* unvarnished ⟨*truth*⟩; uncoloured, undistorted ⟨*account*⟩

ụngefragt *Adj.; nicht attr.* unasked

ụngefüge *(geh.) Adj.* **a)** cumbersome ⟨*furniture*⟩; massive, bulky ⟨*chunk, stature*⟩; massive ⟨*wall, stone*⟩; ungainly ⟨*person*⟩; **b)** *(schwerfällig)* ponderous ⟨*style*⟩

ụngehalten *(geh.)* **1.** *Adj.* annoyed (**über** + *Akk.*, **wegen** about); *(entrüstet)* indignant. **2.** *adv.* indignantly; ⟨*reply, say*⟩ in an aggrieved tone

ụngeheizt *Adj.* unheated

ụngehemmt **1.** *Adj.* **a)** uninhibited ⟨*person*⟩; **b)** *(uneingeschränkt)* unrestricted, unimpeded ⟨*movement*⟩; *(fig.)* unrestrained ⟨*joy, anger, etc.*⟩. **2.** *adv.* **a)** without inhibition; **b)** *(uneingeschränkt)* ⟨*develop*⟩ unhindered, without hindrance; *(fig.)* ⟨*cry, laugh, drink, etc.*⟩ without restraint

ụngeheuer **1.** *Adj.* enormous; immense; tremendous ⟨*strength, energy, effort, enthusiasm, fear, success, pressure, etc.*⟩; vast, immense ⟨*fortune, knowledge*⟩; *(schrecklich)* terrible *(coll.)*, terrific *(coll.)* ⟨*pain, rage*⟩; **ungeheure Ausgaben** an enormous amount of expense. **2.** *adv.* tremendously; terribly *(coll.)* ⟨*difficult, clever*⟩

Ụngeheuer **das;** **~s, ~** *(auch fig.)* monster

ungeheuerlich **1.** *Adj.* monstrous; outrageous. **2.** *adv. (ugs.)* terribly *(coll.)*

Ungeheuerlichkeit **die; ~, ~en** **a)** *o. Pl.* monstrous nature; outrageousness; **b)** *(Vorgang)* monstrous *or* outrageous thing

ụngehindert *Adj.* unimpeded

ụngehobelt **1.** *Adj.* **a)** unplaned ⟨*wood*⟩; **b)** *(grob)* uncouth. **2.** *adv.* uncouthly

ụngehörig **1.** *Adj.* improper ⟨*behaviour*⟩; *(frech)* impertinent ⟨*tone, answer*⟩. **2.** *adv.* improperly; *(frech)* impertinently

ụngehorsam *Adj.* disobedient (**gegenüber** to)

Ụngehorsam **der** disobedience (**gegenüber** to)

ụngehört *Adj.; nicht attr.* unheard

Ụngeist **der;** *o. Pl. (geh. abwertend)* pernicious ideology

ụngekämmt *Adj.* uncombed

ụngeklärt *Adj.* **a)** unsolved ⟨*question, problem*⟩; unknown ⟨*cause*⟩; **die Angelegenheit ist noch ~:** the matter has yet to be cleared up; **b)** *(ungereinigt)* untreated ⟨*sewage*⟩

ụngekrönt *Adj. (auch fig.)* uncrowned

ụngekündigt *Adj.* **in ~er Stellung** not under notice *postpos.*

ụngekünstelt **1.** *Adj.* natural; unaffected. **2.** *adv.* naturally; unaffectedly

ụngekürzt *Adj.* unabridged ⟨*edition, book*⟩; uncut ⟨*film, speech*⟩

ụngeladen *Adj.* **a)** unloaded ⟨*gun, camera*⟩; **b)** *(nicht eingeladen)* uninvited ⟨*guest*⟩

ụngelegen **1.** *Adj.* inconvenient, awkward ⟨*time*⟩; ⟨*visit etc.*⟩ at an awkward *or* inconvenient time; **das kommt mir sehr ~/nicht ~:** that is very inconvenient *or* awkward/quite convenient for me. **2.** *adv.* inconveniently; **komme ich ~?** have I come at an inconvenient *or* awkward time?

Ụngelegenheit **die** inconvenience; **jmdm. große ~en machen** *od.* **bereiten** inconvenience sb. greatly

ụngelegt *Adj. in* **kümmere dich nicht um ~e Eier** *(ugs.)* don't cross your bridges before you get to them

ụngelenk **1.** *Adj.* clumsy; ungainly. **2.** *adv.* clumsily

ụngelenkig *Adj.* stiff-jointed

ụngelernt *Adj.* unskilled

Ụngelernte **der/die;** *adj. Dekl.* unskilled worker

ụngeliebt *Adj.* unloved; *(verhüll.: verhaßt)* hateful, odious ⟨*task*⟩; odious ⟨*school etc.*⟩

ụngelogen *Adv. (ugs.)* honestly

ụngelöscht *Adj. (Chemie)* unslaked ⟨*lime*⟩

Ụngemach **das; ~[e]s** *(geh. veralt.)* trouble

ụngemacht *Adj.* unmade

ụngemein **1.** *Adj.; nicht präd.* exceptional ⟨*progress, popularity*⟩; tremendous ⟨*advantage, pleasure*⟩. **2.** *adv.* exceptionally; **~ fleißig** extraordinarily industrious; **das freut mich ~:** that pleases me no end *(coll.)*

ụngemütlich **1.** *Adj.* **a)** uninviting, cheerless ⟨*room, flat*⟩; uncomfortable, unfriendly ⟨*atmosphere*⟩; **b)** *(unangenehm)* unpleasant ⟨*situation*⟩; **es wird jetzt ~:** things are getting nasty; **es wurde ihnen zu ~:** things got too unpleasant for them. **2.** *adv.* uncomfortably ⟨*furnished*⟩; **hier sitzt es sich ~:** it's not comfortable sitting here

ụngenannt *Adj.* anonymous; **ein Ungenannter** an anonymous person

ụngenau **1.** *Adj.* **a)** inaccurate ⟨*measurement, estimate, thermometer, translation, etc.*⟩; imprecise, inexact ⟨*definition, formulation, etc.*⟩; *(undeutlich)* vague ⟨*memory, idea, impression*⟩; **b)** *(nicht sorgfältig)* careless ⟨*work, worker*⟩. **2.** *adv.* **a)** inaccurately; ⟨*define*⟩ imprecisely, inexactly; ⟨*remember*⟩ vaguely; **die Uhr geht ~:** the clock does not keep good time; **b)** *(nicht sorgfältig)* ⟨*work*⟩ carelessly

Ụngenauigkeit **die** **a)** *o. Pl.* inaccuracy; *(einer Definition)* imprecision; inexactness; **b)** *(etwas Ungenaues)* inaccuracy

ungeniert ['ʊnʒeni:ɐ̯t] **1.** *Adj.* free and easy; uninhibited; **er war ganz ~:** he was not at all embarrassed *or* concerned. **2.** *adv.* openly; ⟨*yawn*⟩ unconcernedly; *(ohne Scham)* ⟨*undress etc.*⟩ without any embarrassment

ungenießbar *Adj.* **a)** *(nicht eßbar)* inedible; *(nicht trinkbar)* undrinkable; **b)** *(fig. ugs.)* unbearable ⟨*person*⟩; **er ist heute ~:** he's in a foul mood today *(sl.)*

ụngenügend **1.** *Adj.* inadequate; **die Note „~"/ein Ungenügend** *(Schulw.)* the/an 'unsatisfactory' [mark]. **2.** *adv.* inadequately

ụngenutzt, ụngenützt *Adj.* unused; unexploited ⟨*resource, energy*⟩; **eine Gelegenheit ~ vorübergehen lassen** let an opportunity slip *or* pass by

ụngepflegt *Adj.* neglected ⟨*garden, park, car, etc.*⟩; unkempt ⟨*person, appearance, hair*⟩; uncared-for ⟨*hands*⟩

ụngerade *Adj.* odd ⟨*number*⟩

ụngerecht **1.** *Adj.* unjust, unfair (**gegen, zu, gegenüber** to). **2.** *adv.* unjustly; unfairly

ungerechterweise *Adv.* unjustly; unfairly; **er verdient ~ genausoviel wie sie** he earns as much as she does, which is unfair

ụngerechtfertigt *Adj.* unjustified; unwarranted

Ụngerechtigkeit **die; ~, ~en** injustice; **der Vorwurf der ~:** the reproach of being unjust; **so eine ~!** how unjust *or* unfair!

ụngeregelt *Adj.* irregular; disorganized

ụngereimt *Adj.* **a)** *(nicht stimmig)* inconsistent; illogical; *(ugs. abwertend: sinnlos, verworren)* muddled; **b)** *(reimlos)* unrhymed

Ụngereimtheit **die; ~, ~en** *(Unstimmigkeit)* inconsistency; *(ugs. abwertend: Unsinnigkeit, Verworrenheit)* muddle

ụngern *Adv.* reluctantly; **etw. ~ tun** not like *or* dislike doing sth.; **Würdest du das bitte tun? – Ungern** Would you do that, please? – I'd rather not

ụngerufen *Adv.* without being called

ụngerührt *Adj.* unmoved

ụngesalzen *Adj.* unsalted

ụngesättigt *Adj. (Chemie)* unsaturated; **mehrfach ~:** polyunsaturated

ụngesäuert *Adj.* unleavened ⟨*bread*⟩

ụngeschält *Adj.* unpeeled ⟨*fruit*⟩; unstripped ⟨*tree-trunk*⟩; **~er Reis** paddy rice

ụngeschehen *Adj. in* **etw. ~ machen** undo sth.

Ụngeschick **das** clumsiness; **~ läßt grüßen!** *(ugs.)* butter-fingers!

Ụngeschicklichkeit **die; ~, ~en** **a)** *o. Pl.* clumsiness; ineptitude; **b)** *(etwas Ungeschicktes)* piece of clumsiness; *(Fehler)* clumsy mistake

ụngeschickt **1.** *Adj.* clumsy; awkward ⟨*movement, formulation, etc.*⟩; **technisch ~:** technically inept. **2.** *adv.* clumsily; ⟨*bow, express oneself, etc.*⟩ awkwardly; **sich ~ anstellen** show a lack of skill; show oneself to be inept

ụngeschlacht *(geh.)* **1.** *Adj.* **a)** *(unförmig, massig)* huge and ungainly ⟨*man, animal*⟩; huge, clumsy ⟨*hands*⟩; clumsy, ungainly ⟨*limbs, movement*⟩; massive ⟨*building etc.*⟩; **b)** *(grob, unkultiviert)* coarse; uncouth. **2.** *adv.* in an uncouth way

ụngeschlechtlich *(Biol.)* **1.** *Adj.* asexual. **2.** *adv.* asexually

ụngeschliffen **1.** *Adj.* **a)** uncut ⟨*diamond etc.*⟩; **b)** *(fig. abwertend)* unrefined ⟨*behaviour, manners*⟩. **2.** *adv. (fig. abwertend)* in an unrefined manner

ụngeschmälert *Adj. (geh.)* undiminished; in full measure *postpos.; (voll anerkannt)* appreciated to the full *postpos.*

ụngeschminkt **1.** *Adj.* **a)** not made-up *pred.*; without make-up *postpos.*; **b)** *(fig.)* unvarnished ⟨*truth*⟩; uncoloured ⟨*account*⟩. **2.** *adv.* without holding anything back; **jmdm. ~ seine Meinung sagen** give sb. one's honest opinion

ụngeschoren *Adj.* **a)** unshorn; **b)** *nicht attr. (fig.)* **~ bleiben** be left in peace; be spared; **~ davonkommen** get away with it; *(ohne Schaden)* get away unscathed

ụngeschrieben *Adj.* unwritten

ụngeschützt *Adj.* unprotected; *(Wind und Wetter ausgesetzt)* exposed

ụngesehen *Adj.; nicht attr.* unseen

ụngesellig **1.** *Adj.* **a)** unsociable; **b)** *(Zool.)* non-gregarious. **2.** *adv. (Zool.)* non-gregariously

ụngesetzlich **1.** *Adj.* unlawful; illegal. **2.** *adv.* unlawfully; illegally

Ụngesetzlichkeit **die** illegality

ụngesittet **1.** *Adj.* uncivilized. **2.** *adv.* in an uncivilized manner

ụngestalt *Adj.* **a)** *(geh.)* shapeless; **b)** *(veralt.: mißgestaltet)* misshapen

ụngestempelt *Adj.* unstamped ⟨*licence etc.*⟩; uncancelled ⟨*stamp*⟩

ụngestillt *Adj. (geh.)* unquenched, unslaked ⟨*thirst*⟩; unsatisfied, unsated ⟨*curiosity, desire, greed*⟩

ụngestört *Adj.* undisturbed; uninterrupted ⟨*development*⟩; **~ arbeiten** work in peace *or* without interruption

ụngestraft **1.** *Adj.; nicht attr.* unpunished. **2.** *adv.* with impunity

ungestüm ['ʊngəʃty:m] *(geh.)* **1.** *Adj.* impetuous, tempestuous ⟨*person, embrace, nature, etc.*⟩; wild ⟨*imagination*⟩; violent, fierce ⟨*wind*⟩; stormy ⟨*sea*⟩. **2.** *adv.* impetuously

Ụngestüm **das; ~[e]s** impetuosity

ụngesühnt *Adj. (geh.)* unatoned

ụngesund **1.** *Adj. (auch fig.)* unhealthy; *(fig.: übermäßig)* excessive ⟨*ambition, activity*⟩; **Rauchen ist ~:** smoking is bad for you *or* for your health. **2.** *adv.* unhealthily; **er lebt sehr ~:** he lives *or* leads a very unhealthy life

ungesüßt ['ʊngəzy:st] *Adj.* unsweetened

ụngetan *Adj.* still to be done *postpos.*; **etw. ~ lassen** leave sth. undone

ụngeteilt *Adj.* **a)** undivided; **b)** *(fig.)* unrestricted, absolute ⟨*power*⟩; undivided ⟨*attention, interest*⟩; *(einmütig)* unanimous; universal ⟨*approval, agreement, etc.*⟩

ụngetreu *Adj. (geh.)* disloyal

ụngetrübt *Adj.* unclouded, perfect ⟨*happiness*⟩; unalloyed ⟨*pleasure*⟩; unspoilt, perfect ⟨*days, relationship*⟩; **seine Freude blieb**

nicht lange ~: his pleasure did not long remain unsullied

Ungetüm ['ʊngəty:m] **das**; ~s, ~e monster

ụngeübt *Adj.* unpractised ⟨*hand*⟩; **in etw. ~ sein** lack practice in sth.

ụngewaschen *Adj.* unwashed

ụngewiß *Adj.* uncertain; **eine Fahrt ins Ungewisse** a journey into the unknown; **über etw.** *(Akk.)* **im ungewissen sein** be uncertain *or* unsure about sth.; **jmdn. [über etw.** *(Akk.)***] im ungewissen lassen** leave sb. in the dark *or* keep sb. guessing [about sth.]

Ụngewißheit die uncertainty; **in ~ sein** be in a state of uncertainty

ụngewöhnlich 1. *Adj.* **a)** unusual; **b)** *(sehr groß)* exceptional ⟨*strength, beauty, ability, etc.*⟩; outstanding ⟨*achievement, success*⟩. **2.** *adv.* **a)** *(unüblich)* ⟨*behave*⟩ abnormally, strangely; **b)** *(enorm)* exceptionally

ụngewohnt 1. *Adj.* unaccustomed ⟨*exertion, heat, cold, load, etc.*⟩; unaccustomed, unusual ⟨*sight, time*⟩; *(nicht vertraut)* unfamiliar ⟨*method, work, surroundings, etc.*⟩; **sie sagte es mit ~er Schärfe** she said it with a sharpness [that was] unusual for her; **die Arbeit ist ihr** *od.* **für sie noch ~**: she is still not used to *or* familiar with the work. **2.** *adv.* unusually

ụngewollt 1. *Adj.* unwanted; *(unbeabsichtigt)* unintentional; inadvertent. **2.** *adv.* unintenionally; inadvertently

ụngezählt *Adj.* **a)** *nicht präd. (unzählig)* countless; **b)** *(nicht gezählt)* uncounted

Ungeziefer ['ʊngətsi:fɐ] **das**; ~s vermin *pl.*

ụngezogen 1. *Adj.* naughty; badly behaved; bad ⟨*behaviour*⟩; *(frech)* cheeky; **zu jmdm. ~ sein** behave badly towards sb.; be cheeky to sb. **2.** *adv.* naughtily; ⟨*behave*⟩ badly

Ụngezogenheit die; ~, ~en **a)** *o. Pl.* naughtiness; bad behaviour; **b)** *(ungezogene Bemerkung)* **~en** insolent remarks; **das ist eine ~**: that's very naughty/cheeky

ụngezügelt 1. *Adj.* unbridled. **2.** *adv.* without restraint

ụngezwungen 1. *Adj.* natural, unaffected ⟨*person, behaviour, cheerfulness*⟩; *(nicht förmlich)* informal, free and easy ⟨*tone, conversation, etc.*⟩. **2.** *adv.* ⟨*behave*⟩ naturally, unaffectedly; ⟨*talk*⟩ freely

Ụngezwungenheit die; ~ *s.* **ungezwungen 1**: naturalness; unaffectedness; informality

ụngiftig *Adj.* non-poisonous; non-toxic ⟨*gas, substance*⟩

Ụnglaube[n] der a) disbelief; incredulity; **b)** *(Rel.)* unbelief

unglaubhaft *Adj.* implausible

ụngläubig 1. *Adj.* **a)** disbelieving; incredulous; **~er Thomas** doubting Thomas; **b)** *(Rel.)* unbelieving. **2.** *adv.* incredulously; in disbelief

Ụngläubige der/die *(Rel.)* unbeliever

unglaublich 1. *Adj.* **a)** incredible; **b)** *(ugs.: sehr groß)* incredible *(coll.)*, fantastic *(coll.)* ⟨*speed, amount, luck, etc.*⟩. **2.** *adv. (ugs.: äußerst)* incredibly *(coll.)*; *(empörend)* ⟨*behave*⟩ in an incredible fashion *(coll.)*

ụnglaubwürdig *Adj.* implausible; untrustworthy, unreliable ⟨*witness etc.*⟩

ụngleich 1. *Adj.* **a)** unequal; unequal, different ⟨*sizes*⟩; odd, unmatching ⟨*socks, gloves, etc.*⟩; *(unähnlich)* dissimilar ⟨*characters etc.*⟩; odd ⟨*couple*⟩; **a [ist] ~ b** *(Math.)* a is not equal to *or* does not equal b; **b)** *(ungleichmäßig)* uneven ⟨*distribution etc.*⟩. **2.** *adv.* **a)** unequally; **~ geartet** of different dispositions; **b)** *(ungleichmäßig)* unevenly. **3.** *Adv. (mit Komparativ)* far ⟨*larger, more difficult*⟩; *(unvergleichlich)* incomparably ⟨*better, more beautiful*⟩. **4.** *Präp. mit Dat. (geh.)* unlike

Ụngleichgewicht das imbalance

Ụngleichheit die a) *o. Pl.* inequality; **b)** *(Unterschied)* difference; dissimilarity

ụngleichmäßig 1. *Adj.* uneven. **2.** *adv.* **a)** unevenly; **b)** *(verschieden)* **~ lang** of different lengths

ụngleichnamig *Adj.* **a)** *(Math.)* ⟨*fractions*⟩ with different denominators; **b)** *(Physik)* opposite ⟨*poles*⟩

Ụnglück das; ~[e]s, ~e **a)** *(Unfall)* accident; *(Flugzeug~, Zug~)* crash; accident; *(Mißgeschick)* mishap; **das ist [doch] kein ~!** that's not a disaster; it doesn't really matter; **b)** *o. Pl. (Not)* misfortune; *(Leid)* suffering; distress; **jmdn. ins ~ stürzen** bring ruin *or* disaster on sb.; **sich ins ~ stürzen, in sein ~ rennen** rush headlong into disaster *or* to one's ruin; **es ist ein ~, daß ...**: it is a real shame *or* a great pity that ...; **c)** *(Pech)* bad luck; misfortune; **~ haben** be unlucky; **das bringt ~**: that's unlucky; **zum ~**: unfortunately; **zu allem ~**: to make matters worse; **das ~ wollte es, daß ...**: as luck would have it ...; **~ im Spiel, Glück in der Liebe** unlucky at cards, lucky in love; **d)** *(Schicksalsschlag)* misfortune; **ein ~ kommt selten allein** *(ugs.)* it never rains but it pours

ụnglücklich 1. *Adj.* **a)** *(traurig)* unhappy; unhappy, unrequited ⟨*love*⟩; **er ist ~ darüber, daß ...**: he is unhappy that ...; **mach dich nicht ~!** don't do it!; **b)** *(nicht vom Glück begünstigt)* unfortunate ⟨*person*⟩; *(bedauernswert, arm)* hapless ⟨*person, animal*⟩; **ich Unglücklicher/Unglückliche!** *(geh.)* poor me!; woe is me! *(literary)*; **der/die Unglückliche** the unfortunate *or* poor man/woman; **c)** *(ungünstig, ungeschickt)* unfortunate ⟨*moment, combination, meeting, etc.*⟩; unhappy ⟨*end, choice, solution*⟩; unfortunate, unhappy ⟨*coincidence, formulation*⟩; clumsy ⟨*movement*⟩; *(unverdient)* unlucky ⟨*defeat*⟩; **[bei** *od.* **in etw.** *(Dat.)***] eine ~e Hand haben** get it wrong [when doing sth.]; **eine ~e Figur abgeben** cut a sorry figure. **2.** *adv.* **a)** unhappily; **~ verliebt sein** be unhappy in love; **b)** *(ungünstig)* unfortunately; *(ungeschickt)* unhappily, clumsily ⟨*translated, expressed*⟩; **~ enden** come to an unfortunate end; ⟨*love affair*⟩ end unhappily; **er stürzte so ~, daß ...**: he fell so awkwardly that ...; he had such a bad fall that ...

unglücklicherweise *Adv.* unfortunately

Ụnglücks·botschaft die bad news *sing.*; bad tidings *pl.*

ụnglück·selig *Adj.* **a)** *(bedauernswert)* unfortunate, hapless ⟨*person*⟩; **b)** *(verhängnisvoll)* unfortunate, fateful ⟨*coincidence, combination*⟩; ill-starred, fateful ⟨*time*⟩; fateful ⟨*predilection*⟩

Ụnglücks-: **~fall der** accident; **~rabe der** *(ugs.)* unlucky sort *(coll.)*; luckless individual *(coll.)*; **~stelle die** scene of an/the accident; **~zahl die** unlucky number

Ụngnade die *in* **[bei jmdm.] in ~** *(Akk.)* **fallen/in ~** *(Dat.)* **sein** fall/be out of favour [with sb.]

ụngnädig 1. *Adj.* bad-tempered; grumpy; *(geh.: schlimm)* unkind ⟨*fate*⟩. **2.** *adv.* in a bad-tempered way; grumpily

ụngültig *Adj.* invalid; void *(esp. Law)*; spoilt ⟨*vote, ballot-paper*⟩; disallowed ⟨*goal*⟩; **~e Banknoten** banknotes which are not legal tender; **eine Ehe/ein Tor für ~ erklären** annul a marriage/disallow a goal

Ụngunst die a) *(geh. veralt.)* disfavour; **b)** *in* **zu jmds. ~en** to sb.'s disadvantage

ụngünstig 1. *Adj.* **a)** unfavourable; unfavourable, poor ⟨*climate, weather*⟩; *(unglücklich)* unfortunate ⟨*consequence*⟩; unfortunate, bad ⟨*shape, layout*⟩; *(unvorteilhaft)* unfavourable, unflattering ⟨*light, perspective, impression*⟩; unflattering ⟨*cut of dress*⟩; inconvenient ⟨*position*⟩; *(schädlich)* harmful ⟨*effect*⟩; **b)** *(unpassend)* inconvenient ⟨*time*⟩; *(ungeeignet)* inappropriate, inconvenient ⟨*time, place*⟩; unsuitable ⟨*colour etc.*⟩. **2.** *adv.* **a)** unfavourably; badly ⟨*designed, laid out*⟩; *(unvorteilhaft)* unflatteringly ⟨*cut*⟩; **sich ~ auswirken** have a harmful effect; **b)** *(unpassend, ungeeignet)* inconveniently

ụngut *Adj.* **a)** uneasy ⟨*feeling, premonition*⟩; negative ⟨*impression, expectation*⟩; *(unangenehm)* unpleasant ⟨*after-taste, recollection, memories*⟩; **b)** *in* **nichts für ~!** no offence [meant]! *(coll.)*

unhaltbar *Adj.* **a)** untenable ⟨*thesis, statement, etc.*⟩; **b)** *(unerträglich)* unbearable, intolerable ⟨*conditions, situation*⟩; **c)** *(Ballspiele)* unstoppable ⟨*shot, goal, etc.*⟩

ụnhandlich *Adj.* unwieldy

Ụnheil das disaster; **~ anrichten** *od.* **stiften** wreak havoc

unheilbar 1. *Adj.* incurable. **2.** *adv.* incurably; **~ krank** suffering from an incurable disease *postpos.*; incurably ill

ụnheil·voll *Adj.* disastrous; *(verhängnisvoll)* fateful; ominous ⟨*development*⟩

ụnheimlich 1. *Adj.* **a)** eerie ⟨*story, figure, place, sound*⟩; eerie, uncanny ⟨*feeling*⟩; **das/er ist mir ~**: it/he gives me an eerie feeling *or (coll.)* the creeps; **mir ist/wird [es] ~**: I have an eerie *or* uncanny feeling; **b)** *(ugs.) (schrecklich)* terrible *(coll.)* ⟨*coward, idiot, hunger, headache, etc.*⟩; *(enorm)* terrific *(coll.)* ⟨*fun, sum, amount, etc.*⟩. **2.** *adv.* **a)** eerily; uncannily; **b)** *(ugs.; äußerst, sehr)* terribly *(coll.)* ⟨*fat, nice, etc.*⟩; terrifically *(coll.)* ⟨*important, large*⟩; incredibly *(coll.)* ⟨*quick, long*⟩; **~ viel** an incredible *or* a terrific amount *(coll.)*; **es macht ~ Spaß** it's terrific fun *(coll.)*

ụnhöflich 1. *Adj.* impolite. **2.** *adv.* impolitely

Ụnhöflichkeit die impoliteness

Ụnhold der; ~[e]s, ~e **a)** fiend; demon; **b)** *(abwertend: böser Mensch)* monster

unhörbar 1. *Adj.* inaudible. **2.** *adv.* inaudibly

ụnhygienisch 1. *Adj.* unhygienic. **2.** *adv.* unhygienically

uni ['yni] *indekl. Adj.* plain, single-colour ⟨*material etc.*⟩; plain ⟨*tie*⟩

Uni ['ʊni] **die**; ~, ~s *(ugs.)* university

UNICEF ['u:nitsɛf] **die**; ~: UNICEF

ụni·farben *Adj. s.* **uni**

Uniform ['ʊnifɔrm] **die**; ~, ~en uniform; **[Staats]bürger in ~**: soldier [in the Bundeswehr]; citizen in uniform; **die ~ ausziehen** *(fig.)* put aside one's uniform; leave the service

uniformieren *tr. V.* uniform; **uniformiert** in uniform *postpos.*; uniformed

Uniformierte der/die; *adj. Dekl.* man/woman in uniform; *(Polizist)* uniformed [police]man/woman

Unikat [uni'ka:t] **das**; ~[e]s, ~e *s.* **Unikum a**

Unikum ['u:nikʊm] **das**; ~s, **Unika** *od.* **~s a)** *(geh.)* **ein ~ sein** be unique; **ein botanisches ~**: a unique botanical specimen; **b)** *(ugs.: Original)* [real] character

ụninteressant *Adj.* **a)** uninteresting; *(nicht von Belang)* of no interest *postpos.*; unimportant; **nicht ~**: quite interesting; **b)** *(nicht lohnend, nicht attraktiv)* untempting, unattractive ⟨*offer*⟩; **[für jmdn.] ~ sein** be of no interest [to sb.]

ụninteressiert *Adj.* uninterested; not interested (**an +** *Dat.* in); **er ist politisch völlig ~**: he is not at all interested in politics

Union [u'nio:n] **die**; ~, ~en union; **die ~** *(Bundesrepublik Deutschland)* the Union of Christian Democrats and Christian Socialists; the CDU and CSU

Unions·republik die republic [of the USSR]

unisono [uni'zo:no] *Adv. (Musik; auch fig.)* in unison; *(einmütig)* unanimously

universal *Adj.* universal; all-embracing ⟨*education*⟩

Universal-: **~erbe der** sole heir; **~genie das** *(fig.)* universal genius; **~lexikon das** general encyclopaedia

universell [univɛr'zɛl] **1.** *Adj.* universal. **2.** *adv.* universally; **~ gebildet sein** have an all-embracing education

Universität [univɛrzi'tɛ:t] **die; ~, ~en** university; **die ~ Marburg, die Marburger ~:** the University of Marburg; Marburg University; **an der ~** ⟨*meet, study, etc.*⟩ at university; **auf die ~ gehen** *(ugs.),* **die ~ besuchen** go to university

Universitäts-: ~bibliothek die university library; **~buch·handlung die** university bookshop *or (Amer.)* bookstore; **„~buchhandlung C. F. Meyer"** 'C. F. Meyer, university booksellers'; **~dozent der** university lecturer; **~klinik die** university hospital; **~stadt die** university town; **~studium das** study *no art.* at university

Universum [uni'vɛrzʊm] **das; ~s** universe

ụnkameradschaftlich 1. *Adj.* uncomradely. **2.** *adv.* in an uncomradely way

Unke ['ʊnkə] **die; ~, ~n a)** fire-bellied toad; **b)** *(ugs. abwertend: Schwarzseher[in])* Jeremiah; prophet of doom

ụnken *itr. V. (ugs.)* prophesy doom [and destruction] *(joc.)*

ụnkenntlich *Adj.* unrecognizable ⟨*person, face*⟩; indecipherable ⟨*writing, stamp*⟩

Ụnkenntlichkeit die; ~: unrecognizable state; *(einer Schrift, eines Stempels)* indecipherable state; **bis zur ~ entstellt** disfigured to the point of being unrecognizable

Ụnkenntnis die; *o. Pl.* ignorance; **~ auf einem Gebiet** ignorance of a subject; **etw. aus ~ tun** do sth. from *or* out of ignorance; **jmdn. [über etw.** *(Akk.)***] in ~ lassen** leave sb. in ignorance [of sth.]; **~ schützt nicht vor Strafe** ignorance [of the law] is no excuse *or* defence

Ụnken·ruf der *(fig.)* prophecy of doom

ụnkeusch *(geh.)* **1.** *Adj.* unchaste. **2.** *adv.* unchastely

Ụnkeuschheit die unchastity *no art.*

ụnklar 1. *Adj.* **a)** *(undeutlich)* unclear; indistinct; *(fig.: unbestimmt)* vague ⟨*feeling, recollection, idea*⟩; **b)** *(nicht klar verständlich)* unclear; **c)** *(nicht durchschaubar)* unclear ⟨*origin, situation, etc.*⟩; *(ungewiß)* uncertain ⟨*outcome*⟩; **sich** *(Dat.)* **über etw.** *(Akk.)* **im ~en sein** be unclear *or* unsure about sth.; **ich bin mir noch im ~en, ob ...:** I am still not sure *or* certain whether ...; **jmdn. über etw.** *(Akk.)* **im ~en lassen** keep sb. guessing about sth.

Ụnklarheit die a) *o. Pl. (Undeutlichkeit)* lack of clarity; indistinctness; **b)** *o. Pl. (Unverständlichkeit)* lack of clarity (*Gen.* in); **c)** *o. Pl. (Undurchschaubarkeit, Ungewißheit)* uncertainty; **es herrscht noch ~ darüber** it is still uncertain; **d)** *(unklarer Punkt)* unclear *or* outstanding point; **falls noch ~en bestehen** if anything is still unclear

ụnklug 1. *Adj.* unwise. **2.** *adv.* unwisely

ụnkollegial 1. *Adj.* inconsiderate *or* unhelpful [to one's colleagues]; **er ist [sehr] ~:** he is not [at all] a good colleague. **2.** *adv.* not ⟨*behave*⟩ like a good colleague

ụnkompliziert 1. *Adj.* uncomplicated, straightforward ⟨*person, mechanism, etc.*⟩; straightforward, simple ⟨*matter, case, problem*⟩; simple ⟨*fracture*⟩ *(Med.).* **2.** *adv.* ⟨*express*⟩ straightforwardly, simply

ụnkontrollierbar *Adj.* impossible to check *or* supervise *postpos.; (nicht zu beherrschen)* uncontrollable

ụnkontrolliert *Adj.* **a)** unsupervised; ⟨*route*⟩ without check-points; **b)** *(unbeherrscht)* uncontrolled ⟨*emotions, feelings, outburst*⟩; intemperate ⟨*words*⟩

ụnkonventionell 1. *Adj.* unconventional. **2.** *adv.* unconventionally

ụnkonzentriert 1. *Adj.* lacking in concentration *postpos.;* **du bist heute sehr ~:** you aren't concentrating today. **2.** *adv.* without concentrating; **sie arbeitet sehr ~:** she doesn't concentrate at all on her work

Ụnkosten *Pl.* **a)** [extra] expense *sing.;* expenses; **mit großen ~ verbunden sein** involve a great deal of expense; **sich in ~ stürzen** dig deep into one's pocket; [really] lash out *(coll.);* **sich in geistige ~ stürzen** *(scherzh.)* strain one's grey matter *(coll.);* **b)** *(ugs.: Ausgaben)* costs; expenditure *sing.*

Ụnkosten·beitrag der contribution towards expenses

Ụnkraut das a) *o. Pl.* weeds *pl.;* **~ vergeht nicht** *(ugs. scherzh.)* it would take a great deal to finish off his/her/our sort *(coll.);* **b)** *(Art)* weed

Ụnkraut·vertilgungsmittel das weed-killer

ụnkritisch 1. *Adj.* uncritical. **2.** *adv.* uncritically

ụnkultiviert *Adj.* uncultivated

unkụ̈ndbar *Adj.* permanent ⟨*position, contract*⟩; irredeemable ⟨*loan*⟩; **er ist ~:** he cannot be given notice

ụnkundig *Adj. (geh.)* ignorant; **einer Sache** *(Gen.)* **~ sein** have no knowledge of sth.; **des Lesens/Schreibens/Deutschen ~:** unable to read/to write/to speak German

ụnlängst *Adv. (geh.)* not long ago; recently; **noch ~, ~ noch** only recently

ụnlauter *Adj. (geh.)* dishonest; **~er Wettbewerb** *(Rechtsspr.)* unfair competition

ụnleidlich 1. *Adj.* tetchy. **2.** *adv.* tetchily

unlẹsbar *Adj.* unreadable

ụnleserlich 1. *Adj.* illegible. **2.** *adv.* illegibly

unleugbar 1. *Adj.* undeniable; indisputable. **2.** *adv.* undeniably; indisputably

ụnliebsam 1. *Adj.* unpleasant; **~es Aufsehen erregen** attract the wrong sort of attention. **2.** *adv.* **er ist ~ aufgefallen** he made a bad impression

ụnlogisch 1. *Adj.* illogical. **2.** *adv.* illogically

Ụnlust die *(Widerwille)* reluctance; *(Lustlosigkeit)* lack of enthusiasm; **mit ~:** with reluctance/without enthusiasm

ụnlustig 1. *Adj.* listless; *(ohne Begeisterung)* unenthusiastic. **2.** *adv.* listlessly; *(ohne Begeisterung)* unenthusiastically

ụnmännlich *(abwertend)* **1.** *Adj.* unmanly; *(weibisch)* effeminate. **2.** *adv.* in an unmanly way

ụnmaßgeblich *Adj.* of no consequence *postpos.;* inconsequential; **nach meiner ~en Meinung** *(scherzh.)* in my humble opinion

ụnmäßig 1. *Adj.* **a)** *(übermäßig, maßlos)* immoderate; excessive; **~ im Essen/Trinken sein** eat/drink to excess; **~ in seinen Ansprüchen/Forderungen sein** make excessive claims/demands; **b)** *(enorm)* tremendous ⟨*desire, thirst, fear, etc.*⟩. **2.** *adv.* **a)** *(übermäßig, allzusehr)* excessively; ⟨*eat, drink*⟩ to excess; **~ viel essen/Geld ausgeben** eat/spend far too much; **b)** *(überaus, sehr)* tremendously *(coll.),* terribly ⟨*surprised, pleased, fond, etc.*⟩

Ụnmäßigkeit die immoderation *no art.*

Ụnmenge die mass; enormous number/amount; **eine ~ Geld/Bücher, eine ~ von** *od.* **an Geld/Büchern** an enormous amount of money/number of books; **er trinkt ~n [von] Tee** he drinks enormous quantities *or (coll.)* gallons of tea

Ụnmensch der brute; **ich bin/man ist ja kein ~** *(ugs.)* I'm not inhuman

ụnmenschlich 1. *Adj.* **a)** inhuman; brutal; subhuman, appalling ⟨*conditions*⟩; **b)** *(entsetzlich)* terrible *(coll.),* appalling ⟨*pain, heat, suffering, etc.*⟩. **2.** *adv.* **a)** in an inhuman way; **b)** *(entsetzlich)* appallingly *(coll.)*

ụnmerklich 1. *Adj.* imperceptible. **2.** *adv.* imperceptibly

ụnmißverständlich 1. *Adj.* **a)** *(eindeutig)* unambiguous; **b)** *(offen, direkt)* blunt ⟨*answer, refusal*⟩; unequivocal ⟨*language*⟩. **2.** *adv.* **a)** *(eindeutig)* unambiguously; **b)** *(offen, direkt)* bluntly; unequivocally

ụnmittelbar 1. *Adj.* **a)** *nicht präd.* immediate ⟨*vicinity, past, future*⟩; immediate, next-door ⟨*neighbour etc.*⟩; **in ~er Strandnähe** right next to the beach; **aus ~er Nähe** ⟨*shoot*⟩ at close quarters, from point-blank range; **b)** *(direkt)* direct ⟨*contact, connection, influence, etc.*⟩; immediate ⟨*cause, consequence, predecessor, successor*⟩. **2.** *adv.* **a)** immediately; right ⟨*behind, next to*⟩; **~ bevorstehen** be imminent; be almost upon us *etc.;* **b)** *(direkt)* directly; **ich fahre von dort ~ zum Bahnhof** I'll go straight from there to the station; **etw. ~ erleben** experience sth. at first hand

ụnmöbliert *Adj.* unfurnished

ụnmodern 1. *Adj.* old-fashioned; *(nicht modisch)* unfashionable; **~ werden** go out of fashion. **2.** *adv.* in an old-fashioned way; *(nicht modisch)* unfashionably

unmọ̈glich 1. *Adj.* **a)** impossible; **ich verlange ja nichts Unmögliches [von dir]** I'm not asking [you] for the impossible; **es ist mir ~:** it is impossible for me; **du machst es ihm/mir ~[, zu ...]** you are making it impossible for him/me [to ...]; **b)** *(ugs.: nicht akzeptabel, unangebracht)* impossible ⟨*person, behaviour, colour, ideas, place, etc.*⟩; **~ aussehen** look ridiculous; **jmdn./sich ~ machen** make a fool of sb./oneself; make sb./oneself look ridiculous; **sich bei jmdm. ~ machen** lose sb.'s respect; **c)** *(ugs.: erstaunlich, seltsam)* incredible; **an den ~sten Orten** in the most impossible *or* incredible places. **2.** *adv. (ugs.)* ⟨*behave*⟩ impossibly; ⟨*dress*⟩ ridiculously; **~ angezogen sein** be wearing impossible clothes. **3.** *Adv. (ugs.: unter keinen Umständen)* **ich/es** *usw.* **kann ~ ...:** I/it *etc.* can't possibly ...; **mehr ist ~ zu erreichen** it's impossible to do any more; **das geht ~:** that's out of the question

Ụnmoral die immorality *no art.*

ụnmoralisch 1. *Adj.* immoral. **2.** *adv.* immorally

ụnmotiviert 1. *Adj.* unmotivated. **2.** *adv.* without reason; for no reason

ụnmündig *Adj.* **a)** under-age; **~ sein** be under age *or* a minor; **b)** *(fig.: geistig unselbständig)* dependent

Ụnmündigkeit die; ~ *(fig.)* dependence

ụnmusikalisch *Adj.* unmusical

Ụnmut der *(geh.)* displeasure; annoyance; **seinen ~ an jmdm. auslassen** take it out on sb.

ụnnachahmlich 1. *Adj.* inimitable. **2.** *adv.* inimitably

ụnnachgiebig *Adj.* intransigent; **in diesem Punkt ~ sein** be uncompromising in this respect; refuse to yield on this point

Ụnnachgiebigkeit die intransigence

ụnnachsichtig 1. *Adj.* merciless; unmerciful; unrelenting ⟨*severity*⟩. **2.** *adv.* mercilessly; ⟨*punish*⟩ unmercifully

unnạhbar *Adj.* unapproachable

ụnnatürlich 1. *Adj.* unnatural; forced ⟨*laugh*⟩; artificial ⟨*material*⟩; ⟨*death*⟩ from unnatural causes; violent ⟨*death*⟩. **2.** *adv.* unnaturally; ⟨*laugh*⟩ in a forced way; ⟨*speak*⟩ affectedly; **er trinkt/schläft ~ viel** he drinks/sleeps an abnormal amount

Ụnnatürlichkeit die unnaturalness; *(von Material)* artificiality

ụnnormal 1. *Adj.* abnormal. **2.** *adv.* abnormally

ụnnötig 1. *Adj.* unnecessary; needless, pointless ⟨*heroism*⟩; **~ zu sagen, daß ...:** needless to say ... **2.** *adv.* unnecessarily

ụnnütz 1. *Adj.* useless ⟨*stuff, person, etc.*⟩; pointless ⟨*talk*⟩; wasted ⟨*words*⟩; pointless, wasted ⟨*expense, effort*⟩; vain ⟨*attempt*⟩; **es ist ~, darüber zu streiten** it is no use arguing about it. **2.** *adv. (unnötig)* needlessly

UNO ['u:no] **die: die ~:** the UN

ụnökonomisch 1. *Adj.* uneconomical. **2.** *adv.* uneconomically; in an uneconomical way

unordentlich 1. *Adj.* **a)** untidy; **b)** *(ungeregelt)* disorderly ⟨*life*⟩. **2.** *adv.* untidily; ⟨*tie, treat, etc.*⟩ carelessly

Unordnung die disorder; mess; **so eine ~!** what a mess *or* muddle!; **in dem Zimmer herrschte eine fürchterliche ~:** the room was terribly untidy *or* in a terrible mess *(coll.)*; **etw. in ~ bringen** muddle *or* mess sth. up; **in ~ geraten** get into a mess *or* muddle; *(fig.)* ⟨*equilibrium*⟩ become upset

unorthodox 1. *Adj.* unorthodox. **2.** in an unorthodox way

Unpaarhufer der *(Zool.)* odd-toed ungulate

unpaarig *(Biol.)* **1.** *Adj.* unpaired; azygous. **2.** *adv.* dissimilarly

unparteiisch 1. *Adj.* impartial. **2.** *adv.* impartially

Unparteiische der/die; *adj. Dekl. (Sport) s.* **Schiedsrichter a**

unpassend 1. *Adj.* inappropriate; unsuitable ⟨*dress etc.*⟩. **2.** *adv.* inappropriately; unsuitably ⟨*dressed etc.*⟩

unpassierbar *Adj.* impassable

unpäßlich ['ʊnpɛslɪç] *Adj.* indisposed

Unpäßlichkeit die; ~, ~en indisposition

Unperson die unperson

unpersönlich 1. *Adj.* impersonal; distant, aloof ⟨*person*⟩. **2.** *adv.* impersonally; ⟨*answer, write*⟩ in impersonal terms

Unpersönlichkeit die; *o. Pl.* impersonal nature

unpolitisch *Adj.* unpolitical; apolitical

unpopulär *Adj.* unpopular

unpraktisch 1. *Adj.* unpractical. **2.** *adv.* in an unpractical way

unproblematisch 1. *Adj.* unproblematic; straightforward; **nicht ganz ~:** not without its problems. **2.** *adv.* without any problems

unproduktiv 1. *Adj.* unproductive. **2.** *adv.* unproductively

unpünktlich 1. *Adj.* **a)** unpunctual ⟨*person*⟩; **b)** *(verspätet)* late, unpunctual ⟨*payment*⟩. **2.** *adv.* late

Unpünktlichkeit die lateness; lack of punctuality

unqualifiziert 1. *Adj.* **a)** unqualified, unskilled ⟨*person*⟩; unskilled ⟨*work*⟩; **b)** *(abwertend: nicht fundiert)* inept ⟨*remark, criticism*⟩. **2.** *adv. (abwertend)* ineptly

unrasiert *Adj.* unshaven; **~ und fern der Heimat** *(scherzh.)* away from it all and looking pretty disreputable

Unrast die; *o. Pl. (geh.)* restlessness

Unrat der; ~[e]s *(geh.)* garbage *(lit. or fig.)*; refuse *(Brit.)*; **~ wittern** smell a rat *(fig.)*

unrationell 1. *Adj.* inefficient. **2.** *adv.* inefficiently

unrealistisch 1. *Adj.* unrealistic. **2.** *adv.* unrealistically

unrecht 1. *Adj.* wrong; **auf ~e Gedanken kommen** get wicked ideas. **2.** *adv.* wrongly; **~ tun** do wrong; *s. auch* **Unrecht a**

Unrecht das; *o. Pl.* **a)** *in* **unrecht haben** be wrong; **jmdm. unrecht tun** do sb. an injustice; do wrong by sb.; **unrecht bekommen** be shown to be in the wrong; **jmdm. unrecht geben** disagree with sb.; **b)** wrong; **im ~ sein** be [in the] wrong; **sich ins ~ setzen** put oneself in the wrong; **ihm ist ein ~ geschehen** he has been wronged; **zu ~:** wrongly; **nicht zu ~** *(wohlbegründet)* not without [good] reason

unrechtmäßig 1. *Adj.* unlawful; illegal. **2.** *adv.* unlawfully; illegally

unredlich *(geh.)* **1.** *Adj.* dishonest. **2.** *adv.* dishonestly

Unredlichkeit die a) *o. Pl.* dishonesty; **b)** *(Handlung)* dishonest act

unreell *Adj.* unfair ⟨*deal, price*⟩

unreflektiert 1. *Adj. (geh.)* unthinking; *(spontan)* spontaneous ⟨*tradition*⟩. **2.** *adv.* without thinking; unthinkingly

unregelmäßig 1. *Adj.* irregular. **2.** *adv.* irregularly

Unregelmäßigkeit die irregularity

unregierbar *Adj.* ungovernable

unreif *Adj.* **a)** unripe; **b)** *(nicht erwachsen)* immature

Unreife die *s.* **unreif a, b:** unripeness; immaturity

unrein *Adj.* **a)** *(auch fig.)* impure; bad ⟨*breath, skin*⟩; *(nicht sauber)* dirty, polluted ⟨*water, air*⟩; unclear ⟨*sound*⟩; **b)** *(Rel.)* unclean; **c)** *in* **etw. ins ~e schreiben** make a rough copy of sth.; write sth. [out] in rough; **ins ~e sprechen** *od.* **reden** *(ugs. scherzh.)* talk off the top of one's head

Unreinheit die a) *o. Pl. s.* **unrein a:** impurity; badness; dirtiness; polluted state; lack of clarity; **b) ~en der Haut** skin disorders

unrentabel 1. *Adj.* unprofitable. **2.** *adv.* unprofitably

unrettbar 1. *Adj.* unsavable; beyond hope *pred.* **2.** *adv.* irretrievably ⟨*lost*⟩

unrichtig 1. *Adj.* incorrect; inaccurate. **2.** *adv. (fehlerhaft)* incorrectly

Unrichtigkeit die a) *o. Pl. (das Unzutreffendsein)* incorrectness; inaccuracy; **b)** *o. Pl. (Fehlerhaftigkeit)* incorrectness; **c)** *(etw. Unzutreffendes, Fehler)* inaccuracy

Unruh ['ʊnru:] **die; ~, ~en** *(Technik)* balance[-wheel] *(of clock)*

Unruhe die a) *(auch fig.)* unrest; *(Lärm)* noise; commotion; *(Unrast)* restlessness; agitation; *(Besorgnis)* anxiety; disquiet; **unter den Zuschauern entstand ~:** the audience became restless; **b)** *(Unfrieden)* unrest; **~ stiften** stir up trouble; **c)** *Pl. (Tumulte)* disturbances; unrest *sing.*

Unruhe-: ~herd der seat of unrest; trouble-spot; **~stifter der** *(abwertend)* trouble-maker

unruhig 1. *Adj.* **a)** restless; *(besorgt)* anxious; *(nervös)* agitated; jittery; *(fig.)* choppy ⟨*sea*⟩; busy ⟨*pattern*⟩; busy, eventful ⟨*life*⟩; unsettled, troubled ⟨*time*⟩; **er ist ein ~er Geist** he's a restless creature; **hier ist es mir zum Arbeiten viel zu ~:** there is too much going on [for me] to work here; **b)** *(laut)* noisy ⟨*area etc.*⟩; **c)** *(ungleichmäßig)* uneven ⟨*breathing, pulse, running, etc.*⟩; fitful ⟨*sleep, motion*⟩; disturbed ⟨*night*⟩; unsettled ⟨*life*⟩. **2.** *adv.* **a)** restlessly; *(besorgt)* anxiously; **hier geht es sehr ~ zu** there is too much going on here; **b)** *(ungleichmäßig)* ⟨*breathe, run*⟩ unevenly; ⟨*sleep*⟩ fitfully

unrühmlich 1. *Adj.* inglorious; ignominious. **2.** *adv.* ignominiously

unrund *Adj. (Technik)* **a)** not perfectly round *pred.*; **b)** *(ungleichmäßig)* uneven, rough ⟨*running of engine*⟩

uns [ʊns] **1. a)** *Akk. des Personalpron.* **wir** us; **b)** *Dat. des Personalpron.* **wir; gib es ~:** give it to us; **gib ~ das Geld** give us the money; **wie geht es ~ heute?** *(fam.)* how are we today? *(joc.)*; **kommst du zu ~?** are you coming to our place? *(coll.)*; **Freunde von ~:** friends of ours; **von ~ aus** as far as we're concerned; **bei ~:** at our home *or (coll.)* place; *(in der Heimat)* where I/we live *or* come from; **bei ~ gegenüber, gegenüber von ~:** opposite us *or* our house. **2.** *Reflexivpron. der 1. Pers. Pl.* **a)** *refl.* ourselves; **wir schämen ~:** we are ashamed [of ourselves]; **wir waschen ~/~ die Hände** we are washing [ourselves]/our hands; **von ~ aus** *(aus eigenem Antrieb)* on our own initiative; **b)** *reziprok* one another; **wir kennen ~ schon** we know one another; we've met; **wir haben ~ gestritten** we had an argument *or* quarrel

unsachgemäß 1. *Adj.* improper. **2.** *adv.* improperly

unsachlich 1. *Adj.* unobjective; **~ werden** lose one's objectivity. **2.** *adv.* without objectivity

Unsachlichkeit die lack of objectivity

unsagbar, unsäglich [ʊn'zɛ:klɪç] *(geh.)* **1.** *Adj.* indescribable; unutterable. **2.** *adv.* indescribably; unutterably

unsanft 1. *Adj.* rough; hard ⟨*push, impact*⟩. **2.** *adv.* roughly; **~ geweckt werden** be rudely awoken; **jmdn. ~ zurechtweisen** reprimand sb. curtly *or* rudely

unsauber 1. *Adj.* **a)** *(schmutzig)* dirty; **b)** *(nachlässig)* untidy, sloppy ⟨*work, writing, etc.*⟩; **c)** *(unklar)* unclear ⟨*sound*⟩; *(ungenau)* inexact, woolly ⟨*definition*⟩; **d)** *(unlauter)* shady ⟨*practice, deal, character, etc.*⟩; underhand, dishonest ⟨*method, means, intention*⟩; *(Sport: unfair)* unsporting, unfair ⟨*play*⟩. **2.** *adv.* **a)** *(nachlässig)* untidily; carelessly; **b)** *(unklar)* ⟨*sing, play*⟩ inaccurately; **c)** *(Sport: unfair)* unsportingly; unfairly

Unsauberkeit die; *o. Pl.* **a)** dirtiness; lack of cleanliness; **b)** *(Nachlässigkeit)* untidiness; sloppiness; **c)** *(Unklarheit)* lack of clarity; *(Ungenauigkeit)* woolliness; **d)** *(Unehrlichkeit)* shadiness; *(Sport: Unfairneß)* unfairness

unschädlich *Adj.* harmless; **~ machen** render harmless, neutralize ⟨*toxic substance, germ. etc.*⟩; put ⟨*weapon, person*⟩ out of action; render ⟨*bomb etc.*⟩ safe; *(verhüll.: durch Tötung)* eliminate ⟨*person*⟩

unscharf 1. *Adj.* **a)** blurred, fuzzy ⟨*photo, picture*⟩; **b)** *(ungenau)* woolly ⟨*formulation*⟩; **die Grenzen sind ~:** there are no clear-cut borderlines; **c)** *(ein ~es Bild ergebend)* ⟨*lens, optical instrument*⟩ with poor definition; *(falsch eingestellt)* out-of-focus. **2.** *adv.* **a)** blurred; **durch diese Brille sehe ich alles ganz ~:** everything looks blurred *or* out of focus [to me] through these spectacles; **b)** *(ungenau)* unclearly

unschätzbar *Adj.* inestimable ⟨*value etc.*⟩; invaluable ⟨*service*⟩; priceless ⟨*riches etc.*⟩

unscheinbar *Adj.* inconspicuous; nondescript; unspectacular ⟨*plumage, blossom*⟩

unschicklich *(geh.)* **1.** *Adj.* unseemly; improper. **2.** *adv.* improperly

unschlagbar *Adj.* unbeatable ⟨*opponent, prices, etc.*⟩

Unschlitt ['ʊnʃlɪt] **das; ~[e]s, ~e** *(veralt.)* tallow

unschlüssig *Adj.* undecided *pred.*; undecisive ⟨*gesture, attitude*⟩; **ich bin [mir] noch ~, ob ...:** I cannot decide whether ...

unschön 1. *Adj.* **a)** ugly; unattractive ⟨*colour, voice*⟩; **b)** *(unerfreulich, unfair)* unpleasant, nasty ⟨*business, incident, weather, conduct, etc.*⟩; ugly ⟨*scene*⟩. **2.** *adv.* **a)** unattractively; **b)** *(unfreundlich, unfair)* badly

Unschuld die; *o. Pl.* **a)** innocence; **wegen erwiesener ~:** having been proved innocent; **seine Hände in ~ waschen** *(fig.)* wash one's hands in innocence; **b)** *(Naivität)* innocence; *(Jungfräulichkeit)* virginity; **in aller ~:** in all innocence; **eine ~ vom Lande** *(ugs. scherzh.)* a naïve country girl

unschuldig 1. *Adj.* **a)** innocent; **an etw.** *(Dat.)* **~ sein** be not guilty of sth.; **er ist an dem Unfall völlig ~:** he was in no way responsible for the accident; **b)** *(unverdorben)* innocent; **ein ~es Mädchen** a virgin; **er/sie ist noch ~:** he/she is still a virgin; **den Unschuldigen/die Unschuldige spielen** play the innocent. **2.** *adv.* innocently

Unschulds-: ~beteuerung die protestation of innocence; **~lamm das** *(spött.)* little innocent; **sie sind auch keine ~lämmer** they're no angels; **~miene die** innocent expression; **mit ~miene** with an air of innocence

unschwer *Adv. (geh.)* easily; without difficulty

unselbständig 1. *Adj.* **a)** dependent [on other people]; **sei doch nicht immer so ~!** try to be a bit more independent!; **b)** *(abhängig)* [financially/economically] dependent; not self-supporting *pred.*; **~e Arbeit** [paid] employment. **2.** *adv.* **a) [sehr] ~ denken/handeln** not think [at all] for oneself *or* independently/not act [at all] on one's own *or* independently; **b)** *(abhängig)* **~ beschäftig-**

te Personen *od.* **Beschäftigte** persons in employment; employed persons
Unselbständigkeit die a) lack of independence; **b)** *(Abhängigkeit)* dependence
unselig *Adj. (geh.)* wretched ⟨*fate, person, etc.*⟩; [extremely] unfortunate ⟨*situation*⟩; ill-starred ⟨*inheritance*⟩; *(verhängnisvoll)* disastrous ⟨*journey, decision, etc.*⟩
[1]**unser** ['ʊnzɐ] *Possessivpron. der 1. Pers. Pl.* our; **Vater** ~ *(bibl.)* Our Father; **das ist ~s** *od. (geh.)* **~es** *od. (geh.)* **das ~e** that is ours; **sein Wagen stand neben ~[e]m** *od.* **unsrem** his car was next to ours; **die Unseren** our family; **wir haben das Unsere getan** we have done our share *or* part
[2]**unser** *Gen. des Personalpronomens* **wir** *(geh.)* of us; **wir waren ~ drei** there were three of us; **erbarme dich ~!** have mercy upon us!; **in ~ aller/beider Interesse** in the interest of all/both of us
unser·einer, unsereins *Indefinitpron. (ugs.)* the likes of us *pl.*; our sort *(coll.)*
unserer·seits *Adv.* for our part
unseres·gleichen *indekl. Indefinitpron.* people *pl.* like us; *attr.* **Menschen ~:** people like us
unseret·halben, unseret·wegen *Adv. s.* **unsertwegen**
unseret·willen *Adv. s.* **unsertwillen**
unserige *subst. Possessivpron. s.* **unsrige**
unseriös *(abwertend)* **1.** *Adj.* **a)** not [quite] the proper thing *pred.*; casual; ⟨*appearance, manner*⟩; **b)** *(niveaulos)* low-quality ⟨*newspaper*⟩; down-market ⟨*publisher*⟩; **c)** *(unlauter)* shady, dubious ⟨*practice, deal*⟩; *(unredlich)* questionable, dishonest ⟨*method etc.*⟩; *(nicht reell)* dubious ⟨*firm, pseudo-scientist, faith-healer*⟩; dishonest, shady ⟨*business man*⟩. **2.** *adv.* **a)** ⟨*behave, dress*⟩ casually; **b)** *(unlauter, unredlich)* dishonestly; unfairly
unser·seits *s.* **unsererseits**
unsers·gleichen *s.* **unseresgleichen**
unsert·wegen *Adv.* **a)** because of us; on our account; **b)** *(was uns angeht)* as far as we are concerned
unsert·willen *Adv.* **in um ~:** for our sake[s]
unsicher 1. *Adj.* **a)** *(gefährlich)* unsafe; dangerous; *(gefährdet)* at risk *pred.*; insecure ⟨*job*⟩; **einen Ort ~ machen** *(scherzh.)* honour a place with one's presence *(joc.)*; *(sich vergnügen)* have a good time in a place; *(sein Unwesen treiben)* get up to one's tricks in a place; **b)** *(unzuverlässig)* uncertain, unreliable ⟨*method*⟩; unreliable ⟨*source, person*⟩; **c)** *(zögernd)* uncertain, hesitant ⟨*step*⟩; *(zitternd)* unsteady, shaky ⟨*hand*⟩; *(nicht selbstsicher)* insecure; diffident; unsure of oneself *pred.*; **ich fühle mich ~:** I don't feel sure of myself; **er ist im Rechnen noch ~:** he still lacks confidence in arithmetic; **jmdn. ~ machen** put sb. off his/her stroke; **d)** *(keine Gewißheit habend)* unsure; uncertain; **[sich** *(Dat.)***] ~ sein[, ob ...]** ⟨*person*⟩ be unsure *or* uncertain [whether ...]; **e)** *(ungewiß)* uncertain; **das ist mir zu ~:** that's too uncertain *or (coll.)* dodgy for my liking. **2.** *adv. (mit Schwierigkeiten)* ⟨*walk, stand, etc.*⟩ unsteadily; **~ fahren** drive without [much] confidence; **b)** *(nicht selbstsicher)* ⟨*smile, look*⟩ diffidently
Unsicherheit die a) *o. Pl. (Gefährlichkeit)* dangerousness; *(Gefahren)* dangers *pl.*; **b)** *o. Pl. (Unzuverlässigkeit)* uncertainty; unreliability; **c)** *o. Pl. (Zaghaftigkeit)* unsureness; *(der Schritte o. ä.)* unsteadiness; **d)** *o. Pl. (fehlende Selbstsicherheit)* insecurity; lack of [self-]confidence; **e)** *o. Pl. (Ungewißheit)* uncertainty; **f)** *o. Pl. (der Arbeitsplätze)* insecurity; *(des Friedens)* instability; **g)** *(Unwägbarkeit)* uncertainty
Unsicherheits·faktor der element of uncertainty
unsichtbar *Adj.* invisible **(für** to)
Unsinn der; *o. Pl.* **a)** nonsense; **rede doch keinen ~!** don't talk nonsense *or* rubbish!; **es wäre ~ zu glauben, ...:** it would be ridiculous to believe ...; **b)** *(Unfug)* tomfoolery; fooling about *no art.*; **~ machen** *od.* **treiben** mess *or* fool about; **mach [ja] keinen ~:** don't do anything silly; no messing about
unsinnig 1. *Adj.* **a)** nonsensical ⟨*statement, talk, etc.*⟩; absurd, ridiculous ⟨*demand etc.*⟩; **b)** *(ugs.: übermäßig)* terrible *(coll.)* ⟨*rage, fear, thirst, etc.*⟩. **2.** *adv.* **a)** foolishly; stupidly; **b)** *(ugs.: übermäßig)* insanely *(coll.)*, terribly *(coll.)* ⟨*expensive*⟩
Unsitte die bad habit; *(allgemein verbreitet)* bad practice
unsittlich 1. *Adj.* indecent. **2.** *adv.* indecently; **sich jmdm. ~ nähern** make indecent advances to sb.
unsolid[e] 1. *Adj.* **a)** flimsy ⟨*structure*⟩; shoddy ⟨*work, repair*⟩; *(fig.)* superficial ⟨*education*⟩; **b)** *(ausschweifend)* dissolute ⟨*person, life*⟩. **2.** *adv.* **a)** flimsily ⟨*made*⟩; shoddily ⟨*executed*⟩; **b)** *(ausschweifend)* **~ leben** live a dissolute life
unsozial 1. *Adj.* unsocial ⟨*policy, measure, rent, etc.*⟩; antisocial ⟨*behaviour*⟩. **2.** *adv.* unsocially; ⟨*behave*⟩ antisocially
unsportlich 1. *Adj.* **a)** unathletic ⟨*person*⟩; **b)** *(unfair)* unsporting, unsportsmanlike ⟨*behaviour, play*⟩. **2.** *adv. (unfair)* in an unsporting way
unsr... *s.* [1]**unser**
unsrer·seits *s.* **unsererseits**
unsres·gleichen *s.* **unseresgleichen**
unsrige ['ʊnzrɪgə] *Possessivpron. (geh. veralt.)* **der/die/das ~:** ours; our one; **das Unsrige** *(unser Anteil)* our share *or* part; *(unser Besitz)* what is/was ours; **die Unsrigen** our family *sing.*
unstatthaft *Adj.* inadmissible
unsterblich 1. *Adj.* immortal; *(fig.)* undying ⟨*love*⟩; **seine Kompositionen sind ~** *(fig.)* his compositions will live for ever. **2.** *adv. (ugs.: außerordentlich)* incredibly *(coll.)*; **sich ~ in jmdn. verlieben** fall madly in love with sb.; **sich ~ blamieren** make a complete ass of oneself
Unsterbliche der/die; *adj. Dekl.* immortal
Unsterblichkeit die immortality
Unstern der; *o. Pl. (geh.)* unlucky star; **unter einem ~ stehen** be ill-starred
unstet *(geh.)* **1.** *Adj.* **a)** *(ruhelos)* restless ⟨*person, glance, thoughts, etc.*⟩; unsettled ⟨*life*⟩; **b)** *(unbeständig)* vacillating ⟨*person, nature*⟩; *(labil)* unstable ⟨*person, character*⟩. **2.** *adv. (ruhelos)* restlessly
unstimmig *Adj.* inconsistent [with the facts]; **[in sich] ~:** inconsistent
Unstimmigkeit die; ~, ~en a) *o. Pl.* inconsistency; **b)** *(etw. Unstimmiges)* discrepancy; **c)** *(Meinungsverschiedenheit)* difference [of opinion]
unstreitig 1. *Adj.* indisputable. **2.** *adv.* indisputably
unstrittig 1. *Adj.* **a)** uncontentious; **b)** *s.* **unstreitig 1. 2.** *adv. s.* **unstreitig 2**
Unsumme die vast *or* huge sum
unsympathisch *Adj.* uncongenial, disagreeable ⟨*person*⟩; unpleasant ⟨*characteristic, nature, voice*⟩; **er ist mir ~/nicht ~:** I find him disagreeable/quite likeable; I don't like/I quite like him; **der Plan ist mir ~:** the plan is not to my liking
unsystematisch 1. *Adj.* unsystematic. **2.** *adv.* unsystematically
untad[e]lig 1. *Adj.* impeccable ⟨*behaviour, reputation, etc.*⟩; irreproachable ⟨*person, life*⟩. **2.** *adv.* impeccably; irreproachably
Untat die misdeed; evil deed
untätig *Adj.* idle; **~ herumsitzen/zusehen** sit around doing nothing/stand idly by
Untätigkeit die idleness; inactivity
untauglich *Adj.* **a)** unsuitable ⟨*applicant*⟩; **~er Versuch** *(Rechtsw.)* attempt doomed to failure; **b)** *(für Militärdienst)* unfit [for service] *postpos.*
unteilbar *Adj.* **a)** indivisible; **b)** *(Math.: nicht dividierbar)* prime ⟨*number*⟩
unten ['ʊntn̩] *Adv.* **a)** down; **hier/da ~:** down here/there; **weiter ~:** further down; **nach ~** *(auch fig.)* downward; **der Weg nach ~:** the way down; **mit dem Gesicht nach ~:** face downwards; **von ~:** from below; **~ liegen** be down below; *(darunter)* lie underneath; **[im Bett] ~ schlafen** sleep in the bottom; **b)** *(in Gebäuden) (im Erdgeschoß)* downstairs; *(im Hochhaus)* on the bottom floor; **nach ~:** downstairs; **hier ~:** down here; **der Aufzug fährt nach ~/kommt von ~:** the lift *(Brit.) or (Amer.)* elevator is going down/coming up; **c)** *(am unteren Ende, zum unteren Ende hin)* at the bottom; **nach ~ [hin]** towards the bottom; **~ [links] auf der Seite/im Schrank** at the bottom [left] of the page/cupboard; **in der dritten Zeile von ~:** on the third line from the bottom; **die Abbildung ~ links** the illustration bottom left; *(als Bildunterschrift)* **„~ [rechts]"** 'below [right]'; *(auf einem Karton o. ä.)* **„~"** 'other side up'; **wo** *od.* **was ist [bei dem Karton] ~?** which is the bottom [of the cardboard box]?; **sich ~ herum waschen** wash one's nether regions *or* lower parts *(joc.)*; **~ am Tisch** *(fig.)* at the bottom of the table; **100 km weiter ~ am Fluß** 100 km. further downstream; **zwei Häuser weiter ~:** two houses further down [the road]; **d)** *(an der Unterseite)* underneath; **e)** *(in einer Hierarchie, Rangfolge)* **ziemlich weit/ganz ~ auf der Liste** rather a long way down/right at the bottom of the list; **f)** *([weiter] hinten im Text)* below; **weiter ~:** further on; below; **wie ~ angeführt** as stated below; **g)** *(ugs.: im Süden)* **~ in Sizilien/im Süden** down in Sicily/in the south; **hier/dort ~:** down here/there [in the south]; **weiter ~:** further south
unten·drunter *Adv. (ugs.)* underneath [it/them]
unten-: ~durch *Adv.* through underneath; *s. auch* **durchsein**; **~erwähnt, ~genannt** *Adj.; nicht präd.* undermentioned *(Brit.)*; mentioned below *postpos.*; **von den Untengenannten** of the undermentioned *(Brit.)*; of those mentioned below; **~herum, ~rum** *Adv. (ugs.)* down below; **~stehend** *Adj.; nicht präd.* following; given below *postpos.*
unter ['ʊntɐ] **1.** *Präp. mit Dat.* **a)** *(Lage, Standort, Abhängigkeit, Unterordnung)* under; **~ jmdm. wohnen** live below sb.; **unter der Devise ...:** according to the motto ...; **b)** *(weniger, niedriger usw. als)* **Mengen ~ 100 Stück** quantities of less than 100; *s. auch* **Durchschnitt b; Gefrierpunkt; Preis a; Wert a; c)** *(während)* **~ Mittag/Tags/der Woche** *(bes. südd.)* at *or* around midday/during the day/during the week; **d)** *(modal)* **~ Angst/Tränen** in *or* out of fear/in tears; **~ Zittern** trembling; **~ dem Beifall der Menge** applauded by the crowd; *s. auch* **Aufbietung a; Einbeziehung; Schmerz a; Verwendung a; e)** *(aus einer Gruppe)* among[st]; **~ anderem** among[st] other things; **einer ~ 40 Bewerbern** one of *or* among[st] 40 applicants; **f)** *(zwischen)* among[st]; **~ sich** by themselves; **~ uns gesagt** between ourselves *or* you and me; **g)** *(Zustand)* **~ Druck/Strom stehen** be under pressure/be live; *s. auch* **Dampf a; leiden a, b; h) ~ dem Datum des 1. März 1850** *(veralt.)* on 1 March 1850. **2.** *Präp. mit Akk.* **a)** *(Richtung, Ziel, Abhängigkeit, Unterordnung)* under; **sich ~ einen Baum setzen** sit under a tree; **die Scheuer war bis ~ die Decke mit Heu gefüllt** the barn was full of hay right up to the roof; **b)** *(niedriger als)* **~ Null sinken** drop below zero; **c)** *(zwischen)* among[st]; **er geht zu wenig ~ Menschen** he has too little to do with people; **~ Strom/Dampf setzen** switch on/put under steam. **3.** *Adv.* less than; **~ 30**

[Jahre alt] sein be under 30 [years of age]; **ein Kind von ~ 4 Jahren** a child of less than *or* under four years

ụnter... *Adj.* **a)** lower; bottom; *(ganz unten)* bottom; **das ~e/~ste Stockwerk** the lower/ bottom storey; **das Unterste zuoberst kehren** *(ugs.)* turn everything upside down; **b)** lower ⟨*Rhine, Nile, etc.*⟩; **c)** *(in der Rangfolge o. ä.)* lower; lesser ⟨*authority*⟩; **die ~en Klassen der Schule** the junior classes *or* forms of the school; **d)** *(der Oberfläche abgekehrt)* **die ~e Seite [von etw.]** the bottom [of sth.]; **auf der ~en Seite** underneath

ụnter-, Ụnter-: ~ab·teilung die a) department; **b)** *(Bot.)* subdivision; **~arm der** forearm; **~art die** *(Biol.)* subspecies; **~bau der;** *Pl.* **~bauten a)** *(Fundament)* foundations *pl.;* **b)** *o. Pl. (Grundlage, Basis)* foundation; basis; **c)** *(Sockel)* base; **d)** *(Straßenbau, Eisenb.)* road-bed; **~bauch der** *(Anat.)* lower abdomen; **~belegt** *Adj.* under-subscribed; half-empty ⟨*hotel, hospital, etc.*⟩; **~belegung die** under-subscription; **~belichten**[1] *tr. V. (Fot.)* underexpose; **geistig ~belichtet sein** *(fig. salopp)* be a bit thick *or (coll.)* dim; **~belichtung die** *(Fot.)* underexposure; **~beschäftigung die;** *o. Pl. (Wirtsch.)* underemployment; **~besetzt** *Adj.* understaffed; **~bett das** underblanket; **~bewerten**[2] *tr. V.* undervalue; underrate; mark ⟨*gymnast, skater*⟩ too low; **die Mark wurde ~bewertet** the mark was undervalued; **~bewertung die** *s.* **~bewerten:** undervaluation; underrating *no pl.;* **~bezahlen**[3] *tr. V.* underpay; **~bezahlung die** underpayment

unter-, Unter-: ~bieten *unr. tr. V.* **a)** *(weniger fordern)* undercut **(um** by); **etw. ist [im Niveau] kaum noch zu ~bieten** *(fig.)* sth. is simply rock-bottom [in quality]; **b)** *(bes. Sport)* beat ⟨*record*⟩; **jmds. Rekord ~bieten** be faster than sb.; **~bịnden** *unr. tr. V.* stop; **~bịndung die** ending; stopping; **~bleiben** *unr. itr. V.; mit sein* **etw. ~bleibt** sth. does not occur *or* happen; **das hat zu ~bleiben!** this must stop

Ụnter·boden der *(Kfz-W.)* under-side

Ụnterboden- *(Kfz-W.)*: **~schutz der** underseal; **~wäsche die** underbody wash; **der Wagen braucht eine ~wäsche** the under-side of the car needs washing

unter·brẹchen *unr. tr. V.* interrupt; break ⟨*journey, silence*⟩; interrupt, break off ⟨*negotiations, studies*⟩; interrupt, cut off ⟨*electricity supply*⟩; terminate ⟨*pregnancy*⟩; **die Telefonverbindung ist unterbrochen worden** the telephone connection has been cut; **wir sind unterbrochen worden** *(im Telefongespräch)* we've been cut off

Unter·brẹchung die *s.* **unterbrechen:** interruption; break *(Gen.* in); termination

unter·breiten *tr. V. (geh.)* present; **Vorschläge ~:** put suggestions *or* proposals forward

ụnter|bringen *unr. tr. V.* **a)** put; **sie konnten die Sachen nicht alle im Kofferraum ~:** they couldn't get *or* fit all the things in the boot *(Brit.) or (Amer.)* trunk; **er wußte nicht, wo er dieses Gesicht ~ sollte** *(fig.)* he knew the face but couldn't quite place it; **b)** *(beherbergen)* put up; **die Kinder sind gut untergebracht** the children are well looked after; **c)** *(ugs.)* **jmdn. bei einer Firma/beim Film/als Lehrling ~:** get sb. a job in a company/in films/as an apprentice; **d)** *(ugs.: einen Interessenten finden für)* place

Ụnterbringung die; ~, **~en** accommodation *no indef. art.*

[1] *ich unterbelichte, unterbelichtet, unterzubelichten*

[2] *ich unterbewerte, unterbewertet, unterzubewerten*

[3] *ich unterbezahle, unterbezahlt, unterzubezahlen*

ụnter|buttern *tr. V. (ugs.)* **a)** *(unterdrücken)* push aside *(fig.);* **b)** *(zusätzlich verbrauchen)* use up

Ụnter·deck das lower deck

unter·der·hạnd *Adv.* on the quiet ; **etw. ~ erfahren** hear sth. on the grape-vine; **jmdm. etw. ~ mitteilen** tell sb. sth. secretly

unter·dẹssen *s.* **inzwischen**

Ụnter·druck der; *Pl.* **~drücke** *(Physik, Technik)* low pressure

unter·drụ̈cken *tr. V.* **a)** suppress; hold back ⟨*comment, question, answer, criticism, etc.*⟩; **ein unterdrücktes Kichern** suppressed giggling; **b)** *(niederhalten)* suppress ⟨*revolution etc.*⟩; oppress ⟨*minority etc.*⟩

Unter·drụ̈cker der *(abwertend)* oppressor

Unterdrụ̈ckung die; ~, **~en a)** *(das Unterdrücken)* suppression; **b)** *(das Unterdrücktwerden, -sein)* oppression

ụnter·durchschnittlich 1. *Adj.* below average. **2.** *adv.* below the average; **~ verdienen** have below average earnings; **~ häufig** with below average frequency

unter·einạnder *Adv.* **a)** *(räumlich)* one below the other; **b)** *(miteinander)* among[st] ourselves/themselves *etc.;* **sie vertrugen sich gut ~:** they had a good relationship with each other; **die Leitungen ~ verbinden** join the wires together; **sich** *(Dat.)* **~ helfen** help each other *or* one another

untereinạnder-: ~|liegen *unr. itr. V.* lie *or* be one below *or* underneath the other; **~|stehen** *unr. itr. V.* **im Fahrplan stehen die einzelnen Stationen ~:** the timetable lists the individual stations one below the other

ụnter-, Ụnter-: ~entwickelt *Adj.* underdeveloped; **~ernährt** *Adj.* undernourished; suffering from malnutrition *postpos.;* **~ernährung die** malnutrition

unter-, Unter-: ~fahren *unr. tr. V.* drive *or* go under; **~fạngen 1.** *unr. refl. V. (geh.)* **a)** *(wagen)* dare; venture; **b)** *(sich erdreisten)* have the audacity; **2.** *unr. tr. V. (Bauw.)* underpin; **~fạngen das;** ~s *(geh.)* venture; undertaking

ụnter|fassen *tr. V. (ugs.)* **a)** *(einhaken)* **jmdn. ~:** take sb.'s arm; **sie gingen untergefaßt** they walked arm in arm; **b)** *(stützen)* support

unter·fẹrtigen *tr. V. (Amtsspr.)* sign

Unterfẹrtiger der; ~s, ~, **Unterfẹrtigte der/die;** *adj. Dekl. (Amtsspr.)* signatory

unter-, Unter-: ~fọrdern *tr. V.* **jmdn. [mit etw.] ~fordern** ask *or* demand too little of sb. [with sth.]; **~führen** *tr. V. (Schrift- u. Druckw.)* put ditto marks for; **~führung die** underpass; *(für Fußgänger)* subway *(Brit.);* [pedestrian] underpass *(Amer.)*

Ụnter·funktion die *(Med.)* hypofunction; **[eine] ~ der Schilddrüse** thyroid insufficiency

unter·fụ̈ttern *tr. V.* **a)** line ⟨*garment*⟩; **b)** *(unterlegen)* **Fliesen mit einer Dämmschicht ~:** back tiles with a layer of insulating material

Ụnter·gang der a) *(Sonnen~, Mond~ usw.)* setting; **b)** *(von Schiffen)* sinking; **c)** *(das Zugrundegehen)* decline; *(plötzlich)* destruction; *(von Personen)* downfall; *(der Welt)* end; **der ~ des Römischen Reiches** the fall of the Roman Empire; **er war ihr ~:** he was her ruin; **der Alkohol war ihr ~:** alcohol was the ruin of her *or* was her downfall; **vom ~ bedroht sein** be threatened by destruction; **etw. geht seinem ~ entgegen** sth. is heading for disaster; **etw. ist dem ~ geweiht** sth. is doomed

Ụntergangs·stimmung die feelings *pl.* of doom

ụnter·gärig [-gɛːrɪç] *Adj.* bottom-fermented ⟨*beer*⟩; bottom-fermenting ⟨*yeast*⟩

unter·gẹben *Adj.* subordinate

Untergẹbene der/die; *adj. Dekl.* subordinate; **jmds. ~r sein** be subordinate to sb.; **die ~n des Königs** the subjects of the king

ụnter-, Ụnter-: ~|gehen *unr. itr. V.; mit sein* **a)** ⟨*sun, star, etc.*⟩ set; ⟨*ship*⟩ sink, go down; ⟨*person*⟩ drown, go under; *(fig.)* **sein Stern ist im Untergehen** his star is on the wane; **die Musik ging/seine Worte gingen in dem Lärm ~:** the music was/his words were drowned by *or* lost in the noise; **jmd. geht im Gedränge** *od.* **Gewühl ~:** sb. gets lost in the crowds; **b)** *(zugrunde gehen)* come to an end; **davon geht die Welt nicht ~:** it's not the end of the world; **~geordnet 1.** *s.* **unterordnen; 2.** *Adj.* **a)** *(weniger wichtig)* secondary ⟨*role, importance, etc.*⟩; subordinate ⟨*position, post, etc.*⟩; **b)** *(Sprachw.)* subordinate; **~geschoß das** basement; **~gestell das a)** *(Fahrgestell)* undercarriage; **b)** *(salopp scherzh.: Beine)* legs *pl.;* **~gewicht das;** *o. Pl.* underweight; **[5 kg] ~gewicht haben** be [5 kilos] underweight; **~gewichtig** *Adj.* underweight

unter-, Unter-: ~gliedern *tr. V.* subdivide; **~gliederung die** subdivision; [1]**~graben** *unr. tr. V.* undermine *(fig.)*

ụnter-, Ụnter-: [2]**~graben** *unr. tr. V.* dig in; **~grenze die** lower limit; **~grund der a)** *(bes. Landw.)* subsoil; **b)** *(Bauw.: Baugrund)* foundation; **c)** *(Farbschicht)* background; **d)** *o. Pl. (bes. Politik)* underground; **in den ~grund gehen** go underground; **im ~grund** underground

Ụntergrund-: ~bahn die underground [railway] *(Brit.);* subway *(Amer.);* **mit der ~bahn fahren** travel on the *or* by underground *(Brit.) or (Amer.)* subway; **~bewegung die** *(Politik)* underground movement

ụnter-, Ụnter-: ~gründig *Adj.* hidden ⟨*connection, sense*⟩; **~|haken** *tr. V. (ugs.)* **jmdn. ~haken** take sb.'s arm; **mit jmdm. ~gehakt gehen** walk arm in arm with sb.; **sich ~haken** link arms; **~halb 1.** *Adv.* below; **weiter ~halb** further down; **~halb von** below; **2.** *Präp. mit Gen.* below; **~halt der;** *o. Pl.* **a)** living; **b)** *(~haltszahlung)* maintenance; **c)** *(Instandhaltung[skosten])* upkeep; [1]**~|halten** *unr. tr. V. (ugs.)* hold underneath

[2]**unter·hạlten 1.** *unr. tr. V.* **a)** *(versorgen)* support; **b)** *(instand halten)* maintain ⟨*building*⟩; **c)** *(betreiben)* run, keep ⟨*car, hotel*⟩; **d)** *(pflegen)* maintain, keep up ⟨*contact, correspondence*⟩; **e)** entertain ⟨*guest, audience*⟩; **ein ~des Buch** an entertaining book. **2.** *unr. refl. V.* **a)** talk; converse; **mit ihm kann man sich gut ~:** he is easy to talk to; one can have a pleasant conversation with him; **b)** *(sich vergnügen)* enjoy oneself; **habt ihr euch gut ~?** did you have a good time?

unterhạltsam *Adj.* entertaining

ụnterhalts-, Ụnterhalts-: ~an·spruch der maintenance claim; claim for maintenance; **~berechtigt** *Adj.* entitled to maintenance *postpos.;* **~kosten** *Pl.* maintenance *sing.;* **~pflicht die** obligation to pay maintenance; **~pflichtig** *Adj.* obliged to pay maintenance *postpos.;* **~zahlung die** maintenance payment

Unterhạltung die a) *o. Pl. (Versorgung)* support; **b)** *o. Pl. (Instandhaltung)* maintenance; upkeep; **etw. ist in der ~ sehr teuer** the maintenance *or* upkeep of sth. is very expensive; **c)** *o. Pl. (Aufrechterhaltung)* maintenance; **d)** *(Gespräch)* conversation; **e)** *(Zeitvertreib)* entertainment; **ich wünsche gute** *od.* **angenehme ~:** enjoy yourself/ yourselves; **ich schreibe zu meiner eigenen ~ Geschichten** I write stories for my own enjoyment

Unterhạltungs-: ~elektronik die; *o. Pl.* home electronics *sing., no art. (for entertainment purposes);* **~kosten** *Pl.* maintenance costs; *(Kfz-W.)* running costs; **~lektüre die** light reading *no art.;* **~literatur die** popular fiction; **~musik die** light

music; **~sendung die** entertainment programme
unter·handeln *itr. V. (bes. Politik)* negotiate (**über** + *Akk.* on)
Unter·händler der *(bes. Politik)* negotiator
Unter·handlung die *(bes. Politik)* negotiation
Unter·haus das *(Parl.)* lower house *or* chamber; *(in Großbritannien)* House of Commons; Lower House
Unter·hemd das vest *(Brit.)*; undershirt *(Amer.)*
unter·höhlen *tr. V.* **a)** hollow out; erode; **b)** *(untergraben)* undermine *(fig.)*
Unter·holz das; *o. Pl.* underwood; undergrowth
Unter·hose die *(Herren~)* [under]pants *pl.*; *(Damen~)* panties; knickers *(Brit.)*; briefs *pl.*; **lange ~n** long underpants; long johns *(coll.)*
unter·irdisch 1. *Adj.* underground; underground, subterranean ⟨*river, spring, etc.*⟩. **2.** *adv.* underground
unter·jochen *tr. V.* subjugate
Unter·jochung die; **~**: subjugation
unter|jubeln *tr. V. (ugs.)* **jmdm. etw. ~**: palm sth. off on sb.
unter·kellern *tr. V.* **das Haus ist nicht unterkellert** the house doesn't have a cellar
unter-, Unter-: ~kiefer der lower jaw; **~kleid das** [full-length] slip; **~kleidung die** underwear; **~|kommen** *unr. itr. V.; mit sein* **a)** *(Unterkunft finden)* find accommodation; **b)** *(ugs.: eine Stelle finden)* find *or* get a job; **c)** *(ugs.: Interesse finden)* **er versuchte, mit seiner Story woanders ~zukommen** he tried to get his story accepted somewhere else; **d)** *(bes. südd., österr.: begegnen)* **so etwas/ein solcher Dummkopf ist mir noch nicht ~gekommen** I've never come across 'anything like it/such a 'fool; **~kommen das**; **~s, ~**: accommodation *no indef. art.*; **~körper der** lower part of the body; **~|kriechen** *unr. itr. V.; mit sein (ugs.)* find shelter; **bei jmdm. ~kriechen** put up at sb.'s *(coll.)*; **~|kriegen** *tr. V. (ugs.)* **a)** *(entmutigen, besiegen)* bring *or* get down; **sich nicht ~kriegen lassen** not let things get one down; **b)** *s.* **unterbringen a, c**
unter-, Unter-: ~kühlen *tr. V.* **jmdn. ~kühlen** reduce sb.'s temperature [below normal]; **er war stark ~kühlt** he was suffering from hypothermia *or* exposure; **~kühlt** *Adj.* dry, factual ⟨*style*⟩; cool ⟨*person*⟩; icy ⟨*tone*⟩; **~kühlung die** reduction of body temperature; **er mußte mit ~kühlungen in ein Krankenhaus gebracht werden** he was taken to hospital suffering from exposure *or* hypothermia
Unterkunft ['ʊntɐkʊnft] **die**; **~, Unterkünfte** [...kʏnftə] accommodation *no indef. art.*; lodging *no indef. art.*; **eine gute ~ haben** have good accommodation *or* lodgings; **~ und Frühstück** bed and breakfast; **~ und Verpflegung** board and lodging; **die Unterkünfte der Soldaten** the soldiers' quarters
Unter·lage die a) *(Schreib~, Matte o.ä.)* pad; *(für eine Schreibmaschine usw.)* mat; *(unter einer Matratze, einem Teppich)* underlay; *(zum Schlafen usw.)* base; **ich brauche eine feste ~ zum Schreiben** I need something to rest my paper on so that I can write; **sorgen Sie für eine gute ~** *(ugs. scherzh.)* make sure you've got something in your stomach; **b)** *Pl. (Akten, Papiere)* documents; papers
Unter·länge die descender
Unter·laß der *in* **ohne ~**: incessantly
unter·lassen *unr. tr. V.* refrain from [doing]; **Zwischenrufe sind zu ~**: no heckling; **unterlaß gefälligst diese Albernheiten** *(ugs.)* kindly stop being so silly; **warum haben Sie es ~, die Angelegenheit zu melden?** why did you omit *or* fail to report the matter?
Unterlassung die; **~, ~en** omission; failure; **~ der Deklination** *(Sprachw.)* omission of declensional inflexion
Unterlassungs-: ~klage die *(Rechtsw.)* application for a restrictive injunction; **~sünde die** *(ugs.)* sin of omission
Unter·lauf der lower reaches *pl.*
unter·laufen 1. *unr. tr. V.; mit sein* **a)** occur; **jmdm. ist ein Fehler/Irrtum ~**: sb. made a mistake; **b)** *(ugs.: begegnen) s.* **unterkommen d. 2.** *unr. tr. V.* **a)** evade; get round; **b)** *(bes. Fuß-, Handball)* **einen Gegner ~**: charge an opponent who is in the air and knock him to the ground; **c)** *mit sein* ⟨*skin tissue*⟩ suffuse with blood; **das Auge war mit Blut** *od.* **blutig ~**: the eye was completely bloodshot
¹unter|legen *tr. V.* **a)** *(unter etw. legen)* put under[neath]; **jmdm. etw. ~**: put sth. under[neath] sb.; **einer Henne** *(Dat.)* **Eier [zum Brüten] ~**: set a hen [on eggs]; **b) einem Text einen anderen Sinn ~**: read another meaning into a text
²unter·legen *tr. V.* **a)** *(mit Stoff, Watte o.ä.)* underlay (**mit** with); **b) einem Film Musik ~**: put music to a film; **einer Melodie einen Text ~**: put words to a tune
³unter·legen 1. *2. Part. v.* **unterliegen. 2.** *Adj.* inferior; **jmdm. ~ sein** be inferior to sb. (**an** + *Dat.* in); **jmdm. zahlenmäßig ~ sein** be outnumbered by sb.
Unterlegene der/die; *adj. Dekl.* loser
Unter-: ~leib der a) *(unterer Bauchteil)* lower abdomen; **b)** *(verhüll.: weibliche Geschlechtsteile)* pudenda; **~leibs·schmerzen** *Pl.* abdominal pain *sing.*; **~lid das** lower [eye]lid
unter·liegen *unr. itr. V.* **a)** *mit sein (besiegt werden)* lose; be beaten *or* defeated; **in einem Kampf ~**: lose a fight; **die unterlegene Mannschaft** the losing team; **b)** *(unterworfen sein)* be subject to; **es unterliegt keinem Zweifel, daß ...**: there is *or* can be no doubt that ...; **einer Täuschung ~**: be mistaken *or* deceived
Unter·lippe die lower lip
unterm *Präp. + Art.* = **unter dem**
unter·malen *tr. V.* accompany; **etw. mit Musik ~**: accompany sth. with music
Unter·malung die; **~, ~en** accompaniment (*Gen.* to)
unter·mauern *tr. V.* **a)** *(mit Mauern stützen)* underpin; **b)** *(mit Argumenten, Fakten absichern)* back up; support
Untermauerung die; **~, ~en a)** underpinning; *(Mauerwerk)* foundation; **b)** *(stützende Argumente)* back-up; support
unter-, Unter-: ~|mengen *tr. V.* mix in; **~mensch der** *(abwertend)* **a)** *(brutaler Mensch)* brute; **b)** *(ns.: minderwertiger Mensch)* inferior person; subhuman creature; **~miete die**; *o. Pl.* subtenancy; sublease; **bei jmdm. in** *od.* **zur ~miete wohnen** be sb.'s subtenant; lodge with sb.; **jmdn. in** *od.* **zur ~miete nehmen** sublet to sb.; **~mieter der** subtenant; lodger
unterminieren [ʊntɐmi'ni:rən] *tr. V.* undermine
unter|mischen *tr. V.* mix in
untern *(ugs.) Präp. + Art.* = **unter den**
unter·nehmen *unr. tr. V.* **a)** *(durchführen)* undertake; make; make ⟨*attempt*⟩; take ⟨*steps*⟩; **b)** *(Unterhaltsames machen, eingreifen)* do; **viel zusammen ~**: do many things together; **etwas gegen die Mißstände ~**: do something about the bad state of affairs
Unter·nehmen das; **~s, ~ a)** *(Vorhaben)* enterprise; venture; undertaking; *(militärische Operation)* operation; **b)** *(Firma)* enterprise; concern
unternehmend *Adj.* enterprising; active
Unternehmens-: ~berater der management consultant; **~form die** form *or* type of enterprise; **~führung die, ~leitung die** management; **~politik die** management policy
Unternehmer der; **~s, ~**: employer; *(in der Industrie)* industrialist
unternehmerisch 1. *Adj.* entrepreneurial. **2.** *adv.* ⟨*think*⟩ in an entrepreneurial *or* business-like way
Unternehmerschaft die; **~, ~en** employers *pl.*
Unternehmertum das; **~s a)** employers *pl.*; **b)** *(das Unternehmersein)* enterprise *no art.*
Unternehmung die; **~, ~en** *s.* **Unternehmen**
Unternehmungs·geist der; *o. Pl.* spirit of enterprise; **er war voller ~**: he was full of initiative
unternehmungs·lustig *Adj.* active; **sie ist sehr ~**: she is always out doing things
unter-, Unter-: ~offizier der a) non-commissioned officer; **~offizier vom Dienst** duty NCO; **b)** *o. Pl. (Dienstgrad)* corporal; **~ordnen 1.** *tr. V.* subordinate; **jmdm./einem Ministerium ~geordnet sein** be [made] subordinate to sb./a ministry; **2.** *refl. V.* **sich [anderen] nicht ~ordnen können** not be able to accept a subordinate role; **die Politik hat sich der Moral ~zuordnen** politics has to be subordinated to morality; **~ordnend** *Adj. (Sprachw.)* subordinating ⟨*conjunction*⟩; **~ordnung die a)** subordination; **b)** *(Sprachw.)* hypotaxis; **c)** *(Biol.: ~gruppe)* suborder; **~pfand das** *(geh.)* pledge (**für** of); **~|pflügen** *tr. V.* plough in *or* under; **~prima die** *(Schulw. veralt.)* eighth year *(of a Gymnasium)*; **~primaner der** *(Schulw. veralt.)* pupil in the eighth year *(of a Gymnasium)*; **~privilegiert** *Adj. (geh.)* underprivileged; **~privilegierte der/die**; *adj. Dekl. (geh.)* underprivileged person; **die ~privilegierten** the underprivileged; **~punkt der a)** subsidiary point; **b)** *(unter einem Buchstaben o. ä.)* dot underneath
unter·queren *tr. V.* cross under
unter·reden *refl. V. (geh.)* confer (**mit** with)
Unterredung die; **~, ~en** discussion; **er bat ihn um eine ~**: he asked to see him to discuss something [with him]
unter·repräsentiert *Adj.* under-represented
Unterricht ['ʊntɐrɪçt] **der**; **~[e]s, ~e** instruction; *(Schul~)* teaching; *(Schulstunden)* classes *pl.*; lessons *pl.*; **der ~ ist beendet** classes *or* lessons are over; **jmdm. ~ [in Musik** *usw.***] geben** give sb. [music *etc.*] lessons; teach sb. [music]; **bei jmdm. ~ [in Russisch] nehmen** have [Russian] lessons from sb.; **zu spät zum ~ kommen** be late for class
-unterricht der: Geschichts-/Musik- *usw.* **~**: history/music *etc.* teaching; *(Unterrichtsstunde)* history/music *etc.* lesson; *s. auch* **Englischunterricht**
unterrichten 1. *tr. V.* **a)** *(lehren)* teach; **er unterrichtet Englisch** he teaches English; **sie unterrichtet ihre Kinder im Malen** she is teaching her children how to paint; **b)** *(informieren)* inform (**über** + *Akk.* of, about); **ich bin bestens/schlecht unterrichtet** I am fully/not well informed. **2.** *itr. V. (Unterricht geben)* teach. **3.** *refl. V. (sich informieren)* inform oneself (**über** + *Akk.* about)
unterrichtlich *Adj.; nicht präd.* instructional ⟨*purpose, problem*⟩; teaching ⟨*success, work*⟩
unterrichts-, Unterrichts-: ~einheit die *(Päd.)* teaching unit; **~fach das** subject; **~frei** *Adj.* free ⟨*day, hour*⟩; **der Samstag ist ~frei** there are no lessons on Saturday; **nächsten Samstag haben wir ~frei** there is no school this Saturday; **~methode die** teaching method; **~stoff der** subject-matter; **~stunde die** lesson; period
Unterrichtung die; **~, ~en** instruction; *(Information)* information

Ụnter·rock der a) [half] slip; b) *s.* Unterkleid

ụnter|rühren *tr. V.* stir in

ụnters *Präp.* + *Art.* = unter das

unter·sagen *tr. V.* forbid; prohibit; **der Arzt untersagte ihm, Alkohol zu trinken** the doctor ordered him not to drink any alcohol; **Rauchen ist strengstens untersagt** smoking is strictly prohibited

Ụnter·satz der *s.* Untersetzer

unter-, Unter-: ~schätzen *tr. V.* underestimate ‹*amount, effect, meaning, distance, etc.*›; underrate ‹*writer, performer, book, performance, talent, ability*›; **~schätzung die** underestimation; **~scheidbar** *Adj.* distinguishable; **~scheiden 1.** *unr. tr. V.* distinguish; **Weizen von Roggen nicht ~scheiden können** not be able to tell the difference between wheat and rye *or* tell wheat from rye; **die Zwillinge sind kaum zu ~scheiden** you can hardly tell the twins apart; **2.** *unr. itr. V.* distinguish; differentiate; **zwischen Richtigem und Falschem ~scheiden** tell the difference between right and wrong; **3.** *unr. refl. V.* differ (**durch** in, **von** from); **sich durch nichts ~scheiden** be in no way different; **sich dadurch ~scheiden, daß ...:** differ in that ...; **in diesem Punkt ~scheiden sich die Parteien überhaupt nicht** on this point there is no difference at all between the parties; **~scheidung die** *(Vorgang)* differentiation; *(Resultat)* distinction

Unterscheidungs-: ~merkmal das distinguishing feature; **~vermögen das;** *o. Pl.* ability to distinguish; discernment

ụnter-, Ụnter-: ~schenkel der shank; lower leg; **~schicht die** *(Soziol.)* lower class; **der ~schicht angehören** be a member of the lower classes *pl.*; **¹~|schieben** *unr. tr. V.* push under[neath]

²unter·schieben *unr. tr. V.* **a)** *(heimlich zuschieben)* **jmdm. etw. ~:** foist sth. on sb.; **b)** *(unterstellen)* **jmdm. etw. ~:** attribute sth. falsely to sb.

Ụnter·schied der; ~[e]s, ~e difference; **es lebe der kleine ~!** *(ugs. scherzh.)* vive la petite différence!; **das ist ein ~ wie Tag und Nacht** it's like the difference between black and white; **es ist [schon] ein [großer] ~, ob ...:** it makes a [big] difference whether ...; **bei der Beurteilung der Schüler ~e machen** use different methods when assessing the pupils; **ohne ~ der Rasse/des Geschlechts** without regard to *or* discrimination against race/sex; **im ~ zu ihm/zum ~ von ihm** in contrast to him; **zwischen Arbeit und Arbeit ist noch ein ~** *(ugs.)* there is work and there is work *(coll.)*

unter·schieden *Adj.* different

ụnterschiedlich 1. *Adj.* different; *(uneinheitlich)* variable; varying. **2.** *adv.* **[sehr/ganz] ~:** in [very/quite] different ways; **~ hohe Erträge** yields of varying amount; **etw. sehr ~ einschätzen** give greatly varying estimates of sth.

Ụnterschiedlichkeit die; ~, ~en difference (*Gen.* between); *(Uneinheitlichkeit)* variability

ụnterschieds·los 1. *Adj.* uniform; equal ‹*treatment*›. **2.** *adv.* ‹*treat*› equally; *(ohne Benachteiligung)* without discrimination

¹ụnter|schlagen *unr. tr. V.* cross ‹*legs*›; fold ‹*arms*›

²unter·schlagen 1. *unr. tr. V.* embezzle, misappropriate ‹*money, funds, etc.*›; *(unterdrücken)* intercept ‹*letter*›; withhold, suppress ‹*fact, news, information, etc.*›. **2.** *unr. itr. V.* **er hat ~:** he embezzled money

Unterschlagung die; ~, ~en *s.* **²unterschlagen:** embezzlement; misappropriation; withholding; suppression; **~en begehen** embezzle sums of money/funds *etc.*

Ụnter·schlupf der; ~[e]s, ~e shelter; *(Versteck)* hiding-place; hide-out

ụnter|schlupfen *(südd.),* **ụnter|schlüpfen** *itr. V.; mit sein (ugs.)* hide out; *(Obdach finden)* take shelter (**vor** + *Dat.* from)

unter·schneiden *unr. tr. V. ([Tisch]tennis)* chop

Ụnter·schnitt der *([Tisch]tennis)* back spin; underspin

unter·schreiben 1. *unr. itr. V.* sign; **mit vollem Namen ~:** sign one's full name. **2.** *unr. tr. V.* sign; **diese Behauptung kann ich nicht ~** *(fig. ugs.)* I cannot subscribe to *or* approve this statement

unter·schreiten *unr. tr. V.* fall below; **wir haben die veranschlagten Summen/Kosten um 2 Prozent unterschritten** we stayed 2 per cent below the estimated amounts/costs

Ụnter·schrift die a) signature; **seine ~ unter etw.** *(Akk.)* **setzen** put one's signature to sth.; sign sth.; **b)** *(Bild~)* caption

Ụnterschriften-: ~aktion die petition; **~liste die** list of signatures; **~mappe die** signature folder

ụnter·schriftlich *Adv.* by one's signature; **~ bestätigt** signed

ụnterschrifts-: ~berechtigt *Adj.* **~berechtigt sein** be authorized to sign; have power to sign; **~reif** *Adj.* ready to be signed *pred.*; **ein ~reifer Vertrag** a contract which is ready to be signed

ụnterschwellig [-ʃvɛlɪç] **1.** *Adj.* subliminal. **2.** *adv.* subliminally

ụnter-, Ụnter-: ~see·boot das submarine; **~seite die** under-side; *(eines Stoffes)* wrong side; **~sekunda die** *(Schulw. veralt.)* sixth year *(of a Gymnasium)*; **~sekundaner der** *(Schulw. veralt.)* pupil in the sixth year *(of a Gymnasium)*; **~|setzen** *tr. V.* put underneath; **~setzer der** mat; *(für Gläser)* coaster; *(für Bügeleisen)* stand

untersetzt *Adj.* stocky

ụnter|sinken *unr. itr. V.; mit sein* sink

unter·spülen *tr. V.* undermine and wash away

ụnterst ... *s.* **unter ...**

Ụnter·stand der a) *(Schutzbunker)* dugout; **b)** *(Unterschlupf)* shelter

¹ụnter|stehen *unr. itr. V.; südd., österr., schweiz. mit sein* take shelter

²unter|stehen 1. *unr. itr. V.* **jmdm. ~:** be subordinate *or* answerable to sb.; **jmdm. untersteht eine Abteilung** sb. is responsible for a department; **diese Ämter ~ dem Ministerium** these offices are under the control of *or* come under the ministry; **ständiger Kontrolle ~:** be under constant supervision. **2.** *unr. refl. V.* dare; **untersteh dich!** [don't] you dare!; **was ~ Sie sich!** how dare you!

¹ụnter|stellen 1. *tr. V.* **a)** *(zur Aufbewahrung)* keep; store ‹*furniture*›; **b)** *(unter etw.)* put underneath. **2.** *refl. V.* take shelter

²unter·stellen *tr. V.* **a)** *(jmdm. unterordnen, übertragen)* **jmdm. ein Sachgebiet/eine Abteilung ~:** put sb. in charge of a subject/a department; **die Behörde ist dem Ministerium unterstellt** the office is under the ministry; **b)** *(annehmen, vermuten)* assume; suppose; **ich unterstelle [einmal], daß ...:** I'll [first of all] assume that ...; **c)** *(unterschieben)* **jmdm. böse Absichten/ schlechte Motive** *usw.* **~:** insinuate *or* imply that sb.'s intentions/motives are bad; **was ~ Sie mir?** what are you trying to accuse me of?

Unter·stellung die a) subordination (**unter** + *Akk.* to); **b)** *(falsche Behauptung)* insinuation

unter·steuern *itr. V. (Kfz-W.)* understeer

unter·streichen *unr. tr. V.* **a)** underline; **b)** *(hervorheben)* emphasize; **das kann ich nur ~!** I can only agree with that!

Unter·streichung die; ~, ~en a) underlining; **b)** *(das Betonen)* emphasizing

Ụnter·stufe die *(Schulw.)* lower school

unter·stützen *tr. V.* support; **vom Staat unterstützte Einrichtungen** state-funded institutions; **das Mittel unterstützt den Heilungsprozeß** the medicine promotes the healing process

Unter·stützung die a) support; **der Plan fand bei vielen ~:** the plan was supported by many; **b)** *(finanzielle Hilfe)* allowance; *(für Arbeitslose)* [unemployment] benefit *no art.*; **staatliche ~:** state aid

Unterstützungs·empfänger der person receiving [unemployment] benefit/an allowance

unter·suchen *tr. V.* **a)** *(zu erkennen suchen)* examine; **b)** *(überprüfen)* test (**auf** + *Akk.* for); **c)** *(ärztlich)* examine; **sich ärztlich ~ lassen** have a medical examination *or* check-up; **jmdn. auf seine Arbeitsfähigkeit [hin] ~:** test sb.'s fitness for work; **d)** *(aufzuklären suchen)* investigate; **einen Fall gerichtlich ~:** try a case [in court]; **e)** *(durchsuchen)* search (**auf** + *Akk.*, **nach** for)

Untersuchung die; ~, ~en a) *s.* **untersuchen:** examination; test; investigation; search; **b)** *(wissenschaftliche Arbeit)* study

Untersuchungs-: ~aus·schuß der investigating committee; *(für Unfälle usw.)* committee of inquiry; **~ergebnis das** *(der Polizei, des Gerichts)* results *pl.* of an/the investigation; *(Med.)* results *pl.* of a/the test; **~gefängnis das** prison *(for people awaiting trial)*; **~haft die** imprisonment *or* detention while awaiting trial; **jmdn. in ~haft nehmen** commit sb. for trial; **in ~haft sein** *od.* **sitzen** be held on remand; **~häftling der** prisoner awaiting trial; remand prisoner; **~kommission die** *s.* **~ausschuß**; **~zimmer das** examination room

unter·tags *Adv. (bes. österr.)* during the day

ụntertan [-ta:n] *Adj.* **in sich** *(Dat.)* **jmdn./etw. ~ machen** *(geh.)* subjugate sb./dominate sth.; **jmdm./einer Sache ~ sein** *(veralt.)* be dominated by sb./be subject to sth.

Ụntertan der; ~s *od.* **~en, ~en** *(hist.)* subject

Ụntertanen·geist der; *o. Pl. (abwertend)* servile *or* subservient spirit

ụntertänig [-tɛ:nɪç] **1.** *Adj.* subservient; **Ihr ~ster Diener** *(veralt.)* your most obedient *or* humble servant. **2.** *adv.* subserviently

Ụnter·tasse die saucer; **fliegende ~** *(fig.)* flying saucer

ụnter|tauchen 1. *itr. V.; mit sein* **a)** *(im Wasser)* dive [under]; **b)** *(verschwinden)* disappear; **c)** *(unerkannt leben)* disappear; go underground; **er mußte vor der Gestapo [bei Freunden] ~:** he had [to seek shelter with friends] to hide from the Gestapo. **2.** *tr. V.* duck

Ụnter·teil das *od.* **der** bottom part

unter·teilen *tr. V.* **a)** *(aufteilen)* divide; **b)** *(einteilen, gliedern)* subdivide

Unter·teilung die; ~, ~en [sub]division

Ụnter·temperatur die subnormal temperature of the body; **der Patient hat ~:** the patient's temperature is below normal

ụnter-, Ụnter-: ~tertia die *(Schulw. veralt.)* fourth year *(of a Gymnasium)*; **~tertianer der** *(Schulw. veralt.)* pupil in the fourth year *(of a Gymnasium)*; **~titel der a)** subtitle; **b)** *(Bildunterschrift)* caption; **~ton der** *(auch Physik, Musik)* undertone; **~tourig** [~tu:rɪç] *(Technik)* **1.** *Adj.* ‹*driving*› with *or* at low revs *(coll.)*. **2.** *adv.* at low revs *(coll.)*

unter·treiben *unr. itr. V.* play things down

Untertreibung die; ~, ~en understatement

unter·tunneln *tr. V.* tunnel under; tunnel through *or* under ‹*mountain*›

ụnter-, Ụnter-: ~vermieten *tr., itr. V.* sublet; **~vermietung die** subletting; **~versichern** *tr. V.* under-insure; **~versicherung die** under-insurance; **~versorgen** *tr. V.* under-supply; **ärztlich ~versorgt sein** not be given proper medical treatment;

~versorgung die under-supply (**mit** of); **die ~versorgung der Zellen mit Sauerstoff** the under-supply of the cells with oxygen
unter·wandern *tr. V.* infiltrate; **kommunistisch unterwandert** infiltrated by communists
Unter·wanderung die infiltration *no indef. art.*
unterwärts ['ʊntɐvɛrts] *Adv. (ugs.)* underneath
Unter·wäsche die; *o. Pl.* underwear
Unter·wasser-: ~jagd die *(Tauchsport)* underwater harpooning; **~massage die** underwater massage
unterwegs *Adv.* **a)** *(auf dem Wege irgendwohin)* on the *or* one's/its way; **er ist den ganzen Tag/geschäftlich viel ~:** he is away all day/a great deal on business; **bei ihr ist etwas Kleines ~** *(ugs.)* she is expecting [a happy event]; **b)** *(auf, während der Reise)* on the way; **sie waren vier Wochen ~:** they travelled for four weeks; the journey took them four weeks; **sie schickten eine Karte von ~:** they sent a card while they were away; **c)** *(nicht zu Hause)* out [and about]
unter·weisen *unr. tr. V. (geh.)* instruct (**in** + *Dat.* in)
Unter·weisung die instruction
Unter·welt die; ~ *(griech. Myth., Verbrechermilieu)* underworld
unter·weltlich *Adj.* underworld *attrib.*
unter·werfen 1. *unr. tr. V.* **a)** subjugate ⟨*people, country*⟩; **b)** *(unterziehen)* subject (*Dat.* to); **jmds. Post einer genauen Kontrolle ~:** make a close scrutiny of sb.'s correspondence; **c)** *(abhängig machen)* **jmdm./einer Sache unterworfen sein** be subject to sb./sth. **2.** *unr. refl. V.* **sich [jmdm./einer Sache] ~:** submit [to sb./sth.]
Unterwerfung die; ~, **~en a)** *(das Unterwerfen)* subjugation (**unter** + *Akk.* to); **b)** *(das Sichunterwerfen)* submission (**unter** + *Akk.* to)
unterwürfig [-vʏrfɪç] *(abwertend)* **1.** *Adj.* obsequious. **2.** *adv.* obsequiously
Unterwürfigkeit die; ~ *(abwertend)* obsequiousness
unter·zeichnen 1. *tr. V.* sign. **2.** *refl. V. (veralt.)* sign
Unter·zeichner der, Unterzeichnete der/die; *adj. Dekl. (Amtsspr.)* signatory
Unterzeichnung die signing
Unter·zeug das; *o. Pl. (ugs.)* underwear
¹unter|ziehen *unr. tr. V.* **a)** put ⟨*underwear, jumper, etc.*⟩ on underneath; **b)** *(Kochk.: vermengen)* fold in
²unter·ziehen 1. *unr. refl. V.* **sich einer Sache** *(Dat.)* **~:** undertake sth.; **sich einer Operation** *(Dat.)* **~:** undergo *or* have an operation. **2.** *unr. tr. V.* **etw. einer Untersuchung/Überprüfung/Reinigung** *(Dat.)* **~:** examine/check/clean sth.
Untiefe die a) *(seichte Stelle)* shallow; **b)** *(große Tiefe)* depth
Untier das monster; **dieses ~ von einer Katze** *(scherzh.)* this beast of a cat
untilgbar *Adj. (geh.)* lasting; indelible ⟨*impression, memory*⟩
Untote der/die zombie; *(Vampir)* vampire; **die ~n** the undead
untragbar *Adj.* unbearable; intolerable; **wirtschaftlich/finanziell ~:** no longer economically/financially viable
Untragbarkeit die; ~**:** intolerableness
untrainiert *Adj.* untrained; *(nicht mehr trainiert)* out of training *postpos.*
untrennbar *Adj.* inseparable
untreu *Adj.* **a)** disloyal; **jmdm. ~ werden** be disloyal to sb.; **du bist uns ~ geworden** *(scherzh.)* you've abandoned us *(joc.)*; **sich selbst ~ werden** be untrue to oneself; **seinen Grundsätzen ~ werden** abandon one's principles; **b)** *(in der Ehe, Liebe)* unfaithful; **jmdm. ~ werden** be unfaithful to sb.
Untreue die a) disloyalty; **b)** *(in der Ehe, Liebe)* unfaithfulness; **c)** *(Rechtsspr.: Veruntreuung)* embezzlement
untröstlich *Adj.* inconsolable; **ich bin ~, daß ...:** I am extremely sorry that ...
untrüglich *Adj.* unmistakable
untüchtig *Adj.* incompetent
Untugend die bad habit
untunlich *Adj. (veralt.)* impracticable; not sensible; *(unklug)* imprudent
untypisch 1. *Adj.* untypical (**für** of). **2.** *adv.* unusually
unüberbietbar *Adj.* unparalleled
unüberbrückbar *Adj.* irreconcilable ⟨*differences, contradictions*⟩
unüberhörbar *Adj.* unmistakable
unüberlegt 1. *Adj.* rash. **2.** *adv.* rashly
Unüberlegtheit die; ~, **~en a)** *o. Pl.* rashness; **b)** *(unüberlegte Handlung)* rash act
unüberschaubar *s.* **unübersehbar 1 b, 2**
unübersehbar 1. *Adj.* **a)** *(offenkundig)* conspicuous; obvious; **b)** *(sehr groß)* enormous; immense. **2.** *adv. (sehr)* extremely
unübersetzbar *Adj.* untranslatable
unübersichtlich 1. *Adj.* unclear; confusing ⟨*arrangement*⟩; blind ⟨*bend*⟩; broken ⟨*country etc.*⟩; *(fig.)* confused ⟨*affair, matter, conditions, etc.*⟩. **2.** *adv.* unclearly; confusingly ⟨*arranged*⟩
Unübersichtlichkeit die; ~**: die ~ der Karte/des Geländes** the unclear map/ broken country
unübertragbar *Adj.* non-transferable; not transferable *pred.*
unübertrefflich 1. *Adj.* superb. **2.** *adv.* superbly
unübertroffen *Adj.* unsurpassed
unüberwindbar, unüberwindlich *Adj.* insuperable, insurmountable ⟨*problem, fear, mistrust, etc.*⟩; invincible ⟨*opponent*⟩
unüblich *Adj.* not usual *or* customary *pred.*; unusual
unumgänglich *Adj.* [absolutely] necessary
Unumgänglichkeit die; ~**:** absolute necessity
unumschränkt ['ʊn|ʊmʃrɛŋkt] *Adj.* absolute; **~ herrschen** have absolute rule
unumstritten *Adj.* undisputed
unumwunden ['ʊn|ʊmvʊndn̩] **1.** *Adj.* frank. **2.** *adv.* frankly; openly
ununterbrochen 1. *Adj.* incessant. **2.** *adv.* incessantly
unveränderbar, unveränderlich *Adj.* unchangeable, unchanging ⟨*law, principle*⟩; constant ⟨*quantity etc.*⟩; permanent ⟨*mark, scar*⟩; *(nicht zu verändern)* unalterable
Unveränderlichkeit die; ~**:** *s.* **unveränderlich:** unchangeableness; unchangingness; constancy; permanence; unalterableness
unverändert *Adj.* unchanged ⟨*appearance, weather, condition*⟩; unaltered, unrevised ⟨*edition etc.*⟩; **in seinem Aussehen war er ~:** he had not changed in [his] appearance
unverantwortlich. 1. *Adj.* irresponsible. **2.** *adv.* irresponsibly
Unverantwortlichkeit die; ~**:** irresponsibility
unverarbeitet *Adj.* **a)** raw, unprocessed ⟨*material*⟩; crude ⟨*iron, oil, etc.*⟩; **b)** *(nicht bewältigt)* raw ⟨*impression*⟩; raw, undigested ⟨*thoughts*⟩
unveräußerlich *Adj.* **a)** *(geh.)* inalienable ⟨*rights, principles*⟩; **b)** *(unverkäuflich)* ⟨*property*⟩ not for sale
unverbaubar *Adj.* ⟨*view*⟩ that cannot be spoiled *or* obstructed
unverbesserlich *Adj.* incorrigible
unverbildet *Adj.* unspoiled
unverbindlich 1. *Adj.* **a)** *(nicht bindend)* not binding *pred.*; without obligation *postpos;* ⟨*information*⟩ without guarantee of correctness; **b)** *(zurückhaltend, reserviert)* non-committal ⟨*answer, words*⟩; detached, impersonal ⟨*attitude, person*⟩. **2.** *adv.* ⟨*send, reserve*⟩ without obligation
Unverbindlichkeit die; ~, **~en a)** *o. Pl.* *(eines Angebots usw.)* freedom from obligation; *(einer Person)* detached *or* impersonal manner; **die ~ der Auskunft** the fact that the information is not guaranteed correct; **b)** *(unverbindliche Äußerung)* non-committal remark
unverblümt [ʊnfɛɐ̯'bly:mt] **1.** *Adj.* blunt; undisguised, open ⟨*distrust*⟩. **2.** *adv.* bluntly
unverbraucht *Adj.* untouched; unspent ⟨*energy*⟩; fresh ⟨*air*⟩; **sie ist noch jung und ~:** she is still young and full of energy
unverbrüchlich [ʊnfɛɐ̯'brʏçlɪç] *Adj. (geh.)* inviolable; steadfast
unverbürgt *Adj.* unconfirmed ⟨*report, news, etc.*⟩
unverdächtig 1. *Adj.* free from suspicion *postpos.* **2.** *adv.* in a way that does/did not arouse suspicion
unverdaulich *Adj.* indigestible
unverdaut *Adj.* undigested
unverdient 1. *Adj.* undeserved ⟨*luck, praise*⟩; undeserved, unjust ⟨*accusation, punishment, etc.*⟩. **2.** *adv.* undeservedly
unverdientermaßen *Adv.* undeservedly
unverdorben *Adj.* unspoilt
Unverdorbenheit die; ~ *(von Früchten, Speisen usw.)* freshness; *(sittliche ~)* innocence
unverdrossen 1. *Adj.* undeterred; *(unverzagt)* undaunted. **2.** *adv.* **~ weitermachen** carry on undaunted
unverdünnt *Adj.* undiluted; **er trinkt Whisky ~:** he drinks whisky neat
unverehelicht *Adj. (bes. Amtsspr.)* unmarried
unvereinbar *Adj.* incompatible (**mit** with)
Unvereinbarkeit die; ~**:** incompatibility (**mit** with)
unverfälscht 1. *Adj.* genuine; unadulterated ⟨*wine etc.*⟩; pure ⟨*dialect*⟩; unaltered ⟨*custom, text*⟩. **2.** *adv.* in pure/unaltered form
unverfänglich *Adj.* harmless
unverfroren 1. *Adj.* insolent; impudent. **2.** *adv.* insolently; impudently
Unverfrorenheit die; ~, **~en a)** *o. Pl. (Art)* insolence; impudence; **b)** *(Äußerung)* insolent remark; impertinence
unvergänglich *Adj.* immortal ⟨*fame*⟩; unchanging ⟨*beauty*⟩; abiding ⟨*recollection*⟩
Unvergänglichkeit die *s.* **unvergänglich:** immortality; unchangingness; abidingness
unvergessen *Adj.* unforgotten
unvergeßlich 1. *Adj.* unforgettable; **dieses Erlebnis wird mir ~ bleiben** *od.* **sein** I shall never forget this experience. **2.** *adv.* unforgettably
unvergleichbar *Adj.* incomparable (*Dat.* to, with)
unvergleichlich 1. *Adj.* incomparable (*Dat.* to, with). **2.** *adv.* incomparably
unverhältnismäßig *Adv.* unusually
unverheiratet *Adj.* unmarried
unverhofft ['ʊnfɛɐ̯hɔft] **1.** *Adj.* unexpected. **2.** *adv.* unexpectedly; **~ kommt oft** *(Spr.)* always expect the unexpected
unverhohlen 1. *Adj.* unconcealed. **2.** *adv.* openly
unverhüllt 1. *Adj.* **a)** *(ohne Umhüllung)* uncovered; **b)** *(unverhohlen)* unconcealed. **2.** *adv.* openly
unverkäuflich *Adj.* **a)** *(nicht zum Verkauf bestimmt)* **~e Ausstellungsstücke** display items that are not for sale; **diese Vase ist ~:** this vase is not for sale; **~es Muster** free sample; **b)** *(nicht absetzbar)* unsaleable
unverkennbar 1. *Adj.* unmistakable. **2.** *adv.* unmistakably
unverlangt 1. *Adj.* unsolicited ⟨*manuscript, photograph*⟩. **2.** *adv.* **~ eingesandt** unsolicited
unvermählt *Adj. (geh.)* unmarried; unwedded

unvermeidbar *Adj.* unavoidable
unvermeidlich *Adj.* **a)** *(nicht vermeidbar)* unavoidable; *(spött.: obligatorisch)* inevitable; **sich ins Unvermeidliche fügen** submit to *or* accept the inevitable; **b)** *(sich als Folge ergebend)* inevitable
ụnvermindert *Adj., adv.* undiminished
ụnvermittelt 1. *Adj.* sudden; abrupt. **2.** *adv.* suddenly; abruptly
Ụnvermögen das lack of ability; **jmds. ~, etw. zu tun** sb.'s inability to do sth.
ụnvermögend *Adj.* without means *postpos.*
ụnvermutet 1. *Adj.* unexpected. **2.** *adv.* unexpectedly
Ụnvernunft die stupidity
ụnvernünftig 1. *Adj.* stupid; foolish. **2.** *adv.* **er raucht/trinkt ~ viel** he smokes/drinks more than is good for him
ụnveröffentlicht *Adj.* unpublished
ụnverpackt *Adj.* unpacked; unwrapped
ụnverputzt *Adj.* unplastered
ụnverrichtet *Adj. in* **~er Dinge** without having achieved anything
unverrückbar 1. *Adj.* unshakeable; immovable; unalterable ⟨*fact, truth*⟩. **2.** *adv.* unshakeably; immovably; **mein Entschluß steht ~ fest** my decision is absolutely final
ụnverschämt 1. *Adj.* **a)** *(respektlos, impertinent)* impertinent, impudent ⟨*person, manner, words, etc.*⟩; barefaced, blatant ⟨*lie*⟩; **b)** *(ugs.: sehr groß)* outrageous ⟨*price, luck, etc.*⟩. **2.** *adv.* **a)** impertinently; impudently; ⟨*lie*⟩ barefacedly; blatantly; **b)** *(ugs.: sehr)* outrageously ⟨*expensive*⟩; **du siehst ~ gut aus** you are looking disgustingly well *(joc.)*
Ụnverschämtheit die; ~, ~en a) *o. Pl. (Art)* impertinence; impudence; *(einer Lüge)* barefacedness; blatancy; **b)** *(Äußerung o. ä.)* [piece of] impertinence; **das ist eine ~!** that's outrageous!
ụnverschlossen *Adj.* unlocked; unsealed ⟨*letter*⟩
ụnverschuldet *Adj.* **ein ~er Verkehrsunfall** an accident which happened through no fault of one's own; **eine ~e Notlage** a plight which is no fault of one's own
unverschuldetermaßen *Adv.* through no fault of one's own
ụnversehens *Adv.* suddenly
ụnversehrt *Adj.* unscathed; unhurt; *(unbeschädigt)* undamaged
Ụnversehrtheit die; ~: intactness; **körperliche ~:** freedom from bodily harm
ụnversöhnlich *Adj.* irreconcilable
Ụnversöhnlichkeit die irreconcilability
ụnversorgt *Adj.* ⟨*children, family, etc.*⟩ unprovided for
Ụnverstand der foolishness; stupidity; **so ein ~!** what foolishness *or* stupidity!
ụnverstanden *Adj.* misunderstood
ụnverständig *Adj.* without understanding *postpos;* ignorant ⟨*child*⟩
Ụnverständigkeit die lack of understanding
ụnverständlich *Adj.* incomprehensible; *(undeutlich)* unclear ⟨*pronunciation, presentation, etc.*⟩; **es ist [mir] ~, warum er nicht kommt** I cannot *or* do not understand why he hasn't come
Ụnverständlichkeit die incomprehensibility
Ụnverständnis das lack of understanding
ụnverstellt *Adj.* normal ⟨*voice*⟩; unfeigned, genuine ⟨*joy, passion, etc.*⟩
ụnversteuert *Adj.* untaxed ⟨*earnings etc.*⟩; duty-free ⟨*goods, cigarettes*⟩
ụnversucht *in* **nichts ~ lassen** try everything; leave no stone unturned
ụnverträglich *Adj.* **a)** *(unbekömmlich)* indigestible; unsuitable ⟨*medicine*⟩; **b)** *(streitsüchtig)* quarrelsome; **c)** *(nicht harmonierend)* incompatible ⟨*blood groups, medicines, transplant tissue*⟩
Ụnverträglichkeit die *s.* **unverträglich:** indigestibility; unsuitability; quarrelsomeness; incompatibility
ụnvertraut *Adj.* unfamiliar
unvertretbar *Adj.* unjustifiable
ụnverwandt 1. *Adj.* fixed; steadfast ⟨*gaze*⟩. **2.** *adv.* fixedly; steadfastly; **jmdn. ~ anstarren** stare at sb. with a fixed gaze
unverwẹchselbar *Adj.* unmistakable; distinctive
Unverwẹchselbarkeit die distinctiveness
unverwụndbar *Adj.* invulnerable
Unverwụndbarkeit die invulnerability
unverwüstlich *Adj.* indestructible; *(fig.)* irrepressible ⟨*nature, humour*⟩; robust ⟨*health*⟩
Unverwüstlichkeit die; ~: *s.* **unverwüstlich:** indestructibility; irrepressible nature/humour; robustness
ụnverzagt *Adj.* undaunted
unverzeihlich *Adj.* unforgivable; inexcusable
unverzịchtbar *Adj.* indispensable, essential ⟨*goods, requirements, etc.*⟩; essential ⟨*measure*⟩; inalienable ⟨*right*⟩
unverzịnslich *(Bankw.)* interest-free
ụnverzollt *Adj.* undeclared; **~ Ware** goods on which duty has not been paid
unverzüglich 1. *Adj.* prompt; immediate. **2.** *adv.* promptly; immediately
ụnvollendet *Adj.* unfinished
ụnvollkommen 1. *Adj.* **a)** imperfect; **b)** *(unvollständig)* incomplete ⟨*collection, account, etc.*⟩. **2.** *adv.* **a)** imperfectly; **sie beherrscht diese Arbeit nur ~:** she does not have perfect *or* complete command of this work; **b)** *(unvollständig)* incompletely
Ụnvollkommenheit die a) *(Fehlerhaftigkeit)* imperfectness; **b)** *(Unvollständigkeit)* incompleteness
ụnvollständig 1. *Adj.* incomplete. **2.** *adv.* **die Tatsachen nur ~ wiedergeben** give an incomplete rendering of the facts; **~ informiert sein** not be fully informed
Ụnvollständigkeit die incompleteness
ụnvorbereitet *Adj.* unprepared
ụnvoreingenommen 1. *Adj.* unbiased; impartial. **2.** *adv.* impartially
Ụnvoreingenommenheit die impartiality
ụnvorhergesehen 1. *Adj.* unforeseen ⟨*difficulty, event, expenditure*⟩; unexpected ⟨*visit*⟩. **2.** *adv.* **etw. kommt ganz ~:** sth. happens quite unexpectedly; **~ Besuch bekommen** have an unexpected visitor/unexpected visitors
ụnvorhersehbar *Adj.* unforeseeable
ụnvorschriftsmäßig 1. *Adj.* contrary to *or* not in accordance with [the] regulations *postpos.;* **die ~e Anwendung eines Geräts** the improper use of a piece of equipment. **2.** *adv.* contrary to [the] regulations; ⟨*use etc.*⟩ improperly; ⟨*park etc.*⟩ illegally
ụnvorsichtig 1. *Adj.* careless; *(unüberlegt)* rash. **2.** *adv.* carelessly; *(unüberlegt)* rashly
unvorsichtigerweise *Adv.* carelessly; *(unüberlegt)* without thinking
Ụnvorsichtigkeit die *s.* **unvorsichtig 1: a)** *o. Pl. (Art)* carelessness; rashness; **b)** *(Handlung usw.)* **eine ~ begehen** do sth. careless/rash; **die ~ begehen, ...:** be careless/rash enough ...
ụnvorstellbar 1. *Adj.* inconceivable; unimaginable. **2.** *adv.* unimaginably; **~ leiden** suffer terribly
ụnvorteilhaft *Adj.* **a)** *(nicht attraktiv)* unattractive ⟨*figure, appearance*⟩; **das Kleid/die Frisur ist sehr ~ für dich** that dress/hairstyle doesn't suit you in the least; **b)** *(ohne Vorteil)* unfavourable, poor ⟨*purchase, exchange*⟩; unprofitable ⟨*business*⟩
unwägbar *Adj.* imponderable; incalculable ⟨*quantity, behaviour*⟩
Unwägbarkeit die; ~, ~en a) *o. Pl.* imponderability; *(eines Verhaltens)* incalculability; **wegen der ~ der Risiken** because of the incalculable risks; **b)** *(etw. Unwägbares)* uncertainty; imponderability
ụnwahr *Adj.* untrue
ụnwahrhaftig *Adj. (geh.)* untruthful
Ụnwahrheit die a) *o. Pl. (Art)* untruthfulness; **b)** *(Äußerung)* untruth
ụnwahrscheinlich 1. *Adj.* **a)** *(kaum möglich, unglaublich)* improbable; unlikely; **es ist ~, daß er so spät noch kommt** it is unlikely that he'll come so late; **ich halte es für ~[, daß ...:]** I think it [is] unlikely that ...; **b)** *(ugs.: sehr viel)* incredible *(coll.).* **2.** *adv. (ugs.: sehr)* incredibly *(coll.);* **er hat sich ~ gefreut** he was really thrilled *(coll.)*
Ụnwahrscheinlichkeit die improbability
unwạndelbar *(geh.)* **1.** *Adj.* unwavering, steadfast ⟨*loyalty, love, friendship, attitude, etc.*⟩; immutable ⟨*laws*⟩. **2.** *adv.* steadfastly
ụnwegsam *Adj.* [almost] impassable
ụnweiblich *Adj.* unfeminine
unweigerlich [ʊnˈvaigɐlɪç] **1.** *Adj.* inevitable. **2.** *adv.* inevitably
ụnweit 1. *Präp. mit Gen.* not far from. **2.** *Adv.* not far (**von** from)
Ụnwesen das; *o. Pl.* dreadful state of affairs; **sein ~ treiben** *(abwertend)* be up to one's mischief *or* one's tricks
ụnwesentlich 1. *Adj.* unimportant; insignificant. **2.** *adv.* slightly; marginally
Ụnwetter das [thunder]storm
ụnwichtig *Adj.* unimportant; **Geld ist dabei ~:** the money is irrelevant; **etw. ist jmdm.** *od.* **für jmdn. ~:** sth. is unimportant *or* not important to sb.
Ụnwichtigkeit die a) *o. Pl.* unimportance; lack of importance; **b)** *(etw. Unwichtiges)* unimportant thing; triviality
unwiderlegbar 1. *Adj.* irrefutable. **2.** *adv.* irrefutably
unwiderruflich 1. *Adj.* irrevocable. **2.** *adv.* irrevocably
unwidersprọchen *Adj.* unchallenged
unwiderstẹhlich *Adj.* irresistible
Unwiderstẹhlichkeit die; ~: irresistibility
unwiederbrịnglich *(geh.)* **1.** *Adj.* irretrievable. **2.** *adv.* irretrievably
Unwiederbrịnglichkeit die; ~: irretrievability
Ụnwille[n] der; *o. Pl.* displeasure; indignation; **jmds. ~n erregen** *od.* **hervorrufen** incur sb.'s displeasure
ụnwillig 1. *Adj.* indignant; angry; *(widerwillig)* unwilling; reluctant. **2.** *adv.* indignantly; angrily; *(widerwillig)* unwillingly; reluctantly
ụnwillkommen *Adj.* unwelcome
ụnwillkürlich 1. *Adj.* **a)** spontaneous ⟨*cry, sigh*⟩; instinctive ⟨*reaction, movement, etc.*⟩; **b)** *(Physiol.)* involuntary ⟨*movement etc.*⟩. **2.** *adv.* **a)** ⟨*shout etc.*⟩ spontaneously; ⟨*react, move, etc.*⟩ instinctively; **b)** *(Physiol.)* ⟨*move etc.*⟩ involuntarily
ụnwirklich *(geh.)* **1.** *Adj.* unreal. **2.** *adv.* **seine Stimme klang ~ fern** his voice sounded distant and unreal
Ụnwirklichkeit die; ~, ~en unreality
ụnwirksam *Adj.* ineffective
Ụnwirksamkeit die ineffectiveness
ụnwirsch 1. *Adj.* surly; ill-natured. **2.** *adv.* ill-naturedly
ụnwirtlich *Adj.* inhospitable; rough ⟨*weather*⟩
Ụnwirtlichkeit die; ~: inhospitableness; inhospitality; *(des Wetters)* roughness
ụnwirtschaftlich 1. *Adj.* uneconomic ⟨*procedure etc.*⟩; *(nicht sparsam)* uneconomical ⟨*driving etc.*⟩. **2.** *adv.* ⟨*work, drive, etc.*⟩ uneconomically
Ụnwirtschaftlichkeit die economic inefficiency; lack of economy; **der Betrieb mußte wegen ~ geschlossen werden** the firm had to be closed down because it was uneconomic

Ụnwissen das ignorance
ụnwissend *Adj.* **a)** *(unerfahren)* ignorant; innocent ⟨*child*⟩; **b)** *(unbewußt)* unwitting; unknowing
Ụnwissenheit die; ~ **a)** *(Unkenntnis)* ignorance; ~ **schützt nicht vor Strafe** ignorance is no defence; **b)** *(mangelndes Wissen)* lack of education; *(auf einem bestimmten Gebiet)* lack of knowledge
ụnwissenschaftlich 1. *Adj.* unscientific. **2.** *adv.* unscientifically
Ụnwissenschaftlichkeit die; ~: unscientific nature
ụnwissentlich 1. *Adj.* unconscious. **2.** *adv.* unknowingly; unwittingly
ụnwohl *Adv.* **a)** *(nicht wohl)* unwell; **mir ist** ~: I don't feel well; **b)** *(unbehaglich)* uneasy; **mir ist ~ bei dem Gedanken** the thought makes me feel uneasy
Ụnwohlsein das; ~s: indisposition; **ein heftiges ~ überkam ihn** he suddenly felt very unwell
ụnwohnlich *Adj.* uncomfortable; unhomely
Ụnwucht die; ~, ~**en** *(Technik)* imbalance
ụnwürdig *Adj.* **a)** *(verachtungswürdig)* undignified ⟨*person, behaviour*⟩; degrading ⟨*treatment*⟩; **b)** *(unangemessen)* unworthy
Ụnzahl die; *o. Pl.* huge *or* enormous number
unzählbar *Adj.* *(auch Sprachw.)* uncountable
unzählig 1. *Adj.* innumerable; countless. **2.** *adv.* ~ **viele Besucher** a huge *or* an enormous number of visitors
unzähligemal *Adv.* countless times; over and over again
unzähmbar *Adj.* untameable ⟨*animal*⟩; *(fig.)* indomitable ⟨*person*⟩
ụnzart 1. *Adj.* indelicate. **2.** *adv.* indelicately
Unze ['ʊntsə] **die;** ~, ~**n** ounce
Ụnzeit die *in* **zur** ~ *(geh.)* at an inopportune moment
ụnzeitgemäß *Adj.* anachronistic
ụnzensiert *Adj.* uncensored; *(unbenotet)* unmarked; ungraded *(Amer.)*
ụnzerbrechlich *Adj.* unbreakable
ụnzerkaut *Adj.* unchewed
unzerstörbar *Adj.* indestructible
Unzerstörbarkeit die; ~: indestructibility
unzertrennlich *Adj.* inseparable
ụnziemlich *Adj.* *(geh.)* unseemly
ụnzivilisiert *Adj.* *(abwertend)* uncivilized
Ụnzucht die; *o. Pl.* *(veralt.)* **das ist** ~: this is a sexual offence; ~ **[mit jmdm.] treiben** fornicate [with sb.]; ~ **mit Abhängigen/Kindern/Tieren** illicit sexual relations *pl.* with dependants/children/animals; **widernatürliche** ~: unnatural sexual act[s]; **gewerbsmäßige** ~: prostitution
ụnzüchtig 1. *Adj.* obscene ⟨*letter, gesture*⟩. **2.** *adv.* ⟨*touch, approach, etc.*⟩ indecently; ⟨*speak*⟩ obscenely
ụnzufrieden *Adj.* dissatisfied; *(stärker)* unhappy
Ụnzufriedenheit die dissatisfaction; *(stärker)* unhappiness
ụnzugänglich *Adj.* inaccessible ⟨*area, building, etc.*⟩; unapproachable ⟨*character, person, etc.*⟩
Ụnzugänglichkeit die; ~: *s.* **unzugänglich:** inaccessibility; unapproachability
unzukömmlich ['ʊntsu:kœmlɪç] *Adj.* *(österr.)* **a)** *(nicht zukommend)* undeserved; **b)** *(unzulänglich)* inadequate
ụnzulänglich *(geh.)* **1.** *Adj.* insufficient; inadequate. **2.** *adv.* insufficiently; inadequately
Ụnzulänglichkeit die; ~, ~**en a)** *o. Pl.* insufficiency; inadequacy; **b)** *(etw. Unzulängliches)* inadequacy; shortcoming
ụnzulässig *Adj.* inadmissible; undue ⟨*influence, interference, delay*⟩; improper ⟨*method, use, etc.*⟩
Ụnzulässigkeit die inadmissibility
ụnzumutbar *Adj.* unreasonable
Ụnzumutbarkeit die; ~, ~**en a)** *o. Pl.* *(das Unzumutbarsein)* unreasonableness; **b)** *(etw. Unzumutbares)* unreasonable demand
ụnzurechnungsfähig *Adj.* not responsible for one's actions *pred.*; *(geistesgestört)* of unsound mind *postpos*; **für ~ erklärt werden** be certified insane
Ụnzurechnungs·fähigkeit die; *o. Pl.* *(Geistesgestörtheit)* unsoundness of mind
ụnzureichend *Adj.* insufficient; inadequate
ụnzusammenhängend *Adj.* disconnected; incoherent ⟨*words, ideas*⟩
ụnzustellbar *Adj.* *(Postw.)* undeliverable ⟨*mail*⟩; **„falls ~, bitte zurück an Absender"** 'if undelivered, please return to sender'; **„~"**: 'not known [at this address]'
ụnzuträglich *Adj.* *in* **jmdm./einer Sache ~ sein** *(geh.)* be detrimental to sb./sth.
Ụnzuträglichkeit die; ~: detrimental effect; detrimentalness
ụnzutreffend *Adj.* inappropriate; inapplicable; *(falsch)* incorrect; **„Unzutreffendes bitte streichen"** 'please delete as appropriate'
ụnzuverlässig *Adj.* unreliable
Ụnzuverlässigkeit die unreliability
ụnzweckmäßig 1. *Adj.* unsuitable; *(unpraktisch)* impractical. **2.** *adv.* unsuitably; *(unpraktisch)* impractically
Ụnzweckmäßigkeit die *s.* **unzweckmäßig 1:** unsuitability; impracticality
ụnzweideutig 1. *Adj.* unambiguous; unequivocal; **etw. mit ~en Worten sagen** say sth. in no uncertain terms. **2.** *adv.* unambiguously; unequivocally; **jmdm. ~ zu verstehen geben, daß ...:** tell sb. in no uncertain terms that ...
Ụnzweideutigkeit die; *o. Pl.* unambiguousness
ụnzweifelhaft 1. *Adj.* unquestionable; undoubted. **2.** *adv.* unquestionably; undoubtedly
ụ̈ppig 1. *Adj.* **a)** *(voll, dicht)* lush, luxuriant ⟨*vegetation*⟩; thick ⟨*hair, beard*⟩; *(fig.)* sumptuous, opulent ⟨*meal*⟩; rich ⟨*colour*⟩; **b)** *(rundlich, voll)* full ⟨*bosom, lips*⟩; voluptuous ⟨*figure, woman*⟩. **2.** *adv.* luxuriantly; *(fig.)* sumptuously
Ụ̈ppigkeit die; ~: *s.* **üppig 1:** lushness; luxuriance; thickness; sumptuousness; opulence; richness; fullness; voluptuousness
up to date ['ʌp tə 'deɪt] up to date; **er ist modisch ~:** he wears fashionable clothes; he is fashionably dressed
Ur [u:ɐ̯] **der;** ~**[e]s,** ~**e** aurochs
Ur·ab·stimmung die [*esp.* strike] ballot
Ur·adel der ancient nobility
Ur·ahn[e] der a) *(Vorfahr)* oldest known ancestor; **b)** *(veralt.: Urgroßvater)* great-grandfather
Ur·ahne die a) *(Vorfahrin)* oldest known ancestress; **b)** *(veralt.: Urgroßmutter)* great-grandmother
Ural der; ~**[s]** Urals *pl.*; Ural Mountains *pl.*
ur·alt *Adj.* very old; ancient; **in ~en Zeiten** very long ago; **ein Märchen aus ~en Zeiten** a story of long, long ago
Uran [u'ra:n] **das;** ~**s** *(Chemie)* uranium
Uran·erz das uranium ore
Ur·angst die primeval fear
[1]**Uranus** ['u:ranʊs] **der;** ~ *(Astron.)*, [2]**Uranus (der)** *(Myth.)* Uranus *no def. art.*
ur·auf·führen *tr. V.* première, give the first performance of ⟨*play, concerto, etc.*⟩; première ⟨*film*⟩; **uraufgeführt werden** ⟨*film*⟩ have its première
Ur·auf·führung die première; first night *or* performance; *(eines Films)* première; first showing
urban [ʊr'ba:n] *Adj.* *(geh.)* **a)** *(weltmännisch)* urbane; **b)** *(städtisch)* urban
Urbanisation [ʊrbaniza'tsio:n] **die;** ~, ~**en** urbanization
urbanisieren *tr. V.* urbanize
Urbanistik [ʊrba'nɪstɪk] **die;** ~: town planning and urban development *no art.*; *(Studienfach)* urban studies *pl., no art.*
Urbanität [ʊrbani'tɛ:t] **die;** ~: urbanity
urbar *in* **ein Stück Land/einen Sumpf/eine Wüste ~ machen** cultivate a piece of land/reclaim a swamp/desert
Urbarmachung die; ~: *(von Land)* cultivation; *(von Sumpf, Wüste)* reclamation
Ur·bevölkerung die native population; native inhabitants *pl.*
Ur·bild das a) *(Vorbild)* archetype; prototype; **b)** *(Inbegriff, Ideal)* perfect example; epitome
urchig ['ʊrçɪç] *Adj.* *(schweiz.)* *s.* **urig**
Ur·christentum das early Christianity *no art.*
ur·christlich *Adj.* early Christian
ur·deutsch *Adj.* thoroughly *or* totally German
ur·eigen *Adj.*; *nicht präd.* very own; **seine ~en Interessen** his own best interests
Ur·einwohner der native inhabitant; **die australischen ~:** the Australian Aborigines
Ur·eltern *Pl.* original ancestors
Ur·enkel der great-grandson
Ur·enkelin die great-granddaughter
Ur·fassung die original version; original
Ur·fehde die *(MA.)* oath of truce
Ur·form die prototype
Ur·gemeinde die early Christian community
ur·gemütlich 1. *Adj.* *(ugs.)* *(behaglich)* extremely cosy; *(bequem)* extremely comfortable. **2.** *adv.* extremely cosily/comfortably
ur·germanisch *Adj.* proto-Germanic
Ur·geschichte die prehistory
ur·geschichtlich *Adj.* prehistoric
Ur·gesellschaft die primitive society
Ur·gestein das primitive *or* primary rocks *pl.*; **er ist politisches ~** *(fig.)* he is a founding father among politicians
Ur·gewalt die *(geh.)* elemental force
urgieren [ʊr'gi:rən] *tr., itr. V.* *(bes. österr.)* press; urge
Urgroß-: ~eltern *Pl.* great-grandparents; **~mutter die** great-grandmother; **~vater der** great-grandfather
Ur·grund der basis; source; **der ~ alles Seins** the source of all being
Ur·heber der; ~**s,** ~ **a)** *(Initiator)* originator; initiator; **b)** *(bes. Rechtsspr.: Verfasser, Autor)* author
Urheber·recht das copyright
urheber·rechtlich 1. *Adj.* copyright *attrib.* **2.** *adv.* ~ **geschützt** copyright[ed]
Urheberschaft die; ~: authorship
Ur·heimat die original home[land]
urig ['u:rɪç] *Adj.* natural ⟨*person*⟩; real ⟨*beer*⟩; cosy ⟨*pub*⟩; **sie ist einfach ~:** she is just different *or* an original
Urin [u'ri:n] **der;** ~**s,** ~**e** *(Med.)* urine; **etw. im ~ haben** *(salopp)* feel sth. in one's bones; have a gut feeling about sth.
Urinal [uri'na:l] **das;** ~**s,** ~**e** urinal
urinieren *itr. V.* urinate (**an** + *Akk.* against)
Ur·instinkt der basic instinct
Ur·kanton der original canton
Ur·kirche die; *o. Pl.* early Church
Ur·knall der; *o. Pl.* big bang
ur·komisch *Adj.* extremely funny; hilarious
Ur·kraft die elemental force
Ur·kunde die; ~, ~**n** document; *(Bescheinigung, Sieger~, Diplom~ usw.)* certificate
Urkunden·fälschung die forgery *or* falsification of documents/of a/the document
urkundlich 1. *Adj.* documentary. **2.** *adv.* ~ **erwähnt** mentioned in a document/in documents; ~ **übereignen** transfer by deed
Urkunds·beamte der *(Rechtsw.)* registrar

Urlaub der; ~[e]s, ~e holiday[s] *(Brit.)*; vacation; *(bes. Milit.)* leave; ~ **haben** have a holiday/have leave; **[sich** *(Dat.)*] ~ **nehmen** take a holiday; **auf** *od.* **in** *od.* **im** ~ **sein** be on holiday/leave; **in** ~ **gehen/fahren** go on holiday; **unbezahlter** ~: unpaid leave; ~ **von der Familie machen** have a holiday away from one's family; **sie machen** ~: they are on holiday; **sie ist noch nicht aus dem** ~ **zurück** she is still not back from holiday

-urlaub der: **Schweiz~/Österreich~** *usw.* holiday in Switzerland/Austria *etc.*; **Billig~/Neckermann~**: cheap *or* budget/Neckermann holiday

urlauben *itr. V. (ugs.)* holiday; be/go on holiday

Urlauber der; ~s, ~: holiday-maker

-urlauber der: **Sommer~/Winter~/Wochenend~**: summer/winter/weekend holiday-maker; **Billig~/Neckermann~**: person on a cheap *or* budget/Neckermann holiday; **Kreta~/Spanien~**: holiday-maker in *or* on Crete/in Spain

Urlauberin die; ~, ~nen *s.* **Urlauber**

urlaubs-, Urlaubs-: ~**an·schrift die** holiday address; ~**an·spruch der** holiday entitlement; ~**geld das** holiday pay *or* money; *(gespartes Geld)* holiday money; ~**lektüre die** holiday reading *no indef. art.*; ~**ort der**; *Pl.* ~**orte** holiday resort; ~**pläne** *Pl.* holiday plans; ~**reif** *Adj. in* ~**reif sein** *(ugs.)* be ready for a holiday; ~**reise die** holiday [trip]; **eine ~reise ans Meer/ins Gebirge machen** go on holiday to the seaside/go for a holiday in the mountains; ~**reisende der/die** holiday-maker; ~**schein der** *(Milit.)* [leave] pass; ~**sperre die a)** *(Milit.)* ban on leave; **b)** *(österr.)* holiday closure; ~**tag der** day of holiday; **zehn ~tage** ten days' holiday; ~**vertretung die** holiday replacement; **er übernimmt die ~vertretung seines Chefs** he stands in *or* deputizes for his boss when the latter is on holiday; ~**zeit die a)** *(Ferienzeit)* holiday period *or* season; **b)** *(Zeit des eigenen Urlaubs)* holiday

Ur·laut der elemental sound; *(schrill)* elemental cry

Ur·mensch der prehistoric *or* primitive man *no art., no pl.*; early hominid *(as tech. term)*

Ur·meter das *(hist.)* standard metre

Urne ['ʊrnə] **die**; ~, ~n **a)** urn; **b)** *(Wahl~)* [ballot-]box; **zu den ~n gerufen werden** be called to the polls; **c)** *(Verlosungs~)* box; *(Lostrommel)* drum

Urnen-: ~**feld das** urnfield; ~**fried·hof der** urn cemetery; cinerarium; ~**grab das** urn grave

Urologe [uro'lo:gə] **der**; ~n, ~n, **Urologin die**; ~, ~nen urologist

urologisch *Adj.; nicht präd.* urological

Ur·oma die *(fam.)* great-granny *(coll./child lang.)*

Ur·opa der *(fam.)* great-grandpa *(coll./child lang.)*

ur·plötzlich 1. *Adj.* extremely sudden. **2.** *adv.* quite suddenly

Ur·quell der *(geh.)* [primary] source

Ur·sache die cause; **aus unbekannter** ~: for no apparent reason; for reasons *pl.* as yet unknown; **die ~ für etw.** the cause of sth.; the reason for sth.; **alle ~ haben, etw. zu tun** have every reason to do sth.; **keine ~!** don't mention it; you're welcome; **kleine ~, große Wirkung** *(Spr.)* great oaks from little acorns grow *(prov.)*

ur·sächlich *Adj.* causal; **in ~em Zusammenhang stehen** be causally related **(mit** to); ~ **für etw. sein** be the cause of sth.

Ur·sächlichkeit die; ~, ~en causality

Ur·schlamm der, Ur·schleim der primeval slime; **vom ~ an** *(ugs.)* from the very beginning

Ur·schrei der *(Psych.)* primal scream

Ur·schrift die original

ur·schriftlich *Adj.* original ‹*version etc.*›

Ur·sendung die *(Rundf.)* first broadcast performance

Ur·sprache die a) *(Sprachw.: Grundsprache)* protolanguage; **b)** *(Originalsprache)* original language; **in der** ~: in the original

Ur·sprung der origin; **vulkanischen ~s sein** be of volcanic origin; **seinen ~ in etw.** *(Dat.)* **haben** originate from sth.

ur·sprünglich 1. *Adj.* **a)** *(anfänglich)* original ‹*plan, price, form, material, etc.*›; initial ‹*reaction, trust, mistrust, etc.*›; **b)** *(unverfälscht, natürlich)* natural. **2.** *adv.* **a)** *(anfänglich)* originally; initially; **b)** *(unverfälscht, natürlich)* naturally

Ursprünglichkeit die; ~: naturalness

Ursprungs·land das *(einer Ware)* country of origin *(Commerc.)*; *(einer Person)* native land; *(einer Bewegung, Sitte, Religion usw.)* birthplace

urst [u:ɐ̯st] *Adv. (DDR Jugendspr.)* terrifically *(coll.)*

Urständ ['u:ɐ̯ʃtɛnt] **die** *in* **[fröhliche] ~ feiern** be [coming] back with a vengeance

Ur·strom·tal das *(Geol.)* glacial valley

Ur·suppe die *(Biol.)* primordial soup

Urteil das; ~s, ~e judgement; *(Ansicht)* opinion; *(Strafe)* sentence; *(Gerichts~)* verdict; **das ~ lautete auf 10 Jahre Freiheitsstrafe** the sentence was ten years' imprisonment; **über jmdn. das ~ sprechen** pass *or* pronounce judgement on sb.; **sich** *(Dat.)* **selbst das ~ sprechen** sentence oneself; **sich** *(Dat.)* **ein ~ bilden** form an opinion **(über** + *Akk.* about); **ein ~ über etw. fällen** pass *or* pronounce judgement on sth.

Ur·teilchen das *s.* [2]**Quark**

urteilen *itr. V.* form an opinion; judge; **nach etw.** ~: form an opinion *or* judge according to sth.; **nach seinem Äußeren zu** ~: to judge from his appearance; **über etw./jmdn.** ~: judge sth./sb.; give one's opinion on sth./sb.; **hart** ~: give a harsh opinion; judge harshly; **fachmännisch** ~: give an expert opinion; ~ **Sie selbst** judge for yourself/yourselves

urteils-, Urteils-: ~**begründung die** opinion; reasons *pl.* for judgement; ~**fähig** *Adj.* competent *or* able to judge *postpos.*; ~**fähigkeit die**; *o. Pl.* competence *or* ability to judge; ~**findung die** *(Rechtsspr.)* reaching a/the verdict *no art*; ~**kraft die**; *o. Pl.* [power of] judgement; ~**spruch der** judgement; *(Strafe)* sentence; *(der Geschworenen)* verdict; ~**verkündung die** pronouncement of judgement; ~**vermögen das**; *o. Pl.* competence *or* ability to judge

Ur·text der original

Ur·tierchen das protozoan

urtümlich ['u:ɐ̯ty:mlɪç] *Adj.* natural ‹*landscape etc.*›; primitive ‹*culture etc.*›; *(urweltlich)* primeval ‹*plant, animal, landscape*›

Uruguay [uru'gua:i] **(das)**; ~s Uruguay

Uruguayer [uru'gua:jɐ] **der**; ~s, ~: Uruguayan

Ur·ur-: ~**enkel der** great-great-grandson; ~**enkelin** *die* great-great-granddaughter; ~**groß·mutter die** great-great-grandmother; ~**groß·vater der** great-great-grandfather

Ur·väter·zeit die olden days *or* times *pl.*

Ur·vertrauen das *(Päd., Psych.)* sense of basic trust

Ur·viech das *(salopp scherzh.)* real character

Ur·vogel der *(Paläont.)* archaeopteryx

Ur·volk das original people

Ur·wald der primeval forest; **tropischer Urwald** tropical forest; jungle

ur·weltlich *Adj.* primeval

ur·wüchsig ['u:ɐ̯vy:ksɪç] *Adj.* natural ‹*landscape, power*›; earthy ‹*language, humour*›

Urwüchsigkeit die; ~: *s.* **urwüchsig**: naturalness; earthiness

Ur·zeit die primeval times *pl.*; **vor ~en** in ages past; **seit ~en** since primeval times; *(ugs.: seit längerer Zeit)* since the year dot *(coll.)*

ur·zeitlich *Adj.* primeval

Ur·zelle die primeval cell; *(fig.)* initial germ

Ur·zeugung die abiogenesis; spontaneous generation

Ur·zustand der original state

USA [u:|ɛs'|a:] *Pl.* USA

Usambara·veilchen [uzam'ba:ra-] **das** African violet

Usance [y'zã:s] **die**; ~, ~n, *(schweiz.)*, **Usanz** [u'zants] **die**; ~, ~en *(bes. Kaufmannsspr.)* practice

usf. *Abk.* **und so fort** etc.

Usurpator [uzʊr'pa:tɔr] **der**; ~s, ~en [...pa'to:rən] usurper

usurpieren *tr. V.* usurp

Usus ['u:zʊs] **der**; ~ *(ugs.)* custom; **das ist hier so** ~: that's the custom here

usw. *Abk.* **und so weiter** etc.

Utensil [utɛn'zi:l] **das**; ~s, ~ien [...iən] piece of equipment; ~**ien** equipment *sing.*

Uterus ['u:terʊs] **der**; ~, **Uteri** [... ri] *(Anat.)* uterus

Utilitarismus [utilita'rɪsmʊs] **der**; ~ *(Philos.)* utilitarianism *no art.*

utilitaristisch *Adj.* utilitarian

Utopia [u'to:pia] **(das)**; ~s Utopia

Utopie [uto'pi:] **die**; ~, ~n **a)** *(Idealvorstellung)* utopian dream; **b)** *(ideale Gesellschaftsform)* utopia; *(literarisches Werk)* utopian *or* futuristic work

utopisch *Adj.* utopian

Utopist der; ~en, ~en, **Utopistin die**; ~, ~nen utopian dreamer; *(Autor[in])* utopian [author]

utopistisch *Adj.* [absurdly] utopian

u. U. *Abk.* **unter Umständen**

UV *Abk.* **Ultraviolett** UV

UV-: ~**-Filter der** *(Fot.)* UV filter; ultraviolet filter; ~**-Strahlen** *Pl.* UV rays; ultraviolet rays

Ü-Wagen der *(Rundf., Ferns.)* OB van or vehicle

Uz [u:ts] **der**; ~es, ~e *(ugs.)* joke

u. Z. *Abk. (bes. DDR)* **unserer Zeitrechnung** AD

uzen *tr., itr. V. (ugs.)* tease; kid

Uz·name der *(ugs.)* nickname

V

v, V [fau] **das**; ~, ~: v, V

v. *Abk.* **von** *(in Familiennamen)* von

V *Abk.* **Volt** V

Vabanque·spiel [va'bã:k-] **das**; *o. Pl. (geh.)* dangerous *or* risky game

Vademekum [vade'me:kʊm] **das**; ~s, ~s *(geh. veralt.)* vade-mecum

vag [va:k] *s.* **vage**

Vagabund [vaga'bʊnt] **der**; ~en, ~en *(veralt.)* vagabond

vagabundieren *itr. V.* **a)** live as a vagabond/as vagabonds; **b)** *mit sein (umherziehen)* wander *or* travel around
Vagant [va'gant] **der;** ~**en,** ~**en** goliard
Vaganten·dichtung die; *o. Pl. (Literaturw.)* goliardic poetry *or* verse
vage 1. *Adj.* vague. **2.** *adv.* vaguely
Vagheit die; ~: vagueness
Vagina [va'gi:na] **die;** ~, **Vaginen** *(Anat.)* vagina
vaginal *Adj. (Anat.)* vaginal
vakant [va'kant] *Adj.* vacant
Vakanz [va'kants] **die;** ~, ~**en** *(geh.)* vacancy
Vakuum ['va:kuʊm] **das;** ~**s, Vakua** ['va:kua] *od.* **Vakuen** [... kuən] *(bes. Physik, auch fig.)* vacuum; **im** ~: in a vacuum
vakuum·verpackt *Adj.* vacuum-packed
Valentins·tag ['va:lɛnti:ns-] **der** [St] Valentine's Day
Valenz [va'lɛnts] **die;** ~,~**en a)** *(Sprachw.)* valency; **b)** *(Chemie)* valence; valency *(Brit.)*
Valet [va'lɛt] **das;** ~**s,** ~**s** *(veralt., noch scherzh.)* farewell
Valuta [va'lu:ta] **die;** ~, **Valuten** *(Wirtsch., Bankw.)* foreign currency
Vamp [vɛmp] **der;** ~**s,** ~**s** vamp
Vampir ['vampi:ɐ] **der;** ~**s,** ~**e a)** vampire; **b)** *(Tier)* vampire [bat]
Vandale der *s.* **Wandale**
Vanille [va'nɪljə] **die;** ~: vanilla
Vanille-: ~**eis das** vanilla ice-cream; ~**geschmack der** vanilla flavour; **Eis mit** ~**geschmack** vanilla-flavoured ice-cream; ~**pudding der** vanilla pudding; ~**zucker der** vanilla sugar
Vanillin [vani'li:n] **das;** ~**s** vanillin
variabel [va'ria:bl] **1.** *Adj.* variable. **2.** *adv.* variably
Variabilität [variabili'tɛ:t] **die;** ~ *(geh.)* variability
Variable [va'ria:blə] **die;** *adj. Dekl. (Math., Physik)* variable
Variante [va'riantə] **die;** ~, ~**n** *(geh.)* variant; variation
Variation [varia'tsio:n] **die;** ~, ~**en** *(auch Musik)* variation (*Gen.,* **über, zu** on)
Varietät [varie'tɛ:t] **die;** ~, ~**en** *(bes. Biol.)* variety
Varieté [varie'te:] **das;** ~**s,** ~**s** variety theatre; *(Aufführung)* variety show; **ins** ~ **gehen** go to a variety show
variieren *tr., itr. V.* vary
Vario·objektiv ['va:rio-] **das** *(Fot.)* zoom lens
Vasall [va'zal] **der;** ~**en,** ~**en** *(hist., auch fig. abwertend)* vassal
Vasallen·staat der *(abwertend)* vassal state
Väschen ['vɛ:sçən] **das;** ~**s,** ~: [little] vase
Vase ['va:zə] **die;** ~, ~**n** vase
Vasektomie [vəzɛkto'mi] **die;** ~, ~**n** *(Med.)* vasectomy
Vaseline [vaze'li:nə] **die;** ~: Vaseline **(P)**
Vasen·malerei die vase-painting
vasomotorisch [vazomo'to:rɪʃ] *Adj. (Physiol.)* vaso-motor
Vater ['fa:tɐ] **der;** ~**s, Väter** ['fɛ:tɐ] **a)** father; **er ist** ~ **von drei Kindern** he is the father of three children; **er ist** ~ **geworden** he has become a father; **ein werdender** ~ *(scherzh.)* an expectant father *(joc.)*; **grüßen Sie Ihren Herrn** ~**!** remember me to your father; **er ist ganz der** ~: he is just like his father; **er ist der [geistige]** ~ **dieser Idee** *(fig.)* he thought up this idea; this idea is his; **die Väter der amerikanischen Verfassung** *(fig.)* the [founding] fathers of the American constitution; ~ **Staat** *(scherzh.)* the State; ~ **Rhein** *(dichter.)* the Rhine; Father Rhine *(literary)*; **Heiliger** ~ *(kath. Kirche)* Holy Father; **ach, du dicker** ~ *(ugs.)* oh my goodness!; oh heavens!; **b)** *(Tier)* sire; **c)** *o. Pl. (Rel.)* Father; **Gott** ~: God the Father
Väterchen ['fɛ:tɐçən] **das;** ~**s,** ~ **a)** *(Koseform)* daddy *(coll.)*; **b) [altes]** ~: little old man; **c)** ~ **Frost** *(scherzh.)* Jack Frost
Vater-: ~**figur die** father-figure; ~**freuden** *Pl.* ~**freuden entgegensehen** *(meist scherzh.)* be expecting a happy event; be going to be a father; ~**haus das** *(geh.)* parental home; **das** ~**haus verlassen** leave one's parents' house; ~**land das;** *Pl.* ~**länder** fatherland
vaterländisch [-lɛndɪʃ] *Adj. (geh.)* patriotic; **der Große Vaterländische Verdienstorden** *(DDR)* the Order of Patriotic Merit
Vaterlands-: ~**liebe die** *(geh.)* love of one's fatherland; patriotism; ~**verräter der** *(abwertend)* traitor to one's fatherland
väterlich ['fɛ:tɐlɪç] **1.** *Adj.* **a)** *nicht präd. (vom Vater)* his/her *etc.* father's; *(verallgemeinernd)* the father's; *(eines Vaters)* paternal ‹*line, love, instincts, etc.*›; **das** ~**e Geschäft übernehmen** take over one's father's business; **die** ~**en Pflichten** the duties of a father; **b)** *(fürsorglich)* fatherly. **2.** *adv.* in a fatherly way
väterlicherseits *Adv.* on the/his/her *etc.* father's side; **meine Großeltern** ~: my paternal grandparents; my grandparents on my father's side
Väterlichkeit die; ~: fatherliness; *(väterliche Gefühle)* fatherly feeling
vater-, Vater-: ~**los** *Adj.* fatherless; ~**los aufwachsen** grow up without a father; ~**mord der** patricide; ~**mörder der a)** patricide; **b)** *(veralt. scherzh.: Stehkragen)* choker [collar]; ~**schaft die;** ~, ~**en** fatherhood; *(bes. Rechtsw.)* paternity; ~**schafts·klage die** paternity suit; ~**stadt die** *(geh.)* home town; ~**stelle die: bei** *od.* **an jmdm.** ~**stelle vertreten** take the place of a father to sb.; ~**tag der** Father's Day *no def. art.*; ~**tier das** *(Landw.)* sire; ~**unser das;** ~**s,** ~: Lord's Prayer; **das** ~**unser sprechen** say the Lord's Prayer; **drei** ~**unser beten** say three Our Fathers
Vati ['fa:ti] **der;** ~**s,** ~**s** *(fam.)* dad[dy] *(coll.)*
Vatikan [vati'ka:n] **der;** ~**s** Vatican
vatikanisch *Adj.; nicht präd.* Vatican
Vatikan·stadt die; *o. Pl.* Vatican City
V-Ausschnitt ['fau-] **der** V-neck
VB *Abk.* **Verhandlungsbasis: VB 7800 DM** 7,800 marks o.n.o *(Brit.)*
v. Chr. *Abk.* **vor Christus** BC
VEB [faue:'be:] *(DDR) Abk.* **Volkseigener Betrieb**
Vegetarier [vege'ta:riɐ] **der;** ~**s,** ~, **Vegetarierin die;** ~, ~**nen** vegetarian
vegetarisch 1. *Adj.* vegetarian. **2.** *adv.* **er ißt** *od.* **lebt** *od.* **ernährt sich** ~: he is a vegetarian; he lives on a vegetarian diet
Vegetarismus der; ~: vegetarianism *no art.*
Vegetation [...'tsio:n] **die;** ~, ~**en** vegetation *no indef. art.*
vegetativ [vegeta'ti:f] *Adj.* **a)** *(Biol.: ungeschlechtlich)* vegetative; **b)** *(Physiol., Biol.: unbewußt ablaufend)* autonomic
vegetieren *itr. V. (oft abwertend)* vegetate; **am Rande der Existenz** ~: eke out a miserable existence
vehement [vehe'mɛnt] *(geh.)* **1.** *Adj.* vehement. **2.** *adv.* vehemently
Vehemenz [...'mɛnts] **die;** ~ *(geh.)* vehemence
Vehikel [ve'hi:kl] **das;** ~**s,** ~ **a)** *(oft abwertend: Auto)* vehicle; **ein altes/klappriges** ~: an old crock *(sl.)*; **b)** *(geh.: Ausdrucksmittel)* vehicle
Veilchen ['failçən] **das;** ~**s,** ~ **a)** *(Blume)* violet; **wie ein** ~ **im Verborgenen blühen** be modesty itself; go unnoticed; *s. auch* **blau; b)** *(ugs. scherzh.: blaues Auge)* black eye; shiner *(sl.)*
veilchen-, Veilchen-: ~**blau** *Adj.* violet; ~**duft der** violet fragrance *or* scent; ~**strauß der** bunch *or* bouquet of violets
Veits·tanz ['faits-] **der;** *o. Pl.* St Vitus's dance; **einen** ~ **kriegen** *(ugs.) od.* **aufführen** *(fig.)* kick up a terrible fuss
Vektor ['vɛktɔr] **der;** ~**s,** ~**en** [-'to:rən] *(Math., Physik)* vector
Vektor·rechnung die; *o. Pl.* vector algebra; *(im weiteren Sinne)* vector analysis
velar [ve'la:ɐ] *(Sprachw.)* **1.** *Adj.* velar. **2.** *adv.* ‹*pronounce*› as a velar sound
Velar der; ~**s,** ~**e, Velar·laut der** *(Phon.)* velar sound
Velo ['ve:lo] **das;** ~**s,** ~**s** *(schweiz.)* bicycle; bike *(coll.)*
[1]**Velours** [və'lu:ɐ] **der;** ~ [və'lu:ɐs], ~ [və'lu:ɐs] *(Stoff)* velour[s]
[2]**Velours das;** ~ [və'lu:ɐs], ~ [və'lu:ɐs], **Velours·leder das** suede
Vene ['ve:nə] **die;** ~, ~**n** *(Anat.)* vein
Venedig [ve'ne:dɪç] **(das);** ~**s** Venice
Venen·entzündung die phlebitis *no indef. art.*
venerisch [ve'ne:rɪʃ] *Adj. (Med.)* venereal
Venezianer [vene'tsia:nɐ] **der;** ~**s,** ~, **Venezianerin die;** ~, ~**nen** Venetian
venezianisch *Adj.* Venetian
Venezolaner [venetso'la:nɐ] **der;** ~**s,** ~, **Venezolanerin die;** ~, ~**nen** Venezuelan
venezolanisch *Adj.* Venezuelan
Venezuela [vene'tsue:la] **(das);** ~**s** Venezuela
Venia legendi ['ve:nia le'gɛndi] **die;** ~ ~ *(geh.) authorization to teach at university after habilitation*
venös *Adj. (Med.)* venous
Ventil [vɛn'ti:l] **das;** ~**s,** ~**e** valve; *(fig.)* outlet; **b)** *(einer Orgel)* pallet
Ventilation [vɛntila'tsio:n] **die;** ~, ~**en** ventilation
Ventilator [vɛnti'la:tɔr] **der;** ~**s,** ~**en** [...la'to:rən] ventilator
ventilieren *tr. V. (geh.)* consider
[1]**Venus** ['ve:nʊs] **die;** ~ *(Astron.)*, [2]**Venus (die)** *(Myth.)* Venus *no def. art.*
Venus·hügel der *(Anat.)* mons Veneris
verabfolgen *tr. V. (Papierdt. veralt.) s.* **verabreichen**
verabreden 1. *tr. V.* arrange; **ein Erkennungszeichen** ~: agree on a sign to recognize each other by; **am verabredeten Ort** at the agreed place. **2.** *refl. V.* **sich im Park/zum Tennis/für den folgenden Abend** ~: arrange to meet in the park/for tennis/next evening; **sich mit jmdm.** ~: arrange to meet sb.; **mit jmdm. verabredet sein** have arranged to meet sb.; *(formell)* have an appointment with sb.; *(mit dem Freund/der Freundin)* have a date with sb. *(coll.)*
Verabredung die; ~, ~**en a)** *(Absprache)* arrangement; **eine** ~ **treffen** arrange to meet *or* a meeting; **wie auf** ~: as if by arrangement; **b)** *(verabredete Zusammenkunft)* appointment; **eine** ~ **absagen** call off a meeting *or* an engagement; **ich habe eine** ~: I am meeting sb.; *(formell)* I have an appointment; *(mit meinem Freund/meiner Freundin)* I have a date *(coll.)*; **eine** ~ **für den Abend haben** have an engagement in the evening
verabreichen *tr. V.* administer ‹*medicine*›; give ‹*injection, thrashing*›
Verabreichung die; ~, ~**en** administration; administering
verabsäumen *tr. V. (Papierdt.)* neglect; omit
verabscheuen *tr. V.* detest; loathe
verabscheuenswürdig *Adj. (geh.)* detestable; loathsome
verabschieden 1. *tr. V.* **a)** say goodbye to; **sie wurde am Bahnhof verabschiedet** she was seen off at the station; **der Staatsgast wurde auf dem Bonner Flughafen verabschiedet** the official guest was given a farewell at the airport in Bonn; **b)** *(aus dem Dienst)* retire ‹*general, civil servant, etc.*›; **c)** *(annehmen)* adopt ‹*plan, budget*›; pass ‹*law*›. **2.** *refl. V.*

sich [von jmdm.] ~: say goodbye [to sb.]; *(formell)* take one's leave [of sb.]
Verabschiedung die; ~, ~en a) leave-taking; **b)** *(aus dem Dienst)* retirement; **c)** *(eines Plans, Etats)* adoption; *(eines Gesetzes)* passing
verabsolutieren *tr. V.* make absolute
verachten *tr. V.* despise; **ihre Süßspeisen sind nicht zu ~:** her sweets are not to be scoffed at *or (coll.)* sneezed at
Verächter [fɛɐ̯'|ɛçtɐ] **der; ~s, ~:** opponent; critic
verächtlich [fɛɐ̯'|ɛçtlɪç] **1.** *Adj.* **a)** *(abschätzig)* contemptuous; **b)** *(verachtenswürdig)* contemptible; despicable; **jmdn./etw. ~ machen** disparage sb./sth.; run sb./sth. down. **2.** *adv.* contemptuously
Verächtlichkeit die; ~: contempt; contemptuousness
Verächtlich·machung die; ~ *(Papierdt.)* disparagement
Verachtung die; ~: contempt; **seine ~ aller** *od.* **für alle Konventionen** his contempt for all forms of convention; **jmdn. mit ~ strafen** treat sb. with contempt
verachtungs·voll *(geh.) s.* **verächtlich 1 a, 2**
veralbern *tr. V.* **a)** *(aufziehen)* **jmdn. ~:** make fun of sb.; **willst du mich ~?** are you trying to make fun of me?; **b)** *(verspotten)* mock
verallgemeinern *tr., itr. V.* generalize
Verallgemeinerung die; ~, ~en generalization
veralten *itr. V.; mit sein* become obsolete; **veraltete Methoden/Wörter** obsolete *or* antiquated methods/obsolete *or* archaic words
Veranda [vɛ'randa] **die; ~, Veranden** veranda; porch
veränderbar *Adj.* changeable; *(Physik)* variable; **nicht mehr ~:** unalterable
veränderlich *Adj.* **a)** changeable ⟨*weather*⟩; variable ⟨*character, star*⟩; **das Barometer steht auf ~:** the barometer says 'changeable'; **b)** *(veränderbar)* variable
Veränderliche die; ~n, ~n *(Math.)* variable
Veränderlichkeit die; ~, ~en *s.* **veränderlich:** changeability; variability
verändern 1. *tr. V.* change; **der Bart verändert ihn stark** the beard makes him look very different. **2.** *refl. V.* **a)** *(anders werden)* change; **sich zu seinem Vorteil/Nachteil ~:** change for the better/worse; *(nur im Aussehen)* look better/worse; **b)** *(die Stellung wechseln)* **sich [beruflich] ~:** change one's job
Veränderung die change *(Gen.* in); **an etw.** *(Dat.)* **eine ~ vornehmen** change sth.; **berufliche ~:** change of job; **bei uns ist eine ~ eingetreten** our situation has changed
verängstigen *tr. V.* frighten; scare; **völlig verängstigt** terrified
verankern *tr. V.* fix ⟨*tent, mast, pole, etc.*⟩; *(mit einem Anker)* anchor; *(fig.)* embody ⟨*right etc.*⟩
Verankerung die; ~, ~en a) *(das Befestigen)* fixing; *(mit einem Anker)* anchoring; *(fig.)* embodiment; **b)** *(Halterung)* anchorage; fixture
veranlagen *tr.V. (Steuerw.)* assess **(mit** at)
veranlagt *Adj.* **künstlerisch/praktisch/romantisch ~ sein** have an artistic bent/be practically minded/have a romantic disposition; **ein homosexuell ~er Mann** a man with homosexual tendencies
Veranlagung die; ~, ~en a) [pre]disposition; **seine homosexuelle/künstlerische/praktische/romantische ~:** his homosexual tendencies *pl.*/artistic bent/practical nature/romantic disposition; **er hat eine ~ zur Fettsucht** he has a tendency towards obesity; **b)** *(Steuerw.)* assessment
veranlassen *tr. V.* **a)** cause; induce; **was hat dich zu diesem Schritt/dieser Bemerkung veranlaßt?** what caused *or* led you to take this step/make this remark?; **ich fühlte mich veranlaßt einzugreifen** I felt obliged to intervene; **b)** *(dafür sorgen, daß etw. getan wird)* **etw. ~:** see to it that sth. is done *or* is carried out; **ich werde alles Weitere/das Nötige ~:** I will take care of *or* see to everything else/I will see [to it] that the necessary steps are taken
Veranlassung die; ~, ~en a) reason, cause **(zu** for); **äußere ~:** outward reason; **b) auf jmds. ~ [hin]** on sb.'s orders
veranschaulichen *tr. V.* illustrate
Veranschaulichung die; ~, ~en illustration; **zur ~:** as an illustration/as illustrations
veranschlagen *tr. V.* estimate **(mit** at); **etw. zu hoch/niedrig ~:** overestimate/underestimate sth.
Veranschlagung die; ~, ~en estimate
veranstalten *tr. V.* **a)** *(stattfinden lassen)* organize; hold, give ⟨*party*⟩; hold ⟨*auction*⟩; do ⟨*survey*⟩; **b)** *(ugs.: machen, aufführen)* make ⟨*noise, fuss*⟩
Veranstalter der; ~s, ~, Veranstalterin die; ~, ~nen organizer
Veranstaltung die; ~, ~en a) *(das Veranstalten)* organizing; organization; **b)** *(etw., was veranstaltet wird)* event
Veranstaltungs·kalender der calendar of events; *(für kürzeren Zeitraum)* diary of events
verantworten 1. *tr. V.* **etw. ~:** take responsibility for sth.; **ich kann das vor Gott/mir selbst/meinem Gewissen nicht ~:** I cannot be responsible for that before God/I cannot justify it to myself/I cannot square that with my conscience. **2.** *refl. V.* **sich für etw. ~:** answer for sth.; **sich vor jmdm. ~:** answer to sb.; **sich vor Gericht für etw. ~:** answer to the courts for sth.; **der Angeklagte hat sich wegen Mordes zu ~:** the accused faces a charge of murder
verantwortlich *Adj.* responsible; **der ~e Redakteur** the managing editor; **der für den Einkauf ~e Mitarbeiter** the person responsible for purchasing; **ich fühle mich dafür ~, daß alles klappt** I feel responsible for making sure that everything goes off all right; **für etw. ~ zeichnen** be responsible for *or* in charge of sth.; **jmdm. [gegenüber] ~ sein** be responsible to sb.; **jmdn. für etw. ~ machen** hold sb. responsible for sth.
Verantwortlichkeit die; ~, ~en responsibility
Verantwortung die; ~, ~en a) responsibility **(für** for); **die Eltern haben** *od.* **tragen die ~ für ihre Kinder** the parents have *or* bear the responsibility for their children; **die ~ für etw. übernehmen** take *or* accept [the] responsibility for sth.; **ich tue es auf deine ~:** you must take responsibility; on your own head be it; **in eigener ~:** on one's own responsibility; off one's own bat *(Brit.)*; **jmdn. [für etw.] zur ~ ziehen** call sb. to account [for sth.]; **die Gruppe hat die ~ für den Anschlag übernommen** the group has accepted *or* admitted responsibility for the attack; **b)** *o. Pl. (~sgefühl)* sense of responsibility
verantwortungs-, Verantwortungs-: ~bewußt *Adj.* responsible; **er handelt sehr ~bewußt** he acts in a very responsible manner; **~bewußtsein das;** *o. Pl.,* **~gefühl das;** *o. Pl.* sense of responsibility; **~los** *Adj.* irresponsible; **~losigkeit die; ~:** irresponsibility; **~voll** *Adj.* responsible
veräppeln [fɛɐ̯'|ɛpl̩n] *tr. V. (ugs.)* **jmdn. ~:** have *(Brit. coll.) or (Amer. coll.)* put sb. on; **willst du mich ~?** are you having *(Brit. coll.) or (Amer. coll.)* putting me on?
verarbeiten *tr. V.* **a)** use; **~de Industrie** processing industry; **im** *od.* **vom Gehirn verarbeitet** *(fig.)* processed by the brain; **etw. zu etw. ~:** make sth. into sth.; use sth. to make sth.; **b)** *(verdauen)* digest ⟨*food*⟩; **c)** *(geistig bewältigen)* digest, assimilate ⟨*film, experience, impressions*⟩; come to terms with ⟨*disappointment*⟩
-verarbeitend *adj.* -processing
verarbeitet *Adj.* **gut/schlecht** *usw.* **~:** well/badly *etc.* finished ⟨*suit, dress, car, etc.*⟩
Verarbeitung die; ~, ~en a) *(das Verarbeiten)* use; **b)** *(Art der Fertigung)* finish; **Schuhe in erstklassiger ~:** shoes with a first-class finish
-verarbeitung die -processing
verargen *tr. V. (geh.)* **jmdm. etw. ~:** hold sth. against sb.
verärgern *tr. V.* annoy; **verärgert wandte er sich ab** he turned away in annoyance
Verärgerung die; ~, ~en annoyance; **aus ~ über die verspätete Einladung nahm er an dem Empfang nicht teil** he did not attend the reception, because he was annoyed about the late invitation
verarmen *itr. V.; mit sein* become poor *or* impoverished; **verarmte Provinzen/verarmter Adel** impoverished provinces/aristocracy
Verarmung die; ~: impoverishment
verarschen *tr.V. (derb)* **jmdn. ~:** take the piss *(coarse) or (Brit. sl.)* mickey out of sb.; **willst du mich ~?** are you taking the piss *(coarse) or (Brit. sl.)* mickey?
verarzten *tr. V. (ugs.)* patch up *(coll.)* ⟨*person*⟩; fix *(coll.)* ⟨*wound, injury, etc.*⟩
verästeln [fɛɐ̯'|ɛstl̩n] *refl. V. (auch fig.)* branch out
Veräst[e]lung die; ~, ~en *(auch fig.)* ramification
verätzen *tr. V.* corrode ⟨*metal etc.*⟩; burn ⟨*skin, face, etc.*⟩
Verätzung die corrosion; *(der Haut)* burn
verausgaben 1. *tr. V. (Papierdt.)* spend. **2.** *refl. V.* wear oneself out; **sie hat sich total verausgabt** *(finanziell)* she has completely spent out
veräußerlich *Adj. (bes. Rechtsspr.)* alienable; **nicht ~:** inalienable
veräußern *tr. V. (bes. Rechtsspr.)* dispose of, sell ⟨*property*⟩; alienate ⟨*right*⟩
Veräußerung die *(bes. Rechtsspr.) (von Eigentum)* disposal; sale; *(eines Rechts)* alienation
Verb [vɛrp] **das; ~s, ~en** *(Sprachw.)* verb
Verba *s.* **Verbum**
verbacken *unr. tr. V.* use ⟨*flour, butter, sugar, etc.*⟩ [in baking]
verbal [vɛr'ba:l] *Adj.* **1.** *(auch Sprachw.)* verbal. **2.** *adv.* verbally
Verbal·injurie die; ~ *(auch Rechtsw.)* verbal injury
verbalisieren *tr. V. (geh.)* verbalize
verballhornen [fɛɐ̯'balhɔrnən] *tr. V.* corrupt ⟨*word, phrase*⟩
Verballhornung die; ~, ~en misuse; corruption
Verbal-: ~phrase die *(Sprachw.)* verbal phrase; **~substantiv das** *(Sprachw.)* verbal noun
Verband der a) *(Binde)* bandage; dressing; **einen ~ anlegen** apply a dressing; **b)** *(von Vereinen, Clubs o. ä.)* association; **c)** *(Milit.: vereinigte Truppenteile)* unit; **d)** *(Milit.: Fahrzeug~, Flugzeug~)* formation; **e)** *(Gruppe)* group; unit
Verband-: ~kasten der first-aidbox; **~material das** dressing materials *pl.*; **~päckchen das** packet of dressings
Verbands·kasten *usw. s.* **Verbandkasten** *usw.*
Verband[s]·stoff der dressing [material]
Verband·zeug das first-aid things *pl.*
verbannen *tr. V. (auch fig.)* banish
Verbannte der/die; *adj. Dekl.* exile
Verbannung die; ~, ~en banishment; exile; **in die ~ gehen** go into exile
Verbannungs·ort der place of exile

verbarrikadieren 1. *tr. V.* barricade. 2. *refl. V.* barricade oneself
verbauen *tr. V.* a) *(versperren)* obstruct; block; **jmdm./sich die Zukunft ~** *(fig.)* spoil sb.'s/one's prospects for the future; b) *(abwertend: unschön bebauen)* spoil; c) *(zum Bauen verwenden)* use; **sein ganzes Geld ~** *(fig.)* use [up] one's entire money for *or* on building
verbauern *itr. V.; mit sein* become a country bumpkin
verbeamten *tr. V.* make ‹*person*› a civil servant; *(fig. abwertend)* [over-]bureaucratize
verbeißen 1. *unr. tr. V.* a) *(unterdrücken)* suppress ‹*pain, laughter, anger, feelings*›; hold back ‹*tears etc.*›; b) *(bes. Jägerspr.: beschädigen)* bite; chew. 2. *refl. V.* **sich in etw. ~**: bite into sth.; ‹*dog*› sink its teeth into sth.; *(fig.)* get stuck into sth. *(sl.)*
verbellen *tr. V. (Jägerspr.)* **der Jagdhund verbellte den Bock** the hunting dog barked to show where the buck was
verbergen *unr. tr. V.* a) *(verstecken, auch fig.)* hide; conceal; **jmdn. vor der Polizei verborgen halten** harbour sb.; **sich ~**: hide; **sein Gesicht in den Händen ~**: bury *or* hide one's face in one's hands; b) *(verheimlichen)* hide; **jmdm. etw. ~, etw. vor jmdm. ~**: keep sth. from sb.; **ich will dir nicht ~, daß ...**: I want you to know that ...; I want to make it clear that ...
verbessern 1. *tr. V.* a) improve ‹*machine, method, quality*›; improve [up]on, better ‹*achievement*›; beat ‹*record*›; reform ‹*schooling, world*›; b) *(korrigieren)* correct. 2. *refl. V.* a) improve; **er hat sich im Skilauf stark verbessert** his skiing has improved a great deal; b) *([beruflich] aufsteigen)* better oneself
Verbesserung die a) improvement; **eine ~ der Lage** an improvement in the situation; b) *(Korrektur)* correction
verbesserungs·fähig *Adj.* capable of improvement *postpos.*; **es ist noch ~**: it could be improved [on]
Verbesserungs·vorschlag der suggestion for improvement
verbeugen *refl. V.* bow (**vor** + *Dat.* to)
Verbeugung die; ~, ~en bow; **eine ~ vor jmdm. machen** bow to sb.
verbeulen *tr. V.* dent
verbiegen 1. *unr. tr. V.* bend. 2. *unr. refl. V.* bend; buckle; **eine verbogene Wirbelsäule** a curved spine
Verbiegung die bending; buckling; *(der Wirbelsäule)* curvature
verbiestern [fɛɐ̯ˈbiːstɐn] *tr. V. (bes. nordd.: verwirren)* confuse; bewilder
verbiestert *Adj. (ugs.)* grumpy
verbieten 1. *unr. tr. V.* a) forbid; **jmdm. etw. ~**: forbid sb. sth.; **du hast mir gar nichts zu ~**: you have no right to forbid me [to do] anything; **sie hat ihm das Haus verboten** she forbade him to enter the house; **der Arzt hat mir das Rauchen verboten** the doctor forbade me to smoke; **„Betreten des Rasens/Rauchen verboten"!** 'keep off the grass'/'no smoking'; **das verbietet mir mein Ehrgefühl** *(fig.)* my sense of honour prevents me from doing that; **das verbietet mir mein Geldbeutel** *(fig. scherzh.)* my resources don't run to that; b) *(für unzulässig erklären)* ban; **so viel Ignoranz müßte verboten werden** *(scherzh.)* such ignorance ought not to be allowed *(joc.)*. 2. *unr. refl. V.* **sich [von selbst] ~**: be out of the question
verbilden *tr. V.* bring up wrongly, miseducate ‹*person*›; **verbildeter Geschmack** *(abwertend)* misguided taste
verbilligen 1. *tr. V.* bring down *or* reduce the cost of; bring down *or* reduce the price of, reduce ‹*goods*›; **verbilligte Butter/Waren** butter at a reduced price/reduced goods; **verbilligter Eintritt** reduced admission. 2. *refl. V.* become *or* get cheaper; ‹*goods*› come down in price, become *or* get cheaper
Verbilligung die *(von Kosten)* reduction; **eine ~ der Einfuhren** a reduction in the cost of imports; **zur ~ der Einfuhren** to reduce the cost of imports
verbimsen [fɛɐ̯ˈbɪmzn̩] *tr. V. (ugs.)* bash; hit
verbinden 1. *unr. tr. V.* a) *(bandagieren)* bandage; dress; **jmdm./sich den Fuß ~**: bandage *or* dress sb.'s/one's foot; **jmdn./sich ~**: dress sb.'s/one's wounds; b) *(zubinden)* bind; **jmdm. die Augen ~**: blindfold sb.; **mit verbundenen Augen** blindfold[ed]; c) *(zusammenfügen)* join ‹*wires, lengths of wood, etc.*›; join up ‹*dots*›; d) *(zusammenhalten)* hold ‹*parts*› together; e) *(in Beziehung bringen)* connect (**durch** by); link ‹*towns, lakes, etc.*› (**durch** by); **ein paar ~de Worte sprechen** *(fig.)* say a few words as a link; f) *(verknüpfen)* combine ‹*abilities, qualities, etc.*›; **die damit verbundenen Anstrengungen/Kosten** *usw.* the effort/cost *etc.* involved; g) *auch itr. (telefonisch)* **jmdn. [mit jmdm.] ~**: put sb. through [to sb.]; **Moment, ich verbinde** one moment, I'll put you through; **falsch verbunden sein** have got the wrong number; h) *auch itr. (in bezug auf menschliche Beziehungen)* **er war ihr freundschaftlich verbunden** he was bound to her by ties of friendship; **uns verbindet nichts mehr** nothing holds us together any longer; **gemeinsame Erlebnisse ~**: shared experiences draw people together; i) *(assoziieren)* associate (**mit** with); j) *(geh. veralt.)* **jmdm. [für etw.] verbunden sein** be obliged to sb. [for sth.]. 2. *unr. refl. V.* a) *(zusammenkommen) (auch Chemie)* combine (**mit** with); b) *(in Zusammenhang stehen)* be connected *or* associated (**mit** with); c) *(sich zusammentun)* join [together]; join forces; **sich zu einer Koalition ~**: join together *or* join forces to form a coalition *or* in a coalition; d) *(in Gedanken)* be associated (**mit** with); **mit dieser Melodie sind für mich schöne Erinnerungen verbunden** this tune has happy memories for me
verbindlich 1. *Adj.* a) *(freundlich)* friendly; *(entgegenkommend)* forthcoming; **eine ~e Verkäuferin** an obliging sales assistant; **~sten Dank!** *(geh.)* a thousand thanks; b) *(bindend)* obligatory; compulsory; binding ‹*agreement, decision, etc.*›. 2. *adv.* a) *(freundlich)* in a friendly manner; *(entgegenkommend)* in a forthcoming manner; b) **~ zusagen** definitely agree; **jmdm. etw. ~ zusagen** make sb. a firm offer of sth.
Verbindlichkeit die; ~, ~en a) *o. Pl. (Freundlichkeit)* friendliness; *(Entgegenkommen)* forthcomingness; b) *o. Pl. (verpflichtender Charakter)* obligatory *or* compulsory nature; **rechtlich [gesehen] keine ~ haben** have no binding force in law; c) *(freundliche Äußerung, Handlung)* friendly remark/act; *(entgegenkommende Äußerung, Handlung)* forthcoming comment/gesture; **ein paar ~en sagen** say a few friendly words; d) *meist Pl. (Pflicht)* obligation; commitment; e) *Pl. (Kaufmannsspr.: Schulden)* liabilities (**gegen** to)
Verbindung die a) *(das Verknüpfen)* linking; b) *(Zusammenhalt)* join; connection; c) *(verknüpfende Strecke)* link; **die kürzeste ~ zwischen zwei Punkten** the shortest line between two points; d) *(Anschluß durch Telefon, Funk)* connection; **keine ~ mit jmdm./einem Ort bekommen** not be able to get through to sb./a place; **unsere ~ wurde unterbrochen** we were cut off; e) *(Verkehrs~)* connection (**nach** to); **die ~ zur Außenwelt** connections *pl.* with the outside world; f) *(Kombination)* combination; **in ~ mit etw.** in conjunction with sth.; g) *(Bündnis)* association; **eheliche ~** *(geh.)* marriage; **eine ~ mit jmdm. eingehen** enter into association with sb.; *(erotisch)* begin a liaison with sb.; h) *(Kontakt)* contact; **sich mit jmdm. in ~ setzen, ~ mit jmdm. aufnehmen** get in touch *or* contact with sb.; contact sb.; **in ~ bleiben** keep in touch; **die ~ mit jmdm./etw. nicht abreißen lassen** not lose touch *or* contact with sb./sth.; **seine ~en spielen lassen** pull a few strings *(coll.)*; i) *(Zusammenhang)* connection; **jmdn. mit etw. in ~ bringen** connect sb. with sth.; j) *(Studenten~)* society; *(für Männer)* fraternity *(Amer.)*; *(für Frauen)* sorority *(Amer.)*; **eine schlagende ~**: a duelling society *or* *(Amer.)* fraternity; k) *o. Pl. (das Zusammenfügen)* joining; l) *(das Zusammengefügtwerden)* bonding; m) *(bes. Chemie) (Stoff)* compound; *(Prozeß)* combination
Verbindungs-: **~linie die** a) *(verbindende Linie)* connecting line; b) *(Milit.)* communication line; line of communication; **~mann der**; *Pl.* **~männer** *od.* **~leute** intermediary; *(Agent)* contact [man] (**zu** with); **~offizier der** *(Milit.)* liaison officer; **~straße die** link road; **~stück das** connecting piece; **~student der** member of a students' society; *s. auch* **Verbindung j**; **~tür die** connecting door
Verbiß der *(Jägerspr.)* damage caused by browsing animals
verbissen 1. *2. Part. v.* **verbeißen**. 2. *Adj.* a) *(hartnäckig)* dogged; doggedly determined; b) *(verkrampft)* grim. 3. *adv.* a) *(hartnäckig)* doggedly; with dogged determination; b) *(verkrampft)* grimly; c) *(ugs.: engherzig)* **etw. nicht so ~ sehen** not take sth. so seriously
Verbissenheit die; ~: doggedness; dogged determination
verbitten *unr. refl. V.* **sich** *(Dat.)* **etw. ~**: refuse to tolerate sth.; **ich verbitte mir diesen Ton** I will not be spoken to in that tone of voice; **das möchte ich mir verbeten haben** I will not have it
verbittern *tr. V.* embitter; make bitter; **verbittert** embittered; bitter
Verbitterung die; ~, ~en bitterness; embitterment
verblassen *itr. V.; mit sein* a) *(auch fig. geh.)* fade; b) *(die Leuchtkraft verlieren)* ‹*star etc.*› fade, pale; ‹*sky*› grow dim; *(fig.)* pale; ‹*memory*› fade
Verbleib der; ~[e]s *(geh.)* a) *(Ort)* whereabouts *pl.*; b) *(das Verbleiben)* staying; **ein weiterer ~**: a longer stay
verbleiben *unr. itr. V.; mit sein* a) *(sich einigen)* **wie seid ihr denn nun verblieben?** what did you arrange?; **wir sind so verblieben, daß er sich bei mir meldet** we left it that he would contact me; b) *(geh.: bleiben)* remain; stay; **niemand wußte, wo Sie verblieben waren** nobody knew where you were; **im Amt ~**: remain *or* continue in office; c) *(im Briefschluß)* remain; **... verbleibe ich Ihr ...**: ... I remain, Yours truly, ...; **ich verbleibe mit freundlichen Grüßen Ihr ...**: I remain, Yours sincerely, ...; d) *(übrigbleiben)* remain; **etw. verbleibt jmdm.** sb. has sth. left
verbleichen *unr. od. regelm. itr. V.; mit sein* a) *(auch fig.) (blaß werden)* fade; b) *(allmählich erlöschen)* ‹*moon*› grow pale
verbleien [fɛɐ̯ˈblaiən] *tr. V. (Technik)* lead ‹*petrol*›
verblenden *tr. V.* a) blind; **ein verblendeter Revolutionär** a blind revolutionary; b) *(Archit.: verkleiden)* face ‹*wall, façade, etc.*›
Verblendung die; ~, ~en a) blindness; b) *(bes. Archit.: Verkleidung)* facing
verbleuen *tr. V. (ugs.)* bash *or* beat up; do over *(sl.)*
Verblichene [fɛɐ̯ˈblɪçənə] **der/die**; *adj. Dekl. (geh.)* deceased; **unser teurer Verblichener** our dear departed brother/leader/friend *etc.*
verblöden *itr. V.; mit sein* a) *(veralt.:*

schwachsinnig werden) become feeble-minded; **b)** *(ugs.: stumpfsinnig werden)* become a zombie *(coll.)*

verblüffen [fɛɐ̯'blʏfn̩] *tr. (auch itr.) V.* astonish; amaze; astound; *(verwirren)* baffle; **seine Offenheit verblüfft** his openness is astonishing; **ich war über seine Antwort verblüfft** I was taken aback by his answer

verblüffend **1.** *Adj.* astonishing; amazing; astounding. **2.** *adv.* astonishingly; amazingly; astoundingly

Verblüffung die; ~, ~en astonishment; amazement

verblühen *itr. V.; mit sein (auch fig.)* fade; **sie war schon verblüht** *(geh.)* her beauty had already faded

verblümt [fɛɐ̯'bly:mt] **1.** *Adj.* oblique. **2.** *adv.* **sich ~ ausdrücken** express oneself in a roundabout *or* an oblique way

verbluten *itr. (auch refl.) V.; mit sein* bleed to death

verbocken *tr. V. (ugs.)* botch; bungle; make a botch-up of

verbohren *refl. V. (ugs.)* become obsessed **(in + *Akk.*** with)

verbohrt *Adj. (abwertend)* pigheaded; stubborn; obstinate; *(unbeugsam)* inflexible

Verbohrtheit die; ~ *(abwertend)* pigheadedness; stubbornness; obstinacy; *(Unbeugsamkeit)* inflexibility

[1]**verborgen** *tr. V.* lend out

[2]**verborgen** **1.** *2. Part. v.* **verbergen. 2.** *Adj.* **a)** *(abgelegen)* secluded; **b)** *(nicht sichtbar)* hidden; **es wird ihm nicht ~ bleiben** he shall hear of it; *(nicht entgehen)* it will not escape his notice; **im Verborgenen** out of the public eye; **im Verborgenen blühen** flourish undetected

Verborgenheit die; ~ *(Abgelegenheit)* seclusion

Verbot das; ~[e]s, ~e ban *(Gen.,* **von** on); **er hat gegen mein ausdrückliches ~ geraucht** he smoked although I had expressly forbidden him to do so; **trotz ärztlichen ~s** against doctor's orders

Verbots-: ~schild das; *Pl.* **~schilder a)** sign *(prohibiting sth.)*; **b)** *(Verkehrsw.)* prohibitive sign; **~tafel die** [large] sign *(prohibiting sth.)*

verbrämen [fɛɐ̯'brɛ:mən] *tr. V.* **a)** *(einfassen)* trim **(mit** with); **b)** *(verschleiern)* dress up *(fig.)*; **wissenschaftlich verbrämter Unsinn** nonsense dressed up as scientific fact

verbraten *unr. tr. V. (salopp)* blow *(sl.)* ⟨*money*⟩ **(für** on)

Verbrauch der; ~[e]s a) consumption; **die Seife ist sparsam im ~:** the soap is economical to use; **zum alsbaldigen ~ bestimmt** for immediate consumption; **b)** *(verbrauchte Menge)* consumption **(von, an + *Dat.*** of)

verbrauchen **1.** *tr. V.* **a)** *(verwenden)* use; consume ⟨*food, drink*⟩; use up ⟨*provisions*⟩; spend ⟨*money*⟩; consume, use ⟨*fuel*⟩; *(fig.)* use up ⟨*strength, energy*⟩; **das Auto verbraucht 10 Liter [auf 100 Kilometer]** the car does 10 kilometres to the litre; **b)** *(verschleißen)* wear out ⟨*clothing, shoes, etc.*⟩; **die Luft in den Räumen ist verbraucht** the air in the rooms is stale. **2.** *refl. V. (sich abarbeiten)* wear oneself out; **verbraucht aussehen** look worn out *or* exhausted

Verbraucher der; ~s, ~: consumer

verbraucher-: ~feindlich *Adj.* not in the interests of consumers *postpos.*; **~freundlich** *Adj.* favourable to consumers *postpos.*

Verbraucherin die; ~, ~nen consumer

Verbraucher-: ~preis der consumer price; **~schutz der** consumer protection

Verbrauchs·gut das consumer item; **Verbrauchsgüter** consumer goods

Verbrauch[s]·steuer die *(Steuerw.)* excise [tax]

verbrechen *unr. tr. V. (scherzh.)* **ich habe nichts verbrochen!** I haven't been up to *or* haven't done anything!; **was hast du verbrochen?** what have you been up to *or* been doing?; **wer hat denn dieses Gedicht verbrochen?** who's responsible for *or* who's the perpetrator of this poem?

Verbrechen das; ~s, ~ *(auch Untat)* crime **(an + *Dat.*, gegen** against)

Verbrechens·bekämpfung die combating of crime; combating crime *no art.*; **für die aktive ~:** for actively combating crime

Verbrecher der; ~s, ~: criminal; **du kleiner ~!** *(scherzh.)* you little rascal!

Verbrecher-: ~album das *(veralt.) s.* **~kartei; ~bande die** gang *or* band of criminals

Verbrecherin die; ~, ~nen criminal

verbrecherisch *Adj.* criminal

Verbrecher-: ~jagd die *(ugs.)* chase after a/the criminal/criminals; **~kartei die** criminal records *pl.*; **~syndikat das** criminal syndicate

Verbrechertum das; ~s criminality

verbreiten **1.** *tr. V.* **a)** *(bekannt machen)* spread ⟨*rumour, lies, etc.*⟩; **er verbreitete, daß ...:** he spread it about that ...; **eine Nachricht über den Rundfunk ~:** broadcast an item of news on the radio; **b)** *(weitertragen)* spread ⟨*disease, illness, etc.*⟩; disperse ⟨*seeds, spores, etc.*⟩; **c)** *(erwecken)* radiate ⟨*optimism, happiness, calm, etc.*⟩; spread ⟨*fear*⟩; **ihre Gewalttaten verbreiteten überall Entsetzen** their deeds of violence horrified everyone. **2.** *refl. V.* **a)** *(bekannt werden)* ⟨*rumour*⟩ spread; **b)** *(sich ausbreiten)* ⟨*smell, illness, religion, etc.*⟩ spread; **c)** *(häufig abwertend: sich äußern)* go on **(über + *Akk.*** about)

verbreitern **1.** *tr. V.* widen; *(fig.)* broaden ⟨*basis*⟩. **2.** *refl. V.* widen out; get wider

Verbreiterung die; ~, ~en a) widening; **b)** *(Stelle)* widened section

Verbreitung die; ~, ~en a) *s.* **verbreiten 1 a, b, c:** spreading; broadcasting; dispersal; radiation; **nicht für allgemeine ~ bestimmt** not [intended] for general circulation; **b)** *(Ausbreitung)* spread

Verbreitungs·gebiet das area of distribution; *(einer Tierart)* range

verbrennen **1.** *unr. itr. V.; mit sein* **a)** burn; ⟨*person*⟩ burn to death; **die Dokumente sind verbrannt** the documents were destroyed by fire; **es riecht verbrannt** *(ugs.)* there's a smell of burning; **b)** *(verkohlen)* burn; **der Kuchen ist verbrannt** the cake got burnt; **c)** *(ausdorren)* scorch; **d)** *(Chemie: sich umwandeln)* be converted **(zu** into). **2.** *tr. V.* **a)** *(ins Feuer geben)* burn; burn, incinerate ⟨*rubbish*⟩; cremate ⟨*dead person*⟩; **b)** *(verletzen)* burn; **sich** *(Dat.)* **an der heißen Suppe die Zunge ~:** burn *or* scald one's tongue on the hot soup; **sich** *(Dat.)* **den Mund** *od. (derb)* **das Maul** *od. (salopp)* **die Schnauze ~** *(fig.)* say too much; *s. auch* **Finger b; c)** *(ugs.: verbrauchen)* use ⟨*gas, electricity, etc.*⟩; **d)** *(Chemie: umwandeln)* convert

Verbrennung die; ~, ~en a) *s.* **verbrennen 2 a:** burning; incineration; cremation; **b)** *(Kfz-W.)* combustion; **c)** *(Wunde)* burn

Verbrennungs·motor der internal-combustion engine

verbriefen *tr. V.* attest

verbringen *unr. tr. V.* **a)** spend ⟨*time, holiday, weekend, year, etc.*⟩; **b)** *(Papierdt.: bringen)* take

verbrüdern *refl. V.* avow friendship and brotherhood; ⟨*troops*⟩ fraternize **(mit** with); *(Politik)* ally oneself/itself

Verbrüderung die; ~, ~en avowal of friendship and brotherhood; *(von Truppen)* fraternization; *(Politik)* alliance

verbrühen *tr. V.* scald; **sich** *(Dat.)* **den Arm ~:** scald one's arm; **sich ~:** scald oneself

Verbrühung die; ~, ~en a) *(das Verbrühen)* scalding; **b)** *(Wunde)* scald

verbuchen *tr. V. (Kaufmannnsspr., Finanzw.)* enter; *(fig.)* notch up ⟨*success, score, etc.*⟩; **etw. auf einem Konto/im Haben ~:** credit sth. to an account/enter sth. on the credit side

verbuddeln *tr. V. (ugs.)* bury

Verbum ['vɛrbʊm] **das; ~s, Verben** *od. (Sprachw. veralt.)* **Verba** verb

verbummeln *tr. V. (ugs., oft abwertend)* **a)** *(verbringen)* waste, fritter away ⟨*time, day, afternoon, etc.*⟩; **sie wollten einmal einen ganzen Tag ~:** they wanted to spend a whole day lazing around doing nothing; **b)** *(vergessen)* forget [all] about; clean forget; *(verlieren)* lose; *(verlegen)* mislay

Verbund der; ~[e]s, ~e a) *(Wirtsch.)* association; **im ~ arbeiten** co-operate; **b)** *(Technik)* composite

Verbund·bau·weise die composite construction

verbünden [fɛɐ̯'bʏndn̩] *refl. V.* form an alliance

Verbundenheit die; ~: closeness **(mit** to); *(mit einem Ort, einer Tradition)* attachment **(mit** to); **aus alter ~:** for the sake of old ties/attachments; **in herzlicher ~:** with deepest sympathy

verbündet *Adj.* **[miteinander] ~:** in alliance *postpos.*

Verbündete der/die; *adj. Dekl.* ally

Verbund-: ~glas das *(Technik)* laminated glass; **~netz das** grid [system]; **~stein der** interlocking paving-stone

verbürgen **1.** *refl. V. (bürgen)* vouch **(für** for); **sich für die Kosten ~:** accept liability for the costs. **2.** *tr. V.* **a)** *(garantieren)* guarantee; **verbürgte Rechte** established rights; **b)** *nur im Perf., Plusq. u. im 2. Part. gebr. (authentisieren)* verify; authenticate

verbürgerlichen **1.** *itr. V.; mit sein* become bourgeois. **2.** *tr. V.* make bourgeois

verbüßen *tr. V.* serve ⟨*sentence*⟩

Verbüßung die; ~: serving

verchromen *tr. V.* chromium-plate

Verdacht [fɛɐ̯'daxt] **der; ~[e]s, ~e** *od.* **Verdächte** [fɛɐ̯'dɛçtə] suspicion; **mein ~ hat sich bestätigt/war begründet** my suspicion was confirmed/was well founded; **der ~ der Polizei fiel auf/richtete sich gegen ...:** the police suspected ...; **ein ~ stieg in mir auf** I began to suspect something *or* to be suspicious; **er wurde wegen ~s der Steuerhinterziehung verhaftet** he was arrested on suspicion of tax evasion; **~ schöpfen** become suspicious; **jmdn. auf [einen] bloßen ~ hin verhaften lassen** have sb. arrested purely on suspicion; **wen hast du in ~?** who do you suspect?; **ich geriet in [den] ~, das Geld gestohlen zu haben** I was suspected of having stolen the money; **er ist über jeden ~ erhaben** he is above suspicion; **bei dem Patienten besteht ~ auf Meningitis** the patient is suspected of having meningitis; **etw. auf ~ tun** *(ugs.)* do sth. just in case

verdächtig [fɛɐ̯'dɛçtɪç] **1.** *Adj.* suspicious; **sich ~ machen** arouse suspicion; **er ist dringend der Tat ~:** he is strongly suspected of being the perpetrator. **2.** *adv.* suspiciously

-verdächtig a) *(unter Verdacht stehend)* suspected of ...; **mord~:** suspected of murder; **b)** *(erwarten lassend)* expected to ...; **ein hit~es Lied** a song expected to be a hit; **der medaillen~e Sportler** the sportsman expected to win a/the medal

Verdächtige der/die; *adj. Dekl.* suspect

verdächtigen *tr. V.* suspect *(Gen.* of)

Verdächtigte der/die; *adj. Dekl.* suspect

Verdächtigung die; ~, ~en suspicion

Verdachts·moment das incriminating factor

verdammen *tr. V.* **a)** *(verwerfen)* condemn; *(Rel.)* damn ⟨*sinner*⟩; **[Gott] verdamm' mich!** damn it *(coll.)*; **b)** *(zwingen)* condemn **(zu** to); **das ist zum Scheitern verdammt** it is doomed to failure

verdämmern *(geh.)* **1.** *itr. V.; mit sein* fade. **2.** *tr. V.* drowse away

Verdammnis die; ~ *(christl. Theol.)* damnation *no art.*

verdammt 1. *Adj.; nicht präd.* **a)** *(salopp abwertend)* bloody *(Brit. sl.)*; damned *(coll.)*; ~ **[noch mal** *od.* **noch eins]!** damn [it all] *(coll.)*; bloody hell *(Brit. sl.)*; ~ **und zugenäht!** damn and blast [it]! *(coll.)*; **so ein ~er Mist!** bloody hell *(Brit. sl.)*; **b)** *(ugs.: sehr groß)* **einen ~en Hunger haben** be damned hungry *(coll.)*; **[ein] ~es Glück haben** be damn[ed] lucky *(coll.)*. **2.** *adv. (ugs.: sehr)* damn[ed] *(coll.)* ‹*cold, heavy, beautiful, etc.*›; **ich mußte mich ~ beherrschen** I had to keep a bloody good grip on myself *(Brit. coll.)*

Verdammte der/die; *adj. Dekl.* damned person/man/woman; **die ~n** the damned

Verdammung die; ~, **~en** condemnation; damnation

verdammungs·würdig *(geh.)* **1.** *Adj.* damnable. **2.** *adv.* damnably

verdampfen 1. *itr. V.; mit sein* evaporate; vaporize; *(fig.)* ‹*anger*› abate; ‹*person*› make oneself scarce *(coll.)*. **2.** *tr. V.* evaporate; vaporize

verdanken *tr. V.* **jmdm./einer Sache etw. ~:** owe sth. to sb./sth.; **ich verdanke meiner Frau wertvolle Anregungen** I have to thank my wife for valuable suggestions; **daß Sie bei uns sind, verdanken wir ...:** it is thanks *or* due to ... that you are here with us

verdarb [fɛɐ̯ˈdarp] *1. u. 3. Pers. Sg. Prät. v.* **verderben**

verdaten *tr. V. (DV)* convert into data; *(erfassen)* store away on computer

verdattert [fɛɐ̯ˈdatɐt] *(ugs.) Adj. (überrascht)* flabbergasted; *(verwirrt)* dazed; stunned; ~ **dastehen** stand there flabbergasted/in a daze

verdauen [fɛɐ̯ˈdauən] **1.** *tr. V. (auch fig.)* digest; *(fig.)* get over ‹*bad experience, shock, blow of fate*›; *(Boxerjargon)* take ‹*blow*›. **2.** *itr. V.* digest [one's food]

verdaulich [fɛɐ̯ˈdaulɪç] *Adj.* digestible

Verdaulichkeit die; ~: digestibility

Verdauung die; ~: digestion

Verdauungs-: ~beschwerden *Pl.* digestive trouble *sing.*; **~spaziergang der** *(ugs.)* after-dinner walk; **~störung die** poor digestion *no pl.*; **~trakt der** *(Anat.)* digestive *or* alimentary tract

Verdeck das; ~[e]s, ~e top; hood *(Brit.)*; *(bei Kinderwagen)* hood; **mit offenem ~ fahren** drive with the top *or* hood down

verdecken *tr. V.* **a)** *(nicht sichtbar sein lassen)* hide; cover; **jmdm. die Sicht ~:** block sb.'s view; **b)** *(verbergen)* cover; conceal; *(fig.)* conceal ‹*intentions etc.*›

verdenken *unr. tr. V.* **jmdm. etw. nicht ~ [können]** not [be able to] hold sth. against sb.; **kann man ihnen verdenken, daß sie ... hassen?** can one blame them for hating ...?

Verderb der; ~s **a)** *(von Lebensmitteln)* spoilage; **b)** *s.* **Gedeih**

verderben 1. *unr. itr. V.; mit sein* ‹*food, harvest*› go bad *or* off, spoil; **verdorbene Lebensmittel** food which has gone bad *or* off. **2.** *unr. tr. V.* **a)** *(unbrauchbar machen)* spoil; *(stärker)* ruin; **daran ist nichts mehr zu ~:** it's in a pretty sorry state anyway; **b)** *(zunichte machen)* ruin; spoil ‹*appetite, enjoyment, fun, etc.*›; **jmdm. die gute Laune ~:** spoil sb.'s good mood; **jmdm. den Abend ~:** ruin sb.'s evening; **c)** *(geh.: negativ beeinflussen)* corrupt; deprave; **er will es mit niemandem ~:** he tries to please everybody; he likes to keep in with everybody. **3.** *unr. refl. V.* **sich** *(Dat.)* **den Magen/die Augen ~:** give oneself an upset stomach/ruin one's eyesight

Verderben das; ~s undoing; ruin; *(Theol.)* destruction; **sie sind ins/in ihr ~ gerannt** they rushed headlong towards ruin

verderben·bringend *Adj.* disastrous ‹*policy*›; deadly ‹*weapon, disease, etc.*›

Verderber der; ~s, ~: destroyer; **ein ~ der Jugend** a corrupter of youth

verderblich *Adj.* **a)** perishable ‹*food*›; **leicht ~:** highly perishable; **b)** *(unheilvoll)* pernicious; *(moralisch schädlich)* corrupting; pernicious ‹*influence, effect, etc.*›

Verderblichkeit die; ~: *s.* **verderblich:** perishableness; perniciousness; corrupting effect

verderbt *Adj.* **a)** *(geh. veralt.: verdorben)* corrupt; depraved; **b)** *(Literaturw.)* illegible

Verderbtheit die; ~ *(geh. veralt.: Verdorbenheit)* corruptness; depravity

verdeutlichen *tr. V.* **etw. ~:** make sth. clear; *(erklären)* explain sth.; **etw. näher ~:** clarify sth. further

verdeutschen *tr. V.* **a)** *(veralt.: übersetzen)* translate into German; *(eindeutschen)* Germanize ‹*name*›; **b)** *(ugs.: erläutern)* put ‹*facts etc.*› more plainly; translate ‹*instruction, officialese, etc.*› into everyday *or* ordinary language

verdichten 1. *refl. V.* ‹*fog, smoke*› thicken, become thicker; *(fig.)* ‹*suspicion, rumour*› grow; ‹*feeling*› intensify. **2.** *tr. V.* **a)** *(Physik, Technik)* compress; *(fig.)* condense ‹*events etc.*› **(zu** into); **b)** *(ausbauen)* increase the density of ‹*road network, public transport*›

verdicken 1. *refl. V.* ‹*hard skin*› thicken, become thicker; *(anschwellen)* ‹*finger, jaw, etc.*› swell. **2.** *tr. V.* thicken ‹*sauce*›; *(gelieren lassen)* cause ‹*fruit juice etc.*› to set

Verdickung die; ~, **~en a)** thickening; *(Schwellung)* swelling; **b)** *(verdickte Stelle) (einer Arterie)* thickened section; *(Schwellung)* swelling

verdienen 1. *tr. V.* **a)** *(in Form von Geld)* earn; **sauer/ehrlich verdientes Geld** hard-/honestly-earned money; **b)** *(wert sein)* deserve; **er verdient kein Vertrauen** he doesn't deserve to be trusted; **er hat es nicht besser/nicht anders verdient** he didn't deserve any better/anything else; **womit habe ich das verdient?** what have I done to deserve that?; **er hat die verdiente Strafe bekommen** he got the punishment he deserved. **2.** *itr. V.* **beide Eheleute ~:** husband and wife are both wage-earners *or* are both earning; **gut ~:** have a good income

Verdiener der; ~s, ~: wage-earner; **die Mutter ist der ~:** the mother is the breadwinner

¹Verdienst der income; earnings *pl.*

²Verdienst das; ~[e]s, ~e merit; **sich** *(Dat.)* **etw. als** *od.* **zum ~ anrechnen** take the credit for sth.; **er hat sich** *(Dat.)* **große ~e um die Stadt erworben** he made a great contribution to the town

Verdienst-: ~aus·fall der loss of earnings; **~kreuz das** *national decoration awarded for service to the community*; **~orden der** order of merit

verdienst·voll 1. *Adj.* **a)** *(lobenswert)* commendable; **b)** *nicht präd. (verdient)* ‹*person*› of outstanding merit. **2.** *adv. (lobenswert)* commendably

verdient 1. *Adj.* **a)** ‹*person*› of outstanding merit; **sich um etw. ~ machen** render outstanding services to sth.; **b)** *(gerecht, zustehend)* well-deserved. **2.** *adv.* deservedly

verdientermaßen *Adv.* deservedly

Verdikt [vɛrˈdɪkt] **das;** ~[e]s, ~e *(geh.)* verdict

verdingen *unr. od. regelm. refl. V. (veralt.)* go into service **(bei** with); go to work **(bei** for)

verdinglichen *(Philos.) tr. V.* reify

Verdinglichung die; ~, **~en** *(Philos.)* reification

verdolmetschen *tr. V. (ugs.)* interpret, translate *(Dat.* for)

verdonnern *tr. V. (salopp)* sentence; **zu einem Bußgeld verdonnert werden** be ordered to pay a fine; **jmdn. dazu ~, etw. zu tun** order *or* make sb. do sth. [as a punishment]; **jmdn. zu einer Strafarbeit ~:** give sb. an imposition

verdoppeln 1. *tr. V.* double; *(fig.)* double, redouble ‹*efforts etc.*›. **2.** *refl. V.* double

Verdoppelung die; ~, **~en** doubling

verdorben [fɛɐ̯ˈdɔrbn̩] *2. Part. v.* **verderben**

Verdorbenheit die; ~: depravity

verdorren [fɛɐ̯ˈdɔrən] *itr. V.; mit sein* wither [and die]; ‹*meadow*› scorch

verdrängen *tr. V.* **a)** *(wegdrängen)* drive out ‹*inhabitants*›; *(fig.: ersetzen)* displace; **das Schiff verdrängt 15 000 Tonnen** the ship displaces 15,000 tons; **jmdn. aus seiner Stellung ~:** oust sb. from his/her job; **b)** *(Psych.)* repress/*(bewußt)* suppress ‹*experience, desire, etc.*›

Verdrängung die; ~, **~en a)** *s.* **verdrängen a:** driving out; displacement; ousting; **b)** *(Psych.)* repression; *(bewußt)* suppression

Verdrängungs·wettbewerb der *(Kaufmannsspr.)* competition for markets

verdrecken *(ugs. abwertend)* **1.** *tr. V.* make filthy dirty. **2.** *itr. V.; mit sein* get *or* become filthy dirty

verdrehen *tr. V.* **a)** twist ‹*joint*›; roll ‹*eyes*›; **den Hals ~:** twist one's head round; **sich** *(Dat.)* **den Hals ~:** crick one's neck; **jmdm. das Handgelenk ~:** twist sb.'s wrist; *s. auch* **Kopf e; b)** *(ugs. abwertend: entstellen)* twist ‹*words, facts, etc.*›; distort ‹*sense*›

verdreht *Adj. (ugs. abwertend)* crazy

Verdrehtheit die; ~ *(ugs. abwertend) (Verrücktheit)* craziness; *(Verwirrung)* confusion

verdreifachen *refl., tr. V.* treble; triple

verdreschen *unr. tr. V. (ugs.)* thrash

verdrießen [fɛɐ̯ˈdriːsn̩] *unr. tr. V. (geh.)* irritate; annoy; **es sich nicht ~ lassen** *(geh.)* not be put off

verdrießlich 1. *Adj.* **a)** *(mißmutig)* morose; **b)** *(geh., veralt.: unangenehm)* irksome ‹*task, matter, etc.*›. **2.** *adv. (mißmutig)* morosely

Verdrießlichkeit die; ~, **~en a)** *o. Pl. (Mißmut)* moroseness; **b)** *meist Pl. (unangenehmer Vorgang)* irksome thing/matter *etc.*

verdroß [fɛɐ̯ˈdrɔs] *1. u. 3. Pers. Sg. Prät. v.* **verdrießen**

verdrossen 1. *2. Part. v.* **verdrießen. 2.** *Adj. (mißmutig)* morose; *(mißmutig und lustlos)* sullen. **3.** *adv. (mißmutig)* morosely; *(mißmutig und lustlos)* sullenly

Verdrossenheit die; ~ *s.* **verdrossen 2:** moroseness; sullenness

verdrücken *(ugs.)* **1.** *tr. V.* **a)** *(essen)* polish off *(coll.)*; **b)** *(verknautschen)* crumple ‹*clothes*›. **2.** *refl. V.* slip away

Verdruß [fɛɐ̯ˈdrʊs] **der; Verdrusses, Verdrusse** annoyance; *(Unzufriedenheit)* dissatisfaction; discontentment; **jmdm. ~ bereiten** annoy sb.

verduften *itr. V.; mit sein* **a)** *(Duft verlieren)* ‹*coffee*› lose its aroma; ‹*aroma*› go; **b)** *(salopp: sich entfernen)* hop it *(Brit. sl.)*; clear off *(coll.)*

verdummen 1. *tr. V.* **jmdn. ~:** dull sb.'s mind. **2.** *itr. V.; mit sein* become stultified

Verdummung die; ~ **a) die ~ der Massen zum Ziel haben** be aimed at dulling the mind of the masses; **b)** *(das Dummwerden)* stultification

verdunkeln 1. *tr. V.* **a)** darken; *(vollständig)* black out ‹*room, house, etc.*›; **b)** *(verdecken)* darken; *(fig.)* cast a shadow on ‹*happiness etc.*›; **c)** *(bes. Rechtsw.)* obscure ‹*facts, situation, etc.*›. **2.** *refl. V.* darken; grow darker; *(fig.)* ‹*expression etc.*› darken

Verdunkelung die; ~, **~en a)** *(das Verdunkeln)* darkening; *(vollständig)* black-out; **b)** *(Vorrichtung)* black-out blind[s]/curtain[s]; **c)** *o. Pl. (bes. Rechtsw.)* obscuring; obscuration

Verdunkelungs·gefahr die; *o. Pl. (Rechtsw.)* danger of suppression of evidence

Verdunklung die; ~, ~en *s.* **Verdunkelung**
verdünnen *tr. V.* **a)** dilute; *(mit Wasser)* water down; dilute; thin [down] ⟨*paint etc.*⟩; **b)** *(dünner machen)* taper [off] ⟨*stick etc.*⟩; **c)** *(Militärjargon)* reduce the number of ⟨*troops etc.*⟩ [in an/the area]
verdünnisieren *refl. V. (salopp)* clear off *(coll.)*
Verdünner der; ~s, ~, **Verdünnungsmittel das** thinner; *(in der Industrie)* diluent
Verdünnung die; ~, ~en **a)** dilution; *(der Luft)* rarefaction; **b)** *(chem. Mittel)* thinner
verdunsten 1. *itr. V.; mit sein* evaporate. **2.** *tr. V.* evaporate; ⟨*plant*⟩ transpire ⟨*water*⟩
Verdunstung die; ~: evaporation
verdursten *itr. V.; mit sein (auch fig.)* die of thirst
verdüstern 1. *tr. V.* darken; *(fig. geh.)* cast a shadow across. **2.** *refl. V.* darken; grow dark; *(fig.)* darken
verdutzt [fɛɐ̯ˈdʊtst] *Adj.* taken aback *pred.*; nonplussed; *(verwirrt)* baffled; ~ **hielt er inne** taken aback *or* nonplussed, he paused
Verdutztheit die; ~: bafflement
verebben *itr. V.; mit sein (geh.)* subside
veredeln *tr. V.* **a)** *(geh.)* ennoble; improve ⟨*taste*⟩; **b)** *(Technik)* refine; beneficiate ⟨*coal*⟩; **c)** *(Gartenbau)* graft
Vered[e]lung die; ~, ~en **a)** *(geh.)* ennoblement; *(des Geschmacks)* improvement; **b)** *(Technik)* refinement; *(von Kohle)* beneficiation; **c)** *(Gartenbau)* grafting
verehelichen *refl. V. (Papierdt., veralt.)* **sich jmdm.** ~: marry sb.; **Else Müller, verehelichte Meyer** Else Meyer, née Müller
Verehelichung die; ~, ~en *(Papierdt., veralt.)* marriage (**mit** to)
verehren *tr. V.* **a)** *(vergöttern)* venerate; revere; **[sehr] verehrte Anwesende!** Ladies and Gentlemen; *(in Briefanreden)* **verehrte gnädige Frau!** [Dear] Madam; **verehrte Frau Müller!** Dear Frau Müller; **b)** *(geh.: bewundern)* admire; *(ehrerbietig lieben)* worship; adore; **c)** *(scherzh.: schenken)* give; **darf ich Ihnen dieses Buch ~?** may I make you a little gift of this book?
Verehrer der; ~s, ~, **Verehrerin die;** ~, ~en admirer
Verehrung die; *o. Pl.* **a)** veneration; reverence; **b)** *(Bewunderung)* admiration
verehrungs·würdig *Adj.* admirable
vereidigen [fɛɐ̯ˈ|aidɪɡn̩] *tr. V.* swear in; **einen Zeugen vor Gericht** ~: swear in a witness; **jmdn. auf etw.** *(Akk.)* ~: make sb. swear to sth.; **ein vereidigter Sachverständiger** a sworn expert
Vereidigung die; ~, ~en swearing in
Verein der; ~[e]s, ~e **a)** organization; *(zur Förderung der Denkmalspflege usw.)* society; *(der Kunstfreunde usw.)* association; society; *(Sport~)* club; *(fig. ugs.)* crowd *(coll.)*; *(kleiner)* bunch *(coll.)*; **b) im ~ [mit]** in conjunction with; together with; **in trautem ~ [mit]** *(scherzh.)* in an unlikely twosome/group [with]
vereinbar *Adj.; nicht attr.* compatible (**mit** with); **nicht** ~: incompatible; **etw. ist mit etw. nur schwerlich** ~: it is difficult to reconcile sth. with sth.
vereinbaren *tr. V.* **a)** *(festlegen)* agree; arrange ⟨*meeting etc.*⟩; **b)** *(harmonieren)* **[nicht] zu ~ sein, sich [nicht] ~ lassen** be [in]compatible *or* [ir]reconcilable; **etw. mit etw. [nicht] ~ können** [not] be able to reconcile sth. with sth.
Vereinbarung die; ~, ~en **a)** *(das Festlegen)* agreeing; *(eines Termins usw.)* arranging; **b)** *(Abmachung)* agreement; **eine ~ treffen** come to an agreement
vereinbarungs·gemäß 1. *Adj.* as agreed/arranged *postpos.* **2.** *adv.* as agreed/arranged
vereinen 1. *tr. V.* **a)** *(zusammenfassen)* unite; merge ⟨*businesses*⟩ (**zu** into); **b)** *(harmonisieren)* reconcile; **c)** *(besitzen)* combine; **er vereint alle Kompetenzen in seiner Hand** he combines all responsibilities. **2.** *refl. V.* **a) sich zu gemeinsamem Handeln ~:** join forces; **b)** *(vorhanden sein)* combine; **in ihr ~ sich Geist und Anmut** in her, beauty and intellect are united
vereinfachen *tr. V.* simplify
Vereinfachung die; ~, ~en simplification
vereinheitlichen *tr. V.* standardize
Vereinheitlichung die; ~, ~en standardization
vereinigen 1. *tr. V.* **a)** *(zusammenschließen)* unite; merge ⟨*businesses*⟩; **b)** *(zusammenfassen)* bring together; **alle Ämter sind in einer Person vereinigt** all offices are held by the same person; **die Mehrheit der Stimmen auf sich ~:** receive the majority of the votes. **2.** *refl. V.* **a)** *(sich zusammenschließen)* unite; ⟨*organizations, firms*⟩ merge; *(fig.)* be combined; **b)** *(zusammentreffen)* assemble (**zu** for); ⟨*rivers*⟩ meet, merge; **Fulda und Werra ~ sich zur Weser** the Fulda and the Werra meet and form the Weser; **c)** *(geh.: sich paaren)* couple
vereinigt *Adj.* **Vereinigte Arabische Emirate** United Arab Emirates; **Vereinigtes Königreich [Großbritannien und Nordirland]** United Kingdom [of Great Britain and Northern Ireland]; **Vereinigte Staaten [von Amerika]** United States *sing.* [of America]
Vereinigung die a) *(Rechtsw.)* organization; **b)** *(Zusammenschluß)* uniting; *(von Unternehmen)* merging; **c)** *(geh.: Koitus)* union; **d)** *(Zusammentreffen)* assembly; *(von Flüssen)* meeting; merging
Vereinigungs-: ~freiheit die *s.* **Koalitionsfreiheit; ~menge die** *(Math.)* union of sets
vereinnahmen *tr. V. (Kaufmannsspr.)* take; collect ⟨*dividend*⟩; *(fig.)* monopolize
vereinsamen *itr. V.; mit sein* become [increasingly] lonely *or* isolated
Vereinsamung die; ~: loneliness; isolation
Vereins-: ~freiheit die freedom of association; **~kamerad der** fellow club *etc.* member; **~lokal das** club's *etc.* local pub *(Brit. coll.)*/meeting room; **~meier der** *(ugs. abwertend)* [real] clubman; enthusiast for club life; **~meierei die;** *o. Pl. (ugs. abwertend)* enthusiasm for club life
vereinzeln *tr. V.* **a)** *(geh.)* isolate; **b)** *(Forstw., Landw.)* thin out
vereinzelt 1. *Adj.; nicht präd.* occasional; isolated, occasional ⟨*shower, outbreak of rain, etc.*⟩; **in ~en Fällen** in isolated cases. **2.** *adv. (zeitlich)* occasionally; now and then; *(örtlich)* here and there
Vereinzelung die; ~, ~en isolation
vereisen 1. *itr. V.; mit sein* freeze *or* ice over; ⟨*wing*⟩ ice up; ⟨*lock*⟩ freeze up; **eine vereiste Fahrbahn** an icy carriageway. **2.** *tr. V. (Med.)* freeze
Vereisung die; ~, ~en **a)** freezing *or* icing over; *(einer Tragfläche)* icing up; *(eines Schlosses)* freezing up; **b)** *(Med.)* freezing
vereiteln *tr. V.* thwart; prevent; thwart, foil ⟨*attempt, plan, etc.*⟩; thwart, frustrate ⟨*efforts, intentions, etc.*⟩
Vereitelung die; ~ *s.* **vereiteln:** thwarting; prevention; foiling; frustrating
vereitern *itr. V.; mit sein* go septic; **vereitert sein** be septic; **dieser Zahn ist vereitert** this tooth has an abscess
Vereiterung die suppuration; *(eines Zahns)* abscess
verekeln *tr. V.* **jmdm. etw. ~:** put sb. off sth.
verelenden *itr. V.; mit sein (geh., Soziol.)* sink into poverty
Verelendung die; ~, ~en *(geh., Soziol.)* impoverishment
Verelendungs·theorie die *(Soziol.)* theory of the pauperization of the proletariat
verenden *itr. V.; mit sein* perish; die
verengen 1. *refl. V.* narrow; become narrow; ⟨*pupils*⟩ contract; ⟨*blood-vessel*⟩ constrict, become constricted. **2.** *tr. V.* make narrower; narrow; restrict, narrow ⟨*field of vision etc.*⟩; make ⟨*circle, loop*⟩ smaller
Verengung die; ~, ~en **a)** *(das [Sich]verengen)* narrowing; *(eines Blutgefäßes)* constriction; **b)** *(verengte Stelle)* narrow part
vererben 1. *tr. V.* **a)** leave, bequeath ⟨*property*⟩ (*Dat.*, **an** + *Akk.* to); *(fig.: schenken)* bequeath *(joc.)* (*Dat.* to); **b)** *(Biol., Med.)* transmit, pass on ⟨*characteristic, disease*⟩; pass on ⟨*talent*⟩ (*Dat.*, **auf** + *Akk.* to). **2.** *refl. V. (Biol., Med.)* ⟨*disease, tendency*⟩ be passed on *or* transmitted (**auf** + *Akk.* to)
vererblich *Adj.* heritable ⟨*goods, property*⟩
Vererbung die; ~, ~en *(Biol., Med.)* heredity *no art.*; **das ist ~:** it runs in the family
Vererbungs·lehre die genetics *sing., no art.*
verewigen 1. *tr. V.* immortalize; *(andauern lassen)* perpetuate ⟨*situation etc.*⟩; preserve ⟨*text*⟩ for posterity. **2.** *refl. V. (ugs.: Spuren hinterlassen)* leave one's mark
[1]**verfahren 1.** *unr. refl. V.* lose one's way. **2.** *unr. tr. V.* use up ⟨*petrol*⟩; **50 DM mit dem Taxi ~:** spend 50 marks on a taxi/taxis. **3.** *unr. itr. V.; mit sein* **a)** *(handeln)* proceed; **b)** *(umgehen)* **mit jmdm./etw. ~:** deal with sb./sth.
[2]**verfahren** *Adj.* dead-end ⟨*situation*⟩
Verfahren das; ~s, ~ **a)** procedure; *(Technik)* process; *(Methode)* method; **b)** *(Rechtsw.)* proceedings *pl.*
Verfahrens-: ~frage die question *or* matter of procedure; procedural question *or* matter; **~technik die** process engineering *no art.*; **~weise die** procedure; method of proceeding; modus operandi
Verfall der; *o. Pl.* **a)** decay; dilapidation; *(fig.: der Preise, einer Währung)* collapse; **mit der Pensionierung begann sein gesundheitlicher ~:** on retirement his health started to deteriorate; **b)** *(Auflösung)* decline; **sittlicher ~:** moral degeneracy; **c)** *(das Ungültigwerden)* expiry
-verfall der: Dollar-/Währungs-~: collapse of the dollar/currency; **Preis-~:** collapse of prices
verfallen *unr. itr. V.; mit sein* **a)** *(baufällig werden)* fall into disrepair; become dilapidated; **b)** *(körperlich)*⟨*strength*⟩ decline; **der Kranke verfiel zusehends** the patient went into a rapid decline; **c)** *(untergehen)* ⟨*empire*⟩ decline; ⟨*morals, morale*⟩ deteriorate; **d)** *(ungültig werden)* expire; **e)** *(hörig werden)* **jmdm. ~:** become a slave; **einem Irrtum ~:** fall a victim to an error; **dem Alkohol ~:** become addicted to alcohol; **jmdm. ~ sein** be completely captivated by sb.; **f)** *(geraten)* **in einen Schlummer ~:** sink into a doze; **in den alten Fehler/Ton ~:** make the same old mistake/adopt the same old tone; **g)** *(übergehen)* **in seinen Dialekt ~:** lapse into one's dialect; **das Pferd verfiel in [einen] Trab** the horse broke into a trot; **h) auf jmdn./etw. ~:** think of sb./sth.; **auf einen sonderbaren Gedanken ~:** hit upon a strange idea; **warum seid ihr gerade auf uns ~?** what made you turn to us?; **i)** *(zufallen)* **dem Staat ~:** be forfeited to the state
Verfalls-: ~datum das use-by date; *(ugs.: Mindesthaltbarkeitsdatum)* best-before date; **~erscheinung die** symptom of decline (*Gen.* in); *(in der Sprache)* sign of deterioration
verfälschen *tr. V.* distort, misrepresent ⟨*statement, message*⟩; falsify, misrepresent ⟨*facts, history, truth*⟩; falsify ⟨*painting, banknote*⟩; adulterate ⟨*wine, milk, etc.*⟩
Verfälschung die *s.* **verfälschen:** distortion; misrepresentation; falsification; adulteration

verfangen 1. *unr. refl. V.* get caught; *(fig.)* become entangled (**in** + *Dat.* in); **sich in Widersprüchen ~** *(fig.)* contradict oneself. **2.** *unr. itr. V.* have the desired effect; **wenig/nicht ~:** have little/no effect; **solche Tricks ~ bei mir nicht** such tricks cut no ice with me *(sl.)*; such tricks won't get you/him *etc.* anywhere *or* won't work with me

verfänglich [fɛɐ̯'fɛŋlɪç] *Adj.* awkward, embarrassing ‹*situation, question, etc.*›; incriminating ‹*evidence, letter, etc.*›

verfärben 1. *refl. V.* change colour; ‹*washing*› become discoloured; ‹*leaves*› turn; **sich rot ~:** change colour to red/be stained red/turn red. **2.** *tr. V.* discolour

Verfärbung die a) *(das [Sich]verfärben)* change of colour; **b)** *(verfärbte Stelle)* discoloration; discoloured patch

verfassen *tr. V.* write; write, compose ‹*poetry*›; write, draw up ‹*document, law, etc.*›; draw up ‹*resolution*›

Verfasser der; ~s, ~, Verfasserin die; ~, ~nen writer; *(eines Buchs, Artikels usw.)* author; writer

Verfasserschaft die; ~: authorship

Verfassung die a) *(Politik)* constitution; **b)** *o. Pl. (Zustand)* state [of health/mind]; **in guter/schlechter ~ sein** be in good/poor shape; **in bester ~:** on top form; **nicht in der ~ sein, Witze zu machen** not be in a joking mood; be in no mood to joke *or* to make jokes

verfassung·gebend *Adj.; nicht präd.* constituent ‹*assembly, power, etc.*›

verfassungs-, Verfassungs-: ~änderung die constitutional amendment; **~beschwerde die** *(Rechtsw.)* complaint about an infringement/infringements of the constitution *(committed by the State)*; **~bruch der** breach of the constitution; **~feindlich** *Adj.* anticonstitutional; **~gericht das** constitutional court; **~konform** *Adj.; nicht attr.* in conformity with the constitution; **~mäßig 1.** *Adj.* constitutional; **2.** *adv.* constitutionally; in accordance with a/the constitution; **~schutz der a)** defence *or* protection of the constitution; **b)** *(Ämter)* authorities responsible for the defence *or* protection of the constitution

verfaulen *itr. V.; mit sein* rot; *(fig.)*‹*system, social order*› decay; *(fig.: moralisch)* degenerate

verfechten *unr. tr. V. (eintreten für)* advocate, champion ‹*theory, hypothesis, etc.*›; uphold ‹*view*›; *(verteidigen)* defend

Verfechter der, Verfechterin die; ~, ~nen advocate; champion

verfehlen *tr. V.* **a)** *(verpassen)* miss ‹*train, person, etc.*›; **b)** *(vorbeigehen)* miss ‹*goal, target, etc.*›; **er hat seinen Beruf verfehlt** *(fig.)* he has missed his true vocation *or* is in the wrong job; **eine verfehlte Politik** *(fig.)* an unsuccessful policy; *s. auch* **Thema a**

Verfehlung die; ~, ~en misdemeanour; *(Rel.: Sünde)* transgression

verfeinden *refl. V.* **sich ~ mit** make an enemy of; **verfeindet sein** be enemies; **sie hatten sich wegen einer Kleinigkeit verfeindet** they had fallen out over a trifling matter

verfeinern [fɛɐ̯'fainɐn] **1.** *tr. V.* improve; refine ‹*method, procedure, sense*›. **2.** *refl. V.* improve; ‹*method, procedure, sense*› be refined

Verfeinerung die; ~, ~en a) *s.* **verfeinern 1, 2:** improvement; refinement; **etw. zur ~ tun** do sth. as a refinement; **b)** *(etwas Verfeinertes)* refinement

verfemen *tr. V. (geh.)* outlaw ‹*person, act*›; *(verbieten)* ban; *(innerhalb einer Gruppe)* ostracize ‹*person*›

Verfemte der/die; *adj. Dekl. (geh.)* outlaw; *(fig.)* ostracized person

verfertigen *tr. V.* produce; make; produce ‹*document*›

Verfertigung die production

verfestigen 1. *tr. V.* harden; *(verstärken)* reinforce; strengthen. **2.** *refl. V.* harden; *(verstärkt werden)* be reinforced *or* strengthened; *(sich etablieren)* become firmly established (**zu** + *Dat.* as)

Verfestigung die hardening; *(Verstärkung)* reinforcement; strengthening

verfetten *itr. V.; mit sein* become [too] fat

verfeuern *tr. V.* **a)** burn; **alles Holz verfeuert haben** have used up all the wood; **b)** *(verschießen)* fire; **alle Munition war verfeuert** all the ammunition had been used up

verfilmen *tr. V.* **a)** film; make a film of; **der Roman wird jetzt verfilmt** the novel is now being made into a film; **b)** *(auf Mikrofilm aufnehmen)* microfilm

Verfilmung die; ~, ~en a) *(das Verfilmen)* filming; **b)** *(Film)* film [version]

verfilzen *itr. V.; mit sein* ‹*fabric, garment*› felt; become felted; ‹*hair*› become matted

verfinstern 1. *tr. V.* obscure ‹*sun etc.*›. **2.** *refl. V. (auch fig.)* darken

Verfinsterung die; ~, ~en darkening

verflachen 1. *itr. V.; mit sein* ‹*ground*› flatten *or* level out, become flatter; ‹*water*› become shallow; *(fig.)* ‹*discussion*› become superficial *or* trivial. **2.** *refl. V.* ‹*ground*› flatten *or* level out. **3.** *tr. V.* flatten; level

verflechten *unr. tr. V.* interweave; intertwine; interlace; *(verwickeln)* involve; **[eng/innig] miteinander verflochten sein** *(fig.)* be [closely/intimately] interlinked

Verflechtung die; ~, ~en interconnection; *(Verwicklung)* involvement; **eine gegenseitige finanzielle ~:** a financial link-up

verfliegen 1. *unr. refl. V.* ‹*pilot*› lose one's way; ‹*aircraft*› get off course. **2.** *unr. itr. V.; mit sein* **a)** *(verschwinden)* ‹*smoke*› disperse, vanish; ‹*scent, smell*› fade, disappear; ‹*mood, tiredness*› evaporate; **b)** *(sich verflüchtigen)* ‹*alcohol etc.*› evaporate; **c)** *(vorübergehen)* ‹*time*› fly by; ‹*anger*› pass

verfließen *unr. itr. V.; mit sein* **a)** *(verschwimmen)* merge; ‹*colours*› run; **b)** *(geh.: vergehen)* go by; pass

verflixt [fɛɐ̯'flɪkst] *(ugs.)* **1.** *Adj.* **a)** *(ärgerlich)* akward, unpleasant ‹*situation, business, etc.*›; **b)** *(abwertend: verdammt)* blasted *(Brit.)*; blessed; confounded; **~ [noch mal]!, ~ noch eins!, ~ und zugenäht!** [damn and] blast *(Brit. coll.)*; **c)** *nicht präd. (sehr groß)* **er hat ~es Glück gehabt** he was damned lucky *(coll.)*. **2.** *adv. (sehr)* damned *(coll.)*; **das sieht ~ nach Betrug aus** that looks damned close to fraud *(coll.)*

verflossen 1. *2. Part. v.* **verfließen. 2.** *Adj. (ugs.)* former; **seine ~e Freundin** his ex-girlfriend; **mein Verflossener/meine Verflossene** my ex *(coll.)*

verfluchen *tr. V.* curse

verflucht 1. *Adj. (salopp)* **a)** *(verdammt)* damned *(coll.)*; bloody *(Brit. sl.)*; **verflucht [noch mal]!, verflucht und zugenäht!** *(derb)* damn [it] *(coll.)*; **b)** *nicht präd. (sehr groß)* **wir hatten ~es Glück/Pech** we were damned lucky/unlucky *(coll.)*. **2.** *adv. (sehr)* damned *(coll.)*

verflüchtigen 1. *tr. V. (bes. Chemie)* evaporate. **2.** *refl. V.* **a)** *(in Gas übergehen)* ‹*alcohol etc.*› evaporate; **b)** *(sich auflösen)* disperse; ‹*smell*› disappear; *(fig.)* ‹*fear, astonishment*› subside; ‹*cheerfulness, mockery*› vanish; ‹*time of youth*› be dissipated; **c)** *(ugs. scherzh.: sich davonmachen)* make oneself scarce *(coll.)*

verflüssigen *(bes. Chemie, Physik)* **1.** *tr. V.* liquefy. **2.** *refl. V.* liquefy; become liquid

Verflüssigung die; ~, ~en liquefaction

verfolgen *tr. V.* **a)** pursue; hunt, track ‹*animal*›; **jmdn. auf Schritt und Tritt ~:** follow sb. wherever he/she goes; **der Gedanke daran verfolgte ihn** *(fig.)* the thought of it haunted him; **vom Pech verfolgt sein** *(fig.)* be dogged by bad luck; **jmdn. mit Blicken** *od.* **den Augen ~** *(fig.)* follow sb. with one's eyes; **b)** *(bedrängen)* plague; **jmdn. mit Bitten ~:** badger sb. with requests; **er verfolgte sie mit seiner Eifersucht** because he was jealous, he would not leave her in peace; **c)** *(bedrohen)* persecute; **politisch verfolgt sein** *od.* **werden** be a victim of political persecution; **d)** *(folgen)* follow ‹*path etc.*›; **e)** *(zu verwirklichen suchen)* pursue ‹*policy, plan, career, idea, purpose, etc.*›; **f)** *(beobachten)* follow ‹*conversation, events, trial, developments, etc.*›; **g) etw. [strafrechtlich] ~:** prosecute sth.

Verfolger der; ~s, ~, Verfolgerin die; ~, ~nen pursuer; *(Häscher)* persecutor

Verfolgte der/die; *adj. Dekl.* victim of persecution

Verfolgung die; ~, ~en a) *(das Hinterhereilen)* pursuit; **die ~ aufnehmen** take up the chase; **b)** *(Bedrohung)* persecution; **c)** *s.* **verfolgen e:** pursuance; **d) [strafrechtliche] ~:** prosecution

Verfolgungs-: ~jagd die pursuit; chase; **~rennen das** *(Radsport)* pursuit race; **~wahn der** *(Psych.)* persecution mania

verformbar *Adj.* malleable; workable

verformen 1. *tr. V.* **a)** make ‹*object*› go out of shape; distort; **b)** *(Technik)* work ‹*steel, plastic, etc.*›. **2.** *refl. V.* go out of shape; distort; become distorted

Verformung die distortion

verfrachten *tr. V.* transport; *(mit dem Schiff)* ship; **jmdn. ins Bett/in einen Streifenwagen ~** *(fig.)* bundle sb. into bed/into a patrol car

verfranzen [fɛɐ̯'frantsn̩] *refl. V.* **a)** *(Fliegerjargon)* stray off course; **b)** *(ugs.: sich verirren)* lose one's way

verfremden *tr. V.* **[jmdm.] etw. ~:** make sth. [appear] unfamiliar [to sb.]; *(Theaterw., Kunstw.)* distance sth. [from sb.]

Verfremdung die; ~, ~en *(Theaterw., Kunstw.)* alienation; distancing

Verfremdungs·effekt der *(Theaterw.)* alienation *or* distancing effect

[1]**verfressen** *unr. tr. V. (salopp)* blow *(sl.)* ‹*money*› on food

[2]**verfressen** *Adj. (salopp abwertend)* piggish *(coll.)*; greedy

Verfressenheit die; ~ *(salopp abwertend)* piggishness *(coll.)*; greediness

verfroren *Adj.* **a)** *(durchgefroren)* frozen; freezing cold; **b)** *(leicht frierend)* sensitive to the cold; **~ sein** feel the cold

verfrühen *refl. V.* arrive *or* come *or* be too early; **diese Maßnahme halte ich für verfrüht** I consider this measure to be premature

verfügbar *Adj.* available; **nicht ~:** unavailable

Verfügbarkeit die; ~: availability

verfügen 1. *tr. V. (anordnen)* order; *(dekretieren)* decree; **in seinem Testament ~, daß ...:** decree in one's will that .... **2.** *itr. V.* **a)** *(bestimmen)* **über etw.** *(Akk.)* **[frei] ~ können** be free to decide what to do with sth.; **über jmdn. ~:** tell sb. what to do; **bitte ~ Sie über mich!** *(geh.)* I am at your disposal; **b)** *(haben)* **über etw.** *(Akk.)* **~:** have sth. at one's disposal; **über gute Beziehungen/große Erfahrung ~:** have good connections/great experience. **3.** *refl. V. (veralt., scherzh.: sich begeben)* proceed

Verfügung die; ~, ~en a) *(Anordnung)* order; *(Dekret)* decree; **eine ~ erlassen** issue a decree; **seine letztwilligen ~en** his last will and testament; **~en treffen** make provision *sing.*; **„~ von Todes wegen"** *(Amtsspr.)* 'Last Will and Testament'; *s. auch* **einstweilig; b)** *o. Pl. (Disposition)* **etw. zur ~ haben** have sth. at one's disposal; **jmdm. etw. zur ~ stellen** put sth. at sb.'s disposal; **sein Amt zur ~ stellen** offer to give up one's post *or* office; **jmdm. zur ~ stehen** be at sb.'s disposal; **sich zur ~ halten** hold oneself ready

Verfügungs·gewalt die power of disposal; ~ **über etw.** *(Akk.)* **haben** *(fig.)* have power over sth.

verführen 1. *tr. V.* **a)** *(verleiten)* tempt; **jmdn. zum Trinken** ~: encourage sb. to take up drinking; **jmdn. zu einem Bier** ~ *(scherzh.)* tempt sb. to a beer; **b)** *(sexuell)* seduce. **2.** *itr. V.* **zu etw.** ~: be a temptation to sth.

Verführer der seducer

Verführerin die seductress

verführerisch 1. *Adj.* **a)** *(verlockend)* tempting; **b)** *(aufreizend)* seductive. **2.** *adv.* **a)** *(verlockend)* temptingly; **b)** *(aufreizend)* seductively

Verführung die a) temptation; **b)** *(sexuell)* seduction; **c)** *(Reiz)* enticement

verfüttern *tr. V.* **a)** feed (+ *Dat.* to); **b)** *(verbrauchen)* use [up] as animal/bird food

Vergabe die allocation; *(eines Auftrages)* placing; awarding; *(eines Stipendiums, eines Preises)* award

vergackeiern [fɛɐ̯'gak|aiɐn] *tr. V. (salopp)* **jmdn.** ~: pull sb.'s leg *(coll.)*

vergaffen *refl. V. (ugs.)* **sich in jmdn.** ~: fall for sb.

vergällen [fɛɐ̯'gɛlən] *tr. V.* **a)** *(verderben)* spoil ⟨*enjoyment etc.*⟩; sour ⟨*life*⟩; **b)** *(bes. Chemie)* denature; denaturalize

vergaloppieren *refl. V. (ugs.)* drop a clanger *(sl.)*; *(zu schnell vorgehen)* fall over oneself

vergammeln *(ugs.)* **1.** *itr. V.; mit sein* ⟨*food*⟩ go bad. **2.** *tr. V.* waste ⟨*time*⟩; **den ganzen Sonntag im Bett** ~: idle away the whole of Sunday in bed

vergammelt *Adj. (ugs. abwertend)* scruffy *(coll.)*; tatty *(coll.)*; tatty *(coll.)*, decrepit ⟨*vehicle*⟩

vergangen [fɛɐ̯'gaŋən] **1.** *2. Part. v.* **vergehen. 2.** *Adj.; nicht präd.* **a)** *(vorüber, vorbei)* bygone, former ⟨*times, years, etc.*⟩; **die ~e Sitzung** the previous *or* last meeting; **b)** *(letzt...)* last ⟨*year, Sunday, week, etc.*⟩; **c)** *(ehemalig)* former

Vergangenheit die; ~, ~**en a)** *o. Pl. (Zeit)* past; **die jüngste** ~: the recent past; **etw. gehört der** ~ **an** sth. is a thing of the past; **einen Strich unter die** ~ **ziehen** let bygones be bygones; **b)** *(Leben)* past; *(einer Stadt usw.)* past; history; **eine Frau mit** ~: a woman with a past; **c)** *(Grammatik)* past tense

Vergangenheits·bewältigung die; *o. Pl.* coming to terms with the past

vergänglich [fɛɐ̯'gɛŋlɪç] *Adj.* transient; transitory; ephemeral; **alles Irdische ist** ~: all earthly things will pass away

Vergänglichkeit die; ~: transience; transitoriness

vergären 1. *unr. od. regelm. tr. V.* ferment **(zu** into). **2.** *unr. od. regelm. itr. V.; mit sein (bes. Chemie)* ferment

vergasen *tr. V.* **a)** *(bes. Physik)* gasify; **b)** *(töten)* gas

Vergaser der; ~s, ~ *(Kfz-W.)* carburettor

vergaß [fɛɐ̯'ga:s] *1. u. 3. Pers. Sg. Prät. v.* **vergessen**

Vergasung die; ~, ~**en a)** *(von Kohle)* gasification; **b)** *(Tötung)* gassing; **c) bis zur** ~ *(ugs.)* ad nauseam

vergattern *tr. V. (bes. Milit.)* remind ⟨*soldier*⟩ of his duties; *(fig.)* reprimand; **jmdn.** ~, **etw. zu tun** *(fig.)* enjoin sb. to do sth.; **jmdn. zu Stillschweigen** ~ *(fig.)* swear sb. to silence

vergeben *unr. tr. V.* **a)** *auch itr. (geh.: verzeihen)* forgive; **jmdm. etw.** ~: forgive sb. [for] sth.; **b)** throw away ⟨*chance, goal, etc.*⟩; **einen Elfmeter** ~: waste a penalty; **c)** *(geben)* place ⟨*order*⟩ **(an** + *Akk.* with); award ⟨*grant, prize*⟩ **(an** + *Akk.* to); **seine Töchter sind alle schon** ~: his daughters are all married [*or* engaged] already; **b) sich** *(Dat.)* **etwas/nichts** ~: lose/not lose face

vergebens 1. *Adv.* in vain; vainly. **2.** *adj.* **es war** ~: it was of *or* to no avail

vergeblich 1. *Adj.* futile; vain, futile ⟨*attempt, efforts*⟩; **alles Bitten/Zureden war** ~: all pleading/encouragement was of *or* to no avail; no amount of pleading/encouragement did any good. **2.** *adv.* in vain; vainly

Vergeblichkeit die; ~: futility

Vergebung die; ~, ~**en** *(geh.)* forgiveness

vergegenständlichen *(bes. Philos.) tr. V.* reify; hypostatize

vergegenwärtigen [od. ---'---] *refl. V.* **sich** *(Dat.)* **etw.** ~: imagine sth.; *(erinnern)* recall sth.

Vergegenwärtigung die; ~, ~**en** *s.* **vergegenwärtigen:** imagining; recalling

vergehen 1. *unr. itr. V.; mit sein* **a)** *(verstreichen)* ⟨*time*⟩ pass [by], go by; **es vergeht kein Tag, an dem er nicht anruft** not a day passes by without him ringing up *(Brit.) or (coll.)* phoning; **wie [doch] die Zeit vergeht!** how time flies!; **b)** *(nachlassen)* ⟨*pain*⟩ wear off, pass; ⟨*pleasure*⟩ fade; **ihr verging der Appetit** she lost her appetite; **c)** *(sich verflüchtigen)* ⟨*cloud, scent*⟩ disappear; ⟨*fog*⟩ lift; **d)** *(geh.: sterben)* pass away; die; **e)** *(verschmachten)* die **(vor** + *Dat.* of); **vor Sehnsucht** ~: pine away. **2.** *unr. refl. V.* **a)** *(verstoßen)* **sich gegen das Gesetz** ~: violate the law; **sich an fremdem Eigentum** ~ *(geh.)* steal another's property; **b)** *(sexuell)* **sich an jmdm.** ~: commit indecent assault on sb.; indecently assault sb.

Vergehen das; ~s, ~: crime; *(Rechtsspr.)* offence

vergeigen *(ugs.) tr. V.* botch up ⟨*test, performance, etc.*⟩; lose ⟨*game, match*⟩

vergeistigt *Adj.* spiritual

vergelten *unr. tr. V.* repay **(durch** with); **jmdm. etw.** ~: repay sb. for sth.; **jmds. Freundlichkeit** ~: return sb.'s kindness; **eine Niederlage blutig** ~: take bloody revenge for a defeat; **vergelt's Gott!** God bless you!

Vergeltung die a) repayment; **b)** *(Rache)* revenge; ~ **an jmdm./etw. üben** take revenge on sb./sth.; **die** ~ **eines Unrechts** the avenging of a wrong

Vergeltungs-: ~maßnahme die retaliatory measure; **~schlag der** retaliatory strike

vergesellschaften *tr. V.* socialize

Vergesellschaftung die; ~, ~**en** socialization

vergessen [fɛɐ̯'gɛsn̩] **1.** *unr. tr. (auch itr.) V.* forget; *(liegenlassen)* forget; leave behind; **seine Umgebung/sich völlig** ~: become totally engrossed; **er wird noch einmal seinen Kopf** ~ *(ugs.)* he'd forget his head if it wasn't screwed on; **... und nicht zu** ~ **Tante Erna ...:** and not forgetting Aunt Erna; **das kannst du** ~! *(ugs.)* forget it!; you can forget about that!; **auf etw.** *(Akk.)* ~ *(südd., österr.)* forget sth.. **2.** *refl. V. (sich nicht beherrschen)* forget oneself

Vergessenheit die; ~: oblivion; **in** ~ **geraten** fall into oblivion

vergeßlich [fɛɐ̯'gɛslɪç] *Adj.* forgetful

Vergeßlichkeit die; ~: forgetfulness

vergeuden [fɛɐ̯'gɔydn̩] *tr. V.* waste; squander, waste ⟨*money*⟩

Vergeudung die; ~, ~**en** waste; squandering; **so eine** ~! what a waste!

vergewaltigen *tr. V.* **a)** rape; **b)** *(fig.)* oppress ⟨*nation, people*⟩; violate ⟨*truth, conscience, law, language, etc.*⟩

Vergewaltigung die; ~, ~**en a)** rape; **b)** *s.* **vergewaltigen b:** oppression; violation

vergewissern [fɛɐ̯gə'vɪsɐn] *refl. V.* make sure (+ *Gen* of); **der Lehrer vergewisserte sich durch Fragen, ob ...:** the teacher ascertained by asking questions whether ...

Vergewisserung die; ~: ascertainment; **nur zur** ~: just as a check

vergießen *unr. tr. V.* **a)** *(verschütten)* spill; **b) Tränen** ~: shed tears; **viel Schweiß** ~: sweat blood *(fig.)*; *s. auch* **Blut**

vergiften *tr. V. (auch fig.)* poison

Vergiftung die; ~, ~**en a)** *(das Vergiften)* poisoning; ~ **durch Nahrungsmittel** food poisoning; **b)** *(Erkrankung)* poisoning; ~**en behandeln** treat cases of poisoning; **an einer** ~ **sterben** die of poisoning

Vergil [vɛr'gi:l] **(der)** Virgil

vergiß [fɛɐ̯'gɪs] *Imper. Sg. v.* **vergessen**

Vergiß·mein·nicht das; ~[e]s, ~[e] forget-me-not

vergißt *2. u. 3. Pers. Sg. Präs. v.* **vergessen**

vergittern *tr. V.* put a grille on ⟨*window etc.*⟩; *(mit Stangen)* put bars over ⟨*window etc.*⟩; **ein vergittertes Fenster** a barred window

verglasen *tr. V.* glaze; **das Fenster neu** ~: put new glass in the window

Verglasung die; ~, ~**en a)** *o. Pl.* glazing; **b)** *(Glasscheiben)* panes *pl.* of glass

Vergleich der; ~[e]s, ~e **a)** comparison; **dieser** ~ **drängt sich einem geradezu auf** one cannot help making this comparison; **dieser** ~ **hinkt** this is a poor comparison; **das ist doch kein** ~! there is no comparison; **einen** ~ **anstellen** *od.* **ziehen** draw *or* make a comparison; **er hält dem** ~ **mit seinem Bruder nicht stand** he doesn't compare *or* stand comparison with his brother; **im** ~ **zu** *od.* **mit etw.** in comparison with sth.; compared with *or* to sth.; **etw. zum** ~ **heranziehen** use sth. by way of comparison; **b)** *(Sprachw.)* simile; **c)** *(Rechtsw.)* settlement; **einen** ~ **schließen** reach a settlement

vergleichbar *Adj.* comparable

Vergleichbarkeit die; ~: comparability

vergleichen 1. *tr. V.* compare **(mit** with, to); **die Uhrzeit** ~: check that one has the correct time; **das ist [doch gar] nicht zu** ~: that [really] doesn't stand comparison *or* compare; **vergleiche Seite 77** compare page 77; ~**de Literaturwissenschaft** comparative literature. **2.** *refl. V.* **a) sich mit jmdm.** ~: compete with sb.; **b)** *(Rechtsw.)* reach a settlement; settle

Vergleichs-: ~form die *(Sprachw.)* comparative/superlative form; **~kampf der** *(Sport)* friendly match; **~maß·stab der** standard *or* yardstick of comparison; **~möglichkeit die** opportunity for comparison; **~partikel die** *(Sprachw.)* comparative particle; **~verfahren das** *(Rechtsw.)* composition proceedings *pl.*; **~weise** *Adv.* comparatively

vergletschern *itr. V.; mit sein* become glaciated; **vergletschert** glaciated

verglimmen *unr. od. regelm. itr. V.; mit sein* ⟨*fire etc.*⟩ [die down and] go out; ⟨*cigarette, embers*⟩ go out

verglühen *itr. V.; mit sein* ⟨*log, wick, fire, etc.*⟩ smoulder and go out; ⟨*glow of sunset*⟩ fade; ⟨*satellite, rocket, wire, etc.*⟩ burn out

vergnügen [fɛɐ̯'gny:gn̩] **1.** *refl. V.* enjoy oneself; have a good time; **sich beim Tanzen** ~: enjoy oneself dancing. **2.** *tr. V.* amuse

Vergnügen das; ~s, ~: pleasure; *(Spaß)* fun; **ein teueres** ~ *(ugs.)* an expensive bit of fun *(coll.)*; **ein kindliches** ~ **bei etw. empfinden** take a childlike pleasure *or* delight in sth.; **es ist mir ein** ~: it's a pleasure; **es war mir ein** ~, **Sie kennenzulernen** it was a pleasure meeting you; **das** ~ **ist ganz meinerseits** *od.* **auf meiner Seite** the pleasure is all mine; **mit wem habe ich das** ~? with whom do I have the pleasure of speaking?; **etw. macht jmdm. [großes]** ~: sth. gives sb. [great] pleasure; sb. enjoys sth. [very much]; **sich ein** ~ **daraus machen, etw. zu tun** derive pleasure from doing sth.; **ich wünsche dir viel** ~: I hope you have a good time *or* enjoy yourself; **viel** ~! *(auch iron.)* have fun!; **mit [dem größten]** ~: with [the greatest of] pleasure; **etw. aus reinem** ~ *od.* **nur zum** ~ **tun** do sth. just for the fun of it *or* for pleasure; **zu meinem** ~: to my great joy

vergnüglich 1. *Adj.* amusing, entertaining ⟨*play, programme*⟩. **2.** *adv.* amusingly; entertainingly
vergnügt 1. *Adj.* **a)** *(in guter Laune)* cheerful; happy ⟨*smile*⟩; merry ⟨*group of people*⟩; **b)** *(unterhaltsam)* enjoyable. **2.** *adv. (in guter Laune)* cheerfully; ⟨*smile*⟩ happily
Vergnügtheit die; ~: cheerfulness
Vergnügung die; ~, ~en a) *(Zeitvertreib)* pleasure; **b)** *(Veranstaltung)* entertainment
vergnügungs-, Vergnügungs-: ~fahrt die pleasure-trip; **~industrie die** entertainment industry; **~lokal das** bar providing entertainment; *(Nachtlokal)* night-club; **~park der** amusement park; **~reise die** pleasure-trip; **~steuer die** entertainment tax; **~sucht die;** *o. Pl. (oft abwertend)* craving for pleasure; **~süchtig** *Adj.* pleasure-hungry; **~viertel das** pleasure district
vergolden *tr. V.* **a)** gold-plate ⟨*jewellery etc.*⟩; *(mit Blattgold)* gild ⟨*statue, dome, etc.*⟩; *(mit Gold bemalen)* paint ⟨*statue, dome, etc.*⟩ gold; *(fig.)* ⟨*evening sun*⟩ bathe ⟨*roof-tops etc.*⟩ in gold; **b)** *(geh.: verklären)* brighten up
vergönnen *tr. V.* grant; **es war ihm nicht vergönnt** it was not granted him
vergotten *tr. V.* deify
vergöttern [fɛɐ̯ˈgœtɐn] *tr. V.* idolize
Vergötterung die; ~, ~en idolization
vergöttlichen *tr. V. (göttlich machen)* deify; *(als Gott verehren)* worship [as God]
vergraben 1. *unr. tr. V.* bury; **sein Gesicht in beide Hände** *od.* **in beiden Händen ~:** bury one's face in one's hands. **2.** *unr. refl. V.* ⟨*animal*⟩ bury itself **(in +** *Akk. od. Dat.* in); *(fig.)* withdraw from the world; hide oneself away; **sich in die Arbeit/in seine Bücher ~** *(fig.)* bury oneself in one's work/books
vergrämen *tr. V.* **a)** antagonize; **b)** *(Jägerspr.)* scare [off]
vergrämt *Adj.* care-worn
vergraulen *tr. V. (ugs.)* put off; **jmdm. etw. ~:** put sb. off sth.
vergreifen *unr. refl. V.* **a) sich im Ton/Ausdruck ~:** adopt the wrong tone/use the wrong expression; **sich in der Wahl seiner Mittel ~:** choose *or* select the wrong means; **b) sich an etw.** *(Dat.)* **~** *(an fremdem Eigentum)* misappropriate sth.; **sich an der Kasse ~:** put one's hand in the till *(euphem.)*; **c)** *(tätlich werden)* **sich an jmdm. ~:** assault sb.; *(geschlechtlich mißbrauchen)* [indecently] assault sb.; **ich werde mich an der Maschine nicht ~** *(ugs.)* I'm not touching the machine; **d)** *(danebengreifen)* ⟨*musician*⟩ play a wrong note
vergreisen *itr. V.; mit sein* **a)** go senile; **vergreist** senile; **b)** *(überaltern)* ⟨*population*⟩ age
Vergreisung die; ~ a) senescence; **b)** *(Überalterung)* ageing
vergriffen 1. *2. Part. v.* **vergreifen. 2.** *Adj.* out of print *pred.*
vergröbern [fɛɐ̯ˈgrø:bɐn] **1.** *tr. V.* coarsen. **2.** *refl. V.* become coarser
Vergröberung die; ~, ~en coarsening; **die Boulevardpresse arbeitet mit ~en** the popular press operates with crude generalizations
vergrößern [fɛɐ̯ˈgrø:sɐn] **1.** *tr. V.* **a)** *(erweitern)* extend ⟨*room, area, building, etc.*⟩; increase ⟨*distance*⟩; **sein Repertoire ~:** extend *or* increase *or* enlarge one's repertoire; **b)** *(vermehren)* increase; **das Übel ~:** make the trouble worse; **c)** *(größer reproduzieren)* enlarge ⟨*photograph etc.*⟩. **2.** *refl. V.* **a)** *(größer werden)* ⟨*firm, business, etc.*⟩ expand; **eine krankhaft vergrößerte Leber** a pathologically enlarged liver; **b)** *(zunehmen)* increase; **c)** *(ugs.: durch Umzug)* give oneself more space. **3.** *itr. V.* ⟨*lens etc.*⟩ magnify
Vergrößerung die; ~, ~en a) *s.* **vergrößern 1, 2: extension; increase; enlargement; expansion; **b)** *(Foto)* enlargement; **in 100facher ~:** enlarged 100fold
Vergrößerungs-: ~apparat der *(Fot.)* enlarger; **~glas das** magnifying glass; **~spiegel der** magnifying mirror
vergucken *refl. V. (ugs.)* **a)** *(sich verlieben)* **sich in jmdn./etw. ~:** fall for sb./sth. *(coll.)*; **b)** *(falsch sehen)* be mistaken [about what one saw]
Vergünstigung die; ~, ~en privilege
vergüten *tr. V.* **a)** *(erstatten)* **jmdm. etw. ~:** reimburse sb. for sth.; **jmdm. seine Unkosten/Auslagen ~:** reimburse sb. for his/her costs/reimburse *or* refund sb.'s expenses; **b)** *(bes. Papierdt.: bezahlen)* remunerate, pay for ⟨*work, services*⟩; **etw. ~:** pay for sth.
Vergütung die; ~, ~en a) *(Rückerstattung) (von Unkosten)* reimbursement; *(von Auslagen)* reimbursement; refunding; **b)** *(Geldsumme)* remuneration
verh. *Abk.* **verheiratet** m.
verhackstücken *tr. V. (ugs.)* **a)** *(abwertend: kritisieren)* ⟨*critic etc.*⟩ tear *or* pull to pieces; **b)** *(nordd.: besprechen)* discuss
verhaften *tr. V.* arrest; **Sie sind verhaftet** you are under arrest
verhaftet *Adj.* **einer Sache** *(Dat.)* **~ sein** be trapped in sth.
Verhaftete der/die; *adj. Dekl.* person under arrest; man/woman under arrest; arrested man/woman
Verhaftung die; ~, ~en arrest
verhageln *itr. V.; mit sein* be destroyed by hail; *s. auch* **Petersilie**
verhaken 1. *tr. V.* **a)** *(zuhaken)* hook up; **b)** *(in etw. haken)* hook ⟨*needle etc.*⟩ **(in +** *Dat.* in). **2.** *refl. V.* ⟨*person*⟩ get hooked *or* caught up; ⟨*zip*⟩ get caught
verhallen *itr. V.; mit sein* ⟨*sound*⟩ die away; **[ungehört] ~** *(fig.)* ⟨*call, words, etc.*⟩ go unheard *or* unheeded
¹verhalten 1. *unr. refl. V.* **a)** *(reagieren)* react; **sich still** *od.* **ruhig ~:** keep quiet; **ich verhielt mich abwartend** I decided to wait and see; **b)** *(sich benehmen)* behave; **c)** *(beschaffen sein)* be; **die Sache verhält sich nämlich so** this is how things stand *or* the matter stands; **d)** *(im Verhältnis stehen)* **a verhält sich zu b wie x zu y** a is to b as x is to y; **die beiden Größen ~ sich zueinander wie 1:10** the two values are in a ratio of 1:10. **2.** *unr. tr. V.* **a)** *(geh.: zurückhalten)* restrain, contain ⟨*anger*⟩; restrain ⟨*mockery*⟩; contain ⟨*laughter*⟩; hold back ⟨*tears, urine*⟩; **b)** *(Reiten) s.* **²parieren c; c)** *auch itr. (geh.)* **[den Schritt] ~:** slow down; check one's pace; *(stehenbleiben)* stop
²verhalten 1. *Adj.* **a)** *(unterdrückt)* restrained; **mit ~em Tempo** at a measured pace; **mit ~en Schritten** treading quietly; **mit ~em Atem** with bated breath; **b)** *(dezent)* restrained, subdued, muted ⟨*colours*⟩; muted, soft ⟨*notes, voice, etc.*⟩; **c)** *(zurückhaltend)* reserved; **eine ~e Fahrweise** a cautious way of driving. **2.** *adv.* **a)** *(unterdrückt)* in a restrained manner; **b)** *(zurückhaltend)* in a reserved manner; **~ fahren** drive cautiously; **c)** *(dezent)* ⟨*speak, play, etc.*⟩ softly
Verhalten das; ~s behaviour; *(Vorgehen)* conduct
verhaltens-, Verhaltens-: ~forschung die; *o. Pl.* behavioural research *no art.*; *(Ethologie)* ethology *no art.*; **~gestört** *Adj. (Psych.)* ⟨*person, child*⟩ with a behavioural disorder; **~maß·regel die;** *meist Pl.* rule of conduct; **~maßregeln für den Notfall** rules governing emergencies; **~muster das** behaviour pattern; pattern of behaviour; **~störung die;** *meist Pl. (Psych.)* behavioural disorder; **~therapie die** behavioural therapy; **~weise die** behaviour; **~weisen** behaviour patterns; patterns of behaviour
Verhältnis [fɛɐ̯ˈhɛltnɪs] **das; ~ses, ~se a) ein ~ von drei zu eins** a ratio of three to one; **im ~ zu früher** in comparison with *or* compared to earlier times; **der Aufwand stand in keinem ~ zum Erfolg** the expenditure was out of all proportion to the result; **b)** *(persönliche Beziehung)* relationship **(zu** with); **zwischen uns** *(Dat.)* **herrscht ein vertrautes ~:** we are on intimate terms; **ein gutes ~ zu jmdm. haben** get on well with sb.; **er hat** *od.* **findet kein [rechtes] ~ zur Musik** he cannot relate to music; **c)** *(ugs.: intime Beziehung)* affair; relationship; **mit jmdm. ein ~ haben** have an affair with sb.; **ein ~ mit jmdm. beenden** break up with sb.; break off a relationship with sb.; **d)** *(ugs.) (Geliebte)* lady-friend; *(Geliebter)* man; **e)** *Pl. (Umstände)* conditions; **in bescheidenen** *od.* **einfachen/gesicherten ~sen leben** live in modest circumstances/be financially secure; **aus bescheidenen** *od.* **einfachen ~sen kommen** come from a humble background; **sie kommt aus kleinen ~sen** she comes from a lower middle-class background; **über seine ~se leben** live beyond one's means
verhältnis-, Verhältnis-: ~gleichung die *(Math.)* proportion; **~mäßig** *Adv.* relatively; comparatively; **~wahl die** proportional representation; **~wahl·recht das;** *o. Pl.* [system of] proportional representation; **~wort das;** *Pl.* **~wörter** *(Sprachw.)* preposition
verhandeln 1. *itr. V.* **a)** negotiate **(über +** *Akk.* about); **b)** *(strafrechtlich)* try a case; *(zivilrechtlich)* hear a case; **das Gericht verhandelt gegen die Terroristen** the court is trying the terrorists. **2.** *tr. V.* **a) etw. ~:** negotiate over sth.; **b)** *(strafrechtlich)* try ⟨*case*⟩; *(zivilrechtlich)* hear ⟨*case*⟩
Verhandlung die a) *(Besprechung)* **~en** negotiations; **mit jmdm. in ~ stehen** be negotiating with sb.; be [involved *or* engaged] in negotiations *pl.* with sb.; **zu ~en bereit sein** be open to negotiation *sing.*; **b)** *(strafrechtlich)* trial; *(zivilrechtlich)* hearing; **die ~ gegen X** the trial of X
verhandlungs-, Verhandlungs-: ~basis die *s.* **~grundlage; ~bereit** *Adj.* ready *or* willing to negotiate *pred.*; **~bereitschaft die;** *o. Pl.* readiness *or* willingness to negotiate; **~gegen·stand der** subject for/under negotiation; **kein ~gegenstand sein** not be a matter for negotiation; **~grundlage die** basis for negotiation[s]; **~partner der** opposite number [in the negotiations]; **die beiden ~partner** *(die miteinander verhandeln)* the two sides in the negotiations; **~tisch der** negotiating table; **~weg der** *in* **auf dem ~weg** by negotiation
verhangen *Adj.* overcast
verhängen *tr. V.* **a)** *(zuhängen)* cover **(mit** with); **b)** *(anordnen)* impose ⟨*fine, punishment*⟩ **(über +** *Akk.* on); declare ⟨*state of emergency, state of siege*⟩; *(Sport)* award, give ⟨*penalty etc.*⟩
Verhängnis [fɛɐ̯ˈhɛŋnɪs] **das; ~ses, ~se** undoing; **jmdm. zum ~ werden** be sb.'s undoing; **das ~ brach über ihn herein** disaster overtook him
verhängnis·voll *Adj. (unheilvoll)* disastrous; fatal, disastrous ⟨*mistake, weakness, hesitation, etc.*⟩; *(schicksalsschwer)* fateful
Verhängung die; ~, ~en imposition; *(des Ausnahme-, Belagerungszustandes)* declaration
verharmlosen *tr. V.* play down
Verharmlosung die; ~, ~en playing down
verhärmt [fɛɐ̯ˈhɛrmt] *Adj.* care-worn
verharren *itr. V. (geh.)* **a)** *(innehalten)* remain; *(plötzlich, kurz)* pause; **b)** *(beharren)* **auf seinem Standpunkt ~:** persist in one's view; **in Resignation/Gleichgültigkeit ~:** remain resigned/indifferent
verharschen *itr. V.; mit sein* ⟨*snow*⟩ form a crust; ⟨*wound*⟩ form a scab

verhärten [fɛɐ̯'hɛrtn̩] **1.** *tr. V.* **a)** *(festigen)* harden ‹*material etc.*›; **b)** *(unbarmherzig machen)* harden; make ‹*person*› hard. **2.** *refl. V.* **a)** *(hart werden)* ‹*tissue*› become hardened; ‹*tumour*› become scirrhous; **b)** *(gefühllos werden)* harden one's heart (**gegen** against); **die Fronten haben sich verhärtet** the positions of the opposing parties have become entrenched

Verhärtung die; ~, ~**en a)** hardening; **b)** *(fig.)* becoming hardened; **die ~ der Positionen auf beiden Seiten** the hardening of attitudes on both sides

verhaspeln *refl. V. (ugs.)* **a)** *(sich versprechen)* stumble over one's words; **b)** *(sich verwickeln)* become *or* get tangled up

verhaßt *Adj.* hated; detested; **es war ihm ~:** he hated *or* detested it; **nichts ist mir so ~ wie ...:** there is nothing I detest so much as ...

verhätscheln *tr. V. (ugs.)* pamper

Verhätschelung die; ~, ~**en** *(ugs.)* pampering

Verhau [fɛɐ̯'hau̯] **der** *od.* **das;** ~**[e]s,** ~**e a)** tangle of branches; *(Dickicht)* thicket; **b)** barrier [made of branches]; *(bes. Milit.)* entanglement

verhauen *(ugs.)* **1.** *unr. tr. V.* **a)** *(verprügeln)* beat up; *(als Strafe)* beat; **jmdm. den Hintern ~:** give sb.'s bottom a good smack[ing]; **b)** *(falsch machen)* make a mess of; muck up *(Brit. sl.)*. **2.** *unr. refl. V. (sich verrechnen)* make a mistake *or* slip; **sich bei etw. mächtig ~:** slip up badly in sth.

verheben *unr. refl. V.* do oneself an injury [while lifting sth.]

verheddern [fɛɐ̯'hɛdɐn] *refl. V.* **a)** *(hängenbleiben)* **sich in etw.** *(Dat.)* **~:** get tangled up in sth.; **b)** *(sich verhaspeln)* get muddled up

verheeren [fɛɐ̯'he:rən] *tr. V.* devastate; lay waste [to]

verheerend *Adj.* **a)** *(katastrophal)* devastating; disastrous; **b)** *(ugs.: scheußlich)* ghastly *(coll.)*; dreadful *(coll.)*

Verheerung die; ~, ~**en** devastation *no pl.*; ~**[en] anrichten** cause devastation; wreak havoc

verhehlen *tr. V. (geh.)* conceal; hide; **jmdm. etw. ~:** conceal *or* hide sth. from sb.; **ich kann/will** *od.* **möchte [es] nicht ~, daß ...:** there is no denying/I have no wish to deny that ...

verheilen *itr. V.; mit sein* ‹*wound*› heal [up]

verheimlichen *tr. V.* **[jmdm.] etw. ~:** keep sth. secret [from sb.]; conceal or hide sth. [from sb.]

Verheimlichung die; ~, ~**en** concealment

verheiraten 1. *refl. V.* get married; **sich mit jmdm. ~:** marry sb.; get married to sb.; **er ist mit seiner Firma/Gitarre verheiratet** *(fig.)* he has no time for anything except his company/guitar. **2.** *tr. V. (veralt.)* marry (**mit, an** + *Akk.* to); **er hatte zwei Töchter zu ~:** he had two daughters to marry off

Verheiratete der/die; *adj. Dekl.* married person; married man/woman; ~ *Pl.* married people; married men/women

Verheiratung die; ~, ~**en** marriage

verheißen *unr. tr. V. (geh.; auch fig.)* promise; **man verhieß ihm eine große Zukunft** a great future was predicted for him; **nichts Gutes ~:** not bode *or* augur well

Verheißung die; ~, ~**en** *(geh.)* promise

verheißungs·voll 1. *Adj.* promising; **ein ~er Anfang** a promising *or* an auspicious start. **2.** *adv.* full of promise

verheizen *tr. V.* **a)** burn; use as fuel; **b)** *(abwertend: rücksichtslos einsetzen)* burn out ‹*athlete, skier, etc.*›; use ‹*troops*› as cannon-fodder; run ‹*employee, subordinate, etc.*› into the ground

verhelfen *unr. itr. V.* **jmdm./einer Sache zu etw. ~:** help sb./sth. to get/achieve sth.; **jmdm. zur Flucht/zum Sieg ~:** help sb. to escape/win

verherrlichen *tr. V.* glorify ‹*war, violence, deed, etc.*›; extol ‹*virtues, leader, etc.*›; celebrate ‹*nature, freedom, peace, etc.*›

Verherrlichung die; ~, ~**en** *s.* **verherrlichen:** glorification; extolling; celebration

verhetzen *tr. V.* incite; stir up; **die verhetzten Massen** the inflamed masses

Verhetzung die; ~, ~**en** incitement; stirring up

verheult [fɛɐ̯'hɔylt] *Adj. (ugs.)* ‹*eyes*› red from crying; ‹*face*› puffy *or* swollen from crying

verhexen *tr. V. (auch fig.)* bewitch; cast a spell on; **jmdn. in etw.** *(Akk.)* **~:** turn sb. into sth. [by magic]; **es ist wie verhext: kaum setze ich mich hin, klingelt das Telefon** there seems to be a jinx on me today: the moment I sit down, the telephone rings

verhindern *tr. V.* prevent; prevent, avert ‹*war, disaster, etc.*›; **es ließ sich nicht ~, daß er losfuhr** he couldn't be prevented from driving off; no one could stop him [from] driving off; **er ist [dienstlich] verhindert** he is prevented from coming [by business commitments]; he is unable to come [for business reasons]; **ein verhinderter Künstler/Schauspieler** *(ugs.)* a would-be artist/actor

Verhinderung die; ~, ~**en** *s.* **verhindern:** prevention; averting

verhohlen [fɛɐ̯'ho:lən] *Adj.* concealed; **kaum ~e Neugier** ill-concealed curiosity

verhöhnen [vɛr'hø:nən] *tr. V.* mock; deride; ridicule

verhohnepipeln [fɛɐ̯'ho:nəpi:pl̩n] *tr. V. (ugs.)* send up *(coll.)*

Verhohnepipelung die; ~, ~**en** send-up *(coll.)*

Verhöhnung die; ~, ~**en a)** mockery; ridiculing; **b)** *(Äußerung)* mocking remark

verhökern [fɛɐ̯'hø:kɐn] *tr. V. (salopp)* flog *(Brit. sl.)*

Verhör [fɛɐ̯'hø:ɐ̯] **das;** ~**[e]s,** ~**e** interrogation; questioning; *(bei Gericht)* examination; **jmdn. ins ~ nehmen** interrogate *or* question sb.; *(fig.)* grill *or* quiz sb.

verhören 1. *tr. V. (befragen)* interrogate; question; *(bei Gericht)* examine. **2.** *refl. V. (falsch hören)* mishear; hear wrongly; **Hier ist niemand. Du mußt dich verhört haben** There's nobody here. You must have been hearing things

verhornen *itr. V.; mit sein* keratinize; ‹*skin*› become horny

verhüllen *tr. V.* **a)** *(verbergen)* cover; *(fig.)* disguise; mask; **eine verhüllte Drohung** *(fig.)* a veiled threat; **b)** *(umgeben)* enshroud; **Wolken verhüllten die Bergspitzen** the mountain-tops were veiled *or* shrouded in cloud

verhüllend *Adj. (Literaturw.)* euphemistic

Verhüllung die; ~, ~**en** covering; *(fig.)* disguising

verhundertfachen *tr., refl. V.* increase a hundredfold

verhungern *itr. V.; mit sein* die of starvation; starve [to death]; **ich bin am Verhungern** *(ugs.)* I'm starving *(fig. coll.)*; **Verhungernde** *Pl.* people starving to death; **verhungert aussehen** look half-starved

verhunzen [fɛɐ̯'hʊntsn̩] *tr. V. (ugs. abwertend)* ruin; mess up; ruin ‹*landscape, townscape, etc.*›

verhüten *tr. V.* prevent; prevent, avert ‹*disaster*›; **der Himmel verhüte, daß ...:** heaven forbid that ...; ~, **daß jmd. etw. tut** prevent sb. [from] doing sth.

Verhüterli das; ~**s,** ~**s** *(ugs. scherzh.)* French letter

verhütten *tr. V.* smelt

Verhüttung die; ~, ~**en** smelting

Verhütung die; ~, ~**en** prevention; *(Empfängnis~)* contraception

Verhütungs-: ~**maßnahmen** *Pl.* contraceptive precautions; ~**mittel das** contraceptive

verhutzelt [fɛɐ̯'hʊts l̩t] *Adj. (ugs.)* wizened ‹*person, face*›; shrivelled ‹*fruit, plant*›

verifizieren [verifi'tsi:rən] *tr. V.* verify

Verifizierung die; ~, ~**en** verification

verinnerlichen *tr. V. (Soziol., Psych.)* internalize

verinnerlicht *Adj. (vergeistigt)* spiritualized; *(introvertiert)* introverted

Verinnerlichung die; ~, ~**en** *(Soziol., Psych.)* internalization

verirren *refl. V.* **a)** *(abkommen)* get lost; lose one's way; ‹*animal*› stray; **verirrte Gewehrkugeln** *(fig.)* stray bullets; **b)** *(irgendwohin gelangen)* stray (**in, an** + *Akk.* into)

Verirrung die; ~, ~**en** aberration

veritabel [veri'ta:bl̩] *Adj.; nicht präd. (geh.)* veritable; real

verjagen *tr. V.* chase away; *(fig.)* dispel ‹*thoughts, cares, etc.*›; **jmdn. von Haus und Hof ~:** drive sb. out of house and home

verjähren [fɛɐ̯'jɛ:rən] *itr. V.; mit sein* come under the statute of limitations; **dieses Verbrechen ist inzwischen verjährt** this crime was committed too long ago to be punishable now

Verjährung die; ~, ~**en** limitation; **für Verbrechen wie Völkermord gibt es keine ~:** there is no statute of limitations for crimes like genocide

Verjährungs·frist die limitation period

verjazzen *tr. V.* play in a jazz style; jazz up

verjubeln *tr. V. (ugs.)* blow *(sl.)* ‹*money*›

verjüngen [fɛɐ̯'jʏŋən] **1.** *tr. V.* rejuvenate ‹*person, skin, etc.*›; *(jünger aussehen lassen)* make ‹*person*› look younger; recruit younger blood into ‹*team, company, etc.*›. **2.** *refl. V. (schmaler werden)* taper; become narrower; narrow

Verjüngung die; ~, ~**en a)** *(Jüngerwerden)* rejuvenation; **eine ~ des Politbüros** a recruitment of younger blood into the politburo; **b)** *(Schmalerwerden)* tapering; narrowing

Verjüngungs·kur die: ich fühle mich reif für eine ~: I feel in need of being rejuvenated; **die neue Freundin wirkt auf ihn wie eine ~:** his new girl-friend has given him a new lease of life

verjuxen *tr. V. (ugs.)* **a)** *(verjubeln)* blow *(sl.)* ‹*money*›; **b)** *(verulken)* poke fun at

verkabeln *tr. V.* connect up [by cable]

Verkabelung die; ~, ~**en** installation of cables (*Gen.* in)

verkalken *itr. V.; mit sein* **a)** ‹*tissue*› calcify, become calcified; ‹*arteries*› become hardened; ‹*bone*› thicken; ‹*pipe, kettle, coffee-machine, etc.*› fur up; **b)** *(ugs.: senil werden)* become senile; **er ist schon ziemlich verkalkt** he is already pretty gaga *(sl.)*

verkalkulieren *refl. V.* **a)** *(falsch berechnen)* miscalculate; **b)** *(falsch einschätzen)* miscalculate; make a miscalculation

Verkalkung die; ~, ~**en a)** *s.* **verkalken a:** calcification; hardening; thickening; furring-up; **b)** *(ugs.: Senilität)* senility

verkannt [fɛɐ̯'kant] *2. Part. v.* **verkennen**

verkanten 1. *tr. V.* tilt; edge ‹*ski*›. **2.** *itr., refl. V. (sich festklemmen)* get jammed

verkappt *Adj.* disguised; ~**e Anarchisten** anarchists in disguise

verkarsten *itr. V.; mit sein* be karstified

Verkarstung die; ~, ~**en** karstification

verkatert [fɛɐ̯'ka:tɐt] *Adj. (ugs.)* hung-over *(coll.)*; ~ **aufwachen** wake up with a hang-over

Verkauf der a) sale; *(das Verkaufen)* sale; selling; **zum ~ stehen** be [up] for sale; **etw. zum ~ anbieten** offer sth. for sale; **b)** *o. Pl. (Kaufmannsspr.)* sales *sing. or pl., no art.*

verkaufen 1. *tr. V. (auch fig.)* sell (*Dat.*, **an** + *Akk.* to); **sie verkauft ihren Körper** she's a prostitute; **„zu verkaufen"** 'for sale'. **2.** *refl. V.* **a)** ‹*goods*› sell; **sich schlecht/gut ~** ‹*goods*› sell badly/well; **b)** *(ugs.: falsch kaufen)* make a bad buy; **ich habe mich bei den**

Möbeln verkauft the furniture was a bad buy

Verkäufer der, Verkäuferin die a) seller; vendor *(formal);* **b)** *(Berufsbez.)* sales *or* shop assistant; salesperson; *(im Außendienst)* salesman/saleswoman; salesperson

verkäuflich *Adj.* **a)** *(zum Verkauf geeignet)* saleable; marketable; **schwer/leicht ~ sein** be hard/easy to sell; **b)** *(zum Verkauf bestimmt)* for sale *postpos.;* **dieses Mittel ist frei ~:** this medicine is available over the counter

verkaufs-, Verkaufs-: ~aus·stellung die exhibition and sale of works; **~automat der** vending-machine; **~förderung die** sales promotion; **~leiter der** sales manager; **~offen** *Adj.* **der ~offene Samstag** *od.* **Sonnabend** Saturday on which *or* when the shops are open all day; **~personal das** sales staff; **~preis der** retail price; **~schlager der** big seller; *(Buch)* best seller; **~stand der** stall

Verkehr der; ~s a) traffic; **den ~ regeln** regulate *or* control the [flow of] traffic; **etw. dem [öffentlichen] ~ übergeben** open sth. to public use; **aus dem ~ ziehen** take ⟨*coin, banknote*⟩ out of circulation; take ⟨*product*⟩ off the market; **jmdn. aus dem ~ ziehen** *(ugs. scherzh.)* put sb. out of circulation *(joc.);* **in [den] ~ bringen** put ⟨*coin, banknote*⟩ into circulation; **b)** *(Kontakt)* contact; communication; **diplomatischer ~:** diplomatic relations *pl.;* **keinen ~ mit jmdm. pflegen/den ~ mit jmdm. abbrechen** not/no longer associate with sb.; **c)** *(Geschlechts~)* intercourse

verkehren 1. *itr. V.* **a)** *auch mit sein (fahren)* run; ⟨*aircraft*⟩ fly; **der Dampfer verkehrt zwischen Hamburg und Helgoland** the steamer plies *or* operates *or* goes between Hamburg and Heligoland; **der Bus verkehrt alle 15 Minuten** the bus runs *or* goes every 15 minutes; there's a bus every 15 minutes; **b)** *(in Kontakt stehen)* **mit jmdm. ~:** associate with sb.; **wir ~ nur noch über unsere Anwälte/schriftlich miteinander** we only deal with each other through our solicitors/we only have written correspondence with each other; **c)** *(zu Gast sein)* **bei jmdm. ~:** visit sb. regularly; **in einem Lokal ~:** frequent a pub *(Brit. coll.);* **in den besten Kreisen ~:** move in the best circles; **d)** *(verhüll.: koitieren)* have intercourse; **sexuell ~:** have sexual intercourse. **2.** *tr. V. (verdrehen)* turn **(in +** *Akk.* into); **jmds. Absicht ~:** reverse sb.'s intentions; **den Sinn einer Aussage ins Gegenteil ~:** twist the meaning of a statement right round. **3.** *refl. V. (sich verwandeln)* turn **(in +** *Akk.* into); **sich ins Gegenteil ~:** change to the opposite

verkehrs-, Verkehrs-: ~ader die traffic artery; **~ampel die** traffic lights *pl.;* **~amt das** tourist information office; **~aufkommen das** volume of traffic; **~beruhigt** *Adj. (Verkehrsw.)* **~beruhigte Zone, ~beruhigter Bereich** *zone in which traffic is limited to a walking pace and pedestrians have priority;* **~betrieb der;** *meist Pl.* transport services *pl.;* **~büro das** tourist office; **~chaos das** traffic chaos *no indef. art.;* chaos *no indef. art.* on the roads; **~dichte die** traffic density; **~erziehung die** road safety training; **~flug·zeug das** commercial aircraft; **~fluß der** flow of traffic; **~funk der** radio traffic service; **~gefährdung die** constituting *no art.* a hazard to other traffic; **eine ~gefährdung darstellen** be *or* constitute a hazard to other traffic; **~hindernis das** obstruction to traffic; **~insel die** traffic island; refuge; **~knoten·punkt der** [traffic] junction; **~kontrolle die** traffic check; **~lage die a)** *(Situation)* traffic situation; **b)** *(Ortslage)* situation with regard to road and rail links; **eine gute ~lage haben** be well situated with regard to road and rail links; **~lärm der** traffic noise; **~meldung die** traffic announcement *or* flash; **~minister der** minister of transport; **~ministerium das** ministry of transport; **~mittel das** means of transport; **die öffentlichen ~mittel** public transport *sing.;* **~netz das** transport system; **~opfer das** road accident *or* traffic accident victim; **~polizei die** traffic police *pl.;* **~polizist der** traffic policeman; **~regel die;** *meist Pl.* traffic regulation; **~reich** *Adj.* busy ⟨*crossing, street, etc.*⟩; **~schild das;** *Pl.* **~schilder** traffic sign; road sign; **~sicher** *Adj.* roadworthy ⟨*vehicle, condition*⟩; **~sicherheit die;** *o. Pl.* road safety; *(eines Fahrzeugs)* roadworthiness; **~sprache die** lingua franca; **~stockung die** traffic hold-up; **~sünder der** *(ugs.)* traffic offender; **~teil·nehmer der** road-user; **~tote der/die;** *meist Pl.* person killed on the roads; **weniger ~tote** fewer deaths on the roads; **~unfall der** road accident; **~unterricht der** road safety instruction; **~verbindung die** transport link; **~verhältnisse** *Pl.* **a)** *(~verbindungen)* transport links; **b)** *(~lage)* traffic conditions; **~weg der** traffic route; **~widrig 1.** *Adj.* contrary to road traffic regulations *postpos.;* **2.** *adv.* contrary to road traffic regulations; **~zeichen das** traffic sign; road sign

verkehrt 1. *Adj.* wrong; **das ist gar nicht so ~:** that's not such a bad idea; **es ist sicher nicht ~, das zu tun** there's no harm in doing that; **an den Verkehrten/die Verkehrte kommen** *od.* **geraten** *(ugs.)* come to the wrong person. **2.** *adv.* wrongly; **alles ~ machen** do everything wrong; **sich ~ verhalten** do the wrong thing; *s. auch* **herum a**

Verkehrung die; ~, ~en reversal; **eine ~ ins Gegenteil** a change to the opposite

verkeilen 1. *tr. V.* wedge. **2.** *refl. V.* become wedged **(in +** *Akk.* in); **sich ineinander ~:** become wedged together

verkennen *unr. tr. V.* fail to recognize; misjudge ⟨*situation*⟩; fail to appreciate ⟨*efforts, achievement, etc.*⟩; **es ist nicht zu ~, daß ...:** it cannot be denied *or* is undeniable that ...; **ihre Absicht war nicht zu ~:** her intention was unmistakable; **ein verkanntes Genie** an unrecognized genius

Verkennung die; ~, ~en *s.* **verkennen:** failure to recognize/appreciate; misjudgement; **in völliger ~ der Situation** completely misjudging the situation

verketten *refl. V.* become interlinked

Verkettung die; ~, ~en *(von Zufällen usw.)* chain

verketzern *tr. V.* denounce

Verketzerung die; ~, ~en denunciation

verkitschen *tr. V.* turn ⟨*novel, film, etc.*⟩ into kitsch; sentimentalize ⟨*song, tune, etc.*⟩

verkitten *tr. V.* fill ⟨*crack, hole, joint, etc.*⟩; put putty round ⟨*window*⟩

verklagen *tr. V.* sue; take proceedings against; take to court; **eine Firma auf Schadenersatz ~:** sue a company for damages

verklammern *tr. V. (Med.)* close ⟨*wound*⟩ with a clamp/clamps

verklappen *tr. V.* dump ⟨*waste*⟩ [at sea]

Verklappung die; ~, ~en dumping [at sea]

verklären 1. *tr. V. (auch Rel.)* transfigure. **2.** *refl. V. (auch fig.)* be transfigured; ⟨*eyes*⟩ shine blissfully

verklärt 1. *Adj.* transfigured, blissful ⟨*expression, face, etc.*⟩. **2.** *adv.* blissfully

Verklärung die transfiguration

verklausulieren [fɛɐ̯klauzu'li:rən] *tr. V.* **a)** *(mit Klauseln versehen)* hedge ⟨*contract etc.*⟩ with qualifying clauses; **b)** *(verbergen)* hedge ⟨*admission of guilt etc.*⟩ round with qualifications; **in verklausulierter Form** in a roundabout way

Verklausulierung die; ~, ~en a) *(das Verklausulieren)* involved formulation; **b)** *(Formulierung)* qualification

verkleben 1. *itr. V.; mit sein* stick together; **der Pinsel ist verklebt** the bristles of the brush are stuck together. **2.** *tr. V.* **a)** *(zusammenkleben)* stick ⟨*eyelids, eyelashes*⟩ together; **verklebte Hände/Haare** sticky hands/matted *or* sticky hair; **b)** *(zukleben)* seal up ⟨*hole*⟩; **eine Wunde mit Heftpflaster ~:** cover a wound with sticking-plaster; **c)** *(festkleben)* stick [down] ⟨*floor-covering etc.*⟩; **das Schaufenster mit Papier ~:** paper over the shop-window; **d)** *(verbrauchen)* use up ⟨*posters, rolls of wallpaper, etc.*⟩

verkleckern *tr. V. (ugs.)* spill

verkleiden *tr. V.* **a)** disguise; *(kostümieren)* dress up; **sich ~:** disguise oneself/dress [oneself] up; **b)** *(umhüllen, verdecken)* cover; *(verschalen)* line; face ⟨*façade*⟩

Verkleidung die a) *o. Pl.* disguising; *(das Kostümieren)* dressing up; **b)** *(Kostüm) (als Tarnung)* disguise; *(bei einer Party usw.)* fancy dress; **c)** *s.* **verkleiden b:** covering; lining; facing; **d)** *(Umhüllung)* cover

verkleinern [fɛɐ̯'klainɐn] **1.** *tr. V.* **a)** *(kleiner machen)* make smaller; reduce the size of; **den Abstand ~:** reduce *or* decrease the distance; **etw. in verkleinertem Maßstab darstellen** represent sth. on a smaller scale; scale sth. down; **b)** *(verringern)* reduce ⟨*size, number, etc.*⟩; **c)** *(schmälern)* belittle ⟨*person, achievements*⟩; minimize ⟨*importance, significance*⟩; **d)** *(kleiner reproduzieren)* reduce ⟨*photograph etc.*⟩. **2.** *refl. V.* **a)** *(ugs.: sich einschränken)* ⟨*company etc.*⟩ move to smaller premises; ⟨*family etc.*⟩ move to a smaller place; **b)** *(kleiner werden)* ⟨*space, area, etc.*⟩ become smaller; **c)** *(sich verringern)* ⟨*number*⟩ decrease, grow smaller; ⟨*circle of friends*⟩ grow smaller, shrink. **3.** *itr. V.* ⟨*lens etc.*⟩ make things look *or* appear smaller

Verkleinerung die; ~, ~en reduction in size; making smaller; *(des Formats, der Anzahl, des Maßstabs, durch eine Linse)* reduction; *(das Kleinerwerden)* becoming smaller

Verkleinerungs·form die *(Sprachw.)* diminutive form

verkleistern *tr. V. (ugs.)* **a)** *(zukleben)* fill ⟨*crack, hole*⟩; *(fig.)* cover up; **b)** *(zusammenkleben)* make into a sticky mass

verklemmen *refl. V.* get *or* become stuck; ⟨*door, window*⟩ jam, get *or* become jammed

verklemmt 1. *Adj.* inhibited. **2.** *adv.* in an inhibited manner

Verklemmtheit die; ~: inhibitedness

verklickern *tr. V. (salopp)* **jmdm. etw. ~:** make sth. clear to sb.; spell sth. out to sb.; *(erklären)* explain sth. to sb. in every detail

verklingen *unr. itr. V.; mit sein* ⟨*sound, voice, song, etc.*⟩ fade away; *(fig.)* ⟨*mood*⟩ wear off

verklumpen *itr. V.; mit sein* ⟨*gravy, sauce, etc.*⟩ go lumpy

verknacken *tr. V. (salopp)* **jmdn. zu Gefängnis/einer Geldstrafe ~:** put sb. inside *(sl.)*/slap a fine on sb. *(coll.);* **er wurde zu 18 Monaten verknackt** he got 18 months; **er wurde wegen ein paar Brüchen verknackt** he was done for a couple of break-ins *(sl.)*

verknacksen [fɛɐ̯'knaksn̩] *refl. V. (ugs.)* twist, sprain ⟨*ankle, wrist*⟩; **sich** *(Dat.)* **den Fuß ~:** twist *or* sprain one's ankle

verknallen 1. *tr. V. (ugs.: verschießen)* let off ⟨*firework*⟩; use up ⟨*ammunition*⟩; **zu Silvester werden unglaubliche Summen verknallt** incredible amounts of money are squandered on fireworks on New Year's Eve. **2.** *refl. V. (ugs.: sich verlieben)* fall head over heels in love **(in +** *Akk.* with); **in jmdn. verknallt sein** be crazy about sb. *(coll.)*

verknappen 1. *tr. V.* cut back [on] ⟨*imports*⟩; **das würde das Wasser noch weiter ~:** that would create even more water shortages. **2.** *refl. V.* run short

Verknappung die; ~, ~en cutting back (*Gen.* on); *(der Liquidität)* loss

verkneifen *unr. refl. V. (ugs.)* **a)** **sich** *(Dat.)* **eine Frage/Bemerkung ~:** bite back a question/remark; **ich konnte mir das Lachen/ein Lächeln kaum ~:** I could hardly keep a straight face; I could hardly stop myself laughing/smiling; **b)** *(verzichten)* manage *or* do without; **es sich** *(Dat.)* **~, etw. zu tun** stop oneself doing sth.

verkniffen 1. *2. Part. v.* **verkneifen. 2.** *Adj.* strained ⟨*expression*⟩; pinched ⟨*mouth, lips*⟩. **3.** *adv.* in a strained manner; **~ grinsen** force a grin

verknittern *tr. V.* crumple; **ein verknittertes Gesicht** *(fig.)* a wrinkled face

verknöchern [fɛɐ̯'knœçɐn] *itr. V.; mit sein* ⟨*person*⟩ become fossilized

verknorpeln *itr. V.; mit sein (Med.)* become cartilaginous

Verknorpelung die; ~, ~en cartilaginification

verknoten 1. *tr. V.* **a)** *(verknüpfen)* tie; knot; **zwei Fäden [miteinander] ~:** tie two threads together; **b)** *(festbinden)* tie **(an +** *Akk.* to). **2.** *refl. V.* become knotted

verknüpfen 1. *tr. V.* **a)** *(knoten)* tie; knot; **die beiden Fäden miteinander ~:** tie *or* knot the two threads together; **b)** *(zugleich tun)* combine; **c)** *(in Beziehung setzen)* link; *(unwillkürlich)* associate. **2.** *refl. V.* be associated

Verknüpfung die; ~, ~en a) *s.* **verknüpfen 1:** tying; knotting; combination; linking; association; **b)** *(Knoten)* knots *pl.*

verknusen [fɛɐ̯'knu:zn̩] *in* **jmdn./etw. nicht ~ können** *(ugs.)* not be able to stick *(sl.) or* stand sb./sth.

verkochen 1. *itr. V.;* mit sein **a)** *(verdampfen)* boil away; **b)** *(breiig werden, zerfallen)* boil down to a pulp. **2.** *tr. V.* boil **(zu +** *Dat.* to make)

[1]verkohlen 1. *itr. V.* char; become charred. **2.** *tr. V.* burn ⟨*wood*⟩ to charcoal; char

[2]verkohlen *tr. V. (ugs.) s.* **veräppeln**

[1]verkommen *unr. itr. V.; mit sein* **a)** *(verwahrlosen)* go to the dogs; *(moralisch, sittlich)* go to the bad; ⟨*child*⟩ go wild; **im tiefsten Elend ~:** sink deeper and deeper into poverty; **b)** *(verfallen)* ⟨*building etc.*⟩ go to rack and ruin, fall into disrepair, become dilapidated; ⟨*garden*⟩ run wild; ⟨*area*⟩ become run down; **c)** *(herabsinken)* degenerate **(zu** into); **d)** *(verderben)* ⟨*food*⟩ go bad; ⟨*wine, beer*⟩ go off

[2]verkommen 1. *2. Part. v.* **[1]verkommen. 2.** *Adj.* depraved; **ein ~es Subjekt** a dissolute character

Verkommenheit die; ~: depravity

verkomplizieren *tr. V.* complicate

verkonsumieren *tr. V. (ugs.)* get through; consume

verkoppeln *tr. V.* couple; ⟨*spacecraft*⟩ link up

Verkoppelung die; ~, ~en coupling; *(von Flugkörpern)* link-up

verkorken 1. *tr. V.* cork [up]. **2.** *itr. V.; mit sein (Bot.)* suberize

verkorksen [fɛɐ̯'kɔrksn̩] *(ugs.)* **1.** *tr. V.* make a mess of; mess up; **eine verkorkste Gesellschaft** a screwed-up society *(sl.).* **2.** *refl. V.* **sich** *(Dat.)* **den Magen ~:** upset one's stomach

verkörpern 1. *tr. V.* **a)** *(als Schauspieler)* play [the part of]; **b)** *(bilden)* embody; ⟨*person*⟩ embody, personify. **2.** *refl. V.* be embodied **(in +** *Dat.* in)

Verkörperung die; ~, ~en embodiment; *(Mensch)* embodiment; personification

verkosten *tr. V.* **a)** *(bes. österr.: kosten)* try; taste; **b)** *(prüfend schmecken)* taste ⟨*wine*⟩

verköstigen [fɛɐ̯'kœstɪgn̩] *tr. V.* feed; provide with meals

Verköstigung die; ~, ~en a) *o. Pl.* feeding; **die ~ der Kinder** the provision of the children with meals; **b)** *(Kost)* foods; meals *pl.*

verkrachen *refl. V. (ugs.)* fall out

verkracht *Adj.* failed; **er war ein ~er Student** he had been a failure at university/college; *s. auch* **Existenz c**

verkraften *tr. V.* cope with; **sie hat dieses Erlebnis nie verkraftet** she's never come to terms with this experience

verkrallen *refl. V.* dig one's fingers **(in +** *Akk.* into); *(festhalten)* cling **(in +** *Akk./Dat.* to)

verkramen *tr. V. (ugs.)* mislay

verkrampfen *refl. V.* ⟨*muscle*⟩ become cramped; ⟨*person*⟩ go tense, tense up; **verkrampft sitzen/lächeln** sit tensed up/smile tensely

Verkrampfung die; ~, ~en tenseness; tension

verkratzen *tr. V.* scratch; **sich** *(Dat.)* **die Beine ~:** scratch one's legs

verkrebst [fɛɐ̯'kre:pst] *Adj. (ugs.)* cancerous

verkriechen *unr. refl. V.* ⟨*animal*⟩ creep [away]; ⟨*person*⟩ hide [oneself away]; **sich unter die** *od.* **der Bank ~:** crawl *or* creep under the bench; **sich ins Bett ~** *(ugs.)* crawl into bed *(coll.);* **am liebsten hätte ich mich [in den hintersten Winkel] verkrochen** I'd have liked to crawl away and hide in a corner; I wished the ground would open and swallow me up

verkrümeln *refl. V. (ugs.: sich entfernen)* slip off *or* away

verkrümmen 1. *refl. V.* double up; ⟨*spine*⟩ become curved. **2.** *tr. V.* bend ⟨*finger etc.*⟩

verkrümmt *Adj.* bent ⟨*person*⟩*;* crooked ⟨*finger*⟩*;* curved ⟨*spine*⟩

Verkrümmung die crookedness; **~ der Wirbelsäule** curvature of the spine

verkrüppeln 1. *itr. V.; mit sein* ⟨*tree*⟩ become stunted; **verkrüppelt** stunted. **2.** *tr. V.* cripple ⟨*person*⟩*;* **verkrüppelte Arme/Füße** deformed arms/crippled feet

Verkrüppelung die; ~, ~en deformity

verkrusten *itr. V.; mit sein* form a crust; ⟨*wound*⟩ form a scab; **mit Blut verkrustet** encrusted with blood

verkühlen *refl. V.* catch a chill

Verkühlung die chill

verkümmern *itr. V.; mit sein* **a)** ⟨*person, animal*⟩ go into a decline; ⟨*plant etc.*⟩ become stunted; ⟨*muscle, limb*⟩ waste away, atrophy; **seelisch ~** ⟨*person*⟩ become emotionally stunted; **b)** ⟨*talent, emotional life, etc.*⟩ wither away; ⟨*strength*⟩ decline, fade; ⟨*relationship*⟩ become less close; ⟨*trade, initiative*⟩ dwindle

Verkümmerung die; ~, ~en *s.* **verkümmern b:** withering away; declining; fading; becoming less close; dwindling

verkünden *tr. V.* announce; pronounce ⟨*judgement*⟩*;* promulgate ⟨*law, decree*⟩*;* ⟨*sign, omen*⟩ presage; **die Menschenrechte ~:** proclaim the rights of man; **seine Miene verkündete nichts Gutes** *(fig.)* his expression did not augur well

verkündigen *tr. V. (geh.)* **a)** *(predigen)* preach; **b)** *(bekanntmachen)* announce; proclaim; *(mit Nachdruck sagen)* announce; **c)** *(ankündigen)* ⟨*sign, omen*⟩ presage

Verkündigung die a) *(das Predigen)* preaching; **b)** *(Bekanntmachung)* announcement; proclamation; **c)** *(das Wort Gottes)* word of God; **die kirchliche ~:** the Church's message

Verkündung die; ~, ~en announcement; *(von Urteilen)* pronouncement; *(von Gesetzen, Verordnungen)* promulgation

verkuppeln *tr. V.* pair off **(mit** with)

verkürzen 1. *tr. V.* **a)** *(verringern)* reduce; *(abkürzen)* shorten; **die Linie erscheint verkürzt** this line appears foreshortened; **b)** *(abbrechen)* cut short ⟨*stay, life*⟩*;* put an end to, end ⟨*suffering*⟩*;* **verkürzte Arbeitszeit** reduced *or* shorter working hours *pl.;* **c)** **sich** *(Dat.)* **die Zeit ~:** while away the time; make the time pass more quickly; **jmdm. die Winterabende ~:** help sb. while away the winter evenings. **2.** *refl. V. (kürzer werden)* become shorter; shorten; ⟨*perspective*⟩ become foreshortened. **3.** *itr. V. (Ballspiele)* close the gap **(auf +** *Akk.* to)

Verkürzung die *s.* **verkürzen 1 a, b:** shortening; reduction; foreshortening; cutting short; ending; **eine ~ der Arbeitszeit** a reduction in working hours; **starkes Rauchen hat eine ~ der Lebenserwartung um ... zur Folge** heavy smoking reduces life expectancy by ...

verlachen *tr. V.* laugh at; **etw. als Unsinn ~:** ridicule sth. as nonsense

verladen *unr. tr. V.* **a)** *(laden)* load; **b)** *(ugs.: betrügen)* **jmdn. ~:** take sb. for a ride *(sl.);* con sb. *(sl.); (Ballspiele)* out-trick sb.

Verlade·rampe die loading platform

Verladung die loading

Verlag [fɛɐ̯'la:k] **der; ~[e]s, ~e** publishing house *or* firm; publisher's; **in welchem ~ ist das Buch erschienen?** who published the book?; who is the publisher of the book?

verlagern 1. *tr. V.* shift ⟨*weight, centre of gravity*⟩*; (an einen anderen Ort)* move; *(fig.)* transfer; shift ⟨*emphasis*⟩. **2.** *refl. V. (auch fig.)* shift; ⟨*area of high/low pressure etc.*⟩ move

Verlagerung die moving; **eine ~ des Schwergewichts** *(fig.)* a shift in emphasis

Verlags-: ~anstalt die publishing house *or* firm; firm of publishers; **~buch·händler der** publisher; **~haus das** publishing house *or* firm; **~programm das** [publisher's] list; **~wesen das** publishing *no art.*

verlanden *itr. V.; mit sein* silt up

Verlandung die silting up

verlangen 1. *tr. V.* **a)** *(fordern)* demand; *(wollen)* want; **man kann von ihm nicht ~, daß er alles bezahlt** one can't ask *or* expect him to pay everything; **das ist zuviel verlangt** that's asking too much; that's too much to expect; **du verlangst Unmögliches** you're asking the impossible; **die Firma verlangt [von den Bewerbern] EDV-Kenntnisse** the company asks for [applicants with] a knowledge of computers; **die Rechnung ~:** ask for the bill; **von jedem wird Pünktlichkeit verlangt** everyone is required *or* expected to be punctual; **b)** *(nötig haben)* ⟨*task etc.*⟩ require, call for ⟨*patience, knowledge, experience, skill, etc.*⟩*;* **diese Aufgabe verlangt den ganzen Menschen** this task makes demands of the whole person; **c)** *(gebieten)* ⟨*situation, decency*⟩ demand; **d)** *(berechnen)* charge; **sie verlangte 200 Mark von ihm** she charged him 200 marks; **wieviel verlangst du dafür?** how much are you asking for it?; **e)** *(sehen wollen)* ask for, ask to see ⟨*passport, driving-licence, etc.*⟩*;* **f)** *(am Telefon)* ask for; ask to speak to; **du wirst am Telefon verlangt** you're wanted on the phone *(coll.);* **g)** *unpers. (geh.)* **es verlangt mich, ihn noch einmal zu sehen** I long *or* yearn to see him again. **2.** *itr. V. (geh.)* **a)** *(bitten)* **nach einem Arzt/Priester** *usw.* **~:** ask for a doctor/priest *etc.;* **nach einem Glas Wasser ~:** ask for a glass of water; **b)** *(sich sehnen)* **nach jmdm./etw. ~:** long for sb./sth.

Verlangen das; ~s, ~ a) *(Bedürfnis)* desire **(nach** for); **ein starkes ~ nach Schokolade haben** *od.* **verspüren** have a craving for chocolate; **b)** *(Forderung)* demand; **auf ~:** on request; **auf jmds. ~:** at sb.'s request

verlängern [fɛɐ̯'lɛŋɐn] **1.** *tr. V.* **a)** *(länger machen)* lengthen, make longer ⟨*skirt, sleeve, etc.*⟩*;* extend ⟨*flex, cable, road, etc.*⟩*; s. auch* **Arm a; Rücken a; b)** *(länger gültig sein lassen)* renew ⟨*passport, driving-licence, etc.*⟩*;* extend, renew ⟨*contract*⟩*;* **c)** *(länger dauern lassen)* extend, prolong ⟨*stay, life, suffering, etc.*⟩ **(um** by); **ein verlängertes**

Wochenende a long weekend; **d)** *(verdünnen)* add water *etc.* to ⟨*sauce, gravy, etc.*⟩ *(to make it go further)*; **e)** *(Ballspiele)* touch ⟨*cross, corner-kick, etc.*⟩ on. **2.** *refl. V.* **a)** *(länger werden)* become longer; ⟨*stay, life, suffering, etc.*⟩ be prolonged (**um** by); *(länger gültig bleiben)* ⟨*contract etc.*⟩ be extended. **3.** *itr. V. (Ballspiele)* touch [the ball] on; **mit dem Kopf ~:** head [the ball] on

Verlängerung die; ~, ~en a) *s.* **verlängern 1 a–c:** lengthening; renewal; extension; prolongation; **b)** *(Ballspiele)* extra time *no indef. art.*; *(nachgespielte Zeit)* injury time *no indef. art.*; **in der/nach ~:** in/after extra time; **c)** *(Teilstück)* extension

Verlängerungs·schnur die extension lead *or (Amer.)* cord

verlangsamen 1. *tr. V.* **die Fahrt** *od.* **das Tempo/seine Schritte ~:** reduce speed/slacken one's pace; slow down. **2.** *refl. V.* slow down; ⟨*pace*⟩ slacken

Verlangsamung die; ~, ~en slowing down; *(des Tempos)* slackening; **zu einer ~ des Tempos gezwungen sein** be forced to slow down

Verlaß der *in* **auf jmdn./etw. ist [kein] ~:** sb./sth. can[not] be relied *or* depended [up]on; **auf ihn ist kein ~:** you can't rely *or* depend on him

[1]verlassen 1. *unr. refl. V. (vertrauen)* rely, depend (**auf** + *Akk.* on); **er verläßt sich darauf, daß du kommst** he's relying on you to come; **darauf kannst du dich ~/worauf du dich ~ kannst** you can depend on *or* be sure of that. **2.** *unr. tr. V.* **a)** leave; **die Patientin konnte das Bett ~:** the patient was able to get up; **b)** *(sich trennen von)* desert; abandon; forsake; leave, desert ⟨*wife, family, etc.*⟩; **Großvater hat uns für immer ~** *(verhüll.)* grandfather has been taken from us *(euphem.)*; **und da/dann verließen sie ihn** *(ugs.)* and after that I/he *etc.* was at a loss; **der Mut/alle Hoffnung hatte mich ~** *(fig.)* my courage/all hope had deserted me

[2]verlassen 1. *2. Part. v.* **[1]verlassen. 2.** *Adj.* deserted ⟨*street, square, village, etc.*⟩; empty ⟨*house*⟩; *(öd)* desolate ⟨*region etc.*⟩; **einsam und ~:** all alone; **~ daliegen** be deserted

Verlassenheit die; ~: desertedness; *(Öde)* desolation; **ein Gefühl von ~:** a feeling of desolation

verläßlich [fɛɐ̯ˈlɛslɪç] **1.** *Adj.* reliable; reliable, dependable ⟨*person*⟩. **2.** *adv.* reliably

Verläßlichkeit die; ~: reliability; *(eines Menschen)* reliability; dependability

verlästern *tr. V.* malign

Verlaub [fɛɐ̯ˈlaup] **der** *in* **mit ~** *(geh.)* with your permission; **mit ~ [gesagt** *od.* **zu sagen]** if you will pardon *or* forgive my saying so

Verlauf der; ~[e]s, Verläufe course; **im ~e des Sommers/ihrer Rede** during *or* in the course of the summer/her speech; **der glückliche ~ der Revolution** the fortunate outcome of the revolution

verlaufen 1. *unr. itr. V.; mit sein* **a)** *(sich erstrecken)* run; **b)** *(ablaufen)* ⟨*test, rehearsal, etc.*⟩ go; ⟨*party etc.*⟩ go off; **es ist alles gut ~:** everything went [off] well; **die Untersuchung ist ergebnislos ~:** die investigation yielded no results; **c)** ⟨*butter, chocolate, etc.*⟩ melt; ⟨*make-up, ink*⟩ run. **2.** *unr. itr. (auch refl.) V.; mit sein (sich verlieren)* ⟨*track, path*⟩ disappear (**in** + *Dat.* in). **3.** *unr. refl. V.* **a)** *(sich verirren)* get lost; lose one's way; **b)** *(auseinandergehen)* ⟨*crowd etc.*⟩ disperse; **c)** *(abfließen)* ⟨*floods*⟩ subside

Verlaufs·form die *(Sprachw.)* progressive *or* continuous form

verlausen *itr. V.; mit sein* become infested with lice; **verlaust** louse-ridden; infested with lice *postpos.*

verlautbaren 1. *tr. V.* announce [officially]; **offen ~:** state openly; **die Ärzte verlautbarten, daß ...:** the doctors issued a bulletin to the effect that .... **2.** *itr. V.; mit sein (geh.)* become known; **es verlautbarte, der Staatschef sei krank** it was reported *or* said that the head of state was ill

Verlautbarung die; ~, ~en announcement; *(inoffizielle Meldung)* [unofficial] report

verlauten 1. *tr. V.* announce; **er hütete sich davor, ein Wort davon zu ~:** he was careful not to say a word about it. **2.** *itr. V.; mit sein* be reported; **wie verlautet** according to reports; **aus amtlicher Quelle verlautet, daß ...:** official reports say that ...; **über ihr Privatleben ließ sie nichts ~:** she let nothing be known about her private life

verleben *tr. V.* **a)** *(verbringen)* spend; **b)** *(ugs.: verbrauchen)* spend ⟨*money*⟩ on everyday needs

verlebendigen *tr. V.* make ⟨*text, past, etc.*⟩ come alive; imbue ⟨*portrait, figure*⟩ with life

verlebt *Adj.* dissipated

[1]verlegen 1. *tr. V.* **a)** *(nicht wiederfinden)* mislay; **b)** *(verschieben)* postpone (**auf** + *Akk.* until); *(vor~)* bring forward (**auf** + *Akk.* to); **einen Termin ~:** alter an appointment; **c)** *(verlagern)* move; transfer ⟨*patient*⟩; **die Handlung ins 18. Jahrhundert ~:** transpose *or* shift the action to the 18th century; **d)** *(legen)* lay ⟨*cable, pipe, carpet, etc.*⟩; **e)** *(versperren)* block, bar ⟨*way etc.*⟩; block off ⟨*retreat*⟩; **jmdm. den Weg ~:** block *or* bar sb.'s way; **f)** *(veröffentlichen)* publish. **2.** *refl. V. (sich ausrichten)* take up ⟨*subject, activity, occupation, etc.*⟩; resort to ⟨*guesswork, flattery, silence, lying, etc.*⟩; **sich auf eine andere Taktik ~:** change [one's] tactics; resort to a different tactic

[2]verlegen 1. *Adj.* **a)** embarrassed; **b) um etw. ~ sein** *(etw. nicht zur Verfügung haben)* be short of sth.; *(etw. benötigen)* be in need of sth.; **nicht/nie um Worte/eine Ausrede ~ sein** not/never be at a loss for words/an excuse. **2.** *adv.* in embarrassment

Verlegenheit die; ~, ~en a) *o. Pl. (Befangenheit)* embarrassment; **in ~ geraten** get *or* become embarrassed; **jmdn. in ~ bringen** embarrass sb.; **b)** *(Unannehmlichkeit)* embarrassing situation; **in finanzieller ~ sein** be in financial difficulties; be financially embarrassed; **ich bin nie in die ~ gekommen** I've never been in that embarrassing situation

Verlegenheits·lösung die makeshift solution

Verleger der; ~s, ~, Verlegerin die; ~, ~nen publisher; *s. auch* **-in**

verlegerisch 1. *Adj.; nicht präd.* publishing; **~e Kenntnisse** knowledge of publishing; **~e Anstrengungen** efforts on the part of the publishers. **2.** *adv.* from the publishing standpoint

Verlegung die; ~, ~en a) *(Verschiebung)* postponement; *(Vor~)* bringing forward *no art.*; **um eine ~ des Termins bitten** ask to change the appointment; **b)** *s.* **[1]verlegen 1 c:** moving; transfer; transposition; shifting; **c)** *(von Kabeln, Rohren, Teppichen usw.)* laying

verleiden *tr. V.* **jmdm. etw. ~:** spoil sth. for sb.

Verleih der; ~[e]s, ~e a) *o. Pl. (das Verleihen)* hiring out; *(von Autos)* renting *or* hiring out; **b)** *(Unternehmen)* hire firm *or* company; *(Film~)* distribution company; *(Video~)* video library; *(Auto~)* rental *or* hire firm

verleihen *unr. tr. V.* **a)** hire out; rent *or* hire out ⟨*car*⟩; *(umsonst)* lend [out]; **b)** *(überreichen)* award; bestow, confer ⟨*award, honour*⟩; **jmdm. einen Orden/Titel ~:** decorate sb./confer a title on sb.; **jmdm. die Ehrenbürgerrechte ~:** give sb. the freedom of the city/town; **c)** *(verschaffen)* give; lend; **er verlieh seinen Worten mit Drohungen Nachdruck** he used threats to lend weight to his words

Verleiher der; ~s, ~: hirer; *(Film~)* distributor

Verleihung die; ~, ~en a) *s.* **verleihen a:** hiring out; renting out; lending [out]; **b)** *s.* **verleihen b:** awarding; bestowing; conferring; *(Zeremonie)* award; conferment; bestowal

verleimen *tr. V.* glue

verleiten *tr. V.* **jmdn. dazu ~, etw. zu tun** lead *or* induce sb. to do sth.; *(verlocken)* tempt *or* entice sb. to do sth.; **jmdn. zum Trinken/Stehlen ~:** lead sb. into drinking/stealing; **sich zu voreiligen Schlußfolgerungen ~ lassen** allow oneself to be led into drawing hasty conclusions

Verleitung die: sie beschuldigte ihn der ~ zum Meineid she accused him of inducing *or* encouraging her to commit perjury; **das wäre ~ zum Diebstahl** it would be encouraging theft

verlernen *tr. V.* forget; **das Kochen ~:** forget how to cook; **sie hat das Lachen verlernt** *(fig.)* she has forgotten how to laugh

[1]verlesen 1. *unr. tr. V.* read out. **2.** *unr. refl. V. (falsch lesen)* make a mistake/mistakes in reading; **er hat sich wohl ~:** he must have read it wrongly

[2]verlesen 1. *2. Part. v.* **[1]verlesen. 2.** *unr. tr. V. (auslesen)* sort ⟨*fruit, vegetables*⟩

Verlesung die; ~, ~en reading out

verletzbar *Adj.* **leicht ~ sein** be easily hurt

Verletzbarkeit die; ~: seine ~ war groß he was very easily hurt; **sie kannte meine ~:** she knew how easily I could be hurt

verletzen [fɛɐ̯ˈlɛtsn̩] *tr. V.* **a)** *(beschädigen)* injure; *(durch Schuß, Stich)* wound; **ich habe mich am Kopf/mir das Bein verletzt** I injured *or* hurt my head/leg; **b)** *(kränken)* hurt, wound ⟨*person, feelings*⟩; **verletzte Eitelkeit/verletzter Stolz** injured *or* wounded vanity/pride; **eine ~de Bemerkung** a wounding remark; **sich in seinem Stolz verletzt fühlen** feel that one's pride has been hurt *or* has taken a blow; **c)** *(verstoßen gegen)* violate; infringe; infringe ⟨*regulation*⟩; break ⟨*agreement, law*⟩; **das Wahlgeheimnis ~:** breach the secrecy of the vote; **den guten Geschmack ~:** offend against good taste; **d)** *(eindringen in)* violate ⟨*frontier, airspace, etc.*⟩

verletzlich *Adj.* vulnerable; *(empfindlich)* sensitive

Verletzlichkeit die; ~: vulnerability; *(Empfindlichkeit)* sensitivity

Verletzte der/die; *adj. Dekl.* injured person; casualty; *(durch Schuß, Stich)* wounded person; **die ~n** the injured/wounded; the casualties; **bei dem Unfall gab es einen Toten und zwei ~:** one person died and two were injured in the accident; **es gab keine ~n bei der Demonstration** nobody was hurt during the demonstration

Verletzung die; ~, ~en a) *(Wunde)* injury; **eine ~ am Knie haben** have an injury to one's knee *or* an injured knee; **b)** *(Kränkung)* hurting; wounding; **c)** *s.* **verletzen c:** violation; infringement; breaking; **d)** *(Grenz~, Luftraum~ usw.)* violation

verleugnen *tr. V.* deny; disown ⟨*friend, relation*⟩; **er kann seine Herkunft nicht ~:** it is obvious where he comes from; **sich selbst ~:** go against *or* betray one's principles

Verleugnung die denial; *(eines Freundes, Verwandten)* disownment

verleumden [fɛɐ̯ˈlɔymdn̩] *tr. V.* slander; *(schriftlich)* libel

Verleumder der; ~, ~: slanderer; *(schriftlich)* libeller

verleumderisch *Adj.* slanderous; *(in Schriftform)* libellous

Verleumdung die; ~, ~en a) *o. Pl.* slander; *(in Schriftform)* libelling; **b)** *(Bemerkung usw.)* slander; *(in Schriftform)* libel

Verleumdungs·kampagne die smear campaign

verlieben *refl. V.* fall in love (**in** + *Akk.* with); **ein verliebtes Pärchen** a pair of lovers; **jmdm. verliebte Blicke zuwerfen** make eyes at sb.; **er ist ganz verliebt in seine Idee** *(fig.)* he is infatuated with his idea; **zum Verlieben sein/aussehen** *(ugs.)* be/look perfectly sweet

Verliebte der/die; *adj. Dekl.* lover; **die beiden ~n** the [two] lovers

Verliebtheit die; ~: being *no art.* in love; **die ~ dauerte bei ihr nur drei Wochen** she was only in love for three weeks; **in ihrer ~ hatte sie ...:** being so much in love, she had ...

verlieren [fɛɐ̯'li:rən] **1.** *unr. tr. V.* lose; ⟨*plant, tree*⟩ lose, shed ⟨*leaves*⟩; **sich** *(Dat.)* **verloren vorkommen** feel lost; **für jmdn./etw. verloren sein** be lost to sb./sth.; **die Katze verliert Haare** the cat is moulting; **nichts [mehr] zu ~ haben** have nothing [more] to lose; **jmdn./etw. verloren geben** give sb./sth. up for lost; **das hat hier nichts verloren** it has no business to be here. **2.** *unr. itr. V.* lose; **an etw.** *(Dat.)* **~:** lose sth.; **sie hat an Reiz verloren** she has lost some of her attraction; **bei jmdm. ~:** become less highly regarded by sb. **3.** *unr. refl. V.* **a)** *(weniger werden)* ⟨*enthusiasm*⟩ subside; ⟨*reserve etc.*⟩ disappear; **b)** *(entschwinden)* vanish; ⟨*sound*⟩ die away; **c)** *(sich verirren)* lose one's way; get lost; **d)** *(sich hingeben)* **er war in Gedanken verloren** he was lost in thought; **e)** *(abschweifen)* digress; **sich in Detailschilderungen ~:** digress into detailed descriptions

Verlierer der; ~s, ~: loser; **ein schlechter ~:** a bad loser; **der ~ des Autoschlüssels** the person who has lost the car key

Verlies [fɛɐ̯'li:s] **das; ~es, ~e** dungeon

verloben 1. *refl. V.* become *or* get engaged, *(arch.)* become betrothed (**mit** to); **verlobt sein** be engaged. **2.** *tr. V. (veralt.)* **jmdn. mit jmdm. ~:** betroth sb. to sb. *(arch.)*

Verlöbnis [fɛɐ̯'lø:pnɪs] **das; ~ses, ~se** *(geh.)* engagement, *(arch.)* betrothal (**mit** to)

Verlobte der/die; *adj. Dekl.* **mein ~r** my fiancé *or (arch.)* betrothed; **meine ~:** my fiancée *or (arch.)* betrothed; **die ~n** the engaged *or (arch.)* betrothed couple

Verlobung die; ~, ~en engagement; betrothal *(arch.)*; *(Feier)* engagement party

Verlobungs·anzeige die engagement announcement

verlocken *tr. V. (geh.)* tempt; entice; **der See verlockt zum Baden** the lake tempts *or* entices one to bathe in it

verlockend *Adj.* tempting; enticing; **das Wetter war nicht gerade ~:** the weather wasn't exactly enticing

Verlockung die temptation; enticement; **der ~ widerstehen** resist the temptation

verlogen [fɛɐ̯'lo:gn̩] *(abwertend)* **1.** *Adj.* lying, mendacious ⟨*person*⟩; false ⟨*morality, phrases, romanticism, etc.*⟩; insincere ⟨*compliment*⟩. **2.** *adv.* mendaciously; falsely

Verlogenheit die; ~, ~en *(eines Menschen)* mendacity; *(einer Moral, Romantik, von Phrasen usw.)* falseness; *(von Komplimenten)* insincerity

verlohnen *(geh.)* **1.** *refl. (auch itr.) V.* be worth while; **es verlohnt sich nicht, das zu tun** it is not worth [while] doing that. **2.** *tr. (od. veralt. itr.) V.* **das verlohnt die/***(veralt.)* **der Mühe nicht** it is not worth the trouble

verlor [fɛɐ̯'lo:ɐ̯] *1. u. 3. Pers. Sg. Prät. v.* **verlieren**

verloren 1. *2. Part. v.* **verlieren. 2.** *Adj.* lost; **[eine] ~e Mühe** a wasted effort; **Laß uns aufhören! Die Sache ist ~:** Let's give up! It's hopeless; **er ist ~:** that's the end of him now; **ohne meine Brille bin ich ~** *(fig.)* I'm lost without my glasses; **~e Eier** poached eggs; **der ~e Sohn** *(bibl.)* the Prodigal Son

verloren|gehen *unr. itr. V.; mit sein* **a)** *(abhanden kommen)* get lost; **deine Postkarte muß wohl verlorengegangen sein** your postcard must have got lost *or* gone astray; **durch diesen Umweg ging uns/ging viel Zeit verloren** we lost a lot of time/a lot of time was lost by this detour; **ein verlorengegangenes Buch** a lost book; a book that has gone missing; **an dir ist ein Künstler verlorengegangen** you ought to have been an artist; you would have made a good artist; **b)** *(nicht gewonnen werden)* ⟨*war, battle, etc.*⟩ be lost

Verlorenheit die; ~: loneliness; isolation

verlöschen *unr. itr. V.; mit sein* ⟨*light, fire, etc.*⟩ go out; ⟨*comet, shooting star*⟩ die

verlosen *tr. V.* raffle

Verlosung die; ~, ~en raffle; draw; *(Ziehung)* draw; *(Vorgang)* raffling

verlottern [fɛɐ̯'lɔtɐn] *itr. V.; mit sein (abwertend)* ⟨*building, town, area, etc.*⟩ become run-down; ⟨*person*⟩ go to seed; ⟨*firm, business*⟩ go downhill, go to the dogs

Verlust der; ~[e]s, ~e loss (**an** + *Dat.* of); **bei ~** in the case *or* event of loss; **schwere ~e erleiden** ⟨*army etc.*⟩ suffer heavy losses *or* casualties; **etw. mit ~ verkaufen** sell sth. at a loss

Verlust·geschäft das loss-making deal *or* transaction; **sonst mache ich ein ~:** otherwise I'll be making a loss

verlustieren *refl. V. (scherzh.)* amuse oneself; **wir haben uns auf der Party verlustiert** we had fun *or* enjoyed ourselves at the party; **sich mit jmdm. im Bett ~:** have a good time in bed with sb.

verlustig *Adj.* **in einer Sache** *(Gen.)* **~ gehen** *(Papierdt.)* lose sth.; *(verwirken)* forfeit *or* lose sth.

verlust-, Verlust-: ~liste die list of casualties and losses; *(fig.)* casualty list; **~meldung die** casualty report; **~reich** *Adj.* **a)** *(mit vielen Toten)* ⟨*battle etc.*⟩ involving heavy losses; **b)** *(mit finanziellen ~en)* heavily loss-making ⟨*product, project, etc.*⟩

vermachen *tr. V.* **jmdm. etw. ~:** leave *or* bequeath sth. to sb.; *(fig.: schenken, überlassen)* give sth. to sb.; let sb. have sth.

Vermächtnis [fɛɐ̯'mɛçtnɪs] **das; ~ses, ~se a)** *(Rechtspr.: Legat)* bequest; legacy; *(fig.)* legacy; **b)** *(Letzter Wille)* last wish

vermählen [fɛɐ̯'mɛ:lən] *(geh.)* **1.** *refl. V.* **sich [jmdm. od. mit jmdm.] ~:** marry *or* wed [sb.]; *(fig.)* be wedded (**mit** to); **frisch vermählt** newly married. **2.** *tr. V. (veralt.)* **seine Tochter mit jmdm. ~:** marry one's daughter to sb.; give one's daughter to sb. in marriage

Vermählte der/die; *adj. Dekl., meist Pl. (geh.)* bridegroom/bride; **die ~n** the bride and bridegroom; **die beiden frisch ~n** the newly-married couple; the newly-weds *(coll.)*

Vermählung die; ~, ~en *(geh.)* **a)** marriage; wedding; **b)** *(Fest)* wedding ceremony

vermaledeit [fɛɐ̯male'dait] *Adj.; nicht präd. (ugs. veralt.)* damned; blasted *(Brit.)*

vermännlichen *tr. V.* masculinize

vermarkten *tr. V.* **a)** *(als Ware verkaufen)* exploit commercially; **b)** *(Wirtsch.)* market ⟨*goods etc.*⟩

Vermarktung die; ~, ~en a) commercial exploitation; **b)** *(Wirtsch.)* marketing

vermasseln [fɛɐ̯'masl̩n] *tr. V. (salopp)* **a)** *(verderben)* muck up *(Brit. sl.)*; mess up; ruin; **b)** *(verhauen)* make a cock-up *(Brit. sl.) or* mess of ⟨*exam etc.*⟩

Vermassung die; ~, ~en *(abwertend)* loss of individuality

vermauern *tr. V.* **a)** *(zumauern)* wall up ⟨*entrance*⟩; brick up ⟨*hole, window, etc.*⟩; **b)** *(verbrauchen)* use up ⟨*bricks, sand, etc.*⟩ in building a/the wall *etc.*

vermehren 1. *tr. V. (größer machen)* increase (**um** by). **2.** *refl. V.* **a)** *(größer werden)* increase; **b)** *(sich fortpflanzen)* reproduce; ⟨*bacterium, virus*⟩ multiply

vermehrt 1. *Adj.* increased. **2.** *adv.* increasingly; **~ auftreten** occur with increasing frequency

Vermehrung die; ~, ~en a) increase (*Gen.* in); **b)** *(Fortpflanzung)* reproduction; *(von Bakterien, Viren)* multiplying

vermeidbar *Adj.* avoidable; **die Niederlage wäre ~ gewesen** the defeat could have been avoided

vermeiden *unr. tr. V.* avoid; **es läßt sich nicht ~:** it is unavoidable; **es ~, etw. zu tun** avoid doing sth.; **er hatte gehofft, daß der Krieg zu ~ sei** he had hoped that war could be avoided; **ein Gegentor ~:** avoid conceding a goal

Vermeidung die; ~, ~en avoidance

vermeinen *tr. V. (geh.)* think; **er vermeinte, ihre Stimme zu hören** he thought he heard her voice

vermeintlich [fɛɐ̯'maintlɪç] **1.** *Adj.; nicht präd.* supposed. **2.** *adv.* supposedly

vermelden *tr. V.* report; ⟨*report*⟩ announce

vermengen 1. *tr. V.* **a)** *(mischen)* mix (**miteinander** together); **b)** *(durcheinanderbringen)* mix up; confuse. **2.** *refl. V. (sich mischen)* mingle

vermenschlichen *tr. V.* anthropomorphize

Vermenschlichung die; ~, ~en anthropomorphization

Vermerk [fɛɐ̯'mɛrk] **der; ~[e]s, ~e** note; *(amtlich)* remark; *(Stempel)* stamp; *(im Kalender)* entry

vermerken *tr. V.* **a)** *(notieren)* make a note of; note [down]; *(in Akten, Wachbuch usw.)* record; **das sei aber nur am Rande vermerkt** but that is only by the way; **b)** *(feststellen)* note; *s. auch* **übel 2 b**

¹vermessen 1. *unr. tr. V.* measure; survey ⟨*land, site*⟩. **2.** *unr. refl. V.* **a)** *(falsch messen)* measure wrongly; **b)** *(geh.: sich anmaßen)* **sich ~, etw. zu tun** presume *or* have the presumption to do sth.; **wie konnte er sich ~!** what presumption!

²vermessen *Adj. (geh.)* presumptuous; **darf ich so ~ sein anzunehmen, daß ...:** may I be so bold as to assume that ...

Vermessenheit die; ~, ~en *(geh.)* presumption; presumptuousness; **das ist eine große ~ von dir** that is very presumptuous of you

Vermessung die measurement; *(Land~)* surveying

vermiesen *tr. V. (ugs.)* **jmdm. etw. ~:** spoil sth. for sb.; **jmdm. die Laune/das Vergnügen ~:** spoil sb.'s mood/enjoyment

vermieten *tr. (auch itr.) V.* rent [out], let [out] ⟨*flat, room, etc.*⟩ (**an** + *Akk.* to); hire [out] ⟨*boat, car, etc.*⟩; **wir ~ auch an Studenten** we also rent *or* let to students; **„Zimmer zu ~"** 'room to let'

Vermieter der landlord

Vermieterin die landlady

Vermietung die; ~, ~en *s.* **vermieten:** renting [out]; letting [out]; hiring [out]

vermindern 1. *tr. V.* reduce; decrease; reduce, lessen ⟨*danger, stress*⟩; lessen ⟨*admiration, ability*⟩; lower ⟨*resistance*⟩; reduce ⟨*debt*⟩. **2.** *refl. V.* decrease; ⟨*influence, danger*⟩ decrease, diminish; ⟨*resistance*⟩ diminish

vermindert *Adj.* **a) ~e Zurechnungsfähigkeit** *(Rechtsw.)* diminished responsibility; **b)** *(Mus.)* diminished

Verminderung die *s.* **vermindern 1:** reduction; decreasing; lessening; lowering; **eine ~ der Einnahmen** a decrease in revenues

verminen *tr. V.* mine

vermischen 1. *tr. V.* mix (**miteinander** together); blend ⟨*teas, tobaccos, etc.*⟩; **Wahres und Erdachtes miteinander ~:** mingle truth and fiction. **2.** *refl. V.* mix; *(fig.)* mingle; ⟨*races, animals*⟩ interbreed; **unter der Rubrik „Vermischtes"** under the heading 'Miscellaneous'

Vermischung die *s.* **vermischen:** mixing; blending; *(fig.)* mingling

vermissen *tr. V.* **a)** *(sich sehnen nach)* miss; **b)** *(nicht haben)* **ich vermisse meinen Ausweis** my identity card is missing; **nach dem Brand wurde er vermißt** he was unaccounted for after the fire; **ich vermisse in deiner Küche einen Kühlschrank** I notice that you do not have a fridge in your kitchen; **etw. ~ lassen** lack sth.; be lacking in sth.; **er gilt als** *od.* **ist vermißt** *(fig.)* he is listed as a missing person; **der vermißte Soldat** the missing soldier; **man hat dich in der Vorlesung vermißt** your absence from the lecture was noticed

Vermißte der/die; *adj. Dekl.* missing person

Vermißten·anzeige die ~ [von jmdm.] erstatten report sb. [as] missing

vermitteln 1. *itr. V.* mediate, act as [a] mediator (**in** + *Dat.* in); **~d eingreifen** act as [a] mediator; **~de Worte** conciliating words. **2.** *tr. V.* **a)** *(herbeiführen)* arrange; negotiate ⟨*transaction, cease-fire, compromise*⟩; **b)** *(besorgen)* **jmdm. eine Stelle ~:** find sb. a job; find a job for sb.; **jmdm. ein Haus ~:** locate a house for sb.; **c)** *(als Mittler tätig sein für)* **das Arbeitsamt vermittelt die Arbeitskräfte an die Firmen** the job centre *(Brit.) or (Amer.)* employment office places workers with firms; **d)** *(weitergeben)* impart ⟨*knowledge, insight, values, etc.*⟩; communicate, pass on ⟨*message, information, etc.*⟩; convey, give ⟨*feeling*⟩; pass on ⟨*experience*⟩; **jmdm. ein genaues Bild von etw. ~:** convey a precise picture of sth. to sb.; **jmdm. Bildung ~:** educate sb.

vermittels[t] *Präp. mit Gen. (Papierdt.)* by means of; **~ eines Wörterbuchs** with the help of a dictionary

Vermittler der; ~s, ~ a) *(Mittler)* mediator; **b)** *(Träger) s.* **vermitteln 2 d:** imparter; communicator; conveyer; **c)** *(von Berufs wegen)* agent; **der ~ eines Geschäfts** the negotiator of a transaction

Vermittler·rolle die role of mediator

Vermittlung die; ~, ~en a) *(Schlichtung)* mediation; **seine ~ anbieten** offer to mediate; **b)** *s.* **vermitteln 2 a:** arrangement; negotiation; **durch die ~ eines Beamten** through the good offices of an official; **c)** *(das Besorgen)* **die ~ einer Stelle** finding a job for sb.; **die ~ eines Hauses für jmdn.** locating a house for sb.; **d)** *s.* **vermitteln 2 d:** imparting; communicating; passing on; conveying; **e)** *(Telefonzentrale)* exchange; *(in einer Firma)* switchboard; *(Telefonist)* operator

Vermittlungs-: ~aus·schuß der mediation committee [between the two houses of parliament]; **~gebühr die** commission

vermöbeln *tr. V. (ugs.)* beat up; *(als Strafe)* thrash

vermodern *itr. V.; mit sein* decay; rot

vermöge *Präp. mit Gen. (geh.)* by virtue of

vermögen *(geh.) unr. tr. V.* **etw. zu tun ~:** be able to do sth.; be capable of doing sth.; **er vermochte [es] nicht, mich zu überzeugen** he was not able to convince me; **wir werden alles tun, was wir [zu tun] ~:** we will do everything we can; **wer vermöchte zu sagen, ob ...:** who can say whether ...; **er vermochte nichts dagegen** he could do nothing to prevent it

Vermögen das; ~s, ~ a) *o. Pl. (geh.: Fähigkeit)* ability; **b)** *(Besitz)* fortune; **er hat ~:** he has money; he is a man of means; **das kostet ja ein ~** *(ugs.)* it costs a fortune; **sein ganzes ~:** all his money

vermögend *Adj.* wealthy; well-off; **sie ist eine ~e Frau** she is a woman of means *or* a wealthy woman

Vermögens-: ~ab·gabe die capital levy; **~bildung die** *(wider) creation of wealth by participation of employees in savings and share-ownership schemes;* **~steuer die** wealth tax

Vermögen·steuer die *s.* Vermögenssteuer

vermögens-, Vermögens-: ~verhältnisse *Pl.* financial circumstances; **~werte** *Pl.* investments; **~wirksam 1.** *Adj.* ⟨*saving*⟩ under the employee's savings scheme; **~wirksame Leistungen** employer's contributions to employees' savings schemes; **2.** *adv.* ⟨*invest*⟩ profitably

vermummen [fɛɐ̯ˈmʊmən] *tr. V.* **a)** *(einhüllen)* wrap up [warmly]; **b)** *(verbergen)* disguise; **vermummte Jugendliche** masked youths

Vermummung die; ~, ~en a) *o. Pl.* **zur ~ hatten wir ...:** in order to disguise ourselves we had ...; **~ soll unter Strafe gestellt werden** wearing a mask is to be made a punishable offence; **b)** *(Kleidung)* disguise

Vermummungs·verbot das ban on wearing masks [during demonstrations]

vermurksen *tr. V. (ugs.)* mess up; muck up *(Brit. sl.)*

vermuten *tr. V.* suspect; **das ist zu ~:** that is what one would suppose *or* expect; we may assume that; **die Untersuchung läßt ~, daß ...:** the investigation leads one to suppose that ...; **ich vermute/vermutete ihn in der Bibliothek** I suspect *or* presume he is/supposed *or* presumed he was in the library

vermutlich 1. *Adj.* probable; probable, likely ⟨*result*⟩; **der ~e Täter** the suspect. **2.** *Adv.* presumably; *(wahrscheinlich)* probably; **[ja,] ~:** [yes,] I suppose so

Vermutung die; ~, ~en supposition ; *(Verdacht)* suspicion; **es liegt die ~ nahe, daß ...:** it seems a likely supposition that ...; there are grounds for supposing that ...; **die ~ haben, daß ...:** presume *or* suppose that ...

vernachlässigen *tr. V.* **a)** neglect; **b)** *(unberücksichtigt lassen)* ignore; disregard

Vernachlässigung die; ~, ~en neglect; *(das Nichtberücksichtigen)* disregard; **unter ~ dieser Erkenntnisse** ignoring these perceptions

vernageln *tr. V.* nail up, cover ⟨*hole etc.*⟩; **mit Brettern vernagelt** boarded up

vernähen *tr. V.* **a)** stitch [up] ⟨*tear, wounds*⟩; **den Faden gut ~:** sew the thread in firmly; **b)** *(beim Nähen verbrauchen)* use up ⟨*thread, material*⟩

vernarben *itr. V.; mit sein* [form a] scar; heal *(lit. or fig.)*

Vernarbung die; ~, ~en formation of a scar; **die ~ der Wunde dauerte Wochen** the wound took weeks to form a scar

vernarren *refl. V.* **sich in jmdn./etw. ~:** become besotted *or* infatuated with sb./sth.; **in jmdn./etw. vernarrt sein** be infatuated with *or (coll.)* crazy about sb./be crazy *(coll.)* abouth sth.

Vernarrtheit die; ~, ~en infatuation (**in** + *Akk.* with)

vernaschen *tr. V.* **a)** *(für Süßigkeiten ausgeben)* spend on sweets *(Brit.) or (Amer.)* candy; **b)** *(salopp: geschlechtlich verkehren mit)* lay ⟨*girl*⟩ *(sl.)*; **c)** *(salopp: bezwingen, ausschalten)* wipe the floor with *(sl.)* ⟨*opponent, competitors*⟩

vernebeln *tr. V.* shroud ⟨*area*⟩ in fog; *(mit Rauch)* cover ⟨*area*⟩ with a smoke-screen; *(fig.)* obscure ⟨*facts*⟩; **jmdm. das Gehirn ~** *(fig.)* ⟨*alcohol*⟩ befuddle sb.'s brain

Vernebelung die; ~, ~en shrouding in fog/smoke; *(fig.: des Kopfes)* befuddling; clouding; *(der Tatsachen)* obscuration

vernehmbar *Adj. (geh.)* audible

vernehmen *unr. tr. V.* **a)** *(geh.: hören, erfahren)* hear; **über seine Absichten nichts ~ lassen** not say anything *or* keep quiet about one's intentions; **b)** *(verhören)* question; *(vor Gericht)* examine

Vernehmen das *in* **dem/allem ~ nach** from what/all that one hears; **sicherem ~ nach** according to reliable sources

vernehmlich 1. *Adj.* [clearly] audible. **2.** *adv.* audibly; **laut und ~:** loud and clear

Vernehmung die; ~, ~en questioning; *(vor Gericht)* examination

vernehmungsfähig *Adj.* in a condition *or* fit to be questioned/examined *postpos.*

verneigen *refl. V. (geh.)* bow (**vor** + *Dat.* to, *(literary)* before)

Verneigung die; ~, ~en *(geh.)* bow

verneinen *tr. (auch itr.) V.* **a)** say 'no' to ⟨*question*⟩; answer ⟨*question*⟩ in the negative; **er verneinte [es]** he said 'no'; **eine ~de Antwort** a negative answer; an answer in the negative; **er schüttelte ~d den Kopf** he shook his head to say 'no'; **b)** *(ablehnen)* reject; **c)** *(Sprachw.)* negate

Verneinung die; ~, ~en a) ~ einer Frage negative answer to a question; **b)** *(Ablehnung)* rejection; **c)** *(Sprachw.)* negation

Verneinungs-: ~fall der *in* **im ~falle** *(Papierdt.)* should the answer be in the negative; **~wort das;** *Pl.* **~wörter** *(Sprachw.)* negative [word]

vernetzen *tr. V. (Chemie, Technik)* interlink

vernichten *tr. V.* destroy; exterminate ⟨*pests, vermin*⟩

vernichtend 1. *Adj.* crushing ⟨*defeat*⟩; shattering ⟨*blow*⟩; *(fig.)* devastating ⟨*criticism*⟩; devastating, withering ⟨*glance*⟩. **2.** *adv.* **den Feind ~ schlagen** inflict a crushing defeat on the enemy

Vernichtung die; ~, ~en destruction; *(von Schädlingen)* extermination

Vernichtungs-: ~lager das extermination camp; **~potential das** destructive potential; **~waffe die** weapon of annihilation

verniedlichen *tr. V.* trivialize ⟨*matter, situation, etc.*⟩; play down ⟨*guilt, error*⟩

Verniedlichung die; ~, ~en trivialization

Vernissage [vɛrnɪˈsaːʒə] **die; ~, ~n** *(geh.)* private view *(of contemporary artist's exhibition)*

Vernunft [fɛɐ̯ˈnʊnft] **die; ~:** reason; **gegen alle [Regeln der] ~:** contrary to all [dictates of] common sense; **ohne ~ handeln** act rashly *or* without thinking; **~ annehmen, zur ~ kommen** see reason; come to one's senses; **jmdn. zur ~ bringen** make sb. see reason

vernunft-, Vernunft-: ~begabt *Adj.* rational; **~ehe die, ~heirat die** marriage of convenience

vernünftig [fɛɐ̯ˈnʏnftɪç] **1.** *Adj.* **a)** sensible; **es wäre das ~ste gewesen, zu ...:** the most sensible thing would have been to ...; **mit ihm kann man kein ~es Wort reden** one can't have a sensible conversation with him; **b)** *(ugs.: ordentlich, richtig)* decent; **einen ~en Beruf lernen** learn a proper trade. **2.** *adv.* **a)** sensibly; **über etw.** *(Akk.)* **~ diskutieren** have a sensible discussion about sth.; **b)** *(ugs.: ordentlich, richtig)* ⟨*talk, eat*⟩ properly; ⟨*dress*⟩ sensibly

vernünftigerweise *Adv.* sensibly; **etw. ~ tun** ⟨*person*⟩ have the [good] sense to do sth.

Vernunft·mensch der [purely] rational person

vernunft·widrig 1. *Adj.* irrational. **2.** *adv.* irrationally

veröden 1. *itr. V.; mit sein* **a)** *(menschenleer werden)* become deserted; **verödet** deserted ⟨*houses, streets, etc*⟩; **b)** *(unfruchtbar werden)* ⟨*land*⟩ become barren *or* desolate. **2.** *tr. V. (Med.)* treat ⟨*varicose veins*⟩ by injection

Verödung die; ~, ~en *s.* **veröden:** desertion; desolation; *(Med.)* injection treatment

veröffentlichen *tr. V.* publish

Veröffentlichung die; ~, ~en publication

verordnen *tr. V.* **[jmdm. etw.] ~:** prescribe [sth. for sb.]; **der Arzt hat mir Bettruhe verordnet** the doctor ordered me to stay in bed

Verordnung die prescribing; prescription

verpachten *tr. V.* lease

Verpächter der landlord; lessor *(Law)*

Verpachtung die; ~, ~en leasing

verpacken *tr. V.* pack; wrap up ⟨*present, parcel*⟩; **etw. als Geschenk ~:** gift-wrap sth.

Verpackung die a) *o.Pl.* packing; **b)** *(Umhüllung)* packaging *no pl.*; wrapping

Verpackungs·material das packaging [material]

verpassen *tr. V.* **a)** miss ⟨*train, person, entry (Mus.), chance, etc.*⟩; **b)** *(ugs.: geben)* **jmdm. etw. ~:** give sb. sth.; **jmdm. eins ~:** clout sb. one *(coll.)*

verpatzen *tr. V. (ugs.)* make a mess of; muck up *(Brit. sl.)*; botch ⟨*job*⟩; **du hast mir alles verpatzt** you've spoilt it all for me; **eine verpatzte Gelegenheit** a wasted opportunity

verpennen *(salopp)* **1.** *itr. V.* oversleep. **2.** *tr. V.* **a)** *(vergessen)* forget; **b)** *(verschlafen)* sleep through ⟨*morning etc.*⟩

verpennt *Adj. (salopp)* half asleep *pred.*; *(fig.)* dozy ⟨*place*⟩; **total ~:** in a complete sleepy daze

verpesten *tr. V. (abwertend)* pollute

Verpestung *(abwertend)* **die; ~, ~en** pollution

verpetzen *tr. V. (abwertend)* **jmdn. [beim Lehrer** *usw.*] **~:** tell *or (sl.)* split on sb. [to the teacher *etc.*]

verpfänden *tr. V.* pawn ⟨*article*⟩; mortgage ⟨*house*⟩; *(fig.)* pledge ⟨*word, honour*⟩

Verpfändung die pawning; *(von Hausbesitz)* mortgaging; mortgage

verpfeifen *unr. tr. V. (ugs. abwertend)* grass *or* split on ⟨*person*⟩ *(sl.)* **(bei** to); sing about ⟨*plan etc.*⟩ *(sl.)*

verpflanzen *tr. V.* **a)** transplant ⟨*tree, bush*⟩; *(fig.)* uproot and move ⟨*person*⟩; **b)** *(Med.)* transplant ⟨*heart etc.*⟩; graft ⟨*skin*⟩

Verpflanzung die; ~, ~en a) transplanting; **b)** *(Med.)* transplant[ing]; *(von Haut)* graft

verpflegen *tr. V.* cater for; feed; **sich selbst ~:** cater for oneself; **nur kalt/im Heim verpflegt werden** only be served cold food/be served one's food in the hostel

Verpflegung die; ~, ~en a) *o.Pl.* catering *no indef. art.* (*Gen.* for); **b)** *(Nahrung)* food; **Unterkunft und ~:** board and lodging

Verpflegungs·kosten *Pl.* cost *sing.* of food *or* meals

verpflichten 1. *tr. V.* **a)** oblige; commit; *(festlegen, binden)* bind; *(durch Eid)* swear; **jmdn. auf die Verfassung ~:** make sb. swear *or* promise to uphold the constitution; **zur Verschwiegenheit verpflichtet** sworn to secrecy; **der Kauf des ersten Bandes verpflichtet zur Abnahme des gesamten Werkes** purchase of the first volume is a commitment *or* obliges one to take the complete work; **sich verpflichtet fühlen [, etw. zu tun]** feel obliged [to do sth.]; **das verpflichtet dich zu nichts** that doesn't commit you to anything; **jmdm. verpflichtet sein** be indebted to sb.; **ich bin Ihnen zu Dank verpflichtet** I am indebted *or* obliged to you; **b)** *(einstellen, engagieren)* engage ⟨*actor, manager, etc.*⟩; *(Sport)* sign ⟨*player*⟩; **jmdn. ans Stadttheater/nach Berlin ~:** take sb. on *or* engage sb. at the Municipal Theatre/for Berlin. **2.** *refl. V.* undertake; promise; **sich zu einer Zahlung ~:** commit oneself to making a payment; **sich vertraglich ~:** sign a contract; bind oneself by contract; **sich bei der Bundeswehr auf 8 Jahre ~:** sign on with the [Federal] Armed Forces for eight years

Verpflichtung die; ~, ~en a) obligation; commitment; **eine ~ übernehmen** take on an obligation *or* a commitment; **[finanzielle] ~en** [financial] commitments; liabilities; **dienstliche/gesellschaftliche** *usw.* **~en** official/social *etc.* commitments; **ich habe keine anderweitigen ~en** I am not otherwise engaged; I have no other engagements; **b)** *(Engagement)* engaging; engagement; *(Sport: eines Spielers)* signing

verpfuschen *tr. V. (ugs.)* make a mess of; muck up *(Brit. sl.)*; **sich** *(Dat.)* **das Leben/die Karriere ~:** make a mess of one's life/career

verpissen *refl. V. (salopp)* piss off *(Brit. sl.)*; beat it *(sl.)*

verplanen *tr. V.* **a)** *(falsch planen)* get the plans wrong for; **b)** *(festlegen, einteilen)* book ⟨*person, time*⟩ up; commit ⟨*money, reprint*⟩; **er hat sein Geld/seine Freizeit schon verplant** his money is already fully committed/his spare time is fully booked

verplappern *refl. V. (ugs.)* blab *(coll.)*; let the cat out of the bag

verplaudern 1. *tr. V.* chat away ⟨*time*⟩; spend ⟨*time*⟩ chatting. **2.** *refl. V.* go on chatting too long

verplempern [fɛɐ̯'plɛmpɐn] *(ugs.)* **1.** *tr. V.* fritter away. **2.** *refl. V.* fritter away one's time/opportunities

verplomben *tr. V.* seal

Verplombung die; ~, ~en a) sealing; **b)** *(Plombe)* seal

verpönt *Adj.*: scorned; *(tabu)* taboo

verpoppen *tr. V.* popularize; *(aufmöbeln)* jazz up

verprassen *tr. V.* squander, *(sl.)* blow ⟨*money, fortune*⟩

verprellen *tr. V.* alienate

verproviantieren 1. *tr. V.* supply with food *or* provisions. **2.** *refl. V.* stock up [with food *or* provisions]

verprügeln *tr. V.* beat up; *(zur Strafe)* thrash

verpuffen *itr. V.; mit sein* go phut; *(fig.)* fizzle out; ⟨*joke*⟩ fall flat

verpulvern *tr. V. (ugs.)* blow *(sl.)* ⟨*money*⟩; *(allmählich)* fritter away ⟨*money*⟩

verpuppen *refl. V. (Zool.)* pupate

Verputz der plaster; *(auf Außenwänden)* rendering; *(Rauhputz)* roughcast

verputzen *tr. V.* **a)** *(mit Putz versehen)* plaster; render ⟨*outside wall*⟩; *(mit Rauhputz)* roughcast; **b)** *(ugs.: aufessen)* polish off *(coll.)* ⟨*food*⟩

Verputzer der; ~s, ~: plasterer

verqualmen 1. *itr. V.; mit sein* ⟨*cigar, cigarette*⟩ go out. **2.** *tr. V. (ugs. abwertend)* fill ⟨*room*⟩ with smoke; **verqualmt** smoke-filled

verquält [fɛɐ̯'kvɛ:lt] *Adj.* tormented; in torment *or* agony *pred.*

verquatschen *(ugs.)* **1.** *tr. V.* natter away *(coll.)* ⟨*time*⟩; spend ⟨*time*⟩ nattering *(coll.)*. **2.** *refl. V.* blab *(coll.)*; let the cat out of the bag

verquer 1. *Adj.* **a)** *(schief)* angled, crooked ⟨*position*⟩; **b)** *(absonderlich)* weird, outlandish ⟨*idea*⟩. **2.** *adv.* **a)** *(schief)* at an angle; crookedly; **b)** *(absonderlich)* ⟨*behave*⟩ weirdly; **c) jmdm. geht etw./alles ~:** sth./everything is going wrong for sb.

verquicken [fɛɐ̯'kvɪkn̩] *tr. V.* combine

Verquickung die; ~, ~en combination

verquirlen *tr. V.* mix [with a whisk]; whisk

verquollen [fɛɐ̯'kvɔlən] *Adj.* swollen

verrammeln *tr. V.* barricade

verramschen *tr. V. (ugs. abwertend) s.* **verschleudern a**

verrannt [fɛɐ̯'rant] *Adj.* obsessed

Verrat der; ~[e]s betrayal **(an +** *Dat.* of); **~ begehen** *(Politik)* commit [an act of] treason; **~ an jmdm. begehen** betray sb.

verraten 1. *unr. tr. V.* **a)** betray ⟨*person, cause*⟩; betray, give away ⟨*secret, plan, etc.*⟩ **(an +** *Akk.* to); **wer hat dir das Versteck ~?** who told you about the hiding-place?; **~ und verkauft sein** be well and truly in the soup *or* sunk *(coll.)*; **b)** *(ugs.: mitteilen)* **jmdm. den Grund** *usw.* **~:** tell sb. the reason *etc.*; **c)** *(erkennen lassen)* show, betray ⟨*feelings, surprise, fear, etc.*⟩; show ⟨*influence, talent*⟩; **d)** *(zu erkennen geben)* give ⟨*person*⟩ away. **2.** *unr. refl. V.* **a)** ⟨*person*⟩ give oneself away; **b)** *(sich zeigen)* show itself; be revealed

Verräter [fɛɐ̯'rɛ:tɐ] **der; ~s, ~:** traitor (*Gen.*, **an +** *Dat.* to)

Verräterei die; ~, ~en treachery

Verräterin die; ~, ~en traitress

verräterisch *Adj.* **a)** treacherous ⟨*plan, purpose, act, etc.*⟩; **b)** *(erkennen lassend)* tell-tale, give-away ⟨*look, gesture*⟩; **die Röte in ihrem Gesicht war ~:** her red face gave her away

verrauchen 1. *itr. V.; mit sein* ⟨*smoke, cloud, etc.*⟩ clear [away], disappear; *(fig.)* ⟨*anger etc.*⟩ blow over, subside. **2.** *tr. V.* spend ⟨*money*⟩ on smoking

verräuchern *tr. V.* fill with smoke; **verräuchert** smoke-filled; smoky

verraucht *Adj.* smoke-filled; smoky

verrauschen *itr. V.; mit sein* die *or* fade [away]

verrechnen 1. *tr. V.* include, take into account ⟨*amount etc.*⟩; *(gutschreiben)* credit ⟨*cheque etc.*⟩ to another account. **2.** *refl. V. (auch fig.)* miscalculate; make a mistake/mistakes

Verrechnung die settlement **(mit** by means of); **„nur zur ~"** *(Bankw.)* 'not negotiable'; 'a/c payee [only]'

Verrechnungs-: ~einheit die *(Wirtsch.)* clearing unit; **~scheck der** *(Wirtsch., Bankw.)* crossed cheque

verrecken *itr. V.; mit sein (salopp)* die [a miserable death]; **das tu ich ums Verrecken nicht** there's no way I'll do that

verregnen *itr. V.; mit sein* be spoilt *or* ruined by rain; **verregnet** rainy, wet ⟨*spring, summer, holiday, etc.*⟩; ⟨*harvest*⟩ spoilt by rain

verreiben *unr. tr. V.* rub in

verreisen *itr. V.; mit sein* go away; **verreist sein** be away

verreißen *unr. tr. V.* **a)** *(ugs.)* tear ⟨*book, play, etc.*⟩ to pieces; **b)** *(ugs.: beim Lenken)* **den Wagen/die Lenkung/das Steuer ~:** snatch at the steering; *(als Ausweichmanöver* swerve

verrenken [fɛɐ̯'rɛnkn̩] *tr. V.* **a)** *(verletzen)* dislocate; **sich** *(Dat.)* **den Fuß ~:** twist one's ankle; **b)** *(biegen)* **sich** *od.* **seine Glieder ~:** go into *or* perform contortions

Verrenkung die; ~, ~en a) *(Verletzung)* dislocation; **b)** *(Biegung des Körpers)* contortion; **~en machen** go into *or* perform contortions

verrennen *unr. refl. V.* get on the wrong track *or* off course; **sich in etw.** *(Akk.)* **~:** become obsessed with sth.

verrenten *tr. V. (Amtsspr.)* retire [on a pension]

Verrentung die; ~, ~en *(Amtsspr.)* retirement [on a pension]

verrichten *tr. V.* perform ⟨*work, duty, etc.*⟩; **seine Notdurft ~:** relieve oneself

Verrichtung die the carrying out; performance; **gute ~!** *(scherzh. wenn jmd. zur Toilette geht)* have fun!; **die täglichen ~en** one's daily tasks

verriegeln *tr. V.* bolt

Verriegelung die; ~, ~en a) *(das Verriegeln)* bolting; **b)** *(Vorrichtung)* bolt mechanism; *(Schloß)* lock

verringern [fɛɐ̯'rɪŋɐn] **1.** *tr. V.* reduce. **2.** *refl. V.* decrease

Verringerung die; ~: reduction; decrease (*Gen.*, **von** in)

verrinnen *unr. itr. V.; mit sein* **a)** *(versickern)* seep away; **b)** *(geh.: verstreichen)* pass [by]; ⟨*year, month*⟩ elapse, pass

Verriß der *(ugs.)* damning review *or* criticism **(über +** *Akk.* of)

verrocken *tr. V.* produce a rock arrangement of ⟨*piece*⟩

verrohen 1. *tr. V.* brutalize. **2.** *itr. V.; mit sein* become brutal

Verrohung die; ~, ~en brutalization

verrosten *itr. V.; mit sein* rust; **verrostet** rusty

verrotten *itr. V.; mit sein* rot; ⟨*building etc.*⟩ decay

verrucht [fɛɐ̯'ru:xt] *Adj.* **a)** *(veralt.: ruchlos)* despicable; **b)** *(scherzh.: verworfen)* disreputable, seedy ⟨*quarter etc.*⟩

Verruchtheit die; ~: **a)** despicableness; **b)** *(scherzh.: Verworfenheit)* disreputableness; seediness

verrücken *tr. V.* move; shift

verrückt *(ugs.)* **1.** *Adj.* **a)** mad; ~ **werden** go mad *or* insane; **jmdn. ~ machen** drive sb. mad; **mach dich doch nicht ~!** don't get yourself into a state!; **du bist wohl ~!** you must be mad *or* crazy!; **bei diesem Lärm kann man ja ~ werden!** this noise is enough to drive you mad *or (coll.)* round the bend; **wie ~:** like mad *or (coll.)* crazy; **ich werde ~!** I'll be blowed *(sl.) or (coll.)* damned; **~ spielen** *(salopp)* ⟨*person*⟩ act crazy *(coll.)*; ⟨*car, machine, etc.*⟩ play up *(coll)*; ⟨*watch, weather*⟩ go crazy; **b)** *(überspannt, ausgefallen)* crazy ⟨*idea, fashion, prank, day, etc.*⟩; **so was Verrücktes!** what a crazy idea!; **c)** *(begierig, geil)* crazy; **sie macht die Männer ~:** she drives men crazy [with desire]; **auf jmdn.** *od.* **nach jmdm/auf etw.** *(Akk.)* **~ sein** be crazy *(coll.) or* mad about sb./sth. **2.** *adv.* crazily; ⟨*behave*⟩ crazily *or* like a madman; ⟨*paint, dress, etc.*⟩ in a mad *or* crazy way

Verrückte der/die; *adj. Dekl. (ugs.)* madman/madwoman; lunatic

Verrücktheit die; ~, ~**en a)** *o.Pl.* madness; insanity; *(Überspanntheit)* craziness; **b)** *(irre Handlung)* act of madness; folly; *(überspannte Idee)* crazy idea

Verrückt·werden das *(ugs.) in* **zum ~ sein** be enough to drive you mad *or (coll.)* round the bend; **es ist zum ~ mit ihm** he's enough to drive anyone scatty *(Brit. sl.)*

Verruf der *in* **in ~ kommen** *od.* **geraten** fall into disrepute; **jmdn./etw. in ~ bringen** bring sb./sth. into disrepute

verrufen *Ad.* disreputable

verrühren *tr. V.* stir together; mix

verrunzelt *Adj.* wrinkled

verrußen 1. *itr. V.; mit sein* become sooty; ⟨*sparking-plug*⟩ soot up; **verrußt** sooty; *(von Ruß bedeckt)* covered in soot *postpos.* **2.** *tr. V.* make sooty

verrutschen *itr. V.* slip

Vers [fɛrs] **der;** ~**es,** ~**e** verse; *(Zeile)* line; **~e schreiben** *od. (ugs.)* **schmieden** write verse *or* poetry; **etw. in ~e setzen** *od.* **bringen** put sth. into verse; **ein Epos in ~en** a verse epic; **sich** *(Dat.)* **einen ~ auf etw.** *(Akk.)***/darauf machen** *(fig.)* make sense of sth./put two and two together

versachlichen *tr. V.* make [more] objective

Versachlichung die; ~: **zur ~ der Diskussion beitragen** help to make the discussion more objective

versacken *itr. V.; mit sein (ugs.)* **a)** sink; **b)** *(fig.)* s. **versumpfen b, c**

versagen 1. *itr. V.* fail; ⟨*machine, engine*⟩ stop [working], break down; **menschliches Versagen** human error; **ihre Stimme versagte** her voice failed. **2.** *tr. V. (geh.) (nicht gewähren)* **jmdm./sich etw. ~:** deny *or* refuse sb. sth./deny oneself sth.; **ein Kind blieb ihr versagt** a child was denied her; **es war ihm versagt, das mitzuerleben** circumstances did not allow him to witness it; **ich konnte es mir nicht ~, darauf zu antworten** I could not refrain from answering; *s. auch* **Dienst d. 3.** *refl. V.* **sich jmdm. ~:** refuse to give oneself *or* surrender to sb.

Versager der; ~**s,** ~: failure

Versagung die; ~, ~**en** refusal

versalzen 1. *unr. tr. V.* **a)** put too much salt in/on; **die Suppe ist versalzen** there is too much salt in the soup; the soup is too salty; **b)** *(fig. ugs.)* spoil; **jmdm. etw. ~:** spoil sth. for sb.; *s. auch* **Suppe. 2.** *itr. V.; mit sein (bes. Ökologie; Bodenk.)* become salty

versammeln 1. *tr. V.* assemble; gather [together]; **seine Leute um sich ~:** gather one's people around one. **2.** *refl. V.* assemble; *(weniger formell)* gather; **sich um jmdn./etw. ~:** gather round sb./sth.; **vor versammelter Belegschaft sprechen** speak to the assembled staff; *s. auch* **Mannschaft c**

Versammlung die a) meeting; *(Partei~)* assembly; *(unter freiem Himmel, bes. politisch)* rally; **auf einer ~ sprechen** speak at a meeting/rally; **b)** *(Gremium)* assembly; **gesetzgebende/verfassunggebende ~:** legislative/constituent assembly; **c)** *o.Pl. (das Sichversammeln)* assembly; bringing together *no art.*

Versammlungs-: ~freiheit die; *o.Pl.* freedom of assembly; **~lokal das** meeting-place

Versand der; ~**[e]s a)** dispatch; **zum ~ fertigmachen** prepare for dispatch; **b)** *(Abteilung)* dispatch department; **c)** *(ugs.:~haus)* mail-order firm

Versand·buch·handel der mail-order trade

versanden *itr. V.; mit sein* **a)** fill with sand; ⟨*harbour etc.*⟩ silt up; *(mit Sand bedeckt werden)* be covered with sand; **b)** *(fig. ugs.)* peter *or* fizzle out

Versand: ~geschäft das, ~handel der mail-order business; **~haus das** mail-order firm; **~haus·katalog der** mail-order catalogue; **~kosten** *Pl.* dispatch costs; carriage *sing.*; *(Post u. Verpackung)* postage and packing

Versatz-: ~amt das *(südd.; österr.)* pawnshop; **~stück das a)** *(Theater)* [movable] piece of scenery; set piece; **b)** *(fig.)* cliché; hackneyed idea; **c)** *(österr.: Pfand)* security

versaubeuteln *tr. V. (ugs.)* **a)** *(verderben)* mess up; **b)** *(verlieren, verlegen)* lose; mislay

versauen *tr. V. (salopp)* **a)** *(verschmutzen)* mess up; make mucky *(coll.)*; **b)** *(verderben)* foul up *(coll.)*

versauern *itr. V.; mit sein (ugs.)* waste away; stagnate

versaufen 1. *unr. tr. V. (salopp)* drink one's way through. **2.** *unr.itr. V.; mit sein* **a)** *(ugs.: ertrinken)* drown; **b)** *(Bergmannsspr.)* flood

versäumen *tr. V.* **a)** *(verpassen)* miss; lose ⟨*time, sleep*⟩; **da hast du nichts/nicht viel versäumt** you didn't miss anything/miss much; **den versäumten Schlaf nachholen** catch up on lost sleep; **b)** *(vernachlässigen, unterlassen)* neglect ⟨*duty, task*⟩; **das Versäumte/Versäumtes nachholen** make up for *or* catch up on what one has neglected *or* failed to do; **er versäumte [es] nicht, X zu erwähnen** he did not omit *or* fail to mention X

Versäumnis das; ~**ses,** ~**se** omission; **die ~se der Eltern gegenüber ihren Kindern** the parents' sins of omission towards their children

verschachern *tr. V. (abwertend)* sell off

verschachtelt *Adj.* higgledy-piggledy ⟨*streets, town*⟩; **ein ~er Satz** *(fig.)* an encapsulated sentence

verschaffen *tr. V.* **jmdm. Arbeit/Geld/Unterkunft** *usw.* **~:** provide sb. with work/money/accommodation *etc.*; get sb. work/money/accommodation *etc.*; **sich** *(Dat.)* **etw. ~:** get hold of sth.; obtain sth.; **sich** *(Dat.)* **Respekt ~:** gain respect; **sich Gewißheit ~:** make sure *or* certain; **es verschaffte mir die Möglichkeit, zu ...:** it gave me the opportunity to ...; **was verschafft mir die Ehre?** *(iron.)* to what do I owe this honour?

verschalen *tr. V.* line ⟨*wall, shaft, etc.*⟩ [with boards]; *(bedecken)* board up ⟨*window, hole*⟩

Verschalung die; ~, ~**en a)** *(das Verschalen)* lining; boarding; *(eines Fensters)* boarding up; **b)** *(Produkt)* lining; *(aus Brettern)* boarding

verschämt [fɛɐ̯'ʃɛ:mt] **1.** *Adj.* bashful. **2.** *adv.* bashfully

verschandeln *tr. V. (ugs.)* spoil; ruin; **das Gebäude verschandelt die Landschaft** the building is a blot on the landscape

Verschandelung die; ~, ~**en** *(ugs.)* ruination *no indef. art.*; **eine solche ~ der Gegend** ruining the area like this

verschanzen 1. *refl. V. (Milit.)* take up a [fortified] position; *(in einem Graben)* entrench oneself; dig [oneself] in; *(in einem Gebäude)* barricade oneself **(in** + *Dat.* into); **sich in seinem Büro/hinter einer Zeitung ~** *(fig.)* take refuge in one's office/take cover *or* hide behind a newspaper; **sich hinter einer Ausrede/seiner Müdigkeit ~** *(fig.)* hide behind an excuse/use one's tiredness as an excuse **2.** *tr. V. (Milit.)* fortify

Verschanzung die; ~, ~**en** *(Milit.)* fortification; *(in Gräben)* entrenchment

verschärfen 1. *tr. V.* **a)** *(steigern)* intensify ⟨*conflict, difference, desire, etc.*⟩; increase, step up ⟨*pace, pressure*⟩; **b)** *(strenger machen)* tighten ⟨*law, control, restriction, etc*⟩; make ⟨*penalty*⟩ more severe; **c)** *(verschlimmern)* make ⟨*unemployment etc.*⟩ worse; aggravate ⟨*situation, crisis, etc.*⟩. **2.** *refl. V.* **a)** *(sich steigern)* ⟨*pace, pressure, etc.*⟩ increase; ⟨*pain, tension, conflict, difference*⟩ intensify; **b)** *(sich verschlimmern)* get worse

verschärft 1. *Adj.; nicht präd.* **a)** *(gesteigert)* increased ⟨*pressure*⟩; intensified ⟨*conflict*⟩; more intense ⟨*training*⟩; **b)** *(strenger)* tighter, stricter ⟨*control, check, restriction*⟩; more severe ⟨*reprimand, punishment*⟩; **c)** *(schlimmer geworden)* aggravated. **2.** *adv. (strenger)* more strictly

Verschärfung die; ~, ~**en** *s.* **verschärfen 1a–c:** intensification; increase; tightening; greater severity; aggravation; worsening

verscharren *tr. V.* bury *(just below the surface)*; bury ⟨*person*⟩ in a shallow grave

verschätzen 1. *refl. V.* **sich in etw.** *(Dat.)* **~:** misjudge sth.; **wenn du dich da mal nicht verschätzt!** unless you've got it all wrong!. **2.** *tr. V.* misjudge

verschauen *refl. V. (österr. ugs.) s.* **vergucken a**

verschaukeln *tr. V. (ugs.)* **jmdn. ~:** take sb. for a ride *(sl.)*

verscheiden *unr.itr. V.; mit sein (geh.)* pass away

verscheißen *(derb)* **1.** *unr. tr. V.* cover with shit *(coarse)*; **verschissene Unterhosen** shitty *(coarse)* underpants. **2.** *unr. itr. V. in* **bei jmdm. verschissen haben** *(fig.)* have had it as far as sb. is concerned *(coll.)*

verscheißern *tr. V. (derb)* **jmdn. ~:** have *(Brit. coll.) or (Amer. coll.)* put sb. on; **du willst mich wohl ~!** pull the 'other one[, it's got bells on] *(sl.)*

verschenken 1. *tr. V.* **a)** give away; **etw. an jmdn. ~:** give sth. to sb.; **b)** *(ungewollt vergeben)* waste ⟨*space*⟩; give away ⟨*points*⟩; **den Sieg ~:** throw away one's chance of winning. **2.** *refl. V. (geh.)* **sich [an jmdn.] ~:** throw oneself away [on sb.]

verscherbeln [fɛɐ̯'ʃɛrbl̩n] *tr. V. (ugs.)* flog *(Brit. sl.)* *(Dat.,* **an** + *Akk.* to)

verscherzen *refl. V.* **sich** *(Dat.)* **etw. ~:** lose *or* forfeit sth. [through one's own folly]

verscheuchen *tr. V.* chase away *(lit. or fig.)*; *(durch Erschrecken)* frighten *or* scare away

verscheuern *tr. V. (ugs.)* flog *(Brit. sl.)* *(Dat.,* **an** + *Akk.* to)

verschicken *tr. V.* **a)** *s.* **versenden; b) jmdn. zur Kur/an die See** *usw.* **~:** send sb. away to take a cure/to the seaside *etc.*

Verschickung die a) *s.* **Versendung; b)** *(zur Erholung)* sending away [for health reasons] *no indef. art.*

verschiebbar *Adj.* **a)** movable; *(verstellbar)* adjustable; **b)** *(aufschiebbar)* which can be put off *postpos., not pred.*

Verschiebe·bahnhof der marshalling yard

verschieben 1. *unr. tr. V.* **a)** shift; move; **die Grenze wurde um 5 km nach Süden verschoben** the boundary was moved five kilometres to the south *or* further south; **die Perspektive/das ganze Bild ~** *(fig.)* alter *or* change the perspective/the whole picture; **b)** *(aufschieben)* put off, postpone **(auf +** *Akk.* till); **etw. um eine Woche/auf unbestimmte Zeit ~:** postpone sth. for a week/indefinitely; *s. auch* **besorgen c; c)** *(ugs.: illegal verkaufen)* traffic in ⟨*goods*⟩; *(beiseite schaffen)* move illegally; **Waren/Devisen ins Ausland ~:** smuggle goods/currency to a foreign country. **2.** *unr. refl. V.* **a)** get out of place; *(rutschen)* slip; *(Geol.)* ⟨*continent etc.*⟩ shift; **das Kräfteverhältnis hat sich verschoben** *(fig.)* the balance of power has shifted; **b)** *(erst später stattfinden)* be postponed **(um** for); ⟨*start*⟩ be put back *or* delayed **(um** by)

Verschiebung die a) movement; *(fig.: Änderung)* alteration, shift *(Gen.* in); **die ~ der Kontinente** *(Geol.)* the continental shift; **b)** *(zeitlich)* postponement; **c)** *(ugs.: illegaler Handel)* trafficking **(von** in); *(ins Ausland)* smuggling

verschieden 1. *2. Part. v.* **verscheiden. 2.** *Adj.* **a)** *(nicht gleich)* different **(von** from); **er hat zwei ~e Socken an** he is wearing two odd socks *or* two socks that don't match; **das ist von Fall zu Fall/von Land zu Land ~:** that varies from one case to another/from country to country; **b)** *nicht präd. (vielfältig)* various; **auf ~e Weise** in various ways; **die ~sten ...:** all sorts of ...; **die ~sten Theorien** the most diverse theories; **in den ~sten Farben** in the most varied colours; in a whole variety of colours; **die ~en ...:** the various ...; **c)** *alleinstehend* **~e** various people; **~e der Anwesenden** several of those present; **~es** various things *pl.*; **„Verschiedenes"** 'miscellaneous'; *(Tagesordnungspunkt)* 'any other business'. **3.** *adv.* differently; **~ groß** of different sizes *postpos.*; different-sized; ⟨*people*⟩ of different heights; **~ schwer/lang** of different weights/lengths *postpos.*

verschieden·artig 1. *Adj.* different in kind *pred.*; *(mehr als zwei)* diverse; **~e Werkzeuge** tools of various [different] kinds; **~e Mittel anwenden** use various different means. **2.** *adv.* diversely; *(auf verschiedene Weise)* in various different ways; **sehr ~ interpretiert werden** be subjected to very diverse interpretations

Verschiedenartigkeit die; ~: difference in nature; *(unter mehreren)* diversity; **die ~ der beiden Systeme** the different nature of the two systems

verschiedene·mal *Adv.* on various occasions

verschiedenerlei *unbest. Gattungsz.; indekl.:* **a)** *attr.* various different; **b)** *alleinstehend* various different things; **~ Käse** various different kinds of cheese

verschieden·farbig 1. *Adj.* different-coloured; of different colours *postpos.* **2.** *adv.* ⟨*paint etc*⟩ in different colours

Verschiedenheit die; ~, ~en difference; dissimilarity; *(unter mehreren)* diversity; *(Unterschied)* difference

verschiedentlich *Adv.* on various occasions

verschießen 1. *unr. tr. V.* **a)** *(als Geschoß verwenden)* fire ⟨*shell, cartridge, etc.*⟩; **b)** *(verbrauchen)* use up ⟨*ammunition*⟩; **verschossene/nicht verschossene Patronen** spent/unspent *or* live cartridges; *s. auch* **Pulver b; c) einen Strafstoß ~** *(Fußball)* miss with a penalty. **2.** *unr. refl. V. (ugs.)* **[in jmdn.] verschossen sein** be madly in love [with sb.] *(coll.).* **3.** *unr. itr. V.; mit sein (verblassen)* fade

verschiffen *tr. V.* ship ⟨*goods, coal*⟩; transport ⟨*troops, emigrants, etc.*⟩ by ship

Verschiffung die; ~, ~en shipment; *(von Personen)* transportation [by ship]

verschimmeln *itr. V.; mit sein* go mouldy; **verschimmelt** mouldy

[1]verschlafen 1. *unr.itr. (auch refl.)V.* oversleep. **2.** *unr. tr. V.* **a)** *(schlafend verbringen)* sleep through ⟨*morning, journey, etc.*⟩; **sein halbes Leben ~:** doze away half one's life; **b)** *(versäumen)* sleep through ⟨*concert*⟩; not wake up in time for ⟨*appointment*⟩; not wake up in time to catch ⟨*train, bus*⟩; *(einschlafen und versäumen)* fall asleep and miss; **c)** *(ugs.: vergessen)* forget about ⟨*appointment etc.*⟩

[2]verschlafen *Adj.* **a)** half-asleep; **b)** *(fig.: ruhig, langweilig)* sleepy ⟨*town, village*⟩

Verschlag der shed; *(angebaut)* lean-to; *(für Kaninchen)* hutch

[1]verschlagen *unr. tr. V.* **a) [jmdm.] die Seite ~:** lose sb.'s place *or* page; **die Seite ~** *(im eigenen Buch)* lose one's place *or* page; **b) jmdm. den Appetit ~:** rob sb. of his/her appetite; **jmdm. die Sprache** *od.* **Rede/den Atem ~:** leave sb. speechless/take sb.'s breath away; **c)** *(Ballspiele)* mishit ⟨*ball*⟩; **d) das Leben/Schicksal hat ihn nach X ~:** the vagaries of life caused/fate caused him to end up in X; **vom Sturm an eine Küste ~ werden** be driven on to a coast by the gale; **es hat ihn nach Berlin ~:** he landed [up] *or* ended up in Berlin.

[2]verschlagen 1. *Adj.* **a)** *(abwertend: gerissen)* sly; shifty; **b)** *(bes. nordd.: lauwarm)* lukewarm; tepid. **2.** *adv. (abwertend: gerissen)* slyly; shiftily

Verschlagenheit die; ~ *(abwertend)* slyness; shiftiness

verschlammen *itr. V.* become *or* get muddy; ⟨*ditch, river*⟩ silt up; **verschlammt** muddy

verschlampen *(ugs., bes. südd.)* **1.** *tr. V.* succeed in losing *(iron.).* **2.** *itr. V.; mit sein (abwertend)* ⟨*person*⟩ let oneself go; ⟨*house etc.*⟩ get into a bad state; **verschlampt** slovenly; in a slovenly state *postpos.*

verschlanken *tr. V. (Wirtschaftsjargon)* trim [down], reduce ⟨*production etc.*⟩

verschlechtern 1. *tr. V.* make worse. **2.** *refl. V.* get worse; deteriorate; **sich [finanziell/wirtschaftlich** *usw.***] ~:** be worse off [financially/economically *etc.*]; **er hat sich verschlechtert** he is worse off [now]

Verschlechterung die; ~, ~en worsening, deterioration *(Gen.* in); **der Wohnungswechsel bedeutet für ihn keine ~:** his change of flat *(Brit.) or (Amer.)* apartment leaves him no worse off

verschleiern 1. *tr. V.* **a)** veil; *(fig.)* cover, veil ⟨*sky, moon, etc.*⟩; obscure ⟨*view*⟩; cloud ⟨*consciousness*⟩; **Dunst verschleierte die Berge** *(fig.)* a veil of mist hid the mountains; **Tränen verschleierten ihre Augen** *od.* **ihr den Blick** *(fig.)* she could scarcely see through her tears; her vision was blurred by tears; **b)** *(fig.: verbergen)* draw a veil over, cover up ⟨*deception, facts, scandal, etc.*⟩; hide ⟨*intentions*⟩. **2.** *refl. V.* ⟨*vision etc.*⟩ become blurred; ⟨*sky*⟩ cloud over

verschleiert 1. *Adj.* veiled; misty ⟨*vision etc.*⟩; fogged ⟨*photograph*⟩; **mit ~er Stimme** in a husky voice; *(vor Rührung)* in a voice choked with emotion. **2.** *adv.* **ohne Brille sieht er [alles] nur ~:** without [his] glasses he sees everything as in a mist

Verschleierung die; ~, ~en a) *o. Pl.* veiling; **ohne ~:** without a veil; **b)** *(fig.: von Sachverhalten, Motiven)* covering up

Verschleierungs·taktik die cover-up tactics *pl.*

verschleifen *unr. tr. V.* smooth; *(fig.)* slur ⟨*consonants, vowels*⟩

verschleimt *Adj.* congested with phlegm *postpos.*

Verschleimung die; ~, ~en mucous congestion

Verschleiß [fɛɐ̯'ʃlais] **der; ~es, ~e a)** *(Abnutzung)* wear *no indef. art.*; wear and tear *sing., no indef. art*; **der Auspuff unterliegt einem sehr hohen/raschen ~:** the exhaust is subject to a great deal of wear and tear/does not last very long; **einen höheren ~ haben** wear more rapidly; have a higher rate of wear; **b)** *(Verbrauch)* consumption **(an +** *Dat.* of); **einen hohen ~ an etw.** *(Dat.)* **haben** use up a large amount of sth.; **sie hat einen unheimlichen ~ an Männern** *(ugs. scherzh.)* she gets through men at an incredible rate *(coll.)*; **c)** *(österr. veralt.: Vertrieb)* sale; retailing

verschleißen 1. *unr. itr. V.; mit sein* wear out. **2.** *unr. tr. V.* **a)** wear out; *(fig.)* run down, ruin ⟨*one's nerves, one's health*⟩; use up ⟨*energy, ability, etc.*⟩; **verschlissen** worn ⟨*material, suit, etc.*⟩; worn out ⟨*machine parts etc.*⟩; **sich ~:** wear oneself out; use up all one's energy **(bei** on); **b)** *(ugs. scherzh.: verbrauchen)* get through ⟨*men friends, cleaning-women, etc.*⟩. **3.** *unr. (auch regelm.) tr. V. (österr. veralt.: verkaufen)* sell; retail

Verschleißer der; ~s, ~ *(österr. veralt.)* retailer

Verschleiß·erscheinung die sign of wear; *(an einem Menschen)* sign of wear and tear *or* exhaustion

verschleppen *tr. V.* **a)** carry off ⟨*valuables, animals*⟩; take away ⟨*person*⟩; *(bes. nach Übersee)* transport ⟨*convicts, slaves, etc.*⟩; **in die Sklaverei verschleppt werden** be carried off into slavery; **b)** *(weiterverbreiten)* carry, spread ⟨*disease, bacteria, mud, etc.*⟩; **c)** *(verzögern)* delay; *(in die Länge ziehen)* draw out; **d)** *(unbehandelt lassen)* let ⟨*illness*⟩ drag on [and get worse]; **verschleppte Krankheit** illness aggravated by neglect

Verschleppung die; ~, ~en *s.* **verschleppen: a)** carrying off; transportation; **b)** carrying; spreading; **c)** delaying; drawing out; **d)** aggravation by neglect

verschleudern *tr. V.* **a)** *(billig verkaufen)* sell dirt cheap; *(mit Verlust)* sell at a loss; **b)** *(abwertend: verschwenden)* squander

verschließbar *Adj.* **a)** closable; **[luftdicht] ~:** sealable ⟨*container etc.*⟩; **b)** *(abschließbar)* lockable ⟨*suitcase, drawer, etc.*⟩

verschließen 1. *unr. tr. V.* **a)** close ⟨*package, tin, pores, mouth, etc*⟩; close up ⟨*blood-vessel, aperture, etc.*⟩; stop ⟨*bottle*⟩; put a/the bung in ⟨*barrel*⟩; *(mit einem Korken)* cork ⟨*bottle*⟩ ; **hermetisch verschlossen** hermetically sealed; **etw. luftdicht ~:** make sth. airtight; put an airtight seal on sth.; **die Augen/Ohren [vor etw.** *(Dat.)***] ~** *(fig.)* close one's eyes *or* be blind/turn a deaf ear *or* be deaf [to sth.]; **b)** *(abschließen)* lock ⟨*door, cupboard, drawer, etc.*⟩; lock up ⟨*house etc.*⟩; *s. auch* **Tür; c)** *(wegschließen)* lock away **(in +** *Dat. od. Akk.* in); **d)** *(versperren)* bar ⟨*way etc.*⟩; **viele berufliche Möglichkeiten blieben ihm verschlossen** many possible professions remained barred *or* closed to him. **2.** *unr. refl. V.* **a) sich jmdm. ~:** be closed to sb.; ⟨*person*⟩ shut oneself off from sb.; **er verschloß sich** he shut up like a clam; **der tiefere Sinn verschloß sich ihm** the deeper meaning remained obscure to him; *s. auch* **verschlossen 2; b)** *in* **sich einer Sache** *(Dat.)* **~:** close one's mind to sth.; *(ignorieren)* ignore sth.

verschlimmbessern *tr. V. (ugs. scherzh.)* make worse with so-called corrections

Verschlimmbesserung die; ~, ~en *(ugs. scherzh.)* so-called correction *(which is wrong)*; **das ist eine ~!** that so-called correction has made things worse

verschlimmern 1. *tr. V.* make worse; aggravate ⟨*state of health*⟩. **2.** *refl. V.* get worse; worsen; ⟨*position, conditions*⟩ deteriorate, worsen

Verschlimmerung die; ~, ~en worsening

verschlingen 1. *unr. tr. V.* **a)** [inter]twine

⟨*threads, string, etc.*⟩ **(zu** into); **miteinander ~**: intertwine ⟨*threads, ropes, etc.*⟩; **b)** *(essen, fressen)* devour ⟨*food*⟩; *(fig.)* devour, consume ⟨*novel, money, etc.*⟩; **jmdn. mit den Augen ~**: devour sb. with one's eyes; **die tobende See verschlang das Schiff** the raging sea engulfed the ship. **2.** *unr. refl. V.* **sich ineinander ~**: become entwined *or* intertwined; *s. auch* **verschlungen**

verschlissen *2. Part. v.* **verschleißen 2**

verschlossen 1. *2. Part. v.* **verschließen. 2.** *Adj. (wortkarg)* taciturn, tight-lipped; *(zurückhaltend)* reserved

Verschlossenheit die; ~: taciturnity; *(Zurückhaltung)* reserve

verschlucken 1. *tr. V.* **a)** swallow ⟨*food, bone, word, etc.*⟩; *(fig.)* absorb, deaden ⟨*sound*⟩; absorb, eliminate ⟨*rays*⟩; **b)** *(fig.: unterdrücken)* choke back ⟨*anger, tears*⟩; hold back ⟨*remark*⟩. **2.** *refl. V.* choke; **er verschluckte sich beim Essen/Lachen** he choked over his food/with laughing

verschludern *tr. V. (ugs. abwertend)* **1.** *tr. V.* **a)** *(verlieren)* lose; *(verlegen)* mislay; **b)** *(vergeuden)* waste ⟨*material*⟩; throw away ⟨*money*⟩; **c)** *(verderben)* ruin, mess up ⟨*exercise book*⟩ **2.** *itr. V.* go to rack and ruin

verschlungen 1. *2. Part. v.* **verschlingen. 2.** *Adj.* entwined ⟨*ornamentation*⟩; winding ⟨*path etc.*⟩; **er saß mit ~en Armen da** he sat there with arms folded

Verschluß der a) *(am BH, an Schmuck usw.)* fastener; fastening; *(an Taschen, Schmuck)* clasp; *(an Schuhen, Gürteln)* buckle; *(am Schrank, Fenster, Koffer usw.)* catch; *(an Flaschen)* top; *(Stöpsel)* stopper; *(Schraub~)* [screw-]top; [screw-]cap; *(Tank~)* cap; **b)** *(einer Feuerwaffe)* breechblock; **c)** *(einer Kamera)* shutter; **d)** *(Med.: einer Arterie)* blockage; occlusion; **e)** *in* **unter ~ sein/bleiben** be under lock and key; **etw. unter ~ halten** keep sth. under lock and key *or* locked away

verschlüsseln *tr. V.* [en]code

Verschlüsselung die; ~, ~en [en]coding

Verschluß: ~kappe die top; cap; **~laut der** *(Sprachw.)* stop; **~sache die** [item of] confidential information; **~sachen** condidential information *sing.*

verschmachten *itr. V.; mit sein (geh.)* fade away **(vor** + *Dat.* from); *(vor Sehnsucht)* pine away

verschmähen *tr. V. (geh.)* spurn; **verschmähte Liebe** unrequited love

verschmälern 1. *tr. V.* narrow; make narrower **(um** by). **2.** *refl. V.* narrow; become narrower

verschmausen *tr. V. (ugs. scherzh.)* dig *or* tuck into *(coll.)*; *(aufessen)* eat up

verschmelzen 1. *unr. tr. V.* **a)** fuse ⟨*metals*⟩; *(fig.)* fuse, merge **(zu** into, to form); **Kupfer und Zink zu Messing ~**: fuse copper and zinc to make brass; **b)** *(verschweißen)* weld together ⟨*metal parts*⟩. **2.** *unr. itr. V.; mit sein* ⟨*metals, cells*⟩ fuse; *(fig.)* ⟨*firms, images, towns, etc.*⟩ merge **(zu** into, to form); **zu einem Ganzen ~**: blend into one

Verschmelzung die, ~, ~en a) fusing, fusion *(lit. or fig.)* **(zu** into); *(von Städten, Firmen usw.)* merging, merger **(zu** into, to form); **b)** *(Verschweißung)* weld

verschmerzen *tr. V.* get over ⟨*defeat, disappointment*⟩

verschmieren *tr. V.* **a)** smear ⟨*window etc.*⟩; *(beim Schreiben)* mess up ⟨*paper*⟩; scrawl all over ⟨*page*⟩; **b)** *(verteilen)* spread ⟨*butter etc.*⟩; smudge ⟨*ink*⟩; **c)** *(verbrauchen)* use up ⟨*butter, oil, plaster, etc.*⟩; **d)** *(zuschmieren)* fill [in] ⟨*crack, hole, etc.*⟩

verschmitzt [fɛɐ̯ˈʃmɪtst] **1.** *Adj.* mischievous; roguish. **2.** *adv.* mischievously; roguishly

Verschmitztheit die; ~: mischievousness; roguishness

verschmoren *itr. V.; mit sein (ugs.)* burn; **es riecht verschmort** there's a smell of burning *or* a burnt smell

verschmust [fɛɐ̯ˈʃmu:st] *Adj. (ugs.)* ⟨*child, cat, etc.*⟩ that always wants to be cuddled; **er ist [sehr] ~**: he always wants to be cuddled

verschmutzen 1. *itr. V.; mit sein* ⟨*material*⟩ get dirty; ⟨*river etc.*⟩ become polluted. **2.** *tr. V.* dirty, soil ⟨*carpet, clothes*⟩; pollute ⟨*air, water, etc.*⟩

Verschmutzung die; ~, ~en a) *(der Umwelt)* pollution; **b)** *(von Stoffen, Teppichen usw.)* soiling; **c)** *(Schmutz)* dirt *no. pl.*; **~en** [cases *pl.* of] soiling *sing.*

verschnaufen *itr. (auch refl.) V.* have *or* take a breather

Verschnauf·pause die breather; rest; **eine ~ einlegen** have *or* take a breather

verschneiden *unr. tr. V.* **a)** *(durch Schneiden verderben)* cut ⟨*hair, roses, etc.*⟩ all wrong; ruin ⟨*wood, material, film*⟩ by bad/wrong cutting; **b)** *(mischen)* blend ⟨*rum, whisky, etc.*⟩; **c)** *(kastrieren)* castrate, geld ⟨*animal*⟩

verschneit *Adj.* snow-covered *attrib.*; covered with snow *postpos.*

Verschnitt der; ~[e]s, ~e a) *o.Pl. (das Mischen)* blending; **b)** *(Mischung)* blend **(aus** of); *(fig., meist abwertend)* mixture; combination; **c)** *(Abfall)* waste; *(von Holz usw.)* off-cuts *pl.*

-verschnitt der: ein James-Bond-~: a second-rate James Bond

verschnörkelt *Adj.* ornate

Verschnörkelung die; ~, ~en ornamentation; *(Schnörkel)* flourish

verschnupft [fɛɐ̯ˈʃnʊpft] **1.** *Adj.* **a)** suffering from a cold *postpos.*; **[ganz] ~ sein** have a [bad] cold; **b)** *(fig. ugs.: gekränkt)* peeved *(coll.)*. **2.** *adv.* in a peeved way *(coll.)*; peevishly

verschnüren *tr. V.* tie up **(zu** into)

Verschnürung die; ~, ~en a) *o. Pl. (das Verschnüren)* tying up; **b)** *(Schnur)* string

verschollen [fɛɐ̯ˈʃɔlən] *Adj.* missing; **er ist ~**: he has disappeared; *(wird vermißt)* he is missing; **sie ließ ihren Mann für ~ erklären** she had her husband declared missing, presumed dead; **er galt seit langem als ~**: for a long time it had been thought he had disappeared

verschonen *tr. V.* spare; **von etw. verschont bleiben** be spared by sth.; escape sth.; **jmdn. mit etw. ~**: spare sb. sth.

verschönen *tr. V.* brighten up

verschönern [fɛɐ̯ˈʃø:nɐn] *tr. V.* brighten up

Verschönerung die; ~, ~en brightening up; beautification *(joc.)*

Verschonung die sparing; **er flehte um ~ seines Lebens/der Kinder** he pleaded that his life/the children be spared

verschorfen *itr. V.; mit sein* form a scab; **eine verschorfte Wunde** a wound with a scab

verschrammen 1. *tr. V.* scratch. **2.** *itr. V.; mit sein* scratch; get scratched

verschränken [fɛɐ̯ˈʃrɛŋkn̩] *tr. V.* fold ⟨*arms*⟩; cross ⟨*legs*⟩; clasp ⟨*hands*⟩; **mit verschränkten Armen/Händen** with one's arms folded/hands clasped

Verschränkung die; ~, ~en *s.* **verschränken**: folding; crossing; clasping

verschrauben *tr. V.* screw on; **[miteinander] ~**: screw together

Verschraubung die; ~, ~en a) *o. Pl. (das Verschrauben)* screwing [together]; **b)** *(Schraubverbindung)* screw fixing

verschrecken *tr. V.* frighten *or* scare [off *or* away]

verschreiben 1. *unr. tr. V.* **a)** *(verbrauchen)* use up ⟨*paper, ink, pencils, etc.*⟩; **b)** *(Med.: verordnen)* prescribe ⟨*medicine, treatment, etc.*⟩; **jmdm. ein Medikament ~**: prescribe a medication for sb.; **sich** *(Dat.)* **etw. für** *od.* **gegen sein Rheuma ~ lassen** get the doctor to prescribe sth. for one's rheumatism; **c)** *in* **sich/seine Seele dem Teufel ~**: give oneself/sell one's soul to the devil; **d)** *(falsch schreiben)* write incorrectly *or* wrongly. **2.** *unr. refl. V.* **a)** *(einen Fehler machen)* make a slip of the pen; **sich beim Datum ~**: make a mistake when writing the date; **b)** *(sich widmen)* **sich einer Sache** *(Dat.)* **~**: devote oneself to sth.

Verschreibung die; ~, ~en prescription; **mit der ~ von Pillen allein is es nicht getan** it is not enough simply to prescribe pills

verschreibungs·pflichtig *Adj.* available only on prescription *postpos.*

verschrie[e]n [fɛɐ̯ˈʃri:[ə]n] *Adj.* notorious **(wegen** for); **als etw. ~ sein** have the reputation of being sth. **(bei** with)

verschroben [fɛɐ̯ˈʃro:bn̩] **1.** *Adj.* eccentric, cranky ⟨*person*⟩; cranky, weird ⟨*ideas*⟩. **2.** *adv.* eccentrically; weirdly

Verschrobenheit die; ~, ~en eccentricity

verschrotten *tr. V.* scrap

Verschrottung die; ~, ~en scrapping

verschrumpeln *itr. V.; mit sein (ugs.)* go shrivelled; **verschrumpelt** shrivelled

verschüchtern *tr. V.* intimidate; **verschüchtert** timid; *(adverbial)* timidly

verschulden 1. *tr. V.* be to blame for ⟨*accident, death, etc.*⟩; *(Fußball usw.)* give away ⟨*goal, corner*⟩; **sein Unglück selbst ~**: have only oneself to blame for one's misfortune. **2.** *refl. V.* get into debt; **er hat sich dafür hoch ~ müssen** he had to borrow heavily to do that; **sich auf Jahre hinaus ~**: incur debts/a debt that will take years to pay off

Verschulden das; ~s guilt; **durch eigenes/fremdes ~**: through one's own/someone else's fault; **ohne mein ~**: through no fault of my own

verschuldet *Adj.* **a)** in debt *postpos.* **(bei** to); **hoch ~**: deeply in debt; **b)** *(belastet)* mortgaged; **hoch ~**: heavily mortgaged

Verschuldung die; ~, ~en indebtedness *no. pl.*; **die hohe ~ des Staates** the state's heavy debts *pl.*

Verschulung die; ~, ~en organization on school lines

verschusselt *Adj. (ugs.) s.* **schusselig**

verschütten *tr. V.* **a)** spill; **b)** *(begraben)* bury ⟨*person*⟩ [alive]; submerge, bury ⟨*road etc.*⟩; *(fig.)* submerge; **die verschütteten Bergleute** the trapped miners; **ein Verschütteter** one of those buried/trapped; **die Verschütteten** those buried/trapped; **verschüttete Erinnerungen** memories buried in the subconscious

verschütt|gehen *unr. itr. V.; mit sein (ugs.)* do a vanishing trick *or* disappearing act *(coll.)*; *(salopp: umkommen)* go for a burton *(Brit. sl.)*

verschwägert [fɛɐ̯ˈʃvɛ:gɐt] *Adj.* related by marriage *postpos.*

verschweigen *unr. tr. V.* conceal ⟨*truth etc.*⟩; *(verheimlichen)* keep quiet about; **jmdm. etw. ~**: hide *or* conceal sth. from sb.; **du verschweigst mir doch etwas** you're keeping something from me; *s. auch* **verschwiegen 2**

verschweißen *tr. V.* weld [together]; **etw. mit etw. ~**: weld sth. to sth.

verschwenden *tr. V.* waste **(an** + *Akk.* on); **du verschwendest deine Worte** you are wasting your breath; **sie verschwendete keinen Blick an ihn** she did not give him a single glance

Verschwender der; ~s, ~ *(von Geld)* spendthrift; *(von Dingen)* wasteful person

verschwenderisch 1. *Adj.* **a)** wasteful, extravagant ⟨*person*⟩; ⟨*life*⟩ of extravagance; **b)** *(üppig)* lavish; sumptuous. **2.** *adv.* **a)** wastefully, extravagantly; **sie geht ~ mit ihrem Geld um** she is lavish *or* extravagant with her money; **b)** *(üppig)* lavishly; sumptuously

Verschwẹndung die; ~, ~**en** wastefulness; extravagance; **so eine ~!** what a waste!; ~ **von Steuergeldern** waste *or* squandering of taxpayers' money

Verschwẹndungs·sucht die; *o. Pl.* love of extravagance; squandermania *(coll.)*

verschwiegen 1. *2. Part. v.* **verschweigen. 2.** *Adj.* **a)** *(diskret)* discreet; *s. auch* **Grab; b)** *(still, einsam)* secluded ‹*place, bay*›; quiet ‹*restaurant etc.*›; **auf dem ~en Örtchen** *(ugs. scherzh.)* in the smallest room *(joc.)*

Verschwiegenheit die; ~: secrecy; *(Diskretion)* discretion; *s. auch* **Siegel b**

verschwịmmen *unr. itr. V.; mit sein* blur; become blurred; **die Zeilen/Buchstaben verschwammen mir vor den Augen** the lines/letters swam in front of my eyes; **ineinander/in eins ~:** merge into one another/into one; *s. auch* **verschwommen 2**

verschwịnden *unr. itr. V.; mit sein* **a)** disappear; vanish; ‹*pain, spot, etc.*› disappear, go [away]; **seine Zahnschmerzen sind von selbst verschwunden** his toothache went away *or* stopped of its own accord; **die Maus verschwand in ihrem Loch** *od.* **in ihr Loch** the mouse disappeared into its hole; **es ist besser, wir ~/laß uns hier ~:** we'd better/let's make ourselves scarce *(coll.)*; **verschwinde [hier]!** off with you!; go away!; hop it! *(sl.)*; **ich muß mal ~** *(ugs. verhüll.)* I have to pay a visit *(coll.) or (Brit. coll.)* spend a penny; **der Müll muß hier ~:** this rubbish must be removed; **jmdn. ~ lassen** take sb. away; *(in einer Anstalt usw.)* put sb. away; *(ermorden)* eliminate sb.; do away with sb.; **etw. ~ lassen** *(wegzaubern)* ‹*conjurer*› make sth. disappear *or* vanish; *(stehlen)* help oneself to sth. *(coll.)*; *(verstecken)* hide sth.; *(unterschlagen, beiseite schaffen)* dispose of sth.; **Zigaretten in seiner Tasche/Karten in seinem Ärmel ~ lassen** slip cigarettes into one's pocket/cards up one's sleeve; **b)** *(verborgen sein)* **unter etw.** *(Dat.)* **~:** disappear under sth.; be hidden by sth.; **c) neben jmdm./etw. ~** *(sehr klein wirken)* be dwarfed by sb./sth.; *(unbedeutend wirken)* pale into insignificance beside sb./sth.

verschwịndend 1. *Adj.* tiny. **2.** *adv.* **~ klein** tiny; minute; **~ wenig** a tiny amount

verschwistert [fɛɐ̯ˈʃvɪstɐt] *Adj.* **[miteinander] ~ sein** *(Bruder u. Schwester sein)* be brother and sister; *(Brüder u. Schwestern sein)* be brothers and sisters; *(Brüder/Schwestern sein)* be brothers/sisters

verschwịtzen *tr. V.* **a)** make ‹*shirt, dress, etc.*› sweaty; **verschwitzt** sweaty; **total verschwitzt** soaked in sweat *or* perspiration; **b)** *(ugs.: vergessen)* forget; **ich habe es völlig verschwitzt** I clean forgot

verschwollen [fɛɐ̯ˈʃvɔlən] *Adj.* swollen

verschwọmmen 1. *2. Part. v.* **verschwimmen. 2.** *Adj.* blurred ‹*photograph, vision*›; blurred, hazy ‹*outline*›; vague, woolly ‹*idea, concept, formulation, etc.*›; vague ‹*hope*›. **3.** *adv.* ‹*express, formulate, refer*› vaguely; ‹*remember*› hazily; **ich sehe alles ganz ~:** everything looks blurred to me

Verschwọmmenheit die; ~, ~**en** *s.* **verschwommen 2:** blurring; haziness; vagueness; woolliness

verschworen 1. *2. Part. v.* **verschwören. 2.** *Adj.* **a)** *(fest zusammenhaltend)* sworn; **ein ~er Haufen** a band of blood-brothers; **b)** *in* **einer Idee/Sache** *(Dat.) usw.* **~ sein** be dedicated to an idea/a cause *etc.*

verschwören *unr. refl. V.* **a)** conspire, plot **(gegen** against); **alles scheint sich gegen uns verschworen zu haben** *(fig.)* everything seems to have conspired against us; **b)** *(sich verschreiben)* **sich jmdm./einer Sache ~:** dedicate *or* devote oneself to sb./sth.; *s. auch* **verschworen**

Verschworene der/die; *adj. Dekl.,* **Verschwörer der;** ~**s,** ~, **Verschwörerin die;** ~, ~**nen** conspirator

verschwörerisch 1. *Adj.* conspiratorial. **2.** *adv.* conspiratorially

Verschwörung die; ~, ~**en** conspiracy; plot

versehen 1. *unr. tr. V.* **a)** *(ausstatten)* provide; equip ‹*car, factory, machine, etc.*›; **b)** *(ausüben, besorgen)* perform ‹*duty etc.*›; **bei jmdm. den Haushalt ~:** keep house for sb.; **c)** *(innehaben)* hold ‹*post, job*›; **d)** *(kath. Kirche)* administer the last rites *or* sacraments to ‹*dying person*›. **2.** *unr. refl. V.* **a)** *(einen Fehler machen)* make a slip; slip up; **b)** *in* **ehe man sich's versieht** before you know where you are; **ehe ich mich's versah** before I knew what was happening

Versehen das; ~**s,** ~: oversight; slip; **aus ~:** by mistake; inadvertently

versehentlich 1. *Adv.* by mistake; inadvertently. **2.** *adj.; nicht präd.* inadvertent

versehrt [fɛɐ̯ˈzeːɐ̯t] *Adj.* disabled

Versehrte der/die; *adj. Dekl.* disabled person; **die ~n** the disabled

Versehrten·sport der sport *no art.* for the disabled

versẹlbständigen *refl. V.* become independent; **sich zu einer eigenen wissenschaftlichen Disziplin ~:** become an independent scientific discipline

Versẹlbständigung die; ~, ~**en** gaining *or* achievement of independence

versẹnden *unr. (auch regelm.) tr. V.* send ‹*letter, parcel*›; send out ‹*invitations*›; dispatch ‹*goods*›

Versẹndung die *s.* **versenden:** sending; sending out; dispatch

versẹngen *tr. V.* scorch; singe ‹*hair*›

versẹnkbar *Adj.* *(Technik)* foldaway ‹*sewing-machine*›; telescopic ‹*aerial*›

versẹnken 1. *tr. V.* **a)** sink ‹*ship*›; sink, dump ‹*waste*›; lower ‹*body, coffin*›; **das eigene Schiff ~:** scuttle one's ship; **b)** *(verschwinden lassen)* lower, retract ‹*aerial, rostrum, etc.*›; sink ‹*nail, rivet*› [flush]; countersink ‹*screw*›; **die Hände in die Taschen ~:** sink one's hands [deep] into one's pockets. **2.** *refl. V. (fig.)* **sich in etw.** *(Akk.)* **~:** immerse oneself *or* become engrossed in sth.; **sich in den Anblick von etw. ~:** lose oneself in the contemplation of sth.

Versẹnkung die a) *s.* **versenken 1 a, b:** sinking; dumping; lowering; scuttling; retraction; countersinking; **b)** *(fig.: das Sichversenken)* immersion, absorption **(in +** *Akk.* in); **mystische ~:** mystic contemplation; **c)** *(Theater)* trap; **in der ~ verschwinden** *(fig. ugs.)* vanish from the scene; sink into oblivion; **aus der ~ auftauchen** *(fig. ugs.)* reemerge on the scene

Vẹrs·epos das epic poem

Vẹrse·schmied der *(scherzh., abwertend)* rhymester; poetaster

versessen [fɛɐ̯ˈzɛsn̩] *Adj.* **auf jmdn./etw. ~ sein** be dead keen on *or* crazy about sb./sth. *(coll.)*; **auf peinlichste Genauigkeit ~:** obsessed with scrupulous accuracy; **darauf ~ sein, etw. zu tun** be dying to do sth.

versẹtzen 1. *tr. V.* **a)** move; transfer, move ‹*employee*›; *(auf einen anderen Platz)* move ‹*pupil*› [to another seat]; *(in die nächsthöhere Klasse)* move ‹*pupil*› up, *(Amer.)* promote ‹*pupil*› **(in +** *Akk.* to); *(umpflanzen)* transplant, move ‹*plant*›; *(fig.)* transport **(in +** *Akk.* to); **sich ins vorige Jahrhundert versetzt fühlen** *(fig.)* be taken back to the last century; **b)** *(nicht geradlinig anordnen)* stagger; **versetzt angeordnet sein** be staggered; **c)** *(verpfänden)* pawn; **d)** *(verkaufen)* sell; **e)** *(ugs.: vergeblich warten lassen)* stand ‹*person*› up *(coll.)*; **f)** *(vermischen)* mix; **g)** *(erwidern)* retort; **h) etw. in Bewegung/Tätigkeit ~:** set sth. in motion/operation; **jmdn. in Erstaunen/Unruhe/Angst/Begeisterung ~:** astonish sb./make sb. uneasy/frighten sb./fill sb. with enthusiasm; **jmdn. in die Lage ~, etw. zu tun** put sb. in a position to do sth.; **jmdm. einen Stoß/Fußtritt/Schlag** *usw.* **~:** give sb. a push/kick/deal sb. a blow *etc.*; **jmdm. eine** *od.* **eins ~** *(ugs.)* belt sb. one *(coll.)*. **2.** *refl. V.* **sich an jmds. Stelle** *(Akk.) od.* **in jmds. Lage** *(Akk.)* **~:** put oneself in sb.'s position *or* place; **sich in jmdn. ~:** put oneself in sb.'s shoes *or* position

Versẹtzung die; ~, ~**en a)** moving; *(einer Pflanze)* transplanting; *(eines Schülers)* moving up, *(Amer.)* promotion **(in +** *Akk.* to); *(eines Angestellten)* transfer; move; *(fig.)* transporting; **b)** *(Verpfändung)* pawning; **c)** *(Verkauf)* selling; sale; **d)** *(das Mischen)* mixing; *s. auch* **Ruhestand**

Versẹtzungs-: ~konferenz die *(Schulw.)* *staff meeting to discuss moving pupils to higher classes;* **~zeugnis das** *(Schulw.)* end-of-year report *(confirming pupil's move to a higher class)*

verseuchen *tr. V. (auch fig.)* contaminate; **radioaktiv ~:** contaminate with radioactivity

Verseuchung *(auch fig.)* **die;** ~, ~**en** contamination

Vẹrs·fuß der *(Verslehre)* [metrical] foot

Versịcherer der; ~**s,** ~: insurer

versịchern 1. *tr. V.* **a)** *(als wahr hinstellen)* assert, affirm ‹*sth.*›; **etw. hoch und heilig/eidesstattlich ~:** swear blind to sth./attest sth. in a statutory declaration; **jmdm. etw.** *od. (geh.)* **jmdn. einer Sache** *(Gen.)* **~:** assure sb. of sth.; **jmdm.** *od. (geh.)* **jmdn. ~, daß ...** assure sb. that ...; **seien Sie versichert, daß ...** *(geh.)* you may rest assured that ...; **b)** *(vertraglich schützen)* insure **(bei** with); **sein Leben ist hoch/mit 50 000 DM versichert** his life is assured *or* insured for a large sum/50,000 marks. **2.** *refl. V. (geh.)* **a) sich jmds./einer Sache ~:** make sure *or* certain of sb./sth.; **b)** *(veralt.: sich bemächtigen)* **sich einer Sache** *(Gen.)* **~:** seize sth.

Versịcherte der/die; *adj. Dekl.* insured [person]

Versịcherung die a) *(Beteuerung)* assurance; **eine eidesstattliche ~:** a statutory declaration; **b)** *(Schutz durch Vertrag)* insurance; *(Vertrag)* insurance [policy] **(über +** *Akk.* for); *(ugs.: Beitrag, Prämie)* insurance [premium]; **eine ~ abschließen** take out an insurance [policy]; **c)** *(Gesellschaft)* insurance [company]

versịcherungs-, Versịcherungs-: ~agent der insurance broker; **~beitrag der** insurance premium; **~betrug der** insurance fraud; **~fall der** event giving rise to a claim; **~gesellschaft die** insurance company; **~karte die a)** *(Sozialversicherung)* insurance *or* contribution card; **b)** *(Kfz.-Versicherung)* **die grüne ~karte** the green card; **~kaufmann der** insurance salesman; **~mathematiker der** actuary; **~nehmer der** policy-holder; **~pflichtig** *Adj.* **a)** *(Sozialversicherung)* ‹*person*› liable for [insurance] contributions; ‹*earnings*› subject to [insurance] contributions; **b)** *(individuell)* subject to compulsory insurance *postpos.*; **~police die, ~schein der** insurance policy; **~schutz der** insurance cover; **~summe die** sum insured

versịckern *itr. V.; mit sein* **a)** ‹*river etc.*› drain *or* seep away; **b)** *(fig.: enden)* ‹*conversation*› fade away; ‹*money*› drain away

versieben *tr. V. (ugs.)* **a)** *(verlegen)* mislay; **b)** *(verderben)* ruin; waste ‹*chance*›

versiegeln *tr. V.* **a)** seal; **jmdm. den Mund** *od.* **die Lippen ~** *(fig.)* seal sb.'s lips; silence sb.; **b)** *(lackieren, überziehen)* seal ‹*floor, paintwork, etc.*›

Versiegelung die; ~, ~**en a)** *o. Pl. (das Versiegeln)* sealing; **b)** *(Siegel)* seal; **c)** *(Schutzschicht)* protective coating; seal

versiegen *itr. V.; mit sein (geh.)* dry up; run dry; ‹*tears*› cease [to flow]; *(fig.)* peter out; ‹*energy*› run out; **sein nie ~der Humor** his inexhaustible fund of humour

versiert [vɛr'ziːɐ̯t] *Adj.* experienced [and knowledgeable]; **in etw.** *(Dat.)* **~ sein** be well versed in sth.
Versiertheit die; **~:** experience (**in** + *Dat.* in); *(Wissen)* knowledge (**in** + *Dat.* of)
versifft [fɛr'zɪft] *Adj. (ugs.)* dirty
versilbern *tr. V.* **a)** silver-plate; *(dichter.)* silver; **b)** *(ugs.: verkaufen)* turn into cash; flog *(Brit. sl.)*
versinken *unr. itr. V.; mit sein* **a)** sink; **im Schlamm/Schnee ~:** sink into the mud/snow; **in den Wellen ~:** sink beneath the waves; **im Moor ~:** be sucked into the bog; **ich wäre am liebsten im Erdboden versunken** I wished the ground would [open and] swallow me up; **die Stadt versank im Dunkel** *(fig. geh.)* darkness descended over the town; **eine versunkene Kultur** *(fig.)* a long-vanished civilization; **b)** *(fig.)* **~ in** (+ *Akk.*) become immersed in *or* wrapped up in ⟨*memories, thoughts*⟩; subside, lapse into ⟨*melancholy, silence, etc.*⟩; **in Gedanken versunken, nickte er** deep *or* lost in thought, he nodded; **er war ganz in ihren Anblick versunken** he was completely absorbed in looking at her
versinnbildlichen *tr. V.* symbolize
Versinnbildlichung die; **~, ~en** symbolic representation
Version [vɛr'zioːn] **die;** **~, ~en** version
versippt *Adj.* related by marriage *postpos.* (**mit** to)
versklaven *tr. V.* enslave
Versklavung die; **~, ~en** enslavement
Vers·maß das metre
versnoben *itr. V.; mit sein (abwertend)* become snobbish; turn into a snob; **versnobt** snobbish
versoffen [fɛɐ̯'zɔfn̩] **1.** *2. Part. v.* **versaufen. 2.** *Adj. (salopp abwertend)* boozy *(coll.)*
versohlen *tr. V. (ugs.)* belt ⟨*person, backside, etc.*⟩; **er muß mal ordentlich versohlt werden** he needs a good hiding *(coll.)*
versöhnen [fɛɐ̯'zøːnən] **1.** *refl. V.* **sich [miteinander] ~:** become reconciled; make it up; **sich mit jmdm. ~:** make it up with sb.; **sich mit seinem Schicksal ~:** come to terms with one's fate. **2.** *tr. V.* reconcile; **jmdn. mit jmdm. ~:** reconcile sb. with sb.; **jmdn. mit seinem Schicksal ~:** reconcile sb. to his/her fate; **b)** *(besänftigen)* placate; appease
versöhnlich 1. *Adj.* **a)** conciliatory; **b)** *(erfreulich)* positive; optimistic. **2.** *adv.* **a)** in a conciliatory way; ⟨*say*⟩ in a conciliatory tone; **b)** *(erfreulich)* ⟨*end*⟩ positively, optimistically
Versöhnlichkeit die; **~: a)** conciliatory nature; **b)** *(Erfreulichkeit)* positive nature; optimism
Versöhnung die; **~, ~en a)** reconciliation; **b)** *(das Besänftigen)* appeasement; **zu ihrer ~:** in order to placate her
Versöhnungs·fest das *(jüd. Rel.)* Day of Atonement
versonnen 1. *Adj.* dreamy; *(in Gedanken versunken)* lost in thought *postpos.* **2.** *adv.* dreamily; *(in Gedanken)* lost in thought
Versonnenheit die, **~;** dreaminess
versorgen *tr. V.* **a)** supply; **jmdn. mit etw. ~:** supply *or* provide sb. with sth.; **danke, ich bin noch versorgt** I still have plenty, thank you; **seid ihr da drüben noch alle [mit Getränken] versorgt?** have you all got enough to drink over there?; are we looking after you over there?; **hast du den Hund/die Blumen schon versorgt?** have you fed the dog/watered the flowers?; **ich muß mich für die Reise mit Lesestoff ~:** I must get myself something to read on the journey; **das Gehirn ist nicht ausreichend mit Blut versorgt** the blood-supply to the brain is not sufficient; **b)** *(unterhalten, ernähren)* provide for ⟨*children, family*⟩; **er hat eine Familie zu ~:** he has a family to support *or* provide for; **versorgt sein** be provided for; **c)** *(sorgen für)* look after; attend to, see to ⟨*heating, garden, etc.*⟩; **er versorgt sich selbst** he looks after himself; he does his own housework; **sie versorgt ihn** *od.* **versorgt ihm den Haushalt** she keeps house for him; **jmdn. ärztlich ~:** give sb. medical care; *(kurzzeitig)* give sb. medical attention
Versorger der; **~s, ~, Versorgerin die;** **~, ~nen** breadwinner; provider
Versorgung die; **~, ~en a)** *o. Pl.* supply[ing]; **die ~ einer Stadt/eines Gebiets/eines Organs mit etw.** the supply of sth. to a town/an area/an organ; **die ~ der Insel erfolgt auf dem Luftwege** the island is supplied by air; supplies reach the island by air; **die ~ des Hundes/der Blumen übernehmen** see to the feeding of the dog/watering of the flowers; **b)** *(Unterhaltung, Ernährung)* support[ing]; **zur ~ einer Familie ausreichen** be enough to provide for *or* support a family; **die ~ der Kriegerwitwen/der pensionierten Beamten** making provision for war widows/retired civil servants; **c)** *(Bedienung, Pflege)* care; **die ~ des Haushalts** the housekeeping; **die ~ der Heizung/des Gartens** seeing *or* attending to the heating/garden; **die ~ der Heimbewohner ist gut** the people living in the home are well looked after; **ärztliche ~:** medical care *or* treatment; *(kurzzeitig)* medical attention; **die ~ der Wunde** the treatment of the wound; **d)** *(Bezüge)* maintenance; *(Sozialhilfe)* benefit
Versorgungs-: ~anspruch der entitlement to benefit/maintenance; **~ausgleich der** *(Rechtsw.)* maintenance settlement; **~lage die** supply situation (**bei** with regard to); **~netz das** supply network *or* grid
verspachteln *tr. V.* **a)** fill, put filler in ⟨*holes, cracks*⟩; **b)** *(ugs.: aufessen)* scoff *(coll.)*
verspannen 1. *refl. V.* ⟨*muscle*⟩ tense up; **verspannt** taut ⟨*muscle*⟩; *(völlig verkrampft)* seized-up ⟨*back*⟩. **2.** *tr. V.* brace ⟨*mast etc.*⟩
Verspannung die a) *(Med.: der Muskulatur)* tension; **b)** *(eines Mastes o. ä.)* bracing; *(Seile)* stays *pl.*
verspäten *refl. V.* be late; **ich habe mich leider etwas/[um] fünf Minuten verspätet** I am unfortunately a little/five minutes late
verspätet *Adj.* late ⟨*arrival, rose, butterfly*⟩; belated ⟨*greetings, thanks*⟩; **~ eintreffen** *od.* **ankommen** arrive late
Verspätung die; **~, ~en** lateness; *(verspätetes Eintreffen)* late arrival; **[fünf Minuten] ~ haben** be [five minutes] late; **eine fünfminütige ~:** a five-minute delay; **mit [fünfminütiger] ~ abfahren/ankommen** leave/arrive [five minutes] late; **seine** *od.* **die ~ aufholen** make up the lost time; **mit dreimonatiger ~:** three months late
verspeisen *tr. V. (geh.)* consume; partake of
verspekulieren 1. *refl. V.* make a bad speculation; back the wrong horse *(fig.)*; **wenn du gedacht hast, ich vergesse das, hast du dich verspekuliert** *(ugs.)* if you thought I would forget about it, you've got another think coming *(coll.)*. **2.** *tr. V.* lose through speculation
versperren *tr. V.* **a)** block ⟨*road, entrance*⟩; obstruct ⟨*view*⟩; **jmdm. den Weg/die Sicht ~:** block sb.'s path/block *or* obstruct sb.'s view; **b)** *(bes. österr.: abschließen)* lock
verspiegeln *tr. V.* **a)** cover ⟨*wall*⟩ with mirrors; **b)** *(beschichten)* cover with a reflective surface
verspielen 1. *tr. V.* **a)** gamble away; *(fig.: vertun, verwirken)* squander, throw away ⟨*opportunity, chance*⟩; forfeit ⟨*right, credibility, sb.'s trust, etc*⟩; **b)** *(spielend verbringen)* spend ⟨*hours, day*⟩ playing. **2.** *itr. V.* **in [bei jmdm.] verspielt haben** *(ugs.)* have had it [so far as sb. is concerned] *(coll.)*. **3.** *refl. V.* play a wrong note/wrong notes
verspielt 1. *Adj. (auch fig.)* playful; fanciful, fantastic ⟨*form, design, etc.*⟩; **das Kleid ist/wirkt etwas zu ~:** the dress is/seems a little too fanciful. **2.** *adv.* playfully *(lit. or fig.)*; ⟨*dress, designed*⟩ fancifully, fantastically
verspießern *itr. V.; mit sein (abwertend)* become typically bourgeois
verspinnen *unr. tr. V.* spin ⟨*wool*⟩ (**zu** into)
versponnen 1. *2. Part. v.* **verspinnen. 2.** *Adj.* eccentric, odd ⟨*person*⟩; odd, weird ⟨*idea*⟩
Versponnenheit die; **~:** eccentricity; oddness; *(einer Idee)* weirdness
verspotten *tr. V.* mock; ridicule
Verspottung die; **~, ~en** mocking; ridiculing
versprechen 1. *unr. tr. V.* **a)** promise; **jmdm. etw. ~:** promise sb. sth.; **was er verspricht, hält er auch** he keeps his promises; **versprich [mir], pünktlich zu sein** *od.* **daß du pünktlich bist** promise [me] you will be on time; **sich jmdm. ~** *(veralt.)* promise oneself to sb.; **seine Miene/sein Blick versprach nichts Gutes** his expression/glance was ominous; **b) sich** *(Dat.)* **etw. von etw./jmdm. ~:** hope for sth. *or* to get sth. from sth./sb.; **ich würde mir nicht zuviel davon ~:** I wouldn't set my hopes too high. **2.** *unr. refl. V.* make a slip/slips of the tongue; **ich habe mich nur versprochen** it was just a slip of the tongue [on my part]
Versprechen das; **~s, ~:** promise; **jmdm. das ~ geben, etw. zu tun** promise sb. *or* give sb. a promise to do sth.
Versprecher der; **~s, ~:** slip of the tongue; **ein Freudscher ~:** a Freudian slip
Versprechung die; **~, ~en** promise
versprengen *tr. V.* **a)** *(bes. Milit.)* disperse; scatter; **versprengte Soldaten** soldiers who have/had lost contact with their units; **b)** *(verspritzen)* sprinkle ⟨*water*⟩
verspritzen *tr. V.* **a)** spray; **darüber ist schon viel Tinte verspritzt worden** *(fig.)* a lot of ink has been spilt over that; **b)** *(bespritzen)* spatter ⟨*windscreen, coat, etc.*⟩
versprühen *tr. V.* spray; **Funken ~:** send out a shower of sparks; **Geist** *od.* **Witz ~** *(fig.)* show sparkling wit; scintillate
verspüren *tr. V.* feel; **Lust/keine Lust zu etw./Verlangen/kein Verlangen nach etw. ~:** have *or* feel a desire/no desire for sth.
verstaatlichen *tr. V.* nationalize
Verstaatlichung die; **~, ~en** nationalization
verstädtern [fɛɐ̯'ʃtɛːtɐn] *itr. V.; mit sein* become urbanized
Verstädterung die; **~, ~en** urbanization
Verstand der; **~[e]s** *(Fähigkeit zu denken)* reason *no art.*; *(Fähigkeit, Begriffe zu bilden)* mind; *(Vernunft)* [common] sense *no art.*; **Tiere haben keinen ~:** animals do not have the power *or* faculty of reason; **der menschliche ~:** the human mind; **mein** *od.* **der ~ sagt mir, daß ...:** reason *or* common sense tells me that ...; **wenn du deinen ~ gebraucht hättest** if you had used your brain *or* had been thinking; **er hat einen klaren ~:** he has a lucid mind; **ich hätte ihm mehr ~ zugetraut** I thought he would have had more sense; **er mußte all seinen ~ zusammennehmen** he had to summon up all his mental powers *or* rack his brains; **manchmal zweifle ich an seinem ~:** I sometimes doubt his sanity; **bei klarem ~ bleiben** keep one's mental faculties; **~ und Vernunft** understanding and reason; **~ und Gefühl** head and heart; **das schreckliche Erlebnis hat ihren ~ verwirrt** the terrible experience threw her mind into confusion; **ich verliere noch den ~:** I'll go out of my mind; **hast du denn den ~ verloren** *(ugs.)* have you taken leave of your senses?; are you out of your mind?; **du bist wohl nicht [ganz] bei ~!** *(ugs.)* you must be out of your mind!; **das geht**

über meinen ~: that's beyond me; **der Schmerz hat ihn um den ~ gebracht** the pain drove him out of his mind; **seinen ~ versaufen** *(salopp)* drink oneself stupid; **etw. mit ~ trinken/essen/rauchen** really savour sth. [while drinking/eating/smoking it]; *s. auch* **Glück a; Sinn g**

verstandes-, Verstandes-: ~kraft die mental *or* intellectual powers *pl.*; **~mäßig 1.** *Adj.* rational; intellectual ‹*inferiority, superiority*›; **2.** *adv.* rationally; intellectually ‹*inferior, superior*›; **mensch der** rational person

verständig [fɛɐ̯ˈʃtɛndɪç] **1.** *Adj.* sensible; intelligent. **2.** *adv.* sensibly; intelligently

verständigen [fɛɐ̯ˈʃtɛndɪgn̩] **1.** *tr. V.* notify, inform (**von, über** + *Akk.* of). **2.** *refl. V.* **a)** make oneself understood; **sich mit jmdm. ~**: communicate with sb.; **b)** *(sich einigen)* **sich [mit jmdm.] über/auf etw.** *(Akk.)* **~**: come to an understanding *or* reach agreement [with sb.] about *or.* on sth.

Verständigkeit die; ~: understanding; intelligence

Verständigung die; ~, ~en a) notification; **b)** *(das Sichverständlichmachen)* communication *no art.*; **wegen des Lärms war eine ~ praktisch unmöglich** because of the noise, it was almost impossible to make oneself understood; **c)** *(Einigung)* understanding; **eine Politik der ~**: a policy of rapprochement; **über diesen Punkt kam es zu keiner ~**: no agreement was reached on this point

Verständigungs-: ~bereitschaft die; *o. Pl.* readiness to come to an understanding; **~schwierigkeit die** difficulty of communication

verständlich 1. *Adj.* **a)** comprehensible; *(deutlich)* clear ‹*pronunciation, presentation, etc.*›; **[leicht] ~**: easily understood; **schwer ~**: difficult to understand; *(bei Lärm)* difficult to make out; **sich ~ machen** make oneself understood; **sich seinen Zuhörern ~ machen** get [one's message] across to one's listeners; **jmdm. etw. ~ machen** make sth. clear to sb.; **b)** *(begreiflich, verzeihlich)* understandable; **seine Verärgerung ist mir durchaus ~**: I can fully understand his annoyance. **2.** *adv.* comprehensibly; in a comprehensible way; *(deutlich)* ‹*speak, express oneself, present*› clearly

verständlicher·weise *Adv.* understandably

Verständlichkeit die; ~: comprehensibility; clarity

Verständnis das; ~ses, ~se understanding; **dem Leser das ~ erleichtern** make it easier for the reader to understand; **ein ~ für Kunst/Musik** an appreciation of *or* feeling for art/music; **ich habe volles ~ dafür, daß ...**: I fully understand that ...; **für so etwas habe ich kein ~**: I have no time for that kind of thing; **für die Unannehmlichkeiten bitten wir um [Ihr] ~**: we ask for your forbearance *or* we apologize for the inconvenience caused

verständnis-, Verständnis-: ~innig 1. *Adj.* knowing, meaningful ‹*glance*›; **2.** *adv.* knowingly; meaningfully; **~los 1.** *Adj.* uncomprehending; **der modernen Kunst steht er völlig ~los gegenüber** he has no understanding of *or* feeling for modern art at all; **2.** *adv.* uncomprehendingly; **~losigkeit die** incomprehension; **voller ~losigkeit** uncomprehendingly; with a complete lack of understanding; **~voll 1.** *Adj.* understanding; **2.** *adv.* understandingly

verstärken 1. *tr. V.* **a)** strengthen; **die Socken sind an den Fersen verstärkt** the socks have reinforced heels; **b)** *(zahlenmäßig)* reinforce ‹*troops, garrison, etc.*› (**um** by); enlarge, augment ‹*orchestra, choir*› (**um** by); **die Truppen auf 1500 Mann ~**: bring the troops up to a strength of 1,500 men; **c)** *(intensiver machen)* intensify, increase ‹*effort, contrast*›; strengthen, increase ‹*impression, suspicion*›; *(größer machen)* increase ‹*pressure, voltage, effect, etc.*›; *(lauter machen)* amplify ‹*signal, sound, guitar, etc.*›. **2.** *refl. V.* increase; *s. auch* **verstärkt**

Verstärker der; ~s, ~: amplifier

verstärkt 1. *Adj.; nicht präd.* **a)** increased; *(größer)* greater ‹*efforts, vigilance, etc.*›; **in ~em Maße** to a greater *or* increased extent; **b)** *(zahlenmäßig)* enlarged, augmented ‹*orchestra, choir, etc.*›; reinforced *(Mil.)*‹*unit*›. **2.** *adv.* to an increased extent

Verstärkung die; ~, ~en a) strengthening; **b)** *(zahlenmäßig)* reinforcement *(esp. Mil.)*; *(eines Orchesters usw.)* enlargement; **c)** *(Intensivierung, Zunahme)* increase (*Gen.* in); *(der Lautstärke)* amplification; **zur ~ einer Sache** *(Gen.)* to increase/amplify sth.; **d)** *(zusätzliche Person[en])* reinforcements *pl.*; **e)** *(verstärkendes Element)* reinforcement

verstauben *itr. V.; mit sein* get dusty; gather dust *(lit. or fig.)*; *s. auch* **verstaubt**

verstäuben [fɛɐ̯ˈʃtɔybn̩] *tr. V.* spray ‹*insecticide etc.*›

verstaubt *Adj.* dusty; covered in dust *postpos.*; *(fig. abwertend)* old-fashioned; outmoded

verstauchen *tr. V.* sprain; **sich** *(Dat.)* **den Fuß/die Hand ~**: sprain one's ankle/wrist

Verstauchung die; ~, ~en sprain

verstauen *tr. V.* pack (**in** + *Dat. od. Akk.* in[to]); *(bes. im Boot/Auto)* stow (**in** + *Dat. od. Akk.* in); **etw. auf dem Boden/in einem** *od.* **einen Schrank ~**: put *or (coll.)* stash sth. away in the loft/a cupboard; **etw. in der Hosentasche ~**: stuff sth. into one's trouser pocket; **er verstaute seine Familie im Auto** *(scherzh.)* he packed his family into the car

Versteck das; ~[e]s, ~e hiding-place; *(eines Flüchtlings, Räubers usw.)* hide-out: **~ spielen** play hide-and-seek; **[vor jmdm./voreinander** *od.* **mit jmdm./miteinander] ~ spielen** *(fig.)* hide *or* keep things [from sb./one another]

verstecken 1. *tr. V.* hide (**vor** + *Dat.* from); **jmdn. versteckt halten** keep sb. hidden; **das Haus war in einem Wäldchen versteckt** the house was tucked away in a small wood. **2.** *refl. V.* **sich [vor jmdm./etw.] ~**: hide [from sb./sth.]; **sich versteckt halten** be [in] hiding; *(versteckt bleiben)* remain in hiding; **ich möchte bloß wissen, wo sich meine Brille schon wieder versteckt hat** I should love to know where my glasses have got to; **sich vor** *od.* **neben jmdm. nicht zu ~ brauchen** *od.* **nicht ~ müssen** *(fig.)* not need to fear comparison with sb.; **das ist eine Leistung, mit der er sich nicht ~ muß** it is a performance of which he has no need to be ashamed; **sich vor** *od.* **neben jmdm. ~ müssen** *(fig.)* not be able to compare with sb.; not be a patch on sb. *(coll.)*; **sich hinter seinem Chef/seinen Vorschriften** *usw.* **~** *(fig.)* use one's boss *(coll.)*/one's rules and regulations to hide behind; *s. auch* **versteckt**

Verstecken das; ~s hide-and-seek *no art.*

Versteck·spiel das game of hide-and-seek; *(fig.)* charade; pretence

versteckt *Adj.* hidden; concealed ‹*polemics*›; veiled ‹*threat*›; *(heimlich)* secret ‹*malice, activity, etc.*›; disguised ‹*foul*›; *(verstohlen)* furtive ‹*glance, smile*›

verstehen 1. *unr. tr. V.* **a)** *(wahrnehmen)* understand; make out; **ich konnte ihn bei dem Lärm nicht ~**: I couldn't make out what he was saying because of the noise; **man versteht [vor Lärm] sein eigenes Wort nicht** one cannot hear oneself speak; **er war am Telefon gut/schlecht/kaum zu ~**: it was easy/difficult/barely possible to understand *or* make out what he was saying on the telephone; **b)** *auch itr. (begreifen, interpretieren)* understand; **das mußt du schon ~**: you must understand *or* see that; **ich verstehe** I understand; I see; **[ich habe] verstanden** understood; I've got it; **wir ~ uns schon** we understand each other; we see eye to eye; **das verstehe [nun] einer!** what is one supposed to make of that?; **du bleibst hier, verstanden** *od.* **verstehst du!** you stay here, understand!; **jmdm. etw. zu ~ geben** give sb. to understand sth.; **das ist in dem Sinne** *od.* **so zu ~, daß ...**: it is supposed to mean that ...; **wie soll ich das ~?** how am I to interpret that?; what am I supposed to make of that?; **jmdn./etw. falsch ~**: misunderstand sb./sth.; **versteh mich bitte richtig** *od.* **nicht falsch** please don't misunderstand me *or* get me wrong; **wenn ich [es] recht verstehe** if I understand rightly; **falsch verstandene Loyalität** misunderstood loyalty; **etw. unter etw.** *(Dat.)* **~**: understand sth. by sth.; **was ~ Sie darunter?** what do you think that means?; **jmdn./sich als etw. ~**: see sb./oneself as sth.; consider sb./oneself to be sth.; **er will sich als Christ verstanden wissen** he wants to be seen as *or* to be considered a Christian; *s. auch* **Bahnhof; Spaß b; c)** *(beherrschen, wissen)* **es ~, etw. zu tun** know how to do sth.; **er versteht zu genießen** he knows how to enjoy himself *or* things; **er versteht eine Menge von Autos** he knows a lot about cars; he is quite an expert on cars; **davon verstehe ich nichts/nicht viel** I don't know anything/know much about it. **2.** *unr. refl. V.* **a) sich mit jmdm. ~**: get on with sb.; **sie ~ sich** they get on well together; **b)** *(selbstverständlich sein)* **das versteht sich [von selbst]** that goes without saying; **versteht sich!** *(ugs.)* of course!; **c)** *(Kaufmannsspr.: gemeint sein)* **der Preis versteht sich einschließlich Mehrwertsteuer** the price is inclusive of VAT; **d) sich auf Pferde/Autos** *usw. (Akk.)* **~**: know what one is doing with horses/cars; know all about horses/cars; **er versteht sich aufs Dichten** he knows how to write poetry; **e) sich zu etw. ~** *(veralt.)* agree [reluctantly] to sth.

versteifen 1. *tr. V.* **a)** stiffen ‹*collar, part of body, etc.*›; **b)** *(Bauw.: abstützen)* shore up ‹*wall, house, excavation, etc.*›; brace ‹*fence*›. **2.** *itr. V.; mit sein* stiffen [up]; become stiff. **3.** *refl. V.* **a)** stiffen [up]; become stiff; **b)** *in* **sich auf etw.** *(Akk.)* **~**: insist on sth.

Versteifung die; ~, ~en a) stiffening; **b)** *(Bauw.)* shoring [up]

versteigen *unr. refl. V.* **a)** *(sich verirren)* get lost [while climbing]; *(nicht mehr herunterkönnen)* get stuck; get into difficulties; **b) sich zu einer Behauptung/zu Angriffen gegen jmdn.** *usw.* **~**: have the presumption to make an assertion/attacks on sb. *etc.*; **wie konnte ich mich zu solcher Schwärmerei ~?** how could I get so carried away?; *s. auch* **verstiegen 2**

versteigern *tr. V.* auction; **etw. ~ lassen** put sth. up for auction; **auf einer Auktion meistbietend versteigert werden** be sold to the highest bidder at an auction

Versteigerung die a) auction *no indef. art.*; **zur ~ kommen** *od.* **gelangen** *(Amtsspr.)* be auctioned; **b)** *(Veranstaltung)* auction; **auf einer ~**: at an auction

versteinern 1. *itr. V.; mit sein* ‹*plant, animal*› fossilize, become fossilized; ‹*wood etc.*› petrify, become petrified; *(fig. geh.)* ‹*person*› go rigid; ‹*expression, face*› harden, become stony; **sie blieb [wie] versteinert stehen** she stopped in her tracks, as rigid as a statue. **2.** *refl. V. (geh.)* ‹*face, features*› harden

Versteinerung die; ~, ~en a) *(das Versteinern)* fossilization; *(von Holz)* petrification; **b)** *(Fossil)* fossil

verstellbar *Adj.* adjustable

verstellen 1. *tr. V.* **a)** *(falsch plazieren)* misplace; put [back] in the wrong place; **b)** *(anders einstellen)* adjust ‹*seat etc.*›; alter [the adjustment of] ⟨*mirror etc.*⟩; reset ⟨*alarm clock, points, etc.*⟩; **der Sitz läßt sich in der Höhe ~:** the seat can be adjusted for height; **c)** *(versperren)* block, obstruct ⟨*entrance, exit, view, etc.*⟩; **er verstellte mir den Weg** he blocked my path; he stood in my way; **[jmdm.] den Blick für etw. ~** *(fig.)* obscure sb.'s view of sth.; **d)** *(zur Täuschung verändern)* disguise, alter ⟨*voice, handwriting*⟩. **2.** *refl. V.* **a)** *(seine Einstellung, Position verändern)* alter; *(so daß es falsch eingestellt ist)* get out of adjustment; **b)** *(sich anders geben als man ist)* pretend; play-act; **sich vor jmdm. ~:** pretend to sb.

Verstellung die play-acting; pretence; *(der Stimme, Schrift)* disguising; alteration

Verstellungs·kunst die [art of] play-acting *no. pl.*

versteppen *itr. V.; mit sein* become steppe

versterben *unr. itr. V.; mit sein (geh.)* die; pass away; **mein verstorbener Mann** my late husband; *s. auch* **Verstorbene**

versteuern *tr. V.* pay tax on

verstiegen 1. *2. Part. v.* **versteigen. 2.** *Adj.* whimsical ⟨*idealist, person*⟩; extravagant, fantastic ⟨*idea, expectation, etc.*⟩; wild ⟨*dream, desire*⟩

Verstiegenheit die; ~, ~en a) *o. Pl.* extravagance; **b)** *(etw. Verstiegenes)* extravagant *or* fantastic idea/remark

verstimmen 1. *tr. V.* **a)** *(Musik)* put ⟨*instrument*⟩ out of tune; **b)** *(schlechtgelaunt machen)* put ⟨*person*⟩ in a bad mood; *(verärgern)* annoy. **2.** *refl. V.* get *or* go out of tune

verstimmt *Adj.* **a)** *(Musik)* out of tune *pred.*; **b)** *(verärgert)* put out, peeved, disgruntled (**über** + *Akk.* by, about); **ein ~er Magen** an upset stomach

Verstimmung die disgruntled *or* bad mood; **eine leichte ~ hinterlassen** leave a slight sense of annoyance

verstockt 1. *Adj.* obdurate; stubborn. **2.** *adv.* obdurately; stubbornly

Verstocktheit die; ~: obduracy; stubbornness

verstohlen [fɛɐ̯ˈʃto:lən] **1.** *Adj.* furtive; surreptitious. **2.** *adv.* furtively; surreptitiously

verstolpern *tr. V. (Sportjargon)* stumble and miss ⟨*ball, chance, etc.*⟩

verstopfen 1. *tr. V.* block; **verstopft sein** ⟨*pipe, drain, jet, nose, etc.*⟩ be blocked (**durch, von** with); *(Med.: keinen Stuhlgang haben)* be constipated; **die vielen Autos ~ die Altstadt** the large number of cars causes congestion in the old quarter. **2.** *itr. V.; mit sein* become blocked

Verstopfung die; ~, ~en *(Med.: Stuhl~)* constipation

verstorben [fɛɐ̯ˈʃtɔrbn̩] *2. Part. v.* **versterben**

Verstorbene der/die; *adj. Dekl. (geh.)* deceased

verstören *tr. V.* distress

verstört *Adj.* distraught; **einen ~en Eindruck machen** appear distraught *or* distressed

Verstörtheit die; ~: distressed *or* distraught state; distress

Verstoß der violation, infringement (**gegen** of); **~ gegen die Etikette/den guten Geschmack** breach of etiquette/offense against good taste

verstoßen 1. *unr. tr. V.* disown; **aus dem Elternhaus ~ werden** be turned out of one's parents' house; **ein Verstoßener** an outcast. **2.** *unr. itr. V.* **gegen etw. ~:** infringe *or* contravene sth.; **gegen die Etikette/den guten Geschmack ~:** commit a breach of etiquette/offend against good taste

Verstoßung die; ~, ~en disowning; *(aus dem Elternhaus)* turning out

verstrahlen *tr. V.* **a)** radiate; **b)** *(radioaktiv verseuchen)* contaminate with radiation

Verstrebung die; ~, ~en struts *pl.*; *(einzelne Strebe)* strut

verstreichen 1. *unr. tr. V.* **a)** *(verteilen)* apply, put on ⟨*paint*⟩; spread ⟨*butter etc.*⟩; **b)** *(verbrauchen)* use [up] ⟨*paint*⟩; **c)** *(zustreichen)* fill ⟨*hole, crack*⟩. **2.** *unr. itr. V.; mit sein (geh.)* ⟨*time*⟩ pass [by]

verstreuen *tr. V.* **a)** *(verteilen)* scatter; put down ⟨*bird food, salt*⟩; *(unordentlich)* strew; **seine Kleider lagen im ganzen Zimmer verstreut** his clothes were scattered *or* strewn all over the room; **verstreute Gehöfte/Aufsätze** isolated *or* scattered farms/isolated essays; **b)** *(versehentlich)* spill

verstricken 1. *tr. V.* **a)** *(verbrauchen)* use ⟨*wool*⟩ [in knitting]; **b)** *(geh.: verwickeln)* **jmdn. in etw.** *(Akk.)* **~:** involve sb. in sth.; draw sb. into sth.; **in etw.** *(Akk.)* **verstrickt [sein]** [be] mixed up *or* involved in sth. **2.** *refl. V.* **a)** *(falsch stricken)* make a mistake/mistakes [in knitting]; **b)** *(fig.)* **sich in etw.** *(Akk.)* **~:** become entangled *or* caught up in sth.

Verstrickung die; ~, ~en involvement (**in** + *Akk.* in)

verströmen *tr. V.* exude

verstrubbeln *tr. V. (ugs.)* tousle

verstümmeln *tr. V.* mutilate; *(fig.)* garble ⟨*report*⟩; chop, mutilate ⟨*text*⟩; mutilate, do violence to ⟨*name*⟩; **sich selbst ~:** maim oneself

Verstümmelung die; ~, ~en mutilation; *(Selbst~)* self-mutilation; *(fig.: einer Meldung usw.)* garbling

verstummen *itr. V.; mit sein (geh.)* fall silent; ⟨*music, noise, conversation*⟩ cease; *(allmählich)* die *or* fade away; *(fig.)* ⟨*rumour, question*⟩ go away; **er verstummte vor Schreck** he broke off, terrified; **jmdn. zum Verstummen bringen** silence sb.; **jeder Zweifel verstummte** *(fig.)* every doubt was stilled

Versuch der; ~[e]s, ~e a) attempt; **beim ~, etw. zu tun** in attempting to do sth.; **er hat es gleich beim ersten ~ geschafft** he made it *or* succeeded at the first attempt; **er hat schon mehrmals den ~ gemacht zu ...:** he has already made several attempts to ...; **das käme auf einen ~ an** we'll have to try it and see; **einen ~ wäre es wert** it's worth a try; **ich will noch einen letzten ~ mit ihm/damit machen** I'd like to give him/it one more try; **b)** *(Experiment)* experiment (**an** + *Dat.* on); *(Probe)* test; **c)** *(literarisches Produkt)* attempt; **seine ersten lyrischen/literarischen ~e** his first attempts at poetry/literature; **„~ über das Schöne"** 'Essay on Beauty'; **d)** *(Rugby)* try; **einen ~ erzielen** *od.* **legen** score a try

versuchen 1. *tr. V.* **a)** try; attempt; **versuch's doch!** *(drohend)* just you try!; *(ermunternd)* just try it!; **es mit jmdm./etw. ~:** give sb./sth. a try; **es bei jmdm. ~:** try sb.; **versuchter Mord** *(Rechtsspr.)* attempted murder; **laß mich mal ~, ob ...:** *(ugs.)* let me [try and] see if ...; *s. auch* **Glück a; b)** *(auch bibl.: in Versuchung führen)* tempt; **versucht sein, etw. zu tun** be tempted to do sth. **2.** *tr., itr. V. (probieren)* **den Kuchen/von dem Kuchen ~:** try the cake/some of the cake. **3.** *refl. V.* **sich in/an etw.** *(Dat.)***/auf einem Instrument/als etw. ~:** try one's hand at sth./at playing an instrument/at being sth.

Versucher der; ~s, ~: *(bibl.)* tempter

versuchs-, Versuchs-: ~anordnung die set-up for an/the experiment/for experiments; **~anstalt die** research institute; **~ballon der a)** *(Met.)* sounding-balloon; **b)** *(fig.)* try-out; *(Gerücht, Vorschlag usw.)* feeler; **einen ~ballon [auf]steigen lassen** fly a kite *(fig.)*; put out feelers *(fig.)*; **~gelände das** testing-ground; *(für nukleare Waffen usw.)* test site; **~kaninchen das** *(fig.)* guinea-pig; **~person die** *(bes. Med., Psych.)* test *or* experimental subject; **~stadium das** experimental stage; **~tier das** experimental animal; **~weise 1.** *Adv.* on a trial basis; as an experiment; **2.** *adj.; nicht präd.* experimental; **~zweck der** experimental purpose; **zu ~zwecken gehaltene Tiere** animals kept for experiments

Versuchung die; ~, ~en temptation; **jmdn. in ~ führen** lead sb. into temptation *(esp. Rel.)*; put sb. in the way of temptation; **in ~** *(Akk.)* **kommen** *od.* **geraten[, etw. zu tun]** be *or* feel tempted [to do sth.]

versumpfen *itr. V.* **a)** become marshy *or* boggy; **versumpft** marshy; boggy; **b)** *(ugs. abwertend: verwahrlosen)* go to seed *or* to the dogs; **c)** *(ugs.; lange bleiben und trinken)* stay out late boozing *(coll.)*

versündigen *refl. V.* **sich an jmdm./etw. ~:** sin against sb./sth.; **sich an seiner Gesundheit ~:** abuse one's health; **versündige dich nicht!** *(als Antwort)* what a [wicked] thing to say/do!

Versunkenheit die; ~ *(geh.)* [state of] contemplation; deep meditation; **in seiner ~ hatte er ihr Kommen gar nicht bemerkt** he was so deep in thought *or* so engrossed that he had not noticed her coming

versüßen *tr. V.* **jmdm./sich etw. ~** *(fig.)* make sth. more pleasant for sb./oneself; *(erträglicher machen)* make sth. more bearable for sb./oneself

vertäfeln *tr. V.* panel

Vertäfelung die; ~, ~en panelling

vertagen 1. *tr. V.* adjourn ⟨*meeting, debate, etc.*⟩ (**auf** + *Akk.* until); postpone ⟨*decision, verdict*⟩ (**auf** + *Akk.* until). **2.** *refl. V.* ⟨*court*⟩ adjourn; ⟨*meeting*⟩ be adjourned

vertändeln *tr. V. (auch Sport)* fritter away ⟨*time, chance*⟩

vertäuen [fɛɐ̯ˈtɔyən] *tr. V. (Seemannsspr.)* moor

vertauschen *tr. V.* **a)** exchange; switch; reverse, switch ⟨*roles*⟩; reverse, transpose ⟨*poles*⟩; **etw. mit** *od.* **gegen etw. ~:** exchange sth. for sth.; **die Kanzel mit dem Ministersessel ~:** exchange the pulpit for a ministerial post; **die Buchstaben eines Wortes ~:** transpose *or* switch round the letters in a word; **b)** *(verwechseln)* mix up

Vertauschung die; ~, ~en a) exchange; *(von Buchstaben, Polen usw.)* transposition; *(von Rollen)* reversal; switching; **b)** *(Verwechslung)* mixing up; **eine ~:** a mix-up

Vertäuung die; ~, ~en *(Seemannsspr.)* mooring

verteidigen [fɛɐ̯ˈtaidɪgn̩] **1.** *tr. V.* defend; **der Angeklagte wird sich selbst ~:** the accused will conduct his own defence. **2.** *itr. V. (Ballspiele)* defend; *(Verteidiger sein)* be a defender

Verteidiger der; ~s, ~, Verteidigerin, die; ~, ~nen a) *(auch Sport)* defender; **[als] ~ spielen** *(Sport)* play as a defender; **b)** *(Rechtsw.)* defence counsel

Verteidigung die, ~, ~en *(auch Sport, Rechtsw.)* defence; **zur ~ seiner Meinung/der Stadt bereit sein** be ready to defend one's opinion/the town; **jmdn. in die ~ drängen** force sb. on [to] the defensive

Verteidigungs-: ~bereitschaft die; *o. Pl.* readiness to defend; **~bündnis das** defensive alliance; **~drittel das** *(Eishockey)* defence zone; **~haushalt der** defence budget; **~minister der** minister of defence; **~ministerium das** ministry of defence; **~rede die** *(vor Gericht)* speech for the defence; *(Apologie)* apologia; **~waffe die** defensive weapon

verteilen 1. *tr. V.* **a)** *(austeilen)* distribute, hand out ⟨*exercise books, leaflets, prizes, etc.*⟩ (**an** + *Akk.* to, **unter** + *Akk.* among); share [out], distribute ⟨*money, food*⟩ (**an** + *Akk.* to, **unter** + *Akk.* among); allocate ⟨*work*⟩; cast, allocate ⟨*parts*⟩; **Karten an die Spieler ~:** deal out cards to the players; **ein Drama mit verteilten Rollen lesen** read a play with each part allocated to a different person; **b)** *(an verschiedene Plätze bringen)* distribute ⟨*weight etc.*⟩ (**auf** + *Akk.* over); spread ⟨*cost*⟩ (**auf** + *Akk.* among); distribute, spread out ‹*cushions etc.*›; **Flüchtlinge auf drei Lager ~:** divide up refugees and send them to three camps; **c)** *(verstreichen, verstreuen, verrühren usw.)* distribute, spread ‹*butter, seed, dirt, etc.*›. **2.** *refl. V.* **a)** spread out; **b)** *(sich ausbreiten, verteilt sein)* be distributed (**auf** + *Akk.* over)

Verteiler der; ~s, ~ a) *(Person)* distributor; **b)** *(Technik: Zündverteiler)* distributor; **c)** *(Bürow.)* distribution list; **„~"** 'copies to'

Verteiler·schlüssel der *(Bürow.)* distribution list

Verteilung die distribution; *(der Rollen, der Arbeit)* allocation; **etw. zur ~ bringen** *(Papierdt.)* distribute sth.; **zur ~ kommen** *od.* **gelangen** *(Papierdt.)* be distributed

vertelefonieren *tr. V. (ugs.)* spend ‹*time*› telephoning *or* on the phone; spend ‹*money*› on telephoning

verteuern 1. *tr. V.* make ‹*goods*› more expensive. **2.** *refl. V.* become more expensive; **die Lebenshaltung verteuert sich** the cost of living is going up

Verteuerung die increase *or* rise in price; **die ~ des Kaffees** the increase in the price of coffee

verteufeln *tr. V.* condemn; denigrate

verteufelt 1. *Adj. (ugs.)* **a)** *(verzwickt)* extremely tricky ‹*situation, business*›; **b)** *nicht präd. (äußerst)* fiendish ‹*thirst, pain, etc.*› **2.** *adv. (ugs.)* damned; fiendishly ‹*cold*›; terribly *(coll.)* ‹*similar*›; **~!** damn!

Verteufelung die; ~, ~en condemnation; denigration

vertiefen 1. *tr. V.* **a)** deepen (**um** by); make deeper; **eine vertiefte Stelle** a depression; a hollow; **b)** *(intensivieren)* deepen ‹*knowledge, understanding, love*›; deepen, strengthen ‹*dislike, friendship, collaboration, etc.*›; **ein vertieftes Verständnis** a deeper understanding. **2.** *refl. V.* **a)** deepen; become deeper; **b)** *(sich konzentrieren)* **sich ~ in** (+ *Akk.*) bury oneself in ‹*book, work, etc.*›; become deeply involved in ‹*conversation*›; **in etw.** *(Akk.)* **vertieft sein** be engrossed *or* absorbed in sth.; **in Gedanken vertieft** deep in thought; **c)** *(intensiver werden)* ‹*friendship*› deepen; ‹*relations*› become closer; ‹*hate, conflict*› deepen, become more intense

Vertiefung die; ~, ~en a) deepening; *(von Freundschaft, Abneigung)* deepening; strengthening; *(von Zusammenarbeit, Beziehungen)* strengthening; *(von Wissen)* consolidation; reinforcement; *(von Haß, Konflikten)* intensification; **b)** *(in Gedanken)* absorption (**in** + *Akk.* in); **c)** *(Mulde)* depression; hollow

vertieren *itr. V.; mit sein* become brutalized; **vertiert** brutalized

vertikal [vɛrti'ka:l] **1.** *Adj.* vertical; **in ~er Richtung** vertically. **2.** *adv.* vertically

Vertikale die; ~; ~n a) *(Linie)* vertical line; **b)** *o. Pl. (Lage)* **die ~:** the vertical *or* perpendicular; **etw. in die ~ bringen** *od.* **bewegen** move sth. into a vertical position

Vertiko ['vɛrtiko] **das,** *auch* **der; ~s, ~s** *small decorated cabinet with a drawer and display shelf on top*

vertilgen *tr. V.* **a)** *(vernichten)* exterminate ‹*vermin*›; kill off ‹*weeds*›; **b)** *(ugs.: verzehren)* devour, *(joc.)* demolish ‹*food*›

Vertilgung die; ~, ~en a) *(von Ungeziefer)* extermination; *(von Unkraut)* killing off; **b)** *(ugs.: das Verzehren)* demolition *(joc.)*

Vertilgungs·mittel das *(gegen Unkraut)* weed-killer; *(gegen Insekten)* pesticide

vertippen 1. *refl. V.* **a)** make a typing mistake/typing mistakes; *(auf der Rechenmaschine, dem Tastentelefon usw.)* press the wrong number; **b)** *(im Lotto, Toto, bei Vorhersagen)* get it wrong. **2.** *tr. V.* mistype ‹*word*›; type ‹*word, letter*› wrongly; *(auf der Rechenmaschine, dem Tastentelefon usw.)* get ‹*number*› wrong

vertonen *tr. V.* set ‹*text, poem*› to music; set, write the music to ‹*libretto*›; add sound to ‹*slides*›; add a sound-track to ‹*film*›

Vertonung die; ~, ~en a) setting [to music]; **die ~ eines Librettos** writing the music to a libretto; **die ~ von Dias/eines Films** adding sound to slides/a sound-track to a film; **b)** *(Werk)* setting

vertrackt [fɛɐ̯'trakt] *(ugs.) Adj.* **a)** complicated, involved ‹*situation, business, etc.*›; tricky, intricate ‹*job*›; **b)** *(ärgerlich)* confounded; infuriating; **das ~e Gefühl haben, daß ...:** have a nasty feeling that ...

Vertracktheit die; ~, ~en *(ugs.)* **a)** complexity; **b)** *(Ärgerlichkeit)* maddening *or* infuriating nature

Vertrag der; ~[e]s, Verträge [...trɛ:gə] contract; *(zwischen Staaten)* treaty; **mündlicher ~:** verbal agreement; **laut ~:** according to the terms of the contract; **ein ~ auf drei Jahre** a three-year contract; **jmdn. unter ~ nehmen** contract sb.; put sb. under contract; **[bei jmdm.] unter ~ stehen** be under contract [to sb.]

vertragen 1. *unr. tr. V.* **a)** endure; tolerate *(esp. Med.)*; *(aushalten, leiden können)* stand; bear; take ‹*joke, criticism, climate, etc.*›; **die Pflanze verträgt keinen Zug/kann Sonne ~:** the plant will not tolerate draughts/can tolerate some sun; **Rauch/Lärm/Belastungen/Aufregung schlecht ~:** not be able to stand too much smoke/noise/strain/excitement; **das Klima [nicht] gut ~:** [not] be able to take the climate; **ich vertrage keinen Kaffee/kein fettes Essen** coffee/fatty food disagrees with me; **den Wein/das Medikament habe ich gut vertragen** I was able to drink the wine/take the medicine with no ill effects; **sie verträgt dieses Medikament schlecht/nicht** this medicine doesn't really agree with her/does not agree with her at all; **ich könnte jetzt einen Whisky ~** *(ugs.)* I could do with *or* wouldn't say no to a whisky; **er verträgt eine Menge [Alkohol]/nichts/nicht viel** *(ugs.)* he can hold a lot of drink *(coll.)*/can't hold his drink/can't hold much drink; **er verträgt keine Kritik/keinen Spaß** he cannot take criticism/a joke; **ich kann alles ~, nur nicht das** I can put up with anything but not that; **die Sache verträgt keinen Aufschub** *(geh.)* the matter brooks no delay; **b)** *(landsch.: abtragen)* wear out. **2.** *unr. refl. V.* **a) sich mit jmdm. ~:** get on *or* along with sb.; **sich gut [miteinander] ~:** get on well together; **er verträgt sich mit keinem** he never gets on with anybody; **sie ~ sich wieder** they are friends again; they have made it up; **wir wollen uns wieder ~:** let's make it up *or* let bygones be bygones; **so Kinder, nun vertragt euch wieder** come on children, stop squabbling and call a truce; *s. auch* [2]**Pack;** **b)** *(passen)* **sich mit etw. ~:** go with sth.; **die Farben ~ sich nicht [miteinander]** the colours do not go together; **wie verträgt sich das mit seinen christlichen Überzeugungen** how does this square with his Christian convictions?; **so ein Verhalten verträgt sich nicht mit seinem liberalen Anspruch** such behaviour is not consistent with his liberal pretensions

vertraglich 1. *Adj.* contractual. **2.** *adv.* contractually; by contract

verträglich [fɛɐ̯'trɛ:klıç] *Adj.* **a)** digestible ‹*food*›; **leicht/schwer ~:** easily digestible/indigestible; **ein gut ~es Medikament** a drug which has no side-effects; **b)** *(umgänglich)* good-natured; easy to get on with *pred.*

Verträglichkeit die; ~, ~en a) digestibility; **die ~ eines Medikaments** a drug's lack of side-effects; **b)** *(Umgänglichkeit)* good nature

vertrags-, Vertrags-: ~abschluß der completion of [a/the] contract; **~bruch der** breach of contract; **~brüchig** *Adj.* in breach of contract *postpos.*; **~brüchig werden/sein** be in breach of contract

vertrag·schließend *Adj.; nicht präd.* contracting

vertrags-, Vertrags-: ~entwurf der draft contract/treaty; **~gemäß** *adv.* as per contract; as stipulated in the contract; **~händler der** authorized *or* appointed dealer; **~partner der** party to a/the contract; **unser ~partner** our contractual partner; **~schluß der** *s.* **~abschluß; ~spieler der** *(Fußball)* semi-professional *(under contract to a club)*; **~werk das** major agreement; *(international)* treaty; **~werkstatt die** authorized garage

vertrauen *itr. V.* **jmdm./einer Sache ~:** trust sb./sth.; **auf etw.** *(Akk.)* **~:** [put one's] trust in sth.; **auf sein Glück ~:** trust to luck; **ich vertraue darauf, daß ...:** I am confident *or* have confidence that ...; **auf Gott ~:** put one's trust in God

Vertrauen das; ~s trust; confidence; **~ zu jmdm./etw. haben/fassen** have/come to have confidence in sb./sth.; trust/come to trust sb./sth.; **er hat kein ~ zu sich selbst** he has no confidence in himself *or* self-confidence; **er hat mein volles ~:** I have complete confidence in him; **jmdm. [sein] ~ schenken** put one's trust in sb.; **jmdm. das** *od.* **sein ~ entziehen** withdraw the trust *or* confidence one has/had [placed] in sb.; **jmds. ~ enttäuschen/erschüttern** betray sb.'s trust/destroy sb.'s confidence [in one]; **das Parlament sprach dem Kanzler das ~ aus** parliament passed a vote of confidence in the Chancellor; **sein ~ in jmdn./etw. setzen** put *or* place one's trust in sb./sth.; **sein** *od.* **das ~ zu jmdm. verlieren** lose confidence in sb.; **im ~ [gesagt]** [strictly] in confidence; between you and me; **im ~ auf etw.** *(Akk.)* trusting to *or* in sth.; **im ~ darauf, daß ...:** trusting that ...; **ein Mann seines ~s** a man whom he trusts; **jmdn. ins ~ ziehen** take sb. into one's confidence

vertrauen·erweckend *Adj.* inspiring *or* that inspires confidence *postpos.*; **einen ~en Eindruck machen** inspire confidence [by one's/it's appearance]; look trustworthy

vertrauens-, Vertrauens-: ~arzt der independent examining doctor *(working for health service, health insurance, etc.)*; **~beweis der** show of confidence (**für** in); **~bildend** *Adj.* **~bildende Maßnahmen** measures designed to build up trust; **~bruch der** breach of trust; *(wenn man Vertrauliches weitersagt)* breach of confidence; **~frage die** *(Parl.)* question of confidence; **die ~frage stellen** ask for a vote of confidence; **~frau die a)** spokeswoman (*Gen.* for); representative; **b)** *(in der Gewerkschaft)* [union] representative; *(in einer Fabrik o.ä.)* shop steward; **~krise die** crisis of confidence; **~lehrer der** *(Schulw.)* liaison teacher *(liaising between staff and pupils)*; **~mann der a)** *Pl.* **~männer** *od.* **~leute** spokesman (*Gen.* for); representative; **b)** *Pl.* **~leute** *(in der Gewerkschaft)* [union] representative; *(in einer Fabrik o. ä.)* shop steward; **~person die** person in a position of trust; **~sache die** matter *or* question of trust; **~sache sein** be a matter *or* question of trust; **~selig** *Adj.* all too trustful *or* trusting; **~seligkeit die;** *o. Pl.* excessive trustfulness; **~stellung die** position of trust; **~verhältnis das** relationship based on trust; **~voll 1.** *Adj.* trusting ‹*relationship*›; ‹*collaboration, co-operation*› based on trust; *(zuversichtlich)* confident; **2.** *adv.* trustingly; *(zuversichtlich)* confidently; **sich ~voll an jmdn. wenden** turn to sb. with complete confidence; **~würdig** *Adj.* trustworthy; **~würdigkeit die** trustworthiness

vertrauern *tr. V. (geh.)* spend ‹*time*› in grieving

vertraulich 1. *Adj.* **a)** confidential; **b)** *(freundschaftlich, intim)* familiar ⟨*manner, tone, etc.*⟩; intimate ⟨*mood, conversation, whisper*⟩; **er wird gleich ~:** he gets familiar straight away. **2.** *adv.* **a)** confidentially; in confidence; **b)** *(freundschaftlich, intim)* in a familiar way; familiarly

Vertraulichkeit die; ~, ~en a) *o. Pl.* confidentiality; **b)** *(vertrauliche Information)* confidence; **c)** *o. Pl. (distanzloses Verhalten)* familiarity; *(Intimität)* intimacy; **d)** *(vertrauliche Handlung)* act of familiarity; *(Äußerung)* familiar remark

verträumen *tr. V.* [day-]dream away ⟨*time*⟩

verträumt 1. *Adj.* dreamy; **sie ist zu ~:** she lives too much in a world of dreams. **2.** *adv.* dreamily; idyllically ⟨*situated*⟩

Verträumtheit die; ~: dreaminess; *(idyllischer Charakter)* idyllic nature

vertraut [fɛɐ̯'traut] *Adj.* **a)** close ⟨*friend etc.*⟩; intimate ⟨*circle, conversation, etc.*⟩; **sie sind sehr/ein wenig ~ miteinander** they are very close/quite friendly; **mit jmdm. ~ werden** become very friendly *or* close friends with sb.; **auf ~em Fuße** on intimate terms; **b)** *(bekannt)* familiar; **jmdm. ~ sein/werden** be/become familiar to sb.; **er ist mit Pferden ~:** he knows about horses; **mit etw. gut/wenig ~ sein** be well acquainted/have little knowledge of sth.; **jmdn./sich mit etw. ~ machen** familiarize sb./oneself with sth.; **mit diesem Gedanken solltest du dich ~ machen** you should get used to this idea

Vertraute der/die; *adj. Dekl.* close friend; **enger ~:** intimate friend

Vertrautheit die; ~ *s.* **vertraut:** closeness; intimacy; familiarity

vertreiben *unr. tr. V.* **a)** drive out **(aus** of); *(wegjagen)* drive away ⟨*animal, smoke, clouds, etc.*⟩ **(aus** from); **aus der Heimat vertrieben werden** be driven out of *or* expelled from one's homeland; **die vertriebenen Juden** the exiled *or* expelled Jews; **von Haus und Hof vertrieben werden** be turned out of house and home; **jmdn. aus seinem Amt ~:** oust sb. from office; **jmdn. [von seinem Platz] ~:** take sb.'s seat; **bleiben Sie doch ruhig sitzen, ich wollte Sie nicht ~:** please don't get up, I didn't mean to take your place *or* chase you away; **die Müdigkeit/Sorgen ~** *(fig.)* fight off tiredness/drive troubles away; *s. auch* **Zeit a; b)** *(verkaufen)* sell

Vertreibung die; ~, ~en driving out; *(das Wegjagen)* driving away; *(aus dem Amt)* ousting; *(aus der Heimat)* expulsion

vertretbar *Adj.* defensible ⟨*risk etc.*⟩; tenable, defensible ⟨*standpoint*⟩; justifiable ⟨*costs*⟩

vertreten 1. *unr. tr. V.* **a)** stand in *or* deputize for ⟨*colleague etc.*⟩; ⟨*teacher*⟩ cover for ⟨*colleague*⟩; **er läßt sich von seinem Staatssekretär ~:** he is sending his permanent secretary as his representative; **b)** *(eintreten für, repräsentieren)* represent ⟨*person, firm, interests, constituency, country, etc.*⟩; *(Rechtsw.)* act for ⟨*person, prosecution, etc.*⟩; **er läßt sich durch einen Anwalt ~:** he is getting a lawyer to act for him; **den Fall vertritt Rechtsanwalt Müller** the lawyer defending the case is Müller; **~ sein** be represented **(mit, durch** by); *(anwesend sein)* be present; **schwach/stark ~:** poorly/well represented; **c)** *(einstehen für, verfechten)* support ⟨*point of view, principle*⟩; hold ⟨*opinion*⟩; advocate ⟨*thesis etc.*⟩; pursue ⟨*policy*⟩; **er vertritt den Standpunkt** *od.* **die Meinung, daß ...:** he takes *or* holds the view that ...; **etw. zu ~ haben** be responsible for sth.; **d) jmdm. den Weg ~:** bar sb's way. **2.** *unr. refl. V.* **sich** *(Dat.)* **den Fuß ~:** twist one's ankle; **sich** *(Dat.)* **die Füße** *od.* **Beine ~** *(ugs.: sich Bewegung verschaffen)* stretch one's legs

Vertreter der; ~s, ~ a) *(Stell~)* deputy; stand-in; *(eines Arztes)* locum *(coll.)*; **b)** *(Interessen~, Repräsentant)* representative; *(Handels~)* sales representative; commercial traveller; **ein ~ für Staubsauger** a traveller in vacuum cleaners; **c)** *(Verfechter, Anhänger)* supporter; advocate; **d)** *(ugs. abwertend: Kerl, Bursche)* **du bist ein übler/sauberer ~!** you're a nasty piece of work *(coll.)*/a fine one! *(iron.)*

Vertreterin die; ~, ~nen *s.* **Vertreter a–c**

Vertretung die; ~, ~en a) deputizing; **jmds. ~ übernehmen** stand in *or* deputize for sb.; ⟨*doctor*⟩ act as locum for sb. *(coll.)*; **in ~ von Herrn N.** in place of *or* standing in for Mr. N.; **in ~ unterschreiben** sign as a proxy; **in ~ M. Schmidt** *(am Schluß eines Briefes usw.)* p.p. M. Schmidt; **b)** *(Vertreter[in])* deputy; stand-in; *(eines Arztes)* locum *(coll.)*; **ich brauche für morgen eine ~:** I need somebody to take my place *or* stand in for me tomorrow; *(als Lehrer)* I need cover for tomorrow; **c)** *(Delegierte[r])* representative; *(Delegation)* delegation; **eine diplomatische ~:** a diplomatic mission; **die deutsche ~** *(Sport)* the German team *or* squad; **d)** *(Handels~)* [sales] agency; *(Niederlassung)* agency; branch; **e)** *(Interessen~)* representation; **f)** *(Verfechtung)* advocacy

Vertretungs·stunde die *(Schulw.)* cover lesson

vertretungs·weise *Adv.* as a [temporary] replacement *or* stand-in

Vertrieb der a) *o. Pl.* sale; marketing; **b)** *(Abteilung)* sales [department]

Vertriebene der/die; *adj. Dekl.* expellee [from his/her homeland]

Vertriebs·gesellschaft die sales *or* marketing company

vertrimmen *tr. V. (ugs.)* wallop *(sl.)*

vertrinken *unr. tr. V.* spend ⟨*money*⟩ on drink

vertrocknen *itr. V.; mit sein* dry up; *(fig.)* ⟨*person*⟩ wither, shrivel up

vertrödeln *tr. V. (ugs. abwertend)* dawdle away, waste ⟨*time*⟩

vertrösten *tr. V.* put ⟨*person*⟩ off **(auf +** *Akk.* until)

Vertröstung die prevarication

vertrotteln *itr. V.; mit sein* go gaga *(sl.)*; **vertrottelt** gaga

vertun 1. *unr. tr. V.* waste; **die Mühe war vertan** it was a waste of effort. **2.** *unr. refl. V. (ugs.)* make a slip; **wenn du dich da mal nicht vertust!** I think you're a bit wide of the mark there

vertuschen *tr. V.* hush up ⟨*scandal etc.*⟩; keep ⟨*truth etc.*⟩ secret

Vertuschung die; ~, ~en hushing up; **eine ~:** a hush-up *or* cover-up

verübeln *tr. V.* **jmdm. eine Äußerung** *usw.* **~:** take sb.'s remark *etc.* amiss; **Sie werden es mir nicht ~, wenn ich ....** I hope you won't take it amiss *or* mind if I ...; **das kann man ihm kaum ~:** one can hardly blame him for that

verüben *tr. V.* commit ⟨*crime etc.*⟩; **Streiche ~:** get up to pranks

verulken *tr. V. (ugs.)* make fun of; take the mickey out of *(Brit. coll)*; **du willst mich wohl ~!** you're pulling my leg *(coll.)*

verunfallen *itr. V.; mit sein (Amtsspr., bes. schweiz.)* have an accident

Verunfallte der/die; *adj. Dekl. (Amtsspr., bes. schweiz.)* accident victim

verunglimpfen [fɛɐ̯'ʊnglɪmpfn̩] *tr. V. (geh.)* denigrate ⟨*person, etc.*⟩; sully ⟨*honour, name, memory*⟩

Verunglimpfung die; ~, ~en *(geh.) s.* **verunglimpfen:** denigration; sullying

verunglücken *itr. V.; mit sein* **a)** have an accident; ⟨*car etc.*⟩ be involved in an accident; **mit dem Auto/Flugzeug ~:** be in a car/an air accident *or* crash; **beim Segeln ~:** have a sailing accident *or* an accident while sailing; **der verunglückte Fahrer** the driver involved in the accident; **b)** *(scherzh.: mißlingen)* go wrong; ⟨*attempt*⟩ fail; ⟨*cake, sauce, etc.*⟩ be a disaster; **verunglückt** unsuccessful

Verunglückte der/die; *adj. Dekl.* accident victim; casualty

verunmöglichen [*od.* --'---] *tr. V. (bes. schweiz.)* **[jmdm.] etw. ~:** make sth. impossible [for sb.]

verunreinigen 1. *tr. V.* **a)** pollute; contaminate ⟨*water, milk, flour, oil*⟩; **~de Stoffe** pollutants/contaminants; **b)** *(geh.: beschmutzen)* dirty, soil ⟨*clothes, floor, etc.*⟩; *(durch Fäkalien)* foul ⟨*pavement etc.*⟩. **2.** *refl. V. (verhüll.)* soil oneself

Verunreinigung die a) *o. Pl.* pollution; *(von Wasser, Milch, Mehl, Öl)* contamination; **b)** *(Stoff)* pollutant/contaminant; **c)** *o. Pl. (von Kleidern, Fußböden usw.)* soiling; *(von Straßen usw.)* fouling

verunsichern *tr. V.* **jmdn. ~:** make sb. feel unsure *or* uncertain; *(so daß er sich gefährdet fühlt)* undermine sb.'s sense of security; **verunsichert** insecure; *(nicht selbstsicher)* unsure of oneself

Verunsicherung die a) *(das Verunsichern)* **die argumentative ~ der Richter** making the judges uncertain by means of argument; **zur ~ der Bevölkerung dienen** serve to undermine the people's sense of security; **b)** *(Unsicherheit)* [feeling of] insecurity

verunstalten [fɛɐ̯'ʊnʃtaltn̩] *tr. V.* disfigure; **du verunstaltest dich mit dieser Frisur** this hair-style spoils your looks *or* makes you look terrible

Verunstaltung die; ~, ~en disfigurement

veruntreuen *tr. V.* embezzle

Veruntreuung die; ~, ~en embezzlement

verunzieren *tr. V.* spoil the look of

verursachen *tr. V.* cause; **es hat ihm viel Arbeit verursacht** it caused *or* gave him a great deal of work

Verursacher der; ~s, ~: cause; person responsible; **der ~ des Unfalls** the person responsible for the accident

Verursacher·prinzip das *principle that the person who causes damage must bear the cost*

Verursachung die; ~: causing

verurteilen *tr. V.* **a)** pass sentence on; sentence; **jmdn. zu Gefängnis** *od.* **einer Haftstrafe/drei Monaten Haft ~:** sentence sb. to imprisonment/to three months' imprisonment; **jmdn. zu einer Geldstrafe ~:** impose a fine on sb.; **jmdn. zum Tode ~:** sentence *or* condemn sb. to death; **jmdn. wegen Diebstahl** *usw.* **~:** sentence sb. for theft *etc.*; **der zum Tode Verurteilte** the condemned man; **zum Scheitern verurteilt sein** *(fig.)* be condemned to failure *or* bound to fail; **zum Schweigen verurteilt sein** *(fig.)* be condemned to silence; **b)** *(fig.: negativ bewerten)* condemn ⟨*behaviour, action*⟩

Verurteilte der/die; *adj. Dekl.* convicted man/woman

Verurteilung die; ~, ~en a) sentencing; **eine ~ zu fünf Jahren Zuchthaus** a sentence of five years' imprisonment; **b)** *(fig.)* condemnation

veruzen *tr. V. (ugs.) s.* **verulken**

Verve ['vɛrvə] **die; ~:** *(geh.)* enthusiasm; verve; **mit ~:** enthusiastically

vervielfachen 1. *tr. V.* greatly increase; *(multiplizieren)* multiply ⟨*number*⟩; **wir müssen unsere Anstrengungen ~:** we must redouble our efforts. **2.** *refl. V.* multiply [several times]; *(fig.)* ⟨*efforts*⟩ be redoubled

Vervielfachung die; ~, ~en multiplication; *(fig.: der Anstrengungen)* redoubling

vervielfältigen *tr. V.* duplicate, make copies of ⟨*document etc.*⟩

Vervielfältigung die; ~, ~en a) duplicating; copying; **b)** *(Kopie)* copy

Vervielfältigungs·zahl·wort das *(Sprachw.)* multiplicative

vervollkommnen [fɛɐ̯ˈfɔlkɔmnən] **1.** *tr. V.* perfect. **2.** *refl. V.* become perfected
Vervollkommnung die; ~, ~**en** perfecting; *(Zustand)* perfection
vervollständigen 1. *tr. V.* complete; *(vollständiger machen)* make ‹*library etc.*› more complete. **2.** *refl. V.* become complete/more complete
Vervollständigung die; ~, ~**en** completion/making more complete
[1]**verwachsen** *Adj.* deformed
[2]**verwachsen** *unr. itr. V.; mit sein* **a)** ‹*wound, scab*› heal [up *or* over]; **b)** *(zusammenwachsen)* grow together (**mit** with); **zu etw.** ~: grow together to form sth.; grow into sth.; **c)** *(fig.)* grow closer (**mit** to); **zu einer Gemeinschaft** ~: grow into a community; **sich mit seiner Umwelt** ~ **fühlen** feel at one with one's environment
Verwachsung die; ~, ~**en** deformity
verwackeln *(ugs.)* **1.** *tr. V.* make ‹*picture*› blurred; **verwackelt** blurred; shaky. **2.** *itr. V.; mit sein* turn out blurred
verwählen *refl. V.* misdial; dial the wrong number
verwahren 1. *tr. V.* **a)** keep [safe]; *(verstauen)* put away [safely]; **b)** *(gefangen halten)* detain, hold ‹*person*›. **2.** *refl. V.* protest
verwahrlosen *itr. V.; mit sein* **a)** get in a bad state; ‹*house, building*› fall into disrepair, become dilapidated; ‹*garden, hedge*› grow wild, become overgrown; ‹*person*› let oneself go, *(coll.)* go to pot; **etw.** ~ **lassen** neglect sth.; allow sth. to get in a bad state; **verwahrlost** neglected; overgrown ‹*hedge, garden*›; dilapidated ‹*house, building*›; unkempt ‹*person, appearance, etc.*›; *(in der Kleidung)* ragged ‹*person*›; **b)** *(sittlich* ~*)* fall into bad ways; **[sittlich] verwahrlost** depraved
Verwahrlosung die; ~: *(eines Gebäudes)* dilapidation; *(einer Person)* advancing decrepitude; *(sittliche* ~*)* decline into depravity; **[Zustand der]** ~: state of dilapidation/decrepitude/depravity
Verwahrung die a) keeping [in a safe place]; **etw. in** ~ **geben/nehmen/haben** give/take sth. into safe keeping/hold sth. in safe keeping; **jmdm. etw. in** ~ **geben** give sth. to sb. for safe keeping; **b)** *(Arrest)* detention *no def. art.*; **c)** *(Einspruch, Protest)* protest
verwaisen *itr. V.* be orphaned; become an orphan; **verwaist** orphaned ‹*child*›; *(fig.)* lonely, deserted ‹*person, place*›; unoccupied ‹*house*›; vacant ‹*professorship*›
verwalken *tr. V. (ugs.) s.* **vertrimmen**
verwalten *tr. V.* **a)** *(betreuen)* administer, manage ‹*estate, property, etc.*›; run, look after ‹*house*›; hold ‹*money*› in trust; **b)** *(leiten)* run, manage ‹*hostel, kindergarten, etc.*›; *(regieren)* administer ‹*area, colony, etc.*›; govern ‹*country*›; **die Kanalinseln** ~ **sich selbst** the Channel Islands are self-governing; **c)** *(versehen)* hold ‹*office*›; carry out, perform ‹*task, duty*›; **d)** *(bürokratisch beherrschen)* **eine verwaltete Gesellschaft** a bureaucratized society
Verwalter der; ~**s,** ~, **Verwalterin die;** ~, ~**nen** administrator; *(eines Amts usw.)* manager; *(eines Nachlasses)* trustee
Verwaltung die; ~, ~**en a)** *(Betreuung, Leitung)* administration; management; **etw. unter staatliche** ~ **stellen** put sth. under State control; **in eigener** ~: under one's own control; **b)** *(eines Gebiets)* administration; *(eines Landes)* government; **unter britischer** ~: under British administration *or* rule; **c)** *(eines Amtes)* tenure; *(einer Aufgabe)* performance; **d)** *(Organ, Behörde, Apparat)* administration; *(eines Betriebes)* management; **die öffentliche/staatliche** ~: the public/state authority
Verwaltungs-: ~**apparat der** administrative machine; ~**beamte der** administrative official; administrator; ~**bezirk der** administrative district; ~**gebühr die** administrative charge *or* fee; ~**gericht das** administrative court; ~**kosten** *Pl.* administrative costs; ~**organ das** administrative organ; ~**rat der a)** governing body; administrative council; **b)** *(schweiz. Wirtsch.)* board of directors
verwamsen [fɛɐ̯ˈvamzn̩] *tr. V. (ugs.)* wallop *(coll.)* ‹*child*›
verwandelbar *Adj.* convertible
verwandeln 1. *tr. V.* **a)** convert (**in** + *Akk.*, **zu** into); *(völlig verändern)* transform (**in** + *Akk.*, **zu** into); **er ist/ich fühlte mich wie verwandelt** he's/I felt a different person *or* transformed; **das Sofa läßt sich in ein Bett** ~: the sofa can be converted into a bed; **der Prinz wurde in einen Frosch verwandelt** the prince was turned *or* transformed into a frog; **b)** *(Ballspiele)* score from ‹*corner, free kick*›; convert ‹*penalty*›. **2.** *refl. V.* **sich in etw.** *(Akk.) od.* **zu etw.** ~: turn *or* change into sth.; *(bei chemischen Vorgängen usw.)* be converted into sth.; **die Raupe verwandelt sich in einen Schmetterling** the caterpillar metamorphoses into a butterfly. **3.** *itr. V. (Ballspiele)* **er verwandelte [zum 2:0]** he scored [to make it 2–0]
Verwandlung die; ~, ~**en a)** *(das Verwandeln)* conversion (**in** + *Akk.*, **zu** into); *(völlige Veränderung)* transformation (**in** + *Akk.*, **zu** into); **b)** *(das Sichverwandeln)* transformation; *(Metamorphose)* metamorphosis
Verwandlungs·künstler der quick-change artist
[1]**verwandt** [fɛɐ̯ˈvant] *2. Part. v.* **verwenden**
[2]**verwandt** *Adj.* **a)** *(auch fachspr.)* related (**mit** to); **mit jmdm.** *od. (schweiz.)* **jmdm.** ~ **sein** be related to sb.; **b)** *(fig.: ähnlich)* similar ‹*views, ideas, forms*›
Verwandte der/die; *adj. Dekl.* relative; relation
Verwandten·besuch der *(Besuch bei Verwandten)* visit to relatives; *(Besuch von Verwandten)* visit from *or* by relatives; **einen** ~ **machen** visit relatives; **wir erwarten** ~: we are expecting relatives
Verwandtschaft die; ~, ~**en a)** relationship (**mit** to); *(fig.: Ähnlichkeit)* affinity; **zwischen ihnen besteht keine** ~: they are not related [to one another]; **b)** *o. Pl. (Verwandte)* relatives *pl.*; relations *pl.*; **die ganze** ~: all one's relatives; **eine große** ~ **haben** have a large number of relatives; **zur** ~ **gehören** be one of the family
verwandtschaftlich 1. *Adj.* family ‹*ties, relationships, etc.*›. **2.** *adv.* ~ **miteinander verbunden sein** be related [to each other]
Verwandtschafts-: ~**grad der** degree of relationship; ~**verhältnis das** family relationship; **in einem** ~**verhältnis zu jmdm. stehen** be related to sb.
verwanzen 1. *itr. V.; mit sein* **verwanzt** bug-ridden. **2.** *tr. V. (fig.)* bug
verwarnen *tr. V.* warn, caution (**wegen** for)
Verwarnung die; ~, ~**en** warning; caution
verwaschen *Adj.* **a)** washed out, faded ‹*jeans, material, inscription, etc.*›; **b)** *(blaß)* washy, watery ‹*colour*›; blurred ‹*lines, contours*›; **c)** *(fig.)* wishy-washy ‹*idea, formulation*›
verwässern *tr. V. (auch fig.)* water down; **verwässert schmecken** taste watery
Verwässerung die *(auch fig.)* watering down
verweben 1. *tr. V.* **a)** weave with; use [for weaving]; **b)** *auch unr.* **[miteinander]** ~: interweave ‹*threads*›; **etw. in etw.** *(Akk.)* ~ *(auch fig.)* weave sth. into sth.; **mit etw. verwoben** *(fig.)* bound *or* caught up with sth. **2.** *unr. refl. V. (dichter.)* **sich [zu etw.]** ~: become interwoven [to form *or* into sth.]
verwechselbar *Adj.* mistakable (**mit** for); **leicht** ~: easily confused (**mit** with)
verwechseln *tr. V.* **a) [miteinander]** ~: confuse ‹*two things/people*›; **du mußt da irgendetwas** ~: you must be getting mixed up; **er verwechselt immer rechts und links** he always gets mixed up between *or* mixes up right and left; **etw. mit etw./jmdn. mit jmdm.** ~: mistake sth. for sth./sb. for sb.; confuse sth. with sth./sb. with sb.; **Entschuldigung, ich habe Sie [mit jemandem] verwechselt/ich habe die Tür[en] verwechselt** sorry, I thought you were *or* I mistook you for somebody else/I've got the wrong door; **jmdm. zum Verwechseln ähnlich sehen** be the spitting image of sb.; **leicht mit etw. zu** ~ **sein** be easily confused with sth.; **nicht zu** ~ **mit ...:** not to be confused with ...; **b)** *(vertauschen)* mix up; **jemand hat meinen Regenschirm verwechselt** somebody has taken my umbrella by mistake
Verwechslung die; ~, ~**en a)** [case of] confusion; mistake; **um** ~**en auszuschließen** to avoid any possibility of confusion; **b)** *(Vertauschung)* mixing up; **eine** ~: a mix-up
verwegen 1. *Adj.* daring; *(auch fig.)* audacious. **2.** *adv. (auch fig.)* audaciously
Verwegenheit die; ~, ~**en a)** *o. Pl.* daring; *(auch fig.)* audacity; **b)** *(Tat)* act of daring
verwehen 1. *tr. V.* **a)** *(zudecken)* cover [over] ‹*track, path*›; **der Wind verwehte die Spur im Sand** the wind covered up the track in the sand; **vom Schnee verweht** covered in snow; **b)** *(wegwehen)* blow away; scatter; **vom Winde verweht** *(fig.)* gone with the wind. **2.** *itr. V.; mit sein (geh.)* **im Wind** ~: drift away *or* be lost on the wind
verwehren *tr. V.* **jmdm. etw.** ~: refuse *or* deny sb. sth.; **jmdm.** ~, **etw. zu tun** bar sb. from doing sth.; *(verbieten)* forbid sb. to do sth.; **es verwehrt uns die Sicht** *(fig.)* it obstructs our view
Verwehung die; ~, ~**en** [snow]drift
verweichlichen 1. *itr. V.; mit sein* grow soft; **ein verweichlichter Mensch** a weakling. **2.** *tr. V.* make soft; **ein verweichlichter Junge** a mollycoddled boy
Verweichlichung die; ~, ~**en a)** *(Vorgang)* **die** ~ **der Jugendlichen verhindern** prevent young people from becoming soft; **b)** *(Zustand)* softness; **eine solche Lebensweise führt zur** ~: this way of life makes one soft
Verweigerer der; ~**s,** ~ **a)** rebel; dissident; **b)** *(des Kriegsdienstes usw.)* objector (*Gen.* to)
verweigern 1. *tr. V.* refuse; **jmdm. die Erlaubnis/eine Hilfeleistung** ~: refuse sb. permission/assistance; **„Annahme verweigert"** 'delivery refused'; **die Aussage/einen Befehl/die Nahrungsaufnahme** ~: refuse to make a statement/to obey an order/to take food; **den Kriegsdienst** ~: refuse to do military service; be a conscientious objector; **[jmdm.] den Gehorsam** ~: refuse to obey [sb.]; **ein Hindernis** ~ *(Pferdesport)* refuse at a jump. **2.** *refl. V.* object; refuse to co-operate; **sich jmdm./einer Sache** ~: refuse to accept sb./sth.; **sich der Gesellschaft** ~: contract out of society; **sich jmdm. [sexuell]** ~ *(geh.)* refuse [to have sexual intercourse with] sb. **3.** *itr. V.* **a)** *(ugs.: den Kriegsdienst* ~*)* refuse [to do military service]; be a conscientious objector; **b)** *(Pferdesport)* refuse
Verweigerung die; ~, ~**en** refusal; *(Protest)* protest; ~ **des Kriegsdienstes** refusal to do military service; conscientious objection
Verweil·dauer die the length of stay; time spent (*Gen.* by); **die** ~ **der Speisen im Magen** the period during which food remains in the stomach
verweilen *itr. V. (geh.)* stay; *(länger als nötig)* linger; **verweile doch** tarry awhile *(literary)*; **bei einem Thema/Gedanken** ~ *(fig.)* dwell on a theme/thought
verweint [fɛɐ̯ˈvaint] *Adj.* tear-stained ‹*face*›; ‹*eyes*› red with tears *or* from crying;

⟨*person*⟩ with a tear-stained face; **sie sah ~ aus/war ~**: she looked as if she had been crying/she had a tear-stained face

Verweis der; ~es, ~e a) reference (**auf** + *Akk.* to); *(Quer~)* cross-reference; **b)** *(Tadel)* reprimand; rebuke; **jmdm. einen ~ erteilen** *od.* **aussprechen** reprimand *or* rebuke sb.

verweisen *unr. tr. V.* **a) jmdn./einen Fall** *usw.* **an jmdn./etw. ~** *(auch Rechtsspr.)* refer sb./a case *etc.* to sb./sth.; **b)** *(wegschicken)* **jmdn. von der Schule/aus dem Saal ~**: expel sb. from the school/send sb. out of the room; **jmdn. des Landes ~**: exile *or (Hist.)* banish sb.; **einen Spieler vom Platz ~**: send a player off [the field]; **c)** *(Sport)* **jmdn. auf den zweiten Platz ~**: relegate sb. to *or* push sb. into second place; **d)** *auch itr. (hinweisen)* **[jmdn.] auf etw.** *(Akk.)* **~**: refer [sb.] to sth.; *(durch Querverweis)* cross-refer [sb.] to sth.

verwelken *itr. V.; mit sein* ⟨*flower, leaf*⟩ wilt; *(fig.)* ⟨*fame*⟩ fade; **verwelkt** wilted ⟨*flowers*⟩; withered ⟨*hands, face*⟩; *(fig.)* faded ⟨*beauty*⟩

verweltlichen 1. *tr. V.* secularize. **2.** *itr. V.; mit sein (geh.)* become worldly *or* secularized

Verweltlichung die; ~, ~en secularization

verwendbar *Adj.* usable (**zu, für** for); **es ist mehrfach ~**: it has several uses *or* applications

Verwendbarkeit die; ~: usability

verwenden 1. *unr. od. regelm. tr. V.* **a)** use (**zu, für** for); **ich kann es nicht mehr ~** *od.* **zu nichts mehr ~**: it is no use to me any more; **jmdn./etw. als etw. ~**: use *or* employ sb./sth. as sth.; **b)** *(aufwenden)* spend ⟨*time*⟩ (**auf** + *Akk.* on); **viel Energie/Mühe auf etw.** *(Akk.)* **~**: put a lot of energy/effort into sth.; **du solltest mehr Sorgfalt auf deine Schularbeiten ~**: you should take more care with *or* over your school-work. **2.** *unr. od. regelm. refl. V. (geh.)* **sich [bei jmdm.] für jmdn./etw. ~**: intercede [with sb.] for sb./use one's influence [with sb.] on behalf of sth.

Verwendung die; ~, ~en a) use; **bei ~ dieses Materials** when using this material; **~ finden** be used; **unter ~ einer Sache** *(Gen.) od.* **von etw.** using sth.; **~/keine ~ für etw. haben** have a/no use for sth.; **etw. in ~ nehmen** *(österr.)* put sth. into use *or* service; **b)** *(geh.: Fürbitte)* intercession

verwendungs-, Verwendungs-: ~fähig *Adj.* employable; *(als Soldat usw.)* fit for service *postpos.*; **~möglichkeit die** [possible] application *or* use; **~weise die** application; **es hängt von der ~weise ab** it depends how it is used; **~zweck der** application; purpose; **„~zweck“** *(auf Zahlkarten usw.)* 'as payment for'

verwerfen 1. *unr. tr. V.* **a)** reject; dismiss ⟨*thought*⟩; **etw. als unsittlich ~**: condemn sth. as [being] immoral; **einen Antrag/Vorschlag** *usw.* **~**: reject *or* turn down an application/suggestion *etc.*; **b)** *(Rechtsw.)* dismiss ⟨*appeal, action*⟩; overturn, quash ⟨*judgement*⟩; **c)** *(geh., bibl.: verstoßen)* reject ⟨*person, people*⟩. **2.** *unr. refl. V.* **a)** *(sich verziehen)* warp; **b)** *(Geol.)* fault; **c)** *(Kartenspiel)* put down the wrong cards/cards

verwerflich *(geh.)* **1.** *Adj.* reprehensible. **2.** *adv.* reprehensibly

Verwerflichkeit die; ~ *(geh.)* reprehensibility; reprehensible *or* despicable nature

Verwerfung die; ~, ~en *(Geol.)* fault

verwertbar *Adj.* utilizable; usable

Verwertbarkeit die; ~: usability; **etw. auf seine ~ untersuchen** examine sth. to see if it can/could be utilized

verwerten *tr. V.* utilize, use (**zu** for); make use of, exploit ⟨*suggestion, experience, knowledge, etc.*⟩; put ⟨*idea*⟩ into practice; *(bes. kommerziell)* exploit ⟨*idea, invention, place, etc.*⟩; **es ist noch zu ~**: it can still be put to good use

Verwertung die utilization; use; *(bes. kommerziell)* exploitation

verwesen *itr. V.; mit sein* decompose

verweslich *Adj.* decomposable

Verwesung die; ~: decomposition; **in ~ übergehen** start to decompose

verwestlichen *itr. V.; mit sein* become westernized

verwetten *tr. V.* spend ⟨*money*⟩ on betting; **seinen Kopf für etw. ~**: bet anything on sth.

verwichsen *tr. V. (ugs.)* beat ⟨*person*⟩ up; *(zur Strafe)* give ⟨*person*⟩ a hiding *(coll.)*

verwickeln 1. *refl. V.* **a)** get tangled up *or* entangled; **b)** *(sich verfangen)* **sich in etw.** *(Akk. od. Dat.)* **~**: get caught [up] in sth.; **sich in Widersprüche ~** *(fig.)* tie oneself up in contradictions. **2.** *tr. V.* involve; **in etw.** *(Akk.)* **verwickelt werden/sein** get/be mixed up *or* involved in sth.

verwickelt 1. *Adj.* involved; complicated. **2.** *adv.* in an involved *or* a complicated way

Verwicklung die; ~, ~en complication

verwiegen *unr. refl. V.* get the weight wrong

verwildern *itr. V.* **a)** ⟨*garden*⟩ become overgrown, go wild; ⟨*domestic animal*⟩ go wild, return to the wild; ⟨*plant*⟩ go *or* grow wild; **b)** *(unkultiviert werden)* ⟨*person*⟩ turn wild; *(verwahrlosen)* go to seed; let oneself go

verwildert *Adj.* **a)** overgrown ⟨*garden*⟩; ⟨*animal, plant*⟩ which has gone wild; **b)** *(unkultiviert)* unkempt, dishevelled ⟨*person, appearance, etc.*⟩; *(ungehobelt)* uncouth ⟨*person*⟩; *(ausschweifend)* morally decadent ⟨*person, society*⟩

Verwilderung die; ~, ~en a) return to the wild [state]; **die ~ des Gartens schreitet weiter fort** the garden is continuing to get more and more overgrown; **b)** *(geh.: von Menschen)* reversion to a primitive state; **die ~ der Sitten** moral decadence

verwinden *unr. tr. V. (geh.)* get over

verwinkelt *Adj.* [narrow and] winding ⟨*street, corridor*⟩; ⟨*flat, old quarter*⟩ full of nooks and crannies

verwirken *tr. V. (geh.)* forfeit

verwirklichen 1. *tr. V.* realize ⟨*dream*⟩; realize, put into practice ⟨*plan, proposal, idea, etc.*⟩; carry out ⟨*project, intention*⟩. **2.** *refl. V.* **a)** ⟨*hope, dream*⟩ be realized *or* fulfilled; **b)** *(sich voll entfalten)* **sich [selbst] ~**: realize one's [full] potential; fulfil oneself

Verwirklichung die; ~, ~en realization; *(eines Wunsches, einer Hoffnung)* fulfilment; **er begann mit der ~ seines Plans** he started to put his plan into practice; **jmdm. bei der ~ eines Projekts helfen** help sb. carry out a project

verwirren 1. *tr. V.* entangle, tangle up ⟨*thread etc.*⟩; tousle, ruffle ⟨*hair*⟩. **2.** *tr. (auch itr.) V.* confuse; bewilder; **jmds. Geist ~** *(geh.)* upset sb.'s mental balance; **das verwirrt [den Zuhörer] nur** it is only confusing [for the listener]; **verwirrt** confused; bewildered; **„Träume ich?“, dachte er verwirrt** 'Am I dreaming?' he thought in confusion *or* bewilderment; **~d** bewildering; **~d viele Möglichkeiten** a bewildering number of possibilities. **3.** *refl. V.* ⟨*thread etc.*⟩ become entangled; ⟨*hair*⟩ become tousled *or* ruffled; ⟨*person, mind*⟩ become confused; *(fig.: kompliziert werden)* become confused *or* complicated

Verwirr·spiel das deliberate confusion *no indef. art.*; **ein ~ mit jmdm. treiben** use intentionally confusing tactics on sb.; **zu einem ~ für jmdn. werden** confuse sb. completely

Verwirrtheit die; ~: [state of] confusion *or* bewilderment

Verwirrung die; ~, ~en confusion; **jmdn. in ~ bringen** make sb. confused *or* bewildered; **in ~ geraten** become confused *or* bewildered; **im Zustand geistiger ~**: in a disturbed *or* confused mental state

verwirtschaften *tr. V.* squander ⟨*money*⟩ by mismanagement

verwischen 1. *tr. V.* smudge ⟨*signature, writing, etc.*⟩; smear ⟨*paint*⟩; **alle Spuren ~** *(fig.)* cover up all [one's] tracks. **2.** *refl. V.* become blurred

verwissenschaftlichen *tr. V.* make ⟨*teaching, life*⟩ highly scientific; put ⟨*research, procedure*⟩ on a scientific basis

verwittern *itr. V.; mit sein* weather

Verwitterung die; ~, ~en weathering

verwitwet [fɛɐ̯'vɪtvət] *Adj.* widowed; **Frau Meier, ~e Schmidt** Mrs Meier, the widow of the late Mr Schmidt

verwohnen *tr. V.* ruin, make a mess of ⟨*house, flat*⟩; **das Zimmer sieht verwohnt aus** the room looks badly knocked about

verwöhnen [fɛɐ̯'vø:nən] *tr. V.* spoil; **~ Sie sich mit einer Tasse X-Kaffee!** treat yourself to a cup of X coffee; **das Schicksal hat ihn nicht gerade verwöhnt** *(fig.)* fate has not exactly smiled upon him

verwöhnt *Adj.* spoilt; *(anspruchsvoll)* discriminating; ⟨*taste, palate*⟩ of a gourmet

Verwöhnung die; ~: spoiling

verworfen [fɛɐ̯'vɔrfn̩] **1.** *2. Part. v.* **verwerfen. 2.** *Adj. (geh.)* depraved ⟨*person*⟩; dastardly ⟨*act*⟩

Verworfenheit die; ~: depravity

verworren [fɛɐ̯'vɔrən] *Adj.* confused, muddled ⟨*ideas, situation, etc.*⟩; confused ⟨*sound*⟩

Verworrenheit die; ~: confused nature; confusion

verwundbar *Adj.* open to injury *pred.*; *(fig.)* vulnerable; **eine sehr ~e Stelle treffen** *(fig.)* touch a very sensitive spot

Verwundbarkeit die vulnerability

[1]**verwunden** *2. Part. v.* **verwinden**

[2]**verwunden** *tr. V.* wound; injure; *(fig. geh.)* wound ⟨*person, feelings, etc.*⟩

verwunderlich *Adj.* surprising

verwundern 1. *tr. V.* **a)** surprise; *(erstaunen)* astonish; **verwundert** surprised/astonished (**über** + *Akk.* at); *adv.* in surprise *or* wonderment/astonishment; **b)** *in* **zu/nicht zu ~ sein** be surprising/not surprising; be a/no wonder. **2.** *refl. V.* be surprised (**über** + *Akk.* at); *(erstaunt sein)* be astonished (**über** + *Akk.* at)

Verwunderung die; ~: surprise; *(Staunen)* astonishment; **jmdn. in ~ setzen** surprise/astonish sb.

Verwundete der/die; *adj. Dekl.* wounded person; casualty; **die ~n** the wounded

Verwundung die; ~, ~en a) wounding; **b)** *(Wunde, Verletzung)* wound

verwunschen *Adj.* enchanted; bewitched

verwünschen *tr. V.* **a)** curse; **b)** *(veralt.) s.* **verzaubern a**

verwünscht *Adj.* **a)** *(vermaledeit)* accursed; wretched; **b)** *(verzaubert)* enchanted; bewitched

Verwünschung die; ~, ~en a) *(das Verfluchen)* cursing; **b)** *(Fluch)* curse; oath; **c)** *(veralt.) s.* **Verzauberung a**

verwurschteln [fɛɐ̯'vʊrʃtl̩n], **verwursteln** *(ugs.)* **1.** *tr. V.* get ⟨*thing*⟩ in a muddle *or* a tangle. **2.** *refl. V.* get in a muddle *or* a tangle

verwurzelt *Adj.* [deeply] rooted; **in etw.** *(Dat.)* **~ sein** have one's roots in sth.; *(in der Tradition, im Glauben usw.)* be [deeply] rooted in *or* committed to sth.

Verwurzelung die; ~: deep rootedness (**mit, in** + *Dat.* in); **trotz seiner ~ in der Tradition** although deeply rooted in tradition

verwüsten *tr. V.* devastate

Verwüstung die; ~, ~en devastation; **die ~en des Krieges** the ravages of war

verzagen *itr. V.; mit sein od. haben* despair; lose heart; **verzagt sein** be despondent

Verzagtheit die; ~: despondency; despair
verzählen *refl. V.* miscount; **ich verzähle mich dauernd** I keep losing count
verzahnen *tr. V.* connect up (**mit** to); *(fig.)* link, dovetail (**mit** with); **miteinander verzahnt** *(fig.)* interconnected
Verzahnung die; ~, ~**en** connection; *(fig.)* link
verzanken *refl. V. (ugs.)* **sich [mit jmdm. wegen etw.]** ~: fall out [with sb. over sth.]
verzapfen *tr. V.* **a)** *(landsch.: zapfen)* pull, draw ⟨*beer etc.*⟩; **b)** *(Tischlerei)* tenon; **c)** *(ugs. abwertend)* **Blödsinn** *od.* **Mist** ~: come out with *or* produce rubbish
verzärteln [fɛɐ̯'tsɛ:ɐtl̩n] *tr. V.* mollycoddle
Verzärtelung die; ~: mollycoddling
verzaubern *tr. V.* **a)** cast a spell on; bewitch; **jmdn. in etw.** *(Akk.)* ~: transform sb. into sth.; **eine verzauberte Prinzessin** a bewitched princess; **b)** *(fig.)* enchant
Verzauberung die; ~, ~**en a)** casting of a/the spell (*Gen.* on); **b)** *(fig.)* enchantment
verzehnfachen *tr., refl. V.* increase tenfold
Verzehr [fɛɐ̯'tse:ɐ̯] **der;** ~**[e]s** consumption; **zum alsbaldigen** ~ **bestimmt** for immediate consumption
Verzehr·bon der meal voucher; *(für Getränke)* drinks voucher
verzehren 1. *tr. V. (auch fig. geh.)* consume; ⟨*illness etc.*⟩ exhaust, debilitate ⟨*person*⟩; consume, drain [away] ⟨*strength*⟩; **der Gram verzehrt sie** she is consumed with grief. **2.** *refl. V. (geh.)* ⟨*energy etc.*⟩ be consumed; ⟨*person*⟩ eat one's heart out; **sich [in Sehnsucht] nach jmdm.** ~: pine away for sb.; **sich in ohnmächtiger Wut** ~: be consumed with *or* by helpless rage
Verzehr·zwang der obligation to order *(in a restaurant)*
verzeichnen *tr. V.* **a)** *(falsch zeichnen)* draw wrongly; **b)** *(aufführen)* list; *(eintragen)* enter; *(registrieren)* record; **der Ort ist auf der Karte nicht verzeichnet** the place is not [marked] on the map; **das Wörterbuch verzeichnet das Wort nicht** the dictionary does not list *or* include the word; **große Erfolge/Verluste zu** ~ **haben** have scored great successes/suffered great losses; **Fortschritte/Erfolge sind nicht zu** ~: no progress was made/there were no successes; **c)** *(fig. geh.: zur Kenntnis nehmen)* note; **d)** *auch itr. (Optik)* ⟨*lens*⟩ distort
Verzeichnis [fɛɐ̯'tsaiçnɪs] **das;** ~**ses,** ~**se** list; *(Register)* index; **ein** ~ **der lieferbaren Titel** a list *or* catalogue of available titles
verzeihen *unr. tr., itr. V.* forgive; *(entschuldigen)* excuse ⟨*behaviour, remark, etc.*⟩; **jmdm. [etw.]** ~: forgive sb. [sth. *or* for sth.]; **es sei dir verziehen, ich will es [dir]** ~: you are *or* shall be forgiven; **ich kann es mir nicht** ~**, daß ich das nicht verhindert habe** I can't *or* I'll never forgive myself for not preventing it; **das ist nicht zu** ~: that's unforgivable/inexcusable; **kannst du mir noch einmal** ~**?** *(auch iron.)* can you ever forgive me?; ~ **Sie [bitte] die Störung** pardon the intrusion; [please] excuse me for disturbing you; ~ **Sie [bitte], können Sie mir sagen ...?** excuse me, could you tell me ...?
verzeihlich *Adj.* forgivable; excusable; **kaum** ~: almost unforgivable
Verzeihung die; ~: forgiveness; ~**, können Sie mir sagen, ...?** excuse me, could you tell me ...?; ~**!** sorry!; **jmdn. um** ~ **bitten** apologize to sb.; **ich bitte vielmals um** ~: I do apologize *or* [do] beg your pardon
verzerren 1. *tr. V.* **a)** contort ⟨*face etc.*⟩ (**zu** into); **b)** *(zerren, überdehnen)* **sich** *(Dat.)* **einen Muskel/eine Sehne** ~: pull *or* strain a muscle/tendon; **c)** *(akustisch, optisch)* distort ⟨*sound, image*⟩; **etw. verzerrt darstellen** *(fig.)* present a distorted account *or* picture of sth.; **seine Stimme klang verzerrt** his voice sounded distorted. **2.** *itr. V.* ⟨*loudspeaker, mirror, etc.*⟩ distort. **3.** *refl. V.* ⟨*face, features*⟩ become contorted (**zu** into)
Verzerrung die; ~, ~**en a)** *(des Gesichts usw.)* contortion; **b)** *(eines Muskels usw.)* strain; pull; **c)** *(des Klangs, eines Bildes, der Realität usw.)* distortion
[1]**verzetteln 1.** *tr. V.* fritter away ⟨*time, money*⟩; dissipate ⟨*energy*⟩. **2.** *refl. V.* dissipate one's energies; try to do too many things at once
[2]**verzetteln** *tr. V. (auf Zettel schreiben)* put ⟨*words etc.*⟩ on slips
Verzettelung die; ~, ~**en** *(auf Zettel)* transfer to slips
Verzicht [fɛɐ̯'tsɪçt] **der;** ~**[e]s,** ~**e a)** renunciation (**auf** + *Akk.* of); **ich bin zum** ~ **auf meinen Anteil bereit** I am prepared to give up my share; **auf etw.** *(Akk.)* ~ **leisten** *(geh.)* renounce sth.; **b)** *(auf Reichtum, ein Amt usw.)* relinquishment (**auf** + *Akk.* of)
verzichten *itr. V.* do without; ~ **auf** (+ *Akk.*) *(auskommen ohne)* do without; *(sich enthalten)* refrain *or* abstain from; *(aufgeben)* give up ⟨*share, smoking, job, etc.*⟩; renounce ⟨*inheritance*⟩; renounce, relinquish ⟨*right, privilege*⟩; *(opfern)* sacrifice ⟨*holiday, salary*⟩; **wenn es nicht mehr für alle reicht, verzichte ich freiwillig** if there isn't enough for everybody I will gladly go without; **auf weitere Ansprüche** ~: waive *or* relinquish further claims; **auf den Thron** ~: renounce one's right to the throne; **auf einen Ministersessel** ~: refuse a ministerial post; **ich verzichte auf deine Hilfe/Ratschläge** I can do without *or* you can keep your help/advice; **[nein danke,] ich verzichte** not for me[, thanks]; **darauf möchte ich nicht [mehr]** ~: I wouldn't be without it now; **darauf kann ich** ~ *(iron.)* I can do without that; **auf eine Strafanzeige** ~: not bring a charge; **ich könnte dazu noch einiges sagen, aber ich will darauf** ~: I could add a few things to that, but I will refrain; **auf eine förmliche Vorstellung** ~: dispense with a formal introduction
Verzicht[s]·erklärung die waiver; disclaimer
[1]**verziehen** *2. Part. v.* **verzeihen**
[2]**verziehen 1.** *unr. tr. V.* **a)** screw up ⟨*face, mouth, etc.*⟩; **er verzog sein Gesicht zu einer Grimasse/zu einem spöttischen Lächeln** he pulled a face *or* grimaced/put on a derisive smile; *see also* **Miene; b)** *(schlecht erziehen)* spoil; **so ein verzogener Bengel!** what a badly brought up *or* spoilt brat!; **c)** *(Ballspiele)* mishit ⟨*ball*⟩; **d)** *(Landw.)* thin out ⟨*seedlings etc.*⟩. **2.** *unr. refl. V.* **a)** twist; be contorted; **sein Gesicht verzog sich zu einer Grimasse** his face twisted *or* screwed itself into a grimace; **b)** *(aus der Form geraten)* go out of shape; ⟨*wood*⟩ warp; **ein verzogener Rahmen** a distorted frame; **total verzogen sein** be completely out of shape; **c)** *(wegziehen)* ⟨*clouds, storm*⟩ move away, pass over; ⟨*fog, mist*⟩ disperse; **d)** *(ugs.: weggehen)* take oneself off; **ich verziehe mich jetzt [ins Bett]** I'm off to bed now; **verzieh dich!** *(salopp)* clear *(coll.) or (sl.)* push off. **3.** *unr. itr. V.; mit sein* move [away]; **„Empfänger [unbekannt] verzogen"** 'no longer at this address'
verzieren *tr. V.* decorate
Verzierung die; ~, ~**en** decoration; **überflüssige** ~**en** superfluous ornamentation *sing.*; **brich dir [bloß/nur] keine** ~ **ab!** *(fig. ugs.)* don't make [such] a fuss!
verzinsen 1. *tr. V.* pay interest on ⟨*sum, capital, etc.*⟩; **etw. mit 6%** ~: pay 6% interest on sth. **2.** *refl. V.* **sich [mit 6%]** ~: yield *or* bear [6%] interest
verzinslich *Adj.* bearing *or* yielding interest *postpos., not pred.* (**mit, zu** at a rate of)
Verzinsung die; ~, ~**en** [payment of] interest (*Gen.* on)
verzögern 1. *tr. V.* **a)** delay (**um** by) ; delay, postpone ⟨*departure etc.*⟩; **den Baubeginn um zwei Jahre** ~: put back the start of building work [by] two years; **b)** *(verlangsamen)* slow down. **2.** *refl. V.* be delayed (**um** by). **3.** *itr. V.* slow down; decelerate
Verzögerung die; ~, ~**en a)** delaying; delay (*Gen.* in); **b)** *(Verlangsamung)* slowing down; *(Technik)* deceleration; **c)** *(Verspätung)* delay; hold-up
Verzögerungs·taktik die delaying tactics *pl.*
verzollen *tr. V.* pay duty on
Verzollung die; ~, ~**en** payment of duty (*Gen.* on)
verzücken *tr. V. (geh.)* enrapture; send into ecstasies; **verzückt** enraptured; in rapture; *(ekstatisch)* ecstatic; **mit verzückter Miene** with a look of ecstasy [on his/her face]
verzuckern *tr. V.* **a)** sugar ⟨*almonds*⟩; *(kandieren)* candy ⟨*fruit*⟩; **b)** *(fig.) s.* **versüßen**
Verzückung die; ~: ecstasy; rapture; **in** ~ **geraten** go into ecstasies
Verzug der; ~**[e]s a)** delay; ~ **der Zahlung** delay in payment; late payment; **[mit etw.] im** ~ **sein/in** ~ **kommen** *od.* **geraten** be/fall behind [with sth.]; **jmdn./etw. in** ~ **bringen** delay sb./sth.; hold sb. up/put sth. back; **ohne** ~: without delay; **b) es ist Gefahr im** ~ *(ugs.)* danger is imminent
Verzugs·zinsen *Pl.* interest *sing.* on arrears *or* for late payment
verzweifeln *itr. V.; meist mit sein* despair; **über etw./jmdn.** ~: despair at sth./of sb.; **am Leben/an den Menschen** ~: despair of life/humanity; **es ist zum Verzweifeln!** it's enough to drive you to despair; **es ist zum Verzweifeln mit dir** you're enough to drive anyone to despair
verzweifelt 1. *Adj.* **a)** despairing ⟨*person, animal*⟩; ~ **sein** be in despair *or* full of despair; **ich bin [ganz] verzweifelt** *(ratlos)* I'm at my wit's end; **b)** desperate ⟨*situation, attempt, effort, struggle, etc*⟩. **2.** *adv.* **a)** *(entmutigt)* despairingly; **b)** *(sehr angestrengt)* desperately
Verzweiflung die; ~ despair; **etw. aus** ~ **tun** do sth. out of despair; **jmdn. zur** ~ **treiben/bringen** drive sb. to despair
Verzweiflungs·tat die act of despair
verzweigen *refl. V.* branch [out]; **ein weit verzweigtes System/Netz** *(fig.)* a widely branching system/network; **das Unternehmen ist stark verzweigt** *(fig.)* the firm is very diversified
Verzweigung die; ~, ~**en a)** branching; **b)** *(schweiz.) (Gabelung)* fork; *(Kreuzung)* crossroads *sing.*; *(Autobahn~)* intersection
verzwickt [fɛɐ̯'tsvɪkt] *(ugs.) Adj.* tricky; complicated
Vesper ['fɛspɐ] **die;** ~, ~**n a)** vespers *pl.*; **in die** *od.* **zur** ~ **gehen** go to vespers; **b)** *auch* **das;** ~**s,** ~ *(südd.: Zwischenmahlzeit)* snack; ~ **machen** have a snack
Vesper·brot das *(südd.)* sandwiches *pl.*
vespern *(bes. südd.)* **1.** *itr. V.* have a snack. **2.** *tr. V.* **etw.** ~: have a snack of sth.
Vestibül [vɛsti'by:l] **das;** ~**s,** ~**e** *(veralt.)* vestibule
Vesuv [ve'zu:f] **der;** ~**s** Vesuvius
Veteran [vete'ra:n] **der;** ~**en,** ~**en** *(auch fig.)* veteran
Veterinär [veteri'nɛ:ɐ̯] **der;** ~**s,** ~**e** veterinary surgeon
Veterinär·medizin die; *o. Pl. s.* **Tiermedizin**
Veto ['ve:to] **das;** ~**s,** ~**s** veto; **ein** ~ **gegen etw. einlegen** veto sth.
Veto·recht das right of veto
Vetter ['fɛtɐ] **der;** ~**s,** ~**n** cousin
Vettern·wirtschaft die; *o. Pl. (abwertend)* nepotism
Vexier·bild [vɛ'ksi:ɐ̯-] **das** puzzle picture
V-förmig ['fau-] *Adj.* V-shaped
vgl. *Abk.* **vergleiche** cf.

v. H. *Abk.* **vom Hundert** per cent
VHB *Abk.* **Verhandlungsbasis: ~ 800 DM** 800 marks o.n.o. *(Brit.)*
VHS *Abk.* **Volkshochschule**
via ['vi:a] *Präp.* via
Viadukt [via'dʊkt] **das** *od.* **der; ~[e]s, ~e** viaduct
Vibraphon [vibra'fo:n] **das; ~s, ~e** *(Musik)* vibraphone
Vibration [vibrə'tsio:n] **die; ~, ~en** vibration
Vibrato [vi'bra:to] **das, ~s, ~s** *od.* **Vibrati** *(Musik)* vibrato
Vibrator der; ~s, Vibratoren vibrator
vibrieren [vi'bri:rən] *itr. V.* vibrate; ‹*voice*› quiver, tremble
video-, Video- ['vi:deo-]: video
Video das; ~s, ~s *(ugs.)* video
Video-: ~auf·zeichnung die video recording; **~band das;** *Pl.* **~bänder** videotape; **~clip** [~klɪp] **der; ~s, ~s** video; **~film der** video [film]; **~kamera die** video camera; **~kassette die** video cassette; **~recorder der** video recorder; **~technik die** video technology *no art.*
Videothek [vi:deo'te:k] **die; ~, ~en** video library
Viech [fi:ç] **das; ~[e]s, ~er a)** *(ugs., oft abwertend: Tier)* creature; **b)** *(derb abwertend: Mensch)* bastard *(coll.)*
Viecherei die; ~, ~en *(ugs.)* hard grind *or* slog
Vieh [fi:] **das; ~[e]s a)** *(Nutztiere)* livestock *sing. or pl.;* **jmdn. wie ein Stück ~ behandeln** treat sb. like an animal; **b)** *(Rind~)* cattle *pl.;* **c)** *(derb abwertend: Mensch)* bastard; **d)** *(ugs.: Tier)* creature
Vieh-: ~bestand der stocks *pl.* of animals/cattle; **wie hoch ist der ~bestand dieses Betriebs?** how much livestock does this farm have?; **~futter das** animal/cattle feed *or* fodder; **~händler der** livestock/cattle dealer; **~hirt der** herdsman; *(von Rindern)* cowherd
viehisch 1. *Adj.* **a)** *(abwertend: brutal)* brutish; **b)** *(ugs.: immens)* terrible *(coll.)* ‹*fear, stupidity, pain*›. **2.** *adv.* **a)** *(abwertend)* ‹*beat, torment*› brutally; **b)** *(ugs.)* ‹*hurt*› like hell *(coll.);* **~ kalt** perishing cold *(coll.)*
Vieh-: ~markt der livestock/cattle market; **~salz das;** *o. Pl.* rock salt; *(als Streusalz)* road salt; **~stall der** cowshed; **~tränke die** cattle-trough; **~treiber der** [cattle] drover; **~waggon der** cattle-truck; **~wirtschaft die;** *o. Pl.* livestock farming *no art.;* **~zeug das** *(ugs.)* **a)** *(Kleinvieh)* animals *pl.;* **b)** *(abwertend: lästige Tiere)* creatures *pl.;* **~zucht die;** *o. Pl.* [live]stock/cattle breeding *no art.;* **~züchter der** [live]stock/cattle breeder
viel [fi:l] **1.** *Indefinitpron. u. unbest. Zahlw.* **a)** *Sg.* a great deal of; a lot of *(coll.);* **so/wie/nicht/zu ~:** that/how/not/too much; **~[es]** *(viele Dinge, vielerlei)* much; **er weiß ~es, aber nicht alles** he knows a great deal, but not everything; **ich kann mich an ~es nicht mehr erinnern** there's much I can't remember; **der ~e Regen** all the rain; **sein ~es Geld** all his money; **gleich ~ Geld/Wasser** the same amount of money/water; **gleich ~ verdienen** earn the same; **in ~er Hinsicht** *od.* **Beziehung** in many respects; **um ~es jünger** a great deal younger; **das ist ein bißchen [sehr] ~!** that's rather too much; **~ Erfreuliches** a great many pleasant things; **er hat in ~em recht** he is right on many points; **er ist nicht ~ über fünfzig** he is not much more than *or* much over fifty; **b)** *Pl.* many; **gleich ~[e]** the same number of; **~e hundert** many hundreds of; **die ~en Bäume/Menschen/Probleme** all the trees/people/problems; **seine ~en Kinder** all his children; **~e** *(viele Menschen)* many people; **das wissen nicht ~e** not many people know that; **das wissen ~e nicht** many people don't know that. **2.** *Adv.* **a)** *(oft, lange)* a great deal; a lot *(coll.);* **man redet ~ vom Fortschritt** there is much *or (coll.)* a lot of talk of progress; **er spielt ~ Golf** he plays a lot of golf; **er fährt [nicht] ~ Rad** he does[n't do] a lot of cycling; **b)** *(wesentlich)* much; a great deal; a lot *(coll.);* **es geht ihm sehr ~ besser** he is very much better; **~ mehr/weniger** much more/less; **~ zu klein** much too small
viel-, Viel-: ~befahren *Adj., präd. getrennt geschrieben* busy, much-used ‹*road*›; **~beschäftigt** *Adj., präd. getrennt geschrieben* very busy; **~besucht** *Adj., präd. getrennt geschrieben* much-frequented ‹*restaurant, etc.*›; much-visited ‹*resort, museum, etc.*›; **~deutig** [~dɔytɪç] **1.** *Adj.* ambiguous; **2.** *adv.* ambiguously; **~deutigkeit die; ~:** ambiguity; **~eck das** polygon; **~ehe die** polygamy *no art.*
vielerlei *indekl. unbest. Gattungsz.* **a)** *attr.* many different; all kinds *or* sorts of; **b)** *subst.* all kinds *or* sorts of things
vieler·orts *Adv.* in many places
viel-, Viel-: ~fach 1. *Adj.* **a)** multiple; **die ~fache Menge** many times the amount; **ein ~facher Millionär** a multimillionaire; **er ist ~facher Weltmeister** he has been world champion many times over; **auf ~fachen Wunsch unserer Zuschauer** at the request of many of our viewers; **b)** *(vielfältig)* manifold; many kinds of; **2.** *adv.* many times; *(ugs.: oft)* often; frequently; **ein ~fach geäußerter Wunsch** a wish many times expressed; **~fache das; ~n;** *adj. Dekl.* **a) ein ~faches** many times the amount/number; **die Preise werden ein ~faches von dem betragen, was ...:** the prices will be many times greater than ...; **um ein ~faches** many times over; **um ein ~faches schneller/teurer** many times faster/more expensive; **b)** *(Math.)* multiple; **~falt die; ~:** diversity; wide variety; **~fältig** [~fɛltɪç] **1.** *Adj.* many and diverse; **2.** *adv.* in many different ways; **~farbig,** *(österr.)* **~färbig** *Adj.* multicoloured; **~flach das; ~[e]s, ~e** polyhedron; **~fraß der a)** *(ugs.: Mensch)* glutton; [greedy-]guts *sing. (sl.);* **b)** *(Tier)* wolverine; **~gefragt** *Adj., präd. getrennt geschrieben* **ein ~gefragter Artikel** *usw.* an article *etc.* that is in great demand *or* much in demand; **ein ~gefragter Spezialist** a specialist who is in great demand; **~gekauft** *Adj., präd. getrennt geschrieben* widely-bought; **~gelesen** *Adj., präd. getrennt geschrieben* much-read; **~gepriesen** *Adj., präd. getrennt geschrieben* much-praised; **~geschmäht** *Adj., präd. getrennt geschrieben (geh.)* much-maligned; much-abused; **~gestaltig** *Adj.* varied *or* diversified in form *postpos.;* **~gestaltig sein** be varied *or* diversified in form; have many different forms; **~götterei** [~gœtə'rai] **die; ~:** polytheism *no art.*
vielleicht [fi'laiçt] **1.** *Adv.* **a)** perhaps; maybe; **~ kommt er morgen** perhaps *or* maybe he will come tomorrow; he might come tomorrow; **du hast dich ~ geirrt** perhaps you were wrong; you may have been mistaken; **~, daß alles nur ein Mißverständnis war** perhaps it was all just a misunderstanding; **hast du den Schirm ~ im Büro liegenlassen?** could it be that you left your umbrella in the office?; **b)** *(ungefähr)* perhaps; about; **ein Mann von ~ fünfzig Jahren** a man of perhaps *or* about fifty. **2.** *Partikel* **a) kannst du mir ~ sagen, ...?** could you possibly tell me ...?; **hast du ~ meinen Bruder gesehen?** have you seen my brother by any chance? **b)** *(wirklich)* really; **ich war ~ aufgeregt** I was terribly excited *or* as excited as anything *(coll.);* **du bist ~ ein Blödmann!** what a stupid idiot you are! *(coll.);* **c)** *(ich bitte dringend, daß ...)* **~ hilfst du mir mal!** would you mind helping me!; **d)** *(etwa)* **ist das ~ eine Lösung?** is that supposed to be a solution?; **ist das ~ dein Ernst?** you don't mean that, do you?
viel-, Viel-: ~mals *Adv.* **ich bitte ~mals um Entschuldigung** I'm very sorry; I do apologize; **sie läßt ~mals grüßen** she sends her best regards *or* wishes; **danke ~mals** thank you very much; many thanks; **~männerei** [~mɛnə'rai] **die; ~:** polyandry *no art.;* **~mehr** [*od.* -'-] *Konj. u. Adv.* rather; *(im Gegenteil)* on the contrary; **~sagend 1.** *Adj.* meaningful; **2.** *adv.* meaningfully; **~schichtig** *Adj.* multi-layered; *(fig.: komplex)* complex; **~schreiber der** *(abwertend)* [over-]prolific writer; **~seitig 1.** *Adj.* versatile ‹*person*›; varied ‹*work, programme, etc.*›; **auf ~seitigen Wunsch** by popular request; **diese Küchenmaschine ist sehr ~seitig** this food processor has many uses; **2.** *adv.* **~seitig begabt sein** be versatile; **sich ~seitig verwenden lassen** have many uses; **~seitigkeit die; ~** *s.* **~seitig 1:** versatility; variedness; **Kombiwagen sind vor allem wegen ihrer ~seitigkeit so beliebt** estate cars are popular above all because of their many uses; **~sprachig** Adj. multilingual; polyglot; **~staaterei** [~ʃta:tə'rai] **die; ~** *s.* **Partikularismus; ~stimmig 1.** *Adj.* many-voiced; **ein ~stimmiger Chor** a choir of many voices; **2.** *adv.* in many voices; **~versprechend 1.** *Adj.* [very] promising; **2.** *adv.* [very] promisingly; **~völker·staat** [-'---] **der** multinational state; **~weiberei** [~vaibə'rai] **die; ~:** polygyny *no art.;* polygamy *no art.;* **~zahl die;** *o. Pl.* large number; multitude
vier [fi:ɐ] *Kardinalz.* four; **alle ~e von sich strecken** *(ugs.)* put one's feet up; **auf allen ~en** *(ugs.)* on all fours; *s. auch* **acht**
Vier die; ~, ~en four; **eine ~ schreiben/bekommen** *(Schulw.)* get a D; *s. auch* **[1]Acht; Zwei**
vier-, Vier~ *(s. auch* **acht-, Acht-): ~achser der; ~s, ~:** four-axle vehicle; **~achsig** *(Technik)* four-axle *attrib.;* **~ sein** have four axles; **~achtel·takt** [-'---] **der** *(Musik)* four-eight time; **~augen·gespräch das** *(ugs.)* private talk *or* discussion; **~beiner der; ~s, ~** *(ugs.)* four-legged friend; **~beinig** *Adj.* four-legged; **~blättrig** *Adj.* four-leaf *attrib.;* four-leaved; **~eck das** quadrilateral; *(Rechteck)* rectangle; *(Quadrat)* square; **~eckig** *Adj.* quadrilateral; *(rechteckig)* rectangular; *(quadratisch)* square
Vierer der; ~s ~ a) *(Rudern)* four; **b)** *(ugs.: im Lotto)* four winning numbers *pl.;* **c)** *(ugs.: Ziffer, beim Würfeln)* four; **d)** *(landsch.: Schulnote)* D; **e)** *(ugs.: Autobus)* [number] four; **f)** *(Golf)* foursome
Vierer·bob der four-man bob
viererlei *Gattungsz.; indekl.* **a)** *attr.* four kinds *or* sorts of; four different ‹*sorts, kinds, sizes, possibilities*›; **b)** *subst.* four [different] things
vier·fach *Vervielfältigungsz.* fourfold; quadruple; **der ~e Olympiasieger** quadruple Olympic winner; *s. auch* **achtfach**
Vier·fache das; ~n; *adj. Dekl.* **um das ~** fourfold; by four times the amount; **die Preise sind um das ~ gestiegen** the prices have quadrupled *or* increased four times; **sie verlangen das ~ des normalen Tarifs** they are demanding four times the normal rate; *s. auch* **Achtfache**
vier-, Vier-: ~farben·druck [-'---] **der;** *Pl.* **-drucke a)** *o. Pl. (Verfahren)* four-colour printing *no art.;* **b)** *(einzelnes Stück)* four-colour print; **~farb[en]·stift der** four-colour pen **~flach das; ~[e]s, ~e, ~flächner** [~flɛçnɐ] **der** *(Math.)* tetrahedron; **~füßer** [~fy:sɐ] **der; ~s, ~** *(Zool.)* quadruped; **~füßig** *Adj.* **a)** four-legged; **b)** *(Verslehre)* tetrameter; **~füßig sein** be a tetrameter; **~gang·getriebe das** *(Technik)* four-speed gearbox; **~händig** [~hɛndɪç] **1.** *Adj.; nicht präd.* **~händiges Klavierspiel**

üben practise piano duets *or* duets on the piano; **2.** *adv.* ⟨*play*⟩ as a duet; **~händig Klavier spielen** play a duet/duets on the piano; **~hundert** *Kardinalz.* four hundred; **~jährig** *Adj. (4 Jahre alt)* four-year-old *attrib.*; four years old *pred.*; *(4 Jahre dauernd)* four-year *attrib.*; *s. auch* **achtjährig; ~jährlich 1.** *Adj.* four-yearly; *s. auch* **achtjährlich; 2.** *adv.* every four years

Vierkant-: ~eisen das square iron; **~holz das** squared timber; **~schlüssel der** square-section key

vier·köpfig *Adj.* four-headed ⟨*monster*⟩; ⟨*family, staff*⟩ of four

Vierling der; ~s, ~e quadruplet

vier-, Vier-: ~mal *Adv.* four times; *s. auch* **achtmal; ~malig** *Adj.; nicht präd.* **nach ~maliger Aufforderung** at the fourth request; after being asked four times; *s. auch* **achtmalig; ~master der; ~s, ~:** four-master; **~motorig** *Adj.* four-engined ⟨*aircraft etc.*⟩; **~rad·an·trieb der** *(Kfz-W.)* four-wheel drive; **~räd[e]rig** [~rɛ:d[ə]rɪç] *Adj.* four-wheeled; **~schrötig** [~ʃrø:tɪç] *Adj.* thickset; **~seitig** *Adj.* **a)** four-sided ⟨*figure, object, etc.*⟩; four-page *attrib.* ⟨*letter, article, etc.*⟩; **b)** *(zwischen vier Beteiligten)* quadripartite ⟨*agreement, talks, etc.*⟩; **~sitzer der; ~s, ~:** four-seater; **~spänner** [~ʃpɛnɐ] **der; ~s, ~:** four-in-hand; **~spännig 1.** *Adj.* four-horse ⟨*coach, carriage, etc.*⟩; **2.** *adv.* with a team of four horses; **~spurig 1.** *Adj.* four-lane ⟨*road, motorway*⟩; **~spurig sein** have four lanes; **2.** *adv.* **~spurig befahrbar sein** have all four lanes open; **eine Straße ~spurig ausbauen** widen a road into four lanes; **~stellig** *Adj.* four-figure *attrib.*; *s. auch* **achtstellig; ~sterne·general** [-'-----] **der** *(Militärjargon)* four-star general; **~sterne·hotel** [-'----] **das** four-star hotel; **~stimmig 1.** *Adj.* four-part ⟨*harmony, song, etc.*⟩; four-voice ⟨*choir, group*⟩; **2.** *adv.* **etw. ~stimmig singen** sing sth. in four voices; **~stöckig** *Adj.* four-storey; *s. auch* **achtstöckig; ~stündig** *Adj.; nicht präd.* four-hour *attrib.*; *s. auch* **achtstündig**

viert [fi:ɐt] *in* **wir waren zu ~:** there were four of us; **zu ~ verreisen** go away *or* on holiday in a foursome; *s. auch* [2]**acht**

viert... *Ordinalz.* fourth; *s. auch* **acht...**

vier-, Vier-: ~tägig *Adj.* four-day *attrib.*; *s. auch* **achttägig; ~takter der; ~s, ~** *(Auto)* car with a four-stroke engine; *(Motor)* four-stroke engine; **~takt·motor der** *(Kfz-W.)* four-stroke engine; **~tausend** *Kardinalz.* four thousand

Vierte der/die; *adj. Dekl.* fourth; *s. auch* **Achte**

vier-: ~teilen *tr. V.* quarter; **~teilig** *Adj.* four-part ⟨*serial, documentary, etc.*⟩; **~teilig sein** be in four parts

viertel ['fɪrtl] *Bruchz.* quarter; **ein ~ Pfund/eine ~ Million** a quarter of a pound/million

Viertel ['fɪrtl] **das** (*schweiz. meist* **der**); **~s, ~ a)** quarter; **ein ~ Leberwurst** *(ugs.)* a quarter of liver sausage; **ein ~ Wein** *(ugs.)* a quarter-litre of wine; **~ vor/nach eins** [a] quarter to/past one; **drei ~:** three-quarters; **um ~ /drei ~ acht** *(landsch.)* at [a] quarter past seven/at [a] quarter to eight; *s. auch* **akademisch 1; b)** *(Musik)* crotchet *(Brit.)*; quarter note *(Amer.)*; **c)** *(Stadtteil)* quarter; district

viertel-, Viertel-: ~drehung die quarter-turn; **~finale das** *(Sport)* quarter-final; **sich für das ~finale qualifizieren** qualify for the quarter-finals; **~jahr das** three months *pl.*; **~jährlich 1.** *Adj.* quarterly; **2.** *adv.* quarterly; every three months; **~kreis der** quadrant; **~liter der** quarter of a litre; **~note die** *(Musik)* crotchet *(Brit.)*; quarter note *(Amer.)*; **~pause die** crotchet rest *(Brit.)*; quarter rest *(Amer.)*; **~pfund das** quarter [of a] pound; **~stunde die** quarter of an hour; **~stündig** *Adj.; nicht präd.* quarter-of-an-hour; fifteen-minute; **~stündlich 1.** *Adj.; nicht präd.* quarter-hourly; every quarter of an hour *postpos.*; **2.** *adv.* every quarter of an hour; **~ton der;** *Pl.* **~töne** *(Musik)* quarter tone

viertens ['fi:ɐtns] *Adv.* fourthly; *s. auch* **zweitens**

Viertonner der; ~s, ~: four-tonner

viertürig [-ty:rɪç] *Adj.* four-door *attrib.*; **~ sein** have four doors

Vierung die; ~, ~en *(Archit.)* crossing

Vier·viertel·takt [-'---] **der** *(Musik)* four-four time

Vierwaldstätter See, *(schweiz.:)* **Vierwaldstättersee der** Lake Lucerne

vier-, Vier-: ~wöchig *Adj.* four-week [-long]; **~zehn** ['fɪr-] *Kardinalz.* fourteen; *s. auch* **achtzehn; ~zehnjährig** *Adj. (14 Jahre alt)* fourteen-year-old *attrib.*; fourteen years old *pred.*; *(14 Jahre dauernd)* fourteen-year *attrib.*

vierzehnt... ['fɪr-] *Ordinalz.* fourteenth; *s. auch* **acht...**

vier-, Vier- ['fɪr-]: **~zehn·tägig** *Adj.; nicht präd.* two-week; **unser ~zehntägiger Urlaub** our two-week *or* two weeks' *or* fortnight's holiday; **~zehn·täglich 1.** *Adj.; nicht präd.* fortnightly; **2.** *adv.* fortnightly; every two weeks

vierzig ['fɪrtsɪç] *Kardinalz.* forty; *s. auch* **achtzig**

vierziger ['fɪrtsɪgɐ] *indekl. Adj.; nicht präd.* **die ~ Jahre** the forties; *s. auch* **achtziger**

[1]**Vierziger** ['fɪrtsɪgə] **der; ~s, ~ a)** *(40jähriger)* forty-year-old; **b)** *(ugs.: Autobus)* number forty; **c)** *(Wein)* '40's vintage

[2]**Vierziger die; ~, ~** *(ugs.)* **a)** *(Briefmarke)* forty-pfennig/-schilling *etc.* stamp; **b)** *(Zigarre)* forty-pfennig cigar; **c)** *(Glühbirne)* 40-watt bulb

[3]**Vierziger** *Pl.* forties; *s. auch* [3]**Achtziger**

Vierzigerin die; ~, ~nen forty-year-old

vierzig·jährig ['fɪrtsɪç-] *Adj. (40 Jahre alt)* forty-year-old *attrib.*; forty years old *pred.*; *(40 Jahre dauernd)* forty-year *attrib.*

vierzigst ... ['fɪrtsɪçst ...] *Ordinalz.* fortieth; *s. auch* **acht ...**

Vierzig·stunden·woche die forty-hour week

vier-, Vier-: ~zimmer·wohnung die four-room flat *(Brit.) or (Amer.)* apartment; **~zylinder der** *(ugs.)* four-cylinder; **~zylinder·motor der** four-cylinder engine

Vietnam [viɛt'nam] **(das); ~s** Vietnam

Vietnamese [viɛtna'me:zə] **der; ~n, ~n, Vietnamesin, die; ~, ~nen** Vietnamese

vietnamesisch 1. *Adj.* Vietnamese. **2.** *adv.* **wir waren ~ essen** we went to a Vietnamese restaurant *or* for a Vietnamese meal; *s. auch* **deutsch; Deutsch;** [2]**Deutsche**

Vietnamisierung die; ~: Vietnamization

Vietnam·krieg der; *o. Pl.* Vietnam war

vif [vi:f] *(veralt.)* **1.** *Adj.* lively; brisk. **2.** *adv.* briskly

Vigil [vi'gi:l] **die; ~, ~ien** *(kath. Kirche)* vigil

Vignette [vɪn'jɛtə] **die; ~, ~n** vignette

Vikar [vi'ka:ɐ] **der; ~s, ~e a)** *(kath. Kirche)* locum tenens; **b)** *(ev. Kirche)* ≈ [trainee] curate

Viktimologie [vɪktimologi:] **die; ~:** victimology *no art.*

Viktoria [vɪk'to:ria] **(die)** Victoria

viktorianisch 1. *Adj.* Victorian. **2.** *adv.* in a Victorian manner

Villa ['vɪla] **die; ~, Villen** villa

Villen·viertel das exclusive residential district

Vinaigrette [vinɛ'grɛtə] **die; ~, ~n** vinaigrette [dressing]

Viola ['vi̯o:la] **die; ~, Violen** *(Musik)* viola

violett [vi̯o'lɛt] purple; violet

Violett das; ~s, ~e *od. ugs.* **~s** purple; violet; *(im Spektrum)* violet

Violine [vi̯o'li:nə] **die; ~, ~n** *(Musik)* violin

Violinist der; ~en, ~en, Violinistin, die; ~, ~nen violinist

Violin-: ~konzert das violin concerto; **~schlüssel der** treble clef

Violon·cello [vi̯olɔn'tʃɛlo] **das** violoncello

Viper ['vi:pɐ] **die; ~, ~n** viper; adder

Viren *s.* **Virus**

Virologie [virolo'gi:] **die; ~:** virology *no art.*

virtuell [vɪr'tu̯ɛl] **1.** *Adj.; nicht präd.* **a)** potential; **b)** *(DV, Optik)* virtual ⟨*memory, image*⟩. **2.** *adv.* virtually

virtuos [vɪr'tu̯o:s] **1.** *Adj.* virtuoso ⟨*performance etc.*⟩. **2.** *adv.* in a virtuoso manner

Virtuose [vɪr'tu̯o:zə] **der; ~n, ~n** virtuoso

Virtuosität die; ~: virtuosity

virulent [viru'lɛnt] *Adj. (Med., geh.)* virulent

Virus ['vi:rʊs] **das; ~, Viren** ['vi:rən] virus

Virus·infektion die virus infection

Visa *s.* **Visum**

Visage [vi'za:ʒə] **die; ~, ~n** *(salopp abwertend)* mug *(sl.)*; *(Miene)* expression

vis-à-vis [viza'vi:] **1.** *Präp. mit Dat.* opposite. **2.** *Adv.* opposite; **~ von etw./jmdm.** opposite sth./sb.

Visavis [viza'vi:] **das; ~** [viza'vi:(s)], **~** [viza'vi:s] **mein ~:** the person opposite me; **jmdn. zum ~ haben** have sb. opposite one

Visen *s.* **Visum**

Visier [vi'zi:ɐ] **das; ~s, ~e a)** *(am Helm)* visor; **das ~ herunterlassen** *(fig.)* put up one's guard; **mit offenem ~ kämpfen** *(fig.)* fight out in the open; **b)** *(an der Waffe)* backsight; **jmdn. ins ~ nehmen** *(fig. ugs.)* start to keep close tabs on sb.

visieren *itr. V.* take aim

Vision [vi'zi̯o:n] **die; ~, ~en** vision

visionär [vizi̯o'nɛ:ɐ] **1.** *Adj.* visionary. **2.** *adv.* in a visionary manner

Visite [vi'zi:tə] **die; ~, ~n a)** round; **~ machen** do one's round; **um 10 Uhr war ~:** at 10 o'clock, the doctor did his round; **b)** *(veralt.: Besuch)* visit; **zu einer ~:** on a visit

Visiten·karte die visiting-card; **diese gepflegten Grünanlagen sind eine gute ~ für die Stadt** these well-tended parks and gardens are a good advertisement for the town; **seine ~ hinterlassen** *(fig.)* leave one's visiting-card *(joc.)*

Visit·karte die *(österr.) s.* **Visitenkarte**

viskos [vɪs'ko:s], **viskös** [vɪs'kø:s] *Adj.* *(Chemie)* viscous

Viskose [vɪs'ko:zə] **die; ~** *(Chemie)* viscose

Viskosität die; ~ *(Chemie)* viscosity

visuell [vi'zu̯ɛl] *(geh.)* **1.** *Adj.* visual. **2.** *adv.* visually

Visum ['vi:zʊm] **das; ~s, Visa** ['vi:za] *od.* **Visen** ['vi:zn̩] visa

Visum·zwang der; *o. Pl.* visa requirement

vital [vi'ta:l] **1.** *Adj.* **a)** *(voller Energie)* vital; energetic; vigorous; **~ sein** be full of life *or* vigour; **b)** *(wichtig)* vital. **2.** *adv. (voller Energie)* energetically

Vitalität die; ~: vitality

Vitamin [vita'mi:n] **das; ~s, ~e a)** vitamin; **b) ~ B** *(ugs. scherzh.)* connections *pl.*; **etw. durch ~ B kriegen** get sth. through knowing the right people

vitamin-, Vitamin-: ~arm *Adj.* ⟨*food, diet, etc.*⟩ low in vitamins; **~gehalt der** vitamin content; **~mangel der;** *o. Pl.* vitamin deficiency; **~reich** *Adj.* rich in vitamins *postpos.*; vitamin-rich; **~stoß der** large dose of vitamins; **~tablette die** vitamin tablet *or* pill

Vitrine [vi'tri:nə] **die; ~, ~n** display case; show-case; *(Möbel)* display cabinet

Vivi·sektion [vivi-] **die** *(bes. Med.)* vivisection *no art.*

vivi·sezieren *tr. V. (bes. Med.)* vivisect

Vize ['fi:tsə] **der; ~s, ~s** *(ugs.)* number two *(coll.)*

Vize-: ['vi:tsə] **~kanzler der** vice-chancellor; **~könig der** viceroy; **~präsident der** vice-president

Vlies [fli:s] **das; ~es, ~e** fleece

V-Mann ['fau-] **der; ~[e]s, V-Männer** *od.* **V-Leute** contact [man]; *(Informant)* informer

Vogel ['fo:gl] **der; ~s, Vögel** ['fø:gl] **a)** bird; **friß, ~, oder stirb!** *(ugs.)* [you can] like it or lump it! *(coll.)*; **der ~ ist ausgeflogen** *(ugs.)* the bird has flown; **[mit etw.] den ~ abschießen** *(ugs.)* take the biscuit [with sth.] *(coll.)*; **einen ~ haben** *(salopp)* be off one's rocker *or* head *(sl.)*; **jmdm. den ~ zeigen** tap one's forehead at sb. *(as a sign that one thinks he/she is stupid)*; **b)** *(salopp, oft scherzh.: Mensch)* character; **ein seltsamer** *od.* **komischer ~:** an odd bird *or* character; **c)** *(Fliegerspr.: Flugzeug)* machine

Vogel-: ~bauer das *od.* **der** birdcage; **~beer·baum der** rowan[-tree]; mountain ash; **~beere die** rowan-berry

Vögelchen ['fø:glçən] **das; ~s, ~:** little *or* small bird

Vogel-: ~dreck der *(ugs.)* bird droppings *pl.*; **~ei das** bird's egg

Vögelei die; ~, ~en *(derb)* screwing *(coarse)*

vogel-, Vogel-: ~flug der flight of the birds; **~frei** *Adj. (hist.)* outlawed; **jmdn./etw. für ~frei erklären** outlaw sb./sth.; **~futter das** bird food; **~häuschen das** bird-house; **~käfig der** birdcage; **~kunde die;** *o. Pl.* ornithology *no art.*

vögeln ['fø:gln] *tr., itr. V. (derb)* screw *(coarse)*; **jmdn./mit jmdm. ~:** screw sb.

Vogel-: ~nest das bird's nest; **~perspektive die** bird's eye view; **Manhattan aus der ~perspektive** a bird's-eye view of Manhattan; **~scheuche** [~ʃɔyçə] **die; ~, ~n** scarecrow; **~schutz der** protection of birds; **~-Strauß-Politik** [--'----] **die;** *o. Pl.* head-in-the-sand-policy; **~-Strauß-Politik treiben** pursue a policy of burying one's head in the sand; **~warte die** ornithological institute; **~zug der** bird migration

Vogesen [vo'ge:zn] *Pl.* Vosges [Mountains]

Vöglein ['fø:glain] **das; ~s, ~:** little bird

Vogt [fo:kt] **der; ~[e]s, Vögte** ['fø:ktə] *(hist.) (eines Gutes, einer Burg usw.)* steward; *(Land~)* governor

Vogtei [fo:k'tai] **die; ~, ~en** *(hist.) s.* **Vogt:** *(Amt)* stewardship; governorship; *(Sitz)* steward's office; governor's residence

Vokabel [vo'ka:bl] **die; ~, ~n** *od. österr. auch* **das; ~s, ~:** word; vocabulary item; **~n** vocabulary *sing.*; vocab *sing. (Sch. coll.)*

Vokabel·heft das vocabulary *or (coll.)* vocab book

Vokabular das; ~s, ~e vocabulary

vokal *Adj. (Musik)* vocal

Vokal [vo'ka:l] **der; ~s, ~e** *(Sprachw.)* vowel

Vokalisation die; ~, ~en *(Musik)* vocalization

vokalisch *(Sprachw.)* **1.** *Adj.* vocalic; **mit ~em Anlaut** beginning with a vowel. **2.** *adv.* **~ auslauten** end in *or* with a vowel

Vokalismus der; ~ *(Sprachw.)* vocalism

Vokalist der; ~en, ~en, Vokalistin die; ~, ~nen vocalist

Vokal·musik die vocal music

Vokativ ['vo:kati:f] **der; ~s, ~e** *(Sprachw.)* vocative

Volant [vo'lã:] **der,** *schweiz., österr. meist* **das; ~s, ~s a)** *(an Kleidungsstücken)* flounce; **b)** *(Lenkrad)* steering-wheel

Voliere [vo'liɛ:rə] **die; ~, ~n** aviary

Volk [fɔlk] **das; ~[e]s, Völker** ['fœlkɐ] **a)** people; **das ~ der Kurden** the Kurdish people; **das irische und das deutsche ~:** the Irish and German peoples; **b)** *o. Pl. (Bevölkerung)* people *pl.*; *(Nation)* people *pl.*; nation; **im ~e** among the people; **das ~ befragen** ask the people *or* nation; **das arbeitende/unwissende ~:** the working people/the ignorant masses *pl.*; **c)** *o. Pl. (einfache Leute)* people *pl.*; **ein Mann aus dem ~:** a man of the people; **dem ~ aufs Maul schauen** listen to the way the ordinary man speaks; **d)** *o. Pl. (ugs.: Leute)* people *pl.*; **viel junges ~:** many young people; **sich unters ~ mischen** go among the people; **etw. unters ~ bringen** make sth. [known to the] public; **e)** *o. Pl. (Gruppe)* lot; crowd *(coll.)*; **die Spatzen sind ein freches ~** *(fig.)* sparrows are a cheeky lot; **f)** *(Bienen~)* colony

Völkchen ['fœlkçən] **das; ~s, ~:** lot; crowd *(coll.)*

völker-, Völker-: ~ball der *ball game in which two teams try to get the other side's players out by hitting them with a ball;* **~bund der;** *o. Pl.* League of Nations; **~familie die;** *o. Pl. (geh.)* family of nations; **~freundschaft die;** *o. Pl.* international friendship *no art.*; **~kunde die;** *o. Pl.* ethnology *no art.*; **~kundler** [~kʊntlɐ] **der; ~s, ~:** ethnologist; **~mord der** genocide; **~recht das;** *o. Pl.* international law *no art.*; **~rechtlich 1.** *Adj.; nicht präd.* ⟨*issue, problem, etc.*⟩ of international law; **~rechtliche Verträge** agreements in *or* under international law; **die ~rechtliche Anerkennung eines Staates** the recognition of a state under international law; **2.** *adv.* ⟨*settle*⟩ in accordance with international law; ⟨*control, regulate*⟩ by international law; ⟨*recognize*⟩ under international law

Völkerschaft die; ~, ~en people; *(Volksstamm)* tribe

völker-, Völker-: ~verbindend ⟨*idea, event*⟩ which brings nations together; **der ~verbindende Charakter des Sports** the ability of sport to bring nations together; **~verständigung die** international understanding; understanding between nations; **~wanderung die a)** *(hist.)* migration of peoples; völkerwanderung; **b)** *(ugs.)* mass migration; *(Zug)* mass progression

völkisch *Adj. (veralt., bes. ns.)* national

volk·reich *Adj.* heavily populated

volks-, Volks-: ~ab·stimmung die plebiscite; **~armee die** People's Army; **~armist** [~armɪst] **der; ~en, ~en** member of the People's Army; **~auf·stand der** national uprising; **~aus·gabe die** *(veralt.)* popular edition; **~befragung die** *(Politik)* referendum; **~begehren das** *(Politik)* petition for a referendum; **~belustigung die** public entertainment; **~brauch der** popular custom; **~bücherei die** public library; **~demokratie** people's democracy; **~deutsche der/die;** *adj. Dekl.* ethnic German; **~dichtung die** *(Literaturw.)* folk literature *no indef. art.*; **eine ~dichtung** a piece of folk literature; **~eigen** *Adj. (DDR)* publicly *or* nationally owned; **~er Betrieb** publicly *or* nationally owned company; **~eigentum das** *(DDR)* national[ly owned] property; **~einkommen das** *(Wirtsch.)* national income; **~empfinden das: das [gesunde] ~empfinden** popular sentiment *or* opinion; **~entscheid der** *(Politik)* referendum; **~etymologie die** *(Sprachw.)* folk *or* popular etymology; **~feind der** enemy of the people; **~fest das** public festival; *(Jahrmarkt)* fair; **~front die** *(Politik)* popular front; **~gemeinschaft die** *(bes. ns.)* national community; **~gemurmel das** *(ugs. scherzh.)* mutterings *pl.*; **~genosse der** *(ns.)* national comrade; **~gerichts·hof der** *(ns.)* People's Court; **~gesundheit die** public health; **~glaube[n] der** *(Volksk.)* popular belief; **~held der** folk hero; **~hoch·schule die** adult education centre; **ein Kurs an der ~hochschule** an adult education class; **~initiative die** *(schweiz. Politik)* petition for a referendum; **~kammer die** *(DDR)* **die ~kammer** the Volkskammer; the People's Chamber; **~kunde die** folklore; **~kundler der; ~s, ~:** folklorist; **~kundlich** *Adj.* folkloric; **~kundliche Bücher** books on folklore; **~kunst die;** *o. Pl.* folk art; **~lied das** folk-song; **~märchen das** folk-tale; **~masse die a) die ~massen** the people; the masses; **b)** *(versammeltes Volk)* crowd [of people]; **~medizin die;** *o. Pl.* folk medicine *no art.*; **~mund der;** *o. Pl.* **im ~mund wird das ... genannt** in the vernacular it is called ...; **~musik die** folk-music; **~nahrungs·mittel das** staple food; **~polizei die;** *o. Pl. (DDR)* People's Police; **~polizist der** *(DDR)* People's Policeman; member of the People's Police; **~rede die** *(veralt.)* public address *or* speech; **~ reden halten** *(ugs. abwertend)* make a long speech; **halt keine ~reden!** no speechifying! *(coll.)*; no long speeches!; **~republik die** People's Republic; **die ~republik China** the People's Republic of China; **~schicht die;** *meist Pl.* social class; **~schule die a)** *(Bundesrepublik Deutschland und Schweiz veralt.) school providing basic primary and secondary education;* **b)** *(österr.)* primary school; **~schüler der, ~schülerin die** pupil at a 'Volksschule'; **~schullehrer der** teacher at a 'Volksschule'; **~seele die;** *o. Pl.* soul of the people; **die russische ~seele** the soul of the Russian people; **~seuche die** national epidemic; **~souveränität die** *(Politik)* sovereignty of the people; **~sprache die** vernacular [language]; **~stamm der** tribe; **~stück das** *(Theater)* folk play; **~sturm der;** *o. Pl. (ns.) German territorial army created towards the end of World War II to help defend the fatherland;* **~tanz der** folk-dance; **~tracht die** traditional costume; *(eines Landes)* national costume; **~trauer·tag der** *(Bundesrepublik Deutschland)* national remembrance day; **~tribun der** *(hist.)* tribune [of the people]

Volkstum das; ~: national character; *(Traditionen)* national customs and traditions

volkstümlich ['fɔlksty:mlɪç] **1.** *Adj.* popular; **ein ~er Politiker** a politician of the people *or* with the common touch; **der ~e Name einer Pflanze** the vernacular name of a plant; **~e Preise** popular prices; **eine ~e Einführung** an introduction readily comprehensible to the layman; **sich ~ geben** act the man/woman of the people. **2.** *adv.* **~ schreiben** write in terms readily comprehensible to the layman

volks-, Volks-: ~verdummung die *(ugs. abwertend)* deliberate deception of the public; **~verhetzung die** incitement of the people; **~vermögen das** *(Wirtsch.)* national wealth; **~versammlung die a)** public meeting; **b)** *(Parlament)* national assembly; **~vertreter der** representative of the people; **~vertretung die** representative body of the people; **~wahl die** *(DDR Politik)* general election; **~weise die** folk-tune; **~weisheit die** old saying; **~wirt der** economist; **~wirtschaft die** national economy; *(Fach)* economics *sing., no art.*; **~wirtschaftler der; ~s, ~:** economist; **~wirtschaftlich 1.** *Adj.* economic; **2.** *adv.* economically; **~wirtschaftslehre die;** *o. Pl.* economics *sing., no art.*; **~wohl das** welfare *or* well-being of the people; **~zählung die** [national] census; **~zorn der** public anger; **~zugehörigkeit die** ethnic origin

voll [fɔl] **1.** *Adj.* **a)** full; **der Saal ist ~ Menschen** the room is full of people **ein Korb ~ [roter] Äpfel** a basket full of [red] apples; **~ von** *od.* **mit etw. sein** be full of sth.; **das Glas ist halb ~:** the glass is half full; **beide Hände ~ haben** have both hands full; **~ [von] Dankbarkeit sein** be full of *or* filled with gratitude; **~ Güte/Tatkraft sein** be full of goodness/vigour; **den Kopf ~ haben** *(ugs.)* be preoccupied (**mit** with); **der Saal ist brechend/gestopft ~** *(ugs.)* the room is jam-packed *(coll.)*; **die Straßen lagen ~ Schnee** *(ugs.)* the streets were deep in snow; **jeder bekam einen Korb ~:** everybody received a basketful; mit ~en Backen kauen eat with bulging cheeks; aus dem ~en schöpfen draw on abundant *or* plentiful resources; aus dem ~en leben *od.* wirtschaften live off *or* on the fat of the land; ~e Pulle *od.* ~[es] Rohr *(salopp)* ‹*drive*› flat out; das Radio auf ~e Pulle drehen *(salopp)* turn the radio on full blast *(coll.)*; *s. auch* Lob; Mund; b) *(salopp: betrunken)* plastered *(sl.)*; canned *(Brit. sl.)*; c) *(üppig)* full ‹*figure, face, lip*›; thick ‹*hair*›; ample ‹*bosom*›; im Gesicht ~er geworden sein have filled out *or* be fuller in the face; d) *(ganz, vollständig)* full; complete ‹*seriousness, success*›; etw. mit ~em Recht tun be quite right to do sth.; einen ~en Tag/Monat warten wait a full *or* whole day/month; in ~er Fahrt at full speed; in ~em Gange sein be in full swing; die ~ Wahrheit the full *or* whole truth; mit dem ~en Namen unterschreiben sign one's full name *or* one's name in full; das Dutzend ist ~: it's a round dozen; ~es/~stes Verständnis für jmdn. haben have full/the fullest understanding for sb.; ~e Gewißheit über etw. *(Akk.)* haben be completely certain about sth.; der Mond ist ~: the moon is full; jmdn. nicht für ~ nehmen not take sb. seriously; in die ~en gehen *(ugs.)* go all out; s. auch Brust a; Hals b; Kehle a; e) *(kräftig)* full, rich ‹*taste, aroma*›; rich ‹*voice*›; f) *(ugs.: bei Uhrzeitangaben)* die Uhr schlug ~: the clock struck the hour; fünf nach ~: five past the hour. 2. *adv.* a) *(völlig, ganz)* fully; ~ und ganz completely; etw. ~ auslasten make full use of sth.; ~ verantwortlich für etw. sein be wholly responsible *or* bear full responsibility for sth.; ~ arbeiten *(ugs.)* work full-time; er ist mir ~ in die Seite gefahren *(salopp)* he drove straight into my side; b) *(kräftig)* richly; ~ klingen have a full, rich sound; *s. auch* voller

volladen *unr. tr. V., trennbar* load up completely; vollgeladen fully laden

Voll·akademiker der university graduate

voll·auf [*od.* '--] *Adv.* completely; fully; ~ genügen/reichen be quite enough

vollaufen *unr. itr. V., trennbar* fill up; etw. ~ lassen fill sth. [up]; sich ~ lassen *(salopp)* get completely paralytic *or* canned *(Brit. sl.)*

voll-, Voll-: ~automatisch 1. *Adj.* fully automatic; 2. *adv.* fully automatically; **~bad das** bath; **~bart der** full beard; **~bärtig** *Adj.* ‹*man*› with a full beard; **~beschäftigung die**; *o. Pl. (Wirtsch.)* full employment *no art.*; **~besitz der**: im ~besitz seiner [geistigen und körperlichen] Kräfte sein be in full possession of one's [mental and physical] faculties; **~bild das** *(Med.)* complete picture; **~blut das** a) thoroughbred; b) *(Med.)* whole blood; **~blut-** true; er ist ein ~blutpolitiker/-schauspieler he is a true politician/actor *or* a politician/actor through and through; **~blüter** [~bly:tɐ] **der**; ~s, ~: thoroughbred; **~blütig** *Adj.* thoroughbred ‹*horse*›; *(fig.)* full-blooded ‹*person*›; **~bremsung die**: eine ~bremsung machen put the brakes full on; **~bringen** [-'--] *unr. tr. V. (geh.)* accomplish; achieve; es ist vollbracht *(bibl.)* it is finished; **~busig** [~bu:zıç] full-bosomed; buxom; **~dampf der**; *o. Pl. (Seemannsspr.)* full steam; mit ~dampf at full steam *or* speed; *(fig. ugs.)* flat out

Völle·gefühl ['fœlə-] **das**; *o. Pl.* feeling of fullness

voll·enden 1. *tr. V.* complete; finish; mit vollendetem *od.* dem vollendeten 16. Lebensjahr on reaching the age of 16 *or* completing one's sixteenth year; vollendeter Mord/Landesverrat consummated murder/treason; sein Leben ~ *(fig. geh. verhüll.)* pass away; depart this life; *s. auch* vollendet. 2. *refl. V. (geh.) (seinen Abschluß finden)* ‹*process, transformation, etc.*› reach its conclusion; *(vollkommen werden)* reach [its] completion

vollendet 1. *Adj.* accomplished ‹*performance*›; perfect ‹*gentleman, host, manners, reproduction*›; vollendete Gegenwart/Vergangenheit/Zukunft *(Sprachw.)* perfect/pluperfect/future perfect; *s. auch* Tatsache. 2. *adv.* ‹*play*› in an accomplished manner; ~ schön sein be perfectly beautiful

vollends ['fɔlɛnts] *Adv.* completely; ~ für Behinderte ist das unzumutbar for disabled people in particular *or* especially it is unreasonable

Voll·endung die a) completion; kurz vor der ~ stehen be nearing completion; mit/nach ~ des 65. Lebensjahres on reaching the age of 65 *or* completing one's sixty-fifth year; b) *(geh.: Krönung)* culmination; c) *o. Pl. (Vollkommenheit)* perfection

voller *indekl. Adj.* full of; *(erfüllt von)* full of; filled with; sein Anzug war ~ Flecken his suit was covered with stains; ein Leben ~ Arbeit a life full of *or* filled with work; ~ Widersprüche sein be full of contradictions

Völlerei [fœlə'rai] **die**; ~, ~en *(abwertend)* gluttony *no pl., no art.*

volley ['vɔli] *Adv. (bes. Fußball, Tennis)* on the volley

Volley·ball der volleyball

voll-, Voll-: ~fett *Adj.* full-fat; **~|fressen** *unr. refl. V.* ‹*animal*› eat its fill; *(derb: sich satt essen)* ‹*person*› stuff oneself *or* one's face *(sl.)*; ~ gefressen sein *(derb)* ‹*person*› be stuffed *(sl.)*; **~führen** [-'--] *tr. V.* perform, execute ‹*somersault, movement*›; perform ‹*dance, deed*›; **~|füllen** *tr. V.* fill up; **~gas das**; *o. Pl.* ~gas geben put one's foot down; ~gas fahren drive flat out; mit ~gas at full throttle; **~|gießen** *unr. tr. V.* a) *(füllen)* fill [up]; b) *(ugs.: begießen)*; den Teppich/sich *(Dat.)* die Hose mit Rotwein *usw.* ~: spill red wine *etc.* all over the carpet/one's trousers; **~gummi·reifen der** solid rubber tyre; **~idiot der** *(salopp abwertend)* complete idiot *(coll.)*

völlig ['fœlıç] 1. *Adj.*; *nicht präd.* complete; total. 2. *adv.* completely; totally; du hast ~ recht you are absolutely right; das ist ~ unmöglich that is absolutely impossible; mit etw. ~ einverstanden sein be in complete agreement with sth.

voll-, Voll-: ~inhaltlich 1. *Adj.*; *nicht präd.* complete; full; 2. *adv.* fully; **~jährig** *Adj.* of age *pred.*; ~jährig werden come of age; attain one's majority; sie hat zwei ~jährige Kinder she has two children who are of age; **~jährigkeit die**; ~: majority *no art.*; **~jurist der** [fully-]qualified lawyer *(who has attained the qualifications necessary to become a judge)*; **~kasko·versicherung die** fully comprehensive insurance; **~klimatisiert** *Adj.* fully air-conditioned

voll·kommen 1. *Adj.* a) [-'-- *od.* '---] *(vollendet)* perfect; b) ['---] *(vollständig)* complete; total. 2. ['---] *adv.* completely; totally

Vollkommenheit die; ~: perfection

voll-, Voll-: ~korn·brot das wholemeal *(Brit.) or (Amer.)* wholewheat bread; **~|laden** *s.* volladen; **~|laufen** *s.* vollaufen; **~|machen** 1. *tr. V.* a) *(ugs.: füllen)* fill up; um das Maß ~zumachen *(fig.)* to crown *or* cap it all; b) *(ugs.: beschmutzen)* etw. ~machen get or make sth. dirty; [sich *(Dat.)*] die Hosen/Windeln ~machen mess one's pants/nappy; c) *(vollständig machen)* complete; das Dutzend ~machen make up a round dozen; **~macht die**; ~, ~en a) authority; jmdm. [die] ~macht geben/erteilen give/grant sb. power of attorney; seine ~macht[en] überschreiten exceed one's authority; in ~macht per procurationem; b) *(Urkunde)* power of attorney; **~mast** *Adv. (Seemannsspr.)* full mast; auf ~mast at full mast; ~mast flaggen hoist a flag/flags to full mast; **~matrose der** able-bodied seaman; **~milch die** full-cream milk; **~milch·schokolade die** full-cream milk chocolate; **~mond der**; *o. Pl.* full moon; es ist/wir haben heute ~mond there is a full moon tonight; bei ~mond at full moon; **~mond·gesicht das** *(ugs.)* moon face; **~mundig** 1. *Adj.* a) *(voll im Geschmack)* full-bodied ‹*wine, flavour, etc.*›; b) *(abwertend: wichtigtuerisch)* pompous; 2. *adv. (abwertend: wichtigtuerisch)* pompously; **~narkose die** *(Med.)* general anaesthetic; unter ~narkose under a general anaesthetic; **~|packen** *tr. V.* pack full; **~pension die**; *meist o. Art.*; *o. Pl.* full board *no art.*; **~pfropfen** *tr. V. (auch fig.)* cram full; mit etw. ~gepfropft sein be crammed full of sth.; **~|pumpen** *tr. V.* pump up ‹*tyre*›; fill up ‹*reservoir*›; sich *(Dat.)* mit Tabletten/Drogen ~pumpen *(fig. ugs.)* pump oneself full of tablets/drugs; **~|qualmen** *tr. V. (ugs.)* fill with smoke; **~rausch der**: sich *(Dat.)* einen ~rausch antrinken get completely drunk; etw. im ~rausch tun do sth. while completely drunk; **~reif** *Adj.* fully ripe; **~|saufen** *unr. refl. V. (salopp)* get completely plastered *(sl.)*; **~|saugen** *regelm. (auch unr.) refl. V.* ‹*leech*› suck itself full (mit of); ‹*sponge*› become saturated (mit with); **~|schlagen** 1. *unr. itr. V.*; *mit sein (Seemannsspr.)* become swamped; 2. *unr. tr. V. (salopp)* sich *(Dat.)* den Bauch [mit etw.] ~schlagen stuff oneself *or* one's face [with sth.] *(sl.)*; **~schlank** *Adj.* with a fuller figure *postpos., not pred.*; ein Modell für ~schlanke Damen a model for the fuller figure; ~schlank sein have a fuller figure; **~|schmieren** *(ugs.) tr. V.* a) *(beschmutzen)* smear; sich *(Dat.)* das ganze Gesicht mit etw. ~schmieren get *or* smear sth. all over one's face; b) *(abwertend: ~schreiben, ~malen)* scrawl/draw all over ‹*wall etc.*›; fill ‹*exercise book etc.*› with scrawl; die Mauern mit Parolen ~schmieren scrawl *or* daub slogans all over the walls; **~|schreiben** *unr. tr. V.* fill [with writing]; **~sperrung die** *(Verkehrsw.)* complete closure; **~|spritzen** *tr. V.* jmdn./etw. ~spritzen splash water *etc.* all over sb./sth.; *(mit Schlauch usw.)* spray water *etc.* all over sb./sth.; jmdn./etw. mit etw. ~spritzen splash sth. all over sb./sth.; *(mit Schlauch usw.)* spray sth. all over sb./sth.; **~ständig** 1. *Adj.* complete; full ‹*text, address, etc.*›; nicht ~ständig incomplete; 2. *adv.* completely; ‹*list*› in full; **~ständigkeit die**; ~: completeness; der ~ständigkeit halber for the sake of completeness; **~|stopfen** 1. *tr. V. (ugs.)* stuff *or* cram full; jmdn. mit Fakten ~stopfen *(fig.)* pump sb. full of facts; 2. *refl. V. (ugs.)* stuff oneself *or* one's face *(sl.)*; **~streckbar** [-'--] *Adj.* (Rechtsw.) enforceable; implementable ‹*sentence*›; **~strecken** [-'--] *tr. V.* enforce ‹*penalty, fine, law*›; carry out ‹*sentence*› (an + *Dat.* on); die ~streckende Gewalt the executive [power]; ein Testament ~strecken execute a will; **~strecker** [-'--] **der**; ~s, ~ *(des Gesetzes)* enforcer; *(eines Testaments)* executor; **~streckung** [-'--] **die**; ~, ~en *s.* vollstrecken: enforcement; carrying out; execution

Vollstreckungs·befehl der *(Rechtsw.)* enforcement order; writ of execution

voll-, Voll-: ~|tanken *tr. (auch itr.) V.* fill up; bitte ~tanken fill it up, please; **~tönend** 1. *Adj.* sonorous; 2. *adv.* sonorously; **~treffer der** direct hit; ein ~treffer sein *(fig.)* hit the bull's eye; **~trunken** *Adj.* completely *or* blind drunk; in ~trunkenem Zustand in a state of total inebriation; **~trunkenheit die** total inebriation *or* intoxication; **~verb das** *(Sprachw.)* full verb; **~versammlung die** general meeting; **~waise die** orphan; **~wertig** *Adj.* full ‹*job, member*›; [fully] adequate ‹*replace-*

ment, substitute, nourishment, diet›; **~zählig** [~tsɛ:lɪç] *Adj.* complete; **wir bitten um ~zähliges Erscheinen** we request everyone to attend; **sie waren ~zählig erschienen** they had turned out in full strength; **als wir ~zählig [versammelt] waren** when everyone was present

voll·ziehen 1. *unr. tr. V.* carry out ‹*instruction, action, will*›; carry out ‹*sentence*› **(an** + *Dat.* on); execute, carry out ‹*order*›; perform ‹*sacrifice, ceremony, sexual intercourse*›; **die Ehe ~:** consummate the marriage; **die ~de Gewalt** the executive [power]; **2.** *unr. refl. V.* take place; **in ihm hatte sich eine Wandlung ~zogen** a change had come over him *or* taken place in him

Voll·zug der *s.* **vollziehen 1:** carrying out; execution; performance; consummation

Vollzugs-: ~anstalt die penal institution; **~beamte der** [prison] warder; **~meldung die** *report that an instruction has been carried out*

Volontär [volɔn'tɛ:ɐ̯] **der; ~s, ~e** trainee *(receiving a low salary in return for training)*

Volontariat [volɔnta'rja:t] **das; ~[e]s, ~e a)** *(Zeit)* period of training; **b)** *(Stelle)* traineeship; *s. auch* **Volontär**

Volontärin die; ~, ~nen *s.* **Volontär**

volontieren *itr. V.* work as a trainee **(bei** with); *s. auch* **Volontär**

Volt [vɔlt] **das; ~** *od.* **~[e]s, ~:** *(Physik, Elektrot.)* volt

Volte ['vɔltə] **die; ~, ~n a)** *(beim Kartenspiel)* sleight of hand; **die** *od.* **eine ~ schlagen** *(fig.)* do a volte-face *or* an about-turn; **b)** *(Reiten, Fechten)* volte

voltigieren [vɔlti'ʒi:rən] *itr. V.* perform acrobatics on horseback

Volt·meter das; ~s, ~ *(Elektrot.)* voltmeter

Volumen [vo'lu:mən] **das; ~s, ~:** volume

Volumen-: ~gewicht das *s.* **Volumgewicht; ~prozent das** *s.* **Volumprozent**

Volum·gewicht das weight per [unit] volume

voluminös [volumi'nø:s] *Adj.* voluminous; bulky ‹*tome*›

Volum·prozent das per cent by volume

vom [fɔm] *Präp. + Art.* **a) = von dem; b)** *(räumlich)* from the; **links/rechts ~ Eingang** to the left/right of the entrance; **~ Stuhl aufspringen** jump up out of one's chair; **c)** *(zeitlich)* **~ Morgen bis zum Abend** from morning till night; **~ ersten Januar an** [as] from the first of January; **d)** *(zur Angabe der Ursache)* **das kommt ~ Rauchen/Alkohol** that comes from smoking/drinking alcohol; **müde ~ Arbeiten/wund ~ Liegen** tired from working/sore from lying; **jmdn. ~ Sehen kennen** know sb. by sight

Vom·hundert·satz der percentage

von [fɔn] *Präp. mit Dat.* **a)** *(räumlich)* from; **nördlich/südlich ~ Mannheim** to the north/south of Mannheim; **rechts/links ~ mir** on my right/left; **~ hier an** *od. (ugs.)* **ab** from here on[ward]; **~ Mannheim aus** from Mannheim; **etw. ~ etw. [ab]wischen/[ab]brechen/[ab]reißen** wipe/break/tear sth. off sth.; *s. auch* **aus 2 c; her a;** [1]**vorn; b)** *(zeitlich)* from; **~jetzt an** *od. (ugs.)* **ab** from now on; **~ heute/morgen an** [as] from today/tomorrow; starting today/tomorrow; **~ Kindheit an** from *or* since childhood; **in der Nacht ~ Freitag auf** *od.* **zu Samstag** during Friday night *or* the night of Friday to Saturday; **das Brot ist ~ gestern** it's yesterday's bread; *s. auch* **her b; klein 1 b;** [1]**Mal; c)** *(anstelle eines Genitivs)* of; **ein Stück ~ dem Kuchen** a slice of the cake; **acht ~ hundert/zehn** eight out of a hundred/ten; **ein Teufel ~ einem Vorgesetzten** a devil of a boss *(coll.)*; **die Stimme ~ Caruso** *(ugs.)* Caruso's voice; **d)** *(zur Angabe des Urhebers, der Ursache, beim Passiv)* by; **der Roman ist ~ Fontane** the novel is by Fontane; **müde ~ der Arbeit sein** be tired from work[ing]; **etw. ~ seinem Taschengeld kaufen** buy sth. with one's pocket-money; **sie hat ein Kind ~ ihm** she has a child by him; *s. auch* **wegen 2; e)** *(zur Angabe von Eigenschaften)* of; **eine Fahrt ~ drei Stunden** a three-hour drive; **Kinder [im Alter] ~ vier Jahren** children aged four; **~ bester Qualität** of the best quality; **ein Mann/eine Frau ~ Charakter** a man/woman of character; **~ größter Bedeutung/Wichtigkeit sein** be of the utmost importance; **f)** *(bestehend aus)* of; **ein Ring ~ Gold** a ring of gold; **g)** *(als Adelsprädikat)* von; **Alexander ~ Humboldt** Alexander von Humboldt; **mit einer ~ verheiratet sein** *(ugs.)* be married to a woman with a title; **h)** *(in bezug auf)* **er ist ~ Beruf Lehrer** he is a teacher by profession; **klein ~ Statur sein** be small in stature; *s. auch* **her c; i)** *(über)* about; **~ diesen Dingen spricht man besser nicht** it's better not to speak of such things *s. auch* **Haus g; davon; wovon**

von·einander *Adv.* from each other *or* one another; **sich ~ trennen** separate *or* part from each other; **sie sind ~ enttäuscht** they are disappointed in each other *or* in one another; **sie halten viel ~:** they think highly of each other

vonnöten [fɔn'nø:tn̩] *Adj.* *in* **~ sein** be necessary

vonstatten [fɔn'ʃtatn̩] *Adv.* *in* **~ gehen** proceed; **der Umzug kann am 15. Juni ~ gehen** the removal can go ahead on 15 June

[1]**Vopo** ['fo:po] **der; ~s, ~s** *(ugs.) s.* **Volkspolizist**

[2]**Vopo die; ~** *(ugs.) s.* **Volkspolizei**

vor [fo:ɐ̯] **1.** *Präp. mit Dat.* **a)** *(räumlich)* in front of; *(weiter vorn)* ahead of; in front of; *(nicht ganz so weit wie)* before; *(außerhalb)* outside; **~ einem Hintergrund von ...:** against a background of ...; **zwei Schritte ~ jmdm. gehen** walk two paces ahead of *or* in front of sb.; **kurz/200 m ~ der Abzweigung** just/200 m. before the turn-off; **~ der Stadt/den Toren der Stadt** outside the town/the gates of the town; **etw. ~ sich haben** *(fig.)* have sth. before one; **das liegt noch ~ mir** *(fig.)* I still have that to come *or* have that ahead of me; **b)** *(zeitlich)* before; **~ Christus** before Christ; B C; **es ist fünf [Minuten] ~ sieben** it is five [minutes] to seven; **c)** *(bei Reihenfolge, Rangordnung)* before; **knapp ~ jmdm. siegen** win just ahead *or* in front of sb.; **d)** *(in Gegenwart von)* before; in front of; **etw. ~ Zeugen erklären** state sth. before *or* in the presence of witnesses; **sie tanzte ~ ausverkauftem Haus** she danced before *or* to a full house; **e)** *o. Art. (auf Grund von)* with; **~ Freude strahlen** beam with joy; **~ Kälte zittern** shiver with cold; **~ Hunger/Durst umkommen** die of hunger/thirst; **~ Arbeit/Schulden nicht mehr aus und ein wissen** not know which way to turn for work/debts; **f) ~ fünf Minuten/10 Jahren/Wochen** *usw.* five minutes/ten years/weeks ago; **heute/gestern/morgen ~ einer Woche** a week ago today/yesterday/tomorrow. **2.** *Präp. mit Akk.* in front of; **keinen Schritt ~ die Tür tun** *od.* **setzen** not set foot outside the door; **er fuhr bis ~ die Haustür** he drove right up to the front door; **~ sich hin** to oneself; **still ~ sich hin arbeiten** work away quietly; *s. auch* **davor; wovor. 3.** *Adv. (voran)* forward; **Freiwillige ~!** volunteers to the front!; **~ und zurück** backwards and forwards

vor·ab *Adv.* beforehand

Vorab·druck der; *Pl.* **Vorabdrucke a)** *o. Pl.* preprinting; **b)** *(gedruckter Text)* preprint

Vor·abend der evening before; *(fig.)* eve; **das war am ~:** that was the evening before

Vor·ahnung die premonition; presentiment; **dunkle/schlimme ~en** dark forebodings

vor·an [fo'ran] **1.** *Adv. (vorwärts)* forward[s]. **2.** *Präp. mit Dat., nachgestellt* ahead; first; **dem Festzug ~:** at the head of the parade; **allem ~:** first and foremost

voran-: ~|bringen *unr. tr. V.* make progress with ‹*work, project, etc.*›; **die Sache des Friedens ~bringen** advance *or* further the cause of peace; **jmdn./etw. ein gutes Stück ~bringen** bring sb./sth. a good step further; **~|gehen** *unr. itr. V.; mit sein* **a)** go first *or* ahead; **jmdm. ~gehen** go ahead of sb.; **[jmdm.] mit gutem Beispiel ~gehen** *(fig.)* set [sb.] a good example; **b)** *(Fortschritte machen)* make progress; **rasch/nur schleppend ~gehen** make rapid/only slow progress; **es geht mit der Arbeit/dem Schreiben nicht [so recht] ~:** the work/writing is not making [much] progress; **c)** *s.* **vorausgehen b; ~|kommen** *unr. itr. V.; mit sein* **a)** make headway; **gut ~kommen** make good headway *or* progress; **b)** *(Fortschritte machen)* make progress; **die Arbeit kommt gut/nicht ~:** the work is making good progress *or* coming along well/not making any progress; **beruflich ~kommen** get on in one's job

Vor·ankündigung die advance announcement; **ohne ~:** without any advance *or* prior notice

Vor·anmeldung die booking; *(für einen Kursus)* registration

voran-: ~|schreiten *unr. itr. V.; mit sein* *(geh.)* **a)** lead the way; **b)** *(fortschreiten)* progress; advance; **~|stellen** *tr. V.* place *or* put first; **dem Buch ist eine Einleitung ~gestellt** the book starts *or* begins with an introduction; **~|treiben** *unr. tr. V.* push ahead

Vor·anzeige die advance announcement

Vor·arbeit die preliminary work *no pl.*

vor|arbeiten 1. *itr. V.* put in some hours in advance; **einen Tag/zwei Tage ~:** work a day/two days in advance. **2.** *refl. V.* work one's way forward; **sich auf den zweiten Platz ~:** work one's way up to second place

Vor·arbeiter der foreman

vor·aus 1. [-'-] *Präp. mit Dat., nachgestellt* in front; **jmdm. weit ~ sein** be a long way in front *or* far ahead of sb.; **jmdm./seiner Zeit ~ sein** *(fig.)* be ahead of sb./one's time. **2.** *Adv.* **a) im ~** ['--] in advance; **b)** *(Seemannsspr.)* ahead; **Volldampf ~!** full steam ahead!

voraus-, Voraus-: ~|ahnen *tr. V.* have a presentiment of; **~ahnen, daß ...:** have a presentiment that ...; **~|berechnen** *tr. V.* *(auch fig.)* calculate in advance; **~|bestimmen** *tr. V.* determine in advance; **~|eilen** *itr. V.; mit sein* hurry on ahead **jmdm. ~eilen** hurry on ahead of sb.; **~|fahren** *unr. itr. V.; mit sein: s.* **vorfahren c; ~|gehen** *unr. itr. V.; mit sein* **a)** go [on] ahead; **ihm geht der Ruf ~, sehr streng zu sein** *(fig.)* he has the reputation of being very strict; **b)** *(zeitlich)* **einem Ereignis ~gehen** precede an event; **dem Entschluß gingen lange Überlegungen ~:** the decision was preceded by *or* followed lengthy deliberations; **~gegangene Mißerfolge** previous failures; **wie im ~gehenden bereits dargestellt worden ist** as has already been shown above; **~|haben** *unr. tr. V.* **jmdm./einer Sache etw. ~haben** have the advantage of sth. over sb./sth.; **er hat ihm [an diplomatischem Geschick] viel/nichts ~:** he has a great/no advantage over him [with regard to diplomatic skill]; **~|laufen** *unr. itr. V.; mit sein* run on ahead *or* in front; **~|planen 1.** *itr. V.* plan ahead; **2.** *tr. V.* **etw. ~planen** plan sth. in advance; **~sage die** *s.* **Vorhersage; ~|sagen** *tr. V.* predict; **jmdm. die Zukunft ~sagen** foretell *or* predict sb.'s future; **~|schauen** *itr. V.* look ahead; **~schauende Planung/Politik** foresighted planning/policy; **~|schicken** *tr. V.* **a)** send [on] ahead; **b)** *(einleitend sagen)* say first; **ich muß folgendes ~schicken** I must start *or* begin by saying the following; ~**sehbar** *Adj.* foreseeable; ~|**sehen** *unr. tr. V.* foresee; **das war [doch] ~zusehen/ließ sich nicht ~sehen** that was foreseeable/unforeseeable; ~|**setzen** *tr. V.* **a)** *(als gegeben ansehen)* assume; **etw. als bekannt ~setzen** assume sth. is known; **er setzte stillschweigend/als selbstverständlich ~, daß ...:** he took it for granted that ...; **Ihr Einverständnis ~setzend** assuming *or* provided that you agree; **~gesetzt, [daß] ...:** provided [that] ...; **b)** *(erfordern)* require ‹*skill, experience, etc.*›; presuppose ‹*good organization, planning, etc.*›; **~setzung die; ~, ~en a)** *(Annahme)* assumption; *(Prämisse)* premiss; **b)** *(Vorbedingung)* prerequisite; **unter der ~setzung, daß ...:** on condition *or* on the pre-condition that ...; **etw. zur ~setzung haben/machen** have sth. as/make sth. a pre-condition *or* prerequisite; **er hat die besten ~setzungen für den Job** he has the best qualifications for the job; **~sicht die** foresight; **aller ~sicht nach** in all probability; **in weiser ~sicht** *(scherzh.)* with great foresight; **~sichtlich 1.** *Adj.; nicht präd.* anticipated; expected; **2.** *adv.* probably; **der Abflug wird sich ~sichtlich verzögern** the departure is expected to be delayed; **~zahlung die** advance payment

Vor·bau der; *Pl.* **~ten a)** porch; **b)** *o. Pl. (salopp scherzh.: Busen)* [well-developed] bust

vor|bauen *itr. V.* make provision; **der kluge Mann baut vor** *(Spr.)* a wise man makes provision for the future; **um vorzubauen, habe ich gleich gesagt, daß ...:** to avoid any problems, I said straight away that ...

Vor·bedacht der *in* **mit** *od. (seltener)* **aus ~:** intentionally; deliberately

Vor·bedingung die [pre-]condition; **~en stellen** set pre-conditions

Vorbehalt ['fo:ɐ̯bəhalt] **der; ~[e]s, ~e** reservation; **etw. nur unter ~ tun** do sth. only with reservations; **unter dem ~, daß ...:** with the reservation that ...; **ohne ~:** unreservedly; without reservation

vor|behalten *unr. tr. V.* reserve; **sich** *(Dat.)* **etw. ~:** reserve oneself sth.; reserve sth. [for oneself]; **sich** *(Dat.)* **das Recht ~, etw. zu tun** reserve the right to do sth.; **„Änderungen ~"** 'subject to alterations'; **alle Rechte ~** *(Druckw.)* all rights reserved; **jmdm. ~ sein/bleiben** ‹*decision*› be left [up] to sb.; ‹*discovery, revision work, etc.*› be left to sb.; **die ersten Sitzreihen waren den Ehrengästen ~:** the first rows of seats were reserved for the guests of honour

vorbehaltlich *Präp. mit Gen. (Papierdt.)* subject to

vorbehalt·los 1. *Adj.* unreserved; unconditional. **2.** *adv.* unreservedly; without reservation[s]

vor·bei *Adv.* **a)** *(räumlich)* past; by; **der Wagen war schon [an uns] ~:** the car was already past [us] *or* had already gone past *or* by [us]; **an etw.** *(Dat.)* **~:** past sth.; **[wieder] ~!** missed [again]!; **b)** *(zeitlich)* past; over; *(beendet)* finished; over; **es ist acht Uhr ~** *(ugs.)* it is past *or* gone eight o'clock; **~ ist ~:** what's past is past; *s. auch* **aus 2 a**

vorbei-: ~|**bringen** *unr. tr. V. (ugs.)* drop off; drop round with; **kannst du mir das Buch heute abend ~bringen?** can you drop the book off at my place this evening?; ~|**dürfen** *unr. itr. V. (ugs.)* be allowed past *or* by; **an jmdm./etw. ~dürfen** be allowed past *or* by sb./sth.; **darf/dürfte ich mal bitte ~?** can/could I come *or* get past *or* by, please?; ~|**fahren 1.** *unr. itr. V.; mit sein* **a)** drive/ride past; pass; **an jmdm. ~fahren** drive/ride past *or* pass sb.; **b)** *(ugs.: einen kurzen Besuch machen)* **[bei jmdm./der Post] ~fahren** drop in *(coll.)* [at sb.'s/at the post office]; **2.** *tr. V. (ugs.)* **kannst du mich schnell beim Bahnhof ~fahren?** can you just run me to the station?; *(absetzen)* can you just drop me off at the station?; ~|**führen** *itr. V.* ‹*path, road, etc.*› go *or* run past; **an etw.** *(Dat.)* **~führen** go *or* run past sth.; **daran führt kein Weg ~** *(fig.)* there's no getting around it; ~|**gehen** *unr. itr. V.; mit sein* **a)** pass; go past; **an jmdm./etw. ~gehen** pass *or* go past sb./sth.; **der Schuß/Schlag ist [am Ziel] ~gegangen** the shot/blow missed [its mark *or* target]; **an der Wirklichkeit ~gehen** *(fig.)* miss the truth; **im Vorbeigehen** *(auch fig.)* in passing; **b)** *(ugs.: einen kurzen Besuch machen)* **[bei jmdm./der Post] ~gehen** drop in *(coll.)* [at sb.'s/at the post office]; **c)** *(vergehen)* pass; **keine Gelegenheit ~gehen lassen** not let an *or* let no opportunity slip *or* pass; **d)** *(Sport)* **an jmdm. ~gehen** pass *or* go past *or* overtake sb.; ~|**kommen** *unr. itr. V.; mit sein* **a)** pass; **an etw.** *(Dat.)* **~kommen** pass sth.; **b)** *(ugs.: einen kurzen Besuch machen);* **[bei jmdm.] ~kommen** drop in *(coll.)* [at sb.'s]; **c)** *(vorbeigehen, -fahren können)* get past *or* by; **daran kommt man nicht ~** *(fig.)* there's no getting around *or* away from that; ~|**können** *unr. itr. V. (ugs.)* be able to get past *or* by; ~|**lassen** *unr. tr. V. (ugs.)* let past *or* by; **jmdn. an etw.** *(Dat.)* **~lassen** let sb. past *or* by sth.; ~|**marschieren** *itr. V.; mit sein* march past; **an jmdm./etw. ~marschieren** march past sb./sth.; ~|**müssen** *unr. itr. V. (ugs.)* have to pass *or* go past; **an jmdm./etw. ~müssen** have to pass *or* go past sb./sth.; ~|**planen** *itr. V.* **an etw.** *(Dat.)* **~planen** plan without regard to sth.; ~|**reden** *itr. V.* **an etw.** *(Dat.)* **~reden** talk round sth. without getting to the point; **am Wesentlichen ~reden** miss the essential point; **aneinander ~reden** talk at cross purposes; ~|**schießen 1.** *unr. itr. V.* **a)** *(danebenschießen)* miss; **[am Ziel] ~schießen** miss [the target]; **b)** *mit sein (vorbeifahren, -fliegen)* ‹*car etc.*› shoot past; **an jmdm./etw. ~schießen** shoot past sb./sth.; **2.** *unr. tr. V.* **den Ball am Tor ~schießen** shoot wide of the goal; ~|**ziehen** *unr. itr. V.; mit sein* pass by; *(überholen)* pass; go past; overtake; **an jmdm./etw. ~ziehen** pass by sb./sth.; *(jmdn./etw. überholen)* pass *or* go past *or* overtake sb.

vor·belastet *Adj.* handicapped **(durch** by); **erblich ~ sein** have an inherited defect

Vor·bemerkung die preliminary remark

vor|bereiten *tr. V.* **a)** prepare; **jmdn./sich auf** *od.* **für etw. ~:** prepare sb./oneself for sth.; **sich [in Latein] nicht vorbereitet haben** not be prepared [in Latin]; **auf diese Reaktion war ich nicht vorbereitet!** I was unprepared for that reaction!; **b)** *(die Vorarbeiten machen für)* prepare for; **ein Fest/eine Reise ~:** prepare for *or* make preparations for a party/trip

Vor·bereitung die; ~, ~en preparation; **~en [für** *od.* **zu etw.] treffen** make preparations for sth.; **in ~ sein** be in preparation

Vor·besitzer der previous owner

Vor·besprechung die a) preliminary discussion[s *pl.*]; **b)** *(Rezension)* advance review

vor|bestellen *tr. V.* order in advance

Vor·bestellung die advance order

vor·bestimmt *Adj.* predestined

vor·bestraft *Adj. (Amtsspr.)* with a previous conviction/previous convictions *postpos., not pred.*; **[zweimal/mehrfach] ~ sein** have [two/several] previous convictions

Vor·bestrafte der/die; *adj. Dekl.* person with a previous conviction/previous convictions

vor|beten 1. *itr. V.* lead the prayer/prayers. **2.** *tr. V.* **a) jmdm. das Vaterunser** *usw.* **~:** say the Lord's Prayer *etc.* [aloud] to sb.; **b)** *(ugs.)* reel off ‹*list, text, explanation, etc.*›

Vorbeuge·haft die preventive custody

vor|beugen 1. *tr. V.* bend ‹*head, upper body*› forward; **sich ~:** lean *or* bend forward. **2.** *itr. V.* **einer Sache** *(Dat.) od.* **gegen etw. ~:** prevent sth.; **einer Gefahr ~:** avert a danger; **~de Maßnahmen** preventive measures; **Vorbeugen ist besser als Heilen** *(Spr.)* prevention is better than cure *(prov.)*

Vor·beugung die prevention **(gegen** of); **zur ~:** as a preventive

Vorbeugungs·maßnahme die preventive measure

Vor·bild das model; **jmdm. als ~ dienen** serve sb. as a model; **jmdm. ein gutes ~ sein** be a good example to sb.; set sb. a good example; **sich** *(Dat.)* **jmdn./etw. zum ~ nehmen** take sb. as a model *or* model oneself on sb./take sth. as a model

vor·bildlich 1. *Adj.* exemplary. **2.** *adv.* in an exemplary way *or* manner

Vor·bildung die; *o. Pl.* **die nötige/theoretische ~ besitzen** have the necessary knowledge and training/the theoretical background; **über eine mangelhafte ~ verfügen** have inadequate knowledge and training; have an inadequate background

vor|bohren *tr. V.* pre-drill

Vor·bote der harbinger

vor|bringen *unr. tr. V.* say; **eine Frage/Forderung/ein Anliegen ~:** ask a question/make a demand/express a desire; **Argumente ~:** present *or* state arguments; **Beweise ~:** produce evidence; **dagegen läßt sich viel ~:** there's much to be said against it

vor·christlich *Adj.* pre-Christian; **das dritte ~e Jahrhundert** the third century before Christ

Vor·dach das canopy

vor|datieren *tr. V.* **a)** postdate ‹*cheque, letter, etc.*›; **b)** *(zurückdatieren)* antedate

vor|dem *[od.* '--*] Adv.* **a)** *(geh.: zuvor)* before; **b)** *(veralt.: früher)* in [the] olden days

Vor·denker der *(Politikjargon)* guiding intellectual force

vorder... ['fɔrdɐ...] *Adj.; nicht präd.* front; **die ~en Reihen** the front rows; **die ~sten Reihen** the rows at the very front; **der Vordere Orient** the Middle East

vorder-, Vorder-: **~achse die** front axle; **~ansicht die** front view; **~asien (das)** the Middle East; the Near East; **~bein das** foreleg; **~gebäude das** front building; **~grund der** foreground; **im ~grund stehen** *(fig.)* be prominent *or* to the fore; **bei seiner Entscheidung standen diese Überlegungen im ~grund** *(fig.)* these considerations were uppermost in his mind when taking his decision; **etw. in den ~grund stellen** *od.* **rücken** *(fig.)* give priority to sth.; place special emphasis on sth.; **in den ~grund treten** *od.* **rücken** *(fig.)* come to the fore; **sich in den ~grund spielen** *od.* **schieben** *od.* **drängen** *(fig.)* push oneself forward; **~gründig** [~ɡrʏndɪç] **1.** *Adj.* superficial; **2.** *adv.* superficially; **~hand** *Adv.* for the time being; for the present; **~haus das** house facing the street/square *etc.*

Vorder·indien (das) the Indian Peninsula

vorder-, Vorder-: **~lader der** *(Waffenkunde)* muzzle-loader; **~lastig** *Adj.* bow-heavy ‹*ship*›; nose-heavy ‹*aircraft*›; **~lauf der** *(Jägerspr.)* foreleg; **~mann der;** *Pl.* **~männer** person in front; **ihr/sein ~mann** the person in front of her/him; **jmdn. auf ~mann bringen** *(ugs.)* lick sb. into shape; **den Garten/Haushalt auf ~mann bringen** *(ugs.)* get the garden/house ship-shape; **~pfote die** front paw; **~rad das** front wheel; **~rad·antrieb der** front-wheel drive; **~reifen der** front tyre; **~seite die** front; *(einer Münze, Medaille)* obverse; **~sitz der** front seat

vorderst... *s.* **vorder...**

Vorder-: **~steven der** *(Seemannsspr.)* stem; **~teil das** *od* **der** front [part]; **~zahn der** front tooth

vor|drängen *refl. V.* push [one's way] forward *or* to the front; *(fig.)* push oneself forward; **sich bis an etw.** *(Akk.)* **~:** push [one's way] forward to sth.; **sich an der Kasse/in der Schlange ~:** push to the front at the check-out/push to the front of the queue *or (Amer.)* line

vor|dringen *unr. itr. V.; mit sein* push forward; advance; **in den Weltraum ~:** push forward into space; **bis zu jmdm. ~** *(fig.)* reach sb.; get as far as sb.

vor·dringlich 1. *Adj.* **a)** priority *attrib.* ⟨*treatment*⟩; **eine ~e Angelegenheit** a matter of priority; **b)** *(dringlich)* urgent; **unser ~stes Anliegen ist es, ...:** our main *or* overriding concern is ... **2.** *adv.* **a)** as a matter of priority; **b)** as a matter of urgency

Vor·druck der; *Pl.* **Vordrucke** form

vor·ehelich *Adj.* pre-marital

vor·eilig 1. *Adj.* rash. **2.** *adv.* rashly; **~ den Schluß ziehen, daß ...:** jump to the conclusion that ...

vor·einander *Adv.* **a)** one in front of the other; **b)** *(einer dem anderen gegenüber)* opposite each other; face to face; **Geheimnisse ~ haben/Gefühle ~ verbergen** have secrets/hide feelings from each other; **Hochachtung/Furcht ~ haben** have great respect for each other/be afraid of each other

vor·eingenommen *Adj.* prejudiced; biased; **für/gegen jmdn. ~ sein** be prejudiced in sb.'s favour/against sb.; **jmdm. gegenüber ~ sein** be prejudiced towards sb.

Vor·eingenommenheit die; ~, ~en prejudice; bias; **politische ~:** political bias

vorenthalten[1] *unr. tr. V.* **jmdm. etw. ~:** withhold sth. from sb.; **jmdm. eine Nachricht ~:** keep *or* withhold news from sb.

Vor·entscheidung die preliminary decision; **mit diesem Tor war eine ~ gefallen** this goal decided the course of the match

vor·erst [*od.* -'-] *Adv.* for the present; for the time being

Vor·essen das *(schweiz.)* stew

vor|exerzieren *tr. V. (ugs.)* demonstrate

vorfabriziert *adj.* pre-fabricated; *(fig.)* ready-made ⟨*opinion, solution*⟩

Vorfahr [-faːɐ̯] **der; ~en** *od. selten* **~s, ~en, Vorfahre der; ~n, ~n** forefather; ancestor

vor|fahren *unr. itr. V.; mit sein* **a)** *(ankommen)* drive/ride up; **vor dem Hotel/Haus ~:** drive/ride up outside the hotel/house; **b)** *(weiter nach vorn fahren)* ⟨*person*⟩ drive *or* move forward; ⟨*car*⟩ move forward; **c)** *(vorausfahren)* drive *or* go on ahead

Vor·fahrt die; *o. Pl. (Verkehrsw.)* right of way; **„~ beachten/gewähren!"** 'give way'; **weil er die ~ nicht beachtete** because he failed to give way; **jmdm. die ~ nehmen** fail to give way to sb.

Vorfahrt[s]-: ~schild das *(Verkehrsw.)* right-of-way sign; **~straße die** main road; **~zeichen das** *(Verkehrsw.) s.* **~schild**

Vor·fall der a) incident; occurrence; **b)** *(Med.)* prolapse

vor|fallen *unr. itr. V.; mit sein* **a)** *(sich ereignen)* happen; occur; **ist etwas [Besonderes] vorgefallen?** has anything [special] happened?; **b)** *(nach vorn fallen)* fall forward

vor|feiern *tr., itr. V.* celebrate early *or* ahead of time

Vor·feld das a) *(eines Flughafens)* apron; **b)** *(Basketball)* front court; **c)** *(fig.)* **im ~:** in advance; **im ~ des Parteitages** in the run-up to the party conference

Vor·film der supporting film

vor|finden 1. *unr. tr. V.* find. **2.** *unr. refl. V.* be to be found

vor|flunkern *tr. V. (ugs.)* **jmdm. ~, daß ...:** spin sb. a yarn that ...; **sie flunkerte ihm irgend etwas vor** she told him some fib or other

Vor·form die early form

Vor·freude die anticipation; **voller ~ auf etw.** *(Akk.)* **sein** be full of [happy] anticipation of sth.

Vor·frühling der early spring

vor|fühlen *itr. V.* **bei jmdm. ~:** sound sb. out; **ich habe bei ihnen vorgefühlt, was ...:** I sounded them out about *or* as to what ...

vor|führen *tr. V.* **a)** bring forward; **jmdn. dem Richter ~:** bring sb. before the judge; **er wurde zur Vernehmung vorgeführt** he was brought for questioning; **b)** *(zeigen)* show; **wann führst du uns deinen Freund vor?** when are you going to introduce your boy-friend to us?; **c)** *(demonstrieren)* demonstrate; **jmdm. etw. ~:** demonstrate sth. to sb.; **d)** *(darbieten)* show ⟨*film, slides, etc.*⟩; present ⟨*circus act, programme*⟩; perform ⟨*play, trick, routine*⟩

Vorführ·gerät das *(Projektor)* projector

Vor·führung die a) bringing forward; **der Richter ordnete die ~ des Gefangenen an** the judge ordered the prisoner to be brought forward; **b)** *(das Zeigen)* showing; exhibiting; **c)** *(das Demonstrieren)* demonstration; **d)** *(das Darbieten) s.* **vorführen d:** showing; presentation; performance; **e)** *(Veranstaltung) s.* **vorführen d:** show; presentation; performance

Vorführ·wagen der demonstration car *or* model

Vor·gabe die a) *(Sport)* handicap; **b)** *(Richtlinie)* guideline

Vorgabe·zeit die *(Wirtsch.)* [target] time for the job/project *etc.*

Vor·gang der a) occurrence; event; **chemische/physikalische** *usw.* **Vorgänge** chemical/physical *etc.* processes; **b)** *(Amtsspr.)* file; **der ~ XY** the file on XY

Vorgänger [-gɛŋɐ] **der; ~s, ~, Vorgängerin die; ~, ~nen** *(auch fig.)* predecessor

Vor·garten der front garden

vor|gaukeln *tr. V.* **jmdm. ~, daß ...:** lead sb. to believe that ...; **jmdm. eine heile Welt ~:** lead sb. to believe in a perfect *or* an ideal world

vor|geben *unr. tr. V.* **a)** *(vortäuschen)* pretend; **b)** *(Sport)* **jmdm. eine Runde/50 m/15 Punkte ~:** give sb. a lap [start]/[a start of] 50 m/[a lead of] 15 points; **c)** *(im voraus festlegen)* set in advance; **vorgegebene Normen/Werte** pre-determined standards/pre-set values; **ein vorgegebenes Programm** a pre-set programme

Vor·gebirge das promontory

vor·geblich *Adj.; adv. s.* **angeblich**

vor·gedruckt *Adj.* pre-printed

vor·gefaßt *Adj.; nicht präd.* preconceived

vorgefertigt *Adj. s.* **vorfabriziert**

Vor·gefühl das presentiment; **im ~ solchen Glücks** in anticipation of such happiness

vor|gehen *unr. itr. V.; mit sein* **a)** *(ugs.: nach vorn gehen)* go forward; **an die Tafel/zum Altar ~:** go up to the blackboard/the altar; **b)** *(vorausgehen)* go on ahead; **jmdn. ~ lassen** let sb. go first; **c)** ⟨*clock*⟩ be fast; *s. auch* **nachgehen d; d)** *(einschreiten)* **gegen jmdn./etw. ~:** take action against sb./sth.; **gesetzlich gegen jmdn./etw. ~:** take legal action *or* proceedings against sb./sth.; **mit etw./mit Strenge gegen jmdn./etw. ~:** use sth. on/take strict measures against sb./sth.; **e)** *(verfahren)* proceed; **f)** *(sich abspielen)* happen; go on; **was geht hier vor?** what is happening *or* going on here?; **in jmdm. ~:** go on inside sb.; **mit ihm war eine Veränderung vorgegangen** there had been a change in him; a change had taken place in him; **g)** *(Vorrang haben)* have priority; come first; **allem anderen ~:** have priority *or* take precedence over everything else

Vor·gehen das; ~s action

vor·gelagert *Adj.* **die [der Küste] ~en Inseln** the offshore islands; the islands situated off the coast

vor·genannt *Adj.; nicht präd. (Amtsspr.)* aforementioned; aforesaid

Vor·geplänkel das preliminary skirmishing *no indef. art.*

Vor·gericht das *s.* **Vorspeise**

Vor·geschichte die a) *o. Pl.* prehistory *no art.;* **b)** *(Begebenheiten)* history

vor·geschichtlich *Adj.* prehistoric

Vor·geschmack der; *o. Pl.* foretaste

vor·geschritten *Adj. (geh.)* late ⟨*hour*⟩; advanced ⟨*age*⟩

Vor·gesetzte der/die; *adj. Dekl.* superior

Vor·gespräch das preliminary discussion

vor·gestern *Adv.* the day before yesterday; **~ mittag/~ abend/~ früh** the day before yesterday at midday/the evening before last/the morning of the day before yesterday; **er ist von ~** *(ugs.)* he is old-fashioned *or* behind the times; **Ansichten/Konventionen von ~** *(ugs.)* old-fashioned *or* outdated views/conventions

vor·gestrig *Adj.; nicht präd.* of the day before yesterday *postpos.*

vor|glühen *tr., itr. V. (Kfz-W.)* pre-heat

vor|greifen *unr. itr. V.* **a) jmdm. [bei** *od.* **in/mit etw.] ~:** anticipate sb. *or* jump in ahead of sb. [in/with sth.]; **einer Sache** *(Dat.)* **~:** anticipate sth.; **b)** *(in einer Erzählung)* jump ahead

Vor·griff der anticipation **(auf +** *Akk.* of); *(bei einer Erzählung)* jump *or* leap ahead **(auf +** *Akk.* to); **im ~ auf etw.** *(Akk.)* in anticipation of sth.

vor|haben *unr. tr. V.* intend; *(geplant haben)* plan; **er hat eine Reise vor** *od.* **er hat vor, eine Reise zu machen** he intends going on a journey/plans to go on a journey; **hast du heute abend etwas vor?** have you anything planned *or* any plans for this evening?; are you doing anything this evening?; **wenn du nichts Besseres vorhast** if you have nothing better to do; **er hat Großes mit seinem Sohn vor** he has great plans for his son

Vor·haben das; ~s, ~ *(Plan)* plan; *(Projekt)* project

Vor·halle die *(eines Tempels)* portico; *(Eingangshalle)* entrance hall; *(eines Theaters, Hotels)* foyer

vor|halten 1. *unr. tr. V.* **a)** hold up; **sich** *(Dat.)* **etw. ~:** hold sth. [up] in front of oneself; **jmdn. mit vorgehaltener Schußwaffe bedrohen** threaten sb. at gunpoint; *s. auch* **Hand f; b)** *(zum Vorwurf machen)* **jmdm. etw. ~:** reproach sb. for sth. **2.** *unr. itr. V. (ugs., auch fig.)* last

Vor·haltungen *Pl.* **jmdm. [wegen etw.] ~ machen** reproach sb. [for sth.]

Vor·hand die; *o. Pl.* **a)** *(Sport, bes. Tennis)* forehand; *s. auch* **Rückhand; b)** *(beim Pferd)* forehand; **c)** *(Kartenspiel)* lead; **in der ~ sein** have the lead

vorhanden [-'handn̩] *Adj.* existing; *(verfügbar)* available; **~ sein** exist *or* be in existence/be available; **ein Vorratsraum ist hier leider nicht ~:** unfortunately there is no store-room here; **von dieser Sorte ist noch genügend ~:** there's still plenty of this sort left

Vorhanden·sein das; ~s existence

Vor·hang der *(auch Theater)* curtain; **viele Vorhänge bekommen** *(Theater)* get a large number of curtain-calls; *s. auch* **eisern 1a**

Vorhänge·schloß das padlock

Vorhang-: ~stange die curtain-rod; **~stoff der** curtain material; curtaining

Vor·haut die foreskin; prepuce

vor|heizen *tr. V.* put the heating on in ⟨*room etc.*⟩ [to warm it up in advance]; **im vorgeheizten Ofen** in a pre-heated oven

vor·her [*od.* -'-] beforehand; *(davor)* before; **am Abend ~:** [on] the evening before; [on] the previous evening; **das ist drei Wochen ~ passiert** it happened three weeks earlier *or* before

vorher-, Vorher-: ~|bestimmen *tr. V.* determine in advance; predetermine; **alles ist vom Schicksal/von Gott ~bestimmt**

[1] *ich enthalte vor (od. seltener: vorenthalte), vorenthalten, vorzuenthalten*

everything is foreordained by fate/preordained by God; **~bestimmung die;** *o. Pl.* predetermination; *(Prädestination)* predestination; **~|gehen** *unr. itr. V.; mit sein* **in den ~gehenden Wochen** in the preceding weeks; in the weeks before; **wie im ~gehenden erläutert** as explained above

vorherig *[od. '---] Adj.; nicht präd.* prior ⟨*notice, announcement, warning*⟩; previous ⟨*discussion, agreement*⟩; **um ~e Bezahlung bitten** request payment in advance

Vor·herrschaft die; *o. Pl.* supremacy; dominance

vor|herrschen *itr. V.* predominate; **die ~de Meinung/der ~de Geschmack** the predominant *or* prevailing opinion/taste

vorher-, Vorher-: ~sage die prediction; *(des Wetters)* forecast; **~|sagen** *tr. V.* predict; forecast ⟨*weather*⟩; **~sehbar** *Adj. s.* **voraussehbar; ~|sehen** *unr. tr. V. s.* **voraussehen**

vor|heucheln *tr. V.* **[jmdm.] etw. ~:** feign sth. [to sb.]; **er heuchelte ihr Liebe vor** he pretended to love her

vor·hin [*od.* -'-] *Adv.* a short time *or* while ago; **sie ist ~ erst angekommen** she has only just arrived; **das ist der Junge von ~** *(ugs.)* that's the boy who we saw a short time ago *or* just now

vor·hinein *Adv. in* **im ~** *(bes. österr.)* in advance

Vor·hof der a) *(Anat.)* atrium; **b)** *(vorderer Hof)* forecourt; **für uns war es schon der ~ zur Seligkeit** *(fig.)* to us it was almost perfect bliss

Vor·hölle die; *o. Pl. (kath. Rel.)* limbo *no art.*

Vor·hut die; ~, **~en** advance guard; *(fig.)* vanguard

vorig *Adj.* **a)** *nicht präd.* last; **b)** *(schweiz.) (übrig)* left over *postpos.*; *(verfügbar)* spare; **etw. ~ lassen** leave sth. over; **~e Zeit haben** have some spare time

vor·industriell *Adj.* pre-industrial

Vor·jahr das previous year

vor·jährig *Adj.* of the previous year

vor|jammern *tr. V. (ugs.)* **jmdm. etw. ~:** moan *or* whine to sb. about sth.

Vor·kämpfer der pioneer; **ein ~ der Freiheit** a pioneering champion of freedom

vor|kauen *tr. V. (fig. ugs.)* spell out; **jmdm. etw. ~:** spell sth. out for sb.; spoon-feed sth. to sb.

Vorkaufs·recht das *(Rechtsw.)* right of first refusal

Vorkehr [-ke:ɐ̯] **die;** ~, **~en** *(schweiz.)* precaution

Vorkehrungen *Pl.* precautions; **~ [gegen etw.] treffen** take precautions [against sth.]

Vor·kenntnis die background knowledge

vor|knöpfen *tr. V. (ugs.)* **sich** *(Dat.)* **jmdn. [ordentlich/kräftig] ~:** give sb. a [proper/good] talking-to *(coll.)*

vor|kochen *tr., itr. V.* cook in advance

vor|kommen *unr. itr. V.; mit sein* **a)** *(sich ereignen)* happen; **daß mir so etwas nicht wieder vorkommt!** I hope I never experience anything like that again; **so etwas ist mir noch nie vorgekommen** nothing like that has ever happened to me before; **b)** *(vorhanden sein)* occur; **das Tier/die Pflanze kommt nur im Gebirge vor** the animal/plant is found only in the mountains; **in einer Erzählung ~** ⟨*character, figure*⟩ appear in a story; **c)** *(erscheinen)* seem; **das Lied kommt mir bekannt vor** I seem to know the song; **es kam mir [so] vor, als ob ...:** I felt *or* it seemed as if ...; **du kommst dir wohl schlau vor** I suppose you think you're clever; **das kommt dir nur so vor** it just seems like that to you; **ich komme mir überflüssig vor** I feel [as if I am] superfluous; **wie kommst du mir eigentlich vor?** *(ugs.)* who do you think you are?; **d)** *(ugs.: nach vorne kommen)* come forward; **an die Tafel ~:** come up to the blackboard; **e)** *(hervorkommen)* come out; **hinter/unter etw.** *(Dat.)* **~:** come out from behind/under sth.; **unter dem Schnee ~** ⟨*flower*⟩ come up out of the snow

Vorkommen das; **~s, ~ a)** *o. Pl. (das Auftreten)* occurrence; *(einer Krankheit)* incidence; **b)** *(Geol.: Lagerstätte)* deposit

Vorkommnis [-kɔmnɪs] **das;** **~ses, ~se** incident; occurence

vor|kosten *tr. V.* sample in advance

Vor·kriegszeit die pre-war period

vor|laden *unr. tr. V.* summon; summon, subpoena ⟨*witness*⟩

Vor·ladung die summons; **eine ~ vor Gericht** a summons to appear in court; **eine gerichtliche/polizeiliche ~:** a court/police summons; **die ~ eines Zeugen beantragen** apply for a witness to be summoned *or* subpoenaed

Vor·lage die a) *o. Pl.; s.* **vorlegen 1a:** presentation; showing; production; submission; tabling; introduction; **gegen ~ einer Sache** *(Gen.)* on production *or* presentation of sth.; **b)** *(Entwurf)* draft; *(Gesetzentwurf)* bill; **c)** *(Muster)* pattern; *(Modell)* model; **~n zum Stricken** knitting patterns; **etw. von einer ~ abschreiben** copy sth.; **etw. als ~ benutzen** use sth. as a model; **nach einer/ohne ~ zeichnen** draw from/without a model; **d)** *(Ballspiele, bes. Fußball)* forward pass; **eine ~ geben/schlagen** make a forward pass; lay the ball forward; **e)** *o. Pl. (Skisport)* vorlage; forward lean; **f)** *(Kaufmannsspr.)* advance; **[für etw.] in ~ treten** advance the money [for sth.]

Vor·land das; *o. Pl.* **a)** *(vor einem Gebirge)* foothills *pl.*; **b)** *(Deich~)* foreshore

vor|lassen *unr. tr. V.* **a)** *(ugs.: den Vortritt lassen)* **jmdn. ~:** let sb. go first *or* in front; **b)** *(empfangen)* admit; let in

vor|laufen *unr. itr. V.; mit sein (ugs.)* **a)** *(ugs.: nach vorn laufen)* run forward; **b)** *s.* **vorauslaufen**

Vor·läufer der precursor; forerunner

vor·läufig 1. *Adj.* temporary; provisional ⟨*diagnosis, settlement, result, successor*⟩; interim ⟨*order, agreement*⟩. **2.** *adv.* for the time being; for the present; **jmdn. ~ festnehmen** detain sb. temporarily; take sb. into temporary custody

vor·laut 1. *Adj.* forward. **2.** *adv.* forwardly

vor|leben *tr. V.* **jmdm. etw. ~:** set sb. an example of sth. [in the way one lives]

Vor·leben das; *o. Pl.* past life; past

Vorlege-: ~besteck das [set of] serving cutlery; **~gabel die** serving fork; **~löffel der** serving spoon

vor|legen 1. *tr. V.* **a)** present; show, produce ⟨*certificate, identity card, etc.*⟩; show ⟨*sample*⟩; submit ⟨*evidence*⟩; table, introduce ⟨*parliamentary bill*⟩; *(veröffentlichen)* publish; **jmdm./sich eine Frage ~:** pose sb./oneself a question; **c)** *(anbringen vor)* **eine Kette/einen Riegel ~:** put a chain on *or* across/a bolt across; **d)** *(geh.: aufgeben)* serve ⟨*food*⟩; **jmdm. etw. ~:** serve sb. with sth.; serve sth. to sb.; **e)** *(bes. Fußball)* **jmdm./sich den Ball ~:** lay the ball on for sb./tap the ball on; **f) ein scharfes Tempo ~:** set a fast pace. **2.** *refl. V.* lean forward

Vorleger der; **~s, ~** *(vor der Badewanne, dem Waschbecken)* mat; *(vor dem Bett)* rug

Vor·leistung die advance concession

vor|lesen *unr. tr., itr. V.* read aloud *or* out; read ⟨*story, poem, etc.*⟩ aloud; **jmdm. [etw.] ~:** read [sth.] to sb.; **lies schon vor!** read it out!; read out what it says!; **aus seinen Werken ~:** read from one's works

Vor·lesung die lecture; *(~sreihe)* series *or* course of lectures

Vorlesungs·verzeichnis das lecture timetable

vor·letzt... *Adj.; nicht präd.* last but one; next to last; penultimate ⟨*page, episode, etc.*⟩; **mein ~es Exemplar** my last copy but one; my next to last copy; **~es Mal** the time before last; **im ~en Jahr/Sommer** the year/summer before last; **seit ~er Woche** since the week before last

Vor·liebe die preference; [special] fondness *or* liking; **eine ~ für jmdn./etw. haben** be fond of sb./be fond of *or* partial to sth.; **etw. mit ~ tun** particularly like doing sth.

vorlieb|nehmen *unr. itr. V.* **mit jmdm./etw. ~:** put up with sb./sth.; *(sich mit jmdm./etw. begnügen)* make do with sb./sth.

vor|liegen *unr. itr. V.* **a) jmdm. ~** ⟨*application, complaint, plans, etc.*⟩ be with sb.; **das Beweismaterial liegt dem Gericht vor** the evidence is before *or* has been submitted to the court; **die Ergebnisse liegen uns noch nicht vor** we do not have the results yet; **die mir ~de Ausgabe/~den Ergebnisse** the edition/results in front of me; **im ~den Fall, in ~dem Fall** in the present case; **b)** *(bestehen)* be [present]; exist; ⟨*symptom*⟩ be present; ⟨*book*⟩ be available; **gegen ihn liegt nichts vor** there is nothing against him; **hier liegt ein Irrtum/Mißverständnis vor** there is a mistake/misunderstanding here; **ein Verschulden des Fahrers liegt nicht vor** the driver is/was not to blame; **c)** *südd., österr., schweiz. mit sein (ugs.: vorgelegt sein)* ⟨*chain, bolt, etc.*⟩ be on *or* across

vor|lügen *unr. tr. V. (ugs.)* **jmdm. etwas ~:** lie to sb.; **er hat uns vorgelogen, daß er die Prüfung bestanden habe** he lied to us, pretending he had passed the examination

vorm [fo:ɐ̯m] *Präp. + Art.* **a) = vor dem; b)** *(räumlich)* in front of the; **c)** *(zeitlich, bei Reihenfolge, Rangordnung)* before the; **~ Frühstück** before breakfast

vor|machen *tr. V. (ugs.)* **a)** *(vorführen)* **jmdm. etw. ~:** show sb. sth.; **ihm macht niemand was vor** there is no one better than him; no one can teach him anything; **b)** *(vortäuschen)* **jmdm. etwas ~:** kid *(coll.) or* fool sb.; **mir kannst du nichts ~:** you can't kid *(coll.) or* fool me; **wir wollen uns nichts ~:** let's not kid *(coll.) or* fool ourselves; **mach mir doch nichts ~:** don't try and kid me *(coll.)*; **der läßt sich von keinem was ~:** he's nobody's fool; *s. auch* **Dunst b; X**

Vor·macht die; *o. Pl.* supremacy *no art.*

Vormacht·stellung die; *o. Pl.* [position of] supremacy *no art.*; **sich** *(Dat.)* **eine ~ sichern** secure [a position of] supremacy

vormalig [-ma:lɪç] *Adj.; nicht präd.* former

vormals [-ma:ls] *Adv.* formerly

Vor·mann der; *Pl.* **Vormänner** foreman

Vor·marsch der *(auch fig.)* advance; **auf dem** *od.* **im ~ sein** ⟨*army*⟩ be advancing *or* on the advance; *(fig.)* ⟨*ideas, new development, etc.*⟩ be gaining ground

Vor·märz der; *o. Pl. (hist.) period in German history from 1815 until the March 1848 revolution*

vor|merken *tr. V.* make a note of; **ein Zimmer ~ lassen** reserve a room; **ich habe Sie für den Kurs/für Montag vorgemerkt** I've put you down for the course/for Monday

Vor·mieter der previous tenant

vor·mittag *Adv.* **heute/morgen/Freitag ~:** this/tomorrow/Friday morning

Vor·mittag der morning; **am [späten] ~:** [late] in the morning; **am frühen ~:** during the first part of the morning

vor·mittäglich *Adj.; nicht präd.* morning

vor·mittags *Adv.* in the morning

Vormittags·stunde die morning hour

Vor·monat der previous *or* preceding month

Vor·mund der; *Pl.* **Vormunde** *od.* **Vormünder** guardian; **einen ~ bestellen** appoint a guardian; **ich brauche keinen ~** *(fig.)* I don't need anyone telling me what to do

Vormundschaft die; ~, **~en** guardianship; **die ~ über** *od.* **für jmdn. übernehmen** become sb.'s guardian; **jmdn. unter jmds. ~ stellen** place sb. under sb.'s guardianship

Vormundschafts·gericht das *court dealing with matters of guardianship*

¹vorn ['fɔrn] *Adv.* at the front; **das Zimmer liegt nach ~ [raus]** *(ugs.)* the room faces the front; **~ am Haus/in der Schlange** at the front of the house/queue *or (Amer.)* line; **ganz ~ sitzen** sit right at the front; **das Kleid wird ~ zugeknöpft** the dress buttons up at the front *or* in front; **~ im Bild** in the foreground of the picture; **nach ~ schauen** look in front *or* to the front; **nach ~ gehen/kommen** go/come to the front; **~ im Buch** at the front of the book; **[gleich] da ~:** [just] over there; **weiter ~:** up ahead; a bit further on; **der Wind/Schlag kam von ~:** the wind/blow came from the front; **noch einmal von ~ anfangen** start afresh; start from the beginning again; **es geht wieder von ~ los** it is starting all over again; **von ~ bis hinten** *(ugs.)* from beginning to end; **das ist von ~ bis hinten gelogen** it's all lies from beginning to end

²vorn [fo:ɐ̯n] *Präp. + Art. (ugs.)* = **vor den**

Vor·name der first *or* Christian name

vorne *Adv. s.* ¹**vorn**

vornehm ['fo:ɐ̯ne:m] **1. Adj. a)** *(nobel)* noble ⟨*character, behaviour, gesture, etc.*⟩; **~e Gesinnung** noble-mindedness; **b)** *(der Oberschicht angehörend, kultiviert)* distinguished; **zur ~en Welt/Gesellschaft/zu den ~en Kreisen gehören** be part of high society; **~e Blässe/~es Getue** genteel pallor/behaviour; **c)** *(von adliger Herkunft)* noble; **d)** *(elegant)* exclusive ⟨*district, hotel, restaurant, resort*⟩; elegant ⟨*villa, clothes*⟩; elegant, distinguished ⟨*appearance*⟩; **e)** *nicht präd.* **~st...** *(geh.: vorrangig)* primary ⟨*duty, task, function, source of income, etc.*⟩. **2.** *adv.* **a)** *(nobel)* nobly; **b)** *(elegant)* elegantly

vor|nehmen *unr. tr. V.* **a) sich** *(Dat.)* **etw. ~:** plan sth.; **sich** *(Dat.)* **~, etw. zu tun** plan to do sth.; **sich** *(Dat.)* **~, mit dem Rauchen aufzuhören** resolve to give up smoking; **b)** *(ugs.: sich beschäftigen mit)* get busy with; **nimm dir ein Buch vor und lies!** pick up a book and read!; **c)** *(ugs.: zur Rede stellen)* **sich jmdn. ~:** give sb. a talking-to *(coll.)*; **d)** *(durchführen)* carry out, make ⟨*examination, search, test*⟩; perform ⟨*action, ceremony*⟩; make ⟨*correction, change, division, choice, selection*⟩; take ⟨*measurements*⟩

Vornehmheit die; ~: *s.* **vornehm 1a–d:** nobility; exclusivity; elegance; **seine ~ beeindruckte sie** she was impressed by his distinguished manner; **die ~ seiner Erscheinung** his distinguished appearance

vornehmlich *Adv. (geh.)* above all; primarily

Vornehm·tuerei [*od.* ----'-] **die; ~** *(abwertend)* affectation

vor|neigen *tr., refl. V.* lean forward; **in vorgeneigter Haltung** bent forward

vorne·weg *Adv. s.* **vorweg**

vorn-: ~herein *in* **von** *od. (schweiz.)* **zum** *od.* **im ~herein** from the start *or* beginning; **~über** *Adv.* forwards

vornüber|fallen *unr. itr. V.; mit sein* fall forwards

Vor·ort der suburb

Vorort·zug der suburban train

Vor·platz der forecourt

Vor·posten der *(Milit., auch fig.)* outpost

vor|preschen *itr. V.; mit sein (fig.)* rush ahead

Vor·programm das supporting programme

vor|programmieren *tr. V. (auch fig.)* preprogramme

vor|ragen *itr. V.* project; jut out

Vor·rang der; *o. Pl.* **a) [den] ~ [vor jmdm./etw.] haben** have priority *or* take precedence [over sb./sth.]; **jmdn. mit ~ bedienen** give sb. priority service; **jmdm./einer Sache den ~ geben** give sb./sth. priority; **b)** *(bes. österr.: Vorfahrt)* right of way

vorrangig [-raŋɪç] **1.** *Adj.* priority *attrib.* ⟨*treatment, task, objective*⟩; **~ sein** be a matter of priority *or* of prime importance; **von ~er Bedeutung** of prime *or* utmost importance; **jmds. ~es Anliegen/Ziel sein** be sb.'s primary concern/goal; **zu den ~sten Aufgaben gehören** be one of the prime *or* most important tasks. **2.** *adv.* **jmdn. ~ behandeln** give sb. priority treatment; **etw. ~ erledigen** deal with sth. as a matter of priority

Vorrang·stellung die position of prime importance; *(eines Landes)* supremacy

Vor·rat der supply, stock **(an** + *Dat.* of); **etw. auf ~ kaufen/herstellen** stock up with *or* on sth./produce stocks of sth.; **ein ~ an Witzen** *(fig.)* a stock of jokes; **solange der ~ reicht** while stocks last

vorrätig [-rɛ:tɪç] *Adj.* in stock *postpos.*; **etw. ~ haben** have sth. in stock; **etw. nicht ~ haben** be out of [stock of] sth.

Vorrats-: ~kammer die pantry; larder; **~keller der** cellar store-room; **~raum der** store-room

Vor·raum der anteroom

vor|rechnen *tr. V.* **jmdm. etw. ~:** work sth. out *or* calculate sth. for sb.; **jmdm. seine Fehler ~** *(fig.)* enumerate sb.'s mistakes

Vor·recht das privilege

Vor·rede die a) *(Vorwort)* preface; foreword; **b)** *(einleitende Worte)* introductory remarks *pl.*; **sich nicht lange bei** *od.* **mit der ~ aufhalten** not take long over the introductions

Vor·redner der previous speaker; **mein ~:** the previous speaker

vor|reiten *unr. itr. V.; mit sein* ride on ahead

Vor·reiter der: den ~ machen, ~ sein lead the way

Vor·richtung die device

vor|rücken 1. *tr. V.* move forward; advance ⟨*chess piece*⟩. **2.** *itr. V.; mit sein* move forward; *(Milit.)* advance; **mit dem Turm ~** *(Schach)* advance the rook; **auf den 5. Platz ~:** move up to fifth place; **zu vorgerückter Stunde** *(geh.)* at a late hour

Vor·ruhestand der early retirement

Vor·ruhestands·regelung die regulation enabling employees to take early retirement

Vor·runde die *(Sport)* preliminary *or* qualifying round

vors *Präp. + Art.* **a) = vor das; b)** in front of the; **jmdm. ~ Auto laufen** run in front of sb.'s car

vor|sagen *tr. V.* **a)** *auch itr.* **jmdm. [die Antwort] ~:** tell sb. the answer; *(flüsternd)* whisper the answer to sb.; **b)** *(aufsagen)* recite; **sich** *(Dat.)* **etw. ~:** recite sth. to oneself

Vor·saison die start of the season; early [part of the] season

Vor·satz der intention; **den ~ fassen, etw. zu tun** resolve to do sth.; make a resolution to do sth.; **den ~ haben, etw. zu tun** intend to do sth.; have the intention of doing sth.; **mit ~:** with intent; **der Weg zur Hölle ist mit guten Vorsätzen gepflastert** *(Spr.)* the road to hell is paved with good intentions *(prov.)*

Vorsatz·blatt das *(Buchw.)* endpaper

vorsätzlich [-zɛtslɪç] **1.** *Adj.* intentional; deliberate; wilful ⟨*murder, arson, etc.*⟩. **2.** *adv.* intentionally; deliberately

Vor·schau die preview

Vor·schein der *in* **etw. zum ~ bringen** reveal sth.; bring sth. to light; **zum ~ kommen** appear; *(entdeckt werden)* come to light; **sie griff in ihre Tasche und brachte eine Tüte zum ~:** she delved into her pocket and produced a bag; **wieder zum ~ kommen** reappear

vor|schieben 1. *unr. tr. V.* **a)** push ⟨*bolt*⟩ across; *s. auch* **Riegel a; b)** *(nach vorn schieben)* push forward; **den Kopf/die Schultern ~:** stick one's head forward/put one's shoulders forward; **die Unterlippe ~:** stick out one's bottom lip; **c)** *(für sich handeln lassen)* **jmdn. ~:** use sb. as a front man; **d)** *(als Vorwand nehmen)* use as a pretext *or* excuse; **die Verabredung war nur vorgeschoben** the appointment was only an excuse. **2.** *unr. refl. V.* push forward; ⟨*air mass, glacier*⟩ advance

vor|schießen *unr. tr. V.* **jmdm. Geld ~:** advance sb. money

vor|schlafen *unr. itr. V. (ugs.)* stock up on sleep

Vorschlag der suggestion; proposal; **das ist ein** *od.* **das nenn' ich einen ~!:** what a good *or (coll.)* great suggestion *or* idea!; **auf ~ von ...:** at the suggestion of ...; **ein ~ zur Güte** *(scherzh.)* a conciliatory proposal

vor|schlagen *unr. tr. V.* **[jmdm.] etw. ~:** suggest *or* propose sth. [to sb.]; **jmdn. für/als etw. ~:** propose sb. for/as sth.

Vorschlag·hammer der sledge-hammer

vor|schmecken *itr. V.* **der Knoblauch schmeckt vor** there is too strong a taste of garlic; it tastes too strongly of garlic; **das Gewürz soll nicht ~:** [the flavour of] the spice should not stand out

vor·schnell *Adj., adv. s.* **voreilig**

vor·schreiben *unr. tr. V.* stipulate, lay down, set ⟨*conditions*⟩; lay down ⟨*rules*⟩; prescribe ⟨*dose*⟩; **er wollte uns ~, was wir zu tun hätten** he wanted to tell us *or* dictate to us what to do; **ich lasse mir [von dir] nichts ~:** I won't be told what to do [by you]; I won't be dictated to [by you]; **das Gesetz schreibt vor, daß ...:** the law lays down *or* provides that ...; **wie es der Brauch vorschreibt** as custom dictates *or* demands; **die vorgeschriebene Geschwindigkeit/Zahl/Dosis** the prescribed speed/number/dose

Vor·schrift die instruction; order; *(gesetzliche od. amtliche Bestimmung)* regulation; **ich lasse mir von dir keine ~en machen** I won't be told what to do by you; I won't be dictated to by you; **das ist ~:** that's/those are the regulations; **das verstößt** *od.* **ist gegen die ~:** it's against the rules *or* regulations; **die Medizin nach ~ einnehmen** take the medicine as directed; **Dienst nach ~ machen** work to rule

vorschrifts·mäßig 1. *Adj.* correct; proper. **2.** *adv.* correctly; properly

Vor·schub der *in* **jmdm./einer Sache ~ leisten** encourage sb./encourage *or* promote *or* foster sth.

Vorschul·alter das pre-school age

Vor·schule die nursery school

Vorschul·erziehung die pre-school education

vor·schulisch *Adj.* pre-school

Vor·schuß der advance; **er bekam 500 Mark ~:** he received an advance of 500 marks

Vorschuß·lorbeeren *Pl.* premature praise *sing.*

vor|schützen *tr. V.* plead as an excuse; **wichtige Geschäfte/Krankheit ~:** pretend one has important business/feign illness; **Unwissenheit ~:** plead ignorance; *s. auch* **Müdigkeit**

vor|schwärmen *tr. V.* **jmdm. von jmdm./etw. ~:** rave about sb./sth. to sb. *(coll.)*

vor|schweben *itr. V.* **jmdm. schwebt etw./jmd. vor** sb. has sth./sb. in mind

vor|schwindeln *tr. V. (ugs.)* **jmdm. ~, daß ...:** kid sb. that ... *(coll.)*; **sie wollte den anderen nichts ~:** she didn't want to kid the others *(coll.)*

vor|sehen 1. *unr. tr. V.* **a)** *(planen)* plan; **wie vorgesehen** as planned; **die Eröffnung ist für den 21. März vorgesehen** the opening is scheduled *or* planned for 21 March; **b)** *(einsetzen, verwenden wollen)* **etw. für/als etw. ~:** intend sth. for/as sth.; **die Gelder sind für den Neubau einer Schule vorgesehen** the money is earmarked for the building of a school; **jmdn. für/als etw. ~:** designate sb.

for/as sth.; **c)** *(festlegen)* ‹*law, plan, contract, etc.*› provide for. **2.** *unr. refl. V. (sich in acht nehmen)* **sich [vor jmdm./etw.] ~:** be careful [of sb./sth.]; **sieh dich vor dem Hund vor** be careful of *or* mind the dog; **sieh dich vor, daß du nicht krank wirst** be careful *or* take care you don't become ill

Vọrsehung die; ~: Providence *no art.*

vọr|setzen *tr. V.* **a)** *(nach vorn setzen)* move forward; **den rechten/linken Fuß ~:** put one's right/left foot forward; **sich ~** *(ugs.)* come/go and sit at the front; **b)** *(zu essen, trinken geben)* **jmdm. etw. ~:** serve sb. sth.; *(fig.)* serve *or* dish sb. up sth.

Vọr·sicht die; *o. Pl.* care; *(bei Risiko, Gefahr)* caution; care; *(Umsicht)* circumspection; caution; **hier ist ~ geboten/nötig** caution/care is advisable/needed here; **alle ~ außer acht lassen** throw [all] caution to the winds; **zur ~:** as a precaution; to be on the safe side; **er ist mit ~ zu genießen** *(ugs.)* you should be wary of *or* careful with him; **was er sagt, ist mit ~ zu genießen** *(ugs.)* what he says should be taken with caution; **~!** be careful!; watch *or* look out!; **„~, Glas"** 'glass – handle with care'; **„~, bissiger Hund"** 'beware of the dog'; **~ an der Bahnsteigkante** stand back from the edge of the platform; **„~, Stufe!"** 'mind the step!'; **„~, Steinschlag"** 'danger, falling rocks'; **„~, frisch gestrichen"** 'wet paint'; **~ ist die Mutter der Porzellankiste** *(ugs.)*, **~ ist besser als Nachsicht** *(ugs. scherzh.)* better safe than sorry

vọrsichtig [-zɪçtɪç] **1.** *Adj.* careful; *(bei Risiko, Gefahr)* cautious; careful; *(umsichtig)* circumspect; cautious; guarded ‹*remark, hint, question, optimism*›; cautious, conservative ‹*estimate*›; **sei ~!** be careful!; take care! **2.** *adv.* carefully; with care; **~ optimistisch** guardedly *or* cautiously optimistic; **etw. ~ andeuten** hint at sth. cautiously; **~ geschätzt** at a conservative estimate

vọrsichts·halber *Adv.* as a precaution; to be on the safe side

Vọrsichts·maßnahme die precautionary measure; precaution

Vọr·silbe die [monosyllabic] prefix

vọr|singen 1. *unr. tr. V.* **[jmdm.] etw. ~:** sing sth. [to sb.]; **ich singe euch die erste Strophe vor** I'll sing you the first verse. **2.** *unr. itr. V.* **a) [jmdm.] ~:** sing [to sb.]; **wenn er ~ soll** when he has to sing in public *or* in front of people; **b)** *(zur Prüfung)* have *or* take a singing test; **bei der Oper ~:** audition for *or* have an audition with the opera company

vọr·sintflutlich *Adj. (ugs.)* antiquated

Vọr·sitz der chairmanship; **den ~ haben** *od.* **führen** be the chairman; be in the chair; *(im Gericht)* preside over the trial; **er hat** *od.* **führt bei der Tagung den ~:** he is chairing the conference; **den ~ übernehmen** *(eines Vereins)* take over the chairmanship *or* presidency; *(bei einer Tagung, Sitzung)* take the chair; **unter dem ~ von ...:** under the chairmanship of ...

vọr|sitzen *unr. itr. V.* **einer Versammlung/Kommission** *(Dat.)* **~:** chair a *or* preside over a meeting/commission

Vọrsitzende der/die; *adj. Dekl.* chair[person]; *(bes. Mann)* chairman; *(Frau auch)* chairwoman

Vọr·sorge die; *o. Pl.* precautions *pl.*; *(für den Todesfall, Krankheit, Alter)* provisions *pl.*; *(Vorbeugung)* prevention; **~ treffen** take precautions **(gegen** against)/make provisions **(für** for); **für den Fall einer Krankheit ~ treffen** make provisions in case of illness; **~ treffen, daß ...:** take precautions/make provisions so that ...

vọr|sorgen *itr. V.* **für etw. ~:** make provisions for sth.; provide for sth.

Vọrsorge·untersuchung die *(Med.)* medical check-up

vọrsorglich 1. *Adj.* precautionary ‹*measure, check-up, etc.*›. **2.** *adv.* as a precaution; to be on the safe side

Vọr·spann der *(Film, Ferns.)* opening credits *pl.*

Vọr·speise die starter; hors d'œuvre

vọr|spiegeln *tr. V.* **jmdm. ~, daß ...:** delude sb. into believing that ...; **er spiegelte ihnen eine Notlage vor** he deluded them into believing *or* led them to believe that he was in a plight; **Unwissenheit/Krankheit ~:** feign ignorance/illness

Vọr·spiegelung die: das ist [eine] ~ falscher Tatsachen these are falsehoods presented as if they were facts; **unter ~ falscher Tatsachen** under false pretences

Vọr·spiel das a) *(Theater)* prologue; *(Musik)* prelude; **b)** *(vorm Geschlechtsakt)* foreplay; **c)** *(als Prüfung)* practical examination; *(bei Bewerbungen)* audition

vọr|spielen 1. *tr. V.* **a) jmdm. ein Musikstück/eine Szene ~:** play a piece of music to *or* for sb./act out *or* perform a scene for *or* in front of sb.; **b)** *(vorspiegeln)* **jmdm. etw. ~:** feign sth. to sb.; **spiel uns doch nichts vor!** don't try and fool us!; **jmdm. Theater/eine Komödie ~:** put on an act for sb. **2.** *itr. V.* **a) jmdm. ~:** play to *or* for sb.; **einer Jury ~:** perform in front of a jury; **b)** *(bei einer Bewerbung)* audition, have an audition **(bei** for); **jmdn. ~ lassen** audition sb.

Vọr·sprache die *(österr.)* visit **(bei** to)

vọr|sprechen 1. *unr. tr. V.* **a)** *(zum Nachsprechen)* **jmdm. etw. ~:** pronounce *or* say sth. first for sb.; **einem Zeugen den Eid ~:** say the oath for the witness to repeat; **b)** *(zur Prüfung)* recite. **2.** *unr. itr. V.* **a)** *(zur Prüfung)* recite one's examination piece; *(bei Bewerbungen)* audition; **am Staatstheater ~:** audition for the State Theatre; **jmdn. ~ lassen** audition sb.; **b)** *(einen Besuch machen)* **bei jmdm. [in einer Angelegenheit] ~:** call on sb. about a matter; **bei** *od.* **auf einer Behörde ~:** call at an office

vọr·springen *unr. itr. V.; mit sein* **a)** *(ugs.)* **hinter einem Auto ~:** jump out from behind a car; **b)** *(weit hervorstehen)* jut out; project; **ein ~des Kinn** a prominent chin

Vọr·sprung der a) *(vorspringender Teil)* projection; *(Fels~)* ledge; **b)** *(räumlicher, zeitlicher Vorteil)* lead; **einen [knappen] ~ [vor jmdm.] haben** have a [slight] lead [over sb.]; be [slightly] ahead [of sb.]; **jmdm. einen ~ geben** give sb. a start; **jmdm. zehn Schritte/einen zehnminütigen ~ geben** give sb. ten paces'/ten minutes' start

Vọr·stadt die suburb; **in der ~ wohnen** live in the suburbs

vọr·städtisch *Adj.* suburban

Vọr·stand der a) *(leitendes Gremium) (einer Firma)* board [of directors]; *(eines Vereins, einer Gesellschaft)* executive committee; *(einer Partei)* executive; **im ~ sein** be on the board/executive committee/executive; **b)** *(Leiter)* chairman

Vọrstands·mitglied das *s.* **Vorstand a:** member of the board; board member; member of the executive committee; member of the executive

vọr|stehen *unr. itr. V.* **a)** *(hervorstehen)* ‹*house, roof, etc.*› project, jut out; ‹*teeth, chin*› stick out; ‹*cheek-bones*› be prominent; **~de Zähne/Augen** buck-teeth *or* projecting teeth/bulging eyes; **b)** *(geh.: leiten)* **einer Institution/dem Haushalt ~:** be the head of an institution/the household; **einem Geschäft/einer Abteilung ~:** be in charge of *or* run a business/department

vọrstehend *Adj.* above *attrib.* ‹*explanation, remarks, etc.*›; **im ~en** above; **das Vorstehende** the above

Vọrsteher der; ~s, ~: head; *(einer Schule)* headmaster; *(einer Gemeinde)* chairman; *(eines Klosters)* abbot

Vọrsteher·drüse die prostate [gland]

Vọrsteherin die; ~, ~nen head; *(einer Schule)* headmistress; *(eines Klosters)* abbess

Vọrsteh·hund der pointer; *(langhaarig)* setter

vọrstell·bar *Adj.* conceivable; imaginable; **es ist durchaus/[nur] schwer ~, daß ...:** it is quite/scarcely conceivable that ...

vọr|stellen 1. *tr. V.* **a)** *(nach vorn stellen)* put ‹*leg, foot, etc.*› out *or* forward; **die Uhr [um eine Stunde] ~:** put the clock forward [one hour]; **b)** *(bekannt machen mit; auch fig.)* introduce; **jmdn./sich jmdm. ~:** introduce sb./oneself to sb.; **c)** *(bei Bewerbung)* **sich ~:** come/go for [an] interview; **sich beim Personalleiter ~:** go for an interview with the personnel director; **d)** *(darstellen)* represent; **er stellt etwas vor** *(ugs.) (sieht gut aus)* he looks good; *(gilt als Persönlichkeit)* he is somebody; **e)** *(zur Untersuchung)* **sich dem Arzt ~:** go to see the doctor. **2.** *refl. V.* **a) sich** *(Dat.)* **etw. ~:** imagine sth.; **stell dir vor, wir würden gewinnen** imagine we won; **ja, stell dir vor!** just imagine!; **ich habe mir das Wochenende ganz anders vorgestellt** the weekend was not at all what I had imagined; **ich kann ihn mir gut als Lehrer ~:** I can easily imagine *or* see him as a teacher; **was haben Sie sich** *(Dat.)* **als Preis vorgestellt?** what price did you have in mind?; **man stelle sich** *(Dat.)* **bitte einmal vor, daß ...:** just imagine that ...; **das muß man sich** *(Dat.)* **[ein]mal ~!** just imagine *or* picture it!; **b) sich** *(Dat.)* **unter etw.** *(Dat.)* **etw. ~:** understand sth. by sth.; **darunter kann ich mir nichts ~:** it doesn't mean anything to me

vọrstellig ['fo:ɐ̯ʃtɛlɪç] *Adj.* *in* **bei jmdm./etw. ~ werden** *(Papierdt.)* approach sb./sth.

Vọr·stellung die a) *(Begriff)* idea; **jmdm. eine ~ von etw. geben** give sb. an idea of sth.; **sich** *(Dat.)* **von jmdm./etw. eine ~ machen** picture sb./sth.; **er macht sich** *(Dat.)* **keine ~ [davon], welche Mühe das kostet** he has no idea how much effort that costs; **das entspricht ganz/nicht meinen ~en** that is exactly/not what I had in mind; **b)** *o. Pl. (Phantasie)* imagination; **das geht über alle ~ hinaus** it is unimaginable; **c)** *(Aufführung)* performance; *(im Kino)* showing; **eine starke/schwache ~ geben** *(fig.)* perform well/badly; **d)** *(das Bekanntmachen)* introduction; **e)** *(Präsentation)* presentation; **f)** *(bei einer Bewerbung)* interview; **zur ~ kommen** come for [an] interview

Vọrstellungs-: ~gespräch das interview; **~kraft die;** *o. Pl.* [powers *pl.* of] imagination; **~vermögen das;** *o. Pl. s.* **~kraft**

Vọr·stopper der *(Fußball)* central defender

Vọr·stoß der advance; **einen ~ in ein Gebiet/in den Weltraum unternehmen** push forward *or* advance into an area/venture into space; **einen ~ bei der Geschäftsleitung unternehmen** *(fig.)* make an approach to management

vọr|stoßen *unr. itr. V.; mit sein* advance; push forward; **in den Weltraum ~:** venture into space

Vọr·strafe die *(Rechtsw.)* previous conviction

Vọrstrafen·register das *s.* **Strafregister**

vọr|strecken *tr. V.* **a)** stretch ‹*arm, hand*› out; stick out ‹*stomach*›; **den Kopf/Hals ~:** crane one's neck forward; **b)** *(auslegen)* advance ‹*money, sum*›

vọr|streichen *unr. tr. V.* **etw. ~:** give sth. an undercoat; undercoat sth.

Vọr·stufe die preliminary stage

vọr|stürmen *itr. V.; mit sein* rush *or* charge forward

Vọr·tag der day before; previous day; **am ~ der Prüfung** the day before *or* on the eve of the examination

vọr|tanzen 1. *tr. V.* **der Tanzlehrer tanzte ihnen den Foxtrott vor** the dancing-teacher showed them *or* demonstrated how to dance the foxtrot. **2.** *itr. V.* demonstrate one's dancing ability; **jmdm. ~:** dance in front of sb.

vor|tasten *refl. V. (auch fig.)* feel one's way forward

vor|täuschen *tr. V.* feign ⟨*interest, illness, etc.*⟩; simulate ⟨*reality etc.*⟩; fake ⟨*crime*⟩

Vor·täuschung die *s.* **vortäuschen:** feigning; simulation; faking; **unter ~ falscher Tatsachen** under false pretences

Vor·teil [*od.* 'fɔrtail] **der a)** advantage; **~e und Nachteile einer Sache gegeneinander abwägen** weigh up the pros and cons *or* the advantages and disadvantages of sth.; **einen ~ aus etw. ziehen** derive an *or* some advantage from sth.; benefit from sth.; **auf seinen [eigenen] ~ bedacht sein** have an eye to the main chance *or* to one's own interests; **jmdm. gegenüber im/sehr im ~ sein** have an/a great advantage over sb.; **[für jmdn.] von ~ sein** be advantageous [to sb.]; **sich zu seinem ~ verändern** change for the better; **b)** *(Fußball, Hockey, Rugby usw.)* advantage; **~ gelten lassen, auf ~ erkennen** ⟨*referee*⟩ play advantage; **c)** *(Tennis)* advantage; **~ Aufschläger** ad in

vorteilhaft 1. *Adj.* advantageous. **2.** *adv.* advantageously; **sich auf etw.** *(Akk.)* **~ auswirken** have a favourable *or* beneficial effect on sth.; **sich ~ kleiden** wear clothes that suit one

Vortrag [-tra:k] **der; ~[e]s, Vorträge** [-trɛ:gə] **a)** *(Rede)* talk; *(wissenschaftlich)* lecture; **einen ~ halten** give a talk/lecture; **b)** *(Darbietung)* presentation; performance; *(eines Gedichts)* recitation; rendering

vor|tragen *unr. tr. V.* **a)** *(darbieten)* perform ⟨*gymnastic routine etc.*⟩; sing ⟨*song*⟩; perform, play ⟨*piece of music*⟩; recite ⟨*poem*⟩; **b)** *(darlegen)* present ⟨*case, matter, request, demands*⟩; lodge, make ⟨*complaint*⟩; express ⟨*wish, desire*⟩; **ich habe ihm die Gründe für meinen Entschluß vorgetragen** I told him the reasons for my decision

Vortragende der/die; *adj. Dekl.* speaker; *(bei wissenschaftlichem Vortrag)* lecturer

Vortrags-: ~reihe die series of lectures/talks; **~reise die** lecture tour

vor·trefflich 1. *Adj.* excellent; splendid; superb ⟨*singer, player, swimmer, etc.*⟩; **~ schmecken** taste excellent *or* superb. **2.** *adv.* excellently; splendidly; ⟨*sing, play, swim, etc.*⟩ superbly; **sich ~ für etw. eignen** be perfectly *or* excellently suited for sth.

Vortrefflichkeit die; ~: excellence

vor|treiben *unr. tr. V.* drive ⟨*tunnel, shaft*⟩

vor|treten *unr. itr. V.; mit sein* step forward

Vor·tritt der; *o. Pl.* **a) jmdm. den ~ lassen** *(auch fig.)* let sb. go first; **Damen haben den ~:** ladies first; **b)** *(schweiz.) s.* **Vorfahrt**

Vortrupp der advance guard; *(fig.)* vanguard

vor|turnen *tr. V.* **[jmdm.] eine Übung ~:** perform a gymnastic exercise [in front of sb.]; *(zur Nachahmung)* demonstrate a gymnastic exercise [to sb.]

Vor·turner der demonstrator [gymnast]

vorüber *Adv.* **a)** *(zeitlich)* over; **~ sein** be over; ⟨*pain*⟩ be gone; ⟨*danger*⟩ be past; **die Gelegenheit ist noch nicht ~:** the opportunity has not yet passed *or* is still there; **das ist aus und ~** *(ugs.)* that is [all] over and done with; **b)** *(räumlich)* past; **an etw.** *(Dat.)* **~:** past sth.

vorüber|gehen *unr. itr. V.; mit sein* **a)** go *or* walk past; pass by; **an jmdm./etw. ~:** go past sb./sth.; pass sb./sth.; *(achtlos)* pass sb./sth. by; **im Vorübergehen** in passing; *(fig.: nebenbei)* in a trice; **b)** *(fig.)* **an jmdm./etw. ~:** ignore sb./sth.; **die Krise ist an uns** *(Dat.)* **vorübergegangen** the crisis passed us by *or* left us untouched; *s. auch* **Kelch a; spurlos 2; c)** *(vergehen)* pass; ⟨*pain*⟩ go; ⟨*storm*⟩ pass, blow over; **das geht vorüber** *(ugs.) (tröstend)* it'll pass; *(scherzh. iron.)* that won't last long; **eine Gelegenheit ~ lassen** let an opportunity slip; miss an opportunity

vorübergehend 1. *Adj.* temporary; passing ⟨*interest, infatuation*⟩; brief ⟨*illness, stay*⟩. **2.** *adv.* temporarily; *(auf kurze Zeit)* for a short time; briefly

Vor·urteil das bias; *(voreilige Schlußfolgerung)* prejudice (**gegen** against, towards); **gegen etw. ~e haben** *od. (geh.)* **hegen** be biased/prejudiced against *or* towards sth.

vorurteils-, Vorurteils-: ~frei, ~los 1. *Adj.* open-minded; **2.** *adv.* open-mindedly; **~losigkeit die; ~:** open-mindedness

Vor·väter *Pl.* forefathers

Vor·vergangenheit die *(Sprachw.)* pluperfect

Vor·verkauf der advance sale of tickets; advance booking; **Karten im ~ besorgen** buy tickets in advance; **im ~ kosten die Karten 20 Mark** the tickets cost 20 marks if bought in advance

Vorverkaufs·kasse die advance ticket-office; *(im Theater)* box-office

vor|verlegen *tr. V.* **a)** *(zeitlich)* bring forward (**auf** + *Akk.* to; **um** by); **b)** *(räumlich)* move forward; *(Milit.)* push forward ⟨*front, position*⟩

vor·veröffentlichen *tr. V.* arrange advance publication of; **vorveröffentlicht werden** appear in advance publication

Vor·verurteilung die condemnation in advance of trial

vor·vor·gestern *Adv. (ugs.)* three days ago; the day before the day before yesterday

vor|wagen *refl. V.* dare to go forward *or* *(Mil.)* advance; **sich zu weit ~:** venture too far forward; *(fig.)* stick one's neck out too far *(coll.)*

Vorwahl die a) *(Politik)* preliminary election; *(in den USA)* primary; **b)** *(Fernspr.)* dialling code

Vor·wahlkampf der *(Polit.)* advance election campaign

Vorwähl·nummer die *(Fernspr.)* dialling code

Vorwand der; ~[e]s, Vorwände pretext; *(Ausrede)* excuse; **etw. zum ~ nehmen** use sth. as a pretext/an excuse; **unter dem ~, daß ...:** giving as one's pretext that ...

vor|wärmen *tr. V.* warm ⟨*bed, room, teapot, etc.*⟩ beforehand; *(bes. Technik)* pre-heat ⟨*air, oven, etc.*⟩

vor|warnen *tr. V.* **jmdn. ~:** give sb. advance warning; warn sb. [in advance]; **vorgewarnt sein** be forewarned

Vor·warnung die [advance] warning; **~ geben** give an early *or* advance warning

vor·wärts *Adv.* forwards; *(weiter)* onwards; *(mit der Vorderseite voran)* facing forwards; **~ marsch!** *(Milit.)* forward, march!; **~!** *(weiter!)* come on!; **den Wagen ~ einparken** park the car nose first; **ein Schritt ~** *(auch fig.)* a step forwards; **mach mal [etwas] ~!** *(ugs.)* get a move on! *(coll.)*; **eine Rolle/ein Salto ~:** a forward roll/somersault; **das Buch kenne ich ~ und rückwärts** I know the book inside out

vorwärts-, Vorwärts-: ~|bringen *unr. tr. V.* advance ⟨*process, cause, plan*⟩; **jmdn. ~bringen** allow sb. to make progress; **~gang der** forward gear; **~|gehen** *unr. itr. V.; mit sein* make progress; **mit der Arbeit will es nicht ~gehen** the work just isn't getting anywhere; **~|kommen** *unr. itr. V.; mit sein* make progress; *(im Beruf, Leben)* get on; get ahead; **~strategie die** strategy of attack; **~verteidigung die** *(Milit.)* forward defence

Vor·wäsche die prewash

Vorwasch·gang der prewash programme

Vor·weg der *in* **im ~[e]** in anticipation

vor·weg *Adv.* **a)** *(vorher)* beforehand; **um es ~ zu sagen ...:** let me say right away ...; **b)** *(voraus)* in front; ahead; **~ marschieren** march at the head of the column; **c)** *(vor allem)* above all

Vorwegnahme die; ~: anticipation

vorweg|nehmen *unr. tr. V.* anticipate; **um das Ergebnis vorwegzunehmen, ...** to come straight to the result ...

Vor·wehe die *(Med.)* early contraction

vor·weihnachtlich 1. *Adj.* pre-Christmas. **2.** *adv.* **~ gestimmt** in a pre-Christmas mood; **~ dekoriert** adorned with Christmas decorations

Vor·weihnachtszeit die pre-Christmas period

vor|weisen *unr. tr. V.* produce; **~ können, vorzuweisen haben** *(fig.)* possess ⟨*knowledge, experience, etc.*⟩

vor|werfen *unr. tr. V.* **a)** *(zum Vorwurf machen)* **jmdm. etw. ~:** reproach sb. with sth.; *(beschuldigen)* accuse sb. of sth.; **jmdm. ~, etw. getan zu haben** reproach sb. with *or* accuse sb. of doing *or* having done sth.; **jmdm. Parteilichkeit/Rücksichtslosigkeit ~:** accuse sb. of being biased/careless; **ich habe mir nichts vorzuwerfen** I've nothing to reproach myself for; **sie haben sich** *(Dat.)* **[gegenseitig] nichts vorzuwerfen** one is as bad as the other; **b)** *(hinwerfen)* **etw. den Tieren [zum Fraß] ~:** throw sth. to the animals [as food]; **c)** *(nach vorn werfen)* throw ⟨*head, ball, etc.*⟩ forward

Vor·werk das a) *(veralt.: eines Guts)* outlying farm; **b)** *(hist.: einer Festung)* outworks *pl.*

vor|wiegen *unr. itr. V.* predominate

vor·wiegend *Adv.* mainly

Vor·wissen das previous *or* existing knowledge; *(über einen bestimmten Sachverhalt)* foreknowledge; prior knowledge

Vor·witz der; *o. Pl.* bumptiousness; *(eines Kindes)* pertness; *(Anmaßung)* presumption; *(Neugier)* excessive curiosity

vor·witzig 1. *Adj.* bumptious; pert ⟨*child*⟩; *(anmaßend)* presumptuous ⟨*speech etc.*⟩; *(neugierig)* curious. **2.** *adv. (anmaßend)* presumptuously

vor|wölben 1. *tr. V.* push out ⟨*stomach etc.*⟩. **2.** *refl. V.* bulge; ⟨*curtain, sail*⟩ billow [out]; **vorgewölbt** puffed-out ⟨*chest*⟩; pouting ⟨*lips*⟩

Vor·wort das; *Pl.* **~e** foreword; preface

Vor·wurf der reproach; *(Beschuldigung)* accusation; **jmdm. etw. zum ~ machen** reproach sb. with sth.; **jmdm. [wegen etw.] einen ~/Vorwürfe machen** reproach sb. [for sth.]; **sich** *(Dat.)* **[wegen etw.] [bittere] Vorwürfe machen** reproach *or* blame oneself [bitterly] [for sth.]; **..., sagte er mit leisem ~ [in der Stimme] ...,** he said in a tone of gentle reproach

vorwurfs·voll 1. reproachful. **2.** *adv.* reproachfully

vor|zählen *tr. V.* **[jmdm.] Geld** *usw.* **~:** count out money *etc.* for sb.

Vor·zeichen das a) *(Omen)* omen; **b)** *(Math.)* [algebraic] sign; **unter anderen/mit veränderten ~** *(fig.)* under different/changed conditions; **c)** *(Musik)* sharp/flat [sign]; *(für Tonart)* key signature

vor|zeichnen *tr. V.* **a)** make a preparatory sketch for ⟨*picture etc.*⟩; **b)** *(zur Nachahmung)* **jmdm. etw ~:** draw sth. for sb. to copy; **c)** *(im voraus festlegen)* lay down, set out ⟨*policy etc.*⟩; *(vorschreiben)* prescribe ⟨*path*⟩

vorzeigbar *Adj.* presentable

vor|zeigen *tr. V.* produce, show ⟨*passport, ticket, etc.*⟩; show ⟨*hands, finger-nails*⟩

Vor·zeit die prehistory; **in grauer ~:** in the dim and distant past

vorzeitig 1. *Adj.* premature ⟨*birth, death, ageing*⟩; early ⟨*retirement*⟩. **2.** prematurely; **~ pensioniert werden** be retired early

Vorzeitigkeit die; ~ *(Sprachw.)* anteriority

vor·zeitlich *Adj.* prehistoric
Vor·zensur die a) preliminary censorship; **b)** *(Schulw.)* classwork mark *(to be combined with examination marks in deciding the final grading)*
vor|ziehen *unr. tr. V.* **a)** *(lieber mögen)* prefer; *(bevorzugen, besser behandeln)* favour, give preference to ⟨*person*⟩; **etw. einer Sache** *(Dat.)* **~:** prefer sth. to sth.; **ich ziehe ihn seinem Bruder vor** I prefer him to *or* like him better than his brother; **das jüngste Kind wird oft [den anderen] vorgezogen** the youngest child is often given preference [over the others]; **b)** *(zuziehen)* draw ⟨*curtain*⟩; **c)** *(vorverlegen)* bring forward ⟨*date*⟩ **(um** by); **der Arzt hat mich vorgezogen** *(ugs.)* the doctor gave me priority; **vorgezogene Wahlen** early elections; **d)** *(nach vorn ziehen)* pull forward; *(Milit.)* move ⟨*troops*⟩ forward
Vor·zimmer das a) outer office; anteroom; **b)** *(österr.: Diele)* hall
Vorzimmer·dame die receptionist
Vor·zug der a) *o. Pl.* preference **(gegenüber** over); **jmdm./einer Sache den ~ geben** prefer sb./sth.; *(Vorrang)* give precedence to sb./sth.; **den ~ haben** be preferred/take precedence; **b)** *(gute Eigenschaft)* good quality; merit; *(Vorteil)* advantage; **c)** *(österr. Schulw.: Auszeichnung)* distinction; **d)** *(Vorrecht, Vergünstigung)* privilege
vorzüglich [fo:ɐ̯'tsy:klɪç] **1.** *Adj.* excellent; first-rate; *(in Briefen)* **mit ~er Hochachtung** *(veralt.)* yours faithfully; your obedient servant *(dated)*; **~ schmecken** taste excellent. **2.** *adv.* excellently; **~ speisen** have an excellent meal
Vorzüglichkeit die; ~, ~en excellence
vorzugs-, Vorzugs-: ~aktie die *(Wirtsch.)* preference share; **~milch die** best quality milk; **~weise** *Adv. (hauptsächlich)* primarily; *(besonders)* especially; particularly; *(am liebsten)* preferably
Vota, Voten *s.* **Votum**
votieren [vo'ti:rən] *itr. V. (geh.)* vote
Votiv·bild das votive picture
Votum ['vo:tʊm] **das; ~s, Vota** *od.* **Voten a)** vote; **b)** *(geh.: Urteil)* judgment
Voyeur [voa'jø:ɐ̯] **der; ~s, ~e** voyeur
VP *Abk. (DDR)* **Volkspolizei**
VR *Abk.* **Volksrepublik**
vulgär [vʊl'gɛ:ɐ̯] **1.** *Adj.* vulgar. **2.** *adv.* in a vulgar way; **er drückt sich sehr ~ aus** he uses very vulgar language
Vulgarität [vʊlgari'tɛ:t] **die; ~, ~en** vulgarity
Vulgär·latein das vulgar Latin
Vulkan [vʊl'ka:n] **der; ~s, ~e** volcano; **wie auf einem ~ leben** be sitting on a powder-keg; *s. auch* **Tanz a**
Vulkan·ausbruch der volcanic eruption
vulkanisch *Adj.* volcanic
Vulkanisier·anstalt die *(veralt.)* vulcanizing plant
vulkanisieren *tr. V.* vulcanize
Vulkanismus der; ~: volcanism *no art.*
Vulva ['vʊlva] **die; ~, Vulven** vulva
v. u. Z. *Abk.* **vor unserer Zeit[rechnung]** BC

W

w, W [ve:] **das; ~s, ~:** w, W
W *Abk.* **a)** **West, Westen** W.; **b)** **Watt** W.
WAA *Abk.* **Wiederaufbereitungsanlage**
Waadt [va(:)t] **die; ~, Waadt·land das** Vaud *no art.*
Waage ['va:gə] **die; ~, ~n** [pair *sing.* of] scales *pl.*; *(Gold~, Apotheker~ usw.)* balance; *(Brücken~)* weighbridge; **etw. mit der ~ wiegen** weigh sth. on the scales; **er bringt 80 kg auf die ~** *(ugs.)* he tips the scales at 80 kilos; **sich** *(Dat.) od.* **einander die ~ halten** balance out; balance one another; *s. auch* **Zünglein b**; **b)** *(Astrol., Astron.)* **[die] ~:** Libra; **er ist [eine] ~:** he is a Libra *or* Libran
waage-, Waage-: ~balken der balance *or* scale beam; **~recht 1.** *Adj.* horizontal; **2.** *adv.* horizontally; **~rechte die;** *adj. Dekl.* **a)** *(Linie)* horizontal line; horizontal; **b)** *o. Pl. (Lage)* horizontal position; **in der ~n** horizontal; level; *(flach liegend)* flat
waag·recht *s.* **waagerecht**
Waag·schale die scale pan; **etw. in die ~schale werfen** *(fig.)* bring sth. to bear
wabb[e]lig ['vab(ə)lɪç] *Adj. (ugs.)* wobbly; flabby ⟨*muscles, flesh*⟩
Wabe ['va:bə] **die; ~, ~n** honeycomb
Waben·honig der comb honey
wabern *itr. V. (geh.)* **a)** ⟨*smoke, mist, cloud*⟩ swirl, drift; ⟨*steam*⟩ billow; *(fig.)* fluctuate; **b)** *(flackern, lodern)* ⟨*flames etc.*⟩ flicker
wach [vax] **1.** *Adj.* **a)** awake; **in ~em** *od.* **im ~en Zustand** in a state of wakefulness; **jmdn. ~ machen** wake sb. up; **jmdn. ~ küssen** wake sb. with a kiss; **sich ~ halten** stay awake; **er wurde früh ~:** he woke up early; **b)** *(aufmerksam, rege)* alert ⟨*mind, eyes, etc.*⟩; attentive ⟨*audience*⟩; lively, keen ⟨*interest*⟩; **mit ~em Verstand** with an alert *or* lively mind. **2.** *adv.* alertly; attentively
Wach-: ~ablösung die changing of the guard/watch; **eine politische ~ablösung** *(fig.)* a change of political leadership; **~boot das** patrol boat; **~dienst der** *(Milit.)* guard *or* sentry duty; *(Seew.)* watch [duty]; **~dienst haben** *(Milit.)* be on guard *or* sentry duty; *(Seew.)* be on watch; have the watch
Wache ['vaxə] **die; ~, ~n a)** *(Wachdienst) (Milit.)* guard *or* sentry duty; *(Seew.)* watch [duty]; *(Seew.: Zeitabschnitt)* watch; **~ haben** *od.* **halten** *(Milit.)* be on guard *or* sentry duty; *(Seew.)* be on watch; have the watch; **~ schieben** *(ugs.)* do sentry duty; **~ gehen** *(Seemannsspr.)* do watch duty; **~ stehen** *(Milit.)* stand on guard; *(Ausschau halten)* keep look-out; **b)** *(Wächter)* guard; *(Milit.: Posten)* sentry; **eine ~ aufstellen** post a guard/sentry; **c)** *(Mannschaft) (Milit.)* guard; *(Seew.)* watch; **d)** *(Wachlokal)* guardroom; *(Gebäude)* guardhouse; *(Polizei~)* police station
wachen *itr. V.* **a)** *(geh.: wach sein)* be awake; **b)** *(um jmdn. zu betreuen)* **bei jmdm. ~:** stay up at sb.'s bedside; sit up with sb.; **c) über etw.** *(Akk.)* **~:** watch over *or* keep an eye on sth.; *(überwachen)* supervise sth.; **er wachte darüber, daß ...:** he watched carefully to ensure that ...
wach-, Wach-: ~habend *Adj.* **~habender Offizier** *(Milit.)* duty officer; *(Seew.)* officer of the watch; **~habende der;** *adj. Dekl. (Milit.)* person on guard; guard; *(Seew.)* watch; **~|halten** *unr. tr. V.* keep ⟨*interest, memory, etc.*⟩ alive
Wachheit die; ~: alertness; *(Scharfsinn)* acuity
Wach-: ~hund der guard-dog; watch-dog; **~lokal das** *(Milit.)* guardroom; **~mann der;** *Pl.* **~männer** *od.* **~leute a)** watchman; **b)** *(österr.: Polizist)* policeman; **~mannschaft die** *(Milit.)* guard detachment
Wacholder [va'xɔldɐ] **der; ~s, ~ a)** juniper; **b)** *(Schnaps) spirit from juniper berries;* ≈ gin
Wacholder-: ~beere die juniper berry; **~schnaps der** *s.* **Wacholder b**
wach-, Wach-: ~posten der *(Milit.)* guard; sentry; **~|rufen** *unr. tr. V.* awaken, rouse ⟨*enthusiasm, ambition, etc.*⟩; evoke, bring back ⟨*memory, past*⟩; **~|rütteln** *tr. V.* rouse *or* shake ⟨*person*⟩ out of his/her apathy; stir ⟨*conscience*⟩
Wachs [vaks] **das; ~es, ~e** wax; **er wurde weich wie ~:** he became really amenable; **~ in jmds. Hand** *od.* **Händen sein** *(fig.)* be like wax in sb.'s hands
Wachs·abdruck der wax impression
wachsam ['vaxza:m] **1.** *Adj.* watchful; vigilant; **sei ~!** be on your guard!. **2.** *adv.* vigilantly
Wachsamkeit die; ~: vigilance
wachs-, Wachs-: ~bild das wax relief; **~bohne die** wax bean
[1]wachsen *unr. itr. V.; mit sein* **a)** grow; ⟨*shadow*⟩ lengthen; ⟨*building*⟩ rise; **sich** *(Dat.)* **einen Bart ~ lassen** grow a beard; **sich** *(Dat.)* **die Haare/die Fingernägel ~ lassen** let one's hair/finger-nails grow long; **ein schlank gewachsener Mann** a slimly-built man; **er ist mit** *od.* **an seiner Verantwortung gewachsen** *(fig.)* he has grown with his responsibilities; **b)** *(fig.: allmählich entstehen)* evolve [naturally]; **eine gewachsene Stadt** a city which has evolved naturally; **eine gewachsene Ordnung** an organic order; **c)** *(fig.: größer werden)* grow; ⟨*wealth, danger, etc.*⟩ grow, increase; ⟨*flood, tide*⟩ rise; ⟨*tension, excitement, anger, astonishment*⟩ grow, mount
[2]wachsen *tr. V.* wax; *(polieren)* wax-polish
wächsern ['vɛksɐn] *Adj. (geh.: bleich)* waxen
Wachs-: ~figur die waxwork; wax figure; **~figuren·kabinett das** waxworks *sing. or pl.*; waxworks museum; **wir waren im ~figurenkabinett** we went to see the waxworks; **~kerze die** wax candle; **~malerei die** encaustic; **~mal·kreide die** wax crayon
Wach·soldat der a) sentry; **b)** *(eines Garderegiments)* Guard
Wachspapier das waxed paper
wächst [vɛkst] *2. u. 3. Pers. Sg. Präsens v.* **wachsen**
Wachs·tafel die wax tablet
Wach·stube die a) *(Milit.)* guardroom; **b)** *(Polizeiwache)* duty room
Wachs·tuch das a) *Pl.* **~tuche** *(Material)* oilcloth; **b)** *Pl.* **~tücher** oilcloth tablecloth
Wachstum ['vakstu:m] **das; ~s** growth; **im ~ zurückgeblieben** stunted ⟨*tree etc.*⟩; underdeveloped ⟨*person*⟩
wachstums-, Wachstums-: ~fördernd *Adj.* promoting growth *postpos.*; **~fördernd wirken** promote growth; **~hemmend** *Adj.* inhibiting growth *postpos.*; **~hemmend wirken** inhibit growth; **~hormon das** growth hormone; **~rate die** *(bes. Wirtsch.)* growth rate; **~störung die** growth disorder
wachs·weich 1. *Adj.* **a)** as soft as butter *postpos.*; **b)** *(fig.: ängstlich, gefügig)* [weak and] submissive
Wacht [vaxt] **die; ~, ~en** *(geh.)* guard *or* sentry duty; **~ haben** *od.* **halten** be on guard *or* sentry duty

Wächte ['vɛçtə] **die; ~, ~n** [snow] cornice
Wachtel ['vaxtl̩] **die; ~, ~n** quail
Wächter ['vɛçtɐ] **der; ~s, ~:** guard; *(Leib~)* bodyguard; *(Nacht~, Turm~)* watchman; *(Park~)* [park-]keeper; *(fig.)* guardian
Wacht-: ~meister der a) *(Dienstgrad der Polizei)* constable *(Brit.);* patrolman *(Amer.);* **b)** *(ugs.: Polizist)* policeman; *(als Anrede)* **Herr ~meister** officer; **c)** *(Milit. hist.)* sergeant; **~posten der** *s.* **Wachposten**
Wach·traum der day-dream; waking dream
Wach[t]·turm der watch-tower
Wach- und Schließgesellschaft die property security company
Wach-: ~zimmer das *(österr.).* [police] duty room; **~zustand der** waking state
wackelig 1. *Adj.* **a)** *(nicht stabil)* wobbly ‹*chair, table, etc.*›; loose ‹*tooth*›; shaky, rickety ‹*structure*›; rickety ‹*car, furniture*›; **b)** *(ugs.: kraftlos, schwach)* frail ‹*person*›; frail, doddery ‹*old person*›; **~ auf den Beinen sein** be a bit shaky on one's feet; **c)** *(fig. ugs.: gefährdet, bedroht)* dodgy *(Brit. coll.)* ‹*business*›; insecure, shaky ‹*job*›; **er steht in der Schule/in Latein ziemlich ~:** things are dodgy for him at school *(Brit. coll.)*/his Latin is somewhat shaky. **2.** *adv.* **~ stehen** be wobbly; *(nicht festgefügt sein)* be shaky/ rickety
Wackel·kontakt der *(Elektrot.)* loose connection
wackeln ['vakl̩n] *itr. V.* **a)** wobble; ‹*post etc.*› move about; ‹*tooth etc.*› be loose; ‹*house, window, etc.*› shake; **mit dem Kopf/ den Ohren/den Hüften ~:** waggle *or* wag one's head/ears/wiggle one's hips; **der Hund wackelte mit dem Schwanz** the dog wagged its tail; **b)** *mit sein (ugs.: gehen)* ‹*person*› totter; **c)** *(ugs.: gefährdet, bedroht sein)* ‹*job, government*› be insecure; ‹*firm*› be in a dodgy *(Brit. coll.) or* shaky state
Wackel·peter der; ~s, ~ *(ugs.)* wobbly jelly
wacker ['vakɐ] *(veralt.)* **1.** *Adj.* **a)** *(rechtschaffen)* upright; decent; *(iron.)* trusty; worthy; **b)** *(tüchtig)* good; **ein ~er Zecher/ Esser** a hearty drinker/eater; **c)** *(tapfer, mutig)* valiant. **2.** *adv.* **a)** *(tapfer)* valiantly; **sich ~ halten/schlagen** put up a good show; **b)** *(tüchtig)* ‹*eat, drink, etc.*› heartily
Wacker·stein der *(veralt.)* lump of rock
wacklig ['vaklɪç] *s.* **wackelig**
Wade ['va:də] **die; ~, ~n** *(Anat.)* calf
Waden-: ~bein das *(Anat.)* fibula; **~krampf der** cramp in one's calf; **einen ~krampf bekommen** get cramp in one's calf; **~wickel der** leg compress
Waffe ['vafə] **die; ~, ~n a)** *(auch fig.)* weapon; *(Feuer~)* firearm; **~n tragen** bear arms; **der Kriegsdienst mit der ~:** service under arms; **unter ~n stehen** *od.* **sein** be under arms; **jmdn. zu den ~n rufen** call sb. to arms; **zu den ~n rufen** issue a call to arms; **die ~n strecken** lay down one's arms; *(fig.)* give up the struggle; **jmdn. mit seinen eigenen ~n schlagen** *(fig.)* defeat sb. with his own arguments; **b)** *o. Pl. (veralt.: Waffengattung)* arm [of the service]
Waffel ['vafl̩] **die; ~, ~n a)** waffle; *(dünne ~, Eis~)* wafer; **b)** *(Eistüte)* cone
Waffel·eisen das waffle-iron
waffen-, Waffen-: ~arsenal das arsenal [of weapons]; *(Versteck)* cache of arms; **~besitz der** possession of a firearm/ firearms; **~bruder der** *(geh.)* brother- *or* comrade-in-arms; **~gang der** *(geh.)* engagement; *(fig.)* clash; **~gattung die a)** *(Truppengattung)* arm [of the service]; **b)** *(Teilstreitkraft)* armed service; **~gewalt die;** *o. Pl.* armed force; **mit ~gewalt** by force of arms; **~handel der** arms trade; arms trading; **~händler der** arms dealer; **~kammer die** *(Milit.)* armoury; **~lager das** arsenal; **~rock der** *(veralt.)* tunic; **~ruhe die** cease-fire; **~schein der** firearms licence; **~schmied der** armourer; **~schmiede die** *(geh.)* armoury; **~schmuggel der** gun-running; **~-SS die** *(ns.) armed divisions of the SS;* Waffen-SS; **~starrend** *Adj. (geh.)* armed to the teeth *postpos.;* **~still·stand der** armistice; [permanent] cease-fire; **~stillstands·abkommen das** armistice agreement; **~stillstands·linie die** cease-fire line; **~technik die** arms technology *no art.*
wägbar ['vɛ:kba:ɐ̯] *Adj.* **nicht ~:** imponderable; **ein kaum ~es Risiko** a risk which it is barely possible to gauge
Wage·mut der; *o. Pl.* daring; audacity
wage·mutig *Adj.* daring; audacious
wagen ['va:gn̩] **1.** *tr. V.* risk; **[es] ~, etw. zu tun** dare to do sth.; **einen Versuch/eine Wette ~:** dare to make an attempt/a bet; risk an attempt/a bet; **eine Bitte/Behauptung ~:** venture a request/statement; **wer nicht wagt, der nicht gewinnt** *(Spr.),* **frisch gewagt ist halb gewonnen** *(Spr.)* nothing ventured, nothing gained; *s. auch* **gewagt 2. 2.** *refl. V.* **sich irgendwohin/nicht irgendwohin ~:** venture somewhere/not dare to go somewhere; **sich an etw.** *(Akk.)* **~:** dare to tackle sth.; venture to tackle sth.
Wagen der; ~s, ~: a) *(PKW)* car; *(Omnibus)* bus; *(LKW)* truck; lorry *(Brit.); (Liefer~)* van; **b)** *(Pferde~)* cart; *(Kutsche)* coach; carriage; *(Plan~)* wagon; *(Zirkus~, Wohn~)* caravan *(Brit.);* trailer *(esp. Amer.);* **der Große ~** *(Astron.)* the Plough; the Big Dipper *(Amer.); (Ursa Major)* the Great Bear; **der Kleine ~** *(Astron.)* the Little Dipper *(Amer.); (Ursa Minor)* the Little Bear; **jmdm. an den ~ fahren** *(fig. ugs.)* give sb. what for *(sl.);* pitch into sb. *(coll.);* **sich [nicht] vor jmds. ~** *(Akk.)* **spannen lassen** *(fig. ugs.)* not let sb. lead one by the nose; **c)** *(Eisenbahn~) (Personen~)* coach; carriage; *(Güter~)* truck; wagon; car *(Amer.); (Straßenbahn~)* car; **d)** *(Kinder~, Puppen~)* pram *(Brit.);* baby carriage *(Amer.); (Sport~)* push-chair *(Brit.);* stroller *(Amer.);* **e)** *(Hand~)* handcart; **f)** *(Einkaufs~)* [shopping] trolley; **g)** *(Schreibmaschinen~)* carriage; **h)** *(Servier~, Tee~)* trolley
wägen ['vɛ:gn̩] *unr. od. regelm. tr. V.* **a)** *s.* **¹wiegen 2; b)** *(geh.: abwägen)* weigh up ‹*pros and cons etc.*›
Wagen-: ~burg die *(hist.)* defensive circle of wagons; **~führer der** tram-driver; **~heber der** jack; **~ladung die** truckload; lorry-load *(Brit.);* **~park der** vehicle pool; **~pflege die** car care; **~plane die** tarpaulin; **~rad das** cartwheel; **~rennen das** *(hist.)* chariot-race; **~schlag der** *(geh.) s.* **~tür; ~schmiere die** cart-grease; **~tür die a)** *(einer Kutsche)* carriage door; **b)** *(eines Autos)* car door; **~wäsche die** car wash
Waggon [va'gɔŋ, *südd., österr.:* va'go:n] **der; ~s, ~s,** *südd., österr.:* **~s, ~e a)** *(Güterwagen)* wagon; truck *(Brit.);* car *(Amer.);* **b)** *(veralt.: Personenwagen)* carriage; coach
waggon·weise *Adv.* by the wagon-load
waghalsig 1. *Adj.* daring; risky ‹*speculation*›; *(leichtsinnig)* reckless ‹*driver, rider*›. **2.** *adv.* daringly; ‹*speculate*› riskily; *(leichtsinnig)* recklessly
Wagnerianer [va:gnə'ri̯a:nɐ] **der; ~s, ~, Wagnerianerin die; ~, ~nen** Wagnerian
wagnerianisch *Adj.* Wagnerian
Wagnis ['va:knɪs] **das; ~ses, ~se** daring exploit *or* feat; *(Risiko)* risk
Wahl [va:l] **die; ~, ~en a)** *o. Pl.* choice; **eine/seine ~ treffen** make a/one's choice; **jmdm. die ~ lassen** let sb. choose; **es gibt/mir bleibt** *od.* **ich habe keine [andere] ~:** there is/I have no choice *or* alternative; **vor die ~ gestellt, nach A oder B zu fahren** faced with the choice between going to A or B; **es stehen drei Menüs zur Wahl** there are three set meals to choose from; **die ~ fiel auf ihn** the choice fell on him; **in die engere ~ kommen** be short-listed *or* put on the short list *(Brit.);* **das Mädchen seiner ~** *(geh.)* his intended; **wer die ~ hat, hat die Qual** *(Spr.)* it's agonizing to have to choose; **b)** *(in ein Gremium, Amt usw.)* election; **die ~[en] zum Bundestag vom 6. März** the election[s] [to the Bundestag] of 6 March; **in Hessen ist ~** *od.* **sind ~en** there are elections in Hessen; **ich werde nicht zur ~ gehen** I am not going to vote; **sich zur ~ stellen** stand *or (Amer.)* run for election; **jmdn. zur ~ vorschlagen** suggest sb. as a candidate; nominate sb.; **seine ~ zum Präsidenten** his election as President *or* to the Presidency; **geheime ~:** secret ballot; **c)** *(Güteklasse)* **erste/zweite/ dritte ~:** best/second/third quality; **die Socken sind zweite ~:** the socks are seconds
Wahl- *in* **~berliner/~bayer** *usw. (scherzh.)* Berliner/Bavarian *etc.* by adoption
Wahl-: ~alter das voting age; **~aus·gang der** election result
wählbar *Adj.* **a)** eligible for election *postpos.;* **diese Partei ist für mich einfach nicht ~:** I just couldn't vote for this party; **b)** *(passiv wahlberechtigt)* eligible to stand for election *postpos.*
wahl-, Wahl-: ~benachrichtigung die polling card; **~berechtigt** *Adj.* eligible *or* entitled to vote *postpos.;* **~berechtigte der/die;** *adj. Dekl.* person entitled to vote; **~beteiligung die** turn-out; **die ~beteiligung lag bei 81%** there was an 81% turnout; **~bezirk der** ward
wählen ['vɛ:lən] **1.** *tr. V.* **a)** choose; *(aus~)* select ‹*station, programme, etc.*›; **seine Worte [sorgfältig/genau] ~:** choose one's words [carefully]; **sich** *(Dat.)* **jmdn. zum Vorbild ~:** take sb. as one's model; model oneself on sb.; *s. auch* **gewählt 2, 3; b)** *(Fernspr.)* dial ‹*number*›; **c)** *(durch Stimmabgabe)* elect; **jmdn. ins Parlament/in den Vorstand ~:** elect sb. to Parliament/to the board; **jmdn. zum Vorsitzenden ~:** elect sb. as chairman; **d)** *(stimmen für)* vote for ‹*party, candidate*›. **2.** *itr. V.* **a)** choose; **zwischen zwei Möglichkeiten** *(Dat.)* **~:** choose between two possibilities; **haben Sie schon gewählt?** *(im Lokal)* are you ready to order?; **b)** *(Fernspr.)* dial; **c)** *(stimmen)* vote; **konservativ/grün ~:** vote Conservative/for the Greens; **wann wird in Hessen gewählt?** when are the elections in Hessen?
Wähler der; ~s, ~: voter
Wähler·auftrag der mandate [given by the electorate]
Wahl·ergebnis das election result
Wählerin die; ~, ~nen voter
Wähler·initiative die a) voters' campaign; **b)** *(Gruppe)* voters' action group
wählerisch *Adj.* choosy; particular (**in** + *Dat.* about); **er war in seiner Ausdrucksweise nicht sehr ~:** his choice of vocabulary was not exactly refined
Wählerschaft die; ~, ~en electorate; **die ~ der SPD** the SPD's voters *pl.;* those who vote for the SPD
Wähler-: ~stimme die vote; **~verzeichnis das** electoral register *or* roll
wahl-, Wahl-: ~fach das *(Schulw.)* optional subject; **~frei** *Adj.* optional; **~gang der** ballot; **~geheimnis das** secrecy *or* confidentiality of the ballot; **~geschenk das** pre-election bonus; **~gesetz das** electoral law; **~heimat die** adopted country/ place of residence; **~helfer der a)** election worker; **b)** *(Unterstützer einer Partei)* supporter *(at election time);* **~kabine die** polling-booth; **~kampf der** election campaign; **~kreis der** constituency; **~leiter der** returning officer *(Brit.);* election official *(Amer.);* **~liste die** list of candidates; **~lokal das** polling-station; **~los 1.** *Adj.*

indiscriminate; random; **2.** *adv.* indiscriminately; at random; **~los durcheinander** ⟨*eat, drink, read*⟩ in any *or (coll.)* any old order; **~mann der;** *Pl.* **~männer** elector *(elected by and representing other voters);* **~möglichkeit die** choice; *(Alternative)* alternative; **~nacht die** election night; **~niederlage die** election defeat; **~periode die** legislative period; *(eines Amtsträgers)* term in office; **~pflicht die** compulsory voting; **~plakat das** election poster; **~programm das** election manifesto; **~propaganda die** election propaganda; **~recht das a)** *o.Pl.* **[aktives] ~recht** right to vote; *(einer Gruppe)* franchise; **[passives] ~recht** right to stand [as a candidate] for election; **b)** *(Rechtsvorschriften)* electoral law; **~rede die** election speech

Wähl·scheibe die *(Fernspr.)* dial

wahl-, Wahl-: ~schein der voting permit *(esp. for postal voter);* **~sieg der** election victory; **~spruch der** motto; **~system das** electoral system; **~tag der** election day; polling day; **~urne die** ballot-box; **~verfahren das** electoral procedure; **~verhalten das** voting habits *pl.;* **~versammlung die** election meeting; **~versprechen das** election promise; **~verteidiger der** *(Rechtsw.) defence lawyer chosen by the defendant;* **~verwandschaft die** *(geh.)* feeling of affinity; **~vorschlag der** nomination; **~weise** *Adv.* as desired; to choice; **~weise ... oder ...:** either ... or ... [as desired]

Wahn [va:n] **der; ~[e]s a)** mania; **b)** *(Täuschung)* delusion; **sie ließ ihn in diesem ~:** she let him go on believing this; **er ist in dem ~ befangen** *od.* **lebt in dem ~, daß ...:** he is labouring under the delusion that ...

wähnen ['vɛ:nən] *tr. V. (geh.)* think [mistakenly]; imagine; **jmdn. in Sicherheit** *od.* **sicher ~:** imagine *or* think sb. is safe

wahn-, Wahn-: ~idee die *s.* **~vorstellung; ~sinn der;** *o. Pl.* **a)** insanity; madness; **jmdn. in den ~sinn treiben** drive sb. insane; **in ~sinn** *od.* **dem ~sinn verfallen** go insane; **b)** *(ugs.: Unvernunft)* madness; lunacy; **das ist ja ~sinn!** that's just crazy!; **c)** *(salopp)* **~sinn!** incredible! *(coll.);* amazing!; **dieser Film ist einfach ~sinn** this film is just fantastic *(coll.);* **~sinnig 1.** *Adj.* **a)** *(geistesgestört)* insane; mad; **~sinnig werden** go insane; **du machst mich noch ~sinnig!** *(ugs.)* you're driving me round the bend *(coll.);* **wie ~sinnig** *(ugs.)* like mad *or (coll.)* crazy; **ich werde ~sinnig!** *(ugs.)* fantastic! *(coll.);* **b)** *(ugs.: ganz unvernünftig)* mad; crazy; **so etwas Wahnsinniges!** what a crazy idea!; **c)** *(ugs.: groß, heftig, intensiv)* terrific *(coll.)* ⟨*effort, speed, etc.*⟩; terrible *(coll.)* ⟨*fright, job, pain*⟩. **2.** *adv. (ugs.)* incredibly *(coll.);* terribly *(coll.);* **ich habe ~sinnig viel zu tun** I'm terribly *or* terrifically busy *(coll.)*

Wahnsinnige der/die; *adj. Dekl.* maniac; madman/madwoman

Wahnsinnig·werden *in* **es ist zum ~/zum ~ mit ihm** it's/he's enough to drive you round the bend *or* up the wall *(coll.)*

Wahn·sinns-: ~idee die a) crazy idea *(coll.);* **b)** *(salopp: großartige Idee)* great *or* fantastic idea *(coll.);* **~tat die** insane act; act of madness

wahn-, Wahn-: ~vorstellung die delusion; **~witz der** lunacy; insanity; **~witzig 1.** *Adj.* **a)** insane; **b)** *(ugs.: allzu groß, stark usw.)* insane, lunatic ⟨*speed*⟩; terrible *(coll.),* awful ⟨*pain*⟩. **2.** *adv. (ugs.)* insanely *(coll.)* ⟨*fast, expensive*⟩; incredibly *(coll.)* ⟨*high*⟩; ⟨*hurt*⟩ like hell *(coll.)*

wahr [va:ɐ̯] **1.** *Adj.* **a)** true; **[das] ist ja gar nicht ~!** that's just not true!; **davon ist kein Wort ~:** there isn't a word of truth in it; **nicht ~?** *translation depends on preceding verb-form;* **du hast Hunger, nicht ~?** you're hungry, aren't you?; **nicht ~, er weiß es doch?** he does know, doesn't he?; **du hast es vergessen, nicht ~?** you've forgotten it, haven't you?; **das darf [doch] nicht ~ sein!** I don't believe it!; **etw. ~ machen** carry sth. out; **so ~ ich hier stehe** as surely as I stand here; **so ~ mir Gott helfe** so help me God; **was ~ ist, muß ~ bleiben** facts are facts; **das ist schon gar nicht mehr ~** *(ugs.)* that was donkey's years ago *(coll.);* **daran ist etwas Wahres** there's a grain of *or* some truth in that; **b)** *nicht präd. (wirklich)* real ⟨*reason, motive, feelings, joy, etc.*⟩; actual ⟨*culprit*⟩; *(echt)* true, real ⟨*friend, friendship, love, art*⟩; *(regelrecht)* veritable ⟨*miracle*⟩; **es war eine ~e Pracht** it was really *or* truly magnificent; **im ~sten Sinne des Wortes** in the truest sense of the word; **das ist nicht das Wahre** *(ugs.)* it's not exactly ideal; it's not quite the thing; **das ist doch das einzig Wahre** *(ugs.)* that's just what the doctor ordered *(coll.);* **s. auch Jakob. 2.** *adv.* **~ sprechen** *(geh.)* speak true *(literary)*

wahren *tr. V. (geh.)* preserve, maintain ⟨*balance, equality, neutrality, etc.*⟩; maintain, assert ⟨*authority, right*⟩; keep ⟨*promise, secret*⟩; *(verteidigen)* defend, safeguard ⟨*interests, rights, reputation*⟩; **Anstand ~:** observe the proprieties; *s. auch* **Distanz b; Form e; [1]Gesicht a; Schein b**

währen ['vɛ:rən] *itr. V. (geh.)* last; **ein lange ~der Prozeß** a process of long duration; **was lange währt, wird endlich gut** *(Spr.)* it will be/was worth it in the end

während ['vɛ:rənt] **1.** *Konj.* **a)** *(zeitlich)* while; **b)** *(adversativ)* whereas. **2.** *Präp. mit Gen.* during; *(über einen Zeitraum von)* for; **~ des ganzen Tages** all day [long]

während·dem *(ugs.),* **während·des** *(geh.),* **während·dessen** *Adv.* in the mean time; meanwhile

wahr|haben *unr. tr. V. in* **etw. nicht ~ wollen** not want to admit sth.

wahrhaft *(geh.)* **1.** *Adj.* true; genuine. **2.** *adv.* truly

wahrhaftig 1. *Adj. (geh.)* truthful ⟨*person*⟩; *(wahr)* true, truthful ⟨*statement*⟩; **der ~e Gott** the true God; **~er Gott!** good God!. **2.** *adv.* really; genuinely; **das habe ich nicht gewollt, ~ nicht!** I didn't want that, really I didn't!; **wirklich und ~:** really and truly

Wahrhaftigkeit die; ~ *(geh.)* truthfulness

Wahrheit die; ~, ~en truth; **die ~ eines Berichts** the accuracy *or* faithfulness of an account; **in ~:** in truth; in reality; **die ~ sagen** *od. (geh.)* **sprechen** tell *or* speak the truth; **um der ~ willen ...** to be truthful ...

wahrheits-; Wahrheits-: ~beweis der proof of truth; **~findung die** *(Rechtsw.)* ascertainment of the truth; **~gehalt der** truth; **~gemäß 1.** *Adj.* truthful; accurate ⟨*information*⟩; **2.** *adv.* truthfully; **~getreu 1.** *Adj.* truthful; faithful, accurate ⟨*account*⟩; **2.** *adv.* truthfully; ⟨*portray*⟩ faithfully, accurately; **~liebe die** love of truth; **~liebend** *Adj.* honest

wahrlich *Adv. (geh.)* really; truly; **~, ich sage euch: ...** *(bibl.)* verily I say unto you, ...

wahrnehmbar *Adj.* perceptible; *(hörbar)* audible

wahr|nehmen *unr. tr. V.* **a)** *(mit den Sinnen erfassen)* perceive; discern; *(spüren)* feel; detect ⟨*sound, smell*⟩; *(bemerken)* notice; be aware of; *(erkennen, ausmachen)* make out; discern; detect, discern ⟨*atmosphere, undertone*⟩; **er nimmt alles, was um ihn herum vorgeht, genau wahr** he takes in everything going on around him; **b)** *(nutzen)* take advantage of ⟨*opportunity*⟩; exploit ⟨*advantage*⟩; exercise ⟨*right*⟩; **die Vorfahrt ~:** exercise one's right of way; **c)** *(vertreten)* look after ⟨*sb.'s interests, affairs*⟩; **d)** *(erfüllen, ausführen)* carry out, perform ⟨*function, task, duty*⟩; fulfil ⟨*responsibility*⟩

Wahrnehmung die; ~, ~en a) perception; *(eines Sachverhalts)* awareness; *(eines Geruchs, eines Tons)* detection; **b)** *(Nutzung) (eines Rechts)* exercise; *(einer Gelegenheit, eines Vorteils)* exploitation; **c)** *(Vertretung)* representation; **in ~ von jmds. Interessen** in sb's interest; **d)** *(einer Funktion, Aufgabe, Pflicht)* performance; execution; *(einer Verantwortung)* fulfilment

Wahrnehmungs·vermögen das; *o. Pl.* faculty of perception

wahr·sagen, wahr|sagen 1. *itr. V.* tell fortunes; **sich** *(Dat.)* **[von jmdm.] ~ lassen** have one's fortune told [by sb.]; **aus den Karten/den Handlinien ~:** read the cards/palms. **2.** *tr. V.* predict, foretell ⟨*future*⟩; **sie hat ihm gewahrsagt, daß er ...:** she predicted that he ...

Wahrsager der; ~s, ~: fortune-teller

Wahrsagerei die; ~: fortune-telling *no def. art.*

Wahrsagerin die; ~, ~nen fortune-teller

Wahrsagung die; ~, ~en prediction

währschaft ['vɛ:ɐ̯ʃaft] *Adj. (schweiz.)* durable ⟨*material*⟩; solid ⟨*roof*⟩; wholesome ⟨*food*⟩; strong ⟨*coffee*⟩; reliable ⟨*workman*⟩

wahrscheinlich 1. *Adj.* probable; likely; **~ klingen** sound plausible; **wenig ~:** not very likely; **das halte ich für das Wahrscheinlichste** I think that's the most likely answer; **nicht im Bereich des Wahrscheinlichen liegen** be beyond the bounds of probability. **2.** *adv.* probably

Wahrscheinlichkeit die; ~, ~en probability *(also Math.);* likelihood; **mit einiger/hoher** *od.* **großer ~:** quite/very probably; **aller ~ nach** in all probability

Wahrscheinlichkeits-: ~grad der degree of probability; **~rechnung die** *(Math.)* probability calculus

Wahrung die; ~: preservation; maintenance; *(eines Versprechens, Geheimnisses)* keeping; *(von Interessen, Rechten, Ruf)* defence; safeguarding; **die ~ des Anstandes** the observation of the proprieties

Währung die; ~, ~en currency

Währungs-: ~block der, *Pl.* **~blöcke** currency bloc; **~einheit die** currency unit; monetary unit; **~reform die** currency reform; **~reserve die** currency reserve; **~schlange die** *(Wirtsch.)* [EEC] currency snake; **~system das** currency system; **~union die** currency union; **Währungs-, Wirtschafts- und Sozialunion** social, economic, and currency union

Wahr·zeichen das symbol; *(einer Stadt, einer Landschaft)* [most famous] landmark

Waise ['vaizə] **die; ~, ~n** orphan; **er/sie ist ~:** he/she is an orphan

Waisen-: ~haus das orphanage; **~kind das** orphan; **~knabe der** *(veralt.)* orphaned boy; **gegen jmdn. der reinste ~knabe sein** *(ugs.)* be a mere novice compared to sb.; **~rente die** orphan's [social] benefit

Wal [va:l] **der; ~[e]s, ~e** whale

Wald [valt] **der; ~[e]s, Wälder** ['vɛldɐ] wood; *(größer)* forest; **die Tiere des ~es** the animals of the forest; **im ~ spazierengehen** go walking in the woods; **viel ~:** a great deal of woodland; **in/durch ~ und Feld** *od.* **Flur** in/through woods and fields; **ein ~ von Masten/Antennen** *(fig.)* a forest of masts/aerials; **ich glaub', ich steh' im ~** *(salopp)* I don't believe this!; you can't be serious!; **den ~ vor [lauter] Bäumen nicht sehen** *(fig.)* not see the wood for the trees; **wie man in den ~ hineinruft, so schallt es heraus** *(Spr.)* you are treated as you treat others

Wald-: ~ameise die wood ant; **~arbeiter der** forestry worker; **~bestand der** forests *pl.;* *(Fläche)* area of forest; **~brand der** forest fire

Wäldchen ['vɛltçən] **das** copse; spinney

Wald·einsamkeit die *(dichter.)* woodland solitude

Wald·erdbeere die wild strawberry

Waldes-: ~rauschen das *(dichter.)* forest

murmurs *pl.*; **~saum der** *(dichter.)* edge of the woods/forest
Wald-: ~frevel der *s.* **Forstfrevel; ~gebiet das** forest area; **~geist der;** *Pl.* ~er woodland sprite; **~gott der** *(Myth.)* forest god; **~horn das** *Pl.* ~hörner French horn; *(Jagdhorn)* [large] hunting-horn
waldig *Adj.* wooded
Wald-: ~land das; *o. Pl.* woodland; **~lauf der: [einen] ~lauf machen** go jogging through the woods; **~lehr·pfad der** woodland nature trail; **~meister der;** *o. pl. (Bot.)* woodruff
Waldorf- ['valdɔrf]-: **~salat der** *(Kochk.)* Waldorf salad; **~schule die** Rudolf Steiner school
wald-, Wald-: ~rand der edge of the woods *or* the forest; **~reich** *Adj.* densely wooded; **~schrat der** hobgoblin; woodland gnome; **~spaziergang der** walk in the woods; **~sterben das** death of the forest [as a result of pollution]; **~stück das** piece of woodland; **~tier das** forest *or* woodland animal
Waldung die; ~, ~en forest
Wald·weg der forest path; *(für Fahrzeuge)* forest track
Wales [weılz] **(das); Wales'** Wales
Wal-: ~fang der; *o. Pl.* whaling *no def. art.*; **auf ~fang gehen/sein** go/be whaling; **~fänger der** whaler; **~fisch der** *(ugs.)* whale
Walhall, Walhalla [val'hal(a)] **(das);** ~s Valhalla
Waliser [va'li:zɐ] **der;** ~s, ~: Welshman
Waliserin die; ~, ~nen Welshwoman
walisisch [va'li:zıʃ] **1.** *Adj.* Welsh; **das Walisische** Welsh. **2.** *adv.* **etw. ~ aussprechen** pronounce sth. the Welsh way
walken ['valkn̩] *tr. V.* full ‹*cloth*›; roll ‹*sheet metal*›; tumble ‹*leather*›
Walküre [val'ky:rə] **die;** ~, ~n *(nord. Myth., fig.)* Valkyrie
Wall [val] **der;** ~[e]s, **Wälle** ['vɛlə] earthwork; embankment; rampart *(esp. Mil.)*; *(fig.)* wall
Wallach ['valax] **der;** ~[e]s, ~e gelding
wallen *itr. V.* **a)** *(brodeln)* boil; **der Zorn brachte sein Blut zum Wallen** *(fig. geh.)* anger made his blood boil; **b)** *(geh.: aufgewühlt sein)* ‹*sea, waves*› seethe, churn; **c)** *mit Richtungsangabe mit sein (geh.)* ‹*mist, steam*› swirl; **d) ~des Haar/~de Gewänder** *(geh.)* flowing hair/robes
wall-, Wall-: ~fahren *itr. V.; mit sein* make a pilgrimage; **~fahrer der, ~fahrerin die** pilgrim; **~fahrt die** pilgrimage; **eine ~fahrt machen** go on a pilgrimage
Wall·fahrts-: ~kirche die pilgrimage church; **~ort der** place of pilgrimage
Wall·graben der moat
Wallis ['valıs] **das;** ~: Valais; **im/aus dem ~:** in/from Valais
Wallone [va'lo:nə] **der;** ~n, ~n Walloon
Wallonien [va'lo:niən] **(das);** ~s Wallonia
Wallonin die; ~, ~nen Walloon
wallonisch *Adj.* Walloon
Wallung die: ~, ~en **a)** *(geh.)* **in ~ sein** be seething *or* churning; **in ~ geraten** start to seethe *or* churn; **in ~ bringen** make ‹*sea, water, etc.*› churn; **b)** *(fig. geh.)* **er** *od.* **sein Blut war/geriet in ~:** he *or* his blood was seething/began to seethe; *(vor Leidenschaft)* his feelings were in turmoil *or* inflamed/became inflamed; **jmdn.** *od.* **jmds. Blut in ~ bringen** *(vor Wut, Ärger)* make sb.'s blood boil; *(vor Leidenschaft)* inflame sb. *or.* sb.'s feelings; **c)** *(Med.) s.* **Hitzewallung**
Walm·dach ['valm-] **das** hipped roof
Wal·nuß ['valnʊs] **die** walnut
Walnuß·baum der walnut tree
walnuß·groß *Adj.* walnut-sized
Walpurgis·nacht [val'pʊrgıs-] **die** Walpurgis Night *no art.*

Wal·roß ['valrɔs] **das;** *Pl.* ~rosse walrus
Wal·statt die *(dichter. veralt.)* field of battle; **auf der ~ bleiben** *(veralt.)* fall in battle
walten ['valtn̩] **1.** *itr. V. (geh.)* **a)** ‹*good sense, good spirit*› prevail; ‹*peace, silence, harmony, etc.*› reign; **rohe Kräfte haben hier gewaltet** brutal forces have been at work here; **Vorsicht/Gnade/Milde/Strenge** *usw.* **~ lassen** exercise caution/mercy/leniency/rigour *etc.*; **Vernunft ~ lassen** be reasonable; **b)** *(veralt.: das Regiment führen)* rule **(über +** *Akk.* over); *s. auch* **Amt b, schalten 2 d. 2.** *tr. V. in* **das walte Gott** *(geh.)/(salopp scherzh.)* **Hugo** may God grant that this be so/I hope to God it is
Walz die; ~: *s.* **Walze e**
Walze ['valtsə] **die;** ~, ~n **a)** roller; *(Straßen~)* [road-]roller; *(Schreib~)* platen; *(Tiefdruck~)* gravure cylinder; **b)** *(eines mechanischen Musikinstruments)* barrel; *(hist.: eines Phonographen)* cylinder; **er spielt immer wieder die alte ~** *(ugs.)* he always comes out with the same old story; **c)** *(Geom.)* cylinder; **d)** *(Walzwerk)* rolling-mill; **e)** *o. Pl. (veralt.) in* **auf der ~ sein/auf die ~ gehen** be on/take to the road; **ein Handwerksbursche auf der ~:** an itinerant journeyman
walzen 1. *tr. V.* roll ‹*field, road, steel, etc.*›. **2.** *itr. V. (veralt., scherzh.)* **a)** *mit Richtungsangabe mit sein (Walzer tanzen)* waltz; **b)** *mit sein (reisen)* rove; *(zu Fuß)* hike
wälzen ['vɛltsn̩] **1.** *tr. V.* **a)** roll ‹*round object*›; heave ‹*heavy object*›; *(drehen)* roll ‹*person etc.*› over; *(fig.)* shove ‹*blame, responsibility*› **(auf +** *Akk.* on); **die Arbeit auf jmdn. ~:** lumber sb. with the work; **b)** *(ugs.: studieren)* pore over ‹*books etc.*›; **c)** *(Kochk.: wenden)* **etw. in Mehl** *usw.* **~:** toss sth. in flour *etc.*; **d)** *(ugs.: diskutieren, nachdenken über)* mull over ‹*plans, problem, etc.*›. **2.** *refl. V.* roll; *(auf der Stelle)* roll about *or* around; *(im Krampf, vor Schmerzen)* writhe around; **sich schlaflos im Bett ~:** toss and turn in bed, unable to sleep; **sich vor Lachen ~** *(ugs.)* fall about laughing; **Menschenmengen wälzten sich durch die Straßen** crowds of people thronged through the streets
walzen·förmig *Adj.* cylindrical
Walzer der; ~s, ~: waltz; **kannst du ~ tanzen?** can you waltz?
Wälzer der; ~s, ~ *(ugs.)* hefty tome
Walzer-: ~musik die waltz music; **~takt der** waltz time
Walz-: ~stahl der rolled steel; **~straße die** *(Technik)* roll train; **~werk das** rolling-mill
Wampe ['vampə] **die;** ~, ~n *(ugs. abwertend)* pot belly
Wams [vams] **das;** ~es, **Wämser** ['vɛmzɐ] **a)** *(hist.: Untergewand zur Rüstung)* gambeson; **b)** *(veralt.: Jacke)* doublet
wand *1. u. 3. Pers. Sg. Prät. v.* **winden**
Wand [vant] **die;** ~, **Wände** ['vɛndə] **a)** wall; *(Trenn~)* partition; **die eigenen vier Wände** one's own four walls; **..., daß die Wände wackeln** *(ugs.)* ... almost fit to raise the roof *(coll.)*; **jmdn. an die ~ stellen** *(verhüll. ugs.)* put sb. up against a wall *(euphem.)*; **da kann man die Wände hochgehen** *(fig.)* it's enough to drive you up the wall *(coll.)*; **jmdn. an die ~ drücken** *(fig.)* push sb. into the background; **jmdn. an die ~ spielen** *(fig.)* outclass sb.; *(durch Manöver ausschalten)* outmanœuvre sb.; **bei ihm redet man gegen eine ~** *(fig.)* talking to him is like talking to a brick wall; **sie wohnen ~ an ~:** they live next door to one another; they are neighbours; **die Wände haben Ohren** *(ugs.)* walls have ears; **b)** *(bewegliche Trenn~)* screen; **spanische ~:** folding screen; **c)** *(eines Behälters, Schiffs)* side; *(eines Zeltes)* wall; side; *(Biol.)* septum; *(Anat.)* wall; **d)** *(Fels~)* face; wall; **e)** *(Wolken~)* bank of cloud

Wandale [van'da:lə] **der;** ~n, ~n **a)** *(hist.)* Vandal; **b)** *(fig.)* vandal
Wandalismus [vanda'lısmʊs] **der;** ~: vandalism
Wand·behang der wall hanging
Wandel ['vandl̩] **der;** ~s change; **im ~ der Zeiten/der Jahrhunderte** through the ages/over the centuries
Wandel·anleihe die *(Bankw.)* convertible loan
wandelbar *Adj.* changeable; variable ‹*size, number*›
Wandel-: ~gang der promenade; *(im Theater)* foyer; **~halle die** lobby; *(im Theater)* foyer
wandeln 1. *refl. V.* change **(in +** *Akk.* into). **2.** *tr. V. (verändern)* change; **etw. in etw.** *(Akk.)* **~** *(geh.)* change *or* turn sth. into sth. **3.** *itr. V.; mit sein (geh.)* stroll; *s. auch* **Leiche; Lexikon a**
Wander-: ~ameise die army ant; **~ausstellung die** touring exhibition; **~bühne die** touring company; **~bursche der** journeyman *(travelling from place to place)*; **~düne die** wandering dune
Wanderer der; ~s, ~: **a)** walker; *(der weite Wege zurücklegt)* rambler; hiker; **b)** *(dichter.: Reisender)* traveller
Wander-: ~falke der peregrine falcon; **~gewerbe das** itinerant trade; **~heuschrecke die** migratory locust
Wanderin die; ~, ~nen *s.* **Wanderer**
Wander-: ~jahr das year of travel; *(eines Handwerkers)* journeyman year; **~karte die** rambler's [path] map; **~kleidung die** rambling *or* hiking clothes *pl.*; **~leben das** unsettled life; *(von Nomaden)* nomadic life; **~lied** ramblers' *or* hikers' song
wandern ['vandɐn] *itr. V.; mit sein* **a)** hike; ramble; *(ohne Angabe des Ziels)* go hiking *or* rambling; **b)** *(ugs.: gehen)* wander *(lit. or fig.)*; *(fig.)* ‹*glance, eyes, thoughts*› roam, wander; **c)** *(ziehen, reisen)* travel; *(ziellos)* roam; ‹*exhibition, circus, theatre*› tour, travel; ‹*animal, people, tribe*› migrate; *(fig.)* ‹*cloud, star*› drift; **~de Stämme** nomadic tribes; **d)** *(sich verlagern)* ‹*glacier, dune, island*› move, shift; *(innerhalb des Körpers)* ‹*kidney etc.*› be displaced; ‹*foreign body*› migrate; **e)** *(ugs.: befördert werden)* land; **in den Papierkorb/Müll** *usw.* **~:** land *or* be thrown in the waste-paper basket/rubbish-bin *etc.*; **g)** *(fig.: weitergegeben werden)* be handed *or* passed on
Wander-: ~niere die *(Med.)* floating kidney; **~pokal der** challenge cup; **~prediger der** itinerant preacher; **~ratte die** brown rat
Wanderschaft die; ~: travels *pl.*; **die Zeit der ~:** the years *pl.* of travel; **auf [der] ~ sein/auf [die] ~ gehen** be on/set off on one's travels; **ein Handwerksbursche auf [der] ~:** a travelling *or* an itinerant journeyman
Wander·schuh der hiking shoe
Wanders·mann der; *Pl.* ~leute *(veralt.)* wayfarer
Wander-: ~stock der staff; **~tag der** day's hike *(for a class or school)*
Wanderung die; ~, ~en **a)** hike; walking tour; *(sehr lang)* trek; **eine ~ machen** go on a hike/tour/trek; **b)** *(Zool., Soziol.)* migration
Wanderungs·bewegung die *(Soziol.)* migration; migratory movement
Wander-: ~verein der ramblers' association; **~vogel der a)** *(ugs.: begeisterter Wanderer)* keen hiker; **b)** *in* **der ~vogel** *(hist.) ramblers' association, founded 1895, precursor of the German youth movement*; **c)** *(Mitglied)* member of the *Wandervogel*; **~weg der** footpath *(constructed for ramblers)*; **~zirkus der** travelling circus
Wand-: ~gemälde das mural; **~haken der** [wall-]hook; **~kalender der** calendar; **~lampe die, ~leuchte die** wall-light
Wandlung die; ~, ~en **a)** change; *(grundle-*

gend) transformation; **b)** *(kath. Rel.)* transubstantiation; *(in der Messe)* consecration of the bread and wine

wạndlungs·fähig *Adj.* adaptable

Wạnd·malerei die mural painting; wall-painting; *(Bild)* mural; wall-painting

Wạndrer der; ~s, ~ *s.* **Wanderer**

Wạndrerin die; ~, ~nen *s.* **Wanderin**

Wạnd-: ~schirm der folding screen; **~schrank der** wall cupboard *or (Amer.)* closet; *(Einbauschrank)* built-in cupboard *or (Amer.)* closet; *(für Kleidung)* built-in wardrobe *or (Amer.)* closet; **~spiegel der** wall mirror; **~tafel die** [wall] blackboard

wandte ['vantə] *1. u. 3. Pers. Prät. v.* **wenden**

Wạnd-: ~teller der wall [display] plate; **~teppich der** wall-hanging; tapestry; **~uhr die** wall clock

Wạndung die; ~, ~en *(von Gefäßen usw.)* side; *(von Organen)* wall

Wạnd-: ~verkleidung die *(außen)* facing; *(innen)* wall covering; *(Täfelung)* wall panelling; **~zeitung die** wall newspaper

Wange ['vaŋə] **die; ~, ~n a)** *(geh.)* cheek; **~ an ~:** cheek to cheek; **ihm stieg das Blut in die ~n** the blood rose to his cheeks; **b)** *(Technik)* cheek; *(einer Treppe)* stringer; *(einer Leiter)* stile

Wạngen·kuß der: jmdm. einen ~ geben kiss sb's cheek

Wạnkel·motor der Wankel engine

Wạnkel·mut der *(geh.)* vacillation

wạnkelmütig [-my:tıç] *Adj.* *(geh.)* vacillating

wanken ['vaŋkn̩] *itr. V.* **a)** *(schwanken)* sway; ⟨*person*⟩ totter; *(unter einer Last)* stagger; **ins Wanken geraten** *od.* **kommen** begin to sway/totter; **nicht ~ und nicht weichen** *(geh.)* not budge an inch; **b)** *mit sein (unsicher gehen)* stagger; totter; **~den Schrittes** *(geh.)* with unsteady gait; **c)** *(geh.: bedroht sein)* ⟨*government, empire, etc.*⟩ totter; **ins Wanken geraten** begin to totter; ⟨*theory, faith, etc.*⟩ become shaky; **ins Wanken bringen** make ⟨*monarchy, government, etc.*⟩ totter; shake ⟨*resolve, faith*⟩; **d)** *(geh.: unsicher sein/werden)* ⟨*person*⟩ waver, vacillate; **[in etw.** *(Dat.)***] ~d werden** begin to waver *or* vacillate [in sth.]; **jmdn. ~d machen** make sb. waver

wann [van] *Adv.* when; **~ kommst du morgen?** when *or* [at] what time are you coming tomorrow?; **~ ist dieses Jahr Ostern?** when *or* on what date does Easter fall this year?; **seit ~ wohnst du dort?** how long have you been living there?; **seit ~ sind Delphine Fische/bin ich dein Laufbursche?** *(iron.)* since when have dolphins been fish/have I been your errand boy?; **bis ~ kann ich noch anrufen?** until when *or* how late can I still phone?; **von ~ an ...?** from when ...?; **von ~ bis ~ gilt es?** for what period is it valid?; **bis ~ ist das Essen fertig?** [by] when will the food be ready?; **ich weiß nicht, ~:** I don't know when; **du kannst kommen, ~ du willst** you can come when[ever] you like; **~ [auch] immer** *(geh.)* whenever

Wạnne die; ~, ~n bath[tub]; *(Öl~)* sump; *(Fot.)* [wash-]tank; **in die ~ steigen** get into the bath

Wạnnen·bad das bath

Wanst [vanst] **der; ~[e]s, Wänste** ['vɛnstə] *(ugs. abwertend)* belly; *(dicker Bauch)* potbelly; **sich den ~ vollschlagen** stuff oneself *(coll.)*

Want [vant] **die; ~, ~en** *(Schiffbau)* shroud

Wanze ['vantsə] **die; ~, ~n** *(Bett~, Abhör~)* bug *(coll.)*

Wappen ['vapn̩] **das; ~s, ~:** coat of arms; **~ oder Zahl?** heads or tails?

Wappen-: ~feld das *(Her.)* quarter; **~kunde die;** *o. Pl.* heraldry *no art.*; **~schild der** *od.* **das** *(Her.)* shield; **~spruch der** motto; **~tier das** heraldic beast

wạppnen *refl. V.* *(geh.)* **a)** forearm oneself; **sich gegen etw. ~:** prepare [oneself] for sth.; **[gegen etw.] gewappnet sein** be forearmed [against sth.]

war [va:ɐ̯] *1. u. 3. Pers. Sg. Prät. v.* **sein**

Waran [va'ra:n] **der; ~s, ~e** *(Zool.)* monitor lizard

warb [varp] *1. u. 3. Pers. Sg. Prät. v.* **werben**

ward [vart] *(geh.) 1. u. 3. Pers. Sg. Prät. v.* **werden**

Ware ['va:rə] **die; ~, ~n a) ~[n]** goods *pl.*; **b)** *(einzelne ~)* article; commodity *(Econ., fig.)*; *(Erzeugnis)* product; **neue ~ bekommen** receive new stock; **die Händler preisen ihre ~n an** the traders are vaunting the excellence of their wares; **heiße ~** *(ugs.)* hot goods; **c)** *(Kaufmannsspr.: Stoff)* material

Waren-: ~an·gebot das supply [of goods]; *(Sortiment)* range of goods; **~annahme die a)** acceptance of goods; **„keine ~annahme"** no deliveries; **b)** *(Annahmestelle)* goods reception; **„~annahme"** 'goods in'; **~auf·zug der** goods lift *(Brit.) or (Amer.)* elevator; **~ausfuhr die** export of goods; **~aus·gabe die a)** issue of goods; **b)** *(Ausgabestelle)* goods collection point; **~begleit·schein der** *(Zollw.)* [customs] bond note; **~bestand der** stock; **~börse die** *(Wirtsch.)* commodity exchange; **~einfuhr die** import of goods; **~haus das** department store; **~korb der** *(Statistik)* basket of goods; **~lager das** *(einer Fabrik o.ä.)* stores *pl.*; *(eines Geschäftes)* stock-room; *(größer)* warehouse; *(Bestand)* stocks *pl.*; **~muster das, ~probe die** sample; **~sendung die** *(Postw.)* parcel containing samples *(sent at a special rate)*; **~test der** product test; **~umsatz der** turnover of goods; **~umschlag der** volume of goods handled; **~zeichen das** trade mark

warf [varf] *1. u. 3. Pers. Sg. Prät. v.* **werfen**

warm [varm]; **wärmer** ['vɛrmɐ], **wärmst ...** ['vɛrmst ...] **1.** *Adj.* **a)** warm; hot ⟨*meal, food, bath, spring*⟩; hot, warm ⟨*climate, country, season, etc.*⟩; **~e Küche** hot food; **das Essen ~ machen/stellen** heat up the food/keep the food warm *or* hot; **im Warmen sitzen/ins Warme kommen** sit in/come into the warm; **~ halten** ⟨*coat, blanket, etc.*⟩ keep one warm; **etw. ~ halten** keep sth. warm; **mir ist/wird ~:** I feel warm/I'm getting warm; *(zu ~)* I feel hot/I'm getting hot; **sich ~ laufen** warm up; **„~"** *(auf Wasserhahn)* 'hot'; **~e Miete** *s.* **Warmmiete; b)** *(herzlich)* warm ⟨*sympathy, appreciation, words, etc.*⟩; *(lebhaft)* enthusiastic ⟨*agreement*⟩; keen, lively ⟨*interest*⟩; **[mit jmdm./etw.] ~ werden** *(ugs.)* warm [to sb./sth.]; **mir wurde ganz ~ ums Herz** *(geh.)* I felt a warm glow [of emotion]; **c)** *(salopp abwertend: homosexuell)* gay *(coll.)*; queer *(sl.)*; **ein ~er Bruder** *(salopp abwertend)* a queer *(sl.)*; a fag *(Amer. sl.)*. **2.** *adv.* warmly; **~ essen/duschen** have a hot meal/shower; **~ sitzen/schlafen** sit/sleep in the warm; **sich ~ anziehen/zudecken** dress up/cover oneself up warmly

warm-, Warm-: ~blut das *cross between heavy and light breeds*; ≈ cross-bred horse; **~blüter** [~bly:tɐ] **der; ~s, ~** *(Zool.)* warm-blooded creature; **~blütig** [~bly:tıç] *Adj.* *(Zool.)* warm-blooded

Warme der; *adj. Dekl.* *(salopp abwertend)* queer *(sl.)*; fag *(Amer. sl.)*

Wärme ['vɛrmə] **die; ~:** warmth; *(Hitze; auch Physik)* heat; **wir haben drei Grad ~:** it is three degrees above zero; **spezifische ~** *(Physik)* specific heat

wärme-, Wärme-: ~austauscher der; ~s, ~ *(Technik)* heat-exchanger; **~belastung die a)** *(Ökologie)* thermal pollution; **b)** *(Technik)* thermal stress; **~beständig** *Adj.* heat-resistant; **~dämmend** *Adj.* insulating [against heat loss]; **~einheit die** thermal unit; **~energie die** thermal energy; **~gewitter das** *(Met.)* heat thunderstorm; **~grad der a)** *Pl.* degrees above zero; **wir hatten ~grade** the temperature was above zero; **b)** *(Temperatur)* temperature; **~haushalt der a)** *(der Erde)* heat balance; **b)** *(des Körpers)* heat regulation; **~isolation die** thermal insulation; **~kraftwerk das** thermal power station; **~lehre die** *(Physik)* theory of heat; *(Thermodynamik)* thermodynamics *sing.*, *no art.*

wärmen 1. *tr. V.* warm; *(aufwärmen)* warm up ⟨*food, drink*⟩; **jmdn./sich/sich [gegenseitig] ~:** warm sb./oneself/each other up. **2.** *itr. V.* be warm; *(warm halten)* keep one warm; **die Sonne wärmt kaum noch** the sun has hardly any warmth now

Wärme-: ~pumpe die *(Technik)* heat pump; **~speicher der** thermal store; **~strahlung die** thermal radiation; **~technik die** heat technology *no art.*; **~verlust der** heat loss

Wạrm·flasche die hot-water bottle

wạrm-, Wạrm-: ~front die *(Met.)* warm front; **~|halten** *unr. refl. V.* *(ugs.)* **sich** *(Dat.)* **jmdn. ~halten** keep on the right side of sb.; **~halte·platte die** hotplate; **~herzig 1.** *Adj.* warm-hearted; **2.** *adv.* warm-heartedly; **~herzigkeit die** warm-heartedness; warmth; **~|laufen** *unr. itr. V.*; *mit sein* warm up; **~laufen lassen** warm up ⟨*engine*⟩; **~luft die;** *o. Pl.* warm air; **~miete die** *(ugs.)* rent inclusive of heating; **es kostet 500 Mark ~miete** the rent, inclusive of heating, is 500 marks

wärmstens ['vɛrmstn̩s] *Adv.* **~ empfehlen** warmly recommend

Warm·wạsser das; *o. Pl.* hot water

Warm·wạsser-: ~bereiter der; ~s, ~: water-heater; boiler; **~heizung die** hot-water heating; **~versorgung die** hot-water supply

Wạrn-: ~blink·anlage die *(am Bahnübergang)* flashing warning lights *pl.*; *(am Kfz)* hazard warning lights *pl.*; **~blinker der** *(ugs.)* hazard warning lights *pl.*; **~blink·leuchte die** flashing warning light; **~dreieck das** *(Kfz-W.)* hazard warning triangle

warnen ['varnən] *tr. (auch itr.) V.* warn **(vor** + *Dat.* of, about); **jmdn. [davor] ~, etw. zu tun** warn sb. against doing sth.; **vor dem Betreten des Eises wird gewarnt** you are warned to beware of thin ice; **die Polizei warnt vor Nebel/vor Taschendieben** the police have issued a fog warning/a warning against pickpockets; **ich bin jetzt gewarnt** I have been warned; I know now to be careful; **ein ~des Beispiel** a cautionary example; **er hob ~d den Zeigefinger** he raised an admonitory finger

Wạrn-: ~kreuz das *(Verkehrsw.)* warning cross; **~lampe die** warning light; **~ruf der a)** warning shout; **b)** *(eines Tiers)* warning cry; **~schild das** warning sign; **~schuß der** warning shot; **~signal das** warning signal; **~streik der** token strike; **~system das** warning system

Wạrnung die; ~, ~en warning **(vor** + *Dat.* of, about); **laß dir das eine ~ sein!** let that be a warning to you!; **das ist meine letzte ~:** that's the last warning I shall give you; I shan't warn you again

Wạrn·zeichen das warning sign; *(Schall~, Leuchtzeichen)* warning signal

Warschau ['varʃau] **(das); ~s** Warsaw

Wạrschauer 1. der; ~s, ~: citizen of Warsaw; *(geborener ~)* native of Warsaw. **2.** *indekl. Adj.* Warsaw; **der ~ Pakt** *od.* **Vertrag** the Warsaw Pact; **die ~-Pakt-** *od.* **Vertrags-Staaten** the Warsaw Pact countries

Warte ['vartə] **die; ~, ~n** *(geh.)* **[hohe] ~:** vantage-point; *(fig.: Standpunkt)* **von jmds. ~ aus [gesehen]** [seen] from sb.'s standpoint

Warte-: ~frau die *(veralt.)* [*esp.* toilet] attendant; **~frist die** *s.* **~zeit b; ~halle die** waiting room; *(Flugw.)* departure lounge;

~liste die waiting list; **auf ~liste** *(Flugw.)* on stand-by
warten ['vartn̩] **1.** *itr. V.* wait **(auf + Akk.** for); **warte mal!** wait a moment!; just a moment!; **na warte!** *(ugs.)* just you wait!; **„bitte warten!“** 'wait'; *(am Telefon)* 'hold the line please'; **da kannst du lange ~!** *(iron.)* you'll have a long wait; you'll be lucky *(iron.)*; **auf sich ~ lassen** take one's/its time; **nicht lange auf sich ~ lassen** not be long in coming; **das lange Warten war völlig umsonst gewesen** the long wait had been all for nothing; **wir wollen mit dem Essen ~, bis alle da sind** we'll hold the meal until everybody's here; **sie wollen mit dem Heiraten noch [etwas] ~:** they want to wait a little before getting married; **darauf habe ich schon lange gewartet** *(iron.)* I've seen that coming [for a long time]; **auf dich/den haben wir gerade noch gewartet** *(iron.)* you were/he was all we needed; **Sie können [gleich] drauf ~:** you might as well wait for it; **so lange ~/mit etw. ~, bis es zu spät ist** leave it/leave sth. until it's too late. **2.** *tr. V.* service ⟨*car, machine, etc.*⟩
Wärter ['vɛrtɐ] **der; ~s, ~:** attendant; *(Tier~, Zoo~, Leuchtturm~)* keeper; *(Kranken~)* orderly; *(Gefängnis~)* warder; *(Schranken~)* crossing-keeper
Warte·raum der waiting-room
Wärter·häuschen das attendant's hut; *(Schranken~)* crossing-keeper's hut
Wärterin die; ~, ~nen *s.* **Wärter**
Warte-: ~saal der waiting-room; **~schleife die** *(Flugw.)* turning loop; **~zeit die a)** wait; **nach einer ~zeit von einer Stunde** after waiting for an hour; **b)** *(festgesetzte Frist)* waiting period; **~zimmer das** waiting-room
-wärts [-vɛrts] *adv.* ⟨*north-, south-, up-, down-, etc.*⟩wards; **seit~:** sideways
Wartung die; ~, ~en service; *(das Warten)* servicing; *(Instandhaltung)* maintenance; **der Wagen muß zur ~:** the car has to go to be serviced *or* go for servicing
wartungs·frei *Adj.* maintenance-free
warum [va'rʊm] *Adv.* why; **~ nicht?** why not?; **~ nicht gleich so?** why not do that in the first place?; **nach dem Warum fragen** ask the reason why
Warze ['vartsə] **die; ~, ~n a)** wart; **b)** *(Brust~)* nipple
Warzen-: ~hof der *(Anat.)* nipple areola; **~schwein das** wart-hog
warzig *Adj.* warty
was [vas] **1.** *Interrogativpron. Nom. u. Akk. u. (nach Präp.) Dat. Neutr.; s. auch (Gen.)* **wessen 1 b** what; **~ kostet das?** what *or* how much does that cost?; **~ ist er [von Beruf]?** what's his job?; **[das ist] gut, ~?** *(ugs.: nicht?)* not bad, eh?; **~ ist?, ~ denn?** *(was ist denn los?)* what is it?; what's up?; **~ denn, willst du etwa schon gehen?** you're not going already, are you?; **ach ~!** *(ugs.)* oh, come on!; of course not!; **für ~ brauchst du es?** *(ugs.)* what do you need it for?; **mit ~ beschäftigt er sich?** *(ugs.)* how does he occupy his time?; **~ der alles weiß!** what a lot he knows!; **~ es [nicht] alles gibt!** *(Ding)* what will they think of next?; *(Ereignis)* the things people will do!; **und ~ nicht alles** *(ugs.)* and so on ad infinitum; **~ [auch] immer** whatever; **~ für ein .../~ für ...:** what sort *or* kind of ...; **~ für ein Auto hat er?,** *(ugs.)* **~ hat er für ein Auto?** what kind of car has he got?; **~ für Möglichkeiten haben wir?** *(ugs.)* what possibilities do we have?; **Hast du den Apfel gegessen? – Was für'n Apfel?** *(ugs.)* Did you eat the apple? – What apple?; **~ für ein Unsinn/Glück/gemeiner Kerl!** *(ugs.)* what nonsense/luck/ *(coll.)* what a mean so-and-so!; **War's ein Sturm? – Und ~ für einer!** Was it a storm? – Not half! *(coll.) or* And then some! *(coll.)*. **2.** *Relativpron. Nom. u. Akk. u. (nach Präp.) Dat. Neutr.; s. auch (Gen.)* **wessen 2 b: a)** **[das,] ~:** what; **alles, was...:** everything *or* all that ...; **alles, ~ ich weiß** all [that] I know; **das Beste, was du tun kannst** the best thing that you can do; **das, ~ du nicht mehr brauchst** the things *pl. or* what you no longer need; **~ er nicht kennt, [das] ißt er nicht** he won't eat anything he doesn't know; **vieles/manches/nichts/dasselbe/etwas, ~ ...:** much/many things/nothing/the same one/something that ...; **~ mich betrifft/das anbelangt, [so] ...:** as far as I'm/that's concerned, ...; **b)** *weiterführend* which; **er hat zugesagt, ~ mich gefreut hat** he agreed, which pleased me; **es hat geregnet, ~ uns aber nicht gestört hat** it rained, but that didn't bother us; **c)** *(ugs.: wer)* **~ ein ganzer Kerl ist, [der] wehrt sich** anyone worth his salt will put up a fight; **d)** *(landsch.: derjenige, der/diejenige, die)* **~ unser Vater ist, der sagt immer ...:** our father always says...; **e)** *(landsch.: der, die, das)* **die Frieda, ~ unsere Jüngste ist** Frieda, who is our youngest. **3.** *Indefinitpron. Nom. u. Akk. u. (nach Präp.) Dat. Neutr. (ugs.)* **a)** *(etwas)* something; *(in Fragen, Verneinungen)* anything; **er hat kaum ~ gesagt** he hardly said anything *or* a thing; **ist ~?** is anything wrong?; **wenn er ~ gesehen hätte ...:** if he had seen anything; **haben die ~ miteinander?** is there something between them?; **so ~:** such a thing; something like that; **nein, so ~!** you don't say!; **so ~ könnte mir nicht passieren** nothing like that could happen to me; **gibt es hier so ~ wie'n Klo?** there isn't a loo *(Brit.) or (Amer.)* john here, is there? *(coll.)*; **er ist so ~ wie'n Professor** he's a professor *or* something of the sort; **so ~ Dummes/Ärgerliches!** how stupid/annoying!; **gibt es ~ Neues?** Is there any news?; **aus ihm wird mal/wird nie ~:** he'll make something of himself/he'll never come to anything; **das will ~ heißen** that really means something; **b)** *(ein Teil)* some; **ich bekomme auch ~:** I get some too; **c)** *(landsch.: ein wenig)* a little; a bit; **noch ~ Geld/Milch** some more money/milk; **~ lauter** a bit louder. **4.** *Adv. (ugs.)* **a)** *(warum, wozu)* why; what ... for; **~ stehst du hier herum?** what are you standing around here for?; **b)** *(wie)* how; **~ hast du dich verändert!** how you've changed; **lauf, ~ du kannst!** run as fast as you can!; **c)** *(inwiefern)* **~ kümmert's dich?** what does it matter to you?
wasch-, Wasch-: ~aktiv *Adj.* detergent; **~an·lage die** washing plant; *(Autowaschanlage)* car-wash; *(Scheibenwaschanlage)* windscreen-washer; **~an·leitung die** washing instructions *pl.*; **~automat der** washing-machine
wasch·bar *Adj.* washable
Wasch-: ~bär der racoon; **~becken das** wash-basin; **~benzin das** cleaning fluid *(with petrol base)*; **~beton der** exposed aggregate concrete; **~brett das** washboard
Wäsche ['vɛʃə] **die; ~, ~n a)** *o. Pl. (zu waschende Textilien)* washing; *(für die Wäscherei)* laundry; **jmdm. die ~ machen** do sb.'s washing; **schmutzige ~ waschen** *(fig.)* wash [one's] dirty linen in public; **b)** *o. Pl. (Unter~)* underwear; **dumm/verdutzt aus der ~ gucken** *(ugs.)* look stupid/flabbergasted; **jmdm. an die ~ gehen/wollen** *(salopp)* go for sb./try to get at sb.; **c)** *(das Waschen)* washing *no pl.*; *(einmalig)* wash; **bei/nach der ersten ~:** when washed for the first time/after the first wash; **in der ~ sein** be in the wash; **etw. in die** *od.* **zur ~ tun** put sth. in the wash; **bei uns ist heute große ~:** we're doing a big wash today; **d)** *(Waschanlage)* washing plant
Wäsche·beutel der laundry-bag
wasch·echt *Adj.* **a)** colour-fast ⟨*textile, clothes*⟩; fast ⟨*colour*⟩; **b)** *(fig.: echt)* genuine; pukka *(coll.)*
Wäsche-: ~garnitur die set of underwear; **~klammer die** clothes-peg *(Brit.)*; clothes-pin *(Amer.)*; **~korb der** laundry-basket; *(für nasse Wäsche)* clothes-basket; **~leine die** clothes-line
waschen 1. *unr. tr. V.* **a)** wash; **sich ~:** wash [oneself]; have a wash; **jmdm./sich die Hände/das Gesicht** *usw.* **~:** wash sb.'s/one's hands/face *etc.*; **Wäsche ~:** do the/some washing; **sich ge~ haben** *(fig. ugs.)* be quite something; **b)** *(fig. ugs.)* launder ⟨*money*⟩. **2.** *unr. itr. V.* do the washing
Wäsche·puff der linen-basket *(Brit.)*, clothes hamper *(Amer.) (with upholstered lid)*
Wäscherei die; ~, ~en laundry
Wäscherin die; ~, ~nen laundrywoman
Wäsche-: ~schleuder die spin-drier; **~spinne die** rotary clothes-drier; **~ständer der** clothes-airer; **~tinte die** marking-ink; **~trockner der a)** *(Maschine)* tumble-drier; **b)** *(Gestell)* clothes-airer; **~zeichen das** linen-mark
wasch-, Wasch-: ~frau die washerwoman; **~gang der** washing cycle; **~gelegenheit die** washing facilities *pl.*; **~hand·schuh der** flannel mitt *(Brit.)*; shower/bath mitt *(Amer.)*; **~küche die a)** laundry-room; **b)** *(ugs.: dichter Nebel)* pea-souper; **~lappen der a)** [face] flannel; washcloth *(Amer.)*; **b)** *(ugs. abwertend) (Weichling)* softie *(coll.)*; *(Feigling)* sissy; **~lauge die** soapy water; soapsuds *pl.*; **~maschine die** washing-machine; **~maschinen·fest** *Adj.* machine-washable; **~mittel das** detergent; **~muschel die** *(österr.)* wash-basin; **~programm das** washing-programme; **~pulver das** washing-powder; **~raum der** washing-room; **~salon der** launderette; laundromat *(Amer.)*; **~schüssel die** washing-bowl; **~straße die** [automatic] car-wash
wäscht [vɛʃt] *3. Pers. Sg. Präsens v.* **waschen**
Wasch-: ~tag der wash-day; **~tisch der** wash-stand
Waschung die; ~, ~en *(Rel., Med.)* ablution
Wasch-: ~wasser das; *o. Pl.* washing water; **~weib das** *(salopp abwertend: Klatschbase)* gossip; **~zettel der** *(Buchw.)* blurb; **~zeug das;** *o. Pl.* washing things *pl.*; **~zwang der** *(Psych.)* obsession with washing oneself
Wasser ['vasɐ] **das; ~s, ~/Wässer** ['vɛsɐ] **a)** *o. Pl.* water; **ins ~ gehen** enter the water; *(zum Schwimmen)* go for a swim; *(verhüll.: sich ertränken)* drown oneself; **warst du schon im ~?** have you been in the water?; *(zum Schwimmen)* have you been for a swim?; **sich über ~ halten** *(auch fig.)* keep one's head above water *(lit. or fig.)*; **direkt am ~:** right by the water; *(am Meer)* right by the sea; **ein Boot zu ~ lassen** put out *or* launch a boat; **auflaufendes/ablaufendes ~:** incoming/outgoing tide; **unter ~ stehen** be under water; be flooded; **etw. unter ~ setzen** flood sth.; **zu ~:** by sea; **ihre Überlegenheit zu ~:** their naval superiority; **der Transport zu ~:** transport by water; **~ treten** paddle *(for therapeutic purposes)*; *(strampeln)* tread water; **b)** *(fig.)* **ins ~ fallen** fall through; **das ~ steht ihm bis zum Hals** he's up to his neck in trouble; *(verschuldet sein)* he's up to his eyes in debt; **reinsten ~s** par excellence; **bis dahin fließt noch viel ~ den Bach** *od.* **Fluß** *od.* **Rhein** *usw.* **hinunter** a lot of water will have flowed under the bridge by then; **nahe am ~ gebaut haben** *(ugs.)* be rather weepy *or* tearful; **mit allen ~n gewaschen sein** know all the tricks; **jmdm. das ~ abgraben** pull the carpet from under sb.'s feet; leave sb. high and dry; **~ ziehen** *(ugs.)* ⟨*stockings, socks*⟩ be at half-mast; **~ hat keine Balken** *(Spr.)* you must

either sink or swim; **stille ~ sind tief** *(Spr.)* still waters run deep *(prov.)*; **die kochen auch nur mit ~** *(ugs.)* they're no different from the rest of us; **bei ~ und Brot sitzen** be doing time [in prison]; **jmdm. nicht das ~ reichen können** not be able to hold a candle to sb.; not be a patch on sb. *(coll.)*; *s. auch* **Mühle a; c)** *Pl.* **Wässer** *(bei Maßangaben unflektiert) (Mineral~, Tafel~)* mineral water; *(Heil~)* water; **d)** *Pl.* **die ~ des Ganges** *(geh.)* the waters of the Ganges; **e)** *o. Pl. (Gewässer)* **ein fließendes/stehendes ~:** a moving/stagnant stretch of water; **f)** *o. Pl. (Schweiß)* sweat; *(Urin)* water; urine; *(Speichel)* saliva; *(Gewebsflüssigkeit)* fluid; **~ lassen** pass water; **sein ~ abschlagen** *(salopp)* have a slash *(sl.)*; **ihm lief das ~ im Munde zusammen** his mouth watered; **~ in den Beinen haben** have fluid in one's legs; *s. auch* **Blut; Rotz a; g)** *Pl.* **Wässer** *(Lösung, Lotion usw.)* lotion; *(Mund~)* mouthwash; *(Duft~)* scent; *(Kölnisch ~)* cologne

wasser-, Wasser-: ~abweisend *Adj.* water-repellent; **~ader die** [underground] watercourse; **~arm** *Adj.* ⟨*area*⟩ suffering from a water shortage; **~aufbereitung die** water treatment; **~bad das** *(Kochk.)* bain-marie; **~ball der a)** beach-ball; **b)** *o. Pl. (Spiel)* water polo; **~baller der; ~s, ~:** water-polo player; **~bau der;** *o. Pl.* hydraulic engineering *no art.*; **~becken das** pool; *(~tank)* water-tank; **~bett das** water-bed; **~büffel der** water-buffalo; **~burg die** moated castle

Wässerchen ['vɛsɐçən] **das; ~s, ~ a) er sieht aus, als könnte er kein ~ trüben** *(fig.)* he looks as though butter wouldn't melt in his mouth; **b)** *s.* **Wasser g; c)** *(scherzh.: Wodka)* vodka

wasser-, Wasser-: ~dampf der steam; **~dicht** *Adj.* **a)** waterproof ⟨*clothing, watch, etc.*⟩; watertight ⟨*container, seal, etc.*⟩; **b)** *(fig. ugs.)* watertight ⟨*alibi, contract*⟩; **~druck der;** *Pl.* **~drücke** water pressure; **~eimer der** bucket; **~fahrzeug das** vessel; water-craft; **~fall der** waterfall; **reden wie ein ~** *(ugs.)* talk non-stop; **~farbe die** water-colour; **~fläche die** expanse of water; **~flasche die** water-bottle; **~floh der** water-flea; **~flugzeug das** seaplane; **~führend** *Adj.* water-bearing; **~gehalt der** water content; **~gekühlt** *Adj.* water-cooled; **~glas das a)** *(Gefäß)* glass; tumbler; *s. auch* **Sturm a; b)** *(Chemie)* water-glass; **~glätte die: bei ~glätte** in wet and slippery conditions; **~graben der a)** ditch; *(um eine Burg)* moat; **b)** *(Reiten, Leichtathletik)* water-jump; **~hahn der** water-tap; faucet *(Amer.)*; **~haushalt der a)** *(Physiol.)* water balance; **b)** *(Ökologie, Bodenk.)* hydrologic balance; **~hose die** *(Met.)* water-spout; **~huhn das** coot

wässerig ['vɛsərɪç] *s.* **wäßrig**

wasser-, Wasser-: ~kasten der water-tank; *(im WC)* cistern; **~kessel der** kettle; **~kopf der** hydrocephalus *(Med.)*; **der ~kopf der Bürokratie** *(fig.)* excessive bureaucracy; **~kraft die** water-power; **~kraftwerk das** hydroelectric power-station; **~kreislauf der** water cycle; **~krug der** water-jug; **~kühlung die** water-cooling system; **mit ~kühlung** water-cooled; **~lache die** puddle [of water]; **~lauf der** watercourse; *(Bach)* stream; **~leiche die** *(ugs.)* body of a drowned person; **~leitung die a)** water-pipe; *(Hauptleitung)* water-main; **unter der/die ~leitung** *(ugs.)* under the tap; **die ~leitung aufdrehen/zudrehen** *(ugs.)* turn the tap on/off; **b)** *(Aquädukt)* aqueduct; **~linie die** *(Schiffahrt)* water-line; **~loch das** water-hole; **~mann der;** *Pl.* **~männer a)** *(Myth.)* merman; **b)** *(Astron., Astrol.)* **[der] ~mann** Aquarius; **c)** *(Astrol.: Mensch)* Aquarian; **~masse die** mass *or* torrent of water; **~melone die** water-melon; **~messer der** water meter; **~mühle die** water-mill

wassern *itr. V.; mit sein (Flugw., Zool.)* land [on the water]; *(Raumf.)* splash down

wässern ['vɛsɐn] **1.** *tr. V.* **a)** *(einweichen)* soak; *(Phot.)* wash ⟨*negative, print*⟩; **b)** *(bewässern)* water. **2.** *itr. V. (geh.)* water; **eine ~de Wunde** a suppurating wound

wasser-, Wasser-: ~nixe die *(Myth.)* water-nymph; **~ober·fläche die** surface of the water; **~pfeife die** hookah; water-pipe; **~pflanze die** aquatic plant; **~pistole die** water-pistol; **~pumpe die** water-pump; **~rad das** water-wheel; **~ratte die a)** water-rat; **b)** *(ugs. scherzh.)* keen swimmer; *(Kind)* water-baby; **~rohr das** water-pipe; **~rohr·bruch der** burst pipe; **~säule die** head of water; **~schaden der** water damage *no pl., no indef. art.*; *(durch Überschwemmung)* flood damage *no pl., no indef. art.*; **~scheide die** *(Geogr.)* watershed; **~scheu** *Adj.* scared of water; **~schlange die** water snake; **~schlauch der** [water-]hose; **~schloß das** *(mit Wassergraben)* moated [residential] castle; *(an einem kleinen See o.ä.)* [residential] castle set on a lake; **~schutz·gebiet das** water conservation area; **~schutz·polizei die** river/lake police; [1]**~ski der** water-ski; **~ fahren** water-ski; [2]**~ski das; ~s** water-skiing *no art.*; **~speier der** *(Archit.)* gargoyle; **~spiegel der a)** *(Oberfläche)* surface [of the water]; **b)** *(Niveau)* water-level; **~spiele** *Pl.* waterworks *pl.*; **~sport der** water-sport *no art.*; **~sportler der** water-sports enthusiast; **~spülung die** flush; flushing system; **~stand der** water-level; **~stands·anzeiger der** water-gauge; **~stands·meldung die** water-level report *(on the radio)*; **~stelle die** watering-place

Wasser·stoff der; *o. Pl.* hydrogen

Wasser·stoff-: ~bombe die hydrogen bomb; **~per·oxid, ~super·oxid das** *(Chemie)* hydrogen peroxide

Wasser-: ~strahl der jet of water; **~straße die** waterway; **~sucht die;** *o. Pl. (Med.)* dropsy; **~tank der** water-tank; **~temperatur die** water-temperature; **~tiefe die** depth of the water; **bei einer ~tiefe von nur 0,50 m** when the water is/was only 0.5 m. deep; **~träger der** water-carrier; *(fig.)* dogsbody *(coll.)*; **~treten das; ~s** treading water *no art.*; **~tropfen der** drop of water; **~turm der** water-tower; **~uhr die a)** water-clock; **b)** *(volkst.: Wassermesser)* water meter; **~verbrauch der** water-consumption; **~verdunster der; ~s, ~:** humidifier; **~verschmutzung die** water-pollution; **~versorgung die** water-supply; **~vogel der** water-bird; aquatic bird; **~vorrat der** water-reserves *pl.*; water-supply; **~waage die** water-level; **~weg der** water-route; **auf dem ~weg** by water; **~welle die** shampoo and set; **~werfer der** water-cannon; **~werk das** waterworks *sing.*; **~wirtschaft die** water-management; **~zähler der** water meter; **~zeichen das** watermark

wäßrig ['vɛs(ə)rɪç] *Adj.* **a)** watery; *s. auch* **Mund; b)** *(Chemie)* aqueous ⟨*solution*⟩

waten ['va:tn̩] *itr. V.; mit sein* wade

Waterkant ['va:tɐkant] **die; ~** *(nordd.)* [North German] coast

watscheln ['vatʃl̩n] *itr. V.; mit sein* waddle

Watschen ['va:tʃn̩] **die; ~, ~** *(bayr., österr. ugs.) s.* **Ohrfeige**

[1]**Watt** [vat] **das; ~[e]s, ~en** mud-flats *pl.*

[2]**Watt das; ~s, ~** *(Technik, Physik)* watt; **die Glühlampe hat 100 ~:** it is a 100-watt light-bulb

Watte ['vatə] **die; ~, ~n** cotton wool; *(als Polsterung)* wadding

Watte·bausch der wad of cotton wool

Watten·meer das tidal shallows *pl. (covering mud-flats)*

wattieren *tr. V.* wad; *(gesteppt)* quilt ⟨*garment*⟩; pad ⟨*shoulder etc.*⟩

wattiert *Adj.* quilted; padded ⟨*shoulder etc., envelope*⟩

Watt·sekunde die *(Physik, Technik)* joule; watt-second

Wat·vogel der *(Zool.)* wading bird; wader

wau, wau [vau, vau] *Interj. (Kindersprr.)* bow-wow; woof-woof

Wauwau der; ~s, ~s *(Kinderspr.)* bow-wow *(child lang.)*

WC [ve:'tse:] **das; ~[s], ~[s]** toilet; WC

WC-Becken das toilet bowl

WDR [ve:de:'ɛr] **der; ~** *Abk.* **Westdeutscher Rundfunk** West German Radio

weben ['ve:bn̩] **1.** *regelm. (geh., fig. auch unr.) tr., itr. V.* weave. **2.** *unr. refl. V. (geh.)* ⟨*legend*⟩ be woven (**um** around)

Weber der; ~s, ~: weaver

Weberei die; ~, ~en a) *o. Pl.* weaving *no art.*; **b)** *(Betrieb)* weaving-mill

Weberin die; ~, ~nen weaver

Weber·knecht der *(Zool.)* daddy-long-legs

Web-: ~fehler der flaw [in the weave]; **~kante die** selvage; **~stuhl der** loom

Wechsel ['vɛksl̩] **der; ~s, ~ a)** *(das Auswechseln)* change; *(Geld~)* exchange; *(Ballspiele) (Seiten~)* change-over; *(Spieler~)* substitution; **fliegender ~** *(Handball, Eishockey)* substitution without stopping play; **b)** *(Aufeinanderfolge)* alternation; **der ~ der Jahreszeiten** the rotation *or* succession of the seasons; **im ~:** alternately; *(bei mehr als zwei)* in rotation; **im ~ mit ...:** alternating with ...; **in täglichem/regelmäßigem ~:** in daily/regular rotation; **im ~ der Zeiten/Jahre/Jahreszeiten** over the ages/years/through the changing seasons; **c)** *(das Überwechseln)* move; *(Sport)* transfer; **d)** *(Bankw.)* bill of exchange (**über + Akk.** for); **e)** *(ugs. veralt.: monatliches Unterhaltsgeld)* monthly allowance; **f)** *(Jägerspr.)* game path

Wechsel-: ~bad das: ein ~bad nehmen, ~bäder machen dip one's feet/arms *etc.* in alternate hot and cold water; **~balg der** changeling; **~beziehung die** interrelation; **in [einer] ~beziehung zueinander** *od.* **miteinander stehen** be interrelated; **~dienst der** shift-work; **im ~dienst arbeiten** work shifts; **~fälle** *Pl.* vicissitudes; ups and downs *(coll.)*; **~geld das;** *o. Pl.* change; **~gesang der** antiphonal chant; *(Art desGesangs)* antiphony *no art.*

wechsel·haft *Adj.* changeable

Wechsel-: ~jahre *Pl.* change of life *sing.*; menopause *sing.*; **in die ~jahre kommen** reach the menopause; **die ~jahre des Mannes** the male menopause; **~kasse die** office issuing change; **~kurs der** exchange rate

wechseln 1. *tr. V.* **a)** change ⟨*subject, socks, job, doctor, etc.*⟩; **das Hemd ~:** change one's shirt; **die Wohnung ~:** move home; **ein Hemd/ein Paar Socken zum Wechseln** a spare shirt/pair of socks; *s. auch* **Besitzer a; b)** *([aus]tauschen)* exchange ⟨*letters, words, glances, etc.*⟩; **mit jmdm. den Platz ~:** change places with sb.; **sie wechselten die Plätze** they changed places; *s. auch* **Ring a; c)** *(um~)* change ⟨*money, note, etc.*⟩ (**in + Akk.** into); **kannst du mir 100 Mark ~?** can you change 100 marks for me?; **einen Hunderter in fünf Zwanziger/einen Schein in Münzen/Mark in Lire ~:** change a hundred for five twenties/a note into coins/marks into lire. **2.** *itr. V.* **a)** *(sich ändern)* change; **auf Rot ~** ⟨*traffic-light*⟩ change to red; **mit ~dem Erfolg** with varying success; **~de Bewölkung, ~d wolkig** *od.* **bewölkt** *(bei Wettervorhersagen)* variable cloud; **Wind aus ~den Richtungen** wind variable; **b)** *mit sein (über~)* move; *(Jägerspr.)* ⟨*game*⟩ change its habitat; **über die Grenze ~:** get across the frontier; c) ([sich] ab~) alternate; (aufeinanderfolgen) succeed one another; Geschlechtsverkehr mit [häufig] ~den Partnern sexual intercourse with frequent changes of partner; d) (herausgeben) ich kann nicht ~: I haven't any change

wẹchsel-, Wẹchsel-: ~objektiv das (Fot.) interchangeable lens; ~rahmen der picture-frame (with a removable back); ~schicht die alternating shift; in ~schicht arbeiten work alternate shifts; ~schritt der change-over step; ~seitig 1. Adj. mutual; ~seitiger Zusammenhang interconnection; ~seitige Abhängigkeit interdependence; 2. adv. mutually; sich ~seitig beeinflussen influence each other; ~seitigkeit die reciprocity; ~spiel das interplay; das ~spiel des Zufalls (geh.) the vagaries pl. of chance; ~ständig Adj. (Bot.) alternate ⟨leaves⟩; ~strom der (Elektrot.) alternating current; ~stube die bureau de change; ~voll Adj. chequered ⟨history⟩; ein ~volles Leben/Schicksal a life full of vicissitudes; ~wähler der (Politik) floating voter; ~warm Adj. (Zool.) cold-blooded; ~weise Adv. alternately; ~wirkung die interaction

Wechsler ['vɛkslɐ] der; ~s, ~ (bibl.) money-changer

Wẹck·dienst der [telephone] alarm call service

wecken ['vɛkn̩] tr. V. a) jmdn. [aus dem Schlaf] ~: wake sb. [up]; der Kaffee weckte seine Lebensgeister (fig.) the coffee revived his spirits; b) (fig.: hervorrufen) arouse, awaken ⟨interest, curiosity⟩; arouse ⟨anger⟩; awaken ⟨desire, misgiving⟩

[1]**Wẹcken** das; ~s morning call; (Mil.) reveille

[2]**Wẹcken** der; ~s, ~ (südd., österr.) a) (Brötchen) oblong roll; b) (Brot) oblong loaf

Wẹcker der; ~s, ~ a) alarm clock; jmdm. auf den ~ gehen od. fallen (ugs.) get on sb.'s nerves; b) (ugs.: Uhr) big fat watch

Wẹck·glas (Wz) das; Pl. ~gläser preserving-jar

Wẹck·ruf der morning call

Wẹdel der; ~s, ~ a) (Staub~) feather-duster; b) (Palm~, Farn~) [palm/fern] frond

wẹdeln 1. itr. V. a) ⟨tail⟩ wag; [mit dem Schwanz] ~ ⟨dog⟩ wag its tail; (winken) mit der Hand/einem Tuch ~: wave one's hand/a handkerchief; b) mit Richtungsangabe mit sein (Ski) wedel. 2. tr. V. Krümel vom Tisch ~: flap crumbs off the table

weder ['ve:dɐ] Konj. ~ A noch B neither A nor B

weg [vɛk] Adv. a) away; (verschwunden, ~gegangen) gone; ~ sein be away; (~gegangen) be gone; er ist schon seit einer Stunde ~: he left an hour ago; ~ sein (fig. ugs.) (eingeschlafen sein) have dropped off; (bewußtlos sein) be out [cold]; er war sofort ~: he was out like a light; [von jmdm./etw.] ~ sein (fig. ugs.) be knocked sideways [by sb./sth.] (coll.); [immer] ~ damit! [let's] chuck it away (coll.); ~ mit dir! away or off with you!; ~ da! get away from there!; Hände ~ [von meiner Kamera]! hands off [my camera]!; Kopf ~! move your head!; [nur] ~ von hier!, nichts wie ~! let's hop it (sl.); let's make ourselves scarce (coll.); und ~ ist/war er, und schon ist/war er ~: and he is/was gone; weit ~: far away; a long way away; weit ~ von der Schule a long way from the school; 100 Meter von der Straße ~: 100 metres from the road; s. auch Fenster; b) von ... ~ (ugs.: unmittelbar von) straight off or from; von der Schule ~ eingezogen werden be conscripted straight from school; c) über einen Schock/Schrecken usw. ~ sein (ugs.) have got over a shock/fright etc.

Weg [ve:k] der; ~[e]s,~e a) (Fuß~) path; (Feld~) track; „kein öffentlicher ~" 'no public right of way'; am ~[e] by the wayside; er kennt hier ~ und Steg (geh.) he knows every inch of this area; b) (Zugang) way; (Passage, Durchgang) passage; sich (Dat.) einen ~ durch etw. bahnen clear a path or way through sth.; jmdm. im ~[e] stehen od. (auch fig.) sein be in sb.'s way; einer Sache (Dat.) im ~[e] stehen (fig.) stand in the way of sth.; sich (Dat.) selbst im ~[e] stehen (fig.) be one's own worst enemy; geh [mir] aus dem ~[e]: get out of the or my way; jmdm. aus dem ~[e] gehen (fig.) keep out of sb's way; avoid sb.; einer Gefahr/Situation/Diskussion usw. aus dem ~[e] gehen (fig.) keep clear of a danger/avoid a situation/discussion etc.; jmdn./etw. aus dem ~[e] räumen (fig.) get rid of sb./sth.; jmdm. den ~ abschneiden head sb. off; jmdm. den ~ versperren, sich jmdm. in den ~ stellen, jmdm. in den ~ treten block sb.'s path; c) (Route, Verbindung) way; route; [jmdn.] nach dem ~ fragen ask [sb.] the way; wir haben denselben ~: we're going the same way; wohin/woher des ~[e]s? (veralt., scherzh.) wither goest/whence comest thou? (arch./joc.); des ~es kommen (geh.) draw near; approach; seines ~es od. seiner ~e gehen (geh.) go on one's way; eigene od. seine eigenen ~e gehen (fig.) go one's own way; das liegt auf dem/meinem ~: that's on the/my way; er ist mir über den ~ gelaufen (fig. ugs.) I ran or bumped into him; jmdm. nicht über den ~ trauen (fig.) not trust sb. an inch; neue ~e beschreiten od. gehen (fig.) break new ground; den ~ der Tugend verlassen leave the path of virtue; den ~ des geringsten Widerstands gehen take the line of least resistance; hier trennen sich unsere ~e (auch fig.) this is where we part company; seinen ~ machen (fig.) make one's way [in the world]; d) (Strecke, Entfernung) distance; (Gang) walk; (Reise) journey; es sind 2 km/10 Minuten ~: it is a distance of two kilometres/it is ten minutes' walk; zwei Stunden ~: two hours' journey; er hat noch einen weiten ~ vor sich (Dat.) he still has a long way to go; den ~ abkürzen take a short cut; auf dem kürzesten ~: by the shortest route; auf halbem ~[e] (auch fig.) half-way; sich auf den ~ machen set off; jmdm. einen guten Ratschlag mit auf den ~ geben (fig.) give sb. some good advice for his/her future life; etw. in die ~e leiten get sth. under way; jmdn. auf seinem letzten ~ begleiten (geh.) accompany sb. on his/her last journey; auf dem besten ~ sein, etw. zu tun (meist iron.) be well on the way towards doing sth.; er ist od. befindet sich auf dem ~[e] der Besserung he's on the road to recovery; viele ~e führen nach Rom (Spr.) all roads lead to Rome; e) (ugs.: Besorgung) errand; einen ~ machen do or run an errand; jmdm. einen ~ abnehmen run an errand for sb.; f) (Methode) way; (Mittel) means; ich sehe keinen anderen ~: I can't see any alternative; auf diesem ~[e] by this means; in this way; auf schnellstem ~[e] as speedily as possible; auf legalem/diplomatischem ~[e] through legal/diplomatic channels; auf friedlichem/gütlichem ~[e] by peaceful/amicable means; auf schriftlichem ~[e] by letter; auf kaltem ~[e] (ugs.) without bothering about the niceties

Wẹg·bereiter der; ~s, ~: forerunner; er war ein ~ des Sozialismus he helped pave the way for socialism

wẹg-: ~|blasen unr. tr. V. blow away; wie weggeblasen sein have vanished; ~|bleiben unr. itr. V.; mit sein a) (nicht kommen) stay away; (nicht nach Hause kommen) stay out; b) (ugs.: aussetzen) ⟨engine⟩ stop; ⟨electricity⟩ go off; mir blieb die Luft ~: I was left gasping; c) (ugs.: weggelassen werden) be left out; ~|bringen unr. tr. V. a) take away; (zur Reparatur, Wartung usw.) take in; b) (ugs., bes. südd.) s. ~kriegen; ~|denken unr. tr. V. sich (Dat.) etw. ~denken imagine sth. is not there; er ist aus unserem Team nicht [mehr] ~zudenken I/we can't imagine our team without him; ~|diskutieren tr. V. es läßt sich nicht ~diskutieren its existence cannot be argued away; ~|dürfen unr. itr. V. be allowed to go away; (ausgehen dürfen) be allowed to go out; ich darf hier nicht ~: I can't leave here

Wẹge·geld das a) mileage charge; b) (veralt.: Straßenzoll) road toll

Wegelagerei die; ~: highway robbery

Wẹgelagerer der; ~s, ~: highwayman

wẹgen 1. Präp. mit Gen., in bestimmten Fällen auch mit Dat./mit endungslosem Nomen a) (zur Angabe einer Ursache, eines Grundes) because of; owing to; ~ des schlechten Wetters, (geh.) des schlechten Wetters ~: because of the bad weather; [nur] ~ Peter/(ugs.) euch all because of Peter/you; ~ Hochwasser[s] owing to flooding; von Berufs ~: for professional reasons; ~ mir (ugs., bes. südd.) because of me; (was mich betrifft) as far as I'm concerned; ~ Umbau[s] geschlossen closed for alterations; ~ Mangel[s] an Beweisen owing to lack of evidence; b) (zur Angabe eines Zwecks, Ziels) for [the sake of]; ~ einer Tagung nach X fahren go to X for a conference; er ist ~ dringender Geschäfte verreist he's away on urgent business; c) (um ... willen) for the sake of; ~ der Kinder/(ugs.) dir for the children's/your sake; d) (bezüglich) about; regarding; ich habe ~ morgen noch eine Frage I've another question about tomorrow. 2. in von ~! (ugs.) you must be joking!; von ~ lauwarm/billig! lukewarm/cheap? not on your life!

Wegerich ['ve:gərɪç] der; ~s, ~e (Bot.) plantain

Wẹges·rand der (geh.) am ~: by the wayside

wẹg-, Wẹg-: ~|essen unr. tr. V. eat up; jmdm. alles ~essen eat up all sb.'s food; ~|fahren 1. unr. itr. V.; mit sein a) leave; (im Auto) drive off; (losfahren) set off; wann seid ihr in Kiel ~gefahren? when did you leave Kiel?; b) (irgendwohin fahren) go away. 2. unr. tr. V. drive away; (mit dem Handwagen/Boot/Schubkarren) take away; ~fall der; o. Pl. ending; (Einstellung) discontinuation; in ~fall kommen (Papierdt.) be discontinued; ~|fallen unr. itr. V.; mit sein be discontinued; (nicht mehr zutreffen) ⟨reason⟩ no longer apply; (weggelassen werden) be omitted; ~|fegen tr. V. (auch fig.) sweep away; ~|fliegen unr. itr. V.; mit sein fly away; (~geschleudert/~geblasen werden) fly off; ~|führen tr., itr. V. lead away; das führt vom Thema weg this takes us away from the subject

Wẹg·gab[e]lung die fork [in the path/road]

Wẹg·gang der departure

wẹg|geben unr. tr. V. a) etw. zur Reparatur ~: take sth. to be repaired; ich gebe meine Wäsche weg I send my washing to the laundry; b) (verschenken) give away

Wẹg·gefährte der (auch fig.) fellow-traveller

wẹg-: ~|gehen unr. itr. V. a) leave; (ugs.: ausgehen) go out; (ugs.: ~ziehen) move away; von jmdm. ~gehen leave sb.; geh ~! go away!; geh mir [bloß] ~ damit! (ugs.) you can keep that!; b) (verschwinden) ⟨spot, fog, etc.⟩ go away; c) (sich entfernen lassen) ⟨stain⟩ come out; d) (ugs.: verkauft werden) sell; ~|gießen unr. tr. V. pour away; ~|gucken itr. V. s. ~sehen; ~|haben unr. tr. V. (ugs.) a) have got rid of ⟨dirt, stain, etc.⟩; etw. ~haben wollen want to get rid of sth.; b) (bekommen haben) have got ⟨punishment, cold, etc.⟩; einen ~haben (betrunken *sein)* have had one too many *(coll.); (nicht bei Verstand sein)* be off one's rocker *(sl.); s. auch* **Fett a; Teil b; c)** *(können, wissen)* **in Literatur/auf einem Gebiet [et]was ~haben** know a thing or two about literature/on a subject; **d)** *(begriffen haben)* **er hatte es sofort ~:** he immediately got the hang of it *(coll.); s. auch* **Ruhe f; ~|holen** *(ugs.)* **1.** *tr. V.* take away; **2.** *refl. V.* **sich** *(Dat.)* **was ~holen** catch something; **~hören** *itr. V.* not listen; **er konnte nicht ~hören** he couldn't help listening; **~|jagen** *tr. V.* chase away; **~|kommen** *unr. itr. V.; mit sein* **a)** get away; *(~gehen können)* manage to go out; **mach, daß du [hier] ~kommst!** *(ugs.)* come on, hop it! *(sl.);* make yourself scarce! *(coll.);* **b)** *(abhanden kommen)* go missing; **c) gut/schlecht** *usw.* **[bei etw.] ~kommen** *(ugs.)* come off well/badly *etc.* [in sth.]; **d)** *(ugs.: davon ~)* get off; **e)** *(ugs.) s.* **hinwegkommen; f)** *(ugs.: loskommen)* **von jmdm. ~kommen** get away from sb.; **vom Rauchen ~kommen** give up smoking; **~|können** *unr. itr. V.* **a)** be able to leave *or* get away; *(ausgehen können)* be able to go out; **b)** *(~geworfen werden können)* **die Zeitung kann ~:** the paper can be thrown away

Weg·kreuz das wayside cross

weg-: ~|kriegen *tr. V.* get rid of ⟨*cold, pain, etc.*⟩; get out, get rid of ⟨*stain*⟩; shift, move ⟨*stone, tree-trunk*⟩; **er ist von seinem Spielzeug kaum ~zukriegen** you can hardly tear him away from his toys; **~|lassen** *unr. tr. V.* **a) jmdn. ~lassen** let sb. go; *(ausgehen lassen)* let sb. go out; **b)** *(auslassen)* leave out; omit; **die Soße ~lassen** do without the sauce; give the sauce a miss; **~|laufen** *unr. itr. V.; mit sein* run away **(von, vor +** *Dat.* from); **von zu Hause ~laufen** run away from home; **seine Frau ist ihm ~gelaufen** *(ugs.)* his wife has gone *or* run off and left him *(coll.);* **die Arbeit läuft [dir] nicht ~** *(ugs.)* the work will keep; **~|legen** *tr. V. (beiseite legen)* put aside; *(an seinen Platz legen)* put away; *(aus der Hand legen)* put down; **~|leugnen** *tr. V. (ugs.)* deny ⟨*sth.*⟩ out of existence; **~|loben** *tr. V.* **jmdn. ~loben** get rid of sb. by singing his/her praises; **~|machen** *(ugs.)* **1.** *tr. V.* get rid of; remove ⟨*wart*⟩; delete ⟨*comma etc.*⟩; **[sich** *(Dat.)***] ein Kind ~machen lassen** *(salopp)* get rid of a baby *(before birth);* **2.** *itr. V.; mit sein (landsch.: wegziehen)* go off; **~|müssen** *unr. itr.V.* **a)** have to leave; *(loskommen müssen)* have to get away; **ich muß kurz ~:** I've got to go out for a short while; **b)** *(entfernt werden müssen)* have to be removed; ⟨*furniture etc.*⟩ have to be moved; *(~gebracht werden müssen)* ⟨*letter etc.*⟩ have to go; *(~geworfen werden müssen)* have to be thrown away; **du mußt da ~:** you'll have to move; **der Diktator muß ~:** the dictator must go; **~|nehmen** *unr. tr. V.* **a)** *(entfernen)* take away; remove; move ⟨*head, arm*⟩; **nimm die Finger da ~!** [keep your] fingers off!; **[das/etwas] Gas ~nehmen** take one's foot off/ease up on the accelerator; **b)** *(entziehen, entwenden)* **jmdm. etw. ~nehmen** take sth. away from sb.; *(einem Besitzer)* **er hat mir das Buch ~genommen** he's taken my book; **dem Freund die Freundin ~nehmen** pinch one's friend's girl-friend *(coll.);* **jmdm. den Turm** *usw.* **~nehmen** *(Schachspiel)* take sb.'s rook *etc.;* **du nimmst mir das [ganze] Licht ~:** you're in my light; **c)** *(beanspruchen, einnehmen)* take up ⟨*space, time*⟩; **~|packen** *tr. V.* put away; **~|putzen** *tr. V.* **a)** clean off ⟨*marks etc.*⟩; **b)** *(ugs.: aufessen, trinken)* polish off *(coll.)*

Weg·rand der wayside; **Blumen/Gasthöfe am ~:** wayside flowers/inns

weg-: ~|rationalisieren *tr. V.* cut ⟨*staff, jobs*⟩ as part of a rationalization programme; **~|räumen** *tr. V.* clear away ⟨*dishes, rubbish, snow, etc.*⟩; remove ⟨*obstacles, difficulties*⟩; *(an seinen Platz tun)* tidy *or* put away; **~|rennen** *unr. itr. V.; mit sein (ugs.)* run away **(vor +** *Dat.* from); **~|schaffen** *tr. V.* get rid of; *(~räumen)* clear away; *(~bringen)* take away; **~|schauen** *itr. V. (bes. südd., österr., schweiz.)* look away; **~|scheren** *refl. V.* clear off *(coll.);* **~|schicken** *tr. V.* **a)** send off ⟨*letter, parcel*⟩; **b)** send ⟨*person*⟩ away; **~|schieben** *unr. tr. V.* push away; **~|schleichen** *unr. itr., refl. V.; itr. mit sein* creep away; **~|schleppen 1.** *tr. V.* **a)** *(wegtragen)* carry *or* lug off *or* away; **b)** *(abschleppen)* tow ⟨*car, rig, etc.*⟩ away; **2.** *refl. V.* drag oneself away; **~|schließen** *untr. tr. V.* lock away; **~|schmeißen** *unr. tr. V. (ugs.)* chuck away *(coll.);* **~|schnappen** *tr. V. (ugs.)* **jmdm. etw. ~schnappen/vor der Nase ~schnappen** snatch sth. away from sb./from under sb.'s nose; **jmdm. die Freundin ~schnappen** pinch sb.'s girl-friend *(coll.);* **~|schütten** *tr. V.* pour away; **~|sehen** *unr. itr. V.* **a)** look away; **b)** *(ugs.) s.* **hinwegsehen; ~|sollen** *unr. itr. V.* **er soll jetzt ~:** he is to *or* should leave now; **diese Sachen sollen ~:** these things are to go; **das Plakat soll ~:** the poster is to be removed; **~|spülen** *tr. V.* **a)** wash away; **b)** *(ugs.: spülen)* wash up; **~|stecken** *tr. V.* **a)** put away; **b)** *(fig. ugs.: hinnehmen)* take, accept ⟨*blow*⟩; swallow ⟨*insult*⟩; **einen ~stecken** *(derb)* have a poke *(coarse);* **~|stellen** *tr. V.* put away; move ⟨*car*⟩ out of the way; *(beiseite stellen)* put aside; **~|stoßen** *unr. tr. V.* push *or* shove away

Weg·strecke die stretch [of road]; *(Entfernung)* distance

weg-: ~|tragen *unr. tr. V.* carry away; **~|treten 1.** *unr. tr. V.* kick away; **2.** *unr. itr. V.; mit sein* step away; *(zurücktreten)* step back; *(Milit.)* dismiss; **~getreten!** *(Milit.)* dismiss!; **[etwas] ~getreten sein** *(fig. ugs.)* be [somewhat] distracted; **~|tun** *unr. tr. V. (ugs.)* **a)** put away; **b)** *(wegwerfen)* throw away

Wegweiser der; ~s, ~ a) signpost; **b)** *(fig.: Buch)* guide

weg-: ~|werfen *unr. tr. V. (auch fig.)* throw away; **das ist doch ~geworfenes Geld** *(ugs.)* that's money down the drain *(coll.);* **~werfend** *Adj.* dismissive ⟨*gesture, remark*⟩

Weg·werf-: ~flasche die disposable *or* non-returnable bottle; **~gesellschaft die** *(abwertend)* throw-away society; **~mentalität die** *(abwertend)* use-and-throw-away attitude

weg-: ~|wischen *tr. V.* wipe away; *(fig.)* erase ⟨*memory*⟩; dispel ⟨*fear, doubt*⟩; dismiss ⟨*objection*⟩; **~|wollen** *unr. itr. V.* want to go *or* leave; *(loskommen wollen)* want to get away; *(ausgehen wollen)* want to go out; *(verreisen wollen)* want to go away; **~|zaubern** *tr. V.* spirit away; **wie weggezaubert sein** have vanished into thin air

Weg·zehrung die *(geh.)* provisions *pl.* for the journey

weg-: ~|zerren *tr. V.* drag away; **~|ziehen 1.** *unr.tr. V.* pull away; pull *or* draw back ⟨*curtain*⟩; pull off ⟨*blanket*⟩; **jmdm. den Stuhl ~ziehen:** pull away sb.'s chair [from under him/her]; **2.** *unr. itr. V.; mit sein* **a)** *(umziehen)* move away; **aus X ~ziehen** leave X; move from X; **b)** *(wandern)* ⟨*animals, nomads, etc.*⟩ leave [on their migration]

Weg·zug der move; **nach ihrem ~ aus Berlin** after moving [away] from Berlin

¹weh *Interj. (veralt.)* **o ~:** alas; **~ mir!** woe is me! *(arch.)*

²weh [veː] **1.** *Adj.* **a)** *nicht präd. (ugs.: schmerzend)* sore; **einen ~en Finger haben** have a sore *or* bad finger; **b)** *(geh.: schmerzlich)* painful; **ein ~es Lächeln** a sad smile. **2.** *adv.* **a)** *(ugs.)* **~ tun** hurt; **mir tut der Magen/Rücken/Kopf ~:** my stomach/back/head is aching *or* hurts; **mir tut der Hals ~:** my throat is sore; **jmdm./sich ~ tun** hurt sb./oneself; **b)** *(geh.: schmerzlich)* **ihr ist ~ ums Herz** her heart aches; she is sore at heart; **ein ~es Gefühl** an aching feeling

Weh das; ~[e]s *(geh.)* sorrow; grief

wehe *Interj.* woe betide you/him *etc.;* **~ [dir], wenn du ...:** woe betide you if you ...

¹Wehe [ˈveːə] **die; ~, ~n: die ~n setzten ein** the contractions started; she went into labour; **~n haben** have contractions; **in den ~n liegen** be in labour

²Wehe die; ~, ~n drift

wehen 1. *itr. V.* **a)** *(blasen)* blow; **b)** *(flattern)* flutter; **ihre Haare wehten im Wind** her hair was blowing about in the wind; **mit ~den Rockschößen** with coat-tails flapping; **c)** *mit sein* ⟨*leaves, snowflakes, scent*⟩ waft. **2.** *tr. V.* blow

weh-, Weh-: ~klage die *(geh.)* lamentation; **~klagen** *itr. V. (geh.)* lament; **über etw.** *(Akk.)* **~klagen** lament *or* bewail sth.; **~leidig** *(abwertend)* **1.** *Adj.* **a)** *(überempfindlich)* soft; **sei nicht so ~leidig!** don't be so soft *or* such a sissy; **b)** *(weinerlich)* whining *attrib.;* **ein ~leidiges Gesicht machen** look sorry for oneself; **2.** *adv.* self-pityingly; *(weinerlich)* whiningly; **~mut die; ~** *(geh.)* melancholy *or* wistful nostalgia; **~mütig 1.** *Adj.* melancholically *or* wistfully nostalgic; **2.** *adv.* with melancholy *or* wistful nostalgia

wehmuts·voll *(geh.) s.* **wehmütig**

¹Wehr die; ~, ~en a) *in* **sich [gegen jmdn./etw.] zur ~ setzen** make a stand [against sb./sth.]; resist [sb./sth.]; **b)** *s.* **Feuer~; c)** *s.* **~macht**

²Wehr das; ~[e]s, ~e weir

Wehr-: ~beauftragte der *parliamentary commissioner for the armed forces;* **~bereichs·kommando das** military district command

Wehr·dienst *der; o. Pl.* military service *no art.;* **zum ~ einberufen werden** be called up; **seinen ~ ableisten** do one's military service

wehr·dienst-, Wehr·dienst-: ~pflichtig *Adj. s.* **wehrpflichtig; ~verweigerer der; ~s, ~:** conscientious objector; **~verweigerung die** conscientious objection

wehren 1. *refl. V.* **a)** *(körperlich Widerstand leisten)* defend oneself; put up a fight; **sich tapfer/mit aller Kraft ~:** defend oneself *or* resist bravely/with all one's might; *s. auch* **Haut a; b)** *(sich verwahren)* **sich gegen etw. ~:** fight against sth.; **gegen so etwas weiß ich mich zu ~:** I know how to deal with that sort of thing; **c)** *(sich sträuben)* **sich [dagegen] ~, etw. zu tun** resist having to do sth. **2.** *itr. V. (geh.: einschreiten gegen)* **jmdm./einer Sache ~:** fight sb./fight [against] sth. **3.** *tr. V. (geh. veralt.) s.* **verwehren**

wehr-, Wehr-: ~ersatz·dienst der *s.* **Ersatzdienst; ~erziehung die** *(bes. DDR)* defence education; **~experte der** defence expert; **~fähig** *Adj.* fit for military service *postpos.;* **~gang der;** *Pl.* **~gänge** *(hist.)* battlemented parapet; **~haft** *Adj.* **a)** *(fähig, sich zu verteidigen)* able to defend oneself *postpos.;* **b)** *(befestigt)* fortified; **~kirche die** fortified church; **~kraft die;** *o. Pl.* military strength; **~kraft·zersetzung die** *(Milit., bes. ns.)* undermining of military strength; **~los** *Adj.* defenceless; **jmdm./einer Sache ~los ausgeliefert sein** be defenceless against sb./sth.; **~losigkeit die; ~:** defencelessness; **~macht die;** *o. Pl.* armed forces *pl.;* **~mann der a)** *Pl.* **~männer** *od.* **~leute** *s.* **Feuerwehrmann; b)** *Pl.* **~männer** *(schweiz.: Soldat)* soldier; **~paß der** service record [book]; **~pflicht die;** *o. Pl.* military service; conscription; **die allgemeine ~pflicht** compulsory military service; **~pflichtig** *Adj.* liable for military service *postpos;* **~pflichtige der;** *adj.*

Dekl. person liable for military service; **~sold der** military pay; **~übung die** reserve duty [re]training exercise

Weh·weh das; ~s, ~s *(Kinderspr.)* hurt; **hast du ein ~?** have you hurt yourself?

Wehwehchen das; ~s, ~: little complaint

Weib [vaip] **das; ~[e]s, ~er a)** *(veralt.: weibliches Wesen, ugs.: Frau)* woman; female *(derog.)*; **sie ist ein tolles ~:** she's a bit of all right *(coll.)*; **b)** *(veralt., noch scherzh.: Ehefrau)* wife; **~ und Kind [haben]** [have a] wife and family; **er nahm sie zum ~[e]** he took her for his wife

Weibchen das; ~s, ~ a) *(weibliches Tier)* female; **b)** *(abwertend: Frau)* female; **er degradiert sie zum ~:** he reduces her to the role of dumb female; **c)** *(veralt., noch fam. scherzh.: Ehefrau)* little woman *(joc.)*

Weiber-: ~feind der woman-hater; misogynist; **~geschichten** *Pl. (salopp)* affairs; **~held der** *(ugs.)* lady-killer; **~wirtschaft die;** *o. Pl. (abwertend)* **das ist ja hier die reinste ~wirtschaft** the whole place seems to be run by women *or* females

weibisch *(abwertend)* **1.** *Adj.* womanish; effeminate. **2.** *adv.* womanishly; effeminately

weiblich 1. *Adj.* **a)** female; **b)** *(für die Frau typisch)* feminine; **c)** *(Sprachw.)* feminine ⟨*noun, declension, gender*⟩; *(Verslehre)* female ⟨*rhyme*⟩. **2.** *adv.* femininely

Weiblichkeit die; ~ a) *(weibliche Art)* femininity; **b)** *(Gesamtheit der Frauen)* women *pl.*; **die holde ~** *(veralt.)* the fair sex

Weibs-: ~bild das a) *(ugs.)* woman; **b)** *(salopp abwertend)* female; **~stück das** *(salopp abwertend)* bitch *(sl.)*

weich [vaiç] **1.** *Adj.* **a)** *(auch fig.)* soft; soft, mellow ⟨*sound, voice*⟩; **ein ~es Ei** a soft-boiled egg; **ein Ei ~ kochen** soft-boil an egg; **ein ~es Herz** *od.* **Gemüt haben** be soft-hearted; **~ werden** *(ugs.)* soften; weaken; **b)** *(nicht scharf u. streng)* soft, gentle ⟨*features*⟩; gentle ⟨*mouth, face*⟩. **2.** *adv.* softly; ⟨*brake*⟩ gently; **~ landen** *od.* **aufsetzen** make a soft landing; *s. auch* **betten 1 a**

Weich·bild das: wir nähern uns dem ~ der Stadt we're approaching the outskirts of the town; **noch im ~ der Stadt liegen** be still just in[side] the town

¹Weiche die; ~, ~n a) *(Flanke)* flank; **b)** *o. Pl. (Weichheit)* softness

²Weiche die; ~, ~n points *pl. (Brit.)*; switch *(Amer.)*; **die ~ stellen** set the points; **die ~n [für etw.] stellen** *(fig.)* set the course [for sth.]

¹weichen 1. *itr. V.; mit sein (weich werden)* soak. **2.** *tr. V. (ein~)* soak

²weichen *unr. itr. V.; mit sein* **a)** *(sich entfernen)* move; **nicht von jmds. Seite ~:** not move from *or* leave sb.'s side; **das Blut wich aus ihrem Gesicht** *(geh.)* the blood drained from her face; **b)** *(Platz machen)* **vor jmdm./einer Sache ~:** give way to sb./sth.; **dem Feind ~:** retreat from the enemy; **vor jmdm./etw. zur Seite ~:** step *or* move out of the way of sb./sth.; **die Bäume sind dem Neubau gewichen** the trees have gone to make room for the new building; **die Spannung wich großer Erleichterung** *(fig.)* [the] tension gave way to great relief; *s. auch* **wanken a; c)** *(nachlassen)* subside; **die Angst/Spannung wich von ihm** the fear/tension left him

Weichen·steller der pointsman *(Brit.)*; switchman *(Amer.)*

weich·gekocht *Adj. (präd. getrennt geschrieben)* soft-boiled ⟨*egg*⟩

Weichheit die; ~ a) *(auch fig.)* softness; *(eines Tons, der Stimme)* mellowness; **die ~ seines Gemüts** *(fig.)* his soft-heartedness; **b)** *s.* **weich 1 b:** softness; gentleness

weich-, Weich-: ~herzig 1. *Adj.* soft-hearted; **2.** *adv.* soft-heartedly; **~herzigkeit die; ~:** soft-heartedness; **~holz das** softwood; **~käse der** soft cheese

weichlich 1. *Adj.* soft; *(ohne innere Festigkeit)* weak. **2.** *adv.* softly

Weichling der; ~s, ~e *(abwertend)* weakling

weich-, Weich-: ~|machen *tr. V. (ugs.)* soften up; **~macher der** *(Chemie, Technik)* plasticizer; **~schalig** *Adj.* soft-shelled ⟨*crustacean*⟩; soft-skinned ⟨*fruit*⟩

Weichsel ['vaiksl] **die; ~:** Vistula

Weichsel·kirsche die *(landsch.) s.* **Sauerkirsche**

Weich-: ~spüler der; ~s, ~ *(Werbespr.)*, **~spülmittel das** [fabric] softener; **~teile** *Pl.* **a)** *(Anat.)* soft parts; **b)** *(ugs.: Genitalien)* privates; **~tier das;** *meist Pl.* mollusc; **~zeichner der** *(Fot.)* soft-focus lens

¹Weide ['vaidə] **die; ~, ~n** willow

²Weide die; ~, ~n pasture; **auf der ~ sein** be at pasture; **die Kühe auf die** *od.* **zur ~ treiben** drive the cows to pasture

Weide-: ~fläche die pasture; **~land das** pasture [land]; grazing land

weiden 1. *itr., tr. V.* graze. **2.** *refl. V.* **a)** *(geh.: sich erfreuen)* **er** *od.* **sein Auge weidete sich an dem herrlichen Anblick** he feasted his eyes on the glorious sight; **b)** *(abwertend: schadenfroh beobachten)* gloat over; revel in; **sich an jmds. Schmerz** *(Dat.)* **~:** gloat over sb.'s pain

Weiden-: ~baum der willow tree; **~gerte die** willow rod; *(zum Korbflechten)* osier; *(kleiner)* wicker; **~kätzchen das** willow catkin

Weide-: ~platz der pasture; **~wirtschaft die** pastoral farming *no art.*

weidlich *Adv.* **etw. ~ ausnutzen** make full use of sth.; **sich ~ über etw. lustig machen** have a good laugh at sth.; **sie mußten sich ~ plagen** they really had to slave away

Weid·mann der; *Pl.* **~männer** *(geh.)* huntsman; hunter

weid·männisch 1. *Adj.* hunting, huntsman's *attrib.* ⟨*expression, terminology, customs*⟩. **2.** *adv.* in the manner of a huntsman; like a huntsman

Weidmanns·heil *Interj.* good hunting

Weid·werk das; *o. Pl.* [art of] hunting

weid·wund *Adj.* **ein ~ geschossenes Tier** an animal shot in the belly [and fatally wounded]

weigern ['vaigɐn] **1.** *refl. V.* refuse; **sich ~, etw. zu tun** refuse to do sth. **2.** *tr. V. (veralt.: ver~)* **jmdm. etw. ~:** refuse *or* deny sb. sth.

Weigerung die; ~, ~en refusal

Weih·bischof der *(kath. Kirche)* suffragan bishop

¹Weihe die; ~, ~n a) *(Rel.: Einweihung)* consecration; dedication; **b)** *(kath. Kirche: Priester~, Bischofs~)* ordination; **die niederen/höheren ~n** *(hist.)* the minor/major orders; **c)** *(geh.: Erhabenheit)* solemnity

²Weihe die; ~, ~n *(Zool.)* harrier

weihen *tr. V.* **a)** *(Rel.: durch Weihe heiligen)* consecrate; **b)** *(kath. Kirche: ordinieren)* ordain; **jmdn. zum Priester/Bischof ~:** ordain sb. priest/consecrate sb. bishop; **c)** *(Rel.: durch Weihe zueignen)* dedicate (*Dat.* to); **d)** *(geh.: preisgeben)* **dem Tod[e]/dem Untergang geweiht sein** be doomed to die/to fall; **e)** *(geh.: widmen)* dedicate

Weiher der; ~s, ~ *(bes. südd.)* [small] pond

Weihe·stätte die *(geh.)* holy place

weihe·voll *Adj. (geh.)* solemn

Weih-: ~gabe die *(bes. kath. Kirche)* votive offering; **~nacht die;** *o. Pl. (geh.) s.* **Weihnachten**

weihnachten *itr. V. (unpers.)* **es weihnachtet bereits/es fängt an zu ~:** Christmas has already started/Christmas is starting

Weihnachten das; ~, ~: Christmas; **frohe** *od.* **fröhliche** *od.* **gesegnete ~!** Merry *or* Happy Christmas!; **grüne ~:** Christmas without snow; **zu** *od. (bes. südd.)* **an/über ~:** at *or* for/over Christmas

weihnachtlich 1. *Adj.* Christmassy. **2.** *adv.* **~ geschmückt/gedeckt sein** be decorated/set for Christmas; **ihr war ~ zumute** she was in a Christmassy mood

Weihnachts-: ~abend der Christmas Eve; **~baum der** Christmas tree; **~einkauf der;** *meist Pl.* Christmas purchase; **~einkäufe** Christmas shopping *sing.*; **~feier die** Christmas party; **~feiertag der: der erste/zweite ~feiertag** Christmas Day/Boxing Day; **~ferien** *Pl.* Christmas holidays; **~fest das** Christmas; **~gans die** Christmas goose; **~gebäck das** Christmas biscuits *pl. (Brit.) or (Amer.)* cookies *pl.*; **~geld das** Christmas bonus; **~geschäft das** Christmas trade; **~geschenk das** Christmas present *or* gift; **~geschichte die** Christmas story; **~gratifikation die** Christmas bonus; **~karte die** Christmas card; **~lied das** Christmas carol; **~mann der;** *Pl.* **~männer a)** Father Christmas; Santa Claus; **b)** *(ugs.: Dummkopf)* silly idiot *(coll.)*; **~markt der** Christmas fair; **~spiel das** *(Literaturw.)* nativity play; **~stern der a)** Christmas star; **b)** *(Pflanze)* poinsettia; **~stollen der** Christmas Stollen; **~tag der** *s.* **~feiertag; ~zeit die** Christmas time; **in der ~zeit** at Christmas time

Weih-: ~rauch der incense; **jmdm. ~rauch streuen** *(geh.)* eulogize sb.; **~wasser das** *(kath. Kirche)* holy water; **~wasserbecken das** *(kath. Kirche)* stoup

weil [vail] *Konj.* because

weiland *Adv. (veralt.) (vormals)* formerly; *(einst)* once

Weilchen das; ~s little while

Weile die; ~: while; **eine ganze** *od. (geh.)* **geraume ~:** a good while; **eine ~ dauern** take a while; **vor einer ~:** a while ago; **damit hat es noch [gute] ~** *(geh.)* there is still [plenty of] time; *s. auch* **¹Ding c; eilen 1 a**

weilen *itr. V. (geh.) (ver~)* stay; *(sein)* be; **zu Besuch bei jmdm. ~:** be on a visit to sb.; be visiting sb.; **er weilt nicht mehr unter uns** *(Dat.) od.* **unter den Lebenden** *(verhüll.)* he is no longer among *or* with us

Weiler der; ~s, ~: hamlet

Weimarer Republik die Weimar Republic

Wein [vain] **der; ~[e]s, ~e a)** wine; **im ~ ist** *od.* **liegt Wahrheit** *(Spr.)* in vino veritas; **jmdm. reinen ~ einschenken** *(fig.)* tell sb. the truth; **neuen ~ in alte Schläuche füllen** *(fig.)* pour new wine into old bottles *(prov.)*; **b)** *o. Pl. (Reben)* vines *pl.*; **wilder ~:** Virginia creeper; **c)** *o. Pl. (~trauben)* grapes *pl.*

Wein-: ~[an]bau der; *o. Pl.* wine-growing *no art.*; **~bauer der** wine-grower; **~beere die a)** grape; **b)** *(südd., österr., schweiz.: Rosine)* raisin; **~beißer der** *(österr.)* **a)** *(Gebäck)* iced ginger biscuit; **b)** *(~kenner)* wine connoisseur; **~berg der** vineyard; **~berg·schnecke die** [edible] snail; **~brand der** brandy

weinen 1. *itr. V.* cry; *(aus Trauer, Kummer)* cry; weep; **um jmdn. ~:** cry *or* weep for sb.; **über jmdn./etw. ~:** cry over *or* about sb./sth.; **vor Glück/Wut ~:** cry with happiness/anger; **vor Freude ~:** cry *or* weep for *or* with joy; **es ist zum Weinen** it's enough to make you weep; **es ist zum Weinen mit dir** *(ugs.)* you're enough to make anyone weep; **leise ~d abziehen** *(fig. ugs.)* leave with one's tail between one's legs. **2.** *tr.V.* shed ⟨*tears*⟩; **sich** *(Dat.)* **die Augen rot ~:** make one's eyes red with crying; **sich in den Schlaf ~:** cry oneself to sleep

weinerlich 1. *Adj.* tearful; weepy; **ein ~es Gesicht machen** look on the verge of tears *or* as if one is about to cry. **2.** *adv.* tearfully

wein-, Wein-: ~essig der wine vinegar; **~faß das** wine barrel *or* cask; **~flasche** winebottle; **~garten der** vineyard; **~gegend die** wine-growing region; **~geist der;** *o. Pl.* ethyl alcohol; ethanol; **~glas das** wineglass; **~gut das** vineyard; **~händ-**

ler der wine-merchant; **~handlung die** wine-merchant's; **~hauer der** *(österr.)* wine-grower; **~jahr das** vintage; **~karte die** wine-list; **~keller der** wine-cellar; **~kenner der** wine connoisseur; **~königin die** wine queen *(representing a particular wine region for the year)*; **~krampf der** crying fit; fit of crying; **~küfer der** cellarman; **~lese die** grape harvest; **~lokal das** wine bar; **~probe die** wine-tasting [session]; **~rebe die a)** grapevine; **b)** *(Ranke)* [grapevine] shoot; **~rot** *Adj.* wine-red; wine-coloured; **~schaum·creme die** *(Kochk.)* zabaglione; **~selig** *Adj.* merry on *or* with wine *pred.*; **in ~seliger Stimmung sein** be merry on *or* with wine; **~stein der;** *o. Pl.* cream of tartar; **~stock der;** *Pl.* **~stöcke** [grape]vine; **~straße die** wine route; **~stube die** wine bar; **~traube die** grape; **~trinker der** wine-drinker; **~verkoster der** wine-taster

weise ['vaizə] **1.** *Adj.* wise; **ein Weiser** a wise man; **die drei Weisen aus dem Morgenland** the three Wise Men from the East. **2.** *adv.* wisely

-weise *(bei Mengen- und Maßangaben)* by the ...; **kilo~/meter~/liter~/eimer~** *usw.* by the kilo/metre/litre/bucketful *etc.*; in kilos/metres/litres/bucketfuls *etc.*; **monats~/wochen~/stunden~:** by the month/week/hour; **paar~:** in pairs

Weise die; ~, ~n a) *(Art, Verfahren)* way; **auf diese/andere ~:** this way/ [in] another way; **auf die eine oder andere ~:** in one way or another; **auf meine ~:** in my own way; **auf geheimnisvolle ~:** in a mysterious manner; mysteriously; **in gewisser ~:** in certain respects; **in keiner ~:** in no way; **b)** *(Melodie)* tune; melody

weisen 1. *unr. tr. V.* **a)** *(geh.: zeigen)* show; **jmdm. etw. ~:** show sb. sth.; *s. auch* **Tür; b)** *(ver~)* **jmdn. aus dem Zimmer ~:** send sb. out of the room; **jmdn. aus dem Land/von der Schule ~:** expel sb. from the country/ from the school; **etw. von sich ~** *(fig.)* reject sth.; *s. auch* **Hand f; Schranke b. 2.** *unr. itr. V. (irgendwohin zeigen)* point; **mit der Hand auf etw.** *(Akk.)* **~:** point to sth.; **nach Norden ~:** point North; **eine Idee, die in die Zukunft weist** a forward-looking idea

Weisheit die; ~, ~en a) *o. Pl.* wisdom; **die ~ mit Löffeln gefressen haben** *(ugs.)* know it all; know all the answers; **er hat die ~ [auch] nicht mit Löffeln gefressen** *(ugs.)* he is not all that bright; **der ~ letzter Schluß** the answer to everything; **mit seiner ~ am Ende sein** be at one's wit's end; **b)** *(Erkenntnis)* wise insight; *(Spruch)* wise saying; **deine ~en kannst du für dich behalten** *(spött.)* you can keep your pearls of wisdom to yourself

Weisheits·zahn der wisdom tooth

weis|machen *tr. V. (ugs.)* **das kannst du mir nicht ~!** you can't expect me to swallow that!; **du willst mir doch nicht ~, daß ...?** you're not trying to make me believe *or* *(coll.)* to kid me that ...; **er läßt sich** *(Dat.)* **nichts ~:** you can't fool him; he's not to be fooled; **das kannst du anderen ~!** tell that to the marines *(coll.)*

[1]**weiß** [vais] *1. u. 3. Pers. Sg. Präsens v.* **wissen**

[2]**weiß** *Adj.* **a)** white; **~e Ostern/Weihnachten** Easter with snow/white Christmas; **das Weiße Meer** the White Sea; **Weißer Sonntag** *(christl. Kirche)* Low Sunday; **der ~e Sport** tennis; **er/sie ist ~ geworden** his/her hair has turned white; *s. auch* **Fleck b; Haus a; Tod; Weste; b)** *(Kaufmannsspr.)* unbranded ⟨*product*⟩

Weiß das; ~[e]s, ~: white

weis-, Weis-: ~sagen *tr. V.* **a)** *auch itr. (prophezeien)* prophesy; foretell; **b)** *(ahnen lassen)* forebode; **~sager der** prophet; **~sagerin die** prophetess; **~sagung die; ~, ~en** prophecy

weiß-, Weiß-: ~bier das *light, highly effervescent, top-fermented beer made from wheat and barley;* weiss beer; **~blech das** tin plate; **~blond** *Adj.* ash-blond/-blonde; **~brot das** white bread; **ein ~brot** a white loaf; **~buch das** *(Politik)* White Paper; **~dorn der** hawthorn

[1]**Weiße die; ~, ~n a)** *o. Pl.* whiteness; **b)** *s.* [1]**Berliner 1**

[2]**Weiße der/die;** *adj. Dekl.* white; white man/woman

Weiße-Kragen-Kriminalität die white-collar crime *no art.*

weißeln *(südd., österr., schweiz.),* **weißen** *tr. V.* paint white; *(tünchen)* whitewash

weiß-, Weiß-: ~gardist der *(hist.)* member of the White Guard; **~glühend** *Adj.* white-hot; **~glut die** white heat; **jmdn. [bis] zur ~glut bringen** *od.* **reizen** *od.* **treiben** *(ugs.)* make sb. livid *(Brit. coll.)*; **~gold das** white gold; **~haarig** *Adj.* white-haired; **~haarig sein** have white hair; **~herbst der** ≈ rosé wine; **~käse der** *(bes. nordd.) s.* **Quark; ~kohl der,** *(bes. südd., österr.)* **~kraut das** white cabbage

weißlich *Adj.* whitish

Weiß-: ~macher der whitener; **~rußland** *(das)* White Russia

weißt *2. Pers. Sg. Präsens v.* **wissen**

weiß-, Weiß-: ~tanne die silver fir; **~wal der** white whale; **~wand·reifen der** whitewall tyre; **~|waschen** *unr. tr. V. (ugs.)* **jmdn./sich ~waschen** clear sb.'s/one's name; **~wein der** white wine; **~wurst die** veal sausage

Weisung die; ~, ~en a) *(geh., sonst Amtsspr.)* instruction; *(Direktive)* directive; **auf** *od.* **nach ~ [von jmdm.]** on *or* in accordance with [sb.'s] instructions; **~ geben/erhalten/haben, etw. zu tun** give/receive/have instructions to do sth.; **b)** *(Rechtsw.)* [court] order; **jmdm. die ~ erteilen, etw. zu tun** order sb. to do sth.

weisungs-, Weisungs-: ~befugnis die authority to issue instructions/directives; **~gebunden** *Adj.* subject to instructions/directives *postpos.*; **~gemäß** *Adv.* in accordance with instructions; as instructed

weit [vait] **1.** *Adj.* **a)** *(räumlich ausgedehnt)* wide; *(fig.)* broad ⟨*concept*⟩; **in die ~e Welt ziehen** go out into the big wide world; **~e Kreise** *od.* **Teile der Bevölkerung** *(fig.)* large *or* broad sections of the population; **im ~eren Sinn** *(fig.)* in the broader sense; **das Weite suchen** *(fig.)* take to one's heels; *s. auch* **Feld e; b)** *(locker sitzend)* wide; **jmdm. zu ~ sein** ⟨*clothes*⟩ be too loose on sb.; **einen Rock [in der Taille] ~er machen** let out a skirt [at the waist]; **c)** *(streckenmäßig ausgedehnt, lang)* long ⟨*way*⟩; **einen ~en Blick [über die Gegend] haben** have a wide view [over the area]. **2.** *adv.* **a)** *(räumlich ausgedehnt)* **~ geöffnet** wide open; **~ verbreitet** widespread; **~ herumgekommen sein** have got around a good deal; have travelled widely; **~ und breit war niemand zu sehen** there was no one to be seen anywhere; **den besten Fisch ~ und breit kriegst du in diesem Restaurant** this restaurant has the best fish for miles around; **b)** *(streckenmäßig ausgedehnt, lang)* far; **~er** further; farther; **am ~esten** [the] furthest *or* farthest; **es ist noch ~:** it is still a long way; **sehr ~ gehen** walk a very long way; **hast du es ~?** do you have far to go?; **~ [entfernt** *od.* **weg] wohnen** live a long way away *or* off; live far away; **zwei Häuser ~er wohnen** live two houses further *or* farther on; **15 km ~ [von hier]** 15 km. away [from here]; **5,80 Meter ~ springen** jump [a distance of] 5.80 metres; **von ~em** from a distance; **von ~ her** from far away; **es würde zu ~ führen, das alles jetzt zu analysieren** it would be too much to analyse it all now; **das geht zu ~** *(fig.)* that is going too far; **etw. zu ~ treiben, es mit etw. zu ~ treiben** *(fig.)* overdo sth.; carry sth. too far; **mit etw. [nicht] ~ kommen** *(fig.)* [not] get far with sth.; **so ~, so gut** so far, so good; *s. auch* **entfernt a; hersein c; c)** *(zeitlich entfernt)* **~ nach Mitternacht** well past midnight; **~ zurückliegen** be a long way back *or* a long time ago; **d)** *(in der Entwicklung)* far; **sehr ~ mit etw. sein** have got a long way with sth.; **wie weit seid ihr?** how far have you got?; **wir wollen es gar nicht erst so ~ kommen lassen** we do not want to let it come to that; **so ~ ist es schon mit dir gekommen?** have things come to that with you?; **er wird es einmal ~ bringen** he will go far one of these days; **~ fortgeschritten** *od.* **gediehen sein** be far advanced; **e)** *(weitaus)* far; **jmdn. ~ übertreffen** surpass sb. by far *or* by a long way; **bei ~em** by far; by a long way; **bei ~em nicht!** not by a long way!; **bei ~em nicht so gut wie ...:** nowhere near as good as ...; **das ist bei ~em nicht alles** that's not all by a long way; **bei ~em hübscher als ...:** far prettier than ...; **etw. bei ~em übertreffen** far exceed sth.; *s. auch* **gefehlt 2; weiter**

-weit *Adj., adv.* **europa~/hessen~:** throughout Europe/Hessen *postpos.*

weit-, Weit-: ~ab *Adv.* far away; **~aus** *Adv.* far ⟨*better, worse, etc.*⟩; **der ~aus beste** *od.* **~aus der beste Reiter** by far *or* far and away the best rider; **~bekannt** *Adj.; präd. getrennt geschrieben* widely known; **~blick der;** *o. Pl.* far-sightedness; **politischen ~blick haben** be politically far-sighted; **ihm fehlt der ~blick** he lacks vision; **~blickend** *Adj.* far-sighted

Weite die; ~, ~n a) *(räumliche Ausdehnung)* expanse; **b)** *(bes. Sport: Entfernung)* distance; **c)** *(eines Kleidungsstückes)* width; **d)** *(Größe, Durchmesser)* width

weiten 1. *tr. V.* widen. **2.** *refl. V.* widen; ⟨*pupil*⟩ dilate; *(fig.)* ⟨*chest*⟩ swell

weiter *Adv.* **a)** *s.* **weit 2; b)** further; farther; **halt, nicht ~!** stop, don't go any further; **~!** go on!; **er hat immer ~ gelacht/geschwatzt** he carried on laughing/chattering; **nur immer ~ so!** keep it up!; **und so ~:** and so on; **und so ~ und so fort** and so on and so forth; **c)** *(~hin, anschließend)* then; **was geschah ~?** what happened then *or* next?; **d)** *(außerdem, sonst)* **~ nichts, nichts ~:** nothing more *or* else; **~ weiß ich nichts von der Sache** that's all I know about it; **ich brauche ~ nichts** I don't need anything else; there's nothing else I need; **er wollte ~ nichts als ...:** all he wanted was ...; **Was ist los? – Ach, nichts ~:** What's the matter – Oh, nothing in particular; **das macht ~ nichts** *od.* **ist nicht ~ schlimm** it isn't that important; it doesn't really matter; **wenn es ~ nichts ist** if that's all

weiter... *Adj.; nicht präd. (zusätzlich)* further; **~e zwei Jahre warten** wait a further two years *or* two more years; **ohne ~e Umstände** without any fuss; **die ~e Entwicklung abwarten** await further developments; **im ~en Verlauf zeigte sich, daß ...:** it later became clear that ...; **bis auf ~es** for the time being; **„bis auf ~es geschlossen"** 'closed until further notice'; **des ~en** *(geh.)* furthermore; *s. auch* **ohne 1 c**

weiter-, Weiter-: ~|arbeiten *itr. V.* continue *or* carry on working; **~|bestehen** *unr. itr. V.* continue to exist; **~|bilden** *tr. V. s.* **fortbilden; ~bildung die;** *o. Pl. s.* **Fortbildung; ~|bringen** *unr. tr. V.* **die Diskussion/Auskunft/sein Ratschlag brachte uns nicht ~:** the discussion/information/his advice did not get us any further [forward]; **~|entwickeln** *tr., refl. V.* develop [further]; **er hat sich im letzten Jahr auffallend ~entwickelt** he has matured noticeably in the last year; **~entwicklung die** [further] development; **~|erzählen** *tr. V.* **a)** continue telling; **b)** *(~sagen)* pass on; **erzähl**

das nicht ~: don't tell anyone; ~|fahren *unr. itr. V.; mit sein* continue [on one's way]; *(~ reisen)* travel on; ~fahrt die; *o. Pl.* continuation of one's journey; angenehme ~fahrt! enjoy the rest of your journey; auf der ~fahrt nach X trafen wir ...: continuing our journey to X we met ...; ~flug der; *o. Pl.* connecting flight; onward flight; auf unserem ~flug as we continued our flight; Passagiere zum ~flug nach New York passengers continuing on to New York; ~|führen 1. *tr. V.* a) *(fortführen)* continue; b) *(voranbringen)* das führt uns nicht ~: that does not get us any further *or* anywhere; 2. *itr. V.* continue; ~führende Schulen secondary schools; ~gabe die; *o. Pl.* a) passing on; b) *(Sport)* pass; ~|geben *unr. tr. V.* a) pass on; b) *(Sport)* pass; ~|gehen *unr. itr. V.; mit sein* a) go on; bitte ~gehen, nicht stehenbleiben! please move along *or* keep moving, don't stop!; b) *(sich fortsetzen, noch nicht aufhören)* continue; go on; der Weg geht nicht ~: the path does not go any further; die Geschichte/Sache geht ~: there's more to come; das Leben geht ~: life goes on; so kann es nicht ~gehen it cannot go on like this; so kann es mit uns nicht ~gehen we cannot go on like this; wie soll es denn nun ~gehen? what is going to happen now?; ~|helfen *unr. itr. V.* jmdm. [mit etw.] ~helfen help sb. [with sth.]; ~hin *Adv.* a) *(immer noch)* still; b) *(künftig)* in future; etw. ~hin tun continue to do sth. [in future]; c) *(außerdem)* in addition; ~|kommen *unr. itr. V.; mit sein* a) get further; mach, daß du ~kommst *(ugs.)* clear off *(coll.)*; b) *(Fortschritte machen)* make progress *or* headway; im Leben/Beruf ~kommen get on in life/one's career; ~|können *unr. itr. V. (ugs.)* a) be able to go on; geradeaus können wir nicht ~: we can't go *or* get any further straight on; b) *(bei einer Aufgabe)* nicht ~können get stuck; be unable to go on; ~|laufen *unr. itr. V.; mit sein* a) *(~gehen)* walk on; carry on walking; b) *(in Betrieb bleiben, auch fig.)* keep going; c) *(fortgeführt werden)* continue; ⟨*agreement, insurance*⟩ run; ~|leben *itr. V.* a) *(am Leben bleiben)* go on living; b) *(seine Existenz fortsetzen)* continue *or* carry on one's life; c) *(nach dem Tod fortleben)* live on; ~|leiten *tr. V.* pass on ⟨*news, information, etc.*⟩; forward ⟨*letter, parcel, etc.*⟩; ~|machen *(ugs.)* 1. *itr. V.* carry on; go on; ~machen! *(Milit.)* carry on; as you were; 2. *tr. V.* etw. ~machen carry on with sth.; ~|müssen *unr. itr. V. (ugs.)* have to be on one's way; ich muß ~: I must be on my way; ~|reden *itr. V.* go on *or* carry on talking; sie ließ mich nicht ~reden she would not let me carry on [with what I was saying]; ~|reichen *tr. V.* pass on; ~reise die; *o. Pl. s.* ~fahrt

weiters *Adv. (österr.) s.* ferner

weiter-: ~|sagen *tr. V.* pass on; sag es nicht weiter don't tell anyone; ~|schicken *tr. V.* forward; send on; send ⟨*person*⟩ on; ~|sehen *unr. itr. V.* see; morgen werden wir ~sehen we'll see what we can do tomorrow; ~|spielen *tr., itr. V.* a) go on *or* carry on playing; der Schiedsrichter ließ ~spielen the referee allowed play to continue; b) *(Sport: abspielen)* pass; ~|sprechen *unr. itr. V.* go on *or* carry on speaking *or* talking

Weiterungen *Pl.* complications; difficulties

weiter-, Weiter-: ~|verarbeiten *tr. V.* process; ~verarbeitung die processing; ~|verfolgen *tr. V.* follow up ⟨*clue, case, etc.*⟩; continue to follow ⟨*developments, events, etc.*⟩; pursue further ⟨*idea, line of thought, etc.*⟩; ~verkauf der resale; nicht zum ~verkauf bestimmt not for resale; ~|verkaufen *tr. V.* resell; ~|wissen *unr. itr. V.* a) nicht [mehr] ~wissen be at one's wit's end; b) *(bei einem Rätsel, einer Aufgabe usw.)* be stuck; ~|wollen *unr. itr. V. (ugs.)* want to go on; das Pferd wollte nicht ~: the horse would not go any further; ~|zahlen *tr., auch itr. V.* continue *or* go on paying; continue to pay; das Gehalt wird ~gezahlt the salary continues to be paid; ~|ziehen *unr. itr. V., mit sein* move on

weit-, Weit-: ~gehend; weiter gehend *od.* weitgehender, weitestgehend *od.* weitgehendst 1. *Adj.* extensive, wide, sweeping ⟨*powers*⟩; far-reaching ⟨*support, concessions, etc.*⟩; wide ⟨*support, agreement, etc.*⟩; general ⟨*renunciation*⟩; 2. *adv.* to a large *or* great extent; ~gereist *Adj.; präd. getrennt geschrieben* widely travelled; ~her *Adv. (geh.)* from afar; ~herzig 1. *Adj.* generous; liberal ⟨*interpretation*⟩; 2. *adv.* generously; ⟨*interpret*⟩ liberally; ~hin *Adv.* a) *(weit umher)* for miles around; b) *(weitgehend)* to a large *or* great extent; ~läufig 1. *Adj.* a) *(ausgedehnt)* extensive; *(geräumig)* spacious; b) *(entfernt)* distant; c) *(ausführlich)* lengthy; long-winded; 2. *adv.* a) *(ausgedehnt)* spaciously; b) *(entfernt)* distantly; c) *(ausführlich)* at length; long-windedly; ~maschig *Adj.* wide-meshed; ~räumig 1. *Adj.* spacious ⟨*room, area, etc.*⟩; wide ⟨*gap, space*⟩; 2. *adv.* spaciously; etw. ~räumig umfahren give sth. a wide berth; ~reichend 1. *Adj.* a) long-range; b) *(umfangreich und gewichtig)* far-reaching ⟨*importance, consequences*⟩; sweeping ⟨*changes, powers*⟩; extensive ⟨*relations, influence*⟩; ~reichende Freiheiten a large *or* great degree of freedom; 2. *adv.* extensively; to a large extent; ~schuß der *(Sport)* long-range shot; ~schweifig 1. *Adj.* long-winded; 2. *adv.* long-windedly; ~sicht die far-sightedness; ~sichtig 1. *Adj.* long-sighted; *(fig.)* far sighted; 2. *adv. (fig.)* far-sightedly; ~sichtigkeit die; ~ long-sightedness; *(fig.)* far-sightedness; ~springen *unr. itr. V.; mit sein; nur im Inf. u. Part. gebr. (Sport)* do the long jump *(Brit.) or* broad jump *(Amer.)*; ~sprung der *(Sport)* long jump *(Brit.)*; broad jump *(Amer.)*; ~verbreitet *Adj.; präd. getrennt geschrieben* widespread; common; common ⟨*plant, animal*⟩; ~verzweigt; *Adj.; präd. getrennt geschrieben* extensive ⟨*network*⟩; ⟨*firm*⟩ with many [different] branches; eine ~verzweigte Verwandtschaft haben have numerous branches in one's family; ~winkel·objektiv das wide-angle lens

Weizen ['vaitsn̩] der; ~s wheat

Weizen-: ~bier das *s.* Weißbier; ~brot das wheat bread; ein ~brot a wheat loaf; a loaf of wheat bread; ~keim der wheat germ *no pl.*; ~keim·öl das wheat-germ oil; ~mehl das wheat flour

welch [vɛlç] 1. *Interrogativpron.* a) *(bei Wahl aus einer unbegrenzten Menge)* what; aus ~em Grund? for what reason?; ~e Folgen wird das haben? what will be the consequences of that?; um ~e Zeit? [at] what time?; b) *(bei Wahl aus einer begrenzten Menge) (adj.)* which; *(subst.)* which one; an ~em Tag/in ~em Jahr? on which day/in which year?; ~e Folgen auch immer whatever the consequences; ~er/~e/~es auch immer whichever one; ~er/~e/~es von [den] beiden which of the two; c) *(geh.: was für ein)* what a; *(oft unflektiert)* ~ reizendes Geschöpf! what a charming creature!; ~ ein Zufall/Glück! what a coincidence/how fortunate!. 2. *Relativpron. (bei Menschen)* who; *(bei Sachen)* which; *(unflektiert, Papierdt.)* X, Y und Z, ~ letztere/letzterer/letzteres ...: X, Y, and Z, the latter of whom/which ... 3. *Indefinitpron.* some; ich habe keine Seife – hast du ~e? I have no soap – have you any?; es gibt ~e, die behaupten, daß ... *(ugs.)* there are some [people] *or* those who claim that ...

welcher·art *Adv.* what kind of; es ist gleichgültig, ~ seine Überlegungen waren it's irrelevant what his considerations were

welcher·lei *indekl. Interrogativadj.* whatever

Welfe ['vɛlfə] der; ~n, ~n *(hist.)* Guelph

welk [vɛlk] *Adj.* withered ⟨*skin, hands, etc.*⟩; wilted ⟨*leaves, flower*⟩; limp ⟨*lettuce*⟩; shrivelled ⟨*breasts*⟩; sein Gesicht sah ~ aus his face looked old and tired

welken *itr. V.; mit sein* ⟨*plant, flower*⟩ wilt; *(fig.)* ⟨*beauty*⟩ fade; ⟨*woman*⟩ age

Well·blech das corrugated iron

Wellblech·dach das corrugated-iron roof

Welle ['vɛlə] die; ~, ~n a) *(auch fig.)* wave; sein Grab in den ~n finden *(geh.)* go to *or* find a watery grave; grüne ~ *(Verkehrsw.)* linked *or* synchronised traffic lights; grüne ~ bei 70 km/h traffic lights phased *or* synchronized for 70 km per hour; [hohe] ~n schlagen *(fig.)* cause a [major] stir; die weiche ~ *(fig. ugs.)* the soft approach *or* line; b) *(im Haar)* wave; sich *(Dat.)* ~n legen lassen have one's hair waved; c) *(Physik)* wave; *(Rundf.: Frequenz)* wavelength; d) *(Technik)* shaft; e) *(wellenförmige Erhebung)* undulation; f) *(Gymnastik)* circle

wellen 1. *tr. V. (wellig formen)* wave ⟨*hair*⟩; corrugate ⟨*iron, metal*⟩. 2. *refl. V.* a) *(wellig sein)* ⟨*hair*⟩ be wavy; ⟨*ground, carpet*⟩ undulate; ⟨*stairs*⟩ be uneven; b) *(wellig werden)* ⟨*carpet, stairs*⟩ become uneven

wellen-, Wellen-: ~bad das artificial wave pool; ~bereich der *(Rundf.)* waveband; ~berg der crest [of a/the wave]; ~brecher der breakwater; ~förmig 1. *Adj.* wavy ⟨*line, outline, seam, etc.*⟩; wavelike ⟨*motion, movement, etc.*⟩; 2. *adv.* ⟨*be propagated*⟩ in the form of waves *or* as waves; ~gang der; *o. Pl.* swell; ein starker/leichter ~gang a strong/light swell; bei starkem ~gang in heavy seas; ~länge die *(Physik)* wavelength; [mit jmdm.] auf der gleichen ~länge liegen *(fig. ugs.)* be on the same wavelength [as sb.]; ~linie die wavy line; ~reiten das surfing *no art.*; ~sittich der budgerigar; ~tal das trough [of a/the wave]

Well·fleisch das boiled belly pork

Well·horn·schnecke die whelk

wellig *Adj.* wavy ⟨*hair*⟩; undulating ⟨*scenery, hills, etc.*⟩; uneven ⟨*surface, track, etc.*⟩

Well·pappe die corrugated cardboard

Welpe ['vɛlpə] der; ~n, ~n *(Hund)* whelp; pup; *(Wolf, Fuchs)* whelp; cub

Wels [vɛls] der; ~es, ~e catfish

welsch [vɛlʃ] *Adj.* a) *(schweiz.)* die ~e Schweiz French[-speaking] Switzerland; b) *(veralt.: romanisch)* Latin; c) *(veralt. abwertend: fremdländisch)* foreign

welsch-, Welsch-: ~land das *(schweiz.)* French[-speaking] Switzerland; ~schweizer der *(schweiz.)* French[-speaking] Swiss [man]; ~schweizerisch *Adj. (schweiz.)* French Swiss

Welt [vɛlt] die; ~, ~en a) *o. Pl.* world; auf der ~: in the world; in der ganzen ~ bekannt sein be known world-wide *or* all over the world; eine Reise um die ~: a round-the-world tour; die schönste Frau der Welt the most beautiful woman in the world; in seiner eigenen ~ leben live in a world of one's own; die Alte/Neue ~: the Old/New World; die dritte/vierte ~ the Third/Fourth World; zwölf Mark, das ist doch nicht die ~! *(ugs.)* twelve marks, that's not the earth! *(coll.)*; nicht die ~ kosten *(ugs.)* not cost the earth *(coll.)*; die ~ ist klein *od.* ein Dorf *(scherzh.)* it's a small world; davon geht die ~ nicht unter *(ugs.)* it's not the end of the world; auf die *od.* zur ~ kommen be born; auf der ~ sein have been born; aus aller ~: from all over the world; nicht aus der ~ sein *(ugs.)* not be at the other end of the earth;

in aller ~: throughout the world; all over the world; **in alle ~:** all over the world; **um nichts in der ~, nicht um alles in der ~:** not for anything in the world *or* on earth; **um alles in der ~** *(ugs.)* for heaven's sake; **die ganze ~** *(fig.)* the whole world; **so etwas hat die ~ noch nicht gesehen** *(fig. ugs.)* it is/was incredible *or* fantastic *(coll.)*; **alle ~** *(fig. ugs.)* the whole world; everybody; **vor aller ~** *(fig. ugs.)* in front of everybody; **eine verkehrte ~:** a topsy-turvy world; **mit sich und der ~ zufrieden sein** be content with life; **aus der ~ schaffen** resolve ‹*problem, dispute, etc.*›; **Kinder in die ~ setzen** *(ugs.)* have children; **Gerüchte in die ~ setzen** start rumours; **wer/was/wo/warum in aller ~ ...?** *(ugs.)* who/what/where/why on earth ...?; **er/sie ist nicht von dieser ~** *(geh.)* he/she is not of this world; **zur ~ bringen** bring into the world; give birth to; **eine Dame/ein Mann von ~:** a woman/man of the world; **die gelehrte ~:** the world of scholars; **die vornehme ~:** high society; *s. auch* **Brett d; nobel 1 b; b)** *(~all)* universe; *(Planetensystem)* planetary system; *(Sternensystem)* galaxy; **uns trennen ~en** *(fig.)* we are worlds apart

wẹlt-, Wẹlt-: ~abgeschieden *Adj.* remote; **~all das** universe; cosmos; **~anschaulich 1.** *Adj.; nicht präd.* ideological; **2.** *adv.* ideologically; **~anschauung die** world-view; Weltanschauung; **~atlas der** atlas of the world; **~aus·stellung die** world fair; **~bank die;** *o. Pl.* World Bank; **~bekannt** *Adj.* known all over the world *pred.*; world-famous ‹*artist, author, etc.*›; **~berühmt** *Adj.* world-famous; **~best...** *Adj.; nicht präd.* world's best *attrib.*; best ... in the world; **der/die Weltbeste** the world champion; **~bẹst·leistung die** *(Sport)* world record; **~bẹst·zeit die** *(Sport)* world record time; **~bewegend 1.** *Adj.* world-shaking; **nicht ~bewegend sein** *(ugs. spött.)* be nothing to write home about *(coll.)*; **2.** *adv.* **er spielt nicht [gerade] ~bewegend** *(ugs. spött.)* his playing isn't [exactly] anything to write home about *(coll.)*; **~bild das** world view; conception of the world; **~bürger der** citizen of the world; cosmopolite

Wẹlten·bummler der; ~s, ~, Wẹlten·bummlerin die; ~, ~nen globe-trotter

Wẹlt·erfolg der world-wide success

Wẹlter·gewicht das welterweight

wẹlt-, Wẹlt-: ~erschütternd *s.* **~bewegend; ~flucht die;** *o. Pl.* withdrawal from the world; **~fremd 1.** *Adj.* unworldly; **2.** *adv.* unrealistically; **~frieden der** world peace; **~geist der;** *o. Pl. (Philos.)* world spirit; **~geistliche der** *(kath. Kirche)* secular priest; **~geltung die** international standing; **~gericht das** *(Rel.)* Last Judgement; **~geschichte die a)** *o. Pl.* world history *no art.*; **in der ~geschichte umherreisen** *(ugs. scherzh.)* travel around all over the place; **b)** *(Werk)* history of the world; **~geschichtlich 1.** *Adj.* **ein ~geschichtliches Ereignis, ein Ereignis von ~geschichtlicher Bedeutung** an important event in world history; **2.** *adv.* **~geschichtlich gesehen** *od.* **betrachtet** [viewed] from the point of view of world history; **~gesụndheits·organisation die** World Health Organization; **~gewandt** *Adj.* sophisticated; **~handel der;** *o. Pl.* world trade; **~herrschaft die;** *o. Pl.* world domination; **~hịlfs·sprache die** international auxiliary language; **~karte die** map of the world; **~kind das** *(dichter.)* worldling; **~klasse die** world class; **~klasse sein, zur ~klasse gehören** be world-class; **~klug 1.** *Adj.* worldly-wise; **2.** *adv.* in a worldly-wise manner; **~krieg der** world war; **der erste** *od.* **Erste/zweite** *od.* **Zweite ~krieg** the First/Second World War; World War I/II; **~kugel die** globe

weltlich *Adj.* **a)** *(irdisch, sinnlich)* worldly; **b)** *(nicht geistlich)* secular

wẹlt-, Wẹlt-: ~literatur die world literature *no art.*; **~macht die** world power; **~mann der;** *Pl.* **~männer** man of the world; **~männisch** [~mɛnɪʃ] **1.** *Adj.* sophisticated; **2.** *adv.* in a sophisticated manner; **~marke die** international make; **~markt der** *(Wirtsch.)* world market; **~meer das** ocean; **die sieben ~meere** the seven seas; **~meister der** world champion; **die Mannschaft ist ~meister** the team are world champions; **~meisterschaft die** world championship; **die ~meisterschaft im Fußball** the [football] World Cup; **~offen 1.** *Adj.* **a)** *(aufgeschlossen)* open-minded; **b)** *(für alle Welt offen)* open to the world *postpos.*; **2.** *adv.* open-mindedly; **~öffentlichkeit die: die Meinung der ~öffentlichkeit** world opinion; **an die ~öffentlichkeit appellieren** make an appeal to the people of the world; **~ordnung die** world order; **~politik die** world politics *pl.*; **~politisch 1.** *Adj.; nicht präd.* **~politische Auswirkungen/Bedeutung haben** have an effect on world politics/be important in world politics; **das ~politische Klima** the climate in world politics; **2.** *adv.* in terms of *or* from the point of view of world politics; **~raum der** space *no art.*

Wẹltraum-: ~fahrer der space traveller; **~fahrt die** space travel *no art.*; **~station die** space station

wẹlt-, Wẹlt-: ~reich das empire; **~reise die** world tour; **eine ~reise machen** go round the world; **~reisende der/die** globe-trotter; **~rekord der** world record; **~rekordler der** world record holder; **~religion die** world religion; **~revolution die** world revolution; **~ruf der;** *o. Pl.* world-wide reputation; **~ruf haben** have a world-wide reputation; **von ~ruf** with a world-wide reputation *postpos., not pred.*; **~schmerz der;** *o. Pl.* world-weariness; Weltschmerz; **~sịcherheitsrat der** *(Pol.)* [United Nations] Security Council; **~sprache die** world language; **~stadt die** cosmopolitan city; **~star der** international star; **~umsegler der** circumnavigator of the globe; **~umspannend** *Adj.* global; **~untergang der** end of the world; **~untergangs·stimmung die** mood of black despair; *(in der Natur)* **es herrschte ~untergangsstimmung** it was as if the end of the world were approaching; **~ụraufführung die** world première; **~verbesserer der; ~s, ~** *(iron.)* **ein ~verbesserer** someone who thinks he/she can set the world to rights; **~weit 1.** *Adj.; nicht präd.* world-wide; **2.** *adv.* throughout *or* all over the world; **~wirtschaft die** world economy; **~wịrtschafts·krise die** world economic crisis; **~wunder das: die Sieben ~wunder** the Seven Wonders of the World; **etw. wie ein ~wunder anstaunen** stare at sth. as if it were from another planet; **~zeit·uhr die** clock showing times around the world

wem [ve:m] *Dat. von* **wer 1.** *Interrogativpron.* to whom; who ... to; **wem hast du das Buch geliehen?** to whom did you lend the book?; who did you lend the book to?; **mit/von/zu ~:** with/from/to whom; who ... with/from/to. **2.** *Relativpron.* the person to whom ...; the person who ... to; **~ der Schal gehört** the person to whom the scarf belongs; the person the scarf belongs to; **~ so etwas nicht selbst passiert ist** anyone to whom this has never happened; **~ es auch [immer]** *od.* **~ immer es passiert ist** *(geh.)* whoever it was it happened to. **3.** *Indefinitpron. (ugs.: jemandem)* to somebody *or* someone; **gehört das ~?** does this belong to anybody?; **telefoniert sie mit ~?** is she on the phone to somebody? *(coll.)*

Wẹm·fall der dative [case]

wen [ve:n] *Akk. von* **wer 1.** *Interrogativpron.* whom; who *(coll.)*; **an/für ~:** to/for whom ...; who ... to/for; **an ~ schreibst du?** to whom are you writing? who are you writing to?; **~ von ihnen kennst du?** which [one] of these do you know?. **2.** *Relativpron.* the person whom; **~ das nicht überzeugt** anyone who is not convinced by that; **~ [auch] immer** *(geh.)* whoever; no matter whom. **3.** *Indefinitpron. (ugs.: jemanden)* somebody; someone; **suchst du ~?** are you looking for somebody?

¹Wende die; ~, ~n a) *(Veränderung)* change; **eine ~ zum Besseren/Schlechteren** a change for the better/worse; **b)** *in* **um die ~ des Jahrhunderts** at the turn of the century; **c)** *(Turnen)* front vault; **d)** *(Seemannsspr.)* turn

²Wẹnde der; ~n, ~n Wend

Wẹnde·hals der *(ugs. abwertend)* turncoat; renegade

Wẹnde·kreis der a) *(Geogr.)* tropic; **der nördliche ~, der ~ des Krebses** the Tropic of Cancer; **der südliche ~, der ~ des Steinbocks** the Tropic of Capricorn; **b)** *(Kfz-W.)* turning circle

Wẹndel die; ~, ~n *(Technik)* coil

Wẹndel·treppe die spiral staircase

Wẹnde-: ~manöver das turning manœuvre; **~marke die** *(Sport)* turning mark

¹wẹnden 1. *tr., auch itr. V. (auf die andere Seite)* turn [over]; toss ‹*pancake, cutlet, etc.*›; *(in die entgegengesetzte Richtung)* turn [round]; **einen Mantel ~:** turn a coat inside out; **bitte ~!** please turn over; *s. auch* **drehen 1 a. 2.** *itr. V.* **a)** turn [round]; **b)** *(Seemannsspr.)* tack. **3.** *refl. V.* **sich zum Besseren/Schlechteren ~:** take a turn for the better/worse; **das Glück hat sich gewendet** *(geh.)* his/her *etc.* luck has turned; *s. auch* **Blatt e**

²wẹnden 1. *unr. (auch regelm.) tr. V.* **a)** *(in eine andere Richtung drehen)* turn; **den Kopf ~:** turn one's head; **keinen Blick von jmdm. ~:** not take one's eyes off sb.; **er wandte seine Schritte nach links** *(geh.)* he turned his steps to the left; **b)** *(geh.: auf~)* spend; **viel Zeit/Geld an** *od.* **auf etw.** *(Akk.)* **~:** spend a great deal of time/money on sth.; **viel Mühe an** *od.* **auf etw.** *(Akk.)* **~:** take a great deal of trouble over sth. **2.** *unr. (auch regelm.) refl. V.* **a)** ‹*person*› turn; **das Glück hat sich von ihm gewandt** *od.* **gewendet** *(fig. geh.)* his good fortune deserted him; **b)** *(sich richten)* **sich an jmdn. [um Rat/Hilfe] ~:** turn to sb. [for advice/help]; **sich mit einer Bitte an jmdn. ~:** ask a favour of sb.; **ich habe mich schriftlich dorthin gewandt** I've written there; **an wen soll ich mich ~?** whom should I approach?; **sich an eine höhere Instanz/die richtige Adresse ~:** go to a higher authority/the right address; **das Buch wendet sich an junge Leser** *(fig.)* the book is addressed to *or* intended for young readers; **sich gegen jmdn./etw. ~:** oppose sb./sth.; **c)** *(geh.: sich anschicken)* **sich zum Gehen/zur Flucht ~:** get ready *or* prepare to go/flee

Wẹnde-: ~platz der turning area; **~punkt der** turning-point; *(Geom.: einer Kurve)* point of inflexion

wẹndig 1. *Adj.* **a)** agile; nimble; manœuvrable ‹*vehicle, boat, etc.*›; **b)** *(gewandt)* astute. **2.** *adv.* **a)** *(beweglich)* agilely; nimbly; **b)** *(gewandt)* astutely

Wẹndigkeit die; ~ a) agility; nimbleness; *(eines Flugzeugs)* manœuvrability; **b)** *(Gewandtheit)* astuteness

Wẹndung die; ~, ~en a) *(Änderung der Richtung)* turn; **eine ~ um 180°** a 180° turn; **b)** *(Veränderung)* change; **eine unerwartete/entscheidende ~:** an unexpected/decisive turn of events; **eine ~ zum Besseren/Schlechteren** a turn for the better/worse; **c)** *(Biegung)* bend; **d)** *(Rede~)* expression

Wẹn·fall der accusative [case]

wenig ['ve:nɪç] **1.** *Indefinitpron. u. unbest. Zahlw.* **a)** *Sing.* little; **sie besitzt nur ~ Schmuck** she owns only a little *or* doesn't own much jewellery; **das ~e Geld reicht nicht aus** this small amount of money is not enough; **~ Zeit/Geld haben** not have much *or* have little time/money; **das ist ~:** that isn't much; **dazu kann ich ~ sagen** I can't say much about that; **nicht ~ Mühe/Arbeit/Zeit kosten** take quite a lot of effort/work/time; **zu ~ Zeit/Geld haben** not have enough time/money; **ein Exemplar/50 Mark zu ~:** one copy too few/50 marks too little; **nur ~es** only a little; **um [ein] ~es älter** *(veralt.)* a little older; **b)** *Pl.* a few; **es sind nur noch ~e Wochen bis ...:** there are only a few weeks to go until ...; **bis auf ~e/mit ~en Ausnahmen** apart from/with a few exceptions; **nur ~ Leute waren unterwegs** only a few people were about; **~ Chancen haben, etw. zu tun** have little chance of doing sth.; **sie hatte ~ Bücher/Freunde** she had few books/friends; **mit ~en Worten** in a few words; **die ~en, die davon wußten** the few who knew about it; **nur ~e haben teilgenommen** only a few took part; **einer von** *od.* **unter ~en** one of only a few; **nicht ~e** quite a few. **2.** *Adv.* little; **nur ~ besser** only a little better; **er war ~ erbaut** he was not particularly pleased; **wir waren nicht ~ erstaunt/erfreut** we were more than a little astonished/pleased; **~ mehr** not much more; **das ist ~ nett von ihr** that is not very nice of her; **ein ~:** a little; **ein ~ zusammensitzen/ausruhen** sit together for a little while/rest a little; **das nützt [mir] ~:** it won't do [me] much good; **ich komme nur ~ in die Stadt** I don't often get into town; **wir gehen ~ ins Theater** we don't go much to the theatre

weniger **1.** *Komp. von* **wenig;** *Indefinitpron. u. unbest. Zahlw.* (+ *Sg.*) less; (+ *Pl.*) fewer; **immer ~:** less and less; **du wirst [ja] immer ~** *(ugs.)* you're wasting away. **2.** *Komp. von* **wenig;** *Adv.* less; **es kommt ~ auf Quantität als auf Qualität an** quantity is less important than quality; **~ schön als praktisch** more practical than attractive; **das ist ~ angenehm/erfreulich/schön** that is not very pleasant/pleasing/nice; **nichts ~ als ...:** nothing less than ...; **je mehr ich darüber nachdenke, um so ~ überzeugt es mich** the more I think about it, the less it convinces me; *s. auch* **mehr 1. 3.** *Konj.* less; **fünf ~ drei** five, take away three

Wenigkeit die; **~:** small amount; **meine ~** *(scherzh.)* yours truly

wenigst... 1. *Sup. von* **wenig;** *Indefinitpron. u. unbest. Zahlw.* least; **damit habe ich die ~e Arbeit** *od.* **am ~sten Arbeit** that gives me the least work; **am ~en** least; **sie hat am ~en [geschenkt] bekommen** she received the fewest presents; **in den ~en Fällen/für die ~en Menschen** in very few cases/for very few people; **nur die ~en** only very few; **das ~e, was wir tun können** the least we can do; **das ist noch das ~e, ...:** worse still, ... **2.** *Sup. von* **wenig;** *Adv.* **am ~en** the least; **das hätte ich am ~en erwartet** that's the last thing I should have expected; **das konnte sie am ~en leiden** it was what she hated most

wenigstens *Adv.* at least

wenn [vɛn] *Konj.* **a)** *(konditional)* if; **außer ~:** unless; **und [selbst] ~:** even if; **~ es sein muß, komme ich mit** If I have to, I'll come along; **~ es nicht anders geht** if there's no other way; **~ du schon rauchen mußt** if you 'must smoke; **~ nicht, dann nicht** if not, it doesn't matter; **~ das Wörtchen ~ nicht wär' [, wär' mein Vater Millionär]** *(scherzh.)* if only, if only; **b)** *(temporal)* when; **jedesmal,** *od.* **immer, ~:** whenever; **~ du dich erst einmal eingearbeitet hast ...:** once you've got used to the work ...; **c)** *(konzessiv)* **wenn ... auch** even though; **~ es auch schwer ist** even though it is hard; **und ~ es [auch] noch so spät ist ...:** no matter how late it is ...; however late it is ...; **[und] ~ auch!** *(ugs.)* even so; all the same; **d)** *(in Wunschsätzen)* if only; **~ ich doch** *od.* **nur** *od.* **bloß wüßte, ob ...:** if only I knew whether ...; **~ er doch käme!** if only he would come

Wenn das; **~s, ~** *od. (ugs.)* **~s: das ~ und Aber, die ~[s] und Aber[s]** the ifs and buts

wenn·gleich *Konj. (geh.)* even though; although

wenn·schon *Adv.* **~ [nicht] ..., dann ...:** even if [not] ..., then ...; **[na** *od.* **und] ~!** *(ugs.)* so what?; **~, dann ...:** if that's how it is, then ...; **~, dennschon** *(ugs.)* if you're going to do something, you may as well do it properly; no half measures!

[1]**Wenzel** ['vɛntsl̩] *(der)* Wenceslas

[2]**Wenzel der;** **~s, ~** *(Kartenspiele)* jack; knave

wer [ve:ɐ̯] *Nom. Mask. u. Fem.; s. auch (Gen.)* **wessen;** *(Dat.)* **wem;** *(Akk.)* **wen 1.** *Interrogativpron.* who; **~ alles ist dabeigewesen?** which people were there?; who was there?; **~ von ...:** which of; **~ weiß wieviel/wie oft/wie lange** *usw.* who knows how much/how often/how long *etc.*; **~ da?** *(Milit.)* who goes there?; **was glaubt er eigentlich, ~ er ist?** who does he think he is?. **2.** *Relativpron.* the person who; *(jeder, der)* anyone *or* anybody who; **~ es auch [immer]** *od.* **~ immer es getan hat** *(geh.)* whoever did it. **3.** *Indefinitpron. (ugs.: jemand)* someone; somebody; *(in Fragen, Konditionalsätzen)* anyone; anybody; **ist da ~?** is anyone there?; **hat ~ nach mir gefragt?** did anyone ask for me?; **~ sein** be somebody

Werbe-: ~abteilung die advertising *or* publicity department; **~agentur die** advertising agency; **~aktion die** advertising campaign; **~feldzug der** advertising campaign; **~fernsehen das** television commercials *pl.*; **~film der** advertising *or* promotional *or* publicity film; **~funk der** radio commercials *pl.*; **~gag der** publicity gimmick *(coll.)*; **~geschenk das** [promotional] free gift; **~kampagne die** *s.* **~feldzug; ~leiter der** advertising manager

werben ['vɛrbn̩] **1.** *unr. itr. V.* **a)** advertise; **für etw. ~:** advertise sth.; **für eine Partei ~:** canvass for a party; **b)** *(geh.: sich bemühen)* **~ um** try to enlist ‹*subscribers, helpers, etc.*›; recruit ‹*soldier, mercenary, etc.*›; **um Wählerstimmen ~:** seek to attract votes; **um jmds. Gunst/Freundschaft ~:** court sb.'s favour/friendship; **um eine Frau ~:** court a woman. **2.** *unr. tr. V.* attract ‹*readers, customers, etc.*›; recruit ‹*soldiers, volunteers, members, staff, etc.*›

werbe-, Werbe-: ~schrift die prospectus; advertising brochure; **~slogan der** advertising slogan; **~spot der** commercial; advertisement; ad *(coll.)*; **~sprache die;** *o. Pl.* advertising jargon; **~text der** advertising copy *no. pl.*; **~texter der** advertising copy-writer; **~träger der** advertising medium; **~trommel die** *in* **[für jmdn./etw.] die ~ rühren** *od.* **schlagen** beat *or* thump the drum [for sb./sth.]; **~wirksam 1.** *Adj.* effective ‹*advertisement etc.*›; **~wirksam sein** be good publicity *or* a good advertisement; **dieser Slogan ist wenig ~wirksam** this slogan is not very effective publicity *or* not a very effective advertisement; **2.** *adv.* effectively ‹*worded etc.*›

Werbung die; **~, ~en a)** *o. Pl. (Reklame, Propaganda)* advertising; **für etw. ~ machen** advertise sth.; **für ein neues Buch/einen Kandidaten viel ~ machen** give a lot of publicity to a new book/a candidate; **b)** *o. Pl.: s.* **Werbeabteilung; c)** *(geh.: Bemühen um jmds. Gunst)* courtship *no pl.*

Werbungs·kosten *Pl. (Steuerw.)* advertising costs

Werde·gang der a) *(Laufbahn)* career; **b)** *(Entwicklungsgang)* development

werden ['ve:ɐ̯dn̩] **1.** *unr. itr. V.; mit sein; 2. Part.* **geworden a)** become; get; **älter ~:** get *or* grow old[er]; **du bist aber groß/schlank geworden!** you've grown so tall/slim; **wahnsinnig** *od.* **verrückt ~:** go mad; **gut ~:** turn out well; **das muß anders ~:** things have to change; **wach ~:** wake up; **rot ~:** go *or* turn red; **das Wetter wurde schlechter** the weather got worse; **er ist 70 [Jahre alt] geworden** he has had his 70th birthday *or* has turned 70; **heute soll es/wird es heiß ~:** it's supposed to get/it's going to be hot today; **mir wird übel/heiß/schwindelig** I feel sick/I'm getting hot/dizzy; **Arzt/Professor ~:** become a doctor/professor; **was willst du einmal ~?** what do you want to be when you grow up?; **Vater ~:** become a father; **erster/letzter ~:** be *or* come first/last; **das Kind wird ein Junge** the baby is going to be a boy; **was soll das ~?** what is that going to be?; **eine ~de Mutter** a mother-to-be; an expectant mother; **b)** *(sich entwickeln)* **zu etw. ~:** become sth.; **das Wasser wurde zu Eis** the water turned into ice; **was soll aus dir ~?** what is to become of you?; **aus Liebe wurde Haß** love turned into hate; **aus ihm ist nichts/etwas geworden** he hasn't got anywhere/has got somewhere in life; **daraus wird nichts ~** nothing will come of it/that!; **Von wegen! Daraus wird nichts!** You must be joking! No chance!; **c)** *(unpers.) (sich einem bestimmten Zeitpunkt nähern)* **es wird [höchste] Zeit** it is [high] time; **es wird ein Jahr, seit ...:** it will be a year since ...; **es wird 10 Uhr** it is nearly 10 o'clock; **es wird Tag/Nacht** day is dawning/night is falling; **es wird Herbst** autumn is coming; **d)** *(entstehen)* come into existence; **es werde Licht!** *(bibl.)* let there be light!; **jeder Tag, den Gott ~ läßt** every day that God gives *or* grants us; **was nicht ist, [das] kann noch ~:** things can change; **im Werden sein** be coming into being; **e)** *(ugs.)* **sind die Fotos [etwas] geworden?** have the photos turned out [well]?; **wird's bald?** *(ugs.)* hurry up!; **was soll nur ~?** what's going to happen now?; **nicht mehr** *od.* **wieder ~** *(salopp)* flip one's lid *(sl.)*; **ich werd' nicht mehr** *od.* **wieder!** *(salopp)* well, I'm blowed! *(sl.)*; **f)** *(geh. veralt.: widerfahren)* **ihm soll [sein] Recht ~:** he shall have justice. **2.** *Hilfsverb; 2. Part.* **worden a)** *(zur Bildung des Futurs)* **wir ~ uns um ihn kümmern** we will take care of him; **dem werd' ich's zeigen!** *(ugs.)* I'll show him *(coll.)*; **dir werd' ich helfen!** *(ugs.)* I'll give you what for *(coll.)*; **wer wird denn gleich weinen!** you're not going to cry, are you?; **Sie ~ entschuldigen** *(ugs.)* excuse me[, please]; **es wird gleich regnen** it is going to rain any minute; **wir ~ nächste Woche in Urlaub fahren** we are going on holiday next week; **b)** *(als Ausdruck der Vermutung)* **es wird um die 80 Mark kosten** it will cost around 80 marks; **sie ~ [wohl] im Garten sein** they are probably in the garden; **er wird doch nicht [etwa] krank sein?** he wouldn't be ill, would he?; **sie wird schon wissen, was sie tut** she must know what she's doing; **c)** *(zur Bildung des Passivs)* **du wirst gerufen** you are being called; **er wurde gebeten** he was asked; **ihm wurde gesagt** he was told; **es wurde gelacht/gesungen/getanzt** there was laughter/singing/dancing; **jetzt wird aber geschlafen!** right, it's time to go to sleep now!; **unser Haus wird renoviert** our house is being renovated; **d)** *(zur Umschreibung des Konjunktivs)* **was würdest du tun?** what would you do?; **würdest du bitte etwas für mich besorgen?** would you mind getting something for me?; **ich würde kommen** I would come

Wer·fall der nominative [case]

werfen ['vɛrfn̩] **1.** *unr. tr. V.* **a)** throw; drop ‹*bombs*›; **die Tür ins Schloß ~:** slam the door shut; **jmdn. aus dem Saal ~** *(fig. ugs.)*

throw sb. out of the hall; **eine Frage in die Debatte ~** *(fig.)* throw *or* inject a question into the debate; **neue Waren auf den Markt ~** *(fig.)* bring new products on to the market; **Bilder an die Wand ~** *(fig.)* project pictures on the wall; **einen kurzen Blick in den Spiegel/in die Zeitung ~** *(fig.)* cast a glance in the mirror/at the paper; **b)** *(ruckartig bewegen)* throw; **den Kopf in den Nacken ~:** throw *or* toss one's head back; **die Arme in die Höhe ~:** throw one's arms up; **c)** *(erzielen)* throw; **eine Sechs ~:** throw a six; **ein Tor ~** *(Handball, Wasserball)* shoot *or* throw a goal; **d)** *(Ringen, Judo: nieder~)* throw, floor ‹*opponent*›; **e)** *(bilden)* **Falten ~:** wrinkle; crease; **Blasen ~:** bubble; **[einen] Schatten ~:** cast [a] shadow; **f)** *(gebären)* give birth to. **2.** *unr. itr. V.* **a)** throw; **mit etw. [nach jmdm.] ~:** throw sth. [at sb.]; **mit Geld/Fremdwörtern/Schimpfwörtern** *usw.* **um sich ~** *(fig.)* throw [one's] money around/bandy foreign words about/bandy curses *etc.* about; **b)** *(Junge kriegen)* give birth; ‹*dog, cat*› litter. **3.** *unr. refl. V.* **a)** throw oneself; **sich vor einen Zug ~:** throw oneself under a train; **sich jmdm. in die Arme/zu Füßen ~:** throw oneself into sb.'s arms/at sb.'s feet; **sich auf eine neue Aufgabe ~** *(fig.)* throw oneself into a new task; **sich in die** *od.* **seine Kleider ~** *(fig.)* throw on one's clothes; **b)** *(sich verziehen)* buckle; ‹*wood*› warp

Wẹrfer der; ~s, ~: thrower; *(Baseball)* pitcher; *(Cricket)* bowler

Werft [vɛrft] **die; ~, ~en** shipyard; dockyard; *(Flugw.)* hangar

Wẹrft·arbeiter der shipyard worker

Werg [vɛrk] **das; ~[e]s** tow

Werk [vɛrk] **das; ~[e]s, ~e a)** *o. Pl. (Arbeit)* work; **am ~[e] sein** be at work; **sich ans ~ machen, ans ~ gehen** set to *or* go to work; **ins ~ setzen** carry out ‹*attack, strategy, etc.*›; put ‹*agreement, plan, etc.*› into effect; set ‹*arrangements, events*› in motion; **zu ~e gehen** *(geh.)* proceed; **b)** *(Tat)* work; **~e der Nächstenliebe** works of charity; **das ist dein ~!** that is your doing *or* handiwork; **du tätest ein gutes ~, wenn ...** *(scherzh.)* you would be doing me/him/us *etc.* a favour if ...; **c)** *(geistiges, künstlerisches Erzeugnis)* work; **ein neues ~ beginnen** begin a new piece of work; **d)** *(Betrieb, Fabrik)* factory; plant; works *sing. or pl.*; *(Belegschaft)* works *sing. or pl.*; **ab ~:** ex works; **e)** *(Trieb~)* mechanism; **das ~ einer Uhr/Orgel** the works *pl.* of a clock/organ

wẹrk-, Wẹrk- *(Betrieb) s.* **werk[s]-, Werk[s]-:**

Wẹrk·bank die; *Pl.* **~bänke** work-bench

wẹrkeln *itr. V.* **a)** *(bes. südd., österr.)* work; **b)** *(herumbasteln)* potter around *or* about

wẹrken *itr. V.* work

Wẹrken das; ~s *(Schulw.)* handicraft

wẹrk-, Wẹrk-: ~getreu 1. *Adj.* faithful to the spirit of the original *postpos.*; **eine ~getreue Inszenierung** a production which is/was faithful to the original; **2.** *adv.* ‹*stage, present, produce*› in a manner faithful to the original; **~lehrer der** [handi]craft teacher; **~meister der** foreman

Wẹrk[s]-: ~angehörige der/die factory *or* works employee; **~arzt der** factory *or* works doctor; **~bücherei die** factory *or* works library

Wẹrk·schutz der a) factory *or* works security; **b)** *(Personen)* factory *or* works security service

wẹrk[s]-, Wẹrk[s]-: ~eigen *Adj.* factory- *or* company-owned; **~fahrer der** *(Motorsport)* works driver; **~gelände das** factory *or* works premises *pl.*; **~halle die** workshop; **~kantine die** works canteen; **~leitung die** factory *or* works management; **~spionage die** industrial espionage

Wẹrk-: ~statt die; ~statt, ~stätten, ~stätte die workshop; *(Kfz-W.)* garage; **~stoff der** material; **~stoff·prüfung die** testing of materials; material-testing; **~stück das** workpiece; **~student der** *(veralt.)* working student; **~verkehr der** works transport

Wẹrk[s]·wohnung die company-owned flat *(Brit.) or (Amer.)* apartment

wẹrk-, Wẹrk-: ~tag der working day; workday; **~tags** *Adv.* on weekdays; **~tätig** *Adj.* working; **~tätige der/die;** *adj. Dekl.* worker; **die Zahl der ~tätigen** the number of people in work; **~treue die** faithfulness to the original; **~unterricht der** [handi]craft instruction *no art.*; *(Unterrichtsstunde)* [handi]craft lesson; *s. auch* **Englischunterricht; ~verzeichnis das** *(Musik)* catalogue of works; **~zeug das;** *Pl.* **~zeuge a)** *(auch fig.)* tool; **b)** *o. Pl. (Gesamtheit)* tools *pl.*

Wẹrkzeug-: ~kasten der tool-box; **~macher der** tool-maker; **~maschine die** machine tool

Wermut ['ve:ɐ̯mu:t] **der; ~[e]s, ~s a)** *(Pflanze)* wormwood; **b)** *(Wein)* vermouth

Wẹrmut-: ~bruder *(ugs. abwertend),* **~penner** *(salopp abwertend)* **der** wino *(sl.)*

Wẹrmuts·tropfen der *(geh.)* drop of bitterness

Wẹrmut·wein der vermouth

wert [ve:ɐ̯t] *Adj.* **a)** *(geh.)* esteemed; *(als Anrede)* **~e Genossen!** my dear comrades; **Ihr ~es Schreiben** *(Kaufmannsspr. veralt.)* your esteemed letter; **wie ist Ihr ~er Name, bitte?** *(geh.)* may I have your name, please?; **b)** *in* **etw. ~ sein** be worth sth.; **das ist nichts ~:** this is worth nothing *or* worthless; **der Teppich ist sein Geld nicht ~:** the carpet is not worth the money; **jmds./einer Sache ~ sein** deserve sb./sth.; **das ist nicht der Erwähnung ~:** this is not worth mentioning; **Berlin ist immer eine Reise ~:** Berlin is always worth a visit; **jmdn./etw. einer Sache** *(Gen.)* **[für] ~ erachten** *(geh.)* consider sb./sth. worthy of sth.; *s. auch* **Rede c**

Wert der; ~[e]s, ~e a) *(Preis)* value; **im ~ steigen/fallen** increase/decrease in value; **an ~ gewinnen/verlieren** gain/lose in value; **im ~[e] von ...:** worth ...; **etw. unter [seinem] ~ verkaufen** sell sth. for less than its value; **b)** *(positive Bedeutung)* value; **einer Sache** *(Dat.)* **großen ~ beimessen** attach great value to sth.; **sich** *(Dat.)* **seines [eigenen] ~es bewußt sein** be conscious of one's own importance; **das hat [doch] keinen ~!** *(ugs.: ist sinnlos)* there's no point; **~ auf etw.** *(Akk.)* **legen** set great store by *or* on sth.; **c)** *(Zahlen~)* value; *(als Ergebnis)* result; **d)** *Pl. (~sachen)* valuable objects; objects of value; **e)** *(Briefmarke)* denomination; **f)** *Pl. (~papiere)* securities

wẹrt-, Wẹrt-: ~arbeit die high-quality workmanship; **~beständig** *Adj.* of lasting value *postpos.*; stable ‹*currency, investment, etc.*›; **~beständig bleiben/sein** retain its value; **~brief der** *(Postw.)* registered letter

wẹrten *tr., itr. V.* **a)** judge; assess; **etw. als besondere Leistung ~:** rate sth. as a special achievement; **etw. als Erfolg/Mißerfolg ~:** regard sth. as *or* consider sth. a success/failure; **etw. hoch/gering ~:** rate sth. highly/not rate sth. very highly; **diese Leistung kann nicht hoch genug gewertet werden** this achievement cannot be regarded highly enough; **etw. kritisch/moralisch ~:** judge sth. critically/from a moral point of view; **b)** *(Sport)* **etw. hoch/niedrig ~:** award high/low points to sth.; **der schlechteste Sprung wird nicht gewertet** the worst jump is not counted

wẹrt·frei 1. *Adj.* detached; impartial; neutral ‹*term*›. **2.** *adv.* with detachment; impartially

Wẹrt·gegenstand der valuable object; object of value; **Wertgegenstände** valuables

-wẹrtig *(Chemie, Sprachw.)* -valent; **zwei~/drei~:** bivalent/trivalent

Wẹrtigkeit die; ~, ~en *(Chemie, Sprachw.)* valency *(Brit.)*; valence *(Amer.)*

wẹrt-, Wẹrt-: ~los *Adj.* worthless; valueless; **~marke die** stamp; *(Essenmarke usw.)* ticket; **~maßstab der** standard [of value]; **~minderung die** depreciation; reduction in value; **~paket das** *(Postw.)* registered parcel; **~papier das** *(Wirtsch.)* security; **~papier·börse die** stock exchange; **~sache die;** *meist Pl.* valuable item *or* object; **~sachen** valuables; **~schätzung die** *(geh.)* esteem; high regard; **~sendung die** *(Postw.)* registered item; **~steigerung die** appreciation; increase in value; **~system das** system of values; value system

Wẹrtung die; ~, ~en judgement; *(Sport)* **er erreichte ~en über 16** he was given scores [of] over 16; **noch in der ~ sein** be still in the competition/race *etc.*

wẹrt-, Wẹrt-: ~urteil das value-judgement; **~voll** *Adj.* valuable; *(moralisch)* estimable ‹*person, quality*›; **~vorstellung die** [concept *sing.* of] values *pl.*; **~zeichen das** stamp; **~zuwachs der** appreciation [in value]

Wẹr·wolf der *(Myth.)* werewolf

wes [vɛs] *Gen. v.* **wer** *(veralt.) s.* **wessen;** *s. auch* **Brot a; Geist c**

Wesen ['ve:zn̩] **das; ~s, ~ a)** *o. Pl. (Natur)* nature; *(Art, Charakter)* character; nature; **ein freundliches/kindliches ~ haben** have a friendly/childlike nature *or* manner; **von liebenswürdigem ~ sein** have a pleasant nature; **b)** *(Mensch)* creature; soul; **ein weibliches/männliches ~:** a woman *or* female/a man *or* male; **c)** *(Lebe~)* being; creature; **es war kein menschliches ~ zu sehen** there was not a [living] soul in sight; **ein höheres ~:** a higher being; **das höchste ~:** the Supreme Being; **d)** *(Philos.)* essence; **e)** *o. Pl. (veralt.: Tun u. Treiben)* hustle and bustle; **sein ~ treiben** ‹*child*› romp *or* play around; ‹*ghost*› be abroad, go around; ‹*thief*› be at work; **viel ~s/kein ~ [aus** *od.* **um** *od.* **von etw.] machen** *(ugs.)* make a lot of fuss/not make a fuss [about sth.]

wesenhaft *(geh.)* **1.** *Adj.* intrinsic. **2.** *adv.* intrinsically

wesens-, Wesens-: ~art die nature; character; **~eigen** *Adj.* characteristic; **jmdm./einer Sache ~eigen sein** be characteristic of sb./sth.; **~fremd** *Adj.* foreign to sb.'s/sth.'s nature *postpos.*; **~gemäß** *Adj.* **etw. ist jmdm. [nicht] ~gemäß** sth. is [not] in keeping with sb.'s nature; **~verwandt** *Adj.* who are similar in character *or* nature *postpos., not pred.*; **~verwandt sein** be similar in character *or* nature; **~zug der** trait; characteristic

wesentlich 1. *Adj.* fundamental **(für** to); **sich auf das Wesentliche beschränken** limit oneself to [the] essentials; **von ~er Bedeutung** of considerable importance; **im ~en** essentially. **2.** *adv. (weit, um vieles)* considerably; much; **es wäre mir ~ lieber, wenn wir ...:** I would much rather we ...; **sich von etw. ~ unterscheiden** be very *or* considerably different from sth.; **nichts ~ Neues enthalten** contain nothing substantially new

Wẹs·fall der genitive [case]

wes·halb *Adv. s.* **warum**

Wesir [ve'zi:ɐ̯] **der; ~s, ~e** vizier

Wespe ['vɛspə] **die; ~, ~n** wasp

Wẹspen-: ~nest das wasp's nest; **in ein ~nest stechen** *(fig. ugs.)* stir up a hornets' nest; **sich in ein ~nest setzen** *(fig.)* bring a hornets' nest [down] about one's ears; **~stich der** wasp sting; **~taille die** wasp-waist

wẹssen *Gen. von* **wer** *u.* **was 1.** *Interrogativpron.* **a)** *(von* **wer)** whose; **b)** *(von* **was) ~ wird er beschuldigt?** what is he accused of?;

~ **hat er sich schuldig gemacht** what is he guilty of?. **2.** *Relativpron.* **a)** (*von* **wer**) ~ **er gedachte, war seine Mutter** the person [whom] he was thinking about was his mother; **b)** (*von* **was**) **[das,]** ~ **er sich rühmt, ist ...:** what he prides himself on is ...

wessent·wegen *Interrogativadv. (geh.)* on whose account; because of whom

wessent·willen *Interrogativadv. in* **um** ~ *(geh.)* for whose sake

Wessi ['vɛsi] **der;** ~**s,** ~**s** *(salopp, bes. berlin.)* West German

Wessi·land (das) *(salopp, bes. berlin.)* West Germany

[1]**West** [vɛst] *o. Art.; o. Pl.* **a)** *(bes. Seemannsspr., Met.)* west; *s. auch* **Westen a; b)** *(Gebiet)* West; *s. auch* [1]**Ost b; c)** *(Politik)* West; *s. auch* [1]**Ost c; d)** *einem Subst. nachgestellt (westlicher Teil, westliche Lage)* West; *s. auch* [1]**Süd c**

[2]**West der;** ~**[e]s,** ~**e** *(Seemannsspr.)* westerly; *(dichter.)* west wind

[3]**West** *o. Art.; o. Pl. (ugs.:* ~**geld)** **in** ~ **bezahlen** pay in West German marks; **zehn Mark** ~**:** ten West German marks

West·afrika (das) West Africa

West-Berlin, Westberlin (das) West Berlin

West·berliner 1. der West Berliner. **2.** *Adj.; nicht präd.* West Berlin

west-, West-: ~**besuch der** *(ugs.)* visitor/visitors *pl.* from West Germany; ~**besuch haben** have a visitor/visitors from West Germany; ~**deutsch 1.** *Adj.* **a)** *(Politik)* West German; **b)** *(Geogr.)* Western German; **2.** *adv.* in a Western German manner; ~**deutsche der/die a)** *(Politik)* West German; **b)** *(Geogr.)* Western German; ~**deutschland (das) a)** *(Politik)* West Germany; **b)** *(Geogr.)* Western Germany

Weste ['vɛstə] **die;** ~, ~**n** waistcoat *(Brit.)*; vest *(Amer.)*; **eine schuß-** *od.* **kugelsichere** ~**:** a bullet-proof vest; **eine weiße** *od.* **reine** *od.* **saubere** ~ **haben** *(ugs.)* have a clean record; **jmdm. etw. unter die** ~ **jubeln** *(fig. ugs.)* shift *or* push sth. on to sb.

Westen der; ~**s a)** *(Richtung)* west; **nach** ~**:** westwards; to the west; **im/aus** *od.* **von** *od.* **vom** ~**:** in/from the west; *s. auch* **Norden a; b)** *(Gegend)* West; **im** ~**:** in the West; **der Wilde** ~**:** the Wild West; *s. auch* **Norden b; c)** *(Geogr.)* **der** ~ the West; d) *(Politik)* **der** ~ *(Westeuropa u. die USA)* the West; *(die BRD)* the West; West Germany

Westen·tasche die waistcoat *(Brit.) or (Amer.)* vest pocket; **etw. wie seine** ~ **kennen** *(ugs.)* know sth. like the back of one's hand *or* inside out

Westentaschen·format das *in* **in** *od.* **im** ~**:** pocket-size[d] ‹*calculator etc.*›; *(ugs. spött. fig.)* small-time ‹*politician etc.*›; tinpot ‹*dictator*›

Western der; ~**[s],** ~**:** western

West·europa (das) Western Europe

west·europäisch *Adj.* West[ern] European; ~**e Zeit** Greenwich Mean Time

Westfale [-'fa:lə] **der;** ~**n,** ~**n** Westphalian

Westfalen (das); ~**s** Westphalia

Westfälin [-'fɛ:lɪn] **die;** ~, ~**nen** Westphalian

westfälisch *Adj.* Westphalian; **der W**~**e Friede** *(hist.)* the Treaty of Westphalia; *s. auch* **deutsch; Deutsch a; badisch**

west-, West-: ~**fernsehen das** *(ugs.)* West German television; ~**flanke die** *(Milit., Geogr.)* western flank; *(Met.)* western edge; ~**geld das;** *o. Pl. (ugs.)* West German money; ~**germanisch** *Adj.* West Germanic; ~**gote der** West Goth; Visigoth; ~**hang der** western slope

West·indien (das) the West Indies *pl*

west·indisch *Adj.* West Indian

West·küste die west[ern] coast

Westler der; ~**s,** ~, **Westlerin die;** ~, ~**nen** *(ugs.)* West German

westlich 1. *Adj.* **a)** *(im Westen)* western; **15 Grad** ~**er Länge** 15 degrees west [longitude]; **das** ~**e Frankreich** western France; ~**st** westernmost; **der** ~**ste Punkt** the most westerly point; **b)** *(nach, aus dem Westen)* westerly; **c)** *(aus dem Westen kommend, für den Westen typisch)* Western, **d)** *(Politik)* Western; *s. auch* **östlich 1 d. 2.** *adv.* westwards; ~ **von ...:** [to the] west of ... **3.** *(Präp. mit Gen.)* [to the] west of

west-, West-: ~**mächte** *Pl. (Politik)* Western powers; ~**mark die;** ~, ~ *(ugs.)* West German mark; [1]~**nordwest** [--'-] *o. Pl.; o. Art. (Seemannsspr., Met.)* west-north-west; *s. auch* [1]**Nord a;** [2]~**nordwest** [--'-] **der** *(Seemannsspr.)* west-north-wester[ly]; ~**nordwesten** [--'--] **der** west-north-west; *s. auch* **Norden a;** ~**östlich 1.** *Adj.* west-to-east; from west to east *postpos.* **2.** *adv.* [from] west to east

West·preußen (das) West Prussia

west-, West-: ~**reise die** *(DDR)* trip to the West; ~**seite die** western side; ~**sender der** *(ugs.)* radio station in the West; [1]~**südwest** [--'-] *o. Pl.; o. Art. (Seemannsspr., Met.)* west-south-west; *s. auch* [1]**Nord a;** [2]~**südwest** [--'-] **der** *(Seemannsspr.)* west-south-wester[ly]; ~**südwesten** [--'--] **der** west-south-west; *s. auch* **Norden a;** ~**teil der** western part; ~**wall der;** *o. Pl. (hist.)* Siegfried Line; ~**wärts** *Adv.* **a)** *(nach Westen)* [to the] west; **b)** *(im Westen)* in the west; ~**wind der** west[erly] wind; ~**zone die** *(hist.)* Western zone

wes·wegen *Adv. s.* **warum**

Wett-: ~**annahme die** betting-office; bookmaker's; ~**bewerb der;** ~**[e]s,** ~**e a)** competition; **in einem** ~**bewerb siegen** win a competition; **sehr gut im** ~**bewerb liegen** have a good chance of winning the competition; **außer** ~**bewerb laufen** run as an unofficial competitor; **b)** *o. Pl. (Wirtsch.: Konkurrenz)* competition *no indef. art.*; **unlauterer** ~**bewerb** *(Rechtsw.)* unfair competition; ~**bewerber der** competitor

wettbewerbs-, Wettbewerbs-: ~**bedingung die** competition condition; ~**bedingungen** conditions *or* terms of a/the competition; ~**beschränkung die** *(Wirtsch.)* restraint of trade; ~**fähig** *Adj.* competitive; ~**verzerrung die** *(Wirtsch.)* distortion of normal trading conditions

Wett·büro das betting-office; bookmaker's

Wette ['vɛtə] **die;** ~, ~**n** bet; **die** ~ **ging um 100 Mark** the bet was 100 marks; **was gilt die** ~**?** how much do you want to bet?; what do you bet?; **eine** ~ **[mit jmdm.] abschließen** make a bet [with sb.]; **[ich gehe] jede** ~ **[ein], daß ...:** I bet you anything [you like] that ...; **mit jmdm. um die** ~ **laufen** *od.* **rennen** race sb.; **die Jungen schwammen um die** ~**:** the boys raced each other at swimming; **um die** ~ **arbeiten/singen** *(fig.)* try to outdo each other at hard work/singing

Wett·eifer der competitiveness

wett·eifern *itr. V.* **mit jmdm. [um etw.]** ~**:** compete with sb. [for sth.]; **miteinander** ~**:** compete with each other

wetten *itr. V.* bet; **mit jmdm.** ~**:** have a bet with sb.; **mit jmdm. um etw.** ~**:** bet sb. sth.; **auf etw.** *(Akk.)* ~**:** bet on sth.; put one's money on sth.; **[wollen wir]** ~**?** [do you] want to bet?; ~ **[daß]?** *(ugs.)* you can bet on it; it's a dead cert *(Brit. sl.) or (Amer. coll.)* surefire thing; **ich wette hundert zu eins, daß ...** *(ugs.)* I'll bet [you] a hundred to one that ...; **so haben wir nicht gewettet** *(ugs.)* that was not the deal *or* not what we agreed; **auf Platz/Sieg** ~**:** make a place bet/bet on a win. **2.** *tr. V.* **10 Mark** ~**:** bet 10 marks

[1]**Wetter das;** ~, ~ **a)** *o. Pl.* weather; **bei jedem** ~**:** in all weathers; **es ist schönes** ~**:** the weather is good *or* fine; **was haben wir heute für** ~**?** what's the weather like today?; **falls das** ~ **es zuläßt** weather permitting; **nach dem** ~ **sehen** see what the weather is like; **bei solchem** ~ **jagt man keinen Hund vor die Tür** the weather is/was not fit for a dog to be out in; **ein** ~ **zum Eierlegen** *(salopp)* fantastic *or* marvellous weather *(coll.)*; **bei jmdm. gut** ~ **machen** *(fig. ugs.)* get on the right side of sb.; butter sb. up; **um gut[es]** ~ **bitten** *(fig. ugs.)* try to make it up; **b)** *(Un*~*)* storm; **alle** ~**!** *(veralt.)* by Jove!; **c)** *Pl. (Bergbau)* **schlagende** ~**:** firedamp

[2]**Wetter der;** ~**s,** ~**:** better

wetter-, Wetter-: ~**amt das** meteorological office; ~**aussichten** *Pl.* weather outlook *sing.*; ~**bericht der** weather report; *(Voraussage)* weather forecast; ~**besserung die** improvement in the weather; ~**beständig** *Adj.* weatherproof

Wetterchen das; ~**s** *(ugs.)* fantastic *(coll.) or* lovely weather

wetter-, Wetter-: ~**dienst der** weather *or* meteorological service; ~**fahne die** weather-vane; ~**fest** *Adj.* weather-resistant; ~**fleck der** *(österr.)* weather-proof cape; ~**frosch der a)** *(ugs.) tree frog kept as a means of predicting the weather;* **b)** *(scherzh.)* weatherman; ~**fühlig** *Adj.* sensitive to [changes in] the weather *postpos.*; ~**fühligkeit die;** ~**:** sensitivity to [changes in] the weather; ~**gott der** weather god; ~**hahn der** weathercock

Wetterin die; ~, ~**nen** better

wetter-, Wetter-: ~**karte die** weather-chart; weather-map; ~**kunde die** meteorology *no art.*; ~**lage die** weather situation; *(fig.)* situation; climate; ~**lampe die** *(Bergbau)* safety lamp; ~**leuchten** *itr. V. (unpers.)* **es** ~**leuchtet** there is summer lightning; **es begann zu** ~**leuchten** flashes of [summer] lightning began to appear; ~**leuchten das;** ~**s** sheet *(esp. summer)* lightning *no indef. art.*; *(fig.)* first ominous signs *pl.*; ~**mantel der** *s.* **Regenmantel**

wettern *itr. V. (ugs.: schimpfen)* curse; **gegen** *od.* **über etw./jmdn.** ~**:** loudly denounce sth./sb.

wetter-, Wetter-: ~**prognose die** weather forecast; ~**regel die** saying about the weather; ~**satellit der** weather satellite; ~**schacht der** *(Bergbau)* ventilation shaft; ~**scheide die** weather *or* meteorological divide; ~**seite die** windward side; side exposed to the weather; ~**station die** weather-station; ~**sturz der** sudden fall in temperature; ~**um·schlag der** change in the weather; ~**vorhersage die** weather forecast; ~**warte die** weather station; ~**wendisch** *Adj. (abwertend)* capricious; unpredictable

wett-, Wett-: ~**fahrt die** race; **eine** ~**fahrt machen** have a race; ~**kampf der** competition; **jmdn. zum** ~**kampf auffordern** challenge sb. to a contest; ~**kämpfer der** competitor; ~**lauf der** race; **einen** ~**lauf machen** run a race; **ein** ~**lauf mit der Zeit/dem Tod** *(fig.)* a race against time/with death; ~**läufer der** runner; ~**machen** *tr. V. (ugs.)* **a)** *(ausgleichen)* make up for; **etw. durch etw.** ~**machen** make up for sth. with sth.; *(wiedergutmachen)* make good ‹*loss, mistake, etc.*›; **b)** *(sich erkenntlich zeigen für)* do something in return for; ~**rennen das** *(auch fig.)* race; **ein** ~**rennen machen** have *or* run a race; ~**rüsten das;** ~**s** arms race; ~**schwimmen das;** ~**s** swimming contest; ~**streit der** contest; *(fig.)* conflict; **mit jmdm./etw. in** ~**streit liegen/treten** be competing/compete with sb./sth.; ~**streiten** *unr. itr. V.; nur im Inf. gebr.* compete

wetzen ['vɛtsn̩] **1.** *tr. V.* sharpen; whet; **der Vogel wetzt seinen Schnabel an einem Stein** the bird rubs its beak on a stone. **2.** *itr. V.; mit sein (ugs.)* dash

Wetz-: ~**stahl der** steel; ~**stein der** whetstone

WEZ *Abk.* **Westeuropäische Zeit** GMT
WG [veː'geː] **die; ~, ~s** *Abk.* **Wohngemeinschaft**
WGB [veːgeː'beː] **der; ~s** *Abk.* **Weltgewerkschaftsbund** WFTU
Whiskey ['vɪski] **der; ~s ~s** whiskey; [American/Irish] whisky
Whisky ['vɪski] **der; ~s, ~s** whisky; **ein ~ mit Eis/[mit] Soda** whisky on the rocks/and soda
Whist [vɪst] **das; ~[e]s** whist
wich [vɪç] *1. u. 3. Pers. Sg. Prät. v.* **weichen**
Wichs [vɪks] **der; ~es, ~e,** *(österr.:)* **die; ~, ~en** *(Studentenspr.)* **in [vollem/voller] ~ erscheinen** appear in full regalia *or* full [gala] dress
Wichse die; ~, ~n *(ugs.)* **a)** *(Schuhcreme)* [shoe-]polish; **b)** *o. Pl. (Schläge)* a hiding *(coll.)*; **dann kriegst du** *od.* **dann gibt's ~:** you'll get a good hiding *(coll.)*
wichsen 1. *tr. V. (ugs.)* **a)** polish; **b)** *(landsch.: schlagen)* **jmdn. ~:** give sb. a good hiding *(coll.)*; **jmdm. eine ~:** box sb.'s ears. **2.** *itr., tr. V. (derb: masturbieren)* wank *(Brit. coarse)*; jerk off *(coarse)*
Wichser der; ~s, ~: *(derb)* wanker *(vulg.)*
Wicht [vɪçt] **der; ~[e]s, ~e a)** *(fam.: kleines Kind)* little rascal *or* imp *(joc.)*; **b)** *(abwertend: männliche Person)* [insignificant] creature; **armer ~:** poor devil
Wichtel der; ~s, ~ a) *s.* **Wichtelmännchen; b)** *(bei den Pfadfinderinnen)* brownie
Wichtel·männchen das gnome; *(Kobold)* goblin
wichtig ['vɪçtɪç] *Adj.* important; **nimm die Sache nicht so ~:** don't take the matter so seriously; **es ist mir ~ zu wissen, ob ...:** it is important to me to know if ...; **nichts Wichtigeres zu tun haben[, als ...]** *(auch iron.)* have nothing better to do [than ...]; **das ~ste ist, daß du schweigst** the most important thing is that you remain silent; **Wichtiges zu tun haben** have important things to do; **sich ~ machen** *od.* **tun** *(ugs. abwertend)* be full of one's own importance; **sich mit etw. ~ machen** be pompous about sth.; **sich** *(Dat.)* **~ vorkommen** *(ugs. abwertend)* be full of oneself; **sich sehr ~ nehmen** *(ugs.)* be full of self-importance
Wichtigkeit die; ~ importance; **einer Sache** *(Dat.)* **[große/besondere] ~ beimessen** *od.* **beilegen** attach [great/particular] importance to sth.
Wichtigtuer [-tuːɐ] **der; ~s, ~** *(ugs. abwertend)* pompous ass
Wichtigtuerei die; ~, ~en *(ugs. abwertend)* pomposity; pompousness *no pl.*
wichtigtuerisch 1. *Adj.* self-important; pompous. **2.** *adv.* in a self-important manner; ⟨*behave, act*⟩ pompously
Wicke ['vɪkə] **die; ~, ~n** vetch; *(im Garten)* sweet pea
Wickel der; ~s, ~: compress; **jmdm. einen ~ machen** put a compress on sb.; **jmdn. am** *od.* **beim ~ haben/nehmen** *(fig. ugs.)* have/grab sb. by the scruff of his/her neck
Wickel-: ~gamasche die puttee; **~kind das** baby; infant; **~kommode die** baby's changing-table
wickeln *tr. V.* **a)** *(schlingen)* wind; **Wolle zu einem Knäuel ~:** wind wool into a ball; **etw. auf/um etw.** *(Akk.)* **~:** wind sth. on to sth./round sth.; **b)** *(eindrehen)* **sich/jmdm. die Haare ~:** put one's/sb.'s hair in curlers *or* rollers; **c)** *(ein~)* wrap; **etw./jmdn./sich in etw.** *(Akk.)* **~:** wrap sth./sb./oneself in sth.; **er hat sich [fest] in seinen Mantel gewickelt** he wrapped his coat tightly [a]round himself; **d)** *(windeln)* **ein Kind ~:** change a baby's nappy; **der Kleine ist frisch gewickelt** the baby has had his nappy changed; **e)** *(bandagieren)* bandage; **f)** *(aus~)* unwrap; **etw./jmdn./sich aus etw. ~:** unwrap sth./sb./oneself from sth.; **das Buch aus dem Papier ~:** take the book out of the wrapping-paper; **g)** *(ab~)* unwind ⟨*thread, wool, etc.*⟩ **(von** from); **h)** *in* **schief** *od.* **falsch gewickelt sein** *(ugs.)* be very much mistaken
Wickel-: ~rock der wrapover skirt; **~tisch der** baby's changing-table
Wicklung die; ~, ~en *(Elektrot.)* winding
Widder ['vɪdɐ] **der; ~s, ~ a)** *(Tier)* ram; **b)** *(Astron., Astrol.)* Aries; **sie/er ist [ein] ~:** she/he is [an] Aries
wider ['viːdɐ] *Präp. mit Akk.* **a)** *(geh., veralt.)* against; **b)** *(geh.: entgegen)* contrary to; **~ [alles] Erwarten** contrary to [all] expectations; **~ besseres Wissen/alle Vernunft** against one's better knowledge/all reason; **~ Willen** against one's will
wider-, Wider-: ~borstig 1. *Adj.* unruly, unmanageable ⟨*hair*⟩; *(fig.)* rebellious ⟨*person*⟩; unruly, rebellious ⟨*child*⟩; **sich ~borstig zeigen** be rebellious; **2.** *adv.* rebelliously; **~fahren** [--'--] *unr. itr. V.; mit sein (geh.)* **etw. ~fährt jmdm.** sth. happens to sb.; **jmdm. ~fährt eine große Freude/ein schweres Leid** sb. experiences great joy/great sorrow; **ihm ist [ein] Unrecht ~fahren** he has been done an injustice; **jmdm. Gerechtigkeit ~fahren lassen** see that justice is done to sb.; **~haken der** barb; **~hall der** echo; *(fig.)* **[bei jmdm.] ~hall finden** meet with a [positive] response [from sb.]; **großen ~hall finden** meet with a wide response; **~|hallen** *itr. V.* echo; resound **(von** with); **der Schuß hallte von den Bergwänden wider** the shot echoed from the mountainsides; **~legen** [--'--] *tr. V.* **etw. ~legen** refute *or* disprove sth.; **jmdn. ~legen** prove sb. wrong; **~legung** [--'--] **die; ~, ~en** refutation
widerlich *(abwertend)* **1.** *Adj.* **a)** *(ekelerregend)* revolting; repulsive; **~ schmecken/riechen** taste/smell revolting; **b)** *(höchst unsympathisch, kaum erträglich)* repugnant, repulsive ⟨*person, behaviour, etc.*⟩; awful ⟨*headache etc.*⟩. **2.** *adv.* **a)** *(ekelerregend)* revoltingly; **b)** *(verabscheuungswürdig)* ⟨*behave, act*⟩ in a repugnant *or* repulsive manner; **c)** *(unangenehm)* awfully ⟨*cold, hot, sweet, etc.*⟩
Widerlichkeit die; ~, ~en *(abwertend)* **a)** *o. Pl.* repulsiveness; **b)** *Äußerung/Handlung)* revolting remark/action
Widerling der; ~[e]s, ~e *(abwertend)* repulsive creature
widern ['viːdɐn] *tr., itr. V. (veralt.) s.* **ekeln 2**
wider-, Wider-: ~natürlich *Adj.* unnatural; **~part der; ~[e]s, ~e** *(geh.)* adversary; **jmdm. ~part bieten** resist sb.; **~raten** [--'--] *unr. itr. V. (geh. veralt.)* **jmdm. ~raten, etw. zu tun** advise sb. against doing sth.; **~rechtlich 1.** *Adj.* illegal; unlawful; **~rechtliches Betreten eines Geländes/Gebäudes** trespass[ing] on a property/unlawful *or* illegal entry to a building; **2.** *adv.* illegally; unlawfully; **~rechtlichkeit die** illegality; unlawfulness; **~rede die a)** argument; contradiction; **keine ~rede!** don't argue!; no arguing!; **ohne ~rede** without [any] argument *or* protest; **b)** *s.* **Gegenrede a; ~rist der** *(Zool.)* withers *pl.*; **~ruf der** *(einer Aussage)* retraction; *(eines Befehls, einer Anordnung, Erlaubnis usw.)* revocation; withdrawal; **[bis] auf ~ruf** until revoked *or* cancelled; **~rufen** [--'--] *unr. tr., auch itr. V.* retract, withdraw ⟨*statement, claim, confession, etc.*⟩; revoke, cancel ⟨*order, permission, etc.*⟩; repeal ⟨*law*⟩; **~ruflich 1.** *Adj.* revocable ⟨*permission, power of attorney*⟩; **2.** *adv.* until further notice; **~sacher der; ~s, ~, ~sacherin die; ~, ~nen** *(geh.)* adversary; opponent; **~schein der** *(geh.)* reflection; **~setzen** [--'--] *refl. V.* **sich jmdm./einer Sache ~setzen** oppose sb./sth.; **sich einer Aufforderung ~setzen** refuse to comply with a demand; **~setzlich** [*od.* --'--] **1.** *Adj.* rebellious; **sich ~setzlich zeigen** be rebellious; **2.** *adv.* rebelliously; **~setzlichkeit** [*od.* --'---] **die; ~, ~en a)** *o. Pl. (Haltung)* rebelliousness; **b)** *(Handlung)* rebellious action; **~sinn der;** *o. Pl.* absurdity; **~sinnig** *Adj.* absurd; **~spenstig** [~ʃpɛnstɪç] **1.** *Adj.* unruly; rebellious; wilful; unruly, unmanageable ⟨*hair*⟩; stubborn ⟨*horse, mule, etc.*⟩; **2.** *adv.* wilfully; rebelliously; **~spenstigkeit die; ~, ~en a)** *o. Pl. (Haltung)* unruliness; rebelliousness; wilfulness; *(von Haaren)* unruliness; unmanageableness; *(von Pferden usw.)* stubborness; **b)** *(Handlung)* unruly *or* rebellious *or* wilful behaviour *no pl.*; **~|spiegeln, ~spiegeln** [--'--] **1.** *tr. V.* reflect; *(als Spiegelbild)* mirror; *(fig.)* reflect; **2.** *refl. V.* be reflected; *(als Spiegelbild)* be mirrored; *(fig.)* be reflected; **~sprechen** *unr. itr. V.* **a)** *(Einwände erheben)* contradict; **jmdm./einer Sache/sich [selbst] ~sprechen** contradict sb./sth./oneself; **der Betriebsrat hat der Entlassung ~sprochen** the works committee has opposed the dismissal; **b)** *(im Gegensatz stehen zu)* contradict, be inconsistent with ⟨*facts, truth, etc.*⟩; **sich** *(Dat.)* **~sprechende Aussagen/Nachrichten** conflicting statements/news reports; **~spruch der a)** *o. Pl. (Widerrede, Protest)* opposition; protest; **es erhob sich allgemeiner ~spruch** there was a general protest; **nicht den geringsten ~spruch dulden** not tolerate the slightest argument; **auf ~spruch stoßen** meet with opposition *or* protests; **etw. ohne ~spruch hinnehmen** accept sth. without argument; **b)** *(etw. Unvereinbares)* contradiction; **ein ~spruch in sich** *(Dat.)* **[selbst] sein** be a contradiction in terms; **sich** *(Akk.)* **in ~sprüche verwickeln** get entangled *or* caught up in contradictions; **in ~spruch zu** *od.* **mit etw. stehen** contradict sth.; be contradictory to sth.; **in ~spruch zu etw. geraten** come into conflict with sth.; **c)** *(Philos.)* contradiction; **~sprüchlich 1.** *Adj.* contradictory ⟨*news, statements, etc.*⟩; inconsistent ⟨*behaviour, attitude, etc.*⟩; **2.** *adv.* **er verhielt sich sehr ~sprüchlich** his behaviour was very inconsistent; **~sprüchlichkeit die; ~, ~en a)** *o. Pl. (Eigenschaft)* contradictoriness; inconsistency; **b)** *(Äußerung, Handlung)* contradiction; **~spruchs·los 1.** *Adj.; nicht präd.* unprotesting; uncontradicting; **2.** *adv.* without opposition *or* protest
Wider·stand der a) resistance **(gegen** to); **jmdm./einer Sache ~ leisten** resist sb./sth.; put up resistance to sb./sth.; **an jmds. ~** *(Dat.)* **scheitern** collapse in the face of sb.'s resistance; **bei jmdm. auf ~ stoßen** meet with *or* encounter resistance from sb.; **zum bewaffneten ~ aufrufen** call [people] to arms; **b)** *(Hindernis)* opposition; **allen Widerständen zum Trotz** despite all opposition; *s. auch* **Weg c; c)** *o. Pl. (~bewegung)* **der ~:** the Resistance; **d)** *(Mech., Elektrot.)* resistance; *(Elektrot.: Schaltungselement)* resistor
widerstands, Widerstands-: ~bewegung die resistance movement; **~fähig** *Adj.* robust; resistant ⟨*material etc.*⟩; hardy ⟨*animal, plant*⟩; **~fähig gegen** *od.* **gegenüber etw. sein** be resistant to sth.; **~fähigkeit die;** *o. Pl.* robustness; *(von Material usw.)* resistance; *(von Tier, Pflanze)* hardiness; **~fähigkeit gegen etw.** resistance to sth.; **~kämpfer der** resistance fighter; **~kraft die;** *o. Pl.* resistance; **~los 1.** *Adj.* without resistance *postpos.*; **2.** *adv.* without resistance
wider-, Wider-: ~stehen *unr. itr. V.* **a)** *(nicht nachgeben)* **[jmdm./einer Sache] ~stehen** resist [sb./sth.]; **b)** *(standhalten)* **jmdm./einer Sache ~stehen** withstand sb./sth.; **~streben** *itr. V.* **a)** *(zuwider sein)* **etw. ~strebt jmdm.** sb. dislikes *or* detests sth.; **das ~strebt meinem Taktgefühl** that goes against my sense of tact; **es ~strebt jmdm.,**

etw. zu tun sb. dislikes doing sth. *or* is reluctant to do sth.; **b)** *(geh.: sich widersetzen)* **einer Sache** *(Dat.)* **~streben** oppose sth.; **~d nachgeben/einwilligen** give in/agree reluctantly; **~streben das** reluctance; **trotz anfänglichem ~streben** after some initial reluctance; **~streit der;** *o. Pl.* conflict; **in** *od.* **im ~streit mit etw. leben/stehen** be/live in conflict with sth.; **~streitend** *Adj.; nicht präd.* conflicting; **~wärtig** [~vɛrtɪç] *(abwertend)* **1.** *Adj.* **a)** *(unangenehm)* disagreeable, unpleasant ‹*conditions, situation, etc.*›; **b)** *(ekelhaft, abscheulich)* revolting, repugnant ‹*smell, taste, etc.*›; objectionable, offensive ‹*person, behaviour, attitude, etc.*›; **das ist mir ~wärtig** I find that offensive *or* objectionable; **~wärtig riechen/schmecken** smell/taste revolting; **2.** *adv.* ‹*behave, act, etc.*› in an objectionable *or* offensive manner; **~wärtigkeit die; ~, ~en a)** *o. Pl.* offensiveness; objectionableness; repulsiveness; **b)** *(Umstand)* disagreeable *or* unpleasant circumstance; **~wille der** aversion **(gegen** to); **einen ~willen gegen jmdn./etw. haben** *od.* **empfinden** have/experience an aversion to sb./sth.; **etw. mit ~willen essen/tun** eat sth. with distaste/do sth. with reluctance *or* reluctantly; **~willig 1.** *Adj.; nicht präd. (unwillig)* reluctant; unwilling; **2.** *adv.* reluctantly; unwillingly; **etw. nur ~willig tun** do sth. only with reluctance; **~wort das;** *Pl.* **~worte: ~worte geben** answer back; **etw. ohne [ein] ~wort tun** do sth. without argument *or* protest; **keine ~worte dulden** not tolerate any argument; **keine ~worte!** no arguments!

widmen ['vɪtmən] **1.** *tr. V.* **a)** *(zueignen)* **jmdm. ein Buch/Gedicht/eine Sinfonie** *usw.* **~:** dedicate a book/poem/symphony *etc.* to sb.; **b)** *(verwenden für/auf)* **etw. jmdm./einer Sache ~:** devote sth. to sb./sth.; **jmdm./einer Sache seine Liebe/Aufmerksamkeit ~:** give sb./sth. one's love/attention. **2.** *refl. V.* *(sich beschäftigen mit)* **sich jmdm./einer Sache ~:** attend to sb./sth.; *(ausschließlich)* devote oneself to sb./sth.; **heute kann ich mich dir ganz ~:** I can devote myself to you entirely today

Widmung die; ~, ~en dedication **(an +** *Akk.* to)

widrig ['vi:drɪç] *Adj.* unfavourable, adverse ‹*wind, circumstances, fate, etc.*›

widrigen·falls *Adv. (bes. Amtsspr.)* otherwise

Widrigkeit die; ~, ~en adversity

wie 1. *Interrogativadv.* **a)** *(auf welche Art u. Weise)* how; **~ heißt er/das?** what is his/its name?; what is he/that called?; **~ [bitte]?** [I beg your] pardon?; *(entrüstet)* I beg your pardon!; **~ war das?** *(ugs.)* what was that?; what did you say?; **~ meinen?** *(scherzh.)* [I beg your] pardon?; **~ kommt es, daß ...?** how is it that ...?; **~ das?** *(ugs.)* how did that come about?; **~ käme ich denn dazu?** why should I?; **b)** *(durch welche Merkmale gekennzeichnet)* **~ war das Wetter?** what was the weather like?; how was the weather?; **~ ist dein neuer Chef?** what is your new boss like? *(coll.);* how is your new boss? *(coll.);* **~ geht es ihm?** how is he?; **~ war es in Spanien?** what was Spain like?; what was it like in Spain?; **~ findest du das Bild?** what do you think of the picture?; **~ gefällt er dir?** how do you like him?; **~ wär's mit ...:** how about ...; **~ wäre es, wenn du dir die Schuhe putztest?** how about [you] cleaning your shoes?; **Gott, ~ du aussiehst!** God, just look at yourself!; **c)** *(in welchem Grade)* how; **~ lange/groß/hoch/oft?** how long/big/high/often?; **~ sehr haben wir uns das gewünscht!** how badly we wanted that!; **~ spät ist es?** what time is it?; **wie alt bist du?** how old are you?; **~ er läuft!** how fast he runs!; **und ~!** and how! *(coll.);* **d)** *(ugs.: nicht wahr)* **das hat dir Spaß gemacht, ~?** you enjoyed that, didn't you?; **das ärgert dich wohl, ~?** that does annoy you, doesn't it? **2.** *Relativadv.* **[die Art,] ~ er es tut** the way *or* manner in which he does it; **die Preise steigen in dem Maße, ~ die Löhne erhöht werden** prices are rising at the same rate as wages; **~ man es auch [immer] macht, es ist ihr nie recht** whatever you do *or* whichever way you do it she's never happy with it; **~ er das wieder geschafft hat!** he's done it again – how does he manage it? **3.** *Konj.* **a)** *Vergleichspartikel* as; **[so] ... ~ ...:** as ... as ...; **das Buch ist so unterhaltend ~ lehrreich** the book is as entertaining as it is instructive; **er kam so schnell ~ möglich** he came as quickly as possible; **~ gewöhnlich** *od.* **üblich/immer** as usual/always; **ein Mann ~ er** a man like him; **es geht dir [so] ~ mir** you're like me; **er macht es [genauso] ~ du** he does it [just] like you [do]; **~ durch ein Wunder** as if by a miracle; **er kann spielen ~ kein zweiter** no one can touch him when it comes to playing; **ich fühlte mich ~ ...:** I felt as if I were ...; **„N" ~ „Nordpol"** N for November; **b)** *(zum Beispiel)* like; such as; **Entwicklungsländer ~ [zum Beispiel] Somalia oder Tansania** developing countries such as Somalia or Tanzania [for example]; **~ folgt** as follows; **~ schon der Name sagt** as the name already implies; **~ wenn** as if *or* though; **c)** *(und, sowie)* as well as; both; **Männer ~ Frauen** men as well as women; both men and women; **d)** *(temporal: als)* **~ ich an seinem Fenster vorbeigehe, höre ich ihn singen** as I pass by his window I hear him singing; **~ ich die Tür öffne, steht doch tatsächlich Christine vor mir** when I open the door, who is standing there but Christine; **e)** *(ugs.: außer)* **wir hatten nichts ~ Ärger [damit]** we had nothing but trouble [with it]; **nichts ~ hin!** come on, let's go!; *s. auch* **nichts; f)** *(nicht standardsprachlich: als)* than

Wiedehopf ['vi:dəhɔpf] **der; ~[e]s, ~e** hoopoe

wieder ['vi:dɐ] *Adv.* **a)** *(erneut)* again; **je/nie ~:** ever/never again; **~ mal** *od* **mal ~ ins Kino gehen** go to the cinema again some time; **immer ~,** *(geh.)* **~ und ~:** again and again; time and [time] again; **es regnet schon ~:** it's raining again; **das Buch ist ~ ein Bestseller** the book is another best seller; **nie ~ Krieg!** no more war!; **wie du ~ aussiehst!** just look at yourself again!; **was ist denn jetzt schon ~ los?** what's happened 'now?; **b)** *(unterscheidend: noch)* **einige ..., andere ... und ~ andere ...:** some ..., others ..., and yet others ...; **das ist ~ etwas anderes** that is something else again; **c)** *(drückt Rückkehr in früheren Zustand aus)* again; **alles ist ~ beim alten** everything is back as it was before; **etw. ~ an seinen Platz zurückstellen** put sth. back in its place; **ich bin gleich ~ da** I'll be right back *(coll.);* I'll be back in a minute; **willst du schon ~ gehen?** are you going already?; **gib es ihm ~ zurück** *(ugs.)* give it back to him!; **d)** *(andererseits, anders betrachtet)* **das ist auch ~ wahr** that's true enough; **da hast du auch ~ recht** you're right there; **so schlimm ist es auch ~ nicht** it's not as bad as all that; **e)** *(meinerseits, deinerseits usw.)* in turn; **f)** *(auch)* likewise; also; **g)** *(ugs.: noch)* **wie heißt er ~?** what's his name again?; **wo/wann war das [gleich] ~?** where/when was that again?

wieder-, Wieder-: ~aufbau der; *o. Pl.* reconstruction; rebuilding; **der wirtschaftliche ~aufbau** economic recovery; **~auf|bauen**[1] *tr. V.* reconstruct; rebuild; **~auf|bereiten**[1] *tr. V.* recycle; *(bes. Kerntechnik)* reprocess; **~aufbereitung die** recycling; *(bes. Kerntechnik)* reprocessing; **~aufbereitungs·anlage die** recycling plant; *(Kerntechnik)* reprocessing plant; **~auf|führen**[1] *tr. V.* revive ‹*play*›; rerun, reshow ‹*film*›; **~aufführung die** *(eines Theaterstücks)* revival; *(eines Films)* rerun; **~aufnahme die a)** resumption; *(von Beziehungen)* re-establishment; **die ~aufnahme eines Verfahrens** *(Rechtsspr.)* the resumption *or* reopening of proceedings; **b)** *(als Mitglied)* readmittance; **c)** *(eines Theaterstücks)* revival; **~aufnahme·verfahren das** *(Rechtsspr.)* retrial; **~auf|nehmen**[1] *unr. tr. V.* **a)** *(erneut beginnen mit)* resume; take up ‹*subject, idea*› again; re-establish ‹*relations, contact*›; **ein Verfahren ~aufnehmen** *(Rechtsspr.)* reopen a case; **b)** *(als Mitglied)* readmit; **~auf|richten**[1] *tr. V.* give fresh heart to ‹*person*›; **~aufrüstung die** rearmament; **~auf|tauchen**[1] *itr. V.; mit sein* turn up again

wieder-, Wieder-: ~beginn der recommencement; resumption; **~|bekommen** *unr. tr. V.* get back; **du bekommst das Buch ~:** you'll get the book back; **~|beleben** *tr. V.* revive, resuscitate ‹*person*›; *(fig.)* revive, resurrect ‹*friendship, custom, etc.*›; **~belebungs·versuch der** attempt at resuscitation; **bei jmdm. ~belebungsversuche machen** attempt to revive *or* resuscitate sb.; **~bewaffnung die** rearmament; **~|bringen** *unr. tr. V.* bring back

Wieder·einsetzung die reinstatement

wieder-, Wieder-: ~|entdecken *tr. V.* rediscover; **~entdeckung die** rediscovery; **~|erkennen** *unr. tr. V.* recognize; **er war kaum ~zuerkennen** he was almost unrecognizable; **~|erobern** *tr. V.* recapture ‹*territory*›; regain ‹*position, title, etc.*›; **~eroberung die** *s.* **~erobern:** recapture; regaining; **~|eröffnen** *tr. V.* reopen; **~eröffnung die** reopening; **~|erwecken** *tr. V.* revive; bring back *or* restore to life; *(fig.)* revive; reawaken; **~|finden 1.** *unr. tr. V.* find again; *(fig.)* regain ‹*composure, dignity, courage, etc.*›; **2.** *unr. refl. V.* **die Handschuhe/Schlüssel** *usw.* **haben sich ~gefunden** the gloves/keys *etc.* have been found; **~gabe die a)** *(Darstellung, Schilderung)* report; account; **b)** *(Übersetzung)* rendering; **c)** *(Reproduktion; in Ton u. Bild)* reproduction; **d)** *(Aufführung)* rendition; **~|geben** *unr. tr. V.* **a)** *(zurückgeben)* give back; return; **b)** *(berichten)* report; give an account of; *(wiederholen)* repeat; *(ausdrücken)* express; *(zitieren)* quote; **etw. gekürzt ~geben** give a shortened version of sth.; **c)** *(übersetzen)* render; **d)** *(darstellen)* portray; depict; **die Gebirge sind auf der Landkarte in Braun ~gegeben** the mountains are shown in brown on the map; **e)** *(hörbar, sichtbar machen)* reproduce; **~geburt die a)** *(Rel.)* reincarnation; **b)** *o. Pl. (christl. Rel., fig. geh.)* rebirth; **~|gewinnen** *unr. tr. V.* recover ‹*lost item, money, etc.*›; regain ‹*composure, equilibrium, etc.*›

wieder·gut|machen[2] *tr. V.* make good; put right; **den Schaden ~** *(bezahlen)* pay for the damage; **das ist nicht wiedergutzumachen** that cannot be put right; **ein nicht wiedergutzumachendes Unrecht** an irreparable injustice

Wieder·gutmachung die; ~, ~en a) reparation; **die ~ des Unrechts fordern** demand that the injustice be made good; **b)** *(Leistung)* compensation

wieder|haben *untr. tr. V. (auch fig.)* have back

wieder-, Wieder-: ~her|stellen[3] *tr. V.* **a)** re-establish ‹*contact, peace*›; **b)** *(reparieren)* restore ‹*building*›; **c)** *(wieder gesund machen)* **jmdn. ~herstellen** restore sb. to health; get sb. on his/her feet again; **~herstellung die a)** re-establishment; **b)** *(Wiederinstandsetzung)* restoration; **c)** *(Gene-*

[1] *ich baue/bereite usw. wieder auf*
[2] *ich mache wieder gut*
[3] *ich stelle wieder her*

sung) recovery; **bis zu seiner völligen ~herstellung** until he has completely recovered *or* is fully restored to health; **~holbar** *Adj.* repeatable; **das ist nicht ~holbar** it cannot be repeated; **~holen 1.** *tr. V.* **a)** repeat; replay ⟨*football match*⟩; retake ⟨*penalty kick*⟩; resit, retake ⟨*exam*⟩; **eine Wahl ~holen** hold an election again; rehold an election; **b)** *(nochmals sagen)* repeat, reiterate ⟨*question, demand, offer, etc.*⟩; **c)** *(repetieren)* revise ⟨*lesson, vocabulary, etc.*⟩; **2.** *refl. V.* **a)** *(wieder dasselbe sagen)* repeat oneself; **b)** *(erneut geschehen)* happen again; **c)** *(wiederkehren)* be repeated; recur

wieder|holen *tr. V.* fetch *or* get back

wiederholt 1. *Adj.; nicht präd.* repeated; **zum ~en Male** yet again. **2.** *adv.* repeatedly

Wiederholung die; ~, ~en a) repetition; *(eines Fußballspiels usw.)* replay; *(eines Freistoßes, Elfmeters usw.)* retaking; *(einer Sendung)* repeat; *(einer Aufführung)* repeat performance; **eine ~ der Wahl ist notwendig** the election must be held again *or* reheld; **b)** *(des Schuljahrs, einer Prüfung usw.)* repeating; **eine ~ der Prüfung ist nicht möglich** it is not possible to resit *or* retake the exam; **c)** *(von Fragen, Forderungen, Angeboten usw.)* repetition; reiteration; **d)** *(von Lernstoff)* revision

Wiederholungs-: ~fall der *in* **im ~fall** *(bes. Amtsspr.)* in the event of [any] recurrence; **~täter der** *(Kriminologie)* habitual offender; **~zahlwort das** *(Sprachw.)* multiplicative; **~zeichen das** *(Musik)* repeat sign

Wieder·hören das *in* **[auf] ~!** goodbye! *(at end of telephone call)*

Wieder·instandsetzung die reconstruction

wieder-, Wieder-: ~|käuen [-kɔyən] **1.** *itr. V.* ruminate; chew the cud; **2.** *tr. V.* **a)** chew again; **b)** *(fig. abwertend)* rehash; **~käuer der; ~s, ~:** ruminant; **~kehr die; ~** *(geh.)* **a)** *(Rückkehr)* return; **b)** *(Wiederholung)* recurrence; *(Jahrestag)* anniversary; **~|kehren** *itr. V.; mit sein (geh.)* **a)** *(zurückkehren)* return; **b)** *(sich noch einmal ereignen)* come again; **eine nie ~kehrende Gelegenheit** a chance that will never come again; the chance of a lifetime; **c)** *(sich wiederholen)* be repeated; recur; **~|kommen** *unr. itr. V.; mit sein* **a)** *(zurückkommen)* return; come back; **b)** *(noch einmal kommen)* come back *or* again; **c)** *(sich noch einmal ereignen)* ⟨*opportunity, past*⟩ come again; **~|kriegen** *tr. V. (ugs.) s.* **~bekommen; ~kunft** [~kʊnft] **die; ~** *(geh.)* return; **die ~kunft Christi** the Second Coming of Christ; **~schauen das** *in* **[auf] ~schauen!** *(südd., österr.)* goodbye!; **~|sehen** *unr. tr. V. (auch fig.)* see again; **sich überraschend ~sehen** see each other *or* meet again unexpectedly; **~sehen das; ~s, ~:** reunion; **~ mit Berlin/der Heimat** return to Berlin/one's homeland; **sie stießen auf ein baldiges ~sehen an** they drank to seeing each other again soon; **~sehen macht Freude** *(scherzh.)* I'd like to have it back some time; **[auf] ~sehen!** goodbye!; **jmdm. auf ~sehen sagen** say goodbye to sb.; **[auf] ~sehen nächsten Monat/in London** goodbye until we meet again next month/in London

Wiedersehens·freude die; *o. Pl.* pleasure of seeing sb./each other again

wieder-, Wieder-: ~täufer der *(Rel.)* anabaptist; **~|tun** *unr. tr. V.* do again; **~um** *Adv.* **a)** *(erneut)* again; **b)** *(andererseits)* on the other hand; **so weit würde ich ~um nicht gehen** I wouldn't, however, go that far; **c)** *(meiner-, deinerseits usw.)* in turn; **~|vereinigen** *tr. V.* reunify ⟨*country*⟩; **~vereinigung die** reunification; **~verheiratung die** remarriage; **~|verwenden** *unr. od. regelm. tr. V.* reuse; **~verwendung die** reuse; **~vorlage die;** *o. Pl. (bes. Amtsspr.) in* **zur ~vorlage** for resubmission; to be resubmitted; **~wahl die** re-election; **sich zur ~wahl stellen** stand *or* run for re-election; **~|wählen** *tr. V.* reelect

Wiege ['vi:gə] **die; ~, ~n** *(auch fig.)* cradle; **seine ~ stand in Sachsen** *(geh.)* he was born in Saxony; his birthplace was in Saxony; **es ist ihm nicht an der ~ gesungen worden, daß ...:** he would never have dreamt *or* could never have foreseen that ...; **eine solche Karriere ist ihm nicht an der ~ gesungen worden** he would never have dreamt of such a career; **von der ~ an** *(geh.)* from the day he/she was born; **von der ~ bis zur Bahre** *(scherzh.)* from the cradle to the grave

Wiege·messer das chopping-knife *(with curved blade used by rocking to and fro)*

[1]wiegen 1. *unr. itr. V.* weigh; **was** *od.* **wieviel wiegst du?** how much do you weigh?; what weight *or* how heavy are you?; **schwer ~** *(fig.)* carry weight. **2.** *unr. tr. V.* weigh; **etw. gut/knapp ~:** weigh sth. generously/short; **gewogen und zu leicht befunden** *(fig.)* weighed [in the balance] and found wanting

[2]wiegen 1. *tr. V.* **a)** *(schaukeln, hin u. her bewegen)* rock; shake ⟨*head*⟩ *(in doubt)*; **die Hüften ~:** sway one's hips; **einen ~den Gang haben** have a rolling gait; **b)** *(zerkleinern)* chop [up] *(with a Wiegemesser)*. **2.** *refl. V.* ⟨*boat, cradle, etc.*⟩ rock; ⟨*person, branch, etc.*⟩ sway; **sich in den Hüften ~:** sway one's hips; **sich in der Hoffnung ~, daß ...:** cherish *or* nurture the hope that ...

Wiegen-: ~fest das *(geh.)* birthday; **~lied das** lullaby; cradle-song

wiehern ['vi:ɐn] *itr. V.* **a)** whinny; *(lauter)* neigh; **b)** *(fig. ugs.)* **vor Lachen ~:** roar with laughter; **[das ist ja] zum W~!** that's a scream! *(sl.)*; **sich ~d auf die Schenkel schlagen** slap one's thigh with a bellow of laughter; **~des Gelächter** uproarious laughter

Wien ['vi:n] **(das); ~s** Vienna

[1]Wiener der; ~s, ~: Viennese

[2]Wiener *Adj.* Viennese; **~ Würstchen** wiener; frankfurter; **~ Schnitzel** Wiener schnitzel; **der ~ Kongreß** the Congress of Vienna; **die ~ Sängerknaben/Philharmoniker** the Vienna Boys' Choir/Vienna Philharmonic

[3]Wiener die; ~, ~: wiener [sausage]

Wienerin die; ~, ~nen Viennese

wienerisch *Adj.* Viennese; **das Wienerische** the Viennese dialect

wienern *tr. V. (ugs.)* polish; shine

wies ['vi:s] *1. u. 3. Pers. Sg. Prät. v.* **weisen**

Wiese ['vi:zə] **die; ~, ~n** meadow; *(Rasen)* lawn; **auf der grünen ~** *(fig.)* out in the [open] country

Wiesel ['vi:zl] **das; ~s, ~:** weasel; **wie ein ~ laufen** run like a hare; *s. auch* **flink 1**

wiesel·flink 1. *Adj.* nimble. **2.** *adv.* quick as a flash

wieseln *itr. V.; mit sein* scurry

Wiesen-: ~blume die meadow flower; **~grund der** *(geh.)* meadowland; **~schaum·kraut das** lady's smock

wie·so *Interrogativadv.* why

wie·viel [*od.* '--] *Interrogativpron.* (+ *Sg.*) how much; (+ *Pl.*) how many; **~ Uhr ist es?** what time is it?; **~ auch immer** however much; **Seite ~?** *(ugs.)* what page?

wie·viel·mal [*od.* -'--] *Interrogativadv.* how many times

wievielt [*od.* '--] *in* **zu ~ [wart ihr]?** how many [of you were there]?

wievielt... [*od.* '--] *Interrogativadj.* **zum ~en Mal bitte ich dich das nun?** how many times *or* how often have I asked you?; **als ~er Läufer ist er durchs Ziel gekommen?** in what position did he finish?; **die ~e Querstraße ist das von hier aus?** how many turnings is that from here?; **der ~e Band?** which number volume?; **beim ~en Versuch hat es geklappt?** how many attempts did it take?; **der Wievielte ist heute?** what is the date today?; **am Wievielten?** [on] what date?

wie·weit *Interrogativadv.* to what extent; how far

wie·wohl *Konj. (geh. veralt.)* although

Wigwam ['vɪkvam] **der; ~s, ~s** wigwam

Wikinger ['vi:kɪŋɐ] **der; ~s, ~:** Viking

wild [vɪlt] **1.** *Adj.* **a)** wild; rugged, wild ⟨*countryside, area, etc.*⟩; untouched, uncultivated ⟨*land, soil*⟩; wild, unruly ⟨*hair, beard, etc.*⟩; **Geranien kommen ~ vor** geraniums grow wild; **~e Triebe** rank shoots; **~es Fleisch** *(Med.)* proud flesh; **b)** *(nicht [behördlich] genehmigt, nicht angemeldet)* unauthorized; illegal; **~e Taxis** unlicensed taxis; **~es Parken** illegal parking; **in ~er Ehe leben** *(veralt.)* live in sin; **~er Streik** wildcat strike; **c)** *(heftig, gewaltig)* wild ⟨*panic, flight, passion, desire, etc.*⟩; fierce ⟨*battle, anger, determination, look*⟩; **~ auf etw.** *(Akk.)* **sein** *(ugs.)* be mad *or* crazy about sth. *(coll.)*; **~ auf jmdn.** *od.* **nach jmdm. sein** *(ugs.)* be mad *or* crazy *or* wild about sb. *(coll.)*; *s. auch* **Jagd e; d)** *(wütend)* furious ⟨*cursing, shouting, etc.*⟩; **~ werden** get furious; **jmdn. ~ machen** make sb. furious; infuriate sb.; **den ~en Mann spielen** *(ugs.)* get heavy *(coll.)*; **e)** *(unbändig, ungestüm)* wild, unruly ⟨*child*⟩; **f)** *(maßlos, wüst)* wild ⟨*speculation, claim, rumour, accusation*⟩; vile ⟨*oaths, curses*⟩; **halb so** *od.* **nicht so ~ sein** *(ugs.)* not be as bad as all that *(coll.)*; **g)** *nicht präd. (primitiv)* savage; wild; *(abwertend: unzivilisiert)* uncivilized; **ein ~er Haufen** a pack of savages; **der Wilde Mann** *(Myth.)* the wild man of the woods. **2.** *adv.* **a)** wildly; **die Haare hingen ihr ~ ins Gesicht** her hair hung wildly about her face; **alles ging ~ durcheinander** everything was in chaos; **~ bewegtes Wasser** turbulent water; **~ entschlossen sein** *(ugs.)* be absolutely determined; **wie ~ um sich schlagen** hit out *or* lash out wildly; **wie ~** *(ugs.)* like mad *(coll.)*; **b)** *(ordnungswidrig)* illegally; **~ zelten/bauen** camp/build in an unauthorized place

Wild das; ~[e]s a) *(Tiere, Fleisch)* game; **b)** *(einzelnes Tier)* [wild] animal

Wild-: ~bach der mountain torrent; **~bahn die** *in* **in freier ~bahn** in the wild; **~bret** [~brɛt] **das;~s** *(geh.)* game; **~dieb der** poacher

Wilde der/die; *adj. Dekl.* savage; **wie ein ~r/eine ~/die ~n** *(ugs.)* like a mad thing/like mad things *(coll.)*

Wild·ente die wild duck

Wilderei die; ~, ~en poaching *no pl., no art.*

Wilderer der; ~s, ~: poacher

wildern 1. *itr. V.* **a)** poach; go poaching; **b)** ⟨*cat, dog*⟩ kill game. **2.** *tr. V.* poach

wild-, Wild-: ~fang der wild creature; **er ist ein kleiner ~fang** he is a wild little thing; **sie war ein richtiger ~fang** she was a real tomboy; **~fremd** *Adj.* completely strange; **~fremder Mensch/~fremde Leute** complete stranger/strangers; **~gans die** wild goose; **~gehege das** game enclosure

Wildheit die; ~: wildness; *(eines Volkes usw.)* savageness

wild-, Wild-: ~hüter der gamekeeper; **~katze die** wild cat; **~lebend** *Adj.; nicht präd.* wild; living in the wild *postpos.*; **~leder das** suede; **~ledern** *Adj.* suede

Wildnis die; ~, ~se wilderness

wild-, Wild-: ~park der game park; **~pferd das** wild horse; **~pflanze die** wild plant; **~romantisch** *Adj.* wild and romantic; romantically wild; **~sau die** wild sow; **~schaden der** damage *no pl., no indef. art.* caused by game

wild-, Wild-: ~schwein das wild boar; **~wachsend** *Adj.; nicht präd.* wild;

~wasser das; *Pl.* ~: mountain torrent; **~wasser·rennen das** wild-water racing; *(einzelne Veranstaltung)* wild-water race; **~wechsel der a)** *(Weg, Pfad)* game path; **b)** *o. Pl. (Vorgang)* game crossing; **~west** -'vɛst] *o. Art.; o. Pl.* the Wild West; **~west·film der** western; Wild West film; **~wuchs der** rank growth

Wilhelm ['vɪlhɛlm] **(der)** William; **Wilhelm der Eroberer** William the Conqueror; *s. auch* **Friedrich Wilhelm**

wilhelminisch [vɪlhɛl'mi:nɪʃ] *Adj.* Wilhelminian

will [vɪl] *1. u. 3. Pers. Sg. Präsens v.* **wollen**

Wille der; ~ns will; *(Wunsch)* wish; *(Absicht)* intention; **der ~ zur Macht** the will to power; **guter/böser ~**: goodwill/ill will; **es war kein böser ~ von mir** there was no ill-will intended; **etw. aus freiem ~n tun** do sth. of one's own free will; **seinen ~n durchsetzen** get one's own way; **sie hat den festen ~n, es zu tun** she firmly intends to do it; **er hat seinen eigenen ~n** he has a mind of his own; **sie ist voll guten ~ns** she is very well-intentioned; **laß ihm seinen ~n** let him have his way; **beim besten ~n nicht** not with the best will in the world; **wo ein ~ ist, ist auch ein Weg** *(Spr.)* where there's a will, there's a way *(prov.)*; **Letzter ~**: will; last will and testament *(formal)*; **mit ~n** intentionally; **ich mußte wider ~n lachen** I couldn't help laughing; **jmdm. zu ~n sein** *(geh.)* do sb.'s bidding; **sie war ihm zu ~n** *(veralt.)* she let him have his way with her

willen *Präp. mit Gen. in* **um jmds./einer Sache ~**: for sb.'s/sth.'s sake

Willen der; ~s *s.* **Wille**

willen·los 1. *Adj.* will-less; **völlig ~ sein** have no will of one's own. **2.** *adv.* will-lessly

Willenlosigkeit die; ~: lack of will

willens *Adj. in* **~ sein, etw. zu tun** *(geh.)* be willing to do sth.; **ich bin nicht ~, es zu tun** I have no intention of doing it

willens-, Willens-: **~akt der** act of will; **~anstrengung die** effort of will; **unter größter ~anstrengung** by a huge effort of will; **~bildung die: die politische ~bildung** the formulation of political demands and objectives; **~erklärung die** *(bes. Rechtsw.)* declaration of intent; **~freiheit die**; *o. Pl.* freedom of will; **~kraft die**; *o. Pl.* will-power; strength of will; **~schwach** *Adj.* weak-willed; **~schwäche die**; *o. Pl.* weakness of will; **~stark** *Adj.* strong-willed; **~stärke die**; *o. Pl.* strength of will

willentlich ['vɪləntlɪç] **1.** *Adj.; nicht präd.* deliberate. **2.** *adv.* deliberately; on purpose

willfahren[1] [*od.* '---] *itr. V. (geh.)* **[jmdm.] ~**: obey [sb.]; do sb.'s bidding; **jmds. Bitte** *(Dat.)* **~**: comply with sb.'s request

willfährig ['vɪlfɛ:rɪç *od.* -'--] *Adj.* compliant; **jmdm. ~ sein** submit to sb.'s will; **sich** *(Dat.)* **jmdn. ~ machen** make sb. submit to one's will

Willfährigkeit [*od.* -'---] **die**; ~ *(geh.)* compliance

Williams Christ·birne ['vɪljamz 'krɪst-] **die** Bartlett pear

willig 1. *Adj.* willing; obedient ‹*horse*›; *s. auch* [1]**Geist a. 2.** *adv.* willingly

will·kommen *Adj.* welcome; **jmdm. ~ sein** be welcome to sb.; **~ zu Hause/in Mannheim!** welcome home/in Mannheim!; **jmdn. ~ heißen** welcome sb.; **ich möchte Sie herzlich ~ heißen** a very warm welcome to you

Will·kommen das *od. (selten)* **der**; ~s, ~: welcome; **jmdm. ein herzliches ~ bereiten** *od.* **bieten** give sb. a warm welcome

Willkommens-: **~gruß der** welcome; **~trunk der** welcoming drink

[1] *ich willfahre, willfahrt od. gewillfahrt, zu willfahren*

Will·kür die; ~: arbitrary use of power; *(einer Entscheidung, Handlung o. ä.)* arbitrariness; **jmds. ~** *(Dat.)* **preisgegeben** *od.* **ausgeliefert sein** be at sb.'s mercy; **das ist die reine ~**: that is purely arbitrary

Willkür-: **~akt der** arbitrary act; **~herrschaft die** tyranny

willkürlich 1. *Adj.* arbitrary; *(vom Willen gesteuert)* voluntary ‹*muscle, movement, etc.*›. **2.** *adv.* arbitrarily; *(vom Willen gesteuert)* voluntarily

Willkür·maßnahme die arbitrary measure

wimmeln ['vɪmḷn] *itr. V.* **a)** *(sich bewegen)* **Insekten/Ratten ~ dort** the place is swarming with insects/rats; **b)** *(voll sein)* **von Menschen ~**: be teeming *or* swarming with people; **von Fischen/Läusen/Ungeziefer ~**: be teeming with fish/swarming with lice/vermin; **in dem Artikel wimmelt es von Fehlern** the article is teeming with mistakes

wimmern ['vɪmɐn] *itr. V.* whimper; **zum Wimmern [sein]** *(ugs.)* [be] simply pathetic

Wimpel ['vɪmpḷ] **der**; ~s, ~: pennant

Wimper ['vɪmpɐ] **die**; ~, ~n **a)** [eye]lash; **ohne mit der ~ zu zucken** without batting an eyelid; **b)** *(Biol.)* cilium

Wimpern·tusche die mascara

Wimper·tierchen das ciliate; infusorian

Wind [vɪnt] **der**; ~[e]s, ~e **a)** wind; **bei ~ und Wetter** in all weathers; **[schnell] wie der ~**: like the wind; **b)** *(fig.)* **hier weht [jetzt] ein schärferer/anderer/frischer ~** *(ugs.)* things have tightened up a lot here [now]/things are different here [now]/there's a much fresher feel to the place [now]; **wissen/merken, woher der ~ weht** *(ugs.)* know/notice which way the wind's blowing; **~ machen** *(ugs.)* brag; **viel ~ um etw. machen** *(ugs.)* make a great fuss about sth.; **~ von etw. bekommen** *od.* **kriegen** *(ugs.)* get wind of sth.; **jmdm. den ~ aus den Segeln nehmen** *(ugs.)* take the wind out of sb.'s sails; **sich** *(Dat.)* **den ~ um die Nase** *od.* **Ohren wehen lassen** *(ugs.)* see a bit of life *or* the world; **gegen den/mit dem ~ segeln** swim against/with the tide; **etw. in den ~ schlagen** turn a deaf ear *or* pay no heed to sth.; **in den ~ reden** waste one's breath; **alle Appelle waren in den ~ gesprochen** all appeals were in vain; **in alle [vier] ~e** in all directions; **ihre Kinder sind in alle ~e zerstreut** her children are scattered to the four corners of the earth; **sein Mäntelchen nach dem ~e hängen** be a trimmer; **wer ~ sät, wird Sturm ernten** *(Spr.)* sow the wind and reap the whirlwind *(prov.)*; **c)** *(Blähung)* wind; **einen ~ fahren lassen** break wind

Wind-: **~beutel der a)** *(Gebäck)* cream puff; **b)** *(abwertend: Person)* frivolous and irresponsible person; **~bö[e] die** gust of wind

Winde die; ~, ~n **a)** *Technik)* winch; **b)** *(Bot.)* bindweed; convolvulus

Wind·ei das wind egg; *(fig. abwertend)* dud

Windel ['vɪndḷ] **die**; ~, ~n nappy *(Brit.)*; diaper *(Amer.)*; **damals lagst du noch in [den] ~n** you were still in nappies then; **noch in den ~n liegen** *od.* **stecken** *(fig.)* ‹*project etc.*› still be in its infancy

Windel·höschen das nappy pants *pl.*

windeln *tr. V.* **ein Baby ~**: put a baby's nappy *(Brit.) or (Amer.)* diaper on

windel·weich *Adj. (ugs.)* soft; **jmdn. ~ schlagen** *od.* **hauen** beat the living daylights out of sb. *(coll.)*

[1]**winden 1.** *unr. tr. V.* **a)** *(geh.)* make ‹*wreath, garland*›; **Blumen zu einem/in einen Kranz ~**: bind flowers into a wreath; make a wreath out of flowers; **etw. um etw. ~**: wind sth. around sth.; **jmdm. etw. aus der Hand ~**: wrest sth. from sb.'s hand; **b)** *(mit einer Winde bewegen)* winch. **2.** *unr. refl. V.* **a)** ‹*plant, tendrils*› wind (**um** around); ‹*snake*› coil [itself], wind itself (**um** around); **b)** *(sich krümmen)* writhe; **sich vor Schmerzen/in Krämpfen ~**: writhe in pain/convulsions; **sich vor Verlegenheit ~**: squirm with embarrassment; **sich vor Lachen ~**: fall about laughing; **sich ~ wie ein Aal** *(fig.)* try to wriggle out of it; **c)** *(sich schlängeln)* ‹*path, river*› wind [its way]; **sich durch etw. ~**: wind one's/its way through sth.

[2]**winden** *itr. V.; unpers.* **es windet** it's windy

Windes·eile die in **in** *od.* **mit ~**: in next to no time; **sich in ~ verbreiten** spread like wildfire

wind-, Wind-: **~fang der** porch; **~geschützt** *Adj.* sheltered from the wind *postpos.*; sheltered; **diese Pflanzen müssen ~geschützt stehen** these plants must be kept sheltered from the wind; **~geschwindigkeit die** wind speed; **~harfe die** wind harp; aeolian harp; **~hauch der** breath of wind; **~hose die** *(Met.)* whirlwind; **~hund der a)** greyhound; **Afghanischer ~hund** Afghan hound; **b)** *(ugs. abwertend)* careless and unreliable sort *(coll.)*

windig *Adj.* **a)** windy; **b)** *(ugs. abwertend)* shady; dubious ‹*excuse, morality*›; empty ‹*words, talk, hope*›

Wind-: **~jacke die** wind-cheater *(Brit.)*; windbreaker *(Amer.)*; **~jammer der**; *Pl.* ~ *(Seemannsspr.)* windjammer; **~kanal der a)** *(Technik)* wind tunnel; **b)** *(an der Orgel)* wind trunk; **~licht das** table lantern *(with candle in glass container)*; **~mühle die** windmill; **gegen** *od.* **mit ~mühlen kämpfen** *(fig.)* tilt at windmills; **~mühlen·flügel der** windmill sail; **~pocken** *Pl.* chickenpox *sing.*; **~rad das a)** wind wheel; **b)** *s.* **~rädchen**; **~rädchen das** windmill; **~richtung die** wind direction; **~rose die** compass card

Winds·braut die; *o. Pl. (dichter.)* gale; *(Wirbelwind)* whirlwind

wind-, Wind-: **~schatten der** lee; **~schief** *Adj. (oft abwertend)* crooked; **~schlüpfig, ~schnittig** *Adj.* streamlined; **~schutz·scheibe die** windscreen *(Brit.)*; windshield *(Amer.)*; **~spiel das** [small] greyhound; **~stärke die** force of the wind; **~stärke 7/9** *usw.* wind force 7/9 *etc.*; **~still** *Adj.* windless; still; **es war völlig ~still** there was no wind at all; **ein ~stilles Plätzchen** a sheltered spot; a spot out of the wind; **~stille die** calm; **es herrschte völlige ~stille** there was no wind at all; **~stoß der** gust of wind; **~surfer der** windsurfer; **~surfing das** windsurfing *no art.*

Windung die; ~, ~en **a)** *(Krümmung)* bend; *(eines Flusses)* meander; *(des Darms, Gehirns)* convolution; **b)** *(spiralförmiger Verlauf)* spiral; *(einer Spule o. ä.)* winding; **c)** *(schlangenartige Bewegung)* wriggling

Wind·zug der; *o. Pl.* breeze

Wingert ['vɪŋɐt] **der**; ~s, ~e *(westmd., schweiz.) s.* **Weinberg**

Wink [vɪŋk] **der**; ~[e]s, ~e **a)** *(Zeichen)* sign; *(mit dem Kopf)* nod; **b)** *(Hinweis)* hint; *(Ratschlag)* tip; hint; *(an die Polizei)* tip-off; **ein ~ mit dem Zaunpfahl** *(scherzh.)* a strong hint

winke *in:* **~, ~ machen** *(Kindersp.)* wave

Winkel ['vɪŋkḷ] **der**; ~s, ~ **a)** *(Math.)* angle; **toter ~**: blind spot; **b)** *(Ecke; auch fig.)* corner; **in allen Ecken und ~n suchen** search every nook and cranny; **c)** *(Ort)* corner; spot; **d)** *(Werkzeug)* [carpenter's] square; *(T-förmig)* T-square; **e)** *(milit. Rangabzeichen)* chevron; **f)** *(~eisen)* angle-iron

winkel-, Winkel-: **~advokat der** *(abwertend)* shady lawyer; **~eisen das** *(Technik)* angle-iron; **~förmig** *Adj.* angled; **~funktion die** *(Math.)* trigonometrical function; **~halbierende die**; *adj. Dekl. (Math.)* bisector of a/the angle

winkelig *Adj.* twisty ‹*streets*›; **ein ~es Haus** a house full of odd corners

Wịnkel-: ~maß das measure of angle; **~messer der** protractor; **~zug der;** *meist Pl.* shady trick *or* move

wịnken 1. *itr. V.* **a)** wave; **jmdm. ~:** wave to sb.; **mit etw. ~:** wave sth.; **mit dem Kopf ~:** nod [one's head]; **b)** *(auffordern heranzukommen)* **jmdm. ~:** beckon sb. over; **einem Taxi ~:** hail a taxi; **c)** *(in Aussicht stehen)* **etw. winkt jmdm.** sth. is in prospect for sb.; **dem Sieger winkt eine Flasche Sekt** the winner will receive a bottle of champagne. **2.** *tr. V.* **a)** *(heran~)* beckon; **jmdn. zu sich ~:** beckon sb. over [to one]; **der Polizist winkte den Wagen zur Seite** the policeman waved the car over [to the side]; **b)** *(signalisieren)* signal

Wịnker der; ~s, ~ trafficator; indicator

wịnklig *Adj. s.* **winkelig**

winseln ['vɪnzl̩n] *itr. V.* **a)** ‹*dog*› whimper; **b)** *(abwertend)* whine; **um Gnade/sein Leben ~:** whine and beg for mercy/one's life

Winter ['vɪntɐ] **der; ~s, ~:** winter; **über den ~:** over [the] winter; *s. auch* **Frühling**

wịnter-, Wịnter-: ~abend der winter['s] evening; **~anfang der** beginning of winter; **am 22. Dezember ist ~anfang** 22 December is the first day of winter; **~einbruch der** onset of winter; **~fahr·plan der** winter timetable; **~fell das** winter coat; **~fest** *Adj.* **a)** winter *attrib.* ‹*clothing*›; **ein ~festes Haus** a house that can withstand the rigours of winter; **b)** *s.* **~hart; ~frucht die;** *o. Pl. s.* **~getreide; ~garten der** conservatory; **~getreide das** *(Landw.)* winter grain; **~halb·jahr das: während des ~halbjahrs/im ~halbjahr** from October to March; **~hart** *Adj. (Bot.)* hardy; **~hilfswerk das;** *o. Pl. (ns.) relief organization in Nazi Germany providing clothes, fuel, food, etc. for the needy;* **~jasmin der** winter jasmine; **~kleid das a)** *(auch fig.)* winter dress; **b)** *(Zool.)* winter coat; *(von Vögeln)* winter plumage; **~kleidung die** winter clothes *pl. or* clothing; **~landschaft die** winter landscape

wịnterlich 1. *Adj.* wintry; winter *attrib.* ‹*clothing, break*›. **2.** *adv.* **~ kalt/öde** cold/bare and wintry; **~ warm angezogen** dressed in warm winter clothes

Wịnter-: ~luft die; *o. Pl.* winter air; **~mantel der** winter coat; **~mode die** winter fashions *pl.; (eines Modehauses)* winter collection; **~monat der** winter month; **~nacht die** winter['s] night; **~olympiade die** Winter Olympics *pl.;* **~quartier das a)** *(Milit.)* winter quarters *pl.;* **b)** *(Zool.)* wintering grounds *pl.;* **~reifen der** winter tyre; **~ruhe die** *(Zool.)* winter dormancy; **~ruhe halten** have a period/periods of winter inactivity

wịnters *Adv.* in winter

Wịnter-: ~saat die *(Landw.) (Saatgut)* winter seed; *(Pflanzen)* young winter corn; **~sachen** *Pl.* winter things; **~saison die** winter season

Wịnters·anfang der *s.* **Winteranfang**

Wịnter-: ~schlaf der *(Zool.)* hibernation; **~schlaf halten** hibernate; **~schluß·verkauf der** winter sale[s *pl.*]; **~schuh der** winter shoe; **~semester das** winter semester; **~sonnen·wende die** winter solstice; **~spiele** *Pl.* Winter Games; **die Olympischen ~spiele** the Winter Olympics; **~sport der** winter sports *pl.;* **in den ~sport fahren** go on a winter sports holiday; **~sportler der** winter sportsman

Wịnters·zeit die *s.* **Winterzeit**

Wịnter-: ~tag der winter['s] day; **~urlaub der** winter holiday; **~wetter das** winter weather; **~zeit die;** *o. Pl.* winter-time; **zur ~zeit** in [the] winter-time

Winzer ['vɪntsɐ] **der; ~s, ~, Wịnzerin die; ~, ~nen** winegrower

winzig ['vɪntsɪç] **1.** *Adj.* tiny; tiny, minute ‹*portion, writing*›. **2.** *adv.* **er schreibt ~:** he has tiny *or* minute writing; **~ klein** tiny; minute

Wịnzigkeit die; ~, ~ a) *o. Pl.* tininess; minuteness; **b)** *(Kleinigkeit)* tiny thing; triviality

Winzling ['vɪntslɪŋ] **der; ~s, ~e** tiny person/animal/thing; **er/sie/es ist ein ~:** he/she/it is a tiny little thing

Wipfel ['vɪpfl̩] **der; ~s, ~:** tree-top

Wippe ['vɪpə] **die; ~, ~n** see-saw

wịppen *itr. V.* bob up and down; *(hin und her)* bob about; *(auf einer Wippe)* see-saw; **er ließ das Kind auf den Knien ~:** he bounced the child [up and down] on his knees; **er wippte in den Knien** he bobbed up and down, bending at the knees; **mit dem Fuß ~:** jiggle one's foot up and down; **mit dem Schwanz ~:** jerk its tail up and down

wir [viːɐ] *Personalpron.; 1. Pers. Pl. Nom.* we; **~ beide** *od.* **beiden** we two; the two of us; **sie weiß mehr als ~:** she knows more than we do; she knows more than us *(coll.);* **nicht nur ~ würden profitieren** we shouldn't be the only ones to profit; **Wer hat das getan? – Wir nicht!** Who did it? – It wasn't us! *or* We didn't!; **Wer kommt mit? – Wir!** Who's coming? – We are!; **Wer ist es? – Wir sind's!** Who is it? – It's us!; **wie fühlen ~ uns heute?** *(zu einem Patienten)* how are we feeling today?; *s. auch (Gen.)* **unser;** *(Dat.)* **uns;** *(Akk.)* **uns**

wirb [vɪrp] *Imperativ Sg. v.* **werben**

Wirbel ['vɪrbl̩] **der; ~s, ~ a)** *(kreisende Bewegung) (im Wasser)* whirlpool; vortex; *(in der Luft)* whirlwind; *(kleiner)* eddy; *(von Rauch, beim Tanz)* whirl; **alles drehte sich in einem ~ um ihn** everything was whirling round him; **ein ~ der Leidenschaft** *(fig.)* a whirlpool of passions; **b)** *(Trubel)* hurly-burly; **der ~ der Ereignisse** the whirl of events; **c)** *(Aufsehen)* fuss; **um jmdn./etw. ~ machen** make a fuss about sb./sth.; **d)** *(Anat.)* vertebra; **e)** *(Haar~)* crown; *(vorne)* cow-lick; **f)** *(Trommel~)* [drum] roll; **g)** *(Musik, bei Streichinstrumenten)* tuning-peg

Wịrbellose *Pl.; adj. Dekl. (Zool.)* invertebrates

wịrbeln 1. *itr. V.* **a)** *mit sein* whirl; ‹*water, snowflakes*› swirl; **jmdm. durch den Kopf ~** *(fig.)* ‹*thoughts*› race through sb.'s head; **b)** *auch mit sein (in kreisender Bewegung sein)* ‹*propeller, wheel, etc.*› whirl; **c)** *(einen Wirbel schlagen)* ‹*drum*› roll; ‹*drummer*› beat a roll. **2.** *tr. V.* swirl ‹*leaves, dust*›; whirl ‹*dancer*›

Wịrbel-: ~säule die *(Anat.)* vertebral column; spinal column; **~sturm der** cyclone; **~tier das** *(Zool.)* vertebrate; **~wind der** whirlwind; *(fig., meist scherzh.)* bundle of energy

wirbt [vɪrpt] *3. Pers. Sg. Präsens v.* **werben**

wird [vɪrt] *3. Pers. Sg. Präsens v.* **werden**

wirf [vɪrf] *Imperativ Sg. v.* **werfen**

wịrft *3. Pers. Sg. Präsens v.* **werfen**

wirken ['vɪrkn̩] **1.** *itr. V.* **a)** *(eine Wirkung haben)* have an effect; **wirkt die Tablette schon?** is the tablet beginning to take effect yet?; **es wirkte erst nach einer Stunde** it only took effect after an hour; **schmerzstillend/einschläfernd ~:** have a pain-killing/soporific effect; **gegen etw. ~:** be effective against sth.; **bei jmdm. ~:** have an effect on sb.; **seine Worte wirkten ermutigend** his words were encouraging; **ihre Heiterkeit wirkte ansteckend** her cheerfulness was infectious; **lassen Sie die Farben und Klänge auf sich ~:** let the colours and sounds sink in; **Sauerstoff wirkt dabei als Katalysator** oxygen acts as a catalyst; **b)** *(erscheinen)* seem; appear; **neben ihm wirkt sie ausgesprochen klein** she seems decidedly small beside him; **sie wirkt sehr nett** she seems very nice; **er wirkt auf mich sehr sympathisch** I find him very congenial; **c)** *(beeindrucken)* ‹*person*› make an impression **(auf + Akk.** on); ‹*picture, design, etc.*› be effective; **d)** *(tätig sein)* work; **da wirkt ein verborgener Mechanismus** a hidden mechanism is operating there. **2.** *tr. V.* **a)** *(geh.: bewirken, vollbringen)* bring about; do ‹*good, harm*›; *s. auch* **Wunder a; b)** *(Textilw.)* knit

Wịrker der; ~s, ~: knitter

Wirkerei die; ~, ~en a) *o. Pl. (Herstellung)* knitting; **b)** *(Betrieb)* knitwear factory

Wịrkerin die; ~, ~nen knitter

wịrklich 1. *Adj.* real; actual, real ‹*event, incident, state of affairs*›; real, true ‹*friend*›. **2.** *Adv.* really; *(in der Tat)* actually; really; **nein, ~?** no, really?; **er ist es ~:** it really is him; **~ und wahrhaftig** really and truly

Wịrklichkeit die; ~, ~en reality; **~ werden** become a reality; ‹*dream*› come true; **in ~:** in reality; **auf den Boden der ~ zurückkehren** come back down to earth *(fig.)*

wịrklichkeits-, Wịrklichkeits-: ~fern 1. *Adj.* unrealistic; **2.** *adv.* unrealistically; **~form die** *(Sprachw.)* indicative; **~fremd 1.** *Adj.* unrealistic; **er ist ~fremd** he is out of touch with reality; **2.** *adv.* unrealistically; **~getreu 1.** *Adj.* faithful; **2.** *adv.* faithfully; **~nah 1.** *Adj.* realistic; **2.** *adv.* realistically; **~sinn der;** *o. Pl.* sense of realism

wirksam ['vɪrkzaːm] **1.** *Adj.* effective; **mit dem 1. Juli ~ werden** *(Amtsspr.)* take effect from 1 July. **2.** *adv.* effectively

Wịrksamkeit die; ~: effectiveness

Wịrk·stoff der active agent

Wịrkung die; ~, ~en a) effect **(auf + Akk.** on); **ohne ~ bleiben** have no effect; **seine ~ verfehlen** fail to have the desired effect; **seine ~ tun** ‹*drug, medicine, etc.*› take effect; ‹*treatment, therapy*› be effective; **mit ~ vom 1. Juli** *(Amtsspr.)* with effect from 1 July; **b)** *(Physik)* action

wịrkungs-, Wịrkungs- : ~bereich der a) area of activity; **sie fühlte sich in ihrem häuslichen ~bereich wohl** she felt quite happy in her domestic domain; **b)** *(Milit.)* range; **~dauer die: eine kurze/lange ~dauer haben** be effective for a short/long period; **~feld das** sphere of activity; **~grad der** effectiveness; *(Technik)* efficiency; **~los 1.** *Adj.* ineffective; **2.** *adv.* ineffectively; **~losigkeit die; ~:** ineffectiveness; **~mechanismus der** mode of action; **~stätte die** *(geh.)* work-place; **~voll 1.** *Adj.* effective; **2.** *adv.* effectively; **~weise die** *(eines Wirkstoffs)* mode of action; **die ~weise eines Mechanismus/ökonomischer Gesetze** the way a mechanism works/economic laws operate

Wịrk·waren *Pl.* knitwear *sing.; (Strümpfe, Socken)* hosiery *sing.*

wirr [vɪr] **1. a)** *(unordentlich)* tousled ‹*hair, beard*›; tangled ‹*ropes, roots*›; **ein ~es Durcheinander** a chaotic muddle; **b)** *(unklar, verwirrt)* confused; muddled, confused ‹*thoughts*›; **mir war ~ im Kopf** my head was reeling. **2.** *adv.* **a)** *(unordentlich)* **das Haar hing ihr ~ ins Gesicht** her tousled hair hung over her face; **alles lag ~ durcheinander** everything lay in a chaotic muddle; **b)** *(verworren)* **sie träumte ~:** she had confused dreams; **~ reden** talk in a confused way; **c)** *(verwirrt)* in confusion

Wịrren *Pl.* turmoil *sing.*

Wịrr·kopf der *(abwertend)* muddle-headed person; **ein ~ sein** be muddle-headed

wịrr·köpfig 1. *Adj.* muddle-headed. **2.** *adv.* muddle-headedly

Wirrnis ['vɪrnɪs] **die; ~, ~se** *(geh.)* confusion; **die ~se der Revolution** the chaos *sing.* of the revolution

Wirrsal ['vɪrzaːl] **das; ~[e]s, ~e** *od.* **die; ~, ~e** *(geh.) s.* **Wirrnis**

Wịrrwarr [-var] **der; ~s** chaos; *(von Stimmen)* clamour; *(von Meinungen)* welter; *(von Haaren, Wurzeln, Vorschriften)* tangle

Wirsing ['vɪrzɪŋ] **der; ~s, Wịrsing·kohl der** savoy [cabbage]

Wirt [vɪrt] **der; ~[e]s, ~e a)** landlord; *s. auch* **Rechnung; b)** *(Biol.)* host
Wirtel ['vɪrtl̩] **der; ~s, ~** *s.* **Spinnwirtel**
Wịrtin die; ~, ~nen landlady
Wịrtschaft die; ~, ~en a) economy; *(Geschäftsleben)* commerce and industry; **in die ~ gehen** become a business man/woman; **die freie ~:** the free market economy; **b)** *(Gast~)* public house; pub *(Brit. coll.)*; bar *(Amer.)*; **c)** *(Haushalt)* household; **jmdm. die ~ führen** keep house for sb.; **d)** *o. Pl. (ugs. abwertend: Unordnung)* mess; shambles *sing.*; **e)** *(landwirtschaftlicher Betrieb)* [small] farm; **f)** *o. Pl. (das Haushalten)* housekeeping
wịrtschaften 1. *itr. V.* **a) mit dem Geld gut ~:** manage one's money well; **mit Verlust/Gewinn ~:** run at a loss/profit; **wenn weiter so gewirtschaftet wird wie bisher** if things continue to be run as they have been up to now; **b)** *(sich zu schaffen machen)* busy oneself. **2.** *tr. V.* **eine Firma konkursreif/in den Ruin ~:** bring a company to the brink of bankruptcy/ruin a company; **er hat den Hof zugrunde gewirtschaftet** he brought the farm to rack and ruin
Wịrtschafter der; ~s, ~ a) *(Wirtsch.: Unternehmer)* entrepreneur; *(Industrieller)* industrialist; **b)** *(in landwirtschaftlichem Betrieb)* farm manager
Wịrtschafterin die; ~, ~nen housekeeper
Wịrtschaftler der; ~s, ~ a) *s.* **Wirtschaftswissenschaftler; b)** *s.* **Wirtschafter a**
wịrtschaftlich 1. *Adj.* **a)** *nicht präd. (die Wirtschaft betreffend)* economic; **b)** *nicht präd. (finanziell)* financial; **c)** *(sparsam, rentabel)* economical. **2.** *adv.*; *s. Adj.* **a, b, c:** economically; financially
Wịrtschaftlichkeit die; ~: economic viability
wịrtschafts-, Wịrtschafts-: ~abkommen das economic agreement; **~aufschwung der** economic upturn; **~berater der** economic adviser; **~beziehungen** *Pl.* economic relations; **~block der;** *Pl.* **~blöcke** economic bloc; **~buch das** *s.* **Haushaltsbuch; ~flüchtling der** economic refugee; **~form die** economic system; **~führer der** leading figure in commerce and industry; **~führung die** *(eines Landes)* management of the economy; *(eines Betriebs)* financial management; **~gebäude** *Pl.* domestic offices; **~geld das;** *o. Pl. s.* **Haushaltsgeld; ~gemeinschaft die** economic community; **~geographie die** economic geography *no art.*; **~gymnasium das** *grammar school placing emphasis on economics, law, and business studies*; **~hilfe die** economic aid *no indef. art.*; **~hoch·schule die** business school *or* college; **~ingenieur der** industrial engineer; **~jahr das** *s.* **Geschäftsjahr; ~kapitän der** captain of industry; **~krieg der** economic war; *(Kriegsführung)* economic warfare; **~kriminalität die** economic crime *no art.*; **~krise die** economic crisis; **~lage die** economic situation; **~leben das** economic life; *(Geschäftsleben)* business life; **ein Mann aus dem ~leben** a man from the business world; **~lenkung die** economic control; **~minister der** minister for economic affairs; **~ministerium das** ministry of economic affairs; **~ordnung die** economic system; **~politik die** economic policy; **~politisch 1.** *Adj.; nicht präd.* relating to economic policy *postpos.*; economic policy *attrib.* ⟨*measures, decisions*⟩; **2.** *adv.* from the point of view of economic policy; **~prüfer der** auditor; **~recht das;** *o. Pl.* commercial law; **~spionage die** industrial espionage; **~system das** economic system; **~teil der** business section; **~union die** economic union; *s. auch* **Währungsunion; ~verband der** employers' association; **~wachstum das** economic growth; **~wissenschaft die;** *meist Pl.* economics *sing., no art.*; economic science *no art.*; **~wissenschaftler der** economist; **~wunder das** *(ugs.)* economic miracle; **~zeitung die** financial newspaper; **~zweig der** economic sector
Wịrts: ~haus das pub *(Brit. coll.)*; *(mit Unterkunft)* inn; pub *(Brit. coll.)*; **~leute** *Pl.* landlord and landlady; **~pflanze die** *(Biol.)* host plant; **~stube die** bar
Wisch [vɪʃ] **der; ~[e]s, ~e** *(salopp abwertend)* piece *or* bit of paper
wịschen 1. *itr., tr. V.* wipe; **etw. von etw. ~:** wipe sth. off *or* from sth.; **er wischte sich** *(Dat.)* **die Stirn** he wiped his brow; **sich** *(Dat.)* **den Schlaf aus den Augen ~:** wipe the sleep from one's eyes; **mit der Hand/einem Lappen über den Tisch ~:** wipe the table with one's hand/a cloth; **versehentlich mit dem Ärmel über die Zeichnung ~:** accidentally brush one's sleeve across the drawing; **Staub ~:** do the dusting; dust; **jmdm. eine ~** *(ugs.)* give sb. a clout round the face. **2.** *itr. V.; mit sein (huschen)* ⟨*person*⟩ slip; ⟨*mouse, lizard*⟩ scurry; ⟨*cat*⟩ dart
Wịscher der; ~s, ~ *s.* **Scheibenwischer**
Wischiwaschi [vɪʃi'vaʃi] **das; ~s** *(salopp abwertend)* wish-wash
Wịsch-: ~lappen der, ~tuch das; *Pl.* **~tücher** cloth
Wisent ['vi:zɛnt] **der; ~s, ~e** wisent; aurochs
Wismut ['vɪsmu:t] **das; ~[e]s** bismuth
wispern ['vɪspɐn] *itr., tr. V.* whisper
wịß-, Wịß-: ~begier, ~begierde die; *o. Pl.* thirst for knowledge; **~begierig** *Adj.* eager for knowledge; ⟨*child*⟩ eager to learn
wissen ['vɪsn̩] **1.** *unr. tr. V.* know; **ich weiß [es]** I know; **ich weiß [es] nicht** I don't know; **etw. genau ~:** know sth. for certain; **ich weiß [mir] keinen anderen Rat/kein größeres Vergnügen, als ...:** I can't think of anything other/I know of no greater pleasure than ...; **soviel ich weiß** as far as I know; **ich weiß ein gutes Lokal** I know [of] a good pub *(Brit. coll.)*; **er weiß es nicht anders** he knows no better; **er weiß immer alles besser** he always knows better; **ich wüßte nicht, daß ich dich um deinen Rat gebeten hätte** I am not aware of having asked your advice; **nicht, daß ich wüßte** not so far as I know; not that I know of; **ich möchte nicht ~, wieviel das gekostet hat** I hardly dare think how much it cost; **woher soll ich das ~?** how should I know?; **weißt du [was], wir fahren einfach dorthin** I'll tell you what, let's just go there; **jmdn. etw. ~ lassen** let sb. know sth.; **ein ~der Blick/ein ~des Lächeln** a knowing look/smile; **nicht mehr weiter ~:** not know what to do next; **was weiß ich** *(ugs.)* I don't know; **man kann nie ~** *(ugs.)* you never know; **gewußt, wie!** *(ugs.)* it's easy when you know how; **was ich nicht weiß, macht mich nicht heiß** *(Spr.)* what I don't know doesn't hurt me; **von jmdm./etw. nichts [mehr] ~ wollen** want to have nothing [more] to do with sb./sth.; **jmd. will es ~** *(ugs.)* sb. wants to put himself/herself to the test; **er tut, als sei es wer weiß wie wichtig** *(ugs.)* he behaves as if it were incredibly important *(coll.)*; **dies und noch wer weiß was alles** *(ugs.)* this and heaven knows what else [too]; **ich hätte wer weiß was darum gegeben** *(ugs.)* I'd have given almost anything for it; **ich weiß sie in Sicherheit/glücklich** *(geh.)* I know she's safe/happy; **ich wußte ihn in Gefahr** *(geh.)* I knew him to be in danger; **ich wollte diese Äußerung nicht als Vorwurf verstanden ~** *(geh.)* I didn't mean what I said to be taken as a reproach; **sich zu benehmen ~:** know how to behave oneself; **er wußte zu berichten, daß ...:** he was able to report that ...; **ich weiß nichts mit ihm anzufangen ~:** he isn't my type of person; **Sie müssen ~, daß ...** *(erklärend)* I should tell you that ...; **ich weiß ihren Namen nicht mehr** I can't remember her name; **weißt du noch, wie arm wir damals waren?** do you remember how poor we were then?; *s. auch* **Glocke a; Gott a, b; Stunde a. 2.** *unr. itr. V.* **von etw./um etw. ~:** know about sth.; **ich weiß von nichts** I don't know anything about it
Wịssen das; ~s knowledge; **ein großes ~ haben** be very knowledgeable; **meines/unseres ~s:** to my/our knowledge; **ohne jmds. ~:** without sb.'s knowledge; **mit jmds. ~:** with sb.'s knowledge; **wider** *od.* **gegen besseres ~:** against one's better judgement; **nach bestem ~ und Gewissen** to the best of one's knowledge and belief; **~ ist Macht** *(Spr.)* knowledge is power *(prov.)*
Wịssenschaft die; ~, ~en science; **die ~ hat ...:** science has ...; **in der ~ tätig sein** be a scientist; **etw. ist eine ~ für sich** *(ugs.)* there's a real art to sth.
Wịssenschafter der; ~s, ~ *(österr. u. schweiz. seltener)*, **Wịssenschaftler der; ~s ~, Wịssenschaftlerin die; ~, ~nen** academic; *(Natur~)* scientist
wịssenschaftlich 1. *Adj.* scholarly; *(natur~)* scientific; **~er Assistent** ≈ assistant lecturer; **~er Rat** ≈ lecturer; assistant professor *(Amer.)*. **2.** *adv.* in a scholarly manner; *(natur~)* scientifically; **das ist ~ nicht haltbar** that is not scientifically tenable; **~ arbeiten** *(als Wissenschaftler tätig sein)* work as a scholar/scientist
Wịssenschaftlichkeit die; ~ *s.* **wissenschaftlich:** scholarliness; scientific rigour; **die ~ einer Untersuchung in Frage stellen** question whether a piece of research has been conducted in a proper scholarly/scientific manner
Wịssenschafts-: ~betrieb der; *o.Pl. (ugs.)* academic activity; *(in den Naturwissenschaften)* scientific activity; **~theorie die** *o. Pl.* philosophy of science
wịssens-, Wịssens-: ~drang der; *o. Pl.*, **~durst der;** *o. Pl.* thirst for knowledge; **~gebiet das** area *or* field of knowledge; **~lücke die** gap in sb's knowledge; **~stand der** state of knowledge; **~wert** *Adj.* **~wert sein** be worth knowing; **eine ~werte Tatsache** a fact worth knowing; **das Buch enthält viel Wissenswertes** the book contains a great deal of valuable and interesting information
wissentlich ['vɪsn̩tlɪç] **1.** *Adj.; nicht präd.* deliberate. **2.** *adv.* knowingly; deliberately
witschen ['vɪtʃn̩] *itr. V.; mit sein (ugs.)* slip
Wittelsbacher ['vɪtl̩sbaxɐ] **der; ~s, ~** *(hist.)* Wittelsbach
wittern ['vɪtɐn] **1.** *itr. V.* sniff the air. **2.** *tr. V.* get wind of; scent; *(fig.: ahnen)* sense
Wịtterung die; ~, ~en a) *(Wetter)* weather *no indef. art*; **b)** *(Jägerspr.) (Geruchssinn)* sense of smell; *(Geruch)* scent; **~ nehmen, die ~ aufnehmen** pick up the scent; **~ von etw. bekommen** *(auch fig.)* get wind of sth.; **c)** *(Spürsinn)* **eine/keine ~ für etw. haben** have a/no instinct for sth.
wịtterungs-, Wịtterungs-: ~bedingt *Adj.* caused by the weather *postpos.*; **~einfluß der;** *meist Pl.* effect of the weather; **~um·schlag der** change in the weather; **~verhältnisse** *Pl.* weather conditions
Witwe ['vɪtvə] **die; ~, ~n** widow; **~ werden** be widowed; **grüne ~** *(ugs. scherzh.) suburban housewife left alone at home during the day while her husband is at work*
Wịtwen-: ~rente die widow's pension; **~schaft die; ~:** widowhood; **~schleier der** widow's veil; **~tröster der** *(ugs. scherzh.)* skirt-chaser *(coll.)* with a preference for widows; **~verbrennung die** suttee
Wịtwer der; ~s, ~: widower; **~ werden** be widowed
Wịtwerschaft die; ~: widowhood

Witz [vɪts] **der;** ~es, ~e **a)** joke; **~e reißen** *(ugs.)* crack jokes; **das ist der [ganze] ~:** that's the whole point; **der ~ ist nämlich der, daß ...:** the thing about it is that ...; **ich mache keine ~e** I'm not joking; **das soll wohl ein ~ sein** you/he *etc.* must be joking; **mach keine ~e!** come off it! *(coll.)*; **b)** *o. Pl. (Geist, Esprit, veralt.: Klugheit)* wit; **mit ~:** wittily

Witz-: ~blatt das humorous magazine; **~blatt·figur die** joke figure; **~bold** [~bɔlt] **der;** ~es, ~e joker; *(der jmdm. einen Streich spielt)* practical joker; prankster

Witzelei die; ~, ~en **a)** *o. Pl.* teasing; **b)** *meist Pl. (witzelnde Bemerkung)* joke

witzeln ['vɪtsl̩n] *itr. V.* joke **(über** + *Akk.* about)

Witz·figur die a) *(in Witzen)* joke character; **b)** *(ugs. abwertend)* figure of fun; **du ~!** you clown!

witzig 1. *Adj.* **a)** *(spaßig)* funny; amusing; **b)** *(ugs.: seltsam)* funny; odd; **c)** *(einfallsreich)* imaginative. **2.** *adv.; s. Adj.* **a, b, c:** amusingly; oddly; imaginatively

Witzigkeit die; ~ **a)** wit; **von umwerfender ~ sein** be hilariously funny; **b)** *s.* **Witz b**

witz·los 1. *Adj.* **a)** *(ohne Witz)* dull; **b)** *(ugs.: sinnlos)* pointless. **2.** *adv. (ohne Witz)* unimaginatively

WM *Abk.* **Weltmeisterschaft**

WNW *Abk.* **Westnordwest[en]** WNW

wo [vo:] **1.** *Adv.* **a)** *(interrogativ)* where; **wo gibt's denn so was!** *(ugs.)* who ever heard of such a thing!; *s. auch* **ach 1 e; hindenken; b)** *(relativisch)* where; *(temporal)* when; **überall, wo** wherever; **wo immer er auch sein mag** wherever he may be; **c)** *(indefinit) (ugs.)* somewhere; **wenn du ihn ~ sehen solltest** if you should see him anywhere. **2.** *Konj.* **a)** *(da, weil)* seeing that; **b)** *(obwohl)* although; when; **c)** *(falls)* **wo möglich** if possible; **wo nicht ..., so doch ...:** if not ..., then ...

wo·anders *Adv.* somewhere else; elsewhere; **sie ist mit ihren Gedanken ganz ~:** she's miles away *(coll.)*

wob [vo:p] *1. u. 3. Pers. Sg. Prät. v.* **weben**

wo·bei *Adv.* **a)** *(interrogativ)* **~ hast du sie ertappt?** what did you catch her doing?; **~ ist es kaputtgegangen?** how did it get broken?; **b)** *(relativisch)* **er gab sechs Schüsse ab, ~ einer der Täter getötet wurde** he fired six shots – one of the criminals was killed; **soviel zu den Statistiken, ~ [aber] zu beachten ist, daß ...:** that concludes our remarks on the statistics, though it should be noted that ...; **sie sagte nein, ~ (indem) sie vermied, mich anzusehen** she said 'no', avoiding looking at me as she did so; *NB The word occurs in North German coll. usage in two parts, e.g.* **wo hast du sie bei ertappt?**

Woche ['vɔxə] **die;** ~, ~n week; **in dieser/der nächsten/der letzten ~:** this/next/last week; **heute in/vor einer ~:** a week today/a week ago today; **zweimal die** *od.* **in der ~:** twice a week

Wochen-: ~bett das: im ~bett liegen be lying in; **im ~bett sterben** die soon after childbirth; **~blatt das** weekly

Wochenend-: ~aus·gabe die weekend edition; **~bei·lage die** weekend supplement

wochen-, Wochen-: ~ende das weekend; **schönes ~ende!** have a nice weekend!; **~end·haus das** weekend house; **~fluß der;** *o. Pl. (Med.)* lochia; **~karte die** weekly season ticket; **~lang 1.** *Adj.; nicht präd.* lasting weeks *postpos;* **2.** *adv.* for weeks [on end]; **~lohn der** weekly wages *pl.;* **~markt der** weekly market; **~schau die** *(bes. früher)* weekly newsreel; **~schrift die** weekly; **~stunde die** *(Schulw.)* period per week; **~tag der** weekday *(including Saturday);* **welcher ~tag ist heute?** what day of the week is it?; **~tags** *Adv.* on weekdays [and Saturdays]

wöchentlich ['vœçn̩tlɪç] **1.** *Adj.* weekly. **2.** *adv.* weekly; **es werden ~ ca. 50 Briefe beantwortet** some fifty letters are answered every week; **~ einmal** once a week; **wir treffen uns ~:** we meet once a week

-wöchentlich 1. *Adj.* -weekly. **2.** *adv.* every ... weeks; *s. auch* **achtwöchentlich**

wochen·weise *Adv.* for a week at a time

Wochen·zeitung die weekly newspaper

-wöchig [-vœçɪç] **a)** *(... Wochen alt)* ... -week-old; **ein achtwöchiges Kind** an eight-week-old baby; **b)** *(... Wochen dauernd)* ... week's/weeks'; ... -week; **eine vierwöchige Kur** a four-week course of treatment; **mit dreiwöchiger Verspätung** three weeks late

Wöchnerin ['vœçnərɪn] **die;** ~, ~nen woman who has just given birth; puerpera *(Med.)*

Wöchnerinnen·station die maternity ward

Wodka ['vɔtka] **der;** ~s, ~s vodka

wo·durch *Adv.* **a)** *(interrogativ)* how; **~ unterscheidet sie sich von den anderen?** in what way is she different from the others?; **b)** *(relativisch)* as a result of which; **alles, ~ er sich verletzt fühlen könnte** anything that might offend him; *s. auch* **wobei** *NB*

wo·fern *Konj. (veralt.)* provided that

wo·für *Adv.* **a)** *(interrogativ)* for what; **~ brauchst du es?** what do you need it for?; **~ hältst du mich?** what do you take me for?; **~ interessierst du dich?** what are you interested in?; **b)** *(relativisch)* for which; **er ist nicht das, ~ er sich ausgibt** he's not what he claims to be; *s. auch* **wobei** *NB*

wog [vo:k] *1. u. 3. Pers. Sg. Prät. v.* **wiegen**

Woge ['vo:gə] **die;** ~, ~n *(auch fig.)* wave; **die ~n glätten** *(fig.)* pour oil on troubled waters

wo·gegen 1. *Adv.* **a)** *(interrogativ)* against what; what ... against; **~ ist sie allergisch?** what is she allergic to?; **b)** *(relativisch)* against which; which ... against; **..., ~ nichts einzuwenden ist** to which there is no objection; *s. auch* **wobei** *NB.* **2.** *Konj.* whereas

wogen ['vo:gn̩] *itr. V. (geh.)* ‹sea› surge; *(fig.)* ‹corn› wave; ‹crowd› surge; ‹battle› rage; **mit ~dem Busen** *(fig.)* with heaving bosom

wo·her *Adv.* **a)** *(interrogativ)* where ... from; **~ weißt du das?** how do you know that?; **~ kennst du ihn?** where do you know him from?; **[ach] ~ denn!, ach ~!** *(ugs.)* good heavens, no!; not at all!; **~ bist du so braun?** how did you get so brown?; **b)** *(relativisch)* where ... from; *s. auch* **wobei** *NB*

wohin *Adv.* **a)** *(interrogativ)* where [... to]; **~ damit?** *(ugs.)* where shall I put it/them?; **~ so spät/eilig?** where are you/is he *etc.* going so late/in such a hurry?; **b)** *(relativisch)* where; **er ging ins Zimmer, ~ ihm die anderen folgten** he went into the room, and the others followed him in; **c)** *(indefinit)* **ich muß mal ~** *(ugs. verhüll.)* I've got to pay a visit *or* a call *(euphem.)*; *s. auch* **wobei** *NB*

wo·hinein *Adv. s.* **worein**

wo·hingegen *Konj.* whereas

wo·hinter *Adv.* **a)** *(interrogativ)* behind what; what ... behind; **~ habt ihr euch versteckt?** what did you hide behind?; **b)** *(relativisch)* behind which; *s. auch* **wobei** *NB*

wohl [vo:l] **1.** *Adv.* **a)** *(gesund)* well; **jmdm. ist nicht ~, jmd. fühlt sich nicht ~:** sb. does not feel well; **b)** *(behaglich)* at ease; happy; **es sich ~ sein lassen** spoil oneself; **mir ist nicht recht ~ bei der Sache** the whole thing makes me a bit uneasy; **laß es dir ~ ergehen!** enjoy yourself!; **leb ~!/leben Sie ~!** farewell!; **~ oder übel** whether I/you *etc.* want to or not; **c)** *(durchaus)* well; **ich bin mir dessen ~ bewußt** I'm quite *or* perfectly conscious of that; **d)** *(ungefähr)* about; **~ 100 Gäste** 100 or so guests; about 100 guests; **e)** *(veralt.: gewiß)* **sehr ~[, der** *od.* **mein Herr]** certainly[, sir]; very good [, sir]; **f) besser, am besten** *(geh.: gut)* well; **er tat es, ~ wissend, daß ...:** he did it knowing full well that ...; **g)** *(jedoch)* **..., ~ aber ...:** but ...; however ...; **hier gibt es keine Ratten, ~ aber Mäuse** there are no rats here, but there are mice; **h)** *(geh. veralt.)* **~ dem, der ...!** happy the man who ...; **~ dir, daß du das nicht machen mußt** count yourself lucky not to have to do that; **i)** *(zwar)* **~ versprach ich hinzugehen, aber ...:** I may have promised to go, but ... **2.** *Partikel* **a)** *(vermutlich)* probably; **er wird ~ bald kommen** I imagine he'll come soon; **~ kaum** hardly; **du bist ~ nicht recht bei Verstand?** have you taken leave of your senses?; **dir ist ~ schlecht?** aren't you feeling well?; **was/warum/wie ~?** but what/why/how?; **na** *od.* **ja, was/warum/wie ~?** need you ask what/why/how?; **das mag ~ sein** that may well be; **es wird ~ gleich Schluß sein** I imagine it's nearly over; **das wird ~ so sein** that's probably the case; **ich habe ~ nicht recht gehört** I don't think I could have heard right; **b)** *(verstärkend)* **wirst du ~ herkommen!** will you come here!; **siehst du ~!** there, you see!; **man wird doch ~ fragen dürfen** there's nothing wrong in asking, is there?

Wohl das; ~[e]s welfare; well-being; **das allgemeine/öffentliche ~:** the public good; **zu jmds. ~:** for sb.'s benefit *or* good; **auf jmds. ~ trinken** drink sb.'s health; **[auf] dein ~!** your health!; **zum ~!** cheers!; **das ~ und Weh[e]** *(geh.)* the weal and woe

wohl-, Wohl-: ~an [-'-] *Interj. (veralt.)* [well,] come now; **~anständig** *(veralt.)* **1.** *Adj.* respectable; proper ‹behaviour›; **2.** *adv.* respectably; ‹behave› properly; **~auf** [-'-] *Adj., nicht attr. (geh.)* **~auf sein** be well *or* in good health; **~aus·gewogen** *Adj. (geh.)* well-balanced; **~bedacht** *(geh.)* **1.** *Adj.* well-considered; [carefully] considered ‹reply, judgement›; well *or* carefully thought-out ‹plan›; **2.** *adv.* in a carefully considered way; with careful consideration; **~befinden das** well-being; **~begründet** *(geh.) Adj.* well-founded; *(berechtigt)* well-justified; **~behagen das** sense of well-being; **mit ~behagen** with a sense of well-being; **etw. mit ~behagen essen** eat sth. with relish; **~behalten** *Adj.* safe and well ‹person›; undamaged ‹thing›; **~bekannt** *Adj.* well-known; **~beleibt** *Adj. (geh.)* corpulent; **~beraten** *Adj.* well-advised; **~bestallt** *Adj. (geh.)* well-established; **~dosiert** *(geh.)* **1.** *Adj.* carefully measured; **2.** *adv.* in a carefully measured way; **~durchdacht** *Adj.* carefully thought-out; **~ergehen das** *s.* **~befinden; ~erzogen** *Adj.* well brought-up; **~erzogenheit die;** ~ *(geh.)* good upbringing; *(gute Manieren)* good manners *pl.;* **~fahrt die;** *o. Pl.* **a)** *(geh.: Wohlergehen)* welfare; **b)** *(öffentliche Fürsorge)* **von der ~fahrt betreut werden** be looked after by the welfare services; **von der ~fahrt leben** *(ugs.)* live on welfare

Wohlfahrts-: ~marke die *(Postw.)* charity stamp; **~pflege die;** *o. Pl.* social welfare *no art.;* **~staat der** welfare state

wohl-, Wohl-: ~feil 1. *Adj.* **a)** *(preiswert)* inexpensive; **b)** *(geistlos, platt)* trite; **2.** *adv.* cheaply; **etw. ~feil verkaufen/erstehen** sell/buy sth. cheap; **~geboren** *Adj. (veralt.)* **Euer Wohlgeboren** Your Honour; **Seiner Wohlgeboren** to His Honour; **~gefallen das** pleasure; **sein ~gefallen an jmdm. haben** have a great liking for sb.; **an etw.** *(Dat.)* **~gefallen finden** take pleasure in sth.; **sich in ~gefallen auflösen** *(scherzh.) (ein gutes Ende finden)* end well; ‹difficulties, misunderstandings› be cleared up; *(entzweigehen, auseinanderfallen)* ‹clothes, book, etc.› fall apart; *(verschwinden)* vanish into thin air;

~gefällig 1. *Adj.* **a)** *(Wohlgefallen ausdrückend)* ‹*smile, look*› of pleasure; **b)** *(veralt.: angenehm)* pleasing; agreeable; **2.** *adv.* **a)** *(mit Wohlgefallen)* with pleasure; **b)** *(veralt.: angenehm)* **die Speisen ~gefällig darreichen** serve the food in a way that is pleasing *or* agreeable to the eye; **~geformt** *Adj.* well-formed; **~gefühl das;** *o. Pl.* sense of well-being; **~gelitten** *Adj. (geh.)* well-liked; **~gemerkt** *Adv.* please note; mark you; **~gemut** [~gəmu:t] *(geh.)* **1.** *Adj.* cheerful; **2.** *adv.* cheerfully; **~genährt** *Adj. (meist spött.)* well-fed; **~geordnet** *Adj. (geh., Math.)* well-ordered; **~geraten** *Adj. (geh.)* fine *attrib.* ‹*child*›; successful ‹*piece of work, translation, etc.*›; **ihre Kinder sind ~geraten** their children have turned out well; **~geruch der** *(geh.)* pleasant *or* agreeable aroma; *(von Blumen)* agreeable fragrance; **alle ~gerüche Arabiens** *(scherzh. od. iron.)* all the perfumes of Arabia; **~gesetzt** *Adj. (geh.)* well-turned ‹*compliment*›; well-chosen ‹*words*›; well-worded ‹*speech*›; **~gesinnt** *Adj.* well-disposed; **jmdm./einer Sache ~gesinnt sein** be well-disposed towards sb./sth.; **der Wettergott war uns nicht ~gesinnt** the weather was unkind to us; **~gestalt** *(veralt.)*, **~gestaltet** *(geh.) Adj.* well-shaped; well-proportioned ‹*body*›; **~getan 1.** *2. Part. v.* **~tun; 2.** *Adj. in* **~getan sein** *(veralt.)* be well done; **~habend** *Adj.* prosperous; **~habenheit die; ~:** prosperity

wohlig 1. *Adj.; nicht präd.* pleasant; agreeable; *(gemütlich)* cosy. **2.** *adv.* ‹*sigh, purr, etc.*› with pleasure; ‹*stretch oneself*› luxuriously

wohl, Wohl-: ~klang der *(geh.)* melodious *or* pleasing sound; **~klingend** *Adj. (geh.)* melodious; **~laut der** *(geh.) s.* **~klang; ~leben das;** *o. Pl. (geh.)* good living; **~meinend** *Adj. (geh.)* well-meaning; **~proportioniert** *Adj. (geh.)* well-proportioned; **~riechend** *Adj. (geh.)* fragrant; **~schmeckend** *Adj. (geh.)* delicious; **~sein das: [zum] ~sein!** your health!; **~stand der;** *o. Pl.* prosperity; **zu ~stand gelangen** achieve a degree of prosperity; **bei dir ist wohl der ~stand ausgebrochen!** *(scherzh.)* have you won the pools *or* something?

Wohlstands-: ~gesellschaft die; *o. Pl. (abwertend)* affluent society; **~kriminalität die** *(Rechtsspr.)* crime characteristic of the affluent society; **~müll der** *(abwertend)* refuse produced by the affluent society

wohl, Wohl-: ~tat die a) *(gute Tat)* good deed; *(Gefallen)* favour; **jmdm. eine ~tat erweisen** do sb. a good turn; **auf die ~taten anderer angewiesen sein** be dependent on the kindness of others; **b)** *o. Pl. (Genuß)* blissful relief; **~täter der** benefactor; **~täterin die** benefactress; **~tätig** *Adj.* charitable; **~tätigkeit die;** *o. Pl.* charity; charitableness

Wohltätigkeits-: ~basar der charity bazaar; **~konzert das** charity concert; **~veranstaltung die** charity event

wohl-, Wohl-: ~temperiert *Adj. (geh.)* **a)** ‹*room*› at a pleasant temperature; ‹*wine*› at the correct temperature; **b)** *(Mus.)* **das ~temperierte Klavier** the Well-Tempered Clavier; **~tuend 1.** *Adj.* agreeable; **eine ~tuende Wirkung haben** have a beneficial effect; **2.** *adv.* agreeably; **~|tun** *unr. itr. V.* **a)** *(guttun)* **etw. tut jmdm. ~:** sth. does sb. good; **b)** *(veralt.: Wohltaten erweisen)* **jmdm. ~tun** show sb. kindness; **~überlegt 1.** *Adj.* well-considered; carefully considered ‹*decision*›; **2.** *adv.* in a carefully considered way; with careful consideration; **~verdient** *Adj.* well-earned, well-deserved ‹*reward, honour, success, etc.*›; well-deserved ‹*punishment, fate*›; **~verhalten das** good behaviour *no indef. art.*; **~versehen** *Adj. (geh.)* well-provided (**mit** with); **~verstanden** *Adv. (geh.) s.* **~gemerkt; ~verwahrt** *Adj.* safely stored; *(unter Verschluß)* safely locked away; **~weislich** [~vaislıç] *Adv.* deliberately; **~|wollen** *unr. itr. V.* **jmdm. ~wollen** wish sb. well; **~wollen das; ~s** goodwill; **jmdn. mit ~wollen betrachten** regard sb. benevolently; **~wollend 1.** *Adj.* benevolent; favourable ‹*judgement, opinion*›; **2.** *adv.* benevolently; ‹*judge, consider*› favourably

Wohn-: ~anhänger der caravan; trailer *(Amer.)*; **~anlage die** residential estate; **~bau der;** *Pl.* **~bauten** residential building; **~bereich der** living-rooms *pl.*; *(eines Zimmers)* living area; **~bezirk der a)** residential district; **b)** *(DDR)* district; **~block der;** *Pl.* **~s,** *(schweiz.)* **~blöcke** residential block

wohnen *itr. V.* live; *(kurzfristig)* stay; *(fig. dichter.)* dwell; **sie ~ sehr hübsch** they have a lovely home; *(der Lage nach)* they live in a lovely spot; **ich wohne in der Leibnizstraße 7** I live/am staying at [number] 7 Leibnizstrasse; **wo ~ Sie?** where do you live/where are you staying?

wohn-, Wohn-: ~fläche die living-space; **eine Wohnung mit 50 m² ~fläche** a flat *(Brit.) or (Amer.)* apartment with 50 sq.m. floor area; **~gebäude das** residential building; **~gebiet das, ~gegend die** residential area; **~geld das** housing benefit; **~gemeinschaft die** group sharing a flat *(Brit.) or (Amer.)* apartment/house; **unsere ~gemeinschaft** the group who share our flat *(Brit.) or (Amer.)* apartment/house; **in einer ~gemeinschaft leben** live in a shared flat *(Brit.) or (Amer.)* apartment/house; share a flat *(Brit.) or (Amer.)* apartment/house; **in diesem Haus wohnt eine studentische ~gemeinschaft/wohnen nur ~gemeinschaften** a group of students is sharing this house/the flats *(Brit.) or (Amer.)* apartments in this house are all shared; **~haft** *Adj.* resident (**in** + *Dat.* in); **~haus das** [dwelling-]house; **~heim das** *(für Alte, Behinderte)* home; *(für Obdachlose, Lehrlinge)* hostel; *(für Studenten)* hall of residence; **~komplex der** residential complex; **~küche die** combined kitchen and living-room; **~kultur die;** *o. Pl.* style of home furnishing; **~lage die: unsere ~lage ist optimal** our house/flat *(Brit.) or (Amer.)* apartment is ideally situated; **in ruhiger/guter ~lage** in a quiet/good area; **~landschaft die** *(bes. Werbesprache) arrangement of furniture etc. to give an impressive 'landscape' effect*

wohnlich 1. *Adj.* homely. **2.** *adv.* **~ eingerichtet** furnished in a homely way

Wohnlichkeit die; ~: homeliness

Wohn-: ~mobil das; ~s, ~e motor home; motor caravan; **~ort der;** *Pl.* **~e** place of residence; **~raum der a)** living-room; **b)** *o. Pl. (~fläche)* living space; **~siedlung die** residential estate; *(mit gleichartigen Häusern)* housing estate; **~silo der** *od.* **das** *(abwertend)* [anonymous] tower block *or* high-rise block; **~sitz der** place of residence; domicile *(formal)*; **seinen ~sitz in Hamburg haben** live *or (formal)* be domiciled in Hamburg; **ohne festen ~sitz** of no fixed abode; **ohne festen ~sitz sein** have no fixed abode; **~stube die** *(landsch.)* living-room

Wohnung die; ~, ~en a) flat *(Brit.)*; apartment *(Amer.)*; *(Wohneinheit)*; home; dwelling *(formal)*; **b)** *o. Pl. (Unterkunft)* lodging; **freie ~ haben** have free lodging; **~ nehmen** *(veralt.)* take up residence

Wohnungs-: ~amt das housing department; **~bau der;** *o. Pl.* housing construction; **der soziale ~bau** *(Amtsspr.)* public-sector house-building; **~inhaber der** occupant *(of a dwelling)*; **~markt der** housing market; **~miete die** rent; **~not die;** *o. Pl.* housing crisis; serious housing shortage; **~schlüssel der** key to the flat *(Brit.) or (Amer.)* apartment; **~suche die** search for a flat *(Brit.) or (Amer.)* apartment; **auf ~suche sein** be flat-hunting; **~suchende der/die;** *adj. Dekl.* person looking for a flat *(Brit.) or (Amer.)* apartment; **~tausch der** flat-swap *(coll.)*; exchange of flats *(Brit.) or (Amer.)* apartments; **~tür die** door of the flat *(Brit.) or (Amer.)* apartment

Wohnung-: ~suche *s.* **Wohnungssuche; ~suchende** *s.* **Wohnungssuchende**

Wohnungs·wechsel der move to a new flat *(Brit.) or (Amer.)* apartment

Wohn-: ~verhältnisse *Pl.* living conditions; **~viertel das** residential district; **~wagen der** caravan; trailer *(Amer.)*; **~zimmer das a)** living-room; **b)** *(Einrichtung)* set of living-room furniture

wölben ['vœlbn̩] **1.** *tr. V.* curve; arch ‹*brows, shoulders*›; cup ‹*hand*›; bend ‹*metal*›; vault, arch ‹*roof, ceiling*›; **eine gewölbte Decke** a vaulted ceiling; **die Brust ~:** swell out one's chest. **2.** *refl. V.* curve; ‹*sky, bridge, ceiling*› arch; ‹*chest*› swell; ‹*stomach, muscles*› bulge; ‹*metal*› bend, buckle; **eine gewölbte Stirn** a domed forehead

Wölbung die; ~, ~en curve; *(einer Decke, des Himmels)* arch; vault; *(von Augenbrauen)* arch; *(eines Bauches, Muskels)* bulge

Wolf [vɔlf] **der; ~[e]s, Wölfe** ['vœlfə] **a)** wolf; **ein ~ im Schafspelz sein** *(fig.)* be a wolf in sheep's clothing; **mit den Wölfen heulen** *(fig. ugs.)* run with the pack; **unter die Wölfe geraten** *(fig.)* be ruthlessly exploited; **b)** *(ugs.: Fleisch~)* mincer; **jmdn. durch den ~ drehen** *(fig. salopp)* put sb. through the mill; **c)** *o. Pl. (volkstüml.: Wundsein)* intertrigo *no art. (Med.)*; *soreness caused by the rubbing of areas of the skin against each other;* **sich** *(Dat.)* **einen ~ laufen** make oneself sore between the legs through walking too much

Wölfin ['vœlfın] **die; ~, ~nen** [wolf] bitch

wölfisch *Adj.* wolfish; ravenous ‹*hunger*›

Wölfling ['vœlflıŋ] **der; ~s, ~e** Cub

Wolfram ['vɔlfram] **das; ~s** *(Chemie)* tungsten

Wolfs-: ~hund der *(volkstüml.)* Alsatian [dog]; **Irischer ~hund** Irish wolfhound; **~hunger der** *(ugs.)* ravenous hunger; **ich habe einen ~hunger!** I'm ravenous!; **~kind das** *(Myth.)* wolf child; **~milch die** *(Bot.)* spurge; **~rachen der** *(volkstüml.)* cleft palate; **~spinne die** wolf spider

Wolga ['vɔlga] **die; ~:** Volga

Wölkchen ['vœlkçən] **das; ~s, ~:** small cloud

Wolke ['vɔlkə] **die; ~, ~n** *(auch Mineral.)* cloud; **'ne ~ sein** *(berlin. salopp)* be fantastic *(coll.)*; **auf ~n** *od.* **in den ~n schweben** *(fig.)* have one's head in the clouds; **aus allen ~n fallen** *(fig. ugs.)* be completely stunned; **eine ~ von Tüll** billows of tulle

wolken-, Wolken-: ~bank die; *Pl.* **~bänke** bank of cloud; **~bildung die** formation of cloud; **es wird zu stärkerer ~bildung kommen** it will become very cloudy *or* overcast; **~bruch der;** *Pl.* **~brüche** cloudburst; **~bruch·artig** *Adj.* torrential; **~decke die** [unbroken] cloud *no indef. art.*; **die ~decke riß auf** the clouds broke; **~feld das;** *meist Pl. (Met.)* cloud field; **~fetzen der;** *meist Pl.* wisp of cloud; **~kratzer der** skyscraper; **~kuckucks·heim das** cloud-cuckoo-land; **im ~kuckucksheim** in cloud-cuckoo-land; **~los** *Adj.* cloudless; **~schleier der** veil of cloud; **~verhangen** *Adj.* overcast; **~wand die** wall of cloud

wolkig *Adj.* **a)** *(auch Fot., Chemie, Mineral.)* cloudy; **b)** *(unklar, verschwommen)* vague; vague, hazy ‹*idea, concept*›

Woll·decke die [woollen] blanket

Wolle ['vɔlə] **die; ~, ~n a)** wool; *(fig.: Haar)* hair; **in der ~ gefärbt** dyed-in-the-wool; **sich in die ~ kriegen** *(fig. ugs.)* quarrel (wegen over); **sich in der ~ haben** *od.* **liegen** *(fig. ugs.)* be at loggerheads; **b)** *(Jägerspr.)* hair; *(von Hasen, Kaninchen)* fur

[1]**wollen** *Adj.; nicht präd.* woollen

[2]**wollen 1.** *unr. Modalverb; 2. Part.* **~ a) etw. tun ~** *(den Wunsch haben, etw. zu tun)* want to do sth.; *(die Absicht haben, etw. zu tun)* be going to do sth.; **wir wollten gerade gehen** we were just about to go; **das Buch habe ich immer lesen ~:** I've always wanted to read that book; **ich will lieber zu Hause bleiben** I'd rather stay at home; **was will man da machen?** *(ugs.)* what can you do?; **ohne es zu ~:** without intending to; **ich wollte Sie fragen, ob ...:** I wanted to ask you if ...; **wenn Sie bitte Platz nehmen ~:** would you like to take a seat/take your seats?; **~ Sie mich entschuldigen?** would you excuse me?; **wenn ich mich darum auch noch kümmern wollte, ...:** if I were to see to that as well, then ...; **na gut, ich will [mal] nicht so sein** *(ugs.)* all right, I don't want to be awkward; **dann will ich nichts gesagt haben** *(ugs.)* I take it all back; **das will ich meinen!** *(ugs.)* I absolutely agree; **wir ~ sehen** we'll see; **b)** *(in Aufforderungen)* **man wolle bitte darauf achten, daß ...:** please note that ...; **wollt ihr Ruhe geben/damit aufhören!** *(ugs.)* will you be quiet/stop that!; **~ Sie bitte so freundlich sein und das heute noch erledigen** would you be so kind as to do it today; **c)** *(in bezug auf bezweifelte Behauptungen)* **er will ein Dichter sein** he claims to be a poet; **sie will es [nicht] gesehen haben** she claims [not] to have seen it; **d)** *(sich in der gewünschten Weise verhalten)* **die Wunde will nicht heilen** the wound [just] won't heal; **der Motor wollte nicht anspringen** the engine wouldn't start; **es will nicht gelingen** it just won't work; **es will mir nicht einleuchten, daß ...:** I can't really see that ...; **e)** *(müssen)* **etw. will getan sein** sth. needs *or (coll.)* has got to be done; **das will gelernt sein** it has to be learned; **f)** *(einen bestimmten Zweck, eine bestimmte Funktion haben)* be intended to; **die Aktion will die Leute über ... aufklären** the purpose of the campaign is to inform people about ...; **g) das will nichts heißen/nicht viel sagen** that doesn't mean anything/much. **2.** *unr. itr. V.* **a) du mußt nur ~, dann geht es auch** you only have to want to enough *or* have the will, then it's possible; **ob du willst oder nicht** whether you want to or not; **ganz wie du willst** just as you like; **wenn du willst, könnten wir ...:** if you want [to], we could ...; **du kannst es halten, wie du willst** you can do just as you like; **das ist, wenn man so will, ...:** that is, if you like, ...; **[na] dann ~ wir mal!** *(ugs.)* [right,] let's get started!; **b)** *(ugs.: irgendwohin zu gehen wünschen)* **ich will nach Hause/ans Meer** I want to go home/to go to the seaside; **ich will hier raus** I want to get out of here; **zu wem ~ Sie?** whom do you want to see?; **er wollte zum Theater** he wanted to become an actor; **c)** *verneint (ugs.: funktionieren)* **der Motor will nicht** the engine won't go; **seine Beine/Gelenke/Augen ~ nicht mehr** his legs/joints/eyes just aren't up to it any more. **3.** *unr. tr. V.* **a)** want; **das wollte ich nicht** I didn't mean to do that; **das habe ich nicht gewollt** I never meant that to happen; **~, daß jmd. etw. tut** want sb. to do sth.; **er will nicht, daß du ihm hilfst** he doesn't want you to help him; **er wollte nur euer Bestes** he only wanted what's best for you; **er will es nicht anders** he wouldn't have it any other way; **da ist nichts [mehr] zu ~** *(ugs.)* there's nothing we/you *etc.* can do about it; **was du nicht willst, daß man dir tu', das füg auch keinem anderen zu** *(Spr.)* do as you would be done by *(prov.)*; **ich wollte, er wäre hier/es wäre vorbei** I wish he were here/it were over; **b)** *(ugs.: zum Gedeihen brauchen)* need; **c)** *(ugs.: schaden)* **jmdm. nichts ~ können** be unable to harm sb.; **was kann sie mir schon ~?** what can she do to me?

Woll·gras das cotton grass

wollig *Adj.* woolly

Woll-: ~jacke die woollen cardigan; **~kleid das** woollen dress; **~knäuel das** ball of wool; **~sachen** *Pl.* woollen things; woollies *(coll.)*; **~socke die;** *meist Pl.* woollen sock; **~stoff der** woollen cloth; **~strumpf der;** *meist Pl.* woollen stocking; *(Kniestrumpf)* woollen sock

Wollust ['vɔlʊst] **die; ~, Wollüste** ['vɔlʏstə] *(geh.)* lust; *(Sinnlichkeit)* sensuality; *(großes Vergnügen)* delight; **etw. mit wahrer ~ tun** take great delight in doing sth.

wollüstig ['vɔlʏstɪç] *(geh.)* **1.** *Adj.* lustful; *(sinnlich)* sensual. **2.** *Adj.* lustfully; *(sinnlich)* sensually

wo·mit *Adv.* **a)** *(interrogativ)* **~ schreibst du?** what do you write with?; *(more formal)* with what do you write?; **~ habe ich das verdient?** what have I done to deserve that?; **b)** *(relativisch)* **~ du schreibst** which *or* that you write with; *(more formal)* with which you write; **~ ich nicht sagen will, daß ...:** by which I don't mean to say that ...; **~ er nicht gerechnet hatte, war ...:** what he had not reckoned with was ...; **~ du es auch machst, ...:** whatever you do it with ...; *s. auch* **wobei** *NB*

wo·möglich *Adv.* possibly

wo·nach *Adv.* **a)** *(interrogativ)* after what; what ... after; **~ suchst du?** what are you looking for?; **~ riecht es?** what does it smell of?; **~ richtet ihr euch?** what do you go by?; **~ verlangte er?** what did he ask for?; **b)** *(relativisch)* after which; which ... after; **alles, ~ er verlangte** all he asked for; **etwas, ~ sie sich sehnte** something she longed for; **eine Vorschrift, ~ ...:** a regulation according to which ...; *s. auch* **wobei** *NB*

Wonne ['vɔnə] **die; ~, ~n** *(geh.)* bliss *no pl.*; ecstasy; *(etw., was Freude macht)* joy; delight; **es war eine ~, ihr zuzuhören** she was a joy *or* delight to listen to; **das Kind ist ihre ganze ~:** the child is her great joy; **es ist eine wahre ~:** it's sheer delight; **Würdest du helfen? – Aber mit ~!** *(scherzh.)* Would you help? – Of course, I'd be delighted!

Wonne-: ~monat *(geh.)*, **~mond** *(veralt.)* **der** May *no art.*; **im ~monat [Mai]** in the merry month of May; **~proppen der** *(ugs. scherzh.)* chubby cherub

wonnig *Adj.* sweet

woran [vo'ran] *Adv.* **a)** *(interrogativ)* **~ hast du dich verletzt?** what did you hurt yourself on?; **~ hat sie sich gelehnt?** what did she lean against?; **man weiß nicht, ~ man ist** you don't know where you are; **~ ist sie gestorben?** what did she die of?; **~ denkst du?** what are you thinking of?; **b)** *(relativisch)* **nichts, ~ man sich verletzen/lehnen könnte** nothing one could hurst oneself on/one could lean against; **alles, ~ er sich erinnern konnte** everything he could remember

worauf [vo'rauf] **a)** *(interrogativ)* **~ sitzt er?** what is he sitting on?; **~ wartest du?** what are you waiting for?; **~ will er hinaus?** what is he getting at?; **b)** *(relativisch)* **es gab nichts, ~ er sich hätte setzen können** there was nothing for him to sit on; **etwas, ~ ich schreiben kann** something to write on; **etwas, ~ man sich verlassen kann** something one can rely on; **etwas, ~ ich Sie hinweisen sollte, ist ...:** something I ought to point out to you is ...; **das einzige, ~ es jetzt ankommt** the only thing that matters now; **es gab nichts, ~ er sich hätte freuen können** there was nothing for him to look forward to; **c)** *(relativisch: woraufhin)* whereupon

worauf·hin *Adv.* **a)** *(interrogativ)* **~ hat er das getan?** what made him do it?; what was the cause of his doing it?; **b)** *(relativisch)* whereupon

woraus [vo'raus] *Adv.* **a)** *(interrogativ)* **~ ist der Zitat?** where is the quotation from?; **~ trinken wir den Wein?** what shall we drink the wine from?; **~ ist das Gewebe?** what is the fabric made of?; **~ schließt du das?** what do you infer that from?; **b)** *(relativisch)* **es gab nichts, ~ wir den Wein hätten trinken können** there was nothing for us to drink the wine out of; **es gab nichts, ~ sie Werkzeuge machen konnten** there was nothing for them to make tools from; **..., ~ ich schließe, daß ...** ... from which I conclude that ...

worden ['vɔrdn̩] *2. Part. v.* **werden 2**

worein [vo'rain] *Adv.* **a)** *(interrogativ)* in what; what ... in; **b)** *(relativisch)* in which; which ... in; **..., ~ sie sich schickte ...,** to which she resigned herself; ..., which she resigned herself to

worin [vo'rɪn] *Adv.* **a)** *(interrogativ)* in what; what ... in; **~ willst du es verschicken?** what do you want to send it in?; **ich weiß nicht, ~ der Unterschied liegt** I don't know what the difference is; **b)** *(relativisch)* in which; which ... in; **..., ~ ich mit dir übereinstimme** ..., which I agree with you on

Work·shop ['wɜːkʃɔp] **der; ~s, ~s** workshop

World·cup ['wɜːldkʌp] **der** *(Sport)* World Cup

Wort [vɔrt] **das; ~[e]s, Wörter** ['vœrtɐ] *od.* **~e a)** *Pl.* **Wörter,** *(auch:)* **~e** word; **~ für ~:** word for word; **DM 1000 (in ~en: tausend)** DM 1,000 (in words: one thousand); **in des ~es wahrster Bedeutung, im wahrsten Sinne des ~es** in the truest sense of the word; **Liebe ist ein großes ~:** love is a big word; **das treffende** *od.* **passende ~:** the right word; **b)** *Pl.* **~e** *(Äußerung)* word; **zwischen uns ist kein böses ~ gefallen** not a harsh word has passed between us; **das ist das erste ~, das ich [davon] höre** that's the first I've heard of it; **mir fehlen die ~e** I'm lost for words; **davon ist kein ~ wahr** not a word of it is true; **darüber ist kein ~ gefallen** not a word was said about it; **spar dir deine ~e!** don't waste your breath!; **in ~ und Tat** in word and deed; **eine Sprache in ~ und Schrift beherrschen** have a written and spoken command of a language; **das ~ an jmdn. richten** address sb.; **ein paar ~e sprechen** say a few words; **ein ~ mit jmdm. sprechen** have a word with sb.; **bei ihm ist jedes zweite ~ Geld** he's always talking about money; **nicht viele ~e machen** not beat about the bush; **ich verstehe kein ~:** I don't understand a word [of it]; **auf ein ~!** *(veralt.)* Can I have a word with you?; **auf jmds. ~e hören** listen to what sb. says; **etw. in ~e fassen** put sth. into words; **mit einem ~:** in a word; **mit anderen ~en** in other words; **ich glaube dir aufs ~:** I can well believe it; **jmdn. [nicht] zu ~ kommen lassen** [not] let sb. get a word in; **kein ~ mehr!** not another word!; **etw. mit keinem ~ erwähnen** not say a word about sth.; not mention sth. at all; **man verstand sein eigenes ~ nicht** you could not hear yourself speak; **die ~e gut zu setzen wissen** *(geh.)* have a way with words; **jmdm. aufs ~ folgen** *od.* **gehorchen** obey sb.'s every word; **dein ~ in Gottes Ohr!** let's hope you're right!; **ein ~ gab das andere** one thing led to another; **hast du [da noch] ~e?** what do you say to that?; **das ist das letzte/mein letztes ~:** that's the/my last word on the matter; **[immer] das letzte ~ haben wollen/müssen** want to have/have to have the last word; **Dr. Meyer hat das ~:** it's Dr Meyer's turn to speak; **das ~ ergreifen** *od.* **nehmen** start to speak; **das ~ führen** be the main speaker; **das große ~ haben** *od.* **führen** talk big; **jmdm. das ~ geben** *od.* **erteilen/entziehen** call upon sb. to speak/to finish speaking; **jmdm. das ~ verbieten** forbid sb. to speak; **einer Sache das ~ reden** *(geh.)* speak out in favour of sth.; **für jmdn. ein [gutes] ~ einle-**

gen put in a [good] word for sb.; **jmdm. das ~ aus dem Munde nehmen** take the words out of sb.'s mouth; **jmdm. das ~ im Munde herumdrehen** twist sb.'s words; **kein ~/kein weiteres ~ über etw.** *(Akk.)* **verlieren** not spend time discussing sth./not say another word about sth.; **jmdm. ins ~ fallen** interrupt sb.; **ums ~ bitten** ask to speak; **sich zu ~ melden** indicate one's wish to speak; **c)** *Pl.* **~e** *(Spruch)* saying; *(Zitat)* quotation; **geflügelte ~e** well-known sayings and quotations; **das bekannte ~ Schillers** the well-known quotation from Schiller; **d)** *Pl.* **~e** *(geh.: Text)* words *pl.*; **in ~ und Bild** in words and pictures; **das geschriebene/gedruckte ~:** the written/printed word; **e)** *Pl.* **~e** *(Versprechen)* word; **[sein] ~ halten** keep one's word; **sein ~ brechen** break one's word; **jmdm. sein ~ [auf etw.** *(Akk.)***] geben** give sb. one's word [on sth.]; **auf mein ~!** I give you my word; **jmdn. beim ~ nehmen** take sb. at his/her word; **[bei jmdm.] im ~ sein** have made a promise [to sb.]; **f)** *o. Pl. (christl. Rel., Theol.)* Word

wọrt-, Wọrt-: ~art die *(Sprachw.)* part of speech; **~bedeutung die** word-meaning; meaning of a/the word; **~bildung die** *(Sprachw.)* word-formation; **~bruch der** breaking one's word *no art.*; **~brüchig** *Adj.* **~brüchig werden** break one's word

Wörtchen ['vœrtçən] **das; ~s, ~:** little word; **noch ein ~ mit jmdm. zu reden haben** *(ugs.)* have a bone to pick with sb.; **[bei** *od.* **in etw.** *(Dat.)***] ein ~ mitzureden haben** *(ugs.)* have some say [in sth.]

Wọ̈rter-: ~buch das dictionary; **~verzeichnis das** word index

wọrt-, Wọrt-: ~familie die *(Sprachw.)* word family; **~feld das** *(Sprachw.)* word field; **~fetzen** *Pl.* scraps of conversation; **~forschung die** lexicology *no art.*; **~führer der/~führerin, die** spokesman/spokeswoman; spokesperson; **sich zum ~führer einer Gruppe/Sache machen** make oneself the spokesman of a group/cause; **~gefecht das** battle of words; **~geklingel das** *(abwertend)* fine-sounding verbiage; **~geplänkel das** banter *no indef. art.*; **~geschichte die** etymology *no art.*; **~getreu 1.** *Adj.* word-for-word; **2.** *adv.* word for word; **~gewaltig 1.** *Adj.* powerfully eloquent; **2.** *adv.* with powerful eloquence; **~gewandt 1.** *Adj.* eloquent; **2.** *adv.* eloquently; **~gottes·dienst der** *(christl. Kirche) service centred on the sermon and readings from the Scriptures;* **~gut das;** *o. Pl.* vocabulary; **~hülse die** *(abwertend)* [empty] cliché; **~inhalt der** *(Sprachw.)* word-meaning; meaning of a/the word; **~karg 1.** *Adj.* taciturn ⟨*person*⟩; laconic ⟨*reply, greeting, etc.*⟩; **ein ~karger Mann** a man of few words; **2.** *adv.* taciturnly; ⟨*reply, greet, etc.*⟩ laconically; **~kargheit die** *s.* **~karg:** taciturnity; laconicism; **~klauberei** [~klaubə'rai] **die; ~, ~en** quibbling; **solche ~en ändern nichts an der Tatsache, daß ...:** such quibbles do not alter the fact that ...; **~laut der;** *o. Pl.* wording; **im [vollen] ~laut** verbatim

Wọ̈rtlein das; ~s, ~ *s.* **Wörtchen**

wörtlich ['vœrtlıç] **1.** *Adj.* **a)** *(wortgetreu)* word-for-word; *s. auch* **Rede e**; **b)** *(der eigentlichen Bedeutung entsprechend)* literal. **2.** *adv.* **a)** *(wortgetreu)* word-for-word; ⟨*copy, repeat*⟩ verbatim, word-for-word; **das hat sie ~ gesagt** those were her very words; **b)** *(der eigentlichen Bedeutung entsprechend)* literally

wọrt-, Wọrt-: ~los 1. *Adj.* silent; wordless; unspoken ⟨*agreement, understanding*⟩; **2.** *adv.* without saying a word; **~meldung die: gibt es noch ~meldungen?** does anyone else wish to speak?; **es liegen keine weiteren ~meldungen vor** no one else wishes to speak; **~reich 1.** *Adj.* **a)** *(mit vielen Worten)* verbose; **b)** *(reich im Wortschatz)* **eine ~reiche Sprache** a language with a rich vocabulary; **2.** *adv. (mit vielen Worten)* verbosely; ⟨*apologize, thank*⟩ profusely; **~schatz der** vocabulary; **~schöpfung die a)** word-coining *no art.*; **b)** *(Wort)* neologism; new coinage; **~schwall der;** *o. Pl.* torrent of words; **~sinn der;** *o. Pl.* sense of a word/the word[s]; **~spiel das** play on words; *(mit ähnlich klingenden Wörtern)* pun; play on words; **~stamm der** *(Sprachw.)* stem of a/the word; **~stellung die** *(Sprachw.)* word order; **~streit der** *s.* **~gefecht; ~ungetüm das** over-long monstrosity of a word; **~wahl die;** *o. Pl.* choice of word; **~wechsel der** exchange of words; **mit jmdm. einen ~wechsel haben** exchange words with sb.; **~witz der** pun; **~wörtlich 1.** *Adj.* word-for-word; **2.** *adv.* word for word; **etw. ~ nehmen** take sth. literally

worụ̈ber *Adv.* **a)** *(interrogativ)* over what ...; what ... over; **~ bist du gestolpert?** what did you trip over?; **~ lachst du?** what are you laughing about?; **b)** *(relativisch)* over which; which ... over; **es gibt nichts, ~ wir sprechen könnten** we have nothing to talk about

worụm *Adv.* **a)** *(interrogativ)* around what; what ... around; **~ bat er?** what did he ask for?; **~ geht es denn?** what is it about then?; **b)** *(relativisch)* around which; which ... around; **alles, ~ er bat** everything he asked for

worụnter *Adv.* **a)** *(interrogativ)* under what; what ... under; **~ leidet er?** what is he suffering from?; **b)** *(relativisch)* under which; which ... under; **etwas, ~ er besonders leidet, ist ...** something he particularly suffers from is ...

wo·sẹlbst *Adv. (veralt.)* where

Wotan ['vo:tan] **(der)** Wotan

wo·vọn *Adv.* **a)** *(interrogativ)* from where; where ... from; **~ soll er leben?** what is he supposed to live on?; **~ redest du?** what are you talking about?; **~ ist er müde/krank?** what has made him tired/ill?; **b)** *(relativisch)* from which; which ... from; **das, ~ er sprach** what he was talking about; *s. auch* **wobei NB**

wo·vọr *Adv.* **a)** *(interrogativ)* in front of what; what ... in front of; **~ stand er?** what was he standing in front of?; **~ hast du Angst?** what are you afraid of?; **b)** *(relativisch)* in front of which; which ... in front of; **das, ~ er sie gewarnt hatte** what he had warned her about; **das einzige, ~ ich Angst habe** the only thing I am afraid of; *s. auch* **wobei NB**

wo·zụ *Adv.* **a)** *(interrogativ)* to what; what ... to; *(wofür)* what ... for; **~ brauchst du das Geld?** what do you need the money for?; **~ hast du dich entschlossen?** what have you decided [on]?; **~ hat sie ihn gezwungen?** what did she force him to do?; **~ diese Umstände?** why all this fuss?; **~ denn?** *(zu welchem Zweck)* what for?; *(als Ausdruck der Ablehnung)* why should I/you *etc.?*; **weißt du, ~ das gut sein soll?** do you know what the point of it is supposed to be?; **b)** *(relativisch)* **dann habe ich gebügelt, ~ ich keine Lust hatte** then I did some ironing, which I had no inclination to do; **~ du dich auch entschließt** whatever you decide on; **er will studieren, ~ er allerdings das Abitur braucht** he wants to go to university but for that he needs the Abitur; *s. auch* **wobei NB**

Wrack [vrak] **das; ~[e]s, ~s** *od.* **~e** wreck; *(fig.: Mensch)* [physical] wreck; **ein seelisches/nervöses ~** *(fig.)* a mental/nervous wreck

wrang [vraŋ] *1. und 3. Pers. Sg. Prät. v.* **wringen**

Wrasen ['vra:zn̩] **der; ~s, ~** *(nordd.)* steam

wringen ['vrıŋən] *unr. tr. V. (bes. nordd.)* wring

WS *Abk.* **Wintersemester**

WSV *Abk.* **Winterschlußverkauf**

WSW *Abk.* **Westsüdwest[en]** WSW

Wucher ['vu:xɐ] **der; ~s** profiteering; *(beim Verleihen von Geld)* usury; **18 Prozent Zinsen: das ist ja ~!** 18 per cent interest: that's extortionate!; **[mit etw.] ~ treiben** profiteer [on sth.]; *(beim Verleihen von Geld)* charge an extortionate rate/extortionate rates of interest [on sth.]

Wụcher·blume die chrysanthemum

Wụcherer der; ~s, ~: profiteer; *(beim Verleihen von Geld)* usurer

wụchern *itr. V.* **a)** *auch mit sein (stark wachsen)* ⟨*plants, weeds, etc.*⟩ proliferate, run wild; *(fig.)* be rampant; **eine ~de Geschwulst** a cancerous tumour; **krebsartig ~** *(fig.)* grow like a cancer; **eine ~de Phantasie** *(fig.)* an imagination that runs wild; **b)** *(Wucher treiben)* **[mit etw.] ~:** profiteer [on sth.]; *(beim Verleihen von Geld)* lend [sth.] at extortionate interest rates

Wụcher·preis der extortionate price

Wụcherung die; ~, ~en growth

Wụcher·zins der; *meist Pl.* extortionate rate of interest

wuchs [vu:ks] *1. u. 3. Pers. Sg. Prät. v.* **wachsen**

Wụchs der; ~es a) *(Wachstum)* growth; **b)** *(Gestalt)* stature; **klein/groß von ~ sein** ⟨*person*⟩ be small/tall in stature

Wucht [vʊxt] **die; ~ a)** force; *(von Schlägen)* power; weight; **mit voller ~:** with full force; **mit voller ~ zuschlagen** hit with all one's might; **b)** *in* **eine ~ sein** *(salopp)* be absolutely fantastic *(coll.)*; **c)** *(bes. ostmd.: Schläge)* beating; *(als Strafe für Kind)* hiding *(coll.)*; beating

wụchten *tr. V.* heave

wụchtig 1. *Adj.* **a)** *(voller Wucht)* powerful; mighty; **b)** *(schwer, massig)* massive. **2.** *adv.* powerfully

Wụ̈hl·arbeit die *(fig.)* subversive activities *pl.*; subversion

wühlen ['vy:lən] **1.** *itr. V.* **a)** *(graben)* dig; *(mit der Schnauze, dem Schnabel)* root **(nach** for); ⟨*mole*⟩ tunnel, burrow; **er wühlte in ihren Locken** he tousled her hair; **b)** *(ugs.: suchen)* rummage [around] **(nach** for); **c)** *(fig.: Wühlarbeit leisten)* engage in subversive activities *or* subversion **(gegen** against); **d)** *(ugs.: schwer arbeiten)* graft *(Brit. sl.)*; slave away. **2.** *tr. V.* burrow; tunnel out ⟨*burrow*⟩. **3.** *refl. V.* **sich in etw.** *(Akk.)***/durch etw. ~:** burrow into/through sth.; **die Autos wühlten sich durch den Schlamm** the cars churned their way through the mud

Wụ̈hler der; ~s, ~ a) *(Zool.)* cricetine; **b)** *(fig.: Subversiver)* subversive; **c)** *(ugs.: fleißig Arbeitender)* grafter *(Brit. sl.)*

Wụ̈hl-: ~maus die one of the Microtinae *(the voles and lemmings)*; *(Kleine ~maus)* European pine vole; *(Schermaus)* European water vole; **~tisch der** *(ugs.)* bargain counter

Wulst [vʊlst] **der; ~[e]s, Wülste** ['vʏlstə] *od.* **~e a)** bulge; *(Fett~)* roll of fat; *(an einer Flasche, einem Reifen)* bead; **b)** *(Heraldik)* wreath; **c)** *(Archit.)* torus

wụlstig *Adj.* bulging; thick ⟨*lips*⟩

wumm [vʊm] *Interj.* boom

wummern ['vʊmɐn] *itr. V.* ⟨*machine, engine*⟩ hum; **mit den Fäusten gegen etw. ~:** drum one's fists against sth.

wund [vʊnt] *Adj.* sore; **sich ~ laufen** walk until one's feet are sore; **ich habe mir die Finger ~ geschrieben** *(ugs.)* I've worn my fingers to the bone with all that writing; *s. auch* **Fuß b; Punkt d; reiben 1 a**

Wụnd-: ~arzt der *(hist.)* surgeon; **~brand der;** *o. Pl. (Med.)* gangrene

Wụnde die; ~, ~n wound; **alte ~n wieder**

aufreißen *(fig.)* open up old wounds; **der Krieg hat dem Land tiefe ~n geschlagen** *(fig.)* the war has left deep scars on the country; *s. auch* **Salz**

wụnder *Adv. (ugs.)* **er denkt, er sei ~ wer** he thinks he's really something; **sie glaubt, sie sei ~ wie klug** she thinks she's ever so *or* oh so clever *(coll.)*; **er glaubt, ~ was geleistet zu haben** he thinks he's achieved something fantastic *(coll.)*; **ich dachte, ~ was es da alles zu sehen gibt** I thought there would be all sorts of fantastic things to see; **er bildet sich ~ was darauf ein** he's terribly pleased with himself about it *(coll.)*

Wụnder das; ~s, ~ a) miracle; **~ tun** work *or* perform miracles; **~ wirken** *(fig. ugs.)* work wonders; **o ~!** wonders will never cease!; **ein/kein ~ sein** *(ugs.)* be a/no wonder; **was ~, wenn ...?** small *or* no wonder that ...; **er wird sein blaues ~ erleben** *(ugs.)* he's in for a nasty shock; **b)** *(etw. Außergewöhnliches, Erstaunliches)* wonder; **ein ~ an ...** *(Dat.)* a miracle of ...; **ein technisches ~:** a technological marvel

wụnderbar 1. *Adj.* **a)** *(übernatürlich erscheinend)* miraculous; **das grenzt ans Wunderbare** it's bordering on the miraculous; **auf ~e Weise** miraculously; **b)** *(sehr schön, herrlich)* wonderful; marvellous. **2.** *adv.* *(sehr schön, herrlich)* wonderfully; marvellously; **b)** *(ugs.: sehr)* wonderfully

wụnder-, Wụnder-: ~ding das; *Pl.* **~dinge** amazing thing; *(ugs.: Gegenstand)* wonder; **~doktor der** *(spött.)* miracle-working doctor; **~glaube der** belief in miracles; **~gläubig** *Adj.* ⟨*person*⟩ who believes in miracles; **~gläubig sein** believe in miracles; **~heiler der** faith-healer; **~heilung die** miraculous cure; **~hübsch 1.** *Adj.* wonderfully pretty; **2.** *adv.* quite beautifully; **~kerze die** sparkler; **~kind das** child prodigy; **~knabe der** boy prodigy; **~lampe die** magic lamp; **~land das** wonderland

wụnderlich 1. *Adj.* strange; odd. **2.** *adv.* strangely; oddly

Wụnderlichkeit die; ~, ~en a) *o. Pl.* strangeness; oddness; **b)** *(etwas Wunderliches)* oddity

Wụnder·mittel das miracle cure **(gegen** for)

wụndern 1. *tr. V.* surprise; **mich wundert** *od.* **es wundert mich, daß ...:** I'm surprised that ...; **es würde** *od.* **sollte mich [nicht] ~, wenn ...:** I should [not] be surprised *or* it would [not] surprise me if ... **2.** *refl. V.* **sich über jmdn./etw. ~:** be surprised at sb./sth.; **du wirst dich [noch mal] ~** *(ugs.)* you're in for a shock; you've got a surprise in store; **ich muß mich doch sehr über dich ~:** I really am surprised at you

wụnder|nehmen *unr. tr. V. (geh.)* **etw. nimmt jmdn. wunder** sth. surprises sb.

wụnders *Adv. (ugs.) s.* **wunder**

wụndersam *(geh.)* **1.** *Adj.* strange. **2.** *adv.* **ihr wurde ~ zumute** she had a strange feeling

wụnder-, Wụnder- : ~schön 1. *Adj.* simply beautiful; *(herrlich)* simply wonderful; **2.** *adv.* quite beautifully; *(einwandfrei)* perfectly; **~tat die** miracle; **~täter der** miracle-worker; **~tätig** *Adj.* miraculous; **~tier das** strange and wonderful animal; **~tüte die** surprise packet; **~voll 1.** *Adj.* wonderful; marvellous; **2.** *adv.* wonderfully; marvellously; **~waffe die** superweapon; **~welt die** wonderworld; **~werk das** marvel

wụnd-, Wụnd-: ~fieber das *(Med.)* traumatic fever; wound fever; **~infektion die** *(Med.)* wound infection; **~|liegen** *unr. refl. V.* get bedsores **(an + *Dat.* on)**; **sich** *(Dat.)* **den Rücken ~liegen** get bedsores on one's back; **~mal das;** *Pl.* **~male** *(bes. Rel.)* scar; **die ~male Christi** Christ's stigmata; **~pflaster das** sticking-plaster; **~rand der;** *meist Pl. (Med.)* edge of a/the wound; **~rose die** *(Med.)* St Anthony's fire; erysipelas *(Med.)*; **~sein das** soreness; **~starrkrampf der** *(Med.)* tetanus

Wunsch [vʊnʃ] **der; ~[e]s, Wünsche** ['vʏnʃə] **a)** wish **(nach** to have); *(Hoffen, Sehnen)* desire **(nach** for); **sich** *(Dat.)* **einen ~ erfüllen/versagen** grant/deny oneself something one wants; **haben Sie [sonst] noch einen ~?** will there be anything else?; **jmds. ~ und Wille sein** be something sb. most earnestly desires; **auf jmds. ~:** at sb.'s wish; **auf allgemeinen ~ [hin]** in response to popular demand; **alles geht** *od.* **läuft nach ~:** everything's going as we want/he wants *etc.*; **dein ~ ist mir Befehl** *(scherzh.)* your wish is my command; **der ~ ist der Vater des Gedankens** *(scherzh.)* the wish is father to the thought; *s. auch* **fromm c; b)** *Pl.* *(zu bestimmten Anlässen)* wishes; **mit den besten/herzlichsten Wünschen** with best/warmest wishes; **beste Wünsche zum Geburtstag** many happy returns of the day

wụ̈nschbar *Adj. (bes. schweiz.)* desirable

Wụnsch-: ~bild das desired ideal; **~denken das** wishful thinking

Wünschel- ['vʏnʃl̩-]: **~rute die** divining rod; **~rutengänger der** diviner

wünschen ['vʏnʃn̩] *tr. V.* **a) sich** *(Dat.)* **etw. ~:** want sth.; *(im stillen)* wish for sth.; **jmdm. Erfolg/nichts Gutes/den Tod ~:** wish sb. success/no good/wish sb. dead; **er wünschte sich** *(Dat.)* **ein Rad zum Geburtstag** he asked for a cycle for his birthday; **du darfst dir [von mir] etwas ~:** you can have a present [from me] - what would you like?; **sich** *(Dat.)* **jmdn. als** *od.* **zum Freund ~:** want to have sb. as a friend; **alles, was du dir nur ~ kannst** everything you could wish for; **er war so, wie man sich** *(Dat.)* **einen Lehrer wünscht** he was just as one would want a teacher to be; **was wünschst du dir?** what would you like?; **ich wünschte, du wärest hier** I wish you were here; **jmdn. weit fort ~:** wish sb. far away; **ich wünschte mich auf eine einsame Insel** I wished I were on a desert island; **b)** *(in formelhaften Wünschen)* wish; **jmdm. alles Gute/frohe Ostern ~:** wish sb. all the best/a happy Easter; **jmdm. gute Nacht ~:** wish *or* bid sb. good night; **sie wünschte ihm gute Besserung** she said she hoped he would soon get better; **c)** *auch itr. V. (begehren)* want; **was ~ Sie?, Sie ~?** *(von einem Bediensteten gesagt)* yes, madam/sir?; *(von einem Kellner gesagt)* what would you like?; *(von einem Verkäufer gesagt)* can I help you?; **er wünscht, daß du gehst** he wants you to go; **ganz, wie Sie ~:** just as you like; **solange Sie es ~:** as long as you wish *or* like; **die gewünschte Auskunft** the information asked for; **ich wünsche das nicht** I do not wish it; **dein Chef wünscht dich zu sprechen** your boss would like to speak to you; **etw. läßt [viel]/läßt nichts zu ~ übrig** sth. leaves a great deal/nothing to be desired; **es verlief alles wie gewünscht** everything went as we/he *etc.* had wanted

wụ̈nschens·wert *Adj.* desirable

wụnsch-, Wụnsch-: ~form die *(Sprachw.) s.* **Optativ; ~gegner der** *(bes. Sport)* ideal opponent; **~gemäß 1.** *Adv.* as desired; *(einer Bitte gemäß)* as requested; **2.** *adj.; nicht präd.* **die ~gemäße Ausführung eines Auftrags** the performance of a task as desired/requested; **~kind das** wanted child; **~konzert das** request concert; *(im Rundfunk)* request programme; **~los 1.** *Adj.* [perfectly] contented; perfect ⟨*happiness*⟩; **2.** *adv.* **~los glücklich sein** be perfectly contented; **~satz der** *(Sprachw.)* optative sentence; **~traum der** wishful dream; *(unrealistisch)* pipe-dream; **~vorstellung die** wishful notion; **~zettel der** list of things one would like; *(zum Geburtstag o. ä.)* list of presents one would like

wupp [vʊp], **wụpp·dich, wụpps** *Interj. (ugs.)* woomph *(coll.)*

wurde ['vʊrdə] *1. u. 3. Pers. Sg. Prät. v.* **werden**

würde ['vʏrdə] *1. u. 3. Pers. Sg. Konjunktiv II v.* **werden**

Wụ̈rde die; ~, ~n a) *o. Pl.* dignity; **seine ~ bewahren** preserve one's dignity; **sich in seiner ~ verletzt fühlen** feel that one's dignity has been affronted; **etw. mit ~ tragen** bear sth. with dignity; *(scherzh.)* bear up well in spite of sth.; **unter jmds. ~ sein** be beneath sb.'s dignity; **unter aller ~ sein** be beneath contempt; **b)** *(Rang)* rank; *(Amt)* office; *(Titel)* title; *(Auszeichnung)* honour; **die ~ eines Professors** the title of professor; **zu höchsten ~n gelangen** attain high office

wụ̈rde·los 1. *Adj.* undignified; *(schimpflich)* disgraceful. **2.** *adv.* in an undignified way; *(schimpflich)* disgracefully

Wụ̈rdelosigkeit die; ~ *s.* **würdelos:** lack of dignity; disgracefulness

Wụ̈rden·träger der dignitary

wụ̈rde·voll 1. *Adj.* dignified. **2.** *adv.* with dignity

wụ̈rdig 1. *Adj.* **a)** *(würdevoll)* dignified; **b)** *(wert)* worthy; suitable ⟨*occasion*⟩; **jmds./einer Sache [nicht] ~ sein** [not] be worthy of sb./sth.; **sich jmds. /einer Sache [nicht] ~ erweisen** *od.* **zeigen** prove oneself [not] worthy of sb./sth. **2.** *adv.* **a)** *(würdevoll)* with dignity; ⟨*dressed*⟩ in a dignified manner; **b)** *(angemessen)* worthily; ⟨*celebrate*⟩ in a/the appropriate manner; **jmdn. ~ zu vertreten wissen** make a worthy deputy for sb.

wụ̈rdigen *tr. V.* **a)** *(anerkennen, beachten)* recognize; *(schätzen)* appreciate; *(lobend hervorheben)* acknowledge; **etw. zu ~ wissen** appreciate sth.; **b)** *(für wert halten)* **jmdn. einer Sache** *(Gen.)* **~:** deem sb. worthy of sth.; **jmdn. keines Blickes/keiner Antwort ~:** not deign to look at/answer sb.

Wụ̈rdigkeit die; ~ a) *(Würde)* dignity; **b)** *(Wert)* worth

Wụ̈rdigung die; ~, ~en *s.* **würdigen a:** recognition; appreciation; acknowledgement; **in ~ einer Sache** *(Gen.)* in recognition of sth.

Wurf [vʊrf] **der; ~[e]s, Würfe** ['vʏrfə] **a)** throw; *(beim Baseball)* pitch; *(beim Kegeln)* bowl; *(gezielt aufs Tor)* shot; **b)** *o. Pl. (das Werfen)* throwing/pitching/bowling; **zum ~ ausholen** draw back one's arm ready to throw; **beim ~:** when throwing/pitching/bowling; **c)** *(Zool.)* litter; **d)** *(gelungenes Werk)* successful work; success; **mit dieser Erfindung ist ihm ein großer ~ gelungen** this invention has been a great success for him

Wụrf·bahn die trajectory

Würfel ['vʏrfl] **der; ~s, ~ a)** *(auch Math.)* cube; **Gemüse/Fleisch in ~ schneiden** dice vegetables/meat; **b)** *(Spiel~)* dice; die *(formal)*; **die ~ sind gefallen** *(fig.)* the die is cast

Wụ̈rfel·becher der dice-cup

Wụ̈rfel·muster das check pattern

wụ̈rfeln 1. *itr. V.* throw the dice; *(mit Würfeln spielen)* play dice; **du bist mit Würfeln dran** it's your turn to throw; **hast du schon gewürfelt?** have you already thrown *or* had your throw?; **um etw. ~:** play dice for sth.; **darum ~, wer anfangen soll** throw a/the dice to see who should start. **2.** *tr. V.* **a)** throw; **b)** *(in Würfel schneiden)* dice ⟨*vegetables, meat*⟩

Wụ̈rfel-: ~spiel das a) *(Glücksspiel)* dice; *(einzelne Partie)* game of dice; **b)** *(Brettspiel)* dice game; **~zucker der;** *o. Pl.* cube sugar; lump sugar

Wụrf-: ~geschoß das missile; **~kreis der** *(Sport)* throwing-circle; **~scheibe die** discus; **~sendung die** *s.* **Postwurfsendung; ~speer der, ~spieß der** *(hist.)* spear; **~taube die** *(Schießsport)* clay pigeon; **~tauben·schießen das** *(Schießsport)* clay-pigeon shooting *no art.*

Würge-: ~engel der *(bes. christl. Rel.)* Angel of Death; **~griff der** *(auch fig.)* stranglehold; **~mal das**; *Pl.* **~male** *od.* **~mäler** strangle *or* strangulation mark

würgen ['vʏrgn̩] **1.** *tr. V.* **a)** strangle; throttle; *(fig.)* ‹*tie, collar*› strangle; **~de Angst** *(fig.)* choking fear; **b)** *(ugs.: zwängen)* **etw. in etw.** *(Akk.)* **~**: stuff sth. into sth. **2.** *itr. V.* **a)** *(Brechreiz haben)* retch; **b)** *(mühsam schlucken)* **an etw.** *(Dat.)* **~**: have to force sth. down; *s. auch* [2]**hängen 1 d**

Würger der; ~s, ~ a) strangler; **b)** *(Zool.)* shrike

[1]**Wurm** [vʊrm] **der; ~[e]s, Würmer** ['vʏrmɐ] worm; *(Made)* maggot; **von Würmern befallen sein** have worms/be maggoty; **da ist** *od.* **sitzt der ~ drin** *(fig. ugs.)* there's something wrong there; **jmdm. die Würmer aus der Nase ziehen** *(fig. ugs.)* get sb. to spill the beans *(fig. sl.)*; **den ~** *od.* **Würmer baden** *(ugs. scherzh.)* be fishing

[2]**Wurm das; ~[e]s, Würmer** *(fam.)* little mite

wurmen *tr., auch itr. V. (ugs.)* **jmdn. ~**: rankle with sb.; **so was wurmt [einen] schon** that sort of thing rankles

Wurm·fort·satz der *(Anat.)* appendix

wurmig *Adj.*, **wurm·stichig** *Adj.* worm-eaten; *(madig)* maggoty

Wurscht [vʊrʃt] *(ugs.)* *in* **jmdm. ist jmd./etw. ~**: sb. doesn't care about sb./sth.; **das ist mir vollkommen** *od.* **völlig ~**: I couldn't care less about that; **ach, mir ist alles ~!** oh, what do I care!

wurscht·egal *Adj. (ugs.) s.* **wurstegal**

Wurst [vʊrst] **die; ~, Würste** ['vʏrstə] **a)** sausage; **es geht um die ~** *(fig. ugs.)* the crunch has come; **mit der Wurst nach der Speckseite** *od.* **dem Schinken werfen** *(fig. ugs.)* use a sprat to catch a mackerel *(fig. coll.)*; **b)** *(wurstähnliches Gebilde)* roll; **den Teig zu einer ~ formen** roll the dough into a sausage shape; **eine ~ machen** *(fam.)* do a big one *(child lang.)*; **c)** *(ugs.) s.* **Wurscht**

Wurst·brot das open sausage sandwich; *(mit Streichwurst)* open meat-spread sandwich; *(zusammengeklappt)* sausage/meat-spread sandwich

Würstchen ['vʏrstçən] **das; ~s, ~ a)** [small] sausage; **Frankfurter/Wiener ~**: frankfurter/wienerwurst; **heiße ~**: hot sausages; **b)** *(ugs., oft abwertend)* nobody; *(hilfloser Mensch)* poor soul; **ein armes ~**: a poor soul; **c) [ein] ~ machen** *(Kinderspr.)* do [poo]poos *(child lang.)*

Würstchen·bude die sausage-stand

wurst·egal *Adj. (ugs.) in* **~ sein** not matter in the slightest; **das ist mir ~**: I couldn't care less [about that]

Wurstel ['vʊrstl̩] **der; ~s, ~** *(bayr., österr.)* clown

Würstel ['vʏrstl̩] **das; ~s, ~** *(bes. österr.)* sausage

Wurstelei die; ~, ~en *(ugs. abwertend)* pottering about *no pl.*

wursteln *itr. V. (ugs.)* **1.** potter; **an etw.** *(Dat.)* **~**: potter about with sth. **2.** *refl. V.* **sich durchs Leben ~**: muddle [along] through life

Wurst-: ~finger der; *meist Pl.* podgy finger; **~haut die** sausage-skin

wurstig *(ugs.)* **1.** *Adj.* couldn't-care-less *attrib.* ‹*attitude, behaviour, reply*›; **er ist ein ~er Typ** *od.* **ist ~**: he couldn't care less about anything. **2.** *adv.* in a couldn't-care-less way

Wurstigkeit die; ~ *(ugs.)* couldn't-care-less attitude

Wurst-: ~salat der *piquant salad with pieces of sausage, onion rings, boiled eggs and/or cheese*; **~suppe die** sausage soup; **~waren** *Pl.* sausages; **~zipfel der** end of a/the sausage

württembergisch ['vʏrtəmbɛrgɪʃ] *Adj.* of/from Württemberg; *s. auch* **badisch**

Würze ['vʏrtsə] **die; ~, ~n a)** *(Gewürz)* spice; seasoning; **b)** *(Aroma)* aroma; *(fig.)* spice; *s. auch* **Kürze c**

Wurzel ['vʊrtsl̩] **die; ~, ~n a)** *(auch fig.)* root; **~[n] fassen** take root; **~n schlagen** take root; *(fig.: heimisch werden)* put down roots; **ich stehe hier schon so lange, daß ich bald ~n schlage** *(scherzh.)* I've been standing here so long I'll soon grow roots; **seine ~n in etw.** *(Dat.)* **haben** *(fig.)* have its roots in sth.; **die ~ allen Übels** *(fig.)* the root of all evil; **das Übel an der ~ fassen** *od.* **packen** *(fig.)* strike at the root of the problem; **etw. mit der ~ ausrotten** *(fig.)* eradicate sth. completely; **b)** *(Math.)* root; **~n ziehen** calculate roots; **aus einer Zahl die ~ ziehen** extract the [square] root of a number; **die dritte ~ aus** *od.* **von 8** the cube root of 8; **c)** *(bes. nordd.)* carrot; **d)** *(der Hand)* wrist; *(des Fußes)* ankle; *(eines Nagels, der Nase)* root; **e)** *(Sprachw.)* root

Wurzel-: ~ballen der root ball; **~behandlung die** *(Zahnmed.)* root treatment; **~bürste die** stiff brush; *(zum Scheuern)* [stiff] scrubbing-brush *or (Amer.)* scrub-brush

Würzelchen ['vʏrtsl̩çən] **das; ~s, ~**: rootlet

Wurzel·haut·entzündung die *(Med.)* periodontitis *no indef. art.*

wurzelig *Adj.* full of roots *postpos.*

Wurzel·knolle die tuber

wurzel·los *Adj.* without roots *postpos.*; *(auch fig.)* rootless

Wurzel·losig·keit die; ~: lack of roots; *(fig.)* rootlessness

wurzeln *itr. V.* **a)** *(Wurzeln schlagen)* take root; **flach ~**: have shallow roots; **das Mißtrauen wurzelt tief in ihm** *(fig.)* his mistrust is deep-rooted; **b) in etw.** *(Dat.)* **~** *(seinen Ursprung haben in)* be rooted in sth.; *(verursacht sein durch)* have its roots in sth.

Wurzel-: ~sproß der *(Bot.)* root sucker; **~stock der**; *Pl.* **~stöcke a)** *(Bot.)* rootstock; rhizome; **b)** *(eines Baumes)* stump and roots *pl.*; **~werk das**; *o. Pl.* roots *pl.*

würzen ['vʏrtsn̩] *tr. V.* season; *(fig.)* spice; **Humor würzt das Leben** *(fig.)* humour is the spice of life

würzig 1. *Adj.* tasty; full-flavoured ‹*beer, wine*›; aromatic ‹*fragrance, smell, tobacco*›; tangy ‹*air*›; *(scharf)* spicy. **2.** *adv.* **sie kocht nicht ~ genug** she doesn't use enough seasoning

Würzigkeit die; ~ *s.* **würzig 1**: tastiness; full flavour; aromatic fragrance; tanginess; spiciness

wusch [vu:ʃ] *1. u. 3. Pers. Sg. Prät. v.* **waschen**

Wuschel·haar das *(ugs.)* frizzy *or* fuzzy hair

wuschelig *Adj. (ugs.)* frizzy; fuzzy

Wuschel·kopf der *(ugs.)* **a)** *(Haar)* shock *or* mop of frizzy *or* fuzzy hair; **b)** *(Mensch)* frizzy-haired *or* fuzzy-haired man/girl *etc.*; man/girl *etc.* with frizzy *or* fuzzy hair

wuscheln ['vʊʃl̩n] *tr., itr. V.* tousle; **in jmds. Haar ~**: tousle sb.'s hair

wuselig *Adj. (bes. südd., md.)* busy; bustling

wuseln ['vu:zl̩n] *itr. V. (bes. südd., md.)* **a)** *mit sein (sich flink bewegen)* scurry; **b)** *(sich beschäftigen)* bustle around

wußte ['vʊstə] *1. und 3. Pers. Sg. Prät. v.* **wissen**

wüßte ['vʏstə] *1. und 3. Pers. Sg. Konjunktiv II v.* **wissen**

Wust [vu:st] **der; ~[e]s** *(abwertend)* jumble; *(fig.)* welter; **ein ~ von Daten/Vorschriften** a mass of data/regulations

wüst [vy:st] **1.** *Adj.* **a)** *(öde)* desolate; **b)** *(unordentlich)* chaotic; tangled, tousled ‹*hair, beard, etc.*›; wild ‹*appearance*›; **ein ~es Durcheinander herrschte dort** it was utter chaos *or* an utter shambles there; **c)** *(abwertend: wild, ungezügelt)* wild; furious ‹*fight, shoot-out*›; **d)** *(abwertend: unanständig)* rude; coarse ‹*oath, abuse*›; **e)** *(abwertend: furchtbar, abscheulich)* terrible; foul *(sl.)*, terrible *(coll.)* ‹*weather*›. **2.** *adv.* **a)** *(unordentlich)* chaotically; **das Haar hing ihr ~ ins Gesicht** her hair straggled down over her face; **b)** *(abwertend: wild, ungezügelt)* wildly; **sie haben's ~ getrieben** they had a wild time; **c)** *(abwertend: unanständig)* ‹*swear, abuse sb.*› coarsely; **d)** *(abwertend: furchtbar, abscheulich)* terribly; **sie haben ihn ~ zugerichtet** they really knocked him about

Wüste die; ~, ~n desert; *(Eis~)* waste; *(fig.)* wasteland; **jmdn. in die ~ schicken** *(ugs.)* give sb. the push *(coll.)*

wüsten *itr. V.* **mit etw. ~**: squander sth.

Wüstenei die; ~, ~en a) *(Einöde)* wasteland; **b)** *(scherzh.: Unordnung)* shambles *sing.*; chaos *no indef. art.*

Wüsten-: ~fuchs der fennec; **~klima das** desert climate; **~sand der** desert sand[s *pl.*]; **~schiff das** *(dichter.)* ship of the desert

Wüstling der; ~s, ~e *(abwertend)* lecher; debauchee

Wut [vu:t] **die; ~**: rage; fury; **auf jmdn. eine ~ haben** be furious with sb.; **seine ~ an jmdm. auslassen** vent one's rage *or* fury on sb.; **in ~ geraten** *od.* **kommen** get furious; **jmdn. in ~ bringen** infuriate sb.; **eine ~ im Bauch haben** *(ugs.)* be livid *(Brit. coll.)*

Wut-: ~an·fall der fit of rage; **~ausbruch der** outburst of rage *or* fury

wüten ['vy:tn̩] *itr. V. (auch fig.)* rage; *(zerstören)* wreak havoc

wütend 1. *Adj.* **a)** furious; angry ‹*voice, mob*›; **auf** *od.* **über jmdn. ~ sein** be furious with sb.; **er war ~ auf sie, weil sie ihn warten ließ** he was furious with her for keeping him waiting; **über etw.** *(Akk.)* **~ sein** be furious about sth.; **b)** *(sehr groß, heftig)* raging ‹*pain, hatred, etc.*›; fierce ‹*proponent, defender*›. **2.** *adv.* **a)** furiously; in a fury; **b)** *(heftig)* furiously

wut·entbrannt 1. *Adj.* infuriated; furious. **2.** *adv.* in a fury

Wüterich ['vy:tərɪç] **der; ~s, ~e** *(abwertend)* hot-tempered person; *(Gewaltmensch)* brute

wut·schnaubend 1. *Adj.* snorting with rage *pred.* **2.** *adv.* snorting with rage

Wutz [vʊts] **die; ~, ~en** *od.* **der; ~en, ~en** *(bes. westmd.)* pig

Wz *Abk.* **Warenzeichen** TM; ®

X

[1]**x, X** [ɪks] **das; ~, ~**: x, X; **Herr/die Stadt X** Mr X/the town of X; **jmdm. ein X für ein U vormachen** *(fig.)* dupe sb.; **er läßt sich** *(Dat.)* **kein X für ein U vormachen** you can't fool him; he's not easily fooled; *s. auch* **a, A**

[2]**x** *unbest. Zahlwort (ugs.)* umpteen *(coll.)*

x-Achse die *(Math.)* x-axis

Xanthippe [ksan'tɪpə] **die; ~, ~n** *(abwertend)* harridan

X-Beine *Pl.* knock-knees; ~ **haben** have knock-knees; be knock-kneed
x-beinig *Adj.* knock-kneed
x-beliebig *Adj. (ugs.)* **irgendein ~er/irgendeine ~e/irgendein ~es** any old *(coll. attrib.)*; **jeder ~e Ort** any old place *(coll.)*; **der Ort ist ~:** any old place will do *(coll.)*; **denk dir eine ~e Zahl** think of a number, any old number *(coll.)*; **irgendwelche ~en Leute** just anybody; **ich tue das nicht für jeden ~en** I don't do it for just anybody
X-Chromosom das *(Biol.)* X-chromosome
x-fach 1. *Vervielfältigungsz.* **die ~e Menge** *(Math.)* x times the amount; *(ugs.)* umpteen times the amount *(coll.)*. **2.** *adv. (ugs.)* ~ **erprobt sein** have been tested umpteen times *(coll.) or* any number of times
X-fache das; ~n: das ~ einer Zahl *(Math.)* X times a number; **das ~ seines normalen Einkommens** *(ugs.)* umpteen times his normal income *(coll.)*
X-Haken der picture-hook
x-mal *Adv. (ugs.)* umpteen times *(coll.)*; any number of times
X-Strahlen *Pl. (Physik)* X-rays
x-t... *Ordinalz.* **a)** *(Math.)* xth; **b)** *(ugs.)* umpteenth *(coll.)*
x-te·mal *Adv. in* **das ~** *(ugs.) (beim x-tenmal)* the umpteenth time *(coll.)*; *(zum x-tenmal)* for the umpteenth time *(coll.)*
x-ten·mal *Adv. in* **zum ~** *(ugs.)* for the umpteenth time *(coll.)*; **beim ~** *(ugs.)* the umpteenth time *(coll.)*
Xylophon [ksylo'fo:n] **das; ~s, ~e** xylophone

Y

y, Y ['ʏpsilɔn] **das; ~, ~:** y, Y; *s. auch* **a, A**
y-Achse die *(Math.)* y-axis
Yacht *s.* **Jacht**
Yankee ['jɛnki] **der; ~s, ~s** *(oft abwertend)* Yankee *(Brit. coll.)*; Yank *(Brit. coll.)*
Y-Chromosom das *(Biol.)* Y-chromosome
Yen [jɛn] **der; ~[s] ~[s]** yen
Yeti ['je:ti] **der; ~s, ~s** yeti
Yoga *s.* **Joga**
Yogi[n] *s.* **Jogi[n]**
Youngster ['jʌŋstə] **der; ~s, ~[s]** *(Sport)* youngster
Yo-Yo [jo'jo: *od.* 'jo:'jo:] **das; ~s, ~s** yo-yo
Ypsilon ['ʏpsilɔn] **das; ~[s], ~s** y, Y; *(im griechischen Alphabet)* upsilon
Ysop ['i:zɔp] **der; ~s, ~e** hyssop
Yucca ['jʊka] **die; ~, ~s** yucca

Z

z, Z [tsɛt] **das; ~, ~:** z, Z; *s. auch* **a, A**
zach [tsax] *Adj. (bes. ostmd.)* timid
zack [tsak] *Interj. (salopp)* ~! ~! *(beeil dich)* get a move on! *(coll.)*; make it snappy! *(coll.)*; **bei ihm muß alles ~, ~ gehen** he likes things done at the double; **und ~, ~ war's fertig** and in a flash it was done
Zack *in* **auf ~ sein** *(ugs.) (tüchtig sein)* be on the ball *(coll.) or* one's toes; *(funktionieren)* be in good shape; **jmdn./etw. auf ~ bringen** *(ugs.)* knock sb./sth. into shape *(coll.)*
Zacke die; ~, ~n point; *(eines Bergkamms, eines Diagramms)* peak; *(einer Säge, eines Kamms)* tooth; *(einer Gabel, Harke)* prong
zacken *tr. V.* serrate; pink ⟨*cloth, seam, hem*⟩; **mit gezacktem Rand** with a serrated edge
Zacken der; ~s, ~ a) *s.* **Zacke; b)** *(fig.)* **sich** *(Dat.)* **keinen ~ aus der Krone brechen** *(ugs.)* not lose face; **dir bricht kein ~ aus der Krone, wenn du mithilfst!** *(ugs.)* it wouldn't hurt you to help out; **einen [kleinen] ~ [in der Krone] haben** *(ugs.)* be [a bit] tipsy
zackig 1. *Adj.* **a)** *(gezackt)* jagged; *(mit kleinen, regelmäßigen Zacken)* serrated; **b)** *(schneidig)* dashing; smart; rousing ⟨*music*⟩; brisk ⟨*orders, tempo*⟩; lively ⟨*organization*⟩. **2.** *adv.* **a)** *(gezackt)* jaggedly; **b)** *(schneidig)* smartly; ⟨*play music*⟩ rousingly; **..., aber mach ein bißchen ~!** ..., and make it snappy! *(coll.)*
zag [tsa:k] *(geh.)* **1.** *Adj.* timid; *(fig.)* tentative ⟨*hope*⟩. **2.** *adv.* timidly; *(fig.)* tentatively
zagen *itr.V. (geh.)* hesitate (**vor** + *Dat.* in the face of); **zögern und ~:** keep hesitating; **~d** hesitant[ly]
zaghaft 1. *Adj.* timid; *(zögernd)* hesitant; tentative. **2.** *adv.* timidly; *(zögernd)* hesitantly; tentatively
Zaghaftigkeit die; ~: timidity; *(Zögern)* hesitancy
Zagheit die; ~ *(geh.)* timidity
zäh [tsɛ:] **1.** *Adj.* **a)** *(fest)* tough; heavy ⟨*dough, soil*⟩; *(dickflüssig)* glutinous; viscous ⟨*oil*⟩; **b)** *(schleppend)* sluggish, dragging ⟨*conversation*⟩; **c)** *(widerstandsfähig)* tough ⟨*person*⟩; **d)** *(beharrlich)* tenacious; tough ⟨*negotiations*⟩; dogged ⟨*resistance*⟩; **mit ~em Fleiß** by dint of sheer hard work. **2.** *adv.* **a)** *(schleppend)* sluggishly; **b)** *(beharrlich)* tenaciously; ⟨*resist*⟩ doggedly
Zäheit die; ~ a) *(Festigkeit)* toughness; *(des Teigs, Bodens)* heaviness; *(Dickflüssigkeit)* glutinousness; *(von Öl)* viscosity; **b)** *(schleppendes Tempo)* sluggishness; **c)** *(Widerstandsfähigkeit)* toughness; *(der Konstitution)* robustness; **d)** *(Beharrlichkeit)* tenacity; *(des Widerstands)* doggedness
zäh·flüssig *Adj.* glutinous; viscous ⟨*oil*⟩; thick ⟨*soup*⟩; heavy ⟨*dough*⟩; *(fig.: langsam)* slow-moving ⟨*traffic*⟩; **die Verhandlungen waren ~** *(fig.)* the negotiations were hard going
Zäh·flüssigkeit die; *o. Pl.* glutinousness; *(von Öl)* viscosity; *(von Soße, Suppe)* thickness
Zähigkeit die; ~ a) *(Widerstandsfähigkeit)* toughness; **b)** *(Beharrlichkeit)* tenacity; **mit ~:** tenaciously
Zahl ['tsa:l] **die; ~, ~en** number; *(Ziffer)* numeral; *(Zahlenangabe, Geldmenge)* figure; **er nannte keine ~en** he did not give any figures; **in die/aus den roten ~en kommen** go into/get out of the red; **in den roten/schwarzen ~en** in the red/black; **mit ~en umgehen können** be good with figures; **[fünf/sieben] an der ~:** [five/seven] in number; **in großer ~:** in great numbers; **Leiden ohne** *od. (veralt.)* **sonder ~:** suffering beyond measure
Zahl·adjektiv das numeral adjective
zahlbar *Adj. (Kaufmannsspr.)* payable
zählbar *Adj.* countable
zählebig *Adj.* hardy ⟨*plant, animal*⟩; **ein ~es Vorurteil** a prejudice which dies hard
zahlen 1. *tr. V.* **a)** pay ⟨*price, amount, rent, tax, fine, etc.*⟩ (**an** + *Akk.* to); **jmdm. 200 Mark ~, 200 Mark an jmdn. ~:** pay sb. 200 marks; **einen hohen Preis ~** *(auch fig.)* pay a high price; **b)** *(ugs.: für eine Dienstleistung)* pay for ⟨*taxi, repair, etc.*⟩; **jmdm. etw. ~:** pay for sth. for sb.; **zahlst du mir ein Bier?** will you buy me a beer?. **2.** *itr. V.* pay; **er will nicht ~:** he won't pay [up]; **er zahlt noch an seinem Auto** he is still paying off his car; **in Dollar** *od.* **mit Dollars ~:** pay in dollars; **~ bitte!** *(im Lokal)* [can I/we have] the bill, please!; **die Firma zahlt gut/schlecht** the firm pays well/badly
zählen ['tsɛ:lən] **1.** *itr. V.* **a)** count; **ich zähle bis drei** I'll count up to three; **b)** *(geh.: vorhanden sein)* **nach Tausenden/Millionen ~:** number thousands/millions; **c)** *(gehören)* **zu einer Gruppe** *usw.* **~:** be one of *or* belong to a group *etc.*; **diese Tage zählten zu den schönsten seines Lebens** these days were among *or* were some of the most wonderful in his life; **d)** *(gültig/wichtig sein)* count; **die Pause zählt nicht als Arbeitszeit** the break does not count as working time; **bei ihm** *od.* **für ihn zählt nur Erfolg** for him the only thing that counts is success; **e)** *(vertrauen)* **auf jmdn./etw. ~:** count on sb./sth. **2.** *tr. V.* **a)** count; **Geld auf den Tisch ~:** count money out on to the table; **b)** *(geh.: eine bestimmte Anzahl haben)* number; **die Stadt zählt 500 000 Einwohner** the town has 500,000 inhabitants; **er zählt 90 Jahre** he is 90 years of age; **seine Tage sind gezählt** *(fig.)* his/its days are numbered; **c)** *(als zugehörig betrachten)* **jmdn. zu seinen Freunden ~:** count sb. among one's friends; **d)** *(wert sein)* be worth; **e)** *(werten)* **das Tor wurde nicht gezählt** the goal was not counted *or* didn't count
zahlen-, Zahlen-: ~folge die sequence *or* series of numbers; **~gedächtnis das** memory for figures; **~kombination die** combination *(for a lock)*; **~lotterie die, ~lotto das** *lottery in which entrants guess which set of figures will be drawn at random from a fixed sequence of numbers*; **~mäßig 1.** *Adj.*; *nicht präd.* numerical; **2.** *adv.* numerically; **~mystik die** numerology *no art.*; **~schloß das** combination lock
Zähler der; ~s, ~ a) *(Meßgerät)* meter; **b)** *(Math.)* numerator
Zähler·stand der meter reading; **den ~ ablesen** read the meter
zahl-, Zahl-: ~grenze die fare stage; **~karte die** *(Postw.)* paying-in slip; **~kellner der** *waiter to whom payment is made*; **~los** *Adj.* countless; innumerable
Zahl·meister der *(auch fig.)* paymaster; *(auf Schiffen)* purser
zahl·reich 1. *Adj.* numerous; large ⟨*family, group, audience*⟩; **seine ~e Nachkommenschaft** his numerous descendants. **2.** *adv.* in large numbers
Zahl·tag der pay-day
Zahlung die; ~, ~en payment; **etw. in ~ nehmen/geben** *(Kaufmannsspr.)* take/give sth. in part-exchange; take sth. as a trade-in/trade sth. in
Zählung die; ~, ~en counting; **eine ~:** a count

zahlungs-, Zahlungs-: ~an·weisung die *postal order paid by the postman to the payee in person;* **~auf·forderung die** notice to pay; demand for payment; **~aufschub der** deferment of payment; **~bedingungen** *Pl. (Wirtsch.)* terms of payment; **~befehl der** *(Rechtsspr. veralt.)* order to pay; **~bilanz die** *(Wirtsch.)* balance of payments; **~empfänger der** payee; **~erleichterung die** easy terms *pl.;* **~fähig** *Adj.* solvent; **~fähigkeit die;** *o. Pl.* solvency; **~frist die** period for payment; credit period; **~kräftig** *Adj. (ugs.)* affluent; **~mittel das** means of payment; **~termin der** date for payment **(für** of); **~unfähig** *Adj.* insolvent; **~unfähigkeit die** insolvency; **~verkehr der;** *o. Pl.* payments *pl.;* transactions *pl.;* **~weise die** method of payment (*Gen.* for); **~ziel das** *(Kaufmannsspr.) s.* **~frist**

Zähl·werk das counter

Zahl-: ~wort das; *Pl.* **~wörter** *(Sprachw.)* numeral; **~zeichen das** numeral

zahm [tsa:m] **1.** *Adj. (auch fig.)* tame. **2.** *adv. (auch fig.)* tamely

zähmen ['tsɛ:mən] *tr. V.* **a)** *(auch fig.)* tame; subdue ⟨*forces of nature*⟩; **b)** *(geh.)* restrain ⟨*curiosity, impatience, etc.*⟩

Zähmung die; ~, **~en** taming

Zahn [tsa:n] **der;** ~**[e]s, Zähne** ['tsɛ:nə] **a)** tooth; *(Raubtier~)* fang; *(an einer Briefmarke usw.)* serration; **Zähne** *(an einer Briefmarke usw.)* perforations; **sich** *(Dat.)* **einen ~ ziehen lassen** have a tooth out; **die dritten Zähne** *(scherzh.)* dentures; **b)** *(fig.)* **der ~ der Zeit** *(ugs.)* the ravages *pl.* of time; **der ~ der Zeit hat an diesem Haus genagt** *(ugs.)* time has left its mark on this house; **jmdm. diesen** *od.* **den ~ ziehen** *(ugs.)* put paid to this idea [of sb.'s] *(coll.);* **[jmdm.] die Zähne zeigen** *(ugs.)* show [sb.] one's teeth; **die Zähne zusammenbeißen** *(ugs.)* grit one's teeth; **sich** *(Dat.)* **an jmdm./etw. die Zähne ausbeißen** *(ugs.)* get nowhere with sb./sth.; **lange Zähne machen, mit langen Zähnen essen** *(ugs.)* make a face over one's food; **jmdn. auf den ~ fühlen[, ob ...]** *(ugs.)* sound sb. out [to see whether ...]; **bis an die Zähne bewaffnet** armed to the teeth; **etw. mit Zähnen und Klauen verteidigen** *(ugs.)* defend sth. tooth and nail; **c)** *(ugs.: Geschwindigkeit)* **einen ganz schönen ~ draufhaben** be going like the clappers *(sl.);* **mit einem höllischen ~:** at a hell of a lick *(sl.);* **einen ~ zulegen** *(ugs.)* get a move on *(coll.);* **d)** *(Jugendspr. veralt.)* piece *or* bit of skirt *(sl.);* **ein steiler ~:** a piece of hot stuff *(sl.)*

zahn-, Zahn-: ~arzt der dentist; *(mit chirurgischer Ausbildung)* dental surgeon; **~ärztlich 1.** *Adj.; nicht präd.* dental ⟨*treatment etc.*⟩; **~ärztlicher Befund** dentist's findings *pl.;* **2.** *adv.* **jmdn. ~ärztlich behandeln** give sb. dental treatment; **~ärztlich empfohlen** recommended by dentists; **~behandlung die** dental treatment; **~bein das;** *o. Pl. (Biol.)* dentine; **~belag der** [dental] plaque; **~bürste die** toothbrush

Zahn·creme die *s.* **Zahnpasta**

zähne-, Zähne-: ~fletschend *Adj.* baring its/their teeth *postpos.; (knurrend)* snarling; **~klappern das** chattering teeth *pl.; s. auch* **heulen b; ~klappernd** *Adj.* with chattering teeth *postpos.;* **~knirschend** *adv.* gnashing one's teeth; cursing silently; **~knirschend nachgeben** give in with bad grace *or* under protest

zahnen *itr. V.* ⟨*baby*⟩ be teething

zahn-, Zahn-: ~ersatz der denture; **~fäule die** tooth decay; dental caries *(Med.);* **~fleisch das** gum; *(als Ganzes)* gums *pl.;* **auf dem ~fleisch gehen** *(fig. ugs.)* be absolutely knackered *(Brit. sl.);* be tuckered [out] *(Amer. coll.);* **~fleisch·bluten das** bleeding gums *pl.;* **~füllung die** filling; **~hals der** neck of a/the tooth; **~heilkunde die** dentistry *no art.;* **~klinik die** dental clinic; **~krone die** crown [of a/the tooth]; **~laut der** *(Sprachw.)* dental; **~los** *Adj.* toothless; **~lücke die** gap in one's teeth; **~medizin die** dentistry *no art.;* **~pasta** [~pasta] **die; ~, ~pasten** toothpaste; **~pflege die** dental care; **~prothese die** dentures *pl.;* [set *sing.* of] false teeth *pl.;* **~pulver das** tooth-powder; **~putz·becher der** tooth-mug; **~rad das** gearwheel; *(für Ketten)* sprocket; **~rad·bahn die** rack-railway; **~schmelz der** enamel; **~schmerzen** *Pl.* toothache *sing.;* **~seide die** dental floss; **~spange die** [tooth-] brace; **~stein der;** *o. Pl.* tartar; **~stocher der; ~s, ~:** toothpick; **~stumpf der** [tooth-]stump; **~techniker der** dental technician; **~wal der** toothed whale; **~weh das;** *o. Pl. (ugs.)* toothache; **~wurzel die** root of a/the tooth

Zähre ['tsɛ:rə] **die; ~, ~n** *(dichter. veralt.)* tear[-drop]

Zaire [za'i:r] **(das); ~s** Zaire

Zairer [za'i:rɐ] **der; ~s, ~:** Zairese

Zampano ['tsampano] **der; ~s, ~s** golden boy; **er ist ein richtiger ~:** everything just falls into his lap

Zander ['tsandɐ] **der; ~s, ~:** zander

Zange ['tsaŋə] **die; ~, ~n a)** *(Werkzeug)* pliers *pl.; (Eiswürfel~, Wäsche~, Zucker~)* tongs *pl.; (Geburts~)* forceps *pl.; (Kneif~)* pincers *pl.; (Loch~)* punch; **eine ~:** a pair of pliers/tongs/forceps/pincers/a punch; **jmdn. in die ~ nehmen** *(fig. ugs.)* put the screws on sb.; *(Fußballjargon)* crowd sb. out; **jmdn. in der ~ haben** *(fig. ugs.)* have sb. where one wants him/her; **b)** *(bei Tieren)* pincer

Zangen·geburt die forceps delivery

Zank [tsaŋk] **der; ~[e]s** squabble; row; **[um** *od.* **über etw.** *(Akk.)*] **in ~ geraten** start squabbling [over sth.]

Zank·apfel der bone of contention

zanken 1. *refl. (auch itr.) V.* squabble, bicker (**um** *od.* **über** + *Akk.* over). **2.** *itr. V. (bes. ostmd.: schimpfen)* **[mit jmdm.] ~:** scold [sb.]

Zänkerei die; ~, ~en [minor] squabbling *no pl. or* squabbles *pl.*

zänkisch *Adj.* quarrelsome

Zäpfchen ['tsɛpfçən] **das; ~s, ~ a)** suppository; **b)** *(Anat.)* uvula

Zäpfchen-R das; ~ *(Sprachw.)* uvular r

zapfen ['tsapfn̩] *tr. V.* tap, draw ⟨*beer, wine*⟩; **kannst du mir zwei Pils ~?** can you draw me two Pils?

Zapfen der; ~s, ~ a) *(Bot.)* [pine-/fir-]cone; **b)** *(Stöpsel)* bung; **c)** *(Eis~)* icicle; **d)** *(Holzverarb.)* tenon

Zapfen·streich der *(Milit.)* **a)** *(Signal)* last post *(Brit.);* taps *pl. (Amer.);* **der Große ~:** the tattoo; **b)** *o. Pl. (Ende der Ausgehzeit)* time for return to barracks

Zapfer der; ~s, ~: barman

Zapf-: ~hahn der tap; **~säule die** petrol-pump *(Brit.);* gasoline pump *(Amer.)*

zappelig *Adj. (ugs.)* **a)** wriggly; fidgety ⟨*child*⟩; **b)** *(nervös)* jittery *(coll.)*

zappeln ['tsapl̩n] *itr. V.* wriggle; ⟨*child*⟩ fidget; **mit den Beinen/Armen ~:** wave one's legs/arms about; **jmdn. ~ lassen** *(fig. ugs.)* keep sb. on tenterhooks; *(im unklaren lassen)* keep sb. guessing

Zappelphilipp der; ~s, ~e *od.* **~s** *(ugs.)* fidgety child; fidget

zappenduster ['tsapn̩'du:stɐ] *Adj. (ugs.)* pitch-dark; **es ist ~** *(fig.)* things look black *or* hopeless

Zar [tsa:ɐ̯] **der; ~en, ~en** *(hist.)* Tsar

Zaren·reich das *(hist.)* tsardom

Zarewitsch [tsa're:vɪtʃ] **der; ~[e]s, ~e** *(hist.)* Tsarevitch

Zarge ['tsargə] **die; ~, ~n a)** *(Rahmen)* frame; **b)** *(eines Saiteninstruments)* side-wall; rib

Zarin die; ~, ~nen *(hist.)* Tsarina

Zarismus der; ~ *(hist.)* tsarism *no art.*

zaristisch *Adj. (hist.)* tsarist

zart [tsa:ɐ̯t] **1.** *Adj.* **a)** delicate; soft ⟨*skin*⟩; tender ⟨*bud, shoot*⟩; fragile, delicate ⟨*china*⟩; fine ⟨*silk, lace*⟩; delicate, frail ⟨*health, constitution, child*⟩; **im ~en Alter von sechs Jahren** *(geh.)* at the tender age of six; **das ist nichts für ~e Seelen** *od.* **Gemüter** it is not at all suitable for sensitive souls; **b)** *(weich)* tender ⟨*meat, vegetables*⟩; soft ⟨*filling*⟩; fine ⟨*biscuits*⟩; **c)** *(leicht)* gentle ⟨*kiss, touch*⟩; delicate ⟨*colour, complexion, fragrance, etc.*⟩; soft ⟨*pastel colours*⟩; soft, gentle ⟨*voice, sound, tune*⟩; **d)** *(einfühlsam, zärtlich)* tender ⟨*care, feelings*⟩; **e)** *(zurückhaltend)* delicate ⟨*reference*⟩; gentle ⟨*hint*⟩; faint ⟨*smile*⟩. **2.** *adv.* **a)** *(empfindlich)* delicately; **b)** *(leicht)* delicately ⟨*coloured, fragrant*⟩; ⟨*kiss, touch*⟩ gently; **c)** *(zärtlich, einfühlsam)* tenderly; **d)** *(zurückhaltend)* ⟨*hint*⟩ gently; ⟨*smile*⟩ faintly

zart-, Zart-: ~besaitet *Adj.* highly sensitive; **~bitter** *Adj.* plain ⟨*chocolate*⟩; **~blau** *Adj.* pale blue; **~fühlend 1.** *Adj.* tactful; **2.** *adv.* tactfully; **~gefühl das** tact; delicacy of feeling

Zartheit die; ~ a) delicacy; *(der Haut)* softness; *(von Porzellan)* fragility; *(von Spitzen, Seide)* fineness; *(der Gesundheit, Konstitution, eines Kindes)* delicateness; *(Sensibilität)* sensitivity; **b)** *(von Fleisch, Gemüse)* tenderness; **c)** *(Leichtheit) (eines Kusses, einer Berührung)* gentleness; *(einer Farbe, des Teints, eines Dufts)* delicacy; *(der Stimme, des Tons, einer Melodie)* softness; gentleness; **d)** *(Zärtlichkeit)* tenderness; **e)** *(Zurückhaltung)* delicacy

zärtlich ['tsɛ:ɐ̯tlɪç] **1.** *Adj.* tender; loving; **~ werden** *(verhüll.)* start petting; **b)** *(geh.: fürsorglich)* loving; caring. **2.** *adv.* **a)** *(liebevoll)* tenderly; lovingly; **b)** *(geh.: fürsorglich)* lovingly; caringly

Zärtlichkeit die; ~, ~en a) *o. Pl. (Zuneigung)* tenderness; affection; **b)** *meist Pl. (Liebkosung)* caress; **es kam zu ~en zwischen ihnen** they became intimate; **~en austauschen** become intimate; **c)** *o. Pl. (Fürsorglichkeit)* loving care

zart·rosa *Adj.* pale pink

Zaster ['tsastɐ] **der; ~s** *(salopp)* dough *(sl.)*

Zäsur [tsɛ'zu:ɐ̯] **die; ~, ~en a)** *(Verslehre, Musik)* caesura; **b)** *(geh.)* *(Einschnitt)* break; *(Wendepunkt)* turning-point

Zauber ['tsaubɐ] **der; ~s, ~ a)** *(auch fig.)* magic; *(magische Handlung)* magic trick; *(Bann)* [magic] spell; **einen großen ~ auf jmdn. ausüben** have a great fascination for sb.; **er ist ihrem ~ erlegen** he has fallen under her spell; **der ~ des Verbotenen** the fascination of what is forbidden; *s. auch* **faul 1 c; b)** *o. Pl. (ugs. abwertend: Aufheben)* fuss; **ich halte nichts von dem ganzen ~:** the whole palaver means nothing to me *(coll.);* **c)** *(ugs.) o. Pl. (Zeug)* stuff

Zauberei die; ~, ~en a) *o. Pl. (das Zaubern)* magic; **b)** *(Zaubertrick)* magic trick

Zauberer der; ~s, ~: magician

zauber-, Zauber-: ~flöte die: „Die ~flöte" 'The Magic Flute'; **~formel die** magic spell; *(fig.: Patentlösung)* magic formula; panacea; **~haft 1.** *Adj.* enchanting; delightful; **2.** *adv.* enchantingly; delightfully

Zauberin die; ~, ~nen a) sorceress; **b)** *(Zauberkünstlerin)* conjurer

zauberisch *(geh.)* **1.** *Adj.* **a)** *(traumhaft)* magical; **b)** *(bezaubernd)* enchanting. **2.** *adv.* **a)** *(traumhaft)* magically; **b)** *(bezaubernd)* enchantingly

zauber-, Zauber-: ~kraft die magic[al] *or* supernatural powers *pl.;* **~kräftig** *Adj.; nicht präd.* with magic properties *postpos., not pred.;* **ein ~kräftiger Trank** a magic potion; **~kunst die a)** *o. Pl.* magic *no art.;* *(eines Bühnenkünstlers)* magic *no art.;* conjuring *no art.;* **b)** *meist Pl. (magische Fähigkeit)* magic; **~künstler der** conjurer; magician

zaubern 1. *itr. V.* **a)** *(Zauberkraft ausüben)* do magic; **ich kann doch nicht ~!** *(ugs.)* I can't work miracles; **b)** *(Zaubertricks ausführen)* do conjuring tricks. **2.** *tr. V. (auch fig.)* conjure; conjure up ⟨*palace, horse, etc.*⟩; **eine Taube aus dem Hut ~:** produce a dove out of a hat; **ein vorzügliches Essen auf den Tisch ~** *(fig.)* conjure up an excellent meal

Zauber-: ~stab der magic wand; **~trank der** magic potion; **~trick der** conjuring trick

Zauderer der; ~s, ~: waverer; ditherer

zaudern ['tsaudɐn] *itr. V. (geh.)* delay; **mit etw. ~:** delay in doing sth.; **zu lange ~:** procrastinate for too long

Zaum [tsaum] **der; ~[e]s, Zäume** ['tsɔymə] **a)** bridle; **b)** *(geh.)* **jmdn./etw. im ~ halten** keep sb./sth. in check *or* under control; **sich/seine Zunge im ~ halten** restrain *or* control oneself/control one's tongue; **seine Gefühle/Leidenschaften im ~ halten** control one's feelings/passions

zäumen ['tsɔymən] *tr. V.* bridle ⟨*horse*⟩

Zaum·zeug das bridle

Zaun [tsaun] **der; ~[e]s, Zäune** ['tsɔynə] fence; **einen Streit/Krieg vom ~ brechen** *(fig.)* suddenly start a quarrel/war

Zaun-: ~gast der onlooker; **~könig der** *(Zool.)* wren; **~pfahl der** fence-post; *s. auch* **Wink b; ~winde die** *(Bot.)* hedge bindweed

Zausel der; ~s, ~ *(landsch. abwertend)* fellow; **ein alter ~:** an old buffer *(sl.)*

zausen ['tsauzn̩] *tr. V. (auch fig.)* ruffle; ruffle, tousle ⟨*hair*⟩

z. B. *Abk.* **zum Beispiel** e.g.

z. b. V. *Abk.* **zur besonderen Verwendung**

ZDF [tsɛtlde:'lɛf] **das; ~** *Abk.* **Zweites Deutsches Fernsehen** Second German Television Channel

Zebra ['tse:bra] **das; ~s, ~s** *(Zool.)* zebra

Zebra·streifen der zebra crossing *(Brit.);* pedestrian crossing

Zebu ['tse:bu] **der** *od.* **das; ~s, ~s** *(Zool.)* zebu

Zech·bruder der *(ugs. abwertend)* **a)** drinking pal *(coll.);* **b)** *(Trinker)* boozer *(coll.);* tippler

Zeche die; ~, ~n a) *(Rechnung)* bill *(Brit.);* check *(Amer.);* **eine hohe ~ machen** run up a large bill; **die ~ prellen** *(ugs.)* leave without paying [the bill]; **die ~ bezahlen müssen** *(fig.)* have to foot the bill *or* pay the price; **b)** *(Grube)* pit; mine

zechen ['tsɛçn̩] *itr. V. (veralt., scherzh.)* tipple

Zecher der; ~s, ~ *(veralt., scherzh.)* tippler

Zech-: ~gelage das *(veralt., scherzh.)* drinking bout; **~genosse der** *(veralt., scherzh.)* drinking companion; **~kumpan der** *(ugs. abwertend)* drinking pal *(coll.);* **~preller der; ~s, ~** *person who leaves without paying the bill;* bill-dodger; **~prellerei die; ~, ~en** *leaving without paying the bill;* bill-dodging; **~tour die** *(ugs.)* pub crawl *(Brit. coll.);* **eine ~tour unternehmen** go on a pub crawl *(Brit. coll.);* bar-hop *(Amer. coll.)*

Zecke ['tsɛkə] **die; ~, ~n** *(Zool.)* tick

Zeder ['tse:dɐ] **die; ~, ~n** cedar

Zedern·holz das cedarwood

Zeh [tse:] **der; ~s, ~en, Zehe die; ~, ~n a)** toe; **jmdm. auf die Zehen treten** *(auch fig.)* tread on sb.'s toes; **b)** *(Knoblauch~)* clove

Zehen-: ~nagel der toe-nail; **~spitze die: auf ~spitzen** on tiptoe; **sich auf die ~spitzen stellen** stand on tiptoe

zehn [tse:n] *Kardinalz.* ten; *s. auch* [1]**acht**

Zehn die; ~, ~en ten; *s. auch* [1]**Acht a, d, e, g**

zehn-, Zehn- *(s. auch* **acht-, Acht-**): **~eck das** decagon; **~eckig** *Adj.* decagonal; **~ender der; ~s, ~** *(Jägerspr.)* ten-pointer

Zehner der; ~s, ~ a) *(ugs.: Geldschein, Münze)* ten; **b)** *(ugs.: Autobus)* number ten; **c)** *(Math.)* ten; **die ~ addieren** add up the tens; **d)** *(Sprungturm)* ten-metre platform; *s. auch* **Achter d**

Zehner·karte die ticket for ten trips/visits etc.

zehnerlei *Gattungsz.; indekl.* **a)** *attr.* ten kinds *or* sorts of; ten different ⟨*sorts, sizes, etc.*⟩; **b)** *subst.* ten [different] things

Zehner-: ~packung die packet of ten; **~stelle die** *(Math.)* **in der ~stelle** in the tens; **~system das** *(Math.) s.* **Dezimalsystem; ~ziffer die** *(Math.)* figure in the tens

zehn·fach *Vervielfältigungsz.* tenfold; **die ~e Menge** ten times the quantity; *s. auch* **achtfach**

Zehnfache das; *adj. Dekl.* **das ~:** ten times as much; **um ein ~s/um das ~:** ten times; *s. auch* **Achtfache**

zehn-, Zehn-: ~finger·system das; *o. Pl.* touch[-typing] system; **im ~fingersystem schreiben** touch-type; **~flach das; ~[e]s, ~e, ~flächner der** *(Math.)* decahedron; **~jahres·feier, ~jahr·feier die** tenth anniversary celebration; **~jährig** *Adj. (10 Jahre alt)* ten-year-old *attrib.;* ten years old *postpos.; (10 Jahre dauernd)* ten-year *attrib.; s. auch* **achtjährig; ~jährlich 1.** *Adj.* ten-yearly; **2.** *adv.* every ten years; *s. auch* **achtjährlich; ~kampf der** *(Sport)* decathlon; **~kämpfer der** decathlete; **~mal** *Adv.* ten times; **und wenn du dich ~mal langweilst** it doesn't matter 'how bored you are; *s. auch* **achtmal; ~malig** *Adj.; nicht präd.* **nach ~maligem Läuten** after ringing ten times; *s. auch* **achtmalig; ~mark·schein der** ten-mark note; **~pfennig·[brief]·marke die** ten-pfennig stamp; **~pfennig·stück das** ten-pfennig piece; **~seitig** *Adj.* ten-sided; ten-page *attrib.* ⟨*letter, article, etc.*⟩; **~stöckig** *Adj.* ten-storey ⟨*building*⟩; *s. auch* **achtstöckig**

zehnt [tse:nt] *in* **wir waren zu ~:** there were ten of us; *s. auch* [2]**acht**

zehnt... *Ordinalz.* tenth; *s. auch* **acht...**

zehn-: ~tägig *Adj. (10 Tage alt)* ten-day-old *attrib.; (10 Tage dauernd)* ten-day *attrib.; s. auch* **achttägig; ~tausend** *Kardinalz.* ten thousand; **die oberen Zehntausend** *(fig.: die vornehmen Leute)* the élite of society

[1]**Zehnte der; ~n, ~n** *(hist.)* tithe

[2]**Zehnte der/die;** *adj. Dekl.* tenth; *s. auch* **Achte**

zehn·teilig *Adj.* ten-piece ⟨*tool-set etc.*⟩; ten-part ⟨*serial*⟩; *s. auch* **achtteilig**

zehntel ['tse:ntl̩] *Bruchz.* tenth; *s. auch* **achtel**

Zehntel das *(schweiz. meist* **der**); **~s, ~:** tenth

Zehntel-: ~liter der tenth of a litre; **~sekunde die** tenth of a second

zehntens *Adv.* tenthly

Zehn·tonner der; ~s, ~: ten-tonner

zehren ['tse:rən] *itr. V.* **a)** *(leben)* **von etw. ~:** live on *or* off sth.; **von Erinnerungen** *usw.* **~** *(fig.)* sustain oneself on memories *etc.;* **b)** *(geh.: schwächen)* drain sb.'s strength; take it out of sb.; **c)** *(zusetzen)* **an jmdm./jmds. Kräften ~:** wear sb. down/sap sb.'s strength

Zehr·geld das *(veralt.)* money for the journey

Zeichen ['tsaiçn̩] **das; ~s, ~ a)** *(Gebärde)* sign; *(Laut, Wink)* signal; **das ~ zum Angriff** the signal to attack; **jmdm. ein ~ geben** signal to sb.; **zum ~, daß ...:** to show that ...; as a sign that ...; **zum** *od.* **als ~ ihrer Versöhnung** as a sign *or* token of their reconciliation; **b)** *(Markierung)* mark; *(Waren~)* [trade] mark; *(am Briefkopf)* reference; **sein ~ unter ein Schriftstück setzen** initial a document; **seines/ihres ~s** *(veralt., scherzh.)* by trade/profession; **[ein] ~ setzen** set an example; point the way; **c)** *(Symbol)* sign; *(Chemie, Math., auf Landkarten usw.)* symbol; *(Satz~)* punctuation mark; *(Musik)* accidental; **das ~ des Kreuzes** the sign of the cross; **d)** *(An~)* sign; indication; *(einer Krankheit)* sign; symptom; **ein ~ dafür, daß ...:** a [sure] sign that ...; **wenn nicht alle ~ trügen** unless I am very much mistaken; **es geschehen noch ~ und Wunder** wonders will never cease *(iron.);* **die ~ der Zeit erkennen** see which way the wind's blowing *(fig.);* **d)** *(Tierkreis~)* sign [of the zodiac]; **ich bin im ~ des Krebses** *usw.* **geboren** I was born under the sign of Cancer *etc.;* **im** *od.* **unter dem ~ von etw. stehen** *(geh.)* be much influenced by sth.

zeichen-, Zeichen-: ~block der; *Pl.* **~blöcke** *od.* **~s** sketch-pad; **~brett das** drawing-board; **~dreieck das** set-square; **~erklärung die** legend; **~feder die** drawing-pen; **~haft** *(geh.)* **1.** *Adj.* symbolic; **2.** *adv.* symbolically; **~heft das** drawing-book; **~kohle die** charcoal *(in stick form);* **~lehrer der** drawing teacher; **~papier das** drawing-paper; **~setzung die** punctuation; **~sprache die** sign language; **~stift der** drawing-pencil; **~trick·film der** animated cartoon; **~unterricht der** drawing lessons *pl.; (Schulfach)* art *no art.; s. auch* **Englischunterricht; ~winkel der** set-square

zeichnen 1. *tr. V.* **a)** *(malen, darstellen)* draw; *(fig.)* portray ⟨*character*⟩; **ein Bild von dem Geschehen ~** *(fig.)* describe what happened; **b)** *(markieren)* **das Fell ist schön/auffallend gezeichnet** the fur has beautiful/striking markings; **er war vom Alter/von der Krankheit gezeichnet** *(fig.)* age/sickness had left its mark on him; **ein vom Tode Gezeichneter** *(fig. geh.)* a man already bearing the mark of death; **c)** *(bes. Kaufmannsspr.)* sign ⟨*cheque*⟩; subscribe for ⟨*share, loan*⟩. **2.** *itr. V.* **a)** draw; **ich zeichne schon länger daran** I have been working on this drawing for quite a while; **b)** *(bes. Kaufmannsspr.: unterschreiben)* sign; **für etw. [verantwortlich] ~** *(fig.)* be responsible for sth.

Zeichner der; ~s, ~, Zeichnerin die; ~, ~nen a) graphic artist; *(Technik)* draughtsman/-woman; **b)** *(Kaufmannsspr.)* subscriber

zeichnerisch 1. *Adj.* ⟨*fault*⟩ of draughtsmanship; ⟨*talent*⟩ as a draughtsman/-woman *or* for drawing; **exakte ~e Wiedergabe** exact portrayal in a drawing. **2.** *adv.* **~ begabt sein** have a talent for drawing; **etw. ~ darstellen** make a drawing of sth.

Zeichnung die; ~, ~en a) drawing; *(fig.: von Figuren)* portrayal; **b)** *(bei Tieren und Pflanzen)* markings *pl.;* **c)** *(Kaufmannsspr.)* subscription

zeichnungs·berechtigt *Adj. (Kaufmannsspr.)* with signatory powers *postpos.;* **~ sein** have signatory powers

Zeige·finger der index finger; forefinger; **der erhobene ~** *(fig.)* the wagging *or* monitory finger

zeigen ['tsaign̩] **1.** *tr. V.* point; **[mit dem Finger/einem Stock] auf jmdn./etw. ~:** point [one's finger/a stick] at sb./sth.; **nach Norden/zwölf ~:** point [to the] north/to twelve o'clock. **2.** *tr. V.* show; **jmdm. etw. ~:** show sb. sth.; show sth. to sb.; **jmdm. sein Zimmer ~:** show sb. to his/her room; **dem werd' ich's ~!** *(ugs.)* I'll show him!; **er hat es allen seinen Konkurrenten gezeigt** *(ugs.)* he showed all his competitors just how it was done; **zeig mal, was du kannst** show [us] what you can do. **3.** *refl. V.* **a)** *(sich sehen lassen)* appear; **er zeigt sich selten in der Öffentlichkeit** he is rarely seen in public; **mit ihr kann man sich überall ~:** you can take her anywhere; **er wollte sich von seiner besten Seite ~:** he wanted to show himself to advantage; **b)** *(sich erweisen)* prove to be; **es wird sich ~, wer daran schuld war** time will tell who was responsible; **es hat sich gezeigt, daß ...:** it turned out that ...; **sich als etw. ~:** prove *or* turn out to be sth.

Zeiger der; ~s, ~: pointer; *(Uhr~)* hand

Zeige·stock der; *Pl.* ~stöcke pointer

Zeig·finger der *(schweiz.) s.* Zeigefinger

zeihen ['tsaiən] *unr. tr. V. (geh.)* **jmdn. einer Sache** *(Gen.)* ~: indict sb. of sth.

Zeile ['tsailə] **die;** ~, ~**n a)** line; **jmdm. ein paar ~n schreiben** drop sb. a line; **vielen Dank für Ihre ~:** many thanks for your letter; **mit zwei ~n Abstand** with double spacing; **zwischen den ~n lesen** *(fig.)* read between the lines; **b)** *(Reihe)* row; *(des Fernsehbildes)* line

Zeilen-: **~ab·stand der** [line] spacing; *(in gedrucktem Text)* leading; **~bau·weise die** ribbon development; **~gieß·maschine die** Linotype (P) machine; **~honorar das** payment by the line; **~sprung der** *(Verslehre)* enjambment

-zeilig [-tsailıç] -line; **zwei~ sein** have two lines

Zeisig ['tsaizıç] **der;** ~s, ~e *(Zool.)* siskin

zeit [tsait] *Präp. mit Gen.* **in ~ meines** *usw.*/**unseres** *usw.* **Lebens** all my *etc.* life/our *etc.* lives

Zeit die; ~, ~**en a)** *o. Pl.* time *no art.;* **im Laufe der ~:** in the course of time; **mit der ~:** with time; in time; *(allmählich)* gradually; **die ~ arbeitet für/gegen jmdn.** time is on sb.'s side/is against sb.; **die ~ heilt alle Wunden** *(Spr.)* time is a great healer; **kommt ~, kommt Rat** *(Spr.)* take your time and you'll find an answer; **keine ~ verlieren dürfen** have no time to lose; **die ~ drängt** time is pressing; there is [precious] little time; **~ ist Geld** *(Spr.)* time is money *(prov.);* **sich** *(Dat.)* **die ~ [mit etw.] vertreiben** pass the time [with/doing sth.]; **jmdm. ~/drei Tage** *usw.* **~ lassen** give sb. time/three days *etc.;* **sich** *(Dat.)* **~ lassen** *od.* **nehmen** take one's time; **sich** *(Dat.)* **für jmdn./etw. ~ nehmen** make time for sb./sth.; **etw. hat ~, mit etw. hat es ~:** there's no hurry about sth.; **auf ~ spielen** *(Sportjargon)* play for time; *s. auch* **nachtschlafend; sparen; stehlen; totschlagen; b)** *(~punkt)* time; **ihre/seine ~ ist gekommen** *(geh. verhüll.)* her/his time has come; **außer der ~, außerhalb der üblichen ~:** at an unusual time; **seit der** *od.* **dieser ~:** since that time; **um diese ~:** at this time; **vor der ~:** prematurely; early; **zu jeder ~:** at any time; **zur rechten ~:** at the right time; **wer nicht kommt zur rechten ~, der muß essen was übrigbleibt** *(Spr.)* the early bird catches the worm *(prov.);* **zu welcher ~?** at what time?; when?; **zu bestimmten ~en** at certain times; **alles zu seiner ~:** all in good time; **es ist/wird [langsam] ~** *od.* **ist an der ~:** it's time/[just] about time; **es ist [aller]höchste ~[, daß wir uns wehren]** it's high time [we fought back]; **von ~ zu ~:** from time to time; **zur ~:** at the moment; at present; **c)** *(~abschnitt, Lebensabschnitt)* time; period; *(Geschichtsabschnitt)* age; period; **die schönste ~ des Lebens** *od.* **im Leben** the best time of one's life; **er hat ~en, in denen ...:** he has times *or* periods when ...; **die erste ~:** at first; **auf ~:** temporarily; **ein Vertrag auf ~:** a fixed-term contract; **ein Zug der ~:** a feature of the times; **mit der ~ gehen** move with the times; **der Geist der ~:** the spirit of the age; **die ~, als es noch kein Telefon gab** the days *pl.* before there were telephones; **andere ~en, andere Sitten** things are different now; **in früheren ~en** in former times; in the old days; **zu meiner ~:** in my day; **in der nächsten ~, in nächster ~:** in the near future; **für alle ~:** for ever; for all time; **in der letzten** *od.* **in letzter** *od.* **in jüngster ~:** recently; **zu allen ~en** always; at all times; **zu keiner ~:** at no time; never; **hier bin ich die längste ~ gewesen** *(ugs.)* I've been here for long enough; **seit ewigen ~en** *(ugs.)* for ages *(coll.);* **seit undenklichen ~en** from time immemorial; **vor ~en** *(dichter.)* long ago; in days gone by; **zu ~en von jmdm./etw.** in sb.'s day/at the time of sth.; *s. auch* **lieb 1 d; d)** *(Sport: ~raum)* time; **gute ~en laufen** do good times; **die ~ bei etw. stoppen** time sth.; **e)** *(Sport: Wettbewerbsdauer)* **einen Vorsprung über die ~ bringen** retain one's lead until the end of the game; **über die ~ kommen** *(Boxen)* go the distance; **f)** *(Sprachw.)* tense

zeit-, Zeit-: **~ab·schnitt der** period; **~alter das** age; era; **~an·gabe die a)** statement regarding time; **er konnte keine genaue ~angabe machen** he could not be precise about the time; **b)** *(Sprachw.)* expression of time; **~an·sage die** *(im Radio)* time check; *(am Telefon)* speaking clock; **~arbeit die** *(Wirtsch.)* temporary work; work as a temp *(coll.);* **~auf·wand der: viel ~aufwand erfordern** take up a great deal of time; **den ~aufwand verringern** reduce the time needed; **~bedingt** *Adj.* arising from prevailing circumstances *postpos.; (vorübergehend)* temporary; **~begriff der** concept of time; **~bestimmung die** *(Sprachw.)* expression of time; **~bombe die** *(auch fig.)* time bomb; **~dauer die** duration; **~dokument das** contemporary document; **~druck der;** *o. Pl.* pressure of time; **unter ~druck** under pressure; **unter ~druck stehen/in ~druck kommen** be/become pressed for time; be/come under pressure [of time]; **~ein·teilung die** timing; **mit seiner ~einteilung nie zurechtkommen** never succeed in organizing one's time properly

Zeiten-: **~folge die** *(Sprachw.)* sequence of tenses; **~wende die** turning-point in history

zeit-, Zeit-: **~erscheinung die** transient phenomenon; **~ersparnis die** time-saving; **das bedeutete keine ~ersparnis** it did not save any time; **~faktor der;** *o. Pl.* time factor; **~form die** *(Sprachw.)* tense; **in der ~form der Gegenwart** in the present tense; **~gebunden** *Adj.* characteristic of its/their time *postpos.;* **~gebunden sein** be an expression *or* a reflection of its/their time; **~gefühl das;** *o. Pl.* sense of time; **~geist der;** *o. Pl.* spirit of the age; **~gemäß** *Adj.* *(modern)* up-to-date; *(aktuell)* topical ‹*theme*›; contemporary ‹*views*›; *(in der Vergangenheit)* in keeping with the period *postpos.;* **~genosse der, ~genossin die a)** contemporary; **b)** *(Mitmensch)* fellow man/woman; **ein seltsamer ~genosse** a strange individual *(coll.);* **prominente ~genossen waren anwesend** leading figures [of the day] were present; **~genössisch** [~gənœsıʃ] *Adj.* contemporary; **~geschehen das: das [aktuelle] ~geschehen** current events *pl.;* **~geschichte die;** *o. Pl.* **a) die ~geschichte** the modern age; our age; **b)** *(Disziplin)* contemporary history *no art.;* **~geschichtlich 1.** *Adj.; nicht präd.* **a)** *(zeitlich)* contemporary ‹*source etc.*›; **b)** *(fachlich)* **~geschichtlicher Unterricht** contemporary-history teaching; **2.** *adv.* **a)** historically; **b)** *(fachlich)* from the point of view of contemporary history; **~geschmack der;** *o. Pl.* contemporary taste; **~gewinn der;** *o. Pl. s.* ~ersparnis; **~gleich 1.** *Adj.* **a)** simultaneous; **b)** *(Sport)* ‹*runners etc.*› with the same time; **2.** *adv.* simultaneously; **sie kamen ~gleich ins Ziel** *(Sport)* they finished with the same time

zeitig *Adj., adv.* early

zeitigen *tr. V. (geh.)* produce, yield ‹*result, success, etc.*›; provoke, precipitate ‹*uproar*›

zeit-, Zeit-: **~karte die** *(Verkehrsw.)* season ticket; **~kritik die;** *o. Pl.* appraisal *or* analysis of contemporary issues; **~kritisch 1.** *Adj.* ‹*essay, article, film*› analysing contemporary issues; **~kritische Themen** contemporary issues; **2.** *adv.* ‹*examine*› in the light of contemporary issues; **~lang die** *in* **eine ~lang** for a while *or* a time; **~läuf[t]e** [~lɔyf(t)ə] *Pl. (geh.)* times; **über alle ~läuf[t]e hinweg** for all time; **~lebens** *Adv.* all one's life

zeitlich 1. *Adj.* **a)** ‹*length, interval*› in time; chronological ‹*order, sequence*›; **in großem/kurzem ~en Abstand** at long/short intervals; **b)** *(Rel.)* temporal; **das Zeitliche segnen** *(verhüll.)* pass on *(euphem.); (scherzh.)* come to grief. **2.** *adv.* **a)** with regard to time; **ich kann es ~ nicht einrichten** I can't fit it in time-wise *(coll.);* **wenn es der Beruf ~ erlaubt** if one's job leaves enough time

zeit-, Zeit-: **~lohn der** *(Wirtsch.)* time-work rate; *(Stundenlohn)* hourly rate; **~los 1.** *Adj.* timeless; classic ‹*fashion, shape*›; **2.** *adv.* timelessly; **~los eingerichtet** furnished in a classic *or* timeless style; **~lupe die;** *o. Pl. (Film) in* **in ~lupe** in slow motion; **~lupen·tempo das** *in* **im ~lupentempo** at a crawl; at a snail's pace; **~mangel der;** *o. Pl.* lack of time; **aus ~mangel, wegen ~mangel[s]** owing to lack of time; **~maß das** speed; *(von Musik usw.)* tempo; **~messer der** timepiece; **~nah[e] 1.** *Adj.* topical ‹*play etc.*›; ‹*teaching, syllabus*› relevant to the present day; **2.** *adv.* topically; **~nehmer der, ~nehmerin die** timekeeper; **~not die;** *o. Pl.* **in ~not geraten** *od.* **kommen** become pressed for time; **in ~not machte er einen falschen Zug** *(Schach)* in time pressure he made a wrong move; **~plan der** schedule; **~punkt der** moment; **zum jetzigen ~punkt** at the present moment; at this point in time; **~raffer der** *(Film)* time-lapse; **etw. im ~raffer zeigen** show sth. speeded up; **~raubend** *Adj.* time-consuming; **~raum der** period; **über einen ~raum von fünf Tagen** for a period of five days; **~rechnung die** calendar; **vor unserer ~rechnung** BC; before Christ; **unserer/christlicher ~rechnung** AD; Anno Domini; **~schrift die** magazine; *(bes. wissenschaftlich)* journal; periodical; **~soldat der** *soldier serving for a fixed period;* **~spanne die** period; **~springen das** *(Pferdesport)* jumping against the clock; **~strafe die** *(Sport)* sending off for a specified time; *(im Eishockey)* penalty; **~strömung die** prevailing trend; **~umstände** *Pl.* prevailing circumstances; **die damaligen ~umstände** the circumstances prevailing at the time

Zeitung die; ~, ~**en** [news]paper; **[die] ~ lesen** read the paper; **bei einer ~ arbeiten** work for a newspaper; **er ist von der ~** *(ugs.)* he's from the press; **eine Anzeige in die ~ setzen** put an advertisement in the paper

Zeitungs-: **~abonnement das** newspaper subscription; **~annonce die, ~anzeige die** newspaper advertisement; **~artikel der** newspaper article; **~ausschnitt der** newspaper cutting; **~austräger der** newspaper-deliverer; **~ente die** *(ugs.)* false [newspaper] report; canard; **~frau die** newspaper-seller; *(Austrägerin)* newspaper-deliverer; **~inserat das** newspaper advertisement; **~leser der** newspaper-reader; **~meldung die** newspaper report; **~notiz die** newspaper item; **~papier das a)** *(alte Zeitung[en])* newspaper; **b)** *(unbedruckt)* newsprint; **~ständer der** newspaper-rack; **~träger der** *s.* ~austräger; **~verkäufer der** newspaper-seller; news-vendor; **~wissenschaft die** *(Hochschulw.)* journalistic studies *pl., no art.*

zeit-, Zeit-: **~unterschied der** time difference; **~verschwendung die** waste of time; **[reine** *od.* **pure] ~verschwendung sein** be a [pure *or* complete] waste of time; **~vertreib der;** ~[e]s, ~e pastime; **zum ~vertreib** to pass the time; **~weilig 1.** *Adj.; nicht präd.* temporary; **2.** *adv.* **a)** *(vorüber-*

gehend) temporarily; for a time; **b)** *(gelegentlich)* occasionally; at times; **~weise** *Adv.* **a)** *(gelegentlich)* occasionally; at times; *(von Zeit zu Zeit)* from time to time; **~weise Regen** occasional rain; **b)** *(vorübergehend)* for a time; for a while; **~wende die a) vor/nach der ~wende** BC/AD; before Christ/Anno Domini; **um die ~wende** about the time of the birth of Christ; **b)** *s.* **Zeitenwende; ~wort das;** *Pl.* **~wörter** *(Sprachw.)* verb; **~zeichen das** *(Rundf., Funkw.)* time signal; **~zone die** time zone; **~zünder der** time fuse

zelebrieren [tsele'bri:rən] *tr. V.* **a)** *(kath. Kirche)* celebrate ‹mass›; conduct ‹*service, wedding*›; **b)** *(feierlich ausführen)* make ‹*meal, event, etc.*› into a ritual; **c)** *(ehren)* honour

Zelebrität [tselebri'tɛ:t] **die; ~, ~en** *(geh.)* celebrity

Zelle ['tsɛlə] **die; ~, ~n** cell; *(Telefon~)* [tele]phone booth *or (Brit.)* box; **die [kleinen] grauen ~n** *(scherzh.)* one's grey matter *sing.*

Zeller der; ~s *(österr. ugs.)* celeriac

Zell-: ~gewebe das *(Biol.)* cell tissue; **~gift das** *(Biol., Med.)* cytotoxin; **~kern der** *(Biol.)* cell nucleus; **~stoff der a)** cellulose; **b)** *(Material)* cellulose wadding; **~teilung die** *(Biol.)* cell division

Zellulitis [tsɛlu'li:tɪs] **die; ~, Zellulitiden** [tsɛluli'ti:dn̩] *(Med.)* cellulitis

Zelluloid [tsɛlu'lɔyt] **das; ~[e]s** celluloid

Zellulose [tsɛlu'lo:zə] **die; ~, ~n** cellulose

Zell·wolle die rayon

Zelt [tsɛlt] **das; ~[e]s, ~e** tent; *(Fest~)* marquee; *(Zirkus~)* big top; **das himmlische ~** *(fig. dichter.)* the canopy of heaven *(literary);* **seine ~e irgendwo aufschlagen** *(fig.)* settle down somewhere; **seine ~e abbrechen** *(fig.)* up sticks *(sl.);* decamp

zelten *itr. V.* camp; **wir waren ~:** we went camping; **„Zelten verboten"** 'no camping'

Zelt-: ~lager das camp; **~pflock der** tentpeg; **~plane die** tarpaulin; **~platz der** camping site; campsite

Zement [tse'mɛnt] **der; ~[e]s, ~e** cement

Zement·boden der concrete floor

zementieren *tr. V.* **a)** cement; **zementierte Wege** concrete paths; **b)** *(fig.: festlegen)* make ‹*division, situation, etc.*› permanent; **weiter zementiert werden** ‹*prejudice, opinion*› become further entrenched

Zen [zɛn] **das; ~[s], Zen-Buddhismus der** *(Rel.)* Zen [Buddhism] *no art.*

Zenit [tse'ni:t] **der; ~[e]s** zenith; **im ~ stehen** be at its zenith; **er stand im ~ seines Ruhms** *(fig. geh.)* he was at the peak of his fame

zensieren [tsɛn'zi:rən] **1.** *tr. V.* **a)** *(Schulw.)* mark, *(Amer.)* grade ‹*essay etc.*›; **b)** *(der Zensur unterziehen)* censor ‹*article, film, etc.*›. **2.** *itr. V. (Schulw.)* **streng/milde ~:** mark *or (Amer.)* grade severely/leniently

Zensierung die; ~, ~en *(Schulw.)* marking; grading *(Amer.)*

Zensor ['tsɛnzɔr] **der; ~s, ~en** [tsɛn'zo:rən] censor

Zensur [tsɛn'zu:ɐ̯] **die; ~, ~en a)** *(Schulw.: Note)* mark; grade *(Amer.);* **~en austeilen** *(fig.)* mete out praise and blame *(literary);* **b)** *(Kontrolle)* censorship; **c)** *(Behörde)* censors *pl.*

zensurieren *tr. V. (österr.) s.* **zensieren 1 b**

Zentaur [tsɛn'tauɐ̯] **der; ~en, ~en** *(Myth.)* centaur

Zenti- [tsɛnti-]: **~gramm** [--'gram] **das** centigram; **~liter** [--'li:tɐ] **der,** *auch:* **das** centilitre; **~meter** [--'me:tɐ] **der,** *auch:* **das** centimetre; **~meter·maß das** [centimetre] measuring-tape

Zentner ['tsɛntnɐ] **der; ~s, ~ a)** centner; metric hundredweight; **b)** *(österr., schweiz.)* centner; 100 kilograms

zentner-, Zentner-: ~gewicht das a) *o. Pl.* centner *or* fifty-kilogram weight; *(fig.: große Last)* massive weight; **~last die** hundredweight load; **ihr fiel eine ~last vom Herzen** *(fig.)* that was a load off her mind; **~schwer 1.** *Adj.* weighing over a hundredweight *postpos., not pred.; (äußerst schwer)* massively heavy; **2.** *adv.* **~schwer auf jmdm. lasten** *(fig.)* weigh heavily on sb.; **~weise** *Adv.* by the hundredweight

zentral [tsɛn'tra:l] **1.** *Adj.* central. **2.** *adv.* centrally

Zentral·afrikanische Republik die Central African Republic

Zentral·bank die; *Pl.* **~en** *(Finanzw.)* central bank

zentral·beheizt *Adj.* centrally heated; *(durch Fernwärme)* heated by a district heating system

Zentrale die; ~, ~n a) *(zentrale Stelle)* head *or* central office; *(der Polizei, einer Partei)* headquarters *sing. or pl.; (Funk~)* control centre; *(fig.: Mittelpunkt)* centre; **das Gehirn ist die ~ für das Nervensystem** the brain is the control centre of the nervous system; **b)** *(Telefon~)* [telephone] exchange; *(eines Hotels, einer Firma o. ä.)* switchboard; **c)** *(Geom.)* line passing through the centres of two circles

Zentral·heizung die central heating

Zentralisation [tsɛntraliza'tsio:n] **die; ~, ~en** centralization

zentralisieren *tr. V.* centralize

Zentralisierung die; ~, ~en centralization

Zentralismus der; ~: centralism *usu. no art.*

zentralistisch 1. *Adj.* centralist. **2.** *adv.* centralistically

Zentral-: ~komitee das Central Committee; **~nerven·system das** *(Anat.)* central nervous system; **~organ das** official organ

Zentren *s.* **Zentrum**

zentrieren 1. *tr. V.* centre **(um** on). **2.** *refl. V.* **sich um etw. ~:** be centred around sth.

Zentrierung die; ~, ~en centring

zentrifugal [tsɛntrifu'ga:l] *(Physik)* **1.** *Adj.* centrifugal. **2.** *adv.* centrifugally

Zentrifugal·kraft die *(Physik)* centrifugal force

Zentrifuge die; ~, ~n centrifuge

zentripetal [tsɛntripe'ta:l] *(Physik)* **1.** *Adj.* centripetal. **2.** *adv.* centripetally

Zentripetal·kraft die *(Physik)* centripetal force

Zentri·winkel ['tsɛntrivɪŋkl̩] **der** *(Geom.)* central angle

Zentrum ['tsɛntrʊm] **das; ~s, Zentren** centre; **im ~:** at the centre; *(im Stadt~)* in the town/city centre; **im ~ des öffentlichen Interesses stehen** *(fig.)* be the focus of public interest

Zephir ['tse:fɪr] **der; ~s, ~e** *(dichter. veralt.)* zephyr

Zeppelin ['tsɛpəli:n] **der; ~s, ~e** Zeppelin

Zepter ['tsɛptɐ] **das,** *auch:* **der; ~s, ~:** sceptre; **das ~ übernehmen** *(fig.)* take the helm; **das ~ führen** *od. (scherzh.)* **schwingen** *(fig.)* wield the sceptre

zerbeißen *unr. tr. V.* bite in two; ‹*flea, mosquito, etc.*› bite ‹*person etc.*› all over

zerbersten *unr. itr. V.; mit sein* burst apart; **zerborstene Mauern** smashed walls

zerbomben *tr. V.* bomb to pieces; destroy by bombing; **zerbombt** bombed ‹*streets, houses*›

zerbrechen 1. *unr. itr. V.; mit sein* break [into pieces]; smash [to pieces]; ‹*glass*› shatter; *(fig.)* ‹*marriage, relationship*› break up; **an seinem Kummer ~** *(fig. geh.)* be broken down by grief. **2.** *unr. tr. V.* break; smash, shatter ‹*dishes, glass*›

zerbrechlich *Adj.* **a)** fragile; **„Vorsicht, ~!"** 'fragile; handle with care'; **b)** *(zart, schwach)* frail

Zerbrechlichkeit die; ~ a) fragility; **b)** *(Zartheit, Schwachheit)* frailty

zerbröckeln 1. *itr. V.; mit sein (auch fig.)* crumble away. **2.** *tr. V.* break into small pieces

zerbröseln 1. *itr. V.; mit sein* crumble. **2.** *tr. V.* crumble up

zerdehnen *tr. V.* **a)** *(dehnen)* stretch [out of shape]; **b)** *(verlängern)* draw out ‹*plot, scenes*›; drawl ‹*word, vowel*›

zerdeppern [tsɛɐ̯'dɛpɐn] *tr. V. (ugs.)* smash ‹*window, china, glass*›

zerdrücken *tr. V.* **a)** *(zerquetschen)* mash ‹*potatoes, banana*›; **b)** *(zusammendrücken)* squash ‹*fly etc.*›; stub out ‹*cigarette*›; **eine Träne ~** *(fig. spöttisch)* shed a tear; **c)** *(ugs.: zerknittern)* crease ‹*clothes*›

Zeremonie [tseremo'ni:] **die; ~, ~n** ceremony; *(fig.)* ritual

Zeremoniell [tseremo'ni̯ɛl] **das; ~s, ~e** ceremonial

Zeremonien·meister der master of ceremonies

zerfahren 1. *Adj.* distracted; scrappy ‹*play*›. **2.** *adv.* distractedly; ‹*play*› scrappily, without concentration

Zerfall der; ~[e]s, Zerfälle a) *o. Pl.* disintegration; *(eines Organismus, fig.: der Moral)* breakdown; *(einer Leiche)* decomposition; *(eines Gebäudes)* decay; **b)** *(Kernphysik)* decay

[1]**zerfallen** *unr. itr. V.; mit sein* **a)** *(auch fig.)* disintegrate **(in + Akk., zu** into); ‹*building*› fall into ruin, decay; ‹*corpse*› decompose, decay; **~de Mauern/Ruinen** crumbling walls/ruins; **zu Staub ~:** crumble into dust; **Moral und Kultur waren ~** *(fig.)* morals and culture had broken down *or* fallen into decay; **b)** *(unterteilt sein)* **in Phasen/Teile** *usw.* **~:** be divided into phases/parts *etc.;* **c)** *(Kernphysik)* decay

[2]**zerfallen** *Adj.* **mit jmdm. ~ sein** have fallen out with sb.; **mit sich und der Welt ~ sein** be at odds with oneself and the world

Zerfalls·produkt das *(bes. Kernphysik)* decay product

zerfasern *itr. V.; mit sein* fray

zerfetzen *tr. V.* **a)** *(zerstören)* rip *or* tear to pieces; rip *or* tear up ‹*letter etc.*› **(in + Akk.** into); *(fig.)* tear apart ‹*body, limb*›; **b)** *(kritisieren)* tear ‹*book, play, etc.*› to pieces *or* shreds

zerfleddern *tr. V.* wear out ‹*book etc.*›; **das Buch ist zerfleddert** the book is falling apart

zerfleischen *tr. V.* tear ‹*person, animal*› limb from limb; **sich ~** *(auch fig.)* tear each other apart; ‹*country*› tear itself apart

Zerfleischung die; ~, ~en tearing apart *no art.*

zerfließen *unr. itr. V.; mit sein* **a)** *(schmelzen)* melt [away]; **in** *od.* **vor Mitleid ~** *(fig.)* dissolve with pity; **das Geld ist ihr unter den Händen zerflossen** the money ran through her fingers *(fig.);* **b)** *(auseinanderfließen)* ‹*paint, ink*› run; ‹*shapes*› dissolve; **~de Konturen/Grenzen** blurred outlines/limits

zerfransen 1. *itr. V.; mit sein* fray. **2.** *tr. V.* fray; *(zerreißen)* tear

zerfressen *unr. tr. V.* **a)** *(fressen)* eat away; ‹*moth etc.*› eat holes in; **von Motten ~:** moth-eaten; **b)** *(zersetzen)* corrode ‹*metal*›; eat away ‹*bone*›; **Kummer/Eifersucht zerfrißt ihm das Herz** *(fig.)* he is consumed with grief/jealousy

zerfurchen *tr. V.* **a)** rut ‹*track etc.*›; **b)** furrow ‹*brow, face*›

zergehen *unr. itr. V.; mit sein* melt; *(in Wasser, im Mund)* ‹*tablet etc.*› dissolve; **auf der Zunge ~:** melt in the mouth

zergliedern *tr. V.* **a)** dissect ‹*plant, animal, corpse*›; **b)** analyse ‹*behaviour, process, etc.*›; **Sätze ~:** parse sentences

Zergliederung die a) dissection; **b)** *(Analyse)* analysis; *(von Sätzen)* parsing

zergrübeln *refl. V.* **sich** *(Dat.)* **den Kopf** *od.* **das Hirn ~:** rack one's brains

zerhacken *tr. V.* chop up **(zu** into); *(in Wut)* hack to pieces

zerhauen *unr. tr. V.* chop up
zerkauen *tr. V.* chew [up]
zerkleinern [tsɛɐ̯'klainɐn] *tr. V.* chop up ⟨*vegetables, meat, wood*⟩; *(zerkauen)* chew up ⟨*food*⟩; *(zermahlen)* crush ⟨*rock etc.*⟩
Zerkleinerung die; ~, ~**en** chopping up; *(Zerkauung)* chewing; *(Zermahlung)* crushing
zerklüftet *Adj.* fissured ⟨*landscape*⟩; craggy ⟨*mountains*⟩; deeply indented ⟨*coastline*⟩
zerknallen 1. *itr. V.; mit sein* burst [with a bang]. **2.** *tr. V.* burst ⟨*bag etc.*⟩ [with a bang]
zerknautschen *tr. V. (ugs.)* crumple
zerknicken 1. *tr. V.* snap. **2.** *itr. V.; mit sein* snap
zerknirscht 1. *Adj.* remorseful. **2.** *adv.* remorsefully
Zerknirschung die; ~: remorse
zerknittern *tr. V.* crease; crumple; **ein zerknittertes Gesicht** a wrinkled face
zerknüllen *tr. V.* crumple up [into a ball]
zerkochen 1. *itr. V.; mit sein* get overcooked; **zu Brei** ~: cook to a pulp; **zerkocht** overcooked. **2.** *tr. V.* overcook
zerkratzen *tr. V.* scratch
zerkrümeln 1. *tr. V.* crumble up. **2.** *itr. V.; mit sein* break into crumbs; crumble
zerlassen *unr. tr. V. (Kochk.)* melt
zerlegen *tr. V.* **a)** *(auseinandernehmen)* dismantle; take to pieces; strip, dismantle ⟨*engine*⟩; **etw. in seine Bestandteile** ~: reduce sth. to its component parts; **einen Lichtstrahl in die Farben des Spektrums** ~: split up a ray of light into the colours of the spectrum; **b)** *(zerschneiden)* cut up ⟨*animal, meat*⟩; carve ⟨*joint*⟩; dissect ⟨*corpse*⟩
zerlesen *unr. tr. V.* read ⟨*book etc.*⟩ again and again until it looks worn out; **ein [völlig]** ~**es Exemplar** a well-thumbed copy
zerlumpt *Adj.* ragged ⟨*clothes, person*⟩; ~ **sein** ⟨*clothes*⟩ be in tatters, be torn; ~ **herumlaufen** go about in rags
zermahlen *unr. tr. V.* grind
zermalmen [tsɛɐ̯'malmən] *tr. V.* crush
zermartern *refl. V.* **in sich** *(Dat.)* **den Kopf** *od.* **das Hirn** ~: rack one's brains
zermürben *tr. V.* wear ⟨*person*⟩ down; ~**d** wearing; trying
Zermürbung die wearing down *no art.*; *(Milit.)* attrition
Zermürbungs·krieg der war of attrition
zernagen *tr. V.* gnaw away
zerpflücken *tr. V.* **a)** pick ⟨*flower, lettuce, etc.*⟩ apart; **b)** *(fig.: kritisch analysieren)* pull ⟨*play, book, etc.*⟩ to pieces; destroy ⟨*alibi, reputation*⟩
zerplatzen *itr. V.; mit sein* burst; **vor Wut** ~ *(fig.)* explode [with anger]
zerquetschen *tr. V.* crush; mash ⟨*potatoes*⟩; **es kostet 20 Mark und ein paar Zerquetschte** *(ugs.)* it costs 20 marks and a bit
zerraufen *tr. V.* tousle ⟨*hair*⟩
Zerr·bild das distorted image
zerreden *tr. V.* talk over and over; do *or* flog ⟨*subject*⟩ to death *(coll.)*
zerreiben *unr. tr. V.* crush ⟨*spices, paint colours, etc.*⟩; grind ⟨*corn*⟩; *(fig.)* crush, wipe out ⟨*enemy*⟩
zerreißen 1. *unr. tr. V.* **a)** *(auseinanderreißen)* tear up; *(in kleine Stücke)* tear to pieces; ⟨*animal*⟩ tear ⟨*prey*⟩ limb from limb; dismember ⟨*prey*⟩; break ⟨*thread*⟩; **ich könnte ihn** ~! I could tear him limb from limb!; **sich [fast]** ~ **[um jmdn.]** [nearly] kill oneself [for sb. *or* to help sb.]; **ich kann mich nicht** ~: I can't be in two places at once; **Schüsse zerrissen die Stille** shots rent the silence; **b)** *(beschädigen)* tear ⟨*stocking, trousers, etc.*⟩ **(an** + *Dat.* on). **2.** *unr. itr. V.; mit sein* **a)** *(auseinandergehen)* ⟨*thread, string, rope*⟩ break; **die Bande zwischen ihnen waren zerrissen** *(fig.)* the bonds between them had parted; **ihre Nerven war zum Zerreißen gespannt** her nerves were stretched to breaking-point; **b)** *(kaputtgehen)* ⟨*paper, cloth, etc.*⟩ tear; **zerrissene Kleider/Schuhe** ragged clothes/worn-out shoes
Zerreiß·probe die acid test
zerren ['tsɛrən] **1.** *tr. V.* **a)** drag; **etw. an die Öffentlichkeit** ~ *(fig.)* drag sth. into the limelight; **b) sich** *(Dat.)* **einen Muskel/eine Sehne** ~: pull a muscle/tendon. **2.** *itr. V.* **an etw.** *(Dat.)* ~: tug *or* pull at sth.
zerrinnen *unr. itr. V.* melt; *(fig.)* ⟨*time, years*⟩ pass; **seine Hoffnungen/Träume/Pläne zerrannen [in nichts]** *(geh.)* his hopes/dreams vanished/plans came to nothing; **jmdm. unter den Händen/Fingern** ~: slip through sb.'s fingers
zerrissen [tsɛɐ̯'rɪsn̩] **1.** *2. Part. v.* **zerreißen. 2.** *Adj.* **[innerlich]** ~: at odds with oneself
Zerrissenheit die; ~: inner turmoil
Zerr·spiegel der distorting mirror
Zerrung die; ~, ~**en** pulled muscle; *(Sehnen~)* pulled tendon
zerrupfen *tr. V.* tear to bits
zerrütten [tsɛɐ̯'rʏtn̩] *tr. V.* ruin ⟨*health*⟩; shatter ⟨*nerves*⟩; ruin, wreck ⟨*marriage*⟩; **aus zerrütteten Familienverhältnissen stammen** come from a broken home; **die Finanzen sind zerrüttet** the finances are in a disastrous state
Zerrüttung die; ~, ~**en** *(der Gesundheit)* ruining; *(der Nerven)* shattering; *(einer Ehe)* [irretrievable] breakdown; *(einer Familie)* break-up
Zerrüttungs·prinzip das *(Rechtsw.)* principle of irretrievable breakdown *(of a marriage)*
zersägen *tr. V.* saw up
zerschellen *itr. V.; mit sein* be dashed *or* smashed to pieces
[1]**zerschlagen 1.** *unr. tr. V.* smash ⟨*plate, windscreen, etc.*⟩; smash up ⟨*furniture*⟩; *(fig.)* smash ⟨*spy ring etc.*⟩; crush ⟨*enemy, attack*⟩; break up ⟨*cartel*⟩. **2.** *unr. refl. V.* ⟨*plan, deal*⟩ fall through
[2]**zerschlagen** *Adj.* worn out; whacked *(Brit. coll.)*; tuckered [out] *(Amer. coll.)*; shattered *(Brit. coll.)*
Zerschlagung die; ~, ~**en** smashing; destruction; *(eines Gegners, Widerstands)* crushing; **die** ~ **der Kartelle** the breaking up of cartels
zerschmelzen *unr. itr. V.; mit sein (auch fig.)* melt
zerschmettern *tr. V.* smash; shatter ⟨*glass, leg, bone*⟩; *(fig.)* crush ⟨*army, enemy*⟩
zerschneiden *unr. tr. V.* **a)** *(schneiden)* cut; *(in Stücke)* cut up; *(in zwei Teile)* cut in two; carve ⟨*joint*⟩; **von tiefen Furchen zerschnitten** deeply rutted; **b)** *(verletzen)* cut [into] ⟨*skin etc.*⟩
zerschnippeln *tr. V. (ugs.)* cut up *or* snip into small pieces
zerschunden [tsɛɐ̯'ʃʊndn̩] *Adj.* covered in scratches *postpos.*
zersetzen 1. *tr. V.* **a)** *(auflösen)* corrode ⟨*metal*⟩; decompose ⟨*organism*⟩; **b)** *(untergraben)* subvert ⟨*ideals*⟩; undermine ⟨*morale*⟩; ~**de Schriften** subversive writings. **2.** *refl. V.* decompose; ⟨*wood, compost*⟩ rot
Zersetzung die; ~, ~**en a)** *s.* **zersetzen 2:** decomposition; rotting; **b)** *s.* **zersetzen 1 b:** subversion; undermining
Zersetzungs·prozeß der process of decomposition
zersiedeln *tr. V. (Amtsspr.)* overdevelop ⟨*area*⟩; spoil ⟨*area*⟩ by overdevelopment
Zersied[e]lung die overdevelopment
zerspalten *unr. (auch regelm.) tr. V. (auch fig.)* split [up]; *(Chemie)* break down ⟨*compounds*⟩ **(in** + *Akk.* into)
zersplittern 1. *itr. V.; mit sein* ⟨*wood, bone*⟩ splinter; ⟨*glass*⟩ shatter; **das Land war in viele Kleinstaaten zersplittert** the country was fragmented into many small states. **2.** *tr. V.* splinter; shatter ⟨*glass*⟩
zersprengen *tr. V.* **a)** *(sprengen)* blow up; *(in Stücke)* blow to pieces; **b)** *(auseinandertreiben)* scatter ⟨*army*⟩
zerspringen *unr. itr. V.; mit sein* **a)** shatter; *(Sprünge bekommen)* crack; *(fig.)* ⟨*heart*⟩ burst **(vor** + *Dat.* with); **der Kopf wollte mir** ~ **vor Schmerzen** my head was splitting; I had a splitting headache; **b)** *(geh.: zerreißen)* ⟨*string etc.*⟩ break
zerstampfen *tr. V.* **a)** *(zerkleinern)* pound, crush ⟨*spices etc.*⟩; mash ⟨*potatoes*⟩; **b)** *(beschädigen)* trample down ⟨*field etc.*⟩
zerstäuben *tr. V.* spray
Zerstäuber der; ~**s**, ~: atomizer
zerstechen *unr. tr. V.* **a)** *(stechen)* sting all over; ⟨*mosquitoes*⟩ bite all over; **b)** *(beschädigen)* jab holes in ⟨*cushion etc.*⟩; puncture, slit ⟨*tyre*⟩; **ihre Venen sind ganz zerstochen** her veins are covered in needle-marks
zerstieben *unr. (auch regelm.) itr.V.; mit sein (geh.)* scatter; ⟨*crowd*⟩ disperse; *(fig.)* ⟨*sadness, nightmare*⟩ vanish; **in alle Winde** ~: disappear without trace
zerstörbar *Adj.* destructible; **leicht** ~ **sein** be easily destroyed *or* broken
zerstören *tr. V.* destroy; ⟨*hooligan*⟩ smash up, vandalize ⟨*telephone-box etc.*⟩; *(fig.)* ruin ⟨*landscape, health, life*⟩; dash, destroy ⟨*hopes, dreams*⟩; wreck, destroy ⟨*marriage*⟩; **durch ein Feuer/Erdbeben zerstört** destroyed in *or* by a fire/an earthquake; ~**de Gewalt** destructive power; **zerstörte Städte** ruined cities
Zerstörer der; ~**s**, ~ **a)** *(Schiff)* destroyer; **b)** *(Person)* destroyer; wrecker; *(Rowdy)* vandal
zerstörerisch 1. *Adj.* destructive. **2.** *adv.* ~ **wirken** have a destructive effect
Zerstörung die destruction; *(durch Rowdies)* smashing up; vandalization; *(der Gesundheit, Existenz)* ruin[ation]; *(einer Ehe)* wrecking; destruction; *(von Hoffnungen)* dashing; destruction
Zerstörungs·wut die destructive frenzy
zerstoßen *unr. tr. V.* crush ⟨*berries etc.*⟩; *(im Mörser)* pound, crush ⟨*peppercorns etc.*⟩
zerstreiten *unr. refl. V.* **sich mit jmdm.** ~: fall out with sb.; **untereinander zerstritten sein** be at loggerheads
zerstreuen 1. *tr. V.* **a)** scatter; *(auseinandertreiben)* disperse ⟨*crowd*⟩; *(fig.)* **zerstreut liegende Gehöfte** scattered farms; **in alle Welt zerstreut** scattered to the four winds; **b)** *(unterhalten)* **jmdn./sich** ~: entertain sb./oneself; *(ablenken)* take sb.'s/one's mind off things; **sich ein wenig** ~: enjoy oneself a little; **sich mit** *od.* **durch etw.** ~: pass the time with sth.; **c)** *(beseitigen)* allay ⟨*fear, doubt, suspicion*⟩; dispel ⟨*worry, concern*⟩. **2.** *refl. V.* disperse; *(schneller)* scatter
zerstreut 1. *Adj.* distracted; *(vergeßlich)* absent-minded; **ein** ~**er Professor** *(ugs. scherzh.)* an absent-minded professor. **2.** *adv.* absent-mindedly
Zerstreutheit die; ~: absent-mindedness
Zerstreuung die; ~, ~**en** diversion; *(Unterhaltung)* entertainment; ~ **suchen** look for a distraction [to take one's mind off things]
zerstückeln *tr. V.* break ⟨*sth.*⟩ up into small pieces; *(zerschneiden)* cut *or* chop sth. up into small pieces; dismember ⟨*corpse*⟩
Zerstückelung die; ~, ~**en** breaking up; *(Zerschneidung)* cutting *or* chopping up; *(einer Leiche)* dismembering
zerteilen 1. *tr. V.* divide into pieces; *(zerschneiden)* cut into pieces; cut up; **das Schiff zerteilte die Wellen** *(fig.)* the ship sliced through the waves. **2.** *refl. V.* part
zerteppern [tsɛɐ̯'tɛpɐn] *s.* **zerdeppern**
Zertifikat [tsɛrtifi'ka:t] **das;** ~**[e]s**, ~**e** certificate; ~ **Deutsch als Fremdsprache** diploma in German as a foreign language
zertrampeln *tr. V.* trample all over ⟨*flower-bed etc.*⟩; trample ⟨*child etc.*⟩ underfoot

zertrennen *tr. V.* take apart; unpick ⟨*dress*⟩
zertreten *unr. tr. V.* stamp on; stamp out ⟨*cigarette, match*⟩; stamp on, crush ⟨*insect*⟩ underfoot
zertrümmern *tr. V.* smash; smash, shatter ⟨*glass*⟩; smash up ⟨*furniture*⟩; wreck ⟨*car, boat*⟩; reduce ⟨*building, city*⟩ to ruins
Zervelat·wurst [tsɛrvə'la:t-] **die** cervelat [sausage]
zerwühlen *tr. V.* churn up ⟨*bedclothes, soil*⟩; make a mess of, tousle ⟨*hair*⟩
Zerwürfnis [tsɛɐ̯'vʏrfnɪs] **das; ~ses, ~se** *(geh.)* quarrel; dispute; *(Bruch)* rift
zerzausen *tr. V.* ruffle; ruffle, tousle ⟨*hair*⟩; **zerzaust aussehen** look dishevelled; **vom Wind zerzauste Bäume** windswept trees
Zeter das *in* **~ und Mord[io] schreien** *(ugs.)* scream blue murder *(sl.)*; raise hell *(coll.)*
zetern ['tse:tɐn] *itr. V. (abwertend) (schimpfen)* scold [shrilly]; *(sich beklagen)* moan **(über +** *Akk.* about); **gegen den Sittenverfall ~:** declaim against the decay of morals
Zettel ['tsɛtl̩] **der; ~s, ~:** slip *or* piece of paper; *(mit einigen Zeilen)* note; *(Bekanntmachung)* notice; *(Formular)* form; *(Kassen~)* receipt; *(Hand~)* leaflet; *(Stimm~)* [ballot-]paper
Zettel-: ~kasten der index on slips of paper; **~wirtschaft die** *(ugs. abwertend)* jumble of bits of paper
Zeug [tsɔyk] **das; ~[e]s, ~e a)** *o. Pl. (ugs., oft abwertend: Sachen)* stuff; **fürchterliches ~ träumen** dream awful things; **sie hat** *od.* **in ihr steckt das ~ zu etw.** *(fig.)* she has what it takes to be sth. *or* has the makings of sth.; **was das ~ hält** *(fig. ugs.)* for all one's worth; ⟨*drive*⟩ hell for leather; **sich [für jmdn./etw. mächtig** *od.* **tüchtig] ins ~ legen** *(fig.)* do one's utmost [for sb./sth.]; **b)** *o. Pl. (ugs.: Unsinn)* **dummes/albernes ~** *(Gerede)* nonsense; rubbish; **dummes ~ machen** mess about; **c)** *(Kleidung)* things *pl.*; **jmdm. etwas am ~ flicken** *(ugs.)* pin something on sb.; **d)** *(veralt.: Tuch)* cloth
Zeuge ['tsɔygə] **der; ~n, ~n** witness; **~ von etw. sein/werden** be a witness to sth.; witness sth.; **~ der Anklage/Verteidigung** *(Rechtsw.)* witness for the prosecution/defence; **die ~n Jehovas** the Jehovah's Witnesses; **die Ruinen sind ~n der Vergangenheit** *(fig.)* the ruins bear witness to the past
[1]**zeugen** *itr. V.* give evidence; testify; **von etw. ~** *(fig.)* testify to sth.; *(zeigen)* display sth.; **das zeugt nicht gerade für seine Uneigennützigkeit** *(fig.)* that doesn't say much for his unselfishness
[2]**zeugen** *tr. V.* procreate; ⟨*man*⟩ father ⟨*child*⟩; *(fig.)* engender; bring about; **Kinder ~:** reproduce; have children
Zeugen·aussage die testimony; witness's statement
Zeugenschaft die; ~: testimony
Zeugen-: ~stand der *o. Pl.* witness-box *(Brit.)*; witness stand *(Amer.)*; **~vernehmung die** examination of the witness/witnesses
Zeug·haus das *(bes. Milit. hist.)* armoury
Zeugin die; ~, ~nen witness
Zeugnis das; ~ses, ~se a) *(Schulw.)* report; **~ der Reife** *s.* **Abiturzeugnis; b)** *(Arbeits~)* reference; testimonial; **ich kann ihm nur das beste ~ ausstellen** *(fig.)* I can't speak too highly of him; **c)** *(Gutachten)* certificate; **d)** *(geh.: Beweis)* evidence; **~se einer früheren Kulturstufe** evidence *or* testimony of an earlier stage of civilization; **e)** *(veralt.: Aussage)* testimony; **falsches ~ ablegen** bear false witness
Zeugs das; ~ *(ugs. abwertend)* stuff; *(einzelne Dinge)* things *pl.*
Zeugung die; ~, ~en procreation; *(eines Kindes)* fathering
zeugungs-, Zeugungs-: ~akt der act of procreation *or* reproduction; **~fähig** *Adj.* fertile; **~fähigkeit die;** *o. Pl.* fertility

Zeus (der) Zeus
ZGB *Abk. (DDR, Schweiz)* **Zivilgesetzbuch**
z. Hd. *Abk.* **zu Händen; zu Handen** *(österr.)* attn.
Zibebe [tsi'be:bə] **die; ~, ~n** *(österr., südd.)* sultana
Zichorie [tsɪ'ço:ri̯ə] **die; ~:** chicory
Zicke ['tsɪkə] **die; ~, ~n a)** *(Ziege)* she- *or* nanny-goat; **b)** *(Schimpfwort) s.* **Ziege b; c)** *Pl. (ugs.: Dummheiten)* stupid tricks; monkey business *(sl.)*; **~n machen** mess about; *(Schwierigkeiten machen)* make trouble; **mach bloß keine ~n!** none of your monkey business! *(sl.)*
zickig *(ugs. abwertend)* **1.** *Adj.* prim; *(prüde)* prudish. **2.** *adv.* primly; *(prüde)* prudishly
Zicklein das; ~s, ~: kid
Zickzack der; ~[e]s, ~e zigzag; **im ~:** in a zigzag; **sie fuhren im ~ durch den Verkehr** they zigzagged through the traffic
Zick·zack·kurs der zigzag line; **im ~:** in a zigzag [line]
Ziege ['tsi:gə] **die; ~, ~n a)** goat; **b)** *(Schimpfwort: Frau)* **dumme** *od.* **blöde ~:** stupid cow *(sl. derog.)*; **eingebildete ~:** stuck-up female *(derog.)*
Ziegel ['tsi:gl̩] **der; ~s, ~ a)** brick; **b)** *(Dach~)* tile
Ziegel·dach das tiled roof
Ziegelei die; ~, ~en brickworks *sing.*
ziegel·rot *Adj.* brick-red
Ziegel·stein der brick
Ziegen-: ~bart der goat's beard; *(ugs.: Spitzbart)* goatee beard; **~bock der** he- *or* billy-goat; **~käse der** goat's cheese; **~leder das** goatskin; **~milch die** goat's milk; **~peter der; ~s, ~** *(ugs.)* mumps *sing.*
zieh [tsi:] *1. u. 3. Pers. Sg. Prät. v.* **zeihen**
Zieh-: ~brunnen der draw-well; **~eltern** *Pl. (veralt.)* foster-parents
ziehen ['tsi:ən] **1.** *unr. tr. V.* **a)** pull; *(sanfter)* draw; *(zerren)* tug; *(schleppen)* drag; **jmdn. an sich ~:** draw sb. to one; **jmdn. am Ärmel ~:** pull sb. by the sleeve; **sie zogen ihn mit Gewalt ins Auto** they dragged him into the car by force; **er zog die Knie bis unters Kinn** he drew his knees up under his chin; **das Auto nach rechts/links ~:** pull the car over to the left/right; **das Flugzeug nach oben/unten ~:** put the plane into a climb/descent; **die Rolläden nach oben ~:** roll up the shutters; **ein Hemd** *usw.* **durchs Wasser ~:** give a shirt *etc.* a quick rinse; **die Gardinen vor das Fenster ~:** draw the curtains [across the window]; **Perlen auf eine Schnur ~:** thread pearls/beads on to a string; **den Hut ins Gesicht ~:** pull one's hat down over one's face; **einen Pullover über das Hemd ~:** put a pullover on over one's shirt; **b)** *(fig.)* **es zog ihn zu ihr/zu dem Ort** he felt drawn to her/to the place; **es zog ihn in die Ferne** he felt an urge to travel; **alle Blicke auf sich ~:** attract *or* capture all the attention; **jmds. Zorn/Unwillen** *usw.* **auf sich ~:** incur sb.'s anger/displeasure *etc.*; **etw. nach sich ~:** result in sth.; entail sth.; **gewisse Folgen nach sich ~:** have certain consequences; **c)** *(heraus~)* pull out ⟨*nail, cork, organ-stop, etc.*⟩; extract ⟨*tooth*⟩; take out, remove ⟨*stitches, splinter*⟩; draw ⟨*cord, sword, pistol*⟩; **den Ring vom Finger ~:** pull *or* take one's ring off one's finger; **den Hut ~:** raise *or* doff one's hat; **etw. aus der Tasche ~:** take sth. out of one's pocket; *(aus Automaten)* **Zigaretten/Süßigkeiten** *usw.* **~:** get cigarettes/sweets *etc.* from a slot-machine; **die [Quadrat]wurzel ~** *(Math.)* extract the square root; **d)** *(dehnen)* stretch ⟨*elastic etc.*⟩; stretch out ⟨*sheets etc.*⟩; *s. auch* **Blase a;** [1]**Faden; e)** *(Gesichtspartien bewegen)* make ⟨*face, grimace*⟩; **die Augenbrauen nach oben ~:** raise one's eyebrows; **die Stirn in Falten ~:** wrinkle *or* knit one's brow; *(mißmutig)* frown; **die Mundwinkel nach unten ~:** pull down the corners of one's mouth; **f)** *(bei Brettspielen)* move ⟨*chess-man etc.*⟩; **g)** *(einatmen)* **Luft durch die Nase ~:** breathe *or* draw in air; **er zog den Rauch in die Lungen** he inhaled the smoke [into his lungs]; **h)** *(zeichnen)* draw ⟨*line, circle, arc, etc.*⟩; **i)** *(anlegen)* dig ⟨*trench*⟩; build ⟨*wall*⟩; erect ⟨*fence*⟩; put up ⟨*washing-line*⟩; run, lay ⟨*cable, wires*⟩; draw ⟨*frontier*⟩; trace ⟨*loop*⟩; follow ⟨*course*⟩; **sich** *(Dat.)* **einen Scheitel ~:** make a parting [in one's hair]; **j)** *(auf~)* grow ⟨*plants, flowers*⟩; breed ⟨*animals*⟩; **den Burschen werde ich mir noch ~** *(ugs.)* I'll knock the lad into shape yet *(coll.)*; **k)** *(verblaßt; auch als Funktionsverb)* draw ⟨*lesson, conclusion, comparison*⟩; *s. auch* **Konsequenz a; Rechenschaft; Verantwortung a; l)** *(herstellen)* make ⟨*candles*⟩; draw ⟨*wire, pipes*⟩; **m)** *(spannen)* mount ⟨*picture*⟩ **(auf +** *Akk.* to); fit ⟨*string*⟩ **(auf +** *Akk.* to); **n)** *(beim Sprechen)* draw out ⟨*vowel*⟩; **o)** *(in sich aufnehmen)* ⟨*plant*⟩ draw [up] ⟨*water, nourishment*⟩ **(aus** from); *(gewinnen)* extract ⟨*oil, ore*⟩ **(aus** from); **Profit/Nutzen aus etw. ~** *(fig.)* derive profit/benefit from sth.; **p)** *(Finanzw.)* **einen Wechsel auf jmdn. ~:** draw a bill on sb.; **q)** *(schlagen)* **jmdm. etw. über den Kopf ~:** hit sb. over the head with sth.; **r)** *(Waffenkunde)* rifle ⟨*barrel*⟩. **2.** *unr. itr. V.* **a)** *(reißen)* pull; **an etw.** *(Dat.)* **~:** pull on sth.; **der Hund zieht an der Leine** the dog is straining at the leash; **an einem** *od.* **am gleichen** *od.* **an demselben Strang** *od.* **Strick ~** *(fig.)* be pulling in the same direction; **b)** *(funktionieren)* ⟨*stove, pipe, chimney*⟩ draw; **ausgezeichnet/nicht richtig ~** *(Kfz-W.)* ⟨*car, engine*⟩ pull really well/not pull properly; **c)** *mit sein (um~)* move **(nach, in +** *Akk.* to); **aufs Land ~:** move [out] into the country; **zu jmdm. ~:** move in with sb.; **d)** *mit sein (gehen)* go; *(marschieren)* march; *(umherstreifen)* roam; rove; *(fortgehen)* go away; leave; ⟨*fog, clouds*⟩ drift; **durch etw. ~:** pass through sth.; **in den Krieg ~:** go *or* march off to war; **an die Front ~:** move up to the front; **jmdn. ungern ~ lassen** be sorry to see sb. go; **die Schwalben ~ nach Süden** the swallows are flying southwards; **e)** *(saugen)* draw; **an einer Zigarette/Pfeife ~:** draw on a cigarette/pipe; **an einem Strohhalm ~:** suck at a straw; **laß mich mal an deiner Zigarette ~:** let me have a puff of your cigarette; **f)** ⟨*tea, coffee*⟩ draw; **g)** *(Kochk.)* simmer; **h)** *(unpers.)* **es zieht [vom Fenster her]** there's a draught [from the window]; **es zieht mir an den Beinen** there's a draught round my legs; **i)** *(ugs.: ankommen)* sell; ⟨*trick*⟩ work; **das zieht bei mir nicht** that won't wash *or* won't cut any ice with me *(coll.)*; **j)** *(schmerzen)* **es zieht [mir] im Rücken** I've got backache; **~de Schmerzen** aches; **ein leichtes/starkes Ziehen im Bauch** a slight/intense stomach-ache. **3.** *unr. refl. V.* **a)** *(sich erstrecken)* ⟨*road*⟩ run, stretch; ⟨*frontier*⟩ run; **eine Narbe zog sich über sein ganzes Gesicht** there was a scar right across his face; **der Weg** *o. ä.* **zieht sich** *(ugs.)* the journey *etc.* goes on and on; **b)** *(sich ver~)* warp; get out of shape
Zieher der; ~s, ~ *(salopp)* pickpocket
Zieh-: ~harmonika die piano accordion; **~kind das** *(veralt.)* foster-child; **~mutter die** *(veralt.)* foster-mother
Ziehung die; ~, ~en draw; **die ~ des Hauptgewinns** the draw for the main prize
Zieh·vater der a) *(veralt.)* foster-father; **b)** *(fig.)* sponsor; patron
Ziel [tsi:l] **das; ~[e]s, ~e a)** *(Punkt, Ort)* destination; **am ~ der Reise angelangen** reach the end of one's journey; reach one's destination; **mit unbekanntem ~ abreisen** leave for an unknown destination; **b)** *(Sport)* finish; *(~linie)* finishing-line; *(Pferderennen)* finishing-post; **im ~:** at the finish; **das ~ er-**

reichen finish; **als erster das ~ erreichen** *od.* **durchs ~ gehen** finish first; cross the finishing-line first; ⟨*horse*⟩ be first past the [finishing-]post; **c)** *(~scheibe; auch Milit.)* target; **[weit] über das ~ [hinaus]schießen** *(fig. ugs.)* go over the top; overstep the mark; **d)** *(Zweck)* aim; goal; **sein ~ erreichen** achieve one's objective *or* aim; **[das] ~ unserer Bemühungen ist es, ... zu ...:** the object of our efforts is to ...; **mit dem ~, etw. zu tun** with the aim of doing sth.; **sich** *(Dat.)* **ein ~ setzen** *od.* **stecken** set oneself a goal; **sich** *(Dat.)* **etw. zum ~ setzen** set oneself *or* take sth. as one's aim; **etw. zum ~ haben** have sth. as one's/its goal; **Beharrlichkeit führt zum ~:** if at first you don't succeed, try, try, and try again; **e)** *(Ende)* **einer Sache** *(Dat.)* **ein ~ setzen** put an end to sth.

ziel-, Ziel-: ~bahn·hof der destination; **~band das;** *Pl.* **~bänder** *(Sport)* finishing-tape; **~bewußt 1.** *Adj.* purposeful; determined; **sehr ~bewußt sein** know exactly where one is going; **2.** *adv.* purposefully; determinedly

zielen *itr. V.* **a)** *(mit einer Waffe)* aim (**auf +** *Akk.*, **nach** at); **genau ~:** take careful aim; **ein gut gezielter Schuß/Wurf** an accurate *or* well-aimed shot/throw; **b)** *(sich richten)* **auf jmdn./etw. ~** ⟨*reproach, plan, efforts, etc.*⟩ be aimed at sb./sth.

zielend *Adj. (Sprachw.)* transitive

ziel-, Ziel-: ~fern·rohr das telescopic sight; **~foto das** *(Sport)* photograph of a/the finish; photo-finish photograph; **~gerade die** *(Sport)* finishing-straight; **~gerichtet 1.** *Adj.* purposeful; **2.** *adv.* purposefully; **~gruppe die** target group; **~kamera die** *(Sport)* photo-finish camera; **~linie die** *(Sport)* finishing-line; **~los 1.** *Adj.* aimless; **2.** *adv.* aimlessly; **~losigkeit die; ~:** aimlessness; **~richter der** finish judge; **~scheibe die** *(auch fig.)* target (*Gen.* for); **~setzung die; ~, ~en** aims *pl.*; objectives *pl.*; **~sicher 1.** *Adj.* **a)** *(treffsicher)* accurate; **b)** *(~gerichtet)* decisive, purposeful ⟨*steps*⟩; confident ⟨*grip*⟩; **2.** *adv.* **a)** *(treffsicher)* accurately; **b)** *(~gerichtet)* decisively; *(zuversichtlich)* confidently; **~sicherheit die;** *o. Pl.* accuracy; **~sprache die** *(Sprachw.)* target language; **~strebig 1.** *Adj.* **a)** purposeful; **b)** *(energisch)* single-minded ⟨*person*⟩; **2.** *adv.* **a)** purposefully; **b)** *(energisch)* single-mindedly; **~strebigkeit die; ~** *s.* **~strebig: a)** purposefulness; **b)** single-mindedness

ziemen ['tsi:mən] *(veralt.)* **1.** *refl. V.* be seemly; **das ziemt sich einfach nicht** that just is not done *(coll.)*. **2.** *itr. V.* **jmdm./einer Sache ~:** befit sb./sth.; be fitting for sb./sth.

Ziemer der; ~s, ~ *s.* **Ochsenziemer**

ziemlich 1. *Adj. (ugs.)* fair, sizeable ⟨*quantity, number*⟩; **eine ~e Frechheit/Weile** quite a cheek/while; **mit ~er Lautstärke** quite loudly; **er kommt mit ~er Sicherheit** he is more or less certain to come; **ich weiß mit ~er Sicherheit, daß ...:** I am fairly *or* reasonably certain that ... **2.** *adv.* **a)** quite; fairly; *(etwas intensiver)* pretty; **du kommst ~ spät** you're rather late; **~ viele Leute** quite a few people; **b)** *(ugs.: fast)* pretty well; more or less; **er ist so ~ in meinem Alter** he's more or less my age

ziepen ['tsi:pn̩] *(bes. nordd.)* **1.** *itr. V.* **es ziepte ihr im Kreuz** she had a twinge in her back. **2.** *tr. V.* tweak (**an +** *Dat.* by); **jmdn. an den Haaren ~:** give sb.'s hair a tug

Zier [tsi:ɐ̯] **die; ~** *(veralt.) s.* **Zierde**

Zierat ['tsi:ra:t] **der; ~[e]s, ~e** *(geh.)* ornament[ation]; **bloßer ~ sein** be purely ornamental; **reich an ~en** richly decorated *or* ornamented

Zierde die; ~, ~n *(auch fig.)* ornament; embellishment; **zur ~:** as decoration; **jmdm. zur ~ gereichen** *(fig.)* be a credit to sb.; **[die] ~ des Landes** *(fig.)* the pride of the nation; **eine ~ des Landes** *(fig.)* one of the country's jewels

Zier·decke die ornamental bedspread

zieren 1. *tr. V. (geh.)* adorn; decorate ⟨*room*⟩. **2.** *refl. V.* be coy; *(sich bitten lassen)* need some coaxing *or* pressing; **zier dich nicht so!** don't make such a fuss!; don't be so coy!

Ziererei die; ~, ~en *(abwertend)* coyness *no indef. art., no pl.*; *(Zögern)* hedging *no indef. art., no pl.*; *(Pose)* posturing *no indef. art.*

Zier-: ~garten der ornamental garden; *(Blumengarten)* flower-garden; **~leiste die** [decorative] moulding; *(an der Decke)* cornice; *(am Auto)* trim

zierlich 1. *Adj.* dainty; delicate; petite, dainty ⟨*woman, figure*⟩. **2.** *adv.* daintily; delicately

Zierlichkeit die; ~: daintiness; delicateness; *(einer Frau, Gestalt)* petiteness; daintiness

Zier-: ~pflanze die ornamental plant; **~stich der** *(Handarb.)* ornamental stitch; **~strauch der** ornamental shrub

Ziffer ['tsɪfɐ] **die; ~, ~n a)** *(Zahlzeichen)* numeral; *(in einer mehrstelligen Zahl)* digit; figure; **arabische/römische ~n** arabic/roman numerals; **b)** *(Unterabschnitt)* subsection; clause

Ziffer·blatt das dial; face

-zig, zig [tsɪç] *unbest. Zahlwort (ugs.)* umpteen *(coll.)*

Zigarettchen das; ~s, ~ *(ugs.)* ciggy *(coll.)*

Zigarette [tsiga'rɛtə] **die; ~, ~n** cigarette

Zigaretten-: ~asche die cigarette-ash; **~automat der** cigarette-machine; **~etui das** cigarette-case; **~kippe die** cigarette-end; **~länge die** *(ugs.) in* **auf** *od.* **für eine ~länge** just for a smoke; **~papier das** cigarette-paper; **~pause die** *(ugs.)* break for a smoke; **~raucher der** cigarette-smoker; **~schachtel die** cigarette-packet; **~spitze die** cigarette-holder

Zigarillo [tsiga'rɪlo] **der** *od.* **das; ~, ~s** cigarillo; small cigar

Zigarre [tsi'garə] **die; ~, ~n a)** cigar; **b)** *(ugs.: Rüffel)* telling-off; rocket *(Brit. sl.)*; **jmdm. eine ~ verpassen** give sb. a dressing down *or (Brit. sl.)* rocket

Zigarren-: ~ab·schneider der cigar-cutter; **~asche die** cigar-ash; **~raucher der** cigar-smoker; **~stummel der** cigar-stub

Zigeuner [tsi'gɔynɐ] **der; ~s, ~, Zigeunerin, die; ~, ~nen a)** gypsy; **b)** *(ugs.: Tramp)* vagabond

Zigeuner-: ~kapelle die gypsy band; **~musik die** gypsy music; **~primas der** leading fiddle-player [of a gypsy band]; **~schnitzel das** *(Kochk.) veal or pork escalope in a spicy sauce with green peppers, tomato, etc.*; **~sprache die** Romany [language]

zig·mal *Adv. (ugs.)* umpteen times *(coll.)*

zigst ... *(ugs.)* umpteenth *(coll.)*

zig·tausend *unbest. Zahlwort (ugs.)* umpteen thousand *(coll.)*

Zikade [tsi'ka:də] **die; ~, ~n** *(Zool.)* cicada

Zimbal ['tsɪmbal] **das; ~s, ~e** *od.* **~s** *(Musik)* cimbalom

Zimbel ['tsɪmbl̩] **die; ~, ~n** *(Musik)* cymbal

Zimmer ['tsɪmɐ] **das; ~s, ~:** room; **auf/in sein ~ gehen** go to one's room

Zimmer-: ~antenne die indoor aerial *or (Amer.)* antenna; **~arbeit die** carpentry *no indef. art.*; **~ arbeiten** carpentry work *sing.*; **~brand der** room fire; **~decke die** ceiling

Zimmerer der; ~s, ~: carpenter

Zimmer-: ~flucht die; *Pl.* **~en** suite [of rooms]; **~hand·werk das** carpentry *no art.*; **~kellner der** room waiter; **~laut·stärke die** domestic listening level; **das Radio auf ~lautstärke stellen** turn the radio down to a reasonable volume [so as not to disturb the neighbours]; **~linde die** African hemp; **~mädchen das** chambermaid; **~mann der;** *Pl.* **~leute** carpenter; **~meister der** master carpenter

zimmern 1. *tr. V.* make ⟨*shelves, coffin, etc.*⟩. **2.** *itr. V.* do carpentry; **an einem Regal ~:** be making a bookshelf

Zimmer-: ~nummer die room number; **~pflanze die** house-plant; indoor plant; **~suche die** room-hunt; **bei der ~suche** when room-hunting; **auf ~suche sein** be looking for a room; **~temperatur die** room temperature; **~theater das** studio theatre; **~vermittlung die** accommodation office

zimperlich ['tsɪmpɐlɪç] *(abwertend)* **1.** *Adj.* timid; *(leicht angeekelt)* squeamish; *(prüde)* prissy; *(übertrieben rücksichtsvoll)* over-scrupulous; **sei nicht ~ mit ihnen** don't go easy on them. **2.** *s. Adj.:* timidly; squeamishly; prissily; over-scrupulously; **die Polizei ging nicht gerade ~ mit ihr um** the police didn't exactly treat her with kid gloves

Zimperlichkeit die; ~, ~en *(abwertend)* timidity; *(Neigung zum Ekel)* squeamishness; *(Prüderie)* prissiness; *(übertriebene Rücksicht)* over-scrupulousness; excessive scruples *pl.*

Zimt [tsɪmt] **der; ~[e]s, ~e a)** cinnamon; **b)** *(ugs. abwertend: Zeug)* rubbish; **so ein ~!** what a load of rubbish! *(coll.)*

Zimt-: ~stange die cinnamon stick; **~ziege die** *(Schimpfwort: Frau)* cow *(sl. derog.)*

[1]**Zink** [tsɪŋk] **das; ~[e]s** zinc

[2]**Zink der; ~[e]s, ~en** *(Musik)* cornetto

Zink-: ~blech das zinc [sheet]; **~blende die** zinc blende

Zinke die; ~, ~n prong; *(eines Kammes)* tooth; *(Holzverarb.)* dovetail

zinken *tr. V. (ugs.)* mark ⟨*cards*⟩

Zinken der; ~s, ~ a) *(Gaunerspr.)* [crook's/beggar's] secret sign *or* mark; **b)** *(ugs. scherzh.: Nase)* conk *(sl.)*

Zink-: ~leim·verband der *(Med.)* Unna's paste dressing; **~salbe die** *(Med.)* zinc oxide ointment

Zinn [tsɪn] **das; ~[e]s a)** *(Metall)* tin; **b)** *(Gegenstände)* pewter[ware]

Zinne die; ~, ~n a) merlon; **~n** battlements; **b)** *(schweiz.: Dachterrasse)* roof terrace

Zinn-: ~figur die pewter figure; *(~soldat o. ä.)* tin figure; **~gießer der** pewterer

Zinnie ['tsɪni̯ə] **die; ~, ~n** *(Bot.)* zinnia

Zinn·kraut das; *o. Pl.* common horsetail

Zinnober [tsɪ'no:bɐ] **der; ~s, ~ a)** cinnabar; **b)** *o. Pl.; österr.:* **das; ~s** *(~rot)* vermilion; **c)** *o. Pl. (salopp abwertend) (wertloses Zeug)* junk; rubbish; *(Unsinn)* twaddle; **~ machen** make a big fuss

zinnober·rot *Adj.* vermilion

Zinn-: ~soldat der tin soldier; **~teller der** pewter plate

Zins [tsɪns] **der; ~es, ~en** *od.* **~e a)** *Pl.* **~en** *(Geld)* interest; **~en tragen** *od.* **bringen** earn interest; **zu 8% ~en** at 8% interest; **bei einem ~ von 8%** at 8% interest; **die ~en sind gestiegen** interest rates have gone up; **jmdm. etw. mit ~en** *od.* **mit ~ und Zinseszins zurückzahlen** *(fig.)* make sb. pay dearly for sth.; **b)** *Pl.* **~e** *(südd., österr., schweiz.: Miet~)* rent

Zins·erhöhung die increase in the rate of interest

Zinses·zins der; ~es, ~en compound interest

zins-, Zins-: ~fuß der interest rate; **~günstig** *(Finanzw.)* **1.** *Adj.* at a favourable rate of interest *postpos.*; low-interest ⟨*credit, loan*⟩; high-interest, high-yield ⟨*savings scheme, investment, etc.*⟩; **2.** *adv.* at a favourable rate of interest; **~los 1.** *Adj.* interest-free; **2.** *adv.* free of interest; **~pflichtig** *Adj.* liable to interest *postpos.*; **... ist ~pflichtig** interest is payable on ...; **~politik die** policy on interest rates; **~rech-**

nung die calculation of interest; ~**satz der** interest rate; ~**senkung die** reduction of interest rates

Zionismus [tsio'nɪsmʊs] **der;** ~: Zionism *no art.*

Zionist der, Zionistin, die; ~, ~**nen** Zionist

zionistisch *Adj.* Zionist

Zipfel ['tsɪpfl] **der;** ~**s,** ~ *(einer Decke, eines Tisch-, Handtuchs usw.)* corner; *(Wurst~, eines Halstuchs)* [tail-]end; *(einer ~mütze)* point; *(Spitze eines Sees usw.)* tip

zipfelig *Adj.* uneven ⟨*hem*⟩; ⟨*coat, skirt*⟩ with an uneven hem

Zipfel·mütze die [long-]pointed cap

Zipp ® [tsɪp] **der;** ~**s,** ~**s** *(österr.)* zip

Zipperlein ['tsɪpɐlain] **das;** ~ *(ugs. veralt.)* gout

Zipp·verschluß der *(österr.)* zip-fastener

Zirbel- ['tsɪrbl]: ~**drüse die** *(Biol.)* pineal gland; ~**kiefer die** Swiss [stone] pine; arolla pine

Zirconium *(fachspr.) s.* **Zirkonium**

zirka ['tsɪrka] *Adv.* about; approximately

Zirkel ['tsɪrkl] **der;** ~**s,** ~ **a)** *(Gerät)* [pair *sing.* of] compasses *pl.;* **b)** *(Kreis, Gruppe; beim Pferdesport; DDR: Arbeitsgemeinschaft)* circle; **c)** *s.* **Zirkeldefinition; Zirkelschluß**

Zirkel-: ~**definition die** circular definition; ~**kasten der** compasses-case

zirkeln 1. *tr. V. (genau abmessen)* measure out precisely; **gezirkelt** precisely laid out; **er zirkelte den Ball genau in die linke obere Ecke** *(Fußballjargon)* he placed the ball with precision in the top left-hand corner. **2.** *itr. V. (ugs.: sehr genau arbeiten)* try to get things just right

Zirkel·schluß der circular argument

Zirkonium [tsɪr'ko:nium] **das;** ~**s** zirconium

zirkular [tsɪrku'la:ɐ] *(Physik, Fot.)* **1.** *Adj.* circular **2.** *adv.* circularly

Zirkulation [tsɪrkula'tsio:n] **die,** ~, ~**en a)** circulation; **b)** *(Fechten)* circular parry

zirkulieren *itr. V.; auch mit sein* circulate

Zirkumflex [tsɪrkʊm'flɛks] **der;** ~**es,** ~**e** *(Sprachw.)* circumflex

Zirkus ['tsɪrkʊs] **der;** ~, ~**se a)** circus; **b)** *(ugs.) o. Pl. (Trubel)* hustle and bustle; *(Krach)* to-do; rumpus *(coll.); (Umstände)* **mach nicht so einen** ~**!** don't make such a fuss!

Zirkus-: ~**pferd das** circus horse; ~**vorstellung die** circus performance; ~**zelt das** big top

zirpen ['tsɪrpn] *itr. V.* chirp

Zirren *s.* **Zirrus**

Zirrhose [tsɪ'ro:zə] **die;** ~, ~**n** *(Med.)* cirrhosis

Zirrus ['tsɪrʊs] **der;** ~, ~ *od.* **Zirren, Zirrus·wolke die** *(Met.)* cirrus [cloud]

zirzensisch [tsɪr'tsɛnzɪʃ] *Adj.* circus *attrib.*

zisalpin [tsɪsal'pi:n] *Adj.* cisalpine

Zischelei die; ~, ~**en** whispering

zischeln ['tsɪʃln] *tr. V.* whisper angrily

zischen ['tsɪʃn] **1.** *itr. V.* **a)** hiss; ⟨*hot fat*⟩ sizzle; **b)** *mit sein* hiss; *(ugs.: flitzen)* whizz. **2.** *tr. V.* **a)** *(zischend sprechen)* hiss; **b) ein Bier/einen** ~ *(ugs.)* knock back a beer *(coll.)*/knock one back *(coll.)*

Zisch·laut der *(Sprachw.)* sibilant

Ziseleur [tsize'lø:ɐ] **der;** ~**s,** ~**e** engraver

Ziselier·arbeit die engraving; *(von Gold, Silber)* chasing *no indef. art.; (Produkt)* piece of engraved/chased work

ziselieren [tsize'li:rən] *tr., itr. V.* engrave; chase ⟨*gold, silver*⟩

Ziselierer der; ~**s,** ~ *s.* **Ziseleur**

Ziselierung die; ~, ~**en** engraving; *(von Gold, Silber)* chasing

Zisterne [tsɪs'tɛrnə] **die;** ~, ~**n** [underground] tank *or* cistern

Zisterzienser [tsɪstɛr'tsiɛnzɐ] **der;** ~**s,** ~, **Zisterzienserin die,** ~, ~**nen** Cistercian [monk/nun]

Zisterzienser·orden der Cistercian order

Zitadelle [tsita'dɛlə] **die;** ~, ~**n** citadel

Zitat [tsi'ta:t] **das;** ~**[e]s,** ~**e** quotation **(aus** from); **falsches** ~: misquotation

Zitaten-: ~**sammlung die** collection of quotations; ~**schatz der** store of quotations

Zither ['tsɪtɐ] **die;** ~, ~**n** zither

Zither·spieler der zither-player

zitieren [tsi'ti:rən] *tr., itr. V.* **a)** quote **(aus, nach** from); *(Rechtsspr.: anführen)* cite; **..., ich zitiere: „..."** ... and I quote: '...'; *(wie er usw. sich ausdrückt)* '...', as he *etc.* puts it; **falsch** ~: misquote; **b)** *(vorladen, rufen)* summon **(vor** before, **zu** to)

Zitronat [tsitro'na:t] **das;** ~**[e]s** candied lemon-peel

Zitrone [tsi'tro:nə] **die;** ~, ~**n** lemon; **jmdn. ausquetschen wie eine** ~ *(ugs.) (ausfragen)* pump sb.; *(ausbeuten)* bleed sb. dry

zitronen-, Zitronen-: ~**falter der** brimstone butterfly; ~**gelb** *Adj.* lemon-yellow; ~**limonade die** lemonade; ~**melisse die** lemon balm; ~**presse die** lemon-squeezer; ~**saft der** lemon-juice; ~**säure die** *(Chemie)* citric acid; ~**schale die** lemon-peel

Zitrus·frucht ['tsitrʊs-] **die** citrus fruit

Zitter-: ~**aal der** electric eel; ~**gras das** quaking grass

zittern ['tsɪtɐn] *itr. V.* **a)** tremble **(vor + *Dat.*** with); *(vor Kälte)* shiver; ⟨*needle, arrow, leaf, etc.*⟩ quiver; *(flimmern)* ⟨*air*⟩ shimmer; *(beben)* ⟨*walls, windows*⟩ shake; **mit** ~**der Stimme** in a trembling *or* quavering voice; **b)** *(Angst haben)* tremble; quake; **vor jmdm./etw.** ~: be terrified of sb./sth.; **er zittert vor der Prüfung** he's scared stiff *(coll.)* about the exam; **mit Zittern und Zagen** in fear and trembling; **um jmdn./etw.** ~: be very worried about sb./sth.; **für jmdn.** ~: be anxious for sb.; **c)** *mit sein (salopp: gehen)* **nach Hause** ~: slope off home *(sl.)*

Zitter-: ~**pappel die** aspen; ~**partie die** *(Sportjargon, auch fig.)* nail-biting affair; ~**rochen der** torpedo ray

zittrig 1. *Adj.* shaky; doddery ⟨*old man*⟩. **2.** *adv.* shakily

Zitze ['tsɪtsə] **die;** ~, ~**n** teat

Zivi ['tsi:vi] **der;** ~**s,** ~**s** *(ugs.) s.* **Zivildienstleistende**

zivil [tsi'vi:l] **1.** *Adj.* **a)** civilian ⟨*life, population*⟩; non-military ⟨*purposes*⟩; civil ⟨*aviation, marriage, law, defence*⟩; *s. auch* **Ersatzdienst; b)** *(annehmbar)* decent; reasonable. **2.** *adv.* decently; reasonably

Zivil das; ~**s a)** civilian clothes *pl.;* **Polizist in** ~: plain-clothes policeman; **b)** *(schweiz.: Familienstand)* marital status

Zivil-: ~**beruf der** civilian profession *or* job; ~**bevölkerung die** civilian population; ~**courage die** courage of one's convictions; ~**diener der** *(österr.) s.* **Ersatzdienstleistende;** ~**dienst der;** *o. Pl. s.* **Ersatzdienst;** ~**dienst·leistende der;** ~**n,** ~**n;** *adj. Dekl.,* ~**dienstler** [~di:nstlɐ] **der,** ~**s,** ~ *(ugs.) s.* **Ersatzdienstleistende;** ~**ehe die** civil marriage; ~**flug·hafen der** civil airport; ~**gericht das** civil court; ~**gesetz·buch** *(schweiz., DDR)* civil code

Zivilisation [tsiviliza'tsio:n] **die;** ~, ~**en** civilization; **eine hohe/niedrige** ~: a high/low level of civilization; **fortschreitende** ~: progressively increasing degree of civilization

Zivilisations·krankheit die disease of modern civilization *or* society

zivilisations·müde *Adj.* weary of modern civilization *postpos.*

zivilisatorisch [tsiviliza'to:rɪʃ] **1.** *Adj.* ⟨*development, level, standard*⟩ of civilization. **2.** *adv.* with regard to civilization

zivilisieren *tr. V.* civilize

zivilisiert 1. *Adj.* civilized. **2.** *adv.* in a civilized way

Zivilist der; ~**en,** ~**en** civilian

Zivil-: ~**kammer die** *(Rechtsw.) chamber for civil matters;* ~**klage die** *(Rechtsw.)* private action *or* prosecution; ~**kleidung die** civilian clothes *pl;* ~**leben das** civilian life; ~**luft·fahrt die** civil aviation; ~**person die** civilian; ~**prozeß der** *(Rechtsw.)* civil action; ~**prozeß·ordnung die** *(Rechtsw.)* civil procedure; ~**recht das;** *o. Pl.* civil law; ~**richter der** civil judge; ~**sache die** *(Rechtsw.)* civil case; ~**schutz der** civil defence; ~**trauung die** civil wedding; ~**verfahren das** *(Rechtsw.)* civil proceedings *pl.*

ZK [tsɛt'ka:] **das;** ~**s,** ~**s** *Abk.* **Zentralkomitee**

Zloty ['zlɔti] **der;** ~**s,** ~**s** zloty

Znüni ['tsny:ni] **der** *od.* **das;** ~**s,** ~**s** *(schweiz.)* mid-morning snack

Zobel ['tso:bl] **der;** ~**s,** ~: sable

Zobel·pelz der sable [fur]

zockeln ['tsɔkln] *s.* **zuckeln**

Zofe ['tso:fə] **die;** ~, ~**n** *(hist.)* lady's maid

Zoff [tsɔf] **der;** ~**s** *(ugs.)* rowing *(coll.);* squabbling; ~ **machen** cause trouble; **mit jmdm.** ~ **haben** have a set-to with sb.

zog *1. u. 3. Pers. Sg. Prät. v.* **ziehen**

zögerlich ['tsø:gɐlɪç] **1.** *Adj.* hesitant; tentative. **2.** *adv.* hesitantly; tentatively

zögern *itr. V.* hesitate; **ich zögere nicht zu behaupten, daß ...:** I have no hesitation in saying that ...; **mit der Antwort** ~: hesitate before answering; **mit der Abreise** ~: delay one's departure; **ohne zu** ~: without hesitation; **nach einigem Zögern** after a moment's hesitation; ~**d vorangehen** proceed hesitantly

Zögling ['tsø:klɪŋ] **der;** ~**s,** ~**e** *(veralt.)* boarding pupil; boarder

Zölibat [tsøli'ba:t] **das** *od.* **der;** ~**[e]s,**~**e** celibacy *no art.*

[1]**Zoll** [tsɔl] **der;** ~**[e]s, Zölle** ['tsœlə] **a)** *(Abgabe)* [customs] duty; **auf dieser Ware liegt kein/ein hoher** ~: there is no duty/a high rate of duty on this article; **die Zölle senken** reduce rates of duty *or* [customs] tariffs; **b)** *(hist.: Benutzungsgebühr)* toll; ~ **erheben** charge a toll; **c)** *o. Pl. (Behörde)* customs *pl.*

[2]**Zoll der;** ~**[e]s,** ~: inch; **ein Nagel von 2** ~: a two-inch nail; **von 4** ~ **Durchmesser** 4 inches in diameter; **keinen** ~ **nachgeben** *od.* **weichen** *(fig.)* not give *or* budge an inch; **jeder** ~ *od.* ~ **für** ~ **ein Gentleman** *(fig.)* every inch a gentleman

zoll-, Zoll-: ~**abfertigung die** customs clearance; **die** ~**abfertigung passieren** go through custom; **bei der** ~**abfertigung** at the customs; ~**amt das** customs house *or* office; ~**aus·land das** *region outside one's own customs area;* ~**beamte der,** ~**beamtin die** customs officer; ~**breit** *Adj.* inch-wide; ~**breit der;** ~, ~: **keinen** ~**breit zurückweichen** *(fig.)* not budge an inch

zollen *tr. V. (geh.)* **jmdm. etw.** ~: accord sb. sth.; **jmdm. Respekt/Bewunderung** ~: show sb. respect/admiration; **jmdm. Lob** ~: bestow praise upon sb.; **jmdm. Anerkennung** ~: give sb. recognition; **jmdm. Beifall** ~: applaud sb.; **jmdm./einer Sache Tribut** ~: pay tribute to sb./sth.

zoll-, Zoll-: ~**erklärung die** customs declaration; ~**fahndung die** customs investigation; ~**formalität die** customs formality; ~**frei 1.** *Adj.* duty-free; free of duty *pred.;* **2.** *adv.* free of duty; ~**gebiet das** customs area; **sich auf britischem** ~**gebiet befinden** be in the British customs area; ~**grenz·bezirk der** frontier area under customs surveillance; ~**grenze die** limit of a/the customs area; ~**inland das** domestic customs area; ~**kontrolle die** customs examination *or* check; **zur** ~**kontrolle gehen** go to customs for clearance

Zöllner ['tsœlnɐ] **der;** ~**s,** ~ **a)** *(ugs. veralt.)* customs officer; **b)** *(hist.: Steuereintreiber)* tax-collector; *(bibl.)* publican

zoll-, Zoll-: **~pflichtig** *Adj.* dutiable; **~schranke die** customs barrier; **~station die, ~stelle, die** customs post; **~stock der** folding rule; **~union die** customs union; **~verein** *der (hist.)* **der Deutsche ~verein** the German customs union; the Zollverein
Zombie ['tsɔmbi] **der; ~[s], ~s** zombie
Zone ['tso:nə] **die; ~, ~n a)** zone; *(für Telefongespräche)* charge zone; *(für öffentlichen Nahverkehr)* fare zone; **b) die ~** *(ugs. veralt.)* East Germany
Zonen-: **~grenze die a) die ~grenze** *(ugs. veralt.)* the East German border; **b)** *(hist.: zwischen Besatzungszonen)* zonal frontier; **~rand·gebiet das** area along the East German border; **~zeit die** zone time
Zoo [tso:] **der; ~s, ~s** zoo; **im/in den ~:** at/to the zoo
Zoo·handlung die pet shop
Zoologe [tsoo'lo:gə] **der; ~n, ~n** zoologist
Zoologie die; ~: zoology *no art.*
Zoologin die; ~, ~nen zoologist
zoologisch 1. *Adj.* zoological; **~er Garten** zoological gardens *pl.;* **~er Bedarf** *pet foods and accessories pl.* **2.** *adv.* zoologically; **~ interessiert/beschlagen** interested in/knowledgeable about zoology
¹Zoom [zu:m] **das; ~s, ~s** *(Film, Fot.: Objektiv)* zoom
²Zoom der; ~s, ~s *(Film: Aufnahme)* zoom shot
zoomen ['zu:mən] *itr., tr. V. (Film)* zoom
Zoom·objektiv das *(Film, Fot.)* zoom lens
Zoo-: **~technik die** *(DDR)* zootechnics *sing., no art.;* **~techniker der** *(DDR)* zootechnics expert; **~tier das** zoo animal; **~wärter der** zookeeper
Zopf [tsɔpf] **der; ~[e]s, Zöpfe** ['tsœpfə] **a)** plait; *(am Hinterkopf)* pigtail; **sich** *(Dat.)* **Zöpfe flechten** plait one's hair [into pigtails]; **falscher ~:** false braid; **einen alten ~ abschneiden** *(fig.)* put an end to an antiquated custom *or* practice; **b)** *(Backwerk)* plait
Zopf·band das; *Pl.* **~bänder** pigtail ribbon
Zöpfchen ['tsœpfçən] **das; ~s, ~:** small plait/pigtail
Zopf-: **~muster das** cable pattern; **~spange die** hair-slide *(Brit.),* barnette *(Amer.) (for a pigtail);* **~stil der;** *o. Pl. (Kunstwiss.) plain style of the late 18th century;* **~zeit die,** *o. Pl. (Kunstwiss.)* age of the Zopfstil
Zorn [tsɔrn] **der; ~[e]s** anger; *(stärker)* wrath; fury; **ihn packte der ~:** he flew into a rage; **einen ~ auf jmdn. haben** *(ugs.)* be furious with sb.; **jmds. ~ erregen** anger sb.; **der ~ der Götter** the wrath of the Gods; **vor ~ kochen** be boiling with rage; **gerechter ~:** righteous anger; **im ~:** in a rage; in anger
Zorn-: **~ader die** *in* **jmdm. schwillt die ~ader** *(geh.)* sb. flies into a rage; **~ausbruch der** angry outburst; fit of rage
Zornes-: **~ader** *s.* **Zornader; ~falte die** *(geh.)* vertical line [on the brow]; angry furrow; **~röte die** *(geh.) in* **jmdm. die ~röte ins Gesicht treiben** make sb. flush with anger; **jmdm. steigt die ~röte ins Gesicht** sb. flushes with anger
zornig 1. *Adj.* furious; **~ über etw.** furious about sth.; **~ auf** *od.* **über jmdn.** furious with sb. **2.** *adv.* furiously
Zorn·röte die *s.* **Zornesröte**
Zote ['tso:tə] **die; ~, ~n** dirty joke
Zoten·reißer der; ~s, ~ *(abwertend)* teller of dirty jokes
zotig 1. *Adj.* smutty; dirty ⟨*joke*⟩. **2.** *adv.* smuttily
Zotte ['tsɔtə] **die; ~, ~n a)** *(Haarbüschel)* shaggy tuft [of hair]; **b)** *(Anat.)* villus
Zottel ['tsɔtḷ] **die; ~, ~n** *(ugs.)* **a)** *s.* **Zotte a; b)** *Pl. (abwertend: Haare)* shaggy locks
Zottel·haar das *(ugs.)* shaggy *or* unkempt hair
zottelig 1. *Adj.* shaggy. **2.** *adv.* **die Haare hingen ihr ~ ins Gesicht** her hair hung shaggily over her face
Zottel·kopf der *(ugs.)* **a)** *(Frisur)* shaggy hair; **b)** *(Person)* shaggy-haired type
zotteln *itr. V.; mit sein (ugs.)* saunter; amble
Zottel·trab der jogtrot
zottig *Adj.* shaggy
ZPO [tsɛtpe:'o:] **die; ~** *Abk.* **Zivilprozeßordnung**
Z-Soldat der *(Militärjargon) s.* **Zeitsoldat**
Ztr. *Abk.* **Zentner** cwt.
zu [tsu:] **1.** *Präp. mit Dat.* **a)** *(Richtung)* to; **zu ... hin** towards ...; **er kommt zu mir** *(besucht mich)* he is coming to my place; **b)** *(zusammen mit)* with; **zu dem Käse gab es Wein** there was wine with the cheese; **das paßt nicht zu Bier/zu dem Kleid** that doesn't go with beer/with that dress; **c)** *(Lage)* at; **zu beiden Seiten** on both sides; **zu seiner Linken** *(geh.)* on his left; **es ist zu Wasser und zu Lande zu erreichen** it can be reached by water and overland; **er kam zu dieser Tür herein** he came in by this door; **der Dom zu Speyer** *(veralt.)* Speyer Cathedral; **er wurde zu Köln geboren** *(veralt.)* he was born in Cologne; **das Gasthaus zu den drei Eichen** the Three Oaks Inn; **der Graf zu Mansfeld** the Count of Mansfeld; **d)** *(zeitlich)* at; **zu Weihnachten** at Christmas; **was schenkst du ihnen zu Weihnachten** what will you give them for Christmas?; **er will zu Ostern verreisen** he wants to go away for Easter; **zu Anfang des Jahres** at the beginning of the year; **zu dieser Stunde** at this time; **zu meiner Zeit** in my day; *s. auch* **Lebzeiten; e)** *(Art u. Weise)* **zu meiner Zufriedenheit/Überraschung** to my satisfaction/surprise; **zu seinem Vorteil/Nachteil** to his advantage/disadvantage; **zu niedrigen Preisen** at low prices; **zu deutsch** *(fig.)* in plain German; in words of one syllable; *(bei Mengenangaben o. ä)* **zu Dutzenden/zweien** by the dozen/in twos; **sie sind zu einem Drittel/zu 50 % arbeitslos** a third/50 % of them are jobless; **zu einem großen Teil** largely; to a large extent; **f)** *(ein Zahlenverhältnis ausdrückend)* **ein Verhältnis von 3 zu 1** a ratio of 3 to 1; **das Ergebnis war 2 zu 1** the result was 2–1 *or* 2 to 1; **g)** *(einen Preis zuordnend)* at; for; **Stoff zu zwanzig Mark der Meter** cloth at *or* for twenty marks a metre; **fünf Briefmarken zu fünfzig [Pfennig]** five 50-pfennig stamps; **h)** *(eine Zahlenangabe zuordnend)* **ein Faß zu zehn Litern** a ten-litre barrel; **Portionen zu je einem Pfund** portions weighing a pound each; **i)** *(Zweck)* for; **zu einer weiteren Behandlung nach X fahren** go to X for further treatment; **sie sagte das zu seiner Beruhigung** she said it to allay his fears; **Stoff zu einem Kleid** material for a dress; **j)** *(Ziel, Ergebnis)* into; **zu etw. werden** turn into sth.; **die Kartoffeln zu einem Brei zerstampfen** mash the potatoes into a puree; **das hat ihn zu meinem Freund gemacht** that made him my friend; **zu Staub zerfallen** crumble into dust; **k)** *(über)* about; on; **sich zu etw. äußern** comment on sth.; **zu welchem Thema spricht er?** what is he going to speak about?; **was sagst du zu meinem Vorschlag?** what do you say to my proposal?; **l)** *(gegenüber)* **freundlich/häßlich zu jmdm. sein** be friendly/nasty to sb.; **Liebe zu jmdm. empfinden** have feelings of love towards sb.; *s. auch* **zum; zur. 2.** *Adv.* **a)** *(allzu)* too; **zu sehr** too much; **er ist zu alt, um diese Reise zu unternehmen** he is too old to undertake this journey; **das ist ja zu schön/komisch!** that's really wonderful/hilarious!; that's too wonderful/hilarious for words!; **b)** *nachgestellt (Richtung)* towards; **der Grenze zu** towards the border; **dem Fenster zu stand ein Polizist** a policeman stood over towards the window; **c)** *(ugs.) elliptisch* **Augen/Tür zu!** shut your eyes/the door!; **d)** *(ugs.: Aufforderung)* **nur zu!** *(fang/fangt an!)* get going!; get down to it!; *(mach/macht weiter!)* get on with it!; **dort gehst du richtig, nur zu!** you're going the right way, just keep going!; **Wir sind fertig. – Na, dann zu!** We're ready. – Right, let's go!. **3.** *Konj.* **a)** *(mit Infinitiv)* to; **ich bat ihn zu helfen** I asked him to help; **du hast zu gehorchen** you must obey; **was gibt's da zu lachen?** what is there to laugh about?; **er ist heute nicht zu sprechen** he is not available today; **die Wände sind noch zu streichen** the walls still have to be painted; **das ist nicht zu glauben** it is unbelievable; **Haus zu verkaufen/vermieten** house for sale/to let; **b)** *(mit 1. Part.)* **die zu gewinnenden Preise** the prizes to be won; **die zu erledigende Post** the letters *pl.* to be dealt with
zu·aller·erst *Adv.* first of all; *(hauptsächlich)* above all else
zu·aller·letzt *Adv.* last of all
zu|arbeiten *itr. V.* **jmdm. ~:** assist sb. [with preparatory work]
zu|bauen *tr. V.* **a)** develop, build on ⟨*land*⟩; **b)** *(ugs.: versperren)* block ⟨*entrance, door*⟩; obstruct ⟨*view*⟩
Zubehör ['tsu:bəhø:ɐ̯] **das; ~[e]s, ~e** *od. schweiz.* **~den** accessories *pl.; (eines Staubsaugers, Mixers o. ä.)* attachments *pl.; (Ausstattung)* equipment; **mit allem ~:** with all accessories *pl.;* fully equipped ⟨*workshop, kitchen, etc.*⟩
zu|beißen *unr. itr. V.* bite; **einen Hund ärgern, bis er zubeißt** tease a dog until he bites one
zu|bekommen *unr. tr. V.* get ⟨*suitcase, door, etc.*⟩ shut; get the top on ⟨*bottle*⟩; get ⟨*clothes, buttons*⟩ done up; manage to repair ⟨*leak*⟩; manage to mend ⟨*hole*⟩
Zuber ['tsu'bɐ] **der; ~s, ~** *(bes. südd.)* tub
zu|bereiten *tr. V.* prepare ⟨*meal, food, cocktail, etc.*⟩; make up ⟨*medicine, ointment*⟩; *(kochen)* cook ⟨*fish, meat, etc.*⟩
Zu·bereitung die; ~, ~en preparation; *(von Arznei)* making up; *(Kochen)* cooking
zu|betonieren *tr. V.* concrete over; cover in concrete
Zu·bett·gehen das; ~s: vorm/beim ~: before/on going to bed
zu|bewegen 1. *tr. V.* **etw. auf jmdn./etw. ~:** move sth. towards sb./sth. **2.** *refl. V.* **sich auf etw. ~:** move towards sth.
zu|billigen *tr. V.* **jmdm. etw. ~:** grant *or* allow sb. sth.; **jmdm. ~, daß er in gutem Glauben gehandelt hat** accept that sb. acted in good faith; **dem Angeklagten mildernde Umstände ~:** allow the accused's plea of extenuating circumstances
Zu·billigung die; ~, ~en granting; allowing; **er wurde unter ~ mildernder Umstände für schuldig befunden** he was found guilty but with extenuating circumstances
zu|binden *unr. tr. V.* tie [up]
zu|blinzeln *itr. V.* **jmdm. ~:** wink at sb.
zu|bringen *unr. tr. V.* **a)** *(verbringen)* spend; **b)** *(landsch.) s.* **zubekommen**
Zu·bringer der; ~s, ~ *(Verkehrsw.)* **a)** *(Straße)* access *or* feeder road; **b)** *(Verkehrsmittel)* shuttle; *(Flughafenbus o. ä.)* courtesy bus
Zu·brot das; *o. Pl.* bit extra *or* on the side; **er ist auf ein ~ angewiesen** he is forced to earn a bit on the side
zu|buttern *tr., itr. V. (ugs.)* chip in *(coll.)*
Zucchetto [tsu'kɛto] **der; ~s, Zucchetti** *(schweiz.),* **Zucchino** [tsu'ki:no] **der; ~s, Zucchini** courgette *(Brit.);* zucchini *(Amer.)*
Zucht [tsʊxt] **die; ~, ~en a)** *o. Pl. (Züchtung) (von Tieren)* breeding; *(von Pflanzen)* cultivation; breeding; *(von Bakterien, Perlen)* culture; **b)** *(Zuchtergebnis) (von Tieren)* breed; *(von Pflanzen)* variety; strain; *(von Bakterien)* culture; strain; **ein Pferd aus deutscher ~:** a German-bred horse; **Pflan-**

zen/Tiere aus meiner ~: plants which I have grown/animals which I have bred; **c)** *(Einrichtung)* breeding establishment; *(für Pferde)* stud; *(für Pflanzen)* plant-breeding establishment; **d)** *o. Pl. (geh.: Disziplin)* discipline; **für ~ und Ordnung sorgen** keep order; **jmdn. in strenge ~ nehmen** take sb. firmly in hand

Zụcht-: ~bulle der breeding bull; **~eber der** breeding boar

züchten ['tsʏçtn̩] *tr. V. (auch fig.)* breed; cultivate ⟨*plants*⟩; culture ⟨*bacteria, pearls*⟩

Zụ̈chter der; ~s, ~, Zụ̈chterin, die; ~, ~nen breeder; *(von Pflanzen)* grower [of new varieties]; plant-breeder

Zụcht·haus das a) *(Gefängnis)* [long-stay] prison; penitentiary *(Amer.)*; **b)** *o. Pl. (Strafe)* [severest form of] imprisonment; imprisonment in a penitentiary *(Amer.)*; *(mit Zwangsarbeit)* penal servitude *(hist.)*

Zụchthäusler [-hɔyslɐ] **der; ~s, ~** *(veralt.)* convict

Zụchthaus·strafe die [severe] prison sentence; sentence to a penitentiary *(Amer.)*; **eine lebenslange ~:** life imprisonment; a life sentence

Zụcht·hengst der stud-horse; breeding stallion

zụ̈chtig *(veralt.)* **1.** *Adj.* demure. **2.** *adv.* demurely

züchtigen ['tsʏçtɪgn̩] *tr. V. (geh.)* beat; thrash; *(fig.: bestrafen)* castigate

Zụ̈chtigung die; ~, ~en *(geh.)* beating; thrashing; *(fig.: Bestrafung)* castigation; **körperliche ~:** corporal punishment

zụcht·los *(veralt.)* **1.** *Adj.* undisciplined; *(unzüchtig)* licentious. **2.** *adv.* without discipline; in an undisciplined way; *(unzüchtig)* licentiously

Zụchtlosigkeit die; ~, ~en *(veralt.)* **a)** *o. Pl.* lack of discipline; *(Unzüchtigkeit)* licentiousness; **b)** *(Verhalten)* impropriety

Zụcht-: ~perle die cultured pearl; **~tier das** breeding animal

Zụ̈chtung die; ~, ~en a) *(das Züchten)* breeding; *(von Pflanzen)* cultivation; **b)** *(Zuchtergebnis)* strain

zuck [tsʊk] *s.* **ruck, zuck**

zuckeln ['tsʊkl̩n] *itr. V.; mit sein* saunter; amble; *(schleppend)* trail; ⟨*cart etc.*⟩ trundle

Zụckel·trab der *(ugs.)* jogtrot

zụcken *itr. V.; mit Richtungsangabe mit sein* twitch; ⟨*body, arm, leg, etc.*⟩ jerk; *(vor Schreck)* start; ⟨*flames*⟩ flicker, flare up; ⟨*light, lightning*⟩ flicker, flash; ⟨*whip*⟩ flick (**nach** at); ⟨*dragon-fly*⟩ flick; ⟨*clock-hand*⟩ jerk; **er zuckte zur Seite** he jumped to one side; **mit der Hand ~:** jerk one's hand; **mit den Achseln/Schultern ~:** shrug one's shoulders; **er ertrug den Schmerz, ohne auch nur zu ~:** he bore the pain without even flinching; **es zuckte in seinem Gesicht/um ihren Mund** his face twitched/there was a twitch around her mouth

zücken ['tsʏkn̩] *tr. V.* draw ⟨*sword, dagger, knife*⟩; *(scherzh.)* take out, produce ⟨*wallet, notebook, camera, etc.*⟩

Zụcker der; ~s, ~ a) sugar; **~ sein** *(fig. salopp)* be fabulous *(coll.)*; **b)** *o. Pl. (Medizinjargon) s.* **Blutzuckerspiegel; c)** *o. Pl. (ugs.: ~krankheit)* diabetes; **~ haben** be a diabetic

Zụcker·bäcker der *(veralt., bes. südd., österr.)* confectioner

Zụckerbäcker·stil der; *o. Pl. (Archit.)* wedding-cake style

Zụcker·brot das *in* **mit ~ und Peitsche** with a carrot and a stick

zụcker-, Zụcker-: ~dose die sugar bowl; **~erbse die** edible-podded *or* mange-tout pea; **~guß der** icing; **~hut der** sugar loaf; **~krank** *Adj.* diabetic; **~krankheit die** diabetes

Zụckerl das; ~s, ~[n] *(südd., österr.)* sweet *(Brit.)*; candy *(Amer.)*; *(fig.)* sweetener; enticement

Zụcker-: ~lecken das *s.* **Honiglecken; ~lösung die** sugar solution; *(sirupartig)* syrup

zụckern *tr. V.* sugar

zụcker-, Zụcker-: ~puppe die *(ugs.)* sweet little thing; sweetie *(coll.)*; **~rohr das** sugar cane; **~rübe die** sugar beet; **~schlecken das** *s.* **Honiglecken; ~stange die** stick of rock; **~streuer der** sugar-caster; **~süß 1.** *Adj.* as sweet as sugar *postpos.*; beautifully sweet; *(fig. abwertend)* saccharine, sugary ⟨*picture, smile, etc.*⟩; **2.** *adv.* **~süß lächeln** *(fig. abwertend)* give a saccharine *or* sugary smile; **~wasser das** *o. Pl.* sugar-water; **~watte die** candy-floss; **~zange die** sugar-tongs *pl.*; **~zeug das;** *o. Pl. (veralt.)* sweet things *pl.*; confectionery

zụckrig *Adj.* sugary

Zụckung die; ~, ~en twitch; **letzte ~en** death throes

Zụ·decke die *(ugs.)* cover

zụ|decken *tr. V.* cover up; cover [over] ⟨*well, ditch*⟩; **sich ~:** tuck oneself up; **gut/warm zugedeckt** well/warmly tucked up

zu·dẹm *Adv. (geh.)* moreover; furthermore

zụ|denken *unr. tr. V. (geh.)* **jmdm. etw. ~:** intend sth. for sb.

zụ|diktieren *tr. V.* **jmdm. etw. ~:** impose sth. on sb.

zụ|drehen 1. *tr. V.* **a)** *(abdrehen)* turn off ⟨*tap, heating, water, gas*⟩; *(schließen)* screw ⟨*valve, container*⟩ shut; **b)** *(zuwenden)* **jmdm. den Kopf/Rücken ~:** turn one's head towards/one's back on sb. **2.** *refl. V.* **sich jmdm./etw. ~:** turn to *or* towards sb./sth.

zụ·dringlich 1. *Adj.* pushy *(coll.)*, pushing ⟨*person, manner*⟩; *(sexuell)* importunate ⟨*person, manner*⟩; prying ⟨*glance*⟩; **er wurde ~:** he began to force his attentions on her/me/*etc.* **2.** *adv.* importunately

Zụ·dringlichkeit die; ~, ~en a) *o. Pl.* pushiness *(coll.)*; *(in sexueller Hinsicht)* importunate manner; **b)** *(Handlung)* **~en** insistent advances *or* attentions

zụ|drücken 1. *tr. V.* press shut; push ⟨*door*⟩ shut; **er drückte ihr die Gurgel** *od.* **Kehle zu** he choked *or* throttled her; **sie drückte ihm** *(dem Toten)* **die Augen zu** she closed his eyes. **2.** *itr. V.* press

zụ|eignen *tr. V. (geh.)* **jmdm. etw. ~:** dedicate sth. to sb.

Zụ·eignung die; ~, ~en dedication

zụ|eilen *itr. V.; mit sein* **auf jmdn./etw. ~:** hurry *or* rush towards sb./sth.

zu·ein·ạnder *Adv.* to one another; **Liebe ~ empfinden** have feelings of love towards one another; **gut/schlecht ~ passen** ⟨*things*⟩ go well together/not match; ⟨*people*⟩ be well-/ill-suited

zueinạnder-: ~|finden *unr. itr. V.* come together; *(fig.: sich einigen)* find common ground; **~|halten** *unr. itr. V.* stick together; **~|kommen** *unr. itr. V.; mit sein* meet up; get together; **~|stehen** *unr. itr. V.* stand by one another; stick together

zụ|erkennen *unr. tr. V.* **jmdm. ein Recht ~:** grant sb. a right; **jmdm. eine Entschädigung/einen Preis ~:** award sb. compensation/a prize; **jmdm. einen Titel ~:** confer a title on sb.

Zụerkennung die; ~, ~en *(eines Rechts)* granting; *(einer Entschädigung, eines Preises)* award; *(eines Titels)* conferring

zu·ẹrst *Adv.* **a)** first; **ich muß ~ einmal etwas essen** I must have something to eat first; **er war ~ da** he was here first; he was the first to come; **wer ~ kommt, wird ~ bedient** first come, first served; **mit dem Kopf ~ ins Wasser springen** jump into the water head first; **b)** *(anfangs)* at first; to start with; **c)** *(erstmals)* first; for the first time

Zụ·erwerb der *s.* **Nebenerwerb**

Zụerwerbs·betrieb der *(Landw.) holding which does not provide an adequate income without supplementation from non-agricultural work*

zụ|fächeln *tr. V.* **jmdm. etw. ~:** waft sth. towards sb.; **jmdm./sich Kühlung ~:** fan sb./oneself

zụ|fahren *unr. itr. V.; mit sein* **a)** *(sich zubewegen)* **auf jmdn./etw. ~:** head towards sb./sth.; *(zusteuern)* drive at *or* aim for sb./sth.; **auf jmdn./etw. zugefahren kommen** come towards sb./sth.; **b)** *(ugs.: los-, weiterfahren)* get a move on *(coll.)*; **fahr zu!** step on it! *(coll.)*

Zụ·fahrt die a) *o. Pl.* access [for vehicles]; **die ~ zum Stadion erfolgt über die B 27** the stadium is approached along the B 27; **b)** *(Straße, Weg)* access road; *(zum Haus)* driveway

Zụfahrts·straße die access road; **~ zur Innenstadt** road leading to the town centre

Zụ·fall der chance; *(zufälliges Zusammentreffen von Ereignissen)* coincidence; **es war [ein] reiner ~:** it was pure chance *or* coincidence; **der ~:** chance; **es ist kein ~, daß ...:** it is no accident that ...; **durch ~:** by chance *or* accident; **ich habe durch ~ gesehen, wo sie es versteckt hat** I happened to see where she hid it; **daß wir uns dort begegneten, war ~:** our meeting there was a coincidence; **das ist aber ein ~/was für ein ~!** what a coincidence!; **der ~ wollte es, daß das Seil riß** by a stroke of fate *or* as chance would have it, the rope broke; **der ~ hat uns dorthin geführt** fate led us there; **etw. dem ~ überlassen** leave sth. to chance; **das verdankt er nur einem ~:** he owes it to chance

zụ|fallen *unr. itr. V.; mit sein* **a)** *(sich schließen)* ⟨*door etc.*⟩ slam shut; ⟨*eyes*⟩ close; **ihm fielen [vor Müdigkeit] die Augen zu** his eyelids were drooping [with tiredness]; **b)** *(zuteil werden, zukommen)* **jmdm. ~** ⟨*task*⟩ fall to sb.; ⟨*prize, inheritance*⟩ go to sb.; **ihm fällt alles nur so zu** everything just drops into his lap; **die Verantwortung fällt ihm zu** the responsibility is his

zụ·fällig 1. *Adj.* accidental; chance *attrib.* ⟨*meeting, acquaintance*⟩; random ⟨*selection*⟩; **~e Ereignisse/Prozesse** *(Math.)* random events/processes. **2.** *adv.* by chance; **ich bin ~ hier vorbeigekommen** I just happened to be passing; **wissen Sie ~, wie spät es ist?** *(ugs.)* do you by any chance know the time?; **~ habe ich den Brief bei mir** as it happens, I have the letter on me; **es ist nicht ~ so, daß ...:** it is no accident *or* coincidence that ...

zufälliger·wẹise *Adv. s.* **zufällig 2**

Zụ·fälligkeit die a) *o. Pl.* accidental nature; fortuitousness; *(des Zusammentreffens von Ereignissen)* coincidental nature; **b)** *(zufälliges Ereignis)* coincidence; chance occurrence

Zụfalls-: ~auswahl die random selection; **~bekanntschaft die** chance acquaintance; **~ergebnis das** chance result; **~fund der** chance find; **~generator der** *(Musik)* random generator; **~größe die** *(Math.) s.* **~variable; ~treffer der** fluke; **~variable die** *(Math.)* random variable; **~zahl die** *(Math.)* random number; **~ziffer die** *(Math.)* random digit

zụ|fassen *itr. V.* **a)** *(zugreifen)* make a snatch *or* grab; **b)** *(ugs.) s.* **zupacken b**

zụ|fliegen *unr. itr. V.; mit sein* **a) auf jmdn./etw. ~:** fly towards sb./sth.; **es kam auf mich zugeflogen** it came flying towards me; **b)** *(geflogen kommen)* **jmdm. ~** ⟨*bird*⟩ fly into sb.'s house; **ihm fliegen die Herzen zu** *(fig.)* all hearts surrender to his charms; **ihr fliegt in der Schule alles nur so zu** *(fig.)* schoolwork comes easily to her; **die Einfälle fliegen ihm nur so zu** *(fig.)* he is never short of inspiration; **c)** *(ugs.: zufallen)* ⟨*door, window, etc.*⟩ slam shut

zụ|fließen *unr. itr. V.; mit sein* **a) einer Sache** *(Dat.)* **~:** flow towards sth.; *(in etw. hin-*

einfließen) flow into sth.; **b)** *(zukommen)* **jmdm./einer Sache ~** ⟨*money etc.*⟩ go to sb./ sth.

Zu·flucht die refuge (**vor** + *Dat.* from); *(vor Unwetter o. ä.)* shelter (**vor** + *Dat.* from); **[seine] ~ zu etw. nehmen** *(fig.)* resort to sth.

Zufluchts-: ~ort der, ~stätte die place of refuge; sanctuary

Zu·fluß der a) *o. Pl. (das Zufließen)* inflow; supply; *(fig.)* influx; **b)** *(Gewässer)* feeder stream/river

zu|flüstern *tr. V.* **jmdm. etw. ~:** whisper sth. to sb.

zu·folge *Präp. mit Dat.; nachgestellt* according to; **sein Vorschlag, dem ~ das Haus versteigert werden soll** his proposal that the house should be put up for auction

zu·frieden 1. *Adj.* contented; *(befriedigt)* satisfied; **mit etw. ~ sein** be satisfied with sth.; **bist du jetzt ~?** are you satisfied [now]?; **ein ~es Gesicht machen** look contented *or* satisfied; **wir können ~ sein** we can't complain; **ich bin es ~** *(veralt.)* it's all right with me. **2.** *adv.* contentedly

zufrieden|geben *unr. refl. V.* be satisfied; **sich mit etw. nicht ~ wollen** refuse to accept sth.; **damit gebe ich mich nicht zufrieden** I cannot accept that

Zufriedenheit die; ~: contentment; *(Befriedigung)* satisfaction; **zu meiner vollen ~:** to my complete satisfaction

zufrieden|lassen *unr. tr. V.* **jmdn./etw. ~:** leave sb./sth. alone; **laß mich damit zufrieden!** stop going on at me about it! *(coll.)*

zufrieden|stellen *tr. V.* satisfy

zufriedenstellend 1. *Adj.* satisfactory. **2.** *adv.* satisfactorily

zu|frieren *unr. itr. V.; mit sein* freeze over

zu|fügen *tr. V.* **a) jmdm. etw. ~:** inflict sth. on sb.; **jmdm. Schaden/[ein] Unrecht ~:** do sb. harm/an injustice; **jmdm. eine Beleidigung/Kränkung ~:** insult/hurt sb.; *s. auch* **wollen; b)** *(hinzufügen)* **etw. einer Sache** *(Dat.)* **~:** add sth. to sth.

Zufuhr [ˈtsuːfuːɐ̯] **die; ~:** supply; *(Material)* supplies *pl.*; **die ~ milder Meeresluft** the stream of mild sea air

zu|führen 1. *itr. V.* **auf etw.** *(Akk.)* **~:** lead towards sth. **2.** *tr. V.* **a)** *(zuleiten)* **einer Sache** *(Dat.)* **etw. ~:** supply sth. to sth.; supply sth. with sth.; **dem Motor Kraftstoff ~:** supply fuel to the engine; supply the engine with fuel; **b)** *(bringen)* **einer Firma Kunden/ einer Partei Mitglieder ~:** bring new customers to a firm/new members to a party; **die Stute dem Hengst ~:** bring the mare to the stallion; **etw. seiner eigentlichen Bestimmung ~:** devote sth. to its proper purpose; **jmdn. der gerechten Strafe ~:** ensure that sb. gets condign punishment

Zu·fuß·gehen das; ~s walking

Zug [tsuːk] **der; ~[e]s, Züge** [ˈtsyːgə] **a)** *(Bahn)* train; *(Straßenbahn)* tram *(Brit.)*; streetcar *(Amer.) (consisting of two or more cars)*; *(Last~)* truck *or (Brit.)* lorry and trailer; **ich nehme lieber den ~** *od.* **fahre lieber mit dem ~:** I prefer to go by train *or* rail; **jmdn. vom ~ abholen/zum ~ bringen** meet sb. off/take sb. to the train; **jmdn. in den ~ setzen** *(ugs.)* put sb. on the train; **b)** *(Gespann von Zugtieren)* team; **ein ~ Ochsen** a team *or* yoke of oxen; **c)** *(Kolonne)* column; *(Umzug)* procession; *(Demonstrations~)* march; *(Vogelschar)* flock; **d)** *(das Ziehen)* pull; traction *(Phys.)*; *(fig.)* **das ist der ~ der Zeit** this is the modern trend *or* the way things are going; **die Sache hat einen ~ ins Lächerliche** there's something ridiculous about it; **dem ~ des Herzens folgen** follow the promptings of one's heart; **e)** *(Vorrichtung)* pull; *(einer Posaune)* slide; **f)** *(Wanderung)* migration; *(Streif~, Beute~, Diebes~)* expedition; **g)** *(beim Brettspiel)* move; **du bist am ~:** it's your move; **etw. ~ um ~ erledigen** *(fig.)* deal with sth. step by step; **Leistung/Erfüllung ~ um ~** *(Rechtsw.)* simultaneous performance; **zum ~e kommen** *(fig.)* get a chance; **h)** *(Schluck)* swig *(coll.)*; mouthful; *(großer Schluck)* gulp; **einen tiefen ~ [von etw.] nehmen** take a big gulp *or (literary)* deep draught [of sth.]; **das Glas auf einen** *od.* **in einem ~ leeren** empty the glass at one go; **einen Roman in einem ~ durchlesen** *(fig.)* read a novel at one sitting; **er hat einen guten ~** *(ugs.)* he can really knock it back *(coll.)*; **etw. in vollen Zügen genießen** *(fig.)* enjoy sth. to the full; **i)** *(beim Rauchen)* pull; puff; drag *(coll.)*; **j)** *(Atem~)* breath; **in tiefen** *od.* **vollen Zügen** in deep breaths; **in den letzten Zügen liegen** *(ugs.)* be at death's door; *(fig. scherzh.)* ⟨*car, engine, machine*⟩ be at its last gasp; ⟨*project etc.*⟩ be on the last lap; **k)** *o. Pl. (Zugluft; beim Ofen)* draught; **im ~ sitzen** sit in a draught; **der Kamin hat einen schlechten/ guten ~:** the fire draws badly/well; **l)** *(Gesichts~)* feature; trait; *(Wesens~)* characteristic; trait; **seine Züge** his features; **in ihrem Gesicht lag ein ~ von Strenge** there was a hint of severity in her face; **die Stadt trägt noch dörfliche Züge** the town still has something of the village about it; **das ist ein charakteristischer ~ an ihm** it is a characteristic of his; **das war kein schöner ~ von ihr** that did her no credit; **m)** *(landsch.: Schublade)* drawer; **n)** *(Bewegung eines Schwimmers/ Ruderers)* stroke; **o)** *(ugs.: Disziplin)* discipline; **jmdn. gut im ~ haben** have sb. well trained *or* under control; **in etw.** *(Dat.)* **ist ~** *(ugs.)* sth. has punch; **~ in etw.** *(Akk.)* **bringen** get sth. organized; **p)** *(Milit.: Einheit)* platoon; **q)** *(Schulw.: Zweig)* side; **r)** *(Höhen~)* range; chain; **die Züge des Odenwalds** the hills of the Odenwald; **s)** *(Abluftrohr)* flue; **t)** *(Schrift~; Strich)* stroke; **mit klaren Zügen geschrieben** written in a clear hand; **in großen/groben Zügen** *(fig.)* in broad outline

Zu·gabe die a) *(Geschenk)* [free] gift; **b)** *(im Konzert, Theater)* encore; **c)** *o. Pl. (das Zugeben)* addition; **unter sparsamer ~ von Wasser** adding water sparingly

Zug·ab·teil das [train] compartment *(Brit.)*

Zu·gang der a) *(Weg)* access; *(Eingang)* entrance; **b)** *(das Betreten, Hineingehen)* access; **~ verboten!** no admittance!; **er hat jederzeit ~ zum Chef** he can see the boss *(coll.)* at any time; **c)** *(fig.)* access; **~ zu jmdm./etw. finden** be able to relate to sb./ sth.; **d)** *o. Pl. (das Hinzukommen) (von Personen)* intake; *(von Patienten)* admission; *(Zuwachs)* increase (**von** in); **e)** *(Person, Sache) (Patient)* new admission; *(Soldat)* new recruit; *(Buch)* [new] accession; *(Ware)* new stock item

zu·gange *in* **irgendwo/mit jmdm./einer Sache ~ sein** *(ugs.)* be busy *or* occupied somewhere/with sb./sth.

zugänglich [ˈtsuːgɛŋlɪç] *Adj.* **a)** *(Zugang bietend)* accessible; *(geöffnet)* open; **schwer ~:** difficult to reach *pred.*; **die Zimmer sind von der Terrasse her ~:** the rooms can be reached from the terrace; **b)** *(zur Verfügung stehend)* available *(Dat.,* **für** to); *(verständlich)* accessible *(Dat.,* **für** to); **schwer ~es Material** material that is difficult to obtain; **c)** *(aufgeschlossen)* approachable ⟨*person*⟩; **für neue Ideen** *usw.* **~ sein** be amenable *or* receptive to new ideas *etc;* **allem Schönen** *od.* **für alles Schöne ~ sein** respond to all that is beautiful

Zugänglichkeit die; ~ a) accessibility; **schlechte ~:** difficulty of access; **b)** *(Aufgeschlossenheit)* receptiveness (**gegenüber** to)

Zug-: ~an·schluß der [train] connection; **~begleiter der a)** *(Schaffner)* guard; **b)** *(Faltblatt)* train schedule leaflet; **~brücke die** drawbridge

zu·geben *unr. tr. V.* **a)** *(hinzufügen)* add *(Dat.* to); **[jmdm.] etw. ~:** give [sb.] sth. as an extra; **der Sänger gab noch ein Lied zu** the singer sang another song as an encore; **b)** *(gestehen, zugestehen)* admit; admit, confess ⟨*guilt, complicity*⟩*;* admit to, confess to ⟨*deed, crime*⟩*;* **sie gab zu, es gestohlen zu haben** she admitted stealing it *or* having stolen it; **ich gebe zu, daß ich mich geirrt habe** I admit [that] I was wrong; **gib's doch endlich zu!** come on, admit it!; **du wirst mir ~** *od.* **du wirst doch ~ müssen, daß ...:** you have to admit that ...; **es war, zugegeben, viel Glück dabei** true, there was a lot of luck involved; **c)** *(erlauben)* allow; permit; **er wollte nicht ~, daß ich allein reise** he would not allow me to *or* let me travel alone

zu·gegebener·maßen *Adv.* admittedly

zu·gegen *Adj. in* **~ sein** *(geh.)* be present

zu|gehen *unr. itr. V.; mit sein* **a)** *(sich nähern)* **auf jmdn./etw. ~:** approach sb./sth.; **sie sollten endlich aufeinander ~** *(fig.)* they should try to come together at last; **dem Ende ~:** be coming to an end; **es geht auf Weihnachten zu** it is coming up to for Christmas; **er geht schon auf die Achtzig zu** he is coming up to eighty; **b)** *(ugs.: vorangehen)* get a move on *(coll.)*; step on it *(coll.)*; **c)** *(Amtsspr.)* **jmdm. ~:** be sent to sb.; **jmdm. etw. ~ lassen** send sth. to sb.; **d)** *unpers. (geschehen, verlaufen)* **hier/dort geht es ... zu** things are ... here/there; **ich weiß, wie es zugegangen ist** I know what went on; **auf dem Fest ging es fröhlich zu** it was very jolly at the party; **es müßte seltsam ~, wenn das nicht gelänge** something remarkable would have to happen for that not to succeed; **es geht nicht mit rechten Dingen zu** there is something fishy going on *(coll.)*; **e)** *(ugs.: sich schließen)* close; shut; **f)** *(ugs.: sich schließen lassen)* **die Tür/der Knopf geht nicht zu** the door will not shut/the button will not fasten; **der Reißverschluß geht schwer zu** the zip is difficult to do up; **g)** *s.* **zulaufen e**

Zu·geherin die; ~, ~nen, Zu·geh·frau die *(bes. südd., österr.)* cleaning lady; *(Haushaltshilfe)* home help

zu|gehören *itr. V. (geh.)* **jmdm./einer Sache ~:** belong to sb./sth.

zu·gehörig *Adj.* belonging to it/them *postpos., not pred.*; *(begleitend)* accompanying; **der Kreis und die ~en Gemeinden** the district and the communities belonging to it; **einer Sache** *(Dat.)* **~:** belonging to sth.; **sich jmdm./einer Sache** *(Dat.)* **~ fühlen** have a feeling of belonging [to sb./sth.]

Zugehörigkeit die; ~: belonging (**zu** to); *(Mitgliedschaft)* membership (**zu** of)

Zugehörigkeits·gefühl das; *o. Pl.* sense of belonging

zu·geknöpft *Adj. (fig. ugs.)* tight-lipped; *(nicht zugänglich)* unapproachable

Zügel [ˈtsyːgl̩] **der; ~s, ~ a)** rein; **ein Pferd am ~ führen** lead a horse by the reins; **einem Pferd in die ~ fallen** stop a horse by seizing the reins; **b)** *(fig.)* **die ~ [fest] in der Hand haben** be [firmly] in control; have things [firmly] under control; **die ~ straffer anziehen** tighten up on things; **jmdm./seiner Phantasie** *usw.* **~ anlegen** clamp down on sb./curb one's imagination *etc.;* **die ~ schießen lassen** let things take their course; **die ~ schleifen lassen** *od.* **lockern** slacken the reins

zügel·los *(fig.)* **1.** *Adj.* unrestrained; unbridled ⟨*rage, passion*⟩*;* limitless ⟨*ambition*⟩; frantic ⟨*rush, retreat*⟩*;* **ein ~es Leben führen** live a life of licentious indulgence. **2.** *adv.* without restraint; **~ leben** live a life of licentious indulgence

Zügellosigkeit die; ~, ~en lack of restraint; *(Unzüchtigkeit)* licentiousness

zügeln *tr. V.* **a)** rein [in] ⟨*horse*⟩*;* **b)** *(fig.)* curb, restrain ⟨*feeling, desire, curiosity, etc.*⟩*;* **sich ~:** restrain oneself

Zügelung die; ~, ~en curbing; restraining
Zu·gereiste der/die; *adj. Dekl.* newcomer
zu|gesellen *refl. V.* **sich jmdm./einer Sache ~:** join sb./sth.
Zu·geständnis das concession (**an** + *Akk.* to)
zu|gestehen *unr. tr. V.* **a)** *(anerkennen)* grant ⟨*right, claim, share, etc.*⟩; allow ⟨*discount, commission, time*⟩; **jmdm. ~, etw. zu tun** give sb. permission to do sth.; **b)** *(zugeben)* admit; concede; **du wirst mir ~ müssen, daß ...:** you have to admit that ...
zu·getan 1. *2. Part. v.* **zutun. 2.** *Adj.* **in jmdm. [herzlich] ~ sein** *(geh.)* be [very] attached to sb.; **den schönen Künsten ~ sein** have a penchant for the fine arts
Zu·gewinn der gain (**an** + *Dat.* in)
Zugewinn·gemeinschaft die *(Rechtsw.) separate property with equal division of property acquired after marriage*
Zu·gezogene der/die; *adj. Dekl.* newcomer
zug·fest *Adj.* tensile ⟨*steel etc.*⟩; **sehr ~ sein** have great tensile strength
Zug·führer der **a)** *(Eisenb.)* guard; **b)** *(Milit.)* platoon sergeant
zu|gießen *unr. tr., itr. V.* add (*Dat.* to); **darf ich [dir] ~?** may I top you up *(Brit. coll.) or (Amer. coll.)* put a top on it?
zugig *Adj.* draughty, *(im Freien)* windy ⟨*corner etc.*⟩
zügig ['tsy:gɪç] **1.** speedy; rapid; **mit ~er Geschwindigkeit, in ~er Fahrt** at a good *or* brisk speed. **2.** *adv.* speedily; rapidly
Zügigkeit die; ~: speediness; rapidity
Zug·kraft die **a)** *(Physik) (verformend)* tensile force; *(beschleunigend)* traction force; **b)** *(fig.)* attraction
zug·kräftig *Adj.* effective ⟨*publicity*⟩; powerful ⟨*argument*⟩; convincing ⟨*evidence*⟩; influential ⟨*name*⟩; catchy ⟨*title, slogan*⟩; **ein ~er Schauspieler/Film** an actor who/film which is a big draw; **~ sein** ⟨*film, actor, etc.*⟩ be a big draw
zu·gleich *Adv.* at the same time; **er ist Maler und Dichter ~:** he is both a painter and a poet
Zug-: ~luft die; *o. Pl.* draught; **~luft [ab]bekommen** be in a draught; **~maschine** die tractor; **~nummer** die **a)** *s.* **Zugpferd b**; **b)** *(Eisenb.)* train number; **~personal** das train crew; **~pferd** das **a)** *(Pferd)* draught-horse; **b)** *(fig.: Attraktion)* big draw; crowd-puller; **c)** *(treibende Kraft)* dynamo; **~pflaster** das *(Med.)* cantharidal plaster
zu|greifen *unr. itr. V.* **a)** take hold; **er kann nicht richtig ~:** he cannot grasp things properly; **rasch ~:** make a quick grab; **b)** *(sich bedienen)* help oneself; *(fig.: handeln)* take action; **er sah seine Chance und griff zu** *(fig.)* he saw his chance and acted at once; **c)** *(fleißig arbeiten)* **[hart** *od.* **kräftig] ~:** [really] knuckle down to it; **wenn viele Hände mit ~:** when plenty of people lend a hand
Zu·griff der **a)** grasp; **sich dem ~ der Polizei entziehen** escape the clutches of the police; **b)** *(Zugang)* access (**auf** + *Akk.* to)
zu·grunde *Adv.* in **a) ~ gehen** *(sterben)* die (**an** + *Dat.* of); *(zerstört werden)* be destroyed (**an** + *Dat.* by); ⟨*marriage*⟩ founder (**an** + *Dat.* owing to); ⟨*person*⟩ go under; *(finanziell)* be ruined; ⟨*company*⟩ go to the wall; **an sich selbst ~ gehen** destroy oneself; **~ richten** destroy; *(finanziell)* ruin ⟨*company, person*⟩; **b) etw. ~ legen** use sth. as a basis; **etw. einer Sache** *(Dat.)* **~ legen** base sth. on sth.; **etw. liegt einer Sache ~:** sth. is based on sth.; **das diesem Urteil ~ liegende Gesetz** the law which gives rise to this verdict
Zugrunde·legung die; **~: unter** *od.* **bei ~ dieser Umstände** on the basis of these facts
Zugs- *(österr.) s.* **Zug-**
Zug-: ~schaffner der ticket inspector; **~telefon** das train telephone; **~tier** das draught animal
zu|gucken *itr. V. (ugs.) s.* **zusehen**
Zug·unglück das train crash
zu·gunsten 1. *Präp. mit Gen.* in favour of; **eine Sammlung ~ der Flutopfer** a collection for the flood victims. **2.** *Adv.* **~ von** in favour of
zu·gut *in* **etw. ~ haben** *(schweiz., südd.)* be owed sth.; **du hast [bei mir] 10 Mark ~:** you've got ten marks to come [from me]
zu·gute *Adv. in* **jmdm. seine Jugend/Unerfahrenheit** *usw.* **~ halten** *(geh.)* take sb.'s youth/inexperience *etc.* into consideration; make allowances for sb.'s youth/inexperience *etc.*; **sich** *(Dat.)* **etwas/viel auf etw.** *(Akk.)* **~ tun** *od.* **halten** *(geh.)* be proud/very proud of sth.; **jmdm./einer Sache ~ kommen** stand sb./sth. in good stead; **jmdm. etw. ~ kommen lassen** let sb. have the benefit of *or* let sb. benefit from sth.
Zug-: ~verbindung die **a)** *(Eisenbahnverbindung)* rail *or (Amer.)* railroad service; **b)** *(Zuganschluß)* [train] connection; **~verkehr** der rail *or (Amer.)* railroad traffic; **~vogel** der migratory bird; **~zeit** *(Zool.)* die period of migration; **~zwang** der **a)** *(fig.)* pressure to take action; **unter ~zwang stehen, in ~zwang sein** be under pressure to take action; **jmdn. in ~zwang bringen** put sb. under pressure; **b)** *(Schach)* zugzwang
zu|haben *unr. itr. V. (ugs.)* **a)** ⟨*shop, office*⟩ be shut *or* closed; **wir haben montags zu** we are closed on Mondays; **b)** *(zubekommen haben)* **endlich hat sie den Koffer/Reißverschluß zu** at last she's managed to shut the suitcase/do up the zip
zu|haken *tr. V.* hook up; do up the hooks on
zu|halten 1. *unr. tr. V.* hold closed; *(nicht öffnen)* keep closed; **jmdm./sich die Augen/den Mund** *usw.* **~:** put one's hand[s] over sb.'s/one's eyes/mouth *etc.*; **sich** *(Dat.)* **die Nase ~:** hold one's nose. **2.** *itr. V.* **auf etw.** *(Akk.)* **~:** head for sth.
Zuhälter ['tsu:hɛltɐ] der; ~s, ~: pimp
Zuhälterei die; ~: pimping; *(Rechtsw.)* living off the earnings of prostitution
zu·handen 1. *Adj.* **jmdm. ~ sein** be available to sb.; be at sb.'s disposal. **2.** *Präp. mit Gen. (österr., schweiz.)* **~ Herrn B** for the attention of Herr B. **3.** *Adv. (österr., schweiz.)* **~ von Herrn B** for the attention of Herr B
zu|hängen *tr. V.* cover ⟨*window, cage*⟩
zu|hauen 1. *unr. itr. V.* **a)** *(ugs.)* bang *or* slam ⟨*door, window*⟩ shut; **b)** *(behauen)* hew into shape. **2.** *unr. itr. V. (ugs.)* hit *or* strike out
zu·hauf *Adv. (geh.)* in great numbers
Zu·hause das; ~s home
zu|heilen *itr. V.; mit sein* heal [over]
Zuhilfenahme [tsu'hɪlfəna:mə] die; **~:** utilization; **ohne/unter ~ einer Sache** *(Gen.)***/von etw.** without/with the aid of sth.
zu·hinterst *Adv.* right at the back; **~ in der Schublade/auf dem Regal** right at the back of the drawer/of the shelf
zu|hören *itr. V.* **jmdm./einer Sache ~:** listen to sb./sth.; **nun hör mal zu** now listen; *(leicht drohend)* now [you] listen here; **er kann gut ~:** he's a good listener
Zu·hörer der, **Zu·hörerin** die listener; **sie merkte, daß sie einen Zuhörer hatte** she noticed that somebody was listening
Zuhörerschaft die; ~: audience
zu·innerst *Adv. (geh.)* deep down; in one's heart of hearts; **~ aufgewühlt** moved to the depths of one's soul
zu|jubeln *itr. V.* **jmdm. ~:** cheer sb. [on]
Zu·kauf der additional purchase/purchases; **~ an Grund und Boden** purchase of more land
zu|kehren *tr. V.* turn (*Dat.* to); **jmdm. den Rücken/das Gesicht ~:** turn one's back on sb./one's face towards sb.
zu|klappen 1. *tr. V.* close; fold ⟨*penknife*⟩ shut; *(mit Wucht)* slam ⟨*lid*⟩ shut. **2.** *itr. V.; mit sein* ⟨*window, lid, etc.*⟩ click to *or* shut; *(mit Wucht)* slam shut
zu|kleben *tr. V.* **a)** *(verschließen)* seal ⟨*letter, envelope*⟩; **b)** *(bekleben)* cover
zu|klinken *tr. V.* [click] shut
zu|knallen *(ugs.)* **1.** *tr. V.* slam. **2.** *itr. V.; mit sein* slam
zu|kneifen *unr. tr. V.* squeeze ⟨*eye[s]*⟩ shut; shut ⟨*eye[s]*⟩ tight; shut ⟨*mouth*⟩ tightly
zu|knöpfen *tr. V.* button up
zu|knoten *tr. V.* knot; tie up
zu|kommen *itr. V.; mit sein* **a)** *(sich nähern)* **auf jmdn. ~:** approach sb.; *(zu jmdm. kommen)* come up to sb.; **er/der Stier/das Auto kam direkt auf mich zu** he/the bull/the car came straight towards me; **er ahnte nicht, was noch auf ihn ~ sollte** *(fig.)* he had no idea what he was in for; **die Dinge auf sich ~ lassen** *(fig.)* take things as they come; **wir werden in der Angelegenheit noch auf Sie ~:** we shall be coming back to you on this matter; **b)** *(geh.) (zuteil/übermittelt werden)* **jmdm. ~:** reach sb.; ⟨*inheritance*⟩ come to sb.; **jmdm. etw. ~ lassen** *(schicken)* send sb. sth.; *(schenken)* give sb. sth.; **jmdm./einer Sache Pflege/Aufmerksamkeit ~ lassen** devote care/attention to sth.; **c)** *(gebühren)* **jmdm. kommt etw. zu/nicht zu** sb. is entitled/not entitled to sth.; sb. has a right/no right to sth.; *(etw. ist jmdm. angemessen/nicht angemessen)* sth. befits/does not befit sb.; **dir kommt diese Entscheidung nicht zu** this decision is not up to you; this is not your decison; **d)** *(beizumessen sein)* **dieser Entdeckung kommt große Bedeutung zu** great significance must be attached to this discovery
zu|korken *tr. V.* cork
zu|kriegen *tr. V. (ugs.) s.* **zubekommen**
Zukunft ['tsu:kʊnft] die; ~, **Zukünfte** ['tsu:kynftə] **a)** future; **das wird die ~ lehren** time will tell; **für alle ~:** for all time; **~/keine ~ haben** have a/no future; **in naher/ferner ~:** in the near *or* immediate/distant future; **in ~:** in future; **einer Sache** *(Dat.)* **gehört die ~:** the future belongs to sth.; **seine [politische] ~ schon hinter sich** *(Dat.)* **haben** *(scherzh.)* be over the hill [politically]; **mit/ohne ~:** with/without a future; **ich wünsche Ihnen alles Gute für Ihre weitere ~:** I wish you all the best for the future; **b)** *(Grammatik)* future [tense]; **erste** *od.* **unvollendete/zweite** *od.* **vollendete ~:** future/future perfect [tense]
zu·künftig 1. *Adj.* future. **2.** *Adv.* in future
Zukünftige der/die; *adj. Dekl. (ugs.)* **mein ~r/meine ~:** my husband/wife-to-be; my intended *(joc.)*
zukunfts-, Zukunfts-: ~aussichten *Pl.* prospects for the future; **~forschung** die futurology *no art.*; **~musik** die *(fig.) in* **~musik sein** be very much in the future; *(als utopisch anzusehen sein)* be pie in the sky; **~perspektive** die prospects *pl.* for the future; future prospects *pl.*; **~roman** der novel set in the future;**~sicherung** die safeguarding *no art.* the future; **etwas für die ~sicherung tun** do something to secure *or* safeguard the future
zukunft[s]·weisend *Adj.* forward-looking; pointing the way forward *postpos.*
zu|lächeln *itr. V.* **jmdm./sich ~:** smile at sb./each other
zu|lachen *itr. V.* **jmdm. ~:** give sb. a friendly laugh
Zulage die *(vom Arbeitgeber)* extra pay *no indef. art.*; additional allowance *no indef. art.*; *(vom Staat)* benefit
zu·lande *Adv. in* **bei jmdm. ~:** where sb. comes from; in sb.'s country
zu|langen *itr. V.* **a)** *(ugs.: sich bedienen)* tuck in *(coll.)*; **b)** *(ugs.: zupacken)* [really] knuckle down to it

zu|länglich *(geh.)* **1.** *Adj.* adequate. **2.** *adv.* adequately

zu|lassen *unr. tr. V.* **a)** *(erlauben, dulden)* allow; permit; **solches Unrecht darf man nicht ~:** such injustice must not be permitted; **ich lasse keine Ausnahme zu** I do not allow *or* permit any exceptions; **das läßt nur einen/keinen anderen Schluß zu** that permits of *or* allows only one/no other conclusion; **b)** *(teilnehmen lassen)* admit; **jmdn. bei etw. ~:** admit sb. to sth.; **c)** *(mit einer Erlaubnis, Lizenz usw. versehen)* **jmdn. als Arzt ~:** register sb. as a doctor; **eine Partei ~** *(Politik)* permit a party to exist; **der Anwalt ist beim Amtsgericht Mannheim zugelassen** the lawyer is registered to practise at Mannheim district court; **jmdn. zum Studium/zum Studium der Medizin ~:** accept sb. at university/to study medicine; **jmdn. zu einer Prüfung ~:** allow *or* permit sb. to take an examination; **der Bulle ist zur Zucht zugelassen** the bull is registered for breeding; **d)** *(zur Benutzung, zur Anwendung, zum Verkauf usw. freigeben)* allow; permit; **ein Medikament ~:** approve a medicine [for sale]; **für den öffentlichen Verkehr/für Autobahnen [nicht] zugelassen sein** [not] be authorized for use on public highways/motorways *(Brit.)* or *(Amer.)* freeways; **e)** *(Kfz-W.)* register ⟨*vehicle*⟩; **auf jmdn./jmds. Namen zugelassen sein** be registered in sb.'s name; **f)** *(geschlossen lassen)* leave closed *or* shut; leave ⟨*letter*⟩ unopened; leave ⟨*collar, coat*⟩ fastened [up]

zu·lässig *Adj.* permissible; admissible ⟨*appeal*⟩; **~e [Höchst]geschwindigkeit** [maximum] permissible speed; [upper] speed limit

Zulässigkeit die; ~ permissibility; *(einer Berufung)* admissibility

Zulassung die; ~, ~en a) *(Erlaubnis, Lizenz)* **~ als Arzt** registration as a doctor; **~ zur Teilnahme/zur Prüfung beantragen** apply for permission to attend/to take *or* *(Brit.)* sit an examination; **ihm ist die ~ zum Studium/zum Medizinstudium erteilt worden** he has been accepted at university/to study medicine; **b)** *(Freigabe)* approval; authorization; **c)** *(Kfz-W.)* registration; **d)** *(Kfz-W. ugs.) s.* **Kraftfahrzeugschein**

zulassungs·pflichtig *Adj.* liable *or* subject to registration *postpos.*

Zulassungs·stelle die vehicle registration office

Zu·lauf der a) *o. Pl.* **[großen** *od.* **starken** *od.* **viel] ~ haben** ⟨*shop, restaurant, etc.*⟩ enjoy a large clientele, be very popular; ⟨*doctor, lawyer*⟩ have a large practice, be very much in demand; **mehr** *od.* **größeren ~ haben** ⟨*shop, restaurant, etc.*⟩ enjoy an increased clientele, be more popular; ⟨*doctor, lawyer*⟩ have a larger practice, be more in demand; **der ~ war so groß, daß das Gastspiel verlängert werden mußte** the guest performance was so popular that its run had to be extended; **b)** *(zulaufende Menge)* inflow; **c)** *(Rohr, Leitung)* intake

zu|laufen *unr. itr. V.; mit sein* **a) auf jmdn./etw. ~** *(auch fig.)* run towards sb./sth.; **auf jmdn./etw. zugelaufen kommen** come running towards sb./sth.; **einer Sache** *(Dat.)* **~** *(geh.)* run towards sth.; **b) jmdm. ~** ⟨*cat, dog, etc.*⟩ adopt sb. as a new owner; **ein zugelaufener Hund** a stray dog that has adopted us/them *etc.*; **c)** *(hinzulaufen)* ⟨*water etc.*⟩ run in; **warmes Wasser ~ lassen** run [some] warm water in; **e)** *(sich verjüngen)* taper; **spitz/konisch/keilförmig ~:** taper to a point; **f)** *(ugs.: schnell laufen)* get one's skates on *(Brit. sl.)*; get a move on *(coll.)*

zu|legen 1. *refl. V.* **sich** *(Dat.)* **etw. ~:** get oneself sth.; **er hat sich einen Bart zugelegt** *(ugs.)* he has grown a beard; **sich einen Künstlernamen ~:** adopt a pseudonym. **2.** *itr. V. (ugs.)* **a)** *(sein Tempo steigern)* step on it *(coll.)*; **b)** *(wachsen, stärker werden)* ⟨*sales, output, turnover, etc.*⟩ increase; **der Dollar hat [um vier Pfennige] zugelegt** the dollar has risen [four pfennigs]; **sie könnten bei Neuwahlen ~:** the could improve their position if there were fresh elections. **3.** *tr. V. (ugs.)* add; **wenn meine Eltern noch 100 Mark ~, kann ich mir das Fahrrad kaufen** if my parents put in a hundred marks, I can afford the bicycle; **einen Schritt/***(ugs.:)* **Zahn ~:** get a move on *(coll.)*

zu·leid[e] *in* **jmdm. etwas/nichts ~ tun** hurt *or* harm sb./not [do anything to] hurt *or* harm sb.; *s. auch* **Fliege a**

zu|leiten *tr. V.* **a)** feed; supply; supply ⟨*nourishment*⟩; feed ⟨*signal*⟩; channel ⟨*sewage*⟩; **b)** *(zukommen lassen)* send; forward

Zu·leitung die a) *o. Pl.* supply; **b)** *o. Pl. (Übersendung, Zustellung)* sending; forwarding; **c)** *(Rohr, Kabel usw.)* feed line

zu·letzt *Adv.* **a)** *(zum Schluß, nach allem anderen)* last [of all]; **~ liest du es noch einmal durch** finally, read it through again; **an sich selbst denkt sie immer ~:** she always thinks of herself last; **sich** *(Dat.)* **etw. für ~ aufheben** save sth. till last; **b)** *(als letzter/letzte/letztes)* last; **er kommt immer ~:** he always comes last; he is always [the] last; **das ~ geborene Kind** the child born last; **c)** *(fig.: am wenigsten)* least of all; **darauf wäre ich ~ gekommen** that's the last thing I should have thought of; **nicht ~:** not least; **d)** *(das letzte Mal)* last; **ich habe ihn ~ gestern abend gesehen** I last saw him yesterday evening; **e)** *(schließlich, am Ende)* in the end; **bis ~:** [right up] to *or* until the end

zu·liebe *Adv.* **jmdm./einer Sache ~:** for sb.'s sake/for the sake of sth.

Zu·liefer·betrieb der supplier *(Gen.* to)

zu|löten *tr. V.* solder; solder up ⟨*hole*⟩

Zu·luft die; *o. Pl. (Technik)* incoming air

zum [tsʊm] *Präp. + Art.* **a) = zu dem; b)** *(räumlich: Richtung)* to the; **ein Fenster ~ Hof** a window on to *or* facing the yard; **~ Hof liegen** face the yard; **wo geht es ~ Stadion?** which is the way to the stadium?; **c)** *(räumlich: Lage)* **etw. ~ Fenster hinauswerfen** throw sth. out of the window; **die Gaststätte „Z~ Lamm"** the 'Lamb Inn'; **d)** *(Zusammengehörigkeit, Hinzufügung)* **Milch ~ Tee/Sahne ~ Kuchen nehmen** take milk with [one's] tea/have cream with one's cake; **e)** *(zeitlich)* at the; **spätestens ~ 15. April** by 15 April at the latest; **~ Schluß/richtigen Zeitpunkt** at the end/the right moment; **f)** *(Zweck)* **ein Gerät ~ Schneiden** an instrument for cutting [with]; **hol dir was ~ Schreiben** get something to write with; **~ Spaß/Vergnügen** for fun/pleasure; **~ Lesen braucht er eine Brille** he needs glasses for reading; **~ Schutz** as *or* for protection; **etw. ~ Essen/Lesen** *(österr.)* sth. to eat/read; **~ Schwimmen gehen** go swimming; **g)** *(Folge)* **~ Nachteil des Kunden** to the disadvantage of the customer; **~ Ärger/Leidwesen seines Vaters** to the annoyance/sorrow of his father; **~ Nutzen der Allgemeinheit** for the benefit of the general public; **es ist ~ Verrücktwerden** it is enough to drive you mad; **das ist gar nicht ~ Lachen** it's no laughing matter; *(in bezug auf etwas Sichtbares)* it's nothing to laugh at; **h)** *(sonstige Verwendungen)* **jmdn. ~ Direktor ernennen/~ Kanzler wählen** appoint sb. director/elect sb. chancellor; **~ Dieb werden** become a thief; **sich** *(Dat.)* **etw. ~ Ziel setzen** set oneself sth. as a goal; **~ ersten, ~ zweiten, ~ dritten!** *(bei Versteigerung)* going, going, gone!; **~ Funk/Fernsehen/Film wollen** want to go *or* get into radio/television/films

zu|machen 1. *tr. V.* close; shut; fasten, do up ⟨*dress*⟩; seal ⟨*envelope, letter*⟩; turn off ⟨*tap*⟩; put the top on ⟨*bottle*⟩; *(stillegen)* close *or* shut down ⟨*factory, mine, etc.*⟩; **den Laden ~** *(ugs.: auflösen)* shut up shop; **ich habe kein Auge zugemacht** I didn't sleep a wink. **2.** *itr. V.* **a)** close; shut; **der Laden hat zugemacht** *(ugs.)* the place has closed down; **b)** *(ugs., bes. nordd.: sich beeilen)* get a move on *(coll.)*

zu·mal 1. *Adv.* especially; particularly; **~ da ...:** especially *or* particularly since ... **2.** *Konj.* especially *or* particularly since

zu|marschieren *itr. V.; mit sein* **auf jmdn./etw. ~:** march towards sb./sth.

zu|mauern *tr. V.* wall *or* brick up

zu·meist *Adj.* in the main; for the most part

zu|messen *unr. tr. V. (geh.)* **a)** *(zuteilen)* **jmdm. seine Essensration ~:** issue sb. with his food ration; **ihm war nur eine kurze Zeit für seine Lebensarbeit zugemessen** *(fig.)* he was only allotted a few short years for his life's work; **b)** *s.* **beimessen**

zumindest *Adv.* at least; **so schien es ~:** at least, that is how it seemed; **~ hätte er sich entschuldigen müssen** he should at least have apologized

zumutbar *Adj.* reasonable; **das ist ihm kaum/durchaus/nicht ~:** one can scarcely/quite well/not expect that of him; **das ist ihr körperlich nicht ~:** that is asking too much of her physically; **im Rahmen des Zumutbaren** within the bounds of what is reasonable

Zumutbarkeit die; ~: reasonableness

zu·mute *Adj. in* **jmdm. ist unbehaglich/elend** *usw.* **~:** sb. feels uncomfortable/wretched *etc.*; **mir war merkwürdig ~:** I had a peculiar *or* strange feeling; **mir wurde ganz komisch ~:** I felt quite funny; a funny feeling came over me; **ich kann mir gut vorstellen, wie dir ~ ist** I can well imagine how you feel; **mir war nicht danach ~:** I didn't feel like it *or* in the mood; **mir war nicht nach Lachen/Ironie ~:** I did not feel in the mood for laughing/irony; **mir war zum Weinen ~:** I felt like crying

zu|muten *tr. V.* **a)** *(abverlangen)* **jmdm. etw. ~:** expect *or* ask sth. of sb.; **willst du mir etwa ~, daß ich die ganze Zeit herumsitze und warte?** do you expect me to *or* are you asking me to sit around here the whole time and wait?; **diesen kleinen Umweg können wir ihm schon ~:** I do not think this small detour would be asking too much of him; **diese Arbeit möchte ich ihm nicht ~:** I would not like to ask him to do this work *or* impose this work on him; **das ist ihm durchaus/nicht zuzumuten** it is perfectly reasonable to/one cannot expect *or* ask that of him; **seinem Körper/seinem Wagen zuviel ~:** overtax oneself physically/ask too much of one's car; **sich** *(Dat.)* **etw. ~:** undertake sth.; **sich zuviel ~:** take on too much; overdo it; **b)** *(antun)* **jmdm. etw. ~:** expect sb. to put up with sth.; **diesen Lärm können wir den Nachbarn nicht ~:** we cannot expect the neighbours to put up with this noise; **so eine winzige Schrift kann man keinem ~:** nobody can be expected to read such tiny writing; **diesen Anblick wollte ich ihm nicht ~:** I wanted to spare him this sight

Zumutung die; ~, ~en a) *(Ansinnen)* unreasonable demand; imposition; **eine ~ sein** be unreasonable; **etw. als [eine] ~ empfinden** consider sth. unreasonable; **b)** *(Belästigung)* imposition; **etw. ist [einfach] eine ~:** sth. is [simply *or* just] too much; **eine ~ für jmdn. sein** be an imposition on sb.; **der Film/die Schauspielerin war eine ~:** the film/actress was appalling; **das Essen war eine ~:** the meal was an affront

zu·nächst 1. *Adv.* **a)** *(als erstes)* first; *(anfangs)* at first; **~ einmal** first; **~ ..., zum zweiten ..., zum dritten ..., schließlich ...:** firstly *or* in the first place *or* for one thing ..., secondly ..., thirdly ..., lastly ...; **b)** *(im Moment, vorläufig)* for the moment; for the time being. **2.** *Präp. + Dat. (geh.)* next to; **jmdm./einer Sache ~:** next to sb./sth.

zu|nageln *tr. V.* nail up; **etw. mit Brettern ~:** board sth. up

zu|nähen *tr. V.* sew up; *s. auch* **verdammt 1 a; verflixt 1 b**

Zunahme ['tsu'na:mə] **die; ~, ~n** increase (*Gen.*, **an** + *Dat.* in)

Zu·name der surname; last name

Zünd·blättchen das percussion cap

zündeln ['tsʏndl̩n] *itr. V. (bes. südd., österr.; auch fig.)* play with fire

zünden ['tsʏndn̩] **1.** *tr. V.* ignite ‹*gas, fuel, etc.*›; detonate ‹*bomb, explosive device, etc.*›; let off ‹*fireworks*›; fire ‹*rocket*›. **2.** *itr. V.* ‹*rocket, engine*› fire; ‹*candle, lighter, match*› light; ‹*gas, fuel, explosive*› ignite; *(fig.)* arouse enthusiasm; **bei ihm hat es gezündet** *(ugs.)* he's cottoned *or* caught on *(coll.)*; the penny's dropped *(coll.)*; **der ~de Funke** *(auch fig.)* the igniting spark

zündend *Adj. (fig.)* stirring, rousing ‹*speech, song, effect, tune, etc.*›; exciting ‹*rhythm*›

Zunder ['tsʊndɐ] **der; ~s a)** tinder; **trocken wie ~:** dry as tinder; tinder-dry; **b)** *(fig. ugs.) in* **jmdm. ~ geben** lay into sb. *(coll.)*; **~ kriegen** get it in the neck *(coll.)*

Zünder der; ~s, ~ a) *(Waffent.)* igniter; *(für Bombe, Mine)* detonator; **b)** *Pl. (österr.)* matches

Zünd-: ~holz das *(bes. südd., österr.)* match; **~holz·schachtel die** *(bes. südd., österr.)* matchbox; **~hütchen das** percussion cap; **~kabel das** *(Kfz-W.)* ignition lead; *(from coil to distributor)* coil lead; *(from distributor to plugs)* plug lead; **~kapsel die** *s.* **Sprengkapsel; ~kerze die** spark[ing]-plug; **~plättchen das** percussion cap; **~schloß das** *(Kfz-W.)* ignition [lock]; **der Schlüssel steckt im ~schloß** the key is in the ignition; **~schlüssel der** *(Kfz-W.)* ignition key; **~schnur die** fuse; **~spule die** spark coil; **~stoff der** *(fig.)* fuel for conflict; **zum ~stoff eines Konflikts werden** become the trigger for a conflict; **die Rede enthält einigen ~stoff** the speech contains some explosive material

Zündung die; ~, ~en a) *s.* **zünden 1:** ignition; detonation; letting off; firing; **b)** *(Kfz-W.: Anlage)* ignition; **die ~ einstellen** adjust the timing

Zünd·verteiler der *(Kfz-W.)* distributor

Zünd·zeitpunkt der *(Kfz-W.)* ignition time; **den ~ einstellen/verstellen** set/alter the ignition timing

zu|nehmen 1. *unr. itr. V.* **a)** increase (**an** + *Dat.* in); ‹*moon*› wax; **an Größe/Länge** *usw.* **~:** increase in size/length *etc.*; **an Erfahrung/Macht ~:** gain [in] experience/power; **in ~dem Maße** to an increasing extent *or* degree; increasingly; **mit ~dem Alter** with advancing age; **die Tage nehmen zu** the days are drawing out *or* getting longer; **b)** *(schwerer werden)* put on *or* gain weight; **er hat [um] ein Kilo zugenommen** he has put on *or* gained a kilo. **2.** *unr. tr. (auch itr.) V. (Handarb.)* increase

zunehmend *Adv.* increasingly; **sich ~ vergrößern/verschlechtern** get increasingly bigger/worse

zu|neigen 1. *itr. V.* incline *or* be inclined towards; **ich neige mehr dieser Ansicht/Auffassung zu** I tend *or* incline more towards this view. **2.** *refl. V.* **a)** *(geh.: sich angezogen fühlen von)* be *or* feel drawn to; **er ist ihr sehr/in Liebe zugeneigt** he is attracted to *or* fond of her/is drawn to her by feelings of love and affection; **der den Künsten zugeneigte Fürst** the prince, who is/was fond of the arts; **b)** *(sich neigen nach)* **jmdm./einer Sache ~:** lean towards sb./sth.; **sich dem/seinem Ende ~** *(fig.)* draw to a close

Zu·neigung die; ~, ~en affection; **[eine] starke ~ zu jmdm. haben/empfinden** have/feel [a] strong *or* deep affection for *or* towards sb.; **~ zu jmdm. fassen** become fond of sb.

Zunft [tsʊnft] **die; ~, Zünfte** ['tsʏnftə] *(hist.)* guild; **die ~ der Bäcker** the bakers' guild; **die ~ der Journalisten** *(scherzh.)* the journalistic fraternity; **zu welcher ~ gehört er?** *(scherzh.)* what does he do for a living?

zünftig ['tsʏnftɪç] **1.** *Adj.* **a)** *(ugs.)* proper; **eine ~e Tracht Prügel/Ohrfeige** a good thrashing/box on the ears; **er sieht richtig ~ aus in seiner Tracht** he really looks the genuine article in his costume; **ein ~es Bier trinken** drink a decent beer; **b)** *(hist.)* guild *attrib.* ‹*craftsman, traditions, etc.*›. **2.** *adv. (ugs.)* properly; **~ Skat spielen** have a decent game of skat

Zunge ['tsʊŋə] **die; ~, ~n a)** tongue; **einen bitteren Geschmack auf der ~ haben** have a bitter taste in one's mouth; **dem Hund hing die ~ heraus** the dog's tongue was hanging out; **[jmdm.] die ~ herausstrecken** put one's tongue out [at sb.]; **auf der ~ zergehen** melt in one's mouth; **mit der ~ anstoßen** *(ugs.)* lisp; **b)** *(fig.)* **mit schwerer ~** with a thick tongue; in a slurred voice; **eine spitze** *od.* **scharfe/lose ~ haben** have a sharp/loose tongue; **mit doppelter** *od.* **gespaltener ~ sprechen** *(geh.)* be two-faced; **böse ~n behaupten, daß ...:** malicious gossip has it that ...; malicious tongues are saying that ...; **seine ~ hüten** *od.* **zügeln** *od.* **im Zaum halten** guard *or* mind one's tongue; **der Wein hatte ihm die ~ gelöst** the wine had loosened his tongue; **ich mußte mir auf die ~ beißen** I had to bite my tongue; **lieber beiße ich mir die ~ ab** *(ugs.)* I would bite my tongue off first; **der Name liegt mir auf der ~:** the name is on the tip of my tongue; **etw. auf der ~ haben** have sth. on the tip of one's tongue; **sich** *(Dat.)* **die ~ abbrechen** tie one's tongue in knots; **bei dem Namen bricht man sich** *(Dat.)* **die ~ ab** that name is a real tongue-twister; **jmdm. leicht** *od.* **glatt von der ~ gehen** trip easily off sb.'s tongue; **Liebe ist ein Wort, das mir nur schwer von der ~ geht** I find it difficult to say the word 'love'; **er ließ den Namen/das Wort auf der ~ zergehen** he rolled the name/word around his tongue; **mit [heraus]hängender ~:** with [one's/its] tongue hanging out; **er hat eine feine** *od.* **verwöhnte ~** *(fig.)* he has a delicate palate; **c)** *(eines Blasinstruments)* reed; *(einer Orgel)* tongue; *(einer Waage)* needle; pointer; *(eines Schuhs)* tongue; **d)** *(geh.: Sprache)* tongue

züngeln ['tsʏŋl̩n] *itr. V.* **a)** ‹*snake etc.*› dart its tongue in and out; **b)** *mit Richtungsangabe mit sein* ‹*flame*› flicker; dart; ‹*water*› lick; **die Flammen züngelten aus dem Dach** tongues of flame leapt up out of the roof

zungen-, Zungen-: ~brecher der *(ugs.)* tongue-twister; **~fertig 1.** *Adj.* eloquent; **2.** *adv.* eloquently; **~fertigkeit die** *o. Pl.* eloquence; **~kuß der** French kiss; **~schlag der** way *or* manner of speaking; **ein falscher ~schlag** a slip of the tongue; **~spitze die** tip of the tongue; **~spitzen-R das** *(Sprachw.)* apical R; **~wurst die** tongue sausage

Zünglein ['tsʏnlain] **das; ~s, ~ a)** [little] tongue; **b)** *(einer Waage)* [small] needle *or* pointer; **das ~ an der Waage sein** *(fig.)* tip the scales

zu·nichte *Adj. in* **etw. ~ machen** ruin sth.; **jmds. Hoffnungen ~ machen** shatter *or* dash sb.'s hopes; **jmds. Anstrengungen/Pläne ~ machen** ruin *or* wreck sb.'s efforts/plans; **~ werden/sein** be ruined/shattered *or* dashed/ruined *or* wrecked

zu|nicken *itr. V.* **jmdm./sich ~:** nod to sb./one another

zu·nutze *Adj. in* **sich** *(Dat.)* **etw. ~ machen** *(nutzen)* make use of sth.; *(ausnutzen)* take advantage of sth.

zu·oberst *Adv.* [right] on [the] top; **ganz ~:** right on [the] top; on the very top; *s. auch* **unter... a**

zuordenbar *Adj.* **a)** relatable; **einander ~e Elemente** elements that can be related to each other; **b)** *(sich zurechnen lassend)* assignable; **einer Sache** *(Dat.)* **~ sein** be classifiable as sth.

zu|ordnen *tr. V.* **a)** relate (*Dat.* to); **einem Bild ein Wort ~:** relate a word to a picture; **einer Sache** *(Dat.)* **eine Zahl/einen Wert ~:** assign a number/value to sth.; **b)** *(zurechnen)* **jmdn./etw. einer Sache** *(Dat.)* **~:** classify sb./sth. as belonging to sth.; **Organismen, die sich den Tieren ~ lassen** organisms which can be classified as animals; **c)** *(zuweisen)* assign (*Dat.* to); **d)** *(beimessen)* attribute, attach (*Dat.* to)

Zu·ordnung die a) relating; **die ~ x→y** *(Math.)* the relation x→y; **b)** *(Zurechnung)* classification; **c)** *(Zuweisung)* assigning, assignment (*Dat.* to)

zu|packen *itr. V.* **a)** grab it/them; **fest ~ können** be able to grab things and grip them tightly; **der Hund stellte den Dieb und packte zu** the dog caught the thief and sank its teeth into him *(fig.)*; **bei dem günstigen Angebot habe ich zugepackt** the offer was a good one and I jumped at it; **b)** *(fig.: energisch ans Werk gehen)* knuckle down to it; **er hat eine sehr ~de Art** he has a very vigorous, purposeful manner

zu·paß *Adv. in* **jmdm. ~ kommen** come [to sb.] at just the right time *or* moment

zupfen ['tsʊpfn̩] **1.** *itr. V.* **an etw.** *(Dat.)* **~:** pluck *or* pull at sth.; **sich** *(Dat.)* **am Ohrläppchen ~:** pull [at] one's ear lobe; **an einer Gitarre/an den Saiten ~:** pluck a guitar/the strings. **2.** *tr. V.* **a) etw. aus/von** *usw.* **etw. ~:** pull sth. out of/from *etc.* sth.; **sie zupfte ihm ein paar Fusseln vom Pullover** she pulled *or* picked a few pieces of fluff off his pullover; **b)** *(auszupfen)* pull out; pluck ‹*eyebrows*›; pull up ‹*weeds*›; **c)** pluck ‹*string, guitar, tune*›; **d) jmdn. am Ärmel/Bart ~:** pull *or* tug [at] sb.'s sleeve/beard

Zupf-: ~geige die *(veralt.)* guitar; **~instrument das** plucked [string] instrument

zu|pflastern *tr.V.* pave over

zu|pressen *tr. V.* press shut

zu|prosten *itr. V.* **jmdm. ~:** drink sb.'s health; raise one's glass to sb.

zur [tsu:ɐ̯] *Präp.* + *Art.* **a) = zu der; b)** *(räumlich, fig.: Richtung)* to the; **~ Schule/Arbeit gehen** go to school/work; **ein Fenster ~ Straße** a window on to the street; **~ Straße liegen** face the street; **wo geht es ~ Post?** which is the way to the post office?; **c)** *(räumlich: Lage)* **~ Tür hereinkommen** come [in] through the door; **~ Rechten** to *or* on the right; **die Gaststätte „Zur Rose"** the 'Rose Inn'; **d)** *(Zusammengehörigkeit, Hinzufügung)* **~ Hasenkeule empfehle ich einen Rotwein** I recommend a red wine with the haunch of hare; **e)** *(zeitlich)* at the; **~ Stunde/Zeit** at the moment; at present; **~ Adventszeit** at Advent time; **~ Jahreswende** at New Year; **rechtzeitig ~ Buchmesse** in [good] time for the book fair; **f)** *(Zweck)* **ein Gerät ~ Zerkleinerung von Gemüse** a device for chopping up vegetables; **~ Entschuldigung** by way of [an] excuse; **~ Inspektion in die Werkstatt müssen** have to go in for a check-up; **g)** *(Folge)* **~ vollen Zufriedenheit ihres Chefs** to the complete satisfaction of her boss; **~ allgemeinen Erheiterung** to everybody's amusement; **h)** *(sonstige Verwendungen)* **sie wurde ~ Direktorin ernannt/~ Präsidentin gewählt** she was appointed director/elected president; **~ Diebin werden** become a thief; **die Wahlen ~ Knesseth** elections to the Knesset

zu|raten *unr. itr. V.;* **ich würde/kann dir nur ~:** I would advise you to do so/I can only recommend it; **auf jmds. Zuraten [hin]** on sb.'s advice *or* recommendation; **ich möchte [dir] weder zu- noch abraten** I should not like to advise you one way or the other

zu|raunen *tr. V.* **jmdm. etw. ~:** whisper sth. to sb.

Zürcher ['tsʏrçɐ] **1.** *indekl. Adj.; nicht präd.* Zurich *attrib.* **2. der;** ~s, ~: inhabitant/native of Zurich; **er ist ~:** he is from Zurich; *s. auch* **Kölner**

zürcherisch *Adj.* Zurich *attrib.*; **~ sein** ⟨*area:*⟩ belong to *or* be part of Zurich

zu|rechnen *tr. V.* **a)** *(zuordnen)* **jmdn./etw. einer Sache** *(Dat.)* **~:** class sb./sth. as belonging to sth.; **solche Wörter rechnen wir den Adverbien zu** such words are classed as adverbs; **b)** *(anlasten, zuschreiben)* **jmdm. etw. ~:** attribute *or* ascribe sth. to sb.; **die Folgen hast du dir selbst zuzurechnen** you've only got yourself to blame for the consequences; **c)** *(hinzufügen)* **etw. einer Sache** *(Dat.)* **~:** add sth. to sth.

zurechnungs·fähig *Adj.* **a)** sound of mind *pred.*; **b)** *(Rechtsw.: schuldfähig)* responsible [for one's actions]

Zurechnungs·fähigkeit die; *o. Pl.* **a)** soundness of mind; **b)** *(Rechtsw.: Schuldfähigkeit)* responsibility [for one's actions]

zurecht-, Zurecht-: ~|**biegen** *unr. tr. V.* bend into shape; **er wird die Sache schon wieder ~biegen** *(fig.)* he will get things straightened out *or* sorted out again; **im Internat werden sie den Jungen schon ~biegen** *(fig.)* they will soon lick the boy into shape at boarding-school; ~|**finden** *unr. refl. V.* find one's way [around]; **sich in einem Fahrplan/Kursbuch ~:** find one's way around a timetable; **er findet sich im Leben/in der Welt nicht [mehr] ~:** he is not able to cope with life/the world [any longer]; ~|**kommen** *unr. itr. V.; mit sein* **a)** get on (**mit** with); **wir kommen gut miteinander ~:** we get on well [with each other]; **mit etw. ~kommen** cope with sth.; **ich komme auch ohne Geschirrspülmaschine/mit meinem Gehalt [ganz gut] ~:** I manage *or* cope *or* get on [very well] without a dishwasher/on my salary; **mit einem Problem/den Kindern ~kommen** cope with *or* handle a problem/the children; **b)** *(ugs.: rechtzeitig kommen)* come in time; ~|**legen** *tr. V.* **a)** lay out [ready]; **jmdm. etw. ~legen** lay sth. out ready for sb.; **sich** *(Dat.)* **den Ball ~legen und schießen** spot the ball and shoot; **b)** *(fig.)* get ready; prepare; **sich** *(Dat.)* **ein Gegenargument/eine Erwiderung ~gelegt haben** have a counter-argument/reply ready; ~|**machen** *tr. V. (ugs.)* **a)** *(vorbereiten)* get ready; **b)** *(herrichten)* do up; **c) jmdn./sich ~:** get sb. ready/get [oneself] ready; *(schminken)* make sb. up/put on one's make-up; **sich** *(Dat.)* **die Haare ~machen** do one's hair; ~|**rücken** *tr. V.* put *or* set ⟨*chair, crockery, etc.*⟩ in place; straighten ⟨*tie*⟩; adjust ⟨*spectacles, hat, etc.*⟩; *(fig.: richtigstellen, korrigieren)* put straight; **jmdm. einen Stuhl ~rücken** put *or* set a chair in place for sb.; *s. auch* **Kopf a;** ~|**schneiden** *unr. tr. V.* cut to size/shape; trim ⟨*fringe, beard, hedge*⟩; *(herstellen)* cut out (**aus** of); ~|**setzen 1.** *tr. V.* adjust ⟨*spectacles, hat, etc.*⟩; **2.** *refl. V.* settle oneself; ~|**stellen** *tr. V.* put *or* set ⟨*chair, crockery, etc.*⟩ in place; ~|**stutzen** *tr. V.* trim ⟨*hedge, beard, hair etc.*⟩; **jmdn./etw. ~stutzen** *(fig.)* sort *or* straighten sb. out/get *or* knock sth. into shape; ~|**weisen** *unr. tr. V.* rebuke; reprimand ⟨*pupil, subordinate, etc.*⟩; **~weisung die** *s.* **~weisen:** rebuke; reprimand

zu|reden *itr. V.* **jmdm. ~:** persuade sb.; *(ermutigen)* encourage sb.; **jmdm. gut ~:** encourage sb.; **gutes Zureden** persuasion; **erst nach langem Zureden** only after a great deal of persuasion

zu·reichend *(geh.) s.* **zulänglich**

zu|reiten 1. *unr. tr. V.* break [in] ⟨*horse*⟩. **2.** *unr. itr. V.; mit sein* **auf jmdn./etw. ~:** ride towards sb./sth.; **auf jmdn./etw. zugeritten kommen** come riding towards sb./sth.

Zürich ['tsy:rɪç] **(das);** ~s Zurich

zürich·deutsch 1. *Adj.* Zurich-German. **2.** *adv.* in Zurich German; *s. auch* **deutsch; Deutsch**

Zürich·see der Lake [of] Zurich

zu|richten *tr. V.* **a)** *(verletzen)* injure; **sie haben ihn übel zugerichtet** they [really] knocked him about; **übel zugerichtet** badly injured; **b)** *(beschädigen)* make a mess of; **c)** *(landsch.: zubereiten, vorbereiten)* prepare; *(Technik: zuschneiden)* cut to size/shape; **d)** *(Lederherstellung, Kürschnerei, Textilind.)* dress, finish ⟨*leather, fur, etc.*⟩; **e)** *(Druckw.)* make ready

zu|riegeln *tr. V.* bolt

zürnen ['tsʏrnən] *itr. V. (geh.)* **jmdm. ~:** be angry with sb.

zurren ['tsʊrən] *tr. V. (Seemannsspr.)* lash down

Zur·schau·stellung die exhibition; display

zu·rück *Adv.* back; **ich bin gleich [wieder] ~:** I'll be right back *(coll.)*; **sei bitte zum Essen ~:** please be back in time for lunch/dinner *etc;* **einen Schritt ~ machen** take a step backwards; **~!** get *or* go back!; **„~ an Absender"** 'return to sender'; **... und 10 Pfennig ~:** ... and 10 pfennigs change; *s. auch* **Dank a; hin d; Natur a; b)** *(weiter hinten; auch fig.)* behind; **[mit etw.] ~ sein** *(fig.: im Rückstand)* be behind [with sth.]

Zurück das *in* **es gibt [für jmdn.] kein ~ [mehr]** there is no going back [for sb.]

zurück-, Zurück-: ~|**begleiten** *tr. V.* **jmdn. ~begleiten** accompany sb. back; ~|**behalten** *unr. tr. V.* **a)** keep [back]; retain; **b)** *(nicht mehr loswerden)* be left with ⟨*scar, heart defect, etc.*⟩; ~|**bekommen** *unr. tr. V.* get back; **Sie bekommen noch 10 Mark ~:** you get 10 marks change; **er bekommt es von mir [doppelt] ~** *(fig.)* I'll pay him back [twice over]; ~|**beordern** *tr. V.* order back; ~|**besinnen** *unr. refl. V.* **sich auf etw.** *(Akk.)* **~besinnen** remember sth.; think back to sth.; ~|**beugen 1.** *tr. V.* bend back; **2.** *refl. V.* lean *or* bend back; ~|**bilden** *refl. V. (Biol.)* **a)** ⟨*swelling*⟩ go down; ⟨*uterus*⟩ contract; ⟨*symptoms*⟩ disappear; *(atrophieren)* ⟨*limb, organ, etc.*⟩ atrophy; **b)** *(im Laufe der Stammesentwicklung)* ⟨*limb, organ*⟩ be lost; ~|**bleiben** *unr. itr. V.; mit sein* **a)** remain *or* stay behind; **b)** *(nicht mithalten)* lag behind; *(fig.)* fall behind; **hinter den Erwartungen ~bleiben** fall short of expectations; **in seiner Entwicklung ~bleiben** ⟨*child*⟩ be retarded *or* backward in its development; **c)** *(bleiben)* remain; **von der Krankheit ist [bei ihm] nichts ~geblieben** the illness has left no lasting effects [on him]; **d)** *(wegbleiben)* stay *or* keep back; *s. auch* **zurückgeblieben;** ~|**blenden** *itr. V. (Film; auch fig.)* flash back; **in/auf etw.** *(Akk.)* **~blenden** flash back to sth.; ~|**blicken** *itr. V.* **a)** look back (**auf** + *Akk.* at); *(sich umblicken)* look back *or* round; **b)** *(fig.)* **auf etw.** *(Akk.)* **~blicken** look back on sth.; ~|**bringen** *unr. tr. V.* **a)** *(wieder herbringen)* bring back; return; *(wieder hinbringen)* take back; return; **jmdn. ins Leben/in die Wirklichkeit ~bringen** *(fig.)* bring sb. back to life/reality; **b)** *(ugs.: zurückwerfen)* set back; ~|**datieren** *tr. V.* antedate, backdate ⟨*letter, cheque, etc.*⟩; antedate ⟨*event, artefact, etc.*⟩; ~|**denken** *unr. itr. V.* think back (**an** + *Akk.* to); **so weit ich ~denken kann** as far as I can remember *or* recall; ~|**drängen** *tr. V.* force back; drive back ⟨*enemy*⟩; **den Drogenmißbrauch ~drängen** *(fig.)* fight drug abuse; ~|**drehen** *tr. V.* **a)** turn back; turn down ⟨*heating, volume, etc.*⟩; **das Rad der Geschichte ~drehen** *(fig.)* turn back the wheel of history; **b)** *(rückwärts drehen)* turn backwards; ~|**dürfen** *unr. itr. V.* be allowed [to go] back *or* to return; **das Fleisch darf nicht in die Kühltruhe ~:** the meat must not go back in the freezer; ~|**eilen** *itr. V.; mit sein* hurry back; ~|**erbitten** *unr. tr. V. (geh.)* **etw. ~erbitten** ask for sth. to be returned; **etw. von jmdm. ~erbitten** ask sb. to return sth.; ~|**erhalten** *unr. tr. V. (geh.)* be given back; get back; **anliegend erhalten Sie ihre Bewerbungsunterlagen ~:** please find enclosed your application, which we are returning to you; ~|**erinnern** *refl. V.* **sich an etw.** *(Akk.)* **~erinnern** remember *or* recall sth.; ~|**erlangen** *tr. V. (geh.)* regain; ~|**erobern** *tr. V.* win back ⟨*votes, majority, etc.*⟩; regain ⟨*power, position, etc.*⟩; recapture ⟨*territory, town, etc.*⟩; ~|**erstatten** *tr. V.* refund; **jmdm. etw. ~erstatten** refund sth. to sb.; ~|**erwarten** *tr. V.* **jmdn. ~erwarten** expect sb. back; ~|**fahren 1.** *unr. itr. V.; mit sein* **a)** go back; return; *(als Autofahrer)* drive back; *(mit dem Fahrrad, Motorrad usw.)* ride back; **b)** *(nach hinten fahren)* go back[wards]; **c)** *(zurückweichen)* start back; *(entsetzt)* recoil; **2.** *unr. tr. V.* **a) jmdn./etw. ~fahren** drive sb./sth. back; **b)** *(Technikjargon)* reduce the output of ⟨*power plant, refinery, etc.*⟩; cut back ⟨*delivery, production, budget, etc.*⟩; ~|**fallen** *unr. itr. V.; mit sein* **a)** fall back; **b)** *(nach hinten fallen)* fall back[wards]; **c)** *(fig.: in Rückstand geraten)* fall behind; **d)** *(fig.: auf einen niedrigeren Rang)* drop (**auf** + *Akk.* to); **e)** *(fig.: in einen früheren Zustand)* **in etw.** *(Akk.)* **~fallen** fall back into sth.; **in den alten Trott ~fallen** slip back into the old routine; **f)** *(fig.)* **an jmdn. ~fallen** ⟨*property*⟩ revert to sb.; **g)** *(fig.)* **auf jmdn. ~fallen** ⟨*actions, behaviour, etc.*⟩ reflect [up]on sb.; **deine Gemeinheiten werden eines Tages auf dich [selbst] ~fallen** your meanness will recoil [up]on you one day; ~|**finden** *unr. itr. V.* find one's way back; ~|**fliegen 1.** *unr. itr. V.; mit sein* fly back; **2.** *unr. tr. V.* **jmdn./etw. ~fliegen** fly sb./sth. back; ~|**fließen** *unr. itr. V.; mit sein* flow back; ~|**fordern** *tr. V.* **etw. ~fordern** ask for sth. back; *(nachdrücklicher)* demand sth. back; ~|**fragen** *itr. V.* answer with a question; **„...?" fragte er ~:** '...?', he asked in return; ~|**führen 1.** *tr. V.* **a) jmdn. ~führen** take sb. back; **b)** *(zurückbewegen)* **etw. ~führen** move sth. back; return sth.; **c) etw. auf etw.** *(Akk.)* **~führen** *(auf Ursprung)* trace sth. back to sth.; *(auf Ursache)* attribute sth. to sth.; put sth. down to sth.; *(auf einfachere Form)* reduce sth. to sth.; **2.** *itr. V.* lead back; **es führt kein anderer Weg ~:** there is no other way back; ~|**geben 1.** *unr. tr. V.* **a)** give back; return; hand in ⟨*driver's licence, membership card*⟩; return ⟨*goods, unused ticket, etc.*⟩; relinquish ⟨*mandate, office, etc.*⟩; take back ⟨*defective goods*⟩; give back ⟨*freedom*⟩; **jmdm. ~geben** give sth. back to sb.; return sth. to sb.; **b)** *(erwidern)* reply; **2.** *unr. tr. (auch itr.) V. (Ballspiele)* **a)** return ⟨*ball, puck, service, pass, throw*⟩; **[den Ball] an jmdn. ~geben** return the ball to sb.; **b)** *(nach hinten geben)* **[den Ball] ~geben** pass the ball back; **~geblieben 1.** *2. Part. v.* **zurückbleiben; 2.** *Adj.* retarded; ~|**gehen** *unr. itr. V.; mit sein* **a)** go back; return; *(sich zurückbewegen)* ⟨*pick-up arm, indicator, needle, etc.*⟩ return; **b)** *(nach hinten gehen)* go back; ⟨*enemy*⟩ retreat; **in die Geschichte/bis in die Jahre meiner Kindheit ~gehen** *(fig.)* go back into history/to the years of my childhood; **c)** *(verschwinden)* ⟨*bruise, ulcer*⟩ disappear; ⟨*swelling, inflammation*⟩ go down; ⟨*pain*⟩ subside; **d)** *(sich verringern)* decrease; go down; ⟨*fever*⟩ abate; ⟨*flood*⟩ subside; ⟨*business*⟩ fall off; **e)** *(zurückgeschickt werden)* be returned *or* sent back; **ein Essen ~gehen lassen** send a meal back; **f) auf jmdn. ~gehen** *(jmds. Werk sein)* go back to sb.; *(von jmdm. abstammen)* originate from *or* be descended from sb.; **der Name geht auf ein lateinisches Wort ~:** the name comes from a Latin word; **g)** *(sich zurückbewegen lassen)* ⟨*lever etc.*⟩ go back; **~|gewinnen** *unr. tr. V.* **a)** win back; regain ⟨*confidence, title, strength, freedom, etc.*⟩; **b)** *(Wirtsch.)* reclaim, recover ⟨*raw materials etc.*⟩; **~gezogen 1.** *2. Part. v.* **zurückziehen; 2.** *Adj.* secluded; **3.** *adv.* **~gezogen leben** lead a withdrawn life; *(an abgelegenem Ort)* live a secluded life; **~gezogenheit die; ~:** seclusion; **~|greifen** *unr. itr. V.* **auf jmdn./etw. ~greifen** fall back on sb./sth.; **~|haben** *unr. tr. V.* have back; **hast du es inzwischen ~?** have you got it back yet?; **ich will es ~haben** I want it back; **~|halten 1.** *unr. tr. V.* **a) jmdn. ~halten** hold sb. back; **eine dringende Angelegenheit hielt mich in Köln ~:** an urgent matter kept *or* detained me in Cologne; **er war durch nichts ~zuhalten** there was no stopping him; nothing would stop him; **b)** *(am Vordringen hindern)* keep back ⟨*crowd, mob, etc.*⟩; **c)** *(behalten)* withhold ⟨*news, letter, parcel, etc.*⟩; **d)** *(nicht austreten lassen)* hold back ⟨*tears etc.*⟩; **sein Wasser ~halten** hold one's water; **e)** *(von etw. abhalten)* **jmdn. ~halten** stop sb.; **jmdn. von etw. ~halten** keep sb. from sth.; **jmdn. davon ~halten, etw. zu tun** stop sb. doing sth.; keep sb. from doing sth.; **2.** *unr. refl. V.* **a)** *(sich zügeln, sich beherrschen)* restrain *or* control oneself; **b)** *(nicht aktiv werden)* **sich in einer Diskussion ~halten** keep in the background in a discussion; **3.** *unr. itr. V.* **mit etw. ~halten** *(etw. nicht äußern)* keep sth. to oneself; **~haltend 1.** *Adj.* **a)** reserved; subdued, muted ⟨*colour*⟩; **b)** *(kühl, reserviert)* cool, restrained ⟨*reception, response*⟩; **c)** *(Wirtsch.: schwach)* slack ⟨*demand*⟩; **d)** *(sparsam)* **mit etw. ~haltend** ⟨*person*⟩ who is/was sparing with sth.; sparing with sth. *pred.*; **2.** *adv.* **a)** ⟨*behave*⟩ with reserve *or* restraint; **eine ~haltend gemusterte Tapete** a wallpaper with a subdued pattern; **b)** *(kühl, reserviert)* coolly; **das Publikum/Bonn reagierte ~haltend** the public's response was cool/Bonn's response was cautious; **sich ~haltend zu etw. äußern** be cautious in one's comments on sth.; **~haltung die;** *o. Pl.* **a)** reserve; **~haltung üben** *(geh.)* exercise restraint; **sich** *(Dat.)* **~haltung auferlegen** *(geh.)* adopt an attitude of reserve; **b)** *(Kühle, Reserviertheit)* coolness; reserve; **ein Buch mit ~haltung aufnehmen** give a book a cool reception; **c)** *(Wirtsch.: geringe Kaufbereitschaft)* caution; **~|holen** *tr. V.* **a)** fetch back; get back ⟨*money*⟩; bring back ⟨*satellite, missile*⟩; **jmdn. ~holen** bring sb. back; **b)** *(~rufen)* call back; **~|kämmen** *tr. V.* comb back; backcomb; **seine ~gekämmten Haare** his backcombed hair; **~|kaufen** *tr. V.* buy back; repurchase; **~|kehren** *itr. V.; mit sein* return; come back **(von, aus** from); **zu jmdm. ~kehren** return *or* go back to sb.; **~|klappen** *tr. V.* tip back ⟨*seat*⟩; lift back ⟨*lid*⟩; fold back ⟨*flap*⟩; **~|kommen** *unr. itr. V.; mit sein* **a)** come back; return; ⟨*letter*⟩ come back, be returned; **b)** *(zurückgelangen)* get back; **c) ~kommen auf** (+ *Akk.*) come back to ⟨*subject, question, point, etc.*⟩; **auf ein Angebot ~kommen** come back on an offer; **d)** *(ugs.: zurückbefördert werden)* go back; **~|können** *unr. itr. V.* be able to go back *or* return; **nicht ans Ufer ~können** not be able to get back to the bank; **jetzt können wir nicht mehr ~** *(fig.)* there's no going *or* turning back now; **~|kriegen** *tr. V. s.* **~bekommen; ~|lassen** *unr. tr. V.* **a)** leave; **b)** *(zurückkehren lassen)* **jmdn. ~lassen** allow sb. to return; let sb. return; **~|lassung die; ~: unter ~lassung einer Sache/jmds.** leaving sth./sb. behind; **~|laufen** *unr. itr. V.; mit sein* **a)** run back; **b)** *(ugs.: zurückgehen)* come/go back; **c)** *(sich zurückbewegen)* run back; **das Tonband ~laufen lassen** run the tape back; **~|legen 1.** *tr. V.* **a)** put back; **b)** *(nach hinten beugen)* lean *or* lay ⟨*head*⟩ back; **c)** *(reservieren)* put aside, keep **(***Dat.***, für** for); **d)** *(sparen)* put away; put by; **e)** *(hinter sich bringen)* cover ⟨*distance*⟩; **2.** *refl. V.* lie back; *(sich ~lehnen, ~neigen)* lean back; **~|lehnen** *refl. V.* lean back; **~|liegen** *unr. itr. V.* **a) das Ereignis/das liegt einige Jahre ~:** the event took place/that was several years ago; **in den ~liegenden Jahren** in the past [few] years; **b)** *(bes. Sport)* be behind; **mit 2 : 3 Toren ~liegen** be 3–2 behind; **~|melden** *refl. V.* report back **(bei** to); **~|müssen** *unr. itr. V.* **a)** have to go back *or* return; **b)** *(zurückbefördert werden müssen)* have to go back; **~|nehmen** *unr. tr. V.* **a)** take back; **b)** *(widerrufen)* take back; **ich nehme alles ~ [und behaupte das Gegenteil** *(scherzh.)***]** I take it all back; **c)** *(rückgängig machen)* revoke, rescind ⟨*decision, ban, etc.*⟩; withdraw ⟨*complaint, legal action*⟩; **einen Zug ~nehmen** *(Brettspiele)* take a move back; **~|pfeifen** *unr. tr. V.* **a)** whistle ⟨*dog*⟩ back; **b)** *(fig. salopp)* **jmdn. ~pfeifen** call sb. off; **~|prallen** *itr. V.; mit sein* **a)** bounce back **(von** off); ⟨*bullet*⟩ ricochet **(von** from); **b)** *(fig.)* start back; *(entsetzt)* recoil; **~|rechnen** *itr. V.* reckon back; **~|reichen 1.** *tr. V.* hand back; **2.** *itr. V.* go back **(in +** *Akk.* to); **~|rollen 1.** *tr. V.* **a)** roll back; **b)** *(nach hinten rollen)* roll back[wards]; **2.** *itr. V.; mit sein* **a)** roll back; **b)** *(nach hinten rollen)* roll back[wards]; **~|rufen 1.** *unr. tr. V.* **a)** call back; recall ⟨*ambassador*⟩; **jmdn. ins Leben ~rufen** *(fig.)* bring sb. back to life; **b)** *(anrufen)* call *or (Brit.)* ring back; **c) jmdm./sich etw. ins Gedächtnis** *od.* **in die Erinnerung ~rufen** remind sb. of sth./call sth. to mind; **d)** *(als Antwort, nach hinten rufen)* call *or* shout back; **e)** *(Wirtsch.)* recall ⟨*defective goods, car, etc.*⟩; **2.** *unr. itr. V. (anrufen)* call *or (Brit.)* ring back; **~|schalten** *itr. V.* **a)** switch *or* turn back; **b)** *(beim Autofahren)* change down; **~|schaudern** *itr. V.; mit sein* shrink back **(vor +** *Dat.* from); **~|schauen** *itr. V. (bes. südd., österr., schweiz.) s.* **~blicken; ~|scheuen** *itr. V.; mit sein s.* **²~schrecken; ~|schicken** *tr. V.* send back; **~|schieben** *unr. tr. V.* **a)** push back; draw back ⟨*bolt, curtains*⟩; **b)** *(nach hinten schieben)* push back[wards]; **~|schlagen 1.** *unr. tr. V.* **a)** *(nach hinten schlagen)* fold back ⟨*cover, hood, etc.*⟩; turn down ⟨*collar*⟩; *(zur Seite schlagen)* pull *or* draw back ⟨*curtains*⟩; **b)** *(durch einen Schlag zurückbefördern)* hit back; *(mit dem Fuß)* kick back; **c)** *(zum Rückzug zwingen, abwehren)* beat off, repulse ⟨*enemy, attack*⟩; **2.** *unr. itr. V.* **a)** hit back; ⟨*enemy*⟩ strike back, retaliate; **b)** *mit sein* ⟨*pendulum*⟩ swing back; ⟨*starting-handle*⟩ kick back; ⟨*wave*⟩ crash back; **c) auf etw.** *(Akk.)* **~schlagen** *(fig.)* have repercussions on sth.; **~|schneiden** *unr. tr. V.* cut back ⟨*plant, shoot, etc.*⟩; **~|schrauben** *tr. V.* reduce ⟨*demand, wage, consumption, etc.*⟩; lower ⟨*expectations*⟩; **¹~|schrecken** *tr. V.* **jmdn. ~schrecken** deter sb.; **²~|schrecken** *regelm., veralt. unr. itr. V.; mit sein* **a)** shrink back; recoil; **b) vor etw.** *(Dat.)* **~schrecken** *(fig.)* shrink from sth.; **er schreckt vor nichts ~:** he will stop at nothing; **~|sehnen** *refl. V.* **sich nach der Geborgenheit seines Elternhauses ~sehnen** long to return to the security of one's parents' home; **sich zu jmdm./nach Italien ~sehnen** long to be back with sb./in Italy; **~|senden** *unr. od. regelm. tr. V. (geh.) s.* **~schicken; ~|setzen 1.** *tr. V.* **a)** put back; **b)** *(nach hinten setzen)* move back; **c)** *(zurückfahren)* move back; reverse; back; **d)** *(benachteiligen)* **jmdn. ~setzen** neglect sb.; **sich ~gesetzt fühlen** feel neglected; **2.** *refl. V.* **a)** sit down again **(an +** *Akk.* at); **b)** *(sich weiter nach hinten setzen)* move back; **3.** *itr. V. (zurückfahren)* move back[wards]; reverse; back; **~setzung die; ~, ~en** neglect; *(Kränkung)* insult; slight; **~|spielen** *tr. V. (Ballspiele)* **den Ball ~spielen** pass *or* play the ball back; **~|springen** *unr. itr. V.; mit sein* **a)** jump back; ⟨*indicator needle etc.*⟩ spring back; ⟨*ball*⟩ bounce back; **b)** *(nach hinten springen)* jump back[wards]; **c)** *(weiter hinten liegen)* be set back; **~|stecken 1.** *tr. V.* **a)** put back; **b)** *(nach hinten stecken)* move back; **2.** *itr. V. (ugs.)* lower one's sights; **~|stehen** *unr. itr. V.* **a)** stand back; be set back; **b)** *(fig.: übertroffen werden)* be left behind; **hinter jmdm. ~stehen** take second place to sb.; **c)** *(fig.: verzichten)* miss out; **~|stellen 1.** *tr. V.* **a)** put back; **b)** *(nach hinten stellen)* move back; **c)** *(niedriger einstellen)* turn down ⟨*heating*⟩; put back ⟨*clock*⟩; **d)** *(reservieren)* put aside, keep **(***Dat.***, für** for); **e)** *(vorläufig befreien)* **jmdn. vom Wehrdienst ~stellen** defer sb.'s military service; defer sb. *(Amer.)*; **sollen wir ihn schon einschulen oder noch ~stellen lassen?** shall we start him at school now or delay it a while?; **f)** *(aufschieben)* postpone; defer; **g)** *(hintanstellen)* put aside ⟨*reservations, doubts, etc.*⟩; **h)** *(österr.: ~geben)* return; **2.** *refl. V.* go *or* get back; **stell dich an deinen Platz ~!** get back in *or* go back to your place!; **~|stoßen 1.** *unr. tr. V.* **a)** push back; **b)** *(von sich stoßen)* push away; **2.** *unr. itr. V.; mit sein s.* **~setzen 3; ~|streifen** *tr. V.* pull back; pull up ⟨*sleeve*⟩; **~|stufen** *tr. V.* downgrade **(in +** *Akk.* to); **~|treten** *unr. itr. V.* **a)** *mit sein* step back; **bitte von der Bahnsteigkante ~treten** please stand back from the edge of the platform; **b)** *mit sein (von einem Amt)* resign; step down; ⟨*government*⟩ resign; **als Vorsitzender/von einem Amt ~treten** step down as chairman/resign from an office; **c)** *mit sein (von einem Vertrag, einer Vereinbarung usw.)* withdraw **(von** from); back out **(von** of); **d)** *mit sein (fig.: in den Hintergrund treten)* become less important; fade in importance; **hinter/gegenüber etw.** *(Dat.)* **~treten** take second place to sth.; **~|tun** *unr. tr. V.* put back; **~|übersetzen** *tr. V.* translate back; **~|verfolgen** *tr. V.* trace back; **~|verlangen** *tr. V.* demand back; **~|versetzen 1.** *tr. V.* **a)** move *or* transfer back; **b)** *(fig.)* take *or* transport back; **2.** *refl. V.* think oneself back **(in +** *Akk.* to); **~|weichen** *unr. itr. V.; mit sein* draw back **(vor +** *Dat.* from); back away; *(~schrecken)* shrink back, recoil **(vor +** *Dat.* from); **er wich keinen Schritt/Zentimeter ~:** he stood his ground; **~|weisen** *unr. tr. V.* **a)** send back; **jmdn. an der Grenze ~weisen** turn sb. back at the frontier; **b)** *(abweisen, nicht akzeptieren)* reject ⟨*proposal, question, demand, application, etc.*⟩; turn down, refuse ⟨*offer, request, invitation, help, etc.*⟩; turn away ⟨*petitioner, unwelcome guest*⟩; **c)** *(sich verwahren gegen)* repudiate ⟨*accusation, claim, etc.*⟩; **~weisung die** *s.* **~weisen a–c:** sending back; turning back; rejection; turning down; refusal; turning away; repudiation; **~|wenden** *unr. od. regelm. tr. u. refl. V.* turn back; **~|werfen 1.** *unr. tr. V.* **a)** throw back; **den Kopf/sein Haar ~werfen** throw *or* toss one's head back/toss one's hair back; **b)** *(reflektieren)* reflect ⟨*light, sound*⟩; **c)** *(Milit.)* repulse ⟨*enemy*⟩; **d)** *(fig.: in einer Entwicklung)* set back; **2.** *unr. refl. V.* throw oneself back; **~|wirken** *itr. V.* react **(auf +** *Akk.* [up]on); **~|wollen 1.** *unr. itr. V.* want to go back; **2.** *unr. tr. V. (ugs.)* **etw. ~wollen** want sth. back; **~|zahlen** *tr. V.* pay back; **~|ziehen 1.** *unr. tr. V.* **a)** pull back; draw back ⟨*bolt, curtains, one's hand, etc.*⟩; **es zieht ihn in die Heimat/zu ihr ~** *(fig.)* he is drawn back to his homeland/to her; **b)** *(abziehen, zurückbeordern)* withdraw, pull back ⟨*troops*⟩; withdraw, recall ⟨*ambassador*⟩; **c)** *(rückgängig machen)* withdraw; cancel ⟨*or-*

der, instruction›; **d)** *(wieder aus dem Verkehr ziehen)* withdraw ‹*coin, stamp, etc.*›; **2.** *unr. refl. V.* withdraw (**aus, von** from); ‹*troops*› withdraw, pull back; **sich von** *od.* **aus der Politik/aus dem Showgeschäft/aus dem Berufsleben ~ziehen** retire from politics/show business/professional life; **sich aufs Land/in sein Zimmer ~:** retreat to the country/retire to one's room; *s. auch* **zurückgezogen; 3.** *unr. itr. V.; mit sein* go back; return; **~|zucken** *itr. V.; mit sein* flinch; *(erschrocken)* start back; **mit der Hand ~zucken** jerk one's hand away

Zu·ruf der shout; **durch ~ wählen/abstimmen** vote by acclamation

zu|rufen *unr. tr. V.* **jmdm. etw. ~:** shout sth. to sb.

Zu·sage die a) *(auf eine Einladung hin)* acceptance; *(auf eine Stellenbewerbung hin)* offer; **b)** *(Versprechen)* promise; undertaking; **jmdm. die** *od.* **seine ~ geben, etw. zu tun** promise sb. that one will do sth.; **ich kann Ihnen keine ~n machen** I cannot make you any promises

zu|sagen 1. *itr. V.* **a)** *(auf eine Einladung hin)* **[jmdm.] ~/fest ~:** accept/give sb. a firm acceptance; **b)** *(auf ein Angebot hin)* accept; **sie haben fest zugesagt** *(auf eine Stellenbewerbung hin)* they made me/him *etc.* a firm offer [of a job]; **c)** *(gefallen)* **jmdm. ~:** appeal to sb. **2.** *tr. V.* **a)** promise; **jmdm. etw. ~:** promise sb. sth.; **sein Kommen ~:** promise to come; **jmdm. sein Kommen ~:** promise sb. that one will come; **b)** *s.* **Kopf a**

zusammen [tsu'zamən] *Adv.* together; **wir bestellten uns ~ eine Flasche Wein** we ordered a bottle of wine between us; **wir haben ~ ein Auto** we own a car between us; **alle/alles ~:** all together; **ihr seid alle ~ Feiglinge!** *(ugs.)* you're cowards, the whole lot of you *(coll.)*; **guten Abend/schöne Ferien** *usw.* **~!** *(ugs.)* good evening/have a good holiday, everyone *or* all of you!; **er verdient mehr als alle anderen ~:** he earns more than the rest of us/them put together

zusammen-, Zusammen-: ~arbeit die; *o. Pl.* co-operation *no indef. art.*; **~|arbeiten** *itr. V.* co-operate; work together; *(kollaborieren)* collaborate; **mit ihm könnte ich nicht ~arbeiten** I could not work with him; **~|ballen 1.** *tr. V.* **[zu einem Klumpen] ~ballen** make into a ball; **2.** *refl. V.* mass together; **dunkle Wolken ballten sich ~:** dark clouds loomed; **~ballung die** concentration; **eine ~ von Städten** a conglomeration of towns; **~|bauen** *tr. V.* assemble; put together; **~|beißen** *unr. tr. V.* **die Zähne ~beißen** clench one's teeth together; *s. auch* **Zahn b; ~|bekommen** *unr. tr. V.* **a)** get together, raise ‹*money, rent, etc.*›; manage to collect ‹*signatures*›; **b)** *(zusammengesetzt/~gebaut usw. bekommen)* get together; **c)** *(fig. ugs.)* remember; **~|betteln** *tr. V.* **sich** *(Dat.)* **etw. ~betteln** manage to collect sth. by begging; **~|binden** *unr. tr. V.* tie together; **jmdm. die Hände auf dem Rücken ~binden** tie sb.'s hands behind his/her back; **sich** *(Dat.)* **das Haar ~binden** tie one's hair; **~|bleiben** *unr. itr. V.; mit sein* stay together; **~|brauen 1.** *tr. V. (ugs.)* concoct ‹*drink*›; **2.** *refl. V. (fig.)* ‹*storm, bad weather, trouble, etc.*› be brewing; ‹*disaster*› loom; **da braut sich was ~:** there's something brewing there; **~|brechen** *unr. itr. V.; mit sein* **a)** *(einstürzen)* collapse; **b)** *(zu Boden sinken)* ‹*person, animal*› collapse; *(fig.)* ‹*person*› break down; **nervlich ~brechen** have a nervous breakdown; **c)** *(fig.)* collapse; ‹*order, communications, system, telephone network*› break down; ‹*theory*› collapse, break down; ‹*traffic*› come to a standstill, be paralysed; ‹*attack, front, resistance*› crumble; **für ihn brach eine Welt ~:** his whole world collapsed; **~|bringen** *unr. tr. V.* **a)** bring together; bring ‹*chemicals*› into contact with each other; **die Ziege mit einem Bock ~bringen** put the nanny-goat together with a billy-goat; **jmdn. mit jmdm. ~bringen** bring sb. together with sb.; **b)** *(ugs., bes. südd.) s.* **~bekommen; ~bruch der a)** *(eines Menschen)* collapse; *(psychisch, nervlich)* breakdown; **dem ~bruch nahe sein** be near to collapse/breakdown; **b)** *(fig.) s.* **~brechen c:** collapse; breakdown; crumbling; **es kam zu einem ~bruch des Verkehrs** traffic came to a standstill *or* was paralysed; **~|drängen 1.** *tr. V.* push together; herd ‹*crowd*› together; *(fig.)* condense ‹*story, report, facts, etc.*›; **2.** *refl. V.* crowd together; *(fig.)* be concentrated **(auf** + *Akk.* into); **~|drücken** *tr. V.* **a)** press together; *(komprimieren)* compress ‹*gas*›; **b)** *(zerdrücken)* crush; **~|fahren 1.** *unr. itr. V.; mit sein* **a)** collide (**mit** with); **zwei Autos sind ~gefahren** two cars have collided [with each other]; **b)** *(~zucken)* start; jump; **2.** *unr. tr. V. (ugs.)* smash up ‹*vehicle*›; run over ‹*person, animal*›; **~fall der** coincidence; **~|fallen** *unr. itr. V.; mit sein* **a)** collapse; **in sich ~fallen** *(auch fig.)* collapse; ‹*fire*› die down; **das ganze Lügengebäude fiel in sich ~** *(fig.)* the whole tissue of lies fell apart; **b)** *(~sinken, schrumpfen)* **[in sich] ~fallen** ‹*cake*› sink [in the middle]; ‹*froth, foam, balloon, etc.*› collapse; **c)** ‹*person*› become emaciated; **d)** *(zeitlich)* **[zeitlich] ~fallen** coincide; fall at the same time; **e)** *(räumlich)* coincide; **~|falten** *tr. V.* fold up; **~|fassen** *tr. V.* **a)** put together; **einzelne Verbände in einer Dachorganisation ~fassen** bring individual associations together in one umbrella organization; **b)** *(in eine kurze Form bringen)* summarize; **etw. in einem Satz ~fassen** sum sth. up *or* summarize sth. in one sentence; **~fassend kann man sagen ...:** to sum up *or* in summary, one can say ...; **~fassung die** *s.* **~fassen a, b:** putting together; bringing together; summary; **~|fegen** *tr. V. (bes. nordd.)* sweep together; **~|finden** *unr. refl. V.* **a)** get together; **b)** *(zusammentreffen)* meet up; **~|flicken** *tr. V.* **a)** *(auch fig.)* patch up; **b)** *s.* **~stoppeln; ~|fließen** *unr. itr. V.; mit sein* ‹*rivers, streams*› flow into each other, join up; *(fig.)* ‹*colours*› run together; ‹*sounds*› blend together; **~fluß der** confluence; **~|fügen 1.** *tr. V.* fit together; **was Gott ~gefügt hat, das soll der Mensch nicht scheiden** what therefore God hath joined together, let not man put asunder; **2.** *refl. V.* fit together; **sich zu einem Ganzen ~fügen** fit together to form a whole; **~|führen** *tr. V.* bring together; **getrennte Familien wieder ~führen** reunite divided families; **~|gehen** *unr. itr. V.; mit sein* **a)** *(sich verbünden, sich zusammentun)* join forces (**mit** with); *(fusionieren)* ‹*firms*› merge; **b)** *(zusammenpassen)* go together; **c)** *(ugs.: zusammenlaufen, ~fließen usw.)* join up; meet; **d)** *(ugs.: sich zusammenfügen, verbinden usw. lassen)* fit together; meet; **~|gehören** *itr. V.* belong together; **~gehörig** *Adj.* [closely] related *or* connected ‹*subjects, problems, etc.*›; matching *attrib.* ‹*pieces of tea service, cutlery, etc.*›; **die ~gehörigen Teile/Fotos** the parts/photographs which belong together; **~gehörigkeit die; ~: tiefe ~gehörigkeit mit jmdm. fühlen** have a deep sense *or* feeling of unity with sb.; **die beiden verbindet ein starkes Gefühl der ~gehörigkeit** the two of them are joined by a strong sense *or* feeling of belonging together; **~gehörigkeits·gefühl** *das; o. Pl.* sense *or* feeling of belonging together; **~genommen** *Adj.; nicht attr.* **alle diese Dinge ~genommen** all these things together; **~gewürfelt** *Adj.* oddly assorted; **ein bunt ~gewürfelter Haufen** a motley collection of people; **~|haben** *unr. tr. V. (ugs.)* have got together; **~halt der;** *o. Pl.* cohesion; **keinen/einen guten ~halt haben** have no/good cohesion; **~|halten 1.** *unr. tr. V.* **a)** hold together; **b)** *(beisammenhalten)* keep together; **sein Geld ~halten** be careful with one's money; **2.** *unr. itr. V.* **a)** hold together; **b)** *(fig.)* ‹*friends, family, etc.*› stick together; **~hang der** connection; *(einer Geschichte, Rede)* coherence; *(Kontext)* context; **was er sagte, hatte keinen ~hang** what he said was incoherent; **in [keinem] ~hang mit etw. stehen** be [in no way] connected with sth.; **die historischen/gesellschaftlichen ~hänge kennen** know the historical/social context; **etw. mit etw. in ~hang bringen** connect sth. with sth.; make a connection between sth. and sth.; **im ~hang mit ...:** in connection with ...; **etw. aus dem ~hang lösen/reißen** take sth. out of [its] context; **~|hängen** *unr. itr. V.* **a)** be joined [together]; **in ~hängenden Sätzen** in coherent sentences; **~hängender Text** continuous text; **~hängend erzählen** relate in a coherent manner; **b)** *(fig.)* **mit etw. ~hängen** *(zu etw. eine Beziehung haben)* be related to sth.; *(durch etw. [mit] verursacht sein)* be the result of sth.; **das hängt damit ~, daß ...:** that is connected with *or* has to do with the fact that ...; **die damit ~hängenden Fragen** the related issues; **~hang·los 1.** *Adj.* incoherent, disjointed ‹*speech, story, etc.*›; **~hanglos nebeneinanderstehen** stand disconnectedly side by side; **2.** *adv.* ‹*speak*› incoherently; **~|hauen** *unr. tr. V. (ugs.)* **a)** *(zerschlagen)* smash up; **b)** *(verprügeln)* **jmdn. ~hauen** beat sb. up; **c)** *(abwertend: nachlässig anfertigen)* knock together ‹*furniture*›; knock off *(coll.)* ‹*homework, task, etc.*›; **~|heften** *tr. V.* **a)** staple together; *(Buchbinderei)* stitch together; **b)** *(Schneiderei)* tack *or* baste together; **~|kauern** *refl. V.* huddle [up]; **sich ängstlich ~kauern** cower; **~|kaufen** *tr. V.* buy; **~|kehren** *tr. V. (bes. südd.) s.* **~fegen; ~klappbar** *Adj.* folding; **~klappbar sein** fold up; **~|klappen 1.** *tr. V.* **a)** fold up; **b)** *(zusammenschlagen)* **die Hacken/Absätze ~klappen** click one's heels; **2.** *itr. V.; mit sein (ugs.)* collapse; **~|klauben** *tr. V. (südd., österr.)* gather together; **~|kleben** *tr., itr. V.* stick together; **~|kneifen** *unr. tr. V.* press ‹*lips*› together; screw ‹*eyes*› up; **~|knüllen** *tr. V.* crumple up; *(fest)* screw up; **~|kommen** *unr. itr. V.; mit sein* **a)** meet; **mit jmdm. ~kommen** meet sb.; **b)** *(zueinanderkommen; auch fig.)* get together; **c)** *(zusammentreffen, gleichzeitig auftreten)* occur *or* happen together; **heute kommt bei mir aber auch alles ~!** *(ugs.)* everything's going wrong at once today!; **d)** *(sich summieren, sich sammeln)* accumulate; **da werden schon so an die 50 Leute ~kommen** there are sure to be getting on for 50 people there altogether; **~|koppeln** *tr. V.* couple together; dock ‹*spacecraft*›; **~|krachen** *itr. V.; mit sein (ugs.)* **a)** collapse with a crash; **er ist mit dem Stuhl ~gekracht** he crashed to the floor with the chair; **b)** *(zusammenstoßen)* ‹*vehicles*› crash [into each other], collide [with each other]; **mit einem Auto ~krachen** crash *or* collide with a car; **~|krampfen** *refl. V.* ‹*hands*› clench; ‹*stomach, chest*› tighten; **es krampfte sich in mir alles ~:** I tensed up inside; **~|kratzen** *tr. V. (ugs.)* scrape together ‹*money, savings, etc.*›; **~|kriegen** *tr. V. (ugs.) s.* **~bekommen; ~|krümmen** *refl. V.* double up; writhe

Zusammenkunft [tsu'zamənkʊnft] **die; ~, Zusammenkünfte** [... kʏnftə] meeting

zusammen-: ~|läppern *refl. V. (ugs.)* mount up; **~|laufen** *unr. itr. V.; mit sein* **a)** ‹*people, crowd*› gather, congregate; **b)** *(zusammenfließen)* ‹*rivers, streams*› flow into each other, join up; **c)** *(sich sammeln)* ‹*water, oil, etc.*› collect; **d)** *(sich vereinigen)* converge; *(Geom.)* intersect; **e)** *(ineinanderlau-*

fen) ⟨*colours*⟩ run together; ~|**leben** *itr. V.* live together; ~|**leben das;** *o. Pl.* living together *no art.;* **das eheliche/menschliche ~leben** married life/man's social existence; ~|**legen 1.** *tr. V.* **a)** put *or* gather together; **b)** *(zusammenfalten)* fold [up]; **c)** *(miteinander verbinden)* amalgamate, merge ⟨*classes, departments, etc.*⟩; combine ⟨*events*⟩; **d)** put ⟨*patients, guests, etc.*⟩ together [in the same room]; **e)** *(aneinanderlegen)* fold ⟨*hands, arms*⟩; **2.** *itr. V.* club together; pool our/your/their money; ~|**leimen** glue *or* stick together; ~|**lesen** *unr. tr. V.* gather; ~|**nähen** *tr. V.* **a)** sew together; **etw. mit etw. ~nähen** sew sth. to sth.; **b)** *(durch Nähen reparieren)* sew up; ~|**nehmen 1.** *unr. tr. V.* **a)** summon *or* muster up ⟨*courage, strength, understanding*⟩; collect ⟨*thoughts, wits*⟩; *s. auch* **~genommen; 2.** *unr. refl. V.* get *or* take a grip on oneself; **nimm dich ~!** pull yourself together!; ~|**packen 1.** *tr. V.* pack up; *(zusammen verpacken)* pack up together; **2.** *itr. V.* pack up; ~|**passen** *itr. V.* ⟨*colours, clothes, furniture*⟩ go together; ⟨*persons*⟩ be suited to each other; **mit etw. ~passen** go with sth.; ~|**phantasieren** *refl. V. (ugs.)* **sich** *(Dat.)* **etw. ~phantasieren** dream up sth.; invent sth.; *(im Fieber)* imagine

Zusạmmenprall der; ~**[e]s,** ~**e** collision; *(fig.)* clash

zusạmmen-, Zusạmmen-: ~|**prallen** *itr. V.; mit sein* collide (**mit** with); *(fig.)* clash; ~|**pressen** *tr. V.* **a)** squeeze; *(komprimieren)* compress ⟨*gas*⟩; **b)** *(aneinanderpressen)* press ⟨*lips, hands*⟩ together; ~|**raffen** *tr. V.* gather up ⟨*possessions, papers, etc.*⟩; bundle up ⟨*clothes*⟩; ~|**rasseln** *itr. V.; mit sein (ugs.) s.* **~krachen b;**~|**rechnen** *tr. V.* add up; **einen Betrag mit einem anderen ~rechnen** add one amount to another; ~|**reimen** *refl. V. (ugs.)* **a) sich** *(Dat.)* **etw. ~reimen** work sth. out [for oneself]; **ich kann mir das nur so ~reimen** that's the only way I can make sense of it; **b)** *(~passen, ~gehören)* **wie reimt sich das ~?** how does that tally?; ~|**reißen** *unr. refl. V. (ugs.) s.* **~nehmen 2;** ~|**ringeln** *refl. V.* ⟨*snake*⟩ coil itself up; ~|**rollen 1.** *tr. V.* roll up; **2.** *refl. V.* ⟨*cat, dog, etc.*⟩ curl up; ⟨*hedgehog*⟩ roll [itself] up [into a ball]; ~|**rotten** *refl. V. (abwertend)* ⟨*crowds, groups, etc.*⟩ band together; ⟨*youths*⟩ gang together *or* up; *(in Aufruhr)* form a mob; **~rottung die;** ~, ~**en** *(abwertend)* gathering; **auf der Straße kam es zu ~rottungen** mobs [of hooligans] gathered in the street; ~|**rücken 1.** *tr. V.* move ⟨*chairs, tables, etc.*⟩ together; **2.** *itr. V.; mit sein (auch fig.)* move closer together; ~|**rufen** *unr. tr. V.* call together; ~|**sacken** *itr. V.; mit sein (ugs.)* **a)** *(einstürzen)* **[in sich] ~sacken** collapse; **b)** *(zu Boden sinken)* ⟨*person*⟩ collapse; **c)** *(eine schlaffe Haltung annehmen)* **[in sich] ~sacken** slump; ~|**scharen** *refl. V.* gather; **~schau die;** *o. Pl.* survey; **aus der ~schau beider ergibt sich ...:** looking at *or* viewing the two together shows ...; ~|**scheißen** *unr. tr. V. (salopp)* **jmdn. ~scheißen** tear sb. off a strip *(sl.)*; ~|**schlagen 1.** *unr. tr. V.* **a)** strike *or* bang together; clap ⟨*hands*⟩ [together]; **die Hacken ~schlagen** click one's heels; **b)** *(verprügeln)* beat up; **c)** *(zertrümmern)* smash up *or* to pieces; **d)** *(zusammenfalten)* fold up; **2.** *unr. itr. V.; mit sein* **über jmdm./etw. ~schlagen** engulf sb./sth.; *(fig.)* ⟨*disaster, misfortune*⟩ overtake sb./sth.; ~|**schließen 1.** *unr. refl. V.* join together; ⟨*firms*⟩ merge, amalgamate; **sich im Kampf für/gegen etw. ~schließen** unite in the struggle for/against sth.; **2.** *unr. tr. V.* lock together; **~schluß der** joining together; union; *(von Firmen)* merger; amalgamation; ~|**schmelzen** *unr. itr. V.; mit sein* melt [away]; *(fig.)* ⟨*supplies, savings, etc.*⟩ dwindle (**auf** + *Akk.* to); ~|**schneiden** *unr. tr. V. (Film, Ferns., Rundf.: kürzen)* cut; ~|**schnüren** *tr. V.* **a)** tie up (**zu** in); **b)** *(einschnüren)* lace in ⟨*waist*⟩; **der Anblick schnürte mir das Herz ~** *(geh.)* the sight tore at my heart[-strings]; ~|**schrecken** *unr. od. regelm. itr. V.; mit sein* start; jump; ~|**schreiben** *unr. tr. V.* **a)** write together; **b)** *(abwertend: verfassen)* dash off ⟨*report, letter, etc.*⟩; **was für einen Unsinn hast du denn da ~geschrieben!** what a lot of rubbish you've written there; **~schreibung die** writing together *or* as one word; **beachten Sie bitte die ~schreibung solcher Bezeichnungen** please remember that such terms are written together *or* as one word; ~|**schrumpfen** *itr. V.; mit sein* shrivel [up]; *(fig.)* dwindle; ~|**schustern** *tr. V. (ugs. abwertend)* cobble together; ~|**schweißen** *tr. V.* weld together; **etw. mit etw. ~schweißen** weld sth. to sth.; **die Gefahr hat sie noch enger ~geschweißt** *(fig.)* the danger forged even stronger bonds between them; ~|**sein** *unr. itr. V.; mit sein; Zusschr. nur im Inf. u. Part.* **a)** be together; **b)** *(zusammenleben)* be *or* live together; **mit jmdm. ~sein** be *or* live with sb.; **~sein das a)** being together *no art.;* **b)** *(Treffen)* get-together; ~|**setzen 1.** *tr. V.* **a)** put together; **Steine zu einem Mosaik ~setzen** put stones together to make a mosaic; **b)** *(herstellen)* make; **ein ~gesetztes Wort/Verb** a compound word/verb; **c)** *(zusammenbauen, -montieren)* assemble; put together; **d)** *(beieinander sitzen lassen)* seat *or* put together; **jmdn. mit jmdm. ~setzen** seat *or* put sb. next to sb.; **2.** *refl. V.* **a) sich aus etw. ~setzen** be made up *or* composed of sth.; **wie setzt sich das Gremium ~?** how is the committee made up?; **b)** *(sich zueinander setzen)* sit together; **sich mit jmdm. ~setzen** sit next to sb.; **c)** *(zu einem Gespräch)* get together; **~setzung die;** ~, ~**en a)** *o. Pl.* putting together; **b)** *(Aufbau)* composition; **„~setzung: ...“** *(als Aufschrift auf Medikamentenpackung)* 'ingredients: ...'; **c)** *(Sprachw.)* compound; ~|**sinken** *unr. itr. V.; mit sein* **a) [in sich] ~sinken** collapse; ⟨*fire*⟩ die down; ⟨*dough*⟩ sink; **b)** *(zu Boden sinken)* **[in sich] ~sinken** slump to the ground; *(eine schlaffe Haltung einnehmen)* slump; **ohnmächtig/tot ~sinken** collapse in a faint/fall down dead; ~|**sitzen** *unr. itr. V.* **a)** sit together; **mit jmdm. ~sitzen** sit next to sb.; **b)** *(miteinander verbunden sein)* be joined together; ~|**sparen** *tr. V.* save up; **sich** *(Dat.)* **ein Auto/Fahrrad ~sparen** save up and buy a car/bicycle; **~spiel das a)** *o. Pl. (von Musikern)* ensemble playing; *(von Darstellern)* ensemble acting; *(einer Mannschaft)* teamwork; **b)** *(fig.)* interplay; ~|**spielen** *itr. V.* **a)** play together; ⟨*actors*⟩ act together; **mit jmdm. ~spielen** play/act with sb.; **b)** *(fig.)* ⟨*forces, influences, etc.*⟩ work together, combine; ~|**stauchen** *tr. V.* **a)** compress; **b)** *(fig. ugs.)* **jmdn. ~stauchen** tear sb. off a strip *(sl.)*; ~|**stecken 1.** *tr. V.* **a)** fit together; join up ⟨*extension cables*⟩; **b)** *(mit einer Nadel, Spange usw.)* pin together; *s. auch* **Kopf a; 2.** *itr. V. (ugs.)* be together; ~|**stehen** *unr. itr. V.* **a)** stand together; **mit jmdm. ~stehen** stand with sb.; **b)** *(fig.: zusammenhalten)* stand by one another; ~|**stellen 1.** *tr. V.* **a)** put together; **b)** *(aus einzelnen Teilen gestalten)* put together ⟨*programme, film, book, menu, exhibition, team, delegation*⟩; draw up ⟨*list, timetable*⟩; compile ⟨*report, broadcast*⟩; work out ⟨*route, tour*⟩; make up ⟨*bouquet, flower arrangement*⟩; **c)** *(in einer Übersicht, Liste usw.)* draw together; compile ⟨*facts, data*⟩; **d)** *(kombinieren)* combine; **2.** *refl. V.* stand together; **~stellung die a)** *s.* **~stellen 1b:** putting together; drawing up; compilation; working out; making up; **b)** *(Übersicht)* survey; *(von Tatsachen, Daten)* compilation; **c)** *(Kombination)* combination; ~|**stimmen** *itr. V.* **a)** ⟨*instruments*⟩ harmonize; ⟨*colours, furniture*⟩ match, go together; **mit etw. ~stimmen** go with sth.; **b)** *(stimmig sein)* agree (**mit** with); ~|**stoppeln** *tr. V. (abwertend)* cobble together; **~stoß der** collision; *(fig.)* clash (**mit** with); **bei dem ~stoß [der beiden Züge]** in the collision [between the two trains]; ~|**stoßen** *unr. itr. V.; mit sein* collide (**mit** with); **wir stießen mit den Köpfen ~:** we banged *or* bumped our heads; ~|**strömen** *itr. V.; mit sein* **a)** ⟨*rivers, streams*⟩ flow into one another, join up; **b)** *(zusammenlaufen, -kommen)* congregate; ~|**stückeln** *tr. V. (ugs.)* patch together; ~|**stürzen** *itr. V.; mit sein* collapse; ⟨*mine shaft, roof*⟩ cave in, collapse; ~|**suchen** *tr. V.* collect bit by bit; hunt out ⟨*information*⟩ bit by bit; ~|**tragen** *unr. tr. V.* collect; ~|**treffen** *unr. itr. V.; mit sein* **a)** meet; **mit jmdm. ~treffen** meet sb.; **b)** *(zeitlich)* coincide; **~treffen das a)** meeting; **b) ein merkwürdiges ~treffen von Zufällen** a peculiar set of coincidences; ~|**treiben** *unr. tr. V.* herd together; ~|**treten** *unr. itr. V.; mit sein* meet (**zu** for); ⟨*parliament*⟩ assemble; ~|**trommeln** *tr. V. (ugs.)* round up; ~|**tun** *(ugs.)* **1.** *unr. tr. V.* put together; **2.** *unr. refl. V.* get together (**mit** with); ~|**wachsen** *unr. itr. V.; mit sein* grow together; join [up]; ⟨*bones*⟩ knit together; *(fig.)* ⟨*towns*⟩ merge into one; **~gewachsen sein** be joined; ⟨*bones*⟩ have knitted together; ~|**werfen** *unr. tr. V. (ugs.)* lump together; ~|**wirken** *itr. V.* combine; ~|**zählen** *tr. V.* add up; ~|**ziehen 1.** *unr. tr. V.* **a)** draw *or* pull together; draw *or* pull ⟨*noose, net*⟩ tight; **die Brauen ~ziehen** knit one's brows; **die Säure zieht einem den Mund ~:** the sourness makes you pucker up your mouth; **b)** *(konzentrieren)* mass ⟨*troops, police*⟩; **c)** *(addieren)* add up *or* together; *(zusammenfassen)* simplify ⟨*mathematical expression*⟩; **2.** *unr. refl. V.* **a)** ⟨*skin, muscle, heart*⟩ contract; ⟨*face*⟩ tighten up; ⟨*wound*⟩ close up; **b)** *s.* **~brauen 2; 3.** *unr. itr. V.; mit sein* move in together; **mit jmdm. ~ziehen** move in with sb.; ~|**zimmern** *tr. V. (ugs.)* knock together; *(fig. abwertend)* cobble together; ~|**zucken** *itr. V.; mit sein* start; jump

Zụ·satz der a) addition; **unter ~ von etw.** while adding sth.; **ohne ~ von ...:** without the addition of ...; without adding ...; **b)** *(Zugesetztes, Additiv)* additive; **c)** *(zusätzlicher Teil)* addition; *(zu einem Vertrag)* rider; additional clause; *(Nachtrag)* addendum; *(zu einem Brief)* postscript; *(zu einem Testament)* codicil

Zusatz·bremsleuchte die *(Kfz-W.)* high-level brake light

zusätzlich ['tsu:zɛtslɪç] **1.** *Adj.* additional; **2.** *adv.* in addition

zu·schạnden *Adv.* *in* **etw. ~ machen** wreck *or* ruin sth.; **ein Auto ~ fahren/ein Pferd ~ reiten** wreck a car/ruin a horse by bad riding; **~ werden** be wrecked *or* ruined

zụ|schanzen *tr. V. (ugs.)* **jmdm./sich etw. ~:** wangle sth. for sb./oneself *(coll.)*

zụ|schauen *itr. V. (südd., österr., schweiz.) s.* **zusehen**

Zụ·schauer der, Zụ·schauerin die; ~, ~**nen** spectator; *(im Theater, Kino)* member of the audience; *(an einer Unfallstelle)* onlooker; *(Fernseh~)* viewer; **die ~:** the spectators; the crowd *sing.; (im Theater, Kino)* the audience *sing.; (an einer Unfallstelle)* the onlookers; *(Fernseh~)* the audience *sing.;* the viewers

Zuschauer·raum der auditorium

zụ|schaufeln *tr. V.* fill in [with a shovel/shovels]

zụ|schicken *tr. V.* send; **jmdm. etw. ~:** send sth. to sb.; send sb. sth.; **sich** *(Dat.)* **etw. ~ lassen** send for sth.

zu|schieben *unr. tr. V.* **a)** push ‹*drawer, door*› shut; **den Riegel ~:** put the bolt across; **b)** *(fig.: zuweisen)* **jmdm. die Schuld/Verantwortung ~:** lay the blame/responsibility on sb.

zu|schießen 1. *unr. tr. V.* **a) jmdm. den Ball ~:** kick *or* pass the ball to sb.; **b)** *(als Zuschuß geben)* contribute **(zu** towards); **Geld zu etw. ~:** contribute [money] *or* put money towards sth.; **jmdm. 200 Mark ~:** give sb. 200 marks towards it. **2.** *unr. itr. V.; mit sein* **auf jmdn./etw. zugeschossen kommen** come shooting towards sb.

Zu·schlag der a) additional *or* extra charge; *(für Nacht-, Feiertagsarbeit, Arbeitserschwernisse)* additional *or* extra payment; **der Intercity-Zug kostet [5 Mark] ~:** you have to pay a supplement [of 5 marks] on an intercity train; **b)** *(Eisenb.)* supplement ticket; **c)** *(bei einer Versteigerung)* acceptance of a/the bid; **der ~ erfolgt an Herrn X** *od.* **wird Herrn X erteilt** the lot is knocked down to Mr X *or* goes to Mr X; **d)** *(bei Ausschreibung eines Auftrags)* acceptance of a/the tender; **jmdm. den ~ für etw. geben** give sb. the contract for sth.; **den ~ bekommen** *od.* **erhalten** get the contract

zu|schlagen 1. *unr. tr. V.* **a)** bang or slam ‹*door, window, etc.*› shut; close ‹*book*›; *(heftig)* slam ‹*book*› shut; **b) jmdm. etw. ~** *(bei einer Versteigerung)* knock sth. down to sb.; *(bei Ausschreibung eines Auftrags, durch Gerichtsbeschluß)* award sth. to sb.; **c)** *(angliedern)* annex *(Dat.* to); **d)** *(als Zuschlag erheben)* add on; **das Porto wird dem Preis zugeschlagen** the price does not include postage. **2.** *unr. itr. V.* **a)** *mit sein* ‹*door, trap*› slam *or* bang shut; **b)** *(einen Schlag führen)* throw a blow/blows; *(losschlagen)* hit *or* strike out; *(fig.)* ‹*army, police, murderer*› strike; **er schlug kräftig zu** he threw a powerful blow; **schlag doch zu!** [go on,] hit it/me/him *etc.;* **c)** *(salopp: zugreifen)* jump at it; *(beim Essen)* have a good nosh-up *(sl.); (beim Trinken)* knock it back *(coll.)*

zuschlag·pflichtig [-'pflɪçtɪç] *Adj. (Eisenb.)* ‹*train*› on which on supplement is payable

Zuschlag·stoff der *(Hüttenw.)* flux; *(Bauw.)* aggregate

zu|schließen 1. *unr. tr. V.* lock. **2.** *unr. itr. V.* lock up

zu|schnappen *itr. V.* **a)** *mit sein* snap shut; **b)** *(zubeißen)* snap; **der Hund schnappt zu, wenn man ihn neckt** if you tease him the dog will snap at you

zu|schneiden *unr. itr. V.* cut out ‹*material etc.*› **(zu, für** for); saw ‹*plank, slat*› to size; cut out ‹*dress, jacket*›; **auf jmdn./etw. zugeschnitten sein** *(fig.)* be tailor-made for sb./sth.; **auf jmds. Geschmack zugeschnitten** geared to sb.'s taste

zu|schneien *itr. V.; mit sein* snow in *or* up

Zu·schnitt der a) *(von Kleidung)* cut; *(fig.)* character; *(Format)* calibre; **b)** *o. Pl. (das Zuschneiden) (von Kleidung)* cutting [out]; *(von Platten usw.)* sawing to size

zu|schnüren *tr. V.* tie up; **sich** *(Dat.)* **die Schuhe ~:** tie *or* do up one's shoes; *s. auch* **Kehle**

zu|schrauben *tr. V.* screw the lid *or* top on ‹*jar, flask*›; screw ‹*lid, top*› on

zu|schreiben *unr. tr. V.* **a) jmdm./einem Umstand etw. ~:** attribute sth. to sb./a circumstance; **jmdm. das Verdienst/die Schuld an etw.** *(Dat.)* **~:** credit sb. with/blame sb. for sth.; **das hast du dir selbst zuzuschreiben** you only have yourself to blame [for this]; **jmdm./einer Sache eine Eigenschaft ~:** ascribe a characteristic *or* quality to sb./sth.; credit sb./sth. with a quality; **b)** *(überschreiben)* **einem Konto eine Summe ~:** transfer a sum to an account

Zu·schrift die letter; *(auf eine Anzeige)* reply

zu·schulden *Adv.* **sich** *(Dat.)* **[irgend] etw. ~ kommen lassen** do [any] wrong

Zu·schuß der contribution **(zu** towards); *(regelmäßiger ~)* allowance; **[staatlicher] ~:** state subsidy **(für, zu** towards); **ich gebe dir einen kleinen ~:** I'll give you something towards it

Zuschuß·betrieb der subsidized concern

zu|schustern *(ugs.) tr. V.* **a) jmdm. einen Posten** *usw.* **~:** organize a job *etc.* for sb.; **b)** *(zuschießen)* contribute **(zu** towards)

zu|schütten *tr. V.* **a)** fill in ‹*ditch etc.*›; **b)** *(ugs. hinzufügen)* pour on, add ‹*water etc.*›

zu|sehen *unr. itr. V.* **a)** watch; **jmdm. [bei einem Spiel/beim Arbeiten** *usw.*] **~:** watch sb. [playing a game/working *etc.*]; **bei näherem Zusehen** on closer examination; if you look more closely; **vom [bloßen] Zusehen** [simply] by watching; **er mußte ~, wie sein Haus niederbrannte** he had to stand by and watch his house burn down; **wir dürfen diesem Unrecht nicht tatenlos ~:** we cannot stand idly by and allow this injustice; **b)** *(dafür sorgen, sich darum bemühen)* make sure; see to it; **sieh zu, daß ...:** see that ...; make sure that ...; **er soll ~, wie er das hinkriegt** he'll just have to manage somehow; **sieh zu, wo du bleibst!** you're on your own

zusehends ['tsu:ze:ənts] *Adv.* visibly

Zu·seher der *(österr.) s.* **Zuschauer**

zu·sein *unr. itr. V. mit sein; Zusschr. nur im Inf. u. Partizip* **a)** ‹*door, window*› be shut; ‹*shop*› have shut; **b)** *(ugs.: betrunken sein)* be tight *(coll.)*

zu|senden *unr. od. regelm. tr. V. s.* **zuschicken**

Zu·sendung die a) *(das Zusenden)* sending; **ich bitte um ~ des Vertrages** I would ask that the contract be sent to me; **b)** *(Zugesandtes) (Brief)* letter; *(Paket)* parcel; *(Warensendung)* consignment

zu|setzen 1. *tr. V.* **a) [zu] einem Stoff etw. ~:** add sth. to a substance; **b)** *(zuzahlen)* pay out; **er hat nichts [mehr] zuzusetzen** *(fig.)* he has no strength left in him. **2.** *itr. V. (ugs.)* **jmdm. ~:** *(jmdn. angreifen)* go for sb.; *(beim Verhör)* grill sb.; *(jmdn. bedrängen)* pester *or* badger sb.; ‹*mosquitoes etc.*› plague sb.; ‹*illness, heat*› take a lot out of sb.; ‹*death, divorce*› be a heavy blow for sb.; **einer Sache** *(Dat.)* **~** *(beschädigen)* damage sth.

zu|sichern *tr. V.* **jmdm. etw. ~:** promise sb. sth.; assure sb. of sth.

Zu·sicherung die promise; assurance

zu|sperren *(südd., österr.)* **1.** *tr. V.* lock. **2.** *itr. V.* lock up

Zu·spiel das; *o. Pl. (Ballspiele)* passing; *(einzelner Spielzug)* pass

zu|spielen 1. *itr. V. (Ballspiele)* pass. **2.** *tr. V.* **a)** *(Ballspiele)* **jmdm. den Ball ~:** pass the ball to sb.; **b)** *(fig.: zukommen lassen)* **der Presse Informationen ~:** leak information to the press

zu|spitzen 1. *tr. V.* **a)** sharpen to a point; **b)** *(fig.: verschärfen)* aggravate ‹*position, crisis*›; intensify ‹*competition, conflict, etc.*›; **c)** *(fig.: pointieren)* make ‹*question, answer*› pointed. **2.** *refl. V.* become aggravated

Zu·spitzung die; ~, ~en a) *(fig.: Verschärfung)* aggravation; *(der Konkurrenz, eines Konflikts)* intensification; **b)** *(fig.: Pointierung)* pointed emphasis

zu|sprechen 1. *unr. tr. V.* **a) er sprach ihr Trost/Mut zu** his words gave her comfort/courage; **sich** *(Dat.)* **selbst Mut ~:** give oneself courage; **b)** *(zuerkennen)* **jmdm. ein Erbe** *usw.* **~:** award sb. an inheritance *etc.;* **die Kinder der Mutter/dem Vater ~:** award custody of the children to the mother/father; **c)** *(zuschreiben)* **jmdm./einer Sache etw. ~:** ascribe sth. to sb./sth. **2.** *unr. itr. V.* **a)** *(zureden)* **jmdm. ermutigend/tröstend** *usw.* **~:** speak encouragingly/comfortingly to sb.; **b)** *(geh.)* **dem Essen/den Getränken ~:** partake of the food/drinks

Zu·spruch der; *o. Pl. (geh.)* **a)** *(Zureden)* words *pl.;* **Worte des ~s** *(tröstend)* words of comfort; *(ermutigend)* words of encouragement; **b)** *(Anklang)* **[bei jmdm.] ~ finden** be popular [with sb.]

Zu·stand der a) condition; *(bes. abwertend)* state; **in rohem/gefrorenem ~:** in the raw/frozen state; raw/frozen; **in flüssigem ~:** in liquid form; **in betrunkenem ~:** while under the influence of alcohol; **in bewußtlosem ~:** in a state of unconsciousness; unconscious; **geistiger/gesundheitlicher ~:** state of mind/health; **der ~ des Patienten** the patient's condition; **er war in einem schlimmen ~:** he was in a bad way; **Zustände kriegen** *od.* **bekommen** *(ugs.)* have a fit *(coll.);* **b)** *(Stand der Dinge)* state of affairs; situation; **Zustände** conditions; **das sind ja [schöne] Zustände!** that's a fine state of affairs!; these are fine goings-on!; **das ist doch kein ~!** that just won't do *(coll.); s. auch* **Rom**

zu·stande *Adv. in:* **~ bringen** manage to do; [manage to] bring about ‹*agreement, coalition, etc.*›; **~ kommen** come into being; *(geschehen)* take place; **es wollte kein Gespräch ~ kommen** it was impossible to get a conversation going

zu·ständig *Adj.* **a)** appropriate, proper, relevant ‹*authority, office, etc.*›; **das ~e Gericht** the court of jurisdiction; **von ~er Seite** by the proper authority; **[für etw.] ~ sein** *(verantwortlich)* be responsible [for sth.]; *(kompetent)* be competent [to deal with sth.]; ‹*court*› have jurisdiction [in sth.]; **dafür sind wir nicht ~:** it's not our responsibility/we are not competent to decide that; **b)** *(österr. Amtsspr.)* **nach Wien ~ sein** be domiciled in Vienna

Zuständigkeit die; ~, ~en *(Verantwortlichkeit)* responsibility; *(Kompetenz)* competence; *(eines Gerichts)* jurisdiction

Zuständigkeits·bereich der *(Verantwortlichkeit)* area of responsibility; *(Kompetenz)* range of competence; **das fällt in den ~ des Innenministeriums** it is within the responsibility/competence of the Ministry of the Interior

Zustands-: ~passiv das *(Sprachw.)* passive of condition; **~verb das** *(Sprachw.)* verb describing a state

zu·statten *Adv. in* **jmdm./einer Sache ~ kommen** be a help *or* be useful to sb./for sth.; *(von Vorteil sein)* be of advantage to sb./sth.

zu|stecken *tr. V.* **a)** pin up ‹*tear*›; pin together ‹*curtains etc.*›; **b)** *(heimlich geben)* **jmdm. etw. ~:** slip sb. sth.

zu|stehen *unr. itr. V.* **etw. steht jmdm. zu** sb. is entitled to sth.; **ein Urteil über ihn steht mir nicht zu** it is not for me to judge him

zu|steigen *unr. itr. V.; mit sein* get on; **ist noch jemand zugestiegen?** *(im Bus)* any more fares, please?; *(im Zug)* ≈ tickets, please!

zu|stellen *tr. V.* **a)** block ‹*entrance, passage, etc.*›; **b)** *(bringen)* deliver ‹*letter, parcel, etc.*›; **jmdm. etw. ~:** deliver sth. to sb.; *(zuschicken)* send sb. sth.; **jmdm. ein Schriftstück ~:** serve a writ on sb.

Zu·steller der; ~s, ~: deliverer; *(Postbote)* postman

Zu·stellung die delivery; *(Zusendung)* submission

zu|steuern 1. *itr. V.; mit sein* **auf jmdn./etw. ~:** head for sb./sth.; **einer Sache** *(Dat.)* **~:** head for sth. **2.** *tr. V.* **a) etw. auf jmdn./etw. ~:** steer *or* drive sth. towards sb./sth.; **b)** *(ugs.) s.* **beisteuern**

zu|stimmen *itr. V.* agree; **jmdm. [in einem Punkt] ~:** agree with sb. [on a point]; **~d nicken** nod in agreement; **einer Sache** *(Dat.)* **~:** agree to sth.; **einem Gesetzentwurf ~** ‹*parliament*› pass *or* approve a bill; **dem kann ich nur ~:** I quite agree

Zu·stimmung die *(Billigung)* approval (zu

of); *(Einverständnis)* agreement **(zu** to, with); *(Plazet)* consent **(zu** to); **[allgemeine] ~ finden** meet with [general] approval; **die ~ der Eltern** the parents' consent; **jmdm. seine ~ zu etw. geben** give sb. one's consent to *or* for sth.; **nicht ohne/nur mit jmds. ~:** not without/only with the agreement *or* consent of sb.

zu|stopfen *tr. V.* **a)** plug, stop up ⟨*hole, crack*⟩; plug ⟨*ears*⟩; **b)** *(mit Nadel und Faden)* darn, mend ⟨*hole*⟩

zu|stöpseln *tr. V.* **a)** put a stopper in ⟨*bottle*⟩; *(mit Korken);* put a cork in, cork ⟨*bottle*⟩; **b)** put a plug in ⟨*basin*⟩; plug ⟨*drain etc.*⟩

zu|stoßen 1. *unr. tr. V.* push ⟨*door etc.*⟩ shut; *(mit dem Fuß, heftig)* kick ⟨*door etc.*⟩ shut. **2.** *unr. itr. V.* **a)** strike out; *(mit einem Messer usw.)* make a stab; stab; ⟨*snake etc.*⟩ strike; **b)** *mit sein* **jmdm. ~:** happen to sb.; **wenn mir etwas zustößt** if anything should happen to me

zu|streben *itr. V.; mit sein* **einer Sache** *(Dat.) od.* **auf etw.** *(Akk.)* **~:** make for sth.; *(fig.)* strive for *or* aim at sth.

Zu·strom der a) *(von Luft, fig.: Geld usw.)* flow; **b)** *(von Menschen)* influx; stream; **starken** *od.* **großen ~ haben** have a great influx of people

zu|stürmen *itr. V.; mit sein* **auf jmdn./etw. ~:** charge towards sb./sth.

zu|stürzen *itr. V.; mit sein* **auf jmdn./etw. ~/zugestürzt kommen** rush/come rushing towards sb./sth.; *(direkt heran)* rush/come rushing up to sb./sth.

zu|tage *Adv. in:* **~ kommen** *od.* **treten** become visible *(lit. or fig.);* ⟨*stream*⟩ come to the surface; *(ans Licht kommen)* ⟨*documents etc.*⟩ come to light, be revealed; ⟨*story*⟩ come out, be made public; *(fig.: erkennbar werden)* become evident; ⟨*differences etc.*⟩ come into the open; **etw. ~ bringen** *od.* **fördern** *(aus der Tasche usw.)* produce sth.; *(fig.: erkennbar machen)* bring sth. to light; reveal sth.; **offen** *od.* **klar ~ liegen** be perfectly clear *or* evident

Zu·tat die ingredient

zu·teil *Adv. (geh.) in* **jmdm./einer Sache ~ werden** be granted *or* accorded to sb./sth.; **ihm wurde die Ehre ~, die Ansprache halten zu dürfen** he was accorded the honour of giving the address; **jmdm. etw. ~ werden lassen** accord sb. sth.; bestow sth. on sb.; **einer Sache** *(Dat.)* **mehr Aufmerksamkeit ~ werden lassen** devote more attention to sth.

zu|teilen *tr. V.* **a) jmdm. jmdn./etw. ~:** allot *or* assign sb./sth. to sb.; **b)** *(als Ration)* **jmdm. seine Portion ~:** mete out his/her share to sb.; **den Kindern das Essen ~:** ration *or* share out the food to the children; **die zugeteilte Menge** the allocated amount

Zu·teilung die a) allotting, assigning **(an +** *Akk.* to); **b)** *(als Ration)* sharing out, allocation **(an +** *Akk.* to); *(eines Mandats, Quartiers)* allocation, assignment **(an +** *Akk.* to); **es gab Fleisch nur auf ~:** meat was only to be had on rations; **c)** *(Ration)* allocation, ration **(an +** *Dat.* of)

zuteilungs·reif *Adj. (Wirtsch.)* mature

zu·tiefst *Adv.* profoundly; **~ verletzt** deeply hurt *or* offended

zu|tragen 1. *unr. refl. V. (geh.)* take place; occur. **2.** *unr. tr. V.* **jmdm. etw. ~:** carry sth. to sb. *(fig.: mitteilen)* report sth. to sb.; **jmdm. Nachrichten/Gerüchte** *usw.* **~:** pass on news/rumours *etc.* to sb.

Zu·träger der, Zu·trägerin die informer

zuträglich ['tsu:trɛ:klɪç] *Adj.* healthy ⟨*climate*⟩; **jmdm./einer Sache ~ sein** be good for sb./sth.; be beneficial to sb./sth.

Zuträglichkeit die; ~: beneficial effect; *(des Klimas)* healthiness

zu|trauen *tr. V.* **jmdm. etw. ~:** believe sb. [is] capable of [doing] sth.; **den Mut hätte ich ihm gar nicht zugetraut** I should never have thought he had the courage; **ich hätte ihm mehr Taktgefühl zugetraut** I should have thought he had more tact; **ihm ist alles zuzutrauen** I wouldn't put anything past him; **das hätte ich ihm nicht zugetraut** I should never have thought it of him; **das ist ihm [durchaus] zuzutrauen** I could [well] believe it of him; **sich** *(Dat.)* **etw. ~:** think one can do *or* is capable of doing sth.; **trau dir nicht zuviel zu** don't take on too much; don't overdo it; **er traut sich** *(Dat.)* **zuwenig zu** he has too little self-confidence

Zutrauen das; ~s confidence, trust **(zu** in); **~ zu sich selbst** self-confidence

zutraulich 1. *Adj.* trusting; trustful. **2.** *adv.* trustingly; trustfully

Zutraulichkeit die; ~: trust[fulness]

zu|treffen *unr. itr. V.* **a)** be correct; **der Vorwurf trifft zu** the reproach is justified; **b) auf** *od.* **für jmdn./etw. ~:** apply to sb./sth.

zutreffend 1. *Adj.* **a)** correct; *(treffend)* accurate; **es ist ~, daß ...:** it is correct *or* the case that ...; **b)** *(geltend)* applicable; relevant; **Zutreffendes bitte ankreuzen** please mark with a cross where applicable. **2.** *adv.* correctly; *(treffend)* accurately

zu|treiben *unr. itr. V.; mit sein* **jmdm./einer Sache ~, auf jmdn./etw. ~** *(auch fig.)* be carried along *or* drift towards sb./sth.

zu|trinken *unr. itr. V.* **jmdm. ~:** raise one's glass and drink to sb.

Zu·tritt der entry; admittance; **„kein ~", „~ verboten"** 'no entry'; 'no admittance'; **jmdm. den ~ verweigern** refuse sb. admission; **~ [zu etw.] haben** have access [to sth.]

zu|tun *unr. tr. V.* **kein Auge ~:** not sleep a wink

Zu·tun das; ~s *in* **ohne jmds. ~:** without sb.'s being involved; **es geschah ohne mein ~:** I had nothing to do with it

zu·ungunsten *Präp. mit Gen.* to the disadvantage of

zu·unterst *Adv.* right at the bottom; *s. auch* **ober... a**

zuverlässig ['tsu:fɛɐ̯lɛsɪç] **1.** *Adj.* reliable; *(verläßlich)* dependable ⟨*person*⟩. **2.** *adv.* **a)** reliably; **er arbeitet sehr ~:** he is a very reliable worker; **b)** *(mit Gewißheit)* ⟨*confirm*⟩ with certainty; ⟨*know*⟩ for sure, for certain

Zuverlässigkeit die; ~: reliability; *(Verläßlichkeit)* dependability

Zuversicht [tsu:'fɛɐ̯zɪçt] **die; ~:** confidence

zuversichtlich 1. *Adj.* confident; **sich ~ geben** express one's confidence. **2.** *adv.* confidently

Zuversichtlichkeit die; ~: confidence

zuviel 1. *indekl. Indefinitpron.* **a)** too much; **viel ~:** far *or* much too much; **das ist mir ~:** that's too much for me; **seine dauernden Besuche werden mir allmählich ~:** his constant visits are getting me down *(coll.);* **~ des Guten, des Guten ~:** too much of a good thing; **was ~ ist, ist ~:** enough is enough; there must be a limit; **~ kriegen** *(ugs.)* blow one's top *(coll.); (bei jmds. Worten)* see red; **das ist ~ gesagt** that's going too far; that's an exaggeration; **b)** *(ugs.: zu viele)* too many. **2.** *adv.* **a)** too much; **das ist genau einmal ~:** that is once too often

Zu·viel das; ~s excess **(an +** *Dat.* of)

zu·vor *Adv.* before; **tags/im Jahr ~:** the day/year before

zu·vorderst *Adv.* right at the front

zuvörderst [tsu'fœrdɐst] *Adv. (veralt.)* first and foremost

zuvor|kommen *unr. itr. V.; mit sein* **a) jmdm. ~:** beat sb. to it; get there first; **b) einer Sache** *(Dat.)* **~:** anticipate *or* forestall sth.

zuvorkommend 1. *Adj.* obliging; *(höflich)* courteous. **2.** *adv.* obligingly; *(höflich)* courteously

Zuvorkommenheit die; ~: courteousness; courtesy

Zu·wachs der; ~es, Zuwächse ['tsu:vɛksə] increase *(Gen.,* **an +** *Dat.* in); **~ an Besuchern/Mitgliedern** increase in the number of visitors/members; **wirtschaftlicher ~:** economic growth; **die Familie hat ~ bekommen** there has been an addition to the family; **der Mantel ist auf ~ genäht** the coat has been made [on the large side] to allow room to grow into

-zuwachs der increase in ⟨*income, capital, exports, votes, expenditure, productivity, population, etc.*⟩; **Lohn-/Gehalts~:** wage/salary increase

zu|wachsen *unr. itr. V.; mit sein* **a)** ⟨*wound*⟩ heal [over]; **b)** *(bewachsen/überwachsen werden)* become overgrown; **mit etw. zugewachsen sein** be overgrown with sth.; **c)** *(zuteil werden)* **jmdm./einer Sache ~:** fall *or* be granted to sb./sth.

Zuwachs·rate die *(bes. Wirtsch.)* growth rate

Zu·wanderer der immigrant

zu|wandern *itr. V.; mit sein* immigrate

Zu·wanderung die immigration

zu|warten *itr. V.* wait

zu·wege *Adv. in* **etw. ~ bringen** [manage to] achieve sth.; **gut/schlecht ~ sein** *(ugs.)* be in good shape/a bad way

zu·weilen *Adv. (geh.)* now and again; at times

zu|weisen *unr. tr. V.* **jmdm. etw. ~:** allocate *or* allot sb. sth.

zu|wenden 1. *unr. od. regelm. refl. V.* **a) sich jmdm./einer Sache ~** *(auch fig.)* turn to sb./sth.; *(sich widmen)* devote oneself to sb./sth.: **b)** *(geh.: gehen)* **er wandte sich dem Ausgang zu** he moved towards the exit. **2.** *unr. od. regelm. tr. V.* **a) jmdm./einer Sache etw. ~:** turn sth. to[wards] sb./sth.; **jmdm. den Rücken ~:** turn one's back on sb.; **b)** *(geben, zuteil werden lassen)* **jmdm. Geld ~:** give *or* donate money to sb.

Zu·wendung die a) *o. Pl. (Aufmerksamkeit)* [loving] attention *or* care; **b)** *(Geldgeschenk)* gift of money; *(Unterstützung)* [financial] contribution; *(Geldspende)* donation; **auf ~en angewiesen sein** be dependent on financial support *sing. or* contributions

zu·wenig 1. *indekl. Indefinitpron.* **a)** too little; **viel ~:** far too little; **das ist mir ~:** that is too little *or* not enough for me; **b)** *(ugs.: zu wenige)* too few; not enough. **2.** *adv.* too little; **~ schlafen/sich ~ bewegen** get too little *or* not get enough sleep/exercise

zu|werfen *unr. tr. V.* **a)** slam ⟨*door, lid*⟩; **b) jmdm. etw. ~:** throw sth. to sb.; throw sb. sth.; **jmdm. einen bösen/giftigen Blick ~:** look daggers at sb.; *s. auch* **Ball a; Blick a; Kußhand**

zuwider 1. *Adj.* **a) jmdm. ~ sein** be repugnant to sb.; **Spinat ist mir äußerst ~:** I absolutely detest spinach; **b)** *(geh.: nicht förderlich)* **jmdm./einer Sache** *(Dat.)* **~ sein** ⟨*circumstances, weather, etc.*⟩ be against sb./sth. **2.** *Präp. mit Dat.; nachgestellt* contrary to *attrib.*

zuwider-, Zuwider-: ~|handeln *itr. V.* **dem Gesetz/einer Vorschrift** *usw.* **~handeln** contravene *or* infringe the law/a regulation *etc.*; **einer Anordnung/einem Verbot ~handeln** defy an instruction/a ban; **~handelnde der/die;** *adj. Dekl.* offender; **~|laufen** *unr. itr. V.; mit sein* **einer Sache** *(Dat.)* **~laufen** go against *or* run counter to sth.

zu|winken *itr. V.* **jmdm./einander ~:** wave to sb./one another

zu|zahlen *tr. V.* pay ⟨*five marks etc.*⟩ extra; **einen Betrag ~:** pay an additional sum

zu|zählen *tr. V.* **a)** *(dazurechnen)* add on; **b)** *(zurechnen)* **etw. einem Gebiet/Zeitalter ~:** assign sth. to an area/era

zu·zeiten *Adv. (geh.) s.* **zuweilen**

zu|ziehen 1. *unr. tr. V.* **a)** pull ⟨*door*⟩ shut; draw ⟨*curtain*⟩; pull *or* draw ⟨*knot, net*⟩ tight; do up ⟨*zip*⟩; **b)** call in ⟨*expert, special-*

ist⟩. **2.** *unr. refl. V.* **a) sich** *(Dat.)* **eine Krankheit/Infektion ~:** catch an illness/contract an infection; **sich** *(Dat.)* **einen Schädelbruch ~:** sustain a fracture of the skull; **sich** *(Dat.)* **jmds. Zorn/Vorwürfe ~:** incur sb.'s anger/reproaches; **b)** *(sich schließen)* ⟨*knot, noose*⟩ tighten, get tight. **3.** *unr. itr. V.; mit sein* move here *or* into the area

Zu·zug der a) influx; **b)** *(Genehmigung)* settlement permit

zuzüglich ['tsu:tsy:klɪç] *Präp. mit Gen.* plus; **400 Mark ~ [der] Heizungskosten** 400 marks plus *or* not including heating

Zuzugs·genehmigung die settlement permit

zu|zwinkern *itr. V.* **jmdm. ~:** wink at sb.

zwacken ['tsvakn̩] *tr., auch itr. V. (ugs.) s.* **zwicken**

zwang [tsvaŋ] *1. u. 3. Pers. Sg. Prät. v.* **zwingen**

Zwang der; ~[e]s, Zwänge ['tsvɛŋə] **a)** *o. Pl.* compulsion; **unter ~ handeln** act under duress; **Kinder ohne ~ erziehen** bring children up without constraint; **auf jmdn. ~ ausüben** exert pressure on sb.; force sb.'s hand; **der ~ der Verhältnisse** the force of circumstance[s]; **soziale Zwänge** social constraints; the constraints of society; **unmittelbarer ~** *(Rechtsspr.)* direct coercion; **das ist freiwilliger ~** *(iron.)* it's voluntary but compulsory; **b)** *(unwiderstehlicher Drang)* irresistible urge; **aus einem ~ [heraus] handeln** act under a compulsion *or* on an irresistible impulse; **c)** *(Beschränkung)* constraint; compulsion; **sich** *(Dat.)* **~ antun** *od.* **auferlegen** restrain oneself; exercise self-restraint; **tu dir keinen ~ an!** feel free!; don't force yourself! *(iron.)*; **ohne [jeden] ~:** without any constraint; ⟨*speak*⟩ [quite] freely *or* openly; **d)** *o. Pl. (Pflicht, Verpflichtung)* obligation; **es besteht kein ~ zur Teilnahme/zum Kauf** there is no obligation to take part/to buy anything

zwängen ['tsvɛŋən] **1.** *tr. V.* squeeze; **Bücher in seine Aktentasche ~:** cram books into one's brief-case. **2.** *refl. V.* squeeze [oneself]

zwanghaft 1. *Adj.* **a)** compulsive; *(als Ausdruck einer Zwangsneurose)* obsessive; **~e Vorstellung** obsession; **b)** *s.* **gezwungen 2. 2.** *adv.* **a)** compulsively; **b)** *s.* **gezwungen 3**

zwanglos 1. *Adj.* **a)** informal; casual, free and easy ⟨*behaviour*⟩; **b)** *(unregelmäßig)* haphazard ⟨*arrangement*⟩; **in ~er Folge** at irregular intervals. **2.** *adv.* **a)** informally; freely; **es ging dort ziemlich ~ zu** things were pretty free and easy there; **b)** *(unregelmäßig)* haphazardly ⟨*arranged*⟩

Zwanglosigkeit die; ~ a) informality; **b)** *(Unregelmäßigkeit)* haphazard *or* casual manner

zwangs-, Zwangs-: ~anleihe die *(Wirtsch.)* compulsory loan; **~arbeit die;** *o. Pl.* forced labour; **~ernährung die** force-feeding *no indef. art.*; **~handlung die** *(Psych.)* compulsive act; **~herrschaft die** tyranny; despotism; **~jacke die** strait-jacket; **~lage die** predicament; **jmdn. in eine ~lage bringen** put sb. in a predicament; **~läufig** [-lɔyfɪç] **1.** *Adj.* inevitable; **2.** *adv.* inevitably; **~maßnahme die** coercive measure; sanction; **~neurose die** *(Psych.)* compulsion *or* obsessive-compulsive neurosis; **~räumung die** [enforced] eviction; **~versteigern** *tr. V., nur im Inf. u. Part. (Rechtsw.)* put up for compulsory auction; **~versteigerung die** *(Rechtsw.)* [compulsory] auction; **~vollstreckung die** *(Rechtsw.)* [compulsory] execution; **~vorstellung die** *(Psych.)* obsession; **~weise 1.** *Adv.* compulsorily; *(mit Gewalt)* by force; **2.** *adj.* compulsory; enforced ⟨*evacuation etc.*⟩; **~weise Ernährung** force-feeding

zwanzig ['tsvantsɪç] *Kardinalz.* twenty; *s. auch* **achtzig**

Zwanzig die; ~, ~en twenty

zwanziger *indekl. Adj.; nicht präd.* **die ~ Jahre** the twenties; *s. auch* **achtziger**

¹Zwanziger der; ~s, ~ a) *(20jähriger)* twenty-year-old; *(Mann von 20 bis 29)* man in his twenties; **b)** twenty-mark/franc/schilling *etc.* note; *s. auch* **¹Achtziger b, c**

²Zwanziger die; ~, ~ *(ugs.)* twenty-pfennig/centimes/schilling *etc.* stamp

³Zwanziger *Pl.* twenties; **die goldenen** *od.* **wilden ~:** the roaring twenties; **in den ~n sein** be in one's twenties

zwanzig·jährig *Adj. (20 Jahre alt)* twenty-year-old *attrib.*; *(20 Jahre dauernd)* twenty-year *attrib.*; *s. auch* **achtjährig**

Zwanzig·mark·schein der twenty-mark note

Zwanzig·pfennig·marke die twenty-pfennig stamp

zwanzigst ... *Ordinalz.* twentieth; *s. auch* **acht...; achtzigst...**

zwar [tsva:ɐ̯] *Adv.* **a)** admittedly; **ich war ~ dabei, habe aber trotzdem nichts gesehen** I was indeed *or* I 'was there, but I didn't see anything; **ich weiß es ~ nicht genau, aber ...:** I'm not absolutely sure [I admit,] but ...; **b)** *in* **und ~:** to be precise; **er ist Zahnarzt, und ~ ein guter** he is a dentist, and a good one at that; **ich komme heute, und ~ um fünf Uhr** I'm coming today, at five o'clock [to be precise]; **verschwinde hier, und ~ sofort!** clear off *(coll.)*, and I mean now!

Zweck [tsvɛk] **der; ~[e]s, ~e a)** purpose; **zu diesem ~:** for this purpose; **zum ~ der Fortbildung** for the purposes of further education; **was ist der ~ Ihrer Reise?** what is the purpose of your journey?; **seinen ~ erfüllen** serve its purpose; **Geld für einen guten/wohltätigen ~:** money for a good cause/for a charity; **das ist [nicht] der ~ der Übung** *(ugs.)* that is [not] the object *or* point of the exercise; *s. auch* **heiligen a; Mittel a; b)** *(Sinn)* point; **es hat keinen/wenig ~ [, das zu tun]** it's pointless *or* there is no point/there is little *or* not much point [in doing that]; **ohne [jeden] Sinn und ~:** completely pointless

zweck-, Zweck-: ~bau der; *Pl.* **~bauten** functional building; **~dienlich 1.** *Adj.* appropriate; helpful, relevant ⟨*information etc.*⟩; **wäre es nicht ~dienlicher, wenn ...?** wouldn't it be more to the point if ...?; **2.** *adv.* **~dienlich verwendet werden** be used for an appropriate purpose; **~entfremden** *tr. V.* use for another purpose; *(durch Umbau)* convert sth. to another use; *(für den falschen Zweck)* misuse; **etw. als etw. ~entfremden** use sth. as sth.; **die Gelder sind ~entfremdet [verwendet] worden** the money has been diverted from its proper use; **~entfremdung die** use/conversion for another purpose; *(von Geldern)* diversion [from its proper use]; **~entsprechend 1.** *Adj.* appropriate; suitable; **2.** *adv.* appropriately; **~frei 1.** *Adj.* ⟨*research*⟩ without any specific purpose; pure ⟨*science*⟩; **2.** *adv.* without any specific purpose; **~gebunden** *Adj. (Finanzw.)* [to be used] for a specified purpose

zweckhaft 1. *Adj.* purposeful; **nicht ~ sein** have no purpose. **2.** *adv.* purposefully; with purpose

zweck-, Zweck-: ~los *Adj.* pointless; **~losigkeit die; ~:** pointlessness; **~mäßig 1.** *Adj.* appropriate; expedient ⟨*behaviour, action*⟩; functional ⟨*building, fittings, furniture*⟩; **2.** *adv.* appropriately ⟨*arranged, clothed*⟩; ⟨*act*⟩ expediently; ⟨*equip, furnish*⟩ functionally; **~mäßigkeit die** appropriateness; *(einer Handlung)* expediency; *(eines Gebäudes)* functionalism; **~optimismus der** expedient optimism; **~propaganda die** [calculated *or* targeted] propaganda

zwecks *Präp. mit Gen. (Papierdt.)* for the purpose of; **~ Heirat** with a view to marriage

zweck·voll *Adj.; adv. s.* **zweckmäßig**

zwei [tsvai] *Kardinalz.* two; **wir ~:** we two; the two of us; **sie gehen ~ und** *od.* **zu ~en nebeneinander** they are walking in pairs; **sie waren/kamen zu ~en** there were two of them/two of them came; **für ~ essen/arbeiten** eat enough for two/do the work of two people; **dazu gehören immer noch ~!** *(ugs.)* it takes two [to do that]!; **das ist so sicher, wie ~ mal ~ vier ist** *(ugs.)* it's as sure as eggs is eggs *(coll.)*; *s. auch* **¹acht**

Zwei die; ~, ~en a) *(Zahl)* two; **b)** *(Schulnote)* B; **eine ~ schreiben/bekommen** get a B; **er hat die Prüfung mit ~ bestanden** he got a B in the examination; *s. auch* **¹Acht a, d, e, g**

zwei-, Zwei- *(s. auch* **acht-, Acht-**): **~ad[e]rig** *Adj.* *(Elektrot.)* two-core; **~bändig** *Adj.* two-volume; **~beiner der; ~s, ~** *(scherzh.)* human [being]; **~bettzimmer das** twin-bedded room; **~deutig** [-dɔytɪç] **1.** *Adj.* **a)** ambiguous; equivocal ⟨*smile*⟩; **b)** *(fig.: schlüpfrig)* suggestive ⟨*remark, joke*⟩; ⟨*novel, film, etc.*⟩ full of double entendre; **2.** *adv.* **a)** ambiguously; ⟨*smile*⟩ equivocally; **b)** *(fig.: schlüpfrig)* suggestively; **~deutigkeit die; ~, ~en a)** *o. Pl.* ambiguity; *(fig.: Schlüpfrigkeit)* suggestiveness; **b)** *(zweideutige Äußerung)* ambiguity; *(schlüpfrige Äußerung)* double entendre; **~dimensional** [~dimɛnzi̯ona:l] **1.** *Adj.* two-dimensional; **2.** *adv.* two-dimensionally; in two dimensions; **~drittel·mehrheit die** two-thirds majority; **~ein·halb** *Bruchz.* two and a half

Zweier der; ~s, ~ a) *(ugs. Schulnote)* **einen ~ haben/schreiben** get a B; **b)** *(ugs.: Münze)* two-pfennig piece; **c)** *(Ruderboot)* pair; **im ~ ohne Steuermann** in the coxless pairs; **d)** *(Golf)* twosome; *(Wettkampf)* single; twosome

zweierlei *Gattungsz.; indekl.* **a)** *attr.* two sorts *or* kinds of; two different ⟨*sizes, kinds, etc.*⟩; odd ⟨*socks, gloves*⟩; **mit ~ Maß messen** use double standards; **auf ~ Art** in two different ways; **b)** *subst.* two [different] things; **es ist ~, ob man es sagt oder [ob man es] auch tut** it is one thing to say it and another [thing] to do it; **Ordnung und Ordnung sind ~:** there is order and order

zwei-, Zwei-: ~fach *Vervielfältigungsz.* double; *(~mal, um den Faktor 2)* twice; **die ~fache Menge/Länge** double *or* twice the amount/length; **in ~facher Vergrößerung/Verkleinerung** enlarged to twice its size/reduced to half-size; **der ~fache Vater** the father of two; **in ~facher Hinsicht** in two respects; **~fach gesichert** double-locked; **~fach gegen die Vorschriften verstoßen** infringe the regulations in two ways; **etw. ~fach vergrößern/verkleinern** enlarge sth. to twice its size/reduce sth. to half-size; *s. auch* **achtfach; ~fache das;** *adj. Dekl.* **das ~fache kosten** cost twice as much; cost double [the amount]; **ein Foto um das ~fache vergrößern** enlarge a photo to twice its size; *s. auch* **Achtfache; ~familien·haus das** two-family house; duplex *(esp. Amer.)*; **~farbig 1.** *Adj.* two-coloured; two-tone ⟨*scarf, paintwork, etc.*⟩; **2.** *adv.* in two colours

Zweifel ['tsvaifl̩] **der; ~s, ~:** doubt **(an +** *Dat.* about); **in ~ geraten, ~ bekommen** become doubtful; **ich habe keinen ~ daran/[gewisse] ~ daran, daß ...:** I am in no doubt that/in some doubt whether ...; **ich habe da so meine ~** *od.* **bin [mir] darüber im ~:** I have my doubts about that; **ich bin mir noch im ~, ob ...:** I am still uncertain whether ...; **etw. in ~ ziehen** question sth.; **[für jmdn.] außer ~ stehen** be beyond doubt [as far as sb. is concerned]; **über jeden** *od.* **allen ~ erhaben sein** be beyond any shadow of a doubt; **er ließ keinen ~ daran, daß ...:** he left no doubt [in anyone's mind] that ...; **jmdn. [über etw.** *(Akk.)*] **[nicht] im ~ lassen** leave sb. in [no] doubt [about sth.]; **daran** *od.* **darüber besteht kein ~, daran gibt es keinen ~:** there is no doubt about it; **mir kommen ~:** I am beginning to have my doubts; **kein ~, ...:** there is/was no doubt about it, ...; **ohne ~:** without [any] doubt; **im ~:** in case of doubt; if in doubt

zweifelhaft *Adj.* **a)** doubtful; **b)** *(fragwürdig)* dubious; *(suspekt)* suspicious

zweifel·los *Adv.* undoubtedly; without [any] doubt

zweifeln *itr. V.* doubt; **wenn man zweifelt** if one is in doubt *or* has any doubts; **an jmdm./etw. ~:** doubt sb./sth.; have doubts about sb./sth.; **man hat lange daran gezweifelt** it has long been in doubt *or* uncertain; **~ daran, daß ..., ~, ob ...:** doubt whether ...; **er hat nie daran gezweifelt, daß ...:** he never doubted that ...; **daran ist nicht zu ~:** there can be no doubt about it

zweifels-, Zweifels-: ~fall der case of doubt; doubtful *or* problematic case; **im ~fall[e]** in case of doubt; if in doubt; **~frei 1.** *Adj.* definite; **~frei sein** be beyond doubt; **2.** *adv.* beyond [any] doubt; **~ohne** *Adv.* undoubtedly; without doubt

zwei·flammig *Adj.* two-burner ⟨*cooker*⟩

Zweifler der; ~s, ~, Zweiflerin die; ~, ~nen doubter

zweiflerisch 1. *Adj.* doubtful; *(skeptisch)* sceptical. **2.** *adv.* doubtfully; *(skeptisch)* sceptically

zweiflüg[e]lig *Adj.* two-winged

Zwei·fronten·krieg der war on two fronts; **einen ~ führen** *(fig.)* fight on two fronts

Zweig [tsvaik] **der; ~[e]s, ~e a)** [small] branch; *(meist ohne Blätter)* twig; **auf keinen grünen ~ kommen** *(ugs.)* not get anywhere; *(finanziell)* not become well off; **b)** *(einer Familie)* branch; **c)** *(Unterabteilung, Branche) (einer Wissenschaft usw.)* branch; *(eines Gymnasiums usw.)* side

Zweig·betrieb der subsidiary; *(Filiale)* branch

zwei-, Zwei-: ~geschlechtig *Adj. (Biol.)* hermaphroditic; bisexual; **~geschossig** *Adj., adv. s.* **~stöckig; ~gespann das a)** pair of horses/oxen; **b)** *(Wagen)* carriage and pair; **c)** *(fig.)* duo; two-man band; **~gestrichen** *Adj. (Musik)* two-line ⟨*octave*⟩; **das ~gestrichene A** the A two above middle C; **das ~gestrichene C** the C above middle C; **~geteilt** *Adj.* divided; divided in two *postpos.*

Zweig·geschäft das branch

zwei·gleisig 1. *Adj.* two-track; double-track; *(fig.)* two-way ⟨*therapy, treatment*⟩. **2.** *adv.* **a)** ⟨*run*⟩ on two tracks; **eine Strecke ~ ausbauen** add a second track [to a section]; **b)** *(fig.)* **~ fahren** follow a dual-track policy

Zweig-: ~stelle die branch [office]; **~werk das** subsidiary plant

zwei·händig [-hɛndɪç] **1.** *Adj.* two-handed. **2.** *adv.* ⟨*hold on, catch ball, etc.*⟩ with both hands; ⟨*type, play*⟩ with two hands

Zweiheit die; ~ *(geh.)* duality

zwei-, Zwei-: ~höck[e]rig *Adj.* two-humped; **~hundert** *Kardinalz.* two hundred; **~jährig** *Adj.* **a)** *(zwei Jahre alt)* two-year-old *attrib.*; *(zwei Jahre dauernd)* two-year *attrib.*; **b)** *(Bot.)* biennial ⟨*plant*⟩; *s. auch* **achtjährig; ~jährlich 1.** *Adj.* two-yearly *attrib.*; biennial; *s. auch* **achtjährlich; 2.** *adv.* every two years; biennially; **~kammer·system das** *(Politik)* bicameral system; **~kampf der a)** single combat; *(Duell)* duel; **jmdn. im ~kampf töten** kill sb. in single combat/a duel; **b)** *(Sport)* man-to-man tussle; duel; **~keim·blättrig** *Adj. (Bot.)* dicotyledonous; **~köpfig** *Adj.* **a)** two-headed; **b)** *(aus zwei Personen bestehend)* two-person *attrib.*; of two [people] *postpos.*; **~kreis·bremse die** *(Kfz-W.)* dual-circuit braking system; **~mal** *Adv.* twice; **das wird er sich** *(Dat.)* **~mal überlegen** he'll think twice about that; *s. auch* **achtmal; ~malig** *Adj.* **nach ~maligem Versuch** after trying twice; after two tries; *s. auch* **achtmalig; ~mark·stück das** two-mark piece; **~monats·schrift die** bimonthly [periodical]; **~motorig** *Adj.* twin-engined; **~parteien·system das** two-party system; **~pfennig·stück das** two-pfennig piece; **~phasen·strom der** *(Physik, Elektrot.)* two-phase current; **~phasig** *Adj. (Physik, Elektrot.)* two-phase; **~-plus-vier-Gespräche** *Pl. (Politik)* two plus four talks; **~polig** *Adj. (Physik, Elektrot.)* double-pole; two-core ⟨*cable*⟩; two-pin ⟨*plug, socket*⟩; **~rad das** two-wheeler; **~räd[e]rig** *Adj.* two-wheeled; **~reiher der** double-breasted suit/coat/jacket; **~reihig 1.** *Adj.* **a)** in two rows *postpos.*; double ⟨*chain*⟩; **b)** *(mit zwei Knopfreihen)* double-breasted ⟨*suit, coat*⟩; **2.** *adv.* in two rows

Zweisamkeit die; ~, ~en togetherness; partnership

zwei-, Zwei-: ~schläfrig *Adj.* double ⟨*bed*⟩; **~schneidig** *Adj.* double-edged; **ein ~schneidiges Schwert** *(fig.)* a double-edged sword; **~seitig 1.** *Adj.* **a)** double-sided; two-sided; **b)** *(zwei Seiten lang)* two page ⟨*letter, article, etc.*⟩; **c)** *(bilateral)* bilateral ⟨*treaty, agreement, etc.*⟩; **2.** *adv.* **a)** on two *or* both sides; **~seitig tragbar** reversible ⟨*anorak, coat*⟩; **b)** *(bilateral)* bilaterally; **~silbig 1.** *Adj.* two-syllable *attrib.*; **2.** *adv.* ⟨*pronounced*⟩ as two syllables; **~sitzer der** two-seater; **~sitzig** *Adj.* two-seater *attrib.*; **~spaltig 1.** *Adj.* two-column; *s. auch* **achtspaltig; 2.** *adv.* ⟨*printed, set*⟩ in two columns; **~spänner der** carriage and pair; **~spännig 1.** *Adj.* drawn by two horses *postpos.*; **2.** *adv.* **~spännig fahren** drive [in] a carriage and pair; **~sprachig 1.** *Adj.* bilingual; ⟨*sign*⟩ in two languages; **2.** *adv.* bilingually; ⟨*written*⟩ in two languages; ⟨*published*⟩ in a bilingual edition; **~sprachigkeit die; ~:** bilingualism; **~spurig 1.** *Adj.* **a)** two-lane ⟨*road, motorway*⟩; *(Eisenb.)* double-track ⟨*railway*⟩; **b)** two-track ⟨*vehicle*⟩; **c)** two- *or* twin-track ⟨*recording*⟩; **2.** *adv.* **a)** in two lanes; **~spurig ausbauen** make ⟨*road*⟩ dual carriageway; dual ⟨*road*⟩; widen ⟨*railway*⟩ to two tracks; **b)** ⟨*record*⟩ on two tracks; **~stellig** *Adj.* two-figure *attrib.* ⟨*number, sum*⟩; **~stellige Stimmenverluste** loss of more than 10% of votes; **~stimmig 1.** *Adj.* two-part *attrib.*; **2.** *adv.* in two parts; **~stöckig 1.** *Adj.* two-storey *attrib.*; **~stöckig sein** have two storeys *or* floors; **ein ~stöckiges Bett** a bunk-bed; **2.** *adv.* ⟨*build*⟩ two storeys high; **~strahlig** *Adj.* twin-engined ⟨*jet aircraft*⟩; **~stündig** *Adj.* two-hour *attrib.*; *(Schulw.)* double-period *attrib.* ⟨*test, examination*⟩; **nach ~stündiger Wartezeit** after waiting for two hours; **~stündlich 1.** *Adj.* two-hourly *attrib.*; **2.** *adv.* every two hours

zweit ['tsvait] *in* **wir waren zu ~:** there were two of us; **sie sind zu ~ verreist** the two of them went away together; **sie schlafen je zu ~ in den Zimmern** they sleep two to a room; **zu ~ lebt man billiger als allein** two can live cheaper than one; *s. auch* **²acht**

zweit... *Ordinalz.* **a)** second; **jeder ~e [der] Einwohner** every other *or* second inhabitant; **jeder ~e** every other one; **b)** *(zweitbest...)* second; **~er Klasse fahren/liegen** travel second-class/be in a second-class hospital bed; **c)** *(ander..., weiter...)* second; other; **ich habe noch einen ~en** I have a second one; *(als Ersatz)* I have a spare; **wie kein ~er** as no one else can; like nobody else; **ein ~er Al Capone** *(fig.)* a second Al Capone; *s. auch* **erst...**

zwei-, Zwei-: ~tägig *Adj. (2 Tage alt)* two-day-old *attrib.*; *(2 Tage dauernd)* two-day *attrib.*; *s. auch* **achttägig; ~täglich 1.** *Adj.* **in ~täglichem Wechsel** on a two-day rota; **2.** *adv.* every two days; **~takter der; ~s, ~** *(Kfz-W.)* **a)** *(Motor)* two-stroke engine; **b)** *(ugs.: Fahrzeug)* two-stroke; **~takt·motor der** *(Kfz-W.)* two-stroke engine

zweit·ältest... *Adj.* second oldest; **der/die Zweitälteste** the second oldest

zwei·tausend *Kardinalz.* two thousand

Zwei·tausender der *mountain more than two thousand metres high*

Zweit·ausfertigung die [second] copy; duplicate

zweit·best... *Adj.* second best; **der/die Zweitbeste** the second best

Zwei·teiler der a) *(Badeanzug, Kleid)* two-piece; *(Kostüm, Anzug)* two-piece suit; **b)** *(Ferns.)* two-part film/programme

zwei·teilig *Adj.* two-piece ⟨*suit, bathing-suit, suite, etc.*⟩; two-part ⟨*film, programme*⟩; two-volume ⟨*dictionary, novel*⟩; *s. auch* **achtteilig**

zweite·mal *Adv.* **das ~:** for the second time

zweiten·mal *Adv.* **zum ~:** for the second time; **beim ~:** the second time [round]

zweitens *Adv.* secondly; in the second place

Zweite[r]-Klasse-Abteil das second-class compartment

zweit-, Zweit-: ~frisur die wig; **~größt...** *Adj.* second biggest *or* largest; **~klassig 1.** *Adj.* second-rate; **als ~klassig behandelt werden** be treated as a second-class citizen/as second-class citizens; **2.** *adv.* **die Mannschaft hat nur ~klassig gespielt** the team's performance was second-rate; **~kläßler der; ~s, ~** *(südd., schweiz.)* pupil in second class of primary school; second-year pupil; **~plazierte der/die;** *adj. Dekl. (Sport)* runner-up; **~rangig** [-raŋɪç] *Adj.* **a)** *(nicht vordringlich)* of secondary importance *postpos.*; **von ~rangiger Bedeutung sein** be of secondary importance; **b)** *(~klassig)* second-rate; **~schlüssel der** second *or* spare key; **~stimme die** second vote

zwei·türig *Adj.* two-door ⟨*car*⟩; ⟨*room*⟩ with two doors

Zweit-: ~wagen der second car; **~wohnung die** second home

zwei-, Zwei-: ~viertel·takt [~'fɪrtl-] **der** *(Musik)* two-four time; **im ~vierteltakt** in two-four time; **~wertig** *Adj.* **a)** *(Chemie)* bivalent; **b)** *(Sprachw.)* two-place *attrib.*; **~wöchentlich 1.** *Adj.* fortnightly; **2.** *adv.* every fortnight *or* two weeks; *s. auch* **achtwöchentlich; ~wöchig** *Adj. (zwei Wochen alt)* two-week-old *attrib.*; *(2 Wochen dauernd)* two-week *attrib.*; fortnight's *attrib.*; **~zeiler der; ~s, ~:** couplet; **~zeilig** *Adj.* two-line *attrib.*; *(Maschinenschreiben)* **in ~zeiligem Abstand** double-spaced; **~zeiliger Leerraum** double-spacing; **~zimmerwohnung** [-'----] **die** two-room flat *(Brit.)* *or (Amer.)* apartment; **~zügig** *Adj.* ⟨*school*⟩ with two main subject areas

Zwerch·fell ['tsvɛrç-] **das** *(Anat.)* diaphragm

zwerchfell·erschütternd 1. *Adj.* side-splitting; screamingly funny. **2.** *adv.* side-splittingly, screamingly ⟨*funny*⟩

Zwerg [tsvɛrk] **der; ~[e]s, ~e a)** dwarf; **b)** *(Garten~)* gnome; **c)** *(abwertend: unbedeutender Mensch)* [little] squirt *(coll.)*; wretch

zwergenhaft *Adj.* dwarfish

Zwerg·huhn das bantam

Zwergin die; ~, ~nen dwarf

zwerg-, Zwerg-: ~pudel der miniature *or* toy poodle; **~schule die** single-class school; **~staat der** miniature state; **~wuchs der** *(Biol.)* dwarfism *no art.*;

stunted growth *no art.*; **~wüchsig** [~vy:ksıç] *Adj. (Biol.)* dwarf-like ⟨*race, people*⟩; dwarf, miniature ⟨*tree, plant*⟩

Zwetsche ['tsvɛtʃə] **die; ~, ~n a)** damson plum; **b)** *(Baum)* damson plum[-tree]

Zwetschen-: ~baum der damson plum-tree; **~kern der** plum-stone; **~kuchen der** plum-flan; **~mus das** plum purée; **~schnaps der, ~wasser das;** *Pl.* **~wässer** plum brandy

Zwetschge ['tsvɛtʃgə] **die; ~, ~n** *(bes. südd., schweiz.) s.* **Zwetsche**

Zwetschken·knödel ['tsvɛtʃkn̩-] **der** *(Kochk.)* plum dumpling

Zwickel ['tsvıkl̩] **der; ~s, ~ a)** *(Schneiderei)* gusset; **b)** *(Archit.)* spandrel; *(einer Kuppel)* pendentive; **c)** *(salopp) s.* **Zweimarkstück**

zwicken ['tsvıkn̩] **1.** *tr., auch itr. V. (bes. südd., österr.)* **a)** pinch; **jmdm.** *od.* **jmdn. in den Arm ~:** pinch sb.'s arm; **b)** *(plagen)* **jmdn. ~:** give sb. twinges; **es zwickte und zwackte ihn überall** he had twinges *or* little aches and pains all over. **2.** *itr. V.* ⟨*trousers, skirt*⟩ pinch

Zwicker der; ~s, ~: pince-nez

Zwick·mühle die a) double mill; **b)** *(fig.: Dilemma)* dilemma; **in der ~ sitzen** *od.* **sein** *od.* **stecken** be in a dilemma

Zwie·back ['tsvi:bak] **der; ~[e]s, ~e** *od.* **Zwiebäcke** ['tsvi:bɛkə] rusk; *(unzählbar)* rusks *pl.*

Zwiebel ['tsvi:bl̩] **die; ~, ~n a)** onion; *(Blumen~)* bulb; **b)** *(ugs. scherzh.: Taschenuhr)* pocket watch; turnip *(sl.)*; **c)** *(ugs. scherzh.: Haarknoten)* bun

Zwiebel-: ~kuchen der *(Kochk.)* onion pie; **~muster das** onion pattern

zwiebeln *tr. V. (ugs.)* keep on at ⟨*person*⟩; give ⟨*person*⟩ a hard time

Zwiebel-: ~ring der onion ring; **~schale die** onion-skin; **~suppe die** onion soup; **~turm der** onion tower

zwie-, Zwie-: ~fach *Adj.; adv. (veralt.) s.* **zweifach; ~fältig** *Adj.; adv. (veralt.) s.* **zweifach; ~gespräch das** *(geh.)* dialogue; **~laut der** *(Sprachw.)* diphthong; **~licht das;** *o. Pl.* **a)** *(Dämmerlicht)* twilight; **b)** *(Mischung von Dämmer- und Kunstlicht)* half-light *(that is unpleasant for the eye)*; **c) ins ~licht geraten** *(fig.)* become suspect; ⟨*person*⟩ come under suspicion; **~lichtig** *Adj.* shady; dubious; **~spalt der; ~[e]s, ~e** *od.* **~spälte** [~ʃpɛltə] **a)** *([innerer] Widerspruch)* [inner] conflict; **in einen ~spalt geraten** get into a state of conflict; **b)** *(Kluft)* rift; split; **~spältig** [~ʃpɛltıç] *Adj.* conflicting ⟨*mood, feelings*⟩; discordant ⟨*impression*⟩; *(widersprüchlich)* contradictory ⟨*nature, attitude, person, etc.*⟩; **~spältigkeit die; ~:** conflicting *or* contradictory nature; **~sprache die** *(geh.)* dialogue; **mit jmdm./etw. ~sprache halten** commune with sb./sth.; **~tracht die** *(geh.)* discord; **~tracht säen** sow the seeds of discord

Zwille ['tsvılə] **die; ~, ~n** *(nordd.)* **a)** *s.* **Astgabel; b)** *(Schleuder)* catapult

Zwilling ['tsvılıŋ] **der; ~s, ~e a)** twin; **b)** *Pl. (Astrol.)* Gemini; the Twins; **er/sie ist [ein] ~:** he/she is a Gemini

Zwillings-: ~bruder der twin brother; **~geburt die** twin birth; **~paar das** pair of twins; **~schwester die** twin sister

Zwing·burg die fortress, stronghold *(for the subjugation of the population)*

zwingen ['tsvıŋən] **1.** *unr. tr. V.* **a)** force; **jmdn. zu etw. ~, jmdn. [dazu] ~, etw. zu tun** force *or* compel sb. to do sth.; make sb. do sth.; **jmdn. zu einem Geständnis ~:** force sb. into a confession *or* to make a confession; **sich zu etw. gezwungen sehen** find oneself forced *or* compelled to do sth.; **man kann ihn nicht dazu ~:** he can't be forced *or* made to do it; **b)** *(geh.)* **jmdn. in/auf** *usw.* **etw.** *(Akk.)* **~:** force sb. into/on to *etc.* sth. **2.** *unr. refl. V.* force oneself; **sich [dazu] ~, etw. zu tun** force oneself to do sth.; **sich zum Schreiben/Essen ~:** force oneself to write/make oneself eat; *s. auch* **gezwungen 2, 3**

zwingend *Adj.* compelling ⟨*reason, logic*⟩; conclusive ⟨*proof, argument*⟩; imperative, absolute ⟨*necessity*⟩

Zwinger der; ~s, ~ a) *(Hunde~)* kennel; *(ganze Anlage, auch Zucht)* kennels *pl.*; **b)** *(Gehege)* compound; enclosure; *(für Bären)* bear-pit

zwinkern ['tsvıŋkɐn] *itr. V.* **[mit den Augen] ~:** blink; *(als Zeichen)* wink; **jmdn. ~d ansehen** wink at sb.; look at sb. with a wink

zwirbeln ['tsvırbl̩n] *tr. V.* twirl; twist

Zwirn [tsvırn] **der; ~[e]s, ~e** [strong] thread *or* yarn

Zwirns·faden der [strong] thread

zwischen ['tsvıʃn̩] *Präp. mit Dat./Akk.* **a)** *(räumlich, zeitlich, fig.)* between; **b)** *(räumlich: unter, inmitten)* among[st]

zwischen-, Zwischen-: ~akt der interlude; **~akt·musik die** incidental music; *(einzelnes Stück)* entr'acte; **~applaus der** spontaneous applause *(during a performance)*; **~aufenthalt der** stopover; **~bemerkung die** interjection; **~bescheid der** provisional notification; *(Entscheidung)* interim decision; **~bilanz die** *(Wirtsch.)* interim balance; *(fig.)* provisional appraisal; **~blutung die** *(Med.)* intermenstrual *or* mid-cyclical bleeding; **~buch·handel der** wholesale book trade; **~deck das** *(Schiffbau)* **a)** 'tween-deck; **b)** *(Raum)* 'tween-decks *sing.*; **im ~deck** 'tween-decks; **~ding das** *s.* **Mittelding; ~drin** [-'-] *Adv. (ugs.) s.* **~durch a; ~durch** [-'-] *Adv.* **a)** *(zeitlich)* between times; *(zwischen zwei Zeitpunkten)* in between; *(von Zeit zu Zeit)* from time to time; *(in der ~zeit)* in the mean time; **das mache ich mal irgendwann ~durch** I'll fit that in whenever I have time; **iß nicht so viel ~durch** don't eat so much between meals; **b)** *(räumlich)* here and there; **~eis·zeit die** interglacial period; **~ergebnis das** interim result; *(einer Untersuchung)* interim findings *pl.*; *(Sport)* latest score; **~examen das** *s.* **~prüfung; ~fall der** incident; **es kam zu schweren/blutigen ~fällen** there were serious/violent incidents; **~frage die** question; **jmdm. eine ~frage stellen** interrupt sb. to ask a question; **~gas das;** *o. Pl. (Kfz-W.)* **~gas geben** *od.* **mit ~gas schalten** double-declutch; **~gericht das** *(Kochk.)* entrée *(Brit.)*; **~geschoß das** mezzanine; **~größe die** intermediate size; *(bei Schuhen)* half-size; **~handel der** *(Wirtsch.)* intermediate trade; *(Großhandel)* wholesale trade; *(~händler)* middleman; **~händler der** *(Wirtsch.)* middleman; *(fig.)* go-between; **~hirn das** *(Anat.)* diencephalon; **~hoch das** *(Met.)* ridge of high pressure; **~kiefer[knochen] der** *(Anat.)* intermaxillary; premaxilla; **~|landen** *itr. V.; mit sein* **in X ~landen** land in X on the way; **~landung die** stopover; **~lauf der** *(Sport)* [intermediate] heat; **~lösung die** interim solution; **~mahlzeit die** snack [between meals]; **~menschlich 1.** *Adj.* interpersonal ⟨*relations*⟩; ⟨*contacts*⟩ between people; **2.** *adv.* on a personal level; **~musik die** musical interlude; **~prüfung die** intermediate examination; **~raum der** space; gap; *(Lücke)* gap; **eine Zeile ~raum lassen** leave a space of one line; *(Maschinenschreiben)* double-space; **~reich das** *(geh.)* twilight world; **~ruf der** interruption; **viele ~rufe** a great deal of heckling *sing.*; **~rufer der** heckler; **~runde die** *(Sport)* intermediate round; **~satz der** *(Sprachw.)* parenthetic clause; parenthesis; **~|schalten** *tr. V. (Elektrot.)* insert ⟨*resistance, amplifier, etc.*⟩ in a circuit; **~spiel das** *(Musik-, Theaterstück)* intermezzo; *(in einem Solokonzert/Gesangsstück)* linking passage; *(fig.)* interlude; **~spurt der** *(Sport)* spurt; burst [of speed]; **~staatlich** *Adj.* international; **~stadium das** intermediate stage; **~station die a)** stop; stopping-place; **b)** *(~aufenthalt)* stop; **dort machten wir einen Tag ~station** we stopped there for a day; **~stecker der** *(Elektrot.)* adaptor; **~stück das** connecting *or* middle piece; *(Verbindungsstück)* connector; *(Adapter)* adapter; **~stufe die** intermediate stage; **~summe die** subtotal; **~text der** linking text; **~ton der** shade; nuance; *(fig.)* nuance; **~tür die** connecting door; **~wand die** dividing wall; partition; **~wirt der** *(Biol., Med.)* intermediate host; **~zeit die a)** interim; *(länger)* intervening period; **in der ~zeit** in the mean time; **b)** *(Sport)* split time; **~zeitlich** *Adv. (bes. Amtsspr.)* in the mean time; **~zeugnis das** *(Schulw.)* intermediate report; *(Arbeitswelt)* [intermediate] performance appraisal

Zwist [tsvıst] **der; ~[e]s, ~e** *(geh.)* strife *no indef. art.*; *(Fehde)* feud; dispute; **in** *od.* **im ~ leben** live in a state of strife; **den alten ~ begraben** bury the hatchet

Zwistigkeit die; ~, ~en *(geh.)* dispute

zwitschern ['tsvıtʃɐn] **1.** *itr. (auch tr.) V.* chirp. **2.** *tr. V. in* **einen ~** *(salopp)* have a drink

Zwitter ['tsvıtɐ] **der; ~s, ~** *(Biol., Med.)* hermaphrodite; **ein ~ aus A und B** *(fig.)* a cross between A and B

Zwitter·stellung die ambiguous position

zwittrig *Adj. (Biol., Med.)* hermaphroditic

zwo [tsvo:] *Kardinalz. (ugs.; bes. zur Verdeutlichung) s.* **zwei**

zwölf [tsvœlf] *Kardinalz.* twelve; **~ Uhr mittags/nachts** [twelve o'clock] midday/midnight; **es ist fünf [Minuten] vor ~** *(fig.)* we are on the brink; *s. auch* [1]**acht**

Zwölf die; ~, ~en twelve; *s. auch* [1]**Acht a, e, g**

zwölf-, Zwölf- twelve-; *s. auch* **acht-, Acht-**

Zwölf-: ~eck das *(Geom.)* dodecagon; **~ender der; ~s, ~ a)** *(Jägerspr.)* royal [stag]; **b)** *(scherzh. veralt.) soldier with twelve years service*

Zwölfer der; ~s, ~: twelve; *s. auch* **Achter c, d**

zwölferlei *Gattungsz.; indekl.* **a)** *attr.* twelve sorts *or* kinds of; twelve different ⟨*sorts, sizes, etc.*⟩; **b)** *subst.* twelve [different] things

zwölf-, Zwölf-: ~fach *Vervielfältigungsz.* twelvefold; **die ~fache Menge** twelve times the quantity; *s. auch* **achtfach; ~fache das;** *adj. Dekl.;* **das ~fache** twelve times as much; **um ein ~faches** *od.* **um das ~fache** twelve times; *s. auch* **Achtfache; ~finger·darm der** *(Anat.)* duodenum; **~finger·darm·geschwür das** *(Med.)* duodenal ulcer; **~jährig** *Adj. (12 Jahre alt)* twelve-year-old *attrib.*; twelve years old *pred.*; *(12 Jahre dauernd)* twelve-year *attrib.*; *s. auch* **achtjährig; ~kampf der** *(Turnen)* twelve-exercise event; **~mal** *Adv.* twelve times; *s. auch* **achtmal; ~meilen·zone** [-'----] **die** twelve-mile zone

zwölft [tsvœlft] *in* **wir waren zu ~:** there were twelve of us; *s. auch* [2]**acht**

zwölft... *Ordinalz.* twelfth; *s. auch* **acht...**

zwölf·tausend *Kardinalz.* twelve thousand

zwölf·teilig *Adj.* twelve-piece ⟨*set*⟩; twelve-part ⟨*serial etc.*⟩; *s. auch* **achtteilig**

zwölftel *Bruchz.* twelfth; *s. auch* **achtel**

Zwölftel das *(schweiz. meist* **der) ~s, ~:** twelfth

zwölftens *Adv.* twelfthly

Zwölf·ton·musik die twelve-tone music

zwot... [tsvo:t...] *Ordinalz. (ugs.; bes. bei Datumsangaben) s.* **zweit...**

zwotens *Adv. (ugs.)* secondly

Zyan [tsya:n] **das; ~s** *(Chemie)* cyanogen

Zyanid [ts̮y̆a'ni:t] **das; ~s, ~e** *(Chemie)* cyanide

Zyan·kali das; ~s *(Chemie)* potassium cyanide

Zyklen *s.* **Zyklus**

zyklisch ['ts̮y:klɪʃ] **1.** *Adj.* cyclic[al]. **2.** *adv.* cyclically; as a cycle

Zykloide [ts̮yklo'i:də] **die; ~, ~n** *(Math.)* cycloid

Zyklon [ts̮y'klo:n] **der; ~s, ~e** *(Met.)* cyclone

Zyklop [ts̮y'klo:p] **der; ~en,~en** *(griech. Myth.)* Cyclops

Zyklopen·mauer die *(Archäol., Bauw.)* Cyclopean wall

zyklothym [ts̮yklo'ty:m] *Adj. (Psych., Med.)* cyclothymic

Zyklotron ['ts̮y:klotro:n] **das; ~s, ~s** *od.* **~e** *(Kernphysik)* cyclotron

Zyklus ['ts̮y:klʊs] **der; ~, Zyklen** *(auch Math.)* cycle

Zylinder [ts̮i'lɪndɐ] **der; ~s, ~ a)** *(Geom., Technik)* cylinder; *(einer Lampe)* chimney; **b)** *(Hut)* top hat

Zylinder-: ~hut der top hat; **~kopf der** cylinder head

zylindrisch 1. *Adj.* cylindrical. **2.** *adv.* cylindrically

Zyniker der; ~s, ~, Zynikerin die; ~, ~nen cynic

zynisch ['ts̮y:nɪʃ] **1.** *Adj.* cynical. **2.** *adv.* cynically

Zynismus der; ~, Zynismen a) *o. Pl.* cynicism; **b)** *(Äußerung)* cynical remark

Zypern ['ts̮y:pɐn] **(das); ~s** Cyprus

Zyprer ['ts̮y:prɐ] **der; ~s, ~, Zyprerin die; ~, ~nen** Cypriot

Zypresse [ts̮y'prɛsə] **die; ~, ~n** cypress

Zypriot [ts̮ypri'o:t] **der; ~en, ~en, Zypriotin die; ~, ~nen** Cypriot

zypriotisch, zyprisch *Adj.* Cypriot

Zyste ['ts̮ʏstə] **die; ~, ~n** *(Med.)* cyst

Zytologie [ts̮ytolo'gi:] **die; ~** *(Biol.)* cytology *no art.*

z. Z., z. Zt. *Abk.* **zur Zeit**

A

[1]A, [1]a [eɪ] *n., pl.* **As** *or* **A's a)** *(letter)* A, a, *das;* **from A to Z** von A bis Z; **A road** Straße 1. Ordnung; ≈ Bundesstraße, *die;* **b) A** *(Mus.)* A, a, *das;* **A sharp** ais, Ais, *das;* **A flat** as, As, *das;* **c)** *(example)* A, a; **if A says to B:...:** wenn A zu B sagt:...; **d)** *(Naut.)* **A 1** in erstklassigem Zustand; **e) A 1** *(coll.)* eins a *(ugs.);* **I'm feeling absolutely A 1** ich fühle mich eins a *(ugs.) od.* erstklassig; **f)** *(paper size)* **A 1, A 2, A 3,** *etc.* [DIN] A 1, A 2, A 3 *usw.;* **a pad of A 4 [paper]** ein [DIN-]A 4-Block; **g)** *(Sch., Univ.: mark)* Eins, *die;* **he got an A [in French]** er bekam [in Französisch] „sehr gut" *od.* eine Eins

[2]A *abbr.* **answer**

[2]a [ə, *stressed* eɪ] *indef. art.* **a)** ein/eine/ein; **he is a gardener/a Frenchman** er ist Gärtner/Franzose; **she did not say a word** sie sagte kein Wort; *see also* **many 1 b; quite; such 1 a; b)** *(per)* pro; **£40 a year** 40 Pfund pro Jahr; **it's 20p a pound** es kostet 20 Pence das Pfund; **two a penny** zwei Stück [für] einen Penny; **six a side** sechs auf jeder Seite

AA *abbr.* **a)** *(Brit.)* **Automobile Association** *britischer Automobilklub;* **b) anti-aircraft** Flugabwehr-; Fla-; **AA gun** Flak, *die;* **c) Alcoholics Anonymous**

AB *abbr.* **a) able rating** *or* **seaman; b)** *(Amer. Univ.)* **Bachelor of Arts**

aback [əˈbæk] *adv.* **be taken ~:** erstaunt sein; **I've never seen her so taken ~:** ich habe sie noch nie so betroffen gesehen

abacus [ˈæbəkəs] *n., pl.* **~es** *or* **abaci** [ˈæbəsaɪ] Abakus, *der*

abandon [əˈbændən] **1.** *v. t.* **a)** *(forsake)* verlassen ‹*Ort*›; verlassen, im Stich lassen ‹*Person*›; aussetzen ‹*Kind, Tier*›; aufgeben ‹*Prinzip*›; stehenlassen ‹*Auto*›; aufgeben, fallenlassen ‹*Gedanken, Plan*›; **~ hope** die Hoffnung aufgeben; **~ ship** das Schiff verlassen; **~ ship!** alle Mann von Bord!; **b)** *(surrender)* **~ sth. to the enemy** etw. dem Feind übergeben *od.* überlassen; **c)** *(yield)* **~ oneself to sth.** sich einer Sache *(Dat.)* hingeben; **d)** *(give up)* ablegen ‹*Gewohnheit*›; abbrechen ‹*Spiel*›; sich trennen von ‹*Reichtümern, Besitz*›; hingeben *(geh.)* ‹*Reichtum, Geld und Gut*›. **2.** *n., no pl.* Unbekümmertheit, *die;* Ungezwungenheit, *die;* **with ~:** unbekümmert; ungezwungen

abandoned [əˈbændənd] *adj.* **a)** *(deserted)* verlassen, ausgesetzt ‹*Kind, Tier*›; **~ property** herrenloses Gut; **b)** *(profligate)* verworfen, verkommen ‹*Person*›; lasterhaft ‹*Benehmen*›

abandonment [əˈbændənmənt] *n., no pl.* **a)** *(giving up) (of right, claim)* Preisgabe, *die;* Abtretung, *die; (of plan, property)* Aufgabe, *die;* **b)** *(carefreeness)* Zwanglosigkeit, *die;* Unbekümmertheit, *die;* **c)** *(self-surrender)* Sichgehenlassen, *das;* Hingabe, *die* **(to** an **+** *Akk.*)

abase [əˈbeɪs] *v. t.* demütigen, erniedrigen ‹*Person*›; **~ oneself** sich erniedrigen

abashed [əˈbæʃt] *adj.* beschämt; verlegen; **feel ~:** beschämt sein; **be ~ [by sth.]** sich [durch etw.] aus der Fassung bringen lassen

abate [əˈbeɪt] *v. i.* [an Stärke *od.* Intensität] abnehmen; nachlassen; ‹*Zorn, Eifer, Sturm:*› abflauen, nachlassen

abatement [əˈbeɪtmənt] *n., no pl.* Abnahme, *die;* Nachlassen, *das; (of a nuisance)* Beseitigung, *die; see also* **noise abatement; smoke abatement**

abattoir [ˈæbətwɑ:(r)] *n.* Schlachthof, *der; ([part of] building)* Schlachthaus, *das*

abbess [ˈæbɪs] *n.* Äbtissin, *die*

abbey [ˈæbɪ] *n.* **a)** Abtei, *die;* **b)** *(church)* Abteikirche, *die;* **the A~** *(Brit.)* die Abteikirche von Westminster

abbot [ˈæbət] *n.* Abt, *der*

abbreviate [əˈbri:vɪeɪt] *v. t.* abkürzen ‹*Wort usw.*›; **~ 'Saint' to 'St'** Saint mit St abkürzen

abbreviation [əbri:vɪˈeɪʃn] *n. (of word etc.)* Abkürzung, *die*

ABC [eɪbi:ˈsi:] *n.* **a)** *(alphabet)* ABC, *das;* **as easy as ~:** kinderleicht; **b)** *(fig.: rudiments)* ABC, *das;* Einmaleins, *das*

abdicate [ˈæbdɪkeɪt] *v. t.* abdanken; **~ [the throne]** auf den Thron verzichten; dem Thron entsagen *(geh.);* **~ one's rights** auf seine Rechte verzichten

abdication [æbdɪˈkeɪʃn] *n. (by monarch)* Abdankung, *die;* Thronverzicht, *der;* **the ~ of his rights** der Verzicht auf seine Rechte

abdomen [ˈæbdəmɪn, æbˈdəʊmɪn] *n. (Anat.)* Bauch, *der;* Unterleib, *der;* Abdomen, *das (fachspr.)*

abdominal [æbˈdɒmɪnl] *adj. (Anat.)* Bauch-; Abdominal- *(fachspr.)*

abduct [əbˈdʌkt] *v. t.* entführen

abduction [əbˈdʌkʃn] *n.* Entführung, *die*

abeam [əˈbi:m] *adv. (Naut.)* querab; dwars; **~ of the ship** dwarsschiffs

abed [əˈbed] *adv. (arch.)* im Bett; zu Bett *(veralt.)*

Aberdeen [ˈæbədi:n] *n.* **~ [Angus]** Angusrind, *das;* **~ [terrier]** Scotchterrier *od.* Schottische Terrier, *der*

Aberdonian [æbəˈdəʊnɪən] **1.** *adj.* aus Aberdeen; Aberdeener. **2.** *n.* Aberdeener, *der/*Aberdeenerin, *die*

aberrant [əˈberənt] *adj.* abweichend, *(bes. fachspr.)* anomal ‹*Verhalten, Exemplar*›

aberration [æbəˈreɪʃn] *n.* **a)** *(straying, lit. or fig.)* Abweichung, *die; (deviation)* Abweichung, *die;* Anomalie, *die (bes. fachspr.); (lapse, moral slip)* Verirrung, *die;* **mental ~[s** *pl.*] geistige Verirrung; **b)** *(Optics, Astron.)* Aberration, *die*

abet [əˈbet] *v. t.,* **-tt-** *(support)* helfen (+ *Dat.*); unterstützen; **aid and ~:** Beihilfe leisten (+ *Dat.*); **aiding and ~ting [a criminal]** *(Law)* Beihilfe [bei einem Verbrechen]

abeyance [əˈbeɪəns] *n.* **a)** *(suspension)* **be in/fall into ~:** zeitweilig außer Kraft sein/treten; **b)** *(Law)* **be in ~** ‹*[Adels]titel:*› [vorübergehend] abgeschafft sein

abhor [əbˈhɔ:(r)] *v. t.,* **-rr-** hassen; *(loathe)* verabscheuen

abhorrence [əbˈhɒrəns] *n.* **a)** *no pl. (loathing)* Abneigung, *die* **(of** gegen); Abscheu, *der* **(of** vor + *Dat.*); **hold sth. in ~:** einen Abscheu vor etw. *(Dat.)* haben; **b)** *(detested thing)* Greuel, *der*

abhorrent [əbˈhɒrənt] *adj. (disgusting)* abscheulich ‹*Benehmen, Gedanke, Person*›; **be ~ to sb.** jmdm. zuwider sein

abide [əˈbaɪd] **1.** *v. i.,* **abode** [əˈbəʊd] *or* **~d: a)** *usu.* **~d: ~ by** befolgen ‹*Gesetz, Regel, Vorschrift*›; [ein]halten ‹*Versprechen*›; **b)** *(continue)* fortdauern; fortbestehen; *(remain)* bleiben; verweilen *(geh.).* **2.** *v. t.* **a)** *(tolerate)* ertragen; **I can't ~ dogs** ich kann Hunde nicht ausstehen; **b)** *(submit to)* hinnehmen ‹*Urteil, Entscheidung, Kritik*›

abiding [əˈbaɪdɪŋ] *attrib. adj.* bleibend, beständig ‹*Liebe*›; dauerhaft ‹*Verbindung, Freundschaft*›

ability [əˈbɪlɪtɪ] *n.* **a)** *(capacity)* Können, *das;* Fähigkeit, *die;* **have the ~ to do sth.** etw. können *od. (geh.)* vermögen; **make use of one's ~** *or* **abilities** seine Fähigkeiten einsetzen; **have the ~ to type/do shorthand** maschineschreiben können/Kurzschrift beherrschen *od.* können; **to the best of my ~:** soweit es in meinen Kräften steht; **b)** *no pl. (cleverness)* Intelligenz, *die;* **she is a girl of great ~:** sie ist ein sehr intelligentes Mädchen; **it depends on his ~ at school** es hängt von seinen Leistungen in der Schule ab; **c)** *(talent)* Begabung, *die;* Talent, *das;* Anlagen *Pl.;* **he shows** *or* **has great musical ~:** er ist musikalisch sehr begabt; **she has a natural ~ for teaching** sie hat eine natürliche Begabung zur Lehrerin

abject [ˈæbdʒekt] *adj.* **a)** *(miserable)* elend; erbärmlich; **in the most ~ poverty** in bitterster Armut; **b)** *(self-abasing, submissive)* unterwürfig

abjectly [ˈæbdʒektlɪ] *adv.* **a)** *(miserably)* erbärmlich; **b)** *(submissively)* unterwürfig

abjectness [ˈæbdʒektnɪs] *n., no pl.* **a)** *(misery)* Erbärmlichkeit, *die;* **b)** *(submissiveness)* Unterwürfigkeit, *die*

abjuration [æbdʒʊəˈreɪʃn] *n. (of belief, religion)* Abschwören, *das*

abjure [əbˈdʒʊə(r)] *v. t.* abschwören (+ *Dat.*) ‹*Glauben, Religion*›; sich lossagen von ‹*Theorie, Weltanschauung*›

ablative [ˈæblətɪv] *(Ling.)* **1.** *adj.* Ablativ-; **~ case** Ablativ, *der.* **2.** *n.* Ablativ, *der; see also* **absolute c**

ablaut [ˈæblaʊt] *n. (Ling.)* Ablaut, *der*

ablaze [əˈbleɪz] *pred. adj.* in Flammen; **be ~:** in Flammen stehen; *(fig.)* glühen **(with** vor + *Dat.*); **be ~ with light** hell erleuchtet sein

able [ˈeɪbl] *adj.* **a) be ~ to do sth.** etw. können; **I'd love to come but I don't know if I'll be ~ [to]** ich würde sehr gern kommen, aber ich weiß nicht, ob es mir möglich sein wird; **I think you'd be better/more ~ to do it than I would** ich glaube, Sie sind eher dazu in der Lage als ich; **b)** *(competent)* fähig; tüchtig; *(talented)* begabt; fähig

able: ~bodied [ˈeɪblbɒdɪd] *adj.* kräftig; stark; tauglich ‹*Soldat, Matrose*›; **~ ˈrating, ~ ˈseaman** *ns.* Vollmatrose, *der*

ablution [ə'blu:ʃn] *n., usu. in pl.* **a)** *(ceremony)* Waschung, *die;* Ablution, *die (Rel.); (joc.: washing)* Wäsche, *die;* **perform one's ~s** sich waschen; **b)** *in pl.* sanitäre Anlagen

ably ['eɪblɪ] *adv.* geschickt; gekonnt

abnormal [æb'nɔ:ml] *adj.* **a)** *(deviant)* abnorm ‹*Gestalt, Größe*›; a[b]normal ‹*Interesse, Verhalten*›; **mentally/physically ~:** geistig/physisch anomal *od.* krank; **b)** *(irregular)* ungewöhnlich; a[b]normal

abnormality [æbnɔ:'mælɪtɪ] *n.* **a)** *(deviation)* Abnormität, *die;* Anomalie, *die;* **b)** *(irregularity)* Ungewöhnlichkeit, *die;* Regelwidrigkeit, *die;* Abnormität, *die*

abnormally [æb'nɔ:məlɪ] *adv. (untypically)* ungewöhnlich; abnorm; *(unusually)* ungewöhnlich

Abo ['æbəʊ] *n., pl.* **~s** *(Austral. sl. derog.)* Eingeborene, *der/die*

aboard [ə'bɔ:d] **1.** *adv. (on or in ship etc.)* an Bord; **a bus with 30 passengers ~:** ein Bus mit 30 Fahrgästen; **all ~!** alle Mann an Bord!; *(bus, train)* alle[s] einsteigen! **2.** *prep.* an Bord; **~ an ocean liner** an Bord eines Überseedampfers; **~ the bus/train** im Bus/Zug; **~ ship** an Bord

¹abode [ə'bəʊd] *n. (formal/joc.: dwelling-place)* Wohnstätte, *die;* Bleibe, *die;* **of no fixed ~:** ohne festen Wohnsitz

²abode *see* **abide**

abolish [ə'bɒlɪʃ] *v. t.* abschaffen; abschaffen, aufheben ‹*Gesetz*›

abolishment [ə'bɒlɪʃmənt], **abolition** [æbə'lɪʃn] *ns.* Abschaffung, *die; (of law)* Abschaffung, *die;* Aufhebung, *die; (of slavery)* Abschaffung, *die;* Abolition, *die*

abolitionist [æbə'lɪʃənɪst] *n.* Abolitionist, *der; attrib.* abolitionistisch

'A-bomb *n.* Atombombe, *die*

abominable [ə'bɒmɪnəbl] *adj.* abscheulich; scheußlich; widerwärtig; **the A~ Snowman** der Schneemensch; der Yeti

abominably [ə'bɒmɪnəblɪ] *adv.* abscheulich; scheußlich; widerwärtig

abominate [ə'bɒmɪneɪt] *v. t.* verabscheuen

abomination [əbɒmɪ'neɪʃn] *n.* **a)** *no pl. (abhorrence)* Abscheu, *der* (**of** vor + *Dat.*); **b)** *(object of disgust)* Abscheulichkeit, *die*

aboriginal [æbə'rɪdʒɪnl] **1.** *adj.* **a)** einheimisch ‹*Pflanze, Tier, Bevölkerung*›; **the ~ inhabitants of this region** die Ureinwohner *od.* die Urbevölkerung dieser Region; **b)** *(in Australia)* **A~ tribes** Aboriginesstämme; **A~ customs** Brauchtum der Aborigines. **2.** *n.* Ureinwohner, *der; (in Australia)* **A~:** [australischer] Ureinwohner

aborigine [æbə'rɪdʒɪnɪ] *n.* Ureinwohner, *der;* Urbewohner, *der; (in Australia)* **A~:** [australischer] Ureinwohner

abort [ə'bɔ:t] **1.** *v. i.* **a)** *(Med.)* eine Fehlgeburt haben; abortieren *(Med.);* **b)** *(fail)* mißlingen; scheitern. **2.** *v. t.* **a)** *(Med.)* **~ a baby** eine Schwangerschaftsunterbrechung durchführen; [ein Baby] abtreiben; **~ a woman** bei einer Frau eine Schwangerschaftsunterbrechung durchführen; **b)** *(fig.: end)* vorzeitig beenden; abbrechen ‹*Projekt, Unternehmen*›; **c)** *(Aeronaut., Astronaut.)* abbrechen; aufgeben ‹*Rakete*›

abortion [ə'bɔ:ʃn] *n.* **a)** *(deliberate)* Schwangerschaftsunterbrechung, *die;* Abtreibung, *die;* **have/get an ~:** die Schwangerschaft unterbrechen lassen; **back-street ~:** illegale Abtreibung *(durch Engelmacherin);* **b)** *(involuntary)* Früh- *od.* Fehlgeburt, *die;* Abort, *der (Med.);* **c)** *(monstrosity)* Mißgeburt, *die*

abortionist [ə'bɔ:ʃənɪst] *n.* abtreibender Arzt/abtreibende Ärztin; **back-street ~:** Engelmacherin, *die*/Engelmacher, *der (ugs.)*

abortive [ə'bɔ:tɪv] *adj.* mißlungen ‹*Plan*›; fehlgeschlagen ‹*Versuch*›; **be ~:** ein Fehlschlag sein

abound [ə'baʊnd] *v. i.* **a)** *(be plentiful)* reichlich *od.* in Hülle und Fülle vorhanden sein *od.* dasein; **b) ~ in sth.** an etw. *(Dat.)* reich sein; **the English language ~s in idioms** die englische Sprache ist reich an Redensarten; **~ with** voll sein von; wimmeln von ‹*Lebewesen*›

about [ə'baʊt] **1.** *adv.* **a)** *(all around)* rings[her]um; *(here and there)* überall; **all ~** ringsumher; **strewn/littered ~ all over the room** überall im Zimmer verstreut; **there must be some kitchen utensils ~:** irgendwo müssen hier ein paar Küchengeräte herumliegen; **b)** *(near)* **be ~:** dasein; hiersein; **is John ~?** ist John da?; **there was nobody ~:** es war niemand da; **c) be ~ to do sth.** gerade etw. tun wollen; im Begriff sein, etw. zu tun; *(Amer.: intend)* beabsichtigen, etw. zu tun; **I was just ~ to go shopping when ...:** ich wollte gerade einkaufen gehen, als ...; **d)** *(active)* **be out and ~:** aktiv sein; etwas unternehmen; **be up and ~:** aufsein *(ugs.);* **e)** *(approximately)* ungefähr; **[at] ~ 5 p.m.** ungefähr um *od.* gegen 17 Uhr; **Here I am! – And ~ time too!** *(coll.)* Hier bin ich. – Langsam wird es auch Zeit!; **it's ~ time somebody told him a thing or two** *(coll.)* langsam wird es Zeit, daß ihm mal jemand die Meinung sagt; **I've had [just] ~ enough of this** *(coll.)* ich habe [endgültig] genug *od.* *(salopp)* die Nase voll davon; **f)** *(round)* herum; rum *(ugs.);* **the battery is the wrong way ~:** die Batterie ist falsch [herum] eingebaut; **~ turn!,** *(Amer.)* **~ face!** *(Mil.)* kehrt!; *see also* **about-turn; g)** *(in rotation)* **[week and] week ~:** in wöchentlichem Wechsel; **[turn and] turn ~:** abwechselnd; **we take turn ~ at [the] cooking** wir wechseln uns mit dem Kochen ab. *See also* **bring about; come about; go about 1; set about. 2.** *prep.* **a)** *(all around)* um [... herum]; **there was litter lying ~ the park/streets** überall im Park/auf den Straßen lag der Abfall herum; **walk ~ the garden** im Garten herumgehen; **man ~ town** *see* **town a; b)** *(with)* **have sth. ~ one** etw. [bei sich] haben; **have you got a match ~ you?** haben Sie vielleicht ein Streichholz?; *see also* **¹wit b; c)** *(concerning)* **a talk/an argument/a question ~ sth.** ein Gespräch über etw. *(Akk.)*/Streit wegen etw./eine Frage zu etw.; **talk/laugh ~ sth.** über etw. *(Akk.)* sprechen/lachen; **cry ~ sth.** wegen etw. weinen; **know ~ sth.** von etw. wissen; **what was it ~?** worum ging es?; **what is/was all that ~?** worum geht/ging es denn?; *see also* **¹do 1b; what 5a; d)** *(occupied with)* **be ~ sb.'s business** für jmdn. arbeiten *od.* tätig sein; **what are you/is he ~?** was hast du/hat er vor?; was führst du/führt er im Schilde?; **mind what you're ~:** paß auf!; sieh dich vor!; sei vorsichtig!; **be quick/brief ~ it** beeil dich!; *(in speaking)* fasse dich kurz!; **while you're ~ it** da Sie gerade dabei sind. *See also* **go about 2**

about-'face, about-'turn 1. *ns. (lit. or fig.)* Kehrtwendung, *die.* **2.** *vs. i.* kehrtmachen; **~!** kehrt!

above [ə'bʌv] **1.** *adv.* **a)** *(position)* oben; oberhalb; *(higher up)* darüber; *(on top)* oben; *(upstream)* weiter oben; **up ~:** oben; droben *(bes. südd.);* **from ~:** von oben [herab]; **~ right** rechts oben; oben rechts; **b)** *(direction)* nach oben; hinauf; *(upstream)* stromauf[wärts]; **c)** *(earlier in text)* weiter oben; **see ~, p. 123** siehe oben, S. 123; **d)** *(upstairs) (position)* oben; *(direction)* nach oben; **the flat/floor ~:** die Wohnung/das Stockwerk *od.* die Etage darüber *od.* über uns/ihnen *usw.;* **on the floor ~:** eine Etage höher; **e)** *(in heaven)* [droben] im Himmel; **from ~:** vom Himmel [herab *od.* hoch]. **2.** *prep.* **a)** *(position)* über (+ *Dat.*); *(upstream from)* oberhalb (+ *Gen.*); **my brother is head and shoulders ~ me** mein Bruder ist zwei Köpfe größer als ich; *(fig.)* mein Bruder ist mir haushoch überlegen; **~ the general noise was heard ...:** durch den allgemeinen Lärm hindurch konnte man ... hören; **~ oneself** *(in high spirits)* übermütig; aufgekratzt *(ugs.); (conceited)* größenwahnsinnig *(ugs.);* **~ board** einwandfrei; korrekt; *see also* **average 1a; ¹ground 1a, b; head 1b; par a, d; b)** *(direction)* über (+ *Akk.*); **the sun rose ~ the horizon** am Horizont ging die Sonne auf; **c)** *(more than)* über (+ *Akk.*); **will anyone go ~ £2,000?** bietet jemand mehr als 2 000 Pfund?; **he valued honour ~ life** er stellte die Ehre über das Leben; **be ~ criticism/suspicion/reproach** über jede Kritik/jeden Verdacht/allen Vorwurf erhaben sein; **that's ~ me** das ist mir zu hoch *(ugs.);* **you ought to be ~ all that at your age** du solltest in deinem Alter über so etwas stehen *(ugs.);* **~ all [else]** vor allem; insbesondere; *see also* **over 1g; station 1d; d)** *(ranking higher than)* über (+ *Dat.*); **she's in the class ~ me** sie ist eine Klasse über mir *od.* höher als ich. **3.** *adj. (earlier)* obig ‹*Erklärung, Aufzählung, Ziffern*›; *(~-mentioned)* obengenannt. **4.** *n.* **the ~:** das Obige; *(person[s])* der/die Obengenannte/die Obengenannten

above-mentioned [ə'bʌvmenʃnd], **above-named** [ə'bʌvneɪmd] *adjs.* obengenannt; obenerwähnt

abracadabra [æbrəkə'dæbrə] *n.* Abrakadabra, *das;* Hokuspokus, *der*

abrade [ə'breɪd] *v. t. (scrape off)* abschaben; abschürfen ‹*Haut*›

abrasion [ə'breɪʒn] *n.* **a)** *(Med.)* Abschürfung, *die;* **b)** *(graze)* Hautabschürfung, *die*

abrasive [ə'breɪsɪv] **1.** *adj.* **a)** scheuernd; Scheuer-; *(scratchy)* kratzig; **b)** *(fig.: harsh)* aggressiv; herausfordernd ‹*Ton*›; **an ~ remark** eine barsche Bemerkung. **2.** *n.* Scheuermittel, *das;* Schleifmittel, *das (Technik)*

abreast [ə'brest] *adv.* **a)** nebeneinander; Seite an Seite; **walk/ride three ~:** zu dritt nebeneinander gehen/fahren; **b)** *(fig.)* **keep ~ of** *or* **with sth.** sich über etw. *(Akk.)* auf dem laufenden halten

abridge [ə'brɪdʒ] *v. t.* **a)** *(condense)* kürzen; **b)** *(curtail)* einschränken; beschneiden ‹*Rechte, Freiheiten, Privilegien*›

abridg[e]ment [ə'brɪdʒmənt] *n.* **a)** *(shortening)* Kürzung, *die;* **b)** *(summary) (of text)* Kurzfassung, *die; (of book)* Epitome, *die (Literaturw.);* Abriß, *der*

abroad [ə'brɔ:d] *adv.* **a)** *(overseas)* im Ausland; *(direction)* ins Ausland; **have you ever been ~?** waren Sie schon mal im Ausland?; **are you going ~?** fahren Sie ins Ausland?; **from ~:** aus dem Ausland; **b)** *(widely)* in alle Richtungen; **the news was spread ~ that ...:** überall verbreitete sich die Nachricht, daß ...; *(at large)* **there is a rumour ~ that ...:** es geht ein Gerücht um, daß ...

abrogate ['æbrəgeɪt] *v. t.* annullieren ‹*Vertrag*›; aufheben, außer Kraft setzen ‹*Gesetz, Vorschrift*›

abrogation [æbrə'geɪʃn] *n., no pl. see* **abrogate:** Annullierung, *die;* Aufhebung, *die;* Außerkraftsetzung, *die*

abrupt [ə'brʌpt] *adj.* **a)** *(sudden)* abrupt, plötzlich ‹*Ende, Abreise, Wechsel*›; **come to an ~ halt** ‹*Fahrzeug:*› plötzlich *od.* abrupt anhalten; **b)** *(disconnected)* zusammenhanglos ‹*Schreibstil*›; **c)** *(brusque)* schroff, barsch ‹*Art, Ton*›; **d)** *(steep)* jäh, steil ‹*Abhang*›; stark ‹*Gefälle*›; *(fig.)* plötzlich ‹*Zunahme, Abnahme, Anstieg, Rückgang*›

abruptly [ə'brʌptlɪ] *adv.* **a)** *(suddenly)* abrupt; plötzlich; **b)** *(disconnectedly)* zusammenhanglos; unzusammenhängend; **c)** *(brusquely)* schroff; barsch; **d)** *(steeply)* jäh; steil; *(fig.)* plötzlich ‹*zunehmen, abnehmen*›

abruptness [ə'brʌptnɪs] *n., no pl. see* **abrupt: a)** Plötzlichkeit, *die;* **b)** Zusammenhanglosigkeit, *die;* **c)** Schroffheit, *die;* Barschheit, *die;* **d)** Steilheit, *die;* Jähe, *die (veralt.); (fig.)* Plötzlichkeit, *die*

abscess [ˈæbsɪs] *n. (Med.)* Abszeß, *der*

abscond [əbˈskɒnd] *v. i.* **a)** *(depart)* sich entfernen; [heimlich] verschwinden *(ugs.)*; **b)** *(flee)* flüchten; fliehen

abseil [ˈæbseɪl, ˈæbzaɪl] *(Mount.)* **1.** *v. i.* abseilen. **2.** *n.* Abseilen, *das*

absence [ˈæbsəns] *n.* **a)** Abwesenheit, *die; (from work)* Fernbleiben, *das;* **his ~s from school** sein Fehlen in der Schule; **how long was your ~ from home?** wie lange waren Sie von zu Hause fort?; **~ makes the heart grow fonder** Abwesenheit verstärkt die Zuneigung; *see also* **ˈleave b**; **b)** *(lack)* **the ~ of sth.** der Mangel an etw. *(Dat.)*; das Fehlen von etw.; **in the ~ of concrete evidence** mangels konkreter Beweise; **c) ~ [of mind]** Geistesabwesenheit, *die;* Zerstreutheit, *die*

absent 1. [ˈæbsənt] *adj.* **a)** abwesend; **be ~:** nicht dasein; **be ~ from school/work** in der Schule/am Arbeitsplatz fehlen; **for all those ~ from the last meeting** für alle, die beim letzten Treffen nicht anwesend waren; **I'm afraid he's ~ in America at the moment** er ist zur Zeit leider in Amerika; **he's ~ on leave** er ist auf Urlaub; **be ~ without leave** sich unerlaubt entfernt haben; **~ voter** Briefwähler, *der*/-wählerin, *die;* **b)** *(lacking)* **be ~:** fehlen; **c)** *(abstracted)* geistesabwesend; zerstreut. **2.** [əbˈsent] *v. refl.* **~ oneself [from sth.]** [einer Sache *(Dat.)*] fernbleiben

absentee [æbsənˈtiː] *n.* Fehlende, *der/die;* Abwesende, *der/die;* **there were a few ~s** ein paar fehlten; **~ landlord** nicht auf seinem Gut lebender Gutsherr

absenteeism [æbsənˈtiːɪzm] *n., no pl.* [häufiges] Fernbleiben; *(without good reason)* Krankfeiern, *das (ugs.)*

absently [ˈæbsəntlɪ] *adv.* [geistes]abwesend

absent-minded [æbsəntˈmaɪndɪd] *adj.* geistesabwesend; *(habitually)* zerstreut

absent-mindedly [æbsəntˈmaɪndɪdlɪ] *adv.* geistesabwesend

absent-mindedness [æbsəntˈmaɪndɪdnɪs], **absentness** [ˈæbsəntnɪs] *ns., no pl.* Geistesabwesenheit, *die; (habitual)* Zerstreutheit, *die*

absinth [ˈæbsɪnθ] *n.* **a)** *(liqueur)* **~[e]** Absinth, *der;* **b)** *(essence)* Wermutextrakt, *der;* **c)** *(Bot.: wormwood)* Wermut, *der*

absolute [ˈæbsəluːt, ˈæbsəljuːt] *adj.* **a)** *(complete, not relative)* absolut; unumstößlich ⟨*Beweis, Tatsache*⟩; unbestreitbar ⟨*Tatsache*⟩; ausgemacht ⟨*Lüge, Schurkerei, Skandal*⟩; *(unconditional)* fest ⟨*Versprechen*⟩; streng ⟨*Verpflichtung*⟩; **~ alcohol** reiner Alkohol; *see also* **zero 1 c**; **b)** *(unrestricted)* absolut ⟨*Monarchie, Herrscher*⟩; uneingeschränkt ⟨*Macht*⟩; unumschränkt ⟨*Herrscher*⟩; **~ majority** absolute Mehrheit; **c)** *(Ling.)* absolut ⟨*Verb*⟩; *(uninflected)* ungebeugt; unflektiert; **ablative ~:** Ablativus absolutus, *der;* **accusative/genitive/nominative ~:** absoluter Akkusativ/Genitiv/Nominativ; **~ construction** absolute Konstruktion; **d)** *(Philos.)* absolut; **the ~:** das Absolute

absolutely [ˈæbsəluːtlɪ, ˈæbsəljuːtlɪ] *adv.* **a)** absolut; strikt ⟨*ablehnen*⟩; völlig ⟨*verrückt*⟩; entschieden ⟨*bestreiten*⟩; ausgesprochen ⟨*kriminell, schlimm, ekelhaft*⟩; **you're ~ right!** du hast völlig recht; **b)** *(positively)* regelrecht; **I say ~ no** ich sage entschieden nein; **~ not!** auf keinen Fall!; **c)** *(unconditionally)* mit absoluter Sicherheit ⟨*behaupten, glauben, beweisen*⟩; strikt ⟨*sich weigern*⟩; **d)** *(without qualification, independently)* absolut; **e)** *(Ling.)* absolut; **f)** [æbsəˈluːtlɪ] *(coll.: yes indeed)* hundertprozentig *(ugs.)*

absolute: ~ ˈpitch *n. (Mus.) (ability)* absolutes Gehör; *(standard)* absolute Tonhöhe; **~ temperature** *n. (Phys.)* absolute Temperatur

absolution [æbsəˈluːʃn, æbsəˈljuːʃn] *n.* **a)** *(release)* Lossprechung, *die* **(from** von); *(forgiveness of wrongdoing)* Vergebung, *die;* **b)** *(Relig.) (forgiveness)* Vergebung, *die; (release)* Erlaß, *der* **(from** *Gen.*); **the priest pronounced ~:** der Priester erteilte [die] Absolution

absolutism [ˈæbsəluːtɪzm, ˈæbsəljuːtɪzm] *n., no pl. (Polit.)* Absolutismus, *der*

absolve [əbˈzɒlv] *v. t.* **a)** *(release)* **~ from** entbinden von ⟨*Pflichten*⟩; vergeben ⟨*Sünde, Verbrechen*⟩; lossprechen von ⟨*Schuld*⟩; *(Relig.)* Absolution erteilen (+ *Dat.*); **b)** *(acquit)* freisprechen *(Rechtsw.)*

absorb [əbˈsɔːb, əbˈzɔːb] *v. t.* **a)** aufsaugen ⟨*Flüssigkeit*⟩; aufnehmen ⟨*Flüssigkeit, Nährstoff, Wärme*⟩; resorbieren *(Med.)*; absorbieren *(fachspr.)*; *(fig.)* in sich aufnehmen ⟨*Wissen*⟩; **~ a price increase** Mehrkosten auffangen; **b)** *(reduce in strength)* absorbieren; abfangen ⟨*Schlag, Stoß*⟩; **c)** *(incorporate)* absorbieren ⟨*Chemikalie*⟩; eingliedern, integrieren ⟨*Abteilung, Gemeinde*⟩; inkorporieren *(Rechtsw.)* ⟨*Gemeinde*⟩; **be ~ed by** *or* **into the crowd** von der Menge verschluckt werden; **d)** *(consume)* aufzehren ⟨*Kraft, Zeit, Vermögen*⟩; aufnehmen ⟨*Importe, Arbeitskräfte*⟩; **e)** *(engross)* ausfüllen ⟨*Person, Interesse, Gedanken*⟩

absorbed [əbˈsɔːbd, əbˈzɔːbd] *adj.* versunken; **be/get ~ in sth.** in etw. *(Akk.)* vertieft sein/sich in etw. *(Akk.)* vertiefen; **be/get ~ in sb.** von jmdm. gefangengenommen sein/werden; **he's totally ~ in his passion/work** er geht völlig in seiner Leidenschaft/Arbeit auf; **be/get ~ by sth./sb.** von etw./jmdm. [völlig] in Anspruch genommen sein/werden

absorbency [əbˈsɔːbənsɪ, əbˈzɔːbənsɪ] *n.* Saugfähigkeit, *die*

absorbent [əbˈsɔːbənt, əbˈzɔːbənt] **1.** *adj.* saugfähig; absorbierend *(fachspr.)*; **~ cotton** *(Amer.)* Watte, *die.* **2.** *n. (substance)* Absorbens *(Chemie, Med.)*; *(material)* absorbierendes Material

absorbing [əbˈsɔːbɪŋ, əbˈzɔːbɪŋ] *adj.* faszinierend

absorption [əbˈsɔːpʃn, əbˈzɔːpʃn] *n.* **a)** *(incorporation, physical process)* Absorption, *die (fachspr.)*; Resorption, *die (Med.)*; **b)** *(of department, community)* Integration, *die; (of effort)* Aufnahme, *die; (of goods)* Abnahme, *die;* **c)** *(engrossment) (in reading, watching)* Versunkenheit, *die;* **their ~ in each other** ihr vollkommenes Aufgehen ineinander

abstain [əbˈsteɪn] *v. i.* **a)** enthaltsam sein; **~ from sth.** sich einer Sache *(Gen.)* enthalten; **b) ~ [from voting]** sich der Stimme enthalten

abstainer [əbˈsteɪnə(r)] *n.* **a)** Antialkoholiker, *der;* Abstinenzler, *der;* **b)** *(in vote)* **an ~:** *jmd., der sich der Stimme enthält*

abstemious [əbˈstiːmɪəs] *adj.*, **abstemiously** [əbˈstiːmɪəslɪ] *adv.* enthaltsam

abstemiousness [əbˈstiːmɪəsnɪs] *n., no pl.* Enthaltsamkeit, *die*

abstention [əbˈstenʃn] *n.* **a)** Enthaltung, *die;* **~ from sex** sexuelle Enthaltsamkeit; **b) ~ from the vote/from voting** Stimmenthaltung, *die;* **how many ~s were there?** wie viele Personen enthielten sich der Stimme?

abstinence [ˈæbstɪnəns] *n.* **a)** *(abstaining)* Abstinenz, *die;* **total ~:** völlige Abstinenz; **b)** *(moderation)* Entsagung, *die*

abstinent [ˈæbstɪnənt] *adj.* abstinent

abstract 1. [ˈæbstrækt] *adj.* abstrakt; **~ noun** *(Ling.)* Abstraktum, *das;* **the ~:** das Abstrakte; **in the ~:** abstrakt; **~ expressionism** *see* **action painting. 2.** *n.* **a)** *(summary)* Zusammenfassung, *die;* Abstract, *das (fachspr.)*; *(of book)* Inhaltsangabe, *die;* **b)** *(idea)* Abstraktum, *das;* **c)** *(Art)* abstraktes [Kunst]werk. **3.** [æbˈstrækt] *v. t.* **a)** *(remove)* wegnehmen; *(euphem.: steal)* entwenden, *(ugs.)* stibitzen **(from** aus); **b)** *(summarize)* zusammenfassen ⟨*Bericht, Referat*⟩

abstracted [æbˈstræktɪd] *adj.*, **abstractedly** [æbˈstræktɪdlɪ] *adv.* [geistes]abwesend

abstraction [æbˈstrækʃn] *n.* **a)** *(removal)* Entnahme, *die; (euphem.: stealing)* Entwendung, *die;* **b)** *no pl. (absence of mind)* Geistesabwesenheit, *die;* Zerstreutheit, *die;* **c)** *(idea)* Abstraktion, *die;* **he talks in ~s** er spricht in abstrakten Begriffen

abstractly [ˈæbstræktlɪ] *adv.* abstrakt

abstractness [ˈæbstræktnɪs] *n., no pl.* Abstraktheit, *die*

abstractor [æbˈstræktə(r)] *n. Verfasser[in] von Abstracts*

abstruse [æbˈstruːs] *adj.*, **abstrusely** [æbˈstruːslɪ] *adv.* abstrus

abstruseness [æbˈstruːsnɪs] *n., no pl.* Abstrusität, *die*

absurd [əbˈsɜːd] *adj.* absurd; *(ridiculous)* lächerlich; **the theatre of the ~:** das absurde Theater

absurdity [əbˈsɜːdɪtɪ] *n.* Absurdität, *die*

absurdly [əbˈsɜːdlɪ] *adv.* lächerlich; **he is ~ afraid of ...:** er hat eine krankhafte Angst vor (+ *Dat.*) ...

abundance [əˈbʌndəns] *n.* **a) [an] ~ of sth.** eine Fülle von etw.; **an ~ of love/energy** ein Übermaß an Liebe/Energie *(Dat.)*; **in ~:** in Hülle und Fülle; **b)** *(profusion)* Überfluß, *der;* **c)** *(wealth)* Reichtum, *der*

abundant [əˈbʌndənt] *adj.* reich ⟨*Auswahl*⟩; übergroß ⟨*Interesse, Begeisterung*⟩; **an ~ supply of fish/fruit** Fisch/Obst im Überfluß; **~ proof/reason** mehr als genug Beweise/Gründe; **be ~:** überreichlich vorhanden sein; **~ in reich an** (+ *Dat.*)

abundantly [əˈbʌndəntlɪ] *adv.* überreichlich; **I made it ~ clear that ...:** ich habe es überdeutlich zum Ausdruck gebracht, daß ...

abuse 1. [əˈbjuːz] *v. t.* **a)** *(misuse)* mißbrauchen ⟨*Macht, Recht, Autorität, Vertrauen*⟩; *(maltreat)* peinigen, quälen ⟨*Tier*⟩; schaden (+ *Dat.*) ⟨*Motor*⟩; **sexually ~:** sexuell mißbrauchen; **b)** *(insult)* beschimpfen. **2.** [əˈbjuːs] *n.* **a)** *(misuse)* Mißbrauch, *der;* **b)** *(unjust or corrupt practice)* Mißstand, *der;* **c)** *(insults)* Beschimpfungen *Pl.*; **a term of ~:** ein Schimpfwort

abusive [əˈbjuːsɪv] *adj.* beleidigend; **~ language** Beleidigungen; Beschimpfungen; **become** *or* **get ~:** ausfallend werden

abut [əˈbʌt] **1.** *v. i.*, **-tt- a)** *(border)* **~ on** grenzen an (+ *Akk.*); **b)** *(end)* **~ on/against** stoßen *od.* angrenzen an (+ *Akk.*); *(rest)* **~ on** ruhen auf (+ *Dat.*). **2.** *v. t.* **a)** *(border on)* angrenzen an (+ *Akk.*); **b)** *(end on)* anstoßen an (+ *Akk.*)

abutment [əˈbʌtmənt] *n.* Widerlager, *das*

abysmal [əˈbɪzml] *adj.* **a)** *(bottomless)* unergründlich ⟨*Tiefe*⟩; *(fig.)* grenzenlos ⟨*Unwissenheit*⟩; **b)** *(coll.: bad)* katastrophal *(ugs.)*

abyss [əˈbɪs] *n. (lit. or fig.)* Abgrund, *der;* **the ~ of space/the sea** die unendliche Tiefe des Weltraums/der See

Abyssinia [æbɪˈsɪnɪə] *pr. n. (Hist.)* Abessinien *(das)*

AC *abbr. (Electr.)* **alternating current** Ws

a/c *abbr.* **account**

acacia [əˈkeɪʃə] *n. (Bot.)* Akazie, *die;* **[false] ~:** Robinie, *die*

academe [ˈækədiːm] *n. (literary)* Akademie, *die; (university)* Alma mater, *die;* **the grove[s] of A~:** die akademischen Gefilde

academic [ækəˈdemɪk] **1.** *adj.* **a)** *(scholarly)* akademisch; wissenschaftlich ⟨*Fach, Studium*⟩; **an ~ person/thinker** ein Theoretiker; **he's better on the ~ side** das Theoretische liegt ihm mehr; **b)** *(of university etc.)* akademisch; **~ year** Universitätsjahr, *das;* **c)** *(abstract, formal)* akademisch. **2.** *n.* Wissenschaftler, *der*/Wissenschaftlerin, *die; (scholar)* Gelehrte, *der/die*

academical [ækə'demɪkl] **1.** *adj.* akademisch. **2.** *n. in pl.* akademische Tracht
academically [ækə'demɪkəlɪ] *adv.* **a)** *(intellectually)* wissenschaftlich; **be ~ very able** große intellektuelle Fähigkeiten haben; **b)** *(educationally)* **~ [speaking]** was die akademische Ausbildung betrifft
academician [əkædə'mɪʃn] *n.* Akademiemitglied, *das*
academy [ə'kædəmɪ] *n.* **a)** *(society)* Akademie, *die;* **Royal A~ [of Arts]** *Akademie der Künste in Großbritannien;* **b)** *(school)* höhere Bildungsanstalt; *(college)* Akademie, *die*
acanthus [ə'kænθəs] *n. (Bot.)* Akanthus, *der;* Bärenklau, *die od. der*
ACAS ['eɪkæs] *abbr. (Brit.)* **Advisory Conciliation and Arbitration Service** *staatliche Schlichtungsstelle*
accede [æk'si:d] *v. i.* **a)** *(assent)* zustimmen (**to** *Dat.*); **b)** beitreten (**to** *Dat.*) ⟨*Abkommen, Bündnis*⟩; antreten ⟨*Amt*⟩; **~ [to the throne]** den Thron besteigen
accelerate [ək'seləreɪt] **1.** *v. t.* beschleunigen; erhöhen ⟨*Geschwindigkeit, Notwendigkeit*⟩. **2.** *v. i.* sich beschleunigen; ⟨*Auto[fahrer], Läufer:*⟩ beschleunigen; ⟨*Autofahrer:*⟩ Gas geben *(ugs.)*
acceleration [əkselə'reɪʃn] *n.* Beschleunigung, *die;* **the ~ of economic growth** das verstärkte wirtschaftliche Wachstum
accelerator [ək'seləreɪtə(r)] *n.* **a)** *(Motor Veh.)* **~ [pedal]** Gas[pedal], *das;* **b)** *(Phys.)* Beschleuniger, *der*
accent 1. ['æksənt] *n.* **a)** *(prominence by stress)* Akzent, *der; (mark)* Akzent, *der;* Akzentzeichen, *das;* **b)** *(pronunciation)* Akzent, *der; (note in sb.'s voice)* Unterton, *der;* **c)** *in pl. (speech)* Ton[fall], *der;* **d)** *(Mus.)* Akzent, *der;* **e)** *(rhythmical stress)* Betonung, *die;* **f)** *(emphasis)* Akzent, *der;* **the ~ is on ...:** der Akzent liegt auf (+ *Dat.*) ...; **g)** *(distinctive character)* Gepräge, *das;* **h)** *(contrasting detail)* [Farb]akzent, *der.* **2.** [ək'sent] *v. t. (stress, lit. or fig.)* betonen; *(mark)* mit Akzent[en] versehen
accentual [ək'sentjʊəl] *adj.* akzentuierend
accentuate [ək'sentjʊeɪt] *v. t.* betonen; vertiefen ⟨*Eindruck, Erinnerung, Feindschaft*⟩; verstärken ⟨*Schmerz, Kummer*⟩
accentuation [əksentjʊ'eɪʃn] *n.* Betonung, *die*
accept [ək'sept] *v. t.* **a)** *(be willing to receive)* annehmen; aufnehmen ⟨*Mitglied*⟩; *(take formally)* entgegennehmen ⟨*Dank, Spende, Auszeichnung*⟩; übernehmen ⟨*Verantwortung, Aufgabe*⟩; *(agree to)* annehmen ⟨*Vorschlag, Plan, Heiratsantrag, Einladung*⟩; **~ sb. for a job/school** jmdm. eine Einstellungszusage geben/jmdn. in eine Schule aufnehmen; **~ sb. for a course** jmdn. in einen Lehrgang aufnehmen; **~ sb. on to the staff** jmdn. in die Belegschaft aufnehmen; **~ sb. into the Church/the family** jmdn. in die Kirche/in die Familie aufnehmen; **get sth. ~ed** dafür sorgen, daß etw. angenommen wird; **~ sth. for publication** etw. zur Veröffentlichung annehmen; **b)** *(approve)* akzeptieren; **he is ~ed in the best circles** er ist in den besten Kreisen eingeführt; **~ sb. as a member of the group** jmdn. als Mitglied der Gruppe anerkennen; **c)** *(acknowledge)* akzeptieren; **it is ~ed that ...:** es ist unbestritten, daß ...; **an ~ed fact** eine anerkannte Tatsache; **an ~ed opinion** eine verbreitete Ansicht; **~ sb. for what he is** jmdn. so nehmen, wie er ist; **d)** *(believe)* **~ sth. [from sb.]** [jmdm.] etw. glauben; **e)** *(heed)* beherzigen ⟨*Rat, Warnung*⟩; **f)** *(tolerate)* hinnehmen; **you'll just have to ~ us as we are** du mußt uns nun einmal nehmen, wie wir sind; **~ losing a job** sich mit einer Kündigung abfinden; **he won't ~ that** er wird das nicht ohne weiteres hinnehmen; **g)** *(Commerc.)* annehmen ⟨*Scheck*⟩
acceptability [əkseptə'bɪlɪtɪ] *n., no pl.* Annehmbarkeit, *die; (of salary, price, risk)* Angemessenheit, *die; (agreeableness)* Annehmlichkeit, *die*
acceptable [ək'septəbl] *adj.* **a)** *(suitable, reasonable)* akzeptabel; **damaged banknotes are not ~:** beschädigte Banknoten können nicht angenommen werden; **b)** *(agreeable)* annehmbar ⟨*Preis, Gehalt*⟩; angenehm ⟨*Person*⟩; **would the salary be ~ to you?** wäre das Gehalt annehmbar für Sie?
acceptably [ək'septəblɪ] *adv.* **a)** *(suitably, agreeably)* angenehm ⟨*nahe, wenig*⟩; **be ~ priced** nicht zu teuer sein; **b)** *(reasonably)* vernünftig; **she sings ~ well** sie singt ganz akzeptabel; **c)** *(adequately, tolerably)* hinreichend
acceptance [ək'septəns] *n.* **a)** *(willing receipt)* Annahme, *die; (of gift, offer)* Annahme, *die;* Entgegennahme, *die; (of duty, responsibility)* Übernahme, *die; (in answer)* Zusage, *die; (welcome)* Aufnahme, *die; (agreement)* Annahme, *die;* Zustimmung, *die* (**of** zu); **[letter of] ~:** schriftliche Zusage, *die;* **she gave her ~ to his proposal of marriage** sie gab ihm ihr Jawort; **b)** *no pl. (approval)* Billigung, *die;* **c)** *no pl. (acknowledgement)* Anerkennung, *die; (of excuse, explanation)* Annahme, *die;* **that fact has gained general ~:** diese Tatsache wird allgemein anerkannt; **d)** *no pl. (heeding)* Beachtung, *die;* **e)** *no pl. (toleration) (of a fact)* Hinnahme, *die; (of behaviour)* Duldung, *die;* **f)** *(Commerc.: [engagement to honour] bill etc.)* Akzept, *das*
access ['ækses] *n.* **a)** *no pl., no art. (entering)* Zutritt, *der* (**to** zu); *(by vehicles)* Einfahren, *das* (**into** in + *Akk.*); **this doorway is the only means of ~:** diese Tür ist der einzige Zugang; **'no entry except for ~'** „Anlieger[verkehr] frei"; **b)** *(admission)* **gain** *or* **obtain** *or* **get ~:** Einlaß finden; **c)** *no pl. (opportunity to use or approach)* Zugang, *der* (**to** zu); **d)** *(accessibility)* **easy/difficult of ~:** leicht/schwer zugänglich; **e)** *(way [in])* Zugang, *der; (road)* Zufahrt, *die; (door)* Eingang, *der*
accessary [ək'sesərɪ] **1.** *n. see* **accessory 2 d. 2.** *adj.* beteiligt (**to** an + *Dat.*)
accessibility [əksesɪ'bɪlɪtɪ] *n., no pl.* **a)** *(reachability)* **the easy ~ of the beach** der leichte Zugang zum Strand; **b)** *(approachability, availability, understandability)* Zugänglichkeit, *die*
accessible [ək'sesɪbl] *adj.* **a)** *(reachable)* **[more] ~ [to sb.]** [besser] erreichbar [für jmdn.]; **b)** *(available, open, understandable)* zugänglich (**to** für)
accession [ək'seʃn] *n.* **a)** Amtsantritt, *der; (to position, estate)* Übernahme, *die* (**to** *Gen.*); **~ to the throne** Thronbesteigung, *die;* **b)** *(being added)* Zugang, *der;* **c)** *(thing added)* **new ~s to the library** Neuerwerbungen der Bibliothek; **d)** *(joining)* Beitritt, *der* (**to** zu)
accessory [ək'sesərɪ] **1.** *adj.* **~ [to sth.]** zusätzlich [zu etw.]. **2.** *n.* **a)** *(accompaniment)* Extra, *das;* **b)** *in pl. (attachments)* Zubehör, *das;* **one of the accessories** eines der Zubehörteile; **c)** *(dress article)* Accessoire, *das;* **d)** **~ [to a crime]** Mittäter [bei einem Verbrechen]; **~ before the fact** Anstifter, *der;* **~ after the fact** Begünstiger, *der*
'access road *n.* Zufahrtsstraße, *die*
accidence ['æksɪdəns] *n. (Ling.)* Formenlehre, *die*
accident ['æksɪdənt] *n.* **a)** *(unlucky event)* Unfall, *der;* **road ~:** Verkehrsunfall, *der;* **meet with/have an ~:** einen Unfall erleiden/haben; **~ rate** Unfallziffer, *die;* **b)** *(chance)* Zufall, *der; (unfortunate chance)* Unglücksfall, *der;* **by ~:** zufällig; **by an** *or* **some ~ of fate** durch eine Laune des Schicksals; **c)** *(mistake)* Versehen, *das;* **by ~:** versehentlich; **d)** *(mishap)* Mißgeschick, *das;* **chapter of ~s** *(coll.)* Pechsträhne, *die;* **have a chapter of ~s** vom Pech verfolgt sein; **~s will happen** das kommt schon mal vor
accidental [æksɪ'dentl] **1.** *adj. (fortuitous)* zufällig; *(unintended)* unbeabsichtigt; **~ death** Tod durch Unfall. **2.** *n. (Mus.)* Akzidens, *das (fachspr.);* Vorzeichen, *das*
accidentally [æksɪ'dentəlɪ] *adv. (by chance)* zufällig; *(by mistake)* versehentlich
'accident-prone *adj.* **~ person** Unfäller, *der (Psych.);* **be ~:** vom Pech verfolgt sein
acclaim [ə'kleɪm] **1.** *v. t. (welcome)* feiern; *(hail as)* **~ sb. king** jmdn. zum König ausrufen. **2.** *n., no pl.* **a)** *(welcome)* Beifall, *der;* **b)** *(approval)* Anerkennung, *die*
acclamation [æklə'meɪʃn] *n.* **a)** *no pl. (approval of plan or proposal)* Beifall, *der;* **b)** *usu. in pl. (shouting)* Beifallsbekundung, *die*
acclimatisation, acclimatise *see* **acclimatiz-**
acclimatization [əklaɪmətaɪ'zeɪʃn] *n. (lit. or fig.)* Akklimatisation, *die*
acclimatize [ə'klaɪmətaɪz] *v. t. (lit. or fig.)* akklimatisieren; **~ sth./sb. to sth.** etw./jmdn. an etw. *(Akk.)* gewöhnen; **~ oneself, get** *or* **become ~d** sich akklimatisieren; **~ oneself** *or* **get** *or* **become ~d to sth.** sich an etw. *(Akk.)* gewöhnen
accolade ['ækəleɪd, ækə'leɪd] *n. (gesture)* Akkolade, *die; (fig.) (praise)* **~[s]** Lob, *das; (approval, acknowledgement)* Anerkennung, *die*
accommodate [ə'kɒmədeɪt] *v. t.* **a)** *(lodge)* unterbringen; *(hold, have room for)* Platz bieten (+ *Dat.*); **b)** *(oblige)* gefällig sein (+ *Dat.*)
accommodating [ə'kɒmədeɪtɪŋ] *adj. (obliging)* zuvorkommend; *(compliant)* entgegenkommend
accommodatingly [ə'kɒmədeɪtɪŋlɪ] *adv. (obligingly)* zuvorkommend
accommodation [əkɒmə'deɪʃn] *n.* **a)** *no pl. (lodgings)* Unterkunft, *die;* **can you provide us with [some] ~ for the night?** können Sie uns ein Nachtquartier besorgen?; **~ is very expensive in Oxford** Wohnungen/Zimmer sind in Oxford sehr teuer; **b)** *(space)* **there is ~ for 500 people in this auditorium** in diesem Auditorium haben *od.* finden 500 Personen Platz; **c)** *in pl. (Amer.: lodgings)* Unterkunft, *die*
accommo'dation address *n.* Gefälligkeitsadresse, *die*
accompaniment [ə'kʌmpənɪmənt] *n.* **a)** *(lit. or fig.; also Mus.)* Begleitung, *die;* **b)** *(thing)* Begleiterscheinung, *die*
accompanist [ə'kʌmpənɪst] *n. (Mus.)* Begleiter, *der*/Begleiterin, *die*
accompany [ə'kʌmpənɪ] *v. t. (go along with; also Mus.)* begleiten; **the ~ing booklet** die beiliegende Broschüre
accomplice [ə'kʌmplɪs, ə'kɒmplɪs] *n.* Komplize, *der*/Komplizin, *die*
accomplish [ə'kʌmplɪʃ, ə'kɒmplɪʃ] *v. t. (perform)* vollbringen ⟨*Tat*⟩; erfüllen ⟨*Aufgabe*⟩; *(complete)* vollenden ⟨*Kunstwerk, Bauwerk*⟩; *(achieve)* erreichen; verwirklichen ⟨*Ziel, Wunsch*⟩
accomplished [ə'kʌmplɪʃt, ə'kɒmplɪʃt] *adj.* fähig; **he is an ~ speaker/dancer** er ist ein erfahrener Redner/vollendeter Tänzer
accomplishment [ə'kʌmplɪʃmənt, ə'kɒmplɪʃmənt] *n.* **a)** *no pl. (completion)* Vollendung, *die; (of deed)* Ausführung, *die; (of task)* Erfüllung, *die; (of aim)* Verwirklichung, *die;* **b)** *(achievement)* Leistung, *die; (skill)* Fähigkeit, *die*
accord [ə'kɔ:d] **1.** *v. i.* **~ [with sth.]** [mit etw.] übereinstimmen. **2.** *v. t. (formal: grant)* **~ sb. sth.** jmdm. etw. gewähren. **3.** *n.* **a)** *(volition)* **of one's own ~:** aus eigenem Antrieb; von selbst; **of its own ~:** von selbst; **b)** *(harmonious agreement)* Übereinstimmung, *die;* **with one ~:** geschlossen; **c)** *(harmony)* Harmonie, *die;* **be in ~ with** harmonieren mit; **d)** *(treaty)* Übereinkunft, *die*

accordance [əˈkɔːdəns] *n.* **in ~ with** in Übereinstimmung mit; gemäß (+ *Dat.*)

according [əˈkɔːdɪŋ] *adv.* **a) ~ as** *(depending on how)* je nachdem wie; *(depending on whether)* je nachdem ob; **b) ~ to** nach; **act ~ to the rules** sich an die Regeln halten; **~ to how** je nachdem wie; **~ to him** *(opinion)* seiner Meinung nach; *(account)* nach seiner Aussage; **~ to circumstances/the season** den Umständen/der Jahreszeit entsprechend

accordingly [əˈkɔːdɪŋlɪ] *adv.* *(as appropriate)* entsprechend; *(therefore)* folglich

accordion [əˈkɔːdɪən] *n.* Akkordeon, *das;* **~ pleats** Plisseefalten

accost [əˈkɒst] *v. t.* ansprechen

account [əˈkaʊnt] **1.** *v. t.* *(consider)* halten für; ansehen als. **2.** *n.* **a)** *(Finance)* *(reckoning)* Rechnung, *die;* *(statement)* Auflistung, *die;* Aufstellung, *die;* *(invoice)* Rechnung, *die;* **money of ~** *(Finance)* Rechnungseinheit, *die;* **~ rendered** *see* **render e; keep ~s/the ~s** Buch/die Bücher führen; **settle** *or* **square ~s with sb.** *(lit. or fig.)* mit jmdm. abrechnen; **on ~:** auf Rechnung; a conto; **on one's [own] ~:** auf eigene Rechnung; auf eigenes Risiko; *(fig.)* von sich aus; **don't change your plans on my ~:** ändert nicht meinetwegen eure Pläne; **on ~ of** wegen; **on no ~, not on any ~:** auf [gar] keinen Fall; **b)** *(at bank, shop)* Konto, *das;* **an ~ with** *or* **at a bank** ein Konto bei einer Bank; **pay sth. into one's ~:** etw. auf sein Konto einzahlen; **draw sth. out of one's ~:** etw. von seinem Konto abheben; **on ~:** auf Rechnung; **joint ~:** gemeinsames Konto; Gemeinschaftskonto, *das; see also* **close 3 b; credit 2 c; credit account; deposit account; open 3 c; savings account; c)** *(statement of facts)* Rechenschaft, *die;* **give** *or* **render an ~ for sth.** über etw. *(Akk.)* Rechenschaft ablegen; **call sb. to ~:** jmdn. zur Rechenschaft ziehen; **give a good ~ of oneself** seinen Mann stehen; **d)** *(consideration)* **take ~ of sth., take sth. into ~:** etw. berücksichtigen; **take no ~ of sth./sb., leave sth./sb. out of ~:** etw./jmdn. unberücksichtigt lassen *od.* nicht berücksichtigen; **e)** *(importance)* **of some/little/no ~:** von/von geringer/ohne Bedeutung; **f)** *(performance)* Interpretation, *die;* **g)** *(report)* **an ~ [of sth.]** ein Bericht [über etw. *(Akk.)*]; **give a full ~ of sth.** ausführlich über etw. *(Akk.)* berichten *od.* Bericht erstatten; **by** *or* **from all ~s** nach allem, was man hört; **h)** *(advantage)* **turn sth. to [good] ~:** aus etw. Nutzen *od.* Vorteil ziehen

~ for *v.t.* **a)** *(give reckoning)* Rechenschaft *od.* Rechnung ablegen über *(+ Akk.);* **b)** *(explain)* erklären; **I can't ~ for that** ich kann mir das nicht erklären; **c)** *(represent in amount)* ausmachen; ergeben; **d)** *(kill, destroy, capture)* zur Strecke bringen

accountability [əkaʊntəˈbɪlɪtɪ] *n., no pl.* Verantwortlichkeit, *die* (**to** gegenüber)

accountable [əˈkaʊntəbl] *adj.* verantwortlich; *(explicable)* erklärlich; **be ~ to sb.** jmdm. Rechenschaft schuldig sein; **be ~ for sth.** für etw. verantwortlich sein

accountancy [əˈkaʊntənsɪ] *n., no pl.* Buchhaltung, *die*

accountant [əˈkaʊntənt] *n.* [Bilanz]buchhalter, *der*/[Bilanz]buchhalterin, *die; see also* **chartered accountant**

accounting [əˈkaʊntɪŋ] *n.* **a)** *no pl.* *(Commerc.)* Buchführung, *die;* **b)** *(explanation)* **there's no ~ for it** das ist nicht zu erklären; **there's no ~ for taste[s]** über Geschmack läßt sich [nicht] streiten

acˈcount number *n.* Kontonummer, *die*

accredit [əˈkredɪt] *v. t.* **a)** *(vouch for)* bestätigen; **b)** *(send as representative)* **be ~ed to sb.** bei jmdm. akkreditiert sein

accredited [əˈkredɪtɪd] *adj.* anerkannt ‹*Schule, Anstalt, Buch, Regierung*›; akkreditiert ‹*Botschafter, diplomatisches Korps*›

accretion [əˈkriːʃn] *n.* **a)** *(combination)* Verschmelzung, *die;* **b)** *(growth)* Wachstum, *das;* *(of power)* Anwachsen, *das*

accrue [əˈkruː] *v. i.* ‹*Zinsen:*› auflaufen; **~ to sb.** ‹*Macht, Ansehen:*› jmdm. zuwachsen; ‹*Reichtümer, Einnahmen:*› jmdm. zufließen

accrued [əˈkruːd] *adj.* anfallend ‹*Ausgaben, Gewinne*›; aufgelaufen ‹*Schulden, Zinsen*›; entstanden ‹*Vorteile, Kontakte*›

accumulate [əˈkjuːmjʊleɪt] **1.** *v. t.* *(gather)* sammeln; machen, *(fachspr.)* akkumulieren ‹*Vermögen*›; *(in a pile)* zusammentragen; *(along the way)* einsammeln; *(produce)* einbringen ‹*Zinsen, Gewinne, Undank, Kritik*› (**for sb.** jmdm.); **it's amazing how much stuff you ~ in the space of a year** es ist erstaunlich, wieviel Zeug sich bei einem in einem Jahr so ansammelt. **2.** *v. i.* ‹*Menge, Staub:*› sich ansammeln; ‹*Schnee, Geld:*› sich anhäufen; ‹*Schlamm:*› sich absetzen

accumulation [əkjuːmjʊˈleɪʃn] *n.* [An]sammeln, *das;* *(being accumulated)* Anhäufung, *die;* *(growth)* Zuwachs, *der* (**of** an + *Dat.*); *(mass)* Menge, *die*

accumulator [əˈkjuːmjʊleɪtə(r)] *n.* **a)** *(Electr.)* Akkumulator, *der;* Akku, *der (ugs.);* Sammler, *der;* **b)** *(bet)* Kumulativwette, *die*

accuracy [ˈækjʊrəsɪ] *n.* Genauigkeit, *die*

accurate [ˈækjʊrət] *adj.* genau; akkurat *(geh.);* *(correct)* richtig; getreu ‹*Wiedergabe*›; **the description of the man turned out to be completely ~:** die Beschreibung des Mannes erwies sich als völlig korrekt; **is the clock ~?** geht die Uhr richtig *od.* genau?

accurately [ˈækjʊrətlɪ] *adv.* *(precisely)* genau; exakt; *(correctly)* richtig; korrekt; *(faithfully)* getreu; genau; **the landscape is represented ~:** die Landschaft ist naturgetreu dargestellt

accursed, *(arch.)* **accurst** [əˈkɜːst] *adj.* **a)** *(ill-fated)* verflucht; verwünscht; **b)** *(involving misery)* unselig; **c)** *(coll.: detestable)* verflixt *(ugs.);* verdammt *(ugs.)*

accusation [ækjuːˈzeɪʃn] *n.* **a)** *(accusing)* Anschuldigung, *die* (**of** gegen); Anklage, *die (Rechtsw.);* *(being accused)* Beschuldigung, *die;* **b)** *(charge)* Vorwurf, *der;* **make an ~/make ~s about sb./sth.** eine Anschuldigung/Anschuldigungen gegen jmdn./wegen etw. vorbringen

accusative [əˈkjuːzətɪv] *(Ling.)* **1.** *adj.* Akkusativ-; akkusativisch; **~ case** Akkusativ, *der.* **2.** *n.* Akkusativ, *der; see also* **absolute c**

accusatory [əˈkjuːzətərɪ] *adj.* anklagend ‹*Blick, Stimme, Schweigen*›

accuse [əˈkjuːz] *v. t.* *(charge)* beschuldigen; bezichtigen *(geh.);* *(indict)* anklagen; **~ sb. of cowardice** jmdm. Feigheit vorwerfen; **what are you accusing me of?** wessen beschuldigt *od.* bezichtigt ihr mich?; was werft ihr mir vor?; **the children were ~d of stealing apples** die Kinder wurden beschuldigt, Äpfel gestohlen zu haben; **~ sb. of theft/murder** jmdn. wegen Diebstahl[s]/Mord[es] anklagen; jmdn. des Diebstahls/Mordes anklagen *(geh.);* **the ~d** der/die Angeklagte/die Angeklagten

accuser [əˈkjuːzə(r)] *n.* Ankläger, *der*/Anklägerin, *die*

accusing [əˈkjuːzɪŋ] *adj.* anklagend; **point an ~ finger at sb.** *(lit. or fig.)* anklagend mit dem Finger auf jmdn. zeigen

accusingly [əˈkjuːzɪŋlɪ] *adv.* anklagend; *(reproachfully)* vorwurfsvoll

accustom [əˈkʌstəm] *v. t.* **~ sb./sth. to sth.** jmdn./etw. an etw. *(Akk.)* gewöhnen; **~ sb. to doing sth.** jmdm. daran gewöhnen, etw. zu tun; **grow/be ~ed to sth.** sich an etw. *(Akk.)* gewöhnen/an etw. *(Akk.)* gewöhnt sein; **I'm not ~ed to being called rude names** ich bin nicht gewohnt, daß man mich beschimpft

accustomed [əˈkʌstəmd] *attrib. adj.* gewohnt; üblich

ace [eɪs] **1.** *n.* **a)** *(Cards, Tennis)* As, *das;* **~ of trumps/diamonds** Trumpf-/Karoas, *das;* **b)** *(fig.)* **an ~ up one's sleeve** ein Trumpf in der Hand; **play one's ~:** seinen Trumpf ausspielen; **c)** *(champion, outstanding person)* As, *das;* *(pilot)* erfolgreicher Kampfflieger; **d)** *(hair's breadth)* **he was within an ~ of doing it/of winning** er hätte es um ein Haar getan/hätte um ein Haar gewonnen. **2.** *adj.* *(coll.)* klasse *(ugs.);* spitze *(ugs.)*

acerbic [əˈsɜːbɪk] *adj.* scharf ‹*Worte, Kritik, Zunge*›; rauh ‹*Umgangston, Temperament*›

acerbity [əˈsɜːbɪtɪ] *n., no pl. see* **acerbic:** Schärfe, *die;* Rauheit, *die*

acetate [ˈæsɪteɪt] *n.* *(Chem.)* Acetat, *das;* **~ fibre/silk** Acetatfaser/-seide, *die*

acetic [əˈsiːtɪk] *adj.* *(Chem.)* essigsauer; **~ acid** Essigsäure, *die*

acetone [ˈæsɪtəʊn] *n.* Aceton, *das*

acetylene [əˈsetɪliːn] *n.* Acetylen, *das*

ache [eɪk] **1.** *v. i.* **a)** schmerzen; weh tun; **whereabouts does your leg ~?** wo tut [dir] das Bein weh?; **I'm aching all over** mir tut alles weh; **her heart ~s with love** *(fig.)* das Herz tut ihr weh vor Liebe; **b)** *(fig.: long)* **~ for sb./sth.** sich nach jmdm./etw. verzehren; **~ to do sth.** darauf brennen, etw. zu tun. **2.** *n.* Schmerz, *der;* **~s and pains** Wehwehchen, *die*

achievable [əˈtʃiːvəbl] *adj.* *(accomplishable)* durchführbar; *(attainable)* erreichbar ‹*Ziel, Standard*›

achieve [əˈtʃiːv] *v. t.* zustande bringen; ausführen ‹*Aufgabe, Plan*›; erreichen ‹*Ziel, Standard, Absicht*›; herstellen, herbeiführen ‹*Frieden, Harmonie*›; erzielen ‹*Rekord, Leistung, Erfolg*›; erfüllen ‹*Zweck*›; finden ‹*Seelenfrieden*›; es bringen zu, erlangen ‹*Berühmtheit, Anerkennung*›; erlangen ‹*gutes Aussehen*›; **he ~d great things** er hat Großes geleistet; **he's ~d what he set out to do** er hat erreicht, was er sich *(Dat.)* vorgenommen hat; **he'll never ~ anything [in life]** er wird es [im Leben] nie zu etwas bringen

achievement [əˈtʃiːvmənt] *n.* **a)** *no pl. see* **achieve:** Zustandebringen, *das;* Ausführung, *die;* Erreichen, *das;* Herstellung, *die;* Herbeiführung, *die;* Erzielen, *das;* Erfüllung, *die;* Finden, *das;* Erlangen, *das;* **the task is impossible of ~:** die Aufgabe ist undurchführbar; **for these people ~ is measured in terms of money** für diese Leute wird Erfolg am Geld gemessen; **b)** *(thing accomplished)* Leistung, *die;* Errungenschaft, *die*

Achilles [əˈkɪliːz] *pr. n.* Achilles *(der); see also* **ˈheel 1 a; tendon**

achy [ˈeɪkɪ] *adj.* **feel ~:** Schmerzen haben; **I feel ~ all over** mir tut alles weh

acid [ˈæsɪd] **1.** *adj.* **a)** *(sour)* sauer; *(fig.: biting)* bissig; **b)** *(Chem., Agric., Geol.)* sauer ‹*Reaktion, Lösung, Boden, Gesteine*›. **2.** *n.* **a)** Säure, *die;* **b)** *(sl.: LSD)* Acid, *das*

acid: **~ drop** *n.* *(Brit.)* saurer *od.* saures Drops; **~-head** *n.* *(sl.)* Säurekopf, *der (salopp);* LSD-Schlucker, *der (salopp)*

acidic [əˈsɪdɪk] *adj.* **a)** *(sour)* säuerlich; *(fig.)* bissig; **b)** *(Chem., Agric., Geol.)* sauer

acidity [əˈsɪdɪtɪ] *n.* Säure, *die;* Acidität, *die (fachspr.);* Säuregrad, *der;* *(excessive)* Übersäuerung, *die;* *(fig.)* Bissigkeit, *die*

acidly [ˈæsɪdlɪ] *adv.* *(fig.)* bissig

acidosis [æsɪˈdəʊsɪs] *n., pl.* **acidoses** [æsɪˈdəʊsiːz] *(Med.)* Acidose, *die*

acid: **~ rain** *n.* saurer Regen; **~ test** *n.* Goldprobe, *die;* *(fig.)* Feuerprobe, *die*

acknowledge [əkˈnɒlɪdʒ] *v. t.* **a)** *(admit)* zugeben, eingestehen ‹*Tatsache, Notwendigkeit, Fehler, Schuld*›; *(accept)* sich bekennen zu ‹*einer Verantwortung, Pflicht, Schuld*›; anerkennen ‹*Schulden*›; *(take notice of)* grüßen ‹*Person*›; *(recognize)* anerkennen ‹*Autorität, Recht, Forderung, Notwendigkeit*›; **an ~d expert** ein anerkannter Fachmann; **he won't ~ himself beaten** er gibt sich nicht geschlagen; **~ sb./sth. [as** *or* to be] sth. jmdn./etw. als etw. anerkennen; **he was ~d [as] the world's greatest living poet** er galt als der Welt größter lebender Dichter; ~ **sb. [as] capable of doing sth.** jmdn. für fähig halten, etw. zu tun; **b)** *(express thanks for)* sich erkenntlich zeigen für ⟨*Dienste, Bemühungen, Gastfreundschaft*⟩; erwidern ⟨*Gruß*⟩; **c)** *(confirm receipt of)* bestätigen ⟨*Empfang, Bewerbung*⟩; ~ **a letter** den Empfang eines Briefes bestätigen

acknowledg[e]ment [ək'nɒlɪdʒmənt] *n.* **a)** *(admission of a fact, necessity, error, guilt)* Eingeständnis, *das; (acceptance of a responsibility, duty, debt)* Bekenntnis, *das* (**of** zu); *(recognition of authority, right, claim)* Anerkennung, *die;* **b)** *(thanks, appreciation) (of services, friendship)* Dank, *der* (**of** für); *(of greetings)* Erwiderung, *die;* **a grateful ~ of the services you have rendered to the community** eine dankbare Anerkennung Ihrer Verdienste um die Gemeinschaft; **c)** *(confirmation of receipt)* Bestätigung [des Empfangs/einer Bewerbung]; **letter of ~:** Bestätigungsschreiben, *das;* **d)** *(author's)* Danksagung, *die;* **'~s'** „Dank"

acme ['ækmɪ] *n.* Gipfel, *der;* Höhepunkt, *der*

acne ['æknɪ] *n. (Med.)* Akne, *die*

acolyte ['ækəlaɪt] *n.* **a)** *(Eccl.)* Ministrant, *der;* Meßdiener, *der;* **b)** *(fig.: follower)* Gefolgsmann, *der*

aconite ['ækənaɪt] *n. (Bot.)* Eisenhut, *der;* Sturmhut, *der;* Akonit, *das (fachspr.)*

acorn ['eɪkɔ:n] *n.* Eichel, *die*

acoustic [ə'ku:stɪk] *adj.* **a)** akustisch; **b)** *(Mus.)* ~ **guitar** Konzertgitarre, *die; (in pop, folk, etc.)* akustische Gitarre

acoustically [ə'ku:stɪkəlɪ] *adv.* akustisch

acoustics [ə'ku:stɪks] *n. pl.* **a)** *(properties)* Akustik, *die;* akustische Verhältnisse *Pl.;* **b)** *constr. as sing. (science)* Akustik, *die*

acquaint [ə'kweɪnt] *v.t.* ~ **sb./oneself with sth.** jmdn./sich mit etw. vertraut machen; **be ~ed with sb.** mit jmdm. bekannt sein

acquaintance [ə'kweɪntəns] *n.* **a)** *no pl.* Vertrautheit, *die;* ~ **with sb.** Bekanntschaft mit jmdm.; **a passing ~:** eine flüchtige Bekanntschaft; **make the ~ of sb.** jmds. Bekanntschaft machen; jmdn. kennenlernen; **b)** *(person)* Bekannte, *der/die; (collectively)* Bekannte *Pl.;* **a wide ~:** ein großer Bekanntenkreis; viele Bekannte

acquiesce [ækwɪ'es] *v.i.* einwilligen (**in** in + *Akk.*); *(under pressure)* sich fügen; **you must not ~ in everything [they say]** du mußt nicht allem zustimmen [,was sie sagen]

acquiescence [ækwɪ'esəns] *n.* **a)** *no pl. (acquiescing)* Einwilligung, *die* (**in** in + *Akk.*); *(state)* Ergebenheit, *die;* **b)** *(assent)* Zustimmung, *die*

acquiescent [ækwɪ'esənt] *adj.* fügsam; ergeben

acquire [ə'kwaɪə(r)] *v.t.* **a)** sich *(Dat.)* anschaffen ⟨*Gegenstände*⟩; *(gain)* erwerben ⟨*Land, Besitz, Wohlstand, Kenntnisse*⟩; sammeln ⟨*Erfahrungen*⟩; ernten ⟨*Lob*⟩; **b)** *(take on)* annehmen ⟨*Tonfall, Farbe, Aussehen, Gewohnheit*⟩; **last year the orchestra ~d a new leader** letztes Jahr erhielt das Orchester einen neuen Konzertmeister; **I have ~d a few unwanted pounds** ich habe leider ein paar Pfund[e] zugenommen; **~d characteristics** *(Biol.)* erworbene Eigenschaften; ~ **the habit of smoking** sich *(Dat.)* das Rauchen angewöhnen; ~ **a taste for sth.** Geschmack an etw. *(Dat.)* gewinnen; **this wine is an ~d taste** an diesen Wein muß man sich erst gewöhnen

acquirement [ə'kwaɪəmənt] *n. see* **acquisition a**

acquisition [ækwɪ'zɪʃn] *n.* **a)** *(of goods, wealth, land)* Erwerb, *der; (of knowledge)* Aneignung, *die;* Erwerb, *der; (of attitude, habit)* Annahme, *die;* **b)** *(thing)* Anschaffung, *die*

acquisitive [ə'kwɪzɪtɪv] *adj.* raffsüchtig; ~ **instinct** Sammeltrieb, *der;* **the ~ society** die nach Besitz strebende Gesellschaft

acquisitiveness [ə'kwɪzɪtɪvnɪs] *n., no pl.* Raffgier, *die*

acquit [ə'kwɪt] *v.t.,* **-tt- a)** *(Law)* freisprechen; ~ **sb. of sth.** jmdn. von etw. freisprechen; **he was ~ted on all three charges** er wurde in allen drei Anklagepunkten freigesprochen; **b)** *(discharge)* ~ **oneself of** erfüllen ⟨*Pflichten*⟩; ~ **oneself well** seine Sache gut machen; **if you ~ yourself well in the test** wenn du in der Prüfung gut abschneidest

acquittal [ə'kwɪtl] *n.* **a)** *(Law)* Freispruch, *der;* **b)** *(performance)* Erfüllung, *die;* Erledigung, *die*

acre ['eɪkə(r)] *n.* **a)** *(measure)* Acre, *der;* ≈ Morgen, *der;* **b)** *in pl. (land)* Grund und Boden, *der;* **broad ~s** weites Land

acreage ['eɪkərɪdʒ] *n.* **what is the ~ of your estate?** wieviel Land *od.* wie viele Morgen hat Ihr Gut?; **a farm of small ~:** ein Hof mit kleiner Anbaufläche

acrid ['ækrɪd] *adj.* beißend ⟨*Geruch, Dämpfe, Rauch*⟩; bitter ⟨*Geschmack*⟩

acrimonious [ækrɪ'məʊnɪəs] *adj.* bitter; aggressiv ⟨*Haltung*⟩; bissig ⟨*Bemerkung*⟩; erbittert ⟨*Streit, Diskussion*⟩

acrimoniously [ækrɪ'məʊnɪəslɪ] *adv.* bitter; erbittert ⟨*angreifen*⟩

acrimony ['ækrɪmənɪ] *n., no pl.* Bitterkeit, *die; (of attitude)* Aggressivität, *die; (of comment, criticism, etc.)* Bissigkeit, *die; (of argument, discussion)* Erbitterung, *die*

acrobat ['ækrəbæt] *n. (lit. or fig.)* Akrobat, *der*/Akrobatin, *die;* **a mental/intellectual ~:** ein Geistesakrobat

acrobatic [ækrə'bætɪk] *adj. (lit. or fig.)* akrobatisch

acrobatics [ækrə'bætɪks] *n., no pl.* Akrobatik, *die;* **mental ~:** Gehirnakrobatik, *die*

acronym ['ækrənɪm] *n.* Akronym, *das;* Initialwort, *das*

across [ə'krɒs] **1.** *adv.* **a)** *(to intersect)* [quer] darüber; **b)** *(from one side to the other)* darüber; *(in crossword puzzle)* waagerecht; *(from here to there)* hinüber; **go ~ to the enemy** *(fig.)* zum Feind übergehen; **measure** *or* **be 9 miles ~:** 9 Meilen breit sein; **c)** *(on the other side)* drüben; ~ **there/here** [da] drüben/hier drüben; ~ **from** gegenüber von; **just ~ from us there is a little shop** bei uns ist gleich gegenüber ein kleiner Laden; **d)** *with verbs (towards speaker)* herüber-; *(away from speaker)* hinüber-; **swim ~:** herüber-/hinüberschwimmen. **2.** *prep.* **a)** *(crossing)* über (+ *Akk.*); **right ~ the field** quer über das Feld; **a double yellow line ~ an entrance** eine gelbe Doppellinie vor einer Einfahrt; **b)** *(from one side to the other of)* über (+ *Akk.*); **we went ~ the Atlantic** wir überquerten den Atlantik; **protest meetings ~ Canada** Protestversammlungen in ganz Kanada; ~ **the board** pauschal; **an ~-the-board pay rise** eine pauschale *od.* generelle Lohnerhöhung; **c)** *(on the other side of)* auf der anderen Seite (+ *Gen.*); ~ **the ocean/river** jenseits des Meeres/Flusses

acrostic [ə'krɒstɪk] *n.* Akrostichon, *das*

acrylic [ə'krɪlɪk] **1.** *adj.* aus Acryl *nachgestellt;* Acryl-. **2.** *n.* Acryl, *das*

act [ækt] **1.** *n.* **a)** *(deed)* Tat, *die; (official action)* Akt, *der;* **an ~ of God** höhere Gewalt; **an ~ of mercy** ein Gnadenakt; **an ~ of kindness** ein Akt *od.* Zeichen der Güte; **an ~ of folly** eine Dummheit; **Acts [of the Apostles]** *(Bibl.) constr. as sing.* Apostelgeschichte, *die;* **b)** *(process)* **be in the ~ of doing sth.** gerade dabei sein, etw. zu tun; **he was caught in the ~ [of stealing]** er wurde [beim Stehlen] auf frischer Tat ertappt; **they were caught in the [very] ~:** sie wurden in flagranti ertappt; **c)** *(in a play)* Akt, *der;* Aufzug, *der (geh.);* **a five-~ play** ein Drama in fünf Akten; **a one-~ play** ein Einakter; **d)** *(theatre performance)* Akt, *der;* Nummer, *die; (performer)* Darsteller, *der*/Darstellerin, *die;* **the ~ consisted of four jugglers** die Truppe bestand aus vier Jongleuren; **e)** *(pretence)* Theater, *das;* Schau, *die (ugs.);* **it's all an ~ with her** sie tut nur so; **put on an ~** *(coll.)* eine Schau abziehen *(ugs.);* Theater spielen; **get into the** *or* **in on the ~** *(sl.)* in das Geschäft einsteigen; mitmischen *(ugs.);* **f)** *(decree)* Gesetz, *das;* **Act of Parliament** Parlamentsakte, *die.* **2.** *v.t.* **a)** *(perform)* spielen ⟨*Stück*⟩; **b)** *(play role of)* spielen ⟨*Rolle*⟩; **he's a famous film producer and really ~s the part** *(fig.)* er ist ein berühmter Filmproduzent und benimmt sich auch so; *see also* **¹fool 1 b. 3.** *v.i.* **a)** *(perform actions)* handeln; reagieren; ~ **upon the instructions you were given** folgen Sie den Anweisungen wie gegeben; ~ **[up]on sb.'s advice** jmds. Rat[schlag] *(Dat.)* folgen; ~ **quickly** schnell reagieren *od.* handeln; **b)** *(behave)* sich verhalten; *(function)* ~ **as sb.** als jmd. fungieren *od.* tätig sein; ~ **as sth.** als etw. dienen; **c)** *(perform special function)* ⟨*Person:*⟩ handeln; ⟨*Gerät, Ding:*⟩ funktionieren; ⟨*Substanz, Mittel:*⟩ wirken; ~ **for** *or* ~ **on behalf of sb.** für jmdn. *od.* in jmds. Auftrag tätig werden; jmdn. vertreten; ~ **to prevent sth.** ⟨*Vorrichtung, Gerät:*⟩ zur Verhütung von etw. dienen; **d)** *(perform play etc.; lit. or fig.)* spielen; schauspielern *(ugs.);* **she wants to ~ on stage/in films** sie will zum Theater/Film; **e)** *(have effect)* ~ **on sth.** auf etw. *(Akk.)* wirken *od.* einwirken

~ **'out** *v.t.* **a)** vorspielen, nachmachen ⟨*Bewegungen, Handlung*⟩; **b)** *(Psych.)* abreagieren ⟨*Spannung, Ärger*⟩

~ **'up** *v.i. (coll.)* Theater machen *(ugs.);* ⟨*Auto, Magen:*⟩ Zicken machen *(ugs.),* verrückt spielen *(salopp);* **the kids have been ~ing up like mad today** die Kinder haben heute total verrückt gespielt *(salopp)*

acting ['æktɪŋ] **1.** *adj. (temporary)* stellvertretend; *(in charge)* geschäftsführend; amtierend. **2.** *n., no pl. (Theatre etc.)* die Schauspielerei; **she's studying ~:** sie ist auf der Schauspielschule; **an ~ career** eine Karriere als Schauspieler; **she does a lot of ~ in her spare time** sie spielt in ihrer Freizeit viel Theater

action ['ækʃn] *n.* **a)** *(doing sth.)* Handeln, *das;* **what kind of ~ do you think is necessary?** welche Schritte *od.* Maßnahmen halten Sie für notwendig?; **his quick ~ saved the boy's life** sein schnelles Eingreifen rettete dem Jungen das Leben; **a man of ~:** ein Mann der Tat; **take ~:** Schritte *od.* etwas unternehmen; Maßnahmen ergreifen; **see sth. in ~:** etw. in Betrieb sehen; **put a plan into ~:** einen Plan in die Tat umsetzen; **come into ~:** in die Tat umgesetzt werden; **put sth. out of ~:** etw. außer Betrieb setzen; **be/be put out of ~:** außer Betrieb sein/gesetzt werden; **a film full of ~:** ein Film mit viel Handlung; **b)** *(effect)* **the ~ of salt on ice** die Wirkung von Salz auf Eis; **c)** *(act)* Tat, *die;* **your ~ was totally inappropriate in the circumstances** deine Reaktion war unter diesen Umständen ganz und gar unangemessen; **she is impulsive in her ~s** sie handelt sehr impulsiv; **d)** *(Theatre)* Handlung, *die;* Geschehen, *das;* **where the ~ is** *(sl.)* wo was los ist *(ugs.);* **hey, man, where's the ~?** *(sl.)* du, sag mal, wo ist hier was los? *(ugs.);* **get a piece of the ~** *(sl.)* mitmachen; **e)** *(legal process)* [Gerichts]verfahren, *das;* **bring an ~ against sb.** eine Klage *od.* ein Verfahren gegen jmdn. anstrengen; **f)** *(fighting)* Gefecht, *das;* Kampf, *der;* **he died in ~:** er ist [im Kampf] gefallen; **go into ~:** Kampfhandlungen aufnehmen; **we all went into ~** *(fig.)* wir machten uns alle an die Arbeit; **g)** *(movement)* Bewegung, *die; (mechanism)* Mechanismus, *der; (of piano, organ)* Mechanik, *die*

actionable ['ækʃənəbl] *adj.* [gerichtlich] verfolgbar *od.* strafbar

action: ~ committee, ~ group *ns.* [Eltern-/Bürger- *usw.*]initiative, *die;* **~ painting** *n.* Action-painting, *das;* abstrakter Expressionismus; **~ 'replay** *n.* Wiederholung [in Zeitlupe]; **~ stations** *n. pl. (Mil.; also fig.)* Stellung, *die;* **go to ~ stations** Stellung beziehen; **~ stations!** in die Stellungen!

activate ['æktɪveɪt] *v. t.* **a)** in Gang setzen ‹*Vorrichtung, Mechanismus*›; auslösen ‹*Mechanismus*›; **~d by concern for public morality** getrieben von der Sorge um die öffentliche Moral; **b)** *(Chem., Phys.)* aktivieren; **~d carbon** *or* **charcoal** Aktivkohle, *die*

activation [æktɪ'veɪʃn] *n.* Aktivierung, *die*

active ['æktɪv] *adj.* **a)** aktiv; wirksam ‹*Kraft, Mittel*›; praktisch ‹*Gebrauch, Versuch, Kenntnisse*›; tätig ‹*Vulkan*›; rege ‹*Verstand, Gesellschaft*›; **a very ~ child** ein sehr lebhaftes Kind; **take an ~ interest in sth.** reges Interesse an etw. *(Dat.)* zeigen; regen Anteil an etw. *(Dat.)* nehmen; **take an ~ part in sth.** sich aktiv an etw. *(Dat.)* beteiligen; **he's still ~ as an author** er arbeitet noch als Schriftsteller; **maintain an ~ knowledge of current affairs** im politischen Tagesgeschehen auf dem laufenden bleiben; **~ carbon** Aktivkohle, *die;* **on ~ service** *or (Amer.)* **duty** *(Mil.)* im aktiven Dienst; *see also* **'list 1 a; b)** *(Ling.)* aktiv[isch]; **~ voice** Aktiv, *das;* Tatform, *die*

actively ['æktɪvlɪ] *adv.* aktiv; **be ~ engaged in sth.** intensiv mit etw. beschäftigt sein; **be ~ interested in sth.** ein reges Interesse an etw. *(Dat.)* zeigen

activeness ['æktɪvnɪs] *n., no pl.* Aktivität, *die; (of mind)* Regsamkeit, *die; (of person)* Regheit, *die*

activist ['æktɪvɪst] *n.* Aktivist, *der/*Aktivistin, *die*

activity [æk'tɪvɪtɪ] *n.* **a)** *no pl.* Aktivität, *die;* **military ~:** militärischer Einsatz; **~ in the field of reform** reformerische Aktivitäten; **b)** *(diligence)* aktive Tätigkeit; rege [Mit]arbeit; **c)** *usu. in pl. (action)* Aktivität, *die; (occupation)* Betätigung, *die;* **she has so many social activities** sie ist gesellschaftlich so aktiv; **classroom activities** schulische Tätigkeiten; **outdoor activities** Betätigung an der frischen Luft; **a new sporting ~:** eine neue Sportart; **~ holiday** Aktivurlaub, *der;* **some activities offered by the youth centre** einige Veranstaltungen des Jugendzentrums

actor ['æktə(r)] *n.* **a)** Schauspieler, *der;* **b)** *see* **actress**

actress ['æktrɪs] *n.* Schauspielerin, *die*

actual ['æktʃʊəl] *adj.* **a)** *(real)* eigentlich, tatsächlich ‹*Lage, Gegebenheiten*›; wirklich ‹*Name, Gegenstand*›; konkret ‹*Beispiel*›; **what was the ~ time of his arrival?** wann genau ist er angekommen?; **what is the ~ position now?** wie ist eigentlich der Stand der Dinge?; **it's an ~ fact** das ist eine Tatsache *od.* ein Faktum; **in ~ fact** tatsächlich; **no ~ crime was committed** es wurde kein eigentliches Verbrechen begangen; **b)** *(current)* derzeitig; **the ~ situation** der gegenwärtige Stand der Dinge

actuality [æktʃʊ'ælɪtɪ] *n.* **a)** *(reality)* Wirklichkeit, *die;* Realität, *die;* **the ~ of the situation** die reale *od.* wirkliche Lage; **in ~:** in Wirklichkeit; **when her dream became an ~:** als ihr Traum Wirklichkeit wurde; **b)** *(realism)* Aktualität, *die*

actually ['æktʃʊəlɪ] *adv. (in fact)* eigentlich; *(by the way)* übrigens; *(believe it or not)* sogar; **~, to tell you the truth ...:** also, um die Wahrheit zu sagen, ...; **~, I must be going** ich muß jetzt wirklich gehen; **I'm ~ quite capable of looking after myself** im übrigen bin ich gut in der Lage, für mich selbst zu sorgen; **he ~ had the cheek to suggest ...:** er hatte tatsächlich die Unverfrorenheit, vorzuschlagen ...

actuarial [æktʃʊ'eərɪəl] *adj.* versicherungsmathematisch

actuary ['æktʃʊərɪ] *n.* Versicherungsmathematiker, *der;* Aktuar, *der*

actuate ['æktʃʊeɪt] *v. t. (activate)* antreiben ‹*Maschine*›; in Bewegung setzen ‹*Vorgang*›; auslösen ‹*Mechanismus, Reaktion*›

actuation [æktʃʊ'eɪʃn] *n. (of machine)* Antrieb, *der; (of mechanism)* Auslösen, *das*

acumen ['ækjʊmen] *n.* Scharfsinn, *der;* **business ~:** Geschäftssinn, *der;* **political ~:** politische Klugheit

acupuncture ['ækjʊpʌnktʃə(r)] *n. (Med.)* Akupunktur, *die*

acute [ə'kju:t] *adj.,* **~r** [ə'kju:tə(r)], **~st** [ə'kju:tɪst] **a)** *(penetrating)* scharf ‹*Kritik*›; genau ‹*Beobachtung*›; wach ‹*Bewußtsein*›; **b)** *(Geom.)* **~ angle** spitzer Winkel; **c)** *(Med.)* akut ‹*Krankheit, Stadium*›; **d)** *(critical)* akut ‹*Gefahr, Knappheit, Situation, Mangel*›; **e)** *(keen)* fein ‹*Geruchssinn*›; heftig ‹*Schmerz*›; **f)** *(Ling.)* **~ accent** Akut, *der;* **g)** *(sharp)* scharf ‹*Schneide*›; fein ‹*Spitze*›

acutely [ə'kju:tlɪ] *adv.* **a)** *(penetratingly)* genau[estens] ‹*sich bewußt sein, durchdenken, beobachten*›; **b)** *(Med.)* akut; **he is ~ ill with pneumonia** er hat eine akute Lungenentzündung; **c)** *(critically)* äußerst; *(keenly)* äußerst; überaus; intensiv ‹*fühlen*›

acuteness [ə'kju:tnɪs] *n., no pl.* **a)** *(of criticism)* Schärfe, *die; (of observation)* Genauigkeit, *die; (of understanding)* Scharfsinn, *der;* **b)** *(Med.)* Akutheit, *die;* **c)** *(of pain, sensation)* Heftigkeit, *die;* **d)** *(of sense, hearing, etc.)* Feinheit, *die;* **e)** *(of cutting edge)* Schärfe, *die; (of point)* Feinheit, *die*

AD *abbr.* **Anno Domini** n. Chr.; *(bes. DDR)* u. Z.

ad [æd] *n. (coll.)* Annonce, *die;* Inserat, *das;* **small ad** Kleinanzeige, *die;* **TV ads** Werbespots im Fernsehen

adage ['ædɪdʒ] *n.* Sprichwort, *das*

adagio [ə'dɑ:dʒɪəʊ] *(Mus.)* **1.** *adv.* adagio. **2.** *adj.* Adagio-; langsam; ruhig. **3.** *n., pl.* **~s** Adagio, *das*

Adam ['ædəm] *pr. n. (first man)* Adam *(der);* **he doesn't know me from ~:** er hat keine Ahnung, wer ich bin

adamant ['ædəmənt] *adj.* unnachgiebig; **be ~ that ...:** darauf bestehen, daß ...

Adam's 'apple *n.* Adamsapfel, *der*

adapt [ə'dæpt] **1.** *v. t.* **a)** *(adjust)* anpassen **(to** *Dat.***)**; umbauen ‹*Auto*›; variieren ‹*Frisur, Kleidung*›; umstellen ‹*Maschine*› **(to** auf + *Akk.***)**; **this room can easily be ~ed to individual tastes** dieses Zimmer läßt sich leicht auf den persönlichen Geschmack abstimmen; **your eyes will quickly ~ themselves to the dark** deine Augen werden sich schnell an die Dunkelheit gewöhnen; **~ oneself to sth.** sich an etw. *(Akk.)* gewöhnen; **this furnace can be ~ed to take coal or oil** dieser Ofen läßt sich auf Kohle oder Öl einstellen; **be ~ed for doing sth.** darauf eingestellt sein, etw. zu tun; **b)** *(modify)* adaptieren, bearbeiten ‹*Text, Theaterstück*›; **~ed for TV by ...:** für das Fernsehen bearbeitet von ...; **~ sth. from sth.** etw. nach etw. bearbeiten. **2.** *v. i.* **a)** ‹*Tier, Auge:*› sich anpassen **(to** an + *Akk.***)**; **b)** *(to surroundings, circumstances)* sich gewöhnen **(to** an + *Akk.***)**

adaptability [ədæptə'bɪlɪtɪ] *n., no pl. (to way of life or environment)* Anpassungsfähigkeit, *die* **(to** *or* **for** an + *Akk.***)**

adaptable [ə'dæptəbl] *adj.* anpassungsfähig; vielseitig ‹*Maschine*›; flexibel ‹*Planung*›; **be ~ to** *or* **for sth.** an etw. *(Akk.)* angepaßt werden können

adaptation [ædəp'teɪʃn] *n.* **a)** *no pl.* Anpassung, *die* **(to** an + *Akk.***)**; *(of garment)* Veränderung, *die; (of system, machine)* Umstellung, *die* **(to** auf + *Akk.***)**; **b)** *(version)* Adap[ta]tion, *die; (of story, text)* Bearbeitung, *die;* **c)** *(Biol.)* Adaptation, *die;* Anpassung, *die*

adapter, adaptor [ə'dæptə(r)] *n. (device)* Adapter, *der;* **a four-socket ~:** eine Vierfachsteckdose

ADC *abbr. (Mil.)* **aide-de-camp**

add [æd] **1.** *v. t.* hinzufügen **(to** *Dat.***)**; hinzufügen, anfügen ‹*weitere Worte*›; beisteuern ‹*Ideen, Vorschläge*› **(to** zu**)**; dazusetzen ‹*Namen, Zahlen*›; **~ two and two** zwei und zwei zusammenzählen; **~ two numbers together** zwei Zahlen addieren; **~ the flour to the liquid** geben Sie das Mehl in die Flüssigkeit; **we have ~ed a number of new books to our collection** wir haben unsere Sammlung um ein paar neue Bücher erweitert. **2.** *v. i.* **~ to** vergrößern ‹*Schwierigkeiten, Einkommen*›; verbessern ‹*Ruf*›; **~ [together] to give** *or* **make the desired amount** zusammen den gewünschten Betrag ergeben

~ 'up 1. *v. i.* **a)** **these figures ~ up to** *or* **make 30 altogether** diese Zahlen ergeben zusammen[gezählt] 30; **these things ~/it ~s up** *(fig. coll.)* all diese Dinge summieren sich/das summiert sich alles; **~ up to sth.** *(fig.)* auf etw. hinauslaufen; **b)** *(make sense)* einen Sinn ergeben. **2.** *v. t.* zusammenzählen

added ['ædɪd] *attrib. adj.* zusätzlich; **~ to this** außerdem; obendrein

addendum [ə'dendəm] *n., pl.* **addenda** [ə'dendə] *(thing to be added)* Nachtrag, *der;* Addendum, *das (veralt.); (addition)* Zusatz, *der; in pl. (in book etc.)* Addenda *Pl.*

adder ['ædə(r)] *n. (Zool.)* Viper, *die*

addict 1. [ə'dɪkt] *v. t.* **be ~ed** süchtig sein; **become ~ed [to sth.]** [nach etw.] süchtig werden; **be ~ed to alcohol/smoking/drugs** alkohol-/nikotin-/drogensüchtig sein. **2.** ['ædɪkt] *n.* Süchtige, *der/die; (fig. coll.)* [begeisterte] Anhänger, *der/*Anhängerin, *die;* **become an ~:** süchtig werden; **drug/heroin ~s** Drogen-/Heroinsüchtige *Pl.;* **a TV ~** *(fig. coll.)* ein Fernsehnarr

addiction [ə'dɪkʃn] *n.* Sucht, *die; (fig. coll.)* Fimmel, *der (ugs.);* **an ~ to sth.** die Sucht nach etw.; **~ to heroin** Heroinsucht, *die*

addictive [ə'dɪktɪv] *adj.* **be ~:** süchtig machen; *(fig. coll.)* zu einer Sucht werden

'adding machine *n.* Rechenmaschine, *die*

addition [ə'dɪʃn] *n.* **a)** *no pl.* Hinzufügen, *das; (of ingredient)* Dazugeben, *das; (adding up)* Addieren, *das; (process)* Addition, *die;* **in ~:** außerdem; **in ~ to** zusätzlich zu; **b)** *(thing added)* Ergänzung, *die* **(to** zu**)**; **we are expecting a new ~ to our family** wir erwarten Familienzuwachs

additional [ə'dɪʃənl] *adj.* zusätzlich; **~ details** weitere Einzelheiten

additionally [ə'dɪʃənəlɪ] *adv.* außerdem

additive ['ædɪtɪv] **1.** *n.* Zusatz, *der.* **2.** *adj.* zusätzlich; *(to be added)* weiter

addled ['ædld] *adj.* **a)** *(rotten)* verdorben; faul; **b)** *(muddled)* verwirrt ‹*Gedanken*›; benebelt ‹*Kopf*›

address [ə'dres] **1.** *v. t.* **a)** **~ sth. to sb./sth.** etw. an jmdn./etw. richten; **you must ~ your complaint to ...:** richten Sie Ihre Beschwerde an (+ *Akk.*) ...; **~ oneself to sb./sth.** sich an jmdn./etw. wenden; **b)** *(mark with ~)* adressieren **(to** an + *Akk.***)**; mit Anschrift versehen; **c)** *(speak to)* anreden ‹*Person*›; sprechen zu ‹*Zuhörern*›; **~ sb. as sth.** jmdn. mit etw. *od.* als etw. anreden; **d)** *(give attention to)* angehen ‹*Problem*›; **e)** *(apply)* **~ oneself to sth.** sich zu etw. anschicken. **2.** *n.* **a)** *(on letter or envelope)* Adresse, *die;* Anschrift, *die; (place of residence)* Wohnsitz, *der;* **of no fixed ~:** ohne festen Wohnsitz; **b)** *(discourse)* Ansprache, *die;* Rede, *die;* **c)** *(skill)* Gewandtheit, *die;* **d)** *in pl. (courteous approach)* Werben, *das;* **pay one's ~es to sb.** jmdm. den Hof machen; **e)** *(Computing)* Adresse, *die*

ad'dress-book *n.* Adressenbüchlein, *das*

addressee [ædre'si:] *n.* Adressat, *der/*Adressatin, *die;* Empfänger, *der/*Empfängerin, *die*

ad'dress-label *n.* Adressenaufkleber, *der*

adduce [ə'dju:s] *v.t.* anführen

adenoids ['ædɪnɔɪdz] *n. pl. (Med.)* Rachenmandel- *od.* Nasenpolypen *Pl.;* Rachenmandelwucherungen *Pl.*

adept ['ædept, ə'dept] **1.** *adj.* geschickt **(in, at** in + *Dat.*). **2.** *n.* Kenner, *der*/Kennerin, *die;* Meister, *der*/Meisterin, *die*

adequacy ['ædɪkwəsɪ] *n., no pl.* **a)** *(sufficiency)* Adäquatheit, *die;* Angemessenheit, *die;* **b)** *(suitability)* Eignung, *die;* **c)** *(bare sufficiency)* Zulänglichkeit, *die;* **d)** *(proportionateness)* **the ~ of sth. to sth.** die Angemessenheit einer Sache für etw.

adequate ['ædɪkwət] *adj.* **a)** *(sufficient)* ausreichend; angemessen ⟨*Bezahlung, Wohnraum*⟩; **b)** *(barely sufficient)* hinreichend; zulänglich; **my grant is ~ and no more** mein Stipendium reicht gerade so aus; **c)** *(suitable)* angemessen; **he couldn't find ~ words** ihm fehlten die richtigen *od.* passenden Worte; **d)** *(proportionate)* **~ [to sth.]** einer Sache *(Dat.)* angemessen

adequately ['ædɪkwətlɪ] *adv.* **a)** *(sufficiently)* ausreichend; **are you ~ prepared for your exam?** haben Sie sich auf die Prüfung in ausreichender Weise vorbereitet?; **these children are not ~ nourished** diese Kinder sind unterernährt; **b)** *(barely sufficiently)* hinreichend; zulänglich; **c)** *(suitably)* angemessen ⟨*gekleidet, qualifiziert usw.*⟩

adhere [əd'hɪə(r)] *v.i.* **a)** *(stick)* haften, *(by glue)* kleben **(to** an + *Dat.*); **~ [to each other]** ⟨*zwei Dinge:*⟩ zusammenkleben; **b)** *(give support)* **~ to sth./sb.** an jmdm./einer Sache festhalten; **~ to a party/policy** eine Partei/Politik unterstützen; **c)** *(keep)* **~ to** festhalten an (+ *Dat.*) ⟨*Programm, Brauch, Gewohnheit*⟩; sich halten an (+ *Akk.*) ⟨*Abmachung, Versprechen, Regel*⟩; **we must ~ strictly to the schedule** wir müssen uns genau an den Zeitplan halten

adherence [əd'hɪərəns] *n., no pl.* **a)** *(to party, leader, policy)* Unterstützung, *die* **(to** *Gen.*); **b)** *(to programme, agreement, promise, schedule)* Einhalten, *das* **(to** *Gen.*); *(to decision, tradition, principle)* Festhalten, *das* **(to** an + *Dat.*); *(to rule)* Befolgen, *das* **(to** *Gen.*)

adherent [əd'hɪərənt] *n.* Anhänger, *der*/Anhängerin, *die*

adhesion [əd'hi:ʒn] *n.* **a)** *no pl. (sticking)* Haften, *das* **(to** an + *Dat.*); *(by glue)* Kleben, *das* **(to** an + *Dat.*); **b)** *no pl. (support)* Unterstützung, *die* **(to** *Gen.*); *(to agreement)* Einhalten, *das* **(to** *Gen.*)

adhesive [əd'hi:sɪv] **1.** *adj. (adherent)* klebrig; gummiert ⟨*Briefmarke, Umschlag*⟩; Klebe⟨*band, -schicht*⟩; **be ~:** kleben/gummiert sein; **~ plaster** Heftpflaster, *das; see also* **tape 1 a. 2.** *n.* Klebstoff, *der;* Klebemittel, *das*

ad hoc [æd 'hɒk] **1.** *adv.* ad hoc. **2.** *adj.* Ad-hoc-

adieu [ə'dju:] **1.** *int.* adieu; leb/lebt wohl; **we bid** *or* **wish you ~:** leb/lebt wohl. **2.** *n., pl.* **~s** *or* **~x** [ə'dju:z] Adieu *od.* Lebewohl, *das*

ad infinitum [æd ɪnfɪ'naɪtəm] *adv.* ad infinitum *(geh.);* ohne Ende

adipose ['ædɪpəʊs] *adj.* adipös *(fachspr.);* verfettet; **~ tissue** Fettgewebe, *das*

adjacent [ə'dʒeɪsənt] *adj.* angrenzend; Neben-; **~ to** *(position)* neben (+ *Dat.*); *(direction)* neben (+ *Akk.*); **he sat in the ~ room** er saß im Zimmer nebenan

adjectival [ædʒɪk'taɪvəl] *adj. (Ling.)* adjektivisch; **~ endings** Adjektivendungen

adjective ['ædʒɪktɪv] *n. (Ling.)* Adjektiv, *das;* Eigenschaftswort, *das*

adjoin [ə'dʒɔɪn] **1.** *v.t.* grenzen an (+ *Akk.*); **the room ~ing ours** das Zimmer neben unserem. **2.** *v.i.* aneinandergrenzen; nebeneinanderliegen; **an ~ing field** ein angrenzendes *od.* benachbartes Feld; **in the ~ing room** im Zimmer daneben *od.* nebenan

adjourn [ə'dʒɜ:n] **1.** *v.t. (break off)* unterbrechen; *(put off)* aufschieben. **2.** *v.i. (suspend proceedings)* sich vertagen; **let's ~ to the sitting-room/***(coll.)* **pub** begeben wir uns ins Wohnzimmer/*(ugs.)* in die Kneipe

adjournment [ə'dʒɜ:nmənt] *n. (suspending) (of court)* Vertagung, *die; (of meeting)* Unterbrechung, *die*

adjudge [ə'dʒʌdʒ] *v.t. (pronounce)* **~ sb./sth. [to be] sth.** jmdn./etw. für etw. erklären *od.* befinden

adjudicate [ə'dʒu:dɪkeɪt] *v.i. (in court, tribunal)* als Richter tätig sein; *(in contest)* Preisrichter sein **(at** bei, in + *Dat.*)

adjudication [ədʒu:dɪ'keɪʃn] *n.* **a)** *(judging)* Beurteilung, *die;* **expert ~:** Expertenmeinung, *die;* **b)** *(decision)* Entscheidung, *die*

adjudicator [ə'dʒu:dɪkeɪtə(r)] *n.* Schiedsrichter, *der*/Schiedsrichterin, *die; (in contest)* Preisrichter, *der*/Preisrichterin, *die*

adjunct ['ædʒʌŋkt] *n.* **a)** Anhängsel, *das; (effect)* Neben- *od.* Begleiterscheinung, *die;* **b)** *(Ling.)* Adjunkt, *das*

adjuration [ædʒʊə'reɪʃn] *n.* [inständige] Bitte; Beschwörung, *die*

adjure [ə'dʒʊə(r)] *v.t.* inständig bitten; beschwören

adjust [ə'dʒʌst] **1.** *v.t.* **a)** richtig [an]ordnen ⟨*Gegenstände, Gliederung*⟩; ändern ⟨*Gegebenheiten*⟩; zurechtmachen ⟨*Frisur*⟩; zurechtrücken ⟨*Hut, Krawatte*⟩; *(regulate)* regulieren, regeln ⟨*Geschwindigkeit, Höhe usw.*⟩; [richtig] einstellen ⟨*Gerät, Mechanismus, Bremsen, Vergaser, Motor, Zündung*⟩; *(adapt)* entsprechend ändern ⟨*Plan, Bedingungen*⟩; angleichen ⟨*Gehalt, Lohn, Zinsen*⟩; **~ sth. [to sth.]** etw. [an etw. *(Akk.)*] anpassen *od.* [auf etw. *(Akk.)*] einstellen; **please ~ your watches** bitte stellen Sie Ihre Uhren richtig; **'do not ~ your set'** „Störung"; **b)** *(assess)* berechnen ⟨*Schaden*⟩; regulieren ⟨*Versicherungsansprüche*⟩; eichen ⟨*Maß, Gewicht*⟩; **such discrepancies can be ~ed** solche Unstimmigkeiten können ausgeglichen *od.* beigelegt werden. **2.** *v.i.* **~ [to sth.]** sich [an etw. *(Akk.)*] gewöhnen *od.* anpassen; ⟨*Gerät, Maschine usw.:*⟩ sich [auf etw. *(Akk.)*] einstellen lassen; **the eye soon ~s to the dark** das Auge gewöhnt sich schnell an die Dunkelheit; **~ to new conditions/a requirement** sich auf neue Verhältnisse/eine Forderung einstellen

adjustable [ə'dʒʌstəbl] *adj.* einstellbar **(to** auf + *Akk.*); verstellbar, justierbar ⟨*Gerät*⟩; regulierbar ⟨*Temperatur*⟩

adjustment [ə'dʒʌstmənt] *n.* **a)** *(of layout, plan)* Ordnung, *die; (of things)* Anordnung, *die; (of device, engine, machine)* Einstellung, *die; (of hair, clothing)* Zurechtmachen, *das; (to situation, life-style)* Anpassung, *die* **(to** an + *Akk.*); *(of eye)* Adaption, *die;* Gewöhnung, *die;* **some ~s are necessary on your car engine** an Ihrem Motor muß einiges neu *od.* richtig eingestellt werden; **she made a few minor ~s to her manuscript** sie brachte an ihrem Manuskript ein paar kleinere Korrekturen an; **b)** *(of insurance claim, damage)* Schadensfestsetzung, *die;* **c)** *(settlement) (of claims or damages)* Regulierung, *die;* **d)** *(device)* Einstellvorrichtung, *die*

adjutant ['ædʒʊtənt] *n.* **a)** *(Mil.)* Adjutant, *der;* **b)** *(Ornith.)* **~ [bird]** Indischer Marabu

ad lib [æd 'lɪb] *adv.* zwanglos, nach Belieben

ad-lib 1. *adj. (unprepared, improvised)* Stegreif-, improvisiert ⟨*Rede, Vortrag*⟩; **give an ~ rendering** improvisieren. **2.** *v.i.,* **-bb-** *(coll.)* improvisieren

Adm. *abbr.* **admiral** Adm.

'adman *n.* Werbe-, Reklamefachmann, *der*

admin ['ædmɪn] *n. (coll.)* Verwaltung, *die;* **an ~ problem** ein Verwaltungsproblem

administer [æd'mɪnɪstə(r)] *v.t.* **a)** *(manage)* verwalten; führen ⟨*Geschäfte, Regierung*⟩; regieren ⟨*Land*⟩; **b)** *(give, apply)* spenden ⟨*Trost*⟩; leisten, gewähren ⟨*Hilfe, Unterstützung*⟩; austeilen, verabreichen ⟨*Schläge, Prügel*⟩; verabreichen, geben ⟨*Medikamente*⟩; spenden, geben ⟨*Sakramente*⟩; anwenden ⟨*Disziplinierungsmaßnahmen*⟩; **~ justice [to sb.]** [über jmdn.] Recht sprechen; **~ punishment to sb.** jmdn. bestrafen; **~ an oath to sb.** jmdn. vereidigen; jmdm. einen Eid abnehmen; **~ treatment to sb.** jmdn. behandeln

administration [ədmɪnɪ'streɪʃn] *n.* **a)** *(management, managing)* Verwaltung, *die;* **b)** *(giving, applying) (of sacraments)* Spenden, *das;* Geben, *das; (of discipline)* Anwendung, *die; (of medicine)* Verabreichung, *die; (of aid, relief)* Gewährung, *die;* **~ of justice** Rechtspflege, *die;* **~ of an oath** Eidesabnahme, *die;* **c)** *(ministry, government)* Regierung, *die; (Amer.: President's period of office)* Amtszeit, *die;* **d)** *(Law)* **~ of the estate** Nachlaßverwaltung, *die;* Vermögensverwaltung, *die*

administrative [əd'mɪnɪstrətɪv] *adj.* Verwaltungs-; administrativ ⟨*Angelegenheit, Geschick, Fähigkeit*⟩; **~ work** Verwaltungsarbeit, *die;* **an ~ job** ein Verwaltungsposten

administrator [əd'mɪnɪstreɪtə(r)] *n.* **a)** *(manager)* Administrator, *der;* Verwalter, *der; (sb. capable of organizing)* Organisator, *der;* **b)** *(performing official duties)* Verwaltungsbeamte/-angestellte, *der;* **c)** *(of deceased person's estate)* Verwalter, *der;* Testamentsvollstrecker, *der*

admirable ['ædmərəbl] *adj.* bewundernswert; erstaunlich; *(excellent)* vortrefflich; ausgezeichnet

admirably ['ædmərəblɪ] *adv.* bewundernswert; erstaunlich; *(excellently)* vortrefflich

admiral ['ædmərəl] *n.* **a)** Admiral, *der;* **A~ of the Fleet** *(Brit.)* Großadmiral, *der;* **b)** *(butterfly)* **red ~:** Admiral, *der*

Admiralty ['ædmərəltɪ] *n.* **~ [Board]** *britisches Marineministerium*

admiration [ædmə'reɪʃn] *n., no pl.* **a)** Bewunderung, *die* **(of, for** für); **b)** *(object of ~)* **be the ~ of sb.** von jmdm. bewundert werden

admire [əd'maɪə(r)] *v.t.* bewundern **(for** wegen)

admirer [əd'maɪərə(r)] *n.* Bewunderer, *der*/Bewunderin, *die; (suitor)* Verehrer, *der*/Verehrerin, *die*

admiring [əd'maɪərɪŋ] *adj.*, **admiringly** [əd'maɪərɪŋlɪ] *adv.* bewundernd

admissibility [ədmɪsɪ'bɪlɪtɪ] *n., no pl.* Zulässigkeit, *die*

admissible [əd'mɪsɪbl] *adj.* **a)** akzeptabel ⟨*Plan, Vorschlag*⟩; erlaubt, zulässig ⟨*Abweichung, Schreibung*⟩; **b)** *(Law)* zulässig; **that is not ~ evidence** das ist kein vor Gericht zugelassener Beweis *od.* zugelassenes Beweisstück

admission [əd'mɪʃn] *n.* **a)** *(entry)* Zutritt, *der;* **~ to university** Zulassung [zum Studium] an einer Universität; **~ costs** *or* **is 50p** der Eintritt kostet 50 Pence; **charge for ~:** Eintrittspreis, *der;* **b)** *(charge)* Eintritt, *der;* **c)** *(confession)* Eingeständnis, *das* **(of, to** *Gen.*); **by** *or* **on one's own ~:** nach eigenem Eingeständnis

admission: ~ fee, ~ price *ns.* Eintrittspreis, *der;* **~ money** *n.* Eintrittsgeld, *das;* **~ ticket** *n.* Eintrittskarte, *die*

admit [əd'mɪt] **1.** *v.t.,* **-tt- a)** *(let in)* hinein-/hereinlassen; **persons under the age of 16 not ~ted** kein Zutritt für Jugendliche unter 16 Jahren; **~ sb. to a school/club** jmdn. in eine Schule/einen Klub aufnehmen; **'this ticket ~s two'** „Eintrittskarte für zwei Personen"; **b)** *(accept as valid)* **if we ~ that argument/evidence** wenn wir davon ausgehen, daß dieses Argument zutrifft/daß diese Beweise erlaubt sind; **c)** *(acknowledge)* zugeben; eingestehen; **~ sth. to be true** zugeben *od.* eingestehen, daß etw. wahr ist; ~ **to being guilty/drunk** zugeben, schuldig/betrunken zu sein; **d)** *(have room for)* Platz bieten (+ *Dat.*). **2.** *v.i.*, **-tt-:** ~ **of sth.** etw. zulassen *od.* erlauben

admittance [əd'mɪtəns] *n.* Zutritt, *der;* **no ~ [except on business]** Zutritt [für Unbefugte] verboten

admittedly [əd'mɪtɪdlɪ] *adv.* zugegeben[ermaßen]; ~ **he is very young** zugegeben, er ist sehr jung

admixture [əd'mɪkstʃə(r)] *n.* **a)** *no pl. (mixing)* [Ver]mischen, *das;* Vermengen, *das;* **b)** *(ingredient)* Zusatz, *der;* Beimischung, *die*

admonish [əd'mɒnɪʃ] *v.t.* ermahnen; *(reproach)* ermahnen; tadeln

admonishment [əd'mɒnɪʃmənt], **admonition** [ædmə'nɪʃn] *ns.* Ermahnung, *die; (reproach)* Ermahnung, *die;* Tadel, *der*

ad nauseam [æd 'nɔ:sɪæm, æd 'nɔ:zɪæm] *adv.* bis zum Überdruß

ado [ə'du:] *n., no pl., no art.* **without more or with no further ~:** ohne weiteres Aufhebens

adobe [ə'dəʊbɪ, ə'dəʊb] *n. (brick)* Adobe, *der;* ungebrannter Lehmziegel

adolescence [ædə'lesns] *n., no art.* die Zeit des Erwachsenwerdens; die Adoleszenz *(Med.)*

adolescent [ædə'lesnt] **1.** *n.* Heranwachsende, *der/die.* **2.** *adj.* heranwachsend ‹*Person*›; pubertär ‹*Benehmen*›

adopt [ə'dɒpt] *v.t.* **a)** adoptieren; aufnehmen ‹*Tier*›; **we ~ed a refugee family** wir übernahmen die Patenschaft für eine Flüchtlingsfamilie; **b)** *(take over)* annehmen, übernehmen ‹*Kultur, Sitte*›; annehmen ‹*Glaube, Religion*›; **c)** *(take up)* übernehmen, sich aneignen ‹*Methode*›; einnehmen ‹*Standpunkt, Haltung*›; **that's not the right attitude to ~:** das ist nicht die richtige Einstellung; **d)** *(approve)* annehmen; billigen; **the meeting ~ed the motion** die Versammlung stimmte dem Antrag zu

adoption [ə'dɒpʃn] *n.* **a)** Adoption, *die;* **b)** *(taking over) (of culture, custom)* Annahme, *die;* Übernahme, *die; (of belief)* Annahme, *die;* **c)** *(taking up) (of method)* Aneignung, *die;* Übernahme, *die; (of point of view)* Einnahme, *die;* **d)** *(approval)* Annahme, *die*

adoptive [ə'dɒptɪv] *adj.* adoptiert; ~ **son/mother** Adoptivsohn, *der*/-mutter, *die*

adorable [ə'dɔ:rəbl] *adj.*, **adorably** [ə'dɔ:rəblɪ] *adv.* bezaubernd; hinreißend

adoration [ædə'reɪʃn] *n.* **a)** Verehrung, *die;* **b)** *(worship of gods etc.)* Anbetung, *die*

adore [ə'dɔ:(r)] *v.t.* **a)** innig *od.* über alles lieben; **his adoring girlfriend/fans** seine schmachtende Freundin/schmachtenden Fans; **b)** *(coll.: like greatly)* ~ **sth.** für etwas schwärmen; ~ **doing sth.** etw. sehr, sehr gern *od. (ugs.)* für sein Leben gern tun; **c)** *(worship)* anbeten ‹*Götter usw.*›

adorn [ə'dɔ:n] *v.t.* schmücken; ~ **oneself** sich schön machen

adornment [ə'dɔ:nmənt] *n.* **a)** *no pl.* Verschönerung, *die;* **b)** *(ornament)* Verzierung, *die;* ~**s** Schmuck, *der*

adrenal [ə'dri:nl] *(Anat.)* **1.** *adj.* ~ **glands** Nebennieren *Pl.* **2.** *n.* Nebenniere, *die*

adrenalin, *(Amer.* **P)** [ə'drenəlɪn] *n. (Physiol., Med.)* Adrenalin, *das*

Adriatic [eɪdrɪ'ætɪk] *pr. n.* ~ **[Sea]** Adriatisches Meer; Adria, *die*

adrift [ə'drɪft] *pred. adj.* **a) be ~:** treiben; **cut a boat ~:** die Halteleine eines Bootes durchschneiden; **b)** *(fig.: exposed)* verloren; preisgegeben; **turn sb. ~:** jmdn. sich *(Dat.)* selbst überlassen

adroit [ə'drɔɪt] *adj.* geschickt; gewandt; **be ~ at sth./doing sth.** gewandt *od.* geschickt in etw. *(Dat.)* sein

adroitly [ə'drɔɪtlɪ] *adv.* geschickt; gewandt

adroitness [ə'drɔɪtnɪs] *n., no pl.* Geschicklichkeit, *die;* Gewandtheit, *die*

adulation [ædjʊ'leɪʃn] *n., no pl. (praise)* Beweihräucherung, *die; (admiration of person)* Vergötterung, *die*

adult ['ædʌlt, ə'dʌlt] **1.** *adj.* erwachsen ‹*Person*›; reif ‹*Verhalten*›; ausgewachsen ‹*Tier, Pflanze*›; **this play is suitable only for ~ audiences** dieses Stück ist nur für Erwachsene geeignet; **behave in an ~ manner** sich wie ein Erwachsener benehmen. **2.** *n.* Erwachsene, *der/die;* **'~s only'** „Nur für Erwachsene"; ~ **education** Erwachsenenbildung, *die*

adulterate [ə'dʌltəreɪt] *v.t.* verunreinigen; panschen ‹*Wein, Milch*›

adulteration [ədʌltə'reɪʃn] *n.* Verunreinigung, *die; (of wine, milk)* Panschen, *das*

adulterer [ə'dʌltərə(r)] *n.* Ehebrecher, *der*

adulteress [ə'dʌltərɪs] *n.* Ehebrecherin, *die*

adulterous [ə'dʌltərəs] *adj.* ehebrecherisch

adultery [ə'dʌltərɪ] *n., no pl.* Ehebruch, *der*

adulthood ['ædʌlthʊd, ə'dʌlthʊd] *n., no pl.* Erwachsenenalter, *das;* **reach ~:** erwachsen werden

adumbrate ['ædəmbreɪt] *v.t.* **a)** *(outline)* umreißen; skizzieren; **b)** *(suggest faintly)* andeuten; **c)** *(foreshadow)* ankündigen

advance [əd'vɑ:ns] **1.** *v.t.* **a)** *(move forward)* vorrücken lassen; **b)** *(put forward)* vorbringen ‹*Plan, Meinung, These*›; **c)** *(bring forward)* vorverlegen ‹*Termin*›; **d)** *(promote)* befördern; **e)** *(further)* fördern; ~ **one's own interests** [nur] die eigenen Interessen verfolgen; **f)** *(pay before due date)* vorschießen; ~ **sb. a week's pay** jmdm. einen Wochenlohn [als] Vorschuß geben; *(loan)* **the bank ~d me two thousand pounds** die Bank lieh mir zweitausend Pfund; **g)** *(increase)* erhöhen. **2.** *v.i.* **a)** *(move forward; also Mil.)* vorrücken; ‹*Prozession:*› sich vorwärts bewegen; ~ **towards sb./sth.** ‹*Person:*› auf jmdn./etw. zugehen; **he ~d towards me** er kam auf mich zu; **b)** *(fig.: make progress)* Fortschritte machen; vorankommen; **c)** *(increase)* steigen. **3.** *n.* **a)** *(forward movement)* Vorrücken, *das; (fig.: progress)* Fortschritt, *der;* **any ~ on £30?** [bietet] jemand mehr als 30 Pfund?; **b)** *usu. in pl. (personal overture)* Annäherungsversuch, *der;* **c)** *(payment beforehand)* Vorauszahlung, *die; (on salary)* Vorschuß, *der* **(on** auf + *Akk.*); *(loan)* Darlehen, *das;* **d) in ~:** im voraus; **be in ~ of one's age** seiner Zeit voraus sein; **send sb./sth. in ~:** jmdn./etw. vorausschicken

advanced [əd'vɑ:nst] *adj.* fortgeschritten; **he has ~ ideas** er hat Ideen, die seiner Zeit voraus sind; **be ~ in years** in fortgeschrittenem Alter sein; ~ **level** *see* **A level;** ~ **studies** weiterführende Studien

advance 'guard *n. (lit. or fig.)* Vorhut, *die*

advancement [əd'vɑ:nsmənt] *n., no pl.* **a)** *(promotion)* Aufstieg, *der;* **b)** *(furtherance)* Förderung, *die*

advance: ~ 'notice *n.* **a week's ~ notice** Benachrichtigung eine Woche [im] voraus; **give sb. ~ notice of sth.** jmdn. im voraus von etw. in Kenntnis setzen; **~ 'payment** *n.* Vorauszahlung, *die*

advantage [əd'vɑ:ntɪdʒ] *n.* **a)** *(better position)* Vorteil, *der;* **give sb. an ~ over sb.** für jmdn. einen Vorteil gegenüber jmdm. bedeuten *od.* ein Vorteil gegenüber jmdm. sein; **gain an ~ over sb.** sich *(Dat.)* einen Vorteil gegenüber jmdm. verschaffen; **have an ~ over sb.** jmdm. gegenüber im Vorteil sein; **take [full/unfair] ~ of sth.** etw. [voll/unfairerweise] ausnutzen; **take ~ of sb.** jmdn. ausnutzen; *(euphem.: seduce)* jmdn. mißbrauchen; **don't let them take ~ of you** laß dich nicht von ihnen ausnutzen; **have the ~ of sb.** [jmdm. gegenüber] in der besseren Position sein; **we shall show our range of products to ~:** wir werden unser Sortiment vorteilhaft ausstellen; **be seen to better ~:** vorteilhafter aussehen; **b)** *(benefit)* Vorteil, *der;* **'ability to type [would be] an ~':** „Schreibmaschinenkenntnisse von Vorteil"; **it could be done/we could do it with ~:** es wäre von Vorteil, wenn es getan würde/wenn wir es täten; **be to one's ~:** für jmdn. von Vorteil sein; **something to your ~:** etwas, was für dich von Vorteil ist; **turn sth. to [one's] ~:** etw. ausnutzen; **c)** *(Tennis)* Vorteil, *der;* ~ **in/out** Vorteil Aufschläger/Rückschläger

advantageous [ædvən'teɪdʒəs] *adj.* vorteilhaft ‹*Verfahren, Übereinkunft*›; günstig ‹*Lage*›; **be [mutually] ~:** [für beide Seiten] von Vorteil sein; **be ~ to sb.** für jmdn. von Vorteil sein

advantageously [ædvən'teɪdʒəslɪ] *adv.* **we could ~ discuss this** es wäre von Vorteil, wenn wir das besprächen; **be ~ placed** günstig gelegen sein; **compare ~ with sth.** gegenüber etw. günstig abschneiden

advent ['ædvənt] *n., no pl.* **a)** *(of thing)* Beginn, *der;* Anfang, *der;* **before the ~ of the railways** vor dem Aufkommen der Eisenbahn; **b)** *no art.* **A~** *(season)* Advent, *der*

adventitious [ædvən'tɪʃəs] *adj.* zufällig

adventure [əd'ventʃə(r)] *n.* Abenteuer, *das;* **in a spirit of ~:** voller Abenteuerdrang

ad'venture playground *n. (Brit.)* Abenteuerspielplatz, *der*

adventurer [əd'ventʃərə(r)] *n.* Abenteurer, *der; (derog.: speculator)* Glücksritter, *der*

adventuress [əd'ventʃərɪs] *n.* Abenteu[r]erin, *die*

adventurism [əd'ventʃərɪzm] *n., no pl.* Abenteuerlust, *die;* Wagemut, *der; (Polit.)* Abenteuerpolitik, *die*

adventurous [əd'ventʃərəs] *adj.* **a)** *(venturesome)* abenteuerlustig; ~ **spirit** Abenteurergeist, *der;* **b)** *(filled with adventures)* abenteuerlich; **c)** *(enterprising)* kühn

adverb ['ædvɜ:b] *n. (Ling.)* Adverb, *das;* Umstandswort, *das;* ~ **of time/place** Zeit-/Ortsadverb, *das*

adverbial [əd'vɜ:bɪəl] *adj. (Ling.)* adverbial

adverbially [əd'vɜ:bɪəlɪ] *adv. (Ling.)* adverbial

adversary ['ædvəsərɪ] *n. (enemy)* Widersacher, *der*/Widersacherin, *die; (opponent)* Kontrahent, *der*/Kontrahentin, *die*

adverse ['ædvɜ:s] *adj.* **a)** *(hostile)* ablehnend **(to** gegenüber); **an ~ response** eine abschlägige Antwort; **b)** *(unfavourable)* ungünstig ‹*Bedingung, Entwicklung*›; negativ ‹*Bilanz, Urteil*›; nachteilig ‹*Auswirkung*›; **developments ~ to our interests** für unsere Interessen nachteilige Entwicklungen; **c)** *(contrary)* widrig ‹*Wind, Umstände*›

adversely ['ædvɜ:slɪ] *adv.* **a)** *(hostilely)* ablehnend; **b)** *(unfavourably)* nachteilig

adversity [əd'vɜ:sɪtɪ] *n.* **a)** *no pl.* Not, *die;* **in ~:** in der Not; in Notzeiten; **b)** *usu. in pl. (misfortune)* Widrigkeit, *die*

advert ['ædvɜ:t] *(Brit. coll.) see* **advertisement**

advertise ['ædvətaɪz] **1.** *v.t.* werben für ‹*Güter, Waren*›; *(by small ad)* inserieren ‹*Auto, Haus*›; ausschreiben ‹*Stelle*›; **~ one's intentions** seine Absichten bekanntgeben; **~ one's presence** seine Anwesenheit bekanntmachen. **2.** *v.i.* werben; *(in newspaper)* inserieren; annoncieren; **~ on television** Werbung im Fernsehen machen; **~ for sb./sth.** jmdn./etw. [per Inserat] suchen

advertisement [əd'vɜ:tɪsmənt] *n.* Anzeige, *die;* **TV ~:** Fernsehspot, *der;* **classified ~:** Kleinanzeige, *die* ; **his behaviour is not a good ~ for the firm** *(fig.)* sein Verhalten ist für das Unternehmen keine gute Reklame

advertiser ['ædvətaɪzə(r)] *n. (in newspaper)* Inserent, *der*/Inserentin, *die; (on radio, TV)* Auftraggeber/Auftraggeberin [der Werbesendung]

advertising ['ædvətaɪzɪŋ] *n., no pl., no indef. art.* Werbung, *die;* **~ agency/campaign** Werbeagentur, *die*/-kampagne, *die*

advice [əd'vaɪs] *n.* **a)** *no pl., no indef. art. (counsel)* Rat, *der;* **seek ~ from sb.** bei jmdm. Rat suchen; **my ~ to you would be ...:** ich würde dir raten ...; **he doesn't listen to ~:** er hört nicht auf Ratschläge; **on sb.'s ~:** auf jmds. Rat *(Akk.)* hin; **a piece of ~:** ein Rat[schlag]; **give sb. a piece** *or* **bit** *or* **word of ~:** jmdm. einen guten Rat geben; **if you ask** *or* **want my ~:** wenn du meinen Rat hören willst; **take ~ [from sb.]** [jmdn.] um Rat fragen; **take sb.'s ~:** jmds. Rat *(Dat.)* folgen; **take legal ~:** sich juristisch beraten lassen; **b)** *(formal notice)* Bescheid, *der;* Avis, *der od. das (Kaufmannsspr.)*

advisability [ədvaɪzə'bɪlɪtɪ] *n., no pl.* Ratsamkeit, *die;* **consider the ~ of doing sth.** erwägen, ob es ratsam ist, etw. zu tun

advisable [əd'vaɪzəbl] *adj.* ratsam

advise [əd'vaɪz] **1.** *v. t.* **a)** *(offer advice to)* beraten; **please ~ me** bitte geben Sie mir einen Rat; **~ sb. to do sth.** jmdm. raten, etw. zu tun; **~ sb. not to do** *or* **against doing sth.** jmdm. abraten, etw. zu tun; **what would you ~ me to do?** wozu würdest du mir raten?; **b)** *(recommend)* **~ sth.** zu etw. raten; **c)** *(inform)* unterrichten, informieren (**of** über + *Akk.*); **keep me ~d** halten Sie mich auf dem laufenden. **2.** *v. i.* **a)** raten; **~ on sth.** bei etw. beraten; **please ~:** erbitte Rat; **b)** *(Amer.: consult)* **~ with sb.** sich mit jmdm. beraten

advised [əd'vaɪzd] *adj.* **[well-]~:** wohl überlegt; **be well/better ~:** ‹*Person:*› wohlberaten/besser beraten sein

advisedly [əd'vaɪzɪdlɪ] *adv.* bewußt

adviser, advisor [əd'vaɪzə(r)] *n.* Berater, *der*/Beraterin, *die*

advisory [əd'vaɪzərɪ] *adj.* beratend; **~ committee** Beratungsausschuß, *der;* **in an ~ capacity** in beratender Funktion

advocaat [ædvə'kɑ:t] *n.* Eierlikör, *der*

advocacy ['ædvəkəsɪ] *n., no pl.* **sb.'s ~ of sth.** jmds. Engagement *od.* Eintreten für etw.

advocate 1. ['ædvəkət] *n.* *(of a cause)* Befürworter, *der*/Befürworterin, *die;* Fürsprecher, *der*/Fürsprecherin, *die; (for a person)* Fürsprecher, *der*/Fürsprecherin, *die; (Law: professional pleader)* [Rechts]anwalt, *der*/[Rechts]anwältin, *die;* **Faculty of A~s** [schottische] Anwaltskammer, *die;* **Lord A~:** [schottischer] Generalstaatsanwalt, *der.* **2.** ['ædvəkeɪt] *v. t.* **a)** *(recommend)* befürworten; empfehlen; **~ a policy** für eine Politik eintreten; **~ that ...:** dafür plädieren, daß ...; **b)** *(defend)* verteidigen; eintreten für

advt. *abbr.* **advertisement**

adze *(Amer.:* **adz**) [ædz] *n.* Dechsel, *die*

Aegean [i:'dʒi:ən] *pr. n.* **~ [Sea]** Ägäisches Meer

aegis ['i:dʒɪs] *n.* **a)** *(auspices)* **under the ~ of sb./sth.** unter der Ägide *(geh.) od.* Schirmherrschaft von jmdm./etw.; **b)** *(protection)* Schutz, *der*

Aeneid ['i:nɪɪd] *n.* Äneis, *die*

aeon ['i:ən] *n.* *(age)* Äon, *der (geh.)*

aerate ['eəreɪt] *v. t.* **a)** *(charge with gas)* [mit Kohlendioxyd] anreichern; **~d water** kohlensaures Wasser; **b)** *(Agric., Hort.)* durchlüften

aerial ['eərɪəl] **1.** *adj.* **a)** *(in the air)* Luft-; **~ root** Luftwurzel, *die;* **~ cableway** *or* **ropeway** *or* **railway** Seilbahn, *die;* **b)** *(atmospheric)* atmosphärisch; **c)** *(Aeronaut.)* Luft-; **~ bombardment** Bombardierung [aus der Luft]; **~ photograph/photography** Luftaufnahme, *die*/Luftaufnahmen; **~ spraying** Besprühung aus der Luft. **2.** *n.* Antenne, *die*

aero- [eərə] *in comb.* Aero-

aerobatics [eərə'bætɪks] *n.* **a)** *no pl.* Kunstflug, *der;* Aerobatik, *die;* **b)** *pl. (feats of flying skill)* fliegerische Kunststücke

aerobic [eə'rəʊbɪk] *adj.* aerob *(Biol.)*

aerobics [eə'rəʊbɪks] *n., no pl.* Aerobic, *das*

aerodrome ['eərədrəʊm] *n.* *(Brit. dated)* Aerodrom, *das (veralt.);* Flugplatz, *der*

aerody'namic *adj.* aerodynamisch

aerody'namics *n., no pl.* Aerodynamik, *die*

aero-engine ['eərəʊendʒɪn] *n.* *(Aeronaut.)* Flug[zeug]motor, *der*

'aerofoil *n.* Tragfläche, *die;* Tragflügel, *der (fachspr.); (on car)* Heckspoiler, *der*

'aerogram[me] *see* **air letter**

aeronautic [eərə'nɔ:tɪk], **aeronautical** [eərə'nɔ:tɪkl] *adj.* aeronautisch

aeronautics [eərə'nɔ:tɪks] *n., no pl.* Aeronautik, *die*

aeroplane ['eərəpleɪn] *n.* *(Brit.)* Flugzeug, *das*

aerosol ['eərəsɒl] *n.* **a)** *(spray)* Spray, *der od. das; (container)* **~ [spray]** Spraydose, *die;* **b)** *(system of particles)* Aerosol, *das*

'aerospace *n., no pl., no art.* Erdatmosphäre und Weltraum; *(technology)* Luft- und Raumfahrt, *die*

aesthete ['i:sθi:t] *n.* Ästhet, *der*/Ästhetin, *die*

aesthetic [i:s'θetɪk] **1.** *adj.* ästhetisch; schöngeistig ‹*Person, Epoche*›. **2.** *n.* **the Hegelian ~:** die Hegelsche Ästhetik

aesthetically [i:s'θetɪkəlɪ] *adv.* ästhetisch

aestheticism [i:s'θetɪsɪzm] *n., no pl.* Ästhetizismus, *der*

aesthetics [i:s'θetɪks] *n., no pl.* Ästhetik, *die*

aether *see* **ether b**

aetiology [i:tɪ'ɒlədʒɪ] *n.* *(Med., Philos.)* Ätiologie, *die*

AF *abbr.* **audio frequency**

afar [ə'fɑ:] *adv.* **~ [off]** weit fort; in weiter Ferne; **from ~:** aus der Ferne

AFC *abbr.* *(Brit.)* **Association Football Club** *Fußballverein*

affability [æfə'bɪlɪtɪ] *n., no pl.* Freundlichkeit, *die;* **the boss's back-slapping ~:** die joviale Leutseligkeit des Chefs

affable ['æfəbl] *adj.* freundlich; **he is on ~ terms with everyone** er versteht sich mit allen gut

affably ['æfəblɪ] *adv.* freundlich

affair [ə'feə(r)] *n.* **a)** *(concern, matter)* Angelegenheit, *die;* **it's not my ~:** es geht mich nichts an; **that's 'his ~:** das ist seine Sache; **the Dreyfus ~:** die Dreyfus-Affäre; **b)** *in pl. (everyday business)* Geschäfte *Pl.;* [tägliche] Arbeit; *(business dealings)* Geschäfte *Pl.;* **state of ~s** Lage, *die; see also* **current 1 c; foreign c; state 1 d; c)** *(love ~)* Affäre, *die;* **have an ~ with sb.** eine Affäre *od.* ein Verhältnis mit jmdm. haben; **d)** *(occurrence)* Geschichte, *die (ugs.);* Angelegenheit, *die;* **e)** *(coll.: thing)* Ding, *das;* **our house is a tumbledown ~:** unser Haus ist eine Bruchbude *(ugs.);* **f) ~ of honour** Ehrenhandel, *der*

¹affect [ə'fekt] *v. t.* *(pretend to have)* nachahmen; imitieren; *(pretend to feel or do)* vortäuschen; spielen; **the boy ~ed indifference** der Junge tat so, als sei es ihm gleichgültig; **~ to do sth.** vorgeben, etw. zu tun

²affect *v. t.* **a)** *(produce effect on)* sich auswirken auf (+ *Akk.*); **damp had ~ed the spark-plugs** Feuchtigkeit hatte die Zündkerzen in Mitleidenschaft gezogen; **plant growth is ~ed by the amount of rainfall** das Wachstum der Pflanzen wird von der Niederschlagsmenge beeinflußt; **b)** *(emotionally)* betroffen machen; **be ~ed by sth.** von etw. betroffen sein; **c)** ‹*Vorschrift:*› betreffen; ‹*Krankheit:*› infizieren; befallen ‹*Pflanze*›

affectation [æfek'teɪʃn] *n.* **a)** *(studied display)* Verstellung, *die; (artificiality)* Affektiertheit, *die;* **b)** *no pl. (pretence)* **~ of sth.** Vortäuschung von etw.

affected [ə'fektɪd] *adj.* affektiert; gekünstelt ‹*Sprache, Stil*›

affectedly [ə'fektɪdlɪ] *adv.* affektiert

affectedness [ə'fektɪdnɪs] *n., no pl.* Affektiertheit, *die*

affecting [ə'fektɪŋ] *adj.* rührend; ergreifend

affectingly [ə'fektɪŋlɪ] *adv.* in ergreifender Weise; rührend

affection [ə'fekʃn] *n.* **a)** *(kindly feeling)* Zuneigung, *die;* **have** *or* **feel ~ for sb./sth.** für jmdn. Zuneigung empfinden/an etw. *(Dat.)* hängen; **gain** *or* **win sb.'s ~s** jmds. Zuneigung gewinnen; **she was held in great ~ by many people** viele hatten sie in ihr Herz geschlossen; **have a place in sb.'s ~s** einen festen Platz in jmds. Herzen einnehmen; **lots of love and ~** *(close of letter)* alles Liebe und Gute; **b)** *(Med.: illness)* Affektion, *die*

affectionate [ə'fekʃənət] *adj.* anhänglich ‹*Person, Kind, [Haus]tier*›; liebevoll ‹*Umarmung*›; zärtlich ‹*Lächeln, Erinnerung*›; **your ~ son** *(in letter)* Dein Dich liebender Sohn

affectionately [ə'fekʃənətlɪ] *adv.* liebevoll; **yours ~:** viele Grüße und Küsse

affidavit [æfɪ'deɪvɪt] *n.* *(Law)* **[sworn] ~:** eidesstattliche Versicherung; **swear an ~:** eine eidesstattliche Versicherung abgeben

affiliate [ə'fɪlɪeɪt] **1.** *v. t.* **a)** *(attach)* **be ~d to** *or* **with sth.** an etw. *(Akk.)* angegliedert *od.* angeschlossen sein; **the organization is not politically ~d** die Organisation ist politisch nicht gebunden; **b)** *(adopt)* aufnehmen ‹*Mitglied*›; angliedern ‹*Vereinigung*›; **be an ~d member of an organization** einer Organisation angeschlossen sein. **2.** *n.* *(person)* assoziiertes Mitglied; *(organization)* Zweigorganisation, *die;* Affiliation, *die (Wirtsch.)*

affiliation [əfɪlɪ'eɪʃn] *n.* Angliederung, *die* (**to, with** an + *Akk.*); **~ order** *gerichtliche Feststellung der Vaterschaft und Festsetzung der Unterhaltsverpflichtung für ein nichteheliches Kind*

affinity [ə'fɪnɪtɪ] *n.* **a)** *(relationship)* Verwandtschaft, *die* (**to** mit); **b)** *(liking)* Neigung, *die* (**for** zu); **feel an ~ to** *or* **for sb./sth.** sich zu jmdm./etw. hingezogen fühlen; **c)** *(structural resemblance)* Affinität, *die;* Verwandtschaft, *die; (fig.)* Verwandtschaft, *die* (**with, to** mit); **the ~ of sth. to** *or* **with sth.** die Affinität von etw. zu etw.

affirm [ə'fɜ:m] **1.** *v. t.* *(assert)* bekräftigen ‹*Absicht*›; beteuern ‹*Unschuld*›; *(state as a fact)* bestätigen; **~ sth. to sb.** jmdm. etw. versichern. **2.** *v. i.* *(Law) ohne religiöse Beteuerung schwören*

affirmation [æfə'meɪʃn] *n.* **a)** *(of intention)* Bekräftigung, *die; (of fact)* Bestätigung, *die; (of quality)* Versicherung, *die;* **b)** *(Law)* eidesstattliche Erklärung

affirmative [ə'fɜ:mətɪv] **1.** *adj.* affirmativ; bestätigend ‹*Erklärung*›; bejahend, zustimmend ‹*Antwort*›; **~ vote** Jastimme, *die.* **2.** *n.* Bejahung, *die;* **answer in the ~:** bejahend antworten; **the answer is in the ~:** die Antwort ist „ja" *od.* positiv

affirmative 'action *n.* *(Amer.)* positive Diskriminierung *(fachspr.);* Bevorzugung, *die*

affirmatively [ə'fɜ:mətɪvlɪ] *adv.* **answer ~:** bejahend antworten

affix 1. [ə'fɪks] *v. t.* **a)** *(fix)* **~ sth. to sth.** etw. an etw. *(Dat.)* befestigen; **the stamp had not been properly ~ed to the letter** die Marke war nicht richtig auf den Brief geklebt worden; **b)** *(impress)* aufdrücken; **~ one's stamp/seal upon sth.** seinen Stempel/sein Siegel auf etw. *(Akk.)* drücken; **c)** *(add)* beifügen; **~ one's signature [to sth.]** seine Unterschrift [unter etw. *(Akk.)*] setzen. **2.** ['æfɪks] *n.* *(Ling.)* Affix, *das*

afflict [ə'flɪkt] *v. t.* *(physically)* plagen; *(mentally)* quälen; peinigen; **be ~ed with sth.** von etw. befallen sein

affliction [ə'flɪkʃn] *n.* **a)** *no pl. (distress)* Bedrängnis, *die;* **endure sorrow and ~:** Kummer und Leid ertragen; **b)** *(cause of distress)* Leiden, *das;* **bodily ~s** körperliche Gebrechen

affluence ['æflʊəns] *n., no pl.* **a)** *(wealth)* Reichtum, *der;* **b)** *(plenty)* Überfluß, *der*

affluent ['æfluənt] **1.** *adj.* **a)** *(wealthy)* reich; **the ~ society** die Überflußgesellschaft; **b)** *(abounding)* reichhaltig; **~ in** reich an (+ *Dat.*). **2.** *n.* *(of river)* Nebenfluß, *der;* *(of lake)* Zufluß, *der*

afford [ə'fɔ:d] *v. t.* **a)** sich *(Dat.)* leisten; **be able to ~ sth.** sich *(Dat.)* etw. leisten können; **be able to ~:** aufbringen können ⟨*Geld*⟩; erübrigen können ⟨*Zeit*⟩; **be able to ~ to do sth.** es sich *(Dat.)* leisten können, etw. zu tun; **sb. can ill ~ sth.** jmd. kann sich *(Dat.)* etw. kaum leisten; **we can well ~ to look critically at our dietary habits** uns täte es sehr gut, sich *(Dat.)* die eigenen Eßgewohnheiten einmal kritisch zu betrachten; **b)** *(provide)* bieten; gewähren ⟨*Schutz*⟩; bereiten ⟨*Vergnügen*⟩; **~ sb. sth.** jmdm. etw. bieten/gewähren/bereiten

affordable [ə'fɔ:dəbl] *adj.* erschwinglich

afforest [ə'fɒrɪst] *v. t.* aufforsten

afforestation [əfɒrɪ'steɪʃn] *n.* Aufforstung, *die*

affray [ə'freɪ] *n.* Schlägerei, *die*

affront [ə'frʌnt] **1.** *v. t.* *(insult)* beleidigen; *(offend)* kränken; vor den Kopf stoßen *(ugs.).* **2.** *n.* *(insult)* Affront, *der* *(geh.)* **(to** gegen); Beleidigung, *die* **(to** *Gen.*); *(offence)* Kränkung, *die* **(to** *Gen.*)

Afghan ['æfgæn] **1.** *adj.* afghanisch; *see also* **English 1. 2.** *n.* **a)** *(person)* Afghane, *der*/Afghanin, *die;* **b)** *(language)* Afghanisch, *das;* *see also* **English 2 a**

Afghan 'hound *n.* Afghane, *der*

Afghanistan [æf'gænɪstɑ:n] *pr. n.* Afghanistan *(das)*

aficionado [əfɪsjə'nɑ:dəʊ] *n., pl.* **~s** Liebhaber, *der*/Liebhaberin, *die*

afield [ə'fi:ld] *adv.* **far ~** *(direction)* weit hinaus; *(place)* weit draußen; **we didn't go farther ~ than ...:** wir gingen nicht weiter hinaus als bis zu ...; **from as far ~ as** von so weit her wie; **go too far ~** *(fig.)* sich zu weit entfernen

afire [ə'faɪə(r)] *pred. adj.* **[set] ~:** in Brand [setzen *od.* stecken]; **be ~:** in Flammen stehen

aflame [ə'fleɪm] *pred. adj.* **be ~:** in Flammen stehen

afloat [ə'fləʊt] *pred. adj.* **a)** *(floating)* über Wasser; flott ⟨*Schiff*⟩; **get a boat ~:** ein Boot flott machen; **b)** *(at sea)* auf See; **be ~:** auf dem Meer treiben; **c)** *(awash)* **be ~:** unter Wasser stehen

afoot [ə'fʊt] *pred. adj.* **a)** *(astir)* auf den Beinen; **b)** *(under way)* im Gange; **set ~:** in Gang setzen; aufstellen ⟨*Plan*⟩; **plans were ~ to ...:** es gab Pläne, zu ...; **there's trouble ~:** es gibt Ärger

aforementioned [ə'fɔ:menʃnd], **aforesaid** [ə'fɔ:sed] *adjs.* obenerwähnt *od.* -genannt

aforethought [ə'fɔ:θɔ:t] *adj.* **with malice ~:** mit Vorbedacht

a fortiori [eɪ fɔ:tɪ'ɔ:raɪ] *adv.* erst recht

afoul [ə'faʊl] *adv.* *(Amer.)* verwickelt **(of** in + *Akk.*); **fall** *or* **run ~ of sth.** sich in etw. *(Akk.)* verwickeln; *(fig.)* mit etw. in Konflikt geraten

afraid [ə'freɪd] *pred. adj.* **[not] be ~ [of sb./sth.]** [vor jmdm./etw.] [keine] Angst haben; **be ~ lest ...:** befürchten, daß ...; **be ~ to do sth.** Angst davor haben, etw. zu tun; **be ~ of doing sth.** Angst haben, etw. zu tun; **I'm ~ [that] we must assume that ...:** leider müssen wir annehmen, daß ...; **I'm ~ so/not** ich fürchte ja/nein

afresh [ə'freʃ] *adv.* von neuem; **every word has been translated ~:** jedes Wort ist neu übersetzt worden

Africa ['æfrɪkə] *pr. n.* Afrika *(das);* *see also* **black 1 c**

African ['æfrɪkən] **1.** *adj.* afrikanisch; **sb. is ~:** jmd. ist Afrikaner/Afrikanerin. **2.** *n.* **a)** Afrikaner, *der*/Afrikanerin, *die;* **b)** *(Amer.: Negro)* Neger, *der*/Negerin, *die*

African 'violet *n.* *(Bot.)* Usambaraveilchen, *das*

Afrikaans [æfrɪ'kɑ:ns] *n.* Afrikaans, *das;* *see also* **English 2 a**

Afrikaner [æfrɪ'kɑ:nə(r)] *n.* Afrika[a]nder, *der*/Afrika[a]nderin, *die*

Afro ['æfrəʊ] **1.** *adj.* Afro-; **~ look** Afro-Look, *der.* **2.** *n., pl.* **~s** Afro-Look, *der*

Afro- [æfrəʊ] *in comb.* afro-/Afro-

Afro-A'merican **1.** *adj.* afroamerikanisch. **2.** *n.* Afroamerikaner, *der*/-amerikanerin, *die*

aft [ɑ:ft] *adv.* *(Naut., Aeronaut.)* achtern; **go ~:** nach achtern gehen

after ['ɑ:ftə(r)] **1.** *adv.* **a)** *(later)* danach; **two days ~:** zwei Tage danach *od.* später; **soon/shortly ~:** bald/kurz danach *od.* darauf; **long ~:** lange danach; **b)** *(behind)* hinterher. **2.** *prep.* **a)** *(following in time)* nach; **~ six months** nach sechs Monaten; **~ you** nach Ihnen; **~ you with the salt** *(coll.)* kann ich das Salz nach dir haben?; **time ~ time** wieder und wieder; **day ~ day** Tag für Tag; **it is a quarter ~ ten o'clock** *(Amer.)* es ist Viertel nach zehn; **b)** *(behind)* hinter (+ *Dat.*); *(in pursuit of)* **be/shout ~ sb.** hinter jmdm. hersein/herrufen; **what are you ~?** was suchst du denn?; *(to questioner)* was willst du wirklich wissen?; **she's only ~ his money** sie ist nur hinter seinem Geld her; **c)** *(about)* **ask ~ sb./sth.** nach jmdm./etw. fragen; **d)** *(next in importance to)* nach; **e)** *(in spite of)* nach; **~ all** schließlich; **so you've come ~ all!** du bist also doch gekommen!; **I think I'll have a beer ~ all** ich glaube, ich trinke doch ein Bier; **so we took the train ~ all** wir haben den Zug schließlich doch genommen; **f)** *(as a result of)* **~ what has happened** nach dem, was geschehen ist; **~ seeing that film/reading that book** nach diesem Film/diesem Buch; **g)** *(in allusion to, in imitation of)* nach; **named ~:** benannt nach; **a picture ~ Rubens** ein Bild im Stil von Rubens. **3.** *conj.* nachdem. **4.** *adj.* **a)** *(later)* später; **in ~ years** in späteren Jahren; **b)** *(Naut.)* Achter-

after: **~birth** *n.* Nachgeburt, *die;* **~-care** *n., no pl.* *(after hospital stay)* Nachbehandlung, *die;* *(after prison sentence)* Resozialisierung, *die;* **~-'dinner speaker** *n.* Tischredner, *der;* **~-'dinner speech** *n.* Tischrede, *die;* **~-effect** *n., usu. in pl.* Nachwirkung, *die;* **~life** *n.* Leben nach dem Tod

aftermath ['ɑ:ftəmæθ, 'ɑ:ftəmɑ:θ] *n., no pl.* Nachwirkungen *Pl.;* **the ~ of the war** die Folgen *od.* Auswirkungen des Krieges; **in the ~ of sth.** nach etw.

afternoon [ɑ:ftə'nu:n] *n.* Nachmittag, *der;* *attrib.* Nachmittags-; **in the ~:** nachmittags; **this/tomorrow ~:** heute/morgen nachmittag; **during the ~:** im Laufe des Nachmittags; **[early/late] in the ~:** am [frühen/späten] Nachmittag; *(regularly)* [früh/spät] nachmittags; **at three in the ~:** um drei Uhr nachmittags; **on Monday ~s/~:** Montag nachmittags/[am] Montag nachmittag; **one ~:** eines Nachmittags; **~s, of an ~:** nachmittags; **the other ~:** neulich nachmittags; **~, all!** *(coll. greeting)* Tag, zusammen!; *see also* **good 1 m**

afters ['ɑ:ftəz] *n. pl.* *(Brit. coll.)* Nachtisch, *der*

after: **~-sales service** *n.* Kundendienst, *der;* **~shave** *n.* After-shave, *das;* **~shock** *n.* Nachbeben, *das;* **~-taste** *n.* Nachgeschmack, *der;* **~thought** *n.* nachträglicher Einfall; nachträgliche Idee; **be added as an ~thought** erst später hinzukommen

afterwards ['ɑ:ftəwədz] *(Amer.:* **afterward** ['ɑ:ftəwəd]) *adv.* danach

again [ə'gen, ə'geɪn] *adv.* **a)** *(another time)* wieder; **see a film ~:** einen Film noch einmal sehen; **play/sing a tune ~:** eine Melodie noch einmal spielen/singen; **not ~!** nicht schon wieder!; **~ and ~, time and [time] ~:** immer wieder; **back ~:** wieder zurück; **go back there ~:** wieder dorthin gehen; **as much ~:** noch einmal soviel; **half as much/many ~:** noch einmal halb soviel/so viele; **come ~** *(coll.: would you say that again?)* wie bitte?; **b)** *(besides)* **[there] ~:** außerdem; **c)** *(on the other hand)* **[then/there] ~:** andrerseits

against [ə'genst, ə'geɪnst] *prep.* **a)** *(in opposition to, to the disadvantage of, in contrast to)* gegen; **those ~ the motion** diejenigen, die gegen den Antrag sind; **as ~:** gegenüber; **be ~ sb.'s doing sth.** dagegen sein, daß jmd. etw. tun darf; **b)** *(into collision with, in contact with)* gegen; **lean sth. ~ sth.** etw. gegen etw. lehnen; **c)** *(in preparation for)* gegen; **protect sth. ~ frost** etw. vor Frost schützen; **save money ~ a rainy day** Geld für schlechte Zeiten sparen; **be warned ~ sth./doing sth.** vor etw. *(Dat.)* gewarnt werden/davor gewarnt werden, etw. zu tun; **d)** *(in return for)* gegen; **rate of exchange ~ the dollar** Wechselkurs des Dollar

agape [ə'geɪp] *adj.* **with mouth ~:** mit offenem Mund; **be ~** ⟨*Person:*⟩ den Mund aufsperren **(with** vor)

agaric ['ægərɪk] *n.* *(Bot.)* Blätterpilz, *der*

agate ['ægət] *n.* *(Min.)* Achat, *der*

agave [ə'geɪvɪ] *n.* *(Bot.)* Agave, *die*

age [eɪdʒ] **1.** *n.* **a)** Alter, *das;* **the boys' ~s are 7, 6, and 3** die Jungen sind 7, 6 und 3 Jahre alt; **what ~ are you?, what is your ~?** wie alt bist du?; **at the ~ of** im Alter von; **at what ~:** in welchem Alter; **be six years of ~:** sechs Jahre alt sein; **children of six years of ~ and under** Kinder [im Alter] von sechs Jahren und darunter; **when I was your ~:** als ich so alt war wie du; **he looks his ~:** man sieht ihm sein Alter an; **come of ~:** mündig *od.* volljährig werden; *(fig.)* den Kinderschuhen entwachsen; **be over ~:** eine vorgeschriebene Altersgrenze überschritten haben; **be/look under ~:** zu jung sein/aussehen; **she's now of an ~ when she ...:** sie ist jetzt in dem Alter, in dem sie ...; **be** *or* **act your ~** *(coll.)* sei nicht so kindisch; **b)** *(advanced age)* Alter, *das;* **her ~ is catching up with her** sie merkt jetzt doch, daß sie alt wird; **her face was wrinkled with ~:** ihr Gesicht war vom Alter zerfurcht; **~ before beauty** *(joc.)* Alter vor Schönheit; **c)** *(generation)* Generation, *die;* **d)** *(great period)* Zeitalter, *das;* **wait [for] ~s** *or* **an ~ for sb./sth.** *(coll.)* eine Ewigkeit auf jmdn./etw. warten; **take/be ~s** *or* **an ~** *(coll.)* eine Ewigkeit dauern; **she took ~s looking for the book** *(coll.)* sie suchte eine Ewigkeit nach dem Buch; **I'll be ~s yet** *(coll.)* ich brauche noch eine Ewigkeit. **2.** *v. t.* **a)** altern lassen; altern *(selten);* **sth. ~s sb./sth. prematurely** etw. läßt jmdn./etw. frühzeitig alt werden; **b)** *(mature)* reifen lassen; altern *(fachspr.)* **3.** *v. i.* altern

aged **1.** *adj.* **a)** [eɪdʒd] **be ~ five** fünf Jahre alt sein; **a boy ~ five** ein fünfjähriger Junge; **b)** [eɪdʒd] *(matured)* gealtert ⟨*Wein, Käse, Brandy*⟩; **c)** ['eɪdʒɪd] *(elderly)* bejahrt. **2.** ['eɪdʒɪd] *n. pl.* **the ~:** die alten Menschen

'age-group *n.* Altersgruppe, *die*

ageism ['eɪdʒɪzm] *n.* Diskriminierung auf Grund des Alters

ageless ['eɪdʒlɪs] *adj.* nicht alternd ⟨*Person*⟩; *(eternal)* zeitlos

'age-long *adj.* jahrhundertelang

agency ['eɪdʒənsɪ] *n.* **a)** *(action)* Handeln, *das;* **through/by the ~ of sth.** durch [die Einwirkung von] etw.; **through/by the ~ of sb.** durch jmds. Vermittlung; **b)** *(business establishment)* Geschäftsstelle, *die;* *(news/advertising ~)* Agentur, *die;* *(United Nations department)* *(major)* Sonderorganisation, *die;* *(minor)* Unterorganisation, *die*

agenda [ə'dʒendə] *n.* *(lit. or fig.)* Tagesordnung, *die*

agent ['eɪdʒənt] *n.* **a)** [treibende] Kraft;

(Ling.) Agens, *das;* **be a free ~:** sein eigener Herr sein; **b)** *(substance)* Mittel, *das;* **an oxidizing ~:** ein Oxidationsmittel; **c)** *(one who acts for another)* Vertreter, *der/*Vertreterin, *die;* **d)** *(spy)* Agent, *der/*Agentin, *die*

agent provocateur [ɑ:ʒɑ̃ prɒvɒkəˈtɜ:(r)] *n., pl.* **agents provocateurs** [ɑ:ʒɑ̃ prɒvɒkəˈtɜ:(r)] Agent provocateur, *der*

ˈ**age-old** *adj.* uralt

agglomerate [əˈglɒməreɪt] *v. t.* agglomerieren

agglomeration [əglɒməˈreɪʃn] *n. (mass)* Agglomeration, *die (bes. fachspr.);* Anhäufung, *die*

aggrandizement [əˈgrændɪzmənt] *n., no pl.* Vergrößerung, *die; (of power, influence)* Ausdehnung, *die;* **his personal ~:** die Glorifizierung seiner Person

aggravate [ˈægrəveɪt] *v. t.* **a)** verschlimmern ‹*Krankheit, Zustand, Situation*›; verschärfen ‹*Streit*›; **b)** *(coll.: annoy)* aufregen; ärgern; **be ~d by sth.** sich über etw. *(Akk.)* ärgern *od.* aufregen

aggravating [ˈægrəveɪtɪŋ] *adj. (coll.)* ärgerlich; lästig ‹*Kind, Lärm*›

aggravation [ægrəˈveɪʃn] *n., no pl.* **a)** Verschlimmerung, *die; (of dispute)* Verschärfung, *die;* **b)** *(coll.: annoyance)* Ärger, *der;* Aufregung, *die*

aggregate 1. [ˈægrɪgət] *n.* **a)** *(sum total)* Gesamtmenge, *die; (assemblage)* Ansammlung, *die;* **in the ~:** in seiner/ihrer Gesamtheit; **b)** *(Building)* [Beton]zuschlag, *der;* **c)** *(Geol.)* Aggregat, *das.* **2.** *adj. (collected into one)* zusammengefügt; *(collective)* gesamt; **the ~ amount** der Gesamtbetrag. **3.** [ˈægrɪgeɪt] *v. t.* **a)** verbinden ‹*Material, Stoff*› **(into** zu); ansammeln ‹*Reichtum*›; **b)** *(unite)* vereinigen; *(coll.: amount to)* sich [insgesamt] belaufen auf (+ *Akk.*); **audiences aggregating 7 million** insgesamt 7 Millionen Zuhörer/Zuschauer

aggregation [ægrɪˈgeɪʃn] *n.* Ansammlung, *die;* Aggregation, *die (bes. fachspr.)*

aggression [əˈgreʃn] *n.* **a)** *no pl.* Aggression, *die;* **b)** *(unprovoked attack)* Angriff, *der;* **c)** *no pl. (Psych.)* Aggression, *die*

aggressive [əˈgresɪv] *adj.* aggressiv; angriffslustig ‹*Kämpfer*›; heftig ‹*Angriff*›

aggressively [əˈgresɪvlɪ] *adv.* aggressiv, herausfordernd ‹*handeln, reagieren*›; *(forcefully)* aggressiv, wirkungsvoll, dynamisch ‹*verkaufen, anbieten*›; **the product was marketed ~:** die Werbung für das Produkt hatte Biß

aggressiveness [əˈgresɪvnɪs] *n., no pl.* Aggressivität, *die*

aggressor [əˈgresə(r)] *n.* Aggressor, *der*

aggrieve [əˈgri:v] *v. t.* **a)** *(treat unfairly)* ungerecht behandeln; **feel [oneself] much ~d at** *or* **over sth.** sich durch etw. ungerecht behandelt fühlen; **b) ~d** *(resentful)* verärgert; *(offended)* gekränkt

aggro [ˈægrəʊ] *n., no pl. (Brit. sl.)* Zoff, *der (ugs.);* Krawall, *der;* **they are looking for ~:** sie suchen Streit

aghast [əˈgɑ:st] *pred. adj. (horrified)* bestürzt; erschüttert; *(terrified)* erschrocken; **we stood ~ as ...:** wir standen wie versteinert, als ...

agile [ˈædʒaɪl] *adj.* beweglich; agil *(geh.);* flink, behend[e] ‹*Bewegung*›

agility [əˈdʒɪlɪtɪ] *n., no pl.* Behendigkeit, *die;* Flinkheit, *die;* Gewandtheit, *die; (fig.)* [geistige] Behendigkeit *od.* Beweglichkeit

agitate [ˈædʒɪteɪt] **1.** *v. t.* **a)** *(shake)* schütteln; *(stir up)* aufrühren; **b)** *(disturb)* beunruhigen; erregen. **2.** *v. i.* **~ for/against sth.** für/gegen etw. agitieren

agitation [ædʒɪˈteɪʃn] *n.* **a)** *(shaking)* Schütteln, *das; (stirring up)* Aufrühren, *das;* **b)** *(emotional disturbance)* Erregung, *die;* **c)** *(campaign)* Agitation, *die*

agitator [ˈædʒɪteɪtə(r)] *n.* **a)** Agitator, *der;* **b)** *(device)* Rührwerk, *das*

AGM *abbr.* **Annual General Meeting** JHV

agnostic [ægˈnɒstɪk] **1.** *adj.* agnostizistisch. **2.** *n.* Agnostiker, *der/*Agnostikerin, *die*

agnosticism [ægˈnɒstɪsɪzm] *n., no pl.* Agnostizismus, *der*

ago [əˈgəʊ] *adv.* **ten years ~:** vor zehn Jahren; **[not] long ~:** vor [nicht] langer Zeit; **that was a long while ~:** das war vor langer Zeit; **how long ~ is it that ...?** wie lange ist es her, daß ...?; **no longer ~ than last Sunday** nicht vor letztem Sonntag; *(only last Sunday)* erst letzten Sonntag

agog [əˈgɒg] *pred. adj.* gespannt **(for** auf + *Akk.*); **be ~ to hear the news** gespannt darauf sein, die Neuigkeiten zu hören

agonize [ˈægənaɪz] **1.** *v. i.* **a)** *(suffer agony)* Todesqualen erleiden; **b)** *(fig.: struggle)* ringen; **~ over sth.** sich *(Dat.)* den Kopf über etw. *(Akk.)* zermartern. **2.** *v. t.* quälen; **an ~d scream** ein qualerfüllter Schrei; **an agonizing wait** *(fig.)* eine qualvolle Wartezeit

agony [ˈægənɪ] *n.* Todesqualen *Pl.;* **suffer ~/agonies** Todesqualen erleiden; **die in ~:** qualvoll sterben; **in an ~ of indecision/anticipation** *(fig.)* in qualvoller Unentschlossenheit/Erwartung; **death ~, last ~:** Agonie, *die;* Todeskampf, *der*

agony: ~ aunt *n. (coll.)* Briefkastentante, *die (ugs. scherzh.);* **~ column** *n. (Brit. coll.)* **a)** *Zeitungsspalte für private Mitteilungen („Persönliches");* **b)** *(advice column) Spalte für die „Briefkastentante"*

agoraphobia [ægərəˈfəʊbɪə] *n. (Psych.)* Agoraphobie, *die;* Platzangst, *die*

agrarian [əˈgreərɪən] *adj.* Agrar-; *(relating to agricultural matters)* agrarisch

agree [əˈgri:] **1.** *v. i.* **a)** *(consent)* einverstanden sein; **~ to** *or* **with sth./to do sth.** mit etw. einverstanden sein/damit einverstanden sein, etw. zu tun; **we can only ~ to differ** *or* **disagree** wir können nur darin übereinstimmen, daß wir nicht übereinstimmen; **b)** *(hold similar opinion)* einer Meinung sein; **they ~d [with me]** sie waren derselben Meinung [wie ich]; **~ with sb. about** *or* **on sth./that ...:** jmdm. in etw. *(Dat.)* zustimmen/jmdm. darin zustimmen, daß ...; **I ~:** stimmt; **I couldn't ~ more** ich bin völlig deiner Meinung; **do you ~ with what I say?** stimmst du darin mit mir überein?; **c)** *(reach similar opinion)* **~ on sth.** sich über etw. *(Akk.)* einigen; **we could not ~ on how ...:** wir konnten uns nicht darüber einigen, wie ...; **d)** *(harmonize)* übereinstimmen; **sth. ~s with sth.** etw. stimmt mit etw. überein; **make ~:** zur Übereinstimmung bringen; **~ closely** weitgehend übereinstimmen; **e)** *(suit)* **~ with sb.** jmdm. bekommen; **f)** *(Ling.)* übereinstimmen. **2.** *v. t.* **a)** *(reach agreement about)* vereinbaren; **b)** *(consent to)* **~ sth.** einer Sache *(Dat.)* zustimmen

agreeable [əˈgri:əbl] *adj.* **a)** *(pleasing)* angenehm ‹*Überraschung, Person, Abend, Stimme*›; erfreulich ‹*Anblick*›; **b)** *(coll.: willing to agree)* **be ~ [to sth.]** [mit etw.] einverstanden sein

agreeableness [əˈgri:əbəlnɪs] *n., no pl.* **the ~ of his company** seine angenehme Gesellschaft; **the ~ of the taste/climate** der angenehme Geschmack/das angenehme Klima

agreeably [əˈgri:əblɪ] *adv.* angenehm; **~ surprised** angenehm überrascht; **we were ~ entertained** wir wurden auf angenehme Weise *od.* nett unterhalten

agreed [əˈgri:d] *adj.* einig; vereinbart ‹*Summe, Zeit*›; **be ~ that .../about sth.** sich *(Dat.)* darüber einig sein, daß .../ sich *(Dat.)* über etw. *(Akk.)* einig sein; **it was ~ that ...:** man war sich *(Dat.)* darüber einig, daß ...; **~!** einverstanden!

agreement [əˈgri:mənt] *n.* **a)** Übereinstimmung, *die; (mutual understanding)* Übereinkunft, *die;* **be in ~ [about sth.]** sich *(Dat.)* [über etw. *(Akk.)*] einig sein; **I'm in ~ with what you say** ich stimme darin mit dir überein; **enter into an ~:** eine Übereinkunft treffen; **come to** *or* **reach an ~ with sb. [about sth.]** mit jmdm. eine Einigung [über etw. *(Akk.)*] erzielen; **b)** *(treaty)* Abkommen, *das;* **c)** *no pl., no indef. art. (state of harmony)* Übereinstimmung, *die;* **d)** *(Law)* Abkommen, *das;* Vertrag, *der;* **legal ~:** rechtliche Vereinbarung; **e)** *(Ling.)* Übereinstimmung, *die*

agribusiness [ˈægrɪbɪznɪs] *n.* ≈ Agrarindustrie, *die*

agrichemical [ˈægrɪkemɪkl] *n.* Agrochemikalie, *die*

agricultural [ægrɪˈkʌltʃərl] *adj.* landwirtschaftlich; **~ worker** Landarbeiter, *der*

agriculturalist [ægrɪˈkʌltʃərəlɪst] *see* **agriculturist**

agriculture [ˈægrɪkʌltʃə(r)] *n.* Landwirtschaft, *die*

agriculturist [ægrɪˈkʌltʃərɪst] *n.* Landwirtschaftsexperte, *der; (farmer)* Landwirt, *der*

agrimony [ˈægrɪmənɪ] *n. (Bot.)* Odermennig, *der*

aground [əˈgraʊnd] *pred. adj.* auf Grund gelaufen; **go** *or* **run ~:** auf Grund laufen

ague [ˈeɪgju:] *n. (fever)* Wechselfieber, *das (veralt.); (shivering fit)* Schüttelfrost, *der*

ah [ɑ:] *int.* ach; *(of pleasure)* ah

aha [ɑ:ˈhɑ:] *int.* aha

ahead [əˈhed] *adv.* **a)** *(further forward in space)* voraus; **the way ~ was blocked** der Weg vor uns/ihnen *usw.* war versperrt; **~ of sb./sth.** vor jmdm./etw.; **right** *or* **straight ~ of us** *(directly in line)* genau vor uns *(Dat.);* **keep going straight ~** *(straight forwards)* gehen Sie immer geradeaus; **b)** *(fig.)* **be ~ of the others** den anderen voraus sein; **be ~ on points** nach Punkten führen; **get ~:** vorwärts kommen; **c)** *(further forward in time)* **~ of us lay three days of intensive training** vor uns lagen drei Tage intensives Training; **Britain is eight hours ~ of Los Angeles** in Großbritannien ist es acht Stunden später als in Los Angeles; **finish ~ of schedule** *or* **time** früher als geplant fertig werden; **get home ~ of sb.** eher *od.* früher nach Hause kommen als jmd.; **we've got ~ of ourselves** *(fig.)* wir sind zu schnell vorgegangen; **there is no point in looking too far ~:** es hat keinen Sinn, zu weit in die Zukunft zu planen. *See also* **go ahead**

ahoy [əˈhɔɪ] *int. (Naut.)* ahoi

AI *abbr.* **a) artificial intelligence** KI; **b) artificial insemination** KB

aid [eɪd] **1.** *v. t.* **a) ~ sb. [to do sth.]** jmdm. helfen[, etw. zu tun]; **~ed by** unterstützt von; **the finances have been ~ed by donations** die Finanzen sind durch Spenden aufgebessert worden; *see also* **abet; b)** *(promote)* fördern. **2.** *n.* **a)** *no pl. (help)* Hilfe, *die;* **come to sb.'s ~, go to the ~ of sb.** jmdm. zu Hilfe kommen; **with the ~ of sth./sb.** mit Hilfe einer Sache *(Gen.)*/mit jmds. Hilfe; mit Hilfe von etw./jmdm.; **in ~ of sb./sth.** zugunsten von jmdm./etw.; **what's [all] this in ~ of?** *(coll.)* wozu soll das [Ganze *od.* alles] gut sein?; *see also* **foreign aid; b)** *(source of help)* Hilfsmittel, *das* **(to** für)

aide [eɪd] *n.* **a)** *see* **aide-de-camp; b)** *(assistant)* Berater, *der/*Beraterin, *die*

aide-de-camp [eɪddəˈkɑ̃:] *n., pl.* **aides-de-camp** [eɪddəˈkɑ̃:] *(Mil.)* Adjutant, *der*

aide-mémoire [ˈeɪdmemwɑ:(r)] *n. (aid to memory)* Gedächtnisstütze, *die*

Aids [eɪdz] *n., no pl., no art.* Aids *(das)*

aikido [ˈaɪkɪdəʊ] *n. (Sport)* Aikido, *das*

ail [eɪl] *v. t. (trouble)* plagen; **what ~s him?** was ist mit ihm?

ailing [ˈeɪlɪŋ] *adj. (sickly)* kränkelnd; kränklich

ailment [ˈeɪlmənt] *n.* Gebrechen, *das;* **minor ~:** leichte Erkrankung

aim [eɪm] **1.** *v. t.* ausrichten ‹*Schußwaffe, Rakete*›; **~ sth. at sb./sth.** etw. auf jmdn./

etw. richten; **that remark was not ~ed at you** *(fig.)* diese Bemerkung war nicht gegen Sie gerichtet; **~ a blow/shot/book at sb.** nach jmdm. schlagen/auf jmdn. schießen/ein Buch nach jmdm. werfen. **2.** *v. i.* **a)** zielen; **~ at sth./sb.** auf etw./jmdn. zielen; **~ high/wide** [zu] hoch/[zu] weit zielen; **~ high** *(fig.)* sich *(Dat.)* ein hohes Ziel stecken *od.* setzen; **b)** *(intend)* **~ to do sth.** *or* **at doing sth.** beabsichtigen, etw. zu tun; **please ~ to be back by 4 p.m.** versuche bitte, gegen 16 Uhr zurück zu sein; **~ at** *or* **for sth.** *(fig.)* etw. anstreben; **I'm not quite sure what you're ~ing at** *(fig.)* ich weiß nicht recht, worauf Sie hinauswollen. **3.** *n.* **a)** Ziel, *das;* **his ~ was true** er hatte genau gezielt; **take ~ [at sth./sb.]** [auf etw./jmdn.] zielen; **take ~ at the target** das Ziel anvisieren; **b)** *(purpose)* Ziel, *das*

aimless ['eɪmlɪs] *adj.* ziellos ‹*Leben, Aktivität*›; sinnlos ‹*Vorhaben, Beschäftigung*›; heillos ‹*Verwirrung*›

aimlessly ['eɪmlɪslɪ] *adv.* ziellos

aimlessness ['eɪmlɪsnɪs] *n.* Ziellosigkeit, *die*

ain't [eɪnt] *(sl.)* **a) = am not, is not, are not;** *see* **be; b) = has not, have not;** *see* **have 2**

air [eə(r)] **1.** *n.* **a)** Luft, *die;* **take the ~:** [frische] Luft schöpfen *(geh.);* **be/go on the ~:** senden; ‹*Programm, Sendung:*› gesendet werden; **be/go off the ~:** nicht/nicht mehr senden; ‹*Programm:*› beendet sein/werden; **be in the ~** *(fig.) (be spreading)* ‹*Gerücht, Idee:*› in der Luft liegen; *(be uncertain)* ‹*Plan, Projekt:*› in der Luft hängen; **by ~:** mit dem Flugzeug; **travel by ~:** fliegen; **send a letter by ~:** einen Brief mit *od.* per Luftpost schicken; **from the ~:** aus der Vogelperspektive; **b)** *(breeze)* Lüftchen, *das;* **c)** *(appearance)* **there was an ~ of absurdity about the whole exercise** die ganze Übung hatte etwas Absurdes; **his newspaper stories have the ~ of fiction** seine Zeitungsgeschichten haben etwas Fiktives; **d)** *(bearing)* Auftreten, *das; (facial expression)* Miene, *die;* **~s and graces** Allüren *Pl. (abwertend);* **give oneself** *or* **put on ~s** sich aufspielen; **e)** *(Mus.)* Melodie, *die.* **2.** *v. t.* **a)** *(ventilate)* lüften ‹*Zimmer, Matratze, Kleidung*›; **b)** *(finish drying)* nachtrocknen ‹*Wäsche*›; **c)** *(parade)* zur Schau tragen; **d)** *(make public)* [öffentlich] darlegen; zur Schau tragen ‹*Kenntnisse*›. **3.** *v. i. (be ventilated)* lüften

air: ~ bag *n.* Airbag, *der;* Luftsack, *der;* **~ base** *n. (Air Force)* Luftwaffenstützpunkt, *der;* **~-bed** *n.* Luftmatratze, *die;* **~borne** *adj.* **~borne bacteria** in der Luft befindliche Bakterien; **~borne freight** Luftfracht, *die;* **~borne troops** Luftlandetruppen *Pl.;* **be ~borne** sich in der Luft befinden; **become ~borne** sich in die Luft erheben; **~ brake** *n.* Druckluftbremse, *die; (flap)* Luftbremse, *die;* **~ brick** *n.* Lüftungsstein, *der (Bauw.);* **~brush** *n.* Spritzpistole, *die;* **~-bubble** *n.* Luftblase, *die;* **~ bus** *n.* Airbus, *der;* **~-conditioned** *adj.* klimatisiert; **~-conditioner** *n.* Klimaanlage, *die;* **~-conditioning** *n., no pl.* Klimatisierung, *die; (system)* Klimaanlage, *die;* **~-cooled** *adj.* luftgekühlt; **~ corridor** *n. (Aeronaut.)* Luftkorridor, *der;* **~ cover** *n.* Deckung aus der Luft

aircraft ['eəkrɑːft] *n., pl. same* Luftfahrzeug, *das; (aeroplane)* Flugzeug, *das*

'aircraft-carrier *n. (Navy)* Flugzeugträger, *der*

air: ~ crew *n.* Besatzung, *die;* Flugpersonal, *das;* **~-cushion** *n.* **a)** Luftkissen, *das;* **b) ~ vehicle** Luftkissenfahrzeug, *das*

Airedale ['eədeɪl] *n.* Airedaleterrier, *der*

airer ['eərə(r)] *n.* Wäscheständer, *der*

air: ~ fare *n.* Flugpreis, *der;* **~ ferry** *n. (aircraft)* [im Pendelluftverkehr eingesetztes] Flugzeug; *(service)* Pendelluftverkehr, *der;* **~field** *n.* Flugplatz, *der;* **~-filter** *n.* Luftfilter, *der;* **~foil** *n. (Amer.) see* **aerofoil; ~ force** *n.* Luftstreitkräfte *Pl.;* Luftwaffe, *die;* **~frame** *n. (Aeronaut.)* Flugwerk, *das;* **~gun** *n.* Luftgewehr, *das;* **~ hostess** *n.* Stewardeß, *die*

airily ['eərɪlɪ] *adv. (flippantly)* leichthin

airiness ['eərɪnɪs] *n., no pl. (flippancy)* Unbekümmertheit, *die*

airing ['eərɪŋ] *n.* Auslüften, *das;* **these clothes need a good ~:** diese Kleider müssen gründlich gelüftet werden; **give a problem an ~** *(fig.)* ein Problem an die Öffentlichkeit bringen; **~ cupboard** Trockenschrank, *der*

airless ['eəlɪs] *adj.* stickig ‹*Zimmer, Büro*›; windstill ‹*Nacht*›

air: ~ letter *n.* Luftpostleichtbrief, *der;* Aerogramm, *das;* **~lift 1.** *n.* Luftbrücke, *die* **(of** für); **2.** *v. t.* auf dem Luftweg *od.* über eine Luftbrücke transportieren; **~line** *n.* Fluggesellschaft, *die;* Fluglinie, *die;* **~line pilot** [für eine Fluggesellschaft fliegender] Pilot; **~ liner** *n.* Verkehrsflugzeug, *das;* **~lock** *n.* **a)** *(stoppage)* Luftblase, *die;* **b)** *(of spacecraft etc.)* Luftschleuse, *die;* **~ mail** *n.* Luftpost, *die;* **by ~ mail** mit *od.* per Luftpost; **~-mail** *v. t.* mit *od.* per Luftpost befördern; **~man** ['eəmən] *n., pl.* **~men** ['eəmən] Flieger, *der;* **~-minded** *adj.* am Fliegen interessiert; **~miss** *n. (Aeronaut.)* Beinahezusammenstoß, *der;* **~plane** *(Amer.) see* **aeroplane; ~ pocket** *n. (Aeronaut.)* Luftloch, *das;* **~ pollution** *n.* Luftverschmutzung, *die;* **~port** *n.* Flughafen, *der;* **~ power** *n.* Schlagkraft der Luftwaffe; **~ pressure** *n.* Luftdruck, *der;* **~ pump** *n.* Luftpumpe, *die;* **~ raid** *n.* Luftangriff, *der;* **~-raid precautions** Luftschutz, *der;* **~-raid shelter** Luftschutzraum, *der;* **~-raid warden** Luftschutzwart, *der;* **~ rifle** *n.* Luftgewehr, *das;* **~screw** *n. (Aeronaut.)* Luftschraube, *die (Technik);* **~-sea 'rescue** *n.* Seenotrettungseinsatz aus der Luft; **~ship** *n.* Luftschiff, *das;* **~sick** *adj.* luftkrank; **~sickness** *n.* Luftkrankheit, *die;* **~space** *n.* Luftraum, *der;* **~ speed** *n. (Aeronaut.)* Eigengeschwindigkeit, *die;* **~-stream** *n. (Meteorol.)* Luftströmung, *die;* **~strip** *n.* Start-und-Lande-Bahn, *die;* **~ terminal** *n.* [Air-]Terminal, *der od. das;* **~tight** *adj.* luftdicht; **~time** *n.* Sendezeit, *die;* **~-to-~** *adj.* Luft-Luft-; **~-to-~ refuelling** Betanken in der Luft; **~ traffic** *n. (Aeronaut.)* Flugverkehr, *der;* **~-traffic control** *(Aeronaut.)* Flugsicherung, *die;* **~-traffic controller** *(Aeronaut.)* Fluglotse, *der;* **~waves** *n. pl.* Äther, *der;* **~way** *n.* **a)** *(Aeronaut.)* Luftstraße, *die;* **b)** *(Anat.)* Luftröhre, *die;* **c)** *(ventilation shaft)* Lüftungsschacht, *der;* **~woman** *n.* Fliegerin, *die;* **~worthy** *adj. (Aeronaut.)* lufttüchtig

airy ['eərɪ] *adj.* **a)** luftig ‹*Büro, Zimmer*›; windig ‹*Küste*›; **b)** *(poet.: lofty)* **the ~ mountain** der in luftige Höhen hinaufragende Berg; **c)** *(superficial)* vage; *(flippant)* leichtfertig

airy-fairy [eərɪ'feərɪ] *adj. (coll. derog.)* aus der Luft gegriffen ‹*Plan*›; versponnen ‹*Idee, Vorstellung*›

aisle [aɪl] *n.* Gang, *der; (lateral section of church)* Seitenschiff, *das;* **have the audience rolling in the ~s** *(coll.)* das Publikum dazu bringen, daß es sich vor Lachen kugelt; **walk down the ~ with sb.** *(fig.)* mit jmdm. vor den Traualtar treten

aitch [eɪtʃ] *n.* H, h, *das;* **drop one's ~es** das h [im Anlaut] nicht aussprechen

Aix-la-Chapelle [eɪkslɑːʃæ'pel] *pr. n.* Aachen *(das)*

ajar [ə'dʒɑː(r)] *pred. adj.* **be** *or* **stand [slightly] ~:** einen [winzigen] Spaltbreit offenstehen; **leave ~** offenlassen

a.k.a. *abbr. (Amer.)* **also known as** al.

akimbo [ə'kɪmbəʊ] *adv.* **with arms ~:** die Arme in die Seite gestemmt

akin [ə'kɪn] *pred. adj.* **a)** verwandt; **look ~:** sich *(Dat.)* ähnlich sehen; **b)** *(fig.)* ähnlich; **be ~ to sth.** einer Sache *(Dat.)* ähnlich sein

à la [ɑː lɑː] *prep.* à la; **~ russe** [ɑː lɑː 'ruːs] auf russische Art

alabaster ['æləbɑːstə] **1.** *n.* Alabaster, *der.* **2.** *adj.* alabastern; **an ~ sculpture** eine Alabasterskulptur

à la carte [ɑː lɑː 'kɑːt] **1.** *adv.* à la carte. **2.** *adj.* **the ~ menu** das Menü à la carte

alack [ə'læk] *int. (arch.)* o weh; **~-a-day** ach und weh

alacrity [ə'lækrɪtɪ] *n., no pl.* Eilfertigkeit, *die;* **accept with ~:** mit [großer] Bereitwilligkeit annehmen

Aladdin's [ə'lædɪnz]: **~ cave** *n. Ort, an dem man Kostbarkeiten in großer Fülle findet;* **~ lamp** *n.* Aladins Wunderlampe

à la mode [ɑː lɑː 'məʊd] *adj.* **a)** in Mode; à la mode *(veralt.);* **be ~:** Mode sein; **b)** *(Cookery)* in Wein geschmort; **c)** *(Amer. Gastr.)* **pie ~:** Kuchen mit Eis

alarm [ə'lɑːm] **1.** *n.* **a)** Alarm, *der;* **give** *or* **raise the ~:** Alarm schlagen; **b)** *(fear)* Angst, *die; (uneasiness)* Besorgnis, *die;* **jump up in ~:** erschreckt aufspringen; **spread ~ and despondency** allgemeine Angst und Mutlosigkeit erzeugen; **c)** *(mechanism)* Alarmanlage, *die; (of ~ clock)* Weckmechanismus, *der; (signal)* Warnsignal, *das;* **sound the ~:** die Alarmanlage betätigen; **d)** *see* **alarm clock. 2.** *v. t.* **a)** *(make aware of danger)* aufschrecken; *(call into action)* alarmieren; **b)** *(cause anxiety to)* beunruhigen

a'larm clock *n.* Wecker, *der*

alarming [ə'lɑːmɪŋ] *adj.* alarmierend

alarmingly [ə'lɑːmɪŋlɪ] *adv.* in alarmierendem Maße

alarmist [ə'lɑːmɪst] **1.** *n.* Panikmacher, *der.* **2.** *adj.* ‹*Reden, Behauptungen*› von Panikmachern

alarum [ə'lɑːrəm] *n.* **~s and excursions** *(joc.)* Lärm und Getümmel

alas [ə'læs, ə'lɑːs] **1.** *int.* ach. **2.** *adv. (unfortunately)* leider Gottes

Alaska [ə'læskə] **a)** *pr. n.* Alaska *(das);* **b)** *n. (Cookery)* **baked ~:** ≈ Überraschungsomelett, *das;* Omelette surprise, *die*

Albania [æl'beɪnɪə] *pr. n.* Albanien *(das)*

Albanian [æl'beɪnɪən] **1.** *adj.* albanisch; **sb. is ~:** jmd. ist Albaner/Albanerin; *see also* **English 1. 2.** *n.* **a)** *(person)* Albaner, *der/*Albanerin, *die;* **b)** *(language)* Albanisch, *das; see also* **English 2 a**

albatross ['ælbətrɒs] *n. (Ornith., Golf)* Albatros, *der*

albeit [ɔːl'biːɪt] *conj. (literary)* wenn auch; obgleich *(geh.)*

albinism ['ælbɪnɪzm] *n., no pl.* Albinismus, *der*

albino [æl'biːnəʊ] *n., pl.* **~s** Albino, *der*

Albion ['ælbɪən] *n. (literary/poet.)* Albion, *das;* **perfidious ~:** das perfide Albion

album ['ælbəm] *n.* **a)** Album, *das;* **b)** *(record, set of records)* Album, *das;* **four-record ~:** Kassette mit vier Langspielplatten; **c)** *(record-holder)* Kassette, *die*

albumen ['ælbjʊmɪn] *n.* **a)** Albumen, *das (Zool.);* Eiweiß, *das;* **b)** *(Bot.)* Nährgewebe, *das*

alchemist ['ælkəmɪst] *n.* Alchimist, *der;* Alchemist, *der*

alchemy ['ælkəmɪ] *n., no pl. (lit. or fig.)* Alchimie, *die;* Alchemie, *die*

alcohol ['ælkəhɒl] *n.* Alkohol, *der*

alcoholic [ælkə'hɒlɪk] **1.** *adj.* alkoholisch; **~ smell/taste** Alkoholgeruch, *der/*-geschmack, *der;* **~ stupor** Vollrausch, *der.* **2.** *n.* Alkoholiker, *der/*Alkoholikerin, *die*

Alcoholics A'nonymous *n.* die Anonymen Alkoholiker

alcoholism ['ælkəhɒlɪzm] *n., no pl.* Alkoholismus, *der;* Trunksucht, *die*

alcove ['ælkəʊv] *n.* Alkoven, *der; (in garden wall, hedge)* Nische, *die*

aldehyde ['ældɪhaɪd] *n. (Chem.)* Aldehyd, *der; (acetaldehyde)* Acetaldehyd, *der*

alder ['ɔ:ldə(r)] *n. (Bot.)* Erle, *die;* ~ **buckthorn** Faulbaum, *der*

alderman ['ɔ:ldəmən] *n., pl.* **aldermen** ['ɔ:ldəmən] **a)** Stadtrat, *der;* Alderman, *der;* Ratsherr, *der (veralt.);* **b)** *(Amer., Austral.) gewähltes Mitglied einer Stadtverwaltung*

ale [eɪl] *n.* **a)** Ale, *das;* **b)** *(Hist.)* Bier, *das*

aleatoric [eɪlɪə'tɔ:rɪk], **aleatory** ['eɪlɪətərɪ] *adjs.* aleatorisch

'**alehouse** *n. (Hist.)* [Bier]schenke, *die*

alert [ə'lɜ:t] **1.** *adj.* **a)** *(watchful)* wachsam; **be ~ for trouble** auf der Hut sein; **be ~ to sth.** mit etw. rechnen; **b)** *(physically lively)* lebhaft; *(mentally lively)* aufgeweckt; *(attentive)* **the ~ listener** der aufmerksame Zuhörer. **2.** *n.* **a)** *(warning)* Alarmsignal, *das;* **b)** *(state of preparedness)* Alarmbereitschaft, *die;* **air-raid ~:** Fliegeralarm, *der;* **be on the ~ [for/against sth.]** [vor etw. *(Dat.)*] auf der Hut sein. **3.** *v. t.* alarmieren; **~ sb. [to sth.]** jmdn. [vor etw. *(Dat.)*] warnen

alertly [ə'lɜ:tlɪ] *adv.* aufmerksam

alertness [ə'lɜ:tnɪs] *n., no pl.* Wachsamkeit, *die;* **~ of mind** geistige Beweglichkeit

A level ['eɪ levl] *n. (Brit. Sch.)* **a)** ≈ Abitur, *das;* Abschluß der Sekundarstufe II; **take one's ~s** ≈ das Abitur machen; **b)** *attrib.* ≈ Abitur-; **~ French** ≈ Französisch als Abiturfach; **~ papers** ≈ Abiturarbeiten

alexandrine [ælɪg'zændraɪn] *n. (Pros.)* Alexandriner, *der*

alfalfa [æl'fælfə] *n. (Bot.)* Luzerne, *die;* Alfalfa, *die*

alfresco [æl'freskəʊ] **1.** *adv.* im Freien. **2.** *adj.* ⟨*Unterhaltung, Essen*⟩ im Freien

alga ['ælgə] *n., pl.* **~e** ['ældʒi:, 'ælgi:] *(Bot.)* Alge, *die*

algebra ['ældʒɪbrə] *n. (Math.)* Algebra, *die*

algebraic [ældʒɪ'breɪk] *adj. (Math.)* algebraisch

Algeria [æl'dʒɪərɪə] *pr. n.* Algerien *(das)*

Algerian [æl'dʒɪərɪən] **1.** *adj.* algerisch; **sb. is ~:** jmd. ist Algerier/Algerierin. **2.** *n.* Algerier, *der*/Algerierin, *die*

Algiers [æl'dʒɪəz] *pr. n.* Algier *(das)*

algorithm ['ælgərɪðm] *n. (Math., Computing)* Algorithmus, *der*

alias ['eɪlɪəs] **1.** *adv.* alias. **2.** *n.* angenommener Name; *(of criminal)* falscher Name

alibi ['ælɪbaɪ] *n.* Alibi, *das; (coll.: excuse)* Ausrede, *die*

Alice ['ælɪs] *n.* **an ~-in-Wonderland situation** eine völlig groteske Situation

alien ['eɪlɪən] **1.** *adj.* **a)** *(strange)* fremd; **be ~ to sb.** jmdm. fremd sein; **b)** *(foreign)* ausländisch; *(from another world)* außerirdisch; **c)** *(different)* **be ~ from sth.** einer Sache *(Dat.)* fremd sein; **d)** *(repugnant)* **be ~ to sb.** jmdm. zuwider sein; **e)** *(contrary)* **cruelty was ~ to her nature** Grausamkeit lag ihr völlig fern; **Fascism is ~ to our democratic beliefs** der Faschismus steht in krassem Gegensatz zu unserer demokratischen Überzeugung. **2.** *n.* **a)** *(Admin.: foreigner)* Ausländer, *der*/Ausländerin, *die;* **b)** *(a being from another world)* Außerirdische, *der/die*

alienate ['eɪlɪəneɪt] *v. t.* **a)** *(estrange)* befremden ⟨*Person*⟩; zerstören ⟨*Zuneigung*⟩; verlieren ⟨*Unterstützung*⟩; **his gaffes have ~d many of his supporters** durch seine Ausrutscher hat er sich *(Dat.)* viele seiner Anhänger entfremdet; **feel ~d from society** sich der Gesellschaft entfremdet fühlen; **b)** *(divert)* entziehen (**from** *Dat.*)

alienation [eɪlɪə'neɪʃn] *n., no pl.* **a)** Entfremdung, *die;* **b)** *(Theatre)* Verfremdung, *die*

¹**alight** [ə'laɪt] *v. i.* **a)** aussteigen; **~ from a vehicle** aus einem Fahrzeug aussteigen; **~ from a horse** von einem Pferd absitzen; **b)** ⟨*Vogel:*⟩ sich niedersetzen; ⟨*Flugzeug, Schneeflocken:*⟩ landen

²**alight** *pred. adj. (on fire)* **be/catch ~:** brennen; **set sth. ~:** etw. in Brand setzen; **the upper storey was well ~:** das obere Stockwerk brannte lichterloh

align [ə'laɪn] *v. t.* **a)** *(place in a line)* ausrichten; **the posts must be ~ed** die Pfosten müssen in einer Linie ausgerichtet werden; **b)** *(bring into line)* in eine Linie bringen; **~ the wheels** *(Motor Veh.)* die Spur einstellen

alignment [ə'laɪnmənt] *n.* **a)** Ausrichtung, *die;* **in/out of ~:** [genau] ausgerichtet/nicht richtig ausgerichtet; **the wheels are in/out of ~** *(Motor Veh.)* die Spur ist richtig/falsch eingestellt; **b)** *(Polit.)* Gruppierung, *die;* Ausrichtung, *die*

alike [ə'laɪk] **1.** *pred. adj.* ähnlich; *(indistinguishable)* [völlig] gleich. **2.** *adv.* gleich; in gleicher Weise; **winter and summer ~:** Sommer wie Winter; **all of us ~ are concerned, this concerns us all ~:** es geht uns alle gleichermaßen an

alimentary [ælɪ'mentərɪ] *adj.* Nahrungs-; alimentär *(Med.);* **~ organ/system** Verdauungsorgan/-system, *das*

alimentary ca'nal *n. (Anat.)* Verdauungskanal, *der*

alimentation [ælɪmən'teɪʃn] *n., no pl.* Ernährung, *die*

alimony ['ælɪmənɪ] *n.* Unterhaltszahlung, *die*

alive [ə'laɪv] *pred. adj.* **a)** lebendig; lebend; **stay ~:** am Leben bleiben; **if I'm still ~ in thirty years' time** wenn ich in dreißig Jahren noch am Leben bin; **any man ~:** jeder x-beliebige; **no man ~:** kein Mensch auf der ganzen Welt; **man ~!** *(coll.)* Menschenskind!; **keep one's hopes ~:** nicht die Hoffnung verlieren; **keep sb.'s hopes ~:** jmdn. noch hoffen lassen; **keep a matter ~:** eine Sache offenhalten; **the issue is still ~:** die Angelegenheit ist immer noch offen; **come ~:** wieder aufleben; ⟨*Ereignis:*⟩ wieder lebendig werden; **b)** *(Electr.)* eingeschaltet ⟨*Mikrophon*⟩; **be/become ~** ⟨*Draht:*⟩ unter Strom stehen/gesetzt werden; **c)** *(aware)* **be ~ to sth.** sich *(Dat.)* einer Sache *(Gen.)* bewußt sein; **he's always ~ to new ideas** er ist neuen Ideen gegenüber immer aufgeschlossen; **d)** *(brisk)* rege; munter; **be ~ and kicking** gesund und munter sein; **look ~!** ein bißchen munter!; **e)** *(swarming)* **be ~ with sth.** von etw. wimmeln

alkali ['ælkəlaɪ] *n., pl.* **~s** *or* **~es** *(Chem.)* Alkali, *das;* **~ metal** Alkalimetall, *das*

alkaline ['ælkəlaɪn] *adj. (Chem.)* alkalisch; **~ earth** Erdalkali, *das;* alkalische Erde

all [ɔ:l] **1.** *attrib. adj.* **a)** *(entire extent or quantity of)* ganz; **~ England** ganz England; **~ day** den ganzen Tag; **~ the snow/milk/food** der ganze *od.* aller Schnee/die ganze *od.* alle Milch/das ganze *od.* alles Essen; **~ the family** die ganze Familie; **for ~ that** trotz allem; **~ his life** sein ganzes Leben; **~ my money** all mein Geld; mein ganzes Geld; **stop ~ this noise/shouting!** hör mit dem Krach/Geschrei auf!; **what's ~ this noise/shouting about?** was soll der [ganze] Krach/das [ganze] Geschrei?; **thank you for ~ your hard work** danke für all deine Anstrengungen; **get away from it ~:** einmal von allem abschalten; **that says it ~:** das sagt alles; **~ hail!** Heil!; **b)** *(entire number of)* alle; **~ the books** alle Bücher; **~ my books** all[e] meine Bücher; **in ~ our houses** in allen unseren Häusern; **where are ~ the glasses?** wo sind all die Gläser *od. (ugs.)* die ganzen Gläser?; **~ ten men** alle zehn Männer; **we ~ went to bed** wir gingen alle schlafen; **aren't we ~?** trifft das nicht für uns alle zu?; **~ you children can stay here** ihr Kinder könnt alle hierbleiben; **~ the others** alle anderen; **~ those present** alle Anwesenden; **be ~ things to ~ men** es allen recht machen [wollen]; **~ Goethe's works** sämtliche Werke Goethes; **why he of ~ people?** warum ausgerechnet er?; **of ~ the nitwits!** so ein Schwachkopf!; **~ manner of things** alles mögliche; **~ manner of sausages** die verschiedensten Wurstsorten; **people of ~ ages** Menschen jeden Alters; **with ~ her faults** trotz all ihrer Fehler; **All Fools' Day** der 1. April; **All Saints' Day** Allerheiligen; **All Souls' Day** Allerseelen; **c)** *(any whatever)* jeglicher/jegliche/jegliches; **d)** *(greatest possible)* **in ~ innocence** in aller Unschuld; **with ~ speed** so schnell wie möglich. *See also* **four 2c**; **kind 1a**; **that 2a**; **time 1a, b, f**; **way 1a. 2.** *n.* **a)** *(~ persons)* alle; **~ present** alle Anwesenden; **one and ~:** [alle] ohne Ausnahme; **goodbye, one and ~!** Wiedersehen, alle zusammen!; **~ and sundry** Krethi und Plethi; **~ of us** wir alle; **the happiest/most beautiful of ~:** der/die Glücklichste/die Schönste unter allen; **the best pupils of ~:** die besten Schüler [von allen]; **most of ~:** am meisten; **he ran fastest of ~:** er lief am schnellsten; **b)** *(every bit)* **~ of it/the money** alles/das ganze *od.* alles Geld; **c)** **~ of** *(coll.: as much as)* **be ~ of seven feet tall** gut sieben Fuß groß sein; **d)** *(~ things)* alles; **~ that I possess** alles, was ich besitze; **~ I need is the money** ich brauche nur das Geld; **not ~ of the missing antiques have been recovered** nicht alle [der] fehlenden Antiquitäten sind wiedergefunden worden; **when ~ is said and done** alles in allem; **~ is lost** alles ist verloren; **~ is not lost** es ist nicht alles verloren; **he wants ~ or nothing** er will alles oder nichts; **it's ~ or nothing** es geht ums Ganze; **that is ~:** das ist alles; **it is not ~ it might be** es läßt zu wünschen übrig; **the most beautiful of ~:** der/die/das Schönste von allen; **most of ~:** am meisten; **for ~ you say, I still like her** trotz allem, was du sagst, mag ich sie immer noch; **give one's ~:** sein Letztes geben; **lose one's ~:** sein ganzes Hab und Gut verlieren; **it was ~ but impossible** es war fast unmöglich; **it was ~ I could do not to laugh** ich konnte mir das Lachen kaum verbeißen; **~ in ~:** alles in allem; **sb's ~ in ~:** jmds. Ein und Alles; **it's ~ the same** *or* **~ one to me** es ist mir ganz egal *od.* völlig gleichgültig; **that's ~ very well** *or* **fine** das ist alles schön und gut; **sth. and ~:** mitsamt etw.; **can I help you at ~?** kann ich Ihnen irgendwie behilflich sein?; **I do not know at ~:** ich weiß wirklich nicht; **I do not care at ~:** es ist mir völlig gleich; **you are not disturbing me at ~:** du störst mich nicht im geringsten; **were you surprised at ~?** warst du denn überrascht?; **if you go to Venice at ~:** wenn du überhaupt nach Venedig fährst; **is he there at ~?** ist er überhaupt da?; **he is not stupid at ~:** er ist keineswegs dumm; **he is not at ~ stupid** er ist gar nicht *od.* überhaupt nicht dumm; **she has no talent at ~:** sie hat gar *od.* überhaupt kein Talent; **nothing at ~:** gar nichts; **not at ~ happy/well** überhaupt nicht glücklich/gesund; **not at ~!** überhaupt nicht!; *(acknowledging thanks)* gern geschehen!; nichts zu danken!; **if at ~:** wenn überhaupt; **in ~:** insgesamt; *see also* **time 1c**; **e)** *(Sport)* **two [goals] ~:** zwei zu zwei; *(Tennis)* **thirty ~:** dreißig beide. **3.** *adv.* ganz; **~ but** fast; **he ~ but fell down** er wäre fast heruntergefallen; **dressed ~ in white** ganz in Weiß [gekleidet]; **~ the better/worse [for that]** um so besser/schlimmer; **I feel ~ the better for it** das hat mir wirklich gutgetan; **~ the more reason to do sth.** um so mehr sollte man etw. tun; **~ at once** *(suddenly)* plötzlich; *(simultaneously)* alle[s] zugleich; **~ too soon** allzu schnell; **go ~ serious** *(coll.)* ganz ernst werden; **be ~ 'for sth.** *(coll.)* sehr für etw. sein; **her latest play is ~ about ...:** in ihrem jüngsten Stück geht es um ...; **be ~ 'in** *(exhausted)* total *od.* völlig erledigt sein *(ugs.);* **go ~ out [to do sth.]** alles daransetzen[, etw. zu tun]; **be ~ ready [to go]** *(coll.)*

fertig [zum Weggehen] sein *(ugs.)*; **sth. is ~ right** etw. ist in Ordnung; *(tolerable)* etw. ist ganz gut; **did you get home ~ right?** sind Sie gut nach Hause gekommen?; **I'm ~ right** mir geht es ganz gut; **work out ~ right** gutgehen; klappen *(ugs.)*; **that's her, ~ right** das ist sie, ganz recht; **yes, ~ right** ja, gut; **is it ~ right if I go in?** kann ich reingehen?; **it's ~ right for you/him** *etc.*, **but ...** *(coll.)* es paßt dir/ihm *usw.*, aber ...; **it's ~ right by** *or* **with me** das ist mir recht; **lie ~ round the room** überall im Zimmer herumliegen; **it was agreed ~ round that ...:** alle waren [damit] einverstanden, daß ...; **order drinks ~ round** Getränke für alle bestellen; **better ~ round** in jeder Hinsicht besser; **be ~ there** *(coll.)* voll dasein *(ugs.)*; **I don't think he's ~ there** *(coll.)* ich glaube, er ist nicht ganz da *(ugs.)*; **~ the same** trotzdem; **it's ~ the same to me** es ist mir einerlei; **if it's ~ the same to you** wenn du nichts dagegen hast; **the All Blacks** *(coll.) die neuseeländische Rugbynationalmannschaft; see also* **along 1 a, 2 d; over 1 h, j, 2 c; set 4 d; square 2 f; that 4**

Allah ['ælə] *pr. n.* Allah *(der)*

all: ~-A'merican *adj.* **the ~-American football team** die beste Footballmannschaft der ganzen USA; **the ~-American boy** der typisch amerikanische Junge; **~-around** *(Amer.) see* **all-round**

allay [ə'leɪ] *v. t.* **a)** vermindern; trüben, dämpfen ‹*Freude, Glück*›; zerstreuen ‹*Besorgnis, Befürchtungen*›; **b)** *(alleviate)* stillen ‹*Hunger, Durst*›; lindern ‹*Schmerz*›

all: ~-'clear *n.* Entwarnung, *die;* **sound the ~-clear** entwarnen; **~-day** *adj.* ganztägig ‹*Ausflug, Versammlung*›

allegation [ælɪ'geɪʃn] *n.* Behauptung, *die;* **make ~s against sb.** Beschuldigungen gegen jmdn. erheben; **reject all ~s of corruption** jeglichen Vorwurf der Korruption zurückweisen

allege [ə'ledʒ] *v. t.* **~ that ...:** behaupten, daß ...; **~ criminal negligence** den Vorwurf grober Fahrlässigkeit erheben

alleged [ə'ledʒd] *adj.*, **allegedly** [ə'ledʒɪdlɪ] *adv.* angeblich

allegiance [ə'li:dʒəns] *n.* Loyalität, *die* **(to** gegenüber); **swear ~ to king and country** dem König und dem Vaterland Treue schwören; **oath of ~:** Treueeid, *der;* **some supporters changed their ~ from Liverpool to Everton** einige Fans sind von Liverpool zu Everton umgeschwenkt

allegorical [ælɪ'gɒrɪkl] *adj.* allegorisch

allegory ['ælɪgərɪ] *n.* Allegorie, *die; (emblem)* Sinnbild, *das*

allegro [æ'leɪgrəʊ, æ'legrəʊ] *(Mus.)* **1.** *adv.* allegro. **2.** *n., pl.* **~s** Allegro, *das*

all-e'lectric *adj.* vollelektrisch; **our house is ~:** in unserem Haus ist alles elektrisch

'all-embracing *adj.* alles umfassend

Allen key, (P) ['ælən ki:] *n.* Inbusschlüssel, *der* Ⓦ

allergic [ə'lɜ:dʒɪk] *adj.* allergisch **(to** gegen)

allergy ['ælədʒɪ] *n.* **a)** *(Med.)* Allergie, *die* **(to** gegen); **b)** *(fig. coll.)* **have an ~ to sth.** auf etw. *(Akk.)* allergisch reagieren

alleviate [ə'li:vɪeɪt] *v. t.* abschwächen

alleviation [əli:vɪ'eɪʃn] *n., no pl.* Abschwächung, *die*

[1]alley ['ælɪ] *n.* **a)** [schmale] Gasse; *(between flower-beds or gardens)* Pfad, *der; (avenue)* Allee, *die;* **be up sb.'s ~** *(coll.)* jmds. Fall sein *(ugs.)*; **this problem is just** *or* **right up his ~** *(coll.)* für dieses Problem ist er genau der Richtige; **b) skittle ~:** Kegelbahn, *die*

[2]alley *see* **[2]ally**

'all-fired *(Amer. sl.) adj., adv.* verdammt

alliance [ə'laɪəns] *n.* Bündnis, *das; (league)* Allianz, *die;* **~ with other groups would increase our influence** ein Bündnis mit anderen Gruppen würde unseren Einfluß vergrößern; **in ~ with sb./sth.** im Verein mit jmdm./etw.

allied ['ælaɪd] *adj.* **be ~ to** *or* **with sb./sth.** mit jmdm./etw. verbündet sein; **German is more closely ~ to English than to French** das Deutsche ist mit dem Englischen enger verwandt als mit dem Französischen; **the A~ Powers** die Alliierten

alligator ['ælɪgeɪtə(r)] *n. (Zool.)* Alligator, *der; (skin)* Krokodilleder, *das*

'alligator clip *n.* Krokodilklemme, *die*

all: ~-important *adj.* entscheidend; **~-in** *adj.* Pauschal-; **it costs £350 ~-in** es kostet 350 Pfund alles inklusive; **~-in wrestling** Freistilringen, *das*

alliteration [əlɪtə'reɪʃn] *n.* Stabreim, *der;* Alliteration, *die*

alliterative [ə'lɪtərətɪv] *adj.* stabreimend; alliterierend

'all-night *adj.* die ganze Nacht dauernd ‹*Sitzung*›; nachts durchgehend geöffnet ‹*Gaststätte*›

allocate ['æləkeɪt] *v. t.* zur Verfügung stellen ‹*Geld, Mittel*›; **~ sth. to sb./sth.** jmdm./einer Sache etw. zuweisen *od.* zuteilen

allocation [ælə'keɪʃn] *n.* Verteilung, *die; (ration)* Zuteilung, *die*

allot [ə'lɒt] *v. t.*, **-tt-: ~ sth. to sb.** jmdm. etw. zuteilen; **you will be ~ted fifty pounds** es werden Ihnen fünfzig Pfund bewilligt; **we ~ted two hours to the task** wir haben zwei Stunden für diese Arbeit vorgesehen; **~ shares** Aktien ausgeben

allotment [ə'lɒtmənt] *n.* **a)** Zuteilung, *die;* **b)** *(Brit.: plot of land)* Gartenparzelle, *die;* ≈ Schrebergarten, *der;* **c)** *(share)* Anteil, *der*

allow [ə'laʊ] **1.** *v. t.* **a)** *(permit)* **~ sth.** etw. erlauben *od.* zulassen *od. (förmlicher)* gestatten; **~ sb. to do sth.** jmdm. erlauben, etw. zu tun; **be ~ed to do sth.** etw. tun dürfen; **will you be ~ed to?** darfst du?; **~ sb./oneself sth.** jmdm./sich etw. erlauben; **sb. is ~ed sth.** jmdm. ist etw. erlaubt; **~ sth. to happen** zulassen, daß etw. geschieht; **~ yourself to be convinced** lassen Sie sich überzeugen; **~ sb. in/out/past/through** jmdn. hinein-/hinaus-/vorbei-/durchlassen; **you are not ~ed in/out/past/through** Sie dürfen nicht hinein/hinaus/vorbei/durch; **~ sb. a discount/5 % interest** jmdm. Rabatt/5 % Zinsen geben; **b)** *(agree)* zugeben; **c)** *(Law)* bestätigen ‹*Anspruch*›; **~ the appeal** der Berufung *(Dat.)* stattgeben; **d)** *(Sport)* **the referee ~ed the goal** der Schiedsrichter gab das Tor. **2.** *v. i.* **~ of sth.** etw. zulassen *od.* erlauben; **~ for sth.** etw. berücksichtigen; **we started very early, to ~ for delays** wir begannen sehr früh, um etwaige Verzögerungen auffangen zu können

allowable [ə'laʊəbl] *adj.* zulässig

allowance [ə'laʊəns] *n.* **a)** Zuteilung, *die; (money for special expenses)* Zuschuß, *der;* **your luggage ~ is 44 kg.** Sie haben 44 kg Freigepäck; **tax ~:** Steuerfreibetrag, *der;* **clothing ~:** Kleidergeld, *das;* **b) make ~s for sth./sb.** etw./jmdn. berücksichtigen; **make ~ for errors** eventuelle Fehler einkalkulieren; **c)** *(Commerc.)* Ermäßigung, *die*

alloy ['ælɔɪ, ə'lɔɪ] **1.** *n.* Legierung, *die; (inferior metal added)* unedles Metall; **~ steel** Sonderstahl, *der.* **2.** *v. t.* legieren; *(debase)* geringhaltiger machen

all: ~-'powerful *adj.* allmächtig; **~-purpose** *adj.* Universal-; Allzweck-; **~-round** *adj.* Allround-; **~-'rounder** *n.* Allroundtalent, *das; (Sport)* Allroundspieler, *der/-spielerin, die*

'allspice *n.* Pimentbaum, *der; (berry)* Piment, *der*

'all-time *adj.* **~ record** absoluter Rekord; **~ favourites** *or* **greats** unvergessene Publikumslieblinge; **~ high/low** höchster/niedrigster Stand aller Zeiten

allude [ə'lju:d, ə'lu:d] *v. i.* **~ to sth./sb.** sich auf etw./jmdn. beziehen; *(covertly)* auf etw./jmdn. anspielen

allure [ə'ljʊə(r)] **1.** *v. t.* locken; *(fascinate)* faszinieren; **~ sb. to do sth.** jmdn. dazu verlocken, etw. zu tun; **~d by thoughts of stardom** durch die Aussicht auf eine glänzende Karriere verlockt. **2.** *n., no pl.* Verlockung, *die; (personal charm)* Charme, *der*

allurement [ə'ljʊəmənt] *n.* Verlockung, *die; (charm)* **she displayed all her ~s** sie ließ all ihre Reize spielen

alluring [ə'ljʊərɪŋ] *adj.* verlockend; **an ~ appeal** eine Verlockung

allusion [ə'lju:ʒn, ə'lu:ʒn] *n.* **a)** Hinweis, *der;* **in an ~ to** unter Bezugnahme auf (+ *Akk.*); **b)** *(covert reference)* Anspielung, *die* **(to** auf + *Akk.*)

allusive [ə'lju:sɪv, ə'lu:sɪv] *adj.* **be ~ to sth.** auf etw. *(Akk.)* anspielen

alluvial [ə'lu:vɪəl] *adj. (Geol.)* angeschwemmt; **~ soil** Alluvialboden, *der*

'all-weather *attrib. adj.* Allwetter-

[1]ally 1. [ə'laɪ, 'ælaɪ] *v. t.* **~ oneself with sb./sth.** sich mit jmdm./etw. verbünden; *see also* **allied. 2.** ['ælaɪ] *n.* Verbündete, *der/die;* **my old friend and ~:** mein alter Freund und Kampfgefährte; **the Allies** die Alliierten

[2]ally ['ælɪ] *n. (besonders schöne)* Murmel *(aus Alabaster od. Glas)*

Alma Mater [ælmə 'meɪtə(r), ælmə 'mɑ:tə(r)] *n.* Alma mater, *die*

almanac ['ɔ:lmənæk, 'ɒlmənæk] *n.* Almanach, *der*

almighty [ɔ:l'maɪtɪ] **1.** *adj.* **a)** allmächtig; **the A~:** der Allmächtige; **God A~!** *(sl.)* großer Gott!; **he acts as if he were God A~:** er tut, als ob er der liebe Gott selber wäre; **b)** *(sl.: very great, hard, etc.)* mächtig. **2.** *adv. (sl.)* mächtig

almond ['ɑ:mənd] *n.* **a)** Mandel, *die;* **sweet/bitter ~:** Süß-/Bittermandel, *die;* **~ eyes** Mandelaugen; **b)** *(tree)* Mandelbaum, *der*

almoner ['ɑ:mənə(r)] *n. (Brit.)* Sozialbetreuer, *der/-betreuerin, die (eines Krankenhauses)*

almost ['ɔ:lməʊst] *adv.* fast; beinahe; **she ~ fell** sie wäre fast gefallen

alms [ɑ:mz] *n., no pl.* Almosen, *das*

'almshouse *n.* Armenhaus, *das*

aloe ['æləʊ] *n.* **a)** Aloe, *die;* **b)** *in pl. (Pharm.)* Aloe, *die;* Aloesaft, *der*

aloft [ə'lɒft] *adv.* **a)** *(position) (literary)* hoch droben *(dichter.)*; *(Naut.)* [oben] in der Takelage *od.* im Rigg; **b)** *(direction) (literary)* empor *(dichter.)*; *(Naut.)* in die Takelage; in das Rigg; **go ~:** in die Takelage *od.* in das Rigg klettern; aufentern *(Seemannsspr.)*

alone [ə'ləʊn] **1.** *pred. adj.* allein; alleine *(ugs.)*; **be [all] ~:** [ganz] allein sein; **she likes to be ~ sometimes** manchmal ist sie gern [für sich] allein; **when his parents died he was left ~ [in the world]** als seine Eltern starben, stand er ganz allein da; **he was not ~ in the belief that ...:** er stand nicht allein mit der Überzeugung, daß ...; er war nicht als einziger davon überzeugt, daß ...; **go it ~:** etw. im Alleingang tun; *see also* **[2]leave e; 'let 1 a. 2.** *adv.* allein; **you ~ can help me** nur du *od.* du allein kannst mir helfen; **the problem/money was his ~:** es war einzig und allein sein Problem/Geld; **this fact ~:** schon allein dies

along [ə'lɒŋ] **1.** *prep.* **a)** *(position)* entlang (+ *Dat.*); **~ one side of the street** auf der einen Straßenseite; **all ~ the wall** die ganze *od.* an der ganzen Mauer entlang; **b)** *(direction)* entlang (+ *Akk.*); **walk ~ the riverbank/street** am Ufer *od.* das Ufer/die Straße entlanglaufen; **creep ~ a wall** eine Mauer *od.* an einer Mauer entlangschleichen. **2.** *adv.* **a)** *(onward)* weiter; **he came running ~:** er kam herbei- *od.* angelaufen; **leaves carried ~ by the wind** vom Wind fortgetragenes Laub; **he saw the train steaming ~ in the distance** er sah den Zug in der Ferne vorbei- *od.* vorüberdampfen; **the snake was slithering ~ in the tall grass** die Schlange glitt durch das hohe Gras; **b)** *(with one)* **bring/take sb./sth. ~:** jmdn./etw. mitbringen/mitnehmen; **c)** *(there)* **I'll be ~ shortly/ as soon as I can** ich komme gleich/sobald ich kann; **d) all ~:** die ganze Zeit [über]

alongside [əlɒŋ'saɪd] **1.** *adv.* daneben; längsseits *(Seemannsspr.)*; **~ the quay** am Kai; **~ of** *see* **2. 2.** *prep. (position)* neben (+ *Dat.*); längsseits *(Seemannsspr.)* (+ *Gen.*); *(direction)* neben (+ *Akk.*); längsseits heran an *(Seemannsspr.)* (+ *Akk.*); *(fig.)* neben (+ *Dat.*); **work ~ sb.** mit jmdm. zusammen arbeiten/*(fig.)* zusammenarbeiten

aloof [ə'lu:f] **1.** *adv.* abseits; **stand ~ from the others** abseits der anderen stehen; **hold ~ from sb.** sich von jmdm. fernhalten; sich abseits von jmdm. halten; **keep ~:** Distanz wahren; **keep ~ from sb.** sich von jmdm. absondern *od.* fernhalten. **2.** *adj.* distanziert; reserviert

aloofness [ə'lu:fnɪs] *n., no pl.* Reserviertheit, *die;* Distanz[iertheit], *die*

aloud [ə'laʊd] *adv.* laut; **read [sth.] ~:** [etw.] vorlesen; **think ~:** laut denken

alp [ælp] *n. (pasture)* Alp, *die; see also* **Alps**

alpaca [æl'pækə] *n.* **a)** *(Zool.)* Alpaka, *das;* **b)** *(wool)* Alpaka, *das;* Alpakawolle, *die; (fabric)* Alpaka, *der*

alpenhorn ['ælpənhɔ:n] *n.* Alphorn, *das*

alpenstock ['ælpənstɒk] *n.* Bergstock, *der*

alpha ['ælfə] *n.* **a)** *(letter)* Alpha, *das;* **the A~ and Omega** das A und O; **b)** *(Sch., Univ.: mark)* Eins, *die*

alphabet ['ælfəbet] *n.* Alphabet, *das;* Abc, *das;* **the phonetic/Cyrillic ~:** das phonetische/kyrillische Alphabet

alphabetical [ælfə'betɪkl] *adj.* alphabetisch; **in ~ order** in alphabetischer Reihenfolge; alphabetisch geordnet

alphabetically [ælfə'betɪkəlɪ] *adv.* alphabetisch; nach dem Alphabet

alphabetize ['ælfəbetaɪz] *v.t.* alphabetisieren; nach dem Alphabet ordnen

alpha: ~ particles *n. pl. (Phys.)* Alphateilchen *Pl.*; **~ rays** *n. pl. (Phys.)* Alphastrahlen *Pl.*

alpine ['ælpaɪn] **1.** *adj.* **a)** alpin; Hochgebirgs-; **~ region/climate/vegetation** Hochgebirgsregion, *die*/-klima, *das*/alpine Vegetation; **~ flowers** Alpen-, Gebirgsblumen; **~ garden** Alpengarten, *der;* Alpinum, *das;* **~ skiing/event** alpiner Skisport/Wettbewerb; **b) A~:** Alpen-. **2.** *n. (Bot.)* Alpenblume, *die;* [Hoch]gebirgspflanze, *die*

Alpinist, alpinist ['ælpɪnɪst] *n.* Alpinist, *der*/Alpinistin, *die*

Alps [ælps] *pr. n. pl.* **the ~:** die Alpen

already [ɔ:l'redɪ] *adv.* schon; **it's ~ 8 o'clock** *or* **8 o'clock ~:** es ist schon 8 Uhr; **He's here. – A~?** Er ist hier. – Schon [so früh]?; **she's ~ got ten children** sie hat schon *od.* bereits zehn Kinder

Alsace [æl'sæs] *pr. n.* Elsaß, *das;* **~-Lorraine** Elsaß-Lothringen *(das)*

Alsatian [æl'seɪʃn] **1.** *adj.* elsässisch. **2.** *n.* **a)** *(person)* Elsässer, *der*/Elsässerin, *die;* **b)** *(dog)* [deutscher] Schäferhund

also ['ɔ:lsəʊ] *adv.* auch; *(moreover)* außerdem; **I'm going, and John is ~ going** *or* **John is going ~:** ich gehe, und John geht auch *od.* ebenfalls; **he's writing a book and ~ translating one** er schreibt ein Buch und übersetzt auch *od.* außerdem eines; **he's writing and ~ translating a book** er schreibt ein Buch und übersetzt es auch

'also-ran *n.* **be an ~** ⟨*Hund, Pferd:*⟩ [immer nur] hintere Plätze/einen hinteren Platz belegen; **he remained an ~ all his life** *(fig.)* er kam sein ganzes Leben lang auf keinen grünen Zweig *(ugs.)*

altar ['ɔ:ltə(r), 'ɒltə(r)] *n.* **a)** *(Communion table)* Altar, *der;* **lead sb. to the ~** *(fig.)* jmdn. zum Traualtar führen; **b)** *(for sacrifice)* Opferstätte, *die;* Opfertisch, *der*

'altar-piece *n.* Altarbild, -gemälde, *das*

alter ['ɔ:ltə(r), 'ɒltə(r)] **1.** *v.t.* **a)** *(change)* ändern; verändern ⟨*Stadt, Wohnung*⟩; **That's wrong. It will have to be ~ed** Das ist falsch. Es muß geändert werden; **have a dress ~ed** ein Kleid ändern lassen; **b)** *(Amer.: castrate, spay)* sterilisieren. **2.** *v.i.* sich verändern; **he has ~ed a lot since then** *(in appearance)* er hat sich seitdem stark verändert; *(in character)* er hat sich seitdem sehr geändert

alteration [ɔ:ltə'reɪʃn, ɒltə'reɪʃn] *n.* Änderung, *die; (of text)* Abänderung, *die; (of house)* Umbau, *der;* **without any ~** ohne jede Änderung; **we're having some ~s done to the house** wir bauen um; bei uns wird umgebaut

altercation [ɔ:ltə'keɪʃn, ɒltə'keɪʃn] *n.* Auseinandersetzung, *die;* Streiterei, *die*

alter ego [æltər 'egəʊ, æltər 'i:gəʊ] *n., pl.* **~s** Alter ego, *das (geh.)*

alternate 1. [ɔ:l'tɜ:nət, ɒl'tɜ:nət] *adj.* **a)** *(in turn)* sich abwechselnd; **John and Mary come on ~ days** John und Mary kommen abwechselnd einen um den anderen Tag; *(together)* John und Mary kommen jeden zweiten Tag; **she goes shopping and goes to work on ~ Saturdays** sie geht abwechselnd jeden zweiten Samstag arbeiten und einkaufen; **~ leaves** *(Bot.)* wechselständige Blätter; **~ angles** *(Math.)* Wechselwinkel *Pl.*; **b)** *see* **alternative 1. 2.** *n.* **a)** *(deputy)* Vertreter, *der*/Vertreterin, *die;* **b)** *(substitute)* Alternative, *die.* **3.** ['ɔ:ltəneɪt, 'ɒltəneɪt] *v.t.* abwechseln lassen; **she has only two summer dresses, so she ~s them** sie hat nur zwei Sommerkleider, deshalb trägt sie sie abwechselnd; **he ~s his days off and** *or* **with his working days** er hat abwechselnd einen Tag frei und geht einen Tag zur Arbeit. **4.** *v.i.* sich abwechseln; alternieren *(fachspr.)*

alternately [ɔ:l'tɜ:nətlɪ, ɒl'tɜ:nətlɪ] *adv.* abwechselnd

'alternating current *n. (Electr.)* Wechselstrom, *der*

alternation [ɔ:ltə'neɪʃn, ɒltə'neɪʃn] *n.* Wechsel, *der;* **~ of generations** *(Biol.)* Generationswechsel, *der*

alternative [ɔ:l'tɜ:nətɪv, ɒl'tɜ:nətɪv] **1.** *adj.* alternativ; Alternativ-; **~ possibility** Ausweich- *od.* Alternativmöglichkeit, *die;* **~ suggestion** Alternativ- *od.* Gegenvorschlag, *der;* **~ route** Alternativstrecke, *die; (to avoid obstruction etc.)* Ausweichstrecke, *die;* **we'll try to get you on an ~ flight** wir werden versuchen, Ihren Flug umzubuchen; **the ~ society** die alternative Gesellschaft; **~ medicine** Alternativmedizin, *die.* **2.** *n.* **a)** *(choice)* Alternative, *die;* Wahl, *die;* **if I had the ~:** wenn ich vor die Wahl *od.* Alternative gestellt würde; wenn ich vor der Wahl *od.* Alternative stünde; **we have no ~ [but to ...]** wir haben keine andere Wahl[, als zu ...]; **that left me** *or* **I was left with no ~:** mir blieb keine andere Wahl; **b)** *(possibility)* Möglichkeit, *die;* **we have two ~s: either we press forward or we turn back** wir haben zwei Möglichkeiten: weiterzufahren oder umzukehren; **there is no [other] ~:** es gibt keine Alternative *od.* andere Möglichkeit; **what are the ~s?** welche Alternativen gibt es?

alternatively [ɔ:l'tɜ:nətɪvlɪ, ɒl'tɜ:nətɪvlɪ] *adv.* oder aber; **or ~:** oder aber auch

alternator ['ɔ:ltəneɪtə(r), 'ɒltəneɪtə(r)] *n. (Electr.)* Wechselstromgenerator, *der*

although [ɔ:l'ðəʊ] *conj.* obwohl; **~ quite clever, he still makes mistakes** obwohl er ziemlich klug ist, macht er trotzdem *od.* doch Fehler

altimeter ['æltɪmi:tə(r)] *n.* Höhenmesser, *der*

altitude ['æltɪtju:d] *n. (height)* Höhe, *die;* **what is our ~?** wie hoch sind wir?; **at what ~ are we flying?** wie hoch *od.* in welcher Höhe fliegen wir?; **from this ~:** aus dieser Höhe; **what is the ~ of ...?** wie hoch liegt ...?; **at an ~ of 2,000 ft.** ≈ in einer Höhe von 600 Metern; **at high ~:** in großer Höhe; **gain/lose ~:** [an] Höhe gewinnen/verlieren

alto ['æltəʊ] *n., pl.* **~s** *(Mus.) (voice, part)* Alt, *der; (male singer)* Alt, *der;* Altist, *der;* Altsänger, *der; (female singer)* Alt, *der;* Altistin, *die;* Altsängerin, *die;* **~ saxophone/ clarinet** Altsaxophon, *das*/Altklarinette, *die;* **~ clef** Altschlüssel, *der*

altogether [ɔ:ltə'geðə(r)] **1.** *adv.* völlig; *(on the whole)* im großen und ganzen; *(in total)* insgesamt; **not ~ [true/convincing]** nicht ganz [wahr/überzeugend]. **2.** *n.* **in the ~** *(coll.)* im Evas-/Adamskostüm

altruism ['æltrʊɪzm] *n., no pl.* Altruismus, *der;* Uneigennützigkeit, *die*

altruist ['æltrʊɪst] *n.* Altruist, *der (geh.)*

altruistic [æltrʊ'ɪstɪk] *adj.*, **altruistically** [æltrʊ'ɪstɪkəlɪ] *adv.* altruistisch; uneigennützig

alum ['æləm] *n. (Chem.)* Alaun, *der*

alumina [ə'lju:mɪnə] *n.* Aluminiumoxyd, *(fachspr.)* -oxid, *das;* Tonerde, *die*

aluminium [æljʊ'mɪnɪəm] *n. (Brit.)* Aluminium, *das*

aluminize [ə'lju:mɪnaɪz] *v.t.* aluminieren

aluminum [ə'lu:mɪnəm] *(Amer.) see* **aluminium**

alumna [ə'lʌmnə] *n., pl.* **~e** [ə'lʌmni:] *(Amer.)* Absolventin, *die*

alumnus [ə'lʌmnəs] *n., pl.* **alumni** [ə'lʌmnaɪ] *(Amer.)* Absolvent, *der;* **we are both alumni of Harvard** wir sind beide ehemalige Harvard-Studenten

alveolar [æl'vɪələ(r), ælvɪ'əʊlə(r)] *adj.* **a)** *(Anat.)* **~ ridge** Alveolarfortsatz, *der;* **b)** *(Phonet.)* alveolar; Alveolar-

always ['ɔ:lweɪz, 'ɔ:lwɪz] *adv. (at all times)* immer; *(repeatedly)* ständig; [an]dauernd *(ugs.)*; *(whatever the circumstances)* jederzeit; **he ~ comes on Monday** er kommt immer am Montag; **he is ~ making fun of other people** er macht sich dauernd *od.* ständig über andere lustig; **don't worry, I can ~ sleep on the floor** keine Sorge, ich kann jederzeit *od.* ohne weiteres auf dem Fußboden schlafen; **you can ~ come by train if you prefer** ihr könnt ja auch mit der Bahn kommen, wenn euch das lieber ist

alyssum ['ælɪsəm] *n. (Bot.)* Steinkraut, *das*

Alzheimer's disease ['æltshaɪməz dɪzi:z] *n.* Alzheimer-Krankheit, *die*

AM *abbr.* **amplitude modulation** AM

am *see* **be**

a.m. [eɪ'em] **1.** *adv.* vormittags; **[at] one/four ~:** [um] ein/vier Uhr nachts *od.* morgens *od.* früh; **[at] five/eight ~:** [um] fünf/acht Uhr morgens *od.* früh; **[at] nine ~:** [um] neun Uhr morgens *od.* früh *od.* vormittags; **[at] ten/eleven ~:** [um] zehn/elf Uhr vormittags. **2.** *n.* Vormittag, *der;* **Monday/this ~:** Montag/heute vormittag

amalgam [ə'mælgəm] *n.* **a)** *(lit. or fig.: mixture)* Mischung, *die;* **b)** *(alloy)* Amalgam, *das*

amalgamate [ə'mælgəmeɪt] **1.** *v.t.* vereinigen; verschmelzen *(geh.)*; amalgamieren *(geh.)* ⟨*Rassen*⟩; zusammenlegen ⟨*Abteilungen*⟩; fusionieren ⟨*Firmen*⟩. **2.** *v.i.* sich vereinigen; ⟨*Firmen:*⟩ fusionieren; ⟨*Abteilungen:*⟩ zusammengelegt werden

amalgamation [əmælgə'meɪʃn] *n.* **a)** *(action)* Vereinigung, *die; (of races)* Verschmelzung, *die (geh.)*; Amalgamierung, *die (geh.)*; *(of firms)* Fusion, *die; (of departments)* Zusammenlegung, *die;* **b)** *(result)* Vereinigung, *die;* **his 'theory' is an ~ of various ideas** seine „Theorie" besteht aus einer Mischung *od.* *(geh.)* ist ein Amalgam der verschiedensten Ideen

amanuensis [əmænjʊ'ensɪs] *n., pl.* **amanuenses** [əmænjʊ'ensi:z] Sekretär, *der*

amaryllis [æmə'rılıs] *n. (Bot.)* **a)** *(plant of genus A~)* Amaryllis, *die;* **b)** *(plant of related genus)* Amaryllisgewächs, *das*

amass [ə'mæs] *v.t.* [ein]sammeln; **what a lot of books you have ~ed over the years!** was für eine Menge Bücher sich bei dir während der Jahre angesammelt *od.* angehäuft hat!; **~ a [large] fortune** ein [großes] Vermögen anhäufen

amateur ['æmətə(r)] *n.* **a)** *(non-professional)* Amateur, *der;* **b)** *(derog.: trifler)* Amateur, *der;* Dilettant, *der;* **c)** *attrib.* Amateur-; Laien-; **~ actor/theatre** Amateur- *od.* Laienschauspieler/Amateur- *od.* Laientheater; **when he retired he took up ~ photography/writing** als Rentner fing er an zu fotografieren/schriftstellern

amateurish ['æmətərıʃ] *adj. (derog.)* laienhaft; amateurhaft

amateurishness ['æmətərıʃnıs] *n.* Dilettantismus, *der*

amateurism ['æmətərızm] *n., no pl.* Amateursport, *der; (as qualifying principle)* Amateurstatus, *der*

amatory ['æmətərı] *adj.* erotisch; Liebes-; **~ poems/letters/affairs** Liebesgedichte/-briefe/-affären; **~ advances** amouröse Avancen *(geh.)*

amaze [ə'meız] *v.t.* verblüffen; verwundern; **be ~d [by sth.]** [über etw. *(Akk.)*] verblüfft *od.* verwundert sein

amazement [ə'meızmənt] *n., no pl.* Verblüffung, *die;* Verwunderung, *die*

amazing [ə'meızıŋ] *adj. (remarkable)* erstaunlich; *(astonishing)* verblüffend; **'~ value'** „sensationell günstig"

amazingly [ə'meızıŋlı] *adv.* **a)** *as sentence-modifier (remarkably)* erstaunlicherweise; *(astonishingly)* verblüffenderweise; **b)** erstaunlich; **~ stupid** außerordentlich *od. (ugs.)* selten dumm

[1]**Amazon** ['æməzən] *pr. n.* **the ~:** der Amazonas *od. (veralt.)* Amazonenstrom

[2]**Amazon** *n.* **a)** *(Mythol.: female warrior)* Amazone, *die;* **b)** *(fig.)* Mannweib, *das (abwertend);* Amazone, *die (veralt.)*

ambassador [æm'bæsədə(r)] *n.* **a)** Botschafter, *der*/Botschafterin, *die; (on particular mission)* Sonderbotschafter, *der;* Gesandte, *der (hist.);* **~ to a country/court** Botschafter in einem Land/an einem Hof; **b)** *(messenger)* Abgesandte, *der/die;* Beauftragte, *der/die*

ambassadorial [æmbæsə'dɔ:rıəl] *adj.* Botschafter-; eines/des Botschafters *nachgestellt; (of envoy)* Gesandten-; eines/des Gesandten *nachgestellt*

amber ['æmbə(r)] **1.** *n.* **a)** Bernstein, *der;* **b)** *(traffic light)* Gelb, *das;* **when the ~ is flashing** bei gelbem Blinklicht. **2.** *adj.* Bernstein-; aus Bernstein *nachgestellt; (colour)* bernsteinfarben; gelb ‹*Verkehrslicht*›

ambergris ['æmbəgrıs, 'æmbəgri:s] *n.* Amber, *der;* Ambra, *die*

ambiance [ɑ̃bı'ɑ̃s] *see* **ambience**

ambidexterity [æmbıdeks'terıtı] *see* **ambidextrousness**

ambidextrous [æmbı'dekstrəs] *adj.* beidhändig; ambidexter *(fachspr.)*

ambidextrously [æmbı'dekstrəslı] *adv.* beidhändig

ambidextrousness [æmbı'dekstrəsnıs] *n., no pl.* Beidhändigkeit, *die*

ambience ['æmbıəns] *n.* Ambiente, *das (geh.);* Milieu, *das;* Atmosphäre, *die;* **the ~ of the theatre** das Ambiente des Theaters; das Theatermilieu; die Theateratmosphäre

ambient ['æmbıənt] *adj.* Umgebungs-; **~ pressure/air** Umgebungsdruck, *der*/-luft, *die*

ambiguity [æmbı'gju:ıtı] *n.* Zweideutigkeit, *die;* Doppelsinnigkeit, *die (geh.); (having several meanings)* Mehrdeutigkeit, *die;* Ambiguität, *die (Sprachw.)*

ambiguous [æm'bıgjʊəs] *adj.* zweideutig; doppelsinnig *(geh.); (with several meanings)* mehrdeutig; ambig *(Sprachw.);* nicht eindeutig klassifizierbar ‹*Pflanze, Tier*›; **her smile was ~:** ihr Lächeln war zweideutig

ambiguously [æm'bıgjʊəslı] *adv.* zweideutig; doppelsinnig *(geh.); (with several meanings)* mehrdeutig; ambig *(Sprachw.);* **smile ~:** zweideutig lächeln

ambiguousness [æm'bıgjʊəsnıs] *n., no pl.* Zweideutigkeit, *die;* Doppelsinnigkeit, *die (geh.); (having several meanings)* Mehrdeutigkeit, *die*

ambit ['æmbıt] *n.* Gebiet, *das;* Bereich, *der;* **the ~ of sb.'s experience/competence** jmds. Erfahrungs-/Kompetenz- *od.* Zuständigkeitsbereich

ambition [æm'bıʃn] *n.* Ehrgeiz, *der; (aspiration)* Ambition, *die;* Wunsch, *der;* **you can never fulfil every ~:** man kann nie all seine Ambitionen verwirklichen

ambitious [æm'bıʃəs] *adj.* ehrgeizig; ambitioniert *(geh.)* ‹*Person*›; **she was very ~ for him to succeed** ihr ganzer Ehrgeiz war es, daß er Erfolg hatte; **be ~ to do sth.** von dem Ehrgeiz erfüllt sein, etw. zu tun

ambitiously [æm'bıʃəslı] *adv.* voller Ehrgeiz; von Ehrgeiz erfüllt

ambitiousness [æm'bıʃəsnıs] *n., no pl.* Ehrgeiz, *der;* ehrgeiziges Streben; **the ~ of his proposal/the new project** das Ehrgeizige an seinem Plan/an dem neuen Projekt

ambivalence [æm'bıvələns] *n., no pl.* Ambivalenz, *die*

ambivalent [æm'bıvələnt] *adj.* ambivalent

amble ['æmbl] **1.** *v.i.* **a)** ‹*Reiter:*› im Paßgang reiten; ‹*Pferd:*› im Paßgang gehen; *(ride at easy pace)* im Schritt reiten; **b)** *(fig.: walk slowly)* schlendern; gemütlich gehen. **2.** *n.* **a)** Paßgang, *der;* **b)** *(fig.)* Schlendern, *das*

ambrosia [æm'brəʊzıə] *n., no pl.* Ambrosia, *die*

ambulance ['æmbjʊləns] *n.* **a)** *(vehicle)* Krankenwagen, *der;* Ambulanz, *die; (Mil.)* Sanitätswagen, *der;* Sanka, *der (bes. Soldatenspr.);* **b)** *(Mil.: mobile hospital)* Feldlazarett, *das;* Ambulanz, *die*

ambulance: ~-chaser *n. (Amer.) Anwalt oder sein Agent, der Unfallopfer dazu überredet, auf Schadenersatz zu klagen;* **~ driver** *n.* Fahrer eines/des Krankenwagens; **~-man** *n.* Sanitäter, *der;* **~ service** *n.* Rettungsdienst, *der;* **~ worker** *n.* Sanitäter, *der*/Sanitäterin, *die*

ambulant ['æmbjʊlənt] *adj.* gehfähig ‹*Patient*›; ambulant ‹*Behandlung*›

ambush ['æmbʊʃ] **1.** *n. (concealment)* Hinterhalt, *der; (troops concealed)* im Hinterhalt liegende Truppe; **lie in ~** *(lit. or fig.)* im Hinterhalt liegen; **arrange an ~:** einen Überfall aus dem Hinterhalt führen. **2.** *v.t.* [aus dem Hinterhalt] überfallen

ameliorate [ə'mi:lıəreıt] **1.** *v.t.* verbessern. **2.** *v.i.* sich verbessern; besser werden

amelioration [əmi:lıə'reıʃn] *n.* [Ver]besserung, *die*

ameliorative [ə'mi:lıərətıv] *adj.* verbessernd; bessernd ‹*Einfluß*›; **~ measures/effect** Verbesserungsmaßnahmen *Pl.*/-effekt, *der*

amen [ɑ:'men, eı'men] **1.** *int.* amen; **say '~' to sth.** ja und amen zu etw. sagen. **2.** *n.* Amen, *das*

amenability [əmi:nə'bılıtı] *n., no pl.* **a)** *(responsiveness)* Zugänglichkeit, *die* **(to** für); **b)** *(of phenomenon etc.)* Unterworfenheit, *die* **(to** unter + *Akk.*); **c)** *(responsibility)* Verantwortlichkeit, *die* **(to** gegenüber); **our ~ to the law** daß wir dem Gesetz gehorchen müssen

amenable [ə'mi:nəbl] *adj.* **a)** *(responsive)* zugänglich, aufgeschlossen ‹*Person*› **(to** *Dat.*); **he simply isn't ~ to reason/advice** er ist Vernunftgründen/Ratschlägen einfach nicht zugänglich; **~ to kindness** für Freundlichkeit empfänglich; **b)** *(subject)* unterworfen ‹*Sache*› **(to** *Dat.*); **be ~ to the laws of nature/rules of grammar** den Naturgesetzen/Regeln der Grammatik unterworfen sein *od.* gehorchen; **c)** *(responsible)* **be ~ to the law** dem Gesetz gehorchen müssen

amend [ə'mend] *v.t. (correct)* berichtigen; *(improve)* abändern, ergänzen ‹*Gesetzentwurf, Antrag*›; ändern ‹*Verfassung*›; [ver]bessern ‹*Situation*›

amendment [ə'mendmənt] *n. (to motion)* Abänderungsantrag, *der; (to bill)* Änderungsantrag, *der; (to Constitution)* Änderung, *die* **(to** *Gen.*); Amendement, *das (Dipl.); (of situation)* [Ver]besserung, *die*

amends [ə'mendz] *n. pl.* **make ~ [to sb.]** es [bei jmdm.] wiedergutmachen; **make ~ for sth.** etw. wiedergutmachen

amenity [ə'mi:nıtı] *n.* **a)** *no pl. (pleasantness)* Annehmlichkeiten *Pl.;* **b)** *(pleasant feature) (of residence)* Attraktivität, *die;* Wohnqualität, *die; (of locality)* Attraktivität, *die;* Reiz, *der;* **the amenities of a town** die kulturellen und Freizeiteinrichtungen einer Stadt; **social amenities** öffentliche Freizeiteinrichtungen; **with every ~, including showers, central heating, etc.** mit allem Komfort inklusive Duschen, Zentralheizung usw.

amenity: ~ bed *n. (Brit.)* ≈ Privatbett [in einem öffentlichen Krankenhaus]; **~ centre** *n.* Freizeitzentrum, *das*

America [ə'merıkə] *pr. n.* **a)** Amerika *(das);* **b) the ~s** Nord-, Süd- und Mittelamerika

American [ə'merıkən] **1.** *adj.* amerikanisch; **sb. is ~:** jmd. ist Amerikaner/Amerikanerin; **~ English** amerikanisches Englisch; **~ studies** Amerikanistik, *die; see also* **English 1; legion b. 2.** *n.* **a)** *(person)* Amerikaner, *der*/Amerikanerin, *die;* **b)** *(language)* Amerikanisch, *das; see also* **English 2 a**

American: ~ 'football *n.* Football, *der;* **~ 'Indian 1.** *n.* Indianer, *der*/Indianerin, *die;* **2.** *adj.* indianisch

Americanisation, Americanise *see* **Americaniz-**

Americanism [ə'merıkənızm] *n.* **a)** *(Ling.)* Amerikanismus, *der;* **b)** *(attachment)* Amerikanertum, *das*

Americanization [əmerıkənaı'zeıʃn] *n.* **a)** Amerikanisierung, *die;* **b)** *(naturalization)* Einbürgerung [in Amerika]

Americanize [ə'merıkənaız] *v.t.* **a)** amerikanisieren; **b)** *(naturalize)* [in Amerika] einbürgern

American: ~ 'organ *n. (Mus.)* amerikanische Orgel; **~ plan** *n. (Amer. Hotel Managem.)* Vollpension, *die*

Amerindian [æmə'rındıən] *adj. (American Indian)* indianisch; *(Eskimo)* eskimoisch; **~ languages** Indianer-/Eskimosprachen; **~ peoples** Indianer/Eskimo[s]

amethyst ['æmıθıst] *n.* Amethyst, *der*

amiability [eımıə'bılıtı] *n., no pl. see* **amiable:** Umgänglichkeit, *die;* Freundlichkeit, *die;* Entgegenkommen, *das*

amiable ['eımıəbl] *adj.* umgänglich; freundlich ‹*Person*›; entgegenkommend ‹*Haltung*›; **be in an ~ mood** gut gelaunt sein

amiably ['eımıəblı] *adv.* freundlich; **be ~ disposed towards sb./sth.** jmdm./einer Sache wohlgesinnt sein

amicability [æmıkə'bılıtı] *n., no pl.* Freundschaftlichkeit, *die*

amicable ['æmıkəbl] *adj.* freundschaftlich ‹*Gespräch, Beziehungen*›; gütlich ‹*Einigung*›; friedlich ‹*Lösung*›; **~ relations with one's neighbours** ein freundnachbarliches Verhältnis

amicably ['æmıkəblı] *adv.* in [aller] Freundschaft; **get on ~ with one's neighbours** mit seinen Nachbarn gut auskommen

amid [ə'mıd] *prep.* inmitten; *(fig.: during)* bei; **~ the fighting** mitten im Gefecht

amidships [əˈmɪdʃɪps] *(Amer.:* **amidship** [əˈmɪdʃɪp]) *adv. (position)* mittschiffs; Mitte Schiff *(Seemannsspr.); (direction)* [nach] mittschiffs; **hit sb.** ~ *(fig. coll.)* jmdn. in den Bauch schlagen/treffen
amidst [əˈmɪdst] *see* **amid**
amino acid [əmiːnəʊ ˈæsɪd] *n. (Chem.)* Aminosäure, *die*
Amish [ˈɑːmɪʃ, ˈeɪmɪʃ, ˈæmɪʃ] *adj.* Amisch; **the ~ Mennonites** die Amischen
amiss [əˈmɪs] **1.** *pred. adj.* **a)** *(wrong)* verkehrt; falsch; **is anything ~?** stimmt irgend etwas nicht?; ist irgend etwas nicht in Ordnung?; **b)** *(out of place)* fehl am Platz[e]; unangebracht. **2.** *adv.* **take sth. ~:** etw. übelnehmen; **come** *or* **go ~:** ungelegen kommen; **a glass of wine would not come** *or* **go ~:** ein Glas Wein wäre nicht verkehrt
amity [ˈæmɪtɪ] *n.* Freundschaft, *die;* gutes Einvernehmen
ammeter [ˈæmɪtə(r)] *n. (Electr.)* Amperemeter, *das;* Strommesser, *der*
ammo [ˈæməʊ] *n., no pl. (Mil. coll.)* Muni, *die (Milit. ugs.)*
ammonia [əˈməʊnɪə] *n.* Ammoniak, *das;* ~ **water** Salmiakgeist, *der;* Ammoniaklösung, *die*
ammunition [æmjʊˈnɪʃn] *n., no pl., no indef. art. (lit. or fig.)* Munition, *die*
amnesia [æmˈniːzɪə] *n. (Med.)* Amnesie, *die;* Gedächtnisschwund, *der*
amnesty [ˈæmnɪstɪ] *n.* Amnestie, *die;* **grant an ~ to sb.** jmdn. amnestieren; **they were released under an ~:** sie wurden im Rahmen einer Amnestie freigelassen
amniocentesis [æmnɪəʊsenˈtiːsɪs] *n. (Med.)* Fruchtwasserentnahme, *die*
amoeba [əˈmiːbə] *n., pl.* **~s** *or* **~e** [əˈmiːbiː] *(Zool.)* Amöbe, *die*
amok [əˈmɒk] *adv.* **run ~:** Amok laufen
among[st] [əˈmʌŋ(st)] *prep.* **a)** unter (+ *Dat.; seltener:* + *Akk.*); ~ **us/you/friends** unter uns/euch/Freunden; ~ **other things** unter anderem; ~ **others** unter anderen; **b)** *(in/into the middle of, surrounded by)* zwischen (+ *Dat./Akk.*); **hide ~ the bushes** sich im Gebüsch verstecken; **~ tall trees** inmitten hoher Bäume; **she was sitting ~ her children** sie saß im Kreise ihrer Kinder; **there are some weeds ~ the flowers** zwischen den Blumen wächst Unkraut; **a village ~ the hills** ein Dorf in den Bergen; **I saw him ~ the crowd** ich habe ihn in der Menge gesehen; **c)** *(in the practice or opinion of, in the number of)* unter (+ *Dat.*); ~ **men/scientists** unter Männern/Wissenschaftlern; **who is the tallest ~ you?** wer ist der größte von *od. (geh.)* unter euch?; **I count him ~ my friends** ich zähle ihn zu meinen Freunden; **that painting is reckoned ~ his best works** das Bild zählt zu seinen besten Werken; **d)** *(between)* unter (+ *Dat.; seltener:* + *Akk.*); **share the sweets ~ yourselves** teilt euch die Bonbons; **we only have five pounds ~ us** wir haben zusammen nur fünf Pfund; **he distributed his wealth ~ the poor** er verteilte sein Vermögen an die *od.* unter die *od.* unter den Armen; **e)** *(reciprocally)* **they often quarrel ~ themselves** sie streiten oft miteinander; sie streiten sich oft; **we often disagree ~ ourselves** wir sind [untereinander] oft verschiedener Meinung; **f)** *(jointly)* ~ **you/them** *etc.* gemeinsam; zusammen
amoral [eɪˈmɒrəl] *adj.* amoralisch
amorous [ˈæmərəs] *adj.* verliebt; amourös ⟨*Abenteuer, Beziehung*⟩; ~ **glances** verliebte Blicke; ~ **advances** Annäherungsversuche *Pl.;* amouröse Avancen *Pl. (veralt., scherzh.);* **an ~ novel/poem** ein Liebesroman/-gedicht; **be ~ of sb.** *(literary)* in jmdn. verliebt sein
amorously [ˈæmərəslɪ] *adv.* verliebt
amorousness [ˈæmərəsnɪs] *n., no pl.* Verliebtheit, *die*
amorphous [əˈmɔːfəs] *adj.* **a)** *(shapeless, unorganized)* formlos; amorph ⟨*Masse*⟩; *(fig.)* chaotisch ⟨*Stil*⟩; **b)** *(Min., Chem.)* amorph
amortization [əmɔːtaɪˈzeɪʃn] *n. (Finance)* **a)** *(of assets)* Abschreibung, *die;* **b)** *(of debt, mortgage)* Tilgung, *die;* Amortisation, *die*
amortize [əˈmɔːtaɪz] *v. t. (Finance)* abschreiben ⟨*Vermögenswerte*⟩; tilgen, amortisieren ⟨*Schuld, Hypothek*⟩
amount [əˈmaʊnt] **1.** *v. i.* ~ **to sth.** sich auf etw. *(Akk.)* belaufen; *(fig.)* auf etw. *(Akk.)* hinauslaufen; einer Sache *(Dat.)* gleichkommen; **the cost/debts/fees/profits ~ed to ...:** die Kosten/Schulden/Gebühren/Gewinne beliefen sich auf ... *(Akk.);* **all these arguments/proposals don't ~ to much** diese Argumente/Vorschläge bringen alle nicht viel; **my savings don't ~ to very much** meine Ersparnisse sind nicht gerade groß; **what this all ~s to is that ...:** zusammenfassend kann man sagen, daß .... **2.** *n.* **a)** *(total)* Betrag, *der;* Summe, *die; (full significance)* volle Bedeutung *od.* Tragweite; **b) the ~ of a bill** die Höhe einer Rechnung; **c)** *(quantity)* Menge, *die;* **an ~ of rain/patience** eine Menge Regen/Geduld; **large ~s of money** beträchtliche Geldsummen; **a tremendous ~ of** *(coll.)* wahnsinnig viel *(ugs.);* **no ~ of money will make me change my mind** und wenn man mir noch soviel Geld gibt: meine Meinung werde ich nicht ändern; **no ~ of talking will settle the matter** soviel wir auch darüber reden, wir werden zu keinem Ergebnis kommen; *see also* **any 1 e**
amour [əˈmʊə(r)] *n.* Affäre, *die;* Liebschaft, *die*
amour propre [æmʊə ˈprɒpr] *n., no pl.* **a)** *(self-esteem)* Ehrgefühl, *das;* Selbstachtung, *die;* **b)** *(vanity)* Eitelkeit, *die*
amp [æmp] *n.* **a)** *(Electr.)* Ampere, *das;* **b)** *(coll.: amplifier)* Verstärker, *der*
ampere [ˈæmpeə(r)] *n. (Electr.)* Ampere, *das*
ampersand [ˈæmpəsænd] *n.* Et-Zeichen, *das*
amphetamine [æmˈfetəmɪn, æmˈfetəmiːn] *n.* Amphetamin, *das*
amphibian [æmˈfɪbɪən] **1.** *adj.* **a)** *(Zool.)* amphibisch; ~ **animal** amphibisches Lebewesen; Amphibie, *die;* Lurch, *der;* **b)** *(Mil.) see* **amphibious b. 2.** *n.* **a)** *(Zool.)* Amphibie, *die;* Lurch, *der;* **b)** *(vehicle)* Amphibienfahrzeug, *das*
amphibious [æmˈfɪbɪəs] *adj.* **a)** *(Biol.)* amphibisch; **toads are ~:** Kröten sind Amphibien; **b)** *(operating on land or water)* amphibisch; zu Lande und zu Wasser einsetzbar; ~ **vehicle/tank/aircraft** Amphibienfahrzeug, *das*/-panzer, *der*/-flugzeug, *das;* ~ **warfare/operations/forces** amphibische Kriegsführung/Operationen/Streitkräfte
amphitheatre *(Amer.:* **amphitheater**) [ˈæmfɪθɪətə(r)] *n.* **a)** Amphitheater, *das;* **b)** *(Geog.: hollow)* Kessel, *der;* **c)** *(fig.: arena)* Schauplatz, *der*
amphora [ˈæmfərə] *n., pl.* **~e** [ˈæmfəriː] *or* **~s** Amphora, Amphore, *die*
ample [ˈæmpl] *adj.,* **~r** [ˈæmplə(r)], **~st** [ˈæmplɪst] **a)** *(spacious)* weitläufig ⟨*Garten, Räume*⟩; groß ⟨*Ausdehnung*⟩; *(extensive, abundant)* reichhaltig ⟨*Mahl, Bibliographie*⟩; ausführlich, umfassend ⟨*Behandlung eines Themas*⟩; weitreichend, umfassend ⟨*Vollmachten, Machtbefugnisse*⟩; **b)** *(enough)* ~ **room/food** reichlich Platz/zu essen; **this hall is ~ in size for the party** dieser Saal bietet reichlich Platz für die Feier; **c)** *(stout)* üppig ⟨*Busen*⟩; stattlich ⟨*Erscheinung*⟩
amplification [æmplɪfɪˈkeɪʃn] *n.* **a)** *(Phys.)* Verstärkung, *die;* **b)** *(enlargement)* weitere *od.* zusätzliche Erläuterungen; **c)** *(of knowledge, wisdom, etc.)* Erweiterung, *die;* Vertiefung, *die*
amplifier [ˈæmplɪfaɪə(r)] *n.* Verstärker, *der*
amplify [ˈæmplɪfaɪ] **1.** *v. t.* **a)** verstärken ⟨*Ton*⟩; **b)** *(enlarge on)* weiter ausführen, näher *od.* ausführlicher erläutern ⟨*Erklärung, Bericht*⟩; **c)** *(enhance)* erweitern, vertiefen ⟨*Wissen, Kenntnisse*⟩. **2.** *v. i.* auf Einzelheiten *(Akk.)* eingehen; ~ **on sth.** etw. näher erläutern
amplitude [ˈæmplɪtjuːd] *n.* **a)** *(Electr.)* Amplitude, *die;* Schwingungsweite, *die;* ~ **modulation** Amplitudenmodulation, *die;* **b)** *(Phys.)* Amplitude, *die;* größte Ausschlagweite; **c)** *no pl. (breadth)* Breite, *die;* Weite, *die; (abundance)* Fülle, *die; (wide range)* Breite, *die*
amply [ˈæmplɪ] *adv. (spaciously, abundantly)* reichlich ⟨*breit, belohnen*⟩; zur Genüge ⟨*zeigen, demonstrieren*⟩
ampoule [ˈæmpuːl] *n.* Ampulle, *die*
amputate [ˈæmpjʊteɪt] *v. t.* amputieren
amputation [æmpjʊˈteɪʃn] *n.* Amputation, *die*
amputee [æmpjʊˈtiː] *n.* Amputierte, *der/die*
amuck [əˈmʌk] *see* **amok**
amulet [ˈæmjʊlɪt] *n. (lit. or fig.)* Amulett, *das*
amuse [əˈmjuːz] *v. t.* **a)** *(interest)* unterhalten; **keep a child ~d** ein Kind richtig beschäftigen; **~ oneself with sth.** sich mit etw. beschäftigen; **children are ~d by the most simple things** Kinder sind mit den einfachsten Dingen zufrieden; **~ oneself by doing sth.** sich *(Dat.)* die Zeit damit vertreiben, etw. zu tun; **b)** *(make laugh or smile)* belustigen; amüsieren; **be ~d by** *or* **at sth.** sich über etw. *(Akk.)* amüsieren
amusement [əˈmjuːzmənt] *n.* Belustigung, *die; (pastime)* Freizeitbeschäftigung, *die;* **all the ~s on offer at the seaside** das gesamte Freizeitangebot am Meer; **in the ~s** in der Spielhalle
aˈmusement arcade *n.* Spielhalle, *die*
amusing [əˈmjuːzɪŋ] *adj.*, **amusingly** [əˈmjuːzɪŋlɪ] *adv.* amüsant
[1]an [ən, *stressed* æn] *indef. art. see also* **[2]a:** ein/eine/ein; **an elephant/Englishman** ein Elefant/Engländer; **an hour/historical play** eine Stunde/ein historisches Stück; **an LP** eine LP
[2]an [æn] *conj. (arch./dial.)* so *(veralt.);* ~ **I meet him** so ich ihn treffe
anabolic steroid [ænəbɒlɪk ˈstɪərɔɪd, ænəbɒlɪk ˈsterɔɪd] *n. (Physiol.)* anaboles Steroid; Anabolikum, *das*
anachronism [əˈnækrənɪzm] *n.* Anachronismus, *der*
anachronistic [ənækrəˈnɪstɪk] *adj.* anachronistisch; zeitwidrig
anaconda [ænəˈkɒndə] *n. (Zool.)* Anakonda, *die*
anaemia [əˈniːmɪə] *n., no pl. (Med.)* Blutarmut, *die;* Anämie, *die; see also* **pernicious**
anaemic [əˈniːmɪk] *adj. (Med.)* blutarm; anämisch; *(fig.)* blutleer; saft- und kraftlos
anaerobic [æneəˈrəʊbɪk] *adj. (Biol.)* anaerob
anaesthesia [ænɪsˈθiːzɪə] *n. (Med.) (absence of sensation)* Empfindungslosigkeit, *die;* Anästhesie, *(fachspr.)* Anaesthesia, *die; (artificially induced)* Narkose, *die;* **general ~:** [Voll]narkose, *die;* Allgemeinanästhesie, *die (fachspr.);* **local ~:** örtliche Betäubung; Lokalanästhesie, *die (fachspr.)*
anaesthetic [ænɪsˈθetɪk] **1.** *adj. (Med.)* anästhetisch; betäubend. **2.** *n.* Anästhetikum, *das;* **give sb. an ~:** jmdm. eine Narkose geben; *(local)* jmdn. betäuben; **be under an ~:** in Narkose liegen; **general ~:** Narkotikum, *das;* Narkosemittel, *das;* **local ~:** Lokalanästhetikum, *das*
anaesthetist [əˈniːsθətɪst] *n. (Med.)* Anästhesist, *der*/Anästhesistin, *die;* Narkose[fach]arzt, *der*/-ärztin, *die*
anaesthetization [əniːsθətaɪˈzeɪʃn] *n.* Betäubung, *die; (fig.)* Abstumpfung, *die* (to gegenüber)

anaesthetize [əˈniːsθətaɪz] *v. t.* narkotisieren; betäuben; anästhesieren *(fachspr.); (fig.)* abstumpfen (**to** gegenüber); **become ~d to sth.** *(fig.)* gegenüber etw. abstumpfen
anagram [ˈænəgræm] *n.* Anagramm, *das*
anagrammatic [ænəgrəˈmætɪk], **anagrammatical** [ænəgrəˈmætɪkl] *adj.* anagrammatisch
anal [ˈeɪnl] *adj.* **a)** *(Anat.)* anal; Anal-; After-; **~ region** Analbereich, *der;* **~ canal** Afterkanal, *der;* **b)** *(Psych.)* **~ stage** anale Phase; **~ eroticism** Analerotik, *die*
analgesia [ænælˈdʒiːzɪə] *n. (Med.)* Analgesie, *die*
analgesic [ænælˈdʒiːsɪk] *(Med.)* **1.** *adj.* analgetisch. **2.** *n.* Analgetikum, *das*
analog *(Amer.) see* **analogue**
analogical [ænəˈlɒdʒɪkl] *adj.* **a)** analog; Analogie-; **~ reasoning** Analogiedenken, *das;* **b)** *(expressing analogy)* metonymisch ⟨*Wort, Ausdruck*⟩
analogous [əˈnæləgəs] *adj.* vergleichbar; analog; **be ~ to sth.** einer Sache *(Dat.)* entsprechen
analogously [əˈnæləgəslɪ] *adv.* analog
analogue [ˈænəlɒg] *n.* Entsprechung, *die;* Analogon, *das (geh.);* **~ computer** Analogrechner, *der;* **~ watch** Analoguhr, *die*
analogy [əˈnælədʒɪ] *n.* **a)** *(agreement; also Ling.)* Analogie, *die;* **b)** *(similarity)* Parallele, *die;* Analogie, *die;* **draw an ~ between/with** eine Parallele ziehen zwischen (+ *Dat.*)/zu; **c)** *(Logic)* Analogie, *die;* **use an argument by ~/argue by ~:** einen Analogieschluß/Analogieschlüsse ziehen
analysable [ˈænəlaɪzəbl] *adj.* analysierbar; zerlegbar ⟨*Satz*⟩
analyse [ˈænəlaɪz] *v. t.* **a)** analysieren; kritisch untersuchen ⟨*Literatur*⟩; **b)** *(Chem.)* untersuchen (**for** auf + *Akk.*); **c)** *(Ling.)* [zer]gliedern; **d)** *(Psych.)* analysieren *(fachspr.);* psychoanalytisch behandeln; **get ~d** sich einer [Psycho]analyse unterziehen
analysis [əˈnælɪsɪs] *n., pl.* **analyses** [əˈnælɪsiːz] **a)** Analyse, *die; (Chem., Med.: of sample)* Untersuchung, *die; (statement)* Analyse, *die;* [Lage]beurteilung, *die;* **in the final** *or* **last** *or* **ultimate ~:** letzten Endes; **b)** *(Math.)* Analysis, *die;* **c)** *(Psych.)* Analyse, *die*
analyst [ˈænəlɪst] *n.* **a)** Laboratoriumsingenieur, *der;* Laborfachmann, *der (ugs.);* **b)** *(Econ., Polit., etc.)* Experte, *der;* Fachmann, *der;* **c)** *(Psych.)* Analytiker, *der*/Analytikerin, *die*
analytic [ænəˈlɪtɪk] *adj.* analytisch
analytical [ænəˈlɪtɪkl] *adj.* **a)** analytisch ⟨*Methode, Sprache, Begabung*⟩; **b) ~ geometry** analytische Geometrie
analytically [ænəˈlɪtɪkəlɪ] *adv.* analytisch
analyze *(Amer.) see* **analyse**
anapaest *(Amer.:* **anapest***)* [ˈænəpiːst] *n. (Pros.)* Anapäst, *der*
anaphora [əˈnæfərə] *n. (Lit.)* Anapher, *die*
anarchic [əˈnɑːkɪk], **anarchical** [əˈnɑːkɪkl] *adj.* anarchisch; *(anarchistic)* anarchistisch
anarchism [ˈænəkɪzm] *n., no pl.* Anarchismus, *der*
anarchist [ˈænəkɪst] *n.* Anarchist, *der*/Anarchistin, *die*
anarchistic [ænəˈkɪstɪk] *adj.* anarchistisch
anarchy [ˈænəkɪ] *n., no pl.* Anarchie, *die; (fig.: disorder)* Chaos, *das*
anathema [əˈnæθəmə] *n.* **a)** *no pl., no art. (detested thing)* ein Greuel; **be ~ to sb.** jmdm. verhaßt *od.* ein Greuel sein; **b)** *no pl., no art. (accursed thing)* **be ~:** verflucht sein; **c)** *(curse of God)* Fluch, *der; (curse of Church)* Anathema, *das;* Kirchenbann, *der*
anathematize [əˈnæθəmətaɪz] **1.** *v. t.* verdammen; verfluchen; ⟨*Kirche, Papst:*⟩ in den Bann tun. **2.** *v. i.* fluchen
anatomical [ænəˈtɒmɪkl] *adj.*, **anatomically** [ænəˈtɒmɪkəlɪ] *adv.* anatomisch
anatomist [əˈnætəmɪst] *n.* Anatom, *der; (dissector)* Anatomiegehilfe, *der; (fig.)* Sezierer, *der;* Analytiker, *der*
anatomize [əˈnætəmaɪz] *v. t.* sezieren; *(fig.)* analysieren; sezieren
anatomy [əˈnætəmɪ] *n., no pl.* **a)** Anatomie, *die; (dissection)* Sektion, *die;* **b)** *(joc.: body)* Anatomie, *die (scherzh.);* **a certain part of his ~:** ein bestimmter Körperteil; **c)** *(fig.: analysis)* Anatomie, *die;* Analyse, *die*
ANC *abbr.* **African National Congress** ANK
ancestor [ˈænsestə(r)] *n.* Vorfahr, *der;* Ahn[e], *der; (fig.)* Ahn[e], *der*
ancestral [ænˈsestrəl] *adj.* angestammt ⟨*Grundbesitz, Land*⟩; **~ portraits** Ahnenbilder
ancestry [ˈænsestrɪ] *n.* **a)** *(lineage)* Abstammung, *die;* Herkunft, *die;* **b)** *(ancestors)* Vorfahren *Pl.;* **c)** *no pl. (ancient descent)* Familientradition, *die*
anchor [ˈæŋkə(r)] **1.** *n.* Anker, *der;* **lie at ~:** vor Anker liegen; **come to** *or* **cast** *or* **drop ~:** vor Anker gehen; **weigh ~:** den Anker lichten; *see also* **drag 2 e. 2.** *v. t.* **a)** verankern; vor Anker legen; *(secure)* befestigen (**to** an + *Dat.*); **b)** *(fig.)* **be ~ed to sth.** an etw. *(Akk.)* gefesselt sein. **3.** *v. i.* ankern
anchorage [ˈæŋkərɪdʒ] *n.* **a)** *(place for anchoring)* Ankerplatz, *der;* Ankergrund, *der (geh.);* **b)** *(anchoring, lying at anchor)* Ankern, *das;* **c)** *(fig.)* [Rück]halt, *der*
anchorite [ˈæŋkəraɪt] *n. (lit. or fig.)* Einsiedler, *der*
anchor: ~man *n.* **a)** *(Sport) (in tug-of-war)* hinterster *od.* letzter Mann; *(in relay race)* Schlußläufer, *der; (Mountaineering)* Seilletzte, *der;* **he is the ~man of the company** *(fig.)* er ist die Stütze der Firma; **b)** *(Telev., Radio)* Moderator, *der;* Redakteur im Studio, *der;* **~-ring** *n.* Ankerring, *der*
anchovy [ˈæntʃəvɪ, ænˈtʃəʊvɪ] *n.* An[s]chovis, *die;* Sardelle, *die*
anchovy: ~ 'pear *n.* Anchovisbirne, *die;* **~ 'toast** *n.* Toast mit An[s]chovispaste
ancien régime [ɑ̃sjɛ̃ reɪˈʒiːm] *n., pl.* **anciens régimes** [ɑ̃sjɛ̃ reɪˈʒiːm] Ancien régime, *das; (fig.)* alte Regierungsform
ancient [ˈeɪnʃənt] **1.** *adj.* **a)** *(belonging to past)* alt; *(pertaining to antiquity)* antik; **~ Rome/Greece** das alte *od.* antike Rom/Griechenland; **in ~ times** im Altertum; **~ history** Alte Geschichte, *die* ; **that's ~ history; everybody knows it** *(fig.)* das ist längst ein alter Hut *(ugs.),* jeder weiß das; **the ~ Greeks** die alten Griechen; **A~ Greek** Altgriechisch, *das;* **~ Egypt** Altägypten *(das);* **b)** *(old)* alt; historisch ⟨*Gebäude usw.*⟩; **~ monument** *(Brit. Admin.)* [offiziell anerkanntes] historisches Denkmal; [offiziell anerkannte] historische Stätte; **~ lights** *(Law) Fenster, die mindestens 20 Jahre lang Lichtzutritt hatten, der nicht durch bauliche Maßnahmen behindert werden darf.* **2.** *n.* **a) the ~s** Menschen der Antike; *(authors)* die Schriftsteller der Antike; **b) the A~ of Days** *(literary)* der Allvater; **c)** *(arch.: old man)* Alte, *der*
anciently [ˈeɪnʃəntlɪ] *adv.* in alten Zeiten; *(in antiquity)* in der Antike; im Altertum
ancillary [ænˈsɪlərɪ] **1.** *adj.* **a)** *(auxiliary)* **be ~ to sth.** für etw. Hilfsdienste leisten; **be ~ to medicine** eine Hilfswissenschaft der Medizin sein; **b)** *(subordinate)* zweitrangig; **~ industries** Zulieferindustrien; **~ services** Hilfeleistungen; **~ worker** Hilfskraft, *die;* **~ subject** Nebenfach, *das; a* **network of ~ roads** ein Netz von Verbindungsstraßen. **2.** *n. (Brit.)* Hilfskraft, *die*
and [ənd, *stressed* ænd] *conj.* **a)** und; **two hundred ~ forty** zweihundert[und]vierzig; **a knife, fork, ~ spoon** Messer, Gabel und Löffel; **there are books ~ books** es gibt Bücher und Bücher; es gibt sone Bücher und solche *(salopp);* **two ~ two are four** zwei und zwei ist *od.* sind vier; **[by] two ~ two** in Zweierreihen; **~/or** und/oder; **b)** *expr. condition* und; **take one more step ~ I'll shoot** noch einen Schritt, und ich schieße; **do that ~ you'll regret it** wenn du das tust, wirst du es noch bedauern; **c)** *expr. continuation* und; **she cried ~ cried** sie weinte und weinte; **he tried ~ tried to open it** er versuchte immer wieder, es zu öffnen; **for weeks ~ weeks/years ~ years** wochen-/jahrelang; **for miles ~ miles** meilenweit; **better ~ better** immer besser
andante [ænˈdæntɪ] *(Mus.)* **1.** *adv.* andante; gemessen; langsam. **2.** *adj.* langsam; ruhig. **3.** *n.* Andante, *das*
Andean [ænˈdiːən] *adj. (Geog.)* Anden-
Andes [ˈændiːz] *pr. n. pl.* Anden *Pl.*
andiron [ˈændaɪən] *n.* Feuerbock, *der*
Andorra [ænˈdɔːrə] *pr. n.* Andorra *(das)*
Andrew [ˈændruː] *pr. n. (as name of saint)* Andreas *(der)*
androgynous [ænˈdrɒdʒɪnəs] *adj. (Biol.)* zwittrig
anecdotal [ˈænɪkdəʊtəl] *adj.* anekdotisch; anekdotenhaft
anecdote [ˈænɪkdəʊt] *n.* Anekdote, *die;* **he is never without a witty ~:** er ist nie um eine witzige Geschichte verlegen
anemia, anemic *(Amer.) see* **anaem-**
anemometer [ænɪˈmɒmɪtə(r)] *n. (Meteorol.)* Anemometer, *das;* Windmesser, *der*
anemone [əˈnemənɪ] *n.* Anemone, *die; (pasque-flower)* Kuhschelle, *die; see also* **sea anemone; wood anemone**
aneroid [ˈænərɔɪd] *adj.* **~ barometer** Aneroidbarometer, *das*
anesthesia *etc. (Amer.) see* **anaesthesia** *etc.*
anew [əˈnjuː] *adv.* **a)** aufs neue; erneut; **let's start ~:** fangen wir noch einmal von vorne an; **b)** *(in a new form)* neu; **he decided to start life ~ in Australia** er beschloß, in Australien ein neues Leben zu beginnen
angel [ˈeɪndʒl] *n.* **a)** *(lit. or fig.)* Engel, *der;* **evil ~:** böser Geist; **good ~:** guter Engel; **be on the side of the ~s** *(fig.)* auf der Seite der Guten stehen; **be an ~ and ...** *(coll.)* sei so lieb und ...; *see also* **guardian angel; b)** *(Commerc. coll.)* Finanzier, *der*
angel: ~ cake *n., no pl.* Biskuitkuchen, *der;* **~-fish** *n.* Kaiserfisch, *der;* Engelfisch, *der*
angelic [ænˈdʒelɪk] *adj.* **a)** *(of angel[s])* Engels-; **b)** *(like angel[s])* engelhaft; engelgleich *(geh.);* **an ~ child** ein Kind wie ein Engel; **she looked ~:** sie sah wie ein Engel aus
angelica [ænˈdʒelɪkə] *n.* **a)** *(Bot., Cookery, Med.)* Angelika, *die;* Engelwurz, *die;* **b)** *(candied)* kandierte Angelika
angelus [ˈændʒɪləs] *n. (RC Ch.)* Angelus, *der od. das;* **~ bell** Angelusläuten, *das*
anger [ˈæŋgə(r)] **1.** *n., no pl. (wrath)* Zorn, *der* (**at** über + *Akk.*); *(fury)* Wut, *die* (**at** über + *Akk.*); **be filled with ~:** erzürnt/wütend sein; **in [a moment of] ~:** im Zorn/in der Wut. **2.** *v. t.* verärgern; *(infuriate)* erzürnen *(geh.)*/wütend machen; **be ~ed by sth.** über etw. *(Akk.)* verärgert/erzürnt/wütend sein
angina [pectoris] [ænˈdʒaɪnə (ˈpektərɪs)] *n., no pl. (Med.)* Angina pectoris, *die*
Angle [ˈæŋgl] *n.* Angehöriger/Angehörige des Volksstammes der Angeln; **the ~s** die Angeln
[1]**angle 1.** *n.* **a)** *(Geom.)* Winkel, *der;* **acute/obtuse/right ~:** spitzer/stumpfer/rechter Winkel; **at an ~ of 60°** im Winkel von 60°; **at an ~:** schief; **at an ~ to the wall** schräg zur Wand; **b)** *(corner)* Ecke, *die; (recess)* Winkel, *der;* **c)** *(direction)* Perspektive, *die;* Blickwinkel, *der; (fig.)* Gesichtspunkt, *der;* Aspekt, *der;* **the photo isn't taken from a flattering ~:** die Aufnahme ist aus einem unvorteilhaften [Blick]winkel gemacht; **the committee examined the matter from various ~s** der Ausschuß prüfte die

Angelegenheit von verschiedenen Seiten; **looking at it from a commercial ~:** aus kaufmännischer Sicht betrachtet; unter kaufmännischen Gesichtspunkten. **2.** *v. t.* **a)** [aus]richten; **b)** *(coll.: bias)* färben ‹*Nachrichten, Formulierung*›. **3.** *v. i.* [im Winkel] abbiegen; **the road ~s sharply to the left** die Straße biegt scharf nach links ab

²angle *v. i.* angeln; *(fig.)* ~ **for sth.** sich um etw. bemühen; ~ **for compliments** nach Komplimenten fischen; ~ **for an opportunity** eine Gelegenheit suchen

'angle brackets *n. pl.* spitze Klammern

angled ['æŋgəld] *adj.* *(angular)* eckig ‹*Form, Figur*›; *(placed obliquely)* schief; *(fig. coll.)* tendenziös, gefärbt ‹*Bericht, Kommentar*›; **acute-/obtuse-/right-~:** spitz-/stumpf-/rechtwinklig

angle: ~dozer ['æŋgldəʊzə(r)] *n.* Seitenräumer, *der;* **~-iron** *n.* Winkeleisen, *das;* **~-parking** *n.* Schrägparken, *das*

angler ['æŋglə(r)] *n.* **a)** Angler, *der*/Anglerin, *die;* **b)** ~[-**fish**] Angler, *der;* Seeteufel, *der*

Anglican ['æŋglɪkən] **1.** *adj.* anglikanisch. **2.** *n.* Anglikaner, *der*/Anglikanerin, *die*

Anglicanism ['æŋglɪkənɪzm] *n., no pl.* Anglikanismus, *der*

Anglicism ['æŋglɪsɪzm] *n.* **a)** *(word or idiom)* Anglizismus, *der;* **b)** *(Englishness)* englische Eigenart

Anglicize ['æŋglɪsaɪz] *v. t.* anglisieren

angling ['æŋglɪŋ] *n.* Angeln, *das*

Anglist ['æŋglɪst] *n.* Anglist, *der*/Anglistin, *die*

Anglistics [æŋ'glɪstɪks] *n., no pl.* Anglistik, *die*

Anglo- [æŋgləʊ] *in comb.* anglo-/Anglo-; **he's an ~-Cypriot** er ist Zyprer britischer Herkunft

Anglo-A'merican **1.** *adj.* angloamerikanisch; **an ~ agreement** ein englisch-/britisch-amerikanischer Vertrag. **2.** *n.* Angloamerikaner, *der*/Angloamerikanerin, *die*

Anglo-'Catholic **1.** *n.* Anglokatholik, *der*/Anglokatholikin, *die.* **2.** *adj.* anglokatholisch

Anglo-'French **1.** *adj.* englisch-/britisch-französisch; *(Ling.)* anglofranzösisch; anglonormannisch. **2.** *n.* *(Ling.)* Anglonormannisch, *das;* Anglofranzösisch, *das*

Anglo-'German *adj.* englisch-/britisch-deutsch

Anglo-'Indian **1.** *adj.* angloindisch. **2.** *n.* Anglo-Inder, *der*/Anglo-Inderin, *die*

Anglomania [æŋgləʊ'meɪnɪə] *n.* Anglomanie, *die*

Anglo-'Norman **1.** *adj.* anglonormannisch. **2.** *n.* *(dialect)* Anglonormannisch, *das*

Anglophile ['æŋgləʊfaɪl] **1.** *n.* Anglophile, *der/die.* **2.** *adj.* anglophil

Anglophobia [æŋgləʊ'fəʊbɪə] *n.* Anglophobie, *die*

anglophone ['æŋgləʊfəʊn] **1.** *adj.* anglophon. **2.** *n.* Anglophone, *der/die*

Anglo-'Saxon **1.** *n.* Angelsachse, *der*/Angelsächsin, *die;* *(language)* Angelsächsisch, *das;* *(Amer. coll.: English)* Englisch, *das.* **2.** *adj.* angelsächsisch; *(Amer. coll.: English)* englisch

Angola [æŋ'gəʊlə] *pr. n.* Angola *(das)*

Angolan [æn'gəʊlən] **1.** *adj.* angolanisch; **sb. is ~:** jmd. ist Angolaner/Angolanerin. **2.** *n.* Angolaner, *der*/Angolanerin, *die*

angora [æŋ'gɔ:rə] *n.* Angora‹*katze, -ziege, -kaninchen*›; ~ **[wool]** Angorawolle, *die;* Mohair, *der*

angrily ['æŋgrɪlɪ] *adv.* verärgert; *(stronger)* zornig

angry ['æŋgrɪ] *adj.* **a)** böse; verärgert ‹*Person, Stimme, Geste*›; *(stronger)* zornig; wütend; **be ~ at** *or* **about sth.** wegen etw. böse sein; **he was ~ at being asked** er war verärgert darüber, daß man ihn fragte; **be ~ with** *or* **at sb.** mit jmdm. *od.* auf jmdn. böse sein; sich über jmdn. ärgern; **be in an ~ mood** schlechter Laune *od.* böse sein; **get ~:** böse werden; **get** *or* **make sb. ~:** jmdn. verärgern; *(stronger)* jmdn. wütend machen; **b)** *(fig.)* drohend, bedrohlich ‹*Wolke, Himmel*›; **c)** *(inflamed and painful)* böse, schlimm ‹*Riß, Wunde*›; **an ~ red** eine entzündliche Röte

angst [æŋst] *n.* neurotische Angst; *(remorse)* Schuldgefühl, *das*

ångström ['æŋstrɜ:m] *n.* *(Phys.)* Ångström, *das;* ~ **unit** Ångströmeinheit, *die*

anguish ['æŋgwɪʃ] *n., no pl.* Qualen *Pl.;* **he shuddered with ~:** er erschauerte vor Schmerz

anguished ['æŋgwɪʃt] *adj.* qualvoll; gequält ‹*Herz, Gewissen*›

angular ['æŋgjʊlə(r)] *adj.* **a)** *(having angles)* eckig ‹*Gebäude, Struktur, Gestalt*›; **b)** *(lacking plumpness, stiff)* knochig ‹*Körperbau*›; kantig ‹*Gesicht*›; **c)** *(measured by angle)* angular; winklig; ~ **momentum** *(Phys.)* Drehimpuls, *der;* Drall, *der;* ~ **motion** *(Phys.)* Kreisbewegung, *die;* ~ **velocity** *(Phys.)* Winkelgeschwindigkeit, *die;* *(Electr.)* Kreisfrequenz, *die;* *(Mech.)* Umlauf- *od.* Drehgeschwindigkeit, *die*

angularity [æŋgjʊ'lærɪtɪ] *n., no pl.* Eckigkeit, *die;* **the ~ of his handwriting** seine eckige Handschrift

anhydride [æn'haɪdraɪd] *n.* *(Chem.)* Anhydrid, *das*

anhydrous [æn'haɪdrəs] *adj.* *(Chem.)* [kristall]wasserfrei; nichtwäßrig

aniline ['ænɪli:n, 'ænɪlaɪn, 'ænɪlɪn] *n.* Anilin, *das;* ~ **dye** künstlicher Farbstoff, *der;* *(made from ~)* Anilinfarbstoff, *der*

animal ['ænɪməl] **1.** *n.* **a)** Tier, *das;* *(quadruped)* Vierbeiner, *der;* *(any living being)* Lebewesen, *das;* ~ **rights** *das Recht der Tiere auf Leben und Unversehrtheit;* ~ **rights activists** aktive Tierschützer; **domestic ~:** Haustier, *das; see also* **kingdom d; b)** *(fig. coll.)* **there is no such ~ as a 'typical' criminal** so etwas wie den „typischen" Verbrecher gibt es gar nicht; **that's a queer sort of ~:** das ist 'ne Sorte für sich *(ugs.);* **c)** *(fig.: animal instinct; brute)* Tier, *das;* **don't be such an ~!** benimm dich doch mal wie ein Mensch!. **2.** *adj.* **a)** tierisch; ~ **behaviour/breeding** Tierverhalten, *das*/Tierzucht, *die;* ~ **spirits** Lebensfreude, *die;* **b)** *(from animals)* tierisch ‹*Produkt, Klebstoff, Öl*›; **c)** *(carnal, sexual)* körperlich ‹*Bedürfnisse, Triebe, Wünsche*›; tierisch, animalisch ‹*Veranlagung, Natur*›

animalcule [ænɪ'mælkju:l] *n.* Mikroorganismus, *der*

'animal-lover *n.* Tierfreund, *der*/-freundin, *die*

animate **1.** ['ænɪmeɪt] *v. t.* **a)** *(enliven)* beleben; **b)** *(inspire)* anregen; *(to do sth. mischievous)* animieren; ~ **sb. with enthusiasm** jmdn. mit Begeisterung erfüllen; **he was ~d by a passion for truth** er war von einer leidenschaftlichen Wahrheitsliebe beseelt; **c)** *(breathe life into)* mit Leben erfüllen. **2.** ['ænɪmət] *adj.* beseelt ‹*Leben, Körper*›; belebt ‹*Objekt, Welt*›; lebendig ‹*Seele*›

animated ['ænɪmeɪtɪd] *adj.* lebhaft ‹*Diskussion, Unterhaltung, Ausdruck, Gebärde*›; lebendig ‹*Darstellung, Kunstwerk*›; ~ **cartoon** Zeichentrickfilm, *der*

animatedly ['ænɪmeɪtɪdlɪ] *adv.* lebhaft

animation [ænɪ'meɪʃn] *n.* **a)** *no pl.* Lebhaftigkeit, *die;* **b)** *(Cinemat.)* Animation, *die*

animator ['ænɪmeɪtə(r)] *n.* *(Cinemat.)* Animator, *der*/Animatorin, *die*

animism ['ænɪmɪzm] *n., no pl.* *(Relig.)* Animismus, *der*

animosity [ænɪ'mɒsɪtɪ] *n.* Animosität, *die* *(geh.),* Feindseligkeit, *die* **(against, towards** gegen)

anion ['ænaɪən] *n.* *(Phys.)* Anion, *das*

anise ['ænɪs] *n.* *(Bot.)* Anis, *der*

aniseed ['ænɪsi:d] *n.* Anis[samen], *der*

anisette [ænɪ'zet] *n.* Anislikör, *der;* Anisette, *der*

ankle ['æŋkl] *n.* *(joint)* Fußgelenk, *das;* *(part of leg)* Knöchelgegend, *die;* Fessel, *die*

ankle: ~-deep *adj.* knöcheltief; **~ sock** *n.* Socke, *die;* *(esp. for children)* Söckchen, *das*

anklet [æŋklɪt] *n.* **a)** Fußkettchen, *das;* **b)** *(Amer.) see* **ankle sock**

annalist ['ænəlɪst] *n.* Annalist, *der*

annals ['ænəlz] *n. pl.* *(lit. or fig.)* Annalen *Pl.;* **in the ~ of human history** in der Geschichte *od.* in den Annalen der Menschheit

Anne [æn] *pr. n.* *(Hist., as name of ruler, saint, etc.)* Anna *(die)*

anneal [ə'ni:l] *v. t.* ausglühen ‹*Stahl*›; kühlen ‹*Glas*›

annelid ['ænəlɪd] *n.* *(Zool.)* Ringelwurm, *der*

annex **1.** [ə'neks] *v. t.* **a)** *(add)* angliedern **(to** *Dat.***)**; anbauen ‹*Gebäude*›; *(append)* anfügen ‹*Bemerkungen*› **(to** *Dat.***)**; **b)** *(incorporate)* annektieren ‹*Land, Territorium*›; *(coll.: take without right)* sich *(Dat.)* unter den Nagel reißen *(ugs.)* ‹*Gegenstände*›; **c)** *(attach) (as an attribute)* zuschreiben **(to** *Dat.***)**; verbinden **(to mit)**; *(as a condition)* verbinden **(to mit)**; *(as a consequence)* binden, knüpfen **(to an +** *Akk.***)**. **2.** ['æneks] *n.* *(supplementary building)* Anbau, *der;* Anexbau, *der (selten);* *(built-on extension)* Erweiterungsbau, *der;* *(appendix) (to document)* Zusatz, *der;* Annex, *der (geh.);* *(to treaty)* Anhang, *der;* Annex, *der (geh.)*

annexation [ænɪk'seɪʃn] *n.* **a)** *(of land)* Annexion, *die;* Annektierung, *die;* **b)** *(as an attribute)* Verknüpfung, *die* **(to mit)**

annexe *see* **annex 2**

annihilate [ə'naɪəleɪt] *v. t.* **a)** vernichten ‹*Armee, Flotte, Bevölkerung, Menschheit*›; zerstören ‹*Stadt, Land*›; **b)** *(fig.)* zunichte machen; am Boden zerstören ‹*Person*›

annihilation [ənaɪə'leɪʃn] *n.* **a)** *see* **annihilate:** Vernichtung, *die;* Zerstörung, *die;* *(fig.)* Verderben, *das;* Untergang, *der;* **the party's ~:** der Untergang der Partei; **b)** *(Phys.)* Paarvernichtung, *die*

anniversary [ænɪ'vɜ:sərɪ] *n.* Jahrestag, *der;* **wedding ~:** Hochzeitstag, *der;* **the university celebrated its 500th ~:** die Universität feierte ihr 500jähriges Jubiläum *od.* Bestehen; **the ~ of Shakespeare's birth** [die Wiederkehr von] Shakespeares Geburtstag; **the ~ of his death** sein Todestag

Anno Domini [ænəʊ 'dɒmɪnaɪ] **1.** *adv.* nach Christi Geburt; ~ **62** [im Jahre] 62 nach Christi Geburt. **2.** *n.* *(coll.)* das Alter

annotate ['ænəteɪt] *v. t.* kommentieren; mit Anmerkungen versehen

annotation [ænə'teɪʃn] *n.* *(act)* Kommentierung, *die;* *(comment)* Anmerkung, *die*

announce [ə'naʊns] *v. t.* bekanntgeben; ansagen ‹*Programm*›; *(over Tannoy etc.)* durchsagen; *(in newspaper)* anzeigen ‹*Heirat usw.*›; *(make known the approach of; fig.: signify)* ankündigen

announcement [ə'naʊnsmənt] *n.* Bekanntgabe, *die;* *(over Tannoy etc.)* Durchsage, *die;* **they made an ~ over the radio that ...:** sie gaben im Radio bekannt, daß ...; **did you read the ~ of his death in the paper?** haben Sie seine Todesanzeige in der Zeitung gelesen?

announcer [ə'naʊnsə(r)] *n.* Ansager, *der*/Ansagerin, *die;* Sprecher, *der*/Sprecherin, *die*

annoy [ə'nɔɪ] *v. t.* **a)** ärgern; **his late arrival ~ed me** ich habe mich über sein spätes Kommen geärgert; **her remarks ~ everybody** ihre Bemerkungen sind allen lästig; **b)** *(harass)* schikanieren

annoyance [ə'nɔɪəns] *n.* Verärgerung, *die;* *(nuisance)* Plage, *die;* **[much] to my/his ~:**

[sehr] zu meiner/seiner Verärgerung; **a look of ~:** ein Blick der Verärgerung; **having a pub next door to one's house is a constant ~:** wenn man eine Kneipe nebenan hat, ist das ein ständiges Ärgernis

annoyed [ə'nɔɪd] *adj.* **be ~ [at *or* with sb./sth.]** ärgerlich [auf *od.* über jmdn./über etw.] sein; **be ~ to find that ...:** sich darüber ärgern, daß ...; **he got very ~:** er hat sich darüber sehr geärgert

annoying [ə'nɔɪɪŋ] *adj.* ärgerlich; lästig ⟨*Gewohnheit, Person*⟩; **the ~ part of it is that ...:** das Ärgerliche daran *od.* was einen daran ärgert ist, daß ...

annual ['ænjʊəl] **1.** *adj.* **a)** *(reckoned by the year)* Jahres-; **~ income/subscription/rent/turnover/production/leave/salary** Jahreseinkommen, *das*/-abonnement, *das*/-miete, *die*/-umsatz, *der*/-produktion, *die*/-urlaub, *der*/-gehalt, *das;* **~ rainfall** jährliche Regenmenge; **b)** *(recurring yearly)* [all]jährlich ⟨*Ereignis, Feier*⟩; Jahres⟨*bericht, -hauptversammlung*⟩; **c)** *(Bot.)* einjährig, *(fachspr.)* annuell ⟨*Pflanze*⟩; **~ ring** *(Bot.)* Jahresring, *der.* **2.** *n.* **a)** *(Bot.)* einjährige Pflanze; **b)** *(Bibliog.)* Jahrbuch, *das;* Jahresschrift, *die; (of comic etc.)* Jahresalbum, *das*

annually ['ænjʊəlɪ] *adv. (per year)* jährlich; *(once a year)* [all]jährlich

annuity [ə'nju:ɪtɪ] *n. (grant, sum payable)* Jahresrente, *die; (investment)* Rentenversicherung, *die*

annul [ə'nʌl] *v. t.*, **-ll-** *(abolish)* annullieren, für ungültig erklären ⟨*Gesetz, Vertrag, Ehe, Testament*⟩; auflösen ⟨*Vertrag*⟩

annular ['ænjʊlə(r)] *adj.* ringartig; ringförmig

annulment [ə'nʌlmənt] *n. (of law, treaty, marriage, will)* Annullierung, *die; (of treaty also)* Auflösung, *die*

Annunciation [ənʌnsɪ'eɪʃn] *n.* **a)** *(Eccl.)* **the ~:** Mariä Verkündigung; **Feast of the ~:** Fest der Verkündigung Mariä; **b) a~:** Ankündigung, *die*

annunciator [ə'nʌnsɪeɪtə(r)] *n. (indicator)* [elektrische] Anzeige

annus mirabilis [ænəs mɪ'rɑ:bɪlɪs] *n., no pl.* Wunderjahr, *das;* wundersames Jahr

anode ['ænəʊd] *n. (Electr.)* Anode, *die*

anodize ['ænədaɪz] *v. t.* anodisieren; **anodizing** anodische Behandlung

anodyne ['ænədaɪn] **1.** *adj. (Med.)* schmerzstillend; analgetisch *(fachspr.); (fig.)* wohltuend; *(soothing)* einlullend; **the ~ aspects of modern life** die Segnungen des modernen Lebens *(iron.).* **2.** *n. (Med.)* Schmerzmittel, *das;* Analgetikum, *das; (fig.)* Wohltat, *die*

anoint [ə'nɔɪnt] *v. t. (esp. Relig.)* salben; **~ sb. king** jmdn. zum König salben

anomalous [ə'nɒmələs] *adj.* **a)** *(abnormal)* anomal, anormal ⟨*Lage, Verhältnisse, Zustand*⟩; ungewöhnlich ⟨*Situation, Anblick*⟩; **b)** *(Ling.: irregular)* unregelmäßig

anomalously [ə'nɒmələslɪ] *adv.* **a)** außergewöhnlich; **b)** *(Ling.)* unregelmäßig ⟨*deklinieren, konjugieren*⟩

anomaly [ə'nɒməlɪ] *n.* Anomalie, *die;* Absonderlichkeit, *die; (exception)* Ausnahme, *die*

anon [ə'nɒn] *adv.* **a)** *(arch./literary: soon)* bald; **b)** *(coll.: later)* später; **more of that ~!** mehr davon später!; **see you ~:** bis später [dann]

anon. [ə'nɒn] *abbr.* **anonymous [author]** anon.

anonymity [ænə'nɪmɪtɪ] *n.* Anonymität, *die*

anonymous [ə'nɒnɪməs] *adj.* anonym

anonymously [ə'nɒnɪməslɪ] *adv.* anonym; **he phoned ~:** er machte einen anonymen Anruf; **he dresses rather ~:** er kleidet sich sehr unauffällig

anorak ['ænəræk] *n.* Anorak, *der*

anorexia [ænə'reksɪə] *n.* Anorexie, *die (Med.);* Appetitlosigkeit, *die;* Magersucht, *die (volkst.);* **~ nervosa** [ænəreksɪə nɜ:'vəʊsə] nervöse Anorexie *(Med.);* Anorexia nervosa, *die (Med.)*

another [ə'nʌðə(r)] **1.** *pron.* **a)** *(additional)* noch einer/eine/eins; ein weiterer/eine weitere/ein weiteres; **yet ~:** noch einer/eine/eins; **one thing leads to ~:** eines ergibt sich aus dem anderen; **We have lots of apples. Please have ~:** Wir haben eine ganze Menge Äpfel. Nimm dir doch noch einen; **send a copy to the customer and keep ~ for reference** schicken Sie eine Kopie an den Kunden, und eine weitere nehmen Sie für unsere Unterlagen; **there's one school in the neighbourhood already and ~ [which is] being built** es gibt schon eine Schule in der Gegend, und eine zweite ist gerade im Bau; **b)** *(counterpart)* wieder einer/eine/eins; **such ~:** noch so einer/so eine/so eins; **c)** *(Brit. Law)* **X versus Y and ~:** X gegen Y und andere; **d)** *(different)* ein anderer/eine andere/ein anderes; **she ran off with/married ~:** sie brannte mit einem anderen durch *(ugs.)*/heiratete einen anderen; **making a mistake is one thing, but lying deliberately is quite ~:** einen Fehler zu machen ist eine Sache, aber absichtlich zu lügen ist ganz etwas anderes; **they said one to ~:** sie sagten zueinander; **in one way or ~:** so oder so; irgendwie; **for one reason or ~:** aus irgendeinem Grund; **A. N. Other** *(Brit.)* N. N.; *see also* **one 1 f, 3 b. 2.** *adj.* **a)** *(additional)* noch einer/eine/eins; ein weiterer/eine weitere/ein weiteres; **give me ~ chance** gib mir noch [einmal] eine Chance; **after ~ six weeks** nach weiteren sechs Wochen; **~ 100 pounds** weitere 100 Pfund; **he didn't say ~ word** er sagte nichts mehr; **he hasn't ~ day to live** er hat keinen Tag länger zu leben; **he hasn't ~ penny left** er hat keinen Pfennig mehr; **it'll take ~ few years** es wird noch ein paar Jahre [länger] dauern; **b)** *(a person like)* ein neuer/eine neue/ein neues; ein zweiter/eine zweite/ein zweites; **~ Chaplin** ein neuer *od.* zweiter Chaplin; **c)** *(different)* ein anderer/eine andere/ein anderes; **ask ~ person** fragen Sie jemand anderen *od.* anders; **~ time, don't be so greedy** sei beim nächsten Mal nicht so gierig; **I'll do it ~ time** ich tu's ein andermal; **[and] [there's] ~ thing** [und] noch etwas; **it's one thing to make a request, ~ thing to order** zu bitten ist eine Sache, zu befehlen eine andere; **that's quite ~ problem** das ist wieder ein anderes Problem; **~ place** *(Brit. Parl.)* die andere Kammer [dieses Parlaments]; *see also* **tomorrow a**

anschluss ['ænʃlʊs] *n. (Hist.)* Anschluß, *der;* **the ~ of Austria by Germany** der Anschluß Österreichs [an Deutschland]

answer ['ɑ:nsə(r)] **1.** *n.* **a)** *(reply)* Antwort, *die* **(to** auf + *Akk.*); *(reaction)* Reaktion, *die;* **I tried to phone him, but there was no ~:** ich habe versucht, ihn anzurufen, aber es hat sich niemand gemeldet; **do you have any ~ to the accusations made against you?** haben Sie irgend etwas auf die Anschuldigungen gegen Sie zu erwidern?; **there is no ~ to that** dem ist nichts mehr hinzuzufügen; **by way of [an] ~:** als Antwort; **in ~ to sth.** als Antwort *od.* Reaktion auf etw. *(Akk.);* **he always has an ~ [ready]** er hat immer eine Antwort parat; **make ~** *(formal)* [eine] Antwort geben; **b)** *(to problem)* Lösung, *die* **(to** *Gen.*); *(to calculation)* Ergebnis, *das;* **have** *or* **know all the ~s** *(coll.)* alles wissen. **2.** *v. t.* **a)** beantworten ⟨*Brief, Frage*⟩; antworten auf (+ *Akk.*) ⟨*Frage, Hilferuf, Einladung, Inserat*⟩; *(react to)* erwidern ⟨*Geste, Schlag*⟩; *(respond to)* eingehen auf (+ *Akk.*) ⟨*Angebot, Vorschlag*⟩; eingehen auf (+ *Akk.*), erfüllen ⟨*Bitte*⟩; sich stellen zu ⟨*Beschuldigung*⟩; erhören ⟨*Gebet*⟩; erfüllen ⟨*Wunsch*⟩; **~ sb.** jmdm. antworten; **~ me!** antworte [mir]!; **~ a question** eine Frage beantworten; auf eine Frage antworten; **b) ~ the door/bell** an die Tür gehen; **c)** *(be satisfactory for)* genügen (+ *Dat.*); entsprechen (+ *Dat.*); **the flat ~ed his purpose very well** die Wohnung entsprach *od.* genügte seinen Anforderungen vollauf; **her desires were fully ~ed** ihren Wünschen wurde vollauf entsprochen; *see also* **telephone 1. 3.** *v. i.* **a)** *(reply)* antworten; **~ to sth.** sich zu etw. äußern; **b)** *(be responsible)* **~ for sth.** für etw. die Verantwortung übernehmen; **~ to sb.** jmdm. [gegenüber] Rechenschaft ablegen; **one day you will have to ~ for your crimes** eines Tages wirst du dich für deine Verbrechen verantworten müssen; **he has a lot to ~ for** er hat vieles zu verantworten; **c)** *(correspond)* **~ to a description** einer Beschreibung *(Dat.)* entsprechen; **d)** *(be satisfactory)* **~ for a purpose/intention** sich für einen Zweck/ein Vorhaben eignen; **e) ~ to the name of ...:** auf den Namen ... hören; **f) ~ back** *(coll.)* widersprechen; Widerworte haben *(ugs.);* **he's always ready to ~ back** er gibt einem gern Kontra *(ugs.);* **don't ~ back!** keine Widerworte!

answerable ['ɑ:nsərəbl] *adj. (responsible)* **be ~ to sb.** jmdm. [gegenüber] verantwortlich sein; **be ~ for sb./sth.** für jmdn./etw. verantwortlich sein

answering: ~ machine *n. (Teleph.)* Anrufbeantworter, *der;* **~ service** *n. (Teleph.)* Fernsprechauftragsdienst, *der*

ant [ænt] *n.* Ameise, *die;* **white ~:** Termite, *die;* weiße Ameise *(volkst.);* **have ~s in one's pants** *(sl.)* nicht stillsitzen können

antacid [ænt'æsɪd] *n.* Antazidum, *das*

antagonism [æn'tægənɪzm] *n.* Feindseligkeit, *die* **(towards, against** gegenüber); *(between two)* Antagonismus, *der (geh.);* **the ~ between the two families** die Feindschaft zwischen den beiden Familien

antagonist [æn'tægənɪst] *n.* Gegner, *der*/Gegnerin, *die; (in debate etc.)* Kontrahent, *der*/Kontrahentin, *die*

antagonistic [æntægə'nɪstɪk] *adj.* feindlich ⟨*Mächte, Prinzipien*⟩; feindselig ⟨*Kritik*⟩; antagonistisch, gegensätzlich ⟨*Interessen*⟩; **be ~ to sth.** im Gegensatz zu etw. stehen; ⟨*Person:*⟩ etw. ablehnen; **be ~ to sb.** mit jmdm. verfeindet sein

antagonize [æn'tægənaɪz] *v. t.* **a)** *(evoke hostility or enmity of)* sich *(Dat.)* zum Feind machen; vor den Kopf stoßen *(ugs.);* **b)** *(counteract)* entgegenwirken (+ *Dat.*); **~ one another** sich gegenseitig bekämpfen

antarctic [ænt'ɑ:ktɪk] **1.** *adj.* antarktisch; **A~ explorer** Antarktisforscher, *der;* **A~ Circle/Ocean** südlicher Polarkreis/Südpolarmeer, *das.* **2.** *n.* **the A~:** die Antarktis

Antarctica [ænt'ɑ:ktɪkə] *n.* die Antarktis

ante ['æntɪ] **1.** *n. (in poker etc.)* Einsatz, *der;* **up the ~** *(fig. coll.)* den Einsatz erhöhen. **2.** *v. t.* setzen; **~ [up] £10** 10 Pfund setzen; **can you ~ up £1,000 to buy this plot of land?** können Sie 1000 Pfund zum Kauf dieses Grundstücks aufbringen?

'ant-eater *n. (Zool.)* Ameisenfresser, *der*

antecedent [æntɪ'si:dənt] **1.** *adj.* vorher-, vorausgehend ⟨*Faktoren, Elemente, Prinzipien*⟩; **be ~ to sth.** einer Sache *(Dat.)* vorausgehen. **2.** *n.* **a)** *(preceding event)* früherer Umstand; vorangegangenes Ereignis; *(preceding thing)* Vorläufer, *der;* **b)** *in pl. (past history)* **sb.'s ~s** jmds. Vorleben

antechamber ['æntɪtʃeɪmbə(r)] *n.* Vorzimmer, *das*

antedate [æntɪ'deɪt] *v. t.* **a)** *(precede)* voraus-, vorangehen (+ *Dat.*); **b)** *(give earlier date to)* zurückdatieren

antediluvian [æntɪdɪ'lju:vɪən, æntɪdɪ'lu:vɪən] *adj. (lit. or fig.)* vorsintflutlich

antelope ['æntɪləʊp] *n.* **a)** *(Zool.)* Antilope, *die;* **b)** *(leather)* Antilopenleder, *das*

antenatal [æntɪ'neɪtl] *adj.* **a)** *(concerning*

pregnancy) Schwangerschafts-; Schwangeren-; ~ **care** Schwangerenfürsorge, *die;* ~ **clinic** Klinik für werdende Mütter; **b)** *(before birth)* vorgeburtlich; prä- *od.* antenatal *(fachspr.)*

antenna [æn'tenə] *n.* **a)** *pl.* ~e [æn'teni:] *(Zool.)* Fühler, *der;* Antenne, *die (fachspr.);* **b)** *pl.* ~s *(Amer.: aerial)* Antenne, *die*

antepenultimate [æntɪpɪ'nʌltɪmət] *adj.* drittletzt...

ante-post [æntɪ'pəʊst] *adj. (Horse-racing)* ~ **betting** Wetten vor dem Renntag

anterior [æn'tɪərɪə(r)] *adj.* **a)** *(to the front)* vorder...; **be in an ~ position** vorn sein; **b)** *(prior)* früher...; **be ~ to sth.** einer Sache *(Dat.)* vorausgehen

ante-room ['æntɪru:m, 'æntɪrʊm] *n.* Vorraum, *der; (waiting room)* Warteraum, *der*

antheap ['ænthi:p] *n.* Ameisenhaufen, *der;* Ameisenhügel, *der;* **this human** ~ *(fig.)* dieses Menschengewimmel

anthem ['ænθəm] *n.* **a)** *(Eccl. Mus.)* Chorgesang, *der;* **b)** *(song of praise)* Jubel-, Preisgesang, *der (geh.);* Hymne, *die; see also* **national anthem**

anther ['ænθə(r)] *n. (Bot.)* Staubbeutel, *der*

anthill ['ænthɪl] *see* **antheap**

anthologist [æn'θɒlədʒɪst] *n.* Herausgeber, *der*/Herausgeberin, *die* [einer Anthologie/von Anthologien]

anthology [æn'θɒlədʒɪ] *n. (of poetry, prose, songs) (by different writers)* Anthologie, *die; (by one writer)* Auswahl, *die*

anthracite ['ænθrəsaɪt] *n.* Anthrazit, *der*

anthrax ['ænθræks] *n., no pl., no indef. art. (Med., Vet. Med.)* Milzbrand, *der;* Anthrax, *der (fachspr.)*

anthropocentric [ænθrəpəʊ'sentrɪk] *adj.* anthropozentrisch

anthropoid ['ænθrəpɔɪd] **1.** *adj.* **a)** *(manlike)* menschenähnlich; anthropoid; ~ **ape** Menschenaffe, *der;* **b)** *(coll. derog.: apelike)* affenartig *(abwertend).* **2.** *n.* Anthropoid[e], *der;* Menschenaffe, *der*

anthropological [ænθrəpə'lɒdʒɪkl] *adj.* anthropologisch

anthropologist [ænθrə'pɒlədʒɪst] *n.* Anthropologe, *der*/Anthropologin, *die*

anthropology [ænθrə'pɒlədʒɪ] *n., no pl.* Anthropologie, *die*

anthropomorphic [ænθrəpəʊ'mɔ:fɪk] *adj.* anthropomorphisch

anti ['æntɪ] **1.** *prep.* gegen; **be ~ sth.** gegen etw. sein; Gegner von etw. sein. **2.** *adj.* ablehnend; **young people are all so ~ these days** die jungen Leute heutzutage sind gegen alles *od.* lehnen einfach alles ab. **3.** *n.* Gegner, *der;* Widersacher, *der*

anti- [æntɪ] *pref.* anti-/Anti-

anti-'aircraft *adj. (Mil.)* Flugabwehr-; ~ **gun** Flak, *die;* ~ **battery** Flakbatterie, *die*

antibiotic [æntɪbaɪ'ɒtɪk] **1.** *adj.* antibiotisch. **2.** *n.* Antibiotikum, *das*

'antibody *n. (Physiol.)* Antikörper, *der*

antic ['æntɪk] *n. (trick)* Mätzchen, *das (ugs.); (of clown)* Possen, *der*

Antichrist ['æntɪkraɪst] *n.* Antichrist, *der*

anticipate [æn'tɪsɪpeɪt] *v. t.* **a)** *(expect)* erwarten; *(foresee)* voraussehen; ~ **rain/trouble** mit Regen/Ärger rechnen; **b)** *(discuss or consider before due time)* vorwegnehmen; antizipieren; **don't ~ your income** gib dein Einkommen nicht im voraus aus; **c)** *(forestall)* ~ **sb./sth.** jmdm./einer Sache zuvorkommen

anticipation [æntɪsɪ'peɪʃn] *n., no pl.* Erwartung, *die;* **in ~ of sth.** in Erwartung einer Sache *(Gen.);* **she was looking forward to the event with ~:** sie sah dem Ereignis erwartungsvoll entgegen; **thanking you in ~:** Ihnen im voraus dankend

anticipatory [æn'tɪsɪpətərɪ] *adj.* vorwegnehmend

anti'clerical *adj.* antiklerikal; kirchenfeindlich

anticli'mactic *adj.* [auf enttäuschende Weise] abfallend; **the film has an ~ ending** der Film hat ein enttäuschendes Ende

anti'climax *n.* **a)** *(ineffective end)* Abstieg, *der;* Abfall, *der;* **b)** *(Lit.)* Antiklimax, *die*

anti'clockwise **1.** *adv.* gegen den Uhrzeigersinn. **2.** *adj.* gegen den *od.* entgegen dem Uhrzeigersinn *nachgestellt;* linksläufig *(Technik);* **in an ~ direction** gegen den *od.* entgegen dem Uhrzeigersinn

anticor'rosive *adj.* Rostschutz-

anti'cyclone *n. (Meteorol.)* Hochdruckgebiet, *das;* Antizyklone, *die (Met.)*

antidepressant [æntɪdɪ'presənt] *n. (Med.)* Antidepressivum, *das*

antidote ['æntɪdəʊt] *n.* Gegengift, -mittel, *das* (**for, against** gegen); *(fig.)* Gegenmittel, *das* (**to** gegen)

'antifreeze *n.* Gefrierschutzmittel, *das;* Frostschutzmittel, *das*

antigen ['æntɪdʒən] *n. (Physiol.)* Antigen, *das*

'anti-hero *n.* Antiheld, *der*

anti'histamine *n. (Med.)* Antihistamin[ikum], *das*

'antiknock *n. (Motor Veh.)* Antiklopfmittel, *das*

Antilles [æn'tɪli:z] *pr. n. pl.* Antillen *Pl.*

antimacassar [æntɪmə'kæsə(r)] *n.* Schonbezug, *der*

'antimatter *n. (Phys.)* Antimaterie, *die*

antimony ['æntɪmənɪ] *n.* Antimon, *das*

antinomy [æn'tɪnəmɪ] *n.* Antinomie, *die*

'anti-novel *n.* Antiroman, *der*

anti'nuclear *adj.* Anti-Atom[kraft]-

'antiparticle *n. (Phys.)* Antiteilchen, *das*

antipathetic [æntɪpə'θetɪk], **antipathetical** [æntɪpə'θetɪkl] *adj.* **a)** *(averse, opposed)* **be ~ to sb./sth.** jmdm./einer Sache abgeneigt sein; eine Antipathie gegen jmdn./etw. haben; **b)** *(arousing antipathy)* **be ~ to sb.** jmdm. zuwider sein

antipathy [æn'tɪpəθɪ] *n.* Antipathie, *die;* Abneigung, *die;* ~ **to** *or* **for sb./sth.** Abneigung gegen jmdn./etw.

anti-person'nel *adj.* gegen Menschen gerichtet; ~ **bomb** Splitterbombe, *die;* ~ **mine** Schützenmine, *die*

antiperspirant [æntɪ'pɜ:spɪrənt] **1.** *adj.* schweißhemmend; ~ **spray** Deodorantspray, *der od. das.* **2.** *n.* Antitranspirant, *das*

antiphonal [æn'tɪfənəl] *adj. (Eccl. Mus.)* ~ **singing** Wechselgesang, *der*

antipodal [æn'tɪpədl] *adj. (Australasian)* australisch und ozeanisch

antipodean [æntɪpə'di:ən] *adj. see* **antipodal**

antipodes [æn'tɪpədi:z] *n. pl.* entgegengesetzte *od.* antipodische Teile der Erde; *(Australasia)* Australien und Ozeanien

'antipope *n. (Hist.)* Gegenpapst, *der*

antiquarian [æntɪ'kweərɪən] **1.** *adj.* **a)** *(of antiquity)* antik; Altertums-; ~ **research** Altertumsforschung, *die;* ~ **writings** antike Schriften; ~ **society** Gesellschaft für Altertumsforschung; **b)** ~ **bookshop** *or* **bookseller's** Antiquariat, *das;* Antiquariatsbuchhandlung, *die;* ~ **bookseller** Antiquar, *der;* Antiquariatsbuchhändler, *der.* **2.** *n. (collector)* Antiquitätensammler, *der*

antiquarianism [æntɪ'kweərɪənɪzm] *n., no pl.* Liebhaberei für Altertümer; Altertümelei, *die (auch abwertend)*

antiquary ['æntɪkwərɪ] *n. see* **antiquarian 2**

antiquated ['æntɪkweɪtɪd] *adj.* *(old-fashioned)* antiquiert; veraltet; *(out of date)* überholt

antique [æn'ti:k] **1.** *adj.* **a)** antik ‹*Möbel, Schmuck usw.*›; *(as an antique)* antiquarisch ‹*Wert, Bedeutung*›; **furniture of ~ design** Möbel im antiken Stil; **b)** *(existing since old times)* antik ‹*Philosophie, Literatur, Kultur, Volk, Kunst, Ideen*›; *(antiquated)* altertümlich ‹*Sprache, Ansicht, Verhalten*›. **2.** *n.* Antiquität, *die;* ~ **dealer** Antiquitätenhändler, *der*/-händlerin, *die;* ~ **shop** Antiquitätenladen, *der*

antiquity [æn'tɪkwɪtɪ] *n.* **a)** *no pl. (ancientness)* Alter, *das;* **a city/law/fossil of great ~:** eine uralte Stadt/ein uraltes Gesetz/Fossil; **b)** *no pl., no art. (old times)* Altertum, *das;* Antike, *die; (the ancients)* Antike, *die;* **in ~:** im Altertum; in der Antike; **c)** *in pl. (ancient relics)* Altertümer *Pl.; (ancient customs)* altertümliche Bräuche

antirrhinum [æntɪ'raɪnəm] *n. (Bot.)* Löwenmaul, *das*

anti-'Semite *n.* Antisemit, *der*/-semitin, *die;* Judenfeind, *der*/-feindin, *die*

anti-Se'mitic *adj.* antisemitisch; judenfeindlich

anti-Semitism [æntɪ'semɪtɪzm] *n., no pl.* Antisemitismus, *der;* Judenhaß, *der*

anti'sepsis *n., no pl. (Med.)* Antisepsis, *die*

anti'septic **1.** *adj.* **a)** antiseptisch; keimtötend; **b)** *(scrupulously clean)* aseptisch; keimfrei; *(sterile)* keimfrei; steril; *(fig.: unfeeling)* gefühllos. **2.** *n.* Antiseptikum, *das*

anti'social *adj.* **a)** asozial; **b)** *(unsociable)* ungesellig ‹*Person*›; unwirtlich ‹*Ort*›

anti'static *adj.* antistatisch

anti-'tank gun *n. (Mil.)* Panzerabwehrkanone, *die*

antithesis [æn'tɪθəsɪs] *n., pl.* **antitheses** [æn'tɪθəsi:z] **a)** *(thing)* Gegenstück, *das* (**of, to** zu); **these two concepts are the ~ of each other** diese beiden Begriffe sind Gegensätze; **b)** *(state)* Gegensatz, *der; (Rhet.: contrast of ideas)* Antithese, *die;* **stand in ~ to sth.** einer Sache *(Dat.)* antithetisch gegenüberstehen; **the ~ of** *or* **between two things** der Gegensatz zwischen zwei Dingen

antithetic [æntɪ'θetɪk], **antithetical** [æntɪ'θetɪkl] *adj.* **a)** *(opposite)* gegensätzlich; *(consisting of opposites)* antithetisch; **be ~ to sth.** zu einer Sache im Gegensatz stehen; **b)** *(Rhet.)* antithetisch

anti'toxin *n. (Med.)* Antitoxin, *das*

anti'trust *adj. (Amer.)* Kartell-; Antitrust-; ~ **law** Kartellgesetz, *das*

antivivisectionism [æntɪvɪvɪ'sekʃənɪzm] *n., no pl.* Ablehnung der Vivisektion

antivivisectionist [æntɪvɪvɪ'sekʃənɪst] *n.* Vivisektionsgegner, *der*/-gegnerin, *die*

antler ['æntlə(r)] *n. (branch of horn)* Geweihsprosse, *die; (horn)* Stange, *die (Jägerspr.);* **a pair of ~s** ein Geweih *od. (Jägerspr.)* Gehörn

antonym ['æntənɪm] *n.* Antonym, *das;* Gegen[satz]wort, *das*

antonymous [æn'tɒnɪməs] *adj.* antonym

Antwerp ['æntwɜ:p] *pr. n.* Antwerpen *(das)*

anus ['eɪnəs] *n. (Anat.)* After, *der;* Anus, *der*

anvil ['ænvɪl] *n. (also Anat.)* Amboß, *der*

anxiety [æŋ'zaɪətɪ] *n.* **a)** *(state)* Angst, *die; (concern about future)* Sorge, *die* (**about** wegen); **anxieties** Sorgen *Pl.;* **cause sb. ~:** jmdm. angst/Sorgen machen; **b)** *(desire)* Verlangen, das (**for** nach); **his ~ to do sth.** sein Verlangen danach, etw. zu tun; **c)** *(Psych.)* Angst, *die;* Angstzustand, *der*

anxious ['æŋkʃəs] *adj.* **a)** *(troubled)* besorgt; **days of ~ waiting** Tage bangen Wartens; **be ~ about sth./sb.** um etw./jmdn. besorgt sein; **we were all so ~ about you** wir haben uns *(Dat.)* alle solche Sorgen um Sie gemacht; **b)** *(eager)* sehnlich; **be ~ for sth.** ungeduldig auf etw. *(Akk.)* warten; **have an ~ desire to do sth.** ängstlich darauf bedacht sein, etw. zu tun; **he is ~ to please** er ist bemüht zu gefallen; **he is ~ to learn another language** er will unbedingt noch eine Sprache lernen; **c)** *(worrying)* **an ~ time** eine Zeit banger Sorge; **two ~ days of waiting** zwei Tage bangen Wartens

anxiously ['æŋkʃəslɪ] *adv.* **a)** besorgt; **b)** *(eagerly)* sehnsüchtig; **always ~ eager to help** immer eifrig darauf bedacht, zu helfen

any ['enɪ] **1.** *adj.* **a)** *(some)* [irgend]ein/eine;

have you ~ wool/~ statement to make? haben Sie Wolle/[irgend]eine Erklärung abzugeben?; **if you have ~ difficulties** wenn du irgendwelche Schwierigkeiten hast; **not ~:** kein/keine; **that isn't ~ way to behave** das ist keine Art, sich zu benehmen; **without ~:** ohne jeden/jede/jedes; **if you've ~ spare time** *or* **time to spare** wenn du Zeit hast *od.* hättest; **we haven't ~ time to lose** wir haben keine Zeit zu verlieren; **have you ~ idea of the time?** hast du eine Ahnung, wie spät es ist?; **~ news of Peter yet?** schon was von Peter gehört?; **b)** *(one)* ein/eine; **there isn't ~ hood on this coat** dieser Mantel hat keine Kapuze; **a book without ~ cover** ein Buch ohne Deckel; **c)** *(all)* jeder/jede/jedes; **to avoid ~ delay** um jede Verzögerung zu vermeiden; **d)** *(every)* jeder/jede/jedes; **~ and every** jeder/jede/jedes beliebige; **~ fool knows that!** das weiß doch jedes Kind!; **~ time** *or* **on ~ occasion [when] I went there** jedesmal *od.* immer, wenn ich dort hinging; **[at] ~ time** jederzeit; **[at] ~ time of day** zu jeder Tageszeit; **e)** *(whichever)* jeder/jede/jedes [beliebige]; **choose ~ [one] book/~ books you like** suchen Sie sich *(Dat.)* irgendein Buch/irgendwelche Bücher aus; **choose ~ two numbers** nimm zwei beliebige Zahlen; **do it ~ way you like** machen Sie es, wie immer Sie wollen; **cook the meat [in] ~ way/[for] ~ length of time you wish** kochen Sie das Fleisch, wie/solange Sie wollen; **visit us [at] ~ time** besuchen Sie uns, wann [immer] Sie wollen; **[at] ~ time/day/minute [now]** jederzeit/jeden Tag/jede Minute; **~ moment now the bomb will explode** die Bombe wird jeden Moment explodieren; **you can count on him ~ time** *(coll.)* du kannst dich jederzeit auf ihn verlassen; **I'd prefer Mozart ~ day** *(coll.)* ich würde Mozart allemal *(ugs.) od.* jederzeit vorziehen; **not [just] ~ house** nicht irgendein beliebiges Haus; **take ~ amount you wish** nehmen Sie, soviel Sie wollen; **~ amount of** jede Menge *(ugs.)*; **the room was filled with ~ amount of decorations/~ number of film stars** das Zimmer war reich geschmückt/in dem Zimmer war ein Heer von Filmstars; *see also* **¹case a; old 1 d; rate 1 f; f)** *(an appreciable)* ein nennenswerter/eine nennenswerte/ein nennenswertes; **she didn't stay ~ length of time** sie ist nicht sehr lange geblieben; **he couldn't walk ~ distance without feeling exhausted** er konnte keine längere Strecke gehen, ohne sich erschöpft zu fühlen; **if he drinks ~ amount he gets roaring drunk** wenn er einmal etwas mehr trinkt, ist er gleich sternhagelvoll *(salopp)*. **2.** *pron.* **a)** *(some) in condit., interrog., or neg. sentence (replacing sing. n.)* einer/eine/ein[e]s; *(replacing collect. n.)* welcher/welche/welches; *(replacing pl. n.)* welche; **not ~:** keiner/keine/kein[e]s/*Pl.* keine; **without ~:** ohne; **I need to buy some sugar, we haven't got ~ at the moment** ich muß Zucker kaufen, wir haben im Augenblick keinen; **Here are some sweets. Would you like ~?** Hier sind ein paar Bonbons. Möchtest du welche?; **they ate all the cake and didn't leave ~ for us** *or* **without leaving ~ for us** sie haben den ganzen Kuchen gegessen und uns nichts übriggelassen; **hardly ~:** kaum welche/etwas; **Tea? No, I don't want ~ at the moment, thanks** Tee? Nein danke, im Moment nicht; **not known to ~ except ...:** keinem *od.* niemandem bekannt außer ...; **Here is a list of the books I need. Do you have ~ of them in stock?** Hier ist eine Liste mit den Büchern, die ich brauche. Haben Sie [irgend]welche davon vorrätig?; **I haven't seen ~ of my friends for years** ich habe seit Jahren keinen von meinen Freunden gesehen; **is there ~ of that cake left?** ist noch etwas [von dem] Kuchen übrig?; **is there ~ of you who would be willing to help?** wäre irgend jemand von Ihnen bereit zu helfen?; **he is not having ~ of it** *(fig. coll.)* er will nichts davon wissen; **b)** *(no matter which)* irgendeiner/irgendeine/irgendein[e]s/irgendwelche *Pl.*; **you have to pick a number between 1 and 10, ~ you like** du mußt eine Zahl zwischen 1 und 10 ziehen, irgendeine; **you can choose three books, ~ [of them] you like** Sie können sich *(Dat.)* drei Bücher aussuchen, egal welche; **Which numbers? – Any between 1 and 10** Welche Zahlen? – Irgendwelche zwischen 1 und 10. **3.** *adv.* **do you feel ~ better today?** fühlen Sie sich heute [etwas] besser?; **if it gets ~ colder** wenn es noch kälter wird; **he didn't seem ~ [the] wiser after that** danach schien er auch nicht klüger zu sein; **I can't wait ~ longer** ich kann nicht [mehr] länger warten; **the occasional jokes do not make the book ~ [the] less boring** durch die gelegentlichen Witze wird das Buch keineswegs interessanter; **I don't feel ~ [the] better** mir ist kein bißchen wohler; **not ~ too happy about it** nicht gerade glücklich darüber; *see also* **more 1 a, 3 d, i**

'anybody *n. & pron.* **a)** *(whoever)* jeder; **~ and everybody** jeder Beliebige; **b)** *(somebody)* [irgend]jemand; **how could ~ be so cruel?** wie kann man nur so grausam sein?; **there wasn't ~ willing to help** es war niemand bereit zu helfen; **there's never ~ at home when I phone** es ist nie jemand zu Hause, wenn ich anrufe; **I've never seen ~ who ...:** ich habe noch keinen gesehen, der ...; **he is a match for ~ with his strength** bei seiner Kraft kann er sich mit jedem *od.* jedermann messen; **~ but** jeder[mann] außer; **The score is 1 : 1. It's ~'s match now** Es steht 1 : 1. Das Spiel ist jetzt offen; **what will happen is ~'s guess** was geschehen wird, [das] weiß keiner; **he's not [just] ~:** er ist nicht [einfach] irgendwer; **c)** *(important person)* jemand; wer *(ugs.)*; **everybody who was ~ was there** alles, was Rang und Namen hatte, war da

'anyhow *adv.* **a)** *see* **anyway**; **b)** *(haphazardly)* irgendwie; **he dresses ~:** er kleidet sich ohne Überlegung; **the furniture was arranged ~:** die Möbel waren wahllos irgendwo hingestellt; **all ~:** ganz unordentlich

'anyone *see* **anybody**

'anyplace *(Amer. coll.) see* **anywhere**

'anything 1. *n. & pron.* **a)** *(whatever thing)* was [immer]; alles, was; **you may do ~ you wish** Sie können [alles] tun, was Sie möchten; **~ and everything** alles mögliche; **b)** *(something)* irgend etwas; **is there ~ wrong with you?** fehlt Ihnen [irgend] etwas?; **have you done ~ silly?** hast du [irgend] etwas Dummes gemacht?; **can we do ~ to help you?** können wir Ihnen irgendwie helfen?; **I don't want ~ [further] to do with him** ich möchte nichts [mehr] mit ihm zu tun haben; **I've never seen ~ like it in my life** ich habe noch nie in meinem Leben so etwas gesehen; **he can hardly see ~ without his glasses** ohne seine Brille kann er kaum etwas sehen; **c)** *(a thing of any kind)* alles; **~ like that** so etwas; **as ... as ~** *(coll.)* wahnsinnig ... *(ugs.)*; **not for ~ [in the world]** um nichts in der Welt; **I will do ~ in my power to help you** ich werde alles tun, was in meiner Macht steht, um Ihnen zu helfen; **the temperature is ~ from 30 to 40 degrees** die Temperatur liegt irgendwo zwischen 30 und 40 Grad; **~ but** *(~ except)* alles außer; *(far from)* alles andere als; **Cheap? The house was ~ but!** Billig war das Haus? Von wegen!; **prices are rising like ~** *(coll.)* die Preise steigen wie nur was *od.* wie verrückt *(ugs.)*; **we don't want [just] ~:** wir wollen nicht einfach irgend etwas [Beliebiges]. **2.** *adv.* **not ~ like as ... as** keineswegs so ... wie

'anyway *adv.* **a)** *(in any case, besides)* sowieso; **we wouldn't accept your help ~:** wir würden von Ihnen sowieso keine Hilfe annehmen; **b)** *(at any rate)* jedenfalls; **~, I must go now** wie dem auch sei, ich muß jetzt gehen

'anywhere 1. *adv.* **a)** *(in any place) (wherever)* überall, wo; wo [immer]; *(somewhere)* irgendwo; **can you see my bag ~?** siehst du meine Tasche irgendwo?; **the price could be ~ between £30 and £40** der Preis könnte irgendwo zwischen 30 Pfund und 40 Pfund liegen; **not ~ near as ... as** *(coll.)* nicht annähernd so ... wie; **~ but ...:** überall, außer ...; überall, nur nicht ...; **[just] ~:** überall; **not just ~:** nicht überall; **b)** *(to any place) (wherever)* wohin [auch immer]; *(somewhere)* irgendwohin; **have you ever been ~ by plane?** sind Sie je mit dem Flugzeug [irgendwohin] geflogen?; **I wouldn't go ~ near that island again** ich würde nicht wieder auch nur in die Nähe der Insel fahren; **~ but ...:** überallhin, außer ...; überallhin, nur nicht ...; **[just] ~:** [einfach] irgendwohin. **2.** *pron.* **if there's ~ you'd like to see** wenn es irgend etwas gibt, was du sehen möchtest; **have you found ~ to live yet?** haben Sie schon eine Wohnung gefunden?; **is there ~ we can stay for the night?** können wir hier irgendwo übernachten?; **there's never ~ open for milk after 6 p.m.** nach 18 Uhr kann man nirgends mehr Milch bekommen; **~ but ...:** überall, außer ...; überall, nur nicht ...; **[just] ~:** irgendein x-beliebiger Ort; **from ~ hot** von irgendwo, wo es warm ist; **from ~ in the world** aus aller Welt

aorta [eɪ'ɔ:tə] *n. (Anat.)* Aorta, *die*

apace [ə'peɪs] *adv. (arch./literary)* rasch; geschwind *(veralt.)*

apart [ə'pɑ:t] *adv.* **a)** *(separately)* getrennt; **with one's legs ~:** mit gespreizten Beinen; **a few problems ~:** einige Probleme ausgenommen; **~ from ...** *(except for)* außer ...; bis auf ... (+ *Akk.*); *(in addition to)* außer ...; **everybody ~ from one person** alle außer einem; **he took me ~ in order to speak to me alone** er nahm mich zur Seite, um allein mit mir zu sprechen; **a race ~:** ein Volk für sich; **b)** *(into pieces)* auseinander; **he took the engine ~:** er nahm den Motor auseinander; **the toy came ~ in his hands** das Spielzeug zerbrach in seinen Händen; **take ~** *(fig.) (criticize)* auseinandernehmen *(ugs.)* ‹*Theaterstück, Theoretiker, Politiker*›; *(analyse)* zergliedern; *(coll.: defeat)* vernichtend schlagen; **take a poem/play/book ~:** ein Gedicht/Stück/Buch zergliedern *od.* [im einzelnen] analysieren; **c) ~ [from]** *(to a distance)* weg [von]; *(at a distance)* **ten kilometres ~:** zehn Kilometer voneinander entfernt; **they have moved far ~ from each other** sie sind weit voneinander weggezogen; **they are miles** *or* **worlds ~ [from each other] in their tastes** zwischen ihren Geschmäkkern liegen Welten

apartheid [ə'pɑ:theɪt] *n., no pl., no art.* Apartheid, *die; (fig.)* Diskriminierung, *die*

apartment [ə'pɑ:tmənt] *n.* **a)** *(room)* Apartment, *das;* Appartement, *das;* **~s** *(in a mansion etc.)* Räume; Räumlichkeiten *Pl.*; **b)** *(Amer.) see* **¹flat; ~ house** Appartementhaus, *das*

apathetic [æpə'θetɪk] *adj.* apathisch (**about** gegenüber); *(not feeling emotion)* gleichgültig

apathetically [æpə'θetɪkəlɪ] *adv.* apathisch; *(without emotion)* gleichgültig

apathy ['æpəθɪ] *n., no pl.* Apathie, *die* (**about** gegenüber); *(lack of emotion)* Gleichmut, *der*

ape [eɪp] **1.** *n.* **a)** *(tailless monkey)* [Menschen]affe, *der; (monkey)* Affe, *der;* **man is descended from the ~s** der Mensch stammt vom Affen ab; **b)** *(imitator)* Nachahmer, *der;* Nachäffer, *der (abwertend)*; **c)** *(apelike person)* Affe, *der;* **go ~** *(sl.)* verrückt werden *(ugs.)*; durchdrehen *(ugs.)*. **2.** *v. t.* nachahmen; nachäffen *(abwertend)*

apelike ['eɪplaɪk] *adj.* wie ein Affe *nachgestellt*
Apennines ['æpɪnaɪnz] *pr. n. pl.* Apenninen *Pl.*
aperçu [æpɜː'sjuː] *n.* **a)** *(summary)* kurzer Überblick **(of** über + *Akk.*); **b)** *(insight)* Aperçu, *das*
aperient [ə'pɪərɪənt] **1.** *adj.* abführend; **this preparation is mildly/strongly ~:** dieses Präparat ist ein schwaches/starkes Abführmittel. **2.** *n.* Abführmittel, *das*
aperitif [əperɪ'tiːf] *n.* Aperitif, *der*
aperture ['æpətʃə(r)] *n.* **a)** *(opening)* Öffnung, *die;* **b)** *(Optics, Photog., etc.)* Blende, *die*
APEX ['eɪpeks] *abbr.* **Advance Purchase Excursion** *reduzierter Flugtarif bei Vorauszahlung*
apex *n., pl.* **~es** *or* **apices** ['eɪpɪsiːz] *(tip)* Spitze, *die; (of heart, lung, etc.)* Spitze, *die;* Apex, *der (fachspr.); (fig.)* Gipfel, *der;* Höhepunkt, *der*
apfelstrudel ['æpfəlstruːdl] *n.* Apfelstrudel, *der*
aphasia [ə'feɪzɪə] *n. (Med.)* Aphasie, *die*
aphid ['eɪfɪd] *n. (Zool.)* Blattlaus, *die*
aphorism ['æfərɪzm] *n.* *(pithy statement)* Aphorismus, *der; (maxim)* Maxime, *die*
aphoristic [æfə'rɪstɪk] *adj.* aphoristisch
aphrodisiac [æfrə'dɪzɪæk] *(Med.)* **1.** *adj.* aphrodisisch. **2.** *n.* Aphrodisiakum, *das*
apiarist ['eɪpɪərɪst] *n.* Bienenzüchter, *der;* Imker, *der*
apiary ['eɪpɪərɪ] *n.* Bienenhaus, *das*
apices *pl. of* **apex**
apiece [ə'piːs] *adv.* je; **we took two bags ~:** wir nahmen je zwei Beutel; **they cost a penny ~:** die kosten einen Penny das Stück; **books/five books at £1 ~:** jedes Buch ein Pfund/fünf Bücher zu je einem Pfund
apish ['eɪpɪʃ] *adj.* **a)** *(apelike)* affenartig; **b)** *(imitative)* sklavisch [nachahmend]; **c)** *(silly)* affig *(ugs.)*
aplenty [ə'plentɪ] *adv.* in [Hülle und] Fülle
aplomb [ə'plɒm] *n.* Sicherheit [im Auftreten]; Aplomb, *der (geh.)*
apocalypse [ə'pɒkəlɪps] *n.* **a)** *(event)* Apokalypse, *die;* **b)** *(Relig.) (revelation)* Offenbarung, *die; (book)* Apokalypse, *die;* Offenbarung, *die*
apocalyptic [əpɒkə'lɪptɪk], **apocalyptical** [əpɒkə'lɪptɪkl] *adj.* **a)** *(dramatic)* apokalyptisch; **b)** *(Relig.) (of revelation)* apokalyptisch; *(of book)* Offenbarungs-; der Offenbarung *nachgestellt*
Apocrypha [ə'pɒkrɪfə] *n. (Bibl.)* Apokryphen *Pl.*
apocryphal [ə'pɒkrɪfl] *adj.* **a)** *(of doubtful origin)* apokryph; zweifelhaft; *(invented)* apokryph; unecht; **b)** *(of the Apocrypha)* apokryph
apogee ['æpədʒiː] *n.* **a)** *(highest point)* Höhepunkt, *der;* Gipfel[punkt], *der;* **b)** *(Astron.)* Apogäum, *das;* Erdferne, *die*
apolitical [eɪpə'lɪtɪkl] *adj.* apolitisch; unpolitisch
Apollo [ə'pɒləʊ] *pr. n.* Apoll[o], *der*
apologetic [əpɒlə'dʒetɪk] *adj.* **a)** entschuldigend; **~ words** Worte der Entschuldigung; **an ~ person** jmd., der sich dauernd entschuldigt; **he wrote a very ~ letter** er schrieb einen Brief, in dem er sich vielmals entschuldigte; **he was most ~ about ...:** er entschuldigte sich vielmals für ...; **b)** *(diffident)* zaghaft ‹*Lächeln, Ton*›; zurückhaltend, bescheiden ‹*Wesen, Art*›
apologetically [əpɒlə'dʒetɪkəlɪ] *adv.* **a)** entschuldigend; **he wrote very ~ to say that he ...:** er schrieb mit großem Bedauern, daß er ...; **b)** *(diffidently)* zaghaft; bescheiden
apologetics [əpɒlə'dʒetɪks] *n., no pl.* Apologetik, *die*
apologia [æpə'ləʊdʒɪə] *n.* Apologie, *die*
apologist [ə'pɒlədʒɪst] *n.* Apologet, *der/* Apologetin, *die*
apologize [ə'pɒlədʒaɪz] *v.i.* **a)** sich entschuldigen; **~ to sb. for sth./sb.** sich bei jmdm. für etw./jmdn. entschuldigen; **b)** *(defend one's actions)* sich rechtfertigen
apology [ə'pɒlədʒɪ] *n.* **a)** Entschuldigung, *die;* **make an ~ [to sb.] for sth.** sich für etw. [bei jmdm.] entschuldigen; **an ~ to sb. for sth.** eine Entschuldigung bei jmdm. für etw.; **you owe him an ~/he deserves an ~ from you** Sie müssen sich bei ihm entschuldigen; **please accept our apologies** wir bitten vielmals um Entschuldigung; **she was full of apologies for her mistake** sie entschuldigte sich vielmals für ihren Fehler; **b)** *(defence)* Rechtfertigung, *die;* **c)** *(poor substitute)* **an ~ for a ...:** ein erbärmliches Exemplar von ...; **what's this ~ for a meal?** was ist denn das für eine kärgliche *od.* armselige Mahlzeit?
apoplectic [æpə'plektɪk] *adj.* apoplektisch; **~ stroke** *or* **fit** Schlaganfall, *der*
apoplexy ['æpəpleksɪ] *n.* Apoplexie, *die (fachspr.);* Schlaganfall, *der;* **a fit of ~:** ein Schlaganfall
apostasy [ə'pɒstəsɪ] *n.* Apostasie, *die*
apostate [ə'pɒstət] **1.** *n.* Abtrünnige, *der/die;* Renegat, *der;* Apostat, *der (Rel.).* **2.** *adj.* abtrünnig; [von einer Partei/Glaubensrichtung] abgefallen
a posteriori [eɪ pɒsterɪ'ɔːraɪ] **1.** *adv.* a posteriori. **2.** *adj.* aposteriorisch
apostle [ə'pɒsl] *n. (lit. or fig.)* Apostel, *der;* **the A~s** die [zwölf] Apostel; **A~s' Creed** Apostolisches Glaubensbekenntnis; Apostolikum, *das (fachspr.)*
apostolic [æpə'stɒlɪk] *adj.* apostolisch
apostrophe [ə'pɒstrəfɪ] *n.* **a)** *(sign)* Apostroph, *der;* Auslassungszeichen, *das;* **b)** *(Rhet.: exclamatory passage)* Apostrophe, *die*
apostrophize [ə'pɒstrəfaɪz] *v.t.* apostrophieren
apothecary [ə'pɒθɪkərɪ] *n.* **a)** *(arch.)* Apotheker, *der/*Apothekerin, *die;* **b) apothecaries' measure/weight** Apothekermaß/-gewicht, *das*
apotheosis [əpɒθɪ'əʊsɪs] *n., pl.* **apotheoses** [əpɒθɪ'əʊsiːz] **a)** *(deification)* Apotheose, *die (auch fig.);* Vergöttlichung, *die;* **b)** *(deified ideal)* Gott, *der/*Göttin, *die;* **c)** *(ultimate point)* Gipfelpunkt, *der;* Apotheose, *die (geh.)*
appal (*Amer.:* **appall**) [ə'pɔːl] *v.t.*, **-ll-** *(dismay)* entsetzen; *(terrify)* erschrecken; **your behaviour ~s me!** ich bin entsetzt über dein Benehmen!; **obscenity ~s her** sie empört sich über Obszönitäten
appalling [ə'pɔːlɪŋ] *adj.* *(dismaying)* entsetzlich; *(terrifying)* schrecklich; *(coll.: unpleasant)* fürchterlich; scheußlich
apparatchik [æpə'rɑːtʃɪk] *n., pl.* **~s** *or* **~i** [æpə'rɑːtʃɪkiː] Apparatschik, *der*
apparatus [æpə'reɪtəs] *n.* *(equipment)* Gerät, *das; (gymnastic ~)* Geräte *Pl.; (machinery, lit. or fig.)* Apparat, *der;* **a piece of ~:** ein Apparat
apparel [ə'pærəl] **1.** *n.* Kleidung, *die;* Gewänder *Pl. (geh.).* **2.** *v.t.*, *(Brit.)* **-ll-** *(arch.)* gewanden *(veralt.);* kleiden *(auch fig.)*
apparent [ə'pærənt] *adj.* **a)** *(clear)* offensichtlich ‹*Ziel, Zweck, Wirkung, Begeisterung, Interesse*›; offenbar ‹*Bedeutung, Wahrheit*›; **it soon became ~ that ...:** es zeigte sich bald, daß ...; **the meaning was/became clearly ~ to all of us** die Bedeutung war/wurde uns allen deutlich klar; **heir ~:** recht- *od.* gesetzmäßiger Erbe; **he is the heir ~ to the throne** er ist der rechtmäßige Thronfolger; **b)** *(seeming)* scheinbar; **be only ~:** nur scheinbar sein; **this was only the ~ truth** das schien nur die Wahrheit zu sein
apparently [ə'pærəntlɪ] *adv.* **a)** *(clearly)* offensichtlich; offenbar; **b)** *(seemingly)* scheinbar; **he was not asleep, but only ~ so** er schien nur zu schlafen
apparition [æpə'rɪʃn] *n.* **a)** *(appearance)* [Geister]erscheinung, *die;* **b)** *(ghost)* Gespenst, *das*
appeal [ə'piːl] **1.** *v.i.* **a)** *(Law etc.)* Einspruch erheben *od.* einlegen **(to** bei**)**; **~ to a court** bei einem Gericht Berufung einlegen; **~ against sth.** gegen etw. Einspruch/Berufung einlegen; **~ from a judgement** gegen ein Urteil Berufung einlegen; **b)** *(refer)* **~ to** verweisen auf ‹*Erkenntnisse, Tatsachen*›; **c)** *(make earnest request)* **~ to sb. for sth./to do sth.** jmdn. um etw. ersuchen/jmdn. ersuchen, etw. zu tun; **I ~ to you to give generously** ich appelliere an Sie *od.* ich ersuche Sie, großzügig zu spenden; **d)** *(address oneself)* **~ to sb./sth.** an jmdn./etw. appellieren; **this type of music ~s to the senses rather than the intellect** solche Musik spricht eher das Gefühl an als den Verstand; **e)** *(be attractive)* **~ to sb.** jmdm. zusagen; **how does that ~?** könnte dir das gefallen? **this music does not ~ to their tastes** diese Musik ist nicht ihr Geschmack; **f)** *(Cricket)* Einspruch erheben. **2.** *v.t.* überweisen ‹*Sache, Fall usw.*›. **3.** *n.* **a)** *(Law etc.)* Einspruch, *der* **(to** bei); *(to higher court)* Berufung, *die* **(to** bei); **an ~ against** *or* **from a judgement** Berufung gegen eine Entscheidung; **lodge an ~ with sb.** bei jmdm. Einspruch/Berufung einlegen; **acquittal on ~:** Freispruch in der Berufung; **right of ~:** Einspruchs-/Berufungsrecht, *das;* **there is no ~ against this decision** gegen diese Entscheidung gibt es keine Einspruchs-/Berufungsmöglichkeit; **Court of A~:** Berufungsgericht, *das;* Appellationsgericht, *das (veralt.);* **b)** *(reference)* Berufung, *die;* Verweisung, *die;* **make an ~ to sth.** sich auf etw. *(Akk.)* berufen; auf etw. *(Akk.)* verweisen; **c)** *(imploring request)* Appell, *der;* Aufruf, *der;* **an ~ to sb. for sth.** eine Bitte an jmdn. um etw.; **make an ~ to sb.** eine dringende Bitte an jmdn. richten; an jmdn. appellieren; **d)** *(addressing oneself)* Appell, *der;* Aufruf, *der;* **make an ~ to sb.** einen Appell an jmdn. richten; **the ~ of the music is to the senses rather than the intellect** die Musik spricht eher das Gefühl an als den Verstand; **e)** *(attraction)* Reiz, *der;* Anziehungskraft, *die;* **a Rolls-Royce has a certain class ~:** ein Rolls Royce ist etwas für Standesbewußte; **f)** *(Cricket)* Einspruch, *der*
appealable [ə'piːləbl] *adj.* gerichtlich anfechtbar; appellabel *(veralt.)*
appealing [ə'piːlɪŋ] *adj.* **a)** *(imploring)* flehend; **b)** *(attractive)* ansprechend ‹*Farbe, Geschichte, Stil*›; verlockend ‹*Essen, Idee*›; reizvoll ‹*Haus, Beruf, Baustil*›; angenehm ‹*Stimme, Charakter*›
appealingly [ə'piːlɪŋlɪ] *adv.* ansprechend
appear [ə'pɪə(r)] *v.i.* **a)** *(become visible, be seen, arrive)* erscheinen; ‹*Licht, Mond:*› auftauchen; ‹*Symptom, Darsteller:*› auftreten; *(present oneself)* auftreten; *(Sport)* spielen; **he was ordered to ~ at the police station/before the court** er wurde zum Polizeirevier geladen/vom Gericht vorgeladen; **he ~ed in court charged with murder** er stand wegen Mordes vor Gericht; **b)** *(occur)* vorkommen; ‹*Irrtum:*› vorkommen, auftreten; ‹*Ereignis:*› vorkommen, eintreten; *(be manifest)* ‹*Einstellung, Meinung:*› sich zeigen; **c)** *(seem)* **~ [to be] ...:** scheinen ... [zu sein]; **try to ~ relaxed** versuch, entspannt zu erscheinen; **you could at least ~ to be interested** du könntest zumindest so tun, als ob du interessiert wärest; **~ to do sth.** scheinen, etw. zu tun; **she only ~s to be asleep** es hat nur den Anschein, als schlafe sie; **d)** *(be published)* erscheinen; herauskommen
appearance [ə'pɪərəns] *n.* **a)** *(becoming visible)* Auftauchen, *das; (of symptoms)* Auftreten, *das; (arrival)* Erscheinen, *das; (of performer, speaker, etc.)* Auftritt, *der;* **make an** *or* **one's ~:** erscheinen; **make a public ~:**

in der Öffentlichkeit auftreten; **put in an ~:** sich sehen lassen; **b)** *(look)* Äußere, *das;* **outward ~:** äußere Erscheinung; **~s** Äußerlichkeiten *Pl.;* **the house had a shabby ~:** das Haus hatte ein schäbiges Aussehen; **his ~ of being nervous** sein nervöses Auftreten; **to judge by ~s, to all ~s** allem Anschein nach; **for the sake of ~s, to keep up ~s** um den Schein zu wahren; **c)** *(semblance)* Anschein, *der;* **~s to the contrary, ...:** entgegen allem Anschein ...; **~s can be deceptive** der Schein trügt; **d)** *(occurrence)* Auftreten, *das;* Vorkommen, *das;* **e)** *(publication)* Veröffentlichung, *die;* Erscheinen, *das*

appease [ə'pi:z] *v. t.* **a)** *(make calm)* besänftigen; *(Polit.)* beschwichtigen; **b)** *(soothe)* lindern ‹*Leid, Schmerz, Not*›; mildern ‹*Beunruhigung, Erregung*›; *(satisfy)* befriedigen ‹*Verlangen, Lust*›; stillen ‹*Hunger, Durst*›

appeasement [ə'pi:zmənt] *n. see* **appease:** Besänftigung, *die;* Beschwichtigung, *die;* Linderung, *die;* Milderung, *die;* Befriedigung, *die;* Stillen, *das*

appellant [ə'pelənt] *(Law)* **1.** *n.* Berufungskläger, *der*/-klägerin, *die;* Appellant, *der (veralt.).* **2.** *adj.* Berufungs-; Appellations- *(veralt.)*

appellate [ə'pelət] *adj. (Law)* Berufungs-; Appellations- *(veralt.);* **~ judge/hearing** Berufungsrichter, *der*/-verfahren, *das*

appellation [æpə'leɪʃn] *n. (name, nomenclature)* Bezeichnung, *die; (way of addressing)* Anrede, *die*

append [ə'pend] *v. t.* **~ sth. to sth.** etw. an etw. *(Akk.)* anhängen; *(add)* etw. einer Sache *(Dat.)* anfügen; **~ one's signature to a document** seine Unterschrift unter ein Dokument setzen

appendage [ə'pendɪdʒ] *n.* **a)** Anhängsel, *das; (addition)* Anhang, *der;* **he feels as if he has become a mere ~ to the household** er fühlt sich im Haus nur noch als fünftes Rad am Wagen; **b)** *(accompaniment)* Zu-, Beigabe, *die* **(to** zu**)**

appendectomy [æpen'dektəmɪ], **appendicectomy** [əpendɪ'sektəmɪ] *n. (Med.)* Blinddarmoperation, *die (volkst.);* Appendektomie, *die (fachspr.)*

appendices *pl. of* **appendix**

appendicitis [əpendɪ'saɪtɪs] *n.* Blinddarmentzündung, *die (volkst.);* Appendizitis, *die (fachspr.)*

appendix [ə'pendɪks] *n., pl.* **appendices** [ə'pendɪsi:z] *or* **~es a)** Anhang, *der* **(to** zu**)**; **b)** *(Anat.)* **[vermiform] ~:** Blinddarm, *der (volkst.);* Wurmfortsatz [des Blinddarms]

appertain [æpə'teɪn] *v. i.* **~ to sth.** *(relate)* sich auf etw. *(Akk.)* beziehen; *(belong)* zu etw. gehören; *(be appropriate)* zu etw. dazugehören

appetite ['æpɪtaɪt] *n.* **a)** Verlangen, *das* **(for** nach**)**; **~ for knowledge** Wissensdrang, *der;* Wissensdurst, *der;* **~ for life** Lebenshunger, *der;* Lebensgier, *die;* **b)** *(desire to satisfy need)* Appetit, *der* **(for** auf + *Akk.***)**; **~ for sex** Lust auf Sex

appetizer ['æpɪtaɪzə(r)] *n.* Appetitanreger, *der; (on menu)* Vorspeise, *die;* **act as an/be an ~:** appetitanregend wirken

appetizing ['æpɪtaɪzɪŋ] *adj.* appetitlich ‹*Anblick, Speise, Geruch*›; appetitanregend ‹*Getränk, Geschmack*›

appetizingly ['æpɪtaɪzɪŋlɪ] *adv.* appetitanregend

applaud [ə'plɔ:d] **1.** *v. i.* applaudieren; [Beifall] klatschen. **2.** *v. t.* applaudieren (+ *Dat.*); Beifall spenden (+ *Dat.*); *(approve of, welcome)* billigen ‹*Entschluß*›; *(praise)* loben, anerkennen ‹*Versuch, Bemühungen*›

applause [ə'plɔ:z] *n.* Applaus, *der; (praise)* Lob, *das;* Anerkennung, *die;* **give ~:** Applaus *od.* Beifall spenden; **get ~:** Applaus *od.* Beifall ernten

apple ['æpl] *n.* Apfel, *der;* **the ~ of sb.'s eye** *(fig.)* jmds. Liebling

apple: **~ 'brandy** *n.* Apfelschnaps, *der;* **~-cart** *n.* **upset the ~-cart** *(fig.)* die Pferde *od.* Gäule scheu machen *(ugs.);* **~-'green 1.** *adj.* apfelgrün; **2.** *n.* Apfelgrün, *das;* **~jack** *(Amer.) see* **~ brandy; ~-'pie** *n.* gedeckte Apfeltorte; **~-pie bed** *Bett, in dem das Bettuch aus Scherz so gefaltet ist, daß man die Beine nicht ausstrecken kann;* **in ~-pie order** picobello *(ugs.);* tadellos in Ordnung; **~ 'sauce** *n.* Apfelmus, *das;* **~-tree** *n.* Apfelbaum, *der*

appliance [ə'plaɪəns] *n. (utensil)* Gerät, *das; (aid)* Hilfsmittel, *das; (fire-engine)* Feuerlöschfahrzeug, *das*

applicability [æplɪkə'bɪlɪtɪ] *n.* **a)** Anwendbarkeit, *die* **(to** auf + *Akk.***)**; **b)** *(appropriateness)* Eignung, *die* **(to** für**)**

applicable ['æplɪkəbl, ə'plɪkəbl] *adj.* **a)** anwendbar **(to** auf + *Akk.***)**; **b)** *(appropriate)* geeignet; angebracht; zutreffend ‹*Fragebogenteil usw.*›; **the ~ documents** die entsprechenden Unterlagen

applicant ['æplɪkənt] *n.* Bewerber, *der*/Bewerberin, *die* **(for** um**)**; *(claimant)* Antragsteller, *der*/Antragstellerin, *die*

application [æplɪ'keɪʃn] *n.* **a)** *(putting)* Auftragen, *das* **(to** auf + *Akk.***)**; *(administering)* Anwendung, *die; (of heat, liquids)* Zufuhr, *die; (employment; of rule etc.)* Anwendung, *die;* **the ~ of new technology** der Einsatz neuer Technologien; **this rule is of** *or* **has universal ~:** diese Regel beansprucht allgemeine Gültigkeit; **b)** *(request)* Bewerbung, *die* **(for** um**)**; *(for passport, licence, etc.)* Antrag, *der* **(for** auf + *Akk.***)**; **~ form** Antragsformular, *das;* **available on ~:** auf Anfrage erhältlich; **~ for a passport** Antrag auf Erteilung eines Passes; **c)** *(diligence)* Fleiß, *der* **(to** bei**)**; *(with enthusiasm)* Eifer, *der* **(to** für**)**; **d)** *(Med.: lotion, poultice, etc.)* Mittel, *das*

applicator ['æplɪkeɪtə(r)] *n.* Applikator, *der*

appliqué [æ'pli:keɪ] **1.** *n.* Applikationsstickerei, *die.* **2.** *adj.* appliziert

apply [ə'plaɪ] **1.** *v. t.* **a)** anlegen ‹*Verband*›; auftragen ‹*Creme, Paste, Farbe*› **(to** auf + *Akk.***)**; zuführen ‹*Wärme, Flüssigkeit*› **(to** *Dat.***)**; **~ the brakes** bremsen; die Bremse betätigen; **~ gentle pressure to the tube** drücken Sie leicht auf die Tube; **~ pressure to sb.** *(fig.)* jmdn. unter Druck setzen; **b)** *(make use of)* anwenden; **applied linguistics/mathematics** angewandte Sprachwissenschaft/Mathematik; **c)** *(devote)* richten, lenken ‹*Gedanken, Überlegungen, Geist*› **(to** auf + *Akk.***)**; verwenden ‹*Zeit, Energie*› **(to** auf + *Akk.***)**; **~ oneself [to sth.]** sich *(Dat.)* Mühe geben [mit etw.]; sich [um etw.] bemühen; **~ oneself to a task** sich an eine Aufgabe machen. **2.** *v. i.* **a)** *(have relevance)* zutreffen **(to** auf + *Akk.***)**; *(be valid)* gelten; **things which don't ~ to us** Dinge, die uns nicht betreffen; **b)** *(address oneself)* **~ [to sb.] for sth.** [jmdn.] um etw. bitten *od. (geh.)* ersuchen; *(for passport, licence, etc.)* [bei jmdm.] etw. beantragen; *(for job)* sich [bei jmdm.] um etw. bewerben

appoint [ə'pɔɪnt] *v. t.* **a)** *(fix)* bestimmen; festlegen ‹*Zeitpunkt, Ort*›; **~ that ...:** anordnen, daß ...; **b)** *(choose for a job)* einstellen; *(assign to office)* ernennen; **~ sb. [to be** *or* **as] sth./to do sth.** jmdn. zu etw. ernennen/jmdn. dazu berufen, etw. zu tun; **~ sb. to sth.** jmdn. in etw. *(Akk.)* einsetzen; **he was ~ed governor** er wurde zum Gouverneur bestellt *od.* ernannt; **~ sb. one's heir** jmdn. als seinen Erben einsetzen

appointed [ə'pɔɪntɪd] *adj.* **a)** *(fixed)* vereinbart; verabredet; **b) well/badly ~:** gut/schlecht ausgestattet *od.* eingerichtet ‹*Zimmer usw.*›

appointee [əpɔɪn'ti:] *n.* Ernannte, *der/die;* Berufene, *der/die*

appointment [ə'pɔɪntmənt] *n.* **a)** *(fixing)* Festlegung, *die;* Festsetzung, *die;* **b)** *(assigning to office)* Ernennung, *die;* Berufung, *die; (Law)* Verfügung, *die* **(of** über + *Akk.***)**; *(being assigned to office)* Ernennung, *die* **(as** zum/zur**)**; *(to job)* Einstellung, *die;* **~ to a position** Berufung auf einen Posten; **by ~ to Her Majesty the Queen, makers of fine confectionery** königlicher Hoflieferant für feines Konfekt; **c)** *(office)* Stelle, *die;* Posten, *der;* **a teaching ~:** eine Stelle als Lehrer/Lehrerin; **d)** *(arrangement)* Termin, *der;* **dental ~:** Termin beim Zahnarzt; **make an ~ with sb.** sich *(Dat.)* von jmdm. einen Termin geben lassen; **by ~:** nach Anmeldung; mit Voranmeldung; **e)** *usu. in pl. (equipment etc.)* Ausstattung, *die*

apportion [ə'pɔ:ʃn] *v. t.* **a)** *(allot)* **~ sth. to sb.** jmdm. etw. zuteilen; **b)** *(portion out)* [gleichmäßig] verteilen **(among** an + *Akk.***)**; aufteilen **(among** unter + *Akk.***)**

apportionment [ə'pɔ:ʃnmənt] *n.* **a)** *(allotting)* Zuteilung, *die* **(to** an + *Akk.***)**; **b)** *(portioning out)* Verteilung, *die* **(among** an + *Akk.***)**; Aufteilung, *die* **(among** unter + *Akk.***)**

apposite ['æpəzɪt] *adj. (appropriate)* passend; geeignet; *(well-chosen)* treffend; **~ to sth.** zutreffend auf etw. *(Akk.);* **these remarks are very ~ to the matter** diese Bemerkungen treffen die Sache genau

appositely ['æpəzɪtlɪ] *adv. (appropriately)* in passender *od.* geeigneter Weise

appositeness ['æpəzɪtnɪs] *n., no pl. (appropriateness)* Angemessenheit, *die*

apposition [æpə'zɪʃn] *n. (Ling.)* Apposition, *die;* **in ~ [to sth.]** in Apposition [zu etw.]

appraisal [ə'preɪzl] *n. (evaluation)* Bewertung, *die;* Beurteilung, *die; (of property)* Taxierung, *die;* Schätzung, *die;* **what ~ do you give/what is your ~ of the situation?** wie beurteilen Sie die Situation?

appraise [ə'preɪz] *v. t. (evaluate)* bewerten; *(value)* schätzen; taxieren; **can you ~ the extent of the damage?** können Sie das Ausmaß des Schadens abschätzen?

appreciable [ə'pri:ʃəbl] *adj. (perceptible)* nennenswert ‹*Unterschied, Einfluß*›; spürbar ‹*Veränderung, Wirkung, Erfolg*›; merklich ‹*Verringerung, Anstieg*›; *(considerable)* beträchtlich; erheblich

appreciably [ə'pri:ʃəblɪ] *adv. (perceptibly)* spürbar ‹*verändern*›; merklich ‹*sich unterscheiden*›; *(considerably)* beträchtlich; erheblich

appreciate [ə'pri:ʃɪeɪt, ə'pri:sɪeɪt] **1.** *v. t.* **a)** *([correctly] estimate value or worth of)* [richtig] einschätzen; *(understand)* verstehen; *(be aware of)* sich *(Dat.)* bewußt sein (+ *Gen.*); *(be receptive to)* Gefallen finden an (+ *Dat.*); **~ that/what ...:** verstehen, daß/was ...; **b)** *(be grateful for)* anerkennen; schätzen; *(enjoy)* genießen; **I'd really ~ that** das wäre sehr nett von dir; **a stamped addressed envelope would be ~d** bitte einen frankierten Rückumschlag beilegen. **2.** *v. i.* im Wert steigen

appreciation [əpri:ʃɪ'eɪʃn, əpri:sɪ'eɪʃn] *n.* **a)** *([right] estimation)* [richtige] Einschätzung; *(understanding)* Verständnis, *das* **(of** für**)**; *(awareness)* Bewußtsein, *das; (sensitivity)* Sinn, *der* **(of** für**)**; **b)** *(gratefulness)* Dankbarkeit, *die; (enjoyment)* Gefallen, *das* **(of** an + *Dat.***)**; **in grateful ~ of** *or* **for your help** in dankbarer Anerkennung Ihrer Hilfe; **c)** *(rise in value)* Wertsteigerung, *die;* **d)** *(review)* [positive] Kritik; Würdigung, *die*

appreciative [ə'pri:ʃətɪv] *adj.* **a) be ~ of sth./sb.** *(aware of)* fähig sein, etw./jmdn. [richtig] einzuschätzen; **she is very ~ of music** sie hat viel Sinn für Musik; **be ~ of sb.'s plight** für jmds. Not Verständnis aufbringen; **b)** *(grateful)* dankbar **(of** für**)**; *(approving)* anerkennend

apprehend [æprɪ'hend] *v. t.* **a)** *(arrest)* festnehmen; fassen; **b)** *(perceive)* wahrnehmen; vernehmen ⟨*Stimme, Geräusch*⟩; einsehen ⟨*Wahrheit*⟩; *(understand)* erfassen; begreifen; **c)** *(anticipate)* vorausahnen; befürchten ⟨*Unglück*⟩

apprehension [æprɪ'henʃn] *n.* **a)** *(arrest)* Festnahme, *die;* Verhaftung, *die;* **b)** *(uneasiness)* Besorgnis, *die;* **c)** *(conception)* Auffassung, *die;* Ansicht, *die* (**of** über + *Akk.*); *(understanding)* Verständnis, *das*

apprehensive [æprɪ'hensɪv] *adj.* *(uneasy)* besorgt; ~ **of sth.** besorgt wegen etw.; **be ~ of doing sth.** ein ungutes Gefühl haben, etw. zu tun; **be ~ that ...:** befürchten, daß ...; ~ **for sb./sb.'s safety** besorgt um jmdn./jmds. Sicherheit

apprehensively [æprɪ'hensɪvlɪ] *adv.* *(uneasily)* besorgt

apprehensiveness [æprɪ'hensɪvnɪs] *n.* Besorgnis, *die* (**of** wegen); ~ **that ...:** Sorge, daß ...; ~ **for sb./sb.'s safety** Besorgtheit um jmdn./jmds. Sicherheit

apprentice [ə'prentɪs] **1.** *n.* *(learner)* Lehrling, *der* (**to** bei); *(to a painter)* Schüler, *der* (**to** *Gen.*); *(beginner)* Neuling, *der;* Anfänger, *der;* *(jockey)* angehender Jockey. **2.** *v. t.* in die Lehre geben (**to** bei); **be ~d [to sb.]** [bei jmdm.] in der Lehre sein *od.* in die Lehre gehen; **become ~d** eine Lehre beginnen

apprenticeship [ə'prentɪsʃɪp] *n.* *(training)* Lehre, *die* (**to** bei); *(learning period)* Lehrzeit, *die;* Lehrjahre *Pl.;* **serve an/one's ~:** eine/seine Lehre machen; *(fig.)* ein/sein Volontariat machen

apprise [ə'praɪz] *v. t.* unterrichten; in Kenntnis setzen; ~ **sb. that ...:** jmdn. darüber unterrichten *od.* davon in Kenntnis setzen, daß ...; ~ **sb. of sth.** jmdn. über etw. *(Akk.)* *od.* von etw. unterrichten; **be ~d of sth.** über etw. *(Akk.)* unterrichtet sein

appro ['æprəʊ] *n.* *(Brit.)* **on ~** *(Commerc. coll.)* = **on approval;** *see* **approval b**

approach [ə'prəʊtʃ] **1.** *v. i.* *(in space)* sich nähern; näher kommen; ⟨*Soldaten:*⟩ [her]anrücken; ⟨*Sturm usw.:*⟩ aufziehen; *(in time)* nahen; **the train now ~ing platform 1** der auf Gleis 1 einfahrende Zug; **the time is fast ~ing when you will have to ...:** es wird nicht mehr lange dauern und du mußt ... **2.** *v. t.* **a)** *(come near to)* sich nähern (+ *Dat.*); *(set about)* herangehen an (+ *Akk.*); angehen ⟨*Problem, Aufgabe, Thema*⟩; **b)** *(be similar to)* verwandt sein (+ *Dat.*); **c)** *(approximate to)* nahekommen (+ *Dat.*); **the temperature/weight ~es 100 °C/50 kg** die Temperatur/das Gewicht beträgt nahezu 100 °C/50 kg; **a performance ~ing perfection** eine an Perfektion grenzende Aufführung; **few writers can ~ Shakespeare** wenige Dichter reichen an Shakespeare heran; **d)** *(appeal to)* sich wenden an (+ *Akk.*); **e)** *(attempt to influence)* herantreten an (+ *Akk.*); **f)** *(make advances to)* sich heranmachen an (+ *Akk.*). **3.** *n.* **a)** [Heran]nahen, *das;* *(treatment)* Ansatz, *der* (**to** zu); *(attitude)* Einstellung, *die* (**to** gegenüber); **a new ~:** eine neue Sicht; **b)** *(similarity)* Ähnlichkeit, *die* (**to** mit); **c)** *(approximation)* Annäherung, *die;* **some sort of ~ to a timetable** ein ungefährer Zeitplan; **d)** *(appeal)* Herantreten, *das* (**to** an + *Akk.*); **make an ~ to sb. concerning sth.** wegen etw. an jmdn. herantreten; sich wegen etw. an jmdn. wenden; **e)** *(attempt to influence)* Vorstoß, *der* (**to** bei); **f)** *(advance)* Annäherungsversuche; **make ~es to sb.** Annäherungsversuche bei jmdm. machen; **g)** *(access)* Zugang, *der;* *(road)* Zufahrtsstraße, *die;* *(fig.)* Zugang, *der;* **h)** *(Aeronaut.)* Landeanflug, *der;* Approach, *der*

approachability [əprəʊtʃə'bɪlɪtɪ] *n.* **a)** *(friendliness)* Umgänglichkeit, *die;* *(receptiveness)* Empfänglichkeit, *die;* **b)** *(accessibility)* Zugänglichkeit, *die*

approachable [ə'prəʊtʃəbl] *adj.* **a)** *(friendly)* umgänglich; *(receptive)* empfänglich; **b)** *(accessible)* zugänglich; erreichbar

ap'proach road *n.* Zufahrtsstraße, *die*

approbate ['æprəbeɪt] *v. t.* *(Amer.)* genehmigen; approbieren *(veralt.)*

approbation [æprə'beɪʃn] *n.* *(sanction)* Genehmigung, *die;* *(Relig.)* Approbation, *die;* *(approval)* Zustimmung, *die;* Einverständnis, *das;* **parental ~:** elterliches Einverständnis; Einwilligung der Eltern; **meet with/get sb.'s ~:** jmds. Zustimmung finden

appropriate 1. [ə'prəʊprɪət] *adj.* *(suitable)* geeignet (**to, for** für); *(peculiar)* eigen (**to** *Dat.*); **I feel it is ~ on such an occasion to say a few words** ich halte es für angebracht, bei einem solchen Anlaß ein paar Worte zu sagen; **a style ~ to a man of his age and importance** ein Stil, der einem Mann in seinem Alter und seiner Stellung entspricht; **the ~ authority** die zuständige Behörde. **2.** [ə'prəʊprɪeɪt] *v. t.* **a)** *(take possession of)* sich *(Dat.)* aneignen; sich bemächtigen (+ *Gen.*); *(take to oneself)* ~ **sth. [to oneself]** etw. in [seinen] Besitz nehmen; etw. mit Beschlag belegen; **b)** *(reserve)* ~ **sth. [to/for sth.]** etw. [zu/für etw.] bestimmen

appropriately [ə'prəʊprɪətlɪ] *adv.* gebührend; passend ⟨*dekoriert, gekleidet, genannt*⟩

appropriateness [ə'prəʊprɪətnɪs] *n., no pl.* Angemessenheit, *die;* *(of remarks, words)* Angebrachtheit, *die*

appropriation [əprəʊprɪ'eɪʃn] *n.* Besitzergreifung, *die;* *(taking to oneself)* Aneignung, *die;* Mit-Beschlag-Belegen, *das;* *(reservation)* Bestimmung, *die*

approval [ə'pru:vl] *n.* **a)** *(sanctioning)* *(of plan, project, expenditure)* Genehmigung, *die;* *(of proposal, reform, marriage)* Billigung, *die;* *(agreement)* Zustimmung, *die;* Einwilligung, *die* (**for** in + *Akk.*); **letter of ~:** Genehmigungsschreiben, *das;* **b)** *(esteem)* Lob, *das;* Anerkennung, *die;* **does the plan meet with your ~?** findet der Plan Ihre Zustimmung?; **murmurs of ~:** zustimmendes Gemurmel; **on ~** *(Commerc.)* zur Probe; *(to view)* zur Ansicht

approve [ə'pru:v] **1.** *v. t.* **a)** *(sanction)* genehmigen ⟨*Plan, Projekt, Ausgaben*⟩; billigen ⟨*Vorschlag, Reform, Heirat*⟩; *(commend)* loben; anerkennen; **~d hotel** empfohlenes Hotel; **~d school** *(Brit. Hist.)* Erziehungsheim, *das;* Besserungsanstalt, *die* *(veralt.)*; **b)** *(find good)* gutheißen; für gut halten. **2.** *v. i.* ~ **of** billigen; zustimmen (+ *Dat.*) ⟨*Plan*⟩; einverstanden sein mit ⟨*Tätigkeiten, Gewohnheiten, Verhalten*⟩; **they don't ~ of her going out with boys** sie sind nicht damit einverstanden, daß sie mit Jungen ausgeht

approving [ə'pru:vɪŋ] *adj.* zustimmend, beipflichtend ⟨*Worte*⟩; anerkennend, bewundernd ⟨*Blicke*⟩

approvingly [ə'pru:vɪŋlɪ] *adv.* *see* **approving:** zustimmend; anerkennend

approx. [ə'prɒks] *abbr.* **approximately** ca.

approximate 1. [ə'prɒksɪmət] *adj.* *(fairly correct)* ungefähr *attr.;* **the figures given here are only ~:** dies hier sind nur ungefähre Zahlen. **2.** [ə'prɒksɪmeɪt] *v. t.* **a)** *(make similar)* ~ **sth. to sth.** etw. einer Sache *(Dat.)* anpassen; **b)** *(come near to)* nahekommen (+ *Dat.*); annähernd erreichen (+ *Akk.*). **3.** *v. i.* **sth. ~s to sth.** etw. gleicht einer Sache *(Dat.)* annähernd

approximately [ə'prɒksɪmətlɪ] *adv.* *(roughly)* ungefähr; *(almost)* fast; **the answer is ~ correct** die Antwort stimmt ungefähr; **very ~:** ganz grob

approximation [əprɒksɪ'meɪʃn] *n.* **a)** Annäherung, *die* (**to** an + *Dat.*); Angleichung, *die* (**to** an + *Dat.*); **b)** *(estimate)* Annäherungswert, *der;* **at** *or* **as a rough ~ I'd say ...:** grob geschätzt würde ich sagen ...

appurtenances [ə'pɜ:tɪnənsɪz] *n. pl.* **a)** *(belongings, appendages)* Zubehör, *das;* **he had all the ~s of 'the good life'** er hatte alles, was zum „guten Leben" gehört; **... and all the ~s:** ... mit allem Zubehör; **b)** *(accessories)* Attribute

APR *abbr.* **annualized percentage rate** Jahreszinssatz, *der*

Apr. *abbr.* **April** Apr.

après-ski [æpreɪ'ski:] *n., no pl.* Après-Ski, *der;* *attrib.* Après-Ski-

apricot ['eɪprɪkɒt] **1.** *n.* **a)** *(fruit, tree)* Aprikose, *die;* ~ **jam** Aprikosenmarmelade, *die;* ~ **brandy** Apricot-Brandy, *der;* Aprikosenlikör, *der;* **b)** *(colour)* Aprikosenfarbe, *die;* Apricot, *das.* **2.** *adj.* aprikosenfarben

April ['eɪprəl] *n.* April, *der;* ~ **fool** April[s]narr, *der;* **make an ~ fool of sb.** jmdn. in den April schicken; **'A~ fool!'** „April, April!"; ~ **Fool's Day** der 1. April; ~ **showers** typisches Aprilwetter; *see also* **August**

a priori [eɪ praɪ'ɔ:raɪ] **1.** *adv.* von vornherein; a priori *(Philos.)*. **2.** *adj.* apriorisch

apron ['eɪprən] *n.* **a)** *(garment)* Schürze, *die;* **be tied to sb.'s ~ strings** jmdm. an der Schürze *od.* am Schürzenzipfel hängen; **b)** *(on airfield)* Vorfeld, *das;* **c)** *(Theatre)* ~ **[stage]** Vorbühne, *die*

apropos [æprə'pəʊ, 'æprəpəʊ] **1.** *adv.* **a)** *(to the purpose)* passend; *(just when wanted)* zur Hand; **b)** ~ **of** *(in respect of)* in bezug auf (+ *Akk.*); hinsichtlich (+ *Gen.*); **c)** *(incidentally)* apropos; übrigens; da wir gerade davon sprechen. **2.** *adj.* passend; treffend ⟨*Bemerkung*⟩. **3.** *prep.* *(coll.)* apropos

apse [æps] *n.* *(Archit.)* Apsis, *die*

apt [æpt] *adj.* **a)** *(suitable)* passend ⟨*Ausdruck, Geschenk*⟩; angemessen ⟨*Reaktion*⟩; treffend ⟨*Zitat, Bemerkung*⟩; **b)** *(tending)* **be ~ to do sth.** dazu neigen, etw. zu tun; **c)** *(quick-witted)* begabt (**at** für); **be ~ at doing sth.** eine Gabe dafür haben, etw. zu tun

aptitude ['æptɪtju:d] *n.* **a)** *(propensity)* Neigung, *die;* *(ability)* Begabung, *die;* **linguistic ~:** Sprachbegabung, *die;* **learning ~:** Lernfähigkeit, *die;* ~ **test** Eignungstest, *der;* **b)** *(suitability)* Eignung, *die*

aptly ['æptlɪ] *adv.* passend; ~ **chosen words** treffend gewählte Worte

aptness ['æptnɪs] *n., no pl.* **a)** *(suitability)* Angemessenheit, *die;* **the ~ of his replies** die Treffsicherheit seiner Antworten; **b)** *(tendency)* Neigung, *die;* **c)** *(quick-wittedness)* Begabung, *die* (**at** für)

aqualung ['ækwəlʌŋ] *n.* Tauchgerät, *das*

aquamarine [ækwəmə'ri:n] **1.** *n.* **a)** *(colour)* Aquamarin, *das;* **b)** *(stone)* Aquamarin, *der.* **2.** *adj.* aquamarin[farben]

aquaplane ['ækwəpleɪn] **1.** *v. i.* **a)** ⟨*Reifen:*⟩ aufschwimmen; ⟨*Fahrzeug:*⟩ [durch Aquaplaning] ins Rutschen geraten; **b)** *(use ~)* Wasserski laufen. **2.** *n.* Monoski, *der;* Wasserski, *der*

aquaplaning ['ækwəpleɪnɪŋ] **a)** Aquaplaning, *das;* **b)** *(Sport)* Wasserski, *das*

aqua regia [ækwə 'ri:dʒɪə] *n.* *(Chem.)* Königswasser, *das;* Goldscheidewasser, *das*

aquarelle [ækwə'rel] *n.* *(technique)* Aquarellmalerei, *die;* *(product)* Aquarell, *das*

Aquarian [ə'kweərɪən] *n.* *(Astrol.)* Wassermann, *der*

aquarium [ə'kweərɪəm] *n., pl.* **~s** *or* **aquaria** [ə'kweərɪə] Aquarium, *das*

Aquarius [ə'kweərɪəs] *n.* *(Astrol., Astron.)* der Wassermann; der Aquarius; *see also* **Aries**

aquatic [ə'kwætɪk] **1.** *adj.* **a)** aquatisch; Wasser-; ~ **plant/bird** Wasserpflanze, *die*/-vogel, *der;* **b)** *(Sport)* Wassersport-; ~ **sports** Wassersportarten. **2.** *n.* **a)** *(plant)* Wasserpflanze, *die;* *(animal)* Wassertier, *das;* **b)** *in pl.* *(Sport)* Wassersport, *der*

aquatint ['ækwətɪnt] *n.* *(technique)* Aquatinta, *die;* *(product)* Aquatintaarbeit, *die*

aqueduct ['ækwɪdʌkt] *n.* Aquädukt, *der od. das*

aqueous ['eɪkwɪəs, 'ækwɪəs] *adj.* *(containing water, watery)* wässerig; wäßrig; aquatisch *(fachspr.)*; ~ **vapour/content** Wasserdampf/-gehalt, *der*

aqueous 'humour *n.* *(Anat.)* Kammerwasser, *das;* Humor aquosus *(fachspr.)*

aquifer ['ækwɪfə(r)] *n.* *(Geol.)* wasserführende Schicht

aquilegia [ækwɪ'li:dʒɪə] *n.* *(Bot.)* [Gemeine] Akelei

aquiline ['ækwɪlaɪn] *adj.* adlerartig; Adler-; ~ **eye/nose** Adlerauge, *das*/-nase, *die*

Arab ['ærəb] **1.** *adj.* arabisch; ~ **horse** Araber, *der.* **2.** *n.* **a)** Araber, *der*/Araberin, *die;* **desert** ~: Beduine, *der;* **b)** *(Arabian horse)* Araber, *der;* **c) street a~**: Betteljunge, *der*

arabesque [ærə'besk] *n.* **a)** Arabeske, *die;* **b)** *(Ballet)* Arabesque, *die*

Arabia [ə'reɪbɪə] *pr. n.* Arabien *(das)*

Arabian [ə'reɪbɪən] **1.** *adj.* arabisch; **the ~ Nights** Tausendundeine Nacht. **2.** *n.* Araber, *der*/Araberin, *die*

Arabic ['ærəbɪk] **1.** *adj.* arabisch; **gum a~**: Gummiarabikum, *das;* **a~ numerals** arabische Ziffern; *see also* **English 1. 2.** *n.* Arabisch, *das; see also* **English 2 a**

arabis ['ærəbɪs] *n.* *(Bot.)* Gänsekresse, *die*

Arabist ['ærəbɪst] *n.* Arabist, *der*/Arabistin, *die*

arable ['ærəbl] **1.** *adj.* bebaubar, landwirtschaftlich nutzbar ⟨*Land*⟩; ~ **land** Ackerland, *das;* ~ **crops** landwirtschaftliche Nutzpflanzen. **2.** *n.* Ackerland, *das*

Araby ['ærəbɪ] *pr. n.* *(poet.)* Arabien *(das)*

arachnid [ə'ræknɪd] *n.* *(Zool.)* Spinnentier, *das;* **the ~s** die Spinnentiere *od.* *(fachspr.)* Arachn[o]iden

Araldite, (P) ['ærəldaɪt] *n.* Araldit, *das* Ⓦⓩ

Aramaic [ærə'meɪɪk] **1.** *adj.* aramäisch. **2.** *n.* Aramäisch, *das*

araucaria [ærɔ:'keərɪə] *n.* *(Bot.)* Araukarie, *die*

arbiter ['ɑ:bɪtə(r)] *n.* *(judge)* Richter, *der;* *(arbitrator)* Vermittler, *der;* *(controller)* Herr, *der,* *(geh.)* Gebieter, *der* (**of** über + *Akk.*)

arbitrage ['ɑ:bɪtrɑ:ʒ] *n.* *(St. Exch.)* Arbitrage, *die*

arbitrarily ['ɑ:bɪtrərɪlɪ] *adv.* **a)** *(at random)* willkürlich; arbiträr *(geh.)*; *(capriciously)* aus einer Laune heraus; **b)** *(unrestrainedly)* rücksichtslos; **c)** *(despotically)* willkürlich

arbitrariness ['ɑ:bɪtrərɪnɪs] *n., no pl.* **a)** *(randomness)* Willkür, *die;* Willkürlichkeit, *die;* Arbitrarität, *die* *(geh.)*; *(capriciousness)* Launenhaftigkeit, *die;* **b)** *(unrestrainedness)* Rücksichtslosigkeit, *die;* **c)** *(despotism)* Willkür, *die*

arbitrary ['ɑ:bɪtrərɪ] *adj.* **a)** *(random)* willkürlich; arbiträr; *(capricious)* launenhaft; launisch ⟨*Idee*⟩; **b)** *(unrestrained)* rücksichtslos ⟨*Vorgehen, Bestrafung, Wesen, Haltung*⟩; **c)** *(despotic)* willkürlich; ~ **rule** Willkürherrschaft, *die*

arbitrate ['ɑ:bɪtreɪt] **1.** *v. t.* schlichten, beilegen ⟨*Streit*⟩; ~ **a difference of opinion** eine Meinungsverschiedenheit beseitigen. **2.** *v. i.* ~ **[upon sth.]** [in einer Sache] vermitteln *od.* als Schiedsrichter fungieren; ~ **between parties** zwischen Parteien vermitteln

arbitration [ɑ:bɪ'treɪʃn] *n.* Vermittlung, *die;* *(in industry)* Schlichtung, *die;* **go to** ~: einen Schlichter anrufen *od.* einschalten; ⟨*Konflikt:*⟩ einem Schlichter vorgelegt werden; **take sth. to** ~: etw. einem Schlichter vorlegen

arbitrator ['ɑ:bɪtreɪtə(r)] *n.* *(mediator)* Vermittler, *der;* *(in industry)* Schlichter, *der;* *(arbiter)* Schiedsrichter, *der;* *(judge)* Richter, *der*

[1]**arbor** ['ɑ:bə(r)] *n.* *(axle)* Welle, *die;* Spindel, *die;* *(Amer.: tool-holder)* Dorn, *der;* Aufsteckhalter, *der;* Träger, *der*

[2]**arbor** *(Amer.) see* **arbour**

Arbor Day ['ɑ:bə deɪ] *n.* *(Amer., Austral.)* Tag des Baumes

arboreal [ɑ:'bɔ:rɪəl] *adj.* *(of trees)* Baum-; *(inhabiting trees)* Baum-; auf Bäumen lebend; **be** ~: auf Bäumen leben

arboretum [ɑ:bə'ri:təm] *n., pl.* **arboreta** [ɑ:bə'ri:tə] *or* *(Amer.)* **~s** Arboretum, *das;* Baumgarten, *der*

arboriculture ['ɑ:bərɪkʌltʃə(r)] *n.* Baumzucht, *die*

arbor vitae [ɑ:bə 'vaɪti:, ɑ:bə 'vi:taɪ] *n.* *(Bot.)* Lebensbaum, *der*

arbour ['ɑ:bə(r)] *n.* *(Brit.)* Laube, *die*

arbutus [ɑ:'bju:təs] *n.* Arbutus, *der;* Erdbeerbaum, *der;* **trailing** ~ *(Amer.)* kriechende Heide

arc [ɑ:k] *n.* **a)** [Kreis]bogen, *der;* **b)** *(Electr.)* Lichtbogen, *der;* ~ **lamp,** ~ **light** Lichtbogenlampe, *die;* ~ **welding** Lichtbogen-, Elektroschweißung, *die*

arcade [ɑ:'keɪd] *n.* Arkade, *die;* **shopping** ~: Einkaufspassage, *die*

Arcadian [ɑ:'keɪdɪən] *adj.* arkadisch

arcane [ɑ:'keɪn] *adj.* geheimnisvoll; undurchschaubar; **an ~ secret** ein verborgenes Geheimnis

[1]**arch** [ɑ:tʃ] **1.** *n.* Bogen, *der;* *(curvature; of foot)* Wölbung, *die;* *(of bridge)* Bogen, *der;* Joch, *das;* *(vault)* Gewölbe, *das.* **2.** *v. i.* sich wölben; ⟨*Ast, Glied:*⟩ sich biegen. **3.** *v. t.* **a)** *(furnish with ~)* mit Bogen versehen; **~ed gateway** Torbogen, *der;* **~ed in the Gothic manner** mit gotischem/gotischen Bogen; **b)** *(form into ~)* beugen ⟨*Rücken, Arm*⟩; **the cat ~ed its back** die Katze machte einen Buckel

[2]**arch** *adj.* schelmisch; kokett

arch- *pref.* Erz-; **~-villain** Erzschurke, *der;* Erzgauner, *der*

archaeological [ɑ:kɪə'lɒdʒɪkl] *adj.* archäologisch; ~ **dig** [Aus]grabung, *die*

archaeologist [ɑ:kɪ'ɒlədʒɪst] *n.* Archäologe, *der*/Archäologin, *die;* Altertumsforscher, *der*/-forscherin, *die*

archaeology [ɑ:kɪ'ɒlədʒɪ] *n.* Archäologie, *die;* Altertumskunde, *die;* **marine/industrial** ~: Unterwasser-/Industriearchäologie, *die*

archaic [ɑ:'keɪɪk] *adj.* *(out of use)* veraltet; archaisch; *(antiquated)* altertümlich; überholt ⟨*Methode, Gesetz*⟩; **an ~ typewriter** *(coll.)* eine museumsreife *od.* vorsintflutliche Schreibmaschine

archaically [ɑ:'keɪɪkəlɪ] *adv.* *(in out-of-use style)* altertümlich, *(deliberately)* altertümelnd ⟨*sich ausdrücken, schreiben*⟩

archaism ['ɑ:keɪɪzm] *n.* Archaismus, *der*

archangel ['ɑ:keɪndʒl] *n.* Erzengel, *der*

arch'bishop *n.* Erzbischof, *der*

arch'bishopric *n.* **a)** *(office)* Amt des Erzbischofs; **b)** *(diocese)* Erzbistum, *das*

arch'deacon *n.* Archi-, Erzdiakon, *der*

arch'deaconry, arch'deaconship *ns.* Archidiakonat, *das od. der*

arch'diocese *see* **archbishopric b**

arch'duchess *n.* *(Hist.)* Erzherzogin, *die*

arch'duke *n.* *(Hist.)* Erzherzog, *der*

arch-'enemy *n.* *(chief enemy)* Erzfeind, *der;* *(the Devil) see* **arch-fiend**

archeology *etc.* *(Amer.) see* **archaeology** *etc.*

archer ['ɑ:tʃə(r)] *n.* **a)** Bogenschütze, *der;* **b)** *(Astrol.)* **the A~**: der Schütze; **under the sign of the A~**: im Zeichen des Schützen

'archer-fish *n.* Schützenfisch, *der*

archery ['ɑ:tʃərɪ] *n., no pl.* Bogenschießen, *das*

archetypal ['ɑ:kɪtaɪpl] *adj.* *(original)* archetypisch *(geh.)*; *(typical)* typisch; prototypisch; **he was the ~ film director** er war der Prototyp des Regisseurs

archetype ['ɑ:kɪtaɪp] *n.* *(original)* Urfassung, *die;* Archetyp, *der;* *(typical specimen)* Prototyp, *der;* Archetyp, *der*

arch-'fiend *n.* Erzfeind, *der;* Satan, *der*

archiepiscopal [ɑ:kɪɪ'pɪskəpl] *adj.* erzbischöflich

archiepiscopate [ɑ:kɪɪ'pɪskəpət] *n. see* **archbishopric a**

Archimedes [ɑ:kɪ'mi:di:z] *n.* **~' principle** *(Phys.)* das Archimedische Prinzip

archipelago [ɑ:kɪ'peləgəʊ] *n., pl.* **~s** *or* **~es** Archipel, *der;* *(islands)* Inselgruppe, *die;* *(sea)* Inselmeer, *das*

architect ['ɑ:kɪtekt] *n.* **a)** *(designer)* Architekt, *der*/Architektin, *die;* Baumeister, *der* *(geh.)*; **naval** ~: Schiffskonstrukteur, *der;* Schiffbauer, *der; see also* **landscape architect; b)** *(maker, creator)* Schöpfer, *der;* *(fig.)* Urheber, *der;* **the ~ of one's own fate/fortune** seines [eigenen] Glückes Schmied

architectonic [ɑ:kɪtek'tɒnɪk] *adj.* **a)** architektonisch; **b)** *(constructive)* schöpferisch ⟨*Fähigkeiten, Kraft*⟩

architectural [ɑ:kɪ'tektʃərl] *adj.* architektonisch; ~ **style** Baustil, *der*

architecture ['ɑ:kɪtektʃə(r)] *n.* **a)** Architektur, *die;* Baukunst, *die* *(geh.)*; *(style)* Bauweise, *die;* Architektur, *die;* **naval/railway/bridge** ~: Schiff[s]-/Eisenbahn-/Brückenbau, *der;* **b)** *(structure, lit. or fig.)* Konstruktion, *die;* **c)** *(Computing)* [System]architektur, *die*

architrave ['ɑ:kɪtreɪv] *n.* *(beam)* Architrav, *der;* Epistylion, *das;* *(moulding)* Archivolte, *die*

archival [ɑ:'kaɪvəl] *adj.* archivalisch

archive ['ɑ:kaɪv] **1.** *n., usu. in pl.* Archiv, *das.* **2.** *v. t.* archivieren

archivist ['ɑ:kɪvɪst] *n.* Archivar, *der*/Archivarin, *die*

archly ['ɑ:tʃlɪ] *adv.* schelmisch; kokett

archness ['ɑ:tʃnɪs] *n., no pl.* Schalkhaftigkeit, *die;* *(of woman)* Koketterie, *die*

arch-'traitor *n.* Erzverräter, *der*

'archway *n.* *(vaulted passage)* Gewölbegang, *der;* Tunnel, *der;* *(arched entrance)* Durchgang, *der;* Torbogen, *der*

arctic ['ɑ:ktɪk] **1.** *adj.* *(lit. or fig.)* arktisch; **A~ Circle/Ocean** nördlicher Polarkreis/Nordpolarmeer, *das.* **2.** *n.* **a) the A~**: die Arktis; **b)** *(Amer.: overshoe)* hoher Überschuh

arctic: ~ **'fox** *n.* Polarfuchs, *der;* ~ **'tern** *n.* Küstenseeschwalbe, *die*

ardency ['ɑ:dənsɪ] *n., no pl.* Eifer, *der* (**in** bei); *(of feeling, desire, etc.)* Leidenschaftlichkeit, *die;* Heftigkeit, *die;* *(of admiration, prayer, belief, poem)* Inbrunst, *die*

Ardennes [ɑ:'den] *pr. n. pl.* Ardennen *Pl.*

ardent ['ɑ:dənt] *adj.* **a)** *(eager)* begeistert ⟨*Anhänger, Theaterbesucher, Interesse, Gefolgsmann*⟩; *(fervent)* glühend ⟨*Bewunderer, Leidenschaft*⟩; hitzig ⟨*Temperament, Wesen*⟩; brennend ⟨*Wunsch*⟩; feurig ⟨*Rede, Liebhaber*⟩; leidenschaftlich ⟨*Gedicht, Liebesbrief, Anbetung*⟩; innigst, *(geh.)* inbrünstig ⟨*Hoffnung, Liebe*⟩; **b)** ~ **spirits** geistige Getränke *Pl.*

ardently ['ɑ:dəntlɪ] *adv.* *(eagerly)* begeistert; *(fervently)* glühend; **hope** ~: inbrünstig *(geh.)* *od.* inständig hoffen

ardour (*Brit.;* *Amer.:* **ardor**) ['ɑ:də(r)] *n.* *(warm emotion)* Leidenschaft, *die;* *(passionate emotion)* Inbrunst, *die* *(geh.)*; *(fervour)* Eifer, *der;* ~ **for reform/learning** Reformeifer, *der*/Wissensdurst, *der*

arduous ['ɑ:djʊəs] *adj.* schwer, anstrengend ⟨*Aufgabe, Arbeit, Unterfangen*⟩; hart ⟨*Arbeit, Tag, Zeit*⟩; beschwerlich ⟨*Reise, Aufstieg, Fahrt*⟩

arduously ['ɑ:djʊəslɪ] *adv.* *(laboriously)* beschwerlich

arduousness ['ɑ:djʊəsnɪs] *n., no pl.* *(difficulty)* Mühe, *die;* Beschwerlichkeit, *die*

[1]**are** [ɑ:(r)] *n.* Ar, *das*

[2]**are** *see* **be**

area ['eərɪə] *n.* **a)** *(surface measure)* Flächenausdehnung, *die;* **the floor ~ is 15 square**

metres der Fußboden hat eine Fläche von 15 Quadratmetern; **what is the ~ of your farm?** wie groß ist Ihr Hof?; **b)** *(region)* Gelände, *das; (of wood, marsh, desert)* Gebiet, *das; (of city, country)* Gegend, *die; (of skin, wall, etc.)* Stelle, *die;* **a poor ~ of the town** eine arme Gegend der Stadt; **it happened in this ~:** es ereignete sich hier in der Nähe; **in the Hamburg ~:** im Hamburger Raum; **in the ~ of ...** *(fig.)* um ... herum; **an ~ of ground** ein Grundstück *od.* Gelände *od.* Areal; **c)** *(defined space)* Bereich, *der;* **parking/picnic/sports ~:** Park-/Picknick-/Sportplatz, *der;* **no-smoking ~:** Nichtraucherzone, *die;* **d)** *(subject field)* Gebiet, *das;* **in the ~ of electronics/medicine** auf dem Gebiet *od.* im Bereich der Elektronik/Medizin; **e)** *(scope)* Raum, *der;* **~ of choice** Wahlmöglichkeiten *Pl.;* **~ of responsibility** Verantwortungsbereich, *der;* **f)** *(sunken court)* Vorhof, *der*

areaway ['eərɪəweɪ] *(Amer.) see* **area f**

areca ['ærɪkə, ə'ri:kə] *n.* Arekapalme, *die;* **~-nut** Arekanuß, *die*

arena [ə'ri:nə] *n. (at circus, bullfight)* Arena, *die; (in equestrianism)* Dressurviereck, *das; (fig.: scene of conflict)* Bühne, *die;* Schauplatz, *der; (fig.: sphere of action)* Bereich, *der;* **the political ~:** die politische Arena; **enter the ~** *(fig.)* die Arena betreten; auf den Plan treten; **~ stage** Arenabühne, *die;* **~ theatre** Arenatheater, *das*

aren't [ɑ:nt] *(coll.)* = **are not;** *see* **be**

areola [ə'ri:ələ] *n., pl.* **~e** [ə'ri:əli:] *(Anat.) (of nipple)* Warzenhof, *der; (of eye) an die Pupille grenzender Teil der Iris*

argent ['ɑ:dʒənt] *(esp. Her.)* **1.** *n.* Silber, *das.* **2.** *adj.* silbern

Argentina [ɑdʒən'ti:nə] *pr. n.* Argentinien *(das)*

Argentine ['ɑ:dʒəntaɪn] **1.** *pr. n.* **the ~:** Argentinien *(das).* **2.** *adj.* argentinisch

Argentinian [ɑ:dʒən'tɪnɪən] **1.** *adj.* argentinisch; **sb. is ~:** jmd. ist Argentinier/Argentinierin. **2.** *n.* Argentinier, *der*/Argentinierin, *die*

argillaceous [ɑ:dʒɪ'leɪʃəs] *adj. (of clay)* tonig; tonhaltig; *(like clay)* tonartig

argle-bargle [ɑ:gl'bɑ:gl] *see* **argy-bargy**

argon ['ɑ:gɒn] *n. (Chem.)* Argon, *das*

argonaut ['ɑ:gənɔ:t] *n.* **a)** *(Zool.)* Papierboot, *das;* **b) A~** *(Mythol.)* Argonaut, *der*

argosy ['ɑ:gəsɪ] *n. (Hist./poet.: merchant-vessel)* Handelsschiff, *das*

argot ['ɑ:gəʊ] *n.* Argot, *das od. der;* **thieves' ~:** Rotwelsch, *das;* **that class/group has its own ~:** diese Klasse/Gruppe hat ihren eigenen Jargon *od.* Slang

arguable ['ɑ:gjʊəbl] *adj.* **a)** fragwürdig ⟨*Angelegenheit, Punkt*⟩; **it's not an ~ point at all** das ist überhaupt keine Frage; **it's ~ whether ...:** es ist noch die Frage, ob ...; **b) it is ~ that ...** *(can reasonably be argued that)* man kann sich auf den Standpunkt stellen, daß ...

arguably ['ɑ:gjʊəblɪ] *adv.* möglicherweise

argue ['ɑ:gju:] **1.** *v. t.* **a)** *(maintain)* **~ that ...:** die Ansicht vertreten, daß ...; **b)** *(treat by reasoning)* darlegen ⟨*Grund, Standpunkt, Fakten*⟩; **I don't want to ~ the point now** lassen wir für den Moment diesen Punkt noch ungeklärt; **~ sth. away** etw. wegdiskutieren; **c)** *(persuade)* **~ sb. into doing sth.** jmdn. dazu überreden, etw. zu tun; **~ sb. out of doing sth.** [es] jmdm. ausreden, etw. zu tun; **d)** *(prove)* **~ sb. [to be] sb./sth.** der Beweis dafür sein, daß jmd. jmd./etw. ist; **e)** *(indicate)* **~ sth.** von etw. zeugen. *See also* **toss 3 a. 2.** *v. i.* **~ with sb.** sich mit jmdm. streiten; **~ against sb.** jmdm. widersprechen; **~ for/against sth.** für/gegen etw. eintreten; sich für/gegen etw. aussprechen; **~ about sth.** sich über/um etw. *(Akk.)* streiten; **none of your arguing!** keine Widerrede!

argument ['ɑ:gjʊmənt] *n.* **a)** *(reason)* Begründung, *die;* **~s for/against sth.** Argumente für/gegen etw.; **b)** *no pl. (reasoning process)* Argumentieren, *das;* **the powers of logical ~:** das Vermögen, logisch zu argumentieren; **assume sth. for ~'s sake** etw. rein theoretisch annehmen; **c)** *(debate)* Auseinandersetzung, *die;* **get into an ~/get into ~s with sb.** mit jmdm. in Streit geraten; **d)** *(summary)* Kurzfassung, *die;* Zusammenfassung, *die;* **e)** *(Math.)* Argument, *das*

argumentation [ɑ:gjʊmen'teɪʃn] *n.* **a)** *no pl. (reasoning)* Argumentieren, *das;* **his powers of ~:** seine Fähigkeit, zu argumentieren; **b)** *(debate)* Gezänk, *das*

argumentative [ɑ:gjʊ'mentətɪv] *adj.* **a)** *(fond of arguing)* widerspruchsfreudig; *(quarrelsome)* streitlustig; streitsüchtig; **b)** *(logical)* argumentativ

Argus ['ɑ:gəs] *n.* **a)** *(butterfly)* Augenfalter, *der;* **b)** *(Ornith.)* Arguspfau, *der*

argy-bargy [ɑ:dʒɪ'bɑ:dʒɪ] *(joc.)* **1.** *n.* Hickhack, *der od. das (ugs.);* Streiterei, *die.* **2.** *v. i.* sich herumstreiten *(ugs.)* **(about** über + *Akk.)*

aria ['ɑ:rɪə] *n. (Mus.)* Arie, *die*

[1]**Arian** ['eərɪən] *n. (Astrol.)* Widder, *der*

[2]**Arian** *see* **Aryan**

arid ['ærɪd] *adj.* **a)** *(dry; also fig.)* trocken ⟨*Klima, Land*⟩; **b)** *(barren)* dürr; karg; **c)** *(Geog.)* arid; **~ zone** Trockengürtel, *der*

aridity [ə'rɪdɪtɪ] *n., no pl.* **a)** *(dryness of land, heat; also fig.)* Trockenheit, *die; (Geog.)* Aridität, *die;* **b)** *(barrenness)* Kargheit, *die*

aridness ['ærɪdnɪs] *see* **aridity**

Aries ['eəri:z] *n. (Astrol., Astron.)* der Widder; der Aries; **under [the sign of] ~, the Ram** im Zeichen des Aries *od.* des Widders; **he/she is an ~:** er/sie ist [ein] Widder; **first point of ~:** Frühlingspunkt, *der;* Widderpunkt, *der*

aright [ə'raɪt] *adv.* recht ⟨*hören, sich erinnern*⟩

arise [ə'raɪz] *v. i.,* **arose** [ə'rəʊz], **arisen** [ə'rɪzn] **a)** *(originate)* entstehen; *(literary: be born)* geboren werden; **hatred has ~n in their hearts** Haß ist in ihren Herzen aufgekeimt *(geh.);* **b)** *(present itself)* auftreten; ⟨*Gelegenheit:*⟩ sich bieten; **a crisis has ~n in Turkey** in der Türkei ist es zu einer Krise gekommen; **new hopes have** *or* **hope has ~n that ...:** man hat wieder Hoffnung geschöpft, daß ...; **c)** *(result)* **~ from** *or* **out of sth.** von etw. herrühren; auf etw. *(Akk.)* zurückzuführen sein; **d)** *(Hist.: stand up)* **~, Sir Robert!** erhebt Euch, Sir Robert!; **e)** ⟨*Sonne, Nebel:*⟩ aufsteigen; **f)** ⟨*See, Sturm:*⟩ anschwellen; **g)** *(rise from the dead)* auferstehen

aristocracy [ærɪ'stɒkrəsɪ] *n.* Aristokratie, *die; (fig.)* **an ~ of ...:** eine Elite von ...

aristocrat ['ærɪstəkræt] *n.* Aristokrat, *der*/Aristokratin, *die;* **an ~ among wines** *(fig.)* ein besonders edler Wein

aristocratic [ærɪstə'krætɪk] *adj.* **a)** aristokratisch; Aristokraten-; adelig; Adels-; **b)** *(grand)* exklusiv ⟨*Luxus, Pracht etc.*⟩; *(distinguished)* vornehm ⟨*Aussehen, Auftreten*⟩; *(refined)* kultiviert; fein ⟨*Manieren, Sitten*⟩; *(stylish, fine)* edel ⟨*Qualität, Geschmack, Gesichtszüge, Wein, Möbel*⟩

aristocratically [ærɪstə'krætɪkəlɪ] *adv.* aristokratisch

Aristotelian [ærɪstə'ti:lɪən] *adj.* aristotelisch

Aristotle ['ærɪstɒtl] *pr. n.* Aristoteles *(der)*

[1]**arithmetic** [ə'rɪθmətɪk] *n.* **a)** *(science)* Arithmetik, *die;* **b)** *(computation)* Rechnen, *das;* **mental ~:** Kopfrechnen, *das;* **there are several mistakes in your ~:** du hast dich mehrmals verrechnet

[2]**arithmetic** [ærɪθ'metɪk], **arithmetical** [ærɪθ'metɪkl] *adj.* arithmetisch; **arithmetical progression** arithmetische Progression; *(sequence/series)* arithmetische Folge/Reihe

ark [ɑ:k] *n.* **sth. looks as if it came [straight] out of the ~:** etw. sieht vorsintflutlich aus; *see also* **Noah's ark**

[1]**arm** [ɑ:m] *n.* **a)** *(limb)* Arm, *der;* **~ in ~ [with each other]** Arm in Arm; **[be] at ~'s length [from]** auf Armeslänge [entfernt sein von]; **remain** *or* **keep at ~'s length from sb.** *(fig.)* eine gewisse Distanz zu jmdm. wahren; **as long as sb.'s ~** *(fig.)* ellenlang; **cost sb. an ~ and a leg** *(fig.)* jmdn. eine Stange Geld kosten *(ugs.);* **on sb.'s ~:** an jmds. Arm *(Dat.);* **under one's ~:** unter dem Arm; **a babe** *or* **a child in ~s** ein kleines Kind; **in sb.'s ~s** in jmds. Armen; **fall into each other's ~s** sich *(Dat.)* in die Arme fallen; **take sb. in one's ~s** jmdn. in die Arme nehmen *od. (geh.)* schließen; **the lovers were found dead in each other's ~s** die beiden Liebenden wurden eng umschlungen tot aufgefunden; **with open ~s** *(lit. or fig.)* mit offenen Armen; **within ~'s reach** *(lit. or fig.)* in Reichweite; **be within ~'s reach of safety** fast in Sicherheit sein; **b)** *(sleeve)* Ärmel, *der; (support)* Armlehne, *die;* **c)** *(branch)* Ast, *der;* **d)** *(~-like thing)* Arm, *der*

[2]**arm** **1.** *n.* **a)** *usu. in pl. (weapon)* Waffe, *die;* **possession/export of ~s** Waffenbesitz/-export, *der;* **~s race** Rüstungswettlauf, *der;* **small ~s** Handfeuerwaffen; **bear ~s** *(be armed)* bewaffnet sein; *(serve as soldier)* Waffen tragen; **in ~s** bewaffnet; **lay down one's ~s** die Waffen niederlegen; **take up ~s** zu den Waffen greifen; **under ~s** bewaffnet; unter Waffen; **up in ~s** *(lit.)* kampfbereit; **be up in ~s about sth.** *(fig.)* wegen etw. in Harnisch *od.* aufgebracht sein; **b)** *in pl. (heraldic device)* Wappen, *das; (inn-sign)* **'The King's/Waterman's Arms'** ≈ „Zum König/Fährmann"; *see also* **coat of arms; c)** *in pl. (military profession)* Kriegs- *od.* Militärdienst, *der;* **d)** *(military grouping)* Waffengattung, *die.* **2.** *v. t.* **a)** *(furnish with weapons)* bewaffnen; mit Waffen ausrüsten ⟨*Schiff*⟩; **b)** *(furnish with tools etc.)* ausrüsten; bewaffnen *(fig.);* **~ oneself with sth.** sich mit etw. wappnen; **~ed with all advantages/virtues** mit allen Vorteilen/Tugenden ausgestattet; **c)** *(make able to explode)* scharf machen ⟨*Bombe usw.*⟩

armada [ɑ:'mɑ:də] *n.* Armada, *die*

armadillo [ɑ:mə'dɪləʊ] *n., pl.* **~s** *(Zool.)* Gürteltier, *das*

Armageddon [ɑ:mə'gedən] *n.* Armageddon, *das (geh.)*

armament ['ɑ:məmənt] *n.* **a)** *(weapons etc.)* **~[s]** Kriegsgerät, *das;* **b)** *(force)* Streitmacht, *die;* **c)** *no pl. (process) (of persons)* Bewaffnung, *die; (of boat)* Ausrüstung, *die*

armature ['ɑ:mətʃə(r)] *n.* **a)** *(Biol.: defensive covering)* Schutzkleid, *das;* **b)** *(sculptor's framework)* Knebel, *der;* Reiter, *der;* **c)** *(Magn., Electr.)* Anker, *der*

arm: **~band** *n.* Armbinde, *die;* **~chair 1.** *n.* Sessel, *der;* **2.** *adj.* **~chair politician/strategist** politischer Amateur/Amateurstratege, *der;* **~chair critic** Hobby- *od.* Amateurkritiker, *der;* **~chair travel** Reisen in der Phantasie

armed [ɑ:md] *adj.* bewaffnet; mit Geschützen bestückt ⟨*Schiff*⟩; **~ forces** Streitkräfte *Pl.;* **~ neutrality** bewaffnete Neutralität

-armed *adj. in comb. (with arms)* mit ... Armen; *(with sleeves)* -ärm[e]lig; **long-/brown-~:** mit langen/braunen Armen; **two-~:** zweiarmig

Armenia [ɑ:'mi:nɪə] *pr. n.* Armenien *(das)*

Armenian [ɑ:'mi:nɪən] **1.** *adj.* armenisch; **sb. is ~:** jmd. ist Armenier/Armenierin; *see also* **English 1. 2.** *n.* **a)** *(person)* Armenier, *der*/Armenierin, *die;* **b)** *(language)* Armenisch, *das; see also* **English 2 a**

armful ['ɑ:mfʊl] *n.* **an ~ of fruit** ein Armvoll Obst; **with an ~ of gifts** mit einem Arm voll Geschenken; **flowers by the ~:** ganze Arme voll Blumen

'**armhole** *n.* Armloch, *das*

armistice ['ɑːmɪstɪs] *n. (cessation from hostilities; also fig.)* Waffenstillstand, *der; (short truce)* Waffenruhe, *die;* **A~ Day** *Gedenktag des Endes des 1. Weltkriegs*
armless ['ɑːmlɪs] *adj. (without arms)* ohne Arme; armlos; *(without sleeves)* ohne Ärmel; ärmellos
armlet ['ɑːmlɪt] *n. (band)* Armbinde, *die; (bracelet)* Armring, *der;* Armreif, *der*
'arm-lock *n. (Wrestling)* Armschlüssel, *der*
armor *(Amer.) see* **armour**
armorer *(Amer.) see* **armourer**
armorial [ɑː'mɔːrɪəl] *adj.* Wappen-; heraldisch; ~ **bearings** Wappen, *das;* Wappenschild, *der*
armory *(Amer.) see* **armoury**
armour ['ɑːmə(r)] *(Brit.)* **1.** *n.* **a)** *no pl. (Hist.)* Rüstung, *die;* **suit of ~:** Harnisch, *der;* **b)** *no pl. (steel plates)* Panzerung, *die;* Panzer, *der;* **c)** *no pl. (~ed vehicles)* Panzerfahrzeuge; **d)** *(steel plate)* **~[-plate]** Panzerplatte, *die;* Panzerblech, *das;* **~-clad** gepanzert; Panzer-; **e)** *no pl. (protective covering)* Panzer, *der.* **2.** *v. t. (furnish with protective cover)* ausrüsten; armieren ⟨*Kabel*⟩; *(toughen)* panzern ⟨*Glas*⟩; *(with steel plates)* verkleiden; **~ed car/train** gepanzerter Wagen/Zug; Panzerwagen/-zug, *der;* **~ed cable** bewehrtes *od.* armiertes Kabel; **~ed division** Panzerdivision, *die;* **~ed glass** Panzerglas, *das*
armourer ['ɑːmərə(r)] *n. (Brit.) (maker of arms etc.)* Waffenschmied, *der (hist.);* Waffentechniker, *der*
armoury ['ɑːmərɪ] *n. (Brit.)* **a)** *(array of weapons)* Waffenarsenal, *das; (fig.)* Arsenal, *das;* **one of the strongest weapons in the British ~:** eine der stärksten britischen Waffen; **b)** *(arsenal)* [Waffen]arsenal, *das;* Waffenkammer, *die;* **c)** *(Amer.: drill hall)* Exerzierhalle, *die*
arm: ~pit *n.* Achselhöhle, *die;* **~-rest** *n.* Armlehne, *die*
army ['ɑːmɪ] *n.* **a)** *(fighting force)* Heer, *das;* **standing ~:** stehendes Heer; **mercenary ~:** Söldnerheer, *das;* **Napoleon's ~:** die Armee Napoleons; **b)** *no pl., no indef. art. (military profession)* Militär, *das;* **be in the ~:** beim Militär sein; **go into** *or* **join the ~:** zum Militär gehen; *(as a career)* die Militärlaufbahn einschlagen; **leave the ~:** aus dem Militärdienst ausscheiden; **c)** *(large number)* Heer, *das;* **an ~ of workmen/officials/ants** ein Heer von Arbeitern/Beamten/Ameisen
army: ~ corps *n.* Armeekorps, *das;* **A~ List** *n. (Brit.)* Rangliste des Heeres; **~-worm** *n.* Heerwurm, *der*
arnica ['ɑːnɪkə] *n.* Arnika, *die*
aroma [ə'rəʊmə] *n. (fragrance)* Duft, *der*
aromatic [ærə'mætɪk] **1.** *adj. (fragrant)* aromatisch *(auch Chem.);* duftend ⟨*Blütenblätter, Nelken usw.*⟩; *(pleasant)* angenehm würzig. **2.** *n.* Duftstoff, *der*
arose *see* **arise**
around [ə'raʊnd] **1.** *adv.* **a)** *(on every side)* **[all] ~:** überall; **he waved his arms ~:** er ruderte mit den Armen; **all ~ there was nothing but trees** ringsumher *od.* ringsherum gab es nichts als Bäume; **b)** *(round)* herum; **come ~ to sb.'s house** bei jmdm. vorbeikommen; **show sb. ~:** jmdn. herumführen; **pass the hat ~:** den Hut herumgehen lassen; **have to get ~ to doing sth.** [endlich] einmal daran denken müssen, etw. zu tun; **look ~, have a look ~:** sich [ein bißchen] umsehen *od.* umschauen; **c)** *(coll.: near)* in der Nähe; **have you seen my hat ~?** hast du irgendwo meinen Hut gesehen?; **we'll always be ~ when you need us** wir werden immer dasein, wenn du uns brauchst; **d)** *(coll.: in existence)* vorhanden; **there's not/you don't see much leather ~ these days** zur Zeit gibt es/sieht man nur wenig Leder; **e)** *(in various places)* **ask/look ~:** herumfragen/-schauen; **travel ~ within England** in England herumreisen; **he's been ~** *(fig.)* er ist viel herumgekommen. *See also* **go around; hang around. 2.** *prep.* **a)** um [... herum]; rund um; **they had their arms ~ each other** sie hielten sich umschlungen; **darkness closed in ~ us** die Dunkelheit umfing uns *(geh.) od.* schloß uns ein; **he wore a coat ~ his shoulders** er hatte einen Mantel um die Schultern gelegt; **b)** *(here and there in)* **we went ~ the town** wir gingen durch die Stadt; **~ the garden you'll find ...:** im Garten findet man ...; **c)** *(here and there near)* **~ London** um London herum; **d)** *(round)* um [... herum]; **~ the back of the house** *(position)* hinter dem Haus; *(direction)* hinter das Haus; **e)** *(approximately at)* **~ 3 o'clock** ungefähr um 3 Uhr; gegen 3 Uhr; **I saw him somewhere ~ the station** ich habe ihn irgendwo am Bahnhof gesehen; **f)** *(approximately equal to)* etwa; ungefähr; **sth. [costing] ~ £2** etw. für um die *od.* ungefähr 2 Pfund
arousal [ə'raʊzl] *n.* **a)** *(awakening)* Aufwachen, *das;* **b)** *(excitement, also sexual)* Erregung, *die; (calling into existence) (of interest, enthusiasm)* Erweckung, *die; (of hatred, passion)* Erregung, *die*
arouse [ə'raʊz] *v. t.* **a)** *(awake)* [auf]wecken; **~ sb. from his sleep** jmdn. aus dem Schlaf reißen; **b)** *(excite)* erregen; *(call into existence)* erwecken ⟨*Interesse, Begeisterung*⟩; erregen ⟨*Haß, Leidenschaften usw.*⟩; **be sexually ~d by sth./sb.** durch etw./jmdn. sexuell erregt werden; **~ suspicion** Verdacht erregen
arpeggio [ɑː'pedʒɪəʊ] *n., pl.* **~s** *(Mus.)* Arpeggio, *das*
arr. *abbr.* **a)** *(Mus.)* **arranged by** Arr.; **b) arrives** Ank.
arrack ['ærək] *n.* Arrak, *der*
arraign [ə'reɪn] *v. t. (indict)* vor Gericht bringen, anklagen **(for** wegen); *(accuse)* beschuldigen; **~ sb. for sth.** jmdm. die Schuld an etw. *(Dat.)* geben
arraignment [ə'reɪnmənt] *n. (indictment)* Anklageerhebung, *die; (accusation)* Beschuldigung, *die;* **the ~ of them, their ~:** die Anklageerhebung gegen sie
arrange [ə'reɪndʒ] **1.** *v. t.* **a)** *(order)* anordnen; *(adjust)* in Ordnung bringen; **the seating was ~d so that ...:** die Sitzreihen waren so angeordnet, daß ...; **b)** *(Mus., Radio, etc.: adapt)* bearbeiten; **c)** *(settle beforehand)* ausmachen, vereinbaren ⟨*Termin*⟩; **~ the catering for a party** sich um Essen und Trinken für eine Feier kümmern; **d)** *(plan)* planen ⟨*Urlaub*⟩; aufstellen ⟨*Stundenplan*⟩; **don't ~ anything for next Saturday** nimm dir für nächsten Sonnabend nichts vor; **e)** *(resolve)* beilegen; ins reine bringen ⟨*Beziehungen*⟩. **2.** *v. i.* **a)** *(plan)* sorgen **(for** für); **~ for sb./sth. to do sth.** veranlassen *od.* dafür sorgen, daß jmd./etw. etw. tut; **can you ~ to be at home when ...?** kannst du es so einrichten, daß du zu Hause bist, wenn ...?; **~ about sth.** etw. in die Wege leiten; **she ~d about getting him a work permit** sie leitete alles in die Wege, damit er eine Arbeitserlaubnis bekam; **b)** *(agree)* **they ~d to meet the following day** sie verabredeten sich für den nächsten Tag; **~ with sb. about sth.** sich mit jmdm. über etw. *(Akk.)* einigen; **~ with sb. about doing sth.** sich mit jmdm. darüber einigen, etw. zu tun
arrangement [ə'reɪndʒmənt] *n.* **a)** *(ordering, order)* Anordnung, *die; (thing ordered)* Arrangement, *das;* **seating-~:** Anordnung der Sitze; **b)** *(Mus., Radio, etc.: adapting, adaptation)* Bearbeitung, *die;* Arrangement, *das;* **a guitar ~:** eine Bearbeitung *od.* ein Arrangement für Gitarre; **c)** *(settling beforehand)* Vereinbarung, *die;* Übereinkunft, *die; (of plans)* Aufstellung, *die;* **by ~:** nach Vereinbarung *od.* Absprache; **d)** *in pl. (plans)* Vorkehrungen; **make ~s** Vorkehrungen treffen; **we have made ~s for you to be picked up from the airport** wir haben veranlaßt, daß Sie vom Flughafen abgeholt werden; **holiday ~s** Urlaubsvorbereitungen; **~s about security** Sicherheitsvorkehrungen; **e)** *(agreement)* Vereinbarung, *die;* **make an ~ to do sth.** vereinbaren *od.* die Vereinbarung treffen, etw. zu tun; **the ~ is that ...:** die Vereinbarung lautet, daß ...; **f)** *(resolution)* Einigung, *die;* **make an ~:** eine Einigung erzielen; **I'm sure we can come to some ~ about ...:** wir können uns sicher irgendwie einigen über (+ *Akk.*) ...
arrant ['ærənt] *adj.* Erz⟨*lump, -schurke, -lügner, -feigling*⟩; dreist ⟨*Lüge, Mißbrauch, Anmaßung*⟩; unverhüllt ⟨*Grobheit, Heuchelei, Begierde*⟩; **~ nonsense** barer Unsinn
arras ['ærəs] *n.* A[r]razzo, *der*
array [ə'reɪ] **1.** *v. t. (formal: dress)* kleiden; schmücken; **~ sb. in sth.** jmdn. in etw. *(Akk.)* kleiden *od. (geh.)* hüllen; **~ sth. with sth.** etw. mit etw. schmücken. **2.** *n. (ordered display)* Reihe, *die*
arrears [ə'rɪəz] *n. pl. (debts)* Schulden *Pl.;* Rückstände *Pl.; (remainder)* **there were huge ~ of work to be done/letters to be answered** es war noch eine Menge Arbeit aufzuholen/es mußten noch zahlreiche Briefe beantwortet werden; **the work on the building is badly in ~:** man ist mit den Arbeiten an dem Gebäude beträchtlich in Verzug [geraten]; **be in ~ with sth.** mit etw. im Rückstand sein; **be paid in ~:** rückwirkend bezahlt werden
arrest [ə'rest] **1.** *v. t.* **a)** *(stop)* aufhalten; zum Stillstand bringen ⟨*Fluß*⟩; **~ judgement** *(Law)* ein/das Urteil aufheben; **b)** *(seize)* verhaften, *(temporarily)* festnehmen ⟨*Person*⟩; beschlagnahmen ⟨*Sache*⟩; **c)** *(catch)* erregen ⟨*Aufmerksamkeit, Interesse*⟩; *(catch attention of)* fesseln; faszinieren. **2.** *n.* **a)** *(stoppage)* Stillstand, *der;* **~ of judgement** *(Law)* Aussetzung des/eines Verfahrens; **cardiac ~:** Herzstillstand, *der;* **b)** *(legal apprehension) (of person)* Verhaftung, *die; (temporary)* Festnahme, *die; (of thing)* Beschlagnahme, *die;* **under ~:** festgenommen; **he was put under police/military ~:** er wurde in Polizeigewahrsam genommen/unter Arrest gestellt
arrestable [ə'restəbl] *adj.* **be an ~ act/offence** ein Grund zur Festnahme sein
arris ['ærɪs] *n. (Archit.)* [Dach]grat, *der*
arrival [ə'raɪvl] *n.* **a)** Ankunft, *die; (fig.: at decision etc.)* Gelangen, *das* **(at** zu); *(of mail etc.)* Eintreffen, *das; (coming)* Kommen, *das;* Nahen, *das;* **it marked his ~ in the literary world** damit hat er sich in der literarischen Welt etabliert; **b)** *(appearance)* Auftauchen, *das;* **the ~ of buds in springtime** das Sprießen der Knospen im Frühling; **c)** *(person)* Ankömmling, *der; (thing)* Lieferung, *die;* **new ~** *(coll.: new-born baby)* Neugeborene, *das;* **how's the new ~?** *(coll.)* wie geht's dem neuen Erdenbürger?; **new ~s** Neuankömmlinge; **late ~s at the theatre** verspätet eintreffende Theaterbesucher
arrive [ə'raɪv] *v. i.* **a)** ankommen; **~ at a conclusion/an agreement** zu einem Schluß/einer Einigung kommen; **we've ~d at stalemate** wir sind in eine Sackgasse geraten; **the train is just arriving** der Zug läuft gerade ein; **b)** *(establish oneself)* es schaffen; arrivieren *(geh.);* **with this book he ~d** mit diesem Buch hat er es geschafft; **c)** *(be brought)* eintreffen; *(coll.: be born)* ankommen; **what time does the mail usually ~?** wann kommt die Post normalerweise?; **d)** *(come)* ⟨*Stunde, Tag, Augenblick:*⟩ kommen; **the time has ~d when ...:** jetzt ist der Zeitpunkt gekommen, wo ...
arrogance ['ærəgəns] *n., no pl.* Arroganz, *die; (presumptuousness)* Anmaßung, *die;* Überheblichkeit, *die*
arrogant ['ærəgənt] *adj.* arrogant; *(presumptuous)* überheblich; anmaßend

arrogantly ['ærəgəntlɪ] *adv.* arrogant; penetrant ⟨*überlegen, stolz*⟩; *(presumptuously)* anmaßend; überheblich; anmaßenderweise ⟨*behaupten, verlangen*⟩

arrogate ['ærəgeɪt] *v. t. (claim)* ~ **sth. to oneself** etw. für sich in Anspruch nehmen; sich *(Dat.)* etw. anmaßen

arrow ['ærəʊ] **1.** *n. (missile)* Pfeil, *der; (pointer)* [Hinweis-, Richtungs]pfeil, *der;* **as straight as an ~:** schnurgerade. **2.** *v. t.* mit einem Pfeil/mit Pfeilen markieren

arrow: ~-head *n.* **a)** Pfeilspitze, *die;* **b)** *(Bot.)* Pfeilkraut, *das;* **~-root** *n.* **a)** *(plant)* Pfeilwurz, *die;* **b)** *(starch)* Arrowroot, *das (Stärkemehl)*

[1]**arse** [ɑ:s] *n. (coarse)* Arsch, *der (derb);* **move your ~!** sei nicht so lahmarschig! *(derb)*

[2]**arse** *see* [1]**ass 2**

arse: ~-hole *n. (coarse)* Arschloch, *das (derb);* **~-licking** *n., no pl. (coarse)* Arschkriecherei, *die (derb);* Schleimscheißerei, *die (derb)*

arsenal ['ɑ:sənl] *n. (store)* [Waffen]arsenal, *das;* Waffenlager, *das; (fig.)* Arsenal, *das*

arsenic ['ɑ:sənɪk] *n. (Chem.)* **a)** Arsenik, *das;* **b)** *(element)* Arsen, *das*

arson ['ɑ:sn] *n.* Brandstiftung, *die*

arsonist ['ɑ:sənɪst] *n.* Brandstifter, *der*/Brandstifterin, *die*

art [ɑ:t] *n.* **a)** Kunst, *die;* **the ~s** *see* **fine art c; b)** *(skill, skilled activity)* Kunst, *die;* **works of ~:** Kunstwerke *Pl.;* **~ needlework/music/film** künstlerische Handarbeit/Kunstmusik/Kunstfilm; **~s and crafts** Kunsthandwerk, *das;* Kunstgewerbe, *das;* **he is a master of his ~:** er ist ein Meister [in] seiner Kunst; **translation is an ~:** Übersetzen ist eine Kunst; **c)** *in pl. (branch of study)* Geisteswissenschaften; **he's an ~s student** er studiert Geisteswissenschaften; **faculty of ~s** philosophische Fakultät; **he has an ~s degree** er hat das Abschlußexamen der philosophischen Fakultät [gemacht]; **Bachelor/Master of Arts** Bakkalaureus/Magister der philosophischen Fakultät; **d)** *(knack)* Kunst, *die; (stratagem)* Kunstgriff, *der;* Kniff, *der (ugs.);* **an ~ in itself** eine Kunst für sich; **e)** *(cunning)* List, *die*

'**art college** *see* **art school**

art deco [ɑ:t 'dekəʊ] *n., no pl.* Art deco, *die*

artefact, artifact ['ɑ:tɪfækt] *n.* Artefakt, *das*

arterial [ɑ:'tɪərɪəl] *adj.* **a)** *(of artery)* arteriell; **b)** *(principal)* Haupt-; **~ road** Hauptverkehrsstraße, *die*

arteriosclerosis [ɑ:tɪərɪəʊsklə'rəʊsɪs] *n., pl.* **arterioscleroses** [ɑ:tɪərɪəʊsklə'rəʊsi:z] *(Med.)* Arteriosklerose, *die (fachspr.);* Arterienverkalkung, *die*

artery ['ɑ:tərɪ] *n.* **a)** *(Anat.)* Arterie, *die;* Schlagader, *die;* **b)** *(fig.: road etc.)* [Haupt]verkehrsader, *die*

artesian [ɑ:'ti:zɪən, ɑ:'ti:ʒən] *adj.* **~ well** artesischer Brunnen

'**art-form** *n. (form of composition)* Kunstform, *die;* [Kunst]gattung, *die; (medium of expression)* Kunst[form], *die*

artful ['ɑ:tfl] *adj.* schlau; raffiniert; **~ dodger** Schlawiner, *der*

artfully ['ɑ:tfəlɪ] *adv.* schlau; raffiniert

artfulness ['ɑ:tflnɪs] *n., no pl.* Schlauheit, *die;* Raffiniertheit, *die*

'**art gallery** *n.* Kunstgalerie, *die*

arthritic [ɑ:'θrɪtɪk] *(Med.)* **1.** *adj.* arthritisch; **she's got ~ joints in her fingers** sie hat Arthritis in den Fingergelenken. **2.** *n.* Arthritiker, *der*/Arthritikerin, *die*

arthritis [ɑ:'θraɪtɪs] *n. (Med.)* Arthritis, *die (fachspr.);* Gelenkentzündung, *die*

arthropod ['ɑ:θrəpɒd] *n. (Zool.)* Gliederfüßler, *der;* **the ~s** die Arthropoden

Arthur ['ɑ:θə(r)] *pr. n.* **King ~:** König Artus

artic [ɑ:'tɪk] *n. (coll.)* Zug, *der (ugs.);* Sattelschlepper, *der (ugs.)*

artichoke ['ɑ:tɪtʃəʊk] *n.* **[globe] ~:** Artischocke, *die;* **Jerusalem ~:** Topinambur, *der; (edible part)* Topinamburwurzel, *die*

article ['ɑ:tɪkl] **1.** *n.* **a)** *(of constitution, treaty)* Artikel, *der; (of creed)* Glaubensartikel, *der; (of indictment)* [Anklage]punkt, *der; (of agreement)* [Vertrags]punkt, *der; (of the law)* Paragraph, *der; (in dictionary etc.)* Eintrag, *der;* **~s [of association]** Satzung, *die;* **~s of apprenticeship/employment** Lehr-/Arbeitsvertrag, *der;* **~ of faith** *(fig.)* Glaubensbekenntnis, *das (fig.);* **b)** *(in magazine, newspaper)* Artikel, *der; (in technical journal)* Beitrag, *der;* Aufsatz, *der;* **c)** *(Ling.)* Artikel, *der;* Geschlechtswort, *das;* **definite/indefinite ~:** bestimmter/unbestimmter Artikel; **d)** *(particular part, thing)* Artikel, *der;* **woollen ~s [of clothing]** Wollsachen; **an ~ of furniture/clothing** ein Möbel-/Kleidungsstück; **an ~ of value** ein Wertgegenstand; **toilet ~s** Toilettenartikel. **2.** *v. t.* in die Lehre geben **(to bei)**; **be ~d to sb.** bei jmdm. in der Lehre sein

articled ['ɑ:tɪkld] *adj.* **~ clerk** Rechtspraktikant, *der*/-praktikantin, *die;* ≈ Rechtsreferendar, *der*/-referendarin, *die*

articulate 1. [ɑ:'tɪkjʊlət] *adj.* **a)** *(clear)* verständlich; **b)** *(eloquent)* redegewandt; **be ~/not very ~:** sich gut/nicht sehr gut ausdrücken [können]; **c)** *(jointed)* gegliedert; Glieder-; *(distinctly joined)* aus Einzelgliedern; mit Gelenken. **2.** [ɑ:'tɪkjʊleɪt] *v. t.* **a)** *usu. in pass.* durch Gelenke/ein Gelenk verbinden; **~d lorry** Sattelzug, *der;* Sattelschlepper, *der (ugs.);* **b)** *(pronounce)* [deutlich] aussprechen; *(utter, express)* artikulieren; in Worte fassen. **3.** *v. i.* **a)** *(speak distinctly)* artikuliert sprechen; deutlich sprechen; **~ clearly** klar und deutlich sprechen; **b)** *(speak)* sprechen; **c)** *(form a joint)* **~ with sth.** mit etw. ein Gelenk bilden

articulately [ɑ:'tɪkjʊlətlɪ] *adv.* **a)** *(clearly)* klar; deutlich; **b)** *(coherently)* klar; **he expresses himself very ~:** er drückt sich sehr klar aus

articulateness [ɑ:'tɪkjʊlətnɪs] *n., no pl. (clarity)* Deutlichkeit, *die; (coherence)* Klarheit, *die*

articulation [ɑ:tɪkjʊ'leɪʃn] *n.* **a)** *(clear speech)* deutliche Aussprache; **his ~ is good** er hat eine deutliche Aussprache; **b)** *(coherent speech)* flüssige Ausdrucksweise; *(act of speaking)* Artikulation, *die;* [Laut]bildung, *die*

artifice ['ɑ:tɪfɪs] *n.* **a)** *(cunning)* List, *die;* Raffinement, *das (geh.);* **b)** *(device)* Trick, *der;* List, *die;* **c)** *(skill)* Geschick, *das;* Geschicklichkeit, *die*

artificial [ɑ:tɪ'fɪʃl] *adj.* **a)** *(not natural)* künstlich; Kunst-; *(not real)* unecht; imitiert; *(artificially produced)* künstlich; Kunst-; synthetisch [hergestellt]; **~ sweetener** Süßstoff, *der;* **~ limb** Prothese, *die;* **~ eye** Glasauge, *das;* **b)** *(affected, insincere)* gekünstelt; unecht; **she's ~ and two-faced** sie verstellt sich; **~ politeness** gekünstelte *od.* gespielte Höflichkeit; **she wore an ~ smile for the cameras** für die Fotografen setzte sie ein einstudiertes Lächeln auf; **her ~ enthusiasm** ihre gespielte Begeisterung

artificial: ~ ho'rizon *n.* Kreiselhorizont, *der;* **~ insemi'nation** *n.* künstliche Besamung; **~ in'telligence** *n.* künstliche Intelligenz

artificiality [ɑ:tɪfɪʃɪ'ælɪtɪ] *n., no pl.* **a)** *(unnaturalness)* Künstlichkeit, *die;* **b)** *(unreality)* Unechtheit, *die;* **c)** *(affectedness)* Affektiertheit, *die;* Geziertheit, *die; (formality)* Förmlichkeit, *die; (insincerity)* Gekünsteltheit, *die*

artificial: ~ 'kidney *see* **kidney machine; ~ 'language** *n.* Kunstsprache, *die*

artificially [ɑ:tɪ'fɪʃəlɪ] *adv.* **a)** *(unnaturally)* künstlich; unnatürlich; **the food has been ~ flavoured** die Lebensmittel sind mit künstlichem Geschmacksstoff versetzt; **~ produced diamonds/pearls** synthetische Diamanten/künstliche Perlen; **b)** *(affectedly, insincerely)* affektiert; geziert; **she's always so ~ polite** ihre Höflichkeit ist immer so gekünstelt

artificialness [ɑ:tɪ'fɪʃəlnɪs] *see* **artificiality**

artificial respi'ration *n.* künstliche Beatmung

artillery [ɑ:'tɪlərɪ] *n.* Artillerie, *die*

artilleryman [ɑ:'tɪlərɪmən] *n., pl.* **artillerymen** [ɑ:'tɪlərɪmən] Artillerist, *der*

artisan ['ɑ:tɪzn, ɑ:tɪ'zæn] *n.* [Kunst]handwerker, *der*

artist ['ɑ:tɪst] *n.* **a)** *(exponent of a fine art)* Künstler, *der*/Künstlerin, *die; (fig.)* Künstler, *der*/Künstlerin, *die;* Könner, *der*/Könnerin, *die;* **he's an ~ in words/rhetoric** er ist ein Wort-/Redekünstler; **she's an ~ in cookery** sie ist eine Kochkünstlerin; **he's a real ~ at his job** er ist ein echter Könner seines Fachs; **b)** *see* **artiste**

artiste [ɑ:'ti:st] *n.* Artist, *der*/Artistin, *die;* Künstler, *der*/Künstlerin, *die;* **circus ~s** Zirkusartisten *Pl.*

artistic [ɑ:'tɪstɪk] *adj.* **a)** *(of art)* Kunst-; künstlerisch; **~ movements such as Expressionism** Kunstrichtungen, zum Beispiel der Expressionismus; **the ~ world** die Welt der Kunst; **b)** *(of artists)* Künstler-; künstlerisch; **~ circles** Künstlerkreise; **c)** *(made with art)* kunstvoll; Kunst-; **~ designs** kunstvolle Muster; **a truly ~ piece of poetry/writing** ein dichterisches/schriftstellerisches Kunstwerk; **d)** *(naturally skilled in art)* künstlerisch veranlagt *od.* begabt; **she's quite ~:** sie ist künstlerisch ziemlich begabt; **have ~ leanings** künstlerische Neigungen haben; **e)** *(appreciative of art)* kunstverständig; **~ sense** Kunstverständnis, *das;* **~ feeling** Sinn für Kunst

artistically [ɑ:'tɪstɪkəlɪ] *adv.* **a)** *(in art)* künstlerisch; in der Kunst; *(from an artist's viewpoint)* künstlerisch [gesehen]; **b)** *(with art)* kunstvoll ⟨*geschmückt, gestaltet*⟩; **c)** künstlerisch ⟨*begabt, veranlagt*⟩; **be ~ interested/appreciative** an Kunst interessiert sein/einen Sinn für Kunst haben

artistry ['ɑ:tɪstrɪ] *n., no pl.* **a)** *(artistic pursuit)* künstlerisches Schaffen; **b)** *(artistic ability)* künstlerische Fähigkeit[en]; künstlerisches Geschick; *(artistic quality)* Kunst, *die;* künstlerischer Wert

artless ['ɑ:tlɪs] *adj.* **a)** *(guileless)* arglos; **~ piety** schlichte Frömmigkeit; **b)** *(simple)* schmucklos; schlicht; **~ beauty/grace** natürliche Schönheit/Anmut

artlessly ['ɑ:tlɪslɪ] *adv.* **a)** *(guilelessly)* arglos; **b)** *(simply)* schmucklos; schlicht

artlessness ['ɑ:tlɪsnɪs] *n., no pl.* **a)** *(guilelessness)* Arglosigkeit, *die;* **b)** *(simplicity)* Schmucklosigkeit, *die;* Schlichtheit, *die*

art: ~ nouveau [ɑ: nu:'vəʊ] *n.* Jugendstil, *der;* **~ paper** *n.* Kunstdruckpapier, *das;* **~ school** *n.* Kunsthochschule, *die;* **~work** *n.* Illustrationen *Pl.;* Bildmaterial, *das*

arty ['ɑ:tɪ] *adj. (coll.)* auf Künstler machend; **he's an ~ type** er ist so ein Künstlertyp; **~ furniture** auf Kunst gemachte Möbel; **an ~ design** ein pseudokünstlerisches Muster; **~-[and-]crafty** *(joc.)* auf Kunstgewerbe gemacht

arum ['eərəm] *n. (Bot.)* Aronstab, *der;* **~ lily** Zimmercalla, *die*

Aryan ['eərɪən] **1.** *adj.* indogermanisch; arisch *(veralt.).* **2.** *n.* **a)** *(language)* Indogermanisch, *das;* Arisch, *das (veralt.);* **b)** *(person)* Arier, *der*/Arierin, *die (bes. ns.);* Indogermane, *der*/Indogermanin, *die*

as [əz, *stressed* æz] **1.** *adv. in main sentence (in same degree)* **as ... [as ...]** so ... [wie ...]; **as soon as possible** so bald wie möglich; **almost as tall as ...:** fast so groß wie ...; **half as much** halb soviel; **you know as well as I do that ...:** Sie wissen genauso gut wie ich, daß ...; **they did as much as they could** sie taten, was sie konnten; **as good a ... [as ...]** ein so guter ... [wie ...]/eine so gute ... [wie ...]/ein so gutes ... [wie ...]. **2.** *rel. adv. or conj. in subord. clause* **a)** *expr. degree* **[as** *or* **so] ... as ...:** [so ...] wie ...; **as ... as possible** so ... wie möglich; **as ... as you can** so ...[, wie] Sie können; **come as quickly as you can** kommen Sie, so schnell Sie können; **quick as a flash** blitzschnell; **as recently as [this morning]** erst [heute morgen]; **as early as [tomorrow]** schon *od.* bereits *od.* gleich [morgen]; **b)** *(though)* **... as he** *etc.* **is/was** obwohl er *usw.* ... ist/war; **intelligent as she is/was, ...:** obwohl sie ziemlich intelligent ist/war, ...; **safe as it might be, ...:** obwohl es vielleicht ungefährlich ist, ...; **c)** *(however much)* **try as he might/would, he could not concentrate** sosehr er sich auch bemühte, er konnte sich nicht konzentrieren; **push/strain/pull as he might/would, ...:** wie sehr er auch drückte/sich anstrengte/zog, ...; **d)** *expr. manner* wie; **as you may already have heard, ...:** wie Sie vielleicht schon gehört haben, ...; **as we are all well aware, ...:** wie wir alle sehr wohl wissen, ...; **as we had hoped/expected ...:** wie erhofft/erwartet, ...; **as it were** sozusagen; gewissermaßen; **as you were!** Kommando zurück!; **e)** *expr. time* als; während; **as and when** wann immer; **as we climbed the stairs** als wir die Treppe hinaufgingen; **as we were talking** während wir uns unterhielten; **he knew her as a teenager** er kannte sie schon, als sie noch ein Teenager war; **f)** *expr. reason* da; **as we're now all assembled** da wir jetzt vollzählig sind; **g)** *expr. result* **so ... as to ...:** so ... zu; **would you be so kind as to help us?** würden Sie so freundlich sein und uns helfen?; **h)** *expr. purpose* **so as to ...:** um ... zu; **i)** *expr. illustration* wie [z. B.]; **industrial areas, as the north-east of England for example** Industriegebiete wie z. B. der Nordosten Englands. **3.** *prep.* **a)** *(in the function of)* als; **as an artist** als Künstler; **speaking as a parent, ...:** als Mutter/Vater ...; **b)** *(like)* wie; **he's treated as an outcast** er wird wie ein Ausgestoßener behandelt; **they regard him as a fool** sie halten ihn für einen Dummkopf. **4.** *rel. pron. (which)* **fool as he was he did not notice the obvious dangers** dumm, wie er war, sah er die Gefahren nicht; **as is our custom** wie immer; **they danced, as was the custom there** sie tanzten, wie es dort Sitte war; **he was shocked, as were we all** er war wie wir alle schockiert; **it was him/the earthquake as did it** *(uneducated)* er ist's gewesen/das Erdbeben war's; **the same as ...:** der-/die-/dasselbe wie ...; **such as** wie zum Beispiel; **they enjoy such foreign foods as ...:** sie essen gern ausländische Lebensmittel wie ... **5. as far** *see* **far 1 d; as for ...:** was ... angeht *od.* betrifft *od.* anbelangt; **as from ...:** von ... an; **you will receive a pension as from your 60th birthday** vom 61. Lebensjahr an bekommen Sie Rente; **you are dismissed as from today** Sie sind mit sofortiger Wirkung entlassen; **as [it] is** wie die Dinge liegen; wie es aussieht; **I'll take the dress as it is** ich nehme das Kleid, wie es ist; **the place is untidy enough as it is** es ist schon liederlich genug[, wie es jetzt ist]; **as of ...** *(Amer.)* von ... an; **as of 31 December annually** am 31. 12. jeden Jahres; **as to** hinsichtlich (+ *Gen.*); **nothing further was mentioned as to holiday plans** von Urlaubsplänen wurde nichts weiter gesagt; **as was** wie es einmal war; **Miss Tay as was** das frühere Fräulein Tay; **as yet** bis jetzt; noch; **as yet the plan is only under discussion** der Plan wird noch diskutiert; *see also* **if 1 a; much 2, 3 e, g; per b; regard 1 c, d; soon c, d; such 1 a, b, 2; [2]well 2 g**

a.s.a.p. *abbr.* **as soon as possible**

asbestos [æz'bestɒs, æs'bestɒs] *n.* **a)** *(fabric)* Asbest, *der;* **b)** *(mineral)* Amiant, *der*

asbestosis [æzbes'təʊsɪs, æsbes'təʊsɪs] *n., no pl. (Med.)* Asbestose, *die (fachspr.);* Staublungenerkrankung, *die;* **suffer from ~:** eine Staublunge haben

ascend [ə'send] **1.** *v. i.* **a)** *(go up)* hinaufgehen *od.* -steigen; *(climb up)* hinaufklettern; *(by vehicle)* hinauffahren; *(come up)* heraufkommen; **the lift ~ed** der Aufzug fuhr nach oben; **Christ ~ed into heaven** Christus fuhr auf gen Himmel *(geh.);* **~ in the lift** mit dem Aufzug hinauffahren; **b)** *(rise)* [höher]steigen; aufsteigen; **the helicopter ~ed slowly** der Hubschrauber stieg langsam höher; **the water ~s to above the level of this line** das Wasser steigt über die Marke; **c)** *(slope upwards)* ⟨*Hügel, Straße:*⟩ ansteigen; **the stairs ~ very steeply** die Treppe ist sehr steil; **d)** *(in quality, rank, etc.)* aufsteigen; **e)** *(in pitch)* höher werden. **2.** *v. t.* **a)** *(go up)* hinaufsteigen, hinaufgehen ⟨*Treppe, Leiter, Berg*⟩; **~ a rope** an einem Seil hochklettern; **b)** *(come up)* **we saw a fireman ~ing the ladder towards us** wir sahen einen Feuerwehrmann die Leiter heraufsteigen; **c)** *(go along)* hinauffahren ⟨*Straße*⟩; **d) ~ the throne** den Thron besteigen

ascendancy [ə'sendənsɪ] *n., no pl.* beherrschender Einfluß; Vorherrschaft, *die;* **gain/have the ~ over sb.** die Vorherrschaft über jmdn. gewinnen/haben

ascendant [ə'sendənt] *n.* **a)** *(Astrol.)* Aszendent, *der;* **b) in the ~:** im Aufsteigen begriffen; **his popularity was now firmly in the ~:** seine Beliebtheit nahm beständig zu

ascension [ə'senʃn] *n.* **a)** *(going up)* Auffahrt, *die;* **right ~** *(Astron.)* Rektaszension, *die;* **b) [the] A~** *(Relig.)* [Christi] Himmelfahrt

A'scension Day *n.* Himmelfahrtstag, *der*

ascent [ə'sent] *n.* **a)** *(going up, rise; also fig.)* Aufstieg, *der;* **our ~ in the lift/up the hill** unsere Auffahrt mit dem Lift/unser Aufstieg den Berg hinauf; **b)** *(way; also fig.)* Aufstieg, *der;* **c)** *(slope)* Steigung, *die;* **d)** *(steps)* Aufgang, *der*

ascertain [æsə'teɪn] *v. t.* feststellen; ermitteln ⟨*Fakten, Daten*⟩

ascertainable [æsə'teɪnəbl] *adj.* feststellbar; zu ermittelnd ⟨*Daten, Fakten*⟩

ascertainment [æsə'teɪnmənt] *n.* Feststellung, *die; (of facts, data)* Ermittlung, *die; (of information)* Beschaffung, *die*

ascetic [ə'setɪk] **1.** *adj.* asketisch. **2.** *n.* **a)** Asket, *der*/Asketin, *die;* **b)** *(Relig. Hist.)* Eremit, *der;* Klausner, *der*

ascetically [ə'setɪkəlɪ] *adv.* asketisch

asceticism [ə'setɪsɪzm] *n., no pl.* Askese, *die*

ascribe [ə'skraɪb] *v. t.* zuschreiben (to *Dat.*); **~ sth. to sth./sb.** *(regard as belonging)* etw. einer Sache/jmdm. zuschreiben; *(attribute, impute)* etw. auf etw./jmdn. zurückführen

ascription [ə'skrɪpʃn] *n. see* **ascribe:** Zuschreiben, *das;* Zurückführen, *das*

asepsis [eɪ'sepsɪs] *n., no pl.* **a)** *(absence of sepsis)* Asepsis, *die;* Keimfreiheit, *die (fachspr.);* **b)** *(aseptic method)* Aseptik, *die (fachspr.);* keimfreie Wundbehandlung

aseptic [eɪ'septɪk] *adj.* aseptisch

asexual [eɪ'sekʃʊəl] *adj.* **a)** *(without sexuality)* asexuell; **b)** *(Biol.: without sex)* asexual; ungeschlechtig; **~ reproduction** ungeschlechtliche Vermehrung

[1]ash [æʃ] *n.* **a)** *(tree)* Esche, *die;* **b)** *(wood)* Eschenholz, *das. See also* **mountain ash**

[2]ash *n.* **a)** *(powdery residue)* Asche, *die;* **layer of ~:** Ascheschicht, *die;* **cigarette ~:** Zigarettenasche, *die;* **sweep up the ~[es]** die Asche auffegen; **b)** *in pl. (remains)* Asche, *die;* **in ~es** in Schutt und Asche; *see also* **sackcloth; c)** *(Cricket)* **the Ashes** *imaginäre Trophäe für den Gewinner einer Serie von Vergleichswettkämpfen zwischen den Mannschaften Englands und Australiens*

ashamed [ə'ʃeɪmd] *adj., usu. pred.* beschämt; **we were ~:** wir schämten uns *od.* waren beschämt; **be ~ [of sb./sth.]** sich [jmds./einer Sache wegen] schämen; **you ought to be ~ of yourselves for telling lies** ihr solltet euch schämen zu lügen; **be/feel ~ for sb./sth.** sich für jmdn./etw. schämen; **be ~ to do sth.** sich schämen, etw. zu tun; **I'm ~ to have to say/admit that I told a white lie** ich muß leider *od.* zu meiner Schande zugeben, daß ich eine Notlüge erzählt habe; **he was not ~ to stand up and say that ...:** er schämte sich nicht, aufzustehen und zuzugeben, daß ...

ash: ~-bin *n.* Mülleimer, *der;* **~ blonde 1.** *adj.* aschblond; **2.** *n.* Aschblonde, *der/die;* **~-can** *(Amer.) see* **~-bin**

ashen ['æʃn] *adj.* **a)** *(ash-coloured)* aschfarben; aschfahl ⟨*Gesicht*⟩; **~ grey** aschgrau; **b)** *(of ashes)* aus Asche; Asche-

ashore [ə'ʃɔ:(r)] *adv. (position)* an Land; am Ufer; *(direction)* an Land; ans Ufer; **go/be ~:** an Land gehen/sein

'ash-pan *n.* Aschkasten, *der*

ashram ['æʃrəm] *n.* Ashram, *das od. der*

ash: ~-tray *n.* Aschenbecher, *der;* **~-tree** *see* **[1]ash a; Ash 'Wednesday** *n.* Aschermittwoch, *der;* **~-wood** *see* **[1]ash b**

Asia ['eɪʃə] *pr. n.* Asien *(das);* **~ 'Minor** Kleinasien *(das)*

Asian ['eɪʃən, 'eɪʒən], **Asiatic** [eɪʃɪ'ætɪk] **1.** *adj.* asiatisch. **2.** *n.* Asiat, *der*/Asiatin, *die*

aside [ə'saɪd] **1.** *adv.* beiseite; zur Seite; **stand ~!** treten Sie zur Seite!; **I pulled the curtain ~:** ich zog den Vorhang zur Seite; **~ from sb./sth.** *(Amer.)* außer jmdm./etw.; **take sb. ~:** jmdn. beiseite nehmen. **2.** *n.* **a)** *(in a play)* Apart, *das;* Beiseitesprechen, *das;* **b)** *(incidental remark)* [beiläufige] Bemerkung

asinine ['æsɪnaɪn] *adj. (stupid)* dämlich; **don't be so ~:** sei kein Esel

asininity [æsɪ'nɪnɪtɪ] *n.* Dämlichkeit, *die*

ask [ɑ:sk] **1.** *v. t.* **a)** fragen; **~ [sb.] a question** [jmdm.] eine Frage stellen; **~ sb.'s name** nach jmds. Namen fragen; **~ sb. [sth.]** jmdn. [nach etw.] fragen; **I was ~ed some awkward questions by the boss** der Chef stellte mir einige unangenehme Fragen; **~ sb. about sth.** jmdn. nach etw. fragen; **I ~ you!** *(coll.)* ich muß schon sagen!; **if you ~ me** *(coll.)* [also,] wenn du mich fragst; **~ me another** *(coll.)* frag mich was Leichteres *(ugs.);* **b)** *(seek to obtain)* **~ sth.** um etw. bitten; **~ sb.'s advice on sth.** jmdn. wegen etw. um Rat fragen; **how much are you ~ing for that car?** wieviel verlangen Sie für das Auto?; **~ a favour of sb., ~ sb. a favour** jmdn. um einen Gefallen bitten; **~ sb. to do sth.** jmdn. [darum] bitten, etw. zu tun; **you have only to ~:** du brauchst es nur zu sagen; **~ a lot of sb.** viel von jmdm. verlangen; **it's ~ing a lot** es ist viel verlangt; **~ing price** geforderter Preis; **it's yours for the ~ing** du kannst es gern haben; **c)** *(invite)* einladen; **~ sb. to dinner** jmdn. zum Essen einladen; **~ sb. out** jmdn. einladen; **the boss ~ed me up to his office** der Chef hat mich gebeten, in sein Büro hinaufzukommen. **2.** *v. i.* **you may well ~:** du hast allen Grund zu fragen; **~ after sb./sth.** nach jmdm./etw. fragen; **~ after sb.'s health** fragen, wie es jmdm. [gesundheitlich] geht; **~ for sth./sb.** etw./jmdn. verlangen; **~ for it** *(sl.: invite trouble)* es herausfordern; es so *od.* nicht anders haben wollen; *see also* **trouble 1 a**

askance [ə'skæns, ə'skɑ:ns] *adv.* **a)** *(sideways)* von der Seite; **b)** *(suspiciously)* **look ~ [at sb./sth.]** [über jmdn./etw.] befremdet sein

askew [ə'skju:] **1.** *adv.* schief; *(awry)* **the wind had blown all her clothes ~:** der Wind hatte ihre ganze Kleidung in Unordnung gebracht. **2.** *pred. adj.* schief; *(awry)* in Unordnung

asleep [ə'sli:p] *pred. adj.* **a)** *(lit. or fig.)* schlafend; *(euphem.: dead)* entschlafen *(geh.)*; **be/lie ~:** schlafen; **he seems to be ~:** er scheint zu schlafen; **fall ~:** einschlafen; **has the government fallen ~?** *(fig.)* schläft die Regierung?; **the old man fell ~** *(euphem.)* der alte Mann schlief [für immer] ein; **b)** *(numb)* eingeschlafen ‹*Arm, Bein*›
asocial [eɪ'səʊʃl] *adj.* *(antisocial)* asozial; *(not social)* ungesellig; asozial; *(coll.: inconsiderate)* rücksichtslos
asp [æsp] *n.* *(Zool.)* *(Vipera aspis)* Aspisviper, *die;* *(Naja haje)* Uräusschlange, *die*
asparagus [ə'spærəgəs] *n.* Spargel, *der;* **~ fern** *(Bot.)* Asparagus, *der*
aspect ['æspekt] *n.* **a)** Aspekt, *der;* **b)** *(expression)* Gesichtsausdruck, *der;* *(appearance)* **[physical] ~:** Erscheinungsbild, *das;* **c)** *(position looking in a given direction)* Lage, *die;* *(front)* Seite, *die;* **have a southern ~:** nach Süden liegen; **d)** *(Ling., Astrol.)* Aspekt, *der*
aspectual [æ'spektjʊəl] *adj.* *(Ling.)* aspektisch
aspen ['æspən] *n.* *(Bot.)* Espe, *die*
asperity [æ'sperɪtɪ] *n., no pl.* **a)** *(harshness)* Schroffheit, *die;* **b)** *(roughness)* Rauheit, *die*
aspersion [ə'spɜ:ʃn] *n.* Verunglimpfung, *die;* **cast ~s on sb./sth.** jmdn./etw. in den Schmutz ziehen
asphalt ['æsfælt] **1.** *n.* Asphalt, *der.* **2.** *v. t.* asphaltieren
asphyxia [æ'sfɪksɪə] *n., no pl.* *(Med.)* Asphyxie, *die (fachspr.)*; schwere Atemstörung; Erstickung, *die*
asphyxiate [æ'sfɪksɪeɪt] *(Med.)* **1.** *v. t.* ersticken; **be ~d by sth.** an etw. *(Dat.)* ersticken. **2.** *v. i.* ersticken
asphyxiation [æsfɪksɪ'eɪʃn] *n.* *(Med.)* Erstickung, *die;* **death by ~** Erstickungstod, *der*
aspic ['æspɪk] *n.* *(jelly)* Aspik, *der*
aspidistra [æspɪ'dɪstrə] *n.* *(Bot.)* Schusterpalme, *die;* Aspidistra, *die (fachspr.)*
aspirant [ə'spaɪərənt, 'æspərənt] **1.** *adj.* aufstrebend. **2.** *n.* Aspirant, *der*/Aspirantin, *die;* Bewerber, *der*/Bewerberin, *die;* **an ~ to high office** ein Bewerber für ein hohes Amt
aspirate 1. ['æspərət] *adj.* *(Phonet.)* aspiriert; behaucht. **2.** *n.* *(Phonet.)* Aspirata, *die;* behauchter [Verschluß]laut. **3.** ['æspəreɪt] *v. t.* **a)** *(Phonet.)* aspirieren; **b)** *(draw by suction)* absaugen
aspiration [æspə'reɪʃn] *n.* **a)** Streben, *das;* Aspiration, *die (geh.)*; **your ~[s] for** *or* **after success** dein Streben nach Erfolg; **have ~s to sth.** nach etw. streben; **b)** *(Phonet.)* Aspiration, *die;* Behauchung, *die*
aspire [ə'spaɪə(r)] *v. i.* **~ to** *or* **after sth.** nach etw. streben; **~ to be sth.** danach streben, etw. zu sein; **I once ~d to be an actor** ich wollte einmal [unbedingt] Schauspieler werden
aspirin ['æspərɪn] *n.* *(Med.)* Aspirin ®, *das;* Kopfschmerztablette, *die*
aspiring [ə'spaɪərɪŋ] *adj.* aufstrebend
[1]**ass** [æs] **1.** *n.* *(Zool.; also fig.)* Esel, *der;* **make an ~ of oneself** sich blamieren. **2.** *v. i.* *(sl.)* **~ about** *or* **around** herumalbern *(ugs.)*
[2]**ass** *(Amer.)* *see* [1]**arse**
assail [ə'seɪl] *v. t.* **a)** angreifen; **b)** *(fig.)* in Angriff nehmen ‹*Hindernis, Aufgabe*›; **~ sb. with questions/insults** jmdn. mit Fragen/Beleidigungen überschütten; **I was ~ed with doubts** mich überkamen Zweifel; **the noise ~ed our ears** der Lärm dröhnte in unseren Ohren
assailant [ə'seɪlənt] *n.* Angreifer, *der*/Angreiferin, *die*
assassin [ə'sæsɪn] *n.* **a)** Mörder, *der*/Mör-…rin, *die;* **b)** *(Hist.)* Assassine, *der*
…**sinate** [ə'sæsɪneɪt] *v. t.* ermorden; **be** …inem Attentat zum Opfer fallen
…**ssination** [əsæsɪ'neɪʃn] *n.* Mord, *der* (**of** an + *Dat.*); **~ attempt** Attentat, *das* (**on** auf + *Akk.*); *see also* **character assassination**
assault [ə'sɔ:lt] **1.** *n.* **a)** Angriff, *der;* *(fig.)* Anschlag, *der;* *(euphem.: rape)* Vergewaltigung, *die;* **verbal ~s** verbale Angriffe; **b)** *(Mil.)* Sturmangriff, *der;* **~ craft** Sturmboot, *das;* **~ course** *Hindernisstrecke für die Truppenausbildung;* **c)** *(Law)* [Androhung einer] Tätlichkeit; *see also* **battery b. 2.** *v. t.* **a)** *(lit. or fig.)* angreifen; *(euphem.: rape)* vergewaltigen; mißbrauchen *(geh.)*; **b)** *(Mil.)* stürmen; angreifen
assay [ə'seɪ] **1.** *n.* **a)** Probe, *die;* **A~ Office** *[amtliches] Labor für die Analyse von Edelmetallen o. ä.;* **b)** *(Chem.)* Analyse, *die.* **2.** *v. t.* **a)** prüfen ‹*Metall, Erz*›; **b)** *(Chem.)* analysieren; **c)** *(show on ~)* enthalten
assemblage [ə'semblɪdʒ] *n.* **a)** *(of things, persons)* Ansammlung, *die;* **b)** *(process)* *(bringing together)* Zusammentragen, *das;* *(fitting together)* Zusammensetzen, *das;* *(coming together)* Zusammenkunft, *die*
assemble [ə'sembl] **1.** *v. t.* **a)** zusammentragen ‹*Beweise, Material, Sammlung*›; zusammenrufen ‹*Menschen*›; **a team was ~d, and work began** ein Team wurde zusammengestellt, und die Arbeit begann; **b)** *(fit together)* zusammenbauen. **2.** *v. i.* sich versammeln
assembly [ə'semblɪ] *n.* **a)** *(coming together, meeting, deliberative body)* Versammlung, *die;* *(in school)* *(tägliche Versammlung aller Schüler und Lehrer zur)* Morgenandacht; **b)** *(fitting together)* Zusammenbau, *der;* Montage, *die;* **c)** *(assembled unit)* Einheit, *die*
as'sembly line *n.* Fließband, *das;* **work/be produced on an ~:** am Fließband arbeiten/produziert werden
assent [ə'sent] **1.** *v. i.* zustimmen; **~ to sth.** einer Sache *(Dat.)* zustimmen. **2.** *n.* Zustimmung, *die;* **royal ~:** Zustimmung des Königs/der Königin; **by common ~:** nach allgemeiner Auffassung
assert [ə'sɜ:t] *v. t.* **a)** geltend machen; **~ oneself** sich durchsetzen; **b)** *(declare)* behaupten; beteuern ‹*Unschuld*›
assertion [ə'sɜ:ʃn] *n.* **a)** Geltendmachen, *das;* **b)** *(declaration)* Behauptung, *die;* **~ of innocence** Unschuldsbeteuerung, *die;* **make an ~:** eine Behauptung aufstellen
assertive [ə'sɜ:tɪv] *adj.* energisch ‹*Person*›; bestimmt ‹*Ton, Verhalten*›; fest ‹*Stimme*›; *(dogmatic)* rechthaberisch
assertiveness [ə'sɜ:tɪvnɪs] *n., no pl.* Bestimmtheit, *die;* *(dogmatism)* Rechthaberei, *die*
assess [ə'ses] *v. t.* **a)** *(evaluate)* einschätzen; beurteilen; **b)** *(value)* schätzen; taxieren; **c)** *(fix amount of)* festsetzen ‹*Steuer, Bußgeld usw.*› (**at** auf + *Akk.*); **d)** *(tax)* veranlagen
assessment [ə'sesmənt] *n.* **a)** *(evaluation)* Einschätzung, *die;* Beurteilung, *die;* **b)** *(valuation)* Schätzung, *die;* Taxierung, *die;* **c)** *(fixing amount of damages or fine)* Festsetzung, *die;* *(of tax)* Veranlagung, *die;* **d)** *(tax to be paid)* Steuerbescheid, *der*
assessor [ə'sesə(r)] *n.* **a)** *(tax inspector)* ≈ Finanzbeamte, *der*/Finanzbeamtin, *die;* **b)** *(adviser to judge)* *(als Beisitzer fungierender)* Sachverständiger
asset ['æset] *n.* **a)** Vermögenswert, *der;* **my [personal] ~s** mein [persönlicher] Besitz; **b)** *(fig.)* *(useful quality)* Vorzug, *der* (**to** für); *(person)* Stütze, *die;* *(thing)* Hilfe, *die*
'asset-stripping *n.* *(Commerc.)* *Ankauf unrentabler Unternehmen, von denen einzelne Teile gewinnbringend weiterverkauft werden*
asseverate [ə'sevəreɪt] *v. t.* beteuern
asseveration [əsevə'reɪʃn] *n.* Beteuerung, *die*
assiduity [æsɪ'dju:ɪtɪ] *n.* **a)** *no pl.* *(diligence)* Eifer, *der;* *(conscientiousness)* Gewissenhaftigkeit, *die;* **b)** *(obsequious attention)* Beflissenheit, *die*
assiduous [ə'sɪdjʊəs] *adj.* **a)** *(diligent)* eifrig; *(conscientious)* gewissenhaft; **we made ~ efforts** wir unternahmen alle Anstrengungen; **b)** *(obsequiously attentive)* beflissen
assiduously [ə'sɪdjʊəslɪ] *adv.* **a)** *(diligently)* gewissenhaft; **b)** *(with obsequious attentiveness)* beflissen
assiduousness [ə'sɪdjʊəsnɪs] *see* **assiduity a**
assign [ə'saɪn] **1.** *v. t.* **a)** *(allot)* **~ sth. to sb.** jmdm. etw. zuweisen; **b)** *(appoint)* zuteilen; **~ sb. to a job/task** jmdn. mit einer Arbeit/Aufgabe betrauen; **~ sb. to do sth.** jmdn. damit betrauen, etw. zu tun; **~ sb. to a post** jmdn. auf einen Posten berufen; **c)** *(specify)* festsetzen ‹*Zeit, Datum, Grenzwert*›; **d)** *(ascribe)* angeben; **~ a cause to sth.** einen Grund für etw. angeben; **~ an event to a date** ein Ereignis einer Zeit zuschreiben. **2.** *n.* *(Law)* Rechtsnachfolger, *der*
assignable [ə'saɪnəbl] *adj.* **a)** *(allottable)* zuteilbar; **be ~ to sb.** jmdm. zugeteilt werden können; **b)** *(specifiable)* bestimmbar; **c)** *(ascribable)* angebbar
assignation [æsɪg'neɪʃn] *n.* **a)** *(appointment)* **sb.'s ~ to a job/task** jmds. Betrauung mit einer Arbeit/Aufgabe; **sb.'s ~ to a post** jmds. Berufung auf einen Posten; **b)** *(allotment)* Zuteilung, *die;* *(of property)* Übereignung, *die;* **c)** *(attribution)* Zuordnung, *die;* **d)** *(Amer.: illicit lovers' meeting)* Stelldichein, *das;* **~ house** Bordell, *das*
assignee [əsaɪ'ni:] *n.* **a)** *(agent)* Bevollmächtigte, *der/die;* **b)** *see* **assign 2**
assignment [ə'saɪnmənt] *n.* **a)** *(allotment)* Zuteilung, *die;* *(of property)* Übereignung, *die;* *(document)* Übereignungsurkunde, *die;* **b)** *(task)* Aufgabe, *die;* *(Amer. Sch. and Univ.)* Arbeit, *die;* Aufgabe, *die;* **c)** *(attribution)* *(of date)* Bestimmung, *die;* *(of reason, cause)* Aufgabe, *die*
assimilate [ə'sɪmɪleɪt] *v. t.* **a)** *(make like)* angleichen; **~ sth. with** *or* **to sth.** etw. an etw. *(Akk.)* angleichen; **b)** *(absorb)* *(Biol.)* assimilieren; **c)** *(fig.)* aufnehmen ‹*Informationen, Einflüsse usw.*›; **d)** *(Ling.)* angleichen
assimilation [əsɪmɪ'leɪʃn] *n.* **a)** *(making or becoming like)* Angleichung, *die* (**to, with** an + *Akk.*); **b)** *(Biol.: absorbing)* Assimilation, *die;* **c)** *(fig.)* *(of information, influences, etc.)* Aufnahme, *die;* *(of people)* Integration, *die;* **d)** *(Ling.)* Assimilation, *die*
assist [ə'sɪst] **1.** *v. t.* *(help)* helfen (+ *Dat.*); voranbringen ‹*Vorgang, Prozeß*›; **~ sb. to do** *or* **in doing sth.** jmdm. helfen, etw. zu tun; **~ sb. with sth.** jmdm. bei etw. helfen. **2.** *v. i.* **a)** *(help)* helfen; **~ with sth./in doing sth.** bei etw. helfen/helfen, etw. zu tun; **b)** *(take part)* mitarbeiten; **~ in sth.** an etw. *(Dat.)* mitarbeiten; **~ in an operation** bei einer Operation assistieren
assistance [ə'sɪstəns] *n., no pl.* Hilfe, *die;* **give ~ to sb.** jmdm. behilflich sein; jmdm. helfen; **be of ~ [to sb.]** [jmdm.] behilflich sein; [jmdm.] helfen
assistant [ə'sɪstənt] **1.** *n.* *(helper)* Helfer, *der*/Helferin, *die;* *(subordinate)* Mitarbeiter, *der*/Mitarbeiterin, *die;* *(of professor, artist)* Assistent, *der*/Assistentin, *die;* *(in shop)* Verkäufer, *der*/Verkäuferin, *die.* **2.** *attrib. adj.* **~ manager** stellvertretender Geschäftsführer; **~ editor** Redaktionsassistent, *der;* **~ professor** *(Amer.)* ≈ Assistenzprofessor, *der*
assizes [ə'saɪzɪz] *n. pl.* *(Brit. Law Hist.)* *regelmäßige Gerichtstage in den verschiedenen Grafschaften*
associate 1. [ə'səʊʃɪət, ə'səʊsɪət] *n.* **a)** *(partner)* Partner, *der*/Partnerin, *die;* Kompagnon, *der;* *(colleague)* Kollege, *der*/Kollegin, *die;* *(companion)* Gefährte, *der*/Gefährtin, *die (geh.)*; Kamerad, *der*/Kameradin, *die;* *(of gangster)* Komplize, *der*/Kom-

plizin, *die;* **b)** *(subordinate member)* außerordentliches Mitglied. **2.** *adj.* beigeordnet; *(allied)* verwandt; außerordentlich ‹*Mitglied usw.*›; **~ judge** Beisitzer, *der;* **~ professor** *(Amer.)* ≈ außerordentlicher Professor. **3.** [ə'səʊʃɪeɪt, ə'səʊsɪeɪt] *v. t.* **a)** *(join)* in Verbindung bringen; **be ~d** in Verbindung stehen; **b)** *(connect in the mind)* in Verbindung bringen; assoziieren *(Psych.)*; **~ sth. with sth.** etw. mit etw. assoziieren *(Psych.) od.* verbinden; **c) ~ oneself with sth.** sich einer Sache *(Dat.)* anschließen. **4.** *v. i.* **~ with sb.** mit jmdm. verkehren *od.* Umgang haben; *(for common purpose)* sich zusammenschließen

associateship [ə'səʊʃɪətʃɪp, ə'səʊsɪətʃɪp] *n.* außerordentliche Mitgliedschaft

association [əsəʊsɪ'eɪʃn] *n.* **a)** *(organization)* Verband, *der;* Vereinigung, *die;* **an ~ of residents** eine Vereinigung von Anwohnern; **articles** *or* **deeds of ~:** Satzung, *die;* **b)** *(mental connection)* Assoziation, *die;* **~ of ideas** Gedankenassoziation, *die;* **have ~s for sb.** bei jmdm. Assoziationen hervorrufen; **c) A~ football** *(Brit.)* Fußball, *der;* **d)** *(connection)* Verbindung, *die;* **e)** *(contact with people)* Kontakt, *der;* *(co-operation)* Zusammenarbeit, *die;* **business ~:** geschäftliche Zusammenarbeit

associative [ə'səʊʃɪətɪv, ə'səʊsɪətɪv] *adj.* assoziativ

assonance ['æsənəns] *n.* *(Pros.)* Assonanz, *die*

assorted [ə'sɔ:tɪd] *adj.* gemischt ‹*Bonbons, Sortiment*›; **cardigans of ~ kinds** verschiedenerlei Strickjacken; **an ~ bunch of people** ein zusammengewürfelter Haufen Leute; *see also* **ill-assorted**

assortment [ə'sɔ:tmənt] *n.* Sortiment, *das;* **a good ~ of hats [to choose from]** eine gute Auswahl an Hüten; **an ~ of ideas** eine Reihe von Ideen; **an odd ~ of players** eine seltsame Mischung von Spielern

Asst. *abbr.* **Assistant** Ass.

assuage [ə'sweɪdʒ] *v. t.* stillen; *(soothe)* besänftigen ‹*Person, Ärger*›; lindern ‹*Schmerz, Sorge*›

assume [ə'sju:m] *v. t.* **a)** voraussetzen; ausgehen von; **~ sb.'s innocence** von jmds. Unschuld ausgehen; jmds. Unschuld voraussetzen; **he's not so stupid as we ~d him to be** er ist nicht so dumm, wie wir angenommen haben; **b)** *(undertake)* übernehmen ‹*Amt, Pflichten*›; **c)** *(take on)* annehmen ‹*Namen, Rolle*›; gewinnen ‹*Aspekt, Bedeutung*›; **under an ~d name** unter einem Decknamen; **d)** *(formal: put on oneself)* anlegen *(geh.)* ‹*Gewand*›; **e)** *(simulate)* vortäuschen ‹*Freude, Trauer, Unwissenheit*›

assuming [ə'sju:mɪŋ] *adj.* **a) ~ that ...:** vorausgesetzt, daß ...; **b)** *(presumptuous)* anmaßend

assumption [ə'sʌmpʃn] *n.* **a)** Annahme, *die;* **going on the ~ that ...:** vorausgesetzt, daß ...; **b)** *(undertaking)* Übernahme, *die;* **~ of power/office** Macht-/Amtsübernahme, *die;* **c)** *(simulation)* Vortäuschung, *die;* *(of look, air)* Aufsetzen, *das;* **with an ~ of indifference** mit scheinbarer Gleichgültigkeit; **d) the A~** *(Relig.)* Mariä Himmelfahrt

assurance [ə'ʃʊərəns] *n.* **a)** Zusicherung, *die;* **I give you my ~ that ...:** ich versichere Ihnen, daß ...; **I can give you no ~ that ...:** ich kann Ihnen nicht versprechen, daß ...; **b)** *no pl. (self-confidence)* Selbstsicherheit, *die;* **c)** *no pl. (certainty)* Sicherheit, *die;* **d)** *no pl. (impudence)* Dreistigkeit, *die;* **e)** *no pl. (Brit.: insurance)* Versicherung, *die*

assure [ə'ʃʊə(r)] *v. t.* **a)** versichern (+ *Dat.*); **you're safe now, I ~ you** ich versichere dir, du bist jetzt in Sicherheit; **~ sb. of sth.** jmdn. einer Sache *(Gen.)* versichern *(geh.)*; **b)** *(convince)* **~ sb./oneself** jmdn./sich überzeugen; **c)** *(make certain or safe)* gewährleisten; **d)** *(Brit.: insure)* versichern

assured [ə'ʃʊəd] *adj.* gesichert ‹*Tatsache*›; gewährleistet ‹*Erfolg*›; **be ~ of sth.** sich *(Dat.)* einer Sache *(Gen.)* sicher sein

assuredly [ə'ʃʊərɪdlɪ] *adv.* gewiß; gewißlich *(geh., veralt.)*

Assyrian [ə'sɪrɪən] **1.** *adj.* assyrisch. **2.** *n.* Assyrer, *der*/Assyrerin, *die*

aster ['æstə(r)] *n.* Aster, *die;* **China ~:** Sommeraster, *die*

asterisk ['æstərɪsk] **1.** *n.* Sternchen, *das;* Asteriskus, *der (Druckw.).* **2.** *v. t.* mit einem Sternchen versehen

astern [ə'stɜ:n] *adv. (Naut., Aeronaut.)* achtern; *(towards the rear)* achteraus; **~ of sth.** hinter etw. *(Dat.)*; **full speed ~!** volle Kraft zurück!; **go ~:** achteraus fahren; **fall ~:** achteraus sacken

asteroid ['æstərɔɪd] *n. (Astron.)* Asteroid, *der*

asthma ['æsmə] *n. (Med.)* Asthma, *das*

asthmatic [æs'mætɪk] *(Med.)* **1.** *adj.* asthmatisch. **2.** *n.* Asthmatiker, *der*/Asthmatikerin, *die*

astigmatism [ə'stɪgmətɪzm] *n. (Med., Optics)* Astigmatismus, *der*

astir [ə'stɜ:(r)] *pred. adj.* in Bewegung; *(out of bed)* auf den Beinen; *(excited)* in Aufruhr

astonish [ə'stɒnɪʃ] *v. t.* erstaunen; **you ~ me** *(iron.)* wer hätte das gedacht; **he was ~ed to hear that ...:** er war erstaunt zu hören, daß ...

astonishing [ə'stɒnɪʃɪŋ] *adj.* erstaunlich

astonishingly [ə'stɒnɪʃɪŋlɪ] *adv.* erstaunlich; *as sentence-modifier* **~ [enough], no one has yet ...:** erstaunlicherweise hat noch niemand ...

astonishment [ə'stɒnɪʃmənt] *n., no pl.* Erstaunen, *das;* **in utter ~:** äußerst erstaunt

astound [ə'staʊnd] *v. t.* verblüffen; [sehr] überraschen; **you ~ me** *(iron.)* das überrascht mich aber sehr

astounding [ə'staʊndɪŋ] *adj.* erstaunlich

astrakhan [æstrə'kæn] *n. (fleece, cloth)* Astrachan, *der*

astral ['æstrl] *adj.* astral; **~ body** Astralleib, *der;* **~ spirits** Sterngeister

astray [ə'streɪ] **1.** *adv.* in die Irre; **sb. goes ~:** jmd. verirrt sich; **sth. goes ~** *(is mislaid)* etw. wird verlegt; *(is lost)* etw. geht verloren; **lead ~:** irreführen; **go/lead ~** *(fig.)* in die Irre gehen/führen; *(into sin)* vom rechten Weg abkommen/abbringen. **2.** *pred. adj.* **be ~:** sich verirrt haben; *(fig.: be in error)* sich irren; ‹*Rechnung:*› abwegig sein

astride [ə'straɪd] **1.** *adv.* rittlings ‹*sitzen*›; breitbeinig ‹*stehen*›; **with one's legs ~:** mit gespreizten Beinen; **~ of sth.** rittlings auf etw. *(Dat./Akk.).* **2.** *prep.* **a)** rittlings auf (+ *Dat.*); **b)** *(extending across)* zu beiden Seiten (+ *Gen.*)

astringency [ə'strɪndʒənsɪ] *n., no pl.* Schärfe, *die;* *(of wine, fruit)* Säure, *die;* *(severity)* Schärfe, *die;* *(of judgement)* Strenge, *die*

astringent [ə'strɪndʒənt] **1.** *adj.* **a)** herb, streng ‹*Geruch, Geschmack*›; stechend, beißend ‹*Geruch*›; sauer ‹*Obst, Wein*›; **b)** *(styptic)* adstringierend *(Med.)*; blutstillend; **c)** *(severe)* scharf; beißend; streng ‹*Urteil*›. **2.** *n.* Adstringens, *das*

astro- [æstrəʊ] *in comb.* astro-/Astro-

astrologer [ə'strɒlədʒə(r)] *n.* Astrologe, *der*/Astrologin, *die*

astrological [æstrə'lɒdʒɪkl] *adj.* astrologisch

astrology [ə'strɒlədʒɪ] *n., no pl.* Astrologie, *die*

astronaut ['æstrənɔ:t] *n.* Astronaut, *der*/Astronautin, *die*

astronautical [æstrə'nɔ:tɪkl] *adj.* astronautisch; **~ research** Weltraumforschung, *die;* **~ engineering** Raumfahrttechnik, *die*

astronautics [æstrə'nɔ:tɪks] *n., no pl.* Astronautik, *die;* Raumfahrt, *die*

astronomer [ə'strɒnəmə(r)] *n.* Astronom, *der*/Astronomin, *die*

astronomical [æstrə'nɒmɪkl] *adj.,* **astronomically** [æstrə'nɒmɪkəlɪ] *adv. (lit. or fig.)* astronomisch

astronomy [ə'strɒnəmɪ] *n., no pl.* Astronomie, *die*

astrophysical [æstrəʊ'fɪzɪkl] *adj.* astrophysikalisch

astrophysicist [æstrəʊ'fɪzɪsɪst] *n.* Astrophysiker, *der*/Astrophysikerin, *die*

astrophysics [æstrəʊ'fɪzɪks] *n., no pl.* Astrophysik, *die*

astute [ə'stju:t] *adj.* scharfsinnig ‹*Beobachter, Bemerkung*›; *(skilful)* geschickt

astutely [ə'stju:tlɪ] *adv.* scharfsinnig ‹*bemerken, entscheiden*›; *(skilfully)* geschickt

astuteness [ə'stju:tnɪs] *n., no pl.* Scharfsinnigkeit, *die;* *(skill)* Geschick, *das*

asunder [ə'sʌndə(r)] *adv. (literary)* auseinander; **tear sth. ~:** etw. zerreißen

asylum [ə'saɪləm] *n.* Asyl, *das;* **grant sb. ~:** jmdm. Asyl gewähren; **seek ~:** um Asyl bitten *od.* nachsuchen; **political ~:** politisches Asyl

asymmetric [æsɪ'metrɪk, eɪsɪ'metrɪk], **asymmetrical** [æsɪ'metrɪkl, eɪsɪ'metrɪkl] *adj.* asymmetrisch; unsymmetrisch; **asymmetric bars** *(Sport)* Stufenbarren, *der*

asymmetry [æ'sɪmɪtrɪ, eɪ'sɪmɪtrɪ] *n.* Asymmetrie, *die*

asynchronous [eɪ'sɪŋkrənəs] *adj.* asynchron; **~ motor** Asynchronmotor, *der*

at [ət, *stressed* æt] *prep.* **a)** *expr. place* an (+ *Dat.*); **at the station** am Bahnhof; **at the baker's/butcher's/grocer's** beim Bäcker/Fleischer/Kaufmann; **at the chemist's** in der Apotheke/Drogerie; **at the supermarket** im Supermarkt; **at my mother's** bei meiner Mutter; **at home** zu Hause; **at the party** auf der Party; **at the office/hotel** im Büro/Hotel; **at school** in der Schule; **at Dover** in Dover; **b)** *expr. time* **at Christmas/Easter/Whitsun** [zu *od.* an] Weihnachten/Ostern/Pfingsten; **at six o'clock** um sechs Uhr; **at midnight** um Mitternacht; **at midday** am Mittag; mittags; **at dawn** im Morgengrauen; **at [the age of] 40** mit 40; im Alter von 40; **at this/the moment** in diesem/im Augenblick *od.* Moment; **at any time** jederzeit; **at irregular intervals** in unregelmäßigen Abständen; **at the first attempt** beim ersten Versuch; **c)** *expr. price* **at £2.50 [each]** zu *od.* für [je] 2,50 Pfund; **petrol is charged at 5p per mile** die Benzinkosten werden mit 5 Pence pro Meile berechnet; **d) she's still 'at it** sie ist immer noch dabei; **at that** *(at that point)* dabei; *(at that provocation)* daraufhin; *(moreover)* noch dazu; *(nevertheless)* trotzdem; **this is where it's at** *(coll.)* da ist was los *(ugs.). See also* **all 2 d**

atavism ['ætəvɪzm] *n.* Atavismus, *der*

atavistic [ætə'vɪstɪk] *adj.* atavistisch

ataxia [ə'tæksɪə] *n., no pl. (Med.)* Ataxie, *die;* **locomotor ~:** lokomotorische Ataxie

ate *see* **eat**

atheism ['eɪθɪɪzm] *n., no pl.* Atheismus, *der*

atheist ['eɪθɪɪst] *n.* Atheist, *der*/Atheistin, *die*

Athenian [ə'θi:nɪən] **1.** *adj.* athenisch; **the ~ people** die Athener; **~ history** die Geschichte Athens. **2.** *n.* Athener, *der*/Athenerin, *die*

Athens ['æθɪnz] *pr. n.* Athen *(das)*

atherosclerosis [æθərəʊsklə'rəʊsɪs] *n., pl.* **atheroscleroses** [æθərəʊsklə'rəʊsi:z] *(Med.)* Atherosklerose, *die*

athlete ['æθli:t] *n.* Athlet, *der*/Athletin, *die;* Sportler, *der*/Sportlerin, *die;* *(runner, jumper)* Leichtathlet, *der*/Leichtathletin, *die;* **~'s foot** *(Med.)* Athletenfuß, *der (fachspr.)*; Fußpilz, *der*

athletic [æθ'letɪk] *adj.* sportlich; *(robust)* athletisch; **~ sports** Leichtathletik, *die;* **any reasonably ~ person** jeder einigermaßen sportliche Mensch; **the goalkeeper made an ~ save** der Torwart zeigte eine Glanzparade

athletically [æθ'letɪkəlɪ] *adv.* sportlich; athletisch ‹*gebaut*›

athleticism [æθ'letɪsɪzm] *n., no pl.* Sportlichkeit, *die*

athletics [æθ'letɪks] *n., no pl.* **a)** Leichtathletik, *die;* **b)** *(Amer.: physical sports)* Sport, *der*

at-'home *n. festgesetzter Tag, an dem man zu festgesetzter Zeit zwanglos Gäste empfängt;* Jour fixe, *der (veralt.)*

athwart [ə'θwɔ:t] **1.** *adv.* **a)** *(literary: from side to side)* quer (to zu); **b)** *(Naut.)* dwars. **2.** *prep.* **a)** *(literary: from side to side of)* quer über (+ *Dat./Akk.*); **b)** *(Naut.)* dwars zu

Atlantic [ət'læntɪk] **1.** *adj.* atlantisch; ~ **Ocean** Atlantischer Ozean; ~ **coast** Atlantikküste, *die.* **2.** *pr. n.* Atlantik, *der*

atlas ['ætləs] *(also Anat.)* Atlas, *der;* ~ **of the world** Weltatlas, *der*

atmosphere ['ætməsfɪə(r)] *n.* **a)** *(lit. or fig.)* Atmosphäre, *die;* **the ~ of the Earth** die Erdatmosphäre; **b)** *(air in a place)* Luft, *die*

atmospheric [ætmə'sferɪk] *adj.* **a)** atmosphärisch; ~ **moisture** Luftfeuchtigkeit, *die;* **b)** *(fig.: evocative)* stimmungsvoll

atmospherics [ætmə'sferɪks] *n. pl. (Radio)* atmosphärische Störungen

atoll ['ætɒl, ə'tɒl] *n.* Atoll, *das*

atom ['ætəm] *n.* **a)** Atom, *das;* **b)** *(fig.)* **not an ~ of truth** kein Körnchen Wahrheit; **not a single ~ of evidence** nicht der Schatten eines Beweises

'atom bomb *see* **atomic bomb**

atomic [ə'tɒmɪk] *adj. (Phys.)* Atom-

atomic: ~ **'bomb** *n.* Atombombe, *die;* ~ **'energy** *n., no pl.* Atomenergie, *die;* ~ **'mass** *see* ~ **weight;** ~ **'number** *n. (Phys., Chem.)* Kernladungszahl, *die;* Ordnungszahl, *die;* ~ **'power** *n., no pl.* Atomkraft, *die;* ~ **'warfare** *n., no pl.* Atomkrieg, *der;* ~ **'weight** *n. (Phys., Chem.)* Atomgewicht, *das*

atomization [ætəmaɪ'zeɪʃn] *n.* Atomisierung, *die; (of liquid)* Zerstäubung, *die*

atomize ['ætəmaɪz] *v.t.* atomisieren; zerstäuben ‹*Flüssigkeit*›

atomizer ['ætəmaɪzə(r)] *n.* Zerstäuber, *der*

atonal [eɪ'təʊnl, ə'təʊnl] *adj. (Mus.)* atonal

atone [ə'təʊn] *v.i.* es wiedergutmachen; ~ **for sth.** etw. wiedergutmachen

atonement [ə'təʊnmənt] *n.* **a)** *(atoning)* Buße, *die; (reparation)* Wiedergutmachung, *die;* **make ~ for sth.** für etw. Buße tun; **b)** *(Relig.)* Versöhnung, *die;* **Day of A~:** Versöhnungsfest, *das;* Jom Kippur, *der;* **the A~:** das Sühneopfer [Christi]

atonic [ə'tɒnɪk] *adj. (Phonet., Pros.)* unbetont; atonisch *(veralt.)*

atop [ə'tɒp] **1.** *adv.* obendrauf; ~ **of sth.** [oben] auf etw. *(Dat./Akk.).* **2.** *prep.* [oben] auf (+ *Dat./Akk.*)

atrium ['eɪtrɪəm] *n., pl.* **atria** ['eɪtrɪə] *or* **~s a)** *(Anat.)* Vorhof, *der;* Atrium, *das (fachspr.);* **b)** *(Roman Ant.)* Atrium, *das*

atrocious [ə'trəʊʃəs] *adj.* grauenhaft; scheußlich ‹*Wetter, Benehmen*›

atrociously [ə'trəʊʃəslɪ] *adv.* grauenhaft; scheußlich ‹*sich benehmen*›

atrocity [ə'trɒsɪtɪ] *n.* **a)** *no pl. (extreme wickedness)* Grauenhaftigkeit, *die;* **b)** *(atrocious deed)* Greueltat, *die (geh.);* Grausamkeit, *die;* **c)** *(coll.: repellent thing)* Widerwärtigkeit, *die*

atrophy ['ætrəfɪ] **1.** *n.* **a)** *(Med.)* Atrophie, *die (Med.);* Verkümmerung, *die;* **muscular ~:** Muskelatrophie, *die (Med.);* Muskelschwund, *der;* **b)** *(emaciation)* Abmagerung, *die; (fig.)* Verfall, *der.* **2.** *v.i.* atrophieren *(Med.);* verkümmern

atropine ['ætrəpɪn, 'ætrəpi:n] *n. (Med.)* Atropin, *das*

attach [ə'tætʃ] **1.** *v.t.* **a)** *(fasten)* befestigen (**to** an + *Dat.*); anhängen ‹*Wagen*› (**to** an + *Dat.*); **please find ~ed a copy of the letter** beigeheftet ist eine Kopie des Briefes; **b)** *(join)* **~ oneself to sth./sb.** sich einer Sache/jmdm. anschließen; **c)** *(assign)* **be ~ed to sth.** einer Sache *(Dat.)* zugeteilt sein; **is there a car ~ed to the job?** ist die Stelle mit einem Dienstwagen verbunden?; **the research unit is ~ed to the university** die Forschungsabteilung ist der Universität *(Dat.)* angegliedert; **d)** *(fig.: ascribe)* zuschreiben; **~ no blame to sb.** jmdm. keine Schuld geben; **I can't ~ a name to that face** ich kann diesem Gesicht keinen Namen zuordnen; **e)** *(attribute)* beimessen; ~ **importance/meaning to sth.** einer Sache *(Dat.)* Gewicht/Bedeutung beimessen; **f)** *(Law)* pfänden ‹*Eigentum*›; festnehmen ‹*Person*›. **2.** *v.i.* **no blame ~es to sb.** jmdn. trifft keine Schuld; **suspicion ~es to sb.** der Verdacht fällt auf jmdn.

attachable [ə'tætʃəbl] *adj.* **a) be ~ to sth.** an etw. *(Dat.)* befestigt werden können; **b)** *(Law)* pfändbar ‹*Gut, Ware*›

attaché [ə'tæʃeɪ] *n.* Attaché, *der;* **cultural/military/press/naval ~:** Kultur-/Militär-/Presse-/Marineattaché, *der*

at'taché case *n.* Diplomatenkoffer, *der*

attached [ə'tætʃt] *adj. (emotionally)* **be ~ to sb./sth.** an jmdm./etw. hängen; **become ~ to sb./sth.** jmdn./etw. liebgewinnen

attachment [ə'tætʃmənt] *n.* **a)** *(act or means of fastening)* Befestigung, *die;* **the ~ of a recording device to a telephone** der Anschluß eines Aufnahmegerätes an ein Telefon; **b)** *(accessory)* Zusatzgerät, *das;* **blender ~:** Mixaufsatz, *der;* **c)** *(ascribing)* Zuordnung, *die;* **the ~ of blame would be premature at this stage** es wäre in diesem Stadium verfrüht, jmdm. die Schuld zu geben; **d)** *(attribution)* Beimessung, *die;* **e)** *(affection)* Anhänglichkeit, *die* (**to** an + *Akk.*); **his ~ to that party** seine Sympathie für diese Partei; **have an ~ for sb.** an jmdm. hängen; **f)** *(Law)* Pfändung, *die*

attack [ə'tæk] **1.** *v.t.* **a)** angreifen; *(ambush, raid)* überfallen; *(fig.: criticize)* attackieren; **a woman was ~ed and raped** eine Frau wurde überfallen und vergewaltigt; **b)** *(affect)* ‹*Krankheit:*› befallen; **c)** *(start work on)* in Angriff nehmen; **she ~ed the washing-up** sie machte sich an den Abwasch; **d)** *(take action against)* vorgehen gegen; **e)** *(act harmfully on)* angreifen ‹*Metall, Oberfläche*›. **2.** *v.i.* angreifen; **~ in strength** in großer Zahl angreifen. **3.** *n.* **a)** *(on enemy)* Angriff, *der; (on person)* Überfall, *der; (fig.: criticism)* Attacke, *die;* Angriff, *der;* **air ~:** Luftangriff, *der;* **be under ~:** angegriffen werden; **come under ~ from all directions** *(fig.)* von allen Seiten attackiert *od.* angegriffen werden; **b)** *(start)* Inangriffnahme, *die* (**on** *Gen.*); **make a spirited ~ on sth.** etw. beherzt in Angriff nehmen; **c)** *(of illness, lit. or fig.)* Anfall, *der;* **the girls got an ~ of the giggles** die Mädchen mußten furchtbar kichern; **d)** *(Sport)* Angriff, *der;* **e)** *(Mus.)* [präziser] Einsatz; *(on piano)* Anschlag, *der;* Attacke, *die (Jazz)*

attacker [ə'tækə(r)] *n. (also Sport)* Angreifer, *der*/Angreiferin, *die*

attacking [ə'tækɪŋ] *adj.* offensiv ‹*Spielweise, Spieler*›; angreifend ‹*Truppen*›

attain [ə'teɪn] **1.** *v.t.* erreichen ‹*Ziel, Wirkung*›; **~ power** an die Macht gelangen; **the author ~ed his ambition** der Autor erreichte sein Ziel; **she ~ed her hope** ihre Hoffnung erfüllte sich. **2.** *v.i.* **~ to sth.** zu etw. gelangen; **~ to success** Erfolg haben; **~ to power** an die Macht gelangen

attainability [əteɪnə'bɪlɪtɪ] *n., no pl.* Erreichbarkeit, *die*

attainable [ə'teɪnəbl] *adj.* erreichbar ‹*Ziel*›; realisierbar ‹*Hoffnung, Ziel*›

attainder [ə'teɪndə(r)] *n. (Hist.)* Verlust von Recht und Besitz *(als Folge eines Todesurteils oder der Ächtung)*

attainment [ə'teɪnmənt] *n.* **a)** *no pl.* Verwirklichung, *die;* **be impossible of ~:** unmöglich zu erreichen sein; **b)** *(thing attained)* Leistung, *die*

attar ['ætə(r)] *n.* Rosenöl, *das;* Attar, *der (veralt.)*

attempt [ə'tempt] **1.** *v.t.* **a)** versuchen; **~ to do sth.** versuchen, etw. zu tun; **b)** *(try to accomplish)* sich versuchen an (+ *Dat.*); *(try to conquer)* angreifen; **candidates should ~ 5 out of 10 questions** die Kandidaten sollten 5 von 10 Fragen zu beantworten versuchen. **2.** *n.* Versuch, *der;* **make an ~ at sth.** sich an etw. *(Dat.)* versuchen; **make an ~ to do sth.** den Versuch unternehmen, etw. zu tun; **he will make an ~ on the 800 m record tonight** er wird heute abend einen Rekordversuch über 800 m unternehmen; **make an ~ on sb.'s life** ein Attentat *od.* einen Mordanschlag auf jmdn. verüben

attend [ə'tend] **1.** *v.i.* **a)** *(give care and thought)* aufpassen; *(apply oneself)* **~ to sth.** auf etw. *(Akk.)* achten; *(deal with sth.)* sich um etw. kümmern; **everyone had their own tasks to ~ to** jeder mußte sich um seine eigenen Aufgaben kümmern *od.* sich seinen eigenen Aufgaben widmen; **b)** *(be present)* anwesend sein; **~ at sth.** bei etw. anwesend sein; **the chiropodist ~s on Wednesdays** der Fußpfleger ist [immer] mittwochs da; **c)** *(wait)* bedienen; aufwarten *(veralt.);* **~ on sb.** jmdn. bedienen; jmdm. aufwarten *(veralt.).* **2.** *v.t.* **a)** *(be present at)* teilnehmen an (+ *Dat.*); *(go regularly to)* besuchen; **his lectures are well ~ed** seine Vorlesungen werden gut besucht; **b)** *(follow as a result from)* sich ergeben aus; **be ~ed by sth.** etw. zur Folge haben; **c)** *(accompany)* verbunden sein mit; **may good luck ~ you** *(formal)* möge das Glück dir hold sein *(geh.);* **d)** *(wait on)* bedienen; aufwarten *(veralt.)* (+ *Dat.*); **e)** ‹*Arzt:*› behandeln

attendance [ə'tendəns] *n.* **a)** *(being present)* Anwesenheit, *die; (going regularly)* Besuch, *der* (**at** *Gen.*); **regular ~ at school** regelmäßiger Schulbesuch; **your ~ record is very poor** Sie haben reichlich oft gefehlt; **b)** *(number of people present)* Teilnehmerzahl, *die;* **there was only a small ~ for sth.** etw. wurde nur schwach besucht; **~s at churches are declining** die Zahl der Kirchenbesucher geht zurück; **c) be in ~:** anwesend sein; **the ladies in ~:** die anwesenden Damen; **in close ~:** in unmittelbarer Nähe. *See also* **dance 2 a**

attendance: ~ **allowance** *n. (Brit.) Sozialversicherungsleistung für Personen, die die Pflege einer pflegebedürftigen Person besorgen;* ~ **centre** *n. (Brit.)* Jugendarrestanstalt *(in der Freizeitarrest verbüßt wird)*

attendant [ə'tendənt] **1.** *n.* **a)** *(person providing service)* **[lavatory] ~:** Toilettenmann, *der*/Toilettenfrau, *die;* **[cloakroom] ~:** Garderobenmann, *der*/Garderobenfrau, *die;* **museum ~:** Museumswärter, *der;* **b)** *(member of entourage)* Begleiter, *der*/Begleiterin, *die.* **2.** *adj.* begleitend; **~ circumstances** Begleitumstände; **its ~ problems/risks** die damit verbundenen Probleme/Risiken; **be ~ upon sth.** mit etw. verbunden sein

attender [ə'tendə(r)] *n. (person present)* Anwesende, *der/die;* **regular ~s will know ...:** wer regelmäßig teilnimmt, wird wissen, ...

attention [ə'tenʃn] **1.** *n.* **a)** *no pl.* Aufmerksamkeit, *die;* **your careful ~ would be much appreciated** ich wäre Ihnen dankbar, wenn Sie gut aufpassen würden; **pay ~ to sb./sth.** jmdn./etw. beachten; **pay ~!** gib acht!; paß auf!; **hold sb.'s ~:** jmds. Interesse wachhalten; **attract [sb.'s] ~:** [jmdn.] auf sich aufmerksam machen; **catch sb.'s ~:** jmds. Aufmerksamkeit erregen; **bring sth. to sb.'s ~:** jmds. Aufmerksamkeit auf etw. *(Akk.)* lenken; jmdn. auf etw. *(Akk.)* aufmerksam machen; **call** *or* **draw sb.'s ~ to sb./sth.** jmds.

Aufmerksamkeit auf jmdn./etw. lenken; jmdn. auf jmdn./etw. aufmerksam machen; **~ Miss Jones** *(on letter)* zu Händen [von] Miss Jones; **b)** *no pl. (consideration)* **give sth. one's personal ~:** sich einer Sache *(Gen.)* persönlich annehmen; **we are giving your enquiry our fullest ~:** wir bearbeiten Ihre Anfrage mit der größten Sorgfalt; **c)** *in pl. (ceremonious politeness)* Aufmerksamkeit, *die;* **show sb. little ~s** jmdm. kleine Aufmerksamkeiten erweisen; **pay [one's] ~s to sb.** jmdm. den Hof machen *(veralt.);* **d)** *(Mil.)* Grundstellung, *die;* Habachtstellung, *die;* **stand to ~:** stillstehen; strammstehen. **2.** *int.* **a)** Achtung!; **~ all shipping** Achtung! An alle Schiffe!; **b)** *(Mil.)* stillgestanden!

attentive [əˈtentɪv] *adj.* **a)** *(paying attention)* aufmerksam; **be ~ to sth.** auf etw. *(Akk.)* achten; **b)** *(heedful)* **be more ~ to one's studies** sich gewissenhafter seinen Studien widmen; **be [more] ~ to sb.'s warnings** auf jmds. Warnungen hören; **c)** *(assiduous)* aufmerksam; **he was very ~ to the ladies** er war den Damen gegenüber sehr aufmerksam *od.* zuvorkommend

attentively [əˈtentɪvlɪ] *adv.* aufmerksam

attentiveness [əˈtentɪvnɪs] *n., no pl.* Aufmerksamkeit, *die*

attenuate [əˈtenjʊeɪt] *v. t.* **a)** *(make thin)* dünn machen; dünnflüssig machen ⟨*Öl*⟩; **b)** *(reduce, lit. or fig.)* abschwächen; dämpfen ⟨*Schall, Ton*⟩; **c)** *(Electr.)* [ab]schwächen; dämpfen ⟨*Welle, Schwingung*⟩

attenuation [ətenjʊˈeɪʃn] *n. see* **attenuate a, b, c:** Verdünnung, *die;* Abschwächung, *die;* Dämpfung, *die*

attest [əˈtest] **1.** *v. t. (certify validity of)* bestätigen; beglaubigen ⟨*Unterschrift, Urkunde*⟩. **2.** *v. i. (bear witness)* **~ to sth.** etw. bezeugen; *(fig.)* von etw. zeugen

attestation [ætɪˈsteɪʃn] *n.* Bestätigung, *die*

Attic [ˈætɪk] **1.** *adj.* attisch; **~ dialect** attischer Dialekt; **~ salt** *or* **wit** attisches Salz; attischer Witz. **2.** *n.* attischer Dialekt

attic *n.* **a)** *(storey)* Dachgeschoß, *das;* oberstes Stockwerk; **b)** *(room)* Dachboden, *der; (habitable)* Dachkammer, *die;* Mansarde, *die*

attire [əˈtaɪə(r)] **1.** *n., no pl.* Kleidung, *die.* **2.** *v. t.* kleiden; **be ~d in sth.** in etw. *(Akk.)* gekleidet sein; **~ oneself** sich kleiden

attitude [ˈætɪtju:d] *n.* **a)** *(posture, way of behaving)* Haltung, *die;* **in a defensive/threatening ~:** in abwehrender/drohender Haltung; **strike an ~:** eine Haltung einnehmen; **b)** *(mode of thinking)* **~ [of mind]** Einstellung, *die* (**to[wards]** zu); **c)** *(Aeron.)* Fluglage, *die*

attitudinize [ætɪˈtju:dɪnaɪz] *v. i.* sich in Szene setzen

attn. *abbr.* **for the attention of** z. H[d].

attorney [əˈtɜ:nɪ] *n.* **a)** *(legal agent)* Bevollmächtigte, *der/die;* **power of ~:** Vollmacht, *die;* **b)** *(Amer.: lawyer)* [Rechts]anwalt, *der/*[Rechts]anwältin, *die; see also* **district attorney**

Attorney-ˈGeneral *n., pl.* **Attorneys-General** *oberster Justizbeamter bestimmter Staaten;* ≈ Generalbundesanwalt, *der (Bundesrepublik Deutschland); (in USA)* ≈ Justizminister, *der*

attract [əˈtrækt] *v. t.* **a)** *(draw)* anziehen; auf sich *(Akk.)* ziehen ⟨*Interesse, Blick, Kritik*⟩; ⟨*Köder, Attraktion:*⟩ anlocken; **the party launched a publicity campaign to ~ new members** die Partei startete eine Werbekampagne, um neue Mitglieder zu gewinnen; **b)** *(arouse pleasure in)* anziehend wirken auf (+ *Akk.*); **what ~s me about the girl** was ich an dem Mädchen anziehend finde; **c)** *(arouse interest in)* reizen (**about** an + *Dat.*); **I am ~ed by that idea** der Gedanke reizt mich

attractant [əˈtræktənt] *n.* Lockmittel, *das*

attraction [əˈtrækʃn] *n.* **a)** Anziehung, *die; (force, lit. or fig.)* Anziehung[skraft], *die;* **I cannot see the ~ of going to horror films** ich kann nichts Besonderes daran finden, in Gruselfilme zu gehen; **the possibility of promotion has little ~ for me** die Möglichkeit, befördert zu werden, reizt mich nur wenig; **b)** *(fig.: thing that attracts)* Attraktion, *die; (charm)* Verlockung, *die;* Reiz, *der;* **c)** *(Ling.)* Attraktion, *die*

attractive [əˈtræktɪv] *adj.* **a)** anziehend; **~ power/force** Anziehungskraft, *die;* **b)** *(fig.)* attraktiv; reizvoll ⟨*Vorschlag, Möglichkeit, Idee*⟩

attractively [əˈtræktɪvlɪ] *adv.* reizvoll

attractiveness [əˈtræktɪvnɪs] *n., no pl.* Attraktivität, *die*

attributable [əˈtrɪbjʊtəbl] *adj.* **be ~ to sb./sth.** jmdm./einer Sache zuzuschreiben sein; **this comment is not ~:** dieser Kommentar muß anonym bleiben

attribute 1. [ˈætrɪbju:t] *n.* **a)** *(quality)* Attribut, *das;* Eigenschaft, *die;* **punctuality is not one of her ~s** Pünktlichkeit ist nicht gerade eine ihrer Stärken; **b)** *(symbolic object)* Attribut, *das;* **c)** *(Ling.)* Attribut, *das.* **2.** [əˈtrɪbju:t] *v. t. (ascribe, assign)* zuschreiben (**to** *Dat.*); *(refer)* zurückführen (**to** auf + *Akk.*)

attribution [ætrɪˈbju:ʃn] *n. (ascribing, assigning)* Zuordnung, *die* (**to** *Dat.*); *(referring)* Zurückführung, *die* (**to** auf + *Akk.*)

attributive [əˈtrɪbjʊtɪv] *adj.*, **attributively** [əˈtrɪbjʊtɪvlɪ] *adv. (Ling.)* attributiv

attrition [əˈtrɪʃn] *n., no pl.* **a)** *(wearing down)* Zermürbung, *die;* **war of ~** *(lit. or fig.)* Zermürbungskrieg, *der;* **b)** *(friction, abrasion)* Abrieb, *der*

attune [əˈtju:n] *v. t.* **a)** *(bring into accord)* aufeinander abstimmen; **b)** *(fig.: make accustomed)* gewöhnen (**to** an + *Akk.*); **be ~d to sth.** auf etw. *(Akk.)* eingestellt sein

atypical [eɪˈtɪpɪkl, əˈtɪpɪkl] *adj.* atypisch; untypisch

aubergine [ˈəʊbəʒi:n] *n.* Aubergine, *die*

aubrietia [ɔ:ˈbri:ʃə] *n. (Bot.)* Blaukissen, *das;* Aubrietie, *die (fachspr.)*

auburn [ˈɔ:bən] *adj.* rötlichbraun

auction [ˈɔ:kʃn] **1.** *n.* **a)** Auktion, *die;* Versteigerung, *die;* **sell sth. by ~:** etw. durch Versteigerung verkaufen; **be put up for ~:** zur Versteigerung kommen; versteigert werden; **Dutch ~:** Abschlag, *der;* **b)** *(Cards)* Bieten, *das.* **2.** *v. t.* versteigern

auctioneer [ɔ:kʃəˈnɪə(r)] *n.* Auktionator, *der/*Auktionatorin, *die*

audacious [ɔ:ˈdeɪʃəs] *adj. (daring)* kühn; verwegen; *(impudent)* dreist

audaciously [ɔ:ˈdeɪʃəslɪ] *adv. (daringly)* kühn; *(impudently)* dreist

audacity [ɔ:ˈdæsɪtɪ] *n., no pl.* **a)** *(daringness)* Kühnheit, *die;* Verwegenheit, *die;* **b)** *(impudence)* Dreistigkeit, *die*

audibility [ɔ:dɪˈbɪlɪtɪ] *n.* Hörbarkeit, *die*

audible [ˈɔ:dɪbl] *adj.* hörbar; **every word was ~ through the wall** man konnte jedes Wort durch die Wand hören; **the child's voice was scarcely ~:** die Stimme des Kindes war kaum zu hören

audibly [ˈɔ:dɪblɪ] *adv.* hörbar; **whisper sth. quite ~:** etw. recht vernehmlich flüstern

audience [ˈɔ:dɪəns] *n.* **a)** *(listeners, spectators)* Publikum, *das;* **cinema/concert ~s have increased** die Zahl der Kino-/Konzertbesucher hat zugenommen; **b)** *(formal interview)* Audienz, *die* (**with** bei); **private ~:** Privataudienz, *die;* **c)** *(readers)* Publikum, *das;* Leserkreis, *der*

audio [ˈɔ:dɪəʊ] *adj.* Ton-; **~ frequency** Tonfrequenz, *die;* **~ range** Hörbereich, *der;* **~ equipment** Phonoausstattung, *die*

audio: ~ engineer *n.* Toningenieur, *der/*-ingenieurin, *die;* **~ typist** *n.* Phonotypist, *der/*-typistin, *die;* **~-ˈvisual** *adj.* audiovisuell *(fachspr.)*

audit [ˈɔ:dɪt] **1.** *n.* **~ [of the accounts]** Rechnungsprüfung, *die (Wirtsch.);* **the ~ of the firm's books** die Revision der Firmengeschäftsbücher. **2.** *v. t.* **a)** prüfen; **b)** *(Amer.: attend)* als Gasthörer belegen

audition [ɔ:ˈdɪʃn] **1.** *n. (singing)* Probesingen, *das; (dancing)* Vortanzen, *das; (acting)* Vorsprechen, *das;* **~s are being held today** heute ist Probesingen/Vortanzen/Vorsprechen. **2.** *v. i. (sing)* vorsingen; probesingen; *(dance)* vortanzen; *(act)* vorsprechen; **~ for a part** für eine Rolle vorsprechen. **3.** *v. t.* vorsingen/vortanzen/vorsprechen lassen

auditor [ˈɔ:dɪtə(r)] *n.* Buchprüfer, *der/*-prüferin, *die;* Rechnungsprüfer, *der/*-prüferin, *die*

auditorium [ɔ:dɪˈtɔ:rɪəm] *n., pl.* **~s** *or* **auditoria** [ɔ:dɪˈtɔ:rɪə] Zuschauerraum, *der*

auditory [ˈɔ:dɪtərɪ] *adj.* **a)** *(concerned with hearing)* Gehör-; auditiv *(Med.);* **b)** *(received by the ear)* akustisch; auditiv *(Med.)*

au fait [əʊ ˈfeɪ] *pred. adj.* vertraut (**with** mit); au fait *(geh.); (up to date)* auf dem laufenden

Aug. *abbr.* **August** Aug.

Augean [ɔ:ˈdʒɪ:ən] *adj.* überaus schmutzig; **~ stables** *(lit. or fig.)* Augiasstall, *der*

auger [ˈɔ:gə(r)] *n. (for wood)* Handbohrer, *der;* Stangenbohrer, *der (Technik); (for soil)* Erdbohrer, *der (Technik)*

[1]**aught** [ɔ:t] *n., no pl., no art. (arch./poet.)* [irgend] etwas

[2]**aught** *see* [2]**ought**

augment 1. [ɔ:gˈment] *v. t.* verstärken ⟨*Armee*⟩; verbessern ⟨*Einkommen*⟩; aufstocken ⟨*Fonds, finanzielle Mittel*⟩; **~ed interval** *(Mus.)* übermäßiges Intervall. **2.** *v. i.* zunehmen; ⟨*Reserven:*⟩ zunehmen, anwachsen; ⟨*Lärm:*⟩ zunehmen, anschwellen

augmentation [ɔ:gmənˈteɪʃn] *n., no pl.* **a)** *(enlargement)* Erweiterung, *die; (of funds, finances)* Aufstockung, *die; (growth)* Anstieg, *der;* Zunahme, *die;* **b)** *(Mus.)* Augmentation, *die*

au gratin *see* **gratin**

augur [ˈɔ:gə(r)] **1.** *n.* **a)** *(Roman Ant.)* Augur, *der;* **b)** *(soothsayer)* Augur, *der (geh.).* **2.** *v. t.* **a)** *(portend)* bedeuten; versprechen ⟨*Erfolg*⟩; **b)** *(foretell)* prophezeien (**of, for** *Dat.*). **3.** *v. i.* **~ well/ill for sth./sb.** ein gutes/schlechtes Zeichen für etw./jmdn. sein

augury [ˈɔ:gjʊrɪ] *n.* Vorzeichen, *das*

August [ˈɔ:gəst] *n.* August, *der;* **in ~:** im August; **last/next ~:** letzten/nächsten August; **the first of/on the first of ~** *or* **on ~ [the] first** der erste/am ersten August; **1st ~** *(as date on document)* 1. August; **every ~:** jeden August; jedes Jahr im August; **an ~ day** ein Augusttag; **from ~ to October** von August bis Oktober

august [ɔ:ˈgʌst] *adj.* **a)** *(venerable)* ehrwürdig; *(noble)* erlaucht; **b)** *(majestic)* großartig; eindrucksvoll

[1]**Augustine** [ɔ:ˈgʌstɪn] *pr. n.* Augustinus *(der)*

[2]**Augustine** *n.* Augustiner, *der*

Augustinian [ɔ:gʌˈstɪnɪən] **1.** *adj.* Augustinisch ⟨*Lehre*⟩; **~ monk** Augustinermönch, *der.* **2.** *n. (monk)* Augustiner, *der*

auk [ɔ:k] *n. (Ornith.)* Alk, *der*

auld [ɔ:ld] *adj. (Scot.) see* **old; for ~ lang syne** um der guten, alten Zeiten willen

au naturel [əʊ nætjəˈrel] *adv., pred. adj. (Gastr.)* nature; au naturel

aunt [ɑ:nt] *n.* Tante, *die;* **A~ Sally** *Wurfspiel [auf dem Jahrmarkt], bei dem mit Stöcken oder Bällen auf eine Holzfigur geworfen wird; (target doll)* ≈ Schießbudenfigur, *die; (fig.)* Zielscheibe, *die (fig.);* **my sainted ~!** du liebe Güte!

auntie, aunty [ˈɑ:ntɪ] *n. (coll.)* Tantchen, *das; (with name)* Tante, *die;* **do you love A~ Betty?** magst du die liebe Tante Betty?

au pair [əʊ ˈpeə(r)] **1.** *n.* Au-pair-Mädchen,

das. **2.** *adj.* ~ **girl** Au-pair-Mädchen, *das*
aura ['ɔ:rə] *n., pl.* ~e ['ɔ:ri:] *or* ~s **a)** *(atmosphere, Med.)* Aura, *die;* **have an ~ about one** von einer Aura umgeben sein; **an ~ of mystery** eine Aura des Geheimnisvollen; **b)** *(subtle emanation)* Aura, *die;* Fluidum, *das*
aural ['ɔ:rl] *adj.* akustisch; aural *(Med.)*; ~ **specialist** Ohrenarzt, *der*
aureola [ɔ:'ri:ələ], **aureole** ['ɔ:rɪəʊl] *n. (Art)* Aureole, *die; (around head)* Nimbus, *der*
au revoir [əʊ rə'vwɑ:(r)] **1.** *int.* auf Wiedersehen. **2.** *n.* **say one's ~s** auf Wiedersehen sagen
auricle ['ɔ:rɪkl] *n.* **a)** *(external ear)* Ohrmuschel, *die;* Auricula, *die (Med.)*; **b)** *(Anat.: of heart)* Atrium, *das (fachspr.)*; Vorhof, *der;* Herzohr, *das;* **c)** *(Bot.)* Blattöhrchen, *das;* Aurikel, *die*
auricular [ɔ:'rɪkjʊlə(r)] *adj.* **a)** *(of the ear)* Ohr-; aurikular *(Med.)*; *(by the ear)* akustisch; ~ **witness** Ohrenzeuge, *der;* ~ **confession** *(Relig.)* Ohrenbeichte, *die;* **b)** *(Anat.: of auricle of heart)* Vorhof-
auriferous [ɔ:'rɪfərəs] *adj. (Geol.)* goldhaltig
aurora [ɔ:'rɔ:rə] *n., pl.* ~s *or* ~e [ɔ:'rɔ:ri:] Polarlicht, *das;* ~ **borealis** [bɔ:rɪ'eɪlɪs] Nordlicht, *das;* ~ **australis** [ɔ:'streɪlɪs] Südlicht, *das*
auscultation [ɔ:skəl'teɪʃn] *n., no pl. (Med.)* Auskultation, *die (fachspr.)*; Abhorchen, *das*
auspice ['ɔ:spɪs] *n.* **a)** *in pl.* **under the ~s of sb./sth.** unter jmds./einer Sache Auspizien *(geh.) od.* Schirmherrschaft; **b)** *(sign)* Auspizium, *das (geh.)*; Vorzeichen, *das;* **under favourable ~s** unter günstigen Auspizien *(geh.) od.* Vorzeichen
auspicious [ɔ:'spɪʃəs] *adj.* **a)** *(favourable)* günstig; vielversprechend ⟨*Anfang*⟩; **b)** *(fortunate)* glückhaft *(geh.)*; glücklich
auspiciously [ɔ:'spɪʃəslɪ] *adv.* **a)** *(favourably)* vielversprechend; **b)** *(fortunately)* glücklich
Aussie ['ɒzɪ, 'ɒsɪ] *(coll.)* **1.** *adj.* australisch. **2.** *n.* **a)** Australier, *der*/Australierin, *die;* **b)** *(Australia)* Australien *(das)*
austere [ɒ'stɪə(r), ɔ:'stɪə(r)] *adj.* **a)** *(morally strict, stern)* streng; unbeugsam ⟨*Haltung*⟩; **b)** *(severely simple)* karg; **c)** *(ascetic)* asketisch ⟨*Leben*⟩
austerely [ɒ'stɪəlɪ, ɔ:'stɪəlɪ] *adv.* **a)** *(morally, strictly, sternly)* streng; **b)** *(severely simply)* karg; ~ **simple** karg und schlicht; **c)** *(ascetically)* asketisch ⟨*leben*⟩
austereness [ɒ'stɪənɪs, ɔ:'stɪənɪs] *see* **austerity a, b**
austerity [ɒ'sterɪtɪ, ɔ:'sterɪtɪ] *n.* **a)** *no pl. (moral strictness)* Strenge, *die;* **b)** *no pl. (severe simplicity)* Kargheit, *die;* **c)** *no pl. (lack of luxuries)* wirtschaftliche Einschränkung; Austerity, *die (Wirtsch.)*; **d)** *in pl. (deprivations)* Entbehrungen; *(for religious reasons)* Entsagungen
Australasia [ɒstrə'leɪʃə, ɔ:strə'leɪʃə] *pr. n.* Australien und der südwestliche Pazifik
Australasian [ɒstrə'leɪʃn, ɔ:strə'leɪʃn] *adj.* ~ **peoples/cultures** Völker/Kulturen Australiens und des südwestlichen Pazifiks; ~ **region** australische Region *(Zool.)*
Australia [ɒ'streɪlɪə, ɔ:'streɪlɪə] *pr. n.* Australien *(das)*
Australian [ɒ'streɪlɪən, ɔ:'streɪlɪən] **1.** *adj.* australisch; ~ **bear** Beutelbär, *der;* Koala, *der;* **sb. is ~:** jmd. ist Australier/Australierin; ~ **[National] Rules football** *australische Art des Football.* **2.** *n.* Australier, *der*/Australierin, *die*
Austria ['ɒstrɪə, 'ɔ:strɪə] *pr. n.* Österreich *(das)*; **~-Hungary** *(Hist.)* Österreich-Ungarn *(das)*
Austrian ['ɒstrɪən, 'ɔ:strɪən] **1.** *adj.* österreichisch. **2.** *n.* Österreicher, *der*/Österreicherin, *die*
Austro-Hungarian [ɒstrəʊhʌŋ'geərɪən, ɔ:strəʊhʌŋ'geərɪən] *adj. (Hist.)* österreichisch-ungarisch
autarchic [ɔ:'tɑ:kɪk], **autarchical** [ɔ:'tɑ:kɪkl] *adj.* **a)** *(sovereign)* unabhängig; selbständig; **b)** *(despotic)* despotisch
autarchy ['ɔ:tɑ:kɪ] *n., no pl.* Autarchie, *die (veralt.)*; *(of state, region)* Unabhängigkeit, *die;* Selbständigkeit, *die; (of ruler, government, regime)* unumschränkte Herrschaft
autarky ['ɔ:tɑ:kɪ] *n., no pl.* Autarkie, *die*
authentic [ɔ:'θentɪk] *adj. (reliable; also Mus.)* authentisch; *(genuine)* authentisch; echt; berechtigt ⟨*Anspruch*⟩; unverfälscht ⟨*Akzent*⟩
authentically [ɔ:'θentɪkəlɪ] *adv. (genuinely)* **his accent was ~ upper-class** er sprach im unverfälschten Tonfall der Oberschicht
authenticate [ɔ:'θentɪkeɪt] *v.t.* authentifizieren; ~ **sth.** die Echtheit einer Sache *(Gen.)* bestätigen; ~ **information/a report** eine Information/einen Bericht bestätigen; **I succeeded in authenticating my claim** es gelang mir, meinen Anspruch zu beweisen
authentication [ɔ:θentɪ'keɪʃn] *n., no pl.* Bestätigung der Echtheit; *(of information, report)* Bestätigung, *die*
authenticity [ɔ:θen'tɪsɪtɪ] *n., no pl.* Echtheit, *die;* Authentizität, *die; (of claim)* Berechtigung, *die; (of information, report)* Zuverlässigkeit, *die*
author ['ɔ:θə(r)] **1.** *n.* **a)** *(writer)* Autor, *der*/Autorin, *die; (profession)* Schriftsteller, *der*/Schriftstellerin, *die;* **the ~ of the book/article** der Autor *od.* Verfasser des Buches/Artikels; **the ~s of the 19th century** die Autoren *od.* Schriftsteller des 19. Jahrhunderts; **b)** *(originator)* Vater, *der.* **2.** *v.t. (write)* verfassen
authoress ['ɔ:θərɪs] *n.* Autorin, *die*
authorisation, authorise *see* **authoriz-**
authoritarian [ɔ:θɒrɪ'teərɪən] **1.** *adj.* autoritär. **2.** *n.* autoritäre Person; **be an ~:** autoritär sein
authoritarianism [ɔ:θɒrɪ'teərɪənɪzm] *n., no pl.* Autoritarismus, *der (Psych.)*; autoritäre Einstellung
authoritative [ɔ:'θɒrɪtətɪv] *adj.* **a)** *(recognized as reliable)* autoritativ; maßgebend; zuverlässig ⟨*Bericht, Information*⟩; *(official)* amtlich; **b)** *(commanding)* respekteinflößend
authoritatively [ɔ:'θɒrɪtətɪvlɪ] *adv.* **a)** *(reliably)* zuverlässig ⟨*berichten*⟩; *(officially)* offiziell; **he talked ~ about his specialist field** er sprach als Fachmann über sein Spezialgebiet; **b)** *(commandingly)* mit Bestimmtheit
authoritativeness [ɔ:'θɒrɪtətɪvnɪs] *n., no pl.* **a)** *(reliability)* Zuverlässigkeit, *die; (official nature)* amtlicher Charakter; **b)** *(commanding quality)* Bestimmtheit, *die; (of person)* entschiedenes Auftreten; **the ~ of his manner** seine respekteinflößende Art
authority [ɔ:'θɒrɪtɪ] *n.* **a)** *no pl. (power)* Autorität, *die; (delegated power)* Befugnis, *die;* **have the/no ~ to do sth.** berechtigt *od.* befugt/nicht befugt sein, etw. zu tun; **you have my ~:** Sie haben meine Zustimmung; **have/exercise ~ over sb.** Weisungsbefugnis gegenüber jmdm. haben; **on one's own ~:** in eigener Verantwortung; **[be] in ~:** verantwortlich [sein]; **be under sb.'s ~:** jmdm. [gegenüber] verantwortlich sein; **those in ~:** die Verantwortlichen; **b)** *(person having power)* Autorität, *die; (body having power)* **the authorities** die Behörde[n]; **the highest legal ~:** die höchste rechtliche Instanz; **c)** *(expert, book, quotation)* Autorität, *die; (evidence)* Quelle, *die;* **what is your ~ for your assertion?** worauf stützt du deine Behauptung?; **on the ~ of Darwin** nach Darwin; **have it on the ~ of sb./sth. that ...:** durch jmdn./etw. wissen, daß ...; **have it on good ~ that ...:** aus zuverlässiger Quelle wissen, daß ...; **d)** *no pl. (weight of testimony)* Autorität, *die;* **give** *or* **add ~ to sth.** einer Sache *(Dat.)* Gewicht verleihen; **e)** *no pl. (power to influence)* Autorität, *die;* **f)** *no pl. (masterfulness)* Souveränität, *die*
authorization [ɔ:θəraɪ'zeɪʃn] *n.* Genehmigung, *die;* Autorisation, *die;* **obtain/give ~:** die Genehmigung einholen/erteilen
authorize ['ɔ:θəraɪz] *v.t.* **a)** *(give authority to)* ermächtigen; bevollmächtigen; autorisieren; ~ **sb. to do sth.** jmdn. ermächtigen, etw. zu tun; **entry is permitted only to ~d personnel** Unbefugten ist der Zutritt verboten; **b)** *(sanction)* genehmigen; ~ **sth.** etw. genehmigen; einer Sache *(Dat.)* zustimmen; **the A~d Version** *engl. Fassung der Bibel von 1611*
authorship ['ɔ:θəʃɪp] *n., no pl.* **a)** *no art. (occupation)* Schriftstellerei, *die;* **b)** *(origin)* Autorschaft, *die;* **of unknown ~:** von einem unbekannten Autor *od.* Verfasser
autistic [ɔ:'tɪstɪk] *adj. (Psych., Med.)* autistisch
auto ['ɔ:təʊ] *n., pl.* ~s *(Amer. coll.)* Auto, *das*
auto- [ɔ:təʊ] *in comb.* auto-/Auto-
autobahn ['ɔ:təbɑ:n] *n., pl.* ~s *or* ~en ['ɔ:təbɑ:nən] [deutsche] Autobahn
autobi'ographer *n.* Autobiograph, *der*/Autobiographin, *die*
autobio'graphic, autobio'graphical *adj.* autobiographisch
autobi'ography *n.* Autobiographie, *die*
autocade ['ɔ:təʊkeɪd] *(Amer.) see* **motorcade**
autoclave ['ɔ:təkleɪv] *n.* Autoklav, *der*
autocracy [ɔ:'tɒkrəsɪ] *n.* Autokratie, *die*
autocrat ['ɔ:təkræt] *n.* Autokrat, *der*
autocratic [ɔ:tə'krætɪk] *adj.* autokratisch
'autocross *n., no pl.* Auto-Cross, *das*
Autocue, (P) ['ɔ:təʊkju:] *n.* Teleprompter ®, *der*
autogenous [ɔ:'tɒdʒɪnəs] *adj. (Med., Industry)* autogen; ~ **welding** autogene Schweißung; Autogenschweißen, *das*
'autogiro *n., pl.* ~s Autogiro, *das*
autograph ['ɔ:təgrɑ:f] **1.** *n.* **a)** *(signature)* Autogramm, *das;* **b)** *(manuscript)* Autograph, *das; (signed document)* **the original ~:** das Original. **2.** *v.t.* **a)** *(sign)* signieren; **b)** *(write with one's own hand)* mit eigener Hand schreiben
autogyro *see* **autogiro**
auto-im'mune *adj. (Med.)* autoimmun; ~ **response** Autoimmunantwort, *die*
automat ['ɔ:təmæt] *n. (Amer.)* **a)** *(slot-machine)* [Münz]automat, *der;* **b)** *(cafeteria)* Automatenrestaurant, *das*
automate ['ɔ:təmeɪt] *v.t.* automatisieren
automatic [ɔ:tə'mætɪk] **1.** *adj.* automatisch; ~ **weapons** automatische Waffen; Schnellfeuerwaffen; ~ **writing** automatisches Schreiben; ~ **gear system,** ~ **transmission** Automatikgetriebe, *das;* **his reaction was completely ~:** er reagierte ganz automatisch; **disqualification is ~ after two false starts** die Disqualifikation erfolgt automatisch nach zwei Fehlstarts; ~ **pilot** *see* **autopilot. 2.** *n. (weapon)* automatische Waffe; *(vehicle)* Fahrzeug mit Automatikgetriebe; *(tool, apparatus)* Automat, *der*
automatically [ɔ:tə'mætɪkəlɪ] *adv.* automatisch
automation [ɔ:tə'meɪʃn] *n., no pl.* Automation, *die; (automatic control)* Automatisierung, *die;* automatische Steuerung
automatism [ɔ:'tɒmətɪzm] *n., no pl. (Biol., Med., Psych.)* Automatismus, *der*
automaton [ɔ:'tɒmətən] *n., pl.* ~s *or* **automata** [ɔ:'tɒmətə] Automat, *der*
automobile ['ɔ:təməbi:l] *n. (Amer.)* Auto, *das*
automotive [ɔ:tə'məʊtɪv] *adj.* Kraftfahrzeug-; ~ **industry** Auto[mobil]industrie, *die;* ~ **workers** Arbeiter in der Auto[mobil]industrie; ~ **products** Erzeugnisse der Auto[mobil]industrie

autonomic [ɔ:tə'nɒmɪk] *adj.* **a)** *(Physiol.)* autonom; unbedingt ‹*Reflex*›; **b)** *see* **autonomous**

autonomous [ɔ:'tɒnəməs] *adj.* *(also Philos.)* autonom

autonomy [ɔ:'tɒnəmɪ] *n.*, *no pl.* *(also Philos.)* Autonomie, *die;* ~ **of action** autonomes Handeln

'**autopilot** *n.* Autopilot, *der;* **[fly] on** ~: mit Autopilot [fliegen]

autopsy ['ɔ:tɒpsɪ, ɔ:'tɒpsɪ] *n.* **a)** *(post-mortem)* Autopsie, *die;* Obduktion, *die;* *(fig.)* Manöverkritik, *die;* **b)** *(personal inspection)* Prüfung durch persönliche Inaugenscheinnahme; Autopsie, *die (fachspr.)*

'**autotimer** *n.* [automatische] Schaltuhr

autumn ['ɔ:təm] *n.* *(lit. or fig.)* Herbst, *der;* **in ~ 1969, in the ~ of 1969** im Herbst 1969; **in early/late** ~: im Frühherbst/Spätherbst; **last/next** ~: letzten/nächsten Herbst; ~ **is a beautiful time of the year** der Herbst ist eine schöne Jahreszeit; ~ **weather/fashions** Herbstwetter, *das*/Herbstmoden

autumnal [ɔ:'tʌmnl] *adj.* *(lit. or fig.)* herbstlich; *(blooming or maturing in autumn)* Herbst-; ~ **flower** Herbstblume, *die*

autumn 'crocus *n.* Herbstzeitlose, *die*

auxiliary [ɔ:g'zɪljərɪ] **1.** *adj.* **a)** *(helping)* Hilfs-; auxiliar *(fachspr.);* **be ~ to sth.** etw. unterstützen *od.* fördern; ~ **troops** Hilfstruppen; **b)** *(subsidiary)* zusätzlich; Zusatz-; **c)** *(Ling.)* ~ **verb** Hilfsverb, *das.* **2.** *n.* **a)** Hilfskraft, *die;* **medical** ~: ärztliches Hilfspersonal; **b)** *in pl. (Mil.)* Hilfstruppen; **c)** *(Ling.)* Hilfsverb, *das*

AV *abbr.* **Authorized Version;** *see* **authorized b**

avail [ə'veɪl] **1.** *n.*, *no pl.*, *no art.* Nutzen, *der;* **be of no** ~: nichts nützen; nutzlos *od.* vergeblich sein; **to no** ~: vergebens; **of what ~ is it ...?** was nützt es ...? **2.** *v. i.* **a)** *(be of profit)* etwas nützen *od.* fruchten; **it will not** ~: es wird nichts nützen *od.* fruchten; **b)** *(afford help)* helfen. **3.** *v. t.* nützen; **it will ~ you nothing** es wird dir nichts nützen. **4.** *v. refl.* ~ **oneself of sth.** von etw. Gebrauch machen; ~ **oneself of an opportunity** eine Gelegenheit nutzen

availability [əveɪlə'bɪlɪtɪ] *n.*, *no pl.* Vorhandensein, *das;* **the ~ of sth.** die Möglichkeit, etw. zu bekommen; **I'll find out about the ~ of tickets** ich werde mich erkundigen, ob Karten zu bekommen sind; **the likely ~ of spare parts** die voraussichtliche Lieferbarkeit von Ersatzteilen; **the ~ of accommodation** das Zimmer-/Wohnungsangebot

available [ə'veɪləbl] *adj.* **a)** *(at one's disposal)* verfügbar; **make sth. ~ to sb.** jmdm. etw. zur Verfügung stellen; **be** ~: zur Verfügung stehen; **b)** *(capable of use)* gültig ‹*Fahrkarte, Angebot*›; **c)** *(obtainable)* erhältlich; lieferbar ‹*Waren*›; verfügbar ‹*Unterkunft, Daten*›; **have sth.** ~: etw. zur Verfügung haben; **nobody was ~ for comment** niemand stellte sich für einen Kommentar zur Verfügung

avalanche ['ævəlɑ:nʃ] **1.** *n.* *(lit. or fig.)* Lawine, *die.* **2.** *v. i.* **mud ~d down** eine Lawine von Schlamm stürzte herab

avant-garde [ævɑ̃'gɑ:d] **1.** *adj.* avantgardistisch. **2.** *n.* Avantgarde, *die*

avarice ['ævərɪs] *n.*, *no pl.* Geldgier, *die;* Habsucht, *die;* ~ **for sth.** *(fig.)* Gier nach etw.

avaricious [ævə'rɪʃəs] *adj.* geldgierig; habsüchtig; *(fig.)* gierig **(for** nach); ~ **for power** machtgierig

Ave. *abbr.* **Avenue**

Ave [Maria] ['ɑ:veɪ (mə'ri:ə)] *n.* Ave[-Maria], *das*

avenge [ə'vendʒ] *v. t.* rächen; **be ~d/~ oneself on sb.** sich an jmdm. rächen; **be ~d for sth.** sich für etw. rächen

avenger [ə'vendʒə(r)] *n.* Rächer, *der*/Rächerin, *die (geh.)*

avenue ['ævənju:] *n.* *(broad street)* Avenue, *die;* Boulevard, *der;* *(tree-lined road; Brit.: approach to country house)* Allee, *die;* *(fig.)* Weg, *der* **(to** zu); ~ **of approach** Zugang, *der;* **all ~s of escape were closed** jeder Ausweg war versperrt; *see also* **explore b**

aver [ə'vɜ:(r)] *v. t.*, **-rr-:** beteuern; **what one expert ~s, another denies** was der eine Fachmann mit Nachdruck bestätigt, das bestreitet der andere

average ['ævərɪdʒ] **1.** *n.* **a)** Durchschnitt, *der;* **the ~ is about ...:** der Durchschnitt liegt bei [ungefähr] ...; **on [the *or* an]** ~: im Durchschnitt; durchschnittlich; im Schnitt *(ugs.);* **above/below** ~: über/unter dem Durchschnitt; **law of ~s** Wahrscheinlichkeitsgesetz, *das;* **b)** *(arithmetic mean)* Mittelwert, *der;* **batting** ~ *(Baseball, Cricket)* Durchschnittsleistung als Schlagmann; **bowling** ~ *(Cricket)* Durchschnittsleistung als Werfer; **c)** *(Insurance)* Havarie, *die;* ~ **adjustment** Dispache, *die.* **2.** *adj.* **a)** durchschnittlich; ~ **speed** durchschnittliche Geschwindigkeit; Durchschnittsgeschwindigkeit, *die;* **he is of ~ height** er ist mittelgroß; **b)** *(mediocre)* durchschnittlich; mittelmäßig. **3.** *v. t.* **a)** *(find the ~ of)* den Durchschnitt ermitteln von; **b)** *(amount on ~ to)* durchschnittlich betragen; **the planks ~d three metres in length** die Bretter waren durchschnittlich drei Meter lang; **these things ~ themselves out** so etwas gleicht sich aus; **c)** *(do on ~)* einen Durchschnitt von ... erreichen; **she ~s four novels a year** sie schreibt durchschnittlich vier Romane im Jahr; **the train ~d 90 m.p.h.** der Zug fuhr im Durchschnitt mit 144 Kilometern pro Stunde. **4.** *v. i.* ~ **out at** im Durchschnitt betragen

averagely ['ævərɪdʒlɪ] *adv.* durchschnittlich

averse [ə'vɜ:s] *pred. adj.* **be ~ to *or* from sth.** einer Sache *(Dat.)* abgeneigt sein; **be ~ to *or* from doing sth.** abgeneigt sein, etw. zu tun

aversion [ə'vɜ:ʃn] *n.* **a)** *no pl. (dislike)* Abneigung, *die;* Aversion, *die;* **have/take an ~ to *or* from sth.** eine Abneigung *od.* Aversion gegen etw. haben/bekommen; ~ **therapy** *(Psych.)* Aversionstherapie, *die;* **b)** *(object)* **be sb.'s** ~: jmdm. ein Greuel sein; **my pet ~ is ...:** ein besonderer Greuel ist mir ...

avert [ə'vɜ:t] *v. t.* **a)** *(turn away)* abwenden ‹*Blick, Gesicht, Aufmerksamkeit*›; **b)** *(prevent)* abwenden ‹*Katastrophe, Schaden, Niederlage*›; verhüten ‹*Unfall*›; verhindern ‹*Fehlschlag*›

aviary ['eɪvɪərɪ] *n.* Vogelhaus, *das;* Aviarium, *das*

aviation [eɪvɪ'eɪʃn] *n.*, *no pl.*, *no art.* **a)** *(operating of aircraft)* Luftfahrt, *die;* ~ **fuel** Flugbenzin, *das;* **b)** *(aircraft manufacture)* Flugzeugbau, *der;* ~ **industry** Flugzeugindustrie, *die;* Luftfahrtindustrie, *die*

aviator ['eɪvɪeɪtə(r)] *n.* Flieger, *der*/Fliegerin, *die*

avid ['ævɪd] *adj.* *(enthusiastic)* begeistert; passioniert; **be ~ for sth.** *(eager, greedy)* begierig auf etw. *(Akk.)* sein

avidity [ə'vɪdɪtɪ] *n.*, *no pl.* *(enthusiasm)* Begeisterung, *die;* *(greed)* Begierde, *die*

avidly ['ævɪdlɪ] *adv.* *(enthusiastically)* eifrig; begeistert ‹*annehmen*›; *(greedily)* begierig

avionics [eɪvɪ'ɒnɪks] *n.* **a)** *no pl.* Bordelektronik, *die;* Avionik, *die;* **b)** *constr. as pl.* *(systems)* Bordelektr[on]ik, *die;* Avionik, *die*

avocado [ævə'kɑ:dəʊ] *n.*, *pl.* **~s:** ~ **[pear]** Avocado[birne], *die;* *(tree)* Avocado, *die*

avocation [ævə'keɪʃn] *n.* *(minor occupation)* Nebenbeschäftigung, *die;* *(coll.: vocation)* Beruf, *der*

avocet ['ævəset] *n.* *(Ornith.)* Säbelschnäbler, *der*

avoid [ə'vɔɪd] *v. t.* **a)** *(keep away from)* meiden ‹*Ort*›; ~ **an obstacle/a cyclist** einem Hindernis/Radfahrer ausweichen; ~ **the boss when he's in a temper** geh dem Chef aus dem Weg, wenn er schlechte Laune hat; **b)** *(refrain from)* vermeiden; ~ **doing sth.** vermeiden, etw. zu tun; **you can hardly ~ seeing her** du wirst kaum umhinkönnen, sie zu sehen; **c)** *(escape)* vermeiden; **they wore masks to ~ recognition** sie trugen Masken, um nicht erkannt zu werden; **d)** *(Law)* annullieren

avoidable [ə'vɔɪdəbl] *adj.* vermeidbar; **if it is [at all]** ~: wenn es sich [irgend] vermeiden läßt

avoidance [ə'vɔɪdəns] *n.*, *no pl.* Vermeidung, *die;* **the ~ of accidents** das Vermeiden von Unfällen; die Unfallverhütung; ~ **of death duties** Umgehung der Erbschaftssteuer

avoirdupois [ævədjʊ'pɔɪz] **1.** *adj.* Avoirdupois-. **2.** *n.* **a)** Avoirdupois, *das;* **b)** *(joc.: bodily weight)* Gewicht, *das*

avow [ə'vaʊ] *v. t.* bekennen; ~ **oneself [to be] sth.** sich als etw. bekennen; **an ~ed opponent/supporter** ein erklärter Gegner/Befürworter

avowal [ə'vaʊəl] *n.* Bekenntnis, *das;* **on your own** ~: wie Sie selbst erklärt haben

avowedly [ə'vaʊɪdlɪ] *adv.* erklärtermaßen

avuncular [ə'vʌŋkjʊlə(r)] *adj.* onkelhaft

aw [ɔ:] *int. expr. remonstrance, commiseration* oh; *expr. disgust* bah; **~, bad luck!** so ein Pech!

AWACS ['eɪwæks] *abbr.* **Airborne Warning and Control Systems** AWACS

await [ə'weɪt] *v. t.* erwarten; **disaster ~s us if ...:** uns erwartet eine Katastrophe, wenn ...; **the long ~ed visit** der langersehnte Besuch

awake [ə'weɪk] **1.** *v. i.*, **awoke** [ə'wəʊk], **awoken** [ə'wəʊkn] *(lit. or fig.)* erwachen; **we awoke to the sound of rain on the windows** als wir erwachten, hörten wir den Regen gegen die Fenster prasseln; **one day I shall ~ to find myself a rich man** eines Tages werde ich aufwachen und ein reicher Mann sein; ~ **to sth.** einer Sache *(Gen.)* gewahr werden; **when she awoke to her surroundings** als sie gewahr wurde, wo sie sich befand. **2.** *v. t.*, **awoke, awoken** *(lit. or fig.)* wecken; ~ **sb. to sth.** *(fig.)* jmdm. etw. bewußtmachen; **be awoken to sth.** *(fig.)* einer Sache *(Gen.)* gewahr werden. **3.** *pred. adj.* *(lit. or fig.)* wach; **wide** ~: hellwach; **lie** ~: wach liegen; **be ~ to sth.** *(fig.)* sich *(Dat.)* einer Sache *(Gen.)* bewußt sein

awaken [ə'weɪkn] **1.** *v. t.* *(esp. fig.)* *see* **awake 2. 2.** *v. i.* *(esp. fig.)* *see* **awake 1**

awakening [ə'weɪknɪŋ] *n.* Erwachen, *das;* **a rude ~** *(fig.)* ein böses Erwachen

award [ə'wɔ:d] **1.** *v. t.* *(grant)* verleihen, zuerkennen ‹*Preis, Auszeichnung*›; zusprechen ‹*Sorgerecht, Entschädigung*›; gewähren ‹*Zahlung, Gehaltserhöhung*›; ~ **sb. sth.** jmdm. etw. verleihen/zusprechen/gewähren; **sb. is ~ed sth.** jmdm. wird etw. verliehen/zugesprochen/gewährt; **he was ~ed the prize** der Preis wurde ihm zuerkannt; **the referee ~ed a penalty [to Arsenal]** der Schiedsrichter erkannte auf Strafstoß [für Arsenal]. **2.** *n.* **a)** *(judicial decision)* Schiedsspruch, *der;* **b)** *(payment)* Entschädigung[ssumme], *die;* *(grant)* Stipendium, *das;* **make an ~ to sb.** jmdm. finanzielle Unterstützung gewähren; **c)** *(prize)* Auszeichnung, *die;* Preis, *der*

a'ward-winning *adj.* preisgekrönt

aware [ə'weə(r)] *adj.* **a)** *pred.* *(conscious)* **be ~ of sth.** sich *(Dat.)* einer Sache *(Gen.)* bewußt sein; **be ~ that ...:** sich *(Dat.)* [dessen] bewußt sein, daß ...; **what made you ~ that ...?** woran bemerkten Sie, daß ...?; **the patient was ~ of everything going on around him** der Patient bekam alles mit, was um ihn herum vorging; **as far as I am** ~: soweit ich weiß; **not that I am ~ of** nicht, daß ich wüßte; **b)** *(well-informed)* informiert

awareness [ə'weənɪs] *n., no pl. (consciousness)* Bewußtsein, *das*

awash [ə'wɒʃ] *pred. adj.* auf gleicher Höhe mit dem Wasserspiegel; **be ~** *(flooded)* unter Wasser stehen; *(fig.)* **be ~ with money** im Geld schwimmen

away [ə'weɪ] **1.** *adv.* **a)** *(at a distance)* entfernt; **~ in the distance** weit in der Ferne; **two feet ~ [from sth.]** zwei Fuß entfernt [von etw.]; **play ~** *(Sport)* auswärts spielen; **Christmas is still months ~:** bis Weihnachten dauert es noch Monate; **b)** *(to a distance)* weg; fort; **get ~ from it all** *see* **all 1 a; ~ with you/him!** weg *od.* fort mit dir/ihm!; **throw sth. ~:** etw. wegwerfen *od.* fortwerfen; **~ we go!** los geht's!; **c)** *(absent)* nicht da; **be ~ on business** geschäftlich außer Haus sein; **be ~ [from school] with a cold** wegen einer Erkältung [in der Schule] fehlen; **he's ~ in France/on holiday** er ist zur Zeit in Frankreich/im Urlaub; **d)** *(towards or into non-existence)* **die/fade ~:** verhallen; **gamble one's money ~:** sein Geld verspielen; **drink the evening ~:** den Abend mit Trinken verbringen; **the water has all boiled ~:** das ganze Wasser ist verkocht; **idle one's time ~:** seine Zeit vertrödeln; **e)** *(constantly)* unablässig; **work ~ on sth.** ohne Unterbrechung an etw. *(Dat.)* arbeiten; **laugh ~ at sth.** unablässig über etw. *(Akk.)* lachen; **they were singing ~:** sie sangen aus voller Kehle; **f)** *(without delay)* gleich ⟨*fragen usw.*⟩; **fire ~** *(lit. or fig.)* losschießen *(ugs.)*. **2.** *adj. (Sport)* auswärts *präd.;* Auswärts-; **the next match is ~:** das nächste Spiel ist auswärts; **~ match** Auswärtsspiel, *das;* **~ team** Gastmannschaft, *die*

awe [ɔ:] **1.** *n.* Ehrfurcht, *die* **(of** vor + *Dat.)*; **be** *or* **stand in ~ of sb.** jmdn. fürchten; *(feel respect)* Ehrfurcht vor jmdm. haben; **hold sb. in ~:** jmdn. ehrfürchtig respektieren. **2.** *v.t.* Ehrfurcht einflößen (+ *Dat.*); **be ~d by sth.** sich von etw. beeindrucken *od.* einschüchtern lassen; **be ~d into silence** beeindruckt *od.* eingeschüchtert schweigen; **in an ~d voice** mit ehrfurchtsvoller Stimme

aweigh [ə'weɪ] *pred. adj. (Naut.)* aus dem Grund

'awe-inspiring *adj.* ehrfurchtgebietend; beeindruckend

awesome ['ɔ:səm] *adj.* überwältigend; eindrucksvoll ⟨*Schweigen*⟩; übergroß ⟨*Verantwortung*⟩

awe: ~-stricken, ~-struck *adj.* [von Ehrfurcht] ergriffen; ehrfurchtsvoll ⟨*Ausdruck, Staunen*⟩

awful ['ɔ:fl] *adj.* **a)** furchtbar; fürchterlich; **too ~ for words** *(coll.)* unbeschreiblich schlecht; **be an ~ lot better/worse** *(coll.)* ein ganzes Stück besser/schlechter sein; **not an ~ lot better/worse** *(coll.)* nicht gerade viel besser/schlechter; **an ~ lot of money/people** *(coll.)* ein Haufen Geld/Leute *(ugs.);* **an ~ long time/way** *(coll.)* eine furchtbar lange Zeit/ein furchtbar weiter Weg; **b)** *(commanding reverence)* ehrfurchtgebietend; *(solemnly impressive)* eindrucksvoll; **~ silence** feierliche Stille

awfully ['ɔ:fəlɪ, 'ɔ:flɪ] *adv.* furchtbar; **not ~** *(coll.)* nicht besonders; **thanks ~** *(coll.)* tausend Dank

awfulness ['ɔ:flnɪs] *n., no pl.* **a)** *(terribleness)* Furchtbarkeit, *die;* **b)** *(impressive solemnity)* [eindrucksvolle *od.* ehrfurchtgebietende] Feierlichkeit

awhile [ə'waɪl] *adv.* eine Weile; **not yet ~:** so bald nicht

awkward ['ɔ:kwəd] *adj.* **a)** *(ill-adapted for use)* ungünstig; **be ~ to use** unhandlich sein; **the parcel is ~ to carry** das Paket ist schlecht zu tragen; **b)** *(clumsy)* unbeholfen; **be at an ~ age** in einem schwierigen Alter sein; **c)** *(embarrassing, embarrassed)* peinlich; **feel ~:** sich unbehaglich fühlen; **d)** *(difficult)* schwierig, unangenehm ⟨*Person*⟩; ungünstig ⟨*Zeitpunkt*⟩; schwierig, peinlich ⟨*Lage, Dilemma*⟩; *see also* **customer b**

awkwardly ['ɔ:kwədlɪ] *adv.* **a)** *(badly)* ungünstig ⟨*geformt, angebracht*⟩; **b)** *(clumsily)* ungeschickt, unbeholfen ⟨*gehen, sich ausdrücken*⟩; ungeschickt, unglücklich ⟨*fallen, sich ausdrücken*⟩; **c)** *(embarrassingly)* peinlicherweise; *(embarrassedly)* peinlich berührt; betreten; **d)** *(unfavourably)* ungünstig ⟨*gelegen*⟩

awkwardness ['ɔ:kwədnɪs] *n., no pl. see* **awkward: a)** Unhandlichkeit, *die;* **the ~ of the design puts me off** das ungünstige Design stößt mich ab; **b)** Unbeholfenheit, *die;* **c)** Peinlichkeit, *die;* **a moment of ~:** ein peinlicher Augenblick; **d)** *(of person)* unangenehmes Wesen; *(of situation, position)* Schwierigkeit, *die*

awl [ɔ:l] *n.* Ahle, *die;* Pfriem, *der*

awn [ɔ:n] *n.* Granne, *die*

awning ['ɔ:nɪŋ] *n. (on wagon)* Plane, *die; (on house)* Markise, *die; (of tent)* Vordach, *das; (on ship)* Sonnensegel, *das*

awoke, awoken *see* **awake**

AWOL ['eɪwɒl] *adj. (Mil.)* unerlaubt von der Truppe entfernt; **go ~:** sich unerlaubt von der Truppe entfernen

awry [ə'raɪ] **1.** *adv.* schief; **your coat has pulled your scarf [all] ~:** deine Jacke hat deinen Schal ganz verzogen; **go ~** *(fig.)* schiefgehen *(ugs.);* ⟨*Plan:*⟩ fehlschlagen. **2.** *pred. adj.* schief; unordentlich; **your tie is all ~:** deine Krawatte sitzt ganz schief; **our clothes were all ~:** unsere Kleidung war völlig in Unordnung; **now our plans are utterly ~** *(fig.)* nun sind unsere Pläne völlig fehlgeschlagen; **something must be seriously ~:** da muß doch etwas nicht in Ordnung sein

axe *(Amer.:* **ax)** [æks] **1.** *n.* **a)** Axt, *die;* Beil, *das;* **have an ~ to grind** *(fig.)* sein eigenes Süppchen kochen *(ugs.);* **b)** *(fig.: reduction)* **the ~:** radikale Kürzung; Rotstift, *der;* **on which sector will the ~ fall next?** welcher Sektor wird als nächster dem Rotstift zum Opfer fallen? *See also* **take 1 f. 2.** *v.t. (reduce)* [radikal] kürzen; *(eliminate)* [radikal] einsparen ⟨*Stellen*⟩; *(dismiss)* entlassen; *(abandon)* aufgeben ⟨*Projekt*⟩

axes *pl. of* **axe, axis**

axial ['æksɪəl] *adj.* axial; Achsen-; Axial-

axil ['æksɪl] *n. (Bot.)* Blattachsel, *die; (of tree)* Winkel zwischen Ast und Stamm

axiom ['æksɪəm] *n.* Axiom, *das*

axiomatic [æksɪə'mætɪk] *adj.* axiomatisch; **I have taken it as ~ that ...:** ich gehe von dem Grundsatz aus, daß ...

axis ['æksɪs] *n., pl.* **axes** ['æksi:z] **a)** Achse, *die;* **~ of rotation** Rotationsachse, *die;* **b)** *(Polit.)* Achse, *die;* **the A~** *(Hist.)* die Achse; **the A~ powers** *(Hist.)* die Achsenmächte; **c)** *(Bot.)* Sproßachse, *die;* **d)** *(Anat., Physiol.)* Axis, *der*

axle ['æksl] *n.* Achse, *die*

'axle grease *n.* Wagenschmiere, *die*

[1]ay [aɪ] **1.** *adv.* **a)** *(in voting; arch./dial.)* ja; **answer ay** mit ja antworten; **b)** *(Naut.)* **ay, ay, sir!** jawohl, Herr Kapitän!/Admiral! *etc.* **2.** *n., pl.* **ayes** [aɪz] *(answer)* Ja, *das; (vote)* Jastimme, *die;* **the ayes have it** die Mehrheit ist dafür

[2]ay *int.* **ay me!** *(arch./poet.)* oh jeh!

ayatollah [aɪə'tɒlə] *n.* Ajatollah, *der*

[1]aye *see* **[1]ay**

[2]aye [eɪ] *adv. (arch.: ever)* all[e]zeit *(veralt.);* **for ~:** auf ewig

azalea [ə'zeɪlɪə] *n. (Bot.)* Azalee, *die*

azimuth ['æzɪməθ] *n. (Astron.)* Azimut, *der*

Azores [ə'zɔ:z] *pr. n. pl.* Azoren *Pl.*

Aztec ['æztek] **1.** *adj.* aztekisch. **2.** *n.* **a)** *(person)* Azteke, *der*/Aztekin, *die;* **b)** *(language)* Aztekisch, *das*

azure ['æʒjə(r), 'eɪʒjə(r)] **1.** *n.* **a)** *(sky blue)* Azur[blau], *das;* **b)** *(Her.)* Blau, *das;* **c)** *(literary: unclouded sky)* Azur, *der.* **2.** *adj.* **a)** *(sky-blue)* azurblau; azurn; **b)** *(Her.)* blau

B

B, b [bi:] *n., pl.* **Bs** *or* **B's a)** *(letter)* B, b, *das;* **B road** Straße 2. Ordnung; ≈ Landstraße, *die;* **~ film** *or (Amer.)* **movie** Vorfilm, *der;* **b) B** *(Mus.)* H, h, *das;* **B flat** B, b, *das;* **c)** *(example)* B, b *(ohne Artikel);* **d) B** *(Sch., Univ.: mark)* Zwei, *die;* **he got a B** er bekam „gut" *od.* eine Zwei

B. *abbr.* **a)** *(Univ.)* **Bachelor; b) bishop** Bisch.; *(Chess)* L; **c)** *(on pencil)* **black** B

b. *abbr.* **a) born** geb.; **b)** *(Cricket)* **bowled by** ausgeschlagen durch Tortreffer von

BA *abbr.* **a)** *(Univ.)* **Bachelor of Arts;** *see also* **B.Sc.; b) British Academy** *geisteswissenschaftliche akademische Institution in Großbritannien;* **c) British Association** *naturwissenschaftliche akademische Institution in Großbritannien*

BAA *abbr.* **British Airports Authority** *britische Flughafenbehörde*

baa [bɑ:] **1.** *n.* Blöken, *das.* **2.** *v.i.,* **baaed** *or* **baa'd** [bɑ:d] mähen; blöken

'baa-lamb *n. (child lang.)* Bählämmchen, *das;* Bählamm, *das*

baba ['bɑ:bɑ:] *n.* **[rum] ~:** [Rum]baba, *das; mit Rumsirup getränktes Gebäck*

babble ['bæbl] **1.** *v.i.* **a)** *(talk incoherently)* stammeln; **~ [away** *or* **on]** ⟨*Baby:*⟩ [vor sich *(Akk.)* hin] lallen *od.* plappern; **b)** *(talk foolishly)* [dumm] schwatzen; **a babbling idiot** ein dummer Schwätzer; **c)** *(talk excessively)* **~ away** *or* **on** quasseln *(ugs.);* **d)** *(murmur)* ⟨*Bach:*⟩ plätschern. **2.** *v.t.* **a)** *(divulge foolishly)* ausplaudern; **~ sth. to sb.** etw. bei jmdm. ausplaudern; **b)** *(utter incoherently)* stammeln. **3.** *n.* **a)** *(incoherent speech)* Gestammel, *das; (childish or foolish speech)* Gelalle, *das;* **b)** *(idle talk)* Geschwätz, *das;* **c)** *(murmur of water)* Geplätscher, *das;* **d)** *(Teleph.)* unverständliches Gemurmel

babbler ['bæblə(r)] *n.* **a)** *(chatterer, teller of secrets)* Plaudertasche, *die;* **b)** *(Ornith.)* Timalie, *die;* Lärmdrossel, *die (veralt.)*

babe [beɪb] *n.* **a)** *(inexperienced person)* Anfänger, *der*/Anfängerin, *die;* **be a ~:** noch nicht trocken hinter den Ohren sein *(ugs.);* **b)** *(guileless person)* Lamm, *das;* **~s in the wood** hilflose Lämmchen; **c)** *(Amer. sl.: young woman)* Kleine, *die (ugs.);* **I love you, ~:** ich liebe dich, Kleines; **d)** *(young child)* kleines Kind; **as innocent as a newborn ~:** unschuldig wie ein neugeborenes Kind; *see also* **mouth 1 a**

babel ['beɪbl] *n.* **a)** *(scene of confusion)* Durcheinander, *das;* **b)** *(noisy medley)* **~ of voices** [lautes] Stimmengewirr; **tower of B~** *(fig.)* gigantisches Projekt; **c)** *(confusion of tongues)* babylonisches Sprachengewirr

baboon [bə'bu:n] *n. (Zool.)* Pavian, *der; (fig. derog.: person)* Neandertaler, *der;* Halbaffe, *der*

babushka [bə'bʊʃkə] *n.* Kopftuch, *das*

baby ['beɪbɪ] **1.** *n.* **a)** Baby, *das;* **have a ~/be going to have a ~:** ein Kind bekommen; **she is having a ~ in May** sie bekommt im Mai ein Kind; **she has a young ~:** sie hat ein kleines Baby; **mother and ~ are doing fine** Mutter und Kind sind wohlauf; **a ~ boy/girl** ein kleiner Junge/ein kleines Mädchen; **throw out** *or* **away the ~ with the bathwater** *(fig.)* das Kind mit dem Bade ausschütten; **be left holding** *or* **carrying the ~** *(fig.)* die Sache ausbaden müssen *(ugs.);* der Dumme sein *(ugs.);* **leave sb. carrying the ~** *(fig.)* jmdn. die Sache ausbaden lassen *(ugs.);* **it's your/his** *etc.* **~** *(fig.)* das ist dein/sein *usw.* Bier *(ugs.);* **reference books are Jones's ~:** um Nachschlagewerke muß sich Jones kümmern; **b)** *(youngest member)* Jüngste, *der/die; (male also)* Benjamin, *der;* **the ~ of the family** das Küken der Familie; **c)** *(childish person)* **be a ~:** sich wie ein kleines Kind benehmen; **d)** *(young animal)* Junge, *das;* **~ bird/giraffe** junger Vogel/junge Giraffe; Vogeljunge, *das*/Giraffenjunge, *das;* **e)** *(small thing)* **be a ~:** winzig sein; **~ [car]** Miniauto, *das;* Kleinwagen, *der;* **~ [bottle]** Miniflasche, *die;* **f)** *(sl.: sweetheart)* Schatz, *der; (in pop song also)* Baby, *das;* **g)** *(sl.: young woman)* Kleine, *die (ugs.);* **h)** *(sl.: person)* Typ, *der; (thing)* Ding, *das (ugs.);* **this ~** *(the speaker himself)* unsereiner *(ugs.).* **2.** *v.t.* wie ein kleines Kind behandeln; *(be easy on)* mit Samthandschuhen anfassen

baby: ~ boom *n.* Babyboom, *der;* **~-bouncer** *n. federnd aufgehängter Sitz für Kleinkinder, in dem sie durch Wippen ihre Beine kräftigen sollen;* **~ buggy** *n. (Amer.)* Kinderwagen, *der;* **~ car** *see* **baby 1e;** **~ carriage** *n. (Amer.)* Kinderwagen, *der;* **~ clothes** *n. pl.* Babykleidung, *die;* **~-doll** *adj.* **~-doll pyjamas/nightdress** Babydoll, *das;* **~-face** *n.* **a)** *(face)* Kindergesicht, *das;* **b)** *(person)* Milchgesicht, *das (leicht abwertend);* **~ food** *n.* Babynahrung, *die;* **~ 'grand** *n. (Mus.)* Stutzflügel, *der*

babyhood ['beɪbɪhʊd] *n., no pl.* frühe Kindheit

babyish ['beɪbɪɪʃ] *adj.* kindlich ‹*Aussehen*›; kindisch ‹*Benehmen, Person*›; **don't be so ~:** benimm dich nicht wie ein kleines Kind

baby: ~-minder *n.* Tagesmutter, *die;* **~ powder** *n.* Babypuder, *der;* **~-sit** *v.i., forms as* **sit 1** babysitten *(ugs.);* auf das Kind/die Kinder aufpassen; **she ~-sits for us** sie kommt zu uns zum Babysitten; **~-sitter** *n.* Babysitter, *der;* **~-sitting** *n.* Babysitting, *das;* **~-snatch** *v.i. see* **cradle-snatch;** **~-snatcher** *n.* **a)** Kindesentführer, *der;* **b)** *(fig. coll.) jmd., der mit einer sehr viel jüngeren Person eine Liebesbeziehung eingeht;* **~-snatching** *n.* **a)** Kindesentführung, *die;* **b) You can't ask her out. That would be ~-snatching** *(fig. coll.)* Du kannst sie nicht einladen. Das wäre Verführung einer Minderjährigen *(scherzh.);* **~-talk** *n.* Babysprache, *die;* **~-walker** *n.* Laufstuhl, *der*

baccarat ['bækərɑ:] *n.* Bakkarat, *das*

Bacchanalia [bækə'neɪlɪə] *n. pl.* **a)** *(drunken revelry)* Bacchanal, *das (geh.);* **b)** *(Greek and Roman Ant.)* Bacchanalien *Pl.*

Bacchanalian [bækə'neɪlɪən] **1.** *adj.* bacchantisch. **2.** *n.* Bacchant, *der (geh.)*

baccy ['bækɪ] *n. (coll.)* Tabak, *der*

bachelor ['bætʃələ(r)] *n.* **a)** *(unmarried man)* Junggeselle, *der;* **b)** *(Univ.)* Bakkalaureus, *der;* Bachelor, *der;* **B~ of Arts/Science** Bakkalaureus der philosophischen Fakultät/der Naturwissenschaften

bachelor: ~ flat *n.* Junggesellenwohnung, *die;* **~ girl** *n.* Junggesellin, *die*

bachelorhood ['bætʃələhʊd] *n., no pl.* Junggesellendasein, *das*

bacillary [bə'sɪlərɪ] *adj. (Biol., Med.)* bazillär

bacillus [bə'sɪləs] *n., pl.* **bacilli** [bə'sɪlaɪ] *(Biol., Med.)* **a)** *(rod-shaped bacterium)* Bazillus, *der;* **b)** *(pathogenic bacterium)* Bakterie, *die;* Bazillus, *der (veralt.)*

back [bæk] **1.** *n.* **a)** *(of person, animal)* Rücken, *der;* **stand ~ to ~:** Rücken an Rücken stehen; **give** *or* **make a ~:** sich bücken; **as soon as my ~ was turned** *(fig.)* sowie ich den Rücken gedreht hatte; **behind sb.'s ~** *(fig.) see* **behind 2b;** **be on one's ~:** [auf dem Rücken] liegen; *(fig.: be ill)* im Bett liegen; flachliegen *(salopp);* auf der Nase liegen *(ugs.);* **turn one's ~ on sb.** jmdm. den Rücken zuwenden; *(fig.: abandon sb.)* jmdn. im Stich lassen; **turn one's ~ on sth.** *(fig.)* etw. vernachlässigen; sich um etw. nicht kümmern; **don't turn your ~ on this chance** laß dir diese Chance nicht entgehen; **get** *or* **put sb.'s ~ up** *(fig.)* jmdn. wütend machen; **be glad to see the ~ of sb./sth.** *(fig.)* froh sein, jmdn./etw. nicht mehr sehen zu müssen; **have one's ~ to the wall** *(fig.)* mit dem Rücken zur Wand stehen; **be at sb.'s ~** *(fig.) (in support)* hinter jmdm. stehen; *(in pursuit)* jmdm. auf den Fersen sein; **with sb. at one's ~** *(fig.)* gefolgt von jmdm.; **get off my ~** *(fig. coll.)* laß mich zufrieden; **have sb./sth. on one's ~** *(fig.)* jmdn./etw. am Hals haben *(ugs.);* **you look as if you had the cares of the world on your ~:** du siehst aus, als ob die Sorgen der ganzen Welt auf dir lasten; **put one's ~ into sth.** *(fig.)* sich für etw. mit allen Kräften einsetzen; **you're not exactly putting your ~ into this work** *(fig.)* du strengst dich bei dieser Arbeit nicht genug an; *see also* **break 1c, 2b;** **b)** *(outer or rear surface)* Rücken, *der; (of vehicle)* Heck, *das;* **the car went into the ~ of me** *(coll.)* das Auto ist mir hinten reingefahren *(ugs.);* **with the ~ of one's hand** mit dem Handrücken; **know sth. like the ~ of one's hand** *(fig.)* etw. wie seine Westentasche kennen; **the ~ of one's/the head** der Hinterkopf; **the ~ of the leg** *(below knee)* die Wade; **c)** *(of book) (spine)* [Buch]rücken, *der; (final pages)* Ende, *das;* **at the ~ [of the book]** hinten [im Buch]; **d)** *(of dress)* Rücken, *der; (of knife)* [Messer]rücken, *der;* **e)** *(more remote part)* hinterer Teil; **at the ~ [of sth.]** hinten [in etw. *(Dat.)*]; im hinteren Teil [von etw.]; **f)** *(inside car)* Rücksitz, *der;* Fond, *der (seltener); (of chair)* [Rücken]lehne, *die; (of material)* linke Seite; *(of house, cheque)* Rückseite, *die; (~ wall)* Rückseite, *die;* Rückwand, *die;* **~-to-~ houses** *(Brit.) Häuser, deren Rückseiten eng aneinandergebaut sind;* **~ to front** verkehrt rum; **please get to the ~ of the queue** bitte, stellen Sie sich hinten an; **we squeezed five people into the ~ [of the car]** wir zwängten fünf Personen auf die Rücksitze [des Wagens]; **the coat-hook was on the ~ of the door** der Kleiderhaken befand sich hinten an der Tür; **there's something at the ~ of my mind** ich habe da noch etwas im Hinterkopf; **in ~ of sth.** *(Amer.)* hinter etw. *(Dat.); see also* **beyond 3;** **g)** *(Sport) (player)* Verteidiger, *der; (position)* **he played at ~ this week** diese Woche hat er als Verteidiger gespielt; **h)** *(of ship)* Kiel, *der;* **i) the B~s** *die Uferanlagen hinter einigen Colleges in Cambridge (England).* **2.** *adj., no comp.; superl.* **~most** ['bækməʊst] **a)** *(situated behind)* hinter...; **from the ~most of the three lines** von der hintersten der drei Linien; **b)** *(of the past)* früher; **~ issue** alte Ausgabe; **c)** *(overdue)* rückständig ‹*Lohn, Steuern*›; **d)** *(remote)* abgelegen ‹*Ort, Straße*›; **e)** *(reversed)* **~ motion** Rückwärtsbewegung, *die;* **~ flow** Rückfluß, *der;* **f)** *(Cricket)* **~ play** *das Schlagen des Balles hinter der Schlagmallinie;* **g)** *(Phonet.)* **~ vowel** Hinterzungenvokal, *der.* **3.** *adv.* **a)** *(to the rear)* zurück; **step ~:** zurücktreten; **play ~** *(Cricket)* zurücktreten, um zu schlagen; **b)** *(behind)* zurück; weiter hinten; **we passed a pub two miles ~:** wir sind vor zwei Meilen an einem Pub vorbeigefahren; **~ and forth** hin und her; **~ of sth.** *(Amer.)* hinter etw. *(Dat.);* **c)** *(at a distance)* **the house stands a long way ~ from the road** das Haus steht weit von der Straße zurück; **d)** *(to original position, home)* [wieder] zurück; **I got my letter ~:** ich habe meinen Brief zurückbekommen; **the journey ~:** die Rückfahrt/der Rückflug; **there and ~:** hin und zurück; **e)** *(to original condition)* wieder; **f)** *(in the past)* zurück; **go a long way ~:** weit zurückgehen; **a week/month ~:** vor einer Woche/vor einem Monat; **g)** *(in return)* zurück; **I got a letter ~:** er/sie hat mir wiedergeschrieben. **4.** *v.t.* **a)** *(assist)* helfen (+ *Dat.*); unterstützen ‹*Person, Sache*›; **b)** *(bet on)* wetten *od.* setzen auf (+ *Akk.*) ‹*Pferd, Gewinner, Favorit*›; **~ the wrong/right horse** *(lit. or fig.)* aufs falsche/richtige Pferd setzen *(ugs.);* **~ X to beat Y** darauf wetten, daß X gegen Y gewinnt; **the horse which is most heavily ~ed** das Pferd, auf das am meisten gesetzt wurde; **c)** *(cause to move back)* zurücksetzen [mit] ‹*Fahrzeug*›; rückwärts gehen lassen ‹*Pferd*›; **how did you manage to ~ the car into that lamp-post?** wie hast du es nur fertiggebracht, rückwärts gegen den Laternenpfahl zu fahren?; **~ water** rückwärts rudern; **d)** *(put or act as a ~ to)* [an der Rückseite] verstärken; **e)** *(endorse)* indossieren ‹*Wechsel, Scheck*›; **f)** *(lie at the ~ of)* **~ sth.** hinten an etw. *(Akk.)* grenzen; **g)** *(Mus.)* begleiten. **5.** *v.i.* zurücksetzen; ‹*Wind:*› [sich] gegen den Uhrzeigersinn drehen; **~ into/out of sth.** rückwärts in etw. *(Akk.)*/aus etw. fahren; **~ on to sth.** hinten an etw. *(Akk.)* grenzen; **~ and fill** *(Amer.)* sich hin und her bewegen; *(fig.)* schwanken

~ a'way *v.i.* zurückweichen; *(fig.)* zurückschrecken

~ 'down *v.i. (fig.)* nachgeben; einen Rückzieher machen *(ugs.); see also* **back-down**

~ 'off *see* **~ away**

~ 'out *v.i.* rückwärts herausfahren; *(fig.)* einen Rückzieher machen *(ugs.);* **~ out of sth.** *(fig.)* von etw. zurücktreten

~ 'up 1. *v.t.* unterstützen; untermauern ‹*Anspruch, Geschichte, These*›. **2.** *v.i.* **a)** ‹*Wasser:*› sich [auf]stauen; **b)** *(reverse)* zurücksetzen; **c)** *(Amer.: form queue of vehicles)* sich stauen. *See also* **back-up**

back: ~ache *n., no pl.* Rückenschmerzen *Pl.;* **~-'bench** *n. (Brit. Parl.)* hintere Sitzreihe; **a ~-bench MP** ein Parlamentsabgeordneter [aus den hinteren Reihen]; **~-bencher** [bæk'bentʃə(r)] *n. (Brit. Parl.)* [einfacher] Abgeordneter/[einfache] Abgeordnete; *(derog.)* Hinterbänkler, *der (abwertend);* **~biter** *n.* Verleumder, *der*/Verleumderin, *die;* **~biting** *n.* Verleumdung, *die;* Hetzerei, *die (ugs.);* **~blocks** *n. pl. (Austral., NZ)* ≈ Hinterland, *das; dünn besiedeltes, abgelegenes Land im Landesinneren;* **~-boiler** *n. (Brit.) (hinter dem Ofen o.ä. angebrachter)* Boiler; **~bone** *n.* Wirbelsäule, *die;* Rückgrat, *das (auch fig.); (Amer.: of book)* [Buch]rücken, *der;* **to the ~bone** *(fig.)* durch und durch; **~-breaking** *adj.* äußerst mühsam; gewaltig ‹*Anstrengung*›; **~-breaking work** Knochenarbeit, *die;* **~ 'burner** *n.* **put sth. on the ~ burner** *(fig. coll.)* etw. zurückstellen; **~chat** *n., no pl. (coll.)* [freche] Widerrede; **none of your ~chat!** keine Widerrede!; **~cloth** *n. (Brit. Theatre)* Prospekt, *der;* **~comb** *v.t.* zurückkämmen; **~date** *v.t.* zurückdatieren (to auf + *Akk.*); **~ 'door** *n.* Hintertür, *die (auch fig.);* **~-door** *adj. (fig.)* Hintertreppen- *(abwertend);* **~-down** *n. (coll.)* Rückzieher, *der (ugs.);* **~drop** *see* **~cloth**

backer ['bækə(r)] *n.* Geldgeber, *der; (of horse)* Wetter, *der*

A-D ENGLISH GERMAN

back: ~-fill *v. t.* [wieder] auffüllen; **~fire 1.** ['--] *n.* Fehlzündung, *die;* **2.** [-'-] *v. i.* knallen; *(fig.)* fehlschlagen; **it ~fired on me/him** *etc.* der Schuß ging nach hinten los *(ugs.);* **~-formation** *n. (Ling.) (word)* rückgebildetes Wort; *(action)* Rückbildung, *die*

backgammon ['bækgæmən] *n. (game)* Backgammon, *das;* ≈ Tricktrack, *das;* ≈ Puff, *das*

back: ~ground *n.* **a)** *(lit. or fig.)* Hintergrund, *der; (social status)* Herkunft, *die; (education)* Ausbildung, *die; (experience)* Erfahrung, *die;* **be in the ~ground** im Hintergrund stehen; **he comes from a poor ~ground** er stammt aus ärmlichen Verhältnissen; **against this ~ground** vor diesem Hintergrund; **~ground heating** *Heizung, die automatisch für eine erträgliche Zimmertemperatur sorgt;* **~ground music** Hintergrundmusik, *die;* **b) ~ground [information]** Hintergrundinformation, *die;* **c)** *(Radio)* Störgeräusch, *das;* **~hand** *(Tennis etc.)* **1.** *adj.* Rückhand-; **2.** *n.* Rückhand, *die;* **~-'handed** *adj.* **a) ~-handed slap** Schlag mit dem Handrücken; **~-handed stroke** *(Tennis)* Rückhandschlag, *der;* **b)** *(fig.)* indirekt; zweifelhaft ⟨*Kompliment*⟩; **~hander** *n.* **a)** *(stroke)* Rückhandschlag, *der (Tennis usw.); (blow)* Schlag [mit dem Handrücken]; **b)** *(sl.: bribe)* Schmiergeld, *das*

backing ['bækɪŋ] *n.* **a)** *(material)* Rückenverstärkung, *die;* **leather ~:** Rückseite aus Leder; **the silver ~ of a mirror** die silberne Beschichtung eines Spiegels; **b)** *(support)* Unterstützung, *die;* **the President has a large ~:** der Präsident kann sich auf eine große Anhängerschaft stützen; **c)** *(betting)* **there was much ~ of the favourite** es wurden viele Wetten auf den Favoriten abgeschlossen; **d)** *(Mus.: accompaniment)* Begleitung, *die*

'backlash *n.* Rückstoß, *der; (excessive play in machine)* Spiel, *das; (fig.)* Gegenreaktion, *die;* **a right-wing ~:** eine Gegenbewegung nach rechts

backless ['bæklɪs] *adj.* rückenfrei ⟨*Kleid*⟩

back: ~list *n.* Verzeichnis der lieferbaren Titel; Backlist, *die (Verlagsw.);* **~log** *n.* Rückstand, *der;* **~log of work** Arbeitsrückstand, *der;* **a large ~log of unfulfilled orders** ein großer Überhang an unerledigten Aufträgen; **~marker** *n.* **a)** *(lagging behind other competitors)* Schlußlicht, *das (ugs. fig.);* **b)** *jmd., der ohne Vorgabe od. mit dem größten Handikap startet;* **~ 'number** *n.* **a)** *(of periodical, magazine)* alte Nummer; **b)** *(fig. sl.)* **these methods are a [real] ~ number** diese Methoden sind [reichlich] rückständig; **not every star is a ~ number when he is 60** nicht jeder Star ist mit 60 abgeschrieben; **~pack 1.** *n.* Rucksack, *der;* **2.** *v. i.* mit dem Rucksack [ver]reisen; **~ passage** *n. (Anat. coll.)* After, *der;* **~-'pedal** *v. i.* **a)** die Pedale rückwärts treten; *(brake)* mit dem Rücktritt bremsen; **b)** *(fig.)* einen Rückzieher machen *(ugs.);* **~rest** *n.* Rückenlehne, *die;* **~ 'room** *n.* Hinterzimmer, *das;* **in the ~ room** *(fig.)* hinter verschlossenen Türen; **~room boys** *(coll.)* Experten im Hintergrund *(bes. Wissenschaftler, die an Geheimprojekten arbeiten);* **~scratcher** *n.* Rückenkratzer, *der;* **~scratching** *n. (fig. coll.)* **[mutual] ~scratching** Klüngelei, *die (abwertend);* **~ 'seat** *n.* Rücksitz, *der; (in bus, coach)* hinterer Sitzplatz; **take a ~ seat** *(fig. coll.)* in den Hintergrund treten; **be in the ~ seat** *(fig. coll.)* im Hintergrund stehen; **~-seat driver** *besserwisserischer Beifahrer, der immer dazwischenredet; (fig.)* Neunmalkluge, *der/die;* **~side** *n.* Hinterteil, *das (ugs.);* Hintern, *der (ugs.);* **get [up] off one's ~side** seinen Hintern heben *(ugs.);* **~sight** *n.* Visier, *das;* **~slapping** *adj. (fig.)* plump-vertraulich; **~slider** *n.* Abtrünnige, *der/die;* **~space** *v. i.* die Rücktaste betätigen; **~'stage 1.** *adj.* hinter der Bühne; **~stage activities** *(fig.)* Aktivitäten hinter den Kulissen; **2.** *adv.* **a) go ~stage** hinter die Bühne gehen; **wait ~stage for the artist** hinter der Bühne auf den Künstler warten; **b)** *(fig.)* hinter den Kulissen; **~-'stair[s]** *see* **~-door;** **~ 'stairs** *n. pl.* Hintertreppe, *die;* **~stitch 1.** *v. t. & i.* steppen; **2.** *n.* Steppstich, *der;* **~stitch seam** Steppnaht, *die;* **~ street** kleine Seitenstraße; **from the ~ streets of Naples** ≈ aus den Hinterhöfen Neapels; *see also* **abortion a; abortionist;** **~stroke** *n. (Swimming)* Rückenschwimmen, *das;* **do** *or* **swim the ~stroke** rückenschwimmen; **~ talk** *(Amer.) see* **~chat;** **~track** *v. i.* wieder zurückgehen; *(fig.)* eine Kehrtwendung machen; **~-up** *n.* **a)** *(support)* Unterstützung, *die;* **a racing driver needs a large ~-up crew** ein Rennfahrer muß eine große Crew hinter sich haben; **b)** *(reserve)* Reserve, *die;* **~-up supplies** Vorräte für den Bedarfs- *od.* Notfall; **~-up [copy]** *(Computing)* Sicherungskopie, *die;* **c)** *(Amer.: queue of vehicles)* Stau, *der;* **a ~-up of cars** eine Autoschlange; **d) ~-up light** *(Amer.)* Rückfahrscheinwerfer, *der*

backward ['bækwəd] **1.** *adj.* **a)** *(directed to rear)* rückwärts gerichtet; Rückwärts-; **~ movement** Rückwärtsbewegung, *die;* **the ~ slant to his handwriting** seine nach links geneigte Handschrift; **b)** *(reluctant, shy)* zurückhaltend; **be ~ in coming forward** *(joc.)* sich zurückhalten; **c)** *(slow, retarded)* zurückgeblieben ⟨*Kind*⟩; *(underdeveloped)* rückständig, unterentwickelt ⟨*Land, Region*⟩; **~ in sth.** in etw. *(Dat.)* zurückgeblieben; **~ in his studies** mit seinem Studium im Rückstand. **2.** *adv. see* **backwards**

backwardness ['bækwədnɪs] *n., no pl.* **a)** *(reluctance, shyness)* Zurückhaltung, *die;* **b)** *(of child)* Zurückgebliebenheit, *die; (of country, region)* Rückständigkeit, *die;* **the child's ~ in school** daß das Kind in der Schule zurückgeblieben ist/war

backwards ['bækwədz] *adv.* **a)** nach hinten; **the child fell [over] ~ into the water** das Kind fiel rückwärts ins Wasser; **bend** *or* **fall** *or* **lean over ~ to do sth.** *(fig. coll.)* sich zerreißen, um etw. zu tun *(ugs.);* **b)** *(oppositely to normal direction)* rückwärts; **~ and forwards** *(to and fro, lit. or fig.)* hin und her; **c)** *(into a worse state)* **go ~:** sich verschlechtern; **under his leadership the country is going ~:** unter seiner Führung verschlechtert sich die Lage des Landes; **d)** *(into past)* **look ~:** an frühere Zeiten denken; **e)** *(reverse way)* rückwärts; von hinten nach vorn; **you're doing everything ~:** du machst ja alles verkehrt herum; **know sth. ~:** etw. in- und auswendig kennen

back: ~wash *n.* Rückstrom, *der* **(from** *Gen.***);** *(fig.)* Auswirkungen *Pl.;* **in the ~wash of** *(fig.)* als Folge von; **~water** *n.* totes Wasser; *(fig.)* Kaff, *das (ugs. abwertend);* **this town is too much of a ~water** diese Stadt ist zu provinziell; **~woods** *n. pl.* abgelegene Wälder; unerschlossene Waldgebiete; *(fig.)* hinterste Provinz; **~woodsman** *n.* ≈ Waldbewohner, *der; (uncouth person)* Hinterwäldler, *der (spött.);* **~ 'yard** *n.* Hinterhof, *der;* **in one's own ~ yard** *(fig.)* vor der eigenen Haustür

bacon ['beɪkn] *n.* [Frühstücks]speck, *der;* **~ and eggs** Eier mit Speck; **bring home the ~** *(fig. coll.)* es schaffen; *(der Ernährer sein)* die Brötchen verdienen *(ugs.);* **save one's ~** *(fig.)* die eigene *od.* seine Haut retten

bacteria *pl. of* **bacterium**

bacterial [bæk'tɪərɪəl] *adj.* bakteriell

bactericide [bæk'tɪərɪsaɪd] *n.* Bakterizid, *das*

bacteriological [bæktɪərɪə'lɒdʒɪkl] *adj.* bakteriologisch; **~ warfare** Bakterienkrieg, *der*

bacteriologist [bæktɪərɪ'ɒlədʒɪst] *n.* Bakteriologe, *der*/Bakteriologin, *die*

bacteriology [bæktɪərɪ'ɒlədʒɪ] *n.* Bakteriologie, *die*

bacterium [bæk'tɪərɪəm] *n., pl.* **bacteria** [bæk'tɪərɪə] Bakterie, *die*

bad [bæd] **1.** *adj.,* **worse** [wɜ:s], **worst** [wɜ:st] **a)** schlecht; *(worthless)* wertlos, ungedeckt ⟨*Scheck*⟩; *(counterfeit)* falsch ⟨*Münze, Banknote*⟩; *(rotten)* schlecht, verdorben ⟨*Fleisch, Fisch, Essen*⟩; faul ⟨*Ei, Apfel*⟩; *(unpleasant)* schlecht, unangenehm ⟨*Geruch*⟩; **do a ~ job on sth.** bei etw. schlecht arbeiten; **sth. gives sb. a ~ name** etw. trägt jmdm. einen schlechten Ruf ein; **sb. gets a ~ name** jmd. kommt in Verruf; **she is in ~ health** sie hat eine angegriffene Gesundheit; **she has a ~ complexion** sie hat einen unreinen Teint; **be ~ at doing sth.** etw. nicht gut können; **be a ~ liar** ein schlechter Lügner sein; **[some] ~ news** schlechte *od.* schlimme Nachrichten; **~ breath** Mundgeruch, *der;* **he is having a ~ day** er hat einen schwarzen Tag; **~ business** ein schlechtes Geschäft; **it is a ~ business** *(fig.)* das ist eine schlimme Sache; **in the ~ old days** in den schlimmen Jahren; **not ~** *(coll.)* nicht schlecht; nicht übel; **not so ~** *(coll.)* gar nicht so schlecht *od.* übel; **things weren't so ~** *(coll.)* es war alles nicht so schlimm; **sth. is not a ~ idea** etw. ist keine schlechte Idee; **not half ~** *(coll.)* [gar] nicht schlecht; **sth. is too ~** *(coll.)* etw. ist ein Jammer; **that was too ~ of him** *(coll.)* das war rücksichtslos von ihm; **too ~!** *(coll.)* so ein Pech! *(auch iron.);* **go ~:** schlecht werden; **in a ~ sense** im schlechten Sinne; **b)** *(noxious)* schlecht; schädlich; **it is ~ for you** es ist schlecht für dich; es schadet dir; **c)** *(wicked)* schlecht; *(immoral)* schlecht; verdorben; unmoralisch ⟨*Buch, Heft*⟩; *(naughty)* ungezogen, böse ⟨*Kind, Hund*⟩; **d)** *(offensive)* **[use] ~ language** Kraftausdrücke [benutzen]; **e)** *(in ill health)* **she's ~ today** es geht ihr heute schlecht; **have a ~ arm/finger** einen schlimmen Arm/Finger haben *(ugs.);* **I have a ~ pain** ich habe schlimme Schmerzen; **be in a ~ way** in schlechtem Zustand sein; **f)** *(serious)* schlimm, böse ⟨*Sturz, Krise*⟩; schwer ⟨*Fehler, Krankheit, Unfall, Erschütterung*⟩; hoch ⟨*Fieber*⟩; schrecklich ⟨*Feuer*⟩; **g)** *(coll.: regretful)* **a ~ conscience** ein schlechtes Gewissen; **feel ~ about sth./not having done sth.** etw. bedauern/bedauern, daß man etw. nicht getan hat; **I feel ~ about him/her** ich habe seinetwegen/ihretwegen ein schlechtes Gewissen; **h)** *(Commerc.)* **a ~ debt** eine uneinbringliche Schuld *(Wirtsch.);* **i)** *(Law: invalid)* ungültig. *See also* **book 1a; ¹egg; form 1h; hat b; lot c; luck a; patch 1a; penny c; temper 1a; worse 1; worst 1. 2.** *n.* **a)** *(ill fortune)* Schlechte, *das;* **b)** *(debit)* **be £100 to the ~:** mit 100 Pfund in der Kreide stehen *(ugs.);* **c)** *(ruin)* **go to the ~:** auf die schiefe Bahn geraten. *See also* **worse 3. 3.** *adv. (Amer. coll.) see* **badly**

baddish ['bædɪʃ] *adj.* ziemlich schlecht

baddy ['bædɪ] *n. (coll.)* Schurke, *der;* **the goodies and the baddies** die Guten und die Bösen *(oft iron.)*

bade *see* **bid 1c, d, e**

badge [bædʒ] *n.* **a)** *(as sign of office, membership, support)* Abzeichen, *das; (larger)* Plakette, *die;* **b)** *(symbol)* Symbol, *das;* **c)** *(thing revealing quality or condition)* Kennzeichen, *das*

badger ['bædʒə(r)] **1.** *n.* Dachs, *der.* **2.** *v. t.* **~ sb. [into doing/to do sth.]** jmdm. keine Ruhe lassen[, bis er/sie etw. tut]; **~ sb. with questions** jmdn. mit Fragen löchern *(ugs.);* **don't ~ her out of her wits!** mach sie nicht verrückt! *(ugs.)*

'badger baiting *n.* Dachshetze, *die*

badinage ['bædɪnɑ:ʒ] *n.* Spöttelei, *die*

'bad lands *n. pl. (Amer.)* Badlands *Pl.*

badly ['bædlɪ] *adv.,* **worse** [wɜ:s], **worst**

[wɜ:st] **a)** schlecht; **b)** *(seriously)* schwer ‹*verletzt, beschädigt*›; sehr ‹*schief sein, knarren*›; **he hurt himself ~:** er hat sich *(Dat.)* schwer verletzt; **he has got it ~:** es hat ihn schlimm erwischt *(ugs.)*; **be ~ beaten** schwer verprügelt werden *(ugs.)*; *(in game, battle)* vernichtend geschlagen werden; **c)** *(urgently)* dringend; **want sth. [so] ~:** sich *(Dat.)* etw. [so] sehr wünschen; **d)** *(coll.: regretfully)* **feel ~ about sth.** etw. [sehr] bedauern; **I don't feel too ~ about it** es macht mir nicht soviel aus. *See also* **worse 2; worst 2**

ˈ**bad man** *n. (Amer.)* Bösewicht, *der*

badminton [ˈbædmɪntən] *n.* Federball, *der;* *(als Sport)* Badminton, *das*

ˈ**bad mouth** *n. (Amer. sl.)* Klatsch, *der (ugs.)*

ˈ**bad-mouth** *v. t. (Amer. sl.)* klatschen über (+ *Akk.*) *(ugs.)*

badness [ˈbædnɪs] *n., no pl. see* **bad:** Schlechtigkeit, *die;* Verdorbenheit, *die;* Ungezogenheit, *die;* Ungültigkeit, *die;* **the ~ in him** seine innere Schlechtigkeit

bad-tempered [bædˈtempəd] *adj.* griesgrämig

BAe *abbr.* **British Aerospace** *britisches Unternehmen, das Flugzeuge und Raumschiffe herstellt*

baffle [ˈbæfl] **1.** *v. t.* **a)** *(perplex)* **~ sb.** jmdm. unverständlich sein; jmdn. vor ein Rätsel stellen; **b)** *(stop progress of)* aufhalten. **2.** *n.* **~[-plate]** Prallfläche, *die (Technik);* **~[-board]** *(of loudspeaker)* Schallwand, *die*

baffled [ˈbæfld] *adj.* verwirrt; **be ~:** vor einem Rätsel stehen

bafflement [ˈbæflmənt] *n.* Verwirrung, *die*

baffling [ˈbæflɪŋ] *adj.* rätselhaft

bag [bæg] **1.** *n.* **a)** Tasche, *die; (sack)* Sack, *der; (hand~)* [Hand]tasche, *die; (of plastic)* Beutel, *der; (small paper ~)* Tüte, *die;* **a ~ of cement** ein Sack Zement; **~ and baggage** *(fig.)* mit Sack und Pack; **be a ~ of bones** *(fig.)* nur Haut und Knochen sein; **[whole] ~ of tricks** *(fig.)* Trickkiste, *die (ugs.);* **have exhausted one's [whole] ~ of tricks** sein Pulver verschossen haben *(ugs.);* **leave sb. holding the ~** *(Amer. fig.)* jmdm. den Schwarzen Peter zuschieben; **his nomination is in the ~** *(fig. coll.)* er hat die Nominierung in der Tasche *(ugs.);* **freedom was as good as in the ~** *(coll.)* die Freiheit war so gut wie gewonnen; *see also* **cat a; mixed bag; b)** *(Hunting: amount of game)* Jagdbeute, *die;* Strecke, *die (Jägerspr.);* **make** *or* **secure a good ~** *(lit. or fig.)* reiche Jagdbeute/*(fig.)* Beute machen; **c)** *in pl. (sl.: large amount)* **~s of** jede Menge *(ugs.);* **d)** *in pl. (Brit. sl.: trousers)* Hose, *die;* **e)** *(puffiness)* **have ~s under** *or* **below one's eyes** Tränensäcke haben; **f)** *(sl. derog.: woman)* **[old] ~:** alte Schlampe *(ugs. abwertend);* **g)** *(sl.: current interest, activity)* **what's your ~?** auf was stehst du [zur Zeit]? *(ugs.).* **2.** *v. t.,* **-gg-: a)** *(put in sacks)* in Säcke füllen; einsacken *(fachspr.); (put in plastic bags)* in Beutel füllen; *(put in small paper bags)* in Tüten füllen; eintüten *(fachspr.);* **b)** *(Hunting)* erlegen, erbeuten ‹*Tier*›; **c)** *(claim possession of)* sich *(Dat.)* schnappen *(ugs.); (euphem.: steal)* klauen *(ugs.); (Brit. Sch. sl.: claim)* **~s I go first!** erster!

bagatelle [bægəˈtel] *n.* **a)** *(trifle)* Nebensächlichkeit, *die;* **b)** *(Mus.)* Bagatelle, *die (fachspr.);* kurzes Musikstück

bagel [ˈbeɪgl] *n. hartes, ringförmiges Hefegebäck*

bagful [ˈbægfʊl] *n. see* **bag 1a: a ~ of** ein Sack [voll]/eine Tasche/ein Beutel/eine Tüte [voll]

baggage [ˈbægɪdʒ] *n.* **a)** Gepäck, *das;* **mental/cultural ~** *(fig.)* geistiges/kulturelles Rüstzeug; *see also* **bag 1a; b)** *(Mil.)* Gepäck, *das;* **c)** *(joc.: woman)* Flittchen, *das (abwertend); (saucy girl)* Fratz, *der (ugs.)*

baggage: ~ car *n. (Amer.)* Gepäckwagen, *der;* **~ check** *n.* Gepäckkontrolle, *die;* *(Amer.: ticket)* Gepäckschein, *der;* **~ room** *n. (Amer.)* Gepäckaufbewahrung, *die;* **~ tag** *n. (Amer.)* Kofferanhänger, *der*

bagginess [ˈbægɪnɪs] *n., no pl.* Schlaffheit, *die;* **the ~ of these old trousers** die Ausgebeultheit dieser alten Hose

baggy [ˈbægɪ] *adj.* weit [geschnitten] ‹*Kleid*›; schlaff [herabhängend] ‹*Haut*›; *(through long use)* ausgebeult ‹*Hose*›

Baghdad [bægˈdæd] *pr. n.* Bagdad *(das)*

bag: ~pipe *adj.* Dudelsack-; **~pipe[s]** *n.* Dudelsack, *der;* **~piper** *n.* Dudelsackpfeifer, *der*

baguette [bæˈget] *n.* Baguette, *die;* [französisches] Stangenweißbrot

bah [bɑ:] *int.* bah

Bahamas [bəˈhɑ:məz] *pr. n. pl.* **the ~:** die Bahamainseln

Bahamian [bəˈheɪ:mɪən] **1.** *adj.* bahamisch. **2.** *n.* Bahamer, *der*/Bahamerin, *die*

[1]**bail** [beɪl] **1.** *n.* **a)** Sicherheitsleistung, *die (Rechtsw.); (financial)* Kaution, *die; (personal)* Bürgschaft, *die;* **grant sb. ~:** jmdm. die Freilassung gegen Kaution bewilligen; **give sb. ~ on payment of the sum of ...:** jmdn. gegen eine Kaution in Höhe von ... freilassen; **be [out] on ~:** gegen Kaution auf freiem Fuß sein; **the judge refused ~ to the accused** der Richter lehnte es ab, den Angeklagten gegen Kaution freizulassen; **put** *or* **release sb. on ~:** jmdn. gegen Kaution freilassen; **forfeit one's** *or (coll.)* **jump** *or (coll.)* **skip [one's] ~:** die Kaution verfallen lassen [und nicht vor Gericht erscheinen]; **b)** *(person[s] acting as surety)* Bürge, *der;* **go ~ for sb.** für jmdn. Bürge sein; **go ~ for sb./sth.** *(fig.)* für jmdn./etw. bürgen *od.* geradestehen. **2.** *v. t.* **a)** *(entrust)* anvertrauen; **b)** *(release)* gegen Kaution freilassen; **c)** *(go ~ for)* bürgen für; **~ sb. out** jmdn. gegen Bürgschaft freibekommen; *(fig.)* jmdm. aus der Klemme helfen *(ugs.)*

[2]**bail** *n. (Cricket)* Querstab, *der*

[3]**bail** *v. t. (scoop)* **~ [out]** ausschöpfen

~ out *v. i. (Aeronaut.)* ‹*Pilot:*› abspringen *od.* *(Fliegerspr.)* aussteigen

bailey [ˈbeɪlɪ] *n.* *(wall)* Burgmauer, *die;* *(outer court)* Zwinger, *der; (inner court)* Burghof, *der;* **the Old B~:** das Old Bailey *(oberster Strafgerichtshof für London)*

ˈ**Bailey bridge** *n.* Bailey-Brücke, *die (Brücke aus vorgefertigten Teilen, die in kurzer Zeit errichtet werden kann)*

bailiff [ˈbeɪlɪf] *n.* **a)** ≈ Justizbeamte, *der;* Büttel, *der (veralt.); (performing distraints)* Gerichtsvollzieher, *der; (serving writs)* Gerichtsbote, *der (veralt.);* **b)** *(agent of landlord)* Verwalter, *der;* Vogt, *der (hist.);* **c)** *(Amer. Admin.: court official)* ≈ Gerichtsbeamte, *der*

bailiwick [ˈbeɪlɪwɪk] *n.* **a)** *(Hist.)* Amtsbezirk eines Bailiffs; Vogtei, *die;* **b)** *(joc.)* Reich, *das (fig.)*

bairn [beən] *n. (Scot./N. Engl./literary)* Kind, *das*

[1]**bait** [beɪt] **1.** *v. t.* **a)** mit einem Köder versehen ‹*Falle*›; beködern ‹*Angelhaken*›; **b)** *(torment with dogs)* **~ sth. [with dogs]** die Hunde auf etw. *(Akk.)* hetzen; **the badger was ~ed to death** der Dachs wurde von den Hunden totgebissen; **c)** *(fig.: torment)* herumhacken auf (+ *Dat.*) *(ugs.); (in playful manner)* necken; **~ sb. with questions** jmdm. mit Fragen zusetzen *(ugs.).* **2.** *n. (lit. or fig.)* Köder, *der;* **live ~:** lebender Köder; **rise to** *or* **take the ~** *(fig.)* anbeißen

[2]**bait** *see* [2]**bate**

baize [beɪz] *n. (Textiles)* Fries, *der*

bake [beɪk] **1.** *v. t.* **a)** *(cook)* backen; **~d apple** Bratapfel, *der;* **~d beans** gebackene Bohnen [in Tomatensoße]; **~d potato** [in der Schale] gebackene Kartoffel; **b)** *(harden)* brennen ‹*Ziegel, Keramik*›; ausdörren ‹*Erde, Boden, Land*›. **2.** *v. i.* **a)** backen; gebacken werden; *(fig.: be hot)* **I am baking!** mir ist wahnsinnig heiß! *(ugs.);* **b)** *(be hardened)* ‹*Ziegel, Keramik:*› gebrannt werden; ‹*Boden, Erde:*› ausdorren. **3.** *n. (Amer.: party)* Party [bei der Gebackenes gegessen wird]

bake: ~apple *n. (Can.)* [getrocknete] Moltebeere; **~house** *n.* Backstube, *die*

bakelite [ˈbeɪkəlaɪt] *n.* Bakelit, *das*

baker [ˈbeɪkə(r)] *n.* Bäcker, *der;* **at the ~'s** beim Bäcker; in der Bäckerei; **go to the ~'s** zum Bäcker *od.* zur Bäckerei gehen; **a ~'s dozen** 13 Stück

bakery [ˈbeɪkərɪ] *n.* Bäckerei, *die*

baking [ˈbeɪkɪŋ] *adv.* **it's ~ hot today, isn't it?** eine Hitze wie im Backofen ist das heute, nicht wahr?

baking: ~-dish *n.* Auflaufform, *die;* **~-powder** *n.* Backpulver, *das;* **~-sheet** *n.* Backblech, *das;* **~-soda** *n.* Natron, *das;* **~-tin** *n.* Backform, *die;* **~-tray** *n.* Kuchenblech, *das*

Balaclava [bæləˈklɑ:və] *n.* **~ [helmet]** Balaklavamütze, *die (Wollmütze, die Kopf und Hals bedeckt und nur das Gesicht frei läßt)*

balalaika [bæləˈlaɪkə] *n.* Balalaika, *die*

balance [ˈbæləns] **1.** *n.* **a)** *(instrument)* Waage, *die;* **~[-wheel]** Unruh, *die;* **b) the B~** *(Astrol.)* die Waage; *see also* **archer b; c)** *(fig.)* **be** *or* **hang in the ~:** in der Schwebe sein; **the prisoners' lives are in the ~:** die Zukunft der Gefangenen ist völlig ungewiß; **d)** *(even distribution)* Gleichgewicht, *das; (correspondence)* Übereinstimmung, *die; (due proportion)* ausgewogenes Verhältnis; *(Art: harmony)* Ausgewogenheit, *die;* **strike a ~ between** den Mittelweg finden zwischen (+ *Dat.*); **the ~ of sb.'s mind** jmds. seelisches Gleichgewicht; **~ of power** *see* **power 1f; e)** *(counterpoise)* Gegengewicht, *das;* Ausgleich, *der;* **f)** *(steady position)* Gleichgewicht, *das;* **keep/lose one's ~** das Gleichgewicht halten/verlieren; *(fig.)* sein Gleichgewicht bewahren/verlieren; **off [one's] ~** *(lit. or fig.)* aus dem Gleichgewicht; **throw sb. off [his] ~** *(lit. or fig.)* jmdn. aus dem Gleichgewicht werfen; **g)** *(preponderating weight or amount)* Bilanz, *die;* **the ~ of evidence appears to be in his favour** die Beweise zu seinen Gunsten scheinen zu überwiegen; **h)** *(Bookk.: difference)* Bilanz, *die; (state of bank account)* Kontostand, *der; (statement)* Auszug, *der;* **on ~** *(fig.)* alles in allem; **~ sheet** Bilanz, *die;* **i)** *(Econ.)* **~ of payments** Zahlungsbilanz, *die;* **~ of trade** Handelsbilanz, *die;* **j)** *(surplus amount)* **~ [in hand]** Überschuß, *der;* **you may keep the ~:** der Rest ist für Sie; **k)** *(remainder)* Rest, *der.* **2.** *v. t.* **a)** *(weigh up)* abwägen; **~ sth. with** *or* **by** *or* **against sth. else** etw. gegen etw. anderes abwägen; **b)** *(bring into or keep in ~)* balancieren; auswuchten ‹*Rad*›; **~ oneself** balancieren; **c)** *(equal, neutralize)* ausgleichen; **~ each other, be ~d** sich *(Dat.)* die Waage halten; **d)** *(make up for, exclude dominance of)* ausgleichen; **e)** *(Bookk.)* bilanzieren. **3.** *v. i.* **a)** *(be in equilibrium)* balancieren; **do these scales ~?** ist diese Waage im Gleichgewicht?; **balancing act** *(lit. or fig.)* Balanceakt, *der;* **b)** *(Bookk.)* ausgeglichen sein; bilanzieren *(Kaufmannsspr.)*

balanced [ˈbælənst] *adj.* ausgewogen; ausgeglichen ‹*Person, Team, Gemüt*›

Balaton [ˈbælətɒn] *pr. n.* **Lake ~:** der Plattensee; der Balaton *(DDR)*

balcony [ˈbælkənɪ] *n.* Balkon, *der; (Amer. Theatre: dress circle)* erster Rang

bald [bɔ:ld] *adj.* **a)** kahl ‹*Person, Kopf*›; kahlköpfig, glatzköpfig ‹*Person*›; **he is ~:** er ist kahl[köpfig] *od.* hat eine Glatze; **go ~:** eine Glatze bekommen; **b)** *(plain)* einfach, schmucklos ‹*Stil, Rede, Prosa*›; schlicht ‹*Appell*›; knapp, nackt ‹*Behauptung*›; **c)** *(coll.: worn smooth)* abgefahren ‹*Reifen*›

ˈ**bald eagle** *n.* Weißkopf-Seeadler, *der*

balderdash [ˈbɔ:ldədæʃ] *n., no pl., no indef.*

art. **a)** Unsinn, *der;* dummes Zeug *(ugs.);* **b)** *(jumble of words)* Wortsalat, *der*

bald: ~head *n.* **a)** kahlköpfiger *od.* glatzköpfiger Mensch; Kahlkopf, *der (ugs.);* Glatzkopf, *der (ugs.);* **b)** *(Ornith.)* Amerikanische Pfeifente; **~-'headed** *adj.* glatzköpfig; kahlköpfig

balding ['bɔ:ldɪŋ] *adj.* mit beginnender Glatze *nachgestellt;* **be ~:** kahl werden

baldly ['bɔ:ldlɪ] *adv.* unverhüllt; offen; knapp und klar ⟨*zusammenfassen, umreißen*⟩; **simply and ~:** schlicht und einfach; **to put it ~:** um es geradeheraus zu sagen

baldness ['bɔ:ldnɪs] *n., no pl. see* **bald a, b:** Kahlheit, *die;* Einfachheit, *die;* Schlichtheit, *die;* Knappheit, *die*

'baldpate *see* **baldhead**

baldric ['bɔ:ldrɪk] *n. (Hist.)* Bandelier, *das*

[1]**bale** [beɪl] **1.** *n.* Ballen, *der.* **2.** *v. t. (pack)* in Ballen verpacken; zu Ballen binden ⟨*Heu*⟩

[2]**bale** *n. (arch./poet.)* **a)** *(evil)* Unheil, *das (geh.);* **b)** *(woe)* Elend, *das*

[3]**bale** *see* [3]**bail**

Balearic Islands [bælɪ'ærɪk aɪləndz] *pr. n. pl.* Balearen *Pl.*

baleful ['beɪlfl] *adj.* unheilvoll; *(malignant)* böse

balefully ['beɪlfəlɪ] *adv.* unheilvoll; *(malignantly)* böse

balk [bɔ:k, bɔ:lk] **1.** *n.* **a)** *(ridge)* Rain, *der;* **b)** *(timber beam)* Balken, *der;* **c)** *(tie-beam)* Binderbalken, *der (Bauw.);* ≈ Dachbalken, *der;* **d)** *(hindrance)* Hindernis, *das* **(to** für); **e)** *no indef. art. (Billiards) markierte Fläche auf dem Billardtisch, wo die Kugel nicht direkt gespielt werden darf;* **f)** *(Baseball) Art Foul des Werfers.* **2.** *v. t.* **a)** [be]hindern; **they were ~ed in their plan/undertaking** *etc.* ihr Plan/Unternehmen *usw.* wurde blockiert; **they were ~ed of their prey** sie wurden um ihre Beute gebracht; **b)** *(avoid)* ausweichen (+ *Dat.*) ⟨*Person, Gespräch*⟩; sich entziehen (+ *Dat.*) ⟨*Verantwortung, Aufgabe, Gespräch*⟩. **3.** *v. i.* sich sträuben **(at** gegen); ⟨*Pferd:*⟩ scheuen **(at** vor + *Dat.*)

Balkan ['bɔ:lkn] **1.** *adj.* Balkan-. **2.** *n. pl.* **the ~s** der Balkan; die Balkanländer

Balkanize ['bɔ:lkənaɪz] *v. t.* balkanisieren

[1]**ball** [bɔ:l] **1.** *n.* **a)** Kugel, *die;* **the animal rolled itself into a ~:** das Tier rollte sich [zu einer Kugel] zusammen; **b)** *(Sport, incl. Golf, Polo)* Ball, *der; (Billiards etc., Croquet)* Kugel, *die;* **the ~ is in your court** *(fig.)* jetzt bist du am Zug *(fig.);* **have the ~ at one's feet** *(fig.)* alle Möglichkeiten *od.* Chancen haben; **keep one's eye on the ~** *(fig.)* die Sache im Auge behalten; **keep the ~ rolling** *(fig.)* die Sache in Schwung halten; **start the ~ rolling** *(fig.)* den Anfang machen; **be on the ~** *(fig. coll.)* voll dasein *(salopp); (be alert)* auf Zack sein *(ugs.);* **play ~:** Ball spielen; *(fig. coll.: co-operate)* mitmachen; **play ~ with sb.** mit jmdm. Ball spielen; *(fig. coll.: co-operate)* mit jmdm. zusammenarbeiten; **c)** *(missile)* Kugel, *die;* **d)** *(round mass)* Kugel, *die; (of wool, string, fluff, etc.)* Knäuel, *das;* **two ~s of wool** zwei Wollknäuel *od.* Knäuel Wolle; **~ of clay** Lehmklumpen, *der;* **e)** *(Anat.: rounded part)* Ballen, *der;* **~ of the hand/foot** Hand-/Fußballen, *der;* **f)** *in pl. (coarse: testicles)* Eier *Pl. (derb);* **~s!** *(fig.)* Scheiß! *(salopp abwertend); constr. as sing.* **make a ~s of sth.** *(fig.)* bei etw. Scheiße bauen *(derb).* **2.** *v. t.* zusammenballen; zerknüllen ⟨*Papier*⟩; ballen ⟨*Faust*⟩

~ 'up *v.t. see* **balls up**

[2]**ball** *n. (dance)* Ball, *der;* **give a ~:** einen Ball geben *od.* veranstalten; **have [oneself] a ~** *(fig. sl.)* sich riesig amüsieren *(ugs.);* **open the ~:** den Ball eröffnen; *(fig.)* den Tanz beginnen

ballad ['bæləd] *n.* **a)** Lied, *das; (narrative)* Ballade, *die;* Lied, *das;* **b)** *(poem)* Ballade, *die*

balladry ['bælədrɪ] *n.* Balladendichtung, *die*

ball and 'socket joint *n.* Kugelgelenk, *das*

ballast ['bæləst] *n.* **a)** Ballast, *der;* **be in ~:** auf Ballastfahrt sein *(Seemannsspr.);* **b)** *(fig.: sth. that gives stability)* stabilisierender Faktor; **c)** *(coarse stone etc.)* Schotter, *der*

ball: ~-'bearing *n. (Mech.)* Kugellager, *das;* **~boy** *n.* Balljunge, *der;* **~ clay** *n. (Amer. Min.)* Pfeifenton, *der;* **~cock** *n.* Schwimmer[regel]ventil, *das (Technik);* **~ control** *n.* Ballführung, *die*

ballerina [bælə'ri:nə] *n.* Ballerina, *die;* **prima ~:** Primaballerina, *die*

ballet ['bæleɪ] *n.* Ballett, *das;* **~ dancer** Balletttänzer, *der*/-tänzerin, *die*

ball: ~ game *n.* **a)** Ballspiel, *das;* **b)** *(Amer.)* Baseballspiel, *das;* **a whole new ~ game** *(fig. coll.)* eine ganz neue Geschichte *(ugs.);* **a different ~ game** *(fig. coll.)* eine andere Sache; **~girl** *n.* Ballmädchen, *das*

ballistic [bə'lɪstɪk] *adj.* ballistisch; **~ missile** ballistische Rakete

ballistics [bə'lɪstɪks] *n., no pl.* Ballistik, *die*

ball: ~ joint *see* **ball and socket joint; ~ lightning** *n.* Kugelblitz, *der*

balloon [bə'lu:n] **1.** *n.* **a)** Ballon, *der;* **hot-air ~:** Heißluftballon, *der;* **when the ~ goes up** *(fig.)* wenn es losgeht *(ugs.);* **b)** *(toy)* Luftballon, *der;* **c)** *(coll.: in strip cartoon etc.)* Sprechblase, *die;* **d)** *(drinking-glass)* Schwenker, *der;* Schwenkglas, *das.* **2.** *v. i.* **a)** sich blähen; **b)** *(travel in ~)* im Ballon fahren. **3.** *v. t. (hit, kick)* hoch in die Luft schlagen

balloon 'tyre *n.* Ballonreifen, *der*

ballot ['bælət] **1.** *n.* **a)** *(voting)* Abstimmung, *die;* **[secret] ~:** geheime Wahl; **hold** *or* **take a ~:** abstimmen; **b)** *(vote)* Stimme, *die;* **cast one's ~:** seine Stimme abgeben; **c)** *(ticket, paper)* Stimmzettel, *der.* **2.** *v. i.* abstimmen; **~ for sb./sth.** für jmdn./etw. stimmen. **3.** *v. t.* abstimmen lassen; eine Abstimmung vornehmen bei

ballot: ~-box *n.* Wahlurne, *die;* **~-paper** *n.* Stimmzettel, *der*

ball: ~-park *n. (Amer.)* Baseballfeld, *das;* **your estimate is not in the right ~park** *(fig.)* mit deiner Schätzung liegst du völlig falsch *(ugs.);* **~-pen, ~-point, ~-point 'pen** *ns.* Kugelschreiber, *der;* **~room** *n.* Tanzsaal, *der;* **~room dancing** *n.* Gesellschaftstanz, *der*

'balls up *v.t. (coarse)* Scheiße bauen bei *(derb)*

balls-up ['bɔ:lzʌp] *(coarse) n.* Scheiß, *der (salopp abwertend);* **make a ~ of sth.** bei etw. Scheiße bauen *(derb.)*

bally ['bælɪ] *(Brit. sl. euphem.) adj., adv.* verdammt *(salopp)*

ballyhoo [bælɪ'hu:] *n.* **a)** *(publicity)* [Reklame]rummel, *der (ugs.);* **create a great deal of ~ over sth.** einen großen Rummel um etw. veranstalten *(ugs.);* **b)** *(nonsense)* Geschrei, *das (abwertend)*

balm [bɑ:m] *n.* **a)** *(lit. or fig.)* Balsam, *der;* **b)** *(fragrance)* [aromatischer] Duft; **c)** *(tree)* Balsambaum, *der;* **d)** *(herb)* Melisse, *die;* **~ of Gilead** Gileadbalsam, *der*

balmy ['bɑ:mɪ] *adj.* **a)** *(yielding balm)* Balsam liefernd; **b)** *(fragrant)* wohlriechend; balsamisch *(geh.);* **c)** *(soft, mild)* mild; **d)** *(sl.: crazy)* bescheuert *(salopp);* **e)** *(soothing, healing)* lindernd

baloney *see* **boloney a**

balsa ['bɔ:lsə, 'bɒlsə] *n.* **a)** *(tree)* Balsabaum, *der;* **b)** *(wood)* **~[-wood]** Balsaholz, *das*

balsam ['bɔ:lsəm, 'bɒlsəm] *n.* **a)** *(lit. or fig.; also Med., Chem.)* Balsam, *der;* **Canada ~:** Kanadabalsam, *der;* **b)** *(tree)* Balsambaum, *der;* **c)** *(plant of genus Impatiens)* Springkraut, *das; (garden flower)* Gartenbalsamine, *die; (touch-me-not)* Rührmichnichtan, *das*

balsam 'fir *n.* Balsamtanne, *die*

Balt [bɔ:lt, bɒlt] *n.* Balte, *der*/Baltin, *die*

Baltic ['bɔ:ltɪk, 'bɒltɪk] **1.** *pr. n.* Ostsee, *die.* **2.** *adj.* baltisch; **~ coast** Ostseeküste, *die;* **the ~ Sea** die Ostsee; **the ~ States** das Baltikum

baluster ['bæləstə(r)] *n.* **a)** *(pillar)* Baluster, *der;* Docke, *die;* **b)** *(post)* Geländerpfosten, *der; (balustrade)* Balustrade, *die*

balustrade [bælə'streɪd] *n.* Balustrade, *die*

bamboo [bæm'bu:] *n.* **a)** *(stem)* Bambus, *der;* Bambusrohr, *das;* **b)** *(grass)* Bambus, *der;* **~ curtain** *(Polit.)* Bambusvorhang, *der;* **~ shoots** Bambussprossen

bamboozle [bæm'bu:zl] *v. t. (sl.)* **a)** *(mystify)* verblüffen; **b)** *(cheat)* reinlegen *(ugs.);* **~ sb. into doing sth.** jmdn. [durch Tricks] dazu bringen, etw. zu tun; jmdn. so reinlegen, daß er etw. tut; **~ sb. out of sth.** jmdm. etw. abluchsen *(salopp)*

ban [bæn] **1.** *v. t.,* **-nn-** verbieten; **~ sb. from doing sth.** jmdm. verbieten, etw. zu tun; **he was ~ned from driving/playing** er erhielt Fahr-/Spielverbot; **~ sb. from a place** jmdm. die Einreise/den Zutritt *usw.* verbieten; **~ sb. from a pub/the teaching profession** jmdm. Lokalverbot erteilen/jmdn. vom Lehrberuf ausschließen. **2.** *n.* Verbot, *das;* **place a ~ on sth.** etw. mit einem Verbot belegen; **the ~ placed on these drugs** das Verbot dieser Drogen; **lift the ~ on sth.** das Verbot einer Sache *(Gen.)* aufheben

banal [bə'nɑ:l, bə'næl] *adj.* banal

banality [bə'nælɪtɪ] *n.* Banalität, *die*

banana [bə'nɑ:nə] *n.* **a)** *(fruit)* Banane, *die;* **a hand of ~s** eine Hand Bananen *(fachspr.);* **go ~s** *(Brit. sl.)* verrückt werden *(salopp);* überschnappen *(ugs.);* **b)** *(plant)* Bananenstaude, *die*

banana: ~ republic *n. (derog.)* Bananenrepublik, *die (abwertend);* **~ skin** *n.* Bananenschale, *die;* **~ 'split** *n.* Bananensplit, *das*

band [bænd] **1.** *n.* **a)** Band, *das;* **a ~ of light/colour** ein Streifen Licht/Farbe; **b)** *(range of values)* Bandbreite, *die (fig.);* **income ~:** ≈ Gehaltsstufe, *die;* **c)** *(of frequency or wavelength)* **long/medium ~:** Langwellen-/Mittelwellenband, *das;* **high-frequency ~:** Hochfrequenzbereich, *der;* **d)** *(organized group)* Gruppe, *die; (of robbers, outlaws, etc.)* Bande, *die;* **B~ of Hope** *Organisation jugendlicher Abstinenzler;* **e)** *(of musicians)* [Musik]kapelle, *die; (pop group, jazz ~)* Band, *die;* Gruppe, *die; (dance ~)* [Tanz]kapelle, *die; (military ~)* Militärkapelle, *die; (brass ~)* Blaskapelle, *die;* **if** *or* **when the ~ begins to play** *(fig. coll.)* wenn es ernst wird; **f)** *in pl. (part of legal, clerical, or academic dress)* Beffchen, *das;* **g)** *(ring round bird's leg)* Beringung, *die;* **h)** *(Amer.) (herd)* Herde, *die; (of birds, insects)* Schwarm, *der;* **i)** *in pl. (arch.: sth. that restrains)* Bande *Pl. See also* **beat 1 d. 2.** *v. t.* **a) ~ sth.** ein Band um etw. machen; **b)** *(form into a league)* vereinigen; **c)** *(mark with stripes)* bändern; **~ed** *(Biol.)* Streifen-; gestreift. **3.** *v. i.* **~ together [with sb.]** sich [mit jmdm.] zusammenschließen

bandage ['bændɪdʒ] **1.** *n. (for wound, fracture)* Verband, *der; (for fracture, as support)* Bandage, *die; (for blindfolding)* Binde, *die.* **2.** *v. t.* verbinden ⟨*[offene] Wunde usw.*⟩; bandagieren ⟨*[verstauchtes] Gelenk usw.*⟩

'Band-Aid, (P) *n.* ≈ Hansaplast ⓦⓩ, *das*

b. & b. [bi: ən 'bi:] *abbr.* **bed & breakfast**

'bandbox *n.* Bandschachtel, *die (veralt.);* ≈ Hutschachtel, *die*

bandicoot ['bændɪku:t] *n.* **a)** *(Ind.: rat)* Bandikutratte, *die;* **b)** *(Austral.: marsupial)* Bandikut, *der;* Beuteldachs, *der*

bandit ['bændɪt] *n.* Bandit, *der*

banditry ['bændɪtrɪ] *n.* Banditen[un]wesen, *das*

'bandmaster *n.* Kapellmeister, *der*

bandoleer, bandolier [bændə'lɪə(r)] *n.* Schultergürtel, *der;* Bandelier, *das (veralt.)*

'band-saw n. Bandsäge, die

bandsman ['bændzmən] n., pl. **bandsmen** ['bændzmən] Mitglied der/einer Kapelle/Band

band: ~**stand** n. Musikertribüne, die; (circular) Konzertpavillon, der; ~**wagon** n. Wagen der Musikkapelle; **climb** or **jump on [to] the ~wagon** (fig.) auf den fahrenden Zug aufspringen (fig.); ~**width** n. (Communications) Bandbreite, die

[1]bandy ['bændɪ] v.t. a) (toss to and fro) hin- und herspielen; b) (fig.) herumerzählen (ugs.) ⟨Geschichte⟩; **be bandied from mouth to mouth** von Mund zu Mund gehen; **insults were being bandied about** Beschimpfungen flogen hin und her; c) (discuss) ~ **about** hin und her diskutieren; d) (exchange) wechseln; **they were ~ing blows** sie tauschten Schläge aus; **don't ~ words with me** ich wünsche keine Diskussion

[2]bandy adj. krumm; **he has ~ legs** or **is ~-legged** er hat O-Beine (ugs.); **~-legged person** O-beinige Person (ugs.)

bane [beɪn] n. Ruin, der; **he is the ~ of my life** er ist der Nagel zu meinem Sarg (ugs.)

[1]bang [bæŋ] 1. v.t. a) knallen (ugs.); schlagen; zuknallen (ugs.), zuschlagen ⟨Tür, Fenster, Deckel⟩; ~ **one's head on** or **against the ceiling** mit dem Kopf an die Decke knallen (ugs.) od. schlagen; **I could ~ their heads together** (fig.) ich könnte ihre Köpfe gegeneinanderschlagen; **she ~ed down the receiver** sie knallte den Hörer auf die Gabel (ugs.); **he ~ed the nail in** er haute den Nagel rein (ugs.); see also **brick wall**; b) (sl.: copulate with) bumsen (salopp). 2. v.i. a) (strike) ~ **[against sth.]** [gegen etw.] schlagen od. (ugs.) knallen; ~ **at the door** gegen die Tür hämmern; b) (make sound of blow or explosion) knallen; ⟨Kanonen:⟩ donnern; ⟨Trommeln:⟩ dröhnen; ~ **away at sth.** auf etw. (Akk.) ballern (ugs.); ~ **shut** zuknallen (ugs.); zuschlagen; **a door is ~ing somewhere** irgendwo schlägt eine Tür. 3. n. a) (blow) Schlag, der; **give your radio a good ~:** hau mal kräftig gegen dein Radio (ugs.); b) (noise) Knall, der; **the party went off with a ~** (fig.) die Party war eine Wucht (ugs.). See also **big bang**; **whimper 1.** 4. adv. a) (with impact) mit voller Wucht; b) (explosively) **go ~** ⟨Gewehr, Feuerwerkskörper:⟩ krachen; **the balloon went ~ and exploded** der Ballon explodierte mit einem lauten Knall; c) ~ **goes sth.** (fig.: sth. ends suddenly) aus ist es mit etw.; ~ **went £50** 50 Pfund waren weg; d) ~ **off** (coll.: immediately) sofort; **answer ~ off** wie aus der Pistole geschossen antworten (ugs.); e) (coll.: exactly) genau; **you are ~ on time** du bist pünktlich auf die Minute (ugs.); ~ **on [the] target** genau richtig; ~ **on** genau od. gerade; f) **~-up** (Amer. sl.: first-class) Klasse (ugs.). 5. int. peng

[2]bang 1. v.t. gerade abschneiden ⟨Haare⟩. 2. n. Pony, der

banger ['bæŋə(r)] n. (sl.) a) (sausage) Würstchen, das; b) (firework) Kracher, der (ugs.); c) (car) Klapperkiste, die (ugs.)

Bangladesh [bæŋglə'deʃ] pr. n. Bangladesch (das)

Bangladeshi [bæŋglə'deʃɪ] 1. adj. bangalisch. 2. n. Bangali, der/die

bangle ['bæŋgl] n. Armreif, der

banian ['bænɪən] n. (Bot.) **~[-tree]** Banyanbaum, der

banish ['bænɪʃ] v.t. verbannen (**from** aus); bannen ⟨Furcht⟩

banishment ['bænɪʃmənt] n. Verbannung, die (**from** aus)

banister ['bænɪstə(r)] n. a) (uprights and rail) [Treppen]geländer, das; b) usu. in pl. (upright) Geländerpfosten, der

banjo ['bændʒəʊ] n., pl. ~s or ~es Banjo, das

[1]bank [bæŋk] 1. n. a) (slope) Böschung, die; b) (at side of river) Ufer, das; c) (elevation in bed of sea or river) Bank, die; d) (mass) **a ~ of clouds/fog** eine Wolken-/Nebelbank; **a ~ of snow** eine Schneewehe; e) (artificial slope) Überhöhung, die (Verkehrsw.). 2. v.t. a) (build higher) überhöhen (Verkehrsw.); b) (heap) ~ **[up]** aufschichten; ~ **[up] the fire with coal** Kohlen auf das Feuer schichten; c) in die Kurve legen ⟨Flugzeug, Auto⟩. 3. v.i. a) (rise) ~ **[up]** ⟨Rauch, Wolken:⟩ sich aufschichten; b) ⟨Flugzeug:⟩ sich in die Kurve legen

[2]bank 1. n. a) (Commerc., Finance) Bank, die; **central ~:** Zentralbank, die; **the B~** (Brit.) die Bank von England; **cry/laugh all the way to the ~** (fig. coll.) sich für seinen Erfolg entschuldigen (iron.)/aus seiner Freude über seinen Erfolg keinen Hehl machen; b) (Gaming) Bank, die; see also **blood bank**; **bottle bank**. 2. v.i. a) (keep ~) Bankier sein; b) (keep money) ~ **at/with ...:** ein Konto haben bei ...; c) ~ **on sth.** (fig.) auf etw. (Akk.) zählen. 3. v.t. zur Bank bringen

[3]bank n. a) (row) Reihe, die; b) (tier) ~ **[of oars]** Ruderreihe, die

bankable ['bæŋkəbl] adj. bankfähig; (fig.) erfolgversprechend

bank: ~ **account** n. Bankkonto, das; ~ **balance** n. Kontostand, der; **~-bill** n. (Brit.) Bankakzept, der; (Amer.: banknote) Banknote, die; **~-book** n. Sparbuch, das; ~ **card** n. Scheckkarte, die; ~ **charges** n. pl. Kontoführungskosten; ~ **clerk** n. Bankangestellte, der/die

banker ['bæŋkə(r)] n. (Commerc., Finance) Bankier, der; Banker, der (ugs.); **let me be your ~:** lassen Sie mich Ihnen Geld leihen

banker's: ~ **card** see **bank card**; ~ **'order** see **order 1 o**

bank 'holiday n. a) Bankfeiertag, der; b) (Brit.: public holiday) Feiertag, der

banking ['bæŋkɪŋ] n. Bankwesen, das; **a career in ~:** die Banklaufbahn; **it is ~ practice** es ist banküblich; **new ~ arrangements** neue Bankverhältnisse

bank: ~ **manager** n. Zweigstellenleiter [einer/der Bank]; **~note** n. Banknote, die; Geldschein, der; ~ **raid** n. Banküberfall, der; ~ **rate** n. Diskontsatz, der; **~-robber** n. Bankräuber, der; **~roll** 1. n. finanzielle Mittel Pl.; 2. v.t. finanziell unterstützen

bankrupt ['bæŋkrʌpt] 1. n. a) (Law) Gemeinschuldner, der; **become a ~:** Gemeinschuldner werden; **be declared a ~:** zum Gemeinschuldner erklärt werden; b) (insolvent debtor) Bankrotteur, der. 2. adj. a) bankrott; **go ~:** in Konkurs gehen; Bankrott machen; bankrottieren (veralt.); b) (fig.) **morally ~:** moralisch bankrott (fig.). 3. v.t. bankrott machen

bankruptcy ['bæŋkrʌptsɪ] n. Konkurs, der; Bankrott, der; **go into ~:** in Konkurs gehen; Bankrott machen; ~ **proceedings** Konkursverfahren, das

'bank statement n. Kontoauszug, der

banner ['bænə(r)] 1. n. a) (flag, ensign; also fig.) Banner, das; **join** or **follow the ~ of** dem Banner (+ Gen.) folgen; b) (on two poles) Spruchband, das; Transparent, das; c) (sth. used as symbol) Symbol, das. 2. adj. a) (conspicuous) ~ **headline** Balkenüberschrift, die; b) (Amer.: pre-eminent) herausragend

bannister see **banister**

bannock ['bænək] n. (Scot., N. Engl.) rundes, flaches Brot

banns [bænz] n. pl. Aufgebot, das; **publish/put up the ~:** das Aufgebot verkünden/aushängen; **forbid the ~:** Einspruch [gegen die Eheschließung] erheben

banquet ['bæŋkwɪt] 1. n. Bankett, das (geh.). 2. v.i. a) [festlich] tafeln (geh.); bankettieren (veralt.); **~ing-hall** Bankettsaal, der; b) (carouse) zechen (geh.)

banshee ['bænʃi:] n. (Ir., Scot.) Banshee, die (Myth.); ≈ Weiße Frau

bantam ['bæntəm] n. Zwerg-, Bantamhuhn, das

'bantamweight n. (Boxing etc.) Bantamgewicht, das; (person also) Bantamgewichtler, der

banter ['bæntə(r)] 1. n. a) heiterer Spott; b) (remarks) Spöttelei, die (**on** über + Akk.); (joking back and forth) spöttisches Geplänkel. 2. v.t. aufziehen (**about** mit). 3. v.i. spötteln

Bantu [bæn'tu:] 1. n. a) pl. same or ~s Bantu, der/die; b) (language-group) Bantu, das; Bantusprachen. 2. adj. Bantu-

Bantustan [bæntʊ'stɑ:n] n. (S. Afr.) Bantuheimatland, das

banyan see **banian**

baobab ['beɪəbæb] n. (Bot.) Baobab, der; Affenbrotbaum, der

BAOR abbr. **British Army of the Rhine** Britische Rheinarmee

bap [bæp] n. ≈ Brötchen, das

baptise see **baptize**

baptism ['bæptɪzm] n. Taufe, die; ~ **is the first sacrament** die Taufe ist das erste Sakrament; ~ **of fire** (fig.) Feuertaufe, die; ~ **of blood** (fig.) Bluttaufe, die (Rel.)

baptismal [bæp'tɪzml] adj. Tauf-; ⟨Wiedergeburt, Reinigung⟩ durch die Taufe; ~ **certificate** Taufschein, der; ~ **name** Taufname, der

Baptist ['bæptɪst] 1. n. a) Baptist, der/Baptistin, die; b) **John the ~:** Johannes der Täufer. 2. adj. **the ~ Church/a ~ chapel** die Kirche/eine Kapelle der Baptisten

baptize [bæp'taɪz] v.t. taufen; **be ~d a Catholic/Protestant** katholisch/protestantisch getauft werden; **what name were you ~d by?** auf welchen Namen wurden Sie getauft?

[1]bar [bɑ:(r)] 1. n. a) (long piece of rigid material) Stange, die; (shorter, thinner also) Stab, der; (of gold, silver) Barren, der; **a ~ of soap** ein Stück Seife; **a ~ of chocolate** ein Riegel Schokolade; (slab) eine Tafel Schokolade; b) (Sport) Stab, der; (of high ~) [Reck]stange, die; (of parallel ~s) [Barren]holm, der; (cross~) [Sprung]latte, die; **high** or **horizontal ~:** Reck, das; **parallel ~s** Barren, der; c) (heating element) Heizelement, das (Elektrot.); d) (band) Streifen, der; (on medal) silberner Querstreifen; (Her.) Balken, der; e) (rod, pole) Stange, die; (of cage, prison) Gitterstab, der; **behind ~s** (in prison) hinter Gittern; (into prison) hinter Gitter; f) (barrier, lit. or fig.) Barriere, die (**to** für); **a ~ on recruitment/promotion** ein Einstellungs-/Beförderungsstopp; g) (for refreshment) Bar, die; (counter) Theke, die; h) (Law: place at which prisoner stands) ≈ Anklagebank, die; **the prisoner at the ~:** der/die Angeklagte; **be judged at the ~ of conscience/of public opinion** (fig.) sich vor dem Gewissen/der öffentlichen Meinung verantworten müssen; i) (Law: particular court) Gerichtshof, der; **be called to the ~:** als Anwalt vor höheren Gerichten zugelassen werden; **be called within the ~:** zum Anwalt der Krone ernannt werden; **the Bar** die höhere Anwaltschaft; **the inner ~:** die Anwaltschaft der Krone; **the outer ~:** die Anwälte, die nicht Anwälte der Krone sind; **he was reading for the ~:** er bereitete sich auf die Zulassung als Anwalt vor höheren Gerichten vor; j) (Mus.) Takt, der; **~[-line]** Taktstrich, der; k) (sandbank, shoal) Barre, die; Sandbank, die. 2. v.t., -rr- a) (fasten) verriegeln; **~red window** vergittertes Fenster; b) (keep) ~ **sb. in/out** jmdn. ein-/aussperren; c) (obstruct) sperren ⟨Straße, Weg⟩ (**to** für); ~ **sb.'s way** jmdm. den Weg versperren; d) (prohibit, hinder) verbieten; ~ **sb. from doing sth.** jmdn. daran hindern, etw. zu tun; e) (not consider) unberücksichtigt lassen; f) (mark) mit Streifen versehen; **~red [with colourful stripes]** [bunt]gestreift;

~red with brown braun gestreift; g) *(Law)* ausschließen. 3. *prep.* abgesehen von; ~ any accidents falls nichts passiert; ~ none ohne Einschränkung; bet two to one ~ one *(Racing)* zwei zu eins auf alle außer einem wetten

²**bar** *n. (Meteorol., Phys.)* Bar, *das*

barb [bɑ:b] 1. *n.* a) Widerhaken, *der; (fig.)* Gehässigkeit, *die;* ~s of ridicule gehässige Spötteleien; b) *(of fish)* Bartfaden, *der;* Bartel, *die;* c) *(of feather)* Fahne, *die.* 2. *v. t.* mit Widerhaken versehen

Barbadian [bɑ:'beɪdɪən] 1. *adj.* barbadisch; sb. is ~: jmd. ist Barbadier/Barbadierin. 2. *n.* Barbadier, *der*/Barbadierin, *die*

Barbados [bɑ:'beɪdəʊz, bɑ:'beɪdɒs] *pr. n.* Barbados *(das)*

barbarian [bɑ:'beərɪən] 1. *n. (lit. or fig.)* Barbar, *der.* 2. *adj. (lit. or fig.)* barbarisch; a ~ king ein Barbarenkönig

barbaric [bɑ:'bærɪk] *adj.* barbarisch; primitiv ‹*Kleidung, Schmuck*›

barbarically [bɑ:'bærɪkəlɪ] *adj.* barbarisch

barbarism ['bɑ:bərɪzm] *n.* a) *no pl.* Barbarei, *die; (rudeness also)* Unkultiviertheit, *die;* b) *no pl. (departing from normal standards)* Barbarismus, *der (Sprachw., Kunstwiss.);* c) *(instance)* [barbarische] Grausamkeit

barbarity [bɑ:'bærɪtɪ] *n.* a) *no pl.* Grausamkeit, *die;* he treats criminals with ~: er behandelt Verbrecher äußerst barbarisch; b) *(instance)* Barbarei, *die*

barbarous ['bɑ:bərəs] *adj.* barbarisch

barbarously ['bɑ:bərəslɪ] *adv.* auf barbarische Art und Weise; barbarisch

barbarousness ['bɑ:bərəsnɪs] *n., no pl.* Roheit, *die*

Barbary 'ape *n. (Zool.)* Magot, *der;* Berberaffe, *der*

barbecue ['bɑ:bɪkju:] 1. *n.* a) *(party)* Grillparty, *die;* Barbecue, *das;* b) *(food)* Grillgericht, *das;* Barbecue, *das;* c) *(fireplace with frame)* Grill, *der;* d) *(frame)* Grill, *der;* Bratrost, *der;* Barbecue, *das.* 2. *v. t.* grillen

barbed wire [bɑ:bd 'waɪər] *n.* Stacheldraht, *der;* ~ fence Stacheldrahtzaun, *der*

barbel ['bɑ:bl] *n.* a) *(Zool.)* Barbe, *die;* b) *(filament)* Bartfaden, *der;* Bartel, *der*

'barbell *n.* Hantel, *die*

barber ['bɑ:bə(r)] *n.* Friseur, *der;* Barbier, *der (veralt.);* go to the ~'s zum Friseur gehen; ~'s pole *spiralig rot und weiß gestreifter Stab als Ladenschild des Friseurs*

barberry ['bɑ:bərɪ] *n.* a) *(shrub)* Berberitze, *die;* Sauerdorn, *der;* b) *(berry)* Berberitzenbeere, *die;* Sauerdornbeere, *die*

barber: ~-shop *n. (Amer.)* ~-shop harmony Barbershopharmonie, *die; vokale Harmonik mit paralleler Stimmführung;* ~-shop singing/quartet Barbershopgesang, *der*/-quartett, *das;* ~'s shop *n. (Brit.)* Friseursalon, *der*

barbican ['bɑ:bɪkən] *n. (Hist.)* Barbakane, *die;* Torvorwerk, *das*

barbiturate [bɑ:'bɪtjʊrət] *n. (Chem.)* Barbiturat, *das*

barcarole [bɑ:kə'rəʊl], **barcarolle** [bɑ:kə'rɒl] *n. (Mus.)* Barkarole, *die*

Barcelona [bɑ:sɪ'ləʊnə] *pr. n.* Barcelona *(das);* ~ nut Barcelonanuß, *die (eine Haselnußsorte)*

bar: ~ chart *n.* Stabdiagramm, *das;* ~ code *n.* Strichcode, *der*

bard [bɑ:d] *n.* Barde, *der;* the B~ [of Avon] Shakespeare

bardic ['bɑ:dɪk] *adj.* bardisch *(veralt.)*

bare [beə(r)] 1. *adj.* a) nackt; expose a ~ back to the sun den nackten Rücken der Sonne aussetzen; walk with *or* in ~ feet barfuß gehen; in one's ~ skin nackt [und bloß]; b) *(hatless)* with one's head ~: ohne Hut; c) *(leafless)* kahl; d) *(unfurnished)* kahl; nackt ‹*Boden*›; e) *(unconcealed)* lay ~ sth. etw. aufdecken; f) *(unadorned)* nackt, ungeschminkt ‹*Wahrheit, Tatsache*›; grob ‹*Skizze*›; nackt, kahl ‹*Wand*›; *see also* bone 1 a; g) *(empty)* leer; h) *(scanty)* knapp ‹*Mehrheit*›; [sehr] gering ‹*Menge, Teil*›; i) *(mere)* äußerst ‹*Notwendige*›; karg ‹*Essen, Leben*›; nur gering ‹*Möglichkeit*›; bloß ‹*Gedanke*›; the ~ necessities of life das zum Leben Notwendigste; j) *(without tools)* do sth. with one's ~ hands etw. mit den *od.* seinen bloßen Händen tun; k) *(unprovided with)* ~ of sth. ohne etw.; the land was ~ of any vegetation das Land war völlig vegetationslos. 2. *v. t.* a) *(uncover)* entblößen ‹*Kopf, Arm, Bein*›; ziehen ‹*Schwert*›; bloßlegen ‹*Draht eines Kabels*›; ~ one's back to the sun seinen Rücken der Sonne aussetzen; b) *(reveal)* blecken ‹*Zähne*›; she ~d her heart to him *(fig.)* sie schüttete ihm ihr Herz aus

bare: ~back 1. *adj.* ‹*Reiter, Reiten*› auf ungesatteltem Pferd; 2. *adv.* ohne Sattel; ~faced *adj.,* ~faced[ly] [beə'feɪsɪd(lɪ)] *adv. (fig.)* unverhüllt; ~foot 1. *adj.* barfüßig; he is ~foot er ist barfuß *od.* barfüßig; ~foot doctor Barfußarzt, *der;* 2. *adv.* barfuß; ~'handed 1. *adj.* he was ~handed *(without gloves)* er trug keine Handschuhe; *(without weapon)* er war unbewaffnet; 2. *adv.* mit bloßen Händen; ~'headed 1. *adj.* he was ~headed er trug keine Kopfbedeckung; 2. *adv.* ohne Kopfbedeckung; ~legged *adj.* mit bloßen Beinen

barely ['beəlɪ] *adv.* a) *(only just)* kaum; knapp ‹*vermeiden, entkommen*›; b) *(scantily)* karg

bare-'midriff *adj.* taillenfrei ‹*Kleid*›

bareness ['beənɪs] *n., no pl. see* bare 1 c, d, f: Kahlheit, *die;* Nacktheit, *die;* Kargheit, *die*

bargain ['bɑ:gɪn] 1. *n.* a) *(agreement)* Abmachung, *die;* an unequal ~: ein ungleicher Handel; into the ~, *(Amer.)* in the ~: darüber hinaus; make *or* strike a ~ to do sth. sich darauf einigen, etw. zu tun; I'll make a ~ with you ich mache dir ein Angebot; they got the best of the ~: sie haben den besseren Teil bekommen; a ~'s a ~: was einmal abgemacht ist, gilt; b) *(thing acquired)* Kauf, *der;* a good/bad ~: ein guter/schlechter Kauf; c) *(thing offered cheap)* günstiges Angebot; *(thing acquired cheaply)* guter Kauf; a definite ~: ein absolutes Sonderangebot. *See also* best 3 e; hard 1 a. 2. *v. i.* a) *(discuss)* handeln; ~ for sth. um etw. handeln; b) ~ for *(expect):* more than one had ~ed for mehr als man erwartet hatte; ~ for sth. mit etw. rechnen. 3. *v. t.* ~ away sich *(Dat.)* abhandeln lassen

bargain: ~ 'basement *n.* Tiefgeschoß mit Sonderangeboten; ~ counter *n.* Tisch mit Sonderangeboten

bargaining ['bɑ:gɪnɪŋ] *n.* Handel, *der; (negotiating)* Verhandlungen; ~ position Verhandlungsposition, *die;* ~ counter *(fig.)* Trumpf [für Verhandlungen]; *see also* collective bargaining

bargain: ~ offer *n.* Sonderangebot, *das;* ~ price *n.* Sonderpreis, *der*

barge [bɑ:dʒ] 1. *n.* a) Kahn, *der;* freight/cargo ~: Fracht-/Lastkahn, *der;* b) *(for State occasions)* Prunkschiff, *das (veralt.).* 2. *v. i.* a) *(lurch)* ~ into sb. jmdn. anrempeln; ~ against sth. gegen etw. taumeln; ~ about the house im Haus herumtoben; b) ~ in *(intrude)* hineinplatzen/hereinplatzen *(ugs.);* he ~d in on us er platzte bei uns herein *(ugs.)*

bargee [bɑ:'dʒi:] *(Brit.),* **barge-man** *(Amer.) ns.* Flußschiffer, *der*

'barge-pole *n.* Stake, *die (nordd.);* I wouldn't touch him/that *etc.* with [the end of] a ~! *(fig.)* ich würde ihn/das *usw.* nicht mit der Beißzange anfassen! *(ugs.)*

baritone ['bærɪtəʊn] *(Mus.)* 1. *n.* Bariton, *der; (voice, part also)* Baritonstimme, *die.* 2. *adj.* ~ voice Baritonstimme, *die*

barium ['beərɪəm] *n. (Chem.)* Barium, *das;* ~ meal Kontrastbrei, *der (mit Bariumsulfat)*

¹**bark** [bɑ:k] 1. *n.* a) *(of tree)* Borke, *die;* Rinde, *die;* b) *(for tanning, dyeing)* [Gerber]lohe, *die.* 2. *v. t.* a) *(abrade)* aufschürfen; b) *(strip ~ from)* entrinden

²**bark** 1. *n. (lit. or fig.)* Bellen, *das;* his ~ is worse than his bite *(fig.)* er ist nicht so bissig, wie er tut; ≈ Hunde, die bellen, beißen nicht. 2. *v. i.* a) *(lit. or fig.)* bellen; ~ at sb. jmdn. anbellen; be ~ing up the wrong tree auf dem Holzweg sein; b) ~ at *(abuse)* anblaffen *(salopp);* c) *(speak loudly and curtly)* brüllen; d) *(Amer.: act as tout)* den Ausrufer machen. 3. a) *v.t.* bellen; b) *(bellow)* ~ [out] orders to sb. jmdm. Befehle zubrüllen

³**bark** *n. (poet.: ship)* Schiff, *das*

'barkeep *(Amer.),* **'barkeeper** *n.* Barkeeper, *der; (owner)* Wirt, *der*

barker ['bɑ:kə(r)] *n.* Ausrufer, *der*

barley ['bɑ:lɪ] *n.* Gerste, *die; see also* pearl barley

barley: ~corn *n. (grain)* Gerstenkorn, *das;* ~-mow *n.* Gerstenschober, *der (bes. südd.);* ~ sugar *n.* Gerstenzucker, *der;* ~ water *n.* Gerstenwasser, *das (veralt.)*

barm [bɑ:m] *n.* Hefe, *die;* Bärme, *die (nordd.)*

bar: ~maid *n. (Brit.)* Bardame, *die;* ~man ['bɑ:mən] *n., pl.* ~men ['bɑ:mən] Barmann, *der;* Schankkellner, *der*

bar mitzvah [bɑ:'mɪtzvə] *n.* a) *(boy)* Bar-Mizwa, *der;* b) *(ceremony)* Bar-Mizwa, *die*

barmy ['bɑ:mɪ] *adj. (sl.: crazy)* bescheuert *(salopp)*

barn [bɑ:n] *n.* a) *(Brit.: for grain etc.)* Scheune, *die; (Amer.: for implements etc.)* Schuppen, *der; (Amer.: for animals)* Stall, *der;* b) *(derog.)* [großer, häßlicher] Schuppen

barnacle ['bɑ:nəkl] *n.* a) *(Zool.)* Rankenfüßer, *der;* b) ~ [goose] Weißwangengans, *die*

barn: ~ dance *n.* ≈ Schottische, *der;* ~-door *n.* Scheunentor, *das;* be as big as a ~-door *(fig.)* nicht zu verfehlen sein

barney ['bɑ:nɪ] *n. (coll.)* Krach, *der (ugs.);* have a ~: Krach haben *(ugs.)*

barn: ~-owl *n.* Schleiereule, *die;* ~storm *v. i.* durch die Provinz ziehen *od.* tingeln; ~stormer *n.* tingelnder Schauspieler; *(Amer.: politician)* Politiker [im Wahlkampf in der Provinz]; *(Amer.: aviator)* [Kunstflug]pilot [auf Tournee durch die Provinz]; ~yard *n.* Wirtschaftshof, *der*

barograph ['bærəgrɑ:f] *n.* Barograph, *der*

barometer [bə'rɒmɪtə(r)] *n. (lit. or fig.)* Barometer, *das*

barometric [bærə'metrɪk] *adj.* barometrisch; ~ pressure Luftdruck, *der*

baron ['bærn] *n.* a) *(holder of title)* Baron, *der;* Freiherr, *der;* b) *(merchant)* coal/oil ~: Kohlen-/Ölmagnat, *der;* c) *(powerful person)* Papst, *der (fig.);* press ~: Pressezar, *der;* d) *(Hist.: holder of land)* Baron, *der;* e) *(sirloin)* ~ of beef [ungeteiltes] Lendenstück; Baron, *der (Kochk.)*

baroness ['bærənɪs] *n.* Baronin, *die;* Freifrau, *die; (baron's unmarried daughter)* Baronesse, *die;* Freifräulein, *das*

baronet ['bærənɪt] *n.* Baronet, *der*

baronetcy ['bærənɪtsɪ] *n.* Stand/Titel eines Baronets

baronial [bə'rəʊnɪəl] *adj.* freiherrlich

barony ['bærənɪ] *n.* a) Baronie, *die;* Baronat, *das;* b) *(Scot.: manor)* Landgut, *das*

baroque [bə'rɒk, bə'rəʊk] 1. *n.* Barock, *das.* 2. *adj.* a) barock; ~ painting/literature Barockmalerei/-literatur, *die;* ~ painter/writer Maler/Schriftsteller des Barock; b) *(grotesque)* barock

barouche [bə'ru:ʃ] *n. (Hist.)* Kalesche, *die*

barque [bɑ:k] *n.* Bark, *die*

¹**barrack** ['bærək] *n. usu. in pl., often constr. as sing.* a) *(for soldiers)* Kaserne, *die;* b) *(for temporary housing)* Baracke, *die;* c) *(plain, dull building)* Kaserne, *die*

[2]barrack 1. *v. i.* buhen *(ugs.).* **2.** *v. t.* ausbuhen *(ugs.)*
barrack: ~-room 'lawyer *n.* Feldwebeltyp, *der (abwertend);* **~-'square** *n.* Kasernenhof, *der*
barracouta [bærə'ku:tə], **barracuda** [bærə'ku:də] *n., pl. same or* ~s **a)** *usu.* **-uda** *(seafish)* Barrakuda, *der;* Pfeilhecht, *der;* **b)** *usu.* **-outa** *(food-fish)* Atun, *der*
barrage ['bærɑ:ʒ] *n.* **a)** *(Mil.)* Sperrfeuer, *das; (fig.)* **a ~ of questions/insults** ein Bombardement von Fragen/Beleidigungen; **a ~ of cheers** stürmischer Jubel; **b)** *(artificial barrier)* Talsperre, *die;* Staustufe, *die;* **c)** *(Fencing, Show-jumping, etc.)* Stechen, *das*
'barrage balloon *n.* Sperrballon, *der*
barramundi [bærə'mʌndɪ] *n. (Zool.)* Barramundi, *der*
barre [bɑ:(r)] *n. (Ballet)* Stange, *die*
barrel ['bærl] *n.* **a)** *(vessel)* Faß, *das; (of metal, for oil, fuel, tar, etc.)* Tonne, *die;* Faß, *das; (measure)* Barrel, *das;* **be over a ~** *(fig.)* in der Klemme sitzen *(ugs.);* **have sb. over a ~** *(fig.)* jmdn. in der Zange haben *(ugs.);* **scrape the ~** *(fig.)* das Letzte zusammenkratzen *(ugs.);* **b)** *(revolving cylinder)* Walze, *die;* **c)** *(of pump)* Stiefel, *der; (of engine-boiler)* Trommel, *die; (of pen or pencil)* Schaft, *der;* **d)** *(of gun)* Lauf, *der; (of cannon etc.)* Rohr, *das*
barrel: ~-chested ['bærltʃestɪd] *adj.* **a ~-chested man** ein Mann mit einem breiten, gewölbten Brustkorb; **~house** *n. (Amer.)* Kneipe, *die; attrib.* **~house music** [einfache, laute] Jazzmusik; **~-organ** *n. (Mus.)* Leierkasten, *der;* Drehorgel, *die;* **~ vault** *n. (Archit.)* Tonnengewölbe, *das*
barren ['bærn] **1.** *adj.* **a)** unfruchtbar ⟨*Mensch, Tier, Pflanze, Land*⟩; kinderlos ⟨*Ehe*⟩; gelt *(Jägerspr., Landw.)* ⟨*Wild, Ziege, Rind*⟩; **b)** *(meagre, dull)* nutzlos ⟨*Handlung, Arbeit*⟩; mager ⟨*Ergebnis*⟩; unfruchtbar ⟨*Periode, Beziehung*⟩; fruchtlos ⟨*Diskussion*⟩; **be ~ of results** wenig Erfolg haben. **2.** *n.* **~[s]** Ödland, *das*
barrenness ['bærnnɪs] *n., no pl.* **a)** Unfruchtbarkeit, *die; (of marriage)* Kinderlosigkeit, *die;* **b)** *see* **barren b:** Nutzlosigkeit, *die;* Magerkeit, *die;* Unfruchtbarkeit, *die;* Fruchtlosigkeit, *die*
barrette [bə'ret] *n. (Amer.)* Haarspange, *die*
barricade [bærɪ'keɪd] **1.** *n.* Barrikade, *die;* **a ~ of silence** *(fig.)* eine Mauer des Schweigens. **2.** *v. t.* verbarrikadieren
barrier ['bærɪə(r)] *n.* **a)** *(fence)* Absperrung, *die;* Barriere, *die; (at railway, frontier)* Schranke, *die;* **b)** *(gate of railway-station)* Sperre, *die;* **c)** *(obstacle, lit. or fig.)* Barriere, *die;* **a ~ to progress** ein Hindernis für den Fortschritt; **break the class ~** die Klassenschranken durchbrechen; *see also* **sound barrier**
barrier: ~ cream *n.* Schutzcreme, *die;* **~ reef** *n.* Barrier- *od.* Wallriff, *das*
barring ['bɑ:rɪŋ] *prep.* außer im Falle (+ *Gen.*); **~ accidents** falls nichts passiert; **~ the possibility of rain** falls es nicht vielleicht regnet
barrister ['bærɪstə(r)] *n.* **a)** *(Brit.)* **~[-at-law]** Barrister, *der;* ≈ [Rechts]anwalt/-anwältin vor höheren Gerichten, *der;* **b)** *(Amer.: lawyer)* [Rechts]anwalt, *der*/-anwältin, *die*
barroom ['bɑ:ru:m] *n. (Amer.)* Bar, *die*
[1]barrow ['bærəʊ] *n.* **a)** Karre, *die;* Karren, *der;* **b)** *see* **wheelbarrow**
[2]barrow *n. (Archaeol.)* Hügelgrab, *das*
'barrow-boy *n.* Straßenhändler, *der*
bar 'sinister *n. (Her.)* Bastardfaden, *der*
Bart. *abbr.* **baronet**
'bartender *n.* Barkeeper, *der;* Schankkellner, *der*
barter ['bɑ:tə(r)] **1.** *v. t.* [ein]tauschen; **~ sth. for sth. [else]** etw. für *od.* gegen etw. [anderes] [ein]tauschen; **~ away sth.** etw. verspielen *(fig.).* **2.** *v. i.* Tauschhandel treiben; **they ~ed for cigarettes with books and clothes** sie tauschten Bücher und Kleidung gegen Zigaretten. **3.** *n.* Tauschhandel, *der;* **~ of opinions/ideas** *(fig.)* Gedankenaustausch, *der*
barytes [bə'raɪti:z] *n. (Min.)* Baryt, *der*
basal ['beɪsl] *adj.* **a)** *(Med., Biol.)* basal; **~ cell** Basalzelle, *die;* **b)** *(fundamental)* grundlegend; fundamental. *See also* **metabolism**
basalt ['bæsɔ:lt, bə'sɔ:lt] *n.* Basalt, *der*
bascule ['bæskju:l] *n.* Baskule, *die (veralt.);* **~ bridge** Klappbrücke, *die*
[1]base [beɪs] **1.** *n.* **a)** *(of lamp, pyramid, wall, mountain, microscope)* Fuß, *der; (of cupboard, statue)* Sockel, *der; (fig.) (support)* Basis, *die;* Fundament, *das; (principle)* Ausgangsbasis, *die; (main ingredient)* Hauptbestandteil, *der; (of make-up)* Grundlage, *die; (Photog.: support for film etc.)* Unterlage, *die; (Ling.: root)* Wurzel, *die; (Ling.: primary morpheme)* Stamm, *der;* **shake the very ~ of sth.** *(fig.)* etw. in seinen Grundfesten erschüttern; **glue has a flour ~:** der Hauptbestandteil von Leim ist Mehl; **a sauce which has a tomato ~:** eine Soße auf Tomatenbasis *(Kochk.);* **b)** *(Mil.)* Basis, *die;* Stützpunkt, *der;* **c)** *(Baseball)* Mal, *das;* **get to first ~** *(fig. coll.)* [wenigstens] etwas erreichen; **he didn't get to first ~ with her** er konnte bei ihr überhaupt nicht landen *(ugs.);* **be off ~** *(fig. coll.)* falschliegen *(ugs.);* **d)** *(Archit.)* Basis, *die;* **e)** *(Geom.)* Basis, *die; (of triangle also)* Grundlinie, *die; (of solid also)* Grundfläche, *die;* **f)** *(Chem.)* Base, *die;* **g)** *(Surv.)* Basis, *die;* **h)** *(Math.: number)* Basis, *die;* Grundzahl, *die;* **i)** *(Bot., Zool.)* Basis, *die; (of leaf)* Blattgrund, *der;* **j)** *(Her.)* Schildfuß, *der.* **2.** *v. t.* **a) be ~d on sth.** sich auf etw. *(Akk.)* gründen; **~ sth. on sth.** etw. auf etw. *(Dat.)* aufbauen; **~ one's hopes on sth.** seine Hoffnung auf etw. *(Akk.)* gründen; **a book ~d on newly discovered papers** ein Buch, das auf neu entdeckten Dokumenten basiert; **b)** *in pass. (have chief station or means)* **be ~d in Paris** in Paris wohnen; **a submarine ~d on Malta** ein U-Boot, das seinen Stützpunkt auf Malta hat; **computer-~d accountancy** Buchführung über Computer; **land-~d forces** landgestützte Streitkräfte; **c) ~ oneself on** sich stützen auf (+ *Akk.*)
[2]base *adj.* **a)** *(morally low)* niederträchtig; niedrig ⟨*Beweggrund*⟩; **b)** *(cowardly)* feige; *(selfish)* selbstsüchtig; *(mean)* niederträchtig; **c)** *(degrading)* entwürdigend
baseball ['beɪsbɔ:l] *n.* Baseball, *der*
base: ~ board *n. (Amer.)* Fußleiste, *die;* **~born** *adj. (arch.)* von niederer Herkunft; *(illegitimate)* unehelich; **~ 'coin** *n.* entwertete Münze; **~ hit** *n. (Baseball) Schlag, der dem Schlagmann ermöglicht, das erste Mal zu erreichen*
baseless ['beɪslɪs] *adj.* unbegründet
baselessly ['beɪslɪslɪ] *adv.* grundlos
baselessness ['beɪslɪsnɪs] *n., no pl.* Haltlosigkeit, *die*
base: ~line *n.* Grundlinie, *die;* **~load** *n. (Electr.)* Grundlast, *die*
basely ['beɪslɪ] *adv.* niederträchtig
baseman ['beɪsmən] *n., pl.* **basemen** ['beɪsmən] *(Baseball)* Malspieler, *der*
basement ['beɪsmənt] *n.* Souterrain, *das;* Kellergeschoß, *das; (esp. in department store)* Untergeschoß, *das;* Tiefgeschoß, *das;* **a ~ flat** eine Souterrain- *od.* Kellerwohnung
base 'metal *n.* unedles Metall
baseness ['beɪsnɪs] *n., no pl.* Niedrigkeit, *die;* Niederträchtigkeit, *die*
'base rate *n.* **a)** *(Finance)* Eckzins, *der;* **b)** *(wage)* Grundlohn, *der*
bases *pl. of* **[1]base** *or* **basis**
bash [bæʃ] **1.** *v. t.* [heftig] schlagen; **~ one's head against sth.** sich *(Dat.)* den Kopf [heftig] an etw. *(Dat.)* anschlagen; **~ sth. in** etw. einschlagen; **the car was badly ~ed in** *or* **up** das Auto war völlig verbeult; **~ sb. up** jmdn. zusammenschlagen; **he was badly ~ed up** er wurde schlimm zusammengeschlagen; **queer-~ing** *(sl.)* Zusammenschlagen von Schwulen *(ugs.);* **union-~ing** Einprügeln auf die Gewerkschaften. **2.** *n.* **a)** [heftiger] Schlag; **b)** *(sl.: attempt)* Versuch, *der;* **have a ~ at sth.** etw. [mal] probieren *od.* versuchen; **c)** *(sl.: party)* Fete, *die (ugs.)*
bashful ['bæʃfl] *adj.* **a)** *(shy)* schüchtern; **b)** *(shamefaced)* verschämt
bashfully ['bæʃfəlɪ] *adv. see* **bashful:** schüchtern; verschämt
bashfulness ['bæʃflnɪs] *n., no pl. see* **bashful:** Schüchternheit, *die;* Verschämtheit, *die*
basic ['beɪsɪk] *adj.* **a)** *(fundamental)* grundlegend; **~ structure/principle/element/vocabulary** Grundstruktur, *die*/-prinzip, *das*/-bestandteil, *der*/-wortschatz, *der;* **be ~ to sth.** wesentlich für etw. sein; **have a ~ knowledge of sth.** Grundkenntnisse einer Sache *(Gen.)* haben; **~ problem/reason/issue** Hauptproblem, *das*/-grund, *der*/-sache, *die;* **b)** *(standard minimum)* **~ wages/salary** Grundlohn, *der*/Grundgehalt, *das;* **the length of a ~ working day is 8 hours** ein normaler Arbeitstag dauert 8 Stunden; **c)** *(Chem., Geol.)* basisch. *See also* **basics**
basically ['beɪsɪkəlɪ] *adv.* im Grunde; grundsätzlich ⟨*übereinstimmen*⟩; *(mainly)* hauptsächlich
basic: ~ 'dye *n. (Chem.)* basischer Farbstoff; **B~ 'English** *n.* Basic English, *das; auf einem sehr einfachen Grundwortschatz beruhendes Englisch;* **~ 'industry** *n.* wichtiger Industriezweig
basics ['beɪsɪks] *n. pl.* **stick to the ~:** beim Wesentlichen bleiben; **the ~ of maths/cooking** die Grundlagen der Mathematik/das ABC der Kochkunst; **he doesn't understand the ~ of honesty** er weiß überhaupt nicht, was Ehrlichkeit ist
basic 'slag *n.* Thomasschlacke, *die (Hüttenw.); (finely ground)* Thomasmehl, *das (Landw.)*
basidium [bə'sɪdɪəm] *n., pl.* **basidia** [bə'sɪdɪə] *(Bot.)* Basidie, *die;* Sporenständer, *der*
basil ['bæzɪl] *n. (Bot.)* **[sweet] ~:** Basilikum, *das;* **bush ~:** Buschbasilikum, *das*
basilica [bə'zɪlɪkə] *n. (Archit., Eccl.)* Basilika, *die*
basilisk ['bæzɪlɪsk] *n. (Mythol., Zool.)* Basilisk, *der;* **~ stare** *(fig.)* Basiliskenblick, *der*
basin ['beɪsn] *n.* **a)** Becken, *das; (wash-~)* Waschbecken, *das; (bowl)* Schüssel, *die;* **b)** *(depression)* Becken, *das; (artificial)* Bassin, *das;* Becken, *das;* **c)** *(of river etc.)* Becken, *das;* **the ~ of the Amazon, the Amazon ~:** das Amazonasbecken; **d)** *(harbour)* [Hafen]becken, *das;* **e)** *(valley)* [Tal]kessel, *der;* **f)** *(Geol.)* Becken, *das*
basinful ['beɪsnfʊl] *n.* **ten ~s of water** zehn Schüsseln [voll] Wasser; **have had a ~ of sth.** *(fig. coll.: more than enough)* von etw. die Nase voll haben *(ugs.)*
basis ['beɪsɪs] *n., pl.* **bases** ['beɪsi:z] **a)** *(ingredient)* Grundbestandteil, *der;* **b)** *(foundation, principle, common ground)* Basis, *die;* Grundlage, *die;* **rest on a ~ of conjecture** sich auf Vermutungen gründen; **meet on a purely friendly ~:** einander auf rein freundschaftlicher Basis begegnen; **on a first come first served ~:** nach dem Prinzip „Wer zuerst kommt, mahlt zuerst"; **c)** *(beginning)* Ausgangspunkt, *der*
bask [bɑ:sk] *v. i.* **a)** sich [wohlig] wärmen; sich aalen *(ugs.);* **~ in the sun** sich sonnen; sich in der Sonne aalen *(ugs.);* **b)** *(fig.)* sich sonnen **(in** in + *Dat.)*
basket ['bɑ:skɪt] *n.* **a)** Korb, *der; (of chippan)* Drahteinsatz, *der;* **wire ~:** Drahtkorb, *der;* **b)** *(quantity)* **a ~ [full] of plums/apples** ein Korb [voll] Pflaumen/Äpfel; **sell ~s of**

sth. [ganze] Körbe voll etw. verkaufen; etw. körbeweise verkaufen; **c)** *(protection for hand)* Korb, *der; (Fencing)* Glocke, *die;* **d)** *(of typewriter)* **[type-]~**: Typenkorb, *der;* **e)** *(Basketball)* Korb, *der;* **make** *or* **score a ~**: einen Korb werfen; **f)** *(Econ.)* ~ **of currencies** Währungskorb, *der*
basket: ~ball *n.* Basketball, *der;* ~ **case** *n. (sl.)* Schwerbeschädigte ohne Arme und Beine; *(fig.)* hoffnungsloser Fall; ~ **chair** *n.* Korbsessel, *der;* ~ **clause** *n.* Generalklausel, *die*
basketful ['bɑ:skɪtfʊl] *see* **basket b**
basketry ['bɑ:skɪtrɪ] *see* **basketwork**
basket: ~ **weave** *n.* Panamabindung, *die (Weberei);* **~work** *n. (art)* Korbflechterei, *die; (collectively)* Korbwaren; **a piece of ~work** ein Korbgeflecht; **~work is his hobby** Korbflechten ist sein Hobby
basking 'shark *n.* Riesenhai, *der*
Basle [bɑ:l] **1.** *pr. n.* Basel *(das).* **2.** *attrib. adj.* Baseler
Basque [bæsk, bɑ:sk] **1.** *adj.* baskisch; **the ~ Country** das Baskenland. **2.** *n.* **a)** Baske, *der*/Baskin, *die; (language)* Baskisch, *das;* **b) b~** *(of bodice)* Schößchen, *das;* **c) b~** *(bodice)* Schößchenjacke, *die*
bas-relief ['bæsrɪli:f] *n. (Art)* Basrelief, *das*
[1]**bass** [bæs] *n., pl. same or* **~es** *(Zool.)* Barsch, *der; (Perca fluviatilis)* [Fluß]barsch, *der*
[2]**bass** [bæs] *n. (fibre)* Bast, *der*
[3]**bass** [beɪs] *(Mus.)* **1.** *adj.* Baß-; ~ **voice** Baßstimme, *die.* **2.** *n.* **a)** Baß, *der; (voice, part)* Baß, *der;* Baßstimme, *die; (singer)* Bassist, *der;* Baß, *der;* **b)** *(coll.) (double-~)* [Kontra]baß, *der; (~ guitar)* Baß, *der;* **c) figured** *or* **thorough ~**: Generalbaß, *der; (theory)* Generalbaßlehre, *die; see also* [1]**ground**
bass [beɪs]: ~ **clef** *n. (Mus.)* Baßschlüssel, *der;* ~ **drum** *n.* große Trommel
basset ['bæsɪt] *n.* **~[-hound]** Basset, *der*
bass gui'tar [beɪs] *n.* Baßgitarre, *die*
bassinet [bæsɪ'net] *n.* Stubenwagen, *der;* Korb[kinder]wagen, *der; (cradle)* Korbwiege, *die*
bassist ['beɪsɪst] *n.* Bassist, *der*/Bassistin, *die*
basso ['bæsəʊ] *n., pl.* **~s** *or* **bassi** ['bæsi:] *(Mus.)* Basso, *der*
bassoon [bə'su:n] *n. (Mus.)* Fagott, *das*
bassoonist [bə'su:nɪst] *n. (Mus.)* Fagottist, *der*/Fagottistin, *die*
bass: ~ **player** *n.* Bassist, *der*/Bassistin, *die;* ~ **viol** [beɪs 'vaɪəl] *n.* Gambe, *die;* Kniegeige, *die (veralt.); (Amer.: double-~)* Baßgeige, *die;* Kontrabaß, *der*
bast [bæst] *n.* Bast, *der*
bastard ['bɑ:stəd, 'bæstəd] **1.** *adj.* **a)** unehelich; **b)** *(hybrid)* verfälscht ⟨*Sprache, Stil*⟩; **c)** *(Bot., Zool.)* Bastard-. **2.** *n.* **a)** uneheliches Kind; unehelicher Sohn/uneheliche Tochter; Bastard, *der (hist.);* **b)** *(coll.) (disliked person)* Schweinehund, *der (derb);* Mistkerl, *der (derb); (disliked thing)* Scheißding, *das (derb);* **you old ~!** *(in friendly exclamation)* alter Schwede! *(salopp);* **the poor ~!** *(unfortunate person)* das arme Schwein! *(ugs.)*
bastard: ~ **title** *n. (Printing)* Schmutztitel, *der;* ~ **wing** *n. (Zool.)* Afterflügel, *der*
bastardy ['bɑ:stədɪ, 'bæstədɪ] *n., no pl.* uneheliche Herkunft; Unehelichkeit, *die*
[1]**baste** [beɪst] *v. t. (stitch)* heften; reihen
[2]**baste** *v. t.* **a)** [mit Fett/Bratensaft] begießen ⟨*Fleisch*⟩; **b)** *(thrash, cudgel)* prügeln
bastion ['bæstɪən] *n.* Bastei, *die; (fig.)* Bastei, *die;* Bastion, *die;* Bollwerk, *das*
[1]**bat** [bæt] *n. (Zool.)* Fledermaus, *die;* **blind as a ~** *(fig.)* blind wie ein Maulwurf; **have ~s in the belfry** *(coll.)* einen Dachschaden haben *(ugs.);* **sb. drives like a ~ out of hell** *(sl.)* jmd. fährt, als ob der Teufel hinter ihm her wäre *(ugs.)*
[2]**bat 1.** *n.* **a)** *(Sport)* Schlagholz, *das; (for table-tennis)* Schläger, *der;* **do sth. off one's own ~** *(fig.)* etw. auf eigene Faust tun; **his earnings off his own ~**: das, was er selbst verdient[e]; **carry one's ~** *(Cricket) als Schlagmann während eines Durchgangs nicht ausscheiden;* **right off the ~** *(Amer. fig.)* sofort; **b)** *(act of using ~)* Schlag, *der;* **c)** *usu. in pl. (implement to guide aircraft)* Kelle, *die;* **d)** *(batsman)* Schlagmann, *der.* **2.** *v. i.,* **-tt-: a)** *(Sport)* schlagen; **b)** *(sl.: move)* ~ **around the town** in der Stadt rummachen *(ugs.);* ~ **away** sich wegmachen *(ugs.).* **3.** *v. t.,* **-tt-: a)** schlagen; **b)** *(Baseball)* ~ **in two runs** zwei Läufe holen *(ugs.)*
[3]**bat** *n. (Brit. sl.: pace)* Tempo, *das;* **at an awful ~**: mit einem Affenzahn *(salopp)*
[4]**bat** *v. t.,* **-tt-:** ~ **one's eyes/eyelids** [mit den Augen/Augenlidern] blinzeln *od.* zwinkern; **he never ~ted an eyelid** *(fig.: betrayed no emotion)* er hat nicht mit der Wimper gezuckt; **without ~ting an eyelid** *(fig.)* ohne mit der Wimper zu zucken
batch [bætʃ] *n.* **a)** *(of loaves)* Schub, *der;* **b)** *(of people)* Gruppe, *die;* Schwung, *der (ugs.); (of letters, books, files, papers)* Stapel, *der;* Schwung, *der (ugs.); (of rules, regulations)* Bündel, *das*
batch: ~ **'processing** *n.* Schub-, Stapelverarbeitung, *die;* ~ **production** *n.* Stapelfertigung, *die*
[1]**bate** [beɪt] *v. t.* **with ~d breath** mit angehaltenem *od. (geh.)* verhaltenem Atem; ~ **one's breath** den Atem verhalten *(geh.)*
[2]**bate** *n. (Brit. sl.)* Rage, *die (ugs.);* **be in a [terrible] ~**: [schrecklich] in Rage sein; **get/fly into a ~**: in Rage geraten
bath [bɑ:θ] **1.** *n., pl.* **~s** [bɑ:ðz] **a)** Bad, *das;* **have** *or* **take a ~**: ein Bad nehmen; **b)** *(vessel)* **~[-tub]** Badewanne, *die;* **room with ~**: Zimmer mit Bad; **c)** *usu. in pl. (building)* Bad, *das;* **[swimming-]~s** Schwimmbad, *das;* **d) Order of the B~** *(Brit.)* Orden vom Bade. **2.** *v. t. & i.* baden
bath: B~ brick *n.* Putzstein, *der;* **B~ bun** *n.* ≈ Rosinenbrötchen mit Zuckerguß; **~-cap** *n.* Badekappe, *die;* Bademütze, *die;* ~ **chair** *n.* Rollstuhl, *der;* ~ **cubes** *n. pl.* Badesalz, *das (in Würfelform)*
bathe [beɪð] **1.** *v. t.* **a)** baden; **b)** *(moisten)* baden ⟨*Wunde, Körperteil*⟩; **~d with** *or* **in sweat** schweißüberströmt ⟨*Gesicht, Person*⟩; in Schweiß gebadet ⟨*Person*⟩; **~d with** *or* **in tears** tränenüberströmt; **c)** *(envelop)* **sunlight ~d the gardens** Sonne lag über den Gärten *(geh.);* **~d in sunlight** von der Sonne beschienen. **2.** *v. i.* baden; **go bathing** baden gehen. **3.** *n.* Bad, *das (im Meer usw.);* **take** *or* **have a ~**: baden; ein Bad nehmen
bather ['beɪðə(r)] *n.* **a)** Badende, *der/die;* **b)** *in pl. (Austral.: garment)* Badeanzug, *der*
bathetic [bə'θetɪk] *adj.* bathisch *(geh.)*
bathing ['beɪðɪŋ] *n.* Baden, *das;* '**~ prohibited**' „Baden verboten!"
bathing: ~ **beach** *n.* Badestrand, *der;* ~ **beauty,** ~ **belle** *ns.* Badenixe, *die;* **~-cap** *n.* Badekappe, *die;* Bademütze, *die;* **~-costume** *n.* Badeanzug, *der;* **~-machine** *n. (Hist.)* Badekarren, *der;* **~-suit** *n.* Badeanzug, *der;* **~-trunks** *n. pl.* Badehose, *die*
'**bath-mat** *n.* Badematte, *die*
bathos ['beɪθɒs] *n., no pl. (Lit., Rhet.)* Bathos, *das (geh.);* Umschlag ins Triviale; *(anticlimax)* Antiklimax, *die (Stilk.)*
bath: ~robe *n.* Bademantel, *der;* **~room** *n.* Badezimmer, *das;* ~ **salts** *n. pl.* Badesalz, *das;* **~-time** *n.* Badezeit, *die;* **~-towel** *n.* Badetuch, *das;* **~-tub** *see* **bath 1b;** **~-water** *n.* Badewasser, *das; see also* **baby 1a**
batik ['bætɪk, bə'ti:k] *n.* Batik, *der od. die*
batiste [bə'ti:st] **1.** *n.* Batist, *der.* **2.** *adj.* batisten; ~ **dress/blouse** Batistkleid, *das*/Batistbluse, *die*
batman ['bætmən] *n., pl.* **batmen** ['bætmən] *(Mil.)* [Offiziers]bursche, *der*
baton ['bætn] *n.* **a)** *(staff of office)* Stab, *der;* Baton, *der (veralt.);* **Field Marshal's ~**: Marschallstab, *der;* **b)** *(truncheon)* Schlagstock, *der;* **c)** *(Mus.)* Taktstock, *der;* **conductor's ~**: Dirigentenstab, *der;* **d)** *(for relay race)* [Staffel]stab, *der;* Staffelholz, *das;* **e)** *(Her.)* ≈ Schrägbalken, *der;* ~ **sinister** Bastardfaden, *der*
bats [bæts] *pred. adj. (sl.)* bekloppt *(salopp);* **go ~**: überschnappen *(ugs.)*
batsman ['bætsmən] *n., pl.* **batsmen** ['bætsmən] *(Sport)* Schlagmann, *der;* **~'s wicket** *für den Schlagmann günstige Spielbahn*
battalion [bə'tæljən] *n. (lit. or fig.)* Bataillon, *das;* **~s of** *(fig.)* ganze Bataillone von; **God is for the big ~s** Gott ist mit dem Stärkeren
[1]**batten** ['bætn] **1.** *n.* **a)** *(piece of timber)* Latte, *die;* **b)** *(Naut.)* Latte, *die;* **c)** *(bar, strip of wood)* Leiste, *die.* **2.** *v. t. (Naut.)* ~ **down** [ver]schalken ⟨*Luke*⟩
[2]**batten** *v. i.* **a)** ~ **on sth.** sich an etw. *(Dat.)* gütlich tun; *(grow fat)* sich mästen mit etw.; **b)** *(thrive)* ~ **on** sich mästen auf Kosten *(+ Gen.)*
[1]**batter** ['bætə(r)] **1.** *v. t.* **a)** *(strike)* einschlagen auf *(+ Akk.);* ~ **down/in** einschlagen; ~ **sth. to pieces** etw. zerschmettern *od.* in Stücke schlagen; **he ~ed his head against the wall** er schlug seinen Kopf gegen die Wand; **b)** *(attack with artillery)* beschießen; bombardieren *(Milit. veralt.);* ~ **down** zusammenschießen; **c)** *(fig.: handle severely)* bombardieren; ~ **sb. into exhaustion** jmdn. völlig zermürben; **d)** *(bruise, damage)* übel zurichten; ramponieren *(ugs.);* **~ed baby** mißhandeltes Baby; **~ed wife** mißhandelte Ehefrau; geschlagene Frau; **~ed wives' home** Frauenhaus, *das;* **~ed by the gales** vom Sturm stark beschädigt; **a ~ed car** ein verbeultes Auto. **2.** *v. i.* heftig klopfen; **they ~ed at** *or* **against the door** sie hämmerten gegen die Tür
[2]**batter** *n. (Cookery)* [Back]teig, *der; (for pancake)* [Eierkuchen]teig, *der; (for waffle)* [Waffel]teig, *der*
[3]**batter** *n. (Baseball)* Schlagmann, *der*
battering ram ['bætərɪŋ ræm] *n.* Rammbock, *der*
battery ['bætərɪ] *n.* **a)** *(series; also Mil., Electr.)* Batterie, *die;* **a ~ of specialists** *(fig.)* eine ganze Reihe von Spezialisten; *see also* **recharge 1; b)** *(Law)* **[assault and] ~**: tätlicher Angriff; **c)** *(Psych.)* Testreihe, *die;* **d)** *(Baseball) Werfer und Fänger;* **e)** *(Agric.)* Legebatterie, *die*
battery: **~-charger** *n.* Batterieladegerät, *das;* ~ **'farming** *n.* Batteriehaltung, *die;* ~ **'hen** *n.* Batteriehuhn, *das*
batting ['bætɪŋ] *n. (Sport)* Schlagen, *das; see also* **average 1b**
battle ['bætl] **1.** *n.* **a)** *(fight)* Schlacht, *die;* **the ~ at Amman** die Schlacht bei Amman; **they went out to ~**: sie zogen in die Schlacht; **do** *or* **give ~**: kämpfen; **join ~ with sb.** jmdm. eine Schlacht liefern; **die in ~**: [in der Schlacht] fallen; **b)** *(fig.: contest)* Kampf, *der;* ~ **for life** Kampf ums Überleben; ~ **of words** Wortgefecht, *das;* ~ **of ideas/wits** Wettstreit der Ideen/geistiger Wettstreit; *see also* **fight 2c; c)** *(victory)* Sieg, *der;* **the ~ is to the strong** der Sieg gehört den Starken; **sth./that is half the ~**: mit etw./damit ist schon viel gewonnen. *See also* [1]**pitch 2f. 2.** *v. i.* ~ **with** *or* **against sth.** mit *od.* gegen etw. kämpfen; ~ **for sth.** für etw. kämpfen. **3.** *v. t.* **a)** kämpfen gegen; **b)** ~ **one's way through the crowd** sich durch die Menge kämpfen
battle: ~axe *n.* Streitaxt, *die; (coll.: woman)* Schreckschraube, *die (ugs. abwertend);* **~-cruiser** *n. (Navy)* Schlachtkreuzer, *der;* **~-cry** *n.* Schlachtruf, *der*

battle: ~dress *n. (Mil.) (for general service)* Arbeitsanzug, *der; (for field service)* Kampfanzug, *der;* **~ fatigue** *n.* Frontkoller, *der (ugs.);* Frontneurose, *die;* **~field, ~ground** *ns.* Schlachtfeld, *das;* **~-lines** *n. pl.* Kampflinien
battlement ['bætlmənt] *n., usu. in pl.* **a)** Zinne, *die;* **b)** *(roof)* mit Zinnen bewehrtes Dach
battlemented ['bætlmәntıd] *adj.* mit Zinnen bewehrt
battle: ~ 'royal *n.* [heftiger] Kampf *(auch fig.); (everyone for himself)* Kampf jeder gegen jeden; **~ship** *n.* Schlachtschiff, *das;* **~-weary** *adj.* kampfesmüde
batty ['bætı] *adj. (sl.)* bekloppt *(salopp);* **go** *or* **become ~:** überschnappen *(ugs.)*
'batwing sleeve *n.* Fledermausärmel, *der*
bauble ['bɔ:bl] *n.* **a)** *(trinket)* Flitter, *der;* **little ~s** kleine, wertlose Schmuckstücke; **b)** *(toy)* Spielzeug, *das;* **dolls and other ~s** Puppen und anderes Spielzeug; **c)** *(Hist.: jester's emblem)* Narrenzepter, *das;* **d)** *(worthless thing)* Talmi, *der;* **be a ~/be ~s** Talmi sein
baulk *see* **balk**
bauxite ['bɔ:ksaıt] *n. (Min.)* Bauxit, *der*
Bavaria [bə'veərıə] *pr. n.* Bayern *(das)*
Bavarian [bə'veərıən] **1.** *adj.* bay[e]risch; **sb. is ~:** jmd. ist Bayer/Bayerin. **2.** *n.* **a)** *(person)* Bayer, *der*/Bayerin, *die;* **b)** *(dialect)* Bay[e]risch[e], *das;* Bairisch[e], *das*
bawdily ['bɔ:dılı] *adv.* zweideutig, *(stronger)* obszön ⟨*lachen, schreiben*⟩
bawdiness ['bɔ:dınıs] *n., no pl. see* **bawdy 1:** Zweideutigkeit, *die;* Obszönität, *die*
bawdy ['bɔ:dı] **1.** *adj.* zweideutig, *(stronger)* obszön ⟨*Witz, Geschichte, Sprache*⟩; obszön ⟨*Mensch*⟩. **2.** *n.* Zweideutigkeit, *die; (stronger)* Obszönität, *die*
'bawdy-house *n. (arch.)* Bordell, *das*
bawl [bɔ:l] **1.** *v. t.* brüllen; **~ sth. at sb.** jmdm. etw. zubrüllen; **~ [out] one's wares** seine Waren ausschreien; **~ sb. out** *(coll.)* jmdn. zusammenstauchen *(ugs.).* **2.** *v. i.* brüllen; **~ out to sb.** nach jmdm. brüllen; **~ at sb.** jmdn. anbrüllen
[1]bay *n. (of sea)* Bucht, *die; (larger also)* Golf, *der;* **the Bay of Bengal** der Golf von Bengalen; **Hudson's Bay** die Hudsonbai; **the Bay of Pigs** die Schweinebucht
[2]bay *n.* **a)** *(division of wall)* Joch, *das (Archit.);* **b)** *(space in room)* Erker, *der;* **c)** *(recess, compartment)* Lagerraum, *der; (in barn)* Banse, *die;* **sick-~** *(Navy)* Schiffshospital, *das; (Mil.)* Sanitätsbereich, *der; (in school, college, office)* Krankenzimmer, *das;* **d)** *(of railway line)* ≈ Nebengleis, *das;* **e)** *(platform) Bahnsteig an einem Nebengleis; (in bus-station)* Haltestelle, *die*
[3]bay 1. *n. (bark)* Gebell, *das;* Gelaut, *das (Jägerspr.);* **at ~:** gestellt; **be at ~** *(fig.)* mit dem Rücken zur Wand stehen *(fig.);* **hold** *or* **keep sb./sth. at ~** *(fig.)* jmdn./etw. vom Leib halten; **stand at ~** *(fig.)* sich [den Verfolgern] stellen. **2.** *v.i.* bellen; **~ at sb./sth.** jmdn./etw. anbellen. **3.** *v.t.* anbellen
[4]bay [beı] *n.* **a)** *(Bot.)* Lorbeer[baum], *der;* **b)** *in pl. (wreath)* **[garland of] ~s** Lorbeer[kranz], *der*
[5]bay 1. *adj.* braun ⟨*Pferd*⟩. **2.** *n.* Braune, *der*
bay: ~berry *n.* Pimentbaum, *der;* **~-leaf** *n. (Cookery)* Lorbeerblatt, *das*
bayonet ['beıənıt] **1.** *n.* Bajonett, *das;* Seitengewehr, *das;* **with fixed ~s** mit aufgepflanzten Bajonetten. **2.** *v. t.* mit dem Bajonett *od.* Seitengewehr aufspießen; **~ sb. to death** jmdn. mit dem Bajonett erstechen
bayonet: ~ fitting *n.* Bajonettfassung, *die;* **~ plug** *n.* Stecker mit Bajonettverschluß *od.* -fassung; **~ socket** *n.* Steckdose mit Bajonettfassung
bay: ~ 'rum *n.* Pimentöl, *das;* **~ 'window** *n.* Erkerfenster, *das; (sl.: abdomen)* Spitzkühler, *der (salopp scherzh.)*
bazaar [bə'zɑ:(r)] *n. (oriental market)* Basar, *der; (large shop)* Kaufhaus, *das;* Basar, *der (DDR); (sale)* [Wohltätigkeits]basar, *der*
bazooka [bə'zu:kə] *n. (Mil.)* Bazooka, *die; (smaller)* Panzerfaust, *die*
BBC *abbr.* **British Broadcasting Corporation** BBC, *die*
bbl. *abbr.* **barrels** *(esp. of oil)*
BC *abbr.* **before Christ** v. Chr.; *(bes. DDR)* v. u. Z.
BD *abbr.* **Bachelor of Divinity** Bakkalaureus der Theologie; *see also* **B. Sc.**
BDS *abbr.* **Bachelor of Dental Surgery** Bakkalaureus der Zahnheilkunde; *see also* **B. Sc.**
be [bi:] *v., pres. t.* **I am** [əm, *stressed* æm], *neg. (coll.)* **ain't** [eınt], **he is** [ız], *neg. (coll.)* **isn't** ['ıznt]; **we are** [ə(r), *stressed* ɑ:(r)], *neg. (coll.)* **aren't** [ɑ:nt]; *p. t.* **I was** [wəz, *stressed* wɒz], *neg. (coll.)* **wasn't** ['wɒznt], **we were** [wə(r), *stressed* wɜ:(r), weə(r)], *neg. (coll.)* **weren't** [wɜ:nt, weənt]; *pres. p.* **being** ['bi:ıŋ]; *p. p.* **been** [bın, *stressed* bi:n] **1.** *copula* **a)** *indicating quality or attribute* sein; **she'll be ten next week** sie wird nächste Woche zehn; **she is a mother/an Italian** sie ist Mutter/Italienerin; **being a Frenchman, he naturally took an interest in politics** als Franzose interessierte er sich natürlich für Politik; **not being a cat-lover, I kept well away** da ich nicht gerade ein Katzenfreund bin, hielt ich mich fern; **he is being nice to them/sarcastic** er ist nett zu ihnen/jetzt ist er sarkastisch; **he has always been lazy** er ist schon immer faul gewesen; **be sensible!** sei vernünftig!; **b)** *in exclamation* **was she pleased!** war sie [vielleicht] froh!; **isn't he stupid!** ist er nicht [wirklich] dumm!; **aren't you a big boy!** was bist du schon für ein großer Junge!; **c) will be** *indicating supposition* **[I dare say] you'll be a big boy by now** du bist jetzt sicher schon ein großer Junge; **you'll be relieved to hear that** du wirst erleichtert sein, das zu hören; **d)** *indicating physical or mental welfare or state* sein; sich fühlen; **be ill/unwell** krank sein/sich nicht wohl fühlen; **I am well** es geht mir gut; **I am hot** mir ist heiß; **I am freezing** mich friert; es friert mich; **how are you/is she?** wie geht's *(ugs.)* /geht es ihr?; **e)** *identifying the subject* **he is the person I was speaking of** er ist es, von dem ich sprach; **it is the 5th today** heute haben wir den Fünften; **who's that?** wer ist das?; **it is she, it's her** sie ist's; **it is Joe who came** Joe ist gekommen; **if I were you** wenn ich du *od.* an deiner Stelle wäre; **f)** *indicating profession, pastime, etc.* **be a teacher/a footballer** Lehrer/Fußballer sein; **she wants to be a surgeon** sie möchte Chirurgin werden; **g)** *with possessive* **it is/was hers** es ist/war ihrs; es gehört/gehörte ihr; **this book is your uncle's** dieses Buch gehört deinem Onkel; **h)** *indicating intended recipient* **it's for you** es ist für dich; **i)** *(cost)* kosten; **how much are those eggs?** was kosten die Eier da?; **that will be 76p** das macht 76 Pence; **j)** *(equal)* sein; **two times three is six, two threes are six** zweimal drei ist *od.* sind *od.* gibt sechs; **sixteen ounces is a pound** sechzehn Unzen sind *od.* ergeben ein Pfund; **k)** *(constitute)* ausmachen; bilden; **London is not England** London ist nicht [gleich] England; **l)** *(mean)* bedeuten; **he was everything to her** er bedeutete ihr alles; **seeing is believing** was man [selbst] sieht, glaubt man; **m)** *(represent)* darstellen; stehen für; bedeuten; **let x be 3** [angenommen] x sei 3. **2.** *v. i.* **a)** *(exist)* [vorhanden] sein; existieren; **can such things be?** kann es so etwas geben?; kann so etwas vorkommen?; **I think, therefore I am** ich denke, also bin ich; **there is/are ...:** es gibt ...; **there are no such things** es gibt nichts dergleichen; so etwas gibt es nicht; **once upon a time there was a princess** es war einmal eine Prinzessin; **to be or not to be** Sein oder Nichtsein; **the powers that be** die maßgeblichen Stellen; die da oben *(ugs.);* **for the time being** vorläufig; **Miss Jones that was** das frühere Fräulein Jones; **be that as it may** wie dem auch sei; **b)** *(remain)* bleiben; **I shan't be a moment** *or* **second** ich komme gleich; noch eine Minute; **she has been in her room for hours** sie ist schon seit Stunden in ihrem Zimmer; **let it be** laß es sein; **let him/her be** laß ihn/sie in Ruhe; **c)** *(attend)* sein; **is he here?** ist er hier?; **d)** *indicating position in space or time* **he's upstairs** er ist oben; **how long has he been here?** wie lange ist er schon hier?; **e)** *(be situated)* sein; **Hungary is in the heart of Europe** Ungarn liegt im Herzen Europas; **the chair is in the corner** der Stuhl steht *od.* ist in der Ecke; **here you are** *(on arrival)* da bist du/da seid ihr [ja]; *(on giving sb. sth.)* so, bitte!; **f)** *(happen, occur, take place)* stattfinden; sein; **where will the party be?** wo ist die Party?; wo findet die Party statt?; **g)** *(go, come)* **be off with you!** geh/geht!; **I'm off** *or* **for home** ich gehe jetzt nach Hause; **she's from Australia** sie stammt *od.* ist aus Australien; **are you for London?** wollen Sie nach London?; sind Sie auf dem Weg nach London?; **be on one's way** unterwegs *od.* auf dem Wege sein; **h)** *(on visit etc.)* sein; **have you [ever] been to London?** bist du schon einmal in London gewesen?; **has anyone been?** ist jemand dagewesen?; **has the postman been?** war der Briefträger *od.* die Post schon da?; **i) be for/against sth./sb.** für/gegen etw./jmdn. sein; **How kind she is. She's been and tidied the room** *(coll.)* Wie nett sie ist. Sie hat doch wirklich das Zimmer aufgeräumt; **the children have been at the biscuits** die Kinder waren an den Keksen *(ugs.);* **I've been into this matter** ich habe mich mit der Sache befaßt. **3.** *v. aux.* **a)** *forming passive* werden; **the child was found** das Kind wurde gefunden; **German is spoken in this shop** in diesem Geschäft wird Deutsch gesprochen; **b)** *(arch.) forming past tenses of verbs of motion* sein; **the sun is set** die Sonne ist untergegangen; **when I got there she was gone** als ich hinkam, war sie schon [weg]gegangen; **Christ is risen** *(Relig.)* Christ[us] ist auferstanden *od. (dichter. veralt.)* erstanden; **the prisoner is fled** der Gefangene ist geflohen; **c)** *forming continuous tenses, active* **he is reading** er liest [gerade]; er ist beim Lesen; **I am leaving tomorrow** ich reise morgen [ab]; **the train was departing when I got there** der Zug fuhr gerade ab, als ich ankam; **d)** *forming continuous tenses, passive* **the house is/was being built** das Haus wird/wurde [gerade] gebaut *od.* ist/war im Bau; **e)** *expressing obligation* **be to** sollen; **I am to inform you** ich soll Sie unterrichten; **you are to report to the police** Sie sollen sich bei der Polizei melden; **he is to clean the house thoroughly** er soll das ganze Haus gründlich putzen; **he is to be admired** er ist zu bewundern; **f)** *expressing arrangement* **the Queen is to arrive at 3 p.m.,** die Königin soll um 15 Uhr eintreffen; **he is to be there** er soll dort sein; **I am to go** ich soll gehen; **g)** *expressing possibility* **the car is for sale** das Auto ist zu verkaufen; **it was not to be seen** es war nicht zu sehen; **there was nothing to be seen** es war nichts zu sehen; **I was not to be side-tracked** ich ließ mich nicht ablenken; **h)** *expressing destiny* **they were never to meet again** sie sollten sich nie wieder treffen; **i)** *expressing condition* **if I were to tell you that ..., were I to tell you that ...:** wenn ich dir sagen würde, daß ... **4. bride-/husband-to-be** zukünftige Braut/zukünftiger Ehemann; **mother-/father-to-be** werdende Mutter/werdender Vater; **the be-all and end-all** das A und O
beach [bi:tʃ] **1.** *n.* Strand, *der;* **~ area**

Strandzone, *die;* **on the ~**: am Strand; *attrib.* ~ **hat/suit/shoe** Strandhut/-anzug/-schuh, *der.* **2.** *v. t.* auf [den] Strand setzen ⟨*Schiff usw.*⟩; ans Ufer ziehen ⟨*Boot, Wal*⟩

beach: ~-ball *n.* Wasserball, *der;* **~-comber** ['bi:tʃkəʊmə(r)] *n.* **a)** Strandgutsammler, *der;* **b)** *(wave)* große Brandungswelle; **~-head** *n. (Mil.)* Brückenkopf, *der;* **~ wear** *n.* Strandkleidung, *die*

beacon ['bi:kn] *n.* **a)** Leucht-, Signalfeuer, *das; (Naut.)* Leuchtbake, *die;* **b)** *(Brit.) (hill)* leicht sichtbarer Hügel *(für ein Signalfeuer);* **c)** *(lighthouse, tower, etc.)* Leuchtfeuer, *das;* **d)** *(radio station)* Funkfeuer, *das;* **e)** *(signal light)* Signalleuchte, *die; (for aircraft)* Landelicht, *das;* **f)** *(fig.)* Leitstern, *der*

bead [bi:d] **1.** *n.* **a)** Perle, *die;* **~s** Perlen *Pl.;* Perlenkette, *die;* **tell one's ~s** den Rosenkranz beten; **~s of dew** Tautropfen *od. (geh.)* -perlen; **~s of perspiration** *or* **sweat** Schweißtropfen *od.* -perlen; **b)** *(gun-sight)* Kornspitze, *die;* Korn, *das;* **draw a ~ on sb./sth.** auf jmdn./etw. zielen; **c)** *(tyre edge) see* **beading c**; **d)** *(Archit.) see* **beading b**. **2.** *v. t.* mit Perlen/perlenartiger Verzierung versehen

beading ['bi:dɪŋ] *n.* **a)** Perlenstickerei, *die;* **b)** *(Archit.)* Perl- *od.* Rundstab, *der;* Abdeckstab, *der;* **c)** *(tyre edge)* Wulst, *der od. die*

beadle ['bi:dl] *n. (Brit.) (Hist.: of church)* Kirchendiener, *der; (with more responsibility, esp. Scot.)* Küster, *der; (of university)* Pedell, *der*

beady ['bi:dɪ] *adj.* ~ **eyes** Knopfaugen; **those ~ eyes of hers don't miss anything** ihrem wachsamen Blick entgeht nichts; **I've got my ~ eye on you** ich lasse dich nicht aus den Augen

'**beady-eyed** *adj.* mit Knopfaugen *nachgestellt; (watchful)* mit wachen Augen *nachgestellt*

beagle ['bi:gl] *n.* Beagle, *der*

[1]**beak** [bi:k] *n.* Schnabel, *der; (of turtle, octopus)* Mundwerkzeug, *das; (fig.: large, hooked nose)* Hakennase, *die;* Zinken, *der (salopp)*

[2]**beak** *n. (Brit. sl.)* **a)** *(magistrate, judge)* Kadi, *der (ugs.);* **b)** *(schoolmaster)* Pauker, *der*

beaked [bi:kt] *adj.* geschnäbelt

beaker ['bi:kə(r)] *n.* **a)** *(cup)* Becher, *der;* **b)** *(Chem.)* Becherglas, *das*

'**be-all** *see* **be 4**

beam [bi:m] **1.** *n.* **a)** *(timber etc.)* Balken, *der;* **behold the ~ in thine own eye** *(Bibl.)* sieh den Balken in deinem eigenen Auge; **b)** *(in loom)* Baum, *der;* **c)** *(Agric.: in plough)* Grindel, *der;* Pflugbaum, *der;* **d)** *(in balance)* Waagebalken, *der;* **e)** *(Naut.) (ship's breadth)* [größte] Schiffsbreite; *(side of ship)* [Schiffs]seite, *die;* **~s** Decksbalken; **on the ~**: querschiffs; **on the port ~**: backbords; **broad in the ~** *(fig. coll.)* breithüftig; **f)** *(ray etc.)* [Licht]strahl, *der;* ~ **of light** Lichtstrahl, *der;* **the car's headlamps were on full ~**: die Scheinwerfer des Wagens waren aufgeblendet; **g)** *(Aeronaut., Mil., etc.: guide)* Peil- *od.* Leitstrahl, *der; (course)* **come in on the ~**: auf dem Peil- *od.* Leitstrahl ein- *od.* anfliegen; **be off ~** *(fig. coll.)* danebenliegen *(ugs.);* **be on the ~** *(fig. coll.)* richtigliegen *(ugs.);* **h)** *(smile)* Strahlen, *das.* **2.** *v. t.* **a)** ~ **[forth]** ausstrahlen; **b)** *(broadcast)* aussenden; ausstrahlen ⟨*Wellen, Licht, Rundfunkprogramm*⟩; *(fig.: aim)* ~ **at** [hin]zielen auf (+ *Akk.*); ~ **towards** richten *od.* lenken auf (+ *Akk.*); **this magazine is ~ed at housewives** die Zielleser[schaft] dieser Illustrierten sind Hausfrauen. **3.** *v. i.* **a)** *(shine)* strahlen; glänzen; **b)** *(smile)* strahlen; ~ **at sb.** jmdn. anstrahlen

'**beam-ends** *n. pl.* **the ship is on her ~** das Schiff liegt auf der Seite; **be on one's ~** *(fig.)* pleite *(ugs.) od.* in großer Geldnot sein

beaming ['bi:mɪŋ] *adj.* strahlend

bean [bi:n] **1.** *n.* **a)** Bohne, *die;* **full of ~s** *(fig. coll.)* putzmunter *(ugs.);* quietschlebendig *(ugs.);* **he hasn't [got] a ~** *(fig. sl.)* er hat keinen roten Heller *(ugs.);* **not worth a ~** *(sl.)* nicht die Bohne *od.* keinen Pfifferling wert *(ugs.); see also* **old 1 d**; [1]**spill 1 b**; **b)** *(Amer. sl.: head)* Birne, *die (fig. salopp).* **2.** *v. t. (Amer. sl.: hit)* ~ **sb.** jmdm. eins auf die Birne geben *(salopp)*

bean: ~ bag *n.* **a)** *mit Bohnen gefülltes Säckchen zum Spielen;* **b)** *(cushion)* Knautschsessel, *der;* **~ feast** *n. (Brit. coll.)* Gelage, *das; (employees' annual dinner)* Betriebsfeier, *die*

beano ['bi:nəʊ] *n., pl.* **~s** *(Brit. sl.)* Gelage, *das*

bean: ~pole *n. (lit. or fig.)* Bohnenstange, *die;* **~sprout** *n.* Sojabohnenkeim, *der;* **~stalk** *n.* Bohnenstengel, *der;* **~stick** *n.* Bohnenstange, *die*

[1]**bear** [beə(r)] *n.* **a)** Bär, *der;* **be like a ~ with a sore head** *(coll.)* ein richtiger Brummbär sein *(ugs.);* **b)** *(fig.)* Tolpatsch, *der (ugs.);* **c)** *(Astron.)* **Great/Little B~**: Großer/Kleiner Bär; **d)** *(St. Exch.)* Baissier, *der*

[2]**bear 1.** *v. t.,* **bore** [bɔ:(r)], **borne** [bɔ:n] **a)** *(show)* tragen ⟨*Wappen, Inschrift, Unterschrift*⟩; aufweisen, zeigen ⟨*Merkmal, Spuren, Ähnlichkeit, Verwandtschaft*⟩; ~ **a resemblance** *or* **likeness to sb.** Ähnlichkeit mit jmdm. haben; **b)** *(be known by)* tragen, führen ⟨*Namen, Titel*⟩; **c)** ~ **some/little relation to sth.** einen gewissen/wenig Bezug zu etw. haben; **d)** *(poet./formal: carry)* tragen ⟨*Waffe, Last*⟩; mitgebracht haben, mit sich führen ⟨*Geschenk, Botschaft*⟩; **I was borne along by the fierce current** die starke Strömung trug mich mit [sich]; **be borne in upon sb.** jmdm. klar werden; jmdm. zu[m] Bewußtsein kommen; **e)** *(endure, tolerate)* ertragen, erdulden ⟨*Schmerz, Kummer*⟩; *with neg.* ertragen, aushalten ⟨*Schmerz*⟩; ausstehen, leiden ⟨*Geruch, Lärm*⟩; **he couldn't ~ the misery** er konnte das Elend nicht ertragen; **I can't ~ watching her eat** ich kann ihr beim Essen einfach nicht zusehen; **I can't ~ salami** ich kann Salami einfach nicht ausstehen; **f)** *(sustain)* tragen, übernehmen ⟨*Verantwortlichkeit, Kosten*⟩; auf sich *(Akk.)* nehmen ⟨*Schuld*⟩; tragen, aushalten ⟨*Gewicht*⟩; **g)** *(be fit for)* vertragen; **it does not ~ repeating** *or* **repetition** das läßt sich unmöglich wiederholen; *(is not important)* es lohnt sich nicht, das zu wiederholen; **his language won't ~ repeating** man kann seine [gemeinen] Ausdrücke gar nicht wiederholen; **it will not ~ scrutiny** es hält einer Überprüfung nicht stand; **it does not ~ thinking about** daran darf man gar nicht denken; ~ **comparison with sth.** den *od.* einen Vergleich mit etw. aushalten; einem *od.* dem Vergleich mit etw. standhalten; **h)** *(carry in the mind)* hegen ⟨*Haß, Liebe*⟩; ~ **sb. a grudge** *or* **a grudge against sb.** jmdm. gegenüber nachtragend sein; ~ **sb. malice** *or* **malice towards sb.** jmdm. grollen; einen Groll auf jmdn. hegen; ~ **sth. in mind** an etw. *(Akk.)* denken; etw. nicht vergessen; ~ **in mind that ...**: vergiß nicht, daß ...; merk dir, daß ...; **i)** *(give birth to)* gebären ⟨*Kind, Junges*⟩; *see also* **born**; **j)** *(yield)* tragen ⟨*Blumen, Früchte usw.*⟩; bringen, tragen ⟨*Zinsen*⟩; **his efforts bore no result** *(fig.)* seine Bemühungen hatten *od.* brachten keinen Erfolg; ~ **fruit** *(fig.)* Früchte tragen *(geh.);* **k)** *(bring sth. needed)* leisten ⟨*Hilfe*⟩; ~ **witness** *or* **testimony to sth.** von etw. zeugen *od.* Zeugnis ablegen; ~ **sb. company** jmdm. Gesellschaft leisten; ~ **a hand** helfen; ~ **a hand in an undertaking** bei einem Vorhaben helfen; **l)** *(behave)* ~ **oneself well/with dignity** sich gut betragen *od.* benehmen/Würde zeigen. **2.** *v. i.,* **bore, borne a) the path ~s [to the] left** der Weg führt [nach] links; **he bore right** er hielt sich [nach] rechts; **b) bring to ~**: aufbieten ⟨*Kraft, Energie*⟩; ausüben ⟨*Druck*⟩; **bring one's influence to ~**: seinen Einfluß geltend machen

~ **a'way** *v. t.* wegtragen; davontragen ⟨*Preis usw.*⟩; **be borne away** fort- *od.* davongetragen werden

~ **'down 1.** *v. t.* niederdrücken; überwältigen ⟨*Feind*⟩; **be borne down by the weight of ...**: von der Last (+ *Gen.*) gebeugt sein. **2.** *v. i.* ~ **down on sb./sth.** auf jmdn./etw. zusteuern; sich jmdm./einer Sache schnell nähern; ⟨*Schiff:*⟩ auf jmdn./etw. zu- *od.* lossegeln; ⟨*Wagen:*⟩ auf jmdn./etw. zufahren *od.* -steuern

~ **'off** *see* ~ **away**

~ **on** *see* ~ **upon**

~ **'out** *v. t.* **a)** hinaustragen; **b)** *(fig.)* bestätigen ⟨*Bericht, Erklärung*⟩; ~ **sb. out** jmdm. recht geben; ~ **sb. out in sth.** jmdn. in etw. *(Dat.)* bestätigen

~ **'up 1.** *v. t.* halten; [unter]stützen. **2.** *v. i.* **a)** durchhalten; ausharren *(geh.);* ~ **up well under sth.** etw. gut ertragen; **b)** *(Naut.)* abfallen

~ **upon** *v. t. (relate to)* sich beziehen auf (+ *Akk.*); Bezug haben auf (+ *Akk.*); im Zusammenhang stehen mit; *see also* ~ **2 b**

~ **with** *v. t.* ~ **with sb./sth.** mit jmdm./etw. Nachsicht haben; ~ **with sth. for the time being** etw. vorübergehend auf sich *(Akk.)* nehmen; **if you'll ~ with me a little longer** wenn Sie sich vielleicht noch einen Moment gedulden wollen

bearable ['beərəbl] *adj.* zum Aushalten *nachgestellt;* erträglich ⟨*Situation, Beruf*⟩

bear: ~-baiting *n. (Hist.)* Bärenhatz, *die;* **~ cub** *n.* Bärenjunge, *das*

beard [bɪəd] **1.** *n.* **a)** Bart, *der;* **full ~**: Vollbart, *der;* **small pointed ~**: Spitzbart, *der;* **b)** *(Bot.)* Grannen. **2.** *v. t.* trotzen (+ *Dat.*); Trotz bieten (+ *Dat.*); ~ **the lion in his den** *(fig.)* sich in die Höhle des Löwen wagen

bearded ['bɪədɪd] *adj.* bärtig; **be ~**: einen Bart haben; **a ~ gentleman** ein Herr mit Bart

bearer ['beərə(r)] *n.* **a)** *(carrier)* Träger, *der*/Trägerin, *die; (of letter, message, cheque, banknote)* Überbringer, *der*/Überbringerin, *die;* **cheque to ~**: Inhaberscheck, *der;* **payable to ~**: zahlbar an Überbringer *od.* Inhaber ⟨*Scheck*⟩; **I am the ~ of glad tidings** ich bringe euch eine frohe Botschaft; **b) the ~ of shares/bonds** der Aktionär/Obligationär; **~ share/bond** Inhaberaktie/Inhaberschuldverschreibung, *die*

bear: ~-garden *n. (fig.)* Tollhaus, *das (fig.);* **~-hug** *n.* kräftige Umarmung

bearing ['beərɪŋ] *n.* **a)** *(behaviour)* Verhalten, *das;* Gebaren, *das (geh.); (deportment)* [Körper]haltung, *die;* **b)** *(endurance)* Ertragen, *das;* Erdulden, *das;* **beyond** *or* **past [all] ~**: unerträglich; nicht zum Aushalten; **c)** *(relation)* Zusammenhang, *der;* Bezug, *der;* **consider sth. in all its ~s** etw. in seiner ganzen Tragweite betrachten; **have some/no ~ on sth.** relevant/irrelevant *od.* von Belang/belanglos für etw. sein; **d)** *(significance)* Bedeutung, *die;* [tieferer] Sinn; **the ~ of a remark** die Bedeutung *od.* der Sinn einer Bemerkung; **e)** *(Mech. Engin.)* Lager, *das;* **f)** *(compass ~)* Lage, *die;* Position, *die;* **take a compass ~**: den Kompaßkurs feststellen; **get one's ~s** sich orientieren; *(fig.)* sich zurechtfinden; **I have lost my ~s** *(lit. or fig.)* ich habe die Orientierung verloren; **g)** *(Her.)* Wappenbild, *das*

bearish ['beərɪʃ] *adj.* **a)** brummig; unfreundlich; **b)** *(St. Exch.)* baissierend; auf Baisse spekulierend ⟨*Kapitalanleger*⟩

'**bear market** *n. (St. Exch.)* Markt mit fallenden Preisen; Baissemarkt, *der*

'bearskin *n.* **a)** Bärenfell, *das;* Bärenhaut, *die;* **b)** *(Mil.)* Bärenfellmütze, *die*

beast [bi:st] *n.* Tier, *das; (quadruped)* Vierbeiner, *der; (ferocious, wild)* Bestie, *die; (fig.: brutal person)* roher, brutaler Mensch; Bestie, *die (abwertend); (disliked person)* Scheusal, *das (abwertend);* **it was a ~ of a winter** das war ein scheußlicher Winter; **the B~** *(Bibl.)* das Tier; **man and ~:** Mensch und Tier

beastliness ['bi:stlɪnɪs] *n., no pl. (coll.)* Scheußlichkeit, *die*

beastly ['bi:stlɪ] *adj., adv. (coll.)* scheußlich

beat [bi:t] **1.** *v. t.,* **beat, beaten** ['bi:tn] **a)** *(strike repeatedly)* schlagen ‹*Trommel, Rhythmus, Eier, Teig*›; klopfen ‹*Teppich*›; hämmern ‹*Gold, Silber usw.*›; **~ the dust out of a carpet/cushion** einen Teppich/ein Polster ausklopfen; **~ a path through sth.** sich *(Dat.)* einen Weg durch etw. bahnen; **~ one's breast** *(lit. or fig.)* sich *(Dat.)* an die Brust schlagen; **~ its chest** ‹*Affe:*› sich *(Dat.)* gegen die Brust trommeln; **~ some sense into sb.** jmdm. Vernunft einprügeln; **~ the bounds** *(Brit.)* die Grenzen der Gemarkung abgehen; **~ one's brains** sich *(Dat.)* den Kopf zerbrechen; **~ it** *(sl.)* sich verdrücken *(ugs.);* **~ it!** *(sl.)* hau ab! *(ugs.);* verschwinde!; **b)** *(hit)* schlagen; [ver]prügeln; **be ~en to death** totgeschlagen *od.* -geprügelt werden; **c)** *(defeat)* schlagen ‹*Mannschaft, Gegner*›; *(surmount)* in den Griff bekommen ‹*Inflation, Arbeitslosigkeit, Krise*›; **~ the deadline** den Termin noch einhalten; **d)** *(surpass)* brechen ‹*Rekord*›; übertreffen ‹*Leistung*›; **hard to ~:** schwer zu schlagen; **you can't ~** *or* **nothing ~s French cuisine** es geht [doch] nichts über die französische Küche; **~ that!** das soll mal einer nachmachen!; **~ everything** *(coll.),* **~ the band** *(sl.)* alles in den Schatten stellen; **~ sb. to it** jmdm. zuvorkommen; **can you ~ it?** ist denn das zu fassen?; **e)** *(circumvent)* umgehen; **~ the system** sich gegen das bestehende System durchsetzen; **f)** *(perplex)* **it ~s me how/why ...:** es ist mir ein Rätsel wie/warum ...; **g) ~ time** den Takt schlagen; **h)** *(Hunting)* **~ the bushes/water** den Treiber machen; **i)** *p.p.* **beat: I'm ~** *(coll.: exhausted)* ich bin geschafft *(ugs.) od.* erledigt *(ugs.). See also* **beaten 2. 2.** *v. i.,* **beat, beaten a)** *(throb)* ‹*Herz:*› schlagen, klopfen; ‹*Puls:*› schlagen; **my heart seemed to stop ~ing** ich dachte, mir bleibt das Herz stehen; **b)** ‹*Sonne:*› brennen (**on** auf + *Akk.*); ‹*Wind, Wellen:*› schlagen (**on** auf + *Akk.,* **against** gegen); ‹*Regen, Hagel:*› prasseln, trommeln (**against** gegen); **c) ~ about the bush** um den [heißen] Brei herumreden *(ugs.);* **d)** *(knock)* klopfen, pochen (**at** an + *Dat.*); **e)** *(Naut.)* kreuzen. **3.** *n.* **a)** *(stroke, throbbing)* Schlag, *der;* Schlagen, *das; (rhythm)* Takt, *der;* **his heart missed a ~:** ihm stockte das Herz; **~ [music]** Beat, *der;* Beatmusik, *die;* **b)** *(Mus.)* Schlag, *der; (of metronome, baton)* Taktschlag, *der;* **c)** *(Phys.)* Schwebung, *die;* **d)** *(of policeman, watchman)* Runde, *die; (habitual round)* übliche Runde; *(area)* Revier, *das;* **be off sb.'s [usual] ~** *(fig.)* nicht in jmds. Fach schlagen; **e)** *(Hunting)* Treibjagd, *die;* **f) did you ever see the ~ of that?** *(Amer. sl.)* hast du so etwas schon mal gesehen?; **g)** *(Amer. Journ.: scoop)* Knüller, *der (ugs.)*

~ a'bout *v. i.* [herum]suchen

~ 'back *v. t.* zurückschlagen ‹*Feind*›

~ 'down 1. *v. i.* ‹*Sonne:*› herniederbrennen; ‹*Regen:*› niederprasseln. **2.** *v. t.* **a)** einschlagen ‹*Tür*›; **b)** *(in bargaining)* herunterhandeln

~ 'in *v. t.* einschlagen; demolieren *(ugs.)*

~ 'off *v. t.* abwehren, zurückschlagen ‹*Angriff*›

~ 'out *v. t.* **a)** heraushämmern ‹*Rhythmus, Melodie*›; aushämmern ‹*Metall*›; ausschlagen ‹*Feuer*›; **b)** *(Amer.: defeat)* aus dem Feld schlagen ‹*Konkurrenten*›

~ 'up *v. t.* **a)** zusammenschlagen ‹*Person*›; schlagen ‹*Sahne usw.*›; **b)** *(attract)* anwerben ‹*Rekruten*›

beaten ['bi:tn] **1.** *see* **beat 1, 2. 2.** *adj.* **a) a ~ track** *or* **path** ein Trampelpfad; **off the ~ track** *(remote)* weit abgelegen; weitab vom Schuß *(ugs.);* **he has always kept to the ~ track** *(fig.)* er ist immer in den gewohnten Bahnen geblieben; **go off the ~ track** *(fig.)* vom üblichen Weg abweichen; **b)** *(hammered)* gehämmert ‹*Silber, Gold*›; **c)** *(exhausted, dejected)* erschöpft, *(ugs.)* erledigt ‹*Person*›

beater ['bi:tə(r)] *n.* **a)** *(Cookery)* Rührbesen, *der;* **b)** *(Hunting)* Treiber, *der;* **c)** *(carpet ~)* [Teppich]klopfer, *der*

beatific [bi:ə'tɪfɪk] *adj.* beglückend; *(blissful)* beglückt, selig ‹*Lächeln*›

beatification [bɪætɪfɪ'keɪʃn] *n. (Relig.)* Seligsprechung, *die;* Beatifikation, *die*

beatify [bɪ'ætɪfaɪ] *v. t. (Relig.)* seligsprechen; beatifizieren

beating ['bi:tɪŋ] *n.* **a)** *(punishment)* **a ~:** Schläge *Pl.;* Prügel *Pl.;* **a good ~:** eine gehörige Tracht Prügel *(ugs.);* **b)** *(defeat)* Niederlage, *die;* **give sb. a good ~:** jmdm. eine schwere Niederlage zufügen; **take** *or* **get a [sound] ~:** eine [schwere] Niederlage hinnehmen [müssen]; **c)** *(surpassing)* **take some/a lot of ~:** nicht leicht zu übertreffen sein; seinesgleichen suchen

beatitude [bɪ'ætɪtju:d] *n.* **a)** *(blessedness)* [Glück]seligkeit, *die;* **b)** *in pl.* Seligpreisungen

'beat-up *adj. (coll.)* ramponiert *(ugs.)*

beau [bəʊ] *n., pl.* **~x** [bəʊz] *or* **~s a)** *(ladies' man)* Frauenheld, *der; (fop)* Beau, *der (geh.);* Dandy, *der (geh.);* **b)** *(Amer.: boyfriend)* Galan, *der (veralt.);* Verehrer, *der*

Beaufort scale ['bəʊfət skeɪl] *n. (Meteorol.)* Beaufortskala, *die*

Beaujolais ['bəʊʒəleɪ] *n.* Beaujolais, *der*

beaut [bju:t] *(Austral., NZ, & Amer. sl.)* **1.** *n.* Prachtexemplar, *das; (woman)* Schönheit, *die.* **2.** *adj.* klasse *(ugs.)*

beauteous ['bju:tɪəs] *adj. (poet.)* wunderschön; herrlich

beautician [bju:'tɪʃn] *n.* Kosmetiker, *der*/Kosmetikerin, *die*

beautification [bju:tɪfɪ'keɪʃn] *n.* Verschönerung, *die; (of the body)* Schönheitspflege, *die*

beautiful ['bju:tɪfl] *adj.* [ausgesprochen] schön; wunderschön ‹*Augen, Aussicht, Blume, Kleid, Morgen, Musik, Schmuck*›; *(morally or intellectually impressive)* großartig; **the B~ People** die Hippies; **~ letters** *(Amer.)* Belletristik, *die;* schöne Literatur; **small is ~:** klein ist schön

beautifully ['bju:tɪfəlɪ] *adv.* wunderbar; *(coll.: very well)* prima *(ugs.);* wunderbar, schön ‹*weich, warm*›; **you did [that] ~:** du hast es prima gemacht

beautify ['bju:tɪfaɪ] *v. t.* verschönern; schöner machen; *(adorn)* [aus]schmücken; **~ oneself** sich schönmachen *(ugs.)*

beauty ['bju:tɪ] *n.* **a)** *no pl.* Schönheit, *die; (of action, response)* Eleganz, *die; (of idea, simplicity, sacrifice)* Größe, *die;* **~ is only skin deep** man kann nicht nach dem Äußeren urteilen; **be a thing of ~** wunderschön sein; **b)** *(person or thing)* Schönheit, *die; (animal)* wunderschönes Tier; **she is a real ~:** sie ist wirklich eine Schönheit; **B~ and the Beast** die Schöne und das Tier; **They've just bought a new car. It's a ~:** Sie haben sich *(Dat.)* gerade einen neuen Wagen gekauft. Er ist wunderbar; **c)** *(exceptionally good specimen)* Prachtexemplar, *das;* **that last goal was a ~:** dieses letzte Tor war ein richtiges Bilderbuchtor; **d)** *(beautiful feature)* Schöne, *das;* **her eyes are her great ~:** das Schöne an ihr sind ihre Augen; **the ~ of it/of living in California** das Schöne *od.* Gute daran/am Leben in Kalifornien

beauty: ~ competition, ~ contest *ns.* Schönheitswettbewerb, *der;* **~ parlour** *see* **~ salon; ~ queen** *n.* Schönheitskönigin, *die;* **~ salon** *n.* Schönheitssalon, *der;* Kosmetiksalon, *der;* **~ spot** *n.* Schönheitsfleck, *der; (patch)* Schönheitspflästerchen, *das; (place)* schönes Fleckchen [Erde]; **a local ~ spot** ein Ausflugsziel am Ort; **~ treatment** *n.* Schönheitsbehandlung, *die*

beaux *pl. of* **beau**

beaver ['bi:və(r)] **1.** *n.* **a)** *pl. same or* **~s** Biber, *der;* Biberratte, *die;* **eager ~** *(fig. coll.)* Übereifrige, *der/die; (esp. at school)* Streber, *der*/Streberin, *die;* **b)** *(fur)* Biber[pelz], *der.* **2.** *v. i. (Brit.)* **~ away** schuften *(ugs.);* eifrig arbeiten (**at** an + *Dat.*)

beaver: B~board, (P) *n. (Amer.)* Hartfaserplatte, *die;* **~ lamb** *n.* Biberlamm, *das*

becalmed [bɪ'kɑ:md] *adj.* **be ~** in einer Flaute *od.* Windstille treiben

became *see* **become**

because [bɪ'kɒz] **1.** *conj.* weil; **one of the reasons why she stopped is ~ she was tired** einer der Gründe, warum sie aufhörte, ist, daß sie müde war; **he is popular ~ handsome** er ist beliebt, weil er gut aussieht; **that is ~ you don't know German** das liegt daran, daß du kein Deutsch kannst. **2.** *adv.* **~ of** wegen (+ *Gen.*); **don't come just ~ of me** nur meinetwegen brauchen Sie nicht zu kommen; **~ of which he ...:** weswegen er ...

¹beck [bek] *n. (dial.: brook)* [Wild]bach, *der*

²beck *n. (literary)* **be at sb.'s ~ and call** jmdm. zur Verfügung stehen; **have sb. at one's ~ and call** jmdn. zur Verfügung haben; ganz über jmdn. verfügen können

beckon ['bekn] **1.** *v. t.* **a)** winken; **~ sb. in/over** jmdn. herein-/herbei- *od.* herüberwinken; **b)** *(fig.: invite)* locken; rufen. **2.** *v. i.* **a) ~ to sb.** jmdm. winken *od.* ein Zeichen geben; jmdn. zu sich winken; **b)** *(fig.: be inviting)* locken

become [bɪ'kʌm] **1.** *copula, forms as* **come** werden; **~ a politician/dentist** Politiker/Zahnarzt werden; **~ a hazard/nuisance/rule** zu einem Risiko/zu einer Plage/zur Regel werden; **~ popular/angry** beliebt/böse werden; **~ accustomed** *or* **used to sb./sth.** sich an jmdn./etw. gewöhnen. **2.** *v. i., forms as* **come** werden; **what has ~ of him?** was ist aus ihm geworden?; **what has ~ of that guidebook/courier?** wo ist der Reiseführer geblieben?; **what is to ~ of you?** was soll bloß aus dir werden?. **3.** *v. t., forms as* **come: a)** *see* **befit; b)** *(suit)* **~ sb.** jmdm. stehen; zu jmdm. passen

becoming [bɪ'kʌmɪŋ] *adj.* **a)** *(fitting)* schicklich *(geh.);* geziemend *(geh.);* **it is not ~ for a young lady to ...:** es ziemt sich für eine junge Dame nicht, zu ...; **b)** *(flattering)* vorteilhaft, kleidsam ‹*Hut, Kleid, Frisur*›

becquerel ['bekərel] *n. (Phys.)* Becquerel, *das*

bed [bed] **1.** *n.* **a)** Bett, *das; (without bedstead)* Lager, *das;* **they talked together till ~** *(coll.)* sie unterhielten sich, bis sie ins Bett gingen; **he's very fond of his ~:** er liegt gerne im Bett; **be/lie in ~:** im Bett sein/liegen; **~ and board** *(lodging)* Unterkunft und Verpflegung; *(marital relations)* Tisch und Bett; **~ and breakfast** Zimmer mit Frühstück; **a ~ and breakfast place** eine Frühstückspension; **get into/out of ~:** ins *od.* zu Bett gehen/aufstehen; **go to ~:** zu *od.* ins Bett gehen; **go to ~ with sb.** *(fig.)* mit jmdm. ins Bett gehen *(ugs.);* **the newspaper has gone to ~** *(fig.)* die Zeitung ist im Druck; **make the ~:** das Bett machen; **put sb. to ~:** jmdn. zu *od.* ins Bett bringen; **put a paper to ~** *(fig.)* eine Zeitung in Druck geben; **life isn't a** *or* **is no ~ of roses** *(fig.)* das Leben ist kein reines Vergnügen; **his life isn't exactly a ~ of roses** *(fig.)* er ist nicht gerade auf Rosen gebettet; ~ **of sickness** *(literary)* Krankenlager, *das (geh.)*; **have got out of ~ on the wrong side** *(fig.)* mit dem linken Fuß zuerst aufgestanden sein; **as you make your ~ so you must lie on it** *(prov.)* wie man sich bettet, so liegt man; **take to one's ~:** sich krank ins Bett legen; **be confined to ~:** ans Bett gefesselt sein *(fig.)*; **be brought to ~** *(literary)* niederkommen (**of** mit); entbunden werden (**of** von); **b)** *(flat base)* Unterlage, *die; (of machine)* Bett, *das; (of road, railway, etc.)* Unterbau, *der;* Kies-/Schotterbett, *das; (of billiard-table)* Schieferplatte *(die mit grünem Kammgarntuch bespannt ist)*; **c)** *(in garden)* Beet, *das; (for osiers etc.)* Pflanzung, *die;* **d)** *(of sea, lake)* Grund, *der;* Boden, *der; (of river)* Bett, *das;* **e)** *(layer)* Schicht, *die;* **f)** *(of oysters etc.)* Bank, *die.* **2.** *v. t.*, **-dd-: a)** ins Bett legen; **b)** *(fig. coll.)* beschlafen ⟨*Frau*⟩; **c)** *(plant)* setzen ⟨*Pflanze, Sämling*⟩. **3.** *v. i.*, **-dd-** zu *od.* ins Bett gehen; schlafen gehen; **he ~s with his mistress** *(fig.)* er schläft mit seiner Geliebten

~ **'down 1.** *v. t.* mit Streu versorgen ⟨*Pferd usw.*⟩; **the troops were ~ded down in a barn** die Soldaten wurden über Nacht in einer Scheune einquartiert; **the farmer ~ded down the tramp** der Bauer beherbergte den Landstreicher. **2.** *v. i.* kampieren; **she ~s down with her boy-friend** *(fig.)* sie schläft mit ihrem Freund

~ **'in** *v. t.* einlassen

~ **'out** *v. t.* auspflanzen ⟨*Pflanzen*⟩

B. Ed. [bi: 'ed] *abbr.* **Bachelor of Education** Bakkalaureus der Erziehungswissenschaften; *see also* **B. Sc.**

bedazzle [bɪ'dæzl] *v. t.* **a)** blenden; **b)** *(confuse)* verwirren

bed: ~bug *n.* [Bett]wanze, *die;* **~chamber** *n.* **a)** *(arch.)* Schlafgemach, *das (veralt.)*; Schlafzimmer, *das;* **b) the Royal Bedchamber** das königliche Schlafgemach; **Lady/Gentleman of the Bedchamber** königliche Hofdame/königlicher Kammerjunker; **~clothes** *n. pl.* Bettzeug, *das;* **turn down** *or* **back the ~clothes** das Bett aufdecken

beddable ['bedəbl] *adj. (coll.)* **be ~:** was fürs Bett sein *(ugs.)*

bedding ['bedɪŋ] *n., no pl., no indef. art.* **a)** Matratze und Bettzeug; *(litter)* Streu, *das;* **b)** *(Geol.)* Lagerung, *die;* Schichtung, *die*

'bedding plant *n.* Freilandpflanze, *die*

beddy-byes ['bedɪbaɪz] *n. (child lang.)* Heiabett, *das (Kinderspr.)*; Heia, *die (Kinderspr.)*; **off to ~:** ab in die Heia *od.* ins Heiabett

bedeck [bɪ'dek] *v. t.* schmücken; **~ oneself** sich aufputzen *(abwertend)*; **~ed with flags** mit Fahnen geschmückt; fahnengeschmückt

bedevil [bɪ'devl] *v. t., (Brit.)* **-ll-: a)** *(spoil)* verderben; durcheinanderbringen ⟨*System*⟩; **b)** *(plague, afflict)* heimsuchen; **that family is ~led by bad luck** diese Familie ist vom Pech verfolgt; **c)** *(torment)* quälen; peinigen *(geh.)*; **~ sb.'s life** jmdm. das Leben zur Hölle machen

bed: ~fast *adj. (arch.)* bettlägerig; **~fellow** *n.* Bettgenosse, *der*/-genossin, *die;* **make** *or* **be strange ~fellows** *(fig.)* ⟨*Personen:*⟩ ein merkwürdiges Gespann sein; ⟨*Staaten, Organisationen:*⟩ eine eigenartige Kombination sein; **~-head** *n.* Kopfende des Bettes; **~jacket** *n.* Bettjacke, *die*

bedlam ['bedləm] *n.* Chaos, *das;* Durcheinander, *das;* **absolute ~:** ein totales Chaos *od.* Durcheinander; **it is [like] ~ in here** hier geht es zu wie im Irrenhaus

'bed-linen *n.* Bettwäsche, *die*

bedouin ['bedu:ɪn] *n., pl. same* Beduine, *der*/Beduinin, *die*

bed: ~pan *n.* Bettschüssel, *die;* Bettpfanne, *die;* **~plate** *n.* Grundplatte, *die;* Bodenplatte, *die;* **~post** *n.* Bettpfosten, *der*

bedraggle [bɪ'drægl] *v. t.* [naß und] schmutzig machen; **~d** [naß und] verschmutzt *od.* schmutzig

bed: ~-rest *n.* Bettruhe, *die;* **~ridden** *adj.* bettlägerig; **~rock** *n.* Felssohle, *die; (fig.)* Basis, *die;* Fundament, *das;* **get** *or* **reach down to ~rock** *(fig.)* zum Kern der Sache kommen; einer Sache *(Dat.)* auf den Grund gehen; **~ roll** *n.* zusammengerolltes Bettzeug; **~room** *n.* Schlafzimmer, *das;* **~room comedy/farce** Schlafzimmerkomödie, *die;* **~room scene** Bettszene, *die;* **she has ~room eyes** sie hat einen Schlafzimmerblick *(ugs.)*; **a two-~room[ed] house** ein Haus mit zwei Schlafzimmern; **~-set'tee** *n.* Bettcouch, *die;* **~side** *n.* Seite des Bettes, *die;* **be at the ~side** am Bett sein; **~side table/lamp** Nachttisch, *der*/Nachttischlampe, *die;* **~side reading** Bettlektüre, *die;* **a ~side book** ein Buch als Bettlektüre; **have a good ~side manner** ⟨*Arzt:*⟩ gut mit Kranken umgehen können; **~-sit, ~-'sitter** *ns. (coll.)*, **~-'sitting-room** *n. (Brit.)* Wohnschlafzimmer, *das;* **~socks** *n. pl.* Bettsocken; **~sore** *n.* wundgelegene Stelle; **get ~sores** sich wundliegen; **~spread** *n.* Tagesdecke, *die;* **~stead** ['bedsted] *n.* Bettgestell, *das;* **~straw** *n. (Bot.)* **[Our] Lady's ~straw** Echtes Labkraut; **~table** *n.* Krankentisch, *der;* **~time** *n.* Schlafenszeit, *die;* **it's past the children's ~time** die Kinder müßten schon im Bett sein; **will you have it finished by ~time?** bist du vor dem Schlafengehen damit fertig?; **a ~time story** eine Gutenachtgeschichte; **a novel that makes good ~time reading** ein Roman, den man gut vor dem Einschlafen lesen kann

beduin *see* **bedouin**

'bed-wetting *n.* Bettnässen, *das*

bee [bi:] *n.* **a)** Biene, *die;* **she's such a busy ~** *(fig.)* sie ist so ein fleißiges Mädchen; **as busy as a ~** *(fig.)* bienenfleißig; **have a ~ in one's bonnet** *(fig.)* einen Fimmel *od.* Tick haben *(ugs.)*; **she thinks she's the ~'s knees** *(fig. coll.)* sie hält sich für die Größte *(ugs.)*; **b)** *(Amer.) (meeting) nachbarliche Versammlung zu gemeinsamer Arbeit; (party)* Fest, *das; see also* **spelling-bee**

Beeb [bi:b] *n. (Brit. coll.)* **the ~:** die BBC

beech [bi:tʃ] *n.* **a)** *(tree)* Buche, *die; (Austral.)* Scheinbuche, *die;* **b)** *(wood)* Buche, *die;* Buchenholz, *das; attrib.* buchen

beech: ~-marten *n.* Steinmarder, *der;* **~-mast** *n.* Bucheckern *Pl.;* **~-nut** *n.* [Buch]ecker, *die;* **~wood** *see* **beech b**

'bee-eater *n. (Ornith.)* Bienenfresser, *der*

beef [bi:f] **1.** *n.* **a)** *no pl.* Rindfleisch, *das;* Rind, *das;* **b)** *no pl. (muscles)* Muskeln; **have plenty of ~:** sehr muskulös sein; **there's a great deal of ~ on him** er ist ganz schön mit Muskeln bepackt *(ugs.)*; **c)** *usu. in pl.* **beeves** [bi:vz] *or (Amer.)* **~s** *(ox)* Mastrind, *das;* **d)** *pl.* **~s** *(coll.: complaint)* Mekkerei, *die (ugs.)*. **2.** *v. t.* **~ up** stärken. **3.** *v. i. (sl.)* meckern *(ugs.)* (**about** über + *Akk.*)

beef: ~burger *n.* Beefburger, *der;* **~cake** *n. (Amer. sl.)* Muskeln *Pl.;* Bizeps, *der (ugs.)*; **~ cattle** *n. pl.* Mastrinder; **~eater** *n. (Brit.)* Beefeater, *der;* **~steak** *n.* Beefsteak, *das;* **~steak fungus** Leberpilz, *der;* **~'tea** *n.* Kraftbrühe, *die;* Fleischbrühe, *die*

beefy ['bi:fɪ] *adj.* **a)** *(like beef)* wie Rindfleisch *nachgestellt;* Rindfleisch-; **b)** *(coll.: muscular)* muskulös; *(fleshy)* massig

bee: ~hive *n.* Bienenstock, *der; (rounded)* Bienenkorb, *der; (fig.: scene of activity)* Taubenschlag, *der; (hair-style)* toupierte Hochfrisur; **~-keeper** *n.* Imker, *der*/Imkerin, *die;* Bienenzüchter, *der*/-züchterin, *die;* **~-keeping** *n.* Bienenzucht, *die;* Imkerei, *die;* Bienenhaltung, *die;* **~-line** *n.* **make a ~-line for sth./sb.** schnurstracks auf etw./jmdn. zustürzen

been *see* **be**

beep [bi:p] **1.** *n.* Piepton, *der; (of car horn)* Tuten, *das.* **2.** *v. i.* piepen; ⟨*Signalhorn:*⟩ hupen; **~ at sb.** jmdn. anhupen; **a ~ing sound** ein Piepton

beeper ['bi:pə(r)] *n.* Piepser, *der*

beer [bɪə(r)] *n.* Bier, *das;* **order two ~s** zwei Bier bestellen; **brew various ~s** verschiedene Biere *od.* Biersorten brauen; **life is not all ~ and skittles** *(fig.)* das Leben ist kein reines Vergnügen; **small ~:** Dünnbier, *das (ugs.)*; *(fig.: trifles)* Nebensächlichkeiten *Pl.;* Kleinigkeiten *Pl.;* **that firm's turnover is only small ~:** der Umsatz dieser Firma ist kaum der Rede wert; **he is only small ~:** er hat nichts zu sagen

beer: ~-barrel *n.* Bierfaß, *das;* **~ belly** *n. (coll.)* Bierbauch, *der (ugs.)*; **~-bottle** *n.* Bierflasche, *die;* **~-can** *n.* Bierdose, *die;* **~ cellar** *n.* Bierkeller, *der;* **~-crate** *n.* Bierkasten, *der;* **~-drinker** *n.* Biertrinker, *der;* **~-engine** *n.* Bierpumpe, *die;* **~ garden** *n.* Biergarten, *der;* **~-glass** *n.* Bierglas, *das;* **~ hall** *n.* Bierhalle, *die;* **~house** *n. (Brit.)* Bierschenke, *die;* Bierstube, *die;* **~-making** *n.* Brauerei, *die;* **~-mat** *n.* Bierdeckel, *der;* Bieruntersetzer, *der;* **~ money** *n.* Geld für Getränke; **~-mug** *n.* Bierkrug, *der;* **~-pump** *see* **~-engine; ~-swilling** *adj. (coll.)* biersaufend *(salopp)*

beery ['bɪərɪ] *adj.* **a)** ⟨*Mensch*⟩ mit Bierfahne; **~ taste/smell** Biergeschmack, *der*/Biergeruch, *der;* **b)** *(tipsy)* bierselig

beestings ['bi:stɪŋz] *n. pl. (Agric.)* Biestmilch, *die*

beeswax ['bi:zwæks] *n.* Bienenwachs, *das*

beet [bi:t] *n.* Rübe, *die;* **red ~:** rote Bete *od.* Rübe; **white ~:** weiße Rübe; Wasserrübe, *die;* **~ sugar** Rübenzucker, *der*

[1]**beetle** ['bi:tl] *n.* Käfer, *der;* **as blind as a ~** *(fig.)* blind wie ein Maulwurf

[2]**beetle** *n. (tool)* Holzhammer, *der; (machine)* Kalander, *der*

[3]**beetle** *v. i.* **a)** ⟨*Brauen:*⟩ vorstehen; ⟨*Felsen:*⟩ überhängen, vorstehen; **b) ~ along/off/past** *(sl.)* ⟨*Mensch:*⟩ entlangpesen/abhauen/vorbeirennen *(ugs.)*; ⟨*Auto:*⟩ entlang-/weg-/vorbeibrummen *(ugs.)*

beetle: ~-browed [bi:tl'braʊd] *adj.* finster aussehend; **~ 'brows** *n. pl.* buschige [vorstehende] Augenbrauen; **~-crusher** *n.* Quadratlatschen, *der*

'beetroot *n.* rote Beete *od.* Rübe

beeves *see* **beef 1 c**

befall [bɪ'fɔ:l] **1.** *v. i., forms as* **fall 2** sich begeben *(geh.)*; geschehen. **2.** *v. t., forms as* **fall 2** widerfahren (+ *Dat.*)

befit [bɪ'fɪt] *v. t.*, **-tt-** *(be seemly for)* sich ziemen *od.* gebühren für *(geh.)*; **it ill ~s you to do that** es steht Ihnen schlecht an, das zu tun; **she behaved as ~ted a lady** sie benahm sich, wie es sich für eine Dame gebührte

befitting [bɪ'fɪtɪŋ] *adj.* gebührend *(geh.)*; schicklich ⟨*Benehmen*⟩ *(geh.)*

befog [bɪ'fɒg] *v. t.*, **-gg-: a)** *(confuse)* verwirren; ⟨*Drogen, Alkohol:*⟩ benebeln, umnebeln; **b)** *(obscure)* verunklaren ⟨*Sachverhalt, Thema*⟩

befool [bɪ'fu:l] *v. t.* täuschen; **be ~ed** sich täuschen lassen

before [bɪ'fɔ:(r)] **1.** *adv.* **a)** *(of time)* vorher; zuvor; **the day ~** am Tag zuvor; **long ~:** lange vorher *od.* zuvor; **not long ~:** kurz vorher; **our friendship is less close than ~:** unsere Freundschaft ist nicht mehr so eng wie früher *od.* vorher; **the noise continued as ~:** der Lärm ging nach wie vor weiter; **you should have told me so ~:** das hättest du mir vorher *od.* früher *od.* eher sagen sollen; **I've seen that film ~:** ich habe den Film schon [einmal] gesehen; **I've heard that ~:** das habe ich schon einmal gehört; **I wish I had known that ~:** hätte ich das nur früher gewußt; **I'll give it to you on your birthday and not ~:** ich gebe es dir an deinem Geburtstag und nicht eher; **b)** *(ahead in position)* vor[aus]; **c)** *(in front)* voran; **go/ride ~:** voran- *od.* vorausgehen/-reiten. **2.** *prep.* **a)**

(of time) vor; **the day ~ yesterday** vorgestern; **the year ~ last** vorletztes Jahr; **the year ~ that** das Jahr davor; **the time ~ that** das vorige Mal; **old/die ~ one's time** frühzeitig gealtert/sterben; **it was [well] ~ my time** das war [lange] vor meiner Zeit; **since ~ the operation/war** schon vor der Operation/dem Krieg; **~ now** vorher; früher; **~ Christ** vor Christus; vor Christi Geburt; **he got there ~ me** er war vor mir da; **~ then** vorher; **~ long** bald; **~ leaving, he phoned/I will phone** bevor er wegging, rief er an/bevor ich weggehe, rufe ich an; **~ tax** brutto; vor [Abzug *(Dat.)* der] Steuern; **b)** *(position)* vor (+ *Dat.*); *(direction)* vor (+ *Akk.*); **~ my very eyes** vor meinen Augen; **go ~ a committee/court of law** vor einen Ausschuß/ein Gericht kommen; **be brought/appear ~ the judge** vor den Richter gebracht werden/vor dem Richter erscheinen; **c)** *(under the action of)* vor (+ *Dat.*); **sail ~ the wind** vor dem Wind segeln; *see also* **carry 1 a; d)** *(awaiting)* **have one's future/life ~ one** seine Zukunft/sein Leben noch vor sich *(Dat.)* haben; *(confronting)* **the matter ~ us** das uns *(Dat.)* vorliegende Thema; die Sache, die uns *(Akk.)* betrifft; **the task ~ us** die Aufgabe, die vor uns *(Dat.)* liegt; **the problem ~ them** das Problem, vor dem sie stehen/standen; **e)** *(ahead of in sequence)* vor (+ *Dat.*); **he's ~ her in class** in der Klasse ist er besser als sie; **he puts work ~ everything** die Arbeit ist ihm wichtiger als alles andere; **~ all else she is a teacher** in erster Linie ist sie Lehrerin; **~ everything else** *(as most important)* vor allem; vor allen Dingen; **ladies ~ gentlemen** Damen haben [den] Vortritt; **f)** *(rather than)* vor; **death ~ dishonour** lieber tot als ehrlos; **right ~ might** Macht darf nicht vor Recht gehen. **3.** *conj.* **a)** bevor; **it'll be ages ~ I finish this** es wird eine Ewigkeit dauern, bis ich damit fertig bin; **shortly/long ~ I met you** kurz/lange bevor ich dich kennenlernte; **b)** *(rather than)* bevor; ehe

beforehand [bɪˈfɔːhænd] *adv.* vorher; *(in anticipation)* im voraus; **I found out about it ~**: ich habe es schon vorher herausgefunden; **whereas five minutes ~ it had been sunny, ...**: während die Sonne vor fünf Minuten noch geschienen hatte, ...; **be ~ with** *(early)* vorzeitig tun; *(premature, overhasty)* voreilig sein mit

befoul [bɪˈfaʊl] *v. t.* **a)** verschmutzen ⟨*Gebäude*⟩; verpesten ⟨*Luft*⟩; **b)** *(fig.)* beschmutzen ⟨*Namen*⟩; vergiften ⟨*Atmosphäre*⟩

befriend [bɪˈfrend] *v. t.* **a)** *(act as a friend to)* sich anfreunden mit; **b)** *(help)* sich annehmen (+ *Gen.*)

befuddle [bɪˈfʌdl] *v. t.* **a)** *(make drunk)* benebeln; **b)** *(confuse)* verwirren; konfus machen

beg [beg] **1.** *v. t.*, **-gg- a)** betteln um; erbetteln ⟨*Lebensunterhalt*⟩; **~ one's bread** sich *(Dat.)* sein Brot erbetteln; **b)** *(ask earnestly)* bitten; **he ~ged her not to go** er bat sie, doch nicht zu gehen; **she ~ged to come with us** sie bat darum, mit uns kommen zu dürfen; **~ that sth. be done** darum bitten, daß etw. getan wird; **I ~ to inform you that ...** *(formal)* ich erlaube mir, Sie davon in Kenntnis zu setzen, daß ... *(geh.)*; **I ~ to differ** da bin ich [aber] anderer Meinung; **~ sb. for sth.** jmdn. um etw. bitten; **c)** *(ask earnestly for)* **~ sth.** um etw. bitten; **~ sth. of sb.** etw. von jmdm. erbitten; **~ a favour [of sb.]** [jmdn.] um einen Gefallen bitten; **~ forgiveness** um Verzeihung bitten; **~ leave** *or* **permission to do sth.** um Erlaubnis bitten, etw. tun zu dürfen; *see also* **pardon 1 b; d) ~ the question** *(evade difficulty)* der Frage *(Dat.)* ausweichen. **2.** *v. i.*, **-gg- a)** ⟨*Bettler:*⟩ betteln **(for** um); ⟨*Hund:*⟩ Männchen machen; betteln; **a ~ging letter** ein Bettelbrief; **go [a-]~ging** keinen Abnehmer finden; **b)** *(ask earnestly)* bitten **(for** um); **~ of sb. to do sth.** jmdn. [darum] bitten, etw. zu tun; **~ off** sich entschuldigen [lassen]

began *see* **begin**

begat *see* **beget**

beget [bɪˈget] *v. t.*, **begot** [bɪˈgɒt] *or (arch.)* **begat** [bɪˈgæt], **begotten** [bɪˈgɒtn] **a)** *(arch.: procreate)* zeugen; **God's only begotten son** Gottes eingeborener Sohn; **b)** *(literary: cause)* zeugen; gebären *(geh.)*

beggar [ˈbegə(r)] **1.** *n.* **a)** Bettler, *der*/Bettlerin, *die*; **~s can't be choosers** *(prov.)* man kann es sich *(Dat.)* eben nicht immer aussuchen; **b)** *(coll.: person)* Arme, *der/die*; **poor ~**: armer Teufel; **a poor old ~** ein armer alter Mann; **be a lucky/lazy/cheeky ~**: ein Glückspilz/Faulpelz/frecher Kerl sein *(ugs.)*; **be a funny little ~**: ein drolliger Fratz sein *(ugs.)*. **2.** *v. t.* **a)** an den Bettelstab bringen; arm machen; **b)** *(outshine)* in den Schatten stellen; **~ description** unbeschreiblich sein

beggarly [ˈbegəlɪ] *adj.* erbärmlich; erbarmungswürdig ⟨*Person*⟩; *(fig.)* erbärmlich; *(ungenerous)* engherzig ⟨*Einstellung*⟩; armselig ⟨*Bezahlung*⟩

beggary [ˈbegərɪ] *n.* [Bettel]armut, *die*; **be reduced to ~**: bettelarm werden

begin [bɪˈgɪn] **1.** *v. t.*, **-nn-, began** [bɪˈgæn], **begun** [bɪˈgʌn] **a) ~ sth.** [mit] etw. beginnen; **~ a new bottle** eine neue Flasche anbrechen; **she began life in a small village** sie verbrachte ihre ersten Lebensjahre in einem kleinen Dorf; **~ school** in die Schule kommen; eingeschult werden; **when do you ~ your retirement?** wann gehen Sie in Pension?; **~ doing** *or* **to do sth.** anfangen *od.* beginnen, etw. zu tun; **I began to slip** ich kam ins Rutschen; **I am ~ning to get annoyed** so langsam werde ich ärgerlich; **b) not ~ to do sth.** *(coll.: make no progress towards doing sth.)*: **the film does not ~ to compare with the book** der Film läßt sich nicht annähernd mit dem Buch vergleichen; **she didn't even ~ to grasp it** sie hat es nicht einmal ansatzweise verstanden; **the authorities couldn't even ~ to assess the damage** die Behörden konnten den Schaden nicht einmal grob abschätzen. **2.** *v. i.* **-nn-, began, begun** anfangen; beginnen *(oft geh.)*; **when the world began** als die Erde entstand; **where does the river ~?** wo entspringt der Fluß?; **~ning student** *(Amer.)* Studienanfänger, *der*/-anfängerin, *die*; **~ning next month** vom nächsten Monat an; **~ at the beginning** von vorne anfangen; **~ [up]on sth.** etw. anfangen; **~ with sth./sb.** bei *od.* mit etw./jmdm. anfangen *od.* beginnen; **to ~ with** zunächst *od.* zuerst einmal; **it is the wrong book, to ~ with** das ist schon einmal das falsche Buch

beginner [bɪˈgɪnə(r)] *n.* Anfänger, *der*/Anfängerin, *die*; **~'s luck** Anfängerglück, *das*

beginning [bɪˈgɪnɪŋ] *n.* Anfang, *der*; Beginn, *der*; **at** *or* **in the ~**: am Anfang; **at the ~ of February/the month** Anfang Februar/des Monats; **myths about the ~ of the world** Mythen über die Entstehung der Welt; **at the ~ of the day** zu Beginn des Tages; **from ~ to end** von Anfang bis Ende; von vorn bis hinten; **from the [very] ~**: [ganz] von Anfang an; **have its ~s in sth.** seine Anfänge *od.* seinen Ursprung in etw. *(Dat.)* haben; **small ~s** kleine Anfänge; **[this is] the ~ of the end** [das ist] der Anfang vom Ende; **go back to the ~** wieder von vorne anfangen; **make a ~ with sth.** mit etw. anfangen

begone [bɪˈgɒn, bɪˈgɔːn] *v. i. in imper. and inf. only* **~!** fort!; hinweg! *(veralt.)*; **tell sb. to ~**: jmdm. sagen, daß er sich fortmachen solle

begonia [bɪˈgəʊnɪə] *n. (Bot.)* Begonie, *die*; Schiefblatt, *das*

begorra [bɪˈgɒrə] *int. (Ir.)* Jesses

begot, begotten *see* **beget**

begrudge [bɪˈgrʌdʒ] *v. t.* **a)** *(envy)* **~ sb. sth.** jmdm. etw. mißgönnen; **I don't ~ their buying a car** ich gönne ihnen, daß sie sich *(Dat.)* ein Auto kaufen; **b)** *(give reluctantly)* **I ~ the time/money I have to spend** es ist mir leid um die Zeit/das Geld; **c)** *(be dissatisfied with)* **~ doing sth.** etw. ungern tun; **he did not ~ the fact that ...**: er war nicht darüber verärgert, daß ...

beguile [bɪˈgaɪl] *v. t.* **a)** *(delude)* betören; verführen; **~ sb. into doing sth.** jmdn. dazu verführen, etw. zu tun; **be ~d by sb./sth.** sich von jmdm./etw. täuschen lassen; **b)** *(cheat)* betrügen; **~ sb. [out] of sth.** jmdn. um etw. betrügen; **~ sb. into doing sth.** jmdn. verleiten, etw. zu tun; **c)** *(divert attention from)* vertreiben; *(charm)* bezaubern; *(amuse)* unterhalten

beguiling [bɪˈgaɪlɪŋ] *adj.* verführerisch; betörend ⟨*Einfluß*⟩; verlockend ⟨*Zeitvertreib*⟩

begun *see* **begin**

behalf [bɪˈhɑːf] *n.*, *pl.* **behalves** [bɪˈhɑːvz]: **on** *or (Amer.)* **in ~ of sb./sth.** *(as representing sb./sth.)* für jmdn./etw.; *(more formally)* im Namen von jmdm./etw.; **on** *or (Amer.)* **in sb.'s/my ~**: *(for sb.'s/my benefit)* zugunsten von jmdm./zu meinen Gunsten; **don't fret on my ~**: mach dir meinetwegen keine Sorgen

behave [bɪˈheɪv] **1.** *v. i.* **a)** sich verhalten; sich benehmen; ⟨*Chemikalien:*⟩ reagieren; **how do you ~ under stress?** wie verhältst du dich bei Streß?; **he ~s more like a friend to them** er behandelt sie mehr wie Freunde; **~ well/badly** sich gut/schlecht benehmen *od.* betragen; **~ well/badly towards sb.** jmdn. gut/schlecht behandeln; **my car hasn't been behaving too well of late** mein Auto hat mir in letzter Zeit ziemlich viel Ärger gemacht; **well-/ill-** *or* **badly/nicely ~d** brav/ungezogen/lieb *(ugs.)*; **b)** *(do what is correct)* brav sein; sich benehmen; sich betragen. **2.** *v. refl.* **~ oneself** sich benehmen; **~ yourself!** benimm dich!

behavior *etc. (Amer.) see* **behaviour** *etc.*

behaviour [bɪˈheɪvjə(r)] *n.* **a)** *(conduct)* Verhalten, *das* **(towards** gegenüber); Benehmen, *das* **(towards** gegenüber); *(of child)* Betragen, *das*; **be on one's good/best ~**: sein bestes Benehmen an den Tag legen; **put sb. on his/her best ~**: jmdm. raten, sich gut zu benehmen; **b)** *(moral conduct)* Verhalten, *das*; **his ~ towards her** sein Verhalten ihr gegenüber; **c)** *(of ship)* Seeverhalten, *das*; *(of machine)* Eigenschaften *Pl.*; *(of substance)* Verhalten, *das*; **d)** *(Psych.)* Verhalten, *das*; **~ therapy** Verhaltenstherapie, *die*

behavioural [bɪˈheɪvjərl] *adj.* Verhaltens-; **~ similarities** Ähnlichkeiten im Verhalten

behaviourism [bɪˈheɪvjərɪzm] *n.*, *no pl. (Psych.)* Behaviorismus, *der*

behaviourist [bɪˈheɪvjərɪst] *n. (Psych.)* Behaviorist, *der*/Behavioristin, *die*

behead [bɪˈhed] *v. t.* enthaupten, köpfen ⟨*Person*⟩

beheld *see* **behold**

behest [bɪˈhest] *n.*, *no pl. (literary)* **at sb.'s ~**: auf jmds. Geheiß *(Akk.)*

behind [bɪˈhaɪnd] **1.** *adv.* **a)** *(at rear of sb./sth.)* hinten; **from ~**: von hinten; **be ~**: dahinter sein; **the person ~**: der Hintermann; **come from ~**: von hinten kommen; *(fig.)* aufholen; **he glanced ~ before moving off** er schaute nach hinten, bevor er losfuhr; **you go ahead and we'll follow on ~**: geh du vor, und wir kommen hinterher; **the church tower and the mountain ~** der Kirchturm und der Berg dahinter; **b)** *(further back)* **[be] miles ~**: kilometerweit [zurückliegen]; **[be] years/weeks ~**: Jahre/Wochen im Rückstand *od.* Verzug [sein]; **leave sb. ~**: jmdn. zurücklassen; *(move faster)* jmdn. hinter sich *(Dat.)* lassen; **fall ~**: zurückbleiben; *(fig.)* in Rückstand geraten; **lag ~**: zurückbleiben; *(fig.)* im Rückstand sein; **be ~:** hinten sein; *(be late)* im Verzug sein; **c)** *(in arrears)* **be/get ~ with one's payments/rent** mit seinen Zahlungen/der Miete im Rückstand *od.* Verzug sein/in Rückstand *od.* Verzug geraten; **d)** *(remaining after one's departure)* **leave sth. ~:** etw. zurücklassen; **he left his gloves ~ by mistake** er ließ seine Handschuhe versehentlich liegen; er vergaß seine Handschuhe; **stay ~:** dableiben; *(as punishment)* nachsitzen. **2.** *prep.* **a)** *(at rear of, on other side of; fig.: hidden by)* hinter (+ *Dat.*); **he stepped out from ~ the wall** er trat hinter der Mauer hervor; **he came from ~ her/a bush** er kam von hinten/er kam hinter einem Busch hervor; **one ~ the other** hintereinander; **the person ~ him** sein Hintermann; **~ sb.'s back** *(fig.)* hinter jmds. Rücken *(Dat.)*; **what was ~ his words?** was verbirgt sich hinter seinen Worten?; **b)** *(towards rear of)* hinter (+ *Akk.*); **I don't want to go ~ his back** ich will nicht hinter seinem Rücken handeln; **put ~ one** einen Strich unter die Vergangenheit ziehen; **look ~ the façade** *(fig.)* hinter die Fassade blicken; **c)** *(further back than)* hinter (+ *Dat.*); **they were miles ~ us** sie lagen meilenweit hinter uns *(Dat.)* zurück; **be ~ the times** nicht auf dem laufenden sein; **fall ~ sb./sth.** hinter jmdn./etw. zurückfallen; **lag ~ sb./sth.** hinter jmdm./etw. bleiben; **d)** *(past)* hinter (+ *Dat.*); **my youth is now ~ me** meine Jugend liegt jetzt hinter mir; **all that trouble is ~ me** ich habe den ganzen Ärger hinter mir; **e)** *(later than)* **be/run ~ schedule** im Rückstand *od.* Verzug sein; **~ time** im Rückstand *od.* Verzug; **f)** *(in support of)* hinter (+ *Dat.*); **I'm right ~ you in all you do** ich stehe hinter dir in allem, was du tust; **the man ~ the project** der Mann, der hinter dem Projekt steht; **he has a lot of money ~ him** er verfügt über viel Geld; **g)** *(in the tracks of)* hinter (+ *Dat.*); **he followed ~ her on his bike** er fuhr ihr mit dem Fahrrad hinterher; **h)** *(remaining after departure of)* **she left nothing ~ her but an old photograph** sie hinterließ nichts als eine alte Fotografie. **3.** *n.* *(buttocks)* Hintern, *der (ugs.)*; Hinterteil, *das (ugs.)*

behindhand [bɪ'haɪndhænd] *pred. adj.* **a)** **be/get ~ with one's payments/rent** mit seinen Zahlungen/der Miete im Rückstand *od.* Verzug sein/in Rückstand *od.* Verzug geraten; **I am getting ~ in my work** ich komme mit meiner Arbeit in Verzug; **the farmers are ~ with their harvesting** die Bauern sind mit der Ernte zurück *od.* im Rückstand; **b)** *(out of date, behind time)* zurück; **she is about twenty years ~ in her style of dress/taste in music** sie hinkt der Mode/dem Musikgeschmack etwa zwanzig Jahre hinterher; **c)** *(backward)* **be ~ in sth./doing sth.** mit etw. zurückhaltend *od.* zögerlich sein/etw. zurückhaltend *od.* zögerlich tun

behold [bɪ'həʊld] *v. t.*, **beheld** [bɪ'held] *(arch./literary)* **a)** erblicken *(geh.)*; **b)** *in imper.* siehe/sehet!

beholden [bɪ'həʊldn] *pred. adj.* **be ~ to sb. [for sth.]** jmdm. [für etw.] verpflichtet *od.* verbunden sein

beholder [bɪ'həʊldə(r)] *n.* *(arch./literary)* Betrachter, *der;* Beschauer, *der;* **beauty is in the eye of the ~:** schön ist, was gefällt

behove [bɪ'həʊv] *v. t. impers. (arch./literary)* **it ~s sb. to do sth.** es [ge]ziemt *od.* schickt sich für jmdn., etw. zu tun *(geh.)*; **it ill ~s sb. to do sth.** es steht jmdm. schlecht an, etw. zu tun *(geh.)*

beige [beɪʒ] **1.** *n.* Beige, *das.* **2.** *adj.* beige

being ['bi:ɪŋ] **1.** *pres. part. of* **be. 2.** *n.* **a)** *no pl., no art. (existence)* Dasein, *das;* Leben, *das;* Existenz, *die;* **in ~:** bestehend; **bring sth. into ~:** etw. einführen; **call into ~:** ins Leben rufen; **come into ~:** entstehen; **when the new system comes into ~:** wenn das neue System eingeführt wird; **b)** *(anything, esp. person, that exists)* Wesen, *das;* Geschöpf, *das;* **the Supreme B~:** das höchste Wesen; **c)** *(constitution, nature, essence)* Sein, *das;* **my very ~ cried out in protest** mein Innerstes schrie aus Protest auf

bejewelled *(Amer.:* **bejeweled)** [bɪ'dʒu:əld] *adj.* mit Edelsteinen geschmückt; juwelengeschmückt

belabour *(Brit.; Amer.:* **belabor)** [bɪ'leɪbə(r)] *v. t.* **a)** einschlagen auf (+ *Akk.*); *(fig.)* überhäufen; **b)** *see* **labour 3 b**

belated [bɪ'leɪtɪd] *adj.* verspätet

belatedly [bɪ'leɪtɪdlɪ] *adv.* verspätet; nachträglich

belay [bɪ'leɪ; *Mount. also* 'bi:leɪ] **1.** *v. t.* belegen ⟨*Tau, Seil*⟩; *(Mount.)* anseilen; **~ [there]!** *(Naut.)* belegen!; **~ing-pin** *(Naut.)* Belegklampe, *die.* **2.** *n.* *(Mount.)* Selbstsicherung, *die; (rock)* Felskopf, *der*

bel canto [bel 'kæntəʊ] *n.* *(Mus.)* Belcanto, Belkanto, *der*

belch [beltʃ] **1.** *v. i.* heftig aufstoßen; rülpsen *(ugs.)*; **flames ~ed forth from the furnace** Flammen schlugen aus dem Ofen. **2.** *v. t.* ausstoßen ⟨*Rauch, Flüche usw.*⟩; [aus]speien ⟨*Asche*⟩; **the car exhaust was ~ing fumes** aus dem Auspuff quollen Rauchschwaden. **3.** *n.* Rülpser, *der (ugs.)*

beleaguer [bɪ'li:gə(r)] *v. t.* *(lit. or fig.)* belagern

belfry ['belfrɪ] *n.* Glockenturm, *der; (bell space)* Glockenstube, *die*

Belgian ['beldʒən] **1.** *n.* Belgier, *der*/Belgierin, *die.* **2.** *adj.* belgisch; **sb. is ~:** jmd. ist Belgier/Belgierin

Belgium ['beldʒəm] *pr. n.* Belgien *(das)*

Belgrade [bel'greɪd] *pr. n.* Belgrad *(das)*

belie [bɪ'laɪ] *v. t.*, **belying** [bɪ'laɪɪŋ] *(fail to fulfil)* enttäuschen ⟨*Versprechen, Vorstellung*⟩; *(give false notion of)* hinwegtäuschen über (+ *Akk.*) ⟨*Tatsachen, wahren Zustand*⟩; *(fail to justify)* nicht gerecht werden (+ *Dat.*) ⟨*einer Erwartung, Theorie*⟩; *(fail to corroborate)* im Widerspruch stehen zu

belief [bɪ'li:f] *n.* **a)** Vertrauen, *das;* Glaube[n], *der;* **have great ~ in sth.** großes Vertrauen zu etw. haben; **~ in sth.** Glaube an etw. *(Akk.)*; **beyond** *or* **past ~:** unglaublich; **it is my ~ that ...:** ich bin der Überzeugung, daß ...; **in the ~ that ...:** in der Überzeugung, daß ...; **to the best of my ~:** meines Wissens; **b)** *(Relig.)* Glaube[n], *der*

believable [bɪ'li:vəbl] *adj.* glaubhaft; glaubwürdig

believe [bɪ'li:v] **1.** *v. i.* **a)** **~ in sth.** *(put trust in truth of)* an etw. *(Dat.)* glauben; **I ~ in him** ich vertraue ihm; **I ~ in free medical treatment for all** ich bin für die kostenlose ärztliche Behandlung aller; **I don't ~ in going to the dentist** ich halte nicht viel von Zahnärzten; **b)** *(have faith)* glauben **(in** an + *Akk.*) ⟨*Gott, Himmel usw.*⟩; **c)** *(suppose, think)* glauben; denken; **I ~ so/not** ich glaube schon/nicht; **Mr Smith, I ~:** Herr Smith, nehme ich an. **2.** *v. t.* **a)** **~ sth.** etw. glauben; **I ~d his words** ich glaubte seinen Worten; **I can well ~ it** das glaub' ich gerne; **if you ~ that, you'll ~ anything** wer's glaubt, wird selig *(ugs. scherzh.)*; **[I] don't ~ a word of it** [ich] glaube kein Wort [davon]; **don't you ~ it** glaub das [ja] nicht; **~ it or not** ob du es glaubst oder nicht; **would you ~ [it]** *(coll.)* stell dir mal vor *(ugs.)*; **I'd never have ~d it of her** das hätte ich ihr nie zugetraut; **~ sb.** jmdm. glauben; **I don't ~ you** das glaube ich dir nicht; **they would have us ~ that ...:** sie wollen uns glauben machen, daß ...; **~ [you] me** glaub/glaubt mir!; **I [can] ~ you** ich kann es dir nachfühlen; **I couldn't ~ my eyes/ears** ich traute meinen Augen/Ohren nicht; **b)** *(be of opinion that)* glauben; der Überzeugung sein; **she ~d it to be wrong** sie hielt es für falsch; **he is ~d to be in the London area** man vermutet ihn im Raum London; **people ~d her to be a witch** die Leute hielten sie für eine Hexe; **make ~ [that ...]** so tun, als ob ...

believer [bɪ'li:və(r)] *n.* **a)** Gläubige, *der/die;* **b)** **be a great** *or* **firm ~ in sth.** viel von etw. halten; **I'm a firm ~ in being strict with children** ich bin sehr für eine strenge Kindererziehung; **I'm no great ~ in taking exercise** ich halte nicht viel von körperlicher Bewegung

Belisha beacon [bəli:ʃə 'bi:kn] *n.* *(Brit.)* *gelbes Blinklicht an Zebrastreifen*

belittle [bɪ'lɪtl] *v. t.* herabsetzen; schlechtmachen; schmälern ⟨*Erfolg, Verdienste, Rechte*⟩; **don't ~ yourself** mach dich nicht schlechter, als du bist

belittlement [bɪ'lɪtlmənt] *n.* Herabsetzung, *die;* Schlechtmachen, *das*

bell [bel] **1.** *n.* **a)** Glocke, *die; (smaller)* Glöckchen, *das;* **clear as a ~:** glockenklar; *(understandable)* [ganz] klar und deutlich; **sound as a ~:** kerngesund ⟨*Person*⟩; völlig intakt ⟨*Gerät, Gegenstand*⟩; **b)** *(device to give ~-like sound)* Klingel, *die;* **electric ~:** elektrisches Läutewerk; **c)** *(ringing)* Läuten, *das;* **the ~ has gone** es hat geläutet *od.* geklingelt; **there's the ~:** es läutet *od.* klingelt; **was that the ~?** hat es geläutet *od.* geklingelt?; **d)** *(Boxing)* Gong, *der;* **e)** *(Naut.)* **one ~/eight ~s** ein Glas/acht Glasen; **f)** *(Bot.)* Glöckchen, *das;* Kelch, *der.* **2.** *v. t.* **~ the cat** *(fig.)* der Katze *(Dat.)* die Schelle umhängen *(ugs.)*

belladonna [belə'dɒnə] *n.* **a)** *(Bot.)* Belladonna, *die; (drug)* Atropin, *das;* **b)** **~ lily** Belladonnalilie, *die (südafrik. Amaryllis)*

bell: ~-bottomed *adj.* ausgestellt; **~-boy** *n.* *(Amer.)* [Hotel]boy, *der;* [Hotel]page, *der;* **~-buoy** *n.* *(Naut.)* Glockenboje, *die*

belle [bel] *n.* Schönheit, *die;* Schöne, *die;* **~ of the ball** Ballkönigin, *die*

belles-lettres [bel'letr] *n. pl.* schöngeistige Literatur; Belletristik, *die*

bell: ~flower *n.* Glockenblume, *die;* **~hop** *(Amer. sl.) see* **bell-boy**

bellicose ['belɪkəʊs] *adj.* kriegerisch, kriegslustig ⟨*Stimmung, Nation*⟩; streitsüchtig ⟨*Person*⟩

belligerence [bɪ'lɪdʒərəns], **belligerency** [bɪ'lɪdʒərənsɪ] *n., no pl.* Kriegslust, *die; (of person)* Kampfeslust, *die;* Streitlust, *die*

belligerent [bɪ'lɪdʒərənt] **1.** *adj.* kriegslustig, kriegerisch, kampflustig ⟨*Nation*⟩; streitlustig ⟨*Person, Benehmen*⟩; aggressiv ⟨*Rede*⟩; **~ powers** kriegführende Mächte. **2.** *n.* kriegführendes Land; kriegführende Partei; *(opponent)* Gegner, *der*

bellow ['beləʊ] **1.** *v. i.* ⟨*Tier, Person:*⟩ brüllen; **~ at sb.** jmdn. anbrüllen; **~ for sth./sb.** lauthals nach etw./jmdm. schreien. **2.** *v. t.* **~ out** brüllen ⟨*Befehl*⟩; grölen ⟨*Lied*⟩. **3.** *n.* Brüllen, *das*

bellowing ['beləʊɪŋ] *n.* Gebrüll, *das*

bellows ['beləʊz] *n. pl.* **a)** Blasebalg, *der;* *(Mus.)* Bälge *Pl.*; **a pair of ~:** ein Blasebalg; **b)** *(Phot.)* Balgen, *der*

bell: ~-pull *n.* Glockenzug, *der;* Klingelzug, *der;* **~-push** *n.* Klingeltaster, *der (fachspr.)*; Klingel, *die;* **~-ringer** *n.* Glöckner, *der;* **~-ringing** *n.* Glockenläuten, *das;* **~-rope** *n.* Glockenseil, *das;* **~-shaped** *adj.* glockenförmig; **~-tent** *n.* Rundzelt, *das;* **~-tower** *n.* Glockenturm, *der;* **~-wether** *n.* Leithammel, *der*

belly ['belɪ] **1.** *n.* Bauch, *der; (womb)* Leib, *der; (stomach)* Magen, *der.* **2.** *v. t.* blähen; **the wind bellied [out] the sails** der Wind blähte die Segel. **3.** *v. i.* **~ [out]** ⟨*Segel:*⟩ sich blähen, schwellen

belly: ~ache 1. *n.* Bauchschmerzen *Pl.*; Bauchweh, *das (ugs.)*; **2.** *v. i.* *(sl.)* jammern **(about** über + *Akk.*); **~aching** *n.* *(sl.)* Gejammer, *das (ugs. abwertend)*; **~-button** *n.* *(coll.)* Bauchnabel, *der;* **~-dance** *n.*

Bauchtanz, *der;* **~-dancer** *n.* Bauchtänzerin, *die*

bellyful ['belɪfʊl] *n.* **a ~ of food** eine ordentliche Portion Essen *(ugs.);* **have had a ~ of sth.** *(fig.)* von etw. die Nase voll haben *(ugs.)*

belly: ~-landing *n. (Aeronaut.)* Bauchlandung, *die;* **~-laugh** *n.* dröhnendes Lachen; **he gave a great ~-laugh** er lachte lauthals los

belong [bɪ'lɒŋ] *v. i.* **a)** *(be rightly assigned)* **~ to sb.** jmdm. gehören; **~ to sth.** zu etw. gehören; **power ~s to the workers** *(as slogan)* alle Macht den Arbeitern; **b) ~ to** *(be member of)* **~ to a club** einem Verein angehören; **she ~s to a trade union/the club** sie ist Mitglied einer Gewerkschaft/des Vereins; **~ to a church/the working class/another generation** einer Kirche/der Arbeiterklasse/einer anderen Generation *(Dat.)* angehören; **c)** *(be rightly placed)* **feel that one doesn't ~:** das Gefühl haben, fehl am Platze zu sein *od.* daß man nicht dazugehört; **he doesn't really ~ anywhere** er ist nirgendwo wirklich zu Hause; **a sense of ~ing** ein Zugehörigkeitsgefühl; **where does this ~?** wo gehört das hin?; **the cutlery ~s in this drawer** das Besteck gehört in diese Schublade; **~ outside** nach draußen gehören; **~ together** zusammengehören; **this item doesn't ~ under this heading** dieser Punkt fällt nicht unter diese Rubrik

belongings [bɪ'lɒŋɪŋz] *n. pl.* Habe, *die;* Sachen *Pl.;* **personal ~:** persönlicher Besitz; persönliches Eigentum; **all our ~:** unsere gesamte Habe; unser ganzes Hab und Gut

beloved [bɪ'lʌvɪd] **1.** *adj.* geliebt; lieb; teuer; **be ~** [bɪ'lʌvd] **by** *or* **of sb.** von jmdm. geliebt werden; jmdm. lieb und teuer sein; **in ~ memory of my husband, in memory of my ~ husband** in treuem Angedenken an meinen geliebten *od.* teuren Mann. **2.** *n.* Geliebte, *der/die;* **my ~** *(iron.)* mein Lieber/meine Liebe; **dearly ~** *(Relig.)* liebe Brüder und Schwestern im Herrn; liebe Gemeinde

below [bɪ'ləʊ] **1.** *adv.* **a)** *(position)* unten; unterhalb; *(lower down)* darunter; *(downstream)* weiter unten; **it is on the shelf ~:** es ist auf dem [Regal]brett darunter; **down ~:** unten; drunten *(bes. südd.);* **from ~:** von unten [herauf]; **b)** *(direction)* nach unten; hinunter; hinab *(geh.);* *(downstream)* stromab[wärts]; **if you glance ~:** wenn Sie nach unten blicken *od. (geh.)* hinabblicken; **c)** *(later in text)* unten; **see [p. 123] ~:** siehe unten[, S. 123]; **as described in detail ~:** wie [weiter] unten ausführlich beschrieben; **please sign ~:** bitte hier unterschreiben; **a photo with a caption ~:** ein Foto mit einer Bildunterschrift; **~ left** links unten; unten links; **d)** *(downstairs) (position)* unten; *(direction)* nach unten; *(Naut.)* unter Deck; **go ~:** unter Deck gehen; **the flat/floor ~:** die Wohnung/das Stockwerk *od.* die Etage darunter *od.* unter uns/ihnen *usw.;* **on the floor ~:** eine Etage tiefer; **e)** *(~ zero)* **frosts of ten and twenty ~:** Fröste von zehn und zwanzig Grad unter Null; **f)** *(Relig.)* **on earth ~:** [hier] auf Erden; **here ~:** hienieden *(geh.);* **g)** *(in hell)* drunten. **2.** *prep.* **a)** *(position)* unter (+ *Dat.*); unterhalb (+ *Gen.*); *(downstream from)* unterhalb (+ *Gen.*); **down ~ us was a huge abyss** tief unter uns war ein riesiger Abgrund; **his hair is well ~ shoulder level** sein Haar reicht bis weit über die Schultern; *see also* **average 1 a; par a, d; b)** *(direction)* unter (+ *Akk.*); **the sun sank ~ the horizon** die Sonne ging am Horizont unter; **he went ~ deck** *(Naut.)* er ging unter Deck; **c)** *(ranking lower than)* unter (+ *Dat.*); **she's in the class ~ me** sie ist eine Klasse unter mir *od.* tiefer als ich; **~-zero temperatures** Temperaturen unter Null; **the temperature is well ~ zero** die Temperatur liegt weit unter Null; **~ the breadline** unter dem Existenzminimum; **d)** *(unworthy of)* **it is ~ him** es ist unter seiner Würde

belt [belt] **1.** *n.* **a)** Gürtel, *der; (for carrying tools, weapons, ammunition, etc.)* Gurt, *der; (on uniform)* Koppel, *das;* **he wears both ~ and braces** *(fig.)* er sichert etw. doppelt und dreifach; er glaubt, doppelt genäht hält besser; **hit below the ~** *(lit. or fig.)* unter die Gürtellinie schlagen; **under one's ~** ‹*Essen usw.*› im Bauch; **with a couple of drinks under his ~:** mit ein paar Drinks intus *(ugs.);* **with all those qualifications under his ~:** mit all den Zeugnissen in der Tasche; *see also* **tighten 1 a; b)** *(strip)* Gurt, *der; (of colour, trees)* Streifen, *der; (region)* Gürtel, *der;* **industrial ~:** Industrierevier, *das;* **~ of warm air/low pressure** Warmluft-/Tiefdruckgürtel, *der;* **coal/oil ~:** Kohlerevier, *das*/Ölgebiet, *das;* **c)** *(of machine-gun cartridges)* Gurt, *der;* **d)** *(Mech. Engin.: drive-~)* Riemen, *der;* **e)** *(sl.: heavy blow)* Schlag, *der;* **give sb. a ~:** jmdm. eine runterhauen *(ugs.).* **2.** *v. t. (hit)* schlagen; **I'll ~ you [one]** *(coll.)* ich hau' dir eine runter *(ugs.).* **3.** *v. i. (sl.)* **~ up/down the motorway** über die Autobahn rasen; **he ~ed off as fast as his legs would carry him** er rannte davon, so schnell er konnte

~ along *v. i. (sl.)* rasen *(ugs.)*

~ out *v. t. (sl.)* schmettern; voll herausbringen ‹*Rhythmus*›; *(on piano)* hämmern

~ 'up *v. i.* **a)** *(Amer. coll., Brit. coll. joc.: put seat-belt on)* sich anschnallen; sich angurten; **b)** *(Brit. sl.: be quiet)* die Klappe halten *(salopp)*

belting ['beltɪŋ] *n.* **a) give sb. a [good] ~:** *(coll.)* jmdm. eine [ordentliche] Tracht Prügel verabreichen *(ugs.);* **b)** *(material)* Gürtelstoff, *der; (of leather)* Riemenleder, *das*

belying *see* **belie**

bemoan [bɪ'məʊn] *v. t.* beklagen

bemuse [bɪ'mju:z] *v. t.* verwirren; *(stupefy)* verblüffen

bemused [bɪ'mju:zd] *adj.* verwirrt

bench [bentʃ] *n.* **a)** Bank, *die; (seat across boat)* Ducht, *die; (Sport: for reserves)* Reservebank, *die;* Ersatzbank, *die;* **b)** *(Law)* **on the ~:** auf dem Richterstuhl; **he was given a seat on the ~:** er wurde zum Richter ernannt; **c)** *(office of judge)* Richteramt, *das;* **be raised to the B~:** zum Richter ernannt werden; **d)** *(lawcourt)* **Queen's/King's B~** *(Brit.) Abteilung des obersten Gerichts, die sich mit Kriminalfällen befaßt;* **e)** *(Brit. Parl.)* Bank, *die;* Reihe, *die; see also* **back-bench; cross-bench; front bench; f)** *(work-table)* Werkbank, *die; (gold- or silversmith's)* Werkbrett, *das; (carpenter's)* Hobelbank, *die; (in laboratory)* [Labor]tisch, *der*

bench: ~-mark *n.* Höhenmarke, *die; (fig.)* Maßstab, *der;* Fixpunkt, *der;* **~ 'seat** *n.* Sitzbank, *die;* **~ test** *n.* Test auf dem Prüfstand

[1]bend [bend] **1.** *n.* **a)** *(bending)* Beuge, *die;* Beugung, *die;* **a ~ of the body/the knee** eine Rumpf-/Kniebeuge; **b)** *(curve) (in road)* Kurve, *die;* **there is a ~ in the road** die Straße macht eine Kurve; **a ~ in the river** eine Flußbiegung; **be round the ~** *(fig. coll.)* spinnen *(ugs.);* verrückt sein *(ugs.);* **go round the ~** *(fig. coll.)* überschnappen *(ugs.);* durchdrehen *(ugs.);* **drive sb. round the ~** *(fig. coll.)* jmdn. wahnsinnig *od.* verrückt machen *(ugs.);* **c) the ~s** *(Med. coll.)* Taucherkrankheit, *die.* **2.** *v.t.,* **bent** [bent] **a)** *(force out of straightness)* biegen; verbiegen ‹*Nadel, Messer, Eisenstange, Ast*›; spannen ‹*Bogen*›; beugen ‹*Arm, Knie*›; anwinkeln ‹*Arm, Bein*›; krumm machen ‹*Finger*›; **~ sth. at an angle** etw. umbiegen; **~ sth. back/forward/up/down** etw. nach hinten/vorne/oben/unten biegen; **'please do not ~'** *(on envelope)* „bitte nicht knicken!"; **~ sth. back into shape** etw. zurückbiegen; etw. wieder in Form biegen; **~ the law** *(fig.)* das Gesetz beugen; *see also* **rule 1 a; b)** *(fix)* **be bent on sth.** zu etw. entschlossen sein; auf etw. *(Akk.)* versessen *od.* erpicht sein; **on pleasure bent** *(dated)* vergnügungssüchtig; **~ one's energies on sth.** *(dated)* seine ganze Kraft auf etw. *(Akk.)* verwenden; **~ oneself to sth.** sich auf etw. *(Akk.)* konzentrieren; **c)** *(sl.: pervert)* mißbrauchen; pervertieren; manipulieren ‹*Ergebnis*›; **d)** *(direct)* **we must ~ our steps home** wir müssen unsere Schritte heimwärts lenken *(geh.);* **he bent his mind on** *or* **to the problem** er dachte ernst über das Problem nach; **~ an ear** sich ihm umhören; **e)** *(force to submit)* unterwerfen; gefügig machen; **f)** *(Naut.)* festmachen; befestigen ‹*Tau*›. **3.** *v. i.,* **bent a)** sich biegen; sich krümmen; ‹*Äste:*› sich neigen; **the road ~s** die Straße macht eine Kurve; **the road ~s for two miles** die Straße ist auf zwei Meilen kurvenreich; **the river ~s/~s in and out** der Fluß macht eine Biegung/schlängelt sich; **~ to** *or* **before sb.** *(fig.)* sich jmdm. beugen; **b)** *(bow)* sich bücken; *(fig.)* sich beugen; **catch sb. ~ing** *(fig. coll.)* jmdn. [in einer peinlichen Lage] erwischen

~ 'down *v. i.* sich bücken; sich hinunterbeugen

~ 'over *v. i.* sich nach vorn beugen; sich bücken; *see also* **backwards a**

[2]bend *n.* **a)** *(Naut.)* Knoten, *der;* Schlinge, *die;* **b)** *(Her.)* Schrägbalken, *der;* **~ sinister** schräglinker Balken; Schräglinksbalken, *der*

bendable ['bendəbl] *adj.* biegbar

bended ['bendɪd] *adj.* **on ~ knee[s]** auf [den] Knien

bender ['bendə(r)] *n. (sl.)* Besäufnis, *das (salopp)*

bendy ['bendɪ] *adj. (coll.)* **a)** biegsam; **b)** *(winding)* gewunden ‹*Pfad, Straße*›

beneath [bɪ'ni:θ] **1.** *prep.* **a)** *(unworthy of)* **~ sb.** jmds. unwürdig; unter jmds. Würde *(Dat.);* **~ sb.'s dignity** unter jmds. Würde *(Dat.);* **marry ~ one** nicht standesgemäß heiraten; unter seinem Stand heiraten; **~ contempt** verachtenswert; unter aller Kritik; **b)** *(arch./literary: under)* unter (+ *Dat.*). **2.** *adv. (arch./literary)* darunter

Benedictine **1.** *n.* **a)** [benɪ'dɪktɪn] *(monk/nun)* Benediktiner, *der*/Benediktinerin, *die;* **b) (P)** [benɪ'dɪkti:n] *(liqueur)* Benediktiner, *der.* **2.** *adj.* Benediktiner-

benediction [benɪ'dɪkʃn] *n. (Relig.)* Benediktion, *die;* Segnung, *die;* **pronounce/say the ~** *(before meal)* um den Segen Gottes bitten; *(after meal)* das Dankgebet sprechen *od.* sagen

benefaction [benɪ'fækʃn] *n.* **a)** *(gift)* Spende, *die; (endowment)* Schenkung, *die;* Stiftung, *die;* **b)** *(doing good)* Wohltat, *die*

benefactor ['benɪfæktə(r)] *n.* Wohltäter, *der; (patron)* Stifter, *der;* Gönner, *der*

benefactress ['benɪfæktrɪs] *n.* Wohltäterin, *die; (patroness)* Stifterin, *die;* Gönnerin, *die*

benefice ['benɪfɪs] *n. (Eccl.)* Benefizium, *das*

beneficence [bɪ'nefɪsəns] *n.* Mildtätigkeit, *die; (active kindness)* Güte, *die*

beneficent [bɪ'nefɪsənt] *adj. (showing active kindness)* gütig; *(doing good)* wohltätig; mildtätig

beneficial [benɪ'fɪʃl] *adj.* **a)** nutzbringend; nützlich; vorteilhaft ‹*Einfluß*›; günstig ‹*Klima*›; **be ~ to sth./sb.** zum Nutzen von etw./jmdm. sein; **a good night's sleep is very ~:** ein guter Schlaf ist sehr erholsam; **b)** *(Law)* nutznießerisch; **~ owner** Nießbraucher, *der*

beneficially [benɪ'fɪʃəlɪ] *adv. see* **beneficial a:** nutzbringend; nützlich; vorteilhaft; günstig

beneficiary [benɪ'fɪʃərɪ] *n.* Nutznießer, *der*/Nutznießerin, *die*

benefit ['benɪfɪt] **1.** *n.* **a)** Vorteil, *der;* Vorzug, *der (geh.);* **be of ~ to sb./sth.** jmdm./einer Sache von Nutzen sein; **have the ~ of** den Vorteil *od. (geh.)* Vorzug (+ *Gen.*) haben; **derive ~ from sth., get some ~ from sth.** aus etw. Nutzen ziehen; von etw. profitieren; **not get much ~ from sth.** wenig Nutzen aus etw. ziehen; nicht viel von etw. profitieren; **did you get much ~ from your holiday?** hat dir der Urlaub viel genützt?; **without the ~ of** ohne das Zutun (+ *Gen.*); **with the ~ of** mit Hilfe (+ *Gen.*); **to sb.'s ~:** zu jmds. Nutzen; **for sb.'s ~:** in jmds. Interesse *(Dat.);* im Interesse von jmdm.; **for the ~ of sth.** im Interesse einer Sache *(Gen.);* **for the ~ of future generations** im Interesse künftiger Generationen; **for the ~ of anyone who/all those who ...** *(iron.)* allen/all denen zuliebe, die ... *(iron.);* **give sb. the ~ of the doubt** im Zweifelsfall zu jmds. Gunsten entscheiden; **give sb. the ~ of sth.** jmdm. etw. zugute kommen lassen *(iron.);* **b)** *(allowance)* Beihilfe, *die;* **social security ~:** Sozialhilfe, *die;* Hilfe zum Lebensunterhalt *(Amtsspr.);* **supplementary ~** *(Brit.)* zusätzliche Hilfe zum Lebensunterhalt; **unemployment ~:** Arbeitslosenunterstützung, *die;* **sickness ~:** Krankengeld, *das;* **disablement ~:** Invalidenrente, *die;* **child ~** *(Brit.)* Kindergeld, *das;* **maternity ~:** Mutterschaftsgeld, *das;* **~ club** *or* **society** Versicherungsverein auf Gegenseitigkeit; **c) ~ [performance/match/concert]** Benefizveranstaltung, *die*/-spiel, *das*/-konzert, *das;* **d) without ~ of clergy** *(joc.)* ohne kirchlichen Segen. **2.** *v.t.* **~ sb./sth.** jmdm./einer Sache nützen *od.* guttun; **these facilities/discoveries have ~ed the area/humanity** diese Einrichtungen/Entdeckungen sind dem Gebiet/der Menschheit zugute gekommen *od.* haben dem Gebiet/der Menschheit Nutzen gebracht. **3.** *v.i.* **~ by/from sth.** von etw. profitieren; aus etw. Nutzen ziehen; **~ from experience** aus Erfahrung lernen; **how do I/will my son ~?** was habe ich/hat mein Sohn davon?

benevolence [bɪ'nevələns] *n., no pl. (desire to do good)* Güte, *die; (of ruler)* Milde, *die; (of despot, the authorities)* Wohlwollen, *das*

benevolent [bɪ'nevələnt] *adj.* **a)** *(desiring to do good)* gütig; mild ‹*Herrscher*›; wohlwollend ‹*Behörde, Despot*›; **~ despotism** aufgeklärter Absolutismus; **b)** *attrib. (charitable)* wohltätig, mildtätig ‹*Institution, Verein*›; **c)** *(kind and helpful)* hilfsbereit; **a ~ smile/air** ein gütiges Lächeln/gütiger Gesichtsausdruck

benevolently [bɪ'nevələntlɪ] *adv.* gütig ‹*lächeln*›

Bengali [beŋ'gɔ:lɪ] **1.** *n.* **a)** *(person)* Bengale, *der*/Bengalin, *die;* **b)** *(language)* Bengali, *das.* **2.** *adj.* bengalisch

benighted [bɪ'naɪtɪd] *adj. (fig.)* unwissend, *(ugs.)* unbedarft ‹*Person*›; finster ‹*Gegend, Zeitalter*›; obskur ‹*Philosophie, Politik, Sitten*›

benign [bɪ'naɪn] *adj.* **a)** *(gracious, gentle)* gütig ‹*Person, Aussehen, Verständnis*›; mildtätig ‹*Gabe, Geschenk*›; wohlwollend ‹*Person, Verhalten*›; *(mild)* mild, heilsam ‹*Klima, Sonne*›; *(fortunate)* günstig ‹*Stern, Einfluß, Ergebnis, Aspekt*›; **b)** *(Med.)* gutartig, *(fachspr.)* benigne ‹*Tumor*›

benignity [bɪ'nɪgnɪtɪ] *n., no pl.* **a)** Wohlwollen, *das;* **b)** *(Med.)* Gutartigkeit, *die*

benignly [bɪ'naɪnlɪ] *adv.* gütig; wohlwollend

benison ['benɪzən] *n. (arch.)* Segen, *der*

¹bent [bent] **1.** *see* **¹bend 2, 3. 2.** *n.* Neigung, *die;* Hang, *der;* Schlag, *der;* **have a ~ for sth.** einen Hang zu etw. *od.* eine Vorliebe für etw. haben; **those with** *or* **of an artistic ~:** Menschen mit einer künstlerischen Ader *od.* Veranlagung; **follow one's ~:** seiner Neigung *od.* seinen Neigungen folgen; **to the top of one's ~:** nach Herzenslust. **3.** *adj.* **a)** krumm; gebogen; **b)** *(Brit. sl.: corrupt)* link *(salopp);* nicht ganz sauber *(salopp)* ‹*Händler usw.*›; **c)** *(Brit. sl.: homosexual);* schwul *(ugs.);* andersrum *präd. (ugs.)*

²bent *n. (Bot.)* Straußgras, *das; (stiff flower stalk)* Halm, *der; (heath)* Heide, *die*

benumb [bɪ'nʌm] *v.t.* **a)** gefühllos machen ‹*Glieder*›; **~ed** gefühllos; **~ed with cold** starr vor Kälte; **b)** *(fig.: stupefy)* lähmen; betäuben ‹*Sinne, Gefühle*›; **he was ~ed with panic/grief** er war vor Entsetzen/Kummer gelähmt

Benzedrine, (P) ['benzɪdri:n] *n. (Med.)* Benzedrin, *das*

benzene ['benzi:n] *n. (Chem.)* Benzol, *das;* **~ ring** Benzolring, *der*

benzine ['benzi:n] *n.* Leichtbenzin, *das*

bequeath [bɪ'kwi:ð] *v.t.* **a) ~ sth. to sb.** jmdm. etw. vermachen *od.* hinterlassen; **b)** *(fig.)* überliefern ‹*Märchen, Legende, Zeugnisse*›; vererben ‹*Tradition*›

bequest [bɪ'kwest] *n.* Legat, *das* **(to** an + *Akk.*); **make a ~ to sb. of sth.** jmdm. etw. vermachen

berate [bɪ'reɪt] *v.t.* schelten

bereave [bɪ'ri:v] *v.t.* **a)** *(deprive through death)* **~ A of B** B *(Dat.)* A nehmen; **be ~d [of sb.]** jmdn. verlieren; **a disaster ~d him of his father** er hat seinen Vater durch ein Unglück verloren; **the ~d** der/die Hinterbliebene/die Hinterbliebenen; **b)** *p.p.* **bereft** [bɪ'reft] *(dispossess)* **be bereft of sth.** einer Sache *(Gen.)* beraubt sein

bereavement [bɪ'ri:vmənt] *n.* Trauerfall, *der;* **he sympathized with her in her ~:** er sprach ihr sein Beileid aus; **on account of their recent ~:** auf Grund ihres Trauerfalles

bereft *see* **bereave b**

beret ['bereɪ, 'berɪ] *n.* Baskenmütze, *die; (as military head-dress)* Barett, *das*

bergamot ['bɜ:gəmɒt] *n.* **a)** *(tree)* Bergamotte, *die;* Bergamottenbaum, *der;* **b)** *(perfume)* Bergamottparfüm, *das;* **c)** *(herb)* Zitronenminze, *die;* Pfefferminze, *die;* **~ oil** Bergamottöl, *das*

beriberi [berɪ'berɪ] *n. (Med.)* Beriberi, *die*

berk [bɜ:k] *n. (Brit. sl.)* Dussel, *der (ugs.);* Spinner, *der (ugs.);* Blödmann, *der (salopp)*

Berlin [bɜ:'lɪn] **1.** *pr. n.* Berlin *(das).* **2.** *attrib. adj.* Berliner; *(Ling.)* berlinisch

Berliner [bɜ:'lɪnə(r)] *n.* Berliner, *der*/Berlinerin, *die*

Bermuda [bə'mju:də] *pr. n.* die Bermudainseln; **the ~s** die Bermudas; **~s, ~ shorts** Bermudashorts

Berne [bɜ:n] **1.** *pr. n.* Bern *(das).* **2.** *attrib. adj.* Berner

berry ['berɪ] *n.* Beere, *die; see also* **brown 1**

berserk [bə'sɜ:k, bə'zɜ:k] *adj.* rasend; **go ~:** durchdrehen *(ugs.);* **he went ~ with an axe** er wütete mit einem Beil

berth [bɜ:θ] **1.** *n.* **a)** *(adequate space)* Seeraum, *der (der für ein Schiff erforderlich ist);* **give the rocks a wide ~:** Abstand zu den Felsen halten; gut frei von den Felsen halten *(fachspr.);* **give sb./sth. a wide ~** *(fig.)* jmdm./einer Sache aus dem Weg gehen; einen großen Bogen um jmdn./etw. machen; **b)** *(ship's place at wharf)* Liegeplatz, *der;* **c)** *(sleeping-place) (in ship)* Koje, *die;* Kajütenbett, *das; (in train)* Schlafwagenbett, *das; (in aircraft)* Sleeper, *der;* **a 4-~ caravan** ein Vierpersonenanhänger; **d)** *(job)* Stelle, *die;* **find a cushy ~:** eine bequeme Stelle *od.* einen bequemen Job finden. **2.** *v.t.* festmachen ‹*Schiff*›. **3.** *v.i.* ‹*Schiff:*› festmachen, anlegen

beryl ['berɪl] *n.* Beryll, *der*

beryllium [bɪ'rɪlɪəm] *n. (Chem.)* Beryllium, *das*

beseech [bɪ'si:tʃ] *v.t.,* **besought** [bɪ'sɔ:t] *or* **~ed** *(literary)* flehen um, *(geh.)* erflehen ‹*Gnade, Vergebung*›; anflehen ‹*Person*›; **~ sb. to do sth.** jmdn. anflehen *od.* inständig bitten, etw. zu tun; **~ sb. for sth.** jmdn. um etw. anflehen; **I ~ you** ich flehe dich an

beseeching [bɪ'si:tʃɪŋ] *adj.*, **beseechingly** [bɪ'si:tʃɪŋlɪ] *adv.* flehend; flehentlich *(geh.)*

beset [bɪ'set] *v.t., forms as* **set 1: a)** heimsuchen; plagen; ‹*Probleme, Zweifel, Versuchungen:*› bedrängen; **sth. is ~ with troubles** etw. steckt voller Schwierigkeiten/Probleme; **~ by doubts** von Zweifeln geplagt; **b)** *(hem in)* umgeben; einschließen; *(occupy and make impassable)* belagern; blockieren; versperren; **~ting sin** Untugend, *die*

beside [bɪ'saɪd] *prep.* **a)** *(close to)* neben (+ *Dat.*); an (+ *Dat.*); **~ the sea/lake** am Meer/See; **walk ~ the river** am Fluß entlanggehen; **sit/stand ~ sb.** neben jmdm. sitzen/stehen; **sit down/go and stand ~ sb.** sich neben jmdn. setzen/stellen; **b)** *(compared with)* neben (+ *Dat.*); **c)** *(wide of)* weit entfernt von ‹*Problem, Frage*›; **be ~ the point** nichts damit zu tun haben; **d) ~ oneself with joy/grief** außer sich vor Freude/Kummer

besides [bɪ'saɪdz] **1.** *adv.* außerdem; **he was a historian ~:** er war außerdem noch Historiker; **do/say sth. [else] ~:** sonst noch etw. tun/sagen; **~, we don't need it** außerdem brauchen wir es nicht; **whatever she may have done ~:** was sie sonst noch getan haben mag. **2.** *prep.* außer; **~ us [there were others]** außer uns [waren noch andere da]; **~ my husband and me** außer meinem Mann und mir; **~ which, he was late** und obendrein *od.* außerdem kam er zu spät; **he said nothing ~ that** er sagte weiter *od.* sonst nichts

besiege [bɪ'si:dʒ] *v.t. (lit. or fig.)* belagern; **be ~d with letters/offers/requests/enquiries** mit Briefen/Angeboten/Bitten/Anfragen überschüttet *od.* überhäuft werden

besieger [bɪ'si:dʒə(r)] *n.* Belagerer, *der*

besmear [bɪ'smɪə(r)] *v.t.* verschmieren; **~ed with blood** blutverschmiert

besmirch [bɪ'smɜ:tʃ] *v.t. (lit. or fig.)* beschmutzen *(geh.);* besudeln *(geh.);* **~ sb.'s name** jmds. Namen besudeln *od.* beflecken

besom ['bi:zəm] *n.* [Reisig]besen, *der*

besot [bɪ'sɒt] *v.t.,* **-tt-** betören; **be ~ted by** *or* **with the idea that ...:** von der Idee besessen sein, daß ...; **~ted with alcohol** berauscht *od.* benommen vom Alkohol; **be ~ted by** *or* **with sb.** in jmdn. vernarrt sein

besought *see* **beseech**

bespatter [bɪ'spætə(r)] *v.t.* bespritzen; vollspritzen

bespeak [bɪ'spi:k] *v.t., forms as* **speak 2: a)** *(suggest)* zeugen von; verraten; **b)** *(reserve)* reservieren; vorbestellen

bespectacled [bɪ'spektəkld] *adj.* bebrillt

bespoke [bɪ'spəʊk] **1.** *see* **bespeak. 2.** *attrib. adj.* **~ overcoat** maßgeschneiderter Mantel; **~ boots** Stiefel nach Maß; **~ tailor** Maßschneider, *der*

bespoken *see* **bespeak**

best [best] **1.** *adj. superl. of* **good: a)** best...; **be ~ [of all]** am [aller]besten sein; **the ~ thing about it was ...:** das Beste daran war ...; **the ~ thing to do is to apologize** das beste ist, sich zu entschuldigen; **the very ~ people** die feinen Leute; **may the ~ man win!** auf daß der Beste gewinnt!; **b)** *(most advantageous)* best...; günstigst...; **which** *or* **what is the ~ way?** wie ist es am besten *od.* günstigsten?; **it's ~ to travel via Paris** am besten fährt man über Paris; **think it ~ to do sth.** es für das beste halten, etw. zu tun; **do as you think ~** *or* **what you think is ~:** mach, was du für richtig hältst; **c)** *(greatest)* größt...; **the ~ part of the day/money** der größte Teil des Tages/Geldes; **[for] the ~ part of an hour** fast eine ganze Stunde. **2.** *adv. superl. of* **²well 2:** am besten; **like sth. ~ of all** etw. am liebsten mögen; **as ~ we could**

so gut wir konnten; **as ~ you can** so gut es geht; **you know ~**: Sie müssen es [am besten] wissen; **you'd ~ be going now** am besten gehen Sie jetzt; **he is ~ known for his etchings** er ist vor allem für seine Kupferstiche bekannt; **he is the person ~ able to do it/ to cope** er ist der Fähigste, um das zu tun/ damit fertigzuwerden; **I was not ~ pleased to discover that ...** *(iron.)* ich war gar nicht begeistert, als ich entdeckte, daß ... *(iron.)*. **3.** *n.* **a) the ~**: der/die/das Beste; **the wine was not of the ~**: der Wein war nicht von der besten Qualität; **their latest record is their ~**: ihre letzte Platte ist die beste; **b)** *(clothes)* beste Sachen; Sonntagskleider *Pl.*; **wear one's [Sunday] ~**: seine Sonntagskleider tragen; sich in Schale werfen *(ugs.)*; **c) play the ~ of three [games]** um zwei Gewinnsätze spielen; **the ~ of it is ...** *(also iron.)* das beste daran ist ...; der Witz dabei ist ... *(iron.)*; **get** *or* **have the ~ of it** gut damit fahren; gut dabei wegkommen; **get the ~ out of sth./sb.** das Beste aus etw./jmdm. herausholen; **that's the ~ of having a car** das ist das beste an einem Auto; **he is not in the ~ of health** es geht ihm nicht sehr gut; **bring out the ~ in sb.** jmds. beste Seiten zum Vorschein bringen; **all the ~!** *(coll.)* alles Gute!; **d) the ~** *pl.* die Besten; **they are the ~ of friends** sie sind die besten Freunde; **with the ~ of intentions** in bester Absicht; **from the ~ of motives** aus den edelsten Motiven [heraus]; **get six of the ~** *(coll.)* Prügel beziehen; verdroschen werden *(ugs.)*; **[sb. is] one of the ~** *(coll.)* [jmd. ist] ein feiner Kerl; **she can down a pint of beer/play tennis with the ~ of them** *(coll.)* beim Biertrinken/ Tennisspielen macht ihr keiner was vor *(ugs.)*; **e) at ~**: bestenfalls; **be at one's ~**: in Hochform sein; **an example of modern architecture at its ~**: eines der gelungensten Beispiele moderner Architektur; **[even] at the ~ of times** schon normalerweise; **it is [all] for the ~**: es ist [doch] nur zum Guten; **he did it [all] for the ~**: er hat es [doch] nur gut gemeint; **hope for the ~**: das Beste hoffen; **do one's ~**: sein bestes *od.* möglichstes tun; **he is doing his ~ to ruin me** *(iron.)* er tut sein möglichstes, mich zu ruinieren; **do the ~ you can** machen Sie es so gut Sie können; **it's not good, but it's the ~ I can do** es ist nicht gut, aber mehr kann ich nicht tun; **look one's ~**: möglichst gut aussehen; **make the ~ of oneself** das Beste aus sich machen; **make the ~ of it/things** das Beste daraus machen; **make the ~ of a bad job** *or* **bargain** *(coll.)* das Beste daraus machen; **to the ~ of one's ability** nach besten Kräften; so gut man kann; **to the ~ of my belief/knowledge** meines Wissens; **she wants/has the ~ of everything** sie will immer nur/ hat von allem das Beste. **4.** *v. t. (Sport)* schlagen; *(outwit)* übervorteilen

best: ~-dressed *attrib. adj.* bestgekleidet; **~ 'end** *n. (Gastr.)* Filet, *das;* **~ 'friend** *n.* bester Freund/beste Freundin; **be ~ friends with sb.** sehr gut mit jmdm. befreundet sein; **~-hated** *attrib. adj. (iron.)* bestgehaßt *(iron.)*

bestial ['bestɪəl] *adj. (of or like a beast)* tierisch; *(brutish, barbarous)* barbarisch; *(savage)* brutal; *(depraved)* bestialisch; tierisch

bestiality [bestɪ'ælɪtɪ] *n.* **a)** Bestialität, *die; (savagery)* Brutalität, *die;* **b)** *(sodomy)* Sodomie, *die*

bestir [bɪ'stɜ:(r)] *v. refl.*, **-rr-** sich aufraffen

best: ~-kept *attrib. adj.* bestgepflegt; bestgehütet ⟨*Geheimnis*⟩; **the ~-kept village in England** das schönste Dorf Englands; **~-known** *attrib. adj.* bekanntest...; **~-laid** *attrib. adj.* bestüberlegt ⟨*Pläne*⟩; **~-loved** *attrib. adj.* meistgeliebt; **~ 'man** *n.* Trauzeuge, *der (des Bräutigams)*

bestow [bɪ'stəʊ] *v. t.* verleihen ⟨*Titel*⟩; schenken ⟨*Gunst, Wohlwollen*⟩; zuteil werden lassen ⟨*Ehre, Segnungen*⟩; **~ sth. [up]on sb.** jmdm. etw. verleihen/schenken/zuteil werden lassen

bestowal [bɪ'stəʊəl] *n.* Verleihung, *die* (**[up]on** an + *Akk.*); *(of land)* Schenkung, *die*

'best-quality *attrib. adj.* der Spitzenklasse *nachgestellt;* erstklassig

bestride [bɪ'straɪd] *v. t., forms as* **stride 3** sich rittlings setzen auf (+ *Akk.*); *(position)* rittlings sitzen auf (+ *Dat.*) ⟨*Mauer, Bank*⟩

best: ~ 'seller *n.* Bestseller, *der; (author)* Bestsellerautor, *der;* **~-selling** *attrib. adj.* meistverkauft ⟨*Schallplatte*⟩; **~-selling book/novel** Bestseller, *der;* **a ~-selling author/novelist** ein Bestsellerautor

bet [bet] **1.** *v. t.*, **-tt-**, **~** *or* **~ted a)** wetten; **I ~ him £10** ich habe mit ihm um 10 Pfund gewettet; **he ~ £10 on that horse** er hat 10 Pfund auf das Pferd gesetzt; **b)** *(coll.: be confident)* wetten; **I ~ he's late** wetten, daß er zu spät kommt?; **[I] ~ you I know where he got it from** wetten, daß ich weiß, woher er es hat?; **[you can] ~ your life** darauf kannst du Gift nehmen *(ugs.)*; **[I] ~ you [anything]** ich gehe jede Wette darauf ein; **I'll ~ he tells them he's swum the Channel** ich wette, er erzählt ihnen, daß er den Kanal durchschwommen hat; **~ [you] I 'can** und ob ich kann; **you '~ [I am/I will** *etc.*] und ob; allerdings. **2.** *v. i.*, **-tt-**, **~** *or* **~ted a)** wetten **(for** um); **~ on sth.** auf etw. *(Akk.)* setzen; **b)** *(coll.: be confident)* **the shops will be closed, I'll ~**: ich wette, die Geschäfte sind geschlossen; **[do you] want to ~?** [wollen wir] wetten? *See also* **[1]boot 1 a; bottom 2 b. 3.** *n.* **a)** Wette, *die; (sum)* Wetteinsatz, *der;* **make** *or* **have a ~ with sb. on sth.** mit jmdm. über etw. *(Akk.)* wetten; **accept** *or* **take a ~ on sth.** eine Wette auf etw. *(Akk.)* eingehen; **lay a ~ on sth.** auf etw. *(Akk.)* wetten; **b)** *(fig. coll.: choice)* Tip, *der;* **be a bad/good/ safe ~**: ein schlechter/guter/sicherer Tip sein; **it's a fair ~ that ...**: du kannst ziemlich sicher sein, daß ...; **be sb.'s best ~**: das beste sein; **my ~ is that ...**: ich wette, daß ...

beta ['bi:tə] *n.* **a)** *(letter)* Beta, *das;* **b)** *(Sch., Univ.: mark)* Zwei, *die*

beta-blocker ['bi:təblɒkə(r)] *n. (Med.)* Beta[rezeptoren]blocker, *der*

betake [bɪ'teɪk] *v. refl., forms as* **take 1** *(literary)* sich begeben; **~ oneself somewhere** sich irgendwohin begeben

beta: ~ particles *n. pl. (Phys.)* Betateilchen *Pl.*; **~ rays** *n. pl. (Phys.)* Betastrahlen *Pl.*

betel ['bi:tl] *n. (Bot.)* Betel, *der;* **~-nut** Betelnuß, *die*

bête noire [beɪt 'nwɑ:(r)] *n., pl.* **bêtes noires** [beɪt 'nwɑ:(r)] Greuel, *der*

bethink [bɪ'θɪŋk] *v. refl.*, **bethought** [bɪ'θɔ:t] *(literary)* sich besinnen

betide [bɪ'taɪd] *(literary)* **1.** *v. t.* geschehen (+ *Dat.*) *(veralt., geh.)*; **woe ~ you if ...**: wehe dir, wenn ...; **whatever ~s you** was Ihnen auch immer geschieht. **2.** *v. i.* geschehen

betimes [bɪ'taɪmz] *adv. (literary)* beizeiten

betoken [bɪ'təʊkn] *v. t.* **a)** *(indicate)* ankündigen ⟨*Frühjahr, Krieg*⟩; **b)** *(suggest)* hindeuten auf (+ *Akk.*)

betony ['betənɪ] *n. (Bot.)* Ziest, *der*

betook *see* **betake**

betray [bɪ'treɪ] *v. t.* **a)** verraten **(to** an + *Akk.*); mißbrauchen ⟨*jmds. Vertrauen*⟩; **~ oneself** sich verraten; **~ the fact that ...**: verraten, daß ...; **b)** *(lead astray)* fehlleiten

betrayal [bɪ'treɪəl] *n.* Verrat, *der;* **~ of one's friends/country** Verrat an seinen Freunden/ seinem Vaterland; **an act of ~**: ein Verrat; **a ~ of trust** ein Vertrauensbruch

betroth [bɪ'trəʊð] *v. t. (arch.)* versprechen *(veralt.)*; **be ~ed to sb.** jmdm. versprochen sein *(veralt.)*

betrothal [bɪ'trəʊðl] *n. (arch.)* Verlöbnis, *das*

betrothed [bɪ'trəʊðd] *(arch.)* **1.** *adj.* versprochen *(veralt.)*. **2.** *n.* Anverlobter, *der*/Anverlobte, *die (veralt.)*

better ['betə(r)] **1.** *adj. compar. of* **good 1** besser; **I have something ~ to do** ich habe etwas Besseres zu tun; **do you know of anything ~?** kennst du etwas Besseres?; **that's ~**: so ist's schon besser; **~ and ~**: immer besser; **~ still, let's phone** oder noch besser: Rufen wir doch an; **be much ~** *(recovered)* sich viel besser fühlen; **he is much ~ today** es geht ihm heute schon viel besser; **get ~** *(recover)* auf dem Wege der Besserung sein; **I am/my ankle is getting ~**: mir/meinem Knöchel geht es besser; **so much the ~**: um so besser; **she is none the ~ for it** das hat ihr nichts genützt; **she is much the ~ for having been to university** es hat ihr sehr genützt, daß sie studiert hat; **my ~ feelings/nature** mein besseres Ich; **be ~ than one's word** mehr tun, als man versprochen hat; **my/his ~ half** *(joc.)* meine/seine bessere Hälfte *(scherzh.)*; **the ~ part of sth.** *(greater part)* der größte Teil einer Sache *(Gen.)*; **[for] the ~ part of an hour** fast eine ganze Stunde; **he is no ~ than a criminal** er kommt einem Kriminellen gleich; **she's no ~ than she should be** *(euphem.)* sie ist auch nicht gerade eine Heilige; **on ~ acquaintance** bei näherer Bekanntschaft; *see also* **all 3. 2.** *adv. compar. of* **[2]well 2: a)** *(in a ~ way)* besser; **I hope you do ~ in future** hoffentlich haben Sie in Zukunft mehr Glück; *(by your own efforts)* ich hoffe, daß Sie es in Zukunft besser machen werden; **b)** *(to a greater degree)* mehr; **the ~ to do sth.** um etw. besser tun zu können; **you cannot do ~ than ...**: das beste, was du tun kannst, ist ...; **I like Goethe ~ than Schiller** ich mag Goethe lieber als Schiller; **he is ~ liked than Carter** er ist beliebter als Carter; **c) he would do ~ to ask first** er sollte lieber *od.* besser zuerst fragen; **d) know ~ than ...**: es besser wissen als ...; **you ought to know ~ than to ...**: du solltest es besser wissen und nicht ...; **e) go one ~ [than sb.]**, *(Amer.)* **go sb. one ~**: jmdn. überbieten; **f) you'd ~ not tell her** Sie erzählen es ihr besser nicht; **I'd ~ begin by introducing myself** ich stelle mich besser zuerst einmal vor; **I'd ~ be off now** ich gehe jetzt besser; **hadn't you ~ ask first?** sollten Sie nicht besser zuerst fragen?; **I promise I'll clear up after the party – You'd ~!** Ich verspreche, daß ich nach der Party aufräume – Das will ich aber auch hoffen. *See also* **better off. 3.** *n.* **a)** Bessere, *das;* **we hope for ~**: wir erhoffen uns *(Dat.)* mehr; **get the ~ of sb./sth.** jmdn./ etw. unterkriegen *(ugs.)*; **exhaustion got the ~ of him** seine Erschöpfung machte ihm schwer zu schaffen; **be a change for the ~**: eine vorteilhafte Veränderung sein; **for ~, for worse** in Freud und Leid; **for ~ or for worse** was immer daraus werden wird; **I thought ~ of it** ich habe es mir anders überlegt; **b)** *in pl.* Leute, die höher stehen; **one's ~s** Leute, die über einem stehen *od.* die einem überlegen sind. **4.** *v. t.* **a)** *(surpass)* übertreffen; **b)** *(improve)* verbessern; **~ oneself** *(rise socially)* sich verbessern

'better-class *attrib. adj.* besser, feiner ⟨*Leute*⟩; vornehm ⟨*Vorort, Familie*⟩

betterment ['betəmənt] *n., no pl.* Verbesserung, *die*

better: ~ 'off *adj.* **a)** *(financially)* [finanziell] besser gestellt; **b) he is ~ off than I am** ihm geht es besser als mir; **be ~ off than sb.** besser als jmd. dran sein *(ugs.)*; **be ~ off without sth./sb.** ohne etw./jmdn. besser dran sein; **~-quality** *attrib. adj.* qualitativ besser; **~-than-average** *attrib. adj.* überdurchschnittlich [gut/viel]; **earn a ~-than-average income** überdurchschnittlich viel verdienen

betting ['betɪŋ] **1.** *n.* Wetten, *das;* **there was heavy ~ on that horse** auf das Pferd wurde sehr viel gesetzt; **what's the ~ it rains?** *(fig.)* ob es wohl regnen wird? **2.** *attrib. adj.* Wett-; **I'm not a ~ man** ich wette nicht

'betting office, 'betting-shop *ns.* Wettbüro, *das*

between [bɪ'twi:n] **1.** *prep.* **a)** *(position)* zwischen (+ *Dat.*); *(direction)* zwischen (+ *Akk.*); **it is not far ~ the two places** die beiden Orte liegen nicht weit auseinander; **~ then and now** zwischen damals und jetzt; **~ now and the end of term** bis zum Ende des Trimesters; **there's nothing to choose ~ them** sie unterscheiden sich durch nichts; **[in] ~:** zwischen; **b)** *(amongst)* unter (+ *Dat.*); **the work was divided ~ the volunteers** die Arbeit wurde zwischen den Freiwilligen aufgeteilt; **~ ourselves, ~ you and me** unter uns *(Dat.)* gesagt; **that's [just] ~ ourselves** das bleibt aber unter uns *(Dat.)*; **c)** *(by joint action of)* **~ them/the four of them they succeeded in dislodging the stone** gemeinsam/zu viert gelang es ihnen, den Stein zu lösen; **we ate it up ~ us** wir haben es zusammen *od.* gemeinsam aufgegessen; **d)** *(shared by)* **~ us we had 40p** wir hatten zusammen 40 Pence; **we had three tents ~ the five of us** wir hatten drei Zelte für uns fünf; **there is nothing ~ us** wir haben nichts miteinander; **it's all over ~ us** es ist aus zwischen uns *(Dat.)* *(ugs.)*. **2.** *adv.* **[in] ~:** dazwischen; *(in time)* zwischendurch; **the space ~:** der Zwischenraum

between: ~times, ~whiles *advs.* in der Zwischenzeit

betwixt [bɪ'twɪkst] **1.** *prep. (arch./poet.)* zwischen. **2.** *adv.* **a)** *(arch./poet.)* dazwischen; **b) ~ and between** *(coll.)* zwischen beiden

bevel ['bevl] **1.** *n. (slope)* Schräge, *die;* **~ edge** Schrägkante, *die;* **~ gear** Kegelradgetriebe, *das.* **2.** *v.t., (Brit.)* **-ll-** abschrägen

beverage ['bevərɪdʒ] *n. (formal)* Getränk, *das*

bewail [bɪ'weɪl] *v.t.* beklagen; *(lament)* bejammern

beware [bɪ'weə(r)] *v.t. & i.; only in imper. and inf.* **~ [of] sth./sb.** sich vor jmdm./etw. hüten *od.* in acht nehmen; **~ of doing sth.** sich davor hüten, etw. zu tun; **'~ of black ice/falling masonry'** „Vorsicht, Glatteis/herabfallendes Mauerwerk!"; **'~ of pickpockets'** „vor Taschendieben wird gewarnt": **'~ of the dog'** „Vorsicht, bissiger Hund!"; **~ [of] how ...** darauf achtgeben, wie ...; **~ that you do not succumb to the temptation** hüte dich davor, der Versuchung zu erliegen

bewilder [bɪ'wɪldə(r)] *v.t.* verwirren; **be ~ed by sth.** durch *od.* von etw. verwirrt werden/sein

bewildering [bɪ'wɪldərɪŋ] *adj.* verwirrend

bewilderment [bɪ'wɪldəmənt] *n., no pl.* Verwirrung, *die;* **in total ~:** völlig verwirrt

bewitch [bɪ'wɪtʃ] *v.t.* verzaubern; verhexen; *(fig.)* bezaubern

bewitching [bɪ'wɪtʃɪŋ] *adj.* bezaubernd

bewitchingly [bɪ'wɪtʃɪŋlɪ] *adv.* bezaubernd; **smile ~ at sb.** jmdn. mit einem bezaubernden Lächeln ansehen

beyond [bɪ'jɒnd] **1.** *adv.* **a)** *(in space)* jenseits; *(on other side of wall, mountain range, etc.)* dahinter; **the world ~:** das Jenseits; **b)** *(in time)* darüber hinaus; **c)** *(in addition)* daneben; außerdem; **and nothing ~:** und weiter nichts *od.* nichts weiter. **2.** *prep.* **a)** *(at far side of)* jenseits (+ *Gen.*); **when we get ~ the river, we'll stop** wenn wir den Fluß überquert haben, machen wir halt; **b)** *(in space: after)* nach; **all we saw was ruin ~ ruin** wir sahen eine Ruine nach der anderen; **c)** *(later than)* nach; **she never looks or sees ~ the present** sie sieht *od.* blickt nie über die Gegenwart hinaus; **I shan't wait ~ an hour/~ 6 o'clock** ich warte nicht länger als eine Stunde/nicht länger als bis 6 Uhr; **d)** *(out of reach, comprehension, range)* über ... (+ *Akk.*) hinaus; **it's [far** *or (coll.)* **way] ~ me/him** *etc.* das ist mir/ihm *usw.* [bei weitem] zu schwer; *(incomprehensible)* das ist mir/ihm *usw.* [völlig] unverständlich; **be ~ the power of anyone's imagination** jedermanns Vorstellungsvermögen *(Akk.)* übersteigen; **your work is ~ all praise** Ihre Arbeit kann man nicht genug loben; **~ reproach** tadellos; **that is ~ my powers/competence** das liegt nicht in meiner Macht/überschreitet meine Befugnisse; **be ~ sb.'s capabilities/understanding** jmds. Fähigkeiten/Begriffsvermögen *(Akk.)* übersteigen; **e)** *(surpassing, exceeding)* mehr als; **I succeeded ~ my wildest hopes** mein Erfolg übertraf meine kühnsten Hoffnungen; **they're living ~ their means** sie leben über ihre Verhältnisse; **f)** *(more than)* weiter als; **he can't yet walk ~ a few steps** er kann noch nicht weiter als ein paar Schritte gehen; *see also* **joke 1 a**; **g)** *(besides)* außer; **there's nothing you can do ~ writing to him regularly** Sie können nichts weiter tun, als ihm regelmäßig [zu] schreiben; **~ this/that** weiter. **3.** *n.* **the B~:** das Jenseits; **at the back of ~:** am Ende der Welt

[1]**b.f.** [bi: 'ef] *n. (Brit. euphem.)* Blödmann, *der (salopp)*

[2]**b.f.** *abbr. (Bookk.)* **brought forward** Übertrag

BFPO *abbr.* **British Forces Post Office** *Postdienst der britischen Streitkräfte*

b.h.p. *abbr. (Mech. Engin.)* **brake horsepower**

biannual [baɪ'ænjʊəl] *adj.* halbjährlich

biannually [baɪ'ænjʊəlɪ] *adv.* zweimal jährlich

bias ['baɪəs] **1.** *n.* **a)** *(leaning)* Neigung, *die;* **have a ~ towards** *or* **in favour of sth./sb.** etw./jmdn. bevorzugen; **have a ~ against sth./sb.** gegen etw./jmdn. eingenommen sein; **be of** *or* **have a conservative ~:** konservativ eingestellt sein; **b)** *(prejudice)* Voreingenommenheit, *die;* **be without ~:** unvoreingenommen sein; **c)** *(Statistics)* systematischer Fehler; Bias, *das (fachspr.)*; **d)** *(Dressmaking)* schräger Schnitt; **cut on the ~:** schräg zum Fadenlauf schneiden; **~ binding** Schrägband, *das.* **2.** *v.t.,* **-s-** *or* **-ss-** beeinflussen; **be ~ed towards** *or* **in favour of sth./sb.** für etw./jmdn. eingestellt sein; **they are ~ed in favour of women** sie bevorzugen Frauen; **be ~ed against sth./sb.** gegen etw./jmdn. voreingenommen sein; **a ~ed account** eine gefärbte *od.* tendenziöse Darstellung; **a ~ed jury/judge** befangene Geschworene/ein befangener Richter/eine befangene Richterin

bib [bɪb] **1.** *n.* **a)** *(for baby)* Lätzchen, *das;* **b)** *(of apron etc.)* Latz, *der;* **put on one's best ~ and tucker** *(joc.)* sich in Schale werfen *(ugs.)*. **2.** *v.i.,* **-bb-** *(arch.)* trinken

Bible ['baɪbl] *n.* **a)** *(Christian)* Bibel, *die;* **b)** *(of other religion)* heiliges Buch; *(fig.: authoritative book)* Bibel, *die*

Bible: ~ class *n.* Bibelstunde, *die;* **~ 'oath** *n.* Eid auf die Bibel

biblical ['bɪblɪkl] *adj.* biblisch; Bibel-

bibliographer [bɪblɪ'ɒgrəfə(r)] *n.* Bibliograph, *der*/Bibliographin, *die*

bibliographic [bɪblɪə'græfɪk], **bibliographical** [bɪblɪə'græfɪkl] *adj.* bibliographisch

bibliography [bɪblɪ'ɒgrəfɪ] *n.* **a)** *(list)* Bibliographie, *die;* Schriftenverzeichnis, *das;* **b)** *(study)* Bibliographie, *die*

bibliophile ['bɪblɪəfaɪl] *n.* Bibliophile, *der/die*

bibulous ['bɪbjʊləs] *adj.* trunksüchtig

bicarb ['baɪkɑ:b] *n. (coll.)* Natron, *das*

bicarbonate [baɪ'kɑ:bənеɪt] *n.* **a)** *(Cookery)* **~ [of soda]** Natron, *das;* **b)** *(Chem.)* doppeltkohlensaures Natrium

bicentenary [baɪsen'ti:nərɪ, baɪsen'tenərɪ], **bicentennial** [baɪsen'tenɪəl] **1.** *adjs.* Zweihundertjahr-; **~ celebrations** Zweihundertjahrfeier, *die.* **2.** *ns.* Zweihundertjahrfeier, *die*

biceps ['baɪseps] *n.* **a)** *(Anat.)* Bizeps, *der;* **b)** *(muscularity)* Muskeln *Pl.;* Bizeps, *der (ugs.)*

bicker ['bɪkə(r)] *v.i.* zanken; streiten; **~ with sb. about** *or* **over sth.** sich mit jmdm. um etw. zanken *od.* streiten

bickering ['bɪkərɪŋ] *n.* Gezänk, *das;* Zankerei, *die (ugs.)*

bicycle ['baɪsɪkl] **1.** *n.* **a)** Fahrrad, *das;* **ride a ~:** [mit dem] Fahrrad fahren; radfahren; **by ~:** mit dem [Fahr]rad; **b)** *(attrib.)* Fahrrad-; **~ clip/rack** Hosenklammer, *die*/Fahrradständer, *der;* **~ kick** *(Football)* Fallrückzieher, *der.* **2.** *v.i.* radfahren; **he ~s to work** er fährt mit dem Fahrrad zur Arbeit

bid [bɪd] **1.** *v.t.* **a) -dd-, bid** *(at auction)* bieten; **what am I ~?** was höre ich?; was wird geboten?; **~ up the price** den Preis in die Höhe treiben; **b) -dd-, bid** *(Cards)* reizen; **c) -dd-, bade** [bæd] *or* **bid, bidden** ['bɪdn] *or* **bid** *(arch./poet.: command)* heißen *(geh.)*; **~ sb. do sth.** jmdn. etw. tun heißen; **do as you are ~[den]** tu, was man dich geheißen hat; **d) -dd-, bade** *or* **bid, bidden** *or* **bid** *(invite)* einladen; **he bade her be seated** er bat sie, Platz zu nehmen; **e) -dd-, bade** *or* **bid, bidden** *or* **bid: ~ sb. welcome** jmdn. willkommen heißen; **~ sb. goodbye** sich von jmdm. verabschieden; **~ sb./***(coll.)* **sth. farewell, ~ farewell to sb./***(coll.)* **sth.** jmdm./einer Sache Lebewohl sagen; **~ sb. good day** jmdm. einen guten Tag wünschen. **2.** *v.i.,* **-dd-, bid a)** werben **(for um)**; **the President is ~ding for re-election** der Präsident bewirbt sich um die Wiederwahl; **~ fair to be sth.** etw. zu werden versprechen; **b)** *(at auction)* bieten; **c)** *(Cards)* bieten; reizen. **3.** *n.* **a)** *(at auction)* Gebot, *das;* **make a ~ of £9 for sth.** 9 Pfund für etw. bieten; **b)** *(fig.: attempt)* Bemühung, *die;* **make a ~ for sth.** sich um etw. bemühen; **he made a strong ~ for the Presidency** er griff nach dem Präsidentenamt; **in his absence they made a ~ for power** in seiner Abwesenheit versuchten sie, die Macht an sich *(Akk.)* zu reißen; **a ~ for fame and fortune** ein Versuch, berühmt und reich zu werden; **the prisoner made a ~ for freedom** der Gefangene versuchte, die Freiheit zu erlangen; **his ~ to save the crew failed** sein Versuch, die Besatzung zu retten, scheiterte; **c)** *(Cards)* Ansage, *die;* **make no ~:** passen; **it's your ~:** Sie bieten!

biddable ['bɪdəbl] *adj. (obedient)* fügsam

bidden *see* **bid 1 c, d, e**

bidder ['bɪdə(r)] *n.* Bieter, *der*/Bieterin, *die;* **the highest ~:** der/die Höchstbietende

bidding ['bɪdɪŋ] *n.* **a)** *(at auction)* Steigern, *das;* Bieten, *das;* **open the ~:** das erste Gebot machen; **~ was brisk** es wurde lebhaft *od.* rege geboten; *see also* **force 2 i**; **b)** *(command)* Geheiß, *das (geh.)*; **at sb.'s ~:** auf jmds. Geheiß *(Akk.)*; **do sb.'s ~:** tun, was einem von jmdm. befohlen wird; **c)** *(Cards)* Bieten, *das;* Reizen, *das*

'bidding-prayer *n.* Bittgebet, *das*

bide [baɪd] **1.** *v.t.* **~ one's time** den rechten Augenblick abwarten. **2.** *v.i. (arch./dial.: remain)* ausharren; **~ awhile** *or (Scot.)* **a wee** ein Weilchen warten

bidet ['bi:deɪ] *n.* Bidet, *das*

biennial [baɪ'enɪəl] **1.** *adj.* **a)** *(lasting two years)* zweijährig; bienn *(fachspr.)*, zweijährig ⟨*Pflanze*⟩; **b)** *(once every two years)* zweijährlich. **2.** *n. (Bot.)* zweijährige Pflanze; Bienne, *die (fachspr.)*

biennially [baɪ'enɪəlɪ] *adv.* alle zwei Jahre

bier [bɪə(r)] *n.* Totenbahre, *die*

biff [bɪf] *(sl.)* **1.** *n.* Klaps, *der (ugs.)*; **he gave her a ~ on the head** er haute ihr auf den Kopf. **2.** *v.t.* hauen; **he ~ed me on the head with a book** er hat mir ein Buch auf den Kopf geknallt *(ugs.)*

bifocal [baɪ'fəʊkl] *(Optics)* **1.** *adj.* Bifokal-. **2.** *n. in pl.* Bifokalgläser *Pl.*

bifurcate ['baɪfəkeɪt] **1.** *v.i.* sich gabeln. **2.** *v.t.* gabelförmig teilen

bifurcation [baɪfə'keɪʃn] *n. (division)* Aufspaltung, *die; (point)* Gabelung, *die; (branch)* Zweig, *der*

big [bɪg] **1.** *adj.* **a)** *(in size)* groß; schwer, heftig ⟨*Explosion, Zusammenstoß*⟩; schwer ⟨*Unfall, Niederlage*⟩; hart ⟨*Konkurrenz*⟩; teuer ⟨*Preis*⟩; reichlich ⟨*Mahlzeit*⟩; **earn ~ money** das große Geld verdienen; **he is a ~ man/she is a ~ woman** *(tall)* er/sie ist eine lange Latte *(ugs.); (fat)* er/sie ist wohlbeleibt; **she is a ~ girl** *(joc.: busty)* sie hat einen ganz schönen Balkon *(ugs.);* **the ~ expense of moving house** die hohen Umzugskosten; **~ words** geschraubte Ausdrücke (*see also* **g**); **in a ~ way** *(coll.)* im großen Stil; **he fell in love with her in a ~ way** er verliebte sich heftig in sie; **carry/wield a ~ stick** *(fig.)* den großen Knüppel schwingen *(ugs.);* **b)** *(of largest size, larger than usual)* groß ⟨*Appetit, Zehe, Buchstabe*⟩; **~ game** Großwild, *das;* **Conservatism with a ~ C** *(fig.)* Konservati[vi]smus par excellence *od.* in Reinkultur; **c)** **~ger** *(worse)* schwerer; **the ~ger the crime the more severe the penalty** je schwerer das Verbrechen, desto härter die Strafe; **~gest** *(worst)* größt...; **he is the ~gest liar/idiot** er ist der größte Lügner/Idiot; **d)** *(grown up, elder)* groß; **you're ~ enough to know better** du bist groß *od.* alt genug, um es besser zu wissen; **e)** *(important)* groß; wichtig ⟨*Nachricht, Entscheidung*⟩; **the ~ story in the papers today is ...:** das Hauptthema in den Zeitungen von heute ist ...; **a ~ man** ein wichtiger Mann (*see also* **a**); **the Big Three/Four** *etc.* die Großen Drei/Vier *usw.*; **f)** *(coll.: outstanding)* groß ⟨*Augenblick, Chance*⟩; **what's the ~ hurry?** warum die große Eile?; **g)** *(boastful)* angeberisch *(ugs.);* großspurig *(ugs.);* **get** *or* **grow/be too ~ for one's boots** *or* **breeches** *(coll.)* größenwahnsinnig werden/sein *(ugs.);* **~ talk** Großsprecherei, *die;* **~ talker** Großsprecher, *der*/Großsprecherin, *die;* **~ words** große Worte (*see also* **a**); **h)** *(coll.: generous)* großzügig; nobel *(oft iron.);* **that's ~ of you** *(iron.)* wie nobel!; **i)** *(coll.: keen)* **be ~ on sth.** großen Wert auf etw. *(Akk.)* legen; **j)** *(coll.: popular)* **be ~** ⟨*Schauspieler, Popstar:*⟩ gut ankommen. *See also* **idea e. 2.** *adv.* groß; **come/go over ~:** groß ankommen *(ugs.)* **(with** bei**)**; **talk ~:** groß daherreden *(ugs.);* **think ~:** im großen Stil planen

bigamist ['bɪgəmɪst] *n.* Bigamist, *der*/Bigamistin, *die*

bigamous ['bɪgəməs] *adj.* bigamistisch

bigamy ['bɪgəmɪ] *n.* Bigamie, *die*

big: ~ band *n. (Mus.)* Big Band, *die;* **~ 'bang** *n.* Urknall, *der;* **Big Ben** *n.* Big Ben *(der); Glocke/Uhr im Turm des Parlamentsgebäudes in London;* **Big 'Brother** *n.* der Große Bruder; **~ 'business** *n.* das Großkapital; **~ 'cheese** *n. (coll.: person)* hohes Tier *(ugs.);* **~ 'deal** *see* **'deal 3 a**; **~ 'dipper** *n.* **a)** *(Brit.: at fair)* Achterbahn, *die;* **b)** *(Astron.) see* **dipper d**; **~ end** *n. (Motor Veh.)* Pleuelfuß, *der;* **~ game** *n.* Großwild, *das;* **~-game hunting** Großwildjagd, *die;* **~head** *n. (coll.)* Fatzke, *der (ugs. abwertend);* **~-'headed** *adj. (coll.)* eingebildet; **~-'hearted** *adj.* großherzig

bight [baɪt] *n.* **a)** *(loop)* Schlaufe, *die;* **b)** *(curve) (in coast)* Bucht, *die; (in river)* Krümmung, *die;* Schleife, *die*

big: ~ mouth *n. (fig. coll.)* **a)** [-'-] **have a ~ mouth** ein Schwätzer/eine Schwätzerin sein *(ugs.);* **b)** ['--] **be a ~ mouth** ein Angeber/eine Angeberin sein *(ugs.);* **~ 'name** *n. (person)* Größe, *die;* **~ 'noise** *n. (sl.)* hohes Tier *(ugs.)*

bigot ['bɪgət] *n.* Eiferer, *der*/Eiferin, *die; (Relig.)* bigotter Mensch

bigoted ['bɪgətɪd] *adj.* eifernd; *(Relig.)* bigott

bigotry ['bɪgətrɪ] *n.* eifernde Borniertheit; Fanatismus, *der; (Relig.)* Bigotterie, *die*

big: ~ shot *see* **~ noise**; **~ time** *n.* **be in the ~ time** *(coll.)* eine große Nummer sein *(ugs.);* **make it [in]to** *or* **hit the ~ time** *(sl.)* groß herauskommen *(ugs.);* **~ 'top** *n.* Zirkuszelt, *das;* **~ 'wheel** *n.* **a)** *(at fair)* Riesenrad, *das;* **b)** *(sl.: person)* hohes Tier *(ugs.);* **~wig** *n. (coll.)* hohes Tier *(ugs.)*

bijou ['bi:ʒu:] **1.** *n., pl.* **~x** ['bi:ʒu:] Schmuckstück, *das; (fig.)* Juwel, *das.* **2.** *adj.* exquisit

bike [baɪk] *(coll.)* **1.** *n. (bicycle)* Rad, *das; (motor cycle)* Maschine, *die.* **2.** *v.i. (by bicycle)* radfahren; radeln *(ugs., bes. südd.);* mit dem Fahrrad fahren; *(by motor cycle)* [mit dem] Motorrad fahren

biker ['baɪkə(r)] *n. (cyclist)* Radfahrer, *der*/Radfahrerin, *die; (motor-cyclist)* Motorradfahrer, *der*/Motorradfahrerin, *die*

bikini [bɪ'ki:nɪ] *n.* Bikini, *der;* **~ briefs** Slip, *der*

bilateral [baɪ'lætərl] *adj.* bilateral

bilaterally [baɪ'lætərəlɪ] *adv.* bilateral; **the two countries agreed ~ on disarmament** beide Länder einigten sich darauf abzurüsten

bilberry ['bɪlbərɪ] *n.* Blau-, Heidelbeere, *die*

bile [baɪl] *n.* **a)** *(Physiol.)* Gallenflüssigkeit, *die;* **b)** *(Med.)* Gallenleiden, *das;* **c)** *(fig.: peevishness)* Verdrießlichkeit, *die;* Übellaunigkeit, *die*

bilge [bɪldʒ] *n.* **a)** Bilge, *die;* **b)** *(filth)* angesammelter Schmutz im Kielraum; *(fig. sl.: nonsense)* Quatsch, *der;* Unsinn, *der*

bilge: ~-keel *n.* Kimm- *od.* Bilge[n]kiel, *der;* **~-water** *n.* Bilge[n]wasser, *das*

bilingual [baɪ'lɪŋgwəl] *adj.* zweisprachig; bilingual *(fachspr.)* ⟨*Person*⟩; bilinguisch *(fachspr.)* ⟨*Buch, Ausgabe*⟩

bilingualism [baɪ'lɪŋgwəlɪzm] *n., no pl.* Bilingualismus, *der;* Zweisprachigkeit, *die*

bilious ['bɪljəs] *adj. (Med.)* Gallen-; biliös *(fachspr.); (fig.: peevish)* verdrießlich; **~ attack** Gallenanfall, *der;* Gallenkolik, *die;* **a ~ green** ein unappetitliches Grün

biliousness ['bɪljəsnɪs] *n., no pl.* Gallenbeschwerden *Pl.;* Gallenleiden, *das; (fig.)* Reizbarkeit, *die;* Verdrießlichkeit, *die*

bilk [bɪlk] *v.t.* **a)** *(evade payment to)* prellen ⟨*Gläubiger, Kellner usw.*⟩; **b)** *(evade payment of)* nicht bezahlen ⟨*Schuld, Rechnung usw.*⟩; **~ payment** nicht bezahlen *od.* Zahlung unterlassen; **c)** *(cheat)* betrügen; **~ sb. of sth.** jmdn. um etw. betrügen

[1]**bill** [bɪl] **1.** *n.* **a)** *(of bird)* Schnabel, *der;* **b)** *(promontory)* Landzunge, *die;* **c)** *(Naut.: point of anchor fluke)* Spitze, *die.* **2.** *v.i.* ⟨*Vögel:*⟩ schnäbeln; ⟨*Personen:*⟩ sich liebkosen; **~ and coo** ⟨*Vögel:*⟩ schnäbeln und gurren; ⟨*Personen:*⟩ [miteinander] turteln

[2]**bill** *n.* **a)** *(Hist.: weapon)* Hellebarde, *die;* **b)** *(for lopping)* Hippe, *die*

[3]**bill 1.** *n.* **a)** *(Parl.)* Gesetzentwurf, *der;* Gesetzesvorlage, *die;* **b)** *(note of charges)* Rechnung, *die;* **could we have the ~, please?** wir möchten zahlen; **a ~ for £10** eine Rechnung über 10 Pfund *(Akk.); (amount)* **a large ~:** eine hohe Rechnung; **a ~ of £10** eine Rechnung von 10 Pfund; **c)** *(poster)* Plakat, *das;* **'[stick] no ~s'** „Plakate ankleben verboten"; **d)** *(programme)* Programm, *das;* **what's on the ~?** was steht auf dem Programm?; **top the ~, be top of the ~:** der Star [des Abends *usw.*] sein; **~ of fare** Speisekarte, *die; (fig.)* [bunter] Programmreigen; **e)** *(Law)* Klageschrift, *die;* **f)** *(Amer.: banknote)* Banknote, *die;* [Geld]schein, *der;* **a 50-dollar ~:** ein Fünfzig-Dollar-Schein; **g)** **~ [of exchange]** *(Commerc.)* Wechsel, *der;* Tratte, *die (fachspr.);* **h)** **~ of health** Gesundheitsattest *od.* -zeugnis, *das;* **give sb./sth. a clean ~ of health** *(fig.)* jmdm./einer Sache ein gutes/einwandfreies Zeugnis ausstellen; **~ of lading** Konnossement, *das;* Seefrachtbrief, *der;* **~ of quantities** *(Brit.)* Kostenvoranschlag, *der (Aufstellung der Kosten/Dimensionen eines Bauwerks);* **~ of sale** Kaufvertrag, *der;* Verkaufsurkunde, *die.* **2.** *v.t.* **a)** *(announce)* ankündigen; **he is ~ed to appear next week at the Palace Theatre** er soll nächste Woche im Palace Theatre auftreten; **b)** *(advertise)* durch Anschlag bekanntmachen *od.* bekanntgeben; **c)** *(charge)* eine Rechnung ausstellen (+ *Dat.*); **~ sb. for sth.** jmdm. etw. in Rechnung stellen *od.* berechnen

'billboard *n.* Anschlagbrett, *das od.* -tafel, *die;* Plakattafel, *die;* Reklametafel, *die*

[1]**billet** ['bɪlɪt] **1.** *n.* **a)** *(quarters)* Quartier, *das;* Unterkunft, *die; (for soldiers)* Truppenunterkunft, *die;* Ortsunterkunft, *die;* **b)** *(job)* Stellung, *die;* Posten, *der.* **2.** *v.t.* **a)** *(quarter)* unterbringen, einquartieren **(with, on** bei; **in** in + *Dat.*); **b)** *(provide quarters for)* ⟨*Einwohner:*⟩ ein Quartier stellen (+ *Dat.*)

[2]**billet** *n.* **a)** *(of wood)* Holzscheit, -klotz, *der;* **b)** *(bar)* kleine Metallstange; **c)** *(Archit.)* Spannkeil, *der*

billet-doux [bɪlɪ'du:] *n., pl.* **billets-doux** [bɪlɪ'du:z] Liebesbrief, *der;* Billetdoux, *das (veralt.)*

bill: ~fold *n. (Amer.)* Brieftasche, *die;* **~head** *n.* gedrucktes Rechnungsformular; **~hook** *see* [2]**bill b**

billiard ['bɪljəd]: **~-ball** *n.* Billardkugel, *die;* **~-cue** *n.* Queue, *das;* Billardstock, *der;* **~-player** *n.* Billardspieler, *der;* **~-room** *n.* Billardzimmer, *das*

billiards ['bɪljədz] *n.* Billard[spiel], *das;* **a game of ~:** eine Partie Billard; **bar ~** *(Brit.) Billardspiel, bei dem die Löcher, in die die Kugeln gespielt werden müssen, nicht an den Seiten, sondern über die Tischplatte verteilt sind*

'billiard-table *n.* Billardtisch, *der*

billion ['bɪljən] *n.* **a)** *(thousand million)* Milliarde, *die;* **b)** *(Brit.: million million)* Billion, *die*

billionaire [bɪljə'neə(r)] *n. (Amer.)* Milliardär, *der*

billow ['bɪləʊ] **1.** *n.* **a)** *(wave)* Woge, *die;* **~[s]** *(poet.: sea)* Wogen *Pl. (dichter.);* **b)** *(fig.: surging mass)* Masse, *die;* **a ~ of flame** eine Feuerwalze. **2.** *v.i.* ⟨*Ballon, Segel:*⟩ sich [auf]blähen; ⟨*See, Meer:*⟩ wogen, sich [auf]türmen; ⟨*Rauch:*⟩ in Schwaden aufsteigen; ⟨*Kleid, Vorhang:*⟩ sich bauschen

billowy ['bɪləʊɪ] *adj.* wogend ⟨*See, Kornfeld*⟩; gebläht ⟨*Segel*⟩; in Schwaden ziehend ⟨*Rauch*⟩; bauschig ⟨*Rock*⟩

bill: ~poster, ~sticker *ns.* Plakat[an]kleber, *der*

[1]**billy** ['bɪlɪ] *n. (pot)* Kochgeschirr, *das*

[2]**billy** *n.* **a)** *see* **billy-goat**; **b)** **~ [club]** *(Amer.)* [Gummi]knüppel, *der*

'billycan *see* [1]**billy**

'billy-goat *n.* Ziegenbock, *der*

billy-o ['bɪlɪəʊ] *n. (coll.)* **like ~:** wie verrückt *(ugs.);* **they are fighting like ~:** sie prügeln sich wie die Wilden *(ugs.)*

bimetallic [baɪmɪ'tælɪk] *adj.* bimetallisch; **~ strip** Bimetall, *das;* Bimetallstreifen, *der*

bimonthly [baɪ'mʌnθlɪ] **1.** *adj.* **a)** *(two-monthly)* zweimonatlich; alle zwei Monate erscheinend ⟨*Zeitschrift*⟩/stattfindend ⟨*Treffen, Ereignis*⟩; **b)** *(twice-monthly)* zweimal im Monat erscheinend ⟨*Zeitschrift*⟩/stattfindend ⟨*Treffen, Ereignis*⟩. **2.** *adv.* **a)** *(two-monthly)* alle zwei Monate; **b)** *(twice monthly)* zweimal im Monat

bin [bɪn] *n.* **a)** *(for storage)* Behälter, *der; (for coal)* Kohlenkasten, *der; (for fruit)* [Obst]kiste, *die; (for bread)* Brotkasten, *der; (for wine)* Weinregal, *das;* **b)** *(for rubbish) (inside house)* Abfalleimer, *der;* Mülleimer, *der; (outside house)* Mülltonne, *die; (in public place)* Abfallkorb, *der*

binary ['baɪnərɪ] **1.** *adj.* **a)** binär; zweizählig;

~ **system** binäres System; **b)** *(Math.)* ~ **digit** binäre Ziffer; Dualzahl, *die;* ~ **number** binäre Zahl; **c)** *(Biol.)* ~ **fission** äquale Zellteilung; **d)** *(Mus.)* ~ **form** zweiteilige Form; ~ **measure** gerader Takt; **e)** *(Astron.)* ~ **star** Doppelstern, *der;* **f)** *(Chem.)* ~ **compound** binäre Verbindung; Zweifachverbindung, *die.* **2.** *n. (Astron.)* Doppelstern, *der*

bind [baɪnd] **1.** *v. t.,* **bound** [baʊnd] **a)** *(tie)* fesseln ⟨*Person, Tier*⟩; *(bandage)* wickeln, binden ⟨*Glied, Baum*⟩; verbinden ⟨*Wunde*⟩ **(with** mit); **he was bound hand and foot** er war/wurde an Händen und Füßen gefesselt; **they bound the animal's legs together** sie fesselten das Tier an den Beinen; ~ **sb. to sth.** jmdn. an etw. *(Akk.)* fesseln *od.* binden; ~ **sth. to sth.** etw. an etw. *(Akk.)* binden; **b)** *(fasten together)* zusammenbinden; *(fig.: unite)* verbinden; **c)** ~ **books** Bücher binden; **d) be bound up with sth.** *(fig.)* eng mit etw. verbunden *od.* verknüpft sein; eng mit etw. zusammenhängen; **e)** *(oblige)* ~ **sb./oneself to sth.** jmdn./sich an etw. *(Akk.)* binden; **this agreement** ~**s us** wir sind an diese Abmachung gebunden; **be bound to do sth.** *(required)* verpflichtet sein, etw. zu tun; **be bound by law** von Gesetzes wegen verpflichtet sein; **be bound to secrecy** zur Verschwiegenheit verpflichtet sein; *see also* **honour 1 d; f) be bound to do sth.** *(certain)* etw. ganz bestimmt tun; **it is bound to rain** es wird bestimmt *od.* sicherlich regnen; **g) I'm bound to say that ...** *(feel obliged)* ich muß schon sagen, daß ...; ich fühle mich verpflichtet zu sagen, daß ...; **I'm bound to agree** ich glaube, ich stimme überein; **h)** *(constipate)* verstopfen; **i)** *(Cookery)* binden; **j)** *(indenture)* durch Lehrvertrag binden ⟨*Lehrling*⟩; **he was bound [apprentice] for 3 years** er ging drei Jahre in die Lehre; **k)** *(Law)* ~ **sb. over [to keep the peace]** jmdn. verwarnen *od.* rechtlich verpflichten[, die öffentliche Ordnung zu wahren]; **I'll be bound** *(fig.)* ganz gewiß; auf mein Wort; **l)** *(coll.: bore)* langweilen; ~ **sb. stiff** jmdn. zu Tode langweilen; **m)** *(encircle)* ~ **one's hair with flowers** sich *(Dat.)* Blumen ins Haar binden; **n)** *(edge)* einfassen ⟨*Stoffkante usw.*⟩ **(with** mit). **2.** *v. i.,* **bound a)** *(cohere)* binden; ⟨*Lehm, Ton:*⟩ fest *od.* hart werden; ⟨*Zement:*⟩ abbinden; **b)** *(be restricted)* blockieren; ⟨*Kolben:*⟩ sich festfressen; **the window-frame** ~**s easily** der Fensterrahmen verklemmt sich leicht; **c)** *(coll.: complain)* meckern *(ugs.)* **(about** über + *Akk.*). **3.** *n.* **a)** *(Bot.)* Ranke, *die;* **b)** *(Mus.)* Bindebogen, *der;* Bindungszeichen, *das;* Bindung, *die;* **c)** *(coll.: nuisance)* **be a** ~: recht lästig sein; **what a** ~! wie unangenehm *od.* lästig!; **d) be in a** ~ *(Amer. sl.)* in einer Klemme sitzen *(ugs.)*

binder ['baɪndə(r)] *n.* **a)** *(substance)* Bindemittel, *das;* Binder, *der;* **b)** *(book~)* Buchbinder, *der/*-binderin, *die;* **c)** *(Agric.)* [Mäh]binder, *der;* Bindemäher, *der;* **d)** *(tiebeam)* Bundbalken, *der;* Binderbalken, *der;* **e)** *(cover) (for papers)* Hefter, *der; (for magazines)* Mappe, *die;* **f)** *(bondstone)* Binder, *der;* Bindestein, *der*

bindery ['baɪndərɪ] *n.* Buchbinderei, *die*

binding ['baɪndɪŋ] **1.** *adj.* bindend, verbindlich ⟨*Vertrag, Abkommen*⟩ **(on** für). **2.** *n.* **a)** *(cover of book)* [Buch]einband, *der;* **b)** *(edge) (of carpet, material, etc.)* [Einfaß]band, *das;* Besatz, *der;* **c)** *(on ski)* Bindung, *die*

bindweed ['baɪndwi:d] *n. (Bot.)* Winde, *die*

binge [bɪndʒ] *n. (sl.)* Sauferei, *die (salopp);* **go/be out on a** ~: auf Sauftour gehen/sein *(salopp)*

bingo ['bɪŋgəʊ] **1.** *n., no pl.* Bingo, *das;* ~ **hall** Bingohalle, *die.* **2.** *int.* peng; zack

binnacle ['bɪnəkl] *n. (Naut.)* Kompaßhaus, *das*

binocular [bɪ'nɒkjʊlə(r)] **1.** *adj.* binokular. **2.** *n. in pl.* **[pair of]** ~**s** Fernglas, *das;* Binokular, *das*

bint [bɪnt] *n. (sl. derog.)* Weib[stück], *das*

bio- [baɪəʊ] *in comb.* Bio-; Lebens-

bio'chemical *adj.* biochemisch

bio'chemist *n.* Biochemiker, *der/*Biochemikerin, *die*

bio'chemistry *n.* Biochemie, *die*

biode'gradable *adj.* biologisch abbaubar

'biogas *n.* Biogas, *das*

bio'genesis *n., no pl.* Biogenese, *die*

biogenic [baɪə'dʒenɪk] *adj.* biogenetisch

biographer [baɪ'ɒgrəfə(r)] *n.* Biograph, *der/*Biographin, *die*

biographic [baɪə'græfɪk], **biographical** [baɪə'græfɪkl] *adj.* biographisch

biography [baɪ'ɒgrəfɪ] *n.* Biographie, *die; (branch of literature)* biographische Literatur

biological [baɪə'lɒdʒɪkl] *adj.* biologisch; ~ **control** biologische Schädlingsbekämpfung; ~ **warfare** biologische Kriegführung; Bakterienkrieg, *der*

biologically [baɪə'lɒdʒɪkəlɪ] *adv.* biologisch

biologist [baɪ'ɒlədʒɪst] *n.* Biologe, *der/*Biologin, *die*

biology [baɪ'ɒlədʒɪ] *n.* Biologie, *die*

'biomass *n.* Biomasse, *die*

biometric [baɪə'metrɪk], **biometrical** [baɪə'metrɪkl] *adj.* biometrisch

bionic [baɪ'ɒnɪk] *adj.* bionisch

bionics [baɪ'ɒnɪks] *n.* Bionik, *die*

biopsy ['baɪɒpsɪ] *n.* Biopsie, *die*

'biorhythm *n.* Biorhythmus, *der*

bioscope ['baɪəskəʊp] *n. (S. Afr.)* Filmtheater, *das;* Kino, *das*

'biosphere *n.* Biosphäre, *die*

bio'synthesis *n.* Biosynthese, *die*

biotech'nology *n.* Biotechnik, *die*

bipartisan [baɪpɑ:tɪ'zæn, baɪ'pɑ:tɪzæn] *adj.* Zweiparteien-

bipartite [baɪ'pɑ:taɪt] *adj. (having two parts)* zweiteilig; *(involving two parties)* zweiseitig ⟨*Dokument, Abkommen*⟩

biped ['baɪped] *n.* Bipede, *der;* Zweifüßer, *der*

biplane ['baɪpleɪn] *n.* Doppeldecker, *der*

birch [bɜ:tʃ] **1.** *n.* **a)** *(tree)* Birke, *die;* **b)** *see* **birch-rod. 2.** *v. t.* mit der Rute züchtigen

'birch-bark *n.* Birkenrinde, *die*

birching ['bɜ:tʃɪŋ] *n.* [Tracht] Prügel, *die;* ~ **should be made illegal** die Prügelstrafe sollte verboten werden

'birch-rod *n.* [Birken]rute, *die*

bird [bɜ:d] *n.* **a)** Vogel, *der;* **the** ~ **is** *or* **has flown** *(fig.)* der Vogel ist ausgeflogen *(fig.);* ~**s of a feather flock together** *(prov.)* gleich und gleich gesellt sich gern *(Spr.);* **it's [strictly] for the** ~**s** *(sl.)* das kannste vergessen *(salopp);* **get the** ~ *(be hissed etc.)* ausgepfiffen werden; *(be dismissed)* entlassen werden; **give sb. the** ~ *(hiss sb.)* jmdn. auspfeifen; *(dismiss sb.)* jmdn. entlassen; **kill two** ~**s with one stone** *(fig.)* zwei Fliegen mit einer Klappe schlagen; **a** ~ **in the hand is worth two in the bush** *(prov.)* ein Spatz in der Hand ist besser als eine Taube auf dem Dach *(Spr.);* **like a** ~ *(without difficulty or hesitation)* einfach so; **a little** ~ **told me** mein kleiner Finger sagt mir das; **tell sb. about the** ~**s and the bees** *(euphem.)* jmdm. erzählen, wo die kleinen Kinder herkommen; **b)** *(sl.: girl)* Mieze, *die (salopp);* **c)** *(coll.: person)* Vogel, *der (ugs.);* **a queer** ~: ein komischer Kauz *od.* Vogel; **a gay old** ~: ein lustiger alter Knabe; **d)** *no art. (sl.: imprisonment)* Knast, *der (ugs.);* **do** ~: Knast schieben *(salopp). See also* **early bird**

bird: ~**-bath** *n.* Vogelbad, *das;* ~**brained** *adj. (coll.)* **a)** *(stupid)* gehirnamputiert *(salopp);* ~**brained person** Mensch mit einem Spatzenhirn *(salopp);* **b)** *(flighty)* flatterhaft; ~**cage** *n.* Vogelkäfig, *der;* Vogelbauer, *das od. der;* ~**-call** *n.* Vogelruf, *der; (instrument)* Lockpfeife, *die;* ~**-fancier** *n.* Vogelfreund, *der/*-freundin, *die; (breeder)* Vogelzüchter, *der/*-züchterin, *die*

birdie ['bɜ:dɪ] **1.** *n.* **a)** Vögelchen, *das;* **b)** *(Golf)* Birdie, *das;* ein Schlag unter Par. **2.** *v. t.* einen Schlag unter Par spielen

bird: ~**lime** *n.* Vogelleim, *der;* ~ **of 'paradise** *n.* Paradiesvogel, *der;* ~ **of 'passage** *n. (lit. or fig.)* Zugvogel, *der;* ~ **sanctuary** *n.* Vogelschutzgebiet, *das;* ~**seed** *n.* Vogelfutter, *das;* ~**'s-eye** *n. (Bot.)* Gamander-Ehrenpreis, *der;* ~**'s-eye 'view** *n.* Vogelperspektive, *die;* **have/get a** ~**'s-eye view of sth.** *(lit. or fig.)* etw. aus der Vogelperspektive sehen; ~**'s nest** *n.* Vogelnest, *das;* ~**'s nest soup** Schwalbennestersuppe, *die;* ~**-strike** *n.* Kollision von Flugzeug und Vogel; ~**-table** *n.* Futterstelle für Vögel; ~**-watcher** *n.* Vogelbeobachter, *der/*-beobachterin, *die;* ~**-watching** *n., no pl., no indef. art.* das Beobachten von Vögeln

biretta [bɪ'retə] *n. (Eccl.)* Birett, *das*

Biro, (P) ['baɪrəʊ] *n., pl.* ~**s** Kugelschreiber, *der;* Kuli, *der (ugs.)*

birth [bɜ:θ] *n.* **a)** Geburt, *die;* **at the/at** ~: bei der Geburt; **[deaf] from** *or* **since** ~: von Geburt an [taub]; **date and place of** ~: Geburtsdatum und -ort; **land of my** ~: Land meiner Väter *(geh.);* **give** ~ ⟨*Frau:*⟩ entbinden; gebären *(geh.);* ⟨*Tier:*⟩ jungen; werfen; **she gave** ~ **prematurely** sie hatte eine Frühgeburt; **give** ~ **to a child** von einem Kind entbunden werden; ein Kind gebären *(geh.) od.* zur Welt bringen; **b)** *(coming into existence) (of movement, fashion, etc.)* Aufkommen, *das; (of party, company)* Gründung, *die; (of nation)* Geburt, *die; (of new era)* Anbruch, *der;* Geburt, *die;* **the** ~ **of an idea** die Geburt einer Idee; **come to** ~ geboren werden; ⟨*Ära:*⟩ anbrechen; **give** ~ **to sth.** etw. entstehen lassen; **c)** *(parentage)* Geburt, *die;* Abkunft, *die (geh.);* **of good/low** *or* **humble** ~: aus gutem Hause *od.* guter Familie/von niedriger Abstammung; **of high** ~: von hoher Geburt; [von] edler Abkunft *(geh.);* **be a German by** ~: Deutsche[r] von Geburt sein; [ein] gebürtiger Deutscher/[eine] gebürtige Deutsche sein; **sb.'s right by** ~: jmds. angeborenes Recht

birth: ~ **certificate** *n.* Geburtsurkunde, *die;* ~ **control** *n.* Geburtenkontrolle *od.* -regelung, *die;* ~**day** *n.* Geburtstag, *der;* **when is your** ~**day?** wann haben Sie Geburtstag?; ~**day card** Geburtstagskarte, *die;* ~**day party** Geburtstagsfeier, *die; (with music and dancing)* Geburtstagsparty, *die; (children's)* Kindergeburtstag, *der;* ~**day present** Geburtstagsgeschenk, *das;* ~**day honours** *(Brit.)* Titel- und Ordensverleihungen *Pl. (am offiziellen Geburtstag des britischen Monarchen);* **[be] in his/her** ~**day suit** im Adams-/Evaskostüm [sein]; ~**mark** *n.* Muttermal, *das;* ~**place** *n.* Geburtsort, *der; (house)* Geburtshaus, *das;* ~ **rate** *n.* Geburtenrate *od.* -ziffer, *die;* ~**right** *n.* Geburtsrecht, *das; (right of first-born)* Erstgeburtsrecht, *das;* ~**stone** *n.* Monatsstein, *der*

biscuit ['bɪskɪt] **1.** *n.* **a)** *(Brit.)* Keks, *der;* **coffee and** ~**s** Kaffee und Gebäck; ~ **tin** Keksdose, *die;* **b)** *(Amer.: roll)* [weiches] Brötchen; **c)** *(colour)* Beige, *das;* **d)** *(pottery)* Biskuit, *das. See also* **take 1 c. 2.** *adj.* beige

bisect [baɪ'sekt] *v. t. (into halves)* in zwei Hälften teilen; halbieren; *(into two)* in zwei Teile teilen

bisection [baɪ'sekʃn] *n. (into halves)* Halbierung, *die; (into two)* Zweiteilung, *die*

bisector [baɪ'sektə(r)] *n.* Halbierende, *die*

bisexual [baɪ'seksjʊəl] **1.** *adj.* **a)** *(Biol.)* zwittrig; doppelgeschlechtig; **b)** *(attracted by both sexes)* bisexuell. **2.** *n.* Bisexuelle, *der/die*

bisexuality [baɪseksjʊ'ælɪtɪ] *n., no pl. see* **bisexual 1:** Zwittrigkeit, *die;* Doppelgeschlechtigkeit, *die;* Bisexualität, *die*
bish [bɪʃ] *n. (Brit. sl.)* Fehler, *der*
bishop ['bɪʃəp] *n.* **a)** *(Eccl.)* Bischof, *der; as voc.* Herr Bischof; **b)** *(Chess)* Läufer, *der*
bishopric ['bɪʃəprɪk] *n.* **a)** *(office)* Bischofsamt, *das;* Bischofswürde, *die;* **b)** *(diocese)* Bistum, *das;* Diözese, *die*
'bishop sleeve *n.* Puffärmel, *der*
bismuth ['bɪzməθ] *n. (Chem., Med.)* Wismut, *das*
bison ['baɪsn] *n. (Zool.)* **a)** *(Amer.: buffalo)* Bison, *der;* **b)** *(European)* Wisent, *der*
bisque [bɪsk] **a)** *(porcelain)* Biskuit, *das;* **b)** *(Gastr.)* Fischcremesuppe, *die*
bistort ['bɪstɔ:t] *n. (Bot.)* Wiesenknöterich, *der*
bistro ['bi:strəʊ] *n., pl.* **~s** Bistro, *das*
¹bit [bɪt] *n.* **a)** *(mouthpiece)* Gebiß, *das;* Gebißstange, *die;* **take the ~ between one's teeth** *(fig.)* aufmüpfig werden *(ugs.);* **b)** *(of drill)* [Bohr]einsatz, *der;* Bohrer, *der;* *(of key)* [Schlüssel]bart, *der; (of soldering-iron)* Lötkolben[kopf], *der*
²bit *n.* **a)** *(piece)* Stück, *das; (smaller)* Stückchen, *das;* **a little ~:** ein kleines Stückchen; **a ~ of cheese/wood/coal/sugar** ein bißchen *od.* etwas Käse/ein Stück Holz/etwas Kohle/ein bißchen *od.* etwas Zucker; **a ~ of trouble/luck** ein wenig Ärger/Glück; **the best ~s** die besten Teile; **it cost quite a ~:** es kostete ziemlich viel; **have a ~ of cheek** ein bißchen frech sein; **a ~ of all right** *(coll.)* gar nicht übel *(ugs.);* **a ~ [of stuff]** *(sl.: woman)* ein netter *od.* toller Käfer *(ugs.);* **~ by ~:** Stück für Stück; *(gradually)* nach und nach; **smashed to ~s** in tausend Stücke zersprungen; **sb./sth. is blown to ~s** jmd. wird zerrissen/etw. wird in die Luft gesprengt; **he was thrilled to ~s** *(coll.)* er hat sich wahnsinnig gefreut *(ugs.);* **~s and bobs** Krimskrams, *der (ugs.);* Kram, *der (ugs.);* **~s and pieces** Verschiedenes; **do one's ~:** seinen Teil tun *od.* dazu beitragen; *(fair share also)* das Seine tun; **not a** *or* **one ~** *(not at all)* überhaupt nicht; **sb./sth. is not a ~ of use** jmd. ist zu nichts zu gebrauchen/mit etw. kann man überhaupt nichts anfangen; **it is not a ~ of use complaining** es hat überhaupt keinen Sinn, sich zu beklagen; **not a ~ of it** ganz im Gegenteil; **he is every ~ as clever as you are** er ist genauso schlau wie du; **b) a ~** *(somewhat):* **a ~ tired/late/too early** ein bißchen müde/spät/zu früh; **a little ~, just a ~:** ein klein bißchen; **quite a ~:** um einiges ⟨*besser, stärker, hoffnungsvoller*⟩; **with a ~ more practice** mit etwas mehr Übung; **c) a ~ of** *(rather):* **be a ~ of a coward/bully** ganz schön feige *od.* ein ziemlicher Feigling sein/den starken Mann markieren *(ugs.);* **every politician has to be a ~ of a showman** jeder Politiker muß auch etwas von einem Schauspieler an sich *(Dat.)* haben; **a ~ of a disappointment** eine ganz schöne Enttäuschung; **d)** *(Brit.)* **~s of furniture** [armselige] Möbel; **~s of children** kleine Kinder; **e)** *(short time)* **[for] a ~:** eine Weile; **a little ~, just a ~:** ein klein bißchen; **wait a ~ longer** noch ein Weilchen warten; **f)** *(short distance)* **a ~:** ein Stückchen; **a ~ closer** ein bißchen näher; **a little ~, just a ~:** ein kleines Stückchen; **g)** *(coin)* Münze, *die;* **sixpenny/threepenny ~** *(Brit. Hist.)* Sixpence-/Dreipencestück, *das;* **h)** *(Amer.: 12½ cents)* **two ~s** 25 Cent; **four/six ~s** 50/75 Cent; **i)** *(role)* **a ~ [part]** eine kleine Rolle
³bit *n. (Computing)* Bit, *das*
⁴bit *see* **bite 1, 2**
bitch [bɪtʃ] **1.** *n.* **a)** *(dog)* Hündin, *die; (vixen)* Füchsin, *die;* **b)** *(sl. derog.: woman)* Miststück, *das;* Schlampe, *die (salopp); see also* **son; c)** *(coll.: grumble)* **have a ~ about sth.** über etw. *(Akk.)* meckern *(ugs.).* **2.** *v. i. (coll.)* meckern *(ugs.)* **(about** über + *Akk.).* **3.** *v. t.* **~ sth. [up]** *(coll.)* etw. verpfuschen *(ugs.) od. (salopp)* versauen
bitchy ['bɪtʃɪ] *adj. (coll.)* gemein; gehässig; **be/get ~ about sb.** gehässige Bemerkungen über jmdn. machen/anfangen, gehässige Bemerkungen über jmdn. zu machen
bite [baɪt] **1.** *v. t.,* **bit** [bɪt], **bitten** ['bɪtn] beißen; *(sting)* ⟨*Moskito usw.:*⟩ stechen; **~ one's nails** an den Nägeln kauen; *(fig.)* wie auf Kohlen sitzen; **~ one's lip** *(lit. or fig.)* sich *(Dat.)* auf die Lippen beißen; **he won't ~ you** *(fig. coll.)* er wird dich schon nicht beißen; **I've been bitten** *(fig.: swindled)* ich bin reingelegt worden *(ugs.) od.* hereingefallen; **once bitten twice shy** *(prov.)* einmal und nie wieder!; **~ the hand that feeds one** *(fig.)* sich [seinem Gönner gegenüber] undankbar zeigen; **~ the dust** *(fig.)* daran glauben müssen *(ugs.);* **be bitten with an idea** von einer Idee besessen sein; **what's biting** *or* **bitten you/him?** *(fig. coll.)* was ist mit dir/ihm los?; was hast du/hat er denn? **2.** *v. i.,* **bit, bitten a)** beißen; *(sting)* stechen; ⟨*Rad:*⟩ fassen, greifen; ⟨*Schraube:*⟩ fassen; *(take bait, lit. or fig.)* anbeißen; **b) ~ at sth.** nach etw. schnappen; **c)** *(have an effect)* sich auswirken; greifen; **d) have sth. to ~ on** *(fig.)* etw. haben, worauf man sich stützen kann; **~ on the bullet** *(fig.)* die Zähne zusammenbeißen. **3.** *n.* **a)** *(act)* Biß, *der; (piece)* Bissen, *der; (wound)* Bißwunde, *die; (by mosquito etc.)* Stich, *der;* **he took a ~ of the apple** er biß in den Apfel; **can I have a ~?** darf ich mal [ab]beißen?; **take one ~ at a time** immer nur einen Bissen auf einmal nehmen; **put the bite on [sb.]** *(Amer. sl.)* jmdn. unter Druck setzen; **b)** *(taking of bait)* [An]beißen, *das;* **I haven't had a ~ all day** es hat den ganzen Tag noch keiner angebissen; **wait for a ~:** darauf warten, daß einer *od.* ein Fisch anbeißt; **c)** *(food)* Happen, *der;* Bissen, *der;* **I haven't had a ~ since breakfast** ich habe seit dem Frühstück nichts mehr gegessen; **have a ~ to eat** eine Kleinigkeit essen; **come and have a ~ to eat** komm und iß eine Kleinigkeit *(ugs.);* **d)** *(grip)* **these old tyres have no ~:** diese alten Reifen fassen *od.* greifen nicht [mehr]; **e)** *(incisiveness)* Bissigkeit, *die;* Schärfe, *die;* **we need new laws that will have more ~:** wir brauchen neue Gesetze, die besser greifen; **f)** *(Dent.)* Biß, *der;* normale Bißstellung
~ 'back *v. t.* **~ sth. back** etw. unterdrücken; **~ back one's words/a remark** sich *(Dat.)* seine Worte/eine Bemerkung verkneifen
~ 'off *v. t.* abbeißen; **the dog bit off the man's ear** der Hund hat dem Mann ein Ohr abgebissen; **~ sb.'s head off** *(fig.)* jmdm. den Kopf abreißen; **~ off more than one can chew** *(fig.)* sich *(Dat.)* zuviel zumuten; sich übernehmen
biter ['baɪtə(r)] *n.* **the ~ bit** mit den eigenen Waffen geschlagen; *(in deception also)* der betrogene Betrüger; **it's a case of the ~ bit** wer andern eine Grube gräbt, fällt selbst hinein *(Spr.)*
'bite-size *adj.* mundgerecht
biting ['baɪtɪŋ] *adj. (stinging)* beißend; schneidend ⟨*Kälte, Wind*⟩; *(sarcastic)* scharf ⟨*Angriff, Worte*⟩; beißend ⟨*Kritik*⟩; bissig, sarkastisch ⟨*Bemerkung, Kommentar*⟩
bitten *see* **bite 1, 2**
bitter ['bɪtə(r)] **1.** *adj.* **a)** bitter; **~ orange** *(Bot.)* Pomeranze, *die;* **~ lemon** *(drink)* Bitter lemon, *das;* **b)** *(fig.)* scharf, heftig ⟨*Antwort, Bemerkung, Angriff*⟩; bitter ⟨*Kampf, Kälte, Enttäuschung, Tränen*⟩; verbittert ⟨*Person*⟩; erbittert ⟨*Feind*⟩; scharf, bitterkalt ⟨*Wind, Wetter*⟩; streng ⟨*Winter*⟩; **~ experience** bittere Erfahrung; **to the ~ end** bis zum bitteren Ende; **be/feel ~ [about sth.]** [über etw. *(Akk.)*] bitter *od.* verbittert sein. *See also* **pill b. 2.** *n.* **a)** *(bitterness)* Bitterkeit, *die;* **b)** *in pl. (liquors)* Magenbitter, *der;* **c)** *(Brit.: beer)* bitteres Bier *(halbdunkles, obergäriges Bier)*
bitterly ['bɪtəlɪ] *adv.* bitterlich ⟨*weinen, sich beschweren*⟩; bitter ⟨*erwidern*⟩; erbittert ⟨*kämpfen, sich widersetzen*⟩; scharf ⟨*kritisieren*⟩; **~ cold** bitterkalt; **he ~ resented the unfounded accusations** er war äußerst erbittert über die unbegründeten Beschuldigungen; **be ~ opposed to sth.** ein erbitterter Gegner einer Sache *(Gen.)* sein
bittern ['bɪtən] *n. (Ornith.)* Rohrdommel, *die*
bitterness ['bɪtənɪs] *n., no pl.* Bitterkeit, *die; (of reply, remark, attack)* Schärfe, *die;* Heftigkeit, *die; (of person)* Verbitterung, *die; (of wind)* bittere Kälte
bitter-'sweet *adj. (lit. or fig.)* bittersüß
bitty ['bɪtɪ] *adj.* zusammengestoppelt *(abwertend);* zusammengestückelt
bitumen ['bɪtjʊmən] *n.* Bitumen, *das*
bituminous [bɪ'tju:mɪnəs] *adj.* bituminös; **~ coal** Stein- *od.* Fettkohle, *die;* Bituminit, *das*
bivalve ['baɪvælv] **1.** *adj.* **a)** *(Zool.)* zweischalig ⟨*Muschel*⟩; zweiklappig ⟨*Schale*⟩; **b)** *(Biol.)* zweiklappig ⟨*Frucht*⟩. **2.** *n. (Zool.)* Muschel, *die*
bivouac ['bɪvʊæk] **1.** *n.* Biwak, *das;* Lager, *das.* **2.** *v. i.,* **-ck-** biwakieren; im Freien übernachten
bi-weekly [baɪ'wi:klɪ] **1.** *adj.* **a)** *(two-weekly)* zweiwöchentlich; alle zwei Wochen erscheinend ⟨*Zeitschrift*⟩/stattfindend ⟨*Treffen, Ereignis*⟩; **b)** *(twice-weekly)* zweimal in der Woche erscheinend ⟨*Zeitschrift*⟩/stattfindend ⟨*Treffen, Ereignis*⟩. **2.** *adv.* **a)** *(two-weekly)* alle zwei Wochen; **b)** *(twice weekly)* zweimal in der Woche
biz [bɪz] *n. (coll.)* Geschäft, *das*
bizarre [bɪ'zɑ:(r)] *adj.* bizarr; *(eccentric)* exzentrisch; *(grotesque, irregular)* grotesk
bk. *abbr.* **book** Bch.
blab [blæb] *(coll.)* **1.** *v. i.,* **-bb-** quatschen *(abwertend).* **2.** *v. t.,* **-bb-** ausplaudern
black [blæk] **1.** *adj.* **a)** schwarz; *(very dark)* dunkel; *(dirty)* **as ~ as coal** *or* **ink** kohlrabenschwarz; *see also* **face 1 a; b)** *(dark-clothed)* schwarz [gekleidet]; **c) B~** *(dark-skinned)* schwarz; **B~ man/woman/child** Schwarze, *der*/Schwarze, *die*/schwarzes Kind; **B~ people** Schwarze *Pl.;* **B~ ghettos** von Schwarzen bewohnte Gettos; **B~ Africa** Schwarzafrika *(das);* **d)** *(looking gloomy)* düster; **things look ~:** es sieht böse *od.* düster aus; **~ clouds** dunkle Wolken; **e)** *(fig.: wicked)* schwarz ⟨*Gedanken*⟩; **~ ingratitude** grober Undank; **f)** *(evil)* schändlich; **he is not as ~ as he is painted** er ist nicht so schlecht, wie er dargestellt wird; **get some ~ looks** finster angesehen werden; **give sb. a ~ look** jmdn. finster ansehen; **g)** *(dismal)* **a ~ day** ein schwarzer Tag; **be in a ~ mood** deprimiert sein; **~ despair** tiefe Verzweiflung; **h)** *(macabre)* schwarz ⟨*Witz, Humor*⟩; **i)** *(not to be handled)* bestreikt ⟨*Lastwagen, Schiff*⟩. **2.** *n.* **a)** *(colour)* Schwarz, *das; (in roulette)* Noir, *das;* **b) B~** *(person)* Schwarze, *der/die;* **c)** *(credit)* **[be] in the ~:** in den schwarzen Zahlen [sein]; **d)** *(Bot.: fungus)* Brand, *der;* **e)** *(Snooker)* schwarze Kugel; **f)** *(~ clothes)* **dressed in ~:** schwarz gekleidet. **3.** *v. t.* **a)** *(blacken)* schwärzen; **~ sb.'s eye** jmdm. ein blaues Auge machen; **~ one's face** sich schwarz anmalen; **~ one's shoes** seine Schuhe wichsen; **b)** *(declare ~)* bestreiken ⟨*Betrieb*⟩; boykottieren ⟨*Arbeit*⟩
~ 'out 1. *v. t.* verdunkeln. **2.** *v. i.* das Bewußtsein verlieren. *See also* **black-out**
black: ~ and 'blue *adj.* grün und blau; **~ and 'white 1.** *adj. (in writing)* schwarz auf weiß; *(Cinemat., Photog., etc.)* schwarzweiß; *(fig.: comprising only opposite extremes)* Schwarzweiß-; **2.** *n.* **[sth. is there/**

down] in ~ and white *(in writing)* [etw. steht] schwarz auf weiß [geschrieben]; **this film is in ~ and white** dieser Film ist in Schwarzweiß; **see/portray** *etc.* **things in ~ and white** *(fig.)* schwarzweiß malen; **~-and-white** *adj.* Schwarzweiß-; ~ **'art** *n.* Schwarze Kunst, *die;* Magie, *die;* **~ball** *v. t.* stimmen gegen; **~-beetle** *n. (Zool.)* Küchenschabe, *die;* **~berry** ['blækbərı] *n.* Brombeere, *die;* **go ~berrying** Brombeeren pflücken gehen; **~bird** *n.* Amsel, *die;* **~board** *n.* [Wand]tafel, *die;* ~ **'books** *n. pl.* **be in sb.'s ~ books** bei jmdm. schlecht angeschrieben sein; ~ **'box** *n. (flight recorder)* Flugschreiber, *der; (apparatus with concealed mechanism)* Black box, *die;* ~ **'bread** *n.* Schwarzbrot, *das;* **~buck** *n. (Zool.)* Hirschziegenantilope, *die;* ~ **'cap** *n. (Brit. Law Hist.) gefaltetes Tuch aus schwarzer Seide, das der Richter früher auf dem Kopf trug, wenn er ein Todesurteil verkündete;* **~cap** *n. (Ornith.)* Mönchsgrasmücke, *die;* **~cock** *n. (Ornith.)* Birkhahn, *der;* **B~ Country** *n. (Brit.) Industriegebiet von Staffordshire und Warwickshire;* **~'currant** *n.* schwarze Johannisbeere; **B~ 'Death** *n.* Schwarzer Tod; ~ **'earth** *n. (Geol.)* Schwarzerde, *die;* Tschernosjom, *der od. das (fachspr.);* ~ **e'conomy** *n.* Schattenwirtschaft, *die*

blacken ['blækn] *v. t.* **a)** *(make dark[er])* verfinstern ‹*Himmel*›; *(make black[er])* schwärzen; **the ancient buildings were ~ed by centuries of smoke and grime** die alten Bauwerke waren durch die Jahrhunderte rauch- und rußgeschwärzt; **b)** *(fig.: defame)* verunglimpfen; ~ **sb.'s [good] name** jmds. [guten] Namen beschmutzen; ~ **the picture** schwarzmalen

black: ~ **'eye** *n.* **a)** *(bruised)* blaues Auge *(fig.);* Veilchen, *das (ugs.);* **b)** *(dark)* ~ **eyes** schwarze Augen; **~-eyed** *adj.* schwarzäugig; **be ~-eyed** schwarze Augen haben; **~-face** *n.* **a)** *(sheep)* Schaf mit schwarzem Gesicht; **b)** *(make-up)* Schminke für eine Negerrolle; **~fly** *n. (Zool.)* **a)** *(aphid)* Blattlaus, *die;* **b)** *(thrips)* Schwarze Fliege; **B~ 'Forest** *pr. n.* Schwarzwald, *der;* **B~ Forest 'gateau** *n.* Schwarzwälder [Kirschtorte], *die;* **B~ Friar** *n.* Dominikaner, *der;* ~ **'frost** *see* **frost 1 a;** ~ **grouse** *n. (Ornith.)* Birkhuhn, *das*

blackguard ['blægɑ:d] **1.** *n. (scoundrel)* Schurke, *der;* Lump, *der; (foul-mouthed person)* Schandmaul, *das (geh. abwertend).* **2.** *adj. (scoundrelly)* schurkisch *(veralt.);* gemein; *(foul-mouthed)* unflätig. **3.** *v. t. (call a ~)* ~ **sb.** jmdn. einen Lumpen *od.* Schurken schimpfen; *(abuse)* in unflätiger Weise schimpfen über (+ *Akk.*)

blackguardly ['blægɑ:dlı] *adj.* gemein

black: ~head *n.* **a)** *(Ornith.)* Bergente, *die;* **b)** *(pimple)* Mitesser, *der;* ~ **'hole** *n.* **a)** *(Astron.)* schwarzes Loch; **b)** *(esp. Mil.: gaol)* Bunker, *der;* ~ **'ice** *n.* Glatteis, *das*

blacking ['blækıŋ] *n.* schwarze Schuhcreme

blackish ['blækıʃ] *adj.* schwärzlich

black: ~jack *n.* **a)** *(flag)* schwarze Piratenflagge; **b)** *(Amer.: bludgeon)* Totschläger, *der;* **c)** *(Cards)* Vingt-[et-]un, *das;* **d)** *(vessel)* lederner *(außen mit Teer überzogener)* Trinkbecher; **~lead** ['blækled] **1.** *n.* Graphit, *der;* **2.** *v. t.* schwärzen; **~leg 1.** *n.* **a)** *(Brit.: strike-breaker)* Streikbrecher, *der/*-brecherin, *die;* **b)** *(swindler) jmd., der bei Pferderennen od. anderen Glücksspielen falschspielt;* **2.** *v. i.* Streikbrecher/-brecherin sein; ~ **'letter** *n. (Gothic type)* gotische Schrift; *(Schwabacher type)* Schwabacher [Schrift], *die; (Fraktur)* Fraktur, *die;* ~ **list** *n.* schwarze Liste; **~list** *v. t.* auf die schwarze Liste setzen

blackly ['blæklı] *adv.* **a)** *(darkly, gloomily)* düster; **b)** *(angrily)* finster

black: ~mail 1. *v. t.* erpressen; **~mail sb. into doing sth.** jmdn. durch Erpressung dazu zwingen, etwas zu tun; **2.** *n.* Erpressung, *die;* **sheer/emotional ~mail** glatte/psychologische Erpressung; **B~ Maria** [blæk mə'raıə] *n.* grüne Minna *(ugs.);* ~ **'mark** *n. (fig.)* Makel, *der;* **a ~ mark against sb.** ein Makel, der an jmdm. haftet; ~ **'market** *n.* schwarzer Markt; ~ **marketeer** [blæk mɑ:kı'tıə(r)] *n.* Schwarzhändler, *der/*-händlerin, *die;* ~ **'mass** *n.* **a)** *(Satanist mass)* schwarze Messe; **b)** *(requiem mass)* Totenmesse, *die*

blackness ['blæknıs] *n., no pl.* **a)** *(black colour)* Schwärze, *die;* **the ~ of the sky** das Schwarz des Himmels; **b)** *(darkness)* Finsternis, *die; (fig.: wickedness)* Abscheulichkeit, *die*

'black-out *n.* **a)** Verdunkelung, *die; (Theatre, Radio)* Blackout, *der;* **news ~:** Nachrichtensperre, *die;* **b)** *(Med.)* **I had a ~:** ich verlor das Bewußtsein

black: ~ **'pudding** *n.* Blutwurst, *die;* **B~ 'Rod** *n. (Brit. Parl.) Zeremonienmeister des britischen Oberhauses;* **B~ 'Sea** *pr. n.* Schwarze Meer, *das;* ~ **'sheep** *n. (lit. or fig.)* schwarzes Schaf; **~shirt** *n. (Polit.)* Schwarzhemd, *das;* **~smith** *n.* Schmied, *der;* ~ **spot** *n. (fig.)* schwarzer Fleck; *(dangerous)* Gefahrenstelle, *die;* ~ **'tea** *n.* schwarzer Tee; **~thorn** *n. (Bot.)* Schwarzdorn, *der;* ~ **'tie** *n.* schwarze Fliege *(zur Smokingjacke getragen);* **~top** *n. (Amer. Road Constr.)* Schwarzdecke, *die;* ~ **'velvet** *n. (drink) Mixgetränk mit Champagner und Starkbier;* ~ **'widow** *n. (Zool.)* Schwarze Witwe

bladder ['blædə(r)] *n. (Anat., Zool., Bot.)* Blase, *die*

'bladder-wrack *n. (Bot.)* Blasentang, *der*

blade [bleıd] *n.* **a)** *(of sword, knife, dagger, razor, plane)* Klinge, *die; (of chisel, scissors, shears)* Schneide, *die; (of saw, oar, paddle, spade, propeller)* Blatt, *das; (of paddle-wheel, turbine)* Schaufel, *die;* **b)** *(of grass etc.)* Spreite, *die;* **c)** *(sword)* Schwert, *das;* Klinge, *die (geh. veralt.);* **d)** *(person)* zackiger, schneidiger Bursche *(veralt.)*

blah [blɑ:], **blah-blah** ['blɑ:blɑ:] *n. (coll.)* Blabla, *das*

blahs [blɑ:z] *n. pl. (Amer. coll.)* Frust, *der (ugs.)*

blame [bleım] **1.** *v. t.* **a)** *(hold responsible)* ~ **sb. [for sth.]** jmdm. die Schuld [an etw. *(Dat.)*] geben; **always get ~d for sth.** immer an etw. *(Dat.)* schuld sein sollen; **don't ~ me [if ...]** geben Sie nicht mir die Schuld[, wenn ...]; ~ **sth. [for sth.]** etw. [für etw.] verantwortlich machen; **be to ~ [for sth.]** an etw. *(Dat.)* schuld sein; ~ **sth. on sb./sth.** *(coll.)* jmdn./etw. für etw. verantwortlich machen; **b)** *(reproach)* ~ **sb./oneself** jmdm./sich Vorwürfe machen; **I don't ~ you/him** *(coll.)* ich kann es Ihnen/ihm nicht verdenken; **who can ~ her?** wer kann es ihr verdenken?; **don't ~ yourself** machen Sie sich *(Dat.)* keine Vorwürfe; **have only oneself to ~:** die Schuld bei sich selbst suchen müssen; **blaming oneself never helps** Selbstvorwürfe helfen nichts. **2.** *n.* **a)** *(responsibility)* Schuld, *die;* **lay** *or* **put the ~ on sb. [for sth.]** jmdm. [an etw. *(Dat.)*] die Schuld geben; **bear the ~ [for sth.]** die Schuld [an etw. *(Dat.)*] tragen; **get the ~:** die Schuld bekommen; **take the ~ [for sth.]** die Schuld [für etw.] auf sich *(Akk.)* nehmen; **b)** *(censure)* Tadel, *der*

blameable ['bleıməbl] *adj.* tadelnswert

blameless ['bleımlıs] *adj.*, **blamelessly** ['bleımlıslı] *adv.* untadelig

blameworthy ['bleımwɜ:ðı] *adj.* tadelnswert

blanch [blɑ:nʃ] **1.** *v. t.* **a)** *(whiten)* bleichen; abziehen ‹*Mandeln*›; *(make pale)* erbleichen lassen; **b)** *(Cookery: scald)* blanchieren; überbrühen. **2.** *v. i. (grow pale)* bleich werden

blancmange [blə'mɒnʒ] *n.* Flammeri, *der*

blanco ['blæŋkəʊ] *(Mil.)* **1.** *n., no pl.* weißes Mittel zum Wachsen. **2.** *v. t.* [weiß] wachsen

bland [blænd] *adj. (gentle, suave)* verbindlich; freundlich ‹*Art, Stimmung*›; *(mild)* mild ‹*Luft*›; *(not irritating, not stimulating)* mild ‹*Medizin, Nahrung*›; *(unexciting)* farblos

blandish ['blændıʃ] *v. t. (flatter)* schmeicheln (+ *Dat.*); *(cajole)* beschwatzen

blandishment ['blændıʃmənt] *n. (flattery)* Schmeichelei, *die; (cajolery)* Beschwatzen, *das; (allurement)* Verlockung, *die*

blandly ['blændlı] *adv. (gently)* verbindlich; *(mildly)* mild

blandness ['blændnıs] *n., no pl.; see* **bland:** Verbindlichkeit, *die;* Freundlichkeit, *die;* Milde, *die;* Farblosigkeit, *die*

blank [blæŋk] **1.** *adj.* **a)** leer; kahl ‹*Wand, Fläche*›; **b)** *(empty)* frei; **leave a ~ space** Platz frei lassen; **c)** *(fig.)* leer, ausdruckslos ‹*Gesicht, Blick*›; **look ~:** ein verdutztes Gesicht machen; **give sb. a ~ look** jmdn. verdutzt ansehen. **2.** *n.* **a)** *(space)* Lücke, *die;* **my mind was a ~:** ich hatte ein Brett vor dem Kopf; **his memory was a ~:** er hatte keinerlei Erinnerung; **b)** *(document with ~s)* Vordruck, *der;* **c)** *(lottery ticket)* Niete, *die;* **draw a ~:** eine Niete ziehen; *(fig.)* kein Glück haben; **d)** *(domino) Dominostein mit ein od. zwei Leerfeldern;* **e)** *(cartridge)* Platzpatrone, *die;* **f)** *(Num.)* Schrötling, *der;* **g)** *(dash)* Lücke, *die; (euphemism)* Gedankenstrich, *der;* Punkt, Punkt, Punkt

blank: ~ **'cartridge** *n.* Platzpatrone, *die;* ~ **'cheque** *n.* Blankoscheck, *der; (fig.)* Blankovollmacht, *die;* **give sb. a ~ cheque** *(fig.)* jmdm. freie Hand *od.* eine Blankovollmacht geben

blanket ['blæŋkıt] **1.** *n.* **a)** Decke, *die;* **wet '~** *(fig.)* Trauerkloß, *der (ugs.);* **be born on the wrong side of the ~** *(fig.)* unehelich geboren sein; **b)** *(thick layer)* Decke, *die;* **a ~ of snow** eine Schneedecke; **a ~ of fog/cloud** eine Nebel-/Wolkendecke; **c)** *(Printing)* Gummituch, *das.* **2.** *v. t.* **a)** *(cover)* zudecken; **b)** *(stifle)* ersticken. **3.** *adj.* umfassend; ~ **agreement** Pauschalabkommen, *das;* ~ **term** Allerweltswort, *das*

'blanket stitch *n.* Festonstich, *der*

blankety ['blæŋkıtı] *adj. (euphem.)* ~ **[blank]** verflixt *(ugs.);* **what the ~ blank ...?** was zum Kuckuck ...? *(ugs.);* **call sb./sth. a ~ blank** jmdn./etw. zum Kuckuck wünschen *(ugs.)*

blankly ['blæŋklı] *adv.* verdutzt

blankness ['blæŋknıs] *n., no pl.* **a)** *(of surface etc.)* Leere, *die;* **the ~ of the wall** die kahle Wand; **b)** *(expressionlessness)* Ausdruckslosigkeit, *die;* **the ~ of his expression** sein nichtssagender Gesichtsausdruck

blank: ~ **test** *n.* Blindversuch, *der;* ~ **'verse** *n. (Pros.)* Blankvers, *der*

blanquette [blɑ̃'ket] *n. (Cookery)* [Kalbs]frikassee, *das*

blare [bleə(r)] **1.** *v. i.* ‹*Lautsprecher:*› plärren; ‹*Trompete:*› schmettern. **2.** *v. t.* ~ **[out]** [hinaus]plärren ‹*Worte*›; [hinaus]schmettern ‹*Melodie*›. **3.** *n. (of loudspeaker, radio, voice)* Plärren, *das; (of trumpet, trombone)* Schmettern, *das*

blarney ['blɑ:nı] **1.** *n. (cajoling)* Schmeichelei, *die; (nonsense)* Geschwätz, *das.* **2.** *v. i.* schmeicheln. **3.** *v. t.* ~ **sb.** jmdm. schmeicheln; **don't be ~ed into doing it** laß dich nicht beschwatzen, das zu tun

blasé ['blɑ:zeı] *adj.* blasiert

blaspheme [blæs'fi:m] *v. i.* lästern

blasphemous ['blæsfəməs] *adj.* lästerlich, blasphemisch ‹*Bemerkung, Eid, Fluch*›

blasphemy ['blæsfəmı] *n.* Blasphemie, *die;* ~ **is a sin** Gotteslästerung ist eine Sünde

blast [blɑ:st] **1.** *n.* **a)** *(gust)* **a ~ [of wind]** ein Windstoß; **b)** *(sound)* Tuten, *das;* **he gave a ~ on his trumpet** er ließ seine Trompete erschallen; **give one ~ of the horn** einmal ins Horn stoßen; **c)** *(Metallurgy etc.: air current)* Gebläseluft, *die;* **at full ~** *(fig.)* auf Hochtouren *Pl.;* **d)** *(of explosion)* Druckwelle, *die; (coll.: explosion)* Explosion, *die;* **e)** *(coll.: reprimand)* Standpauke, *die (ugs.).* **2.** *v. t.* **a)** *(blow up)* sprengen ‹*Felsen*›; *(coll.: kick)* donnern ‹*Fußball*›; **b)** *(wither)* verdorren lassen; **c)** *(curse)* **~ you/him!** zum Teufel mit dir/ihm! **3.** *v. i. (coll.: shoot)* **start ~ing away** drauflosschießen (**at** auf + *Akk.*); **4.** *int.* **[oh] ~!** [oh] verdammt!

~ 'off *v. i.* abheben; *see also* **blast-off**

blasted ['blɑːstɪd] *adj. (damned)* verdammt *(salopp);* verflucht *(salopp)*

blast: ~-furnace *n.* Hochofen, *der;* **~-hole** *n.* Sprengloch, *das;* **~-off** *n.* Abheben, *das*

blatancy ['bleɪtənsɪ] *n., no pl. see* **blatant:** Eklatanz, *die;* Unverhohlenheit, *die;* Unverfrorenheit, *die;* Kraßheit, *die;* Lärmen, *das;* Plärren, *das;* Aufdringlichkeit, *die*

blatant ['bleɪtənt] *adj.* **a)** *(flagrant)* eklatant; **b)** *(unashamed)* unverhohlen; unverfroren ‹*Lüge*›; **c)** *(noisy)* lärmend; plärrend ‹*Geräusche, Musikbox*›; **d)** *(visually obtrusive)* aufdringlich

blatantly ['bleɪtəntlɪ] *adv. see* **blatant:** eklatant; unverhohlen; unverfroren; lärmend; plärrend; aufdringlich

¹blaze [bleɪz] **1.** *n.* **a)** *(conflagration)* Feuer, *das;* **it took hours to put out the ~:** es dauerte Stunden, bis das Feuer *od.* der Brand gelöscht war; **b)** *(display)* **a ~ of lights** ein Lichtermeer; **a ~ of colour** eine Farbenpracht; ein Farbenmeer; **c)** *(fig.: full light)* Glanz, *der;* **in a ~ of glory** mit Glanz und Gloria; **d)** *(fig.: outburst)* Ausbruch, *der;* **[in] a ~ of temper** in einem Wutausbruch; **e)** *(sl.)* **go to ~s!** scher dich zum Teufel! *(salopp);* **like ~s** wie verrückt *(ugs.)* ‹*arbeiten, rennen usw.*›; **what the ~s [are you doing]?** was zum Teufel [machst du da]? *(salopp);* **how the ~s am I supposed to ...?** wie zum Teufel soll ich ...? **2.** *v. i.* **a)** *(burn)* brennen; **the house was already blazing when the firemen arrived** das Haus stand schon in Flammen als die Feuerwehr ankam; **a blazing fire** ein helloderndes Feuer; **the blazing sun** die glühende Sonne; **a blazing hot day** ein glühend heißer Tag; **b)** *(be brilliantly lighted)* [er]strahlen; ‹*Schnee:*› glänzen; **c)** *(emit light)* strahlen; **the spotlight ~d down on them** der Scheinwerfer strahlte sie an; **d)** *(fig.: with anger etc.)* ‹*Augen:*› glühen; **a blazing row** ein heftiger Streit; **e)** *(show bright colours)* leuchten

~ a'way *v. i.* **a)** *(shoot)* [drauf]losschießen (**at** auf + *Akk.*); **b)** *(work)* loslegen (**at** mit)

~ 'up *v. i.* **a)** *(burst into ~)* aufflammen; **b)** *(in anger)* aufbrausen

²blaze 1. *n. (on animal's head)* Blesse, *die; (on tree)* Markierung, *die.* **2.** *v. t.* markieren, kennzeichnen ‹*Baum, Weg, Pfad*›; **~ a trail** einen Weg markieren; **~ a** *or* **the trail** *(fig.)* den Weg bahnen

³blaze *v. t. (proclaim)* verkünden; **~ sth. abroad** etw. ausposaunen *(ugs.)*

blazer ['bleɪzə(r)] *n.* Blazer, *der*

blazing 'star *n. (Amer. Bot.)* Prachtscharte, *die*

blazon ['bleɪzn] *v. t.* **a)** *(Her.) (describe) nach den Regeln der Heraldik beschreiben; (paint)* blasonieren; kunstgerecht ausmalen ‹*Wappen*›; **b)** *(fig.) (paint)* ausmalen; *(proclaim)* verkünden

bleach [bliːtʃ] **1.** *v. t.* bleichen ‹*Wäsche, Haar, Knochen*›. **2.** *v. i.* bleichen. **3.** *n. (substance)* Bleichmittel, *das; (process)* Bleiche, *die*

bleaching ['bliːtʃɪŋ]: **~-agent** *n.* Bleichmittel, *das;* **~-powder** *n.* Bleichpulver, *das*

¹bleak [bliːk] *adj.* **a)** *(bare)* öde ‹*Landschaft, Berg, Insel, Ebene, Hügel*›; karg ‹*Zimmer*›; **b)** *(chilly)* rauh; kalt ‹*Wetter, Tag*›; **c)** *(unpromising)* düster; **~ prospect[s]** trübe Aussichten

²bleak *n. (Zool.)* Ukelei, *der*

bleakly ['bliːklɪ] *adv.* **a)** düster ‹*anschauen*›; **b)** kalt ‹*wehen*›

bleakness ['bliːknɪs] *n., no pl.* **a)** *(of prospect)* Düsterkeit, *die;* **b)** *(of weather)* Kälte, *die*

bleary ['blɪərɪ] *adj.* trübe ‹*Augen*›; **look ~-eyed** verschlafen aussehen; einen verschleierten Blick haben

bleat [bliːt] **1.** *v. i.* ‹*Schaf, Kalb:*› blöken; ‹*Ziege:*› meckern; *(fig.)* jammern; *(plaintively)* meckern. **2.** *v. t.* **~ [out]** herunterplärren ‹*Entschuldigungen, Klagen*›. **3.** *n. see* **1:** Blöken, *das;* Geblök, *das;* Meckern, *das; (fig.)* Gejammer, *das (ugs.); (plaintive)* Gemecker, *das (ugs.)*

bled *see* **bleed**

bleed [bliːd] **1.** *v. i.,* **bled** [bled] bluten; **~ for the cause/one's country** für die Sache/die Heimat sein Blut geben *(dichter.).* **2.** *v. t.,* **bled a)** *(draw blood from, lit. or fig.)* zur Ader lassen; **~ sb. white** *(fig.)* jmdn. den letzten Pfennig kosten *(ugs.);* ‹*Erpresser:*› jmdn. bis aufs Hemd ausziehen *(ugs.);* **b)** *(extract fluid, air, etc. from)* entlüften ‹*Bremsen, Heizkörper*›

bleeder ['bliːdə(r)] *n.* **a)** *(haemophiliac)* Bluter, *der;* **b)** *(coarse: unpleasant person)* Scheißer, *der (derb)*

bleeding ['bliːdɪŋ] **1.** *n. (loss of blood)* Blutung, *die.* **2.** *adj. (Brit. coarse: damned)* Scheiß-; **don't stand there the whole ~ time doing nothing!** steh da nicht die ganze Zeit so blöd rum, ohne was zu tun! *(salopp).* **3.** *adv. (Brit. coarse)* **I don't ~ care!** das ist mir scheißegal! *(salopp);* **don't be ~ stupid!** sei doch nicht so saublöd! *(salopp)*

bleeding 'heart *n.* **a)** *(Bot.)* Tränendes Herz; Flammendes Herz; **b)** *(coll.: person)* mitfühlende Seele

bleep [bliːp] **1.** *n.* Piepen, *das;* **two faint ~s** zwei schwache Piepser. **2.** *v. i.* ‹*Geigerzähler, Funksignal:*› piepen. **3.** *v. t.* **~ sb.** jmdn. über seinen Kleinempfänger *od. (ugs.)* Piepser rufen

bleeper ['bliːpə(r)] *n.* Kleinempfänger, *der;* Piepser, *der (ugs.)*

blemish ['blemɪʃ] **1.** *n.* **a)** *(stain)* Fleck, *der; (on fruit)* Stelle, *die;* **b)** *(defect, lit. or fig.)* Makel, *der;* **be without a ~:** makellos sein; **her only ~ was her quick temper** ihr einziger Fehler war ihr aufbrausendes Wesen. **2.** *v. t.* **a)** *(spoil)* verunstalten; **b)** *(fig.)* **~ sth.** einer Sache *(Dat.)* schaden

blench [blenʃ] *v. i.* zurückschrecken

blend [blend] **1.** *v. t.* **a)** *(mix)* mischen ‹*Tabak-, Kaffee-, Teesorten*›; **b)** *(make indistinguishable)* vermischen. **2.** *v. i.* **a)** sich mischen lassen; **pink does not ~ with orange** Rosa verträgt sich nicht mit Orange; **~ in with/into sth.** [gut] zu etw. passen/mit etw. verschmelzen; **b)** ‹*Whisky-, Tee-, Tabaksorten:*› sich [harmonisch] verbinden. **3.** *n. (mixture)* Mischung, *die*

blender ['blendə(r)] *n.* **a)** *(person)* [Ver]mischer, *der;* **b)** *(apparatus)* Mixer, *der;* Mixgerät, *das*

Blenheim ['blenɪm] *pr. n.* **the Battle of ~:** die Schlacht von Höchstädt

bless [bles] *v. t.,* **blessed** [blest] *or* **blest** [blest] **a)** *(consecrate, pronounce blessing on)* segnen; **she did not have a penny to ~ herself with** *(fig.)* sie besaß keinen Pfennig *od. (ugs.)* keinen roten Heller; **they have been ~ed with a son** sie wurden mit einem Sohn gesegnet; **[God] ~ you** Gottes Segen; *(as thanks)* das ist sehr lieb von dir/Ihnen; *(to person sneezing)* Gesundheit!; **goodbye and God ~:** Wiedersehen, [und] mach's/macht's gut!; **~ you, I wouldn't dream of it** mein Gott, ich denke gar nicht daran; **~ me!, I'm blest!, ~ my soul!** du meine Güte! *(ugs.);* **~ me if it isn't Sid** ja das ist doch Sid!; **b)** *(call holy)* preisen; *(attribute one's good fortune to)* **they ~ed their stars/guardian angel that ...:** sie priesen dankbar das Glück/ihren Schutzengel dafür, daß ...

blessed 1. [blest] *p. t. and p. p. of* **bless. 2.** ['blesɪd, *pred.* blest] *adj.* **a) be ~ with sth.** *(also iron.)* mit etw. gesegnet sein; **b)** *(revered)* heilig ‹*Gott, Mutter Maria*›; *(in Paradise)* selig; *(RC Ch.: beatified)* selig; *(blissful)* beglückend; **c)** *attrib. (euphem.: cursed)* verdammt *(salopp)*

blessedness ['blesɪdnɪs] *n., no pl. (happiness)* Glückseligkeit, *die; (enjoyment of divine favour)* Seligkeit, *die*

blessing ['blesɪŋ] *n.* **a)** *(declaration or bestowal of divine favour, grace at table)* Segen, *der;* **do sth. with sb.'s ~** *(fig.)* etw. mit jmds. Segen tun *(ugs.);* **give sb./sth. one's ~** *(fig.)* jmdm./etw. seinen Segen geben *(ugs.);* **b)** *(divine gift)* Segnung, *die;* **count one's ~s** *(fig.)* dankbar sein; **c)** *(fig. coll.: welcome thing)* Segen, *der;* **what a ~!** welch ein Segen!; **be a ~ in disguise** sich schließlich doch noch als Segen erweisen; *see also* **mixed blessing**

blest *see* **bless;** *(poet.) see* **blessed** 2

blether ['bleðə(r)] **1.** *v. i.* schwafeln *(ugs.);* sülzen *(ugs.);* **go on ~ing** weiterschwafeln *od.* -sülzen. **2.** *n.* Geschwafel, *das;* Gesülze, *das (ugs.)*

blew *see* **¹blow 1, 2**

blight [blaɪt] **1.** *n.* **a)** *(plant disease)* Brand, *der; (fig.: malignant influence)* Fluch, *der;* Geißel, *die;* **Fascism – a ~ on the twentieth century** Faschismus – ein Fluch des zwanzigsten Jahrhunderts; **b)** *(fig.: unsightly urban area)* Schandfleck, *der;* **c)** *(Brit.: aphid)* Blattlaus, *die.* **2.** *v. t.* **a)** *(affect with ~)* **be ~ed** von Brand befallen werden/sein; **b)** *(spoil)* beeinträchtigen ‹*Schönheit*›; überschatten ‹*Freude, Leben*›; *(frustrate)* zunichte machen ‹*Hoffnung*›; **a ~ed area** eine heruntergekommene Gegend

blighter ['blaɪtə(r)] *n. (Brit. coll.)* **a) the poor ~:** der arme Kerl; **b)** *(derog.)* Lümmel, *der (abwertend); (thing)* Mistding, *das (salopp)*

blimey ['blaɪmɪ] *interj. (Brit. sl.)* Mensch *(salopp)*

blimp [blɪmp] *n.* **a)** *(Brit.)* **[Colonel] B~:** *Personifikation des stockkonservativen Engländers;* **b)** *(airship)* unstarres Kleinluftschiff

blimpish ['blɪmpɪʃ] *adj.* reaktionär

blind [blaɪnd] **1.** *adj.* **a)** blind ‹*Mensch, Tier*›; **a ~ man/woman** ein Blinder/eine Blinde; **[be] as ~ as a bat** stockblind [sein] *(ugs.);* **~ in one eye** auf einem Auge blind; **go** *or* **become ~:** blind werden; erblinden; **turn a ~ eye [to sth.]** *(fig.)* [bei etw.] ein Auge zudrücken; **b)** *(Aeronaut.)* **~ landing/flying** Blindlandung, *die*/Blindflug, *der;* **c)** *(without foresight)* blind; **a ~ policy** eine kurzsichtige *od.* unbesonnene Politik; **d)** *(unreasoning)* blind ‹*Vorurteil, Weigerung, Gehorsam, Vertrauen*›; **e)** *(oblivious)* **be ~ to sth.** blind gegenüber etw. sein; **f)** *(reckless)* blind ‹*Hast*›; rasend ‹*Geschwindigkeit*›; **g)** *(not ruled by purpose)* blind ‹*Wut, Zorn*›; dunkel ‹*Instinkt*›; kopflos ‹*Panik*›; **h)** *(concealed)* verdeckt ‹*Graben*›; unsichtbar ‹*Hindernis*›; **i)** *(walled up)* blind ‹*Tür, Fenster*›; **j)** *(coll.: drunk)* blau *(ugs.);* **get ~:** sich vollaufen lassen *(ugs.);* **k) a ~** *(sl.: any whatever):* **he doesn't do a ~ thing [to help her]** er rührt keinen Finger[, um ihr zu helfen]; **not a ~ bit of** überhaupt kein/keine; **it didn't do a ~ bit of good** es hat überhaupt nichts genützt; **you didn't take a ~ bit of notice** du hast dich überhaupt nicht darum gekümmert. **2.** *adv.* **a)** blindlings; **the pilot had to fly/land ~:** der Pilot mußte blind fliegen/landen; **b)** *(completely)* **~ drunk** stockbetrunken *(ugs.);* **swear ~:** hoch und heilig versichern; **c)** *(Cookery)* **bake sth. ~:** etw. blind backen. **3.** *n.* **a)** *(screen)* Jalousie, *die; (of cloth)* Rouleau, *das; (of shop)* Markise, *die;* **b)** *(Amer. Hunting: hide)* Jagdschirm, *der;* **c)** *(pretext)* Vorwand, *der; (cover)* Tarnung, *die;* **be a ~ for sth.** als Tarnung für etw. dienen; **d)** *(Brit. sl.: drinking-bout)* **go on a ~:** eine Sauftour machen *(salopp);* **e)** *pl.* **the ~:** die Blinden *Pl.;* **it's [a case of] the ~ leading the ~** *(fig.)* das ist, wie wenn ein Blinder einen Lahmen [spazieren]führt. **4.** *v. t. (lit. or fig.)* blenden; **be ~ed** *(accidentally)* das Augenlicht verlieren; **~ sb. to the fact that ...:** jmdn. gegenüber der Tatsache blind machen, daß ...; **he was ~ed by his infatuation** er war von seiner eigenen Verliebtheit geblendet *od.* verblendet; **~ sb. with science** jmdn. mit großen Worten beeindrucken. **5.** *v. i. (Brit. coll.: go heedlessly)* rasen; **~ along** rumrasen *(ugs.)*

blind: ~ 'alley *n. (lit. or fig.)* Sackgasse, *die;* **~ 'corner** *n.* unübersichtliche Ecke; **~ 'date** *n.* Verabredung mit einem/einer Unbekannten

blinder ['blaɪndə(r)] *n.* **a) play a ~** *(Sport)* sich selbst übertreffen; **b)** *usu. in pl. (Amer.: blinker)* Scheuklappe, *die*

'blindfold 1. *v. t.* die Augen verbinden (+ *Dat.*); **the conjurer asked to be ~ed** der Zauberer bat darum, ihm die Augen zu verbinden. **2.** *adj.* mit verbundenen Augen; **he was ~ all the time** er hatte die ganze Zeit die Augen verbunden; **I could do that ~** *(fig.)* das könnte ich mit verbundenen Augen [tun]. **3.** *n.* Augenbinde, *die*

blind 'gut *n. (Anat.)* Blinddarm, *der*

blinding ['blaɪndɪŋ] *adj.* blendend ⟨*Licht, Sonnenlicht, Blitz*⟩; grell ⟨*Strahl*⟩; **a ~ headache** rasende Kopfschmerzen *Pl.*

blindly ['blaɪndlɪ] *adv.* [wie] blind; wie ein Blinder; *(fig.)* blindlings

blind man's 'buff *n.* Blindekuh *o. Art.*

blindness ['blaɪndnɪs] *n., no pl.* **a)** Blindheit, *die;* **b)** *(lack of foresight)* Blindheit, *die* **(to** gegenüber); *(unreasonableness)* Verblendung, *die*

blind: ~ side *n. (Rugby)* ungeschützte Seite; *(fig.)* schwache Seite *(fig.);* **~ spot** *n. (Anat.)* blinder Fleck; *(Motor Veh.)* toter Winkel; *(fig.: weak spot)* schwacher Punkt; **~worm** *n. (Zool.)* Blindschleiche, *die*

blink [blɪŋk] **1.** *v. i.* **a)** blinzeln; **b)** *(shine intermittently)* blinken; *(shine momentarily)* aufblinken. **2.** *v. t.* **a) ~ back/away one's tears** seine Tränen blinzelnd zurückhalten; **~ one's eyes** mit den Augen zwinkern; **b)** *(fig.: ignore)* die Augen verschließen vor (+ *Dat.*); ignorieren ⟨*Tatsache*⟩. **3.** *n.* **a)** *(blinking)* Blinzeln, *das;* **he gave one or two ~s** er blinzelte ein paarmal; **b)** *(intermittent light)* Blinken, *das; (momentary gleam)* Aufblinken, *das;* **c)** *(sl.)* **be on the ~:** kaputt sein *(ugs.)*

blinker ['blɪŋkə(r)] **1.** *n. in pl.* Scheuklappen; **have/put ~s on** *(lit. or fig.)* Scheuklappen tragen/anlegen. **2.** *v. t.* Scheuklappen anlegen (+ *Dat.*); **this horse has to be ~ed** dieses Pferd muß Scheuklappen tragen; **be ~ed** *(fig.)* borniert sein

blinking ['blɪŋkɪŋ] *(Brit. coll. euphem.)* **1.** *adj.* verflixt *(ugs.);* **it's a ~ nuisance** das ist verdammt ärgerlich *(ugs.).* **2.** *adv.* verflixt *(ugs.);* **I don't ~ [well] care** das kümmert mich verflixt wenig; **it's ~ raining** verflixt [und zugenäht], es regnet

blip [blɪp] **1.** *v. t.,* **-pp-** hauen. **2.** *n.* **a)** *(sound) (of bursting bubble)* leiser Knall; *(on magnetic tape)* leises Knacken; *(act)* Schlag, *der;* **b)** *(Radar: image)* Echozeichen, *das*

bliss [blɪs] *n. (joy)* [Glück]seligkeit, *die;* Glück, *das; (gladness)* Freude, *die;* **his idea of ~:** seine Vorstellung vom Glücklichsein

blissful ['blɪsfl] *adj.* [glück]selig; **~ ignorance** *(iron.)* selige Unwissenheit

blissfully ['blɪsfəlɪ] *adv.* **~ happy** glückselig; **be ~ unaware** *or* **ignorant [of sth.]** *(iron.)* in seliger Unwissenheit [von etw.] sein

blister ['blɪstə(r)] **1.** *n. (on skin, plant, metal, paintwork)* Blase, *die.* **2.** *v. t.* Blasen hervorrufen auf (+ *Dat.*) ⟨*Metall, Anstrich, Haut*⟩. **3.** *v. i.* ⟨*Haut, Pflanze:*⟩ Blasen bekommen; ⟨*Metall, Anstrich:*⟩ Blasen werfen

blistering ['blɪstərɪŋ] *adj.* **a ~ attack** ein erbitterter Angriff; **a ~ criticism** eine ätzende Kritik; **a ~ pace** ein mörderisches Tempo

'blister pack *n.* Sichtpackung, *die*

blithe [blaɪð] *adj.* **a)** *(poet.: joyous)* fröhlich; heiter; **b)** *(casual)* unbekümmert

blithely ['blaɪðlɪ] *adv.* **~ ignore sth.** sich unbekümmert über etw. *(Akk.)* hinwegsetzen

blithering ['blɪðərɪŋ] *adj. (coll.)* **a)** *(utter)* total; völlig; **a ~ idiot** ein alter Idiot *(salopp);* **b)** *(senselessly talkative)* quatschig *(salopp)* ⟨*Kommentator, Journalist*⟩

B. Litt. [bi: 'lɪt] *abbr.* **Bachelor of Letters** Bakkalaureus der Literaturwissenschaften; *see also* **B. Sc.**

blitz [blɪts] *(coll.)* **1.** *n.* **a)** *(Hist.)* Luftangriff, *der* **(on** auf + *Akk.*); **during the [London] ~:** während der Luft- *od.* Bombenangriffe [auf London]; **b)** *(fig.: attack)* Großaktion, *die (fig.);* **have a ~ on one's room** in seinem Zimmer gründlich saubermachen. **2.** *v. t.* [schwer] bombardieren

blizzard ['blɪzəd] *n.* Schneesturm, *der*

bloat [bləʊt] **1.** *v. t.* aufblähen; **dead bodies ~ed by the water** vom Wasser aufgedunsene Leichen. **2.** *v. i.* aufschwellen; aufschwemmen

bloated ['bləʊtɪd] *adj.* **a)** *(with gluttony)* aufgedunsen; **I feel ~:** ich bin voll *(ugs.);* **b) be ~ with pride/wealth** aufgeblasen sein/im Geld schwimmen

bloater ['bləʊtə(r)] *n.* Bückling, *der*

blob [blɒb] *n.* **a)** *(drop)* Tropfen, *der; (small mass)* Klacks, *der (ugs.); (of butter etc.)* Klecks, *der;* **b)** *(spot of colour)* Fleck, *der*

bloc [blɒk] *n. (Polit.)* Block, *der;* **the Eastern ~/Eastern ~ countries** der Ostblock/die Ostblockstaaten; **the Western ~ [countries]** die westlichen Staaten; **the anti-EC ~:** der Anti-EG-Block; **~ vote** *see* **block vote**

block [blɒk] **1.** *n.* **a)** *(large piece)* Klotz, *der;* **~ of wood** Holzklotz, *der;* **b)** *(for chopping on)* Hackklotz, *der;* **c)** *(for beheading on)* Richtblock, *der; (for hammering on, for mounting horse from)* Klotz, *der; (toy building-brick)* Bauklotz, *der;* **be a chip off the old ~:** ganz der Vater sein; **be on the ~** *(Amer.)* zur Versteigerung angeboten werden; **d)** *(large mass of concrete or stone, building-stone)* Block, *der;* **e)** *(sl.: head)* **knock sb.'s ~ off** jmdm. eins überziehen *(salopp);* **f)** *(building)* [Häuser]block, *der;* **~ of flats/offices** Wohnblock, *der*/Bürohaus, *das;* **g)** *(Amer.: area between streets)* Block, *der;* **on this/our ~:** in diesem/unserem Block; **six ~s away** sechs Blocks weiter; **h)** *(large quantity)* Masse, *die;* **a ~ of shares** ein Aktienpaket; **a ~ of seats** mehrere nebeneinanderliegende Sitze; **in the cheapest ~ of seats** im billigsten Block; **i)** *(pad of paper)* Block, *der;* **j)** *(obstruction)* Verstopfung, *die;* **k)** *(traffic jam)* [Verkehrs]stau, *der;* **l)** *(mental barrier)* **a mental ~:** eine geistige Sperre; Mattscheibe *o. Art. (salopp);* **a psychological ~:** ein psychologischer Block; **m)** *(Printing)* Klischee, *das;* **n)** *(pulley)* Block, *der;* **~ and tackle** Flaschenzug, *der;* **o)** *(Athletics)* Startblock, *der.* **2.** *v. t.* **a)** *(obstruct)* blockieren, versperren ⟨*Tür, Straße, Durchgang, Sicht*⟩; verstopfen ⟨*Pfeife, Nase, Abfluß*⟩; blockieren, verhindern ⟨*Fortschritt*⟩; abblocken ⟨*Ball, Torschuß*⟩; **b)** *(Commerc.)* einfrieren ⟨*Investitionen, Guthaben*⟩; **~ed currency** nicht frei konvertierbare Währung; **c)** *(emboss)* prägen

~ 'in *v. t.* ausfüllen ⟨*Umrisse, Zeichnung*⟩; abdecken ⟨*Kamin, Fenster usw.*⟩

~ 'off *v. t.* [ab]sperren ⟨*Straße*⟩; blockieren ⟨*Rohr, Verkehr*⟩

~ 'out *v. t.* ausschließen ⟨*Licht, Lärm*⟩; retuschieren ⟨*Foto*⟩; abdecken ⟨*Matrize, Schablone*⟩

~ 'up *v. t.* verstopfen; versperren, blockieren ⟨*Eingang*⟩

blockade [blɒ'keɪd] **1.** *n.* Blockade, *die.* **2.** *v. t.* blockieren

blockage ['blɒkɪdʒ] *n.* Block, *der; (of pipe, gutter)* Verstopfung, *die*

block: ~board *n.* Tischlerplatte, *die;* **~ 'booking** *n.* Gruppenbuchung, *die;* **~-buster** *n.* **a)** *(bomb)* [große] Fliegerbombe; **b)** *(fig.)* Knüller, *der (ugs.);* **~ 'capital** *n.* Blockbuchstabe, *der;* **~ diagram** *n.* Blockdiagramm, *das;* **~ 'grant** *n.* Pauschalsubvention, *die;* **~head** *n.* Dummkopf, *der (abwertend);* **~ heater** *n.* Nachtspeicherheizung, *die;* **~house** *n.* Blockhaus, *das;* **~ 'letters** *n. pl.* Blockschrift, *die;* **~ 'vote** *n.* Stimmenblock, *der*

bloke [bləʊk] *n. (Brit. coll.)* Typ, *der (ugs.)*

blond [blɒnd] *adj. see* **blonde 1**

blonde [blɒnd] **1.** *adj.* blond ⟨*Haar, Person*⟩; hell ⟨*Teint*⟩. **2.** *n.* Blondine, *die*

blood [blʌd] **1.** *n.* **a)** Blut, *das;* **sb.'s ~ boils** *(fig.)* jmd. ist in Rage; **it makes my ~ boil** es bringt mich in Rage; **sb.'s ~ turns** *or* **runs cold** *(fig.)* jmdm. erstarrt das Blut in den Adern; **draw first ~** *(lit. or fig.)* den ersten Treffer erzielen; **be after** *or* **out for sb.'s ~** *(fig.)* es auf jmdn. abgesehen haben; **taste ~** *(fig.)* Blut lecken; **it's like getting ~ out of** *or* **from a stone** das ist fast ein Ding der Unmöglichkeit; **[a policy of] ~ and iron** Blut und Eisen; **b)** *(relationship)* Blutsverwandtschaft, *die;* **~ is thicker than water** *(prov.)* Blut ist dicker als Wasser; **c)** *(race)* Blut, *das;* Geblüt, *das (geh.);* **of noble ~:** von edlem Geblüt; **fresh** *or* **new ~:** frisches Blut; **young ~:** Nachwuchs, *der;* **sth. is in sb.'s ~:** etw. liegt jmdm. im Blut; **d)** *(passion)* **his ~ is up** er ist in Rage; **do sth. in cold ~:** etw. kaltblütig tun; **[there is] bad ~ [between them]** [es gibt] böses Blut [zwischen ihnen]. **2.** *v. t.* **a) has this hound been ~ed yet?** ist dieser Spürhund schon an Blut gewöhnt?; **b)** *(fig.)* **he was ~ed in the Battle of Leipzig** er bestand seine Feuertaufe in der Völkerschlacht bei Leipzig

blood: ~ and 'thunder *n.* Mord und Totschlag; **~-and-thunder stories** Schauer-und-Schund-Geschichten; **~ bank** *n.* Blutbank, *die;* **~-bath** *n.* Blutbad, *das;* **~-brother** *n. (by birth)* leiblicher Bruder; *(by ceremony)* Blutsbruder, *der;* **~ cell** *n.* Blutkörperchen, *das;* **~ clot** *n.* Blutgerinnsel, *das;* **~ count** *n.* Blutbild, *das;* **carry out a ~ count** das Blutbild bestimmen; **~-curdling** *adj.* grauenerregend; **~ donor** *see* **donor b; ~ feud** *n.* Blutrache, *die;* **~ group** *n.* Blutgruppe, *die;* **~-heat** *n.* Körpertemperatur, *die;* **~hound** *n.* Bluthund, *der; (fig.)* Spürhund, *der*

bloodless ['blʌdlɪs] *adj.* **a)** *(without bloodshed)* unblutig; **a ~ coup** ein unblutiger Staatsstreich; **b)** *(without blood, pale)* blutleer; **c)** *(unemotional)* gefühllos

blood: ~-letting *n. (Med. Hist.; also fig.)* Aderlaß, *der;* **~-lust** *n.* Blutgier, *die;* **~-money** *n.* Blutgeld, *das;* **~ orange** *n.* Blutorange, *die;* **~-poisoning** *n.* Blutvergiftung, *die;* **~ pressure** *n.* Blutdruck, *der;* **~ 'pudding** *n.* ≈ Blutwurst, *die;* **~-red** *adj.* blutrot; **~ relation** *n.* Blutsverwandte, *der/die;* **~ sample** *n.* Blutprobe, *die;* **~shed** *n.* Blutvergießen, *das;* **~shot** *adj.* blutunterlaufen; **~ sports** *n. pl.* Hetzjagd, *die;* **~-stain** *n.* Blutfleck, *der;* **~-stained** *adj. (lit. or fig.)* blutbefleckt; **~-stock** *n.* Vollblutpferde *Pl.;* **~stone** *n.* Blutstein, *der;* **~stream** *n.* Blutstrom, *der;* **~sucker** *n. (leech)* Blutegel, *der; (fig.: extortioner)* Blutsauger, *der;* **~ sugar** *n.* Blutzucker, *der (Med.);* **~ test** *n.* Blutprobe, *die;* **~thirsty** *adj.* blutdürstig *(geh.);* blutrünstig; ~ **transfusion** *n.* Bluttransfusion, *die;* ~-**vessel** *n.* Blutgefäß, *das*

bloody ['blʌdɪ] **1.** *adj.* **a)** blutig; *(running with blood)* blutend; *(like blood)* blutrot; *(loving bloodshed)* blutrünstig; **give sb. a ~ nose** *(lit., or fig. coll.)* jmdm. eins auf die Nase geben; **b)** *(sl.: damned)* verdammt *(salopp);* **you ~ fool!** du Vollidiot! *(salopp);* **~ hell!** verdammt noch mal! *(salopp);* **c)** *(Brit.) as intensifier* einzig; **he didn't leave me a ~ penny** er ließ mir keinen roten Heller; **that/he is a ~ nuisance** das ist vielleicht ein Mist *(salopp)*/der geht einem vielleicht *od.* ganz schön auf den Wecker *(ugs.).* **2.** *adv.* **a)** *(sl.: damned)* verdammt *(salopp);* **don't be so ~ stupid!** sei doch nicht so verdammt blöde! **b)** *(Brit.) as intensifier* verdammt *(salopp);* **not ~ likely!** denkste! *(salopp);* **I don't ~ [well] like it!** ich kann das, verdammt noch mal, nicht leiden! **3.** *v. t.* *(make ~)* blutig machen; *(stain with blood)* mit Blut beflecken

bloody: B~ 'Mary *n.* Bloody Mary, *der od. die (ein Cocktail);* ~-**'minded** *adj.* stur *(ugs.)*

bloom [blu:m] **1.** *n.* **a)** Blüte, *die;* **be in ~:** in Blüte stehen; **have come into ~:** blühen; **b)** *(on fruit)* Flaum, *der;* *(flush)* rosige Gesichtsfarbe; **c)** *(prime)* Blüte, *die;* **come into ~:** erblühen. **2.** *v. i.* blühen; *(fig.: flourish)* in Blüte stehen

bloomer ['blu:mə(r)] *n.* *(Brit.)* **a)** *(coll.: error)* Schnitzer, *der;* **b)** *(loaf)* Langbrot, *das*

bloomers ['blu:məz] *n. pl.* **a)** [Damen]pumphose, *die;* *(coll.: knickers)* Schlüpfer, *der;* **b)** *(Hist.: costume)* weite Damenhose *(zum Radfahren)*

blooming ['blu:mɪŋ] *(sl. euphem.)* **1.** *adj.* verflixt *(ugs.);* **oh, you ~ idiot!** du Trottel! *(ugs.).* **2.** *adv.* verflixt *(ugs.)*

blooper ['blu:pə(r)] *n.* *(Amer. coll.)* [peinlicher] Fehler, *der;* Patzer, *der (ugs.);* **make** *or* **pull a ~:** einen Bock schießen *(ugs.)*

blossom ['blɒsəm] **1.** *n.* **a)** *(flower)* Blüte, *die;* **b)** *no pl., no indef. art. (mass of flowers)* Blüte, *die;* Blütenmeer, *das (geh.);* **be in ~:** in [voller] Blüte stehen *od.* sein; **have come into ~:** blühen. **2.** *v. i.* **a)** blühen; **the trees ~ed early this year** die Baumblüte begann dieses Jahr schon früh; **b)** *(fig.)* blühen; ⟨*Mensch:*⟩ aufblühen; erblühen *(geh.);* **~ [out] into a statesman/poet** sich zu einem Staatsmann/Dichter entwickeln

blot [blɒt] **1.** *n.* **a)** *(spot of ink)* Tintenklecks, *der;* *(stain)* Fleck, *der;* *(blemish)* Makel, *der;* Schandfleck, *der;* **a ~ on the landscape** *(lit. or fig.)* ein Schandfleck in der Landschaft; **b)** *(fig.)* Makel, *der;* **a ~ on sb.'s character** ein Fleck auf jmds. weißer Weste*(fig.);* *see also* **escutcheon. 2.** *v. t.*, **-tt-** **a)** *(dry)* ablöschen ⟨*Tinte, Schrift, Papier*⟩; **b)** *(spot with ink)* beklecksen; verklecksen; *(fig.: disgrace)* beflecken ⟨*Namen, guten Ruf*⟩; **~ one's copy-book** *(fig. coll.)* sich unmöglich machen

~ **'out** *v. t.* **a)** *(obliterate)* einen Klecks machen auf (+ *Akk.*); unleserlich machen ⟨*Schrift*⟩; **b)** *(obscure)* verdecken ⟨*Sicht*⟩; **thick smoke/fog ~ted out the enemy ship/the mountains** dichter Rauch/Nebel verdeckte [die Sicht auf] das feindliche Schiff/die Berge; **c)** auslöschen ⟨*Leben, Menschheit, Erinnerung*⟩; dem Erdboden gleichmachen, ausradieren ⟨*Stadt, Land*⟩

blotch [blɒtʃ] *n.* *(on skin)* Fleck, *der;* *(patch of ink etc.)* Klecks, *der*

blotchy ['blɒtʃɪ] *adj.* *(skin)* fleckig; *(with wet blotches)* verkleckst

blotter ['blɒtə(r)] *n.* **a)** Schreibunterlage, *die;* **b)** *(Amer.)* *(record-book)* Kladde, *die;* *(Police: record of arrests)* [Polizei]register, *das*

blotting-paper ['blɒtɪŋpeɪpə(r)] *n.* Löschpapier, *das*

blotto ['blɒtəʊ] *pred. adj.* *(sl.)* [sternhagel]voll *(salopp)*

blouse [blaʊz] *n.* Bluse, *die*

[1]**blow** [bləʊ] **1.** *v. i.*, **blew** [blu:], **blown** [bləʊn] **a)** ⟨*Wind:*⟩ wehen; ⟨*Sturm:*⟩ blasen; ⟨*Luft:*⟩ ziehen; **there is a gale ~ing out there** es stürmt draußen; **the wind blew in gusts** es wehte ein böiger Wind; der Wind war böig; **there's a draught ~ing** es zieht; **cold air blew down every corridor** auf allen Gängen war es kalt und zugig; **b)** *(exhale)* blasen; **~ on one's tea to cool it** in den Tee pusten, um ihn abzukühlen; **~ on one's hands to warm them** in die Hände hauchen, um sie zu wärmen; **~ hot and cold** *(fig.)* einmal hü und einmal hott sagen; **c)** *(puff, pant)* ⟨*Person:*⟩ schwer atmen, schnaufen; ⟨*Tier:*⟩ schnaufen; **d)** *(eject air and water)* ⟨*Wal:*⟩ spritzen; **e)** *(be sounded by ~ing)* geblasen werden; ⟨*Trompete, Flöte, Horn, Pfeife usw.:*⟩ ertönen; **f)** *(be driven by ~ing)* geblasen *od.* geweht werden; ⟨*Blätter, Schneeflocken, Seifenblasen:*⟩ [durch die Luft] fliegen; **a few leaves blew along the road** einige Blätter wirbelten *od. (dichter.)* tanzten die Straße entlang; **g)** *(melt)* ⟨*Sicherung, Glühfaden:*⟩ durchbrennen; **h)** *(sl.: depart)* abhauen *(salopp).* **2.** *v. t.*, **blew, blown** (*see also* **m**): **a)** *(breathe out)* [aus]blasen, ausstoßen ⟨*Luft, Rauch*⟩; **b)** *(send by ~ing)* **~ sb. a kiss** jmdm. eine Kußhand zuwerfen; **c)** *(drive by ~ing)* treiben; **d)** *(make by ~ing)* blasen ⟨*Glas*⟩; machen ⟨*Seifenblasen*⟩; **e)** *(sound)* blasen ⟨*Trompete, Flöte, Horn, Pfeife usw.*⟩; **~ one's own trumpet** *(fig.)* sein Eigenlob singen; **f)** *(send jet of air at)* anblasen ⟨*Feuer*⟩; *(gently)* anhauchen; **g)** *(clear)* ausblasen ⟨*Ei*⟩; **~ one's nose** sich *(Dat.)* die Nase putzen; [sich] schneuzen *(geh.);* **h)** *(send flying)* schleudern; **~ sth. to pieces** etw. in die Luft sprengen; **it ~s your mind** *(sl.)* da flippst du aus *(ugs.);* **this dope will ~ your mind** *(sl.)* der Stoff hier haut voll rein *(salopp);* **~ one's top** *or (Amer.)* **stack** *(coll.)* in die Luft gehen *(ugs.);* **i)** *(cause to melt)* durchbrennen lassen ⟨*Sicherung, Glühlampe*⟩; durchhauen *(ugs.)* ⟨*Sicherung*⟩; **j)** *(break into)* sprengen, aufbrechen ⟨*Tresor, Safe*⟩; aufbrechen ⟨*Schloß*⟩; **k)** *(sl.: reveal)* verraten ⟨*Plan, Komplizen*⟩; *see also* **cover 1 i;** [2]**gaff; l) be ~n** *(out of breath)* erschöpft sein; **m)** *p. t., p. p.* **~ed** *(sl.: curse)* **[well,] I'm** *or* **I'll be ~ed** ich werde verrückt! *(salopp);* **I'll be ~ed if I'll do it!** ich denk' nicht [im Traum] dran, das zu tun *(ugs.);* **well, I'll be ~ed if it isn't old Sid!** Mensch[enskind], wenn das nicht der alte Sid ist! *(ugs.);* **~ you, Jack!** du kannst mich mal gern haben! *(salopp);* **~ you, Jack, I'm all right** [das ist] dein Pech *od.* Problem *od.* Bier *(ugs.);* **~!** [so ein] Mist! *(ugs.);* **~ the expense** es ist doch Wurscht, was es kostet *(ugs.);* **n)** *(sl.: squander)* verpulvern, verplempern *(ugs.)* ⟨*Geld, Mittel, Erbschaft*⟩; **he blew all his winnings on gambling** er hat seinen ganzen Gewinn verspielt; **he blew all his money on women** er hat sein ganzes Geld für Frauen ausgegeben; **~ it** *(lose opportunity)* es vermasseln *(salopp).* **3.** *n.* **a)** *(wind)* Sturm, *der;* **b)** *(inhaling of fresh air)* **we went outside for a ~:** wir gingen raus, um etwas frische Luft zu schnappen *(ugs.);* **c)** *(~ing of instrument)* **he gave a loud/long ~ on his trumpet** er ließ einen lauten/langen Trompetenstoß erschallen; **d)** *(~ing of nose)* **he gave his nose a [good] ~:** er schneuzte sich [gründlich] *(geh.);* **have a good ~:** putz dir mal ordentlich die Nase

~ **a'way 1.** *v. i.* wegfliegen. **2.** *v. t.* **a)** wegblasen; **b)** *(Amer. sl.: kill by shooting)* umblasen *(ugs.)*

~ **'down 1.** *v. i.* umgeblasen werden. **2.** *v. t.* umblasen

~ **'in 1.** *v. t.* zum Einsturz bringen ⟨*Haus, Mauer*⟩; **the gale blew the windows in** der Sturm drückte die Fenster ein. **2.** *v. i.* **a)** ⟨*Luft:*⟩ hereinkommen; ⟨*Staub:*⟩ hereingeweht werden; **b)** *(coll.: enter)* hereinschneien; hereinplatzen

~ **'off 1.** *v. i.* **a)** weggeblasen werden; **b)** *(Brit. sl.: break wind)* pup[s]en *(fam.).* **2.** *v. t.* wegblasen; ⟨*Explosion:*⟩ wegreißen

~ **'out 1.** *v. t.* **a)** *(extinguish)* ausblasen ⟨*Kerze, Lampe*⟩; **b)** *(by explosion)* **the explosion blew all the windows out** durch die Explosion flogen alle Fensterscheiben raus; **~ sb.'s/one's brains out** jmdm./sich eine Kugel durch den Kopf jagen *(ugs.).* **2.** *v. i.* ⟨*Reifen:*⟩ platzen; ⟨*Kerze, Lampe:*⟩ ausgeblasen werden. **3.** *v. refl.* ⟨*Sturm:*⟩ sich legen. *See also* **blow-out**

~ **'over 1.** *v. i.* umgeblasen werden; ⟨*Streit, Sturm:*⟩ sich legen; **wait till the whole thing ~s over** *(fig.)* warte, bis sich die Sache gelegt hat. **2.** *v. t.* umblasen

~ **'up 1.** *v. t.* **a)** *(shatter)* [in die Luft] sprengen; **b)** *(inflate)* aufblasen ⟨*Ballon*⟩; aufpumpen ⟨*Reifen*⟩; **c)** *(coll.: reprove)* in der Luft zerreißen *(ugs.);* **d)** *(coll.: enlarge)* vergrößern ⟨*Foto, Seite*⟩; **e)** *(coll.: exaggerate)* hochspielen, aufbauschen ⟨*Ereignis, Bericht*⟩. **2.** *v. i.* **a)** *(explode)* explodieren; **b)** *(arise suddenly)* ⟨*Krieg, Konflikt, Sturm:*⟩ ausbrechen; **c)** *(lose one's temper)* [vor Wut] explodieren *(ugs.);* in die Luft gehen *(ugs.).* *See also* **blow-up**

[2]**blow** *n.* **a)** *(stroke)* Schlag, *der;* *(with axe)* Hieb, *der;* *(jolt, push)* Stoß, *der;* **in** *or* **at one ~** *(lit. or fig.)* mit einem Schlag; **come to ~s** handgreiflich werden; **a ~-by-~ description/account** eine Beschreibung/ein Bericht in allen Einzelheiten; **strike a ~ for sb./sth.** *(fig.)* jmdm./einer Sache einen großen Dienst erweisen; **strike a ~ against sb./sth.** *(fig.)* jmdm./einer Sache einen [schweren] Schlag versetzen; **b)** *(disaster)* [schwerer] Schlag, *der (fig.)* **(to** für); Schicksalsschlag, *der;* Tiefschlag, *der;* **come as** *or* **be a ~ to sb.** ein schwerer Schlag für jmdn. sein; **suffer a ~:** einen Schock erleiden

'blow-dry *v.t.* fönen

blower ['bləʊə(r)] *n.* **a)** *(apparatus)* Gebläse, *das;* **b)** *(Brit. coll.: telephone)* **on the ~:** an der Strippe; **get on the ~:** sich an die Strippe hängen; **I spoke to him on the ~ yesterday** ich habe gestern mit ihm telefoniert

blow: ~-fish *n.* Kugelfisch, *der;* ~**fly** *n.* Schmeißfliege, *die;* ~-**hole** *n.* **a)** *(Zool.)* Atemloch, *das;* Spritzloch, *das;* **b)** *(Metallurgy)* Abzugsloch, *das;* ~-**job** *n.* *(coarse)* Blasmusik, *die (fig. vulg.);* **give sb. a ~-job** jmdm. einen blasen *(vulg.);* ~**lamp** *n.* Lötlampe, *die*

blown *see* [1]**blow 1, 2**

blow: ~-out *n.* **a)** *(burst tyre)* Reifenpanne, *die;* **b)** *(coll.: meal)* feudales Essen *(ugs.);* **we had a good ~-out at the Savoy** wir sind im Savoy richtig feudal essen gewesen *(ugs.);* ~**pipe** *n.* *(weapon)* Blasrohr, *das;* *(tool)* Lötrohr, *das (Chemie);* *(Glass-blowing)* Glasmacherpfeife, *die;* ~**torch** *(Amer.) see* ~**lamp;** ~-**up** *n.* *(coll.: enlargement)* Vergrößerung, *die*

blowy ['bləʊɪ] *adj.* windig; *(wind-swept)* stürmisch

blowzy ['blaʊzɪ] *adj.* **a)** *(red-faced)* rotbäckig; **she had a ~, well-fed appearance** sie war pausbäckig und wohlgenährt; **b)** *(coarse-looking)* schlampig; verwildert; **c)** *(slatternly)* schlampig ⟨*Frau*⟩

blub [blʌb] *v. i.*, **-bb-** *(coll.)* heulen *(ugs.);* plärren *(ugs.)*

blubber ['blʌbə(r)] **1.** *n.* **a)** *(whale-fat)* Walspeck, *der;* **b)** *(coll.: weeping)* Geplärr[e], *das (ugs.);* Heulen, *das (ugs.).* **2.** *v.i.* *(coll.: weep)* heulen *(ugs.);* plärren *(ugs.);* jammern

bludgeon ['blʌdʒn] **1.** *n.* Knüppel, *der.* **2.** *v. t.* niederknüppeln; **~ sb. to death** jmdm. [mit einem Knüppel] totschlagen

¹blue [blu:] **1.** *adj.* **a)** blau; **be ~ with cold/rage** blau gefroren/rot vor Zorn sein; *see also* **face 1 a**; **b)** *(depressed)* **be/feel ~**: niedergeschlagen sein/sich bedrückt *od.* deprimiert fühlen; **c)** *(Brit. Polit.: conservative)* konservativ; ≈ schwarz *(ugs.)*; **d)** *(pornographic)* pornographisch; Porno-; **~ film** *or* **movie** Porno[film], *der;* **~ jokes** unanständige Witze. **2.** *n.* **a)** *(colour)* Blau, *das;* **b)** *(blueness)* Bläue, *die;* **c)** *(Snooker)* blaue Kugel; **d)** *(~ clothes)* **dressed in ~**: blau gekleidet; **the boys in ~** *(Brit. coll.: police)* die Blauen *(ugs.)*; **e)** *(Brit. Univ.)* **be a/get a** *or* **one's ~**: die Universität bei Sportwettkämpfen vertreten haben/vertreten; **f)** *(whitener)* Waschblau, *das;* Wäscheblau, *das;* **g)** *(sky)* Himmelsblau, *das;* **out of the ~** *(fig.)* aus heiterem Himmel *(ugs.)*; völlig unerwartet *(ugs.)*; **disappear into the ~** *(fig.)* sich in nichts auflösen; **h)** *(Polit.: Conservative)* Konservative, *der/die;* ≈ Schwarze, *der/die (ugs.)*; **i)** *(butterfly)* Bläuling, *der;* **j)** **the ~s** *(melancholy)* Niedergeschlagenheit; **have the ~s** niedergeschlagen *od.* deprimiert sein; **get the ~s** schwermütig *od.* melancholisch werden; **k)** **the ~s** *(Mus.)* der Blues; **play/sing the ~s** Blues spielen/singen; **play a ~s** einen Blues spielen. **3.** *v. t.* *(make ~)* blau machen; bläuen ‹*Stahl, Wäsche*›

²blue *v. t.* *(Brit. coll.: squander)* verpulvern, verplempern ‹*Geld, Erbe*›

blue: ~ baby *n.* *(Med.)* blausüchtiger Säugling; **~bell** *n.* *(campanula)* [blaue Wiesen]glockenblume, *die;* *(wild hyacinth)* Sternhyazinthe, *die;* **~berry** [blu:bərı] *n.* Heidelbeere, *die;* Blaubeere, *die;* **~-bird** *n.* *(of N. Amer.)* Elfenblauvogel, *der;* *(of S. and S.E. Asia)* Rotkehlhüttensänger, *der;* **~ 'blood** *n.* blaues Blut; **~-'blooded** *adj.* blaublütig; **~ book** *n.* **a)** *(Brit. Parl.)* Blaubuch, *das;* **b)** *(Amer. Polit.) eine Art Who's Who;* **~bottle** *n.* **a)** *(Zool.)* Schmeißfliege, *die;* **b)** *(Bot.)* Kornblume, *die;* **~ 'cheese** *n.* Blauschimmelkäse, *der;* Edelpilzkäse, *der;* **~ 'chip** *n.* *(Poker)* blaue Spielmarke, *die;* **~-chip share** *n.* *(St. Exch.)* erstklassiges Wertpapier; Blue chip, *der (fachspr.)*; **~-'collar** *adj.* **~-collar worker** Arbeiter, *der*/Arbeiterin, *die;* **~-collar union** Arbeitergewerkschaft, *die;* **~-eyed** *adj.* blauäugig; **be ~-eyed** blaue Augen haben; **~-eyed 'boy** *n.* *(fig. coll.)* Goldjunge, *der;* **~fish** *n.* Blaubarsch, *der;* **~ 'fit** *n.* *(coll.)* **have a ~ fit** Zustände kriegen *(ugs.)*; **~ grass** *n.* *(Amer.: Poa pratensis)* Wiesenrispengras, *das;* **~ gum** *n.* *(Bot.)* Blaugummibaum, *der;* Fieberbaum, *der;* **~jacket** *n.* *(fig.)* Blaujacke, *die (ugs.)*; **~ 'jeans** *n. pl.* Blue jeans *Pl.*; **~ 'moon** *n.* **once in a ~ moon** alle Jubeljahre *(ugs.)*; **~ 'mould** *n.* eßbare Schimmelpilze *Pl.*; **~ 'murder** *n.* **cry** *or* **scream ~ murder** *(sl.)* Zeter und Mordio schreien *(ugs.)*

blueness ['blu:nıs] *n., no pl.* Bläue, *die*

blue: ~ 'pencil *n.* *(fig.)* blauer Farbstift; ≈ Rotstift, *der;* **~-'pencil** *v. t.* mit dem Rotstift gehen an ‹*Text*›; zensieren ‹*Nachricht*›; **B~ 'Peter** *n.* *(Naut.)* Blauer Peter; **~print** *n.* **a)** Blaupause, *die;* **b)** *(fig.)* Plan, *der;* Entwurf, *der;* **~ 'ribbon** *n.* **a)** *(ribbon of the Garter)* das blaue Band des Hosenbandordens; **b)** *(distinction)* höchste Auszeichnung; erster Preis; **c)** *(sign of teetotalism) Abzeichen eines Temperenzlervereins;* **~stocking** *n.* Blaustrumpf, *der;* **she was too much of a ~stocking** sie war zu blaustrümpfig; **~ 'streak** *n.* *(coll.)* **he ran like a ~ streak** er rannte wie ein geölter Blitz *(ugs.)*; **~throat** *n.* *(Ornith.)* Blaukehlchen, *das;* **~ tit** *n.* *(Ornith.)* Blaumeise, *die;* **~ 'water** *n.* hohe See; **~ 'whale** *n.* Blauwal, *der*

¹bluff [blʌf] **1.** *n.* *(act)* Täuschungsmanöver, *das;* Bluff, *der (ugs.)*; **it's nothing but a ~**: das ist bloß [ein] Bluff; *see also* **call 2 c. 2.** *v. i. & t.* bluffen *(ugs.)*

²bluff **1.** *n.* *(headland)* Kliff, *das;* Steilküste, *die;* *(inland)* Steilhang, *der.* **2.** *adj.* **a)** *(abrupt, blunt, frank, hearty)* rauhbeinig *(ugs.)*; **b)** *(perpendicular)* steil; schroff ‹*Felswand, Abhang, Küste*›; breit ‹*Schiffsbug*›

bluffness ['blʌfnıs] *n., no pl.* Rauhbeinigkeit, *die (ugs.)*

bluish ['blu:ıʃ] *adj.* bläulich

blunder ['blʌndə(r)] **1.** *n.* [schwerer] Fehler; **make a ~**: einen [schweren] Fehler machen; einen Bock schießen *(ugs.)*. **2.** *v. i.* **a)** *(make mistake)* einen [schweren] Fehler machen; **b)** *(move blindly)* tappen; **he ~ed about the darkened room/down the corridor** er tappte in dem dunklen Zimmer umher/den Flur entlang. **3.** *v. t.* *(mismanage)* falsch machen

blunderbuss ['blʌndəbʌs] *n.* *(Arms Hist.)* Donnerbüchse, *die (veralt.)*

blunt [blʌnt] **1.** *adj.* **a)** stumpf; **a ~ instrument** ein stumpfer Gegenstand; **b)** *(outspoken)* direkt; unverblümt; **he was quite ~ about his opinion/dislike** er machte aus seiner Meinung/Abneigung überhaupt keinen Hehl; **c)** *(uncompromising)* glatt *(ugs.)* ‹*Ablehnung*›. **2.** *v. t.* **~ [the edge of]** stumpf machen ‹*Messer, Schwert, Säge*›; dämpfen ‹*Begeisterung, Mut*›; mildern ‹*Trauer, Enttäuschung*›; **~ the edge of one's appetite** sich *(Dat.)* den Appetit verderben

bluntly ['blʌntlı] *adv.* **a)** *(outspokenly)* direkt, unverblümt ‹*sprechen, antworten*›; **b)** *(uncompromisingly)* glatt ‹*ablehnen*›

bluntness ['blʌntnıs] *n., no pl. see* **blunt 1**: Stumpfheit, *die;* Direktheit, *die;* Unverblümtheit, *die;* **he was shocked by the ~ of her refusal** ihre glatte Absage hat ihn regelrecht schockiert *(ugs.)*

blur [blɜ:(r)] **1.** *v. t., -rr-* **a)** *(smear)* verwischen, verschmieren ‹*Schrift, Seite*›; **b)** *(make indistinct)* verwischen ‹*Schrift, Farben, Konturen*›; **become ~red** ‹*Farben, Schrift:*› verwischt werden; **c)** *(dim)* trüben ‹*Sicht, Wahrnehmung*›; **my vision is ~red** ich sehe alles verschwommen; mir [ver]schwimmt alles vor [den] Augen; **her eyes were ~red by tears** ihre Augen schwammen in Tränen. **2.** *n.* **a)** *(smear)* [verschmierter] Fleck, *der;* **b)** *(dim image)* verschwommener Fleck

blurb [blɜ:b] *n.* Klappentext, *der;* Waschzettel, *der*

blurt [blɜ:t] *v. t.* hervorstoßen ‹*Worte, Beschimpfung*›; **~ sth. out** mit etw. herausplatzen *(ugs.)*

blush [blʌʃ] **1.** *v. i.* **a)** erröten *(geh.)*; rot werden; **make sb. ~**: jmdn. erröten *(geh.) od.* rot werden lassen; **b)** *(be ashamed)* sich schämen **(at** bei). **2.** *n.* **a)** *(reddening)* Erröten, *das (geh.)*; **spare sb.'s ~es** jmdn. nicht in Verlegenheit bringen; **b)** *(rosy glow)* Röte, *die;* **the ~ of dawn** *(literary)* der rosige Schimmer der Morgenröte; **c)** *(glance)* **at [the] first ~**: auf den ersten Blick

blusher ['blʌʃə(r)] *n.* Rouge, *das*

bluster ['blʌstə(r)] **1.** *v. i.* **a)** ‹*Wind:*› tosen, brausen; **b)** ‹*Person:*› herumschreien *(ugs.)*. **2.** *v. t.* **~ one's way out of sth.** etw. lautstark abstreiten; **you can't ~ your way out of this one** diesmal kannst du dich nicht großartig aus der Affäre ziehen. **3.** *n.* **a)** *(blowing of wind)* Tosen, *das;* Brausen, *das;* **b)** *(talk, threats)* Schreierei, *die (ugs.)*; Geschrei, *das (abwertend)*

blustery ['blʌstərı] *adj.* stürmisch ‹*Wetter, Wind*›

BM *abbr.* **a)** *see* **MB**; **b)** **British Museum** Britisches Museum

B. Mus. [bi:'mʌz] *abbr.* **Bachelor of Music** Bakkalaureus der Musik; *see also* **B. Sc.**

BO *abbr.* *(coll.)* **body odour** Körpergeruch, *der*

boa ['bəʊə] *n.* **a)** *(Zool.)* Boa, *die;* *(python)* Riesenschlange, *die;* **b)** *(garment)* Boa, *die*

boa constrictor ['bəʊə kənstrıktə(r)] *n.* Boa constrictor, *die;* *(python)* Riesenschlange, *die*

boar [bɔ:(r)] *n.* **a)** *(male pig)* Eber, *der;* **b)** *(wild)* Keiler, *der;* **c)** *(guinea-pig)* Bock, *der*

board [bɔ:d] **1.** *n.* **a)** Brett, *das;* **as flat as a ~**: flach; ‹*Frau*› flach wie ein Bügelbrett; **bare ~s** bloße Dielen; **b)** *(black~)* Tafel, *die;* **c)** *(notice-~)* Schwarzes Brett; **d)** *(in game)* Brett, *das;* **e)** *(spring~)* [Sprung]brett, *das;* **f)** *(material)* Spanplatte, *die;* **g)** *(meals)* Verpflegung, *die;* **~ and lodging** Unterkunft und Verpflegung; **full ~**: Vollpension, *die;* **h)** *(table)* **a festive ~**: ein festlich gedeckter Tisch; **i)** *(Admin. etc.)* Amt, *das;* Behörde, *die;* **gas/water/electricity ~**: Gas-/Wasser-/Elektrizitätsversorgungsgesellschaft, *die;* **~ [of examiners]** [Prüfungs]kommission, *die;* **~ of inquiry** Untersuchungsausschuß, *der;* **~ of trustees** Kuratorium, *das;* **~ [of interviewers]** Gremium, *das (zur Auswahl von Bewerbern);* *(Univ.)* Berufungskommission, *die;* **~ of trade** *(Amer.)* Handelskammer, *die;* **B~ of Trade** *(Brit. Hist.)* Handelsministerium, *das;* **j)** *(Commerc., Industry)* **~ [of directors]** Vorstand, *der;* *(supervisory ~)* Aufsichtsrat, *der;* *(in public body)* Verwaltungsrat, *der;* **chairman of the ~**: Vorstands-/Aufsichtsrats-/Verwaltungsratsvorsitzende, *der/die;* **k)** *(Naut., Aeronaut., Transport)* **on ~**: an Bord; **on ~ the ship/plane** an Bord des Schiffes/Flugzeugs; **on ~ the train/bus** im Zug/Bus; **go on ~ the train/bus** in den Zug/Bus einsteigen; **take sb. on ~** *(fig. coll.)* jmdn. aufnehmen; **take sth. on ~** *(fig. coll.)* *(consume)* etw. zu sich nehmen; *(accept)* etw. annehmen; **l)** **the ~s** *(Theatre)* die Bühne; **m)** **go by the ~**: ins Wasser fallen; **your high principles will have to go by the ~**: du mußt deine hohen Grundsätze über Bord werfen. *See also* **above 2 a**; **across 2 b. 2.** *v. t.* **a)** *see* **~ up**; **b)** *(provide with lodging)* in Pension nehmen; **c)** *(go on ~)* **~ the ship/plane** an Bord des Schiffes/Flugzeugs gehen; **~ the train/bus** in den Zug/Bus einsteigen; **d)** *(come alongside)* längsseits herankommen an (+ *Akk.*); *(force one's way on ~)* entern; **e)** *(interview)* **~ sb.** mit jmdm. ein Vorstellungsgespräch führen. **3.** *v. i.* **a)** *(lodge)* [in Pension] wohnen **(with** bei); **b)** *(~ an aircraft)* an Bord gehen; **'flight L 5701 now ~ing [at] gate 15'** „Passagiere des Fluges L 5701 bitte zum Flugsteig 15“

~ 'out **1.** *v. i.* in Pension wohnen. **2.** *v. t.* in Pension geben

~ 'up *v. t.* mit Brettern vernageln

boarder ['bɔ:də(r)] *n.* **a)** *(lodger)* Pensionsgast, *der;* **b)** *(Sch.)* Internatsschüler, *der*/-schülerin, *die;* Interne, *der/die (veralt.)*; **c)** *(Naut.)* Enterer, *der*

'board-game *n.* Brettspiel, *das*

boarding ['bɔ:dıŋ]: **~-house** *n.* Pension, *die;* **~-party** *n.* Enterkommando, *das;* **~-pass** *n.* Bordkarte, *die;* **~-school** *n.* Internat, *das*

board: ~ meeting *n.* Vorstands-/Aufsichtsrats-/Verwaltungsratssitzung, *die;* **~room** *n.* Sitzungssaal, *der;* *(fig.: top management)* Vorstandsetage, *die;* **'~sailing** *see* **windsurfing**; **~walk** *n.* *(Amer.)* Bohlenweg, *der;* *(in yard, trench, etc.)* Holzrost, *der*

boast [bəʊst] **1.** *v. i.* prahlen **(of, about** mit); **that's nothing to ~ about** das ist kein Grund zum Prahlen. **2.** *v. t.* prahlen mit; *(possess)* sich rühmen (+ *Gen.*); **our school ~s a fine playing-field** unsere Schule nennt einen sehr schönen Sportplatz ihr eigen. **3.** *n.* **a)** Prahlerei, *die;* **his favourite ~ is that ...**: am liebsten prahlt er damit, daß ...; **b)** *(cause of pride)* Stolz, *der*

boaster ['bəʊstə(r)] *n.* Aufschneider, *der*/Aufschneiderin, *die (ugs.)*

boastful ['bəʊstfl] *adj.* prahlerisch; großspurig ‹*Erklärung, Behauptung*›; **~ stories** Angebergeschichten *(ugs.)*

boastfully ['bəʊstfəlɪ] *adv.* großspurig; **talk ~ of sth.** mit etw. prahlen

boastfulness ['bəʊstfəlnɪs] *n., no pl.* Großspurigkeit, *die*

boat [bəʊt] *n.* **1. a)** Boot, *das;* **ship's ~:** Beiboot, *das;* **go by ~** mit dem Schiff fahren; **push the ~ out** *(fig. coll.)* ein Faß aufmachen *(ugs.);* **be in the same ~** *(fig.)* im gleichen Boot sitzen; *see also* **[1]burn 2 a; miss 2 d; [2]rock 1 b; b)** *(ship)* Schiff, *das;* **c)** *(for sauce etc.)* Sauciere, *die.* **2.** *v. i.* **go ~ing** eine Bootsfahrt machen

boat: ~-deck *n.* Bootsdeck, *das;* **~ drill** *n.* Bootsmanöver, *das*

boater ['bəʊtə(r)] *n.* **a)** *(person)* Bootsfahrer, *der*/-fahrerin, *die;* **b)** *(hat)* steifer Strohhut; Kreissäge, *die (ugs.)*

boatful ['bəʊtfʊl] *n.* Bootsladung, *die*

boat: ~-hook *n.* Bootshaken, *der;* **~-house** *n.* Bootshaus, *das;* **~load** *n.* Bootsladung, *die;* **~man** ['bəʊtmən] *n., pl.* **~men** ['bəʊtmən] **a)** *(hiring)* Bootsverleiher, *der;* **b)** *(providing transport)* Bootsführer, *der;* **~ people** *n. pl.* Boat people *Pl.;* Bootsflüchtlinge; **~ race** *n.* Regatta, *die;* **the B~ Race** die Oxford-Cambridge-Regatta; **~swain** ['bəʊsn] *n.* Bootsmann, *der;* **~swain's chair** Bootsmannsstuhl, *der;* **~-train** *n.* Zug mit Schiffsanschluß

[1]bob [bɒb] **1.** *v. i.,* **-bb- a) ~ [up and down]** sich auf und nieder bewegen; *(jerkily)* auf und nieder schnellen; ‹*[Pferde]schwanz:*› [auf und nieder] wippen; **the poppies ~bed in the breeze** der Mohn wiegte sich im Wind [hin und her]; **a cork was ~bing on the waves** ein Korken tanzte auf den Wellen [auf und nieder]; **~ up** hochschnellen; **b)** *(curtsy)* knicksen. **2.** *n. (curtsy)* Knicks, *der*

[2]bob 1. *n.* **a)** *(weight)* Gewicht, *das;* **b)** *(hairstyle)* Bubikopf, *der.* **2.** *v. t.,* **-bb-** kurz schneiden ‹*Haar*›; **wear one's hair ~bed** einen Bubikopf tragen

[3]bob *n., pl. same (Brit. coll.)* **a)** *(Hist.: shilling)* Schilling, *der; (fig.)* **she's got a few ~, she's not short of a ~ or two** sie hat schon ein paar Mark; **b)** *(5p)* Fünfer, *der (ugs.);* **two/ten ~:** 10/50 Pence

[4]bob *n. (coll.)* **~'s your uncle** die Sache ist geritzt *(ugs.);* fertig ist der Lack *(ugs.)*

[5]bob *n. (~-sled)* Bob, *der*

bobbin ['bɒbɪn] *n.* Spule, *die*

'bobbin-lace *n.* Klöppelspitze, *die*

bobble ['bɒbl] *n.* Pompon, *der;* Bommel, *die (bes. nordd.)*

bobby ['bɒbɪ] *n. (Brit. coll.)* Bobby, *der (ugs.);* Schupo, *der (ugs. veralt.)*

bobby: ~ pin *n. (Amer.)* Haarklemme, *die;* **~ socks** *n. pl.* Söckchen; **~-soxer** ['bɒbɪsɒksə(r)] *n.* Backfisch, *der*

'bobcat *n. (Amer.)* [Rot]luchs, *der*

bob: ~-sled, ~-sleigh *ns.* Bob[schlitten], *der;* **~stay** *n. (Naut.)* Wasserstag, *das;* **~tail** *n. (horse) Pferd mit gestutztem Schwanz; (dog) Hund mit kupiertem Schwanz*

bock [bɒk] *n.* Bock[bier], *das*

bod [bɒd] *n. (Brit. coll.)* Mensch, *der;* **~s** Leute; **odd ~:** seltsamer Typ (ugs.)

bode [bəʊd] **1.** *v. i.* **~ ill/well** nichts Gutes/einiges erhoffen lassen. **2.** *v. t.* **a)** *(foretell)* prophezeien; **b)** *(portend)* bedeuten; **~ no good** nichts Gutes ahnen lassen

bodega [bə'di:gə] *n.* Bodega, *die*

bodice ['bɒdɪs] *n. (part of dress)* Oberteil, *das; (undergarment, part of dirndl)* Mieder, *das*

-bodied [bɒdɪd] *in comb.* von ... Körperbau; **big-~** von großem, schwerem Körperbau; **a wide-~ aircraft** ein Flugzeug mit breitem Rumpf

bodiless ['bɒdɪlɪs] *adj.* körperlos ‹*Gespenst*›; **a ~ head** ein Kopf ohne Rumpf

bodily ['bɒdɪlɪ] **1.** *adj.* körperlich; organisch ‹*Krankheit*›; **~ harm** Körperverletzung, *die;* **~ needs** leibliche Bedürfnisse; **~ organs** Körperorgane. **2.** *adv.* *(as a whole)* ganz; **the audience rose ~:** das Publikum stand geschlossen auf

bodkin ['bɒdkɪn] *n.* **a)** *(needle)* Durchziehnadel, *die;* **b)** *(hairpin)* lange Haarnadel; **c)** *(tool)* Ahle, *die*

body ['bɒdɪ] **1.** *n.* **a)** *(of person)* Körper, *der;* Leib, *der (geh.); (of animal)* Körper, *der;* **bend one's ~ forward** den Oberkörper nach vorne beugen; **the ~ of Christ** der Leib Christi; **enough to keep ~ and soul together** genug, um am Leben zu bleiben; **do sth. ~ and soul** etw. mit aller Kraft tun; **b)** *(corpse)* Leiche, *die;* Leichnam, *der (geh.);* **over my dead ~!** nur über meine Leiche; **c)** *(coll.: person)* Mensch, *der; (woman also)* Person, *die;* **she/he is a very kind ~:** sie ist eine ganz reizende Person/er ist ein sehr netter Kerl; **d)** *(group of persons)* Gruppe, *die; (having a particular function)* Organ, *das; (military force)* [Truppen]verband, *der;* **government ~:** staatliche Einrichtung; **charitable ~:** Wohltätigkeitsorganisation, *die;* **student ~:** Studentenschaft, *die;* **in a ~:** geschlossen; **e)** *(mass)* **a huge ~ of water** große Wassermassen; **f)** *(main portion)* Hauptteil, *der;* **g)** *(Motor Veh.)* Karosserie, *die; (Railw.)* Aufbau, *der; (aircraft fuselage)* Rumpf, *der;* **h)** *(majority)* Gros, *das;* **i)** *(collection)* Sammlung, *die;* **a ~ of knowledge** ein Wissensschatz; **a ~ of facts** Tatsachenmaterial, *das;* **j)** *(of soup or gravy)* Substanz, *die; (of wine)* Körper, *der;* **have no great ~:** nicht sehr gehaltvoll sein/nicht sehr viel Körper haben. *See also* **corporate a; foreign d; heavenly b; politic 1 c. 2.** *v. t.* **~ sth. forth** etw. verkörpern *od.* versinnbildlichen

body: ~-blow *n.* Körperstoß, *der (Boxen); (fig.)* schwerer Schlag; **~-building 1.** *n.* Bodybuilding, *das;* **2.** *adj.* **~-building food** Aufbaukost, *die;* **~-colour** *n.* Deckfarbe, *die;* **~ fluids** *n. pl.* Körperflüssigkeiten; **~guard** *n. (single)* Leibwächter, *der; (group)* Leibwache, *die;* **~ hair** *n.* Körperhaar, *das;* **~ language** *n.* Körpersprache, *die;* **~ odour** *n.* Körpergeruch, *der;* **~ search** *n.* Leibesvisitation, *die;* **~-snatcher** *n.* Leichenräuber, *der;* **~-stocking** *n.* Bodystocking, *der;* **~work** *n., no pl. (Motor Veh.)* Karosserie, *die*

Boer ['bəʊə(r), bʊə(r)] **1.** *n.* Bure, *der*/Burin, *die.* **2.** *adj.* **the ~ War** der Burenkrieg

boffin ['bɒfɪn] *n. (Brit. sl.)* Eierkopf, *der (salopp)*

bog [bɒg] **1.** *n.* **a)** Moor, *das; (marsh, swamp)* Sumpf, *der;* **b)** *(Brit. sl.: lavatory)* Lokus, *der (salopp).* **2.** *v. t.,* **-gg-: be ~ged down** festsitzen *(fig.);* nicht weiterkommen; **get ~ged down in details** *(fig.)* sich in Details verzetteln

bogey ['bəʊgɪ] *n.* **a)** *(Golf: one stroke over par)* Bogey, *das;* **b)** *see* **bogy**

boggle ['bɒgl] *v. i.* **a)** *(be startled)* sprachlos sein; **the imagination ~s at the thought** der Gedanke übersteigt die Vorstellungskraft; **the mind ~s [at the thought]** bei dem Gedanken wird einem schwindlig; **b)** *(hesitate, demur)* **~ at or about sth.** etw. höchst ungern tun

boggy ['bɒgɪ] *adj.* sumpfig; morastig

bog 'oak *n.* Mooreiche, *die*

bogus ['bəʊgəs] *adj.* falsch; gefälscht ‹*Geld, Schmuck, Dokument*›; **~ firm** Schwindelfirma, *die;* **the claim/deal was ~:** die Behauptung/das Geschäft war reiner Schwindel

bogy ['bəʊgɪ] *n.* **a) B~** *(the Devil)* der Gottseibeiuns; **b)** *(evil spirit)* Gespenst, *das;* **~man** Schreckgestalt, *die;* **c)** *(bugbear)* Schreckgespenst, *das;* **d)** *(sl.: piece of dried mucus)* Popel, *der (ugs.)*

Bohemia [bəʊ'hi:mɪə] *pr. n.* Böhmen *(das)*

Bohemian [bəʊ'hi:mɪən] **1.** *adj.* **a)** *(socially unconventional)* unkonventionell; unbürgerlich; **a ~ person** ein Bohemien; **b)** *(Geog.)* böhmisch; **he/she is ~:** er ist Böhme/sie ist Böhmin. **2.** *n.* **a)** *(socially unconventional person)* Bohemien, *der;* **b)** *(native of Bohemia)* Böhme, *der*/Böhmin, *die*

bohemianism [bəʊ'hi:mɪənɪzm] *n., no pl.* unkonventioneller Lebensstil

[1]boil [bɔɪl] **1.** *v. i.* **a)** kochen; *(Phys.)* sieden; **the kettle's ~ing** das Wasser im Kessel kocht; **keep the pot ~ing** *(fig.) (get a living)* sich über Wasser halten; *(keep sth. going)* dafür sorgen, daß es weitergeht; **b)** *(fig.)* ‹*Wasser, Wellen:*› schäumen, brodeln; **c)** *(fig.: be angry)* kochen; schäumen **(with** vor + *Dat.*); **d)** *(fig. coll.: be hot)* sehr heiß sein; **I'm ~ing** mir ist heiß; **be ~ing [hot]** sehr heiß sein; ‹*Wasser:*› kochend heiß sein; **a ~ing hot August day** ein glühendheißer Augusttag. **2.** *v. t.* **a)** kochen; **~ sth. dry** etw. verkochen; **it is necessary to ~ the water** man muß das Wasser abkochen; **~ed potatoes** Salzkartoffeln; **~ the kettle** das Wasser heiß machen; **~ed shirt** gestärktes Frackhemd; **go and ~ your head** *(fig. coll.)* du kannst mir den Buckel herunterrutschen *(salopp);* **b)** *(make by ~ing)* kochen ‹*Seife*›; **~ed sweet** *(Brit.)* hartes [Frucht]bonbon; Hartkaramelle, *die (fachspr.).* **3.** *n.* Kochen, *das;* **come to/go off the ~:** zu kochen anfangen/aufhören; *(fig.)* sich zuspitzen/sich wieder beruhigen; **bring to the ~:** zum Kochen bringen; *(fig.)* auf die Spitze treiben

~ a'way *v. i.* **a)** *(continue boiling)* weiterkochen; **b)** *(evaporate completely)* verkochen

~ 'down 1. *v. i.* einkochen; **~ down to sth.** *(fig.)* auf etw. *(Akk.)* hinauslaufen. **2.** *v. t.* einkochen; *(fig.)* kurz zusammenfassen

~ 'over *v. i.* überkochen

~ 'up 1. *v. t.* kochen. **2.** *v. i.* kochen; *(fig.)* sich zuspitzen

[2]boil *n. (Med.)* Furunkel, *der*

boiler ['bɔɪlə(r)] *n.* **a)** Kessel, *der;* **b)** *(hot-water tank)* Boiler, *der;* **c)** *(for laundry)* [Wasch]kessel, *der*

boiler: ~-house *n.* Kesselhaus, *das;* **~maker** *n.* Kesselschmied, *der;* **~-room** *n.* Kesselraum, *der;* **~ suit** *n.* Overall, *der*

boiling ['bɔɪlɪŋ] **1.** *see* **[1]boil 1, 2. 2.** *n.* **the whole ~** *(sl.)* der ganze Krempel *(ugs.)*

boiling: ~-point *n.* Siedepunkt, *der;* **be at/reach ~-point** *(fig.)* auf dem Siedepunkt sein/den Siedepunkt erreichen; **~-ring** *n.* Kochspirale, *die*

boisterous ['bɔɪstərəs] *adj.* **a)** *(noisily cheerful)* ausgelassen; **b)** *(rough)* wild; rauh ‹*Wind, See, Witterung*›

boisterously ['bɔɪstərəslɪ] *adv. see* **boisterous:** ausgelassen; wild

bold [bəʊld] *adj.* **a)** *(courageous)* mutig; *(daring)* kühn; **b)** *(forward)* keck; kühn ‹*Worte*›; **make so ~ [as to ...]** so kühn sein[, zu ...]; *see also* **brass 1 a; c)** *(striking)* auffallend, kühn ‹*Farbe, Muster*›; kräftig ‹*Konturen*›; fett ‹*Schlagzeile*›; **bring out in ~ relief** deutlich hervortreten lassen; **d)** *(vigorous)* kühn; ausdrucksvoll ‹*Stil, Beschreibung*›; **e)** *(Printing)* fett; *(secondary ~)* halbfett; **in ~ [type]** im Fettdruck

bold: ~-face, ~-faced *see* **bold e**

boldly ['bəʊldlɪ] *adv.* **a)** *(courageously)* mutig; *(daringly)* kühn; **b)** *(forwardly)* dreist; **c)** *(strikingly)* kräftig ‹*hervortreten*›; mit kühnem Schwung ‹*signieren, malen*›; auffällig ‹*mustern*›

boldness ['bəʊldnɪs] *n., no pl.* **a)** *(courage, daring)* Kühnheit, *die;* **b)** *(forwardness)* Dreistigkeit, *die;* **c)** *(strikingness)* Kühnheit, *die; (of description, style)* Ausdruckskraft, *die; (of an outline, of lettering)* Deutlichkeit, *die; (of pattern)* Auffälligkeit, *die*

bole [bəʊl] *n. (trunk)* [Baum]stamm, *der*

bolero [bə'leərəʊ] *n., pl.* **~s** Bolero, *der*

Bolivia [bə'lɪvɪə] *pr. n.* Bolivien *(das)*

Bolivian [bə'lɪvɪən] **1.** *adj.* bolivianisch; **sb. is ~:** jmd. ist Bolivianer/Bolivianerin. **2.** *n.* Bolivianer, *der*/Bolivianerin, *die*

boll [bəʊl] *n.* Samenkapsel, *die*
bollard ['bɒləd] *n. (Brit.)* Poller, *der*
bollocks ['bɒləks] *(coarse)* **1.** *n. pl.* Eier *(derb).* **2.** *int.* Scheiße
'boll-weevil *n.* Baumwollkapselkäfer, *der*
bologna [bə'ləʊnjə] *n. (Amer.)* ~ **[sausage]** ≈ Mortadella, *die*
boloney [bə'ləʊnɪ] *n.* **a)** *(sl.)* Quatsch, *der (ugs.);* **b)** *(Amer.: sausage) see* **bologna**
Bolshevik ['bɒlʃɪvɪk] *n.* **a)** *(Hist.)* Bolschewik, *der;* **b)** *(coll.: revolutionary)* Bolschewist, *der*/Bolschewistin, *die (ugs.)*
Bolshie, Bolshy ['bɒlʃɪ] *adj. (sl.: uncooperative)* aufsässig; rotzig *(salopp)*
bolster ['bəʊlstə(r)] **1.** *n. (pillow)* Nackenrolle, *die; (wedge-shaped)* Keilkissen, *das.* **2.** *v. t. (fig.)* stärken; ~ **sb. up** jmdm. Mut machen; ~ **sth. up** etw. stärken; ~ **up a regime/one's status** ein Regime stützen/seinen Status aufpolieren *(ugs.)*
[1]bolt [bəʊlt] **1.** *n.* **a)** *(on door or window)* Riegel, *der; (on gun)* Kammerverschluß, *der;* **b)** *(metal pin)* Schraube, *die; (without thread)* Bolzen, *der;* **c)** *(of crossbow)* Bolzen, *der;* **shoot one's** ~ *(fig.)* sein Pulver verschießen; **d)** ~ **[of lightning]** Blitz[strahl], *der;* **[like] a** ~ **from the blue** *(fig.)* wie ein Blitz aus heiterem Himmel; **e)** *(sudden dash)* **make a** ~ **for freedom** einen Fluchtversuch machen; **make a** ~ **for it** das Weite suchen. **2.** *v. i.* **a)** davonlaufen; ‹*Pferd:*› durchgehen; ‹*Fuchs, Kaninchen:*› [mit einem Satz] flüchten; ~ **out of the shop** aus dem Laden rennen; **b)** *(Hort., Agric.)* vorzeitig Samen bilden; ‹*Salat, Kohl:*› schießen; **c)** *(Amer. Polit.)* abspringen *(ugs.).* **3.** *v. t.* **a)** *(fasten with* ~*)* verriegeln; ~ **sb. in/out** jmdn. einsperren/aussperren; **b)** *(fasten with* ~*s with/without thread)* verschrauben/mit Bolzen verbinden; ~ **sth. to sth.** etw. an etw. *(Akk.)* schrauben/mit Bolzen befestigen; **c)** *(gulp down)* ~ **[down]** hinunterschlingen ‹*Essen*›; hinunterstürzen ‹*Getränk*›; **d)** aufjagen ‹*Fuchs, Kaninchen usw.*›. **4.** *adv.* ~ **upright** kerzengerade
[2]bolt *v. t. (sift)* sieben
bolt: ~**-hole** *n. (lit. or fig.)* Schlupfloch, *das;* ~**-on** *adj.* aufschraubbar
Bolzano [bɒl'zɑ:nəʊ] *pr. n.* Bozen *(das)*
bomb [bɒm] **1.** *n.* **a)** Bombe, *die;* **go like a** ~ *(fig. coll.)* ein Bombenerfolg sein; **my new car goes like a** ~: mein neues Auto ist die reinste Rakete; **go down a** ~ **with** *(fig. sl.)* ein Bombenerfolg sein bei; **b)** *(sl.: large sum of money)* **a** ~: 'ne Masse Geld *(ugs.);* **c)** *(Amer. coll.: failure)* Reinfall, *der (ugs.).* **2.** *v. t.* bombardieren; ~ **a pub** einen Bombenanschlag auf eine Kneipe verüben. **3.** *v. i.* **a)** Bomben werfen; ~**ing raid** Bombenangriff, *der;* **b)** *(sl.: fail)* durchfallen; **c)** *(sl.: travel fast)* rasen
~ **'out** *v. t.* ausbomben
bombard [bɒm'bɑ:d] *v. t. (Mil.)* beschießen; bombardieren *(veralt.); (fig.)* bombardieren
bombardier [bɒmbə'dɪə(r)] *n. (Brit. Mil.)* Unteroffizier [bei der Artillerie]
bombardment [bɒm'bɑ:dmənt] *n.* Beschuß, *der;* Bombardierung, *die (veralt.); (fig.)* Bombardierung, *die*
bombast ['bɒmbæst] *n., no pl.* Schwulst, *der;* Bombast, *der*
bombastic [bɒm'bæstɪk] *adj.* bombastisch; schwülstig
bomb: ~**-bay** *n.* Bombenschacht, *der;* ~**-disposal** *n.* Räumung von Bomben; ~**-disposal expert** Experte für die Räumung von Bomben; ~**-disposal squad** Bombenräumkommando, *das*
bombe [bɔ̃b] *n. (Gastr.)* Eisbombe, *die*
bomber ['bɒmə(r)] *n.* **a)** *(Air Force)* Bomber, *der (ugs.);* **b)** *(terrorist)* Bombenattentäter, *der*/-attentäterin, *die;* Bombenleger, *der*/-legerin, *die (ugs.)*
'bomber jacket *n.* Bomberjacke, *die*
bombing ['bɒmɪŋ] *n.* Bombardierung, *die*
bomb: ~**-proof** *adj.* bombenfest; ~ **scare** *n.* Bombendrohung, *die;* ~**-shell** *n.* Bombe, *die; (fig.)* Sensation, *die;* **come as a** *or* **be something of a** ~**-shell** wie eine Bombe einschlagen; **a blonde** ~**-shell** eine Superblondine; ~**-site** *n.* Trümmergrundstück, *das; (larger area)* Trümmerfeld, *das*
bona fide [bəʊnə 'faɪdɪ] **1.** *adj. (genuine)* echt; *(sincere)* ehrlich; redlich; ~ **contract** in gutem Glauben abgeschlossener Vertrag; ~ **purchaser** gutgläubiger Erwerber. **2.** *adv. (genuinely)* wahrhaftig; *(sincerely)* ehrlich; redlich; *(in good faith)* in gutem Glauben; bona fide *(geh.)*
bonanza [bə'nænzə] **1.** *n.* **a)** *(unexpected success)* Goldgrube, *die (fig.);* **b)** *(large output)* reiche Ausbeute. **2.** *adj.* äußerst ertragreich ‹*Farm, Geschäftsjahr*›
bon-bon ['bɒnbɒn] *n.* Praliné, *das*
bonce [bɒns] *n. (Brit. sl.: head)* Birne, *die (salopp)*
bond [bɒnd] **1.** *n.* **a)** Band, *das;* **b)** *in pl. (shackles, lit. or fig.)* Fesseln; Bande *(dichter. veralt.);* **c)** *(uniting force)* Band, *das;* **d)** *(adhesion)* **the** ~ **will be instantaneous/unbreakable** die Haftwirkung wird sofort eintreten/die Teile werden absolut fest aneinanderkleben; **e)** *(Commerc.) (debenture)* Anleihe, *die;* Schuldverschreibung, *die; (deed)* Schuldschein, *der;* **goods in** ~: Waren unter Zollverschluß; **f)** *(agreement)* Übereinkommen, *das; (covenant)* Bund, *der;* **my word is [as good as] my** ~: was ich verspreche, das halte ich auch; **g)** *(Insurance)* ≈ Vertrauensschadenversicherung, *die;* **h)** *(Building)* [Mauer]verband, *der;* **English** ~: Blockverband, *der;* **i)** *see* **bond paper; j)** *(Chem.)* Bindung, *die.* **2.** *v. t.* **a)** *(join securely)* zusammenfügen **(to** mit); **b)** *(Building)* im Verband legen; **c)** *(Commerc.)* unter Zollverschluß nehmen; *see also* **bonded a**
bondage ['bɒndɪdʒ] *n., no pl.* Sklaverei, *die (auch fig.); (sexual perversion)* Bondage, *das;* Fesseln, *das;* **in** ~ **to sb.** als jmds. Sklave/Sklavin *(auch fig.)*
bonded ['bɒndɪd] *adj.* **a)** *(Commerc.)* unter Zollverschluß; ~ **goods** Zollagergut, *das;* ~ **warehouse** Zollager, *das;* ~ **debt** fundierte Schuld *(Finanzw.);* **b)** *(cemented, reinforced)* verstärkt
'bond: ~**paper** *n.* Dokumentenpapier, *das; (for general use)* feines Schreibpapier; ~**stone** *n. (Building)* Binder, *der;* ~**-washing** *n. (Finance) Umwandlung von zu versteuernden Dividendengewinnen in steuerfreie Kapitalerträge*
bone [bəʊn] **1.** *n.* **a)** Knochen, *der; (of fish)* Gräte, *die;* ~**s** *(fig.: remains)* Gebeine *Pl. (geh.);* **be chilled to the** ~ *(fig.)* völlig durchgefroren sein; **cut prices to the** ~: die Preise äußerst scharf kalkulieren; **pare expenditure to the** ~: sich radikal einschränken; **work one's fingers to the** ~ *(fig.)* bis zum Umfallen arbeiten; **I feel it in my** ~**s** *(fig.)* ich habe es im Gefühl; **make old** ~**s** *(fig.)* alt werden; **the bare** ~**s** *(fig.)* die wesentlichen Punkte; *(of a story)* die Grundzüge; **close to the** *or* **near the** ~ *(fig.) (indecent)* gewagt; *(destitute)* am Rande des Existenzminimums; **come** *or* **get close to** *or* **near the** ~ *(fig.)* [ziemlich] gewagt sein; *see also* **dry 1 a; b)** *(material)* Knochen, *der; (ivory)* Elfenbein, *das;* **c)** *(stiffener) (in collar)* Kragenstäbchen, *das; (in corset)* Korsettstange, *die;* **d)** *(subject of dispute)* **have/find a** ~ **to pick with sb.** mit jmdm. ein Hühnchen zu rupfen haben *(ugs.)* /einen Grund finden, mit jmdm. Streit anzufangen; ~ **of contention** Zankapfel, *der;* **make no** ~**s about sth./doing sth.** keinen Hehl aus etw. machen/sich nicht scheuen, etw. zu tun. **2.** *v. t.* den/die Knochen herauslösen aus, ausbeinen ‹*Fleisch, Geflügel*›; entgräten ‹*Fisch*›. **3.** *v. i.* ~ **up on sth.** *(Amer. coll.)* etw. büffeln *(ugs.)*
bone: ~ **'china** *n.* Knochenporzellan, *das;* ~**-'dry** *adj.* knochentrocken *(ugs.);* ~**fish** *n. (Amer.)* Grätenfisch, *der;* ~**head** *n. (sl.)* Holzkopf, *der (salopp abwertend);* ~**-headed** *adj. (sl.)* blöd *(ugs. abwertend);* ~**-'idle,** ~ **'lazy** *adjs.* stinkfaul *(salopp);* ~ **marrow** *n. (Anat.)* Knochenmark, *das;* ~**-meal** *n.* Knochenmehl, *das*
boner ['bəʊnə(r)] *n. (sl.)* grober Schnitzer; **pull a** ~: sich *(Dat.)* einen groben Schnitzer leisten
bone: ~**-shaker** *n.* Klapperkiste, *die (salopp);* ~ **'weary** *adj.* völlig erschöpft
bonfire ['bɒnfaɪə(r)] *n.* **a)** *(at celebration)* Freudenfeuer, *das;* **B~ Night** *(Brit.)* [Abend des] Guy Fawkes Day *(mit Feuerwerk);* **b)** *(for burning rubbish)* Feuer, *das;* **make a** ~ **of sth.** *(lit. or fig.)* etw. verbrennen
bongo ['bɒŋgəʊ] *n., pl.* ~**s** *or* ~**es** *(drum)* Bongo, *das od. die*
bonhomie ['bɒnəmi:] *n., no pl.* Bonhomie, *die (geh.);* Jovialität, *die*
bonk [bɒŋk] *(Brit. sl.)* **1.** *v. t.* **a)** hauen; **b)** *(copulate with)* bumsen *(salopp).* **2.** *v. i. (copulate)* bumsen *(salopp)*
bonkers ['bɒŋkəz] *adj. (sl.)* verrückt *(salopp);* wahnsinnig *(ugs.);* **go** ~: überschnappen *(ugs.);* **be** ~: spinnen *(ugs. abwertend)*
bon mot [bɔ̃ 'məʊ, bɒn 'məʊ] *n., pl.* **bons mots** [bɔ̃ 'məʊ, bɒn 'məʊ] Bonmot, *das*
bonnet ['bɒnɪt] *n.* **a)** *(woman's)* Haube, *die;* Bonnet, *das (hist.); (child's)* Häubchen, *das; (Scotch cap)* [Schotten]mütze, *die; see also* **bee a; b)** *(Brit. Motor Veh.)* Motor- *od.* Kühlerhaube, *die*
bonny ['bɒnɪ] *adj.* **a)** *(fine)* prächtig ‹*Bursche, Schiff*›; herrlich ‹*Land, Stadt, Anblick*›; **b)** *(healthy-looking)* prächtig ‹*Baby*›; gesund ‹*Gesicht*›; **c)** *(Scot. and N. Engl.: comely)* hübsch
bonsai ['bɒnsaɪ] *n.* **a)** *(tree)* Bonsai[baum], *der;* **b)** *no pl., no art. (method)* Bonsai, *das*
bonus ['bəʊnəs] *n.* **a)** zusätzliche Leistung; **b)** *(to shareholders, insurance-policy holder)* Bonus, *der; (to employee)* **Christmas** ~: Weihnachtsgratifikation, *die;* **cost-of-living** ~: Teuerungszulage, *die;* **production** ~: Leistungsprämie, *die;* **c)** *(advantage)* Pluspunkt, *der*
bon vivant [bɔ̃ vi:'vɑ̃] *n., pl.* **bon vivants** *or* **bons vivants** [bɔ̃ vi:'vɑ̃] Gourmet, *der;* Feinschmecker, *der*
bon voyage [bɔ̃ vwɑ:'jɑ:ʒ] *int.* glückliche Reise
bony ['bəʊnɪ] *adj.* **a)** *(of bone)* beinern; knöchern; Knochen-; *(like bone)* knochenartig; **b)** *(big-boned)* grobknochig; **c)** *(skinny)* knochendürr *(ugs.);* spindeldürr; **d)** *(full of bones)* grätig ‹*Fisch*›; ‹*Fleisch*› mit viel Knochen; **be** ~: viele Gräten/Knochen haben
boo [bu:] **1.** *int. to surprise sb.* huh; *expr. disapproval, contempt* buh; **he wouldn't say '~' to a goose** er ist sehr schüchtern; **cries of '~'**: Buhrufe. **2.** *n.* Buh, *das (ugs.).* **3.** *v. t.* ausbuhen *(ugs.);* **he was** ~**ed off the stage** er wurde so ausgebuht, daß er die Bühne verließ *(ugs.).* **4.** *v. i.* buhen *(ugs.)*
boob [bu:b] *(Brit. sl.)* **1.** *n.* **a)** *(mistake)* Fehler, *der;* Schnitzer, *der (ugs.);* **b)** *(simpleton)* Dussel, *der (salopp);* Blödian, *der (ugs. abwertend);* **c)** *(breast)* Titte, *die (derb).* **2.** *v. i.* einen Schnitzer machen *(ugs.)*
booboo ['bu:bu:] *(coll.) see* **boob 1 a**
booby ['bu:bɪ] *n.* **a)** Trottel, *der (ugs. abwertend);* **b)** *(Ornith.)* Tölpel, *der*
booby: ~**hatch** *n. (Amer. sl.)* Klapsmühle, *die (salopp);* ~ **prize** *n. Preis für den schlechtesten Teilnehmer an einem Wettbewerb;* ~ **trap** *n.* **a)** *Falle, mit der man jmdm. einen Streich spielen will;* **b)** *(Mil.)* versteckte Sprengladung; ~**-trap** *v. t.* **a)** [für einen Streich] präparieren; **b)** *(Mil.)* **the bomb/the**

door had been ~-trapped die Bombe war präpariert worden/an der Tür war eine versteckte Sprengladung angebracht worden
boodle ['bu:dl] *n. (sl.)* Zaster, *der (salopp); (for bribery)* Schmiergeld, *das (ugs.)*
book [bʊk] **1.** *n.* **a)** Buch, *das;* **in ~ form** in Buchform; als Buch; **be a closed ~ [to sb.]** *(fig.)* [jmdm. *od.* für jmdn.] ein Buch mit sieben Siegeln sein; **the ~ of Job** das Buch Hiob; **the ~ of fate** *(fig.)* das Schicksal; **the ~ of life** *(fig.)* das Buch des Lebens *(Rel.);* das Lebensbuch *(Rel.);* **the [Good] B~** das Buch der Bücher; die Bibel; **throw the ~ at sb.** *(fig.)* jmdn. kräftig zusammenstauchen *(ugs.);* **bring to ~** *(fig.)* zur Rechenschaft ziehen; **in my ~** *(fig.)* meiner Ansicht *od.* Meinung nach; **it won't suit my ~** *(fig.)* es paßt mir nicht; **be in sb.'s good/bad ~s** *(fig.)* bei jmdm. gut/schlecht angeschrieben sein; **that's not in the ~** *(fig. coll.)* das geht nicht; **I can read you like a ~** *(fig.)* ich kann in dir lesen wie in einem Buch; **do sth.** *or* **play it/speak by the ~** *(fig.)* sich an die Regeln halten/ganz korrekte Angaben machen; **speak** *or* **talk like a ~** *(fig.)* sich geschraubt ausdrücken *(ugs. abwertend);* **take a leaf out of sb.'s ~** *(fig.)* sich *(Dat.)* jmdn. zum Vorbild nehmen; **you could take a leaf out of his ~:** du könntest dir von ihm eine Scheibe abschneiden *(ugs.); see also* **black books; open 1k; b)** *(for accounts)* Konto- *od.* Rechnungsbuch, *das; (for notes)* [Notiz]buch, *das; (for exercises)* [Schreib]heft, *das;* **c)** *(telephone directory)* Telefonbuch, *das;* **be in the ~:** im Telefonbuch stehen; **d)** *(coll.: magazine)* Magazin, *das;* Illustrierte, *die;* **e)** *in pl. (records, accounts)* Bücher; **do the ~s** die Abrechnung machen; **balance the ~s** die Bilanz machen *od.* ziehen; *see also* **keep 1h; f)** *in pl. (list of members)* **be on the ~s** auf der [Mitglieds]liste *od.* im Mitgliederverzeichnis stehen; **g)** *(record of bets)* Wettbuch, *das;* **make** *or* **keep a ~ on sth.** Wetten auf etw. *(Akk.)* annehmen; **h) ~ of tickets** Fahrscheinheft, *das;* **~ of stamps/matches** Briefmarkenheft/Streichholzbriefchen, *das;* **~ of samples** Musterbuch, *das;* **i)** *(in poem)* Gesang, *der;* **j)** *(libretto)* Textbuch, *das; (play-script)* Textvorlage, *die;* **~ of words** Textbuch, *das; (fig.)* Arbeitsanweisungen *Pl.* **2.** *v. t.* **a)** *(engage in advance)* buchen ⟨*Reise, Flug, Platz [im Flugzeug]*⟩; [vor]bestellen ⟨*Eintrittskarte, Tisch, Zimmer, Platz [im Theater]*⟩; anmelden ⟨*Telefongespräch*⟩; engagieren, verpflichten ⟨*Künstler, Orchester*⟩; **be fully ~ed** ⟨*Vorstellung:*⟩ ausverkauft sein; ⟨*Flug[zeug]:*⟩ ausgebucht sein; ⟨*Hotel:*⟩ voll belegt *od.* ausgebucht sein; **b)** *(enter in ~)* eintragen; *(for offence)* aufschreiben *(ugs.)* **(for** wegen); **c)** *(issue ticket to)* **we are ~ed on a flight to Athens** man hat für uns einen Flug nach Athen gebucht. **3.** *v. i.* buchen; *(for travel, performance)* vorbestellen
~ 'in 1. *v. i.* sich eintragen; **we ~ed in at the Ritz** wir sind im Ritz abgestiegen. **2.** *v. t.* **a)** *(make reservation for)* Zimmer/ein Zimmer vorbestellen *od.* reservieren für; **we're ~ed in at the Dorchester** unsere Zimmer sind im Dorchester reserviert; **b)** *(register)* eintragen
~ 'up 1. *v. i.* buchen. **2.** *v. t.* buchen; **the guest-house is ~ed up** die Pension ist ausgebucht *od.* voll belegt
bookable ['bʊkəbl] *adj.* **be ~:** vorbestellt werden können; ⟨*Flug, Urlaub:*⟩ gebucht werden können
book: ~binder *n.* Buchbinder, *der*/-binderin, *die;* **~binding** *n., no pl.* Buchbinderei, *die;* **~case** *n.* Bücherschrank, *der;* **~ club** *n.* Buchklub, *der;* Buchgemeinschaft, *die;* **~-ends** *n. pl.* Buchstützen
bookie ['bʊkɪ] *n. (coll.)* Buchmacher, *der*
booking ['bʊkɪŋ] *n.* **a)** Buchung, *die; (of ticket)* Bestellung, *die; (of table, room, seat)* Vorbestellung, *die;* **~ for the concert opens today** der Vorverkauf für das Konzert beginnt heute; **make/cancel a ~:** buchen/eine Buchung rückgängig machen; *(for tickets)* bestellen/abbestellen; **change one's ~:** umbuchen; *(for tickets)* umbestellen; **b)** *(of performer)* Engagement, *das*
booking: ~-clerk *n.* Schalterbeamte, *der*/-beamtin, *die;* Fahrkartenverkäufer, *der*/-verkäuferin, *die;* **~-hall** *n.* Schalterhalle, *die;* **~-office** *n. (in station)* [Fahrkarten]schalter, *der; (in theatre)* [Theater]kasse, *die; (selling tickets in advance)* Vorverkaufsstelle, *die*
bookish ['bʊkɪʃ] *adj.* **a)** *(studious)* gelehrt; *(addicted to reading)* **be ~:** ein Bücherwurm sein; **b)** *(as in books)* schriftsprachlich; papieren *(abwertend)*
book: ~-jacket *n.* Schutzumschlag, *der;* **~keeper** *n.* Buchhalter, *der*/Buchhalterin, *die;* **~keeping** *n.* Buchführung, *die;* Buchhaltung, *die*
booklet ['bʊklɪt] *n.* Broschüre, *die*
book: ~-lover *n.* Bücherfreund, *der;* **~maker** *n. (in betting)* Buchmacher, *der;* **~making** *n., no pl.* **a)** *(in betting)* Buchmacherei, *die;* **b)** *(compiling books)* Kompilation, *die;* **~man** *n.* Literat, *der;* **~mark[er]** *ns.* Lese- *od.* Buchzeichen, *das;* **~mobile** ['bʊkməbi:l] *n. (Amer.)* Fahrbücherei, *die;* **~ page** *n.* **a)** *(in newspaper) Seite mit Buchrezensionen;* ≈ Literaturseite, *die;* **b)** *(page of book)* Buchseite, *die;* **~-plate** *n.* Exlibris, *das;* **~-post** *n., no pl.* Büchersendung, *die;* **~-rest** *n. Halter für das aufgeschlagene Buch;* **~ review** *n.* Buchbesprechung, *die;* **~seller** *n.* Buchhändler, *der*/-händlerin, *die;* **~shelf** *n.* Bücherbord, *das;* **on my ~shelves** in meinen Bücherregalen; **~shop** *n.* Buchhandlung, *die;* Buchladen, *der;* **~stall** *n.* Bücherstand, *der;* **~store** *(Amer.) see* **~shop**
booksy ['bʊksɪ] *adj. (coll.)* hochgestochen *(ugs. abwertend)* ⟨*Stil, Ausdruck, Konversation*⟩; hochgelahrt *(scherzh.)* ⟨*Person*⟩
book: ~ token *n.* Büchergutschein, *der;* **~-trough** *n.* Bücherständer, *der;* **~ value** *n. (Bookk.)* Buchwert, *der;* **~work** *n.* Bücherstudium, *das;* **~worm** *n. (lit. or fig.)* Bücherwurm, *der*
¹boom [bu:m] *n.* **a)** *(for camera or microphone)* Ausleger, *der;* **b)** *(Naut.)* Baum, *der;* **c)** *(floating barrier)* [schwimmende] Absperrung
²boom 1. *v. i.* **a)** dröhnen; ⟨*Kanone, Wellen, Brandung:*⟩ dröhnen, donnern; ⟨*Vogel:*⟩ [dumpf] rufen; **b)** ⟨*Geschäft, Verkauf, Stadt, Gebiet:*⟩ sich sprunghaft entwickeln; ⟨*Preise, Aktien:*⟩ rapide steigen. **2.** *n.* **a)** *(of person)* Gebrüll, *das; (of gun, waves)* Dröhnen, *das;* Donnern, *das; (of bird)* [dumpfes] Rufen; [dumpfer] Ruf; **b)** *(in business)* [sprunghafter] Aufschwung; Boom, *der; (in prices)* [rapider] Anstieg; *attrib.* **a ~ area** ein Gebiet, das sich sprunghaft entwickelt; **a ~ year** ein Boomjahr; **c)** *(period of economic expansion)* Hochkonjunktur, *die;* Boom, *der; attrib.* **the ~ years** die Jahre der Hochkonjunktur
~ 'out 1. *v. i.* ⟨*Stimme:*⟩ dröhnen; ⟨*Kanone:*⟩ donnern, dröhnen. **2.** *v. t.* brüllen ⟨*Kommando, Befehl*⟩
boomerang ['bu:məræŋ] **1.** *n. (lit. or fig.)* Bumerang, *der.* **2.** *v. i. (fig.)* sich als Bumerang erweisen
'boom town *n. Stadt in sprunghaftem Aufschwung*
boon [bu:n] *n.* **a)** *(blessing)* Segen, *der;* Wohltat, *die;* **be a tremendous ~** *or* **a ~ and a blessing to sb.** ein wahrer Segen für jmdn. sein; **b)** *(request, favour)* Gunst, *die (geh.)*
'boon companion *n.* Kumpan, *der*
boondoggle ['bu:ndɒgl] *(Amer.)* **1.** *n.* sinnlose Arbeit. **2.** *v. i.* sinnlos arbeiten
boor [bʊə(r)] *n.* Rüpel, *der (abwertend)*
boorish ['bʊərɪʃ] *adj.,* **boorishly** ['bʊərɪʃlɪ] *adv.* flegelhaft *(abwertend);* rüpelhaft *(abwertend)*
boorishness ['bʊərɪʃnɪs] *n., no pl.* Flegelei, *die (abwertend);* Rüpelei, *die (abwertend)*
boost [bu:st] **1.** *v. t.* **a)** steigern; ankurbeln ⟨*Wirtschaft*⟩; in die Höhe treiben ⟨*Preis, Wert, Aktienkurs*⟩; stärken, heben ⟨*Selbstvertrauen, Moral*⟩; *(increase reputation of)* aufbauen; *(recommend vigorously)* anpreisen; **b)** *(coll.: push from below)* hochschieben; hochheben; **c)** *(Electr.)* erhöhen ⟨*Spannung*⟩; **d)** *(Radio)* verstärken ⟨*Signal*⟩. **2.** *n.* Auftrieb, *der; (increase)* Zunahme, *die;* **give sb./sth. a ~:** jmdn./einer Sache Auftrieb geben; **be given a ~:** Auftrieb erhalten; **give sales/production a ~:** den Verkauf/die Produktion ankurbeln
booster ['bu:stə(r)] *n.* **a)** *(Med.)* **~ [shot** *or* **injection]** Auffrischimpfung, *die;* **b)** *(Astronaut.)* **~ [rocket/motor]** Starthilfsrakete, *die*/Starthilfstriebwerk, *das*
¹boot [bu:t] **1.** *n.* **a)** Stiefel, *der;* **get the ~** *(fig. coll.)* rausgeschmissen werden *(ugs.);* **give sb. the ~** *(fig. coll.)* jmdn. rausschmeißen *(ugs.);* **give sb. a ~ up the backside** *(fig. coll.)* jmdm. den Marsch blasen *(salopp);* **as tough as old ~s** *(fig. sl.)* zäh wie Leder; **put the ~ in** *(sl.)* ihn/sie *usw.* [brutal] treten; **put the ~ in!** *(sl.)* tritt ihn/sie *usw.* zusammen! *(ugs.);* **the ~ is on the other foot** *(fig.)* es ist genau umgekehrt; **you can bet your ~s that ...** *(fig. sl.)* ..., darauf kannst du Gift nehmen *(ugs.); see also* **big 1g; ¹die 1a; heart 1c; b)** *(Brit.: of car)* Kofferraum, *der;* **c)** *(Hist.: torture)* spanischer Stiefel. **2.** *v. t.* **a)** *(coll.)* treten; kicken *(ugs.)* ⟨*Ball*⟩; **~ sb. out** *(fig. coll.)* jmdn. rausschmeißen *(ugs.);* **b)** *(Computing)* **~ [up]** laden
²boot *n.* **to ~:** noch dazu; obendrein
'bootblack *(Amer.) see* **shoeblack**
booted ['bu:tɪd] *adj.* gestiefelt
bootee [bu:'ti:] *n. (infant's)* Babyschuh, *der; (woman's)* Stiefelette, *die*
booth [bu:ð] *n.* **a)** Bude, *die;* **b)** *(telephone ~)* Telefonzelle, *die;* **c)** *(polling-~)* Wahlkabine, *die*
'bootleg 1. *v. t.* schmuggeln; *(sell/make)* schwarz *(ugs.) od.* illegal verkaufen/brennen. **2.** *adj.* geschmuggelt; *(sold/made)* schwarz *(ugs.) od.* illegal verkauft/gebrannt
bootlegger ['bu:tlegə(r)] *n. see* **bootleg 1:** Schmuggler, *der;* Schwarzhändler *der;* Schwarzbrenner, *der*
'bootlicker *n. (derog.)* Speichellecker, *der (abwertend)*
boots [bu:ts] *n. sing. (Brit. dated)* Hausbursche, *der*
boot: ~ sale *n. (Brit.) eine Art Flohmarkt, bei dem die Verkaufsgegenstände im Kofferraum des Autos ausgelegt werden;* **~strap** *n. (Computing)* Bootstrapping, *das;* **~straps** *n. pl.* **pull oneself up** *or* **raise oneself by one's own ~straps** *(fig.)* sich aus eigener Kraft hocharbeiten
booty ['bu:tɪ] *n., no pl.* Beute, *die*
booze [bu:z] *(coll.)* **1.** *v. i.* saufen *(derb).* **2.** *n., no pl.* **a)** *(drink)* Alkohol, *der;* **b)** *(drinking-bout)* Besäufnis, *das (salopp);* **go/be on the ~:** [einen] saufen gehen/saufen *(derb)*
boozer ['bu:zə(r)] *n.* **a)** *(coll.: one who boozes)* Säufer, *der*/Säuferin, *die (derb);* **b)** *(Brit. sl.: public house)* Kneipe, *die (ugs.)*
'booze-up *n. (coll.)* Besäufnis, *das (salopp);* **have a ~:** einen heben *(ugs.)*
boozy ['bu:zɪ] *adj. (coll.)* betrunken; blau *nicht attr. (ugs.); (addicted to drink)* versoffen *(salopp)*
bop [bɒp] *(coll.)* **1.** *v. i. (zur Popmusik)* tanzen. **2.** *n.* Tanz, *der (zur Popmusik);* **have a ~:** tanzen; **put on a ~:** eine Tanzfete *(ugs.)* veranstalten
bopper ['bɒpə(r)] *n. (coll.) jmd., der zur Popmusik tanzt*

borage ['bɒrɪdʒ] *n. (Bot.)* Borretsch, *der*
borax ['bɔːræks] *n. (Chem.)* Borax, *der*
Bordeaux [bɔː'dəʊ] *n., pl. same* [bɔː'dəʊz] Bordeaux[wein], *der*
bordel [bɔː'del], **bordello** [bɔː'deləʊ] *ns., pl. ~s (Amer.)* Bordell, *das*
border ['bɔːdə(r)] **1.** *n.* **a)** Rand, *der; (of table-cloth, handkerchief, dress)* Bordüre, *die;* **b)** *(of country)* Grenze, *die;* **the B~[s]** die Grenze; **north of the B~** *(in Scotland)* in Schottland; **c)** *(flower-bed)* Rabatte, *die; see also* **herbaceous. 2.** *attrib. adj.* Grenz⟨*stadt, -gebiet, -streit*⟩. **3.** *v. t.* **a)** *(adjoin)* [an]grenzen an (+ *Akk.*); **be ~ed by** [an]grenzen an (+ *Akk.*); **b)** *(put a ~ to, act as ~ to)* umranden; einfassen; **c)** *(resemble closely)* grenzen an (+ *Akk.*). **4.** *v. i.* **~ on** *see* **3 a, c**
borderer ['bɔːdərə(r)] *n.* Grenzbewohner, *der*/-bewohnerin, *die*
border: ~land Grenzgebiet, *das; (fig.)* Grenzbereich, *der;* **~line 1.** *n.* Grenzlinie, *die; (fig.)* Grenze, *die;* **2.** *adj.* **sb./sth. is ~line** *(fig.)* jmd. ist/etw. liegt auf der Grenze; **a ~line case/candidate/type** *(fig.)* ein Grenzfall; **B~ terrier** *n.* Borderterrier, *der*
[1]**bore** [bɔː(r)] **1.** *v. t. (make hole in)* bohren; **~ the rock/the wood** ein Loch in das Gestein/das Holz bohren; **~ rock/wood** Gestein/Holz bohren; **~ one's way through sth.** sich durch etw. hindurchbohren. **2.** *v. i. (drill)* bohren (**for** nach). **3.** *n.* **a)** *(of firearm, engine cylinder)* Bohrung, *die (Technik); (of tube, pipe)* Innendurchmesser, *der;* **b)** *(calibre)* Kaliber, *das;* **c)** *see* **borehole**
[2]**bore 1.** *n.* **a)** *(nuisance)* **it's a real ~:** es ist wirklich ärgerlich; **what a ~!** wie ärgerlich!; **she is a real ~:** sie kann einem wirklich auf die Nerven gehen; **b)** *(dull person)* Langweiler, *der (ugs. abwertend).* **2.** *v. t. (weary)* langweilen; **sb. is ~d with sth.** etw. langweilt jmdn.; **sb. is ~d with life** jmdn. ödet alles an *(ugs.);* **I'm ~d** ich langweile mich; ich habe Langeweile; **~ sb. to death** *or* **to tears** *(coll.)* jmdn. zu Tode langweilen
[3]**bore** *n. (tide-wave)* Flutbrandung, *die;* Bore, *die*
[4]**bore** *see* [2]**bear**
boredom ['bɔːdəm] *n., no pl.* Langeweile, *die;* **with a look of utter ~ on one's face** mit einem völlig gelangweilten Gesichtsausdruck
'**borehole** *n.* Bohrloch, *das*
borer ['bɔːrə(r)] *n. (tool)* Bohrer, *der*
boring ['bɔːrɪŋ] *adj.* langweilig
born [bɔːn] **1. be ~:** geboren werden; **I was ~ in England** ich bin *od.* wurde in England geboren; **he was ~ of rich parents** *or* **~ rich** er war das Kind reicher Eltern; **he was ~ into a rich family** er wurde in eine reiche Familie hineingeboren; **a new era was ~:** eine neue Ära brach an; **be ~ again** *(fig.)* wiedergeboren werden; **I wasn't ~ yesterday** *(fig.)* ich bin nicht von gestern *(ugs.);* **there's one ~ every minute** *(coll.)* die Dummen werden nicht alle; **be ~ of sth.** *(fig.)* aus etw. entstehen; **be ~ blind/lucky** blind von Geburt sein/ein Glückskind sein; **be ~ a poet** zum Dichter geboren sein; **be ~ to sth.** *(fig.)* zu etw. geboren *od.* bestimmt sein; **be ~ to command** zum Befehlen geboren sein; **sb. is ~ to be hanged** jmdm. ist ein schlimmes Ende vorbestimmt. **2.** *adj.* **a)** geboren; **you don't know you are ~** *(coll.)* du kannst dich nicht beklagen; **~ again** *(fig.)* wiedergeboren; **in all my ~ days** *(fig. coll.)* in meinem ganzen Leben; mein Lebtag *(ugs. veralt.); see also* **breed 1 c; b)** *(destined to be)* **be a ~ orator** *or* **an orator ~:** der geborene Redner *od.* zum Redner geboren sein; **c)** *(complete)* **a ~ fool** ein völliger Narr
borne *see* [2]**bear**
boron ['bɔːrɒn] *n. (Chem.)* Bor, *das*
borough ['bʌrə] *n.* **a)** *(Brit. Hist.: town with corporation)* Borough, *das; Stadt mit Selbstverwaltung;* **the ~ of Brighton** ≈ die Stadt Brighton; **b)** *(Brit.: town sending members to Parliament)* Borough, *das; Stadt[bezirk] mit Vertretung im Parlament;* **c)** *(Amer.)* **the ~ of ...** *(town)* die Stadt ...; *(village)* die Gemeinde ...
borrow ['bɒrəʊ] **1.** *v. t.* **a)** [sich *(Dat.)*] ausleihen; [sich *(Dat.)*] borgen; entleihen, ausleihen ⟨*Buch, Schallplatte usw. aus der Leihbücherei*⟩; [sich *(Dat.)*] leihen ⟨*Geld von der Bank*⟩; [sich *(Dat.)*] leihen, [sich *(Dat.)*] borgen ⟨*Geld*⟩; **~ sth. from sb.** [sich *(Dat.)*] etw. von *od.* bei jmdm. borgen *od.* [aus]leihen; **b)** *(fig.)* übernehmen ⟨*Idee, Methode, Meinung*⟩; entlehnen ⟨*Wort, Ausdruck aus einer anderen Sprache*⟩; **sb. is living on ~ed time** jmds. Uhr ist abgelaufen. **2.** *v. i.* borgen; *(from bank)* Kredit aufnehmen (**from** bei)
borrowed '**light** *n.* **a)** *(reflected light)* indirektes Licht; **b)** *(internal window)* Innenfenster, *das*
borrower ['bɒrəʊə(r)] *n. (from bank)* Kreditnehmer, *der; (from library)* Entleiher, *der*
borrowing ['bɒrəʊɪŋ] *n. (from bank)* Kreditaufnahme, *die* (**from** bei); *(from library)* Entleihen, *das;* Ausleihen, *das; (fig.)* Übernahme, *die;* **'haute couture' is a ~ from French** „Haute couture" ist eine Entlehnung aus dem Französischen
borsch [bɔːʃ] *n.* Borschtsch, *der*
Borstal ['bɔːstl] *n. (Brit.)* Erziehungsheim, *das;* Besserungsanstalt für jugendliche Straftäter
bortsch [bɔːtʃ] *see* **borsch**
borzoi ['bɔːzɔɪ] *n.* Barsoi, *der*
bosh [bɒʃ] *n., no pl., no indef. art. (sl.)* Quatsch, *der (ugs. abwertend)*
bos'n ['bəʊsn] *see* **boatswain**
Bosnia ['bɒznɪə] *n.* Bosnien *(das)*
Bosnian ['bɒznɪən] *adj.* bosnisch
bosom ['bʊzəm] *n.* **a)** *(person's breast)* Brust, *die;* Busen, *der (dichter. veralt.);* **b)** *(of dress)* ≈ Vorderseite des Oberteils; *(of blouse)* ≈ Vorderteil, *das; (space between breast and garment)* Busen, *der (dichter. veralt.);* **c)** *(fig.: enfolding relationship)* Schoß, *der (geh.);* **in the ~ of one's family** im Schoße der Familie; **a ~ friend** ein guter Freund; ein Busenfreund; **d)** *(fig.: seat of thoughts or emotions)* Brust, *die;* **lay bare one's ~ to sb.** jmdm. sein Herz ausschütten; **e)** *(fig.: surface)* Oberfläche, *die;* **f)** *in pl. (Amer.: breasts)* Busen, *der;* Brüste; **g)** *(Amer.: shirt-front)* Hemdbrust, *die; (as separate garment)* Vorhemd, *das*
bosomy ['bʊzəmɪ] *adj.* vollbusig
Bosphorus ['bɒsfərəs] *pr. n.* Bosporus, *der*
[1]**boss** [bɒs] *n.* **a)** *(metal knob, stud)* Bosse, *die (Kunstwiss.); (on shield)* Schildbuckel, *der od. die;* **b)** *(protuberance)* Verdickung, *die;* **c)** *(Archit.)* Schlußstein, *der*
[2]**boss 1.** *n. (coll.)* **a)** *(master)* Boß, *der (ugs.);* Chef, *der;* **OK, you're the ~:** du bist der Boß; **who's the ~ in your household?** wer bestimmt bei euch zu Hause?; **b)** *(Amer. Polit.)* [Partei]boß, *der (ugs.).* **2.** *v. t. (sl.)* **~ sth.** bei etw. das Sagen haben; **~ sb. [about** *or* **around]** jmdn. herumkommandieren *(ugs.)*
'**boss-eyed** *adj. (coll.)* schielend; **be ~:** schielen
bossiness ['bɒsɪnɪs] *n., no pl.* herrische Art
bossy ['bɒsɪ] *adj. (coll.)* herrisch; **don't be so ~:** hör auf herumzukommandieren *(ugs.)*
bosun, bo'sun ['bəʊsn] *see* **boatswain**
botanical [bə'tænɪkl] *adj.* botanisch; **~ garden[s]** botanischer Garten
botanist ['bɒtənɪst] *n.* Botaniker, *der*/Botanikerin, *die*
botany ['bɒtənɪ] *n., no pl.* Botanik, *die;* Pflanzenkunde, *die*
botch [bɒtʃ] **1.** *n. (bungled work) see* **2 a:** Pfuscherei, *die (ugs. abwertend);* Patzer, *der (ugs.);* **make a ~ of sth.** bei etw. pfuschen *(ugs. abwertend).* **2.** *v. t.* **a)** *(bungle)* pfuschen bei *(ugs. abwertend)* ⟨*Reparatur, Arbeit*⟩; patzen bei *(ugs.)* ⟨*Vortrag, Stabwechsel*⟩; **a ~ed job** eine gepfuschte Arbeit *(ugs. abwertend);* **b)** *(repair badly)* [notdürftig] flicken. **3.** *v. i. see* **2 a:** pfuschen *(ugs. abwertend);* patzen *(ugs.)*
~ 'up *v. t.* **a)** *(bungle)* verpfuschen *(ugs. abwertend);* **b)** *(repair badly)* [notdürftig] flicken
both [bəʊθ] **1.** *adj.* beide; **we ~ like cooking** wir kochen beide gern; **~ these books are expensive** die[se] Bücher sind beide teuer; **~ [the] brothers** beide Brüder; **~ our brothers** unsere beiden Brüder; **~ ways** *(Brit. Racing)* = **each way** *see* **each 1; you can't have it ~ ways** beides [zugleich] geht nicht; *see also* **cut 2 a. 2.** *pron.* beide; **~ [of them] are dead** beide sind tot; **they are ~ dead** sie sind beide tot; **~ of you/them are ...:** ihr seid/sie sind beide ...; **for them ~:** für sie beide; **Love or hate? – B~:** Liebe oder Haß? – Beides; **go along to bed, ~ of you** ihr geht jetzt ins Bett, alle beide. **3.** *adv.* **~ A and B, A and B ~:** sowohl A als [auch] B; **~ brother and sister are dead** sowohl der Bruder als auch die Schwester sind tot; **~ you and I** wir beide; **he and I were ~ there** er und ich waren beide da; **she was ~ singing and playing** sie hat gesungen und zugleich gespielt
bother ['bɒðə(r)] **1.** *v. t.* **a)** *in pass. (take trouble)* **I can't be ~ed [to do it]** ich habe keine Lust[, es zu machen]; **I can't be ~ed with details like that** ich kann mich nicht mit solchen Kleinigkeiten abgeben *od.* befassen; **can't you even be ~ed to dress properly?** kannst du dich nicht einmal richtig anziehen?; **I can't be ~ed with people who ...:** ich habe nichts übrig für Leute, die ...; **b)** *(annoy)* lästig sein *od.* fallen (+ *Dat.*); ⟨*Lärm, Licht:*⟩ stören; ⟨*Schmerz, Wunde, Zahn, Rücken:*⟩ zu schaffen machen (+ *Dat.*); **I'm sorry to ~ you, but ...:** es tut mir leid, daß ich Sie damit belästigen muß, aber ...; **don't ~ me now** laß mich jetzt in Ruhe!; **c)** *(worry)* Sorgen machen (+ *Dat.*); ⟨*Problem, Frage:*⟩ beschäftigen; **I'm not ~ed about him/the money** seinetwegen/wegen des Geldes mache ich mir keine Gedanken; **what's ~ing you/is something ~ing you?** was hast du denn/hast du etwas?; **~ oneself** *or* **one's head about sth.** sich *(Dat.)* über etw. *(Akk.)* den Kopf zerbrechen *(ugs.); see also* **hot 1 f; d)** *(coll.: confound)* **~ it!** wie ärgerlich!; **~ him/her/you/this car!** zum Kuckuck mit ihm/ihr/dir/diesem Auto! **2.** *v. i. (trouble oneself)* **~ to do that** sich damit aufhalten, das zu tun; **don't ~ to do sth.** Sie brauchen etw. nicht zu tun; **she didn't even ~ to ask** sie hielt es nicht mal für nötig, zu fragen; **you needn't have ~ed to come** Sie hätten wirklich nicht zu kommen brauchen; **you needn't/shouldn't have ~ed** das wäre nicht nötig gewesen; **don't ~!** nicht nötig!; **~ with sth./sb.** sich mit etw./jmdm. aufhalten; **~ about sth./sb.** sich *(Dat.)* über etw./jmdn. Gedanken machen. **3.** *n.* **a)** *(nuisance)* **what a ~!** wie ärgerlich!; **it's a real/such a ~:** es ist wirklich lästig; **b)** *(trouble)* Ärger, *der;* **it's no ~ [for me]** es macht mir gar nichts aus; **the children were no ~ at all** wir hatten mit den Kindern überhaupt keine Schwierigkeiten; **have a spot of ~ with sth.** Schwierigkeiten mit etw. haben; **without any ~ at all** ohne irgendwelche Schwierigkeiten; **it's not worth the ~:** es lohnt nicht; **I'm sorry to have put you to all this ~:** es tut mir leid, Ihnen soviel Umstände gemacht zu haben; **if it isn't too much ~:** wenn es nicht zu viel Mühe macht; **go to the ~ of doing sth.** sich *(Dat.)* die Mühe machen, etw. zu tun. **4.** *int. (coll.)* wie ärgerlich!
botheration [bɒðə'reɪʃn] *int. see* **bother 4**
bothersome ['bɒðəsəm] *adj.* lästig; unleidlich ⟨*Kind*⟩
bottle ['bɒtl] **1.** *n.* **a)** Flasche, *die;* **a beer-~:**

eine Bierflasche; **a ~ of beer** eine Flasche Bier; **b)** *(fig. coll.: alcoholic drink)* **be too fond of the ~:** dem Alkohol zu sehr zugetan sein; **be on the ~:** trinken; *see also* **hit 1 k; c)** *(gas cylinder)* **a ~ of gas** eine Gasflasche; **d)** *(Brit. sl.: courage, confidence)* Mumm, *der (ugs.)*; **lose one's ~:** sich *(Dat.)* den Schneid abkaufen lassen *(ugs.)*. **2.** *v. t.* **a)** *(put into ~s)* in Flaschen [ab]füllen; **b)** *(store in ~s)* in Flaschen lagern *od.* aufheben; **~d beer** Flaschenbier, *das;* **~d gas** Flaschengas, *das;* **c)** *(preserve in jars)* einmachen

~ 'up *v. t.* **a)** *(conceal)* in sich *(Dat.)* aufstauen; **b)** *(entrap)* einschließen

bottle: ~ bank *n.* Altglasbehälter, *der;* **~-fed** *adj.* mit der Flasche gefüttert; **~-fed babies** Flaschenkinder

bottleful ['bɒtlfʊl] *n.* **a ~ of shampoo** eine Flasche Schampon

bottle: ~-glass *n.* Flaschenglas, *das;* **~-green 1.** *n.* Flaschengrün, *das;* **2.** *adj.* flaschengrün; **~-neck** *n. (fig.)* Flaschenhals, *der (ugs.)*; *(in production process also)* Engpaß, *der;* **~-opener** *n.* Flaschenöffner, *der;* **~-party** *n.* Bottle-Party, *die;* **~-top** *n.* Flaschenverschluß, *der*

bottom ['bɒtəm] **1.** *n.* **a)** *(lowest part)* unteres Ende; *(of cup, glass, box, chest)* Boden, *der; (of valley, canyon, crevasse, well, shaft)* Sohle, *die; (of canyon, crevasse, well also)* Grund, *der; (of hill, slope, cliff, stairs)* Fuß, *der;* **the ~ of the valley** die Talsohle; **[be] at the ~ of the page/list** unten auf der Seite/Liste [sein]; **[be] in the ~ of the box/glass** am Boden des Kastens/Glases [sein]; unten im Kasten/Glas [sein]; **the ~ of my coat/dress is all muddy** mein Mantel/Kleid ist unten ganz schmutzig; **the book right at the ~ of the pile** das Buch ganz unten im Stapel; **~ up** auf dem Kopf; verkehrt herum; **~s up!** *(coll.)* hoch die Tassen!; **the ~ fell** *or* **dropped out of her world/the market** *(fig.)* für sie brach eine Welt zusammen/der Markt brach zusammen; **knock the ~ out of sth.** *(fig.)* etw. zusammenbrechen lassen; *see also* **false bottom; b)** *(buttocks)* Hinterteil, *das (ugs.)*; Po[dex], *der (fam.)*; **c)** *(of chair)* Sitz, *der;* Sitzfläche, *die;* **d)** *(of sea, lake)* Grund, *der;* **on the ~:** auf dem Grund; **go to the ~:** [ver]sinken; **send a ship to the ~:** ein Schiff in den Grund bohren *od.* versenken; **touch ~:** Grund haben; *(fig.)* den Tiefpunkt erreichen; **e)** *(farthest point)* **at the ~ of the garden/street** hinten im Garten/am Ende der Straße; *see also* **heart 1 b; f)** *(underside)* Unterseite, *die;* **g)** *(fig.)* **start at the ~** ganz unten anfangen; **be ~ of the class/league** der/die Letzte in der Klasse sein/Tabellenletzte[r] sein; **h)** *usu. in pl.* **~[s]** *(of track suit, pyjamas)* Hose, *die;* **i)** *(fig.: basis, origin)* **be at the ~ of sth.** hinter etw. *(Dat.)* stecken *(ugs.)*; einer Sache *(Dat.)* zugrunde liegen; **get to the ~ of sth.** einer Sache *(Dat.)* auf den Grund kommen; **at ~:** im Grunde genommen; **j)** *(Naut.)* Schiffsboden, *der;* **~ up** kieloben; **k)** *(Brit. Motor Veh.)* **in ~:** im ersten Gang. **2.** *adj.* **a)** *(lowest)* unterst...; *(lower)* unter...; **b)** *(fig.: last)* letzt...; **be ~:** der/die/das Letzte sein; **you can bet your/I'd [be willing to] bet my ~ dollar** *(fig. sl.)* jede Wette *(ugs.)*. **3.** *v. i.* **~ [out]** ‹*Preise:*› den tiefsten Stand erreichen; ‹*Rezession, Rückgang:*› den tiefsten Punkt erreichen

bottom: ~ 'dog *see* **underdog; ~ 'drawer** *n. (fig.)* Aussteuer, *die;* **put sth. [away] in one's ~ drawer** etw. für die Aussteuer beiseite legen

bottomless ['bɒtəmlɪs] *adj.* bodenlos; unendlich tief ‹*Meer, Ozean*›; *(fig.: inexhaustible)* unerschöpflich; **the ~ pit** der Abgrund der Hölle

bottom 'line *n. (fig. coll.)* **the ~:** das Fazit

boudoir ['bu:dwɑ:(r)] *n.* Boudoir, *das (veralt.)*; Damenzimmer, *das (veralt.)*

bouffant ['bu:fã] *adj.* voll und duftig, füllig ‹*Haar, Frisur*›; bauschig ‹*Kleidung*›

bough [baʊ] *n.* Ast, *der*

bought *see* **buy 1**

bouillabaisse [bu:jə'beɪs] *n. (Gastr.)* Bouillabaisse, *die*

bouillon ['bu:jɔ̃] *n. (Cookery)* Bouillon, *die;* **~ cube** Brühwürfel, *der*

boulder ['bəʊldə(r)] *n.* Felsbrocken, *der*

'boulder clay *n. (Geol.)* Geschiebelehm, *der; (with many boulders)* Blocklehm, *der*

boulevard ['bu:ləvɑ:d] *n.* Boulevard, *der*

boult *see* **²bolt**

bounce [baʊns] **1.** *v. i.* **a)** ‹*Ball:*› springen; *(on bumpy road)* ‹*Auto:*› holpern; **the ball ~d twice** der Ball sprang zweimal auf; **b)** *(coll.: be rejected by bank)* ‹*Scheck:*› nicht gedeckt sein; **it won't ~:** er ist gedeckt; **c)** *(rush)* **~ about** herumspringen *od.* -hüpfen; **~ into/out of the room** ins/aus dem Zimmer stürmen; **~ in/out** hereinplatzen/hinausstürzen. **2.** *v. t.* **a)** aufspringen lassen ‹*Ball*›; **he ~d the baby on his knee** er ließ das Kind auf den Knien reiten; **b)** *(Amer. sl.: dismiss)* rausschmeißen *(ugs.)*; an die Luft setzen *(ugs.)*. **3.** *n.* **a)** *(rebound)* Aufprall, *der;* **on the ~:** beim Aufprall; **b)** *(rebounding power)* ≈ Elastizität, *die; (fig.: energy)* Schwung, *der;* **there's plenty of/not much ~ in the ball** der Ball springt sehr gut/nicht besonders gut

~ 'back *v. i.* zurückprallen; *(fig.)* ‹*Person:*› [plötzlich] wieder dasein

~ 'off 1. *v. i.* abprallen. **2.** *v. t.* **~ sth. off sth.** etw. von etw. abprallen lassen; **~ off sth.** von etw. abprallen; ‹*Signal:*› von etw. reflektiert werden

bouncer ['baʊnsə(r)] *n. (coll.)* **a)** Rausschmeißer, *der (ugs.)*; **b)** *(Cricket)* hoch aufspringender Ball

bouncing ['baʊnsɪŋ] *adj.* kräftig; stramm

bouncy ['baʊnsɪ] *adj.* **a)** gut springend ‹*Ball*›; federnd ‹*Matratze, Bett*›; **b)** *(fig.: lively)* munter

¹bound [baʊnd] **1.** *n.* **a)** *usu. in pl. (limit)* Grenze, *die;* **within the ~s of possibility** *or* **the possible** im Bereich des Möglichen; **keep sth. within ~s** etw. in Grenzen halten; **increase beyond all ~s** über alle Maßen ansteigen; **the ball is out of ~s** der Ball hat die Spielbahn verlassen; **go beyond the ~s of decency** die Grenzen des Anstands verletzen; **sth. is out of ~s [to sb.]** der Zutritt zu etw. ist [für jmdn.] verboten; **the pub is out of ~s** das Betreten des Lokals ist verboten; **beyond the ~s of human knowledge** jenseits der menschlichen Erkenntnisfähigkeit; **there are no ~s to his ambition** sein Ehrgeiz kennt keine Grenzen; **know no ~s** *(fig.)* keine Grenzen kennen; **keep within the ~s of reason/propriety** vernünftig/im Rahmen bleiben; **b)** *(of territory)* Grenze, *die; see also* **beat 1 a. 2.** *v. t., usu. in pass.* begrenzen; **be ~ed by sth.** durch etw. begrenzt werden; **sth. is ~ed by sth.** *(fig.)* einer Sache *(Dat.)* ist durch etw. Grenzen gesetzt

²bound 1. *v. i. (spring)* hüpfen; springen; **~ with joy** vor Freude hüpfen; **~ into the room** ins Zimmer stürzen; **the dog came ~ing up** der Hund kam angesprungen. **2.** *n. (spring)* Satz, *der;* **at** *or* **with one ~:** mit einem Satz; *see also* **leap 3**

³bound *pred. adj.* **be ~ for home/Frankfurt** auf dem Heimweg/nach Frankfurt unterwegs sein; **homeward ~:** auf dem Weg nach Hause; **where are you ~ for?** wohin geht die Reise?; **all passengers ~ for Zürich** alle Passagiere nach Zürich

⁴bound *see* **bind 1, 2**

boundary ['baʊndərɪ] *n.* Grenze, *die*

bounden ['baʊndn] *attrib. adj.* **~ duty** Pflicht und Schuldigkeit

bounder ['baʊndə(r)] *n. (dated coll.)* Lump, *der (abwertend)*

boundless ['baʊndlɪs] *adj.* grenzenlos

bounteous ['baʊntɪəs] *adj. (rhet.) see* **bountiful**

bountiful ['baʊntɪfl] *adj. (generous)* großzügig; gütig ‹*Gott*›; *(plentiful)* reichlich ‹*Ernte, Gaben, Ertrag*›; **Lady B~:** gute Fee

bountifully ['baʊntɪfəlɪ] *adv. (generously)* großzügig; *(plentifully)* reichlich

bounty ['baʊntɪ] *n.* **a)** *(reward)* Kopfgeld, *das; (for capturing animal)* Fangprämie, *die; (for shooting animal)* Abschußprämie, *die;* **b)** *(Commerc.)* Subvention, *die;* **c)** *(gift)* Gabe, *die*

bouquet [bʊ'keɪ, bəʊ'keɪ, 'bu:keɪ] *n.* **a)** *(bunch of flowers)* Bukett, *das;* [Blumen]strauß, *der;* **bride's ~:** Brautstrauß, *der;* Brautbukett, *das;* **b)** *(fig.: praise)* **get a ~:** gelobt werden; **he gets all the ~s** ihm gilt alles Lob; **be meant as a ~:** als Kompliment gemeint sein; **c)** *(perfume of wine)* Bukett, *das;* Blume, *die*

bouquet garni [bʊkeɪ gɑ:'ni:] *n., pl.* **bouquets garnis** [bʊkeɪ gɑ:'ni:] *(Cookery)* Kräutersträußchen, *das;* Bouquet garni, *das (fachspr.)*

bourbon ['bɜ:bən, 'bʊəbən] *n. (Amer.)* **~ [whiskey]** Bourbon, *der*

bourgeois ['bʊəʒwɑ:] **1.** *n., pl. same* **a)** *(middle-class person)* Bürger, *der*/Bürgerin, *die;* **the ~** *pl.* die bürgerliche Mittelklasse; **b)** *(person with conventional ideas, selfish materialist)* Spießbürger, *der (abwertend)*; Spießer, *der*/Spießerin, *die (abwertend)*; **c)** *(capitalist)* Bourgeois, *der (marx.)*. **2.** *adj.* **a)** *(middle-class)* bürgerlich; **b)** *(conventional, selfishly materialist)* spießbürgerlich *(abwertend)*; **c)** *(capitalistic)* bourgeois *(marx.)*

bourgeoisie [bʊəʒwɑ:'zi:] *n.* **a)** Bürgertum, *das;* **b)** *(capitalist class)* Bourgeoisie, *die (marx.)*

bout [baʊt] *n.* **a)** *(spell)* Periode, *die;* **b)** *(contest)* Wettkampf, *der;* **c)** *(fit)* Anfall, *der;* **~ of temper** Wutanfall, *der;* **he's out on one of his drinking ~s again** er ist mal wieder auf einer seiner Zechtouren *(ugs.)*

boutique [bu:'ti:k] *n.* Boutique, *die*

bovine ['bəʊvaɪn] *adj.* **a)** *(of ox)* Rinder-; **b)** *(of genus Bos)* **be a ~ animal** zu den Stirnrindern gehören; **c)** *(fig.) (heavy)* grob; *(stupid)* erzdumm; *(sluggish)* träge

bovver ['bɒvə(r)] *n. (sl.)* Zoff, *der (ugs.)*

¹bow [bəʊ] **1. a)** *(curve)* Bogen, *der;* **b)** *(weapon)* Bogen, *der;* **have two strings to one's ~:** eine Alternative haben; *see also* **longbow; c)** *see* **saddle-bow; d)** *(Mus.)* Bogen, *der; (stroke)* [Bogen]strich, *der;* **up/down ~** Auf-/Abstrich, *der;* **e)** *(tied knot or ribbon)* Schleife, *die;* **tie the shoe-lace in a ~:** den Schnürsenkel zu einer Schleife binden; **f)** *(Amer.: of spectacle-frame)* Bügel, *der.* **2.** *v. t.* streichen ‹*Violine, Viola usw.*›. **3.** *v. i.* den Bogen führen

²bow [baʊ] **1.** *v. i.* **a)** *(submit)* sich beugen **(to** *Dat.***)**; **b) ~ [down to** *or* **before sb./sth.]** *(bend)* sich [vor jmdm./etw.] verbeugen *od.* verneigen; **c)** *(incline head)* **~ [to sb.]** sich [vor jmdm.] verbeugen; **a ~ing acquaintance with sth.** eine flüchtige Bekanntschaft mit etw.; **~ out** sich formell verabschieden; **~ out of sth.** sich von etw. zurückziehen; *see also* **scrape 2 e. 2.** *v. t.* **a)** *(cause to bend)* beugen; **~ed down by** *or* **with care/responsibilities/age** *(fig.)* von Sorgen/Verpflichtungen niedergedrückt/vom Alter gebeugt; *see also* **knee a; b)** *(show by ~ing)* **he ~ed his acknowledgement of the applause** er verbeugte sich zum Dank für den Applaus; **~ sb. in/out** jmdn. unter Verbeugungen hinein-/hinausgeleiten. **3.** *n.* Verbeugung, *die;* **make one's ~** *(make entrance)* sich vorstellen; *(make exit)* sich [formell] verabschieden; **take a ~:** sich [unter Applaus] verbeugen; **they ought to** *or* **can take a ~** *(fig.)* sie verdienen Hochachtung

³bow [baʊ] *n. (Naut.)* **a)** *usu. in pl.* Bug, *der;* **in the ~s** im Bug; **on the ~:** am Bug; **shot**

across the ~s *(fig.)* Schuß vor den Bug *(ugs.)*; **b)** *(rower)* Bugmann, *der*

bowdlerize ['baʊdləraɪz] *v. t.* zensieren; **a ~d version** eine „gereinigte" Fassung

bowel ['baʊəl] *n.* **a)** *(Anat.)* ~s *pl.*, *(Med.)* ~: Darm, *der;* **b)** *in pl. (interior)* Innere, *das;* **in the ~s of the library/the earth** in den Katakomben der Bibliothek/im Inneren der Erde

bower [baʊə(r)] *n.* **a)** *(enclosed by foliage)* Laube, *die; (summer-house)* Sommerhaus, *das;* **b)** *(poet.) (inner room)* Gemach, *das (geh.); (boudoir)* Boudoir, *das*

'**bower-bird** *n.* Laubenvogel, *der*

[1]**bowl** [bəʊl] *n.* **a)** *(basin)* Schüssel, *die; (shallower)* Schale, *die;* **mixing/washing-up ~**: Rühr-/Abwaschschüssel, *die;* **soup-~**: Suppentasse, *die;* **sugar-~**: Zuckerdose, *die;* **a ~ of water** eine Schüssel/Schale Wasser; **a ~ of soup** eine Tasse Suppe; **b)** *(~-shaped part) schalenförmiger Teil; (of WC)* Schüssel, *die; (of spoon)* Schöpfteil, *der; (of pipe)* [Pfeifen]kopf, *der;* **c)** *(amphitheatre)* Freilufttheater, *das; (Sport)* Stadion, *das;* **d)** *(Amer.: region)* Senke, *die*

[2]**bowl 1.** *n.* **a)** *(ball)* Kugel, *die; (in skittles)* [Kegel]kugel, *die; (in ten-pin bowling)* [Bowling]kugel, *die;* **b)** *in pl. (game)* Bowlsspiel, *das;* Bowls, *das.* **2.** *v. i.* **a)** *(play ~s)* Bowls spielen; *(play skittles)* kegeln; *(play ten-pin bowling)* bowlen; **b)** *(go along)* rollen; **~ along** dahinrollen; **c)** *(Cricket)* werfen. **3.** *v. t.* **a)** *(roll)* rollen lassen; **~ sb./sth. over** jmdn./etw. umwerfen; **~ sb. over** *(fig.)* jmdn. überwältigen *od. (ugs.)* umhauen; **b)** *(Cricket etc.)* werfen; **~ [down] the wicket** das Tor einwerfen; **~ the batsman [out]/side out** den Schlagmann/die Mannschaft ausschlagen

bow [bəʊ]: **~-'legged** *adj.* krummbeinig; O-beinig *(ugs.)*; **be ~-legged** krumme Beine *od. (ugs.)* O-Beine haben; **~-'legs** *n. pl.* krumme Beine; O-Beine *Pl. (ugs.)*

[1]**bowler** ['bəʊlə(r)] *n.* **a)** *(Cricket etc.)* Werfer, *der;* **b)** *(at bowls)* Bowlsspieler, *der*/Bowlsspielerin, *die; (at bowling)* Bowlingspieler, *der*/Bowlingspielerin, *die*

[2]**bowler** *n.* **~ [hat]** Bowler, *der*

'**bowl fire** *n.* Heizsonne, *die*

bowline ['bəʊlɪn] *n.* **a) ~ [knot]** Palstek, *der;* **b)** *(Naut.: rope)* Buline, *die (Seemannsspr.)*

bowling ['bəʊlɪŋ] *n.* **[ten-pin] ~**: Bowling, *das;* **go ~**: bowlen gehen

bowling: ~-alley *n. (for ten-pin ~)* Bowlingbahn, *die; (for skittles)* Kegelbahn, *die;* **~ average** *see* **average 1 b**; **~-crease** *n. (Cricket)* Wurflinie, *die;* **~-green** *n. Rasenfläche für Bowls*

[1]**bowman** ['bəʊmən] *n., pl.* **bowmen** ['bəʊmən] *(archer)* Bogenschütze, *der*

[2]**bowman** ['baʊmən] *n., pl.* **bowmen** ['baʊmən] *(Naut.)* Bugmann, *der*

bowser ['baʊzə(r)] *n. (tanker)* Tankwagen, *der*

bow: ~sprit ['bəʊsprɪt] *n. (Naut.)* Bugspriet, *der od. das;* **~string** ['bəʊstrɪŋ] *n.* Bogensehne, *die;* **~-tie** [bəʊ'taɪ] *n.* Fliege, *die;* [Smoking-/Frack]schleife, *die;* **~-window** [bəʊ'wɪndəʊ] *n.* Erkerfenster, *das*

bow-wow ['baʊwaʊ] **1.** *n.* **a)** *(dog's bark)* Gebell, *das;* **b)** *(child lang.: dog)* Wauwau, *der (Kindersprr.).* **2.** *interj.* wauwau

[1]**box** [bɒks] *n. (Bot.)* **a)** *(tree)* Buchsbaum, *der;* **b)** *(wood)* Buchsbaumholz, *das*

[2]**box 1.** *n.* **a)** *(container)* Kasten, *der; (bigger)* Kiste, *die; (made of cardboard, thin wood, etc.)* Schachtel, *die;* **a ~ of cigars** eine Schachtel Zigarren; **pencil-~**: Federkasten, *der;* **jewellery-~**: Schmuckkasten, *der;* **cigar-~**: Zigarrenkiste, *die;* **cardboard ~**: [Papp]karton, *der; (smaller)* [Papp]schachtel, *die;* **shoe-~**: Schuhkarton, *der;* **~ of matches** Streichholzschachtel, *die;* **b)** *(~ful)* **she emptied the whole ~ of beads on to the floor** sie hat die ganze Schachtel [mit] Perlen auf die Erde geschüttet; **c) the ~** *(coll.: television)* der Kasten *(ugs. abwertend);* die Flimmerkiste *(scherzh.);* **d)** *(coachman's seat)* [Kutsch]bock, *der;* **e)** *(at newspaper office)* ≈ Chiffre, *die;* **f)** *(in theatre etc.)* Loge, *die; (in restaurant etc.)* ≈ Nische, *die;* **g)** *(compartment)* **[loose] ~**: Box, *die; see also* **horse-box**; **h)** *(country house)* Hütte, *die;* **i)** *(casing)* Kasten, *der; (cricketer's etc. shield)* ≈ Suspensorium, *das;* **j)** *(confined area)* Viereck, *das; (enclosed by printed lines)* Kasten, *der;* **k)** *(Footb. coll.: penalty area)* Strafraum, *der;* **l)** *(Baseball)* Box, *die.* **2.** *v. t. see* **1 a**: [in eine Schachtel/in Schachteln *usw.*] verpacken; **~ the compass** *(Naut.)* alle Kompaßpunkte der Reihe nach aufzählen; *(fig.)* einmal die Runde machen

~ 'in *v. t.* **a)** *(enclose in ~)* in einem Gehäuse unterbringen; **b)** *(enclose tightly)* einklemmen; **feel ~ed in** sich eingeengt fühlen

~ 'up *v. t.* **a)** *(enclose in ~) see* **~ 1 a**: [in eine Schachtel/in Schachteln *usw.*] verpacken; **b)** *(confine)* einzwängen; **I'd hate to be ~ed up anywhere with him** ich wäre nur äußerst ungern irgendwo mit ihm eingesperrt

[3]**box 1.** *n. (slap, punch)* Schlag, *der;* **he gave him a ~ on the ear[s]** er gab ihm eine Ohrfeige. **2.** *v. t.* **a)** *(slap, punch)* schlagen; **he ~ed his ears** *or* **him round the ears** er ohrfeigte ihn; **get one's ears ~ed** eine Ohrfeige bekommen; **b)** *(fight with fists)* **~ sb.** gegen jmdn. boxen. **3.** *v. i.* boxen **(with, against** gegen); **~ clever** *(sl.)* auf Draht sein *(ugs.)*

Box and Cox [bɒks ənd 'kɒks] *n. (two persons who take turns)* **like ~**: im ständigen Wechsel; **be like ~**: sich ständig abwechseln

box: ~ barrage *n.* Sperrfeuer, *das;* **~ camera** *n.* Box, *die;* **~car** *n. (Amer. Railw.)* gedeckter [Güter]wagen

boxer ['bɒksə(r)] *n.* **a)** Boxer, *der;* **b)** *(dog)* Boxer, *der*

'**boxer shorts** *n. pl.* Boxershorts *Pl.*

boxful ['bɒksfʊl] *n.* **a ~ of chocolates** *etc.* eine [ganze] Schachtel Pralinen *usw.*

'**box girder** *n.* Kastenträger, *der (Technik)*

boxing ['bɒksɪŋ] *n.* Boxen, *das;* **professional/amateur ~**: Berufs-/Amateurboxen, *das*

boxing: B~ Day *n. (Brit.)* zweiter Weihnachtsfeiertag; **~-glove** *n.* Boxhandschuh, *der;* **~-match** *n.* Boxkampf, *der;* **~-ring** *n.* Boxring, *der*

box: ~ junction *n. (Brit.) gelb markierter Kreuzungsbereich, in den man bei Stau nicht einfahren darf;* **~-kite** *n.* Kastendrachen, *der;* **~ number** *n. (at newspaper office)* Chiffre, *die; (at post office)* Postfach, *das;* **my post office ~ number is ...**: meine Postfachnummer ist ...; **~-office** *n.* Kasse, *die; (fig.)* **be ~-office, be a ~-office success** ein Kassenerfolg sein; **be good/bad ~-office** gut/schlecht ankommen **(among** bei); **~ pew** *n.* geschlossener Chorstuhl; **~-pleat** *n.* Quetschfalte, *die;* **~-room** *n. (Brit.)* Abstellraum, *der;* **~ score** *n.* [tabellarischer] Spielbericht; ≈ Spielbogen, *der;* **~-spanner** *n.* Steckschlüssel, *der;* **~-spring** *n.* Sprungfeder, *die;* **~wood** *see* [1]**box b**

boy [bɔɪ] **1.** *n.* **a)** Junge, *der;* **baby ~**: kleiner Junge; **~s' school** Jungenschule, *die;* **a ~'s name** ein Jungenname; **a little Italian ~**: ein kleiner Italiener; **[my] ~** *(as address)* [mein] Junge; **here/sit/come on ~!** *(to dog)* hier!/sitz!/komm!; **good ~!** *(to dog)* guter Hund!; **the ~s** *(male friends)* die Kumpels *(salopp);* **come on, ~s!** los, Jungs!; **~s will be ~s** so sind Jungs/Männer nun mal; **jobs for the ~s** Vetternwirtschaft, *die (abwertend);* **the Smith ~s** die Jungen von Smiths; *see also* **old boy**; **b)** *(servant)* Boy, *der.* **2.** *int.* **[oh] ~**: Junge, Junge! *(ugs.)*

boy-and-'girl *adj.* teenagerhaft; Teenager‹*romanze, -liebe*›

boycott ['bɔɪkɒt] **1.** *v. t.* boykottieren. **2.** *n.* Boykott, *der*

'**boy-friend** *n.* Freund, *der*

boyhood ['bɔɪhʊd] *n.* Kindheit, *die*

boyish ['bɔɪɪʃ] *adj.* jungenhaft; **she had a ~ haircut/figure** sie hatte einen Knabenhaarschnitt/eine knabenhafte Figur

Boyle's Law ['bɔɪlz lɔ:] *n. (Phys.)* Boyle-Mariotte-Gesetz, *das*

boy: ~meets-'girl *attrib. adj.* Liebes‹*geschichte, -film*›; **~ 'scout** *see* [1]**scout 1 a**

BP *abbr.* **a) boiling-point** SP; **b) British Petroleum** BP; **c)** *(Med.)* **British Pharmacopoeia** *amtliches britisches Arzneimittelverzeichnis*

Bp. *abbr.* **bishop** Bf.

BR *abbr.* **British Rail[ways]** *britische Eisenbahngesellschaft*

Br. *abbr.* **a) British** brit.; **b) Brother** Br.

bra [brɑ:] *n.* BH, *der (ugs.)*

brace [breɪs] **1.** *n.* **a)** *(buckle)* Schnalle, *die; (connecting piece)* Klammer, *die; (Dent.)* [Zahn]spange, *die;* [Zahn]klammer, *die;* **b)** *in pl. (trouser-straps)* Hosenträger; **c)** *pl. same (pair)* **a/two ~ of** zwei/vier; *(derog.)* **a ~ of twins/servants** ein Zwillings-/Dienerpaar; **d)** *(Printing, Mus.)* geschweifte Klammer; Akkolade, *die;* **e)** *(strut)* Strebe, *die;* **f)** *(Naut.)* Brasse, *die. See also* **brace and bit**. **2.** *v. t.* **a)** *(fasten)* befestigen; *(stretch)* spannen; *(string up)* anspannen; *(with struts)* stützen; **~ up one's courage** seinen ganzen Mut zusammennehmen; **b)** *(support)* stützen; **c)** *(Naut.)* brassen. **3.** *v. refl.* **~ oneself [up]** *(fig.)* sich zusammennehmen; **~ oneself [up] for sth.** *(fig.)* sich auf etw. *(Akk.)* [innerlich] vorbereiten

brace and 'bit *n.* Bohrwinde, *die*

bracelet ['breɪslɪt] *n.* **a)** *(band)* Armband, *das; (chain)* Kettchen, *das; (bangle)* Armreif, *der;* **b)** *in pl. (sl.: handcuffs)* Brasselett, *das (Gaunerspr.)*

bracer ['breɪsə(r)] *(coll.: tonic)* Muntermacher, *der (ugs. scherzh.)*

brachial ['breɪkɪəl] *adj. (Anat.)* brachial

bracing ['breɪsɪŋ] *adj.* belebend

bracken ['brækn] *n.* [Adler]farn, *der*

bracket ['brækɪt] **1.** *n.* **a)** *(support, projection)* Konsole, *die; (of iron)* Krageisen, *das; (of stone)* Kragstein, *der; (lamp-support)* Lampenhalter, *der;* **b)** *(mark)* Klammer, *die;* **open/close ~s** Klammer auf/zu; **c)** *(group)* Gruppe, *die;* **social ~**: Gesellschaftsschicht, *die.* **2.** *v. t.* **a)** *(enclose in ~s)* einklammern; **b)** *(couple with brace)* mit einer Klammer verbinden; *(fig.)* in Verbindung bringen

brackish ['brækɪʃ] *adj.* brackig

bract [brækt] *n. (Bot.)* Braktee, *die*

brad [bræd] *n.* [flacher] Drahtstift

bradawl ['brædɔ:l] *n.* [flache] Ahle

brae [breɪ] *n. (Scot.) (bank)* [Ufer]böschung, *die; (hillside)* Hang, *der*

brag [bræg] **1.** *n. (boast, boasting)* Prahlerei, *die;* **his ~ is that ...**: er prahlt damit, daß ... **2.** *v. i.*, **-gg-** prahlen **(about** mit). **3.** *v. t.*, **-gg-** prahlen; **he ~s that he has a Rolls Royce** er prahlt damit, daß er einen Rolls-Royce hat

braggart ['brægət] **1.** *n.* Prahler, *der*/Prahlerin, *die.* **2.** *adj.* prahlerisch

brahmin ['brɑ:mɪn] *n.* Brahmane, *der*

brahminism ['brɑ:mɪnɪzm] *n.* Brahmanismus, *der*

braid [breɪd] **1.** *n.* **a)** *(plait)* Flechte, *die (geh.);* Zopf, *der; (band entwined with hair)* Haarband, *das;* Flechtband, *das (veralt.);* **b)** *(decorative woven band)* Borte, *die;* **c)** *(on uniform)* Litze, *die; (with metal threads)* Tresse, die. **2.** *v. t.* **a)** *(plait; arrange in ~s)* flechten; **b)** zusammenbinden ‹*Haare*›; **c)** *(trim with ~)* mit Borten/Litzen/Tressen besetzen

braiding ['breɪdɪŋ] *n. (bands)* Bänder; *(decorative woven bands)* Borten

Braille [breɪl] *n.* Blindenschrift, *die*

brain [breɪn] **1.** *n.* **a)** Gehirn, *das;* **have [got] sex/food/money on the ~:** nur Sex/Essen/Geld im Kopf haben; **he's got her on the ~:** sie geht ihm nicht aus dem Kopf; **use your ~[s]** gebrauch deinen Verstand; **he's got a good ~:** er ist ein kluger Kopf; **you need ~s for that** dafür braucht man Verstand; **he didn't have the ~s to do it** er war zu dumm, es zu tun; **~ versus brawn** Köpfchen gegen Muskelkraft; *see also* **¹rack 2c; b)** *in pl. (Gastr.)* Hirn, *das;* **c)** *(coll.: clever person)* **she's the ~[s] of the class** sie ist die Intelligenteste in der Klasse; **he's a terrific ~:** er ist wahnsinnig intelligent *(ugs.);* **the ~ behind the business** der Kopf des Unternehmens. **2.** *v.t.* den Schädel einschlagen (+ *Dat.*); **I'll ~ you!** *(coll.)* du kriegst gleich eins auf die Rübe! *(ugs.)*

brain: **~-child** *n. (coll.)* Geistesprodukt, *das;* **that system was my own ~-child** ich war der geistige Vater dieses Systems; **~-drain** *n. (coll.)* Abwanderung [von Wissenschaftlern]; Brain-Drain, *der*

brainless ['breɪnlɪs] *adj. (stupid)* hirnlos

brain: **~ power** *n.* geistige Leistung; **his ~ power will get him far** mit seiner Intelligenz wird er es weit bringen; **~-stem** *n. (Anat.)* Hirnstamm, *der;* **~storm** *n.* **a)** Anfall geistiger Umnachtung; **b)** *(Amer. coll.) see* **~wave b; ~storming** *n.* Brainstorming, *das;* **~s trust** *n.* Expertengremium, *das;* **~ surgeon** *n.* Gehirnchirurg, *der;* **~-teaser** *n.* Denk[sport]aufgabe, *die;* **~ trust** *n. (Amer.)* [beratendes] Expertengremium; Brain-Trust, *der;* **~-twister** *see* **~-teaser; ~wash** *v.t.* einer Gehirnwäsche unterziehen; **~wash sb. into doing sth.** jmdm. [ständig] einreden, etw. zu tun; **~washing** *n.* Gehirnwäsche, *die;* **~wave** *n.* **a)** *(Physiol.)* Hirnstromwelle, *die;* **b)** *(coll.: inspiration)* genialer Einfall; **~work** *n.* Kopfarbeit, *die*

brainy ['breɪnɪ] *adj.* intelligent

braise [breɪz] *v.t. (Cookery)* schmoren

¹brake [breɪk] **1.** *n. (apparatus; coll.: pedal etc.)* Bremse, *die;* **sth. acts as a ~ on sth.** etw. bremst etw.; **apply** *or* **put on the ~s** die Bremse betätigen; *(fig.)* zurückstecken; **put the ~[s] on sth.** *(fig.)* etw. bremsen; **put the ~[s] on spending** die Ausgaben einschränken. **2.** *v.t. & i.* bremsen; **~ hard** scharf bremsen

²brake *n. (Bot.)* Adlerfarn, *der*

³brake *n. (thicket)* Dickicht, *das*

⁴brake *n.* **a)** *(wagonette)* Break, *der od. das;* **b)** *(estate car)* Kombi[wagen], *der*

brake: **~-block** *n.* Bremsklotz, *der;* **~-drum** *n.* Bremstrommel, *die;* **~ fluid** *n.* Bremsflüssigkeit, *die;* **~ horsepower** *n.* Bremsleistung, *die;* Nutzleistung, *die;* **~-light** *n.* Bremslicht, *das;* **~ lining** *n.* Bremsbelag, *der;* **~-pad** *n.* Bremsbelag, *der;* **~-shoe** *n.* Bremsbacke, *die;* **~-van** *n. (Railw.)* Bremswagen, *der*

braking ['breɪkɪŋ] *n.* Bremsen, *das*

'braking distance *n.* Bremsweg, *der*

bramble ['bræmbl] *n.* **a)** *(shrub)* Dornenstrauch, *der;* *(blackberry-bush)* Brombeerstrauch, *der;* **b)** *(fruit)* Brombeere, *die*

Bramley ['bræmlɪ] *n. englischer Kochapfel*

bran [bræn] *n.* Kleie, *die*

branch [brɑːnʃ] **1.** *n.* **a)** *(bough)* Ast, *der;* *(twig)* Zweig, *der;* **b)** *(of nerve, artery, antlers)* Ast, *der;* *(of river)* [Neben]arm, *der;* *(of road, pipe, circuit)* Abzweigung, *die;* *(of railway)* Nebenstrecke, *die;* *(of family [of languages], subject)* Zweig, *der;* *(local establishment)* Zweigstelle, *die;* *(shop)* Filiale, *die.* **2.** *v.i.* **a)** sich verzweigen; **b)** *(tend)* **~ away from sth.** sich von etw. wegentwickeln; **c)** *(diverge)* **~ into sth.** sich in etw. *(Akk.)* aufspalten

~ 'forth *v.i. see* **~ 2a**

~ 'off *v.i.* abzweigen; *(fig.)* sich abspalten

~ 'out *v.i.* **a)** *see* **~ 2a; b)** *(~ off)* abzweigen **(from** von); **c)** *(fig.)* **~ out into sth.** sich auch mit etw. befassen; **~ out on one's own** sich selbständig machen

branch: **~ line** *n. (Railw.)* Nebenstrecke, *die;* **~ office** *n.* Zweigstelle, *die*

brand [brænd] **1.** *n.* **a)** *(trade mark)* Markenzeichen, *das;* *(goods of particular make)* Marke, *die;* *(fig.: type)* Art, *die;* **~ of washing-powder/soap** Waschpulvermarke, *die*/Seifenmarke, *die;* **b)** *(permanent mark, stigma)* Brandmal, *das;* *(on sheep, cattle)* Brandzeichen, *das;* *(on cigar-box, crate)* eingebranntes Zeichen; **~ of Cain** Kainsmal, *das;* **c)** *(burning log etc.)* [Feuer]brand, *der (veralt.);* *(charred log etc.)* verkohltes Holzscheit; *(poet.: torch)* Brand, *der (geh.);* **d)** *(Bot.: blight)* Brand, *der;* **e)** *(poet.: sword)* Schwert, *das.* **2.** *v.t.* **a)** *(burn)* mit einem Brandzeichen markieren ⟨*Tier*⟩; **b)** *(stigmatize [as])* **~ [as]** brandmarken als ⟨*Verräter, Verbrecher usw.*⟩; **c)** *(Brit.: label with trade mark)* mit einem Markenzeichen versehen; **~ed goods** Markenware, *die;* **d)** *(impress)* einbrennen **(upon** *Dat. od.* in + *Akk.*)

'branding-iron *n.* Brandeisen, *das*

brandish ['brændɪʃ] *v.t.* schwenken; schwingen ⟨*Waffe*⟩

brand: **~ name** *n.* Markenname, *der;* **~-'new** *adj.* nagelneu *(ugs.);* brandneu *(ugs.);* **is the car ~-new?** ist der Wagen [fabrik]neu?

brandy ['brændɪ] *n.* Weinbrand, *der*

brandy: **~-ball** *n. (Brit.)* Weinbrandtrüffel, *die;* **~ butter** *n.* ≈ Kognakbutter, *die; Creme aus Butter, Zucker und Brandy;* **~-snap** *n. mit Schlagsahne gefülltes knuspriges Röllchen mit Ingwergeschmack*

brant [brænt] *(Amer.) see* **brent**

'bran-tub *n. mit Kleie o. ä. gefüllte Kiste, aus der man Geschenke herausfischen kann*

¹brash [bræʃ] *adj.* **a)** *(self-assertive)* dreist; *(garish)* auffällig ⟨*Kleidung*⟩; knallig ⟨*Farbe*⟩; **b)** *(rash)* unüberlegt

²brash *n.* **a)** *(loose rock)* **[stone] ~:** Trümmergestein, *das;* **b)** *(loose ice)* Eistrümmer *Pl.*

³brash *n. (Med.)* saures Aufstoßen

brashly ['bræʃlɪ] *adv. see* **¹brash:** dreist; auffällig; unüberlegt

brashness ['bræʃnɪs] *n., no pl. see* **¹brash:** Dreistigkeit, *die;* Unüberlegtheit, *die*

brass [brɑːs] **1.** *n.* **a)** Messing, *das;* **do sth. as bold as ~:** die Unverfrorenheit haben, etw. zu tun; **b)** *(inscribed tablet)* Grabplatte aus Messing; **c) [horse-]~es** Messinggeschirr, *das;* **d) the ~** *(Mus.)* das Blech *(fachspr.);* die Blechbläser; **e)** *see* **brassware; f)** *no pl., no indef. art. (Brit. sl.: money)* Kies, *der (salopp);* **g) [top] ~** *(coll.: officers, leaders of industry etc.)* hohe Tiere *(ugs.).* **2.** *attrib. adj.* Messing-; **~ player** *(Mus.)* Blechbläser, *der.* **3.** *v.t.* **be ~ed off [doing sth.]** *(sl.)* es satt haben[, etw. zu tun] *(ugs.);* **be ~ed off with** *or* **about sb./sth.** *(sl.)* jmdn./etw. satt haben *(ugs.)*

brass 'band *n.* Blaskapelle, *die*

brasserie ['bræsərɪ] *n.* Bierlokal, *das;* *(more fashionable)* Brasserie, *die*

brass: **~ 'farthing** *n.* **not a ~ farthing** kein Pfennig *(ugs.);* **he doesn't care a ~ farthing about it** es interessiert ihn nicht für fünf Pfennige *(ugs.);* **~ hat** *n. (sl.)* hohes Tier *(ugs.)*

brassica ['bræsɪkə] *n. (Bot.)* Kohlpflanze, *die;* Brassica, *die (Bot.)*

brassière ['bræsːeə(r), 'bræzjə(r)] *n. (formal)* Büstenhalter, *der*

brass: **~ 'plate** *n.* Messingschild, *das;* **~ rubbing** *n.* **a)** *no pl., no indef. art.* Frottage, *die (von Messingtafeln);* **b)** *(impression)* Frottage, *die (einer Messingtafel);* **~ 'tacks** *n. pl.* **get** *or* **come down to ~ tacks** *(sl.)* zur Sache kommen; **~ware** *n., no pl.* Messingteile; *(utensils, candlesticks, etc.)* Messinggerät, *das*

brassy ['brɑːsɪ] *adj.* **a)** *(in colour)* messing-; *(in sound)* blechern; **b)** *(impudent)* dreist; *(pretentious)* auffällig

brat [bræt] *n. (derog.: child)* Balg, *das od. der (ugs., meist abwertend);* *(young rascal)* Flegel, *der*

bravado [brə'vɑːdəʊ] *n., pl.* **~es** *or* **~s** Mut, *der;* **be full of ~:** sehr mutig tun; **do sth. out of ~:** so waghalsig sein, etw. zu tun; *(as pretence)* den starken Mann markieren wollen und etw. tun *(ugs.)*

brave [breɪv] **1.** *adj.* **a)** mutig; *(able to endure sth.)* tapfer; **be ~!** nur Mut!/sei tapfer!; **b)** *(literary: splendid)* stattlich; prachtvoll; **make a ~ show** einen prächtigen Anblick bieten; **a ~ new world** eine schöne neue Welt. **2.** *n.* [indianischer] Krieger. **3.** *v.t.* trotzen (+ *Dat.*); mutig gegenübertreten (+ *Dat.*) ⟨*Kritiker, Interviewer*⟩; **~ it out** sich durch nichts einschüchtern lassen

bravely ['breɪvlɪ] *adv.* **a)** mutig; *(showing endurance)* tapfer; **b)** *(literary: splendidly)* stattlich; prachtvoll

bravery ['breɪvərɪ] *n., no pl.* Mut, *der;* *(endurance)* Tapferkeit, *die*

bravo [brɑː'vəʊ] *int.* bravo; **shouts of '~':** Bravorufe

bravura [brə'vʊərə] *n.* Bravour, *die;* **~ piece/passage** *(Mus.)* Bravourstück, *das*

braw [brɔː] *adj. (Scot.)* schön

brawl [brɔːl] **1.** *v.i.* **a)** sich schlagen; **b)** ⟨*Bach:*⟩ rauschen. **2.** *n.* Schlägerei, *die*

brawn [brɔːn] *n.* **a)** *(muscle)* Muskel, *der;* *(muscularity)* Muskeln; **he's got some ~:** er hat ganz schön starke Muskeln; **you need a bit of ~ for that** dafür brauchst du schon ein paar Muskeln; *see also* **brain 1a; b)** *(chopped pig's head)* ≈ Preßkopf, *der;* *(in aspic jelly)* Schweinskopfsülze, *die*

brawny ['brɔːnɪ] *adj.* muskulös

bray [breɪ] **1.** *n. (of ass)* Iah, *das.* **2.** *v.i.* ⟨*Esel:*⟩ iahen, schreien; ⟨*Mensch:*⟩ wiehern

braze [breɪz] **1.** *v.t.* [hart]löten. **2.** *n.* [Hart]lötung, *die*

brazen ['breɪzn] **1.** *adj.* **a)** dreist; *(shameless)* schamlos; **b)** *(of brass)* Messing-; aus Messing *nachgestellt;* messingen *(seltener);* **c)** *(harsh-sounding)* metallisch; **d)** *(brass-coloured)* **~ [yellow]** messinggelb; **a ~ yellow** ein Messinggelb. **2.** *v.t.* **~ [out]** trotzen (+ *Dat.*); **~ it out** durchhalten

'brazen-faced *see* **brazen 1a**

brazenly ['breɪznlɪ] *adv.* dreist; *(shamelessly)* schamlos

brazenness ['breɪznnɪs] *n., no pl.* Dreistigkeit, *die;* *(shamelessness)* Schamlosigkeit, *die*

brazier ['breɪzɪə(r), 'breɪʒə(r)] *n.* Kohlenbecken, *das*

Brazil [brə'zɪl] *n.* **a)** *pr. n.* Brasilien *(das);* **b)** *see* **Brazil nut**

Brazilian [brə'zɪlɪən] **1.** *adj.* brasilianisch; **sb. is ~:** jmd. ist Brasilianer/Brasilianerin. **2.** *n.* Brasilianer, *der*/Brasilianerin, *die*

Bra'zil nut *n.* Paranuß, *die*

breach [briːtʃ] **1.** *n.* **a)** *(violation)* Verstoß, *der* **(of** gegen); **~ of faith/duty** Vertrauensbruch, *der*/Pflichtverletzung, *die;* **~ of the peace** Störung von Ruhe und Ordnung; *(by noise only)* ruhestörender Lärm; **~ of contract** Vertragsbruch, *der;* **~ of promise** Wortbruch, *der;* *(Law Hist.: breaking off an engagement to marry)* Bruch des Eheversprechens; **be in ~ of the regulations** gegen die Verordnungen verstoßen; **b)** *(of relations)* Bruch, *der;* **~ of diplomatic relations** Abbruch der diplomatischen Beziehungen; **c)** *(gap)* Bresche, *die;* *(fig.)* Riß, *der;* **stand in the ~** *(fig.)* in der Schußlinie stehen; **step into the ~** *(fig.)* in die Bresche treten *od.* springen. **2.** *v.t.* eine Bresche schlagen in (+ *Akk.*); **the wall/dike was ~ed** in die Mauer wurde eine Bresche geschlagen/der Deich wurde durchbrochen

bread [bred] **1.** *n.* **a)** Brot, *das;* **a piece of ~ and butter** ein Butterbrot; **[some] ~ and but-**

ter [ein paar] Butterbrote; ~ **and butter** *(fig.)* tägliches Brot; **quarrel with one's ~ and butter** *(fig.)* an dem Ast sägen, auf dem man sitzt; ~ **and circuses** Brot und Spiele; ~ **and milk** heiße Milch mit eingebrocktem Brot; ~ **and water** *(lit. or fig.)* Wasser und Brot; **have one's ~ buttered on both sides** es in jeder Hinsicht gut getroffen haben; **know which side one's ~ is buttered** wissen, wo etwas zu holen ist; *see also* **water 1 b; b)** *(necessary food)* **[daily]** ~: [tägliches] Brot; **break ~ [with sb.]** *(arch.)* das Brot [mit jmdm.] brechen; **eat the ~ of idleness** *(literary)* müßiggehen *(geh.)*; **take the ~ out of sb.'s mouth** *(fig.)* jmdn. seiner Existenzgrundlage berauben; **c)** *(sl.: money)* Kies, *der (salopp).* **2.** *v. t.* panieren

bread: ~-and-butter 'pudding *n.* Brot-und-Butter-Pudding, *der; Auflauf aus Brot, Butter, Zucker, Rosinen usw.*; **~-bin** *n.* Brotkasten, *der;* **~-board** *n.* [Brot]brett, *das;* **~crumb** *n.* Brotkrume, *die;* **~crumbs** *(for coating e.g. fish)* Paniermehl, *das;* **~-fruit** *n.* Brotfrucht, *die;* **~-knife** *n.* Brotmesser, *das;* **~line** *n. (Amer.) Warteschlange bei der Ausgabe kostenloser Nahrungsmittel an Bedürftige;* **live on/below the ~line** *(fig.)* gerade noch/nicht einmal mehr das Notwendigste zum Leben haben; **~-'roll** *n.* Brötchen, *das;* ~ **'sauce** *n. (Gastr.)* [englische] Brotsauce *(Kochk.);* **~-stick** *n. stangenförmiges Gebäck aus Brotteig*

breadth [bredθ] *n.* **a)** *(broadness)* Breite, *die;* **what is the ~ of ...?** wie breit ist ...?; **be 20 metres in ~:** 20 Meter breit sein; **b)** *(extent)* Weite, *die; (range)* **with his ~ of experience/knowledge** bei seiner großen Erfahrung/bei seiner umfassenden Kenntnis; ~ **of mind/vision** *etc. (fig.)* große Aufgeschlossenheit/Einbildungskraft *usw.*

bread: ~ tin Brotbüchse, *die;* **~-winner** *n.* Ernährer, *der*/Ernährerin *die*

¹break [breɪk] **1.** *v. t.,* **broke** [brəʊk], **broken** ['brəʊkn] **a)** brechen; *(so as to damage)* zerbrechen; kaputtmachen *(ugs.);* aufschlagen ⟨*Ei zum Kochen*⟩; zerstören ⟨*Ufer*⟩; zerreißen ⟨*Seil*⟩; *(fig.: interrupt)* unterbrechen; brechen ⟨*Bann, Zauber, Schweigen*⟩; ~ **sth. in two/in pieces** etw. in zwei Teile/in Stücke brechen; ~ **the set** Teile des Satzes einzeln abgeben; **the TV/my watch is broken** der Fernseher/meine Uhr ist kaputt *(ugs.);* **b)** *(crack)* zerbrechen; zertrümmern ⟨*Fundament, Schiffsrumpf*⟩; **c)** *(fracture)* sich *(Dat.)* brechen; *(pierce)* verletzen ⟨*Haut*⟩; **he broke his leg** er hat sich *(Dat.)* das Bein gebrochen; **sth. ~s no bones** *(fig.)* etw. ist nicht so schlimm; **no ~s broken** *(fig.)* es ist nichts passiert; ~ **one's/sb.'s back** *(fig.)* sich/jmdn. kaputtmachen *(ugs.);* ~ **one's back** *(fig.)* sich abstrampeln *(ugs.);* ~ **the back of sth.** *(fig.)* bei etw. das Schwerste hinter sich bringen; ~ **a tooth** sich *(Dat.)* ein Stück vom Zahn abbrechen; ~ **open** aufbrechen; **d)** *(violate)* brechen ⟨*Vertrag, Versprechen*⟩; verletzen, verstoßen gegen ⟨*Regel, Tradition*⟩; nicht einhalten ⟨*Verabredung*⟩; überschreiten ⟨*Grenze*⟩; ~ **the law** gegen das Gesetz verstoßen; **e)** *(destroy)* zerstören, ruinieren ⟨*Freundschaft, Ehe*⟩; **f)** *(surpass)* brechen ⟨*Rekord*⟩; **g)** *(abscond from)* ~ **jail** [aus dem Gefängnis] ausbrechen; ~ **the bounds** ausreißen; ~ **ship** sich beim Landgang absetzen *(ugs.); see also* **cover 1 j; h)** *(weaken)* brechen, beugen ⟨*Stolz*⟩; *(quash)* niederschlagen ⟨*Rebellion, Aufstand*⟩; zusammenbrechen lassen ⟨*Streik*⟩; ~ **sb.'s spirit** jmds. Lebensmut brechen; ~ **sb.'s heart** jmdm. das Herz brechen; **it broke my heart** es brach mir das Herz; ~ **sb.** *(crush)* jmdn. fertigmachen *(ugs.);* ~ **a horse [to the rein]** ein Pferd zureiten; ~ **the habit** es sich *(Dat.)* abgewöhnen; ~ **the smoking/drinking habit** sich *(Dat.)* das Rauchen/Trinken abgewöhnen; ~ **sb. of the smoking habit** jmdm. das Rauchen abgewöhnen; *see also* **make 1 p; i)** *(cushion)* auffangen ⟨*Schlag, jmds. Fall*⟩; abschwächen ⟨*Wind*⟩; **j)** *(make bankrupt)* ruinieren; ~ **the bank** die Bank sprengen; **you mustn't ~ the bank** *(fig. coll.) (spend a lot)* du darfst dich nicht in Unkosten stürzen; *(ruin yourself)* du darfst dich nicht finanziell ruinieren; **it won't ~ the bank** *(fig. coll.)* es kostet kein Vermögen; **k)** *(reveal)* ~ **the news that ...:** melden, daß ...; ~ **the glad/bad news to sb. that ...:** jmdm. die frohe Nachricht mitteilen/jmdm. die schlechte Nachricht beibringen, daß ...; **I don't know how to ~ this news to you, but ...:** ich weiß nicht, wie ich dir das sagen soll, aber ...; **l)** *(use part of)* anbrechen ⟨*Banknote*⟩; **m)** *(unfurl)* entfalten ⟨*Fahne*⟩; **n)** *(solve)* entschlüsseln, entziffern ⟨*Kode, Geheimschrift*⟩; **o)** *(disprove)* entkräften ⟨*Alibi*⟩; **p)** *(Tennis)* ~ **service/sb.'s service** den Aufschlag des Gegners/jmds. Aufschlag durchbrechen. *See also* **broken 2; ¹wind 1 e. 2.** *v. i.,* **broke, broken a)** kaputtgehen *(ugs.);* entzweigehen; ⟨*Faden, Seil:*⟩ [zer]reißen; ⟨*Glas, Tasse, Teller:*⟩ zerbrechen; ⟨*Eis:*⟩ brechen; *(fig.: be interrupted)* unterbrochen werden; **sb.'s heart is ~ing** jmdm. bricht das Herz; ~ **in two/in pieces** entzweibrechen; **the chocolate ~s easily** die Schokolade bricht sich leicht; **b)** *(crack)* ⟨*Fenster-, Glasscheibe:*⟩ zerspringen; **the bows of the ship broke against** *or* **on the rocks** der Bug des Schiffes zerschellte an den Felsen; **my back was nearly ~ing** ich brach mir fast das Kreuz; **c)** *(be destroyed)* ⟨*Freundschaft, Ehe, Bündnis:*⟩ zerbrechen; ⟨*Familienbande:*⟩ zerreißen; **d)** *(sever links)* ~ **with sb./sth.** mit jmdm./etw. brechen; **e)** *(weaken)* gebrochen werden; **until he/his will ~s** bis er zusammenbricht/sein Wille gebrochen ist; **f)** ~ **into** einbrechen in (+ *Akk.*) ⟨*Haus*⟩; aufbrechen ⟨*Safe*⟩; ~ **into laughter/tears** in Gelächter/Tränen ausbrechen; **he broke into a sweat** ihm brach der Schweiß aus; ~ **into a trot/run** *etc.* zu traben/laufen *usw.* anfangen; **sb. ~s into acting/industry** *(coll.)* jmdm. gelingt der Durchbruch in der Schauspielerei/in der Industrie; ~ **into one's capital** sein Kapital angreifen; ~ **into a banknote** eine Banknote anbrechen; ~ **out of prison** *etc.* aus dem Gefängnis *usw.* ausbrechen; **g)** *(escape)* ~ **free** *or* **loose [from sb./sb.'s grip]** sich [von jmdm./aus jmds. Griff] losreißen; ~ **free/loose [from prison]** [aus dem Gefängnis] ausbrechen; **some planks had broken loose** einige Planken waren losgebrochen; **h)** ⟨*Welle:*⟩ sich brechen **(on/against** an + *Dat.*), branden **(on/against** an + *Akk.*/gegen); **i)** ⟨*Wetter:*⟩ umschlagen; **j)** ⟨*Wolkendecke:*⟩ aufreißen; **k)** ⟨*Tag:*⟩ anbrechen; **l)** ⟨*Sturm:*⟩ losbrechen; **m)** *(disperse)* ⟨*Truppen:*⟩ auseinanderlaufen; **n)** *(change tone)* **sb.'s voice ~s** jmd. kommt in den Stimmbruch; *(with emotion)* jmdm. bricht die Stimme; **o)** *(Boxing)* sich aus dem Clinch lösen; **~!** break!; **p)** *(have interval)* ~ **for coffee/lunch** [eine] Kaffee-/Mittagspause machen; **we'll ~ for five minutes** wir machen fünf Minuten Pause; **q)** *(Cricket)* die Richtung beim Aufprall ändern; ≈ Drall haben; **r)** *(become public)* bekanntwerden. **3.** *n.* **a)** Bruch, *der; (of rope)* Reißen, *das;* **a ~ [of service]** *(Tennis)* Break, *der od. das;* **a ~ in the weather** ein Wetterumschlag; **a ~ with sb./sth.** ein Bruch mit jmdm./etw.; ~ **of day** Tagesanbruch, *der;* **at ~ of day** bei Tagesanbruch; **b)** *(gap)* Lücke, *die; (in ground)* Riß, *der;* Spalte, *die; (Electr.: in circuit)* Unterbrechung, *die; (broken place)* Sprung, *der;* **c)** *(escape from prison)* Ausbruch, *der; (sudden dash)* **they made a sudden ~:** sie stürmten plötzlich davon; **they made a ~ for the gateway** sie stürzten zum Tor; **d)** *(interruption)* Unterbrechung, *die;* **e)** *(pause, holiday)* Pause, *die;* **during the commercial ~s on TV** während der Werbespots im Fernsehen; **take** *or* **have a ~:** [eine] Pause machen; **work without a ~:** ohne Pause arbeiten; **tea-~** *(Brit.)* Teepause, *die;* **go away for a weekend ~:** übers Wochenende verreisen; **f)** *(coll.: fair chance, piece of luck)* Chance, *die;* **lucky ~:** große Chance; **that was a bad ~ for him** das war Pech für ihn; **g) [bad] ~** *(coll.) (unfortunate remark)* ungeschickte Bemerkung; *(ill-judged action)* Dummheit, *die;* **h)** *(Electr.)* Unterbrechen, *das (in Gen.);* **i)** *(Cricket)* Richtungsänderung beim Aufprall *etc.*; ≈ Drall, *der;* **j)** *(Billiards etc.)* Serie, *die;* **k)** *(Jazz)* Break, *der od. das*

~ **a'way 1.** *v. t.* ~ **sth. away [from sth.]** etw. [von etw.] losbrechen *od.* abbrechen. **2.** *v. i.* **a)** ~ **away [from sth.]** [von etw.] losbrechen *od.* abbrechen; *(separate itself/oneself)* sich [von etw.] lösen; *(escape)* [aus etw.] entkommen; **he broke away from them** er distanzierte sich von ihnen; *(escaped)* er entkam ihnen; **b)** *(Footb.)* sich freilaufen; **c)** *(get out of control)* ⟨*Auto:*⟩ ausbrechen. *See also* **breakaway**

~ **'down 1.** *v. i.* **a)** *(fail)* zusammenbrechen; ⟨*Verhandlungen:*⟩ scheitern; **b)** *(cease to function)* ⟨*Auto:*⟩ eine Panne haben; ⟨*Telefonnetz:*⟩ zusammenbrechen; **the machine has broken down** die Maschine funktioniert nicht mehr; **c)** *(be overcome by emotion)* zusammenbrechen; **d)** *(Chem.)* aufspalten. **2.** *v. t.* **a)** *(demolish)* aufbrechen ⟨*Tür*⟩; zum Einsturz bringen ⟨*Mauer*⟩; umknicken ⟨*Baum*⟩; **b)** *(suppress)* brechen ⟨*Widerstand*⟩; niederreißen ⟨*Barriere, Schranke*⟩; **c)** *(analyse)* aufgliedern. *See also* **breakdown; broken-down**

~ **'in 1.** *v. i.* **a)** *(intrude forcibly)* einbrechen; *see also* **break-in; b)** *(interrupt)* ~ **in [on sb./sth.]** [jmdn./etw.] unterbrechen. **2.** *v. t.* **a)** *(accustom to habit)* eingewöhnen; einarbeiten ⟨*Lehrling etc.*⟩; *(tame)* zureiten ⟨*Pferd*⟩; abrichten ⟨*Hund*⟩; *(discipline)* zur Disziplin erziehen; **b)** *(wear etc. until comfortable)* einlaufen ⟨*Schuhe*⟩; sich gewöhnen an (+ *Akk.*) ⟨*Brille, Gebiß*⟩; **c)** ~ **the door in** die Tür aufbrechen

~ **into** *see* ~ **2 f**

~ **'off 1.** *v. t.* abbrechen; abreißen ⟨*Faden*⟩; auflösen ⟨*Verlobung*⟩; ~ **it off [with sb.]** sich von jmdm. trennen. **2.** *v. i.* **a)** abbrechen; **b)** *(cease)* aufhören; ⟨*Gespräch, Gesang:*⟩ abbrechen; ⟨*Diskussion, Verfahren:*⟩ abgebrochen werden

~ **'out** *v. i. (escape, appear)* ausbrechen; ⟨*Flecken, Pusteln, Schweißtropfen:*⟩ sich bilden; ~ **out in spots/a rash** *etc.* Pickel/einen Ausschlag *usw.* bekommen; **he broke out in a cold sweat** ihm brach der kalte Schweiß aus

~ **out of** *see* ~ **2 f**

~ **'through** *v. t. & i.* durchbrechen; *see also* **breakthrough**

~ **'up 1.** *v. t.* **a)** *(~ into pieces)* zerkleinern; ausschlachten ⟨*Auto*⟩; abwracken ⟨*Schiff*⟩; aufbrechen ⟨*Erde*⟩; zerbrechen ⟨*Stuhl*⟩; **b)** *(disband)* auflösen; auseinanderreißen ⟨*Familie*⟩; zerstreuen ⟨*Menge*⟩; ~ **it up!** *(coll.)* auseinander!; **c)** *(disconcert)* aus der Fassung bringen; **d)** *(end)* zerstören ⟨*Freundschaft, Ehe*⟩. **2.** *v. i.* **a)** *(~ into pieces, lit. or fig.)* zerbrechen; ⟨*Erde, Straßenoberfläche:*⟩ aufbrechen; ⟨*Eis:*⟩ brechen; **b)** *(disband)* sich auflösen; ⟨*Schule:*⟩ schließen; ⟨*Schüler, Lehrer:*⟩ in die Ferien gehen; **c)** *(be convulsed)* ~ **up [with laughter]** in Gelächter ausbrechen; **d)** *(cease)* abgebrochen werden; *(end relationship)* ~ **up [with sb.]** sich [von jmdm.] trennen; **they broke up last year** sie trennten sich letztes Jahr; **e)** *see* ~ **2 i; f)** *(mentally)* zusammenbrechen. *See also* **break-up**

²break *see* **⁴brake**

breakable ['breɪkəbl] **1.** *adj.* zerbrechlich. **2.** *n. in pl.* zerbrechliche Dinge
breakage ['breɪkɪdʒ] *n.* **a)** *(breaking)* Zerbrechen, *das;* **b)** *(result of breaking)* Bruchschaden, *der;* **~s must be paid for** zerbrochene Ware muß bezahlt werden
break: ~away 1. *n.* **a)** Ausbrechen, *das;* **a ~away from tradition** ein Bruch mit der Tradition; **b)** *(Sport: false start)* Fehlstart, *der;* **c)** *(Rugby) [schnelles] Lösen aus dem Gedränge.* **2.** *adj. (Brit.)* abtrünnig; **~away group** Splittergruppe, *die;* **~ dancing** *n.* Breakdance, *der;* **~down** *n.* **a)** *(fig.: collapse)* **a ~down in the system** *(fig.)* ein Zusammenbruch des Systems; **b)** *(mechanical failure)* Panne, *die; (in machine)* Störung, *die;* **~down service** Pannendienst, *der;* **~down truck/van** Abschleppwagen, *der;* **c)** *(health or mental failure)* Zusammenbruch, *der;* **a ~down in health** ein gesundheitlicher Zusammenbruch; **d)** *(analysis)* Aufschlüsselung, *die;* **e)** *(disintegration)* Aufspaltung, *die;* **~down product** Spaltprodukt, *das (Chemie)*
breaker ['breɪkə(r)] *n.* **a)** *(wave)* Brecher, *der;* **b) [car] ~:** *jmd., der Autos ausschlachtet;* **~'s [yard]** Autofriedhof, *der*
break 'even *v. i.* die Kosten decken; **break-even point** Nutzschwelle, *die (Wirtsch.)*
breakfast ['brekfəst] **1.** *n.* Frühstück, *das;* **for ~:** zum Frühstück; **have sth. for ~:** etw. zum Frühstück essen/trinken; **eat** *or* **have [one's] ~:** frühstücken; **have a cooked ~:** zum Frühstück etwas Warmes essen; *see also* **wedding breakfast. 2.** *v. i.* frühstücken; **we ~ed on bacon and eggs** wir aßen Eier mit Speck zum Frühstück
breakfast: ~ cereal *n.* ≈ Frühstücksflocken *Pl.;* **~ 'television** *n.* Frühstücksfernsehen, *das;* **~-time** *n.* Frühstückszeit, *die*
'break-in *n.* Einbruch, *der;* **there has been a ~ at the bank** in der *od.* die Bank ist eingebrochen worden
'breaking *n.* **~ and entering** *(Law)* Einbruch, *der*
breaking: ~-point *n.* Belastungsgrenze, *die;* **be at ~-point** *(mentally)* die Grenze der Belastbarkeit erreicht haben; **~-strength** *n.* Belastbarkeit, *die*
break: ~neck *adj.* halsbrecherisch; **~-out** *n.* Ausbruch, *der;* **~through** *n.* Durchbruch, *der;* **~-up** *n.* **a)** *(disintegration) (of earth, soil, road surface)* Aufbrechen, *das; (fig.)* Zusammenbruch, *der; (of weather)* Umschlag, *der; (of old structure)* Zerfall, *der;* **b)** *(disbanding, dispersal)* Auflösung, *die;* **c)** *(ceasing)* Ende, *das; (ending of relationship)* Bruch, *der;* **~water** *n.* Wellenbrecher, *der*
bream [bri:m] *n., pl. same (Zool.)* **a)** Brachsen, *der;* **b) [sea-]~** *(Sparidae)* Meerbrassen, *der;* **c)** *(Amer.: sunfish)* Sonnenbarsch, *der*
breast [brest] **1.** *n. (lit. or fig.)* Brust, *die;* **make a clean ~ [of sth.]** *(fig.)* [etw.] offen bekennen. **2.** *v. t.* **a)** *(oppose, confront)* sich entgegenstellen (+ *Dat.*); **b)** *(Brit.: climb)* übersteigen ‹*Mauer, Hindernis*›; besteigen ‹*Berg*›; **~ the waves** gegen die Wellen ankämpfen. *See also* **tape 1 b**
breast: ~bone *n.* Brustbein, *das;* **~ cancer** *n.* Brustkrebs, *der;* **~-fed** *adj.* **be ~-fed** gestillt werden; **~-feed** *v. t. & i.* stillen; **~-feeding** *n.* das Stillen; **~plate** *n. (armour)* Brustharnisch, *der;* **~-'pocket** *n.* Brusttasche, *die;* **~-stroke** *n. (Swimming)* Brustschwimmen, *das;* **do** *or* **swim [the] ~-stroke** brustschwimmen
breath [breθ] *n.* **a)** Atem, *der;* **have bad ~:** Mundgeruch haben; **say sth. below** *or* **under one's ~:** etw. vor sich *(Akk.)* hin murmeln; **draw ~:** Atem holen; **as long as I draw ~:** solange ich atme; **a ~ of fresh air** ein wenig frische Luft; **go out for a ~ of fresh air** frische Luft schnappen gehen; **be a ~ of fresh air in sb.'s life** etwas Abwechslung in jmds. Leben bringen; **waste one's ~:** seine Worte verschwenden; **sth. is the ~ of life to sb.** jmd. kann ohne etw. nicht leben; **she caught her ~:** ihr stockte der Atem; **hold one's ~:** den Atem anhalten; **get one's ~ back** wieder zu Atem kommen; **be out of/short of ~:** außer Atem *od.* atemlos sein/kurzatmig sein; **take ~:** [sich] verschnaufen; **pause for ~:** eine Verschnaufpause machen; **take sb.'s ~ away** *(fig.)* jmdm. den Atem verschlagen; *see also* **save 1 e**; **b)** *(one respiration)* Atemzug, *der;* **take** *or* **draw a [deep] ~:** [tief] einatmen; **in the same ~:** im selben Atemzug; **c)** *(air movement, whiff)* Hauch, *der;* **there wasn't a ~ of air** es regte sich kein Lüftchen; **a ~ of wind** ein Windhauch; **not a ~ of suspicion/rumour** nicht die Spur eines Verdachts/nicht die leiseste Andeutung eines Gerüchts
breathalyse ['breθəlaɪz] *v. t.* ins Röhrchen *od.* in die Tüte blasen lassen *(ugs.)*
breathalyser, (P) *(Amer.:* **breathalyzer***)* ['breθəlaɪzə(r)] *n.* **~ test** Alcotest Ⓦⓩ, *der;* **blow/breathe into a ~ [bag]** ins Röhrchen *od.* in die Tüte blasen *(ugs.)*
breathe [bri:ð] **1.** *v. i.* **a)** *(lit. or fig.)* atmen; **~ in** einatmen; **~ out** ausatmen; **~ into sth.** [sanft] in etw. *(Akk.)* [hinein]blasen; *see also* **neck 1 a**; **b)** *(take breath)* **stop to ~:** eine Verschnaufpause machen; **give me a chance to ~!** laß mich erst wieder zur Besinnung kommen!; **c)** *(blow)* [sanft] wehen. **2.** *v. t.* **a) ~ a breath** einen Atemzug tun; **~ one's last** seinen letzten Atemzug tun; **~ fire** Feuer speien; *(fig.)* Gift und Galle spucken; **~ [in/out]** ein-/ausatmen; **~ new life into sth.** *(fig.)* etw. mit neuem Leben erfüllen; **b)** *(utter)* hauchen; **~ a sigh [of relief]/a sigh of regret** [erleichtert] aufatmen/aufseufzen; **don't ~ a word about** *or* **of this to anyone** sag kein Sterbenswörtchen darüber zu irgend jemandem; **c)** *(show evidence of)* atmen *(geh.);* ausstrahlen
breather ['bri:ðə(r)] *n.* **a)** *(brief pause)* Verschnaufpause, *die; (brief holiday etc.)* Erholungspause, *die;* **take** *or* **have a ~:** eine Verschnaufpause/Erholungspause einlegen; **go out for a ~:** ein wenig frische Luft schöpfen; **b)** *(Motor Veh.)* Entlüfter, *der*
breathing ['bri:ðɪŋ] *n.* Atmen, *das*
breathing: ~-apparatus *n.* **a)** *(Med.)* Beatmungsgerät, *das;* **b)** *(of fireman etc.)* Atemschutzgerät, *das;* **~-space** *n. (time to breathe)* Zeit zum Luftholen; *(pause)* Atempause, *die;* **~-tube** *n.* Atemschlauch, *der*
breathless ['breθlɪs] *adj.* atemlos (**with** vor + *Dat.*); **leave sb. ~** *(lit. or fig.)* jmdm. den Atem nehmen; **we stood ~ while ...:** uns *(Dat.)* stockte der Atem, während ...; **we were ~ with amazement** uns *(Dat.)* blieb vor Staunen die Luft weg *(ugs.)*
breathlessly ['breθlɪslɪ] *adv.* atemlos
breathlessness ['breθlɪsnɪs] *n., no pl.* Atemlosigkeit, *die; (caused by smoking or illness)* Kurzatmigkeit, *die*
breath: ~-taking *adj.* atemberaubend; **~ test** *n.* Alcotest Ⓦⓩ, *der*
breathy ['breθɪ] *adj.* hauchig ‹*Stimme*›
Brechtian ['brektɪən] *adj. (Theatre)* brechtsch
bred *see* **breed 1, 2**
breech [bri:tʃ] *n.* [Geschütz]verschluß, *der*
breech: ~ birth *n. (Med.)* Steißgeburt, *die;* **~-block** *n.* Verschlußblock, *der*
breeches ['brɪtʃɪz] *n. pl.* **a)** *(short trousers)* **[pair of] ~:** [Knie]bundhose, *die;* **[riding-] ~:** Reithose, *die;* Breeches *Pl.;* **b)** *(trousers)* Hose, *die; (knickerbockers)* Knickerbocker *Pl.;* **wear the ~** *(fig.)* die Hosen anhaben *(ugs.); see also* **big 1 g**
'breeches-buoy *n. (Naut.)* Hosenboje, *die*
breech: ~-loader *n.* Hinterlader, *der;* **~-loading** *adj.* Hinterlader-
breed [bri:d] **1.** *v. t.,* **bred** [bred] **a)** *(be the cause of)* erzeugen; hervorrufen; **b)** *(raise)* züchten ‹*Tiere, Pflanzen*›; **bred in the bone** angeboren; **c)** *(bring up)* erziehen; **be bred and born** *or* **born and bred sth.** etw. durch und durch sein; **he was born and bred in London** er ist in London geboren und aufgewachsen; **d)** *(bear)* gebären ‹*Nachkommen*›; *(generate)* hervorbringen ‹*Rasse*›. **2.** *v. i.,* **bred: a)** sich vermehren; ‹*Vogel:*› brüten; ‹*Tier:*› Junge haben; **they ~ like flies** *or* **rabbits** sie vermehren sich wie die Kaninchen; **b)** *(arise)* entstehen; *(spread)* sich ausbreiten. **3.** *n.* **a)** Art, *die; (of animals)* Rasse, *die;* **~s of cattle** Rinderrassen; **the Jersey ~ [of cattle]** das Jerseyrind; **what ~ of dog is that?** zu welcher Rasse gehört dieser Hund?; **b)** *(lineage)* Rasse, *die;* **a noble ~ of men** ein vornehmer Menschenschlag; **c)** *(sort)* Art, *die*
breeder ['bri:də(r)] *n.* Züchter, *der;* **be a ~ of sth.** etw. züchten; **dog-/horse-~:** Hunde-/Pferdezüchter, *der*
'breeder reactor *n. (Nucl. Engin.)* Brutreaktor, *der;* Brüter, *der*
breeding ['bri:dɪŋ] *n.* Erziehung, *die;* **[good] ~:** gute Erziehung; **have ~:** eine gute Erziehung genossen haben
breeding: ~-ground *n. (lit. or fig.)* Brutstätte, *die;* **~ season** *n.* Brutzeit, *die*
[1]**breeze** [bri:z] **1.** *n.* **a)** *(gentle wind)* Brise, *die;* **there is a ~:** es weht eine Brise; **night ~:** nächtliche Brise; **sea ~:** Seebrise, *die;* **b)** *(Meteorol.)* [leichter] Wind. **2.** *v. i. (coll.)* **~ along** dahinrollen; *(on foot)* dahinschlendern; **~ in** hereingeschneit kommen *(ugs.)*
[2]**breeze** *n. (cinders)* Lösche, *die*
[3]**breeze** *n. (Zool.)* Bremse, *die*
'breeze-block *n. (Building)* ≈ Leichtstein, *der*
breezily ['bri:zɪlɪ] *adv. (coll.)* [frisch und] unbekümmert; *(carelessly)* leichthin; unbekümmert
breeziness ['bri:zɪnɪs] *n., no pl. (coll.) (carefree nature)* [frische und] unbekümmerte Art; *(carelessness)* Unbekümmertheit, *die*
breezy ['bri:zɪ] *adj.* **a)** *(windy)* windig; **b)** *(coll.) (brisk and carefree)* [frisch und] unbekümmert; *(careless)* unbekümmert
brent [brent] *n.* **~[-goose]** Ringelgans, *die*
brethren *see* **brother d**
Breton ['bretn] **1.** *adj.* bretonisch; *see also* **English 1. 2.** *n.* **a)** *(language)* Bretonisch, *das; see also* **English 2 a**; **b)** *(person)* Bretone, *der*/Bretonin, *die*
breve [bri:v] *n.* **a)** *(Mus.)* Brevis, *die (veralt.);* Doppelganze, *die;* **b)** *(of short/unstressed vowel)* Halbkreis, *der (zur Kennzeichnung kurzer/unbetonter Vokale)*
breviary ['bri:vɪərɪ] *n. (Eccl.)* Brevier, *das*
brevity ['brevɪtɪ] *n.* Kürze, *die*
brew [bru:] **1.** *v. t.* **a)** brauen ‹*Bier*›; keltern ‹*Apfelwein*›; **~ [up]** kochen ‹*Kaffee, Tee, Kakao usw.*›; aufbrühen ‹*Tee, Kaffee*›; **~ up** *abs.* Tee kochen; [sich *(Dat.)*] einen Tee kochen *od.* aufbrühen; **b)** *(fig.: put together)* **~ [up]** [zusammen]brauen *(ugs.)* ‹*Mischung*›; *(generate)* hervorrufen ‹*Empfindungen*›; *(formulate)* ausbrüten *(ugs.)* ‹*Plan usw.*›. **2.** *v. i.* **a)** ‹*Bier, Apfelwein:*› gären; ‹*Kaffee, Tee:*› ziehen; **b)** *(fig.: gather)* ‹*Unwetter:*› sich zusammenbrauen; ‹*Rebellion, Krieg:*› drohen. **3.** *n.* **a)** Gebräu, *das (abwertend);* *(brewed beer/tea)* Bier, *das*/Tee, *der;* **~ [of tea/coffee]** Tee, *der*/Kaffee, *der;* **b)** *(amount brewed)* ≈ Abfüllung, *die; (of tea etc.)* **we'll have to make another ~:** wir müssen noch einmal aufbrühen
brewer ['bru:ə(r)] *n.* **a)** *(person)* Brauer, *der;* **b)** *(firm)* Brauerei, *die*
brewery ['bru:ərɪ] *n.* Brauerei, *die*
briar *see* [1, 2]**brier**
bribe [braɪb] **1.** *n.* Bestechung, *die;* **a ~ [of £100]** ein Bestechungsgeld [in Höhe von

100 Pfund]; **take a ~/~s** sich bestechen lassen; **he won't accept ~s** er ist unbestechlich; **offer sb. a ~:** jmdn. bestechen wollen. **2.** *v. t.* bestechen; **he won't be ~d** er ist unbestechlich; **~ sb. to do/into doing sth.** jmdn. bestechen, damit er etw. tut

bribery ['braɪbərɪ] *n.* Bestechung, *die;* **open to ~:** bestechlich; käuflich; **be involved in ~:** in einen Bestechungsfall verwickelt sein

bric-à-brac ['brɪkəbræk] *n.* Antiquarisches; *(smaller things)* Nippsachen *Pl.;* **~ collector** ≈ Antiquitätensammler, *der*

brick [brɪk] **1.** *n.* **a)** *(block)* Ziegelstein, *der;* Backstein, *der; (clay)* Lehmziegel, *der;* **~s and mortar** *(buildings)* Gebäude; *(as investment)* Immobilien *Pl.;* **drop a ~** *(fig. sl.)* ins Fettnäpfchen treten *(ugs. scherzh.);* **be *or* come down on sb. like a load *or* ton of ~s** *(coll.)* jmdn. unheimlich fertigmachen *od.* zusammenstauchen *(ugs.);* **b)** *(toy)* Bauklötzchen, *das;* **c)** *(of ice-cream)* Packung, *die;* **d)** *(sl.: person)* feiner Kerl; **you've been a real ~:** du warst ein prima Kumpel *(ugs.).* **2.** *adj.* **a)** Ziegelstein-; Backstein-; **b)** *(red)* ziegelrot. **3.** *v. t.* **~ up/in** zu-/einmauern

brick: ~bat *n.* **a)** Backsteinbrocken, *der;* **b)** *(fig.: uncomplimentary remark)* schlechte Kritik; **greet sb. with ~bats** jmdn. attackieren; **~-built** *adj.* backsteinern; Backstein‹*haus, -mauer*›; **it is ~-built** es ist aus Backstein

brickie ['brɪkɪ] *n. (Brit. sl.)* Maurer, *der*

brick: ~-kiln *n.* Ziegelofen, *der;* **~layer** *n.* Maurer, *der;* **~laying** *n.* Mauern, *das;* **~-red** *adj.* ziegelrot; **~ 'wall** *n.* Backsteinmauer, *die;* **bang one's head against a ~ wall** *(fig.)* mit dem Kopf gegen die Wand rennen *(fig.);* **come up against a ~ wall** *(fig.)* plötzlich vor einer Mauer stehen *(fig.);* **~work** *n.* **a)** *(bricklaying)* Mauern, *das;* **b)** *(structure)* [Backstein]mauerwerk, *das;* **~yard** *n.* Ziegelei, *die*

bridal ['braɪdl] *adj. (of bride)* Braut-; *(of wedding)* Hochzeits-; **~ couple/suite** Brautpaar, *das*/Hochzeitssuite, *die*

bride [braɪd] *n.* Braut, *die*

'bridegroom *n.* Bräutigam, *der*

bridesmaid ['braɪdzmeɪd] *n.* Brautjungfer, *die;* **chief ~:** erste Brautjungfer

¹bridge [brɪdʒ] **1.** *n.* **a)** *(lit. or fig.)* Brücke, *die;* **cross that ~ when you come to it** *(fig.)* alles zu seiner Zeit; *see also* **¹burn 2 a; b)** *(Naut.)* [Kommando]brücke, *die;* **c)** *(of nose)* Nasenbein, *das;* Sattel, *der;* **d)** *(of violin, spectacles)* Steg, *der;* **e)** *(Dent.)* [Zahn]brücke, *die.* **2.** *v. t.* eine Brücke bauen *od.* errichten *od.* schlagen über (+ *Akk.*); **~ the gap** *(fig.)* die Kluft überbrücken

²bridge *n. (Cards)* Bridge, *das*

'bridgehead *n.* Brückenkopf, *der*

'bridging loan *n. (Commerc.)* Überbrückungskredit, *der*

bridle ['braɪdl] **1.** *n.* Zaumzeug, *das;* Zaum, *der.* **2.** *v. t.* **a)** aufzäumen ‹*Pferd*›; **b)** *(fig.: restrain)* zügeln ‹*Zunge*›; im Zaum halten ‹*Leidenschaft*›. **3.** *v. i.* **~ at sth.** sich gegen etw. sträuben *od. (geh.)* stemmen

'bridle-path, 'bridle-road *ns.* Saumpfad, *der; (for horses)* Reitweg, *der*

Brie [bri:] *n.* Brie[käse], *der*

¹brief [bri:f] *adj.* **a)** *(of short duration)* kurz; gering, geringfügig ‹*Verspätung*›; **after a ~ discussion/the ~est of discussions** nach kurzer/ganz kurzer Diskussion; **b)** *(concise)* knapp; **in ~, to be ~:** kurz gesagt; **make *or* keep it ~:** es kurz machen; **be ~:** sich kurz fassen; **the news in ~:** die Nachrichten im Überblick

²brief 1. *n.* **a)** *(Law: summary of facts)* Schriftsatz, *der;* **hold a ~ for sb.** jmdn. als Anwalt [vor Gericht] vertreten; **hold no ~ for sb.** *(fig.)* nicht auf jmds. Seite *(Dat.)* stehen; nicht für jmdn. plädieren *od.* eintreten; **b)** *(Brit. Law: piece of work)* Mandat, *das;* **c)** *(Amer. Law: statement of arguments)* Darlegung der Beweisgründe; **d)** *(instructions)* Instruktionen *Pl.;* Anweisungen *Pl.* **2.** *v. t.* **a)** *(Brit. Law)* mit der Vertretung eines Falles betrauen; **b)** *(Mil.: instruct)* Anweisungen *od.* Instruktionen geben (+ *Dat.*); instruieren; unterweisen; **c)** *(inform, instruct)* unterrichten; informieren

'brief-case *n.* Aktentasche, *die*

briefing ['bri:fɪŋ] *n.* **a)** Briefing, *das; (of reporters or press)* Unterrichtung, *die; (before raid etc.)* Einsatzbesprechung, *die;* **b)** *(instructions)* Instruktionen *Pl.;* Anweisungen *Pl.; (information)* Informationen *Pl.*

briefly ['bri:flɪ] *adv.* **a)** *(for a short time)* kurz; **b)** *(concisely)* knapp; kurz; **[to put it] ~, ...:** kurz gesagt ...

briefness ['bri:fnɪs] *n., no pl.* **a)** *(shortness)* Kürze, *die;* **b)** *(conciseness)* Knappheit, *die*

briefs [bri:fs] *n. pl.* **[pair of] ~:** Slip, *der*

¹brier [braɪə(r)] *n. (Bot.: rose)* Wilde Rose

²brier *n.* **a)** *(pipe)* Bruyèrepfeife, *die;* **b)** *(Bot.: heath)* Baumheide, *die*

'brier-rose *n.* Hundsrose, *die*

brig [brɪg] *n.* **a)** *(Naut.)* Brigg, *die;* **b)** *(Amer. sl.: prison)* Bau, *der (salopp);* Bunker, *der (salopp)*

Brig. *abbr.* **brigadier** Brig.

brigade [brɪ'geɪd] *n.* **a)** *(Mil.)* Brigade, *die;* **the old ~** *(fig.)* die alte Garde; **b)** *(organized or uniformed body)* Einheit, *die*

brigadier[-general] [brɪgə'dɪə(r) ('dʒenrl)] *n. (Mil.)* Brigadegeneral, *der;* Brigadier, *der*

brigand ['brɪgənd] *n.* Bandit, *der;* Brigant, *der (geh.)*

bright [braɪt] **1.** *adj.* **a)** hell ‹*Licht, Stern, Fleck*›; grell ‹*Scheinwerfer[licht], Sonnenlicht*›; strahlend ‹*Sonnenschein, Stern, Augen*›; glänzend ‹*Metall, Augen*›; leuchtend, lebhaft ‹*Farbe, Blume*›; **~ reflection** starke Reflexion *od.* Spiegelung; **~ blue** *etc.* leuchtend blau *usw.;* **~ yellow/red** leuchtend gelb/rot; knallgelb/-rot *(ugs.);* **a ~ day** ein heiterer *od.* strahlender Tag; **~ intervals/periods** Aufheiterungen; **the one ~ spot** *(fig.)* der Lichtblick; **the ~ lights of the city** *(fig.)* der Glanz der Großstadt; **look on the ~ side** *(fig.)* die Sache positiv sehen; **~-eyed and bushy-tailed** *(joc.)* fidel und munter; **b)** *(cheerful)* fröhlich, heiter ‹*Mensch, Charakter, Stimmung*›; strahlend ‹*Lächeln*›; freundlich ‹*Zimmer, Farbe*›; **c)** *(clever)* intelligent; **that wasn't very ~ [of you], was it?** das war nicht gerade intelligent [von dir]!; **he is a ~ boy** er ist ein heller *od.* aufgeweckter Junge; **d)** *(hopeful)* vielversprechend ‹*Zukunft*›; glänzend ‹*Aussichten*›. **2.** *adv.* **a)** hell; **b) ~ and early** in aller Frühe

brighten ['braɪtn] **1.** *v. t.* **~ [up] a)** aufhellen ‹*Farben*›; aufpolieren, zum Glänzen bringen ‹*Metall*›; **b)** *(make more cheerful)* aufhellen, aufheitern ‹*Zimmer*›. **2.** *v. i.* **~ [up] a)** ‹*Himmel:*› sich aufhellen; **the weather *or* it is ~ing [up]** es klärt sich auf; es klart auf *(Met.);* **b)** *(become more cheerful)* ‹*Mensch:*› vergnügter werden; ‹*Augen:*› [auf]leuchten; ‹*Gesicht:*› sich aufhellen; ‹*Aussichten:*› sich verbessern

brightly ['braɪtlɪ] *adv.* **a)** hell ‹*scheinen, glänzen*›; glänzend ‹*poliert*›; **~ lit** hellerleuchtet *präd. getrennt geschrieben;* **~ coloured** leuchtend bunt; **b)** *(cheerfully)* gutgelaunt; strahlend

brightness ['braɪtnɪs] *n., no pl.* **a)** *(of light, star, spot)* Helligkeit, *die; (of sunlight)* Grelle, *die;* Grellheit, *die; (of sun, eyes, star)* Strahlen, *das; (of metal, eyes)* Glanz, *der; (of colours)* Leuchtkraft, *die; (of eyes)* Leuchten, *das;* **the ~ of the reflection** die Stärke der Reflexion; **b)** *(cheerfulness)* Fröhlichkeit, *die;* Heiterkeit, *die;* **c)** *(cleverness)* Intelligenz, *die;* **the ~ of his ideas** seine glänzenden Ideen

¹brill [brɪl] *n., pl. same (Zool.)* Glattbutt, *der*

²brill *adj. (Brit. sl.)* super *(ugs.)*

brilliance ['brɪljəns], **brilliancy** ['brɪljənsɪ] *n., no pl.* **a)** *(brightness) (of light)* Helligkeit, *die; (of star, diamond)* Funkeln, *das; (of flash)* Grelle, *die;* Grellheit, *die; (of colours)* Leuchten, *das;* **b)** *(of person, invention, idea, move, achievement)* Genialität, *die;* **the ~ of his mind** sein genialer Geist; **c)** *(illustriousness)* Glanz, *der*

brilliant ['brɪljənt] **1.** *adj.* **a)** *(bright)* hell ‹*Licht*›; strahlend ‹*Sonne*›; funkelnd ‹*Diamant, Stern*›; leuchtend ‹*Farbe*›; **b)** *(highly talented)* genial ‹*Mensch, Erfindung, Gedanke, Schachzug, Leistung*›; glänzend ‹*Verstand*›; brillant, glänzend ‹*Aufführung, Vorstellung, Idee*›; bestechend ‹*Theorie, Argument*›; **that was ~** *(iron.)* das war gekonnt *od.* intelligent *(iron.);* **c)** *(illustrious)* glänzend ‹*Karriere, Erfolg, Sieg*›; großartig ‹*[Helden]tat*›; **a ~ achievement** eine Glanzleistung. **2.** *n.* Brillant, *der*

brilliantine ['brɪljənti:n] *n.* Brillantine, *die;* Haarpomade, *die*

brilliantly ['brɪljəntlɪ] *adv.* **a)** hell ‹*scheinen, funkeln, schimmern*›; **it was a ~ sunny day** es war ein strahlender Sonnentag; **~ lit** hellerleuchtet *präd. getrennt geschrieben;* **b)** *(with great talent)* brillant; **a ~ thought-out scheme** ein genial ausgedachter Plan; **c)** *(illustriously)* glänzend ‹*erfolgreich sein, triumphieren*›

brim [brɪm] **1.** *n.* **a)** *(of cup, bowl, hollow)* Rand, *der;* **full to the ~:** randvoll; **b)** *(of hat)* [Hut]krempe, *die.* **2.** *v. i.,* **-mm-: be ~ming with sth.** randvoll mit etw. sein; *(fig.)* strotzen vor etw. *(Dat.);* **be ~ming with tears** *(fig.)* ‹*Augen:*› voller Tränen stehen

~ 'over *v. i.* **a)** übervoll sein; **b)** *(fig.)* **he was ~ming over with confidence** er strotzte vor Zuversicht

brim-'full *adj.* **be ~ with sth.** randvoll mit etw. sein; **be ~ of energy/curiosity** *(fig.)* vor Energie *(Dat.)* sprühen/vor Neugierde *(Dat.)* platzen; **be ~ of new ideas** *(fig.)* von neuen Ideen übersprudeln

brimless ['brɪmlɪs] *adj.* ‹*Hut*› ohne Krempe

brindle ['brɪndl], **brindled** ['brɪndld] *adjs.* gestreift ‹*Katze*›; gestromt ‹*Kuh, Hund*›

brine [braɪn] *n. (salt water)* Salzwasser, *das;* Sole, *die; (for preserving)* Pökellake, *die;* [Salz]lake, *die*

bring [brɪŋ] *v. t.,* **brought** [brɔ:t] **a)** bringen; *(as a present or favour)* mitbringen; **~ sth. with one** etw. mitbringen; **I haven't brought my towel** ich habe mein Handtuch nicht mitgebracht *od.* dabei; **he brought the chair nearer** er zog den Stuhl näher heran; **~ sb. before sb.** jmdn. vor jmdn. führen; **what ~s you here?** was führt dich hierher?; **who brought you here?** wer hat Sie hergebracht?; **he brought the car to the front door** er fuhr mit dem Wagen vor; **April brought a change in the weather** der April brachte einen Wetterumschwung mit sich; **~ sb. low** jmdn. erniedrigen; **~ sth. [up]on oneself/sb.** sich selbst/jmdm. etw. einbrocken; **~ a business/country through a crisis** ein Unternehmen/ein Land durch eine Krise führen; **b)** *(result in)* [mit sich] bringen; **the television appeal brought thousands of replies** auf den Aufruf im Fernsehen meldeten sich Tausende; **the distress call brought help within a matter of minutes** auf den Notruf kam Hilfe in Minutenschnelle; **this will ~ shame on you** das wird dir Schande bringen; **~ honour to sb.** jmdm. Ehre machen; **~ tears to sb.'s eyes** jmdm. Tränen in die Augen treiben; **c)** *(persuade)* **~ sb. to do sth.** jmdn. dazu bringen *od.* bewegen, etw. zu tun; **I could not ~ myself to do it** ich konnte es nicht über mich bringen, es zu tun; **d)** *(initiate, put forward)* **~ a charge/legal action against sb.** gegen jmdn. [An]klage erheben/einen Prozeß anstrengen; **~ a case/matter before a court** einen Fall/eine Sache vor Gericht bringen; ~ **a complaint** eine Beschwerde vorbringen; **e)** *(be sold for, earn)* [ein]bringen ⟨*Geldsumme*⟩; **f)** *(adduce)* vorbringen ⟨*Argument*⟩

~ **a'bout** *v. t.* **a)** *(cause to happen)* verursachen; herbeiführen; ~ **it about that ...:** es zustande bringen, daß ...; **b)** *(Naut.)* ~ **the ship about** das Schiff auf Gegenkurs bringen

~ **a'long** *v. t.* **a)** mitbringen; **b)** *see* ~ **on b**

~ **'back** *v. t.* **a)** *(return)* zurückbringen; *(from a journey)* mitbringen; **b)** *(recall)* in Erinnerung bringen *od.* rufen; ~ **sth. back to sb.** ⟨*Musik, Foto usw.:*⟩ jmdn. an etw. *(Akk.)* erinnern; ~ **back memories** Erinnerungen wachrufen *od.* wecken; **c)** *(restore, reintroduce)* wieder einführen ⟨*Sitten, Todesstrafe*⟩; ~ **back the Socialists!** wir wollen die Sozialisten wieder haben; **be brought back to power** wieder an die Macht kommen; ~ **sb. back to health** jmdn. wieder gesund machen; ~ **sb. back to life** jmdn. wiederbeleben; **nothing will ~ him back to life** nichts kann ihn wieder lebendig machen

~ **'down** *v. t.* **a)** herunterbringen; **b)** *(shoot down out of the air)* abschießen; herunterholen *(ugs.)*; **c)** *(land)* herunterbringen ⟨*Flugzeug, Drachen*⟩; **d)** *(kill, wound)* zur Strecke bringen ⟨*Person, Tier*⟩; erlegen ⟨*Tier*⟩; **e)** *(reduce)* senken ⟨*Preise, Inflationsrate, Fieber*⟩; ~ **sb. down to one's own level** jmdn. zu sich *od.* auf sein [eigenes] Niveau herunterziehen; **f)** *(attract)* **that'll ~ a penalty down on you** das wird dir eine Strafe einbringen; **that'll ~ the boss's wrath down on you[r head]** damit werden Sie sich *(Dat.)* den Zorn des Chefs zuziehen; **g)** *(cause to fall)* zu Fall bringen ⟨*Gegner, Fußballer*⟩; einstürzen lassen ⟨*Haus, Mauer*⟩; *(fig.)* stürzen, zu Fall bringen ⟨*Regierung*⟩; *see also* **house 1 i**

~ **'forth** *v. t.* **a)** *(produce)* hervorbringen ⟨*Frucht*⟩; zur Welt bringen ⟨*Kinder, Junge*⟩; **b)** *(fig.)* vorbringen ⟨*Vorschlag, Idee*⟩; auslösen ⟨*Protest, Kritik*⟩

~ **'forward** *v. t.* **a)** nach vorne bringen; ~ **your chairs forward** rücken Sie nach vorn; **b)** *(draw attention to)* vorlegen ⟨*Beweise*⟩; vorbringen ⟨*Argument, Beschwerde*⟩; zur Sprache bringen ⟨*Fall, Angelegenheit, Frage*⟩; **c)** *(move to earlier time)* vorverlegen ⟨*Termin*⟩ **(to** auf + *Akk.***)**; **d)** *(Bookk.)* übertragen; **the amount brought forward** der Übertrag

~ **'in** *v. t.* **a)** hereinbringen; auftragen ⟨*Essen*⟩; einbringen ⟨*Ernte*⟩; **b)** *(introduce)* anschneiden ⟨*Thema*⟩; einführen ⟨*Mode*⟩; einbringen ⟨*Gesetzesvorlage*⟩; **why ~ all that in?** das gehört hier nicht hin; **c)** *(yield)* einbringen ⟨*Verdienst, Summe*⟩; bringen ⟨*Zinsen*⟩; **d)** *(Law)* ~ **in a verdict of guilty/not guilty** einen Schuldspruch fällen/auf Freispruch erkennen; **e)** *(call in)* hinzuziehen, einschalten ⟨*Experten*⟩

~ **'off** *v. t.* **a)** *(rescue)* retten; in Sicherheit bringen; **b)** *(conduct successfully)* zustande *od.* zuwege bringen; ~ **off a coup** einen Coup landen; **we didn't ~ it off** wir haben es nicht geschafft

~ **'on** *v. t.* **a)** *(cause)* verursachen; **brought on by ...** ⟨*Krankheit*⟩ infolge von ...; **b)** *(advance progress of)* wachsen *od.* sprießen lassen ⟨*Blumen, Getreide*⟩; weiterbringen, fördern ⟨*Schüler, Sportler*⟩; **c)** *(on stage etc.)* auftreten lassen; **d)** *(Sport)* bringen *(ugs.)*; einsetzen

~ **'out** *v. t.* **a)** herausbringen; **he put his hand in his pocket and brought out a knife** er griff in die Tasche und zog ein Messer heraus; **b)** *(show clearly)* hervorheben, betonen ⟨*Unterschied*⟩; verdeutlichen ⟨*Bedeutung*⟩; herausbringen ⟨*Farbe*⟩; **c)** *(cause to appear)* herausbringen ⟨*Pflanzen, Blüte*⟩; **the crisis brought out the best in him** die Krise brachte seine besten Seiten zum Vorschein *od.* ans Licht; ~ **sb. out in a rash** bei jmdm. einen Ausschlag verursachen; **d)** *(begin to sell)* einführen ⟨*Produkt*⟩; herausbringen ⟨*Buch, Zeitschrift*⟩

~ **'over** *v. t.* **a)** herüberbringen; **b)** *(convert)* ~ **sb. over to sth.** jmdn. von etw. überzeugen; ~ **sb. over to a cause** jmdn. für eine Sache gewinnen

~ **'round** *v. t.* **a)** mitbringen ⟨*Bekannte, Freunde usw.*⟩; vorbeibringen ⟨*Gegenstände*⟩; **b)** *(restore to consciousness)* wieder zu sich bringen ⟨*Ohnmächtigen*⟩; **c)** *(win over)* überreden; herumkriegen *(ugs.)*; ~ **sb. round to one's way of thinking** jmdn. von seiner Meinung überzeugen; **d)** *(direct)* ~ **a conversation round to sth.** ein Gespräch auf etw. *(Akk.)* bringen *od.* lenken

~ **'through** *v. t.* durchbringen ⟨*Kranken*⟩

~ **'to** *v. t.* **a)** *(restore to consciousness)* wieder zu sich bringen; **b)** *(Naut.)* beidrehen

~ **to'gether** *v. t.* zusammenbringen

~ **'up** *v. t.* **a)** heraufbringen; **b)** *(educate)* erziehen; ~ **sb. up to be economical** jmdn. zur Sparsamkeit erziehen; **I was brought up to believe that ...:** ich wurde in dem Glauben erzogen, daß ...; **c)** *(rear)* aufziehen; großziehen; **d)** *(call attention to)* zur Sprache bringen ⟨*Angelegenheit, Thema, Problem*⟩; **did you have to ~ that up?** mußten Sie davon anfangen?; ~ **up the past** die Vergangenheit aufrühren; **e)** *(vomit)* erbrechen; wieder von sich geben; **f)** *(Law)* ~ **sb. up [before a judge]** jmdn. [einem Richter] vorführen; **g)** *(Mil.)* an die Front bringen ⟨*Truppen, Panzer*⟩; **h)** *(cause to stop)* ~ **sb. up short** jmdn. innehalten lassen. *See also* **'rear 1 b**

bring-and-'buy [sale] *n.* [Wohltätigkeits]basar, *der*

brink [brɪŋk] *n. (lit. or fig.)* Rand, *der;* **shiver on the ~** *(fig.)* mit sich ringen; **be on the ~ of doing sth.** nahe daran sein, etw. zu tun; **be on the ~ of ruin/success** am Rand des Ruins sein *od.* stehen/dem Erfolg greifbar nahe sein; **they were on the ~ of starvation** sie waren kurz vor dem *od.* nahe am Verhungern

briny ['braɪnɪ] *n. (Brit. sl.)* **the ~:** das Meer

briquet, briquette [brɪ'ket] *n.* Brikett, *das*

brisk [brɪsk] *adj.* flott ⟨*Gang, Bedienung*⟩; forsch ⟨*Person, Art*⟩; frisch ⟨*Wind*⟩; *(fig.)* rege ⟨*Handel, Nachfrage*⟩; lebhaft ⟨*Geschäft*⟩; **we set off at a ~ pace** wir marschierten in flottem Tempo los; **we went for a ~ walk** wir machten einen zünftigen Spaziergang; **business was ~:** das Geschäft florierte; **bidding for the lots was ~:** auf die Auktionsstücke wurde eifrig geboten

brisket ['brɪskɪt] *n. (Gastr.)* Bruststück, *das;* Brust, *die;* ~ **of beef** Rinderbrust, *die;*

briskly ['brɪsklɪ] *adv.* flott; flink; **the wind blew ~:** es wehte ein frischer Wind; **sell ~:** sich gut verkaufen

briskness ['brɪsknɪs] *n., no pl. see* **brisk:** Flottheit, *die;* Forschheit, *die;* Flinkheit, *die;* Frische, *die; (fig.)* Lebhaftigkeit, *die;* **the ~ of demand/trade** die rege Nachfrage/der rege Handel

bristle ['brɪsl] **1.** *n.* **a)** Borste, *die;* **be made of ~:** aus Borsten bestehen; **b) ~s** *(of beard)* [Bart]stoppeln. **2.** *v. i.* **a)** ~ **[up]** ⟨*Haare:*⟩ sich sträuben; **the dog's hair ~d [up], the dog ~d** dem Hund sträubte sich *(Dat.)* das Fell; **b)** ~ **with** *(fig.: have many)* strotzen *od.* starren vor (+ *Dat.*); ~ **with difficulties/obstacles** mit Schwierigkeiten/Hindernissen gespickt sein; **c)** ~ **[up]** *(fig.: become angry)* ⟨*Person:*⟩ hochgehen *(ugs.)*, aufgebracht sein

bristly ['brɪslɪ] *adj.* borstig; stopp[e]lig ⟨*Kinn*⟩; ~ **beard** Stoppelbart, *der*

Brit [brɪt] *n. (coll.)* Brite, *der*/Britin, *die;* Engländer, *der*/Engländerin, *die (ugs.)*

Brit. *abbr.* **a) Britain** Gr.-Brit.; Gr.-Br.; **b) British** brit.

Britain ['brɪtn] *pr. n.* Großbritannien *(das);* Britannien *das (hist.; auch Zeitungsjargon)*

Britannia [brɪ'tænjə] *pr. n. (literary)* Britannia, *die (dichter.)*

Briticism ['brɪtɪsɪzm] *n.* Britizismus, *der*

British ['brɪtɪʃ] **1.** *adj.* britisch; **he/she is ~:** er ist Brite/sie ist Britin; **sth. is ~:** etw. ist aus Großbritannien; **the best of ~ [luck]** *(coll.)* na, [dann mal] viel Glück!; *see also* **English 1. 2.** *n. pl.* **the ~:** die Briten

British: ~ Columbia [brɪtɪʃ kə'lʌmbɪə] *pr. n.* Britisch-Kolumbien *(das);* ~ **'Council** *n. britisches Kulturinstitut im Ausland*

Britisher ['brɪtɪʃə(r)] *n.* Brite, *der*/Britin, *die*

British 'Isles *pr. n. pl.* Britische Inseln

Britishism ['brɪtɪʃɪzm] *see* **Briticism**

Briton ['brɪtn] *n.* Brite, *der*/Britin, *die*

Brittany ['brɪtənɪ] *pr. n.* Bretagne, *die*

brittle ['brɪtl] *adj.* **a)** spröde ⟨*Material*⟩; zerbrechlich ⟨*Glas*⟩; schwach ⟨*Knochen*⟩; brüchig ⟨*Gestein*⟩; **b)** *(fig.: insecure)* empfindlich ⟨*Person*⟩; schwach ⟨*Nerven*⟩

brittleness ['brɪtlnɪs] *n., no pl. see* **brittle: a)** Sprödigkeit, *die;* Zerbrechlichkeit, *die;* Schwäche, *die;* Brüchigkeit, *die;* **b)** *(fig.)* Empfindlichkeit, *die;* Schwäche, *die*

bro. *abbr.* **brother** Br.

broach [brəʊtʃ] *v. t.* **a)** anzapfen; anstechen ⟨*Faß*⟩; anbrechen ⟨*Vorräte*⟩; **b)** *(fig.)* zur Sprache bringen ⟨*Vorschlag, Idee*⟩; anschneiden ⟨*Thema*⟩

broad [brɔːd] **1.** *adj.* **a)** breit; *(extensive)* weit ⟨*Ebene, Meer, Land, Felder*⟩; ausgedehnt ⟨*Fläche*⟩; **a river sixty feet ~:** ein sechzig Fuß breiter Fluß; **grow ~er** breiter werden; sich verbreitern; **make sth. ~er** etw. verbreitern; **it's as ~ as it is long** *(fig.)* es ist gehupft wie gesprungen *(ugs.)*; **b)** *(explicit)* deutlich, klar ⟨*Hinweis*⟩; breit ⟨*Lächeln*⟩; **a ~ hint** ein Wink mit dem Zaunpfahl *(scherzh.)*; **c)** *(clear, main)* grob; wesentlich ⟨*Fakten*⟩; **in ~ outline** in groben *od.* großen Zügen; **give the ~ outlines of a plan** einen Plan in groben Zügen erläutern; **draw a ~ distinction between ...:** grob unterscheiden zwischen (+ *Dat.*) ...; *see also* **daylight a**; **d)** *(generalized)* allgemein; **in the ~est sense** im weitesten Sinne; **as a ~ rule/indication** als Faustregel; **e)** *(strongly dialectal)* stark ⟨*Akzent*⟩; breit ⟨*Aussprache*⟩; **he speaks ~ Scots** er spricht breites Schottisch *od.* einen starken schottischen Dialekt; **f)** *(coarse)* derb ⟨*Humor, Geschichte*⟩; **g)** *(tolerant)* großzügig; liberal; vielseitig ⟨*Interessen*⟩; **B~ Church** *liberale Richtung in der Kirche von England;* Broad Church *(fachspr.)*. **2.** *n.* **a)** *(broad part)* breiter Teil; **the ~ of the back** die Schultergegend; **b)** *(Amer. sl.: woman)* Weib, *das (abwertend);* Weibsstück, *das (salopp abwertend)*

broad: ~ 'bean *n.* Saubohne, *die;* dicke Bohne; **~-brimmed** ['brɔːdbrɪmd] *adj.* breitkrempig

broadcast ['brɔːdkɑːst] **1.** *n. (Radio, Telev.)* Sendung, *die; (live)* Übertragung, *die.* **2.** *v. t.*, ~ *or* **~ed, ~: a)** *(Radio, Telev.)* senden; ausstrahlen; übertragen ⟨*Livesendung, Sportveranstaltung*⟩; **b)** *(spread)* aussäen ⟨*Samen*⟩; *(fig.)* verbreiten ⟨*Gerücht, Nachricht*⟩; ausposaunen *(ugs.)* ⟨*Neuigkeit*⟩. **3.** *v. i.*, ~ *or* **~ed** ⟨*Rundfunk-, Fernsehstation:*⟩ senden; ⟨*Redakteur usw.:*⟩ [im Rundfunk/Fernsehen] sprechen. **4.** *adj. (Radio, Telev.)* im Rundfunk/Fernsehen gesendet; Rundfunk-/Fernseh-; **a ~ appeal** ein Aufruf im Rundfunk/Fernsehen

broadcaster ['brɔːdkɑːstə(r)] *n. (Radio, Telev.)* im Rundfunk/Fernsehen auftretende Persönlichkeit; **famous ~s** vom Rundfunk/Fernsehen her bekannte Persönlichkeiten

broadcasting ['brɔːdkɑːstɪŋ] *n., no pl. (Radio, Telev.)* Senden, *das; (of live programmes)* Übertragen, *das;* **written for ~:** für den Rundfunk/das Fernsehen geschrieben; **the early days of ~:** die Anfänge des Rundfunks; **work in ~:** beim Funk arbeiten

broaden ['brɔ:dn] **1.** *v. t.* **a)** verbreitern; **b)** *(fig.)* ausweiten ‹*Diskussion*›; ~ **one's mind** seinen Horizont erweitern; **travel ~s the mind** Reisen bildet. **2.** *v. i.* breiter werden; sich verbreitern; *(fig.)* sich erweitern; **her smile ~ed into a grin** ihr Lächeln verzog sich zu einem breiten Grinsen
'**broad jump** *n. (Amer. Sport)* Weitsprung, *der*
broadly ['brɔ:dlɪ] *adv.* **a)** deutlich ‹*hinweisen*›; breit ‹*grinsen, lächeln*›; **b)** *(in general)* allgemein ‹*beschreiben*›; ~ **speaking** allgemein gesprochen; ~ **based** auf breiter Grundlage *nachgestellt*
broad: ~'minded *adj.* tolerant; **have very ~minded views about sth.** sehr freie Ansichten über etw. *(Akk.)* haben; **~mindedness** [brɔ:d'maɪndɪdnɪs] *n., no pl.* Toleranz, *die*
broadness ['brɔ:dnɪs] *see* **breadth**
broad: ~sheet *n.* **a)** *(Printing)* Einblattdruck, *der;* **b)** *(pamphlet)* Flugblatt, *das;* **~'shouldered** *adj.* breitschultrig; **~side** *n.* **a)** *(Naut.; also fig.)* Breitseite, *die;* **~side on [to sth.]** mit der Breitseite [nach etw.]; **fire [off] a ~side** *(lit. or fig.)* eine Breitseite abfeuern; **b)** *see* **broadsheet; ~sword** *n.* breites Schwert; Pallasch, *der;* **~way** *n.* Hauptstraße, *die;* **B~way** *(Amer.)* der Broadway
brocade [brə'keɪd] *n.* Brokat, *der*
broccoli ['brɒkəlɪ] *n.* **a)** *(heading ~)* Brokkoli, *der;* Spargelkohl, *der;* **b)** *(sprouting ~)* Schößlinge des Spargelkohls
brochure ['brəʊʃə(r), 'brəʊʃjʊə(r)] *n.* Broschüre, *die;* Prospekt, *der*
broderie anglaise ['brəʊdrɪ ã'gleɪz] *n.* Lochstickerei, *die*
¹brogue [brəʊg] *n.* **a)** *(rough shoe)* fester Schuh; **b)** *(decorated outdoor shoe)* Budapester, *der*
²brogue *n. (accent)* irischer Akzent
broil [brɔɪl] *v. t.* braten; *(on gridiron)* grillen; **~ing sun** *(fig.)* brennende Sonne
broiler ['brɔɪlə(r)] *n.* **a)** *(chicken)* Brathähnchen, *das;* [Gold]broiler, *der (DDR);* **b)** *(utensil)* Grill, *der;* Bratrost, *der*
'**broiler house** *n.* Hähnchenmästerei, *die*
broke [brəʊk] **1.** *see* **break 1, 2. 2.** *pred. adj. (coll.)* pleite *(ugs.);* **go ~:** pleite gehen; **go for ~** *(sl.)* alles auf eine Karte setzen; alles riskieren
broken ['brəʊkn] **1.** *see* **break 1, 2. 2.** *adj.* **a)** zerbrochen; gebrochen ‹*Bein, Hals*›; verletzt ‹*Haut*›; abgebrochen ‹*Zahn*›; gerissen ‹*Seil*›; kaputt *(ugs.)* ‹*Uhr, Fernsehen, Fenster*›; ~ **glass** Glasscherben; **get ~:** zerbrechen/brechen/reißen/kaputtgehen; **he got a ~ arm** er hat sich *(Dat.)* den Arm gebrochen; **b)** *(uneven)* uneben ‹*Fläche*›; bewegt ‹*See, Wasser*›; **c)** *(imperfect)* gebrochen; **in ~ English** in gebrochenem Englisch; **d)** *(fig.)* ruiniert ‹*Ehe*›; gebrochen ‹*Mensch, Herz, Stimme*›; unruhig, gestört ‹*Schlaf*›; **come from a ~ home** aus zerrütteten Familienverhältnissen kommen; **in a ~ voice** mit gebrochener Stimme
broken: ~-down *adj.* baufällig ‹*Gebäude*›; kaputt *(ugs.)* ‹*Wagen, Maschine*›; **~-hearted** [brəʊkn'hɑ:tɪd] *adj.* untröstlich; ~ **'line** *n.* gestrichelte Linie
brokenly ['brəʊknlɪ] *adv.* gebrochen
broker ['brəʊkə(r)] *n.* **a)** *(Commerc.: middleman)* Händler, *der;* Kommissionär, *der; (of real estate)* [Immobilien]makler, *der; (stockbroker)* [Börsen]makler, *der;* **b)** *see* **pawnbroker; c)** *(intermediary)* Vermittler, *der;* Unterhändler, *der; see also* **honest a**
brolly ['brɒlɪ] *n. (Brit. coll.)* [Regen]schirm, *der*
bromide ['brəʊmaɪd] *n.* **a)** *(Chem.)* Bromsalz, *das;* **b)** *(fig.) (person)* Langweiler, *der; (remark)* [All]gemeinplatz, *der;* Platitüde, *die (abwertend)*
bromine ['brəʊmi:n] *n. (Chem.)* Brom, *das*
bronchial ['brɒŋkɪəl] *adj. (Anat., Med.)* bronchial; Bronchial-; ~ **tubes** Bronchien; ~ **pneumonia** Bronchopneumonie, *die*
bronchitis [brɒŋ'kaɪtɪs] *n., no pl. (Med.)* Bronchitis, *die*
bronco ['brɒŋkəʊ] *n., pl.* **~s a)** *wildes od. halbwildes Pferd im Westen der USA;* **b)** *(any horse)* Gaul, *der (ugs.)*
bronze [brɒnz] **1.** *n.* **a)** Bronze, *die;* **the B~ Age** die Bronzezeit; **a statuette in ~:** eine Bronzestatuette; **b)** *(colour)* Bronze[farbe], *die;* **c)** *(work of art)* Bronze, *die;* **d)** *(medal)* Bronze, *die.* **2.** *attrib. adj.* Bronze-; *(coloured like bronze)* bronzefarben; bronzen; ~ **medal** Bronzemedaille, *die.* **3.** *v. t.* bräunen ‹*Gesicht, Haut*›. **4.** *v. i.* braun werden
bronzed [brɒnzd] *adj.* [sonnen]gebräunt; braun[gebrannt]
brooch [brəʊtʃ] *n.* Brosche, *die*
brood [bru:d] **1.** *n.* **a)** Brut, *die; (of hen)* Küken *Pl.;* Küchlein *Pl. (veralt.);* **b)** *(joc./derog.: human family)* Sippe, *die;* Sippschaft, *die; (children only)* Brut, *die.* **2.** *v. i.* **a)** *(of person)* [vor sich *(Akk.)* hin] brüten; ~ **over** *or* **upon sth.** über etw. *(Akk.)* [nach]grübeln; über etw. *(Dat.)* brüten; **b)** *(sit)* ‹*Vogel:*› brüten; **c)** *(fig.: hang close)* **thunder clouds ~ed over the valley** Gewitterwolken hingen über dem Tal
'**brood-mare** *n.* Zuchtstute, *die*
broody ['bru:dɪ] *adj.* **a)** brütig; ~ **hen** Glucke, *die;* **b)** *(fig. coll.)* **she is getting** *or* **feeling ~:** in ihr werden Muttergefühle wach; **c)** *(fig.: depressed)* grüblerisch; schwermütig
¹brook [brʊk] *n.* Bach, *der*
²brook *v. t.* dulden; ~ **no nonsense/delay** keinen Unfug/Aufschub dulden
broom [bru:m] *n.* **a)** Besen, *der;* **a new ~** *(fig.)* ein neuer Besen; **a new ~ sweeps clean** *(prov.)* neue Besen kehren gut; **b)** *(Bot.) (Genista)* Ginster, *der; (Cytisus scoparius)* Besenginster, *der*
broom: ~-cupboard *n.* Besenschrank, *der;* **~stick** *n.* Besenstiel, *der*
Bros. *abbr.* **Brothers** Gebr.
broth [brɒθ] *n.* **a)** *(unclarified stock)* Brühe, *die;* **b)** *(thin soup)* Bouillon, *die;* [Fleisch]brühe, *die*
brothel ['brɒθl] *n.* Bordell, *das*
brother ['brʌðə(r)] *n.* **a)** Bruder, *der;* **they are ~ and sister** sie sind Geschwister *od.* Bruder und Schwester; **the ~s Robinson** *or* **Robinson ~s** die Brüder Robinson; **the Marx B~s** die Marx Brothers; **b)** *(friend, associate, fellow member)* Bruder, *der; (in trade union)* Kollege, *der;* **oh ~!** *(sl.)* Junge, Junge!; **be ~s in arms** Kameraden sein; *attrib.* **his ~ doctors/officers** seine Ärztekollegen/Offizierskameraden; **c)** *pl. (Commerc.)* **Hedges B~s** Gebrüder Hedges; **d)** *pl.* **brethren** ['breðrɪn] *(Eccl.)* Bruder, *der*
brotherhood ['brʌðəhʊd] *n.* **a)** *no pl.* Brüderschaft, *die;* brüderliches Verhältnis; **the ~ of all men** *(fig.)* die Gemeinschaft aller Menschen; **b)** *(association)* Bruderschaft, *die; (Amer.: trade union)* Gewerkschaft, *die*
'**brother-in-law** *n., pl.* **brothers-in-law** Schwager, *der*
brotherly ['brʌðəlɪ] *adj.* brüderlich; ~ **love** Bruderliebe, *die*
brought *see* **bring**
brouhaha ['bru:hɑ:hɑ:] *n. (coll.) (noise)* Spektakel, *der (ugs.); (fuss)* Getue, *das*
brow [braʊ] *n.* **a)** *(eye~)* Braue, *die;* **b)** *(forehead)* Stirn, *die;* **c)** *(of hill)* [Berg]kuppe, *die*
'**browbeat** *v. t., forms as* **beat 1** unter Druck setzen; einschüchtern; ~ **sb. into doing sth.** jmdn. so unter Druck setzen, daß er etw. tut; **I refuse to be ~en** ich lasse mich nicht unter Druck setzen
brown [braʊn] **1.** *adj.* braun; **as ~ as berries/a berry** schokoladenbraun. **2.** *n.* **a)** Braun, *das;* **b)** *(Snooker)* braune Kugel; **c)** *(~ clothes)* **dressed in ~:** braun gekleidet. **3.** *v. t.* **a)** bräunen ‹*Haut, Körper*›; **b)** *(Cookery)* [an]bräunen; anbraten ‹*Fleisch*›; **c)** *(Brit. sl.)* **be ~ed off with sth./sb.** etw./jmdn. satt haben *(ugs.);* **be ~ed off with doing sth.** es satt haben, etw. zu tun *(ugs.).* **4.** *v. i.* **a)** ‹*Haut:*› bräunen; **I don't ~ easily** ich werde nicht leicht braun; **b)** *(Cookery)* ‹*Fleisch:*› braun werden
brown: ~ 'ale *n.* dunkles Starkbier; ~ **'bear** *n.* Braunbär, *der;* ~ **'bread** *n.* ≈ Mischbrot, *das; (made with wholemeal flour)* Vollkornbrot, *das;* ~ **'coal** *n.* Braunkohle, *die;* **~-eyed** *adj.* braunäugig; **be ~-eyed** braune Augen haben
brownie ['braʊnɪ] *n.* **a) the B~s** die Wichtel *(Pfadfinderinnen von 7–11 Jahren);* **get ~ points** *(fig. coll.)* Pluspunkte sammeln; **b)** *(goblin)* Heinzelmännchen, *das;* Kobold, *der;* Wichtel, *der;* **c)** *(Amer.: cake) kleiner Schokoladenkuchen oft mit Nüssen*
browning ['braʊnɪŋ] *n. (Cookery) (sugar)* brauner Zucker; *(flour)* braunes Mehl
brownish ['braʊnɪʃ] *adj.* bräunlich
brown: ~-nose *v. i. (Amer. sl.)* hinten reinkriechen *(derb);* ~ **'paper** *n.* Packpapier, *das;* ~ **'rice** *n.* Naturreis, *der;* **B~ shirt** *n. (Hist.)* Braunhemd, *das;* **~stone** *n. (Amer.)* **a)** rotbrauner Sandstein; **b)** *(house)* Sandsteinhaus, *das;* ~ **'study** *n.* **be in a ~ study** geistesabwesend *od.* in Gedanken verloren sein; ~ **'sugar** *n.* brauner Zucker
browse [braʊz] **1.** *v. t.* abgrasen ‹*Weide*›; abfressen ‹*Blätter*›. **2.** *v. i.* **a)** ‹*Vieh:*› weiden; ‹*Wild:*› äsen; ~ **on sth.** etw. fressen; **b)** *(fig.)* ~ **through a book/a magazine** in einem Buch schmökern/in einer Zeitschrift blättern; **I'm just browsing** *(in shop)* ich sehe mich nur mal um. **3.** *n. (fig.)* **have a ~:** sich umsehen; **it's worth a ~:** es ist das Reinschauen wert
Bruges [bru:ʒ] *pr. n.* Brügge *(das)*
bruise [bru:z] **1.** *n.* **a)** *(Med.)* blauer Fleck; **b)** *(on fruit)* Druckstelle, *die.* **2.** *v. t.* **a)** quetschen ‹*Obst, Pflanzen*›; ~ **oneself/one's leg** sich stoßen/sich am Bein stoßen; **he was badly ~d when he fell off his bike** er hat sich *(Dat.)* starke Prellungen zugezogen, als er vom Rad fiel; **the peaches are ~d/easily ~d** die Pfirsiche haben Druckstellen/bekommen leicht Druckstellen; **b)** *(fig.)* mitnehmen. **3.** *v. i.* ‹*Person:*› blaue Flecken bekommen; ‹*Obst:*› Druckstellen bekommen
bruiser ['bru:zə(r)] *n. (coll.)* Schläger, *der (abwertend)*
brunch [brʌnʃ] *n. (coll.)* Brunch, *der;* ausgedehntes, spätes Frühstück
brunette [bru:'net] **1.** *n.* Brünette, *die.* **2.** *adj.* brünett
Brunswick ['brʌnzwɪk] **1.** *pr. n.* Braunschweig *(das).* **2.** *attrib. adj.* Braunschweiger
brunt [brʌnt] *n.* Hauptlast, *die;* **the main** *or* **full ~ of the attack fell on the French** die Franzosen waren der vollen Wucht des Angriffs ausgesetzt; **the ~ of the financial cuts** die Hauptlast der Einsparungen; **bear the ~:** das meiste abkriegen
brush [brʌʃ] **1.** *n.* **a)** Bürste, *die; (for sweeping)* Hand-, Kehrbesen, *der; (with short handle)* Handfeger, *der; (for scrubbing)* [Scheuer]bürste, *die; (for painting or writing)* Pinsel, *der;* **flat ~:** Flachpinsel, *der;* **b)** *(quarrel, skirmish)* Zusammenstoß, *der;* **his first ~ with the law came at an early age** er kam schon früh mit dem Gesetz in Konflikt; **c)** *(light touch)* flüchtige Berührung; **d)** *(tail) (of squirrel)* Rute, *die; (of fox)* Lunte, *die;* **e) give your hair/teeth a ~:** bürste dir die Haare/putz dir die Zähne; **give your shoes/clothes a ~:** bürste deine Schuhe/Kleider ab; **f)** *(Amer., Austral.: undergrowth)* Unterholz, *das;* **g)** *(land covered with undergrowth)* Buschland, *das.* **2.** *v. t.* **a)** *(sweep)* kehren; fegen; abbürsten ‹*Kleidung*›; ~ **one's teeth/hair** sich *(Dat.)*

die Zähne putzen/die Haare bürsten; ~ **the dust from one's coat/the shelf** den Staub vom Mantel bürsten/vom Regal wischen; **b)** *(treat)* bepinseln, bestreichen ‹*Teigwaren, Gebäck*›; **~ed aluminium/fabric** aufgerauhtes Aluminium/aufgerauhter Stoff; **c)** *(touch in passing)* flüchtig berühren; streifen; ~ **one's hand over one's hair/brow** sich *(Dat.)* mit der Hand über das Haar/die Stirn fahren. **3.** *v.i.* ~ **by** *or* **against** *or* **past sb./sth.** jmdn./etw. streifen

~ **a'side** *v.t.* beiseite schieben ‹*Personen, Hindernis*›; abtun, vom Tisch wischen ‹*Einwand, Zweifel, Beschwerde*›

~ **a'way** *v.t.* abwischen, wegwischen ‹*Staub, Schmutz*›; verscheuchen ‹*Insekt*›

~ **'down** *v.t.* abbürsten ‹*Kleidungsstück*›; ~ **oneself down** sich abbürsten; *(with hand)* sich abklopfen

~ **'off** *v.t.* **a)** abbürsten ‹*Schmutz usw.*›; *(with hand or cloth)* abwischen; wegwischen; verscheuchen ‹*Insekt*›; **b)** *(fig.: rebuff)* abblitzen lassen *(ugs.)*; **she ~ed me off** sie gab mir einen Korb; *see also* **brush-off**

~ **'up 1.** *v.t.* **a)** zusammenfegen ‹*Krümel*›; **b)** auffrischen ‹*Sprache, Kenntnisse*›. **2.** *v.i.* ~ **up on** auffrischen. *See also* **brush-up**

'brushfire 1. *n.* Buschfeuer, *das.* **2.** *adj.* *(fig.)* ~ **warfare** begrenzter Krieg *od.* Konflikt

brushless ['brʌʃlɪs] *adj.* schaumlos ‹*Rasiercreme*›

brush: ~-off *n.* Abfuhr, *die;* **give sb. the ~-off** jmdm. einen Korb geben *(ugs.)*; jmdn. abblitzen lassen *(ugs.)*; **~-stroke** *n.* Pinselstrich, *der;* **~-up** *n.* **a) I'll have to give my English a ~-up** ich muß meine Englischkenntnisse auffrischen; **b) have a wash and ~-up** sich frisch machen; **~wood** *n.* **a)** Reisig, *das;* **b)** *(thicket)* Dickicht, *das;* Unterholz, *das;* **~work** *n.* Pinselführung, *die*

brusque [brʊsk, brʌsk] *adj.*, **brusquely** ['brʊsklɪ, 'brʌsklɪ] *adv.* schroff

brusqueness ['brʊsknɪs, 'brʌsknɪs] *n., no pl.* Schroffheit, *die*

Brussels ['brʌslz] *pr. n.* Brüssel *(das)*

Brussels: ~ 'carpet *n.* Brüsseler Teppich; **~ 'lace** *n.* Brüsseler Spitze[n]; **~ 'sprouts** *n. pl.* Rosenkohl, *der;* Kohlsprossen *(österr.)*

brutal ['bru:tl] *adj.* brutal; *(fig.)* brutal, schonungslos ‹*Offenheit*›; bitter ‹*Wahrheit*›

brutalism ['bru:təlɪzm] *n.* **a)** Brutalität, *die;* **b)** *(Art, Archit.)* Brutalismus, *der*

brutality [bru:'tælɪtɪ] *n.* Brutalität, *die*

brutalization [bru:təlaɪ'zeɪʃn] *n.* *(treating brutally)* brutale Behandlung; *(becoming brutalized)* Verrohung, *die*

brutalize ['bru:təlaɪz] **1.** *v.t.* **a)** verrohen lassen; brutalisieren; **b)** *(treat brutally)* brutal behandeln. **2.** *v.i.* verrohen

brutally ['bru:təlɪ] *adv.* brutal; **be ~ frank with sb.** *(fig.)* mit jmdm. schonungslos offen sein

brute [bru:t] **1.** *n.* **a)** *(animal)* Bestie, *die;* **b)** *(brutal person)* Rohling, *der;* brutaler Kerl *(ugs.)*; *(thing)* höllische Sache; **a ~ of a problem** *(fig.)* ein höllisches Problem; **a drunken ~:** ein brutaler Trunkenbold; **an unfeeling ~ of a man** eine gefühllose Bestie; **c)** *(coll.: person)* Kerl, *der (ugs.)*. **2.** *attrib. adj.* *(without capacity to reason)* vernunftlos; irrational; *(merely material)* roh ‹*Gewalt*›; nackt ‹*Tatsachen*›; bitter ‹*Notwendigkeit*›; ~ **beasts** wilde Tiere *Pl.*; **by ~ force** mit roher Gewalt

brutish ['bru:tɪʃ] *adj.* brutal ‹*Flegel*›; tierisch ‹*Leidenschaften, Gelüste*›; **lead a ~ existence** das Leben eines Tieres führen

bryony ['braɪənɪ] *n.* *(Bot.)* Zaunrübe, *die*

BS *abbr.* **a) British Standard** Britische Norm; **b) Bachelor of Surgery** „Bachelor" der Chirurgie; *see also* **B.Sc.**; **c)** *(Amer.)* **Bachelor of Science**; *see also* **B.Sc.**

B.Sc. [bi:es'si:] *abbr.* **Bachelor of Science** Bakkalaureus der Naturwissenschaften; **John Clarke ~:** John Clarke, Bakkalaureus der Naturwissenschaften; **he is a** *or* **has a ~:** ≈ er hat ein Diplom in Naturwissenschaften; **[study for] one's** *or* **a ~ in physics/chemistry** ≈ ein Diplom in Physik/Chemie [machen wollen]

BSI *abbr.* **British Standards Institution** Britischer Normenausschuß

BST *abbr.* **British Summer Time** Britische Sommerzeit

Bt. *abbr.* **baronet**

bubble ['bʌbl] **1.** *n.* **a)** Blase, *die;* *(small)* Perle, *die;* *(fig.)* Seifenblase, *die;* **blow ~s** [Seifen]blasen machen; **the/his ~ has burst** *(fig.)* alles ist wie eine Seifenblase zerplatzt; **b)** *(sound or appearance of boiling)* Brodeln, *das;* **c)** *(domed canopy)* [Glas]kuppel, *die.* **2.** *v.i.* **a)** *(rise in ~s)* ‹*Schlamm:*› in Blasen aufsteigen; *(form ~s)* ‹*Wasser, Schlamm, Lava:*› Blasen bilden; ‹*Suppe, Flüssigkeiten:*› brodeln; *(make sound of ~s)* ‹*Bach, Quelle:*› plätschern; ‹*Schlamm:*› blubbern; **b)** *(fig.)* ~ **with sth.** vor etw. *(Dat.)* übersprudeln

~ **'over** *v.i.* überschäumen; ~ **over with excitement/laughter/joy** *(fig.)* vor Aufregung/Lachen übersprudeln/vor Freude überquellen

~ **'up** *v.i.* ‹*Gas:*› in Blasen aufsteigen; ‹*Wasser:*› aufsprudeln

bubble: ~ and 'squeak *n.* Pfannengericht aus Gemüse und Kartoffeln [mit Fleischresten]; **~ bath** *n.* Schaumbad, *das;* **~ car** *n.* Kabinenroller, *der;* **~ gum** *n.* Bubble-Gum, *der;* Ballonkaugummi, *der;* **~ pack** *n.* Klarsichtpackung, *die*

bubbly ['bʌblɪ] **1.** *adj.* **a)** sprudelnd; schäumend ‹*Bade-, Spülwasser*›; **b)** *(fig. coll.)* quirlig *(ugs.)* ‹*Person*›. **2.** *n.* *(Brit. coll.)* Schampus, *der (ugs.)*

bubonic plague [bju:bɒnɪk 'pleɪg] *n.* *(Med.)* Beulenpest, *die*

buccaneer [bʌkə'nɪə(r)] *n.* Seeräuber, *der;* Freibeuter, *der (auch fig.)*

Bucharest [bju:kə'rest] *pr. n.* Bukarest *(das)*

[1]**buck** [bʌk] **1.** *n.* **a)** *(male)* männliches Tier; Männchen, *das;* *(deer, chamois)* Bock, *der;* *(rabbit, hare)* Rammler, *der;* **b)** *(arch.: dandy)* Geck, *der (abwertend)*; Stutzer, *der (abwertend)*; **c)** *attrib.* ~ **negro** *(sl. derog.)* Negerkerl, *der (salopp abwertend)*; ~ **private** *(Amer. Mil. sl.)* Schütze Arsch *(derb)*. **2.** *v.i.* ‹*Pferd:*› bocken. **3.** *v.t.* **a)** ~ **[off]** ‹*Pferd:*› abwerfen; **b)** *(Amer.: resist)* sich sträuben gegen; sich widersetzen (+ *Dat.*)

[2]**buck** *n.* *(coll.)* **pass the ~ to sb.** *(fig.)* jmdm. den Schwarzen Peter zuschieben; jmdm. die Verantwortung aufhalsen; **the ~ stops here** *(fig.)* die Verantwortung liegt letzten Endes bei mir

[3]**buck** *(coll.)* **1.** *v.i.* ~ **'up a)** *(make haste)* sich ranhalten *(ugs.)*; ~ **up!** los, schnell!; auf, los!; **b)** *(cheer up)* ein fröhliches Gesicht machen; ~ **up!** Kopf hoch! **2.** *v.t.* ~ **'up a)** *(cheer up)* aufmuntern; **we were ~ed up by the good news** die gute Nachricht hat uns aufgemuntert; **b)** ~ **one's ideas up** *(coll.)* sich zusammenreißen

[4]**buck** *n.* *(Amer. and Austral. sl.: dollar)* Dollar, *der;* **make a fast ~:** eine schnelle Mark machen *(ugs.)*

bucked [bʌkt] *adj.* *(coll.)* aufgemuntert; **I was** *or* **felt ~ by it** es hat mich aufgemuntert

bucket ['bʌkɪt] **1.** *n.* **a)** Eimer, *der;* **a ~ of water** ein Eimer [voll] Wasser; **the rain fell in ~s** *(fig.)* es goß wie aus Kübeln *(ugs.)*; es schüttete *(ugs.)*; **kick the ~** *(fig. sl.)* abkratzen *(derb)*; ins Gras beißen *(salopp)*; **b)** *(of water-wheel)* Schaufelkammer, *die.* **2.** *v.i.* **a)** *(pour down)* **the rain is ~ing down** es gießt wie aus Kübeln *(ugs.)*; es schüttet *(ugs.)*; **b)** *(move jerkily)* ‹*Fahrzeug:*› holpern; ‹*Boot:*› schaukeln

bucketful ['bʌkɪtfʊl] *n.* Eimer [voll]; **two ~s of water** zwei Eimer [voll] Wasser

bucket: ~ seat *n.* Schalensitz, *der;* **~-shop** *n.* [nicht ganz seriöses] Maklerbüro; *(for air tickets)* [Hinterhof]reisebüro *(das vor allem Billigflüge vermittelt)*

buckle ['bʌkl] **1.** *n.* Schnalle, *die.* **2.** *v.t.* **a)** zuschnallen; ~ **sth. on** etw. anschnallen; ~ **sth. up** etw. festschnallen *od.* zuschnallen; **b)** *(cause to give way)* verbiegen ‹*Stoßstange, Rad*›. **3.** *v.i.* ‹*Rad, Metallplatte:*› sich verbiegen; ~ **under the weight** unter dem Gewicht nachgeben

~ **to 1.** ['---] *v.t.* ~ **[down] to a task/to work** sich hinter eine Aufgabe klemmen/sich an die Arbeit machen. **2.** [--'-] *v.i.* sich zusammenreißen *(ugs.)*; sich am Riemen reißen *(ugs.)*

buckler ['bʌklə(r)] *n.* *(Hist.)* Rundschild, *der*

buckram ['bʌkrəm] *n.* *(Textiles)* Buckram, *der*

buck 'rarebit *n.* *überbackene Käseschnitte mit pochiertem Ei*

Buck's Fizz [bʌks 'fɪz] *n.* Sekt mit Orangensaft

buckshee ['bʌkʃi:] *(Brit. sl.)* **1.** *adj.* Gratis-; **a ~ trip** eine Reise zum Nulltarif; eine Gratisreise. **2.** *adv.* gratis, umsonst ‹*bekommen, reisen*›; zum Nulltarif ‹*reisen*›

buck: ~shot *n.* grober Schrot; Rehposten, *der;* **~thorn** *n.* *(Bot.)* Kreuzdorn, *der;* **~-tooth** *n.* vorstehender Zahn; Raffzahn, *der (ugs.)*

buckwheat ['bʌkwi:t] *n.* *(Agric.)* Buchweizen, *der*

bucolic [bju:'kɒlɪk] *adj.* bukolisch

bud [bʌd] **1.** *n.* Knospe, *die;* **come into ~/be in ~:** knospen; Knospen treiben; **the trees are in ~:** die Bäume schlagen aus; **nip sth. in the ~** *(fig.)* etw. im Keim ersticken. **2.** *v.i.*, **-dd-** knospen; Knospen treiben; ‹*Baum:*› ausschlagen; **a ~ding painter/actor** *(fig.)* ein angehender Maler/Schauspieler

Buddha ['bʊdə] *n.* Buddha, *der*

Buddhism ['bʊdɪzm] *n.* Buddhismus, *der*

Buddhist ['bʊdɪst] **1.** *n.* Buddhist, *der*/Buddhistin, *die.* **2.** *adj.* buddhistisch

buddleia ['bʌdlɪə] *n.* *(Bot.)* Schmetterlingsstrauch, *der;* Buddleia, *die (fachspr.)*

buddy ['bʌdɪ] *(coll.)* **1.** *n.* Kumpel, *der (ugs.)*. **2.** *v.i.* ~ **up [with sb.]** sich [mit jmdm.] anfreunden

budge [bʌdʒ] **1.** *v.i.* ‹*Person, Tier:*› sich [von der Stelle] rühren; ‹*Gegenstand:*› sich bewegen, nachgeben; *(fig.: change opinion)* nachgeben. **2.** *v.t.* **a)** bewegen; **I can't ~ this screw** ich kriege diese Schraube nicht los; **b)** *(fig.: change opinion)* abbringen; **he refuses to be ~d** er läßt sich nicht umstimmen

budgerigar ['bʌdʒərɪgɑ:(r)] *n.* Wellensittich, *der*

budget ['bʌdʒɪt] **1.** *n.* Budget, *das;* Etat, *der;* Haushalt[splan], *der;* **keep within ~:** seinen Etat nicht überschreiten; **be on a ~:** haushalten *od.* wirtschaften müssen; ~ **meal/holiday** preisgünstige Mahlzeit/Ferien. **2.** *v.i.* planen; ~ **for sth.** etw. [im Etat] einplanen. **3.** *v.t.* [im Etat] einplanen

'budget account *n.* Konto für laufende Zahlungen

budgetary ['bʌdʒɪtərɪ] *adj.* budgetär; Budget‹*beratung, -betrag, -entwurf, -vorlage*›

budget: ~ day *n.* Haushaltsdebattentermin, *der;* **~ speech** *n.* Etatrede, *die*

budgie ['bʌdʒɪ] *n.* *(coll.)* Wellensittich, *der*

budo ['bu:dəʊ] *n.* Budo, *das*

buff [bʌf] **1.** *adj.* gelbbraun. **2.** *n.* **a)** *(coll.: enthusiast)* Fan, *der (ugs.)*; **b) in the ~:** nackt; im Adams-/Evaskostüm *(scherzh.)*; **strip down to the ~:** sich bis auf die Haut ausziehen; **c)** *(colour)* Gelbbraun, *das.* **3.** *v.t.* **a)** *(polish)* polieren, [blank] putzen ‹*Metall, Schuhe usw.*›; **b)** aufrauhen ‹*Leder*›

buffalo ['bʌfələʊ] *n., pl.* ~**es** *or same (Zool.)* Büffel, *der*

[1]**buffer** ['bʌfə(r)] **1.** *n.* **a)** *(Railw.)* Prellbock, *der; (on vehicle; also Chem., fig.)* Puffer, *der;* **b)** *(Computing)* Pufferspeicher, *der.* **2.** *v. t.* dämpfen

[2]**buffer** *n. (sl.)* **old** ~: alter Zausel *(ugs.)*

'**buffer state** *n.* Pufferstaat, *der*

[1]**buffet** ['bʌfɪt] **1.** *n. (blow, lit. or fig.)* Schlag, *der;* ~**s of fate** Schicksalsschläge. **2.** *v. t.* schlagen; ~**ed by the wind/waves** vom Wind geschüttelt/von den Wellen hin und her geworfen

[2]**buffet** ['bʊfeɪ] *n.* **a)** *(Brit.: place)* Büfett, *das;* ~ **car** *(Railw.)* Büfettwagen, *der;* **b)** *(Brit.: meal)* Imbiß, *der;* ~ **lunch/supper/meal** Büfettessen, *das;* **a cold** ~: ein kaltes Büfett; **c)** *(cupboard)* Büfett, *das;* Geschirrschrank, *der; (sideboard)* Anrichte, *die*

buffeting ['bʌfɪtɪŋ] *n.* Schütteln, *das; (fig.)* Schläge; ~**s of fate** Schicksalsschläge

buffoon [bə'fu:n] **1.** *n.* Kasper, *der;* Clown, *der.* **2.** *v. i.* den Clown *od.* Kasper spielen

buffoonery [bə'fu:nərɪ] *n.* Clownerie, *die;* Possenreißerei, *die*

bug [bʌg] **1.** *n.* **a)** Wanze, *die;* **b)** *(Amer.: small insect)* Insekt, *das;* Käfer, *der;* **c)** *(coll.: virus)* Bazillus, *der;* **don't you breathe your** ~**s over me** steck mich nicht an; **d)** *(coll.: disease)* Infektion, *die;* Krankheit, *die;* **catch a** ~: sich *(Dat.)* eine Krankheit *od. (ugs.)* was holen; **I don't want to catch that** ~ **of yours** ich will mich nicht bei dir anstecken; **e)** *(coll.: concealed microphone)* Wanze, *die (ugs.);* **f)** *(coll.: defect)* Macke, *die (salopp);* **we have got all the** ~**s out of the system** wir haben alle Fehler im System beseitigt; **g)** *(coll.: obsession)* Tick, *der (ugs.);* **he has a** ~ **about neatness** er hat einen Ordnungsfimmel *(ugs.);* **then I got the** ~: dann packte es mich; **h)** *(coll.: enthusiast)* Fan, *der (ugs.).* **2.** *v. t.,* **-gg- a)** *(coll.: install microphone in)* verwanzen ⟨*Zimmer*⟩ *(ugs.);* abhören ⟨*Telefon, Konferenz*⟩; ~**ging device** Abhöreinrichtung, *die;* Wanze, *die (ugs.);* **b)** *(sl.) (annoy)* nerven *(salopp);* den Nerv töten (+ *Dat.*) *(ugs.); (bother)* beunruhigen; **what's** ~**ging you?** was ist los mit dir?

bugbear ['bʌgbeə(r)] *n.* **a)** *(annoyance, problem)* Problem, *das;* Sorge, *die;* **b)** *(object of fear)* Schreckgespenst, *das*

bugger ['bʌgə(r)] **1.** *n.* **a)** *(sodomite)* Analverkehr Ausübender; Sodomit, *der;* **b)** *(coarse) (fellow)* Bursche, *der (ugs.);* Makker, *der (salopp); as insult* Scheißkerl, *der (derb);* Arschloch, *das (salopp);* **you lucky** ~: du hast vielleicht ein Schwein *od.* Dusel *(ugs.);* **you poor** ~: du kannst einem leid tun; **play silly** ~**s** Scheiß machen *(derb);* **c)** *(coarse: thing)* Scheißding, *das (derb);* **that door is a** ~ **to open** diese Scheißtür geht immer so schwer auf *(derb);* **d)** *(coarse: damn)* ~! Scheiße! *(derb);* **I don't give a** ~ **what you think** ich gebe einen Scheiß drauf, was du denkst *(derb).* **2.** *v. t.* **a)** anal verkehren mit; **b)** *(coarse: damn)* ~ **you/him** *(dismissive)* du kannst/der kann mich mal *(derb);* ~ **this car/him!** *(angry)* dieses Scheißauto/dieser Scheißkerl! *(derb);* ~ **it!** ach du Scheiße *(derb); (in surprise)* **well,** ~ **me** *or* **I'll be** ~**ed!** ach du Scheiße *od.* meine Fresse! *(derb);* **c)** *(coarse: tire)* **be [completely]** ~**ed** [total] fertig sein *(ugs.)*

~ **a'bout,** ~ **a'round** *(coarse)* **1.** *v. i.* Scheiß machen *(derb);* rumblödeln *(ugs.);* ~ **about with sth.** mit etw. rumfummeln *(ugs.).* **2.** *v. t.* verarschen *(derb)*

~ **'off** *v. i. (coarse)* abhauen *(ugs.);* ~ **off!** hau ab! *(ugs.);* verdufte! *(ugs.);* verpiß dich! *(salopp)*

~ **'up** *v. t. (coarse)* verkorksen *(ugs.)*

bugger-'all *n. (coarse)* rein gar nichts; Null Komma nichts; **be worth** ~ keinen Pfifferling wert sein *(ugs.);* zum Wischen sein *(salopp)*

buggery ['bʌgərɪ] *n.* Analverkehr, *der*

Buggins's turn ['bʌgɪnzɪz tɜ:n] *n. (Brit.)* Ernennung auf Grund von Dienstjahren

buggy ['bʌgɪ] *n.* **a)** *(horse-drawn or motor vehicle)* Buggy, *der;* **b)** *(pushchair)* Sportwagen, *der;* **c)** *(Amer.) see* **baby buggy**

bugle[-horn] ['bju:gl(hɔ:n)] *n.* Bügelhorn, *das*

bugler ['bju:glə(r)] *n.* Hornist, *der*

build [bɪld] **1.** *v. t.,* **built** [bɪlt] **a)** bauen; errichten ⟨*Gebäude, Damm*⟩; mauern ⟨*Schornstein, Kamin*⟩; zusammenbauen *od.* -setzen ⟨*Fahrzeug*⟩; **the house is still being built** das Haus ist noch im Bau; **the house took three years to** ~: der Bau des Hauses dauerte drei Jahre; **he was the man who built the bridge** er war der Erbauer der Brücke; **the house is solidly built** das Haus ist sehr solide; ~ **a fire** [ein] Feuer machen; ~ **sth. from** *or* **out of sth.** etw. aus etw. machen *od.* bauen; **the dinghy was built from a kit** das Dingi entstand aus einem Bausatz; **be sturdily/strongly built** *(fig.)* ⟨*Sache:*⟩ solide gebaut sein; ⟨*Person:*⟩ stämmig/kräftig gebaut sein; **b)** *(fig.)* aufbauen ⟨*System, Gesellschaft, Reich, Zukunft*⟩; schaffen ⟨*bessere Zukunft, Bedingungen, Beziehung*⟩; begründen ⟨*Ruf*⟩; ~ **one's hopes upon sb./sth.** seine Hoffnungen auf jmdn./etw. setzen; ~ **a new career for oneself** sich *(Dat.)* eine neue Existenz aufbauen. **2.** *v. i.,* **built a)** bauen; **b)** *(fig.)* ⟨*Drama, Musik:*⟩ sich steigern **(to** zu); ~ **on one's successes** auf seinen Erfolgen aufbauen. **3.** *n.* Bauweise, *die; (of person)* Körperbau, *der*

~ **'in** *v. t.* einbauen; *see also* **built-in**

~ **into** *v. t.* ~ **sth. into sth.** *(to form part)* etw. in etw. *(Akk.)* einbauen; *(fig.)* ~ **a clause into a contract** eine Klausel in einen Vertrag aufnehmen

~ **on** *v. t.* **a)** aufbauen auf (+ *Dat.*); bebauen ⟨*Gelände*⟩; **b)** *(attach)* ~ **sth. on to sth.** etw. an etw. *(Akk.)* anbauen

~ **'up 1.** *v. t.* **a)** bebauen ⟨*Land, Gebiet*⟩; **b)** *(accumulate)* aufhäufen ⟨*Reserven, Mittel, Kapital*⟩; ~ **up a reputation** sich *(Dat.)* einen Namen machen; ~ **up a fine reputation as a speaker** sich *(Dat.)* einen ausgezeichneten Ruf als Redner erwerben; **c)** *(strengthen)* stärken ⟨*Gesundheit, Widerstandskraft*⟩; widerstandsfähig machen, kräftigen ⟨*Personen, Körper*⟩; **d)** *(increase)* erhöhen, steigern ⟨*Produktion, Kapazität*⟩; verstärken ⟨*Truppen*⟩; stärken ⟨*[Selbst]vertrauen*⟩; ~ **up sb.'s hopes [unduly]** jmdm. [falsche] Hoffnung machen; **e)** *(develop)* aufbauen ⟨*Firma, Geschäft*⟩; *(expand)* ausbauen; ~ **sth. up from nothing** etw. aus dem Nichts aufbauen; ~ **up one's strength** sich kräftigen; ⟨*Athlet:*⟩ seine Muskelkraft trainieren; **f)** *(praise, boost)* aufbauen ⟨*Star, Schauspieler*⟩; **the film was built up to be something marvellous** der Film wurde großartig herausgebracht *od.* angekündigt; **he wasn't half the performer he was built up to be** seine Vorstellung war nicht mal halb so gut wie angekündigt. **2.** *v. i.* **a)** ⟨*Spannung, Druck:*⟩ zunehmen, ansteigen; ⟨*Musik:*⟩ anschwellen; ⟨*Lärm:*⟩ sich steigern **(to** in + *Akk.*); ~ **up to a crescendo** sich zu einem Crescendo steigern; **b)** ⟨*Schlange, Rückstau:*⟩ sich bilden; ⟨*Verkehr:*⟩ sich verdichten, sich stauen. *See also* **build-up; built-up**

builder ['bɪldə(r)] *n.* **a)** Erbauer, *der;* **b)** *(contractor)* Bauunternehmer, *der;* ~**'s labourer** Bauarbeiter, *der;* ~**'s merchant** *(person)* Baustoffhändler, *der; (firm)* Baustoffhandlung, *die*

building ['bɪldɪŋ] *n.* **a)** Bau, *der; (of vehicle)* Zusammenbauen/-setzen, *das;* ~ **commenced three years ago** mit dem Bau wurde vor drei Jahren begonnen; *attrib.* ~ **materials** Baumaterialien; ~ **operations** Baumaßnahmen; ~ **land** Bauland, *das;* **b)** *(structure)* Gebäude, *das; (for living in)* Haus, *das*

building: ~ **contractor** *n.* Bauunternehmer, *der;* ~ **line** *n. (Archit.)* Bauflucht[linie], *die;* ~**-site** *n.* Baustelle, *die;* ~ **society** *n. (Brit.)* Bausparkasse, *die;* ~ **trade** *n.* Baugewerbe, *das*

'**build-up** *n.* **a)** *(publicity)* Reklame[rummel], *der;* Werbung, *die;* **give sb./sth. a good** ~: jmdn./etw. groß ankündigen; **give a film a massive** ~: für einen Film kräftig die Werbetrommel rühren; **b)** *(approach to climax)* Vorbereitungen *Pl.* **(to** für); **c)** *(increase)* Zunahme, *die; (of forces)* Verstärkung, *die;* **a** ~ **of traffic** ein [Verkehrs]stau *od.* eine Stauung

built *see* **build 1, 2**

built: ~**-in** *adj.* **a)** eingebaut; **a** ~**-in cupboard/bookcase/kitchen** ein Einbauschrank/-regal/eine Einbauküche; **b)** *(fig.: instinctive)* angeboren; **the system has** ~**-in safeguards against accidents** *(fig.)* das System hat eine Art eingebauten Schutz gegen Unfälle; *see also* **obsolescence;** ~**-up** *adj.* **a)** bebaut; **a** ~**-up area** ein Wohngebiet; **the speed limit applies in all** ~**-up areas** die Geschwindigkeitsbegrenzung gilt für alle geschlossenen Ortschaften; **b)** *(prefabricated)* vorgefertigt; **c)** ~**-up shoulders** [aus]wattierte *od.* gepolsterte Schultern; **a** ~**-up shoe** ein Schuh mit dickerer Sohle

bulb [bʌlb] *n.* **a)** *(Bot., Hort.)* Zwiebel, *die;* **b)** *(of lamp)* [Glüh]birne, *die;* **c)** *(of thermometer, chemical apparatus)* [Glas]kolben, *der;* **d)** *(of syringe, dropper, horn)* Gummiballon, *der*

bulbous ['bʌlbəs] *adj.* **a)** bauchig ⟨*Form*⟩; bulbös, bulboid ⟨*Schwellung*⟩; ~ **fingers/nose** Wurstfinger/Knollennase, *die;* **b)** *(Bot.)* Zwiebel-; zwiebelartig

Bulgaria [bʌl'geərɪə] *pr. n.* Bulgarien *(das)*

Bulgarian [bʌl'geərɪən] **1.** *adj.* bulgarisch; **he/she is** ~: er ist Bulgare/sie ist Bulgarin; *see also* **English 1. 2.** *n.* **a)** *(person)* Bulgare, *der*/Bulgarin, *die;* **b)** *(language)* Bulgarisch, *das; see also* **English 2 a**

bulge [bʌldʒ] **1.** *n.* **a)** Ausbeulung, *die;* ausgebeulte Stelle; *(in line)* Bogen, *der; (in tyre)* Wulst, *der od. die;* **b)** *(coll.: increase)* Anstieg, *der* **(in** *Gen.*); **c)** *(Mil.)* Frontausbuchtung, *die.* **2.** *v. i.* **a)** *(swell outwards)* sich wölben; **her eyes** ~**d out of her head** *(fig. coll.)* die Augen traten ihr [fast] aus dem Kopf; sie bekam Stielaugen *(ugs.);* **b)** *(be full)* vollgestopft sein **(with** mit)

bulging ['bʌldʒɪŋ] *adj.* prall gefüllt ⟨*Einkaufstasche usw.*⟩; vollgestopft ⟨*Hosentasche, Kiste*⟩; rund ⟨*Bauch*⟩; ~ **eyes** hervortretende Augen; *(in surprise)* staunende Augen

bulk [bʌlk] **1.** *n.* **a)** *(large quantity)* **in** ~: in großen Mengen; **b)** *(large shape)* massige Gestalt; **c)** *(size)* Größe, *die;* **be of great** ~: [sehr] massig sein; **d)** *(volume)* Menge, *die;* Umfang, *der;* **sea water is heavier,** ~ **for** ~, **than fresh water** Seewasser ist, Quantum für Quantum, schwerer als Süßwasser; **e)** *(greater part)* **the** ~ **of the money/goods** der Groß- *od.* Hauptteil des Geldes/der Waren; **the** ~ **of the population/votes** die Mehrheit der Bevölkerung/Stimmen; **f)** *(Commerc.)* **in** ~ *(loose)* lose; unabgefüllt ⟨*Wein*⟩; *(wholesale)* en gros; ~ **transport** Massentransport, *der;* ~ **sales** Großverkauf, *der.* **2.** *v. i.* ~ **large** eine wichtige Rolle spielen. **3.** *v. t.* **a)** *(combine)* zu einer Sendung zusammenstellen; **b)** *(make thicker)* anschwellen lassen; an Umfang zunehmen lassen

bulk: ~ **'buyer** *n.* Großabnehmer, *der;* ~ **'buying** *n.* Großeinkauf, *der;* ~ **'carrier** *n.* Bulkfrachter, *der;* ~ **goods** *n. pl.* Schüttgut, *das;* ~**head** *n.* Schott, *das*

bulkiness ['bʌlkɪnɪs] *n., no pl. (unwieldiness)* Unhandlichkeit, *die*

bulky ['bʌlkɪ] *adj.* sperrig ⟨*Gegenstand*⟩; beleibt ⟨*Person*⟩; massig, wuchtig ⟨*Gestalt, Körper*⟩; unförmig ⟨*Kleidungsstück*⟩; *(un-*

wieldy) unhandlich ‹*Gegenstand, Paket*›; ~ **goods** Sperrgut, *das;* **a ~ book** ein dickes Buch

[1]bull [bʊl] **1.** *n.* **a)** Bulle, *der; (for bullfight)* Stier, *der;* **like a ~ in a china shop** *(fig.)* wie ein Elefant im Porzellanladen; **like a ~ at a gate** wie ein Wilder; **take the ~ by the horns** *(fig.)* den Stier bei den Hörnern fassen *od.* packen; **b)** *(Astrol.)* **the B~:** der Stier; *see also* **archer b; c)** *(whale, elephant)* Bulle, *der;* **d)** *see* **bull's eye a; e)** *(Amer. sl.: policeman)* Bulle, *der (salopp);* **f)** *(St. Exch.)* Haussier, *der.* **2.** *adj.* bullig

[2]bull *n. (RC Ch.)* Bulle, *die*

[3]bull *see* **Irish bull**

[4]bull *n. (sl.)* **a)** *(routine)* [lästige] Routine; *(Mil.: discipline)* Drill, *der;* **b)** *(nonsense)* Geschwafel, *das (ugs. abwertend);* Gesülze, *das (salopp abwertend);* **c)** *(Amer.: blunder)* grober Schnitzer

bull: ~-at-a-gate *adj., adv.* wild; rücksichtslos; **~-calf** *n.* Bullenkalb, *das;* **~dog** *n.* **a)** Bulldogge, *die;* **he's one of the ~dog breed** *(fig.)* er ist hartnäckig und fürchtet sich vor nichts; **~dog clip** Flügelklammer, *die;* **b)** *(Brit. Univ.)* Helfer des Proktors; **~doze** *v.t.* **a)** planieren ‹*Boden*›; mit der Planierraupe wegräumen ‹*Gebäude*›; **~doze a path** mit der Planierraupe einen Weg bahnen; **b)** *(fig.: force)* **~doze sb. into doing sth.** jmdn. dazu zwingen, etw. zu tun; **the Bill was ~dozed through Parliament by the government** *(fig.)* das Gesetz wurde von der Regierung im Parlament durchgeboxt; **~dozer** ['bʊldəʊzə(r)] *n.* Planierraupe, *die;* Bulldozer, *der*

bullet ['bʊlɪt] *n.* [Gewehr-, Pistolen]kugel, *die; see also* **bite 2 d**

bullet: ~-head *n.* [kugel]runder Kopf; Rundkopf, *der;* **~-hole** *n.* Einschuß, *der;* Einschußloch, *das;* **be riddled with ~-holes** von Kugeln durchsiebt sein

bulletin ['bʊlɪtɪn] *n.* Bulletin, *das;* **we will bring you further ~s to keep you informed** wir bringen Ihnen weitere Meldungen, um Sie auf dem laufenden zu halten

'bulletin-board *n. (Amer.)* Anschlagtafel, *die; (Sch., Univ.)* Schwarzes Brett

bullet: ~proof *adj.* kugelsicher; **~proof glass** Panzerglas, *das;* **~ wound** *n.* Schußwunde, *die*

bull: ~fight *n.* Stierkampf, *der;* **~-fighter** *n.* Stierkämpfer, *der;* **~-fighting** *n.* Stierkämpfe; **~finch** *n. (Ornith.)* Gimpel, *der;* **~frog** *n.* Ochsenfrosch, *der;* **~-horn** *n.* Megaphon, *das;* Flüstertüte, *die (ugs. scherzh.)*

bullion ['bʊljən] *n., no pl., no indef. art.* Bullion, *das (fachspr.);* **gold/silver ~:** ungemünztes Gold/Silber; *(ingots)* Gold-/Silberbarren *Pl.*

bullish ['bʊlɪʃ] *adj. (St. Exch.)* haussierend; auf Hausse spekulierend ‹*Kapitalanleger*›; **feel ~:** in Haussestimmung sein; *(fig.)* in optimistischer Stimmung sein

bull: ~ market *n. (St. Exch.)* Haussemarkt, *der;* **~ neck** *n.* Stiernacken, *der;* **~-necked** *adj.* stiernackig; **~-nose[d]** ['bʊlnəʊz(d)] *adj.* abgerundet

bullock ['bʊlək] *n.* Ochse, *der*

bull: ~ point *n. (coll.)* Vorteil, *der;* **~ring** *n.* Stierkampfarena, *die;* **~ session** *n. (esp. Amer.)* zwanglose Diskussionsrunde; *(men only)* Männerrunde, *die (ugs.);* **~'s-eye** *n.* **a)** *(of target)* Schwarze, *das;* **score a ~'s-eye** *(lit. or fig.)* ins Schwarze treffen; **b)** *(boss of glass)* Butzen, *der; (Naut.)* Bullauge, *das; (Archit.)* Ochsenauge, *das;* **c)** *(boiled sweet)* rundes, schwarz-weißes Pfefferminzbonbon; **~shit** *(coarse) n.* Scheiße, *die (salopp abwertend);* **~-terrier** *n.* Bullterrier, *der*

[1]bully ['bʊlɪ] **1.** *n.* **a)** *jmd., der gern Schwächere schikaniert bzw. tyrannisiert; (esp. schoolboy etc.)* ≈ Rabauke, *der (abwertend); (boss)* Tyrann, der; **b)** *(hired ruffian) see* **bully-boy. 2.** *v.t. (persecute)* schikanieren; *(frighten)* einschüchtern; **~ sb. into/out of doing sth.** jmdn. so sehr einschüchtern, daß er etw. tut/läßt

[2]bully *(coll.)* **1.** *adj.* toll *(ugs.);* prima *(ugs.).* **2.** *int.* **~ for you** *(also iron.)* gratuliere!; **~ for him!** *(also iron.)* da muß man ihm gratulieren!

[3]bully *(Hockey)* **1.** *n.* Bully, *das.* **2.** *v.i.* **~ off** das Bully ausführen *(fachspr.)*

bully: ~ beef *n.* Corned beef, *das;* **~-boy** *n.* [angeheuerter] Schläger; **a gang of ~-boys** ein Schlägertrupp

bullying ['bʊlɪɪŋ] **1.** *n.* Schikanieren, *das.* **2.** *adj.* tyrannisch

'bully-off *n. (Hockey)* Bully, *das (fachspr.)*

bulrush ['bʊlrʌʃ] *n.* **a)** *(Bot.)* Teichsimse, *die;* **b)** *(Bibl.)* Rohr, *das*

bulwark ['bʊlwək] *n.* **a)** *(rampart)* Wall, *der;* Bollwerk, *das (auch fig.);* **b)** *(breakwater)* Mole, *die;* **c)** *usu. in pl. (Naut.)* Schanzkleid, *das*

[1]bum [bʌm] *n. (Brit. sl.)* Hintern, *der (ugs.);* Arsch, *der (derb)*

[2]bum *(sl.)* **1.** *n. (Amer.)* **a)** *(tramp)* Penner, *der (salopp abwertend);* Berber, *der (salopp);* **b)** *(lazy dissolute person)* Penner, *der (salopp abwertend);* Gammler, *der (ugs. abwertend);* **c) be on the ~** *(be a vagrant)* rumgammeln *(ugs.);* als Berber leben *(salopp); (cadge)* schnorren *(ugs.).* **2.** *adj.* mies *(ugs.);* schlimm *(ugs.)* ‹*Fuß, Bein usw.*›; **a ~ cheque** ein fauler Scheck *(ugs.).* **3.** *v.i.,* **-mm-** rumgammeln *(ugs.).* **4.** *v.t.,* **-mm-** schnorren *(ugs.)* ‹*Zigaretten usw.*› **(off** bei**); ~ one's way through France** durch Frankreich gammeln *(ugs.)*

bumble ['bʌmbl] *v.i.* zockeln *(ugs.);* **~ about** herumwursteln *(ugs.)*

'bumble-bee *n.* Hummel, *die*

bumbling ['bʌmblɪŋ] *adj.* stümperhaft

bumf [bʌmf] *n. (Brit. sl.)* **a)** *(derog.: papers)* Papierkram, *der (ugs.);* **b)** *(toilet-paper)* Klopapier, *das (ugs.)*

bump [bʌmp] **1.** *n.* **a)** *(sound)* Bums, *der; (impact)* Stoß, *der;* **this car has had a few ~s** der Wagen hat schon einige Dellen abgekriegt; **b)** *(swelling)* Beule, *die;* **c)** *(hump)* Buckel, *der (ugs.);* Hubbel, *der (ugs.);* **d)** *(on skull)* Höcker, *der;* **e)** *(sl.: dancer's forward thrust of abdomen)* Stoß, *der* [mit dem Bauch]; **~s and grinds** erotische Zuckungen. **2.** *adv.* bums; rums, bums; **the car went ~ into the vehicle in front** das Auto bumste gegen das Fahrzeug vor ihm; **be afraid of things that go ~ in the night** Angst vor komischen Geräuschen in der Nacht haben. **3.** *v.t.* **a)** anstoßen; **I ~ed the chair against the wall** ich stieß mit dem Stuhl an die Wand; **b)** *(hurt)* **~ one's head/knee** sich am Kopf/am Knie stoßen. **4.** *v.i.* **a) ~ against sth.** an etw. *(Akk.) od.* gegen etw. stoßen; **~ against sb.** jmdn. anstoßen; **b)** *(move with jolts)* rumpeln; **~ down the stairs** die Treppe runterpurzeln *(ugs.)*

~ into *v.t.* **a)** stoßen an (+ *Akk.*) *od.* gegen; *(with car, shopping trolley, etc.)* fahren gegen ‹*Mauer, Baum*›; **~ into sb.** jmdn. anstoßen; *(with vehicle)* jmdn. anfahren; **I ~ed into the back of another car** ich hatte einen Auffahrunfall; **b)** *(meet by chance)* zufällig [wieder]treffen; **if you ~ into Tom, tell him ...:** wenn dir Tom über den Weg läuft, sag ihm, ...

~ 'off *v.t. (sl.)* kaltmachen *(salopp);* umlegen *(salopp)*

~ up *v.t. (coll.)* aufschlagen ‹*Preise*›; aufbessern ‹*Gehalt*›

bumper ['bʌmpə(r)] **1.** *n.* **a)** *(Motor Veh.)* Stoßstange, *die;* **b)** *(Amer. Railw.)* Puffer, *der;* **c)** *(brim-full glass)* [rand]volles Glas; **d)** *(Cricket)* Schmetterball, *der.* **2.** *adj.* Rekord‹*ernte, -jahr*›; **~ edition** [besonders umfangreiche] Extra- *od.* Sonderausgabe

bumper: ~ car *n.* [Auto]skooter, *der;* **~-to-bumper 1.** *adj.* **a ~-to-bumper traffic jam** ein Stau, bei dem nichts mehr geht/ging; **2.** *adv.* Stoßstange an Stoßstange

bumpkin ['bʌmpkɪn] *n.* **[country] ~:** [Bauern]tölpel, *der (abwertend)*

bumptious ['bʌmpʃəs] *adj.,* **bumptiously** ['bʌmpʃəslɪ] *adv.* wichtigtuerisch

bumptiousness ['bʌmpʃəsnɪs] *n., no pl.* Wichtigtuerei, *die*

bumpy ['bʌmpɪ] *adj.* holp[e]rig ‹*Straße, Fahrt, Fahrzeug*›; uneben ‹*Fläche*›; unruhig ‹*Flug*›

bum: ~ 'rap *n. (Amer. sl.)* Verurteilung unter falscher Anklage; **~'s 'rush** *n. (Amer. sl.)* Rausschmiß, *der (ugs.);* **give sb. the ~'s rush** jmdn. rausschmeißen *(ugs.);* **~ 'steer** *n. (Amer. sl.)* **give sb. a ~ steer** jmdn. in die falsche Richtung lenken

bun [bʌn] *n.* **a)** süßes Brötchen; *(currant ~)* Korinthenbrötchen, *das;* **b)** *(hair)* [Haar]knoten, *der. See also* **oven**

bunch [bʌntʃ] **1.** *n.* **a)** *(of flowers)* Strauß, *der; (of grapes, bananas)* Traube, *die; (of parsley, radishes)* Bund, *das;* **a ~ of roses/parsley** ein Strauß Rosen/Bund Petersilie; **a ~ of keys** ein Schlüsselbund; **b)** *(lot)* Anzahl, *die;* **a whole ~ of ...:** ein ganzer Haufen ... *(ugs.);* **the best** *or* **pick of the ~:** der/die/das Beste [von allen]; **c)** *(sl.: gang)* Bande, *die (ugs.); (group)* Haufen, *der (ugs.);* **look a real ~ of idiots** wie ein Haufen [von] Idioten dastehen *(ugs.).* **2.** *v.t.* **a)** zu einem Strauß/zu Sträußen binden ‹*Blumen*›; bündeln ‹*Radieschen, Spargel*›; zusammendrängen ‹*Personen*›; **the runners were tightly ~ed as they came round the final bend** die Läufer lagen alle dicht beieinander, als sie in die Zielgerade einbogen; **b)** *(gather into folds)* [zusammen]raffen ‹*Kleid*›

~ 'up 1. *v.i.* ‹*Personen:*› zusammenrücken; ‹*Kleid, Stoff:*› sich zusammenknüllen. **2.** *v.t.* zusammenraffen ‹*Kleid*›

bundle ['bʌndl] **1.** *n.* **a)** Bündel, *das; (of papers)* Packen, *der; (of hay)* Bund, *das; (of books)* Stapel, *der; (of fibres, nerves)* Strang, *der;* **tie sth. up in a ~:** etw. zu einem Bündel zusammenbinden; **in ~s** bündelweise; **she's a ~ of mischief/energy/misery** *(fig.)* sie hat nichts als Unfug im Kopf/ist ein Energiebündel/ist ein Häufchen Unglück *od.* Elend; **b)** *(sl.: large amount of money)* Vermögen, *das;* [schöne] Stange Geld *(ugs.);* **c)** *(sl.)* **go a ~ on sb./sth.** von jmdm./etw. begeistert sein. *See also* **nerve 1 b. 2.** *v.t.* **a)** bündeln; **b)** *(throw hastily)* **~ sth. into the suitcase/back of the car** etw. in den Koffer stopfen/hinten ins Auto werfen; **c)** *(put hastily)* **~ sb. into the car** jmdn. ins Auto verfrachten *od.* packen

~ 'off *v.t.* [eilig] schaffen; schicken

~ 'up *v.t.* **a)** *(put in bundles)* bündeln; **b)** *(dress warmly)* einmummeln *(fam.)*

'bun-fight *n. (Brit. sl.)* Teegesellschaft, *die*

bung [bʌŋ] **1.** *n.* Spund[zapfen], *der.* **2.** *v.t.* **a)** verspunden; spunden; **b)** *(sl.: throw)* schmeißen *(ugs.)*

~ 'up *v.t.* **be/get ~ed up** verstopft sein/verstopfen

bungalow ['bʌŋgələʊ] *n.* Bungalow, *der*

'bung-hole *n.* Spundloch, *das*

bungle ['bʌŋgl] **1.** *v.t.* stümpern bei; **~ it/the job** alles vermasseln. **2.** *n.* Stümperei, *die (ugs.)*

bungler ['bʌŋglə(r)] *n.* Stümper, *der (abwertend)*

bungling ['bʌŋglɪŋ] **1.** *adj.* stümperhaft ‹*Versuch*›; **~ person** Stümper, der; **you ~ idiot!** du Trottel! **2.** *n.* Stümperei, *die*

bunion ['bʌnjən] *n. (Med.)* chronische Bursitis bei Hallux valgus *(fachspr.);* ≈ entzündeter Ballen

'bunk [bʌŋk] *n. (in ship, aircraft, lorry)* Koje, *die; (in room, sleeping-car)* Bett, *das;* *(~-bed)* Etagenbett, *das*

²bunk *n. (sl.: nonsense)* Quatsch, *der (salopp);* Mist, *der (salopp)*
³bunk *n. (Brit. sl.)* **do a ~:** türmen *(salopp);* **the cashier did a ~ with the money** der Kassierer brannte mit dem Geld durch *(ugs.)*
'bunk-bed *n.* Etagenbett, *das*
bunker ['bʌŋkə(r)] **1.** *n. (also Mil., Golf)* Bunker, *der.* **2.** *v. t. (Golf)* **be ~ed** im Bunker *od.* Sand liegen; *(fig. coll.)* in der Klemme sitzen *(ugs.)*
bunkum ['bʌŋkəm] *n.* Unsinn, *der*
bunny ['bʌnɪ] *n.* Häschen, *das*
Bunsen burner [bʌnsn 'bɜːnə(r)] *n.* Bunsenbrenner, *der*
¹bunting ['bʌntɪŋ] *n. (Ornith.)* Ammer, *die*
²bunting *n., no pl.* **a)** *(fabric)* Fahnentuch, *das;* **b)** *(flags, decoration)* [bunte] Fähnchen; Wimpel *Pl.*
buoy [bɔɪ] **1.** *n.* **a)** Boje, *die; (buoyant part)* Schwimmkörper, *der;* **b)** *(lifebuoy)* Rettungsring, *der.* **2.** *v. t.* **~ [up]** über Wasser halten; *(fig.: support, sustain)* aufrechterhalten; **I was ~ed [up] by the thought that ...:** der Gedanke, daß ..., hielt mich aufrecht *od.* ließ mich durchhalten
buoyancy ['bɔɪənsɪ] *n.* **a)** *(of body)* Auftrieb, *der;* **b)** *(fig.) (of stock-market prices)* Aufwärtstendenz, *die; (of person)* Schwung, *der;* Elan, *der*
'buoyancy tank *n. (Naut.)* Trimmtank, *der*
buoyant ['bɔɪənt] *adj.* **a)** Auftrieb habend; schwimmend; **be [more] ~:** [einen größeren] Auftrieb haben; [besser] schwimmen; **b)** *(fig.)* rege, lebhaft ⟨*Markt*⟩; heiter, munter ⟨*Person*⟩; federnd ⟨*Schritt*⟩; **share prices were ~ today** die Kurse sind heute gestiegen *od.* hochgegangen; **in ~ spirits** in Hochstimmung
bur [bɜː(r)] *n.* **a)** *(Bot.; also fig.)* Klette, *die;* **b)** *see* **burr a; c)** *see* **burr b**
burble ['bɜːbl] *v. i.* **a)** *(speak lengthily)* **~ [on] about sth.** von etw. ständig quasseln *(ugs.);* **~ [on] incessantly to sb.** jmdm. die Ohren voll schwatzen *(ugs.);* **b)** *(make a murmuring sound)* brummeln *(ugs.);* ⟨*Baby:*⟩ plappern; ⟨*Bach:*⟩ murmeln
burbot ['bɜːbət] *n. (Zool.)* Aalquappe, *die*
burden ['bɜːdn] **1.** *n.* **a)** *(load)* Last, *die; (fig.)* Last, *die;* Bürde, *die (geh.);* **beast of ~:** Lasttier, *das;* **become a ~:** zur Last werden; **be a ~ to sb.** für jmdn. eine Belastung sein; *(less serious)* jmdm. zur Last fallen; **put a fresh ~ upon sb.** ⟨*Person:*⟩ jmdm. eine zusätzliche Last aufladen; ⟨*Sache:*⟩ für jmdn. eine zusätzliche Belastung darstellen; **put too much of a ~ upon sb.** jmdn. überlasten; **the ~ of proof rests with** *or* **on you** Sie tragen die Beweislast; **tax ~:** steuerliche Belastung; Steuerlast, *die;* **b)** *(chief theme)* Schwerpunkt, *der;* Kern, *der;* **c)** *(of song)* Refrain, *der;* **d)** *(Naut.: tonnage)* Tonnage, *die;* Tragfähigkeit, *die.* **2.** *v. t.* belasten; **they were heavily ~ed** sie hatten schwer *od.* eine schwere Last zu tragen; *(fig.)* **~ sb./oneself with sth.** jmdn./sich mit etw. belasten; **~ sb./oneself with too many responsibilities** jmdn./sich zu viel Verantwortung aufladen
burdensome ['bɜːdnsəm] *adj.* schwer ⟨*Last*⟩; *(fig.)* lästig ⟨*Person, Pflicht, Verantwortung*⟩; **become/be ~ to sb.** jmdm. zur Last werden/fallen
burdock ['bɜːdɒk] *n. (Bot.)* Klette, *die*
bureau ['bjʊərəʊ, bjʊə'rəʊ] *n., pl.* **~x** ['bjʊərəʊz, bjʊə'rəʊz] *or* **~s a)** *(Brit.: writing-desk)* Schreibschrank, *der;* Sekretär, *der; (Amer.: chest of drawers)* Kommode, *die;* **b)** *(office)* Büro, *das; (department)* Abteilung, *die; (Amer.: government department)* Dienststelle, *die;* Amt, *das*
bureaucracy [bjʊə'rɒkrəsɪ] *n.* **a)** Bürokratie, *die;* **b)** *(officials)* Beamte *Pl.;* Bürokraten *Pl. (abwertend)*
bureaucrat ['bjʊərəkræt] *n.* Bürokrat, *der*/Bürokratin, *die (abwertend)*
bureaucratic [bjʊərə'krætɪk] *adj.* bürokratisch; **~ mentality** Beamtenmentalität, *die*
bureaucratically [bjʊərə'krætɪkəlɪ] *adv.* bürokratisch
bureau de change [bjʊərəʊ də ʃɑ̃ʒ] *n.* Wechselstube, *die*
burette *(Amer.:* **buret)** [bjʊə'ret] *n. (Chem.)* Bürette, *die*
burg [bɜːg] *n. (Amer. coll.)* Ort, *der*
burgee [bɜː'dʒiː] *n. (Naut.)* [gezackter] Stander; *(triangular)* Wimpel, *der*
burgeon ['bɜːdʒən] *v. i.* **a)** *(begin to grow rapidly)* blühen; **the arts and sciences ~ed** die Künste und Wissenschaften erlebten eine Blütezeit; **b)** *(bud)* ⟨*Pflanze:*⟩ sprießen; ⟨*Baum:*⟩ Knospen treiben, ausschlagen
burger ['bɜːgə(r)] *n. (coll.)* Hamburger, *der*
burgess ['bɜːdʒɪs] *n.* **a)** *(Brit.)* Bürger, *der*/Bürgerin, *die;* **b)** *(Amer.)* Stadtverordnete, *der/die*
burgh ['bʌrə] *n. (Scot. Hist.)* Stadt mit Stadtrechten; freie Stadt
burgher ['bɜːgə(r)] *n.* Bürger, *der*/Bürgerin, *die*
burglar ['bɜːglə(r)] *n.* Einbrecher, *der*
'burglar alarm *n.* Alarmanlage, *die*
burglarize ['bɜːgləraɪz] *(Amer.) see* **burgle 1**
'burglar-proof *adj.* einbruch[s]sicher
burglary ['bɜːglərɪ] *n.* Einbruch, *der; (offence)* [Einbruchs]diebstahl, *der*
burgle ['bɜːgl] **1.** *v. t.* einbrechen in (+ *Akk.*); **the shop/he was ~d** in dem Laden/bei ihm wurde eingebrochen. **2.** *v. i.* einen Einbruch begehen
burgomaster ['bɜːgəmɑːstə(r)] *n.* Bürgermeister, *der (einer holländ. od. fläm. Stadt)*
Burgundy ['bɜːgəndɪ] *pr. n.* Burgund *(das)*
burgundy *n.* **a)** *(wine)* Burgunder[wein], *der;* **b)** *(colour)* Burgunderrot, *das*
burial ['berɪəl] *n.* Bestattung, *die;* Begräbnis, *das; (funeral)* Beerdigung, *die;* Beisetzung, *die (geh.);* **Christian ~:** christliches Begräbnis; **~ at sea** Seebestattung, *die*
burial: ~-ground *n.* Begräbnisstätte, *die;* **~ mound** *n.* Grabhügel, *der;* **~-service** *n.* Trauerfeier, *die*
burin ['bjʊərɪn] *n.* **a)** Stichel, *der;* Punze, *die;* **b)** *(Archaeol.)* Meißel, *der*
burlap ['bɜːlæp] *n.* Sackleinen, *das*
burlesque [bɜː'lesk] **1.** *adj.* burlesk, possenhaft ⟨*Theaterstück*⟩; parodistisch ⟨*Literatur, Rede*⟩; **~ show** Varietévorstellung, *die.* **2.** *n.* **a)** Kabarett, *das;* Varieté, *das;* **b)** *(book, play)* Burleske, *die; (parody)* Parodie, *die;* **c)** *(Amer.: variety show)* Varieté, *das;* Tingeltangel, *das (abwertend).* **3.** *v. t.* parodieren
burly ['bɜːlɪ] *adj.* kräftig; stämmig; stramm ⟨*Soldat*⟩
Burma ['bɜːmə] *pr. n.* Birma *(das)*
Burmese [bɜː'miːz] **1.** *adj.* birmanisch; **sb. is ~:** jmd. ist Birmane/Birmanin; *see also* **English 1. 2.** *n., pl. same* **a)** *(person)* Birmane, *der*/Birmanin, *die;* **b)** *(language)* Birmanisch, *das; see also* **English 2 a**
¹burn [bɜːn] **1.** *n. (on the skin)* Verbrennung, *die; (on material)* Brandfleck, *der; (hole)* Brandloch, *das;* **second-degree ~s** Verbrennungen zweiten Grades. **2.** *v. t.,* **~t** *or* **~ed a)** verbrennen; **~ a hole in sth.** ein Loch in etw. *(Akk.)* brennen; **money ~s a hole in his pocket** *(fig.)* das Geld rinnt ihm nur so durch die Finger; **~ one's boats** *or* **bridges** *(fig.)* alle Brücken hinter sich *(Dat.)* abbrechen; **b)** *(use as fuel)* als Brennstoff verwenden ⟨*Gas, Öl usw.*⟩; heizen mit ⟨*Kohle, Holz, Torf*⟩; verbrauchen ⟨*Strom*⟩; *(use up)* verbrauchen ⟨*Treibstoff*⟩; verfeuern ⟨*Holz, Kohle*⟩; **~ coal in the stove** den Ofen mit Kohle feuern; **this lamp ~s oil** das ist eine Öllampe; **have money to ~** *(fig.)* Geld wie Heu haben; **I haven't got money to ~:** ich bin doch kein Krösus *(ugs.);* **c)** *(injure)* verbrennen; **~ oneself/one's hand** sich verbrennen/sich *(Dat.)* die Hand verbrennen; **he was severely ~t in the fire** er erlitt schwere Brandverletzungen; **~ one's fingers, get one's fingers ~t** *(fig.)* sich *(Dat.)* die Finger verbrennen *(fig.);* **d)** *(spoil)* anbrennen lassen ⟨*Fleisch, Kuchen*⟩; **be ~t** angebrannt sein; **~t toast** verbrannter *od.* schwarzer Toast; **e)** *(cause burning sensation to)* verbrennen; **this curry is ~ing my throat** das Curry verbrennt mir den Hals *od.* brennt mir im Hals; **f)** *(put to death)* **~ sb. [at the stake/alive]** jmdn. [auf dem Scheiterhaufen/bei lebendigem Leibe] verbrennen; **g)** *(fire, harden)* brennen; **~ wood to make** *or* **for charcoal** Holz zu Holzkohle verbrennen; **h)** *(corrode)* ätzen; verätzen ⟨*Haut*⟩; **i)** *(parch)* **the earth was ~ed brown/dry** die Erde war ganz versengt/ausgedörrt. **3.** *v. i.,* **~t** *or* **~ed a)** brennen; **~ to death** verbrennen; **five people ~ed to death in the fire** fünf Menschen kamen in den Flammen um; **may you ~ in hell** in der Hölle sollst du schmoren *(ugs.);* **b)** *(blaze)* ⟨*Feuer:*⟩ brennen; ⟨*Gebäude:*⟩ in Flammen stehen, brennen; **c)** *(give light)* ⟨*Lampe, Kerze, Licht:*⟩ brennen; **~ lower** ⟨*Kerze:*⟩ herunterbrennen; ⟨*Lampe:*⟩ schwach brennen; **d)** *(be injured)* sich verbrennen; **she/her skin ~s easily** sie bekommt leicht einen Sonnenbrand; **e)** *(be spoiled)* ⟨*Kuchen, Milch, Essen:*⟩ anbrennen; **f)** *(feel hot)* brennen; glühen; *(fig.)* [glut]rot sein **(with** vor + *Dat.*); **her cheeks were ~ing with embarrassment** sie lief vor Verlegenheit rot an; **I was ~ing with shame** ich wurde rot vor Scham; **his ears were ~ing** *(fig.)* ihm klangen die Ohren; **g)** *(fig.: be passionate)* **~ with rage/anger** vor Wut/Ärger kochen; **~ with desire/longing [for sb.]** sich vor Verlangen/Sehnsucht [nach jmdm.] verzehren; **be ~ing with curiosity** vor Neugierde sterben; **be ~ing to do sth.** darauf brennen, etw. zu tun; **h)** *(be corrosive)* ätzen; ätzend sein
~ a'way 1. *v. t.* verbrennen; *(by laser etc.)* wegbrennen. **2.** *v. i.* **a)** *(continue to ~)* weiterbrennen; vor sich *(Dat.)* hin brennen; **b)** *(diminish, be destroyed)* verbrennen; ⟨*Kerze, Docht:*⟩ herunterbrennen
~ 'down 1. *v. t.* niederbrennen. **2.** *v. i.* ⟨*Gebäude:*⟩ niederbrennen, abbrennen; *(less brightly)* ⟨*Feuer, Kerze:*⟩ herunterbrennen
~ 'in *v. t. (lit. or fig.)* einbrennen
~ into *v. t.* einbrennen in (+ *Akk.*); **the events were ~t into her memory** *(fig.)* die Ereignisse hatten sich ihrem Gedächtnis *od.* in ihr Gedächtnis eingebrannt
~ 'out 1. *v. t.* **a)** ausbrennen; **the fire ~ed itself out** das Feuer brannte aus *od.* nieder; **b)** *(fig.)* **feel ~ed out** sich erschöpft fühlen; total kaputt sein *(ugs.);* **~ oneself out** sich völlig verausgaben *od. (ugs.)* kaputtmachen; **c) the family was ~ed out of house and home** Haus und Hof der Familie waren abgebrannt; **d)** *(Electr.)* durchbrennen lassen ⟨*Sicherung*⟩; ausbrennen lassen ⟨*Motor*⟩. **2.** *v. i.* **a)** ⟨*Kerze, Feuer:*⟩ erlöschen, ausgehen; ⟨*Rakete, Raketenstufe:*⟩ ausbrennen; **b)** *(Electr.)* durchbrennen
~ 'up 1. *v. t.* **a)** verbrennen; verbrauchen ⟨*Energie*⟩; **~ up the road** *(fig. coll.)* die Straße entlangrasen; **b)** *(Amer.: make furious)* in Wut versetzen; zur Weißglut bringen *(fig.);* fuchsteufelswild machen *(ugs.).* **2.** *v. i.* **a)** *(flash into blaze)* auflodern; **b)** *(be destroyed)* ⟨*Rakete, Meteor, Satellit:*⟩ verglühen
²burn *n. (Scot.)* Bach, *der*
burner ['bɜːnə(r)] *n.* Brenner, *der; see also* **back burner; Bunsen burner**
burning ['bɜːnɪŋ] **1.** *adj.* **a)** brennend; **b)** *(fig.)* glühend ⟨*Leidenschaft, Haß, Wunsch*⟩; brennend ⟨*Wunsch, Frage, Problem*⟩; **sth. is a ~ shame** etw. ist eine wahre Schande *od.* schreit zum Himmel. **2.** *n.* Brennen, *das;* **a smell of ~:** ein Brandgeruch

¹**burning-glass** *n.* Brennglas, *das*
burnish ['bɜ:nɪʃ] *v. t.* polieren
burnt *see* ¹**burn 2, 3**
burnt 'offering *n.* Brandopfer, *das; (fig. joc.: burnt food)* angebranntes Essen
burp [bɜ:p] *(coll.)* **1.** *n.* Rülpser, *der (ugs.); (of baby)* Bäuerchen, *das (fam.);* **emit a loud ~/a series of ~s** laut/mehrmals rülpsen. **2.** *v. i.* rülpsen *(ugs.);* aufstoßen. **3.** *v. t.* ein Bäuerchen machen lassen *(fam.)* ‹*Baby*›
burr [bɜ:(r)] *n.* **a)** *(rough edge)* Grat, *der;* **b)** *(drill)* Bohrer, *der;* **c)** *see* **bur a**
burrow ['bʌrəʊ] **1.** *n.* Bau, *der.* **2.** *v. t.* graben, *(ugs.)* buddeln ‹*Loch, Höhle, Tunnel*›; **~ one's way under/through sth.** einen Weg *od.* Gang unter etw. *(Dat.)* durch/durch etw. graben. **3.** *v. i.* [sich *(Dat.)*] einen Gang graben; sich durchbuddeln *(ugs.);* **~ into sth.** *(fig.)* sich in etw. *(Akk.)* einarbeiten; **~ through sth.** *(fig.)* sich durch etw. hindurchwühlen
bursar ['bɜ:sə(r)] *n. Verwalter der geschäftlichen Angelegenheiten einer Schule/Universität*
bursary ['bɜ:sərɪ] *n.* Kasse, *die; (scholarship)* Stipendium, *das*
burst [bɜ:st] **1.** *n.* **a)** *(split)* Bruch, *der;* **a ~ in a pipe** ein Rohrbruch; **b)** *(of flame)* Auflodern, *das;* **a sudden ~ of flame** eine Stichflamme; **c)** *(outbreak of firing)* Feuerstoß, *der;* Salve, *die;* **d)** *(fig.)* **a ~ of applause/cheering** ein Beifallsausbruch/Beifallsrufe *Pl.;* **there was a ~ of laughter** man brach in Lachen aus; **~ of rage** Wutausbruch, *der;* **~ of enthusiasm** Begeisterungsausbruch, *der;* **a ~ of speed** ein Spurt; **e)** *(explosion)* Explosion, *die;* **a bomb ~:** eine Bombenexplosion. **2.** *v. t.,* **burst** zum Platzen bringen; platzen lassen ‹*Luftballon*›; platzen ‹*Reifen*›; sprengen ‹*Kessel*›; **~ pipe** Rohrbruch, *der;* **the river ~ its banks** der Fluß trat über die Ufer; **he ~ a blood-vessel** ihm ist eine Ader geplatzt; **he [almost] ~ a blood-vessel** *(fig.)* ihn traf [fast] der Schlag; **~ the door open** die Tür aufbrechen *od.* aufsprengen; **~ one's sides with laughing** *(fig.)* vor Lachen beinahe platzen. **3.** *v. i.,* **burst a)** platzen; ‹*Granate, Bombe, Kessel:*› explodieren; ‹*Damm:*› brechen; ‹*Flußufer:*› überschwemmt werden; ‹*Furunkel, Geschwür:*› aufgehen, aufplatzen; ‹*Knospe:*› aufbrechen; **~ open** ‹*Tür, Deckel, Kiste, Koffer:*› aufspringen; **b)** *(be full to overflowing)* **be ~ing with sth.** zum Bersten voll sein mit etw.; **be full to ~ing[-point]** proppenvoll sein *(ugs.);* **be ~ing with pride/impatience** *(fig.)* vor Stolz/Ungeduld platzen; **be ~ing with health** *(fig.)* vor Gesundheit strotzen; **be ~ing with happiness/excitement** *(fig.)* vor Freude/Aufregung außer sich sein; **I can't eat any more. I'm ~ing** *(fig.)* Ich kann nichts mehr essen. Ich platze [gleich] *(ugs.);* **be ~ing to say/do sth.** *(fig.)* es kaum abwarten können, etw. zu sagen/tun; **c)** *(appear, come suddenly)* **~ from sb.'s lips** ‹*Schrei:*› jmds. Lippen entfahren; **~ through sth.** etw. durchbrechen; **the Beatles ~ upon the pop scene in the early sixties** die Beatles wurden Anfang der 60er Jahre in die Popszene katapultiert; **the sun ~ through the clouds** die Sonne brach durch die Wolken
~ 'in *v. i.* hereinplatzen; hereinstürzen; **~ in [up]on sb./sth.** bei jmdm./etw. hereinplatzen
~ into *v. t.* **a)** eindringen in; **we ~ into the room** wir stürzten ins Zimmer; **b)** *(suddenly begin)* **~ into tears/laughter** in Tränen/Gelächter ausbrechen; **~ into flower** [plötzlich] aufblühen; **~ into song** ein Lied anstimmen; **~ into flames** in Brand geraten
~ 'out *v. i.* **a)** herausstürzen; **~ out of a room** aus einem Raum [hinaus]stürmen *od.* stürzen; **b)** *(exclaim)* losplatzen; **c)** *(suddenly begin)* **~ out laughing/crying** in Lachen/Tränen ausbrechen
burton ['bɜ:tn] *n. (Brit. sl.)* **go for a ~** *(be destroyed)* kaputtgehen *(ugs.);* futsch gehen *(salopp); (be lost)* hopsgehen *(salopp);* flötengehen *(salopp); (be killed)* dran glauben müssen *(salopp)*
bury ['berɪ] *v. t.* **a)** begraben; beisetzen *(geh.)* ‹*Toten*›; **~ sb. at sea** jmdn. auf See bestatten; **be dead and buried** *(lit. or fig.)* tot und begraben sein; schon lange tot sein; **where is Marx buried?** wo ist *od.* liegt Marx begraben?; **~ sb. alive** jmdn. lebendig begraben; **b)** *(hide)* vergraben; verbuddeln *(ugs.); (fig.)* begraben; **~ one's differences** *(fig.)* seinen Streit begraben; **~ the hatchet** *or (Amer.)* **tomahawk** *(fig.)* das Kriegsbeil begraben; **~ one's face in one's hands** das Gesicht in den Händen vergraben; **c)** *(bring underground)* eingraben; abdecken ‹*Wurzeln*›; **buried cable** *(Electr.)* Erdkabel; **the houses were buried by a landslide** die Häuser wurden durch einen Erdrutsch verschüttet; **d)** *(plunge)* **~ one's teeth in sth.** seine Zähne in etw. *(Akk.)* graben *od.* schlagen; **~ one's hands in one's pockets** seine Hände in den Taschen vergraben; **sth. buries itself in sth.** etw. bohrt sich in etw. *(Akk.);* **e)** *(involve deeply)* **~ oneself in one's studies/books** sich in seine Studien vertiefen/in seinen Büchern vergraben
burying ['berɪɪŋ]: **~-ground, ~-place** *ns.* Friedhof, *der;* Begräbnisstätte, *die*
bus [bʌs] **1.** *n., pl.* **~es** *(Amer.:* **~ses) a)** [Auto-, Omni]bus, *der;* **go by ~:** mit dem Bus fahren; **b)** *(coll.: car, aircraft)* Kiste, *die (ugs.). See also* **miss 2 d. 2.** *v. i., (Amer.)* **-ss-** mit dem Bus fahren. **3.** *v. t.,* **-ss-** *(Amer.)* mit dem Bus befördern
bus: ~bar *n. (Electr.)* Stromschiene, *die;* **~boy** *n. (Amer.)* Bedienungshilfe, *die;* Abräumer, *der*
busby ['bʌzbɪ] *n. (Brit.)* Kalpak, *der; (worn by guardsmen)* Bärenfellmütze, *die*
bus: ~ company *n.* ≈ Verkehrsbetrieb, *der;* **~-conductor** *n.* Busschaffner, *der;* **~ depot** *see* **~ garage; ~-driver** *n.* Busfahrer, *der;* **~ fare** *n.* [Bus]fahrpreis, *der;* **how much is the ~ fare from A to B?** wieviel kostet die [Bus]fahrt von A nach B?; **~ garage** *n.* Busdepot, *das*
¹**bush** [bʊʃ] *n.* **a)** *(shrub)* Strauch, *der;* Busch, *der; (collect.: shrubs)* Gebüsch, *das;* Gestrüpp, *das; see also* **beat 1 h, 2 c; b)** *(woodland)* Busch, *der;* **go ~** *(Austral.) (leave usual surroundings)* abhauen *(ugs.);* verschwinden *(ugs.); (run wild)* verwildern; *(go berserk)* durchdrehen *(salopp);* **c) ~ [of hair]** [Haar]schopf, *der*
²**bush** *n.* **a)** *(threaded socket)* Gewindeanschluß, *der;* **b)** *(metal lining)* Buchse, *die;* **c)** *(Electr.)* Durchführung, *die*
'**bush-baby** *n. (Zool.)* Galago, *der;* Buschbaby, *das*
bushed [bʊʃt] *adj. (Amer. coll.)* erledigt *(ugs.);* groggy *(ugs.)*
bushel ['bʊʃl] *n.* Bushel, *der;* ≈ Scheffel, *der;* **hide one's light under a ~** *(fig.)* sein Licht unter den Scheffel stellen *(Spr.)*
bushing ['bʊʃɪŋ] *see* ²**bush**
bush: ~ jacket *n.* Safarijacke, *die;* **~ league** *n. (Amer.)* Provinzliga, *die (abwertend);* **B~man** *n.* **a)** *(native)* Buschmann, *der;* **b)** *(language)* Buschmännisch, *das;* **~-ranger** *n. (Austral. Hist.)* Strauchdieb, *der (veralt.);* Buschklepper, *der (veralt.);* **~ 'telegraph** *n. (fig.)* Informationssystem, *das;* **the news spread via the ~ telegraph** die Nachricht sprach sich herum; **~-whacker** *n. (Amer., Austral., NZ: backwoodsman)* Waldsiedler, *der*
bushy ['bʊʃɪ] *adj. (covered with bushes)* buschbewachsen; *(growing luxuriantly)* buschig
busily ['bɪzɪlɪ] *adv.* eifrig
business ['bɪznɪs] *n.* **a)** *(trading operation)* Geschäft, *das; (company, firm)* Betrieb, *der; (large)* Unternehmen, *das;* **b)** *no pl. (buying and selling)* Geschäfte *Pl.;* **on ~:** geschäftlich; **he's in the wool ~:** er ist in der Wollbranche; **~ is brisk** die Geschäfte florieren; **how's ~ with you?** *(lit. or fig.)* was machen die Geschäfte [bei Ihnen]?; **~ is ~** *(fig.)* Geschäft ist Geschäft; **in my ~:** in meiner Branche; **set up in ~:** ein Geschäft *od.* eine Firma gründen; **he's in ~ for himself** er ist selbständig; **go out of ~** pleite gehen *(ugs.);* **go into ~:** Geschäftsmann/-frau werden; **do ~ [with sb.]** [mit jmdm.] Geschäfte machen; **I'm glad we were able to do ~:** ich bin froh, daß wir ins Geschäft gekommen sind; **be in ~:** Geschäftsmann/-frau sein; **we're in ~ [again]** *(fig.)* es kann [wieder] losgehen; **it was ~ as usual** die Geschäfte gingen ihren normalen Gang; **'B~ as usual during alterations'** „Während des Umbaus geht der Verkauf/Betrieb weiter"; **do you want to go into ~ or become a lawyer?** wollen Sie in die Wirtschaft gehen oder Anwalt werden?; **go about one's ~:** seinen Geschäften nachgehen; **c)** *(task, duty, province)* Aufgabe, *die;* Pflicht, *die;* **that is 'my ~/none of 'your ~:** das ist meine Angelegenheit/nicht deine Sache; **that is 'your ~:** das ist deine Sache; **what ~ is it of yours?** was geht Sie das an?; **send sb. about his ~:** jmdn. abblitzen lassen *(ugs.);* jmdm. eine Abfuhr erteilen; **mind your own ~:** kümmere dich um deine [eigenen] Angelegenheiten!; **he has no ~ to do that** er hat kein Recht, das zu tun; **make it one's ~ to do sth.** es sich *(Dat.)* angelegen sein lassen, etw. zu tun *(geh.); (with more effort)* es sich *(Dat.)* zur Aufgabe machen, etw. zu tun; **like nobody's ~** *(coll.)* wie verrückt *(ugs.);* **d)** *(matter to be considered)* Angelegenheit, *die;* **'any other ~'** „Sonstiges"; **the [main] ~ of the day** das [Haupt]anliegen des Tages; **get on with the ~ in hand** zur Sache kommen; **e)** *(difficult matter)* Problem, *das;* **a lengthy ~:** eine langwierige Angelegenheit; **it's going to be a ~ getting the piano down the stairs** das wird noch ein Problem geben, das Klavier die Treppe hinunterzukriegen; **what a ~ [this is]!** was für ein Theater!; **make a [great] ~ of sth.** ein [großes] Problem aus etw. machen; *(make a fuss)* einen [Riesen]wirbel um etw. machen; **f)** *(serious work)* **get down to [serious] ~:** [ernsthaft] zur Sache kommen; *(Commerc.)* an die Arbeit gehen; **mean ~:** es ernst meinen; **~ before pleasure** erst die Arbeit, dann das Vergnügen; **combine ~ and pleasure** das Angenehme mit dem Nützlichen verbinden; **g)** *(derog.: affair)* Sache, *die;* Geschichte, *die (ugs.);* **h)** *no pl. (Theatre)* Gestik und Mimik, *die*
business: ~ address *n.* Geschäftsadresse, *die;* **~ card** *n.* Geschäftskarte, *die;* **~ correspondence** *n.* Geschäftskorrespondenz, *die;* **~ cycle** *n. (Amer.)* Konjunkturzyklus, *der;* **~ end** *n. (coll.) (of tool)* vorderes Ende; *(of hammer etc.)* Kopf, *der; (of rifle etc.)* Lauf, *der;* **~ hours** *n. pl.* Geschäftszeit, *die; (in office)* Dienstzeit, *die;* **~ letter** *n.* Geschäftsbrief, *der;* **~-like** *adj.* geschäftsmäßig ‹*Art*›; sachlich, nüchtern ‹*Untersuchung*›; geschäftstüchtig ‹*Person*›; **~ lunch** *n.* Arbeitsessen, *das;* **~ machine** *n.* Büromaschine, *die;* **~man** *n.* Geschäftsmann, *der;* **~ premises** *n. pl.* Geschäftsräume; **~ school** *n.* kaufmännische Fachschule; **~ studies** *n. pl.* Wirtschaftslehre, *die;* **~ suit** *n.* Straßenanzug, *der;* **~ trip** *n.* Geschäftsreise, *die;* **on a ~ trip** auf Geschäftsreise; **~woman** *n.* Geschäftsfrau, *die*
busker ['bʌskə(r)] *n.* Straßenmusikant, *der*
busking ['bʌskɪŋ] *n.* Musizieren auf Straßen und Plätzen
bus: ~ lane *n. (Brit.)* Busspur, *die;* **~load** *n.* Busladung, *die;* **~man** ['bʌsmən] *n.* **a ~-man's holiday** *(fig.)* praktisch gar keine

Ferien *(weil man dasselbe wie im Berufsalltag tut)*; **~-ride** *n.* Busfahrt, *die;* **B. is only an hour's ~-ride away** B. ist nur eine Busstunde entfernt; **~-route** *n.* Buslinie, *die;* **~ service** *n.* Omnibusverkehr, *der; (specific service)* Busverbindung, *die;* **~ shelter** *n.* Wartehäuschen, *das*
bussing ['bʌsɪŋ] *n., no pl. (Amer.) Busbeförderung von Schulkindern in andere Bezirke zur Förderung der Rassenintegration*
bus: ~-station *n.* Omnibusbahnhof, *der;* **~-stop** *n.* Bushaltestelle, *die*
[1]**bust** [bʌst] *n.* **a)** *(sculpture)* Büste, *die;* **b)** *(upper front of body)* Brust, *die; (woman's bosom)* Busen, *der;* **what ~ are you?, what is your ~ [measurement]?** welche Oberweite haben Sie?
[2]**bust** *(coll.)* **1.** *n.* **a)** *(collapse of trade)* Pleite, *die (ugs.); (general)* Zusammenbruch, *der;* **b)** *(police raid)* Razzia, *die;* **c)** *(Cards)* schlechtes Blatt; **d)** *(drinking-bout)* Sauftour, *die (salopp);* **go on a ~:** auf Sauftour gehen. **2.** *adj.* **a)** *(broken)* kaputt *(ugs.);* **b)** *(bankrupt)* bankrott; pleite *(ugs.);* **go ~:** pleite gehen. **3.** *v. t.,* **~ed** *or* **bust a)** *(burst)* aufplatzen lassen ‹*Koffer usw.*›; *(break)* kaputtmachen *(ugs.);* **~ sth. open** etw. aufbrechen; **b)** *(coll.) (dismiss)* entlassen; *(demote)* degradieren ‹*Unteroffizier usw.*›; *(break up)* auffliegen lassen ‹*Verbrecherring*›; *(arrest)* schnappen *(ugs.);* **c)** *(sl.: punch)* schlagen; hauen *(ugs.);* **~ sb. on the chin/jaw** jmdm. einen Kinnhaken geben *od.* verabreichen. **4.** *v. i.,* **~ed** *or* **bust** kaputtgehen *(ugs.);* ‹*Lineal usw.:*› zerbrechen; ‹*Bleistiftspitze:*› abbrechen; **be laughing fit to ~:** sich halbtot lachen; **~ in half** auseinanderbrechen
~ 'up *v. t.* kaputtmachen *(ugs.)* ‹*Ehe, Partnerschaft*›; **~ a place up** in einem Laden Kleinholz machen *(salopp)*
bustard ['bʌstəd] *n. (Ornith.)* Trappe, *die*
buster ['bʌstə(r)] *n. (sl.) (as address)* Meister *(der) (salopp); (threatening)* Freundchen *(das) (salopp)*
bus: ~ terminal *n.* Busbahnhof, *der;* **~-ticket** *n.* Busfahrkarte, *die;* Busfahrschein, *der*
[1]**bustle** ['bʌsl] **1.** *v. i.* eilig umherlaufen; **~ in/out/about** geschäftig hinein- *od.* herein-/hinaus- *od.* herauseilen/geschäftig hin und her eilen; **the town centre was bustling with activity** im Stadtzentrum herrschte großer Betrieb *od.* ein reges Treiben. **2.** *v. t.* jagen *(ugs.);* treiben *(ugs.).* **3.** *n. (activity)* Betrieb, *der; (of fair, streets also)* geschäftiges *od.* reges Treiben **(of** auf, in + *Dat.*); *(fuss)* Aufregung, *die*
[2]**bustle** *n. (Fashion Hist.)* Turnüre, *die*
bustling ['bʌslɪŋ] *adj.* belebt ‹*Straße, Stadt, Markt usw.*›; emsig, geschäftig ‹*Person, Art*›; rege ‹*Tätigkeit*›
'bust-up *n. (coll.)* Krach, *der (ugs.);* **have a ~:** Krach haben *(ugs.);* sich verkrachen *(ugs.);* **there's going to be a ~:** es wird Krach geben
busty ['bʌstɪ] *adj.* vollbusig
busy ['bɪzɪ] **1.** *adj.* **a)** *(occupied)* beschäftigt; **I'm ~ now** ich habe jetzt zu tun; **keep oneself ~:** sich [selbst] beschäftigen; **keep sb. ~:** jmdn. auf Trab halten; **be ~ at** *or* **with sth.** mit etw. beschäftigt sein; **be ~ in the kitchen** in der Küche zu tun haben; **he was ~ packing** er war mit Packen beschäftigt *od.* war gerade beim Packen; **get ~:** sich an die Arbeit machen; **as ~ as a bee** *(fig.)* bienenfleißig; **b)** *(full of activity)* arbeitsreich ‹*Leben*›; ziemlich hektisch ‹*Zeit*›; belebt ‹*Stadt*›; ausgelastet ‹*Person*›; fleißig ‹*Hände*›; rege ‹*Verkehr*›; **a ~ road** eine verkehrsreiche *od.* vielbefahrene Straße; **the office was ~ all day** im Büro war den ganzen Tag viel los; **I'm/he's a ~ man** ich habe/er hat viel zu tun; **he leads a very ~ life** er ist immer beschäftigt; **it has been a ~ day/week** heute/diese Woche war viel los; **I had a ~ day/week** ich hatte heute/diese Woche viel zu tun; **c)** *(Amer. Teleph.)* besetzt. **2.** *v. refl.* **~ oneself with sth.** sich mit etw. beschäftigen; **~ oneself [in] doing sth.** sich damit beschäftigen, etw. zu tun
busy: ~body *n.* G[e]schaftlhuber, *der (südd., österr.);* Wichtigtuer, *der;* **don't be such a ~body** misch dich nicht überall ein; **~ Lizzie** [bɪzɪ 'lɪzɪ] *n. (Bot.)* Fleißiges Lieschen; **~ signal** *n. (Amer. Teleph.)* Besetztzeichen, *das*
but 1. [bət, *stressed* bʌt] *conj.* **a)** *co-ordinating* aber; **Sue wasn't there, ~ her sister was** Sue war nicht da, dafür aber ihre Schwester; **I can't come today ~ I can come tomorrow** heute kann ich [zwar] nicht kommen, aber [ich kann dafür] morgen [kommen]; **he might have been able to help, ~ then he isn't here** er hätte vielleicht helfen können, aber er ist ja nicht hier; **we tried to do it ~ couldn't** wir haben es versucht, aber nicht gekonnt; **~ surely you must have noticed ...:** aber du hast doch sicherlich bemerkt, ...; **~ I 'did!** hab' ich doch!; **~ then what if the plane is delayed?** aber was ist, wenn das Flugzeug Verspätung hat?; **b)** *correcting after a negative* sondern; **not that book ~ this one** nicht das Buch, sondern dieses; **not only ... ~ also** nicht nur ..., sondern auch; **I can't change the way my son acts, not ~ what I've tried** ich kann das Verhalten meines Sohnes nicht ändern, obwohl ich es schon versucht habe; **I don't doubt ~ that it's true** ich bezweifle nicht, daß es wahr ist; **I don't deny ~ that ...:** ich leugne nicht ab, daß ...; **c)** *subordinating* ohne daß; **never a week passes ~ he phones** keine Woche vergeht, ohne daß er anruft. **2.** *prep.* außer (+ *Dat.*); **all ~ him** alle außer ihm; **no one ~ you** niemand außer dir; nur du; **anyone ~ Jim** alle mit Ausnahme von *od.* alle außer Jim; **all ~ three** alle außer dreien; **the next ~ one/two** der/die/das über-/überübernächste; **the last ~ one/two** der/die/das vor-/vorvorletzte; **nobody, ~ nobody, may leave the room** niemand, aber auch wirklich niemand darf das Zimmer verlassen; *see also* **all 3; anything 1 c; nothing 1 a. 3.** [bət] *adv.* nur; bloß; **they are ~ children** sie sind doch noch Kinder; **if I could ~ talk to her ...:** wenn ich [doch] nur mit ihr sprechen könnte ...; **we can ~ try** wir können es immerhin versuchen. **4.** *rel. pron.* der/die/das nicht; **there is no one ~ knows that ...:** es gibt niemanden, der nicht weiß, daß ... **5.** [bʌt] *n.* Aber, *das;* **no ~s [about it]!** kein Aber!; **there are no ~s about it** da gibt es kein Wenn und kein Aber; *see also* **if 2**
butane ['bju:teɪn] *n. (Chem.)* Butan, *das*
butch [bʊtʃ] **1.** *adj.* betont männlich ‹*Frau, Kleidung, Frisur*›; betont maskulin, *(salopp)* macho ‹*Mann*›; **~ haircut** *(Amer.)* Bürstenschnitt, *der.* **2.** *n. (woman)* kesser Vater *(salopp); (man)* betont maskuliner Typ; Macho, *der (salopp)*
butcher ['bʊtʃə(r)] **1.** *n.* **a)** Fleischer, *der;* Metzger, *der (bes. westmd., südd.);* Schlachter, *der (nordd.);* **~'s [shop]** Fleischerei, *die;* Metzgerei, *die (bes. westmd., südd.);* **~'s meat** Rind-, Schweine- und Hammelfleisch *(im Gegensatz zu Geflügel, Wild und Speck);* **the ~, the baker, the candlestick-maker** *(fig.)* ehrbare Bürger; **have** *or* **take a ~'s [hook] at sb./sth.** *(sl.)* [sich *(Dat.)*] jmdn./etw. angucken *(ugs.); see also* **baker; b)** *(fig.: murderer)* [Menschen]schlächter, *der;* **c)** *(Amer. coll.: vendor)* Verkäufer in Eisenbahnzügen. **2.** *v. t.* schlachten; *(fig.: murder)* niedermetzeln; abschlachten; *(fig.: ruin)* verhunzen *(ugs.),* verunstalten ‹*Text usw.*›
butchery ['bʊtʃərɪ] *n.* **a)** **~ [trade** *or* **business]** Fleischerhandwerk, *das;* **b)** *(fig.: needless slaughter)* Metzelei, *die;* Gemetzel, *das;* **it's sheer ~!** das ist [ja] das reinste Gemetzel!; **c)** *(slaughterhouse)* Schlachthaus, *das*
butler ['bʌtlə(r)] *n.* Butler, *der;* erster Diener
[1]**butt** [bʌt] *n. (vessel)* Faß, *das; (for rainwater)* Tonne, *die*
[2]**butt** *n.* **a)** *(end)* dickes Ende; *(of rifle)* Kolben, *der; (of spear, fishing-rod, etc.)* Schaft, *der;* **b)** *(of cigarette, cigar)* Stummel, *der;* **cigarette ~:** Zigarettenstummel, *der;* Kippe, *die (ugs.);* **c)** *(Amer. sl.: buttocks)* Hintern, *der (ugs.)*
[3]**butt** *n.* **a)** *(object of teasing or ridicule)* Zielscheibe, *die;* Gegenstand, *der;* **be the ~ of ridicule** Zielscheibe des Spottes sein; **make a ~ of sb.** sich über jmdn. lustig machen; **b)** *in pl. (shooting-range)* Schießstand, *der;* Waffenjustierstand, *der;* **c)** *(target)* Schießscheibe, *die;* **d)** *(grouse-shooter's stand)* Schießstand *(beim Moorhuhnschießen)*
[4]**butt 1.** *n. (push) (by person)* [Kopf]stoß, *der; (by animal)* Stoß [mit den Hörnern], *der;* **give sb. a ~ in the stomach** jmdm. mit dem Kopf in den Bauch stoßen. **2.** *v. i.* **a)** *(push with head)* ‹*Person:*› [mit dem Kopf] stoßen; ‹*Stier, Widder, Ziege:*› [mit den Hörnern] stoßen; **b)** *(meet end to end)* **~ against sth.** an etw. *(Akk.)* stoßen. **3.** *v. t.* **a)** *(push with head)* ‹*Person:*› mit dem Kopf stoßen; ‹*Widder, Ziege:*› mit den Hörnern stoßen; **~ sb. in the stomach** jmdm. mit dem Kopf in den Bauch stoßen; **b)** aneinanderfügen; zusammenstoßen lassen; **~ sth. against sth.** etw. mit etw. zusammenstoßen lassen *od.* auf etw. *(Akk.)* stoßen lassen
~ 'in *v. i. (fig. coll.)* dazwischenreden; *(meddle)* sich [ungefragt] einmischen; **may I ~ in?** darf ich mal kurz stören?
butte [bju:t] *n. (Amer. Geog.)* Restberg, *der*
'butt-end *see* [2]**butt a, b**
butter ['bʌtə(r)] **1.** *n.* Butter, *die;* **he looks as if ~ wouldn't melt in his mouth** *(fig.)* er sieht aus, als ob er kein Wässerchen trüben könnte; **melted ~:** zerlassene Butter. **2.** *v. t.* buttern; mit Butter bestreichen; **fine words ~ no parsnips** Worte allein genügen nicht
~ 'up *v. t.* **~ sb. up** jmdm. Honig um den Mund *od.* Bart schmieren *(fig.)*
butter: ~-bean *n.* Gartenbohne, *die; (lima bean)* Mondbohne, *die;* Limabohne, *die;* **~ cream** *n.* Buttercreme, *die;* **~cup** *n. (Bot.)* Butterblume, *die;* **~-dish** *n.* Butterdose, *die;* **~-fingers** *n. sing.* Tolpatsch, *der (beim Fangen usw.)*
butterfly ['bʌtəflaɪ] *n.* **a)** Schmetterling, *der;* **break a ~ on the wheel** *(fig.)* mit Kanonen nach Spatzen schießen; **have butterflies [in one's stomach]** *(fig. coll.)* ein flaues Gefühl im Magen haben; **b)** *(fig.: showy person)* Paradiesvogel, *der; (frivolous woman)* Schmetterling, *der (abwertend);* **c)** *see* **butterfly stroke**
butterfly: ~-nut *n.* Flügelmutter, *die;* **~ stroke** *n. (Swimming)* Delphinstil, *der;* Delphin *(das);* **do** *or* **swim the ~ stroke** delphinschwimmen; **~ valve** *n.* Drosselklappe, *die*
butter: ~-knife *n.* Buttermesser, *das;* **~milk** *n.* Buttermilch, *die;* **~scotch** *n.* Buttertoffee, *das*
buttery ['bʌtərɪ] *n.* Vorratskammer, *die; (Univ.)* ≈ Cafeteria, *die*
buttock ['bʌtək] *n. (of person)* Hinterbacke, *die;* Gesäßhälfte, *die; (of animal)* Hinterbacke, *die;* **~s** Gesäß, *das*
button ['bʌtn] **1.** *n.* **a)** Knopf, *der;* **as bright as a ~:** putzmunter *(ugs.);* **he didn't care** *or* **give a ~ [about it]** *(fig.)* er hat sich den Teufel darum geschert *(ugs.);* **b)** *(of electric bell etc., on fencing foil)* Knopf, *der;* **press** *or* **push the ~:** auf den Knopf drücken; **c)** *(bud)* Auge, *das;* Knopf, *der (südd., österr., schweiz.);* **~ mushroom** Champignon, *der.* **2.** *v. t. (fasten)* zuknöpfen; einknöpfen ‹*Futter*›; **~ one's lip** *(Amer. sl.)* die Klappe hal-

ten *(salopp).* **3.** *v.i.* [zu]geknöpft werden; **this dress ~s down the back** dieses Kleid wird hinten geknöpft

~ **'up 1.** *v.t.* zuknöpfen; *(fig.)* erledigen ⟨*Job*⟩; **have the deal [all] ~ed up** das Geschäft unter Dach und Fach haben *(ugs.)*; **~ed up** *(fig.: taciturn)* zugeknöpft *(ugs.)*; reserviert. **2.** *v.i.* [zu]geknöpft werden

'button-down *adj.* Buttondown⟨*-Kragen*⟩

'buttonhole 1. *n.* **a)** Knopfloch, *das;* **~ stitch** Knopflochstich, *der;* **b)** *(Brit.: flowers worn in coat-lapel)* Knopflochsträußchen, *das; (single flower)* Knopflochblume, *die;* Blume im Knopfloch. **2.** *v.t. (detain)* zu fassen kriegen *(ugs.)*; **he was ~d by X X** hat sich *(Dat.)* ihn geschnappt *(ugs.)*

'button-through *adj.* durchgeknöpft ⟨*Kleid*⟩

buttress ['bʌtrɪs] **1.** *n.* **a)** *(Archit.)* Mauerstrebe, *die;* Mauerstütze, *die; (not built-on)* Strebepfeiler, *der;* **~es** Strebewerk, *das;* **b)** *(support)* Pfeiler, *der;* **c)** *(fig.)* Stütze, *die;* [Eck]pfeiler, *der.* **2.** *v.t.* **~ [up]** [durch Strebepfeiler] stützen; *(fig.)* [unter]stützen; stärken; untermauern ⟨*Argument*⟩

'butt weld *n.* Stumpfschweißnaht, *die*

butty ['bʌtɪ] *n. (coll.)* Butterbrot, *das;* Stulle, *die (nordd.)*

buxom ['bʌksəm] *adj.* drall

buy [baɪ] **1.** *v.t.*, **bought** [bɔːt] **a)** kaufen; lösen ⟨*Fahrkarte*⟩; **~ sb./oneself sth.** jmdm./sich etw. kaufen; **~ and sell goods** Waren an- und verkaufen; **the pound ~s less than it used to** für ein Pfund bekommt man heute weniger als früher; **~ [oneself]/sb. a pint** sich *(Dat.)* einen Halben genehmigen/jmdm. einen Halben ausgeben; **he bought them a round** er spendierte ihnen eine Runde; **money cannot ~ happiness** Glück kann man nicht kaufen; **b)** *(fig.)* erkaufen ⟨*Sieg, Ruhm, Frieden*⟩; einsparen, gewinnen ⟨*Zeit*⟩; **c)** *(bribe)* bestechen; kaufen *(ugs.)*; erkaufen ⟨*Zustimmung*⟩; **d)** *(sl.) (believe)* schlucken *(ugs.)*; glauben; *(accept)* akzeptieren; einverstanden sein mit; **I'll ~ that** *(believe)* das nehm' ich dir ab *(ugs.)*; *(agree)* ja, das glaube ich; **e) ~ it** *(sl.: be killed)*: **we nearly bought it that time** da hätte es uns beinahe erwischt. **2.** *n.* [Ein]kauf, *der;* **be a good ~**: preiswert sein; **plenty of good ~s** viele preiswerte Artikel; **the best ~**: der/die/das Preiswerteste; der preiswerteste Artikel; **this week's best ~ is ...** der Preisschlager der Woche ist ...

~ **'in** *v.t.* **a)** einkaufen, sich eindecken mit ⟨*Vorräte, Fleisch usw.*⟩; **b)** *(at auction)* [durch höheres Gebot] zurückkaufen

~ **into** *v. refl. & i.* **~ [oneself] into a business** sich in ein Geschäft einkaufen

~ **'off** *v.t.* auszahlen ⟨*Forderung*⟩; abfinden ⟨*Anspruchserhebenden*⟩; *(bribe)* bestechen; kaufen *(ugs.)*

~ **'out** *v.t.* auszahlen ⟨*Aktionär, Partner*⟩; aufkaufen ⟨*Firma*⟩

~ **'up** *v.t.* aufkaufen

buyer ['baɪə(r)] *n.* **a)** Käufer, *der*/Käuferin, *die;* **potential ~**: Kaufinteressent, *der;* **b)** *(Commerc.)* Einkäufer, *der*/Einkäuferin, *die;* **c) a ~'s** *or* **~s' market** ein Käufermarkt

buying ['baɪɪŋ] *n., no pl.* Kaufen, *das*

buzz [bʌz] **1.** *n.* **a)** *(of insect)* Summen, *das; (of large insect)* Brummen, *das; (of smaller or agitated insect)* Schwirren, *das;* **b)** *(sound of buzzer)* Summen, *das;* **give one's secretary a ~**: über den Summer seine Sekretärin rufen; **c)** *(of conversation, movement)* Gemurmel, *das;* **d)** *(sl.: telephone call)* [Telefon]anruf, *der;* **give sb. a ~**: jmdn. anrufen; **e)** *(sl.: thrill)* Nervenkitzel, *der (ugs.)*. **2.** *v.i.* **a)** *see* **1 a**: ⟨*Insekt:*⟩ summen/brummen/schwirren; **b)** *(signal with buzzer)* [mit dem Summer] rufen; **c)** *(sound confusedly)* **the court-room ~ed as ...**: im Gerichtssaal erhob sich *od.* hörte man ein Raunen, als ...; **~ with excitement** in heller Aufregung sein; **the rumour set the office ~ing** das Gerücht versetzte das Büro in helle Aufregung; **my ears are ~ing** mir sausen die Ohren. **3.** *v.t. (Aeronaut.)* dicht vorbeifliegen *od. (ugs.)* vorbeizischen an (+ *Dat.*)

~ **a'bout,** ~ **a'round 1.** *v.i.* herumschwirren; herumsurren; *(fig.)* ⟨*Person:*⟩ herumsausen, herumschwirren. **2.** *v.t.* **~ around sth.** um etw. [herum]schwirren; **~ around the room** im Zimmer herumschwirren *od.* umherschwirren

~ **'off** *v.i. (sl.)* abhauen *(salopp)*; abzischen *(salopp)*

buzzard ['bʌzəd] *n. (Ornith.)* **a)** *(Brit.)* Bussard, *der;* **b)** *(Amer.: turkey ~)* Amerikanischer Truthahngeier

buzzer ['bʌzə(r)] *n.* Summer, *der*

buzz: ~-saw *n. (Amer.)* Kreissäge, *die;* **~-word** *n.* Schlagwort, *das*

[1]by [baɪ] **1.** *prep.* **a)** *(near, beside)* an (+ *Dat.*); bei; *(next to)* neben; **by the window/river** am Fenster/Fluß; **the bus-stop by the school** die Haltestelle an der Schule; **she sat by me** sie saß neben mir; **come and sit by me** komm, setz dich zu mir!; **b)** *(to position beside)* zu; **go over by the table/wall** geh zum Tisch/zur Wand!; **come by the fire** komm ans Feuer!; **c)** *(about, in the possession of)* bei; **have sth. by one** etw. bei sich haben; **d)** *(slightly inclining to)* auf (+ *Dat.*); **north-east by east** Nordost auf Ost; **e) by herself** *etc. see* **herself a**; **f)** *(along)* entlang; **by the river** am *od.* den Fluß entlang; **g)** *(via)* über (+ *Akk.*); **to Paris by Dover** nach Paris über Dover; **leave by the door/window** zur Tür hinausgehen/zum Fenster hinaussteigen; **we came by the quickest/shortest route** wir sind die schnellste/kürzeste Strecke gefahren; **h)** *(passing)* vorbei an (+ *Dat.*); **run/drive by sb./sth.** an jmdm./etw. vorbeilaufen/vorbeifahren; **i)** *(during)* bei; **by day/night** bei Tag/Nacht; tagsüber/nachts; **by the light of the moon** im Mondschein; **j)** *(through the agency of)* von; **written by ...**: geschrieben von ...; **by sheer good fortune** durch reines Glück; **k)** *(through the means of)* durch; **they escaped by the back door/a stairway/a ladder** sie flüchteten durch die Hintertür/über eine Treppe/mit[tels] einer Leiter; **he was killed by lightning/a falling chimney** er ist vom Blitz/von einem umstürzenden Schornstein erschlagen worden; **heated by gas/oil** mit Gas/Öl geheizt; gas-/ölbeheizt; **begin/end by doing sth.** damit beginnen/aufhören, etw. zu tun; **by turning the knob** durch Drehen des Griffs; **grab sb. by the collar** jmdn. am Kragen packen; **I knew him by his voice** ich erkannte ihn an seiner Stimme; **I could tell by his face that ...**: ich erkannte an seinem Gesicht, daß ...; **by bus/ship** *etc.* mit dem Bus/Schiff *usw.*; **by air/sea** mit dem Flugzeug/Schiff; **make a living by sth.** sich *(Dat.)* seinen Lebensunterhalt mit *od.* durch etw. verdienen; **have children by sb.** Kinder von jmdm. haben; **l)** *(not later than)* bis; **by now/this time** inzwischen; **by next week she will be in China** nächste Woche ist sie schon in China; **by the time this letter reaches you** bis Dich dieser Brief erreicht; **but by that time all the tickets had been sold** aber bis dahin waren schon alle Karten verkauft; **but by that time it was too late** aber da war es schon zu spät; **by the 20th of the month** bis zum 20. des Monats; **m)** *indicating unit of time* pro; *indicating unit of length, weight, etc.* -weise; **by the second/minute/hour** pro Sekunde/Minute/Stunde; **rent a house by the year** ein Haus für jeweils ein Jahr mieten; **you can hire a car by the day or by the week** man kann sich *(Dat.)* ein Auto tageweise oder wochenweise mieten; **pay sb. by the month** jmdn. monatlich bezahlen; **day by day/month by month, by the day/month** *(as each day etc. passes)* Tag für Tag/Monat für Monat; **cloth by the metre** Stoff am Meter; **sell sth. by the packet/ton/dozen** etw. paket-/tonnenweise/im Dutzend verkaufen; **10 ft. by 20 ft.** 10 [Fuß] mal 20 Fuß; **n)** *indicating amount* **by the thousands** zu Tausenden; **one by one** einzeln; **two by two/three by three/four by four** zu zweit/dritt/viert; **little by little** nach und nach; **o)** *indicating factor* durch; **8 divided by 2 is 4** 8 geteilt durch 2 ist 4; **p)** *indicating extent* um; **wider by a foot** um einen Fuß breiter; **win by ten metres** mit zehn Metern Vorsprung gewinnen; **passed by nine votes to two** mit neun zu zwei Stimmen angenommen; **q)** *(according to)* nach; **by my watch** nach meiner Uhr; **by the left, quick march!** *(Mil.)* im Geschwindschritt – marsch! [Links, zwo, drei, vier!]; **r)** *in oaths* bei; **by [Almighty] God** bei Gott[, dem Allmächtigen]. **2.** *adv.* **a)** *(past)* vorbei; **march/drive/run/flow by** vorbeimarschieren/-fahren/-laufen/-fließen; **b)** *(near)* **close/near by** in der Nähe; **c)** *(aside, in reserve)* auf die Seite; **d) by and large** im großen und ganzen; **by and by** nach und nach; *(in past)* nach einer Weile

[2]by *see* **[2]bye**

[1]bye [baɪ] *int. (coll.)* tschüs *(ugs.)*; **~ [for] now!** bis später!; tschüs! *(ugs.)*

[2]bye *n.* **a)** *(Sport)* **draw a ~ in the first round** spielfrei in die zweite Runde kommen; **b) by the ~ = by the way** *see* **way 1 g**; **c)** *(Cricket) Lauf bei einem Ball, der vom Schlagmann nicht getroffen wurde*

[1]bye-bye [baɪ'baɪ] *int. (coll.)* Wiedersehen *(ugs.)*; **~ [for] now!** [also] tschüs! *(ugs.)*

[2]bye-bye ['baɪbaɪ], **bye-byes** ['baɪbaɪz] *n. (child lang.)* **go [to] ~**: in die Heia gehen *(Kinderspr.)*

bye-law *see* **by-law**

'by-election *n.* Nachwahl, *die*

'bygone 1. *n.* **let ~s be ~s** die Vergangenheit ruhen lassen. **2.** *adj.* **[in] ~ days** [in] vergangene[n] Tage[n]

'by-law *n.* **a)** *(esp. Brit.)* Verordnung, *die;* **the park ~s** die Parkordnung; **b)** *(of company etc.)* Punkt der Richtlinien; *in pl.* Richtlinien *Pl.*

byline *n.* **a)** *(source of income)* Nebenerwerb, *der;* **b)** *(in newspaper) Zeile mit dem Namen des Verfassers*

'bypass 1. *n. (road)* Umgehungsstraße, *die; (channel; also Electr.)* Nebenleitung, *die; (Med.)* Bypass, *der;* **~ surgery** *(Med.)* eine Bypassoperation/Bypassoperationen. **2.** *v.t.* **a)** umleiten ⟨*Flüssigkeit, Gas*⟩; **b) the road ~es the town** die Straße führt um die Stadt herum; **c)** *(avoid)* aus dem Wege gehen (+ *Dat.*); *(fig.: ignore)* übergehen

by-play *n., no pl., no indef. art. (Theatre)* Nebenhandlung, *die*

'by-product *n.* Nebenprodukt, *das*

byre ['baɪə(r)] *n. (Brit.)* Kuhstall, *der*

'by-road *n.* Nebenstraße, *die;* Seitenstraße, *die*

bystander ['baɪstændə(r)] *n.* Zuschauer, *der*/Zuschauerin, *die*

byte [baɪt] *n. (Computing)* Byte, *das*

'byway *n.* Seitenweg, *der*

'byword *n. (proverb)* Spruch, *der;* [Sprich]wort, *das; (person or thing taken as typical or notable example)* Inbegriff, *der* **(for** *Gen.*)

Byzantine [bɪ'zæntaɪn, baɪ'zæntaɪn] *adj.* **a)** byzantinisch; **b)** *(complicated)* undurchschaubar

Byzantium [bɪ'zæntɪəm, baɪ'zæntɪəm] *pr. n.* Byzanz *(das)*

C

C, c [si:] *n., pl.* **Cs** *or* **C's a)** *(letter)* C, c, *das;* **b)** C *(Mus.)* C, c, *das;* **middle C** das eingestrichene c; **C sharp** cis, Cis, *das;* **c)** *(Roman numeral)* C; **d)** *(example)* C, c *(ohne Artikel);* **e) C** *(Sch., Univ.: mark)* Drei, *die;* **he got a C** er bekam „befriedigend" *od.* eine Drei

C. *abbr.* **a) Celsius** C; **b) Centigrade** C; **c)** *(Geogr.)* **Cape; d)** *(Pol.)* **Conservative**

c. *abbr.* **a) circa** ca.; **b) cent[s]** c; **c) century** Jh.; **d) chapter** Kap.; **e) cubic** Kubik-

© *symb.* **copyright** ©

CA *abbr.* **chartered accountant**

ca. *abbr.* **circa** ca.

cab [kæb] *n.* **a)** *(taxi)* Taxi, *das;* Taxe, *die (ugs.);* **b)** *(Hist.: hackney carriage)* [Pferde]droschke, *die;* **c)** *(of lorry, truck)* Fahrerhaus, *das; (of crane)* Fahrerkabine, *die; (of train)* Führerstand, *der*

cabal [kə'bæl] *n.* **a)** *(intrigue)* Intrige, *die;* Kabale, *die (veralt.);* **b)** *(clique, faction)* Clique, *die (abwertend)*

cabaret ['kæbəreɪ] *n.* Varieté, *das;* Cabaret, *das; (more sophisticated)* Kabarett, *das*

cabbage ['kæbɪdʒ] *n.* **a)** Kohl, *der;* **red/white ~:** Rot-/Weißkohl, *der;* **a [head of] ~:** ein Kopf Kohl; ein Kohlkopf; **as big as ~s** riesengroß ‹*Rosen usw.*›; **b)** *(coll.: person)* stumpfsinniger Mensch; Trottel, *der (ugs. abwertend);* **become a ~:** stumpfsinnig werden; vertrotteln *(ugs. abwertend);* **after his accident he became a complete ~:** nach seinem Unfall vegetierte er nur noch dahin

cabbage: ~ lettuce *n.* Kopfsalat, *der;* **~ 'white** *n. (Zool.)* Kohlweißling, *der*

cabbalistic [kæbə'lɪstɪk] *adj.* kabbalistisch

cabby ['kæbɪ] *(coll.),* **'cab-driver** *ns.* Taxifahrer, *der; (of horse-drawn vehicle)* Kutscher, *der*

caber ['keɪbə(r)] *n.* Pfahl, *der;* Stamm, *der;* **tossing the ~:** Baumstammwerfen, *das*

cabin ['kæbɪn] *n.* **a)** *(in ship) (for passengers)* Kabine, *die; (for crew)* Kajüte, *die; (in aircraft)* Kabine, *die;* **b)** *(simple dwelling)* Hütte, *die;* **c)** *(driver's) see* **cab c**

cabin: ~-boy *n. (Naut.)* Kabinensteward, *der;* **~ class** *n.* zweite Klasse; **they travelled ~ class** sie reisten zweiter Klasse; **~ cruiser** *n.* Kajütboot, *das*

cabinet ['kæbɪnɪt] *n.* **a)** Schrank, *der; (in bathroom, for medicines)* Schränkchen, *das; (display ~)* Vitrine, *die; (for radio, TV, etc.)* Gehäuse, *das;* **b) the C~** *(Polit.)* das Kabinett

cabinet: ~-maker *n.* Möbeltischler, *der;* **C~ 'Minister** *n.* Minister, *der;* Mitglied des Kabinetts

cable ['keɪbl] **1.** *n.* **a)** *(rope)* Kabel, *das;* Trosse, *die (Naut.); (of mountain railway)* Seil, *das;* **cut one's ~s** *(fig.)* alle Brücken hinter sich *(Dat.)* abbrechen; **b)** *(Electr., Teleph.)* Kabel, *das;* **c)** *(cablegram)* Kabel, *das;* Überseetelegramm, *das;* **d)** *(Naut.) (chain of anchor)* Ankerkette, *die; (measure)* Kabellänge, *die.* **2.** *v. t. (transmit)* telegraphisch durchgeben, kabeln ‹*Mitteilung, Nachricht*›; *(inform)* **~ sb.** jmdm. kabeln

cable: ~-car *n.* Drahtseilbahn, *die; (in street)* gezogene Straßenbahn; **~gram** *n.* Kabel, *das;* Überseetelegramm, *das;* **~ railway** *n.* Standseilbahn, *die;* **~ stitch** *n.* Zopfmuster, *das;* **~ television** *n.* Kabelfernsehen, *das;* **~way** *n. (double-~ ropeway)* Seilschwebebahn, *die; (gondola type)* Kleinkabinenbahn, *die*

'cabman ['kæbmən] *n., pl.* **cabmen** ['kæbmən] Taxifahrer, *der*

caboodle [kə'bu:dl] *n., no pl. (sl.)* **the whole ~** *(things)* der ganze Kram *(ugs.);* das ganze Gelumpe *(ugs.); (people)* die ganze Bande *(salopp) od.* Sippschaft *(ugs.)*

caboose [kə'bu:s] *n.* **a)** *(on ship)* Kombüse, *die;* **b)** *(Amer.: on train)* Dienstwagen, *der*

'cab-rank *n. (Brit.)* Taxistand, *der;* Droschken[halte]platz, *der (Amtsspr.)*

cabriolet [kæbrɪə'leɪ] *n. (Hist.)* **a)** *(carriage)* Kabriolett, *das;* **b)** *(car)* Kabriolett, *das;* Kabrio, *das (ugs.)*

cacao [kə'kɑ:əʊ, kə'keɪəʊ] *n., pl.* **~s a)** *(seed)* Kakaobohne, *die;* **b)** *(tree)* **~[-tree]** Kakaobaum, *der*

cache [kæʃ] **1.** *n.* **a)** *(hiding-place)* geheimes [Waffen-/Proviant-]lager; Versteck, *das;* **b)** *(things hidden)* Lager, *das;* **make a ~ of sth.** etw. verstecken *od.* in Sicherheit bringen. **2.** *v. t.* verstecken

cachet ['kæʃeɪ] *n.* **a)** *(mark)* Siegel, *das (fig.);* Stempel, *der (fig.);* **b)** *(prestige)* Ansehen, *das;* Distinktion, *die (geh.)*

cack-handed [kæk'hændɪd] *adj. (coll.)* **a)** *(left-handed)* linkshändig; **b)** *(clumsy)* tolpatschig *(ugs.)*

cackle ['kækl] **1.** *n.* **a)** *(clucking of hen)* Gackern, *das;* Gegacker, *das;* **b)** *(laughter)* [meckerndes] Gelächter; *(of woman)* Gegacker, *das (abwertend); (laugh)* **he gave a loud ~:** er prustete los *(ugs.);* **c)** *(talk)* Geschwätz, *das (abwertend);* **cut the ~!** *(coll.)* genug geredet!; Schluß mit dem Geschwätz! *(ugs.).* **2.** *v. i.* **a)** ‹*Henne:*› gackern; **b)** *(laugh)* meckernd lachen; ‹*Frau auch:*› gackern *(ugs.)*

cacophonous [kə'kɒfənəs] *adj.* kakophon *(geh.);* mißtönend *(geh.)*

cacophony [kə'kɒfənɪ] *n.* Kakophonie, *die (geh.);* Mißklang, *der (geh.)*

cactus ['kæktəs] *n., pl.* **cacti** ['kæktaɪ] *or* **~es** Kaktus, *der*

cad [kæd] *n. (dated derog.)* Schuft, *der;* Schurke, *der (veralt.)*

cadaver [kə'dɑ:və(r)] *n. (of animal)* Kadaver, *der; (of human)* Leiche, *die*

cadaverous [kə'dævərəs] *adj.* **a)** *(corpselike)* Kadaver-, Leichen-; **b)** *(deathly pale)* leichenfahl; totenblaß; **c)** *(gaunt)* dürr

caddie ['kædɪ] *(Golf)* **1.** *n.* Caddie, *der.* **2.** *v. i.* **~ for sb.** jmds. Caddie sein; für jmdn. Caddie spielen *(ugs.)*

caddis ['kædɪs]: **~-fly** *n.* Köcherfliege, *die;* Frühlingsfliege, *die;* **~-worm** *n.* Köcherlarve, *die*

[1]caddy ['kædɪ] *n.* Behälter, *der; (tin)* Büchse, *die;* Dose, *die*

[2]caddy *see* **caddie**

cadence ['keɪdəns] *n.* **a)** *(rhythm)* Rhythmus, *der;* **marching/dancing ~:** Marsch-/Tanzrhythmus, *der;* **speech ~:** Sprachmelodie, *die;* **b)** *(close of musical phrase, fall of voice)* Kadenz, *die*

cadenza [kə'denzə] *n. (Mus.)* [Konzert]kadenz, *die*

cadet [kə'det] *n.* **a)** *(Mil. etc.)* Offiziersschüler, *der;* Kadett, *der (veralt.);* **naval/police ~:** Marinekadett/Anwärter für den Polizeidienst; **~ corps** Kadettenkorps; **b)** *(younger brother/son)* jüngerer Bruder/Sohn

cadge [kædʒ] **1.** *v. t.* schnorren *(ugs.);* [sich *(Dat.)*] erbetteln; **could I ~ a lift with you?** können Sie mich vielleicht [ein Stück] mitnehmen? **2.** *v. i.* schnorren *(ugs.)*

cadger ['kædʒə(r)] *n.* Schnorrer, *der (ugs.)*

cadmium ['kædmɪəm] *n.* Kadmium, *das*

cadre ['kɑ:də(r), kɑ:dr] *(Mil., Polit.)* Kader, *der*

caecum ['si:kəm] *n., pl.* **caeca** ['si:kə] *(Anat.)* Blinddarm, *der*

Caesar ['si:zə(r)] *n.* **a)** Cäsar, Caesar *(der); (fig.)* Alleinherrscher, *der;* **b)** *(Med. sl.)* Kaiserschnitt, *der*

Caesarean, Caesarian [sɪ'zeərɪən] *adj. & n.* **~ [birth** *or* **operation** *or* **section]** Kaiserschnitt, *der*

caesura [sɪ'zjʊərə] *n. (Pros.)* Zäsur, *die*

café, cafe ['kæfɪ, 'kæfeɪ] *n.* **a)** Lokal, *das; (tea-room)* Café, *das;* **b)** *(Amer.: bar)* Bar, *die*

café: ~ au lait [kæfeɪ əʊ 'leɪ] *n., no pl.* Kaffee mit Sahne/Milch; Café crème *(schweiz.);* Brauner *(österr.);* **~ society** *n., no pl.* Schickeria, *die*

cafeteria [kæfɪ'tɪərɪə] *n.* Selbstbedienungsrestaurant, *das;* Cafeteria, *die*

caff [kæf] *n. (Brit. sl.)* Café, *das;* **transport ~:** Fernfahrerimbiß, *der*

caffeine ['kæfi:n] *n.* Koffein, *das; (in tea)* T[h]ein, *das*

caftan ['kæftæn] *n.* Kaftan, *der*

cage [keɪdʒ] **1.** *n.* **a)** Käfig, *der; (for small birds)* Bauer, *das;* **b)** *(Mining)* Förderkorb, *der;* **c)** *(of lift)* Fahrkabine, *die.* **2.** *v. t.* einsperren; käfigen *(fachspr.)* ‹*Vögel*›

'cage-bird *n.* Käfigvogel, *der*

cagey ['keɪdʒɪ] *adj. (coll.)* **a)** *(wary)* vorsichtig; **be ~ about sth.** vorsichtig bei etw. sein; sich mit etw. [sehr] zurückhalten; **a ~ buyer** ein wachsamer *od.* mißtrauischer Käufer; **b)** *(secretive, uncommunicative)* zugeknöpft *(ugs.);* **be ~ about saying sth.** mit etw. hinterm Berg halten *(ugs.)*

cagily ['keɪdʒɪlɪ] *adv. (coll.)* vorsichtig; *(shrewdly)* clever *(ugs.);* geschickt

caginess ['keɪdʒɪnɪs] *n. (caution)* Vorsicht, *die; (secretiveness)* Zugeknöpftheit, *die*

cagoule [kə'gu:l] *n.* [leichter, knielanger] Anorak

cagy *see* **cagey**

cahoots [kə'hu:ts] *n. pl. (Amer. sl.)* **a)** *(company, partnership)* **be in ~ with the devil** mit dem Teufel im Bunde stehen; **go into ~ with sb.** sich mit jmdm. verbünden; **b)** *(collusion)* **be in ~ with sb.** mit jmdm. unter einer Decke stecken *(ugs.)*

caiman *see* **cayman**

Cain [keɪn] *pr. n.* Kain *(der);* **raise ~** *(coll.)* Krach schlagen *(ugs.)*

cairn [keən] *n.* **a)** *(pyramid of stones)* Steinpyramide, *die;* Cairn, *der (fachspr.);* **a ~ of stones** ein Steinhaufen; **b)** *(dog)* **~ [terrier]** Cairn-Terrier, *der; schottischer Zwergterrier*

Cairo ['kaɪərəʊ] *pr. n.* Kairo *(das)*

caisson ['keɪsən, kə'su:n] *n.* **a)** *(watertight chamber)* Senkkasten, *der;* Caisson, *der;* **b)** *(floating vessel)* Docktor, *das;* Dockponton, *der*

'caisson-disease *n.* Druckluftkrankheit, *die;* Caissonkrankheit, *die*

cajole [kə'dʒəʊl] *v. t.* **~ sb. into sth./into doing sth.** jmdm. etw. einreden/jmdm. einreden, etw. zu tun; **~ sb. out of doing sth.** jmdm. ausreden, etw. zu tun; **~ sth. out of a person** jmdm. etw. entlocken

cajolery [kə'dʒəʊlərɪ] *n.* Überredungskunst, *die*

cake [keɪk] **1.** *n.* **a)** Kuchen, *der;* **a piece of ~:** ein Stück Kuchen/Torte; **a slice of ~:** eine Scheibe Kuchen; **b)** *(fig.)* **get a slice of the ~:** sein Teil abbekommen; **go** *or* **sell like hot ~s** weggehen wie warme Semmeln *(ugs.);* **a piece of ~** *(coll.)* ein Kinderspiel *(ugs.);* **you cannot have your ~ and eat it** *or* **eat your ~ and have it** beides auf einmal geht nicht; **~s and ale** *(fig.)* reinste Vergnügungen; *see also* **take 1 c; c)** *(compact mass)* **a ~ of soap** ein Riegel *od.* Stück Seife; **a ~ of wax** ein Riegel Wachs; **a ~ of tobacco** ein Plättchen Tabak. **2.** *v. t.* **a)** *(cover)* verkrusten; **~d with dirt/blood** schmutz-/blutverkrustet; **his suit was ~d with mud** sein Anzug war voll Schlamm; **b)** *(form into mass)* **rain ~d the soil** Regen machte die Erde klumpig. **3.** *v. i. (form a mass)* verklumpen

cake: **~-shop** *n.* Konditorei, *die;* **~-slice** *n.* Tortenheber, *der;* **~-stand** *n.* Etagere, *die;* **~-tin** *n.* Kuchenform, *die;* **~walk** *n.* *(dance)* Cakewalk, *der; (easy task)* Kinderspiel, *das (ugs.)*

CAL [kæl] *abbr.* **computer-aided** *or* **computer-assisted learning** computergestütztes Lernen

cal. *abbr.* **calorie[s]** cal.

calabash ['kæləbæʃ] *n.* **a)** *(gourd)* Flaschenkürbis, *der;* **b)** *(pipe, container)* Kalebasse, *die*

calaboose [kælə'bu:s] *n.* *(Amer.)* Gefängnis, *das;* Kittchen, *das (ugs.)*

calamitous [kə'læmɪtəs] *adj.* verhängnisvoll

calamity [kə'læmɪtɪ] *n.* **a)** Unheil, *das;* Unglück, *das;* **calamities of nature** Naturkatastrophen; **b)** *(adversity)* Schicksalsschlag, *der;* **c)** *(distress)* Not, *die;* Elend, *das;* **a ~:** ein Unglück

Calamity 'Jane *n.* Schwarzseherin, *die*

calcification [kælsɪfɪ'keɪʃn] *n.* Verkalkung, *die*

calcify ['kælsɪfaɪ] **1.** *v. i.* verkalken. **2.** *v. t.* verkalken lassen

calcine ['kælsaɪn, 'kælsɪn] **1.** *v. t.* kalzinieren. **2.** *v. i.* kalziniert werden

calcite ['kælsaɪt] *n.* *(Min.)* Kalzit, *der*

calcium ['kælsɪəm] *n.* Kalzium, *das;* Calcium, *das (fachspr.)*

calcium: **~ 'carbide** *n.* Kalziumkarbid, *das;* **~ 'carbonate** *n.* Kalziumkarbonat, *das;* kohlensaures Kalzium

calculable ['kælkjʊləbl] *adj.* berechenbar; kalkulierbar ‹*Risiko*›

calculate ['kælkjʊleɪt] **1.** *v. t.* **a)** *(ascertain)* berechnen; *(by estimating)* ausrechnen; errechnen; **b)** *(plan)* **be ~d to do sth.** darauf abzielen, etw. zu tun; **c)** *(Amer. coll.: suppose, believe)* meinen; schätzen *(ugs.).* **2.** *v. i.* **a)** *(Math.)* rechnen; **b)** **~ on doing sth.** damit rechnen, etw. zu tun

calculated ['kælkjʊleɪtɪd] *adj.* *(deliberate)* vorsätzlich ‹*Handlung, Straftat*›; bewußt ‹*Zurückhaltung, Affront*›; kalkuliert ‹*Risiko*›; *(apt, suitable)* geeignet

calculating ['kælkjʊleɪtɪŋ] *adj.* berechnend; **with a ~ eye** mit berechnendem Blick

calculation [kælkjʊ'leɪʃn] *n.* **a)** *(result)* Rechnung, *die;* **he is out in his ~s** er hat sich verrechnet; **b)** *(calculating)* Berechnung, *die;* **c)** *(forecast)* Schätzung, *die;* **by my ~s** nach meiner Schätzung

calculator ['kælkjʊleɪtə(r)] *n.* **a)** *(person, machine)* Rechner, *der;* **b)** *(set of tables)* Rechentabelle, *die*

calculus ['kælkjʊləs] *n., pl.* **calculi** ['kælkjʊlaɪ] *or* **~es** **a)** *(Math. etc.)* -rechnung, *die;* *(infinitesimal ~)* Infinitesimalrechnung, *die;* **[the] differential/infinitesimal/integral ~:** [die] Differential-/Infinitesimal-/Integralrechnung; **b)** *(Med.)* Stein, *der*

Calcutta [kæl'kʌtə] *pr. n.* Kalkutta *(das)*

caldron *see* **cauldron**

Caledonia [kælɪ'dəʊnɪə] *pr. n.* *(Hist./poet.)* Kaledonien *(das)*

Caledonian [kælɪ'dəʊnɪən] **1.** *adj.* kaledonisch. **2.** *n.* *(joc./Hist.)* Kaledonier, *der*/Kaledonierin, *die*

calendar ['kælɪndə(r)] *n.* **a)** Kalender, *der;* *attrib.* Kalender‹*woche, -monat, -jahr*›; **[church] ~:** Kirchenkalender, *der;* **b)** *(register, list)* Verzeichnis, *das;* *(list of canonized saints)* Heiligenkalender, *der;* *(list of cases for trial)* Prozeßregister, *das;* *(Amer.: list of matters for debate)* Tagesordnung, *die*

calender ['kælɪndə(r)] **1.** *n.* Kalander, *der (Technik).* **2.** *v. t.* kalandern, kalandrieren *(Technik)*

calends ['kælɪndz] *n. pl.* Kalenden *Pl.*

calendula [kə'lendjʊlə] *n.* *(Bot.)* Ringelblume, *die*

¹calf [kɑ:f] *n., pl.* **calves** [kɑ:vz] **a)** *(young of bovine animal)* Kalb, *das;* *(leather)* **~[skin]** Kalbsleder, *das;* **a cow in** *or* **with ~:** eine trächtige Kuh; **b)** *(of deer)* Kalb, *das;* *(of elephant, whale, rhinoceros)* Junge, *das.* *See also* **fat 3; golden calf**

²calf *n., pl.* **calves** *(Anat.)* Wade, *die*

calf: **~ love** *n.* [Jugend]schwärmerei, *die;* **~skin** *n.* Kalbfell, *das;* *(leather)* Kalbsleder, *das*

caliber *(Amer.)* *see* **calibre**

calibrate ['kælɪbreɪt] *v. t.* kalibrieren; eichen, kalibrieren ‹*Meßgerät*›

calibration [kælɪ'breɪʃn] *n.* Kalibrierung, *die;* *(of gauge)* Eichung, *die;* Kalibrierung, *die*

calibre ['kælɪbə(r)] *n.* *(Brit.)* **a)** *(diameter)* Kaliber, *das;* **b)** *(fig.)* Format, *das;* Kaliber, *das;* **a man of your ~:** ein Mann Ihres Kalibers *od.* von Ihrem Format

calico ['kælɪkəʊ] **1.** *n., pl.* **~es** *or (Amer.)* **~s** **a)** Kattun, *der;* **b)** *(Amer.: printed cotton fabric)* Druckkattun, *der.* **2.** *adj.* **a)** Kattun-; kattunen *(geh.);* **b)** *(Amer.: multicoloured)* bunt

California [kælɪ'fɔ:nɪə] *pr. n.* Kalifornien *(das)*

Californian [kælɪ'fɔ:nɪən] **1.** *adj.* kalifornisch. **2.** *n.* Kalifornier, *der*/Kalifornierin, *die*

caliper *see* **calliper**

caliph ['kælɪf, 'keɪlɪf] *n.* *(Hist.)* Kalif, *der*

calisthenics *see* **callisthenics**

calk *see* **caulk**

call [kɔ:l] **1.** *v. i.* **a)** *(shout)* rufen; **~ to sb.** jmdm. zurufen; **~ [out] for help** um Hilfe rufen; **~ [out] for sb.** nach jmdm. rufen; **~ [out] for food/drink** nach Essen/zu trinken verlangen; **~ after sb.** jmdm. hinterherrufen; hinter jmdm. herrufen; **b)** *(pay brief visit)* [kurz] besuchen **(at** *Akk.***);** vorbeikommen *(ugs.)* **(at** bei); ‹*Zug:*› halten **(at in +** *Dat.***);** **~ at a port/station** einen Hafen anlaufen/an einem Bahnhof halten; **~ on sb.** jmdn. besuchen; bei jmdm. vorbeigehen *(ugs.);* **the postman ~ed to deliver a parcel** der Postbote war da und brachte ein Päckchen; **a man has ~ed to read the meter** ein Mann ist da, um den Zähler abzulesen; **~ round** vorbeikommen *(ugs.);* **c)** *(communicate by telephone)* **who is ~ing, please?** wer spricht da, bitte?; **thank you for ~ing** vielen Dank für Ihren Anruf!; *(communicate by radio)* **this is London ~ing** hier spricht *od.* ist London. **2.** *v. t.* **a)** *(cry out)* rufen; aufrufen ‹*Namen, Nummer*›; **b)** *(cry to)* rufen ‹*Person*›; **c)** *(summon)* rufen; *(into the army)* einberufen; *(to a duty, to do sth.)* aufrufen; **~ him into the room** rufen Sie ihn herein!; **be ~ed home/to arms** nach Hause/zu den Waffen gerufen werden; **he was ~ed to his maker** *(literary)* er ist in die Ewigkeit abberufen worden *(geh. verhüllend);* **~ sth. into being** etw. ins Leben rufen; **~ sb.'s bluff** es darauf ankommen lassen *(ugs.);* **that was ~ed in question** das wurde in Frage gestellt *od.* in Zweifel gezogen; **please ~ me a taxi** *or* **~ a taxi for me** bitte rufen Sie mir ein Taxi; **d)** *(communicate with by radio/telephone)* rufen/anrufen; *(initially)* Kontakt aufnehmen mit; **don't ~ us, we'll ~ you** wir sagen Ihnen Bescheid; **e)** *(rouse)* wecken; **f)** *(announce)* einberufen ‹*Konferenz*›; ausrufen ‹*Streik*›; anberaumen ‹*Gerichtstermin*›; **~ a halt to sth.** mit etw. Schluß machen; **time was ~ed by the bartender** der Barmann rief „Feierabend" *od.* *(veralt., geh.)* bot Feierabend; **g)** *(urge)* **duty ~s** die Pflicht ruft; **he was ~ed to preach the Gospel by God** er war von Gott zur Verkündigung des Evangeliums auserwählt; *see also* **attention 1 a; h)** *(nominate)* **he was ~ed to the presidency of the university** er wurde zum Präsidenten der Universität berufen; **be ~ed to witness sth.** als Zeuge bei etw. aufgerufen werden; **i)** *(name)* nennen; **he is ~ed Bob** er heißt Bob; **he doesn't mind if you simply ~ him Bob** er hat nichts dagegen, wenn du ihn einfach Bob nennst *od.* einfach Bob zu ihm sagst; **you can ~ him by his first name** ihr könnt ihn mit Vornamen anreden; **what is it ~ed in English?** wie heißt das auf englisch?; **~ it what you will** wie immer man es auch nennen will; **~ sb. names** jmdn. beschimpfen; **j)** *(consider)* nennen; **I ~ that selfish** das nenne ich egoistisch; **£1.03 – let's ~ it one pound** ein Pfund drei Pence – sagen wir ein Pfund *(ugs.);* **shall we ~ it ten dollars/even?** sagen wir zehn Dollar/, wir sind quitt? *(ugs.);* **~ sth. one's own** etw. sein eigen nennen; **k)** *(Cards etc.)* ansagen; *(in coin-tossing)* sagen; **he ~ed heads and lost** er setzte auf Kopf und verlor. *See also* **account 3 c; ¹bar 1 i; day a; spade a; tune 1 a. 3.** *n.* **a)** *(shout, cry)* Ruf, *der;* **a ~ for help** ein Hilferuf; **he came at my ~:** er kam, als ich rief; **can you give me a ~ at 6 o'clock?** können Sie mich um 6 Uhr wecken?; **remain/be within ~:** in Rufweite bleiben/sein; **on** *or* **at ~:** dienstbereit; **b)** *(of bugle, whistle)* Signal, *das;* *(of drum)* Schlag, *der;* **c)** *(instrument)* Lockinstrument, *das;* Locke, *die (Jägerspr.);* **d)** *(visit)* Besuch, *der;* **make** *or* **pay a ~ on sb., make** *or* **pay sb. a ~:** jmdn. besuchen; jmdm. einen Besuch abstatten *(geh.);* **have to pay a ~** *(coll.: need lavatory)* mal [verschwinden] müssen *(ugs.);* **e)** *(telephone ~)* Anruf, *der;* Gespräch, *das;* **give sb. a ~:** jmdn. anrufen; **make a ~:** ein Telefongespräch führen; **receive a ~:** einen Anruf erhalten; **f)** *(invitation, summons)* Aufruf, *der;* *(by God)* Berufung, *die;* *(Theatre)* Aufruf, *der;* *(by audience)* Hervorruf, *der;* **the ~ of the sea/the wild** der Ruf des Meeres/der Wildnis; **~ of nature** natürlicher Drang; **answer the ~ of duty** der Pflicht gehorchen; **a ~ for unity** ein Aufruf zur Einheit; **a world-wide ~ for disarmament** ein weltweiter Ruf nach Abrüstung; **g)** *(need, occasion)* Anlaß, *der;* Veranlassung, *die;* **what ~ is there for you to worry?** aus welchem Anlaß *od.* Grund sorgen Sie sich?; **h)** *(esp. Comm.: demand)* Abruf, *der;* *(demand made)* Inanspruchnahme, *die;* **a ~ for capital/money** Abruf von Kapital/Geldern; **have many ~s on one's purse/time** finanziell/zeitlich sehr in Anspruch genommen sein; **i)** *(Cards etc.)* Ansage, *die;* **it is your ~** now du mußt ansagen; **was your ~ heads or tails?** hatten Sie Kopf oder Zahl?; **j)** *(St. Exch.)* Kaufoption, *die*

~ a'side *v. t.* beiseite rufen ‹*Person*›

~ a'way *v. t.* wegrufen; abrufen

~ 'back **1.** *v. t.* zurückrufen. **2.** *v. i.* **a)** zurückrufen; **b)** *(come back)* zurückkommen; noch einmal vorbeikommen *(ugs.)*

~ 'down *v. t.* **a)** *(invoke)* herabflehen *(geh.)* ‹*Segen*›; herausfordern ‹*Unwillen, Tadel*›; **~ down curses on sb.'s head** jmdn. verfluchen; **b)** *(reprimand)* ausschimpfen

~ for *v. t.* **a)** *(send for, order)* [sich *(Dat.)*] kommen lassen, bestellen ‹*Taxi, Essen, Getränke, Person*›; **b)** *(collect)* abholen ‹*Person, Gepäck, Güter*›; **'to be ~ed for'** „wird abgeholt"; **c)** *(require, demand)* erfordern; verlangen; **that remark was not ~ed for** die Bemerkung war unangebracht; **this ~s for a celebration** das muß gefeiert werden

~ 'forth *v. t.* hervorrufen ‹*Protest, Kritik*›; zusammennehmen ‹*Mut, Energie*›; beschwören, lebendig werden lassen ‹*Eindrücke, Erinnerungen, Erlebnisse*›

~ 'in **1.** *v. i.* vorbeikommen *(ugs.);* **I'll ~ in on you** ich komme bei dir vorbei *(ugs.);* **I'll ~ in at your office** ich komme bei dir im Büro vorbei *(ugs.).* **2.** *v. t.* **a)** aus dem Verkehr ziehen ‹*Waren, Münzen*›; zurückfordern ‹*Bücher*›; **b)** **~ in a specialist** einen Fachmann/Facharzt zu Rate ziehen

~ 'off *v. t.* *(cancel)* absagen ‹*Treffen, Verabredung*›; rückgängig machen ‹*Geschäft*›; lösen ‹*Verlobung*›; *(stop, end)* abbrechen,

(ugs.) abblasen ⟨*Streik*⟩; ~ **off your dogs!** rufen Sie Ihre Hunde zurück!
~ **on** *see* ~ **[up]on**
~ **'out 1.** *v.t.* alarmieren ⟨*Truppen*⟩; rufen ⟨*Wache*⟩; zum Streik aufrufen ⟨*Arbeitnehmer*⟩. **2.** *v.i. see* ~ **1 a**; ~ **out to warn sb.** jmdm. zurufen, um ihn zu warnen
~ **'up** *v.t.* **a)** *(imagine, recollect)* wachrufen ⟨*Erinnerungen, Bilder*⟩; [herauf]beschwören, erwecken ⟨*böse Erinnerungen, Phantasien*⟩; **b)** *(summon)* anrufen, beschwören ⟨*Teufel, Geister*⟩; **c)** *(by telephone)* anrufen; **I'll ~ you up again** ich rufe Sie wieder an; **d)** *(Mil.)* einberufen; **they were ~ed up to go to Vietnam** sie wurden nach Vietnam einberufen; *see also* **call-up**
~ **[up]on** *v.t.* ~ **upon God** Gott anrufen; ~ **upon sb.'s generosity/sense of justice** an jmds. Großzügigkeit/Gerechtigkeitssinn *(Akk.)* appellieren; ~ **[up]on sb. to do sth.** jmdn. auffordern, etw. zu tun

call: ~-box *n.* Telefonzelle, *die;* Fernsprechzelle, *die (Amtsspr.);* **~-boy** *n.* **a)** *(in theatre)* Gehilfe des Inspizienten/Souffleurs; **b)** *(in hotel)* [Hotel]boy, *der;* **~-button** *n.* Ruftaste, *die*

caller ['kɔ:lə(r)] *n.* **a)** Rufende, *der/die; (visitor)* Besucher, *der*/Besucherin, *die; (on telephone)* Anrufer, *der*/Anruferin, *die;* **b)** *(in bingo, square dance)* Ansager, *der*/Ansagerin, *die*

'call-girl *n.* Callgirl, *das*

calligrapher [kə'lɪgrəfə(r)] *n.* Schönschreiber, *der*/Schönschreiberin, *die; (professional)* Kalligraph, *der*/Kalligraphin, *die*

calligraphy [kə'lɪgrəfɪ] *n.* **a)** *(beautiful handwriting)* Schönschrift, *die;* Kalligraphie, *die; (as an art)* Kalligraphie, *die;* Schönschreiben, *das;* **b)** *(handwriting)* Handschrift, *die;* Hand, *die (geh.)*

calling ['kɔ:lɪŋ] *n.* **a)** *(occupation, profession)* Beruf, *der;* **b)** *(divine summons)* Berufung, *die*

'calling-card *n. (Amer.)* Visitenkarte, *die*

calliper ['kælɪpə(r)] *n.* **a)** *in pl.* **[pair of] ~s** Greifzirkel, *der;* Tasterzirkel, *der;* Taster, *der;* **b)** ~ **[splint]** *(Med.)* Beinschiene, *die;* **c)** **[brake]** **~:** Bremssattel, *der*

callisthenics [kælɪs'θenɪks] *n. pl.* Kallisthenie, *die;* leichte Gymnastik

'call meter *n. (Teleph.)* Gebührenzähler, *der*

callosity [kə'lɒsɪtɪ] *n.* **a)** *no pl.* Schwieligkeit, *die;* **b)** *(lump)* Schwiele, *die*

callous ['kæləs] **1.** *adj. (unfeeling, insensitive)* gefühllos; herzlos ⟨*Handlung, Verhalten*⟩; lieblos ⟨*Leben, Welt*⟩. **2.** *n. see* **callus**

callously ['kæləslɪ] *adv.* herzlos

callousness ['kæləsnɪs] *n., no pl. (want of feeling)* Gefühllosigkeit, *die; (of act, behaviour)* Herzlosigkeit, *die;* **his ~ towards [the feelings of] other people** seine Gleichgültigkeit den Gefühlen anderer gegenüber

'call-over *n.* Namensruf, *der; (of betting-prices)* Verlesen, *das*

callow ['kæləʊ] *adj.* **a)** *(raw, inexperienced)* unreif ⟨*Junge, Student*⟩; grün *(ugs.)* ⟨*Jüngling*⟩; **in my ~ youth** als ich noch jung und unreif war; **b)** *(unfledged)* nackt; kahl

call: ~-sign, ~-signal *ns.* Rufzeichen, *das;* **~-up** *n. (Mil.)* Einberufung, *die*

callus ['kæləs] *n.* **a)** *(Physiol.)* Schwiele, *die;* Kallus, *der (fachspr.);* **b)** *(Med.)* Knochennarbe, *die;* Kallus, *der (fachspr.);* **c)** *(Bot.)* Wundgewebe, *das;* Kallus, *der (fachspr.)*

calm [kɑ:m] **1.** *n.* **a)** *(stillness)* Stille, *die; (serenity)* Ruhe, *die;* **the peaceful ~ of the night** die friedliche Stille der Nacht; **b)** *(windless period)* Windstille, *die;* Kalme, *die (Met.);* **a dead ~:** totale Windstille; **the ~ before the storm** *(lit. or fig.)* die Ruhe vor dem Sturm. **2.** *adj.* **a)** *(tranquil, quiet, windless)* ruhig; **keep ~:** ruhig bleiben; Ruhe bewahren; **keep one's voice ~:** ruhig sprechen; **b)** *(coll.: self-confident)* lässig *(ugs.);* gelassen. **3.** *v.t.* beruhigen ⟨*Person*⟩; besänftigen ⟨*Leidenschaften, Zorn*⟩; ~ **sb. down** jmdn. beruhigen. **4.** *v.i.* ~ **[down]** sich beruhigen; ⟨*Sturm:*⟩ abflauen

calmly ['kɑ:mlɪ] *adv.* ruhig; gelassen

calmness ['kɑ:mnɪs] *n., no pl.* Ruhe, *die; (of water, sea)* Stille, *die*

Calor gas, (P) ['kælə gæs] *n.* Butangas, *das*

calorie ['kælərɪ] *n.* Kalorie, *die*

calorific [kælə'rɪfɪk] *adj.* wärmeerzeugend; ~ **value** Heizwert, *der*

calorimeter [kælə'rɪmɪtə(r)] *n.* Kalorimeter, *das*

calumniate [kə'lʌmnɪeɪt] *v.t.* verleumden

calumny ['kæləmnɪ] **1.** *n.* Verleumdung, *die.* **2.** *v.t.* verleumden

calvados ['kælvədɒs] *n.* Calvados, *der*

Calvary ['kælvərɪ] *n. (place)* Golgatha *(das); (representation)* Kalvarienberg, *der*

calve [kɑ:v] *v.i.* kalben; abkalben *(fachspr.)*

calves *pl. of* [1,2]**calf**

Calvinism ['kælvɪnɪzm] *n.* Kalvinismus, *der*

Calvinist ['kælvɪnɪst] *n.* Kalvinist, *der*/Kalvinistin, *die*

Calvinistic [kælvɪ'nɪstɪk], **Calvinistical** [kælvɪ'nɪstɪkl] *adj.* kalvinistisch

calypso [kə'lɪpsəʊ] *n., pl.* **~s** Calypso, *der*

calyx ['keɪlɪks, 'kælɪks] *n., pl.* **calyces** ['keɪlɪsi:z, 'kælɪsi:z] *or* **-es a)** *(Bot.)* Kelch, *der;* Kalyx, *der (fachspr.);* **b)** *(Anat.)* Kelch, *der*

cam [kæm] *n.* Nocken, *der*

camaraderie [kæmə'rɑ:dərɪ] *n.* Kameradschaft, *die*

camber ['kæmbə(r)] **1.** *n.* **a)** *(convexity)* Wölbung, *die;* **b)** *(Motor Veh.)* Achssturz, *der;* Radsturz, *der.* **2.** *v.t.* wölben; **a ~ed road** eine gewölbte Straße

Cambodia [kæm'bəʊdɪə] *pr. n. (Hist.)* Kambodscha *(das)*

Cambodian [kæm'bəʊdɪən] *(Hist.)* **1.** *adj.* kambodschanisch. **2.** *n.* Kambodschaner, *der*/Kambodschanerin, *die*

Cambrian ['kæmbrɪən] **1.** *adj.* **a)** *(Welsh)* walisisch; Waliser *nicht präd.;* **b)** *(Geol.)* kambrisch. **2.** *n. (Geol.)* Kambrium, *das*

cambric ['kæmbrɪk] *n.* Kambrik[batist], *der*

Cambridge ['keɪmbrɪdʒ]: ~ **blue** *n.* Blaßblau, *das;* Cambridgeblau, *das*

camcorder ['kæmkɔ:də(r)] *n.* Camcorder, *der;* Kamerarecorder, *der*

came *see* come **1**

camel ['kæml] *n. (Zool.)* Kamel, *das*

'camel['s]-hair *n.* Kamelhaar, *das;* ~ **brush** Haarpinsel, *der;* ~ **coat** Kamelhaarmantel, *der*

camellia [kə'mi:lɪə, kə'melɪə] *n. (Bot.)* Kamelie, *die*

cameo ['kæmɪəʊ] *n., pl.* **~s a)** *(carving)* Kamee, *die;* **b)** *(short sketch)* Sketch, *der; (minor role)* [winzige] Nebenrolle

camera ['kæmərə] *n.* **a)** Kamera, *die; (for still pictures)* Fotoapparat, *der;* Kamera, *die;* **be/go on ~:** vor der Kamera sein/vor die Kamera treten; **b)** *(Law)* **in ~:** unter Ausschluß der Öffentlichkeit; *(fig.)* hinter verschlossenen Türen

camera: ~-case *n.* Kameratasche, *die;* **~man** *n.* Kameramann, *der;* **~-shy** *adj.* kamerascheu

Cameroon ['kæməru:n] *pr. n.* Kamerun *(das)*

camiknickers ['kæmɪnɪkəz] *n. pl. (Brit.)* Spitzenhemdhöschen, *das*

camisole ['kæmɪsəʊl] *n. (arch.)* Leibchen, *das;* Mieder, *das;* Kamisol, *das (veralt.)*

camomile ['kæməmaɪl] *n. (Bot.)* Kamille, *die;* ~ **tea** Kamillentee, *der*

camouflage ['kæməflɑ:ʒ] **1.** *n. (lit. or fig.)* Tarnung, *die;* Camouflage, *die (Milit. veralt./fig. geh.).* **2.** *v.t. (lit. or fig.)* tarnen; camouflieren *(veralt./geh.)*

[1]**camp** [kæmp] **1.** *n.* Lager, *das; (Mil.)* Feldlager, *das;* **the world is divided into two opposing ~s** *(fig.)* die Welt teilt sich in zwei entgegengesetzte Lager; *see also* **foot 1 a. 2.** *v.i.* ~ **[out]** campen; *(in tent)* zelten; **go ~ing** Campen/Zelten fahren/gehen

[2]**camp 1.** *adj.* **a)** *(affected)* affektiert, geziert ⟨*Mensch, Art, Benehmen*⟩; **b)** *(exaggerated)* übertrieben, theatralisch ⟨*Gestik, Ausdrucksform*⟩; **c)** *(homosexual)* schwul *(ugs.); (effeminate)* tuntenhaft *(ugs.).* **2.** *n.* Manieriertheit, *die.* **3.** *v.t.* ~ **it up** zu dick auftragen *(ugs.);* ~ **up a part** bei einer Rolle zu dick auftragen *(ugs.)*

campaign [kæm'peɪn] **1.** *n.* **a)** *(Mil.)* Feldzug, *der;* Kampagne, *die (veralt.);* **be on ~:** im Felde stehen *(veralt.);* **b)** *(organized course of action)* Kampagne, *die;* Feldzug, *der;* **publicity ~:** Werbekampagne, *die;* **presidential ~:** Präsidentschaftswahlkampf, *der.* **2.** *v.i.* kämpfen; **the Republican candidate will start ~ing in April** der republikanische Kandidat beginnt seinen Wahlkampf im April

campaigner [kæm'peɪnə(r)] *n.* **a)** Vorkämpfer, *der*/Vorkämpferin, *die;* **b)** *(veteran)* Veteran, *der;* alter Kämpfer; **an old ~:** ein alter Kämpfer *od. (veralt.)* Kämpe

campanology [kæmpə'nɒlədʒɪ] *n.* Kunst des Glockenläutens

campanula [kæm'pænjʊlə] *n.* Glockenblume, *die;* Campanula, *die (fachspr.)*

'camp-bed *n.* Campingliege, *die*

camper ['kæmpə(r)] *n.* **a)** Camper, *der*/Camperin, *die;* **b)** *(vehicle)* Wohnmobil, *das; (adapted minibus)* Campingbus, *der*

camp: ~-fire *n.* Lagerfeuer, *das;* **~-follower** Marketender, *der*/Marketenderin, *die; (fig.: disciple, follower)* Mitläufer, *der*/Mitläuferin, *die*

camphor ['kæmfə(r)] *n.* Kampfer, *der*

camping ['kæmpɪŋ] *n.* Camping, *das; (in tent)* Zelten, *das*

camping: ~-ground *(Amer.) see* ~ **site;** ~ **holiday** *n.* Campingurlaub, *der;* ~ **site** *n.* Campingplatz, *der*

camp: ~site *n.* Campingplatz, *der;* **~-stool** *n.* Campinghocker, *der*

campus ['kæmpəs] *n.* **a)** *(grounds of university)* Campus, *der;* Hochschulgelände, *das;* **b)** *(university)* Hochschule, *die*

CAMRA ['kæmrə] *abbr.* **Campaign for Real Ale**

'camshaft *n.* Nockenwelle, *die*

[1]**can** [kæn] **1.** *n.* **a)** *(milk ~, watering-~)* Kanne, *die; (for oil, petrol)* Kanister, *der; (Amer.: for refuse)* Eimer, *der;* Tonne, *die;* **a ~ of paint** eine Büchse Farbe; *(with handle)* ein Eimer Farbe; **carry** *or* **take the ~ [back]** *(fig. sl.)* die Sache ausbaden *(ugs.);* **b)** *(container for preserving)* [Konserven]dose, *die;* [Konserven]büchse, *die;* **a ~ of tomatoes/sausages** eine Dose *od.* Büchse Tomaten/Würstchen; **~s of food** Lebensmittelkonserven; **a ~ of beer** eine Dose Bier; **a ~ of worms** *(fig.)* eine verzwickte Angelegenheit *(ugs.);* **c)** *(Amer. sl.: lavatory)* Lokus, *der (ugs.);* **d)** *(sl.: prison)* Knast, *der (salopp).* **2.** *v.t.,* **-nn- a)** *(preserve)* konservieren; **b)** *(put into ~)* eindosen; einmachen ⟨*Obst*⟩

[2]**can** *v. aux., only in pres.* **can,** *neg.* **cannot** ['kænət], *(coll.)* **can't** [kɑ:nt], *past* **could** [kʊd], *neg. (coll.)* **couldn't** ['kʊdnt] können; *(have right, be permitted)* dürfen; können; **as much as one ~:** so viel man kann; **as ... as '~ be** wirklich sehr ...; ~ **do** *(coll.)* kein Problem; **he can't be more than 40** er kann nicht über 40 sein; **you can't smoke in this compartment** in diesem Abteil dürfen Sie nicht rauchen; **what you say cannot be true** was du sagst, kann nicht stimmen; **come nearer, I can't hear what you're saying** kommen Sie näher, ich kann Sie nicht verstehen; **could you ring me tomorrow?** könnten Sie mich morgen anrufen?; **how [ever] could you do this to me?** wie konnten Sie mir das bloß antun?; **I could have killed him** ich hätte ihn umbringen können; **[that] could be [so]** das könnte *od.* kann sein

Canada ['kænədə] *pr. n.* Kanada *(das)*
'**Canada goose** *n.* Kanadagans, *die*
Canadian [kə'neɪdɪən] **1.** *adj.* kanadisch; **sb. is ~:** jmd. ist Kanadier/Kanadierin. **2.** *n.* Kanadier, *der*/Kanadierin, *die;* **the French/English ~s** die Franko-/Anglokanadier
canaille [kə'nɑ:i:] *n.* Pöbel, *der (abwertend)*
canal [kə'næl] *n.* **a)** *(watercourse, marking on Mars)* Kanal, *der;* **the Panama C~:** der Panamakanal; **b)** *(Zool., Bot.)* Gang, *der; (alimentary ~)* [Verdauungs]kanal, *der*
ca'nal boat *n. langes, enges Boot zum Befahren der Kanäle; (Hist.: towed barge)* Schleppkahn, *der*
canalize ['kænəlaɪz] *v. t.* kanalisieren ⟨*Fluß*⟩
canalization [kænəlaɪ'zeɪʃn] *n.* Kanalisierung, *die*
canapé ['kænəpɪ] *n. (food)* Cocktailhappen, *der;* Kanapee, *das*
canard [kə'nɑ:d, 'kænɑ:d] *n. (false report)* Ente, *die (ugs.)*
Canaries [kə'neərɪz] *pr. n. pl.* Kanarische Inseln *Pl.;* Kanaren *Pl.*
canary [kə'neərɪ] *n.* Kanarienvogel, *der*
canary: C~ 'Islands *pr. n. pl.* Kanarische Inseln *Pl.;* **~-seed** *n.* Kanariensamen, *der;* **~ 'yellow** *n.* Kanariengelb, *das;* **~-yellow** *adj.* kanariengelb
canasta [kə'næstə] *n. (Cards)* Canasta, *das*
cancan ['kænkæn] *n.* Cancan, *der*
cancel ['kænsl] **1.** *v. t., (Brit.)* **-ll- a)** *(cross out)* streichen ⟨*Wort, Satz, Absatz*⟩; **b)** *(call off)* absagen ⟨*Besuch, Urlaub, Reise, Sportveranstaltung*⟩; ausfallen lassen ⟨*Veranstaltung, Vorlesung, Zug, Bus*⟩; fallenlassen ⟨*Pläne*⟩; *(annul, revoke)* rückgängig machen ⟨*Einladung, Vertrag*⟩; zurücknehmen ⟨*Befehl*⟩; stornieren ⟨*Bestellung, Auftrag*⟩; streichen ⟨*Schuld[en]*⟩; kündigen ⟨*Abonnement*⟩; abbestellen ⟨*Zeitung*⟩; aufheben ⟨*Klausel, Gesetz, Recht*⟩; **the match had to be ~led** das Spiel mußte ausfallen *od.* abgesagt werden; **the boat to Dublin has been ~led** die Fähre nach Dublin fährt *od.* verkehrt nicht; **the lecture has been ~led** die Vorlesung fällt aus; **c)** *(balance, neutralize)* aufheben; **the arguments ~ each other out** die Argumente heben sich gegenseitig auf; **d)** *(deface)* entwerten ⟨*Briefmarke, Fahrkarte*⟩; ungültig machen ⟨*Scheck*⟩; **e)** *(Math.)* aufheben; wegkürzen *(ugs.);* **f)** *(Amer. Mus.)* auflösen. **2.** *v. i., (Brit.)* **-ll- ~ [out]** sich [gegenseitig] aufheben
cancellation [kænsə'leɪʃn] *n. see* **cancel 1: a)** Streichung, *die;* **b)** Absage, *die;* Ausfall, *der;* Ausfallen, *das;* Fallenlassen, *das;* Aufgabe, *die;* Rückgängigmachen, *das;* [Zu]rücknahme, *die;* Stornierung, *die;* Streichung, *die;* Kündigung, *die;* Abbestellung, *die;* Aufhebung, *die;* **c)** Aufhebung, *die;* **d)** Entwertung, *die;* Ungültigmachen, *das;* **e)** Aufhebung, *die;* Wegkürzen, *das (ugs.);* **f)** Auflösung, *die*
cancer ['kænsə(r)] *n.* **a)** *(Med.)* Krebs, *der; (fig.)* Krebsgeschwür, *das;* **~ of the lung** Lungenkrebs, *der;* **b)** **C~** *(Astrol., Astron.)* der Krebs; der Cancer; *see also* **Aries; tropic**
Cancerian [kæn'sɪərɪən] *n. (Astrol.)* Krebs, *der*
cancerous ['kænsərəs] *adj.* Krebs⟨*geschwulst, -geschwür*⟩; krebsartig ⟨*Wucherung, Wachstum*⟩; kanzerös *(fachspr.); (fig.)* bösartig ⟨*Haß, Einfluß*⟩; **~ growth** krebsartige Wucherung
candelabra [kændɪ'lɑ:brə] *n.,* **candelabrum** [kændɪ'lɑ:brəm] *n., pl.* **candelabra** *or (Amer.)* **candelabrums** Leuchter, *der; (large)* Kandelaber, *der*
candid ['kændɪd] *adj.* offen; ehrlich ⟨*Ansicht, Bericht*⟩; **let me be ~ with you** ich will ganz offen mit Ihnen sein
candidacy ['kændɪdəsɪ] *n.* Kandidatur, *die*
candidate ['kændɪdət, 'kændɪdeɪt] *n.* **a)** Kandidat, *der*/Kandidatin, *die;* Anwärter, *der*/Anwärterin, *die;* **a ~ for Mayor** ein Bürgermeisterkandidat/-kandidatin; **he offered himself as a ~ for the position** er bot sich als Kandidat für den Posten an; **~s for a club/for membership** Anwärter für einen Klub/auf Mitgliedschaft; **b)** *(examinee)* Kandidat, *der*/Kandidatin, *die;* **a Ph. D. ~:** ein Promotionskandidat *od.* Promovend; **a ~ for a degree** ein Prüfling *od.* Examinand
candidature ['kændɪdətʃə(r)] *n. (esp. Brit.)* Kandidatur, *die*
candid 'camera *n.* versteckte Kamera
candidly ['kændɪdlɪ] *adv.* offen; ehrlich; **~, I dislike the whole idea** offen gesagt, gefällt mir die Idee gar nicht
candle [kændl] **1.** *n.* **a)** Kerze, *die;* **burn the ~ at both ends** *(fig.)* sich übernehmen; sich *(Dat.)* zuviel aufladen; **she can't** *or* **is not fit to hold a ~ to him** *(fig.)* sie kann ihm nicht das Wasser reichen; **the game is not worth the ~** *(fig.)* die Sache lohnt sich nicht *od.* ist nicht der Mühe *(Gen.)* wert; **b)** *(unit)* **~[-power]** Kerze, *die (veralt.);* Candela, *die. See also* **Roman candle. 2.** *v. t.* gegen das Licht halten, durchleuchten ⟨*Eier*⟩
candle: ~-light *n.* Kerzenlicht, *das;* **by ~-light** bei Kerzenlicht ⟨*lesen*⟩; im Kerzenschein ⟨*geh.*⟩ ⟨*feiern, speisen*⟩; **~-power** *see* **candle 1b; ~stick** *n.* Kerzenhalter, *der; (elaborate)* Leuchter, *der;* **~wick** *n.* **a)** *(of candle)* Kerzendocht, *der;* **b)** *(material)* Frottierplüsch, *der*
candour *(Brit.; Amer.:* **candor)** ['kændə(r)] *n. (frankness)* Offenheit, *die; (honesty)* Ehrlichkeit, *die*
candy ['kændɪ] **1.** *n.* **a)** Kandis[zucker], *der;* **a ~:** ein Stück Kandis[zucker]; **b)** *(Amer.) (sweets)* Süßigkeiten *Pl.; (sweet)* Bonbon, *das od. der.* **2.** *v. t.* kandieren ⟨*Früchte*⟩; **candied lemon/orange peel** Zitronat/Orangeat, *das*
candy: ~-floss *n.* Zuckerwatte, *die;* **~-store** *n. (Amer.)* Süßwarengeschäft, *das;* Bonbonladen, *der (ugs.);* **~-stripe** *n.* Muster mit bunten Streifen [auf weißem Hintergrund]; **~-striped** *adj.* buntgestreift
'**candytuft** *(Bot.) n.* Schleifenblume, *die*
cane [keɪn] **1.** *n.* **a)** *(stem of bamboo, rattan, etc.)* Rohr, *das; (of raspberry, blackberry)* Sproß, *der; see also* **sugar-cane; b)** *(material)* Rohr, *das;* **c)** *(stick)* [Rohr]stock, *der;* **get the ~:** eine Tracht Prügel bekommen; **d)** *(esp. Brit.: walking-stick)* Spazierstock, *der.* **2.** *v. t.* **a)** *(beat)* [mit dem Stock] schlagen; **b)** *(weave)* flechten
cane: ~ chair *n.* Rohrstuhl, *der;* **~-sugar** *n.* Rohrzucker, *der*
canine ['keɪnaɪn, 'kænaɪn] **1.** *adj.* **a)** *(of dog[s])* Hunde⟨*rasse, -gebell, -natur*⟩; **b) ~ tooth** Eck- *od.* Augenzahn, *der.* **2.** *n.* Eckzahn, *der;* Augenzahn, *der*
caning ['keɪnɪŋ] *n.* [Ver]prügeln, *das od.* [Ver]hauen, *das* [mit dem Stock]; **he got a ~:** er kriegte eine Tracht Prügel *(ugs.)* [mit dem Stock]
canister ['kænɪstə(r)] *n.* Büchse, *die;* Dose, *die; (for petrol, oil, DDT, etc.)* Kanister, *der*
canker ['kæŋkə(r)] **1.** *n.* **a)** *(disease) (of dogs, cats, rabbits, etc.)* Ohrräude, *die; (of horses)* Strahlfäule, *die;* **b)** *(fig.: corrupting influence)* [Krebs]geschwür, *das.* **2.** *v. t.* **a)** *(consume with ~)* verrotten; **b)** *(fig.: infect, corrupt)* vergiften ⟨*Gemüt, Gefühl*⟩
cannabis ['kænəbɪs] *n. (Bot.)* Kannabis, *der;* Hanf, *der; (drug)* Haschisch, *das;* Marihuana, *das*
cannabis 'resin *n.* Haschisch, *das;* Cannabisharz, *das (fachspr.)*
canned [kænd] *adj.* **a)** Dosen-; in Dosen *nachgestellt;* **~ fish/meat/fruit** Fisch-/Fleisch-/Obstkonserven *Pl.;* Fisch/Fleisch/Obst in Dosen; **~ beer** Dosenbier; **~ food** [Lebensmittel]konserven *Pl.;* **b)** *(sl.: drunk)* abgefüllt *(ugs.);* **c)** *(sl.: recorded)* aufgezeichnet; **~ music/entertainment** Musikkonserve, *die*/Unterhaltungskonserve, *die*
canner ['kænə(r)] *n.* Konservenfabrikant, *der; (worker)* Arbeiter/Arbeiterin in einer Konservenfabrik
cannery ['kænərɪ] *n.* Konservenfabrik, *die*
cannibal ['kænɪbl] *n.* Kannibale, *der*/Kannibalin, *die;* Menschenfresser, *der*/-fresserin, *die (ugs.);* **these animals are ~s** diese Tiere fressen ihre Artgenossen auf
cannibalise *see* **cannibalize**
cannibalism ['kænɪbəlɪzm] *n.* Kannibalismus, *der;* Menschenfresserei, *die (ugs.); (fig.)* Blutdurst, *der*
cannibalistic [kænɪbə'lɪstɪk] *adj.* kannibalisch
cannibalize ['kænɪbəlaɪz] *v. t.* ausschlachten ⟨*Auto, Flugzeug, Maschine usw.*⟩
cannily ['kænɪlɪ] *adv.* behutsam; vorsichtig; *(shrewdly)* schlau
cannon ['kænən] **1.** *n.* **a)** *(gun)* Kanone, *die;* **b)** *(Brit. Billiards etc.)* Karambolage, *die.* **2.** *v. i. (Brit.)* **a) ~ against sth.** gegen etw. prallen; **~ into sb./sth.** mit etw./jmdm. zusammenprallen; **b)** *(Billiards)* karambolieren
cannonade [kænə'neɪd] *(arch.)* **1.** *n.* Kanonade, *die (veralt.).* **2.** *v. t.* kanonieren *(veralt.)*
cannon: ~-ball *n. (Hist.)* Kanonenkugel, *die;* **~-fodder** *n.* Kanonenfutter, *das (salopp abwertend)*
cannot *see* **²can**
cannula ['kænjʊlə] *n., pl.* **~e** ['kænjʊli:] *or* **~s** *(Med.)* Kanüle, *die*
canny ['kænɪ] *adj.* **a)** *(shrewd)* schlau; bauernschlau *(ugs.); (thrifty)* sparsam; **b)** *(cautious, wary)* vorsichtig, umsichtig; **ca'~** [kɑ-'kænɪ] Bummelstreik, *der;* **c)** trocken ⟨*Humor*⟩
canoe [kə'nu:] **1.** *n.* Paddelboot, *das; (Indian ~, Sport)* Kanu, *das; see also* **¹paddle 2. 2.** *v. i.* paddeln; *(in Indian ~, Sport)* Kanu fahren; **~ down the river** flußabwärts paddeln/im Kanu flußabwärts fahren
canoeing [kə'nu:ɪŋ] *n.* Paddeln, *das; (Sport)* Kanufahren, *das;* Kanusport, *der*
canoeist [kə'nu:ɪst] *n.* Paddelbootfahrer, *der*/-fahrerin, *die; (Sport)* Kanute, *der*/Kanutin, *die;* Kanufahrer, *der*/-fahrerin, *die*
canon ['kænən] *n.* **a)** *(general law, criterion)* Grundregel, *die;* Grundprinzip, *das;* **the ~s of conduct** die Grundregeln des Verhaltens; der Verhaltenskodex; **b)** *(member of cathedral chapter)* Kanoniker, *der;* Kanonikus, *der;* **c)** *(church decree)* Kirchengebot, *das;* **d)** *(list of sacred books)* Kanon, *der; (fig.)* **the Shakespearean ~:** das Gesamtwerk Shakespeares; **e)** *(Mus.)* Kanon, *der*
cañon *see* **canyon**
canonical [kə'nɒnɪkl] **1.** *adj.* **a)** kanonisch ⟨*Gehorsam, Gelübde, Bücher, Schriften*⟩; **~ dress** Priestertracht *od.* -kleidung, *die;* **~ hours** Gebetszeiten *Pl.; (Brit.: for weddings)* Trauzeiten *Pl.;* **b)** *(authoritative, standard)* verbindlich, kanonisch ⟨*Urteil, Werte, Vorschriften*⟩; maßgeblich ⟨*Person*⟩; **c)** *(Mus.)* Kanon⟨*form, -komposition*⟩; ⟨*Musikstück*⟩ in Kanonform; **d)** *(of cathedral chapter or member of it)* Kanoniker-; Chorherren-; **a ~ clergyman** ein Kanoniker *od.* Chorherr. **2.** *n. in pl.* Priesterkleidung, *die*
canonisation, canonise *see* **canoniz-**
canonization [kænənaɪ'zeɪʃn] *n.* Kanonisation, *die;* **~ of saints** Heiligsprechungen
canonize ['kænənaɪz] *v. t.* **a)** kanonisieren ⟨*Heiligen*⟩; heiligsprechen ⟨*Märtyrer*⟩; **he was ~d [a saint]** er wurde heiliggesprochen; **b)** *(regard as saint)* wie einen Heiligen/eine Heilige/Heilige *Pl.* verehren
canon: ~ law *n.* kanonisches Recht; **~ 'regular** *n.* regulierter Chorherr
canoodle [kə'nu:dl] *(sl.)* **1.** *v. i.* [rum]knutschen *(salopp).* **2.** *v. t.* abknutschen *(salopp)*

'can-opener *n.* Dosen-, Büchsenöffner, *der*

canopy ['kænəpɪ] **1.** *n.* **a)** Baldachin, *der (auch fig.); (over entrance)* Vordach, *das;* **the ~ of the heavens** *or* **celestial ~:** das Himmelszelt *od.* himmlische Zelt *(dichter.);* **a ~ of leaves** ein Blätterdach; **b)** *(of parachute)* [Fall]schirmkappe, *die;* **c)** *(of aircraft)* [Kanzel]haube, *die.* **2.** *v. t.* überwölben

[1]cant [kænt] **1.** *v. t.* kippen; ankippen, kanten ⟨*Faß*⟩; **~ off** abschrägen; **~ over** umdrehen; umkippen. **2.** *v. i. (take inclined position, lie aslant)* sich neigen. **3.** *n. (movement)* Ruck, *der; (tilted position)* Schräglage, *die; (bevel)* Schräge, *die*

[2]cant 1. *n.* **a)** *(derog.: language of class, sect, etc.)* Zunftsprache, *die;* Jargon, *der;* Kauderwelsch, *das (abwertend);* **thieves'/beggars' ~:** Rotwelsch, *das;* Gaunersprache, *die;* **b)** *(insincere use of words)* Scheinheiligkeit, *die; (talk)* scheinheiliges Gerede; **c)** *(ephemeral catchwords)* Phrase, *die (abwertend);* **a ~ phrase** eine [leere] Phrase; **~ phrases/terms/words** [leere] Phrasen. **2.** *v. i.* **a)** *see* **1 a:** *(use, speak in ~)* Jargon/Kauderwelsch/Rotwelsch reden; **b)** *(talk with affectation of piety)* [scheinheilig] schwafeln *(abwertend)*

can't [kɑ:nt] *(coll.)* = **cannot;** *see* **[2]can**

Cantab. ['kæntæb] *abbr.* **of Cambridge University** der Universität Cambridge

cantabile [kæn'tɑ:bɪlɪ] *(Mus.)* **1.** *adv.* cantabile. **2.** *adj.* Kantabile⟨*satz, -stil, -ton*⟩; sangbar ⟨*Stück, Musik*⟩. **3.** *n.* Kantabile, *das*

cantaloup[e] ['kæntəlu:p] *n.* Zucker-, Gartenmelone, *die*

cantankerous [kæn'tæŋkərəs] *adj.* streitsüchtig; knurrig *(ugs.)* ⟨*müde od. launische Person*⟩; störrisch ⟨*Esel, altes Auto usw.*⟩; **don't be so ~ on Monday mornings** sei doch nicht immer so eklig *od.* mufflig am Montagmorgen! *(ugs.)*

cantankerously [kæn'tæŋkərəslɪ] *adv. see* **cantankerous: behave** *or* **act ~:** streitsüchtig/knurrig *(ugs.)*/störrisch/mufflig *od.* eklig *(ugs.)* sein

cantankerousness [kæn'tæŋkerəsnɪs] *n., no pl. see* **cantankerous:** Streitsucht, *die;* Knurrigkeit, *die (ugs.);* störrisches Benehmen

cantata [kæn'tɑ:tə] *n. (Mus.)* Kantate, *die*

canteen [kæn'ti:n] *n.* **a)** Kantine, *die;* **b)** *(case of plate or cutlery)* Besteckkasten, *der*

canter ['kæntə(r)] **1.** *n.* Handgalopp, *der;* Kanter, Canter, *der (fachspr.);* **the horse broke into an easy ~:** das Pferd begann leicht zu galoppieren; **win in a ~** *(fig.)* spielend gewinnen. **2.** *v. i.* leicht galoppieren; kantern *(fachspr.).* **3.** *v. t.* in Handgalopp *od.* Kanter gehen lassen ⟨*Pferd*⟩

'Canterbury bell ['kæntəbərɪ bel] *n. (Bot.)* Glockenblume, *die*

canticle ['kæntɪkl] *n.* **a)** Lobgesang, *der;* Canticum, *das (Theol.); (hymn)* Preislied, Hohelied, *das* **b) the C~ of Solomon** *or* **C~s** das Hohe Lied *od.* Hohelied; das Lied der Lieder

cantilever ['kæntɪli:və] *n.* **a)** *(bracket)* Konsole, *die;* Kragplatte, *die;* **b)** *(beam, girder)* Träger, *der*

'cantilever-bridge *n.* Auslegerbrücke, *die*

canto ['kæntəʊ] *n., pl.* **~s** Gesang, *der;* Canto, *der (fachspr.)*

canton ['kæntɒn] *n.* Kanton, *der*

cantonal ['kæntənl] *adj.* kantonal; Kantons-

Cantonese [kæntə'ni:z] **1.** *adj.* kantonesisch; **sb. is ~:** jmd. ist Kantonese/Kantonesin. **2.** *n., pl. same* **a)** *(person)* Kantonese, *der*/Kantonesin, *die;* **b)** *(language)* Kantonesisch *(das)*

cantor ['kæntə(r)] *n.* Kantor, *der*

canvas ['kænvəs] *n.* **a)** *(cloth)* Leinwand, *die; (for tents, tarpaulins, etc.)* Segeltuch, *das;* **under ~:** im Zelt; *(Naut.)* unter Segel; **under full ~:** mit vollen Segeln; **b)** *(Art)* Leinwand, *die; (painting)* Gemälde, *das; (for tapestry and embroidery)* Kanevas, *der;* Gitterleinwand, *die;* **c)** *(of racing-boat)* Segeltuchbezug, *der;* **win by a ~:** mit einer Nasenlänge gewinnen

canvass ['kænvəs] **1.** *v. t.* **a)** *(solicit votes in or from)* Wahlwerbung treiben in ⟨*einem Wahlkreis, Gebiet*⟩; Wahlwerbung treiben bei ⟨*Wählern, Bürgern*⟩; **~ customers** Kunden werben; **they were ~ed on their political views** man versuchte, ihre politischen Ansichten herauszufinden; **b)** *(Brit.: propose)* vorschlagen ⟨*Plan, Idee, Handel*⟩; **c)** *(Amer.: check validity of)* auszählen ⟨*Stimmen*⟩. **2.** *v. i.* werben **(on behalf of** für); **~ for votes** um Stimmen werben; **~ for a seat in Parliament/a job** sich um einen Parlamentssitz/einen Posten bewerben; **~ for an applicant** sich für einen Bewerber einsetzen. **3.** *n.* [Wahl]kampagne, *die; (Amer.: scrutiny of votes)* Auszählung, *die*

canvasser ['kænvəsə(r)] *n.* **a)** *(for votes)* Wahlhelfer, *der*/Wahlhelferin, *die;* **b)** *(salesperson)* Vertreter, *der*/Vertreterin, *die;* **c)** *(Amer.: checker of votes)* Auszähler, *der*/Auszählerin, *die*

canvassing ['kænvəsɪŋ] *n. (for votes)* Wahlwerbung, *die; (Commerc.)* Kundenwerbung, *die; (opinion polling)* Meinungsforschung, *die*

canyon ['kænjən] *n.* Cañon, *der*

CAP *abbr.* **Common Agricultural Policy** gemeinsame Agrarpolitik

cap [kæp] **1.** *n.* **a)** Mütze, *die; (nurse's, servant's)* Haube, *die; (bathing-~)* Badekappe, *die; (with peak)* Schirmmütze, *die; (skull-~)* Kappe, *die;* Käppchen, *das;* **college ~:** *viereckige akademische Kopfbedeckung;* ≈ Barett, *das;* **in ~ and gown** mit Barett und Talar; **if the ~ fits, [he** *etc.* **should] wear it** *(fig.)* wem die Jacke paßt, der soll sie sich *(Dat.)* anziehen; **with ~ in hand** *(fig.)* demütig; **she set her ~ at him** *(fig.)* sie hatte es auf ihn abgesehen; **~ and bells** Narren- *od.* Schellenkappe, *die; see also* **feather 1 a; b)** *(of mushroom)* Hut, *der; (of honeycomb)* Deckel, *der;* **c)** *(device to seal or close)* [Verschluß]kappe, *die; (petrol ~, radiator-~)* Verschluß, *der; (on milk-bottle)* Deckel, *der; (of shoe)* Kappe, *die;* **d)** *(Brit. Sport) Ziermütze als Zeichen der Aufstellung für die [National]mannschaft; (player)* Nationalspieler, *der/*-spielerin, *die;* **get one's ~:** für die [National]mannschaft aufgestellt werden; **e)** *(contraceptive)* Pessar, *das;* **f)** *(explosive)* Zündhütchen, *das; (for toy gun)* Zündplättchen, *das.* **2.** *v. t.,* **-pp- a)** verschließen ⟨*Flasche*⟩; zu-, abdecken ⟨*Brunnen, Bohrloch*⟩; mit einer Schutzkappe versehen ⟨*Zahn*⟩; **b)** *(Brit. Sport: award ~ to)* aufstellen; **he was ~ped ten times for England** er ist zehnmal für die englische Nationalmannschaft aufgestellt worden; **c)** *(crown) (with clouds, snow, mist)* bedecken; *(fig.)* krönen **(by** durch); **~ped with snow** schneebedeckt; **d)** *(follow with sth. even more noteworthy)* überbieten ⟨*Geschichte, Witz usw.*⟩; **to ~ it all** obendrein; **that ~s the lot!** das ist die Höhe!

cap. [kæp] *abbr.* **a)** *(Printing etc.)* **capital** Vers.; **b) chapter** Kap.

capability [keɪpə'bɪlɪtɪ] *n.* **a)** Fähigkeit, *die;* Vermögen, *das (geh.);* **his ~ of understanding difficult texts** sein Verständnis[vermögen] für schwierige Texte; **this plot of land has the ~ for further development** dieses Grundstück läßt sich noch weiter erschließen; **~ for growth** Wachstumschancen *Pl.;* **b)** *in pl. (undeveloped faculty)* Entwicklungsmöglichkeiten *Pl.*

capable ['keɪpəbl] *adj.* **a) be ~ of sth.** ⟨*Person:*⟩ zu etw. imstande sein; **show him what you are ~ of** zeig ihm, wozu du imstande bist *od.* wessen du fähig bist; **he is ~ of any crime** er ist zu jedem Verbrechen fähig; **she is quite ~ of neglecting her duties** sie bringt es durchaus fertig, ihre Pflichten zu vernachlässigen; **be ~ of improvement** verbesserungsfähig sein; **be ~ of misinterpretation** sich leicht falsch interpretieren lassen; leicht falsch interpretiert werden; **it is not ~ of being expressed in a few words** es läßt sich nicht in ein paar Worten ausdrücken; **b)** *(gifted, able)* fähig ⟨*Person, Lehrer usw.*⟩; **~ fingers** geschickte Finger

capably ['keɪpəblɪ] *adv.* gekonnt, kompetent ⟨*leiten, führen*⟩

capacious [kə'peɪʃəs] *adj.* geräumig; groß ⟨*Gedächtnis, Verstand, Appetit*⟩; weit, groß ⟨*Schuhe, Taschen*⟩

capaciousness [kə'peɪʃəsnɪs] *n., no pl. (of room, hall)* Geräumigkeit, *die; (of receptacle)* Größe, *die*

capacitance [kə'pæsɪtəns] *n. (Electr.)* Kapazitanz, *die*

capacitor [kə'pæsɪtə(r)] *n. (Electr.)* Kondensator, *der*

capacity [kə'pæsɪtɪ] *n.* **a)** *(power)* Aufnahmefähigkeit, *die; (to do things)* Leistungsfähigkeit, *die;* **this book is within the ~ of young readers** junge Leser sind mit diesem Buch nicht überfordert; **some have more ~ for happiness than others** manche sind zu größeren Glücksempfindungen fähig als andere; **b)** *no pl. (maximum amount)* Fassungsvermögen, *das;* **the machine is working to ~:** die Maschine ist voll ausgelastet; **a seating ~ of 300** 300 Sitzplätze; **filled to ~** ⟨*Saal, Theater*⟩ bis auf den letzten Platz besetzt; **the film drew ~ houses for ten weeks** zehn Wochen lang waren alle Vorstellungen dieses Films ausverkauft; **the star was cheered by a ~ audience** ein volles Haus jubelte dem Star zu; **c)** *(measure)* Rauminhalt, *der;* Volumen, *das;* **measure of ~:** Hohlmaß, *das;* **d)** *(position)* Eigenschaft, *die;* Funktion, *die;* **in his ~ as critic/lawyer** *etc.* in seiner Eigenschaft als Kritiker/Anwalt *usw.;* **in a civil ~:** als Zivilist; **e)** *(mental power)* **he has a mind of great ~:** er ist ein äußerst fähiger Kopf; **have a ~ for genuine love** echter Liebe *(Gen.)* fähig sein; **f)** *(legal competence)* Geschäftsfähigkeit, *die;* **he does not have any legal ~:** er ist nicht geschäftsfähig; **g)** *(Electr.)* Kapazität, *die*

caparison [kə'pærɪsən] *n., usu. in pl. (horse's trappings)* Schabracke, *die*

[1]cape [keɪp] *n. (garment)* Umhang, *der;* Cape, *das; (part of coat)* Pelerine, *die*

[2]cape *n. (Geog.)* Kap, *das;* **the C~ [of Good Hope]** das Kap der guten Hoffnung; **C~ Horn** Kap Hoorn *(das);* **C~ Town** Kapstadt *(das);* **C~ Verde Islands** Kapverdische Inseln *Pl.*

[1]caper ['keɪpə(r)] **1.** *n.* **a)** *(frisky movement)* Luftsprung, *der;* **cut a ~/~s** einen Luftsprung/Luftsprünge machen; **b)** *(wild behaviour)* Kapriole, *die;* **c)** *(sl.: activity, occupation)* Masche, *die (salopp).* **2.** *v. i.* **~ [about]** [herum]tollen; [umher]tollen

[2]caper *n.* **a)** *(shrub)* Kapernstrauch, *der;* **b)** *in pl. (pickled buds)* Kapern *Pl.*

capercaillie [kæpə'keɪljɪ], **capercailzie** [kæpə'keɪlzɪ] *ns. (Ornith.)* Auerhahn, *der*

capful ['kæpfʊl] *n.* **one ~:** der Inhalt einer Verschlußkappe

capillary [kə'pɪlərɪ] **1.** *adj. (of hairlike diameter)* haardünn; haarfein; Kapillar⟨*gefäß*⟩; *(of hair)* Haar-; **~ tube** Kapillare, *die (fachspr.).* **2.** *n.* Kapillare, *die (fachspr.)*

[1]capital ['kæpɪtl] **1.** *adj.* **a)** Todes⟨*strafe, -urteil*⟩; Kapital⟨*verbrechen*⟩; tödlich ⟨*Irrtum, Fehler, Laster, Torheit*⟩; **b)** *attrib.* groß, Groß-, *(fachspr.)* Versal⟨*buchstabe*⟩; **~ letters** Großbuchstaben; Versalien *(fachspr.);* **'I' is written with a ~ letter** „I" wird groß geschrieben *od.* mit großem I geschrieben; **with a ~ A** *etc.* mit großem A *usw. od. (fachspr.)* mit Versal-A *usw.; (fig.)*

im wahrsten Sinne des Wortes; **c)** *attrib.* *(principal)* Haupt⟨*stadt*⟩; **London is the ~ city of Britain** London ist die Hauptstadt *od.* *(geh.)* Kapitale Großbritanniens; **d)** *(important, leading)* einmalig ⟨*Vorteil, Person, Buch, Vorstellung*⟩; *(dated coll.: excellent, first-rate)* einmalig; famos *(veralt.)* ⟨*Idee*⟩; **~!** tadellos!; famos! *(veralt.)*; **e)** *(Commerc.)* **~ funds/stock** Grundkapital, *das;* **~ sum/expenditure/investment** Kapitalbetrag, *der*/-aufwendungen *Pl.*/-anlage, *die.* **2.** *n.* **a)** *(letter)* Großbuchstabe, *der;* **[large] ~s** Großbuchstaben; Versalien *(fachspr.)*; **small ~s** Kapitälchen *(fachspr.)*; **write one's name in [block] ~s** seinen Namen in Blockbuchstaben schreiben; **b)** *(city, town)* Hauptstadt, *die;* Kapitale, *die (geh.)*; **c)** *(stock, accumulated wealth, its holders)* Kapital, *das;* **personal** *or* **private ~:** Eigenkapital, *das;* **~ and labour** Kapital und Arbeit; *(in non-socialist terminology)* Arbeitgeber und Arbeitnehmer; **make ~ out of sth.** *(fig.)* aus etw. Kapital schlagen

²capital *n.* *(Archit.)* Kapitell, *das;* Kapitäl, *das*

capital: ~ 'gain *n.* Kapitalgewinn, *der;* Kapitalertrag, *der;* **~ 'gains tax** *n.* *(Brit.)* Steuer auf Kapitalgewinn, *die;* **~ goods** *n. pl.* Investitionsgüter *Pl.*

capitalise *see* **capitalize**

capitalism ['kæpɪtəlɪzm] *n.* Kapitalismus, *der;* *(possession of capital)* Kapitalbesitz, *der;* **~ is ...:** der Kapitalismus ist ...

capitalist ['kæpɪtəlɪst] **1.** *n.* Kapitalist, *der*/Kapitalistin, *die.* **2.** *adj.* kapitalistisch; **the ~ class** die Kapitalistenklasse

capitalistic [kæpɪtə'lɪstɪk] *adj.* kapitalistisch

capitalize ['kæpɪtəlaɪz] **1.** *v.t.* **a)** groß schreiben ⟨*Buchstaben, Wort*⟩; **b)** *(convert, compute)* kapitalisieren ⟨*Rente, Reserven*⟩. **2.** *v.i.* *(fig.)* **~ on sth.** von etw. profitieren; aus etw. Kapital schlagen *(ugs.)*

capital: ~ 'levy *n.* Vermögensabgabe, *die;* Kapitalabgabe, *die;* **~ ship** *n.* Großkampfschiff, *das;* **~ sum** *n.* Kapitalbetrag, *der;* **~ territory** *n.* Gebiet der/einer Hauptstadt

capitation [kæpɪ'teɪʃn] *n.* Kopfsteuer, *die*

capi'tation grant *n.* Zuschuß pro Kopf

Capitol ['kæpɪtl] *n.* Kapitol, *das*

capitulate [kə'pɪtjʊleɪt] *v.i.* kapitulieren

capitulation [kəpɪtjʊ'leɪʃn] *n.* Kapitulation, *die*

capo ['kæpəʊ] *n., pl.* **~s** *(Mus.)* Kapodaster, *der*

capon [keɪpn] *n.* Kapaun, *der*

cappuccino [kɑ:pʊ'tʃi:nəʊ] *n., pl.* **~s** Cappuccino, *der*

Capri [kə'pri:] *pr. n.* Capri *(das)*; **~ pants, ~s** Caprihosen *Pl.*

caprice [kə'pri:s] *n.* **a)** *(change of mind or conduct)* Laune, *die;* Kaprice, *die (geh.)*; *(inclination)* Willkür, *die;* **out of sheer ~:** aus einer Laune heraus; **the ~s of English weather** die Launen[haftigkeit] des englischen Wetters; **b)** *(work of art)* Capriccio, *das;* Caprice, *die (geh.)*

capricious [kə'prɪʃəs] *adj.* launisch; kapriziös *(geh.)*; *(irregular, unpredictable)* wechselhaft, launisch ⟨*Wetter*⟩; unberechenbar, schwankend ⟨*System, Markt*⟩

capriciously [kə'prɪʃəslɪ] *adv.* willkürlich

capriciousness [kə'prɪʃəsnɪs] *n., no pl.* Launenhaftigkeit, *die;* *(of actions)* Willkür, *die;* *(of weather)* Wechselhaftigkeit, *die;* Launenhaftigkeit, *die*

Capricorn ['kæprɪkɔ:n] *n.* *(Astrol., Astron.)* der Steinbock; der Capricornus; *see also* **Aries; tropic**

Capricornian [kæprɪ'kɔ:nɪən] *n.* *(Astrol.)* Steinbock, *der*

caps. [kæps] *abbr.* **capital letters** Vers.

capsicum ['kæpsɪkəm] *n.* **a)** *(pod)* Pfefferschote, *die;* **b)** *(plant)* Paprika, *der*

capsize [kæp'saɪz] **1.** *v.t.* zum Kentern bringen. **2.** *v.i.* kentern

capstan ['kæpstən] *n.* **a)** *(barrel for cable)* Winde, *die;* Spill, *das (Seemannsspr.)*; **b)** *(in tape-recorder)* Tonwelle, *die;* Tonrolle, *die*

'capstan lathe *n.* Sattelrevolverdrehmaschine, *die*

'cap stone *n.* *(top stone)* Deckstein, *der;* *(coping)* Mauerkrone, *die*

capsule ['kæpsjʊl] *n.* *(Med., Physiol., Bot., of rocket)* Kapsel, *die*

Capt. *abbr.* **Captain** Kapt.; Hptm.

captain ['kæptɪn] **1.** *n.* **a)** Kapitän, *der;* *(in army)* Hauptmann, *der;* *(in navy)* Kapitän [zur See]; **~ of a ship** Schiffskapitän, *der;* **~ of industry** *(fig.)* Industriekapitän, *der (ugs.)*; **b)** *(head boy/girl at school)* Schulsprecher, *der*/-sprecherin, *die;* **form ~:** Klassensprecher, *der*/-sprecherin, *die;* **c)** *(Sport)* Kapitän, *der;* Spielführer, *der*/-führerin, *die;* **d)** *(Amer.: police rank)* ≈ Polizeidirektor, *der.* **2.** *v.t.* befehligen ⟨*Soldaten, Armee*⟩; **~ a team** Mannschaftskapitän sein; Kapitän einer Mannschaft sein

captaincy ['kæptɪnsɪ] *n.* *(Sport)* Führung, *die*

caption ['kæpʃn] **1.** *n.* **a)** *(heading)* Überschrift, *die;* **b)** *(wording under photograph/drawing)* Bildunterschrift, *die;* *(Cinemat., Telev.)* Untertitel, *der.* **2.** *v.t.* betiteln; mit Bildunterschrift[en] versehen ⟨*Foto, Illustration*⟩; mit Untertiteln versehen ⟨*Film*⟩

captious ['kæpʃəs] *adj.* überkritisch

captivate ['kæptɪveɪt] *v.t.* fesseln *(fig.)*; gefangennehmen *(fig.)*; **she was ~d by his charm/by Tom** sie war von seinem Charme gefesselt/von Tom fasziniert

captivating ['kæptɪveɪtɪŋ] *adj.* bezaubernd; einnehmend ⟨*Lächeln*⟩

captivation [kæptɪ'veɪʃn] *n.* Fesselung, *die (fig.)*; Verzauberung, *die*

captive ['kæptɪv] **1.** *adj.* *(taken prisoner)* gefangen; ⟨*Zustand, Stunden, Ketten*⟩ der Gefangenschaft; **a ~ person** ein Gefangener/eine Gefangene; **a ~ animal** ein Tier in Gefangenschaft; **be taken ~:** gefangengenommen werden; **hold sb. ~:** jmdn. gefangenhalten; **lead/bring sb. ~ somewhere** jmdn. als Gefangenen irgendwohin führen/bringen. **2.** *n.* Gefangener, *der*/Gefangene, *die*

captive: ~ 'audience *n.* unfreiwilliges Publikum; **~ bal'loon** *n.* Fesselballon, *der*

captivity [kæp'tɪvɪtɪ] *n.* Gefangenschaft, *die;* **in [a state of] ~:** in [der] Gefangenschaft; **be held in ~:** gefangengehalten werden

captor ['kæptə(r)] *n.* *(of city, country)* Eroberer, *der;* *(Hist.: of ship)* Kaperer, *der;* **his ~:** der/die ihn gefangennahm

capture ['kæptʃə(r)] **1.** *n.* **a)** *(seizing)* *(of thief etc.)* Festnahme, *die;* *(of town)* Einnahme, *die;* **b)** *(thing or person captured)* Fang, *der;* **c)** *(Chess etc.)* Schlagen, *das.* **2.** *v.t.* **a)** ergreifen, festnehmen ⟨*Person*⟩; [ein]fangen ⟨*Tier*⟩; einnehmen ⟨*Stadt*⟩; holen, ergattern ⟨*Preis*⟩; gefangennehmen ⟨*Phantasie*⟩; erregen ⟨*Aufmerksamkeit*⟩; *(Hist.)* kapern ⟨*Schiff*⟩; **~ sb.'s heart** jmds. Herz gewinnen; **they ~d the city from the Romans** sie nahmen den Römern die Stadt ab; **b)** *(put in permanent form)* einfangen ⟨*Augenblick, Eindruck*⟩; **c)** *(Chess etc.)* schlagen ⟨*Figur*⟩; **d)** *(Computing)* erfassen ⟨*Daten*⟩

Capuchin ['kæpjʊtʃɪn] *n.* *(Franciscan friar)* Kapuziner[mönch], *der*

capuchin: ~ monkey *n.* Kapuzineraffe, *der;* **~ pigeon** *n.* Mönchtaube, *die*

capybara [kæpɪ'bɑ:rə] *n.* *(Zool.)* Capybara, *das;* Wasserschwein, *das*

car [kɑ:(r)] *n.* **a)** *(motor ~)* Auto, *das;* Wagen, *der;* *(official)* Dienstwagen, *der;* **by ~:** mit dem Auto *od.* Wagen; **b)** *(railway-carriage etc.)* Wagen, *der;* **c)** *(Amer.: lift-cage)* Fahrkabine, *die;* **d)** *(of balloon, airship, etc.)* Gondel, *die*

carafe [kə'ræf, kə'rɑ:f] *n.* Karaffe, *die*

caramel ['kærəmel] *n.* **a)** *(toffee)* Karamelle, *die;* Karamelbonbon, *das;* **b)** *(burnt sugar or syrup)* Karamel, *der;* **c)** *(colour)* Karamelfarbe, *die;* bräunliches Gelb

carapace ['kærəpeɪs] *n.* *(of turtle, tortoise)* Rückenschild, *der;* *(of other crustacean)* Schale, *die*

carat ['kærət] *n.* Karat, *das;* **a 22-~ gold ring, a gold ring of 22 ~s** ein 22karätiger Goldring

caravan ['kærəvæn] **1.** *n.* **a)** *(Brit.)* Wohnwagen, *der;* *(used for camping)* Wohnwagen, *der;* Caravan, *der;* **b)** *(company of merchants, pilgrims, etc.)* Karawane, *die.* **2.** *v.i.,* *(Brit.)* **-nn-: go ~ning** Urlaub im Wohnwagen *od.* Caravan machen; **~ through Ireland** im Wohnwagen *od.* Caravan durch Irland fahren

caravan: ~ park, ~ site *ns.* Campingplatz für Wohnwagen

caravel ['kærəvel] *n.* *(Hist.)* Karavelle, *die*

caraway ['kærəweɪ] *n.* Kümmel, *der*

'caraway seed *n.* Kümmelkorn, *das;* *in pl.* Kümmel, *der*

carbide ['kɑ:baɪd] *n.* Karbid, *das;* Carbid, *das (fachspr.)*

carbine ['kɑ:baɪn] *n.* Karabiner, *der*

carbohydrate [kɑ:bə'haɪdreɪt] *n.* *(Chem.)* Kohle[n]hydrat, *das*

carbolic [kɑ:'bɒlɪk] *adj.* Karbol⟨*säure*⟩; **~ soap** Karbolseife, *die*

'car bomb *n.* Autobombe, *die*

carbon ['kɑ:bən] *n.* **a)** Kohlenstoff, *der;* **b)** *(copy)* Durchschlag, *der;* *(paper)* Kohlepapier, *das;* **c)** *(Electr.)* Kohle, *die;* Kohlestift, *der*

carbonade [kɑ:bə'neɪd] *n.* **[beef] ~** *(mit Bier abgeschmeckter)* Rindfleischeintopf

carbonate ['kɑ:bəneɪt] **1.** *n.* Karbonat, *(fachspr.)* Carbonat, *das.* **2.** *v.t.* mit Kohlensäure versetzen ⟨*Getränke*⟩; **a ~d beverage** ein kohlensäurehaltiges Getränk

carbon: ~ 'copy *n.* Durchschlag, *der;* *(fig.)* *(imitation)* Nachahmung, *die;* Abklatsch, *der (abwertend)*; *(identical counterpart)* Ebenbild, *das;* **~ dating** *n.* Radiokarbonmethode, *die;* Radiokohlenstoffmethode, *die;* **~ di'oxide** *n.* *(Chem.)* Kohlendioxid, *das*

carboniferous [kɑ:bə'nɪfərəs] **1.** *adj.* **a)** *(producing coal)* kohlehaltig; **b)** *(Geol.)* Karbon-, Steinkohlen-; **C~ period** Karbon *od.* Steinkohlenformation, *die.* **2.** *n.* *(Geol.)* **the C~** das Karbon

carbonize (carbonise) ['kɑ:bənaɪz] *v.t.* karbonisieren ⟨*Diamanten, Graphit*⟩; verkohlen ⟨*Kohle*⟩; *(to obtain gas)* verkoken ⟨*Kohle*⟩; verschwelen ⟨*Torf, Lignit*⟩; [mit der/einer Färbemasse] beschichten ⟨*Papier, Formulare*⟩

carbon: ~ mo'noxide *n.* *(Chem.)* Kohlenmonoxyd, *(fachspr.)* Kohlenmonoxid, *das;* **~ paper** *n.* Kohlepapier, *das;* **~ 'steel** *n.* Kohlenstoffstahl, *der;* **~ tetra'chloride** *n.* *(Chem.)* Tetrachlorkohlenstoff, *der*

carborundum [kɑ:bə'rʌndəm] *n.* Karborund, *das*

carboy ['kɑ:bɔɪ] *n.* Korbflasche, *die*

carbuncle ['kɑ:bʌŋkl] *n.* **a)** *(stone)* Karfunkel[stein], *der;* **b)** *(abscess)* Karbunkel, *der*

carburettor *(Amer.:* **carburetor)** [kɑ:bə'retə(r)] *n.* Vergaser, *der*

carcass *(Brit. also:* **carcase)** ['kɑ:kəs] *n.* **a)** *(dead body; joc.: live human body)* Kadaver, *der;* *(at butcher's)* Rumpf, *der;* **~ meat** Frischfleisch, *das;* **b)** *(remains)* Überreste *Pl.;* **carcasses of old cars/bikes** Schrottautos/-räder *Pl.;* **c)** *(of ship, fortification, etc.)* Skelett, *das;* *(of new building)* Rohbau, *der;* **d)** *(of tyre)* Karkasse, *die*

carcinogen [kɑ:'sɪnədʒən] *n.* *(Med.)* Karzinogen, *das (fachspr.)*; Krebserreger, *der*

carcinogenic [kɑ:sɪnə'dʒenɪk] *adj.* *(Med.)* karzinogen *(fachspr.)*; krebserregend

carcinoma [kɑːsɪˈnəʊmə] *n., pl.* **carcinomata** [kɑːsɪˈnəʊmətə] *or* ~s *(Med.)* Karzinom, *das*

car: ~ **coat** *n.* Autocoat, *der;* ~ **crash** *n.* Autounfall, *der*

[1]**card** [kɑːd] *n.* **a)** *(playing-~)* Karte, *die;* **read the ~s** Karten lesen; **be on the ~s** *(fig.)* zu erwarten sein; **put [all] one's ~s on the table** *(fig.)* [alle] seine Karten auf den Tisch legen; **have [yet] another ~ up one's sleeve** *(fig.)* noch einen Trumpf in der Hand haben; noch etwas in petto haben *(ugs);* **b)** *in pl. (game)* Karten *Pl.;* **play ~s** Karten spielen; **lose money at ~s** beim Kartenspiel[en] Geld verlieren; **c)** *(~board, post~, visiting ~, greeting ~, ticket, invitation)* Karte, *die;* **let me give you my ~:** ich gebe Ihnen meine Karte; **d)** *(programme at races etc.)* Programm, *das;* **e)** *in pl. (coll.: employee's documents)* Papiere *Pl.;* **ask for/get one's ~s** sich *(Dat.)* seine Papiere geben lassen/seine Papiere kriegen *(ugs.);* **f)** *(person)* Type, *die (ugs.);* **an odd ~:** eine komische Type; **g)** *(coll.: eccentric person)* komischer Vogel *(ugs.)*

[2]**card** *(Textiles)* **1.** *n. (instrument)* Karde, *die;* Kratze, *die.* **2.** *v.t.* karden

cardamom, cardamum [ˈkɑːdəməm] *n.* Kardamom, *das od. der*

card: ~board *n.* Pappe, *die;* Pappkarton, *der; (fig. attrib.)* klischeehaft ‹*Figur*›; **~board box** Karton, *der;* **~-carrying** *adj.* **a ~-carrying member** ein eingetragenes Mitglied; **~-file** *n.* Kartei, *die; (large)* Kartothek, *die;* **~-game** *n.* Kartenspiel, *das*

cardiac [ˈkɑːdɪæk] *adj. (of heart)* Herz-; *(of stomach)* Magen-

cardiac arˈrest *n.* Herzstillstand, *der*

cardigan [ˈkɑːdɪgən] *n.* Strickjacke, *die*

cardinal [ˈkɑːdɪnl] **1.** *adj.* **a)** *(fundamental)* grundlegend ‹*Frage, Doktrin, Pflicht*›; Kardinal‹*fehler, -problem*›; *(chief)* hauptsächlich, Haupt‹*argument, -punkt, -merkmal*›; **b)** *(of deep scarlet)* scharlachfarben; scharlachrot ‹*Farbe*›; ~ **red** scharlachrot. **2.** *n.* **a)** *(Eccl.)* Kardinal, *der;* **b)** *see* **cardinal number**; **c)** *(song-bird)* Kardinal, *der*

cardinal: ~ **number** *n.* Grund-, Kardinalzahl, *die;* ~ **points** *n. pl.* Himmelsrichtungen *Pl.;* ~ **ˈsin** *n.* Todsünde, *die;* ~ **ˈvirtues** *n. pl.* Kardinaltugenden *Pl.;* ~ **ˈvowel** *n. (Phonet.)* Kardinalvokal, *der*

card: ~ **ˈindex** *n.* Kartei, *die;* **~-ˈindex** *v.t.* karteimäßig erfassen *od.* ordnen

carding-machine [ˈkɑːdɪŋməʃiːn] *n.* Karde, *die*

cardio- [kɑːdɪəʊ] *in comb. (Med.)* kardio-/Kardio-

ˈ**cardiogram** *n.* Kardiogramm, *das (Med.)*

ˈ**cardiograph** *n.* Kardiograph, *der (Med.)*

cardiologist [kɑːdɪˈɒlɪgɪst] *n.* Kardiologe, *der*/Kardiologin, *die*

cardiology [kɑːdɪˈɒlədʒɪ] *n.* Kardiologie, *die*

card: ~-playing *n., no pl.* Kartenspielen, *das;* **all forms of ~-playing** alle Formen des Kartenspiels; **~-room** *n.* Spielzimmer, *das;* **~-sharp, ~-sharper** *ns.* Falschspieler, *der;* **~-table** *n.* Kartentisch, *der;* ~ **trick** *n.* Kartentrick, *der;* ~ **vote** *n.* Abstimmung durch Wahlmänner *(in Gewerkschaften)*

care [keə(r)] **1.** *n.* **a)** *(anxiety)* Sorge, *die;* **a life full of ~:** ein Leben voller Sorgen; **cast ~ aside** *(arch./literary)* seine Sorgen vergessen; **she hasn't got a ~ in the world** sie hat keinerlei Sorgen; **b)** *(pains)* Sorgfalt, *die;* **take ~:** sich bemühen; **he takes great ~ over his work** er gibt sich *(Dat.)* große Mühe mit seiner Arbeit; **c)** *(caution)* Vorsicht, *die;* **take ~, have a ~:** aufpassen; **take ~** *or* **have a ~ to do sth.** darauf achten, etw. zu tun; **take more ~!** paß [doch] besser auf!; **take ~ to lock the door** vergiß ja *od.* nur nicht, die Tür abzuschließen; **d)** *(attention)* **medical ~:** ärztliche Betreuung; **old people need special ~:** alte Menschen brauchen besondere Fürsorge; **e)** *(concern)* ~ **for sb./sth.** die Sorge um jmdn./etw.; **f)** *(charge)* Obhut, *die (geh.);* ~ **of,** *(Amer.)* **in ~ of** *(on letter)* per Adresse; bei; **be in ~:** in Pflege sein; **put sb. in ~/take sb. into ~:** jmdn. in Pflege geben/nehmen; **take ~ of sb./sth.** *(ensure safety of)* auf jmdn./etw. aufpassen; *(attend to, dispose of)* sich um jmdn./etw. kümmern; **take ~ of one's appearance** auf sein Äußeres achten; **take ~ of oneself** für sich selbst sorgen; *(as to health)* sich schonen; **take ~ [of yourself]!** mach's gut! *(ugs.);* **that will take ~ of itself** das erledigt sich von selbst. **2.** *v.i.* **a)** ~ **for** *or* **about sb./sth.** *(heed)* sich um jmdn./etw. kümmern; *(feel interest)* sich für jmdn./etw. interessieren; **he ~s only for his own interests** er hat nur seine eigenen Interessen im Sinn; **b)** ~ **for** *or* **about sb./sth.** *(like)* jmdn./etw. mögen; **someone he really ~s for** *or* **about** jemand, der ihm wirklich etwas bedeutet; **he never shows how much he ~s** er zeigt nie die Stärke seiner Zuneigung; **I don't ~ about him** er ist mir völlig gleichgültig; **would you ~ for a drink?** möchten Sie etwas trinken?; **c)** *(feel concern)* **I don't ~ [whether/how/what** *etc.*] es ist mir gleich[, ob/wie/was *usw.*]; **do you ~ if ...:** macht es Ihnen etwas aus, wenn ...; **people who ~:** Leute, die nicht nur an sich selbst denken; **she doesn't appear to ~ [how she dresses]** es scheint ihr gleich zu sein[, wie sie angezogen ist]; **don't you ~?** ist es dir [denn] gleichgültig?; **for all I ~** *(coll.)* von mir aus *(ugs.);* **I couldn't ~ less** *(coll.)* es ist mir völlig einerlei *od. (ugs.)* egal; **I couldn't ~ less about money** *(coll.)* Geld ist mir völlig gleichgültig; **I couldn't/don't ~ a tinker's cuss** *or* **a hoot** *or* **two hoots** *or* **tuppence about him/it** *etc. (coll.)* er/es *usw.* ist mir piepegal *od.* schnuppe *(ugs.);* **what do I ~?** *(coll.)* mir ist es egal *(ugs.);* **not that ˈI ~** *(coll.)* obwohl es mir egal ist *(ugs.);* **who ~s?** *(coll.)* was soll's *(ugs.); see also* **damn 2 b; d)** *(wish)* ~ **to do sth.** etw. tun mögen; **would you ~ to try some cake?** darf ich Ihnen ein Stückchen Kuchen anbieten?; **e)** ~ **for sb./sth.** *(look after)* sich um jmdn./etw. kümmern; **well ~d for** gepflegt; gut versorgt ‹*Person*›; gut erhalten ‹*Auto*›

careen [kəˈriːn] **1.** *v.t. (Naut.)* kielholen. **2.** *v.i.* **a)** *(Naut.: be turned over)* gekielholt werden; krängen; *(fig.)* schwanken; torkeln; **b)** *(Amer.: career)* rasen

career [kəˈrɪə(r)] **1.** *n.* **a)** *(way of livelihood)* Beruf, *der;* **a teaching ~:** der Beruf des Lehrers; **take up a ~ in journalism** *or* **as a journalist** den Beruf des Journalisten ergreifen; **her modelling ~ was finished** sie mußte ihren Beruf als Modell aufgeben; **she's not interested in [having] a ~:** sie interessiert sich nicht für eine Berufslaufbahn; **b)** *(progress in life)* [berufliche] Laufbahn; *(very successful)* Karriere, *die;* **c)** *(swift course)* Rasen, *das;* **in our ~ down the slope** als wir den Abhang hinuntersausten; **in full ~:** in rasendem Lauf; ‹*Wagen, Rennboot*› in voller Fahrt; ‹*Pferd*› in gestrecktem Galopp; **in mid ~:** mittendrin. **2.** *v.i.* rasen; ‹*Pferd, Reiter:*› galoppieren; **go ~ing down the hill** den Hügel hinunterrasen

career: ~ **ˈdiplomat** *n.* Berufsdiplomat, *der;* ~ **girl** *n.* Karrierefrau, *die*

careerist [kəˈrɪərɪst] *n.* Karrieremacher, *der (abwertend)*

career: ~s adviser *n.* Berufsberater, *der*/-beraterin, *die;* **~s [advisory] service** *n.* Berufsberatung, *die;* **~s master/~s mistress** *n. Lehrer, der/Lehrerin, die die Schüler bei der Wahl des Berufs berät;* **~s office** *n.* Berufsberatung[sstelle], *die;* **~s officer** *see* **~s adviser;** ~ **woman** *n.* Karrierefrau, *die*

ˈ**carefree** *adj.* sorgenfrei

careful [ˈkeəfl] *adj.* **a)** *(thorough)* sorgfältig; *(watchful, cautious)* vorsichtig; **[be] ~!** Vorsicht!; **be ~ to do sth.** darauf achten, etw. zu tun; **he was ~ not to mention the subject** er war darum bemüht, das Thema nicht zu erwähnen; **be ~ that ...:** darauf achten, daß ...; **be ~ for sb./sth.** auf jmdn./etw. achten; **he is ~ for his own interests** er achtet darauf, seine eigenen Interessen zu wahren; **be ~ of sb./sth.** *(take care of)* mit jmdm./etw. vorsichtig sein; *(be cautious of)* sich vor jmdm./etw. in acht nehmen; **be ~ of the roads!** paß auf, wenn du über die Straße gehst!; **be ~ how you word the letter** sei vorsichtig bei der Formulierung des Briefes; **be ~ [about] how/what/where** *etc.* darauf achten, wie/was/wo *usw.;* **be ~ about sth.** auf etw. *(Akk.)* achten; **be ~ about sb.** auf jmdn. aufpassen *od.* achten; **they're so ~ about the baby** sie kümmern sich sehr um das Baby; **be ~ about saying too much** darauf achten, nicht zu viel zu sagen; **do be ~ about drinking and driving** bitte sei vorsichtig mit dem Alkohol, wenn du noch fahren mußt; **be ~ with sb./sth.** vorsichtig mit jmdm./etw. umgehen; **he's very ~ with his words** er wählt seine Worte sehr genau; **b)** *(showing care)* sorgfältig; **a ~ piece of work** ein sorgfältig gearbeitetes Stück; **after ~ consideration** nach reiflicher Überlegung; **pay ~ attention to what he says** achte genau auf das, was er sagt

carefully [ˈkeəfəlɪ] *adv. (thoroughly)* sorgfältig; gewissenhaft; *(attentively)* aufmerksam; *(cautiously)* vorsichtig; **watch ~:** gut aufpassen

carefulness [ˈkeəflnɪs] *n., no pl.* Sorgfalt, *die; (caution)* Vorsicht, *die*

careless [ˈkeəlɪs] *adj.* **a)** *(inattentive)* unaufmerksam; *(thoughtless)* gedankenlos; unvorsichtig, leichtsinnig ‹*Fahrer*›; nachlässig ‹*Arbeiter*›; **be ~ about** *or* **of sb./sth.** wenig auf jmdn./etw. achten; **you oughtn't to be so ~ about drinking and driving** du solltest mehr auf deinen Alkoholkonsum achten, wenn du noch fahren mußt; ~ **of sb./sth.** *(unconcerned about)* unbekümmert um jmdn./etw.; ~ **with sb./sth.** unvorsichtig mit jmdm./etw.; **be ~ [about** *or* **of] how/what/where** *etc.* wenig darauf achten, wie/was/wo *usw.;* **b)** *(showing lack of care)* unordentlich, nachlässig ‹*Arbeit*›; gedankenlos ‹*Bemerkung, Handlung*›; unachtsam ‹*Fahren*›; **a [very] ~ mistake** ein [grober] Flüchtigkeitsfehler; **c)** *(nonchalant)* ungezwungen; lässig ‹*Aussehen, Geste*›

carelessly [ˈkeəlɪslɪ] *adv.* **a)** *(without care)* nachlässig; *(thoughtlessly)* gedankenlos; unvorsichtig, leichtsinnig ‹*fahren*›; **b)** *(nonchalantly)* lässig

carelessness [ˈkeəlɪsnɪs] *n., no pl. (lack of care)* Nachlässigkeit, *die; (thoughtlessness)* Gedankenlosigkeit, *die*

caress [kəˈres] **1.** *n.* Liebkosung, *die.* **2.** *v.t.* liebkosen; ~ **[each other]** sich *od.* einander liebkosen

caret [ˈkæret] *n. Korrekturzeichen für fehlende Buchstaben od. Wörter in einem Text*

care: ~taker *n.* **a)** Hausmeister, *der*/-meisterin, *die; (in private house)* Hausverwalter, *der*/-verwalterin, *die;* **b) ~taker government** Übergangsregierung, *die;* **~-worn** *adj.* von Sorgen gezeichnet; **he looked ~-worn** sein Gesicht war von Sorgen gezeichnet

car: ~fare *n. (Amer.)* Fahrgeld, *das;* ~ **ferry** *n.* Autofähre, *die*

cargo [ˈkɑːgəʊ] *n., pl.* **~es** *or (Amer.)* **~s** Fracht, *die;* Ladung, *die;* **a ~ of spices** eine Ladung Gewürze

cargo: ~ boat, ~ ship, ~vessel *ns.* Frachter, *der;* Frachtschiff, *das*

ˈ**carhop** *n. (Amer. coll.) Kellner/Kellnerin in einem Drive-in-Restaurant*

Caribbean [kærɪ'bi:ən] **1.** *n.* **the ~:** die Karibik. **2.** *adj.* karibisch; **the ~ Sea** das Karibische Meer; **~ holiday** Urlaub in der Karibik
caribou ['kærɪbu:] *n., pl. same (Zool.)* Karibu, *der od. das*
caricature ['kærɪkətjʊə(r)] **1.** *n.* Karikatur, *die; (in mime)* Parodie, *die;* **do a ~ of sb.** jmdn. karikieren/parodieren. **2.** *v. t.* karikieren; *(in mime)* parodieren
caricaturist ['kærɪkətjʊərɪst] *n.* Karikaturist, *der*/Karikaturistin, *die; (in mime)* Parodist, *der*/Parodistin, *die*
caries ['keəri:z] *n., pl. same (Med., Dent.)* Karies, *die*
carillon [kə'rɪljən, 'kærɪljən] *n.* Glockenspiel, *das*
caring ['keərɪŋ] *adj.* sozial ⟨*Gesellschaft*⟩; fürsorglich ⟨*Person*⟩
Carinthia [kə'rɪnθɪə] *pr. n.* Kärnten *(das)*
Carinthian [kə'rɪnθɪən] **1.** *n.* Kärntner, *der*/Kärntnerin, *die.* **2.** *adj.* kärntnerisch; **the ~ Lakes** die Kärntner Seen
'**carload** *n.* **a)** Wagenladung, *die;* **people were arriving by the ~** es trafen ganze Wagenladungen von Menschen ein; **b)** *(Amer.) Mindestladung für ermäßigten Frachtbrief*
carman ['kɑ:mən] *n., pl.* **carmen** ['kɑ:mən] [Berufskraft]fahrer, *der*
'**car-mat** *n.* Fußmatte, *die (im Auto)*
Carmelite ['kɑ:mɪlaɪt] **1.** *n. (friar)* Karmelit[er], *der; (nun)* Karmelit[er]in, *die.* **2.** *adj.* Karmeliter-
carmine ['kɑ:maɪn, 'kɑ:mɪn] **1.** *n.* Karmin[rot], *das.* **2.** *adj.* karminrot
carnage ['kɑ:nɪdʒ] *n.* Gemetzel, *das;* **a scene of ~:** ein Schlachtfeld *(fig.);* **the dreadful annual ~ on the roads** das alljährliche schreckliche Blutvergießen auf den Straßen
carnal ['kɑ:nl] *adj.* **a)** *(sensual)* körperlich; sinnlich; fleischlich *(geh.);* **~ desires/sins** sinnliche Begierden/Sünden des Fleisches *(geh.);* **~ lust** Fleischeslust, *die (geh.);* **b)** *(worldly)* profan
carnal 'knowledge *n. (Law)* **have ~ of sb.** mit jmdm. Geschlechtsverkehr haben
¹**carnation** [kɑ:'neɪʃn] *n. (Bot.)* [Garten]nelke, *die*
²**carnation 1.** *n.* Rosarot, *das.* **2.** *adj.* **~ [pink]** [zart]rosa
carnet ['kɑ:neɪ] *n. (of motorist)* Triptyk, *das; (of camper)* Ausweis für Camper
carnival ['kɑ:nɪvl] *n.* **a)** *(festival)* Volksfest, *das;* **~ procession** Festzug, *der;* **b)** *(pre-Lent festivities)* Karneval, *der;* Fastnacht, *die;* Fasching, *der (bes. südd., österr.); (fig.: revelry)* ausgelassenes Fest; **~ procession** Karnevals[um]zug, *der;* **c)** *(Amer.) (circus)* Zirkus, *der; (fun-fair)* Jahrmarkt, *der*
carnivore ['kɑ:nɪvɔ:(r)] *n. (animal)* Fleischfresser, *der;* Karnivore, *der (Zool.); (plant)* fleischfressende Pflanze; Karnivore, *die (Bot.)*
carnivorous [kɑ:'nɪvərəs] *adj.* fleischfressend; karnivor *(Zool., Bot.)*
carob ['kærəb] *n.* **a)** *(pod)* Johannisbrot, *das;* **b)** *(tree)* Johannisbrotbaum, *der*
carol ['kærl] **1.** *n.* **a) [Christmas] ~:** Weihnachtslied, *das;* **~ concert, ~-singing** weihnachtliches Liedersingen; **b)** *(joyous song)* fröhliches Lied. **2.** *v. t., (Brit.)* **-ll- a)** *(sing as carol)* singen ⟨*Weihnachtslied*⟩; **b)** *(sing joyfully)* [fröhlich] singen. **3.** *v. i., (Brit.)* **-ll- a)** Weihnachtslieder singen; **b)** *(sing joyfully)* [fröhlich] singen
carom ['kærəm] *(Amer.)* **1.** *n.* Karambolage, *die;* **~ billiards** Karambolagebillard, *das.* **2.** *v. i. (Billiards)* karambolieren
carotid [kə'rɒtɪd] *(Anat.)* **1.** *adj.* Karotis-; **~ artery** *see* **2. 2.** *n.* Halsschlagader, *die;* Karotis, *die (fachspr.)*
carousal [kə'raʊzl] *n.* Zechgelage, *das*
carouse [kə'raʊz] **1.** *v. i.* zechen *(veralt., noch scherzh.).* **2.** *n. see* **carousal**
carousel [kærʊ'sel, kærʊ'zel] *n.* **a)** *(conveyor system)* Ausgabeband, *das;* **b)** *(Amer.: roundabout)* Karussell, *das*
'**car-owner** *n.* Autobesitzer, *der*
¹**carp** [kɑ:p] *n., pl. same (Zool.)* Karpfen, *der*
²**carp** *v. i.* nörgeln; **~ [on and on] at sb./sth.** an jmdm./etw. [dauernd] herumnörgeln *(ugs.)*
'**car-park** *n.* Parkplatz, *der; (underground)* Tiefgarage, *die; (building)* Parkhaus, *das*
'**car-parking** *n.* Parken, *das;* **~ facilities are available** Parkplätze [sind] vorhanden
Carpathians [kɑ:'peɪθjənz, kɑ:'peɪðjənz] *pr. n. pl.* Karpaten *Pl.*
carpel ['kɑ:pl] *n. (Bot.)* Fruchtblatt, *das;* Karpell, *das (fachspr.)*
carpenter ['kɑ:pɪntə(r)] **1.** *n.* Zimmermann, *der; (for furniture)* Tischler, *der*/Tischlerin, *die; (ship's ~)* Schiffszimmermann, *der.* **2.** *v. t.* zimmern; tischlern ⟨*Regale*⟩
carpentry ['kɑ:pɪntrɪ] *n.* **a)** *(art)* Zimmerhandwerk, *das; (in furniture)* Tischlerhandwerk, *das;* **b)** *(woodwork)* **[piece of] ~:** Tischlerarbeit, *die; (structure)* [Holz]konstruktion, *die*
carpet ['kɑ:pɪt] **1.** *n.* **a)** *(covering)* Teppich, *der;* **[fitted] ~:** Teppichboden, *der;* **stair-~:** [Treppen]läufer, *der;* **be on the ~** *(coll.: be reprimanded)* zusammengestaucht werden *(ugs.); (be under discussion)* zur Debatte stehen; **have sb. on the ~** *(coll.: reprimand sb.)* jmdn. zusammenstauchen *(ugs.);* **sweep sth. under the ~** *(fig.)* etw. unter den Teppich kehren *(ugs.); see also* **red carpet; b)** *(expanse)* **~ of flowers** Blumenteppich, *der;* **~ of grass/snow/leaves** Gras-/Schnee-/Laubdecke, *die.* **2.** *v. t.* **a)** *(cover)* [mit Teppich(boden)] auslegen; *(fig.)* bedecken; **snow ~ed the village in [a layer of] white** Schnee bedeckte das Dorf mit einem weißen Teppich; **b)** *(coll.: reprimand)* **be ~ed for sth.** wegen etw. zusammengestaucht werden *(ugs.)*
carpet: ~-bag *n.* Reisetasche, *die;* **~-bagger** ['kɑ:pɪtbægə(r)] *n.* **a)** politischer Karrieremacher; **b)** *(Hist.) Politiker aus dem Norden der USA, der in den Südstaaten nach dem Sezessionskrieg rasch Karriere machen wollte;* **~-beater** *n.* Teppichklopfer, *der*
carpeting ['kɑ:pɪtɪŋ] *n.* **a)** Teppich[boden], *der;* **some ~ing** ein Stück Teppichboden; **wall-to-wall ~:** Teppichboden, *der;* **stair-~:** [Treppen]läufer, *der;* **b)** *(fig.) see* **carpet 1 b**
carpet: ~-slipper *n.* Hausschuh, *der;* **~-sweeper** *n.* Teppichkehrer, *der;* Teppichkehrmaschine, *die*
car: ~ phone *n.* Autotelefon, *das;* **~ pool** *n.* Fahrgemeinschaft, *die; (of a firm etc.)* Fahrzeugpark, *der;* **~-port** *n.* Einstellplatz, *der*
'**car radio** *n.* Autoradio, *das*
carrel ['kærl] *n.* [abgeteilter] Arbeitsplatz *(in einer Bibliothek/hist.: in einem Kloster)*
carriage ['kærɪdʒ] *n.* **a)** *(horse-drawn vehicle)* Kutsche, *die;* **~ and pair/four/six** *etc.* Zwei-/Vier-/Sechsspänner *usw., der; see also* **drive 2 a; b)** *(Railw.)* [Eisenbahn]wagen, *der;* **c)** *(Mech.)* Schlitten, *der; (of typewriter)* Schlitten, *der;* Wagen, *der;* **d)** *no pl. (conveying, being conveyed)* Transport, *der;* **use for ~:** für den Transport benutzen; **e)** *(cost of conveying)* Frachtkosten *Pl.;* **~ forward** Fracht[kosten] zu Lasten des Empfängers; **~ paid** frachtfrei; **f)** *(bearing)* Haltung, *die. See also* **gun carriage; invalid carriage**
carriage: ~ clock *n.* Reiseuhr, *die;* **~way** *n.* Fahrbahn, *die*
'**car ride** *n.* Autofahrt, *die*
carrier ['kærɪə(r)] *n.* **a)** *(bearer)* Träger, *der;* **~ of good news** Überbringer guter Nachrichten; **b)** *(conductor)* **be the ~ of sth.** etw. transportieren *od.* leiten; **c)** *(hired conveyor of goods or passengers)* Transportunternehmen, *das; (person)* Transportunternehmer, *der;* **firm of ~s** Transportunternehmen, *das;* **d)** *(on bicycle etc.)* Gepäckträger, *der; (for child passenger)* Kindersitz, *der;* **e)** *see* **carrier-bag; f)** *see* **carrier wave; g)** *see* **aircraft-carrier; h)** *(Med.: of disease)* Ausscheider, *der; (Genetics: of characteristic)* Konduktor, *der*
carrier: ~-bag *n.* Tragetasche, *die;* Tragetüte, *die;* **~ pigeon** *n.* Brieftaube, *die;* **by ~ pigeon** mit der Taubenpost; **~ wave** *n. (Phys.)* Trägerwelle, *die*
carrion ['kærɪən] *n.* **a)** *(flesh)* Aas, *das;* **b)** *(fig.: garbage)* Unflat, *der;* Schmutz, *der*
'**carrion crow** *n.* Rabenkrähe, *die; (Corvus corone)* Aaskrähe, *die*
carrot ['kærət] *n.* **a)** Möhre, *die;* Karotte, *die;* **grated ~[s]** geraspelte Möhren *od.* Karotten; **b)** *(fig.)* Köder, *der;* **dangle a ~ in front of sb.'s nose** jmdm. einen Köder vor die Nase halten; **with ~ and stick** mit Zuckerbrot und Peitsche
carroty ['kærətɪ] *adj.* rotblond ⟨*Haare*⟩
carrousel *(Amer.) see* **carousel**
carry ['kærɪ] **1.** *v. t.* **a)** *(transport)* tragen; *(with emphasis on destination)* bringen; überbringen ⟨*Nachrichten*⟩; ⟨*Tornado:*⟩ fegen; ⟨*Strom:*⟩ spülen; ⟨*Verkehrsmittel:*⟩ befördern; **~ sth. with one in a bag** etw. in einer Tasche bei sich haben *od.* tragen; **where do you ~ your purse?** wo hast *od.* trägst du dein Portemonnaie?; **~ sth. in one's head** etw. im Kopf haben; **~ sth. round with one** *(lit. or fig.)* etw. mit sich herumtragen *(ugs.); (fig.)* etw. nicht vergessen können; **~ all before one** *(fig.)* nicht aufzuhalten sein; **b)** *(conduct)* leiten; **~ sth. into effect** etw. in die Tat umsetzen; **c)** *(support)* tragen; *(contain)* fassen; **~ responsibility** Verantwortung tragen; **d)** *(have with one)* **~ [with one]** bei sich haben *od.* tragen; tragen ⟨*Waffe, Kennzeichen*⟩; ⟨*Schiff:*⟩ führen ⟨*Lichter, Segel*⟩; **e)** *(possess)* besitzen ⟨*Autorität, Gewicht*⟩; *see also* **conviction b; f)** *(hold)* **he carries his head in a proud way** er trägt den Kopf hoch; **she carries herself well** sie hat eine gute Haltung; **he carries himself very erect** er hält sich sehr aufrecht; **g)** *(prolong)* **~ sth. to sth.** etw. zu etw. führen; **~ sth. to a close** *or* **an end** etw. zu Ende führen *od.* bringen; **such plans must be carried to their natural conclusions** solche Pläne müssen [bis zum Ende] durchgezogen werden *(ugs.);* **~ modesty/altruism** *etc.* **to excess** die Bescheidenheit/den Altruismus *usw.* bis zum Exzeß treiben; **~ things to extremes** die Dinge auf die Spitze treiben; *see also* **far 1 d; h)** *(transmit)* übertragen ⟨*Krankheit*⟩; **i)** *(Math.: transfer)* im Sinn behalten; **~ one** eins im Sinn; **j)** *(be pregnant with)* erwarten ⟨*Kind*⟩; **she was ~ing his child** sie erwartete ein Kind von ihm; **k)** *(win)* erringen ⟨*Sieg*⟩; bekommen, erhalten ⟨*Belohnung*⟩; gewinnen ⟨*Preis, Wahl*⟩; durchbringen ⟨*Antrag, Gesetzentwurf, Vorschlag*⟩; **the motion is carried** der Antrag ist angenommen; **~ one's point [with sb.]** seine Sache [bei jmdm.] durchsetzen; **~ one's hearers/audience with one** die Zuhörer/das Publikum überzeugen; **~ the day** den Sieg davontragen; **l)** *(involve)* [mit sich] bringen; bringen ⟨*Gewinn, Zinsen*⟩; **discipline carries both advantages and disadvantages** Disziplin hat ihre Vor- und Nachteile; **m)** *(stock)* führen; **n)** *(publish, broadcast)* bringen. **2.** *v. i.* ⟨*Stimme, Laut:*⟩ zu hören sein; ⟨*Geruch:*⟩ zu riechen sein; ⟨*Geschoß, Ball:*⟩ [weit] fliegen
~ a'way *v. t.* forttragen; *(by force)* fortreißen; *(fig.)* **be** *or* **get carried away** *(be inspired)* hingerissen sein **(by** von); *(lose self-control)* sich hinreißen lassen; **don't get carried away!** übertreib's nicht!
~ 'back *v. t.* **a)** *(return)* zurückbringen; **b)** *see* **take back b**
~ 'forward *v. t. (Bookk.)* vortragen
~ 'off *v. t.* **a)** *(from place)* davontragen; *(as*

owner or possessor) mit sich nehmen; *(cause to die)* dahinraffen *(geh.)*; **b)** *(abduct)* entführen ‹*Person*›; **c)** *(win)* gewinnen ‹*Preis, Medaille*›; erringen ‹*Sieg*›; **d)** *(make acceptable)* durchführen; *(cope with)* fertig werden mit; ~ **it/sth. off [well]** es/etw. [gut] zustande bringen

~ **'on 1.** *v. t. (continue)* fortführen ‹*Tradition, Diskussion, Arbeit*›; ~ **on the firm** die Firma übernehmen; ~ **on [doing sth.]** weiterhin etw. tun; **they carried on talking** sie fuhren fort, sich zu unterhalten. **2.** *v. i.* **a)** *(continue)* weitermachen; ~ **on with a plan/project** einen Plan/ein Projekt weiterverfolgen; **b)** *(coll.: behave in unseemly manner)* sich danebenbenehmen *(ugs.)*; *(make a fuss)* Theater machen *(ugs.)*; **c)** ~ **on with sb.** *(flirt)* mit jmdm. flirten; *(have affair)* mit jmdm. ein Verhältnis haben. *See also* **carry-on**

~ **'out** *v. t. (put into practice)* durchführen ‹*Plan, Programm, Versuch*›; in die Tat umsetzen ‹*Plan, Vorschlag, Absicht, Vorstellung*›; ausführen ‹*Anweisung, Auftrag*›; halten ‹*Versprechen*›; vornehmen ‹*Verbesserungen*›; wahr machen ‹*Drohung*›

~ **'over** *v. t.* **a)** *(postpone)* vertagen **(to** auf + *Akk.*); **b)** *(St. Exch.)* prolongieren; **c)** *see* ~ **forward.** *See also* **carry-over**

~ **'through** *v. t.* **a)** *(bring safely through)* ~ **sb. through** jmdm. durchhelfen; **b)** *(complete)* durchführen

'carry-cot *n.* Babytragetasche, *die*

carryings-on [kærɪɪŋz'ɒn] *n. pl. (sl.)* **a)** *(questionable behaviour)* seltsames Treiben; **there are strange** ~ **in that house** in diesem Haus geht Seltsames vor; **b)** *(love affairs)* Affären

carry: ~**-on** *n. (sl.)* **a)** Theater, *das (ugs.)*; **b)** *(flirtation)* Flirt, *der; (love affair)* [Liebes]affäre, *die;* ~**-over** *n. (St. Exch.)* Prolongation, *die*

'carsick *adj.* **children are often** ~: Kindern wird beim Autofahren oft schlecht

cart [kɑ:t] **1.** *n.* Karren, *der;* Wagen, *der;* **horse and** ~: Pferdewagen, *der;* **be [left] in the** ~ *(Brit. coll.)* in der Tinte sitzen *(ugs.)*; **put sb. in the** ~ *(Brit. coll.)* jmdn. in die Bredouille bringen *(ugs.)*; **put the** ~ **before the horse** *(fig.)* das Pferd beim Schwanz aufzäumen. **2.** *v. t.* **a)** *(carry [as] in cart)* karren; **b)** *(fig. sl.: carry with effort)* schleppen; ~ **sth. around with one** etw. mit sich herumschleppen

~ **'off** *v. t. (coll.)* abtransportieren

carte blanche [kɑ:t 'blɑ̃ʃ] *n.* Carte blanche, *die;* unbeschränkte Vollmacht

cartel [kɑ:'tel] *n.* Kartell, *das*

carter ['kɑ:tə(r)] *n.* Fuhrmann, *der*

Cartesian [kɑ:'ti:zjən] *adj.* ~ **coordinates** *(Math.)* kartesische Koordinaten

Carthage ['kɑ:θɪdʒ] *pr. n.* Karthago *(das)*

'cart-horse *n.* Arbeitspferd, *das*

Carthusian [kɑ:'θju:zjən] **1.** *adj.* Kartäuser-. **2.** *n.* Kartäuser, *der*

cartilage ['kɑ:tɪlɪdʒ] *n.* Knorpel, *der*

cartilaginous [kɑ:tɪ'lædʒɪnəs] *adj.* knorpelig

'cart-load *n.* **a)** Wagenladung, *die;* Fuhre, *die;* **by the** ~ fuhrenweise; **b)** *(fig.: large quantity)* **a** ~ **of books** ein Berg von Büchern; ~**s of food** Essen in Hülle und Fülle

cartographer [kɑ:'tɒgrəfə(r)] *n.* Kartograph, *der*/Kartographin, *die*

cartographic [kɑ:tə'græfɪk], **cartographical** [kɑ:tə'græfɪkl] *adjs.* kartographisch

cartography [kɑ:'tɒgrəfɪ] *n.* Kartographie, *die*

carton ['kɑ:tn] *n.* [Papp]karton, *der;* **a** ~ **of milk** eine Tüte Milch; **a** ~ **of detergent** ein Paket Waschpulver; **a** ~ **of cigarettes** eine Stange Zigaretten; **a** ~ **of yoghurt** ein Becher Joghurt

cartoon [kɑ:'tu:n] **1.** *n.* **a)** *(amusing drawing)* humoristische Zeichnung; Cartoon, *der; (satirical illustration)* Karikatur, *die; (sequence of drawings)* [humoristische] Bilderserie; Cartoon, *der;* **b)** *(film)* Zeichentrickfilm, *der;* **c)** *(Art)* Entwurf, *der;* Karton, *der (Kunstwiss.).* **2.** *v. t. (draw amusingly)* karikieren

cartoonist [kɑ:'tu:nɪst] *n.* Cartoonist, *der*/Cartoonistin, *die; (satirical* ~*)* Karikaturist, *der*/Karikaturistin, *die*

cartridge ['kɑ:trɪdʒ] *n.* **a)** *(case for explosive)* Patrone, *die;* **b)** *(spool of film, cassette)* Kassette, *die;* **c)** *(pick-up head)* Tonabnehmer, *der;* **d)** *(ink-container)* Patrone, *die*

cartridge: ~**-belt** *n.* Patronengurt, *der;* ~**-case** *n.* Patronenhülse, *die;* ~ **paper** *n.* *(for drawing)* Zeichenpapier, *das; (for envelopes, gun cartridges) festes, haltbares Papier*

cart: ~**-road,** ~**-track** *ns.* ≈ Feldweg, *der;* ~**-wheel** *n.* **a)** Wagenrad, *das;* **b)** *(Gymnastics)* Rad, *das;* **turn** *or* **do** ~**-wheels** radschlagen; ~**-wright** ['kɑ:traɪt] *n.* Stellmacher, *der*

carve [kɑ:v] **1.** *v. t.* **a)** *(cut up)* tranchieren, aufschneiden ‹*Fleisch, Braten*›; tranchieren ‹*Hähnchen*›; **b)** *(produce by cutting) (from wood)* schnitzen; *(from stone)* meißeln; ~ **sth. out of wood/stone** etw. aus Holz schnitzen/aus Stein meißeln; ~ **sth. in/into/on sth.** etw. in etw. *(Akk.)* [ein]ritzen; ~ **a tunnel in the rock** einen Tunnel in den Fels hauen; ~ **one's way** sich *(Dat.)* seinen Weg hauen; **c)** *(change by cutting)* **he** ~**d a block of wood/stone into a madonna** er schnitzte aus einem Holzblock/meißelte aus einem Steinblock eine Madonna; **d)** *(adorn by cutting)* **the frame was** ~**d with leaves** der Rahmen war mit geschnitzten/in Stein gehauenen Blättern verziert. **2.** *v. i.* **a)** tranchieren; **b)** ~ **in wood/ivory/stone** in Holz/Elfenbein schnitzen/in Stein meißeln; ~ **through sth.** sich *(Dat.)* einen Weg durch etw. hauen

~ **out** *v. t.* heraushauen; ~ **out a tunnel in the rock** einen Tunnel in den Fels hauen *od.* treiben; ~ **out an existence** *(fig.)* sich *(Dat.)* eine Existenz aufbauen

~ **up** *v. t.* aufschneiden ‹*Fleisch*›; aufteilen ‹*Erbe, Land*›; zerstückeln ‹*Leiche*›

carver ['kɑ:və(r)] *n.* **a)** *(in wood)* [Holz]schnitzer, *der; (in stone)* Bildhauer, *der; (of meat)* Trancheur, *der;* **b)** *(knife) see* **carving-knife; c)** *in pl. (knife and fork)* Tranchierbesteck, *das*

carving ['kɑ:vɪŋ] *n.* **a)** *(in or from wood, ivory)* Schnitzerei, *die;* **a** ~ **of a madonna in wood** eine holzgeschnitzte Madonna; **an ivory** ~ **of an elephant** ein aus Elfenbein geschnitzter Elefant; **b)** *(in or from stone)* Skulptur, *die; (on stone)* eingeritztes Bild; *(ornament)* eingeritztes Muster

'carving: ~**-fork** *n.* Tranchiergabel, *die;* ~**-knife** *n.* Tranchiermesser, *das*

'car-wash *n.* Waschanlage, *die*

caryatid [kærɪ'ætɪd] *n., pl.* ~**s** *or* ~**es** [kærɪ'ætɪdi:z] *(Archit.)* Karyatide, *die*

Casanova [kæzə'nəʊvə, kæsə'nəʊvə] *n.* Casanova, *der*

cascade [kæs'keɪd] **1.** *(lit. or fig.)* Kaskade, *die.* **2.** *v. i.* [in Kaskaden] herabstürzen; **her hair** ~**d down her back** *(fig.)* ihr Haar fiel in Kaskaden über ihren Rücken hinab

¹case [keɪs] *n.* **a)** *(instance, matter)* Fall, *der;* **if there is another** ~ **of this happening** wenn das noch einmal vorkommt; **several** ~**s of fire** mehrere Brände; **if it's a** ~ **of your not being able to get here** wenn es nur daran liegt, daß du nicht herkommen kannst; **it's just a** ~ **of concentrating** es ist nur eine Sache der Konzentration; **then that's a different** ~: dann ist das was anderes; **if that's the** ~: wenn das so ist; **it is [not] the** ~ **that ...:** es trifft [nicht] zu *od.* stimmt [nicht], daß ...; **it seems to be the** ~ **that they have ...:** sie scheinen tatsächlich ... zu haben; **as is generally the** ~ **with ...:** wie das normalerweise bei ... der Fall ist; **such being the** ~: deshalb; **as the** ~ **may be** je nachdem; **in** ~ **...:** falls ...; für den Fall, daß ... *(geh.)*; **[just] in** ~ *(to allow for all possibilities)* für alle Fälle; **in** ~ **of fire/complaints/burst pipes/danger** bei Feuer/Reklamationen/Rohrbrüchen/Gefahr; **in** ~ **of emergency** im Notfall; **in** ~ **of the hostages' being released** falls die Geiseln freigelassen werden; **in the** ~ **of** bei; **in the** ~ **of New College** was das New College anbelangt; **in any** ~ *(regardless of anything else)* jedenfalls; **I don't need it in any** ~: ich brauche es sowieso nicht; **we don't want to go to the party and in any** ~ **it's raining** wir haben keine Lust, auf die Party zu gehen, und außerdem regnet es ja; **in no** ~ *(certainly not)* unter keinen Umständen; auf keinen Fall; **in that** ~: in diesem Fall; **in which** ~ **he would ...:** in diesem Fall *od.* dann würde er ...; **b)** *(Med., Police, Soc. Serv., etc., or coll.: person afflicted)* Fall, *der;* **a murder** ~: ein Mordfall; **he is a mental/psychiatric** ~: er ist ein Fall für den Psychiater; **this man is a dangerous** ~: dieser Mann ist gefährlich; **her son is a problem** ~: ihr Sohn ist ein Problemkind; **c)** *(Law)* Fall, *der; (action)* Verfahren, *das;* **which was that** ~ **five years ago?** welcher Fall war das vor fünf Jahren?; **the Dreyfus** ~: der Fall Dreyfus; die Dreyfusaffäre *(hist.)*; **the** ~ **for the prosecution/defence** die Anklage/Verteidigung; **put one's** ~: seinen Fall darlegen; **and that is our** ~: und damit beende ich meine Ausführungen; **d)** *(fig.: set of arguments)* Fall, *der; (valid set of arguments)* **you have no** ~ **there** das ist kein Argument; **there's a** ~ **for doing sth.** es gibt Gründe, die dafür sprechen, daß man etw. tut; **have a [good]** ~ **for doing sth./for sth.** gute Gründe haben, etw. zu tun/für etw. haben; **make out a** ~ **for sth.** Argumente für etw. anführen; **e)** *(Ling.)* Fall, *der;* Kasus, *der (fachspr.)*; **f)** *(fig. coll.) (comical person)* ulkiger Typ *(ugs.)*; *(comical woman)* ulkige Nudel *(ugs.)*

²case 1. *n.* **a)** Koffer, *der; (small)* Handkoffer, *der; (brief-*~*)* [Akten]tasche, *die; (for musical instrument)* Kasten, *der;* **violin** ~: Geigenkasten, *der;* **doctor's** ~: Arzttasche, *die;* **pen and pencil** ~: Federmäppchen, *das;* **b)** *(sheath)* Hülle, *die; (for spectacles, cigarettes)* Etui, *das; (for jewellery)* Schmuckkassette, *die;* Schmuckkästchen, *das;* **c)** *(crate)* Kiste, *die;* ~ **of oranges** Kiste [mit] Apfelsinen; **d)** *(glass box)* Vitrine, *die;* **[display-]**~: Schaukasten, *der;* **e)** *(cover)* Gehäuse, *das; (seed-vessel)* Hülle, *die; (of sausage)* Haut, *die; (of book)* Buchdeckel, *der;* **f)** *(Printing)* Schriftkasten, *der; see also* **lower case; upper case. 2.** *v. t.* **a)** *(box)* verpacken; **b)** *(sl.: examine)* ~ **the joint** sich *(Dat.)* den Laden mal ansehen *(ugs.)*

case: ~**-book** *n.* **a)** *(Law)* Sammlung von Rechtsfällen; **b)** *(Med.)* Sammlung von Krankheitsfällen; **c)** *(of social worker etc.; also fig.)* Fallsammlung, *die;* ~**-bound** *adj.* mit festem Einband *nachgestellt;* **be** ~**-bound** einen festen Einband haben; ~**-ending** *n. (Ling.)* Beugungsendung, *die;* Kasusendung, *die (fachspr.)*; ~**-harden** *v. t.* härten ‹*Metall*›; ~**-hardened** *(fig.)* abgebrüht; ~ **history** *n.* **a)** *(record)* [Vor]geschichte, *die;* **b)** *(Med.)* Krankengeschichte, *die;* ~**-knife** *n.* Fahrtenmesser, *das;* ~**-law** *n. (Law)* Fallrecht, *das;* ~**-load** *n.* Fälle *Pl.;* **he has a heavy** ~**-load, his** ~**-load is heavy** er hat sehr viele Fälle zu bearbeiten; **the [doctor's]** ~**-load** die Anzahl der Patienten; **share the [doctor's]** ~**-load** einen Teil der Patienten übernehmen

casement ['keɪsmənt] *n.* **a)** [Fenster]flügel, *der;* **b)** *(poet.: window)* Fenster, *das*

'casement window *n.* Flügelfenster, *das*

case: ~**-study** *n.* Fallstudie, *die;* ~**work**

n., no pl., no indef. art. [auf den Einzelfall bezogene] Sozialarbeit; Casework, *das (Psychol., Soziol.);* **~worker** *n.* [Einzelfälle betreuender] Sozialarbeiter

cash [kæʃ] **1.** *n., no pl., no indef. art.* **a)** Bargeld, *das;* **payment in ~ only** nur Barzahlung; **pay [in] ~, pay ~ down** bar zahlen; **we haven't got the ~:** wir haben [dafür] kein Geld; **be short of ~:** knapp bei Kasse sein *(ugs.);* **~ on delivery** per Nachnahme; **b)** *(Banking etc.)* Geld, *das;* **can I get ~ for these cheques?** kann ich diese Schecks einlösen?; **you may withdraw £50 in ~:** Sie können 50 Pfund in bar abheben; *see also* **discount 1. 2.** *v.t.* **a)** einlösen ⟨*Scheck*⟩; **b)** *(Bridge)* ausspielen [und den Stich machen] **~ in 1.** ['--] *v.t.* sich *(Dat.)* gutschreiben lassen ⟨*Scheck*⟩; auf die Bank bringen ⟨*Geld, Einnahmen*⟩; **~ in one's checks** *or* **chips** *(fig. coll.)* abkratzen *(salopp).* **2.** [-'-] *v.i.* **~ in on sth.** *(lit. or fig.)* von etw. profitieren

cash: **~-account** *n.* Kassekonto, *das (Buchf.);* **~ and 'carry** *n. Verkaufssystem, bei dem der Kunde bar bezahlt und die Ware selbst nach Hause transportiert;* cash and carry; **~-and-carry store** Cash-and-carry-Laden, *der;* **~-book** *n.* Kassenbuch, *das;* **~-box** *n.* Geldkassette, *die;* **~card** *n.* Geldautomatenkarte, *die;* **~ crop** *n. zum Verkauf bestimmtes landwirtschaftliches Erzeugnis;* **~ desk** *n. (Brit.)* Kasse, *die;* **~ dispenser** *n.* Geldautomat, *der*

cashew ['kæʃu:] *n.* **a)** *(nut) see* **cashew-nut; b)** *(tree)* Nierenbaum, *der (Bot.);* Cashewbaum, *der (Bot.)*

'cashew-nut *n.* Cashewnuß, *die*

'cash-flow *n. (Econ.)* Cash-flow, *der*

[1]**cashier** [kæ'ʃɪə(r)] *n.* Kassierer, *der*/Kassiererin, *die;* **~'s office** Kasse, *die*

[2]**cashier** *v.t.* entlassen; des Amtes entheben *(geh.); (Mil.)* [unehrenhaft] entlassen; kassieren *(veralt.)*

cashmere ['kæʃmɪə(r)] *n.* Kaschmir, *der;* **~ wool/sweater** Kaschmirwolle, *die*/Kaschmirpullover, *der*

cash: **~ payment** *n.* Barzahlung, *die;* **make ~ payment** bar bezahlen; **~point** *n.* Geldautomat, *der;* **~ price** *n.* Barzahlungspreis, *der;* **~ register** *n.* [Registrier]kasse, *die; (in shop also)* [Laden]kasse, *die;* **~ sale** *n.* Bargeschäft, *das*

casing ['keɪsɪŋ] *n.* Gehäuse, *das; (of projectile, cable, tyre)* Mantel, *der*

casino [kə'si:nəʊ] *n., pl.* **~s** Kasino, *das; (for gambling also)* Spielkasino, *das;* Spielbank, *die*

cask [kɑ:sk] *n.* Faß, *das*

casket ['kɑ:skɪt] *n.* **a)** *(box)* Schatulle, *die (veralt.);* Kästchen, *das;* **b)** *(Amer.: coffin)* Sarg, *der*

Caspian Sea [kæspɪən 'si:] *pr. n.* Kaspische Meer, *das;* Kaspisee, *der*

Cassandra [kə'sændrə] *n.* Kassandra, *die*

cassata [kæ'sɑ:tə] *n.* Cassata, *die od. das*

cassava [kə'sɑ:və] *n.* **a)** *(plant)* Maniok, *der;* **b)** *(flour)* Tapioka, *die*

casserole ['kæsərəʊl] **1.** *n.* **a)** *(vessel)* Schmortopf, *der; (oval also)* Bräter, *der; (with long handle)* Kasserolle, *die;* **b)** *(food)* Schmortopf, *der.* **2.** *v.t.* schmoren

cassette [kə'set, kæ'set] *n.* Kassette, *die;* **miniature film ~:** Kleinbildkassette, *die*

cassette: **~-deck** Kassettendeck, *das;* **~ recorder** *n.* Kassettenrecorder, *der*

cassock ['kæsək] *n. (Eccl.)* Soutane, *die*

cast [kɑ:st] **1.** *v.t.,* **cast a)** *(throw)* werfen; **~ sth. adrift** etw. abtreiben lassen; **~ loose** losmachen; **he ~ loose from his family** *(fig.)* er löste sich von seiner Familie; **~ sth. ashore** etw. an Land spülen; **~ an** *or* **one's eye over sth.** einen Blick auf etw. *(Akk.)* werfen; **~ one's eyes round a room** seine Augen *od.* Blicke durch ein Zimmer schweifen lassen; **~ light on sth.** Licht auf etw. *(Akk.)* werfen; *(fig.)* Licht in etw. *(Akk.)* bringen; **~ the line/net** die Angel[schnur]/das Netz auswerfen; **~ a shadow [on/over sth.]** *(lit. or fig.)* einen Schatten [auf etw. *(Akk.)*] werfen; **~ a spell on sb./sth.** jmdn./etw. verzaubern; **~ a vote** seine Stimme abgeben; **~ one's mind back to sth.** an etw. *(Akk.)* zurückdenken; sich an etw. *(Akk.)* erinnern; **~ sth. to the winds** *(fig.)* etw. über Bord werfen *(fig.); see also* **aspersion; lot g; b)** *(shed)* verlieren ⟨*Haare, Winterfell*⟩; abwerfen ⟨*Gehörn, Blätter, Hülle*⟩; **the snake ~s its skin** die Schlange häutet sich; **a horse ~s a shoe** ein Pferd verliert ein Hufeisen; **~ aside** *(fig.)* beiseite schieben ⟨*Vorschlag*⟩; ablegen ⟨*Vorurteile, Gewohnheiten*⟩; vergessen ⟨*Sorgen, Vorstellungen*⟩; fallenlassen ⟨*Freunde, Hemmungen*⟩; sich *(Dat.)* entgehen lassen ⟨*günstige Gelegenheit*⟩; **she ~ aside her books and the academic life** sie kehrte den Büchern und dem akademischen Leben den Rücken; **c)** *(shape, form)* gießen; **d)** *(calculate)* stellen ⟨*Horoskop*⟩; **e)** *(assign role[s] of)* besetzen; **~ Joe as sb./in the role of sb.** jmdn./jmds. Rolle mit Joe besetzen; **~ a play/film** die Rollen [in einem Stück/Film] besetzen. **2.** *n.* **a)** *(Med.)* Gipsverband, *der;* **b)** *(set of actors)* Besetzung, *die;* **c)** *(model)* Abdruck, *der;* **d)** *(throwing of missile etc., throw of dice)* Wurf, *der; (distance of throw)* **a stone's ~:** einen Steinwurf [weit]; **e)** *(Fishing) (throw of net)* Auswerfen, *das; (throw of line)* Wurf, *der;* **f)** *(twist)* **develop a ~:** sich verbiegen; **have a ~ in the** *or* **one's eye** [leicht] schielen; **g)** *(tinge)* Schimmer, *der;* **h)** *(quality)* Zuschnitt, *der;* **~ of mind** Gesinnung, *die;* **~ of features** *or* **countenance** Gesichtsschnitt, *der*

~ a'bout *v.i.* **~ about [to find** *or* **for sth.]** sich [nach etw.] umsehen

~ a'round *see* **~ about**

~ a'way *v.t.* **a)** wegwerfen; **b) be ~ away on an island** auf einer Insel stranden

~ 'down *v.t.* **be ~ down [by sth.]** [wegen etw.] niedergeschlagen sein

~ in *v.i.* **~ in one's lot with sb.** sich mit jmdm. zusammentun

~ 'off 1. *v.t.* **a)** *(abandon)* verlassen ⟨*Kind*⟩; aufgeben ⟨*früheres Leben*⟩; ablegen ⟨*alte Kleider*⟩; *(reject)* den Laufpaß geben (+ *Dat.*) *(ugs.);* **b)** *(Naut.)* losmachen; **c)** *(Knitting)* abketten; **d)** *(Printing)* **~ off [the manuscript]** den Umfang [des Manuskripts] berechnen. **2.** *v.i. (Knitting)* abketten. *See also* **cast-off**

~ 'on *v.t. & i. (Knitting)* anschlagen

~ 'up *v.t.* **a)** *(add)* zusammenzählen; **b)** *(wash up)* an Land spülen

castanet [kæstə'net] *n., usu. in pl. (Mus.)* Kastagnette, *die*

castaway ['kɑ:stəweɪ] *n.* Schiffbrüchige, *der/die*

caste [kɑ:st] *n. (lit. or fig.)* **a)** Kaste, *die;* **b)** *no pl., no art. (class system)* Kastenwesen, *das; (social position)* soziale Stellung; **lose ~:** gesellschaftliches Ansehen einbüßen

castellated ['kæstəleɪtɪd] *adj.* **a)** *(castle-like)* schloßartig; **b)** *(battlemented)* mit Zinnen bewehrt

'caste mark *n.* Kastenzeichen, *das*

caster ['kɑ:stə(r)] *n.* **a)** *see* **castor; b)** *(Printing)* [Schrift]gießmaschine, *die*

castigate ['kæstɪgeɪt] *v.t. (punish)* züchtigen *(geh.); (criticize)* geißeln *(geh.)*

castigation [kæstɪ'geɪʃn] *n. (punishment)* Züchtigung, *die (geh.); (criticism)* Geißelung, *die (geh.)*

Castilian [kə'stɪlɪən] **1.** *adj.* kastilisch; *see also* **English 1. 2.** *n.* **a)** *(person)* Kastilier, *der*/Kastilierin, *die;* **b)** *(language)* Kastilisch, *das; see also* **English 2 a**

casting ['kɑ:stɪŋ] *n.* **a)** *(Metallurgy: product)* Gußstück, *das; (Art)* Abguß, *der;* **b)** *(Theatre, Cinemat.)* Rollenbesetzung, *die*

casting 'vote *n.* ausschlaggebende Stimme *(des Vorsitzenden bei Stimmengleichheit);* **the ~ rests with the manager** die [letzte] Entscheidung hat der Geschäftsführer

cast: **~ 'iron** *n.* Gußeisen, *das;* **~-iron** *adj.* gußeisern; *(fig.)* eisern ⟨*Wille, Konstitution, Magen*⟩; handfest, triftig ⟨*Grund, Entschuldigung*⟩; hieb- und stichfest ⟨*Alibi, Beweis*⟩; hundertprozentig ⟨*Garantie*⟩

castle ['kɑ:sl] **1.** *n.* **a)** *(stronghold)* Burg, *die; (mansion)* Schloß, *das;* **Windsor C~:** Schloß Windsor; **an Englishman's home is his ~:** für den Engländer ist sein Haus wie eine Burg; **~s in the air** *or* **in Spain** Luftschlösser; **b)** *(Chess)* Turm, *der.* **2.** *v.i. (Chess)* rochieren

'cast-off 1. *adj.* abgelegt. **2.** *n. in pl.* abgelegte Sachen; **she didn't want her friend's ~s** *(fig. joc.)* sie wollte nicht die abgelegten Liebhaber ihrer Freundin haben *(ugs.)*

castor ['kɑ:stə(r)] *n.* **a)** *(sprinkler)* Streuer, *der;* **b)** *(wheel)* Rolle, *die;* Laufrolle, *die (Technik)*

castor: **~ 'oil** *n.* Rizinusöl, *das;* Kastoröl, *das (Kaufmannsspr.);* **~ sugar** *n. (Brit.)* Raffinade, *die;* Kastorzucker, *der (selten)*

castrate [kæ'streɪt] *v.t.* **a)** kastrieren; *(fig.)* beschneiden ⟨*Macht*⟩; **b)** *(expurgate)* verstümmeln; kastrieren *(ugs. scherzh.)*

castration [kæ'streɪʃn] *n.* **a)** Kastration, *die; (fig.)* Beschneidung, *die;* **b)** *(expurgation)* Verstümmelung, *die*

castrato [kæ'strɑ:təʊ] *n., pl.* **castrati** [kæ'strɑ:ti:] *(Mus. Hist.)* Kastrat, *der*

casual ['kæʒjʊəl, 'kæzjʊəl] **1.** *adj.* **a)** ungezwungen; zwanglos; leger ⟨*Kleidung*⟩; beiläufig ⟨*Bemerkung*⟩; flüchtig ⟨*Bekannter, Bekanntschaft, Blick*⟩; unbekümmert, unbeschwert ⟨*Haltung, Einstellung*⟩; salopp ⟨*Ausdrucksweise*⟩; lässig ⟨*Auftreten*⟩; gemächlich ⟨*Schritt, Spaziergang*⟩; **I'm just here on a ~ visit** ich habe nur mal vorbeigeschaut *(ugs.);* **be ~ about sth.** etw. auf die leichte Schulter nehmen; **you can't be so ~ about timekeeping** du mußt es mit der Pünktlichkeit schon etwas genauer nehmen; **he's so ~ about his work** er nimmt seine Arbeit einfach nicht richtig ernst; **~ sex** Sex ohne feste Bindung; **b)** *(accidental)* zufällig; **by some ~ coincidence** durch Zufall. **2.** *n.* **a)** *in pl. (clothes)* Freizeitkleidung, *die;* **b)** *see* **casual labourer; c)** *see* **casual shoe**

casual: **~'earnings** *n. pl.* Nebeneinkünfte *Pl.;* **~ 'labour** *n., no pl.* Gelegenheitsarbeit, *die;* **~ 'labourer** *n.* Gelegenheitsarbeiter, *der*

casually ['kæʒjʊəlɪ, 'kæzjʊəlɪ] *adv.* **a)** ungezwungen; zwanglos; beiläufig ⟨*bemerken*⟩; flüchtig ⟨*anschauen*⟩; gemächlich ⟨*wandern, spazierengehen*⟩; lustlos ⟨*Problem anpacken*⟩; salopp ⟨*sich ausdrücken*⟩; leger ⟨*sich kleiden*⟩; **I glanced ~ at the headlines** ich überflog die Schlagzeilen; **I was ~ reading a book** ich blätterte in einem Buch; **he treats/approaches his work too ~:** er nimmt seine Arbeit zu wenig ernst; **b)** *(accidentally)* zufällig

casualness ['kæʒjʊəlnɪs, 'kæzjʊəlnɪs] *n., no pl.* Ungezwungenheit, *die;* Zwanglosigkeit, *die; (of remark)* Beiläufigkeit, *die*

casual 'shoe *n.* Freizeitschuh, *der*

casualty ['kæʒjʊəltɪ, 'kæzjʊəltɪ] *n.* **a)** *(injured person)* Verletzte, *der/die; (in battle)* Verwundete, *der/die; (dead person)* Tote, *der/die;* **b)** *(fig.)* Opfer, *das; (failure)* Versager, *der;* **c)** *no art. (hospital department)* Unfallstation, *die;* **work in ~:** in der Unfallstation arbeiten

casualty: **~ department** *n.* Unfallstation, *die;* **~ list** *n.* Verletztenliste, *die;* Liste der Getöteten/Gefallenen; **~ ward** *n.* Unfallstation, *die*

casuist ['kæʒjʊɪst, 'kæzju:ɪst] *n.* Kasuist, *der (Philos.)*

casuistry ['kæʒjʊɪstrɪ, 'kæzju:ɪstrɪ] *n.* Kasuistik, *die (Philos.)*

cat [kæt] *n.* **a)** Katze, *die;* **she-~** Kätzin, *die;*

[weibliche] Katze; **tom-~:** Kater, *der;* **be as nervous as a ~:** furchtbar ängstlich sein; **play ~ and mouse with sb.** Katz und Maus mit jmdm. spielen *(ugs.);* **when the ~'s away [the mice will play]** *(prov.)* wenn die Katze aus dem Haus ist, tanzen die Mäuse [auf dem Tisch]; **let the ~ out of the bag** *(fig.)* die Katze aus dem Sack lassen; **be like a ~ on hot bricks** wie auf glühenden Kohlen sitzen; **look like something the ~ brought in** *(fig.)* aussehen wie unter die Räuber gefallen; **curiosity killed the ~** *(fig.)* sei nicht so neugierig; **[fight] like ~ and dog** wie Hund und Katze [sein]; **not a ~ in hell's chance** nicht die geringste Chance; **we'll wait and see which way the ~ jumps** *(fig.)* wir warten ab, bis wir sehen, wie der Hase läuft *(ugs.);* **a ~ may look at a king** *(prov.)* das ist doch auch nur ein Mensch; **enough to make a ~ laugh** zum Schreien [komisch] *(ugs.);* **put the ~ among the pigeons** *(fig.)* für Aufregung sorgen; **it would be putting the ~ among the pigeons** es würde einigen Aufruhr verursachen; **rain ~s and dogs** in Strömen regnen; **no room to swing a ~** *(fig.)* kaum Platz zum Umdrehen; **has the ~ got your tongue?** hast du die Sprache verloren?; **b)** *(coll. derog.: malicious woman)* Biest, *das; (sl.: person)* Typ, *der; (sl.: jazz enthusiast)* Jazzfan, *der;* **c)** *(Zool.: member of genus Felis)* Katze, *die;* **the [great] Cats** die Großkatzen; **the ~ family** die Familie der Katzen; **d)** *see* **cat-o'-nine-tails**

cataclysm ['kætəklɪzm] *n.* [Natur]katastrophe, *die;* Kataklysmus, *der (Geol.); (fig.: upheaval)* Umwälzung, *die*

cataclysmic [kætə'klɪzmɪk] *adj.* katastrophal; verheerend; *(fig.)* umwälzend; dramatisch ‹*Umwälzung*›

catacomb ['kætəku:m, 'kætəkəʊm] *n.* **a)** Katakombe, *die;* **b)** *(cellar)* Keller[raum], *der*

catafalque ['kætəfælk] *n.* Katafalk, *der; (movable)* Leichenwagen, *der*

Catalan ['kætəlæn] **1.** *adj.* katalanisch; *see also* **English 1. 2.** *n.* **a)** *(person)* Katalane, *der/*Katalanin, *die;* **b)** *(language)* Katalanisch, *das; see also* **English 2 a**

catalog, cataloger *(Amer.) see* **catalogue, cataloguer**

catalogue ['kætəlɒg] **1.** *n.* Katalog, *der;* **subject ~:** Sachkatalog, *der (Buchw.).* **2.** *v. t.* katalogisieren

cataloguer ['kætəlɒgə(r)] *n.* Bearbeiter/Bearbeiterin des Katalogs

Catalonia [kætə'ləʊnɪə] *pr. n.* Katalonien *(das)*

catalyse ['kætəlaɪz] *v. t. (Chem.; also fig.)* katalysieren

catalysis [kə'tælɪsɪs] *n., pl.* **catalyses** [kə'tælɪsi:z] *(Chem.)* Katalyse, *die*

catalyst ['kætəlɪst] *n. (Chem.; also fig.)* Katalysator, *der;* **act as a ~:** als Katalysator wirken **(to** bei)

catalytic [kætə'lɪtɪk] *adj. (Chem.; also fig.)* katalytisch

catalytic con'verter *n. (Motor Veh.)* Katalysator, *der*

catalyze *(Amer.) see* **catalyse**

catamaran [kætəmə'ræn] *n. (Naut.)* Katamaran, *der*

cat-and-'dog *adj.* **lead a ~ life** wie Hund und Katze leben

catapult ['kætəpʌlt] **1.** *n.* Katapult, *das.* **2.** *v. t.* **a)** *(fling)* katapultieren; **they were ~ed into action** *(fig.)* sie wurden [plötzlich] zum Handeln gezwungen; **the tragedy ~ed us into the depths of despair** die Tragödie stürzte uns in tiefste Verzweiflung; **b)** *(launch)* katapultieren. **3.** *v. i. (be flung)* katapultiert werden

cataract ['kætərækt] *n.* **a)** Katarakt, *der;* Wasserfall, *der; (fig.)* Katarakt, *der;* **b)** *(Med.)* grauer Star; Katarakt[a], *die (fachspr.)*

catarrh [kə'tɑ:(r)] *n.* **a)** *(discharge)* Schleimabsonderung, *die;* **b)** *(inflammation)* Katarrh, *der (Med.)*

catastrophe [kə'tæstrəfɪ] *n.* Katastrophe, *die;* **end in ~:** in einer Katastrophe enden; **mean ~:** eine Katastrophe bedeuten

catastrophic [kætə'strɒfɪk] *adj.,* **catastrophically** [kætə'strɒfɪkəlɪ] *adv.* katastrophal

catatonia [kætə'təʊnɪə] *n. (Psych.)* Katatonie, *die*

catatonic [kætə'tɒnɪk] *adj. (Psych.)* katatonisch

cat: ~ burglar *n.* Fassadenkletterer, *der/*Fassadenkletterin, *die;* **~call 1.** *n.* ≈ Pfiff, *der;* **2.** *v. i.* ≈ pfeifen

catch [kætʃ] **1.** *v. t.,* **caught** [kɔ:t] **a)** *(capture)* fangen; *(lay hold of)* fassen; packen; **~ sb. by the arm** jmdn. am Arm packen *od.* fassen; **~ hold of sb./sth.** jmdn./etw. festhalten; *(to stop oneself falling)* sich an jmdm./etw. festhalten; **he caught hold of me by the throat** er packte mich an der Kehle; **b)** *(intercept motion of)* auffangen; fangen ‹*Ball*›; **he caught the door before it slammed** er hielt die Tür fest, bevor sie zuschlagen konnte; **the brambles kept ~ing our clothes** die Dornenranken verfingen sich immer wieder in unseren Kleidern; **~ a thread** einen Faden vernähen; **get sth. caught** *or* **~ sth. on/in sth.** mit etw. an/in etw. *(Dat.)* hängenbleiben; **I got my finger caught** *or* **caught my finger in the door** ich habe mir den Finger in der Tür eingeklemmt; **get caught on/in sth.** an/in etw. *(Dat.)* hängenbleiben; *see also* **breath a; c)** *(travel by)* nehmen; *(manage to see)* sehen; *(manage to hear)* bekommen ‹*Sender, Sendung*›; *(be in time for)* [noch] erreichen; [noch] kriegen *(ugs.)* ‹*Bus, Zug*›; [noch] erwischen *(ugs.)* ‹*Person*›; **did you ~ her in?** hast du sie zu Hause erwischt? *(ugs.);* **did you ~ the post?** bist du noch rechtzeitig zum Briefkasten gekommen?; **d)** *(surprise)* **~ sb. at/doing sth.** jmdn. bei etw. erwischen *(ugs.)*/[dabei] erwischen, wie er etw. tut *(ugs.);* **~ sb. unawares** jmdn. überraschen; **caught by a sudden fall of the dollar** vom plötzlichen Sturz des Dollars überrascht; **caught in a mist/thunderstorm** vom Nebel/Sturm überrascht; **I caught myself thinking how old she looked** ich ertappte mich bei dem Gedanken, wie alt sie doch aussah; **~ sb. in sth./somewhere** jmdn. in etw. *(Dat.)*/irgendwo antreffen; **you'll never ~ me in this pub again** in diesem Lokal siehst du mich nicht mehr; **~ me!/him!** das wirst du nicht erleben!; *see also* **act 1 b; ¹bend 3 b; ²hop 3 c; e)** *(become infected with, receive)* sich *(Dat.)* zuziehen *od. (ugs.)* holen; **~ sth. from sb.** sich bei jmdm. mit etw. anstecken; **~ [a] cold** sich erkälten/sich *(Dat.)* einen Schnupfen holen; *(fig.)* übel dran sein; **he caught this habit from his wife** *(fig.)* diese Angewohnheit hat er von seiner Frau geerbt *(ugs.);* **he caught that trick from his brother** *(fig.)* diesen Trick hat er von seinem Bruder; **you'll ~ a terrible scolding/beating** *etc.* **from your father** dein Vater wird dich furchtbar ausschimpfen/verprügeln *usw.;* **~ it** *(fig. coll.)* etwas kriegen *(ugs.);* **you'll ~ it from me** du kannst von mir was erleben *(ugs.); see also* **death a; f)** *(arrest)* **~ sb.'s gaze** jmds. Aufmerksamkeit erregen; **~ sb.'s attention/interest** jmds. Aufmerksamkeit erregen/jmds. Interesse wecken; **~ sb.'s fancy** jmdm. gefallen; jmdn. ansprechen; **~ the Speaker's eye** *(Parl.)* das Wort erhalten; **~ sb.'s eye** jmdm. auffallen; jmdn. auf sich *(Akk.)* aufmerksam machen; ‹*Gegenstand:*› jmdm. ins Auge fallen; *(be impossible to overlook)* jmdm. ins Auge springen; **g)** *(hit)* **~ sb. on/in sth.** jmdn. auf/in etw. *(Akk.)* treffen; **~ sb. a blow [on/in sth.]** jmdm. einen Schlag [auf/in etw. *(Akk.)*] versetzen; **h)** *(grasp in thought)* verstehen; mitbekommen; **did you ~ his meaning?** hast du verstanden *od.* mitbekommen, was er meint?; **~ the mood** die Stimmung einfangen; **~ sb.'s likeness** jmdn. treffen; **i)** *see* **~ out a. 2.** *v. i.,* **caught a)** *(begin to burn)* [anfangen zu] brennen; **b)** *(become fixed)* hängenbleiben; ‹*Haar, Faden:*› sich verfangen; **my coat caught on a nail** ich blieb mit meinem Mantel an einem Nagel hängen; **c) ~ at sb.'s sleeve** jmdn. am Ärmel zupfen. **3.** *n.* **a)** *(of ball)* **make [several] good ~es** [mehrmals] gut fangen; **make a ~ with one hand** mit einer Hand fangen; **b)** *(amount caught, lit. or fig.)* Fang, *der;* **you've made a great ~ as far as your house is concerned** *(fig.)* mit eurem Haus habt ihr das große Los gezogen; **sth. is no [great] ~** *(fig.)* etw. ist kein gutes Geschäft; **he was no ~[, matrimonially]** *(fig.)* er war keine gute Partie; **c)** *(trick, unexpected difficulty)* Haken, *der* **(in** an + *Dat.*); **there must be a ~ in it somewhere** da muß irgendwo ein Haken sein; **the ~ is that ...:** der Haken an der Sache ist, daß ...; **~-22** *(coll.)* Dilemma, *das;* **it's ~-22** *(coll.)* es ist ein Teufelskreis; **d)** *(contrivance)* Verschluß, *der; (of door)* Schnapper, *der;* **e)** *(Cricket etc.)* ≈ Fang, *der (Schlagball); Abfangen des Balles, das den Schlagmann aus dem Spiel bringt;* **miss a ~:** einen Ball nicht abfangen; **he is a good ~:** er kann gut fangen

~ 'on *v. i. (coll.)* **a)** *(become popular)* [gut] ankommen *(ugs.);* sich durchsetzen; **b)** *(understand)* begreifen; kapieren *(ugs.)*

~ 'out *v. t.* **a)** *(Cricket etc.) durch Abfangen des Balles aus dem Spiel bringen;* **b)** *(detect in mistake etc.)* [bei einem Fehler] ertappen; **it's not easy to ~ him out** man kann ihm nicht leicht etwas am Zeug flicken *(ugs.);* **he was caught out on a point of form** er stolperte über eine Formsache; **c)** *(take unawares)* erwischen *(ugs.)*

~ 'up 1. *v. t.* **a)** *(reach)* **~ sb. up** jmdn. einholen; *(in quality, skill)* mit jmdm. mitkommen; **b)** *(absorb)* **be caught up in sth.** in etw. *(Dat.)* [völlig] aufgehen; **they were completely caught up in each other** sie waren nur mit sich [selbst] beschäftigt; **c)** *(snatch)* packen; **sth. gets caught up in sth.** etw. verfängt sich in etw. *(Dat.).* **2.** *v. i. (get level)* **~ up** einholen; **~ up with sb.** *(in quality, skill)* mit jmdm. mitkommen; **~ up on sth.** etw. nachholen; **I'm longing to ~ up on your news** ich bin gespannt, was für Neuigkeiten du hast

catch: ~-all *n.* Sammelplatz, *der; (fig.)* Auffangbecken, *das;* **~-all term** Allerweltswort, *das;* **~-as-~-'can** *n.* Catch-as-catch-can, *das;* **play ~-as-~-can** keine Rücksicht nehmen; **~ crop** *n. (Agric.)* Zwischenfrucht, *die*

catcher ['kætʃə(r)] *n.* **a)** Fänger, *der/*Fängerin, *die;* **b)** *(Baseball)* Fänger, *der*

catching ['kætʃɪŋ] *adj.* ansteckend

catchment area ['kætʃmənt eərɪə] *n. (lit. or fig.)* Einzugsgebiet, *das*

catch: ~penny *adj.* **~penny goods** Ramsch, *der (ugs.);* Tinnef, *der (ugs.);* **~-phrase** *n.* Slogan, *der;* **~-points** *n. pl. (Railw.)* Entgleisungsvorrichtung, *die;* **~ question** *n.* Fangfrage, *die;* **~word** *n.* **a)** *(headword)* Kolumnentitel, *der; (rhymeword)* Reimwort, *das; (cue)* Stichwort, *das; (slogan)* Schlagwort, *das;* **b)** *(at foot of page)* Kustos, *der*

catchy ['kætʃɪ] *adj.* **a)** eingängig; **a ~ song** ein Ohrwurm *(ugs.);* **b)** *(attractive)* reizvoll; ansprechend ‹*Farbe, Kleidung*›

'cat-door *n.* Katzentür, *die*

catechise *see* **catechize**

catechism ['kætɪkɪzm] *n. (Relig.)* **a)** *(book)* Katechismus, *der;* **Church C~:** Katechismus der Anglikanischen Kirche; **b)** *(instruction)* [Unterweisung im] Katechismus; *(fig.: questioning)* Befragung, *die;* **put sb.**

through a ~ *(fig.)* jmdn. ins Kreuzverhör nehmen *(fig.)*
catechize ['kætɪkaɪz] *v. t. (Relig.) (instruct)* katechisieren; *(fig.: question)* befragen
categorial [kætɪ'gɔ:rɪəl] *adj.* kategorial *(geh.)*
categorical [kætɪ'gɒrɪkl] *adj.* kategorisch; **he was quite ~ about it** er vertrat in dieser Angelegenheit eine recht entschiedene Haltung; **~ imperative** *(Philos.)* kategorischer Imperativ
categorically [kætɪ'gɒrɪkəlɪ] *adv.* kategorisch
categorize (categorise) ['kætɪgəraɪz] *v. t.* kategorisieren
category ['kætɪgərɪ] *n. (also Philos.)* Kategorie, *die*
cater ['keɪtə(r)] *v. i.* **a)** *(provide or supply food)* **~ [for sb./sth.]** [für jmdn./etw.] [die] Speisen und Getränke liefern; **~ for weddings** Hochzeiten ausrichten; **b)** *(provide requisites etc.)* **~ for sb./sth.** auf jmdn./etw. eingestellt sein; **~ for the needs of the individual** den Bedürfnissen des einzelnen gerecht werden; **~ for all ages** jeder Altersgruppe etwas bieten; **c) ~ to** *(pander)* nachgeben (+ *Dat.*); entgegenkommen (+ *Dat.*)
catercorner ['kætəkɔ:nə(r)], **catercornered** ['kætəkɔ:nəd] *(Amer.) adv., adj.* diagonal
caterer ['keɪtərə(r)] *n.* Lieferant von Speisen und Getränken; Caterer, *der (fachspr.)*; *(for party)* Partyservice, *der*
catering ['keɪtərɪŋ] *n.* **a)** *(trade)* **~ [business]** Gastronomie, *die;* **he is interested in ~ as a career** er interessiert sich beruflich für die Gastronomie; **b)** *(service)* Lieferung von Speisen und Getränken; Catering, *das (fachspr.)*; **who's responsible for the ~ in this hotel?** wer hat in diesem Hotel die Küche unter sich *(Dat.)*?; **do the ~:** für Speisen und Getränke sorgen; **~ firm/service** *see* **caterer**
caterpillar ['kætəpɪlə(r)] *n.* **a)** *(Zool.)* Raupe, *die;* **b) C~ [tractor] (P)** *(Mech.)* Raupenfahrzeug, *das*
caterpillar: ~ 'track, ~ 'tread *ns.* Raupen-, Gleiskette, *die*
caterwaul ['kætəwɔ:l] **1.** *v. i.* ‹*Katze:*› schreien, [laut] miauen; ‹*Sänger:*› jaulen *(abwertend)*. **2.** *n.* Katzengeschrei, *das; (of singer)* Gejaule, *das (abwertend)*; ≈ Katzenmusik, *die (ugs.)*
cat: ~fish *n.* Wels, *der;* **~-flap** *see* **catdoor; ~gut** *n.* Darm, *der; (Med.)* Katgut, *das*
catharsis [kə'θɑ:sɪs] *n., pl.* **catharses** [kə'θɑ:si:z] *(emotional outlet; also Psych.)* Katharsis, *die*
cathartic [kə'θɑ:tɪk] **1.** *adj.* **a)** *(Med.)* abführend; **~ medicine** Abführmittel, *das;* **b)** *(effecting catharsis; also Psych.)* kathartisch. **2.** *n. (Med.)* Abführmittel, *das*
Cathay [kə'θeɪ] *pr. n. (arch./poet.)* China; das Reich der Mitte *(dichter.)*
cathedral [kə'θi:drl] *n.* **~ [church]** Dom, *der;* Kathedrale, *die (bes. in England, Frankreich u. Spanien)*; **Cologne C~:** der Kölner Dom; **Rheims C~:** die Kathedrale von Reims
ca'thedral city *n.* Domstadt, *die*
Catherine ['kæθərɪn] *pr. n. (Hist., as name of ruler etc.)* Katharina *(die)*
'Catherine wheel *n.* **a)** *(firework)* Feuerrad, *das;* **b)** *see* **cart-wheel b; c)** *(Archit.)* Radfenster, *das;* Katharinenfenster, *das (selten)*
catheter ['kæθɪtə(r)] *n. (Med.)* Katheter, *der*
catheterize ['kæθɪtəraɪz] *v. t. (Med.)* katheterisieren
cathode ['kæθəʊd] *n. (Electr.)* Kathode, *die*
'cathode ray *n.* Kathodenstrahl, *der;* **cathode-ray tube** Kathodenstrahlröhre, *die;* Braunsche Röhre
catholic ['kæθəlɪk, 'kæθlɪk] **1.** *adj.* **a)** *(all-embracing)* umfassend; vielseitig ‹*Interessen*›; *(universal, universally applicable)* allgemein; universell ‹*Lehren*›; **b) C~** *(Relig.)* katholisch. **2.** *n.* **C~:** Katholik, *der*/Katholikin, *die*
Catholicism [kə'θɒlɪsɪzm] *n. (Relig.)* Katholizismus, *der*
cation ['kætaɪən] *n. (Phys.)* Kation, *das*
catkin ['kætkɪn] *n. (Bot.)* Kätzchen, *das*
cat: ~lick *n.* Katzenwäsche, *die;* **give oneself a ~lick** Katzenwäsche machen; **~like** *adj.* katzenartig; katzenhaft ‹*Art, Bewegung*›; **~-lover** *n.* Katzenfreund, *der*/-freundin, *die;* **~mint** *n. (Bot.)* Katzenminze, *die;* **~nap** *n.* Nickerchen, *das (ugs.)*; kurzes Schläfchen; **have** *or* **take a ~nap** ein Nickerchen machen *(ugs.)*; **~-nip** *n. (Bot.)* Katzenminze, *die;* **~-o'-'nine-tails** *n.* neunschwänzige Katze; **~'s-'cradle** *n.* **a)** *(game)* Fadenspiel, *das;* **b)** *(string-pattern) Figur beim Fadenspiel;* Fadenspannbild, *das;* **~'s-eye** *n.* **a)** *(stone)* Katzenauge, *das;* **b)** *(Brit.: reflector)* Bodenrückstrahler, *der (Verkehrsw.)*; **~'s-paw** *n.* **a)** *(person)* Handlanger, *der;* Werkzeug, *das (fig.)*; **b)** *(Naut.)* leichte Brise; **~'s pyjamas** *see* **~'s whiskers; ~'s-tail** *n. (Bot.)* Rohrkolben, *der;* **~suit** *n. (woman's)* hautenger einteiliger Hosenanzug; *(infant's)* Overall, *der;* **~'s 'whiskers** *n. pl. (sl.: the best)* **sb. is the ~'s whiskers** jmd. ist der/die Größte *(ugs.)*; **sth. is the ~'s whiskers** etw. ist spitze *(ugs.)*
cattery ['kætərɪ] *n.* Katzenpension, *die*
cattily ['kætɪlɪ] *adv.* gehässig
cattish ['kætɪʃ] *see* **catty**
cattle ['kætl] *n. pl.* Vieh, *das;* Rinder *Pl.;* **sheep and ~:** Schafe und Rinder; **700 head of ~:** 700 Rinder *od.* Stück Vieh
cattle: ~-breeding *n.* Rinderzucht, *die;* Viehzucht, *die;* **~-cake** *n. (Brit. Agric.) konzentriertes, gepreßtes Viehfutter;* ≈ Preßkuchen, *der;* **~-grid** *n. (Brit.)*, **~-guard** *n. (Amer.) mit einem Gitterrost bedeckte Grube als Durchlaß bei Weiden od. Gehegen;* **~man** *n.* **a)** *(tender)* Viehhüter, *der;* **b)** *(breeder)* Viehzüchter, *der;* **~-market** *n.* Viehmarkt, *der; (fig.)* Fleischbeschau, *die (ugs. scherzh.)*; **~-plague** *n.* Rinderpest, *die;* **~-rustler** *n. (Amer.)* Viehdieb, *der;* **~-truck** *n.* Viehtransporter, *der; (Railw.)* Viehwagen, *der*
catty ['kætɪ] *adj.* gehässig; **they're so ~ about their colleague** sie sprechen so gehässig über ihre Kollegin
'catwalk *n.* Laufsteg, *der*
Caucasia [kɔ:'keɪzɪə, kɔ:'keɪʒə] *pr. n.* Kaukasien *(das)*
Caucasian [kɔ:'keɪzɪən, kɔ:'keɪʒn] **1.** *adj.* kaukasisch. **2.** *n.* Kaukasier, *der*/Kaukasierin, *die*
Caucasus ['kɔ:kəsəs] *pr. n.* Kaukasus, *der*
caucus ['kɔ:kəs] *n. (Brit. derog., Amer.)* **a)** *(committee) den Wahlkampf und die Richtlinien der Politik bestimmendes regionales Gremium einer Partei;* **b)** *(party meeting) den Wahlkampf und die Richtlinien der Politik bestimmende Sitzung der regionalen Parteiführung*
caudal ['kɔ:dl] *adj. (Zool.)* **a)** *(of tail)* Schwanz-; *(at tail)* kaudal; **b)** *(of posterior of body)* Kaudal-
caught *see* **catch 1, 2**
cauldron ['kɔ:ldrən, 'kɒldrən] *n.* Kessel, *der*
cauliflower ['kɒlɪflaʊə(r)] *n.* Blumenkohl, *der*
cauliflower: ~ 'cheese *n. (mit Käse)* überbackener Blumenkohl; **~ 'ear** *n.* Blumenkohlohr, *das (Boxerjargon)*
caulk [kɔ:k] *v. t.* kalfatern *(Seemannsspr.)*; abdichten
causal ['kɔ:zl] *adj.* kausal; **~ connection** Kausalzusammenhang, *der;* **~ sentence** Kausalsatz, *der*
causality [kɔ:'zælɪtɪ] *n., no pl. (esp. Ling., Philos.)* Kausalität, *die;* **the law[s] of ~:** das Kausalitätsgesetz
causally ['kɔ:zəlɪ] *adv.* kausal
causation [kɔ:'zeɪʃn] *n.* **a)** *(causing)* Verursachung, *die;* **b)** *(relation of cause and effect)* Kausalität, *die*
causative ['kɔ:zətɪv] *adj.* **a)** verursachend; **b)** *(Ling.)* kausativ
cause [kɔ:z] **1.** *n.* **a)** *(what produces effect)* Ursache, *die* **(of** für *od. Gen.)*; *(person)* Verursacher, *der*/Verursacherin, *die;* **be the ~ of sth.** etw. verursachen; **b)** *(Philos.)* Ursache, *die;* **c)** *(reason)* Grund, *der;* Anlaß, *der;* **~ for/to do sth.** Grund *od.* Anlaß zu etw./, etw. zu tun; **no ~ for concern** kein Grund zur Beunruhigung; **where he saw ~ to do so** wo er es für nötig hielt; **show ~ why ...:** Gründe vorbringen, weshalb ...; **without good ~:** ohne triftigen Grund; **d)** *(object of support)* Sache, *die;* **he died in the ~ of peace** er starb für die Sache des Friedens *od.* für den Frieden; **take up sb.'s ~:** sich für jmds. Sache einsetzen; **freedom is our common ~:** Freiheit ist unser gemeinsames Anliegen *od.* Ziel; **be a lost ~:** aussichtslos sein; verlorene Liebesmühe sein *(ugs.)*; **make common ~ with sb.** mit jmdm. gemeinsame Sache machen; **[in] a good ~:** [für] eine gute Sache; **e)** *(Law) (matter)* Sache, *die; (case)* Fall, *der;* **he lost his ~ in the courts** er hat seinen Prozeß verloren. **2.** *v. t.* **a)** *(produce)* verursachen; erregen ‹*Aufsehen, Ärgernis*›; hervorrufen ‹*Verstimmung, Unruhe, Verwirrung*›; **b)** *(give)* **~ sb. worry/pain** *etc.* jmdm. Sorge/Schmerzen *usw.* bereiten; **~ sb. expense** jmdm. Ausgaben verursachen; **~ sb. trouble/bother** jmdm. Umstände machen; **c)** *(induce)* **~ sb. to do sth.** jmdn. veranlassen, etw. zu tun; **~ the alarm to go off** den Alarm auslösen; **~ sb. to lose concentration** jmdm. die Konzentration nehmen; **~ sb. to be miserable** bewirken, daß sich jemand elend fühlt; **~ sth. to be done** dazu führen, daß etw. getan wird
cause célèbre [kɔ:z seɪ'lebr] *n., pl.* **causes célèbres** [kɔ:z seɪ'lebr] Cause célèbre, *die (geh.)*; aufsehenerregender Fall
causeless ['kɔ:zlɪs] *adj.* grundlos
causeway ['kɔ:zweɪ] *n.* Damm, *der*
caustic ['kɔ:stɪk] **1.** *adj.* **a)** *(sarcastic)* kaustisch *(geh.)*; beißend ‹*Spott*›; bissig ‹*Bemerkung, Worte*›; spitz, scharf ‹*Zunge*›; **b)** *(burning)* ätzend; *(Chem.)* kaustisch; **~ potash/soda** Ätzkali, *das*/Ätznatron, *das.* **2.** *n. (substance)* Ätzmittel, *das;* Kaustikum, *das (Med.)*
caustically ['kɔ:stɪkəlɪ] *adv. (sarcastically)* bissig
cauterisation, cauterise *see* **cauteriz-**
cauterization [kɔ:təraɪ'zeɪʃn] *n. (Med.)* Kauterisation, *die*
cauterize ['kɔ:təraɪz] *v. t. (Med.)* kauterisieren; *(fig.)* abstumpfen
caution ['kɔ:ʃn] **1.** *n.* **a)** Vorsicht, *die;* **use ~:** vorsichtig sein; **b)** *(warning)* Warnung, *die; (warning and reprimand)* Verwarnung, *die;* **by way of a ~:** als Warnung; **act as a ~ to sb.** jmdm. eine Warnung sein; **just a word of ~:** noch ein guter Rat; **c)** *(dated coll.: sb. comical)* **be a ~:** ein Kasper sein *(ugs.)*. **2.** *v. t.* *(warn)* warnen; *(warn and reprove)* verwarnen **(for** wegen**)**; **~ sb. against sth./doing sth.** jmdn. vor etw. *(Dat.)* warnen/davor warnen, etw. zu tun; **~ sb. to/not to do sth.** jmdn. ermahnen, etw. zu tun/nicht zu tun
cautionary ['kɔ:ʃənərɪ] *adj.* [er]mahnend; warnend ‹*Beispiel*›
'caution money *n.* Kaution, *die;* **demand/pay ~:** eine Kaution verlangen/zahlen
cautious ['kɔ:ʃəs] *adj.* vorsichtig; *(circumspect)* umsichtig
cautiously ['kɔ:ʃəslɪ] *adv.* vorsichtig; *(circumspectly)* umsichtig
cavalcade [kævəl'keɪd] *n.* Kavalkade, *die*

(veralt., auch fig.); (convoy of cars) Konvoi, *der; (procession of cars)* Korso, *der*

cavalier [kævəˈlɪə(r)] **1.** *n.* **a)** Kavalier, *der;* **b)** *(Hist.: Royalist)* Kavalier, *der (Anhänger König Karls I.);* **c)** *(arch.: horseman)* Ritter, *der.* **2.** *adj. (offhand)* keck; *(arrogant)* anmaßend

cavalry [ˈkævəlrɪ] *n. constr. as sing. or pl.* Kavallerie, *die; (soldiers in vehicles)* motorisierte Streitkräfte

cavalry: ~man [ˈkævəlrɪmən] *n., pl.* **~men** [ˈkævəlrɪmən] Kavallerist, *der;* **~ officer** *n.* Kavallerieoffizier, *der;* **~ regiment** *n.* Reiterregiment, *das;* **~ sword** *n.* Säbel, *der;* **~ twill** *n.* Kavallerietwill, *der*

¹cave [keɪv] **1.** *n.* Höhle, *die.* **2.** *v. t.* aushöhlen. **3.** *v. i.* Höhlen erforschen

~ ˈin *v. i.* einbrechen; *(fig.) (collapse)* zusammenbrechen; *(submit)* nachgeben. *See also* **cave-in**

²cave [ˈkeɪvɪ] *int. (sl.)* Achtung!; **keep ~:** Schmiere stehen *(salopp)*

caveat [ˈkævɪæt] *n. (warning)* Warnung, *die; (against repetition)* Mahnung, *die;* **~ emptor** [kævɪæt ˈemptɔ:(r)] Ausschluß der Gewährleistung

cave: ~-bear *n. (Zool.)* Höhlenbär, *der;* **~-dweller** *n.* Höhlenbewohner, *der; (fig.)* Wilde, *der;* **~-in** *n.* Einsturz, *der;* **~-man** *see* **~-dweller; ~-painting** *n.* Höhlenmalerei, *die*

caver [ˈkeɪvə(r)] *n.* Höhlenforscher, *der*

cavern [ˈkævən] *n. (cave, lit. or fig.)* Höhle, *die; (artificial)* Kaverne, *die*

cavernous [ˈkævənəs] *adj. (like a cavern)* höhlenartig; herzhaft ‹*Gähnen*›; *(full of caverns)* reich an Höhlen

caviare (caviar) [ˈkævɪɑ:(r), kævɪˈɑ:(r)] *n.* Kaviar, *der;* **it is ~ to the general** *(fig.)* das ist Perlen vor die Säue geworfen *(ugs.)*

cavil [ˈkævɪl] **1.** *v. i., (Brit.)* **-ll-** kritteln *(abwertend);* **~ at/about sth.** etw. bekritteln *(abwertend).* **2.** *n.* unsachlicher Anwurf

caving [ˈkeɪvɪŋ] *n.* Höhlenforschung, *die*

cavity [ˈkævɪtɪ] *n.* Hohlraum, *der; (in tooth)* Loch, *das;* **nasal/oral/uterine ~:** Nasen-/Mund-/Gebärmutterhöhle, *die*

ˈcavity wall *n. (Building)* Hohlmauer, *die*

cavort [kəˈvɔ:t] *v. i. (sl.)* **~ [about *or* around]** herumtollen *(ugs.)*

caw [kɔ:] **1.** *n.* Krächzen, *das.* **2.** *v. i.* krächzen

cay [keɪ] *n.* Riff, *das*

cayenne [keɪˈen] *n.* **~ [ˈpepper]** Cayennepfeffer, *der*

cayman [ˈkeɪmən] *n. (Zool.)* Kaiman, *der*

CB *abbr.* **a) Companion [of the Order] of the Bath** *Mitglied der 3. Klasse des Bathordens;* **b) citizens' band** CB

CBE *abbr.* **Commander [of the Order] of the British Empire** *Träger des Ordens des British Empire 3. Klasse*

CBI *abbr.* **Confederation of British Industry** *britischer Unternehmerverband*

cc [si:ˈsi:] *abbr.* **cubic centimetre(s)** cm^3

CD *abbr.* **a) civil defence; b) Corps Diplomatique** CD; **c) compact disc** CD; **CD player** CD-Spieler, *der*

Cdr. *abbr.* **commander b** Kdt

CE *abbr.* **a) Church of England; b) civil engineer; c) Common Era**

cease [si:s] **1.** *v. i.* aufhören; **he never ~d in his efforts** er gab seine Bemühungen nie auf; **when the storm ~d** als der Sturm sich legte; **~ from sth./from doing sth.** mit etw. aufhören/aufhören, etw. zu tun; **without ceasing** ununterbrochen. **2.** *v. t.* **a)** *(stop)* aufhören; **~ doing** *or* **to do sth.** aufhören, etw. zu tun; **~ to understand** nicht mehr verstehen; **sth. has ~d to exist** etw. existiert *od.* besteht nicht mehr; **we have ~d manufacturing tyres** wir stellen keine Reifen mehr her; **it never ~s to amaze me** ich kann nur immer darüber staunen; **b)** *(end)* aufhören mit; einstellen ‹*Bemühungen, Versuche*›; **~ ˈfire** *(Mil.)* das Feuer einstellen. **3.** *n.* **without ~:** ununterbrochen; ohne Unterbrechung

ˈcease-fire *n.* Waffenruhe, *die; (signal)* Befehl zur Feuereinstellung

ceaseless [ˈsi:slɪs] *adj.* endlos; unaufhörlich ‹*Anstrengung*›; ständig ‹*Wind, Regen, Lärm*›

ceaselessly [ˈsi:slɪslɪ] *adv.* unaufhörlich; endlos ‹*streiten*›

cedar [ˈsi:də(r)] *n.* **a)** Zeder, *die;* **~ of Lebanon** Libanonzeder, *die;* **b)** *see* **cedar-wood**

ˈcedar-wood *n.* Zedernholz, *das*

cede [si:d] *v. t. (surrender)* abtreten ‹*Land, Rechte*› **(to** *Dat.,* an + *Akk.*); einräumen ‹*Privilegien*› **(to** *Dat.*); *(grant)* überlassen ‹*Land*› **(to** *Dat.*); zugestehen ‹*Rechte*› **(to** *Dat.*)

cedilla [sɪˈdɪlə] *n. (Ling.)* Cedille, *die*

Ceefax, (P) [ˈsi:fæks] *n. (Brit.)* Bildschirmtextdienst der BBC

ceilidh [ˈkeɪlɪ] *n. (Scot., Ir.) zwangloses Beisammensein zum Musizieren, Tanzen, Singen und Geschichtenerzählen*

ceiling [ˈsi:lɪŋ] *n.* **a)** Decke, *die; see also* **hit 1 b; b)** *(upper limit)* Maximum, *das;* **~ temperature** maximale Temperatur; **c)** *(Aeronaut.)* Gipfelhöhe, *die;* **d)** *(Meteorol.)* **[cloud] ~:** Wolkenuntergrenze, *die; (height)* Wolkenhöhe, *die*

celandine [ˈseləndaɪn] *n. (Bot.)* **a) [greater] ~:** [Großes] Schöllkraut; **b) [lesser] ~:** Scharbockskraut, *das*

celebrant [ˈselɪbrənt] *n. (Eccl.)* Zelebrant, *der*

celebrate [ˈselɪbreɪt] **1.** *v. t.* **a)** *(observe)* feiern; **b)** *(Eccl.)* zelebrieren, lesen ‹*Messe*›; **the wedding was ~d in St Paul's** die Hochzeit fand in St Paul's statt; **c)** *(extol)* verherrlichen. **2.** *v. i.* **a)** feiern; **b)** *(officiate at Eucharist)* die Eucharistie *od.* das Abendmahl feiern

celebrated [ˈselɪbreɪtɪd] *adj.* gefeiert, berühmt ‹*Person*›; berühmt ‹*Gebäude, Werk usw.*›

celebration [selɪˈbreɪʃn] *n.* **a)** *(observing)* Feiern, *das; (party etc.)* Feier, *die;* **in ~ of** aus Anlaß (+ *Gen.*); *(with festivities)* zur Feier (+ *Gen.*); **the ~ of Easter** *etc.* das Feiern *od.* Begehen des Osterfestes *usw.*; **the ~ on her birthday** ihre Geburtstagsfeier; **the Coronation ~s** die Feierlichkeiten anläßlich der Krönung; **this calls for a ~!** das muß gefeiert werden!; **b)** *(performing)* **the ~ of the wedding/christening** die Trauung[szeremonie]/Taufe; **the ~ of Communion** die Feier der Kommunion; **c)** *(extolling)* Verherrlichung, *die*

celebratory [ˈselɪbreɪtərɪ] *adj.* feierlich; Fest‹*programm, -essen -trunk*›

celebrity [sɪˈlebrɪtɪ] *n.* **a)** *no pl. (fame)* Berühmtheit, *die;* **b)** *(person)* Berühmtheit, *die;* **that ~ of stage and cinema** der Star von Bühne und Leinwand

celeriac [sɪˈlerɪæk] *n.* [Wurzel-, Knollen]sellerie, *der od. die*

celerity [sɪˈlerɪtɪ] *n. (literary)* Schnelligkeit, *die*

celery [ˈselərɪ] *n.* [Bleich-, Stangen]sellerie, *der od. die*

celesta [sɪˈlestə] *n. (Mus.)* Celesta, *die*

celestial [sɪˈlestɪəl] *adj.* **a)** *(heavenly)* himmlisch; **~ realm** Himmelreich, *das;* **b)** *(of the sky)* Himmels-

celibacy [ˈselɪbəsɪ] *n., no art.* Zölibat, *das od. der (Rel.);* Ehelosigkeit, *die*

celibate [ˈselɪbət] **1.** *adj.* zölibatär *(Rel.);* ehelos; **remain ~:** im Zölibat leben *(Rel.);* ehelos bleiben. **2.** *n.* Zölibatär, *der (Rel.)*

cell [sel] *n.* **a)** *(also Biol., Electr.)* Zelle, *die;* **b)** *(enclosed cavity)* Pore, *die; (fig.: compartment of brain)* Gehirnzelle, *die*

cellar [ˈselə(r)] *n.* Keller, *der; (wine storage-place, stock of wine)* [Wein]keller, *der;* **they keep a good ~:** sie haben einen guten Weinkeller

cellist [ˈtʃelɪst] *n. (Mus.)* Cellist, *der*/Cellistin, *die*

cello [ˈtʃeləʊ] *n., pl.* **~s** *(Mus.)* Cello, *das*

Cellophane, cellophane, (P) [ˈseləfeɪn] *n.* Cellophan ⓦⓩ, *das*

cellular [ˈseljʊlə(r)] *adj.* **a)** porös ‹*Mineral, Gestein, Substanz*›; *(Biol.: of cells)* zellular; Zell-; **~ plant** Lagerpflanze, *die;* Zellenpflanze, *die (veralt.);* **b)** *(with open texture)* luftdurchlässig; atmungsaktiv *(Werbespr.)*

cellular: ~ phone *n.* Mobiltelefon, *das;* **~ ˈradio** *n.* Mobilfunk, *der*

cellule [ˈselju:l] *n. (Anat.)* kleine Zelle; Cellula, *die (fachspr.)*

cellulitis [seljʊˈlaɪtɪs] *n. (Med.)* Zellulitis, *die;* Zellgewebsentzündung, *die*

celluloid [ˈseljʊlɔɪd] *n.* **a)** Zelluloid, *das;* **b)** *(cinema films)* Kino, *das;* **~ hero** Leinwandheld, *der*

cellulose [ˈseljʊləʊs, ˈseljʊləʊz] *n.* **a)** *(Chem.)* Zellulose, *die;* **b)** *in popular use* **~ [lacquer]** Lack, *der;* **~ finish** Lackierung, *die*

Celsius [ˈselsɪəs] *adj.* Celsius; **~ scale** Celsiusskala, *die*

Celt [kelt, selt] *n.* Kelte, *der*/Keltin, *die*

celt [selt] *n. (Archaeol.)* Kelt, *der*

Celtic [ˈkeltɪk, ˈseltɪk] **1.** *adj.* keltisch. **2.** *n.* Keltisch, *das*

Celtic: ~ ˈcross *n.* Radkreuz, *das;* **~ ˈfringe** *n. keltische Randgebiete [Großbritanniens]*

cement [sɪˈment] **1.** *n.* **a)** *(Building)* Zement, *der; (mortar)* [Zement]mörtel, *der;* **b)** *(sticking substance)* Klebstoff, *der; (for mending broken vases etc. also)* Kitt, *der; (fig.)* Band, *das;* Kitt, *der.* **2.** *v. t.* **a)** *(unite with binder)* mit Zement/Mörtel zusammenfügen; *(stick together)* zusammenkleben; *(fig.)* zusammenkitten; zementieren ‹*Freundschaft, Beziehung*›; **b)** *(apply cement to)* zementieren/mörteln

cemetery [ˈsemɪtərɪ] *n.* Friedhof, *der*

C. Eng. *abbr.* **chartered engineer**

cenotaph [ˈsenətɑ:f, ˈsenətæf] *n.* Kenotaph, *das;* Zenotaph, *das;* **the C~** *(Brit.) Mahnmal in London für die Gefallenen der beiden Weltkriege*

censer [ˈsensə(r)] *n.* Rauchfaß, *das*

censor [ˈsensə(r)] **1.** *n.* **a)** *(also Roman Hist.)* Zensor, *der;* **get past the ~s** durch die Zensur kommen; **b)** *(judge)* Kritiker, *der;* **c)** *(Psych.)* Zensur, *die.* **2.** *v. t.* **a)** zensieren; **b)** *(make changes in)* abändern

censorious [senˈsɔ:rɪəs] *adj.* [übertrieben] kritisch; [übertrieben] scharf ‹*Kritik, Kritiker*›; **be ~ of sb./sth.** jmdn./etw. scharf kritisieren

censorship [ˈsensəʃɪp] *n.* Zensur, *die*

censure [ˈsenʃə(r)] **1.** *n.* Tadel, *der;* **~ of sth.** Tadel für etw.; **propose a vote of ~:** einen Tadelsantrag stellen. **2.** *v. t.* tadeln

census [ˈsensəs] *n.* Zählung, *die;* **[national] ~:** Volkszählung, *die;* Zensus, *der*

cent [sent] *n.* Cent, *der;* **I don't** *or* **couldn't care a ~ about sth.** *(coll.)* etw. ist mir völlig egal *(ugs.)*

cent. *abbr.* **century** Jh.

centaur [ˈsentɔ:(r)] *n. (Mythol.)* Zentaur, *der;* Kentaur, *der*

centenarian [sentɪˈneərɪən] **1.** *adj.* hundertjährig; *(over 100 years old)* mehr als hundert Jahre alt. **2.** *n.* Hundertjährige, *der/die; (over 100 years old)* über Hundertjährige, *der/die;* **he/she lived to be a ~:** er/sie wurde hundert Jahre alt/über hundert Jahre alt

centenary [senˈti:nərɪ, senˈtenərɪ] **1.** *adj.* **~ celebrations/festival** Hundertjahrfeier, *die.* **2.** *n.* Hundertjahrfeier, *die; (birthday)* 100. Geburtstag

centennial [senˈtenɪəl] **1.** *adj. (100th)* hundertst...; *(lasting 100 years)* hundertjährig; *(occurring every 100 years)* Jahrhundert-. **2.** *n. see* **centenary 2**

center *(Amer.) see* **centre**

centering ['sentərɪŋ] *(Amer.) see* **centring**

centi- ['sentɪ] *pref.* **a)** *(one-hundredth)* Zenti-; **b)** *(one hundred)* Hundert-/hundert-

centigrade ['sentɪgreɪd] *see* **Celsius**

centime ['sɑ̃ti:m] *n.* Centime, *der*

centimetre *(Brit.; Amer.:* **centimeter***)* ['sentɪmi:tə(r)] *n.* Zentimeter, *der*

centipede ['sentɪpi:d] *n.* Hundertfüßer, *der (Zool.);* ≈ Tausendfüßler, *der*

central ['sentrl] **1.** *adj.* zentral; **be ~ to sth.** von zentraler Bedeutung für etw. sein; **in ~ London** im Zentrum von London; **in a ~ situation** in zentraler Lage; **the ~ part** *or* **portion of the apple/the earth** das Innere des Apfels/der Erde; **the ~ part of the town** das Zentrum der Stadt. **2.** *n., no art. (Amer.)* Vermittlung, *die;* **call ~:** die Vermittlung anrufen

Central: ~ African Re'public *pr. n.* Zentralafrikanische Republik; **~ A'merica** *pr. n.* Mittelamerika *(das);* **~ A'merican 1.** *adj.* mittelamerikanisch; **2.** *n.* Mittelamerikaner, *der*/-amerikanerin, *die;* **~ 'Europe** *pr. n.* Mitteleuropa *(das);* **~ Euro'pean 1.** *adj.* mitteleuropäisch; **2.** *n.* Mitteleuropäer, *der*/-europäerin, *die;* **c~ 'heating** *n.* Zentralheizung, *die*

centralisation, centralise *see* **centraliz-**

centralization [sentrəlaɪ'zeɪʃn] *n.* Zentralisierung, *die*

centralize ['sentrəlaɪz] *v.t.* zentralisieren; **~ records** Unterlagen zentral erfassen

central 'locking *n. (Motor Veh.)* Zentralverriegelung, *die*

centrally ['sentrəlɪ] *adv.* **a)** *(in centre)* zentral; **b)** *(in leading place)* an zentraler Stelle

central: ~ 'nervous system *n. (Anat., Zool.)* Zentralnervensystem, *das;* **~ processing unit** *n. (Computing)* Zentraleinheit, *die;* **~ reser'vation** *n.* Mittelstreifen, *der;* **~ 'station** *n. (Railw.)* Hauptbahnhof, *der*

centre ['sentə(r)] *(Brit.)* **1.** *n.* **a)** Mitte, *die; (of circle, globe)* Mitte, *die;* Zentrum, *das;* Mittelpunkt, *der;* **be the ~ of attention** im Mittelpunkt des Interesses stehen; **be in the ~ of things** im Brennpunkt des Geschehens sein; **b)** *(of rotation)* Drehpunkt, *der; (in lathe etc.)* Spitzdocke, *die (Technik);* **c)** *(nucleus)* Zentrum, *das;* **d)** *(serving an area)* Zentrum, *das;* **university careers ~:** Studienberatung, *die;* **e)** *(filling of chocolate)* Füllung, *die;* **f)** *(Polit.)* Mitte, *die;* **left of ~:** links von der Mitte; **g)** *(Sport: player)* Mittelfeldspieler, *der*/-spielerin, *die; (Basketball)* Center, *der; (Football, Hockey: kick or hit)* Flanke, *die;* **he kicked/hit a ~:** er schlug eine Flanke [nach innen]; **h) ~ of attraction** *(Phys.)* Zentrum der Anziehungskraft; **she likes to be the ~ of attraction** *(fig.)* sie steht gern im Mittelpunkt [des Interesses]; **sth. is a [great] ~ of attraction** *(fig.)* etw. ist eine [große] Attraktion; *see also* **gravity d; ²mass 1 f; i)** *see* **centring. 2.** *adj.* mittler...; **~ party** *(Polit.)* Partei der Mitte; **the ~ point of the circle/triangle** der Mittelpunkt des Kreises/Dreiecks. **3.** *v.i.* **~ in sth.** seinen Mittelpunkt in etw. *(Dat.)* haben; **~ on sth.** sich auf etw. *(Akk.)* konzentrieren; **the novel ~s on Prague** Prag steht im Mittelpunkt des Romans; **the discussion ~d on pollution** im Mittelpunkt der Diskussion stand die Umweltverschmutzung; **~ [a]round sth.** um etw. kreisen; sich um etw. drehen. **4.** *v.t.* **a)** *(place in ~)* in der Mitte anbringen; in der Mitte aufhängen ‹*Bild, Lampe*›; zentrieren ‹*Überschrift*›; **b)** *(concentrate)* **be ~d/~ sth. in a place** einen Ort zum Mittelpunkt haben/von etw. machen; **~ sth. on sth.** etw. auf etw. *(Akk.)* konzentrieren; **~ a novel [a]round sth.** etw. in den Mittelpunkt eines Romans stellen; **be ~d [a]round sth.** etw. zum Mittelpunkt haben; **c)** *(Football, Hockey)* [nach innen] flanken

centre: ~-bit *n.* Zentrumbohrer, *der (Technik);* **~-board** *n. (Naut.)* Schwert, *das;* **~ circle** *n. (Football, Basketball, Ice Hockey)* Mittelkreis, *der;* **~-fold** *n.* Faltblatt in der Mitte; **~-'forward** *n. (Sport)* Mittelstürmer, *der*/-stürmerin, *die;* **~-'half** *n. (Sport)* Mittelläufer, *der*/-läuferin, *die; (Football also)* Vorstopper, *der*/-stopperin, *die;* **~-piece** *n. (ornament)* ≈ Tafelschmuck, *der (in der Mitte der Tafel); (principal item)* Kernstück, *das;* **~ 'spread** *n.* Doppelseite in der Mitte; **~ three-'quarter** *n. (Rugby)* Innendreiviertel[spieler], *der*

centrifugal [sen'trɪfjʊgl] *adj.* zentrifugal; **~ force** Zentrifugalkraft, *die;* Fliehkraft, *die*

centrifuge ['sentrɪfju:dʒ] **1.** *n.* Zentrifuge, *die.* **2.** *v.t.* zentrifugieren

centring ['sentrɪŋ] *n. (Building)* Lehrgerüst, *das*

centripetal [sen'trɪpɪtl] *adj.* zentripetal; **~ force** Zentripetalkraft, *die*

centrism ['sentrɪzm] *n. (Polit. etc.)* gemäßigter Kurs; Zentrismus, *der (abwertend)*

centrist ['sentrɪst] *n. (Polit. etc.)* Vertreter/Vertreterin eines gemäßigten Kurses; Zentrist, *der*/Zentristin, *die (abwertend)*

centurion [sen'tjʊərɪən] *n. (Roman Hist.)* Zenturio, *der*

century ['sentʃərɪ] *n.* **a)** *(hundred-year period from a year ..00)* Jahrhundert, *das; (hundred years)* hundert Jahre; **~-old** hundertjährig; **centuries-old** jahrhundertealt; seit Jahrhunderten bestehend ‹*Gebäude usw.*›; **b)** *(Cricket)* hundert Läufe; *(more than a hundred)* über hundert Läufe; **c)** *(hundred)* Hundert, *das;* **a ~ of** hundert; **d)** *(Roman Hist.)* Zenturie, *die*

cephalopod ['sefələpɒd] *n. (Zool.)* Kopffüßer, *der*

ceramic [sɪ'ræmɪk] **1.** *adj.* keramisch; Keramik‹*vase, -kacheln*›. **2.** *n.* Keramik, *die*

ceramics [sɪ'ræmɪks] *n., no pl.* Keramik, *die*

Cerberus ['sɜ:bərəs] *n.* Zerberus, *der*

cereal ['sɪərɪəl] **1.** *n.* **a)** *(kind of grain)* Getreide, *das;* **b)** *(breakfast dish)* Getreideflocken *Pl.* **2.** *adj.* Getreide-; **~ grasses** Getreidepflanzen

cerebellum [serɪ'beləm] *n. (Anat.)* Kleinhirn, *das;* Cerebellum, *das (fachspr.)*

cerebral ['serɪbrl] *adj.* **a)** *(of the brain)* Gehirn‹*tumor, -blutung, -schädigung*›; zerebral *(Anat.);* **b)** *(appealing to intellect, intellectual)* intellektuell

cerebral 'palsy *n. (Med.)* Zerebralparese, *die;* zerebrale Kinderlähmung

cerebrate ['serɪbreɪt] *v.i. (literary)* nachdenken

cerebration [serɪ'breɪʃn] *n.* Gehirntätigkeit, *die*

cerebrum ['serɪbrəm] *n. (Anat.)* Großhirn, *das;* Cerebrum, *das (Anat.)*

ceremonial [serɪ'məʊnɪəl] **1.** *adj.* feierlich; *(prescribed for ceremony)* zeremoniell; **~ clothing** Festkleidung, *die.* **2.** *n.* Zeremoniell, *das*

ceremonially [serɪ'məʊnɪəlɪ] *adv.* feierlich; festlich ‹*gekleidet*›

ceremonious [serɪ'məʊnɪəs] *adj.* formell; förmlich ‹*Höflichkeit*›; *(according to prescribed ceremony)* zeremoniell

ceremoniously [serɪ'məʊnɪəslɪ] *adv.* formell; förmlich; **he bowed ~:** er verbeugte sich mit aller Förmlichkeit

ceremoniousness [serɪ'məʊnɪəsnɪs] *n., no pl.* Förmlichkeit, *die*

ceremony ['serɪmənɪ] *n.* **a)** Feier, *die; (formal act)* Zeremonie, *die;* **opening/prize-giving ~:** Eröffnungsfeier, *die*/Preisverleihung, *die;* **Christmas ~:** Weihnachtsfeier, *die;* **b)** *no pl., no art. (formalities)* Zeremoniell, *das;* **stand on ~:** Wert auf Förmlichkeiten legen; **without [great] ~:** ohne große Förmlichkeit. *See also* **master 1 f**

cerise [sə'ri:z, sə'ri:s] **1.** *adj.* kirschrot; cerise *(fachspr.).* **2.** *n.* Kirschrot, *das;* Cerise, *das (fachspr.)*

cerium ['sɪərɪəm] *n. (Chem.)* Cer, *das;* Zer, *das*

cert [sɜ:t] *n. (Brit. coll.)* **a) that's a ~:** das steht fest; **b)** *(as winner)* todsicherer Tip *(ugs.);* **be tipped as a/look [like] a ~:** als todsicherer Tip gelten; **c)** *(for appointment)* **be a ~ for the job/as the next party leader** die Stelle mit Sicherheit kriegen/mit Sicherheit der nächste Parteiführer werden; **his record makes him a ~ for the team** durch seine Leistung kommt er bestimmt in die Mannschaft

cert. [sɜ:t] *abbr.* **certificate**

certain ['sɜ:tn, 'sɜ:tɪn] *adj.* **a)** *(settled)* bestimmt ‹*Zeitpunkt*›; **b)** *(unerring)* sicher; *(sure to happen)* unvermeidlich; sicher ‹*Tod*›; **the course of the tragedy is ~:** der Verlauf der Tragödie steht fest; **for ~:** bestimmt; **I [don't] know for ~ when ...:** ich weiß [nicht] genau, wann ...; **I can't say for ~ that ...:** ich kann nicht mit Bestimmtheit sagen, daß ...; **make ~ of sth.** *(ensure)* für etw. sorgen; *(examine and establish)* sich einer Sache *(Gen.)* vergewissern; **we made ~ of a seat on the train** wir sicherten uns einen Sitzplatz im Zug; **we made ~ of a timely arrival** wir sorgten dafür, daß wir rechtzeitig ankamen; **the doctor had to make absolutely ~ of his diagnosis** der Arzt mußte in seiner Diagnose absolut sichergehen; **c)** *(indisputable)* unbestreitbar; **d)** *(confident)* sicher; **I'm not ~ of** *or* **about the colour** was die Farbe betrifft, da bin ich mir nicht sicher; **of that I'm quite ~:** dessen bin ich [mir] ganz sicher; **we're not ~ about emigrating** wir wissen nicht [recht], ob wir auswandern sollen/können; **are you ~ of the facts?** sind Sie Ihrer Sache sicher?; **she wasn't ~ about** *or* **of her love for him** sie war [sich *(Dat.)*] nicht sicher, ob sie ihn liebte; **be ~ that ...:** sicher sein, daß ...; **e) be ~ to do sth.** etw. bestimmt tun; **people were ~ to notice that she'd been crying** die Leute würden bestimmt merken, daß sie geweint hatte; **f)** *(particular but as yet unspecified)* bestimmt; **g)** *(slight; existing but probably not already known)* gewiß; **to a ~ extent** in gewisser Weise; **a ~ Mr Smith** ein gewisser Herr Smith

certainly ['sɜ:tnlɪ, 'sɜ:tɪnlɪ] **a)** *(admittedly)* sicher[lich]; *(definitely)* bestimmt; *(clearly)* offensichtlich; **b)** *(in answer)* [aber] gewiß; [aber] sicher; **[most] ~ 'not!** auf [gar] keinen Fall!

certainty ['sɜ:tntɪ, 'sɜ:tɪntɪ] *n.* **a) be a ~:** sicher sein; feststehen; **regard sth. as a ~:** etw. für sicher halten; **it isn't as much of a ~ now as it was** es ist jetzt nicht mehr ganz so sicher; **b)** *(absolute conviction, sure fact, assurance)* Gewißheit, *die;* **~ of** *or* **about sth./sb.** Gewißheit über etw./jmdn.; **~ that ...:** Gewißheit [darüber], daß ...; **with some ~:** mit einiger Sicherheit; **with ~, for a ~:** mit Sicherheit *od.* Bestimmtheit; **have the ~ of accommodation/sunshine** die Gewißheit haben, eine Unterkunft zu bekommen/daß die Sonne scheint

Cert. Ed. [sɜ:t 'ed] *abbr. (Brit.)* **Certificate in Education** ≈ *Berechtigung, an Grund- und Hauptschulen zu unterrichten*

certifiable ['sɜ:tɪfaɪəbl] *adj.* **a)** nachweislich; überprüfbar ‹*Ergebnis*›; **what makes a person ~ as dead?** wann kann jemand für tot erklärt werden?; **b)** *(as insane)* unzurechnungsfähig ‹*Person*›; **~ insanity** Unzurechnungsfähigkeit, *die*

certifiably ['sɜ:tɪfaɪəblɪ] *adv.* **~ [in]sane** [un]zurechnungsfähig

certificate 1. [sə'tɪfɪkət] *n.* Urkunde, *die; (of action performed)* Schein, *der; (Cinemat.) Einblendung zu Beginn eines Films, die angibt, für welches Publikum der Film freigegeben ist;* **doctor's ~:** ärztliches Attest; **teaching ~:** *Zeugnis über eine Ausbildung als Lehrer;* **~ of satisfactory performance** Zeugnis über zufriedenstellende Leistun-

gen; **he gained a ~ of merit in his exam** er bestand die Prüfung mit Auszeichnung. **2.** [sə'tɪfɪkeɪt] *v. t.* zulassen
Certificate of Secondary Edu'cation *n. (Brit. Hist.)* ≈ Volksschulabschluß, *der*
certification [sɜ:tɪfɪ'keɪʃn] *n.* Bestätigung, *die; (as teacher etc.)* Zulassung, *die; (as insane)* Bescheinigung der Unzurechnungsfähigkeit; *(certificate)* Bescheinigung, *die*
certified ['sɜ:tɪfaɪd] *adj.* **a)** zugelassen; **~ as unfit for human habitation** für unbewohnbar erklärt; **she's a ~ driving instructor** sie ist als Fahrlehrerin zugelassen; **state-~**: staatlich anerkannt; **this film is ~ as unsuitable for children** dieser Film ist als nicht jugendfrei eingestuft worden; **b)** *(declared insane)* unzurechnungsfähig
certified: ~ 'cheque *n. (Finance)* bestätigter Scheck; **~ 'mail** *n. (Amer.)* **send sth. by ~ mail** etw. per Einschreiben schicken; **an item of ~ mail** eine Einschreibesendung; **~ public ac'countant** *n. (Amer.)* Wirtschaftsprüfer, *der/*-prüferin, *die*
certify ['sɜ:tɪfaɪ] *v. t.* **a)** bescheinigen; bestätigen; *(declare by certificate)* berechtigen; **~ sb. as competent** jmds. Befähigung bescheinigen *od.* bestätigen; **this is to ~ that ...**: hiermit wird bescheinigt *od.* bestätigt, daß ...; **this building has been certified [as] Crown property** dieses Gebäude ist zum Eigentum der Krone erklärt worden; **certified as a true copy** beglaubigt; **b)** *(declare insane)* für unzurechnungsfähig erklären; **you ought to be certified** *(coll.)* du bist wohl verrückt *(salopp)*
certitude ['sɜ:tɪtju:d] *n.* Gewißheit, *die*
cervical [sɜ:'vaɪkl, 'sɜ:vɪkl] *adj. (Anat.)* **a)** *(of neck)* Hals-; zervikal *(Anat.)*; **b)** *(of cervix)* Gebärmutterhals-; zervikal *(Anat.)*; **~ smear test** [Gebärmutterhals]abstrich, *der*
cervix ['sɜ:vɪks] *n., pl.* **cervices** ['sɜ:vɪsi:z] *(Anat.: of uterus)* Gebärmutterhals, *der*
Cesarean, Cesarian *(Amer.) see* **Caesarean**
cessation [se'seɪʃn] *n.* Ende, *das; (interval)* Nachlassen, *das*
cession ['seʃn] *n.* Abtretung, *die*
cesspit ['sespɪt] *n.* **a)** *(refuse pit)* Abfallgrube, *die;* **b)** *see* **cesspool**
cesspool ['sespu:l] *n.* Senk- *od.* Jauchegrube, *die; (fig.)* Sumpf, *der;* **~ of iniquity** Sündenpfuhl, *der*
cetacean [sɪ'teɪʃn] *n. (Zool.)* Waltier, *das*
Ceylon [sɪ'lɒn] *pr. n. (Hist.)* Ceylon *(das)*
c.f. *abbr.* **carried forward** Vortrag *(Buchf.)*
cf. *abbr.* **compare** vgl.
CFC *abbr. (Chem., Ecol.)* **chlorofluorocarbon** FCKW, *das*
ch. *abbr.* **a) chapter** Kap.; **b) church** K.
cha [tʃɑ:] *see* [3]**char**
cha-cha ['tʃɑ:tʃɑ:] **1.** *n.* Cha-Cha-Cha, *der.* **2.** *v. i.* Cha-Cha-Cha tanzen
Chad [tʃæd] *pr. n.* Tschad, *der*
chafe [tʃeɪf] **1.** *v. t. (make sore)* aufscheuern; wund scheuern; *(rub)* reiben; *(fig.)* reizen; ärgern. **2.** *v. i.* ‹*Mensch, Tier:*› sich scheuern; ‹*Gegenstand:*› scheuern **([up]on, against** an + *Dat.*); **my skin ~s easily** meine Haut wird leicht wund; **~ at** *or* **under sth.** *(fig.)* sich über etw. *(Akk.)* ärgern
chafer ['tʃeɪfə(r)] *n. (Zool.)* [Mai]käfer, *der*
chaff [tʃɑ:f] **1.** *v. t.* **~ sb. about sth.** jmdn. wegen etw. necken *od. (ugs.)* mit etw. aufziehen. **2.** *v. i.* scherzen; flachsen *(ugs.)*. **3.** *n.* **a)** *(banter)* Neckerei, *die;* Flachserei, *die (ugs.)*; **enough of the ~!** genug geflachst! *(ugs.)*; **b)** *(husks of corn, etc.)* Spreu, *die; see also* **wheat**; **c)** *(cattle-food)* Häcksel, *das*
chaffinch ['tʃæfɪnʃ] *n. (Ornith.)* Buchfink, *der*
chagrin ['ʃægrɪn] **1.** *n.* Kummer, *der;* Verdruß, *der;* **much to sb.'s ~**: zu jmds. großen Kummer *od.* Verdruß. **2.** *v. t.* bekümmern; **be** *or* **feel ~ed at** *or* **by sth.** niedergeschlagen *od.* bekümmert sein wegen etw.
chain [tʃeɪn] **1.** *n.* **a)** Kette, *die; (fig.)* Fessel, *die; (of flowers)* Kranz, der; *(to stop skidding)* Schneekette, *die; (jewellery)* [Hals]kette, *die; (barrier)* Sperrkette, *die;* **~ of office** Amtskette, *die;* **be in ~s** in Ketten sein; **be/put on a ~**: an der Kette sein/an die Kette legen; **door-~**: Tür- *od.* Sicherungskette, *die;* **b)** *(series)* Kette, *die;* Reihe, *die;* **~ of events** Reihe *od.* Kette von Ereignissen; **~ of ideas** Gedankenkette, *die;* **~ of mountains** Gebirgskette, *die;* **~ of islands/lakes** Insel-/Seenkette, *die;* **~ of shops/hotels** Laden-/Hotelkette, *die;* **c)** *(measurement)* Chain, *das* (≈ *20 m*). **2.** *v. t. (lit. or fig.)* **~ sb./sth. to sth.** jmdn./etw. an etw. *(Akk.)* [an]ketten; **the dog must be kept ~ed up** der Hund muß an der Kette bleiben
chain: ~-armour *n.* Kettenpanzer, *der;* **~-gang** *n.* Trupp aneinandergeketteter Sträflinge; **~-letter** *n.* Kettenbrief, *der;* **~-link fencing** *n.* Maschendraht, *der;* **~-mail** *n.* Kettenpanzer, *der;* **~ re'action** *n. (Chem., Phys.; also fig.)* Kettenreaktion, *die;* **~-saw** *n.* Kettensäge, *die;* **~-smoke** *v. t. & i.* Kette rauchen *(ugs.)*; **~-smoker** *n.* Kettenraucher, *der/*-raucherin, *die;* **~-smoking** *n.* Kettenrauchen, *das;* **~-stitch** *n.* Kettenstich, *der;* **~ store** *n.* Kettenladen, *der (Wirtsch.)*
chair [tʃeə(r)] **1.** *n.* **a)** Stuhl, *der; (arm~, easy ~)* Sessel, *der;* **take a ~ [please]** bitte nehmen Sie Platz; **hairdresser's ~**: Frisierstuhl, *der;* **b)** *(professorship)* Lehrstuhl, *der; (of authority)* [Thron]sessel, *der;* **c)** *(at meeting)* Vorsitz, *der; (chairman)* Vorsitzende, *der/die;* **be** *or* **preside in/take the ~**: den Vorsitz haben *od.* führen/übernehmen; **leave** *or* **vacate the ~**: den Vorsitz abgeben; **address the ~**: den Vorsitzenden ansprechen. **2.** *v. t.* **a)** *(preside over)* den Vorsitz haben *od.* führen bei; **~ a meeting** den Vorsitz bei einer Versammlung haben *od.* führen; **the meeting was ~ed by ...**: den Vorsitz bei der Versammlung hatte *od.* führte...; **b)** *(Brit.: carry as victor) im Triumph tragen*
chair: ~-back *n.* Rückenlehne, *die;* **~-lift** *n.* Sessellift, *der*
chairman ['tʃeəmən] *n., pl.* **chairmen** ['tʃeəmən] **a)** Vorsitzende, *der/die;* Präsident, *der/*Präsidentin, *die;* **Mr/Madam C~**: Herr Vorsitzender/Frau Vorsitzende; **~ of the firm** Firmenleiter, *der;* **~'s report** Geschäftsbericht, *der; see also* **board 1 j**; **b)** *(master of ceremonies)* Conferencier, *der*
chairmanship ['tʃeəmənʃɪp] *n.* Vorsitz, *der*
chair: ~person *n.* Vorsitzende, *der/die;* **~woman** *n.* Vorsitzende, *die*
chaise [ʃeɪz] *n. (esp. Hist.)* Cab, *das;* **closed** *or* **covered ~**: Chaise, *die*
chaise longue [ʃeɪz 'lɒŋg] *n.* Chaiselongue, *die*
chalcedony [kæl'sedənɪ] *n. (Min.)* Chalzedon, *der*
chalet ['ʃæleɪ] *n.* Chalet, *das*
chalet 'bungalow *n. einem Chalet ähnliches, aber kleineres Haus mit tief heruntergezogenem Satteldach*
chalice ['tʃælɪs] *n. (poet./Eccl.)* Kelch, *der*
chalk [tʃɔ:k] **1.** *n.* Kreide, *die; (Geol.)* Oberkreide, *die;* **a drawing in ~/~s** eine Kreidezeichnung; **as white as ~**: kreidebleich; **by a long ~** *(Brit. coll.)* bei weitem; mit Abstand; **not by a long ~** *(Brit. coll.)* bei weitem nicht; **as different as ~ and cheese** so verschieden wie Tag und Nacht. **2.** *v. t.* mit Kreide schreiben/malen/zeichnen *usw.*
~ 'out *v. t.* [mit Kreide] zeichnen; **she had her future career ~ed out** *(fig.)* ihr künftiger Lebensweg war vorgezeichnet
~ 'up *v. t.* **a)** [mit Kreide] an- *od.* aufschreiben; **b)** *(fig.: register)* zu verzeichnen haben, für sich verbuchen können ‹*Erfolg*›; **c) ~ it up** *(fig.)* es auf die Rechnung setzen; **~ it up to sb.'s account** *(fig.)* es auf jmds. Rechnung setzen
chalk: ~-pit *n.* Kalksteinbruch, *der;* **~-stripe** *n. (Textiles)* Kreidestreifen, *der*
chalky ['tʃɔ:kɪ] *adj.* kalkig
challenge ['tʃælɪndʒ] **1.** *n.* **a)** *(to contest or duel; also Sport)* Herausforderung, *die* **(to** *Gen.*); **issue a ~ to sb.** jmdn. herausfordern; **b)** *(call for a response)* Herausforderung, *die* **(to** an + *Akk.*); **the main ~ facing us today** die größte Herausforderung *od.* Aufgabe für uns heute; **rise to a ~**: sich einer Herausforderung gewachsen zeigen; **pose a ~ to sb.** für jmdn. eine Herausforderung bedeuten; **c)** *(of sentry)* Aufforderung, *die; (call for password)* Anruf, *der;* **d)** *(person, task)* Herausforderung, *die;* **accept a ~**: sich einer Herausforderung *(Dat.)* stellen; **hold a ~ for sb.** einen Reiz für jmdn. haben; **e)** *(Law: exception taken)* Ablehnung, *die; (Amer.: to a vote)* Anfechtung, *die.* **2.** *v. t.* **a)** *(to contest etc.)* herausfordern; **~ sb. to a duel** jmdn. zum Duell [heraus]fordern; **~ sb. to a match/fight/debate** jmdn. zu einem Wettkampf/zum Kampf/zu einem Streitgespräch herausfordern; **~ the world record** versuchen, einen neuen Weltrekord aufzustellen; **b)** *(fig.)* auffordern; **~ sb.'s authority** jmds. Autorität *od.* Befugnis in Frage stellen; **c)** *(demand password etc. from)* ‹*Wachposten:*› anrufen; **d)** *(Law)* **~ a juryman** einen Geschworenen ablehnen; **~ [the] evidence [of a witness]** gegen die Aussage [eines Zeugen] Einspruch erheben; **e)** *(question)* in Frage stellen; anzweifeln; **~ sb.'s right to do sth.** jmds. Recht anzweifeln, etw. zu tun; **~ a belief/principle** eine Glaubenslehre/ein Prinzip in Frage stellen; **~ a verdict** ein Urteil kritisieren; **~ an opinion** einer Ansicht widersprechen; **f)** *(stimulate)* erregen
'challenge cup *n.* Wanderpokal, *der*
challenger ['tʃælɪndʒə(r)] *n.* Herausforderer, *der/*Herausforderin, *die*
challenging ['tʃælɪndʒɪŋ] *adj.* herausfordernd; fesselnd, faszinierend ‹*Problem*›; anspruchsvoll ‹*Arbeit*›
chamber ['tʃeɪmbə(r)] *n.* **a)** *(poet./arch.: room)* Gemach, *das (geh.)*; *(bedroom)* [Schlaf]gemach, *das (geh.)*; **b)** *in pl. (Brit.) (set of rooms)* Geschäftsräume *Pl.; (lawyer's rooms)* ≈ Praxisräume *Pl.; (judge's room)* ≈ Amtszimmer, *das;* **in ~s** ≈ im Amtszimmer; **c)** *(of deliberative or judicial body)* Sitzungszimmer, *das;* Sitzungssaal, *der;* **Upper/Lower C~** *(Parl.)* Ober-/Unterhaus, *das;* **d)** *(Anat.; in machinery, esp. of gun; artificial compartment)* Kammer, *die;* **~ of the heart/eye** Herz-/Augenkammer, *die. See also* **cloud chamber; horror 1 c**
'chamber concert *n.* Kammerkonzert, *das*
chamberlain ['tʃeɪmbəlɪn] *n.* Kammerherr, *der; (of corporation etc.)* [Stadt]kämmerer, *der;* **Lord Great C~ [of England]** *(Brit.) Hofbeamter mit bestimmten zeremoniellen Aufgaben;* **Lord C~ [of the Household]** *(Brit.) Vorsteher des königlichen Hofstaates*
chamber: ~maid *n.* Zimmermädchen, *das;* **~ music** *n.* Kammermusik, *die;* **C~ of 'Commerce** *n.* Industrie- und Handelskammer, *die;* **~ orchestra** *n.* Kammerorchester, *das;* **~-pot** *n.* Nachttopf, *der*
chameleon [kə'mi:lɪən] *n. (Zool.; also fig.)* Chamäleon, *das*
chamfer ['tʃæmfə(r)] **1.** *v. t.* abfasen *(Technik)*. **2.** *n.* Fase, *die (Technik)*
chamois ['ʃæmwɑ:] *n., pl. same* ['ʃæmwɑ:z] **a)** *(Zool.)* Gemse, *die;* **b)** *(leather)* Chamois[leder], *das;* **~-leather** ['ʃæmwɑ:-, 'ʃæmɪ-] Chamoisleder, *das*
chamomile *see* **camomile**
[1]**champ** [tʃæmp] **1.** *v. t.* ‹*Pferd:*› [geräuschvoll] kauen ‹*Futter*›; ‹*Pferd:*› [geräuschvoll] kauen auf (+ *Dat.*) ‹*Gebiß*›; ‹*Person:*› [geräuschvoll] kauen. **2.** *v. i.* [geräuschvoll]

kauen (**on, at** an, auf + *Dat.*); **be ~ing [at the bit] to do sth.** *(fig.)* voll Ungeduld darauf brennen, etw. zu tun

[2]**champ** *(coll.) see* **champion 1 b, c**

champagne [ʃæm'peɪn] *n.* Sekt, *der; (from Champagne)* Champagner, *der*

champagne: ~-coloured *adj.* champagnerfarben; **~ glass** *n.* Sektglas, *das*

champers ['ʃæmpəz] *n. (Brit. coll.)* Schampus, *der (ugs.)*

champion ['tʃæmpɪən] **1.** *n.* **a)** *(defender)* Verfechter, *der*/Verfechterin, *die;* **he is a ~ of the poor** er ist ein Anwalt der Armen; **b)** *(Sport)* Meister, *der*/Meisterin, *die;* Champion, *der;* **the ice-skating/discus ~:** der Meister/die Meisterin im Eiskunstlauf/Diskuswurf; **world ~:** Weltmeister, *der*/-meisterin, *die;* **the world lightweight ~:** der Weltmeister im Leichtgewicht; **c)** *(animal or plant best in contest)* Sieger, *der;* **be a ~:** prämiert *od.* preisgekrönt sein; **d)** *attrib.* **~ dog** preisgekrönter Hund; **~ boxer** Champion im Boxen. **2.** *v.t.* verfechten ⟨*Sache*⟩; **~ a person** sich für eine Person einsetzen. **3.** *adj., adv. (N. Engl. coll.)* klasse *(ugs.)*

championship ['tʃæmpɪənʃɪp] *n.* **a)** *(Sport)* Meisterschaft, *die;* **defend the ~:** den Titel *od.* die Meisterschaft verteidigen; **the world figure-skating ~s** die Weltmeisterschaften im Eiskunstlauf; *attrib.* **~ title/match** Titel, *der*/Titelkampf, *der;* **compete for the ~ title** um den Titel kämpfen; **b)** *(advocacy)* **~ of a cause** Engagement für eine Sache

chance [tʃɑːns] **1.** *n.* **a)** *no art. (fortune)* Zufall, *der; attrib.* Zufalls-; zufällig; **~ encounter** Zufallsbegegnung, *die;* **as ~ would have it** wie der Zufall *od.* das Schicksal es wollte; **leave sth. to ~, let ~ decide** es dem Zufall *od.* Schicksal überlassen; **trust to ~:** auf den Zufall *od.* sein Glück vertrauen; **game of ~:** Glücksspiel, *das;* **the result of ~:** [reiner] Zufall; **pure ~:** reiner Zufall; **by ~** zufällig; durch Zufall; **it's not just ~:** es ist kein Zufall; **b)** *(trick of fate)* Zufall, *der;* **by [any] ~, by some ~ or other** zufällig; **could you by any ~ give me a lift?** könntest du mich vielleicht mitnehmen?; **c)** *(opportunity)* Chance, *die;* Gelegenheit, *die; (possibility)* Chance, *die;* Möglichkeit, *die;* **give sb. a ~:** jmdm. eine Chance geben; **give sb. half a ~:** jmdm. nur die [geringste] Chance geben; **given the ~:** wenn ich *usw.* die Gelegenheit dazu hätte; **give sth. a ~ to do sth.** einer Sache *(Dat.)* Gelegenheit geben, etw. zu tun; **offer sb. the ~ of doing sth.** jmdm. die Möglichkeit *od.* Gelegenheit bieten, etw. zu tun; **get a/the ~ to do sth.** eine/die Gelegenheit haben, etw. zu tun; **~ would be a fine thing!** *(coll.)* keine Chance! *(ugs.);* **have a ~ to do sth., have the ~ of doing sth.** die Gelegenheit *od.* Möglichkeit haben, etw. zu tun; **this is my big ~:** das ist die Chance für mich; **now's your ~!** das ist deine Chance!; **have no ~ of doing** *or* **to do sth.** keine Gelegenheit haben, etw. zu tun; **not have much ~ of doing** *or* **to do sth.** kaum eine Gelegenheit haben, etw. zu tun; **on the [off] ~ of doing sth./that ...:** in der vagen Hoffnung, etw. zu tun/daß ...; **be in with a ~ of doing sth.** [gute] Aussichten haben, etw. zu tun; **stand a ~ of doing sth.** die Chance haben, etw. zu tun; **no ~!** *(coll.)* unmöglich!; ist nicht drin! *(ugs.);* **d)** *in sing. or pl. (probability)* **have a good/fair ~ of doing sth.** gute Aussichten haben, etw. zu tun; **[is there] any ~ of your attending?** besteht eine Chance, daß Sie kommen können?; **what ~ [of a breakthrough] is there?** wie stehen die Chancen [für einen Durchbruch]? **there is every/not the slightest ~ that...:** es ist sehr gut möglich/es besteht keine Möglichkeit, daß ...; **there's a good/fair ~ of its working out** es besteht eine gute Chance, daß es gelingt; **there's little ~ of its being a success** es wird wohl kaum ein Erfolg werden; **the ~s are that ...** es ist wahrscheinlich, daß ...; **the ~s are against it** es ist unwahrscheinlich; **the ~s against its happening are slight** die Chancen, daß es nicht geschieht, sind gering; **the ~s are ten to one against its being a success** die Chancen, daß es ein Erfolg sein wird, stehen [nur] 1 zu 10; **sb.'s ~s are slim** jmds. Aussichten sind gering; **e)** *(risk)* **take one's ~:** es darauf ankommen lassen; **take a ~/~s** ein Risiko/Risiken eingehen; es riskieren; **take a ~ on sth.** es bei etw. auf einen Versuch ankommen lassen. **2.** *v.i.* zufällig geschehen *od.* sich ereignen; **it ~d that ...:** es traf *od.* fügte sich, daß ...; **~ to do sth.** zufällig etw. tun; **she ~d to be sitting there** zufällig saß sie gerade da; **~ [up]on sth./sb.** zufällig auf etw./jmdn. stoßen. **3.** *v.t.* riskieren; **~ it** es riskieren *od.* darauf ankommen lassen; **we'll have to ~ that happening** wir müssen es riskieren; **~ one's arm** *(Brit. coll.)* es riskieren; **~ one's luck** sein Glück versuchen

chancel ['tʃɑːnsl] *n. (Eccl.)* Altarraum, *der; (choir)* Chor, *der*

chancellery ['tʃɑːnsələrɪ] *n. (office)* ≈ Botschaft, *die; (of consul)* Konsulat, *das*

chancellor ['tʃɑːnsələ(r)] *n.* **a)** *(Polit., Law, Univ.)* Kanzler, *der;* **C~ of the Exchequer** *(Brit.)* Schatzkanzler, *der;* **Lord [High] C~** *(Brit.)* Lordkanzler, *der;* **b)** *(chief minister of State)* Kanzler, *der;* **Federal C~:** Bundeskanzler, *der*

chancery ['tʃɑːnsərɪ] *n.* **a)** **C~** *(Brit. Law)* Gerichtshof des Lordkanzlers; **Court of C~** *(Hist.)* Kanzleigericht, *das (veralt.);* **b)** *(Brit. Diplom.)* ≈ Botschaft, *die*/Gesandtschaft, *die;* **c)** *(public records office)* Archiv, *das*

chancy ['tʃɑːnsɪ] *adj.* riskant; gewagt

chandelier [ʃændə'lɪə(r)] *n.* Kronleuchter, *der*

chandler ['tʃɑːndlə(r)] *n. (arch.)* Krämer, *der; see also* **ship's chandler**

change ['tʃeɪndʒ] **1.** *n.* **a)** *(of name, address, life-style, outlook, condition, etc.)* Änderung, *die; (of job, surroundings, government, etc.)* Wechsel, *der;* **there has been a ~ of plan** der Plan ist geändert worden; **sth. undergoes a ~:** etw. ändert sich; *(more profoundly)* etw. verändert sich; **How is she, doctor? – No ~:** Wie geht es ihr, Doktor? – Unverändert; **see a ~ in sb.** eine Veränderung an jmdm. bemerken; **this last year has seen many ~s** das vergangene Jahr hat viele Veränderungen [mit sich] gebracht; **there has been a ~ in sb./sth.** eine Veränderung ist in jmdm. vorgegangen/es hat bei etw. eine Änderung gegeben; **make ~s/a ~:** einiges ändern/etwas verändern (**to, in** an + *Dat.*); **make a ~ [of trains/buses]** umsteigen; **a ~ in the weather** ein Witterungs- *od.* Wetterumschlag; **a ~ for the better/worse** eine Verbesserung/Verschlechterung; **a ~ of air would do her good** eine Luftveränderung täte ihr gut; **a ~ of scene/environment** ein positiver Ortswechsel; **the ~ [of life]** die Wechseljahre; **a ~ of drivers every four hours** ein Fahrerwechsel alle vier Stunden; **a ~ of heart** ein Sinneswandel; **b)** *no pl., no art. (process of changing)* Veränderung, *die;* **be for/against ~:** für/gegen eine Veränderung sein; **~ came slowly** nur allmählich zeigte sich eine Veränderung; **c)** *(for the sake of variety)* Abwechslung, *die;* **[just] for a ~:** [nur so] zur Abwechslung; *(iron.)* zur Abwechslung mal; **make a ~** *(be different)* mal etwas anderes sein (**from** als); **that makes a ~** *(iron.)* das ist ja [et]was ganz Neues!; **a ~ is as good as a rest** *(prov.)* Abwechslung wirkt Wunder; **d)** *no pl., no indef. art. (money)* Wechselgeld, *das;* **[loose** *or* **small] ~:** Kleingeld, *das;* **give ~,** *(Amer.)* **make ~:** herausgeben; **give sb. his/her ~:** jmdm. das Wechselgeld [heraus]geben; **give sb. 40 p in ~:** jmdm. 40 p [Wechselgeld] herausgeben; **can you give me ~ for 50 p?** können Sie mir 50 p wechseln?; **[here is] 15 marks ~:** 15 Mark zurück; **I haven't got ~ for a pound** ich kann auf ein Pfund nicht herausgeben; **[you can] keep the ~:** behalten Sie den Rest; [es] stimmt so; **get no ~ out of sb.** *(fig. coll.)* nichts aus jmdm. rauskriegen *(ugs.);* **e)** **a ~ [of clothes]** *(fresh clothes)* Kleidung zum Wechseln; **f)** *(of moon)* Mondwechsel, *der;* **g)** *usu. in pl. (Bell-ringing)* Schlagtonfolge, *die (Musik);* **ring the ~s** *(fig.)* für Abwechslung sorgen. **2.** *v.t.* **a)** *(switch)* wechseln; auswechseln ⟨*Glühbirne, Batterie, Zündkerzen*⟩; **~ one's clothes** seine Kleider *od.* Kleidung wechseln; sich umziehen; **~ one's address/name** seine Anschrift/seinen Namen ändern; **~ trains/buses** umsteigen; **~ schools/one's doctor** die Schule/den Arzt wechseln; **he's always changing jobs** er wechselt ständig den Job; **~ seats** sich woanders hinsetzen *od.* auf einen anderen Platz setzen (*see also* **c**); **~ the record** eine andere Platte auflegen; **~ the bed** das Bett frisch beziehen; die Bettwäsche wechseln; **~ the baby** das Baby [frisch] wickeln *od.* trockenlegen; **~ ownership** den Besitzer wechseln; *see also* **gear 1 a; hand 1 a, c; horse 1 a; side 1 i;** **b)** *(transform)* verwandeln; *(alter)* ändern; **~ sth./sb. into sth./sb.** etw./jmdn. in etw./jmdn. verwandeln; **she ~d him from a prince into a frog** sie verwandelte den Prinzen in einen Frosch; **marriage ~d his way of life** die Ehe veränderte sein Leben; **you won't be able to ~ him** du kannst ihn nicht ändern; **~ direction** die Richtung ändern; *see also* **colour 1 c; mind 1 b; step 1 e; tune 1 a;** **c)** *(exchange)* eintauschen; **~ seats** die Plätze tauschen (*see also* **a**); **~ seats with sb.** mit jmdm. den Platz tauschen; **~ sth./sb. for sth./sb.** etw./jmdn. für etw./jmdn. eintauschen; **take sth. back to the shop and ~ it for sth.** etw. [zum Laden zurückbringen und] gegen etw. umtauschen; *see also* **place 1 f;** **d)** *(in currency or denomination)* wechseln ⟨*Geld*⟩; **~ one's money into Deutschmarks** sein Geld in DM umtauschen. **3.** *v.i.* **a)** *(alter)* sich ändern; ⟨*Person, Land:*⟩ sich verändern; ⟨*Wetter:*⟩ umschlagen, sich ändern; **has she ~d?** hat sie sich verändert?; *(for the better also)* hat sie sich geändert?; **she'll never ~!** sie wird sich nie ändern!; **wait for the lights to ~:** warten, daß es grün/rot wird; **~ for the better** sich verbessern; **conditions ~d for the worse** die Lage verschlechterte sich; **b)** *(into something else)* sich verwandeln; **he ~d from a prince into a frog** aus dem Prinzen wurde ein Frosch; **the wind ~s from east to west** der Wind dreht von Ost nach West; **Britain ~d to the metric system** Großbritannien führte das metrische System ein; **almost overnight it seemed to ~ from winter to spring** fast über Nacht schien sich der Winter in den Frühling verwandelt zu haben; **c)** *(exchange)* tauschen; **~ with sb.** mit jmdm. tauschen; **d)** *(put on other clothes)* sich umziehen; **~ out of/into sth.** etw. ausziehen/anziehen; **e)** *(take different train or bus)* umsteigen; **where do I ~?** wo muß ich umsteigen?; **all ~!** Endstation! Alles aussteigen!; **~ at Bristol** in Bristol umsteigen

~ 'down *v.i. (Motor Veh.)* herunterschalten

~ 'over *v.i.* **a)** *(to something else)* **~ over from sth. to sth.** von etw. zu etw. übergehen; **the student ~d over to medicine** der Student wechselte zum Fach Medizin über; **they ~d over from one system to another** sie stellten das System auf ein anderes um; **b)** *(exchange places)* die Plätze wechseln; *(Sport)* [die Seiten] wechseln. *See also* **change-over**

~ 'round 1. *v.i.* wechseln; *(Sport)* [die Seiten] wechseln. **2.** *v.t.* umstellen ⟨*Möbel, Tagesordnung[spunkte]*⟩; umräumen ⟨*Zimmer*⟩

~ 'up v. i. *(Motor Veh.)* hochschalten
changeability [tʃeɪndʒə'bɪlɪtɪ] *see* **changeableness**
changeable ['tʃeɪndʒəbl] *adj.* veränderlich; *(irregular, inconstant)* unbeständig ‹*Charakter, Wetter*›; wankelmütig ‹*Person*›; wechselhaft, veränderlich ‹*Wetter*›; wechselnd ‹*Wind, Stimmung*›
changeableness ['tʃeɪndʒəblnɪs] *n., no pl.* Veränderlichkeit, *die; (inconstancy)* Unbeständigkeit, *die; (of person)* Wankelmütigkeit, *die*
'**change[-giving] machine** *n.* Geldwechsler, *der*
changeless ['tʃeɪndʒlɪs] *adj.* unveränderlich
changeling ['tʃeɪndʒlɪŋ] *n.* Wechselbalg, *der*
'**change-over** *n* **a)** Wechsel, *der;* ~ **from sth. to sth.** Umstellung von etw. auf etw. *(Akk.);* **the ~ from one government to the next** der Wechsel von einer Regierung zur nächsten; **the sudden ~ in public opinion** der plötzliche Umschwung der öffentlichen Meinung; **b)** *(Sport: of baton in relay race)* Stabwechsel, *der; (of teams changing ends)* Seitenwechsel, *der*
changing ['tʃeɪndʒɪŋ] **1.** *adj.* wechselnd; sich ändernd. **2.** *n.* **the C~ of the Guard** die Wachablösung *(der brit. Hofwache)*
changing: ~**-cubicle** *n.* Umkleidekabine, *die;* ~**-room** *n. (Brit.)* **a)** *(Sport)* Umkleideraum, *der;* **b)** *(in shop)* Umkleidekabine, *die*
channel ['tʃænl] **1.** *n.* **a)** Kanal, *der; (gutter)* Rinnstein, *der; (navigable part of waterway)* Fahrrinne, *die;* **the C~** *(Brit.)* der [Ärmel]kanal; ~ **of a/the river** Flußbett, *das;* **b)** *(fig.)* Kanal, *der;* **your application will go through the usual ~s** Ihre Bewerbung wird auf dem üblichen Weg weitergeleitet; **you must apply through the official ~s** Sie müssen mit Ihrer Bewerbung den Dienstweg einhalten; **direct sb.'s talents into the right ~:** jmds. Talente in die richtige Bahn lenken; **c)** *(Telev., Radio)* Kanal, *der;* **d)** *(on recording tape etc.)* Spur, *die;* **e)** *(groove)* Rille, *die; (flute)* Kannelüre, *die.* **2.** *v. t., (Brit.)* **-ll-** *(convey)* übermitteln; *(fig.: guide, direct)* lenken, richten (**into** auf + *Akk.*)
Channel: ~ **Islands** *pr. n. pl.* Kanalinseln *Pl.;* ~ **Tunnel** *n.* [Ärmel]kanaltunnel, *der;* ~ **Tunnel rail link** *schnelle Bahnverbindung zwischen London und dem Kanaltunnel*
chant [tʃɑ:nt] **1.** *v. t.* **a)** *(Eccl.)* singen; **b)** *(utter rhythmically)* skandieren. **2.** *v. i.* **a)** *(Eccl.)* singen; **b)** *(utter slogans etc.)* Sprechchöre anstimmen. **3.** *n.* **a)** *(Eccl., Mus.)* Gesang, *der;* **b)** *(sing-song)* Singsang, *der; (slogans)* Sprechchor, *der*
chanterelle [ʃɑ:ntə'rel] *n. (Bot.)* Pfifferling, *der*
chaos ['keɪɒs] *n., no indef. art.* Chaos, *das;* **be in [a state of] [complete] ~:** ein [einziges] Chaos sein; **it's absolute ~:** es herrscht ein totales Chaos; **cause ~:** zu einem Chaos führen
chaotic [keɪ'ɒtɪk] *adj.,* **chaotically** [keɪ'ɒtɪkəlɪ] *adv.* chaotisch
[1]**chap** [tʃæp] *n. (Brit. coll.)* Bursche, *der;* Kerl, *der;* **old ~:** alter Knabe *(ugs.);* **my dear ~:** mein lieber Mann *(ugs.);* **would you ~s lend a hand?** könntet ihr mal helfen, Jungs?; **hello, old ~!** hallo, alter Junge!
[2]**chap 1.** *v. t.,* **-pp-** aufplatzen lassen; **my hands are ~ped** meine Hände sind [ganz] aufgesprungen; **~ped skin** aufgesprungene *od.* rissige Haut. **2.** *n. usu. in pl.* Riß, *der*
[3]**chap** *n. (jaw)* Kinnbacke, *die; (Gastr.: of pig)* Schweinebacke, *die*
chap. *abbr.* **chapter** Kap.
chapat[t]i [tʃə'pætɪ] *n.* [indisches] Fladenbrot
'**chap-book** *n. (Hist.)* Volksbuch, *das*
chapel ['tʃæpl] *n.* **a)** Kapelle, *die;* ~ **of rest** *(Brit.) Raum in einem Bestattungsinstitut, in dem Tote bis zur Beerdigung aufgebahrt werden;* ≈ Kapelle, *die;* **b)** *(Brit.: of Nonconformists)* Kirche, *die;* **c)** *(subordinate to parish church)* ≈ Filialkirche, *die*
chaperon ['ʃæpərəʊn] **1.** *n.* Anstandsdame, *die; (joc.)* Anstandswauwau, *der (ugs. scherzh.).* **2.** *v. t.* beaufsichtigen; *(escort)* begleiten
chaplain ['tʃæplɪn] *n.* Kaplan, *der*
chaplaincy ['tʃæplɪnsɪ] *n.* **a)** Amt eines Kaplans; **b)** *(building)* Haus des/eines Kaplans
chaplet ['tʃæplɪt] *n.* **a)** *(wreath)* Kranz, *der;* **b)** *(string of beads) (RC Ch.)* Rosenkranz, *der; (as necklace)* Perlenkette, *die*
chappie, chappy ['tʃæpɪ] *n. (coll.)* **a nice ~:** ein liebes Kerlchen; **the Czech chappies** die tschechischen Jungs
chaps [tʃæps] *n. pl. (Amer.: overalls)* lederne Beinschützer
chapter ['tʃæptə(r)] *n.* **a)** *(of book)* Kapitel, *das;* **[quote sth.] ~ and verse** [etw.] mit genauer Quellenangabe [zitieren]; **give ~ and verse for sth.** etw. hieb- und stichfest belegen; **b)** *(fig.)* ~ **in** *or* **of sb.'s life** Abschnitt in jmds. Leben; ~ **of history** Kapitel [in] der Geschichte; *see also* **accident d; c)** *(Eccl.)* Kapitel, *das;* **d)** *(Amer.: branch of a society)* Sektion, *die*
chapter: ~ **heading** *n.* [Kapitel]überschrift, *die;* ~ **house** *n.* **a)** Kapitelsaal, *der;* **b)** *(Amer.: for student meetings)* ≈ Klubhaus, *das*
[1]**char** [tʃɑ:(r)] *v. t. & i.,* **-rr-** verkohlen
[2]**char 1.** *n. (Brit.)* Putzfrau, *die.* **2.** *v. i.,* **-rr-** *(be cleaner)* als Putzfrau arbeiten; putzen; ~ **for sb.** bei jmdm. putzen *od.* als Putzfrau arbeiten
[3]**char** *n. (Brit. sl.: tea)* Tee, *der;* **a cup of ~:** eine Tasse Tee
charabanc ['ʃærəbæŋ] *n. (Brit. dated) [offener] Bus für Ausflugsfahrten usw.*
character ['kærɪktə(r)] *n.* **a)** *(mental or moral qualities, integrity)* Charakter, *der; (description of qualities)* Charakterbild, *das;* **be of good ~:** ein guter Mensch sein; einen guten Charakter haben; **a woman of ~:** eine Frau mit Charakter; **strength of ~:** Charakterstärke, *die;* **b)** *(reputation)* Ruf, *der; (testimonial)* Zeugnis, *das;* **c)** *no pl. (individuality, style)* Charakter, *der; (characteristic, esp. Biol.)* Charakteristikum, *das;* **the town has a ~ all of its own** die Stadt hat einen ganz eigenen Charakter; **have no ~:** charakterlos *od.* ohne Charakter sein; **his face has ~:** er hat ein charakter- *od.* ausdrucksvolles Gesicht; **d)** *(in novel etc.)* Charakter, *der; (part played by sb.)* Rolle, *die;* **be in/out of ~** *(fig.)* typisch/untypisch sein; **his behaviour was quite out of ~** *(fig.)* sein Betragen war ganz und gar untypisch für ihn; **act in/out of ~** *(fig.)* sich typisch/untypisch verhalten; **e)** *(coll.: extraordinary person)* Original, *das;* **be [quite] a ~/a real ~:** ein [echtes/richtiges] Original sein; **what a ~!** was für ein Mann/eine Frau!; **f)** *(personage)* Persönlichkeit, *die;* Gestalt, *die; (coll.: individual)* Mensch, *der; (derog.)* Individuum, *das;* **a public ~:** eine Persönlichkeit des öffentlichen Lebens; **g)** *(graphic symbol; Computing)* Zeichen, *das; (set of letters)* Schrift, *die*
character: ~ **actor** *n.* Chargenspieler, *der;* ~ **actress** *n.* Chargenspielerin, *die;* ~ **assassination** *n.* Rufmord, *der;* ~**-building 1.** *n.* Charakterbildung, *die;* **2.** *adj.* charakterbildend
characterisation, characterise *see* **characteriz-**
characteristic [kærɪktə'rɪstɪk] **1.** *adj.* charakteristisch (**of** für). **2.** *n.* **a)** charakteristisches Merkmal; Charakteristikum, *das;* **one of the main ~s** eines der charakteristischsten Merkmale; **b)** *see* **characteristic curve**
characteristically [kærɪktə'rɪstɪkəlɪ] *adv.* in charakteristischer Weise; ~ **American** typisch amerikanisch; ~ **enough for him he ...:** es ist/war typisch *od.* bezeichnend für ihn, daß er ...
characteristic 'curve *n.* Kennlinie, *die*
characterization [kærɪktəraɪ'zeɪʃn] *n.* Charakterisierung, *die*
characterize ['kærɪktəraɪz] *v. t.* charakterisieren
characterless ['kærɪktəlɪs] *adj.* nichtssagend
character: ~ **part** *n. (Theatre)* Charge, *die;* ~ **sketch** *n.* Charakterskizze, *die;* ~ **study** *n.* Charakterstudie, *die*
charade [ʃə'rɑ:d] *n.* Scharade, *die; (fig.)* Farce, *die;* **play [a game of] ~s** Scharade spielen; **be an absolute ~** *(fig.)* die reinste Farce sein
charcoal ['tʃɑ:kəʊl] *n.* **a)** Holzkohle, *die; (for drawing)* Kohle, *die;* **b)** *see* **charcoal grey**
charcoal: ~ **biscuit** *n. Keks mit Holzkohle zur Förderung der Verdauung;* ~**-burner** *n.* Köhler, *der;* ~ **drawing** *n.* Kohlezeichnung, *die;* ~ '**grey** *n.* [Kohlen]grau, *das;* ~ **pencil** *n.* Kohlestift, *der*
chard [tʃɑ:d] *n. (Bot.)* Mangold, *der*
charge [tʃɑ:dʒ] **1.** *n.* **a)** *(price)* Preis, *der; (payable to telephone company, bank, authorities, etc., for services)* Gebühr, *die;* **what's your ~?** wieviel verlangen *od.* berechnen Sie?; **what would the ~ be for doing that?** was würde es kosten, das zu tun?; **is there a ~ for it?** kostet das etwas?; **make a ~ of £1/no ~ for sth.** ein Pfund/nichts für etw. berechnen; **at no extra ~:** ohne Extrakosten; **incidental ~s** Nebenkosten; **b)** *(care)* Verantwortung, *die; (task)* Auftrag, *der; (person entrusted)* Schützling, *der;* **be in ~ of a child** ein Kind betreuen; **the boy was placed in his ~:** der Junge wurde in seine Obhut gegeben; der Junge wurde ihm anvertraut; **the patients in** *or* **under her ~:** die ihr anvertrauten Patienten; **be under sb.'s ~:** unter jmds. Obhut stehen; sich in jmds. Obhut befinden; **leave sb. in [full] ~ of sth.** jmdm. die [volle] Verantwortung für etw. übertragen; **the officer/teacher in ~:** der diensthabende Offizier/der verantwortliche Lehrer; **be in ~:** die Verantwortung haben; **be in ~ of sth.** für etw. die Verantwortung haben; *(be the leader)* etw. leiten; **put sb. in ~ of sth.** jmdn. mit der Verantwortung für etw. betrauen; *(make leader)* jmdm. die Leitung einer Sache *(Gen.)* übertragen; **take ~:** die Verantwortung übernehmen; *(fig. coll.: get out of control)* außer Kontrolle geraten; **take ~ of sth.** *(become responsible for)* etw. übernehmen; *(as deputy)* sich um etw. kümmern; *(for safe keeping)* etw. in Verwahrung nehmen; **the police took ~ of the evidence** die Polizei stellte das Beweisstück sicher; **give sb. in ~** *(Brit.)* jmdn. der Polizei übergeben; **c)** *(Law: accusation)* Anklage, *die;* **make a ~ against sb.** jmdn. beschuldigen; **bring a ~ of sth. against sb.** jmdn. wegen etw. beschuldigen/verklagen; ‹*Staatsanwalt:*› jmdn. wegen etw. anklagen; **press ~s** Anzeige erstatten; **face a ~ [of sth.]** sich [wegen etw.] vor Gericht zu verantworten haben; **on a ~ of** wegen; **[stand] convicted on all six ~s** in allen sechs Anklagepunkten für schuldig befunden [werden]; **what's the ~?** wie lautet die Anklage?; was liegt gegen mich/ihn *usw.* vor?; **lay to sb.'s ~:** jmdm. zur Last legen; **d)** *(allegation)* Beschuldigung, *die;* **e)** *(attack)* Angriff, *der;* Attacke, *die;* **return to the ~** *(fig. etc.)* es erneut versuchen; **f)** *(of explosives etc.)* Ladung, *die; (in blast-furnace etc.)* Gicht, *die;* **g)** *(of electricity)* Ladung, *die;* **put the battery on ~:** die Batterie an das Ladegerät anschließen; **poetry/person with an emotional ~** *(fig.)* von [tiefen] Gefühlen

geprägte Dichtung/geprägter Mensch; **h)** *(directions)* Anweisung, *die; (of judge to jury)* Rechtsbelehrung, *die;* **i)** *(Her.)* Wappenbild, *das.* **2.** *v. t.* **a)** *(demand payment of or from)* ~ **sb. sth.,** ~ **sth. to sb.** jmdm. etw. berechnen; etw. von jmdm. verlangen *(ugs.);* **be ~d** bezahlen müssen; **I wasn't ~d for it** ich mußte nichts dafür bezahlen; mir wurde nichts dafür berechnet; ~ **sb. £1 for sth.** jmdm. ein Pfund für etw. berechnen; **customers are ~d for breakages** Kunden haften für Bruchschäden; ~ **sth. [up] to sb.'s account** jmds. Konto mit etw. belasten; jmdm. etw. in Rechnung stellen; **to whom is the dress to be ~d?** auf wessen Rechnung geht das Kleid?; ~ **it [up] to the firm** stellen Sie das der Firma in Rechnung; **I'd like to ~ this dress** ich möchte dieses Kleid über mein Kreditkonto bezahlen; **b)** *(Law: accuse)* anklagen; ~ **sb. with sth.** jmdn. wegen etw. anklagen; **c)** *(blame)* beschuldigen; bezichtigen; ~ **sb. with doing sth.** jmdn. beschuldigen, etw. getan zu haben; ~ **sb. with being lazy** jmdm. vorwerfen, er/sie sei faul; **d)** *(formal: entrust)* ~ **sb. with sth.** jmdn. mit etw. betrauen; ~ **oneself with sth.** etw. übernehmen; **e)** *(load)* laden ⟨*Gewehr*⟩; beschicken ⟨*Hochofen*⟩; **f)** *(Electr.)* laden; [auf]laden ⟨*Batterie*⟩; **~d with emotion** *(fig.)* voller Gefühl; gefühlsgeladen; **g)** *(rush at)* angreifen; **h)** *(formal: command)* befehlen; ~ **sb. to do sth.** jmdm. befehlen, etw. zu tun; **the judge ~d the jury** der Richter erteilte den Geschworenen Rechtsbelehrung. **3.** *v. i.* **a)** *(attack)* angreifen; **~!** Angriff!; Attacke!; ~ **at sb./sth.** jmdn./etw. angreifen; **he ~d into a wall** *(fig.)* er krachte gegen eine Mauer; **b)** *(coll.: hurry)* sausen

chargeable ['tʃɑ:dʒəbl] *adj.* **a) be ~ to sb.** auf jmds. Kosten gehen; **b)** *(Law)* **be ~ with sth.** wegen einer Sache belangt werden können

charge: ~ **account** *n. (Amer.)* Kreditkonto, *das;* ~ **card** *n.* Kreditkarte, *die*

chargé d'affaires [ʃɑ:ʒeɪ dæ'feə(r)] *n., pl.* **chargés d'affaires** [ʃɑ:ʒeɪ dæ'feə(r)] Chargé d'affaires, *der;* [diplomatischer] Geschäftsträger

charge: **~-hand** *n. (Brit.)* Vorarbeiter, *der*/Vorarbeiterin, *die;* **~-nurse** *n. (Brit.)* Stationsschwester, *die*

charger ['tʃɑ:dʒə(r)] *n.* **a)** *(Mil.: cavalry horse)* [Kavallerie]pferd, *das; (of knight)* Schlachtroß, *das (veralt.);* **b)** *(poet.: horse)* Roß, *das (dichter.);* **c)** *(arch.: dish)* Platte, *die;* **d)** *(Electr.)* [Batterie]ladegerät, *das*

'**charge-sheet** *n.* **a)** *Buch, in dem auf einem Polizeirevier Festnahmen und Beschuldigungen registriert werden;* **b)** *(Mil.)* Anklageschrift, *die*

charily ['tʃeərɪlɪ] *adv.* vorsichtig

chariot ['tʃærɪət] *n. (Hist.) (for fighting or racing)* [zweirädriger] Streitwagen; *(carriage)* [leichter, vierrädriger] Wagen

charioteer [tʃærɪə'tɪə(r)] *n.* Wagenlenker, *der*

charisma [kə'rɪzmə] *n., pl.* **~ta** [kə'rɪzmətə] Charisma, *das*

charismatic [kærɪz'mætɪk] *adj.* charismatisch

charitable ['tʃærɪtəbl] *adj.* **a)** *(generous)* großzügig; **b)** *(lenient)* nachsichtig; großzügig; **c)** *(of or for charity)* karitativ; wohltätig, karitativ ⟨*Organisation, Werke*⟩

charity ['tʃærɪtɪ] *n.* **a)** *(leniency)* Nachsicht, *die;* **b)** *(Christian love)* Nächstenliebe, *die;* **faith, hope, and ~:** Glaube, Hoffnung, Liebe; **c)** *(kindness)* Güte, *die;* **d)** *(beneficence)* Wohltätigkeit, *die;* **live on ~/accept ~:** von Almosen leben/Almosen annehmen; **~ begins at home** *(prov.)* man muß zuerst an die eigenen Leute denken; **give money to ~:** Geld für wohltätige Zwecke spenden; **collect for ~:** für wohltätige Zwecke sammeln; **be in aid of ~:** für einen wohltätigen Zweck sein; **[as] cold as ~:** eiskalt *(fig.);* **e)** *(institution)* wohltätige Organisation; **f)** *(educational trust)* gemeinnützige Bildungseinrichtung

charlady ['tʃɑ:leɪdɪ] *n. (Brit.) see* **²char 1**

charlatan ['ʃɑ:lətən] *n.* Scharlatan, *der*

Charlemagne ['ʃɑ:ləmeɪn] *pr. n.* Karl der Große

Charles [tʃɑ:lz] *pr. n. (Hist., as name of ruler etc.)* Karl *(der)*

Charles's Wain ['tʃɑ:lzɪz weɪn] *n. (Astron.)* der Große Wagen *od.* Bär

charleston ['tʃɑ:lstən] *n.* Charleston, *der*

charley horse ['tʃɑ:lɪ hɔ:s] *n. (Amer. sl.)* Muskelkater, *der*

charlie ['tʃɑ:lɪ] *n.* **be/look a right ~** *(coll.)* dämlich sein/aussehen *(ugs.);* **feel a proper ~** *(coll.)* sich *(Dat.)* richtig blöd *od.* dämlich vorkommen *(ugs.)*

charm [tʃɑ:m] **1.** *n.* **a)** *(act)* Zauber, *der; (thing)* Zaubermittel, *das; (words)* Zauberspruch, *der;* Zauberformel, *die;* **lucky ~:** Glücksbringer, *der;* **work like a ~:** Wunder wirken; **b)** *(talisman)* Talisman, *der;* **c)** *(trinket)* Anhänger, *der;* Berlocke, *die (veralt.);* **d)** *(attractiveness)* Reiz, *der; (of person)* Charme, *der;* **have ~:** ⟨*Person:*⟩ Charme haben; ⟨*Schloß, Buch:*⟩ seinen eigenen Reiz haben; **place of great ~:** reizvoller Ort; **person of great ~:** sehr charmanter Mensch; **turn on the ~** *(coll.)* auf charmant machen *(ugs.).* **2.** *v. t.* **a)** *(captivate)* bezaubern ; **be ~ed with sth.** von etw. bezaubert *od.* begeistert sein; **she can ~ the birds out of the trees** sie kann mit ihrem Charme alles erreichen; **~ed, I'm sure** *(coll. iron.)* [wie] charmant *(iron.);* **b)** *(by magic)* verzaubern; beschwören ⟨*Schlange*⟩; ~ **sth. out of sb.** jmdm. etw. [durch Zauberei] entlocken; **bear** *or* **lead a ~ed life** unter einem Glücksstern geboren sein; ein Glückskind sein

charmer ['tʃɑ:mə(r)] *n. (man)* Charmeur, *der; (woman)* bezauberndes Geschöpf

charming ['tʃɑ:mɪŋ] *adj.* bezaubernd; charmant, bezaubernd ⟨*Person, Lächeln*⟩; **~!** *(iron.)* [wie] charmant! *(iron.)*

charmingly ['tʃɑ:mɪŋlɪ] *adv.* bezaubernd; charmant ⟨*lächeln*⟩

charnel-house ['tʃɑ:nlhaʊs] *n.* Leichenhalle, *die; (for bones)* Beinhaus, *das*

chart [tʃɑ:t] **1.** *n.* **a)** *(map)* Karte, *die;* **naval ~:** Seekarte, *die;* **weather ~:** Wetterkarte, *die;* **b)** *(graph etc.)* Schaubild, *das; (diagram)* Diagramm, *das;* **c)** *(tabulated information)* Tabelle, *die;* **the ~s** *(of pop records)* die Hitliste. **2.** *v. t.* graphisch darstellen; *(map)* kartographisch erfassen; kartographieren; *(fig.: describe)* schildern ⟨*Werdegang, Leben*⟩

'**chart-buster** *n.* Hit, *der*

charter ['tʃɑ:tə(r)] **1.** *n.* **a)** Charta, *die; (of foundation also)* Gründungs- *od.* Stiftungsurkunde, *die; (fig.)* Freibrief, *der;* **grant a ~ to a city** einem Ort das Stadtrecht verleihen; **the Great C~** *(Hist.)* die Magna Charta; **b)** *(deed conveying land)* ≈ [Besitz]urkunde, *die;* **c)** *(privilege, admitted right)* Privileg, *das;* Vorrecht, *das;* **d)** *(Transport)* **be on ~:** gechartert sein. **2.** *v. t. (Transport)* chartern ⟨*Schiff, Flugzeug*⟩; mieten ⟨*Bus*⟩

chartered ['tʃɑ:təd]: ~ **ac'countant** *n. (Brit.)* Wirtschaftsprüfer, *der*/-prüferin, *die;* ~ **'aircraft** *n.* Charterflugzeug, *das;* Chartermaschine, *die;* ~ **engi'neer** *n. (Brit.)* Ingenieur, *der*/Ingenieurin, *die (der/die Mitglied eines Verbands ist);* ~ **lib'rarian** *n. (Brit.)* Bibliothekar, *der*/Bibliothekarin, *die (der/die Mitglied eines Verbands ist);* ~ **sur'veyor** *n. (Brit.)* Vermessungsingenieur, *der*/-ingenieurin, *die (der/die Mitglied eines Verbands ist)*

charter: ~ **flight** *n.* Charterflug, *der;* **~-party** *n. (Transport)* Charterpartie, *die;* ~ **plane** *n. see* **chartered aircraft**

charwoman ['tʃɑ:wʊmən] *n. see* **²char 1**

chary ['tʃeərɪ] *adj.* **a)** *(sparing, ungenerous)* zurückhaltend (**of** mit); **be ~ of doing sth.** zurückhaltend damit sein, etw. zu tun; **b)** *(cautious)* vorsichtig; **be ~ of doing sth.** darauf bedacht sein, etw. nicht zu tun

¹chase [tʃeɪs] **1.** *n.* **a)** Verfolgungsjagd, *die;* **car ~:** Verfolgungsjagd im Auto; **give ~ [to the thief]** [dem Dieb] hinterherjagen; **b)** *(Hunting)* Jagd, *die; (steeplechase)* Jagdrennen, *das;* Steeplechase, *die.* **2.** *v. t. (pursue)* jagen; ~ **sth.** *(fig.)* einer Sache *(Dat.)* nachjagen; hinter etw. *(Dat.)* hersein *(ugs.);* ~ **yourself** *imper. (fig. coll.)* verschwinde *(ugs.).* **3.** *v. i.* ~ **after sb./sth.** hinter jmdm./etw. herjagen; **I've been chasing about all over the place** *(coll.)* ich bin überall herumgerast *(ugs.)*

~ **around** **1.** [--'-] *v. i.* ~ **around after sb.** jmdm. hinterherrennen. **2.** ['---] *v. t.* ~ **around town** in der Stadt herumrennen *(ugs.)*

~ **a'way** *v. t.* wegjagen

~ **'off** *v. i.* davonjagen

~ **round** *see* ~ **around**

~ **'up** *v. t. (coll.)* ausfindig machen

²chase *v. t. (Metalw.)* ziselieren

chaser ['tʃeɪsə(r)] *n.* **a)** *(horse)* Steepler, *der (Reitsport);* **b) drink sth. as a ~** *(coll.)* etw. zum Nachspülen trinken *(ugs.)*

chasm ['kæzm] *n. (lit. or fig.)* Kluft, *die*

chassis ['ʃæsɪ] *n., pl. same* ['ʃæsɪz] *(Motor Veh.)* Chassis, *das;* Fahrgestell, *das*

chaste [tʃeɪst] *adj.* **a)** keusch; **b)** *(decent)* gesittet ⟨*Worte, Ausdruck, Antwort*⟩; **c)** *(restrained)* schlicht ⟨*Erscheinung, Kleidung*⟩

chastely ['tʃeɪstlɪ] *adv. see* **chaste:** keusch; gesittet; schlicht

chasten ['tʃeɪsn] *v. t.* **a)** züchtigen *(geh.);* strafen; **b)** *(fig.)* dämpfen ⟨*Stimmung*⟩; demütigen ⟨*Person*⟩

chastening ['tʃeɪsənɪŋ] *adj.* ernüchternd

chastise [tʃæ'staɪz] *v. t.* **a)** *(punish)* züchtigen *(geh.);* bestrafen; **b)** *(thrash)* züchtigen *(geh.)*

chastisement [tʃæ'staɪzmənt, 'tʃæstɪzmənt] *n.* Züchtigung, *die (geh.);* Strafe, *die*

chastity ['tʃæstɪtɪ] *n., no pl.* Keuschheit, *die;* **vow of ~:** Keuschheitsgelübde, *das*

'**chastity belt** *n.* Keuschheitsgürtel, *der*

chasuble ['tʃæzjʊbl] *n. (Eccl.)* Meßgewand, *das;* Kasel, *die*

chat [tʃæt] **1.** *n.* **a)** Schwätzchen, *das;* Plausch, *der (bes. südd., österr.);* **have a ~ about sth.** sich über etw. *(Akk.)* unterhalten; **b)** *no pl., no indef. art. (~ting)* Geplauder, *das.* **2.** *v. i.,* **-tt-** plaudern; ~ **with** *or* **to sb. about sth.** mit jmdm. von etw. plaudern; sich mit jmdm. über etw. *(Akk.)* unterhalten

~ **'up** *v. t. (Brit. coll.)* **a)** *(amorously)* anmachen *(ugs.);* **b)** *(to elicit information)* sich heranmachen an (+ *Akk.*) *(ugs.)*

château ['ʃætəʊ] *n., pl.* **~x** ['ʃætəʊz] Château, *das;* **~-bottled wine** Schloßabzug, *der*

'**chat show** *n.* Talk-Show, *die*

chattel ['tʃætl] *n., usu. in pl.* **~[s]** bewegliche Habe *(geh.); see also* **good 3 g**

chatter ['tʃætə(r)] **1.** *v. i.* **a)** schwatzen; ⟨*Kind:*⟩ schwatzen, plappern; ⟨*Affe:*⟩ schnattern; **b)** *(rattle)* ⟨*Zähne:*⟩ klappern; **his teeth ~ed** er klapperte mit den Zähnen. **2.** *n.* **a)** Schwatzen, *das; (of child)* Plappern, *das;* Schwatzen, *das; (of monkey)* Schnattern, *das;* **b)** *(of teeth)* Klappern, *das*

chatterbox ['tʃætəbɒks] *n.* Quasselstrippe, *die (ugs.); (child)* Plappermäulchen, *das*

chattily ['tʃætɪlɪ] *adv.* im Plauderton

chattiness ['tʃætɪnɪs] *n., no pl.* Gesprächigkeit, *die;* Schwatzhaftigkeit, *die (abwertend)*

chatty ['tʃætɪ] *adj.* gesprächig; schwatzhaft *(abwertend)*

chauffeur ['ʃəʊfə(r), ʃəʊ'fɜ:(r)] **1.** *n.* Fahrer, *der;* Chauffeur, *der;* **~-driven car** Wagen mit Chauffeur. **2.** *v. t.* fahren; chauffieren *(veralt.)*

chauvinism ['ʃəʊvɪnɪzm] *n., no pl.* Chauvi-

nismus, *der;* **male ~:** männlicher Chauvinismus
chauvinist ['ʃəʊvɪnɪst] *n.* Chauvinist, *der*/Chauvinistin, *die;* **male ~/[male] ~ pig** Chauvinist, *der*/Chauvinistenschwein, *das*
chauvinistic [ʃəʊvɪ'nɪstɪk] *adj.* chauvinistisch
cheap [tʃi:p] **1.** *adj.* **a)** *(inexpensive)* billig; **~ ticket** *(at reduced rate)* verbilligte Fahrkarte; **be ~ and nasty** billiger Ramsch sein; **be ~ at the price** sehr preiswert sein; *(fig.)* es wert sein; **on the ~** *(coll.)* billig; **do it on the ~** *(coll.)* es billig machen *(ugs.);* **b)** *(easily got or made)* billig; **c)** *(worthless)* billig ‹*Aussehen*›; gemein ‹*Lügner*›; schäbig ‹*Verhalten, Betragen*›; **feel ~** *(coll.)* sich *(Dat.)* schäbig vorkommen; **hold ~:** geringschätzen; **make oneself ~:** sich [selbst] herabsetzen; **d)** *(Finance)* billig ‹*Geld*›. **2.** *adv.* billig; **I got it ~:** ich hab's billig gekriegt *(ugs.);* **be going ~:** besonders günstig sein *(ugs.)*
cheapen ['tʃi:pn] **1.** *v. t.* verbilligen; verringern ‹*Kosten*›; *(fig.)* herabsetzen; **~ oneself** sich [selbst] herabsetzen; **feel ~ed** sich gedemütigt fühlen. **2.** *v. i.* billiger werden
'**cheapjack 1.** *n.* Straßenhändler, *der;* billiger Jakob *(ugs.).* **2.** *adj.* Billig-
cheaply ['tʃi:plɪ] *adv. see* **cheap 1:** billig; gemein; schäbig
cheapness ['tʃi:pnɪs] *n., no pl.* niedriger Preis; *(fig.)* Gewöhnlichkeit, *die*
cheat [tʃi:t] **1.** *n.* **a)** *(person)* Schwindler, *der*/Schwindlerin, *die;* **b)** *(act)* Schwindel, *der;* **that's a ~!** das ist Betrug! **2.** *v. t.* **a)** hintergehen; betrügen; **~ sb./sth. [out] of sth.** jmdn./etw. um etw. betrügen; **~ sb. into doing sth.** jmdn. durch Täuschung dazu bringen, etw. zu tun; **b)** *(escape)* **~ sb.** jmdm. entgehen; **~ death** dem Tod entkommen. **3.** *v. i.* betrügen; **~ at cards/at school/in class** beim Kartenspielen mogeln/in der Schule/im Unterricht abschreiben
¹**check** [tʃek] **1.** *n.* **a)** *(stoppage, thing, that restrains)* Hindernis, *das; (restraint)* Kontrolle, *die;* **[hold** *or* **keep sth.] in ~:** [etw.] unter Kontrolle [halten]; **hold** *or* **keep one's temper in ~:** sich beherrschen; **act as a ~ upon sth.** etw. unter Kontrolle halten; **a ~ must be put on sth.** etw. muß unter Kontrolle gebracht werden; **[a system of] ~s and balances** *(Amer.)* ein Kontrollsystem; **b)** *(for accuracy)* Kontrolle, *die;* **make a ~ on sth./sb.** etw./jmdn. überprüfen *od.* kontrollieren; **give sth. a ~:** etw. überprüfen *od.* kontrollieren; **keep a ~ on** überprüfen; kontrollieren; überwachen ‹*Verdächtigen*›; **c)** *(token) (for left luggage)* Gepäckaufbewahrungsschein, *der; (Amer.: in theatre)* Garderobenmarke, *die; (for seat-holder)* Platzkarte, *die; (of verification)* Kontrollzeichen, *das; (Amer.: bill in restaurant etc.)* Rechnung, *die;* **d)** *(rebuff; also Mil.)* Widerstand, *der;* **e)** *(Chess)* Schach, *das;* **be in ~:** im Schach stehen; **put sb. in ~:** jmdm. Schach bieten; **f)** *(Hunting)* Stocken [beim Verlieren der Fährte]; **g)** *(Amer.: counter at cards)* Spielmarke, *die; see also* **cash in 1; h)** *(Amer.) see* **cheque. 2.** *v. t.* **a)** *(restrain)* unter Kontrolle halten; unterdrücken ‹*Ärger, Lachen*›; **~ oneself** sich beherrschen; **b)** *(examine accuracy of)* nachprüfen; nachsehen ‹*Hausaufgaben*›; kontrollieren ‹*Fahrkarte*›; *(Amer.: mark with tick)* abhaken; *(Amer.: deposit)* aufgeben ‹*Gepäck*›; **c)** *(stop; also Mil.)* aufhalten; **d)** *(Chess)* Schach bieten (+ *Dat.*). **3.** *v. i.* **a)** *(test)* **~ on sth.** etw. überprüfen; **~ with sb.** bei jmdm. nachfragen; **just ~ing** *(coll. joc.)* wollte mich nur vergewissern; **b)** *(Amer.: agree)* übereinstimmen; **c)** *(Hunting)* stocken. **4.** *int.* **a)** *(Chess)* Schach; **b)** *(Amer.)* einverstanden
~ 'back *v. i.* nachsehen
~ 'in 1. *v. t.* eintragen; *(at airport)* **~ in one's luggage** sein Gepäck abfertigen lassen *od.* einchecken. **2.** *v. i. (arrive at hotel)* ankommen; *(sign the register)* sich eintragen; *(report one's arrival)* sich melden; *(at airport)* einchecken. *See also* **check-in**
~ 'off *v. t.* abhaken
~ 'out 1. *v. t.* überprüfen. **2.** *v. i.* abreisen; **~ out of a hotel** abreisen; *(pay)* die Hotelrechnung bezahlen; **~ out of the supermarket** im Supermarkt bezahlen; *see also* **check-out**
~ 'over *v. t.* durchsehen
~ 'through *v. t.* kontrollieren; durchsehen ‹*Brief, Rechnung*›
~ 'up *v. i.* überprüfen; **~ up on sb./sth.** jmdn./etw. überprüfen *od.* kontrollieren; **the police will ~ up on you** die Polizei wird Nachforschungen über dich anstellen; *see also* **check-up**
²**check** *n. (pattern)* Karo, *das;* **a shirt of red and white ~:** ein rotweiß kariertes Hemd
checked [tʃekt] *adj. (patterned)* kariert
checker ['tʃekə(r)] *n.* Prüfer, *der*/Prüferin, *die;* Kontrolleur, *der*
'**checkerboard** *n. (Amer.)* Schachbrett, *das*
checkers ['tʃekəz] *n., no pl. (Amer.) see* **draughts**
'**check-in** *n.* Abfertigung, *die; attrib.* Abfertigungs-
'**checking account** *n. (Amer.)* Girokonto, *das*
check: ~-list *n.* Verzeichnis, *das;* Checkliste, *die (Technik, Flugw.);* **~mate** ['tʃekmeɪt] **1.** *n.* [Schach]matt, *das;* **2.** *int.* [schach]matt; **3.** *v. t.* **a)** matt setzen; **b)** *(fig.)* zunichte machen; **~-out** *n.* Abreise, *die; (desk)* Kasse, *die; attrib.* **~-out desk** *or* **point** *or* **counter** Kasse, *die;* **~-point** *n.* Kontrollpunkt, *der;* **~-room** *n. (Amer.)* **a)** *(cloakroom)* Garderobe, *die;* **b)** *(for left luggage)* Gepäckaufbewahrung, *die;* **~-up** *n. (Med.)* Untersuchung, *die;* **get/have a ~-up** untersucht werden; **go to the doctor for a ~-up** sich beim Arzt untersuchen lassen
Cheddar ['tʃedə(r)] *n.* Cheddar[käse], *der*
cheek [tʃi:k] **1.** *n.* **a)** Backe, *die;* Wange, *die (geh.);* **~ by jowl** Seite an Seite; dicht nebeneinander ‹*stehen, wohnen*›; **dance ~ to ~:** Wange an Wange tanzen; **turn the other ~** *(fig.)* die andere Wange darbieten; **b)** *(impertinence)* Frechheit, *die;* **have the ~ to do sth.** die Frechheit *od.* Stirn besitzen, etw. zu tun; **I like your ~** *(iron.)* du hast vielleicht Nerven! *(ugs.);* **none of your ~:** sei nicht so frech; **have plenty of ~:** ziemlich unverschämt sein; **c)** *in pl. (sl.: buttocks)* Hinterbacken *(ugs.).* **2.** *v. t.* **~ sb.** zu jmdm. frech sein
'**cheek-bone** *n.* Backenknochen, *der*
cheekily ['tʃi:kɪlɪ] *adv.* frech; **behave ~:** frech sein
cheekiness ['tʃi:kɪnɪs] *n., no pl.* Frechheit, *die*
'**cheek-pouch** *n. (Zool.)* Backentasche, *die*
cheeky ['tʃi:kɪ] *adj.* frech; **~ girl** freches Ding *(ugs.);* **~ boy** frecher Bengel; **~ devil/monkey** *(coll.)* Frechdachs, *der (ugs.)*
cheep [tʃi:p] **1.** *v. i.* piep[s]en. **2.** *n.* Piep[s]en, *das;* **not a ~ [out of sb.]** *(fig. coll.)* kein Pieps [von jmdm.] *(ugs.)*
cheer [tʃɪə(r)] **1.** *n.* **a)** *(applause)* Beifallsruf, *der;* **give sb. a [big] ~:** jmdn. zujubeln; **give three ~s for sb.** jmdn. [dreimal] hochleben lassen; **two ~s** *(iron.)* ist ja großartig *(iron.);* **b)** *in pl. (Brit. coll.: as a toast)* prost!; **c)** *in pl. (Brit. coll.: thank you)* danke!; **d)** *in pl. (Brit. coll.: goodbye)* tschüs! *(ugs.);* **e)** *(arch.: frame of mind)* **be of good ~:** sei/seid guten Mutes *(geh.).* **2.** *v. t.* **a)** *(applaud)* **~ sth./sb.** etw. bejubeln/jmdm. zujubeln; **b)** *(gladden)* aufmuntern; aufheitern. **3.** *v. i.* jubeln
~ 'on *v. t.* anfeuern ‹*Sportler, Wettkämpfer*›
~ 'up 1. *v. t.* aufheitern. **2.** *v. i.* bessere Laune bekommen; **~ up!** Kopf hoch!
cheerful ['tʃɪəfl] *adj. (in good spirits)* fröhlich; gutgelaunt; *(bright, pleasant)* heiter; erfreulich ‹*Aussichten*›; lustig ‹*Feuer*›; *(willing)* bereitwillig; **make sb. ~:** jmdn. heiter stimmen
cheerfully ['tʃɪəfəlɪ] *adv.* vergnügt; **the fire blazed ~:** das Feuer brannte lustig; **~ assuming that ...** *(iron.)* in der unbekümmerten Annahme, daß ...
cheerily ['tʃɪərɪlɪ] *adv.* fröhlich
cheering ['tʃɪərɪŋ] **1.** *adj.* **a)** *(gladdening)* fröhlich stimmend; **b)** *(applauding)* jubelnd. **2.** *n.* Jubeln, *das*
cheerio [tʃɪərɪ'əʊ] *int.* **a)** *(Brit. coll.: goodbye)* tschüs! *(ugs.);* **b)** *(dated: as a toast)* zum Wohl
'**cheer-leader** *n. jmd., der andere zu Beifall, Hochrufen usw. anfeuert*
cheerless ['tʃɪəlɪs] *adj.* freudlos; düster ‹*Aussichten*›
cheery ['tʃɪərɪ] *adj.* fröhlich
cheese [tʃi:z] *n.* **a)** *(food)* Käse, *der;* **~s** Käsesorten; **b)** *(whole)* Käselaib, *der; (piece)* Stück Käse; **c) say ~!** *(Photog.)* bitte recht freundlich!; **hard ~!** *(dated coll.)* Pech gehabt! *(ugs.). See also* **lemon cheese**
cheese: ~board *n.* Käseplatte, *die;* **~cake** *n.* **a)** Käsetorte, *die;* **b)** *no pl., no indef. art. (coll.)* Pin-up-Girls *Pl.;* **~cloth** *n.* [indischer] Baumwollstoff; **~-cutter** *n. Draht zum Schneiden von Käse;* **~-dish** *n.* ≈ Käseglocke, *die*
cheesed off [tʃi:zd 'ɒf] *adj. (Brit. sl.)* angeödet; **I am ~ with school** die Schule ödet mich an *(ugs.) od.* stinkt mir *(salopp);* **I'm ~:** mir stinkt's! *(salopp)*
cheese: ~-grater *n.* Käseraspel, *die;* **~-paring 1.** *adj.* knauserig; **2.** *n.* Knauserei, *die;* **~ 'straw** *n.* Käsestange, *die*
cheetah ['tʃi:tə] *n. (Zool.)* Gepard, *der*
chef [ʃef] *n.* Küchenchef, *der; (as profession)* Koch, *der*
Chelsea ['tʃelsɪ]: **~ 'bun** *n.* ≈ Rosinenbrötchen, *das;* **~ 'pensioner** *n. Insasse des Chelsea Royal Hospital für alte und kriegsversehrte Soldaten*
chemical ['kemɪkl] **1.** *adj.* chemisch. **2.** *n.* Chemikalie, *die*
chemical: ~ engi'neer *n.* Chemieingenieur, *der*/-ingenieurin, *die;* **~ engi'neering** *n.* Chemotechnik, *die;* **~ firm** *n.* Chemiebetrieb, *der*
chemically ['kemɪkəlɪ] *adv.* chemisch
chemical: ~ 'warfare *n.* chemische Krieg[s]führung; **~ worker** *n.* Chemiearbeiter, *der*/-arbeiterin, *die*
chemise [ʃə'mi:z] *n.* Unterkleid, *das*
chemist ['kemɪst] *n.* **a)** *(person skilled in chemistry)* Chemiker, *der*/Chemikerin, *die;* **b)** *(Brit.: pharmacist)* Drogist, *der*/Drogistin, *die;* **~'s [shop]** Drogerie, *die; (dispensary)* Apotheke, *die; see also* **baker**
chemistry ['kemɪstrɪ] *n., no pl.* **a)** *no indef. art.* Chemie, *die;* **the ~ of iron** die chemischen Eigenschaften des Eisens; **b)** *(fig.)* unerklärliche Wirkungskraft
chemistry: ~ laboratory *n.* Chemiesaal, *der;* **~ set** *n.* Chemiebaukasten, *der*
chemotherapy [kemə'θerəpɪ] *n.* Chemotherapie, *die*
chenille [ʃə'ni:l] *n.* Chenille, *die*
cheque [tʃek] *n.* Scheck, *der;* **write a ~:** einen Scheck ausfüllen; **will you take a ~?** kann ich mit Scheck bezahlen?; **pay by ~:** mit [einem] Scheck bezahlen
cheque: ~-book *n.* Scheckbuch, *das;* **~-book journalism** *n.* Scheckbuchjournalismus, *der;* **~ card** *n.* Scheckkarte, *die*
chequer ['tʃekə(r)] **1.** *n.* Karomuster, *das.* **2.** *v. t.* karieren
'**chequer-board** *n.* Schachbrett, *das*
chequered ['tʃekəd] *adj.* **a)** kariert; **a lawn ~ with sunlight and shade** ein von Licht und Schatten gefleckter Rasen; **b)** *(fig.)* bewegt ‹*Geschichte, Leben, Laufbahn*›

cherish ['tʃerɪʃ] *v.t.* **a)** *(value and keep)* hegen ‹*Hoffnung, Gefühl*›; in Ehren halten ‹*[Erinnerungs]gegenstand*›; ~ **an illusion** sich einer Illusion *(Dat.)* hingeben; ~ **sb.'s memory** jmds. Andenken in Ehren bewahren; **b)** *(foster)* ~ **sb.** [liebevoll] für jmdn. sorgen; **to love and to ~, till death us do part** *(in marriage ceremony)* zu lieben und zu ehren, bis daß der Tod uns scheidet

cheroot [ʃə'ru:t] *n.* Stumpen, *der*

cherry ['tʃerɪ] **1.** *n.* **a)** *(fruit)* Kirsche, *die;* **it's no use having two bites at a ~** *(fig.)* es hat keinen Sinn, das Ganze zweimal durchzuführen; **we may get two bites at the ~** *(fig.)* wir werden vielleicht eine zweite Chance haben; **b)** *(tree)* Kirschbaum, *der.* **2.** *adj.* kirschrot; **a bright ~ red** ein helles Kirschrot

cherry: ~ **blossom** *n.* Kirschblüte, *die;* ~ **'brandy** *n.* Cherry Brandy, *der;* ≈ Kirschlikör, *der;* **~-'pie** *n.* **a)** Kirschkuchen, *der;* **b)** *(Brit.: flower)* Vanillestrauch, *der;* **~-stone** *n.* Kirschkern, *der*

cherub ['tʃerəb] *n.* **a)** *pl.* **~im** ['tʃerəbɪm] *(Theol., of celestial order)* Cherub, *der;* **b)** *pl.* **~s** *(Art)* Putte, *die;* Putto, *der; (child)* Engelchen, *das*

cherubic [tʃɪ'ru:bɪk] *adj.* cherubinisch; engelhaft; ~ **face** Engelsgesicht, *das*

chervil ['tʃɜ:vɪl] *n. (Bot.)* Kerbel, *der*

Cheshire ['tʃeʃə(r), 'tʃeʃɪə(r)]: ~ **'cat** *n.* **grin like a ~ cat** übers ganze Gesicht grinsen; ~ **'cheese** *n.* Cheshirekäse, *der*

chess [tʃes] *n., no pl., no indef. art.* das Schach[spiel]; **play ~:** Schach spielen; **be good at ~:** gut Schach spielen

chess: **~-board** *n.* Schachbrett, *das;* **~-man** *n.* Schachfigur, *die;* **~-player** *n.* Schachspieler, *der*/-spielerin, *die*

chest [tʃest] *n.* **a)** Kiste, *die; (for clothes or money)* Truhe, die; *(treasury; also fig.)* Kasse, *die;* **b)** *(part of body)* Brust, *die; (Anat.)* Brustkorb, *der;* Brustkasten, *der (ugs.);* **cold on the ~:** Bronchitis, *die;* **get sth. off one's ~** *(fig. coll.)* sich *(Dat.)* etw. von der Seele reden; **play [sth.] close to one's ~** *(fig. coll.)* so wenig wie möglich [über etw. *(Akk.)*] erwähnen

-chested ['tʃestɪd] *adj. in comb.* -brüstig; **a broad-~ man** ein Mann mit einem breiten Brustkorb

chesterfield ['tʃestəfi:ld] *n. (sofa)* gepolstertes Sofa *(mit hohen Armlehnen)*

chest: **~-expander** *n.* Expander, *der;* **~-measurement** *n.* Brustumfang, *der;* Brustweite, *die*

chestnut ['tʃesnʌt] **1.** *n.* **a)** *(tree)* Kastanie, *die;* **Spanish** *or* **sweet ~:** Edelkastanie, *die; see also* **horse-chestnut; b)** *(fruit)* Kastanie, *die;* **pull the ~s out of the fire** *(fig.)* die Kastanien aus dem Feuer holen *(ugs.);* **c)** *(colour)* Kastanienbraun, *das;* **d)** *see* **chestnut-wood; e)** *(stale story or topic)* **[old] ~:** alte *od.* olle Kamelle *(ugs.);* **f)** *(horse)* Fuchs, *der.* **2.** *adj. (colour)* **~[-brown]** kastanienbraun

chestnut: **~-tree** *see* **chestnut 1a; ~-wood** *n.* Kastanienholz, *das*

chest of 'drawers Kommode, *die*

chesty ['tʃestɪ] *adj. (coll.)* anfällig *(für Erkältungen);* tief sitzend ‹*Husten*›; **be ~:** es auf der Brust haben *(ugs.);* **you sound rather ~ today** du klingst heute ziemlich erkältet

chevron ['ʃevrən] *n.* **a)** *(badge)* Winkel, *der;* **b)** *(Her.)* Sparren, *der;* Chevron, *der;* **c)** *(traffic-sign)* Winkel *(auf Richtungstafeln o. ä.)*

chew [tʃu:] **1.** *v.t.* kauen; ~ **one's finger-nails** an den [Finger]nägeln kauen; ~ **the rag** *or* **the fat [about sth.]** *(fig.)* [über etw. *(Akk.)*] meckern *(ugs.); see also* **bite off; cud. 2.** *v.i.* kauen (**on** auf + *Dat.*); ~ **on** *or* **over sth.** *(fig.)* sich *(Dat.)* etw. durch den Kopf gehen lassen. **3.** *n.* Kauen, *das*

~ **'out** *v.t. (Amer. coll.)* zusammenstauchen *(ugs.)*

chewing-gum ['tʃu:ɪŋgʌm] *n.* Kaugummi, *der od. das*

chewy ['tʃu:ɪ] *adj.* zäh ‹*Fleisch, Bonbon*›

Chianti [kɪ'æntɪ] *n.* Chianti[wein], *der*

chiaroscuro [kjɑ:rə'skʊərəʊ] *n., pl.* **~s** *(in painting)* Clair-obscur, *das; (fig. also)* Helldunkel, *das*

chic [ʃi:k] **1.** *adj.* schick; elegant. **2.** *n.* Schick, *der*

chicane [ʃɪ'keɪn] *n. (Sport)* Schikane, *die*

chicanery [ʃɪ'keɪnərɪ] *n.* **a)** *no pl. (deception)* Täuschungsmanöver, *das; (legal trickery)* Rechtsverdrehung, *die;* **b)** *(sophistry)* Winkelzug, *der;* Trick, *der*

chichi ['ʃi:ʃi:] **1.** *adj.* überspannt, affektiert ‹*Person, Verhalten*›; extravagant ‹*Gegenstand*›. **2.** *n.* Chichi, *das*

chick [tʃɪk] *n.* **a)** Küken, *das;* **b)** *(coll.: child)* Kleine, *das;* **c)** *(sl.: young woman)* Biene, *die (ugs.)*

chickadee ['tʃɪkədi:] *n. (Ornith.)* Chickadee-Meise, *die*

chicken ['tʃɪkɪn] **1.** *n.* **a)** Huhn, *das; (grilled, roasted)* Hähnchen, *das;* **don't count your ~s [before they are hatched]** *(prov.)* man soll den Pelz nicht verkaufen, ehe man den Bären erlegt hat; **b)** *(coll.: youthful person)* Küken, *das;* **she's no ~** *(is no longer young)* sie ist nicht mehr die Jüngste; *(is experienced)* sie ist kein [kleines] Kind mehr; **c)** *(coll.: game)* **play ~:** eine Mutprobe ablegen; **d)** *(coll.: coward)* Angsthase, *der.* **2.** *adj. (coll.)* feig[e]. **3.** *v.i.* ~ **out** *(sl.)* kneifen; ~ **out of sth.** sich vor etw. *(Dat.)* drücken; vor etw. *(Dat.)* kneifen

chicken: **~-and-'egg** *adj.* Huhn-Ei-‹*Frage*›; **~-breasted** *adj.* hühnerbrüstig; flachbrüstig; **~-feed** *n.* **a)** Hühnerfutter, *das;* **b)** *(fig. coll.)* eine lächerliche Summe; **the firm pays them ~-feed** die Firma zahlt ihnen einen Hungerlohn; **~-hearted** *adj.* feige; hasenfüßig; ~ **'pie** *n.* Hühnerpastete, *die;* **~-pox** *n. (Med.)* Windpocken *Pl.;* **~-run** *n.* Auslauf, *der (Landw.);* ~ **'salad** *n.* Geflügelsalat, *der;* ~ **'soup** *n.* Hühnersuppe, *die;* **~-wire** *n.* Maschendraht, *der*

chick: **~-pea** *n.* Kichererbse, *die;* **~weed** *n. (Bot.)* Vogelmiere, *die;* Hühnerdarm, *der*

chicory ['tʃɪkərɪ] *n.* **a)** *(plant)* Chicorée, *der od. die; (for coffee)* Zichorie, *die; (flower)* Wegwarte, *die;* **b)** *(Amer.: endive)* Endivie, *die*

chide [tʃaɪd], **~d** *or* **chid** [tʃɪd], **~d** *or* **chid** *or* **chidden** ['tʃɪdn] *(arch./literary)* **1.** *v.t.* schelten *(geh.)* (**for** wegen). **2.** *v.i.* schelten *(geh.)*

chief [tʃi:f] **1.** *n.* **a)** *(of state, town, clan)* Oberhaupt, *das; (of party)* Vorsitzende, *der; (of tribe)* Häuptling, *der;* ~ **of state** Staatschef, *der;* **b)** *(of department)* Leiter, *der; (coll.: one's superior, boss)* Chef, *der;* Boss, *der;* ~ **of police** Polizeipräsident, *der;* ~ **of staff** *(of a service)* Generalstabschef, *der; (commander)* Stabschef, *der;* **c) in ~** *postpos.* hauptsächlich; **Colonel-in-C~** Regimentskommandeur, *der;* **d)** *(Her.)* Schildhaupt, *das.* **2.** *adj., usu attrib.* **a)** Ober-; ~ **priest** Oberpriester, *der;* ~ **clerk** Bürochef, *der;* ~ **engineer** erster Maschinist *(Seew.);* **[Lord] C~ Justice** *(Brit.)* [Lord] Oberrichter, *der;* **b)** *(first in importance, influence, etc.)* Haupt-; ~ **reason/aim** Hauptgrund, *der*/-ziel, *das;* **his ~ crime** das Schlimmste, was er sich *(Dat.)* geleistet hat; **his ~ hope** seine größte Hoffnung; **c)** *(prominent, leading)* führend; ~ **culprit** Hauptschuldige, *der/die;* ~ **offender** Haupttäter, *der*/-täterin, *die*

chiefly ['tʃi:flɪ] *adv.* hauptsächlich; vor allem

chieftain ['tʃi:ftən] *n. (of Highland clan)* Oberhaupt, *das; (of tribe)* Stammesführer, *der; (of band of robbers)* Hauptmann, *der (hist.)*

chiff-chaff ['tʃɪftʃæf] *n. (Ornith.)* Zilpzalp, *der*

chiffon ['ʃɪfɒn] **1.** *n. (Textiles)* Chiffon, *der.* **2.** *adj.* Chiffon-

chignon ['ʃi:njɔ̃] *n.* Chignon, *der;* [Haar]knoten, *der*

chihuahua [tʃɪ'wɑ:wə] *n.* Chihuahua, *der*

chilblain ['tʃɪlbleɪn] *n.* Frostbeule, *die*

child [tʃaɪld] *n., pl.* **~ren** ['tʃɪldrən] Kind, *das;* **when I was a ~:** als ich klein war; **a ~'s guide to ...** *(fig.)* ...für Anfänger; **[be] with ~** *(dated)* schwanger [sein]; **the ~ is the father of the man** *(prov.) Einflüsse und Erfahrungen der Kindheit bestimmen den Charakter des Erwachsenen*

child: ~ **abuse** Kindesmißhandlung, *die;* **~-bearing 1.** *n.* Schwangerschaften; **2.** *adj.* gebärfähig; ~ **'benefit** *n. (Brit.)* Kindergeld, *das;* **~birth** *n.* Geburt, *die;* **die in ~birth** bei der Geburt *od.* im Wochenbett sterben; ~ **care** *n.* **a)** Betreuung von Kindern; **b)** *(social services department)* Kinderfürsorge, *die;* ~ **'guidance** *n.* Erziehungsberatung, *die*

childhood ['tʃaɪldhʊd] *n.* Kindheit, *die;* **in ~:** als Kind; **from** *or* **since ~:** schon als Kind; **be in one's second ~:** an Altersschwachsinn leiden

childish ['tʃaɪldɪʃ] *adj.*, **childishly** ['tʃaɪldɪʃlɪ] *adv.* kindlich; *(derog.)* kindisch

childishness ['tʃaɪldɪʃnɪs] *n., no pl.* Kindlichkeit, *die; (derog.)* kindisches Wesen; *(conduct)* kindisches Benehmen

childless ['tʃaɪldlɪs] *adj.* kinderlos

childlike ['tʃaɪldlaɪk] *adj.* kindlich

child: **~-minder** *n. (Brit.)* Tagesmutter, *die;* ~ **'prodigy** *n.* Wunderkind, *das;* **~-proof** *adj.* kindersicher; **~-proof door lock** *(in car)* Kindersicherung, *die;* ~ **psy'chology** *n.* Kinderpsychologie, *die*

children *pl. of* **child**

child: **~'s play** *n., no pl. (fig.)* Kinderspiel, *das;* **it's ~'s play!** es ist ein Kinderspiel!; ~ **'welfare** *n.* Kinderfürsorge, *die*

Chile ['tʃɪlɪ] *pr. n.* Chile *(das)*

Chilean ['tʃɪlɪən] **1.** *adj.* chilenisch; **sb. is ~:** jmd. ist Chilene/Chilenin. **2.** *n.* Chilene, *der*/Chilenin, *die*

Chile: ~ **'pine** *n. (Bot.)* Chilefichte, *die;* ~ **saltpetre** *n.* Chilesalpeter, *der*

chili *see* **chilli**

chill [tʃɪl] **1.** *n.* **a)** *(cold sensation)* Frösteln, *das; (feverish shivering)* Schüttelfrost, *der; (illness)* Erkältung, *die;* **catch a ~:** sich verkühlen *od.* erkälten; **b)** *(unpleasant coldness)* Kühle, *die; (fig.)* Abkühlung, *die;* **take the ~ off [sth.]** etw. leicht erwärmen; **there's a ~ in the air** es ist ziemlich kühl [draußen]; **c)** *(depressing influence)* Ernüchterung, *die;* **her presence at the party cast** *or* **spread a ~ over things** durch ihre Anwesenheit bei der Party entstand eine frostige Atmosphäre; **d)** *(of manner)* Frostigkeit, *die.* **2.** *v.t.* **a)** *(make cold, preserve)* kühlen; **I was ~ed to the marrow** ich war ganz durchgefroren; **b)** *(Metallurgy)* abschrecken. **3.** *v.i.* abkühlen. **4.** *adj. (literary; lit. or fig.)* kühl

chilli ['tʃɪlɪ] *n., pl.* **~es** Chili, *der;* ~ **con carne** [tʃɪlɪ kɒn 'kɑ:nɪ] *(Gastr.)* Chili con carne

chilliness ['tʃɪlɪnɪs] *n., no pl. (lit. or fig.)* Kühle, *die*

chilling ['tʃɪlɪŋ] *adj. (fig.)* ernüchternd; frostig ‹*Art, Worte, Blick*›

chilly ['tʃɪlɪ] *adj.* **a)** *(lit. or fig.)* kühl; **b)** *(feeling somewhat cold)* **I am rather ~:** mir ist ziemlich kühl; *(sensitive to cold)* **I'm rather a ~ person** ich friere ziemlich leicht

Chiltern Hundreds [tʃɪltən 'hʌndrədz] *n. (Brit. Polit.) Kronamt, dessen Übernahme Parlamentariern die Aufgabe ihres Parlamentssitzes ermöglicht;* **apply for the ~:** seinen Unterhaussitz aufgeben

chimaera *see* **chimera**

chime [tʃaɪm] **1.** *n.* **a)** Geläute, *das;* **ring the ~s** die Glocken läuten; **b)** *(set of bells)* Glockenspiel, *das.* **2.** *v.i.* läuten; ‹*Turmuhr:*› schlagen; **chiming clock** Schlaguhr, *die.* **3.** *v.t.* erklingen lassen ⟨*Melodie*⟩; schlagen ⟨*Stunde, Mitternacht*⟩

~ **'in** *v.i.* **a)** *(Mus.)* einstimmen; *(fig.)* übereinstimmen; **b)** *(interject remark)* sich [in die Unterhaltung] einmischen

chimera [kaɪ'mɪərə, kɪ'mɪərə] *n.* **a)** *(hybrid)* [bunte, phantastische] Mischung; *(fanciful conception)* Schimäre, *die;* **b)** *(bogy)* Schimäre, *die;* Schreckgespenst, *das;* **c)** *(Biol.)* Chimäre, *die*

chimerical [kaɪ'merɪkl, kɪ'merɪkl] *adj.* schimärisch *(geh.);* trügerisch

chimney ['tʃɪmnɪ] *n.* **a)** *(of house, factory, etc.)* Schornstein, *der; (of house also)* Kamin, *der (bes. südd.); (of factory or ship also)* Schlot, *der; (above open fire)* Rauchfang, *der;* **the smoke goes up the ~:** der Rauch zieht durch den Kaminschacht ab; **come down the ~:** durch den Schornstein kommen; **smoke like a ~** *(fig.)* wie ein Schlot rauchen; **b)** *(of lamp)* [Lampen]zylinder, *der;* **c)** *(vent of volcano etc.)* Schlot, *der;* **d)** *(Mountaineering)* Kamin, *der*

chimney: ~-breast *n.* Kaminmantel, *der;* **~-corner, ~-nook** *ns.* Sitzecke am Kamin; **~-piece** *n.* Kaminsims, *der;* **~-pot** *n.* ≈ Schornsteinkopf, *der;* **~-stack** *see* **stack 1 d; ~-sweep** *n.* Schornsteinfeger, *der*

chimp [tʃɪmp] *(coll.),* **chimpanzee** [tʃɪmpən'zi:] *ns.* Schimpanse, *der*

chin [tʃɪn] *n.* Kinn, *das;* **keep one's ~ up** *(fig.)* den Kopf nicht hängen lassen; **~ up!** Kopf hoch!; **take it on the ~** *(suffer severe blow)* einen harten Schlag einstecken müssen; *(endure sth. courageously)* es mit Fassung tragen; *see also* **stick out 1 a**

China ['tʃaɪnə] *pr. n.* China *(das)*

china *n.* Porzellan, *das; (crockery)* Geschirr, *das;* **broken ~:** Scherben *Pl.*

china: ~ cabinet *n.* Vitrine, *die;* ~ **'clay** *n.* Porzellanerde, *die;* ~ **cupboard** *n.* Geschirrschrank, *der*

China: ~man ['tʃaɪnəmən] *n., pl.* **~men** ['tʃaɪnəmən] *(derog.)* Chinese, *der;* **c~ shop** *n. see* **bull 1 a;** ~ **'tea** *n.* Chinatee, *der;* **~town** *n.* Chinesenviertel, *das;* **c~ware** *n., no pl.* Porzellan, *das*

chinch[-bug] ['tʃɪntʃ(bʌg)] *n. (Amer.)* **a)** Bettwanze, *die;* **b)** *(destroying grain)* Getreidewanze, *die*

chinchilla [tʃɪn'tʃɪlə] *n.* **a)** *(Zool.)* Chinchilla, *die;* **b)** *(fur)* Chinchilla[pelz], *der;* **c)** *(cat)* Chinchillaperser, *der; (rabbit)* Chinchilla, *das*

chin-chin [tʃɪn'tʃɪn] *int. (Brit.) (greeting)* hallo! *(ugs.); (farewell)* tschüs! *(ugs.);* cheerio!; *(as a toast)* prost!

¹chine [tʃaɪn] *n. (Brit. Geog.: ravine)* ≈ Klamm, *die*

²chine *n.* **a)** *(backbone)* Rückgrat, *das; (Cookery: joint of meat)* Rückenstück, *das;* **b)** *(Geog.: ridge)* Kamm, *der*

Chinese [tʃaɪ'ni:z] **1.** *adj.* chinesisch; **sb. is ~:** jmd. ist Chinese/Chinesin; *see also* **English 1. 2.** *n.* **a)** *pl. same (person)* Chinese, *der*/Chinesin, *die;* **b)** *(language)* Chinesisch, *das; see also* **English 2 a**

Chinese: ~ **'boxes** *n. pl.* Satz ineinanderpassender Schachteln; ~ **'goose** *n.* Höckergans, *die;* ~ **'lantern** *n.* **a)** *(of paper)* Lampion, *der;* **b)** *(Bot.)* Judenkirsche, *die;* ~ **'puzzle** *n.* chinesisches Geduldsspiel; ~ **'white** *n.* Zinkweiß, *das*

Chink [tʃɪŋk] *n. (sl. derog.)* Schlitzauge, *das (abwertend)*

¹chink *n.* **a)** Spalt, *der;* **a ~ in sb.'s armour** *(fig.)* jmds. schwache Stelle; **b) a ~ of light** ein Lichtspalt

²chink 1. *n. (sound) see* **¹clink 1. 2.** *v.i. & t. see* **¹clink 2, 3**

chinless ['tʃɪnlɪs] *adj.* **a)** mit fliehendem Kinn *nachgestellt;* **be ~:** ein fliehendes Kinn haben; **b)** *(fig.)* ~ **wonder** *(Brit. joc.) bornierter Vertreter der Oberschicht*

chinoiserie [ʃɪn'wɑ:zərɪ] *n.* Chinoiserie, *die*

chin: ~-rest *n.* Kinnstütze, *die;* **~-strap** *n. (of helmet)* Kinnriemen, *der; (of bonnet)* Kinnband, *das*

chintz [tʃɪnts] *n.* Chintz, *der*

chintzy ['tʃɪntsɪ] *adj.* auffällig bunt und billig

'chin-wag *(coll.)* **1.** *n.* Schwatz, *der.* **2.** *v.i.* schwatzen

chip [tʃɪp] **1.** *n.* **a)** Splitter, *der;* **have a ~ on one's shoulder** *(fig.)* einen Komplex haben; *see also* **block 1 c; b)** *(of potato)* [Kartoffel]stäbchen, *das;* **c)** *in pl. (Brit.: fried)* Pommes frites *Pl.; (Amer.: crisps)* Kartoffelchips *Pl.;* **d) there is a ~ on this cup/paintwork** diese Tasse ist angeschlagen/etwas Farbe ist abgeplatzt; **e)** *(Gambling)* Chip, *der;* Jeton, *der;* **have had one's ~s** *(Brit. fig. coll.)* erledigt sein *(ugs.);* **when the ~s are down** *(fig. coll.)* wenn's ernst wird; *see also* **cash in 1; f)** *(Electronics)* Chip, *der;* **g)** *(for making baskets)* Span, *der;* ~ **[basket]** *(Brit.)* Spankorb, *der;* **h)** *see* **chip shot. 2.** *v.t.,* **-pp- a)** anschlagen ⟨*Geschirr*⟩; Späne abschlagen von ⟨*Holz*⟩; *(cut or break off)* abschlagen; **the varnish is ~ped** der Lack ist abgeplatzt; **b)** *(cut into ~s)* **~ped potatoes** Kartoffelstäbchen; **c)** ~ **the ball** *(Golf)* den Ball mit einem kurzen Annäherungsschlag auf das Grün bringen; *(Football)* den Ball anheben. **3.** *v.i.,* **-pp-: this china ~s easily** von diesem Porzellan platzt leicht etwas ab

~ **'in** *(coll.)* **1.** *v.i.* **a)** *(interrupt)* sich einmischen; **who asked you to ~ in with your opinion?** wer hat dich nach deiner Meinung gefragt?; **b)** *(contribute money)* etwas beisteuern; ~ **in with £5** sich mit 5 Pfund an etw. *(Dat.)* beteiligen. **2.** *v.t. (contribute)* beisteuern

'chipboard *n.* Spanplatte, *die*

chipmunk ['tʃɪpmʌŋk] *n. (Zool.)* Chipmunk, *das*

chipolata [tʃɪpə'lɑ:tə] *n. kleine, scharf gewürzte Wurst;* Chipolata, *die*

'chip-pan *n.* Friteuse, *die*

chipper ['tʃɪpə(r)] *adj. (Amer.)* fröhlich

chipping ['tʃɪpɪŋ] *n.* Splitter, *der; (stone also)* Steinchen, *das;* **~s** *(Road Constr.)* Splitt, *der;* **'loose ~s'** „Rollsplitt"

chippy ['tʃɪpɪ] *n. (coll.)* Pommes-frites-Bude, *die;* Frittenbude, *die (ugs.)*

chip: ~ **shop** *n. (Brit.) see* **chippy;** ~ **shot** *n. (Golf)* kurzer Annäherungsschlag; *(Footb.)* kurzer Heber

chiropodist [kɪ'rɒpədɪst, ʃɪ'rɒpədɪst] *n.* Fußpfleger, *der*/-pflegerin, *die*

chiropody [kɪ'rɒpədɪ, ʃɪ'rɒpədɪ] *n.* Fußpflege, *die*

chiropractor [kaɪərə'præktə(r)] *n. (Med.)* Chiropraktiker, *der*/-praktikerin, *die*

chirp [tʃɜ:p] **1.** *v.i.* zwitschern; ⟨*Sperling:*⟩ tschilpen; ⟨*Grille:*⟩ zirpen; *(talk merrily)* jubilieren. **2.** *n.* Zwitschern, *das; (of sparrow)* Tschilpen, *das; (of grasshopper)* Zirpen, *das*

~ **'up** *v.i.* munter werden

chirpily ['tʃɜ:pɪlɪ] *adv.,* **chirpy** ['tʃɜ:pɪ] *adj. (coll.)* vergnügt

chirrup ['tʃɪrəp] **1.** *v.i.* zwitschern; ⟨*Sperling:*⟩ tschilpen. **2.** *n.* Zwitschern, *das; (of sparrow)* Tschilpen, *das*

chisel ['tʃɪzl] **1.** *n.* Meißel, *der; (for wood)* Stemmeisen, *das;* Beitel, *der; see also* **cold chisel. 2.** *v.t., (Brit.)* **-ll- a)** meißeln; *(in wood)* hauen; stemmen; **finely ~led features** fein gemeißelte [Gesichts]züge *(geh.);* **b)** *(coll.: defraud)* hereinlegen *(ugs.);* ~ **sb. out of sth.** jmdn. um etw. bringen

chiseller *(Amer.:* **chiseler)** ['tʃɪzələ(r)] *n. (coll.: swindler)* Betrüger, *der*/Betrügerin, *die*

¹chit [tʃɪt] *n.* **a)** *(young child)* Balg, *das od. der (bes. südd.);* Gör, *das (nordd.);* **be a mere ~ of a child** nur ein Kind sein; **b)** *(usu. derog.: woman)* junges Ding; **only a ~ of a girl** noch ein halbes Kind

²chit *n. (note)* Notiz, *die; (certificate)* Zeugnis, *das; (bill)* Rechnung, *die; (receipt)* Quittung, *die; (from doctor)* Krankmeldung, *die*

chit-chat ['tʃɪttʃæt] **1.** *n.* Plauderei, *die.* **2.** *v.i.,* **-tt-** plaudern

chitterling ['tʃɪtəlɪŋ] *n., usu. in pl.* Schweinsdarm, *der*

chivalric ['ʃɪvlrɪk] *adj. (of chivalry)* **the ~ ages** die Ritterzeit

chivalrous ['ʃɪvlrəs] *adj.* ritterlich; ~ **age** Ritterzeit, *die;* ~ **deed** ritterliche Tat

chivalrously ['ʃɪvlrəslɪ] *adv.* ritterlich

chivalry ['ʃɪvlrɪ] *n., no pl.* **a)** Ritterlichkeit, *die;* **b)** *(medieval knightly system)* Rittertum, *das;* **Age of C~:** Ritterzeit, *die;* **the Age of C~ is not dead** es gibt noch richtige Kavaliere

chives [tʃaɪvz] *n. pl.* Schnittlauch, *der*

chiv[v]y ['tʃɪvɪ] *v.t.* hetzen; *(harass)* schikanieren; ~ **sb. into doing sth.** jmdn. drängen, etw. zu tun; ~ **sb. about sth.** jmdn. wegen etw. drängen

~ **a'long** *v.t.* antreiben

chloride ['klɔ:raɪd] *n. (Chem.)* Chlorid, *das; (bleaching agent)* chloridhaltiges Bleichmittel

chlorinate ['klɔ:rɪneɪt] *v.t.* chloren

chlorination [klɔ:rɪ'neɪʃn] *n.* Chlorung, *die*

chlorine ['klɔ:ri:n] *n.* Chlor, *das*

chloroform ['klɒrəfɔ:m] **1.** *n.* Chloroform, *das.* **2.** *v.t.* chloroformieren

chlorophyll ['klɒrəfɪl] *n. (Bot.)* Chlorophyll, *das*

choc [tʃɒk] *n. (Brit. coll.)* Schokopraline, *die*

'choc-ice *n.* Eis mit Schokoladenüberzug

chock [tʃɒk] **1.** *n.* Bremsklotz, *der; (on rail)* Bremsschuh, *der.* **2.** *v.t.* blockieren

'chock-a-block *pred. adj.* vollgepfropft

chocker ['tʃɒkə(r)] *adj. (Brit. sl.)* sauer *(salopp);* **be ~ with** *or* **of sth.** von etw. die Nase gestrichen voll haben *(salopp)*

'chock-full *pred. adj.* gestopft voll *(ugs.);* ~ **with sth.** mit etw. vollgepfropft

chockie ['tʃɒkɪ] *see* **choc**

chocolate ['tʃɒkələt, 'tʃɒklət] **1.** *n.* **a)** Schokolade, *die; (sweetmeat)* Praline, *die;* **drinking ~:** Trinkschokolade, *die;* **b)** *(colour)* Schokoladenbraun, *das.* **2.** *adj.* **a)** *(with flavour of ~)* Schokoladen-; **b)** *(with colour of ~)* **~[-brown]** schokoladenbraun

chocolate: ~ **'biscuit** *n.* Schokoladenkeks, *der;* **~-box 1.** *n.* Pralinenschachtel, *die;* Bonbonniere, *die;* **2.** *adj. (fig.)* kitschig; **~-coated** *adj.* mit Schokoladeüberzug *nachgestellt*

choice [tʃɔɪs] **1.** *n.* **a)** Wahl, *die;* **if the ~ were mine, if I had the ~:** wenn ich die Wahl hätte; **by** *or* **for ~:** am liebsten; **of my/his** *etc.* **~:** meiner/seiner *usw.* Wahl; **take your ~:** suchen Sie sich *(Dat.)* eine/einen/eins aus; wählen Sie; *(truculently)* entscheiden Sie sich; **take one's ~ of sth. from sth.** etw. aus etw. auswählen; **make a [good] ~:** eine [gute] Wahl treffen; **make a careful ~:** sorgfältig [aus]wählen; **give sb. the ~:** jmdm. die Wahl lassen; **the ~ is yours** Sie haben die Wahl; **you have a free ~:** Sie können frei wählen; **do sth. from ~:** etw. freiwillig tun; **if I were given the ~:** wenn man mir die Wahl ließe; **have no ~ but to do sth.** keine andere Wahl haben, als etw. zu tun; **leave sb. no ~:** jmdm. keine [andere] Wahl lassen; **you have several ~s** Sie haben mehrere Möglichkeiten; **b)** *(thing chosen)* **his ~ of wallpaper was ...:** die Tapete, die er sich ausgesucht hatte, war ...; **the curtains were your ~:** die Vorhänge hast du ausgesucht; **this is my ~:** ich habe mich dafür entschieden; *see also* **Hobson's choice; c)** *(variety)* Auswahl, *die;* **there is a ~ of three** es gibt drei zur Auswahl; **be spoilt for ~:** die Qual der Wahl haben; **have a ~:** die Auswahl haben. **2.** *adj.* ausgewählt; auserlesen *(geh.);* ~ **wine** erlesener Wein *(geh.);* ~ **tomatoes/fruit** Tomaten/Obst erster Wahl

choir ['kwaɪə(r)] *n. (also Archit.)* Chor, *der*
choir: **~boy** *n.* Chorknabe, *der;* **~master** *n.* Chorleiter, *der;* **~ practice** *n.* Chorprobe, *die;* **~ school** *n. [Konfessions]schule für Chorknaben;* **~-screen** *n.* Chorschranke, *die;* **~-stall** *see* ˈstall 1 c
choke [tʃəʊk] **1.** *v.t.* **a)** *(lit. or fig.)* ersticken; **a fish-bone was choking him** er drohte an einer Fischgräte zu ersticken; **you'll ~ yourself** du wirst ersticken; **in a voice ~d with emotion** *(fig.)* mit vor Erregung versagender Stimme; **be/get ~d up about sth.** *(fig. coll.)* sich *(Dat.)* etw. sehr zu Herzen nehmen; **b)** *(strangle)* erdrosseln; **~ to death** erdrosseln; **the collar was choking him** der Kragen würgte ihn; **c)** *(fill chock-full)* vollstopfen; *(block up)* verstopfen. **2.** *v.i.* **a)** *(temporarily)* keine Luft [mehr] bekommen; *(permanently)* ersticken (**on** an + *Dat.*); **b)** *(from emotion)* **he almost ~d with rage** er brachte vor Wut fast keinen Ton heraus. **3.** *n.* **a)** *(Motor Veh.)* Choke, *der;* **b)** *(Electr.)* Drosselspule, *die*
~ ˈback *v.t.* unterdrücken ‹*Wut*›; zurückhalten ‹*Tränen*›; hinunterschlucken *(ugs.)* ‹*Wut, Worte*›
~ ˈdown *v.t.* unterdrücken
~ ˈoff *v.t. (fig. coll.)* abwimmeln *(ugs.); (tell off)* einen Rüffel verpassen (+ *Dat.*)
choked [tʃəʊkt] *adj. (coll.: disgusted)* sauer *(salopp)*
choker ['tʃəʊkə(r)] *n. (high collar)* Stehkragen, *der; (necklace)* Halsband, *das*
choler ['kɒlə(r)] *n.* **a)** *(Hist.)* Galle, *die;* **b)** *(poet./arch.)* **in ~:** wutentbrannt; **fit of ~:** Zornesausbruch, *der (geh.)*
cholera ['kɒlərə] *n. (Med.)* Cholera, *die*
choleric ['kɒlərɪk] *adj.* cholerisch
cholesterol [kə'lestərɒl] *n. (Med.)* Cholesterin, *das*
chomp [tʃɒmp] *v.t. see* ˈ**champ**
choo-choo ['tʃu:tʃu:] *n. (child lang./coll.)* Puffpuff, *die (Kindersp.)*
choose [tʃu:z] **1.** *v.t.*, **chose** [tʃəʊz], **chosen** ['tʃəʊzn] **a)** *(select)* wählen; *(from a group)* auswählen; **~ a career** einen Beruf wählen; **~ sb. as** *or* **to be** *or* **for leader** jmdn. zum Anführer wählen; **~ sb. from among ...:** jmdn. unter (+ *Dat.*) *od.* aus ... auswählen; **carefully chosen words** sorgfältig gewählte Worte; **the chosen [few]** *(Theol.)* die [wenigen] Auserwählten; **the chosen people** *or* **race** *(Theol.)* das auserwählte Volk; **b)** *(decide)* **~/~ not to do sth.** sich dafür/dagegen entscheiden, etw. zu tun; **he chose rather to study** er zog es vor zu lernen; **she did not ~ to wear** ˈ**black** sie zog es vor, nicht Schwarz zu tragen; **she did not** ˈ**~ to wear black** sie hat nicht freiwillig Schwarz getragen; **there's nothing/not much/little to ~ between them** sie unterscheiden sich in nichts/nicht sehr/nur wenig voneinander. **2.** *v.i.*, **chose, chosen** wählen; **when I ~:** wenn es mir paßt; **do just as you ~:** machen Sie es so, wie Sie möchten; **~ between ...:** zwischen ... wählen; **~ from sth.** aus etw./*(from several)* unter etw. *(Dat.)* [aus]wählen; **there are several to ~ from** es stehen mehrere zur Auswahl; **he cannot ~ but submit** er hat keine andere Wahl, als nachzugeben; **if you/we** *etc.* **so ~:** wenn Sie/wir *usw.* [es] möchten *od.* wollen; **as you ~:** wie Sie möchten
chooser ['tʃu:zə(r)] *n. see* **beggar 1 a**
choos[e]y ['tʃu:zɪ] *adj. (coll.)* wählerisch
¹**chop** [tʃɒp] **1.** *n.* **a)** Hieb, *der;* **b)** *(of meat)* Kotelett, *das;* **c)** *(coll.)* **get the ~** *(be killed)* abgemurkst werden *(salopp); (be dismissed)* rausgeworfen werden *(ugs.);* **sth. gets the ~:** etw. wird abgeschafft; **give sb. the ~** *(dismiss)* jmdn. rauswerfen *(ugs.); (kill)* jmdn. abmurksen *(salopp);* **be due for the ~:** die längste Zeit existiert haben *(ugs.). See also* **karate chop. 2.** *v.t.*, **-pp- a)** hacken ‹*Holz*›; kleinschneiden ‹*Gemüse, Fleisch, Obst*›; **they ~ped a way through the undergrowth** sie schlugen einen Weg durch das Unterholz; **~ped herbs** gehackte Kräuter; **b)** *(Sport)* schneiden ‹*Ball*›. **3.** *v.i.*, **-pp-: ~ [away] at sth.** auf etw. *(Akk.)* einhacken; **~ through the bone** den Knochen durchhacken
~ ˈdown *v.t.* fällen ‹*Baum*›; umhauen ‹*Busch, Pfosten*›
~ ˈoff *v.t.* abhacken
~ ˈup *v.t.* kleinschneiden ‹*Fleisch, Obst, Gemüse*›; zerhacken ‹*Möbel*›; zerkleinern ‹*Holz*›; **~ped-up parsley** [klein]gehackte Petersilie
²**chop** *n.* **a)** *(jaw)* Kiefer, *der;* **b)** *in pl.* Maul, *das; (coll.: person's mouth)* Klappe, *die (salopp); see also* **lick 1 a**
³**chop** *v.i.*, **-pp-: she's always ~ping and changing** sie überlegt es sich *(Dat.)* dauernd anders; **keep ~ping and changing** ‹*Wetter:*› [sich] dauernd ändern
~ aˈbout *v.i. (coll.)* sprunghaft sein; ‹*Wind:*› umspringen
ˈ**chop-house** *n. (coll.)* Gaststätte, *die*
chopper ['tʃɒpə(r)] *n.* **a)** *(axe)* Beil, *das; (cleaver)* Hackbeil, *das;* **b)** *(coll.: helicopter)* Hubschrauber, *der;* **c)** *in pl. (coll.: teeth)* Beißerchen *(ugs.)*
chopping-board ['tʃɒpɪŋbɔ:d] *n.* Hackbrett, *das*
choppy ['tʃɒpɪ] *adj.* bewegt; kabbelig *(Seemannsspr.)*
ˈ**chopstick** *n.* [Eß]stäbchen, *das*
chop-suey [tʃɒp'su:ɪ, tʃɒp'sju:ɪ] *n. (Gastr.)* Chop-suey, *das*
¹**choral** ['kɔ:rl] *adj.* Chor-; chorisch; **~ piece** Komposition für Chor
chorale (²**choral)** [kɔ:'rɑ:l] *n.* **a)** Choral, *der;* **b)** *(group)* Chor, *der*
choral ['kɔ:rl]: **~ service** *n.* Gottesdienst mit Chorgesang; **~ society** *n.* Gesangverein, *der*
¹**chord** [kɔ:d] *n.* **a)** *(string of harp etc.; also fig.)* Saite, *die;* **strike a [familiar/responsive] ~ with sb.** *(fig.)* bei jmdm. eine Saite zum Erklingen bringen/bei jmdm. Echo finden; **touch the right ~** *(fig.)* den richtigen Ton anschlagen *od.* treffen; **b)** *(Math.)* Sehne, *die; (Aeron.: of wing)* Flügeltiefe, *die*
²**chord** *n. (Mus.)* Akkord, *der;* **common ~:** Dreiklang [mit reiner Quinte]
chore [tʃɔ:(r)] *n.* [lästige] Routinearbeit; **do the [general] household ~s** die üblichen Hausarbeiten erledigen; **writing letters is a ~:** Briefe zu schreiben ist eine lästige Pflicht
chorea [kə'ri:ə] *n. (Med.)* Chorea, *die (fachspr.);* Veitstanz, *der*
choreograph ['kɒrɪəgrɑ:f] *v.t. & i.* choreographieren
choreographer [kɒrɪ'ɒgrəfə(r)] *n.* Choreograph, *der*/Choreographin, *die*
choreographic [kɒrɪə'græfɪk] *adj.* choreographisch
choreography [kɒrɪ'ɒgrəfɪ] *n.* Choreographie, *die*
chorister ['kɒrɪstə(r)] *n.* **a)** *(choirboy)* Chorknabe, *der;* **b)** *(Amer.: leader of choir)* Chorleiter, *der*
chortle ['tʃɔ:tl] **1.** *v.i.* vor Lachen glucksen; *(contemptuously)* [hämisch] kichern. **2.** *n.* Glucksen, *das;* **reply/say with a ~:** glucksend erwidern/sagen
chorus ['kɔ:rəs] **1.** *n.* **a)** Chor, *der;* **they broke [out] into a ~ of ...:** sie fingen an, im Chor ... zu singen/rufen; **say sth. in ~:** etw. im Chor sagen; **the football fans kept up a ~ of 'Scotland'** die Fußballfans hörten nicht auf, im Chor „Scotland" zu rufen; **b)** *(of singers)* Chor, *der; (of dancers)* Ballett, *das;* **be in the ~:** zum Chor/zum Ballett gehören; **c)** *(of popular song)* Chorus, *der;* **d)** *(Mus.: composition)* Chor, *der.* **2.** *v.t.* im Chor singen/sprechen
chorus: **~-girl** *n.* Chorsängerin, *die; (dancer)* [Revue]girl, *das;* **~ line** *n.* Ballett, *das;* **~-master** *n.* Chorleiter, *der*
chose, chosen *see* **choose**
chough [tʃʌf] *n. (Ornith.)* **[Cornish] ~:** Alpenkrähe, *die;* **[alpine] ~** Alpendohle, *die*
choux [ʃu:] *n.* **~ [pastry]** Brandteig, *der*
chow [tʃaʊ] *n.* **a)** *(dog)* Chow-Chow, *der;* **b)** *(Amer. sl.: food)* Futterage, *die (ugs.);* Futter, *das (salopp)*
chowder [tʃaʊdə(r)] *n. (Amer.) Suppe od. Eintopf mit Fisch od. Muscheln, Pökelfleisch od. Schinken, Milch, Kartoffeln u. Gemüse*
Christ [kraɪst] **1.** *n.* Christus *(der); see also* **before 2 a. 2.** *int. (sl.)* **[oh] ~!, ~ almighty!** Herrgott noch mal! *(ugs.)*
Christadelphian [krɪstə'delfɪən] *n.* Christadelphian, *der (Mitglied einer chiliastischen Sekte)*
ˈ**Christ-child** *n.* Christkind, *das*
christen ['krɪsn] *v.t.* **a)** taufen; **she was ~ed Martha** sie wurde [auf den Namen] Martha getauft; **b)** *(coll.: use for first time)* einweihen *(ugs. scherzh.)*
Christendom ['krɪsndəm] *n.*, *no pl., no art.* die christliche Welt; *(Christians)* die Christenheit; die Christen
christening ['krɪsənɪŋ] *n.* Taufe, *die;* **her ~ will be next Sunday** sie wird nächsten Sonntag getauft
Christian ['krɪstjən] **1.** *adj.* christlich. **2.** *n.* Christ, *der*/Christin, *die*
Christian ˈera *n.* **in the first centuries of the ~:** in den ersten Jahrhunderten christlicher Zeitrechnung
Christianity [krɪstɪ'ænɪtɪ] *n.*, *no pl., no art.* das Christentum
Christian: **~ name** *n.* Vorname, *der;* **~ ˈScience** *n.* Christian Science, *die;* Christliche Wissenschaft; **~ ˈScientist** *n.* Christian Scientist, *der;* Christlicher Wissenschafter
Christlike ['kraɪstlaɪk] *adj.* christusgleich
Christmas ['krɪsməs] *n.* Weihnachten, *das od. Pl.;* **merry** *or* **happy ~:** frohe *od.* fröhliche Weihnachten; **what did you get for ~?** was hast du zu Weihnachten bekommen?; **at ~:** [zu *od.* an] Weihnachten
Christmas: **~-box** *n. (Brit.) Geschenk/Trinkgeld zu Weihnachten für den Postboten, Zeitungsjungen usw.;* **~ cake** *n.* Weihnachtskuchen, *der; mit Marzipan und Zuckerguß verzierter, reichhaltiger Gewürzkuchen;* **~ card** *n.* Weihnachtskarte, *die;* **~ ˈcarol** *n.* Weihnachtslied, *das;* **~ ˈDay** *n.* erster Weihnachtsfeiertag; **~ ˈEve** *n.* Heiligabend, *der;* **~ ˈholiday** *n.* Weihnachtsurlaub, *der;* **the ~ holidays** die Weihnachtsferien; **~ present** *n.* Weihnachtsgeschenk, *das;* **~ ˈpudding** *n.* Plumpudding, *der;* **~ ˈrose** *n.* Christrose, *die;* **~ ˈstocking** *n. von den Kindern am Heiligabend aufgehängter Strumpf, den der Weihnachtsmann mit Geschenken füllen soll*
Christmassy ['krɪsməsɪ] *adj.* weihnachtlich; **it doesn't feel very ~:** es herrscht keine rechte Weihnachtsstimmung
Christmas: **~-tide, ~ time** *ns.* Weihnachtszeit, *die;* **at ~-tide** *or* **~ time** in der *od.* zur Weihnachtszeit; **~ tree** *n.* Weihnachtsbaum, *der*
chromatic [krə'mætɪk] *adj.* chromatisch
chromatic ˈscale *n. (Mus.)* chromatische Tonleiter
chromatography [krəʊmə'tɒgrəfɪ] *n. (Chem.)* Chromatographie, *die*
chrome [krəʊm] *n.* **a)** *(chromium-plate)* Chrom, *das;* **b)** *(colour)* Chromgelb, *das*
chrome: **~ ˈsteel** *n.* Chromstahl, *der;* **~ ˈyellow** *n. see* **chrome a**
chromium ['krəʊmɪəm] *n.* Chrom, *das*
chromium: **~-plate 1.** *n.* Chrom, *das;* **2.** *v.t.* verchromen; **~-plated** *adj.* verchromt; **~-ˈplating** *n.* Verchromung, *die*
chromosome ['krəʊməsəʊm] *n. (Biol.)* Chromosom, *das*
chronic ['krɒnɪk] *adj.* **a)** chronisch; **~ sufferers from arthritis** Personen, die an

chronischer Arthritis leiden; **he had been plagued by ~ doubts** ihn hatten ständig Zweifel geplagt; **b)** *(Brit. coll.: bad, intense)* katastrophal *(ugs.)*; **be ~:** eine [einzige] Katastrophe sein *(ugs.)*; **it hurt something ~:** es hat wahnsinnig weh getan *(ugs.)*
chronically ['krɒnɪkəlɪ] *adv.* chronisch; **she was ~ afraid of ...:** sie hatte [eine] chronische Angst vor ...
chronicle ['krɒnɪkl] **1.** *n.* **a)** Chronik, *die;* **b)** *(account)* Schilderung, *die;* **c)** *(Bibl.)* **C~s** Chronik, *die.* **2.** *v. t.* [chronologisch] aufzeichnen; **he ~d these events** er verfaßte eine Chronik dieser Ereignisse
chronicler ['krɒnɪklə(r)] *n.* Chronist, *der*
chronological [krɒnə'lɒdʒɪkl] *adj.*, **chronologically** [krɒnə'lɒdʒɪkəlɪ] *adv.* chronologisch
chronology [krə'nɒlədʒɪ] *n.* Chronologie, *die; (table)* Zeittafel, *die*
chronometer [krə'nɒmɪtə(r)] *n.* Chronometer, *das*
chrysalis ['krɪsəlɪs] *n., pl.* **~es** *or* **chrysalides** [krɪ'sælɪdi:z] *(Zool.)* **a)** *(pupa)* Chrysalide, *die (Zool.)*; Puppe, *die;* **b)** *(case enclosing pupa)* Puppenhülle, *die*
chrysanth [krɪ'sænθ] *n. (coll.) see* **chrysanthemum**
chrysanthemum [krɪ'sænθɪməm] *n. (Bot.)* **a)** *(flower)* Chrysantheme, *die;* **b)** *(plant)* Chrysanthemum, *das;* Wucherblume, *die*
chub [tʃʌb] *n., pl. same (Zool.)* Döbel, *der*
chubby ['tʃʌbɪ] *adj.* **a)** *(plump)* pummelig; rundlich ‹*Gesicht*›; **~ cheeks** Pausbacken *(fam.)*; **b)** *(plump-faced)* pausbäckig
¹chuck [tʃʌk] **1.** *v. t.* **a)** *(coll.: throw)* schmeißen *(ugs.)*; **b) ~ sb. under the chin** jmdm. einen Stups unters Kinn geben; **c)** *(coll.: throw out)* wegschmeißen *(ugs.)*; **~ it!** *(sl.)* hör schon auf [damit]!; **~ the whole thing** alles hinschmeißen. **2.** *n.* **a) give sb. a ~ under the chin** jmdm. einen Stups unters Kinn geben; **b)** *(sl.: dismissal)* **give sb. the ~ [from his/her job]** jmdn. [aus der Firma *usw.*] rausschmeißen *(ugs.)*; **get the ~:** rausfliegen *(ugs.)*
~ a'way *v. t. (coll.)* wegschmeißen *(ugs.)*; *(fig.: waste)* zum Fenster rauswerfen *(ugs.)* ‹*Geld*› (**on** für); vertun ‹*Chance, Gelegenheit*›
~ 'out *v. t. (coll.)* wegschmeißen *(ugs.)*; *(fig.: eject)* rausschmeißen *(ugs.)*
²chuck *n. (of drill, lathe)* Futter, *das*
³chuck *n. (Amer. coll.: food)* Futter, *das (salopp)*
chucker-out [tʃʌkə'raʊt] *n. (coll.)* Rausschmeißer, *der (ugs.)*
chuckle ['tʃʌkl] **1.** *v. i.* **a)** leise [vor sich hin] lachen (**at** über + *Akk.*); **b)** *(exult)* sich *(Dat.)* eins lachen. **2.** *n.* leises, glucksendes Lachen; **have a ~ [to oneself] about sth.** leise über etw. *(Akk.)* vor sich hin lachen
chuckle: ~-head *n.* Schwachkopf, *der (abwertend)*; **~-headed** *adj.* schwachköpfig *(abwertend)*
'chuck-wagon *n. (Amer. coll.) Proviantwagen mit Kochvorrichtung (auf einer Ranch usw.)*
chuff [tʃʌf] *v. i.* puffen *(ugs.)*
chuffed [tʃʌft] *pred. adj. (Brit. sl.)* zufrieden (**about, at, with** über + *Akk.*); **be ~:** sich freuen
chug [tʃʌg] **1.** *v. i.*, **-gg-** ‹*Motor:*› tuckern. **2.** *n.* Tuckern, *das*
chum [tʃʌm] *(coll.) n.* **a)** Kumpel, *der (salopp)*; **be great ~s** dicke Freunde sein *(ugs.)*; **b)** *(Austral., NZ)* **new ~:** Neuling, *der*
~ 'up *v. i.* **~ up [with sb.]** sich [mit jmdm.] anfreunden
chummy ['tʃʌmɪ] *adj. (coll.)* freundlich; **be ~ with sb.** mit jmdm. dick befreundet sein *(ugs.)*
chump [tʃʌmp] *n.* **a)** *(sl.: foolish person)* Trottel, *der (ugs.)*; **b) be off one's ~** *(coll.)* nicht bei Trost sein *(ugs.)*
chump 'chop *n.* ≈ Lammkotelett, *das*
chunk [tʃʌŋk] *n.* dickes Stück; *(broken off)* Brocken, *der; (large amount)* guter Brocken; **~ of wood** Holzklotz, *der*
chunky ['tʃʌŋkɪ] *adj.* **a)** *(containing chunks)* ‹*Orangenmarmelade, Hundefutter*› mit ganzen Stücken; **b)** *(small and sturdy, short and thick)* stämmig; **~ fingers** kurze, dicke Finger; **~ book** kleines, dickes Buch; **c)** *(made of thick, bulky material)* dick ‹*Pullover, Strickjacke*›
Chunnel ['tʃʌnl] *n. (Brit. coll.)* [Ärmel]kanaltunnel, *der*
chunter ['tʃʌntə(r)] *v. i. (coll.)* **a)** *(murmur)* brummeln; brabbeln; **b)** *(grumble)* murren
chupatty *see* **chapat[t]i**
church [tʃɜ:tʃ] *n.* **a)** Kirche, *die;* **in** *or* **at ~:** in der Kirche; **after ~:** nach der Kirche; **go to ~:** in die *od.* zur Kirche gehen; **b) C~** *(body)* die Kirche; **go into the C~:** Geistlicher werden; **the C~ of England** die Kirche von England; **the C~ militant/triumphant** Ecclesia militans/triumphans, *die (Rel.)*
church: ~-goer *n.* Kirchgänger, *der*/-gängerin, *die;* **~-going 1.** *n., no pl.* Kirchenbesuch, *der;* **2.** *attrib. adj.* regelmäßig den Gottesdienst besuchend; **~man** ['tʃɜ:tʃmən] *n., pl.* **~men** ['tʃɜ:tʃmən] **a)** *(member of clergy)* Geistliche, *der;* **b)** *(member of church)* Mitglied der Kirche; **~ 'mouse** *n.* **as poor as a ~ mouse** arm wie eine Kirchenmaus *(ugs. scherzh.)*; **~ parade** *n.* gemeinsamer Kirchgang *(von Soldaten, Pfadfindern usw.)*; **~warden** *n.* **a)** Kirchenvorsteher, *der*/-vorsteherin, *die;* **b)** *(Amer.: church administrator) [für die Finanzen zuständiger] Beauftragter der Protestantischen Episkopalkirche;* **~woman** *n.* [weibliches] Mitglied der Kirche
churchy ['tʃɜ:tʃɪ] *adj.* streng kirchlich; kirchenfromm *(abwertend)*
'churchyard *n.* Kirchhof, *der (veralt.)*; Friedhof, *der (bei einer Kirche)*
churl [tʃɜ:l] *n.* **a)** *(derog.) (ill-bred person)* ungehobelter Kerl *(ugs. abwertend)*; *(surly person)* Griesgram, *der (abwertend)*; **b)** *(arch.) (peasant)* Bauer, *der; (person of low birth)* einfacher *od.* gemeiner Mann
churlish ['tʃɜ:lɪʃ] *adj. (derog.) (ill-bred)* ungehobelt *(abwertend)*; *(surly)* griesgrämig *(abwertend)*
churlishly ['tʃɜ:lɪʃlɪ] *adv. (derog.) see* **churlish:** ungehobelt; griesgrämig
churlishness ['tʃɜ:lɪʃnɪs] *n., no pl. (derog.) see* **churlish:** Ungehobeltheit, *die;* Griesgrämigkeit, *die*
churn [tʃɜ:n] **1.** *n. (Brit.)* **a)** *(for making butter)* Butterfaß, *das;* **b)** *(milk-can)* Milchkanne, *die.* **2.** *v. t.* **a)** verbuttern; **~ butter** buttern; **b)** aufwühlen ‹*Wasser, Schlamm*›. **3.** *v. i.* ‹*Meer:*› wallen *(geh.)*; ‹*Schiffsschraube:*› wirbeln; ‹*Räder:*› durchdrehen; **my stomach was ~ing** mir drehte sich der Magen um
~ 'out *v. t.* massenweise produzieren *(ugs.)*; **he's been ~ing out three books a year** er hat pro Jahr drei Bücher produziert
~ 'up *v. t.* aufwühlen
chute [ʃu:t] *n.* **a)** Schütte, *die; (for persons)* Rutsche, *die;* **escape ~** *(in aircraft)* Notrutsche, *die;* **b)** *(coll.: parachute)* [Fall]schirm, *der*
chutney ['tʃʌtnɪ] *n.* Chutney, *das*
chutzpah ['hʊtspə] *n. (sl.)* Chuzpe, *die (salopp abwertend)*
CI *abbr. (Brit.)* **Channel Islands**
CIA *abbr. (Amer.)* **Central Intelligence Agency** CIA, *der od. die*
ciborium [sɪ'bɔ:rɪəm] *n., pl.* **ciboria** [sɪ'bɔ:rɪə] *(Archit., Eccl.)* Ziborium, *das*
cicada [sɪ'kɑ:də] *n. (Zool.)* Zikade, die
CID *abbr. (Brit.)* **Criminal Investigation Department** C. I. D.; **the ~:** die Kripo
cider ['saɪdə(r)] *n.* ≈ Apfelwein, *der; (from France)* Cidre, *der*
cider: ~ apple *n.* Mostapfel, *der;* **~-press** *n.* Mostpresse, *die*
cig [sɪg] *n. (coll.)* Glimmstengel, *der (ugs.)*
cigar [sɪ'gɑ:(r)] *n.* Zigarre, *die*
cigarette [sɪgə'ret] *n.* Zigarette, *die*
cigarette: ~ card *n.* Zigarettenbild, *das;* **~-case** *n.* Zigarettenetui, *das;* **~-end** *n.* Zigarettenstummel, *der;* **~-holder** *n.* Zigarettenspitze, *die;* **~-lighter** *n.* Feuerzeug, *das; (in car)* Zigarettenanzünder, *der;* **~-packet** *n.* Zigarettenschachtel, *die;* **~-paper** *n.* Zigarettenpapier, *das*
cigar: ~ lighter *n. see* **cigarette-lighter;** **~-shaped** *adj.* zigarrenförmig
cilium ['sɪlɪəm] *n., pl.* **cilia** ['sɪlɪə] *(Biol., Anat.)* Wimper, *die;* Zilie, *die (fachspr.)*
C.-in-C. *abbr. (Mil.)* **Commander-in-Chief**
cinch [sɪntʃ] **1.** *n.* **a)** *(sl.) (easy thing)* Klacks, *der (ugs.)*; Kinderspiel, *das; (Amer.: sure thing)* todsichere Sache *(ugs.)*; **that's a ~:** [das ist] ganz klar! *(ugs.)*; klarer Fall! *(ugs.)*; **b)** *(Amer.: saddle-girth)* Sattelgurt, *der.* **2.** *v. t. (Amer.)* **a)** *(sl.: make certain of)* **~ sth. for sb.** jmdm. etw. sichern; **b)** *(put girth on)* **~ a horse** den Sattelgurt eines Pferdes schnallen
cinchona [sɪŋ'kəʊnə] *n.* **a)** *(Med.)* Chinarinde, *die;* **b)** *(Bot.)* Chinarindenbaum, *der*
cinder ['sɪndə(r)] *n.* **a)** Zinder, *der;* ausgeglühtes Stück Holz/Kohle; **~s** Asche, *die;* **burnt to a ~:** völlig verkohlt; **b)** *(glowing ember)* glühendes Stück Holz/Kohle; **c)** *(slag)* Schlacke, *die*
Cinderella [sɪndə'relə] *n.* **a)** *(person)* Aschenbrödel, *das;* Aschenputtel, *das;* **b)** *(fig.: thing)* Stiefkind, *das*
cinder: ~-path *n.* Schlackenweg, *der (Bauw.)*; **~-track** *n.* Aschenbahn, *die*
cine ['sɪnɪ] *adj.* Schmalfilm-
cine: ~ camera *n.* Filmkamera, *die;* **~ film** *n.* Schmalfilm, *der*
cinema ['sɪnɪmə] *n.* **a)** *(Brit.: building)* Kino, *das;* **go to the ~:** ins Kino gehen; **what's on at the ~?** was gibt's im Kino?; **b)** *no pl., no art. (cinematography)* Kinematographie, *die;* **c)** *(films, film production)* Film, *der;* Kino, *das (seltener)*
'cinema-goer *n. (Brit.)* Kinogänger, *der*/-gängerin, *die*
cinematic [sɪnɪ'mætɪk] *adj.* filmisch; **~ art** Filmkunst, *die*
cinematographic [sɪnɪmætə'græfɪk] *adj.* kinematographisch
cinematography [sɪnɪmə'tɒgrəfɪ] *n., no pl.* Kinematographie, *die*
cineraria [sɪnə'reərɪə] *n. (Bot.)* Zinerarie, *die;* Aschenpflanze, *die*
cinnabar ['sɪnəbɑ:(r)] *n.* Zinnober, *der*
cinnamon ['sɪnəmən] *n.* Zimt, *der; (plant)* Zimtbaum, *der*
cinquefoil ['sɪŋkfɔɪl] *n.* **a)** *(Bot.)* Fingerkraut, *das;* **b)** *(Archit.)* Fünfpaß, *der*
Cinque Ports [sɪŋk 'pɔ:ts] *n. pl.* Cinque Ports *Pl. (hist.; südenglischer Städtebund)*
cipher ['saɪfə(r)] **1.** *n.* **a)** *(code, secret writing)* Chiffre, *die;* Geheimschrift, *die; (key)* Kode, *der; (method)* Chiffrierung, *die;* Kodierung, *die;* **in ~:** chiffriert; **b)** *(symbol for zero)* [Ziffer] Null, *die;* **c)** *(fig.: nonentity)* Nummer, *die;* **d)** *(monogram)* Monogramm, *das.* **2.** *v. t. (put into code)* chiffrieren
circa ['sɜ:kə] *prep.* zirka
circadian [sɜ:'keɪdɪən] *adj. (Physiol.)* zirkadian
circle ['sɜ:kl] **1.** *n.* **a)** *(also Geom.)* Kreis, *der;* **great/small ~** *(Geom., Naut., Aeronaut., Astron.)* Groß-/Kleinkreis, *der;* **fly/stand in a ~:** im Kreis fliegen/stehen; *(inside a ~)* in einem Kreis fliegen/stehen; **run round in ~s** *(fig. coll.)* hektisch herumlaufen *(ugs.)*; **go round in ~s** im Kreis laufen; *(fig.)* sich im Kreis drehen; **~ of friends** Freundeskreis, *der;* **come full ~** *(fig.)* zum Ausgangspunkt zurückkehren; **things have now**

come full ~: der Kreis schließt sich *od.* hat sich geschlossen; **b)** *see* **vicious circle; c)** *(seats in theatre or cinema)* Rang, *der;* **d)** *(Archaeol.)* [Stein]kreis, *der;* **e)** *(Hockey)* Schußkreis, *der.* **2.** *v. i.* kreisen; *(walk in a ~)* im Kreis gehen. **3.** *v. t.* **a)** *(move in a ~ round)* umkreisen; **the aircraft ~d the airport** das Flugzeug kreiste über dem Flughafen; **b)** *(draw ~ round)* einkreisen

~ **'back** *v. i.* auf einem Umweg zurückkehren

~ **'round** *v. i.* kreisen

circlet ['sɜ:klɪt] *n. (of gold etc.)* Reif, *der; (of flowers)* Kranz, *der*

circuit ['sɜ:kɪt] *n.* **a)** *(Electr.)* Schaltung, *die; (path of current)* Stromkreis, *der;* **b)** *(Motor-racing)* Rundkurs, *der;* **c)** *(journey round)* Runde, *die; (by car etc.)* Rundfahrt, *die;* **we made a ~ of the lake** wir machten einen Rundgang/eine Rundfahrt um den See; **d)** *(judge's itinerary)* **dienstliche Rundreise** *(eines Richters, der in Städten in England und Wales in Zivil- u. Strafsachen Gerichtssitzungen abhält); (district visited)* Gerichtsbezirk, *der;* **go on ~:** den Gerichtsbezirk bereisen; **e)** *(sequence of sporting events)* **on the professional tennis/golf ~:** bei den Turnieren der professionellen Tennis-/Golfspieler

circuit: ~ **board** *n. (Computing)* Schaltbrett, *das;* ~**-breaker** *n. (Electr.)* Leistungsschalter, *der; (as protection)* Leistungsschutzschalter, *der;* ~ **diagram** *n. (Electr.)* Schaltplan, *der*

circuitous [sə'kju:ɪtəs] *adj.* umständlich; **the path followed a ~ route** der Pfad machte einen weiten Bogen; **reach sb. by a ~ route** jmdn. auf Umwegen erreichen

circuitry ['sɜ:kɪtrɪ] *n. (Electr.)* Schaltungen *Pl.*

circular ['sɜ:kjʊlə(r)] **1.** *adj.* **a)** *(round)* kreisförmig; ~ **form** Kreisform, *die;* **b)** *(moving in circle)* Kreis‹*bahn, -bewegung*›; **c)** *(Logic)* **that argument is ~:** das ist ein Zirkelschluß *od.* -beweis. **2.** *n. (letter, notice)* Rundbrief, *der;* Rundschreiben, *das; (advertisement)* Werbeprospekt, *der*

circularize (circularise) ['sɜ:kjʊləraɪz] *v. t.* **every household was ~d** jeder Haushalt erhielt ein Rundschreiben/einen Werbeprospekt

circular: ~ **'letter** *n. see* **circular 2;** ~ **'saw** *n.* Kreissäge, *die;* ~ **'tour** *n. (Brit.)* Rundfahrt, *die* **(of** durch)

circulate ['sɜ:kjʊleɪt] **1.** *v. i.* ‹*Blut, Flüssigkeit:*› zirkulieren; ‹*Geld, Gerüchte:*› zirkulieren, in Umlauf sein, kursieren; ‹*Nachrichten:*› sich herumsprechen; ‹*Verkehr:*› fließen; ‹*Personen, Wein usw.:*› herumgehen *(ugs.),* die Runde machen *(ugs.).* **2.** *v. t.* in Umlauf setzen ‹*Gerücht*›; in Verkehr bringen ‹*Falschgeld*›; verbreiten ‹*Nachricht, Information*›; zirkulieren lassen ‹*Aktennotiz, Rundschreiben*›; herumgehen lassen ‹*Buch, Bericht*› **(around** in + *Dat.*)

circulation [sɜ:kjʊ'leɪʃn] *n.* **a)** *(Physiol.)* Kreislauf, *der;* Zirkulation, *die (Med.); (of sap, water, atmosphere)* Zirkulation, *die;* ~ **trouble, poor ~** *(Physiol.)* schlechte Durchblutung; Kreislaufstörungen *Pl.;* **b)** *(of news, rumour, publication)* Verbreitung, *die;* **have a wide ~:** große Verbreitung finden; **that document was not intended for public ~:** das Dokument war nicht für die Öffentlichkeit bestimmt; **c)** *(of notes, coins)* Umlauf, *der;* **withdraw from ~:** aus dem Umlauf ziehen; **put/come into ~:** in Umlauf bringen/kommen; **d)** *(fig.)* **be back in ~:** *(after illness etc.)* wieder auf dem Posten sein; *(after emotional crisis)* wieder am normalen Leben teilnehmen; **be out of ~:** aus dem Verkehr gezogen sein *(ugs. scherzh.);* **e)** *(number of copies sold)* verkaufte Auflage

circulatory [sɜ:kjʊ'leɪtərɪ, 'sɜ:kjʊleɪtərɪ] *adj. (Physiol., Bot.)* Kreislauf-; ~ **system** Kreislauf, *der*

circumcise ['sɜ:kəmsaɪz] *v. t.* beschneiden

circumcision [sɜ:kəm'sɪʒn] *n.* **a)** Beschneidung, *die;* **b) C~** *(Eccl.)* Beschneidung Christi

circumference [sə'kʌmfərəns] *n.* Umfang, *der; (periphery)* Kreislinie, *die;* **be ... in ~:** einen Umfang von ... haben

circumflex ['sɜ:kəmfleks] **1.** *adj.* ~ **accent** Zirkumflex, *der.* **2.** *n.* Zirkumflex, *der*

circumlocution [sɜ:kəmlə'kju:ʃn] *n.* **a)** *no pl. (use of many words)* Weitschweifigkeit, *die; (evasive talk)* Drumherumreden, *das (ugs.);* **without ~:** ohne Umschweife; **b)** *(roundabout expression)* umständliche Formulierung

circumnavigate [sɜ:kəm'nævɪgeɪt] *v. t.* umfahren; *(by sailing-boat)* umsegeln

circumscribe ['sɜ:kəmskraɪb] *v. t. (lay down limits of)* eingrenzen; einschränken ‹*Macht, Handlungsfreiheit usw.*›; **our choice was ~d** unsere Auswahl war begrenzt

circumspect ['sɜ:kəmspekt] *adj.* umsichtig; **we must be ~ about making new investments** neue Investitionen wollen [von uns] genau überlegt sein

circumspection [sɜ:kəm'spekʃn] *n., no pl.* Umsicht, *die*

circumspectly ['sɜ:kəmspektlɪ] *adv.* umsichtig; vorsichtig ‹*sich nähern*›

circumstance ['sɜ:kəmstəns] *n.* **a)** *usu. in pl.* Umstände; **by force of ~[s]** durch den Zwang der Umstände; **in** *or* **under the ~s** unter den gegebenen *od.* diesen Umständen; **in certain ~s** unter [gewissen] Umständen; **under no ~s** unter [gar] keinen Umständen; **b)** *in pl. (financial state)* Verhältnisse; **c)** *no pl. (full detail in narrative)* Detailschilderung, *die;* **d)** *no pl. (ceremony)* Prachtentfaltung, *die;* Gepränge, *das (geh.);* **e)** *(incident, occurrence, fact)* Umstand, *der. See also* **creature c**

circumstantial [sɜ:kəm'stænʃl] *adj.* **a)** ~ **evidence** Indizienbeweise; **the evidence was purely ~:** der Beweis war nur auf Indizien gegründet; **b)** *(detailed)* detailliert

circumvent [sɜ:kəm'vent] *v. t.* umgehen; hinters Licht führen ‹*Gegner, Feind*›

circumvention [sɜ:kəm'venʃn] *n.* Umgehung, *die*

circus ['sɜ:kəs] *n.* **a)** Zirkus, *der; (arena)* Arena, *die;* **b)** *(Brit.: in town)* [runder] Platz

cirque [sɜ:k] *n. (Geog.)* Kar, *das*

cirrhosis [sɪ'rəʊsɪs] *n., pl.* **cirrhoses** [sɪ'rəʊsi:z] *(Med.)* Zirrhose, *die;* ~ **of the liver** Leberzirrhose, *die*

cirrus ['sɪrəs] *n., pl.* **cirri** ['sɪraɪ] *(Meteorol.)* Zirrus, *der*

CIS *abbr.* **Commonwealth of Independent States**

cissy ['sɪsɪ] *see* **sissy**

cist [sɪst] *n. (Archaeol.) (coffin)* [Stein]kistengrab, *das; (burial-chamber)* Kammergrab, *das*

Cistercian [sɪ'stɜ:ʃn] **1.** *n.* Zisterzienser, *der*/Zisterzienserin, *die.* **2.** *adj.* Zisterzienser-

cistern ['sɪstən] *n.* Wasserkasten, *der; (in roof)* Wasserbehälter, *der*

citadel ['sɪtədəl] *n. (fortress)* Zitadelle, *die*

citation [saɪ'teɪʃn] *n.* **a)** *no pl. (citing)* Zitieren, *das;* **b)** *(quotation)* Zitat, *das;* **c)** *(announcement accompanying award)* Text der Verleihungsurkunde; **d)** *(Mil.: mention in dispatch)* lobende Erwähnung

cite [saɪt] *v. t.* **a)** *(quote)* zitieren; anführen ‹*Beispiel*›; **b)** *(Mil.: mention in dispatch)* lobend erwähnen **(for** wegen); **c)** *(Law)* vorladen ‹*Person*›

citizen ['sɪtɪzən] *n.* **a)** *(of town, city)* Bürger, *der*/Bürgerin, *die;* **b)** *(of state)* [Staats]bürger, *der*/-bürgerin, *die;* **he is a British ~:** er ist britischer Staatsbürger *od.* Brite; ~ **of the world** *(fig.)* Weltbürger, *der*/-bürgerin, *die;* **C~s' Advice Bureau** *(Brit.)* Bürgerberatungsstelle, *die;* **~'s arrest** Festnahme durch eine Zivilperson; **~s' band radio** CB-Funk, *der; (radio set)* CB-Funkgerät, *das;* **c)** *(Amer.: civilian)* Zivilist, *der*

citizenry ['sɪtɪzənrɪ] *n.* Bürgerschaft, *die*

citizenship ['sɪtɪzənʃɪp] *n.* Staatsbürgerschaft, *die*

citric acid [sɪtrɪk 'æsɪd] *n. (Chem.)* Zitronensäure, *die*

citron ['sɪtrən] *n.* **a)** *(fruit)* Zitrone, *die;* **b)** *(tree)* Zitronenbaum, *der*

citrus ['sɪtrəs] *n.* **a)** ~ **[fruit]** Zitrusfrucht, *die;* **b)** *(tree)* Zitrusgewächs, *das*

city ['sɪtɪ] *n.* **a)** [Groß]stadt, *die;* **the ~ of Birmingham** die Stadt Birmingham; **the C~:** die [Londoner] City; das Londoner Banken- und Börsenviertel; **Heavenly C~, C~ of God** Himmelreich, *das;* **b)** *(Brit.: town created ~ by charter)* Stadt, *die (Ehrentitel für bestimmte Städte, meist Bischofssitze);* **c)** *(Amer.: municipal corporation)* ≈ Stadtgemeinde, *die;* **d)** *attrib.* [Groß]stadt‹*leben, -verkehr*›; ~ **lights** Lichter der Großstadt; ~ **wall** Stadtmauer, *die;* ~ **workers** Leute, die in der Stadt arbeiten

city: ~ **'centre** *n.* Stadtzentrum, *das;* Innenstadt, *die;* ~ **desk** *n. (Amer.)* Lokalredaktion, *die;* **C~ editor** *n. (Brit.)* Wirtschaftsredakteur, *der;* ~ **editor** *n. (Amer.)* Lokalredakteur, *der;* ~ **'fathers** *n. pl.* Stadtväter *Pl. (ugs. scherzh.);* ~ **'hall** *n. (Amer.)* **a)** Rathaus, *das;* **b)** *no pl., no art. (municipal officers)* die Stadtverwaltung; ~ **'slicker** *n.* **a)** *(derog.: plausible rogue)* raffinierter Großstadttyp *(ugs.);* **b)** *(sophisticated city-dweller)* eleganter Großstädter; **~-state** *n. (Hist.)* Stadtstaat, *der*

civet ['sɪvɪt] *n.* ~ **[-cat]** Zibetkatze, *die*

civic ['sɪvɪk] *adj.* **a)** *(of citizens, citizenship)* [Staats]bürger-; [staats]bürgerlich; **my ~ responsibility** meine Verantwortung als Staatsbürger; **b)** *(of city)* Stadt-; städtisch; ~ **authorities** Stadtverwaltung, *die;* ~ **centre** Verwaltungszentrum der Stadt

civics ['sɪvɪks] *n., no pl.* Gemeinschaftskunde, *die;* Staatsbürgerkunde, *die (DDR)*

civies *see* **civvies**

civil ['sɪvɪl, 'sɪvl] *adj.* **a)** *(not military)* zivil; **in ~ life** im Zivilleben; **the ~ authorities** die Zivilbehörden; **b)** *(polite, obliging)* höflich; **c)** *(Law)* Zivil‹*gerichtsbarkeit, -prozeß, -verfahren*›; zivilrechtlich; **d)** *(of citizens)* bürgerlich; Bürger‹*krieg, -recht, -pflicht*›; **e)** *(defined by enactment)* bürgerlich ‹*Jahr, Zeit*›; **f)** *(not ecclesiastical)* weltlich

civil: ~ **avi'ation** *n.* Zivilluftfahrt, *die;* ~ **de'fence** *n.* Zivilschutz, *der;* ~ **diso'bedience** *n.* ziviler Ungehorsam; ~ **engi'neer** *n.* Bauingenieur, *der*/-ingenieurin, *die;* ~ **engi'neering** *n.* Hoch- und Tiefbau, *der*

civilian [sɪ'vɪljən] **1.** *n.* Zivilist, *der.* **2.** *adj.* Zivil-; **wear ~ clothes** Zivil[kleidung] tragen

civilisation, civilise *see* **civiliz-**

civility [sɪ'vɪlɪtɪ] *n.* **a)** *no pl.* Höflichkeit, *die;* **b)** *in pl.* Höflichkeiten; *(remarks also)* Höflichkeitsfloskeln

civilization [sɪvɪlaɪ'zeɪʃn] *n.* Zivilisation, *die*

civilize ['sɪvɪlaɪz] *v. t.* **a)** zivilisieren; **b)** *(refine)* ~ **sb.** jmdm. Manieren beibringen

civilized ['sɪvɪlaɪzd] *adj.* zivilisiert; *(refined)* kultiviert

civil: ~ **'law** *n.* Zivilrecht, *das;* ~ **'liberty** *n., usu. in pl.* bürgerliche Freiheit; ~ **list** *n. (Brit.)* Zivilliste, *die*

civilly ['sɪvɪlɪ, 'sɪvəlɪ] *adv.* höflich

civil: ~ **'marriage** *n.* Ziviltrauung, *die;* standesamtliche Trauung; ~ **'rights** *n. pl.* Bürgerrechte; ~ **rights movement** Bürgerrechtsbewegung, *die;* ~ **'servant** *n.* ≈ [Staats]beamte, *der*/-beamtin, *die;* **C~ 'Service** *n.* öffentlicher Dienst; ~ **'war** *n.* Bürgerkrieg, *der*

civvies ['sɪvɪz] *n. pl. (Brit. sl.)* Zivil, *das;* Zivilklamotten *Pl. (ugs.)*

Civvy Street ['sɪvɪ stri:t] *n., no pl., no art.* *(Brit. sl.)* das Zivilleben; **get back to ~:** ins Zivilleben zurückkehren

cl. *abbr.* **class** Kl.

[1]**clad** [klæd] *adj.* *(arch./literary)* gekleidet; **walls ~ in ivy** mit Efeu bewachsene Mauern; *see also* **ironclad; ivy-clad**

[2]**clad** *v. t.*, **-dd-** verkleiden

cladding ['klædɪŋ] *n.* Verkleidung, *die*

claim [kleɪm] **1.** *v. t.* **a)** *(demand as one's due property)* Anspruch erheben auf (+ *Akk.*), beanspruchen ‹*Thron, Gebiete*›; fordern ‹*Lohnerhöhung, Schadensersatz*›; beantragen ‹*Arbeitslosenunterstützung, Sozialhilfe usw.*›; abholen ‹*Fundsache*›; **~ one's luggage** sein Gepäck [ab]holen; **b)** *(represent oneself as having)* für sich beanspruchen, in Anspruch nehmen ‹*Sieg*›; **c)** *(profess, contend)* behaupten; **the new system is ~ed to have many advantages** das neue System soll viele Vorteile bieten; **d)** *(need, deserve)* in Anspruch nehmen ‹*Interesse, Aufmerksamkeit*›; **e)** *(result in loss of)* fordern ‹*Opfer, Menschenleben*›. **2.** *v. i.* **a)** *(Insurance)* Ansprüche geltend machen; **b)** *(for costs)* **~ for damages/expenses** Schadenersatz fordern/sich *(Dat.)* Auslagen rückerstatten lassen. **3.** *n.* **a)** Anspruch, *der* **(to** auf + *Akk.*); **lay ~ to sth.** auf etw. *(Akk.)* Anspruch erheben; **make too many ~s on sth.** etw. zu sehr in Anspruch nehmen; **b)** *(assertion)* **make ~s about sth.** Behauptungen über etw. *(Akk.)* aufstellen; **c)** *(pay ~)* Forderung, *die* **(for** nach); **put in a ~ for a pay rise** eine Lohnerhöhung fordern; **d) ~ [for expenses]** Spesenabrechnung, *die* **(for** über + *Akk.*); **~ for damages** Schadenersatzforderung, *die;* **e)** *(Mining)* Claim, *das;* **stake a ~:** ein Claim abstecken; **stake a ~ to sth.** *(fig.)* ein Anrecht auf etw. *(Akk.)* anmelden; **I staked my ~ to the seat** ich habe mir den Platz gesichert; **f)** *(Insurance)* [Versicherungs]anspruch, *der;* **g)** *(in patent)* Patentanspruch, *der*

~ 'back *v. t.* zurückfordern; **~ tax/expenses** *etc.* **back** sich *(Dat.)* Steuern/Spesen *usw.* rückerstatten lassen **(from** von)

claimant ['kleɪmənt] *n.* *(for rent rebate, social security benefit)* Antragsteller, *der*/-stellerin, *die;* *(for inheritance)* Erbberechtigte, *der/die;* **~ to a title** Titelanwärter, *der*/-anwärterin, *die;* **~ to the throne** Thronanwärter, *der*/-anwärterin, *die*

'**claim form** *n.* **a)** *(Insurance)* Antragsformular, *das;* **b)** *(for expenses)* Spesenabrechnungsformular, *das*

clairvoyance [kleə'vɔɪəns] *n., no pl.* Hellsehen, *das*

clairvoyant [kleə'vɔɪənt] **1.** *n.* Hellseher, *der*/Hellseherin, *die.* **2.** *adj.* hellseherisch

clam [klæm] **1.** *n.* Klaffmuschel, *die;* *(Mercenaria mercenaria)* Quahogmuschel, *die;* **shut up like a ~** *(fig.)* ausgesprochen wortkarg werden. **2.** *v. i.*, **-mm-: ~ up** *(coll.)* den Mund nicht [mehr] aufmachen

'**clambake** *n.* *(Amer.)* Picknick *(bes. am Strand, bei dem Muscheln und Fisch auf heißen Steinen gebacken werden)*

clamber ['klæmbə(r)] **1.** *v. i.* klettern; kraxeln *(ugs., bes. südd., österr.)*; ‹*Baby:*› krabbeln; **~ up a wall** auf eine Mauer klettern; eine Mauer hochklettern. **2.** *n.* Kletterei, *die;* Kraxelei, *die (ugs., bes. südd., österr.)*

clamminess ['klæmɪnɪs] *n., no pl. see* **clammy:** Feuchtigkeit, *die;* Klammheit, *die*

clammy ['klæmɪ] *adj.* feucht; kalt und schweißig ‹*Hände, Gesicht, Haut*›; klamm ‹*Kleidung usw.*›; naßkalt ‹*Luft usw.*›; **~ with sweat** klebrig von Schweiß

clamor *(Amer.) see* **clamour**

clamorous ['klæmərəs] *adj.* lärmend ‹*Menge*›; lautstark ‹*Protest, Forderung*›

clamour ['klæmə(r)] *(Brit.)* **1.** *n.* **a)** *(noise, shouting)* Lärm, *der;* lautes Geschrei; **b)** *(protest)* [lautstarker] Protest; *(appeal, demand)* [lautstarke] Forderung **(for** nach). **2.** *v. i.* **a)** *(shout)* schreien; **b)** *(protest, demand)* **~ against sth.** gegen etw. [lautstark] protestieren; **~ for sth.** nach etw. schreien; **~ to be let out** lautstark fordern, herausgelassen zu werden

clamp [klæmp] **1.** *n.* Klammer, *die;* *(for holding)* Schraubzwinge, *die;* *see also* **wheel-clamp. 2.** *v. t.* **a)** klemmen; einspannen ‹*Werkstück*›; *(Med.)* klammern; **~ two pieces of wood together** zwei Holzstücke miteinander verklammern; **b) ~ a vehicle** eine Parkkralle an ein Fahrzeug anbringen. **3.** *v. i.* *(fig.)* **~ down on sb./sth.** gegen jmdn./etw. rigoros vorgehen; **~ down on expenses** die Ausgaben radikal drosseln

'**clamp-down** *n.* rigoroses Vorgehen **(on** gegen); **the credit ~, the ~ on credit** das Anziehen der Kreditbremse

clan [klæn] *n.* **a)** Sippe, *die;* *(of Scottish Highlanders)* Clan, *der;* **b)** *(derog.: group, set)* Clan, *der;* Sippschaft, *die (abwertend)*

clandestine [klæn'destɪn] *adj.*, **clandestinely** [klæn'destɪnlɪ] *adv.* heimlich

clang [klæŋ] **1.** *n.* *(of bell)* Läuten, *das;* *(of hammer)* Klingen, *das;* *(of sword)* Klirren, *das.* **2.** *v. i.* ‹*Glocke:*› läuten; ‹*Hammer:*› klingen; ‹*Schwert:*› klirren

clanger ['klæŋə(r)] *n.* *(Brit. sl.)* Schnitzer, *der (ugs.);* **drop a ~:** sich *(Dat.)* einen Schnitzer leisten *(ugs.)*

clangor *(Amer.) see* **clangour**

clangorous ['klæŋgərəs] *adj.* [laut] schallend

clangour ['klæŋgə(r)] *n.* *(Brit.)* [lauter] Schall

clank [klæŋk] **1.** *n.* Klappern, *das;* *(of sword, chain)* Klirren, *das.* **2.** *v. i.* klappern; ‹*Schwert, Kette:*› klirren; ‹*Kette:*› rasseln. **3.** *v. t.* klirren mit ‹*Schwert, Kette*›

clannish ['klænɪʃ] *adj.* *(derog.)* cliquenbewußt; klüngelnd *(ugs.)*

[1]**clap** [klæp] **1.** *n.* **a)** Klatschen, *das;* **give sb. a ~:** jmdm. applaudieren *od.* Beifall klatschen; **b)** *(slap)* Klaps, *der (ugs.);* **give sb. a congratulatory ~ on the back** jmdm. anerkennend auf die Schulter klopfen; **c) ~ of thunder** Donnerschlag, *der.* **2.** *v. i.*, **-pp-** klatschen. **3.** *v. t.*, **-pp-: a) ~ one's hands** in die Hände klatschen; **~ sth.** etw. beklatschen; **~ sb.** jmdm. Beifall klatschen; **b)** *(slap)* **~ sb. on the back** jmdm. auf die Schulter klopfen; **c)** *(place)* **~ him in prison!** werft ihn ins Gefängnis!; **the prisoner was ~ped in irons** der Gefangene wurde in Ketten gelegt; **~ one's hand over sb.'s mouth** jmdm. den Mund zuhalten; **~ eyes on sb./sth.** jmdn./etw. zu Gesicht bekommen; **d) ~ped out** *(sl.)* schrottreif *(ugs.)* ‹*Auto, Flugzeug*›; kaputt *(ugs.)* ‹*Person, Idee*›

~ on *v. t.* **a)** draufschlagen ‹*Steuern usw.*›; **the airlines ~ped 25 % on the fare** die Fluggesellschaften haben auf den Flugpreis 25% aufgeschlagen; **a preservation order has been ~ped on my house** die haben mein Haus einfach unter Denkmalschutz gestellt *(ugs.);* **b)** *(Naut.)* **~ on sail** mehr Segel setzen *(Seemannsspr.);* **c)** *(put on hastily)* aufstülpen ‹*Hut*›; **~ handcuffs on sb.** jmdm. Handschellen anlegen

[2]**clap** *n.* *(coarse)* Tripper, *der;* **pick up a dose of the ~:** sich *(Dat.)* einen Tripper holen

clapboard ['klæpbɔ:d, 'klæbəd] *n.* *(Amer.)* Schindel, *die*

Clapham ['klæpəm] *n.* **the man on the ~ omnibus** *(Brit.)* der kleine Mann; der Durchschnittsbürger

clapper ['klæpə(r)] *n.* **a)** *(of bell)* Klöppel, *der;* Schwengel, *der;* **b) like the ~s** *(Brit. sl.)* mit einem Affenzahn *od.* Affentempo *(salopp)*

'**clapper-board** *n.* *(Cinemat.)* Synchronklappe, *die*

clapping ['klæpɪŋ] *n., no pl.* Beifall, *der;* Applaus, *der*

claptrap ['klæptræp] *n., no pl.* **a)** *(pretentious assertions)* [leere] Phrasen; **b)** *(coll.: nonsense)* Geschwafel, *das (ugs. abwertend);* Geschwätz, *das (ugs. abwertend)*

claque [klɑ:k, klæk] *n.* Claque, *die*

claret ['klærət] **1.** *n.* roter Bordeauxwein; Claret, *der.* **2.** *adj.* weinrot

clarification [klærɪfɪ'keɪʃn] *n.* **a)** Klärung, *die;* *(explanation)* Klarstellung, *die;* **I should like more ~ on several points** zu einigen Punkten hätte ich gern nähere Erläuterungen; **b)** *(of liquid)* Klärung, *die;* Klären, *das*

clarify ['klærɪfaɪ] *v. t.* **a)** *(make clear)* klären ‹*Situation, Problem usw.*›; *(by explanation)* klarstellen; erläutern ‹*Bedeutung, Gedanken, Aussage, Bemerkung*›; **the discussion helped me to ~ my thoughts about the matter** die Diskussion half mir, mir über die Sache klarzuwerden; **b)** *(purify, make transparent)* reinigen; klären ‹*Abwasser, Flüssigkeit*›

clarinet [klærɪ'net] *n.* *(Mus.)* Klarinette, *die*

clarinettist *(Amer.:* **clarinetist)** [klærɪ'netɪst] *n.* *(Mus.)* Klarinettist, *der*/Klarinettistin, *die*

clarion ['klærɪən] *attrib. adj.* hell klingend; **like a ~ call** wie ein Fanfarenstoß

clarity ['klærɪtɪ] *n., no pl.* Klarheit, *die*

clash [klæʃ] **1.** *v. i.* **a)** scheppern *(ugs.);* ‹*Gangschaltung:*› krachen; ‹*Becken:*› dröhnen; ‹*Schwerter:*› aneinanderschlagen; **b)** *(meet in conflict)* zusammenstoßen; aufeinanderstoßen; **~ with sb.** mit jmdm. zusammenstoßen; **c)** *(disagree)* sich streiten; **~ with sb.** mit jmdm. eine Auseinandersetzung haben; **d)** *(be incompatible)* aufeinanderprallen; ‹*Interesse, Ereignis:*› kollidieren **(with** mit); ‹*Persönlichkeit, Stil:*› nicht zusammenpassen **(with** mit); ‹*Farbe:*› sich beißen *(ugs.)* **(with** mit). **2.** *v. t.* gegeneinanderschlagen. **3.** *n.* **a)** *(of cymbals)* Dröhnen, *das;* *(of swords)* Aneinanderschlagen, *das;* *(of gears)* Krachen, *das;* **b)** *(meeting in conflict)* Zusammenstoß, *der;* **c)** *(disagreement)* Auseinandersetzung, *die;* **d)** *(incompatibility)* Unvereinbarkeit, *die;* *(of personalities, styles, colours)* Unverträglichkeit, *die;* *(of events)* Überschneidung, *die;* **~ of interests** Interessenkonflikt, *der*

clasp [klɑ:sp] **1.** *n.* **a)** Verschluß, *der;* Schließe, *die;* *(of belt)* Schnalle, *die;* **b)** *(embrace)* Umarmung, *die;* **c)** *(grasp)* Griff, *der;* **d)** *(on medal-ribbon)* Ordensspange, *die.* **2.** *v. t.* **a)** *(embrace)* drücken **(to** an + *Akk.*); **the lovers lay ~ed in each other's arms** die Liebenden lagen eng umschlungen; **b)** *(grasp)* umklammern; **~ hands** sich [gegenseitig] bei den Händen fassen; **~ sth. in one's hand** etw. mit der Hand umklammern; **~ one's hands** die Hände falten; **he stood with his hands ~ed behind his back** er stand da, die Hände auf dem Rücken verschränkt

'**clasp-knife** *n.* Klappmesser, *das*

class [klɑ:s] **1.** *n.* **a)** *(in society)* Gesellschaftsschicht, *die;* Klasse, *die (Soziol.);* *(as system)* Klassensystem, *das;* **b)** *(Educ.)* *(group)* Klasse, *die;* *(Sch.: lesson)* Stunde, *die;* *(Univ.: seminar etc.)* Übung, *die;* **teach a ~** *(Univ.)* eine Übung abhalten; **in ~:** im Unterricht; während des Unterrichts; **a French ~:** eine Französischstunde; **the ~ of 1970** *(Amer.)* der Jahrgang 1970; **c)** *(division according to quality)* Klasse, *die;* *(of hotel)* [Hotel]kategorie, *die;* **be in a ~ by itself** *or* **on its own/of one's own** *or* **by oneself** eine Klasse für sich sein; **he's not in the same ~ as ...:** er hat nicht die Klasse von ...; **d)** *(coll.: quality)* Klasse, *die (ugs.);* **there's not much ~ about her** sie hat keine Klasse; **have [no] ~:** [keine] Klasse haben; *attrib.* **a ~ football-player** ein klasse Fußballer *(ugs.);* **e)** *(group, set; also Biol.)* Klasse, *die;* **f)** *(Univ.: of degree)* Prädikat, *das;* **g)** *(Mil.)* [Rekruten]jahrgang, der. 2. *v.t.* einordnen; ~ **sth. as sth.** etw. als etw. einstufen

class: ~-conscious *adj.* klassenbewußt; **~-consciousness** *n.* Klassenbewußtsein, *das;* ~ **distinction** *n.* Klassenunterschied, *der*

classic ['klæsɪk] **1.** *adj.* klassisch. **2.** *n.* **a)** *in pl. (classical studies)* Altphilologie, *die;* **b)** *(writer; follower of ~ models)* Klassiker, *der;* **c)** *(garment)* klassisch-zeitlose Kleidung; **d)** *(book, play, film)* Klassiker, *der;* **e)** *(Brit.: horse-race)* Klassiker [unter den Pferderennen]

classical ['klæsɪkl] *adj.* klassisch; ~ **scholar/studies** Altphilologe, *der*/Altphilologie, *die;* **the ~ period** die Klassik; **the ~ world** die Antike; ~ **education** humanistische [Schul]bildung

classically ['klæsɪkəlɪ] *adv.* klassisch

classicism ['klæsɪsɪzm] *n.* Klassizismus, *der*

classicist ['klæsɪsɪst] *n.* Anhänger des Klassizismus; *(classics scholar)* Altphilologe, *der*/-philologin, *die*

classifiable ['klæsɪfaɪəbl] *adj.* klassifizierbar; **be ~ into five main types** sich in fünf Hauptgruppen einteilen lassen

classification [klæsɪfɪ'keɪʃn] *n.* Klassifikation, *die*

classified ['klæsɪfaɪd] *adj.* **a)** *(arranged in classes)* gegliedert; unterteilt; ~ **advertisement** Kleinanzeige, *die;* ~ **directory** Branchenverzeichnis, *das;* ~ **results** Sportergebnisse; **b)** *(officially secret)* geheim

classify ['klæsɪfaɪ] *v.t.* **a)** klassifizieren; ~ **books by subjects** Bücher nach Fachgebieten [ein]ordnen; **b)** *(designate as secret)* für geheim erklären

classless ['klɑ:slɪs] *adj.* klassenlos ‹*Gesellschaft*›

class: ~-list *n. (Univ.)* Liste der Prüfungsergebnisse; **~-mate** *n.* Klassenkamerad, *der*/-kameradin, *die;* **~-room** *n. (Sch.)* Klassenzimmer, *das;* Klasse, *die;* ~ **'struggle,** ~ **'war** *ns.* Klassenkampf, *der;* **~work** *n.* Arbeit am Studienplatz

classy ['klɑ:sɪ] *adj. (coll.)* klasse *(ugs.);* nobel ‹*Vorort, Hotel*›

clatter ['klætə(r)] **1.** *n.* Klappern, *das;* **the kettle fell with a ~ to the ground** der Kessel fiel scheppernd zu Boden. **2.** *v.i.* **a)** klappern; **b)** *(move or fall with a ~)* poltern. **3.** *v.t.* klappern mit

clause [klɔ:z] *n.* **a)** Klausel, *die;* **b)** *(Ling.)* Teilsatz, *der;* **[subordinate] ~:** Nebensatz, *der;* Gliedsatz, *der*

claustrophobia [klɔ:strə'fəʊbɪə] *n., no pl. (Psych.)* Klaustrophobie, *die*

claustrophobic [klɔ:strə'fəʊbɪk] *adj.* beengend ‹*Ort, Atmosphäre*›; an Klaustrophobie leidend ‹*Person*›

clavicle ['klævɪkl] *n. (Anat.)* Schlüsselbein, *das;* Clavicula, *die (fachspr.)*

claw [klɔ:] **1.** *n.* **a)** *(of bird, animal)* Kralle, *die; (of crab, lobster, etc.)* Schere, *die; (foot with ~)* Klaue, *die;* **the cat bared its ~s** die Katze zeigte die Krallen; **get one's ~s into sb.** *(fig. coll.)* auf jmdm. herumhacken *(ugs.);* **b)** *(of hammer)* Klaue, *die; (of cine camera, projector)* Greifer, *der.* **2.** *v.t.* kratzen; **the two women ~ed each other** die beiden Frauen gingen mit den Fingernägeln aufeinander los; ~ **one's way to the top** sich zum Gipfel durchkämpfen; *(fig.)* sich nach oben durchboxen *(ugs.).* **3.** *v.i.* ~ **at sth.** sich an etw. *(Akk.)* krallen; **she ~ed desperately for the door-handle** sie versuchte verzweifelt, die Türklinke zu fassen

~ **'back** *v.t.* wiedereintreiben ‹*Geld, Unterstützung*›; wieder an sich reißen ‹*Kontrolle*›; wettmachen ‹*Defizit*›

'claw-back *n.* Wiedereintreiben, *das*

clay [kleɪ] *n.* Lehm, *der; (for pottery)* Ton, *der*

clayey ['kleɪɪ] *adj.* lehmig

clay: ~ 'pigeon *n. (Sport)* Tontaube, *die;* ~ **'pigeon shooting** *n.* Tontaubenschießen, *das;* ~ **'pipe** *n.* Tonpfeife, *die*

clean [kli:n] **1.** *adj.* **a)** sauber; frisch ‹*Wäsche, Hemd*›; **b)** *(unused, fresh)* sauber; *(free of defects)* einwandfrei; sauber; **start with/have a ~ sheet** *(fig.)* ganz neu beginnen/eine reine Weste haben *(ugs.);* **he has a ~ record** gegen ihn liegt nichts vor; **make a ~ start** noch einmal neu anfangen; **come ~** *(coll.) (confess)* auspacken *(ugs.); (tell the truth)* mit der Wahrheit [he]rausrücken *(ugs.);* **have ~ hands** *or* **fingers** *(fig.)* eine reine Weste haben *(ugs.);* **c)** *(well-formed, shapely)* makellos ‹*Glieder, Taille*›; **a ship/car with ~ lines** ein Schiff/Auto mit klarer Linienführung; **d)** *(regular, complete)* glatt ‹*Bruch*›; glatt, sauber ‹*Schnitt*›; **make a ~ break [with** *or* **from sth.]** *(fig.)* einen Schlußstrich [unter etw. *(Akk.)*] ziehen; **make a ~ break with sb.** sich endgültig von jmdm. trennen; **make a ~ job of sth.** *(fig. coll.)* etw. vernünftig machen; etw. sauber hinkriegen *(ugs.. auch iron.);* **e)** *(cleanly)* sauber; *(house-trained)* stubenrein, sauber; **f)** *(free from disease)* gesund; *(Relig.: not prohibited)* rein; **g)** *(deft)* sauber; **h)** *(coll.: free from impropriety)* sauber; stubenrein *(scherzh.)*‹*Witz*›; **be good ~ fun** völlig harmlos sein; **keep the jokes ~!** bitte nur stubenreine Witze! *(scherzh.);* **i)** *(sportsmanlike, fair)* sauber; **j)** astrein ‹*Holz*›. **2.** *adv.* **a)** *(completely, outright, simply)* glatt; einfach ‹*vergessen*›; **we're ~ out of whisky** wir haben überhaupt keinen Whisky mehr; **the fox got ~ away** der Fuchs ist uns/ihnen *usw.* glatt entwischt; **b)** *(fairly)* sauber ‹*spielen, kämpfen*›. **3.** *v.t.* saubermachen; putzen ‹*Zimmer, Haus, Fenster, Schuh*›; reinigen ‹*Teppich, Möbel, Käfig, Kleidung, Wunde*›; fegen, kehren ‹*Kamin*›; ausnehmen ‹*Fisch*›; *(with cloth)* aufwischen ‹*Fußboden*›; **~ that dirt off your face** wisch dir den Schmutz aus dem Gesicht!; **~ the house from top to bottom** großen Hausputz halten; **~ one's hands/teeth** sich *(Dat.)* die Hände waschen/sich *(Dat.)* die Zähne putzen; **~ one's plate** *(eat everything)* seinen Teller leer essen. **4.** *v.i.* sich reinigen lassen. **5.** *n.* **this carpet needs/your teeth need a good ~:** dieser Teppich muß gründlich gereinigt werden/du mußt dir gründlich die Zähne putzen; **give your shoes/face/jacket a ~:** putz deine Schuhe/wasch dir das Gesicht/mach deine Jacke sauber

~ **'down** *v.t.* waschen ‹*Auto*›; abwaschen ‹*Tür, Wand*›

~ **'out** *v.t.* **a)** *(remove dirt from)* saubermachen; ausmisten ‹*Stall*›; *(remove rubbish from)* entrümpeln; **b)** *(sl.)* **~ sb. out** jmdn. ausnehmen *(salopp);* **I'm completely ~ed out** ich bin total blank *(ugs.);* **the tobacconist was ~ed out of cigarettes** beim Tabakhändler war alles an Zigaretten aufgekauft worden; **sb. is ~ed out of sherry** jmdm. ist der Sherry ausgegangen. *See also* **clean-out**

~ **'up 1.** *v.t.* **a)** aufräumen ‹*Zimmer, Schreibtisch*›; beseitigen ‹*Trümmer, Unordnung*›; **b) ~ oneself up** sich saubermachen; *(get washed)* sich waschen; **c)** *(coll.: acquire)* absahnen *(ugs.)* ‹*Geld*›; **~ up a fortune** ein Vermögen machen; **d)** *(Mil.)* ausheben ‹*Schlupfwinkel des Feindes*›; **e)** *(fig.)* säubern ‹*Stadt*›; aufräumen mit ‹*Korruption, Laster, Drogenhandel*›. **2.** *v.i.* **a)** aufräumen; **b)** *see* **1 b; c)** *(coll.: make money)* absahnen *(ugs.). See also* **clean-up**

'clean-cut *adj.* klar [umrissen]; **his ~ features** seine klar geschnittenen Gesichtszüge

cleaner ['kli:nə(r)] *n.* **a)** *(person)* Raumpfleger, *der*/-pflegerin, *die; (woman also)* Putzfrau, *die;* Rein[e]machefrau, *die;* **b)** *(vacuum ~)* Staubsauger, *der; (substance)* Reinigungsmittel, *das;* Reiniger, *der;* **c)** *usu. in pl. (dry-~)* Reinigung, *die;* **take sth. to the ~s** etw. in die Reinigung bringen; **take sb. to the ~s** *(sl.)* jmdn. bis aufs Hemd ausziehen *(ugs.)*

cleaning ['kli:nɪŋ]: **~-rag** *n.* Putzlappen, *der;* **~-woman** *n.* Putzfrau, *die*

clean-limbed ['kli:nlɪmd] *adj.* wohlproportioniert; wohlgeformt

cleanliness ['klenlɪnɪs] *n., no pl.* Reinlichkeit, *die;* Sauberkeit, *die;* **~ is next to godliness** *(prov.)* Reinlichkeit ist die erste Tugend nach Gottseligkeit *(veralt.)*

'clean-living *adj.* von untadeligem Lebenswandel *nachgestellt*

¹cleanly [kli:nlɪ] *adv.* sauber; **the bone broke ~:** der Knochen ist glatt gebrochen

²cleanly ['klenlɪ] *adj.* sauber

cleanness ['kli:nnɪs] *n., no pl.* **a)** Sauberkeit, *die;* **b)** *(freshness)* Sauberkeit, *die; (freedom from defects)* Makellosigkeit, *die;* **c)** *(shapeliness)* Wohlgeformtheit, *die;* **the ~ of the ship's lines** die klare Linienführung des Schiffes; **d)** *(regularity of cut or break)* Glätte, *die;* **e)** *(cleanliness)* Sauberkeit, *die;* **the ~ of her habits** ihre Sauberkeit; **f)** *(deftness)* Sauberkeit, *die;* **g)** *(coll.: of joke, entertainment, etc.)* Harmlosigkeit, *die;* **h)** *(of fight, contest, etc.)* Sauberkeit, *die*

'clean-out *n.* **give sth. a ~:** etw. saubermachen; **sth. needs a [good] ~:** etw. muß [gründlich] saubergemacht werden

cleanse [klenz] *v.t.* **a)** *(spiritually purify)* läutern; **~d of** *or* **from sin** von der Sünde befreit; **b)** *(clean)* [gründlich] reinigen; **c)** *(Bibl.)* heilen ‹*Aussatz, Aussätzige*›

cleanser ['klenzə(r)] *n.* **a)** Reinigungsmittel, *das;* Reiniger, *der;* **b)** *(for skin)* Reinigungscreme, *die; (fluid)* Reinigungsmilch, *die*

'clean-shaven *adj.* glattrasiert

cleansing ['klenzɪŋ]: ~ **cream** *n.* Reinigungscreme, *die;* ~ **department** *n.* Stadtreinigung, *die;* ~ **tissue** *n.* Papiertuch, *das*

'clean-up *n.* **a) give sth./oneself a ~:** etw./sich saubermachen; **sth. needs a ~:** etw. muß saubergemacht werden; **b)** *(reducing crime or corruption)* Säuberungsaktion, *die*

clear [klɪə(r)] **1.** *adj.* **a)** klar; rein ‹*Haut, Teint*›; **as ~ as a bell** glockenhell; **b)** *(distinct)* scharf ‹*Bild, Foto, Umriß*›; deutlich ‹*Abbild*›; klar ‹*Ton*›; klar verständlich ‹*Wort*›; **c)** *(obvious, unambiguous)* klar ‹*Aussage, Vorteil, Vorsprung, Mehrheit, Sieg, Fall*›; **you have a ~ duty to report these thefts** es ist eindeutig Ihre Pflicht, diese Diebstähle zu melden; **make oneself ~:** sich deutlich *od.* klar [genug] ausdrücken; **make sth. ~:** etw. deutlich zum Ausdruck bringen; **make it ~ [to sb.] that ...:** [jmdm.] klar und deutlich sagen, daß ...; **let's get this/one thing ~:** laß uns das klarstellen/eins wollen wir klarstellen; **in ~:** im Klartext; **d)** *(free)* frei; *(Horse-riding)* fehlerfrei ‹*Runde*›; **[be] ~ of a place** aus einem Ort heraus[sein]; **~ of debt** schuldenfrei; frei von Schulden; **he is ~ of blame** ihm kann man keinen Vorwurf machen; **be ~ of suspicion** nicht unter Verdacht stehen; **we're in the ~** *(free of suspicion)* auf uns fällt kein Verdacht; *(free of trouble)* wir haben es geschafft; **be three points ~:** drei Punkte Vorsprung haben; **e)** *(complete)* **a ~ six inches** volle sechs Zoll; **three ~ days/lines** drei volle *od.* volle drei Tage/Zeilen; **f)** *(open, unobstructed)* frei; **keep sth. ~** *(not block)* etw. frei halten; **~ of snow** schneefrei; frei von Schnee; **have a ~ run** freie Fahrt haben; **all ~** *(one will not be detected)* die Luft ist rein *(ugs.); see also* **all-clear; the way is [now] ~ [for sb.] to do sth.** *(fig.)* es steht [jmdm.] nichts [mehr] im Wege, etw. zu tun; **g)** *(discerning)* klar; **keep a ~ head** einen klaren *od.* kühlen Kopf bewahren; **a ~ thinker** jmd., der klar denken kann; **h)** *(certain, confident)* **be ~ [on** *or* **about sth.]** sich *(Dat.)* [über etw. *(Akk.)*] im klaren sein; **are you ~ in your own mind**

that ...? sind Sie ganz sicher, daß ...?; **i)** *(without deduction, net)* ~ **profit** Reingewinn, *der. See also* **coast 1 a; conscience. 2.** *adv.* **a)** *(apart, at a distance)* **keep ~ of sth./sb.** etw./jmdn. meiden; **'keep ~'** *(don't approach)* „Vorsicht [Zug *usw.*]"; **please stand** *or* **keep ~ of the door** bitte von der Tür zurücktreten; **move sth. ~ of sth.** etw. von etw. wegräumen; **the driver was pulled ~ of the wreckage** man zog den Fahrer aus dem Wrack seines Wagens; **the driver leaped ~ just before the crash** der Fahrer konnte im Moment vor dem Zusammenstoß noch abspringen; **b)** *(distinctly)* deutlich ‹*sprechen, sehen, hören*›; **c)** *(completely)* **the prisoners had got ~ away** die Häftlinge waren auf und davon *(ugs.)*; **d)** *(Amer.: all the way)* ganz; ~ **through to Boston** direkt bis Boston. **3.** *v. t.* **a)** *(make ~)* klären ‹*Flüssigkeit*›; reinigen ‹*Blut*›; ~ **the air** lüften; *(fig.)* die Atmosphäre reinigen; ~ **one's mind of doubts/anxieties** *(fig.)* seine Zweifel/Ängste loswerden; **he tried to ~ his head** *(fig.)* er versuchte, einen klaren Kopf zu bekommen; ~ **one's conscience** sein Gewissen erleichtern; **b)** *(free from obstruction)* räumen ‹*Straße*›; abräumen ‹*Regal, Schreibtisch*›; reinigen ‹*Pfeife*›; freimachen ‹*Abfluß, Kanal*›; ~ **the streets of snow** den Schnee von den Straßen räumen; ~ **a space for sb./sth.** für jmdn./etw. Platz machen; ~ **one's throat** sich räuspern; ~ **the ground** *(fig.)* die Bahn frei machen; ~ **land [for cultivation]** Land roden [um es urbar zu machen]; *see also* **deck 1 a; way 1 f; c)** *(make empty)* räumen; leeren ‹*Briefkasten*›; ~ **the room** das Zimmer räumen; ~ **the table** den Tisch abräumen; ~ **one's desk** seinen Schreibtisch ausräumen; ~ **a country of bandits** ein Land von Banditen befreien; ~ **the court** den Saal räumen; ~ **one's plate** seinen Teller leer essen; **d)** *(remove)* wegräumen; beheben ‹*Verstopfung*›; ~ **sth. out of the way** etw. aus dem Weg räumen; **e)** *(pass over without touching)* nehmen ‹*Hindernis*›; überspringen ‹*Latte*›; *(pass by)* vorbeikommen; **f)** *(show to be innocent)* freisprechen; ~ **oneself** seine Unschuld beweisen; ~ **sb. of sth.** jmdn. von etw. freisprechen; **seek to ~ oneself of a charge** versuchen, eine Anschuldigung zu widerlegen; ~ **one's name** seine Unschuld beweisen; **g)** *(declare fit to have secret information)* für unbedenklich erklären; **h)** *(get permission for)* ~ **sth. with sb.** etw. von jmdm. genehmigen lassen; *(give permission for)* ~ **a plane for take-off/landing** einem Flugzeug Start-/Landeerlaubnis erteilen; **i)** *(at customs)* ~ **customs** vom Zoll abgefertigt werden; ~ **sth. through customs** etw. [zollamtlich] abfertigen; **j)** *(make as gain)* verdienen ‹*Geld*›; ~ **one's expenses** seine Ausgaben wieder hereinbekommen; **k)** *(pay off)* begleichen ‹*Schuld*›; **l)** *(pass through bank)* ~ **a cheque** einen Scheck verrechnen; **m)** *(get rid of)* ~ **[old] stock** Lagerbestände räumen; **'reduced to ~'** „reduziertes Einzelstück"; **n)** *(Sport: move away)* klären; **the ball was ~ed upfield** der Ball wurde ins Feld hinausgeschlagen. **4.** *v. i.* **a)** *(become clear)* klar werden; sich klären; ‹*Wetter, Himmel:*› aufklaren *(Met.)*, sich aufheitern; *(fig.)* ‹*Gesicht:*› sich aufhellen; **b)** *(disperse)* sich verziehen; ‹*Nebel:*› sich auflösen, sich verziehen; **c)** *(Sport)* klären

~ **a'way 1.** *v. t.* wegschaffen; *(from the table)* abräumen ‹*Geschirr, Besteck*›. **2.** *v. i.* **a)** abräumen; **b)** *(disperse)* ‹*Nebel:*› sich auflösen, sich verziehen

~ **'off 1.** *v. t.* begleichen ‹*Schulden*›; abzahlen, abtragen ‹*Hypothek*›; aufarbeiten ‹*Rückstand*›. **2.** *v. i. (coll.)* abhauen *(salopp)*

~ **'out 1.** *v. t.* ausräumen. **2.** *v. i. (coll.)* verschwinden. *See also* **clear-out**

~ **'up 1.** *v. t.* **a)** beseitigen ‹*Unordnung*›; wegräumen ‹*Abfall*›; aufräumen ‹*Platz, Sachen*›; **b)** *(explain, solve)* klären. **2.** *v. i.* **a)** aufräumen; Ordnung machen; **b)** *(become ~)* ‹*Wetter:*› aufklaren *(Met.)*, sich aufhellen; **c)** *(disappear)* ‹*Symptome, Ausschlag:*› zurückgehen. *See also* **clear-up**

clearance ['klɪərəns] *n.* **a)** *(of obstruction)* Beseitigung, *die; (of old building)* Abriß, *der; (of forest)* Abholzung, *die;* **make a ~:** gründlich aufräumen; **b)** *(of people)* Räumung, *die;* **c)** *(of cheque)* Verrechnung, *die;* Clearing, *das (Finanzw.);* **d)** *(of ship at customs)* Klarierung, *die (Seemannsspr.); (certificate)* [Zoll]papiere *Pl.;* **e)** *(for aircraft to land/take off)* Lande-/Starterlaubnis, *die;* **f)** *(security ~) Einstufung als unbedenklich [im Sinne der Sicherheitsbestimmungen]; (document)* ≈ Sonderausweis, *der;* **g)** *(clear space)* Spielraum, *der; (headroom)* lichte Höhe; **h)** *(Sport)* Abwehr, *die;* **make a poor ~:** schlecht abwehren

clearance: ~ order *n.* Räumungsbefehl, *der;* ~ **sale** *n.* Räumungsverkauf, *der*

clear: ~-cut *adj.* klar umrissen; klar ‹*Sieg, Abgrenzung, Ergebnis, Entscheidung*›; [gestochen] scharf ‹*Umriß, Raster*›; **~-headed** *adj.* besonnen; **remain ~-headed** einen kühlen *od.* klaren Kopf bewahren

clearing ['klɪərɪŋ] *n. (land)* Lichtung, *die*

clearing: ~ bank *n. (Commerc.)* Clearingbank, *die;* **~-house** *n. (Commerc.)* Abrechnungsstelle, *die;* Clearingstelle, *die; (fig.)* Zentrale, *die*

clearly ['klɪəlɪ] *adv.* **a)** *(distinctly)* klar; deutlich ‹*sprechen*›; **b)** *(manifestly, unambiguously)* eindeutig; klar ‹*denken*›; **please explain yourself more ~:** bitte erklären Sie sich deutlicher; **~, immediate action is called for** ohne Frage ist sofortiges Handeln vonnöten

clearness ['klɪənɪs] *n., no pl.* **a)** Klarheit, *die; (of skin, complexion)* Reinheit, *die;* **b)** *(distinctness) (of photograph, outline)* Schärfe, *die; (of articulation, words, reflection)* Deutlichkeit, *die; (of note, sound, image)* Klarheit, *die;* **c)** *(manifestness, unambiguousness)* Eindeutigkeit, *die;* Klarheit, *die; (of argument also)* Schärfe, *die*

clear: ~-out *n.* Entrümpelung, *die;* **have a ~-out** eine Aufräum- *od.* Entrümpelungsaktion starten; **sth. needs a good ~-out** etw. muß einmal gründlich entrümpelt werden; **~-sighted** *adj.* weitsichtig; vorausschauend; ~ **'soup** *n.* klare Brühe

clearstory *(Amer.) see* **clerestory**

clear: ~-thinking *adj.* klardenkend; **~-up** *n.* Aufräumen, *das;* **have a [good] ~-up** [gründlich] aufräumen; **~way** *n. (Brit.)* Straße mit Halteverbot

cleat [kli:t] *n.* **a)** *(to give footing on gangway)* Querleiste, *die; (to prevent rope from slipping)* Klampe, *die (Seemannsspr.);* **b)** *(wedge)* Keil, *der;* **c)** *(to strengthen woodwork)* Leiste, *die;* **d)** *(on boot, shoe)* Stollen, *der*

cleavage ['kli:vɪdʒ] *n.* **a)** *(act of splitting)* Spaltung, *die; (tendency)* Spaltbarkeit, *die; (fig.)* Kluft, *die;* **the sharp ~ of opinions/interests** das deutliche Auseinandergehen der Meinungen/Interessen; **b)** *(coll.: between breasts)* Dekolleté, *das;* **c)** *(Biol.)* Spaltung, *die*

[1]cleave [kli:v] *v. t.,* **clove** [kləʊv] *or* **cleft** [kleft] *or* **~d, cloven** ['kləʊvn] *or* **cleft** *or* **~d** *(literary)* **a)** *(split)* spalten; **b)** *(make way through)* durchpflügen ‹*Wellen, Wasser*›; ~ **one's way through sth.** sich [mühsam] einen Weg durch etw. bahnen. *See also* **[2]cleft 2; cloven 2**

[2]cleave *v. i. (arch.: adhere)* kleben (**to** an + *Dat.*); ~ **to sb./sth.** *(fig.)* jmdm./einer Sache treu bleiben

cleaver ['kli:və(r)] *n.* Hackbeil, *das*

clef [klef] *n. (Mus.)* Notenschlüssel, *der*

[1]cleft [kleft] *n.* Spalte, *die; (fig.)* Kluft, *die*

[2]cleft 1. *see* **[1]cleave. 2.** *adj.* gespalten; ~ **palate** Gaumenspalte, *die;* **be [caught] in a ~ stick** *(fig.)* in der Klemme sitzen *(ugs.)*

clematis ['klemətɪs, klə'meɪtɪs] *n. (Bot.)* Klematis, *die*

clemency ['klemənsɪ] *n., no pl.* **a)** *(mercy)* Milde, *die;* Nachsicht, *die;* **show ~ to sb.** jmdm. gegenüber Milde *od.* Nachsicht walten lassen; **b)** *(of weather, climate)* Milde, *die*

clementine ['klemənti:n, 'kleməntaɪn] *n.* Klementine, *die*

clench [klentʃ] *v. t.* **a)** *(close tightly)* zusammenpressen; ~ **one's fist** *or* **fingers** die Faust ballen; **with one's fist ~ed** *or* **[one's] ~ed fist** mit geballter Faust; **they gave the ~ed-fist salute** sie hoben die geballte Faust zum Gruß; ~ **one's teeth** die Zähne zusammenbeißen; **through ~ed teeth** durch die zusammengebissenen Zähne; **b)** *(grasp firmly)* umklammern; ~ **sth. between one's teeth** etw. zwischen die Zähne klemmen; **c)** *(secure by bending)* umschlagen *(Nagel)*

clerestory ['klɪəstɔ:rɪ] *n.* **a)** *(Archit.)* Lichtgaden, *der;* **b)** *(Amer. Railw.) erhöhter Teil des Daches eines Eisenbahnwagens mit Fenstern od. Luftsaugern*

clergy ['klɜ:dʒɪ] *n. pl.* Geistlichkeit, *die;* Klerus, *der;* **thirty ~:** dreißig Geistliche

clergyman ['klɜ:dʒɪmən] *n., pl.* **~men** ['klɜ:dʒɪmən] Geistliche, *der*

cleric ['klerɪk] *n.* Kleriker, *der*

clerical ['klerɪkl] *adj.* **a)** *(of clergy)* klerikal; geistlich; ~ **collar** Kollar, *das;* **b)** *(of or by clerk)* ~ **duties/task/occupation/work** Büroarbeit, *die;* ~ **error** Schreibfehler, *der;* ~ **staff** Büropersonal, *das;* ~ **worker** Büroangestellte, *der/die;* Bürokraft, *die*

clerihew ['klerɪhju:] *n. (Lit.)* Clerihew, *das*

clerk [klɑ:k] *n.* **a)** Angestellte, *der/die; (in bank)* Bankangestellte, *der/die; (in office)* Büroangestellte, *der/die; (in shop, firm)* kaufmännischer Angestellter/kaufmännische Angestellte; **b)** *(in charge of records)* Schriftführer, *der*/Schriftführerin, *die;* **c)** ~ **of the course** *(Horse-racing)* Assistent der Rennleitung; ~ **of [the] works** *(Building)* Bauleiter, *der;* **d)** *(Eccl.: lay officer)* Küster, *der;* Kirchendiener, *der; (arch./Law: clergyman)* ~ **[in holy orders]** Geistliche, *der;* **e)** *(Brit. Parl.)* Parlamentssekretär, *der;* **f)** *(Amer.: assistant in shop)* Verkäufer, *der*/Verkäuferin, *die; (in hotel)* Hotelangestellte, *der/die*

clever ['klevə(r)] *adj.,* **~er** ['klevərə(r)]; **~est** ['klevərɪst] **a)** gescheit; klug; **be ~ at mathematics/thinking up excuses** gut in Mathematik/findig im Ausdenken von Entschuldigungen sein; **b)** *(skilful, dextrous)* geschickt; **be ~ with one's hands** geschickte Hände haben; **c)** *(ingenious)* brillant, geistreich ‹*Idee, Argument, Rede, Roman, Gedicht*›; geschickt ‹*Verkleidung, Täuschung, Vorgehen*›; glänzend *(ugs.)* ‹*Idee, Erfindung, Mittel*›; **d)** *(smart, cunning)* clever; raffiniert ‹*Schritt, Taktik, Täuschung*›; schlau, gewitzt, raffiniert ‹*Person*›

clever: ~-clever *adj. (derog.)* superklug *(iron.);* **~-clogs** *n. sing., pl. same: see* **clever-sticks;** ~ **Dick** *n. (coll. derog.)* Schlaumeier, *der (ugs.);* **all right, ~ Dick!** schon gut, du Schlaumeier! *(ugs.)*

cleverly ['klevəlɪ] *adv.* **a)** klug; **b)** *(skilfully, dextrously)* geschickt

cleverness ['klevənɪs] *n., no pl.* **a)** Klugheit, *die; (talent)* Begabung, *die* (**at** für); **b)** *(skilfulness, dexterity)* Geschicklichkeit, *die;* **his ~ with his hands** seine handwerkliche Begabung; **c)** *(ingenuity)* Brillanz, *die;* **d)** *(smartness)* Cleverness, *die;* Raffiniertheit, *die; (of person also)* Schläue, *die*

'clever-sticks *n. sing., pl. same (coll. derog.)* Superschlaue, *der/die (iron.)*

clew [klu:] *(Naut.)* **1.** *n. (of hammock)* Schlaufe, *die; (of sail)* [Schot]horn, *das*

(Seemannsspr.). **2.** *v.t.* ~ **up** aufgeien *(Seemannsspr.)*

cliché ['kli:ʃeɪ] *n. (also Printing)* Klischee, *das*

click [klɪk] **1.** *n.* **a)** Klicken, *das;* **b)** *(Ling.)* Schnalzlaut, *der.* **2.** *v.t.* zuschnappen lassen ⟨*Schloß, Tür*⟩; ~ **the shutter of a camera** den Verschluß einer Kamera auslösen; ~ **one's heels/tongue** die Hacken zusammenschlagen/mit der Zunge schnalzen; ~ **finger and thumb** mit Daumen und Finger schnalzen. **3.** *v.i.* **a)** klicken; ⟨*Absätze, Stricknadeln:*⟩ klappern; **b)** *(sl.: agree)* ~ **with sth.** mit etw. übereinstimmen; **c)** *(be successful)* [gut] ankommen *(ugs.); (sl.: fall into context)* **it's just ~ed** ich hab's *(ugs.);* **the name ~ed** ich konnte mit dem Namen etwas anfangen; ~ **with sb.** *(sl.)* mit jmdm. gleich prima auskommen *(ugs.);* **they ~ed immediately** sie kamen gleich prima miteinander aus *(ugs.)*

'click beetle *n.* Schnellkäfer, *der*

client ['klaɪənt] *n.* **a)** *(of lawyer, solicitor, barrister, social worker)* Klient, *der*/Klientin, *die; (esp. of barrister)* Mandant, *der*/Mandantin, *die; (of architect)* Auftraggeber, *der*/-geberin, *die;* **b)** *(customer)* Kunde, *der*/Kundin, *die*

clientele [kli:ɒn'tel] *n. (of shop)* Kundenkreis, *der;* Kundschaft, *die; (of theatre)* Publikum, *das; (of lawyer)* Klientel, *die*

cliff [klɪf] *n. (on coast)* Kliff, *das; (inland)* Felswand, *die*

cliff: ~-hanger *n.* Thriller, *der;* **~-hanging** *adj.* äußerst spannend; atemberaubend

climacteric [klaɪ'mæktərɪk, klaɪmæk'terɪk] **1.** *adj.* **a)** *(critical)* entscheidend; **b)** *(Med.)* klimakterisch. **2.** *n. (Med.)* Klimakterium, *das (fachspr.);* Wechseljahre *Pl.; (fig.)* Wendepunkt, *der*

climactic [klaɪ'mæktɪk] *adj.* ~ **scene/event** Höhepunkt, *der*

climate ['klaɪmət] *n.* Klima, *das:* **the ~ of opinion** *(fig.)* die allgemeine Meinung

climatic [klaɪ'mætɪk] *adj.* klimatisch

climatology [klaɪmə'tɒlədʒɪ] *n., no pl.* Klimatologie, *die;* Klimakunde, *die*

climax ['klaɪmæks] **1.** *n.* **a)** Höhepunkt, *der;* **b)** *(orgasm)* Höhepunkt, *der;* Orgasmus, *der.* **2.** *v.i.* seinen Höhepunkt erreichen; ~ **in sth.** mit etw. seinen Höhepunkt erreichen

climb [klaɪm] **1.** *v.t.* hinaufsteigen ⟨*Treppe, Leiter, Hügel, Berg*⟩; hinaufklettern ⟨*Mauer, Seil, Mast*⟩; klettern auf ⟨*Baum*⟩; ⟨*Auto:*⟩ hinaufkommen ⟨*Hügel*⟩; **this mountain had never been ~ed before** dieser Berg war noch nie zuvor bestiegen worden; **the prisoners escaped by ~ing the wall** die Gefangenen entkamen, indem sie über die Mauer kletterten. **2.** *v.i.* **a)** klettern **(up** auf + *Akk.*); ~ **into/out of** steigen in (+ *Akk.*)/aus ⟨*Auto, Bett*⟩; ~ **aboard** einsteigen; **~ing plants/roses** Kletterpflanzen/-rosen; **b)** ⟨*Flugzeug, Sonne:*⟩ aufsteigen; **c)** *(slope upwards)* ansteigen; **d)** *(in social rank)* aufsteigen. **3.** *n. (ascent)* Aufstieg, *der; (of road)* Steigung, *die; (of aeroplane)* Steigflug, *der;* **the pilot put the plane into a steep ~:** der Pilot zog die Maschine steil nach oben; **the first ~ of Everest** die erste Besteigung des Everest

~ **'down** *v.i.* **a)** hinunterklettern; *(from horse)* absteigen; **b)** *(fig.: retreat, give in)* nachgeben; einlenken; ~ **down over an issue** in einer Frage nachgeben; *see also* **climb-down**

climbable ['klaɪməbl] *adj.* besteigbar

'climb-down *n.* Rückzieher, *der (ugs.)*

climber ['klaɪmə(r)] *n.* **a)** *(mountaineer)* Bergsteiger, *der; (of cliff, rock-face)* Kletterer, *der;* **b)** *(plant)* Kletterpflanze, *die*

climbing: ~-boot *n.* Kletterschuh, *der;* **~-frame** *n.* Klettergerüst, *das;* **~-iron** *n.* Steigeisen, *das*

clime [klaɪm] *n. (literary)* **a)** *in sing. or pl. (region)* Gefilde, *das (geh.);* **b)** *(climate)* Klima, *das*

clinch [klɪntʃ] **1.** *v.t.* **a)** *(confirm or settle conclusively)* zum Abschluß bringen ⟨*Angelegenheit, Meinungsverschiedenheit*⟩; perfekt machen *(ugs.)* ⟨*Geschäft, Handel*⟩; **that ~es it** damit ist der Fall klar; **b)** *see* **clench c. 2.** *n.* **a)** *(Boxing)* Clinch, *der;* **b)** *(coll.: embrace)* Umschlingung, *die;* Clinch, *der (ugs. scherzh.);* **go into a ~:** sich eng umschlingen; in den Clinch gehen *(ugs. scherzh.)*

clincher ['klɪntʃə(r)] *n.* entscheidender Faktor; **be the ~:** den Ausschlag geben

cling [klɪŋ] *v.i.,* **clung** [klʌŋ] **a)** ~ **to sth./sb.** sich an etw./jmdn. klammern; ⟨*Schmutz:*⟩ einer Sache/jmdm. anhaften; ⟨*Staub:*⟩ sich auf etw./jmdn. setzen; ⟨*Klette:*⟩ an etw./jmdm. hängen; ⟨*Schlamm usw.:*⟩ an etw./jmdm. haftenbleiben; **the lovers clung to each other** die Liebenden hielten sich umschlungen; **his sweat-soaked shirt clung to his back** das durchgeschwitzte Hemd klebte ihm am Rücken; **her perfume still ~s to the scarf** der Duft ihres Parfüms haftet noch immer an dem Schal; ~ **together** aneinanderhaften; *(Personen:)* sich aneinanderklammern; **a ~ing dress** ein enganliegendes Kleid; **b)** *(remain stubbornly faithful)* ~ **to sb./sth.** sich an jmdn./etw. klammern

cling: ~ film *n.* Klarsichtfolie, *die;* **~[stone] peach** *n. (Bot.)* Härtling, *der*

clinic ['klɪnɪk] *n.* **a)** *(place)* [Abteilung einer] Klinik; *(occasion)* Sprechstunde, *die;* **b)** *(private hospital)* Privatklinik, *die; (specified hospital)* Klinik, *die;* **dental ~:** Zahnklinik, *die;* **c)** *(medical teaching at bedside)* Klinik, *die;* Klinikum, *das;* **d)** *(Amer.: conference, short course)* Seminar, *das*

clinical ['klɪnɪkl] *adj.* **a)** *(Med.)* klinisch ⟨*Medizin, Tod*⟩; ~ **thermometer** Fieberthermometer, *das;* **b)** *(objective, dispassionate)* nüchtern; *(coldly detached)* kühl; distanziert ⟨*Haltung*⟩; klinisch ⟨*Interesse*⟩; **c)** *(bare, functional)* steril

clinically ['klɪnɪkəlɪ] *adv.* **a)** *(Med.)* klinisch; **b)** *(dispassionately)* nüchtern

¹clink [klɪŋk] **1.** *n. (of glasses, bottles)* Klirren, *das; (of coins, keys)* Klimpern, *das.* **2.** *v.i.* ⟨*Flaschen, Gläser:*⟩ klirren; ⟨*Münzen, Schlüssel:*⟩ klimpern. **3.** *v.t.* klirren mit ⟨*Glas*⟩; klimpern mit ⟨*Kleingeld, Schlüssel*⟩

²clink *n. (sl.: prison)* Knast, *der (salopp);* **be in ~:** im Knast sitzen *(salopp);* **be put in ~:** in den Knast kommen *(salopp)*

clinker ['klɪŋkə(r)] *n.* Schlacke, *die*

'clinker-built *adj.* in Klinkerbauweise [gebaut]; **a ~ boat** ein klinkergebautes Boot *od.* Klinkerboot

¹clip [klɪp] **1.** *n.* **a)** Klammer, *die; (for paper)* Büroklammer, *die; (of pen)* Klipp, *der; (hose-~)* Schelle, *die; (for wires)* Klemme, *die;* **b)** *(piece of jewellery)* Klipp, *der;* Clip, *der;* **c)** *(set of cartridges)* Ladestreifen, *der.* **2.** *v.t., -pp-:* ~ **sth. [on] to sth.** etw. an etw. *(Akk.)* klammern; ~ **papers together** Schriftstücke zusammenklammern; ~ **the leads to the battery terminals** die Kabel an die Batteriepole klemmen

~ **'on 1.** *v.i.* angeklemmt *od.* angesteckt werden; ⟨*Sonnenbrille:*⟩ aufgesteckt werden. **2.** *v.t.* anlegen ⟨*Ohrring*⟩; anstecken ⟨*Brosche, Mikrophon*⟩; aufstecken ⟨*Sonnenbrille*⟩. *See also* **clip-on**

²clip 1. *v.t.,* **-pp- a)** *(cut)* schneiden ⟨*Fingernägel, Haar, Hecke*⟩; scheren ⟨*Wolle*⟩; stutzen ⟨*Flügel*⟩; ~ **sb.'s wings** *(fig.)* jmdm. die Flügel stutzen; ~ **a second off the record** einen Rekord um eine Sekunde unterbieten; **b)** scheren ⟨*Schaf*⟩; trimmen ⟨*Hund*⟩; **c)** lochen, entwerten ⟨*Fahrkarte*⟩; **d)** *(coll.: hit)* ~ **sb.'s ear** jmdm. eins *od.* ein paar hinter die Ohren geben *(ugs.);* ~ **sb. on the jaw** jmdm. einen Kinnhaken verpassen *(ugs.);* ~ **the crash barrier** die Leitplanke streifen; **e)** ~ **one's words/letters** abgehackt sprechen; **f)** *(Amer.: cut from newspaper)* ausschneiden. **2.** *n.* **a)** *(of finger-nails, hedge)* Schneiden, *das; (of dog)* Trimmen, *das; (of sheep)* Schur, *die;* **give the hedge a ~:** die Hecke schneiden; **b)** *(extract from film)* [Film]ausschnitt, *der;* **c)** *(blow with hand)* Schlag, *der;* ~ **round** *or* **on** *or* **over the ear** Ohrfeige, *die;* ~ **on the jaw** Kinnhaken, *der;* **d) be going at a good** *or* **fast** ~ *(coll.)* einen ziemlichen Zahn draufhaben *(ugs.);* **e)** *(quantity of wool)* Schur, *die*

clip: ~board *n.* Klemmbrett, *das;* **~-clop** ['klɪpklɒp] **1.** *n.* Klappern, *das;* Klippklapp, *das;* **2.** *v.i.,* **-pp-** klappern; **~-joint** *n. (sl. derog.)* Nepplokal, *das (ugs. abwertend);* **~-on** *adj.* **a ~-on accessory** ein Accessoire zum Anstecken; **~-on sun-glasses** eine Sonnenbrille zum Aufstecken; **a ~-on handle** ein Griff zum Feststecken

clipped [klɪpt] *adj.* abgehackt ⟨*Wörter*⟩

clipper ['klɪpə(r)] *n.* **a)** *in pl. (for hair)* Haarschneidemaschine, *die;* **b)** *(Naut.)* Klipper, *der*

clipping ['klɪpɪŋ] *n.* **a)** *(piece clipped off)* Schnipsel, *der od. das;* **b)** *(newspaper cutting)* Ausschnitt, *der*

clique [kli:k] *n.* Clique, *die*

cliquey ['kli:kɪ], **cliquish** ['kli:kɪʃ] *adjs. (derog.)* **be ~:** zur Cliquenbildung neigen; **a ~ attitude** eine Neigung zur Cliquenbildung

clitoris ['klɪtərɪs] *n. (Anat.)* Kitzler, *der;* Klitoris, *die (fachspr.)*

cloak [kləʊk] **1.** *n.* **a)** Umhang, *der;* Mantel, *der (hist.); (fig.)* ~ **of snow** Schneedecke, *die;* **under the ~ of darkness** im Schutz der Dunkelheit; **use sth. as a ~ for sth.** etw. als Deckmantel für etw. benutzen; **a ~ of secrecy** ein Mantel des Schweigens; **b)** *in pl. (Brit. euphem.: lavatory)* Toilette, *die.* **2.** *v.t.* **a)** [ein]hüllen; **b)** *(fig.)* **~ed in mist/darkness** in Nebel/Dunkel gehüllt; **sth. is ~ed in secrecy** über etw. *(Akk.)* wird der Mantel des Schweigens gebreitet

cloak: ~-and-'dagger *adj.* mysteriös; Spionage⟨*stück, -tätigkeit*⟩; **~room** *n.* Garderobe, *die; (Brit. euphem.: lavatory)* Toilette, *die;* **~room attendant** Garderobier, *der*/Garderobiere, *die*/Toilettenmann, *der*/-frau, *die*

¹clobber ['klɒbə(r)] *n. (Brit. sl.)* Klamotten *Pl. (salopp)*

²clobber *v.t. (sl.)* **a)** *(hit)* zusammenschlagen; *(fig.)* zur Ader lassen *(ugs. scherzh.);* schröpfen *(ugs.);* **b)** *(defeat, criticize)* in die Pfanne hauen *(salopp)*

cloche [klɒʃ] *n.* **a)** *(Agric., Hort.)* [Frühbeet]abdeckung, *die; (polythene)* Folientunnel, *der;* **b)** ~ **['hat]** Glocke, *die;* Glockenhut, *der*

clock [klɒk] **1.** *n.* **a)** Uhr, *die;* **[work] against the ~:** gegen die Zeit [arbeiten]; **beat the ~ [by ten minutes]** [10 Minuten] früher fertig werden; **put** *or* **turn the ~ back** *(fig.)* die Zeit zurückdrehen; **round the ~:** rund um die Uhr; **hold the ~ on sb.** jmds. Zeit stoppen; **watch the ~** *(fig.)* [dauernd] auf die Uhr sehen *(weil man ungeduldig auf den Arbeitsschluß wartet);* **b)** *(coll.) (speedometer)* Tacho, *der (ugs.); (milometer)* ≈ Kilometerzähler, *der; (taximeter)* Taxameter, *das;* **c)** *(coll.: stop-watch)* Uhr, *die;* **d)** *(Bot.: seedhead)* Haarkelch, *der (Bot.);* **e)** *(Brit. sl.: face)* Visage, *die (salopp abwertend). See also* **o'clock. 2.** *v.t.* **a)** ~ **[up]** zu verzeichnen haben ⟨*Sieg, Zeit, Erfolg*⟩; erreichen ⟨*Geschwindigkeit*⟩; zurücklegen ⟨*Entfernung, Kilometer*⟩; ~ **3.43·7/a personal best** ⟨*Läufer:*⟩ 3:43,7/eine persönliche Bestzeit laufen; **b)** *(coll.: time)* stoppen **(at** mit); **c)** *(sl.: hit)* ~ **sb. [one]** jmdm. eins überbraten *(ugs.)*

~ **'in,** ~ **'on** *v.i.* [bei Arbeitsantritt] stechen *od.* stempeln; **the night shift ~s in** *or* **on at**

8 p.m. die Nachtschicht beginnt abends um acht
~ **'off,** ~ **'out** *v.i.* [bei Arbeitsschluß] stechen *od.* stempeln; **we ~ off or out earlier than usual on a Friday** freitags machen wir früher Feierabend
clock: ~-face *n.* Zifferblatt, *das;* ~ **golf** *n.* Uhrengolf, *das;* **~maker** *n.* Uhrmacher, *der*/-macherin, *die;* ~ **tower** *n.* Uhr[en]turm, *der;* **~-watcher** *n. jmd., der keine Sekunde länger als vorgeschrieben am Arbeitsplatz bleibt;* **~-watching** *n.* ständiges Auf-die-Uhr-Sehen *(weil man ungeduldig auf den Arbeitsschluß wartet)*
'clockwise 1. *adv.* im Uhrzeigersinn. **2.** *adj.* im Uhrzeigersinn *nachgestellt;* rechtsläufig *(Technik);* **in a ~ direction** im Uhrzeigersinn
'clockwork *n.* Uhrwerk, *das;* ~ **[mechanism]** Aufziehmechanismus, *der;* Uhrwerk, *das (veralt.);* **a ~ car** ein Aufziehauto; **as regular as ~** *(fig.)* absolut regelmäßig; **with ~ precision/regularity** *(fig.)* absolut genau/regelmäßig; **go like ~** *(fig.)* klappen wie am Schnürchen *(ugs.)*
clod [klɒd] *n.* **a)** *(lump)* Klumpen, *der; (of earth)* Scholle, *die;* **b)** *(derog.: dolt)* Tölpel, *der (abwertend)*
'clodhopper *n.* **a)** *see* **clod b; b)** *(coll.: shoe)* Elbkahn, der *(ugs. scherzh.);* Quadratlatschen, *der (salopp scherzh.)*
clog [klɒg] **1.** *n.* Holzschuh, *der; ([fashionable] wooden-soled shoe)* Clog, *der.* **2.** *v.t.*, **-gg-: a)** ~ **[up]** verstopfen ‹*Rohr, Poren*›; blockieren ‹*Rad, Maschinerie*›; **be ~ged [up] with sth.** mit etw. verstopft/durch etw. blokkiert sein; **b)** *(impede)* hemmen; *(obstruct)* blockieren; **c)** ~ **[up]** *(encumber)* belasten
'clog-dance *n.* Holzschuhtanz, *der*
cloister ['klɔɪstə(r)] **1.** *n.* **a)** *(covered walk)* Kreuzgang, *der;* **b)** *(convent, monastery; monastic life)* Kloster, *das.* **2.** *v. refl.* ~ **oneself in one's study** *(fig.)* sich in sein Studierzimmer einschließen
cloistered ['klɔɪstəd] *adj.* in einem Kloster lebend; *(fig.)* klösterlich ‹*Abgeschiedenheit, Dasein*›
clone [kləʊn] *(Biol.)* **1.** *n.* Klon, *der; (fig.: copy)* [schlechte] Kopie. **2.** *v.t.* klonen
clonk [klɒŋk] *n. (coll.)* **a)** *(sound)* harter Schlag; **b) get a ~ on the head** eins gegen die Birne kriegen *(ugs.)*
close 1. [kləʊs] *adj.* **a)** *(near in space)* dicht; nahe; **be ~ to sth.** nahe bei *od.* an etw. *(Dat.)* sein; **how ~ is London to the South coast?** wie weit ist London von der Südküste entfernt?; **you're too ~ to the fire** du bist zu dicht *od.* nah am Feuer; **fly ~ to the ground** dicht über dem Boden fliegen; **I wish we lived ~r to your parents** ich wünschte, wir würden näher bei deinen Eltern wohnen; **be ~ to tears/breaking-point** den Tränen/einem Zusammenbruch nahe sein; **be ~ to exhaustion** vor Erschöpfung fast umfallen; **at ~ quarters, the building looked less impressive** aus der Nähe betrachtet, wirkte das Gebäude weniger imposant; **fighting at ~ quarters** der Kampf Mann gegen Mann; **at ~ range** aus kurzer Entfernung; **b)** *(near in time)* nahe **(to** an + *Dat.*); **war is ~:** ein Krieg steht unmittelbar bevor; **c)** *(in near or intimate relation)* eng ‹*Freund, Freundschaft, Beziehung, Zusammenarbeit, Verbindung*›; nahe ‹*Verwandte, Angehörige, Bekanntschaft*›; **be/become ~ to sb.** jmdm. nahestehen/nahekommen; **d)** *(rigorous, painstaking)* eingehend, genau ‹*Untersuchung, Prüfung, Befragung usw.*›; streng, verschärft ‹*Haft, Arrest*›; **pay ~ attention** genau aufpassen; **e)** *(stifling)* stickig ‹*Luft, Raum*›; drückend, schwül ‹*Wetter*›; **f)** *(nearly equal)* hart ‹*[Wett]kampf, Spiel*›; knapp ‹*Ergebnis*›; **a ~ race** ein Kopf-an-Kopf-Rennen; **that was too ~ for comfort** das ging gerade noch gut; **I had a ~ call** *or* **shave** *or* **thing** *(coll.)* ich bin gerade noch davongekommen; **that was a ~ call** *or* **shave** *or* **thing** *(coll.)* das war knapp!; **g)** *(fitting exactly)* genau passend ‹*Kleidungsstück*›; *(nearly matching)* wortgetreu ‹*Übersetzung*›; getreu, genau ‹*Imitation, Kopie*›; groß ‹*Ähnlichkeit*›; **be the ~st equivalent to sth.** einer Sache *(Dat.)* am ehesten entsprechen; **bear a ~ resemblance to sb.** jmdm. sehr ähnlich sehen; große Ähnlichkeit mit jmdm. haben; **h)** *(narrow, confined)* eng ‹*Raum*›; **i)** *(dense)* dicht, fest *(Gewebe);* dicht, undurchdringlich ‹*Dickicht, Gestrüpp*›; eng ‹*Schrift*›; *(fig.)* lückenlos, stichhaltig ‹*Beweisführung, Argument*›; **j)** *(concealed)* verborgen; **keep** *or* **lie ~:** sich verborgen *od.* versteckt halten; *(secret)* **keep sth. ~:** etw. geheimhalten; *(secretive)* **be ~ about sth.** in bezug auf etw. *(Akk.)* verschwiegen sein; **k)** *(niggardly)* knauserig *(ugs. abwertend);* **l)** *(Phonet.)* geschlossen ‹*Vokal*›. **2.** [kləʊs] *adv.* **a)** *(near)* nah[e]; **come ~ to the truth** der Wahrheit nahekommen; **that's the ~st I've ever come to being involved in an accident** so knapp *od. (ugs.)* haarscharf bin ich noch nie einem Unfall entgangen; **be ~ at hand** in Reichweite sein; ‹*Ereignis:*› nahe bevorstehen; ~ **by** in der Nähe; ~ **by the river** in der Nähe des Flusses; nahe am Fluß; **the lamb stayed ~ by its mother's side** das Lamm blieb dicht an der Seite seiner Mutter; ~ **on 60 years** fast 60 Jahre; ~ **on 2 o'clock** kurz vor 2 [Uhr]; ~ **to sb./sth.** nahe bei jmdm./etw.; **don't stand so ~ to the edge of the cliff** stell dich nicht so nah *od.* dicht an den Rand des Kliffs; **come ~ to tears** den Tränen nahe sein; **she came ~ to being the best/the winner** sie wäre fast *od.* beinah[e] die Beste geworden/sie hätte fast *od.* beinah[e] gewonnen; ~ **together** dicht beieinander; **can't you stand ~r together?** könnt ihr nicht etwas mehr zusammenrücken?; **try not to come too ~ together** versucht, einander nicht zu nahe zu kommen; **these deadlines come too ~ together** diese Termine liegen zu nahe zusammen; **it brought them ~r together** *(fig.)* es brachte sie einander näher; ~ **behind** dicht dahinter; **leave sth./stand ~ behind sb./sth.** etw. dicht hinter jmdm./etw. lassen/ dicht hinter jmdm./etw. stehen; **see sth. [from] ~ 'to** *or* **'up** etw. aus der Nähe sehen; **go ~:** es beinahe schaffen; **b)** *(in close manner)* fest *(schließen);* genau ‹*hinsehen*›; **on looking ~r** bei genauerem Hinsehen. **3.** [kləʊz] *v.t.* **a)** *(shut)* schließen, *(ugs.)* zumachen ‹*Augen, Tür, Fenster, Geschäft*›; zuziehen ‹*Vorhang*›; *(declare shut)* schließen ‹*Laden, Geschäft, Fabrik, Betrieb, Werk, Zeche*›; stillegen ‹*Betrieb, Werk, Zeche, Bahnlinie*›; sperren ‹*Straße, Brücke*›; **behind ~d doors** hinter verschlossenen Türen; ~ **one's eyes to sth.** *(fig.)* die Augen vor etw. *(Dat.)* verschließen; **b)** *(conclude)* schließen, beenden ‹*Besprechung, Rede, Diskussion*›; schließen ‹*Versammlung, Sitzung*›; abschließen ‹*Handel, Geschäft*›; ~ **an account** ein Konto auflösen; **the matter is ~d** der Fall *od.* die Sache ist abgeschlossen; **c)** *(make smaller)* schließen *(auch fig.)* ‹*Lücke*›; zustopfen ‹*Riß*›; ~ **the gap between rich and poor** die Kluft zwischen Arm und Reich überwinden; **d)** *(Electr.)* schließen ‹*Stromkreis*›. **4.** [kləʊz] *v.i.* **a)** *(shut)* sich schließen; ‹*Tür:*› zugehen *(ugs.)*, sich schließen; **the door/lid doesn't ~ properly** die Tür/der Deckel schließt nicht richtig; **the valve won't ~:** das Ventil schließt nicht; **b)** ‹*Laden, Geschäft, Fabrik:*› schließen, *(ugs.)* zumachen; *(permanently)* ‹*Betrieb, Werk, Zeche:*› geschlossen *od.* stillgelegt werden; ‹*Geschäft:*› geschlossen werden, *(ugs.)* zumachen; ‹*Theaterstück:*› abgesetzt werden; **c)** *(come to an end)* zu Ende gehen; enden; *(finish speaking)* schließen; **in closing** abschließend; **d)** *(come closer, within striking distance)* sich nähern; aufschließen *(bes. Sport); (join battle)* aufeinandertreffen; aneinandergeraten; **I ~d with him in hand-to-hand fighting** ich fing ein Handgemenge mit ihm an. **5.** *n.* **a)** [kləʊz] *no pl.* Ende, *das;* Schluß, *der;* **come** *or* **draw to a ~:** zu Ende gehen; **bring** *or* **draw sth. to a ~:** einer Sache *(Dat.)* ein Ende bereiten; etw. zu Ende bringen; **at ~ of business** bei Geschäftsschluß; ~ **of play** *(Cricket)* Ende des Spieltages; **b)** [kləʊz] *(Mus.)* Kadenz, *die;* **c)** [kləʊs] *(Brit.: precinct of cathedral)* Domhof, *der; (cul-de-sac)* Sackgasse, *die; (enclosed place)* Hof, *der*
~ [kləʊz] **'down 1.** *v.t.* schließen; *(ugs.)* zumachen; stillegen ‹*Werk, Zeche*›; einstellen ‹*Betrieb, Arbeit*›. **2.** *v.i.* geschlossen werden, zugemacht werden *(ugs.);* ‹*Werk, Zeche:*› stillgelegt werden; *(Brit.)* ‹*Rundfunkstation:*› Sendeschluß haben
~ **'in** *v.i.* ‹*Nacht, Dunkelheit:*› hereinbrechen; ‹*Tage:*› kürzer werden; ~ **in [up]on sb./sth.** *(draw nearer)* sich jmdm./etw. nähern; *(draw around)* jmdn./etw. umzingeln
~ **'off** *v.t.* [ab]sperren; abriegeln
~ **'out** *v.t. (Amer.)* absetzen, abstoßen ‹*Waren*›; auflösen ‹*Betrieb*›
~ **'up 1.** *v.i.* **a)** aufrücken; **b)** ‹*Blume:*› sich schließen; **c)** *(lock up)* abschließen. **2.** *v.t.* abschließen. *See also* **close-up**
close-cropped ['kləʊskrɒpt] *adj.* kurzgeschoren
closed [kləʊzd] *adj.* **a)** *(no longer open)* geschlossen ‹*Laden, Geschäft, Fabrik*›; **we're ~:** wir haben geschlossen; **'~'** „Geschlossen"; **the subject is ~:** das Thema ist [für mich] erledigt; **b)** *(restricted)* [der Öffentlichkeit] nicht frei zugänglich; *(Sport)* nur für Teilnehmer einer bestimmten Gruppe/Klasse offen ‹*Wettbewerb etc.*›; ~ **scholarship** *Stipendium, das nur einer bestimmten Gruppe von Studierenden gewährt wird;* **a women's ~ golf tournament** ein Golfturnier für Damen; **c)** *(Phonet.)* geschlossen ‹*Silbe*›. *See also* **book 1 a**
closed: ~-circuit *adj.* **~-circuit television** interne Fernsehanlage; *(for supervision)* Fernsehüberwachungsanlage, *die*
close-down ['kləʊzdaʊn] *n.* **a)** *(closing)* Schließung, *die; (of works, railway, mine)* Stillegung, *die; (of project, operation)* Einstellung, *die;* **b)** *(Radio, Telev.)* Sendeschluß, *der*
closed: ~ season *(Amer.) see* **close season;** ~ **'shop** *n.* Closed Shop, *der;* **we have** *or* **operate a ~ shop in this factory** in unserer Fabrik besteht Gewerkschaftszwang
close [kləʊs]: **~-fisted** *adj.* geizig; knauserig *(ugs. abwertend);* **~-fitting** *adj.* enganliegend; knapp sitzend ‹*Anzug*›; **~-grained** *adj.* fest ‹*Gewebe*›; fein gemasert ‹*Holz*›; feinnarbig ‹*Leder*›; ~ **'harmony** *n. (Mus.)* enge Lage; **~-hauled** *adj. (Naut.)* hart am Wind segelnd ‹*Schiff*›; **~-knit** *adj.* fest zusammengewachsen
closely ['kləʊslɪ] *adv.* **a)** dicht; **follow me ~:** bleib *od.* geh dicht hinter mir!; **look ~ at** genau betrachten; **look ~ into** *(fig.)* näher untersuchen; **the first explosion was ~ followed by two more** unmittelbar auf die [erste] Explosion folgten zwei weitere; **b)** *(intimately)* eng; **we're not ~ related** wir sind nicht nah miteinander verwandt; **c)** *(rigorously, painstakingly)* genau; genau, eingehend ‹*befragen, prüfen*›; streng, scharf ‹*bewachen*›; **a ~ guarded secret** ein streng *od.* sorgsam gehütetes Geheimnis; **d)** *(nearly equally)* ~ **fought/contested** hart umkämpft; **the contest was ~ fought** man kämpfte hart um den Sieg; **e)** *(exactly)* genau; ~ **resemble sb.** jmdm. sehr ähneln; **f)** *(densely)* dicht; ~ **printed/written** eng bedruckt/beschrieben; ~ **reasoned** *(fig.)* schlüssig

closeness ['kləʊsnɪs] *n.*, *no pl.* **a)** *(nearness in space or time)* Nähe, *die;* **b)** *(intimacy)* Enge, *die;* **the ~ of their friendship** die Tiefe ihrer Freundschaft; **c)** *(rigorousness)* Genauigkeit, *die; (of questioning)* Nachdrücklichkeit, *die; (of guard, watch)* Strenge, *die;* **d)** *(of atmosphere, air)* Schwüle, *die;* **e)** *(of contest, election, etc.)* knapper Ausgang; **f)** *(exactness)* **the ~ of the fit** der genaue Sitz; **the ~ of a translation** die Worttreue einer Übersetzung; **the ~ of the resemblance** die große Ähnlichkeit

close [kləʊs]: **~-range** *adj.* ⟨*Sicht, Betrachtung*⟩ aus nächster Nähe; **~-range weapon** Nahkampfwaffe, *die;* **~-range shots** *(Photog.)* Nahaufnahmen; **~ season** *n.* Schonzeit, *die;* **~-set** *adj.* dicht beieinander liegend ⟨*Augen*⟩; dicht ⟨*Hecke*⟩

closet ['klɒzɪt] *n.* **a)** *(Amer.: cupboard)* Schrank, *der;* **come out of the ~** *(fig.)* sich nicht länger verstecken; **b)** *(water-~)* Klosett, *das*

closeted ['klɒzɪtɪd] *adj.* **be ~ together/with sb.** eine Besprechung/mit jmdm. eine Besprechung hinter verschlossenen Türen haben

close-up ['kləʊsʌp] *n. (Cinemat., Telev.)* **~ [picture/shot]** Nahaufnahme *die; (of face etc.)* Großaufnahme, *die;* **in ~** in Nahaufnahme/Großaufnahme

closing ['kləʊzɪŋ]: **~ date** *n. (for competition)* Einsendeschluß, *der; (to take part)* Meldefrist, *die;* **the ~ date for applications for the job is ...:** Bewerbungen bitte bis zum ... einreichen; **~-time** *n. (of public house)* Polizeistunde, *die; (of shop)* Ladenschlußzeit, *die;* **it's nearly ~-time** es wird gleich geschlossen

closure ['kləʊʒə(r)] *n.* **a)** *(closing)* Schließung, *die; (of factory, pit also)* Stillegung, *die; (of road, bridge)* Sperrung, *die;* **a two-year ~:** eine zweijährige Stillegung; **b)** *(Parl.)* Schluß der Debatte; **c)** *(cap, stopper)* [Flaschen]verschluß, *der*

clot [klɒt] **1.** *n.* **a)** Klumpen, *der;* **a ~ [of blood] had formed over the wound/in the artery** geronnenes Blut hatte die Wunde verschlossen/ein Blutgerinnsel hatte sich in der Arterie gebildet; **b)** *(Brit. sl.: stupid person)* Trottel, *der (ugs. abwertend).* **2.** *v. i.*, **-tt-** ⟨*Blut:*⟩ gerinnen; ⟨*Sahne:*⟩ klumpen

cloth [klɒθ, klɔ:θ] *n.*, *pl.* **~s** [klɒθs, klɔ:ðz] **a)** Stoff, *der;* Tuch, *das;* **~ of gold/silver** gold-/silberdurchwirkter Stoff; **bound in ~** mit Leineneinband *nachgestellt;* **cut one's coat according to one's ~** *(fig.)* sich nach der Decke strecken *(ugs.);* **b)** *(piece of ~)* Tuch, *das; (dish-~)* Spültuch, *das; (table-~)* Tischtuch, *das;* [Tisch]decke, *die; (duster)* Staubtuch, *das;* **c)** *no pl. (clerical profession)* **a gentleman of the ~:** ein Geistlicher; **the ~** *(clergy)* die Geistlichkeit

cloth: **~ binding** *n.* Leineneinband, *der;* **~-bound** *adj.* mit Leineneinband *nachgestellt;* **~-cap** *adj.* **he tried to project a ~-cap image** er versuchte, das Image des [typischen] Arbeiters zu vermitteln; **a ~-cap comedian/entertainer** ein Komiker/Entertainer für die Arbeiterklasse

clothe [kləʊð] *v. t.* kleiden; *(fig.)* **~ one's sentiments/ideas in words** seine Gefühle/Gedanken in Worte kleiden; **the cherry trees were ~d in blossom** die Kirschbäume standen in voller Blüte; **the hills were ~d in snow** die Hügel waren mit Schnee bedeckt

'cloth-eared *adj. (coll. derog.)* schwerhörig

clothes [kləʊðz] *n. pl.* **a)** Kleider *Pl.; (collectively)* Kleidung, *die;* **with one's ~ on** angezogen; **put one's ~ on** sich anziehen; **without any ~ on** völlig unbekleidet; **take one's ~ off** sich ausziehen; **b)** *see* **bedclothes**

clothes: **~-basket** *n.* Wäschekorb, *der;* **~-brush** *n.* Kleiderbürste, *die;* **~-hanger** *n.* Kleiderbügel, *der;* **~-horse** *n.* Wäscheständer, *der;* **~-line** *n.* Wäscheleine, *die;* **~-moth** *n.* Motte, *die;* **~-peg** *(Brit.),* **~-pin** *(Amer.) ns.* Wäscheklammer, *die*

clothier ['kləʊðɪə(r)] *n. (formal)* Herrenausstatter, *der*

clothing ['kləʊðɪŋ] *n.*, *no pl.* Kleidung, *die;* **article of ~:** Kleidungsstück, *das;* **bloodstained ~ was found** blutbefleckte Kleidungsstücke wurden gefunden

clotted cream [klɒtɪd 'kri:m] *see* **Devonshire cream**

cloture ['kləʊtʃə(r)] *(Amer.) see* **closure b**

cloud [klaʊd] **1.** *n.* **a)** Wolke, *die; (collective)* Bewölkung, *die;* **be** *or* **live in the ~s** *(fig.)* auf Wolken *od.* in den Wolken schweben; **walk** *or* **go round with one's head** *or* **have one's head in the ~s** *(fig.) (be unrealistic)* in den Wolken schweben; *(be absent-minded)* mit seinen Gedanken ganz woanders sein; **[be] on ~ seven** *or* **nine** *(fig. coll.)* im sieb[en]ten Himmel [sein] *(ugs.);* **every ~ has a silver lining** *(prov.)* es hat alles sein Gutes; **there wasn't a ~ in the sky** *(lit. or fig.)* es zeigte sich [noch] kein Wölkchen am Himmel; **a ~ on the horizon** *(fig.)* ein Wölkchen am Horizont; **b) ~ of dust/smoke** Staub-/Rauchwolke, *die;* **c)** *(fig.: cause of gloom or suspicion)* dunkle Wolke; **the ~ of suspicion hangs over him** der Schatten des Verdachts liegt auf ihm; **he left under a ~:** unter zweifelhaften Umständen schied er aus dem Dienst. **2.** *v. t.* **a)** verdunkeln ⟨*Himmel*⟩; blind machen ⟨*Fenster[scheibe], Spiegel*⟩; **b)** *(fig.: cast gloom or trouble on)* trüben ⟨*Glück, Freude, Aussicht*⟩; umwölken ⟨*Gesicht, Stirn*⟩; überschatten ⟨*Zukunft*⟩; *(make unclear)* trüben ⟨*Urteilsvermögen, Verstand, Bewußtsein*⟩; verunklaren ⟨*Problem*⟩

~ 'over *v. i.* sich bewölken; ⟨*Spiegel:*⟩ beschlagen; **her face ~ed over** ihr Gesicht verdüsterte sich *(geh.)*

cloud: **~ bank** *n.* Wolkenbank, *die;* **~berry** *n.* Moltebeere, *die;* **~burst** *n.* Wolkenbruch, *der;* **~-capped** *adj.* wolkenverhangen ⟨*Gipfel*⟩; **~ chamber** *n. (Phys.)* Nebelkammer, *die;* **~ cover** *n.* Wolkendecke, *die;* **C~-'cuckoo-land** *n.* Wolkenkuckucksheim, *das (geh.)*

cloudiness ['klaʊdɪnɪs] *n.* **a)** *(of liquid)* Trübheit, *die;* **b)** *(of sky)* Bewölkung, *die*

cloudless ['klaʊdlɪs] *adj.* wolkenlos

cloudy ['klaʊdɪ] *adj.* bewölkt, bedeckt, wolkig ⟨*Himmel*⟩; trübe ⟨*Wetter, Flüssigkeit, Glas*⟩; wolkig ⟨*Edelstein, Mineral*⟩; **it is getting ~:** der Himmel bewölkt sich

clout [klaʊt] **1.** *n.* **a)** *(coll.: hit)* Schlag, *der;* **get a ~ round the ears** eins hinter die Ohren kriegen *(ugs.);* **b)** *(coll.: power, influence)* Schlagkraft, *die;* **c) ~ [nail]** Pappnagel, *der.* **2.** *v. t. (coll.)* hauen *(ugs.);* **~ sb. round the ear/on the head** jmdm. eins hinter die Ohren/auf den Deckel geben *(ugs.);* **~ sb. [one]** jmdm. eine runterhauen *(salopp)*

[1]**clove** [kləʊv] *n.* Brutzwiebel, *die; (of garlic)* [Knoblauch]zehe, *die*

[2]**clove** *n.* **a)** *(spice)* [Gewürz]nelke, *die;* *(plant)* Gewürznelkenbaum, *der;* **oil of ~s** Nelkenöl, *das;* **b) ~ [gillyflower]** Gartennelke, *die*

[3]**clove** *see* [1]**cleave**

'clove hitch *n.* Webeleinenstek, *der*

cloven ['kləʊvn] **1.** *see* [1]**cleave. 2.** *adj.* **~ foot/hoof** Spaltfuß, *der (veralt.)*/ Spalthuf, *der (veralt.); (of devil)* Pferdefuß, *der*

clover ['kləʊvə(r)] *n.* Klee, *der;* **be/live in ~** *(fig.)* wie Gott in Frankreich leben

'clover-leaf *n. (also Road Constr.)* Kleeblatt, *das*

clown [klaʊn] **1.** *n.* **a)** Clown, *der;* **act** *or* **play the ~:** den Clown spielen; **b)** *(ignorant person)* Dummkopf, *der (ugs.); (ill-bred person)* ungehobelter Klotz. **2.** *v. i.* **~ [about** *or* **around]** den Clown spielen *(abwertend)*

clownish ['klaʊnɪʃ] *adj. (derog.)* albern *(abwertend)*

cloy [klɔɪ] **1.** *v. t.* übersättigen; überfüttern; **~ the appetite** sich *(Dat.)* den Appetit verderben; **be ~ed with pleasure** des Vergnügens überdrüssig sein. **2.** *v. i.* seinen Reiz verlieren; an Reiz verlieren

cloying ['klɔɪɪŋ] *adj. (lit. or fig.)* süßlich

cloze [kləʊz] *n.* **~ test** *(Educ.)* Ergänzungstest, *der*

club [klʌb] **1.** *n.* **a)** *(weapon)* Keule, *die; (Indian ~)* [Gymnastik]keule, *die; (golf-~)* Golfschläger, *der;* **b)** *(association)* Klub, *der;* Club, *der;* Verein, *der;* **social ~:** ≈ Vereinsgaststätte, *die; (of firm)* ≈ Gemeinschaftsräume *Pl.;* **Conservative ~:** Club der Konservativen; **join the ~** *(fig.)* mitmachen; **join the** *or* **welcome to the ~!** *(fig.)* du also auch!; **be in the ~** *(Brit. fig. sl.)* ein Kind kriegen *(ugs.);* **put sb. in the ~** *(Brit. fig. sl.)* jmdm. ein Kind machen *(ugs.);* **c)** *(premises)* Klub, *der; (buildings/grounds)* Klubhaus/-gelände, *das;* **d)** *(Cards)* Kreuz, *das;* Treff, *das;* **the ace/seven of ~s** das Kreuzas/die Kreuzsieben; **~s are trumps** Kreuz ist Trumpf. **2.** *v. t.*, **-bb-:** **a)** *(beat)* prügeln; *(with ~)* knüppeln; **b)** *(contribute)* **~ [together]** zusammenlegen ⟨*Geld, Ersparnisse*⟩. **3.** *v. i.*, **-bb-:** **~ together** sich zusammentun; *(in order to buy something)* zusammenlegen

clubbable ['klʌbəbl] *adj.* gesellig

club: **~ chair** *n.* Klubsessel, *der;* **~-foot** *n.* Klumpfuß, *der;* **~house** *n.* Klubhaus, *das;* **~-man** *n.* Klubmensch, *der (jmd., der in seinem Klub/in Klubs zu Hause ist);* Vereinsmeier, *der (abwertend);* **~-moss** *n.* *(Bot.)* Bärlapp, *der; (Selaginella)* Moosfarn, *der;* **~-root** *n.* Kohlhernie, *die;* Knotensucht, *die;* **~ 'sandwich** *n. (Amer.)* Club-Sandwich, *das;* Doppeldecker, *der (ugs.)*

cluck [klʌk] **1.** *n.* Gackern, *das; (to call chicks)* Glucken, *das.* **2.** *v. i.* gackern; *(to call chicks)* glucken

clue [klu:] **1.** *n.* **a)** *(fact, principle)* Anhaltspunkt, *der; (in criminal investigation)* Spur, *die;* **find a ~ to a mystery/problem** einen Zugang zu einem Geheimnis/einem Problem finden; **the fingerprints are a ~ as to who murdered the man** die Fingerabdrücke können auf die Spur des Mörders führen; **b)** *(fig. coll.)* **give sb. a ~:** jmdm. einen Tip geben; **not have a ~:** keine Ahnung haben *(ugs.);* **he never seems to have a ~ about anything** er hat offenbar nie die geringste Ahnung; **c)** *(in crossword)* Frage, *die.* **2.** *v. t.* *(sl.: inform)* **~ sb. up** jmdm. Bescheid sagen; **be ~d up about** *or* **on sth., be ~d in on sth.** über etw. *(Akk.)* Bescheid wissen; **keep sb. ~d up** jmdn. auf dem laufenden halten

clueless ['klu:lɪs] *adj. (coll. derog.)* unbedarft *(ugs.)* ⟨*Person*⟩; **he's completely ~:** er hat absolut keine Ahnung

clump [klʌmp] **1.** *n. (of trees, bushes, flowers)* Gruppe, *die; (of grass)* Büschel, *das;* **a ~ of shrubs** ein Gebüsch. **2.** *v. i.* **a)** *(tread)* stapfen; **b)** *(form ~)* klumpen. **3.** *v. t.* **a)** *(heap, plant together)* zusammengruppieren; in Gruppen anordnen; **b)** *(coll.: hit)* hauen *(ugs.)*

clumsily ['klʌmzɪlɪ] *adv. see* **clumsy:** schwerfällig; unbeholfen; plump

clumsiness ['klʌmzɪnɪs] *n.*, *no pl. see* **clumsy:** Schwerfälligkeit, *die;* Plumpheit, *die*

clumsy ['klʌmzɪ] *adj.* **a)** *(awkward)* schwerfällig, unbeholfen ⟨*Person, Bewegungen*⟩; ungeschickt ⟨*Hände*⟩; plump ⟨*Form, Figur*⟩; tolpatschig ⟨*Heranwachsender*⟩; **b)** *(ill-contrived)* plump ⟨*Verse, Nachahmung*⟩; unbeholfen ⟨*Worte*⟩; primitiv ⟨*Vorrichtung, Maschine, Erfindung*⟩; **c)** *(tactless)* plump

clung *see* **cling**

cluster ['klʌstə(r)] **1.** *n.* **a)** *(of grapes, berries)* Traube, *die; (of fruit, flowers, curls)* Büschel, *das; (of eggs)* Gelege, *das; (of trees, shrubs)* Gruppe, *die;* **b)** *(of stars, cells)* Haufen, *der; (of houses, huts, etc.)* Gruppe, *die;* Haufen, *der; (of coral animals, bees, spectators)* Traube, *die; (of islands)* Gruppe, *die; (of diamonds on brooch)* Kranz, *der;* Besatz, *der;* **c)** *(Ling.)* Cluster, *der.* **2.** *v. t.* **be ~ed with sth.** dicht mit etw. bestanden sein. **3.** *v. i.* **~ [a]round sb./sth.** sich um jmdn./etw. scharen *od.* drängen

¹clutch [klʌtʃ] **1.** *v. t.* umklammern; **the mother ~ed the child to her breast** die Mutter drückte das Kind fest an ihre Brust. **2.** *v. i.* **~ at sth.** nach etw. greifen; *(fig.)* sich an etw. *(Akk.)* klammern; *see also* **straw b. 3.** *n.* **a)** *(tight grasp)* Umklammerung, *die;* **b)** *in pl. (fig.: control)* Klauen; **fall into sb.'s ~es** jmdm. in die Klauen fallen; in jmds. Klauen *(Akk.)* fallen; **get out of sb.'s ~es** sich aus jmds. Klauen befreien; **c)** *(grasping)* **make a ~ at sth./sb.** nach etw./jmdm. greifen; **d)** *(Motor Veh., Mech.)* Kupplung, *die;* **let in the ~, put the ~ in** einkuppeln; **disengage the ~, let the ~ out** auskuppeln; **~ pedal** Kupplungspedal, *das*

²clutch *n. (of eggs)* Gelege, *das; (of chicks)* Brut, *die*

'clutch bag *n.* Unterarmtasche, *die*

clutter ['klʌtə(r)] **1.** *n.* **a)** Durcheinander, *das;* **in a ~:** in einem Durcheinander; völlig verkramt *(ugs.);* **he pushed the ~ into a corner** er schob den ganzen Kram in eine Ecke; **b)** *(on radar screen)* Störflecke *Pl.* **2.** *v. t.* **~ [up] the table/room** überall auf dem Tisch/im Zimmer herumliegen; **be ~ed [up] with sth.** ⟨*Zimmer:*⟩ mit etw. vollgestopft sein; ⟨*Tisch:*⟩ mit etw. übersät sein; **be ~ed [up] with holiday-makers/cabs** von Urlaubern/Taxis wimmeln; **a ~ed room** ein total vollgestopftes Zimmer

cm. *abbr.* **centimetre[s]** cm

CND *abbr. (Brit.)* **Campaign for Nuclear Disarmament** Kampagne für atomare Abrüstung

CO *abbr.* **a) Commanding Officer; b) conscientious objector** KDV

Co. *abbr.* **a)** company Co.; **and Co.** [ənd kəʊ] *(coll.)* und Co. *(ugs.);* **b) county**

c/o *abbr.* **care of** bei; c/o

coach [kəʊtʃ] **1.** *n.* **a)** *(road vehicle)* Kutsche, *die; (state ~)* [Staats]karosse, *die;* **~ and four/six** Vier-/Sechsspänner, *der; see also* **drive 2 a; b)** *(railway carriage)* Wagen, *der;* **c)** *(bus)* [Reise]bus, *der;* **by ~:** mit dem Bus; **d)** *(tutor)* Privat- *od.* Nachhilfelehrer, *der/*-lehrerin, *die; (sport instructor)* Trainer, *der*/Trainerin, *die; (baseball ~)* Coach, *der.* **2.** *v. t.* trainieren; **~ a pupil for an examination** einen Schüler auf eine Prüfung vorbereiten

coach: ~builder *n.* Karosseriebauer, *der;* **~-house** *n.* Remise, *die*

coaching ['kəʊtʃɪŋ] *n., no pl.* **a)** *(teaching)* Privatunterricht, *der;* **b)** *(travelling)* **~ days** Postkutschenzeit, *die;* **~ inn** Herberge einer Poststation *(hist.)*

coach: ~-load *n.* **a ~-load of football supporters** ein Bus voll Fußballanhänger; **~man** ['kəʊtʃmən] *n., pl.* **~men** ['kəʊtʃmən] Kutscher, *der;* **~ party** *n.* Reisegesellschaft, *die;* **~-station** *n.* Busbahnhof, *der;* **~ tour** *n.* Rundreise [im Omnibus], *die;* Omnibusreise, *die;* **~work** *n.* Karosserie, *die*

coagulant [kəʊ'ægjʊlənt] *n. (Med.)* blutgerinnungsförderndes Mittel; Koagulans, *das (fachspr.)*

coagulate [kəʊ'ægjʊleɪt] **1.** *v. t.* gerinnen lassen; koagulieren *(fachspr.).* **2.** *v. i.* gerinnen; koagulieren *(fachspr.)*

coagulation [kəʊægjʊ'leɪʃn] *n.* **a)** *(process)* Gerinnung, *die;* Koagulation, *die (fachspr.);* **b)** *(mass)* Gerinnsel, *das;* Koagulat, *das (fachspr.)*

coal [kəʊl] *n.* **a)** Kohle, *die; (hard ~)* Steinkohle, *die;* **b)** *(piece of ~)* Stück Kohle; **live ~s** Glut, *die;* **heap ~s of fire on sb.'s head** *(fig.)* feurige Kohlen auf jmds. Haupt *(Akk.)* sammeln *(fig.);* **haul** *or* **call sb. over the ~s** *(fig.)* jmdm. die Leviten lesen *(ugs.);* **carry ~s to Newcastle** *(fig.)* Eulen nach Athen tragen *(fig.)*

coal: ~-bed *n.* Kohlenflöz, *der;* **~-black** *adj.* kohlrabenschwarz; **~-box** *n.* Kohlenkasten, *der;* **~-bunker** *n.* Kohlenbunker, *der;* **~-cellar** *n.* Kohlenkeller, *der;* **~-dust** *n.* Kohlenstaub, *der*

coalesce [kəʊə'les] *v. i.* **a)** sich verbinden; eine Verbindung eingehen; **b)** *(unite)* sich vereinigen

coalescence [kəʊə'lesəns] *n.* Verbindung, *die; (fig.)* Vereinigung, *die*

coal: ~-face *n.* Streb, *der;* **at the ~-face** im Streb *od.* vor Ort; **~field** *n.* Kohlenrevier, *das;* **~ fire** *n.* Kohlenfeuer, *das;* **~-fired** *adj.* mit Kohle beheizt; kohlebeheizt; **~-fired power-station** Kohlekraftwerk, *das;* **~ gas** *n.* Leuchtgas, *das;* Stadtgas, *das;* **~-heaver** *n.* Kohlenträger, *der;* **~-hole** *n.* *(Brit.)* **a)** Kohlenbunker, *der;* **b)** *(cellar)* Kohlenkeller, *der;* **~-house** *n.* Kohlenschuppen, *der*

coalition [kəʊə'lɪʃn] *n. (Polit.)* Koalition, *die; (union, fusion)* Zusammenschluß, *der (von Gruppen, Firmen);* **a ~ of plans/projects** eine Planungsgemeinschaft; **a ~ of interests** eine Interessenkoalition

coa'lition government *n.* Koalitionsregierung, *die*

coal: ~ man *n. (coll.)* Kohlenmann, *der (ugs.);* **~ measures** *n. pl. (Geol.)* Kohlevorkommen, *das;* **~-merchant** *n.* Kohlenhändler, *der;* **~-mine** *n.* [Kohlen]bergwerk, *das;* **~-miner** *n.* [im Kohlenbergbau tätiger] Grubenarbeiter; **~-mining** *n.* Kohlenbergbau, *der;* **~-oil** *n. (Amer.)* Paraffin, *das;* **~-scuttle** *n.* Kohleneimer, *der;* Kohlenschütte, *die;* **~-seam** *n.* Kohlenflöz, *der;* **~-shed** *see* **~-house; ~-shovel** *n.* Kohlenschaufel, *die;* **~ tar** *n.* Steinkohlenteer, *der;* **~-tit** *n. (Ornith.)* Tannenmeise, *die*

coaming ['kəʊmɪŋ] *n. (Naut.)* Süllrand, *der*

coarse [kɔ:s] *adj.* **a)** *(inferior)* derb, einfach ⟨*Essen*⟩; **b)** *(in texture)* grob; rauh, grob ⟨*Haut, Teint*⟩; **c)** *(unrefined, rude, obscene)* derb; roh ⟨*Geschmack, Kraft*⟩; primitiv ⟨*Person, Geist*⟩; ungehobelt ⟨*Manieren, Person*⟩; gemein ⟨*Lachen, Witz, Geräusch*⟩

coarse: ~ 'fish *n. (esp. Brit.)* Süßwasserfisch, *der (außer Lachs und Forelle);* **~-grained** *adj.* grob gekörnt ⟨*Sand, Salz, Papier*⟩; grob genarbt ⟨*Leder*⟩; grob gemasert ⟨*Holz*⟩

coarsely ['kɔ:slɪ] *adv. see* **coarse: a)** derb; einfach; **b)** grob; rauh; **c)** derb; roh; primitiv; ungehobelt; gemein

coarsen ['kɔ:sn] **1.** *v. t.* vergröbern. **2.** *v. i.* sich vergröbern

coarseness ['kɔ:snɪs] *n., no pl. see* **coarse: a)** Derbheit, *die;* Einfachheit, *die;* **b)** Grobheit, *die;* Rauheit, *die;* **c)** Derbheit, *die;* Roheit, *die;* Primitivität, *die;* Ungehobeltheit, *die;* Gemeinheit, *die*

coast [kəʊst] **1.** *n.* **a)** Küste, *die;* **on the ~:** an der Küste; **off the ~:** vor der Küste; **the ~ is clear** *(fig.: there is no danger)* die Luft ist rein *(fig.);* **b)** *(Amer.)* **the C~:** die Pazifik- *od.* Westküste der USA; **c)** *(Amer.: slide)* Rodelbahn, *die;* **go for a ~:** rodeln gehen. **2.** *v. i.* **a)** *(ride)* im Freilauf fahren; **b)** *(fig.: progress)* **they are just ~ing along in their work** sie tun bei der Arbeit nur das Nötigste; sie arbeiten nur im Schongang *(ugs.);* **he ~s through every examination** er schafft jede Prüfung spielend; **c)** *(sail)* die Küste entlang fahren; **d)** *(Amer.: toboggan)* hinunterfahren

coastal ['kəʊstl] *adj.* Küsten-; **~ traffic** Küstenschiffahrt, *die*

coaster ['kəʊstə(r)] *n.* **a)** *(mat)* Untersetzer, *der;* **b)** *(tray)* Tablett, *das;* **c)** *(ship)* Küstenmotorschiff, *das;* Kümo, *das;* **d)** *(Amer.: sledge)* Rodelschlitten, *der*

coast: ~guard *n.* **a)** *(person)* Angehörige[r] der Küstenwacht; **b)** *(body of men)* Küstenwache, -wacht, *die;* **~line** *n.* Küste, *die*

coat [kəʊt] **1.** *n.* **a)** Mantel, *der; (man's jacket)* Jackett, *das;* Rock, *der (veralt.);* **turn one's ~** *(fig.)* sein Mäntelchen nach dem Winde hängen *(ugs. abwertend); see also* **cloth a; b)** *(layer)* Schicht, *die;* **c)** *(animal's hair, fur, etc.)* Fell, *das; (of bird)* Federkleid, *das;* **d)** *see* **coating; e)** *(skin, rind, husk)* Schale, *die;* **f)** *(Anat.)* Haut, *die.* **2.** *v. t.* überziehen; *(with paint)* streichen

'coat dress *n.* Mantelkleid, *das*

coated ['kəʊtɪd] *adj.* gestrichen ⟨*Papier*⟩; belegt ⟨*Zunge*⟩; imprägniert ⟨*Stoff*⟩; getönt ⟨*Glas, Linsen*⟩; **~ with dust/sugar** staubbedeckt/mit Zucker überzogen

coat: ~-hanger *n.* Kleiderbügel, *der;* **~-hook** *n.* Kleiderhaken, *der*

coating ['kəʊtɪŋ] *n. (of paint)* Anstrich, *der; (of dust, snow, wax, polish, varnish)* Schicht, *die; (for ceramic glazes)* Überzug, *der*

coat: ~ of 'arms *n.* Wappen, *das;* **~-tails** *n. pl.* Frackschöße

co-author [kəʊ'ɔ:θə(r)] **1.** *n.* Mitautor, *der/*-autorin, *die;* **they were ~s of the book** sie haben das Buch gemeinsam verfaßt. **2.** *v. t.* gemeinsam verfassen ⟨*Buch, Dokument*⟩

coax [kəʊks] *v. t.* überreden; **~ sb. to do sth.** jmdn. überreden *od.* dazu bringen, etw. zu tun; **~ sb. into doing sth.** jmdn. herumkriegen *(ugs.),* etw. zu tun; **~ a fire to burn/an engine into life** ein Feuer/einen Motor in Gang bringen; **~ a smile/some money out of sb.** jmdm. ein Lächeln/etw. Geld entlocken; **~ sb. out of doing sth.** jmdm. ausreden, etw. zu tun

coaxial [kəʊ'æksɪəl] *adj.* koaxial

coaxing ['kəʊksɪŋ] *n.* Überredung, *die;* Zureden, *das*

cob [kɒb] *n.* **a)** *(nut)* Haselnuß, *die;* **b)** *(swan)* männlicher Schwan; **c)** *(horse)* Cob, *die; kleines, stämmiges Pferd;* **d)** *see* **corncob; e)** *(loaf)* rundes Brot

cobalt ['kəʊbɔ:lt, 'kəʊbɒlt] *n.* **a)** *(element)* Kobalt, *das;* **b)** *(pigment, colour)* Kobaltblau, *das*

cobber ['kɒbə(r)] *n. (Austral. and NZ coll.)* Kumpel, *der (ugs.)*

¹cobble ['kɒbl] **1.** *n. (stone)* Pflaster-, Kopfstein, *der;* Katzenkopf, *der;* **rumble over the ~s** über das Kopfsteinpflaster rumpeln. **2.** *v. t.* pflastern ⟨*Straße*⟩; **~d streets** Straßen mit Kopfsteinpflaster

²cobble *v. t. (put together, mend)* flicken; **~ up plans/verses** [sich *(Dat.)*] Pläne zusammenbasteln *(ugs.) od.* zusammenreimen/[sich *(Dat.)*] Gedichte zusammenstoppeln *(ugs.);* **~ together** zusammenbasteln; zusammenmischen ⟨*Essen, Mannschaft*⟩

cobbler ['kɒblə(r)] *n.* **a)** Schuster, *der;* Flickschuster, *der (veralt.);* **b)** *in pl. (Brit. sl.: nonsense)* Scheiße, *die (derb);* Mist, *der (salopp);* **a load of ~s** totaler Mist *(salopp)*

'cobble-stone *see* **¹cobble 1**

Coblenz [kəʊ'blents] *pr. n.* Koblenz *(das)*

'cob-nut *see* **cob a**

cobra ['kɒbrə] *n. (Zool.)* Kobra, *die*

cobweb ['kɒbweb] *n.* **a)** *(network)* Spinnengewebe, *das;* Spinnennetz, *das; (material)* Spinn[en]weben *Pl.;* Spinn[en]fäden *Pl.;* **b)** *in pl. (rubbish)* Hirngespinste *Pl.;* **blow away the ~s** *(fig.)* für einen klaren Kopf sorgen

Coca-Cola, (P) *n.* [kəʊkə'kəʊlə] Coca-Cola ⓦ, *das od. die*

cocaine [kə'keɪn] *n.* Kokain, *das*

coccyx ['kɒksɪks] *n. (Zool.)* Steiß, *der; (Anat.)* Steißbein, *das*

cochineal [kɒtʃɪ'ni:l] *n.* Koschenille, *die*

cochlea ['kɒklɪə] *n. pl.* **cochleae** ['kɒklɪi:] *(Anat.)* Schnecke, *die;* Cochlea, *die (fachspr.)*

[1]**cock** [kɒk] **1.** *n.* **a)** *(bird, lobster, crab, salmon)* Männchen, *das; (domestic fowl)* Hahn, *der; (woodcock)* Waldschnepfe, *die;* **live like fighting ~s** *(fig.)* wie Gott in Frankreich leben; **that ~ won't fight** *(fig.)* das hat keinen Zweck; **b)** *(sl.: man)* Bengel, *der (ugs.);* Bursche, *der (ugs.);* **old ~:** alter Junge *(ugs.);* **c)** *(spout, tap, etc.)* Hahn, *der;* **d)** *(coarse: penis)* Schwanz, *der (salopp);* Pimmel, *der (salopp);* **e)** *(in gun)* Hahn, *der;* **be/start/go off at half ~** *(fig.)* danebengehen *(ugs.);* ein Reinfall sein *(ugs.).* **2.** *v.t.* **a)** *(erect, stand up)* aufstellen, *(fig.)* spitzen ⟨*Ohren*⟩; **~ one's eye at sb.** zu jmdm. hinblicken; *(wink)* jmdm. zublinzeln; **b)** *(bend)* anwinkeln ⟨*Knie-, Handgelenk*⟩; **the parrot ~ed its head [to one side]** der Papagei legte den Kopf auf die Seite; **c)** *(put on slanting)* schief *od.* schräg aufsetzen ⟨*Hut*⟩; *(turn up brim of)* hochstülpen ⟨*Hut*⟩; **a ~ed hat** ein Hut mit hoher Krempe; *(triangular hat)* ein Dreispitz; **knock sb./sth. into a ~ed hat** *(fig.) (destroy)* jmdn./etw. zerschmettern *(fig.); (surpass)* jmdn./etw. weit übertreffen; jmdn./etw. in den Sack stecken *(ugs. fig.);* **d) ~ a/the gun** den Hahn spannen

~ 'up *v.t. (Brit. sl.)* versauen *(salopp); see also* **cock-up**

[2]**cock** *n. (heap)* Haufen, *der*

cockade [kə'keɪd] *n.* Kokarde, *die*

cock-a-doodle-doo [kɒkədu:dl'du:] *n. (crowing)* Kikeriki, *das; (child lang.: cock)* Kikeriki, *der*

cock-a-hoop [kɒkə'hu:p] **1.** *adj.* überschwenglich; *(boastful)* triumphierend; **be ~:** triumphieren. **2.** *adv.* überschwenglich; *(boastfully)* triumphierend

cock-and-'bull story *n.* Lügengeschichte, *die*

cockatoo [kɒkə'tu:] *n. (parrot)* Kakadu, *der*

cockchafer ['kɒktʃeɪfə(r)] *n.* Maikäfer, *der*

'cock-crow *n.* **at ~:** beim ersten Hahnenschrei

cocker [spaniel] ['kɒkə('spænjəl)] *n.* Cockerspaniel, *der*

cockerel ['kɒkərəl] *n.* junger Hahn

cock-eyed ['kɒkaɪd] *adj.* **a)** *(crooked)* schief; **b)** *(absurd)* verrückt; **c)** *(sl.: squinting)* schielend ⟨*Blick*⟩; **be ~:** schielen

'cock-fighting *n.* Hahnenkampf, *der*

cockily ['kɒkɪlɪ] *adv.* anmaßend; frech

cockiness ['kɒkɪnɪs] *n., no pl.* Anmaßung, *die;* Frechheit, *die*

cockle [kɒkl] *n.* **a)** *(bivalve, shell)* Herzmuschel, *die;* **b) warm the ~s of sb.'s heart** es jmdm. warm ums Herz werden lassen

cockney ['kɒknɪ] **1.** *adj.* Cockney-. **2.** *n.* **a)** *(person)* waschechter Londoner/waschechte Londonerin; Cockney, *der;* **b)** *(dialect)* Cockney, *das*

cock: ~ of the 'walk *(fig.)* **be the ~ of the walk** die Szene beherrschen; *(domineer)* den Ton angeben; **~ of the 'wood** *n.* **a)** *(capercaillie)* Auerhahn, *der;* **b)** *(Amer.: woodpecker)* Haubenschwarzspecht, *der;* **~pit** *n.* **a)** *(Aeronaut.)* Cockpit, *das;* [Piloten]kanzel, *die;* **b)** *(in racing-car)* Cockpit, *das; (in boat)* Plicht, *die;* Cockpit, *das;* **c)** *(for cock-fighting)* Hahnenkampfplatz, *der*

cockroach ['kɒkrəʊtʃ] *n.* [Küchen-, Haus-]schabe, *die;* Kakerlak, *der*

cockscomb ['kɒkskəʊm] *n. (Ornith., Bot.)* Hahnenkamm, *der*

cocksure [kɒk'ʃʊə(r)] *adj.* **a)** *(convinced)* todsicher; **b)** *(self-confident)* selbstsicher; *(dogmatic)* selbstgerecht; **be ~ of oneself** sich *(Dat.)* seiner Sache *(Gen.)* [unberechtigterweise] völlig sicher sein

cocktail ['kɒkteɪl] *n.* Cocktail, *der; see also* **fruit cocktail**

cocktail: ~ cabinet *n.* Hausbar, *die;* **~ dress** *n.* Cocktailkleid, *das;* **~ glass** *n.* Cocktailglas, *das;* **~ party** *n.* Cocktailparty, *die;* **~-shaker** *n.* Mixbecher, *der;* **~ stick** *n.* Partystick, *der od. das*

'cock-up *n. (Brit. sl.)* Schlamassel, *der (ugs.);* **make a ~ of sth.** bei etw. Scheiße bauen *(derb)*

cocky ['kɒkɪ] *adj.* anmaßend

coco ['kəʊkəʊ] *see* **coconut a**

cocoa ['kəʊkəʊ] *n.* Kakao, *der*

'cocoa bean *n.* Kakaobohne, *die*

coconut ['kəʊkənʌt] *n.* **a)** *(tree)* Kokospalme, *die;* **b)** *(nut)* Kokosnuß, *die;* **c)** *(sl.: head)* Rübe, *die (derb)*

coconut: ~ 'butter *n.* Kokosfett, *das;* **~ 'matting** *n.* Kokosmatten *Pl.;* **~ milk** *n.* Kokosmilch, *die;* **~ palm** *see* **coconut a;** **~ shy** *n.* Wurfbude, *die*

cocoon [kə'ku:n] **1.** *n.* **a)** *(Zool.)* Kokon, *der;* **b)** *(covering)* Hülle, *die.* **2.** *v.t. (wrap as in ~)* einmummen

[1]**cod** [kɒd] *n., pl. same* Kabeljau, *der; (in Baltic)* Dorsch, *der*

[2]**cod** *(sl.)* **1.** *v.t.,* **-dd-: a)** *(hoax)* vergackeiern *(salopp);* verscheißern *(derb);* **b)** *(parody)* verulken *(ugs.).* **2.** *v.i.,* **-dd-** rumblödeln *(ugs.);* flachsen *(ugs.)*

COD *abbr.* **cash on delivery; collect on delivery** *(Amer.)* p. Nachn.

coda ['kəʊdə] *n. (Mus.)* Koda, *die*

coddle ['kɒdl] *v.t.* **a)** [ver]hätscheln ⟨*Kind*⟩; verwöhnen ⟨*Kranken*⟩; **b)** *(Cookery)* schwach pochieren ⟨*Eier*⟩

code [kəʊd] **1.** *n.* **a)** *(collection of statutes etc.)* Kodex, *der;* Gesetzbuch, *das;* **a ~ of laws** ein Gesetzbuch; eine Gesetzessammlung; **~ of religion/literature/society** religiöse/literarische/gesellschaftliche Normen; **~ of honour** Ehrenkodex, *der;* **~s of behaviour** Verhaltensnormen; Verhaltenskodizes *(geh.);* **b)** *(system of signals)* Kode, Code, *der; (coded word, etc.)* Chiffre, *die;* **be in ~:** verschlüsselt sein; **put sth. into ~:** etw. verschlüsseln; *see also* **genetic a. 2.** *v.t.* chiffrieren, verschlüsseln ⟨*Nachricht*⟩

code: ~-book *n.* Signalbuch, *das;* **~-name** *n.* Deckname, *der;* **~-number** *n.* Kenn-, Tarnzahl, *die;* **~-word** *n.* Kennwort, *das*

codex ['kəʊdeks] *n., pl.* **codices** ['kəʊdɪsi:z] **a)** *(manuscript volume)* Kodex, *der;* **b)** *(of drugs etc.) pharmazeutisches Nachschlagewerk*

'codfish *see* [1]**cod**

codger ['kɒdʒə(r)] *n. (coll.)* Knacker, *der (salopp)*

codicil ['kəʊdɪsɪl] *n.* Kodizill, *das*

codification [kəʊdɪfɪ'keɪʃn] *n.* Kodifizierung, *die;* Kodifikation, *die*

codify ['kəʊdɪfaɪ] *v.t.* kodifizieren ⟨*Gesetze, Rechtsnormen*⟩; festlegen, kodifizieren ⟨*Rechtschreibung, Grammatik*⟩

coding ['kəʊdɪŋ] *n.* **a)** *(action)* Chiffrieren, *das;* **b)** *(result)* verschlüsselte Informationen

codling *n. (fish)* Dorsch, *der*

cod-liver 'oil *n.* Lebertran, *der*

codpiece ['kɒdpi:s] *n. (Hist.)* Hosenlatz, *der*

co-driver ['kəʊdraɪvə(r)] *n.* Beifahrer, *der*/-fahrerin, *die*

cods [kɒdz], **codswallop** ['kɒdzwɒləp] *n. (Brit. sl.)* Stuß, *der (ugs.);* **this is a load of ~:** das ist großer Stuß

coed ['kəʊed] *(esp. Amer. coll.)* **1.** *n.* Studentin, *die.* **2.** *adj.* koedukativ; Koedukations-; **~ school** gemischte Schule

co-edition [kəʊɪ'dɪʃn] *n.* gemeinsame Ausgabe

coeducation [kəʊedjʊ'keɪʃn] *n.* Koedukation, *die*

coeducational [kəʊedjʊ'keɪʃənl] *adj.* koedukativ; Koedukations-

coefficient [kəʊɪ'fɪʃənt] *n. (Math., Phys.)* Koeffizient, *der*

coelacanth ['si:ləkænθ] *n. (Zool.)* Coelacanthus, *der*

coequal [kəʊ'i:kwəl] *(arch./literary) adj.* ebenbürtig *(geh.)*

coerce [kəʊ'ɜ:s] *v.t.* zwingen; **~ sb. into sth.** jmdn. zu etw. zwingen; **~ sb. into doing sth.** jmdn. dazu zwingen, etw. zu tun

coercion [kəʊ'ɜ:ʃn] *n.* Zwang, *der*

coercive [kəʊ'ɜsɪv] *adj.* Zwangs⟨*gewalt, -herrschaft, -gesetz, -maßnahmen*⟩

coexist [kəʊɪg'zɪst] *v.i.* ⟨*Ideen, Überzeugungen:*⟩ nebeneinander bestehen, koexistieren; **~ [together] with sb./sth.** neben jmdm./etw. bestehen; mit jmdm./etw. koexistieren

coexistence [kəʊɪg'zɪstəns] *n.* Koexistenz, *die;* **peaceful ~:** friedliche Koexistenz

coexistent [kəʊɪg'zɪstənt] *adj. (formal)* nebeneinander bestehend ⟨*Systeme, Regierungen*⟩

coextensive [kəʊɪk'stensɪv] *adj. (formal)* **be ~:** übereinstimmen; sich decken

C. of E. [si:əv'i:] *abbr.* **Church of England**

coffee ['kɒfɪ] *n.* **a)** Kaffee, *der;* **drink** *or* **have a cup of ~:** eine Tasse Kaffee trinken; **three black/white ~s** drei [Tassen] Kaffee ohne/mit Milch; **I was invited to ~:** ich bin zum Kaffee[trinken] eingeladen worden; **b)** *(colour)* Kaffeebraun, *das*

coffee: ~ bar *n.* Café, *das; (in department store, university, etc.)* Erfrischungsraum, *der;* **~-bean** *n.* Kaffeebohne, *die;* **~-break** *n.* Kaffeepause, *die;* **~-cup** *n.* Kaffeetasse, *die;* **~ 'essence** *n.* Kaffee-Extrakt, *der;* **~-filter** *n.* Kaffeefilter, *der;* **~-grinder** *n.* Kaffeemühle, *die;* **~-grounds** *n. pl.* Kaffeesatz, *der;* **~-house** *n.* Café, *das; (Hist.)* Kaffeehaus, *das;* **~-machine, ~-maker** *ns.* Kaffeeautomat, *der;* **~-mill** *n.* Kaffeemühle, *die;* **~ morning** *n.* Morgenkaffee, *der (als Wohltätigkeitsveranstaltung);* **~ percolator** *n.* Kaffeemaschine, *die;* **~-pot** *n.* Kaffeekanne, *die;* **~ shop** *n.* Kaffeestube, *die;* Café, *das; (selling ~-beans etc.)* Kaffeegeschäft, *das;* **~ stall** *n.* Kaffeebar, *die; (serving other light refreshments also)* Erfrischungsstand, *der;* **~-table** *n.* Couchtisch, *der;* **~-table book** Bildband [in Luxusausstattung]

coffer ['kɒfə(r)] *n.* **a)** *(box)* Truhe, *die;* **b)** *in pl. (treasure, funds)* **the household ~s** die Privatschatulle; **the ~s of the government** der Staatssäckel *(scherzh.);* **c)** *(Archit.)* Kassette, *die;* **d) ~[dam]** Caisson, *der*

coffin ['kɒfɪn] *n.* Sarg, *der; see also* **nail 1 b**

cog [kɒg] *n. (Mech.)* Zahn, *der;* **be just a ~ [in the wheel/machine]** *(fig.)* bloß ein Rädchen im Getriebe sein

cogency ['kəʊdʒənsɪ] *n. (of argument, reason)* Stichhaltigkeit, *die; (of narration, description, slogan)* Überzeugungskraft, *die*

cogent ['kəʊdʒənt] *adj. (convincing)* überzeugend ⟨*Argument, Grund*⟩; zwingend ⟨*Grund*⟩; *(valid)* stichhaltig ⟨*Kritik, Analyse*⟩

cogently ['kəʊdʒəntlɪ] *adv. see* **cogent:** überzeugend; zwingend; stichhaltig

cogitate ['kɒdʒɪteɪt] *(formal/joc.)* **1.** *v.i.* nachsinnen, nachdenken **(on** über + *Akk.*). **2.** *v.t.* nachsinnen, nachdenken über (+ *Akk.*)

cogitation [kɒdʒɪ'teɪʃn] *n. (formal/joc.)* Nachdenken, *das;* Nachsinnen, *das;* **after much ~:** nach langem Grübeln

cognac ['kɒnjæk] *n.* Cognac, *der* ⓦᶻ

cognate ['kɒgneɪt] *adj. (Ling.)* verwandt

cognisance, cognisant *see* **cogniz-**

cognition [kɒg'nɪʃn] *n.* Erkenntnis, *die*

cognitive ['kɒgnɪtɪv] *adj.* kognitiv ⟨*Fähigkeiten*⟩; Erkenntnis⟨*gehalt, -kräfte*⟩

cognizance ['kɒgnɪzəns] *n. (formal)* **a)** *no pl. (awareness)* Kenntnis, *die;* **have ~ of sth.** von etw. Kenntnis haben; **take ~ of sb./sth.** jmdn./etw. zur Kenntnis nehmen; **b)** *no pl. ([right of] dealing with a matter legally)* Zuständigkeit, *die* **(of** in + *Dat.*)

cognizant ['kɒgnɪzənt] *adj. (formal)* **a)** *(having knowledge)* in Kenntnis **(of** *Gen.*); **b)** *(having jurisdiction)* zuständig **(of** für)

cognoscenti [kɒnjəˈʃenti:, kɒnjəˈʃentɪ] *n. pl.* Kenner

cog: **~-railway** *n. (esp. Amer.)* Zahnradbahn, *die;* **~-wheel** *n.* Zahnrad, *das*

cohabit [kəʊˈhæbɪt] *v. i.* zusammenleben; in eheähnlicher Gemeinschaft leben *(Rechtsspr.)*

cohabitation [kəʊhæbɪˈteɪʃn] *n.* Zusammenleben, *das;* eheähnliche Gemeinschaft *(Rechtsspr.)*

cohere [kəʊˈhɪə(r)] *v. i.* **a)** ‹*Teile, Ganzes, Gruppe:*› zusammenhalten; **b)** ‹*Argumentation, Komposition, Aufsatz:*› in sich *(Dat.)* geschlossen sein

coherence [kəʊˈhɪərəns] *n.* **a)** Zusammenhang, *der;* Kohärenz, *die (geh.); (in work, system, form)* Geschlossenheit, *die;* **b)** *(Phys.)* Kohärenz, *die*

coherent [kəʊˈhɪərənt] *adj.* **a)** *(cohering)* zusammenhängend; **b)** *(fig.)* zusammenhängend; kohärent *(geh.);* in sich *(Dat.)* geschlossen ‹*System, Ganzes, Werk, Aufsatz, Form*›; **a ~ presentation of the facts** eine [in sich *(Dat.)*] stimmige Darlegung der Fakten; **c)** *(Phys.)* kohärent

coherently [kəʊˈhɪərəntlɪ] *adv.* zusammenhängend; im Zusammenhang

cohesion [kəʊˈhi:ʒn] *n.* **a)** *(sticking together)* Zusammenhängen, *das; (of substances)* Haften, *das;* **b)** *(fig.) (of group, state, community)* Zusammenhalt, *der;* Kohäsion, *die (geh.);* **c)** *(Phys.)* Kohäsion, *die*

cohesive [kəʊˈhi:sɪv] *adj.* geschlossen, in sich *(Dat.)* ruhend ‹*Ganzes, Einheit, Form*›; stimmig ‹*Stil, Argument*›; kohäsiv ‹*Masse, Mischung*›

cohort [ˈkəʊhɔ:t] *n.* **a)** *(division of Roman army, band of warriors)* Kohorte, *die;* **b)** *(group)* Gruppe, *die;* **c)** *(Amer.: assistant, colleague)* Helfer, *der*/Helferin, *die*

coiffure [kwɑ:ˈfjʊə(r)] *n.* Frisur, *die;* Coiffure, *die (veralt., geh.)*

coil [kɔɪl] **1.** *v. t.* **a)** *(arrange)* aufwickeln; **the snake ~ed itself round a branch** die Schlange wand sich um einen Ast; **b)** *(twist)* aufdrehen; **the snake ~ed itself up** die Schlange rollte sich auf. **2.** *v. i.* **a)** *(twist)* **~ round sth.** etw. umschlingen; **b)** *(move sinuously)* sich winden; ‹*Rauch:*› sich ringeln. **3.** *n.* **a)** **~s of rope/wire/piping** aufgerollte Seile *Pl.*/aufgerollter Draht/aufgerollte Leitungen *Pl.;* **b)** *(single turn of coiled thing)* Windung, *die;* **c)** *(length of coiled rope etc.)* Stück, *das;* **d)** *(lock of hair)* Locke, *die;* **e)** *(contraceptive device)* Spirale, *die;* **f)** *(Electr.)* Spule, *die*

ˈ**coil spring** *n.* Spiralfeder, *die*

coin [kɔɪn] **1.** *n.* Münze, *die; (metal money)* Münzen *Pl.;* Münzgeld, *das;* **in ~:** in Münzen; **the other side of the ~** *(fig.)* die Kehrseite der Medaille; **pay sb. in his own ~** *(fig.)* jmdm. in *od.* mit gleicher Münze heimzahlen. **2.** *v. t.* **a)** *(invent)* prägen ‹*Wort, Redewendung*›; **..., to ~ a phrase** *(iron.)* ..., um mich ganz originell auszudrücken; **b)** *(make)* prägen ‹*Geld*›; **~ money** *(fig.)* Geld scheffeln; **c)** *(make into money)* münzen *(Gold, Silber usw.)*

coinage [ˈkɔɪnɪdʒ] *n.* **a)** *(system)* Währung, *die;* **b)** *(coins)* Münzen *Pl.;* Hartgeld, *das;* **c)** *(coining)* Prägung, *die;* Prägen, *das;* **d)** *(invention)* Prägung, *die;* **'astronaut' and 'sputnik' are modern ~s** „Astronaut" und „Sputnik" sind Neuprägungen

ˈ**coin-box telephone** *n.* Münzfernsprecher, *der*

coincide [kəʊɪnˈsaɪd] *v. i.* **a)** *(in space)* sich decken; **~ with one another** sich decken; **b)** *(in time)* ‹*Ereignisse, Veranstaltungen:*› zusammenfallen; **c)** *(agree together, concur in opinion)* übereinstimmen **(with** mit); **~ in sth.** in etw. *(Dat.)* übereinstimmen

coincidence [kəʊˈɪnsɪdəns] *n.* **a)** *(being coincident)* Deckungsgleichheit, *die; (of two points)* Zusammenfall, *der;* **b)** *(instance)* Zufall, *der;* **by pure** *or* **sheer ~:** rein zufällig; **it was a happy ~:** es traf sich gut; **by a curious ~:** durch einen merkwürdigen Zufall; **c)** *(of events)* Duplizität der Ereignisse; Koinzidenz, *die*

coincident [kəʊˈɪnsɪdənt] *adj. (formal) (in space)* deckungsgleich ‹*Figuren*›; *(in time or place)* zusammenfallend; *(agreeing)* übereinstimmend; **be ~ with sth.** mit etw. deckungsgleich sein/zusammenfallen/übereinstimmen

coincidental [kəʊɪnsɪˈdentl] *adj.* zufällig; **be ~ with sth.** mit etw. zufällig zusammentreffen

coincidentally [kəʊɪnsɪˈdentəlɪ] *adv.* gleichzeitig; *(by coincidence)* zufälligerweise

coiner [ˈkɔɪnə(r)] *n. (esp. Brit.)* Falschmünzer, *der*

ˈ**coin-operated** *adj.* Münz-

coir [ˈkɔɪə(r)] *n.* Coir, *das od. die;* Kokosfaser, *die*

coition [kəʊˈɪʃn], **coitus** [ˈkəʊɪtəs] *ns. (Med.)* Koitus, *der;* Beischlaf, *der*

coitus interruptus [kəʊɪtəs ɪntəˈrʌptəs] *n.* Coitus interruptus, *der*

Coke, (P) [kəʊk] *n. (drink)* Coke, *das* Ⓦⓩ

[1]**coke** [kəʊk] **1.** *n.* Koks, *der.* **2.** *v. t.* verkoken

[2]**coke** *n. (sl.: cocaine)* Koks, *der (salopp)*

col [kɒl] *n.* [Berg]sattel, *der*

Col. *abbr.* **Colonel** Obst.

col. *abbr.* **column** Sp.

cola [kəʊlə] *n.* Cola, *das od. die (ugs.)*

colander [ˈkʌləndə(r)] *n.* Sieb, *das;* Durchschlag, *der*

cold [kəʊld] **1.** *adj.* **a)** kalt; **I feel ~:** ich friere; mir ist kalt; **her hands/feet were ~:** sie hatte kalte Hände/Füße; **b)** *(without ardour etc.)* kalt ‹*Intellekt, Herz*›; [betont] kühl ‹*Person, Ansprache, Aufnahme, Begrüßung*›; eiskalt ‹*Handlung*›; unterdrückt ‹*Wut*›; **go ~ on sth.** das Interesse an etw. *(Dat.)* verlieren; **leave sb. ~:** jmdn. kaltlassen *(ugs.);* **c)** *(dead)* kalt; **d)** *(sl.: unconscious)* bewußtlos; k.o. *(ugs.);* **he laid him out ~:** er schlug ihn k.o.; **the punch knocked him out ~:** durch den Schlag ging er bewußtlos zu Boden; **e)** *(coll.: at one's mercy)* **have sb. ~:** jmdn. am Kragen haben *(ugs.);* **f)** *(sexually frigid)* [gefühls]kalt; **g)** *(slow to warm)* kalt ‹*Boden*›; **h)** *(Amer.: unrehearsed)* ohne Vorbereitung *nachgestellt;* **i)** *(chilling, depressing)* kalt ‹*Farbe*›; nackt ‹*Tatsache, Statistik*›; **j)** *(uninteresting)* fade ‹*Geschichte*›; **the news is already ~:** für die Sache interessiert sich niemand mehr; **k)** *(Hunting)* kalt ‹*Fährte*›; *(in children's games)* **you're ~ and getting ~er** kalt, noch kälter. **2.** *adv.* **a)** *(in cold state)* kalt; *(Amer.: without preparation)* kühl ‹*handeln*›; **b)** *(Amer. sl.: completely)* voll *(salopp).* **3.** *n.* **a)** Kälte, *die;* **shiver with ~:** vor Kälte *(Dat.)* zittern; **be left out in the ~** *(fig.)* links liegengelassen werden; **b)** *(illness)* Erkältung, *die;* **~ [in the head]** Schnupfen, *der. See also* **blood 1 a, d; catch 1 e; cold turkey; fish 1 c; snap 3 e; water**

cold: **~-blooded** [ˈkəʊldblʌdɪd] *adj.* **a)** wechselwarm ‹*Tier*›; kaltblütig *(selten);* **~-blooded animals** Kaltblüter *Pl.;* wechselwarme Tiere; **b)** *(callous)* kaltblütig ‹*Person, Mord*›; **~ chisel** *n. (Metalw.)* Kaltmeißel, *der;* **~ ˈcomfort** *n.* ein schwacher Trost; **~ cream** *n.* Cold Cream, *die od. das;* **~ cuts** *n. pl.* Aufschnitt, *der;* **~ ˈfeet** *n. (fig.)* **get/have ~ feet** kalte Füße kriegen *(ugs.)*/gekriegt haben *(ugs.);* **~ frame** *n.* Frühbeet, *das;* **~ ˈfront** *n. (Meteorol.)* Kaltfront, *die;* **~-hearted** *adj.* kaltherzig

coldly [ˈkəʊldlɪ] *adv.* [betont] kühl; [eis]kalt ‹*handeln*›

cold ˈmeat *n.* **a)** kaltes Fleisch; **~s** Aufschnitt, *der;* **b)** *(sl.: corpse)* Kadaver, *der (salopp)*

coldness [ˈkəʊldnɪs] *n., no pl.* **a)** Kälte, *die;* **the ~ of the weather** die Kälte; das kalte Wetter; **b)** *(feeling cold)* Frieren, *das; (of hands, feet)* Kälte, *die;* **c)** *(lack of ardour etc.) (of heart, intellect)* Kälte, *die; (of person, attitude, manner, look)* betonte Kühle; **d)** *(of dead body, colour)* Kälte, *die*

cold: **~ ˈshoulder** *n. (fig.)* **give sb. the ~ shoulder** jmdn. schneiden; **get the ~ shoulder from sb.** von jmdm. geschnitten werden; **~-ˈshoulder** *v. t.* schneiden *(fig.);* **~ ˈsteel** *n.* kalter Stahl *(dichter.);* Hieb- und Stichwaffen *Pl.;* **~ ˈstorage** *n.* Kühllagerung, *die;* **put sth. in ~ storage** *(fig.)* etw. auf Eis legen *(fig.);* **~ store** *n.* Kühlhaus, *das;* **~ ˈsweat** *n.* kalter Schweiß; **break out in a ~ sweat** in kalten Schweiß ausbrechen; **~ ˈturkey** *n. (Amer. sl.)* Totalentzug, *der;* Cold turkey, *der (Drogenjargon); attrib.* **the ~ turkey cure/treatment** Totalentzugstherapie, *die;* **~ ˈwar** *n.* kalter Krieg; **~ wave** *n.* Kältewelle, *die;* **~-work** *v. t.* kaltformen ‹*Metall*›

coleslaw [ˈkəʊlslɔ:] *n.* Kohl-, Krautsalat, *der*

coleus [ˈkəʊlɪəs] *n. (Bot.)* Buntnessel, *die*

colic [ˈkɒlɪk] *n.* Kolik, *die*

coliseum [kɒlɪˈsi:əm] *n. (Amer.)* Stadion, *das*

colitis [kəˈlaɪtɪs] *n. (Med.)* Entzündung des Dickdarms; Kolitis, *die (fachspr.)*

collaborate [kəˈlæbəreɪt] *v. i.* **a)** *(work jointly)* zusammenarbeiten; **~ [with sb.] on sth.** zusammen [mit jmdm.] an etw. *(Dat.)* arbeiten; **~ [with sb.] on** *or* **in doing sth.** mit jmdm. bei etw. zusammenarbeiten; **b)** *(cooperate with enemy)* kollaborieren *(abwertend);* zusammenarbeiten

collaboration [kəlæbəˈreɪʃn] *n.* Zusammenarbeit, *die; (with enemy)* Kollaboration, *die (abwertend);* **work in ~ with sb.** mit jmdm. zusammenarbeiten

collaborator [kəˈlæbəreɪtə(r)] *n.* Mitarbeiter, *der*/-arbeiterin, *die; (with enemy)* Kollaborateur, *der*/Kollaborateurin, *die (abwertend);* **they were ~s on this book** sie haben zusammen an diesem Buch gearbeitet

collage [ˈkɒlɑ:ʒ] *n.* Collage, *die*

collapse [kəˈlæps] **1.** *n.* **a)** *(of person) (physical, mental breakdown)* Zusammenbruch, *der; (heart-attack; of lung, blood-vessel, circulation)* Kollaps, *der; (cerebral haemorrhage)* Gehirnschlag, *der;* **b)** *(of tower, bridge, structure, wall, roof)* Einsturz, *der; (of tent)* Zusammenfallen, *das; (of table, chair)* Zusammenbruch, *der;* **c)** *(fig.: failure)* Zusammenbruch, *der; (of negotiations, plans, hopes)* Scheitern, *das; (of civilization, empire, society, system)* Zerfall, *der; (of prices, currency)* Sturz, *der.* **2.** *v. i.* **a)** ‹*Person:*› zusammenbrechen, *(Med.)* kollabieren; ‹*Lunge, Gefäß, Kreislauf:*› kollabieren; **his circulation ~d** er erlitt einen Kreislaufkollaps; **~ into tears** weinend zusammenbrechen; **~ with laughter** *(fig.)* sich vor Lachen kugeln; **b)** ‹*Zelt:*› in sich zusammenfallen; ‹*Tisch, Stuhl:*› zusammenbrechen; ‹*Turm, Brücke, Gebäude, Mauer, Dach:*› einstürzen; **c)** *(fig.: fail)* ‹*Verhandlungen, Pläne, Hoffnungen:*› scheitern; ‹*Zivilisation, Reich, Gesellschaft, System:*› zerfallen; ‹*Geschäft, Unternehmen usw.:*› zusammenbrechen, zugrunde gehen; ‹*Traum:*› zerbrechen; ‹*Preise, Währung:*› [zusammen]stürzen; **d)** *(fold down)* ‹*Fernrohr, Spazierstock:*› sich zusammenschieben lassen; ‹*Regenschirm, Fahrrad, Tisch:*› sich zusammenklappen lassen. **3.** *v. t.* zusammenklappen ‹*Regenschirm, Fahrrad, Tisch*›; zusammenschieben ‹*Fernrohr*›

collapsible [kəˈlæpsɪbl] *adj.* Klapp-, zusammenklappbar ‹*Stuhl, Tisch, Fahrrad*›; Falt-, faltbar ‹*Boot*›; zusammenschiebbar ‹*Fernrohr*›; **it is ~:** es läßt sich zusammenklappen/falten/zusammenschieben

collar ['kɒlə(r)] **1.** *n.* **a)** Kragen, *der;* **with ~ and tie** mit Krawatte; **[surgical] ~:** Halsmanschette, *die;* **hot under the ~** *(fig.) (embarrassed)* verlegen; *(angry)* wütend; **b)** *(for dog)* [Hunde]halsband, *das;* Halsung, *die (Jagdw.);* **c)** *(for horse)* Kumt, *das;* Kummet, *das;* **d)** *(on bolt, pipe, etc.)* Bund, *der.* **2.** *v. t.* **a)** *(seize)* am Kragen kriegen *(ugs.);* schnappen *(ugs.);* **b)** *(sl.: appropriate)* sich *(Dat.)* unter den Nagel reißen *(salopp);* klemmen *(salopp)*

collar: ~-bone *n. (Anat.)* Schlüsselbein, *das;* **~-button** *n.* **a)** *(Brit.)* Hemd[en]knopf, *der;* **b)** *(Amer.: stud)* Kragenknopf, *der;* **~-stud** *n. (esp. Brit.)* Kragenknopf, *der*

collate [kə'leɪt] *v. t.* **a)** *(Bibliog.: compare)* kollationieren *(Buchw.)* ‹*Manuskripte, Druckbögen*›; **~ a copy with the original** eine Abschrift mit dem Original vergleichen; **b)** *(put together)* zusammenstellen ‹*Daten, Beweismaterial*›

collateral [kə'lætərl] **1.** *adj.* **a)** *(subordinate)* nebensächlich ‹*Dinge, Themen*›; *(contributory)* **~ evidence** zusätzliches Beweismaterial; **b) ~ relatives** Verwandte einer Seitenlinie. **2.** *n.* **a)** *(person)* Kollateralverwandte, *der/die (veralt.)* **b)** *(property pledged as guarantee)* **~ [security]** Sicherheiten *Pl.*

collation [kə'leɪʃn] *n.* **a)** Textvergleich, *der;* *(of book or set of sheets)* Kollationierung, *die (Buchw.);* **b)** *(light meal)* Imbiß, *der;* Kollation, *die (veralt., landsch.); (in RC Ch.)* Kollation, *die;* **cold ~:** kaltes Büfett

collator [kə'leɪtə(r)] *n. (Computing)* Mischer, *der*

colleague ['kɒli:g] *n.* Kollege, *der*/Kollegin, *die*

[1]**collect** [kə'lekt] **1.** *v. i.* **a)** *(assemble)* sich versammeln; **b)** *(accumulate)* ‹*Staub, Müll usw.:*› sich ansammeln. **2.** *v. t.* **a)** *(assemble)* sammeln; aufsammeln ‹*Müll, leere Flaschen usw.*›; **~ volunteers** Freiwillige zusammenbringen; **~ [up] one's belongings** seine Siebensachen *(ugs.)* zusammensuchen; **she ~ed a lot of praise/good marks** sie hat viel Lob/viele gute Noten eingeheimst *(ugs.);* **~ dust** Staub anziehen; **b)** *(coll.: fetch, pick up)* abholen ‹*Menschen, Dinge*›; **~ a parcel from the post office** ein Paket bei *od.* auf der Post abholen; **~ sb. from the station** jmdn. am Bahnhof *od.* von der Bahn abholen; **c)** *(get from others)* eintreiben ‹*Steuern, Zinsen, Schulden*›; [wohltätig] sammeln ‹*Geld, Altkleider*›; kassieren ‹*Miete, Fahrgeld*›; beziehen ‹*Zahlungen, Sozialhilfe*›; einsammeln ‹*Fahrkarten*›; **~ on delivery** *(Amer.)* per Nachnahme; **d)** *(as hobby)* sammeln ‹*Münzen, Bücher, Briefmarken, Gemälde usw.*›; **e)** *(regain control of)* **~ one's wits/thoughts** seine Gedanken sammeln; **f)** *(coll. abs.: receive money)* abkassieren *(ugs.)* **(on** bei). **3.** *adj. (Amer.)* **a ~ telephone call** ein R-Gespräch; **a ~ telegram** ein Nachnahmetelegramm. **4.** *adv. (Amer.)* **send a message ~:** eine vom Empfänger zu bezahlende Nachricht senden; **pay for the goods ~:** die Ware bei Lieferung bezahlen; **he called New York ~:** er führte ein R-Gespräch nach New York

[2]**collect** ['kɒlekt] *n. (Eccl.)* Altargebet, *das;* Kollekte, *die (veralt.)*

collected [kə'lektɪd] *adj.* **a)** *(gathered)* gesammelt; **b)** *(calm)* gesammelt; gelassen

collectedly [kə'lektɪdlɪ] *adv.* gesammelt; gelassen

collection [kə'lekʃn] *n.* **a)** *(collecting)* Sammeln, *das; (of rent, fares)* Kassieren, *das; (of taxes, interest, debts)* Eintreiben, *das; (coll.: of goods, persons)* Abholen, *das;* **make** *or* **hold a ~ of old clothes** eine Altkleidersammlung durchführen; **b)** *(amount of money collected)* Sammlung, *die; (in church)* Kollekte, *die;* **take the ~:** einsammeln; **c)** *(of mail)* Abholung, *die; (from post-box)* Leerung, *die;* **d)** *(group collected) (of coins, books, stamps, paintings, etc.)* Sammlung, *die; (of fashionable clothes)* Kollektion, *die; (of people)* Ansammlung, *die;* **e)** *(accumulated quantity)* Ansammlung, *die*

collective [kə'lektɪv] **1.** *adj.* kollektiv *nicht präd.;* gesamt *nicht präd.;* **~ interests** gemeinsame Interessen; Gesamt- *od.* Kollektivinteressen; **~ leadership/responsibility** kollektive Führung/Verantwortung; **~ guilt** Kollektivschuld, *die;* **~ agreement** Tarifvertrag, *der.* **2.** *n.* **a)** Genossenschaftsbetrieb, *der;* **b)** *see* **collective noun**

collective: ~ 'bargaining *n.* Tarifverhandlungen *Pl.;* **~ 'farm** *n.* landwirtschaftliche Produktionsgenossenschaft, LPG, *die (bes. DDR);* Kolchose, *die*

collectively [kə'lektɪvlɪ] *adj.* gemeinsam; **work/act ~:** gemeinsam arbeiten/handeln

collective: ~ 'noun *n. (Ling.)* Kollektivum, *das;* Sammelbegriff, *der;* **~ 'ownership** *n.* Kollektiveigentum, *das* **(of** an + *Dat.*); Gemeineigentum, *das* **(of** an + *Dat.*); **~ se'curity** *n.* kollektive Sicherheit

collectivism [kə'lektɪvɪzm] *n.* Kollektivwirtschaft, *die; (doctrine)* Kollektivismus, *der*

collector [kə'lektə(r)] *n.* **a)** *(of stamps, coins, etc.)* Sammler, *der*/Sammlerin, *die;* *(of taxes)* Einnehmer, *der*/Einnehmerin, *die; (of rent, cash)* Kassierer, *der*/Kassiererin, *die; (of jumble)* Abholer, *der*/Abholerin, *die; see also* **ticket-collector; b)** *(of electric train)* Stromabnehmer, *der*

collector: ~'s item, ~'s piece *ns.* Liebhaberstück, *das;* Sammlerstück, *das*

colleen [kɒ'li:n] *n. (Ir.)* [junges] Mädel

college ['kɒlɪdʒ] *n.* **a)** *(esp. Brit.: independent corporation in university)* College, *das;* **b)** *(small university)* [private] Hochschule; **c)** *(place of further education)* Fach[hoch]schule, *die;* **military/naval ~:** Militär-/Marineakademie; **go to ~** *(esp. Amer.)* studieren; **start ~** *(esp. Amer.)* sein Studium aufnehmen; **d)** *(esp. Brit.: school)* Internatsschule, *die;* Kolleg, *das;* **e)** *(of physicians, surgeons)* [Ärzte]kammer, *die; (of cardinals)* Kollegium, *das*

College: ~ of 'Arms *n. (esp. Brit.)* Heroldsamt, *das;* **~ of Edu'cation** Pädagogische Hochschule; *(for graduates)* Studienseminar, *das*

collegiate [kə'li:dʒət] *adj.* College‹*leben, -system usw.*›; **Oxford has a ~ structure/is a ~ university** die Universität von Oxford ist nach dem Collegesystem organisiert

collide [kə'laɪd] *v. i.* **a)** *(come into collision)* zusammenstoßen **(with** mit); ‹*Schiff:*› kollidieren; **b)** *(be in conflict)* zusammenprallen; kollidieren

collie ['kɒlɪ] *n.* Collie, *der*

collier ['kɒlɪə(r)] *n.* **a)** *see* **coal-miner; b)** *(ship)* Kohlenschiff, *das*

colliery ['kɒljərɪ] *n.* Kohlengrube, *die*

collision [kə'lɪʒn] *n.* **a)** *(colliding)* Zusammenstoß, *der; (between ships)* Kollision, *die;* **come into ~:** zusammenstoßen; ‹*Schiffe:*› in Kollision geraten, kollidieren; **a head-on ~ of a car with a bus** *or* **between a car and a bus** ein Frontalzusammenstoß eines PKW mit einem Bus; **b)** *(fig.)* Konflikt, *der;* Kollision, *die;* **come into ~ with the law** in Konflikt mit dem Gesetz geraten

col'lision course *n. (lit. or fig.)* Kollisionskurs, *der;* **on a ~:** auf Kollisionskurs

collocate ['kɒləkeɪt] **1.** *v. t.* **a)** *(place together)* zusammenstellen; **b)** *(arrange)* [an]ordnen; **c)** *(put in a place)* aufführen; **d)** *(Ling.)* kombinieren, *(fachspr.)* kollokieren ‹*Wörter*›. **2.** *v. i. (Ling.)* kollokieren

collocation [kɒlə'keɪʃn] *n.* Zusammenstellung, *die; (arrangement)* Anordnung, *die; (Ling.: of words)* Kollokation, *die*

collocator ['kɒləkeɪtə(r)] *n. (Ling.)* Kollokator, *der*

colloid ['kɒlɔɪd] *n. (Chem.)* Kolloid, *das*

colloidal [kə'lɔɪdl] *adj. (Chem.)* kolloid[al]

colloquial [kə'ləʊkwɪəl] *adj.* umgangssprachlich; **~ language** Umgangssprache, *die*

colloquialism [kə'ləʊkwɪəlɪzm] *n.* **a)** *(style)* Umgangssprache, *die;* **b)** *(a form)* umgangssprachlicher Ausdruck

colloquially [kə'ləʊkwɪəlɪ] *adv.* umgangssprachlich

colloquium [kə'ləʊkwɪəm] *n., pl.* **colloquia** [kə'ləʊkwɪə] Kolloquium, *das*

colloquy ['kɒləkwɪ] *n. (formal)* **a)** *no pl. (act of conversing)* Konversation, *die;* **b)** *(a conversation)* Unterhaltung, *die*

collusion [kə'lju:ʒn, kə'lu:ʒn] *n.* geheime Absprache; **act in ~ with sb.** mit jmdm. gemeinsame Sache machen

collywobbles ['kɒlɪwɒblz] *n. pl. (coll.)* *(feeling of apprehension)* flaues Gefühl *(ugs.)* [im Magen]; *(stomach-ache)* Bauchschmerzen *Pl.*

Cologne [kə'ləʊn] **1.** *pr. n.* Köln *(das).* **2.** *attrib. adj.* Kölner

cologne *see* **eau-de-Cologne**

Colombia [kə'lɒmbɪə] *pr. n.* Kolumbien *(das)*

Colombian [kə'lɒmbɪən] **1.** *adj.* kolumbianisch. **2.** *n.* Kolumbianer, *der*/Kolumbianerin, *die*

[1]**colon** ['kəʊlən] *n.* Doppelpunkt, *der;* Kolon, *das (veralt.)*

[2]**colon** ['kəʊlən, 'kəʊlɒn] *n. (Anat.)* Grimmdarm, *der*

colonel [kɜ:nl] *n.* **a)** *(highest regimental officer)* Oberst, *der;* **b)** *(member of military junta)* Obrist, *der (abwertend). See also* **blimp a; chief 1 c**

colonial [kə'ləʊnɪəl] *adj.* **a)** *(of colony)* Kolonial-; kolonial; **~ empire** Kolonialreich, *das;* **C~ Office** *(Hist.)* Kolonialministerium, *das;* **b)** *(Amer.: of period of British colonies)* kolonial; Kolonial-; **~ architecture** Kolonialstil, *der*

colonialism [kə'ləʊnɪəlɪzm] *n.* Kolonialismus, *der*

colonialist [kə'ləʊnɪəlɪst] *n.* Kolonialist, *der*/Kolonialistin, *die; attrib.* kolonialistisch

colonic [kəʊ'lɒnɪk] *adj. (Med.)* Kolon-; des Grimmdarms *nachgestellt*

colonisation, colonise *see* **coloniz-**

colonist ['kɒlənɪst] *n.* Siedler, *der*/Siedlerin, *die;* Kolonist, *der*/Kolonistin, *die*

colonization [kɒlənaɪ'zeɪʃn] *n.* Kolonisation, *die;* Kolonisierung, *die*

colonize ['kɒlənaɪz] *v.t.* kolonisieren; besiedeln ‹*unbewohntes Gebiet*›

colonnade [kɒlə'neɪd] *n. (Archit.)* Säulengang, *der;* Kolonnade, *die*

colony ['kɒlənɪ] *n.* Kolonie, *die;* **a ~ of artists/ants** eine Künstlerkolonie/ein Ameisenstaat

colophon ['kɒləfən] *n.* **a)** *(tailpiece)* Kolophon, *der;* **b)** *(on title-page)* Signet, *das*

color *(Amer.) see* **colour**

Colorado beetle [kɒlə'rɑ:dəʊ bi:tl] *n.* Kartoffelkäfer, *der;* Coloradokäfer, *der (fachspr.)*

coloration [kʌlə'reɪʃn] *n.* **a)** *(colouring)* Kolorierung, *die;* **b)** *(colour)* Färbung, *die*

coloratura [kɒlərə'tʊərə, kɒlərə'tjʊərə] *n.* *(Mus.)* Koloratur, *die;* **~ soprano** Koloratursopran, *der*

colored *(Amer.) see* **coloured**

colossal [kə'lɒsl] *adj.* **a)** *(gigantic, huge)* ungeheuer; gewaltig ‹*Bauwerk*›; **b)** *(of or like a colossus)* riesenhaft, kolossal ‹*Mann, Statue*›; **c)** *(coll.: remarkable, splendid)* ungeheuer, *(veralt.)* kolossal ‹*Irrtum, Glücksfall*›

colossus [kə'lɒsəs] *n., pl.* **colossi** [kə'lɒsaɪ] *or* **~es** Koloß, *der*

colostomy [kə'lɒstəmɪ] *n. (Med.)* Kolostomie, *die*

colour ['kʌlə(r)] *(Brit.)* **1.** *n.* **a)** Farbe, *die;* **primary ~s** Grundfarben *Pl.;* Primärfarben *Pl. (fachspr.);* **secondary ~s** Mischfarben *Pl.;* **what ~ is it?** welche Farbe hat es?; **see the ~ of sb.'s money** *(fig.)* Geld sehen *(ugs.);* **b)** *(Art, Her.)* Farbe, *die; (Art: colouring)* Farbe, *die;* Farbgebung, *die;* **a box of ~s** ein Mal- *od.* Tuschkasten; **c)** *(complexion)* [Gesichts]farbe, *die;* **change ~:** die Farbe ändern; *(go red/pale)* rot/blaß werden; **lose/gain ~:** Farbe verlieren/wieder Farbe bekommen; **get one's ~ back** wieder etwas Farbe kriegen; **bring the ~ back to sb.'s cheeks** jmdm. wieder Farbe geben; **he is/feels/looks a bit off ~ today** ihm ist heute nicht besonders gut/er fühlt sich heute nicht besonders gut/er sieht heute nicht besonders gut aus; **have a high ~:** rot im Gesicht sein; ein rotes Gesicht haben; **d)** *(racial)* Hautfarbe, *die;* **e)** *usu. in pl. (appearance, aspect)* Farben *Pl.;* **appear in its true ~s** sich so zeigen, wie es wirklich ist; **see sth. in its true ~s** etw. so sehen, wie es wirklich ist; **f)** *(appearance of reasonableness)* **give** *or* **lend ~ to sth.** etw. glaubhaft *od.* glaubwürdig erscheinen lassen; **g)** *(character, tone, quality, etc.)* Charakter, *der;* Gepräge, *das; (aspect, appearance)* Anstrich, *der;* **add ~ to a story** einer Erzählung Farbe *od.* Kolorit geben; **local ~:** Lokalkolorit, *das;* **h)** *in pl. (ribbon, dress, etc., worn as symbol of party, club, etc.)* Farben *Pl.;* **get** *or* **win one's ~s** *(Brit. Sport)* als Vollmitglied aufgenommen werden; **give sb. his ~s** *(Brit. Sport)* jmdn. als Vollmitglied aufnehmen; **show one's [true] ~s** *or* **oneself in one's true ~s** *(fig.)* sein wahres Gesicht zeigen; **i)** *in pl. (national flag)* Farben *Pl.;* **j)** *(flag)* Fahne, *die; (of ship)* Flagge, *die;* **Queen's/King's/regimental ~:** Regimentsfahne, *die;* **serve with the ~s** *(Hist.)* der Fahne dienen *(veralt.);* **join the ~s** *(Hist.)* den bunten Rock anziehen *(veralt.);* **come off/pass with flying ~s** *(fig.)* glänzend abschneiden; **nail one's ~s to the mast** *(fig.)* Farbe bekennen; sich zu seiner Überzeugung bekennen; **lower one's ~** *(fig.)* zurückstecken; **sail under false ~s** *(fig.)* unter falscher Flagge segeln; **k)** *(Mus.) (timbre, quality)* Klangfarbe, *die. See also* **troop 3. 2.** *v. t.* **a)** *(give ~ to)* Farbe geben (+ *Dat.*); **b)** *(paint)* malen; **~ in** ausmalen ‹*Bild, Figur*›; **~ a wall red** eine Wand rot anmalen; **c)** *(stain, dye)* färben ‹*Material, Stoff*›; **d)** *(disguise)* verstecken; **e)** *(misrepresent)* [schön]färben ‹*Nachrichten, Bericht*›; **f)** *(fig.: influence)* beeinflussen. **3.** *v. i.* **a)** ‹*Blätter, Trauben:*› sich verfärben; **b)** *(blush)* **~ [up]** erröten; rot werden

colouration *(Brit.) see* **coloration**

colour: ~ bar *n.* Rassenschranke, *die;* **~-blind** *adj.* farbenblind; **a ~-blind person** ein Farbenblinder/eine Farbenblinde; **~-blindness** *n.* Farbenblindheit, *die;* **~ code** *n.* Farbkennzeichnung, *die;* **~-coded** *adj.* mit Farbkennzeichnung *nachgestellt*

coloured ['kʌləd] *(Brit.)* **1.** *adj.* **a)** farbig; **yellow-/green-~** gelb/grün; **~ paper** *(for printing or wrapping)* farbiges Papier; *(for making designs)* Buntpapier, *das;* **~ pencil** Farbstift, *der;* **b)** *(of non-white descent)* farbig; **~ people** Farbige *Pl.;* **c)** *(S. Afr.: of mixed descent)* gemischtrassig; gemischtrassisch; **~ people** Mischlinge *Pl..* **2.** *n.* **a)** Farbige, *der/die;* **b)** *(S. Afr.: person of mixed descent)* Mischling, *der*

colour: ~-fast *adj.* farbecht; **~ film** *n.* Farbfilm, *der*

colourful ['kʌləfl] *adj. (Brit.)* bunt; farbenfroh, bunt ‹*Bild, Schauspiel*›; farbig, anschaulich ‹*Sprache, Stil, Bericht*›; buntbewegt ‹*Zeitepoche, Leben*›

colourfully ['kʌləfəlɪ] *adv. (Brit.)* bunt; **~ dressed/striped/painted** buntgekleidet/-gestreift/-bemalt *attr.*

colouring ['kʌlərɪŋ] *n. (Brit.)* **a)** *(action)* Malen, *das;* **~ 'in** Ausmalen, *das;* **b)** *(colours)* Farben *Pl.;* **c)** *(facial complexion)* Teint, *der;* **d)** **~ [matter]** *(in food etc.)* Farbstoff, *der*

colouring-book *n.* Malbuch, *das*

colourless ['kʌləlɪs] *adj. (Brit.)* **a)** *(without colour)* farblos ‹*Flüssigkeit, Gas*›; *(pale)* blaß ‹*Teint*›; *(dull-hued)* grau, düster ‹*Bild, Stoff, Himmel, Meer*›; **b)** *(fig.)* farblos, langweilig ‹*Geschichte, Schilderung, Stil*›; unauffällig ‹*Person*›

colour: ~ magazine *see* **~ supplement; ~ photograph** *n.* Farbfotografie, -aufnahme, *die;* **~ photography** *n.* Farbfotografie, *die;* **~ printing** *n.* Farbdruck, *der;* **~ scheme** *n.* Farb[en]zusammenstellung, *die;* **~-sergeant** *n. (Mil.)* ≈ Hauptfeldwebel, *der;* **~ supplement** *n.* Farbbeilage, *die;* **~ television** *n.* Farbfernsehen, *das; (set)* Farbfernsehgerät, *das;* **~ transparency** *n.* Farbdia, *das*

colt [kəʊlt] *n.* **a)** [Hengst]fohlen, *das; (player in junior team)* Fohlen, *das;* **b)** *(inexperienced person) (girl)* Küken, *das (ugs.); (boy)* junger Dachs *(ugs.) od.* Springer *(ugs.)*

coltsfoot ['kəʊltsfʊt] *n., pl.* **~s** *(Bot.)* Huflattich, *der*

columbine ['kɒləmbaɪn] *n. (Bot.)* Akelei, *die*

Columbus [kə'lʌmbəs] *pr. n.* Kolumbus *(der)*

column ['kɒləm] *n.* **a)** Säule, *die;* **b)** *(in machine)* Ständer, *der; (of tripod)* Säule, *die;* **c)** *(of liquid, vapour, etc.)* Säule, *die;* **~ of mercury/smoke** Quecksilber-/Rauchsäule, *die;* **d)** *(division of page, table, etc.)* Spalte, *die;* Kolumne, *die;* **a ~ of figures** eine Zahlenkolonne; **in two ~s** zweispaltig; **e)** *(in newspaper)* Spalte, *die;* Kolumne, *die;* **the sports ~:** der Sportteil; **the gossip ~:** die Klatschspalte *(ugs. abwertend);* **f)** *(of troops, vehicles, ships)* Kolonne, *die;* **dodge the ~** *(fig. coll.)* sich drücken *(ugs.);* **g)** *(Amer.: party, faction)* Lager, *das*

columnar [kə'lʌmnə(r)] *adj.* säulenförmig

'column-inch *n.* **advertisement of two ~es** ≈ Anzeige von 50 Millimeterzeilen

columnist ['kɒləmɪst] *n.* Kolumnist, *der*/Kolumnistin, *die;* **radio ~:** Rundfunkkommentator, *der*/-kommentatorin, *die*

coma ['kəʊmə] *n.* **a)** *(Med.)* Koma, *das;* **be in a ~:** im Koma liegen; **go into a ~:** ins Koma fallen; **b)** *(fig.: torpor)* Dämmerzustand, *der*

comb [kəʊm] **1.** *n.* **a)** *(also as tech. term)* Kamm, *der; (curry-~)* Striegel, *der;* **b)** *(action)* **give one's hair a ~:** sich *(Dat.)* die Haare kämmen; **c)** *(honey~)* Wabe, *die.* **2.** *v. t.* **a)** kämmen ‹*Haare, Flachs, Wolle*›; **~ sb.'s/one's hair** jmdm./sich die Haare kämmen; jmdn./sich kämmen; **~ sth. out of sb.'s hair** jmdm. etw. aus den Haaren kämmen; **b)** *(curry)* striegeln ‹*Pferd*›; **c)** *(search)* durchkämmen ‹*Gelände, Wald*›

~ 'out *v. t.* **a)** auskämmen ‹*Haare*›; **b)** *(separate for removal)* aussortieren; **c)** *(search)* durchkämmen; durchforsten

combat ['kɒmbæt] **1.** *n.* Kampf, *der;* **single ~:** Einzelkampf, *der; (duel)* Zweikampf, *der.* **2.** *v. t. (fig.: strive against)* bekämpfen. **3.** *v. i. (engage in battle or contest)* kämpfen

'combat aircraft *n.* Kampfflugzeug, *das*

combatant ['kɒmbətənt] **1.** *adj.* zur Kampftruppe gehörend. **2.** *n. (in war)* Kombattant, *der; (in duel)* Kämpfer, *der*

combat: ~ dress *n.* Kampfanzug, *der;* **~ fatigue** *n.* Frontneurose, *die*

combative ['kɒmbətɪv] *adj.*, **combatively** ['kɒmbətɪvlɪ] *adv.* streitlustig

combativeness ['kɒmbətɪvnɪs] *n., no pl.* Streitlust, *die*

combe *(Brit.) see* **coomb**

combed [kəʊmd] *adj.* gekämmt

comber ['kəʊmə(r)] *n. (wave, breaker)* Sturzwelle, *die*

combination [kɒmbɪ'neɪʃn] *n.* **a)** Kombination, *die;* **b)** *(Chem.)* Verbindung, *die;* **c)** *(Brit. Motor Veh.)* Motorrad mit Beiwagen; **d)** *in pl. (dated Brit.: undergarment)* Kombination, *die (veralt.);* Hemdhose, *die (veralt.)*

combi'nation lock *n.* Kombinationsschloß, *das*

combine 1. [kəm'baɪn] *v. t.* **a)** *(join together)* kombinieren; zusammenfügen (**into** zu); vereinigen ‹*Städte*›; **b)** *(possess together)* vereinigen; in sich *(Dat.)* vereinigen ‹*Eigenschaften*›; **c)** *(cause to coalesce)* verbinden ‹*Substanzen*›. **2.** *v. i.* **a)** *(join together, coalesce)* ‹*Stoffe:*› sich verbinden; **b)** *(cooperate)* zusammenwirken; ‹*Parteien:*› sich zusammentun. **3.** ['kɒmbaɪn] *n.* **a)** Konzern, *der; (in socialist economy)* Kombinat, *das;* **b)** *(machine)* **~ [harvester]** Mähdrescher, *der;* Kombine, *die*

combined [kəm'baɪnd] *adj.* vereint; **a ~ operation** eine gemeinsame Operation

combings ['kəʊmɪŋz] *n. pl.* ausgekämmte Haare

combining form [kəm'baɪnɪŋ fɔ:m] *n. (Ling.)* Wortbildungselement, *das*

combo ['kɒmbəʊ] *n., pl.* **~s** Combo, *die*

combust [kəm'bʌst] *v. t.* verbrennen

combustible [kəm'bʌstɪbl] *adj.* **a)** brennbar; **b)** *(fig.)* entflammbar; erregbar

combustion [kəm'bʌstʃn] *n.* Verbrennung, *die;* **~ chamber** *(Mech. Engin.) (of jet engine)* Brennkammer, *die; (of internal-combustion engine)* Verbrennungsraum, *der*

come [kʌm] **1.** *v. i.*, **came** [keɪm], **come** [kʌm] **a)** *(start or move towards or to sth. or sb.)* kommen; **~ here!** komm [mal] her!; **[I'm] coming!** [ich] komme schon!; **~ running** angelaufen kommen; **~ running into the room** ins Zimmer gerannt kommen; **~ laughing into the room** lachend ins Zimmer kommen; **not know whether** *or* **if one is coming or going** nicht wissen, wo einem der Kopf steht; **~, ~!** aber ich bitte dich!; **~ [now]!** *(fig.) (encouraging)* komm!; *(don't be hasty)* [also] komm! *(ugs.);* **b)** *(arrive at a place)* kommen; **they came to a house/town** sie kamen zu einem Haus/in eine Stadt; **he has just ~ from school/America** er ist gerade aus der Schule/aus Amerika gekommen; **let 'em all ~!, ~ one ~ all** *(coll.)* sollen sie doch alle kommen!; **~ and see me soon** besuchen Sie mich bald einmal!; **the news came as a surprise** die Nachricht kam überraschend; **Christmas/Easter is coming** bald ist Weihnachten/Ostern; **c)** *(traverse)* kommen; **he has ~ a long way** er kommt von weit her; **the project has ~ a long way** *(fig.)* das Projekt ist schon weit gediehen; **d)** *(be brought)* kommen; **~ to sb.'s notice** *or* **attention/knowledge** jmdm. auffallen/zu Ohren kommen; **e)** *(enter)* kommen; **the train came into the station** der Zug fuhr in den Bahnhof ein; **f)** *(occur)* kommen; *(in list etc.)* stehen; **the adjective ~s before the noun** das Adjektiv steht vor dem Substantiv; **g)** *(become, be)* **the shoe-laces have ~ undone** die Schnürsenkel sind aufgegangen; **the handle has ~ loose** der Griff ist lose; **it ~s cheaper to buy things in bulk** es ist *od. (ugs.)* kommt billiger, en gros einzukaufen; **it all came right in the end** es ging alles gut aus; **it will all ~ right in the end** es wird schon alles gutgehen; **it ~s easily/naturally to him** das fällt ihm leicht; **what you say ~s to this: ...:** was du sagst, läuft auf Folgendes hinaus: ...; **when it ~s to cooking** wenn es ums Kochen geht; **~ to that, if it ~s to that** wenn es darum geht; **~ to oneself** zu sich selbst kommen; **have ~ to believe/realize that ...:** zu der Überzeugung/Einsicht gelangt sein, daß ...; **we came to know him better** wir lernten ihn allmählich *od.* nach und nach besser kennen; **h)** *(become present)* kommen; **in the coming week/month** kommende Woche/kommenden Monat; **be a**

coming man der kommende Mann sein; **this coming Christmas** Weihnachten dieses Jahr; **she had it coming to her** das hat sie sich *(Dat.)* selbst zu verdanken *(iron.)*; **you've got it coming to you if you go on behaving like that** du kannst dich auf was gefaßt machen, wenn du so weitermachst *(ugs.)*; **i) to ~** *(future)* künftig; **in years to ~:** in künftigen Jahren; **for some time to ~:** [noch] für einige Zeit; **j)** *(be left or willed)* **he has a lot of money coming to him** er erbt einmal viel Geld; **the farm came to him on his father's death** beim Tod seines Vaters bekam er den Hof; **k)** *(be result)* kommen; **that's what ~s of grumbling** das kommt vom Schimpfen; **nothing came of it** es ist nichts daraus geworden; **~ of noble parents** aus adligem Elternhaus stammen; **the suggestion came from him** der Vorschlag war *od.* stammte von ihm; **l)** *(reach, extend)* **the motorway ~s within 10 miles of us** die Autobahn ist nur zehn Meilen von uns entfernt; **m)** *(happen)* **how ~s it that you ...?** wie kommt es, daß du ...?; **how did you ~ to break your leg?** wie hast du dir denn das Bein gebrochen?; **how ~?** *(coll.)* wieso?; weshalb?; **~ what may** komme, was wolle *(geh.)*; ganz gleich, was kommt; **n)** *(be available)* ⟨*Waren:*⟩ erhältlich sein; **this dress ~s in three sizes** dies Kleid gibt es in drei Größen *od.* ist in drei Größen erhältlich; **as tough/clever/stupid as they ~:** zäh/schlau/dumm wie sonstwas *(ugs.)*; **o)** *(sl.: play a part)* **~ the bully with sb.** bei jmdm. den starken Mann markieren *(salopp)*; **don't ~ the innocent with me** spiel mir nicht den Unschuldsengel vor! *(ugs.)*; **don't ~ that game with me** komm mir bloß nicht mit dieser Tour *od.* Masche! *(salopp)*; **~ it strong** [es] übertreiben; **~ it too strong** zu dick auftragen *(ugs.)*; **p) ~ [next] Friday/next week** [nächsten] Freitag/nächste Woche; **it's two years ~ Christmas since we were divorced** Weihnachten sind wir zwei Jahre geschieden; **q)** *(sl.: have orgasm)* kommen *(salopp)*. **2.** *n.* *(sl.: semen)* Soße, *die (derb)*

~ a'bout *v. i.* **a)** passieren; **how did it ~ about that ...?** wie kam es, daß ...?; **b)** *(Naut.)* wenden

~ across 1. [--'-] *v. i.* **a)** *(be understood)* ⟨*Bedeutung:*⟩ verstanden werden; ⟨*Mitteilung, Rede:*⟩ ankommen *(ugs.)*, rüberkommen *(salopp)*; **b)** *(coll.: make an impression)* wirken **(as** wie); **he always wants to ~ across as a tough guy** er will immer den harten Burschen mimen *(ugs.)*; **c) ~ across with** *(coll.: give, hand over)* rausrücken *(ugs.)* ⟨*Geld, Schlüssel*⟩; rausrücken mit *(ugs.)* ⟨*Informationen*⟩. **2.** ['---] *v. t.* **~ across sb./sth.** jmdm./einer Sache begegnen; **have you ~ across my watch?** ist dir meine Uhr begegnet? *(ugs.)*

~ a'long *v. i.* *(coll.)* **a)** *(hurry up)* **~ along!** komm/kommt!; nun mach/macht schon! *(ugs.)*; **b)** *(try harder)* **~ along, now!** nun überleg aber mal!; **c)** *(make progress)* **~ along nicely** gute Fortschritte machen; **her maths is coming along nicely** in Mathematik macht sie recht gute Fortschritte *od.* kommt sie recht gut voran; **d)** *(arrive, present oneself/itself)* ⟨*Person:*⟩ ankommen; ⟨*Gelegenheit, Stelle:*⟩ sich bieten; **he'll take any job that ~s along** er nimmt jeden Job, der sich ihm bietet; **e)** *(to place)* mitkommen **(with** mit)

~ at *v. t.* **a)** herausfinden ⟨*Tatsachen, Wahrheit*⟩; **b)** *(attack)* losgehen auf (+ *Akk.*); **he came at me with a knife** er ging mit einem Messer auf mich los

~ a'way *v. i.* **a)** weggehen; **b)** *(become detached)* sich lösen **(from** von); abgehen *(ugs.)* **(from** von); **c)** *(be left)* **~ away with the impression/feeling that ...:** mit dem Eindruck/Gefühl gehen, daß ...

~ 'back *v. i.* **a)** *(return)* zurückkommen; ⟨*Gedächtnis, Vergangenes:*⟩ wiederkehren; **b)** *(return to memory)* **it will ~ back [to me]** es wird mir wieder einfallen; **c) ~ back [into fashion]** wiederkommen; wieder in Mode kommen; **d)** *(retort)* **~ back at sb. with sth.** jmdm. etw. entgegnen; **the team came back strongly** die Mannschaft spielte glänzend auf. *See also* **come-back**

~ between *v. t.* treten zwischen (+ *Akk.*)

~ by 1. ['--] *v. t.* *(obtain, receive)* kriegen *(ugs.)*; bekommen; **was the money honestly ~ by?** ist das Geld auf ehrliche Weise erworben worden? **2.** [-'-] *v. i.* vorbeikommen

~ 'down *v. i.* **a)** *(collapse)* herunterfallen; runterfallen *(ugs.)*; *(fall)* ⟨*Schnee, Regen, Preis:*⟩ fallen; **the beams came down on my head** die Balken fielen mir auf den Kopf; **b)** *(~ to place regarded as lower)* herunterkommen; runterkommen *(ugs.)*; *(~ southwards)* runterkommen *(ugs.)*; **c)** *(leave university)* **~ down [from Oxford]** sein Studium [in Oxford] abschließen; **when he came down [from Oxford] he got married** als er sein Studium [in Oxford] abgeschlossen hatte, heiratete er; **d)** *(land)* [not]landen; *(crash)* abstürzen; **~ down in a field** auf einem Acker [not]landen/auf einen Acker stürzen; **e)** *(be transmitted)* ⟨*Sage, Brauch:*⟩ überliefert werden; **f) ~ down to** *(reach)* reichen bis; **g) ~ down to** *(be reduced to)* hinauslaufen auf (+ *Akk.*); **h) ~ down to** *(be a question of)* ankommen **(to** auf + *Akk.*); **i)** *(be reduced; suffer change for the worse)* angewiesen sein **(to** auf + *Akk.*); **she has ~ down in the world** sie hat einen Abstieg erlebt; **j)** *(make a decision)* **~ down in favour of sb./sth.** sich zu gunsten jmds./einer Sache entscheiden; **~ down on the side of sb./sth.** sich für jmdn./etw. einsetzen; **k) ~ down on** *(rebuke, pounce on)* fertigmachen *(ugs.)*; **~ down on sb. for sth.** jmdn. wegen etw. rankriegen *(ugs.)*; **l) ~ down with** bekommen ⟨*Krankheit*⟩. *See also* **come-down**; **earth 1 a**

~ 'forth *v. i.* herauskommen

~ 'in *v. i.* **a)** *(enter)* hereinkommen; reinkommen *(ugs.)*; **~ in!** herein!; **this is where we came in** *(fig.)* wie gehabt; **b)** ⟨*Flut:*⟩ kommen; **c)** *(be received)* ⟨*Nachrichten, Bericht:*⟩ hereinkommen; **d)** *(in radio communication)* melden; **C~ in, Tom, ~ in, Tom. Over** Tom melden, Tom melden. Ende; **e)** *(make next contribution to discussion etc.)* sich einschalten; **would you like to ~ in here, Mr Brown?** würden Sie bitte an dieser Stelle fortfahren, Mr. Brown?; **f)** *(become fashionable)* in Mode kommen; aufkommen; **g)** *(become seasonable or available)* reinkommen *(ugs.)*; *see also* **handy b**; **h)** *(gain power, be elected)* an die Regierung kommen; ans Ruder kommen *(ugs.)*; rankommen *(ugs.)*; **i)** *(take specified place in race)* einlaufen als *od.* durchs Ziel gehen als ⟨*erster usw.*⟩; **j)** *(as income)* ⟨*Geld:*⟩ hereinkommen; reinkommen *(ugs.)*; **k)** *(find a place; have a part to play)* **where do I ~ in?** welche Rolle soll ich spielen?; **~ in on sth.** sich an etw. *(Dat.)* beteiligen; **l) ~ in for** erregen ⟨*Bewunderung, Aufmerksamkeit*⟩; auf sich *(Akk.)* ziehen, hervorrufen ⟨*Kritik*⟩

~ into *v. t.* **a)** *(enter)* hereinkommen in (+ *Akk.*); ⟨*Zug:*⟩ einfahren in ⟨*Bahnhof*⟩; ⟨*Schiff:*⟩ einlaufen in ⟨*Hafen*⟩; **b)** *(inherit)* erben ⟨*Vermögen*⟩; **c)** *(play a part)* **wealth does not ~ into it** Reichtum spielt dabei keine Rolle; **where do I ~ into it?** welche Rolle soll ich [dabei] spielen?

~ near *v. t.* **~ near [to] doing sth.** drauf und dran sein, etw. zu tun *(ugs.)*; **he came near [to] committing suicide** er war kurz davor, sich das Leben zu nehmen

~ off 1. [-'-] *v. i.* **a)** *(become detached)* ⟨*Griff, Knopf:*⟩ abgehen; *(be removable)* sich abnehmen lassen; ⟨*Fleck:*⟩ weg-, rausgehen *(ugs.)*; **b)** *(fall from sth.)* runterfallen; **c)** *(emerge from contest etc.)* abschneiden; **d)** *(succeed)* ⟨*Pläne, Versuche:*⟩ Erfolg haben, *(ugs.)* klappen; **the play/experiment/marriage/holiday didn't ~ off** das Stück war kein Erfolg/das Experiment war erfolglos/die Ehe/der Urlaub war ein Reinfall *(ugs.)*; **e)** *(take place)* stattfinden; **their marriage/holiday did not ~ off** aus ihrer Hochzeit/ihrem Urlaub wurde nichts; **f)** *(coll.: have orgasm)* kommen *(salopp)*. **2.** *v. t.* **~ off a horse/bike** vom Pferd/Fahrrad fallen; **~ 'off it!** *(coll.)* nun mach mal halblang! *(ugs.)*

~ on 1. [-'-] *v. i.* **a)** *(continue coming, follow)* kommen; **~ on!** komm, komm/kommt, kommt!; *(encouraging)* na, komm; *(impatient)* na, komm schon; *(incredulous)* ach komm!; **I'll ~ on later** ich komme später nach; **b)** *(make progress)* **my work is coming on very well** meine Arbeit macht gute Fortschritte; mit meiner Arbeit geht es gut voran; **c)** *(begin to arrive)* ⟨*Nacht, Dunkelheit, Winter:*⟩ anbrechen; **the rain came on, it came on to rain** es begann zu regnen; **he thought he had a cold coming on** er glaubte, eine Erkältung zu kriegen; **d)** *(be heard or seen on television etc.)* gegeben werden; **the film/opera** *etc.* **doesn't ~ on till 8 o'clock** der Film/die Oper *usw.* ist erst um 8 Uhr; **e)** *(appear on stage or scene)* auftreten. *See also* **come-on**. **2.** ['--] *v. t. see* **~ upon**

~ 'out *v. i.* **a)** herauskommen; **~ out [on strike]** in den Streik treten; **b)** *(emerge from examination etc.)* **~ out top/second/bottom** am besten/zweitbesten/schlechtesten abschneiden; **c)** *(appear, become visible)* ⟨*Sonne, Knospen, Blumen:*⟩ herauskommen, *(ugs.)* rauskommen; ⟨*Sterne:*⟩ zu sehen sein; **d)** *(be revealed)* ⟨*Wahrheit, Nachrichten:*⟩ herauskommen, *(ugs.)* rauskommen; **the results came out negative** die Resultate waren negativ; **the answer came out wrong** das Ergebnis war falsch; **e)** *(be published, declared, etc.)* herauskommen; rauskommen *(ugs.)*; ⟨*Ergebnisse, Zensuren:*⟩ bekanntgegeben werden; **f)** *(be solved)* ⟨*Aufgabe, Rätsel:*⟩ sich lösen lassen; **g)** *(make début)* debütieren; **h)** *(be released from prison)* rauskommen *(ugs.)*; herauskommen; **i)** *(declare oneself)* **~ out for** *or* **in favour of sth.** sich für etw. aussprechen; etw. befürworten; **~ out against sth.** sich gegen etw. aussprechen; **j)** ⟨*Homosexuelle[r]:*⟩ sich öffentlich zu seiner Homosexualität bekennen; **k)** *(be satisfactorily visible)* herauskommen; **you have ~ out very well in all of these photos** du bist auf allen Fotos gut getroffen; **the photo has not ~ out** das Foto ist nichts geworden; **l)** *(be covered)* **his face came out in pimples** er bekam im ganzen Gesicht Pickel; **she came out in a rash** sie bekam einen Ausschlag; **m)** *(be removed)* ⟨*Fleck, Schmutz:*⟩ rausgehen *(ugs.)*; **n) ~ out with** herausrücken mit *(ugs.)* ⟨*Wahrheit, Fakten*⟩; loslassen *(ugs.)* ⟨*Flüche, Bemerkungen*⟩

~ 'over 1. *v.i.* **a)** *(~ from some distance)* herüberkommen; **b)** *(change sides or opinions)* **~ over to sb./sth.** sich jmdm./einer Sache anschließen; **c)** *see* **~ across 1 b**; **d) she came over funny/dizzy** ihr wurde auf einmal ganz komisch/schwindlig *(ugs.)*; **he came over faint** ihm wurde plötzlich schwarz vor [den] Augen. **2.** *v.t.* *(coll.)* kommen über (+ *Akk.*); **what has ~ 'over him?** was ist über ihn gekommen?

~ 'round *v. i.* **a)** *(make informal visit)* vorbeischauen; **b)** *(recover)* wieder zu sich kommen; **c)** *(be converted)* es sich [anders] *(Dat.)* überlegen; **he came round to my way of thinking** er hat sich meiner Auffassung *(Dat.)* angeschlossen; **d)** *(recur)* **Christmas ~s round again** wir haben wieder Weihnachten

~ 'through 1. *v.i.* durchkommen. **2.** *v.t.* *(survive)* überleben

~ to 1. ['--] *v. t.* **a)** *(amount to)* ⟨*Rechnung,*

Gehalt, Kosten:⟩ sich belaufen auf (+ *Akk.*); **his plans came to nothing** aus seinen Plänen wurde nichts; **he/it will never ~ to much** aus ihm wird nichts Besonderes werden/daraus wird nicht viel; **b)** *(inherit)* erben ⟨*Vermögen*⟩; **~ to oneself** *see* **2**; **c)** *(arrive at)* **what is the world coming to?** wohin ist es mit der Welt gekommen?; **this is what he has ~ to** so weit ist es also mit ihm gekommen. **2.** [-'-] *v.i.* wieder zu sich kommen

~ to'gether *v.i.* ⟨*Menschen:*⟩ zusammenkommen; ⟨*Ereignisse:*⟩ zusammenfallen

~ under *v.t.* **a)** *(be classed as or among)* kommen unter (+ *Akk.*); **b)** *(be subject to)* geraten *od.* kommen unter (+ *Akk.*); **these shops have ~ under new management** diese Läden stehen unter neuer Leitung

~ 'up *v.i.* **a)** *(~ to place regarded as higher)* hochkommen; heraufkommen; *(~ northwards)* raufkommen *(ugs.)*; **he ~s up to London every other weekend** er kommt jedes zweite Wochenende nach London; **b)** *(join university)* **~ up [to Cambridge]** sein Studium [in Cambridge] beginnen; **c) ~ up to sb.** *(approach for talk)* auf jmdn. zukommen; **d) ~ up with sb.** *(get abreast)* jmdn. einholen; **e)** *(arise out of ground)* herauskommen; rauskommen *(ugs.)*; **f)** *(be discussed)* ⟨*Frage, Thema:*⟩ angeschnitten werden, aufkommen; ⟨*Name:*⟩ genannt werden; ⟨*Fall:*⟩ verhandelt werden; **g)** *(present itself)* sich ergeben; **~ up for sale/renewal** zum Kauf angeboten werden/erneuert werden müssen; **coming up** *(coll.: sth. is nearly ready)* kommt gleich; **h) ~ up to** *(reach)* reichen bis an (+ *Akk.*); *(be equal to)* entsprechen (+ *Dat.*) ⟨*Erwartungen, Anforderungen*⟩; **i) ~ up against sth.** *(fig.)* auf etw. *(Akk.)* stoßen; **j) ~ up with** vorbringen ⟨*Vorschlag*⟩; wissen ⟨*Lösung, Antwort*⟩; haben ⟨*Erklärung, Idee*⟩; geben, liefern ⟨*Informationen*⟩

~ upon *v.t.* **a)** *(attack)* kommen über (+ *Akk.*); **disaster/war came upon them** Unheil/Krieg kam über sie *(geh.) od.* brach über sie herein *(geh.)*; **b)** *(meet by chance)* begegnen (+ *Dat.*)

~ with *v.t.* *(be supplied together with)* **this model ~s with ...:** zu diesem Modell gehört ...

'come-back *n.* **a)** *(return to profession etc.)* Comeback, *das;* **b)** *(sl.: retort)* Reaktion, *die;* **I got an immediate ~ from him that ...:** er entgegnete mir darauf sofort, daß ...; **c)** *(means of redress)* **have no ~:** [etw.] nicht beanstanden können

comedian [kə'mi:dɪən] *n.* Komiker, *der*

comedienne [kəmi:dɪ'en, kəmedɪ'en] *n.* Komikerin, *die*

'come-down *n.* *(loss of prestige etc.)* Abstieg, *der*

comedy ['kɒmɪdɪ] *n.* **a)** *(Theatre)* Lustspiel, *das;* Komödie, *die;* **b)** *(humorous incident in life)* komischer Vorfall; **a ~ of errors** eine einzige Kette komischer Irrtümer; **c)** *(humour)* Witz, *der;* Witzigkeit, *die*

come-'hither *attrib. adj.* einladend

comeliness ['kʌmlɪnɪs] *n., no pl.* Ansehnlichkeit, *die*

comely ['kʌmlɪ] *adj.* gutaussehend; ansehnlich

'come-on *n.* *(sl.)* *(lure)* **give sb. the ~:** jmdn. anmachen *(salopp)*

comer ['kʌmə(r)] *n.* **the competition is open to all ~s** an dem Wettbewerb kann sich jeder beteiligen; **the first ~:** derjenige, der zuerst kommt

comestible [kə'mestɪbl] *n. usu. in pl.* Nahrungsmittel, *das*

comet ['kɒmɪt] *n.* *(Astron.)* Komet, *der*

comeuppance [kʌm'ʌpəns] *n.* **get one's ~:** die Quittung kriegen *(fig.)*

comfort ['kʌmfət] **1.** *n.* **a)** *(consolation)* Trost, *der;* **it is a ~/no ~ to know that ...:** es ist tröstlich/alles andere als tröstlich zu wissen, daß ...; **he takes ~ from the fact that ...:** er tröstet sich mit der Tatsache, daß ...; **b)** *(physical well-being)* Behaglichkeit, *die;* **live in great ~:** sehr behaglich *od.* bequem leben; **c)** *(person)* Trost, *der;* **be a ~ to sb.** jmdm. *od.* für jmdn. ein Trost sein; **d)** *(cause of satisfaction)* Tröstung, *die;* **e)** *usu. in pl.* *(things that make life easy)* Komfort, *der o. Pl.;* **with every modern ~** *or* **all modern ~s** mit allem modernen Komfort; **he likes his ~s** er schätzt den Komfort; **creature ~s** leibliches Wohl. *See also* **cold comfort. 2.** *v.t.* trösten; *(give help to)* sich annehmen (+ *Gen.*)

comfortable ['kʌmfətəbl] **1.** *adj.* **a)** *(giving, having, providing comfort)* bequem ⟨*Bett, Sessel, Schuhe, Leben*⟩; komfortabel ⟨*Haus, Hotel, Zimmer*⟩; *(fig.)* ausreichend ⟨*Einkommen, Rente*⟩; **a ~ victory** ein leichter Sieg; **a ~ majority** eine gute Mehrheit; **b)** *(at ease)* **be/feel ~:** sich wohl fühlen; **make yourself ~:** machen Sie es sich *(Dat.)* bequem; **the patient/his condition is ~:** der Patient/er ist schmerzfrei; **c)** *(having an easy conscience)* **she didn't feel very ~ about it** ihr war nicht ganz wohl bei der Sache. **2.** *n.* *(Amer.)* Deckbett, *das*

comfortably ['kʌmfətəblɪ] *adv.* bequem; komfortabel ⟨*eingerichtet*⟩; gut, leicht ⟨*gewinnen*⟩; **they are ~ off** es geht ihnen gut

comforter ['kʌmfətə(r)] *n.* **a)** *(person)* Tröster, *der*/Trösterin, *die;* **b)** *(esp. Brit.: baby's dummy)* Schnuller, *der;* **c)** *(esp. Brit.: woollen scarf)* Schal, *der;* **d)** *(Amer.: warm quilt)* Deckbett, *das*

comforting ['kʌmfətɪŋ] *adj.* beruhigend ⟨*Gedanke*⟩; tröstend ⟨*Worte*⟩; wohlig ⟨*Wärme*⟩; **we gave her a ~ cup of tea** wir gaben ihr zur Beruhigung eine Tasse Tee

comfortless ['kʌmfətlɪs] *adj.* unbequem; ⟨*Hotel, Zimmer*⟩ ohne Komfort; ungemütlich ⟨*Mensch, Leben*⟩; unangenehm ⟨*Gedanke*⟩; unwirtlich ⟨*Landschaft, Welt*⟩

'comfort station *n.* *(Amer.)* öffentliche Toilette; Bedürfnisanstalt, *die (veralt.)*

comfrey ['kʌmfrɪ] *n.* *(Bot.)* Beinwell, *der;* Schwarzwurz, *die*

comfy ['kʌmfɪ] *adj.* *(coll.)* bequem; gemütlich ⟨*Hotel, Zimmer*⟩; **make yourself ~:** mach's dir gemütlich; **are you ~?** sitzt/liegst *usw.* du bequem?

comic ['kɒmɪk] **1.** *adj.* **a)** *(burlesque, funny)* komisch; belustigend; **b)** *(of or in the style of comedy)* humoristisch ⟨*Dichtung, Dichter*⟩; **~ relief** befreiende Komik. **2.** *n.* *(coll.)* **a)** *(comedian)* Komiker, *der*/Komikerin, *die;* **b)** *(periodical)* Comic-Heft, *das;* **c)** *(amusing person)* Witzbold, *der;* ulkiger Vogel *(ugs.)*

comical ['kɒmɪkl] *adj.* ulkig; komisch

comically ['kɒmɪkəlɪ] *adv.* ulkig; komisch

comic: ~ 'opera *n.* *(lit. or fig.)* komische Oper; **~ strip** *n.* Comic, *der;* **~ strips** Comic strips; Comics

coming ['kʌmɪŋ] **1.** *adj. see* **come. 2.** *n.* *(of person)* Ankunft, *die;* *(of time)* Beginn, *der;* *(of institution)* Einführung, *die;* **~s and goings** das Kommen und Gehen

comma ['kɒmə] *n.* Komma, *das*

command [kə'mɑ:nd] **1.** *v.t.* **a)** *(order, bid)* befehlen **(sb.** jmdm.); **he ~ed that the work should be done immediately** er befahl, die Arbeit sofort auszuführen; **b)** *(be in ~ of)* befehligen ⟨*Schiff, Armee, Streitkräfte*⟩; *(have authority over or control of)* gebieten über (+ *Akk.*) *(geh.)*; beherrschen; **c)** *(have at one's disposal)* verfügen über (+ *Akk.*) ⟨*Gelder, Ressourcen, Wortschatz*⟩; **d)** *(restrain)* **~ oneself/one's temper** sich beherrschen; **e)** *(deserve and get)* verdient haben ⟨*Achtung, Respekt*⟩; **he ~s a high fee** er kann ein hohes Honorar verlangen; **f)** überragen ⟨*Küste, Stadt, Bucht, Hafen*⟩; **the hill ~s a fine view** der Berg bietet eine schöne Aussicht. **2.** *v.i.* **a)** *(be supreme)* befehlen; Befehle geben; **b)** *(be in ~)* das Kommando *od.* die Befehlsgewalt haben. **3.** *n.* **a)** Kommando, *das;* *(in writing)* Befehl, *der;* **at** *or* **by sb.'s ~:** auf jmds. Befehl *(Akk.)* [hin]; **at the ~ 'halt'** auf das Kommando „stehenbleiben" [hin]; **word of ~:** Befehl, *der;* Kommando, *das;* **b)** *(exercise or tenure)* Kommando, *das;* Befehlsgewalt, *die;* **be in ~ of an army/ship** eine Armee/ein Schiff befehligen; **the army is under the ~ of General X** die Armee steht unter dem Befehl von General X; **have/take ~ of ...:** das Kommando über (+ *Akk.*) ... haben/übernehmen; **officer in ~:** befehlshabender Offizier; **c)** *(control, mastery, possession)* Beherrschung, *die;* **have a good ~ of French** das Französische gut beherrschen; **all the money at his ~:** das gesamte ihm zur Verfügung stehende Geld; **d)** *(body of troops)* Kommando, *das;* *(district under ~)* Abschnitt, *der;* Befehlsbereich, *der;* *(ship)* Schiff, *das;* **e)** *(Computing)* Befehl, *der*

commandant [kɒmən'dænt] *n.* Kommandant, *der;* **C~-in-Chief** Oberbefehlshaber, *der*

commandeer [kɒmən'dɪə(r)] *v.t.* **a)** *(take arbitrary possession of)* sich *(Dat.)* aneignen; requirieren *(scherzh.)*; **b)** *(seize for military service)* einziehen ⟨*Männer*⟩; beschlagnahmen, requirieren ⟨*Pferde, Vorräte, Gebäude*⟩

commander [kə'mɑ:ndə(r)] *n.* **a)** *(one who commands)* Führer, *der;* Leiter, *der;* **b)** *(naval officer below captain)* Fregattenkapitän, *der;* **c)** *(Police)* Abschnittsleiter, *der;* **d) C~-in-Chief** Oberbefehlshaber, *der.* *See also* **wing commander**

commanding [kə'mɑ:ndɪŋ] *adj.* **a)** gebieterisch ⟨*Persönlichkeit, Erscheinung, Stimme*⟩; imposant, eindrucksvoll ⟨*Statur, Gestalt*⟩; **be in a ~ position** Befehlsbefugnis haben; *(Sport)* stark in Führung liegen; **b)** beherrschend ⟨*Ausblick, Lage*⟩; **~ heights** *(fig.)* Kommandohöhen *Pl.*

commanding 'officer *n.* Befehlshaber, *der*/Befehlshaberin, *die*

commandment [kə'mɑ:ndmənt] *n.* Gebot, *das;* **the Ten C~s** die Zehn Gebote

commando [kə'mɑ:ndəʊ] *n., pl.* **~s a)** *(unit)* Kommando, *das;* Kommandotrupp, *der;* **b)** *(member of ~)* Angehöriger eines Kommando[trupp]s

command: C~ Paper *n.* *(Brit.)* königliche Parlamentsvorlage; **~ performance** *n.* königliche Galavorstellung; **~ post** *n.* Kommandozentrale, *die*

commemorate [kə'meməreɪt] *v.t.* gedenken (+ *Gen.*); **Easter ~s the resurrection of Christ** zu Ostern wird die Wiederauferstehung Christi gefeiert; **in order to ~ the victory** zum Gedenken an den Sieg

commemoration [kəmemə'reɪʃn] *n.* **a)** *(act)* Gedenken, *das;* **in ~ of** zum Gedenken an (+ *Akk.*); **the ~ of sb.'s death** das Gedenken an jmds. Tod *(Akk.)*; **b)** *(church service)* Gedenkgottesdienst, *der*

commemorative [kə'memərətɪv] *adj.* Gedenk-; **~ of** zum Gedenken an (+ *Akk.*)

commence [kə'mens] *v.t.* & *i.* beginnen; **building ~d** mit dem Bau wurde begonnen; **~ to do** *or* **~ doing sth.** beginnen, etw. zu tun

commencement [kə'mensmənt] *n.* Beginn, *der*

commend [kə'mend] *v.t.* **a)** *(praise)* loben; **~ sb. [up]on sth.** jmdn. wegen etw. loben; **~ sb./sth. to sb.** jmdm. jmdn./etw. empfehlen; **be highly ~ed** eine sehr gute Beurteilung bekommen; **b)** *(entrust or commit to person's care)* anvertrauen

commendable [kə'mendəbl] *adj.* lobenswert; löblich

commendably [kə'mendəblɪ] *adv.* lobenswert

commendation [kɒmen'deɪʃn] *n.* **a)** *(praise)* Lob, *das;* *(official)* Belobigung, *die;*

(award) Auszeichnung, *die;* **b)** *(act of commending)* Empfehlung, *die*

commendatory [kə'mendətərɪ] *adj.* lobend

commensurable [kə'menʃərəbl, kə'mensjərəbl] *adj.* **a)** vergleichbar (**with, to** mit); **b)** *(proportionate)* **be ~ with sth.** einer Sache *(Dat.)* entsprechen

commensurate [kə'menʃərət, kə'mensjərət] *adj.* **~ to** *or* **with** entsprechend (+ *Dat.*); **be ~ to** *or* **with sth.** einer Sache *(Dat.)* entsprechen

comment ['kɒment] **1.** *n.* **a)** *(explanatory note, remark)* Bemerkung, *die* (**on** über + *Akk.*); *(marginal note)* Anmerkung, *die* (**on** über + *Akk.*); **no ~!** *(coll.)* kein Kommentar!; **b)** *(criticism)* Rederei, *die (ugs.);* **c)** *no pl. (gossip)* Gerede, *das;* **d)** *(illustration)* Deutung, *die;* Beschreibung, *die.* **2.** *v.i.* **a)** *(make remarks)* **~ on sth.** über etw. *(Akk.)* Bemerkungen machen; **he ~ed that ...:** er bemerkte, daß ...; **b)** *(write explanatory notes)* **~ on a text/manuscript** einen Text/ein Manuskript kommentieren

commentary ['kɒməntərɪ] *n.* **a)** *(series of comments, expository treatise)* Kommentar, *der* (**on** zu); **b)** *(comment)* Erläuterung, *die* (**on** zu); **the sombre factories are a sad ~ upon our civilization** die düsteren Fabriken sind traurige Zeugnisse unserer Kultur; **c)** *(Radio, Telev.)* **[live** *or* **running] ~:** Live-Reportage, *die*

commentate ['kɒmənteɪt] *v.i.* **~ on sth.** etw. kommentieren

commentator ['kɒmənteɪtə(r)] *n.* Kommentator, *der*/Kommentatorin, *die; (Sport)* Reporter, *der*/Reporterin, *die*

commerce ['kɒmɜːs] *n.* Handel, *der; (between countries)* Handel[sverkehr], *der;* **the world of ~:** die Geschäftswelt

commercial [kə'mɜːʃl] **1.** *adj.* **a)** Handels-; kaufmännisch ⟨*Ausbildung*⟩; **the ~ world** die Geschäftswelt; **b)** *(interested in financial return)* kommerziell; **c)** *(impure)* handelsüblich. **2.** *n.* Werbespot, *der;* **during the ~s on TV** während der Fernsehwerbung

commercial: ~ '**art** *n.* Gebrauchs-, Werbegraphik, *die;* ~ '**broadcasting** *n.* Werbefunk und -fernsehen; ~ **college** *n.* Fach[hoch]schule für kaufmännische Berufe; [höhere] Handelsschule; ~ **correspondence** *n.* Handelskorrespondenz, *die*

commercialise *see* **commercialize**

commercialism [kə'mɜːʃəlɪzəm] *n.* Kommerzialismus, *der*

commercialize [kə'mɜːʃəlaɪz] *v.t.* kommerzialisieren; vermarkten

commercially [kə'mɜːʃəlɪ] *adv.* kommerziell

commercial: ~ '**radio** *n.* Werbefunk, *der;* ~ '**television** *n.* kommerzielles Fernsehen; Werbefernsehen, *das;* ~ '**traveller** *n.* Handelsvertreter, *der*/-vertreterin, *die;* ~ **vehicle** *n.* Nutzfahrzeug, *das*

Commie ['kɒmɪ] *n. (sl.)* Rote, *der/die (abwertend)*

commingle [kə'mɪŋgl] *(formal)* **1.** *v.t.* vermischen. **2.** *v.i.* sich vermischen

commis [kɒ'miː] *adj.* **~ chef** Assistenzkoch, *der*

commiserate [kə'mɪzəreɪt] *v.i.* **~ with sb.** mit jmdm. mitfühlen; *(express one's commiseration)* jmdm. sein Mitgefühl aussprechen (**on** zu)

commiseration [kəmɪzə'reɪʃn] *n.* **a)** Mitgefühl, *das;* **b)** *in sing. or pl. (condolence)* Teilnahme, *die;* Beileid, *das*

commissar ['kɒmɪsɑː(r)] *n. (Hist.)* Kommissar, *der*

commissariat [kɒmɪ'seərɪət] *n.* Intendantur, *die*

commissary ['kɒmɪsərɪ, kə'mɪsərɪ] *n.* **a)** *(Mil.)* Verpflegungsoffizier, *der;* **b)** *(Amer.: store for supply of food etc.)* Laden, *der (auf Baustellen, in Lagern, Bergwerken usw.)*

commission [kə'mɪʃn] **1.** *n.* **a)** *(authority)* Vollmacht, *die;* **b)** *(body of persons having authority, department of Commissioner)* Kommission, *die;* **c)** *(command, instruction)* Auftrag, *der;* Anweisung, *die;* **d) Royal C~** *(Brit.)* Königliche [Untersuchungs]kommission; **e)** *(warrant conferring authority)* Ernennung, *die;* Bestellung, *die; (in armed services)* Ernennungsurkunde, *die;* Offizierspatent, *das (veralt.);* **get one's ~:** zum Offizier ernannt werden; **resign one's ~:** aus dem Offiziersdienst ausscheiden; den Dienst quittieren *(veralt.);* **f)** *(pay of agent)* Provision, *die;* **sell goods on ~:** Waren auf Provisionsbasis verkaufen; **g)** *(act of committing crime etc.)* Begehen, *das;* Begehung, *die;* **h) in/out of ~** ⟨*Kriegsschiff*⟩ in/außer Dienst; ⟨*Auto, Maschine, Lift usw.*⟩ in/außer Betrieb. **2.** *v.t.* **a)** beauftragen ⟨*Künstler*⟩; in Auftrag geben ⟨*Gemälde usw.*⟩; **b)** *(empower by commission)* bevollmächtigen; **~ed officer** Offizier, *der;* **c)** *(give command of ship to)* zum Kapitän ernennen; **d)** *(prepare for service)* in Dienst stellen ⟨*Schiff*⟩; **e)** *(bring into operation)* in Betrieb setzen ⟨*Kraftwerk, Fabrik*⟩

commissionaire [kəmɪʃə'neə(r)] *n. (esp. Brit.)* Portier, *der*

commissioner [kə'mɪʃənə(r)] *n.* **a)** *(person appointed by commission)* Beauftragte, *der/die; (of police)* Präsident, *der;* **b)** *(member of commission)* Kommissions-, Ausschußmitglied, *das;* **c)** *(representative of supreme authority)* Kommissar, *der;* **High C~:** Hochkommissar, *der;* **d) C~ for Oaths** Notar, *der*/Notarin, *die*

commit [kə'mɪt] *v.t.*, **-tt-: a)** *(perpetrate)* begehen, verüben ⟨*Mord, Selbstmord, Verbrechen, Raub*⟩; begehen ⟨*Dummheit, Bigamie, Fehler, Ehebruch*⟩; **thou shalt not ~ adultery** *(Bibl.)* du sollst nicht ehebrechen; **b)** *(pledge, bind)* **~ oneself/sb. to doing sth.** sich/jmdn. verpflichten, etw. zu tun; **~ oneself to a course of action** sich auf eine Vorgehensweise festlegen; **c)** *(entrust)* anvertrauen (**to** *Dat.*); **~ sth. to a person/a person's care** jmdm. etw. anvertrauen/etw. jmds. Obhut *(Dat.)* anvertrauen; **~ sth. to the flames/waves** etw. den Flammen/Wellen übergeben *(geh.);* **~ sth. to writing/paper** etw. zu Papier bringen; *see also* **memory a; d)** *(consign to custody)* **~ sb. for trial** jmdn. dem Gericht überstellen; **~ sb. to prison** jmdn. ins Gefängnis einliefern

commitment [kə'mɪtmənt] *n.;* **a)** *(to course of action or opinion)* Verpflichtung (**to** gegenüber); *(by conviction)* Engagement, *das* (**to** für); **b)** *see* **committal a**

committal [kə'mɪtl] *n.* **a)** *(to prison)* Einlieferung, *die; (to hospital)* Einweisung, *die;* **b)** *(to grave)* Bestattung, *die;* **~ service** Bestattungsgottesdienst, *der*

committed [kə'mɪtɪd] *adj.* **a)** verpflichtet (**to** zu); festgelegt (**to** auf + *Akk.*); **b)** *(morally dedicated)* engagiert

committee [kə'mɪtɪ] *n.* Ausschuß, *der (auch Parl.);* Komitee, *das*

com'mittee-man, com'mittee-woman *ns.* Ausschußmitglied, *das*

commode [kə'məʊd] *n.* **a)** *(chest of drawers)* Kommode, *die;* **b)** *(chamber-pot)* **[night-]~:** Nachtstuhl, *der*

commodious [kə'məʊdɪəs] *adj.* geräumig

commodity [kə'mɒdɪtɪ] *n.* **a)** *(utility item)* Gebrauchsgegenstand, *der; (not luxury)* Gebrauchsartikel, *der;* **household ~:** Haushaltsartikel, *der;* **a rare/precious ~** *(fig.)* etwas Seltenes/Kostbares; **b)** *(St. Exch.)* [vertretbare] Ware; *(raw material)* Rohstoff, *der*

commodore ['kɒmədɔː(r)] *n.* **a)** *(naval officer)* Flottillenadmiral, *der;* **b)** *(of squadron)* Kommodore, *der;* **c)** *(of yacht-club)* Präsident, *der*/Präsidentin, *die;* **d)** *(senior captain of shipping line)* Kommodore, *der*

common ['kɒmən] **1.** *adj.*, **~er** ['kɒmənə(r)], **~est** ['kɒmənɪst] **a)** *(belonging equally to all)* gemeinsam ⟨*Ziel, Interesse, Sache, Unternehmung, Vorteil, Merkmal, Sprache*⟩; **~ to all birds** allen Vögeln gemeinsam; *see also* **cause 1d; consent 2a; b)** *(belonging to the public)* öffentlich; **the ~ good** das Gemeinwohl; **a ~ belief** [ein] allgemeiner Glaube; **a ~ prostitute** *or* **harlot** *(arch.)* eine Straßendirne *(veralt.);* **a ~ criminal** ein gewöhnlicher *od.* gemeiner Verbrecher; **have the ~ touch** volkstümlich sein; **c)** *(usual)* gewöhnlich, normal; *(frequent)* häufig ⟨*Vorgang, Erscheinung, Ereignis, Erlebnis*⟩; allgemein verbreitet ⟨*Sitte, Wort, Redensart*⟩; allgemein bekannt ⟨*Marke, Produkt*⟩; *(Bot., Zool.: of the most familiar type)* gemein ⟨*Farnkraut, Sperling usw.*⟩; **a ~ sight** ein ganz gewöhnlicher *od.* alltäglicher Anblick; **such a thing is ~ nowadays** so etwas ist heutzutage ganz normal; *(is frequent)* kommt heutzutage häufig vor; **a word in ~ usage** ein Wort des allgemeinen Sprachgebrauchs; **drugs are in ~ use today** die Einnahme von Drogen ist heute weit verbreitet; **~ honesty/courtesy** [ganz] normale Ehrlichkeit/Höflichkeit; **~ or garden** *(coll.)* ganz gewöhnlich *od.* normal; **a ~ or garden subject/programme** ein Feld-Wald-und-Wiesen-Thema/-Programm *(ugs.);* **a hotel out of the ~ run** ein Hotel, das über dem Durchschnitt liegt; **no ~ mind** ein außergewöhnlicher Kopf *(fig.);* **d)** *(without rank or position)* einfach; gemein *(veralt.); see also* **herd 1b; e)** *(vulgar)* gemein; gewöhnlich *(abwertend),* ordinär *(ugs. abwertend)* ⟨*Ausdrucksweise, Mundart, Aussehen, Benehmen*⟩; **be as ~ as muck** schrecklich ordinär *od.* gewöhnlich sein; **f)** *(Math.)* gemeinsam; **g)** *(Ling.)* **~ noun** Gattungsbegriff, *der;* **~ gender** doppeltes Geschlecht. **2.** *n.* **a)** *(land)* Gemeindeland, *das;* Allmende, *die;* **b) have sth./nothing/a lot in ~ [with sb.]** etw./nichts/viel [mit jmdm.] gemein[sam] haben; **in ~ with most of his friends he wanted ...:** ebenso wie die meisten seiner Freunde wollte er ...; **c)** *(coll.: common sense)* Grips, *der (ugs.);* **use your ~!** denk doch mal ein bißchen nach! *(ugs.)*

common: C~ Agri'cultural Policy *n.* gemeinsame Agrarpolitik [der EG]; ~ '**cold** *n.* Erkältung, *die;* ~ **de'nominator** *n.* *(Math.)* gemeinsame Nenner, *der;* **the least** *or* **lowest ~ denominator** *(lit. or fig.)* der kleinste gemeinsame Nenner; ~ '**entrance** *n. (Brit.) Aufnahmeprüfung für eine Privatschule*

commoner ['kɒmənə(r)] *n.* **a)** *(one of the people)* Bürgerliche, *der/die;* **b)** *(student) Student, der kein Stipendium erhält*

common: ~ '**factor** *n. (Math.)* gemeinsamer Teiler; ~ '**ground** *n.* gemeinsame Basis; ~ '**knowledge** *n.* **it's [a matter of] ~ knowledge that ...:** es ist allgemein bekannt, daß ...; ~ **land** *n.* Gemeindeland, *das;* ~ '**law** *n.* Common Law, *das;* ~**-law** *adj.* **~-law marriage** eheähnliche Gemeinschaft; **she's his ~-law wife/he's her ~-law husband** sie lebt mit ihm/er lebt mit ihr in eheähnlicher Gemeinschaft

commonly ['kɒmənlɪ] *adv.* **a)** *(generally)* im allgemeinen; gemeinhin; **b)** *(vulgarly)* gewöhnlich *(abwertend)*

common: C~ '**Market** *n.* Gemeinsamer Markt; ~ '**multiple** *n. (Math.)* gemeinsames Vielfaches; **the least** *or* **lowest ~ multiple** das kleinste gemeinsame Vielfache

commonness ['kɒmənnɪs] *n., no pl.* **a)** *(usualness)* Gewöhnlichkeit, *die;* Normalität, *die; (frequency)* Häufigkeit, *die;* **b)** *(vulgarity)* Gewöhnlichkeit, *die (abwertend)*

commonplace ['kɒmənpleɪs] **1.** *n. (platitude)* Gemeinplatz, *der; (anything usual or trite)* Alltäglichkeit, *die.* **2.** *adj.* nichtssagend, banal ⟨*Person, Bemerkung, Buch*⟩; alltäglich ⟨*Angelegenheit, Ereignis*⟩

common: C~ 'Prayer *n.* Liturgie, *die (der Kirche von England)*; **the Book of C ~ Prayer** *liturgisches Buch der Kirche von England;* **~-room** *n. (Brit.)* Gemeinschaftsraum, *der; (for lecturers)* Dozentenzimmer, *das*
commons ['kɒmənz] *n. pl.* **a) the [House of] C~:** das Unterhaus; **b)** *(Brit.: common people)* einfache Volk, *das. See also* **short commons**
common: ~ 'sense *n.* gesunder Menschenverstand; **~-sense** *adj.* vernünftig; gesund ⟨*Ansicht, Standpunkt*⟩; **~ stock** *n. (Amer. Finance)* Stammaktien; **~ time** *n. (Mus.)* Viervierteltakt, *der*
commonwealth ['kɒmənwelθ] *n.* **a) the [British] C~ [of Nations]** das Commonwealth; **C~ Day** Commonwealthtag, *der;* **b)** *(independent state)* Staat, *der;* Gemeinwesen, *das; (republic or democratic state)* Republik, *die;* **C~ of Australia** Australischer Bund; **c) the C~** *(Brit. Hist.) die Republik unter Cromwell*
commotion [kə'məʊʃn] *n. (noisy confusion)* Tumult, *der; (insurrection)* Aufruhr, *der;* **make a ~:** einen Tumult *od.* einen großen Spektakel veranstalten
communal ['kɒmjʊnl] *adj.* **a)** *(of or for the community)* gemeindlich; Gemeinde-, kommunal ⟨*Verwaltung*⟩; **~ living/life** Gemeinschaftsleben, *das;* **b)** *(for the common use)* gemeinsam; Gemeinschafts⟨*-küche, -schüssel, -bad, -grab, -zelle, -ehe*⟩
communally ['kɒmjʊnəlɪ] *adv.* gemeinsam; gemeinschaftlich; **be ~ owned** Gemeinschaftsbesitz sein
[1]**commune** ['kɒmju:n] *n.* **a)** Kommune, *die;* **b)** *(territorial division)* Gemeinde, *die;* Kommune, *die*
[2]**commune** [kə'mju:n] *v. i.* **a) ~ with sb./sth.** mit jmdm./etw. Zwiesprache halten *(geh.);* **~ together** miteinander Zwiesprache halten *(geh.);* **b)** *(Amer. Eccl.)* das Abendmahl empfangen; *(RC Ch.)* kommunizieren
communicable [kə'mju:nɪkəbl] *adj.* übertragbar ⟨*Krankheit*⟩; vermittelbar, kommunizierbar ⟨*Ideen, Informationen*⟩
communicant [kə'mju:nɪkənt] *n. (RC Ch.)* Kommunizierende, *der/die; (Protestant Ch.)* Empfänger/Empfängerin des Abendmahls
communicate [kə'mju:nɪkeɪt] **1.** *v. t. (impart, transmit)* übertragen ⟨*Wärme, Bewegung, Krankheit*⟩; übermitteln ⟨*Nachrichten, Informationen*⟩; vermitteln ⟨*Gefühle, Ideen*⟩; **he ~d the plan to his friends** er teilte seinen Freunden den Plan mit. **2.** *v. i.* **a)** *(have common door)* verbunden sein; **communicating rooms** Zimmer mit einer Verbindungstür; **b) ~ with sb.** mit jmdm. kommunizieren; **she has difficulty in communicating** sie hat Kommunikationsschwierigkeiten; **c)** *(RC Ch.)* kommunizieren; *(Protestant Ch.)* das Abendmahl empfangen
communication [kəmju:nɪ'keɪʃn] *n.* **a)** *(imparting of disease, motion, heat, etc.)* Übertragung, *die; (imparting of news, information)* Übermittlung, *die; (imparting of ideas)* Vermittlung, *die;* **~ with the spacecraft/the mainland** die Verbindung zum Raumschiff/Festland; **~ among the deaf and dumb** die Verständigung unter Taubstummen; **b)** *(information given)* Mitteilung, *die* **(to** an + *Akk.*); **c)** *(interaction with sb.)* Verbindung, *die;* **lines of ~:** Verbindungslinien; **means/systems of ~:** Kommunikationsmittel/-systeme; **be in ~ with sb.** mit jmdm. in Verbindung stehen; **d)** *in pl. (conveying information)* Kommunikation, *die; (science, practice)* Kommunikationswesen, *das; (Mil.)* Nachschublinien *Pl.*
communication: ~-cord *n.* Notbremse, *die;* **~ link** *n.* Nachrichtenverbindung, *die;* **~s satellite** *n.* Nachrichten- *od.* Kommunikationssatellit, *der;* **~ theory** *n.* Kommunikationstheorie, *die*

communicative [kə'mju:nɪkətɪv] *adj.* gesprächig; mitteilsam
communion [kə'mju:nɪən] *n.* **a) [Holy] C~** *(Protestant Ch.)* das [heilige] Abendmahl; *(RC Ch.)* die [heilige] Kommunion; **receive** *or* **take [Holy] C~:** das [heilige] Abendmahl/die [heilige] Kommunion empfangen; **b)** *(fellowship)* Gemeinschaft, *die;* **the ~ of saints** die Gemeinschaft der Heiligen; **~ with nature/God** Zwiesprache mit der Natur/mit Gott
communion: ~-cup *n.* Abendmahlskelch, *der;* **~-rail** *n.* Kommunionbank, *die;* **~ service** *n.* Abendmahlsgottesdienst, *der*
communiqué [kə'mju:nɪkeɪ] *n.* Kommuniqué, *das*
communism ['kɒmjʊnɪzm] *n.* Kommunismus, *der;* **C~:** der Kommunismus
communist, Communist ['kɒmjʊnɪst] **1.** *n.* Kommunist, *der*/Kommunistin, *die.* **2.** *adj.* kommunistisch; **the C ~ Party/Manifesto** die Kommunistische Partei/das Kommunistische Manifest; **~-led/-dominated** von Kommunisten angeführt/beherrscht
communistic [kɒmjʊ'nɪstɪk] *adj.* kommunistisch
community [kə'mju:nɪtɪ] *n.* **a)** *(organized body)* Gemeinwesen, *das;* **b)** *(persons living in same place, having common religion, etc.)* **the Jewish ~:** die jüdische Gemeinde; **a ~ of monks** eine Mönchsgemeinde; **c)** *no pl. (public)* Öffentlichkeit, *die;* **the ~ at large** die breite Öffentlichkeit; **d)** *(body of nations)* Gemeinschaft, *die;* **the ~ of nations** die Völkergemeinschaft; **e)** *no pl. (sharedness)* Gemeinschaft, *die;* **a sense of ~:** ein Gemeinschaftsgefühl
community: ~ centre *n.* Gemeindezentrum, *das;* Kulturhaus, *das;* **~ charge** *n. (Brit.)* Gemeindesteuer, *die;* **~ chest** *n. (Amer.)* Sozialfonds, *der (einer Gemeinde);* **~ council** *n. (Brit.)* Gemeinderat, *der;* **~ home** *n. (Brit.)* Jugendhof, *der;* Jugendwerkhof, *der (DDR);* **~ medicine** *n.* Sozialhygiene, *die;* **~ relations** *n. pl.* Verhältnis zwischen den Bevölkerungsgruppen; **~ 'service** *n. [freiwilliger od. als Strafe auferlegter] sozialer Dienst;* **~ singing** *n.* gemeinsames Singen; **~ spirit** *n.* Gemeinschaftsgeist, *der*
commutable [kə'mju:təbl] *adj.* **a)** *(interchangeable)* austauschbar; **b)** *(convertible)* umwandelbar
commutation [kɒmjʊ'teɪʃn] *n.* **a)** *(of punishment)* Umwandlung, *die;* **b)** *(Electr.)* Kommutierung, *die*
commu'tation ticket *n. (Amer.)* Zeitkarte, *die*
commutator ['kɒmjʊteɪtə(r)] *n. (Electr.)* Kommutator, *der;* Stromwender, *der*
commute [kə'mju:t] **1.** *v. t.* **a)** *(change to sth. milder)* umwandeln ⟨*Strafe*⟩ **(to** in + *Akk.*); **b)** *(change to sth. different)* umwandeln; **c)** *(interchange)* austauschen ⟨*Dinge, Begriffe*⟩; **d)** *(make payment)* ablösen ⟨*Verpflichtung, Schulden*⟩ **(for, into** durch). **2.** *v. i.* **a)** *(travel daily)* pendeln; **b)** *(Amer.: hold season ticket)* eine Zeitkarte haben
commuter [kə'mju:tə(r)] *n.* Pendler, *der*/Pendlerin, *die*
com'muter belt *n.* großstädtischer Einzugsbereich
[1]**compact** [kəm'pækt] **1.** *adj.* kompakt; komprimiert ⟨*Stil, Sprache*⟩. **2.** *v. t.* **a)** *(put firmly together)* zusammenpressen; **b)** *(fig.: condense)* zusammenfügen **(into** zu)
[2]**compact** ['kɒmpækt] *n.* **a)** Puderdose [mit Puder(stein)]; **b)** *(Amer.: car)* Kompaktauto, *das;* Kompaktwagen, *der*
[3]**compact** *n. (agreement)* Vertrag, *der;* **a ~ with the devil** ein Pakt mit dem Teufel
compact 'disc *n.* Compact Disc, *die;* Kompaktschallplatte, *die*
compactly [kəm'pæktlɪ] *adv.* kompakt; komprimiert ⟨*ausgedrückt*⟩

compactness [kəm'pæktnɪs] *n., no pl.* Kompaktheit, *die*
[1]**companion** [kəm'pænjən] *n.* **a)** *(one accompanying)* Begleiter, *der*/Begleiterin, *die;* **my travelling ~s** meine Reisebegleiter; **b)** *(associate)* Kamerad, *der*/Kameradin, *die;* Gefährte, *der*/Gefährtin, *die (geh.);* Genosse, *der*/Genossin, *die (veralt.);* **the ~s of his youth** seine Jugendgefährten; **his drinking ~s** seine Zechgenossen *(veralt.) od. (ugs.)* -brüder; **~ in arms** Kampfgefährte, *der;* **c)** *(Brit.: of [knightly] order) unterste Stufe verschiedener [Ritter]orden, z. B.* **C~ of the Bath,** *(nicht ritterlich)* **C~ of Honour/Literature; d)** *(woman living with another)* Gesellschafterin, *die;* **e)** *(handbook)* Ratgeber, *der;* **Gardener's C~:** Ratgeber für den Gartenfreund; **C~ to Music/the Theatre** Musik-/Theaterführer, *der;* **f)** *(matching thing)* Gegenstück, *das;* Pendant, *das; attrib.;* **the ~ volume to ...:** der Begleitband zu ...; **g)** *(Astron.)* Begleiter, *der*
[2]**companion** *n. (Naut.)* **a)** Kajütskappe, *die;* **b)** *(stairs) see* **companion-way**
companionable [kəm'pænjənəbl] *adj.* freundlich
companion: ~ hatch *n. (Naut.)* Luke, *die;* Luk, *das (fachspr.);* **~-ladder** *n. (Naut.)* Niedergang, *der;* **~-set** *n.* Kaminbesteck, *das*
companionship [kəm'pænjənʃɪp] *n.* Gesellschaft, *die; (fellowship)* Kameradschaft, *die;* Freundschaft, *die*
com'panion-way *n. (Naut.)* Niedergang, *der*
company ['kʌmpənɪ] *n.* **a)** *(persons assembled, companionship)* Gesellschaft, *die;* **a ~ of ships** ein Schiffsverband; **expect/receive ~:** Besuch *od.* Gäste *Pl.* erwarten/empfangen; **for ~:** zur Gesellschaft; **two is ~, three is a crowd** zu zweit ist es gemütlich, ein Dritter stört; **keep one's own ~:** für sich bleiben; **he likes his own ~:** er ist gern für sich; **in ~ with sb.** in jmds. Gesellschaft *(Dat.);* **be in ~:** in Gesellschaft sein; **bear** *or* **keep sb. ~:** jmdm. Gesellschaft leisten; **keep ~ with sb.** mit jmdm. verkehren; **part ~ with sb./sth.** sich von jmdm./etw. trennen; **b)** *(companion[s])* **low ~:** schlechte Gesellschaft; **the ~ he keeps** sein Umgang; seine Gesellschaft; **be good/bad** *etc.* **~:** ein guter/schlechter Gesellschafter sein; **c)** *(firm)* Gesellschaft, *die;* Firma, *die;* **~ car** Firmenwagen, *der;* **d)** *(Commerc.)* **Jones and C~:** Jones & Co.; **e)** *(of actors)* Truppe, *die;* Ensemble, *das;* **f)** *(of Guides)* Trupp, *der;* **g)** *(Mil.)* Kompanie, *die;* **~ sergeant-major** Kompaniefeldwebel, *der;* **h)** *(Navy)* **ship's ~:** Besatzung, *die*
comparability [kɒmpərə'bɪlɪtɪ] *n., no pl.* Vergleichbarkeit, *die*
comparable ['kɒmpərəbl] *adj.* vergleichbar **(to, with** mit)
comparably ['kɒmpərəblɪ] *adv.* in vergleichbarer Weise; vergleichbar
comparative [kəm'pærətɪv] **1.** *adj.* **a)** vergleichend ⟨*Anatomie, Sprachwissenschaft usw.*⟩; **~ religion** vergleichende Religionswissenschaft; **b)** *(estimated by comparison)* **the ~ merits/advantages of the proposals** die Vorzüge/Vorteile der Vorschläge im Vergleich; **c)** *(relative)* relativ; **in ~ comfort** relativ *od.* verhältnismäßig komfortabel; **with ~ ease** relativ *od.* verhältnismäßig leicht; **d)** *(Ling.)* komparativ *(fachspr.);* **the ~ degree** der Komparativ; die erste Steigerungsstufe; **a ~ adjective/adverb** ein Adjektiv/Adverb im Komparativ; ≈ ein gesteigertes Adjektiv/Adverb. **2.** *n. (Ling.)* Komparativ, *der;* erste Steigerungsstufe
comparatively [kəm'pærətɪvlɪ] *adv.* **a)** *(by means of comparison)* vergleichend; im Vergleich; **b)** *(relatively)* relativ; verhältnismäßig
compare [kəm'peə(r)] **1.** *v. t.* **a)** vergleichen

(**to, with** mit); ~ **two/three** *etc.* **things** zwei/drei *usw.* Dinge [miteinander] vergleichen; **~d with** *or* **to sb./sth.** verglichen mit *od.* im Vergleich zu jmdm./etw.; **X is not to be ~d to Y** X läßt sich nicht mit Y vergleichen; ~ **notes about sth.** Erfahrungen über etw. *(Akk.)* austauschen; **b)** *(Ling.)* steigern; komparieren *(fachspr.)*. **2.** *v. i.* sich vergleichen lassen. **3.** *n. (literary)* **beyond** *or* **without ~**: unvergleichlich; **lovely beyond ~**: unvergleichlich *od.* einmalig reizvoll

comparison [kəm'pærɪsn] *n.* **a)** *(act of comparing, simile)* Vergleich, *der;* **the ~ of X and** *or* **with Y** ein Vergleich von *od.* zwischen X und Y; **in** *or* **by ~ [with sb./sth.]** im Vergleich [zu jmdm./etw.]; **this one is cheaper in** *or* **by ~**: dieser ist vergleichsweise billiger; **beyond [all] ~**: über jeden Vergleich erhaben; **there's no ~ between them** man kann sie einfach nicht vergleichen; **bear** *or* **stand ~**: einem Vergleich standhalten; **~s are odious** Vergleiche sind immer ungerecht; **b)** *(Ling.)* Steigerung, *die;* **degrees of ~**: Steigerungsstufen

compartment [kəm'pɑ:tmənt] *n.* *(in drawer, desk, etc.)* Fach, *das; (fig.)* Schubfach, *das; (of railway-carriage)* Abteil, *das; (Naut.)* Abteilung, *die*

compartmentalize [kɒmpɑ:t'mentəlaɪz] *v. t.* aufgliedern; *(excessively)* aufsplittern

compass ['kʌmpəs] **1.** *n.* **a)** *in pl.* **[a pair of] ~es** ein Zirkel; **b)** *(for navigating)* Kompaß, *der;* **mariner's ~**: Magnetkompaß, *der;* **the four points of the ~**: die vier Himmelsrichtungen; **c)** *(boundary)* Umkreis, *der;* **d)** *(extent)* Gebiet, *das; (fig.: scope)* Rahmen, *der;* **beyond the ~ of the human mind** jenseits des menschlichen Fassungsvermögens; **in a small ~**: im kleinen Rahmen; **e)** *(Mus.) (of instrument)* Tonraum, *der; (of voice)* Umfang, *der.* **2.** *v. t. (grasp mentally)* erfassen

'compass card *n.* Kompaß-, Windrose, *die*

compassion [kəm'pæʃn] *n., no pl.* Mitgefühl, *das; (Bibl.)* Erbarmen, *das;* **have** *or* **take ~ on sb.** Mitleid mit jmdm. haben

compassionate [kəm'pæʃənət] *adj.* mitfühlend; **on ~ grounds** aus persönlichen Gründen; *(for family reasons)* aus familiären Gründen

compassionate 'leave *n. (Brit.)* Sonderurlaub aus familiären Gründen

compatibility [kəmpætɪ'bɪlɪtɪ] *n., no pl.* *(consistency, mutual tolerance)* Vereinbarkeit, *die; (of people)* Zueinanderpassen, *das; (of equipment etc.)* Aufeinander-Abgestimmtsein, *das;* Zueinanderpassen, *das; (Computing)* Kompatibilität, *die; (of drugs)* Verträglichkeit, *die*

compatible [kəm'pætɪbl] *adj.* *(consistent, mutually tolerant)* vereinbar; zueinander passend ⟨*Menschen*⟩; aufeinander abgestimmt, zueinander passend, *(Computing)* kompatibel ⟨*Geräte, Maschinen*⟩; verträglich ⟨*Medikamente*⟩

compatriot [kəm'pætrɪət, kəm'peɪtrɪət] *n.* Landsmann, *der*/-männin, *die*

compel [kəm'pel] *v. t.*, **-ll-** zwingen; **~ sb. to do sth.** jmdn. [dazu] zwingen, etw. zu tun; **~ sb.'s admiration/respect** jmdm. Bewunderung/Achtung abnötigen; **he felt ~led to tell her** er sah sich gezwungen *od.* genötigt, es ihr zu sagen

compelling [kəm'pelɪŋ] *adj.* bezwingend

compellingly [kəm'pelɪŋlɪ] *adv.* mit bezwingender Überzeugungskraft/Logik *usw.*

compendious [kəm'pendɪəs] *adj.* kompendiarisch *(veralt.)*; kurzgefaßt, knapp ⟨*Buch, Aufzeichnungen*⟩

compendium [kəm'pendɪəm] *n., pl.* **~s** *or* **compendia** [kəm'pendɪə] Abriß, *der;* Kurzfassung, *die; (summary)* Kompendium, *das;* **~ of games** Spielemagazin, *das*

compensate ['kɒmpenseɪt] **1.** *v. i.* **a)** *(make amends for)* **~ for sth.** etw. ersetzen; **~ for injury** *etc.* für Verletzung *usw.* Schaden[s]ersatz leisten; **b)** *(Psych.)* **~ for sth.** etw. kompensieren. **2.** *v. t.* **a) ~ sb. for sth.** jmdn. für etw. entschädigen; **b)** *(Mech.)* ausgleichen ⟨*Pendel*⟩

compensation [kɒmpen'seɪʃn] *n.* **a)** Ersatz, *der; (for damages, injuries, etc.)* Schaden[s]ersatz, *der; (for requisitioned property)* Entschädigung, *die;* Ausgleichszahlung, *die;* **£100 in ~** *or* **by way of ~**: 100 Pfund Schaden[s]ersatz; **but he had the ~ of knowing that ...**: aber er hatte die Genugtuung zu wissen, daß ...; **growing old has its ~s** das Altwerden hat auch seine guten Seiten; **b)** *(Psych.)* Kompensation, *die*

compère ['kɒmpeə(r)] *(Brit.)* **1.** *n.* Conférencier, *der;* Showmaster, *der.* **2.** *v. t.* konferieren ⟨*Show*⟩

compete [kəm'pi:t] *v. i.* konkurrieren (**for** um); *(Sport)* kämpfen; **~ with sb./sth.** mit jmdm./etw. konkurrieren; **he ~d against** *or* **with his rivals for the title** er kämpfte gegen seine *od.* mit seinen Rivalen um den Titel; **~ in a race** an einem Rennen teilnehmen; **be [un]able to ~**: [nicht] konkurrenzfähig sein; **~ with one another** miteinander wetteifern

competence ['kɒmpɪtəns], **competency** ['kɒmpɪtənsɪ] *ns.* **a)** *(ability)* Fähigkeiten *Pl.;* **a high degree of ~ in French** sehr gute Französischkenntnisse; *(of native speaker)* hohe Sprachkompetenz im Französischen; **b)** *(Law)* Zuständigkeit, *die;* **c)** *(Ling.)* Kompetenz, *die*

competent ['kɒmpɪtənt] *adj.* **a)** *(qualified)* fähig; befähigt; **not ~ to do sth.** nicht kompetent, etw. zu tun; **b)** *(effective)* angemessen, adäquat ⟨*Antwort, Kenntnisse*⟩; **c)** *(appropriate)* angemessen; geboten; **d)** *(Law)* zuständig ⟨*Richter, Gericht*⟩; zugelassen ⟨*Zeuge*⟩; zulässig ⟨*Beweismaterial*⟩

competently ['kɒmpɪtəntlɪ] *adv.* sachkundig; kompetent

competition [kɒmpɪ'tɪʃn] *n.* **a)** *(contest)* Wettbewerb, *der; (in magazine etc.)* Preisausschreiben, *das;* **b)** *(those competing)* Konkurrenz, *die; (Sport)* Gegner *Pl.;* **c)** *(act of competing)* Konkurrenz, *die;* **a spirit of ~**: Konkurrenz- *od.* Wettbewerbsdenken, *das;* **be in ~ with sb.** mit jmdm. konkurrieren *od.* im Wettbewerb stehen

competitive [kəm'petɪtɪv] *adj.* **a)** Leistungs-; **~ sports** Wettkampf- *od.* Leistungssport, *der;* **~ spirit** Konkurrenz- *od.* Wettbewerbsdenken, *das;* **a ~ examination** eine Auswahlprüfung; **on a ~ basis** nach Leistung; **b)** *(comparable with rivals)* leistungs-, wettbewerbsfähig ⟨*Preis, Unternehmen*⟩; **a very ~ market** ein Markt mit starker Konkurrenz

competitively [kəm'petɪtɪvlɪ] *adv.* **they were bidding ~**: sie boten um die Wette *(ugs.)*; **these models are ~ priced** der Preis dieser Modelle ist wettbewerbs- *od.* konkurrenzfähig

competitor [kəm'petɪtə(r)] *n.* Konkurrent, *der*/Konkurrentin, *die;* Mitbewerber, *der*/-bewerberin *die (fachspr.)*; *(in contest, race)* Teilnehmer, *der*/-nehmerin, *die; (for job)* Mitbewerber, *der*/-bewerberin, *die;* **our ~s** unsere Konkurrenz

compilation [kɒmpɪ'leɪʃn] *n.* Zusammenstellung, *die;* Kompilation, *die (geh.)*; *(of dictionary, guidebook)* Verfassen, *das*

compile [kəm'paɪl] *v. t.* **a)** *(put together)* zusammenstellen; kompilieren *(geh.)*; verfassen ⟨*Wörterbuch, Reiseführer*⟩; **b)** *(accumulate)* sammeln ⟨*Punkte*⟩

compiler [kəm'paɪlə(r)] *n.* **a)** Verfasser, *der*/Verfasserin, *die;* Kompilator, *der*/Kompilatorin, *die (geh.)*; **b)** *(Computing)* Compiler, *der*

complacency [kəm'pleɪsənsɪ] *n., no pl.* Selbstzufriedenheit, Selbstgefälligkeit, *die*

complacent [kəm'pleɪsənt] *adj.* selbstzufrieden; selbstgefällig

complain [kəm'pleɪn] *v. i. (express dissatisfaction)* sich beklagen *od.* beschweren (**about, at** über + *Akk.*); **~ of sth.** über etw. *(Akk.)* klagen; **his continual ~ing** sein ständiges Klagen; **she ~s of [having] toothache** sie klagt über Zahnschmerzen; **I have nothing to ~ about/of** ich habe keine Beanstandungen/ich kann nicht klagen

complaint [kəm'pleɪnt] *n.* **a)** *(utterance of grievance)* Beanstandung, *die;* Beschwerde, *die;* Klage, *die; (formal accusation, expression of grief)* Klage, *die;* **have/cause grounds for ~**: Grund zur Klage haben/Anlaß zu Beschwerden geben; **b)** *(bodily ailment)* Leiden, *das;* **a heart ~**: ein Herzleiden

complaisance [kəm'pleɪzəns] *n., no pl.* *(formal)* Entgegenkommen, *das; (deference)* Respekt, *der*

complaisant [kəm'pleɪzənt] *adj. (formal)* entgegenkommend

complement 1. ['kɒmplɪmənt] *n.* **a)** *(what completes)* Vervollständigung, *die;* Komplement, *das (geh.)*; **b)** *(full number)* **a [full] ~**: die volle Zahl; *(of people)* die volle Stärke; **the ship's ~**: die volle Schiffsbesatzung; **c)** *(Ling.)* Ergänzung, *die.* **2.** ['kɒmplɪment] *v. t.* ergänzen

complementary [kɒmplɪ'mentərɪ] **a)** *(completing)* ergänzend; **b)** *(completing each other)* einander ergänzend; **they are ~ to one another** sie ergänzen einander

complementary 'colour *n.* Komplementärfarbe, *die*

complete [kəm'pli:t] **1.** *adj.* **a)** vollständig; *(in number)* vollzählig; komplett; **a ~ edition** eine Gesamtausgabe; **the ~ works of Schiller** Schillers sämtliche Werke; **make a ~ confession** ein umfassendes Geständnis ablegen; **a house ~ with contents** ein Haus mit allem Inventar; **b)** *(finished)* fertig; abgeschlossen ⟨*Arbeit*⟩; fertiggestellt ⟨*Gebäude, Bauwerk*⟩; **c)** *(absolute)* völlig; total, komplett ⟨*Idiot, Reinfall, Ignoranz*⟩; absolut ⟨*Chaos, Katastrophe*⟩; vollkommen ⟨*Ruhe*⟩; total, *(ugs.)* blutig ⟨*Anfänger, Amateur*⟩; **a ~ stranger** ein völlig Fremder; **meet with ~ approval** uneingeschränkte Zustimmung finden; **d)** *(accomplished)* perfekt ⟨*Sportler, Reiter, Gentleman usw.*⟩. **2.** *v. t.* **a)** *(finish)* beenden; fertigstellen ⟨*Gebäude, Arbeit*⟩; abschließen ⟨*Vertrag*⟩; **b)** *(make whole)* vervollkommnen, vollkommen machen ⟨*Glück*⟩; vervollständigen, *(geh.)* komplettieren ⟨*Sammlung*⟩; **c)** *(make whole amount of)* vollzählig machen; vollmachen *(ugs.)*; **d)** ausfüllen ⟨*Fragebogen, Formular*⟩

completely [kəm'pli:tlɪ] *adv.* völlig; absolut ⟨*erfolgreich*⟩

completeness [kəm'pli:tnɪs] *n., no pl.* Vollständigkeit, *die; (in numbers)* Vollzähligkeit, *die*

completion [kəm'pli:ʃn] *n.* Beendigung, *die; (of building, work)* Fertigstellung, *die; (of contract)* Abschluß, *der; (of questionnaire, form)* Ausfüllen, *das;* **on ~ of the course** nach Abschluß des Kurses; **on ~ of all the formalities** nach Erledigung aller Formalitäten; **on ~ of the sale** bei Kaufabschluß

com'pletion date *n.* Datum der Fertigstellung/des Vertragsabschlusses

complex ['kɒmpleks] **1.** *adj.* **a)** *(complicated)* kompliziert; **b)** *(composite)* komplex; **c)** *(Ling.)* **a ~ sentence** ein Satzgefüge; **d)** *(Chem., Math.)* komplex. **2.** *n. (also Psych.)* Komplex, *der;* **a [building] ~**: ein Gebäudekomplex; **have a ~ about sth.** *(coll.)* Komplexe wegen etw. haben

complexion [kəm'plekʃn] *n.* Gesichtsfarbe, *die;* Teint, *der; (fig.)* Gesicht, *das;* **of various political ~s** verschiedener politischer Richtungen; **that puts a different ~ on the matter** dadurch sieht die Sache schon anders aus

-complexioned [kəm'plekʃnd] *adj.* *in*

comb. **sallow-/fair-~:** mit gelblichem Teint/mit hellem Teint

complexity [kəm'pleksɪtɪ] *n. see* **complex 1:** Komplexität, *die;* Kompliziertheit, *die*

compliance [kəm'plaɪəns] *n.* **a)** *(action)* Zustimmung, *die* (**with** zu); **act in ~ with sth.** gemäß etw. handeln; **b)** *(unworthy submission)* Unterwürfigkeit, *die;* Willfährigkeit, *die (geh.)*

compliant [kəm'plaɪənt] *adj.* unterwürfig; willfährig *(geh.)*

complicate ['kɒmplɪkeɪt] *v. t.* komplizieren; verkomplizieren

complicated ['kɒmplɪkeɪtɪd] *adj.* kompliziert

complication [kɒmplɪ'keɪʃn] *n.* **a)** Kompliziertheit, *die;* **b)** *(circumstance; also Med.)* Komplikation, *die*

complicity [kəm'plɪsɪtɪ] *n.* Mittäterschaft, *die;* Komplizenschaft, *die* (**in** bei)

compliment 1. ['kɒmplɪmənt] *n.* **a)** *(polite words)* Kompliment, *das;* **pay sb. a ~ [on sth.]** jmdm. [wegen etw.] ein Kompliment machen; **return the ~:** das Kompliment erwidern; *(fig.)* zurückschlagen; **my ~s to the chef** mein Kompliment dem Küchenchef; **b)** *in pl. (formal greetings)* Grüße *Pl.;* Empfehlung, *die;* **my ~s to your parents** eine Empfehlung an Ihre Eltern *(geh.);* **give them my ~s** bitte empfehlen Sie mich ihnen *(geh.);* bitte grüßen Sie sie von mir; **the ~s of the season** Grüße zum Fest; **with the ~s of the management/author** mit den besten Empfehlungen, die Geschäftsleitung/der Verfasser. **2.** ['kɒmplɪment] *v. t. (say polite words to)* **~ sb. on sth.** jmdm. Komplimente wegen etw. machen

complimentary [kɒmplɪ'mentərɪ] *adj.* **a)** *(expressing compliment)* schmeichelhaft; **b)** *(given free as compliment)* Frei-; **a ~ ticket/copy** eine Freikarte/ein Freiexemplar

compline ['kɒmplɪn, 'kɒmplaɪn] *n. (Eccl.)* Komplet, *die*

comply [kəm'plaɪ] *v. i.* **~ with sth.** sich nach etw. richten; **~ with a treaty/conditions** einen Vertrag/Bedingungen erfüllen; **he refused to ~:** er wollte sich nicht danach richten

component [kəm'pəʊnənt] **1.** *n.* **a)** Bestandteil, *der; (of machine)* [Einzel]teil, *das; (in manufacturing)* Teilfabrikat, *das;* **b)** *(Math.)* Komponente, *die.* **2.** *adj.* **a ~ part** ein Bestandteil; **the ~ parts of a car** die [Einzel]teile eines Wagens

comport [kəm'pɔːt] *v. refl. (formal)* sich verhalten

compose [kəm'pəʊz] *v. t.* **a)** *(make up)* bilden; **be ~d of** sich zusammensetzen aus; **b)** *(construct)* verfassen ‹*Rede, Gedicht, Liedertext, Libretto*›; abfassen, aufsetzen ‹*Brief*›; **c)** *(Mus.)* komponieren; **d)** *(Printing)* setzen; **e)** *(arrange)* in Ordnung bringen ‹*Aussehen, Kleider usw.*›; **~ oneself to** *or* **for an action** sich auf eine Handlung konzentrieren; **~ one's thoughts** Ordnung in seine Gedanken bringen; **f)** *(calm)* **~ oneself** sich zusammennehmen; **g)** *(put together)* anordnen, arrangieren ‹*Blumen, Sträucher usw.*›

composed [kəm'pəʊzd] *adj. (calm)* gefaßt

composer [kəm'pəʊzə(r)] *n.* **a)** *(of music)* Komponist, *der*/Komponistin, *die;* **b)** *(of poem etc.)* Verfasser, *der*/Verfasserin, *die*

composite ['kɒmpəzɪt] **1.** *adj.* **a)** zusammengesetzt; **a ~ illustration/photograph** eine Bild-/Fotomontage; **b)** *(Bot.)* **~ flower/plant** Korbblütler, *der;* Komposite, *die (fachspr.).* **2.** *n.* **a)** Gemisch, *das;* Komposition, *die (geh.);* **b)** *(Bot.)* Korbblütler, *der;* Komposite, *die (fachspr.)*

composition [kɒmpə'zɪʃn] *n.* **a)** *(act)* Zusammenstellung, *die; (construction)* Herstellung, *die; (formation of words)* Wortbildung, *die;* Komposition, *die (fachspr.);* **b)** *(constitution) (of soil, etc.)* Zusammensetzung, *die; (mental constitution)* Wesen, *das; (of picture)* Aufbau, *der;* **c)** *(composed thing) (mixture)* Gemisch, *das; (piece of writing)* Darstellung, *die; (essay)* Aufsatz, *der; (piece of music)* Komposition, *die;* **d)** *(construction in writing) (of sentences)* Konstruktion, *die; (of prose, verse)* Verfassen, *das; (literary production)* Schreiben, *das; (Mus.)* Komposition, *die;* Komponieren, *das; (art of ~)* Komposition, *die;* Kompositionslehre, *die;* **e)** *(Printing)* Setzen, *das;* Satz, *der;* **f)** *(formal: compromise)* Abmachung, *die; (with creditors etc.)* Vergleich, *der;* Akkord, *der; (sum paid to creditors)* Vergleichssumme, *die;* **g)** *(formal: of disagreement)* Beilegung, *die*

composition 'floor *n.* Estrich, *der*

compositor [kəm'pɒzɪtə(r)] *n. (Printing)* Schriftsetzer, *der*/-setzerin, *die*

compos mentis ['kɒmpɒs 'mentɪs] *adj.* zurechnungsfähig; bei Trost *(ugs.)*

compost ['kɒmpɒst] **1.** *n.* Kompost, *der; (fig.)* Nährboden, *der.* **2.** *v. t.* kompostieren

compost: ~ heap, ~ pile *ns.* Komposthaufen, *der*

composure [kəm'pəʊʒə(r)] *n.* Gleichmut, *der;* **lose/regain one's ~:** die Fassung verlieren/wiederfinden; **upset sb.'s ~:** jmdn. aus der Fassung bringen

compote ['kɒmpəʊt] *n.* Kompott, *das*

[1]**compound 1.** ['kɒmpaʊnd] *adj.* **a)** *(of several ingredients)* zusammengesetzt; **a ~ substance** eine Verbindung; **b)** *(of several parts)* kombiniert; **a ~ word** ein zusammengesetztes Wort; eine Zusammensetzung; **c)** *(Zool.)* **~ eye** Facettenauge, *das;* **d)** *(Bot.)* zusammengesetzt; **e)** *(Med.)* **~ fracture** komplizierter Bruch; **f)** *(Ling.)* zusammengesetzt ‹*Zeit*›; **~ sentence** Satzreihe, *die.* **2.** *n.* **a)** *(mixture)* Mischung, *die;* **b)** *(Ling.)* Kompositum, *das;* Zusammensetzung, *die;* **c)** *(Chem.)* Verbindung, *die.* **3.** [kəm'paʊnd] *v. t.* **a)** *(mix)* mischen ‹*Bestandteile*›; *(fig.)* vereinigen; *(combine)* zusammensetzen ‹*Wort*›; *(make up)* herstellen ‹*Präparat*›; **be ~ed of ...:** sich aus ... zusammensetzen; **b)** *(increase, complicate)* verschlimmern ‹*Schwierigkeiten, Verletzung usw.*›; **c)** *(formal: settle)* beilegen ‹*Affäre, Meinungsverschiedenheit*›; begleichen ‹*Schulden*›. **4.** *v. i. (formal)* **~ with sb. for sth.** sich mit jmdm. auf etw. *(Akk.)* einigen

[2]**compound** ['kɒmpaʊnd] *n.* **a)** *(enclosed space)* umzäuntes Gebiet *od.* Gelände; **prison ~:** Gefängnishof, *der;* **b)** *(enclosure round building)* Grundstück, *das;* **embassy ~:** Botschaftsgelände, *das*

compound interest [kɒmpaʊnd 'ɪntrɪst] *n. (Finance)* Zinseszinsen *Pl.;* Zinseszins, *der*

comprehend [kɒmprɪ'hend] *v. t.* **a)** *(understand)* begreifen; verstehen; **b)** *(include, embrace)* umfassen

comprehensibility [kɒmprɪhensɪ'bɪlɪtɪ] *n., no pl.* Faßlichkeit, *die;* Verständlichkeit, *die*

comprehensible [kɒmprɪ'hensɪbl] *adj.* faßbar; verständlich; **~ only to specialists** nur Fachleuten *od.* für Fachleute verständlich

comprehensibly [kɒmprɪ'hensɪblɪ] *adv.* verständlich

comprehension [kɒmprɪ'henʃn] *n.* **a)** *(understanding)* Verständnis, *das;* **her behaviour is beyond my ~:** für ihr Benehmen habe ich kein Verständnis; **b) ~ [exercise/test]** Übung zum Textverständnis

comprehensive [kɒmprɪ'hensɪv] **1.** *adj.* **a)** *(inclusive)* umfassend; universal ‹*Verstand*›; allseitig, universal ‹*Begriffsvermögen*›; **b)** *(Sch.)* **~ school** Gesamtschule, *die;* **go ~** ‹*Schule:*› zur Gesamtschule [gemacht] werden; ‹*Stadt:*› die Gesamtschule einführen; **c)** *(Insurance)* Vollkasko-; **~ policy** Vollkaskoversicherung, *die;* **have you ~ insurance?** sind Sie vollkaskoversichert?. **2.** *n. (Sch.)* Gesamtschule, *die*

comprehensively [kɒmprɪ'hensɪvlɪ] *adv.* umfassend; **~ beaten** deutlich geschlagen

comprehensiveness [kɒmprɪ'hensɪvnɪs] *n., no pl.* Allseitigkeit, *die;* **the ~ of the book is surprising** das Buch ist überraschend umfassend

compress 1. [kəm'pres] *v. t.* **a)** *(squeeze)* zusammenpressen (**into** zu); **b)** komprimieren ‹*Luft, Gas, Bericht*›. **2.** ['kɒmpres] *n. (Med.)* Kompresse, *die*

compressed air [kəmprest 'eə(r)] *adj.* Druck-, Preßluft, *die*

compressible [kəm'presɪbl] *adj.* zusammendrückbar; *(Phys.)* kompressibel

compression [kəm'preʃn] *n.* Kompression, *die;* Verdichtung, *die*

compressor [kəm'presə(r)] *n.* Kompressor, *der;* Verdichter, *der*

comprise [kəm'praɪz] *v. t. (include)* umfassen; *(not exclude)* einschließen; *(consist of)* bestehen aus; *(compose, make up)* bilden

compromise ['kɒmprəmaɪz] **1.** *n.* Kompromiß, *der; attrib.* **~ decision/agreement** Kompromißentscheidung/-vereinbarung, *die.* **2.** *v. i.* Kompromisse/einen Kompromiß schließen; **~ with sb. over sth.** mit jmdm. einen Kompromiß in etw. *(Dat.)* schließen; **agree to ~:** einem Kompromiß zustimmen. **3.** *v. t. (bring under suspicion)* kompromittieren; *(bring into danger)* schaden (+ *Dat.*); **~ oneself** sich kompromittieren; **~ one's reputation** seinem Ruf schaden

compromising ['kɒmprəmaɪzɪŋ] *adj.* kompromittierend

comptroller [kən'trəʊlə(r)] *n.* Controller, *der; Mitarbeiter des betriebswirtschaftlichen Rechnungswesens;* **C~ General** ≈ Präsident des Rechnungshofes

compulsion [kəm'pʌlʃn] *n. (also Psych.)* Zwang, *der;* **be under no ~ to do sth.** keineswegs etw. tun müssen

compulsive [kəm'pʌlsɪv] *adj.* **a)** *(also Psych.)* zwanghaft; pathologisch ‹*Lügner*›; **he is a ~ eater/gambler** er leidet unter Eßzwang/er ist dem Spiel verfallen; **b)** *(irresistible)* **this book is ~ reading/this TV programme is ~ viewing** von diesem Buch/dieser Fernsehsendung kann man sich nicht losreißen

compulsively [kəm'pʌlsɪvlɪ] *adv.* **do sth. ~:** etw. wie unter einem [inneren] Zwang tun

compulsorily [kəm'pʌlsərɪlɪ] *adv.* zwangsweise

compulsory [kəm'pʌlsərɪ] *adj.* obligatorisch; **be ~:** obligatorisch *od.* Pflicht sein; **a ~ subject** ein Pflichtfach; **~ purchase** Enteignung, *die*

compunction [kəm'pʌŋkʃn] *n.* Schuldgefühle; Gewissensbisse *Pl.*

computation [kɒmpjʊ'teɪʃn] *n.* Berechnung, *die;* **form of ~:** Rechenart, *die*

compute [kəm'pjuːt] **1.** *v. t.* berechnen (**at** auf + *Akk.*). **2.** *v. i.* **a)** *(make reckoning)* rechnen; **b)** *(use computer)* Computer/einen Computer benutzen

computer [kəm'pjuːtə(r)] *n.* Computer, *der*

computer: ~-aided, ~-assisted *adjs.* computergestützt; **~ 'graphics** *n. pl.* Computergraphik, *die*

computerisation, computerise, computerised *see* **computeriz-**

computerization [kəmpjuːtəraɪ'zeɪʃn] *n.* Computerisierung, *die*

computerize [kəm'pjuːtəraɪz] *v. t.* computerisieren; auf Computer umstellen ‹*Buchhaltung*›

computerized [kəm'pjuːtəraɪzd] *adj.* computerisiert

computer: ~-'operated *adj.* computergesteuert; rechnergesteuert; **~ 'processing** *n.* elektronische Datenverarbeitung; **~ program** *n.* Programm, *das;* **~ programmer** *n.* Programmierer, *der*/Programmiererin, *die;* **~ programming** *n.* Programmieren, *das;* ~ **terminal** *n.* Terminal, *das;* ~ **'typesetting** *n.* Computersatz, *der*

comrade ['kɒmreɪd] *n.* **a)** Kamerad, *der*/Kameradin, *die;* ~**-in-arms** Kampfgefährte, *der;* Waffenbruder, *der (geh.);* **b)** *(Polit.)* Genosse, *der*/Genossin, *die*

comradely ['kɒmreɪdlɪ, 'kɒmrɪdlɪ] *adj.* kameradschaftlich

comradeship ['kɒmreɪdʃɪp, 'kɒmrɪdʃɪp] *n., no pl.* Kameradschaft, *die;* **a spirit of** ~: Kameradschaftsgeist

[1]con [kɒn] *(coll.)* **1.** *n.* Schwindel, *der.* **2.** *v.t.,* **-nn- a)** *(swindle)* reinlegen *(ugs.);* ~ **sb. out of sth.** jmdm. etw. abschwindeln *od. (ugs.)* abgaunern; **b)** *(persuade)* beschwatzen *(ugs.);* ~ **sb. into believing sth.** jmdm. etw. einreden

[2]con *n., adv., prep. see* **[1]pro**

[3]con *n. (coll.: convict)* Knacki, *der (salopp)*

[4]con *v.t.,* **-nn-** *(arch.: study)* sorgfältig durchlesen

concatenation [kənkætɪ'neɪʃn] *n. (lit. or fig.)* Verkettung, *die*

concave ['kɒnkeɪv] *adj.* konkav; ~ **mirror/lens** Konkav- *od.* Hohlspiegel, *der*/Konkavlinse, *die*

concavity [kən'kævɪtɪ] *n.* Konkavität, *die*

conceal [kən'si:l] *v.t.* verbergen (**from** vor + *Dat.*); ~ **the true state of affairs from sb.** jmdm. den wirklichen Sachverhalt verheimlichen; ~ **vital facts** entscheidende Tatsachen unterschlagen

concealed [kən'si:ld] *adj.* verdeckt; ~ **lighting** indirekte Beleuchtung

concealment [kən'si:lmənt] *n. see* **conceal**: Verbergen, *das;* Verheimlichung, *die;* Unterschlagung, *die;* **stay in** ~: sich versteckt halten

concede [kən'si:d] *v.t. (admit, allow)* zugeben; *(grant)* zugestehen, einräumen ‹*Recht, Privileg*›; *(Sport)* abgeben ‹*Punkte, Spiel*› (**to** an + *Akk.*); zulassen ‹*Tor*›; in Kauf nehmen ‹*Elfmeter*›; ~ **[defeat]** *(in election etc.)* seine Niederlage eingestehen

conceit [kən'si:t] *n.* **a)** *no pl. (vanity)* Einbildung, *die;* **b)** *in pl. (Lit.)* Konzetti *Pl.*

conceited [kən'si:tɪd] *adj.* eingebildet

conceitedly [kən'si:tɪdlɪ] *adv.* eingebildet

conceitedness [kən'si:tɪdnɪs] *n.* Einbildung, *die*

conceivable [kən'si:vəbl] *adj.* vorstellbar; **it's scarcely** ~ **that ...:** man kann sich *(Dat.)* kaum vorstellen, daß ...

conceivably [kən'si:vəblɪ] *adv.* möglicherweise; **he cannot** ~ **have done it** er kann es unmöglich getan haben

conceive [kən'si:v] **1.** *v.t.* **a)** empfangen ‹*Kind*›; **b)** *(form in mind)* sich *(Dat.)* vorstellen *od.* denken; haben, kommen auf (+ *Akk.*) ‹*Idee, Plan*›; ~ **a dislike for sb./sth.** eine Abneigung gegen jmdn./etw. entwickeln; ~ **a liking for sb./sth.** Zuneigung zu jmdm./etw. fassen; **when the idea was first** ~**d** als man erstmals auf die Idee kam; **c)** *(think)* meinen; glauben; **d)** *(express)* fassen; ausdrücken. **2.** *v.i.* **a)** *(become pregnant)* empfangen; **b)** ~ **of sth.** sich *(Dat.)* etw. vorstellen

concentrate ['kɒnsəntreɪt] **1.** *v.t.* konzentrieren, zusammenziehen ‹*Truppen, Flotte*›; zusammendrängen ‹*Wissen, Informationen*›; ~ **one's efforts/energies [up]on sth.** seine Bemühungen/Energien auf etw. *(Akk.)* konzentrieren; ~ **one's mind on sth.** sich auf etw. *(Akk.)* konzentrieren; ~ **the mind** jmds. Gedanken ausschließlich beschäftigen. **2.** *v.i.* sich konzentrieren (**on** auf + *Akk.*); ~ **on doing sth.** sich darauf konzentrieren, etw. zu tun. **3.** *n.* Konzentrat, *das; (animal food)* Kraftfutter, *das*

concentrated ['kɒnsəntreɪtɪd] *adj.* konzentriert; geballt ‹*Haß, Eifersucht*›

concentration [kɒnsən'treɪʃn] *n.* **a)** *(also Chem.)* Konzentration, *die;* **power[s] of** ~: Konzentrationsfähigkeit, *die;* Konzentrationsvermögen, *das;* **lose one's** ~: sich nicht mehr konzentrieren können; **b)** *(people brought together)* Ansammlung, *die; (of troops etc.)* Konzentration, *die*

concen'tration camp *n.* Konzentrationslager, *das;* KZ, *das*

concentric [kən'sentrɪk] *adj.* konzentrisch; **the circles were** ~ **with each other** die Kreise hatten einen gemeinsamen Mittelpunkt

concept ['kɒnsept] *n.* **a)** *(notion)* Begriff, *der; (idea)* Vorstellung, *die;* **b)** *(invention)* Idee, *die;* Konzept, *das;* **a new** ~ **in make-up** eine neue Make-up-Idee; ein neues Make-up-Konzept

conception [kən'sepʃn] **a)** *(idea)* Vorstellung, *die* (**of** von); **I had no** ~ **of how ...:** ich hatte keine Vorstellung, wie ...; **the original** ~ **of a picture** die ursprüngliche Konzeption eines Bildes; **b)** *(conceiving)* Vorstellungsvermögen, *das;* **great powers of** ~: ein großes Vorstellungsvermögen; **c)** *(of child)* Empfängnis, *die*

conceptual [kən'septjʊəl] *adj.* begrifflich

conceptualize [kən'septjʊəlaɪz] *v.t.* begrifflich fassen

conceptually [kən'septjʊəlɪ] *adv.* begrifflich; **the plan is** ~ **good** in der Vorstellung *od.* als Idee ist der Plan gut

concern [kən'sɜ:n] **1.** *v.t.* **a)** *(affect)* betreffen; **as** ~**s ..., so far as ... is** ~**ed** was ... betrifft; **all that** ~**s us is whether ...:** uns hat nur zu interessieren, ob ...; **'to whom it may** ~**'** ≈ „Bestätigung"; *(on certificate, testimonial)* ≈ „Zeugnis"; **b)** *(interest)* ~ **oneself with** *or* **about sth.** sich mit etw. befassen; **she does not** ~ **herself with politics** sie kümmert sich nicht um Politik; **c)** *(trouble)* **the news/her health greatly** ~**s me** ich bin über diese Nachricht tief beunruhigt/ihre Gesundheit bereitet mir große Sorgen. **2.** *n.* **a)** *(relation)* **have no** ~ **with sth.** mit etw. nichts zu tun haben; **have a** ~ **in sth.** an etw. *(Dat.)* beteiligt sein *od.* einen Anteil haben; **b)** *(anxiety)* Besorgnis, *die; (interest)* Interesse, *das;* **a matter of general** ~: eine Sache, die alle beunruhigt/eine Sache von allgemeinem Interesse; **an expression of** ~ **on one's face** ein besorgter Gesichtsausdruck; **express** ~: Sorge ausdrücken; **c)** *(matter)* Angelegenheit, *die;* **that's no** ~ **of mine** das geht mich nichts an; **it's his** ~: das ist seine Sache *od.* seine Angelegenheit; **d)** *(firm)* Unternehmen, *das; see also* **going 2 e**

concerned [kən'sɜ:nd] *adj.* **a)** *(involved)* betroffen; *(interested)* interessiert; **the people** ~: die Betroffenen; **the firms/countries** ~: die betroffenen Firmen/Länder; **we are not** ~ **with it** damit haben wir nichts zu tun; **where work/health** *etc.* **is** ~: wenn es um die Arbeit/die Gesundheit *usw.* geht; **as** *or* **so far as I'm** ~: was mich betrifft *od.* anbelangt; **not as far as I'm** ~: von mir aus nicht; **b)** *(implicated)* verwickelt (**in** in + *Akk.*); **c)** *(troubled)* besorgt; **I am** ~ **to hear/learn that ...:** ich höre/erfahre mit Sorge, daß ...; **I was** ~ **at the news** die Nachricht beunruhigte mich; **I am very** ~ **for** *or* **about him/his health** er/seine Gesundheit macht mir Sorgen

concerning [kən'sɜ:nɪŋ] *prep.* bezüglich

concernment [kən'sɜ:nmənt] *n.* **a)** Beteiligung, *die;* **b)** *(anxiety)* Sorge, *die*

concert 1. ['kɒnsət] *n.* **a)** *(of music)* Konzert, *das;* **b)** *(agreement, union)* Übereinkunft, *die;* **work in** ~ **with sb.** mit jmdm. zusammenarbeiten; **c)** *(combined sounds)* Chor, *der;* Konzert, *das;* **in** ~: im Chor. **2.** [kən'sɜ:t] *v.t.* abstimmen ‹*Maßnahmen, Pläne*›

concerted [kən'sɜ:tɪd] *adj.* vereint; gemeinsam; ~ **action** eine konzertierte Aktion; **make a** ~ **effort** mit vereinten Kräften vorgehen

concert: ~**-goer** *n.* Konzertbesucher, *der*/-besucherin, *die;* ~ **'grand** *n.* Konzertflügel, *der;* ~**-hall** *n.* Konzertsaal, *der; (building)* Konzerthalle, *die*

concertina [kɒnsə'ti:nə] **1.** *n. (Mus.)* Konzertina, *die.* **2.** *v.i.* [wie eine Ziehharmonika] zusammengeschoben werden

'concert-master *n. (esp. Amer.)* Konzertmeister, *der*

concerto [kən'tʃɜ:təʊ, kən'tʃeətəʊ] *n., pl.* ~**s** *or* **concerti** [kən'tʃeəti:] *(Mus.)* Konzert, *das*

concert: ~ **overture** *n. (Mus.)* Konzertouvertüre, *die;* ~ **pianist** *n.* Konzertpianist, *der*/-pianistin, *die;* ~ **pitch** *n.* Kammerton, *der*

concession [kən'seʃn] *n.* Konzession, *die; (voluntary yielding)* Zugeständnis, *das*

concessionaire [kənseʃə'neə(r)] *n.* Konzessionär, *der*/Konzessionärin, *die*

concessionary [kən'seʃənərɪ] *adj.* Konzessions-; ~ **rate/fare** ermäßigter Tarif

concessionnaire *see* **concessionaire**

concessive [kən'sesɪv] *adj. (Ling.)* konzessiv; einräumend; **a** ~ **clause** ein Konzessiv- *od.* Einräumungssatz

conch [kɒntʃ, kɒŋk] *n. (Zool.)* Meeresschnecke, *die; (shell)* Gehäuse einer Meeresschnecke

concierge ['kɔ:nsɪeəʒ, 'kɒnsɪeəʒ] *n.* Concierge, *der/die; (in hotel)* Empfangschef, *der*

conciliate [kən'sɪlɪeɪt] *v.t.* **a)** *(reconcile)* in Einklang bringen ‹*Gegensätze, Theorien*›; **b)** *(pacify)* besänftigen; beschwichtigen

conciliation [kənsɪlɪ'eɪʃn] *n.* **a)** *(reconcilement)* Versöhnung, *die;* **b)** *(pacification)* Besänftigung, *die;* Beschwichtigung, *die;* **c)** *(in industrial relations)* Schlichtung, *die;* ~ **board** Schlichtungsausschuß, *der*

conciliator [kən'sɪlɪeɪtə(r)] *n.* Schlichter, *der*/Schlichterin, *die*

conciliatory [kən'sɪljətərɪ] *adj.* versöhnlich; *(pacifying)* beschwichtigend; besänftigend

concise [kən'saɪs] *adj.* kurz und prägnant; knapp, konzis ‹*Stil*›; **be** ~ ‹*Person:*› sich knapp fassen; **a** ~ **dictionary** ein Handwörterbuch

concisely [kən'saɪslɪ] *adv.* kurz und prägnant; knapp, konzis ‹*schreiben*›

conciseness [kən'saɪsnɪs], **concision** [kən'sɪʒn] *ns., no pl.* Kürze, *die;* Prägnanz, *die*

conclave ['kɒnkleɪv] *n.* **a)** *(RC Ch.)* Konklave, *das;* **b)** *(private meeting)* Klausurtagung, *die*

conclude [kən'klu:d] **1.** *v.t.* **a)** *(end)* beschließen; beenden; **b)** *(infer)* schließen; folgern; **c)** *(reach decision)* beschließen; ~ **from the evidence that ...:** auf Grund des Beweismaterials zu dem Schluß kommen, daß ...; **d)** *(agree on)* schließen ‹*Bündnis, Vertrag*›. **2.** *v.i. (end)* schließen

concluding [kən'klu:dɪŋ] *attrib. adj.* abschließend

conclusion [kən'klu:ʒn] *n.* **a)** *(end)* Abschluß, *der;* **in** ~: zum Abschluß; **b)** *(result)* Ausgang, *der;* **c)** *(decision reached)* Beschluß, *der;* **come to a** ~: einen Beschluß fassen; **d)** *(inference)* Schluß, *der;* **draw** *or* **reach a** ~: zu einem Schluß kommen; **e)** *(Logic)* [Schluß]folgerung, *die;* Konklusion, *die (fachspr.);* **f)** *(agreement)* Abschluß, *der*

conclusive [kən'klu:sɪv] *adj.* schlüssig

conclusively [kən'klu:sɪvlɪ] *adv.* abschließend ‹*regeln*›; schlüssig ‹*beweisen, belegen*›; eindeutig ‹*klären*›

conclusiveness [kən'klu:sɪvnɪs] *n., no pl.* Schlüssigkeit, *die*

concoct [kən'kɒkt] *v.t.* zubereiten; zusammenbrauen ‹*Trank*›; *(fig.)* sich *(Dat.)* ausdenken ‹*Geschichte*›; aushecken ‹*Komplott, Intrige usw.*›; sich *(Dat.)* zurechtlegen ‹*Ausrede, Alibi*›

concoction [kən'kɒkʃn] *n.* **a)** *(preparing)* Zubereitung, *die;* **b)** *(drink)* Gebräu, *das; (meal)* Fraß, *der (ugs.)*

concomitant [kən'kɒmɪtənt] *(formal)* **1.** *adj.* begleitend; *(simultaneous)* gleichzeitig; ~ **circumstances** Begleitumstände. **2.** *n.* Begleiterscheinung, *die*

concord ['kɒŋkɔ:d, 'kɒnkɔ:d] *n.* **a)** *(agreement)* Eintracht, *die;* **b)** *(treaty)* Freundschaftsvertrag, *der;* **c)** *(Mus.)* Harmonie, *die;* **d)** *(Ling.)* Kongruenz, *die*

concordance [kən'kɔ:dəns] *n.* **a)** *(formal) (agreement)* Übereinstimmung, *die;* **b)** *(index)* Konkordanz, *die*

concordant [kən'kɔ:dənt] *adj. (formal)* übereinstimmend; **be ~ with sth.** mit etw. übereinstimmen

concordat [kən'kɔ:dæt] *n.* Konkordat, *das*

concourse ['kɒŋkɔ:s, 'kɒnkɔ:s] *n. (of public building)* Halle, *die;* **station ~:** Bahnhofshalle, *die*

concrete ['kɒnkri:t] **1.** *adj. (specific)* konkret; ~ **noun** *(Ling.)* Konkretum, *das.* **2.** *n.* Beton, *der; attrib.* Beton-; aus Beton *präd.* **3.** *v.t.* betonieren; *(embed in ~)* ~ **[in]** einbetonieren

concretely ['kɒnkri:tlɪ] *adv.* konkret

concrete ['kɒnkri:t]: **~-mixer** *n.* Betonmischer, *der;* Betonmischmaschine, *die;* **~ poetry** *n.* konkrete Poesie

concretion [kən'kri:ʃn] *n.* **a)** *no pl. (coalescence)* Verwachsung, *die;* Zusammenwachsen, *das;* **b)** *(Med.)* Konkrement, *das;* **c)** *(Geol.)* Konkretion, *die*

concubine ['kɒŋkjʊbaɪn] *n.* **a)** *(formal: cohabiting mistress)* Konkubine, *die;* **b)** *(secondary wife)* Nebenfrau, *die*

concur [kən'kɜ:(r)] *v.i.,* **-rr-: a)** *(agree)* ~ **[with sb.] [in sth.]** [jmdm.] [in etw. *(Dat.)*] zustimmen *od.* beipflichten; **b)** *(coincide, combine)* zusammenkommen

concurrence [kən'kʌrəns] *n., no pl.* **a)** *(general agreement)* Übereinstimmung, *die;* **b)** *(coincidence)* Zusammentreffen, *das*

concurrent [kən'kʌrənt] *adj.* **a)** gleichzeitig; **be ~ with sth.** gleichzeitig mit etw. stattfinden; ~ **sentences** zu einer Gesamtstrafe zusammengefaßte Einzelstrafen; **b)** *(agreeing)* übereinstimmend; **be ~ with sth.** mit etw. übereinstimmen

concurrently [kən'kʌrəntlɪ] *adv.* **a)** *(simultaneously)* gleichzeitig; **b)** *(Law)* **run ~** ‹*Gefängnisstrafen:*› zu einer Gesamtstrafe zusammengefaßt sein/werden

concuss [kən'kʌs] *v.t.* **be ~ed** eine Gehirnerschütterung haben

concussion [kən'kʌʃn] *n. (Med.)* Gehirnerschütterung, *die;* Konkussion, *die (fachspr.)*

condemn [kən'dem] *v.t.* **a)** *(censure)* verdammen; **b)** *(Law: sentence)* verurteilen; *(fig.)* verdammen; **~ sb. to death/to life imprisonment** jmdn. zum Tode/zu lebenslanger Haft verurteilen; **be ~ed to do sth.** *(fig.)* dazu verdammt sein, etw. zu tun; **c)** *(give judgement against)* aburteilen; **d)** *(show to be guilty)* überführen; **e)** *(declare unfit)* für unbewohnbar erklären ‹*Gebäude*›; für ungenießbar erklären ‹*Fleisch*›

condemnation [kɒndem'neɪʃn] *n.* **a)** *(censure)* Verdammung, *die;* **b)** *(Law: conviction)* Verurteilung, *die*

condemnatory [kən'demnətərɪ] *adj.* verdammend; scharf mißbilligend ‹*Blick*›

condemned [kən'demd] *adj.* **a)** verurteilt; **a ~ man** ein zum Tode Verurteilter; ein Todeskandidat; **b) a ~ house** ein Haus, das auf der Abrißliste steht; **c) ~ cell** Todeszelle, *die*

condensate [kən'denseɪt, 'kɒndənseɪt] *n.* Kondensat, *das*

condensation [kɒnden'seɪʃn] *n.* **a)** *no pl. (condensing)* Kondensation, *die;* **b)** *(what is condensed)* Kondensat, *das; (water)* Kondenswasser, *das;* **c)** *(abridgement)* [Ver]kürzung, *die; (abridged form)* Kurzfassung, *die*

conden'sation trail *n. (Aeronaut.)* Kondensstreifen, *der*

condense [kən'dens] **1.** *v.t.* **a)** komprimieren; **~d milk** Kondensmilch, *die;* **b)** *(Phys., Chem.)* kondensieren; **c)** *(make concise)* zusammenfassen; **in a ~d form** in verkürzter Form. **2.** *v.i.* kondensieren

condenser [kən'densə(r)] *n.* **a)** *(of steam-engine)* Kondensator, *der;* **b)** *(Electr.) see* **capacitor; c)** *(Chem.)* Kühler, *der*

condescend [kɒndɪ'send] *v.i.* **~ to do sth.** geruhen *(geh.),* etw. zu tun; sich dazu herablassen, etw. zu tun; **~ to sb.** jmdn. von oben herab behandeln

condescending [kɒndɪ'sendɪŋ] *adj. (derog.)* herablassend

condescendingly [kɒndɪ'sendɪŋlɪ] *adv. (derog.)* herablassend; von oben herab

condescension [kɒndɪ'senʃn] *n. (derog.: patronizing manner)* Herablassung, *die;* **his air of ~:** sein herablassendes Gebaren

condiment ['kɒndɪmənt] *n.* Gewürz, *das*

condition [kən'dɪʃn] **1.** *n.* **a)** *(stipulation)* [Vor]bedingung, *die;* Voraussetzung, *die;* **make it a ~ that ...:** es zur Bedingung machen, daß ...; **on [the] ~ that ...:** unter der Voraussetzung *od.* Bedingung, daß ...; **b)** *(in pl.: circumstances)* Umstände *Pl.;* **weather/light ~s** Witterungsverhältnisse/Lichtverhältnisse; **under** *or* **in present ~s** unter den gegenwärtigen Umständen *od.* Bedingungen; **living/working ~s** Unterkunfts-/Arbeitsbedingungen; **c)** *(state of being) (of athlete, etc.)* Kondition, *die;* Form, *die; (of thing)* Zustand, *der; (of invalid, patient, etc.)* Verfassung, *die;* **keep sth. in good ~:** etw. in gutem Zustand erhalten; **be out of ~/in [good] ~** ‹*Person:*› schlecht/gut in Form sein; **sb. is in no ~ to do sth.** jmds. Gesundheitszustand erlaubt ihm nicht, etw. zu tun; **she's in no ~ to travel/drive** sie ist nicht reisefähig/fahrtüchtig; **get into ~** *(Sport)* sich in Form *od.* Kondition bringen; **d)** *(Med.)* Leiden, *das;* **have a heart/lung** *etc.* **~:** ein Herz-/Lungenleiden *usw.* haben; herz-/lungenleidend sein. **2.** *v.t.* **a)** *(determine)* bestimmen; **b)** *(make suitable or fit)* in Form bringen ‹*Sportler, Tier, Haar*›; *see also* **air-conditioned; c)** *(accustom)* dressieren ‹*Pferd, Hund*›; **~ sb. to sth.** jmdn. an etw. *(Akk.)* gewöhnen; **be ~ed to do sth.** gewöhnt sein, etw. zu tun; **be ~ed to respond to a stimulus** konditioniert sein, auf einen Reiz zu reagieren; *see also* **reflex 1**

conditional [kən'dɪʃənl] **1.** *adj.* **a)** bedingt; **be ~ [up]on sth.** von etw. abhängen; **b)** *(Ling.)* konditional; bedingend; **~ clause** Konditional- *od.* Bedingungssatz, *der;* **~ mood/tense** Konditional[is], *der.* **2.** *n. (Ling.)* Konditional[is], *der*

conditionally [kən'dɪʃənəlɪ] *adv.* mit *od.* unter Vorbehalt

conditioner [kən'dɪʃənə(r)] *n.* **a)** *see* **air-conditioner; b)** *see* **hair-conditioner**

condole [kən'dəʊl] *v.i. (formal)* **~ with sb. [up]on sth.** jmdm. zu etw. seine Anteilnahme *od.* sein Mitgefühl aussprechen; **~ with sb. on the death of his mother** jmdm. zum Tode seiner Mutter kondolieren

condolence [kən'dəʊləns] *n.* Anteilnahme, *die;* Mitgefühl, *das; (on death)* Beileid, *das;* **offer sb. one's ~s** jmdm. sein Mitgefühl/sein Beileid *od.* seine Teilnahme aussprechen; **letter of ~:** Beileidsbrief, *der;* Kondolenzbrief, *der;* **please accept my ~s** darf ich Ihnen mein Beileid *od.* meine [An]teilnahme aussprechen?

condom ['kɒndəm] *n.* Kondom, *das od. der;* Präservativ, *das*

condominium [kɒndə'mɪnɪəm] *n.* **a)** *(Polit.)* Kondominium, *das;* **b)** *(Amer.: property)* Appartementhaus [mit Eigentumswohnungen]; *(single dwelling)* Eigentumswohnung, *die*

condone [kən'dəʊn] *v.t.* **a)** hinwegsehen über (+ *Akk.*); *(approve)* billigen; **b)** *(Law)* in Kauf nehmen; stillschweigend billigen

condor ['kɒndə(r)] *n. (Ornith.)* Kondor, *der*

conduce [kən'dju:s] *v.i. (formal)* **~ to** förderlich sein (+ *Dat.*); beitragen zu

conducive [kən'dju:sɪv] *adj.* **be ~ to sth.** einer Sache *(Dat.)* förderlich sein; zu etw. beitragen

conduct 1. ['kɒndʌkt] *n.* **a)** *(behaviour)* Verhalten, *das;* **good ~:** gute Führung; **rules of ~:** Verhaltensregeln; **b)** *(way of ~ing)* Führung, *die; (of conference, inquiry, operation)* Leitung, *die;* Durchführung, *die;* **his ~ of the war** seine Kriegsführung; **their ~ of the negotiations** ihre Verhandlungsführung; **c)** *(leading, guidance)* Geleit, *das; see also* **safe conduct. 2.** [kən'dʌkt] *v.t.* **a)** *(Mus.)* dirigieren; **b)** *(direct)* führen ‹*Geschäfte, Krieg, Gespräch*›; durchführen ‹*Operation, Untersuchung*›; leiten ‹*Konferenz*›; **~ one's affairs** seine Geschäfte führen; **c)** *(Phys.)* leiten ‹*Wärme, Elektrizität*›; **d) ~ oneself** sich verhalten; **e)** *(guide)* führen; **~ sb. away [from]** jmdn. wegführen [von]; **a ~ed tour [of a museum/factory]** eine [Museums-/Werks]führung

conduction [kən'dʌkʃn] *n. (Phys.)* Leitung, *die*

conductivity [kɒndək'tɪvɪtɪ] *n. (Phys.)* Leitfähigkeit, *die;* Konduktivität, *die (fachspr.)*

conductor [kən'dʌktə(r)] *n.* **a)** *(Mus.)* Dirigent, *der*/Dirigentin, *die;* **b)** *(of bus, tram)* Schaffner, *der; (Amer.: of train)* Zugführer, *der;* Schaffner, *der (ugs.);* **c)** *(Phys.)* Leiter, *der;* Konduktor, *der (fachspr.);* **~ rail** Strom-, Sammelschiene, *die*

conductress [kən'dʌktrɪs] *n.* Schaffnerin, *die*

conduit ['kɒndɪt, 'kɒndjʊɪt] *n.* **a)** Leitung, *die;* Kanal, *der (auch fig.);* **b)** *(Electr.)* Isolierrohr, *das*

cone [kəʊn] **1.** *n.* **a)** Kegel, *der;* Konus, *der (fachspr.); (traffic ~)* Leitkegel, *der;* Pylon, *der (fachspr.);* Pylone, *die (fachspr.);* **b)** *(Bot.)* Zapfen, *der;* **c) ice-cream ~:** Eistüte, *die;* **d)** *(Anat.)* Zapfen, *der.* **2.** *v.t.* **~ off** [mit Leitkegeln *od.* Pylonen] absperren ‹*Fahrbahn*›

confab ['kɒnfæb] *n. (coll.)* Unterhaltung, *die;* Schwätzchen, *das (ugs.); (discussion)* Besprechung, *die*

confection [kən'fekʃn] *n.* **a)** Konfekt, *das;* **b)** *(mixing, compounding)* Anfertigung, *die;* **c)** *(article of dress)* [Damen]modeartikel, *der*

confectioner [kən'fekʃənə(r)] *n. (maker)* Hersteller von Süßigkeiten; *(retailer)* Süßwarenhändler, *der; (cake decorator)* Konditor, *der;* Zuckerbäcker, *der (veralt., südd., österr.);* **~'s [shop]** Süßwarengeschäft, *das;* **~s' sugar** *(Amer.)* Puderzucker, *der*

confectionery [kən'fekʃənərɪ] *n.* **a)** Süßwaren *Pl.; (cakes etc.)* Konditoreiwaren *Pl.;* **b)** *(shop)* Süßwarengeschäft, *das;* **c)** *(confectioner's art)* Konditorei, *die;* Zuckerbäckerei, *die (veralt., südd., österr.)*

confederacy [kən'fedərəsɪ] *n.* **a)** *(league, alliance)* Bündnis, *das;* **b)** *(conspiracy)* Verschwörung, *die;* **c)** *(body)* Konföderation, *die;* **the [Southern] C~** *(Amer. Hist.)* die Konföderierten

confederate 1. [kən'fedərət] *adj.* **a)** *(allied)* verbündet; **b)** *(Polit.)* konföderiert; **the C~ States** *(Amer. Hist.)* die Konföderierten Staaten von Amerika. **2.** *n.* Verbündete, *der/die; (accomplice)* Komplize, *der*/Komplizin, *die;* **C~** *(Amer. Hist.)* Konföderierte, *der.* **3.** [kən'fedəreɪt] *v.t.* vereinigen. **4.** *v.i.* sich verbünden *od.* zusammenschließen

confederation [kənfedə'reɪʃn] *n.* **a)** *(Polit.)* [Staaten]bund, *der;* **the Swiss C~:** die Schweizerische Eidgenossenschaft; **b)** *(alliance)* Bund, *der;* **C~ of British Industry** *britischer Unternehmerverband*

confer [kən'fɜ(r)] **1.** *v. t.*, **-rr-:** ~ **a title/degree/knighthood [up]on sb.** jmdm. einen Titel/Grad verleihen/jmdn. zum Ritter schlagen; ~ **a quality [up]on sth.** einer Sache *(Dat.)* eine Eigenschaft verleihen. **2.** *v. i.*, **-rr-:** ~ **with sb.** sich mit jmdm. beraten
conference ['kɒnfərəns] *n.* **a)** *(meeting)* Konferenz, *die;* Tagung, *die;* **b)** *(consultation)* Beratung, *die; (business discussion)* Besprechung, *die;* **be in** ~: in einer Besprechung sein
conference: ~**-room** *n.* Konferenzraum, *der; (smaller)* Besprechungszimmer, *das;* ~**-table** *n.* Konferenztisch, *der;* **get round the** ~**-table** *(fig.)* sich an den Verhandlungstisch setzen
conferment [kən'fɜ:mənt] *n.* Verleihung, *die*
confess [kən'fes] **1.** *v. t.* **a)** zugeben; gestehen; **he** ~**ed himself to be the culprit** er gestand, der Schuldige zu sein; **I** ~ **myself a traditionalist** ich bekenne mich als Traditionalist; **b)** *(Eccl.)* beichten; ~ **one's sins to a priest** einem Priester seine Sünden beichten *od.* bekennen; **c)** *(Eccl.)* **the priest** ~**ed the penitent** der Priester nahm dem reuigen Sünder die Beichte ab. **2.** *v. i.* **a)** ~ **to sth.** etw. gestehen; ~ **to being unable to do sth.** gestehen *od.* zugeben, daß man etw. nicht kann; **b)** *(Eccl.)* beichten **(to sb.** jmdm.); ⟨*Priester:*⟩ die Beichte abnehmen
confessed [kən'fest] *adj.* geständig ⟨*Verbrecher*⟩; **a** ~ **homosexual** jemand, der sich dazu bekennt, homosexuell zu sein
confessedly [kən'fesɪdlɪ] *adv.* zugegebenermaßen; *(avowedly)* eingestandenermaßen
confession [kən'feʃn] *n.* **a)** *(of offence etc.)* Geständnis, *das;* **on** *or* **by one's own** ~: nach eigenem Geständnis; **I have a** ~ **to make** ich muß ein Geständnis ablegen; **b)** *(Eccl.: of sins etc.)* Beichte, *die;* ~ **of sins** Sündenbekenntnis, *das;* **hear sb.'s** ~: jmdm. die Beichte abnehmen; **make one's** ~: seine Sünden bekennen; **c)** *(thing confessed)* Geständnis, *das;* **d)** *(Relig.: denomination)* Konfession, *die;* **what** ~ **is he?** welcher Konfession ist er?; **Roman Catholic** *etc.* **by** ~: römisch-katholischer *usw.* Konfession; **e)** *(Eccl.: confessing)* Bekenntnis, *das;* ~ **of faith** Glaubensbekenntnis, *das*
confessional [kən'feʃənl] *(Eccl.)* **1.** *adj. (of confession)* bekennend; *(denominational)* konfessionell; ~ **schools** Konfessionsschulen. **2.** *n.* **a)** *(stall)* Beichtstuhl, *der;* **b)** *(act)* Beichte, *die*
confessor [kən'fesə(r)] *n. (Eccl.)* Beichtvater, *der*
confetti [kən'fetɪ] *n.* Konfetti, *das*
confidant ['kɒnfɪdænt, kɒnfɪ'dænt] *n. masc.* Vertraute, *der*
confidante ['kɒnfɪdænt, kɒnfɪ'dænt] *n. fem.* Vertraute, *die*
confide [kən'faɪd] **1.** *v. i.* ~ **in sb.** sich jmdm. anvertrauen; ~ **to sb. about sth.** jmdm. etw. anvertrauen. **2.** *v. t.* ~ **sth. to sb.** jmdm. etw. anvertrauen; **he** ~**d that he ...:** er gestand, daß er ...
confidence ['kɒnfɪdəns] *n.* **a)** *(firm trust)* Vertrauen, *das;* **have [complete** *or* **every/no]** ~ **in sb./sth.** [volles/kein] Vertrauen zu jmdm./etw. haben; **have [absolute]** ~ **that ...:** [absolut] sicher sein, daß ...; **place** *or* **put one's** ~ **in sb./sth.** sein Vertrauen in jmdn./etw. setzen; auf jmdn./etw. bauen; **b)** *(assured expectation)* Gewißheit, *die;* Sicherheit, *die;* **in full** ~ **of success** voller Erfolgsgewißheit; **c)** *(self-reliance)* Selbstvertrauen, *das;* **d)** *(boldness)* Dreistigkeit, *die;* **e)** *(telling of private matters)* Vertraulichkeit, *die;* **in** ~: im Vertrauen; **this is in [strict]** ~: das ist [streng] vertraulich; **take sb. into one's** ~: jmdn. ins Vertrauen ziehen; **be in sb.'s** ~: jmds. Vertrauen genießen; **f)** *(thing told in* ~*)* Vertraulichkeit, *die*
confidence: ~ **game** *n. (Amer.) see* ~ **trick;** ~ **man** *n.* Trickbetrüger, *der;* Bauernfänger, *der (ugs.);* ~ **trick** *n. (Brit.)* Trickbetrug, *der;* Bauernfängerei, *die (ugs.);* ~ **trickster** *n. (Brit.) see* ~ **man**
confident ['kɒnfɪdənt] *adj.* **a)** *(trusting, fully assured)* zuversichtlich **(about** in bezug auf + *Akk.*); **be** ~ **that [sth. will happen]** sicher sein, daß [etw. geschieht]; **be** ~ **of sth.** auf etw. *(Akk.)* vertrauen; **b)** *(bold)* dreist; **c)** *(self-assured)* selbstbewußt
confidential [kɒnfɪ'denʃl] *adj.* **a)** *(uttered in confidence)* vertraulich; **b)** *(entrusted with secrets)* persönlich; privat; ~ **secretary** Privatsekretär, *der*/-sekretärin, *die*
confidentiality [kɒnfɪdenʃɪ'ælɪtɪ] *n., no pl.* Vertraulichkeit, *die*
confidentially [kɒnfɪ'denʃəlɪ] *adv.* vertraulich
confidently ['kɒnfɪdəntlɪ] *adv.* zuversichtlich
confiding [kən'faɪdɪŋ] *adj.*, **confidingly** [kən'faɪdɪŋlɪ] *adv.* vertrauensvoll
configuration [kənfɪgjʊ'reɪʃn] *n.* **a)** *(arrangement, outline)* Gestaltung, *die;* **b)** *(Astron., Computing)* Konfiguration, *die*
configure [kən'fɪgə(r)] *v. t. (esp. Computing)* konfigurieren
confine [kən'faɪn] *v. t.* **a)** einsperren; eindämmen ⟨*Flut, Feuer usw.*⟩; **be** ~**d to bed/the house** ans Bett/Haus gefesselt sein; **be** ~**d to barracks** keinen Ausgang bekommen; **be** ~**d to a small area** auf ein kleines Gebiet begrenzt sein; **b)** *(fig.)* ~ **sb./sth. to sth.** jmdn./etw. auf etw. *(Akk.)* beschränken; ~ **oneself to sth./doing sth.** sich auf etw. *(Akk.)* beschränken/sich darauf beschränken, etw. zu tun; **c)** *(imprison)* einsperren
confined [kən'faɪnd] *adj.* begrenzt **(to** auf + *Akk.*); **the word is** ~ **to regional use** das Wort wird nur landschaftlich gebraucht
confinement [kən'faɪnmənt] *n.* **a)** *(imprisonment)* Einsperrung, *die; (in asylum)* Einweisung, *die;* **b)** *(being confined)* **put/keep sb. in** ~: jmdn. in Haft nehmen/halten; ~ **in hospital** ein Krankenhausaufenthalt; **animals kept in** ~: gefangengehaltene Tiere; **c)** *(childbirth)* Niederkunft, *die;* **d)** *(limitation)* Beschränkung, *die* **(to** auf + *Akk.*)
confines ['kɒnfaɪnz] *n. pl.* Grenzen
confirm [kən'fɜ:m] *v. t.* **a)** bestätigen; **be** ~**ed in one's suspicions** sich in seinem Verdacht bestätigt sehen; **b)** *(Protestant Ch.)* konfirmieren; einsegnen; *(RC Ch.)* firmen
confirmation [kɒnfə'meɪʃn] *n.* **a)** Bestätigung, *die;* **b)** *(Protestant Ch.)* Konfirmation, *die;* Einsegnung, *die; (RC Ch.)* Firmung, *die;* ~ **class[es]** Konfirmanden-/Firmunterricht, *der;* **c)** *(of Jewish faith)* Konfirmation, *die*
confirmatory [kən'fɜ:mətərɪ] *adj.* bestätigend
confirmed [kən'fɜ:md] *adj.* **a)** *(unlikely to change)* eingefleischt ⟨*Junggeselle*⟩; überzeugt ⟨*Atheist, Vegetarier*⟩; unheilbar ⟨*Trinker, Kranker*⟩; **b)** *(Protestant Ch.)* konfirmiert; *(RC Ch.)* gefirmt
confiscate ['kɒnfɪskeɪt] *v. t.* beschlagnahmen; konfiszieren; ~ **sth. from sb.** jmdm. etw. wegnehmen
confiscation [kɒnfɪs'keɪʃn] *n.* Beschlagnahme, *die;* Konfiskation, *die*
conflagration [kɒnflə'greɪʃn] *n.* Feuersbrunst, *die (geh.);* Großbrand, *der*
conflate [kən'fleɪt] *v. t.* verschmelzen
conflation [kən'fleɪʃn] *n.* Verschmelzung, *die*
conflict 1. ['kɒnflɪkt] *n.* **a)** *(fight)* Kampf, *der; (prolonged)* Krieg, *der;* **come into** ~ **with sb./sth.** mit jmdm./etw. in Konflikt geraten; **be in** ~ **with sb./sth.** *(fig.)* mit jmdm./etw. im Kampf liegen; **b)** *(clashing)* Konflikt, *der;* **a** ~ **of views/interests** ein Meinungs-/Interessenkonflikt; **c)** *(Psych.)* Konflikt, *der.* **2.** [kən'flɪkt] *v. i. (be incompatible)* sich *(Dat.)* widersprechen; ~ **with sth.** einer Sache *(Dat.)* widersprechen; zu einer Sache im Widerspruch stehen
conflicting [kən'flɪktɪŋ] *adj.* sich *(Dat.)* widersprechend
confluence ['kɒnflʊəns] *n.* Zusammenfluß, *der*
conform [kən'fɔ:m] **1.** *v. i.* **a)** entsprechen **(to** *Dat.*); ~ **to a pattern** sich mit einem Muster decken; *(fig.)* einem Muster entsprechen; **those who do not** ~ **will be asked to leave the club** wer sich nicht einfügt, wird aufgefordert, den Klub zu verlassen; **b)** *(comply)* ~ **to** *or* **with sth./with sb.** sich nach etw./jmdm. richten. **2.** *v. t.* ~ **sth. to sth.** etw. an etw. *(Akk.)* anpassen; etw. auf etw. *(Akk.)* abstimmen *(fig.)*
conformation [kɒnfə'meɪʃn] *n.* **a)** *(structure)* Gestalt, *die;* **b)** *(adaptation)* Anpassung, *die* **(to** an + *Akk.*)
conformism [kən'fɔ:mɪzm] *n.* Konformismus, *der*
conformist [kən'fɔ:mɪst] *n.* Konformist, *der*/Konformistin, *die*
conformity [kən'fɔ:mɪtɪ] *n.* Übereinstimmung, *die* **(with, to** mit)
confound [kən'faʊnd] *v. t.* **a)** ~ **it!** verflixt noch mal! *(ugs.);* ~ **him** *or* **the man!** der verflixte Kerl! *(ugs.);* **b)** *(defeat)* vereiteln ⟨*Plan, Hoffnung*⟩; **c)** *(confuse)* verwirren; **d)** *(discomfit)* ins Unrecht setzen; **e)** *(make indistinguishable)* durcheinanderbringen; verwischen ⟨*Unterschied*⟩; **f)** *(mix up mentally)* verwechseln; **g)** *(throw into disorder)* durcheinanderwerfen
confounded [kən'faʊndɪd] *adj.*, **confoundedly** [kən'faʊndɪdlɪ] *adv.* *(coll. derog.)* verdammt
confront [kən'frʌnt] *v. t.* **a)** gegenüberstellen; konfrontieren; ~ **sb. with sth./sb.** jmdn. mit etw./[mit] jmdm. konfrontieren; **he was** ~**ed with** *or* **by an angry mob** er sah sich [mit] einer wütenden Menge konfrontiert; **b)** *(stand facing)* gegenüberstehen (+ *Dat.*); **enemies** ~**ing one another** einander gegenüberstehende Feinde; **find oneself** ~**ed by** *or* **with a problem** sich [mit] einem Problem konfrontiert sehen; **c)** *(face in defiance)* ins Auge sehen (+ *Dat.*); **d)** *(oppose)* widersprechen (+ *Dat.*); *(make comparison)* gegenüberstellen
confrontation [kɒnfrən'teɪʃn] *n.* Konfrontation, *die; (with witnesses)* Gegenüberstellung, *die*
Confucianism [kən'fju:ʃənɪzm] *n., no pl.* Konfuzianismus, *der*
confuse [kən'fju:z] *v. t.* **a)** *(disorder)* durcheinanderbringen; verwirren; *(blur)* verwischen; ~ **the issue** den Sachverhalt unklar machen; **it simply** ~**s matters** das verwirrt die Sache nur; **b)** *(mix up mentally)* verwechseln; ~ **two things** zwei Dinge [miteinander] verwechseln; **c)** *(perplex)* konfus machen; verwirren
confused [kən'fju:zd] *adj.* konfus; wirr ⟨*Gedanken, Gerüchte*⟩; verworren ⟨*Lage, Situation*⟩; *(embarrassed)* verlegen
confusing [kən'fju:zɪŋ] *adj.* verwirrend
confusion [kən'fju:ʒn] *n.* **a)** *(disordering)* Verwirrung, *die; (mixing up)* Verwechslung, *die;* ~ **of tongues** Sprachverwirrung, *die;* **b)** *(state)* Verwirrung, *die; (embarrassment)* Verlegenheit, *die;* **throw sb./sth. into** ~: jmdn./etw. [völlig] durcheinanderbringen; **reply/blush in** ~: verlegen antworten/erröten; **in [total]** ~: in völligem Durcheinander ⟨*fliehen*⟩; [völlig *od.* wild] durcheinander ⟨*daliegen*⟩; **a scene of total** ~: ein totales Chaos
confutation [kɒnfjʊ'teɪʃn] *n.* Widerlegung, *die*
confute [kən'fju:t] *v. t.* widerlegen
conga ['kɒŋgə] *n.* Conga, *die*
congeal [kən'dʒi:l] **1.** *v. i.* **a)** *(coagulate)* ge-

rinnen; ~ **into sth.** *(fig.)* zu etw. erstarren; **b)** *(freeze)* gefrieren. **2.** *v. t.* **a)** *(coagulate)* gerinnen lassen; koagulieren; **b)** *(solidify by cooling)* gefrieren lassen

congenial [kən'dʒi:nɪəl] *adj.* **a)** *(kindred)* geistesverwandt; ~ **spirits** kongeniale Geister; **b)** *(agreeable)* angenehm

congeniality [kəndʒi:nɪ'ælɪtɪ] *n., no pl.* Geistesverwandtschaft, *die*

congenital [kən'dʒenɪtl] *adj.* angeboren; kongenital *(fachspr.)*; **a** ~ **idiot** ein von Geburt an Schwachsinniger; **a** ~ **defect** ein Geburtsfehler

congenitally [kən'dʒenɪtəlɪ] *adv.* von Geburt an

conger ['kɒŋgə(r)] *n. (Zool.)* ~ **[eel]** Meer- *od.* Seeaal, *der*

congest [kən'dʒest] *v. t.* verstopfen

congested [kən'dʒestɪd] *adj.* überfüllt, verstopft ⟨*Straße*⟩; übervölkert ⟨*Stadtviertel*⟩; **my nose is** ~: ich habe eine verstopfte Nase

congestion [kən'dʒestʃn] *n. (of traffic etc.)* Stauung, *die; (overpopulation)* Übervölkerung, *die;* ~ **of the lungs** *(Med.)* Lungenstauung, *die;* **nasal** ~: verstopfte Nase

conglomerate 1. [kən'glɒməreɪt] *v. t. (lit. or fig.)* verschmelzen. **2.** *v. i.* sich zusammenballen; *(fig.)* sich versammeln. **3.** [kən'glɒmərət] *n.* **a)** *(Commerc.)* Großkonzern, *der;* **b)** *(Geol.)* Konglomerat, *das*

conglomeration [kənglɒmə'reɪʃn] *n.* Konglomerat, *das; (collection)* Ansammlung, *die*

Congo ['kɒŋgəʊ] *pr. n. (Geog.: river, country)* Kongo, *der*

Congolese [kɒŋgə'li:z] **1.** *adj.* kongolesisch. **2.** *n.* Kongolese, *der*/Kongolesin, *die*

congratulate [kən'grætjʊleɪt] *v. t.* gratulieren (+ *Dat.*); ~ **sb./oneself [up]on sth.** jmdm./sich zu etw. gratulieren

congratulation [kəngrætjʊ'leɪʃn] **1.** *int.* ~**s!** herzlichen Glückwunsch! **(on** zu). **2.** *n.* **a)** *in pl.* Glückwünsche *Pl.*; **offer sb. one's** ~**s** jmdm. gratulieren; jmdn. beglückwünschen; **b)** *(action)* Gratulation, *die*

congratulatory [kən'grætjʊlətərɪ] *adj.* beglückwünschend; ~ **note/letter** Glückwunschschreiben, *das*/-brief, *der*

congregate ['kɒŋgrɪgeɪt] **1.** *v. i.* sich versammeln; zusammenkommen. **2.** *v. t.* versammeln

congregation [kɒŋgrɪ'geɪʃn] *n.* **a)** *(Eccl.)* Gemeinde, *die;* **b)** *(Brit. Univ.)* ≈ Konzil, *das*

congress ['kɒŋgres] *n.* **a)** *(meeting of heads of state etc.)* Kongreß, *der;* **the C~ of Vienna** der Wiener Kongreß; **a party** ~: ein Parteitag; **b)** *(association)* Verband, *der;* **c)** C~ *(Amer.: legislature)* der Kongreß

congressional [kən'greʃənl] *adj.* Kongreß-; ⟨*Erlaubnis*⟩ des Kongresses; ~ **district** Kongreßwahlbezirk, *der*

Congress: ~**man** ['kɒŋgresmən] *n., pl.* ~**men** ['kɒŋgresmən] *(Amer.)* Kongreßabgeordnete, *der;* ~**woman** *n. (Amer.)* Kongreßabgeordnete, *die*

congruence ['kɒŋgrʊəns], **congruency** ['kɒŋgrʊənsɪ] *n.* **a)** Übereinstimmung, *die;* **b)** *(Geom.)* Kongruenz, *die;* Deckungsgleichheit, *die*

congruent ['kɒŋgrʊənt] *adj.* **a)** *(formal)* übereinstimmend; **b)** *(Geom.)* kongruent; deckungsgleich

congruity [kɒŋ'gru:ɪtɪ] *n.* Übereinstimmung, *die;* Kongruenz, *die (geh.)*

conic ['kɒnɪk] *adj.* Kegel-; ~ **section** Kegelschnitt, *der*

conical ['kɒnɪkl] *adj.* konisch; kegelförmig; *see also* **projection i**

conifer ['kɒnɪfə(r), 'kəʊnɪfə(r)] *n.* Nadelbaum, *der;* Konifere, *die;* ~**s** Nadelhölzer

coniferous [kə'nɪfərəs] *adj.* Nadel-; ~ **tree** Nadelbaum, *der;* Konifere, *die;* ~ **forest** Nadelwald, *der*

conjectural [kən'dʒektʃərl] *adj.* auf Mutmaßungen *(geh.) od.* Vermutungen beruhend; konjektural *(Literaturw.)*; **all this is** ~: all das ist Vermutung; **a** ~ **emendation of a text** eine Konjektur *(Literaturw.)*

conjecturally [kən'dʒektʃərəlɪ] *adv.* auf Grund von Mutmaßungen *(geh.) od.* Vermutungen

conjecture [kən'dʒektʃə(r)] **1.** *n.* **a)** Mutmaßung, *die (geh.)*; Vermutung, *die;* **rely on** ~: sich auf Mutmaßungen *(Akk.)* stützen; **b)** *(Lit.)* Konjektur, *die.* **2.** *v. t.* mutmaßen *(geh.)*; vermuten. **3.** *v. i. (guess)* Mutmaßungen *(geh.) od.* Vermutungen anstellen

conjoin [kən'dʒɔɪn] **1.** *v. t.* verbinden. **2.** *v. i.* sich verbinden

conjoint [kən'dʒɔɪnt] *adj. (formal)* **a)** *(united)* gemeinsam; **b)** *(associated)* Mit-

conjointly [kən'dʒɔɪntlɪ] *adv.* gemeinsam

conjugal ['kɒndʒʊgl] *adj.* ehelich; **the** ~ **state** der Stand der Ehe; ~ **bliss/worries** Eheglück, *das*/Ehesorgen

conjugate 1. ['kɒndʒʊgeɪt] *v. t. (Ling.)* konjugieren. **2.** *v. i.* **a)** *(Ling.)* konjugiert werden; **b)** *(Biol.)* sich paaren *od.* vereinigen. **3.** ['kɒndʒʊgət] *adj.* **a)** gepaart; **b)** *(Ling.)* wurzelverwandt; **c)** *(Math.)* konjugiert. **4.** *n. (Ling.)* wurzelverwandtes Wort

conjugation ['kɒndʒʊ'geɪʃn] *n.* **a)** *(joining together)* Vereinigung, *die;* **b)** *(Ling., Biol.)* Konjugation, *die*

conjunction [kən'dʒʌŋkʃn] *n.* **a)** Verbindung, *die;* **in** ~ **with sb./sth.** in Verbindung mit jmdm./etw.; **b)** *(formal: of events)* Zusammentreffen, *das;* **c)** *(Ling.)* Konjunktion, *die;* Bindewort, *das;* **d)** *(Astrol., Astron.)* Konjunktion, *die*

conjunctivitis [kəndʒʌŋktɪ'vaɪtɪs] *n. (Med.)* Bindehautentzündung, *die;* Konjunktivitis, *die (fachspr.)*

conjure 1. *v. t.* **a)** [kən'dʒʊə(r)] *(formal: beseech)* beschwören; anflehen; **b)** ['kʌndʒə(r)] *(by magic)* beschwören ⟨*Geister*⟩. **2.** ['kʌndʒə(r)] *v. i.* zaubern; **conjuring trick** Zaubertrick, *der;* Zauberkunststück, *das;* **a name to** ~ **with** ein exotischer *od.* geheimnisvoller Name; *(because of great importance)* ein klangvoller Name

~ **'away** *v. t.* wegzaubern

~ **'up** *v. t.* beschwören ⟨*Geister, Teufel*⟩; *(fig.)* heraufbeschwören

conjurer, conjuror ['kʌndʒərə(r)] *n.* Zauberkünstler, *der*/-künstlerin, *die;* Zauberer, *der*/Zauberin, *die*

[1]conk [kɒŋk] *v. i.* ~ **'out** *(coll.)* schlappmachen *(ugs.)*; ⟨*Maschine, Auto usw.:*⟩ den Geist aufgeben *(scherzh.)*, kaputtgehen *(ugs.)*

[2]conk *n. (sl.)* **a)** *(nose)* Zinken, *der (ugs.)*; Rüssel, *der (salopp)*; **b)** *(head)* Rübe, *die (salopp)*; Birne, *die (salopp)*

conker ['kɒŋkə(r)] *n. (horse-chestnut)* [Roß]kastanie, *die;* **play** ~**s** ein Wettspiel mit Kastanien machen

'con-man *(coll.) see* **confidence man**

connect [kə'nekt] **1.** *v. t.* **a)** *(join together)* verbinden **(to, with** mit); *(Electr.)* anschließen **(to, with** an + *Akk.*); **b)** *(join in sequence)* verbinden; verknüpfen; **c)** *(associate)* verbinden; ~ **sth. with sth.** etw. mit etw. verbinden *od.* in Verbindung bringen; **be** ~**ed with sb./sth.** mit jmdm./etw. in Verbindung stehen. **2.** *v. i.* **a)** *(join)* ~ **with sth.** mit etw. zusammenhängen *od.* verbunden sein; ⟨*Zug, Schiff usw.:*⟩ Anschluß haben an etw. *(Akk.)*; **b)** *(form logical sequence)* einen Zusammenhang/Zusammenhänge darstellen; **c)** *(coll.: hit)* einen Haken *usw.* landen **(with** auf, an + *Dat.*)

~ **'up** *v. t.* anschließen

connected [kə'nektɪd] *adj.* **a)** *(logically joined)* zusammenhängend; **sth. is** ~ **with sth.** etw. hängt mit etw. zusammen; etw. hat mit etw. zu tun; **b)** *(related)* verwandt; **he is well** ~: er hat einflußreiche Verwandte

connecting [kə'nektɪŋ]: ~ **door** *n.* Verbindungstür, *die;* ~ **rod** *n. (Mech. Engin.)* Pleuelstange, *die*

connection [kə'nekʃn] *n.* **a)** *(act, state)* Verbindung, *die; (Electr.; of telephone)* Anschluß, *der;* **cut the** ~: die Verbindung abbrechen; **the Italian** ~: die Beziehungen zu Italien; **run in** ~ **with sth.** ⟨*Zug usw.:*⟩ Anschluß haben an etw. *(Akk.)*; **b)** *(fig.: of ideas)* Zusammenhang, *der;* **in this** ~: in diesem Zusammenhang; **in** ~ **with sth.** im Zusammenhang mit etw.: **c)** *(part)* Verbindung, *die;* Verbindungsstück, *das;* **d)** *(train, boat, etc.)* Anschluß, *der;* **miss a** ~: einen Anschluß verpassen; **catch** *or* **make a** ~: einen Anschluß erreichen *od. (ugs.)* kriegen; **e)** *(family relationship)* Verwandtschaft, *die;* **f)** *(person) (relative)* Verwandte, *der/die;* **business** ~**s** Geschäftsbeziehungen; **have** ~**s** Beziehungen haben; **g)** *(personal dealings)* **he has no** ~ **with the firm of this name** er hat keinerlei Verbindung zu dem gleichnamigen Unternehmen; **h)** *(sl.: supplier of narcotics)* Dealer, *der (Jargon)*

connective [kə'nektɪv] *adj.* **a)** verbindend; **b)** *(Anat.)* ~ **tissue** Bindegewebe, *das*

connexion *(Brit.) see* **connection**

conning-tower ['kɒnɪŋtaʊə(r)] *n. (Naut.)* Kommandoturm, *der*

connivance [kə'naɪvəns] *n.* stillschweigende Duldung

connive [kə'naɪv] *v. i.* **a)** ~ **at sth.** *(disregard)* über etw. *(Akk.)* hinwegsehen; etw. stillschweigend dulden; **b)** *(conspire)* ~ **with sb.** mit jmdm. gemeinsame Sache machen **(in bei)**

connoisseur [kɒnə'sɜ:(r)] *n.* Kenner, *der;* **a** ~ **of wine** ein Weinkenner

connotation [kɒnə'teɪʃn] *n.* Assoziation, *die;* Konnotation, *die (Sprachw.)*

connote [kə'nəʊt] *v. t. (formal)* **a)** *(suggest)* suggerieren; **b)** *(signify)* bezeichnen

connubial [kə'nju:bɪəl] *adj.* ehelich; Ehe-

conquer ['kɒŋkə(r)] *v. t.* besiegen ⟨*Gegner, Leidenschaft, Gewohnheit*⟩; erobern ⟨*Land*⟩; bezwingen ⟨*Berg, Gegner*⟩; **I came, I saw, I** ~**ed** ich kam, ich sah, ich siegte

conqueror ['kɒŋkərə(r)] *n.* Sieger, *der*/Siegerin, *die* **(of** über + *Akk.*); *(of a mountain)* Bezwinger, *der; (of a country)* Eroberer, *der;* **[William] the C~**: Wilhelm der Eroberer

conquest ['kɒŋkwest] *n.* **a)** Eroberung, *die;* **the [Norman] C~**: die Eroberung Englands durch die Normannen; **b)** *(territory)* Eroberung, *die;* erobertes Gebiet; **c)** *(fig.: of mountain)* Bezwingung, *die;* Sieg, *der* **(of** über + *Akk.*)

'con-rod *n. (Motor Veh. coll.)* Pleuelstange, *die*

conscience ['kɒnʃəns] *n.* Gewissen, *das;* **have a good** *or* **clear/bad** *or* **guilty** ~: ein gutes/schlechtes Gewissen haben; **have no** ~: gewissenlos sein; **with a clear** *or* **easy** ~: mit gutem Gewissen; guten Gewissens *(geh.)*; **have sth. on one's** ~: wegen etw. ein schlechtes Gewissen haben; **that is still on my** ~: das liegt mir immer noch auf der Seele; **in all** ~: ehrlicherweise; *(without doubt)* zweifellos; **freedom** *or* **liberty of** ~: Gewissensfreiheit, *die;* Freiheit des Gewissens; **a matter of** ~: eine Gewissensfrage

conscience: ~ **clause** *n. (Law)* Gewissensklausel, *die;* ~ **money** *n.* freiwillige Geldbuße; ~**-smitten,** ~**-stricken,** ~**-struck** *adjs.* schuldbewußt

conscientious [kɒnʃɪ'enʃəs] *adj.* pflichtbewußt; *(meticulous)* gewissenhaft; ~ **objector** Wehrdienstverweigerer [aus Gewissensgründen]

conscientiously [kɒnʃɪ'enʃəslɪ] *adv.* pflichtbewußt; *(meticulously)* gewissenhaft

conscientiousness [kɒnʃɪ'enʃəsnɪs] *n., no pl.* Pflichtbewußtsein, *das; (meticulousness)* Gewissenhaftigkeit, *die*

conscious ['kɒnʃəs] **1.** *adj.* **a) be** ~ **of sth.**

sich *(Dat.)* einer Sache *(Gen.)* bewußt sein; **I was ~ that ...:** mir war bewußt, daß ...; **but he is not ~ of it** aber es ist ihm nicht bewußt; **I suddenly became ~ that ...:** mir wurde plötzlich bewußt, daß ...; **b)** *pred. (awake)* bei Bewußtsein *präd.*; **become ~:** wach werden; **become ~ again** wieder zu sich kommen; **c)** *(realized by doer)* bewußt ⟨*Handeln, Versuch, Bemühung*⟩; **d)** *(self-~)* gewollt ⟨*Auftreten, Gehabe*⟩. **2.** *n.* Bewußte, *das (Psych.)*

consciously ['kɒnʃəslɪ] *adv.* bewußt; **be ~ superior** sich *(Dat.)* seiner Überlegenheit *(Gen.)* bewußt sein

consciousness ['kɒnʃəsnɪs] *n., no pl.* **a)** Bewußtsein, *das;* **lose/recover** *or* **regain ~:** das Bewußtsein verlieren/wiedererlangen; bewußtlos werden/wieder zu sich kommen; **b)** *(totality of thought)* Bewußtsein, *das;* **c)** *(perception)* Bewußtsein, *das;* Bewußtheit, *die*

conscript 1. [kən'skrɪpt] *v. t.* einberufen ⟨*Soldaten*⟩; ausheben ⟨*Armee*⟩; **be ~ed into the army** zum Wehrdienst einberufen werden. **2.** ['kɒnskrɪpt] *n.* Einberufene, *der/die;* **an army of ~s** eine Armee von Wehrpflichtigen

conscription [kən'skrɪpʃn] *n. (action)* Einberufung, *die; (compulsory military service)* Wehrpflicht, *die*

consecrate ['kɒnsɪkreɪt] *v. t. (Eccl.; also fig.)* weihen; konsekrieren; **~ sb. a bishop** jmdn. zum Bischof weihen

consecration [kɒnsɪ'kreɪʃn] *n. (Eccl.; also fig.)* Weihe, *die;* Konsekration, *die*

consecutive [kən'sekjʊtɪv] *adj.* **a)** *(following continuously)* aufeinanderfolgend ⟨*Monate, Jahre*⟩; fortlaufend ⟨*Zahlen*⟩; **this is the fifth ~ day that ...:** heute ist schon der fünfte Tag, an dem ...; **b)** *(in logical sequence)* folgerichtig; **c)** *(Ling.)* konsekutiv; Konsekutiv-; **~ clause** Konsekutiv-/Folgesatz, *der*

consecutive interpre'tation *n.* Konsekutivdolmetschen, *das*

consecutively [kən'sekjʊtɪvlɪ] *adv.* hintereinander; fortlaufend ⟨*numeriert*⟩

consensus [kən'sensəs] *n.* Einigkeit, *die;* Konsens[us], *der (geh.); attrib.* ⟨*Politik, Regierungsstil usw.*⟩ des Miteinander *od.* der Gemeinsamkeit; **the general ~ is that ...:** es besteht allgemeiner Konsens *(geh.) od.* allgemeine Einigkeit darüber, daß ...; **the ~ of opinion is in favour of the amendment** die allgemeine Mehrheit *od.* die Mehrheitsmeinung ist für den Änderungsantrag

consent [kən'sent] **1.** *v. i.* zustimmen; **~ to sth.** einer Sache *(Dat.)* zustimmen; in eine Sache einwilligen; **~ to do sth.** einwilligen, etw. zu tun; **~ing adult** erwachsene homosexuelle Person. **2.** *n.* **a)** *(agreement)* Zustimmung, *die* **(to** zu); Einwilligung, *die* **(to** in + *Akk.*); **by common** *or* **general ~:** nach allgemeiner Auffassung; *(as wished by all)* auf allgemeinen Wunsch; **age of ~:** *Alter, in dem man hinsichtlich Heirat und Geschlechtsleben nicht mehr als minderjährig gilt;* ≈ Ehemündigkeitsalter, *das;* **b)** *(permission)* Zustimmung, *die;* Erlaubnis, *die;* **give/refuse [sb.] one's ~:** [jmdm.] seine Zustimmung geben/verweigern

consequence ['kɒnsɪkwəns] *n.* **a)** *(result)* Folge, *die;* **in ~:** folglich; infolgedessen; **in ~ of** als Folge (+ *Gen.*); **as a ~:** infolgedessen; **as a ~ of** infolge (+ *Gen.*); **with the ~ that ...:** mit dem Ergebnis, daß ...; **accept** *or* **take the ~s** die Folgen tragen; **b)** *(importance)* Bedeutung, *die;* **be of no ~:** unerheblich *od.* ohne Bedeutung sein; **nothing of ~:** nichts von Bedeutung; nichts Erhebliches; **persons of [no] ~** *(significant)* [un]bedeutende/*(influential, high-ranking)* [un]wichtige Leute; **he's of no ~:** er ist unbedeutend *od.* unwichtig

consequent ['kɒnsɪkwənt] *adj.* **a)** *(resultant)* daraus folgend; sich daraus ergebend; *(following in time)* darauffolgend; **be ~ [up]on sth.** *(formal)* die Folge einer Sache *(Gen.)* sein; **b)** *(logically consistent)* folgerichtig

consequential [kɒnsɪ'kwenʃl] *adj.* **a)** *(resulting)* daraus folgend; sich daraus ergebend; *(following in time)* darauffolgend; **b)** *(indirectly following)* indirekt; sich indirekt ergebend; **~ damage[s]** Folgeschäden *Pl.*; **c)** *(self-important)* überheblich ⟨*Lächeln, Stimme, Person*⟩

consequentially [kɒnsɪ'kwenʃəlɪ] *adv.* **a)** *(indirectly)* indirekt; **b)** *(self-importantly)* überheblich

consequently ['kɒnsɪkwəntlɪ] *adv.* infolgedessen; folglich

conservancy [kən'sɜ:vənsɪ] *n.* **a)** *(Brit.: conserving body) Behörde, der der Natur-/Gewässerschutz usw. untersteht;* **the Nature C~:** die Naturschutzbehörde; **the Thames C~:** der Themse-Gewässerschutz; **b)** *(preservation)* Naturschutz, *der*

conservation [kɒnsə'veɪʃn] *n.* **a)** *(preservation)* Schutz, *der;* Erhaltung, *die; (wise utilization)* sparsamer Umgang **(of** mit); **wildlife ~:** Schutz wildlebender Tierarten; **b)** *(Phys.)* **~ of energy/momentum** Erhaltung der Energie/des Impulses

conser'vation area *n. (Brit.) (rural)* Landschaftsschutzgebiet, *das; (urban)* unter Denkmalschutz stehendes Gebiet

conservationist [kɒnsə'veɪʃənɪst] *n.* Naturschützer, *der/*-schützerin, *die*

conservatism [kən'sɜ:vətɪzm] *n.* Konservati[vi]smus, *der*

conservative [kən'sɜ:vətɪv] **1.** *adj.* **a)** *(conserving)* erhaltend; konservierend; **~ surgery** konservative Chirurgie; **b)** *(averse to change)* konservativ; **c)** *(not too high)* vorsichtig, eher zu niedrig ⟨*Zahlen, Schätzung*⟩; **at a ~ estimate** nach vorsichtiger *od. (Jargon)* konservativer Schätzung; **d)** *(avoiding extremes)* konservativ ⟨*Geschmack, Ansichten, Baustil*⟩; **e)** *(Brit. Polit.)* konservativ; **the C~ Party** die Konservative Partei. **2.** *n.* **a) C~** *(Brit. Polit.)* Konservative, *der/die;* **b)** *(conservative person)* Konservative, *der/die*

conservatively [kən'sɜ:vətɪvlɪ] *adv.* vorsichtig, eher zu niedrig ⟨*geschätzt*⟩

conservatoire [kən'sɜ:vətwɑ:(r)] *n. (school of music)* Konservatorium, *das; (school of other arts)* Kunsthochschule, *die*

conservatory [kən'sɜ:vətərɪ] *n.* **a)** *(greenhouse)* Wintergarten, *der;* **b)** *(Amer.) see* **conservatoire**

conserve [kən'sɜ:v] **1.** *v. t.* **a)** erhalten ⟨*Gebäude, Kunstwerk, Wälder*⟩; bewahren ⟨*Ideale, Prinzipien*⟩; schonen ⟨*Gesundheit, Kräfte*⟩; **b)** *esp. in p.p. (Phys.)* erhalten ⟨*Energie, Impuls*⟩. **2.** *n. often in pl.* Eingemachte, *das;* **~s** Eingemachtes

consider [kən'sɪdə(r)] *v. t.* **a)** *(look at)* betrachten; *(think about)* **~ sth.** an etw. *(Akk.)* denken; **b)** *(weigh merits of)* denken an (+ *Akk.*); **he's ~ing emigrating** er denkt daran *od.* trägt sich mit dem Gedanken, auszuwandern; **five candidates are being ~ed** fünf Kandidaten sind in der engeren Wahl; **c)** *(reflect)* sich *(Dat.)* überlegen; bedenken; **you must ~ that you/whether or not you ...:** du mußt bedenken *od.* dir überlegen, daß du/ob du ... oder nicht; **just ~!** *(abs.)* überleg [dir das] doch mal!; **d)** *(have opinion)* annehmen; finden; **we ~ that you are not to blame** wir sind der Ansicht *od.* finden, daß Sie nicht schuld sind; **e)** *(regard as)* halten für; **I ~ him [to be** *or* **as] a swindler** ich halte ihn für einen Betrüger; **do you ~ yourself educated?** hältst du dich für gebildet?; **~ yourself under arrest** betrachten Sie sich als verhaftet; **she is ~ed a great beauty** sie gilt als große Schönheit; **f)** *(allow for)* berücksichtigen; **~ other people's feelings** auf die Gefühle anderer Rücksicht nehmen; **all things ~ed** alles in allem

considerable [kən'sɪdərəbl] *adj.* **a)** *(no little)* beträchtlich; erheblich ⟨*Schwierigkeiten, Ärger*⟩; groß ⟨*Freude, Charakterstärke*⟩; eingehend ⟨*Überlegung*⟩; *(Amer.: large)* ansehnlich ⟨*Gebäude, Edelstein*⟩; **b)** *(important)* bedeutend ⟨*Person, Künstler*⟩

considerably [kən'sɪdərəblɪ] *adv.* erheblich; *(in amount)* beträchtlich

considerate [kən'sɪdərət] *adj.* rücksichtsvoll; *(thoughtfully kind)* entgegenkommend; **be ~ to[wards] sb.** rücksichtsvoll gegenüber jmdm. sein; auf jmdn. Rücksicht nehmen

considerately [kən'sɪdərətlɪ] *adv.* rücksichtsvoll; *(obligingly)* entgegenkommend

considerateness [kən'sɪdərətnɪs] *n.* Rücksichtnahme, *die* **(for** auf + *Akk.*); *(obligingness)* Entgegenkommen, *das*

consideration [kənsɪdə'reɪʃn] *n.* **a)** Überlegung, *die; (meditation)* Betrachtung, *die;* **take sth. into ~:** etw. berücksichtigen *od.* bedenken; **give sth. one's ~:** etw. in Erwägung ziehen; **the matter is under ~:** die Angelegenheit wird geprüft; **in ~ of** unter Berücksichtigung (+ *Gen.*); **leave sth. out of ~:** etw. unberücksichtigt lassen; etw. außer Betracht lassen; **b)** *(thoughtfulness)* Rücksichtnahme, *die* **(for** auf + *Akk.*); **show ~ for sb.** Rücksicht auf jmdn. nehmen; **c)** *(sth. as reason)* Gesichtspunkt, *der;* Umstand, *der;* **an important ~:** ein wichtiger Faktor; **d)** *(payment)* Bezahlung, *die;* **for a ~:** gegen Entgelt; **e)** *(Law)* Ausgleich, *der;* Ersatz, *der*

considered [kən'sɪdəd] *adj.* **a) ~ opinion** feste *od.* ernsthafte Überzeugung; **b) be highly ~ [by others]** [bei anderen] in hohem Ansehen stehen

considering [kən'sɪdərɪŋ] *prep.* **~ sth.** wenn man etw. bedenkt; **~ [that] ...:** wenn man bedenkt, daß ...; **that's not so bad, ~** *(coll.)* das ist eigentlich gar nicht mal so schlecht *(ugs.)*

consign [kən'saɪn] *v. t.* **a)** anvertrauen **(to** *Dat.*); **~ a child to its uncle's care** ein Kind in die Obhut seines Onkels geben; **~ sth. to the scrap-heap** *(lit. or fig.)* etw. auf den Schrotthaufen werfen; **~ a letter to the flames** einen Brief dem Feuer übergeben *(geh.)*; **b)** *(Commerc.)* übersenden, *(fachspr.)* konsignieren ⟨*Güter*⟩ **(to** an + *Akk.*); senden ⟨*Brief, Paket*⟩ **(to** an + *Akk.*)

consignment [kən'saɪnmənt] *n. (Commerc.)* **a)** *(consigning)* Übersendung, *die* **(to** an + *Akk.*); Konsignation, *die (fachspr.)* **(to** an + *Akk.*); **~ note** Frachtbrief, *der;* **b)** *(goods)* Sendung, *die; (large)* Ladung, *die*

consist [kən'sɪst] *v. i.* **a) ~ of** bestehen aus; **b) ~ in** bestehen in (+ *Dat.*)

consistence [kən'sɪstəns], **consistency** [kən'sɪstənsɪ] *ns.* **a)** *(density)* Konsistenz, *die; (of thick liquids)* Dickflüssigkeit, *die;* **mixtures of various consistencies** Mischungen verschiedener Konsistenz; **b)** *(being consistent)* Konsequenz, *die;* **~ of style** stilistische Konsistenz

consistent [kən'sɪstənt] *adj.* **a)** *(compatible)* [miteinander] vereinbar; **be ~ with sth.** mit etw. übereinstimmen; mit etw. vereinbar sein; **b)** *(uniform)* beständig; gleichbleibend ⟨*Qualität*⟩; einheitlich ⟨*Verfahren, Vorgehen, Darstellung*⟩; **c)** *(adhering to principles)* konsequent

consistently [kən'sɪstəntlɪ] *adv. (compatibly, in harmony)* in Übereinstimmung ⟨*handeln*⟩; *(uniformly)* einheitlich ⟨*gestalten*⟩; konsistent ⟨*denken*⟩; *(persistently)* konsequent ⟨*behaupten, verfolgen, handeln*⟩

consistory [kən'sɪstərɪ, 'kɒnsɪstərɪ] *n. (RC Ch.)* Konsistorium, *das*

consolation [kɒnsə'leɪʃn] *n.* **a)** *(act)* Tröstung, *die;* Trost, *der;* **words of ~:** Worte des Trostes; tröstende Worte; **a letter of ~:**

ein trostvoller Brief; **b)** *(consoling circumstance)* Trost, *der;* **that's one ~!** das ist tröstlich *od.* ein Trost!

conso'lation prize *n.* Trostpreis, *der*

consolatory [kən'sɒlətərɪ, kən'səʊlətərɪ] *adj.* tröstend, trostvoll **(to** für)

[1]**console** [kən'səʊl] *v. t.* trösten; **~ sb. for a loss** jmdn. über einen Verlust hinwegtrösten

[2]**console** ['kɒnsəʊl] *n.* **a)** *(Mus.)* Spieltisch, *der;* **b)** *(panel)* [Schalt]pult, *das;* **c)** *(cabinet)* Truhe, *die*

consolidate [kən'sɒlɪdeɪt] **1.** *v. t.* **a)** *(strengthen)* festigen ‹*Macht, Stellung*›; *(fig.)* konsolidieren ‹*Stellung, Einfluß, Macht*›; **b)** *(combine)* zusammenlegen ‹*Territorien, Grundstücke, Firmen*›; konsolidieren ‹*Schulden, Anleihen*›. **2.** *v. i.* **a)** *(become solid)* hart werden; **b)** *(merge)* ‹*Firmen:*› fusionieren

consolidation [kənsɒlɪ'deɪʃn] *n., no pl.* **a)** *(strengthening)* Festigung, *die; (fig.)* Konsolidierung, *die;* **b)** *(unification)* Zusammenlegung, *die*

consoling [kən'səʊlɪŋ] *adj.* tröstlich

consommé [kən'sɒmeɪ] *n. (Gastr.)* Kraftbrühe, *die;* Consommé, *die (fachspr.)*

consonance ['kɒnsənəns] *n.* **a)** *(Mus.)* Harmonie, *die; (of two notes)* Konsonanz, *die;* **b)** *(fig. formal)* Übereinstimmung, *die;* **c)** *(Phonet.)* Konsonanz, *die*

consonant ['kɒnsənənt] **1.** *n.* Konsonant, *der;* Mitlaut, *der;* **~ shift** Lautverschiebung, *die.* **2.** *adj.* **a)** *(formal)* **be ~ with** *or* **to sth.** im Einklang mit etw. stehen; **b)** *(Mus.)* konsonant; **c)** *(Phonet.)* gleichklingend

consonantal [kɒnsə'næntl] *adj. (Phonet.)* konsonantisch

[1]**consort** ['kɒnsɔ:t] *n.* Gemahl, *der*/Gemahlin, *die;* **queen ~:** Gemahlin des Königs; Königin, *die (volkst.)*

[2]**consort** [kən'sɔ:t] *v. i.* **a)** *(keep company)* verkehren **(with** mit); **b)** *(arch.: agree)* übereinstimmen **(with, to** mit); **they ~ed ill together** sie paßten schlecht zusammen

[3]**consort** ['kɒnsɔ:t] *n. (Mus.)* Consort, *das*

consortium [kən'sɔ:tɪəm] *n., pl.* **consortia** [kən'sɔ:tɪə] *(association)* Konsortium, *das*

conspectus [kən'spektəs] *n.* Übersicht, *die*

conspicuous [kən'spɪkjʊəs] *adj.* **a)** *(clearly visible)* unübersehbar; **make oneself ~:** dafür sorgen, daß man deutlich sichtbar ist; **leave sth. in a ~ position** etw. sichtbar liegenlassen; **b)** *(noticeable)* auffallend; **be ~:** sehr auffallen; **make oneself ~ by one's absence** durch Abwesenheit auffallen *od. (iron.)* glänzen; **~ expenditure/consumption** Prestigeausgaben/demonstrativer Konsum; **c)** *(obvious, noteworthy)* auffallend ‹*Schönheit*›; herausragend ‹*Tapferkeit*›; **~ for their loyalty** bekannt für ihre Loyalität; **the most ~ example** das augenfälligste Beispiel; das Paradebeispiel

conspicuously [kən'spɪkjʊəslɪ] *adv.* **a)** *(very visibly)* unübersehbar; **b)** *(obviously)* auffallend

conspicuousness [kən'spɪkjʊəsnɪs] *n., no pl.* **a)** *(being clearly visible)* Unübersehbarkeit, *die;* **b)** *(obviousness)* Auffälligkeit, *die*

conspiracy [kən'spɪrəsɪ] *n.* **a)** *(conspiring)* Verschwörung, *die;* **be in ~ against sb.** sich gegen jmdn. verschworen haben; **b)** *(plot)* Komplott, *das;* **form a ~:** ein Komplott schmieden; **~ of silence** verabredetes Stillschweigen; **c)** *(Law)* Verabredung zu einer Straftat; **~ to murder** Mordkomplott, *das*

conspirator [kən'spɪrətə(r)] *n.* Verschwörer, *der*/Verschwörerin, *die*

conspiratorial [kənspɪrə'tɔ:rɪəl] *adj.* verschwörerisch

conspire [kən'spaɪə(r)] *v. i. (lit. or fig.)* sich verschwören

constable ['kʌnstəbl, 'kɒnstəbl] *n.* **a)** *(Brit.) see* **police constable; b)** *(Brit.)* **Chief C~:** ≈ Polizeipräsident, *der*/-präsidentin, *die*

constabulary [kən'stæbjʊlərɪ] **1.** *n.* Polizei, *die; (unit)* Polizeieinheit, *die.* **2.** *adj.* Polizei-

Constance ['kɒnstəns] *pr. n. (Geog.)* Konstanz *(das);* **Lake ~:** der Bodensee

constancy ['kɒnstənsɪ] *n.* **a)** *(steadfastness)* Standhaftigkeit, *die;* **b)** *(faithfulness)* Treue, *die;* **c)** *(unchangingness)* Beständigkeit, *die; (uniformity)* Gleichmäßigkeit, *die*

constant ['kɒnstənt] **1.** *adj.* **a)** *(unceasing)* ständig; anhaltend ‹*Regen*›; **it's ~ laughter when they're around** es wird ununterbrochen gelacht, wenn sie da sind; **be a ~ reminder of sth./sb.** ständig an etw./jmdn. erinnern; **we had ~ rain** es hat dauernd geregnet; **there was a ~ stream of traffic** der Verkehr floß ununterbrochen; **b)** *(unchanging)* gleichbleibend; konstant; **c)** *(steadfast)* standhaft; **be ~ in one's determination** stets an seinem Entschluß festhalten; **d)** *(faithful)* treu; **be ~ [to sb.]** [jmdm.] treu sein. **2.** *n. (Phys., Math.)* Konstante, *die*

constantly ['kɒnstəntlɪ] *adv.* **a)** *(unceasingly)* ständig; **b)** *(unchangingly)* konstant; **c)** *(steadfastly)* standhaft; **d)** *(faithfully)* treu

constellation [kɒnstə'leɪʃn] *n.* Sternbild, *das;* Konstellation, *die (Astron.)*

consternation [kɒnstə'neɪʃn] *n.* Bestürzung, *die; (confusion)* Aufregung, *die;* **in ~:** bestürzt/aufgeregt; **be filled with ~:** sehr bestürzt/aufgeregt sein

constipate ['kɒnstɪpeɪt] *v. t.* zu Verstopfung führen bei; **be ~d** an Verstopfung leiden

constipation [kɒnstɪ'peɪʃn] *n.* Verstopfung, *die;* Konstipation, *die (Med.)*

constituency [kən'stɪtjʊənsɪ] *n.* *(voters)* Wählerschaft, *die (eines Wahlkreises); (area)* Wahlkreis, *der*

constituent [kən'stɪtjʊənt] **1.** *adj. (composing a whole)* **~ part** Bestandteil, *der;* **~ member** Mitglied, *das;* **the ~ gases in air/~ parts of water** die Gase, aus denen Luft/die Teile, aus denen Wasser besteht. **2.** *n.* **a)** *(component part)* Bestandteil, *der;* **b)** *(member of constituency)* Wähler, *der* /Wählerin, *die (eines Wahlkreises)*

constitute ['kɒnstɪtju:t] *v. t.* **a)** *(appoint)* ernennen zu; **~ oneself judge in a matter** sich *(Dat.)* in einer Sache ein Urteil erlauben; **b)** *(form)* sein; **~ a threat to** eine Gefahr sein für; **c)** *(frame)* **be ~d** beschaffen sein; **he is strongly ~d** er hat eine kräftige Konstitution; **d)** *(make up)* bilden; begründen ‹*Anspruch*›; **be ~d of bricks and mortar** aus Ziegelsteinen und Mörtel bestehen; **e)** *(give legal form to)* gründen ‹*Partei, Organisation*›; konstituieren ‹*Versammlung*›

constitution [kɒnstɪ'tju:ʃn] *n.* **a)** *(character of body, mental character)* Konstitution, *die;* **the complex ~ of his mind** die Komplexität seines Geistes; **b)** *(mode of State organization)* Staatsform, *die;* **c)** *(body of principles)* Verfassung, *die;* **written ~:** schriftlich festgelegte Verfassung; **d)** *(giving legal form)* Gründung, *die*

constitutional [kɒnstɪ'tju:ʃənl] **1.** *adj.* **a)** *(of bodily or mental constitution)* konstitutionell; **b)** *(Polit.) (of constitution)* der Verfassung *nachgestellt; (authorized by or in harmony with constitution)* verfassungsmäßig; konstitutionell ‹*Monarchie*›; **~ law** Verfassungsrecht, *das;* **c)** *(essential)* wesentlich; grundsätzlich ‹*Fähigkeit*›. **2.** *n.* Spaziergang, *der*

constitutionality [kɒnstɪtju:ʃə'nælɪtɪ] *n., no pl.* Verfassungskonformität, *die*

constitutionally [kɒnstɪ'tju:ʃənəlɪ] *adv.* **a)** *(in bodily or mental constitution)* konstitutionell; **b)** *(Polit.)* verfassungsmäßig; **c)** *(essentially)* wesentlich

constrain [kən'streɪn] *v. t.* **a)** zwingen; **b)** *(confine)* [auf]halten; *(fig.)* zügeln

constrained [kən'streɪnd] *adj.* gequält; gezwungen ‹*Pose*›; steif ‹*Bewegung, Pose*›

constraint [kən'streɪnt] *n.* **a)** Zwang, *der;* **he felt himself under some ~ to speak** er fühlte sich gezwungen zu sprechen; **b)** *(confinement)* Enge, *die; (limitation)* Einschränkung, *die;* **c)** *(restraint)* Gezwungenheit, *die;* **the atmosphere was one of ~:** die Atmosphäre war gezwungen *od.* steif

constrict [kən'strɪkt] *v. t. (make narrow)* verengen; **road-works are ~ing the flow of traffic** Straßenarbeiten behindern den Verkehrsfluß

constriction [kən'strɪkʃn] *n. (narrowing)* Verengung, *die;* **~ of the neck/throat** Einschnürung des Halses/der Kehle

construct 1. [kən'strʌkt] *v. t.* **a)** *(build)* bauen; *(fig.)* aufbauen; erstellen ‹*Plan*›; entwickeln ‹*Idee*›; **b)** *(Ling.; Geom.: draw)* konstruieren. **2.** ['kɒnstrəkt] *n.* **a)** Konstrukt, *das;* **b)** *(Ling.)* Konstruktion, *die*

construction [kən'strʌkʃn] *n.* **a)** *(constructing)* Bau, *der; (of sentence)* Konstruktion, *die; (fig.) (of empire, kingdom)* Errichtung, *die;* Aufbau, *der; (of plan, syllabus)* Erstellung, *die; (of idea)* Entwicklung, *die;* **~ work** Bauarbeiten *Pl.;* **~ worker** Bauarbeiter, *der;* **of wooden ~:** aus Holz gebaut; **be under ~:** im Bau sein; **b)** *(thing constructed)* Bauwerk, *das; (fig.)* Gebilde, *das;* **a wooden ~:** eine Holzkonstruktion; **c)** *(Ling.; Geom.: drawing)* Konstruktion, *die;* **d)** *(interpretation)* Deutung, *die;* **what ~ would you put upon ...?** wie würden Sie ... interpretieren *od.* auslegen?

constructional [kən'strʌkʃənl] *adj.* Bau‹*vorhaben, -plan, -weise*›; Konstruktions‹*element, -teil, -basis*›; **~ kit** Bausatz, *der;* **~ toy** Spielzeug zum Aufbauen

constructive [kən'strʌktɪv] *adj.* **a)** *(of construction; of structure of building)* konstruktiv; Bau‹*arbeiter, -material, -element, -plan*›; **b)** *(tending to construct)* konstruktiv ‹*Philosophie, Methode*›; schöpferisch ‹*Talent, Intelligenz*›; **c)** *(helpful)* konstruktiv; **d)** *(inferred)* indirekt

constructively [kən'strʌktɪvlɪ] *adv.* **a)** *(in construction)* bautechnisch gesehen; **b)** *(helpfully)* konstruktiv

construe [kən'stru:] *v. t.* **a)** *(Ling.) (combine)* konstruieren; *(analyse)* zerlegen; *(translate)* übersetzen; **b)** *(interpret)* auslegen; auffassen; **I ~d his words as meaning that ...:** ich habe ihn so verstanden, daß ...

consul ['kɒnsl] *n.* Konsul, *der*

consular ['kɒnsjʊlə(r)] *adj. (of State agent)* konsularisch; **~ rank** Rang eines Konsuls

consulate ['kɒnsjʊlət] *n.* **a)** *(period)* Amtszeit [als Konsul]; **b)** *(establishment)* Konsulat, *das;* **c)** *(Roman & French Hist.)* Konsulat, *das*

consulship ['kɒnslʃɪp] *see* **consulate a, c**

consult [kən'sʌlt] **1.** *v. i.* sich beraten **(with** mit); **~ together** sich miteinander beraten. **2.** *v. t.* **a)** *(seek information from)* konsultieren; befragen ‹*Orakel*›; fragen, konsultieren, zu Rate ziehen ‹*Arzt, Fachmann*›; **~ a list/book** in einer Liste/einem Buch nachsehen; **~ one's watch** auf die Uhr sehen; **~ a dictionary** in einem Wörterbuch nachschlagen; **b)** *(consider)* berücksichtigen; bedenken

consultancy [kən'sʌltənsɪ] *n.* **a)** *(of adviser)* Beraterstelle, *die;* **~ fee** Beratungsgebühr, *die;* **b)** *(of physician)* ≈ Chefarztstelle, *die*

consultant [kən'sʌltənt] **1.** *n.* **a)** *(adviser)* Berater, *der* /Beraterin, *die;* **b)** *(physician)* ≈ Chefarzt, *der*/-ärztin, *die.* **2.** *attrib. adj. see* **consulting**

consultation [kɒnsʌl'teɪʃn] *n.* Beratung, *die* **(on** über + *Akk.*); **have a ~ with sb.** sich mit jmdm. beraten; **by ~ of a dictionary/of an expert** durch Konsultation eines Wörterbuchs/Experten; **they are in ~ with the management about wages** sie stehen mit der Betriebsleitung in Lohnverhandlungen; **act in ~ with sb.** in Absprache mit jmdm. handeln

consultative [kən'sʌltətɪv] *adj.* beratend; konsultativ; **work on a ~ basis** *or* **in a ~ capacity for sb.** als Berater für jmdn. arbeiten; **~ document** ≈ Entwurf als Diskussionsgrundlage; *(governmental)* Regierungsentwurf, *der*

consulting [kən'sʌltɪŋ] *attrib. adj.* beratend ⟨*Architekt, Chemiker, Ingenieur*⟩; **~ physician** Konsiliararzt, *der/*-ärztin, *die*

con'sulting-room *n.* Sprechzimmer, *das*

consumable [kən'sju:məbl] *adj.* **a)** *(exhaustible)* kurzlebig ⟨*Konsumgüter*⟩; **b)** *(edible, drinkable)* genießbar

consume [kən'sju:m] *v. t.* **a)** *(use up)* verbrauchen; ⟨*Person:*⟩ aufwenden, ⟨*Sache:*⟩ kosten ⟨*Zeit, Energie*⟩; **b)** *(destroy)* vernichten; *(eat, drink)* konsumieren; verkonsumieren *(ugs.)*; **'nothing is to be ~d on these premises'** „Verzehr von Speisen und Getränken nicht gestattet"; **c)** *(fig.)* **be ~d with love/passion** sich in Liebe/Leidenschaft verzehren; **be ~d with fear/jealousy/envy/longing** sich vor Angst/Eifersucht/Neid/Sehnsucht verzehren *(geh.)*

consumer [kən'sju:mə(r)] *n. (Econ.)* Verbraucher, *der*/Verbraucherin, *die;* Konsument, *der*/Konsumentin, *die; see also* **durable 2**

con'sumer goods *n. pl.* Konsumgüter

consumerism [kən'sju:mərɪzm] *n., no pl., no art.* Konsumerismus, *der*

consumer: ~ pro'tection *n.* Verbraucherschutz, *der;* **~ research** *n.* Verbrauchsforschung, *die;* Konsumforschung, *die;* **~ resistance** *n. see* **sales resistance**

consuming [kən'sju:mɪŋ] *adj.* ganz in Anspruch nehmend, verzehrend *(geh.)* ⟨*Sehnsucht, Ehrgeiz*⟩; **stamp-collecting is a ~ interest of his** sein Interesse am Briefmarkensammeln nimmt ihn ganz in Anspruch

consummate 1. [kən'sʌmət] *adj.* **a)** *(perfect)* vollkommen; **with ~ ease** mühelos; **b)** *(accomplished)* perfekt; **a ~ artist** ein vollendeter Künstler. **2.** ['kɒnsəmeɪt, 'kɒnsjʊmeɪt] *v. t.* vollenden, zum Abschluß bringen ⟨*Diskussion, Geschäftsverhandlungen*⟩; vollziehen ⟨*Ehe*⟩

consummately [kən'sʌmətlɪ] *adj. (highly)* höchst; *(perfectly)* vollendet; *(completely)* völlig

consummation [kɒnsə'meɪʃn] *n.* **a)** *(completion)* Vollendung, *die; (of discussion, business)* Abschluß, *der; (of marriage)* Vollzug, *der;* **b)** *(goal)* Erfüllung, *die; (perfection, perfected thing)* Vollendung, *die*

consumption [kən'sʌmpʃn] *n.* **a)** *(using up, eating, drinking)* Verbrauch, *der* **(of** an + *Dat.*); *(act of eating or drinking)* Verzehr, *der* **(of** von); **~ of electricity/fuel/sugar** Strom-/Kraftstoff-/Zuckerverbrauch, *der;* **~ of alcohol** Alkoholkonsum, *der;* **what is our milk ~?** wieviel Milch verbrauchen wir?; **b)** *(destruction)* Vernichtung, *die; (waste)* Vergeudung, *die;* **c)** *(Econ.)* Verbrauch, *der;* Konsum, *der;* **d)** *(Med. dated)* Schwindsucht, *die (veralt.)*

consumptive [kən'sʌmptɪv] **1.** *adj. (Med. dated)* schwindsüchtig *(veralt.)*. **2.** *n.* Tuberkulosekranke, *der/die;* Schwindsüchtige, *der/die (veralt.)*

cont. *abbr.* **continued** Forts.

contact 1. ['kɒntækt] *n.* **a)** *(state of touching)* Berührung, *die;* Kontakt, *der; (fig.)* Verbindung, *die;* Kontakt, *der;* **point of ~:** Berührungspunkt, *der;* **be in ~ with sth.** etw. berühren; **be in ~ with sb.** *(fig.)* mit jmdm. in Verbindung stehen *od.* Kontakt haben; **come in** *or* **into ~ [with sth.]** [mit etw.] in Berührung kommen; **come into ~ with sb./sth.** *(fig.)* mit jmdm./etw. etwas zu tun haben; **make ~ with sth.** etw. berühren; **make ~ with sb.** *(fig.)* sich mit jmdm. in Verbindung setzen; mit jmdm. Kontakt aufnehmen; **lose ~ with sb.** *(fig.)* den Kontakt mit jmdm. verlieren; **renew ~ [with sb.]** *(fig.)* den Kontakt [mit *od.* zu jmdm.] wiederaufnehmen; **b)** *(Electr.) (connection)* Kontakt, *der;* **make/break a/the ~:** einen/den Kontakt herstellen/unterbrechen; **when the two wires make ~:** wenn die beiden Drähte sich berühren; **c)** *(Med.: person)* Kontaktperson, *die;* **d)** *(adviser etc.)* Verbindung, *die;* Kontakt, *der.* **2.** ['kɒntækt, kən'tækt] *v. t.* **a)** *(get into touch with)* sich in Verbindung setzen mit; **can I ~ you by telephone?** sind Sie telefonisch zu erreichen?; **try to ~ sb.** jmdn. zu erreichen versuchen; **~ your bank manager about the loan** wenden Sie sich bezüglich des Darlehens an den Direktor Ihrer Bank; **~ sb. by letter** sich schriftlich mit jmdm. in Verbindung setzen; **b)** *(begin dealings with)* Kontakt aufnehmen mit

contact: ~ lens *n.* Kontaktlinse, *die;* **~ man** *n.* Kontaktmann, *der;* Mittelsmann, *der;* **~ print** *n. (Photog.)* Kontaktabzug, *der*

contagion [kən'teɪdʒn] *n.* **a)** *(communication of disease)* Ansteckung, *die;* **b)** *(contagious disease)* ansteckende Krankheit; **c)** *(moral corruption)* Seuche, *die (fig.)*

contagious [kən'teɪdʒəs] *adj. (lit. or fig.)* ansteckend; **~ area/water** verseuchtes Gebiet/Wasser; **he is ~/is no longer ~:** er hat eine ansteckende Krankheit/er steckt niemanden mehr an

contain [kən'teɪn] *v. t.* **a)** *(hold as contents, include)* enthalten; *(comprise)* umfassen; **be ~ed within a space/between limits** sich in einem Gebiet/zwischen Grenzen befinden; **b)** *(prevent from moving)* halten; *(prevent from spreading; also Mil.)* aufhalten; eindämmen ⟨*Krankheit*⟩; *(restrain)* unterdrücken; **he could hardly ~ himself for joy** er konnte vor Freude kaum an sich *(Akk.)* halten

container [kən'teɪnə(r)] *n.* Behälter, *der; (cargo ~)* Container, *der;* **cardboard/wooden ~:** Pappkarton, *der*/Holzkiste, *die;* **in cylindrical/circular plastic ~s** in Plastiktrommeln/in [runden] Plastikbehältern

containerize [kən'teɪnəraɪz] *v. t.* in Container verpacken; auf Containertransport umstellen ⟨*Handelsweg, Verfahren*⟩

con'tainer ship *n.* Containerschiff, *das*

containment [kən'teɪnmənt] *n.* Eindämmung, *die; (Mil.)* Aufhalten, *das*

contaminant [kən'tæmɪnənt] *n.* verunreinigende Substanz

contaminate [kən'tæmɪneɪt] *v. t.* **a)** *(pollute)* verunreinigen; *(with radioactivity)* verseuchen; **b)** *(infect, lit. or fig.)* infizieren; *(fig.: spoil)* verseuchen

contamination [kəntæmɪ'neɪʃn] *n. see* **contaminate:** Verunreinigung, *die;* Verseuchung, *die;* Infizierung, *die*

contango [kən'tæŋgəʊ] *n., pl.* **~s** *(Brit. Finance)* Report, *der (Bankw.)*

contemplate ['kɒntəmpleɪt] **1.** *v. t.* **a)** betrachten; *(mentally)* nachdenken über (+ *Akk.*); *see also* **navel; b)** *(expect)* rechnen mit; *(consider)* in Betracht ziehen; **~ sth./doing sth.** an etw. *(Akk.)* denken/daran denken, etw. zu tun; **I wouldn't even ~ the idea** das käme für mich überhaupt nicht in Betracht. **2.** *v. i.* nachdenken

contemplation [kɒntəm'pleɪʃn] *n.* **a)** Betrachtung, *die; (mental)* Nachdenken, *das* **(of** über + *Akk.*); **b)** *(expectation)* Erwartung, *die; (consideration)* Erwägung, *die;* **be in ~:** erwogen werden; **c)** *(meditation)* Kontemplation, *die*

contemplative [kən'templətɪv, 'kɒntəmpleɪtɪv] *adj.* besinnlich; kontemplativ *(geh.)*

contemporaneous [kəntempə'reɪnɪəs] *adj. (formal)* gleichzeitig; *(of the same period)* aus derselben Zeit *nachgestellt*

contemporary [kən'tempərərɪ] **1.** *adj.* **a)** zeitgenössisch; *(present-day)* heutig; zeitgenössisch; **A is ~ with B** A und B finden zur gleichen Zeit statt; **the design is highly/very ~:** das Design ist hochmodern; **b)** *(equal in age)* gleichaltrig; **A is ~ with B** A und B sind gleichaltrig. **2.** *n.* **a)** *(person belonging to same time)* Zeitgenosse, *der*/-genossin, *die* **(to** von); **we were contemporaries** *or* **he was a ~ of mine at university/school** er war ein Studienkollege *od.* Kommilitone/Schulkamerad von mir; **b)** *(person of same age)* Altersgenosse, *der*/-genossin, *die;* **they are contemporaries** sie sind gleichaltrig *od.* Altersgenossen; **he is a ~ of hers** er ist [genau] so alt wie sie

contempt [kən'tempt] *n.* **a)** Verachtung, *die* **(of, for** für); *see also* **familiarity c; b)** *(disregard)* Mißachtung, *die;* **in ~ of all rules** unter Mißachtung aller Regeln; **c)** *(being despised)* **have** *or* **hold sb. in ~:** jmdn. verachten; **bring sb. into ~:** jmdn. in Verruf bringen; **fall into ~:** in Verruf kommen; *see also* **beneath 1 a; d)** *(Law)* Ungehorsam, *der;* **~ of court** *Ungehorsam od. Mißachtung gegenüber der Justiz; (in face of court)* ≈ Ungebühr vor Gericht

contemptible [kən'temptɪbl] *adj.* verachtenswert; **Old C~s** *(coll.) 1914 nach Frankreich geschicktes britisches Expeditionskorps*

contemptibly [kən'temptɪblɪ] *adv.* verachtenswert

contemptuous [kən'temptjʊəs] *adj.* verächtlich; überheblich ⟨*Person*⟩; **be ~ of sth./sb.** etw./jmdn. verachten; **~ of danger/warning** die Gefahr verachtend/alle Warnungen mißachtend; **with** *or* **in ~ disdain** voller Verachtung

contemptuously [kən'temptjʊəslɪ] *adv.* verächtlich

contend [kən'tend] **1.** *v. i.* **a)** *(strive)* **~ [with sb. for sth.]** [mit jmdm. um etw.] kämpfen; **b)** *(struggle)* **be able/have to ~ with** fertig werden können/müssen mit; bewältigen können/müssen ⟨*Post, Hindernis*⟩; ins reine kommen können/müssen mit ⟨*Gewissen*⟩; **I've got enough to ~ with at the moment** ich habe schon so genug um die Ohren *(ugs.)*; **~ with/against the waves** mit den Wellen kämpfen/gegen die Wellen ankämpfen; **c)** *(arch.: argue)* **~ with sb. about sth.** mit jmdm. über etw. streiten. **2.** *v. t.* **~ that ...:** behaupten, daß ...

contender [kən'tendə(r)] *n.* Bewerber, *der*/Bewerberin, *die*

[1]content ['kɒntent] *n.* **a)** *in pl.* Inhalt, *der;* **the ~s of the room had all been damaged** alles im Zimmer war beschädigt worden; **the ~s of this medicine are listed on the packet** die Zusammensetzung dieses Medikaments ist auf der Packung angegeben; **[table of] ~s** Inhaltsverzeichnis, *das;* **something in the ~s of the letter has made her very upset** etwas, was in dem Brief steht, hat sie ganz aus der Fassung gebracht; **b)** *(amount contained)* Gehalt, *der* **(of** an + *Dat.*); **c)** *(capacity)* Fassungsvermögen, *das; (volume)* Volumen, *das;* **d)** *(constituent elements, substance)* Gehalt, *der*

[2]content [kən'tent] **1.** *pred. adj.* zufrieden **(with** mit); **not rest ~ until** nicht zufrieden sein, bis; **not ~ with being late every morning, he also wants a pay rise** nicht genug [damit], daß er jeden Morgen zu spät kommt, er will auch noch eine Gehaltserhöhung; **be ~ to do sth.** bereit sein, etw. zu tun; *(pleased)* etw. gern tun; **I should be well ~ to do so** das würde ich recht gern tun. **2.** *n.* **to one's heart's ~:** nach Herzenslust. **3.** *v. t.* zufriedenstellen; befriedigen; **~ oneself with sth./sb.** sich mit etw./jmdm. zufriedengeben

contented [kən'tentɪd] *adj.* zufrieden **(with** mit); glücklich ⟨*Kindheit, Ehe, Leben*⟩; **be ~ to do sth.** sich damit abfinden, etw. zu tun

contentedly [kən'tentɪdlɪ] *adv.* zufrieden

contentedness [kən'tentɪdnɪs] *n., no pl.* Zufriedenheit, *die*

contention [kən'tenʃn] *n.* **a)** *(dispute)* Streit, *der;* Auseinandersetzung, *die; (rivalry)* Kampf, *der;* **the matter in ~:** die Streitfrage; **sth. is the subject of much ~:** etw. wird heftig diskutiert *od.* ist eine sehr strittige Frage; **be in ~ with sb.** sich mit jmdm. streiten; **b)** *(point asserted)* Behauptung, *die; see also* **¹put 1 f**
contentious [kən'tenʃəs] *adj.* **a)** *(quarrelsome)* streitsüchtig; streitlustig; **b)** *(involving contention)* strittig ‹*Punkt, Frage, Thema*›; umstritten ‹*Verhalten, Argument, Angelegenheit*›
contentiously [kən'tenʃəslɪ] *adv.* provozierend; **a ~ worded question** eine kontrovers formulierte Frage
contentment [kən'tentmənt] *n.* Zufriedenheit, *die;* **smile with ~:** zufrieden lächeln
contest 1. ['kɒntest] *n.* **a)** *(competition)* Wettbewerb, *der; (Sport)* Wettkampf, *der;* **b)** *no pl., no art. (dated/formal)* **a matter of ~:** eine Streitfrage; **engage in ~:** sich auf einen Kampf einlassen. **2.** [kən'test] *v.t.* **a)** *(dispute)* bestreiten; anfechten ‹*Anspruch, Recht*›; in Frage stellen ‹*Behauptung, These*›; **b)** *(fight for)* kämpfen um; **c)** *(Brit.) (compete in)* kandidieren bei; *(compete for)* kandidieren für; **d)** *(Amer.: dispute result of)* anfechten. **3.** *v.i.* **~ with** *or* **against sb./sth.** sich mit jmdm./etw. auseinandersetzen
contestable [kən'testəbl] *adj.* anfechtbar
contestant [kən'testənt] *n.* *(competitor)* Teilnehmer, *der*/Teilnehmerin, *die* **(in** an + *Dat.*, bei); *(in election)* Bewerber, *der*/Bewerberin, *die* **(for** um, für); *(in fight)* Gegner, *der*/Gegnerin, *die*
contestation [kɒntes'teɪʃn] *n.* **a)** *(contesting)* Bestreiten, *das; (of claim, right)* Anfechtung, *die;* **b)** *(disputation)* Streit, *der;* **c)** *(assertion)* Behauptung, *die*
context ['kɒntekst] *n.* **a)** Kontext, *der;* **in/out of ~:** im/ohne Kontext; **this sentence is quoted out of [its proper] ~:** dieser Satz ist aus dem Zusammenhang gerissen; **in this ~:** in diesem Zusammenhang; **b)** *(fig.: ambient conditions)* Umgebung, *die;* **in the ~ of** im Rahmen (+ *Gen.*)
contextual [kən'tekstjʊəl] *adj.* kontextuell
contextualize [kən'tekstjʊəlaɪz] *v.t.* *(place in context)* in einen Kontext einordnen
contiguity [kɒntɪ'gju:ɪtɪ] *n., no pl. (formal)* **a)** *(contact)* Berührung, *die;* **b)** *(proximity)* [unmittelbare] Nähe
contiguous [kən'tɪgjʊəs] *adj.* *(formal) (touching)* sich berührend; *(adjoining, neighbouring)* aneinandergrenzend; **be ~:** sich berühren/aneinandergrenzen/aufeinanderfolgen; **be ~ to sth.** etw. berühren/an etw. *(Akk.)* grenzen
continence ['kɒntɪnəns] *n.* **a)** *(temperance)* Mäßigkeit, *die; (chastity)* [sexuelle] Enthaltsamkeit; **b)** *(Med.)* Kontinenz, *die*
¹continent ['kɒntɪnənt] *n.* Kontinent, *der;* Erdteil, *der;* **the ~s of Europe, Asia, Africa** die Erdteile Europa, Asien, Afrika; **the C~:** das europäische Festland; der Kontinent
²continent *adj.* **a)** *(temperate)* maßvoll; *(chaste)* [sexuell] enthaltsam; **b)** *(Med.)* **be ~:** Harn und Stuhl zurückhalten können
continental [kɒntɪ'nentl] **1.** *adj.* **a)** kontinental; **~ Europe** Kontinentaleuropa *(das);* **b) C~** *(mainland European)* kontinental[europäisch]. **2.** *n.* **C~:** Kontinentaleuropäer, *der*/-europäerin, *die*
continental: ~ 'breakfast *n.* kontinentales Frühstück *(im Unterschied zum englischen Frühstück);* **~ climate** *n.* *(Geog.)* Kontinentalklima, *das;* **~ quilt** *(Brit.) n.* [Stepp]federbett, *das;* **~ 'shelf** *n.* *(Geog.)* Festland[s]sockel, *der*
contingency [kən'tɪndʒənsɪ] *n.* **a)** *(chance event)* Eventualität, *die; (possible event)* Eventualfall, *der;* **b)** *(incidental event)* unvorhergesehenes Ereignis; *(incidental expense)* unvorhergesehene Ausgabe
contingency: ~ fund *n.* Fonds für unvorhergesehene Ausgaben; **~ plan** *n.* Alternativplan, *der*
contingent [kən'tɪndʒənt] **1.** *adj.* **a)** *(fortuitous)* zufällig; **b)** *(incidental)* unvorhergesehen; **c)** *(Philos.)* kontingent; **d)** *(conditional)* abhängig **([up]on** von). **2.** *n.* *(Mil.; also fig.)* Kontingent, *das*
continual [kən'tɪnjʊəl] *adj.* *(frequently happening)* ständig; *(without cessation)* unaufhörlich; **there have been ~ quarrels** es gab ständig *od.* dauernd Streit; **she's a ~ chatterbox** ihr Mundwerk steht nie still *(ugs.)*
continually [kən'tɪnjʊəlɪ] *adv.* *(frequently)* ständig; immer wieder; *(without cessation)* unaufhörlich; **~ tired** immer müde
continuance [kən'tɪnjʊəns] *n.* **a)** *(continuing)* Fortbestand, *der; (of happiness, noise, rain)* Fortdauer, *die; (remaining)* Verbleiben, *das;* **b)** *(Amer. Law)* Vertagung, *die* **(until** auf + *Akk.*)
continuation [kəntɪnjʊ'eɪʃn] *n.* **a)** Fortsetzung, *die;* **a ~ of these good relations** eine Fortdauer dieser guten Beziehungen; **b)** *(St. Exch.)* Reportgeschäft, *das*
continue [kən'tɪnju:] **1.** *v.t.* **a)** fortsetzen; **'to be ~d'** „Fortsetzung folgt"; **'~d on page 2'** „Fortsetzung auf S. 2"; **~ doing** *or* **to do sth.** etw. weiter tun; **it ~d to rain** es regnete weiter; **it ~s to be a problem** es ist weiterhin ein Problem; **'...', he ~d** „...", fuhr er fort; **do ~ what you were saying** sprechen Sie nur weiter!; **I'll ~ the story where I left off** ich werde die Geschichte von da an weitererzählen, wo ich aufgehört habe; **b)** *(Amer. Law)* vertagen **(until** auf + *Akk.*). **2.** *v.i.* **a)** *(persist)* ‹*Wetter, Zustand, Krise usw.:*› andauern; *(persist in doing etc. sth.)* weitermachen *(ugs.);* nicht aufhören; *(last)* dauern; **this tradition still ~s** diesen Brauch gibt es immer noch; dieser Brauch lebt weiter; **if the rain ~s** wenn der Regen anhält; **if you ~ like this/in this manner** wenn Sie so weitermachen *(ugs.);* **how long is his speech likely to ~?** wie lange dauert seine Rede wohl noch?; **~ with sth.** mit etw. fortfahren; **we ~d with the work until midnight** wir arbeiteten weiter bis Mitternacht; **~ with a plan** einen Plan weiterverfolgen; **~ on one's way** seinen Weg fortsetzen; **b)** *(stay)* bleiben; **~ in power** an der Macht bleiben; **~ in control** die Kontrolle behalten; **she ~d in mourning for him all her life** sie trauerte ihr ganzes Leben lang um ihn; **c)** *(not become other than)* weiterhin sein; **he ~s feverish** er hat immer noch Fieber
continued [kən'tɪnju:d] *adj.* fortgesetzt ‹*Bemühungen*›; **~ existence** Weiterbestehen, *das*
continuity [kɒntɪ'nju:ɪtɪ] *n., no pl.* **a)** *(of path, frontier)* ununterbrochener Verlauf; *(unbroken succession, logical sequence, consistency)* Kontinuität, *die;* **b)** *(Cinemat., Telev., Radio) (scenario)* Szenario, *das; (script)* Skript, *das; (linking announcements)* Zwischentext, *der*
conti'nuity girl *n.* Skriptgirl, *das*
continuo [kən'tɪnjʊəʊ] *n., pl.* **~s** *(Mus.)* **a)** *(accompaniment)* Generalbaß, *der;* Basso continuo, *der;* **b)** *(instruments)* Generalbaßinstrumente
continuous [kən'tɪnjʊəs] *adj.* **a)** ununterbrochen; anhaltend ‹*Regen, Sonnenschein, Anstieg*›; ständig ‹*Kritik, Streit, Änderung*›; fortlaufend ‹*Mauer*›; durchgezogen ‹*Linie*›; **b)** *(Ling.)* **~ [form]** Verlaufsform, *die;* **present ~** *or* **~ present/past ~** *or* **~ past** Verlaufsform des Präsens/Präteritums
continuously [kən'tɪnjʊəslɪ] *adv.* *(in space)* durchgehend; nahtlos ‹*aneinanderfügen*›; *(in time or sequence)* ununterbrochen; unablässig, anhaltend ‹*ansteigen*›; ständig ‹*sich ändern*›
continuous 'stationery *n.* Endlosdruck, *der (Druckw.)*
continuum [kən'tɪnjʊəm] *n., pl.* **continua** [kən'tɪnjʊə] Kontinuum, *das*
contort [kən'tɔ:t] *v.t.* verdrehen *(auch fig.);* verzerren ‹*Gesicht, Gesichtszüge*›; verrenken, verdrehen ‹*Körper*›; **his face was ~ed with anger** sein Gesicht war wutverzerrt
contortion [kən'tɔ:ʃn] *n.* Verzerrung, *die; (of body)* Verdrehung, *die;* Verrenkung, *die*
contortionist [kən'tɔ:ʃənɪst] *n.* Schlangenmensch, *der*
contour ['kɒntʊə(r)] *n.* **a)** *(outline)* Kontur, *die;* **b)** *see* **contour line**
contour: ~ line *n.* *(Geog., Surv.)* Höhen[schicht]linie, *die;* **~ map** *n.* Höhenlinienkarte, *die;* **~ ploughing** *n.* *(Agric.)* Konturpflügen, *das*
contra ['kɒntrə] **1.** *prep. & adv.* **pro and ~:** pro und kontra. **2.** *n.* **the pros and ~s** das Pro und Kontra
contraband ['kɒntrəbænd] **1.** *n.* *(smuggled goods)* Schmuggelware, *die;* **~ of war** Konterbande, *die (Völkerrecht).* **2.** *adj.* geschmuggelt; **~ goods** Schmuggelware, *die*
contrabassoon ['kɒntrəbəsu:n] *n.* Kontrafagott, *das*
contraception [kɒntrə'sepʃn] *n.* Empfängnisverhütung, *die*
contraceptive [kɒntrə'septɪv] **1.** *adj.* empfängnisverhütend; kontrazeptiv *(Med.);* **~ device/method** Verhütungsmittel, *das*/-methode, *die.* **2.** *n.* Verhütungsmittel, *das*
contract 1. ['kɒntrækt] *n.* **a)** Vertrag, *der;* **~ of employment** Arbeitsvertrag, *der;* **be under ~ to do sth.** vertraglich verpflichtet sein, etw. zu tun; **exchange ~s** *(Law)* die Vertragsurkunden austauschen; **marriage ~:** Ehevertrag, *der;* **b)** *(Bridge etc.)* Kontrakt, *der;* **c)** *see* **contract bridge. 2.** [kən'trækt] *v.t.* **a)** *(cause to shrink, make smaller)* schrumpfen lassen; *(draw together)* zusammenziehen; verengen ‹*Pupillen*›; **b)** *(form)* **~ marriage** die Ehe eingehen *od.* schließen; **~ a habit** eine Angewohnheit annehmen; **c)** *(become infected with)* sich *(Dat.)* zuziehen; **~ sth. from sb.** sich mit etw. bei jmdm. anstecken; **~ sth. from ...:** an etw. *(Dat.)* durch ... erkranken; **d)** *(incur)* machen ‹*Schulden*›; **e)** *(Ling.)* zusammenziehen ‹*Wort, Silbe*›. **3.** *v.i.* **a)** *(enter into agreement)* Verträge/einen Vertrag schließen; **~ for sth.** etw. vertraglich zusichern; **~ to do sth.** *or* **that one will do sth.** sich vertraglich verpflichten, etw. zu tun; **b)** *(shrink, become smaller, be drawn together)* sich zusammenziehen; ‹*Pupillen:*› sich verengen
~ 'out 1. *v.i.* **~ out [of sth.]** sich [an etw. *(Dat.)*] nicht beteiligen; *(withdraw)* [aus etw.] aussteigen *(ugs.).* **2.** *v.t.* **~ work out [to another firm]** Arbeit [an eine andere Firma] vergeben
contract bridge [kɒntrækt 'brɪdʒ] *n.* Kontraktbridge, *das*
contractile [kən'træktaɪl] *adj.* *(Anat.: capable of contracting)* kontraktil
contraction [kən'trækʃn] *n.* **a)** *(shrinking)* Kontraktion, *die (Physik); (of eye-pupils)* Verengung, *die;* **b)** *(Physiol.: of muscle)* Zusammenziehung, *die;* Kontraktion, *die (Med.);* **c)** *(Ling.)* Kontraktion, *die;* **d)** *(catching)* Ansteckung, *die* **(of** mit); **e)** *(forming)* Annahme, *die; (of marriage)* Schließen, *das;* **~ of debts** Schuldenmachen, *das*
contractor [kən'træktə(r)] *n.* Auftragnehmer, *der*/-nehmerin, *die; see also* **building contractor**
contractual [kən'træktjʊəl] *adj.*, **contractually** [kən'træktjʊəlɪ] *adv.* vertraglich
contradict [kɒntrə'dɪkt] *v.t.* widersprechen (+ *Dat.*)
contradiction [kɒntrə'dɪkʃn] *n.* Widerspruch, *der* **(of** gegen); **in ~ to sth./sb.** im Widerspruch *od.* Gegensatz zu etw./jmdm.; **be a ~ to** *or* **of sth.** im Widerspruch zu etw. stehen; **a ~ in terms** ein Wider-

spruch in sich selbst; eine Contradictio in adjecto *(Rhet.)*

contradictory [kɒntrəˈdɪktərɪ] *adj.* **a)** widersprechend; *(mutually opposed)* widersprüchlich; **that is ~ to what was said last week** das widerspricht dem, was letzte Woche gesagt wurde; **b)** *(inclined to contradict)* widersetzlich; *(inconsistent)* widersprüchlich

contradistinction [kɒntrədɪˈstɪŋkʃn] *n.* Unterscheidung, *die;* **in ~ to sth.** im Unterschied zu etw.

ˈcontra-flow *n.* Gegenverkehr auf einem Fahrstreifen

contralto [kənˈtræltəʊ] *n., pl.* **~s** *(Mus.)* **a)** *(voice)* Alt, *der; (very low)* Kontraalt, *der;* **b)** *(singer)* Altistin, *die;* Alt, *der (selten); (with very low voice)* Kontraalt, *der;* **c)** *(part)* Alt, *der; (for very low voice)* zweiter Alt; Alt II

contraption [kənˈtræpʃn] *n. (coll.) (strange machine)* Apparat, *der (ugs.); (vehicle)* Vehikel, *das; (device)* [komisches] Gerät

contrapuntal [kɒntrəˈpʌntl] *adj. (Mus.)* kontrapunktisch

contrarily *adv.* **a)** [ˈkɒntrərɪlɪ] *(in a contrary manner)* **I think ~:** ich glaube das Gegenteil; **we've decided ~:** wir haben uns für das Gegenteil entschieden; **b)** [kənˈtreərɪlɪ] *(coll.: perversely)* widerspenstig; widerborstig

contrariness [kənˈtreərɪnɪs] *n., no pl. (coll.)* Widerspenstigkeit, *die;* Widerborstigkeit, *die*

contrariwise [kənˈtreərɪwaɪz] *adv.* **a)** *(on the other hand)* andererseits; **b)** *(in the opposite way)* umgekehrt

contrary 1. *adj.* **a)** [ˈkɒntrərɪ] entgegengesetzt; **be ~ to sth.** im Gegensatz zu etw. stehen; **the result was ~ to expectation** das Ergebnis entsprach nicht den Erwartungen; **b)** *(opposite)* entgegengesetzt; *(adverse)* widrig ‹*Wind*›; **c)** [kənˈtreərɪ] *(coll.: perverse)* widerspenstig; widerborstig; **he's ~ by nature** er ist von Natur aus voller Widerspruchsgeist. **2.** [ˈkɒntrərɪ] *n.* **the ~:** das Gegenteil; **be/do completely the ~:** das genaue Gegenteil sein/tun; **go by contraries** anders als erwartet verlaufen; ‹*Traum:*› das Gegenteil bedeuten; ‹*Stimmung:*› [grundsätzlich] konträr sein; **on the ~:** im Gegenteil; **appearances to the ~, ...:** dem äußeren Anschein zum Trotz, ...; **quite the ~:** ganz im Gegenteil. **3.** *adv.* **~ to sth.** entgegen einer Sache; **~ to expectation** wider Erwarten

contrast 1. [kənˈtrɑːst] *v. t.* gegenüberstellen; kontrastieren lassen, [deutlich] voneinander abheben ‹*Farben*›; **~ sth. with sth.** etw. von etw. [deutlich] abheben; **be ~ed with sth.** sich [deutlich] von etw. abheben. **2.** *v. i.* **~ with sth.** mit etw. kontrastieren; sich von etw. abheben. **3.** [ˈkɒntrɑːst] *n.* **a)** *(juxtaposition)* Kontrast, *der* **(with** zu); **what a ~!** welch ein Gegensatz!; **in ~, ...:** im Gegensatz dazu, ...; **[be] in ~ with sth.** im Gegensatz *od.* Kontrast zu etw. [stehen]; **by way of ~:** als Kontrast; **b)** *(thing)* **a ~ to sth.** ein Gegensatz zu etw.; *(person)* **be a ~ to sb.** [ganz] anders sein als jmd.; **c)** *(Photog., Telev., Psych.)* Kontrast, *der;* **d) ~ medium** *(Med.)* Kontrastmittel, *das*

contrasting [kənˈtrɑːstɪŋ] *adj.* gegensätzlich; kontrastierend ‹*Farbe*›; *(very different)* sehr unterschiedlich

contravene [kɒntrəˈviːn] *v. t. (infringe)* verstoßen gegen ‹*Recht, Gesetz*›; zuwiderhandeln (+ *Dat.*) ‹*Beschluß, Rat, Empfehlung*›; *(conflict with)* widersprechen (+ *Dat.*)

contravention [kɒntrəˈvenʃn] *n.* **~ of the law/rules/moral standards** Verstoß gegen das Gesetz/die Regeln/die Moral; **be in ~ of sth.** im Widerspruch zu etw. stehen; **act in ~ of sth.** einer Sache *(Dat.)* zuwiderhandeln

contretemps [ˈkɔ̃trətɑ̃] *n., pl. same* [ˈkɔ̃trətɑ̃z] Mißgeschick, *das;* Malheur, *das (ugs.)*

contribute [kənˈtrɪbjuːt] **1.** *v. t.* **~ sth. [to** *or* **towards sth.]** etw. [zu etw.] beitragen/*(cooperatively)* beisteuern; **~ money towards sth.** für etw. Geld beisteuern/*(for charity)* spenden; **he regularly ~s articles to the 'Guardian'** er schreibt regelmäßig für den „Guardian". **2.** *v. i.* **~ to** *or* **towards a jumble sale** etwas zu einem Trödelmarkt beisteuern; **if only the child would ~ more in class** wenn das Kind nur mehr zum Unterricht beitragen würde; **everyone ~d towards the production** jeder trug etwas zur Aufführung bei; **~ to charity** für karitative Zwecke spenden; **~ to sb.'s misery/disappointment** jmds. Kummer/Enttäuschung vergrößern; **~ to a newspaper** für eine Zeitung schreiben; **he ~d to the 'Encyclopaedia Britannica'** er hat an der Encyclopaedia Britannica mitgearbeitet; **~ to the success of sth.** zum Erfolg einer Sache *(Gen.)* beitragen

contribution [kɒntrɪˈbjuːʃn] *n.* **a)** *(act of contributing)* **make a ~ to a fund** etw. für einen Fonds spenden; **the ~ of clothing and money to sth.** das Spenden von Kleidern und Geld für etw.; **b)** *(thing contributed)* Beitrag, *der; (for charity)* Spende, *die* **(to** für); **~s of clothing and money** Kleider- und Geldspenden; **make a ~ to sth.** einen Beitrag zu etw. leisten

contributor [kənˈtrɪbjʊtə(r)] *n.* **a)** *(giver)* Spender, *der*/Spenderin, *die;* **b)** *(supplier of writings)* Mitarbeiter, *der*/Mitarbeiterin, *die;* **he is a regular ~ [of articles] to the 'Guardian'** er schreibt regelmäßig [Artikel] für den „Guardian"

contributory [kənˈtrɪbjʊtərɪ] *adj.* **a)** *(that contributes)* **a ~ factor to his state of mind/in the poor state of the economy** ein Faktor, der bei seiner geistigen Verfassung/bei der schlechten Wirtschaftslage eine Rolle spielt; **~ funds** Hilfsfonds; **~ negligence** *(Law)* Mitverschulden, *das;* **b)** *(operated by contributions)* **be run on a ~ basis** mit Beiträgen *od.* Spenden finanziert werden; **~ insurance payments** Versicherungspflichtbeiträge

contrite [ˈkɒntraɪt] *adj.* zerknirscht; *(showing contrition)* reuevoll; **~ sigh/tears/words** Seufzer/Tränen/Worte der Reue; **~ apology** zerknirschte Entschuldigung

contritely [ˈkɒntraɪtlɪ] *adv.* zerknirscht

contrition [kənˈtrɪʃn] *n.* Reue, *die;* **~ leads to absolution** Kontrition ist die Voraussetzung für die Absolution *(kath. Theol.);* **hang one's head in ~:** den Kopf reumütig senken

contrivance [kənˈtraɪvəns] *n.* **a)** *(contriving)* Plan, *der;* **deceitful ~s** faule Tricks *(ugs. abwertend);* **b)** *(invention)* Ersinnen, *das; (inventive capacity)* Erfindungsgabe, *die;* **c)** *(device)* Gerät, *das*

contrive [kənˈtraɪv] *v. t.* **a)** *(manage)* **~ to do sth.** es fertigbringen *od.* zuwege bringen, etw. zu tun; **can you ~ to be here by 6 a.m.?** können Sie es einrichten, bis 6 Uhr morgens hier zu sein?; **they ~d to meet** es gelang ihnen, sich zu treffen; **b)** *(devise)* sich *(Dat.)* ausdenken; ersinnen *(geh.);* **~ ways and means of doing sth.** Mittel und Wege finden, etw. zu tun

contrived [kənˈtraɪvd] *adj.* künstlich

control [kənˈtrəʊl] **1.** *n.* **a)** *(power of directing, restraint)* Kontrolle, *die* **(of** über + *Akk.*); *(management)* Leitung, *die;* **~ of the economy** Wirtschaftslenkung, *die;* **board of ~:** Aufsichtsbehörde, *die;* **~ over ecclesiastical matters** höchste Gewalt in kirchlichen Dingen; **governmental ~:** Regierungsgewalt, *die;* **~ of the vehicle/machine is totally automatic** das Fahrzeug/die Maschine hat vollautomatische Steuerung; **have ~ of sth.** die Kontrolle über etw. *(Akk.)* haben; etw. kontrollieren; *(take decisions)* für etw. zuständig sein; **take ~ of** die Kontrolle übernehmen über (+ *Akk.*); **keep ~ of sth.** etw. unter Kontrolle halten; **be in ~ [of sth.]** die Kontrolle [über etw. *(Akk.)*] haben; **be in ~ of the situation** die Situation unter Kontrolle haben; **who's in ~ here?** wer hat hier zu bestimmen?; **be in ~ of education** für das Erziehungswesen zuständig sein; **[go** *or* **get] out of ~** *or* **beyond [sb.'s] ~:** außer Kontrolle [geraten]; **circumstances beyond sb.'s ~:** unvorhersehbare, nicht in jmds. Hand liegende Umstände; **[get sth.] under ~:** [etw.] unter Kontrolle [bringen]; **keep oneself/sth. under ~:** sich/etw. in der Gewalt haben; **everything's under ~** *(fig.)* alles in Ordnung; **lose ~ [of sth.]** die Kontrolle [über etw. *(Akk.)*] verlieren; **lose ~ of the situation** die Situation nicht mehr unter Kontrolle haben; **gain ~ of sth.** etw. unter Kontrolle bekommen; **lose/regain ~ of oneself** die Beherrschung verlieren/wiedergewinnen; **have some/complete/no ~ over sth.** eine gewisse/die absolute/keine Kontrolle über etw. *(Akk.)* haben; **have ~ over oneself** sich in der Gewalt haben; **he has no ~ over himself** er hat sich nicht in der Gewalt; *see also* **flight control; b)** *(standard of comparison)* Kontrollobjekt, *das; (person)* Kontrollperson, *die;* **~ experiment** Kontrollversuch, *der;* **c)** *(device)* Regler, *der;* **~s** *(as a group)* Schalttafel, *die; (of TV, stereo system)* Bedienungstafel, *die;* **at the ~s** an der Schalttafel; **be at the ~s** an der Schalttafel sitzen; ‹*Fahrer, Pilot:*› am Steuer sitzen; *(fig.)* das Steuer in der Hand haben; **d)** *in pl. (means of regulating)* Beschränkung, *die;* Kontrolle, *die;* **impose ~s on imports** Importbeschränkungen einführen; **e)** *(Spiritualism)* Kontrolle, *die (Parapsych.);* Kontrollgeist, *der (Parapsych.);* **f)** *(check-point for rally cars)* Kontrollpunkt, *der.* **2.** *v. t.,* **-ll-: a)** *(have ~ of)* kontrollieren; steuern, lenken ‹*Auto*›; leiten ‹*Firma*›; **you must ~ your dog** Sie müssen Ihren Hund unter Kontrolle halten; **he ~s the financial side of things** er ist für die Finanzen zuständig *od.* hat die Finanzen unter sich; **~ a class** eine Klasse fest im Griff haben; **~ling company** *(Econ.)* Kontrollgesellschaft, *die;* **~ling interest** Mehrheitsbeteiligung, *die (Wirtsch.);* **b)** *(hold in check)* beherrschen; zügeln ‹*Zorn, Ungeduld, Temperament*›; im Zaum halten ‹*Zunge*›; *(regulate)* kontrollieren; regulieren ‹*Geschwindigkeit, Temperatur*›; einschränken ‹*Export, Ausgaben*›; regeln ‹*Verkehr*›; unterdrücken ‹*Gefühlsäußerung*›; **~ yourselves, children!** nehmt euch zusammen, Kinder!; **c)** *(check, verify)* [über]prüfen

control: ~ centre *n.* Kontrollzentrum, *das;* **~ desk** *n.* Schaltpult, *das*

controller [kənˈtrəʊlə(r)] *n.* **a)** *(director)* Leiter, *der*/Leiterin, *die;* Chef, *der*/Chefin, *die (ugs.);* **b)** *see* **comptroller**

control: ~ panel *n.* Schalttafel, *die;* **~ room** *n.* Kontrollraum, *der; (in theatre)* Stellwarte, *die; (Radio, Telev.)* Regieraum, *der; (in power station)* Schaltwarte, *die;* **~ tower** *n.* Kontrollturm, *der;* Tower, *der*

controversial [kɒntrəˈvɜːʃl] *adj. (causing controversy)* umstritten ‹*Mode, Kunstwerk, Gesetz, Idee*›; strittig ‹*Frage, Punkt, Angelegenheit*›; *(given to controversy)* streitsüchtig; *(lacking neutrality)* polemisch

controversy [ˈkɒntrəvɜːsɪ, kənˈtrɒvəsɪ] *n.* Kontroverse, *die;* Auseinandersetzung, *die;* **much ~:** eine längere Kontroverse *od.* Auseinandersetzung; **sth. is beyond ~:** etw. ist unumstritten

controvert [ˈkɒntrəvɜːt, kɒntrəˈvɜːt] *v. t. (formal)* bestreiten; ‹*Argument, Theorie:*› widersprechen (+ *Dat.*)

contuse [kənˈtjuːz] *v. t.* prellen

contusion [kənˈtjuːʒn] *n.* Prellung, *die*

conundrum [kəˈnʌndrəm] *n. (riddle) (auf einem Wortspiel beruhendes)* Rätsel; *(hard question)* Problem, *das;* **pose ~s** Rätsel aufgeben

conurbation [kɒnɜːˈbeɪʃn] *n.* Konurbation, *die (Soziol.);* ≈ Stadtregion, *die*
convalesce [kɒnvəˈles] *v. i.* genesen; rekonvaleszieren *(Med.)*
convalescence [kɒnvəˈlesəns] *n.* Genesung, *die;* Rekonvaleszens, *die (Med.)*
convalescent [kɒnvəˈlesənt] **1.** *adj.* rekonvaleszent *(Med.);* **you'll be ~ for a few weeks** Ihre Genesung wird ein paar Wochen dauern; **~ patient** Rekonvaleszent, *der*/Rekonvaleszentin, *die (Med.).* **2.** *n.* Rekonvaleszent, *der*/Rekonvaleszentin, *die (Med.);* Genesende, *der/die*
convalescent: ~ home, ~ hospital *ns.* Genesungsheim, *das*
convection [kənˈvekʃn] *n. (Phys., Meteorol.)* Konvektion, *die;* **~ current** Konvektionsstrom, *der*
convective [kənˈvektɪv] *adj. (Phys., Meteorol.)* konvektiv
convector [kənˈvektə(r)] *n.* Konvektor, *der*
convene [kənˈviːn] **1.** *v. t.* einberufen. **2.** *v. i.* zusammenkommen; ⟨*Gericht, gewählte Vertreter:*⟩ zusammentreten; ⟨*Konferenz, Versammlung:*⟩ beginnen
convener [kənˈviːnə(r)] *n. (Brit.) jmd., der eine Versammlung einberuft/leitet*
convenience [kənˈviːnɪəns] *n.* **a)** *no pl. (suitableness, advantageousness)* Annehmlichkeit, *die;* **its ~ to** *or* **for the city centre** seine günstige Lage zum Stadtzentrum; **marriage of ~:** Vernunftehe, *die; see also* ¹**flag 1; b)** *(personal satisfaction)* Bequemlichkeit, *die;* Wohlbefinden, *das;* **for sb.'s ~, for ~'s sake** zu jmds. Bequemlichkeit; **is it to your ~?** paßt es Ihnen?; **at your ~:** wann es Ihnen paßt; **at your earliest ~:** möglichst bald; baldmöglichst *(Papierdt.);* **c)** *(advantage)* **be a ~ to sb.** angenehm *od.* praktisch für jmdn. sein; **having a car is such a ~:** ein Auto zu haben ist so angenehm *od.* praktisch; **make a ~ of sb.** jmdn. ausnutzen; **d)** *(advantageous thing)* Annehmlichkeit, *die;* **a car is a [great] ~ to have** es ist [sehr] angenehm *od.* praktisch, ein Auto zu haben; **e)** *(esp. Admin.: toilet)* Toilette, *die;* **public ~** öffentliche Toilette *od. (Amtsspr.)* Bedürfnisanstalt
conˈvenience food *n.* Fertignahrung, *die*
convenient [kənˈviːnɪənt] *adj.* **a)** *(suitable, not troublesome)* günstig; *(useful)* praktisch; angenehm; **be ~ to** *or* **for sb.** günstig für jmdn. sein; **would it be ~ to you?** würde es Ihnen passen?; wäre es Ihnen recht?; **it's not very ~ at the moment** es paßt im Augenblick nicht gut; **if it is not ~ to have us to stay** wenn es ungelegen kommt, daß wir bleiben; **b)** *(of easy access)* **be ~ to** *or* **for sth.** günstig zu etw. liegen; **our house is very ~ to** *or* **for the city centre** wir haben es nicht weit zum Stadtzentrum; **c)** *(opportunely available or occurring)* **a ~ taxi** ein Taxi, das gerade dasteht/angefahren kommt
conveniently [kənˈviːnɪəntlɪ] *adv.* **a)** *(suitably, without difficulty, accessibly)* günstig ⟨*gelegen, angebracht*⟩; leicht ⟨*gesehen werden*⟩; angenehm ⟨*ruhig*⟩; **when can you ~ drop round?** wann paßt es dir *od.* wann kannst du es einrichten, mal vorbeizukommen?; **we're ~ situated for the shops** wir haben es nicht weit zu den Geschäften; **b)** *(opportunely)* angenehmerweise; **very ~, we were only a mile from a garage** glücklicherweise waren wir nur eine Meile von einer Werkstatt entfernt
convenor *see* **convener**
convent [ˈkɒnvənt] *n.* Kloster, *das;* **~ of nuns** Nonnenkloster, *das;* **enter a ~:** ins Kloster gehen
convention [kənˈvenʃn] *n.* **a)** *(a practice)* Brauch, *der;* **it is the ~ to do sth.** es ist Brauch, etw. zu tun; **~s of spelling** Rechtschreibregeln; **b)** *no art. (established customs)* Konvention, *die;* **break with ~:** sich über die Konventionen hinwegsetzen; **c)** *(formal assembly)* Konferenz, *die;* **d)** *(agreement between parties)* Abkommen, *das;* Übereinkunft, *die; (agreement between States)* Konvention, *die (bes. Völkerrecht)*
conventional [kənˈvenʃənl] *adj.* konventionell; *(not spontaneous)* formell; **it is ~ wisdom that ...:** man glaubt allgemein, daß ...; **it is ~ to send flowers** es ist üblich, Blumen zu schicken; **~ weapons** konventionelle Waffen
conventionally [kənˈvenʃənəlɪ] *adv.* konventionell
conventioneer [kənvenʃəˈnɪə(r)] *n. (Amer.)* Konferenzteilnehmer, *der*/-teilnehmerin, *die*
ˈ**convent school** *n.* Klosterschule, *die*
converge [kənˈvɜːdʒ] *v. i.* **~ [on each other]** aufeinander zulaufen; ⟨*Gedanken, Meinungen, Ansichten:*⟩ sich [einander] annähern, *(geh.)* konvergieren; **~ on sb.** auf jmdn. zulaufen; **they ~d on the scene of the accident** sie liefen an Unfallort zusammen
convergence [kənˈvɜːdʒəns] *n.* **a)** Annäherung, *die;* Konvergenz, *die (geh.); (of roads, rivers)* Zusammentreffen, *das;* **at the ~ of the roads** an der Stelle, wo die Straßen zusammentreffen; **b)** *(Math., Biol., Psych.)* Konvergenz, *die*
convergent [kənˈvɜːdʒənt] *adj.* **a)** aufeinander zulaufend; konvergierend *(geh.),* sich einander annähernd ⟨*Meinungen, Gedanken, Ansichten*⟩; **b)** *(Math., Biol., Psych.)* konvergent; **~ lens** *(Optics)* Sammellinse, *die*
conversant [kənˈvɜːsənt] *pred. adj.* vertraut **(with** mit)
conversation [kɒnvəˈseɪʃn] *n.* Unterhaltung, *die;* Gespräch, *das;* Konversation, *die (geh.); (in language-teaching)* Konversation, *die;* **be in ~ [with sb.]** sich [mit jmdm.] unterhalten; **be deep in ~:** in ein Gespräch vertieft sein; **enter into ~ with sb.** mit jmdm. ein Gespräch anfangen *od.* anknüpfen; **make [polite] ~ with sb.** mit jmdm. Konversation machen; **in the course of ~:** im Verlauf des Gesprächs; **come up in ~:** gesprächsweise erwähnt werden; **he hasn't much ~:** man kann sich kaum mit ihm unterhalten; **have a ~ with sb.** mit jmdm. ein Gespräch führen
conversational [kɒnvəˈseɪʃənl] *adj.* gesprächig ⟨*Person*⟩; **talk in ~ tones/in a ~ manner** im Plauderton/ungezwungen sprechen; **~ English** gesprochenes Englisch; **the discussion remained on a casual, ~ level** die Diskussion blieb auf der Ebene einer zwanglosen Unterhaltung
conversationalist [kɒnvəˈseɪʃənəlɪst] *n.* Unterhalter, *der*/Unterhalterin, *die;* **be a/no great ~:** gut/nicht gut Konversation machen können
conversationally [kɒnvəˈseɪʃənəlɪ] *adv.* **'Nice day today', he remarked ~:** „Schöner Tag heute", stellte er fest, um ein Gespräch zu beginnen
converˈsation piece *n. (topic of conversation)* Gesprächsthema, *das*
¹**converse** [kənˈvɜːs] *v. i. (formal)* **~ [with sb.] [about** *or* **on sth.]** sich [mit jmdm.] [über etw. *(Akk.)*] unterhalten
²**converse** [ˈkɒnvɜːs] **1.** *adj.* entgegengesetzt; umgekehrt ⟨*Fall, Situation*⟩. **2.** *n.* **a)** *(opposite)* Gegenteil, *das;* **b)** *(Math.)* Kehrsatz, *der;* **c)** *(Logic)* Konversion, *die*
conversely [kənˈvɜːslɪ] *adv.* umgekehrt
conversion [kənˈvɜːʃn] *n.* **a)** *(transforming)* Umwandlung, *die* **(into** in + *Akk.*); **b)** *(adaptation, adapted building)* Umbau, *der;* **do a ~ on sth.** etw. umbauen; **c)** *(of person)* Bekehrung, *die* **(to** zu); Konversion, *die (Rel.);* **d)** *(to different units or expression)* Übertragung, *die* **(into** in + *Akk.*); **e)** *(Finance, Logic, Theol., Psych., Phys.)* Konversion, *die; (calculation)* Umrechnung, *die; (Rugby, Amer. Footb.)* Erhöhung, *die*
conˈversion table *n.* Umrechnungstabelle, *die*
convert 1. [kənˈvɜːt] *v. t.* **a)** *(transform, change in function)* umwandeln **(into** in + *Akk.*); **b)** *(adapt)* **~ sth. [into sth.]** etw. [zu etw.] umbauen; **c)** *(bring over)* **~ sb. [to sth.]** *(lit. or fig.)* jmdn. [zu etw.] bekehren; **d)** *(to different units or expressions)* übertragen **(into** in + *Akk.*); **e)** *(Finance)* konvertieren; *(calculate)* umrechnen **(into** in + *Akk.*); **f)** *(Rugby, Amer. Footb.)* erhöhen; **g) ~ to one's own use** sich *(Dat.)* aneignen. **2.** *v. i.* **a)** *(be transformable, be changeable in function)* **~ into sth.** sich in etw. *(Akk.)* umwandeln lassen; **b)** *(be adaptable)* sich umbauen lassen; **c)** *(to new method etc.)* umstellen **(to** auf + *Akk.*). **3.** [ˈkɒnvɜːt] *n.* **a)** *(Relig.)* Konvertit, *der*/Konvertitin, *die;* **b)** *(fig.)* **the new ~ s to the Party** die neuen Anhänger der Partei; **he became a ~ to Asian philosophy** er wurde ein Anhänger der asiatischen Philosophie
converter [kənˈvɜːtə(r)] *n.* **a)** *(Metall.)* Konverter, *der;* **b)** *(Electr.)* Umformer, *der*
convertibility [kənvɜːtɪˈbɪlɪtɪ] *n., no pl.* **a)** Umwandelbarkeit, *die;* **b)** *(Finance)* Konvertierbarkeit, *die*
convertible [kənˈvɜːtɪbl] **1.** *adj.* **a) be ~ into sth.** sich in etw. *(Akk.)* umwandeln lassen; **~ sofa** Ausziehcouch, *die;* **b)** *(able to be altered)* **be ~ [into sth.]** sich zu etw. umbauen lassen; **c)** *(Finance)* **be ~ into sth.** in etw. *(Akk.)* konvertierbar sein. **2.** *n.* Kabrio[lett], *das; (with four or more seats)* Kabriolimousine, *die*
convex [ˈkɒnveks] *adj.* konvex; Konvex⟨*linse, -spiegel*⟩
convexity [kənˈveksɪtɪ] *n.* Wölbung, *die;* Konvexität, *die (Optik)*
convey [kənˈveɪ] *v. t.* **a)** *(transport)* befördern; *(transmit)* übermitteln ⟨*Nachricht, Grüße*⟩; **the TV pictures are ~ed by satellite** die Fernsehbilder werden per Satellit übertragen; **b)** *(impart)* vermitteln; **words cannot ~ it** Worte können es nicht wiedergeben; **the message ~ed nothing whatever to me** die Nachricht sagte mir überhaupt nichts; **~ one's meaning to sb.** jmdm. deutlich machen, was man meint; **c)** *(Law)* **~ property [to sb.]** [jmdm.] Eigentum übertragen *od.* überschreiben
conveyance [kənˈveɪəns] *n.* **a)** *(transportation)* Beförderung, *die; (of sound, picture, heat, light)* Übertragung, *die; (of message, greetings)* Übermittlung, *die;* **b)** *(formal: vehicle)* Beförderungsmittel, *das;* **c)** *(Law)* Übertragung, *die;* Überschreibung, *die;* **[deed of] ~:** Übertragungsurkunde, *die*
conveyancing [kənˈveɪənsɪŋ] *n. (Law)* **~ [of property]** [Eigentums]übertragung, *die*
conveyer, conveyor [kənˈveɪə(r)] *n.* Förderer, *der (Technik);* **[bucket] ~:** Becherwerk, *das;* **[chain] ~:** Kettenförderer, *der;* **~ [belt]** *(Industry)* Förderband, *das; (in manufacture also)* Fließband, *das*
convict 1. [ˈkɒnvɪkt] *n.* Strafgefangene, *der/die.* **2.** [kənˈvɪkt] *v. t.* **a)** *(declare guilty)* für schuldig befinden; verurteilen; **be ~ed** verurteilt werden; **b)** *(prove guilty)* **~ sb. of sth.** jmdn. einer Sache *(Gen.)* überführen
conviction [kənˈvɪkʃn] *n.* **a)** *(Law)* Verurteilung, *die* **(for** wegen); **have you [had] any previous ~s?** sind Sie vorbestraft?; **he has no criminal ~s at all** er hat keinerlei Vorstrafen; **b)** *(settled belief)* Überzeugung, *die;* **a vegetarian by ~:** ein überzeugter Vegetarier; **it is their ~ that ...:** sie sind der Überzeugung, daß ...; **her ~ of the existence of God/of his innocence** ihr fester Glaube an die Existenz Gottes/an seine Unschuld; **what are his political ~s?** wie sind seine politischen Anschauungen?; **carry ~:** überzeugend sein; ⟨*Stimme:*⟩ überzeugend klingen
convince [kənˈvɪns] *v. t.* überzeugen; **~ sb.**

that ...: jmdn. davon überzeugen, daß ...; **be ~d that ...:** davon überzeugt sein, daß ...; **manage to ~ oneself that ...:** sich *(Dat.)* einreden, daß ...; **~ sb. of sth.** jmdn. von etw. überzeugen
convincing [kən'vɪnsɪŋ] *adj.* überzeugend; täuschend ⟨*Ähnlichkeit*⟩
convincingly [kən'vɪnsɪŋlɪ] *adv.* überzeugend
convivial [kən'vɪvɪəl] *n.* fröhlich
conviviality [kənvɪvɪ'ælɪtɪ] *n., no pl.* Fröhlichkeit, *die*
convivially [kən'vɪvɪəlɪ] *adv.* fröhlich
convocation [kɒnvə'keɪʃn] *n.* **a)** *(calling together)* Zusammenrufen, *das; (of council, synod)* Einberufung, *die;* **b)** *(assembly)* Versammlung, *die;* **c)** *(Brit. Eccl.)* Provinzialsynode, *die;* **d)** *(Brit. Univ.) universitäre gesetzgebende Versammlung;* ≈ Vollversammlung, *die*
convoke [kən'vəʊk] *v. t.* zusammenrufen; einberufen ⟨*Versammlung, Synode, Rat*⟩
convoluted ['kɒnvəlu:tɪd] *adj.* **a)** *(twisted)* verschlungen; verdreht ⟨*Körperhaltung*⟩; **b)** *(complex)* kompliziert
convolution [kɒnvə'lu:ʃn] *n.* Windung, *die;* **the ~s of the winding road** die Biegungen der kurvenreichen Straße
convolvulus [kən'vɒlvjʊləs] *n. (Bot.)* Winde, *die*
convoy ['kɒnvɔɪ] **1.** *v. t.* Geleitschutz geben (+ *Dat.*). **2.** *n.* Konvoi, *der;* **in ~:** im Konvoi
convulse [kən'vʌls] *v. t.* **a) be ~d** von Krämpfen geschüttelt werden; *(fig.)* **be ~d with laughter** sich vor Lachen biegen *(ugs.);* **be ~d with rage/fury** sich vor Wut krümmen; **b)** *(shake, lit. or fig.)* erschüttern
convulsion [kən'vʌlʃn] *n.* **a)** *in pl.* Schüttelkrampf, *der (Med.);* Krämpfe; *(fig.)* **~s of laughter** Lachkrampf, *der;* **we were in absolute ~s** wir bogen uns förmlich vor Lachen *(ugs.);* **b)** *(shaking, lit. or fig.)* Erschütterung, *die*
convulsive [kən'vʌlsɪv] *adj.*, **convulsively** [kən'vʌlsɪvlɪ] *adv.* konvulsivisch
cony [kəʊnɪ] *n.* **a)** *(rabbit)* Kaninchen, *das;* **b)** *(fur)* Kaninchenfell, *das;* Kanin, *das (Kürschnerei, Mode)*
coo [ku:] **1.** *int. (of person)* oh; *(of dove)* ruckedigu. **2.** *n. (of dove)* **the ~[s]** das Gurren. **3.** *v. i.* gurren; ⟨*Baby:*⟩ gurren *(fig.).* **4.** *v. t. & i.* gurren *(auch fig.)*
cooee ['ku:i:] **1.** *int.* huhu *(ugs.).* **2.** *v. i.* **they ~d to us** sie riefen uns „huhu“ zu
cook [kʊk] **1.** *n.* Koch, *der*/Köchin, *die;* **too many ~s spoil the broth** *(prov.)* viele Köche verderben den Brei *(Spr.).* **2.** *v. t.* **a)** garen *(Kochk.); (concoct and prepare)* kochen; **how would you ~ this piece of meat?** wie würden Sie dieses Stück Fleisch zubereiten?; **~ed in the oven** im Backofen zubereitet *od. (Kochk.)* gegart; **~ed meal** warme Mahlzeit; **how long should one ~ this joint?** wie lange sollte man diesen Braten garen lassen? *(Kochk.); abs.* **do you ~ with gas or electricity?** kochen Sie mit Gas oder mit Strom?; **she knows how to ~:** sie kann gut kochen *od.* kocht gut; **~ sb.'s goose [for him]** *(fig.)* jmdm. alles verderben; **he ~ed his own goose** er hat sich *(Dat.)* alles verdorben *od. (ugs.)* vermasselt; **b)** *(fig. coll.: falsify)* frisieren *(ugs.);* **c)** *(Brit. sl.: fatigue)* **be ~ed** fix und fertig sein *(ugs.).* **3.** *v. i.* kochen; garen *(Kochk.);* **the meat was ~ing slowly** das Fleisch garte langsam; **what's ~ing?** *(fig. coll.)* was liegt an? *(ugs.)*
~ **'up** *v. t.* sich *(Dat.)* ausbrüten, *(ugs.)* aushecken ⟨*Plan*⟩; erfinden ⟨*Geschichte*⟩
cook: ~book *n. see* **cookery book; ~-chill 'food** *n. durch rasche Abkühlung haltbar gemachte Fertiggerichte*
cooker ['kʊkə(r)] *n.* **a)** *(Brit.: appliance)* Herd, *der;* **electric/gas ~:** Elektroherd/ Gasherd, *der;* **b)** *(vessel)* Kochgefäß, *das;* **c)** *(fruit)* **are those apples eaters or ~s?** sind diese Äpfel zum Essen oder zum Kochen?
cookery ['kʊkərɪ] *n.* **a)** Kochen, *das;* **b)** *(Amer.: place)* Küche, *die*
'cookery book *n. (Brit.)* Kochbuch, *das*
cookhouse ['kʊkhaʊs] *n. (Mil.)* Feldküche, *die*
cookie ['kʊkɪ] *n.* **a)** *(Scot.)* Plätzchen, *das;* **b)** *(Amer.: biscuit)* Keks, *der;* **that's the way the ~ crumbles** *(fig. coll.)* es kommt, wie es kommen muß; **c)** *(sl.: person) (woman)* Person, *die; (attractive woman)* Klasseweib, *das (ugs.); (man)* Typ, *der (ugs.)*
cooking ['kʊkɪŋ] *n.* Kochen, *das;* **German ~:** die deutsche Küche; **your ~ is marvellous** du kochst wunderbar; **do one's own ~:** für sich selbst kochen; **do the ~:** kochen
cooking: ~ apple *n.* Kochapfel, *der;* **~ fat** *n.* Bratfett, *das;* **~ salt** *n.* Speisesalz, *das;* **~ sherry** *n. Sherry zum Kochen;* **~ utensil** *n.* Küchengerät, *das;* **~ vessel** *n.* Kochgefäß, *das*
cook: ~out *n. (Amer.)* ≈ Grillparty, *die;* **have a ~out** im Freien kochen; **~-stove** *n. (Amer.)* [Koch]herd, *der*
cool [ku:l] **1.** *adj.* **a)** kühl; luftig ⟨*Kleidung*⟩; **I wait until my tea is ~ enough to drink** ich warte, bis mein Tee so weit abgekühlt ist, daß ich ihn trinken kann; **I am/feel ~:** mir ist kühl; **'store in a ~ place'** „kühl aufbewahren“; **bake in a ~ oven** bei schwacher Hitze backen; **b)** *(unexcited)* **he kept** *or* **stayed ~:** er blieb ruhig *od.* bewahrte die Ruhe; **play it ~** *(coll.)* ruhig bleiben; cool vorgehen *(salopp);* **she's always so ~ about things** sie ist immer so ruhig und besonnen; **he was ~, calm, and collected** er war ruhig und gelassen; **a ~ customer** ein kühler Kopf; **keep a ~ head** einen kühlen Kopf bewahren; *see also* **cucumber; c)** *(unemotional, unfriendly)* kühl; *(calmly audacious)* kaltblütig; unverfroren ⟨*Forderung*⟩; **be a ~ customer** *(fig.)* ganz schön unverschämt sein; **a ~ £3,000/thousand** *(coll.)* glatt 3 000 Pfund/ein glatter Tausender *(ugs.);* **d)** *(Jazz) in der Art des Cool Jazz;* **~ jazz** Cool Jazz, *der;* **e)** *(coll.: excellent)* cool *(salopp);* geil *(salopp).* **2.** *n.* **a)** *(coolness)* Kühle, *die;* **b)** *(cool air, place)* **sit in the ~:** im Kühlen sitzen; **store sth. in the ~:** etw. kühl aufbewahren; **c)** *(coll.: composure)* **keep/lose one's ~:** die Ruhe bewahren/verlieren. **3.** *v. i.* abkühlen; **the weather has ~ed** es ist kühler geworden; **wait until your milk ~s a bit** laß deine Milch etwas abkühlen; *(fig.)* **our relationship has ~ed** unsere Beziehung ist kühler geworden; **the first heat of passion had ~ed** die erste Leidenschaft war verflogen; **~ towards sb./sth.** an jmdm./etw. das Interesse verlieren. **4.** *v. t.* kühlen; *(from high temperature)* abkühlen; *(fig.)* abkühlen ⟨*Leidenschaft, Raserei, Liebe*⟩; **[have to] ~ one's heels** lange warten [müssen]; **~ it!** *(sl.)* reg dich ab! *(ugs.)*
~ **'down 1.** *v. i.* **a)** ⟨*Tee:*⟩ abkühlen; ⟨*Luft:*⟩ sich abkühlen; **b)** *(fig.)* sich beruhigen; **his anger has ~ed down** sein Zorn hat sich gelegt. **2.** *v. t.* abkühlen; *(fig.)* besänftigen; *(disillusion)* ernüchtern
~ **'off 1. a)** *v. i.* abkühlen; **the weather has ~ed off** es ist kühler geworden; **we need a few minutes to ~ off** wir brauchen ein paar Minuten, um uns abzukühlen; **b)** *(fig.)* sich beruhigen; ⟨*Zorn, Begeisterung, Interesse, Leidenschaft:*⟩ sich legen, nachlassen; ⟨*Freundschaft:*⟩ sich abkühlen. **2.** *v. t.* abkühlen; *(fig.)* beruhigen; besänftigen; abkühlen ⟨*Leidenschaft, Begeisterung*⟩
coolant ['ku:lənt] *n.* Kühlmittel, *das; (for cutting-tool)* Schneidflüssigkeit, *die (Technik); (for internal-combustion engine)* Kühlwasser, *das*
cooler ['ku:lə(r)] *n.* **a)** *(vessel)* Kühler, *der;* **b)** *(Amer.: refrigerator)* Kühlschrank, *der;* **c)** *(coll.: prison)* Knast, *der (ugs.)*
'cool-headed *adj.* kühl; nüchtern
coolie ['ku:lɪ] *n.* Kuli, *der*
'coolie hat *flacher Hut [der chinesischen Kulis];* Chinesenhut, *der*
cooling ['ku:lɪŋ]: **~ fan** *n.* Kühlgebläse, *das (Technik);* **~-'off period** *n.* Rücktrittsfrist, *die;* **~ tower** *n.* Kühlturm, *der*
coolly ['ku:llɪ] *adv.* **a)** kühl; **b)** *(fig.) (calmly)* ruhig; *(unemotionally, in unfriendly manner)* kühl; *(impudently)* kaltblütig; unverfroren ⟨*verlangen, fordern*⟩
coolness ['ku:lnɪs] *n., no pl.* Kühle, *die; (fig.) (calmness)* Ruhe, *die; (unemotional nature, unfriendliness)* Kühle, *die; (impudence)* Kaltblütigkeit, *die; (insolence)* Unverfrorenheit, *die*
coomb [ku:m] *n. (Brit.) (on hill-flank) Taleinschnitt an der Seite eines Berges; (short valley)* Schlucht, *die*
coon [ku:n] *n.* **a)** *(Amer.: racoon)* Waschbär, *der;* **b)** *(sl. derog.) (Negro)* Nigger, *der (abwertend); (Negro woman)* Niggerweib, *das (abwertend)*
'coonskin *n. (Amer.)* Waschbärfell, *das;* Waschbär[pelz], *der; (cap)* Waschbärmütze, *die; (jacket)* Waschbärjacke, *die*
coop [ku:p] **1.** *n. (cage)* Geflügelkäfig, *der; (for poultry)* Hühnerstall, *der; (fowl-run)* Auslauf, *der.* **2.** *v. t.* **~ in** *or* **up** einpferchen
co-op ['kəʊɒp] *n. (coll.)* **a)** *(Brit.) (society)* Genossenschaft, *die; (shop)* Konsum[laden], *der;* **b)** *(Amer.) see* **co-operative 2 b**
co-operate [kəʊ'ɒpəreɪt] *v. i.* mitarbeiten (**in** bei); *(with each other)* zusammenarbeiten (**in** bei); *(not obstruct)* mitmachen *(ugs.);* ⟨*Dinge, Ereignisse:*⟩ zusammenwirken; *(Polit., Econ. also)* kooperieren (**in** bei); **~ with sb.** mit jmdm. zusammenarbeiten/kooperieren; **the patient refused to ~:** der Patient verweigerte die Mitarbeit *od.* war nicht kooperativ; **~ with the police** die Polizei unterstützen
co-operation [kəʊɒpə'reɪʃn] *n.* **a)** *see* **co-operate:** Mitarbeit, *die;* Zusammenarbeit, *die;* Kooperation, *die;* **with the ~ of** unter Mitarbeit von; **in ~ with** in Zusammenarbeit mit; **b)** *(Econ.)* Genossenschaft, *die;* **the principle of ~:** das genossenschaftliche Prinzip
co-operative [kəʊ'ɒpərətɪv] **1.** *adj.* **a)** *(offering co-operation)* kooperativ; *(helpful)* hilfsbereit; **b)** *(Econ.)* genossenschaftlich. **2.** *n.* **a)** Genossenschaft, *die;* Kooperative, *die (DDR); (shop)* Genossenschaftsladen, *der;* **workers' ~:** Produktivgenossenschaft, *die;* **b)** *(Amer.: dwelling) gemeinschaftlich gemieteter/gekaufter Wohnraum*
co-operative: ~ shop *n. see* **~ store; ~ society** *n.* Genossenschaft, *die;* **~ store** *n.* Genossenschaftsladen, *der*
co-opt [kəʊ'ɒpt] *v. t.* kooptieren; hinzuwählen; **be ~ed [on] to a committee** von einem Komitee kooptiert werden
co-option [kəʊ'ɒpʃn] *n.* Koop[ta]tion, *die*
co-ordinate 1. [kəʊ'ɔ:dɪnət] *adj.* **a)** *(equal in rank)* gleichrangig; **b)** *(Ling.)* nebengeordnet. **2.** *n.* **a)** *(Math.)* Koordinate, *die;* **b)** *in pl. (clothes)* Kombination, *die.* **3.** [kəʊ'ɔ:dɪneɪt] *v. t.* **a)** koordinieren; **~ one's thoughts** seine Gedanken sammeln *od.* ordnen; **b)** *(Ling.)* **co-ordinating conjunction** koordinierende *od.* nebenordnende Konjunktion
co-ordination [kəʊɔ:dɪ'neɪʃn] *n.* Koordination, *die;* **he lacks ~:** er hat Koordinationsschwierigkeiten
co-ordinator [kəʊ'ɔ:dɪneɪtə(r)] *n.* Koordinator, *der*/Koordinatorin, *die*
coot [ku:t] *n.* **a)** *(Ornith.)* **[bald] ~:** Bläßhuhn, *das;* **be [as] bald as a ~:** völlig kahl sein; **b)** *(coll.: stupid person)* **[silly] ~:** dummes Huhn
co-owner [kəʊ'əʊnə(r)] *n.* Miteigentümer, *der*/-eigentümerin, *die; (of business)* Mitinhaber, *der*/-inhaberin, *die*

[1]**cop** [kɒp] *n.* *(sl.: police officer)* Bulle, *der (salopp)*; Polyp, *der (salopp)*; **she's a ~**: sie ist von der Polente *(salopp)*; **~s and robbers** Räuber und Gendarm

[2]**cop** *(sl.)* **1.** *v. t.*, **-pp-**: **a)** **they ~ped it** *(were captured)* sie sind geschnappt worden *(ugs.)*; *(were killed)* sie mußten dran glauben; **b)** *(hit)* **he ~ped him one under the chin** er hat ihm eins unters Kinn verpaßt *(ugs.)*. **2.** *n.* **it's a fair ~!** guter Fang!; **no ~, not much ~**: nichts Besonderes

~ 'out *v.i.* *(sl.)* **a)** *(escape)* abhauen *(salopp)*; **~ out of society** [aus der Gesellschaft] aussteigen *(ugs.)*; **b)** *(give up)* alles hinwerfen *(ugs.)*; **c)** *(go back on one's promise)* **you can't ~ out like that** du kannst mich/ihn *usw.* doch nicht so hängenlassen *(ugs.)*. *See also* **cop-out**

copartner [kəʊ'pɑ:tnə(r)] *n.* Partner, *der*/Partnerin, *die;* Teilhaber, *der*/-haberin, *die*

copartnership [kəʊ'pɑ:tnəʃɪp] *n.* *(relationship)* Partnerschaft, *die;* Teilhaberschaft, *die;* *(company)* Sozietät, *die*

[1]**cope** [kəʊp] *v. i.* **a)** *(be able to contend)* **~ with sb./sth.** mit jmdm./etw. fertig werden; **~ with a handicapped child** mit einem behinderten Kind zurechtkommen; **b)** *(coll.: deal with sth.)* klarkommen *(ugs.)*; **we must find someone who will ~**: wir brauchen jemanden, der die Sache in die Hand nimmt

[2]**cope** *n.* *(Eccl.)* Pluviale, *das (kath. Kirche)*

Copenhagen [kəʊpn'heɪgn] *pr. n.* Kopenhagen *(das)*

Copernican [kə'pɜ:nɪkn] *adj.* kopernikanisch

copier ['kɒpɪə(r)] *n.* *(machine)* Kopiergerät, *das;* Kopierer, *der (ugs.)*

co-pilot ['kəʊpaɪlət] *n.* Kopilot, *der*/Kopilotin, *die*

coping ['kəʊpɪŋ] *n.* Mauerabdeckung, *die*

'coping-stone *n.* Abdeckplatte, *die*

copious ['kəʊpɪəs] *adj.* *(plentiful)* reichhaltig; voll ‹*Haar*›; *(informative)* umfassend

copiously ['kəʊpɪəslɪ] *adv.* *(plentifully)* reichlich; *(informatively)* umfassend

copiousness ['kəʊpɪəsnɪs] *n.*, *no pl.* *(plentifulness)* Fülle, *die*

'cop-out *n.* *(sl.)* Drückebergerei, *die (ugs. abwertend)*; **that's a ~**: das ist Drückebergerei *(ugs. abwertend)*

[1]**copper** ['kɒpə(r)] **1.** *n.* **a)** Kupfer, *das;* **b)** *(coin)* Kupfermünze, *die;* **a few ~s** etwas Kupfergeld; **it only costs a few ~s** es kostet nur ein paar Pfennige; **c)** *(boiler)* [Kupfer]kessel, *der;* *(for laundry)* Waschkessel, *der.* **2.** *attrib. adj.* **a)** *(made of ~)* kupfern; Kupfer‹*münze, -kessel, -rohr*›; **b)** *(coloured like ~)* kupferfarben; kupfern

[2]**copper** *n.* *(Brit. sl.) see* [1]**cop**

copper: ~ 'beech *n.* Blutbuche, *die;* **~-bottomed** *adj.* gekupfert *(Seew.)* ‹*Schiff*›; ‹*Pfanne*› mit Kupferboden; *(fig.)* *(authentic)* waschecht; *(financially reliable)* todsicher *(ugs.)*; **~-coloured** *adj.* kupferfarben; **~plate 1.** *n.* **a)** *(metal plate)* Kupferplatte, *die;* **b)** *(print)* Kupferstich, *der;* **2.** *adj.* **~plate writing** ≈ Schönschrift, *die; Schreib- und Druckschrift mit dickem Ab- und dünnem Aufstrich*

coppery ['kɒpərɪ] *adj.* kupferfarben; kupfern

coppice ['kɒpɪs] *n.* Wäldchen, *das;* Niederwald, *der (Forstw.)*

'coppice-wood *n.* Unterholz, *das*

copra ['kɒprə] *n.* Kopra, *die*

copse [kɒps] *n. see* **coppice**

'cop-shop *n.* *(Brit. sl.)* Wache, *die;* Revier, *das*

Copt [kɒpt] *n.* Kopte, *der*/Koptin, *die*

Coptic ['kɒptɪk] **1.** *adj.* koptisch. **2.** *n.* *(language)* Koptisch, *das*

copula ['kɒpjʊlə] *n.* *(Ling.)* Kopula, *die*

copulate ['kɒpjʊleɪt] *v.i.* kopulieren

copulation [kɒpjʊ'leɪʃn] *n.* Kopulation, *die*

copy ['kɒpɪ] **1.** *n.* **a)** *(reproduction)* Kopie, *die;* *(imitation)* Nachahmung, *die;* *(with carbon paper etc.)* *(typed)* Durchschlag, *der;* *(written)* Durchschrift, *die;* **write a ~**: eine Abschrift machen; *see also* [2]**fair 1 h; rough copy; b)** *(specimen)* Exemplar, *das;* **have you a ~ of today's 'Times'?** haben Sie die „Times" von heute?; **send three copies of the application** die Bewerbung in dreifacher Ausfertigung schicken; **top ~**: Original, *das;* **c)** *(manuscript etc. for printing)* Druckvorlage, *die;* **supply ~**: die Druckvorlage liefern; **make good ~** *(Journ. coll.: news)* ein klasse Stoff sein *(ugs.)*; **[advertising] ~**: Werbetext, *der.* **2.** *v. t.* **a)** *(make copy of)* kopieren; *(by photocopier)* [foto]kopieren; *(transcribe)* abschreiben; **b)** *(imitate)* nachahmen. **3.** *v. i.* **a)** kopieren; **~ from sb./sth.** jmdn./etw. kopieren; **b)** *(in exam etc.)* abschreiben; **~ from sb./sth.** bei jmdm./aus etw. abschreiben

~ 'out *v. t.* abschreiben

copy: ~-book *n. attrib.* wie im Bilderbuch *nachgestellt;* Bilderbuch‹*landschaft, -wetter*›; *see also* **blot 2 b; ~-cat** *n.* *(coll.)* **you're such a ~-cat!** du mußt immer alles nachmachen!; **~ desk** *n.* *(Amer.)* Redaktionstisch, *der;* **~ editor** *n.* **a)** *see* **copy-reader; b)** *Leiter/Leiterin einer Copy-reader-Abteilung*

copyist ['kɒpɪɪst] *n.* Kopist, *der*

'copy-reader *n.* Redakteur, *der*/Redakteurin, *die (für formale Manuskriptbearbeitung und redaktionelles Korrekturlesen)*

copyright ['kɒpɪraɪt] **1.** *n.* Copyright, *das;* Urheberrecht, *das;* **be out of ~**: gemeinfrei [geworden] sein; **protected by ~**: urheberrechtlich geschützt. **2.** *adj.* urheberrechtlich geschützt; **~ library** *(Brit.)* *Bibliothek, die Anspruch auf ein Freiexemplar jedes in Großbritannien veröffentlichten Buches hat.* **3.** *v. t.* urheberrechtlich schützen

copy: ~ typist *n.* Schreibkraft *(die nur nach schriftlichen Vorlagen arbeitet)*; **~-writer** *n.* [Werbe]texter, *der*/-texterin, *die*

coquetry ['kɒkɪtrɪ, 'kəʊkɪtrɪ] *n.* Koketterie, *die;* *(fig.)* Kokettieren, *das*

coquette [kə'ket] **1.** *n.* Kokette, *die.* **2.** *v. i.* kokettieren

coquettish [kə'ketɪʃ] *adj.* kokett

cor [kɔ:(r)] *int.* *(Brit. sl.)* Mensch! *(salopp)*

coracle ['kɒrəkl] *n.* *(Brit.)* Coracle, *das (Fischerboot aus lederüberzogenem Flechtwerk)*

coral ['kɒrl] **1.** *n.* Koralle, *die.* **2.** *attrib. adj.* korallen; Korallen‹*insel, -riff, -rot*›

cor anglais [kɔ:r 'ɑ̃gleɪ, kɔ:r 'ɒŋgleɪ] *n.* *(Mus.)* **a)** *(instrument)* Englischhorn, *das;* Englisch Horn, *das (fachspr.)*; **b)** *(organstop)* Englisch Horn, *das*

corbel [kɔ:bl] *n.* *(Archit.)* *(of stone)* Kragstein, *der;* *(of timber)* Sattelholz, *das*

'corbel-table *n.* *(Archit.)* Bogenfries, *der*

cord [kɔ:d] *n.* **a)** Kordel, *die;* **b)** *(Anat.) see* **spermatic cord; spinal cord; umbilical cord; vocal cords; c)** *(rib)* Rippe, *die;* *(cloth)* Cord, *der;* **d)** *in pl.* *(trousers)* **[pair of] ~s** Cordhose, *die;* **e)** *(Amer. Electr.: flex)* Kabel, *das*

cordage ['kɔ:dɪdʒ] *n.* *(Naut.)* Tauwerk, *das*

cordate ['kɔ:deɪt] *adj.* *(Biol.)* herzförmig

cordial ['kɔ:dɪəl] **1.** *adj.* herzlich; **a ~ dislike for sb.** eine tiefempfundene Abneigung gegenüber jmdm.. **2.** *n.* *(drink)* Sirup, *der*

cordiality [kɔ:dɪ'ælɪtɪ] *n.*, *no pl.* Herzlichkeit, *die*

cordially ['kɔ:dɪəlɪ] *adv.* herzlich; **~ dislike sb.** eine tiefempfundene Abneigung gegenüber jmdm. haben; **~ yours** mit herzlichen Grüßen

cordillera [kɔ:dɪ'ljeərə] *n.* *(Geog.)* Kettengebirge, *das*

cordite ['kɔ:daɪt] *n.* Kordit, *der*

cordless ['kɔ:dlɪs] *adj.* **a)** *(without cord)* ohne Kordel *nachgestellt;* **b)** *(without flex)* ohne Kabel *nachgestellt*

cordon ['kɔ:dn] **1.** *n.* **a)** *(line of police; also Mil.)* Kordon, *der;* **a ~ of policemen** ein Polizeikordon; *see also* **throw around b; b)** *(fruit-tree)* Schnurbaum, *der;* Kordon, *der.* **2.** *v. t.* **~ [off]** absperren; abriegeln

cordon bleu [kɔ:dɔ̃ 'blɜ:] *n.* Meisterkoch, *der*/-köchin, *die;* **~ cookery** feine Küche

corduroy ['kɔ:dərɔɪ, 'kɔ:djʊrɔɪ] *n.* **a)** *(material)* Cordsamt, *der;* **b)** *in pl.* *(trousers)* Cordsamthose, *die*

core [kɔ:(r)] **1.** *n.* **a)** *(of fruit)* Kerngehäuse, *das;* **b)** *(Geol.)* *(rock sample)* [Bohr]kern, *der;* *(of earth)* [Erd]kern, *der;* **c)** *(Electr.: of soft iron)* [Eisen]kern, *der;* **d)** *(fig.: innermost part)* **get to the ~ of the matter** zum Kern der Sache kommen; **rotten to the ~**: verdorben bis ins Mark; **English to the ~**: durch und durch englisch; **shake sb. to the ~**: jmdn. zutiefst erschüttern; **e)** *(Industry: internal mould)* Kern, *der;* **f)** *(Nucl. Engin.)* Core, *das;* Reaktorkern, *der;* **g)** *(Computing)* Magnetkern, *der;* **h)** *(of rope, electrical cable)* Seele, *die.* **2.** *v. t.* entkernen ‹*Apfel, Birne*›

corer ['kɔ:rə(r)] *n.* Entkerner, *der*

co-respondent [kəʊrɪ'spɒndənt] *n.* Mitbeklagte, *der/die (im Scheidungsprozeß)*

'core time *n.* Kernzeit, *die*

Corfu [kɔ:'fu:] *pr. n.* Korfu *(das)*

corgi ['kɔ:gɪ] *n.* **[Welsh] ~**: Welsh Corgi, *der*

coriander [kɒrɪ'ændə(r)] *n.* Koriander, *der*

cori'ander seed *n.* Koriander, *der*

Corinth ['kɒrɪnθ] *pr. n.* Korinth *(das)*

cork [kɔ:k] **1.** *n.* **a)** *(bark)* Kork, *der;* **b)** *(bottle-stopper)* Korken, *der;* **c)** *(fishing-float)* Schwimmer, *der;* **d)** *attrib.* Kork-. **2.** *v. t.* zukorken; verkorken

~ 'up *v. t.* zukorken; verkorken; **~ up one's emotions** seine Gefühle unterdrücken

corked [kɔ:kt] *adj.* **a)** *(stopped with cork)* verkorkt; **b)** *(impaired)* korkig ‹*Wein*›

corker ['kɔ:kə(r)] *n.* *(coll.)* *(thing)* **that joke was a real ~, that was a ~ of a joke** der Witz war echt Spitze *(ugs.)*; *(person)* **she's/he's a real ~**: sie/er ist einsame Spitze *(ugs.)*

corking ['kɔ:kɪŋ] *adj.* *(coll.)* *(large)* Riesen-; *(excellent)* klasse *(ugs.)*

cork: ~screw 1. *n.* *(bottle-opener)* Korkenzieher, *der;* *(spiral)* Spirale, *die;* **2.** *v. i.* ‹*Flugzeug:*› trudeln; **~'tile** *n.* Korkplatte, *die;* **~-tipped** *adj.* *(Brit.)* ‹*Zigarette*› mit Korkmundstück; **~wood** *n.* **a)** *(wood)* Korkholz, *das;* **b)** *(tree)* Korkholzbaum, *der*

corky ['kɔ:kɪ] *adj.* korkig

corm [kɔ:m] *n.* *(Bot.)* Knolle, *die*

cormorant ['kɔ:mərənt] *n.* *(Ornith.)* Kormoran, *der*

[1]**corn** [kɔ:n] *n.* **a)** *(cereal)* Getreide, *das;* *(esp. rye, wheat also)* Korn, *das;* **[sweet] ~** *(maize)* Mais, *der;* **~ on the cob** [gekochter/gerösteter] Maiskolben; **b)** *(seed)* Korn, *das*

[2]**corn** *n.* *(on foot)* Hühnerauge, *das;* **tread on sb.'s ~s** *(fig.)* jmdm. auf die Hühneraugen treten *(ugs.)*

corn: ~-cob *n.* Maiskolben, *der;* **~crake** ['kɔ:nkreɪk] *n.* *(Ornith.)* Wachtelkönig, *der;* **~ dolly** *n.* Strohpuppe, *die*

cornea ['kɔ:nɪə] *n.* *(Anat.)* Hornhaut, *die;* Cornea, *die (fachspr.)*

corneal ['kɔ:nɪəl] *adj.* *(Anat.)* Korneal- *(fachspr.)*; Hornhaut-

corned beef [kɔ:nd 'bi:f] *n.* Corned beef, *das*

cornelian 'cherry *n.* Kornelkirsche, *die*

corner ['kɔ:nə(r)] **1.** *n.* **a)** Ecke, *die;* *(curve)* Kurve, *die;* **on the ~**: an der Ecke/in der Kurve; **at the ~**: an der Ecke; **~ of the street** Straßenecke, *die;* **sharp ~**: scharfe *od.* enge Kurve; **cut [off] a/the ~**: eine/die Kurve schneiden; **cut ~s** *(fig.)* auf die schnelle arbeiten *(ugs.)*; **cut ~s with sth.** *(fig.)* bei etw. pfuschen *(ugs.)*; **[sth. is] just [a]round the ~**: [etw. ist] gleich um die Ecke; **Christmas is just round the ~** *(fig. coll.)* Weihnachten steht vor der Tür; **turn the ~**: um die Ecke biegen; **he has turned the ~ now** *(fig.)* er ist jetzt über den Berg *(ugs.)*; **b)** *(hollow angle between walls)* Ecke, *die;* *(of mouth, eye)* Winkel, *der;* ~ **of the mouth/eye** Mund-/Augenwinkel, *der;* **drive sb. into a ~:** jmdn. in die Enge treiben; *see also* **paint 2a; tight 1i; c)** *(Boxing, Wrestling)* Ecke, *die;* **d)** *(secluded place)* Eckchen, *das;* Plätzchen, *das;* *(remote region)* Winkel, *der;* **from the four ~s of the earth** aus aller Welt; **e)** *(Hockey/Footb.)* Ecke, *die;* **score from a ~:** eine Ecke verwandeln; **take a ~:** eine Ecke schlagen/treten; **f)** *(Commerc.)* Corner, *der;* Schwänze, *die.* **2.** *v. t.* **a)** *(drive into ~)* in eine Ecke treiben; *(fig.)* in die Enge treiben; **have [got] sb. ~ed** jmdn. in der Falle haben; **b)** *(Commerc.)* ~ **the market in coffee** die Kaffeevorräte aufkaufen; den Kaffeemarkt aufschwänzen *(fachspr.)*. **3.** *v. i.* die Kurve nehmen; ~ **well/badly** eine gute/schlechte Kurvenlage haben; **when ~ing** beim Kurvenfahren

corner: ~ **cupboard** *n.* Eckschrank, *der;* ~ **flag** *n. (Sport)* Eckfahne, *die;* **~-hit** *n. (Hockey)* Eckball, *der;* Eckschlag, *der;* **score [a goal] from a ~-hit** einen Eckball verwandeln; **take a ~-hit** eine Ecke schlagen; **~-kick** *n. (Footb.)* Eckball, *der;* Eckstoß, *der;* **score from a ~-kick** einen Eckstoß verwandeln; **take a ~- kick** eine Ecke treten; ~ **seat** *n.* Ecksitz, *der;* ~ **shop** *n.* Tante-Emma-Laden, *der (ugs.)*; **~stone** *n.* Eckstein, *der; (fig.)* Eckpfeiler, *der*

cornet ['kɔ:nɪt] *n.* **a)** *(Brit.: wafer)* [Eis]tüte, *die;* Eishörnchen, *das;* **b)** *(Mus.) (instrument)* Kornett, *das*

corn: ~ **exchange** *n.* Getreidebörse, *die;* **~field** *n.* Kornfeld, *das; (Amer.)* Maisfeld, *das;* **~flakes** *n. pl.* Corn-flakes *Pl.;* **~flour** *n.* **a)** *(Brit.: ground maize)* Maismehl, *das;* **b)** *(flour of rice etc.)* Stärkemehl, *das;* **~flower** *n.* Kornblume, *die*

cornice ['kɔ:nɪs] *n.* **a)** *(Archit.)* Kranzgesims, *das;* **b)** *(moulding)* Fries, *der (an der Wand unmittelbar unter der Decke)*; **c)** *(Mount.)* [Schnee]wächte, *die*

Cornish ['kɔ:nɪʃ] **1.** *adj.* kornisch. **2.** *n.* Kornisch, *das*

Cornish: ~ **'cream** *see* **Devonshire cream;** ~ **pasty** [kɔ:nɪʃ 'pæstɪ] *n. mit Fleisch, Kartoffeln und Zwiebeln gefülltes Blätterteiggebäck*

corn: ~ **marigold** *n.* Saatwucherblume, *die;* **~starch** *n. (Amer.) see* **~flour a**

cornucopia [kɔ:njʊ'kəʊpɪə] *n.* Füllhorn, *das;* **a ~ of information** *(fig.)* Information in Hülle und Fülle

corny ['kɔ:nɪ] *adj. (coll.) (old-fashioned)* altmodisch ⟨*Witz usw.*⟩; *(trite)* abgedroschen *(ugs.)*; *(sentimental)* schmalzig *(abwertend)*

corolla [kə'rɒlə] *n. (Bot.)* Krone, *die;* Korolla, *die*

corollary [kə'rɒlərɪ] *n. (proposition)* Korollar[ium], *das (Logik)*; *(inference)* Schluß, *der;* Folgerung, *die;* *(consequence)* [logische *od.* natürliche] Folge

corona [kə'rəʊnə] *n., pl.* **~e** [kə'rəʊni:] *or* **~s a)** *(circle of light round sun or moon)* Hof, *der;* *(gaseous envelope of sun)* Korona, *die;* **b)** *(Anat.)* Corona, *die*

coronary ['kɒrənərɪ] **1.** *adj. (Anat.)* koronar. **2.** *n. (Med.) see* **coronary thrombosis**

coronary: ~ **'artery** *n. (Anat.)* Herzkranzarterie, *die;* Koronararterie, *die (fachspr.)*; ~ **throm'bosis** *n. (Med.)* Koronarthrombose, *die*

coronation [kɒrə'neɪʃn] *n.* Krönung, *die*

coroner ['kɒrənə(r)] *n.* Coroner, *der; Beamter, der gewaltsame od. unnatürliche Todesfälle untersucht*

coronet ['kɒrənet] *n.* Krone, *die*

Corp. *abbr.* **a)** *(Mil.)* **corporal** ≈ Uffz.; **b)** *(Amer.)* **corporation**

corpora *pl. of* **corpus**

[1]**corporal** ['kɔ:pərl] *adj.* körperlich

[2]**corporal** *n. (Mil.)* Korporal, *der (hist.; österr.)*; ≈ Hauptgefreite, *der;* ≈ Stabsgefreite, *der (DDR)*

corporate ['kɔ:pərət] *adj.* **a)** *(forming corporation)* körperschaftlich; ~ **body, body ~:** Körperschaft, *die;* juristische Person; **b)** *(of corporation)* körperschaftlich; korporativ

corporately ['kɔ:pərətlɪ] *adv.* körperschaftlich; korporativ

corporation [kɔ:pə'reɪʃn] *n.* **a)** *(civic authority)* **[municipal]** ~: Gemeindeverwaltung, *die;* *(of borough, city)* Stadtverwaltung, *die;* **b)** *(united body)* Körperschaft, *die;* Korporation, *die;* *(artificial person)* juristische Person; ~ **tax** Körperschaftssteuer, *die;* **c)** *(coll.: belly)* Schmerbauch, *der (ugs.)*; Wampe, *die (ugs. abwertend)*

corporative ['kɔ:pərətɪv] *adj.* **a)** *(of civic authorities)* behördlich; *(of united body)* korporativ; *(of artificial body)* körperschaftlich; **b)** *(organized in corporations)* berufsständisch organisiert; korporativ ⟨*Organisation*⟩; *(governed by corporations)* ~ **state** Ständestaat, *der*

corporeal [kɔ:'pɔ:rɪəl] *adj.* **a)** *(bodily)* körperlich; **b)** *(material)* materiell; stofflich

corps [kɔ:(r)] *n., pl. same* [kɔ:z] Korps, *das;* *see also* **diplomatic corps**

corps: ~ **de ballet** [kɔ: də 'bæleɪ] *n.* Corps de ballet, *das;* Ballettkorps, *das;* ~ **diplomatique** [kɔ: dɪpləmæ'ti:k] Corps diplomatique, *das;* diplomatisches Korps

corpse [kɔ:ps] *n.* Leiche, *die;* Leichnam, *der (geh.)*

corpulence ['kɔ:pjʊləns], **corpulency** ['kɔ:pjʊlənsɪ] *n.* Korpulenz, *die*

corpulent ['kɔ:pjʊlənt] *adj.* korpulent

corpus ['kɔ:pəs] *n., pl.* **corpora** ['kɔ:pərə] *(texts)* Sammlung, *die;* Korpus, *das*

Corpus Christi [kɔ:pəs 'krɪstɪ] *n. (Eccl.)* Fronleichnam *(der)*; Fronleichnamsfest, *das*

corpuscle ['kɔ:pəsl] *n.* **a)** *(Phys.)* Korpuskel, *das od. die;* **b)** *(Anat.)* Corpusculum, *das;* **[blood] ~s** Blutkörperchen

corral [kə'rɑ:l] **1.** *n.* **a)** *(Amer.: pen)* Pferch, *der;* **b)** *(Hist.: defensive enclosure)* Wagenburg, *die;* **c)** *(for wild animals)* Korral, *der.* **2.** *v. t.,* **-ll-: a)** *(Hist.: form into ~)* zu einer Wagenburg formieren; **b)** *(confine in ~)* einpferchen; **c)** *(Amer. coll.: acquire)* einsacken *(ugs.)*; mit Beschlag belegen ⟨*Person*⟩

correct [kə'rekt] **1.** *v. t.* **a)** *(amend)* korrigieren; verbessern, korrigieren ⟨*Fehler, Formulierung, jmds. Englisch/Deutsch*⟩; ~ **a few points** einige Punkte richtigstellen; **~ed for spelling mistakes** auf Rechtschreibfehler hin korrigiert; **these glasses should ~ your eyesight/vision** mit dieser Brille müßten Sie richtig sehen können; ~ **the focus** die Bildschärfe richtig einstellen; ~ **me if I'm wrong** ich könnte mich natürlich irren; **I stand ~ed** ich nehme das zurück; **b)** *(counteract)* ausgleichen ⟨*etw. Schädliches*⟩; **c)** *(admonish)* zurechtweisen **(for** wegen); **d)** *(punish)* bestrafen; **e)** *(bring to standard)* korrigieren **(for** hinsichtlich); **f)** *(eliminate aberration from)* korrigieren *(Optik)*. **2.** *adj.* richtig; korrekt; *(precise)* korrekt; akkurat; **that is ~:** das stimmt; **have you the ~ time?** haben Sie die genaue Uhrzeit?; **is that clock ~?** geht die Uhr richtig?; **am I ~ in assuming that ...?** gehe ich recht in der Annahme, daß ...?; **the ~ thing for you to do is to speak to the manager** darüber sollten Sie mit dem Abteilungsleiter sprechen; **what is the ~ thing to do in such a situation?** was soll man in so einer Situation korrekterweise tun?; ~ **to five decimal places** auf fünf Dezimalstellen genau

correcting fluid [kə'rektɪŋ flu:ɪd] *n.* Korrekturflüssigkeit, *die*

correction [kə'rekʃn] *n.* **a)** *(correcting)* Korrektur, *die;* **I speak under ~:** ich sage das mit *od.* unter Vorbehalt; **I'm open to ~:** ich lasse mich korrigieren; **b)** *(corrected version)* **~s to the manuscript** Manuskriptkorrekturen; **the pupils had to write out** *or* **do their ~s** die Schüler mußten die Verbesserung *od.* Berichtigung schreiben; **c)** *(punishment)* Bestrafung, *die;* **house of ~** *(arch.)* Erziehungsheim, *das;* Besserungsanstalt, *die (veralt.)*

corrective [kə'rektɪv] *adj.* korrigierend; **take ~ action** korrigierend eingreifen

correctly [kə'rektlɪ] *adv.* richtig; korrekt; *(precisely)* korrekt; akkurat; **behave very ~:** sich sehr korrekt benehmen

correctness [kə'rektnɪs] *n., no pl. see* **correct 2:** Richtigkeit, *die;* Korrektheit, *die;* Akkuratesse, *die*

corrector [kə'rektə(r)] *n.* Korrektor, *der*/Korrektorin, *die*

correlate ['kɒrɪleɪt] **1.** *v. i.* einander entsprechen; ~ **with** *or* **to sth.** einer Sache *(Dat.)* entsprechen. **2.** *v. t.* ~ **sth. with sth.** etw. zu etw. in Beziehung setzen. **3.** *n.* Korrelat, *das*

correlation [kɒrɪ'leɪʃn] *n.* [Wechsel]beziehung, *die;* Korrelation, *die (bes. Math., Naturw.)*; *(connection)* Zusammenhang, *der*

correlative [kə'relətɪv] *adj.* **a)** *(having correlation)* ~ **[with** *or* **to sth.]** [mit etw.] korrelierend; **be ~ with** *or* **to sth.** mit etw. korrelieren; **b)** *(Ling.)* korrelativ

correspond [kɒrɪ'spɒnd] *v. i.* **a)** *(be analogous, agree in amount)* ~ **[to each other]** einander entsprechen; ~ **to sth.** einer Sache *(Dat.)* entsprechen; **do the classes ~ in number?** sind die Klassen gleich stark?; **b)** *(agree in position)* ~ **[to sth.]** [mit etw.] übereinstimmen; *(be in harmony)* ~ **[with** *or* **to sth.]** [mit etw.] zusammenpassen *od. (geh.)* korrespondieren; **c)** *(communicate)* ~ **with sb.** mit jmdm. korrespondieren; **do you still ~ with your old school-friends?** hast du noch Briefkontakt mit deinen alten Schulfreunden?

correspondence [kɒrɪ'spɒndəns] *n.* **a)** Übereinstimmung **(with,** to mit, **between** zwischen); **the ~ of form with** *or* **to** *or* **and content** die Übereinstimmung von Form und Inhalt; **b)** *(communication, letters)* Briefwechsel, *der;* Korrespondenz, *die;* **be in ~ with sb.** mit jmdm. im Briefwechsel *od.* in Korrespondenz stehen

correspondence: ~ **college** *n.* Fernschule, *die;* ~ **column** *n.* Rubrik „Leserbriefe"; ~ **course** *n.* Fernkurs, *der;* ~ **school** *see* ~ **college**

correspondent [kɒrɪ'spɒndənt] *n.* **a)** Briefschreiber, *der*/-schreiberin, *die;* *(penfriend)* Brieffreund, *der*/-freundin, *die;* *(to newspaper)* Leserbriefschreiber, *der*/-schreiberin, *die;* **be a good/bad ~:** ein fleißiger/fauler Briefschreiber sein; **b)** *(Radio, Telev., Journ., etc.)* Berichterstatter, *der*/-erstatterin, *die;* Korrespondent, *der*/Korrespondentin, *die;* **c)** *(business ~)* Geschäftspartner, *der*/-partnerin, *die;* Korrespondent, *der*/Korrespondentin, *die (Kaufmannsspr.)*

corresponding [kɒrɪ'spɒndɪŋ] *adj.* **a)** entsprechend **(to** *Dat.*); **the number of calories ~ to the amount of energy** die Anzahl der Kalorien, die der Energiemenge entspricht; **b)** ~ **member** korrespondierendes Mitglied

correspondingly [kɒrɪ'spɒndɪŋlɪ] *adv.* entsprechend

corrida [kɒ'ri:də] *n.* Stierkampf, *der;* Corrida, *die*

corridor ['kɒrɪdɔ:(r)] *n.* **a)** *(inside passage)* Flur, *der;* Gang, *der;* Korridor, *der;* *(outside passage)* Galerie, *die;* **in the ~s of power** *(fig.)* in den politischen Schaltstellen; **b)** *(Railw.)* [Seiten]gang, *der*

corridor: ~ **coach** *n. (Railw.)* Durchgangswagen, *der;* ~ **train** *n.* Zug mit Durchgangswagen

corrie ['kɒrɪ] *n. (esp. Scot.)* Kar, *das (Geol.)*

corrigenda [kɒrɪ'dʒendə] *n. pl.* zu verbessernde Fehler; *(in book)* Korrigenda *Pl.*

corroborate [kə'rɒbəreɪt] *v. t.* bestätigen; bekräftigen ‹*Anspruch, Überzeugung*›; *(formally)* [offiziell] bestätigen

corroboration [kərɒbə'reɪʃn] *n. see* **corroborate:** Bestätigung, *die;* Bekräftigung, *die;* **in ~ of sth.** als *od.* zur Bestätigung *od.* Bekräftigung einer Sache *(Gen.)*

corroborative [kə'rɒbərətɪv] *adj.* bekräftigend; bestätigend ‹*Aussage*›; erhärtend ‹*Beweis*›

corrode [kə'rəʊd] **1.** *v. t.* zerfressen; korrodieren, zerfressen ‹*Metall, Gestein*›; *(fig.)* aushöhlen. **2.** *v. i.* zerfressen werden; ‹*Gestein, Metall:*› korrodieren, zerfressen werden; *(fig.)* ausgehöhlt werden

corrosion [kə'rəʊʒn] *n.* Zerfall, *der; (of metal, stone)* Korrosion, *die; (fig.)* Aushöhlung, *die*

cor'rosion-resistant *adj.* korrosionsbeständig

corrosive [kə'rəʊsɪv] **1.** *adj.* zerstörend; korrosiv *(bes. Chemie, Geol.);* ätzend ‹*Chemikalien*›; *(fig.)* zerstörerisch. **2.** *n.* Korrosion verursachender Stoff; *(fig.)* zerstörerische Kraft

corrosiveness [kə'rəʊsɪvnɪs] *n., no pl.* zerstörende Wirkung; *(of chemicals)* ätzende Wirkung; *(fig.)* zersetzende Wirkung

corrugate ['kɒrʊgeɪt] *v. t.* zerfurchen; *(bend into ridges)* wellen; **~d cardboard/paper** Wellpappe, *die;* **~d iron** Wellblech, *das*

corrugation [kɒrʊ'geɪʃn] *n.* **a)** Zerfurchung, *die;* **b)** *(wrinkle, ridge mark)* Furche, *die; (ridge made by bending)* Rille, *die*

corrupt [kə'rʌpt] **1.** *adj.* **a)** *(rotten)* verunreinigt; schlecht; verfault ‹*Körper*›; **b)** *(depraved)* verkommen; verdorben *(geh.); (influenced by bribery)* korrupt; **~ practices** Korruption, *die;* **c)** *(impure)* verdorben, korrumpiert ‹*Sprache*›; *(vitiated)* verfälscht ‹*Text, Buch*›. **2.** *v. t.* **a)** *(taint)* verderben; verschmutzen ‹*Luft, Wasser*›; *(fig.)* zerstören; **b)** *(deprave)* korrumpieren; *(bribe)* bestechen; **c)** *(destroy purity of)* verderben; korrumpieren; *(vitiate)* verfälschen

corruption [kə'rʌpʃn] *n.* **a)** *(decomposition)* Fäulnis, *die;* Verwesung, *die;* **b)** *(moral deterioration)* Verdorbenheit, *die (geh.);* **c)** *(use of corrupt practices)* Korruption, *die;* **d)** *(perversion)* Korrumpierung, *die;* Entstellung, *die; (vitiation)* Verfälschung, die

corruptness [kə'rʌptnɪs] *n., no pl. see* **corrupt 1:** Verunreinigung, *die;* Verfaultheit, *die;* Verkommenheit, *die;* Verdorbenheit, *die (geh.);* Korruptheit, *die;* Korrumpiertheit, *die;* Verfälschung, *die*

corsage [kɔ:'sɑ:ʒ] *n.* **a)** *(bodice)* Korsage, *die;* Mieder, *das;* **b)** *(bouquet)* [Ansteck]sträußchen, *das*

corsair ['kɔ:seə(r)] *n. (Hist.)* Korsar, *der*

corselette ['kɔ:slet] *n.* Korselett, *das*

corset ['kɔ:sɪt] **1.** *n.* **a)** *in sing. or pl. (woman's undergarment)* Korsett, *das;* **b)** *(garment worn for injury etc.)* [Stütz]korsett, *das.* **2.** *v. refl.* sich schnüren. **3.** *v. t. (fig.)* einengen

Corsica ['kɔ:sɪkə] *pr. n.* Korsika *(das)*

Corsican ['kɔ:sɪkən] **1.** *adj.* korsisch; **sb. is ~:** jmd. ist Korse/Korsin. **2.** *n.* **a)** *(person)* Korse, *der*/Korsin, *die;* **b)** *(dialect)* Korsisch, *das*

cortège [kɔ:'teɪʒ] *n. (funeral procession)* Trauerzug, *der*

cortex ['kɔ:teks] *n., pl.* **cortices** ['kɔ:tɪsi:z] *(Bot., Anat., Zool.)* Rinde, *die;* Kortex, *der (fachspr.)*

cortical ['kɔ:tɪkl] *adj. (Bot., Anat., Zool.)* Rinden-; kortikal *(fachspr.)*

cortisone ['kɔ:tɪzəʊn] *n.* Kortison, *das (Med.);* Cortison, *das (fachspr.)*

corundum [kə'rʌndəm] *n.* Korund, *der*

coruscate ['kɒrəskeɪt] *v. i.* funkeln; [auf]blitzen; *(fig.)* glänzen; brillieren

corvette [kɔ:'vet] *n. (Naut.)* Korvette, *die*

[1]**cos** [kɒs] *n.* Römischer Salat; Sommerendivie, *die*

[2]**cos, 'cos** [kɒz] *(coll.) see* **because**

[3]**cos** [kɒs, kɒz] *abbr. (Math.)* **cosine** cos

cosecant [kəʊ'si:kənt] *n. (Math.)* Kosekans, *der*

cosh [kɒʃ] *(Brit. coll.)* **1.** *n.* Totschläger, *der;* Knüppel, *der.* **2.** *v. t.* niederknüppeln

co-signatory [kəʊ'sɪgnətərɪ] **1.** *adj.* mitunterzeichnend. **2.** *n.* Mitunterzeichner, *der*/-unterzeichnerin, *die*

cosily ['kəʊzɪlɪ] *adv.* bequem; gemütlich, behaglich ‹*plaudern, wohnen*›

cosine ['kəʊsaɪn] *n. (Math.)* Kosinus, *der*

cosiness ['kəʊzɪnɪs] *n., no pl. see* **cosy 1 a:** Gemütlichkeit, *die;* Behaglichkeit, *die*

cosmetic [kɒz'metɪk] **1.** *adj. (lit. or fig.)* kosmetisch; **~ surgery** Schönheitschirurgie, *die.* **2.** *n.* Kosmetikum, *das*

cosmetician [kɒzme'tɪʃn] *n. (Amer.)* Kosmetiker, *der*/Kosmetikerin, *die*

cosmic ['kɒzmɪk] *adj. (lit. or fig.)* kosmisch; **~ radiation** *or* **rays** kosmische Strahlung; Höhenstrahlung, *die*

cosmology [kɒz'mɒlədʒɪ] *n. (Astron., Philos.)* Kosmologie, *die (fachspr.)*

cosmonaut ['kɒzmənɔ:t] *n.* Kosmonaut, *der*/Kosmonautin, *die*

cosmopolitan [kɒzmə'pɒlɪtən] **1.** *adj.* kosmopolitisch; weltbürgerlich. **2.** *n.* Kosmopolit, *der*/Kosmopolitin, *die (geh.);* Weltbürger, *der*/-bürgerin, *die*

cosmos ['kɒzmɒs] *n.* **a)** Kosmos, *der;* Weltall, *das;* **b)** *(fig.: system)* Kosmos, *der*

Cossack ['kɒsæk] *n.* Kosak, *der*/Kosakin, *die;* **~ hat** Kosakenmütze, *die;* **~ trousers** Stiefelhose, *die*

cosset ['kɒsɪt] *v. t.* [ver]hätscheln

cost [kɒst] **1.** *n.* **a)** Kosten *Pl.;* **the ~ of bread/gas/oil** der Brot-/Gas-/Ölpreis; **the ~ of heating a house** die Heizkosten für ein Haus; **the ~ of travelling by public transport** die Kosten für die Benutzung der öffentlichen Verkehrsmittel; **regardless of ~, whatever the ~:** ganz gleich, was es kostet; **bear the ~ of sth.** die Kosten für etw. tragen; **do sth. at great/little ~ to sb./sth.** etw. unter großer/geringer finanzieller Belastung für jmdn./etw. tun; **[sell sth.] at ~:** [etw.] zum Selbstkostenpreis [verkaufen]; **b)** *(fig.)* Preis, *der;* **at all ~s, at any ~:** um jeden Preis; **at the ~ of sth.** auf Kosten einer Sache *(Gen.);* **at great ~ in human lives** um den Preis vieler Menschenleben; **whatever the ~:** koste es, was es wolle; **to my/his** *etc.* **~:** zu meinem/seinem *usw.* Nachteil; **as I know to my ~:** wie ich aus bitterer Erfahrung weiß; *see also* [1]**count 2 a; c)** *in pl. (Law)* [Gerichts]kosten *Pl.;* **which party was ordered to pay ~s?** welche Seite hatte die [Gerichts]kosten zu tragen? **in the case A v. B, A was awarded ~s** in der Sache A gegen B wurden A die Kosten erstattet. **2.** *v. t.* **a)** *p. t., p. p.* **cost** *(lit. or fig.)* kosten; **how much does it ~?** was kostet es?; **~ money** Geld kosten; **~ what it may, whatever it may ~:** koste es, was es wolle; **~ sb. sth.** jmdn. etw. kosten; **it'll ~ you** *(coll.)* das wird ein teures Vergnügen; **~ sb. dear[ly]** jmdm. *od.* jmdn. teuer zu stehen kommen; *see also* [1]**arm a; earth 1 f; b)** *p. t., p. p.* **~ed** *(Commerc.: fix price of)* **~ sth.** den Preis für etw. kalkulieren

cost: ~ accountant *n. (Commerc.)* Betriebskalkulator, *der;* **~ accounting** *n. (Commerc.)* Betriebskostenrechnung, *die*

co-star ['kəʊstɑ:(r)] *(Cinemat., Theatre)* **1.** *n.* **be a/the ~:** eine der Hauptrollen/die zweite Hauptrolle spielen; **Bogart and Bacall were ~s** Bogart und Bacall spielten die Hauptrollen. **2.** *v. i.,* **-rr-** eine der Hauptrollen spielen. **3.** *v. t.,* **-rr-: the film ~red Robert Redford** der Film zeigte Robert Redford in einer der Hauptrollen

Costa Rican [kɒstə 'ri:kən] **1.** *adj.* costaricanisch. **2.** *n.* Costaricaner, *der*/Costaricanerin, *die*

cost: ~-'benefit *adj.* Kosten-Nutzen-; **~-effective** *adj.* rentabel

coster[monger] ['kɒstə(mʌŋgə(r))] *n. (Brit.)* Straßenhändler, *der*/-händlerin, *die*

costing ['kɒstɪŋ] *n.* **a)** *(estimation of costs)* Kostenberechnung, *die;* **b)** *(costs)* Kosten *Pl.*

costly ['kɒstlɪ, 'kɔ:stlɪ] *adj.* **a)** teuer; kostspielig; **b)** *(fig.)* **a ~ victory** ein teuer erkaufter Sieg; **a ~ error** ein folgenschwerer Irrtum

cost: ~ of 'living *n.* Lebenshaltungskosten *Pl;* **~-of-living allowance** Ausgleichszulage, *die;* **~-of-living bonus** Teuerungszulage, *die;* **~-of-living index** Lebenshaltungsindex, *der;* **~ price** *n.* Selbstkostenpreis, *der*

costume ['kɒstju:m] **1.** *n.* **a)** Kleidermode, *die; (theatrical ~)* Kostüm, *das;* **the ~ of the nation** die Nationaltracht; **historical ~s** historische Kostüme; **Highland ~:** schottische Tracht; **b)** *(dated: jacket and skirt)* Kostüm, *das.* **2.** *v. t.* ausstatten

costume: ~ ball *n.* Kostümfest, *das;* Kostümball, *der;* **~ designer** *n.* Kostümbildner, *der*/-bildnerin, *die;* **~ 'jewellery** *n.* Modeschmuck, *der;* **~ piece, ~ play** *ns.* Kostümstück, *das*

costumer ['kɒstjʊmə(r)], **costumier** [kɒ'stju:mɪə(r)] *ns.* Kostümschneider, *der*/-schneiderin, *die; (hirer of costumes)* Kostümverleiher, *der*/-verleiherin, *die*

cosy ['kəʊzɪ] **1.** *adj.* **a)** gemütlich; behaglich ‹*Atmosphäre*›; bequem ‹*Sessel*›; **feel ~:** sich wohl *od.* behaglich fühlen; **be ~:** es gemütlich haben; **a ~ feeling** ein Gefühl der Behaglichkeit; **b)** *(derog.: complacent, convenient)* bequem; **they have a very ~ relationship** sie passen zueinander wie ein altes Paar Filzpantoffeln. **2.** *n. see* **egg-cosy; tea-cosy**

~ a'long *v. t. (coll.)* beruhigen

~ 'up to *v. i. (Amer. coll.)* **~ up to the fireplace** es sich *(Dat.)* am Kamin gemütlich machen; **~ up to sb.** mit jmdm. vertraulich werden; *(ingratiate oneself with sb.)* sich bei jmdm. einschmeicheln

cot [kɒt] *n. (Brit.: child's bed)* Kinderbett, *das;* **the baby cried in his ~:** das Baby schrie in seinem Bettchen

cotangent [kəʊ'tændʒənt] *n. (Math.)* Kotangens, *der*

'cot-death *n. (Brit.)* plötzlicher Kindstod; Cot-death, *der (Med.)*

cote [kəʊt] *n.* Stall, *der; see also* **dove-cote**

coterie ['kəʊtərɪ] *n.* Zirkel, *der;* **artistic ~:** Künstlerkreis, *der*

cotoneaster [kətəʊnɪ'æstə(r)] *n. (Bot.)* Zwergmispel, *die*

cottage ['kɒtɪdʒ] *n.* Cottage, *das;* Häuschen, *das*

cottage: ~ 'cheese *n.* Hüttenkäse, *der;* **~ 'hospital** *n. kleines [Land]krankenhaus ohne ständige ärztliche Betreuung;* **~ industry** *n.* Heimarbeit, *die;* **~ loaf** *n. eine Art rundes Weißbrot;* **~ 'pie** *n. mit Kartoffelbrei überbackenes Hackfleisch*

cottager ['kɒtɪdʒə(r)] *n.* Cottagebewohner, *der*/-bewohnerin, *die*

cotter ['kɒtə(r)] *n.* **~[-pin]** Splint, *der*

cotton ['kɒtn] **1.** *n. (substance, plant)* Baumwolle, *die; (thread)* Baumwollgarn, *das; (cloth)* Baumwollstoff, *der.* **2.** *attrib. adj.* Baumwoll-. **3.** *v. i.* **~ 'on** *(coll.)* kapieren *(ugs.);* **~ 'on to** *(coll.) (catch on to)* spitzkriegen *(ugs.); (understand)* kapieren *(ugs.);* **~ to sb.** *(Amer.)* sich mit jmdm. anfreunden

cotton: ~ belt *n. (Geog.)* Baumwollgürtel, *der;* **~ candy** *n. (Amer.)* Zuckerwatte, *die;* **~-gin** *n. (machine)* Egreniermaschine, *die (fachspr.);* **~-mill** *n.* Baumwollspinnerei, *die;* **~-picking** *adj. (Amer. sl.)* verdammt; verflucht; ~ **plant** *n.* Baumwollpflanze, *die;* ~ '**print** *n.* bedruckter Baumwollstoff; ~-**reel** *n.* [Näh]garnrolle, *die;* ~-**spinner** *n.* Baumwollspinner, *der*/-spinnerin, *die;* ~-**spinning** *n.* Baumwollspinnerei, *die;* ~**tail** *n. (Amer. Zool.)* Waldkaninchen, *das;* Baumwollschwanzkaninchen, *das;* ~ '**waste** *n.* Putzwolle, *die;* ~ '**wool** *n.* **a)** Watte, *die;* ~-**wool ball** Wattebausch, *der;* **wrap sb. up** *or* **keep sb. in ~ wool** *(fig.)* jmdn. in Watte packen; **b)** *(Amer.: raw cotton)* Rohbaumwolle, *die*

cottony ['kɒtənɪ] *adj.* baumwollartig ‹*Substanz*›; flaumig, behaart ‹*Blatt*›

cotyledon [kɒtɪ'li:dən] *n. (Bot.)* Keimblatt, *das*

[1]**couch** [kaʊtʃ] **1.** *n.* **a)** *(sofa)* Couch, *die;* **b) doctor's ~:** [Untersuchungs]liege, *die;* **psychiatrist's ~:** Couch [des Psychiaters]; **c)** *(arch./literary: bed)* Lager, *das.* **2.** *v.t.* formulieren; ~**ed in modest terms** in bescheidener Sprache abgefaßt

[2]**couch** [ku:tʃ, kaʊtʃ] *n.* ~[-**grass**] *(Bot.)* Quecke, *die*

couchette [ku:'ʃet] *n. (Railw.)* Liegewagen, *der; (berth)* Liegesitz, *der*

cougar ['ku:gə(r)] *n. (Amer. Zool.)* Puma, *der*

cough [kɒf] **1.** *n. (act of coughing, condition)* Husten, *der;* **give a ~:** husten; **have a [bad] ~:** [einen schlimmen] Husten haben. **2.** *v.i.* **a)** husten; **b)** ‹*Motor:*› stottern; ‹*Gewehr usw.:*› knattern. **3.** *v.t.* ~ **out** [her]aushusten; *(say with cough)* husten; ~ **up** [her]aushusten; *(sl.: pay)* ausspucken *(ugs.);* **come on, ~ up!** na los, spuck's aus!

'**cough-drop** *see* **cough sweet**

coughing ['kɒfɪŋ] *n.* Husten, *das;* Gehuste, *das;* **there was a lot of ~:** es wurde ständig gehustet; **a bout of ~:** ein Hustenanfall

cough: ~ **medicine** *n.* Hustenmittel, *das;* ~ **mixture** *n.* Hustensaft, *der;* ~ **sweet** *n.* Hustenbonbon, *das od. der*

could *see* [2]**can**

couldn't ['kʊdnt] *(coll.)* = **could not;** *see* [2]**can**

coulomb ['ku:lɒm] *n. (Electr.)* Coulomb, *das;* Amperesekunde, *die*

council ['kaʊnsl] *n.* **a)** Ratsversammlung, *die;* **family ~:** Familienrat, *der;* **b)** *(administrative/advisory body)* Rat, *der;* **local ~:** Gemeinderat, *der;* **city/town ~:** Stadtrat, *der;* **c)** *(Eccl.)* Konzil, *das;* **diocesan ~:** Diözesanrat, *der*

council: ~-**chamber** *n.* Sitzungssaal [des Rats]; ~ **estate** *n.* Wohnviertel mit Sozialwohnungen; ~ **flat** *n.* Sozialwohnung, *die;* ~ **house** *n.* Haus des sozialen Wohnungsbaus; ~ **housing** *n.* sozialer Wohnungsbau

councillor ['kaʊnsələ(r)] *n.* Ratsmitglied, *das;* **town ~:** Stadtrat, *der*/-rätin, *die*

council: ~ **man** ['kaʊnslmən] *n., pl.* ~**men** ['kaʊnslmən] [Gemeinde-/Stadt]ratsmitglied, *das (bes. in London und in den USA);* ~ **meeting** *n.* Ratssitzung, *die;* ~ **of 'war** *n. (lit. or fig.)* Kriegsrat, *der;* ~ **school** *(Brit. dated) see* **State school**

counsel ['kaʊnsl] **1.** *n.* **a)** *(consultation)* Beratung, *die;* **take/hold ~ with sb. [about sth.]** sich mit jmdm. [über etw. *(Akk.)*] beraten; **b)** Rat[schlag], *der;* ~ **of perfection** Vollkommenheitsforderung, *die (Rel.); (fig.)* ideale Forderung; **keep one's own ~:** seine Meinung für sich behalten; **c)** *pl. same (Law)* Rechtsanwalt, *der*/-anwältin, *die;* ~ **for the defence** Verteidiger, *der*/Verteidigerin, *die;* ~ **for the prosecution** Anklagevertreter, *der*/-vertreterin, *die;* Staatsanwalt, *der*/-anwältin, *die;* **Queen's/King's C~:** Anwalt/Anwältin der Krone; Kronanwalt, *der*/-anwältin, *die.* **2.** *v.t., (Brit.)* -**ll- a)** *(advise)* beraten; ~ **sb. to do sth.** jmdm. raten *od.* den Rat geben, etw. zu tun; **b)** *(suggest)* ~ **forbearance** *etc.* zur Nachsicht *usw.* raten

counselling *(Amer.:* **counseling)** ['kaʊnsəlɪŋ] *n.* Beratung, *die;* **marriage ~:** Eheberatung, *die*

counsellor, *(Amer.)* **counselor** ['kaʊnsələ(r)] *n.* **a)** Berater, *der*/Beraterin, *die;* **marriage-guidance ~:** Eheberater, *der*/-beraterin, *die;* **[student] ~:** Studienberater, *der*/-beraterin, *die;* **b)** *(Diplom.)* Botschaftsrat, *der*/-rätin, *die;* **c)** *(Law)* ~ **[-at-law]** *(Amer.: barrister)* Rechtsanwalt, *der*/-anwältin, *die;* **d)** *(Brit.)* **C~ of State** Stellvertreter des Königs/der Königin

[1]**count** [kaʊnt] **1.** *n.* **a)** Zählen, *das;* Zählung, *die* ; **keep ~ [of sth.]** [etw.] zählen; **I'm going to keep ~ of the number of times he says 'incredible'** ich werde mitzählen, wie oft er „unglaublich" sagt; **lose ~:** beim Zählen durcheinandergeraten; **lose ~ of sth.** etw. gar nicht mehr zählen können; **have/take/make a ~:** zählen; **on the ~ of three** bei „drei"; **b)** *(sum total)* Ergebnis, *das;* **c)** *(Law)* Anklagepunkt, *der;* **on all ~s** in allen [Anklage]punkten; **on that ~** *(fig.)* in diesem Punkt; **d)** *(Boxing)* Auszählen, *das;* **be out for the ~:** ausgezählt werden; *(fig.)* hinüber sein *(ugs.);* **e)** *(Phys.) (event)* Impuls, *der; (total number)* Impulszahl, *die.* **2.** *v.t.* **a)** zählen; ~ **ten** bis zehn zählen; ~ **the votes** die Stimmen [aus]zählen; ~ **again** nachzählen; ~ **the pennies** *(fig.)* jeden Pfennig umdrehen; sparsam sein; ~ **the cost** *(usu. fig.)* unter den Folgen zu leiden haben; **b)** *(include)* mitzählen; **be ~ed against sb.** gegen jmdn. sprechen; **not ~ing** abgesehen von; **c)** *(consider)* halten für; ~ **oneself lucky** sich glücklich schätzen können; ~ **sb. as one of us/a friend** jmdn. als einen von uns/als Freund betrachten; **I ~ him [as] one of the family** er gehört für mich zur Familie; ~ **sb. among one's friends/clients** jmdn. zu seinen Freunden/Kunden zählen. **3.** *v.i.* **a)** zählen; ~ **from one to ten** von eins bis zehn zählen; ~ **[up] to ten** bis zehn zählen; **b)** *(be included)* zählen; **every moment ~s** jede Sekunde zählt; ~ **against sb.** gegen jmdn. sprechen; **money ~s/looks ~:** Geld/Aussehen ist wichtig; **money is what ~s** Geld ist das, was zählt; ~ **for much/little** viel/wenig zählen; **appearances ~ for a great deal** *or* **a lot** der äußere Schein macht viel aus; **c)** *(conduct a reckoning)* zählen; ~**ing from now** von jetzt an [gerechnet]; ab jetzt

~ '**down 1.** *v.i.* rückwärts zählen. **2.** *v.t.* ~ **sth. down** den *od.* das Countdown für etw. durchführen. *See also* **count-down**

~ '**in** *v.t.* mitrechnen; ~ **sb. in on a venture** jmdn. bei einem Unternehmen einplanen; **shall I ~ you in?** machst/kommst du mit? **you can ~ me in** ich bin dabei

~ **on** *v.t.* ~ **on sb./sth.** sich auf jmdn./etw. verlassen; **you mustn't ~ on winning first prize** du darfst nicht damit rechnen, den ersten Preis zu gewinnen

~ '**out** *v.t.* **a)** *(one by one)* abzählen; **b)** *(exclude)* **[you can] ~ me out** ich komme/mache nicht mit; **c)** *(Boxing)* auszählen; **d)** *(Brit. Parl.)* ~ **the House out** die Sitzung wegen Beschlußunfähigkeit vertagen

~ '**up** *v.t.* zusammenzählen; zusammenrechnen

~ **upon** *see* ~ **on**

[2]**count** *n. (nobleman)* Graf, *der*

countable ['kaʊntəbl] *adj. (also Ling.)* zählbar

'**countdown** *n.* Countdown, *der od. das*

countenance ['kaʊntɪnəns] **1.** *n.* **a)** *(literary: face)* Antlitz, *das (dichter.);* **b)** *(formal: expression)* Gesichtsausdruck, *der;* **change ~:** den Gesichtsausdruck verändern; **keep ~:** keine Miene verziehen; **c)** *(dated/formal: composure)* Haltung, *die;* **keep sb. in ~** *(arch.)* jmdn. ermuntern *od.* aufrichten; **keep one's ~:** Haltung *od.* die Fassung bewahren; **lose ~:** die Fassung verlieren; **put sb. out of ~:** jmdn. aus der Fassung bringen; **d)** *(dated/formal: moral support)* Ermutigung, *die;* [moralische] Unterstützung; **give ~ to sb./sth.** jmdn./etw. unterstützen. **2.** *v.t. (formal) (approve)* billigen; gutheißen; *(support)* unterstützen

[1]**counter** ['kaʊntə(r)] *n.* **a)** *(in shop)* Ladentisch, *der; (in cafeteria, restaurant, train)* Büfett, *das; (in post office, bank)* Schalter, *der;* ~ **clerk** Schalterbeamte, *der*/-beamtin, *die;* **these medicines/weapons can be bought over the ~:** diese Arzneimittel kann man ohne Rezept kaufen/diese Waffen kann man ohne Waffenschein kaufen; **[buy/sell sth.] under the ~** *(fig.)* [etwas] unter dem Ladentisch [kaufen/verkaufen]; **b)** *(small disc for games)* Spielmarke, *die; (token representing coin)* Jeton, *der;* **c)** *(apparatus for counting)* Zähler, *der*

[2]**counter 1.** *adj.* entgegengesetzt; Gegen-/gegen-. **2.** *v.t.* **a)** *(oppose, contradict)* begegnen (+ *Dat.*); **b)** *(meet by ~move)* kontern; zurückschlagen. **3.** *v.i.* **a)** *(make ~move)* antworten; kontern; **b)** *(Boxing)* kontern. **4.** *adv. (in the opposite direction)* in entgegengesetzter Richtung; **go/run ~:** in die falsche Richtung gehen/laufen; **b)** *(contrary)* **act ~ to** zuwiderhandeln (+ *Dat.*); **go ~ to** zuwiderlaufen (+ *Dat.*); **run ~ to** im Widerspruch stehen zu. **5.** *n.* **a)** *(Boxing)* Konter, *der;* **b)** *(~move)* Antwort, *die* **(to** auf + *Akk.*)

[3]**counter** *n. (Naut.)* Gilling, *die*

counter: ~'**act** *v.t.* entgegenwirken (+ *Dat.*); ~'**action** *n.* Gegenwirkung, *die;* ~-**attack** *(lit. or fig.)* **1.** *n.* Gegenangriff, *der;* **2.** *v.t.* ~-**attack sb.** gegen jmdn. einen Gegenangriff richten; **3.** *v.i.* zurückschlagen; ~-**attraction** *n.* **a)** *(rival)* Konkurrenz, *die;* **b)** *(of contrary tendency)* entgegengesetzte Anziehungskraft; ~**balance 1.** *v.t.* ein Gegengewicht bilden zu; *(fig.: neutralize)* ausgleichen; **2.** *n. (lit. or fig.)* Gegengewicht, *das;* ~**blast** *n.* Gegenschlag, *der;* ~**charge** *n.* Gegenbeschuldigung, *die;* Gegenklage, *die (Rechtsspr.);* ~**check** *n.* **a)** *(double check)* Gegenkontrolle, *die;* **b)** *(check that opposes a thing)* Gegenkraft, *die;* ~-**claim** *(Law)* **1.** *n.* Gegenforderung, *die;* **2.** *v.t.* eine Gegenforderung erheben auf (+ *Akk.*); ~-'**clockwise** *see* **anticlockwise;** ~-'**espionage** *n.* Spionageabwehr, *die;* Gegenspionage, *die*

counterfeit ['kaʊntəfɪt, 'kaʊntəfi:t] **1.** *adj.* falsch, unecht ‹*Schmuck*›; falsch, gefälscht ‹*Unterschrift, Münze, Banknote*›; *(fig. literary)* vorgetäuscht ‹*Emotionen*›; ~ **money** Falschgeld, *das.* **2.** *v.t.* **a)** *(forge)* fälschen; **b)** *(fig.: simulate)* vortäuschen

counterfeiter ['kaʊntəfɪtə(r)] *n. (forger)* Fälscher, *der*/Fälscherin, *die*

counter: ~**foil** *n.* Kontrollabschnitt, *der;* ~-**intelligence** *n. see* ~-**espionage;** ~-'**irritant** *n. (Med.)* Hautreizmittel, *das*

countermand [kaʊntə'mɑ:nd] *v.t.* **a)** *(revoke)* widerrufen; **b)** *(cancel order for)* abstellen ‹*Waren*›; ~ **an action/payment** die Anweisung für eine Handlung/Zahlung zurücknehmen; **c)** *(recall)* zurückrufen

counter: ~**measure** *n.* Gegenmaßnahme, *die;* ~**move** *n.* Gegenzug, *der;* ~-**offensive** *n. (Mil.)* Gegenoffensive, *die;* ~-**offer** *n.* Gegenangebot, *das*

counterpane ['kaʊntəpeɪn] *n. (dated)* Tagesdecke, *die*

counter: ~**part** *n.* Gegenstück, *das* **(of** zu); Pendant, *das (geh.)* **(of** zu); ~**point** *n. (Mus.)* Kontrapunkt, *der;* ~**poise** *n.* Gegengewicht, *das;* ~-**pro'ductive** *adj.* das Gegenteil des Gewünschten bewirkend; **sth. is ~-productive** etw. bewirkt das Gegenteil des Gewünschten; ~-**proposal** *n.* Gegenvorschlag, *der;* **C~-Reformation** *n. (Hist.)* Gegenreformation, *die;* ~-**revolution** *n.* Gegenrevolution, *die;*

Konterrevolution, *die (bes. marx.)*; ~-**revolutionary 1.** *adj.* gegenrevolutionär; konterrevolutionär *(bes. marx.)*; **2.** *n.* Konterrevolutionär, *der*/-revolutionärin, *die*; ~**shaft** *n. (Mech. Engin.)* Transmissionswelle, *die*; *(Amer.: layshaft)* Vorgelegewelle, *die*; ~**sign 1.** *v. t.* **a)** *(add signature to)* gegenzeichnen; **b)** *(ratify)* bestätigen; **2.** *n. (Mil.: password)* Parole, *die*; ~'**signature** *n.* Gegenunterschrift, *die*; ~**sink** *v. t.*, ~**sunk** ['kaʊntəsʌŋk] *(Woodw., Metalw.)* **a)** *(bevel off)* senken ‹*Loch*›; **b)** *(sink)* versenken ‹*Schraube*›; ~**stroke** *n.* Gegenschlag, *der*; ~-'**tenor** *n. (Mus.)* Contratenor, *der*; ~**weight** *n.* Gegengewicht, *das*

countess ['kaʊntɪs] *n.* Gräfin, *die*

counting-house ['kaʊntɪŋhaʊs] *n. (dated)* Kontor, *das (veralt.)*

countless ['kaʊntlɪs] *adj.* zahllos; ~ **numbers of** eine zahllose Menge von

countrified ['kʌntrɪfaɪd] *adj.* ländlich

country ['kʌntrɪ] *n.* **a)** Land, *das*; *(fatherland)* Heimat, *die*; **sb.'s [home]** ~: jmds. Heimat; **fight/die for one's** ~: für sein [Vater]land kämpfen/sterben; **farming** ~: Ackerland, *das*; **this is excellent bird-watching** ~: das ist eine Gegend, in der man hervorragend Vögel beobachten kann; **densely wooded** ~: dicht bewaldetes Gebiet; **this is unknown** ~ **to me** *(fig.)* das ist Neuland *od.* unbekanntes Gelände für mich; **[the] Hardy** ~: das Land Hardys; **b)** *(rural district)* Land, *das*; *(countryside)* Landschaft, *die*; ~ **road/air** Landstraße, *die*/Landluft, *die*; ~ **inn** [ländlicher] Gasthof; **[be/live** *etc.***] in the** ~: auf dem Land [sein/leben *usw.*]; **to the** ~: aufs Land; **[go/travel** *etc.***] across** ~: über Land [fahren/reisen *usw.*]; **up** ~: *(Richtung)* ins Landesinnere; *(Lage)* im Landesinneren; **in the** ~ *(Cricket sl.)* weit draußen; **c)** *(Brit.: population)* Volk, *das*; **appeal** *or* **go to the** ~: den Wähler entscheiden lassen

country: ~-**and-'western** *adj.* Country-und-Western-; ~ **club** *n.* Country Club, *der*; ~ '**cousin** *n.* Landei, *das (ugs. abwertend)*; *(woman also)* Landpomeranze, *die (ugs. abwertend)*; ~ '**dance** *n.* Kontertanz, *der*; ~ '**dancing** *n.* Kontertanz, *der*

countryfied *see* **countrified**

country: ~ **folk** *n.* Landbewohner *Pl.*; ~ '**gentleman** *n.* Landbesitzer, *der*; ~ '**house** *n.* Landhaus, *das*; ~ **life** *n.* Landleben, *das*; ~**man** ['kʌntrɪmən] *n., pl.* ~**men** ['kʌntrɪmən] **a)** *(national)* Landsmann, *der*; **[my/her** *etc.***] fellow** ~**man** [mein/ihr *usw.*] Landsmann; **b)** *(rural)* Landbewohner, *der*; ~ **music** *n.* Country-music, *die*; ~ **people** *n. pl.* Landbewohner *Pl.*; ~ '**seat** *n.* Landsitz, *der*; ~**side** *n.* **a)** *(rural areas)* Land, *das*; **the preservation of the** ~**side** die Erhaltung der Landschaft; **b)** *(rural scenery)* Landschaft, *die*; ~-**wide** *adj.* landesweit; ~**woman** *n.* **a)** *(national)* Landsmännin, *die*; **my fellow** ~**woman** meine Landsmännin; **b)** *(rural)* Landbewohnerin, *die*

county ['kaʊntɪ] **1.** *n.* **a)** *(Brit.)* Grafschaft, *die*; *(Amer., Commonwealth)* Verwaltungsbezirk, *der*; **b)** *(Brit.: gentry)* Gentry [der/einer Grafschaft]. **2.** *adj. (Brit.) den Lebensstil reicher Grundbesitzer pflegend*; ≈ junkerhaft

county: ~ '**borough** *n. (Hist./Ir.) Stadt mit dem Status einer Grafschaft*; ~ '**council** *n.* Grafschaftsrat, *der*; ~ '**court** *n. (Law) (Brit.)* Grafschaftsgericht, *das*; *(Amer.) Zivil- und Strafgericht*; ~ '**cricket** *n. (Brit.) Kricketspiele zwischen Grafschaftsauswahlen*; ~ **family** *n. alteingesessene [Adels]familie*; ~ **school** *n. von der Grafschaft bezuschußte öffentliche Schule*; ~ '**seat** *n. (Amer.)* ≈ Bezirksstadt, *die*; ~ '**town** *n. (Brit.) Verwaltungssitz einer Grafschaft*

coup [ku:] *n.* **a)** Coup, *der*; **pull off** *(coll.) or* **make a** ~: einen Coup landen *(ugs.)*; **b)** *see* **coup d'état**

coup: ~ **de grâce** [ku: də 'grɑ:s] *n.* Todesstoß, *der*; ~ **d'état** [ku: deɪ'tɑ:] *n.* Staatsstreich, *der*; ~ **de théâtre** [ku: də teɪ'ɑ:tr] *n.* Theatercoup, *der*

coupé ['ku:peɪ] *(Amer.:* **coupe** [ku:p]) *n. (car)* Coupé, *das*

couple [kʌpl] **1.** *n.* **a)** *(pair)* Paar, *das*; *(married)* [Ehe]paar, *das*; *(dancing)* [Tanz]paar, *das*; **in** ~**s** paarweise; **b) a** ~ **[of]** *(a few)* ein paar; *(two)* zwei; **a** ~ **of people/things/days/weeks** *etc.* ein paar/zwei Leute/Dinge/Tage/Wochen *usw.*; **a** ~ **of times** ein paarmal/zweimal; **c)** *(Mech.)* Kräftepaar, *das*. **2.** *v. t.* **a)** *(associate)* verbinden; **be** ~**d with sth.** mit etw. verbunden sein; **b)** *(fasten together)* koppeln. **3.** *v. i.* sich paaren

~ '**on** *v. t.* ankoppeln

~ **to'gether** *v. t.* ankoppeln; *(fig.)* miteinander in Verbindung bringen

~ '**up** *v. t.* ankoppeln

coupler ['kʌplə(r)] *n. (Mus.)* Koppel, *die*

couplet ['kʌplɪt] *n. (Pros.)* Verspaar, *das*; *(rhyming)* Reimpaar, *das*

coupling ['kʌplɪŋ] *n.* **a)** *(Railw., Mech. Engin.)* Kupplung, *die*; **b)** *(arrangement on gramophone record)* Zusammenstellung, *die*; *(recording on reverse side)* B-Seite, *die*

coupon ['ku:pɒn] *n. (detachable ticket)* Abschnitt, *der*; *(for rationed goods)* Marke, *die*; *(in advertisement)* Gutschein, *der*; Coupon, *der*; *(entry-form for football pool etc.)* Tippschein, *der*; *(voucher)* Gutschein, *der*

courage ['kʌrɪdʒ] *n.* Mut, *der*; **have/lack the** ~ **to do sth.** den Mut haben/nicht den Mut haben, etw. zu tun; **take one's** ~ **in both hands** sein Herz in beide Hände nehmen; **sb. takes** ~ **from sth.** etw. macht jmdm. Mut; **take** ~**!** nur Mut!; **lose** ~: den Mut verlieren; **have the** ~ **of one's convictions** zu seiner Überzeugung stehen

courageous [kə'reɪdʒəs] *adj.* mutig

courageously [kə'reɪdʒəslɪ] *adv.* mutig

courageousness [kə'reɪdʒəsnɪs] *n., no pl.* Mut, *der*

courgette [kʊə'ʒet] *n. (Brit.)* Zucchino, *der*

courier ['kʊrɪə(r)] *n.* **a)** *(Tourism)* Reiseleiter, *der*/-leiterin, *die*; **b)** *(messenger)* Kurier, *der*

course [kɔ:s] **1.** *n.* **a)** *(of ship, plane)* Kurs, *der*; **change [one's]** ~ *(lit. or fig.)* den Kurs wechseln; ~ **[of action]** Vorgehensweise, *die*; **what are our possible** ~**s of action?** welche Möglichkeiten haben wir?; **the most sensible** ~ **would be to ...:** das Vernünftigste wäre, zu ...; **in the ordinary** ~ **of things** *or* **events** unter normalen Umständen; **the** ~ **of nature/history** der Lauf der Dinge/Geschichte; **run** *or* **take its** ~: seinen/ihren Lauf nehmen; **let things take their** ~: den Dingen ihren Lauf lassen; **off/on** ~: vom Kurs abgekommen/auf Kurs; **be on** ~ **for sth.** *(fig.)* auf etw. *(Akk.)* zusteuern; **b) of** ~: natürlich; **[do sth.] as a matter of** ~: [etw.] selbstverständlich [tun]; **c)** *(progression)* Lauf, *der*; **in due** ~: zu gegebener Zeit; **the road is in** ~ **of construction** die Straße wird gerade gebaut; **be in the** ~ **of doing sth.** gerade dabei sein, etw. zu tun; **in the** ~ **of a few minutes** im Laufe von wenigen Minuten; **in the** ~ **of the lesson/the day/his life** im Lauf[e] der Stunde/des Tages/seines Lebens; **in the** ~ **of time/our relationship** im Lauf[e] der Zeit/unserer Beziehung; **d)** *(of river etc.)* Lauf, *der*; **e)** *(of meal)* Gang, *der*; **f)** *(Sport)* Kurs, *der*; *(for race)* Rennstrecke, *die*; **[golf-]**~: [Golf]platz, *der*; **g)** *(Educ.)* Kurs[us], *der*; *(for employee also)* Lehrgang, *der*; *(book)* Lehrbuch, *das*; **a** ~ **of lectures** eine Vorlesungsreihe; **go to** *or* **attend/do a** ~ **in sth.** einen Kurs in etw. *(Dat.)* besuchen/machen; **be/go on a** ~: auf einem Lehrgang sein/zu einem Lehrgang gehen; **h)** *(Med.)* **a** ~ **of treatment** eine Kur; **a** ~ **of tablets** eine Tablettenkur; **i)** *(Building)* Schicht, *die*. **2.** *v. i. (rhet.: flow)* strömen

coursing ['kɔ:sɪŋ] *n. (Sport)* Hetzjagd, *die*

court [kɔ:t] **1.** *n.* **a)** Hof, *der*; *(Brit.: quadrangle)* [Innen]hof [des/eines Colleges] *(in Cambridge)*; *(subdivision of building)* ≈ Halle, *die*; **b)** *(Sport)* Spielfeld, *das*; *(Tennis, Squash also)* Platz, *der*; **c)** *(of sovereign)* Hof, *der*; **the C**~ **of St James's** *(Brit.)* der englische Königshof; **hold** ~ *(fig.)* hofhalten *(scherzh.)*; **d)** *(Law)* Gericht, *das*; *(courtroom)* Gerichtssaal, *der*; ~ **of law** *or* **justice** Gerichtshof, *der*; **go to** ~ **[over sth.]** [wegen *od.* mit etw.] vor Gericht gehen; **take sb. to** ~: jmdn. vor Gericht bringen *od.* verklagen; **appear in** ~: vor Gericht erscheinen; **the case comes up in** ~ **today** der Fall wird heute verhandelt; **settle sth. in** ~: etw. gerichtlich klären; **out of** ~: außergerichtlich; *(fig.)* indiskutabel; **rule/laugh sth. out of** ~ *(fig.)* etw. verwerfen/auslachen; **e)** *(managing body)* Rat, *der*; **f)** *no art. (dated: attentions)* **pay** ~ **to sb.** jmdn. hofieren *(veralt.)*; **pay** ~ **to a woman** einer Frau den Hof machen *(veralt.)*. **2.** *v. t.* **a)** *(woo)* ~ **sb.** jmdn. umwerben; ~**ing couple** Liebespärchen, *das*; **are they** ~**ing?** sind sie ein Pärchen?; **b)** *(Zool., Ornith.)* umwerben; **c)** *(fig.)* suchen ‹*Gunst, Ruhm, Gefahr*›; **he is** ~**ing disaster/danger** er wandelt am Rande des Abgrunds *(fig. geh.)*; ~ **death** sein Leben riskieren

court: ~ **card** *n.* Figurenkarte, *die*; ~ '**circular** *n. (Brit.)* Hofnachrichten *Pl.*; ~ **dress** *n.* Hofkleid, *das*

courteous ['kɜ:tɪəs] *adj.* höflich; ~ **manners** gute Manieren

courteously ['kɜ:tɪəslɪ] *adv.* höflich; **behave** ~: höflich sein

courtesan [kɔ:tɪ'zæn] *n.* Kokotte, *die*; Kurtisane, *die (hist.)*

courtesy ['kɜ:təsɪ] *n.* Höflichkeit, *die*; **drinks were [served] by** ~ **of sb.** die Getränke gingen auf jmds. Kosten; **by** ~ **of the museum** mit freundlicher Genehmigung des Museums; **by** ~ *(with some exaggeration)* mit viel Wohlwollen; *(as mark of politeness)* aus Höflichkeit

courtesy: ~ **call** *n.* Höflichkeitsbesuch, *der*; ~ **light** *n. (Motor Veh.)* Innenbeleuchtung, *die*; ~ **title** *n. Höflichkeitsanrede mit einem höheren Titel, als die betreffende Person besitzt*

'**court-house** *n. (Law)* Gerichtsgebäude, *das*; *(Amer.) Verwaltungsgebäude eines Verwaltungsbezirks [mit Bezirksgefängnis]*

courtier ['kɔ:tɪə(r)] *n.* Höfling, *der*

courtly ['kɔ:tlɪ] *adj.* vornehm; ~ **love** *(Hist.)* Minne, *die*

court: ~ '**martial** *n., pl.* ~**s martial** *(Mil.)* Kriegsgericht, *das*; **be tried by** ~ **martial** vor das/ein Kriegsgericht kommen; ~-'**martial** *v. t., (Brit.)* **-ll-** vor das/ein Kriegsgericht stellen; **C**~ **of Ap'peal** *n. (Brit.)* Berufungsgericht, *das*; ~**room** *n. (Law)* Gerichtssaal, *der*

courtship ['kɔ:tʃɪp] *n.* Werben, *das*

court: ~ **shoe** *n.* Pumps, *der*; ~**yard** *n.* Hof, *der*

cousin ['kʌzn] *n.* **[first]** ~: Cousin, *der*/Cousine, *die*; Vetter, *der*/*(veralt.)* Base, *die*; **[second]** ~: Cousin/Cousine zweiten Grades; **they are** ~**s** sie sind Cousins/Cousinen/Cousin und Cousine; **first** ~ **once removed** *(first* ~*'s child)* Kind eines Cousins/einer Cousine; *(parent's* ~*)* Cousin/Cousine des Vaters/der Mutter; **sth. is first** ~ **to sth.** *(fig.)* etw. ist fast das gleiche wie etw.

couture [ku:'tjʊə(r)] *n.* Couture, *die*; *see also* **haute couture**

couturier [ku:'tjʊərjeɪ] *n.* Couturier, *der*; Modeschöpfer, *der*

couturière [ku:'tjʊərjeə(r)] *n.* Modeschöpferin, *die*

[1]**cove** [kəʊv] *n.* **a)** *(Geog.)* [kleine] Bucht; **b)** *(sheltered recess)* Einbuchtung, *die*

[2]cove *n. (dated Brit. sl.)* Kerl, *der*
coven [kʌvn] *n.* ≈ Hexensabbat, *der; Zusammenkunft von [dreizehn] Hexen*
covenant ['kʌvənənt] **1.** *n.* **a)** formelle Übereinkunft; **b)** *(Law)* [besiegelter] Vertrag; **deed of ~:** Vertragsurkunde, *die;* **c)** *(Bibl.)* Bund, *der.* **2.** *v. i. (also Law)* **~ [with sb.] [for sth.]** [mit jmdm.] [etw.] vertraglich festlegen. **3.** *v. t. (also Law)* [vertraglich] vereinbaren
Coventry ['kɒvəntrı] *n.* **send sb. to ~** *(fig.)* jmdn. [demonstrativ] schneiden
cover ['kʌvə(r)] **1.** *n.* **a)** *(piece of cloth)* Decke, *die; (of cushion, bed)* Bezug, *der; (lid)* Deckel, *der; (of hole, engine, typewriter, etc.)* Abdeckung, *die;* **put a ~ on** *or* **over** zudecken; abdecken ‹*Loch, Fußboden, Grab, Fahrzeug, Maschine*›; beziehen ‹*Kissen, Bett*›; **b)** *(of book)* Einband, *der; (of magazine)* Umschlag, *der; (of record)* [Platten]hülle, *die;* Cover, *das;* **read sth. from ~ to ~:** etw. von vorn bis hinten lesen; **on the [front/back] ~:** auf dem [vorderen/hinteren] Buchdeckel; *(of magazine)* auf der Titelseite/hinteren Umschlagseite; **a removable paper ~:** ein loser Papierumschlag; **c)** *(Post: envelope)* [Brief]umschlag, *der;* **under plain ~:** in neutralem Umschlag; **[send sth.] under separate ~:** [etw.] mit getrennter Post [schicken]; **d)** *in pl. (bedclothes)* Bettzeug, *das;* **e)** *(of pneumatic tyre)* Decke, *die;* **f)** *(hiding-place, shelter)* Schutz, *der;* **take ~ [from sth.]** Schutz [vor etw. *(Dat.)*] suchen; **take ~ from the rain** sich unterstellen; **[be/go] under ~** *(from bullets etc.)* in Deckung [sein/gehen]; **under ~** *(from rain)* überdacht ‹*Sitzplatz*›; regengeschützt; **keep sth. under ~:** etw. abgedeckt halten; **under ~ of darkness** im Schutz der Dunkelheit; **g)** *(Mil.: supporting force)* Deckung, *die;* **fighter ~:** Deckung durch Jagdflugzeuge; *see also* **air cover; h)** *(protection)* Deckung, *die;* **give sb./sth. ~:** jmdm. Deckung geben; **i)** *(pretence)* Vorwand, *der; (false identity, screen)* Tarnung, *die;* **under ~ of charity** unter dem Deckmantel der Barmherzigkeit; **blow sb.'s ~** *(coll.)* jmdn. enttarnen; **j)** *(Hunting)* Deckung, *die;* **break ~:** aus der Deckung herauskommen; **k)** *(Insurance)* **[insurance] ~:** Versicherung, *die;* **get ~ against sth.** sich gegen etw. versichern; **have adequate ~:** ausreichend versichert sein; **l)** *(place laid at table)* Gedeck, *das.* **2.** *v. t.* **a)** bedecken; **~ a book with leather** ein Buch in Leder binden; **~ your mouth while coughing** halte die Hand vor den Mund, wenn du hustest; **~ the table with a cloth** ein Tischtuch auf den Tisch legen; **~ a roof with shingles** ein Dach mit Schindeln decken; **~ a chair with chintz** einen Stuhl mit Chintz beziehen; **~ a pan with a lid/a car with plastic sheeting** eine Pfanne mit einem Deckel/ein Auto mit einer Plastikplane zudecken; **she ~ed her face with her hands** sie verbarg das Gesicht in den Händen; **~ed with blood** blutüberströmt; **the roses are ~ed with greenfly** die Rosen sind voller Blattläuse; **cats are ~ed with fur** Katzen haben ein Fell; **floodwaters ~ed the town** die Stadt war überflutet; **the children were ~ed in mud** die Kinder waren von oben bis unten voller Schlamm; **the car ~ed us with mud** das Auto bespritzte uns von oben bis unten mit Schlamm; **sb. is ~ed in** *or* **with confusion/shame** *(fig.)* jmd. ist ganz verlegen/sehr beschämt; *see also* **glory 1 b; b)** *(conceal, lit. or fig.)* verbergen; *(for protection)* abdecken; **c)** *(travel)* zurücklegen; **d)** *in p.p. (having roof)* überdacht; **~ed market** Markthalle, *die;* **a ~ed wagon** ein Planwagen; **e)** *(deal with)* behandeln; *(include)* abdecken; **~ all possible cases** alle möglichen Fälle abdecken; **an examination ~ing last year's work** eine Prüfung über den Stoff des vergangenen Jahres; **this book does not fully ~ the subject** dieses Buch behandelt das Thema nicht vollständig; **f)** *(Journ.)* berichten über (+ *Akk.*); **g)** *(suffice to defray)* decken; **~ expenses** die Kosten decken; **£10 will ~ my needs for the journey** 10 Pfund werden für die Reisekosten reichen; **h)** *(shield)* decken; **I'll keep you ~ed** ich gebe dir Deckung; **i) ~ oneself** *(fig.)* sich absichern; *(Insurance)* **~ oneself against sth.** sich gegen etw. versichern; **j)** *(aim gun at)* in Schach halten *(ugs.);* **I've got you ~ed** ich habe meine Waffe auf dich gerichtet; **k)** *(command)* kontrollieren ‹*Gelände*›; **l)** ‹*Hengst:*› decken
~ for *v. t.* einspringen für
~ 'in *v. t.* überdachen; *(fill in)* zuschütten
~ 'over *v. t.* zudecken; *(with gold etc.)* überziehen
~ 'up 1. *v. t. (conceal)* zudecken; *(fig.)* vertuschen. **2.** *v. i. (fig.: conceal)* es vertuschen; **~ up for sb.** jmdn. decken. *See also* **cover-up**
'cover address *n.* Deckadresse, *die*
coverage ['kʌvərıdʒ] *n., no pl.* **a)** *(Radio, Telev.: area)* Sendebereich, *der;* **provide a greater ~ of the country** den Sendebereich innerhalb des Landes vergrößern; **b)** *(Journ., Radio, Telev.: treatment)* Berichterstattung, *die* **(of** über + *Akk.*); **newspaper/broadcast ~:** Berichterstattung in der Presse/in Funk und Fernsehen; **give sth. [full/limited] ~:** [ausführlich/kurz] über etw. *(Akk.)* berichten; **c)** *(Advertising)* Abdeckung des Marktes; **d)** *(Insurance)* Deckung, *die*
coverall ['kʌvərɔ:l] *n. usu. in pl. (esp. Amer.)* Overall, *der; (for baby)* Strampelanzug, *der*
cover: ~ charge *n.* [Preis für das] Gedeck; **~ girl** *n.* Covergirl, *das*
covering ['kʌvərıŋ] *n. (material)* Decke, *die; (of billiard-table, aircraft wing)* Bespannung, *die; (of chair, bed)* Bezug, *der*
covering: ~ letter *n.* Begleitbrief, *der;* **~ note** *n.* [kurzes] Begleitschreiben
coverlet ['kʌvəlıt] *n.* Tagesdecke, *die*
cover: ~ note *n. (Insurance)* Deckungskarte, *die;* **~ story** *n.* **a)** *(Journ.)* Titelgeschichte, *die;* **b)** *(espionage)* [zur Tarnung erfundene] Geschichte
covert 1. ['kʌvət] *adj.* versteckt. **2.** ['kʌvət, 'kʌvə(r)] *n. (shelter)* Schlupfwinkel, *der; (thicket)* Dickicht, *das*
covertly ['kʌvətlı] *adv.* versteckt; **glance ~ at sb./sth.** jmdn./etw. verstohlen anschauen
'cover-up *n.* Verschleierung, *die;* **the Watergate ~:** die Watergate-Affäre
covet ['kʌvıt] *v. t.* begehren *(geh.)*
covetous ['kʌvıtəs] *adj. (desirous)* begehrlich *(geh.); (avaricious)* habgierig; **be ~ of sth.** etw. begehren *(geh.)*
covetously ['kʌvıtəslı] *adv.* begehrlich *(geh.)*
covetousness ['kʌvıtəsnıs] *n., no pl.* Begehrlichkeit, *die*
covey ['kʌvı] *n. (Hunting)* Kette, *die (Jägerspr.)*
[1]cow [kaʊ] *n.* **a)** Kuh, *die;* **till the ~s come home** *(fig. coll.)* bis in alle Ewigkeit *(ugs.);* **b)** *(female elephant, whale, etc.)* Kuh, *die;* **~ buffalo/elephant** Büffelkuh, *die*/Elefantenkuh, *die;* **c)** *(sl. derog.: woman)* Kuh, *die (salopp abwertend)*
[2]cow *v. t.* einschüchtern; **~ sb. into submission** jmdn. so einschüchtern, daß er sich unterordnet; **have a ~ed look/appearance** verschüchtert aussehen
coward ['kaʊəd] *n.* Feigling, *der;* **the ~'s way out** die feige Art, sich aus der Affäre zu ziehen
cowardice ['kaʊədıs] *n.* Feigheit, *die; see also* **moral cowardice**
cowardly ['kaʊədlı] *adj.* feig[e]
cow: ~bell *n.* Kuhglocke, *die;* **~boy** *n.* Cowboy, *der; (Brit. coll.: unscrupulous businessman, tradesman, etc.)* Betrüger, *der;* **play Cowboys and Indians** Cowboy und Indianer spielen; **~-catcher** *n. (Amer. Railw.)* Bahnräumer, *der;* Kuhfänger, *der;* **~ dung** *n.* Kuhmist, *der*
cower ['kaʊə(r)] *v. i.* sich ducken; *(squat)* kauern; **~ in fear** sich ängstlich ducken; **stand ~ing in the corner** geduckt in der Ecke stehen
cow: ~-hand *n.* Cowboy, *der;* **~herd** *n.* Kuhhirte, *der;* **~hide** *n.* Rindsleder, *das*
cowl [kaʊl] *n.* **a)** *(of monk)* Kutte, *die;* *(hood)* Kapuze, *die;* **b)** *(of chimney)* Schornsteinaufsatz, *der*
'cow-lick *n.* [Haar]tolle, *die (ugs.)*
cowling ['kaʊlıŋ] *n. (Aeronaut., Motor Veh.)* Motorhaube, *die*
'cowman *n.* Stallknecht, *der*
'co-worker *n.* Kollege, *der*/Kollegin, *die*
cow: ~-parsley *n. (Bot.)* Wiesenkerbel, *der;* **~-pat** *n.* Kuhfladen, *der;* **~pox** *n.* Kuhpocken *Pl.;* **~puncher** ['kaʊpʌnʃə(r)] *n. (Amer.)* Cowboy, *der*
cowrie, cowry ['kaʊrı] *n.* Kaurischnecke, *die; (shell)* Kaurimuschel, *die*
cow: ~-shed *n.* Kuhstall, *der;* **~slip** *n.* **a)** Schlüsselblume, *die;* **b)** *(Amer.: marsh marigold)* Sumpfdotterblume, *die;* **~'s milk** *n.* Kuhmilch, *die*
cox [kɒks] **1.** *n.* Steuermann, *der.* **2.** *v. t. (esp. Rowing)* steuern; **~ a crew** Steuermann einer Mannschaft sein; **~ed four** Vierer mit Steuermann. **3.** *v. i.* steuern
coxcomb ['kɒkskəʊm] *n. (literary/arch.)* Stutzer, *der (veralt.)*
coxless ['kɒkslıs] *adj.* ohne Steuermann
coxswain ['kɒkswein, 'kɒksn] *see* **cox 1**
coy [kɔı] *adj.* gespielt schüchtern; geziert ‹*Benehmen, Ausdruck*›; **play ~:** auf schüchtern machen
coyly ['kɔılı] *adv.* gespielt schüchtern; geziert ‹*sich benehmen*›
coyness ['kɔınıs] *n., no pl.* Schüchternheit, *die; (of behaviour)* Geziertheit, *die*
coyote [kə'jəʊtı, 'kɔıəʊt] *n. (Zool.)* Kojote, *der*
coypu ['kɔıpu:] *n. (Zool.)* Biberratte, *die;* Nutria, *die*
cozily, coziness, cozy *(Amer.) see* **cos-**
cp. *abbr.* **compare** vgl.
Cpl. *abbr.* **Corporal** Korp.
c.p.s. *abbr.* **cycles per second** Hz
CPU *abbr. (Computing)* **central processing unit** ZE
Cr. *abbr.* **a) creditor** Gl.; **b) Councillor** ≈ StR
crab [kræb] **1.** *n.* **a)** Krabbe, *die;* **b)** *(Astrol.)* **the C~** der Krebs; *see also* **archer b; c)** *(Rowing)* **catch a ~:** einen Krebs fangen; **d)** *(Bot.) see* **crab-apple. 2.** *v. i.,* **-bb-** *(coll.)* **~ about sth.** über etw. *(Akk.)* meckern *(ugs.)*
'crab-apple *n.* Holzapfel, *der*
crabbed [kræbd] *adj.* **a)** *(perverse)* starrköpfig; **b)** *(morose)* griesgrämig; **c)** *(badly formed)* unleserlich ‹*Handschrift*›
crabby ['kræbı] *adj. see* **crabbed a, b**
crabwise ['kræbwaız] *adv.* seitwärts [wie eine Krabbe]
crack [kræk] **1.** *n.* **a)** *(noise)* Krachen, *das;* **a ~ of the whip** ein Peitschenknall; **give sb./have a fair ~ of the whip** *(fig.)* jmdm. eine Chance geben/eine Chance haben; **the ~ of doom** *(fig.)* die Posaunen des Jüngsten Gerichts; **b)** *(in china, glass, eggshell, ice, etc.)* Sprung, *der; (in rock)* Spalte, *die; (chink)* Spalt, *der;* **there's a ~ in the ceiling** die Decke hat einen Riß; *see also* **paper over; c)** *(blow)* Schlag, *der;* **d)** *(coll.: try)* Versuch, *der;* **have a ~ at sth./at doing sth.** etw. in Angriff nehmen/versuchen, etw. zu tun; **e) the/at the ~ of dawn** *or* **day** *(coll.)* der/bei Tagesanbruch; **f)** *(coll.: wisecrack)* [geistreicher] Witz; **g)** *(sl.: drug)* Crack, *das.* **2.** *adj. (coll.)* erstklassig. **3.** *v. t.* **a)** *(break, lit. or fig.)* knacken ‹*Nuß, Problem*›; knacken *(salopp)* ‹*Safe, Kode*›; **~ a bottle** *(fig.)* einer Flasche den Hals brechen *(ugs. scherzh.);* ~

sth. open etw. aufbrechen; b) *(make a ~ in)* anschlagen ‹*Porzellan, Glas*›; ~ one's head/skull sich *(Dat.)* den Kopf/Schädel aufschlagen; c) ~ a whip mit einer Peitsche knallen; ~ the whip *(fig.)* Druck machen *(ugs.)*; ~ one's knuckles mit den Knöcheln knacken; d) ~ a joke einen Witz machen; e) *(Chem.: decompose)* kracken. 4. *v. i.* a) ‹*Porzellan, Glas:*› einen Sprung/Sprünge bekommen; ‹*Haut:*› aufspringen, rissig werden; ‹*Eis:*› Risse bekommen; b) *(make sound)* ‹*Peitsche:*› knallen; ‹*Gelenk:*› knakken; ‹*Gewehr:*› krachen; c) *(change)* ‹*Stimme:*› brechen *(geh.)*, versagen (with vor + *Dat.*); his voice is ~ing *(at age of puberty)* er ist im Stimmbruch; d) *(yield under torture etc.)* zusammenbrechen; e) *(coll.)* get ~ing! mach los! *(ugs.)*; let's get ~ing fangen wir endlich an; get ~ing [with sth.] [mit etw.] loslegen *(ugs.)*
~ 'down *v. i. (coll.)* ~ down [on sb./sth.] [gegen jmdn./etw.] [hart] vorgehen; *see also* crack-down
~ 'up *(coll.)* 1. *v. i.* ‹*Flugzeug usw.:*› auseinanderbrechen; ‹*Gesellschaft, Person:*› zusammenbrechen. 2. *v. t.* she/it *etc.* is not all she/it *etc.* is ~ed up to be so toll ist sie/es *usw.* nun auch wieder nicht[, wie sie/es dargestellt wird]; she is ~ed up to be brilliant sie soll brillant sein *(ugs.)*. *See also* crack-up
crack: ~-brained *adj. (coll.)* bescheuert *(salopp abwertend)* ‹*Person*›; hirnrissig *(abwertend)* ‹*Idee usw.*›; ~-down *n. (coll.)* there will be a ~-down man wird hart durchgreifen; have/order a ~-down on sb./sth. drastische Maßnahmen gegen jmdn./etw. ergreifen/anordnen
cracked [krækt] *adj.* a) gesprungen ‹*Porzellan, Ziegel, Glas*›; rissig, aufgesprungen ‹*Haut, Erdboden*›; rissig ‹*Verputz*›; brüchig ‹*Stimme*›; b) *(coll.: crazy)* übergeschnappt *(ugs.)*
cracker ['krækə(r)] *n.* a) *(paper toy)* [Christmas] ~ ≈ Knallbonbon, *der od. das;* b) *(firework)* Knallkörper, *der;* c) *(thin dry biscuit)* Cracker, *der; (Amer.: biscuit)* Keks, *der;* d) *see* crackerjack 2
'crackerjack *(Amer. sl.)* 1. *adj.* phantastisch *(ugs.)*. 2. *n. (person)* As, *das (ugs.)*; *(thing)* Knüller, *der (ugs.)*
crackers ['krækəz] *pred. adj. (Brit. coll.)* übergeschnappt *(ugs.)*; go ~: überschnappen *(ugs.)*
crackle [krækl] 1. *v. i.* knistern; ‹*Maschinengewehr:*› knattern; ‹*Feuer:*› prasseln; ‹*Blätter:*› rascheln; the telephone line/the radio ~s in der Telefonleitung/im Radio knackt es. 2. *n.* Knistern, *das; (of leaves)* Rascheln, *das; (of telephone line)* Knacken, *das; (of machine-gun)* Knattern, *das; (of fire)* Prasseln, *das*
crackling ['kræklɪŋ] *n., no pl., no indef. art. (Cookery)* Kruste, *die*
crackly ['kræklɪ] *adj.* knisternd
'crackpot *n. (coll.)* Spinner, *der*/Spinnerin, *die (ugs.)*; *attrib.* ~ ideas/schemes hirnrissige Ideen/Pläne *(abwertend)*
cracksman ['kræksmən] *n., pl.* cracksmen ['kræksmən] Einbrecher, *der*
'crack-up *n. (coll.)* Zusammenbruch, *der*
Cracow ['krækaʊ] *pr. n.* Krakau *(das)*
cradle [kreɪdl] 1. *n.* a) *(cot, lit. or fig.)* Wiege, *die;* from the ~: von der Wiege an; von Kindesbeinen an; from the ~ to the grave von der Wiege bis zur Bahre; b) *(Building)* Hängebühne, *die; (to support ship)* Stapel, *der;* c) *(Teleph.)* Gabel, *die.* 2. *v. t.* wiegen; ~ sb./sth. in one's arms jmdn. in den Armen halten/etw. im Arm halten
cradle: ~-snatch *v. i. (coll.)* Your boyfriend/girl-friend is much younger than you. You're ~-snatching Dein Freund/deine Freundin ist viel jünger als du. Du vergreifst dich ja an kleinen Kindern *(ugs. scherzh.)*; ~-snatcher *n. (coll.) see* baby-snatcher b; ~-snatching *n. (coll.) see* baby-snatching b; ~-song *n.* Wiegenlied, *das*
craft [krɑːft] *n.* a) *(trade)* Handwerk, *das; (art)* Kunsthandwerk, *das; (in school)* ~[s] Werken, *das;* b) *no pl. (skill)* Kunstfertigkeit, *die;* c) *no pl. (cunning)* List, *die;* be full of ~: sehr gewitzt sein; d) *pl. same (boat)* Boot, *das; (aircraft)* Flugzeug, *das; (spacecraft)* Raumfahrzeug, *das*
craftily ['krɑːftɪlɪ] *adv.* listig
craftiness ['krɑːftɪnɪs] *n., no pl.* Schläue, *die*
craftsman ['krɑːftsmən] *n., pl.* craftsmen ['krɑːftsmən] Handwerker, *der; (skilled person)* a real ~: ein wahrer Künstler
craftsmanship ['krɑːftsmənʃɪp] *n., no pl. (skilled workmanship)* handwerkliches Können; *(performance)* shoddy ~: schludrige Arbeit
'craftwork *n., no pl.* Kunsthandwerk, *das*
crafty ['krɑːftɪ] *adj.* listig; as ~ as a fox schlau wie ein Fuchs
crag [kræg] *n.* Felsspitze, *die*
craggy ['krægɪ] *adj. (rugged)* zerklüftet; zerfurcht ‹*Gesicht*›; *(rocky)* felsig; *(steep)* schroff
crake [kreɪk] *n. (Ornith.)* Ralle, *die*
cram [kræm] 1. *v. t.,* -mm- a) *(overfill)* vollstopfen *(ugs.)*; *(force)* stopfen; ~med with information vollgepackt mit Informationen; ~ people into a bus Leute in einen Bus zwängen; the bus was ~med der Bus war gerammelt voll *(ugs.) od.* war überfüllt; *see also* throat a; b) *(for examination)* ~ pupils mit Schülern pauken *(ugs.)*; ~ up maths Mathe pauken *od.* büffeln *(ugs.)*; c) *(feed to excess)* mästen; ~ poultry *etc.* Geflügel *usw.* mästen *od. (bes. südd.)* stopfen. 2. *v. i.,* -mm- *(for examination)* büffeln *(ugs.)*; pauken *(ugs.)*
~ 'in 1. *v. i.* [sich] herein-/hineindrängen. 2. *v. t.* hineinstopfen
'cram-full *see* chock-full
crammer ['kræmə(r)] *n. (place)* Presse, *die (ugs. abwertend)*; *(person)* [Ein]pauker, *der (ugs.)*
cramp [kræmp] 1. *n.* a) *(Med.)* Krampf, *der;* suffer an attack of ~: einen Krampf bekommen; have ~ [in one's leg/arm] einen Krampf [im Bein/Arm] haben; *see also* writer's cramp; b) *(Woodw.)* Schraubzwinge, *die;* c) *(Building)* ~[-iron] [Bau]klammer, *die.* 2. *v. t.* a) *(confine)* einengen; ~ [up] zusammenpferchen; ~ sb.'s style jmdn. einengen; b) *(restrict)* lähmen ‹*Willen, Eifer, Fleiß, Handel*›
cramped [kræmpt] *adj.* eng ‹*Raum*›; gedrängt ‹*Handschrift*›
crampon ['kræmpən] *(Amer.:* crampoon [kræm'puːn]) *n.* a) *(metal hook)* Kanthaken, *der;* b) *(on boot)* Steigeisen, *das*
cranberry ['krænbərɪ] *n.* Preiselbeere, *die; (Vaccinium oxycoccos)* Moosbeere, *die (Bot.)*; *(Vaccinium macrocarpon)* Großfrüchtige Moosbeere *(Bot.)*; ~ sauce Preiselbeersoße, *die*
crane [kreɪn] 1. *n.* a) *(machine)* Kran, *der;* b) *(Ornith.)* Kranich, *der.* 2. *v. t.* ~ one's neck den Hals recken. 3. *v. i.* den Hals recken; ~ forward den Hals [nach vorn] recken
crane: ~-driver *n.* Kranführer, *der;* ~-fly *n. (Zool.)* Schnake, *die;* ~'s-bill *n. (Bot.)* Storch[en]schnabel, *der*
crania *pl. of* cranium
cranial ['kreɪnɪəl] *adj. (Anat.)* Schädel-; kranial *(fachspr.)*
cranium ['kreɪnɪəm] *n., pl.* crania ['kreɪnɪə] *or* ~s *(Anat.)* Schädel, *der;* Kranium, *das (fachspr.)*; *(bones enclosing the brain)* Hirnschädel, *der*
[1]**crank** [kræŋk] 1. *n. (Mech. Engin.)* [Hand]kurbel, *die.* 2. *v.t. (turn with ~)* ankurbeln
~ 'up *v. t. (Motor Veh.)* ankurbeln
[2]**crank** *n.* Irre, *der/die (salopp)*; health ~: Gesundheitsfanatiker, *der*/-fanatikerin, *die (ugs.)*
crank: ~case *n. (Mech. Engin.)* Kurbelwellengehäuse, *das;* ~pin *n. (Mech. Engin.)* Kurbelzapfen, *der;* ~shaft *n. (Mech. Engin.)* Kurbelwelle, *die*
cranky ['kræŋkɪ] *adj.* a) *(eccentric)* schrullig; verschroben; b) *(ill-tempered)* griesgrämig
cranny ['krænɪ] *n.* Ritze, *die*
[1]**crap** [kræp] *(coarse)* 1. *n.* a) *(faeces)* Scheiße, *die (derb)*; have a ~: scheißen *(derb)*; b) *(nonsense)* Scheiß, *der (salopp abwertend)*; a load of ~: ein Haufen Scheiß *(salopp abwertend)*. 2. *v. i.,* -pp- scheißen *(derb)*
[2]**crap** *n. (Amer.: throw in craps)* Fehlwurf, *der;* Crap, *der;* ~ game Craps, *das*
crape [kreɪp] *n.* [schwarzer] Krepp; *(ribbon)* Trauerflor, *der*
crappy ['kræpɪ] *adj. (coarse)* beschissen *(derb)*; ~ film/café Scheißfilm, *der*/Scheißcafé, *das (derb)*
craps [kræps] *n. pl. (Amer.: dice game)* Craps, *das;* shoot ~: Craps spielen
crash [kræʃ] 1. *n.* a) *(noise)* Krachen, *das;* fall with a ~: mit einem lauten Krach fallen; a sudden ~ of thunder ein plötzlicher Donnerschlag; b) *(collision)* Zusammenstoß, *der;* plane/train ~: Flugzeugunglück, *das*/Eisenbahnunglück, *das;* have a ~: einen Unfall haben; in a [car] ~: bei einem [Auto]unfall; be in a [car] ~: in einen [Auto]unfall verwickelt sein; c) *(Finance etc.)* Zusammenbruch, *der;* the great ~ on Wall Street der große Börsenkrach in der Wall Street; d) *attrib. (intensive)* ~ job Noteinsatz, *der;* ~ measures Sofortmaßnahmen *Pl.* 2. *adv.* krachend; ~, bang, wallop *(coll.)* holterdiepolter *(ugs.)*. 3. *v. i.* a) *(make a noise)* krachen; b) *(go noisily)* krachen; ~ down herunterkrachen; ~ about one's ears *(fig.)* zusammenbrechen; c) *(have a collision)* einen Unfall haben; ‹*Flugzeug, Flieger:*› abstürzen; ~ into sth. gegen etw. krachen; d) *(Finance etc., Computing)* zusammenbrechen. 4. *v. t.* a) *(smash)* schmettern; b) *(cause to have collision)* einen Unfall haben mit; ~ a plane mit dem Flugzeug abstürzen; c) *(pass illegally)* überfahren; he ~ed the lights er fuhr bei Rot über die Ampel; d) *see* gatecrash 1
~ a'bout *v. i.* laut herumtollen
~ 'out *v. i. (sl.)* pennen *(salopp)*; *(go to sleep)* einpennen *(salopp)*
crash: ~ barrier *n.* Leitplanke, *die;* ~ course *n.* Intensivkurs, *der;* ~ diet *n.* radikale Diät; ≈ Nulldiät, *die;* ~-dive 1. *v. t.* schnell untertauchen lassen ‹*U-Boot*›; abstürzen lassen ‹*Flugzeug*›; 2. *v. i.* ‹*Unterseeboot:*› schnell untertauchen; ~-dive on sth. im Sturzflug auf etw. *(Akk.)* herabstoßen; 3. *n. (of submarine)* schnelles Untertauchen; *(of aircraft)* Sturzflug, *der;* ~-helmet *n.* Sturzhelm, *der*
crashing ['kræʃɪŋ] *adj. (coll.)* be a ~ bore wahnsinnig langweilig sein *(ugs.)*
crash: ~-land 1. *v. t.* ~-land a plane mit einem Flugzeug bruchlanden; 2. *v. i.* bruchlanden; ~-landing *n.* Bruchlandung, *die;* ~ pad *n. (youth sl.)* Schlafplatz, *der;* Penne, *die (salopp)*; ~ programme *n.* Sofortprogramm, *das*
crass [kræs] *adj.* kraß; grob ‹*Benehmen*›; haarsträubend ‹*Dummheit, Unwissenheit*›; *(grossly stupid)* strohdumm
crassly ['kræslɪ] *adv.* grob, unfein ‹*sich benehmen*›; grob, kraß ‹*fehldeuten*›
crassness ['kræsnɪs] *n., no pl.* Kraßheit, *die; (of person)* Grobheit, *die; (stupidity)* Dummheit, *die*
crate [kreɪt] 1. *n.* a) *(case)* Kiste, *die;* a ~ of beer/lemonade ein Kasten Bier/Limonade; b) *(sl.: vehicle)* Kiste, *die (ugs.)*. 2. *v. t.* ~ [up] in eine Kiste/in Kisten packen

crater ['kreɪtə(r)] *n.* Krater, *der*

crater 'lake *n.* Kratersee, *der*

cravat [krə'væt] *n. (scarf)* Halstuch, *das; (necktie)* Krawatte, *die*

crave [kreɪv] **1.** *v. t.* **a)** *(beg)* erbitten; erflehen ⟨*Gnade*⟩; **b)** *(long for)* sich sehnen nach. **2.** *v. i.* ~ **for** *or* **after** *see* **1**

craven [kreɪvn] **1.** *adj.* feige; **a ~ coward** ein elender *od.* erbärmlicher Feigling. **2.** *n.* Feigling, *der*

cravenly ['kreɪvnlɪ] *adv.* feige

craving ['kreɪvɪŋ] *n.* Verlangen, *das;* **have a ~ for sth.** ein [dringendes] Verlangen nach etw. haben

craw [krɔ:] *n.* Kropf, *der;* **stick in sb.'s ~** *(fig.)* jmdm. gegen den Strich gehen

crawfish ['krɔ:fɪʃ] *n., pl. same* Languste, *die*

crawl [krɔ:l] **1.** *v. i.* **a)** kriechen; **the baby/insect ~s along the ground** das Baby/Insekt krabbelt über den Boden; **b)** *(coll.: behave abjectly)* kriechen *(abwertend);* **~ to sb.** vor jmdm. buckeln *od.* kriechen; **don't you come ~ing back to me** du brauchst nicht wieder angekrochen zu kommen; **c) be ~ing** *(be covered or filled)* wimmeln **(with** von); **d)** *see* **creep 1 b. 2.** *n.* **a)** Kriechen, *das; (of insect, baby also)* Krabbeln, *das; (slow speed)* Schneckentempo, *das;* **move/go at a ~:** sich im Schneckentempo bewegen/im Schneckentempo fahren; **b)** *(swimming-stroke)* Kraulen, *das;* **do** *or* **swim the ~:** kraulen

crawler ['krɔ:lə(r)] *n.* **a)** *usu. in pl. (baby's overall)* Spielanzug, *der;* **b)** *(coll. derog.: abject person)* Kriecher, *der (abwertend)*

'crawler lane *n.* Kriechspur, *die*

crayfish ['kreɪfɪʃ] *n., pl. same* **a)** Flußkrebs, *der;* **b)** *(crawfish)* Languste, *die*

crayon ['kreɪən] *n.* **a)** *(pencil)* **[coloured] ~:** Buntstift, *der; (of wax)* Wachsmalstift, *der; (of chalk)* Kreidestift, *der;* **b)** *(drawing)* [Kreide]zeichnung, *die*

craze [kreɪz] **1.** *n.* **a)** *(temporary enthusiasm)* Begeisterung, *die;* Fimmel, *der (ugs. abwertend);* **there's a ~ for doing sth.** es ist gerade große Mode, etw. zu tun; **b)** *(mania)* Manie, *die.* **2.** *v. t. usu. in p.p. (make insane)* zum Wahnsinn treiben; **be [half] ~d with pain/grief** *etc.* [halb] wahnsinnig vor Schmerz/Kummer *usw.* sein; **a ~d look/expression [on sb.'s face]** ein vom Wahnsinn verzerrtes Gesicht

crazily ['kreɪzɪlɪ] *adv.* verrückt; *(of motion)* wie verrückt

craziness ['kreɪzɪnɪs] *n., no pl.* Verrücktheit, *die;* **sheer ~:** heller Wahnsinn

crazy ['kreɪzɪ] *adj.* **a)** *(mad)* verrückt; wahnsinnig; **go ~:** verrückt *od.* wahnsinnig werden; **drive** *or* **send sb. ~:** jmdn. verrückt *od.* wahnsinnig machen *(ugs.);* **like ~** *(coll.)* wie verrückt *(ugs.);* **b)** *(coll.: enthusiastic)* **be ~ about sb./sth.** nach jmdm./etw. verrückt sein *(ugs.);* **she's ~ about dancing** sie ist ganz wild aufs Tanzen *(ugs.);* **football/pop-music ~:** verrückt nach Fußball/Popmusik *(ugs.);* **c)** *(sl.: exciting)* irre *(salopp);* **d)** *(of irregular pieces)* **~ paving** gestückeltes Pflaster; **~ quilt** Flickendecke, *die;* **e) lean [over] at a ~ angle** gefährlich schief stehen

'crazy bone *n. (Amer.)* Musikantenknochen, *der*

creak [kri:k] **1.** *n. (of gate, door)* Quietschen, *das; (of floor-board, door, chair)* Knarren, *das.* **2.** *v. i.* ⟨*Tor, Tür:*⟩ quietschen; ⟨*Diele, Tür, Stuhl:*⟩ knarren; ⟨*Gelenke:*⟩ knacken; **the old car ~ed to a halt** der alte Wagen kam quietschend zum Stehen

creaky ['kri:kɪ] *adj.* quietschend ⟨*Tor, Tür*⟩; knarrend ⟨*Stuhl, Treppe, Stiefel, Tür*⟩

cream [kri:m] **1.** *n.* **a)** Sahne, *die;* **b)** *(Cookery) (sauce)* Sahnesoße, *die; (dessert)* Creme, *die; (chocolate)* gefülltes Bonbon; *(biscuit)* gefüllter Keks; **~ of mushroom soup** Champignoncremesuppe, *die;* **custard ~s** Kekse mit Vanillecremefüllung; **c)** *(cosmetic preparation)* Creme, *die;* **d)** *(fig.: best)* Beste, *das;* **the ~ of society** die Creme der Gesellschaft; **the ~ of the applicants** die besten Bewerber; **e)** *(colour)* Creme, *das.* **2.** *adj.* **a) ~[-coloured]** creme[farben]; **b)** *(Cookery)* **~ soup/sauce** Cremesuppe, *die*/Sahnesoße, *die.* **3.** *v. t.* cremig rühren *od.* schlagen; schaumig rühren ⟨*Butter*⟩; **~ed potatoes** Kartoffelpüree, *das*

~ 'off *v. t.* **~ off the best players** die besten Spieler wegschnappen *(ugs.)*

cream: ~ 'bun *n.* ≈ Eclair, *das;* **~ cake** *n.* Cremetorte, *die; (small)* Cremetörtchen, *das; (with whipped cream)* Sahnetorte, *die*/Sahnetörtchen, *das;* **~ 'cheese** *n.* ≈ Frischkäse, *der;* **~ 'cracker** *n.* ≈ Cracker, *der*

creamer ['kri:mə(r)] *n. (Amer.: jug)* Sahnekännchen, *das*

creamery ['kri:mərɪ] *n. (butter-factory)* Molkerei, *die; (shop)* Milchgeschäft, *das*

cream: ~jug *n.* Sahnekännchen, *das;* **~ of 'tartar** *n.* Weinstein, *der;* **~ 'puff** *n.* Windbeutel, *der;* **~ 'tea** *n.* Tee mit Marmeladetörtchen und Sahne

creamy ['kri:mɪ] *adj.* **a)** *(with cream)* sahnig; *(like cream)* cremig; **b) ~[-coloured]** creme[farben]

crease [kri:s] **1.** *n.* **a)** *(pressed)* Bügelfalte, *die; (accidental; in skin)* Falte, *die; (in fabric)* Falte, *die;* Knitter, *der; (in paper)* Kniff, *der;* Knick, *der;* **put a ~ in trousers** Bügelfalten in Hosen bügeln; **b)** *(Cricket)* Linie, *die.* **2.** *v. t. (press)* eine Falte/Falten bügeln in (+*Akk.*); *(accidentally)* knittern; *(extensively)* zerknittern. **3.** *v. i.* Falten bekommen; knittern

~ 'up *v. i. (coll.: in amusement)* sich [vor Lachen] kringeln *(ugs.)*

'crease-resistant *adj.* knitterfrei

create [krɪ'eɪt] **1.** *v. t.* **a)** schaffen; erschaffen *(geh.);* verursachen ⟨*Verwirrung*⟩; machen ⟨*Eindruck*⟩; ⟨*Sache:*⟩ mit sich bringen, ⟨*Person:*⟩ machen ⟨*Schwierigkeiten*⟩; **~ a scene** eine Szene machen; **~ a sensation** für eine Sensation sorgen; **b)** *(design)* schaffen; kreieren ⟨*Mode, Stil*⟩; **c)** *(invest with rank)* ernennen; **~ sb. a peer** jmdn. zum Peer erheben *od.* ernennen. **2.** *v. i. (Brit. coll.: make a fuss)* Theater machen *(ugs.)*

creation [krɪ'eɪʃn] *n.* **a)** *no pl. (act of creating)* Schaffung, *die; (of the world)* Erschaffung, *die;* Schöpfung, *die (geh.);* **b)** *no pl. (all created things)* Schöpfung, *die;* **the wonders of C~:** die Wunder der Schöpfung; **all [of] ~, the whole of ~:** alle Kreatur *(geh.);* alle Geschöpfe; **c)** *no pl. (investing with title, rank, etc.)* Ernennung, *die;* **d)** *(Fashion)* Kreation, *die*

creationism [krɪ'eɪʃənɪzm] *n.* Kreatianismus, *der*

creationist [krɪ'eɪʃənɪst] *n.* Anhänger des Kreatianismus

creative [krɪ'eɪtɪv] *adj.*, **creatively** [krɪ'eɪtɪvlɪ] *adv.* schöpferisch; kreativ

creativeness [krɪ'eɪtɪvnɪs], **creativity** [kri:eɪ'tɪvɪtɪ] *ns., no pl.* Kreativität, *die*

creator [krɪ'eɪtə(r)] *n.* Schöpfer, *der*/Schöpferin, *die;* **the C~:** der Schöpfer

creature ['kri:tʃə(r)] *n.* **a)** *(created being)* Geschöpf, *das;* Kreatur, *die (geh.);* **all living ~s** alle Lebewesen; alle Kreatur *(geh.);* **b)** *(human being)* Geschöpf, *das; (derog.)* Kerl, *der (abwertend); (woman)* **the ~ with the red hair** die mit den roten Haaren *(ugs.);* **lovely ~:** reizendes Geschöpf; **wicked/deserving ~:** böser/verdienstvoller Mensch; **~ of habit** Gewohnheitsmensch, *der;* Gewohnheitstier, *das (scherzh.);* **c)** *(minion, lit. or fig.)* Kreatur, *die (abwertend);* **~s of circumstance** Opfer der Umstände. *See also* **comfort 1 e**

crèche [kreʃ] *n.* [Kinder]krippe, *die*

credence ['kri:dəns] *n.* **a)** *(belief)* Glaube, *der;* **give** *or* **attach ~ to sth./sb.** einer Sache *(Dat.)* /jmdm. Glauben schenken; **lend ~ to sth.** etw. glaubwürdig machen *od.* erscheinen lassen; **gain ~:** an Glaubwürdigkeit gewinnen; **worthy of ~:** glaubwürdig; **b)** *(Eccl.)* **~ [table]** Kredenz, *die*

credential [krɪ'denʃl] *n. usu. in pl. (testimonial)* Zeugnis, *das; (of ambassador)* Beglaubigungsschreiben, *das; (letter[s] of introduction)* Referenzen *Pl.;* **present one's ~s** seine Referenzen vorlegen

credibility [kredɪ'bɪlɪtɪ] *n.* Glaubwürdigkeit, *die;* **~ gap** Mangel an Glaubwürdigkeit

credible ['kredɪbl] *adj.* glaubwürdig ⟨*Mensch, Aussage*⟩; glaubhaft ⟨*Aussage*⟩

credibly ['kredɪblɪ] *adv.* glaubwürdig; glaubhaft

credit ['kredɪt] **1.** *n.* **a)** *no pl. (commendation)* Anerkennung, *die; (honour)* Ehre, *die; (good reputation)* Ansehen, *das* **(with** bei); **give sb. [the] ~ for sth.** jmdm. für etw. Anerkennung zollen *(geh.);* **get [the] ~ for sth.** Anerkennung für etw. finden; **take the ~ for sth.** die Anerkennung für etw. einstecken; **all ~ to her/them for not giving in** alle Achtung, daß sie nicht nachgegeben hat/haben; **[we must give] ~ where ~ is due** Ehre, wem Ehre gebührt; **it is [much** *or* **greatly/little] to sb.'s/sth.'s ~ that ...:** es macht jmdm./einer Sache [große/wenig] Ehre, daß ...; **it is to his ~ that ...:** es ehrt ihn, daß ...; **do ~ to sb./sth., do sb./sth. ~, be a ~ to sb./sth.** jmdm./einer Sache Ehre machen; **reflect [great/little] ~ on sb./sth.** jmdm./einer Sache [große/wenig] Ehre machen; **b)** *in pl. (in book)* Liste der Mitarbeiter und sonstigen Beteiligten; *(in film, play, etc.)* Liste der Mitwirkenden und sonstigen Beteiligten; **~s, ~ titles** *(at beginning of film)* Vorspann, *der; (at end)* Nachspann, *der;* **c)** *no pl., no art. (belief)* Glaube, *der;* **give ~ to sth.** einer Sache *(Dat.)* Glauben schenken; **gain ~:** an Glaubwürdigkeit gewinnen; **d)** *no pl. (Commerc.)* Kredit, *der;* **give [sb.] ~:** [jmdm.] Kredit geben; **deal on ~:** Kredit geben; **buy [sth.] on ~:** [etw.] auf Kredit kaufen; **six months' ~:** Kredit mit sechsmonatiger Laufzeit; **their ~ is excellent** sie sind unbedingt kreditwürdig; **e)** *no pl. (Finance, Bookk.)* Guthaben, *das;* **be in ~** ⟨*Konto:*⟩ im Haben sein; ⟨*Person:*⟩ mit seinem Konto im Haben sein; **get a ~ line** Kredit bekommen; **she has sth. to her ~:** ihr ist etw. gutzuschreiben; **letter of ~:** Kreditbrief, *der;* Akkreditiv, *das (Bankw.);* **f)** *(fig.)* **have sth. to one's ~:** etw. vorzuweisen haben; **we must give him ~ for being able to finish it by tomorrow** wir dürfen annehmen, daß er es bis morgen erledigen kann; **he's cleverer than I gave him ~ for** er ist klüger, als ich dachte; **I gave you ~ for being a kind man** ich habe dich für einen netten Menschen gehalten; **I gave her ~ for better taste** ich hatte ihr einen besseren Geschmack zugetraut; **g)** *(Amer. Educ.)* Schein, *der.* **2.** *v. t.* **a)** *(believe)* glauben; **b)** *(accredit)* **~ sb. with sth.** jmdm. etw. zutrauen; **~ sth. with sth.** einer Sache *(Dat.)* etw. zuschreiben; **c)** *(Finance, Bookk.)* gutschreiben; **~ £10 to sb./sb.'s account** jmdm./jmds. Konto 10 Pfund gutschreiben; **be ~ed with £10** 10 Pfund gutgeschrieben bekommen

creditable ['kredɪtəbl] *adj.* anerkennenswert

creditably ['kredɪtəblɪ] *adv.* achtbar

credit: ~ account *n.* Kreditkonto, *das;* **~ balance** *n.* Guthaben, *das;* **~ card** *n.* Kreditkarte, *die;* **~ note** *n.* Gutschein, *der*

creditor ['kredɪtə(r)] *n.* **a)** *(one to whom debt is owing)* Gläubiger, *der*/Gläubigerin, *die;* **b)** *(one who gives credit for money or goods)* Kreditgeber, *der*/-geberin, *die*

credit: ~ rating *n.* [Einschätzung der] Kreditwürdigkeit; **have a good/bad ~ rating** als kreditwürdig/kreditunwürdig eingeschätzt werden; ~ **sale** *n.* Kreditkauf, *der;* ~ **side** *n. (Finance)* Habenseite, *die; (fig.)* **on the ~ side she has experience** für sie spricht ihre Erfahrung; ~ **squeeze** *n.* Kreditrestriktion, *die;* ~ **'transfer** *n. (Finance)* Banküberweisung, *die;* **~-worthiness** *n.* Kreditwürdigkeit, *die;* **~-worthy** *adj.* kreditwürdig

credo ['kri:dəʊ, 'kreɪdəʊ] *n., pl.* ~s Glaubensbekenntnis, *das;* Kredo, *das*

credulity [krɪ'dju:lɪtɪ] *n., no pl.* Leichtgläubigkeit, *die*

credulous ['kredjʊləs] *adj.* leichtgläubig; naiv ⟨*Erstaunen, Verhalten*⟩

credulously ['kredjʊləslɪ] *adv.* leichtgläubig; **believe sth. too ~:** etw. allzu arglos glauben

creed [kri:d] *n. (lit. or fig.)* Glaubensbekenntnis, *das*

creek [kri:k] *n.* **a)** *(Brit.) (inlet on sea-coast)* [kleine] Bucht; *(small harbour)* [kleiner] Hafen; **b)** *(short arm of river)* [kurzer] Flußarm; **c)** *(Amer.: tributary of river)* Nebenfluß, *der; (Austral., NZ: stream)* Bach, *der;* **d) be up the ~:** *(coll.: be in difficulties or trouble)* in der Klemme *od.* Tinte sitzen *(ugs.); (be wrong)* ⟨*Antwort usw.:*⟩ völlig falsch sein; ⟨*Person:*⟩ auf dem Holzweg sein

creel [kri:l] *n.* Fischkorb, *der*

creep [kri:p] **1.** *v.i.,* **crept** [krept] **a)** kriechen; *(move timidly, slowly, stealthily)* schleichen; ~ **and crawl** *(fig.)* kriechen; **~ing Jesus** *(sl.)* Scheinheilige, *der/die; (fig.: develop gradually)* **~ing inflation/sickness** schleichende Inflation/Krankheit; *(insinuate oneself/itself unobserved)* **~ into sth.** sich in etw. *(Akk.)* einschleichen; **b) make sb.'s flesh ~:** jmdm. eine Gänsehaut über den Rücken jagen; **the thought made my flesh ~:** bei dem Gedanken lief mir eine Gänsehaut über den Rücken. **2.** *n.* **a)** *in pl. (coll.)* **give sb. the ~s** jmdm. nicht [ganz] geheuer sein; **b)** *(sl.: person)* Fiesling, *der (salopp abwertend);* **c)** *(Metallurgy)* Kriechen, *das*

~ **'in** *v.i.* [sich] hinein-/hereinschleichen; *(fig.)* ⟨*Irrtum, Enttäuschung usw.:*⟩ sich einschleichen

~ **'on** *v.i.* **time is ~ing on** die Zeit verrinnt [unaufhaltsam]

~ **'up** *v.i. (approach)* sich anschleichen; ~ **up on sb.** sich an jmdn. anschleichen; *(fig.)* für jmdn. langsam näherrücken

creeper ['kri:pə(r)] *n.* **a)** *(Bot.) (growing along ground)* Kriechpflanze, *die; (growing up wall etc.)* Kletterpflanze, *die;* Rankengewächs, *das;* **b)** *(Ornith.)* [Wald]baumläufer, *der;* **c)** *(coll.: soft-soled shoe) Schuh mit dicker, weicher Sohle;* Leisetreter, *der (scherzh.)*

creepy ['kri:pɪ] *adj.* unheimlich; gruselig, schaurig ⟨*Geschichte, Film*⟩

creepy-crawly [kri:pɪ 'krɔ:lɪ] *(coll./child lang.)* **1.** *n.* **she's got a horror of creepy-crawlies** sie hat eine Heidenangst vor allem, was krabbelt; **there's a ~ in the bath-tub** da krabbelt was in der Badewanne *(ugs.).* **2.** *adj.* krabbelnd ⟨*Insekt*⟩

cremate [krɪ'meɪt] *v.t.* einäschern; kremieren *(schweiz.)*

cremation [krɪ'meɪʃn] *n.* Einäscherung, *die;* Kremation, *die*

crematorium [kremə'tɔ:rɪəm] *n., pl.* **crematoria** [kremə'tɔ:rɪə] *or* ~s Krematorium, *das*

crematory ['kremətərɪ] *n. (Amer.)* Krematorium, *das*

crème: ~ **de la crème** [kreɪm dlɑ:'kreɪm] *n.* Crème de la crème, *die (geh.);* ~ **de menthe** [kreɪm də 'mɑ̃t] *n.* Pfefferminzlikör, *der*

crenellated ['krenəleɪtɪd] *adj.* kreneliert *(veralt.);* mit Zinnen versehen

Creole ['kri:əʊl] **1.** *n.* **a)** *(person)* Kreole, *der/*Kreolin, *die; (of mixed European and Negro descent)* Mulatte, *der/*Mulattin, *die;* **b)** *(language)* Kreolisch, *das.* **2.** *adj.* kreolisch

creosote ['kri:əsəʊt] **1.** *n.* ≈ Holzschutzmittel, *das.* **2.** *v.t.* mit einem Holzschutzmittel behandeln

crêpe [kreɪp] *n.* **a)** Krepp, *der;* **b)** *(crêpe rubber)* Kreppgummi, *der;* ~ **soles** Kreppsohlen *Pl.;* **c)** *(pancake)* dünner Eierkuchen

crêpe: ~ **de Chine** [kreɪp də 'ʃi:n] *n.* Crêpe de Chine, *der;* ~ **'paper** *n.* Kreppapier, *das;* ~ **'rubber** *n.* Kreppgummi, *der;* ~ **Suzette** [kreɪp su:'zet] *n. (Cookery)* Crêpe Suzette, *die*

crept *see* **creep 1**

crescendo [krɪ'ʃendəʊ] *n., pl.* ~s *(Mus.)* Crescendo, *das; (fig.)* Zunahme, *die;* **a ~ of cheers** immer lauter werdende Jubelrufe; **reach a ~** *(fig. coll.)* einen Höhepunkt erreichen

crescent ['kresənt] **1.** *n.* **a)** Mondsichel, *die; (as emblem)* Halbmond, *der;* **~-shaped** halbmondförmig; **b)** *(Brit.: street)* [kleinere] halbkreisförmige Straße; **c)** *(~-shaped object)* Bogen, *der.* **2.** *adj.* halbmondförmig; **the ~ moon** die Mondsichel

cress [kres] *n.* Kresse, *die;* **garden ~:** Gartenkresse, *die; see also* **watercress**

crest [krest] *n.* **a)** *(on bird's or animal's head)* Kamm, *der; (neck of horse)* Genick, *das; (plume of feathers)* Federschopf, *der;* **b)** *(top of mountain or wave)* Kamm, *der; (top of roof)* Dachfirst, *der;* **[be/ride] on the ~ of a** *or* **the wave** *(fig.)* ganz oben [sein/schwimmen]; **c)** *(Her.)* Helmzier, *die; (emblem)* Emblem, *das*

crested ['krestɪd] *adj.* **a)** ⟨*Vogel, Tier*⟩ mit einem Kamm; ~ **tit/lark** Haubenmeise/-lerche, *die;* **b)** ⟨*Siegel, Briefpapier usw.*⟩ mit einem Emblem versehen

'crestfallen *adj. (fig.)* niedergeschlagen

Cretaceous [krɪ'teɪʃəs] **1.** *adj. (Geol.)* Kreide-; kretazeisch *(fachspr.);* **the ~ period** die Kreidezeit. **2.** *n. (Geol.)* Kreide, *die*

Cretan ['kri:tn] **1.** *adj.* kretisch. **2.** *n.* Kreter, *der/*Kreterin, *die*

Crete [kri:t] *pr. n.* Kreta *(das)*

cretin ['kretɪn] *n.* **a)** *(Med.)* Kretin, *der;* **b)** *(coll.: fool)* Trottel, *der (ugs. abwertend)*

cretinous ['kretɪnəs] *adj.* **a)** *(Med.)* kretinoid; **b)** *(coll.: stupid)* schwachsinnig *(abwertend)*

cretonne [krɪ'tɒn, 'kretɒn] *n. (Textiles)* Cretonne, *die od. der*

crevasse [krɪ'væs] *n.* Gletscherspalte, *die*

crevice ['krevɪs] *n.* Spalt, *der; (of skin)* Riß, *der*

crew [kru:] **1.** *n.* **a)** *(of ship, aircraft, etc.)* Besatzung, *die;* Crew, *die; (excluding officers)* Mannschaft, *die;* Crew, *die; (of train)* Personal, *das; (Sport)* Mannschaft, *die;* Crew, *die;* **b)** *(associated body)* Gruppe, *die; (gang of workers)* Kolonne, *die; (set; often derog.)* Haufen, *der;* **a motley ~:** ein bunt zusammengewürfelter Haufen. **2.** *v.i.* die Mannschaft/Mitglied der Mannschaft sein; **he ~s on my boat** er gehört zu meiner Mannschaft. **3.** *v.t.* ~ **a boat** Mitglied der Mannschaft eines Bootes sein

crew: ~ **cut** *n.* Bürstenschnitt, *der;* **~-man** ['kru:mən] *n., pl.* **~-men** ['kru:mən] Besatzungsmitglied, *das;* ~ **neck** *n.* enger, runder Halsausschnitt; **a ~-neck pullover** ein Pullover mit engem, rundem Halsausschnitt

crib [krɪb] **1.** *n.* **a)** *(cot)* Gitterbett, *das;* **b)** *(model of manger-scene; manger)* Krippe, *die;* **c)** *(coll.) (translation)* Klatsche, *die (Schülerspr.); (plagiarism)* **that's a ~:** das ist abgekupfert *(salopp).* **2.** *v.t.,* **-bb-** *(coll.) (plagiarize)* abkupfern *(salopp)*

cribbage ['krɪbɪdʒ] *n. (Cards)* Cribbage, *das*

'crib death *(Amer.) see* **cot-death**

crick [krɪk] **1.** *n.* **a ~ [in one's neck/back]** ein steifer Hals/Rücken. **2.** *v.t.* ~ **one's neck/back** einen steifen Hals/Rücken bekommen

¹cricket ['krɪkɪt] *n. (Sport)* Kricket, *das;* **it's/that's not ~** *(Brit. dated coll.)* das ist nicht die feine Art *(ugs.)*

²cricket *n. (Zool.)* Grille, *die;* **as lively as a ~:** putzmunter *(ugs.)*

cricket: **~-bag** *n. Tasche für das Schlagholz usw.;* ~ **ball** *n.* Kricketball, *der;* ~ **bat** Schlagholz, *das*

cricketer ['krɪkɪtə(r)] *n.* Kricketspieler, *der/*-spielerin, *die*

cricket: ~ **match** *n.* Kricketspiel, *das;* ~ **pitch** *n.* Kricketfeld, *das (zwischen den Toren)*

cri de cœur [kri: də 'kɜ:(r)] *n., pl.* **cris de cœur** [kri: də 'kɜ:(r)] *(complaint)* Stoßseufzer, *der; (appeal)* [verzweifelter] Hilferuf

crier ['kraɪə(r)] *n. (in lawcourt)* Gerichtsdiener, *der (veralt.); (in a town)* Ausrufer, *der*

crikey ['kraɪkɪ] *int. (sl.)* Jesses *(ugs.)*

crime [kraɪm] *n.* **a)** Verbrechen, *das;* **b)** *collect., no pl.* **a wave of ~:** eine Welle von Straftaten; **juvenile ~ is on the increase** die Jugendkriminalität nimmt zu; **lead a life of ~:** ein Krimineller sein; ~ **doesn't pay** Verbrechen lohnen sich nicht; **c)** *(fig. coll.: shameful action)* Sünde, *die*

Crimea [kraɪ'mi:ə] *pr. n.* Krim, *die*

Crimean [kraɪ'mi:ən] *adj.* **the ~ War** der Krimkrieg

crime: ~ **prevention** *n.* Verbrechensverhütung, *die;* **C~ Prevention Officer** *Polizeibeamter, dessen/-beamtin, deren Aufgabe aktive, vorbeugende Verbrechensbekämpfung ist;* ~ **rate** *n.* Kriminalitätsrate, *die;* **~-sheet** *n. (Mil.)* Strafregister, *das;* ~ **story** *n.* Kriminalgeschichte, *die;* ~ **wave** *n.* Welle von Straftaten; **~-writer** *n.* Kriminalschriftsteller, *der/*-schriftstellerin, *die*

criminal ['krɪmɪnl] **1.** *adj.* **a)** *(illegal)* kriminell; strafbar; *(concerned with criminals and crime)* Straf-; ~ **act** *or* **deed/offence** Straftat, *die;* **take ~ proceedings against sb.** strafrechtlich gegen jmdn. vorgehen; ~ **judge** Strafrichter, *der;* **b)** *(guilty of crime)* kriminell; straffällig; ~ **gang** Verbrecherbande, *die;* **c)** *(tending to be guilty of crime)* kriminell; **d)** *(fig. coll.)* kriminell *(ugs.);* **it's ~ to do that** es ist eine Schande, das zu tun; **it's a ~ shame** es ist einfach ungeheuerlich; **it's a ~ waste** es ist eine sträfliche Verschwendung. **2.** *n.* Kriminelle, *der/die*

criminal: ~ **'code** *n.* Strafgesetzbuch, *das;* ~ **'court** *n.* Strafgericht, *das;* Kriminalgericht, *das (veralt.);* **C~ Investi'gation Department** *n. (Brit.)* Kriminalpolizei, *die*

criminality [krɪmɪ'nælɪtɪ] *n.* Kriminalität, *die*

criminal: ~ **'law** *n.* Strafrecht, *das;* ~ **'lawyer** *n.* Anwalt/Anwältin für Strafsachen; ~ **'libel** *n.* [schriftliche] Verleumdung

criminally ['krɪmɪnəlɪ] *adv.* kriminell; *(according to criminal law)* strafrechtlich

criminal 'record *n.* Strafregister, *das;* **have a ~** vorbestraft sein

criminologist [krɪmɪ'nɒlədʒɪst] *n.* Kriminologe, *der/*Kriminologin, *die*

criminology [krɪmɪ'nɒlədʒɪ] *n.* Kriminologie, *die*

crimp [krɪmp] *v.t.* kräuseln; **~ed hair** onduliertes Haar

Crimplene, (P) ['krɪmpli:n] *n.* Crimplene, *das* Ⓦⓩ; *knitterfreier Stoff*

crimson ['krɪmzn] **1.** *adj.* purpurrot; **turn ~:** ⟨*Himmel:*⟩ sich blutrot färben; *(with anger)* ⟨*Mensch:*⟩ rot anlaufen; *(blush)* puterrot werden. **2.** *n.* Purpurrot, *das.* **3.** *v.i.* purpurrot werden

cringe [krɪndʒ] *v.i.* **a)** *(cower)* zusammenzucken; ⟨*Hund:*⟩ sich ducken, kuschen; ~ **at sth.** bei etw. zusammenzucken; ~ **away** *or* **back [from sb./sth.]** [vor jmdm./etw.] zurückschrecken; **it makes me ~:** es läßt mich zusammenzucken; *(in disgust)* da wird mir schlecht; **b)** *(behave obsequiously)* kriechen *(abwertend);* kuschen; ~ **before sb.** vor jmdm. kriechen *od.* kuschen; **go cringing to sb.** zu jmdm. gekrochen kommen

cringing ['krɪndʒɪŋ] *adj.* kriecherisch *(abwertend);* **a ~ person** ein Kriecher *(abwertend)*

crinkle [krɪŋkl] **1.** *n.* Knick, *der; (in fabric)* Knitterfalte, *die; (in hair)* Kräusel, *die; (in skin)* Fältchen, *das.* **2.** *v.t.* knicken; zerknittern ‹*Stoff, Papier*›; kräuseln ‹*Haar*›. **3.** *v.i.* ‹*Stoff, Papier:*› knittern; ‹*Haar:*› sich kräuseln; ‹*Haut:*› Fältchen bekommen; ‹*Papierrand:*› sich wellen

crinkly ['krɪŋklɪ] *adj.* zerknittert ‹*Stoff, Papier*›; gekräuselt ‹*Haar*›; faltig ‹*Haut*›

crinoline ['krɪnəlɪn, 'krɪnəli:n] *n. (Hist.)* Krinoline, *die*

cripes [kraɪps] *int. (dated sl.)* Jesses *(ugs.)*

cripple [krɪpl] **1.** *n. (lit. or fig.)* Krüppel, *der.* **2.** *v.t.* zum Krüppel machen; *(fig.)* lähmen

crippled [krɪpld] *adj.* verkrüppelt ‹*Arm, Baum, Bettler*›; **be ~ with rheumatism** durch Rheuma gelähmt sein; **industry was ~ by the strikes** die Streiks haben die ganze Industrie lahmgelegt; **small firms, ~ by inflation** kleine, durch [die] Inflation geschwächte Firmen; **a ~ ship/plane** ein schwer beschädigtes Schiff/Flugzeug

crippling ['krɪplɪŋ] *adj.* zur Verkrüppelung führend ‹*Krankheit, Verletzung*›; *(fig.)* erdrückend ‹*Preise, Inflationsrate, Steuern, Mieten*›; lähmend ‹*Streik, Schmerzen*›; **deal sb. a ~ blow** *(fig.)* jmdm. einen vernichtenden Schlag versetzen

crisis ['kraɪsɪs] *n., pl.* **crises** ['kraɪsi:z] Krise, *die;* **reach ~ point** einen kritischen Punkt erreichen; **a time of ~:** eine kritische Zeit; **at times of ~:** in Krisenzeiten; **suffer a ~:** eine Krise durchmachen

crisis 'management *n.* Krisenmanagement, *das*

crisp [krɪsp] **1.** *adj.* knusprig ‹*Brot, Keks, Kruste, Speck*›; knackig ‹*Apfel, Gemüse*›; steif ‹*Papier*›; trocken ‹*Herbstblätter, Zweige*›; frisch [gebügelt/gestärkt] ‹*Wäsche*›; [druck]frisch ‹*Banknote*›; verharscht ‹*Schnee*›; *(clearly defined)* scharf ‹*Züge, Umrisse, Kanten*›; *(bracing)* frisch ‹*Brise, Seeluft*›; *(brisk)* knapp [und klar] ‹*Stil*›; frisch [und flott *(ugs.)*] ‹*Auftreten, Erscheinung*›; **~ intonation/speech** klare Intonation/Sprache. **2.** *n.* **a)** *usu. in pl. (Brit.: potato ~)* [Kartoffel]chip, *der;* **b)** *(sth. overcooked)* **be burned to a ~:** verbrannt sein. **3.** *v.t. (make ~)* **~ [up]** aufbacken ‹*Brot*›; knusprig backen ‹*Speck*›; knackig machen ‹*Gemüse*›

'crispbread *n.* Knäckebrot, *das*

crisper ['krɪspə(r)] *n.* Gemüsefach, *das*

crisply ['krɪsplɪ] *adv.* knusprig ‹*gebacken*›; klar ‹*sprechen*›; frisch ‹*gebügelt, gestärkt*›

crispness ['krɪspnɪs] *n., no pl. (of bread, biscuit, bacon)* Knusprigkeit, *die; (of apple, vegetable)* Knackigkeit, *die; (of style)* Knappheit [und Klarheit], *die; (of manner)* Frische [und Knappheit], *die*

crispy ['krɪspɪ] *adj.* knusprig ‹*Brot, Keks, Speck*›; knackig ‹*Apfel, Gemüse*›

crispy 'noodles *n. pl.* gebratene Nudeln

criss-cross ['krɪskrɒs] **1.** *n.* Gewirr, *das.* **2.** *adj.* **~ pattern** Muster aus gekreuzten Linien. **3.** *adv.* kreuz und quer. **4.** *v.t. (intersect repeatedly)* wiederholt schneiden. **5.** *v.i. (move crosswise)* kreuz und quer laufen/fahren/fliegen *usw.; (intersect repeatedly)* kreuz und quer verlaufen

criterion [kraɪ'tɪərɪən] *n., pl.* **criteria** [kraɪ'tɪərɪə] Kriterium, *das;* **by what ~ will the issue be judged?** nach welchen Kriterien wird man die Angelegenheit beurteilen?

critic ['krɪtɪk] *n.* Kritiker, *der*/Kritikerin, *die;* **literary ~:** Literaturkritiker, *der*/-kritikerin, *die*

critical ['krɪtɪkl] *adj.* **a)** kritisch; **be ~ of sb./sth.** jmdn./etw. kritisieren; **cast a ~ eye over sth.** etw. mit kritischen Augen betrachten; **the play received ~ acclaim** das Stück fand die Anerkennung der Kritik; **~ skills/ability** Kritikfähigkeit, *die;* **~ edition** kritische Ausgabe; **b)** *(involving risk, crucial)* kritisch ‹*Zustand, Punkt, Phase*›; entscheidend ‹*Faktor, Test*›; gefährlich ‹*Operation*›

critically ['krɪtɪkəlɪ] *adv.* kritisch; **be ~ important** von entscheidender Bedeutung sein; **be ~ ill** ernstlich krank sein

critical: ~ 'mass *n. (Phys.)* kritische Masse; **~ 'path** *n. (Managem.)* kritischer Pfad *od.* Weg

criticise *see* **criticize**

criticism ['krɪtɪsɪzm] *n.* Kritik, *die* (**of** an + *Dat.*); **come in for a lot of ~:** heftig kritisiert werden; **be open to ~:** für Kritik offen sein; **literary ~:** Literaturkritik, *die*

criticize ['krɪtɪsaɪz] *v.t.* kritisieren (**for** wegen); *(review)* besprechen; rezensieren; **~ sb. for sth.** jmdn. wegen etw. kritisieren

critique [krɪ'ti:k] *n.* Kritik, *die*

critter ['krɪtə(r)] *n. (coll. joc.)* Viech, *das (ugs.); (derog.: person)* Kerl, *der (ugs. abwertend); (female)* Person, *die (abwertend)*

croak [krəʊk] **1.** *n. (of frog)* Quaken, *das; (of raven, person)* Krächzen, *das.* **2.** *v.i.* **a)** ‹*Frosch:*› quaken; ‹*Rabe, Person:*› krächzen; **b)** *(sl.: die)* abkratzen *(salopp).* **3.** *v.t.* krächzen

croaky ['krəʊkɪ] *adj.* krächzend

Croat ['krəʊæt] *n.* **a)** *(person)* Kroate, *der*/Kroatin, *die;* **b)** *(language)* Kroatisch, *das*

Croatia [krəʊ'eɪʃə] *pr. n.* Kroatien *(das)*

Croatian [krəʊ'eɪʃən] **1.** *adj.* kroatisch; **sb. is ~:** jmd. ist Kroate/Kroatin. **2.** *n. see* **Croat**

croc [krɒk] *n. (coll.: crocodile)* Krokodil, *das*

crochet ['krəʊʃeɪ, 'krəʊʃɪ] **1.** *n.* Häkelarbeit, *die;* **~ hook** Häkelhaken, *der.* **2.** *v.t., p.t. and p.p.* **~ed** ['krəʊʃeɪd, 'krəʊʃɪd] häkeln

crocheting ['krəʊʃeɪɪŋ, 'krəʊʃɪɪŋ] *n.* Häkeln, *das; (product)* Häkelarbeit, *die*

[1]crock [krɒk] *n.* **a)** *(pot)* Topf, *der (aus Ton); (jar)* Krug, *der (aus Ton); see also* **gold 1 b; b)** *(broken piece of earthenware)* [Ton]scherbe, *die*

[2]crock *(coll.)* **1.** *n. (person)* Wrack, *das (fig.); (vehicle)* [Klapper]kiste, *die (ugs.).* **2.** *v.i.* **~ up** zusammenklappen. **3.** *v.t.* **~ [up]** den Rest geben (+ *Dat.*) *(ugs.)*

crockery ['krɒkərɪ] *n.* Geschirr, *das*

crocodile ['krɒkədaɪl] *n.* **a)** Krokodil, *das; (skin)* Krokodilleder, *das;* Kroko, *das;* **b)** *(Brit. coll.: line of schoolchildren)* Schulkinder in Zweierreihen; **walk in a ~:** zwei und zwei [hintereinander] gehen

crocodile: ~ clip *n. (Electr.)* Krokodilklemme, *die;* **~ tears** *n. pl.* Krokodilstränen *Pl. (ugs.)*

crocus ['krəʊkəs] *n.* Krokus, *der*

Croesus ['kri:səs] *n.* Krösus, *der;* **be as rich as ~:** ein [wahrer] Krösus sein

croft [krɒft] *n. (Brit.)* **a)** [kleines] Stück Acker-/Weideland; **b)** *(smallholding)* [kleines] Pachtgut

crofter ['krɒftə(r)] *n. (Brit.)* Pächter, *der*/Pächterin, *die*

crofting ['krɒftɪŋ] *n., no pl., no art. (Brit.)* *Bewirtschaftung kleiner Pachtgüter*

croissant ['krwɑːsɑ̃] *n.* Hörnchen, *das*

cromlech ['krɒmlek] *n.* **a)** *see* **dolmen; b)** *(stone circle)* Kromlech, *der*

crone [krəʊn] *n.* **a[n old] ~:** ein altes Weib

crony ['krəʊnɪ] *n.* Kumpel, *der; (drinking companion)* Kumpan, *der;* **they were old cronies** sie waren gute, alte Freunde

crook [krʊk] **1.** *n.* **a)** *(coll.: rogue)* Gauner, *der;* **b)** *(staff)* Hirtenstab, *der; (of bishop)* [Krumm]stab, *der;* **c)** *(hook)* Haken, *der;* **d)** *(of arm)* [Arm]beuge, *die;* **e)** *(curve in river, road, etc.)* Biegung, *die.* **2.** *adj. (Austral. and NZ coll.)* mies *(ugs.); (ill)* krank; *(bad-tempered)* sauer *(ugs.);* **go ~:** sauer werden (**at, on** + *Akk.*). **3.** *v.t.* biegen; **~ one's finger** seinen Finger krümmen; **she has only to ~ her little finger** *(fig. coll.)* sie braucht nur mit dem kleinen Finger zu winken

crooked 1. [krʊkt] *p.t. and p.p. of* **crook 3. 2.** *adj.* **a)** ['krʊkɪd] krumm; schief ‹*Lächeln*›; *(fig.: dishonest)* betrügerisch; **this coin is ~:** diese Münze ist verbogen; **the picture on the wall is ~:** das Bild an der Wand hängt schief; **you've got your hat on ~:** dein Hut sitzt schief; **a ~ person** *(fig.)* ein Gauner; **~ dealings** krumme Geschäfte; **b)** [krʊkt] *(having a transverse handle)* **a ~ stick** ein Krückstock

crookedly ['krʊkɪdlɪ] *adv.* schief; **a tree that has grown ~:** ein krumm gewachsener Baum; *(fig.: dishonestly)* **deal ~:** krumme Geschäfte machen; **~ acquired** unrechtmäßig erworben

crookedness ['krʊkɪdnɪs] *n., no pl.* Verkrümmung, *die; (fig.: dishonesty)* Unehrlichkeit, *die*

croon [kru:n] **1.** *v.t. & i.* [leise] singen; ‹*Popsänger:*› schmachtend singen; schnulzen *(ugs. abwertend).* **2.** *n.* [leises] Singen

crooner ['kru:nə(r)] *n.* *Sänger mit schmachtender Stimme;* Schnulzensänger, *der (ugs. abwertend)*

crop [krɒp] **1.** *n.* **a)** *(Agric.)* [Feld]frucht, *die; (season's total yield)* Ernte, *die; (fig.)* [An]zahl, *die;* **cereal ~:** Getreide, *das;* **get the ~s in** die Ernte einbringen; **arable ~s** Feldfrüchte *Pl.;* **~ of apples** Apfelernte, *die;* **b)** *(of bird)* Kropf, *der;* **c)** *(of whip)* [Peitschen]stiel, *der;* **[hunting-]~:** Jagdpeitsche, *die;* **d)** *(of hair)* kurzer Haarschnitt; *(style)* Kurzhaarfrisur, *die.* **2.** *v.t.,* **-pp-: a)** *(cut off)* abschneiden; *(cut short)* stutzen ‹*Bart, Haare, Hecken, Flügel*›; kupieren ‹*Ohren, Schwanz (bei Hunden od. Pferden)*›; abschneiden ‹*Kante*›; ‹*Tier:*› abweiden ‹*Gras*›; **have one's hair ~ped** sich *(Dat.)* das Haar kurz schneiden lassen; **b)** *(reap)* ernten. **3.** *v.i.,* **-pp-** tragen

~ 'out *see* **~ up b**

~ 'up *v.i.* **a)** *(occur)* auftauchen; *(be mentioned)* erwähnt werden; **b)** *(Geol.)* ausbeißen

crop: ~-dusting *n. (Agric.)* Schädlingsbekämpfung aus der Luft; **~-eared** *adj.* ‹*Tier*› mit gestutzten *od.* kupierten Ohren

cropper ['krɒpə(r)] *n. (coll.: heavy fall)* [schwerer] Sturz; **come a ~:** einen Sturz bauen *(ugs.); (fig.)* auf die Nase fallen *(ugs.)*

crop: ~ rotation *n. (Agric.)* Fruchtfolge, *die;* **~-spraying** *n. (Agric.)* Schädlingsbekämpfung *(mit Sprühmitteln)*

croquet ['krəʊkeɪ, 'krəʊkɪ] *n.* Krocket[spiel], *das*

croquette [krə'ket] *n. (Cookery)* Krokette, *die*

crosier ['krəʊzɪə(r)] *n.* Krummstab, *der*

cross [krɒs] **1.** *n.* **a)** Kreuz, *das; (monument)* [Gedenk]kreuz, *das; (sign)* Kreuzzeichen, *das;* **the C~:** das Kreuz [Christi]; **make the sign of the C~:** das Kreuzzeichen machen; ein Kreuz schlagen; **b)** *(~-shaped thing or mark)* Kreuz[zeichen], *das;* **mark with a ~:** ankreuzen; **c)** *(mixture, compromise)* Mittelding, *das* (**between** zwischen + *Dat.*); Mischung, *die* (**between** aus); **d)** *(trial, affliction, cause of trouble)* Kreuz, *das;* Leid, *das;* **take [up] one's ~:** sein Kreuz auf sich nehmen; **we all have our [little] ~es to bear** wir haben alle unser Kreuz zu tragen; **e)** *(intermixture of breeds)* Kreuzung, *die;* **f)** *(Astron.)* **[Southern] C~:** Kreuz des Südens; Südliches Kreuz; **g)** *(decoration)* Kreuz, *das;* **Grand C~:** Großkreuz, *das;* **h)** *(Footb.)* Querpaß, *der; (Boxing)* Cross, *der;* **i) on the ~:** quer; **j)** *(Dressmaking)* **cut on the ~:** schräg [zum Fadenlauf] zugeschnitten. **2.** *v.t.* **a)** *(place crosswise)* [über]kreuzen; ~ **one's arms/legs** die Arme verschränken/die Beine übereinanderschlagen; ~ **one's fingers** *or* **keep one's fingers ~ed [for sb.]** *(fig.)* [jmdm.] die *od.* den Daumen drücken/halten; ~ **swords [with sb.]** *(fig.)* [mit jmdm.] die Schwerter kreuzen *od.* sich streiten (**on** über + *Akk.*); **I got a ~ed line** *(Teleph.)* es war jemand in der Leitung; **you've got your** *or* **the lines** *or* **wires ~ed** *(fig. coll.)* du hast da etwas falsch verstanden; ~ **a fortune-teller's hand** *or* **palm with silver** einer Wahrsagerin Geld in die Hand drükken; **b)** *(go across)* kreuzen; überqueren ‹*Straße, Gewässer, Gebirge*›; durchqueren ‹*Land, Wüste, Zimmer*›; ~ **the picket line** die Streikpostenkette durchbrechen; ~ **the road** über die Straße gehen; **we can ~** *abs.* die Straße ist frei; wir können gehen/fahren; '~ **now'** „Gehen"; **the bridge ~es the river** die Brücke führt über den Fluß; **the lines ~ each other** die Linien schneiden sich; **a train ~ed the river** ein Zug fuhr über den Fluß; **a plane ~es the desert** ein Flugzeug fliegt über *od.* überfliegt die Wüste; ~ **sb.'s mind** *(fig.)* jmdm. einfallen; **it seems never to have ~ed his mind to do it** es scheint ihm nie in den Sinn gekommen zu sein *od.* es scheint ihm nie der Gedanke gekommen zu sein, es zu tun; ~ **sb.'s path** *(fig.)* jmdm. über den Weg laufen *(ugs.)*; jmdm. begegnen; **c)** *(Brit.)* ~ **a cheque** einen Scheck zur Verrechnung ausstellen; **a ~ed cheque** ein Verrechnungsscheck; **d)** *(make sign of ~ on)* ~ **oneself** sich bekreuzigen; ~ **my heart** Ehrenwort!; **e)** *(thwart)* durchkreuzen ‹*Plan*›; zerstören ‹*Hoffnung*›; vereiteln ‹*Wunsch, Hoffnung*›; **be ~ed in love** Unglück in der Liebe haben; **he ~es me in everything I do** er kommt mir bei allem in die Quere; **f)** *(cause to interbreed)* kreuzen; *(cross-fertilize)* kreuzbefruchten. *See also* **¹bridge 1 a; T a. 3.** *v. i. (meet and pass)* aneinander vorbeigehen; ~ **[in the post]** ‹*Briefe:*› sich kreuzen; **our paths have ~ed several times** *(fig.)* unsere Wege haben sich öfters gekreuzt. **4.** *adj.* **a)** *(transverse)* Quer-; ~ **traffic** kreuzender Verkehr; **b)** *(coll.: peevish)* verärgert; ärgerlich ‹*Worte*›; **sb. will be ~:** jmd. wird ärgerlich *od.* böse werden; **be ~ with sb.** böse auf jmdn. *od.* mit jmdm. sein; **as ~ as two sticks** *(coll.)* unleidlich; **c)** *(Cricket)* ~ **bat** *schräg gehaltenes Schlagholz*

~ **'off** *v. t.* streichen; ~ **a name off a list** einen Namen von einer Liste streichen

~ **'out** *v. t.* ausstreichen

~ **'over** *v. t.* überqueren; *abs.* hinübergehen

cross- *in comb.* **a)** *see* **cross 1 a** Kreuz-; **b)** *see* **cross 4** Quer-; **c)** = **across** quer durch

cross: ~bar *n.* **a)** [Fahrrad]stange, *die;* **b)** *(Footb.)* Querlatte, *die;* **~-beam** *n.* Querbalken, *der;* **~-bench** *n. (Brit. Parl.) quergestellte Bank, auf der die „cross-benchers" sitzen;* **~-bencher** *n.* Abgeordnete, *der/ die weder der Regierungspartei noch der Opposition angehört;* **~bill** *n. (Ornith.)* Kreuzschnabel, *der;* **~-bones** *n. pl.* gekreuzte Knochen *Pl. (unter Totenkopf);* **~bow** *n.* Armbrust, *die;* **~-bred** *adj.* gekreuzt; **~-breed 1.** *n.* Hybride, *die; (animal)* Bastard, *der;* **2.** *v. t.* kreuzen; **~-buttock** *n. (Wrestling)* Hüftwurf, *der;* **~-Channel** *adj.* **~-Channel traffic/ferry** Verkehr/Fähre über den Kanal; **~-check 1.** *n.* Gegenprobe, *die;* **2.** *v. t.* [nochmals] nachprüfen; nachkontrollieren; **~-country 1.** *adj.* Querfeldein-; **~-country running** Crosslauf, *der;* Querfeldeinlauf, *der;* **~-country skiing** Skilanglauf, *der.* **2.** *adv.* querfeldein; **~-cultural** *adj.* interkulturell; **~-current** *n. (lit. or fig.)* Gegenströmung, *die;* **~-examination** *n.* Kreuzverhör, *das;* **undergo** *or* **be under ~-examination** ins Kreuzverhör genommen werden; **~-examine** *v. t.* ins Kreuzverhör nehmen; einem Kreuzverhör unterziehen; **~-eyed** *adj.* [nach innen] schielend; **be ~-eyed** schielen; **~-fertili'zation** *n.* Fremdbestäubung, *die;* Kreuzbefruchtung, *die; (fig.)* gegenseitige Befruchtung; **~-'fertilize** *v. t.* fremdbestäuben; kreuzbefruchten; *(fig.)* sich gegenseitig befruchten; **~-fire** *n. (lit. or fig.)* Kreuzfeuer, *das;* **~-grained** *adj. (fig.)* verquer, vertrackt ‹*Situation, Problem*›; querköpfig ‹*Person*›; **~-head[ing]** *n.* Überschrift, *die*

crossing ['krɒsɪŋ] *n.* **a)** *(act of going across)* Überquerung, *die;* **a Channel ~:** eine Überfahrt über den Kanal; **b)** *(road or rail intersection)* Kreuzung, *die;* **c)** *(pedestrian ~)* Überweg, *der;* **[railway] ~:** Bahnübergang, *der;* **d)** *(in church)* Vierung, *die*

cross-legged ['krɒslegd] *adv.* mit gekreuzten Beinen; *(with feet across thighs)* im Schneidersitz

crossly ['krɒslɪ] *adv. (coll.)* verärgert

crossness ['krɒsnɪs, 'krɔːsnɪs] *n., no pl. (coll.)* Verärgerung, *die*

cross: ~-over *n.* Übergang, *der; (Railw.)* Gleiskreuzung, *die;* **~-patch** *n.* Griesgram, *der;* Miesepeter, *der;* **~-piece** *n.* Querbalken, *der;* **~-ply tyre** *n.* Diagonalreifen, *der;* ~ **'purposes** *n. pl.* **talk at ~ purposes** aneinander vorbeireden; **be at ~ purposes [with sb.]** *(have different aims)* gegensätzliche Vorstellungen haben; *(misunderstand)* [jmdn.] mißverstehen; **~-'question** *v. t.* ins Kreuzverhör nehmen; **~-refer** *v. i.* einen Querverweis machen; **~-'reference 1.** *n.* Querverweis, *der;* **2.** *v. t.* verweisen ‹*Person, Stichwort*› (**to** auf + *Akk.*); mit Querverweisen versehen ‹*Eintrag, Werk*›; **~roads** *n. sing.* Kreuzung, *die; (fig.)* Wendepunkt, *der;* **be at a/the ~roads** *(fig.)* am Scheideweg stehen; **~-section** *n.* Querschnitt, *der; (fig.)* repräsentative Auswahl; **in ~-section** im Querschnitt; **a ~-section of the population** ein Querschnitt durch die Bevölkerung; **~-stitch** *n.* Kreuzstichstickerei, *die; (stitch)* Kreuzstich, *der;* **~-talk** *n. (Communications)* Übersprechen, *das;* **~-town 1.** *adj.* **a ~-town route/road** eine Strecke/ Straße, die quer durch die Stadt führt; **a ~-town bus** ein Bus, der quer durch die Stadt fährt; **2.** *adv. (Amer.)* quer durch die Stadt ‹*gehen, fahren*›; **~-voting** *n. Stimmabgabe für eine andere als die eigene Partei;* **~-walk** *n. (Amer.)* Fußgängerüberweg, *der*

crossways ['krɒsweɪz] *see* **crosswise 2**

'cross-wind *n.* Seitenwind, *der*

crosswise ['krɒswaɪz] **1.** *adj.* Quer-. **2.** *adv.* kreuzweise; *(of one in relation to another)* quer

crossword ['krɒswɜːd] *n.* ~ **[puzzle]** Kreuzworträtsel, *das*

crotch [krɒtʃ] *n.* **a)** *(of tree)* Gabelung, *die;* **b)** *(of trousers, body)* Schritt, *der;* **kick sb. in the ~:** jmdn. zwischen die Beine treten

crotchet ['krɒtʃɪt] *n. (Brit. Mus.)* Viertelnote, *die*

crotchety ['krɒtʃɪtɪ] *adj.* launisch; quengelig ‹*Kind*›

crouch [kraʊtʃ] *v. i.* [sich zusammen]kauern; ~ **down** sich niederkauern; ‹*Person:*› sich hinhocken

¹croup [kruːp] *n. (of horse)* Kruppe, *die*

²croup *n. (Med.)* Krupp, *der*

croupier ['kruːpɪə(r), 'kruːpɪeɪ] *n.* Croupier, *der*

crouton ['kruːtɔ̃] *n. (Gastr.)* Croûton, *der*

crow [krəʊ] **1.** *n.* **a)** *(bird)* Krähe, *die;* **as the ~ flies** Luftlinie; **eat ~** *(Amer. fig.)* zu Kreuze kriechen; **b)** *(cry of cock or infant)* Krähen, *das;* **c)** *see* **crowbar. 2.** *v. i.* **a)** ‹*Hahn, Baby:*› krähen; **b)** *(exult)* ~ **over** [hämisch] frohlocken über (+ *Akk.*)

crow: ~bar *n.* Brechstange, *die;* **~berry** *n. (Bot.)* Krähenbeere, *die*

crowd [kraʊd] **1.** *n.* **a)** *(large number of persons)* Menschenmenge, *die;* **~[s] of people** Menschenmassen *Pl.;* **he would pass in a ~:** er ist passabel; **stand out from the ~:** aus der Menge herausragen; **b)** *(mass of spectators, audience)* Zuschauermenge, *die;* **c)** *(multitude)* breite Masse; **follow the ~** *(fig.)* mit der Herde laufen; **be just one of the ~** *(fig.)* in der Masse untergehen; **d)** *(coll.: company, set)* Clique, *die;* **a strange ~:** ein komischer Haufen; **e)** *(large number of things)* Menge, *die;* **a ~ of thoughts/new ideas** eine Menge Gedanken/ein Haufen neuer Ideen. **2.** *v. t.* **a)** *(collect in a ~)* **be ~ed at a place** sich an einem Ort drängen; **b)** *(fill, occupy, cram)* füllen; ~ **people into a bus/room** Leute in einen Bus/ein Zimmer pferchen; ~ **sth. with sth.** etw. mit etw. vollstopfen; **the port was ~ed with ships** im Hafen lagen die Schiffe dicht an dicht; **the streets were ~ed with people** die Straßen waren voll mit Leuten; **c)** *(fig.: fill)* ausfüllen; **the year was ~ed with incidents** es war ein sehr ereignisreiches Jahr; **d)** *(come close to)* [absichtlich] fast berühren; **e)** *(force)* drängen; ~ **sb. into doing sth.** jmdn. drängen, etw. zu tun; **f)** *(Amer. coll.: approach)* **he's ~ing thirty** er geht auf die Dreißig zu. **3.** *v. i.* **a)** *(collect)* sich sammeln; ~ **around sb./sth.** sich um jmdn./etw. drängen *od.* scharen; **b)** *(force itself)* strömen; **memories were ~ing in [on him]** Erinnerungen stürmten auf ihn ein; ~ **into/through sth.** in (+ *Akk.*)/durch etw. strömen *od.* drängen

~ **'out** *v. t.* herausdrängen; **be ~ed out by sth.** von etw. verdrängt werden

'crowd control *n. Ordnungsdienst bei Großveranstaltungen*

crowded ['kraʊdɪd] *adj.* überfüllt; voll ‹*Programm*›; ereignisreich ‹*Tag, Leben, Karriere*›; ~ **'out** *(coll.)* proppenvoll *(ugs.)*; gerammelt voll *(ugs.)*

'crowd-puller *n. (coll.)* Attraktion, *die*

'crowfoot *n. (Bot.)* Hahnenfuß, *der*

crown [kraʊn] **1.** *n.* **a)** *(of monarch; device, ornament)* Krone, *die;* **the C~:** die Krone; **succeed to the C~:** die Thronfolge antreten; **be heir to the C~:** Thronfolger/-folgerin sein; **the world heavyweight ~:** der Weltmeisterschaftstitel im Schwergewicht; **b)** *(wreath of flowers etc.)* Sieger-, Ehrenkranz, *der;* **c)** *(bird's crest)* Kamm, *der;* **d)** *(of head)* Scheitel, *der; (of arched structure)* Scheitelpunkt, *der; (of arch)* Kappe, *die; (of tree, tooth)* Krone, *die; (of hat)* Kopfteil, *das; (thing that forms the summit)* Gipfel, *der; (fig.)* Krönung, *die;* **e)** *(coin)* Krone, *die.* **2.** *v. t.* **a)** krönen; ~ **sb. king/queen** jmdn. zum König/zur Königin krönen; **b)** *(surmount)* krönen; **the hill was ~ed with trees** die Kuppe des Hügels war mit Bäumen bewachsen; **c)** *(put finishing touch to)* krönen; **to ~ [it] all** zur Krönung des Ganzen; *(to make things even worse)* um das Maß vollzumachen; **d)** *(bring to happy ending)* krönen; **success ~ed his efforts** seine Anstrengungen waren von Erfolg gekrönt; **e)** *(sl.: hit on the head)* einen überbraten *(salopp)* (+ *Dat.*); **f)** *(Draughts)* zur Dame machen; eine Dame bekommen mit; **g)** *(Dent.)* überkronen; eine Krone machen für

crown: ~ 'cap *n.* Kron[en]korken, *der;* **C~ 'Colony** *n.* Kronkolonie, *die;* **C~ 'Court** *n. (Brit. Law)* Krongericht, *das*

crowned [kraʊnd] *adj.* **a)** *(invested with royal crown)* gekrönt; **b)** *(provided with a crown)* mit einer Krone; *see also* **¹head 1 a**

'crown green *n. Bowlingrasen, der in der Mitte höher ist als an den Seiten*

crowning ['kraʊnɪŋ] **1.** *n.* Krönung, *die.* **2.** *adj.* krönend; **her ~ glory is her hair** ihr Haar ist ihre größte Zier

crown: ~ 'jewels *n. pl.* Kronjuwelen; **~ land** *n.* Ländereien *Pl.* der Krone; **~ of 'thorns** *n. (Zool., Relig.)* Dornenkrone, die; **C~ 'prince** *n. (lit. or fig.)* Kronprinz, *der;* **C~ 'princess** *n.* Kronprinzessin, *die*

crow: ~'s-foot *n., usu. in pl.* Krähenfuß, *der;* **~'s-nest** *n. (Naut.)* Krähennest, *das;* Mastkorb, *der*

crozier *see* **crosier**

crucial ['kru:ʃl] *adj.* entscheidend (**to** für)

crucially ['kru:ʃəlı] *adv.* entscheidend; **be ~ important** von entscheidender Wichtigkeit sein

crucible ['kru:sıbl] *n.* [Schmelz]tiegel, *der*

crucifix ['kru:sıfıks] *n.* Kruzifix, *das*

crucifixion [kru:sı'fıkʃn] *n.* Kreuzigung, *die*

cruciform ['kru:sıfɔ:m] *adj.* kreuzförmig

crucify ['kru:sıfaı] *v. t.* **a)** kreuzigen; **b)** *(torment, persecute)* peinigen; verfolgen; *(severely criticize)* verreißen

crud [krʌd] *n. (sl.)* **a)** *(impurity etc.)* Verunreinigung, *die;* Fremdstoff, *der;* **b)** *(nonsense)* Schrott, *der (salopp);* Mist, *der (ugs.)*

crude [kru:d] **1.** *adj.* **a)** *(in natural or raw state)* roh; Roh-; **~ oil/ore** Rohöl, *das*/Roherz, *das;* **b)** *(fig.: rough, unpolished)* primitiv; simpel; grob ‹*Entwurf, Skizze*›; **c)** *(rude, blunt)* ungehobelt, ungeschliffen ‹*Person, Benehmen*›; grob, derb ‹*Worte*›; ordinär ‹*Witz*›; **d)** *(not adjusted or corrected)* unbereinigt ‹*Statistik*›; roh ‹*Ziffer*›. **2.** *n.* Rohöl, *das;* Erdöl, *das*

crudely ['kru:dlı] *adv.* *(roughly)* grob ‹*skizzieren, schätzen, entwerfen*›; *(rudely, bluntly)* ungehobelt, ungeschliffen ‹*sich benehmen*›; derb, plump ‹*sagen*›; ordinär ‹*reden*›

crudeness ['kru:dnıs] *n. no pl.* **a)** *(roughness)* Primitivität, *die; (of theory, design, plan)* Skizzenhaftigkeit, *die;* **b)** *(rudeness, bluntness) (of person, behaviour, manners)* Ungeschliffenheit, *die; (of words)* Derbheit, *die; (of joke)* Geschmacklosigkeit, *die*

crudity ['kru:dıtı] *n.* **a)** *no pl. see* **crudeness; b)** *(crude remark)* Grobheit, *die*

cruel ['kru:əl] *adj.*, *(Brit.)* **-ll-: a)** grausam; **be ~ to sb.** grausam zu jmdm. sein; **be ~ to animals** ein Tierquäler sein; **be ~ to one's dog** seinen Hund quälen; **b)** *(causing pain or suffering)* grausam; unbarmherzig; **be ~ to be kind** in jmds. Interesse unbarmherzig sein müssen

cruelly ['kru:əlı] *adv.* grausam; unbarmherzig ‹*kritisieren*›; **life treated him ~:** das Leben spielte ihm grausam mit

cruelty ['kru:əltı] *n. see* **cruel:** Grausamkeit, *die;* Unbarmherzigkeit, *die;* **~ to animals** Tierquälerei, *die;* **~ to children** Kindesmißhandlung, *die*

cruet ['kru:ıt] *n.* **a)** Essig-/Ölfläschchen, *das;* **b)** *see* **cruet-stand**

'cruet-stand *n.* Menage, *die*

cruise [kru:z] **1.** *v. i.* **a)** *(sail for pleasure)* eine Kreuzfahrt machen; **b)** *(at random)* ‹*Fahrzeug, Fahrer:*› herumfahren; **c)** *(at economical speed)* ‹*Fahrzeug:*› mit Dauergeschwindigkeit fahren; ‹*Flugzeug:*› mit Reisegeschwindigkeit fliegen; **cruising speed** Reisegeschwindigkeit, *die;* **we are now cruising at a height/speed of ...:** wir fliegen nun in einer Flughöhe/mit einer Reisegeschwindigkeit von ...; **d)** *(for protection of shipping)* kreuzen. **2.** *n.* Kreuzfahrt, *die;* **go on** *or* **for a ~:** eine Kreuzfahrt machen

'cruise missile *n.* Marschflugkörper, *der*

cruiser ['kru:zə(r)] *n.* Kreuzer, *der*

'cruiserweight *n. (Boxing etc.)* Halbschwergewicht, *das; (person also)* Halbschwergewichtler, *der*

crumb [krʌm] **1.** *n.* **a)** Krümel, *der;* Brösel, *der; (fig.)* Brocken, *der;* **~s of wisdom** ein bißchen Weisheit; **~s from the rich man's table** *(fig.)* Brosamen, die von des Reichen Tische fallen; **~[s] of comfort** kleiner Trost; **b)** *(soft part of bread)* Krume, *die.* **2.** *v. t.* *(cover with ~s)* panieren

crumble ['krʌmbl] **1.** *v. t.* zerbröckeln ‹*Brot*›; zerkrümeln ‹*Keks, Kuchen*›; **~ sth. into/onto sth.** etw. in/auf etw. *(Akk.)* bröckeln *od.* krümeln. **2.** *v. i.* ‹*Brot, Kuchen:*› krümeln; ‹*Gestein:*› [zer]bröckeln; ‹*Mauer:*› zusammenfallen; *(fig.)* ‹*Hoffnung:*› sich zerschlagen; ‹*Reich, Gesellschaft:*› zerfallen, zugrunde gehen. **3.** *n.* *(Cookery)* **a)** *(dish) mit Streuseln bestreutes und überbackenes [Apfel-, Rhabarber- usw.]dessert;* **b)** *(substance)* Streusel *Pl.*

crumbly ['krʌmblı] *adj.* krümelig ‹*Keks, Kuchen, Brot*›; bröckelig ‹*Gestein, Erde*›

crumbs [krʌmz] *int. (Brit. coll.)* Mensch *(ugs.);* verflixt *(ugs.)*

crummy ['krʌmı] *adj. (sl.)* **a)** *(dirty, unpleasant)* schmuddelig *(ugs.);* verdreckt *(ugs.);* **b)** *(inferior, worthless)* mies *(ugs.)*

crumpet ['krʌmpıt] *n.* **a)** *(cake) weiches Hefeküchlein zum Toasten;* **b)** *(sl.: women)* Weiber *Pl. (salopp);* Miezen *Pl. (salopp);* **a bit/piece of ~:** ein Weib; **c)** *(sl.: head)* Birne, *die (salopp);* Rübe, *die (salopp);* **off one's ~:** übergeschnappt

crumple ['krʌmpl] **1.** *v. t.* **a)** *(crush)* zerdrücken; zerquetschen; **b)** *(ruffle, wrinkle)* zerknittern ‹*Kleider, Papier, Stoff*›; **~ [up] a piece of paper** ein Stück Papier zerknüllen. **2.** *v. i.* ‹*Kleider, Stoff, Papier:*› knittern; **~ [up]** *(fig.)* ‹*Person:*› zusammensinken

'crumple zone *n. (Motor Veh.)* Knautschzone, *die*

crunch [krʌnʃ] **1.** *v. t.* [geräuschvoll] knabbern ‹*Keks, Zwieback*›; [geräuschvoll] nagen an (+ *Dat.*) ‹*Knochen*›. **2.** *v. i.* **a) ~ away [at sth.]** [an etw. *(Dat.)*] herumknabbern *od.* -nagen; **b)** ‹*Schnee, Kies:*› knirschen; ‹*Eis:*› [zer]splittern; **the wheels ~ed on the gravel** der Kies knirschte unter den Rädern; **he ~ed through the snow** er ging durch den knirschenden Schnee. **3.** *n.* **a)** *(crunching noise)* Knirschen, *das;* **b)** *(decisive event)* **when it comes to the ~, when the ~ comes** wenn es hart auf hart geht

crunchy ['krʌnʃı] *adj.* knusprig ‹*Gebäck, Nüsse*›; knackig ‹*Apfel*›

crupper ['krʌpə(r)] *n.* **a)** *(strap)* Schweifriemen, *der;* **b)** *(of horse)* Kruppe, *die*

crusade [kru:'seıd] **1.** *n. (Hist.)* Kreuzzug, *der;* **a ~ against sth.** *(fig.)* ein Feldzug *od.* Kreuzzug gegen etw. **2.** *v. i.* einen Kreuzzug unternehmen; *(fig.)* zu Felde ziehen

crusader [kru:'seıdə(r)] *n.* Kreuzfahrer, *der;* Kreuzritter, *der*

crush [krʌʃ] **1.** *v. t.* **a)** *(compress with violence)* quetschen; auspressen ‹*Trauben, Obst*›; *(kill, destroy)* zerquetschen; zermalmen; **~ to death** zu Tode quetschen; **~ed strawberry** *(colour)* Erdbeerrot, *das;* **b)** *(reduce to powder)* zerstampfen; zermahlen; zerstoßen ‹*Gewürze, Tabletten*›; **c)** *(fig.: subdue, overwhelm)* niederwerfen, niederschlagen ‹*Aufstand*›; vernichten ‹*Feind*›; zunichte machen ‹*Hoffnungen, Wünsche*›; **her angry look ~ed him** vernichtend traf ihn ihr zorniger Blick; **d)** *(crumple, crease)* zerknittern ‹*Kleid, Stoff*›; zerdrücken, verbeulen ‹*Hut*›. **2.** *n.* **a)** *(crowded mass)* Gedränge, *das;* Gewühl, *das;* **b)** *(sl.) (infatuation)* Schwärmerei, *die; (person)* Schwarm, *der (ugs.);* **have/get a ~ on sb.** in jmdn. verknallt sein/sich in jmdn. verknallen *(ugs.);* **c)** *(drink)* Saftgetränk, *das;* **d)** *(coll.: crowded gathering)* Rummel, *der (ugs.)*

crush: ~ bar *n.* Bar, *die (im Foyer eines Theaters);* **~-barrier** *n.* Absperrgitter, *das*

crushing ['krʌʃıŋ] *adj.* niederschmetternd ‹*Antwort*›; vernichtend ‹*Niederlage, Schlag*›

crust [krʌst] *n.* **a)** *(of bread)* Kruste, *die;* Rinde, *die;* **b)** *(hard surface, coating, deposit)* Kruste, *die;* **the earth's ~:** die Erdkruste; **c)** *(of pie)* Teigdeckel, *der;* **d)** *(scab)* Kruste, *die;* Schorf, *der;* **e)** *(fig.: superficial hardness)* Panzer, *der;* **f)** *(in winebottle)* Depot, *das. See also* **¹last 1; upper 1 b**

crustacean [krʌ'steıʃn] *n.* Krusten- *od.* Krebstier, *das;* Krustazee, *die (fachspr.)*

crusted ['krʌstıd] *adj. (having a crust)* verkrustet; abgelagert ‹*Wein*›; **~ snow** Harsch, *der*

crusty ['krʌstı] *adj.* **a)** *(crisp)* knusprig; **b)** *(hard)* hart; **c)** *(irritable, curt)* barsch

crutch [krʌtʃ] *n.* **a)** *(lit. or fig.)* Krücke, *die;* **go about on ~es** an Krücken gehen; **b)** *see* **crotch b**

crux [krʌks] *n., pl.* **~es** *or* **cruces** ['kru:si:z] **a)** *(difficult matter, puzzle)* Rätsel, *das;* harte Nuß *(ugs.);* **the ~ of the matter** der Haken bei der Sache; **b)** *(decisive point)* Kern[punkt], *der;* **the ~ of the matter** der springende Punkt bei der Sache

cry [kraı] **1.** *n.* **a)** *(loud utterance of grief)* Schrei, *der; (loud utterance of words)* Schreien, *das;* Geschrei, *das; (of hounds or wolves)* Heulen, *das;* Geheul, *das; (of birds)* Schreien, *das;* Geschrei, *das;* **a ~ of pain/rage/happiness** ein Schmerzens-/Wut-/Freudenschrei; **a far ~ from ...** *(fig.)* etwas ganz anderes als ...; **be in full ~:** ‹*Hundemeute:*› laut bellend hinter der Beute herhetzen; **be in full ~ after sb.** *(fig.)* jmdn. mit großem Geheul verfolgen; **b)** *(appeal, entreaty)* Appell, *der;* **a ~ for freedom/independence/justice** ein Ruf nach Freiheit/Unabhängigkeit/Gerechtigkeit; **a ~ for mercy** eine flehentliche Bitte um Gnade; **a ~ for help** ein Hilferuf; **c)** *(proclamation of goods or business)* Ausrufen, *das;* **d)** *(public demand)* Ruf, *der;* **e)** *(watchword)* Losung, *die;* Parole, *die; (in battle)* Schlachtruf, *der;* **f)** *(fit or spell of weeping)* **have a good ~:** sich ausweinen; **it will do her good to have a ~:** es wird ihr guttun, sich einmal richtig auszuweinen. **2.** *v. t.* **a)** rufen; *(loudly)* schreien; **b)** *(weep)* weinen; **~ bitter tears over sth.** bittere Tränen wegen etw. weinen *od.* über etw. *(Akk.)* vergießen; **~ one's eyes out** sich *(Dat.)* die Augen ausweinen *od.* aus dem Kopf weinen; **~ oneself to sleep** sich in den Schlaf weinen; **c) ~ one's wares** *(lit. or fig.)* seine Waren anpreisen. **3.** *v. i.* **a)** rufen; *(loudly)* schreien; **~ [out] for sth./sb.** nach etw./jmdm. rufen *od.* schreien; **~ [out] for mercy** um Gnade flehen; **~ [out] for help** um Hilfe schreien; **~ to sb. [to come]** jmdm. zurufen[, er solle kommen *od.* daß er kommen soll]; **~ with pain** vor Schmerz[en] schreien; **sth. cries out for sth.** *(fig.)* etw. schreit nach etw.; **[well,] for ~ing out loud** *(coll.)* das darf doch wohl nicht wahr sein! *(ugs.);* **what's the matter, for ~ing out loud?** was ist los, um Himmels willen?; **~ for the moon** *(fig.)* Unmögliches verlangen; **b)** *(weep)* weinen (**over** wegen); **~ for sth.** nach etw. weinen; *(fig.)* einer Sache *(Dat.)* nachweinen; *see also* **milk 1; c)** ‹*Möwe:*› schreien; ‹*Hund:*› bellen

~ 'down *v. t.* **~ sb./sth. down** jmdn./etw. herabsetzen *od. (ugs.)* miesmachen

~ 'off *v. i.* absagen; einen Rückzieher machen *(ugs.)*

~ 'out *v. i.* aufschreien; *see also* **~ 3a**

~ 'up *v. t.* **~ sth./sb. up** etw./jmdn. hochjubeln *(ugs.) od.* in den Himmel heben *(ugs.);* **it/he wasn't all it/he was cried up to be** so großartig war es/er nun auch wieder nicht

'cry-baby *n.* Heulsuse, *die (ugs.)*

cryer *see* **crier**

crying ['kraııŋ] *adj.* weinend ‹*Kind*›; schreiend ‹*Unrecht*›; dringend ‹*Bedürfnis, Notwendigkeit*›; dringlich ‹*Forderung*›; kraß ‹*Mißverhältnis*›; **it is a ~ shame** es ist eine wahre Schande

cryo- [kraıəʊ] *in comb.* Kryo-/kryo-

cryogenic [kraıəʊ'dʒenık] *adj.* **~ laboratory** Tieftemperaturlabor, *das*

crypt [krıpt] *n.* Krypta, *die*

cryptic ['krıptık] *adj.* **a)** *(secret, mystical)* geheimnisvoll; **b)** *(obscure in meaning)* undurchschaubar; kryptisch

cryptically ['krɪptɪkəlɪ] *adv. see* **cryptic**: geheimnisvoll; undurchschaubar; kryptisch

crypto- [krɪptəʊ] *in comb.* Krypto-

cryptogram ['krɪptəgræm] *n.* verschlüsselter Text; Geheimtext, *der*

cryptographic [krɪptə'græfɪk] *adj.* verschlüsselt; *(employing cryptography)* Verschlüsselungs-

cryptography [krɪp'tɒgrəfɪ] *n.* Kryptographie, *die*

crystal ['krɪstl] **1.** *n.* **a)** *(Chem., Min., etc.)* Kristall, *der;* **b)** *see* **crystal glass. 2.** *adj. (made of ~ glass)* kristallen; **~ bowl/vase** Kristallschale, *die/*-vase, *die*

crystal: ~ 'ball *n.* Kristallkugel, *die;* **I haven't got a ~ ball!** ich bin [doch] kein Hellseher!; **~-clear** *adj.* kristallklar; kristallen *(geh.); (fig.)* glasklar; **make sth. ~-clear** *(fig.)* etw. ganz klar machen; **~-gazing** *n.* Hellseherei, *die;* Kristallomantie, *die (fachspr.);* **~ 'glass** *n.* Bleikristall, *das;* Kristallglas, *das*

crystalline ['krɪstəlaɪn] *adj.* **a)** *(made of crystal)* Kristall-; kristallen; **b)** *(Chem., Min.)* kristallin[isch]

crystallisation, crystallise *see* **crystalliz-**

crystallization [krɪstəlaɪ'zeɪʃn] *n.* Kristallbildung, *die;* Kristallisation, *die; (fig.)* Kristallisierung, *die*

crystallize ['krɪstəlaɪz] **1.** *v.t.* auskristallisieren ⟨*Salze*⟩; kandieren ⟨*Früchte*⟩; **~ one's thoughts** *(fig.)* seinen Gedanken feste Form geben. **2.** *v.i.* kristallisieren; *(fig.)* feste Form annehmen

crystallographer [krɪstə'lɒgrəfə(r)] *n.* Kristallograph, *der/*-graphin, *die*

crystallography [krɪstə'lɒgrəfɪ] *n.* Kristallographie, *die*

c/s *abbr.* **cycle[s] per second** Hz

CSCE *abbr.* **Conference on Security and Co-operation in Europe** KSZE

CSE *abbr. (Brit. Hist.)* **Certificate of Secondary Education**

CS 'gas *n.* CS, *das (fachspr.);* ≈ Tränengas, *das*

ct *abbr.* **a) carat** Kt.; **b) cent** ct., Ct.

cu. *abbr.* **cubic** Kubik-

cub [kʌb] *n.* **a)** Junge, *das; (of wolf, fox, dog)* Welpe, *der;* Junge, *das;* **b) Cub** *see* **Cub Scout; c)** *(Amer.: apprentice)* Lehrling, *der*

Cuba ['kju:bə] *n.* Kuba *(das)*

Cuban ['kju:bn] **1.** *adj.* kubanisch; **sb. is ~:** jmd. ist Kubaner/Kubanerin. **2.** *n.* Kubaner, *der/*Kubanerin, *die*

Cuban 'heel *n.* Blockabsatz, *der*

cubby[-hole] ['kʌbɪ(-həʊl)] *n.* Kämmerchen, *das; (snug place)* Kuschelecke, *die*

cube [kju:b] **1.** *n.* **a)** Würfel, *der;* Kubus, *der (fachspr.);* **b)** *(Math.)* dritte Potenz; Kubus, *der (fachspr.).* **2.** *v.t.* in die dritte Potenz erheben ⟨*Zahl*⟩; hoch drei nehmen; **2 ~d is 8** 2 hoch 3 ist 8; die dritte Potenz von 2 ist 8

cube: ~ 'root *n.* Kubikwurzel, *die;* **the ~ root of 8 is 2** die dritte Wurzel aus 8 ist 2; **~ sugar** *n.* Würfelzucker, *der*

cubic ['kju:bɪk] *adj.* **a)** würfelförmig; **have a ~ form** würfelförmig sein; die Form eines Würfels haben; **b)** *(of three dimensions)* Kubik-; Raum-; **~ content** Rauminhalt, *der;* **~ metre/centimetre/foot/yard** Kubikmeter/-zentimeter/-fuß/-yard, *der;* **c)** *(Math.)* kubisch; **~ equation** Gleichung dritten Grades

cubical ['kju:bɪkl] *adj. see* **cubic a**

cubicle ['kju:bɪkl] *n.* **a)** *(sleeping-compartment)* Alkoven, *der;* **b)** *(for dressing, private discussion, etc.)* Kabine, *die*

cubism ['kju:bɪzm] *n. (Art)* Kubismus, *der*

cubist ['kju:bɪst] *n. (Art)* Kubist, *der/*Kubistin, *die*

cubit ['kju:bɪt] *n. (Hist.)* Elle, *die*

'cub reporter *n. (coll.)* unerfahrener [junger] Reporter/unerfahrene [junge] Reporterin

'Cub Scout *n.* Wölfling, *der*

cuckold ['kʌkəld] *(arch.)* **1.** *n.* Hahnrei, *der (veralt.);* gehörnter Ehemann *(scherzh.).* **2.** *v.t.* Hörner aufsetzen (+ *Dat.*) *(scherzh.);* hörnen *(scherzh.)*

cuckoo ['kʊku:] **1.** *n.* **a)** Kuckuck, *der;* **~ in the nest** *(fig.)* Fremdkörper, *der;* **b)** *(simpleton)* Einfaltspinsel, *der (ugs.);* Heini, *der (ugs.).* **2.** *adj. (sl.)* meschugge *nicht attr. (salopp);* **a ~ notion/idea** eine bekloppte Idee *(salopp)*

cuckoo: ~ clock *n.* Kuckucksuhr, *die;* **~ flower** *n. (Bot.)* **a)** *(lady-smock)* Wiesenschaumkraut, *das;* **b)** *(ragged robin)* Kuckuckslichtnelke, *die;* **~-pint** ['kʊku:pɪnt] *n. (Bot.)* Aron[s]stab, *der*

cucumber ['kju:kʌmbə(r)] *n.* [Salat]gurke, *die;* **be as cool as a ~** taufrisch sein; *(fig.: remain calm)* einen kühlen Kopf behalten

cud [kʌd] *n.* wiedergekäutes Futter; **chew the ~:** wiederkäuen; *(fig.)* vor sich hin grübeln

cuddle ['kʌdl] **1.** *n.* Liebkosung, *die;* enge Umarmung; **give sb. a ~:** jmdn. drücken *od.* in den Arm nehmen; **have a ~:** schmusen. **2.** *v.t.* schmusen mit; hätscheln ⟨*kleines Kind*⟩. **3.** *v.i.* schmusen; **~ up** sich zusammenkuscheln; *(in bed)* sich einmummeln; **he ~d up beside her** er kuschelte sich an ihre Seite

cuddlesome ['kʌdlsəm] *adj.* zum Liebhaben *od.* Schmusen *nachgestellt*

cuddly ['kʌdlɪ] *adj.* **a)** *(given to cuddling)* verschmust; **b)** *see* **cuddlesome**

cuddly 'toy *n.* Plüschtier, *das*

cudgel ['kʌdʒl] **1.** *n.* Knüppel, *der;* **take up the ~s for sb./sth.** *(fig.)* [energisch] für jmdn./etw. eintreten. **2.** *v.t., (Brit.)* **-ll-** knüppeln; **~ one's brains** *(fig.)* sich *(Dat.)* das [Ge]hirn zermartern

[1]cue [kju:] *n. (Billiards etc.)* Queue, *das;* Billardstock, *der*

[2]cue 1. *n.* **a)** *(Theatre)* Stichwort, *das; (Music)* Stichnoten *Pl.; (Cinemat., Broadcasting)* Zeichen zum Aufnahmebeginn; **be/speak/play on ~:** rechtzeitig einsetzen; **enter on ~:** auf das Stichwort hin auftreten; **b)** *(sign when or how to act)* Wink, *der;* Zeichen, *das;* **take one's ~ from sb.** *(lit. or fig.)* sich nach jmdm. richten. **2.** *v.t. (label)* kennzeichnen

[1]cuff [kʌf] *n.* **a)** Manschette, *die;* **off the ~** *(fig.)* aus dem Stegreif; **b)** *(Amer.: trouser turn-up)* [Hosen]aufschlag, *der;* **c)** *in pl. (coll.: handcuffs)* Handschellen *Pl.*

[2]cuff 1. *v.t.* **~ sb.'s ears, ~ sb. over the ears** jmdm. eins hinter die Ohren geben *(ugs.);* **~ sb.** jmdm. einen Klaps geben. **2.** *n.* Klaps, *der;* **give sb. a ~ on the ears** jmdm. eins hinter die Ohren geben *(ugs.)*

'cuff-link *n.* Manschettenknopf, *der*

cuirass [kwɪ'ræs] *n. (armour)* Küraß, *der;* Brustharnisch, *der*

cuisine [kwɪ'zi:n] *n.* Küche, *die;* **French/ Italian** *etc.* **~:** französische/italienische *usw.* Küche

cul-de-sac ['kʌldəsæk] *n., pl.* **culs-de-sac** ['kʌldəsæk] Sackgasse, *die*

culinary ['kʌlɪnərɪ] *adj.* kulinarisch; **the ~ arts** die Kochkunst; **~ herbs/plants** *etc.* Küchenkräuter/-gewächse *usw.*

cull [kʌl] **1.** *v.t.* **a)** *(pick)* pflücken; **b)** *(select)* auswählen; **c)** *(select and kill)* ausmerzen. **2.** *n.* **a)** *(act of ~ing)* Ausmerzung, *die;* **~ of seals** Robbenschlag, *der;* **b)** *(~ed animal)* Merztier, *das*

cullet ['kʌlɪt] *n. (Glass-making)* Glasscherben; Glasbruch, *der*

culm [kʌlm] *n. (Bot.)* Halm, *der*

culminate ['kʌlmɪneɪt] *v.i. (reach highest point, lit. or fig.)* gipfeln; kulminieren; **~ in sth.** in etw. *(Dat.)* seinen Höchststand erreichen

culmination [kʌlmɪ'neɪʃn] *n.* Höhepunkt, *der;* Kulmination, *die (geh.)*

culottes [kju:'lɒt] *n. pl.* Hosenrock, *der*

culpable ['kʌlpəbl] *adj.* schuldig ⟨*Person*⟩; strafbar ⟨*Handlung*⟩; **hold sb. ~:** jmdn. für schuldig halten; **~ negligence** grobe Fahrlässigkeit

culprit ['kʌlprɪt] *n. (guilty of crime)* Schuldige, *der/die;* Täter, *der/*Täterin, *die; (guilty of wrong)* Übeltäter, *der/*-täterin, *die;* Missetäter, *der/*-täterin, *die*

cult [kʌlt] *n.* Kult, *der;* **the ~ of the dead** der Totenkult; *attrib.* Kult⟨*film, -figur usw.*⟩

cultivate ['kʌltɪveɪt] *v.t.* **a)** *(prepare and use for crops)* kultivieren; bestellen, bebauen ⟨*Feld, Land*⟩; *(prepare with cultivator)* mit dem Kultivator bearbeiten; **b)** *(produce by culture)* anbauen, züchten ⟨*Pflanzen*⟩; züchten ⟨*Tiere*⟩; **c)** *(fig.) (improve, develop)* kultivieren ⟨*Stimme, Sprache*⟩; kultivieren, entwickeln ⟨*Geschmack*⟩; kultivieren, verfeinern ⟨*Manieren*⟩; *(pay attention to, cherish)* kultivieren ⟨*Freundschaft, Gefühl, Gewohnheit*⟩; pflegen ⟨*Freundschaft, Verbindung*⟩; entwickeln ⟨*Kunst, Fertigkeit*⟩; betreiben ⟨*Wissenschaft*⟩; **~ sb.** die Verbindung mit jmdm. pflegen; sich *(Dat.)* jmdn. warmhalten *(ugs.);* **~ one's mind** sich bilden; **d)** züchten ⟨*Bakterien*⟩

cultivated ['kʌltɪveɪtɪd] *adj.* **a)** kultiviert; gezüchtet ⟨*Pflanzen*⟩; bebaut ⟨*Land, Feld*⟩; **~ plant** Zuchtpflanze, *die;* **b)** *(fig.)* kultiviert ⟨*Manieren, Sprache, Geschmack*⟩; kultiviert, gebildet ⟨*Person*⟩

cultivation [kʌltɪ'veɪʃn] *n. (lit. or fig.)* Kultivierung, *die; (of a skill)* Entwicklung, *die;* **~ of plants** Anbau von Pflanzen; **~ of land** Landbau, *der;* Pflanzenbau, *der;* **land that is under ~:** Boden, der landwirtschaftlich genutzt wird; **bring land into ~:** Land urbar machen; *(fig.)* **~ of the mind** Bildung, *die*

cultivator ['kʌltɪveɪtə(r)] *n.* **a)** *(person)* Ackerbauer, *der;* **b)** *(implement)* Handkultivator, *der; (machine)* Kultivator, *der;* Grubber, *der*

cultural ['kʌltʃərl] *adj.* kulturell ⟨*Entwicklung, Ereignis, Interessen, Beziehungen*⟩; **~ revolution/anthropology** Kulturrevolution/-anthropologie, *die;* **there are ~ activities** es wird kulturell etwas geboten

culture ['kʌltʃə(r)] **1.** *n.* **a)** Kultur, *die;* **the two ~s** die entgegengesetzten Bereiche Geisteswissenschaft und Naturwissenschaft; **b)** *(intellectual development)* [Geistes]bildung, *die;* Kultur, *die;* **c) physical ~:** Fitneßtraining, *das;* **beauty ~:** Schönheitspflege, *die;* **d)** *(Agric.)* Kultur, *die; (tillage of the soil)* Landbau, *der; (rearing, production)* Zucht, *die;* **methods of ~:** Anbaumethoden *Pl.;* **e)** *(of bacteria)* Kultur, *die.* **2.** *v.t.* züchten ⟨*Bakterien*⟩

cultured ['kʌltʃəd] *adj.* **a)** *(cultivated, refined)* kultiviert; gebildet; **b) ~ pearl** Zuchtperle, *die*

culture: ~ shock *n.* Kulturschock, *der;* **~ vulture** *n. (joc.)* Kulturfanatiker, *der/*-fanatikerin, *die (ugs.)*

culvert ['kʌlvət] *n.* **a)** *(for water)* [unterirdischer] Kanal, *der;* **b)** *(for electric cable)* Kabelkanal, *der*

cum [kʌm] *prep.* **a)** *(Finance)* **~ dividend** mit Dividende; **b)** *(indicating combined nature or function)* **dining-~-sitting-room** Wohn- und Speisezimmer, *das;* **dinner-~-cocktail dress** Abend- und Cocktailkleid, *das*

cumbersome ['kʌmbəsəm] *adj.* lästig, hinderlich ⟨*Kleider*⟩; sperrig ⟨*Gepäck, Pakete*⟩; unhandlich ⟨*Paket*⟩; schwerfällig ⟨*Bewegung, Stil, Arbeitsweise, Ausdruck*⟩; umständlich ⟨*Methode*⟩

cumin ['kʌmɪn] *n. (Bot.)* Kreuzkümmel, *der*

cummerbund ['kʌməbʌnd] *n.* Kummerbund, *der*

cummin *see* **cumin**

cumulate ['kju:mjʊleɪt], **cumulation** [kju:mjʊ'leɪʃn] *see* **accumul-**

cumulative ['kju:mjʊlətɪv] *adj.* **a)** *(in-*

creased by successive additions) kumulativ *(geh.)*; ~ **strength/effect** Gesamtstärke/-wirkung, *die;* ~ **evidence** Häufung von Beweismaterial; **b)** *(formed by successive additions)* zusätzlich; Zusatz-; kumulierend, kumuliert ‹*Bibliographie*›

cumulatively ['kju:mjʊlətɪvlɪ] *adv.* kumulativ

cumulus ['kju:mjʊləs] *n., pl.* **cumuli** ['kju:mjʊlaɪ] *(Meteorol.)* Kumuluswolke, *die*

cuneiform ['kju:nɪɪfɔ:m, 'kju:nɪfɔ:m] *adj.* keilförmig; ‹*Text, Dokument, Inschrift*› in Keilschrift; ~ **writing** Keilschrift, *die*

cunnilingus [kʌnɪ'lɪŋgəs] *n., no pl., no art.* Cunnilingus, *der*

cunning ['kʌnɪŋ] **1.** *n.* **a)** Schläue, *die;* Gerissenheit, *die;* **b)** *(arch.: skill)* Geschicklichkeit, *die;* Geschick, *das.* **2.** *adj.* **a)** schlau; gerissen; **b)** *(arch.: skilful)* geschickt; **c)** *(Amer.: quaint, small)* niedlich

cunningly ['kʌnɪŋlɪ] *adv.* schlau ‹*reden, denken*›; listig ‹*täuschen*›; gerissen ‹*handeln*›; *as sentence modifier* schlauerweise

cunt [kʌnt] *n. (coarse)* **a)** *(female genitals)* Fotze, *die (vulg.);* Möse, *die (vulg.);* **b)** *(derog.) (woman)* Fotze, *die (vulg.);* Schlampe, *die (derb); (man)* Arschloch, *das (derb)*

cup [kʌp] **1.** *n.* **a)** *(drinking-vessel)* Tasse, *die;* **there's many a slip between the ~ and the lip** *(fig.)* da kann immer noch etwas dazwischenkommen; **in one's ~s** *(fig.)* in angetrunkenem Zustand; **b)** *(prize, competition)* Pokal, *der;* **c)** *(cupful)* Tasse, *die;* **a ~ of coffee/tea** eine Tasse Kaffee/Tee; **another ~ of tea** *(fig.)* etwas ganz anderes; **a nasty/nice ~ of tea** *(fig. coll.)* ein fieses Stück *(ugs. abwertend)* /ein netter Typ *(ugs.)*; **it's [not] my ~ of tea** *(fig. coll.)* das ist [nicht] mein Fall *(ugs.)*; **d)** *(flavoured wine etc.)* Bowle, *die;* **e)** *(Eccl.)* Kelch, *der;* **f)** *(fig.: fate, experience)* **his ~ [of happiness/sorrow] was full** er war überglücklich/das Maß seiner Leiden war voll; **g)** *(of brassière)* Körbchen, *das;* **A/B** *etc.* **~:** A-/B-Körbchen *usw.* **2.** *v.t.,* **-pp-: a)** *(take or hold as in ~)* ~ **one's chin in one's hand** das Kinn in die Hand stützen; ~ **water** Wasser [mit der hohlen Hand] schöpfen; **b)** *(make ~-shaped)* hohl machen; ~ **one's hand to one's ear** die Hand ans Ohr halten

cupboard ['kʌbəd] *n.* Schrank, *der*

'cupboard love *n.* geheuchelte Zuneigung; **it's just ~:** es ist nur Getue *(ugs.)*

'cup-cake *n. kleiner [Rühr]kuchen in einem Förmchen aus Papier*

Cup 'Final *n. (Footb.)* Pokalendspiel, *das*

cupful ['kʌpfʊl] *n.* Tasse, *die;* **a ~ of water** eine Tasse Wasser

Cupid ['kju:pɪd] *n. (god)* Amor, *der;* Cupido, *der; (representation)* Amorette, *die;* **~'s bow** Amors Bogen

cupidity [kju:'pɪdɪtɪ] *n., no pl.* Begierde, *die* **(for** nach); Gier, *die* **(for** nach)

cupola ['kju:pələ] *n.* Kuppel, *die; (ceiling of dome)* Kuppel, *die;* Kuppelgewölbe, *das*

cuppa ['kʌpə], **cupper** ['kʌpə(r)] *n. (Brit. coll.)* Tasse Tee

'cup-tie *n.* Pokalspiel, *das*

cur [kɜ:(r)] *n. (derog.)* **a)** *(dog)* Köter, *der (ugs. abwertend);* **b)** *(fig.: person)* [Schweine]hund, *der (derb abwertend)*

curable ['kjʊərəbl] *adj.* heilbar; **the patient is ~:** der Patient kann geheilt werden; **not ~** *(lit. or fig.)* unheilbar

curaçao ['kjʊərəsəʊ] *n.* Curaçao, *der*

curare [kjʊə'rɑ:rɪ] *n.* Curare, *das*

curate ['kjʊərət] *n.* **a)** *(Eccl.)* Kurat, *der;* Hilfsgeistliche, *der;* **b) sth. is a** *or* **like the ~'s egg** *(fig.)* etw. hat seine guten und seine schlechten Seiten

curative ['kjʊərətɪv] *adj.* heilend; Heil-; **be ~:** heilend wirken; heilen

curator [kjʊə'reɪtə(r)] *n.* **a)** *(of museum)* Direktor, *der*/Direktorin, *die;* **b)** *(person in charge)* Verwalter, *der*/Verwalterin, *die*

curb [kɜ:b] **1.** *v.t. (lit. or fig.)* zügeln. **2.** *n.* **a)** *(chain or strap for horse)* Kandare, *die;* **put a ~ on** *(fig.)* an die Kandare nehmen ‹*Person*›; zügeln ‹*Gefühle*›; einschränken ‹*Ausgaben, Einfuhr*›; **b)** *see* **kerb**

'curd cheese *n.* ≈ Quark, *der*

curdle ['kɜ:dl] **1.** *v.t. (lit. or fig.)* gerinnen lassen; *see also* **blood-curdling. 2.** *v.i. (lit. or fig.)* gerinnen

curds [kɜ:dz] *n. pl.* ≈ Quark, *der;* ~ **and whey** Quark [mit Molke]

cure [kjʊə(r)] **1.** *n.* **a)** *(thing that ~s)* [Heil]mittel, *das* **(for** gegen); *(fig.)* Mittel, *das;* **b)** *(restoration to health)* Heilung, *die;* **c)** *(treatment)* Behandlung, *die;* **take a ~ at a spa** in *od.* zur Kur gehen; **d)** *(spiritual charge)* ~ **of souls** Seelsorge, *die.* **2.** *v.t.* **a)** heilen; kurieren; ~ **sb. of a disease** jmdn. von einer Krankheit heilen; **b)** *(fig.)* kurieren; **he was ~d of his bad habits** er wurde von seinen schlechten Gewohnheiten kuriert; ihm wurden seine schlechten Gewohnheiten ausgetrieben; **c)** *(preserve)* haltbar machen ‹*Nahrungsmittel*›; [ein]pökeln ‹*Fleisch*›; räuchern ‹*Fisch*›; trocknen ‹*Häute, Tabak*›; **d)** *(harden)* aushärten ‹*Beton, Kunststoffe*›

'cure-all *n.* Allheilmittel, *das*

curfew ['kɜ:fju:] *n.* **a)** Ausgangssperre, *die;* **b)** *(Hist.: bell)* Abendglocke, *die*

Curia ['kjʊərɪə] *n.* Kurie, *die*

curio ['kjʊərɪəʊ] *n., pl.* **~s** Kuriosität, *die*

curiosity [kjʊərɪ'ɒsɪtɪ] *n.* **a)** *(desire to know)* Neugier[de], *die* **(about** in bezug auf + *Akk.*); ~ **killed the cat** *(fig.)* die Neugier ist schon manchem zum Verhängnis geworden; **b)** *(strange or rare object)* Wunderding, *das;* Rarität, *die; (strange matter)* Kuriosität, *die;* **c)** *no pl. (strangeness)* Fremdartigkeit, *die*

curious ['kjʊərɪəs] *adj.* **a)** *(inquisitive)* neugierig; *(eager to learn)* wißbegierig; **be ~ about sth.** *(eagerly awaiting)* auf etw. *(Akk.)* neugierig sein; **be ~ about sb.** in bezug auf jmdn. neugierig sein; **be ~ to know sth.** etw. gern wissen wollen; **he was ~ to know what ...:** er wollte zu gerne wissen, was ...; **b)** *(strange, odd)* merkwürdig; seltsam; **how [very] ~!** [sehr] seltsam!; **~er and ~er** *(coll.)* es wird immer geheimnisvoller

curiously ['kjʊərɪəslɪ] *adv. see* **curious:** neugierig ‹*fragen, gucken*›; seltsam, merkwürdig ‹*sprechen, sich verhalten*›; **it was ~ quiet** es war merkwürdig still; ~ **[enough]** *(as sentence-modifier)* merkwürdigerweise; seltsamerweise

curiousness ['kjʊərɪəsnɪs] *n., no pl. (inquisitiveness)* Neugier[de], *die; (oddness)* Merkwürdigkeit, *die;* Sonderbarkeit, *die*

curl [kɜ:l] **1.** *n.* **a)** *(of hair)* Locke, *die;* **put one's/sb.'s hair in ~s** sich/jmdm. das Haar locken; **hair in ~s** gelocktes Haar; **hair in tight ~s** Kraushaar, *das;* **b)** *(sth. spiral or curved inwards)* **the ~ of a leaf/wave** ein gekräuseltes Blatt/eine gekräuselte Welle; **a ~ of smoke** ein Rauchkringel; **c)** *(act of curling)* Kräuseln, *das;* **with a ~ of the lip** mit gekräuselten Lippen. **2.** *v.t.* **a)** *(cause to form coils)* locken; *(tightly)* kräuseln; **she ~ed her hair** sie legte ihr Haar in Locken *(Akk.)*; **b)** *(bend, twist)* kräuseln ‹*Blätter, Lippen*›; **the animal ~ed itself into a ball** das Tier rollte sich zu einer Kugel zusammen; **it's enough to ~ your hair** *(fig.)* da stehen einem ja die Haare zu Berge! **3.** *v.i.* **a)** *(grow in coils)* sich locken; *(tightly)* sich kräuseln; **her hair ~s naturally** sie hat Naturlocken; *(tightly)* sie hat eine Naturkrause; **it's enough to make your hair ~** *(fig.)* da stehen einem ja die Haare zu Berge!; **b)** *(move in spiral form)* ‹*Straße, Fluß:*› sich winden, sich schlängeln; **the smoke ~ed upwards** der Rauch stieg in Kringeln hoch

~ **'up 1.** *v.t.* hochbiegen; ~ **oneself up** *(coll.: roll into shape of ball)* sich zusammenrollen; sich einrollen. **2.** *v.i. (coll.: roll into curved shape)*; sich zusammenrollen; sich einrollen; *(fig.: writhe with horror)* erschauern; **he ~ed up on the sofa** er machte es sich *(Dat.)* auf dem Sofa bequem *od. (ugs.)* fläzte sich auf das Sofa; **she ~ed up with a book** sie machte es sich *(Dat.)* mit einem Buch gemütlich

curler ['kɜ:lə(r)] *n.* Lockenwickler, *der;* **in ~s** mit Lockenwicklern

curlew ['kɜ:lju:] *n. (Ornith.)* Brachvogel, *der*

curlicue ['kɜ:lɪkju:] *n.* Schnörkel, *der*

curling ['kɜ:lɪŋ] *n. (game)* Curling, *das;* ≈ Eisschießen, *das*

curling: ~-iron *n.,* *(Brit.)* **~-tongs** *n. pl.* Brennschere, *die; (electrical appliance)* Lockenstab, *der*

curly ['kɜ:lɪ] *adj.* lockig, *(tightly)* kraus ‹*Haar*›; kraus ‹*Salat*›; gewellt, gekräuselt ‹*Blatt*›; Schnörkel‹*schrift, -muster*›, verschnörkelt ‹*Schrift, Muster*›

curly: ~-haired *adj.* lockenköpfig; mit lockigem Haar; **~-head** *n.* Lockenkopf, *der; (with tight curls)* Krauskopf, *der;* **~-headed** *see* **~-haired**

currant ['kʌrənt] *n.* **a)** *(dried fruit)* Korinthe, *die;* **b)** *(fruit)* Johannisbeere, *die; (plant)* Johannisbeerstrauch, *der; see also* **black currant; flowering; red currant**

currency ['kʌrənsɪ] *n.* **a)** *(money)* Währung, *die; (circulation)* Umlauf, *der;* **foreign currencies** Devisen *Pl.;* **withdraw from ~:** aus dem Verkehr ziehen; **b)** *(other commodity)* [Tausch]ware, *die;* Zahlungsmittel, *das;* **c)** *(prevalence) (of word, idea, story, rumour)* Verbreitung, *die; (of expression)* Gebräuchlichkeit, *die;* **gain wide ~:** weite Verbreitung finden; **give ~ to a rumour** ein Gerücht in Umlauf bringen

current ['kʌrənt] **1.** *adj.* **a)** *(in general circulation or use)* kursierend, umlaufend ‹*Geld, Geschichte, Gerücht*›; verbreitet ‹*Meinung*›; gebräuchlich ‹*Wort*›; gängig ‹*Redensart*›; **these coins are no longer ~:** diese Münzen sind nicht mehr in Umlauf; **b)** laufend ‹*Jahr, Monat*›; **in the ~ year** in diesem Jahr; **c)** *(belonging to the present time)* aktuell ‹*Ereignis, Mode*›; Tages‹*politik, -preis*›, derzeitig ‹*Politik, Preis*›; gegenwärtig ‹*Krise, Aufregung*›; ~ **issue/edition** letzte Ausgabe/neueste Auflage; ~ **affairs** Tagespolitik, *die;* aktuelle Fragen. **2.** *n.* **a)** *(of water, air)* Strömung, *die;* **air/ocean ~:** Luft-/Meeresströmung, *die;* **swim against/with the ~:** gegen den/mit dem Strom schwimmen; **upward/downward ~ of air** *(in atmosphere)* Aufwind/Abwind, *der;* **b)** *(Electr.)* Strom, *der; (intensity)* Stromstärke, *die;* **c)** *(running stream)* Strömung, *die;* **d)** *(tendency of events, opinions, etc.)* Tendenz, *die;* Trend, *der;* **the ~ of public opinion** der Trend in der öffentlichen Meinung; **go against/with the ~** gegen den/mit dem Strom schwimmen

'current account *n.* Girokonto, *das; (in balance of payments)* Leistungsbilanz, *die*

currently ['kʌrəntlɪ] *adv.* gegenwärtig; momentan; zur Zeit; **he is ~ writing a book** er schreibt gerade *od.* zur Zeit an einem Buch; **it is ~ thought** *or* **believed that ...:** heute glaubt man, daß ...

curriculum [kə'rɪkjʊləm] *n., pl.* **curricula** [kə'rɪkjʊlə] Lehrplan, *der;* Curriculum, *das;* **be on the ~:** auf dem Lehrplan stehen

curriculum vitae [kərɪkjʊləm 'vi:taɪ] *n.* Lebenslauf, *der*

¹curry ['kʌrɪ] *(Cookery)* **1.** *n.* Curry[gericht], *das.* **2.** *v.t.* mit Curry würzen

²curry *v.t.* **a)** striegeln ‹*Pferd*›; **b)** zurichten ‹*Leder*›; **c)** ~ **favour [with sb.]** sich [bei jmdm.] einschmeicheln *od.* lieb Kind machen *(ugs.)*

curry: ~-comb *n.* Striegel, *der;* **~-powder** *n.* Currypulver, *das;* Curry, *das od. der*

curse [kɜ:s] **1.** *n.* **a)** Fluch, *der;* **be under a ~:**

unter einem Fluch stehen; **put a ~ on sb./sth.** einen Fluch über jmdn./etw. aussprechen; jmdn./etw. mit einem Fluch belegen; **call down ~s [from Heaven] upon sb.** jmdn. verfluchen; **b)** *(profane oath)* Fluch, *der,* Verwünschung, *die;* **bawl ~s at sb.** Flüche gegen jmdn. ausstoßen; **a thousand ~s on this old car** *(joc.)* zum Teufel mit diesem verfluchten alten Auto!; **~s! he's diddled me again** *(joc.)* verflucht! der Kerl hat mich wieder reingelegt *(ugs.)*; **c)** *(great evil)* Geißel, *die;* Plage, *die;* **d)** *(coll.: menstruation)* **the ~:** die Tage *(ugs.)*. **2.** *v. t.* **a)** *(utter ~ against)* verfluchen; **b)** *(as oath)* **~ it/you!** verflucht!; verdammt!; **c)** *(afflict)* strafen; **~d with poverty** mit Armut geschlagen *od.* gestraft. **3.** *v. i.* fluchen (**at** über + *Akk.*); **he started cursing and swearing** er fing an, heftig zu fluchen

cursed ['kɜ:sɪd] *adj.* **a)** *(under a curse)* verflucht; verwünscht; **b)** *(damnable)* verdammt

cursive ['kɜ:sɪv] *adj.* kursiv; **~ writing** Schreibschrift, *die*

cursor ['kɜ:sə(r)] *n.* Läufer, *der; (on screen)* Cursor, *der;* Schreibmarke, *die*

cursorily ['kɜ:sərɪlɪ] *adv.* flüchtig ‹*lesen*›; oberflächlich ‹*untersuchen*›

cursory ['kɜ:sərɪ] *adj.* flüchtig ‹*Blick*›; oberflächlich ‹*Untersuchung, Bericht, Studium*›

curt [kɜ:t] *adj.* *(discourteously brief)* kurz und schroff ‹*Brief, Mitteilung*›; kurz angebunden ‹*Person, Art*›; **he gave a ~ nod and left** er nickte kurz und ging

curtail [kɜ:'teɪl] *v. t.* kürzen; abkürzen ‹*Urlaub*›; beschneiden ‹*Macht*›

curtailment [kɜ:'teɪlmənt] *n.* Kürzung, *die; (of power)* Beschneidung, *die*

curtain ['kɜ:tən] **1.** *n.* **a)** Vorhang, *der; (with net ~s)* Übergardine, *die;* **draw** *or* **pull the ~s** *(open)* die Vorhänge aufziehen; *(close)* die Vorhänge zuziehen; **draw** *or* **pull back the ~s** die Vorhänge aufziehen; **b)** *(fig.)* **a ~ of fog/mist** ein Nebelschleier; **a ~ of smoke/flames/rain** eine Rauch-/Flammen-/Regenwand; **c)** *(Theatre)* Vorhang, *der; (end of play)* Schlußszene, *die; (rise of ~ at start of play)* Aufgehen des Vorhanges; Aktbeginn, *der; (fall of ~ at end of scene)* Fallen des Vorhanges; Aktschluß, *der;* **the ~ rises/falls** der Vorhang hebt sich/fällt; **d)** *see* **curtain-call**; **e)** *see* **Iron Curtain**; **e)** *in pl. (sl.: the end)* Ende, *das;* **that's ~s for him** jetzt ist er erledigt *(ugs.)*. *See also* **safety curtain. 2.** *v. t.* **~ a window** an einem Fenster Vorhänge/einen Vorhang aufhängen *od.* anbringen; **~ off** mit einem Vorhang abteilen; durch einen Vorhang abtrennen

curtain: ~-call *n.* Vorhang, *der;* **get/take a ~-call** einen Vorhang bekommen/vor den Vorhang treten; **~-hook** *n.* Gardinenhaken, *der;* **~ lecture** *n.* Gardinenpredigt, *die;* **~ rail** *n.* Gardinenstange, *die;* **~-raiser** *n.* [kurzes] Vorspiel; *(fig.)* Auftakt, *der;* **~-ring** *n.* Gardinenring, *der;* **~-rod** *n.* Gardinenstange, *die;* **~-runner** *n.* Gardinenröllchen, *das;* **~ track** Gardinenleiste, *die*

curtly ['kɜ:tlɪ] *adv.* kurz ‹*sprechen*›; knapp ‹*schreiben, antworten*›

curtsy (curtsey) ['kɜ:tsɪ] **1.** *n.* Knicks, *der;* **make** *or* **drop a ~ to sb.** vor jmdm. einen Knicks machen. **2.** *v. i.* **~ to sb.** vor jmdm. knicksen *od.* einen Knicks machen

curvaceous [kɜ:'veɪʃəs] *adj. (coll.)* kurvenreich *(ugs.)*; **a ~ figure** eine üppige Figur

curvature ['kɜ:vətʃə(r)] *n.* Krümmung, *die;* **~ of the spine** Rückgratverkrümmung, *die*

curve [kɜ:v] **1.** *v. t.* krümmen. **2.** *v. i.* ‹*Straße, Fluß:*› *(once)* eine Biegung machen; *(repeatedly)* sich winden; ‹*Horizont:*› sich krümmen; ‹*Linie:*› einen Bogen machen *od.* beschreiben; **the road ~s round the town** die Straße macht einen Bogen um die Stadt. **3.** *n.* **a)** Kurve, *die;* **b)** *(surface; ~d form or thing) (of vase, figure)* Rundung, *die;* **there's a ~ in the road/river** die Straße/der Fluß macht einen Bogen *od.* eine Biegung

curved [kɜ:vd] *adj.* krumm; gebogen; gekrümmt ‹*Horizont, Raum, Linie*›

cushion ['kʊʃn] **1.** *n.* **a)** Kissen, *das;* **b)** *(for protection)* Kissen, *das;* Polster, *das;* **c)** *(of billiard-table)* Bande, *die;* **d)** *(of hovercraft)* Luftkissen, *das.* **2.** *v. t.* **a)** [aus]polstern ‹*Stuhl*›; **~ sb. against sth.** *(fig.)* jmdn. gegen etw. schützen; **~ed seats** Polsterstühle; **b)** *(absorb)* dämpfen ‹*Aufprall, Stoß*›

cushy ['kʊʃɪ] *adj. (coll.)* bequem; gemütlich; **a ~ job** *or* **number** ein ruhiger Job

cuss [kʌs] *(coll.)* **1.** *n.* **a)** *(curse)* Fluch, *der;* Beschimpfung, *die;* **sb. does not give** *or* **care a ~:** jmdm. ist es vollkommen schnuppe *(ugs.)*; **he/it is not worth a tinker's ~:** er/es ist keinen Pfifferling *od.* roten Heller wert *(ugs.)*; **b)** *(usu. derog.: person)* Kerl, *der (ugs.)*. **2.** *v. i.* fluchen; schimpfen. **3.** *v. t.* verfluchen; beschimpfen

cussed ['kʌsɪd] *adj. (coll.)* **a)** *(perverse, obstinate)* stur *(ugs.)*; **b)** *(cursed)* verdammt *(ugs.)*; verflixt *(ugs.)*

cussedness ['kʌsɪdnɪs] *n., no pl.* Sturheit, *die;* **from sheer ~:** aus reiner Sturheit

'**cuss-word** *n. (Amer.)* Fluch, *der;* Verwünschung, *die*

custard ['kʌstəd] *n.* **a)** **~ [pudding]** ≈ Vanillepudding, *der;* **b)** *(sauce)* ≈ Vanillesoße, *die*

custard: ~-apple *n.* Zimt-, Rahmapfel, *der;* **~-'pie** *n. (pie) Kuchen mit einer Füllung aus Vanillepudding; (in comedy)* Sahnetorte, *die;* **~-pie comedy** Slapstickkomödie, *die;* **~ powder** *n.* Vanillesoßenpulver, *das*

custodial [kʌs'təʊdɪəl] *adj.* **~ sentence** Freiheitsstrafe, *die*

custodian [kʌs'təʊdɪən] *n. (of public building, of prisoner)* Wärter, *der*/Wärterin, *die;* Aufseher, *der*/Aufseherin, *die; (of park, museum)* Wächter, *der*/Wächterin, *die; (of valuables, traditions, culture, place)* Hüter, *der*/Hüterin, *die; (of child)* Vormund, *der*

custody ['kʌstədɪ] *n.* **a)** *(guardianship, care)* Obhut, *die;* **be in the ~ of sb.** unter jmds. Obhut *(Dat.)* stehen; **put** *or* **place sb./sth. in sb.'s ~:** jmdn./etw. in jmds. Obhut *(Akk.)* geben; **the child is in the ~ of his uncle** sein Onkel hat die Vormundschaft über *od.* für das Kind; **in safe ~:** in sicherer Obhut; **the mother was given** *or* **awarded [the] ~ of the children** die Kinder wurden der Mutter zugesprochen; **b)** *(imprisonment)* **[be] in ~:** in Haft [sein]; **take sb. into ~:** jmdn. verhaften *od.* festnehmen

custom ['kʌstəm] *n.* **a)** Brauch, *der;* Sitte, *die;* **it was his ~ to smoke a cigar after dinner** er pflegte nach dem Essen eine Zigarre zu rauchen; er rauchte gewöhnlich eine Zigarre nach dem Essen; **b)** *in pl. (duty on imports)* Zoll, *der;* **[the] C~s** *(government department)* der Zoll; **c)** *(Law)* Gewohnheitsrecht, *das;* **d)** *(business patronage, regular dealings)* Kundschaft, *die (veralt.)*; **I shall withdraw my ~ from that shop** ich werde in dem Laden nicht mehr kaufen; **we should like to have your ~:** wir hätten Sie gern zum/zur *od.* als Kunden/Kundin; **e)** *(regular customers)* Kundschaft, *die*

customarily ['kʌstəmərɪlɪ] *adv.* in der Regel; üblicherweise

customary ['kʌstəmərɪ] *adj.* **a)** üblich; **b)** *(Law)* gewohnheitsmäßig; Gewohnheits-

custom: ~-built *adj.* spezial[an]gefertigt; **~-built clothes** *(Amer.)* maßgeschneiderte Kleidung; **~ clothes** *n. (Amer.) see* **~-built**

customer ['kʌstəmə(r)] *n.* **a)** Kunde, *der*/Kundin, *die; (of restaurant)* Gast, *der; (of theatre)* Besucher, *der*/Besucherin, *die; (of library)* Benutzer, *der*/Benutzerin, *die;* **b)** *(coll.: person)* Kerl, *der (ugs.)*; **a queer/an awkward ~:** ein schwieriger Kunde *(ugs.)*

'**custom-house** *n.* Zollamt, *das*

customize (customise) ['kʌstəmaɪz] *v. t.* speziell anfertigen; *(alter)* umbauen

'**custom-made** *adj.* spezial[an]gefertigt; maßgeschneidert ‹*Kleidung*›

customs: ~ clearance *n.* Zollabfertigung, *die;* **get ~ clearance for sth.** etw. zollamtlich abfertigen lassen; **~ declaration** *n.* Zollerklärung, *die;* **~ duty** *n.* Zoll, *der;* **~ inspection** *n.* Zollkontrolle, *die;* **~ officer** *n.* Zollbeamter, *der*/-beamtin, *die;* **~ union** *n.* Zollunion, *die*

cut [kʌt] **1.** *v. t.,* **-tt-, cut a)** *(penetrate, wound)* schneiden; **~ one's finger/leg** sich *(Dat. od. Akk.)* in den Finger/ins Bein schneiden; **he ~ himself on broken glass** er hat sich an einer Glasscherbe geschnitten; **he ~ his head open** er schlug sich *(Dat.)* den Kopf auf; **the icy blasts that ~ one to the marrow** *(fig.)* die eisigen Winde, die einem durch und durch *od.* durch Mark und Bein gehen; **the remark ~ him to the quick** *(fig.)* die Bemerkung traf ihn ins Mark; **b)** *(divide) (with knife)* schneiden; durchschneiden ‹*Seil*›; *(with axe)* durchhacken; **~ sth. in half/two/three** etw. halbieren/zweiteilen/dreiteilen; **~ sth. [in]to pieces** etw. in Stücke schneiden/hacken; **~ one's ties** *or* **links** alle Verbindungen abbrechen; alle Brücken hinter sich *(Dat.)* abbrechen; **~ no ice with sb.** *(fig. sl.)* keinen Eindruck auf jmdn. machen; jmdm. nicht imponieren *(ugs.)*; **~ the knot** *(fig.)* das Problem lösen; **c)** *(detach, reduce)* abschneiden; schneiden, stutzen ‹*Hecke*›; mähen ‹*Getreide, Gras*›; **~ (p.p.) flowers** Schnittblumen; **~ one's nails** sich *(Dat.)* die Nägel schneiden; **d)** *(shape, fashion)* schleifen ‹*Glas, Edelstein, Kristall*›; hauen, schlagen ‹*Stufen*›; treiben ‹*Tunnel*›; einhauen ‹*Inschrift*›; **~ a key** einen Schlüssel feilen *od.* anfertigen; **~ figures in wood/stone** Figuren aus Holz schnitzen/aus Stein hauen; **~ a record** eine Schallplatte schneiden; **e)** *(meet and cross)* ‹*Straße, Linie, Kreis:*› schneiden; **the two lines ~ one another at right angles** die beiden Linien schneiden sich im rechten Winkel; **f)** *(fig.: renounce, refuse to recognize)* schneiden; **~ sb. dead** jmdn. wie Luft behandeln; **g)** *(carve)* [auf]schneiden ‹*Fleisch, Geflügel*›; abschneiden ‹*Scheibe*›; **~ (p.p.) loaf** *(Brit. dated)* Schnittbrot, *das;* **h)** *(reduce)* senken ‹*Preise*›; verringern, einschränken ‹*Menge, Produktion*›; mindern ‹*Qualität*›; drosseln ‹*Tempo, Produktion*›; kürzen ‹*Ausgaben, Lohn*›; verkürzen ‹*Arbeitszeit, Urlaub*›; *(cease, stop)* einstellen ‹*Dienstleistungen, Lieferungen*›; abstellen ‹*Strom*›; *(coll.)* aufhören mit ‹*Tätigkeit*›; **these scenes were ~ by the censor** diese Szenen hat die Zensur herausgeschnitten; **i)** *see* **figure 1d**; **j)** *(absent oneself from)* schwänzen ‹*Schule, Unterricht*›; **k) ~ a loss** der Sache *(Dat.)* ein Ende machen *(ehe der Schaden noch größer wird)*; **~ one's losses** höherem Verlust vorbeugen; **l) ~ sth. short** *(lit. or fig.: interrupt, terminate)* etwas abbrechen; **the war ~ short his career** der Krieg hat seine Karriere vorzeitig beendet; **~ sb. short** jmdn. unterbrechen; *(impatiently)* jmdm. ins Wort fallen; **to ~ a long story short** der langen Rede kurzer Sinn; **m)** *(Cards)* abheben; **~ the pack [of cards]** [die Karten] abheben; **n) ~ a tooth** einen Zahn bekommen; **~ one's teeth on sth.** *(fig.)* sich *(Dat.)* die ersten Sporen an etw. *(Dat.)* *od.* mit etw. verdienen; **o) be ~ and dried** genau festgelegt *od.* abgesprochen sein; **her opinions are ~ and dried** ihre Ansichten sind unverrückbar; **p)** *(Cricket, Tennis)* [an]schneiden ‹*Ball*›; **q)** *(Cinemat.)* schneiden; cutten; **r) half ~** *(sl.)* angetrunken. *See also* **cloth a; corner 1a; eye-tooth; [2]fine 1g. 2.** *v. i.,* **-tt-, cut a)** ‹*Messer, Schwert usw.:*› schneiden; ‹*Papier, Tuch, Käse:*› sich schneiden lassen; ~ **into a cake** einen Kuchen anschneiden; ~ **both ways** *(fig.)* ein zweischneidiges Schwert sein *(fig.)*; **b)** *(cross, intersect)* sich schneiden; **c)** *(pass)* ~ **through** *or* **across the field/park** [quer] über das Feld/durch den Park gehen; ~ **across sth.** *(fig.)* sich über etw. *(Akk.)* hinwegsetzen; **d)** *(Cinemat.) (stop the cameras)* abbrechen; *(go quickly to another shot)* überblenden (**to** zu); **the film director cried '~!'** der Regisseur rief: „Schnitt!" *od.* „aus!"; **e)** *(sl.: run)* ~ **along** sich auf die Socken machen *(ugs.)*; ~ **and run** abhauen *(ugs.)*. *See also* **loose 1 a. 3.** *n.* **a)** *(act of cutting)* Schnitt, *der;* **b)** *(stroke, blow) (with knife)* Schnitt, *der; (with sword, whip)* Hieb, *der; (injury)* Schnittwunde, *die;* **the ~ and thrust of politics** *(fig.)* das Spannungsfeld der Politik; **the ~ and thrust of debate** *(fig.)* die Hitze der Debatte; **c)** *(reduction) (in wages)* Kürzung, *die; (in expenditure, budget)* Kürzung, *die;* Streichung, *die;* Einsparung, *die; (in prices)* Senkung, *die; (in time, working hours, holiday, etc.)* Verkürzung, *die; (in services)* Verringerung, *die; (in production, output, etc.)* Einschränkung, *die; (in supply)* Einstellung, *die; (in quality)* Minderung, *die;* **make the ~** *(Sport, esp. Golf)* sich für den weiteren Wettkampf qualifizieren; **d)** *(wounding act or utterance)* Seitenhieb, *der* (**at** gegen); Affront, *der (geh.)*; **the unkindest ~ of all** der schlimmste Schlag; **e)** *(of meat)* Stück, *das;* **f)** *see* **wood-cut; g)** *(coll.: commission, share)* Anteil, *der;* **h)** *(way thing is ~) (of gem)* Schliff, *der; (of hair: style)* [Haar]schnitt, *der;* Frisur, *die; (of clothes)* Schnitt, *der;* **be a ~ above [the rest]** [den anderen] um einiges überlegen sein; **i)** *(in play, book, etc.)* Streichung, *die; (in film)* Schnitt, *der;* **make ~s** Streichungen/Schnitte vornehmen; **j)** *(channel made for river)* Rinne, *die;* Einschnitt, *der. See also* **jib a; short cut**

~ **'away** *v. t. see* ~ **off a**

~ **'back 1.** *v. t.* **a)** *(reduce)* einschränken ‹*Produktion*›; verringern ‹*Investitionen*›; **b)** *(prune)* stutzen. **2.** *v. i.* **a)** *(reduce)* ~ **back on sth.** etw. einschränken; **b)** *(Cinemat.)* zurückblenden. *See also* **cut-back**

~ **'down 1.** *v. t.* **a)** *(fell)* fällen; **b)** *(kill)* töten; ~ **sb. down with a sword** jmdn. mit dem Schwert erschlagen *od. (geh.)* niederstrecken; **c)** *(reduce)* einschränken; ~ **an article down** einen Artikel zusammenstreichen *od.* kürzen; ~ **sb. down to size** *(fig.)* jmdn. auf seinen Platz verweisen. **2.** *v. i.* *(reduce)* ~ **down on sth.** etw. einschränken; ~ **down on tobacco** den Tabakverbrauch einschränken; ~ **down on clothes** die Ausgaben für die Garderobe einschränken

~ **'in 1.** *v. i.* **a)** *(come in abruptly, interpose)* sich einschalten; unterbrechen; ~ **in on sb./sth.** jmdn./etw. unterbrechen; **b)** *(after overtaking)* schneiden; ~ **in in front of sb.** jmdn. schneiden; **c)** *(take dance-partner from another)* ~ **in [on sb.]** [jmdn.] abklatschen; **d)** *(switch itself on)* ‹*Motor usw.:*› sich einschalten. **2.** *v. t.* *(give share of profit to)* beteiligen ‹*Komplizen*›

~ **'off** *v. t.* **a)** *(remove by ~ting)* abschneiden; abtrennen; *(with axe etc.)* abschlagen; **b)** *(interrupt, make unavailable)* abschneiden ‹*Zufuhr*›; streichen ‹*Zuschuß*›; abstellen ‹*Strom, Gas, Wasser*›; unterbrechen ‹*Telefongespräch, Sprecher am Telefon*›; **c)** *(isolate)* abschneiden; **be ~ off by the snow/tide** durch den Schnee/die Flut [von der Außenwelt] abgeschnitten sein; **d)** *(prevent, block)* abschneiden; **their retreat was ~ off** ihnen wurde der Rückzug abgeschnitten; **e)** *(exclude from contact with others)* ~ **sb. off from friends/the outside world** jmdn. von seinen Freunden trennen/von der Außenwelt abschneiden; ~ **oneself off** sich absondern; **f)** *(disinherit)* enterben; ~ **sb. off with a shilling** jmdn. mit einem Apfel und einem Ei abspeisen *(ugs.)*. *See also* **cut-off**

~ **'out 1.** *v. t.* **a)** *(remove by cutting)* ausschneiden; ~ **sth. out of sth.** etw. aus etw. ausschneiden; **b)** *(omit)* [heraus]streichen; **c)** *(stop doing or using)* aufhören mit; ~ **out cigarettes/alcohol/drugs** aufhören, Zigaretten zu rauchen/Alkohol zu trinken/Tabletten zu nehmen; ~ **it** *or* **that out** *(coll.)* hör/hört auf damit!; laß/laßt das sein!; **d)** *(defeat)* ausstechen *(ugs.)* ‹*Rivalen, Konkurrenten, Gegner*›; **e)** *(shape)* zuschneiden ‹*Stoff, Kleid, Leder*›; **f)** *(disconnect electrically)* ausschalten ‹*Motor, Licht*›; abstellen ‹*Motor*›; abschalten ‹*Strom*›; **g)** *(make suitable)* **be ~ out for sth.** für etw. geeignet sein; **he was not ~ out to be a teacher** er war nicht zum Lehrer gemacht; er taugte nicht zum Lehrer; **Peter and Susan seem to be ~ out for each other** Peter und Susan sind füreinander wie geschaffen. **2.** *v. i.* *(cease functioning)* ‹*Motor:*› aussetzen; ‹*Gerät:*› sich abschalten. *See also* **cut-out**

~ **'up 1.** *v. t.* **a)** *(~ in pieces)* zerschneiden; in Stücke schneiden ‹*Fleisch, Gemüse*›; *(chop)* zerhacken; **b)** *(injure)* verletzen; *(fig.: criticize)* zerreißen; ~ **up the enemy** den Feind vernichten; **be ~ up about sth.** *(fig.)* zutiefst betroffen über etw. *(Akk.)* sein. **2.** *v. i.* ~ **up rough** Krach schlagen *(ugs.)*; Radau machen *(ugs.)*

cutaneous [kjuːˈteɪnɪəs] *adj.* Haut-; kutan *(fachspr.)*

cut: ~away *adj.* Schnitt-; **~away model** Schnittmodell, *das;* **~-back** *n. (reduction)* Kürzung, *die; (Cinemat.)* Rückblende, *die*

cute [kjuːt] *adj. (coll.)* **a)** *(Amer.: attractive)* süß, niedlich ‹*Kind, Mädchen*›; entzückend ‹*Stadt, Haus*›; **b)** *(shrewd)* schlau; gerissen; *(ingenious)* raffiniert ‹*Gerät*›; einfallsreich ‹*Person*›; pfiffig ‹*Erklärung*›

cut 'glass *n.* Kristall[glas], *das*

'cut-glass *adj.* Kristall-

cuticle [ˈkjuːtɪkl] *n.* Epidermis, *die (fachspr.)*; Oberhaut, *die; (of nail)* Nagelhaut, *die*

'cuticle-remover *n.* Nagelhautentferner, *der*

cutie [ˈkjuːtɪ] *n. (sl.)* **a)** *(woman)* Süße, *die;* **b)** *(usu. joc. : man)* irrer Typ *(ugs.)*

cutlass [ˈkʌtləs] *n.* **a)** *(Hist.)* Entersäbel, *der;* **b)** *see* **machete**

cutler [ˈkʌtlə(r)] *n.* Messerschmied, *der*

cutlery [ˈkʌtlərɪ] *n.* Besteck, *das*

cutlet [ˈkʌtlɪt] *n.* **a)** *(of mutton or lamb)* Kotelett, *das;* **b) veal ~:** Frikandeau, *das;* **c)** *(minced meat etc. in shape of ~)* Hacksteak, *das;* **nut/cheese/potato ~:** *aus Nüssen/Käse/Kartoffeln hergestelltes Gericht in Form eines Schnitzels od. Koteletts*

cut: ~-off *n.* **a)** Trennung, *die;* **~-off point** Trennungslinie, *die;* **b)** *as tech. term* Ausschaltmechanismus, *der;* Ausschaltung, *die;* **~-out** *n. (Electr.)* Unterbrecher, *der; (figure ~ out of material)* Ausschneidefigur, *die;* **~-out box** *(Amer.) see* **fuse-box; ~-price** *adj.* herabgesetzt; **~-price goods** Waren zu herabgesetzten Preisen; **~-price offer** Billigangebot, *das;* **~-rate** *adj.* verbilligt; herabgesetzt

cutter [ˈkʌtə(r)] *n.* **a)** *(person) (of cloth)* Zuschneider, *der*/-schneiderin, *die; (of stones)* Steinmetz, *der; (of glass, gems)* Schleifer, *der*/Schleiferin, *die; (of films)* Cutter, *der*/Cutterin, *die;* Schnittmeister, *der*/-meisterin, *die; (miner)* Hauer, *der;* **b)** *(machine)* Schneidmaschine, *die;* Schneidwerkzeug, *das; (rotary cutting tool)* Bohrkrone, *die;* Bohrkopf, *der; (cutting stylus)* Cutter, *der;* **c)** *(Naut.)* Kutter, *der*

'cutthroat 1. *n.* **a)** Strolch, *der; (murderer)* Killer, *der (ugs.)*; **b)** *(Amer.: trout)* Purpurforelle, *die.* **2.** *adj.* **a)** mörderisch, gnadenlos ‹*Wettbewerb*›; **b)** ~ **razor** Rasiermesser, *das*

cutting [ˈkʌtɪŋ] **1.** *adj.* beißend ‹*Bemerkung, Antwort*›; schneidend ‹*Wind*›; ~ **edge** Schneide, *die;* ~ **tool** Schneidewerkzeug, *das.* **2.** *n.* **a)** *(esp. Brit.: from newspaper)* Ausschnitt, *der;* **b)** *(esp. Brit.: excavation for railway, road etc.)* Einschnitt, *der;* **c)** *(of plant)* Ableger, *der*

cuttle[fish] [ˈkʌtl(fɪʃ)] *n.* Tintenfisch, *der;* Sepia, *die (fachspr.)*

c.v. *abbr.* **curriculum vitae**

c.w.o. *abbr.* **cash with order** Barzahlung *od.* Kasse bei Auftragserteilung

cwt. *abbr.* **hundredweight** ≈ Ztr.

cyan [ˈsaɪən] **1.** *adj.* grünstichig blau. **2.** *n.* Cyanblau, *das*

cyanide [ˈsaɪənaɪd] *n.* Cyanid, *das*

cyanogen [saɪˈænədʒən] *n. (Chem.)* Cyan, *das*

cybernetics [saɪbəˈnetɪks] *n., no pl.* Kybernetik, *die*

cyclamen [ˈsɪkləmən] *n. (Bot.)* Alpenveilchen, *das;* Zyklamen, *das (fachspr.)*

cycle [ˈsaɪkl] **1.** *n.* **a)** *(recurrent period)* Zyklus, *der; (period of completion)* Turnus, *der;* ~ **of the seasons** Jahreszyklus, *der;* ~ **per second** *(Phys., Electr.)* Schwingung pro Sekunde; Hertz, *das;* **b)** *(recurring series)* Kreislauf, *der; (complete set or series)* Zyklus, *der;* **c)** *(bicycle)* Rad, *das.* **2.** *v. i.* radfahren; mit dem [Fahr]rad fahren

cycle: ~-race *n.* Radrennen, *das;* **~-track** *n.* Rad[fahr]weg, *der; (for racing)* Radrennbahn, *die;* **~way** *see* **~-track**

cyclic [ˈsaɪklɪk], **cyclical** [ˈsaɪklɪkl] *adj.*, **cyclically** [ˈsaɪklɪkəlɪ] *adv.* zyklisch

cyclist [ˈsaɪklɪst] *n.* Radfahrer, *der*/-fahrerin, *die*

cyclo-cross *n.* Querfeldeinrennen, *das*

cyclone [ˈsaɪkləʊn] *n.* *(system of winds)* Tiefdruckgebiet, *das;* Zyklon, *die (fachspr.)*; *(violent hurricane)* Zyklon, *der*

cyclonic [ˈsaɪklɒnɪk] *adj.* Zyklon‹*wind, -stärke*›; ~ **storm** Zyklon, *der*

Cyclops [ˈsaɪklɒps] *n., pl. same or* **~es** *or* **Cyclopes** [saɪˈkləʊpiːz] *(Mythol.)* Zyklop, *der*

cyclotron [ˈsaɪklətrɒn] *n. (Phys.)* Zyklotron, *das*

cygnet [ˈsɪgnɪt] *n.* junger Schwan

cylinder [ˈsɪlɪndə(r)] *n. (also Geom., Motor Veh.)* Zylinder, *der; (of revolver, carding-machine)* Trommel, *die; (for compressed or liquefied gas)* Gasflasche, *die; (of diving-apparatus)* [Sauerstoff]flasche, *die; (of platen press, typewriter, mower)* Walze, *die*

cylinder: ~ block *n.* Motorblock, *der;* **~ head** *n.* Zylinderkopf, *der*

cylindrical [sɪˈlɪndrɪkl] *adj.* zylindrisch; *see also* **projection i**

cymbal [ˈsɪmbl] *n. (Mus.)* Beckenteller, *der;* **~s** Becken *Pl.*

cyme [saɪm] *n. (Bot.)* Trugdolde, *die*

cynic [ˈsɪnɪk] *n.* **a)** Zyniker, *der;* **b) C~** *(Greek philosopher)* Kyniker, *der*

cynical [ˈsɪnɪkl] *adj.* zynisch; bissig ‹*Artikel, Bemerkung, Worte*›; **be ~ about sth.** sich zynisch zu etw. äußern

cynically [ˈsɪnɪkəlɪ] *adv.* zynisch

cynicism [ˈsɪnɪsɪzm] *n.* Zynismus, *der*

cypher *see* **cipher**

cypress [ˈsaɪprɪs] *n.* Zypresse, *die*

Cyprian [ˈsɪprɪən], **Cypriot** [ˈsɪprɪət] **1.** *adjs.* zyprisch; zypriotisch. **2.** *ns.* Zypriot, *der*/Zypriotin, *die;* Zyprer, *der*/Zyprerin, *die*

Cyprus [ˈsaɪprəs] *pr. n.* Zypern *(das)*

Cyrillic [sɪˈrɪlɪk] *adj.* kyrillisch

cyst [sɪst] *n. (Biol., Med.)* Zyste, *die*

cystitis [sɪsˈtaɪtɪs] *n. (Med.)* Zystitis, *die (Med.)*; Blasenentzündung, *die*

cytology [saɪˈtɒlədʒɪ] *n.* Zytologie, *die*

cytoplasm [ˈsaɪtəplæzm] *n. (Biol.)* Zytoplasma, *das*

czar *etc. see* **tsar** *etc.*

Czech [tʃek] **1.** *adj.* tschechisch; **sb. is ~:** jmd. ist Tscheche/Tschechin; *see also* **Eng-**

lish 1. 2. *n.* **a)** *(language)* Tschechisch, *das; see also* **English 2 a; b)** *(person)* Tscheche, *der*/Tschechin, *die*
Czechoslovak [tʃekəʊ'sləʊvæk] *(Hist.) see* Czechoslovakian
Czechoslovakia [tʃekəʊslə'vækɪə] *pr. n. (Hist.)* die Tschechoslowakei
Czechoslovakian [tʃekəʊslə'vækɪən] *(Hist.)* **1.** *adj.* tschechoslowakisch. **2.** *n.* Tschechoslowake, *der*/Tschechoslowakin, *die*
Czech Republic *n.* Tschechische Republik; Tschechien *(das)*

D

D, d [di:] *n., pl.* **Ds** *or* **D's a)** *(letter)* D, d, *das;* **b) D** *(Mus.)* D, d, *das;* **D sharp** dis, Dis, *das;* **D flat** des, Des, *das;* **c)** *(Roman numeral)* D; **d) D** *(Sch., Univ.: mark)* Vier, *die;* **he got a D** er bekam „ausreichend" *od.* eine Vier
D. *abbr.* **a)** *(Amer.)* **Democrat; b) dimensional**
d. *abbr.* **a) daughter** T.; **b) deci-** d; **c) delete** d.; **d) died** gest.; **e)** *(Brit. Hist.)* **penny/pence** d.
'd [d] *(coll.)* = **would, had, should**
DA *abbr. (Amer.)* **District Attorney**
¹dab [dæb] **1.** *n.* **a)** Tupfer, *der;* **b)** *(slight blow, tap)* Klaps, *der; (bird's peck)* Picken, *das;* **c)** *in pl. (Brit. sl.: fingerprints)* Fingerabdrücke *Pl.* **2.** *v. t.,* **-bb- a)** *(press with sponge etc.)* abtupfen; *(press on surface)* **~ sth. on** *or* **against sth.** etw. auf etw. *(Akk.)* tupfen; **b)** *(strike lightly, tap)* **~ sb.** jmdm. einen Klaps geben; **c)** ⟨*Vogel:*⟩ picken. **3.** *v. i.,* **-bb- ~ at sth.** etw. ab- *od.* betupfen
²dab *n. (Zool.)* Kliesche, *die;* Scharbe, *die*
³dab *(Brit. coll.: expert)* **1.** *n.* Könner, *der;* As, *das (ugs.)* **(at** in + *Dat.*). **2.** *adj.* geschickt; **be a ~ hand at cricket/making omelettes** ein As im Kricket/Eierkuchenbacken sein *(ugs.)*
dabble ['dæbl] *v. t.* **a)** *(wet slightly)* befeuchten; *(move in water)* **~ one's feet in the water** mit den Füßen im Wasser planschen; **b)** *(soil, splash)* bespritzen. **2.** *v. i.* *(engage in)* **~ at/in sth.** sich in etw. *(Dat.)* versuchen; in etw. *(Dat.)* dilettieren
dabbler ['dæblə(r)] *n.* Amateur, *der;* Dilettant, *der (abwertend)*
dabchick ['dæbtʃɪk] *n. (Ornith.)* Lappentaucher, *der;* Steißfuß, *der*
dace [deɪs] *n., pl. same (Zool.)* Hasel, *der;* Häsling, *der*
dacha ['dætʃə] *n.* Datscha, *die; (bes. DDR:)* Datsche, *die*
dachshund ['dækshʊnd] *n.* Dackel, *der;* Dachshund, *der (fachspr.)*
dactyl ['dæktɪl] *n. (Pros.)* Daktylus, *der*
dad [dæd] *n. (coll.)* Vater, *der*
Dadaism ['dɑ:dɑ:ɪzm] *n. (Art Hist.)* Dadaismus, *der*
daddy ['dædɪ] *n. (coll.)* **a)** Vati, *der (fam.);* Papi, *der (fam.);* Papa, *der (fam.);* **b)** *(man)* Alte, *der (ugs.);* **c)** *(oldest/most important person)* König, *der (ugs.);* **the ~ of them all** der/die/das Allergrößte *(ugs.)*
daddy-'long-legs *n. sing. (Zool.)* **a)** *(cranefly)* Schnake, *die;* **b)** *(Amer.: harvestman)* Weberknecht, *der;* Kanker, *der*
dado ['deɪdəʊ] *n., pl.* **~s** *or (Amer.)* **~es a)** *(of room-wall)* Sockel, *der;* **b)** *(of column)* Kehle, *die*
daemon ['di:mən] *n.* Dämon, *der*
daffodil ['dæfədɪl] *n.* Gelbe Narzisse; Osterglocke, *die*
daffy ['dæfɪ] *adj. (sl.)* blöd[e] *(ugs.);* dämlich *(ugs.)*
daft [dɑ:ft] *adj.* **a)** *(foolish, wild)* doof *(ugs.);* blöd[e] *(ugs.);* **what a ~ thing to do!** so was Doofes *(ugs.) od.* Blödes *(ugs.)*!; **b)** *(crazy)* verrückt *(ugs.);* übergeschnappt *(ugs.);* **be ~ about sth./sb.** verrückt nach etw./jmdm. sein
dagger ['dægə(r)] *n.* **a)** Dolch, *der;* **be at ~s drawn with sb.** *(fig.)* mit jmdm. auf Kriegsfuß stehen; **look ~s at sb.** jmdn. finster anblicken; jmdm. finstere Blicke zuwerfen; **b)** *(Printing)* Kreuz, *das*
dago ['deɪgəʊ] *n., pl.* **~s** *or* **~es** *(sl. derog.)* **a)** *(Spaniard, Portuguese, Italian)* Welsche, *der (veralt. abwertend);* Kanake, *der (derb abwertend);* **b)** *(any foreigner)* Kanake, *der (derb abwertend)*
daguerreotype [də'gerətaɪp] *n.* Daguerreotypie, *die*
dahlia ['deɪlɪə] *n.* Dahlie, *die*
Dáil [Éireann] [dɔɪl ('eɪrən)] *n. Unterhaus der Republik Irland*
daily ['deɪlɪ] **1.** *adj.* täglich; **~ [news]paper** Tageszeitung, *die;* **the ~ grind [of life]** der Alltagstrott; **on a ~ basis** tageweise. **2.** *adv.* täglich; jeden Tag; *(constantly)* Tag für Tag; täglich. **3.** *n.* **a)** *(newspaper)* Tageszeitung, *die;* **b)** *(Brit. coll.: charwoman)* Reinemachefrau, *die. See also* **bread 1 b; dozen b**
daintily ['deɪntɪlɪ] *adv.* zierlich; anmutig ⟨*gehen, sich bewegen*⟩
daintiness ['deɪntɪnɪs] *n., no pl.* Zierlichkeit, *die; (of movement, manner, etc.)* Anmut, *die*
dainty ['deɪntɪ] **1.** *adj.* **a)** *(of delicate beauty)* zierlich; anmutig ⟨*Bewegung, Person*⟩; zart, fein ⟨*Gesichtszüge*⟩; **b)** *(choice)* delikat, köstlich ⟨*Essen*⟩; **c)** *(having delicate tastes)* empfindsam; feinfühlig.. **2.** *n. (lit. or fig.)* Delikatesse, *die;* Leckerbissen, *der*
dairy ['deərɪ] *n.* **a)** Molkerei, *die;* **b)** *(shop)* Milchladen, *der*
dairy: ~ cattle *n.* Milchvieh, *das;* **~ cream** *n.* [echter] Rahm; [echte] Sahne; **~ farm** *n.* Milchbetrieb, *der;* **~ farmer** *n.* Milchbauer, *der*
dairying ['deərɪɪŋ] *n.* Milchwirtschaft, *die*
dairy: ~maid *n.* Molkereiangestellte, *die;* **~man** ['deərɪmən] *n., pl.* **~men** ['deərɪmən] Milchmann, *der;* **~ produce** *n.,* **~ products** *n. pl.* Molkereiprodukte
dais ['deɪɪs, 'deɪs] *n.* Podium, *das*
daisy ['deɪzɪ] *n.* Gänseblümchen, *das; (oxeye)* Margerite, *die;* **be pushing up [the] daisies** *(fig. sl.)* sich *(Dat.)* die Radieschen von unten ansehen *(salopp); see also* **fresh 1 e**
daisy: ~-chain *n.* Kranz aus Gänseblümchen; **~-wheel** *n.* Typenrad, *das*
dale [deɪl] *n. (literary/N. Engl.)* Tal, *das; see also* **up 2 a**
dalliance ['dælɪəns] *n. (literary)* Tändelei, *die (veralt. geh.)*
dally ['dælɪ] *v. i.* **a)** *(amuse oneself, sport)* **~ with sb.** mit jmdm. spielen *od.* leichtfertig umgehen; *(flirt)* mit jmdm. schäkern *(ugs.) od.* flirten; **~ with an idea** mit einem Gedanken spielen; **b)** *(idle, loiter)* [herum]trödeln *(ugs.);* **~ [over sth.]** mit etw. trödeln *(ugs.)*
Dalmatian [dæl'meɪʃn] *n.* Dalmatiner, *der*
¹dam [dæm] **1.** *n.* **a)** [Stau]damm, *der;* **b)** *(barrier made by beavers)* Damm, *der.* **2.** *v. t.,* **-mm- a)** *(lit. or fig.)* **~ [up/back] sth.** etw. abblocken; **~ [up/back] the flow of words** dem Wortschwall Einhalt gebieten; **~ [up/back] one's feelings** seine Gefühle zurückhalten; **b)** *(furnish or confine with ~)* eindämmen; aufstauen
²dam *n. (Zool.)* Muttertier, *das*
damage ['dæmɪdʒ] **1.** *n.* **a)** *no pl.* Schaden, *der;* **do a lot of ~ to sb./sth.** jmdm./einer Sache großen Schaden zufügen; jmdm. sehr schaden/etw. stark beschädigen; **the ~ is done now** es ist nun einmal passiert; **b)** *no pl. (loss of what is desirable)* **to sb.'s great ~:** zu jmds. großem Leidwesen; **c)** *in pl. (Law)* Schaden[s]ersatz, *der;* **d)** *no pl. (Brit. sl.: cost)* **what's the ~?** was kostet der Spaß? *(ugs.).* **2.** *v. t.* **a)** beschädigen; **smoking can ~ one's health** Rauchen gefährdet die Gesundheit; **b)** *(detract from)* schädigen; **the article ~d his good reputation** der Artikel hat seinem guten Ruf geschadet; **that ~d his chances [of promotion]/his pride** das hat seine [Aufstiegs]chancen geschmälert/seinen Stolz verletzt
damaging ['dæmɪdʒɪŋ] *adj.* schädlich **(to** für)
damask ['dæmәsk] **1.** *n.* **a)** *(material)* Damast, *der;* **b)** *(twilled table-linen)* Damastdecke, *die.* **2.** *adj.* damasten
damask 'rose *n.* Damaszenerrose, *die*
dame [deɪm] *n.* **a) D~** *(Brit.)* Dame *(Titel der weiblichen Träger verschiedener Orden im Ritterstand);* **b) D~** *(literary/poet.: title of woman of rank)* Dame, *die; (title of thing personified as woman)* **D~ Nature** Mutter Natur; **D~ Fortune** Frau Fortuna; **c)** *(arch./poet./joc./Amer. sl.)* Weib, *das;* **d)** *(in pantomime)* komische Alte
damfool ['dæmfu:l] *(coll.)* **1.** *adj.* idiotisch *(ugs.);* blöd *(ugs.);* **~ action/remark** *etc.* Blödsinn, *der (ugs.);* **that was a ~ thing to do!** das war saublöd! *(ugs.).* **2.** *n.* Idiot, *der (ugs.);* Blödmann, *der (salopp)*
dammit ['dæmɪt] *int. (coll.)* verdammt noch mal! *(ugs.);* **as ... as ~:** verdammt ... *(ugs.);* **as near as ~:** jedenfalls so gut wie *(ugs.)*
damn [dæm] **1.** *v. t.* **a)** *(condemn, censure)* verreißen ⟨*Buch, Film, Theaterstück*⟩; **~ with faint praise** durch kühles Lob ablehnen; **b)** *(doom to hell, curse)* verdammen; **c)** *(coll.)* **~ [it], ~ and blast [it]!** verflucht [noch mal]! *(ugs.);* zum Teufel [noch mal]! *(ugs.);* **~ it all!** verdammt noch mal! *(ugs.);* zum Donnerwetter! *(ugs.);* **~ all** *(Brit. sl.)* nicht die Bohne *(ugs.);* **~ you/him!** hol' dich/ihn der Teufel! *(salopp);* **[well,] I'll be** *or* **I'm ~ed** ich werd' verrückt *(ugs.) od.* dreh' durch *(salopp);* **[I'll be** *or* **I'm] ~ed if I know** ich habe nicht die leiseste Ahnung; **[I'll be** *or* **I'm] ~ed if I'll go to meet him** ich werde ihn auf gar keinen Fall *od.* garantiert nicht treffen; **I'm ~ed if I can find it** ich kann es beim besten Willen nicht finden; *see also* **God; d)** *(be the ruin of)* zu Fall bringen. **2.** *n.* **a)** *(curse)* Fluch, *der;* **b) he didn't give** *or* **care a ~ [about it]** ihm war es völlig Wurscht *(ugs.) od.* scheißegal *(salopp);* **I don't give a ~ for that girl** das Mädchen ist mir völlig schnuppe *(ugs.) od.* Wurscht *(ugs.).* **3.** *adj.* verdammt *(ugs.);* Scheiß- *(salopp).* **4.** *adv.* verdammt
damnable ['dæmnəbl] *adj.* gräßlich, scheußlich ⟨*Wetter*⟩; ungeheuerlich ⟨*Lüge, Anschuldigung*⟩; **~ luck** entsetzliches Pech
damnably ['dæmnəblɪ] *adv.* verdammt
damnation [dæm'neɪʃn] **1.** *n.* Verdammnis, *die.* **2.** *int.* verdammt [noch mal]! *(ugs.)*
damned [dæmd] **1.** *adj.* **a)** *(doomed)* verdammt; **b)** *(infernal, unwelcome)* verdammt *(ugs.);* **I can't see a ~ thing in this fog** so'n Mist, ich sehe überhaupt nichts [mehr] bei diesem Nebel *(ugs.);* **I have to walk back in this rain. What a ~ nuisance!** Verdammter Mist! Jetzt muß ich bei dem Regen zurücklaufen! *(ugs.);* **c) do/try one's ~est** sein möglichstes tun. **2.** *adv.* verdammt *(ugs.);* **I should ~ well hope so/think so** das will ich

aber [auch] schwer hoffen *(ugs.)* /stark annehmen. **3.** *n. pl.* **the ~**: die Verdammten
damning ['dæmɪŋ] *adj.* **a)** *(expressing severe criticism)* vernichtend ‹*Urteil, Kritik, Worte*›; **b)** *(that proves guilt)* belastend ‹*Beweise*›
Damocles ['dæməkli:z] *pr. n.* Damokles *(der)*; **sword of ~**: Damoklesschwert, *das*
damp [dæmp] **1.** *adj.* feucht; **a ~ squib** *(fig.)* ein Reinfall. **2.** *v.t.* **a)** befeuchten; [ein]sprengen ‹*Wäsche*›; **b)** *(stifle, extinguish)* dämpfen ‹*Lärm*›; **~ [down] a fire** ein Feuer ersticken; **c)** *(Mus., Phys.)* dämpfen; **d)** *(discourage, depress)* dämpfen ‹*Eifer, Begeisterung*›; **~ sb.'s spirits** jmdm. den Mut nehmen. **3.** *n. (moisture)* Feuchtigkeit, *die*
'**damp course** *see* **damp-proof**
dampen ['dæmpn] *see* **damp 2 a, d**
damper ['dæmpə(r)] *n.* **a)** *(sth. that checks or depresses)* **put a ~ on sth.** einer Sache *(Dat.)* einen Dämpfer aufsetzen; **his presence put a ~ on us** seine Anwesenheit dämpfte unsere Stimmung; **b)** *(Mus.)* Dämpfer, *der;* **c)** *(in vehicle)* Stoßdämpfer, *der;* **d)** *(in flue)* Luftklappe, *die*
dampness ['dæmpnɪs] *n. no pl.* Feuchtigkeit, *die;* **~ in the air** Luftfeuchtigkeit, *die*
'**damp-proof** *adj.* feuchtigkeitsbeständig; **~ course** Sperrschicht, *die (gegen aufsteigende Bodenfeuchtigkeit)*
damsel ['dæmzl] *n. (arch./literary)* Maid, *die (veralt.)*; **a ~ in distress** *(joc.)* eine hilflose junge Dame
damson ['dæmzn] *n.* **a)** *(fruit)* Haferpflaume, *die;* **b)** *(tree)* Haferpflaumenbaum, *der*
damson 'plum *n.* große Haferpflaume
dance [dɑ:ns] **1.** *v.i.* **a)** tanzen; **~ to sb.'s tune** *(fig.)* nach jmds. Pfeife tanzen; **b)** *(jump about, skip)* herumtanzen; **~ about in agony/with rage** vor Schmerzen/Zorn rasen; **~ for joy** vor Freude an die Decke springen; einen Freudentanz aufführen; **c)** *(bob up and down)* tanzen; **the boat was dancing on the waves** das Boot tanzte *od.* schaukelte auf den Wellen. **2.** *v.t.* **a)** tanzen; **~ attendance on sb.** *(fig.)* jmdn. vorn und hinten bedienen *(ugs.)*; um jmdn. herumscharwenzeln *(ugs. abwertend)*; **b)** *(move up and down, dandle)* schaukeln. **3.** *n.* **a)** Tanz, *der;* **lead sb. a [merry] ~** *(fig.)* jmdn. [schön] an der Nase herumführen; **b)** *(party)* Tanzveranstaltung, *die; (private)* Tanzparty, *die;* **c)** *(tune in ~ rhythm)* Tanz, *der;* **light ~ music** leichte Tanzmusik; **d) St. Vitus's ~**: Veitstanz, *der*
dance: ~-band *n.* Tanzkapelle, *die;* **~-floor** *n.* Tanzfläche, *die;* **~-hall** *n.* Tanzsaal, *der*
dancer ['dɑ:nsə(r)] *n.* Tänzer, *der*/Tänzerin, *die*
dancing ['dɑ:nsɪŋ]: **~-girl** *n.* Tänzerin, *die;* **~-master** *n.* Tanzlehrer, *der;* **~-partner** *n.* Tanzpartner, *der*/-partnerin, *die;* **~-step** *n.* Tanzschritt, *der*
dandelion ['dændɪlaɪən] *n.* Löwenzahn, *der; (with seed-head)* Pusteblume, *die (Kinderspr.)*
dander ['dændə(r)] *n. (coll.)* Rage, *die (ugs.)*; **get one's/sb.'s ~ up** in Rage kommen *(ugs.)*/jmdn. in Rage bringen *(ugs.)*
dandify ['dændɪfaɪ] *v.t.* herausputzen
dandle ['dændl] *v.t.* schaukeln
dandruff ['dændrʌf] *n.* [Kopf]schuppen *Pl.*
dandy ['dændɪ] **1.** *n. (person)* Dandy, *der (geh.)*; Geck, *der (abwertend)*; Stutzer, *der (veralt. abwertend)*. **2.** *adj. (coll.)* **[fine and] ~**: prima *(ugs.)*
Dane [deɪn] *n.* Däne, *der*/Dänin, *die*
danger ['deɪndʒə(r)] *n.* Gefahr, *die;* **a ~ to sb./sth.** eine Gefahr für jmdn./etw.; **'~!'** „Vorsicht!"; *(stronger)* „Lebensgefahr!"; **there is [a/the] ~ of war/disease** es besteht Kriegs-/Seuchengefahr; **[a] ~ of invasion** die Gefahr einer Invasion; **in ~**: in Gefahr; **put sb. in ~**: jmdn. in Gefahr bringen; **in ~ of one's life/of death** in Lebensgefahr/Todesgefahr; **be in ~ of doing sth.** ‹*Person:*› Gefahr laufen, etw. zu tun; ‹*Sache:*› drohen, etw. zu tun; **out of ~**: außer Gefahr
danger: ~ level *n.* Gefahrengrenze, *die;* **~ list** *n.* **be on/off the ~ list** in/außer Lebensgefahr sein; **~ money** *n.* Gefahrenzulage, *die*
dangerous ['deɪndʒərəs] *adj.* gefährlich; **~ to health** gesundheitsgefährdend
dangerously ['deɪndʒərəslɪ] *adv.* gefährlich; **he drives ~**: er hat einen gefährlichen Fahrstil; **he's ~ overweight** er hat gefährliches Übergewicht
dangle ['dæŋgl] **1.** *v.i.* baumeln (**from** an + *Dat.*). **2.** *v.t.* baumeln lassen; **~ [the prospect of] sth. in front of sb.** *(fig.)* jmdm. etw. [als Anreiz] in Aussicht stellen
Danish ['deɪnɪʃ] **1.** *adj.* dänisch; **sb. is ~**: jmd. ist Däne/Dänin; *see also* **English 1. 2.** *n.* Dänisch, *das; see also* **English 2 a**
Danish: ~ 'blue *n.* dänischer Blauschimmelkäse; Danablu ®, *der;* **~ 'pastry** *n.* Plunderstück, *das*
dank [dæŋk] *adj.* feucht
Danube ['dænju:b] *pr. n.* Donau, *die*
daphne ['dæfnɪ] *n. (Bot.)* Seidelbast, *der*
dapper ['dæpə(r)] *adj.* *(neat)* adrett; schmuck *(veralt.)*; *(sprightly)* munter
dapple ['dæpl] *v.t.* [be]sprenkeln
dappled ['dæpld] *adj.* gesprenkelt; gefleckt ‹*Pferd, Kuh*›
dapple-'grey 1. *adj.* **~ mare** Apfelschimmelstute, *die.* **2.** *n.* Apfelschimmel, *der*
Darby and Joan [dɑ:bɪ ən 'dʒəʊn] *n., pl.* **Darbies and Joans** *treues, altes Ehepaar;* ≈ Philemon und Baucis *(geh.)*
Darby and 'Joan club *n. (Brit.)* Seniorenclub, *der*
dare [deə(r)] **1.** *v.t.*, *pres.* **he ~** *or* **~s**, *neg.* **~ not**, *(coll.)* **~n't** [deənt] **a)** *(venture)* [es] wagen; sich *(Akk.)* trauen; **if you ~ [to] give away the secret** wenn du es wagst, das Geheimnis zu verraten; **we didn't ~ [to] go any further** wir wagten [es] nicht *od.* trauten uns nicht, noch weiter zu gehen; **we ~ not/~d not** *or (coll.)* **didn't ~ tell him the truth** wir wagen/wagten [es] nicht *od.* trauen/trauten uns nicht, ihm die Wahrheit zu sagen; **you wouldn't ~**: das wagst du nicht; du traust dich nicht; **just you ~!** untersteh dich!; das versuch mal! *(ugs.)*; **don't you ~!** untersteh dich!; wehe!; **how ~ you [do ...]?** wie kannst du es wagen[, ... zu tun]?; **how ~ you!** was fällt dir ein!; *(formal)* was erlauben Sie sich!; **I ~ say** *(supposing)* ich nehme an; *(confirming)* das glaube ich gern; **b)** *(attempt)* wagen ‹*Aufstieg, Flucht*›; sich wagen an (+ *Akk.*) ‹*Projekt, Berg*›; *(take the risk of)* riskieren; herausfordern ‹*Zorn der Götter*›; **c)** *(challenge)* herausfordern; **~ sb. to do sth.** jmdn. dazu aufstacheln, etw. zu tun; **I ~ you!** trau dich!; **I ~ you to** *or* **I bet you ~n't call the boss by his first name** wetten, daß du dich nicht traust, den Chef beim Vornamen zu rufen? **2.** *n. (act of daring)* **do sth. for/as a ~**: etw. als Mutprobe tun; *(challenge)* **Go on! It's a ~!** Los! Sei kein Frosch!
'**daredevil** *n.* Draufgänger, *der*/-gängerin, *die*
daren't [deənt] *(coll.)* = **dare not**
daring ['deərɪŋ] **1.** *adj. (bold)* kühn; waghalsig ‹*Kunststück, Tat*›; *(fearless)* wagemutig. **2.** *n.* Kühnheit, *die*
daringly ['deərɪŋlɪ] *adv. (boldly)* kühn; *(fearlessly)* wagemutig
dark [dɑ:k] **1.** *adj.* **a)** *(without light)* dunkel; dunkel, finster ‹*Nacht, Haus, Straße*›; *(gloomy)* düster; dunkel, finster ‹*Wolke*›; **b)** dunkel ‹*Farbe*›; *(brown-complexioned)* dunkelhäutig; *(dark-haired)* dunkelhaarig; **~-blue/-brown/-green** *etc.* dunkelblau/-braun/-grün *usw.*; *see also* **¹blue 2 e**; **c)** *(evil)* finster; übel ‹*Zauber, Ruf, Fluch*›; düster ‹*Drohung, Bedeutung*›; furchtbar ‹*Grausamkeiten*›; **d)** *(cheerless)* finster; düster ‹*Bild*›; *(sad)* düster ‹*Stimmung, Gedanke*›; *(frowning)* finster; **don't always look on the ~ side of things** sieh doch nicht immer alles so schwarz *od.* düster; **e)** *(obscure)* dunkel; schwierig ‹*Frage*›; **he's a ~ one as far as his plans are concerned** er ist so verschwiegen, was seine Pläne anbelangt; **keep sth./it ~**: etw./es geheimhalten (**from** vor + *Dat.*); **be in ~est Africa** im tiefsten *od.* finstersten Afrika sein. **2.** *n.* **a)** *(absence of light)* Dunkel, *das;* **in the ~**: im Dunkeln; **b)** *no art. (nightfall)* Einbruch der Dunkelheit; **c) the ~** *(fig.: lack of knowledge)* **keep sb./be [kept] in the ~ about/as to sth.** jmdn. über etw. *(Akk.)* im dunkeln lassen/über etw. *(Akk.)* im dunkeln gelassen werden; **a leap in the ~**: ein Sprung ins Ungewisse; **it was a shot in the ~**: es war aufs Geratewohl geraten/versucht
'**Dark Ages** *n. pl.* [frühes] Mittelalter
darken ['dɑ:kn] **1.** *v.t.* **a)** verdunkeln; **the sun had ~ed her skin** die Sonne hatte ihre Haut gebräunt; **b)** *(fig.)* verdüstern; verfinstern ‹*Miene*›; **he was told never to ~ the door of that house again** man sagte ihm, er solle sich in diesem Hause nie wieder blicken lassen. **2.** *v.i.* **a)** ‹*Zimmer:*› dunkel werden; ‹*Wolken, Himmel:*› sich verfinstern; **the day ~ed** es wurde dunkel; **b)** *(fig.)* sich verfinstern
dark: ~ 'glasses *n. pl.* dunkle Brille; **~-haired** *adj.* dunkelhaarig; **~ 'horse** *n.* unbekanntes Pferd; *(fig.: little-known yet successful person)* [erfolgreicher] Außenseiter; *(fig.: secretive person)* **be a ~ horse** ein stilles Wasser sein
darkie *see* **darky**
darkish ['dɑ:kɪʃ] *adj.* ziemlich dunkel
darkly ['dɑ:klɪ] *adv.* **a)** dunkel; **b)** *(ominously)* finster; *(obscurely, dimly)* dunkel
darkness ['dɑ:knɪs] *n., no pl.* **a)** *(dark)* Dunkelheit, *die;* **b)** *(wickedness, ominousness)* Finsterkeit, *die;* **the powers of ~**: die Mächte der Finsternis; **c)** *(obscurity)* Dunkelheit, *die*
'**dark-room** *n.* Dunkelkammer, *die*
darky ['dɑ:kɪ] *n. (coll.)* Schwarze, *der/die*
darling ['dɑ:lɪŋ] **1.** *n.* Liebling, *der;* **she was his ~**: sie war seine Liebste *od.* sein Schatz; **her little ~s** ihre Lieblinge; **you 'are a ~** *(coll.)* du bist ein Schatz. **2.** *adj.* geliebt; *(coll.: delightful)* reizend
¹darn [dɑ:n] **1.** *v.t.* stopfen. **2.** *n.* gestopfte Stelle
²darn *(sl.: damn)* **1.** *v.t.* **~ you** *etc.* **!** zum Kuckuck mit dir *usw.* ! *(salopp)*; **~ [it]** verflixt [und zugenäht]! *(ugs.)*; **~ it all!** verflixt noch mal! *(ugs.)*; **I'll be ~ed** ich werd' nicht mehr *(salopp)*; **I'm** *or* **I'll be ~ed if I'll help you** ich werde dir auf gar keinen Fall helfen; **I'm** *or* **I'll be ~ed if I know** ich habe nicht die leiseste Ahnung *(ugs.)*. **2.** *n. see* **damn 2 b. 3.** *adj.* verflixt *(ugs.)*. **4.** *adv.* verflixt *(ugs.)*; **~ stupid** schrecklich dumm
darned [dɑ:nd] *(sl.)* **1.** *adj.* verflixt *(ugs.)*; **you ~ fool!** du verdammter Narr!; *see also* **damned 1 b, c. 2.** *adv.* verflixt; **don't be so ~ stubborn!** sei nicht so verdammt *od.* furchtbar stur!; *see also* **damned 2**
darning ['dɑ:nɪŋ] *n.* Stopfen, *das;* **there's a lot of ~ to be done** es sind eine Menge Sachen zu stopfen
'**darning-needle** *n.* Stopfnadel, *die*
dart [dɑ:t] **1.** *n.* **a)** *(missile)* Pfeil, *der;* **b)** *(Sport)* Wurfpfeil, *der;* **~s** *sing. (game)* Darts, *das;* **c)** *(Zool.)* Stachel, *der;* **d)** *(rapid motion)* Satz, *der;* **the child made a sudden ~ into the road** das Kind rannte plötzlich auf die Fahrbahn; **e)** *(Dressmaking: tapering tuck)* Abnäher, *der.* **2.** *v.t.* **~ a look at sb.** jmdm. einen Blick zuwerfen; **the toad ~ed its tongue out** die Kröte ließ ihre Zunge herausschnellen. **3.** *v.i.* *(start rapidly)* sausen;

~ towards sth. auf etw. *(Akk.)* zustürzen; **her eyes ~ed towards the staircase** sie warf einen raschen Blick zur Treppe; **the fish ~ed through the water** der Fisch schnellte durch das Wasser
'**dartboard** *n.* Dartscheibe, *die*
dash [dæʃ] **1.** *v.i. (move quickly)* sausen; *(coll.: hurry)* sich eilen; **~ along behind sb./sth.** hinter jmdm./etw. herrasen; **~ away from sb./sth.** von jmdm./etw. wegrasen; **~ down/up [the stairs]** [die Treppe] hinunter-/hinaufstürzen; **~ up to sb./sth.** auf jmdn./etw. zustürzen; **I must just ~ to the loo** ich muß noch [eben] schnell aufs Klo; **~ against sth.** ‹*Wellen usw.*:› gegen etw. peitschen *od.* schlagen. **2.** *v.t.* **a)** *(shatter)* **~ sth. [to pieces]** etw. [in tausend Stücke] zerschlagen *od.* zerschmettern; **b)** *(fling)* schleudern; schmettern; *(splash)* schütten; *(bespatter)* bespritzen (**with** mit); **c)** *(frustrate)* **sb.'s hopes are ~ed** jmds. Hoffnungen haben sich zerschlagen; **d)** *(sl.) see* [2]**darn 1. 3.** *n.* **a) make a ~ for sth.** zu etw. rasen *(ugs.)*; **make a ~ at sb.** auf jmdn. losstürzen *(ugs.)*; **make a ~ for shelter** rasch Schutz suchen; **make a ~ for freedom** plötzlich versuchen, wegzulaufen; **b)** *(horizontal stroke)* Gedankenstrich, *der;* **c)** *(Morse signal)* Strich, *der;* **d)** *(slight admixture)* Schuß, *der;* **a ~ of salt** eine Prise Salz; **add a ~ of colour to sth.** einer Sache *(Dat.)* etwas Farbe geben; **beige with a ~ of brown** beige mit einem Stich ins Braune; **e)** *(vigorous action)* Schwung, *der; (showy appearance etc.)* **cut a ~:** Aufsehen erregen; **f)** *see* **dashboard**
~ a'way 1. *v.i. (rush)* davonjagen; *(coll: hurry)* **they had to ~ away** sie mußten schnell weg; **you're not going to ~ away so soon, surely** du willst doch nicht schon wieder weg. **2.** *v.t.* wegstoßen
~ 'off 1. *v.i. see* **~ away 1. 2.** *v.t.* rasch schreiben
~ 'out *v.t.* **~ sb.'s brains out** jmdm. den Schädel einschlagen
'**dashboard** *n. (Motor Veh.)* Armaturenbrett, *das*
dashed [dæʃt] *see* **darned**
dashing ['dæʃɪŋ] *adj.* schneidig
dastardly ['dæstədlɪ] *adj.* feige; *(malicious)* hinterhältig
data ['deɪtə, 'dɑːtə] *n. pl., constr. as pl. or sing.* Daten *Pl.; see also* **datum**
data: ~ bank, ~base *ns.* Datenbank, *die;* **~ capture** *n.* Datenerfassung, *die;* **~-handling, ~ 'processing** *ns.* Datenverarbeitung, *die;* **~ 'processor** *n.* Datenverarbeitungsanlage, *die;* **~ pro'tection** *n.* Datenschutz, *der;* **~ sheet** *n.* Informationsblatt, *das*
[1]**date** [deɪt] *n. (Bot.)* **a)** *(fruit)* Dattel, *die;* **b)** *(tree) see* **date-palm**
[2]**date 1.** *n.* **a)** Datum, *das; (on coin etc.)* Jahreszahl, *die;* **~ of birth** Geburtsdatum, *das;* **what are his ~s?** von wann bis wann hat er gelebt?; **the last ~ for payment** der letzte Termin für die Zahlung; **b)** *(coll.: appointment)* Verabredung, *die;* **have/make a ~ with sb.** mit jmdm. verabredet sein/sich mit jmdm. verabreden; **go [out] on a ~ with sb.** mit jmdm. ausgehen; *see also* **blind date; c)** *(Amer. coll.: person)* Freund, *der*/Freundin, *die;* **d)** *(period)* [Entstehungs]zeit, *die;* **e) be out of ~:** altmodisch sein; *(expired)* nicht mehr gültig sein; **to ~:** bis heute. *See also* **up to date. 2.** *v.t.* **a)** *(mark with date, refer to a time)* datieren; **~ sth. to a time** etw. einer Zeit zuordnen; **b)** *(coll: make seem old)* alt machen; **c)** *(Amer. coll.: make date with)* **~ [each other]/sb.** miteinander/mit jmdm. gehen *(ugs.)*. **3.** *v.i.* **a) ~ back to/~ from a certain time** aus einer bestimmten Zeit stammen; **b)** *(coll.: become out of date)* aus der Mode kommen
dated ['deɪtɪd] *adj. (coll.)* altmodisch; **a ~ fashion** eine Mode von gestern

date: ~-line *n.* **a)** *(Geog.)* Datumsgrenze, *die;* **b)** *(in newspaper etc.) Zeile, in der das Datum steht;* ≈ Kopf, *der;* **~-palm** *n.* Dattelpalme, *die;* **~-stamp 1.** *n.* Datumsstempel, *der;* **2.** *v.t.* abstempeln; mit einem Datumsstempel versehen
dative ['deɪtɪv] *(Ling.)* **1.** *adj.* Dativ-; dativisch; **~ case** Dativ, *der.* **2.** *n.* Dativ, *der*
datum ['deɪtəm, 'dɑːtəm] *n., pl.* **data** ['deɪtə, 'dɑːtə] **a)** *(premiss)* Datum, *das;* Faktum, *das;* **b)** *(fixed starting-point)* Nullpunkt, *der*
'**datum-line** *n. (Surv.)* Normalnull, *das*
daub [dɔːb] **1.** *v.t.* **a)** *(coat)* bewerfen; verschmieren ‹*Geflecht*›; *(smear, soil)* beschmieren; **b)** *(lay crudely)* schmieren. **2.** *v.i.* ‹*Künstler:*› die Leinwand vollschmieren *(abwertend)*. **3.** *n.* **a)** *(plaster etc.)* Bewurf, *der;* **b)** *(crude painting)* Kleckserei, *die (ugs. abwertend); (large)* Schinken, *der (ugs. abwertend);* **c)** *(smear)* Fleck, *der;* **covered with great ~s of sth.** reichlich mit etw. beschmiert
daughter ['dɔːtə(r)] *n. (lit. or fig.)* Tochter, *die*
'**daughter-in-law** *n., pl.* **daughters-in-law** Schwiegertochter, *die*
daunt [dɔːnt] *v.t.* entmutigen; schrecken *(geh.)*; **nothing ~ed** unverzagt
dauntless ['dɔːntlɪs] *adj.* unerschrocken
dauphin ['dɔːfɪn] *n. (Hist.)* Dauphin, *der*
davenport ['dævnpɔːt] *n.* **a)** *(Brit.: writing-desk)* Sekretär, *der;* **b)** *(Amer.: sofa)* Sofa, *das*
davit ['dævɪt] *n.* [Boots]davit, *der*
Davy [lamp] ['deɪvɪ (læmp)] *n.* Wetterlampe, *die;* Davy-Lampe, *die*
dawdle ['dɔːdl] **1.** *v.i.* bummeln *(ugs.)*. **2.** *v.t.* **~ away** verbummeln *(ugs.)*. **3.** *n. (dawdling)* Bummelei, *die (ugs.); (stroll)* Bummel, *der (ugs.)*
dawn [dɔːn] **1.** *v.i.* **a)** dämmern; **day[light] ~ed** der Morgen dämmerte; der Tag brach an; **b)** *(fig.)* ‹*Zeitalter:*› anbrechen; ‹*Idee:*› aufkommen; ‹*Liebe, Hoffnung:*› erwachen; **until the meaning finally ~ed** bis schließlich der Sinn klar wurde; **sth. ~s on** *or* **upon sb.** etw. dämmert jmdm.; **hasn't it ~ed on you that ...?** ist dir nicht langsam klargeworden, daß ...? **the idea ~ed on her that ...:** ihr kam die Idee, daß ... **2.** *n.* **a)** [Morgen]dämmerung, *die;* **from ~ to dusk** von früh bis spät; **it is ~:** die Dämmerung bricht an; es wird hell; **at ~:** im Morgengrauen; **[the] ~ breaks** der Tag bricht an; **in the ~:** in der Morgendämmerung; **into the ~:** gen Sonnenaufgang *(geh.)*; **b)** *(fig.)* Morgenröte, *die (geh.); (of idea, love, hope)* Keimen, *das (geh.)*; **at the ~ of civilization** in der Morgenröte der Zivilisation *(geh.)*
dawn 'chorus *n.* morgendlicher Gesang der Vögel
dawning ['dɔːnɪŋ] *n.* **a)** Anbruch, *der;* **at the ~ of the day** bei Tagesanbruch; **b)** *(fig.)* Anfänge *Pl.*; **at the ~ of a new era/civilization** bei Anbruch eines neuen Zeitalters/in den Anfängen der Zivilisation
'**dawn raid** *n. (St. Exch.) frühzeitiges, heimliches Aufkaufen von Aktien (um überraschend eine Aktienmehrheit zu erlangen)*
day [deɪ] *n.* **a)** Tag, *der;* **on a ~ like today** an einem Tag wie heute; **all ~ [long]** den ganzen Tag [lang]; **take all ~** *(fig.)* eine Ewigkeit brauchen; **as happy as the ~ is long** äußerst glücklich; **the ~ of ~s** der Tag der Tage; **all ~ and every ~:** tagaus, tagein; **not for many a long ~:** schon lange nicht mehr; **to this ~, from that ~ to this** bis zum heutigen Tag; **as clear as ~:** augenfällig; **for two ~s** zwei Tage [lang]; **what's the ~** *or* **what ~ is it today?** welcher Tag ist heute?; **twice a ~:** zweimal täglich *od.* am Tag; **in a ~/two days** *(within)* in *od.* an einem Tag/in zwei Tagen; **in a ~['s time]/a few ~s[' time]** in einem Tag/in ein paar Tagen; **in six ~s[' time]** in sechs Tagen; **in eight ~s** in genau acht Tagen; **[on] the ~ after/before** am Tag danach/davor; **[on] the ~ after/before sth.** am Tag nach/vor etw. *(Dat.)*; **[on] the ~ after/before we met** am Tag, nach dem/bevor wir uns trafen; **[the] next/[on] the following/[on] the previous ~:** am nächsten/folgenden/vorhergehenden Tag; **the ~ before yesterday/after tomorrow** vorgestern/übermorgen; **the other ~:** neulich; **only the other ~:** erst vor ein paar Tagen; **every other ~:** alle zwei Tage; **from this/that ~ [on]** von heute an/von diesem Tag an; **one ~ he came** eines Tages kam er; **come and see us one ~:** komm irgendwann einmal vorbei; **one ~ ..., the next ...:** heute ..., morgen ...; **one of these [fine] ~s** eines [schönen] Tages; **two ~s ago** vor zwei Tagen; **some ~:** eines Tages; irgendwann einmal; **for the ~:** für einen Tag; **to the ~:** auf den Tag genau; **~ after ~:** Tag für Tag; **~ by ~, from ~ to ~:** von Tag zu Tag; **from one ~ to the next** von einem Tag zum andern; **~ in ~ out** tagaus, tagein; **it's all in the/a ~'s work** das gehört dazu *(ugs.)*; **call it a ~** *(end work)* Feierabend machen; *(more generally)* Schluß machen; *(fig.)* es gut sein lassen *(ugs.)*; **at the end of the ~** *(fig.)* letzten Endes; **early in the ~** *(fig.)* früh; **he's 65 if he's a ~:** er ist mindestens 65; **it's not my ~:** ich habe [heute] einen schlechten Tag; **it's my ~:** ich habe [heute] einen guten Tag; **on his ~:** wenn er seinen guten Tag hat; **that will be the ~** *(iron.)* das möchte ich sehen/erleben *(ugs.)*; **it's been one of those ~s** das war vielleicht ein Tag *(ugs.)*; **soup/dish of the ~:** Tagessuppe, *die*/Stammessen, *das; see also* **any 1 e; good 1 m; late 2 e; make 1 p; off 1 e; b)** *(daylight)* **before/at ~:** vor/bei Tagesanbruch; **c)** *in sing. or pl. (period)* **in the ~s when ...:** zu der Zeit, als ...; **in his/that/Queen Anne's ~:** zu seiner/jener Zeit/zur Zeit der Königin Anne; **in former/earlier ~s** in früheren Zeiten; **these ~s** heutzutage; **in those ~s** damals; zu jener Zeit; **in this ~ and age, at the present ~:** heutzutage; **this ~ and age, the [present] ~:** die heutige Zeit; **have seen/known better ~s** bessere Tage gesehen/gekannt haben; **I have seen the ~ when ...:** zu meiner Zeit ...; **those were the ~s** das waren noch Zeiten; *(iron.)* schöne Zeiten waren das; *see also* **bad 1 a; good 1 d; d)** *in sing. or pl. (lifetime)* **in our ~[s]** zu unserer Zeit; **end one's ~s** seine Tage beenden; **e)** *(time of prosperity)* **in one's ~:** zu seiner Zeit; *(during lifetime)* in seinem Leben; **sth.'s ~ is over** die Zeiten einer Sache *(Gen.)* sind vorbei; **every dog has its ~:** jeder hat einmal seine Chance; **it has had its ~:** es hat ausgedient *(ugs.)*; **f)** *(victory)* **win** *or* **carry the ~:** den Sieg davontragen; **g)** *(~ for regular event)* **Monday is my ~:** montags bin ich an der Reihe *(ugs.)*; **it's my ~ [for doing** *or* **to do sth.]** ich bin an der Reihe[, etw. zu tun]; **whose ~ is it?** wer ist an der Reihe?
-day *adj. suf.* -tägig; **three-~[s]-old** drei Tage alt; **five-~ week** Fünftagewoche, *die*
day: ~-bed *n.* Liegesofa, *das;* **~book** *n. (Commerc.)* Journal, *das;* **~-boy** *n. (Brit.)* externer Schüler; **~break** *n.* Tagesanbruch, *der;* **at ~break** bei Tagesanbruch; **~dream 1.** *n.* Tagtraum, *der;* **lost in a ~dream** traumverloren; **2.** *v.i.* träumen; **~dreamer** *n.* Tagträumer, *der*/-träumerin, *die;* **~-girl** *n. (Brit.)* externe Schülerin; **~light** *n.* **a)** *(light of day)* Tageslicht, *das;* **by ~light** bei Tageslicht; **go on working while it's still ~light** weiterarbeiten, solange es noch hell ist; **~light comes** es wird hell; der Tag bricht an; **it's [already] ~light** es ist [schon] hell; **during the hours of ~light, in ~light** bei Tag[eslicht]; **in broad ~light** am hellichten Tag[e]; **~light saving [time]** Sommerzeit, *die;* **b)** *(dawn)* **at** *or* **by/before ~light** bei/vor Tagesanbruch; **c)** *(fig.)* **bring sth. into the ~light** etw. ans Tageslicht brin-

gen; **I see ~light** ich denke, die Situation lichtet sich; *(understand)* mir geht ein Licht auf *(ugs.)*; **scare/beat the [living] ~lights out of sb.** *(sl.)* jmdn. zu Tode erschrecken/ *(ugs.)* windelweich schlagen; **it's ~light robbery** es ist der reine Wucher; **d)** *(visible interval)* Luft, *die;* **~-long** *attrib. adj.* den ganzen Tag dauernd; **~ nursery** *n.* **a)** *(room)* Kinderzimmer, *das;* **b)** *(school)* Kindergarten, *der;* **~ release** *n.* *(Brit.)* [tageweise] Freistellung zur Fortbildung; **~-return 1.** *attrib. adj.* **~-return ticket** *see* **2; 2.** *n.* Tagesrückfahrkarte, *die;* **~-school** *n.* Tagesschule, *die;* **~ shift** *n.* Tagschicht, *die;* **be on [the] ~ shift** Tagschicht haben; **~time** *n.* Tag, *der;* **in** *or* **during the ~time** während des Tages; tagsüber; **~-to-~** *adj.* [tag]täglich; **~-to-~ life** Alltagsleben, *das;* **~ trip** *n.* Tagesausflug, *der;* **~ tripper** *n.* Tagesausflügler, *der*/-ausflüglerin, *die*

daze [deɪz] **1.** *v. t.* benommen machen; **be ~d** benommen sein (**at** von). **2.** *n.* Benommenheit, *die;* **in a [complete/bit of a] ~:** [völlig/ein wenig] benommen

dazzle ['dæzl] *v. t.* *(lit., or fig.: delude)* blenden; *(fig.: confuse, impress)* überwältigen

dB *abbr.* **decibel[s]** dB

DC *abbr.* **a)** *(Electr.)* **direct current** GS; **b)** *(Geog.)* **District of Columbia** Bundesdistrikt Columbia; **c)** *(Mus.)* **da capo** d.c.

DD *abbr.* **Doctor of Divinity** ≈ Dr. theol.; *see also* **B.Sc.**

D-Day ['di:deɪ] *n.* **a)** *(6 June 1944) Tag der Landung der Alliierten in der Normandie;* **b)** *(starting day)* der Tag X

DDT [di:di:'ti:] *n.* DDT, *das*

deacon ['di:kn] *n.* Diakon, *der*

deaconess ['di:kənɪs] *n.* Diakonin, *die*

deactivate [di:'æktɪveɪt] *v. t.* entschärfen ‹*Bombe*›; desaktivieren ‹*Chemikalie*›; abschalten ‹*Maschine, Motor*›

dead [ded] **1.** *adj.* **a)** tot; tot, abgestorben ‹*Gewebe, Pflanze*›; **[as] ~ as a doornail/as mutton** mausetot *(ugs.)*; **be ~ from the neck up** *(coll.)* gehirnamputiert sein *(salopp)*; **I wouldn't be seen ~ doing sth./in that dress** *(coll.)* ich würde nie im Leben etw. tun/dieses Kleid anziehen *(ugs.)*; **I wouldn't be seen ~ in a place like that** *(coll.)* keine zehn Pferde würden mich an solch einen Ort bringen *(ugs.)*; **~ men tell no tales** *(prov.)* Tote reden nicht; *see also* **body 1 b; bury a; 'go 1 j; b)** *(inanimate, extinct)* tot ‹*Materie*›; erloschen ‹*Vulkan, Gefühl, Interesse*›; ausgestorben ‹*Spezies*›; *(without power)* verbraucht, leer ‹*Batterie*›; ausgebrannt ‹*Glühbirne*›; *(extinguished)* ausgegangen ‹*Zigarette*›; erloschen ‹*Feuer*›; *(not glowing)* ausgeglüht ‹*Kohle, Asche*›; **the fire is ~:** das Feuer ist aus *(ugs.)*; *see also* **dodo; c)** *(dull, lustreless)* stumpf ‹*Haar, Farbe*›; *(without force)* wirkungslos ‹*Gesetz, Politik*›; *(without warmth)* kalt ‹*Stimme, Ton*›; ausgestorben, tot ‹*Stadt*›; *(quiet)* [toten]still ‹*Nacht, Wald, Straße*›; unbelebt, tot ‹*Straße*›; *(unexciting)* öde ‹*Party, Geschmack*›; *(flat)* schal, abgestanden ‹*Getränk*›; **d)** *(inactive, unproductive)* tot ‹*Telefon, Leitung, Saison, Kapital, Ball*›; unfruchtbar ‹*Land, Erde*›; **go ~:** zusammenbrechen; *(lose interest)* Interesse verlieren (**on an** + *Dat.*); **the phone has gone ~:** die Leitung ist tot; **the motor is ~:** der Motor läuft nicht; **a ~ engine** eine Maschine, die/ein Motor, der nicht läuft; **e)** *expr. completeness* plötzlich ‹*Halt*›; völlig ‹*Stillstand*›; genau ‹*Mitte*›; *(coll.: absolute)* absolut; **~ silence** *or* **quiet** Totenstille, *die;* **~ calm** Flaute, *die;* Windstille, *die;* **~ faint** [totenähnliche] Ohnmacht; **~ trouble** große Schwierigkeiten *Pl.*; **a ~ shot** ein unfehlbarer Schütze; **f)** *(benumbed)* taub; *(sleeping)* schlafend; **be ~ to sth.** *(lit. or fig.)* etw. nicht mehr empfinden; **be ~ to shame** gar kein Schamgefühl haben; **be ~ to the world** *(unconscious)* bewußtlos sein; weggetreten sein *(ugs.)*; *(asleep)* tief und fest schlafen; **g)** *(exhausted)* erschöpft; kaputt *(ugs.)*; **I feel absolutely ~:** ich bin völlig erschöpft. **2.** *adv.* **a)** *(completely)* völlig; **~ silent** totenstill; **~ straight** schnurgerade; **~ tired** todmüde; **~ easy** *or* **simple/slow** kinderleicht/ganz langsam; **'~ slow'** „besonders langsam fahren"; **~ drunk** stockbetrunken *(ugs.)*; **~ level** völlig eben; **~ still** regungslos; *(without wind)* windstill; **make ~ certain** *or* **sure of sth.** etw. todsicher machen; **be ~ against sth.** absolut gegen etw. sein; **b)** *(exactly)* **~ on the target** genau im Ziel; **~ on time** auf die Minute; **~ on two [o'clock]** Punkt zwei [Uhr]. *See also* **cut 1 f; stop 2 b. 3.** *n.* **a) in the ~ of winter/night** mitten im Winter/in der Nacht; **it was the ~ of winter** es war mitten im Winter; **b)** *pl.* **the ~:** die Toten *Pl.*

dead: ~-[and-]a'live *adj.* langweilig; öde ‹*Ort, Leben*›; **~-beat 1.** ['-'] *adj.* *(exhausted)* völlig zerschlagen; *(without money)* bettelarm; **2.** ['--] *n.* *(sl.)* *(sponger)* Nassauer, *der (ugs.)*; *(penniless person)* **he is a ~-beat** er ist bettelarm; **~ 'duck** *n.* *(sl.)* **a)** *(person)* Null, *die (ugs.)*; **b)** *(thing)* **it is a ~ duck** das kann man vergessen

deaden ['dedn] *v. t.* dämpfen; abstumpfen ‹*Gefühl*›; betäuben ‹*Nerv, Körperteil, Schmerz*›; **~ sb./sth. to sth.** jmdn./etw. gegen etw. unempfindlich machen

dead: ~ 'end *n.* *(closed end)* Absperrung, *die;* *(street; also fig.)* Sackgasse, *die;* **~-end** *attrib. adj.* **a) ~-end street/road** Sackgasse, *die;* **b)** *(fig.)* aussichtslos; **she's in a ~-end job** in ihrem Job hat sie keine Aufstiegschancen; **he is a ~-end kid** er ist in ärmlichen Verhältnissen aufgewachsen; **~-eye** *n.* *(Naut.)* Jungfer, *die;* **~ head** *n.* *(flowerhead)* verblühte Blüte; **~ 'heat** *n.* totes Rennen; **finish** *or* **end in a ~ heat** unentschieden ausgehen; **~ 'language** *n.* tote Sprache; **~ 'letter** *n.* **a)** *(law)* Gesetz, das nicht angewendet wird; **be a ~ letter** nur noch auf dem Papier bestehen; **b)** *(letter)* unzustellbarer Brief; **~ 'lift** *n.* Gewaltleistung, *die;* **~light** *n.* *(Naut.)* [Seeschlag]blende, *die;* **~line** *n.* **a)** *(line of limit) Linie um ein Gefängnis o. ä., die von den Gefangenen nicht überschritten werden darf;* **b)** *(time-limit)* [letzter] Termin; **meet the ~line** den Termin einhalten; **set a ~line for sth.** eine Frist für etw. setzen

deadliness ['dedlɪnɪs] *n., no pl.* *(fatal quality)* tödliche Wirkung

dead: ~lock 1. *n.* **a)** *(standstill)* völliger Stillstand; **come to a** *or* **reach [a] ~lock/be at ~lock** an einem toten Punkt anlangen/angelangt sein; **the negotiations had reached ~lock** die Verhandlungen waren festgefahren; **b)** *(lock)* einfaches Schloß ohne Feder; **2.** *v. t.* blockieren; **~ 'loss** *n.* **a)** *(complete loss)* [totaler] Verlust; **b)** *(coll.)* *(worthless thing)* totaler Reinfall *(ugs.)*; *(person)* hoffnungsloser Fall *(ugs.)*

deadly ['dedlɪ] **1.** *adj.* **a)** tödlich; *(fig. coll.: awful)* fürchterlich; *(very boring)* todlangweilig; *(very dangerous)* lebensgefährlich; **~ enemy** Todfeind, *der;* **~ fear** Todesangst, *die;* **he looked ~** *(dangerous)* er sah furchterregend aus; **I'm in ~ earnest about this** es ist mir todernst damit; **b)** *(accurate)* [absolut] exakt; **c)** *(Theol.)* **~ sin** Todsünde, *die.* **2.** *adv.* tod-; *(extremely)* äußerst; **~ pale** totenblaß; **~ dull** todlangweilig

deadly 'nightshade *n.* *(Bot.)* Tollkirsche, *die*

dead: ~ man's 'handle *n.* *(Transport)* Sicherheitsfahrschalter, *der;* **~ march** *n.* Trauermarsch, *der;* **~ men** *n. pl.* *(coll.: bottles)* leere Flaschen; tote Marine *(salopp scherzh.)*

deadness ['dednɪs] *n., no pl.* *(numbness)* Gefühllosigkeit, *die;* *(inactivity)* Öde, *die;* Trostlosigkeit, *die*

dead: ~-'on 1. *adj.* [ganz] genau; **he was ~-on with his shot** er hat mit seinem Schuß genau getroffen; **you were ~-on when you said that** du hattest vollkommen recht, als du das sagtest; **2.** *adv.* [ganz] genau; **~pan** *adj.* *(coll.)* unbewegt; **he looked ~pan** *or* **had a ~pan expression** er verzog keine Miene; **~ 'reckoning** *n.* *(Naut.)* Koppeln, *das;* Besteckrechnung, *die;* **D~ 'Sea** *pr. n.* Tote Meer, *das;* **D~ Sea Scrolls** *pr. n. pl.* Schriftrollen von Kumran *od.* vom Toten Meer; **~ weight** *n.* **a)** *(inert mass)* Eigengewicht, *das;* Totgewicht, *das (Technik)*; *(fig.)* schwere Bürde; **b)** *(Naut.: weight of cargo etc.)* Tragfähigkeit, *die;* Deadweight, *das;* **~ 'wood** *n.* **a)** totes Holz; **b)** *(fig.)* **be just ~ wood** völlig überflüssig sein; **get rid of much of the ~ wood** *(persons)* viele Nieten loswerden *(ugs.)*; *(things)* viel Überflüssiges loswerden

deaf [def] **1.** *adj.* **a)** *(without hearing)* taub; **~ and dumb** taubstumm; **~ in one ear** auf einem Ohr taub; **go** *or* **become ~:** taub werden; **b)** *(insensitive)* **musically ~:** unmusikalisch; **be ~ to sth.** kein Ohr für etw. haben; *(fig.)* taub gegenüber etw. sein; **turn a ~ ear [to sth./sb.]** sich [gegenüber etw./jmdm.] taub stellen; **fall on ~ ears** kein Gehör finden. **2.** *n. pl.* **the ~:** die Gehörlosen *Pl.*

deaf: ~-aid *n.* Hörgerät, *das;* **~-and-'dumb alphabet** *or* **language** *n.* Taubstummensprache, *die*

deafen ['defn] *v. t.* **~ sb.** bei jmdm. zur Taubheit führen; **I was ~ed by the noise** *(fig.)* ich war von dem Lärm wie betäubt

deafening ['defənɪŋ] ohrenbetäubend ‹*Lärm, Musik, Geschrei*›

deaf 'mute *n.* Taubstumme, *der/die*

deafness ['defnɪs] *n., no pl.* Taubheit, *die;* **cause ~ in sb.** bei jmdm. zur Taubheit führen

[1]**deal** [di:l] **1.** *v. t.*, **dealt** [delt] **a)** *(Cards)* austeilen; **who ~t the cards?** wer hat gegeben?; **he was ~t four aces** er bekam vier Asse; **b)** *(deliver as share)* **~ sb. sth.** jmdm. etw. zuteil werden lassen *(geh.)*; **c)** *(administer)* versetzen; **~ sb. a blow** *(lit. or fig.)* jmdm. einen Schlag versetzen; **d)** *(distribute)* verteilen. **2.** *v. i.*, **dealt a)** *(do business)* **~ with sb.** mit jmdm. Geschäfte machen; **~ in sth.** mit etw. handeln; **b)** *(occupy oneself)* **~ with sth.** sich mit etw. befassen; *(manage)* mit etw. fertig werden; **this point must be ~t with** dieser Punkt muß behandelt werden; **I'll ~ with the washing-up** ich kümmere mich um den Abwasch; **the play ~s with the Civil War** das Stück handelt vom Bürgerkrieg; **c)** *(associate)* **~ with sb.** mit jmdm. zu tun haben; **d)** *(behave)* **~ gently/circumspectly with sb./sth.** mit jmdm./etw. sanft/vorsichtig umgehen; **e)** *(take measures)* **~ with sb.** mit jmdm. fertig werden. **3.** *n.* **a)** *(coll.: arrangement, bargain)* Geschäft, *das;* **new ~** neue Bedingungen; *(Polit.)* Reformprogramm, *das;* **make a ~ with sb.** mit jmdm. ein Geschäft abschließen; **you've got a good ~ there** da hast du ein gutes Geschäft gemacht; **it's a ~!** abgemacht!; **big ~!** *(iron.)* na und?; **fair ~** *(bargain)* gutes Geschäft; *(treatment)* faire *od.* gerechte Behandlung; **raw** *or* **rough ~** *(treatment)* ungerechte Behandlung; *(bad luck)* Pech, *das;* **b)** *(coll.: agreement)* **make** *or* **do a ~ with sb.** mit jmdm. eine Vereinbarung treffen; **let's stick to our ~:** laß uns bei unserer Abmachung bleiben; **c)** *(Cards)* **it's your ~:** du gibst **~ 'out** *v. t.* verteilen; **~ sth. out to sb.** etw. an jmdn. verteilen

[2]**deal** *n.* **a great** *or* **good ~,** *(coll.)* **a ~:** viel; *(often)* ziemlich viel; **a great** *or* **good ~ of,** *(coll.)* **a ~ of** eine [ganze] Menge, viel; **we resent it a [great/good] ~ that ...** *(coll.)* es ärgert uns ganz schön, daß ... *(ugs.)*

[3]**deal** *n.* *(fir/pine timber)* [Tannen-/Kiefern]holz, *das*

dealer ['di:lə(r)] *n.* **a)** *(trader)* Händler, *der;* **he's a ~ in antiques** er ist Antiquitätenhändler *od.* handelt mit Antiquitäten; **b)** *(Cards)* Geber, *der;* **he's the ~:** er gibt; **c)** *(Stock Exch.)* Börsenmakler, *der*

dealing ['di:lɪŋ] *n.* **have ~s with sb.** mit jmdm. zu tun haben

dealt *see* ¹**deal 1, 2**

dean [di:n] *n.* **a)** *(Eccl.)* Dechant, *der;* Dekan, *der;* **b)** *(in college, university, etc.) (resident fellow) Fellow mit Aufsichts- und Beratungsfunktion; (head of faculty)* Dekan, *der*

deanery ['di:nərɪ] *n.* **a)** *(office)* Dekanat, *das;* **b)** *(house)* Dekanei, *die;* **c)** *(Brit.: group of parishes)* Dekanat, *das*

dear [dɪə(r)] **1.** *adj.* **a)** *(beloved; also iron.)* lieb; geliebt; *(sweet; also iron.)* entzückend; reizend; **my ~ sir/madam** [mein] lieber Herr/[meine] liebe Dame; **my ~ man/woman** guter Mann/gute Frau; **my ~ Jones/child/girl** [mein] lieber Jones/liebes Kind/liebes Mädchen; **sb./sth. is [very] ~ to sb.['s heart]** jmd. liebt jmdn./etw. [über alles]; **sb. holds sb./sth. ~ [to him/to his heart]** jmd./etw. liegt jmdm. [sehr] am Herzen; **run for ~ life** um sein Leben rennen; **my ~est wish** mein innigster *od.* sehnlichster Wunsch; **his ~est ambition** sein höchstes Ziel; **b)** *(beginning letter)* **D~ Sir/Madam** Sehr geehrter Herr/Sehr verehrte gnädige Frau; **D~ Mr Jones/Mrs Jones** Sehr geehrter Herr Jones/Sehr verehrte Frau Jones; **D~ Malcolm/Emily** Lieber Malcolm/Liebe Emily; **D~est Auntie Minnie** Liebste Tante Minnie; **My ~ Smith** *(Brit.: less formal)* Lieber Herr Smith; *(between old schoolfellows etc.)* Lieber Smith; *(Amer.: more formal)* Sehr geehrter Herr Smith; **c)** *(in addressing sb.)* lieb; *(in exclamation)* **~ God!** ach du lieber Gott! *See also* **madam a; sir b; d)** *(expensive)* teuer. **2.** *int.* **~, ~!, ~ me!, oh ~!** [ach] du liebe *od.* meine Güte. **3.** *n.* **a) you 'are a ~** *(coll.)* du bist wirklich lieb; **she is a ~:** sie ist ein Schatz; **b) [my] ~** *(to wife, husband, younger relative)* [mein] Liebling; [mein] Schatz; *(to aunt)* Tantchen *(das); (to little girl/boy)* [meine] Kleine/[mein] Kleiner; *(to man/woman)* guter Mann/gute Frau; **~est** Liebling *(der).* **4.** *adv.* teuer; *see also* **cost 2 a**

dearie ['dɪərɪ] *n.* Kleine, *der/die;* **~ me!** [ach] du liebe *od.* meine Güte

dearly ['dɪəlɪ] *adv.* **a)** *(very fondly, earnestly)* von ganzem Herzen; **I'd ~ love to do sth.** ich würde liebend gern etw. tun; **b)** *(at high price)* teuer; **you'll pay ~ for it** *(fig.)* du wirst teuer dafür bezahlen müssen

dearth [dɜ:θ] *n.* Mangel, *der* **(of** an + *Dat.*); **there is a ~ of sth.** es besteht *od.* herrscht Mangel an etw. *(Dat.);* **there is no ~ of sth.** es fehlt nicht an etw. *(Dat.)*

death [deθ] *n.* **a)** Tod, *der;* **end in/mean ~:** zum Tod führen; **be afraid of ~:** Angst vor dem Tod haben; **after ~:** nach dem Tod; **[as] sure as ~:** todsicher; **meet one's death** den Tod finden *(geh.);* **catch one's ~ [of cold]** *(coll.)* sich *(Dat.)* den Tod holen *(ugs.);* **drink will be the ~ of him** er trinkt sich noch zu Tode; **... to ~:** zu Tode ...; **bleed to ~:** verbluten; **freeze to ~:** erfrieren; **beat sb. to ~:** jmdn. totschlagen; **burn [sb.] to ~:** [jmdn.] verbrennen; **he worked/drank himself to ~:** er hat sich totgearbeitet/totgetrunken *(ugs.);* **I'm scared to ~** *(fig.)* mir ist angst und bange **(about** vor + *Dat.*); **be sick** *or* **tired to ~ of sth.** *(fig.)* etw. gründlich satt haben; **be tickled to ~ by sth.** *(fig.)* sich über etw. totlachen; **be done to ~:** getötet werden; *(fig.)* zu Tode geritten werden; **be worked to ~:** zu Tode geschunden werden; *(fig.)* zu Tode geritten werden; **[fight] to the ~:** auf Leben und Tod [kämpfen]; **be in at the ~** *(in fox-hunting)* dabeisein, wenn der Fuchs getötet wird; *(fig.)* das Ende miterleben; **a fate worse than ~** *(joc.)* das Allerschlimmste; **~ or glory!** Ruhm oder Untergang!; **~ to Fascism!** Tod dem Faschismus!; **D~** *(personified)* der Tod; **be at ~'s door** an der Schwelle des Todes stehen; **feel/look like ~ [warmed up]** *(sl.)* sich wie eine Leiche auf Urlaub fühlen/wie eine Leiche auf Urlaub aussehen *(salopp);* **b)** *(instance)* Todesfall, *der;* **how many ~s were there?** wie viele Tote gab es?

death: ~bed *n.* Totenbett, *das;* Sterbebett, *das; attrib.* auf dem Sterbebett *nachgestellt;* **on one's ~bed** auf dem Sterbebett; **~-blow** *n. (lit. or fig.)* Todesstoß, *der* (to für); **~ cell** *n.* Todeszelle, *die;* **~ certificate** *n. (from authorities)* Sterbeurkunde, *die; (from doctor)* Totenschein, *der;* **~-dealing** *attrib. adj.* todbringend; **~ duty** *n. (Brit. Hist.)* Erbschaftssteuer, *die;* **~-knell** *n. (lit. or fig.)* Totengeläut, *das*

deathless ['deθlɪs] *adj.* unsterblich; *(fig.)* unvergänglich; **~ prose** *(iron.)* hochgestochene Prosa

deathly ['deθlɪ] **1.** *adj.* tödlich; **~ stillness/hush** Totenstille, *die;* **~ pallor** Totenblässe, *die.* **2.** *adv.* tödlich; **~ pale** totenblaß; **~ still/quiet** totenstill

death: ~-mask *n.* Totenmaske, *die;* **~ penalty** *n.* Todesstrafe, *die;* **~ rate** *n.* Sterblichkeitsziffer, *die;* **~-rattle** *n.* Todesröcheln, *das;* **~-ray** *n.* tödlicher Strahl; **~-roll** *n.* Verlustliste, *die; (after battle)* Gefallenenliste, *die;* **~ row** [deθ 'rəʊ] *n.* [Reihe von] Todeszellen; **~ sentence** *n.* Todesurteil *das;* **~'s head** *n.* Totenkopf, *der;* **~ squad** *n.* Todesschwadron, *die;* **~ tax** *(Amer.)* Erbschaftssteuer, *die;* **~-toll** *n.* Zahl der Todesopfer; Blutzoll, *der (geh.);* **~-trap** *n.* lebensgefährliche Sache; **this corner/house/car is a ~-trap** diese Kurve/dieses Haus/Auto ist lebensgefährlich; **~-warrant** *n.* Exekutionsbefehl, *der; (fig.)* Todesurteil, *das;* **~-watch [beetle]** *n. (Zool.)* Totenuhr, *die;* **~-wish** *n. (Psych.)* Todeswunsch, *der*

deb [deb] *n. (coll.)* Debütantin, *die*

débâcle [deɪ'bɑ:kl] *n.* Debakel, *das (geh.)*

debar [dɪ'bɑ:(r)] *v.t.*, **-rr-** ausschließen; **~ sb. from doing sth.** jmdn. davon ausschließen, etw. zu tun

debase [dɪ'beɪs] *v.t.* **a)** verschlechtern; herabsetzen, entwürdigen ⟨*Person*⟩; **~ oneself** sich erniedrigen; **b) ~ the coinage** den Wert der Währung mindern

debatable [dɪ'beɪtəbl] *adj.* **a)** *(questionable)* fraglich; **b) ~ ground** umstrittenes Gebiet

debate [dɪ'beɪt] **1.** *v.t.* debattieren über (+ *Akk.*); **be ~d** diskutiert *od.* debattiert werden. **2.** *v.i.* **~ [up]on sth.** etw. debattieren; **~ about sth.** über etw. *(Akk.)* debattieren *od.* streiten. **3.** *n.* Debatte, *die;* **there was much ~ about whether ...:** es wurde viel darüber debattiert, ob ...

debating [dɪ'beɪtɪŋ]: **~ point** *n. (für die Sache unerheblicher, nur aus rhetorischen Gründen vorgebrachter)* Diskussionspunkt; **~ society** *n. (regelmäßig zusammentretende)* Diskussionsrunde

debauch [dɪ'bɔ:tʃ] *(literary)* **1.** *v.t.* **a)** verderben; **b)** *(seduce)* verführen. **2.** *n.* Gelage, *das*

debauched [dɪ'bɔ:tʃt] *adj.* verderbt *(geh.)*

debauchery [dɪ'bɔ:tʃərɪ] *n. (literary)* Ausschweifung, *die*

debenture [dɪ'bentʃə(r)] *n. (Finance)* Schuldverschreibung, *die*

debilitate [dɪ'bɪlɪteɪt] *v.t.* schwächen

debilitating [dɪ'bɪlɪteɪtɪŋ] *adj.* anstrengend ⟨*Klima*⟩; schwächend ⟨*Krankheit*⟩

debility [dɪ'bɪlɪtɪ] *n.* Schwäche, *die*

debit ['debɪt] **1.** *n. (Bookk.)* Soll, *das; (debit side)* Soll, *das;* Debet, *das;* **~ balance** Lastschrift, *die;* **~ side** *(Finance)* Sollseite, *die.* **2.** *v.t.* belasten; **~ a sum against** *or* **to sb./sb.'s account, ~ sb./sb.'s account with a sum** jmdn./jmds. Konto mit einer Summe belasten

debonair [debə'neə(r)] *adj.* frohgemut

debrief [di:'bri:f] *v.t. (coll.)* befragen *(bei Rückkehr von einem Einsatz usw.)*

debris ['debri:, 'deɪbri:] *n., no pl.* Trümmer *Pl.*

debt [det] *n.* Schuld, *die;* **owe sb. a ~ of gratitude** *or* **thanks** jmdm. Dank schulden; [tief] in jmds. Schuld stehen; **~ of honour** Ehrenschuld, *die;* **National D~:** Staatsverschuldung, *die;* **be in ~:** Schulden haben; verschuldet sein; **get** *or* **run into ~:** in Schulden geraten; sich verschulden; **get out of ~:** aus den Schulden herauskommen; **be in sb.'s ~:** in jmds. Schuld stehen

'**debt collector** *n.* Inkassobevollmächtigte, *der/die;* Schuldeneintreiber, *der (veralt.)*

debtor ['detə(r)] *n.* Schuldner, *der*/Schuldnerin, *die*

debug [di:'bʌg] *v.t.*, **-gg-: a)** entwanzen; **b)** *(fig. coll.) (remove microphones from)* von Wanzen befreien; *(remove defects from)* von Fehlern befreien

debunk [di:'bʌŋk] *v.t. (coll.) (remove false reputation from)* entlarven; *(expose falseness of)* bloßstellen

début (*Amer.:* **debut**) ['deɪbu:, 'deɪbju:] *n.* Debüt, *das;* **make one's ~:** debütieren

débutante (*Amer.:* **debutante**) ['debju:tɑ:nt, 'deɪbju:tɑ:nt] *n.* Debütantin, *die*

Dec. *abbr.* **December** Dez.

decade ['dekeɪd] *n.* Jahrzehnt, *das;* Dekade, *die*

decadence ['dekədəns] *n.* Dekadenz, *die*

decadent ['dekədənt] *adj.* dekadent

decaffeinated [di:'kæfɪneɪtɪd] *adj.* entkoffeiniert; koffeinfrei *(veralt.)*

Decalogue ['dekəlɒg] *n.* **the ~:** der Dekalog; die Zehn Gebote

decamp [dɪ'kæmp] *v.i.* **a)** *(abscond)* verschwinden *(ugs.);* **b)** *(leave camp)* das Lager abbrechen

decant [dɪ'kænt] *v.t.* abgießen; dekantieren ⟨*Wein*⟩; *(fig.)* abladen

decanter [dɪ'kæntə(r)] *n.* Karaffe, *die*

decapitate [dɪ'kæpɪteɪt] *v.t.* **a)** köpfen ⟨*Person, Blume*⟩; enthaupten *(geh.);* **b)** *(Amer.: dismiss)* entlassen

decathlete [dɪ'kæθli:t] *n. (Sport)* Zehnkämpfer, *der*

decathlon [dɪ'kæθlən] *n. (Sport)* Zehnkampf, *der*

decay [dɪ'keɪ] **1.** *v.i.* **a)** *(become rotten)* verrotten; [ver]faulen; ⟨*Zahn:*⟩ faul *od. (fachspr.)* kariös werden; ⟨*Gebäude, Tuch:*⟩ zerfallen; **b)** *(decline)* verfallen; **c)** *(Phys.: decrease)* zerfallen. **2.** *n.* **a)** *(rotting)* Verrotten, *das; (of tooth)* Fäule, *die; (of building)* Zerfall, *der;* Verfall, *der;* **b)** *(decline)* Verfall, *der; (of nation)* Verfall, *der;* Niedergang, *der;* **c)** *(decayed tissue etc.)* Zersetzung, *die;* Fäulnis, *die;* **d)** *(Phys.: decrease)* Zerfall, *der*

decease [dɪ'si:s] *(Law/formal)* **1.** *n.* Ableben, *das (geh.).* **2.** *v.i.* versterben *(geh.);* sterben

deceased [dɪ'si:st] *(Law/formal)* **1.** *adj.* verstorben; **the ~ man** der Tote *od.* Verstorbene; **Jim Fox ~:** der verstorbene Jim Fox. **2.** *n.* Verstorbene, *der/die*

decedent [dɪ'si:dənt] *n. (Amer.)* Verstorbene, *der/die*

deceit [dɪ'si:t] *n. (misrepresentation)* Täuschung, *die;* Betrug, *der; (trick)* Täuschungsmanöver, *das;* Betrügerei, *die; (being deceitful)* Falschheit, *die*

deceitful [dɪ'si:tfl] *adj.* falsch ⟨*Person, Art, Charakter*⟩; hinterlistig ⟨*Trick*⟩; **that was a ~ thing to say** es war hinterlistig, das zu sagen

deceitfully [dɪ'si:tfəlɪ] *adv. see* **deceitful:** falsch; hinterlistig

deceitfulness [dɪ'si:tflnɪs] *n., no pl. see* **deceitful:** Falschheit, *die;* Hinterlistigkeit, *die*

deceive [dɪ'si:v] *v.t.* täuschen; *(be unfaithful to)* betrügen; **if my eyes/ears do not ~ me** wenn ich richtig sehe/höre; **~ sb. into doing sth.** jmdn. [durch Täuschung] dazu bringen, etw. zu tun; **~ oneself** sich täuschen; *(delude oneself)* sich *(Dat.)* etwas vormachen *(ugs.)*; **[let oneself] be ~d** sich täuschen lassen; **[let oneself] be ~d into doing sth.** sich dazu bringen lassen, etw. zu tun
deceiver [dɪ'si:və(r)] *n.* Betrüger, *der*/Betrügerin, *die*
decelerate [di:'seləreɪt] **1.** *v.t.* verlangsamen. **2.** *v.i.* ⟨*Fahrzeug, Fahrer:*⟩ die Fahrt verlangsamen
deceleration [di:selə'reɪʃn] *n.* Verlangsamung, *die*
December [dɪ'sembə(r)] *n.* Dezember, *der; see also* **August**
decency ['di:sənsɪ] *n.* **a)** *(modesty, propriety)* Anstand, *der; (of manners, literature, language)* Schicklichkeit, *die (geh.); (fairness, respectability)* Anständigkeit, *die;* **it is [a matter of] common ~:** es ist eine Frage des Anstands; es gehört sich; **b)** *in pl. (requirements of propriety)* Anstandsregeln *Pl.*
decent ['di:sənt] *adj.* **a)** *(seemly)* schicklich *(geh.)*; anständig ⟨*Person*⟩; **are you ~?** *(coll.)* hast du was an? *(ugs.)*; **b)** *(passable, respectable)* annehmbar; anständig ⟨*Person, ugs. auch Preis, Gehalt*⟩; **do the ~ thing** das einzig Richtige tun; **c)** *(Brit. coll.: kind)* nett; **that is very ~ of you** das ist sehr liebenswürdig von Ihnen; **be ~ about sth.** auf etw. *(Akk.)* nett reagieren
decently ['di:səntlɪ] *adv.* **a)** *(in seemly manner)* anständig; geziemend *(geh.)*; schicklich *(geh.)*; **b)** *(passably, respectably)* annehmbar; **c)** *(Brit. coll.: kindly)* netterweise *(ugs.)*; **behave ~:** sich nett verhalten
decentralisation, decentralise *see* **decentraliz-**
decentralization [di:sentrəlaɪ'zeɪʃn] *n.* Dezentralisierung, *die*
decentralize [di:'sentrəlaɪz] *v.t.* dezentralisieren
deception [dɪ'sepʃn] *n.* **a)** *(deceiving, trickery)* Betrug, *der; (being deceived)* Täuschung, *die;* **use ~:** betrügen; **b)** *(trick)* Betrügerei, *die*
deceptive [dɪ'septɪv] *adj.* trügerisch
deceptively [dɪ'septɪvlɪ] *adv.* täuschend
decibel ['desɪbel] *n.* Dezibel, *das*
decide [dɪ'saɪd] **1.** *v.t.* **a)** *(settle, judge)* entscheiden über (+ *Akk.*); **~ sth. by tossing a coin** etw. durch Werfen einer Münze entscheiden; **~ the winner** entscheiden, wer gewonnen hat; **~ that ...:** entscheiden, daß ...; **b)** *(resolve)* **be ~d** sich entschieden haben; **~ that ...:** beschließen, daß ...; **~ to do sth.** sich entschließen, etw. zu tun. **2.** *v.i.* sich entscheiden (**between** zwischen + *Dat.*, **in favour of** zugunsten von, **against** gegen, **on** für); **~ against/on doing sth.** sich dagegen/dafür entscheiden, etw. zu tun
decided [dɪ'saɪdɪd] *adj.* **a)** *(unquestionable)* entschieden; eindeutig; **he made a ~ effort** er hat sich deutlich *od.* entschieden bemüht; **b)** *(not hesitant)* bestimmt; entschlossen, entschieden ⟨*Haltung, Ansicht*⟩
decidedly [dɪ'saɪdɪdlɪ] *adv.* **a)** *(unquestionably)* entschieden; deutlich; **b)** *(firmly)* bestimmt
decider [dɪ'saɪdə(r)] *n. (game)* Entscheidungsspiel, *das*
deciduous [dɪ'sɪdjʊəs] *adj. (Bot.)* **~ leaves** Blätter, die abgeworfen werden; **~ tree** laubwerfender Baum; ≈ Laubbaum, *der*
decimal ['desɪml] **1.** *adj.* Dezimal-; dezimal; **go ~:** sich auf das Dezimalsystem umstellen. **2.** *n.* Dezimalbruch, *der*
decimal: ~ 'coinage, ~ 'currency *ns.* Dezimalwährung, *die;* **~ 'fraction** *n.* Dezimalbruch, *der*
decimalize (decimalise) ['desɪməlaɪz] *v.t. (express as decimal)* als Dezimalzahl schreiben; *(convert to decimal system)* dezimalisieren
decimal: ~ 'place *n.* Dezimale, *die;* **calculate sth. to five ~ places** etw. auf fünf Stellen nach dem Komma ausrechnen; **~ 'point** *n.* Komma, *das;* **~ system** *n.* Dezimalsystem, *das*
decimate ['desɪmeɪt] *v.t.* dezimieren ⟨*Bevölkerung, Truppe*⟩; drastisch verringern ⟨*Zahl*⟩
decimetre ['desɪmi:tə(r)] *n.* Dezimeter, *der*
decipher [dɪ'saɪfə(r)] *v.t.* entziffern
decipherable [dɪ'saɪfərəbl] *adj.* entzifferbar
decision [dɪ'sɪʒn] *n.* **a)** *(settlement, judgement, conclusion)* Entscheidung, *die* (**on** über + *Akk.*); *(resolve)* Entschluß, *der;* **it's 'your ~:** die Entscheidung liegt ganz bei dir; **come to** *or* **arrive at** *or* **reach a ~:** zu einer Entscheidung kommen; **has there been a ~?** ist eine Entscheidung gefallen?; **make** *or* **take a ~:** eine Entscheidung treffen; **make a firm ~ to do sth.** den festen Entschluß fassen, etw. zu tun; **leave the ~ to sb.** jmdm. die Entscheidung überlassen; **~s, ~s!** immer diese Entscheidungen!; **b)** *no pl. (resoluteness)* Entschlossenheit, *die*
de'cision-making *n.* Beschlußfassung, *die*
decisive [dɪ'saɪsɪv] *adj.* **a)** *(conclusive)* entscheidend; **b)** *(decided)* entschlußfreudig ⟨*Person*⟩; bestimmt ⟨*Charakter, Art*⟩
decisively [dɪ'saɪsɪvlɪ] *adv.* **a)** *(conclusively)* entscheidend; **b)** *(decidedly)* entschlossen
decisiveness [dɪ'saɪsɪvnɪs] *n., no pl.* **a)** *(conclusiveness)* entscheidende Bedeutung; **b)** *(decidedness)* Entschlossenheit, *die*
deck [dek] **1.** *n.* **a)** *(of ship)* Deck, *das;* **above ~:** auf Deck; **below ~[s]** unter Deck; **clear the ~s [for action** *etc.*] das Schiff klarmachen [zum Gefecht *usw.*]; *(fig.)* alles startklar machen; **on ~:** an Deck; **all hands on ~!** alle Mann an Deck!; **it was all hands on ~** *(fig.)* alle packten mit an; **b)** *(of bus etc.)* Deck, *das;* **the upper ~:** das Oberdeck; **c)** *(sunbathing platform)* ≈ Sonnenterrasse, *die;* **d)** *(tape ~)* Tape-deck, *das; (record ~)* Plattenspieler, *der;* **e)** *(sl.: ground)* Boden, *der;* **hit the ~:** auf den Boden schlagen; **f)** *(Amer.: pack)* **a ~ of cards** ein Spiel Karten; **split/shuffle the ~:** die Karten austeilen/mischen. **2.** *v.t.* **~ sth. [with sth.]** etw. [mit etw.] schmücken; **they were ~ed in all their finery** sie waren prächtig herausgeputzt
~ 'out *v.t.* herausputzen ⟨*Person*⟩; [aus]schmücken ⟨*Raum*⟩
deck: ~-chair *n.* Liegestuhl, *der; (on ship)* Liege- *od.* Deckstuhl, *der;* **~-hand** *n. (Naut.)* Decksmann, *der*
deckle ['dekl]: **~-'edge** *n.* Büttenrand, *der;* **~-'edged** *adj.* mit Büttenrand
declaim [dɪ'kleɪm] **1.** *v.i.* **a)** **~ against sb./sth.** gegen jmdn./etw. eifern *od. (ugs.)* wettern; **b)** *(deliver impassioned speech)* eifern; deklamieren *(veralt.)*. **2.** *v.t.* deklamieren ⟨*Gedicht*⟩; verkünden *(geh.)* ⟨*Botschaft*⟩
declamatory [dɪ'klæmətərɪ] *adj.* deklamatorisch ⟨*Stil, Rede, Art*⟩; leidenschaftlich ⟨*Kritik, Worte*⟩
declaration [deklə'reɪʃn] *n.* Erklärung, *die; (at customs)* Deklaration, *die;* Zollerklärung, *die; (of the truth, one's errors)* Eingeständnis, *das;* **~ of love** Liebeserklärung, *die;* **income tax ~:** Einkommensteuererklärung, *die;* **~ of the poll** *or* **election results** Bekanntgabe der Wahlergebnisse; **~ of war** Kriegserklärung, *die;* **make a ~:** eine Erklärung abgeben; *(of guilt)* ein Geständnis ablegen; **D~ of Human Rights** Menschenrechtserklärung, *die*
declare [dɪ'kleə(r)] **1.** *v.t.* **a)** *(announce)* erklären; zugeben ⟨*Schuld, Wissen*⟩; *(state explicitly)* kundtun *(geh.)* ⟨*Wunsch, Absicht*⟩; Ausdruck verleihen (+ *Dat.*) *(geh.)* ⟨*Erwartung, Hoffnung*⟩; *(prove)* bezeugen; **[well,] I [do] ~!** *(dated)* das darf [doch] nicht wahr sein! *(ugs.)*; **b)** *(pronounce)* **~ sth./sb. [to be]** **sth.** etw./jmdn. für etw. erklären; **~ oneself** sich zu erkennen geben; **c)** *(acknowledge)* deklarieren; angeben ⟨*Einkünfte*⟩; *see also* **interest 1 f. 2.** *v.i.* **~ for/against sb./sth.** sich für/gegen jmdn./etw. erklären
declassify [di:'klæsɪfaɪ] *v.t.* freigeben
declension [dɪ'klenʃn] *n. (Ling.)* Deklination, *die*
declination [deklɪ'neɪʃn] *n.* **a)** *(downward bend)* Neigung, *die;* **b)** *(Amer.: refusal)* Ablehnung, *die*
decline [dɪ'klaɪn] **1.** *v.i.* **a)** *(fall off)* nachlassen; ⟨*Moral:*⟩ sinken, nachlassen; ⟨*Preis, Anzahl:*⟩ sinken, zurückgehen; ⟨*Gesundheitszustand:*⟩ sich verschlechtern; ⟨*Reich, Kultur:*⟩ verfallen; **~ in popularity** an Beliebtheit verlieren; **his strength ~d rapidly** seine Kräfte nahmen rasch ab; **b)** *(slope downwards)* abfallen; *(droop)* sich neigen; **c) his declining years** die letzten Jahre seines Lebens; **d)** *(refuse)* **~ with thanks** *(also iron.)* dankend ablehnen. **2.** *v.t.* **a)** *(refuse)* ablehnen; **~ to do sth.** *or* **doing sth.** [es] ablehnen, etw. zu tun; **they ~d to make any comment** sie lehnten jede Stellungnahme ab; **b)** *(Ling.)* deklinieren. **3.** *n.* Nachlassen, *das* (**in** *Gen.*); **a ~ in prices/numbers** ein Sinken der Preise/Anzahl; **the ~ of the empire** der Verfall des Reiches; **~ and fall** Verfall und Untergang; **a ~ in wealth/poverty/the birth rate** eine Abnahme des Wohlstands/ein Rückgang der Armut/der Geburten; **be on the ~:** nachlassen; **he is on the ~:** er ist auf dem absteigenden Ast *(ugs.)*; **be in ~:** rückläufig sein
declutch [di:'klʌtʃ] *v.i. (Motor Veh.)* auskuppeln; **double-~:** Zwischengas geben
decoction [dɪ'kɒkʃn] *n. (product)* Dekokt, *das (Pharm.)*; Abkochung, *die*
decode [di:'kəʊd] *v.t.* dekodieren, dechiffrieren ⟨*Mitteilung, Signal*⟩; entschlüsseln ⟨*Schrift, Hieroglyphen*⟩
decoder [di:'kəʊdə(r)] *n. (Electronics)* Decoder, *der*
décolleté [deɪ'kɒlteɪ] **1.** *adj.* dekolletiert ⟨*Kleid, Dame*⟩. **2.** *n.* Dekolleté, *das*
decolonize (decolonise) [di:'kɒlənaɪz] *v.t.* dekolonisieren
decompose [di:kəm'pəʊz] *v.i.* sich zersetzen
decomposition [di:kɒmpə'zɪʃn] *n.* Zersetzung, *die; (rotting also)* Verrottung, *die*
decompression [di:kəm'preʃn] *n.* Dekompression, *die*
decom'pression: ~ chamber *n.* Dekompressionskammer, *die;* **~ sickness** *n., no pl.* Dekompressionskrankheit, *die*
decongestant [di:kən'dʒestənt] *n. (Med.)* Abschwellung bewirkendes Mittel; **bronchial ~:** ≈ Hustensaft, *der;* **nasal ~:** Nasenspray, *das; (drops)* Nasentropfen *Pl.*
decontaminate [di:kən'tæmɪneɪt] *v.t.* dekontaminieren *(fachspr.)*; entseuchen
decontamination [di:kəntæmɪ'neɪʃn] *n.* Dekontamination, *die (fachspr.)*; Entseuchung, *die*
decontrol [di:kən'trəʊl] *v.t.*, **-ll-** *(Admin.)* freigeben
décor ['deɪkɔ:(r)] *n.* Ausstattung, *die;* Dekor, *der od. das*
decorate ['dekəreɪt] *v.t.* **a)** *(adorn)* schmücken ⟨*Raum, Straße, Baum*⟩; verzieren ⟨*Kuchen, Kleid*⟩; dekorieren ⟨*Schaufenster*⟩; *(with wallpaper)* tapezieren; *(with paint)* streichen; **b)** *(invest with order etc.)* auszeichnen; dekorieren
decorated ['dekəreɪtɪd] *adj.* **a)** geschmückt ⟨*Zimmer*⟩; verziert ⟨*Kuchen*⟩; **b)** *(Archit.)* **D~ style** Decorated style, *der (fachspr.) (Stil der englischen Hochgotik)*
decoration [dekə'reɪʃn] *n.* **a)** Schmücken, *das; (with paint)* Streichen, *das; (with wallpaper)* Tapezieren, *das; (of cake, dress)* Verzieren, *das; (of shop window)* De-

koration, *die;* **b)** *(adornment) (thing)* Schmuck, *der; (in shop window)* Dekoration, *die;* **c)** *(medal etc.)* Auszeichnung, *die;* Dekoration, *die;* **D~ Day** *(Amer.) amerikanischer Heldengedenktag (30. Mai);* **d)** *in pl.* **Christmas ~s** Weihnachtsschmuck, *der*

decorative ['dekərətɪv] *adj.* dekorativ

decorator ['dekəreɪtə(r)] *n.* Maler, *der*/Malerin, *die; (paper-hanger)* Tapezierer, *der*/Tapeziererin, *die;* **[firm of] ~s** Malerbetrieb, *der*

decorous ['dekərəs] *adj.,* **decorously** ['dekərəslɪ] *adv.* schicklich *(geh.)*

decorousness ['dekərəsnɪs] *n., no pl.* Schicklichkeit, *die (geh.)*

decorum [dɪ'kɔ:rəm] *n.* Dekorum, *das (geh. veralt.); (seemliness also)* Schicklichkeit, *die (geh.);* **behave with ~:** sich schicklich benehmen

decoy 1. [dɪ'kɔɪ] *v. t.* **a)** *(allure)* locken; *(ensnare)* betören; **~ sb./sth. into sth.** jmdn./etw. in etw. *(Akk.)* locken; **~ sb./sth. into doing sth.** jmdn./etw. dazu verleiten, etw. zu tun; **b)** *(Hunting)* locken. **2.** [dɪ'kɔɪ, 'di:kɔɪ] *n.* **a)** *(Hunting)* Lockvogel, *der;* **b)** *(person)* Lockvogel, *der;* **c)** *(bait)* Verlokkung, *die*

decrease 1. [dɪ'kri:s] *v. i.* abnehmen; ⟨*Anzahl, Einfuhr, Produktivität:*⟩ abnehmen, zurückgehen; ⟨*Stärke, Gesundheit:*⟩ nachlassen; **~ in value/size/weight/popularity** an Wert/Größe/Gewicht/Popularität verlieren; **~ in price** im Preis fallen; billiger werden. **2.** *v. t.* reduzieren; [ver]mindern ⟨*Wert, Lärm, Körperkraft*⟩; schmälern ⟨*Popularität, Macht*⟩; senken ⟨*Standard, Kaufkraft*⟩. **3.** ['di:kri:s] *n.* Rückgang, *der; (in weight, knowledge, stocks)* Abnahme, *die; (in strength, power, energy)* Nachlassen, *das; (in value, noise)* Minderung, *die; (in standards)* Senkung, *die;* **a ~ in inflation/strength/speed** ein Rückgang der Inflation/ein Nachlassen der Kräfte/eine Minderung der Geschwindigkeit; **be on the ~** *see* **1**

decreasingly [dɪ'kri:sɪŋlɪ] *adv.* immer weniger

decree [dɪ'kri:] **1.** *n.* **a)** *(ordinance)* Dekret, *das;* Erlaß, *der;* **b)** *(Law)* Urteil, *das;* **~ nisi/absolute** vorläufiges/endgültiges Scheidungsurteil. **2.** *v. t. (ordain)* verfügen

decrepit [dɪ'krepɪt] *adj.* altersschwach; *(dilapidated)* heruntergekommen ⟨*Haus, Stadt*⟩; schrottreif ⟨*Auto, Maschine*⟩

decrepitude [dɪ'krepɪtju:d] *n., no pl.* Altersschwäche, *die; (of house)* heruntergekommener Zustand; *(of car, machine)* schrottreifer Zustand

decry [dɪ'kraɪ] *v. t.* verwerfen

dedicate ['dedɪkeɪt] *v. t.* **a)** *(with name of honoured person)* **~ sth. to sb.** jmdm. etw. widmen; **a statue ~d to the memory of ...:** eine Statue zum Gedenken an ...; **b)** *(give up)* **~ one's life to sth.** sein Leben einer Sache *(Dat.)* weihen; **c)** *(devote solemnly)* weihen

dedicated ['dedɪkeɪtɪd] *adj.* **a)** *(devoted)* **be ~ to sth./sb.** nur für etw./jmdn. leben; **b)** *(devoted to vocation)* hingebungsvoll; **a ~ teacher/politician** ein Lehrer/Politiker mit Leib und Seele

dedication [dedɪ'keɪʃn] *n.* **a)** *(act, inscription)* Widmung, *die* **(to** *Dat.***);** *(in book)* Widmung, *die;* Zueignung, *die; (on building, monument)* Inschrift, *die;* **b)** *(devotion)* Hingabe, *die;* **c)** *(ceremony)* Weihe, *die*

deduce [dɪ'dju:s] *v. t.* **~ sth. [from sth.]** etw. [aus etw.] ableiten; auf etw. *(Akk.)* [aus etw.] schließen; **~ from sth. that ...:** aus etw. schließen, daß ...

deducible [dɪ'dju:sɪbl] *adj.* ableitbar, *(Philos.)* deduzierbar **(from** aus**)**

deduct [dɪ'dʌkt] *v. t.* **~ sth. [from sth.]** etw. [von etw.] abziehen

deductible [dɪ'dʌktɪbl] *adj.* **be ~:** einbehalten werden [können]

deduction [dɪ'dʌkʃn] *n.* **a)** *(deducting)* Abzug, *der;* **b)** *(deducing, thing deduced)* Ableitung, *die;* **c)** *(amount)* Abzüge *Pl.;* **a ~ from the price** ein Preisnachlaß

deductive [dɪ'dʌktɪv] *adj.* deduktiv

deductively [dɪ'dʌktɪvlɪ] *adv.* deduktiv

deed [di:d] **1.** *n.* **a)** Tat, *die;* **b)** *(Law)* [gesiegelte] Urkunde; **~ of transfer** Übertragungsurkunde, *die; see also* **covenant 1 b. 2.** *v. t. (Amer.)* **~ sth. to sb.** jmdm. etw. [urkundlich] übertragen

deed: ~-box *n. Kasten zur Aufbewahrung von Urkunden;* ≈ Dokumentenbox, *die;* **~ poll** ['di:d pəʊl] *n. (Law)* einseitiges Rechtsgeschäft *(Rechtsw.)*

deejay [di:'dʒeɪ] *n. (sl.)* Diskjockey, *der*

deem [di:m] *v. t.* erachten für; **[as] I ~ed** wie mir schien; **she is ~ed to be the best singer** sie gilt als die beste Sängerin; **he shall be ~ed to have given his assent** man wird annehmen, daß er seine Zustimmung gegeben hat

deep [di:p] **1.** *adj.* **a)** *(extending far down, going far in, lit. or fig.)* tief; **water ten feet ~:** drei Meter tiefes Wasser; **take a ~ breath/drink** tief Atem holen/einen tiefen Schluck nehmen; **b)** *(lying far down or back or inwards)* tief; **ten feet ~ in water** drei Meter tief unter Wasser; **be ~ in thought/prayer** in Gedanken/im Gebet versunken sein; **be ~ in discussion** mitten in einer Diskussion sein; **be ~ in debt** hoch verschuldet sein; **be standing three ~:** drei hintereinander stehen; **c)** *(profound)* tief ⟨*Grund*⟩; ernst ⟨*Problem, Sache*⟩; gründlich ⟨*Studium, Forschung*⟩; tiefgründig ⟨*Bemerkung*⟩; **give sth. ~ thought** über etw. *(Akk.)* gründlich nachdenken; **he's a ~ one** *(coll.)* er ist ein stilles Wasser *(ugs.);* **in ~ space** [tief] im Weltraum; **d)** *(heartfelt)* tief; aufrichtig ⟨*Interesse, Dank*⟩; **e)** *(low-pitched, intense)* tief; *(full-toned)* volltönend; **the ~-blue sea** das tiefblaue Meer; **f)** *(Cricket) weit vom Schlagmann entfernt. See also* **end 1 f. 2.** *adv.* tief; **still waters run ~** *(prov.)* stille Wasser sind tief *(Spr.);* **~ down** *(fig.)* im Innersten. **3.** *n.* **a)** *(~ part)* **~s** Tiefen *Pl.;* **the ~** *(poet.)* der Ozean; **b)** *(abyss, lit. or fig.)* Tiefe, *die;* **c)** *(Cricket)* **the ~** *äußerer Rand des Spielfeldes*

deep 'breathing *n.* tiefes Atmen; **~ [exercise]** Atemübung, *die*

deepen ['di:pn] **1.** *v. t.* **a)** tiefer machen; vertiefen; **b)** *(make lower)* tiefer werden lassen ⟨*Stimme*⟩; **c)** *(increase, intensify)* vertiefen; intensivieren ⟨*Farbe*⟩. **2.** *v. i.* **a)** tiefer werden; **b)** *(intensify)* sich vertiefen

deep: ~-'freeze 1. *n. (Amer.:* **P)** Tiefkühltruhe, *die; (in shop also)* Tiefkühlbox, *die; (upright)* Gefrierschrank, *der;* **2.** *v. t.* tiefgefrieren; **~-fried** *adj.* fritiert; **~-laid** *adj.* ausgeklügelt; ausgetüftelt

deeply ['di:plɪ] *adv.* **a)** *(to great depth, lit. or fig.)* tief; **drink ~:** einen kräftigen Zug *od.* Schluck nehmen; **b)** tief ⟨*beeindruckt, gerührt, verletzt, getroffen*⟩; äußerst ⟨*interessiert, dankbar, engagiert, selbstbewußt*⟩; **be ~ in love** sehr verliebt sein; **be ~ indebted to sb.** jmdm. sehr zu Dank verpflichtet sein; **sleep ~:** tief *od.* fest schlafen; **read/study ~:** sehr aufmerksam lesen/studieren

deepness ['di:pnɪs] *n., no pl.* Tiefe, *die; (of interest, gratitude)* Ausmaß, *das*

deep: ~-rooted *adj.* tief ⟨*Abneigung*⟩; tiefverwurzelt ⟨*Tradition*⟩; **~-sea** *adj.* Tiefsee-; **~-'seated** *adj.* tief sitzend; **D~ 'South** *n. (Amer.)* tiefer Süden *(die Staaten der USA am Golf von Mexiko)*

deer [dɪə(r)] *n., pl. same* Hirsch, *der; (roe ~)* Reh, *das*

deer: ~-forest *n.* Jagdgehege, *das;* **~-park** *n.* Wildpark, *der;* **~skin** *n.* Rehleder, *das;* **~-stalker** *n.* **a)** *(person)* Jäger *(auf der Pirsch);* **b)** *(hat)* Mütze *(aus Stoff mit einem Schild vorn und hinten);* ≈ Sherlock-Holmes-Mütze, *die*

de-escalate [di:'eskəleɪt] *v. t.* deeskalieren

deface [dɪ'feɪs] *v. t.* verunstalten; verschandeln ⟨*Gebäude*⟩

defacement [dɪ'feɪsmənt] *n.* Verunstaltung, *die; (of building)* Verschandelung, *die*

de facto [di: 'fæktəʊ, deɪ 'fæktəʊ] **1.** *adj.* de facto; **a ~ government** eine De-facto-Regierung. **2.** *adv.* de facto

defamation [defə'meɪʃn, di:fə'meɪʃn] *n.* Diffamierung, *die*

defamatory [dɪ'fæmətərɪ] *adj.* diffamierend; **be ~ about sb.** jmdn. diffamieren

defame [dɪ'feɪm] *v. t.* diffamieren; beschmutzen ⟨*Name, Ansehen*⟩

default [dɪ'fɔ:lt, dɪ'fɒlt] **1.** *n.* **a)** *(lack)* Mangel, *der;* **in ~ of** mangels (+ *Gen.*); in Ermangelung *(geh.)* (+ *Gen.*); **b)** *(Law) (failure to act)* Versäumnis, *das; (failure to appear)* Säumnis, *die od. das;* **judgement by ~:** Versäumnisurteil, *das;* **c)** *(failure to pay)* Verzug, *der; (failure to act or appear)* Ausbleiben, *das; (Sport)* Nichterscheinen, *das;* **~ of payment** Zahlungsverzug, *der;* **lose/go by ~:** durch Abwesenheit verlieren/nicht zur Geltung kommen; **win by ~:** durch Nichterscheinen des Gegners gewinnen. **2.** *v. i.* versagen; **~ on one's payments/debts** seinen Zahlungsverpflichtungen nicht nachkommen

defaulter [dɪ'fɔ:ltə(r), dɪ'fɒltə(r)] *n.* **a)** *(Brit. Mil.)* Straffällige, *der;* **b)** *(who fails to pay)* säumiger Schuldner/säumige Schuldnerin

defeat [dɪ'fi:t] **1.** *v. t.* **a)** *(overcome)* besiegen; *(in battle or match also)* schlagen; ablehnen, zu Fall bringen ⟨*Antrag, Vorschlag*⟩; **b)** *(baffle)* **sth. ~s me** ich kann etw. nicht begreifen; **it ~s me why ...:** ich verstehe einfach nicht, warum ...; *(frustrate)* **the task has ~ed us** diese Aufgabe hat uns überfordert; **~ the object/purpose of sth.** etw. völlig sinnlos machen; **~ one's own object** seine eigenen Pläne durchkreuzen. **2.** *n.* *(being defeated)* Niederlage, *die; (defeating)* Sieg, *der* **(of** über + *Akk.***);** **the ~ of a motion/bill** das Scheitern eines Antrags/Gesetzentwurfs; **admit ~:** seine Niederlage eingestehen

defeatism [dɪ'fi:tɪzm] *n.* Defätismus, *der*

defeatist [dɪ'fi:tɪst] **1.** *n.* Defätist, *der.* **2.** *adj.* defätistisch; **you're so ~ about things** du siehst die Dinge immer so schwarz

defecate ['defəkeɪt] *v. i.* Kot ausscheiden; defäkieren *(Med.)*

defecation [defə'keɪʃn] *n.* Ausscheidung, *die;* Defäkation, *die (Med.)*

defect 1. ['di:fekt, dɪ'fekt] *n.* **a)** *(lack)* Mangel, *der;* **b)** *(shortcoming)* Fehler, *der; (in construction, body, mind, etc. also)* Defekt, *der;* **the ~s in his character, his character ~s** seine Charakterfehler; **he has the ~s of his qualities** er hat die für seine guten Eigenschaften typischen Charakterfehler. **2.** [dɪ'fekt] *v. i.* überlaufen **(to** zu**);** **~ from the cause** sich von der Sache lossagen

defection [dɪ'fekʃn] *n.* Abfall, *der; (desertion)* Flucht, *die;* **~ from the army** Desertion aus der Armee

defective [dɪ'fektɪv] *adj.* **a)** *(faulty)* defekt ⟨*Maschine*⟩; gestört ⟨*Gehirn*⟩; fehlerhaft ⟨*Sprache, Material, Arbeiten, Methode, Plan*⟩; mangelhaft, gestört ⟨*Verdauung, Kreislauf, Wachstum, Entwicklung*⟩; **sb./sth. is ~ in sth.** es mangelt jmdm./einer Sache an etw. *(Dat.);* **have a ~ heart** einen Herzfehler haben; **b)** *(mentally deficient)* geistig gestört; **c)** *(Ling.)* defektiv

defectiveness [dɪ'fektɪvnɪs] *n., no pl.* Fehlerhaftigkeit, *die*

defector [dɪ'fektə(r)] *n.* Überläufer, *der*/-läuferin, *die; (from a cause or party)* Abtrünnige, *der/die; (from army)* Deserteur, *der*

defence [dɪ'fens] *n. (Brit.)* **a)** *(defending)* Verteidigung, *die; (of body against disease)* Schutz, *der;* **in ~ of** zur Verteidigung (+ *Gen.*); **b)** *(thing that protects, means of* *resisting attack)* Schutz, *der;* **c)** *(justification)* Rechtfertigung, *die;* **in sb.'s ~:** zu jmds. Verteidigung; **come to sb.'s ~:** jmdm. zur Seite springen; **d)** *(military resources)* Verteidigung, *die;* **e)** *in pl. (fortification)* Befestigungsanlagen *Pl.; (fig.)* Widerstandskraft, *die;* **sb.'s ~s are down** *(fig.)* jmds. Widerstandskraft ist erschöpft; **f)** *(Law)* Verteidigung, *die;* **the case for the ~:** die Verteidigung; **~ witness** Zeuge/Zeugin der Verteidigung; **g)** *(Sport)* Verteidigung, *die*

de'fence budget *n.* Verteidigungshaushalt, *der*

defenceless [dɪ'fenslɪs] *adj. (Brit.)* wehrlos; **look ~:** hilflos dreinschauen

de'fence mechanism *n. (Physiol., Psych.)* Abwehrmechanismus, *der*

defend [dɪ'fend] **1.** *v. t.* **a)** *(protect)* schützen (**from** vor + *Dat.*); *(by fighting)* verteidigen; **b)** *(uphold by argument, vindicate, speak or write in favour of)* verteidigen; verteidigen, rechtfertigen ‹*Politik, Handeln*›; **c)** *(Sport)* verteidigen ‹*Titel, Tor*›; **d)** *(Law)* verteidigen; **~ oneself** sich selbst verteidigen. **2.** *v. i. (Sport)* verteidigen

defendant [dɪ'fendənt] *n. (Law) (accused)* Angeklagte, *der/die; (sued)* Beklagte, *der/die*

defender [dɪ'fendə(r)] *n.* **a)** *(one who defends)* Verteidiger, *der; (of principle, method, etc.)* Verfechter, *der;* **b)** *(Sport) (of championship)* Titelverteidiger, *der/*-verteidigerin, *die; (of goal)* Verteidiger, *der/*Verteidigerin, *die*

defense, defenseless *(Amer.) see* **defence, defenceless**

defensible [dɪ'fensɪbl] *adj.* **a)** *(easily defended)* wehrhaft; **b)** *(justifiable)* vertretbar

defensive [dɪ'fensɪv] **1.** *adj.* **a)** *(protective)* defensiv ‹*Strategie, Handlung*›; **~ player** Defensivspieler, *der;* **~ wall** Schutzwall, *der;* **~ fortification** Verteidigungsanlage, *die;* **b)** *(by argument)* rechtfertigend; **c)** *(excessively self-justifying)* **he's always so ~ when he's criticized** er will sich immer um jeden Preis rechtfertigen, wenn er kritisiert wird. **2.** *n.* Defensive, *die;* **be/act on the ~:** in der Defensive sein; **she's always so much on the ~:** sie geht immer gleich in die Defensive

defensively [dɪ'fensɪvlɪ] *adv.* **act ~:** sich in übertriebener Weise rechtfertigen

¹defer [dɪ'fɜ:(r)] *v. t.,* **-rr- a)** *(postpone)* aufschieben; **~red annuity** aufgeschobene Rente; **~red payment** Ratenzahlung, *die;* **~red shares/stock** Nachzugsaktien *Pl.;* **b)** *(Amer.: postpone call-up of)* zurückstellen

²defer *v. i.,* **-rr-:** **~ [to sb.]** sich [jmdm.] beugen; **~ to sb.'s wishes** sich jmds. Wünschen fügen

deference ['defərəns] *n.* Respekt, *der;* Ehrerbietung, *die (geh.);* **in ~ to sb./sth.** aus Achtung vor jmdm./etw.; **in ~ to your wishes** Ihren Wünschen entsprechend

deferential [defə'renʃl] *adj.* respektvoll; groß ‹*Respekt*›; **be ~ to sb./sth.** jmdm./einer Sache mit Respekt begegnen

deferentially [defə'renʃəlɪ] *adv.* respektvoll

deferment [dɪ'fɜ:mənt] *n.* **a)** *(deferring)* Aufschub, *der;* **b)** *(Amer.: postponement of call-up)* **have a ~:** zurückgestellt sein

defiance [dɪ'faɪəns] *n.* Aufsässigkeit, *die; (open disobedience)* Mißachtung, *die;* **act of ~:** Herausforderung, *die;* **in ~ of sb./sth.** jmdm./einer Sache zum Trotz

defiant [dɪ'faɪənt] *adj.* aufsässig ‹*Tonfall, Kind, Benehmen*›

defiantly [dɪ'faɪəntlɪ] *adv.* aufsässig

deficiency [dɪ'fɪʃənsɪ] *n.* **a)** *(lack)* Mangel, *der* (**of, in** an + *Dat.*); **mental ~** geistige Behinderung; **nutritional ~:** Ernährungsmangel, *der;* **b)** *(inadequacy)* Unzulänglichkeit, *die;* **c)** *(deficit)* Defizit, *das*

de'ficiency disease *n.* Mangelkrankheit, *die*

deficient [dɪ'fɪʃənt] *adj.* **a)** *(not having enough)* **sb./sth. is ~ in sth.** jmdm./einer Sache mangelt es an etw. *(Dat.);* **be [mentally] ~:** geistig behindert sein; **b)** *(not being enough)* nicht ausreichend; *(in quality also)* unzulänglich

deficit ['defɪsɪt] *n.* Defizit, *das* (**of** an + *Dat.*); **a ~ of manpower** ein Mangel an Arbeitskräften

'deficit spending *n. (Finance)* Defizitfinanzierung, *die*

¹defile 1. [dɪ'faɪl] *v. i.* [hintereinander] marschieren; defilieren *(geh.).* **2.** ['di:faɪl] *n.* **a)** *(narrow way)* Engpaß, *der;* **b)** *(gorge)* Hohlweg, *der*

²defile [dɪ'faɪl] *v. t.* **a)** verschandeln; *(pollute)* verderben ‹*Aussicht*›; verpesten ‹*Luft*›; **b)** *(desecrate)* beflecken ‹*Unschuld, Reinheit*›

defilement [dɪ'faɪlmənt] *n.* **a)** Verschandelung, *die; (of air)* Verpestung, *die;* **b)** *(desecration)* Befleckung, *die*

definable [dɪ'faɪnəbl] *adj. (able to be set forth)* definierbar; erklärbar; **love is not ~ in words** Liebe kann man nicht mit Worten erklären

define [dɪ'faɪn] *v. t.* **a)** *(mark out limits of, make clear)* definieren; festlegen; **be ~d [against sth.]** sich [gegen etw.] abzeichnen; **~ one's position** *(fig.)* Stellung beziehen (**on** zu); **b)** *(set forth essence or meaning of)* definieren; **c)** *(characterize)* charakterisieren

definite ['defɪnɪt] *adj. (having exact limits)* bestimmt; *(precise)* eindeutig, definitiv ‹*Antwort, Entscheidung*›; eindeutig ‹*Beschluß, Verbesserung, Standpunkt*›; eindeutig, klar ‹*Vorteil*›; klar *od.* scharf umrissen ‹*Ziel, Plan, Thema*›; klar ‹*Konzept, Linie, Vorstellung*›; deutlich ‹*Konturen, Umrisse*›; genau ‹*Zeitpunkt*›; entschlossen ‹*Schritte, Stimme, Person*›; **you don't seem to be very ~:** Sie scheinen sich nicht ganz sicher zu sein; **she was so ~ about marrying him** sie war so fest entschlossen, ihn zu heiraten

definitely ['defɪnɪtlɪ] **1.** *adv.* eindeutig ‹*festlegen, größer sein, verbessert, erklären*›; endgültig ‹*entscheiden, annehmen*›; fest ‹*vereinbaren*›; **she's ~ going to America** sie fährt auf jeden Fall nach Amerika. **2.** *int. (coll.)* na, klar *(ugs.)*

definition [defɪ'nɪʃn] *n.* **a)** Definition, *die;* **by ~:** per definitionem *(geh.);* **b)** *(making or being distinct, degree of distinctness)* Schärfe, *die;* **improve the ~ on the TV** den Fernseher schärfer einstellen

definitive [dɪ'fɪnɪtɪv] *adj.* **a)** *(decisive)* endgültig, definitiv ‹*Beschluß, Antwort, Urteil*›; entschieden ‹*Ton, Art*›; entscheidend ‹*Vorsprung*›; **b)** *(most authoritative)* maßgeblich; **c)** *(Philat.)* **~ stamp** Dauermarke, *die*

definitively [dɪ'fɪnɪtɪvlɪ] *adv.* endgültig; definitiv; mit Entschiedenheit ‹*beanspruchen, behaupten*›

deflate [dɪ'fleɪt] **1.** *v. t.* **a)** *(release air etc. from)* **~ a tyre/balloon** die Luft aus einem Reifen/Ballon ablassen; **b)** *(cause to lose conceitedness)* ernüchtern; **~ sb.'s opinion of himself** jmds. Selbsteinschätzung *(Dat.)* einen Dämpfer versetzen *(ugs.);* **c)** *(Econ.)* deflationieren. **2.** *v. i.* **a)** ‹*Reifen:*› Luftdruck verlieren; **b)** *(Econ.)* deflationieren

deflation [dɪ'fleɪʃn] *n. (Econ., Geol.)* Deflation, *die*

deflationary [dɪ'fleɪʃənərɪ] *adj. (Econ.)* deflationär

deflect [dɪ'flekt] **1.** *v. t. (bend)* umleiten ‹*Fluß*›; brechen, beugen ‹*Licht*›; *(cause to deviate)* **~ sb./sth. [from sb./sth.]** jmdn./etw. [von jmdm./einer Sache] ablenken. **2.** *v. i. (bend)* einen Bogen machen; *(deviate)* abbiegen; *(fig.)* abweichen

deflection *see* **deflexion**

deflector [dɪ'flektə(r)] *n.* Deflektor, *der*

deflexion [dɪ'flekʃn] *n. (Brit.)* **a)** *(bending)* Umleitung, *die; (deviation)* Ablenkung, *die; (turn)* Abweichung, *die; (fig.)* Ablenkung, *die;* **b)** *(Phys.)* Ausschlag, *der*

deflower [di:'flaʊə(r)] *v. t.* deflorieren

defocus [di:'fəʊkəs] *v. t.,* **-s-** *or* **-ss-** unscharf machen; *(Phys.)* defokussieren ‹*Strahl*›

defoliant [di:'fəʊlɪənt] *n.* Entlaubungsmittel, *das*

defoliate [di:'fəʊlɪeɪt] *v. t.* entlauben

defoliation [di:fəʊlɪ'eɪʃn] *n.* Entlaubung, *die*

deforestation [di:fɒrɪ'steɪʃn] *n.* Entwaldung, *die;* Abholzung, *die*

deform [dɪ'fɔ:m] **1.** *v. t.* **a)** *(deface)* deformieren; verunstalten; **b)** *(misshape)* verformen. **2.** *v. i.* **a)** *(become disfigured)* entstellt werden; **b)** *(Phys.)* sich verformen

deformation [di:fɔ:'meɪʃn] *n.* **a)** *(disfigurement)* Deformation, *die;* Entstellung, *die;* **b)** *(Phys.)* Verformung, *die*

deformed [dɪ'fɔ:md] *adj.* entstellt ‹*Gesicht*›; verunstaltet ‹*Person, Körperteil*›

deformity [dɪ'fɔ:mɪtɪ] *n. (being deformed)* Mißgestalt, *die; (malformation)* Verunstaltung, *die*

defraud [dɪ'frɔ:d] *v. t.* **~ sb. [of sth.]** jmdn. [um etw.] betrügen

defray [dɪ'freɪ] *v. t.* bestreiten ‹*Kosten*›

defrayal [dɪ'freɪəl], **defrayment** [dɪ'freɪmənt] *ns.* Bestreitung, *die*

defrock [di:'frɒk] *see* **unfrock**

defrost [di:'frɒst] *v.t.* auftauen ‹*Speisen*›; abtauen ‹*Kühlschrank*›; enteisen ‹*Windschutzscheibe, Fenster*›

deft [deft] *adj.* sicher und geschickt

deftly ['deftlɪ] *adv.* sicher und geschickt

deftness ['deftnɪs] *n., no pl.* Geschicklichkeit, *die*

defunct [dɪ'fʌŋkt] *adj.* tot, verstorben ‹*Person*›; *(extinct)* ausgestorben; *(fig.)* defekt ‹*Maschine*›; veraltet ‹*Gesetz*›; eingegangen ‹*Zeitung*›; stillgelegt ‹*Betrieb, Bahnlinie*›; überholt, vergessen ‹*Brauch, Idee, Mode*›

defuse [di:'fju:z] *v. t. (lit. or fig.)* entschärfen

defy [dɪ'faɪ] *v. t.* **a)** auffordern; **~ sb. to do sth.** jmdn. auffordern, etw. zu tun; **b)** *(resist openly)* **~ sb.** jmdm. trotzen *od.* Trotz bieten; *(refuse to obey)* **~ sb./sth.** sich jmdm./einer Sache widersetzen; **c)** *(present insuperable obstacles to)* widerstehen; **it defies explanation** das spottet jeder Erklärung

degeneracy [dɪ'dʒenərəsɪ] *n. (also Biol.)* Degeneration, *die*

degenerate 1. [dɪ'dʒenəreɪt] *v. i.* **a)** **~ [into sth.]** [zu etw.] verkommen *od.* degenerieren; **b)** *(Biol.)* **~ [into sth.]** [zu etw.] verkümmern *od.* degenerieren. **2.** [dɪ'dʒenərət] *adj. (also Biol.)* degeneriert; **become ~:** degenerieren

degeneration [dɪdʒenə'reɪʃn] *n. (also Biol., Med.)* Degeneration, *die*

degradation [degrə'deɪʃn] *n.* **a)** *(abasement)* Erniedrigung, *die;* **b)** *(demotion; also Geol.)* Degradierung, *die;* **c)** *(Biol.)* Degeneration, *die;* **d)** *(Chem.)* Abbau, *der*

degrade [dɪ'greɪd] *v. t.* **a)** *(abase)* erniedrigen; herabsetzen ‹*Ansehen, Maßstab*›; **b)** *(demote)* degradieren; **c)** *(Chem.)* abbauen; **d)** *(Geol.)* zerfallen lassen; erodieren

degrading [dɪ'greɪdɪŋ] *adj.* entwürdigend; erniedrigend

degree [dɪ'gri:] *n.* **a)** *(Math., Phys.)* Grad, *der;* **an angle/a temperature of 45 ~s** ein Winkel/eine Temperatur von 45 Grad; **b)** *(stage in scale or extent)* Grad, *der;* **by ~s** allmählich; **a certain ~ of imagination** ein gewisses Maß an Phantasie; **to a high ~:** in hohem Grade *od.* Maße; **to some** *or* **a certain ~:** [bis] zu einem gewissen Grad; **to the last ~:** in höchstem Grade; **obstinate to a ~:** reichlich widerspenstig *(ugs.);* **to what ~?** [in]wieweit?; **c)** *(relative condition)* Art, *die;* **in its ~:** auf seine Art; **d)** *(step in* *genealogical descent)* [Verwandtschafts]grad, *der;* **e) forbidden** *or* **prohibited ~s** *Verwandtschaftsgrade, die eine Heirat ausschließen;* **f)** *(rank)* Stand, *der;* **g)** *(academic rank)* [akademischer] Grad; **take/receive a ~ in sth.** einen akademischen Grad in etw. *(Dat.)* erwerben/verliehen bekommen; **have a ~ in physics/maths** einen Hochschulabschluß in Physik/Mathematik haben; **h)** *(Ling.)* **~s of comparison** Steigerungsstufen *Pl.;* **positive/comparative/superlative ~:** Positiv, *der*/Komparativ, *der*/Superlativ, *der;* **i)** *(Amer.)* **give sb. the third ~:** jmdn. schonungslos ins Verhör nehmen

degree: ~ ceremony *n.* Feierstunde zur Verleihung der akademischen Würde; **~ course** *n.* Studium, *das;* **~ day** *n.* Tag der Verleihung der akademischen Würde

dehumanize (dehumanise) [di:'hju:mənaɪz] *v.t.* entmenschlichen; dehumanisieren

dehydrate [di'haɪdreɪt] *v.t.* **a)** *(remove water from)* das Wasser entziehen (+ *Dat.*), austrocknen ‹*Körper*›; **~d** dehydratisiert *(fachspr.)*; getrocknet; **b)** *(make dry)* austrocknen

dehydration [di:haɪ'dreɪʃn] *n. see* **dehydrate:** Dehydration, *die (fachspr.);* Austrocknung, *die*

de-ice [di:'aɪs] *v.t.* enteisen

de-icer [di:'aɪsə(r)] *n.* Defroster, *der*

deify ['di:ɪfaɪ] *v.t. (make a god of)* vergotten; deifizieren; *(worship)* vergöttern

deign [deɪn] *v.t.* **~ to do sth.** sich [dazu] herablassen, etw. zu tun

deism ['di:ɪzm] *n.* Deismus, *der*

deist ['di:ɪst] *n.* Deist, *der*/Deistin, *die*

deity ['di:ɪtɪ] *n.* **a)** *(god)* Gottheit, *die;* **the D~:** Gott; die Gottheit *(geh.);* **b)** *(divine status)* Göttlichkeit, *die;* Gottheit, *die (geh.)*

dejected [dɪ'dʒektɪd] *adj.* niedergeschlagen

dejection [dɪ'dʒekʃn] *n.* Niedergeschlagenheit, *die*

delay [dɪ'leɪ] **1.** *v.t.* **a)** *(postpone)* verschieben; **he ~ed his visit for a few weeks** er verschob seinen Besuch einige Wochen; **b)** *(make late)* aufhalten; verzögern ‹*Ankunft, Abfahrt*›; **the train has been seriously ~ed** der Zug hat beträchtliche Verspätung; **c)** *(hinder)* aufhalten; *(retard)* **be ~ed** ‹*Veranstaltung:*› verspätet *od.* später erfolgen. **2.** *v.i.* *(wait)* warten; *(loiter)* trödeln *(ugs.);* **don't ~:** warte nicht damit; **~ in doing sth.** zögern, etw. zu tun. **3.** *n.* **a)** Verzögerung, *die* **(to** bei); **what's the ~ now?** weshalb geht es jetzt nicht weiter?; **without ~:** unverzüglich; **without further ~:** ohne weitere Verzögerung; **b)** *(Transport)* Verspätung, *die;* **trains are subject to ~:** es ist mit Zugverspätungen zu rechnen

delayed-action [dɪleɪd'ækʃn] *adj.* **~ bomb** Bombe mit Zeitzünder; **~ mechanism** *(Photog.)* Selbstauslöser, *der;* **~ drug** Medikament mit Depotwirkung

delectable [dɪ'lektəbl] *adj.* köstlich; **she looked ~:** sie sah reizend aus

delectation [di:lek'teɪʃn] *n.* Ergötzen, *das (geh.);* Vergnügen, *das*

delegate 1. ['delɪgət] *n.* **a)** *(elected representative)* Delegierte, *der/die; (of firm)* Beauftragte, *der/die;* **b)** *(deputy)* Vertreter, *der*/Vertreterin, *die;* **c)** *(member of deputation)* Delegierte, *der/die.* **2.** ['delɪgeɪt] *v.t.* **a)** *(depute)* delegieren; **b)** *(commit)* **~ power/responsibility/a task [to sb.]** Macht/Verantwortlichkeit/eine Aufgabe [an jmdn.] delegieren; **he does not know how to ~:** er will alles selbst erledigen

delegation [delɪ'geɪʃn] *n.* **a)** *(body of delegates)* Delegation, *die;* **b)** *(deputation)* Abordnung, *die;* Delegation, *die;* **c)** *(entrusting of authority to deputy)* Delegation, *die* **(to** an + *Akk.*)

delete [dɪ'li:t] *v.t.* streichen **(from** in + *Dat.*); *(Computing)* löschen; **~ where inapplicable** Nichtzutreffendes streichen

deleterious [delɪ'tɪərɪəs] *adj.* schädlich **(to** für); **~ [to health]** gesundheitsschädlich

deletion [dɪ'li:ʃn] *n.* Streichung, *die; (Computing)* Löschung, *die*

delft [delft] **(delf** [delf]) *n.* **~ [pottery]/tiles** *etc.* Delfter Keramik/Kacheln *usw.*

deliberate 1. [dɪ'lɪbərət] *adj.* **a)** *(intentional)* absichtlich; bewußt ‹*Lüge, Irreführung*›; vorsätzlich ‹*Verbrechen*›; **b)** *(fully considered)* wohlerwogen; [sorgfältig] überlegt; **c)** *(cautious)* behutsam; **d)** *(unhurried and considered)* bedächtig. **2.** [dɪ'lɪbəreɪt] *v.i.* **a)** *(think carefully)* **~ on sth.** über etw. *(Akk.)* [sorgfältig] nachdenken; **b)** *(debate)* **~ over** *or* **on** *or* **about sth.** über etw. *(Akk.)* beraten. **3.** *v.t.* ‹*Gruppe:*› beraten; ‹*Einzelner:*› überlegen

deliberately [dɪ'lɪbərətlɪ] *adv.* **a)** *(intentionally)* absichtlich; mit Absicht; vorsätzlich ‹*ein Verbrechen begehen*›; **b)** *(with full consideration)* **[very] ~:** [ganz] bewußt; **c)** *(in unhurried manner)* bedächtig

deliberation [dɪlɪbə'reɪʃn] *n.* **a)** *(care)* Sorgfalt, *die;* **b)** *(unhurried nature)* Bedächtigkeit, *die;* **c)** *(careful consideration)* Überlegung, *die;* **after much ~:** nach reiflicher Überlegung; **d)** *(discussion)* Beratung, *die*

deliberative [dɪ'lɪbərətɪv] *adj.* beratend

delicacy ['delɪkəsɪ] *n.* **a)** *(tactfulness and care)* Feingefühl, *das;* Delikatesse, *die (geh.);* **b)** *(fineness)* Zartheit, *die;* Feinheit, *die;* **c)** *(weakliness)* Zartheit, *die;* **d)** *(need of discretion etc.)* Delikatheit, *die;* **e)** *(food)* Delikatesse, *die*

delicate ['delɪkət] *adj.* **a)** *(easily injured)* empfindlich ‹*Organ*›; zart ‹*Gesundheit, Konstitution*›; *(sensitive)* sensibel, empfindlich ‹*Person, Natur*›; empfindlich ‹*Waage, Instrument, Verfassung*›; **b)** *(requiring careful handling)* empfindlich; *(fig.)* delikat, heikel ‹*Frage, Angelegenheit, Problem*›; **c)** *(fine, of exquisite quality, subdued)* zart; fein; delikat; *(dainty)* delikat; **d)** *(subtle)* fein; **e)** *(deft, light)* geschickt; zart; **f)** *(tactful)* taktvoll; behutsam

delicately ['delɪkətlɪ] *adv.* fein; **~ put** taktvoll ausgedrückt

delicatessen [delɪkə'tesən] *n.* Feinkostgeschäft, *das;* Delikatessengeschäft, *das*

delicious [dɪ'lɪʃəs] *adj.* köstlich, lecker ‹*Speise, Geschmack*›; köstlich ‹*Anblick, Spaß, Humor*›

deliciously [dɪ'lɪʃəslɪ] *adv.* köstlich; herrlich ‹*kühl, lustig*›

deliciousness [dɪ'lɪʃəsnɪs] *n., no pl.* Köstlichkeit, *die*

delight [dɪ'laɪt] **1.** *v.t.* erfreuen. **2.** *v.i.* **sb. ~s in doing sth.** es macht jmdm. Freude, etw. zu tun; **~ to do sth.** etw. gern tun. **3.** *n.* **a)** *(great pleasure)* Freude, *die;* **~ at sth./at doing sth.** Freude über etw. *(Akk.)* /darüber, etw. zu tun; **~ in sth./in doing sth.** Freude an etw. *(Dat.)* /daran, etw. zu tun; **to my/our ~:** zu meiner/unserer Freude; **sb. takes ~ in doing sth.** es macht jmdm. Freude, etw. zu tun; **b)** *(cause of pleasure)* Vergnügen, *das;* **these cakes are a ~ to eat** diese Kuchen schmecken köstlich

delighted [dɪ'laɪtɪd] *adj.* freudig ‹*Schrei*›; **be ~** ‹*Person:*› hocherfreut sein; **be ~ by** *or* **with** *or* **at sth.** sich über etw. *(Akk.)* freuen; **be ~ to do sth.** sich freuen, etw. zu tun; **we shall be ~ to accept your invitation** wir werden Ihre Einladung gern annehmen

delightedly [dɪ'laɪtɪdlɪ] *adv.* erfreut

delightful [dɪ'laɪtfl] *adj.* wunderbar; köstlich ‹*Geschmack, Klang*›; reizend ‹*Person, Landschaft*›

delightfully [dɪ'laɪtfəlɪ] *adv.* wunderbar; bezaubernd ‹*singen, tanzen, hübsch*›; angenehm ‹*hell, luftig*›

delimit [dɪ'lɪmɪt] *v.t.* begrenzen ‹*Gebiet, Region*›; *(fig.)* eingrenzen

delimitation [dɪlɪmɪ'teɪʃn] *n.* Begrenzung, *die; (fig.)* Eingrenzung, *die*

delineate [dɪ'lɪnɪeɪt] *v.t.* *(draw)* zeichnen; *(describe)* darstellen; **sharply ~d** sich scharf abzeichnend

delinquency [dɪ'lɪŋkwənsɪ] *n.* **a)** *no pl.* Kriminalität, *die;* **b)** *(misdeed)* Straftat, *die*

delinquent [dɪ'lɪŋkwənt] **1.** *n.* *(bes. jugendlicher)* Randalierer, *der.* **2.** *adj.* **a)** *(offending)* kriminell; **b)** *(Amer.: in arrears)* säumig

delirious [dɪ'lɪrɪəs] *adj.* **a)** delirant *(Med.);* **be ~:** im Delirium sein; ≈ phantasieren; **b)** *(wildly excited)* **be ~ [with sth.]** außer sich *(Dat.)* [vor etw. *(Dat.)*] sein; **c)** *(ecstatic, wild)* wahnsinnig; rasend ‹*Zorn, Wut*›

deliriously [dɪ'lɪrɪəslɪ] *adv.* **a)** wie im Delirium; **b)** *(ecstatically)* wahnsinnig

delirium [dɪ'lɪrɪəm] *n.* Delirium, *das*

delirium tremens [dɪlɪrɪəm 'tri:menz] *n., no pl.* Delirium tremens, *das (Med.);* Säuferwahn, *der (veralt.)*

deliver [dɪ'lɪvə(r)] *v.t.* **a)** *(utter)* halten ‹*Rede, Vorlesung, Predigt*›; vorbringen ‹*Worte*›; vortragen ‹*Verse*›; *(pronounce)* verkünden ‹*Urteil, Meinung, Botschaft*›; **b)** *(launch)* werfen ‹*Ball*›; versetzen ‹*Stoß, Schlag, Tritt*›; vortragen ‹*Angriff*›; **c)** *(hand over)* bringen; liefern ‹*Ware*›; zustellen ‹*Post, Telegramm*›; überbringen ‹*Botschaft*›; **~ sth. to the door** etw. ins Haus liefern; **~ [the goods]** *(fig.)* es schaffen *(ugs.); (fulfil promise)* halten, was man versprochen hat; **d)** *(give up)* aushändigen; **stand and ~!** halt, Geld her!; **e)** *(render)* erzählen ‹*Geschichte*›; geben, liefern ‹*Bericht, Beschreibung*›; stellen ‹*Ultimatum*›; geben ‹*Versprechen*›; ablegen ‹*Gelübde*›; **f)** *(Law)* aushändigen ‹*Dokument*›; **g)** *(assist in giving birth, aid in being born)* entbinden; *(give birth to)* gebären; **be ~ed [of a child]** [von einem Kind] entbunden werden; **h)** *(formal: unburden)* **~ oneself of one's opinion** seine Meinung loswerden; **i)** *(save)* **~ sb./sth. from sb./sth.** jmdn./etw. von jmdm./etw. erlösen; **~ us from evil** *(Relig.)* erlöse uns von dem Übel *od.* Bösen *(bibl.)*

~ 'up *v.t.* aushändigen; übergeben

deliverance [dɪ'lɪvərəns] *n.* Erlösung, *die* **(from** von); **~ from captivity** Befreiung aus der Gefangenschaft

delivery [dɪ'lɪvərɪ] *n.* **a)** *(handing over)* Lieferung, *die; (of letters, parcels)* Zustellung, *die;* **there is no charge for ~:** Lieferung frei Haus; **there are no deliveries on Sunday** sonntags wird keine Post zugestellt *od.* ausgetragen; **take ~ of sth.** etw. annehmen; **pay on ~:** bei Lieferung bezahlen; *(Post)* per Nachnahme bezahlen; **b)** Wurf, *der;* **~ of a blow/punch** Schlag, *der;* **c)** *(uttering)* Vortragen, *das; (manner of uttering)* Vortragsweise, *die;* Vortrag, *der;* **d)** *(childbirth)* Entbindung, *die*

delivery: ~ boy *n.* Austräger, *der;* **~ date** *n.* Liefertermin, *der;* **~ girl** *n.* Austrägerin, *die;* **~ man** *n.* Lieferant, *der;* Ausfahrer, *der (landsch.);* **~ note** *n.* Lieferschein, *der;* **~ room** *n. (Med.)* Kreißsaal, *der;* **~ service** *n.* Zustelldienst, *der;* **~ van** *n.* Lieferwagen, *der*

dell [del] *n.* [bewaldetes] Tal; Grund, *der (veralt.)*

delouse [di:'laʊs] *v.t.* entlausen

delphinium [del'fɪnɪəm] *n. (Bot.)* Rittersporn, *der*

delta ['deltə] *n.* **a)** *(of river; Greek letter)* Delta, *das;* **b)** *(Sch., Univ.: mark)* Vier, *die*

delta 'wing *n.* Deltaflügel, *der;* **~ aircraft** Deltaflugzeug, *das*

delude [dɪ'lju:d, dɪ'lu:d] *v.t.* täuschen; **~ sb. into believing that ...:** jmdm. weismachen, daß ...; **stop deluding yourself!** machen Sie sich doch nichts vor!

deluge ['delju:dʒ] **1.** *n.* **a)** *(rain)* sintflutartiger Regen; **b)** *(Bibl.)* **the D~:** die Sintflut; **c)** **~ of complaints/letters** Flut von Beschwer-

den/Briefen. **2.** *v. t.* *(lit. or fig.)* überschwemmen; **~ sb. with questions** jmdn. mit Fragen überschütten
delusion [dɪˈlju:ʒn, dɪˈlu:ʒn] *n.* Illusion, *die;* *(as symptom or form of madness)* Wahnvorstellung, *die;* **be under a ~:** einer Täuschung unterliegen; **be under the ~ that ...:** sich *(Dat.)* der Täuschung hingeben, daß ...; **have ~s of grandeur** größenwahnsinnig sein
delusive [dɪˈlju:sɪv, dɪˈlu:sɪv] *adj.*, **delusively** [dɪˈlju:sɪvlɪ, dɪˈlu:sɪvlɪ] *adv.* trügerisch
de luxe [dəˈlʌks, dəˈlu:ks] *adj.* Luxus-; **~ trade** Handel mit Luxusartikeln
delve [delv] *v. i.* **a)** *(arch./poet.: dig)* graben **(for** nach); **b)** *(search)* **~ into sth. [for sth.]** tief in etw. *(Akk.)* greifen[, um etw. herauszuholen]; **c)** *(research)* **~ into sth.** sich in etw. *(Akk.)* vertiefen; **~ into sb.'s past** in jmds. Vergangenheit nachforschen
Dem. *abbr. (Amer.)* **Democrat** Dem.
demagogue *(Amer.:* **demagog)** [ˈdeməgɒg] *n.* Demagoge, *der*/Demagogin, *die*
demagoguery [ˈdeməgɒgərɪ], **demagogy** [ˈdeməgɒgɪ] *ns.* Demagogie, *die*
demand [dɪˈmɑ:nd] **1.** *n.* **a)** *(request)* Forderung, *die* **(for** nach); **a ~ for sb. to do sth.** eine Forderung, daß jmd. etw. tun soll; **payable on ~:** zahlbar bei Sicht *(Kaufmannsspr.)*; **final ~:** letzte Mahnung; **b)** *(desire for commodity)* Nachfrage, *die* **(for** nach); **by popular ~:** auf vielfachen Wunsch; **sth./sb. is in [great] ~:** etw. ist [sehr] gefragt/jmd. ist [sehr] begehrt; **~ for teachers/clerks** Bedarf an Lehrern/Büroangestellten; **c)** *(claim)* **make ~s on sb.** jmdn. beanspruchen; **make too many ~s on sb.'s patience/time** jmds. Geduld/Zeit zu sehr beanspruchen; **I have many ~s on my time** ich bin zeitlich sehr beansprucht. *See also* **supply 2 a. 2.** *v. t.* **a)** *(ask for, require, need)* verlangen **(of, from** von); fordern ‹*Recht, Genugtuung*›; **~ to know/see sth.** etw. zu wissen/zu sehen verlangen; **he ~ed to be told everything** er wollte unbedingt alles wissen; **~ money with menaces** Geld erpressen; **b)** *(insist on being told)* unbedingt wissen wollen; **he ~ed my business** er fragte mich nachdrücklich, was ich wünschte
demanding [dɪˈmɑ:ndɪŋ] *adj.* anspruchsvoll; *(taxing)* anstrengend ‹*Kind*›; **physically [very] ~:** körperlich [sehr] anstrengend
deˈmand note *n.* **a)** *(Brit.: request for payment)* Zahlungsaufforderung, *die;* **b)** *(Amer.: bill payable at sight)* Sichtwechsel, *der (Bankw.)*
demarcate [ˈdi:mɑ:keɪt] *v. t.* festlegen ‹*Grenze*›; demarkieren *(geh.)*; **~ sth. from sth.** etw. von etw. abgrenzen
demarcation [di:mɑ:ˈkeɪʃn] *n.* *(of frontier)* Demarkation, *die (geh.)*; *(of topics)* Abgrenzung, *die;* **line of ~:** *(frontier)* Demarkationslinie, *die;* *(of topics)* Trennungslinie, *die*
demarˈcation dispute *n.* Streit um die Abgrenzung der Zuständigkeitsbereiche
démarche [ˈdeɪmɑ:ʃ] *n.* *(Diplom.)* Demarche, *die*
demean [dɪˈmi:n] *v. refl.* *(lower one's dignity)* **~ oneself [to do sth.]** sich [dazu] erniedrigen[, etw. zu tun]; **~ oneself by sth./doing sth.** sich durch etw. erniedrigen/sich dadurch erniedrigen, daß man etw. tut
demeaning [dɪˈmi:nɪŋ] *adj.* erniedrigend
demeanour *(Brit.; Amer.:* **demeanor)** [dɪˈmi:nə(r)] *n.* Benehmen, *das*
demented [dɪˈmentɪd] *adj.* wahnsinnig; **be ~ with worry** verrückt vor Angst sein *(ugs.)*; **like somebody ~:** wie ein Wahnsinniger/eine Wahnsinnige
dementedly [dɪˈmentɪdlɪ] *adv.* wie von Sinnen
dementia [dɪˈmenʃə] *(Med.)* Demenz, *die*
demerara [deməˈreərə] *n.* **~ [sugar]** brauner Zucker; Farin, *der*
demerit [di:ˈmerɪt] *n.* **a)** Schwäche, *die;* **b)** *(quality deserving blame)* [Charakter]fehler, *der;* *(action)* Fehlverhalten, *das;* **c)** *(Amer.: mark)* Strafpunkt, *der*
demesne [dɪˈmi:n, dɪˈmeɪn] *n.* *(land attached to mansion etc.)* Grundstück des Landsitzes
demi- [ˈdemɪ] *pref.* Halb-
ˈdemigod *n.* Halbgott, *der*
demijohn [ˈdemɪdʒɒn] *n.* Demijohn, *der (fachspr.)*; Korbflasche, *die*
demilitarisation, demilitarise *see* **demilitariz-**
demilitarization [di:mɪlɪtəraɪˈzeɪʃn] *n.* Entmilitarisierung, *die*
demilitarize [di:ˈmɪlɪtəraɪz] *v. t.* entmilitarisieren
demi-monde [ˈdemɪmɔ̃d] *n.* Demimonde, *die (geh.)*; Halbwelt, *die*
demise [dɪˈmaɪz] *n.* *(death)* Ableben, *das (geh.)*; *(fig.)* Verschwinden, *das;* *(of firm, party, creed, etc.)* Untergang, *der*
demisemiquaver [demɪˈsemɪkweɪvə(r), ˈdemɪsemɪkweɪvə(r)] *n.* *(Brit. Mus.)* Zweiunddreißigstelnote, *die*
demist [di:ˈmɪst] *v. t.* *(Brit.)* trockenblasen; *(with cloth etc.)* trockenreiben
demister [di:ˈmɪstə(r)] *n.* *(Brit.)* Defroster, *der;* Gebläse, *das*
demo [ˈdeməʊ] *n., pl.* **~s** *(coll.)* Demo, *die (ugs.)*
demob [di:ˈmɒb] *(Brit. coll.)* **1.** *v. t.*, **-bb-** aus dem Kriegsdienst entlassen. **2.** *n.* Entlassung aus dem Kriegsdienst
demobilisation, demobilise *see* **demobiliz-**
demobilization [di:məʊbɪlaɪˈzeɪʃn] *n.* Demobilisation, *die;* *(of soldier)* Entlassung aus dem Kriegsdienst
demobilize [di:ˈməʊbɪlaɪz] *v. t.* demobilisieren ‹*Armee, Kriegsschiff*›; aus dem Kriegsdienst entlassen ‹*Soldat*›
democracy [dɪˈmɒkrəsɪ] *n.* Demokratie, *die*
democrat [ˈdeməkræt] *n.* **a)** *(advocate of democracy)* Demokrat, *der*/Demokratin, *die;* **b) D~** *(Amer. Polit.)* Demokrat, *der*/Demokratin, *die*
democratic [deməˈkrætɪk] *adj.* **a)** demokratisch; **b)** *(Amer. Polit.)* **D~ Party** Demokratische Partei
democratically [deməˈkrætɪkəlɪ] *adv.* demokratisch
democratize [dɪˈmɒkrətaɪz] *v. t.* demokratisieren
demographic [di:məˈgræfɪk, deməˈgræfɪk], **demographical** [di:məˈgræfɪkl, deməˈgræfɪkl] *adj.* demographisch
demolish [dɪˈmɒlɪʃ] *v. t.* **a)** *(pull down)* abreißen; *(break to pieces)* zerstören; demolieren; schleifen, niederreißen ‹*Festungsanlagen*›; **~ by bombing** zerbomben; **b)** *(overthrow)* auflösen ‹*Institution*›; abschaffen ‹*System, Privilegien*›; widerlegen, umstoßen ‹*Theorie*›; entkräften ‹*Einwand*›; zerstören ‹*Legende, Mythos*›; **c)** *(joc.: eat up)* verschlingen
demolition [deməˈlɪʃn, di:məˈlɪʃn] *n.* **a)** *see* **demolish a:** Abriß, *der;* Zerstörung, *die;* Demolierung, *die;* Schleifung, *die;* **~ contractors** Abbruchunternehmen, *das;* **due for ~:** abbruchreif; **~ work** Abbruchsarbeit, *die;* **b)** *see* **demolish b:** Auflösung, *die;* Abschaffung, *die;* Widerlegung, *die;* Entkräftung, *die;* Zerstörung, *die*
demon [ˈdi:mən] *n.* **a)** Dämon, *der;* **b)** *(person, animal)* Teufel, *der;* **~ bowler** *(Cricket)* sehr schneller Werfer; **he is a ~ for work** er arbeitet wie ein Besessener
demonetize (demonetise) [di:ˈmʌnɪtaɪz] *v. t.* *(Finance)* demonetisieren *(Bankw.)*; aus dem Umlauf ziehen
demoniac [dɪˈməʊnɪæk] **1.** *adj.* dämonisch; *(possessed)* besessen. **2.** *n.* Besessene, *der/die*
demoniacal [di:məˈnaɪəkl, deməˈnaɪəkl] *adj.* dämonisch
demonic [di:ˈmɒnɪk] *see* **demoniac 1**
demonstrability [demənstrəˈbɪlɪtɪ, dɪmɒnstrəˈbɪlɪtɪ] *n., no pl.* Beweisbarkeit, *die*
demonstrable [ˈdemənstrəbl, dɪˈmɒnstrəbl] *adj.* beweisbar; nachweislich ‹*Schaden*›; **it is ~ that ...:** man kann beweisen, daß ...; es läßt sich nachweisen, daß ...
demonstrably [ˈdemənstrəblɪ, dɪˈmɒnstrəblɪ] *adv.* nachweislich
demonstrate [ˈdemənstreɪt] **1.** *v. t.* **a)** *(by examples, experiments, etc.)* zeigen; demonstrieren; *(show, explain)* vorführen ‹*Vorrichtung, Gerät*›; **b)** *(be proof of)* zeigen; beweisen; **c)** *(logically prove the truth of)* beweisen; nachweisen; **d)** *(prove the existence of)* zeigen ‹*Gefühl, Bedürfnis, Gutwilligkeit*›. **2.** *v. i.* **a)** *(make, take part in, a meeting or procession)* demonstrieren; **b)** *(give a demonstration)* **~ on sth./sb.** etw./jmdn. als Demonstrationsobjekt benutzen
demonstration [demənˈstreɪʃn] *n.* **a)** *(as way of teaching)* Demonstration, *die;* praktische Vorführung; **cookery ~s** Anschauungsunterricht im Kochen; **b)** *(showing of appliances etc.)* Vorführung, *die;* **give sb. a ~ of sth.** jmdm. etw. vorführen; **c)** *(meeting, procession)* Demonstration, *die;* **d)** *(exhibition of feeling etc.)* Ausdruck, *der;* **make a ~ of sth.** etw. zeigen; **e)** *(proof)* Beweis, *der*
demonstrative [dɪˈmɒnstrətɪv] *adj.* **a)** *(with open expression)* offen; unverhohlen ‹*Freude*›; **b)** *(serving to point out or to exhibit)* anschaulich; **c)** *(logically conclusive)* schlüssig ‹*Beweis, Argument*›; **d)** *(Ling.)* Demonstrativ-; hinweisend
demonstrator [ˈdemənstreɪtə(r)] *n.* **a)** *(in a meeting or procession)* Demonstrant, *der*/Demonstrantin, *die;* **b)** *(Commerc.)* Vorführer, *der*/Vorführerin, *die*
demoralisation, demoralise *see* **demoraliz-**
demoralization [dɪmɒrəlaɪˈzeɪʃn] *n.* Demoralisierung, *die*
demoralize [dɪˈmɒrəlaɪz] *v. t.* demoralisieren
demote [di:ˈməʊt] *v. t.* degradieren **(to** zu); zurückstufen ‹*Schüler*›
demotic [dɪˈmɒtɪk] *adj.* **a)** *(popular)* volkstümlich; **b) ~ Greek** Demotike, *die*
demotion [di:ˈməʊʃn] *n.* Degradierung, *die* **(to** zu); *(Sch.)* Zurückstufung, *die*
demur [dɪˈmɜ:(r)] *v. i.*, **-rr-** Einwände erheben; **~ to sth.** gegen etw. Einwände erheben; **~ at doing sth.** Einwände dagegen erheben, etw. zu tun
demure [dɪˈmjʊə(r)] *adj.* **a)** *(affectedly quiet and serious)* betont zurückhaltend; **b)** *(sober)* nüchtern; *(grave, composed)* ernst; gesetzt ‹*Benehmen*›; **c)** *(decorous)* sittsam *(veralt.)*; gesittet ‹*Rede*›
demurely [dɪˈmjʊəlɪ] *adv.* zurückhaltend; **~ dressed** sittsam *(veralt.)* gekleidet
demythologize (demythologise) [di:mɪˈθɒlədʒaɪz] *v. t.* entmythologisieren
den [den] *n.* **a)** *(of wild beast)* Höhle, *die;* **fox's ~:** Fuchsbau, *der;* **Daniel in the lions' ~** *(Bibl.)* Daniel in der Löwengrube; **b)** *(resort of criminals etc.)* **~ of thieves, thieves' ~:** Diebeshöhle, *die;* Diebesnest, *das;* **~ of vice or iniquity** Lasterhöhle, *die (ugs. abwertend)*; **robbers' ~:** Räuberhöhle, *die (veralt.)*; **c)** *(coll.: small room)* Bude, *die (ugs.)*
denationalisation, denationalise *see* **denationaliz-**
denationalization [di:næʃənəlaɪˈzeɪʃn] *n., no pl.* Privatisierung, *die*
denationalize [di:ˈnæʃənəlaɪz] *v. t.* privatisieren
denaturalize (denaturalise) [di:ˈnætʃərəlaɪz] *v. t.* **a)** *(make unnatural)* denaturieren; *(make unfit for drinking etc.)* denaturieren *(Chemie, Physik)*; ungenießbar machen; vergällen *(Chemie)* ‹*Alkohol*›; **~d** de-

naturiert *(Chemie, Physik)*; ungenießbar; **b)** *(deprive of citizenship)* denaturalisieren

denature [di:ˈneɪtʃə(r)] *v. t.* denaturieren

denazification [di:nɑ:tsɪfɪˈkeɪʃn] *n.* Entnazifizierung, *die*

denazify [di:ˈnɑ:tsɪfaɪ] *v. t.* entnazifizieren

dendrochronology [dendrəʊkrəˈnɒlədʒɪ] *n.* Dendrochronologie, *die;* Jahresringforschung, *die*

deniable [dɪˈnaɪəbl] *adj.* bestreitbar; *(refutable)* widerlegbar

denial [dɪˈnaɪəl] *n.* **a)** *(refusal)* Verweigerung, *die; (of request, wish)* Ablehnung, *die;* **b)** *(contradiction)* Leugnen, *das;* **an official ~:** ein offizielles Dementi; **~ of [the existence of] God** Gottesleugnung, *die;* **c)** *(disavowal of person)* Verleugnung, *die*

denier [ˈdenjə(r)] *n.* Denier, *das (Textilw.)*; **20 ~ stockings** 20-den-Strümpfe

denigrate [ˈdenɪgreɪt] *v. t.* verunglimpfen; **~ sb.'s character** jmdn. verunglimpfen *od. (ugs.)* schlechtmachen

denigration [denɪˈgreɪʃn] *n.* Verunglimpfung, *die*

denigratory [ˈdenɪgreɪtərɪ] *adj.* verunglimpfend

denim [ˈdenɪm] *n.* **a)** *(fabric)* Denim ®, *der;* Jeansstoff, *der;* **~ jacket** Jeansjacke, *die;* **b)** *in pl. (garment)* Bluejeans *Pl.*; *(for workman)* Arbeitsanzug, *der/*-hose, *die*

denizen [ˈdenɪzən] *n. (inhabitant, occupant)* Bewohner, *der/*Bewohnerin, *die*

Denmark [ˈdenmɑ:k] *pr. n.* Dänemark *(das)*

denominate [dɪˈnɒmɪneɪt] *v. t.* bezeichnen

denomination [dɪnɒmɪˈneɪʃn] *n.* **a)** *(class of units)* Einheit, *die;* **coins/paper money of the smallest ~:** Münzen/Papiergeld mit dem geringsten Nennwert; **b)** *(Relig.)* Glaubensgemeinschaft, *die;* Konfession, *die;* **c)** *(name, designation)* Bezeichnung, *die;* **d)** *(class, kind)* Art, *die*

denominational [dɪnɒmɪˈneɪʃənl] *adj. (Relig.)* konfessionell; **~ school** Konfessions- *od.* Bekenntnisschule, *die*

denominator [dɪˈnɒmɪneɪtə(r)] *n. (Math.)* Nenner, *der; see also* **common denominator**

denotation [di:nəˈteɪʃn] *n.* **a)** *(marking)* Kennzeichnung, *die;* **b)** *(sign, indication)* Zeichen, *das;* **c)** *(designation)* Bezeichnung, *die;* **d)** *(meaning)* Bedeutung, *die; (esp. Ling.)* Denotation, *die*

denote [dɪˈnəʊt] *v. t.* **a)** *(indicate)* hindeuten auf (+ *Akk.*); **~ that ...:** darauf hindeuten, daß ...; **b)** *(designate)* bedeuten; *(by specified symbol)* bezeichnen; **c)** *(signify)* symbolisieren; bedeuten

dénouement, denouement [deɪˈnu:mɑ̃] *n.* Ausgang, *der;* Auflösung, *die*

denounce [dɪˈnaʊns] *v. t.* **a)** *(inform against)* denunzieren *(abwertend); (accuse publicly)* beschuldigen; *(openly attack)* anprangern; **~ sb. to sb.** jmdn. bei jmdm. denunzieren; **~ sb. as a spy** jmdn. beschuldigen, ein Spion zu sein; **b)** *(terminate)* [auf]kündigen

denouncement [dɪˈnaʊnsmənt] *see* **denunciation**

dense [dens] *adj.* **a)** *(compacted in substance)* dicht; massiv ‹*Körper*›; *(photog.)* undurchlässig ‹*Negativ*›; **b)** *(crowded together)* dichtgedrängt; eng ‹*Schrift*›; **the population is very ~:** die Bevölkerungsdichte ist sehr hoch; **c)** *(stupid)* dumm; **he's pretty ~:** er ist ziemlich schwer von Begriff

densely [ˈdenslɪ] *adv.* dicht; **~ packed** dichtgedrängt

denseness [ˈdensnɪs] *n., no pl.* **a)** Dichte, *die;* **b)** *(stupidity)* Begriffsstutzigkeit, *die*

density [ˈdensɪtɪ] *n.* **a)** *(also Phys.)* Dichte, *die;* **population ~:** Bevölkerungsdichte, *die;* **b)** *(Photog.)* Schwärzung, *die;* Dichte, *die*

dent [dent] **1.** *n.* Beule, *die;* Delle, *die (landsch.)*; *(fig. coll.)* Loch, *das;* **make a ~ in production/in sb.'s savings** ein Loch in die Produktion/in jmds. Ersparnisse reißen; **make a bit of a ~ in sb.'s pride** jmds. Stolz leicht anknacksen *(ugs.)*. **2.** *v. t.* einbeulen; verbeulen; eindellen ‹*Holz, Tisch*› *(ugs.)*; *(fig.)* anknacksen *(ugs.)*; **he ~ed his car in a collision** sein Auto wurde bei einem Zusammenstoß verbeult *od.* eingebeult

dental [ˈdentl] **1.** *adj.* **a)** Zahn-; **~ care** Zahnpflege, *die;* **~ training** Ausbildung in der Zahnheilkunde; **b)** *(Phonet.)* Dental-; **~ consonant** *see* **2. 2.** *n. (Phonet.)* Dental, *der;* Zahnlaut, *der*

dental: ~ floss *n.* Zahnseide, *die;* **~ mechanic** *n.* Zahntechniker, *der/*-technikerin, *die;* **~ surgeon** *n.* Zahnarzt, *der/*-ärztin, *die*

dentate [ˈdenteɪt] *adj. (Bot., Zool.)* gezähnt

dentine [ˈdenti:n] *(Amer.:* **dentin** [ˈdentɪn]) *n. (Med.)* Dentin, *das (fachspr.)*; Zahnbein, *das*

dentist [ˈdentɪst] *n.* Zahnarzt, *der/*-ärztin, *die;* **at the ~['s]** beim Zahnarzt; **~'s chair** Zahnarztstuhl, *der*

dentistry [ˈdentɪstrɪ] *n., no pl.* Zahnheilkunde, *die*

denture [ˈdentʃə(r)] *n.* **~[s]** Zahnprothese, *die;* [künstliches] Gebiß; **partial ~:** Teilprothese, *die*

denuclearize (denuclearise) [di:ˈnju:klɪəraɪz] *v. t.* atomwaffenfrei machen

denudation [di:nju:ˈdeɪʃn] *n. (of valley, slope)* Abholzung, *die; (of tree)* Entlaubung, *die; (fig.)* Entzug, *der; (Geol.)* Denudation, *die (fachspr.)*; Abtragung, *die*

denude [dɪˈnju:d] *v. t.* **a)** abholzen, kahlschlagen ‹*Tal, Hang*›; **~ a tree [of its leaves]** einen Baum entlauben; **~d of trees** abgeholzt; **~ sb. of sth.** *(fig.)* jmdm. etw. entziehen; **b)** *(Geol.)* erodieren *(fachspr.)*

denunciation [dɪnʌnsɪˈeɪʃn] *n.* **a)** Denunziation, *die (abwertend); (public accusation)* Beschuldigung, *die; (act of attacking)* Anprangerung, *die;* **b)** *(of treaty etc.)* [Auf]kündigung, *die*

deny [dɪˈnaɪ] *v. t.* **a)** *(declare untrue)* bestreiten; zurückweisen ‹*Beschuldigung*›; **he denied knowing it** er bestritt, es zu wissen; **it cannot be denied** *or* **there is no ~ing the fact that ...:** es läßt sich nicht bestreiten *od.* leugnen, daß ...; **he denied this to be the case** er bestritt, daß dies der Fall sei; **~ all knowledge of sth.** bestreiten, irgendetwas von etw. zu wissen; **b)** *(refuse)* verweigern; **~ sb. sth.** jmdm. etw. verweigern; **he can't ~ her anything** er kann ihr nichts abschlagen; **recognition was denied [to] him** die Anerkennung blieb ihm versagt; **c)** *(disavow, repudiate; refuse access to)* verleugnen; ablehnen ‹*Verantwortung*›; **d)** *(Relig.)* **~ oneself** *or* **the flesh** sich kasteien

deodorant [di:ˈəʊdərənt] **1.** *adj.* desodorierend; **~ spray** Deo[dorant]spray, *der od. das.* **2.** *n.* Deodorant, *das*

deodorisation, deodorise *see* **deodoriz-**

deodorization [di:əʊdəraɪˈzeɪʃn] *n.* Desodorierung, *die*

deodorize [di:ˈəʊdəraɪz] *v. t.* desodorieren

dep. *abbr.* **a) departs** *(Railw.)* Abf.; *(Aeronaut.)* Abfl.; **b) deputy** stellv.

depart [dɪˈpɑ:t] **1.** *v. i.* **a)** *(go away, take one's leave)* weggehen; fortgehen; sich entfernen *(geh.)*; **b)** *(set out, start, leave)* abfahren; ‹*Schiff auch:*› auslaufen, ablegen; ‹*Flugzeug:*› abfliegen; *(on one's journey)* abreisen; **ready to ~:** abfahrbereit; **c)** *(fig.: deviate)* **~ from sth.** von etw. abweichen; **d)** *(literary: die)* **~ from this life** aus dem Leben *od.* von hinnen scheiden *(geh.)*; **he has ~ed from us** er ist von uns gegangen *(verhüll.)*. **2.** *v. t. (literary)* **~ this life/world** aus dem Leben/aus dieser Welt scheiden *(geh.)*

departed [dɪˈpɑ:tɪd] **1.** *adj.* **a)** *(bygone)* vergangen; **b)** *(deceased)* dahingeschieden *(geh. verhüll.)*. **2.** *n.* **the ~:** der/die Dahingeschiedene; die Dahingeschiedenen *(geh. verhüll.)*

department [dɪˈpɑ:tmənt] *n.* **a)** *(of municipal administration)* Amt, *das; (of State administration)* Ministerium, *das; (of university)* Seminar, *das; (of shop)* Abteilung, *die;* **D~ of Employment/Education** Arbeits-/Erziehungsministerium, *das;* **the shipping ~/personnel ~:** die Versand-/Personalabteilung; **English ~:** anglistisches *od.* englisches Seminar; **history ~:** Seminar *od.* Institut für Geschichte; **~ of pathology** Pathologie, *die;* pathologisches Institut; *(in hospital)* pathologische Abteilung; **b)** *(administrative district in France)* Departement, *das;* **c)** *(fig.: area of activity)* Ressort, *das;* **it's not my ~:** da kenne ich mich nicht aus; *(not my responsibility)* dafür bin ich nicht zuständig

departmental [di:pɑ:tˈmentl] *adj.* **a)** *see* **department a, b:** Amts-; Ministerial-; Seminar-; Abteilungs-; Departement-; **b) be ~:** die Abteilung betreffen

departmentally [di:pɑ:tˈmentəlɪ] *adv. see* **departmental a:** auf Amts-/Ministerial-/Seminar-/Abteilungsebene

deˈpartment store *n.* Kaufhaus, *das*

departure [dɪˈpɑ:tʃə(r)] *n.* **a)** *(going away)* Abreise, *die;* **take one's ~:** sich entfernen *(geh.)*; **after sb.'s ~:** nachdem jmd. weggegangen war/ist; **make a hasty ~:** sich rasch entfernen; **b)** *(deviation)* **~ from sth.** Abweichen von etw.; **c)** *(of train, bus, ship)* Abfahrt, *die; (of aircraft)* Abflug, *der;* **two ~s a day** täglich zwei Abfahrtszeiten; **d)** *(of action or thought)* Ansatz, *der;* **point of ~:** Ansatzpunkt, *der;* **this product is a new ~ for us** mit diesem Produkt schlagen wir einen neuen Weg ein

departure: ~ gate *n.* Flugsteig, *der;* **~ lounge** *n.* Abflughalle, *die;* **~ platform** *n.* [Abfahrt]gleis, *das;* **~ time** *n. (of train, bus)* Abfahrtzeit, *die; (of aircraft)* Abflugzeit, *die*

depend [dɪˈpend] *v. i.* **a) ~ [up]on** abhängen von; **it [all] ~s on whether/what/how ...:** das hängt [ganz] davon ab *od.* kommt ganz darauf an, ob/was/wie ...; **that ~s** es kommt darauf an; **~ing on how ...:** je nachdem, wie ...; **b)** *(rely, trust)* **~ [up]on** sich verlassen auf (+ *Akk.*); *(have to rely on)* angewiesen sein auf (+ *Akk.*); **~ on sb. for help** sich auf jmds. Hilfe verlassen/auf jmds. Hilfe angewiesen sein

dependability [dɪpendəˈbɪlɪtɪ] *n., no pl.* Verläßlichkeit, *die;* Zuverlässigkeit, *die*

dependable [dɪˈpendəbl] *adj.* verläßlich; zuverlässig

dependably [dɪˈpendəblɪ] *adv.* zuverlässig

dependant [dɪˈpendənt] *n.* **a)** Abhängige, *der/die;* **~s** *(Taxation)* abhängige Angehörige; **b)** *(servant)* Bedienstete, *der/die*

dependence [dɪˈpendəns] *n.* **a)** Abhängigkeit, *die;* **~ [up]on sb./sth.** Abhängigkeit von jmdm./etw.; **b)** *(reliance)* **put** *or* **place ~ [up]on sb.** sich auf jmdn. verlassen

dependency [dɪˈpendənsɪ] *n.* **a)** *(country)* Territorium, *das;* **b)** *(condition of being dependent)* Abhängigkeit, *die* **(on** von)

dependent [dɪˈpendənt] **1.** *n. see* **dependant. 2.** *adj.* **a)** *(also Ling., Math.)* abhängig; **be ~ on sth.** von etw. abhängen *od.* abhängig sein; **b) be ~ on** *(be unable to do without)* angewiesen sein auf (+ *Akk.*); abhängig sein von ‹*Droge, Ursache*›; **be ~ on heroin** heroinabhängig sein

depict [dɪˈpɪkt] *v. t.* darstellen

depiction [dɪˈpɪkʃn] *n.* Darstellung, *die*

depilate [ˈdepɪleɪt] *v. t.* enthaaren; depilieren *(Med.)*

depilatory [dɪˈpɪlətərɪ] **1.** *adj.* Enthaarungs-. **2.** *n.* Enthaarungsmittel, *das*

deplete [dɪˈpli:t] *v. t.* **a)** *(reduce in number or amount)* erheblich verringern; **the audience is ~d** die Zuschauerzahl hat sich deutlich verringert; **our stores are ~d** unser Vorrat ist zusammengeschrumpft; **air ~d of oxygen**

Luft mit wenig Sauerstoff; **b)** *(empty)* entleeren; *(exhaust)* erschöpfen
depletion [dɪ'pli:ʃn] *n.* **a)** Verringerung, *die;* **b)** *(emptying)* Entleerung, *die; (exhausting)* Erschöpfung, *die*
deplorable [dɪ'plɔ:rəbl] *adj.* beklagenswert; erbärmlich ‹*Essen, Leistung*›
deplorably [dɪ'plɔ:rəblɪ] *adv.* erbärmlich; ~ **neglected** schändlich verwahrlost
deplore [dɪ'plɔ:(r)] *v.t.* **a)** *(disapprove of)* verurteilen; **b)** *(bewail, regret)* beklagen; **sth. is to be ~d** etw. ist beklagenswert
deploy [dɪ'plɔɪ] **1.** *v.t.* **a)** *(bring into effective action)* einsetzen; **b)** *(Mil.)* einsetzen; *(extend)* ausschwärmen lassen. **2.** *v.i. (Mil.)* eingesetzt werden
deployment [dɪ'plɔɪmənt] *n.* Einsatz, *der*
deponent [dɪ'pəʊnənt] **1.** *adj. (Ling.)* ~ **verb** Deponens, *das.* **2.** *n.* **a)** *(Law)* ≈ Zeuge, *der*/Zeugin, *die;* **b)** *(Ling.)* Deponens, *das*
depopulate [di:'pɒpjʊleɪt] *v.t.* entvölkern
depopulation [di:pɒpjʊ'leɪʃn] *n.* Entvölkerung, *die*
deport [dɪ'pɔ:t] **1.** *v.t.* deportieren; *(from country)* ausweisen. **2.** *v. refl.* sich benehmen
deportation [di:pɔ:'teɪʃn] *n.* Deportation, *die; (from country)* Ausweisung, *die*
deportee [di:pɔ:'ti:] *n.* Deportierte, *der/die; (from country)* Ausgewiesene, *der/die*
deportment [dɪ'pɔ:tmənt] *n.* Benehmen, *das*
depose [dɪ'pəʊz] **1.** *v.t.* absetzen; ~ **sb. from an office** jmdn. eines Amtes entheben. **2.** *v.i. & t. (Law)* [unter Eid] aussagen
deposit [dɪ'pɒzɪt] **1.** *n.* **a)** *(in bank)* Depot, *das; (credit)* Guthaben, *das; (Brit.: at interest)* Sparguthaben, *das;* **make a ~:** etwas einzahlen; **have £70 on ~:** ein [Spar]guthaben von 70 Pfund haben; **b)** *(payment as pledge)* Kaution, *die; (first instalment)* Anzahlung, *die;* **pay** *or* **make** *or* **leave a ~:** eine Kaution zahlen *od.* hinterlegen/eine Anzahlung leisten; **there is a five pence ~ on the bottle** auf der Flasche sind fünf Pence Pfand; **put down a ~ on sth.** eine Anzahlung für etw. leisten; **lose one's ~** *(Polit.)* die Kaution verlieren; **c)** *(for safe keeping)* anvertrautes Gut; **d)** *(natural accumulation) (of sand, mud, lime, etc.; also Med.)* Ablagerung, *die; (of ore, coal, oil)* Lagerstätte, *die; (in glass, bottle)* Bodensatz, *der.* **2.** *v.t.* **a)** *(lay down in a place)* ablegen; abstellen ‹*etw. Senkrechtes, auch Tablett, Teller usw.*›; absetzen ‹*Mitfahrer*›; **b)** *(leave lying)* ‹*Wasser usw.:*› ablagern; **be ~ed** sich ablagern; ~ **a layer of sand/dust over sth.** etw. mit einer Schicht Sand/Staub überziehen; **c)** *(in bank)* deponieren, [auf ein Konto] einzahlen ‹*Geld*›; *(Brit.: at interest)* [auf ein Sparkonto] einzahlen; ~ **money in a bank** Geld bei einer Bank einzahlen; **d)** *(pay as pledge)* anzahlen
de'posit account *n. (Brit.)* Sparkonto, *das*
deposition [depə'zɪʃn, di:pə'zɪʃn] *n.* **a)** *(depositing) (of papers, money, etc.)* Hinterlegung, *die* (**with** bei); *(of mud, coal, ore, etc.)* Ablagerung, *die;* **b)** *(from office)* Absetzung, *die;* **c)** *(Law: giving of evidence, allegation)* [eidliche Zeugen]aussage
depositor [dɪ'pɒzɪtə(r)] *n. (Banking)* Einleger, *der*/Einlegerin, *die*
depository [dɪ'pɒzɪtərɪ] *n.* *(storehouse)* Lagerhaus, *das; (place for safe keeping)* Aufbewahrungsort, *der; (fig.)* Fundgrube, *die*
depot ['depəʊ] *n.* **a)** Depot, *das;* **b)** *(storehouse)* Lager, *das;* **grain ~:** Getreidespeicher, *der;* **c)** **[bus]** ~ *(Brit.)* Depot, *das;* Omnibusgarage, *die; (Amer.: bus station)* Omnibusbahnhof, *der; (Amer.: railway station)* Bahnhof, *der*
deprave [dɪ'preɪv] *v.t.* **a)** *(make bad)* beeinträchtigen; **b)** *(corrupt)* verderben
depraved [dɪ'preɪvd] *adj.* verdorben; lasterhaft ‹*Gewohnheit*›
depravity [dɪ'prævɪtɪ] *n.* Lasterhaftigkeit, *die;* Verderbtheit, *die (geh.);* Verdorbenheit, *die*
deprecate ['deprɪkeɪt] *v.t.* **a)** *(disapprove of)* mißbilligen; **b)** *(plead against)* abzuwenden suchen
deprecation [deprɪ'keɪʃn] *n.* Mißbilligung, *die*
depreciate [dɪ'pri:ʃɪeɪt, dɪ'pri:sɪeɪt] **1.** *v.t.* **a)** *(diminish in value)* abwerten; herabsetzen; abwerten ‹*Währung*›; **b)** *(disparage)* herabsetzen. **2.** *v.i.* an Wert verlieren
depreciation [dɪpri:ʃɪ'eɪʃn, dɪpri:sɪ'eɪʃn] *n.* *(of money, currency, property)* Wertverlust, *der; (of person)* Herabsetzung, *die;* **allowance for ~:** Abschreibung, *die*
depreciatory [dɪ'pri:ʃətərɪ] *adj.* verächtlich; abfällig
depredation [deprɪ'deɪʃn] *n.* **a)** Verwüstung, *die;* **b)** *(ravages of disease etc.)* verheerende Wirkung
depress [dɪ'pres] *v.t.* **a)** *(deject)* deprimieren; **b)** *(push or pull down)* herunterdrücken; *(cause to move to a lower level)* absenken; **c)** *(reduce activity of)* unterdrücken; sich nicht entfalten lassen ‹*Handel, Wirtschaftswachstum*›
depressant [dɪ'presənt] **1.** *adj. (Med.)* beruhigend; sedativ *(fachspr.).* **2.** *n.* **a)** *(influence)* Hemmnis, *das;* **b)** *(Med.)* Beruhigungsmittel, *das;* Sedativ[um], *das (fachspr.)*
depressed [dɪ'prest] *adj.* deprimiert ‹*Person, Stimmung*›; abgesenkt ‹*Gelände, Ebene*›; unterdrückt ‹*Bevölkerung, Völker*› geschwächt ‹*Industrie*›; ~ **area** unter [wirtschaftlicher] Depression leidendes Gebiet
depressing [dɪ'presɪŋ] *adj.* deprimierend
depressingly [dɪ'presɪŋlɪ] *adv.* deprimierend
depression [dɪ'preʃn] *n.* **a)** Depression, *die;* **b)** *(sunk place)* Vertiefung, *die;* **c)** *(Meteorol.)* Tief[druckgebiet], *das;* Depression, *die (fachspr.);* **d)** *(reduction in vigour, vitality)* Schwächung, *die;* **e)** *(Econ.)* **the D~:** die Weltwirtschaftskrise; **economic ~:** Wirtschaftskrise, *die;* Depression, *die;* **f)** *(lowering, sinking)* Senkung, *die; (pressing down)* Herunterdrücken, *das*
depressive [dɪ'presɪv] **1.** *adj.* **a)** *(tending to depress)* bedrückend; deprimierend; **b)** *(Psych.)* depressiv. **2.** *n. (Psych.)* Depressive, *der/die*
depressurize (depressurise) [di:'preʃəraɪz] *v.t.* dekomprimieren
deprival [dɪ'praɪvl] *see* **deprivation a**
deprivation [deprɪ'veɪʃn, di:praɪ'veɪʃn] *n.* **a)** *(being deprived)* Entzug, *der; (of one's rights, liberties, or title)* Aberkennung, *die;* **b)** *(loss of desired thing)* Entbehrung, *die;* **that is a great ~:** das ist ein großer Verlust; **oxygen ~:** Sauerstoffmangel, *der*
deprive [dɪ'praɪv] *v.t.* **a)** *(strip, bereave)* ~ **sb. of sth.** jmdm. etw. nehmen; *(debar from having)* jmdm. etw. vorenthalten; **trees that ~ a house of light** Bäume, die einem Haus das Licht nehmen; **the village was ~d of electricity** das Dorf war ohne Stromversorgung; **he will be ~d of his right to vote** ihm wird das Wahlrecht entzogen werden; ~ **sb. of citizenship** jmdm. die Staatsbürgerschaft aberkennen; ~ **sb. of his command** jmdm. das Kommando entziehen; **am I depriving you of it?** brauchen Sie das gerade?; **be ~d of one's car/books** auf sein Auto/seine Bücher verzichten müssen; **be ~d of light** nicht genug Licht haben; ~ **sb. of a pleasure** jmdm. ein Vergnügen vorenthalten; jmdn. eines Vergnügens berauben *(geh.);* **b)** *(depose)* absetzen; **c)** *(prevent from having normal life)* benachteiligen
deprived [dɪ'praɪvd] *adj.* benachteiligt ‹*Kind, Familie usw.*›
Dept. *abbr.* **Department** Amt/Min./Seminar/Abt.
depth [depθ] *n.* **a)** *(lit. or fig.)* Tiefe, *die;* **at a ~ of 3 metres** in einer Tiefe von 3 Metern; **3 feet in ~:** 3 Fuß tief; **what is the ~ of the pond?** wie tief ist der Teich?; ~ **of thought/meaning** Gedankentiefe, *die*/Bedeutungsgehalt, *der;* **from/in the ~s of the forest/ocean** aus/in der Tiefe des Waldes/des Ozeans; **from the ~s of his soul** aus tiefster Seele; **sink** *or* **fall into the ~s of oblivion/despair** völlig in Vergessenheit/in tiefste Verzweiflung geraten; **sink** *or* **fall to such ~s that ...** *(fig.)* so tief sinken, daß ...; **in the ~s of winter** im tiefen Winter; **great ~ of feeling** große Gefühls- *od.* Ausdruckstiefe; **b)** *(mental profundity)* geistige Tiefe; **c)** **in ~:** gründlich, intensiv ‹*studieren*›; **an in-~ study/analysis** *etc.* eine gründliche Untersuchung/Analyse *usw.*; **defence in ~:** tief gestaffelte Verteidigung; **d)** **be out of one's ~:** nicht mehr stehen können; keinen Grund mehr unter den Füßen haben; *(fig.)* ins Schwimmen kommen *(ugs.);* überfordert sein; **go/get out of one's ~** *(lit. or fig.)* den Grund unter den Füßen verlieren; **don't go out of your ~:** geh nicht zu tief hinein
depth: ~-bomb, ~-charge *ns.* Wasserbombe, *die;* **~-charge** *v.t.* mit Wasserbomben angreifen; ~ **of field** *n. (Photog.)* Schärfentiefe, *die;* ~ **psychology** *n.* Tiefenpsychologie, *die*
deputation [depjʊ'teɪʃn] *n.* Abordnung, *die;* Delegation, *die*
depute 1. [dɪ'pju:t] *v.t.* **a)** *(commit task or authority to)* ~ **sb. to do sth.** jmdn. beauftragen, etw. zu tun; ~ **sth. to sb.** etw. auf jmdn. übertragen; **b)** *(appoint as deputy)* ~ **sb. to do sth.** jmdn. [als Stellvertreter] damit betrauen, etw. zu tun. **2.** ['depju:t] *n. (Scot.: deputy)* Stellvertreter, *der/*-vertreterin, *die*
deputize (deputise) ['depjʊtaɪz] *v.i.* als Stellvertreter einspringen; ~ **for sb.** jmdn. vertreten
deputy ['depjʊtɪ] *n.* **a)** *attrib.* stellvertretend; ~ **sheriff** *(Amer.)* Hilfssheriff, *der;* **b)** *(person appointed to act for another)* [Stell]vertreter, *der/*-vertreterin, *die;* **act as ~ for sb.** jmdn. vertreten; **c)** *(parliamentary representative)* Abgeordnete, *der/die;* Deputierte, *der/die;* **Chamber of Deputies** Abgeordnetenkammer, *die;* **d)** *(Brit.: coal-mine overseer)* Steiger, *der*
derail [dɪ'reɪl, di:'reɪl] *v.t. usu. in pass.* zum Entgleisen bringen; **be ~ed** entgleisen
derailment [dɪ'reɪlmənt, di:'reɪlmənt] *n.* Entgleisung, *die;* **cause the ~ of sth.** etw. zum Entgleisen bringen
derange [dɪ'reɪndʒ] *v.t.* **a)** *(throw into confusion, put out of order)* durcheinanderbringen; *(make insane)* geistig verwirren; **b)** *(disturb, interrupt)* stören
deranged [dɪ'reɪndʒd] *adj.* **[mentally] ~:** geistesgestört
derangement [dɪ'reɪndʒmənt] *n.* **a)** Unordnung, *die;* **cause ~ of** durcheinanderbringen; **b)** **[mental] ~:** Geistesgestörtheit, *die*
Derby ['dɑ:bɪ] *n.* **a)** *(annual horse-race at Epsom)* Derby [in Epsom], *das; (other race or contest)* Derby, *das;* ~ **Day** Tag des Derbys [in Epsom]; **local ~:** Lokalderby, *das;* **b)** **d~** *(Amer.: bowler hat)* Melone, *die*
deregulation [di:regjʊ'leɪʃn] *n.* ~ **of prices/fares** Aufhebung der Preiskontrolle
derelict ['derɪlɪkt] **1.** *adj.* **a)** *(abandoned)* verlassen und verfallen; aufgegeben ‹*Schiff*›; **b)** *(Amer.: negligent)* nachlässig. **2.** *n.* **a)** *(abandoned property)* herrenloses Gut; *(ship)* aufgegebenes Schiff; *(wreck)* [treibendes] Wrack; **b)** *(person)* Ausgestoßene, *der/die*
dereliction [derɪ'lɪkʃn] *n.* **a)** *(abandoning)* Vernachlässigung, *die; (state)* verkommener Zustand; **the building is in a state of ~:** das Gebäude ist verkommen; **b)** *(neglect)* ~ **of duty** Pflichtverletzung, *die*

derestrict [di:rɪ'strɪkt] *v.t.* [wieder] freigeben; ~**ed road** Straße ohne Geschwindigkeitsbeschränkung

derestriction [di:rɪ'strɪkʃn] *n.* Freigabe, *die*

deride [dɪ'raɪd] *v.t. (treat with scorn)* sich lustig machen über (+ *Akk.*); *(laugh scornfully at)* verlachen

de rigueur [də rɪ'gɜ:(r)] *pred. adj.* de rigueur *nicht attr. (veralt.);* unerläßlich

derision [dɪ'rɪʒn] *n.* Spott, *der;* **be an object of** ~: Zielscheibe des Spottes sein; **bring sb./sth. into** ~: jmdn./etw. zum Gespött *od.* lächerlich machen

derisive [dɪ'raɪsɪv] *adj. (ironical)* spöttisch; *(scoffing)* verächtlich

derisively [dɪ'raɪsɪvlɪ] *adv. see* **derisive**: spöttisch; verächtlich

derisory [dɪ'raɪsərɪ, dɪ'raɪzərɪ] *adj.* **a)** *(ridiculously inadequate)* lächerlich; **b)** *(scoffing)* verächtlich; *(ironical)* spöttisch

derivation [derɪ'veɪʃn] *n.* **a)** *(obtaining from a source)* Herleitung, *die;* **b)** *(extraction, origin)* Herkunft, *die; (descent)* Abstammung, *die;* **c)** *(Ling.)* Ableitung, *die;* Derivation, *die (fachspr.); (origin)* Ursprung, *der;* Herkunft, *die*

derivative [dɪ'rɪvətɪv] **1.** *adj.* abgeleitet; *(lacking originality)* nachahmend; epigonal; *(secondary)* indirekt. **2.** *n.* **a)** Abkömmling, *der; (word)* Ableitung, *die;* Derivat[iv], *das (Sprachw.); (chemical substance)* Derivat, *das;* **b)** *(Math.)* Ableitung, *die*

derive [dɪ'raɪv] **1.** *v.t.* **a)** *(get, obtain, form)* ~ **sth. from sth.** etw. aus etw. gewinnen; **he ~s much of his earnings from free-lance work** er bezieht einen großen Teil seines Einkommens aus freiberuflicher Tätigkeit; **the river ~s its name** *or* **the name of the river is ~d from a Greek god** der Name des Flusses geht auf eine griechische Gottheit zurück; **he ~s pleasure from his studies** er hat Freude an seinem Studium; ~ **profit/advantage from sth.** aus etw. Nutzen/seinen Vorteil ziehen; **b)** *(deduce)* ableiten; herleiten; **c)** ~ **one's origin/ancestry/pedigree from sth.** aus etw. stammen. **2.** *v.i.* ~ **from** beruhen auf (+ *Dat.*); **the word ~s from Latin** das Wort stammt *od.* kommt aus dem Lateinischen

dermatitis [dɜ:mə'taɪtɪs] *n. (Med.)* Hautentzündung, *die;* Dermatitis, *die (fachspr.)*

dermatologist [dɜ:mə'tɒlədʒɪst] *n. (Med.)* Hautarzt, *der*/-ärztin, *die;* Dermatologe, *der*/Dermatologin, *die*

dermatology [dɜ:mə'tɒlədʒɪ] *n. (Med.)* Dermatologie, *die*

dern [dɜ:n], **derned** [dɜ:nd] *(Amer.) see* **²darn, darned**

derogate ['derəgeɪt] *v.i. (formal)* ~ **from sth.** etw. schmälern

derogation [derə'geɪʃn] *n. (formal)* Schmälerung, *die* (**from** *Gen.*)

derogatory [dɪ'rɒgətərɪ] *adj.* **a)** *(depreciatory)* abfällig; abschätzig; ~ **sense [of a word]** abwertende Bedeutung [eines Wortes]; **b)** *(tending to detract)* **be** ~ **to sth.** einer Sache *(Dat.)* abträglich sein; **be regarded as** ~: als etwas Ehrenrühriges angesehen werden

derrick ['derɪk] *n.* **a)** *(for moving or hoisting)* [Derrick]kran, *der;* **b)** *(over oil-well)* Bohrturm, *der*

derring-do [derɪŋ'du:] *n. (literary)* Wagemut, *der;* **a deed of** ~: eine wagemutige Tat

derv [dɜ:v] *n. (Brit. Motor Veh.)* Diesel[kraftstoff], *der*

dervish ['dɜ:vɪʃ] *n.* Derwisch, *der*

desalination [di:sælɪ'neɪʃn] *n.* Entsalzung, *die*

descale [di:'skeɪl] *v.t.* entkalken

descant 1. ['deskænt] *n.* **a)** *(Mus.)* Diskant, *der;* **b)** *(poet.: melody)* Weise, *die;* Melodie, *die.* **2.** [dɪ'skænt] *v.i.* **a)** *(formal: talk lengthily)* ~ **upon sth.** sich über etw. *(Akk.)* verbreiten; **b)** *(sing descant)* Diskant singen

'descant recorder *n. (Mus.)* Sopranflöte, *die*

descend [dɪ'send] **1.** *v.i.* **a)** *(go down)* hinuntergehen/-steigen/-klettern/-fahren; *(come down)* herunterkommen; *(sink)* niedergehen (**on** auf + *Dat.*); **the lift ~ed** der Aufzug fuhr nach unten; ~ **in the lift** mit dem Aufzug nach unten fahren; ~ **into hell** zur Hölle hinabsteigen *od.* niederfahren; ~ **on sb.** *(fig.)* über jmdn. hereinbrechen; **night ~ed upon the village** die Nacht senkte sich auf das Dorf herab; **b)** *(slope downwards)* abfallen; **the hill ~s into/towards the sea** der Hügel fällt zum Meer hin ab; **c)** *(in quality, thought, etc.)* herabsinken; ~ **from the general to the particular** vom Allgemeinen zum Besonderen gehen *od.* kommen; **d)** *(in pitch)* fallen; sinken; tiefer werden; ~ **to a low note** auf einen tiefen Ton hinuntergehen; **e)** *(make sudden attack)* ~ **on sth.** über etw. *(Akk.)* herfallen; ~ **on sb.** *(lit., or fig.: arrive unexpectedly)* jmdn. überfallen; ~ **on a country** in ein Land einfallen; **f)** *(fig.: lower oneself)* ~ **to sth.** sich zu etw. erniedrigen; **g)** *(pass by inheritance)* vererbt werden (**to** an + *Akk.*); **h)** *(derive)* abstammen (**from** von); *(have origin)* zurückgehen (**from** auf + *Akk.*); **i)** *(go forward in time)* weitergehen. **2.** *v.t.* **a)** *(go/come down)* hinunter- / heruntergehen / -steigen / -klettern / -fahren; hinab-/herabsteigen *(geh.);* **b)** *(go along)* hinuntergehen/-fahren ‹*Straße*›

descendant [dɪ'sendənt] *n.* Nachkomme, *der;* **be ~s/a ~ of** abstammen von

descended [dɪ'sendɪd] *adj.* **be ~ from sb.** von jmdm. abstammen

descent [dɪ'sent] *n.* **a)** *(going or coming down) (of person)* Abstieg, *der; (of parachute, plane, bird, avalanche)* Niedergehen, *das;* **the ~ of the mountain took us a few hours** für den Abstieg vom Berg brauchten wir einige Stunden; **the D~ from the Cross** die Kreuzabnahme; **b)** *(way)* Abstieg, *der;* **the ~ leading to the river** der Weg hinunter zum Fluß; **c)** *(slope)* Abfall, *der;* **the road made a sharp ~ into the valley** die Straße fiel zum Tal hin steil ab; **the ~ was very steep** das Gefälle war sehr stark; **d)** *(sudden attack)* **the Danes made numerous ~s upon the English coast** die Dänen fielen mehrfach an der englischen Küste ein; **e)** *(decline, fall)* Abstieg, *der;* **f)** *(lineage)* Abstammung, *die;* Herkunft, *die;* **be of Russian/noble ~**: russischer/adliger Abstammung sein; **g)** *(transmission by inheritance)* Herkunft, *die;* **jazz traces its ~ from African music** der Jazz hat seine Ursprünge in afrikanischer Musik

describable [dɪ'skraɪbəbl] *adj.* beschreibbar; **be ~**: zu beschreiben sein; **it's not ~ in words** es ist unbeschreiblich *od.* nicht mit Worten zu beschreiben

describe [dɪ'skraɪb] *v.t.* **a)** *(set forth in words)* beschreiben; schildern; *(distinguish)* bezeichnen; **it can't be ~d in words** es ist unbeschreiblich *od.* nicht mit Worten zu beschreiben; ~ **[oneself] as ...**: [sich] als ... bezeichnen; **sth. can hardly be ~d as ...**: etw. ist kaum ... zu nennen; **b)** *(move in, draw)* beschreiben ‹*Kreis, Bogen, Kurve*›

description [dɪ'skrɪpʃn] *n.* **a)** *(describing, verbal portrait)* Beschreibung, *die;* Schilderung, *die;* **she is beautiful beyond ~**: sie ist unbeschreiblich schön; **he answers [to]** *or* **fits the ~**: er entspricht der Beschreibung *(Dat.);* **b)** *(sort, class)* Art, *die;* **cars of every ~**: Autos aller Art; **c)** *(more or less complete definition)* Beschreibung, *die; (designation)* Bezeichnung, *die*

descriptive [dɪ'skrɪptɪv] *adj.* **a)** anschaulich; beschreibend ‹*Lyrik*›; deskriptiv ‹*Analyse*›; **b)** *(not expressing feelings or judgements; also Ling.)* deskriptiv

descriptively [dɪ'skrɪptɪvlɪ] *adv.* anschaulich ‹*schreiben, sprechen*›; deskriptiv ‹*analysieren*›

descry [dɪ'skraɪ] *v.t. (catch sight of)* erblicken; erspähen; *(fig.: perceive, observe)* erkennen

desecrate ['desɪkreɪt] *v.t.* entweihen; schänden

desecration [desɪ'kreɪʃn] *n.* Entweihung, *die;* Schändung, *die*

desegregate [di:'segrɪgeɪt] *v.t.* die Rassentrennung aufheben an (+ *Dat.*)

desegregation [di:segrɪ'geɪʃn] *n.* Aufhebung der Rassentrennung (**of** an + *Dat.*)

deselect [di:sɪ'lekt] *v.t. (Brit. Polit.)* nicht mehr als Wahlkandidat vorsehen

desensitize (desensitise) [di:'sensɪtaɪz] *v.t. (Med., Phot., Psych.)* desensibilisieren

¹desert [dɪ'zɜ:t] *n.* **a)** *in pl. (what is deserved)* Verdienste *Pl.;* **meet with** *or* **get one's [just] ~s** das bekommen, was man verdient hat; **b)** *(deserving)* Verdienst, *das*

²desert ['dezət] **1.** *n.* Wüste, *die; (fig.)* Einöde, *die;* **the Sahara D~**: die Wüste Sahara; **a cultural ~** *(fig.)* kulturelles Ödland. **2.** *adj.* öde; Wüsten‹*klima, -stamm*›

³desert [dɪ'zɜ:t] **1.** *v.t.* verlassen; im Stich lassen ‹*Frau, Familie usw.*›. **2.** *v.i.* *(run away)* davonlaufen; ‹*Soldat:*› desertieren; ~ **to sb.** zu jmdm. überlaufen

deserted [dɪ'zɜ:tɪd] *adj.* verlassen; **the streets were ~**: die Straßen waren wie ausgestorben

deserter [dɪ'zɜ:tə(r)] *n.* Deserteur, *der;* Fahnenflüchtige, *der/die*

desertion [dɪ'zɜ:ʃn] *n.* Verlassen, *das; (of one's duty)* Vernachlässigen, *das; (Mil.)* Desertion, *die;* Fahnenflucht, *die;* ~ **to the enemy** Überlaufen zum Feind

desert island [dezət 'aɪlənd] *n.* einsame Insel

deserve [dɪ'zɜ:v] **1.** *v.t.* verdienen; **he ~s to win** er verdient [es] zu gewinnen; **he ~s to be punished** er verdient [es], bestraft zu werden; er verdient Strafe; **what have I done to ~ this?** womit habe ich das verdient?; **he got what he ~d** er hat es nicht besser verdient. **2.** *v.i. (formal)* ~ **well of** sich verdient gemacht haben um

deservedly [dɪ'zɜ:vɪdlɪ] *adv.* verdientermaßen; **and ~ so** und das zu Recht; **be ~ punished** zu Recht bestraft werden

deserving [dɪ'zɜ:vɪŋ] *adj.* **a)** *(worthy)* verdienstvoll; **donate money to a ~ cause** Geld für einen guten Zweck geben; **the ~ poor** die unverschuldet Bedürftigen; **b)** *(meritorious)* **be ~ of sth.** etw. verdienen; **people most ~ of help** Leute, die am ehesten Hilfe verdienen

déshabillé [deɪzæ'bi:eɪ] *n.* Nachlässigkeit in der Kleidung; **in ~**: nachlässig gekleidet; *(partly undressed)* halbbekleidet

desiccated ['desɪkeɪtɪd] *adj.* getrocknet; vertrocknet ‹*Person*›; ~ **fruit** Dörr- *od.* Backobst, *das*

desideratum [dɪzɪdə'reɪtəm] *n., pl.* **desiderata** [dɪzɪdə'reɪtə] *(literary)* Desiderat, *das (geh.);* Desideratum, *das (geh.)*

design [dɪ'zaɪn] **1.** *n.* **a)** *(preliminary sketch)* Entwurf, *der;* **~s of costumes** Kostümentwürfe; **a technical ~**: eine technische Zeichnung; **b)** *(pattern)* Muster, *das;* **c)** *no art. (art)* Design, *das;* Gestaltung, *die (geh.);* **d)** *(established form of a product)* Entwurf, *der; (of machine, engine, etc.)* Bauweise, *die;* **e)** *(general idea, construction from parts)* Konstruktion, *die;* **a machine of faulty/good ~**: eine schlecht/gut konstruierte Maschine; **f)** *(mental plan)* Planung, *die;* **argument from ~** *(Theol.)* theologischer Gottesbeweis; **g)** *in pl. (scheme of attack)* **have ~s on sb./sth.** es auf jmdn./etw. abgesehen haben; **h)** *(purpose)* Absicht, *die;* **by ~**: mit Absicht; absichtlich; **i)** *(end in view)* Ziel, *das.* **2.** *v.t.* **a)** *(draw plan of)* entwerfen; konstruieren, entwerfen ‹*Maschine, Fahrzeug, Flugzeug*›; **b)** *(make preliminary* *sketch of)* entwerfen; **c)** *(contrive, plan)* planen; aufstellen ‹*Lehrplan*›; **d)** *(intend)* beabsichtigen; **be ~ed to do sth.** ‹*Maschine, Werkzeug, Gerät:*› etw. tun sollen; **the book is ~ed as an aid to beginners** das Buch ist als Hilfe für Anfänger konzipiert; **e)** *(set apart)* vorsehen; **be ~ed for sb./sth.** für jmdn./etw. gedacht *od.* vorgesehen sein; **f)** *(destine)* bestimmen. **3.** *v.i.* Entwürfe machen

designate 1. ['dezɪgnət] *postpos. adj.* designiert. **2.** ['dezɪgneɪt] *v.t.* **a)** *(serve as name of, describe)* bezeichnen; *(serve as distinctive mark of)* kennzeichnen; **~ sth. A** etw. als A bezeichnen/kennzeichnen; **b)** *(specify, particularize)* angeben; aufzeigen ‹*Fehler, Mangel*›; **c)** *(appoint to office)* designieren *(geh.)*; **be ~d as sb.'s successor** zu jmds. Nachfolger ernannt werden

designation [dezɪg'neɪʃn] *n.* **a)** Bezeichnung, *die;* **b)** *(appointing to office)* Designation, *die*

designedly [dɪ'zaɪnɪdlɪ] *adv.* absichtlich

designer [dɪ'zaɪnə(r)] *n.* Designer, *der*/Designerin, *die; (of machines, buildings)* Konstrukteur, *der*/Konstrukteurin, *die; (of clothes);* Modedesigner, *der*/-designerin, *die; (Theatre: stage ~)* Bühnenbildner, *der*/-bildnerin, *die; attrib.* Modell‹*kleidung, -jeans*›; *see also* **costume designer**

designing [dɪ'zaɪnɪŋ] *adj. (crafty, artful, scheming)* ränkevoll; intrigant

desirability [dɪzaɪərə'bɪlɪtɪ] *n., no pl.* Wünschbarkeit, *die (bes. schweiz.);* **consider the ~ of sth.** erwägen, ob etw. wünschenswert ist

desirable [dɪ'zaɪərəbl] *adj.* **a)** *(worth having or wishing for)* wünschenswert; **'knowledge of French ~'** „Französischkenntnisse erwünscht"; **b)** *(causing desire)* attraktiv; begehrenswert ‹*Frau*›

desire [dɪ'zaɪə(r)] **1.** *n.* **a)** *(wish)* Wunsch, *der* **(for** nach); *(longing)* Sehnsucht, *die* **(for** nach); **~ to do sth.** Wunsch, etw. zu tun; **~ for wealth** Verlangen nach Reichtum; **~ for freedom/peace** Freiheits-/Friedenswille, *der;* **his ~ for adventure** seine Abenteuerlust; **I have no ~ to see him** ich habe nicht den Wunsch, ihn zu sehen; **I have no ~ to cause you any trouble** ich möchte Ihnen keine Unannehmlichkeiten bereiten; **b)** *(request)* Wunsch, *der;* **at your ~:** auf Ihren Wunsch; **c)** *(thing desired)* **she is my heart's ~:** sie ist die Frau meines Herzens; **d)** *(lust)* Verlangen, *das;* **fleshly ~s** fleischliche Begierden. **2.** *v.t.* **a)** *(wish)* sich *(Dat.)* wünschen; *(long for)* sich sehnen nach; **he only ~d her happiness** er wollte nur ihr Glück; **b)** *(request)* wünschen; **as ~d, the door has been painted red** die Tür ist, wie gewünscht, rot gestrichen worden; **the furniture can be arranged as ~d** die Einrichtung kann ganz nach Wunsch gestaltet werden; **what do you ~ me to do?** was habe ich zu tun?; **c)** *(ask for)* **leave much to be ~d** viel zu wünschen übriglassen; **d)** *(sexually)* begehren ‹*Mann, Frau*›; **e)** *(arch.: pray, entreat)* ersuchen *(geh.)*

desirous [dɪ'zaɪərəs] *pred. adj. (formal)* **be ~ to do sth.** den Wunsch haben, etw. zu tun; **be ~ of sth.** etw. wünschen

desist [dɪ'zɪst, dɪ'sɪst] *v.i. (literary)* einhalten *(geh.);* **~ from sth.** von etw. ablassen *(geh.);* **~ in one's efforts to do sth.** von seinen Bemühungen ablassen, etw. zu tun

desk [desk] *n.* **a)** Schreibtisch, *der; (in school)* Tisch, *der; (teacher's raised ~)* Pult, *das;* **~ unit** Schreibplatz, *der;* **~ copy** Arbeitsexemplar, *das;* **~ dictionary** Wörterbuch für den Schreibtisch; **b)** *(compartment) (for cashier)* Kasse, *die; (for reception-ist)* Rezeption, *die;* **information ~:** Auskunft, *die;* **sales ~:** Verkauf, *der;* **c)** *(music-stand)* Notenpult, *das;* **d)** *(section of newspaper office)* Ressort, *das*

desk: ~-bound *adj.* an den Schreibtisch gefesselt *(fig.);* **~ calendar, ~ diary** *ns.* Tischkalender, *der;* **~ editor** *n.* Manuskriptbearbeiter, *der*/-bearbeiterin, *die;* Lektor, *der*/Lektorin, *die;* **~ lamp** *n.* Schreibtischlampe, *die;* **~-top** *adj.* **~-top publishing** Desktop publishing, *das;* **~-top computer** Tischcomputer, *der*

desolate 1. ['desələt] *adj.* **a)** *(ruinous, neglected, barren)* trostlos ‹*Haus, Ort*›; desolat ‹*Zustand*›; **b)** *(solitary)* einsam; **c)** *(uninhabited)* öde; verlassen; **d)** *(forlorn, wretched)* trostlos ‹*Leben*›; arm ‹*Seele*›; verzweifelt ‹*Schrei*›. **2.** ['desəleɪt] *v.t.* **a)** *(depopulate)* entvölkern; **b)** *(devastate)* verwüsten ‹*Land*›; **c)** *(make wretched)* in Verzweiflung stürzen

desolation [desə'leɪʃn] *n.* **a)** *(desolating)* Verwüstung, *die;* **b)** *(neglected, solitary, or barren state)* Öde, *die; (state of ruin)* Verwüstung, *die;* **c)** *(loneliness, being forsaken)* Verlassenheit, *die;* **d)** *(grief, wretchedness)* Verzweiflung, *die*

despair [dɪ'speə(r)] **1.** *n.* **a)** Verzweiflung, *die;* **commit suicide in ~:** aus Verzweiflung Selbstmord begehen; **a cry of ~:** ein Verzweiflungsschrei; **his ~ of ever seeing her again** seine aufgegebene Hoffnung, sie je wiederzusehen; **b)** *(cause)* **be the ~ of sb.** jmdn. zur Verzweiflung bringen *od.* verzweifeln lassen. **2.** *v.i.* **a)** verzweifeln; **b) ~ of doing sth.** die Hoffnung aufgeben, etw. zu tun; **~ of sth.** die Hoffnung auf etw. *(Akk.)* aufgeben

despatch *(Brit.) see* **dispatch**

desperado [despə'rɑ:dəʊ] *n., pl.* **~es** *(Amer.:* **~s)** Desperado, *der*

desperate ['despərət] *adj.* **a)** verzweifelt; *(coll.: urgent)* dringend; **get** *or* **become ~:** verzweifeln; **feel ~:** verzweifelt sein; **be ~ for sth.** etw. dringend brauchen; **he was ~ for a beer** *(coll.)* er lechzte nach einem Bier; **be ~ to do sth.** verzweifelt versuchen, etw. zu tun; **don't do anything ~:** tun Sie nur nichts Unüberlegtes!; **b)** *(staking all on a small chance)* extrem ‹*Maßnahmen, Lösung*›; **a ~ disease must have a ~ remedy** *(fig.)* extreme Situationen erfordern extreme Maßnahmen; **c)** *(extremely dangerous or serious)* verzweifelt ‹*Lage, Situation*›; **things are getting ~:** die Lage wird immer verzweifelter; **d)** *(extremely bad)* schrecklich; **be in ~ need of sth.** etw. äußerst dringend brauchen

desperately ['despərətlɪ] *adv.* **a)** verzweifelt; hoffnungslos ‹*verliebt*›; *(urgently)* dringend; *(recklessly, with extreme energy)* verzweifelt; **be ~ ill** *or* **sick** todkrank sein; **b)** *(appallingly, shockingly, extremely)* schrecklich *(ugs.)*

desperation [despə'reɪʃn] *n.* Verzweiflung, *die;* **out of** *or* **in [sheer] ~:** aus [lauter] Verzweiflung; **be in ~:** verzweifelt sein; **act** *or* **deed of ~:** Verzweiflungstat, *die;* **fight with ~:** verzweifelt kämpfen

despicable ['despɪkəbl] *adj.*, **despicably** ['despɪkəblɪ] *adv.* verabscheuungswürdig

despise [dɪ'spaɪz] *v.t.* verachten; verschmähen *(geh.)* ‹*Geschenke*›; **this is not to be ~d** das ist nicht zu verachten

despite [dɪ'spaɪt] *prep.* trotz; **~ what she said** ungeachtet dessen, was sie sagte; **~ his warning** trotz seiner Warnung

despoil [dɪ'spɔɪl] *v.t. (literary)* berauben **(of** *Gen.*); ausplündern

despoliation [dɪspəʊlɪ'eɪʃn] *n.* Plünderung, *die*

despond [dɪ'spɒnd] *n. (arch.)* **Slough of D~** *(literary)* Pfuhl der Verzweiflung *(dichter.)*

despondency [dɪ'spɒndənsɪ] *n., no pl.* Niedergeschlagenheit, *die;* **view a situation with ~:** einer Lage sehr mutlos gegenüberstehen; **fall into ~:** den Mut verlieren; **answer in a tone of ~:** bedrückt antworten

despondent [dɪ'spɒndənt] *adj.* niedergeschlagen; bedrückt; **be ~ about sth.** wegen etw. *od.* über etw. *(Akk.)* bedrückt sein; **feel ~:** niedergeschlagen sein; **grow** *or* **get ~:** mutlos werden; **don't become ~!** nur Mut!

despondently [dɪ'spɒndəntlɪ] *adv.* niedergeschlagen

despot ['despɒt] *n.* Despot, *der*

despotic [dɪ'spɒtɪk] *adj.*, **despotically** [dɪ'spɒtɪkəlɪ] *adv.* despotisch

despotism ['despətɪzm] *n. (tyranny)* Despotie, *die;* Gewaltherrschaft, *die; (political system)* Despotismus, *der; (fig.: absolute power)* Tyrannei, *die*

dessert [dɪ'zɜ:t] *n.* **a)** süße Nachspeise; **b)** *(Brit.: after dinner)* Dessert, *das;* Nachtisch, *der*

dessert: ~ apple *n.* Dessertapfel, *der;* **~spoon** *n.* Dessertlöffel, *der;* **~spoonful** *n.* Eßlöffel, *der;* **a ~spoonful** ein Eßlöffel; **~ wine** *n.* Dessertwein, *der*

destabilize [di'steɪbɪlaɪz] *v.t. (Polit.)* destabilisieren

destination [destɪ'neɪʃn] *n. (of persons)* Reiseziel, *das; (of goods)* Bestimmungsort, *der; (of train, bus)* Zielort, *der;* **arrive at one's ~:** am Ziel ankommen; **place/port of ~:** Bestimmungsort, *der*/-hafen, *der*

destine ['destɪn] *v.t.* bestimmen; **~ sb. for sth.** jmdn. für etw. bestimmen; ‹*Schicksal:*› jmdn. für etw. vorbestimmen; **be ~d to do sth.** dazu ausersehen *od.* bestimmt sein, etw. zu tun; **we were ~d [never] to meet again** wir sollten uns [nie] wiedersehen; **be ~d for sth.** für etw. bestimmt sein; **qualities which ~d him for leadership** Eigenschaften, die ihn für Führungsaufgaben prädestinierten

destiny ['destɪnɪ] *n.* **a)** Schicksal, *das;* Los, *das;* **find one's ~:** seine Bestimmung finden; **b)** *no art. (power)* das Schicksal

destitute ['destɪtju:t] *adj.* **a)** *(without resources)* mittellos; **the ~ [poor]** die Mittellosen; **b)** *(devoid)* **be ~ of sth.** *(formal)* einer Sache *(Gen.)* bar sein *(geh.)*

destitution [destɪ'tju:ʃn] *n., no pl.* Armut, *die;* Not, *die*

destroy [dɪ'strɔɪ] *v.t.* **a)** *(demolish)* zerstören; kaputtmachen *(ugs.)* ‹*Tisch, Stuhl, Uhr, Schachtel*›; **the paintings were ~ed by fire** die Gemälde wurden durch einen Brand vernichtet; **b)** *(make useless)* vernichten ‹*Ernte, Papiere, Dokumente*›; **c)** *(kill, annihilate)* vernichten ‹*Feind, Insekten*›; **the dog will have to be ~ed** der Hund muß eingeschläfert werden; **d)** *(fig.)* zunichte machen ‹*Hoffnungen, Chancen*›; ruinieren ‹*Zukunft*›; zerstören ‹*Glück, Freundschaft, Schönheit, Macht*›

destroyer [dɪ'strɔɪə(r)] *n.* Zerstörer, *der*

destruct [dɪ'strʌkt] *(Amer.)* **1.** *v.t. & i.* zerstören. **2.** *n.* Zerstörung, *die*

destruction [dɪ'strʌkʃn] *n.* **a)** Zerstörung, *die; (of documents, mankind, a regime, an enemy)* Vernichtung, *die; (of toys, small objects)* Kaputtmachen, *das (ugs.); (of hopes)* Zunichtemachen, *das;* **bring about one's own ~:** sich selbst zugrunde richten; **b)** *(cause of ruin)* Untergang, *der*

destructive [dɪ'strʌktɪv] *adj.* **a)** *(destroying, tending to destroy)* zerstörerisch; verheerend ‹*Sturm, Feuer, Krieg*›; zersetzend ‹*Einfluß, Haltung, Tendenz*›; destruktiv ‹*Mensch*›; **~ urge** Destruktionstrieb, *der (Psych.);* Zerstörungswut, *die;* **b)** *(negative)* destruktiv ‹*Kritik, Vorstellung, Kommentar, Einfluß, Ziel*›

destructively [dɪ'strʌktɪvlɪ] *adv.* zerstörerisch; **behave ~:** sich destruktiv aufführen

destructor [dɪ'strʌktə(r)] *n. (Brit.)* Müllverbrennungsanlage, *die*

desuetude [dɪ'sju:ɪtju:d, 'deswɪtju:d] *n. (literary)* **fall into ~:** in Vergessenheit geraten; ‹*Wort, Sitte:*› außer Gebrauch kommen

desultory ['desəltərɪ] *adj.* **a)** *(going from one subject to another, disconnected)* sprunghaft; zwanglos, ungezwungen ‹*Gespräch*›; **b)** *(unmethodical)* planlos

detach [dɪˈtætʃ] *v.t.* **a)** *(unfasten)* entfernen; ablösen ⟨*Aufgeklebtes*⟩; abbrechen ⟨*Angewachsenes*⟩; abtrennen ⟨*zu Entfernendes*⟩; abnehmen ⟨*wieder zu Befestigendes*⟩; abhängen ⟨*Angekuppeltes*⟩; herausnehmen ⟨*innen Befindliches*⟩; **a couple of pages of the book have become ~ed** einige Seiten des Buches sind lose; **~ oneself from sb.** sich von jmdm. lösen; **b)** *(Mil., Navy)* abkommandieren (**from** aus); detachieren *(veralt.)*

detachable [dɪˈtætʃəbl] *adj.* abnehmbar; herausnehmbar ⟨*Futter*⟩

detached [dɪˈtætʃt] *adj.* **a)** *(impartial)* unvoreingenommen; *(unemotional)* unbeteiligt; **~ garage** freistehende Garage; **b)** *(separate)* **~ house** Einzelhaus, *das;* **~ retina** abgelöste Netzhaut

detachment [dɪˈtætʃmənt] *n.* **a)** *(detaching) see* **detach a:** Entfernen, *das;* Ablösen, *das;* Abbrechen, *das;* Abtrennen, *das;* Abnehmen, *das;* Abhängen, *das;* Herausnehmen, *das;* **b)** *(Mil., Navy)* Abteilung, *die;* Detachement, *das (veralt.);* **c)** *(being aloof)* Abstand, *der;* Distanz, *die;* **d)** *(independence of judgement)* Unvoreingenommenheit, *die*

detail [ˈdiːteɪl] **1.** *n.* **a)** *(item)* Einzelheit, *die;* Detail, *das;* **enter** *or* **go into ~s** ins Detail gehen; auf Einzelheiten eingehen; **a minor ~:** eine Kleinigkeit; **leave the ~s to sb. else** die Kleinarbeit [einem] anderen überlassen; **our correspondent will be giving you the ~s** unser Korrespondent wird [Ihnen] im einzelnen darüber berichten; **plan sth. down to the last ~:** etw. bis ins letzte Detail planen; **but that is a ~** *(iron.)* aber was macht das schon?; **b)** *(dealing with things item by item)* **in ~:** Punkt für Punkt; **have too much ~:** zu sehr ins einzelne *od.* Detail gehen; **we haven't discussed anything in ~ yet** wir haben bisher noch nicht im einzelnen darüber gesprochen; **in great** *or* **much ~:** in allen Einzelheiten; **in greater ~:** [noch] näher; **in minute ~:** haarklein; **go into ~:** ins Detail gehen; auf Einzelheiten eingehen; **attention to ~:** Sorgfalt in den Details; **c)** *(account)* Aufstellung, *die;* **d)** *(in building, picture, etc.)* Detail, *das;* **e)** *(part of picture)* Ausschnitt, *der;* **f)** *(Mil.)* Dienstplan, *der;* **g)** *(body for special duty)* Kommando, *das.* **2.** *v.t.* **a)** *(list)* einzeln aufführen; **be fully ~ed** *(stated, described)* im Detail ausgeführt werden; **b)** *(Mil.)* abkommandieren; einteilen

detailed [ˈdiːteɪld] *adj.* detailliert; eingehend ⟨*Studie*⟩

detain [dɪˈteɪn] *v.t.* **a)** *(keep in confinement)* festhalten; *(take into confinement)* verhaften; **b)** *(delay)* aufhalten; **do not let me ~ you** lassen Sie sich durch mich nicht aufhalten

detainee [dɪteɪˈniː] *n.* Verhaftete, *der/die*

detect [dɪˈtekt] *v.t.* **a)** *(discover presence of)* entdecken; bemerken ⟨*Trauer, Verärgerung*⟩; wahrnehmen ⟨*Bewegung*⟩; aufdecken ⟨*Irrtum, Verbrechen*⟩; durchschauen ⟨*Beweggrund*⟩; feststellen ⟨*Strahlung*⟩; **~ a note of anger in sb.'s voice** eine gewisse Verärgerung aus jmds. Stimme heraushören; **b)** *(reveal guilt of)* **~ sb. in doing sth.** jmdn. bei etw. ertappen

detectable [dɪˈtektəbl] *adj.* feststellbar; wahrnehmbar ⟨*Bewegung*⟩

detection [dɪˈtekʃn] *n.* **a)** *see* **detect a:** Entdeckung, *die;* Bemerken, *das;* Wahrnehmung, *die;* Aufdeckung, *die;* Durchschauen, *das;* Feststellung, *die;* **in order to escape ~:** um nicht entdeckt zu werden; **try to escape ~:** versuchen, unentdeckt zu bleiben; **b)** *(work of detective)* Ermittlungsarbeit, *die*

detective [dɪˈtektɪv] **1.** *n.* Detektiv, *der;* *(policeman)* Kriminalbeamte, *der*/Kriminalbeamtin, *die;* **private ~:** Privatdetektiv, *der.* **2.** *attrib. adj.* Kriminal-; **~ novel** Kriminalroman, *der;* **~ work** Ermittlungsarbeit, *die;* **~ story** Detektivgeschichte, *die*

detector [dɪˈtektə(r)] *n.* **a)** *(device)* Detektor, *der;* *(indicator)* Anzeiger, *der;* **b)** *(Electr.)* [Kristall]detektor, *der*

détente [deɪˈtɑ̃t] *n.* *(Polit.)* Entspannung, *die*

detention [dɪˈtenʃn] *n.* **a)** Festnahme, *die;* *(confinement)* Haft, *die;* **b)** *(Sch.)* Nachsitzen, *das;* *(Mil.)* Arrest, *der (veralt.);* **give sb. two hours' ~:** jmdn. zwei Stunden nachsitzen lassen; **c)** *(delay)* [unfreiwilliger] Aufenthalt

de'tention centre *n.* *(Brit.)* Jugendstrafanstalt, *die*

deter [dɪˈtɜː(r)] *v.t.*, **-rr-** abschrecken; **~ sb. from sth.** jmdn. von etw. abhalten; **~ sb. from doing sth.** jmdn. davon abhalten, etw. zu tun; **the danger did not ~ him** er ließ sich durch die Gefahr nicht abschrecken; die Gefahr schreckte ihn nicht *(geh.);* **be ~red by sth.** sich durch etw. abschrecken lassen

detergent [dɪˈtɜːdʒənt] **1.** *adj.* reinigend. **2.** *n.* Reinigungsmittel, *das;* *(for washing)* Waschmittel, *das;* Detergens, *das (Chemie)*

deteriorate [dɪˈtɪərɪəreɪt] **1.** *v.t.* verschlechtern; verringern, mindern ⟨*Wert*⟩. **2.** *v.i.* sich verschlechtern; ⟨*Haus:*⟩ verfallen, verkommen; ⟨*Holz, Leder:*⟩ verrotten; **his condition** *or* **he has ~d** sein Zustand hat sich verschlechtert; **his work has ~d** seine Arbeit hat nachgelassen; **~ in value** an Wert verlieren

deterioration [dɪtɪərɪəˈreɪʃn] *n.* *see* **deteriorate 2:** Verschlechterung, *die;* Verfall, *der;* Verrottung, *die;* **preserve paintings from ~:** Gemälde vor Schädigungen schützen

determinable [dɪˈtɜːmɪnəbl] *adj.* *(capable of being fixed or ascertained)* bestimmbar; **sth. is ~:** etw. läßt sich bestimmen

determinate [dɪˈtɜːmɪnət] *adj.* **a)** *(limited, finite)* begrenzt; **b)** *(distinct)* bestimmt; **c)** *(definitive)* eindeutig; fest ⟨*Begriff*⟩

determination [dɪtɜːmɪˈneɪʃn] *n.* **a)** *(ascertainment, definition)* Bestimmung, *die;* **b)** *(resoluteness)* Entschlossenheit, *die;* **with [sudden] ~:** [kurz] entschlossen; **he had an air of ~ about him** er wirkte fest entschlossen; **c)** *(intention)* [feste] Absicht; **d)** *(Law: ending)* Ablauf, *der;* **e)** *(judicial decision)* Entscheidung, *die;* **f)** *(fixing beforehand)* Festlegung, *die*

determine [dɪˈtɜːmɪn] **1.** *v.t.* **a)** *(decide)* beschließen; **~ to do sth.** beschließen, etw. zu tun; sich entschließen, etw. zu tun; **b)** *(make decide)* veranlassen; **~ sb. to do sth.** jmdn. dazu veranlassen, etw. zu tun; **c)** *(be a decisive factor for)* bestimmen; entscheiden über (+ *Akk.*); **d)** *(ascertain, define)* feststellen; bestimmen; **e)** *(fix beforehand)* festlegen; **f)** *(Law: end)* beenden. **2.** *v.i.* *(decide)* **~ on doing sth.** beschließen, etw. zu tun; **~ on sth.** sich für etw. entscheiden

determined [dɪˈtɜːmɪnd] *adj.* **a)** *(resolved)* **be ~ to do** *or* **on doing sth.** etw. unbedingt tun wollen; fest entschlossen sein, etw. zu tun; **sb. is ~ that ...:** es ist für jmdn. beschlossene Sache, daß ...; **I am ~ that he shall win** ich werde alles Mögliche tun, daß er siegt; **b)** *(resolute)* entschlossen; resolut ⟨*Person*⟩; **c)** *(fixed)* bestimmt

determinedly [dɪˈtɜːmɪndlɪ] *adv.* entschlossen

determinism [dɪˈtɜːmɪnɪzm] *n.* Determinismus, *der*

deterrence [dɪˈterəns] *n.* Abschreckung, *die*

deterrent [dɪˈterənt] **1.** *adj.* abschreckend. **2.** *n.* Abschreckungsmittel, *das* (**to** für); **~ strategy** Strategie der Abschreckung

detest [dɪˈtest] *v.t.* verabscheuen; **~ doing sth.** es verabscheuen, etw. zu tun

detestable [dɪˈtestəbl] *adj.* verabscheuenswert; verabscheuungswürdig

detestably [dɪˈtestəblɪ] *adv.* abscheulich

detestation [diːteˈsteɪʃn] *n.*, *no pl.* Abscheu, *der* (**of** vor + *Dat.*)

dethrone [diːˈθrəʊn] *v.t.* *(lit. or fig.)* entthronen

dethronement [diːˈθrəʊnmənt] *n.* *(lit. or fig.)* Entthronung, *die*

detonate [ˈdetəneɪt] **1.** *v.i.* detonieren. **2.** *v.t.* zur Explosion bringen; zünden

detonation [detəˈneɪʃn] *n.* **a)** *(detonating)* Detonation, *die;* **b)** *(Motor Veh.)* Klopfen, *das*

detonator [ˈdetəneɪtə(r)] *n.* **a)** *(part of bomb or shell)* Sprengkapsel, *die;* Detonator, *der;* **b)** *(Railw.)* Knallkapsel, *die*

detour [ˈdiːtʊə(r), ˈdeɪtʊə(r)] **1.** *n.* Umweg, *der;* *(in a road, river)* Bogen, *der;* Schleife, *die;* *(diversion)* Umleitung, *die;* **make a ~:** einen Umweg machen. **2.** *v.t.* umleiten

detract [dɪˈtrækt] *v.i.* **~ from sth.** etw. beeinträchtigen; **~ from sb.'s merits** jmds. Verdienste schmälern

detraction [dɪˈtrækʃn] *n.* Beeinträchtigung, *die* (**from** *Gen.*); *(defamation)* Schmähung, *die*

detractor [dɪˈtræktə(r)] *n.* Verleumder, *der*/Verleumderin, *die*

detriment [ˈdetrɪmənt] *n.* Schaden, *der;* **to the ~ of sth.** zum Nachteil *od.* Schaden einer Sache *(Gen.);* **without ~ to** ohne Schaden für; **I know nothing to his ~:** mir ist nichts Nachteiliges über ihn bekannt

detrimental [detrɪˈmentl] *adj.* schädlich; **be ~ to sth.** einer Sache *(Dat.)* schaden *od.* *(geh.)* abträglich sein

detrimentally [detrɪˈmentəlɪ] *adv.* auf schädliche Weise

detritus [dɪˈtraɪtəs] *n.*, *no pl.* **a)** *(debris)* Überbleibsel, *das;* **b)** *(Geol.)* Geröll, *das;* Detritus, *der*

de trop [dəˈtrəʊ] *pred. adj.* fehl am Platz; überflüssig

[1]**deuce** [djuːs] *n.* **a)** *(on dice; arch. Cards)* Zwei, *die;* **b)** *(Tennis)* Einstand, *der*

[2]**deuce** *n.* *(coll.) see* **devil 1 c**

deuced [djuːsɪd, djuːst] *adj., adv.* *(arch.) see* **damned 1 b, c, 2**

deus ex machina [deɪəs eks ˈmɑːkɪnə, diːəs eks ˈmɑːkɪnə] *n.* Deus ex machina, *der*

deuterium [djuːˈtɪərɪəm] *n.* Deuterium, *das*

Deuteronomy [djuːtəˈrɒnəmɪ] *n.* *(Bibl.)* das fünfte Buch Mose

Deutschmark [ˈdɔɪtʃmɑːk] *n.* Deutsche Mark

devaluation [diːvæljuːˈeɪʃn] *n.* **a)** Abwertung, *die;* **b)** *(Econ.)* Abwertung, *die;* Devalvation, *die*

devalue [diːˈvæljuː] *v.t.* **a)** *(reduce value of)* abwerten; **b)** *(Econ.)* abwerten; devalvieren

devastate [ˈdevəsteɪt] *v.t.* verwüsten; verheeren; *(fig.)* niederschmettern

devastating [ˈdevəsteɪtɪŋ] *adj.* verheerend; niederschmetternd ⟨*Nachricht, Analyse*⟩; überwältigend ⟨*Leidenschaft*⟩; vernichtend ⟨*Spielweise, Kritik*⟩

devastation [devəˈsteɪʃn] *n.*, *no pl.* Verwüstung, *die;* Verheerung, *die*

develop [dɪˈveləp] **1.** *v.t.* **a)** *(bring into existence)* entwickeln; aufbauen ⟨*Handel, Handelszentrum*⟩; **the girl had ~ed a mature figure** die Figur des Mädchens war voll entwickelt; **the machine was ~ed from their plans** die Maschine wurde nach ihren Plänen entwickelt; **~ a business from scratch** ein Geschäft neu aufziehen; **b)** *(bring to more evident form)* entwickeln ⟨*Instinkt, Fähigkeiten, Kräfte*⟩; entfalten ⟨*Persönlichkeit, Individualität*⟩; erschließen ⟨*natürliche Ressourcen*⟩; **c)** *(bring to fuller form)* entwickeln; *(expand; make more sophisticated)* weiterentwickeln; ausbauen ⟨*Verkehrsnetz, System, Handel, Verkehr, Position*⟩; wachsen lassen ⟨*Pflanze, Korn*⟩; **~ sth. further** etw. weiterentwickeln; **~ an essay into a book** einen Essay zu einem Buch ausbauen; **a highly ~ed civilization** eine hochentwickelte Zivilisation; **d)** *(begin to exhibit, begin to suffer from)* annehmen ⟨*Ge-*

wohnheit›; bei sich entdecken ‹*Vorliebe*›; bekommen ‹*Krankheit, Fieber, Lust*›; entwickeln ‹*Talent, Stärke*›; erkranken an (+ *Dat.*) ‹*Krebs, Tumor*›; ~ **a taste for sth.** Geschmack an etw. *(Akk.)* finden; **the car ~ed a fault** an dem Wagen ist ein Defekt aufgetreten; **e)** *(Photog.)* entwickeln; **f)** *(construct buildings etc. on, convert to new use)* erschließen; sanieren ‹*Altstadt*›; aufschließen ‹*Schacht*›; **g)** *(Mus.)* durchführen ‹*Thema*›; **h)** *(Chess)* entwickeln; **i)** *(Amer.: make known)* an den Tag bringen. **2.** *v. i.* **a)** *(come into existence, become evident)* sich entwickeln (**from** aus; **into** zu); ‹*Defekt, Symptome, Erkrankungen:*› auftreten; **b)** *(become fuller)* sich [weiter]entwickeln (**into** zu); **c)** *(Amer.: become known)* an den Tag kommen; **it ~ed that ...:** es stellte sich heraus, daß ...

developable [dɪˈveləpəbl] *adj.* entwicklungsfähig; erschließungsfähig ‹*Gebiet*›

developer [dɪˈveləpə(r)] *n.* **a)** *(Photog.) (chemical agent)* Entwickler, *der;* **b)** *(person who develops real estate)* ≈ Bauunternehmer, *der;* **c)** *(person who matures)* **late** *or* **slow ~:** Spätentwickler, *der*

deˈveloping country *n.* Entwicklungsland, *das*

development [dɪˈveləpmənt] *n.* **a)** *(bringing into existence)* Entwicklung, *die* (**from** aus, **into** zu); **b)** *(bringing into more evident form) (of individuality)* Entfaltung, *die; (of heat, gas, vapour)* Entwicklung, *die; (of natural resources etc.)* Erschließung, *die;* **sth. is in the course of ~:** etw. befindet sich in der Entwicklung; **c)** *(bringing into fuller form)* Entwicklung, *die; (expansion)* Ausbau, *der;* Weiterentwicklung, *die;* **be capable of [further] ~:** noch weiter entwicklungsfähig sein; **d)** *(beginning to exhibit)* Entwicklung, die; *(of a talent also)* Entfaltung, *die; (beginning to suffer from)* Beginn, *der;* **e)** *(of land etc.)* Erschließung, *die;* **regional ~:** Regionalplanung, *die;* **f)** *(evolution)* Entwicklung, *die;* **g)** *(full-grown state)* Vollendung, *die;* **h)** *(developed product or form)* **a ~ of sth.** eine Fortentwicklung *od.* Weiterentwicklung einer Sache; **at that time tea-bags were a new ~:** damals waren Teebeutel eine Neuerung; **i)** *(Photog.)* Entwickeln, *das;* Entwicklung, *die;* **j)** *(Mus.)* Durchführung, *die;* **k)** *(Chess)* Entwicklung, *die;* **l)** *(developed land)* **[new] ~:** Neubaugebiet, *das*

developmental [dɪveləpˈmentl] *adj.* Entwicklungs-

deˈvelopment area *n. (Brit.)* Entwicklungsgebiet, *das*

deviance [ˈdi:vɪəns], **deviancy** [ˈdi:vɪənsɪ] *n.* abweichendes Verhalten; Devianz, *die (Soziol.)*

deviant [ˈdi:vɪənt] **1.** *adj.* [von der Norm] abweichend; deviant *(Soziol.)*. **2.** *n.* [von der Norm] Abweichende, *der/die/das;* **a sexual ~:** jmd. mit [von der Norm] abweichendem Sexualverhalten; sexuell devianter Mensch *(Soziol.)*

deviate [ˈdi:vɪeɪt] *v. i. (lit. or fig.)* abweichen

deviation [di:vɪˈeɪʃn] *n.* **a)** *(deviating)* Abweichung, *die;* **b)** *(of compass-needle)* Ablenkung, *die;* Deviation, *die;* **c)** *(Statistics)* **[standard] ~:** [Standard]abweichung, *die*

deviationism [di:vɪˈeɪʃənɪzm] *n. (Polit.)* Abweichlertum, *das*

deviationist [di:vɪˈeɪʃənɪst] *n. (Polit.)* Abweichler, *der*/Abweichlerin, *die*

device [dɪˈvaɪs] *n.* **a)** *(contrivance)* Gerät, *das; (as part of sth.)* Vorrichtung, *die;* **nuclear ~:** atomarer Sprengkörper; **b)** *(plan, scheme)* List, *die;* **rhetorical ~s** rhetorische Kunstgriffe; **c)** *(drawing, design, figure)* Verzierung, *die;* **d)** *(emblematic or heraldic design)* Emblem, *das;* **e)** *(motto)* Motto, *das;* Devise, *die;* **f)** *in pl. (fancy, will)* **leave sb. to his own ~s** jmdn. sich *(Dat.)* selbst überlassen; **be left to one's own ~s** sich *(Dat.)* selbst überlassen sein

devil [ˈdevl] **1.** *n.* **a)** *(Satan)* **the D~:** der Teufel; **b)** *(heathen god)* Götze, *der; (evil spirit, Satan's follower)* Teufel, *der;* **the ~ of greed** der Dämon Habgier; **c)** *or* **D~** *(coll.)* **who/where/what** *etc.* **the ~?** wer/wo/was *usw.* zum Teufel? *(salopp);* **the ~ take him!** hol' ihn der Teufel! *(salopp);* **he's got the ~ in him** er hat den Teufel im Leib *(ugs.);* **the ~!** Teufel auch! *(salopp);* **the ~ knows** weiß der Teufel *(salopp);* **there will be the ~ to pay** da ist der Teufel los *(ugs.);* **go to the ~:** zum Teufel gehen *(salopp);* sich zum Teufel scheren *(salopp);* **[you can] go to the ~!** scher dich zum Teufel! *(salopp);* **work/shout like the ~:** wie ein Besessener arbeiten/schreien; **run/fight like the ~:** wie der Teufel rennen/kämpfen *(ugs.);* **between the ~ and the deep [blue] sea** in einer Zwickmühle *(ugs.);* **~ take it!** verdammt noch mal!; **it was ~ take the hindmost** es galt nur noch: Rette sich, wer kann!; **play the ~ with sb./sth.** jmdm./einer Sache übel mitspielen; **better the ~ one knows** lieber das bekannte Übel; **speak** *or* **talk of the ~ [and he will appear]** wenn man vom Teufel spricht[, kommt er]; *see also* **idle 1 f; needs; d) a** *or* **the ~ of a mess** ein verteufelter Schlamassel *(ugs.);* **be in a ~ of a mess** im dicksten Schlamassel sitzen *(ugs.);* **a** *or* **the ~ of a problem** ein verteufelt schwieriges Problem; **have a ~ of a temper** verteufelt jähzornig sein *(ugs.);* **have the ~ of a time** es verteufelt schwer haben; **be a ~!** sei kein Frosch!; **he is a ~ of a [good] teacher** er ist ein verdammt guter Lehrer *(ugs.);* **this car is the [very] ~ to start** dieses Auto läßt sich verteufelt schwer starten *(ugs.);* **the crossword is a real ~:** das Kreuzworträtsel ist verteufelt schwer *(ugs.);* **e)** *(wicked or cruel person, vicious animal)* Teufel, *der (fig.); (mischievously energetic or self-willed person)* Teufel, *der (fig. ugs.);* Teufelsbraten, *der (ugs. scherzh.); (able, clever person)* As, *das (ugs.);* **he's a ~ with the women** er spielt mit den Frauen; **he's a clever ~:** er ist ein schlauer Hund *(ugs.);* **you ~!** *(ugs.)* du Schlingel!; **a poor ~:** ein armer Teufel; **lucky ~:** Glückspilz, *der (ugs.);* **unlucky ~:** Unglücksrabe, *der (ugs.);* **cheeky/naughty ~:** Frechdachs, *der (fam., meist scherzh.);* **queer** *or* **odd ~:** komischer Kauz; **f)** *(fighting spirit)* Kampfgeist, *der;* **g)** *(Law) [unbezahlter] Gehilfe eines Anwalts;* **h)** *(literary hack) Zuarbeiter eines Schriftstellers;* **i)** *(S.Afr.)* **[dust] ~:** Sandsturm, *der. See also* **due 3 b; Tasmanian 1 b. 2.** *v. t., (Brit.)* **-ll-: a)** *(Cookery) kleingeschnitten und scharf gewürzt braten;* **b)** *(Amer. coll.: harass, worry)* piesacken *(ugs.)*

ˈdevil-fish *n.* **a)** *(angler-fish)* Seeteufel, *der;* **b)** *(Amer.: ray)* Teufelsrochen, *der*

devilish [ˈdevəlɪʃ] **1.** *adj.* **a)** *(of the Devil)* teuflisch ‹*Künste, Zauberei*›; ‹*Erfindung, Lehre*› des Teufels; **b)** *(damnable)* teuflisch. **2.** *adv. (arch. coll.)* verteufelt *(ugs.)*

devilishly [ˈdevəlɪʃlɪ] *adv.* *(diabolically)* teuflisch; *(exceedingly)* verteufelt *(ugs.)*

ˈdevil-may-care *adj.* sorglos-unbekümmert

devilment [ˈdevlmənt] *n.* **a)** *(mischief)* Unfug, *der; (wild spirits)* Übermut, *der;* **be up to some ~:** Unfug treiben *od.* anstellen; **b)** *(devilish phenomenon)* Teufelei, *die*

devilry [ˈdevlrɪ] *n.* **a)** *(black magic)* Teufelskunst, *die;* **b)** *(wickedness, cruelty)* teuflische Bosheit; *(action)* Teufelei, *die;* **c)** *(mischief)* Unfug, *der; (hilarity)* Schabernack, *der;* **out of sheer ~:** aus purem Schabernack

devil: ~'s ˈadvocate *n. (RC Ch.; also fig.)* Advocatus Diaboli, *der;* **~'s ˈcoach-horse** *n. (Brit. Zool.)* Schwarzer *od.* Stinkender Moderkäfer; **~s-on-ˈhorseback** *n. (Gastr.)* Austern in Röllchen aus Frühstücksspeck; Austern auf englische Art; **~'s ˈown** *attrib. adj.* **the ~'s own** ein/eine verteufelt... *(ugs.);* **[take] the ~'s own time** eine verteufelt lange Zeit [dauern] *(ugs.);* **he has the ~'s own luck** er hat verteufeltes Glück *(ugs.)*

devious [ˈdi:vɪəs] *adj.* **a)** *(winding)* verschlungen; **take a ~ route** einen Umweg fahren; **b)** *(unscrupulous, insincere)* verschlagen ‹*Person*›; hinterhältig ‹*Person, Methode, Tat*›

deviously [ˈdi:vɪəslɪ] *adv.* hinterhältigerweise; **behave ~:** sich hinterhältig verhalten

deviousness [ˈdi:vɪəsnɪs] *n., no pl.* Hinterhältigkeit, *die;* Verschlagenheit, *die*

devise [dɪˈvaɪz] *v. t.* *(plan)* entwerfen; schmieden ‹*Pläne*›; kreieren ‹*Mode, Stil*›; ausarbeiten ‹*Programm*›

devoid [dɪˈvɔɪd] *adj.* **~ of sth.** *(lacking)* ohne etw.; bar einer Sache *(Gen.) (geh.); (free from)* frei von etw.

devolution [di:vəˈlu:ʃn] *n.* **a)** *(deputing, delegation)* Übertragung, *die;* Delegieren, *das; (Polit.)* Dezentralisierung, *die;* **b)** *(descent of property, power, etc.)* Übergang, *der* (**on [to]** auf + *Akk.*); **c)** *(Biol.)* Degeneration, *die;* **d)** *(Brit. Polit.) Übertragung von administrativer Unabhängigkeit;* Devolution, *die (fachspr.)*

devolve [dɪˈvɒlv] *v. i.* **a)** *(be transferred)* **~ [up]on sb.** ‹*Pflicht, Verantwortung, Aufgabe:*› jmdm. zufallen; **b)** *(descend)* vererbt werden; **~ to sb.** auf jmdn. übergehen

Devonian [dɪˈvəʊnɪən] **1.** *adj. (Geol.)* devonisch. **2.** *n. (Geol.)* Devon, *das*

Devonshire cream [devnʃɪə ˈkri:m] *n. sehr fetter Rahm;* Dickrahm, *der*

devote [dɪˈvəʊt] *v. t. (consecrate)* widmen; **~ one's thoughts/energy to sth.** sein Denken/seine Energie auf etw. *(Akk.)* verwenden; **~ sums of money to sth.** Geldsummen für etw. bestimmen

devoted [dɪˈvəʊtɪd] *adj.* treu; ergeben ‹*Diener*›; aufrichtig ‹*Freundschaft, Liebe, Verehrung*›; **he is very ~ to his work/his wife** er geht in seiner Arbeit völlig auf/liebt seine Frau innig

devotedly [dɪˈvəʊtɪdlɪ] *adv.* [treu] ergeben; innig ‹*lieben*›

devotee [devəˈti:] *n.* **a)** *(enthusiast)* Anhänger, *der*/Anhängerin, *die; (of music, art)* Liebhaber, *der*/Liebhaberin, *die; (of a person)* Verehrer, *der*/Verehrerin, *die;* **b)** *(pious person)* [fanatischer/glühender] Anhänger/[fanatische/glühende] Anhängerin

devotion [dɪˈvəʊʃn] *n.* **a)** *(addiction, loyalty, devoutness)* **~ to sb./sth.** Hingabe an jmdn./etw.; **~ to music/the arts** Liebe zur Musik/Kunst; **~ to duty** Pflichteifer, *der;* **b)** *(devoting)* Weihung, *die;* **c)** *(divine worship)* Anbetung, *die* (**to** *Gen.*); **d)** *in pl. (prayers)* Gebet, *das;* **be at one's ~s** seine Andacht halten; **book of ~s** Andachtsbuch, *das*

devotional [dɪˈvəʊʃənl] *adj.* fromm; andächtig ‹*Gebet*›; religiös ‹*Literatur, Lied*›; Andachts‹*buch, -übung*›

devour [dɪˈvaʊə(r)] *v. t.* **a)** verschlingen; ‹*Pest:*› dahinraffen *(geh.);* **b)** *(absorb the attention of)* verzehren; **he was ~ed by anxiety** er verzehrte sich vor Angst

devouring [dɪˈvaʊərɪŋ] *adj.* verzehrend ‹*Hunger, Leidenschaft, Feuer*›; verschlingend ‹*Fluten*›; menschenfressend, alles verschlingend ‹*Ungeheuer, Tier*›

devout [dɪˈvaʊt] *adj.* fromm; sehnlich ‹*Wunsch*›; inständig ‹*Hoffnung*›

devoutly [dɪˈvaʊtlɪ] *adv.* in [frommer] Andacht ‹*knien, beten, bekennen*›; inständig ‹*hoffen, wünschen*›

dew [dju:] **1.** *n.* Tau, *der.* **2.** *v. t. (poet./literary)* betauen *(geh.).*

dew: ~berry *n.* Brombeere, *die;* **~-claw** *n.* Afterklaue, *die;* **~-drop** *n.* Tautropfen, *der*

Dewey system [ˈdju:ɪ sɪstəm] *n. (Biliog.)* Dezimalklassifikation, *die*

dewlap ['dju:læp] *n.* *(of animal)* Wamme, *die;* *(of person)* Doppelkinn, *das*
dew: **~-point** *n.* *(Phys.)* Taupunkt, *der;* **~-pond** *n.* *(Brit.) flacher, künstlich angelegter Teich, in dem sich Tau- und Regenwasser sammelt*
dewy ['dju:ı] *adj.* taufeucht; tauig *(geh.)*
'**dewy-eyed** *adj.* naiv; **go all ~** ganz feuchte Augen bekommen
dexter ['dekstə(r)] *adj.* *(Her.)* recht...; dexter *(fachspr.)*
dexterity [dek'sterıtı] *n., no pl.* **a)** *(skill)* Geschicklichkeit, *die;* **~ in argument** Redegewandtheit, *die;* **b)** *(right-handedness)* Rechtshändigkeit, *die*
dexterous[ly] *see* **dextr-**
dextrose ['dekstrəʊs] *n.* *(Chem.)* Traubenzucker, *der;* Dextrose, *die (fachspr.)*
dextrous ['dekstrəs] *adj.* **a)** *(nimble of hand, skilful, clever)* geschickt; **b)** *(using right hand)* rechtshändig
dextrously ['dekstrəslı] *adv.* geschickt; mit großem Geschick
dhow [daʊ] *n.* *(Naut.)* D[h]au, *die*
DHSS *abbr.* *(Brit. Hist.)* **Department of Health and Social Security** *Amt für Gesundheit und Sozialwesen*
dia. *abbr.* **diameter** D.; Durchm.
diabetes [daıə'bi:ti:z] *n., pl. same* *(Med.)* Zuckerkrankheit, *die;* Diabetes, *der (fachspr.)*
diabetic [daıə'betık, daıə'bi:tık] *(Med.)* **1.** *adj.* **a)** *(of diabetes)* diabetisch; **b)** *(having diabetes)* diabetisch *(Med.)*; zuckerkrank; **c)** *(for diabetics)* Diabetiker⟨*nahrung, -schokolade usw.*⟩. **2.** *n.* Diabetiker, *der*/Diabetikerin, *die*
diabolic [daıə'bɒlık], **diabolical** [daıə'bɒlıkl] *adj.* **a)** *(cruel, wicked)* teuflisch; diabolisch; *(coll.: extremely bad)* mörderisch *(ugs.)* ⟨*Hitze*⟩; teuflisch *(ugs.)* ⟨*Kälte, Wetter*⟩; **this child is a ~ nuisance!** *(coll.)* dieses Kind kann einen zur Weißglut treiben! *(ugs.)*; **shopping today was ~** *(coll.)* das Einkaufen heute war die reinste Hölle *(ugs.)*; **b)** *(of the Devil)* diabolisch; teuflisch
diabolically [daıə'bɒlıkəlı] *adv.* *(coll.)* teuflisch *(ugs.)* ⟨*kalt, grausam*⟩; mörderisch *(ugs.)* ⟨*heiß*⟩
diachronic [daıə'krɒnık] *adj.*, **diachronically** [daıə'krɒnıkəlı] *adv.* *(Ling.)* diachronisch
diacritic [daıə'krıtık], **diacritical** [daıə'krıtıkl] **1.** *adj.* **a)** *(distinctive)* distinktiv *(geh.)*; **b)** *(Ling.)* **~ mark** *or* **sign** diakritisches Zeichen. **2.** *n.* *(Ling.)* diakritisches Zeichen
diadem ['daıədem] *n.* Diadem, *das;* *(wreath)* Kranz, *der*
diagnose [daıəg'nəʊz] *v.t.* diagnostizieren ⟨*Krankheit*⟩; feststellen ⟨*Fehler*⟩
diagnosis [daıəg'nəʊsıs] *n., pl.* **diagnoses** [daıəg'nəʊsi:z] **a)** *(of disease)* Diagnose, *die;* **make a ~:** eine Diagnose stellen; **b)** *(of difficulty, fault)* Feststellung, *die*
diagnostic [daıəg'nɒstık] **1.** *adj.* diagnostisch; **~ sign** *(Med.)* Symptom, *das.* **2.** *n.* *(Med.)* Symptom, *das*
diagnostics [daıəg'nɒstıks] *n. sing.* Diagnostik, *die*
diagonal [daı'ægənl] **1.** *adj.* diagonal. **2.** *n.* Diagonale, *die*
diagonally [daı'ægənəlı] *adv.* diagonal
diagram ['daıəgræm] **1.** *n.* **a)** *(sketch)* schematische Darstellung; **I'll make a ~ to show you how to get there** ich zeichne Ihnen auf, wie Sie dorthin kommen; **b)** *(graphic or symbolic representation)* Diagramm, *das;* **c)** *(Geom.)* Diagramm, *das.* **2.** *v.t.*, *(Brit.)* **-mm-** [in einem Diagramm] graphisch darstellen; *(make sketch of)* aufzeichnen
diagrammatic [daıəgrə'mætık] *adj.*, **diagrammatically** [daıəgrə'mætıkəlı] *adv.* diagrammatisch
dial ['daıəl] **1.** *n.* **a)** *(of clock or watch)* Zifferblatt, *das;* **b)** *(of gauge, meter, etc., on radio or television)* Skala, *die;* **c)** **[sun]~:** Sonnenuhr, *die;* **d)** *(Teleph.)* Wählscheibe, *die;* **e)** *(Brit. sl.: face)* Visage, *die (salopp abwertend).* **2.** *v.t.*, *(Brit.)* **-ll-** *(Teleph.)* wählen; **~ [London] direct** [nach London] durchwählen; **~ a call to somewhere/to sb.** irgendwo/bei jmdm. anrufen. **3.** *v.i.*, *(Brit.)* **-ll-** *(Teleph.)* wählen
dialect ['daıəlekt] *n.* Dialekt, *der;* Mundart, *die;* *(of class)* Ausdrucksweise, *die;* *attrib.* **~ expression** mundartlicher *od.* dialektaler Ausdruck
dialectal [daıə'lektl] *adj.* dialektal; mundartlich
dialectic [daıə'lektık] **1.** *n. in sing. or pl. constr. as sing.* Dialektik, *die.* **2.** *adj.* **a)** dialektisch; **b)** *(dialectal)* dialektal; dialektisch
dialectical [daıə'lektıkl] *adj.* **a)** *see* **dialectic 2 a**; **b)** **~ materialism** dialektischer Materialismus
dialling *(Amer.:* **dialing***)* ['daıəlıŋ]: **~ code** *n.* Vorwahl, *die;* Ortsnetzkennzahl, *die (Amtsspr.)*; **~ tone** *n.* Freizeichen, *das;* Wählton, *der (fachspr.)*
dialogue *(Amer.:* **dialog***)* ['daıəlɒg] *n.* Dialog, *der;* **written in ~ [form]** in der Form eines Dialogs geschrieben
'**dial tone** *(Amer.)* *see* **dialling tone**
dialysis [daı'ælısıs] *n., pl.* **dialyses** [daı'ælısi:z] **a)** *(Chem.)* Dialyse, *die;* **b)** *(Med.)* [Hämo]dialyse, *die (fachspr.)*; Blutwäsche, *die*
diameter [daı'æmıtə(r)] *n.* **a)** Durchmesser, *der;* Diameter, *der (Geom.)*; **b)** **a magnification of eight ~s** eine achtfache Vergrößerung; **magnify 2,000 ~s** zweitausendfach vergrößern
diametrical [daıə'metrıkl] *adj.* diametral; **I hold opinions in ~ opposition to his** meine Ansichten sind seinen diametral entgegengesetzt
diametrically [daıə'metrıkəlı] *adv.* **a)** *(in direct opposition)* diametral ⟨*entgegengesetzt, widersprechen*⟩; **b)** *(straight through)* diametrisch
diamond ['daıəmənd] **1.** *n.* **a)** Diamant, *der;* **it was [a case of] ~ cut ~** *(fig.)* da sind die Richtigen aneinandergeraten; **b)** *(figure)* Raute, *die;* Rhombus, *der;* **c)** *(Cards)* Karo, *das;* *see also* **club 1 d**; **d)** *(tool)* [Glaser]diamant, *der;* **e)** *(Baseball) (space enclosed by bases)* Innenfeld, *das;* *(entire field)* Spielfeld, *das. See also* **rough diamond. 2.** *adj.* **a)** *(made of ~[s])* diamanten; *(set with ~[s])* diamantenbesetzt; Diamant⟨*ring, -staub, -schmuck*⟩; **b)** *(rhomb-shaped)* rautenförmig
diamond: **~-drill** *n.* Diamantbohrer, *der;* **~-field** *n.* Diamantlagerstätte, *die;* **~ 'jubilee** *n.* 60jähriges/75jähriges Jubiläum; **~-merchant** *n.* Diamantenhändler, *der*/-händlerin, *die;* **~ mine** *n.* Diamantenbergwerk, *das;* **~-shaped** *adj.* rautenförmig; **~ 'wedding** *n.* diamantene Hochzeit
dianthus [daı'ænθəs] *n.* *(Bot.)* Nelke, *die*
diaper ['daıəpə(r)] *n.* **a)** *(Amer.: nappy)* Windel, *die;* **b)** *(fabric) mit kleinen Rauten o. ä. gemustertes [Jacquard]gewebe*
diaphanous [daı'æfənəs] *adj.* durchsichtig
diaphragm ['daıəfræm] *n.* Diaphragma, *das (fachspr.)*; *(Anat. also)* Zwerchfell, *das;* *(Zool., Bot. also)* Scheidewand, *die;* *(Photog. also)* Blende, *die;* *(contraceptive also)* Pessar, *das;* *(Mech., Teleph. also)* Membran, *die*
diapositive [daıə'pɒzıtıv] *n.* *(Photog.)* Diapositiv, *das*
diarist ['daıərıst] *n.* Tagebuchautor, *der*/-autorin, *die*
diarrhoea *(Amer.:* **diarrhea***)* [daıə'ri:ə] *n.* Durchfall, *der;* Diarrhö[e], *die (Med.)*
diary ['daıərı] *n.* **a)** Tagebuch, *das;* **keep a ~:** [ein] Tagebuch führen; **b)** *(for appointments)* Terminkalender, *der;* **pocket/desk ~:** Taschen-/Tischkalender, *der*
Diaspora [daı'æspərə] *n.* Zerstreuung der Juden; *(persons)* Diaspora, *die*
diastolic [daıə'stɒlık] *adj.* *(Physiol.)* diastolisch
diatonic [daıə'tɒnık] *adj.* *(Mus.)* diatonisch
diatribe ['daıətraıb] *n.* *(speech)* Schmährede, *die;* *(piece of writing)* Schmähschrift, *die*
dibber ['dıbə(r)] *see* **dibble 1**
dibble ['dıbl] **1.** *n.* Pflanzholz, *das.* **2.** *v.t.* [mit dem Pflanzholz] pflanzen
dice [daıs] **1.** *n., pl. same* **a)** *(cube)* Würfel, *der;* **throw ~:** würfeln; **throw ~ for sth.** etw. auswürfeln; **no ~!** *(fig. coll.)* kommt nicht in Frage!; **b)** *in sing. (game)* Würfelspiel, *das;* **play ~:** würfeln; **c)** *in pl. (Cookery)* Würfel *Pl.*; **cut into ~:** würfeln. **2.** *v.i.* würfeln **(for** um); **~ with death** mit seinem Leben spielen. **3.** *v.t.* *(Cookery)* würfeln
dicey ['daısı] *adj.* *(sl.)* riskant; *(unreliable)* unzuverlässig
dichotomy [daı'kɒtəmı, dı'kɒtəmı] *n.* Dichotomie, *die*
dick [dık] *n.* **a)** *(sl.: detective)* Schnüffler, *der (ugs. abwertend)*; **b)** *(coarse: penis)* Schwanz, *der (derb)*; Riemen, *der (derb). See also* **clever Dick; Tom a**
dickens ['dıkınz] *n.* *(coll.)* **what/why/who** *etc.* **the ~ ...:** was/warum/wer *usw.* zum Kuckuck ... *(salopp)*
Dickensian [dı'kenzıən] **1.** *n.* Dickensianer. **2.** *adj.* Dickenssch; **~ conditions** Zustände, wie man sie aus Dickens' Romanen kennt
[1]**dicky (dickey)** ['dıkı] *n.* **a)** *see* **dicky-bird**; **b)** *(Brit. Hist.: seat)* Klappsitz *(im Fond eines Zweisitzers)*; **c)** *(shirt-front)* Vorhemd, *das*
[2]**dicky** *adj.* *(sl.)* mies *(ugs. abwertend)*; klapprig *(ugs.)* ⟨*Herz*⟩
'**dicky-bird** *n.* *(child lang./coll.)* Piepvogel, *der (Kinderspr.)*; *(sl.: word)* **not a ~:** kein Sterbenswörtchen
dicta *pl. of* **dictum**
dictate **1.** [dık'teıt] *v.t. & i.* diktieren; *(prescribe)* vorschreiben; **~ to** Vorschriften machen (+ *Dat.*); **I will not be ~d to** ich lasse mir keine Vorschriften machen. **2.** ['dıkteıt] *n., usu. in pl.* Diktat, *das*
dic'tating-machine *n.* Diktiergerät, *das*
dictation [dık'teıʃn] *n.* Diktat, *das;* **take a ~:** ein Diktat aufnehmen
dictator [dık'teıtə(r)] *n.* *(lit. or fig.)* Diktator, *der;* **be a ~** *(fig.)* diktatorisch sein
dictatorial [dıktə'tɔ:rıəl] *adj.*, **dictatorially** [dıktə'tɔ:rıəlı] *adv.* *(lit. or fig.)* diktatorisch
dictatorship [dık'teıtəʃıp] *n.* *(lit. or fig.)* Diktatur, *die*
diction ['dıkʃn] *n.* Diktion, *die (geh.)*
dictionary ['dıkʃənərı] *n.* Wörterbuch, *das; see also* **walking 1**
dictum ['dıktəm] *n., pl.* **~s** *or* **dicta** ['dıktə] **a)** *(pronouncement, maxim)* Spruch, *der;* Diktum, *das (geh.)*; **b)** *(Law)* richterliche Meinung
did *see* [1]**do**
didactic [dı'dæktık, daı'dæktık] *adj.* **a)** didaktisch; **b)** *(authoritarian)* schulmeisterlich *(abwertend)*
diddle ['dıdl] *v.t.* *(sl.)* übers Ohr hauen *(ugs.)*; **~ sb. out of sth.** jmdm. etw. abluchsen *(salopp)*; **~ sb. into doing sth.** jmdn. so verschaukeln, daß er etw. tut *(ugs.)*
diddums ['dıdəmz] *n.* *(child lang./coll.)* der/die arme Kleine; **[poor little] ~!** armes Kleines!
didn't ['dıdnt] *(coll.)* = **did not**; *see* [1]**do**
dido ['daıdəʊ] *n., pl.* **~s** *or* **~es** *(Amer. coll.)* Mätzchen, *das (ugs.)*
[1]**die** [daı] **1.** *v.i.*, **dying** ['daııŋ] **a)** sterben; ⟨*Tier, Pflanze:*⟩ eingehen, *(geh.)* sterben; ⟨*Körperteil:*⟩ absterben; **be dying** sterben; **~ from** *or* **of sth.** an etw. *(Dat.)* sterben; **~ of grief** vor Kummer sterben; **~ of a heart attack/a brain tumour** einem Herzanfall/

Hirntumor erliegen; ~ **from one's injuries** seinen Verletzungen erliegen; ~ **a rich man** als reicher Mann sterben; ~ **by one's own hand** *(literary)* Hand an sich *(Akk.)* legen *(geh.)*; ~ **in one's bed** im Bett sterben; ~ **in one's boots** *(working)* in den Sielen sterben; ‹*Soldat:*› im Kampf fallen; **sb. would ~ rather than do sth.** um nichts in der Welt würde jmd. etw. tun; **never say ~** *(fig.)* nur nicht den Mut verlieren; **b)** *(fig.)* **be dying for sth.** etw. unbedingt brauchen; **be dying for a cup of tea** nach einer Tasse Tee lechzen; **be dying to do sth.** darauf brennen, etw. zu tun; **I'm dying to know how she ...:** ich möchte zu gerne wissen, wie sie ...; **be dying of boredom/curiosity** vor Langeweile sterben/vor Neugier platzen; ~ **[laughing]** sich totlachen *(ugs.)*; **I [nearly] ~d with** *or* **of embarrassment** es war mir furchtbar peinlich; ~ **with** *or* **of shame** sich zu Tode schämen; **c)** *(disappear)* in Vergessenheit geraten; ‹*Gefühl, Liebe, Ruhm:*› vergehen; ‹*Ton:*› verklingen; ‹*Flamme:*› verlöschen; ‹*Worte, Lächeln:*› ersterben *(geh.)*; **the secret ~d with them** sie haben das Geheimnis mit ins Grab genommen; **d)** *(coll.: cease to function)* ‹*Zeitschrift, Firma:*› eingehen *(ugs.)*; **the engine ~d on me** *(coll.)* der Motor ist mir abgestorben. *See also* **ditch 1; harness 1 b. 2.** *v. t.* **dying: ~ a natural/violent death** eines natürlichen/gewaltsamen Todes sterben; **let the matter ~ a natural death** die Sache langsam einschlafen lassen; **sth. ~s the death** *(coll.)* mit etw. ist nichts mehr *(ugs.)*

~ **a'way** *v. i.* ‹*Laut, Geräusch:*› schwächer werden; ‹*Wind, Zorn:*› sich legen

~ **'back** *v. i.* absterben

~ **'down** *v. i.* ‹*Sturm, Wind, Protest, Aufruhr:*› sich legen; ‹*Flammen:*› kleiner werden; ‹*Feuer:*› herunterbrennen; ‹*Lärm:*› leiser werden; ‹*Kämpfe:*› nachlassen; ‹*Epidemie:*› abklingen

~ **'off** *v. i.* ‹*Pflanzen, Tiere:*› [nacheinander] eingehen; ‹*Blätter:*› [nacheinander] absterben; ‹*Menschen:*› [nacheinander] sterben

~ **'out** *v. i.* aussterben

²die *n.* **a)** *pl.* **dice** [daɪs] *(formal)* Würfel, *der;* **the ~ is cast** die Würfel sind gefallen; **as straight** *or* **true as a ~:** schnurgerade ‹*Weg, Linie*›; *(fig.)* grundehrlich; **b)** *pl.* **~s** *(engraved stamp)* Stempel, *der;* **c)** *pl.* **~s** *(Metalw.)* Gußform, *die; (in drop-forging)* Gesenk, *das;* **d)** *(for cutting threads)* [Gewinde]schneideisen, *das*

die: ~-casting *n.* **a)** *(process)* [Kokillen]guß, *der;* **b)** *(product)* Gußstück, *das;* **~-hard 1.** *n.* hartnäckiger Typ; *(reactionary)* Ewiggestrige, *der/die;* **2.** *adj.* hartnäckig; *(dyed-in-the-wool)* eingefleischt; *(reactionary)* ewiggestrig

diesel ['di:zl] *n.* ~ **[engine]** Diesel[motor], *der;* ~ **[lorry/car]** Diesel, *der;* ~ **[train]** *(Railw.)* Dieseltriebwagen, *der;* ~ **[fuel]** Diesel[kraftstoff], *der*

diesel-e'lectric *adj.* dieselelektrisch

'diesel oil *n.* Dieseltreibstoff, *der*

¹diet ['daɪət] **1.** *n.* **a)** *(for slimming)* Diät, *die;* Schlankheitskur, *die;* **be/go on a ~:** eine Schlankheitskur *od.* Diät machen; **b)** *(Med.)* Diät, *die;* Schonkost, *die;* **c)** *(habitual food)* Kost, *die.* **2.** *v. i.* eine Schlankheitskur *od.* Diät machen

²diet *n. (Polit.)* Reichstag, *der*

dietary ['daɪətərɪ] *adj.* ~ **rules** Diätvorschriften; ~ **habits** Eßgewohnheiten; ~ **deficiencies** mangelhafte Ernährung

dietetic [daɪə'tetɪk] *adj.* Diät-; diätetisch

dietetics [daɪə'tetɪks] *n., no pl.* Ernährungslehre, *die;* Diätetik, *die (fachspr.)*

dietitian (dietician) [daɪə'tɪʃn] *n.* Diätassistent, *der/*-assistentin, *die*

'diet-sheet *n.* Diätplan, *der*

differ ['dɪfə(r)] *v. i.* **a)** *(vary, be different)* sich unterscheiden; **the two accounts of what happened ~ed greatly** die beiden Berichte von den Ereignissen wichen stark voneinander ab; **opinions/ideas ~:** die Meinungen/Vorstellungen gehen auseinander; **tastes/temperaments ~:** die Geschmäcker *(ugs.)* /Temperamente sind verschieden; **people ~:** es sind nicht alle Menschen gleich; ~ **from sb./sth. in that ...:** sich von jmdm./etw. dadurch *od.* darin unterscheiden, daß ...; **b)** *(disagree)* anderer Meinung sein; ~ **with sb. over** *or* **on sth.** über etw. *(Akk.)* anderer Meinung sein als jmd.; *see also* **agree 1 a; beg 1 b**

difference ['dɪfərəns] *n.* **a)** Unterschied, *der;* ~ **in age** Altersunterschied, *der;* **have a ~ of opinion [with sb.]** eine Meinungsverschiedenheit [mit jmdm.] haben; **there is a ~ in her now** *(in appearance)* sie sieht jetzt anders aus; *(in character)* sie hat sich geändert; **it makes a ~:** es ist ein *od. (ugs.)* macht einen Unterschied; **what ~ would it make if ...?** was würde es schon ausmachen, wenn ...?; **the new curtains make a big ~ to the room** mit den neuen Vorhängen sieht das Zimmer schon ganz anders aus; **it makes a ~:** es ist ein *od. (ugs.)* macht einen Unterschied; **as if 'that made any ~:** als ob das etwas ändern würde; **make all the ~ [in the world]** ungeheuer viel ausmachen; **I could [as well] have stayed at home for all the ~ it made** da hätte ich auch gleich zu Hause bleiben können; **make no ~ [to sb.]** [jmdm.] nichts ausmachen; **a holiday with a ~:** Urlaub – einmal anders; **same ~** *(coll.)* ein und dasselbe; **b)** *(between amounts)* Differenz, *die;* **pay the ~:** den Rest[betrag] bezahlen; **split the ~:** sich *(Dat.)* den Rest[betrag] teilen; *(fig.)* einen Kompromiß machen; **c)** *(dispute)* **have a ~ with sb.** mit jmdm. eine Auseinandersetzung haben; **resolve** *or* **settle one's ~s** seine Differenzen beilegen

different ['dɪfərənt] *adj.* verschieden; *(pred. also)* anders; *(attrib. also)* ander...; **be ~ from** *or (esp. Brit.)* **to** *or (Amer.)* **than ...:** anders sein als ...; **the two sisters are very ~ from each other** die beiden Schwestern sind sehr verschieden; **she was totally ~ from** *or* **to what I'd expected** sie war ganz anders, als ich erwartet hatte; ~ **viewpoints/cultures** unterschiedliche Standpunkte/Kulturen; **how are they ~?** worin *od.* wodurch unterscheiden sie sich?; **I feel a ~ person** ich fühle mich wie neu geboren; **I asked several ~ people** ich habe mehrere *od.* verschiedene Leute gefragt; **wear a ~ dress on every occasion** zu jedem Anlaß ein anderes Kleid tragen; **oh, that's ~:** ach so, das ist was anderes; **a holiday that is ~:** Urlaub – einmal anders; **the same, only ~** *(coll.)* fast der-/die-/dasselbe

differential [dɪfə'renʃl] **1.** *adj.* **a)** unterschiedlich; ungleich ‹*Behandlung*›; gestaffelt ‹*Lohn, Kosten*›; unterscheidend ‹*Merkmal*›; ~ **tariffs/duties** *(Commerc.)* Differentialtarife/-zölle; **b)** *(Math.)* ~ **calculus** Differentialrechnung, *die;* ~ **equation** Differentialgleichung, *die;* ~ **coefficient** *see* **derivative 2 b. 2.** *n.* **a)** *(Commerc.)* **[wage] ~:** [Einkommens]unterschied, *der;* **price ~s** Preisunterschiede; **b)** *(Motor Veh.)* Differential[getriebe], *das;* Ausgleichsgetriebe, *das*

differentiate [dɪfə'renʃɪeɪt] **1.** *v. t.* **a)** unterscheiden; **b)** *(Biol.)* herausbilden; **c)** *(Math.)* differenzieren. **2.** *v. i.* **a)** *(recognize the difference)* unterscheiden; differenzieren; **b)** *(treat sth. differently)* einen Unterschied machen; differenzieren

differentiation [dɪfərenʃɪ'eɪʃn] *n.* **a)** Unterscheidung, *die;* Differenzierung, *die;* **b)** *(Biol., Math.)* Differenzierung, *die*

differently ['dɪfərəntlɪ] *adv.* anders **(from,** *esp. Brit.* **to** als); ~ **[to** *or* **from each other]** verschieden; *(with different result, at various times)* unterschiedlich; **they reacted ~ to the news** sie reagierten unterschiedlich auf die Nachricht

differing ['dɪfərɪŋ] *adj.* unterschiedlich

difficult ['dɪfɪkəlt] *adj.* **a)** schwer; schwierig; **a ~ writer** ein schwieriger Schriftsteller; **he finds it ~ to do sth.** ihm fällt es schwer, etw. zu tun; **make things ~ for sb.** es jmdm. nicht leicht machen; **the ~ thing is ...:** die Schwierigkeit ist ...; **b)** *(unaccommodating)* schwierig; **he is being ~:** er macht Schwierigkeiten; **he is ~ to get on with** es ist schwer, mit ihm auszukommen

difficulty ['dɪfɪkəltɪ] *n.* **a)** Schwierigkeit, *die;* **with [great] ~:** [sehr] mühsam; **with the greatest ~:** unter größten Schwierigkeiten; **without [great] ~:** ohne große Probleme; mühelos; **have ~ [in] doing sth.** Schwierigkeiten haben, etw. zu tun; **experience** *or* **have [some] ~ in walking** Beschwerden beim Gehen haben; **b)** *usu. in pl. (trouble)* **be in ~** *or* **difficulties** in Schwierigkeiten sein; **under great difficulties** unter großen Schwierigkeiten; **fall** *or* **get into difficulties** in Schwierigkeiten kommen *od.* geraten

diffidence ['dɪfɪdəns] *n., no pl.* Zaghaftigkeit, *die; (modesty)* Zurückhaltung, *die*

diffident ['dɪfɪdənt] *adj.* zaghaft; *(modest)* zurückhaltend

diffraction [dɪ'frækʃn] *n. (Phys.)* Beugung, *die;* Diffraktion, *die (veralt.)*

diffuse 1. [dɪ'fju:z] *v. t.* verbreiten; diffundieren *(fachspr.)*; **~d lighting/traces** diffuse Beleuchtung/Spuren. **2.** *v. i.* sich ausbreiten **(through** in + *Dat.*); diffundieren *(fachspr.)*. **3.** [dɪ'fju:s] *adj.* **a)** *(dispersed)* diffus; **b)** *(verbose)* weitschweifig; diffus *(fig.)*

diffusion [dɪ'fju:ʒn] *n.* **a)** *(also Anthrop.)* Verbreitung, *die;* **b)** *(Phys.)* Diffusion, *die*

dig [dɪg] **1.** *v. i.*, **-gg-, dug** [dʌg] **a)** graben **(for** nach); **b)** *(Archaeol.: excavate)* Ausgrabungen machen; graben; *(fig.: search)* ~ **for information** versuchen, Informationen zu bekommen; **c)** ~ **at sb.** eine [spitze] Bemerkung über jmdn. machen. **2.** *v. t.*, **-gg-, dug a)** graben; ~ **a hole [in sth.]** ein Loch [in etw. *(Akk.)*] graben; **b)** *(turn up with spade etc.)* umgraben; *(obtain by digging)* ~ **potatoes/peat** Kartoffeln ernten *od. (landsch.)* ausmachen/Torf stechen; **c)** *(Archaeol.)* ausgraben; **d)** *(sl.: appreciate)* stark finden *(Jugendspr.)*; *(understand)* schnallen *(salopp)*. **3.** *n.* **a)** Grabung, *die;* **b)** *(Archaeol. coll.)* Ausgrabung, *die; (site)* Ausgrabungsort, *der;* **c)** *(fig.)* Anspielung, *die* **(at** auf + *Akk.*); **have** *or* **make a ~ at sb./sth.** eine [spitze] Bemerkung über jmdn./etw. machen; **d)** *see* **rib**

~ **'in 1.** *v. i.* **a)** *(Mil.)* sich eingraben; *(fig.)* sich festsetzen; **b)** *(coll.: begin eating, eat)* zulangen *(ugs.)*. **2.** *v. t.* **a)** *(Mil.)* eingraben; ~ **oneself in** sich eingraben; *(fig.)* sich etablieren; **b)** *(thrust)* **the cat dug its claws in** die Katze krallte sich fest; ~ **one's heels** *or* **toes in** *(fig. coll.)* sich auf die Hinterbeine stellen *(ugs.)*; **c)** *(mix with soil)* eingraben

~ **into** *v. t.* **a)** *(+ Akk.)* ‹*Tasche*›; eindringen in (+ *Akk.*) ‹*Materie*›; vordringen in (+ *Akk.*) ‹*Vergangenheit, Geschichte*›; **b)** *(coll.: begin eating)* zulangen bei *(ugs.)*; **c)** *(take from)* ~ **into one's savings** seine Ersparnisse angreifen; **have to ~ into one's pocket** in die Tasche greifen müssen; **d)** *(mix with)* ~ **compost into the soil** Kompost untergraben; **e)** *(embed itself in)* sich graben in (+ *Akk.*)

~ **'out** *v. t. (lit. or fig.)* ausgraben; ~ **sb. out from underneath the debris/out of the wreckage** jmdn. aus den Trümmern bergen

~ **'up** *v. t.* **a)** umgraben ‹*Garten, Rasen, Erde*›; ausgraben ‹*Pflanzen, Knochen, Leiche, Schatz*›; **b)** *(fig.: find)* ausgraben ‹*Fakten, Informationen*›; *(coll. derog.: obtain)* aufgabeln *(ugs.)*

digest 1. [dɪ'dʒest, daɪ'dʒest] *v. t.* **a)** *(assimilate, lit or fig.)* verdauen; **b)** *(consider)* durchdenken. **2.** ['daɪdʒest] *n.* **a)** *(periodical)* Digest, *der od. das (Zeitschrift mit Auszügen aus Büchern od. anderen Zeitschriften);* **b)** *(summary)* Zusammenfassung, *die*

digestible [dɪ'dʒestɪbl, daɪ'dʒestɪbl] *adj.* verdaulich; *(fig.)* verständlich

digestion [dɪ'dʒestʃn, daɪ'dʒestʃn] *n.* Verdauung, *die;* Digestion, *die (Physiol.); (fig.)* [geistige] Verarbeitung

digestive [dɪ'dʒestɪv, daɪ'dʒestɪv] **1.** *adj.* Verdauungs-; ~ **biscuit** *(Brit.) see* **2. 2.** *n. (Brit.: biscuit)* Keks *(aus Vollkornmehl)*

digger ['dɪgə(r)] *n.* **a)** *(Archaeol.)* Ausgräber, *der*/Ausgräberin, *die; (miner)* Bergmann, *der; (gold-~)* Goldgräber, *der;* **b)** *(Mech.)* Bagger, *der; (garden tool)* Grabschaufel, *die;* **trench ~:** Grabenbagger, *der;* **c)** *(coll.) (Australian)* Australier, *der*/Australierin, *die; (New Zealander)* Neuseeländer, *der*/Neuseeländerin, *die*

diggings ['dɪgɪŋz] *n. pl.* **a)** *(Mining)* [Gold]lagerstätte, *die;* **b)** *(Archaeol.)* Ausgrabungsort, *der*

digit ['dɪdʒɪt] *n.* **a)** *(numeral)* Ziffer, *die;* **a six-~ number** eine sechsstellige Zahl; **b)** *(Zool., Anat.) (finger)* Finger, *der; (toe)* Zehe, *die*

digital ['dɪdʒɪtl] *adj.* **a)** *(numerical)* digital; **~ clock/watch** Digitaluhr, *die;* **~ computer** Digitalrechner, *der;* **~ recording** Digitalaufnahme, *die;* **b)** *(Zool., Anat.)* digital

digitize (digitise) ['dɪdʒɪtaɪz] *v. t. (Computing)* digitalisieren

dignified ['dɪgnɪfaɪd] *adj.* würdig; *(self-respecting, stately)* würdevoll

dignify ['dɪgnɪfaɪ] *v. t.* **a)** *(make stately)* Würde verleihen (+ *Dat.*); **b)** *(give distinction to)* Glanz verleihen (+ *Dat.*); auszeichnen ⟨*Person*⟩; **c)** *(give grand title to)* aufwerten *(fig.)*

dignitary ['dɪgnɪtərɪ] *n.* Würdenträger, *der;* **dignitaries** *(notabilities)* Honoratioren; **church ~:** kirchlicher Würdenträger

dignity ['dɪgnɪtɪ] *n.* Würde, *die;* **speak with quiet ~:** ruhig und würdevoll sprechen; **he is not one to stand on his ~:** er hat keine Angst, sich *(Dat.)* etwas zu vergeben; **be beneath one's ~:** unter seiner Würde sein

digress [daɪ'gres, dɪ'gres] *v. i.* abschweifen **(from** von, **on** zu)

digression [daɪ'greʃn, dɪ'greʃn] *n.* Abschweifung, *die; (passage)* Exkurs, *der*

digs [dɪgz] *n. pl. (Brit. coll.)* Bude, *die (ugs.);* **he's in ~:** er hat eine [eigene] Bude *(ugs.)*

dike [daɪk] *n.* **a)** *(flood-wall)* Deich, *der;* **b)** *(ditch)* Graben, *der;* **c)** *(causeway)* Damm, *der;* **d)** *(Mining, Geol.)* Gang, *der; (of igneous rock)* Eruptivgang, *der*

diktat ['dɪktæt] *n.* **a)** *(decree)* Anordnung, *die;* **b)** *(severe settlement)* Diktat, *das*

dilapidated [dɪ'læpɪdeɪtɪd] *adj.* verfallen ⟨*Gebäude*⟩; verwahrlost ⟨*Äußeres, Erscheinung*⟩

dilapidation [dɪlæpɪ'deɪʃn] *n., no pl.* Verfall, *der;* **in a state of ~:** in verwahrlostem Zustand

dilatation [daɪlə'teɪʃn, dɪlə'teɪʃn] *n.* **a)** *see* **dilation; b)** *(Med.)* Dilatation, *die (fachspr.);* Erweiterung, *die*

dilate [daɪ'leɪt, dɪ'leɪt] **1.** *v. i.* **a)** sich weiten; **b)** *(discourse)* ~ **[up]on sth.** sich über etw. *(Akk.)* verbreiten. **2.** *v. t.* ausdehnen; blähen ⟨*Nüstern*⟩

dilation [daɪ'leɪʃn, dɪ'leɪʃn] *n.* Dilatation, *die; (Phys. also)* Ausdehnung, *die; (Med. also)* Erweiterung, *die*

dilatory ['dɪlətərɪ] *adj.* langsam; saumselig *(geh.);* zögernd ⟨*Antwort, Reaktion*⟩; *(causing delay)* **be ~ in** sich *(Dat.)* [viel] Zeit lassen bei

dildo ['dɪldəʊ] *n., pl.* ~s Godemiché, *der*

dilemma [dɪ'lemə, daɪ'lemə] *n. (also Logic)* Dilemma, *das;* **be on the horns of** *or* **faced with a ~:** vor einem Dilemma stehen

dilettante [dɪlɪ'tæntɪ] **1.** *n., pl.* **dilettanti** [dɪlɪ'tænti:] *or* ~s Dilettant, *der*/Dilettantin, *die;* Laie, *der.* **2.** *adj.* dilettantisch; laienhaft ⟨*Interesse*⟩

diligence ['dɪlɪdʒəns] *n.* Fleiß, *der; (purposefulness)* Eifer, *der*

diligent ['dɪlɪdʒənt] *adj.* fleißig; *(purposeful)* eifrig; sorgfältig, gewissenhaft ⟨*Arbeit, Suche*⟩

diligently ['dɪlɪdʒəntlɪ] *adv.* fleißig; *(purposefully)* eifrig; **execute one's duties ~:** seine Pflichten gewissenhaft erfüllen

dill [dɪl] *n. (Bot.)* Dill, *der*

dill: ~ pickle *n. mit Dill eingelegte Gurke usw.;* **~-water** *n.* Dillöl, *das (Pharm.)*

dilly ['dɪlɪ] *n. (sl.)* irre Type *(ugs.); (thing)* irres Ding *(ugs.)*

dilly-dally ['dɪlɪdælɪ] *v. i. (coll.)* **a)** *(dawdle)* trödeln; **b)** *(vacillate)* ~ **over the choice of sth.** sich nicht für etw. entscheiden können; **stop ~ing!** entscheide dich endlich!

diluent ['dɪljʊənt] *n.* Verdünnungsmittel, *das*

dilute 1. [daɪ'lju:t, 'daɪlju:t] *adj.* **a)** verdünnt; **b)** *(washed out)* verwaschen ⟨*Farbe*⟩; *(faded)* verblaßt, ausgebleicht ⟨*Farbe*⟩; **c)** *(fig.)* blaß *(geh.).* **2.** [daɪ'lju:t] *v. t.* **a)** verdünnen; **b)** ausbleichen ⟨*Farbe*⟩; **c)** *(fig.)* abschwächen; entschärfen

dilution [daɪ'lju:ʃn, daɪ'lu:ʃn] *n.* **a)** *(act)* Verdünnen, *das;* **b)** *(state, substance)* Verdünnung, *die;* **c)** *(fig.)* Abschwächung, *die*

dim [dɪm] **1.** *adj.* **a)** schwach, trüb ⟨*Licht, Flackern*⟩; matt, gedeckt ⟨*Farbe*⟩; dämmrig, dunkel ⟨*Zimmer*⟩; undeutlich, verschwommen ⟨*Gestalt*⟩; **grow ~:** schwächer werden; **b)** *(fig.)* blaß; verschwommen; **in the ~ and distant past** in ferner Vergangenheit; **have a ~ suspicion that ...:** den leisen Verdacht haben, daß ...; **have only a ~ understanding of sth.** nur eine ungefähre *od.* vage Vorstellung von etw. haben; **c)** *(indistinct)* schwach, getrübt ⟨*Seh-, Hörvermögen*⟩; **his eyesight/hearing had grown ~:** seine Augen hatten/sein Gehör hatte nachgelassen; **d)** *(coll.) (stupid)* beschränkt; *(clumsy)* ungeschickt; **e) take a ~ view of sth.** *(coll.)* von etw. nicht erbaut sein. **2.** *v. i.,* **-mm-:** *(lit. or fig.)* schwächer werden. **3.** *v. t.,* **-mm- a)** verdunkeln; verdüstern; *(fig.)* trüben; dämpfen; **~ the lights** *(Theatre, Cinemat.)* die Lichter langsam verlöschen lassen; **b)** *(Amer. Motor Veh.)* abblenden

~ 'out *v. t.* **a)** verdunkeln; **b)** *(Theatre)* **~ out the lights on stage** die Bühne abblenden. *See also* **dim-out**

dime [daɪm] *n. (Amer.)* Zehncentstück, *das;* ≈ Groschen, *der (ugs.);* **be a ~ a dozen** *(fig.)* Dutzendware sein *(fig. abwertend);* **it's not worth a ~** *(fig.)* es ist keinen Pfifferling wert *(ugs.);* **~ novel** Groschenroman, *der (abwertend)*

dimension [dɪ'menʃn, daɪ'menʃn] **1.** *n. (lit. or fig.)* Dimension, *die; (measurement)* Abmessung, *die.* **2.** *v. t.* dimensionieren

-dimensional [dɪ'menʃənl, daɪ'menʃənl] *adj. in comb.* -dimensional

diminish [dɪ'mɪnɪʃ] **1.** *v. i.* nachlassen; ⟨*Zahl:*⟩ sich verringern; ⟨*Vorräte, Autorität, Einfluß:*⟩ abnehmen; ⟨*Wert, Bedeutung, Ansehen:*⟩ geringer werden; **~ in value/number** an Wert verlieren/an Zahl *od.* zahlenmäßig abnehmen. **2.** *v. t.* vermindern; verringern; *(fig.)* herabwürdigen ⟨*Person*⟩; schmälern ⟨*Ansehen, Ruf*⟩; beeinträchtigen ⟨*Schönheit, Freundschaft*⟩

diminished [dɪ'mɪnɪʃt] *adj.* geringer ⟨*Wert, Anzahl, Einfluß, Popularität*⟩; vermindert ⟨*Stärke, Fähigkeit*⟩; verringert ⟨*Belegschaft*⟩; verkleinert ⟨*Reich*⟩ ; **[plead] ~ responsibility** *(Law)* [auf] verminderte Zurechnungsfähigkeit [plädieren]; **~ interval** *(Mus.)* vermindertes Intervall

diminishing [dɪ'mɪnɪʃɪŋ] *adj.* sinkend; abnehmend ⟨*Vorräte*⟩; schwindend ⟨*Kraft, Einfluß, Macht*⟩; **law of ~ returns** *(Econ.)* Gesetz vom abnehmenden Ertragszuwachs; Ertragsgesetz, *das*

diminuendo [dɪmɪnjʊ'endəʊ] *(Mus.) n., pl.* ~s Diminuendo, *das*

diminution [dɪmɪ'nju:ʃn] *n. (of number, supplies)* Verringerung, *die; (of value)* Minderung, *die; (of strength, influence)* Schwinden, *das; (of reputation, fame)* Schmälerung, *die; (Mus.)* Diminution, *die*

diminutive [dɪ'mɪnjʊtɪv] **1.** *adj.* **a)** winzig; **b)** *(Ling.)* diminutiv. **2.** *n. (Ling.)* Diminutiv[um], *das*

dimly ['dɪmlɪ] *adv.* schwach; undeutlich ⟨*sehen*⟩; ungefähr ⟨*begreifen*⟩; **I ~ remember it** ich erinnere mich noch dunkel daran

dimmer ['dɪmə(r)] *n.* **a)** Dimmer, *der;* Helligkeitsregler, *der;* **b)** *(Amer. Motor Veh.: switch)* Abblendschalter, *der*

dimness ['dɪmnɪs] *n., no pl.* **a)** Trübheit, *die; (almost darkness)* Halbdunkel, *das;* **b)** *(fig.)* Undeutlichkeit, *die;* Unklarheit, *die*

dimorphic [daɪ'mɔ:fɪk] *adj. (Biol., Chem., Min.)* dimorph

dimorphism [daɪ'mɔ:fɪzm] *n. (Biol., Chem., Min.)* Dimorphie, *die*

'dim-out *n.* **a)** Verdunk[e]lung, *die;* **b)** *(Theatre)* Abblendung, *die*

dimple ['dɪmpl] *n.* Grübchen, *das; (on golf-ball etc.)* kleine Vertiefung

dim: ~-wit *n. (coll.)* Dummkopf, *der (ugs.);* **~-witted** ['dɪmwɪtɪd] *adj. (coll.)* dusselig *(salopp);* dämlich *(ugs. abwertend)*

din [dɪn] **1.** *n.* Lärm, *der.* **2.** *v. t.,* **-nn-:** **~ sth. into sb.** jmdm. etw. einhämmern *od.* einbleuen

din-din[s] ['dɪndɪn(z)] *n. (child lang.)* Freßchen, *das (ugs.)*

dine [daɪn] **1.** *v. i. (at midday/in the evening)* [zu Mittag/zu Abend] essen *od. (geh.)* speisen; dinieren *(geh.);* **~ off/on sth.** etw. [zum Mittag-/Abendessen] verzehren; **~ off sth.** *(eat from)* von etw. speisen. **2.** *v. t.* bewirten; *see also* **wine and dine**

~ 'out *v. i.* **a)** auswärts [zu Mittag/Abend] essen; **b) ~ out on sth.** wegen etw. zum Essen eingeladen werden

diner ['daɪnə(r)] *n.* **a)** Gast, *der (zum Abendessen);* **b)** *(Railw.)* Speisewagen, *der;* **c)** *(Amer.: restaurant)* Restaurant, *das*

ding-a-ling ['dɪŋəlɪŋ] *see* **ting-a-ling**

ding-dong ['dɪŋdɒŋ] **1.** *n.* **a)** Bimbam, *das;* **b)** *(coll.: argument)* Krach, *der (ugs.).* **2.** *adj.* hin- und herwogend. **3.** *adv.* mit Feuereifer

dinghy ['dɪŋgɪ, 'dɪŋɪ] *n.* Ding[h]i, *das; (inflatable)* Schlauchboot, *das*

dingle ['dɪŋgl] *n.* waldiges kleines Tal

dingo ['dɪŋgəʊ] *n., pl.* ~es **a)** *(dog)* Dingo, *der;* **b)** *(Austral. sl.: rogue)* [gemeiner] Hund *(salopp)*

dingy ['dɪndʒɪ] *adj.* schmuddelig

dining ['daɪnɪŋ]: **~ area** *n.* ≈ Eßecke, *die;* **~-car** *n. (Railw.)* Speisewagen, *der;* **~-chair** *n.* Eßzimmerstuhl, *der;* **~-hall** *n.* Speisesaal, *der;* **~-room** *n. (in private house)* Eßzimmer, *das; (in hotel etc.)* Speisesaal, *der;* **~-table** *n.* Eßtisch, *der*

dinkel ['dɪŋkl] *see* **²spelt**

dinkum ['dɪŋkəm] *(Austral. and NZ coll.) adj.* astrein *(ugs.);* **fair ~:** echt *(ugs.);* **[the] ~ oil** die Wahrheit

dinky ['dɪŋkɪ] *adj. (coll.)* **a)** *(Brit.: pretty)* niedlich; **b)** *(Amer.: trifling)* kümmerlich

dinner ['dɪnə(r)] *n.* Essen, *das; (at midday also)* Mittagessen, *das; (in the evening also)* Abendessen, *das; (formal event)* Diner, *das;* **have** *or* **eat [one's] ~:** zu Mittag/Abend essen; **go out to ~:** [abends] essen gehen; *(to friends)* zum [Abend]essen eingeladen sein; **~'s ready!** [das] Essen ist fertig!; **be at** *or* **having** *or* **eating [one's] ~:** gerade beim Essen sein; **have people [in] to** *or* **for ~:** Gäste zum Essen haben

dinner: ~-dance *n. Abendessen mit anschließendem Tanz;* **~-gong** *n.* Gong, *der;* **~-jacket** *n. (Brit.)* Dinnerjacket, *das;*

~ **lady** *n. (Brit.) Serviererin beim Mittagessen in der Schule;* ~-**party** *n.* Abendessen, *das; (more formal)* Abendgesellschaft, *die;* ~-**plate** *n.* flacher Teller; Eßteller, *der;* ~-**service** *n.* Eßgeschirr, *das;* ~-**table** *n.* Eßtisch, *der;* **be at** *or* **seated round the** ~-**table** bei Tisch sitzen; ~-**time** *n.* Essenszeit, *die;* **at** ~-**time** zur Essenszeit; *(12–2 p.m.)* mittags
dinosaur ['daɪnəsɔ:(r)] *n.* Dinosaurier, *der*
dint [dɪnt] *n.* **a) by** ~ **of** durch; **by** ~ **of doing sth.** indem jmd. etw. tut; **b)** *see* **dent 1**
diocesan [daɪ'ɒsɪsən] *adj. (Eccl.)* diözesan; ~ **synod** Diözesansynode, *die*
diocese ['daɪəsɪs] *n. (Eccl.)* Diözese, *die*
dioxide [daɪ'ɒksaɪd] *n. (Chem.)* Dioxid, *das (fachspr.);* Dioxyd, *das*
dip [dɪp] **1.** *v. t.*, **-pp-: a)** [ein]tauchen (**in** in + *Akk.*); **she** ~**ped her hand into the sack** sie griff in den Sack; **b)** *(dye)* in ein Färbemittel tauchen; **c)** *(Agric.)* dippen ⟨*Schaf*⟩; **d)** *(Brit. Motor Veh.)* ~ **one's [head] lights** abblenden; **[drive with** *or* **on]** ~**ped headlights** [mit] Abblendlicht [fahren]. **2.** *v. i.*, **-pp-: a)** *(go down)* sinken; **the sun** ~**ped below the horizon** die Sonne versank hinter dem Horizont; **b)** *(Aeronaut.)* vor dem Steigen plötzlich absacken; **c)** *(incline downwards, lit. or fig.)* abfallen; **the magnetic needle** ~**s** die Magnetnadel neigt sich; **d)** *(go under water)* [ein]tauchen; ~ **under** untertauchen; **e)** *(Brit. Motor Veh.)* abblenden. **3.** *n.* **a)** *(dipping)* [kurzes] Eintauchen; **give sb./sth. a** ~ **in sth.** jmdn./etw. in etw. *(Akk.)* [kurz] eintauchen; *see also* **lucky dip; b)** *(coll.: bathe)* [kurzes] Bad; **c)** *(of stratum)* Fallen, *das (Geol.); (of road)* Senke, *die; (hollow, depression in landscape)* Mulde, *die;* **d)** *(Gastr.)* Dip, *der;* **e)** *(for sheep)* Räudebad, *das;* **f)** *(underworld sl.: pickpocket)* Krebs, *der (Gaunerspr.)*
~ **into** *v. t.* **a)** greifen in (+ *Akk.*); *(put ladle into)* den Löffel tauchen in (+ *Akk.*); *(fig.)* ~ **into one's pocket** *or* **purse** tief in die Tasche greifen; ~ **into one's reserves/savings** seine Reserven antasten/Ersparnisse angreifen; **b)** *(look cursorily at)* einen flüchtigen Blick werfen in (+ *Akk.*); **the book is good for** ~**ping into** man kann das Buch gut in kurzen Abschnitten lesen
Dip. *abbr.* **Diploma** Dipl.
Dip. Ed. [dɪp 'ed] *abbr.* **Diploma in Education** Pädagogikdiplom, *das; see also* **B.Sc.**
diphtheria [dɪf'θɪərɪə] *n. (Med.)* Diphtherie, *die*
diphthong ['dɪfθɒŋ] *n. (Phonet.)* Diphthong, *der (fachspr.);* Doppellaut, *der*
diploma [dɪ'pləʊmə] *n.* **a)** *(Educ.)* Diplom, *das;* **b)** *(conferring honour)* [Ehren]urkunde, *die;* **c)** *(charter)* Charte, *die*
diplomacy [dɪ'pləʊməsɪ] *n. (Polit.; also fig.)* Diplomatie, *die;* **use** ~ *(fig.)* diplomatisch vorgehen
diplomat ['dɪpləmæt] *n. (Polit.; also fig.)* Diplomat, *der*/Diplomatin, *die*
diplomatic [dɪplə'mætɪk] *adj.*, **diplomatically** [dɪplə'mætɪkəlɪ] *adv. (Polit.; also fig.)* diplomatisch
diplomatic: ~ '**bag** *n.* ~ **bags** Kuriergepäck, *das;* ~ **corps** *n.* diplomatisches Korps; ~ **im'munity** *n.* diplomatische Immunität; ~ **service** *n.* diplomatischer Dienst
diplomatist [dɪ'pləʊmətɪst] *see* **diplomat**
dipole ['daɪpəʊl] *n. (Electr., Magn., Chem., Radio)* Dipol, *der*
dipper ['dɪpə(r)] *n.* **a)** *(excavating machine)* Löffelbagger, *der;* **b)** *(Ornith.)* Wasseramsel, *die;* **c)** *(ladle)* Schöpfkelle, *die;* **d)** *(Amer. Astron.)* **Big/Little D**~: Großer/Kleiner Wagen *od.* Bär; **e)** *see* **big dipper a**
dippy ['dɪpɪ] *adj. (sl.)* übergeschnappt *(ugs.);* **go** ~: überschnappen *(ugs.);* **be** ~ **about sb./sth.** verrückt nach jmdm./etw. sein
dip: ~-**stick** *n.* [Öl-/Benzin]meßstab, *der;* ~-**switch** *n. (Brit. Motor Veh.)* Abblendschalter, *der*
dire [daɪə(r)] *adj.* **a)** *(dreadful)* entsetzlich; furchtbar; **b)** *(ominous)* unheilvoll; **c)** *(extreme)* ~ **necessity** dringende Notwendigkeit; **be in** ~ **need of sth.** etw. dringend benötigen *od.* brauchen; **in cases of** ~ **emergency** im äußersten Notfall; **be in** ~ **[financial] straits** in einer ernsten [finanziellen] Notlage sein
direct [dɪ'rekt, daɪ'rekt] **1.** *v. t.* **a)** *(turn)* richten (**to[wards]** auf + *Akk.*); ~ **one's steps towards sth.** seine Schritte nach etw. lenken; ~ **sb.'s attention to sth.** jmds. Aufmerksamkeit auf etw. *(Akk.)* lenken; **the remark/wink was** ~**ed at you** die Bemerkung/das Zwinkern galt dir; ~ **a blow at sb.** nach jmdm. schlagen; **the bomb/missile was** ~**ed at** die Bombe/das Geschoß galt (+ *Dat.*); **government policy is** ~**ed at reducing inflation** die Regierungspolitik ist darauf ausgerichtet, die Inflation einzudämmen; ~ **sb. to a place** jmdm. den Weg zu einem Ort weisen *od.* sagen; ~ **a parcel to sb./an address in L.** ein Paket an jmdn. adressieren/an eine Adresse in L. senden *od.* schicken; **b)** *(control)* leiten; beaufsichtigen ⟨*Arbeitskräfte, Arbeitsablauf*⟩; lenken ⟨*Volksmassen*⟩; regeln, dirigieren ⟨*Verkehr*⟩; **does fate** ~ **our actions?** lenkt das Schicksal unser Tun?; **c)** *(order)* anweisen; ~ **sb. to do sth.** jmdn. anweisen, etw. zu tun; ~ **sth. to be done** *or* **that sth. [should] be done** anordnen, daß etw. zu tun sei; **as** ~**ed [by the doctor]** wie [vom Arzt] verordnet; nach [ärztlicher] Verordnung; **d)** *(Theatre, Cinemat., Telev., Radio)* Regie führen bei; inszenieren; ~**ed by Orson Welles** unter der Regie von Orson Welles. **2.** *adj.* **a)** *(straight, without intermediaries; also Geneal., Logic)* direkt; durchgehend ⟨*Zug*⟩; unmittelbar ⟨*Ursache, Gefahr, Auswirkung*⟩; *(immediate)* unmittelbar, persönlich ⟨*Erfahrung, Verantwortung, Beteiligung*⟩; **be in the** ~ **line of fire** genau in der Schußlinie stehen; **'keep away from** ~ **heat'** „nicht unmittelbar der Hitze aussetzen!"; **b)** *(diametrical)* genau ⟨*Gegenteil*⟩; direkt ⟨*Widerspruch*⟩; diametral ⟨*Gegensatz*⟩; **c)** *(frank)* direkt, offen; glatt ⟨*Absage*⟩; **he's a very** ~ **person** er ist immer sehr direkt *od.* geradeheraus; **be** ~ **with sb.** offen zu jmdm. sein. **3.** *adv.* direkt
direct: ~ '**access** *n. (Computing)* direkter Zugriff; Direktzugriff, *der;* ~ '**action** *n.* direkte Aktion; ~ '**current** *n. (Electr.)* Gleichstrom, *der;* ~ '**flight** *n.* Direktflug, *der;* ~-'**grant school** *n. (Brit. Hist.) staatlich unterstützte Privatschule;* ~ '**hit** *n.* Volltreffer, *der*
direction [dɪ'rekʃn, daɪ'rekʃn] *n.* **a)** *(guidance)* Führung, *die; (of firm, orchestra)* Leitung, *die; (of play, film, TV or radio programme)* Regie, *die; (of play also)* Spielleitung, *die;* **b)** *usu. in pl. (order)* Anordnung, *die; (instruction)* ~**s [for use]** Gebrauchsanweisung, *die;* ~**s for use** *(of machine)* Bedienungsanleitung, *die;* **on** *or* **by sb.'s** ~: auf jmds. Anordnung *(Akk.)* [hin]; **give sb.** ~**s to the museum/to York** jmdm. den Weg zum Museum/nach York beschreiben; **c)** *(point moved towards or from, lit. or fig.)* Richtung, *die;* **from which** ~**?** aus welcher Richtung?; **travel in a southerly** ~**/in the** ~ **of London** in südliche[r] Richtung/in Richtung London reisen; **go in the** ~ **of the tower** in Richtung des Turms gehen; **in the** ~ **of** *(fig.)* in Richtung auf (+ *Akk.*); **sense of** ~: Orientierungssinn, *der; (fig.)* Orientierung, *die;* **lose all sense of** ~ *(lit. or fig.)* jede Orientierung verlieren; **complaints poured in from all** ~**s** *(fig.)* von allen Seiten hagelte es Beschwerden
directional [dɪ'rekʃənl, daɪ'rekʃənl] *adj.* **a)** *(spatial)* Richtungs-; ~ **gyro** Kurskreisel, *der;* **b)** *(directorial)* führend ⟨*Rolle*⟩; steuernd ⟨*Kontrolle*⟩; **c)** *(Communications)* Richt-
direction: ~-**finder** *n. (Communications)* Peilgerät, *das;* ~-**indicator** *n. (Motor Veh.)* [Fahrt]richtungsanzeiger, *der*
directive [dɪ'rektɪv, daɪ'rektɪv] *n.* Weisung, *die;* Direktive, *die*
direct 'labour *n.* **do the work by** ~: die Arbeit mit eigenen Arbeitskräften ausführen
directly [dɪ'rektlɪ, daɪ'rektlɪ] **1.** *adv.* **a)** *(in direct manner)* direkt; unmittelbar ⟨*folgen, verantwortlich sein*⟩; **b)** *(exactly)* direkt; genau; wörtlich ⟨*zitieren, abschreiben*⟩; **c)** *(at once)* direkt; umgehend; **d)** *(shortly)* gleich; sofort. **2.** *conj. (Brit. coll.)* sowie
directness [dɪ'rektnɪs, daɪ'rektnɪs] *n., no pl.* **a)** *(of route, course)* Geradheit, *die;* ~ **of aim** Zielgenauigkeit, *die;* **b)** *(fig.)* Direktheit, *die;* **he replied with** ~ **and honesty** er antwortete offen und ehrlich
di'rect object *n. (Ling.)* direktes Objekt
director [dɪ'rektə(r), daɪ'rektə(r)] *n.* **a)** *(Commerc.)* Direktor, *der*/Direktorin, *die; (of project)* Leiter, *der*/Leiterin, *die;* **board of** ~**s** Aufsichtsrat, *der;* **b)** *(Theatre, Cinemat., Telev., Radio)* Regisseur, *der*/Regisseurin, *die; (Mus., esp. Amer.)* Dirigent, *der*/Dirigentin, *die*
directorate [dɪ'rektərət, daɪ'rektərət] *n.* **a)** *(position, period of service)* Direktorat, *das; (of project)* Leitung, *die;* **b)** *(board of directors)* Direktorium, *das*
director-'general *n., pl.* **directors-general** Generaldirektor, *der*/-direktorin, *die; (Telev., Radio)* ≈ Intendant, *der*/Intendantin, *die*
directorial [dɪrek'tɔ:rɪəl, daɪrek'tɔ:rɪəl] *adj.* **a)** direktorial; **b)** *(Theatre, Cinemat., Telev., Radio)* als Regisseur/Regisseurin *nachgestellt*
directorship [dɪ'rektəʃɪp, daɪ'rektəʃɪp] *n. (Commerc.)* Leitung, *die;* **hold two** ~**s** in zwei Aufsichtsräten sein
directory [dɪ'rektərɪ, daɪ'rektərɪ] *n. (of local residents)* Adreßbuch, *das; (telephone* ~*)* Telefonbuch, *das;* Fernsprechbuch, *das (postamtl.); (of tradesmen etc.)* Branchenverzeichnis, *das;* ~ **enquiries** *(Brit.)*, ~ **information** *(Amer.)* [Fernsprech]auskunft, *die*
direct: ~ **pro'portion** *n.* direkte Proportionalität; ~ **question** *n. (Ling.)* direkter Fragesatz; ~ **speech** *n. (Ling.)* direkte Rede; ~ **tax** *n.* direkte Steuer; ~ **taxation** *n.* direkte Besteuerung
direly ['daɪəlɪ] *adv.* **be** ~ **in need of sth.** etw. dringend brauchen
dirge [dɜ:dʒ] *n.* **a)** *(for the dead)* Grabgesang, *der;* **b)** *(mournful song)* Klagegesang, *der;* Klage, *die (dichter.)*
dirigible ['dɪrɪdʒɪbl, dɪ'rɪdʒɪbl] **1.** *adj.* lenkbar. **2.** *n.* Luftschiff, *das*
dirk [dɜ:k] *n.* [längerer] Dolch
dirndl ['dɜ:ndl] *n.* Dirndl[kleid], *das;* ~ **[skirt]** Dirndlrock, *der*
dirt [dɜ:t] *n., no pl.* **a)** Schmutz, *der;* Dreck, *der (ugs.);* **be covered in** ~: ganz schmutzig sein; *(stronger)* vor Schmutz starren; ~ **cheap** spottbillig; **treat sb. like** ~: jmdn. wie [den letzten] Dreck behandeln *(salopp);* **do sb.** ~ *(fig. sl.)* jmdm. eins auswischen *(ugs.);* **b)** *(soil)* Erde, *die;* **c)** *(fig.) (lewdness)* Schmutz, *der; (worthless thing)* Dreck, *der (salopp abwertend);* Schund, *der (ugs.); (person)* Abschaum, *der;* **give me the** ~ **on him** *(coll.)* sag mir, wo er Dreck am Stecken hat *(ugs.)*
'**dirt-farmer** *n. (Amer.)* [richtiger] Farmer *(der selbst sein Land bestellt)*
dirtiness ['dɜ:tɪnɪs] *n., no pl.* Schmutzigkeit, *die*
dirt: ~ **road** *n. (Amer.)* unbefestigte Straße; ~-**track** *n. (Sport)* Aschenbahn, *die; (made of earth)* ≈ Sandbahn, *die*

dirty ['dɜ:tɪ] **1.** *adj.* **a)** schmutzig; dreckig *(ugs.)*; **get one's shoes/hands ~:** sich *(Dat.)* die Schuhe/Hände schmutzig machen; **get sth. ~:** etw. schmutzig machen; **~ money** Schmutzzulage, *die;* **b)** *(with dark tinge)* schmutzig ‹*Farbe*›; **~ grey colour** schmutziggraue Farbe; **c) ~ weather** stürmisches Wetter; Dreckwetter, *das (ugs. abwertend);* **d)** *(coll.: causing fall-out)* ‹*Kernwaffe:*› mit starkem Fallout; schmutzig *(fig.)*; **e) ~ look** *(coll.)* giftiger Blick; **give sb. a ~ look** jmdn. giftig ansehen; **f)** *(ill-gotten)* schmutzig ‹*Geld*›; **g)** *(fig.: obscene)* schmutzig; schlüpfrig; *(sexually illicit)* **spend a ~ weekend together** ein Liebeswochenende zusammen verbringen; *(lascivious)* **have a ~ mind** eine schmutzige Phantasie haben; **~ old man** alter Lustmolch *(ugs. abwertend);* geiler alter Bock *(salopp abwertend);* **h)** *(despicable, sordid)* schmutzig ‹*Lüge, Gerücht, Geschäft*›; dreckig *(salopp abwertend),* gemein ‹*Lügner, Betrüger*›; *(unsportsmanlike)* unfair; **do the ~ on sb.** *(coll.)* jmdn. [he]reinlegen *(ugs.);* **~ dog** *(fig. sl.)* Schwein, *das (ugs. abwertend);* **~ trick** gemeiner Trick; **play sb. a ~ trick** jmdn. ganz gemein übers Ohr hauen *(ugs.);* **~ work [at the crossroads]** *(coll.)* schmutziges Geschäft; **do sb.'s/the ~ work** sich *(Dat.)* für jmdn./sich *(Dat.)* die Finger schmutzig machen; **get the ~ end of the stick** *(coll.)* der Dumme sein *(ugs.).* **2.** *adv. (sl.)* **~ great** riesig *(ugs.).* **3.** *v. t.* schmutzig machen; beschmutzen

dirty 'word *n.* unanständiges Wort; *(fig.)* Schimpfwort, *das*

disability [dɪsə'bɪlɪtɪ] *n.* **a)** Behinderung, *die; (inability to be gainfully employed)* Invalidität, *die;* Erwerbsunfähigkeit, *die;* **suffer from** *or* **have a ~:** behindert/erwerbsunfähig sein; **b)** *(cause of inability)* Behinderung, *die*

disability: ~ allowance *n.* Erwerbsunfähigkeitsentschädigung, *die;* **~ pension** *n.* Erwerbsunfähigkeitsrente, *die*

disable [dɪ'seɪbl] *v. t.* **a) ~ sb. [physically]** jmdn. zum Invaliden machen; **be ~d by sth.** durch etw. behindert sein; **be permanently ~d by sth.** eine bleibende Behinderung bei etw. davontragen; **strikes which ~ the economy** Streiks, die die Wirtschaft lahmlegen; **b)** *(make unable to fight)* kampfunfähig machen ‹*Feind, Schiff, Panzer, Flugzeug*›; kampfunfähig schlagen ‹*Boxer*›; unbrauchbar machen ‹*Gewehr, Kanone*›

disabled [dɪ'seɪbld] **1.** *adj.* **a)** behindert; **~ ex-serviceman** Kriegsinvalide, *der;* **physically/mentally ~:** körperbehindert/geistig behindert; **b)** *(unable to fight)* kampfunfähig ‹*Schiff, Panzer, Flugzeug, Boxer*›; unbrauchbar ‹*Kanone, Gewehr*›. **2.** *n. pl.* **the [physically/mentally] ~:** die [Körper]behinderten/[geistig] Behinderten

disablement [dɪ'seɪblmənt] *n., no pl.* Behinderung, *die*

disabuse [dɪsə'bju:z] *v. t.* **~ sb. of sth.** jmdn. von etw. abbringen

disadvantage [dɪsəd'vɑ:ntɪdʒ] **1.** *n.* **a)** Nachteil, *der; (state of being disadvantaged)* Benachteiligung, *die;* **be at a ~:** im Nachteil sein; benachteiligt sein; **his inexperience put him at a ~:** er war durch seine mangelnde Erfahrung benachteiligt; **b)** *no pl. (damage)* Schaden, *der;* **be to sb.'s/sth.'s ~:** sich zu jmds. Nachteil/zum Nachteil einer Sache auswirken. **2.** *v. t.* benachteiligen

disadvantaged [dɪsəd'vɑ:ntɪdʒd] *adj.* benachteiligt

disadvantageous [dɪsædvən'teɪdʒəs] *adj.* **a)** nachteilig; ungünstig ‹*Zeitpunkt*›; **be ~ to sb./sth.** für jmdn./etw. von Nachteil sein; **b)** *(unflattering)* unvorteilhaft

disaffected [dɪsə'fektɪd] *adj.* **a)** *(disloyal)* illoyal **(to** gegenüber); **b)** *(estranged)* entfremdet **(from** *Dat.*)

disaffection [dɪsə'fekʃn] *n., no pl.* Entfremdung, *die* **(from** von)

disagree [dɪsə'gri:] *v. i.* **a)** anderer Meinung sein; **~ with sb.** mit jmdm. nicht übereinstimmen; anderer Meinung als jmd. sein; **~ with sth.** mit etw. nicht übereinstimmen; **~ [with sb.] about** *or* **over sth.** sich [mit jmdm.] über etw. *(Akk.)* nicht einig sein; *see also* **agree 1 a; b)** *(quarrel)* eine Auseinandersetzung haben; **c)** *(be mutually inconsistent)* nicht übereinstimmen; **d) ~ with sb.** *(have bad effects on)* jmdm. nicht bekommen

disagreeable [dɪsə'grɪəbəl] *adj.* unangenehm; unappetitlich ‹*Nahrungsmittel*›

disagreeably [dɪsə'grɪəblɪ] *adv.* **a)** unangenehm; **b)** *(bad-temperedly)* übellaunig

disagreement [dɪsə'gri:mənt] *n.* **a)** *(difference of opinion)* Uneinigkeit, *die; (refusal to agree)* **be in ~:** geteilter Meinung sein; **be in ~ with sb./sth.** mit jmdm./etw. nicht übereinstimmen; **b)** *(strife, quarrel)* Meinungsverschiedenheit, *die;* **c)** *(discrepancy)* Diskrepanz, *die*

disallow [dɪsə'laʊ] *v. t.* nicht gestatten; abweisen ‹*Antrag, Anspruch, Klage*›; *(refuse to admit)* nicht anerkennen; nicht gelten lassen; *(Sport)* nicht geben ‹*Tor*›

disambiguate [dɪsæm'bɪgjʊeɪt] *v. t.* eindeutig machen; disambiguieren *(Sprachw.)*

disappear [dɪsə'pɪə(r)] *v. i.* verschwinden; ‹*Brauch, Kunst, Tierart:*› aussterben; ‹*Angst, Ärger, Laune:*› verfliegen; **do a ~ing act** *or* **trick** *(fig.)* spurlos verschwinden

disappearance [dɪsə'pɪərəns] *n.* Verschwinden, *das; (of customs; extinction)* Aussterben, *das*

disappoint [dɪsə'pɔɪnt] *v. t.* enttäuschen; **be ~ed in** *or* **by** *or* **with sb./sth.** von jmdm./etw. enttäuscht sein; **he was ~ed at** *or* **by** *or* **with having failed/the way things had changed** er war enttäuscht [darüber], daß er durchgefallen war/darüber, wie sich die Dinge verändert hatten

disappointing [dɪsə'pɔɪntɪŋ] *adj.* enttäuschend; **how ~!** so eine Enttäuschung!

disappointingly [dɪsə'pɔɪntɪŋlɪ] *adv.* enttäuschend; **~, he only came fourth** enttäuschenderweise wurde er nur vierter

disappointment [dɪsə'pɔɪntmənt] *n.* Enttäuschung, *die;* **come as a ~ to sb.** eine Enttäuschung für jmdn. sein

disapprobation [dɪsæprə'beɪʃn], **disapproval** [dɪsə'pru:vl] *ns.* Mißbilligung, *die;* **show one's/cause ~:** sein Mißfallen zeigen/Mißfallen erregen; **with ~:** mißbilligend; mit Mißbilligung

disapprove [dɪsə'pru:v] **1.** *v. i.* dagegen sein; **~ of sb./sth.** jmdn. ablehnen/etw. mißbilligen; **~ of sb. doing sth.** es mißbilligen, wenn jmd. etw. tut. **2.** *v. t.* mißbilligen

disapproving [dɪsə'pru:vɪŋ] *adj.*, **disapprovingly** [dɪsə'pru:vɪŋlɪ] *adv.* mißbilligend

disarm [dɪ'sɑ:m] **1.** *v. t.* **a)** entwaffnen; entschärfen ‹*Bombe*›; **b)** *(fig.)* entwaffnen; verstummen lassen ‹*Kritik*›; abbauen ‹*Feindseligkeit*›. **2.** *v. i.* abrüsten

disarmament [dɪ'sɑ:məmənt] *n.* Abrüstung, *die;* **~ talks** Abrüstungsgespräche

disarming [dɪ'sɑ:mɪŋ] *adj.* entwaffnend

disarmingly [dɪ'sɑ:mɪŋlɪ] *adv.* entwaffnend

disarrange [dɪsə'reɪndʒ] *v. t.* durcheinanderbringen; zerzausen ‹*Haar*›

disarray [dɪsə'reɪ] **1.** *n.* Unordnung, *die; (confusion)* Wirrwarr, *der;* **fall into ~:** durcheinandergeraten; **be in ~:** in Unordnung sein. **2.** *v. t.* in Unordnung bringen

disassemble [dɪsə'sembl] *v. t.* auseinandernehmen ‹*Maschine*›; abbauen ‹*Gebäude, Anlage*›

disassembly [dɪsə'semblɪ] *n. (of machine)* Auseinandernehmen, *das; (of structure)* Abbau, *der*

disassociation [dɪsəsəʊsɪ'eɪʃn] *see* **dissociation a**

disaster [dɪ'zɑ:stə(r)] *n.* **a)** Katastrophe, *die;* **air ~:** Flugzeugunglück, *das; (with many deaths also)* Flugzeugkatastrophe, *die;* **a railway/mining ~:** ein Eisenbahn-/Grubenunglück; **natural ~:** Naturkatastrophe, *die;* **motorway ~:** schwerer Unfall auf der Autobahn; **end in ~:** in einer Katastrophe enden; **b)** *(complete failure)* Fiasko, *das;* Katastrophe, *die;* **lead to ~:** zu einem Fiasko *od.* einer Katastrophe führen; **prove a ~:** sich als katastrophal erweisen

disaster: ~ area *n.* Katastrophengebiet, *das;* **he/she is a [walking] ~ area** *(fig. coll.)* er/sie ist eine wandelnde Katastrophe *(fig.);* **~ fund** *n.* Nothilfefonds, *der*

disastrous [dɪ'zɑ:strəs] *adj.* katastrophal; verhängnisvoll ‹*Irrtum, Entscheidung, Politik*›; verheerend ‹*Überschwemmung, Wirbelsturm, Feuer*›

disastrously [dɪ'zɑ:strəslɪ] *adv.* katastrophal

disavow [dɪsə'vaʊ] *v. t.* verleugnen; nicht anerkennen ‹*Rechtsprechung, Vereinbarung*›; **~ responsibility for sth.** die Verantwortung für etwas von sich weisen

disavowal [dɪsə'vaʊəl] *n.* Verleugnung, *die*

disband [dɪs'bænd] **1.** *v. t.* auflösen; **the ~ed soldiers** die entlassenen Soldaten. **2.** *v. i.* sich auflösen

disbar [dɪs'bɑ:(r)] *v. t.* **-rr-** *(Law)* die Zulassung entziehen (+ *Dat.*)

disbelief [dɪsbɪ'li:f] *n.* Unglaube, *der;* **be met with ~:** auf Unglauben stoßen; **in ~:** ungläubig

disbelieve [dɪsbɪ'li:v] **1.** *v. t.* **~ sb./sth.** jmdm. nicht glauben *od. (geh.)* keinen Glauben schenken/etw. nicht glauben. **2.** *v. i.* nicht glauben; **~ in sth.** nicht an etw. *(Akk.)* glauben

disbeliever [dɪsbɪ'li:və(r)] *n.* Ungläubige, *der/die;* **be a ~ in sth.** nicht an etw. *(Akk.)* glauben

disburden [dɪs'bɜ:dn] *see* **unburden**

disburse [dɪs'bɜ:s] *v. t.* ausgeben

disbursement [dɪs'bɜ:smənt] *n.* Auszahlung, *die; (expenditure)* Ausgabe, *die*

disc [dɪsk] *n.* **a)** Scheibe, *die;* **b)** *(gramophone record)* [Schall]platte, *die; see also* **compact disc; c)** *(Computing)* **[magnetic] ~:** Magnetplatte, *die;* **floppy ~:** Floppy disk, *die;* Diskette, *die;* **hard ~** *(exchangeable)* [harte] Magnetplatte; *(fixed)* Festplatte, *die;* **d)** *(Anat.)* Bandscheibe, *die; see also* **slipped disc; e)** *(Bot.)* Körbchen, das

discard 1. [dɪ'skɑ:d] *v. t.* **a)** wegwerfen; ablegen ‹*Kleidung*›; fallenlassen ‹*Vorschlag, Idee, Mensch*›; **b)** *(Cards)* abwerfen. **2.** ['dɪskɑ:d] *n.* Ausschuß, *der; (person)* Ausgestoßene, *der/die*

disc: ~ brake *n.* Scheibenbremse, *die;* **~ drive** *n. (Computing)* Diskettenlaufwerk, *das*

discern [dɪ'sɜ:n] *v.t.* wahrnehmen; **sth. can be ~ed** etw. ist zu erkennen; **~ from sth. whether ...:** an etw. *(Dat.)* erkennen, ob ...

discernible [dɪ'sɜ:nɪbl] *adj.* erkennbar; wahrnehmbar ‹*Stimme, Geruch*›; **a ~ pattern has emerged** ein Schema ist erkennbar geworden

discerning [dɪ'sɜ:nɪŋ] *adj.* fein ‹*Gaumen, Ohr, Geschmack*›; scharf ‹*Auge*›; urteilsfähig ‹*Richter, Kritiker*›; kritisch ‹*Leser, Kunde, Zuschauer, Kommentar*›; scharfsichtig ‹*Kritik*›

discernment [dɪ'sɛ:nmənt] *n., no pl. (act of discerning)* Wahrnehmung, *die; (faculty of discerning)* Urteilsfähigkeit, *die*

discharge 1. [dɪs'tʃɑ:dʒ] *v. t.* **a)** *(dismiss, allow to leave)* entlassen **(from** aus); freisprechen ‹*Angeklagte*›; *(exempt from liabilities)* befreien **(from** von); **the patient ~d himself from hospital** der Patient verließ eigenmächtig das Krankenhaus; **b)** *(send out)* abschießen ‹*Pfeil, Torpedo*›; ablassen ‹*Flüssigkeit, Gas*›; absondern ‹*Eiter*›; *(unload* *from ship)* ausschiffen; löschen ‹*Ladung*›; *(Electr.)* entladen; **c)** *(relieve of load)* entladen; löschen ‹*Schiff*›; *(fire)* abfeuern ‹*Gewehr, Kanone*›; **d)** *(acquit oneself of, pay)* erfüllen ‹*Pflicht, Verbindlichkeiten, Versprechen*›; bezahlen ‹*Schulden*›. **2.** *v.i.* **a)** entladen werden; ‹*Schiff auch:*› gelöscht werden; ‹*Batterie:*› sich entladen; ‹*Gewehr:*› losgehen; **b)** *(flow)* münden (**into** in + *Akk.*); **c)** ‹*Wunde, Geschwür:*› eitern. **3.** [dɪsˈtʃɑːdʒ, ˈdɪstʃɑːdʒ] *n.* **a)** *(dismissal)* Entlassung, *die* (**from** aus); *(of defendant)* Freispruch, *der; (exemption from liabilities)* Befreiung, *die; (written certificate of release)* Entlassungsschein, *der; (written certificate of exemption)* Entlastungsschein, *der;* **be granted a full ~ [by the court]** [vom Gericht] in allen Punkten freigesprochen werden; **b)** *(emission)* Ausfluß, *der; (of gas)* Austritt, *der; (of pus)* Absonderung, *die; (Electr.)* Entladung, *die; (of gun)* Abfeuern, *das;* **vaginal ~:** [Scheiden]ausfluß, *der;* **c)** *(of debt)* Begleichung, *die; (of duty)* Erfüllung, *die*

ˈdisc harrow *n. (Agric.)* Scheibenegge, *die*

disciple [dɪˈsaɪpl] *n.* **a)** *(Relig.)* Jünger, *der;* **b)** *(follower)* Anhänger, *der*/Anhängerin, *die;* Jünger, *der (geh., oft scherzh.)*

disciplinarian [dɪsɪplɪˈneərɪən] *n.* Zuchtmeister, *der*/-meisterin, *die (veralt., noch scherzh.); (in school, family also)* [strenger] Erzieher; **he is a poor ~:** er kann nicht für Disziplin sorgen

disciplinary [ˈdɪsɪplɪnərɪ, dɪsɪˈplɪnərɪ] *adj.* Disziplinar-; disziplinarisch; **~ action** Disziplinarmaßnahme, *die;* **~ proceedings** Disziplinarverfahren, *das*

discipline [ˈdɪsɪplɪn] **1.** *n.* **a)** *(order, branch)* Disziplin, *die;* **maintain ~:** die Disziplin aufrechterhalten; **lack of ~:** Mangel an Disziplin; **change ~s** die Disziplin *od.* das Fach wechseln; **b)** *(mental training)* Schulung, *die;* **the ~ of adversity** die strenge Schule der Not; **c)** *(system of rules)* Kanon, *der;* **d)** *(punishment)* Strafe, *die; (physical also)* Züchtigung, *die (geh.); (Relig.)* Kasteiung, *die.* **2.** *v.t.* **a)** disziplinieren; *(train in military exercises)* ausbilden; **you must ~ yourself to eat less** Sie müssen sich zwingen, weniger zu essen; **~ one's emotions/feelings** *etc.* seine Emotionen/Gefühle *usw.* unter Kontrolle halten; **b)** *(punish)* bestrafen; *(physically also)* züchtigen *(geh.); (Relig.)* kasteien

disciplined [ˈdɪsɪplɪnd] *adj.* diszipliniert; **highly/well ~:** sehr diszipliniert; **badly ~:** undiszipliniert

ˈdisc jockey *n.* Diskjockey, *der*

disclaim [dɪsˈkleɪm] *v.t.* **a)** abstreiten; **b)** *(Law)* verzichten auf (+ *Akk.*)

disclaimer [dɪsˈkleɪmə(r)] *n.* Gegenerklärung, *die; (Law)* Verzichterklärung, *die*

disclose [dɪsˈkləʊz] *v.t.* **a)** *(expose to view)* den Blick freigeben auf (+ *Akk.*); **b)** *(make known)* enthüllen; bekanntgeben ‹*Information, Nachricht*›; **research ~d that ...:** Nachforschungen ergaben, daß ...; **he didn't ~ why he'd come** er verriet nicht, warum er gekommen war

disclosure [dɪsˈkləʊʒə(r)] *n.* Enthüllung, *die; (of information, news)* Bekanntgabe, *die;* **for fear of possible ~:** aus Furcht vor einer möglichen Enthüllung; **the newspaper's ~ of bribery** die Enthüllungen der Zeitung über Bestechung

disco [ˈdɪskəʊ] *n., pl.* **~s** *(coll.)* **a)** *(discothèque, party)* Disko, *die;* **b)** *(equipment)* **travelling ~:** rollende Disko

ˈdisco dancing *n.* Diskotanz, *der*

discolor *(Amer.) see* **discolour**

discoloration [dɪskʌləˈreɪʃn] *n.* Verfärbung, *die*

discolour [dɪsˈkʌlə(r)] *(Brit.)* **1.** *v.t.* verfärben; *(fade)* ausbleichen. **2.** *v.i.* sich verfärben; *(fade)* ausbleichen

discolouration *(Brit.) see* **discoloration**

discombobulate [dɪskəmˈbɒbjʊleɪt] *v.t. (Amer. joc.)* durcheinanderbringen

discomfit [dɪsˈkʌmfɪt] *v.t.* **a)** *(baffle, disconcert)* verunsichern; **b)** *(arch.: overwhelm, thwart)* schlagen

discomfiture [dɪsˈkʌmfɪtʃə(r)] *n.* Verunsicherung, *die*

discomfort [dɪsˈkʌmfət] **1.** *n.* **a)** *no pl. (uneasiness of body)* Beschwerden *Pl.;* **cause/give sb. ~:** jmdm. Beschwerden machen; **b)** *no pl. (uneasiness of mind)* Unbehagen, *das;* **c)** *(hardship)* Unannehmlichkeit, *die.* **2.** *v.t.* zu schaffen machen (+ *Dat.*)

discompose [dɪskəmˈpəʊz] *v.t.* aus der Fassung bringen; **appear ~d** einen verstörten Eindruck machen

discomposure [dɪskəmˈpəʊʒə(r)] *n., no pl.* Verstörtheit, *die*

ˈdisco music *n.* Diskomusik, *die*

disconcert [dɪskənˈsɜːt] *v.t.* verstören; irritieren; **I was ~ed to find the gates locked** ich war verwirrt, als ich vor verschlossenen Toren stand

disconcerted [dɪskənˈsɜːtɪd] *adj.* verstört; irritiert

disconcerting [dɪskənˈsɜːtɪŋ] *adj.*, **disconcertingly** [dɪskənˈsɜːtɪŋlɪ] *adv.* irritierend

disconnect [dɪskəˈnekt] *v.t.* **a)** abtrennen; abhängen ‹*Wagen*›; **b)** *(Electr., Teleph.)* **~ the electricity from a house** ein Haus von der Stromversorgung abtrennen; **~ the TV** den Stecker des Fernsehers herausziehen; **the loudspeakers have become ~ed** die Lautsprecher sind nicht mehr angeschlossen; **if you don't pay your telephone bill you will be ~ed** wenn Sie Ihre Telefonrechnung nicht bezahlen, wird Ihr Telefon abgestellt; **operator, I've been ~ed** hallo, Vermittlung, die Verbindung ist unterbrochen; **~ a call** ein Gespräch unterbrechen

disconnected [dɪskəˈnektɪd] *adj.* **a)** abgetrennt; abgestellt ‹*Telefon*›; **is the cooker/TV ~?** ist der Stecker beim Herd/Fernseher herausgezogen?; **b)** *(incoherent)* unzusammenhängend ‹*Rede, Worte*›

disconnectedly [dɪskəˈnektɪdlɪ] *adv.* unzusammenhängend

disconnection, *(Brit.)* **disconnexion** [dɪskəˈnekʃn] *n.* Abtrennung, *die*

disconsolate [dɪsˈkɒnsələt] *adj.*, **disconsolately** [dɪsˈkɒnsələtlɪ] *adv.* untröstlich

discontent [dɪskənˈtent] **1.** *n.* Unzufriedenheit, *die.* **2.** *v.t.* unzufrieden machen

discontented [dɪskənˈtentɪd] *adj.* unzufrieden (**with, about mit**)

discontentment [dɪskənˈtentmənt] *n., no pl.* Unzufriedenheit, *die*

discontinuance [dɪskəntˈtɪnjʊəns], **discontinuation** [dɪskəntɪnjʊˈeɪʃn] *ns.* Einstellung, *die; (of subscription)* Abbestellung, *die; (of treatment)* Abbruch, *der; (of habit)* Aufgabe, *die*

discontinue [dɪskənˈtɪnjuː] *v.t.* **a)** einstellen; abbestellen ‹*Abonnement*›; abbrechen ‹*Behandlung*›; aufgeben ‹*Gewohnheit*›; **b)** *(Commerc.)* **a ~d range** *or* **line** eine auslaufende Serie

discontinuity [dɪskɒntɪˈnjuːɪtɪ] *n.* Bruch, *der;* **a ~ of style** ein stilistischer Bruch

discontinuous [dɪskənˈtɪnjʊəs] *adj.* nicht kontinuierlich; diskontinuierlich *(geh.)*

discontinuously [dɪskənˈtɪnjʊəslɪ] *adv.* mit Unterbrechungen; nicht kontinuierlich

discord [ˈdɪskɔːd] *n.* **a)** Zwietracht, *die; (quarrelling)* Streit, *der;* **b)** *(Mus.) (chord)* Dissonanz, *die; (interval)* Disharmonie, *die; (single note)* Mißton, *der;* **c)** *(harsh noise)* Mißklang, *der*

discordant [dɪˈskɔːdənt] *adj.* **a)** gegensätzlich; **b)** *(dissonant)* mißtönend

discordantly [dɪˈskɔːdəntlɪ] *adv.* **a)** gegensätzlich; **b)** *(dissonantly)* mißtönend

discothèque [ˈdɪskətek] *n.* Diskothek, *die*

discount 1. [ˈdɪskaʊnt] *n. (Commerc.)* Rabatt, *der; (on bill of exchange)* Diskont, *der; (discounting)* Diskontierung, *die;* **give** *or* **offer [sb.] a ~ on sth.** [jmdm.] Rabatt auf etw. *(Akk.)* geben *od.* gewähren; **~ for cash** Skonto, *der od. das;* Rabatt bei Barzahlung; **at a ~:** mit Rabatt; *(St. Exch.)* unter dem Nennwert; *(fig.)* nicht gefragt; **the books were sold at a [big] ~:** die Bücher wurden [weit] unter dem normalen Preis verkauft. **2.** [dɪˈskaʊnt] *v.t.* **a)** *(disbelieve)* unberücksichtigt lassen; *(discredit)* widerlegen ‹*Beweis, Theorie*›; *(underrate)* zu gering einschätzen; *(lessen)* schmälern ‹*Wert*›; *(reduce effect of)* einkalkulieren; **b)** *(Commerc.)* diskontieren ‹*Wechsel*›

ˈdiscount broker *n. (Commerc.)* Wechselmakler, *der*

ˈdiscount: ~ house *n. (Commerc.)* Diskontbank, *die;* **~ shop, ~ store** *ns.* Discountladen, *der;* Discountgeschäft, *das*

discourage [dɪˈskʌrɪdʒ] *v.t.* **a)** *(dispirit)* entmutigen; **be** *or* **become ~d [by sth.** *or* **because of sth.]** sich [durch etw.] entmutigen lassen; **be ~d because ...:** sich entmutigt fühlen, weil ...; **b)** *(advise against)* abraten; **~ sb. from sth.** jmdm. von etw. abraten; **~ sb. from doing sth.** jmdm. davon abraten, etw. zu tun; **c)** *(act against)* zu unterbinden suchen; **d)** *(disapprove of)* nicht gutheißen; **sth. must be ~d** man darf etw. nicht gutheißen; **e)** *(stop)* abhalten ‹*Person*›; verhindern ‹*Handlung*›; **~ sb. from doing sth.** jmdn. davon abhalten, etw. zu tun; **not ~d by fear of reprisals** ohne Furcht vor Vergeltungsmaßnahmen

discouragement [dɪˈskʌrɪdʒmənt] *n.* **a)** Entmutigung, *die;* **b)** *(deterrent)* Abschreckung, *die;* **act as a ~ to sb.** eine abschreckende Wirkung auf jmdn. haben; **c)** *(depression)* Mutlosigkeit, *die*

discouraging [dɪˈskʌrɪdʒɪŋ] *adj.* **a)** *(dispiriting)* entmutigend; **paint a ~ picture of sth.** ein düsteres Bild von etw. malen; **he was rather ~:** er hat mir/ihm/ihr *usw.* wenig Mut gemacht; **the article makes ~ reading** die Lektüre des Artikels ist entmutigend; **b)** *(deterring)* abschreckend

discouragingly [dɪˈskʌrɪdʒɪŋlɪ] *adv.* entmutigend

discourse 1. [ˈdɪskɔːs] *n.* Diskurs, *der;* **hold a ~** *or* **be in ~ with sb.** einen Diskurs mit jmdm. haben *od.* führen. **2.** [dɪˈskɔːs] *v.i.* **~ [upon sth.]** sich [über etw. *(Akk.)*] ausführlich äußern; *(converse)* [über etw.] ausführlich reden

discourteous [dɪsˈkɜːtɪəs] *adj.*, **discourteously** [dɪsˈkɜːtɪəslɪ] *adv.* unhöflich

discourtesy [dɪsˈkɜːtəsɪ] *n.* Unhöflichkeit, *die;* **he did her a ~:** er beging ihr gegenüber eine Unhöflichkeit

discover [dɪˈskʌvə(r)] *v.t.* **a)** *(find, notice, get knowledge of, realize)* entdecken; **b)** *(by search)* herausfinden; **~ a meaning in life** entdecken, daß das Leben einen Sinn hat; **it was never ~ed how ...:** es kam nie heraus, wie ...; **~ sb.'s identity** herausfinden, wer jmd. ist; **as far as I can ~:** soweit ich feststellen kann; **c)** *(Chess)* **~ed check** Abzugsschach, *das*

discoverable [dɪˈskʌvərəbl] *adj.* auffindbar

discoverer [dɪˈskʌvərə(r)] *n.* Entdecker, *der*/Entdeckerin, *die*

discovery [dɪˈskʌvərɪ] *n.* Entdeckung, *die;* **voyage of ~:** Entdeckungsreise, *die;* **for fear of ~** aus Angst, entdeckt zu werden

ˈdisc parking *n. (Brit.)* Parken mit Parkscheibe

discredit [dɪsˈkredɪt] **1.** *n.* **a)** *no pl.* Mißkredit, *der;* **bring ~ on sb./sth., bring sb./sth. into ~:** jmdn./etw. in Mißkredit *(Akk.)* bringen; **be to the ~ of sb.** jmdm. keine Ehre machen; **without any ~ to the firm** ohne die Firma in Mißkredit zu bringen; **b)** *(sb.*

or sth. that ~s) **be a ~ to sb./sth.** jmdm./einer Sache keine Ehre machen; **c)** *no pl. (doubt)* **throw ~ on sth.** etw. unglaubwürdig erscheinen lassen; **fall into ~:** ins Zwielicht geraten. **2.** *v. t.* **a)** *(disbelieve)* keinen Glauben schenken (+ *Dat.*); *(discount as unreliable)* anzweifeln; *(cause to be disbelieved)* unglaubwürdig machen; **careful research has ~ed this theory** sorgfältige Untersuchungen haben diese Theorie zweifelhaft werden lassen; **b)** *(disgrace)* diskreditieren *(geh.)*; in Verruf bringen; **be ~ed** diskreditiert werden *(geh.)*; in Verruf geraten

discreditable [dɪsˈkredɪtəbl] *adj.* unehrenhaft

discreditably [dɪsˈkredɪtəblɪ] *adv.* unehrenhaft; **perform ~ in the examination** bei der Prüfung unrühmlich abschneiden

discreet [dɪˈskriːt] *adj.*, **~er** [dɪˈskriːtə(r)], **~est** [dɪˈskriːtɪst] diskret; taktvoll; *(unobtrusive)* diskret; dezent ‹*Parfüm, Kleidung*›

discreetly [dɪˈskriːtlɪ] *adv.* diskret; dezent ‹*gekleidet*›

discreetness [dɪˈskriːtnɪs] *n., no pl.* Diskretheit, *die*

discrepancy [dɪˈskrepənsɪ] *n.* Diskrepanz, *die;* **there is wide ~ between the statements of the two witnesses** die beiden Zeugenaussagen stimmen bei weitem nicht überein

discrepant [dɪˈskrepənt] *adj.* [voneinander] abweichend

discrete [dɪˈskriːt] *adj.* eigenständig; *(Math., Phys.)* diskret; **a ~ whole** ein Ganzes aus eigenständigen Teilen

discreteness [dɪˈskriːtnɪs] *n., no pl.* Eigenständigkeit, *die*

discretion [dɪˈskreʃn] *n.* **a)** *(prudence)* Umsicht, *die; (reservedness)* Diskretion, *die;* **use ~:** diskret sein; **reach years** *or* **the age of ~:** mündig werden; **~ is the better part of valour** *(prov.)* Vorsicht ist besser als Nachsicht *(ugs. scherzh.)*; Vorsicht ist die Mutter der Weisheit; **b)** *(liberty to decide)* Ermessen, *das;* **leave sth. to sb.'s ~:** etw. in jmds. Ermessen *(Akk.)* stellen; etw. jmds. Entscheidung *(Dat.)* überlassen; **at sb.'s ~:** nach jmds. Ermessen; **be within** *or* **at** *or* **left to sb.'s ~:** in jmds. Ermessen *(Dat.)* liegen; **use one's ~:** nach eigenem Ermessen *od.* Gutdünken handeln; **at ~** *(as one pleases)* nach Gutdünken *od.* Belieben

discretionary [dɪˈskreʃənərɪ] *adj.* Ermessens-; **a ~ grant** *ein Stipendium, das nach Ermessen der Behörden vergeben wird;* **~ powers** Entscheidungsgewalt, *die*

discriminate [dɪˈskrɪmɪneɪt] **1.** *v. t.* unterscheiden. **2.** *v. i.* **a)** *(distinguish, use discernment)* unterscheiden; **~ between [two things]** unterscheiden zwischen [zwei Dingen]; **b) ~ against sb.** jmdn. diskriminieren; **~ in favour of sb.** jmdn. bevorzugen

discriminating [dɪˈskrɪmɪneɪtɪŋ] *adj.* kritisch ‹*Urteil, Auge, Kunde, Kunstsammler*›; fein ‹*Geschmack, Gaumen, Ohr*›

discriminatingly [dɪˈskrɪmɪneɪtɪŋlɪ] *adv.* kritisch; scharfsichtig ‹*kritisieren*›

discrimination [dɪskrɪmɪˈneɪʃn] *n.* **a)** *(act of discriminating)* Unterscheidung, *die;* **b)** *(discernment)* [kritisches] Urteilsvermögen; **c)** *(differential treatment)* Diskriminierung, *die* **(against** *Gen.*); **~ against Blacks/women** Diskriminierung von Schwarzen/Frauen; **~ against foreign imports** die Erschwerung von ausländischen Importen; **~ in favour of** Bevorzugung (+ *Gen.*); **racial ~:** Rassendiskriminierung, *die*

discriminatory [dɪˈskrɪmɪnətərɪ] *adj.* diskriminierend

discursive [dɪˈskɜːsɪv] *adj.*, **discursively** [dɪˈskɜːsɪvlɪ] *adv.* weitschweifig

discursiveness [dɪˈskɜːsɪvnɪs] *n., no pl.* Weitschweifigkeit, *die*

discus [ˈdɪskəs] *n. (Sport)* **a)** Diskus, *der;* **b)** *(event)* Diskuswerfen, *das*

discuss [dɪˈskʌs] *v. t.* **a)** *(talk about)* besprechen; **~ sth. with sb.** etw. mit jmdm. besprechen; **the children were ~ing the wedding** die Kinder sprachen über die Hochzeit; **I'm not willing to ~ this matter at present** ich möchte jetzt nicht darüber sprechen; **b)** *(debate)* diskutieren über (+ *Akk.*); *(examine)* erörtern; diskutieren

discussion [dɪˈskʌʃn] *n.* **a)** *(conversation)* Gespräch, *das; (more formal)* Unterredung, *die;* **after much ~:** nach langen Gesprächen/Unterredungen; **let's have a ~ about it** wir wollen darüber reden *od.* sprechen; **there was some ~ before they ...:** sie besprachen sich miteinander, bevor sie ...; **b)** *(debate)* Diskussion, *die; (examination)* Erörterung, *die;* **come up for ~:** zur Diskussion gestellt werden; **be under ~:** zur Diskussion stehen; **matter** *or* **topic for ~:** Thema *od.* Gegenstand der Diskussion; **hold** *or* **have a ~ with sb.** mit jmdm. diskutieren

discussion: ~ group *n.* Diskussionsrunde, *die;* **~ programme** *n. (Radio, Telev.)* Diskussionssendung, *die*

disdain [dɪsˈdeɪn] **1.** *n.* Verachtung, *die;* **with ~:** verächtlich; **a look of ~:** ein verächtlicher *od.* geringschätziger Blick. **2.** *v. t.* verachten; verächtlich ablehnen ‹*Rat, Hilfe*›; **~ to do sth.** zu stolz sein, etw. zu tun

disdainful [dɪsˈdeɪnfl] *adj.* verächtlich, geringschätzig ‹*Lachen, Ton, Blick, Kommentar*›; **look ~:** verächtlich dreinblicken; **be ~ of advice/simple pleasures** Ratschläge verächtlich ablehnen/einfache Freuden verachten

disdainfully [dɪsˈdeɪnfəlɪ] *adv.* verächtlich; geringschätzig; voll Verachtung ‹*ignorieren*›; **look ~ at sb./sth.** jmdn./etw. verächtlich *od.* geringschätzig ansehen

disease [dɪˈziːz] *n. (lit. or fig.)* Krankheit, *die;* **suffer from a ~:** an einer Krankheit leiden; **the spreading of ~:** die Ausbreitung von Krankheiten

diseased [dɪˈziːzd] *adj. (lit. or fig.)* krank

disembark [dɪsɪmˈbɑːk] **1.** *v. t.* ausschiffen. **2.** *v. i.* von Bord gehen; **wait a long time to ~:** lange auf die Ausschiffung warten

disembarkation [dɪsembɑːˈkeɪʃn] *n. (of troops)* Landung, *die; (of cargo, passengers)* Ausschiffung, *die*

disembodied [dɪsɪmˈbɒdɪd] *adj.* körperlos ‹*Seele, Geist*›; geisterhaft ‹*Stimme*›

disembowel [dɪsɪmˈbaʊəl] *v. t., (Brit.)* **-ll-** die Eingeweide herausnehmen (+ *Dat.*); *(by violence)* den Bauch aufschlitzen (+ *Dat.*)

disenchant [dɪsɪnˈtʃɑːnt] *v. t.* **a)** entzaubern *(geh.)*; **b)** *(disillusion)* ernüchtern; **he became ~ed with sb./sth.** jmd./etw. hat ihn desillusioniert

disenchantment [dɪsɪnˈtʃɑːntmənt] *n. see* **disenchant:** Entzauberung, *die (geh.)*; Ernüchterung, *die* **(with** in bezug auf)

disenfranchise [dɪsɪnˈfræntʃaɪz] *see* **disfranchise**

disengage [dɪsɪnˈgeɪdʒ] **1.** *v. t.* **a)** lösen **(from** aus, von); **~ one's hand** seine Hand frei bekommen; **b)** *(Mech.)* **~ the clutch** auskuppeln; **~ the gear** den Gang herausnehmen; **c)** *(Mil.)* abziehen. **2.** *v. i.* **a)** sich zurückziehen **(from** aus); ‹*Kupplung:*› sich lösen; **b)** *(Mil.)* sich zurückziehen **(from** aus); **c)** *(Fencing)* sich [aus der gegnerischen Bindung] lösen

disengaged [dɪsɪnˈgeɪdʒd] *adj.* **a)** frei; **b)** *(uncommitted)* nicht [politisch] engagiert

disentangle [dɪsɪnˈtæŋgl] **1.** *v. t.* **a)** *(extricate)* befreien **(from** aus); *(fig.)* herauslösen **(from** aus); **b)** *(unravel)* entwirren; *(fig.)* ordnen ‹*Gedanken*›; entwirren ‹*Handlung, Hinweise*›. **2.** *v. i.* sich entwirren

disentanglement [dɪsɪnˈtæŋglmənt] *n. (lit. or fig.)* Entwirrung, *die*

disentomb [dɪsɪnˈtuːm] *v. t.* ausgraben; freilegen

disequilibrium [dɪsiːkwɪˈlɪbrɪəm] *n., no pl.* gestörtes Gleichgewicht; Ungleichgewicht, *das*

disestablishment [dɪsɪˈstæblɪʃmənt] *n.* **the ~ of the Church** die Trennung der Kirche vom Staat

disfavour *(Brit.; Amer.:* **disfavor**) [dɪsˈfeɪvə(r)] **1.** *n.* **a)** *(displeasure, disapproval)* Mißfallen, *das; (condition of being out of favour)* Ungnade, *die;* **incur sb.'s ~:** jmds. Unwillen erregen; **b)** *(disadvantage)* **in sb.'s ~:** zu jmds. Ungunsten. **2.** *v. t.* mißbilligen

disfigure [dɪsˈfɪgə(r)] *v. t.* entstellen; verunstalten ‹*Landschaft*›

disfigurement [dɪsˈfɪgəmənt] *n.* Entstellung, *die; (of countryside)* Verunstaltung, *die*

disfranchise [dɪsˈfræntʃaɪz] *v. t.* die Privilegien entziehen (+ *Dat.*); *(of right to vote)* das Wahlrecht entziehen (+ *Dat.*)

disgorge [dɪsˈgɔːdʒ] *v. t.* **a)** ausspucken; ausspeien *(geh.)*; *(fig.)* ausspeien *(geh.)*; herausgeben ‹*Gefangene, Beute, Eigentum*›; **b)** *(discharge)* ergießen ‹*Wasser*›

disgrace [dɪsˈgreɪs] **1.** *n., no pl.* **a)** *(ignominy)* Schande, *die;* Schmach, *die (geh. emotional); (deep disfavour)* Ungnade, *die;* **bring ~ on sb./sth.** Schande über jmdn./etw. bringen; **send sb. home in ~:** jmdn. wegen ungebührlichen Verhaltens nach Hause schicken; **he had to resign in ~:** er mußte unehrenhaft zurücktreten; **b) be a ~ [to sb./sth.]** [für jmdn./etw.] eine Schande sein. **2.** *v. t.* **a)** *(bring shame on)* ‹*Person:*› Schande machen (+ *Dat.*); ‹*Person, Handlung:*› Schande bringen über (+ *Akk.*); **~ oneself** sich blamieren; ‹*Kind, Hund:*› sich danebenbenehmen *(ugs.)*; **b) be ~d** *(be put out of favour)* in Ungnade fallen; *(be held up to reproach)* bloßgestellt werden

disgraceful [dɪsˈgreɪsfl] *adj.* erbärmlich; miserabel ‹*Handschrift*›; skandalös ‹*Benehmen, Enthüllung, Bedingungen, Verstoß, Behandlung, Tat*›; **what a ~ thing to say/do!** wie kann man nur so etwas Schändliches sagen/tun!; **it's [absolutely** *or* **really** *or* **quite] ~:** es ist [wirklich] ein Skandal; **how ~!** was für eine Schande!; **you look ~:** du siehst ja furchtbar aus! *(ugs.)*

disgracefully [dɪsˈgreɪsfəlɪ] *adv.* erbärmlich; schändlich ‹*verraten, betrügen, behandeln*›; **behave ~:** sich schändlich *od. (geh.)* schimpflich benehmen; **arrive ~ late** *(coll.)* furchtbar spät eintreffen; **she neglected her duties quite ~:** sie vernachlässigte ihre Pflichten geradezu sträflich

disgruntled [dɪsˈgrʌntld] *adj.* verstimmt; **be in a ~ mood** verstimmt sein

disguise [dɪsˈgaɪz] **1.** *v. t.* **a)** verkleiden ‹*Person*›; verstellen ‹*Stimme*›; tarnen ‹*Gegenstand*›; **~ oneself** sich verkleiden; **he ~d himself with a false beard** er tarnte sich mit einem falschen Bart; **b)** *(misrepresent)* verschleiern; **there is no disguising the fact that ...:** es läßt sich nicht verheimlichen, daß ...; **a ~d tax** eine versteckte Steuer; **c)** *(conceal)* verbergen; hinter dem Berg halten mit ‹*Ansichten, Mißbilligung*›; **the herbs ~ the taste of the meat** die Kräuter überdecken den Geschmack des Fleisches. **2.** *n.* Verkleidung, *die; (fig.)* Maske, *die;* **adopt/wear a ~:** eine Verkleidung wählen/verkleidet sein; **wear sth. as a ~:** etw. zur Tarnung tragen; **in the ~ of** verkleidet als; **in ~:** verkleidet; **without any attempt at ~:** ohne irgendeinen Versuch, sich zu tarnen; *see also* **blessing c**

disgust [dɪsˈgʌst] **1.** *n. (nausea)* Ekel, *der* **(at** vor + *Dat.*); *(revulsion)* Abscheu, *der* **(at** vor + *Dat.*); *(indignation)* Empörung, *die* **(at** über + *Akk.*); **in/with ~:** angewidert; *(with indignation)* empört. **2.** *v. t.* anwidern; *(fill with nausea)* anwidern; ekeln; *(fill with indignation)* empören

disgusted [dɪsˈgʌstɪd] *adj.* angewidert; *(nauseated)* angewidert; angeekelt; *(indig-*

nant) empört; **feel ~ at sth./with sb.** angewidert/angeekelt von etw./empört über etw./jmdn. sein
disgustedly [dɪs'gʌstɪdlɪ] *adv.* voller Ekel; angewidert; *(with nausea)* angewidert, angeekelt; *(indignantly)* empört
disgusting [dɪs'gʌstɪŋ] *adj.* widerlich; widerwärtig; *(nauseating also)* ekelhaft; miserabel *(ugs. abwertend)* ⟨*Prüfungsergebnis, schulische Leistungen*⟩; **don't be ~:** sei nicht so geschmacklos
disgustingly [dɪs'gʌstɪŋlɪ] *adv.* widerlich; *(causing nausea also)* ekelhaft; unmöglich *(ugs.)* ⟨*sich kleiden*⟩; *(iron.)* unverschämt ⟨*gut aussehen, reich*⟩
dish [dɪʃ] **1.** *n.* **a)** *(for food)* Schale, *die; (flatter)* Platte, *die; (deeper)* Schüssel, *die;* **b)** *in pl. (crockery)* Geschirr, *das;* **wash** *or (coll.)* **do the ~es** Geschirr spülen; abwaschen; **c)** *(type of food)* Gericht, *das;* **it is [not] my/everybody's ~** *(fig. sl.)* darauf steh' ich [nicht]/darauf steht [nicht] jeder *(ugs.);* **d)** *(coll.: person) (woman, girl)* klasse Frau *(ugs.); (man)* klasse Typ *(ugs.);* **be quite a ~:** eine Wucht sein *(salopp);* **e)** *(receptacle)* Schale, *die; (concavity)* Mulde, *die;* **f)** *(Radio, Telev.)* Parabolantenne, *die.* **2.** *v. t.* **a)** anrichten ⟨*Essen*⟩; **b)** *(coll.) (outmanœuvre)* austricksen *(ugs.); (ruin)* kleinkriegen *(ugs.);* zunichte machen ⟨*Hoffnung, Chancen*⟩
~ 'out *v. t.* **a)** austeilen ⟨*Essen*⟩; **b)** *(coll.: distribute)* verteilen
~ 'up *v. t.* auftragen, servieren ⟨*Essen*⟩; *(fig.)* auftischen *(ugs. abwertend)*
dishabille [dɪsə'bi:l] *see* **déshabillé**
disharmony [dɪs'hɑ:mənɪ] *n. (lit. or fig.)* Disharmonie, *die*
dish: ~cloth *n.* **a)** *(for washing)* Abwaschlappen, *der;* Spültuch, *das;* **b)** *(Brit.: for drying)* Geschirrtuch, *das;* **~-cover** *n.* Cloche, *die (Gastr.); (against flies etc.)* Fliegenglocke, *die*
dishearten [dɪs'hɑ:tn] *v. t.* entmutigen; **be ~ed** den Mut verlieren/verloren haben
disheartening [dɪs'hɑ:tənɪŋ] *adj.,* **dishearteningly** [dɪs'hɑ:tənɪŋlɪ] *adv.* entmutigend
dished [dɪʃt] *adj.* konkav
dishevelled *(Amer.:* **disheveled)** [dɪ'ʃevld] *adj.* unordentlich ⟨*Kleidung*⟩; zerzaust ⟨*Haar, Bart*⟩; ungepflegt ⟨*Erscheinung*⟩
'dish-mop *n.* ≈ Spülbürste, *die*
dishonest [dɪ'sɒnɪst] *adj.* unehrlich ⟨*Person*⟩; unaufrichtig ⟨*Person, Antwort*⟩; unlauter *(geh.)* ⟨*Geschäftsgebaren, Vorhaben*⟩; unredlich ⟨*Geschäftsmann*⟩; unreell ⟨*Geschäft, Gewinn*⟩; **~ goings-on** undurchsichtige Vorgänge; **be ~ with sb.** unehrlich *od.* unaufrichtig gegen jmdn. sein
dishonestly [dɪ'sɒnɪstlɪ] *adv.* unehrlich; unaufrichtig; unlauter *(geh.)* ⟨*handeln*⟩; unredlich ⟨*sich verhalten*⟩
dishonesty [dɪ'sɒnɪstɪ] *n.* Unehrlichkeit, *die;* Unaufrichtigkeit, *die; (of methods)* Unlauterkeit, *die (geh.)*
dishonor *etc. (Amer.) see* **dishonour** *etc.*
dishonour [dɪ'sɒnə(r)] **1.** *n.* Schande, *die;* **bring ~ [up]on the nation/sb.** Schande über die Nation/jmdn. bringen. **2.** *v. t.* **a)** beleidigen; **b)** *(disgrace)* entehren; **~ one's family** seiner Familie *(Dat.)* Schande machen; **c)** *(Commerc.)* nicht honorieren ⟨*Wechsel*⟩; nicht einlösen, zurückgehen lassen ⟨*Scheck*⟩; nicht bezahlen ⟨*Schulden*⟩
dishonourable [dɪ'sɒnərəbl] *adj.* unehrenhaft
dishonourably [dɪ'sɒnərəblɪ] *adv.* in unehrenhafter Weise
dish: ~-rack *n.* Abtropfgestell, *das; (in dishwasher)* Geschirrwagen, *der;* **~-towel** *n.* Geschirrtuch, *das;* **~washer** *n.* **a)** Geschirrspülmaschine, *die;* Geschirrspüler, *der (ugs.);* **b)** *(person)* Geschirrspüler, *der/*-spülerin, *die;* **~-washing** *n.* Geschirrspülen, *das;* **~-washing machine** *see* **~washer a;** **~-water** *n.* Abwaschwasser, *das;* Spülwasser, *das;* **this tea's like ~-water** der Tee schmeckt wie Spülwasser
dishy ['dɪʃɪ] *adj. (Brit. sl.)* klasse *(ugs.)*
disillusion [dɪsɪ'lju:ʒn, dɪsɪ'lu:ʒn] **1.** *n., no pl.* Desillusion, *die* **(with** über + *Akk.*). **2.** *v. t.* ernüchtern; **I don't want to ~ you, but ...:** ich möchte dir nicht deine Illusionen rauben, aber ...
disillusioned [dɪsɪ'lju:ʒnd, dɪsɪ'lu:ʒnd] *adj.* desillusioniert; **become ~ with sth.** seine Illusionen über etw. *(Akk.)* verlieren
disillusionment [dɪsɪ'lju:ʒnmənt, dɪsɪ'lu:ʒnmənt] *n.* Desillusionierung, *die*
disincentive [dɪsɪn'sentɪv] *n.* Hemmnis, *das;* **act as** *or* **be a ~ to sb. to do sth.** jmdn. davon abhalten, etw. zu tun
disinclination [dɪsɪnklɪ'neɪʃn] *n.* Abneigung, *die* **(for, to** gegen)
disincline [dɪsɪn'klaɪn] *v. t.* abgeneigt machen **(for, to** gegen)
disinclined [dɪsɪn'klaɪnd] *adj.* abgeneigt
disinfect [dɪsɪn'fekt] *v. t.* desinfizieren
disinfectant [dɪsɪn'fektənt] **1.** *adj.* desinfizierend. **2.** *n.* Desinfektionsmittel, *das*
disinfection [dɪsɪn'fekʃn] *n.* Desinfektion, *die;* Desinfizierung, *die*
disinfest [dɪsɪn'fest] *v. t.* von Ungeziefer befreien; entwesen *(fachspr.)*
disinformation [dɪsɪnfə'meɪʃn] *n.* Desinformation, *die*
disingenuous [dɪsɪn'dʒenjʊəs] *adj.* unaufrichtig
disingenuously [dɪsɪn'dʒenjʊəslɪ] *adv.* in unaufrichtiger Weise
disinherit [dɪsɪn'herɪt] *v. t.* enterben; *(fig.)* entrechten
disinheritance [dɪsɪn'herɪtəns] *n.* Enterbung, *die*
disintegrate [dɪs'ɪntɪgreɪt] **1.** *v. i.* **a)** zerfallen; ⟨*Straßenbelag:*⟩ aufbrechen; ⟨*Gestein:*⟩ zerbröckeln, zerfallen; *(shatter suddenly)* zerbersten; *(fig.)* sich auflösen; **b)** *(Phys.)* zerfallen. **2.** *v. t.* **a)** zerstören; *(by weathering also)* zerfressen; *(by exploding)* sprengen; *(fig.)* auflösen; **b)** *(Phys.)* spalten
disintegration [dɪsɪntɪ'greɪʃn] *n.* **a)** Zerfall, *der; (of road surface)* Aufbrechen, *das; (fig.)* Auflösung, *die; (of personality)* [allmähliche] Zerstörung; *(of hopes)* Zusammenbruch, *der;* **b)** *(Phys.)* Zerfall, *der*
disinter [dɪsɪn'tɜ:(r)] *v. t.,* **-rr-: a)** ausgraben; **b)** *(fig.)* ans Licht bringen
disinterest [dɪs'ɪntrəst, dɪs'ɪntrɪst] *see* **disinterestedness**
disinterested [dɪs'ɪntrəstɪd, dɪs'ɪntrɪstɪd] *adj.* **a)** *(impartial)* unvoreingenommen; unparteiisch; *(free from selfish motive)* selbstlos; uneigennützig; **b)** *(coll.: uninterested)* desinteressiert
disinterestedly [dɪs'ɪntrəstɪdlɪ, dɪs'ɪntrɪstɪdlɪ] *adv. see* **disinterested:** unvoreingenommen; unparteiisch; selbstlos; uneigennützig; desinteressiert
disinterestedness [dɪs'ɪntrəstɪdnɪs, dɪs'ɪntrɪstɪdnɪs] *n., no pl. see* **disinterested:** Unvoreingenommenheit, *die;* Selbstlosigkeit, *die;* Uneigennützigkeit, *die;* Desinteresse, *das* **(in** an + *Dat.*)
disinterment [dɪsɪn'tɜ:mənt] *n.* **a)** Ausgrabung, *die;* **b)** *(fig.)* Ausgraben, *das*
disinvestment [dɪsɪn'vestmənt] *n. (Econ.)* Desinvestition, *die*
disjoin [dɪs'dʒɔɪn] *v. t.* [voneinander] trennen
disjointed [dɪs'dʒɔɪntɪd] *adj.,* **disjointedly** [dɪs'dʒɔɪntɪdlɪ] *adv.* unzusammenhängend; zusammenhanglos
disjunctive [dɪs'dʒʌŋktɪv] *adj.* **a)** trennend; **b)** *(Ling., Logic)* disjunktiv
disk *see* **disc**
diskette [dɪs'ket] *n. (Computing)* Diskette, *die*
dislike [dɪs'laɪk] **1.** *v. t.* nicht mögen; *(a little stronger)* nicht leiden können; **~ sb./sth. greatly** *or* **intensely** jmdn./etw. ganz und gar nicht leiden können; **I don't ~ it** ich finde es nicht schlecht; **~ doing sth.** es nicht mögen/nicht leiden können, etw. zu tun; etw. ungern tun; **I ~ your having to stay late** ich sehe es nicht gern, daß du lange bleiben mußt. **2.** *n.* **a)** *no pl.* Abneigung, *die* **(of, for** gegen); **she took an instant ~ to him/the house** sie empfand sofort eine Abneigung gegen ihn/das Haus; **have a ~ for sb./sth.** eine Abneigung gegen jmdn./etw. haben *od. (geh.)* hegen; **feel ~ for sb./sth.** jmdn./etw. nicht leiden können; **b)** *(object)* **one of my greatest ~s is ...:** zu den Dingen, die ich am wenigsten leiden kann, gehört ...
dislocate ['dɪsləkeɪt] *v. t.* **a)** *(Med.)* luxieren *(fachspr.);* ausrenken; auskugeln ⟨*Schulter, Hüfte*⟩; **b)** *(fig.)* beeinträchtigen
dislocation [dɪslə'keɪʃn] *n.* **a)** *(Med.)* Luxation, *die (fachspr.);* Ausrenkung, *die; (of shoulder, hip)* Auskugelung, *die;* **b)** *(fig.)* Beeinträchtigung, *die*
dislodge [dɪs'lɒdʒ] *v. t.* entfernen **(from** aus); *(detach)* lösen **(from** von); *(Mil.: drive out)* vertreiben **(from** aus)
disloyal [dɪs'lɔɪəl] *adj.* illoyal **(to** gegenüber); treulos ⟨*Freund, Ehepartner*⟩; **be ~:** nicht loyal sein
disloyalty [dɪs'lɔɪəltɪ] *n.* Illoyalität, *die* **(to** gegenüber); *(to spouse, friend)* Treulosigkeit, *die*
dismal ['dɪzməl] *adj.* trist; düster; trostlos ⟨*Landschaft, Ort*⟩; bedrückend ⟨*Niedergang*⟩; *(coll.: feeble)* kläglich ⟨*Zustand, Leistung, Versuch*⟩; **in a ~ manner/tone of voice** düster/mit bedrückter Stimme; **a ~ failure** ein völliger Reinfall *(ugs.)*
dismally ['dɪzməlɪ] *adv.* trostlos; trübe ⟨*beleuchtet*⟩; kläglich ⟨*fehlschlagen, jammern*⟩
dismantle [dɪs'mæntl] *v. t.* zerlegen; demontieren; *(fig.)* demontieren; abbauen ⟨*Schuppen, Gerüst*⟩; *(permanently)* abreißen, niederreißen ⟨*Gebäude*⟩; schleifen ⟨*Befestigungsanlage*⟩; abwracken ⟨*Schiff*⟩
dismast [dɪs'mɑ:st] *v. t. (Naut.)* entmasten
dismay [dɪs'meɪ] **1.** *v. t.* bestürzen; **he was ~ed to hear that ...:** mit Bestürzung hörte er, daß ...; **he was ~ed at the news** er war bestürzt über die Nachricht. **2.** *n.* Bestürzung, *die* **(at** über + *Akk.*); **he was filled with ~ at the news** die Nachricht erfüllte ihn mit Bestürzung; **watch in** *or* **with ~:** bestürzt zusehen
dismember [dɪs'membə(r)] *v. t.* **a)** verstümmeln; **b)** *(partition)* zersplittern
dismemberment [dɪs'membəmənt] *n.* **a)** Verstümmelung, *die;* **b)** *(partitioning)* Zersplitterung, *die*
dismiss [dɪs'mɪs] *v. t.* **a)** *(send away, ask to leave or disperse)* entlassen; auflösen, aufheben ⟨*Versammlung*⟩; **~!** *(Mil.)* weggetreten!; **b)** *(from employment)* entlassen; **c)** *(from the mind)* verwerfen; *(treat very briefly)* abtun; **d)** *(Law)* abweisen ⟨*Klage*⟩; entlassen ⟨*Geschworene*⟩; **~ with costs** kostenpflichtig abweisen; **e)** *(Cricket)* ausscheiden lassen
dismissal [dɪs'mɪsl] *n.* **a)** Entlassung, *die; (of committee, gathering, etc.)* Auflösung, *die;* Aufhebung, *die;* **she made a gesture of ~ to the servant** sie entließ den Diener mit einer Handbewegung; **b)** *(from employment)* Entlassung, *die;* **give sb. his/her ~:** jmdn. entlassen; **c)** *(from the mind)* Aufgabe, *die; (rejection)* Ablehnung, *die; (very brief treatment)* Abtun, *das;* **d)** *(Law) (of a case)* Abweisung, *die; (of jury)* Entlassung, *die;* **e)** *(Cricket)* Ausscheiden, *das*
dismissive [dɪs'mɪsɪv] *adj.* abweisend; *(disdainful)* abschätzig; **be ~ about sth.** etw. abtun *od.* nicht würdigen
dismissively [dɪs'mɪsɪvlɪ] *adv.* abweisend; *(disdainfully)* abschätzig

dismount [dɪs'maʊnt] 1. *v.i.* absteigen. 2. *v.t.* abwerfen ‹*Reiter*›
disobedience [dɪsə'bi:dɪəns] *n.* Ungehorsam, *der;* **act of ~:** ungehorsames Verhalten; Ungehorsam, *der;* **~ to orders** Nichtbefolgen der Anordnungen
disobedient [dɪsə'bi:dɪənt] *adj.* ungehorsam; **be ~ to orders/to sb.** Anordnungen nicht befolgen/jmdm. nicht gehorchen
disobediently [dɪsə'bi:dɪəntlɪ] *adv.* ungehorsam; **act/behave ~:** ungehorsam sein
disobey [dɪsə'beɪ] *v.t.* nicht gehorchen (+ *Dat.*); nicht befolgen, mißachten ‹*Befehl, Vorschrift usw.*›; übertreten ‹*Gesetz*›; *(Mil.)* den Gehorsam verweigern (+ *Dat.*)
disoblige [dɪsə'blaɪdʒ] *v.t.* **~ sb.** jmds. Wunsch nicht nachkommen
disobliging [dɪsə'blaɪdʒɪŋ] *adj.* ungefällig; **be very/most ~:** wenig/kein bißchen entgegenkommend sein
disorder [dɪs'ɔ:də(r)] 1. *n.* **a)** Unordnung, *die;* Durcheinander, *das;* **everything was in [complete] ~:** alles war ein einziges[, heilloses] Durcheinander; **the meeting broke up in ~:** die Versammlung endete in einem heillosen Durcheinander; **throw sth. into ~:** etw. in Unordnung bringen; **the marchers were thrown into ~:** die Marschierenden gerieten aus der Reihe; **the troops fled in ~:** die Soldaten flohen in ungeordneten Haufen; **leave the house in a state of ~:** das Haus in großer Unordnung hinterlassen; **b)** *(rioting, disturbance)* Unruhen *Pl.;* **c)** *(Med.)* [Funktions]störung, *die;* **suffer from a mental ~:** geisteskrank sein; **a stomach/liver ~:** ein Magen-/Leberleiden; **a blood ~:** eine Blutkrankheit. 2. *v.t.* **a)** in Unordnung bringen; durcheinanderbringen; **b)** verwirren ‹*Geist*›
disordered [dɪs'ɔ:dəd] *adj.* **a)** unordentlich; ungeordnet ‹*Wortschwall, Gedanken[gang]*›; wirr ‹*Phantasie*›; **b)** *(Med.)* gestört; angegriffen ‹*Organ*›; *(mentally unbalanced)* geistesgestört
disorderly [dɪs'ɔ:dəlɪ] *adj.* **a)** *(untidy)* unordentlich; ungeordnet ‹*Denkweise, Ansammlung*›; **b)** *(unruly)* undiszipliniert; disziplinlos; zügellos, unsolide ‹*Lebensweise*›; aufrührerisch ‹*Mob*›; **~ conduct** ungebührliches *od.* ungehöriges Benehmen
dis'orderly house *n.* *(brothel)* öffentliches Haus *(verhüll.); (gambling-den)* Spielhölle, *die (abwertend)*
disorganization [dɪsɔ:gənaɪ'zeɪʃn] *n., no pl.* Desorganisation, *die; (muddle)* Durcheinander, *das;* **cause ~ of sth.** etw. durcheinanderbringen
disorganize [dɪs'ɔ:gənaɪz] *v.t.* durcheinanderbringen; desorganisieren *(geh.)*
disorganized [dɪs'ɔ:gənaɪzd] *adj.* chaotisch; unsystematisch, chaotisch ‹*Arbeiter, Person*›; **he's completely ~:** er geht völlig unsystematisch vor
disorient [dɪs'ɔ:rɪənt, dɪs'ɒrɪənt], **disorientate** [dɪs'ɒrɪənteɪt, dɪs'ɔ:rɪənteɪt] *v.t.* die Orientierung nehmen (+ *Dat.*); *(fig.)* verwirren
disorientated [dɪs'ɒrɪənteɪtɪd, dɪs'ɔ:rɪənteɪtɪd] *adj.* verwirrt; desorientiert
disorientation [dɪsɒrɪən'teɪʃn, dɪsɔ:rɪən'teɪʃn] *n.* *(lit. or fig.)* Verwirrung, *die;* Desorientiertheit, *die*
disoriented [dɪs'ɔ:rɪəntɪd, dɪs'ɒrɪəntɪd] *see* **disorientated**
disown [dɪs'əʊn] *v.t.* **a)** *(repudiate)* verleugnen; **if you do that I'll ~ you** *(joc.)* wenn du das tust, sind wir geschiedene Leute; **b)** *(renounce allegiance to)* nicht anerkennen
disparage [dɪ'spærɪdʒ] *v.t.* **a)** herabsetzen; **b)** *(discredit)* in Verruf bringen; diskreditieren *(geh.)*
disparagement [dɪ'spærɪdʒmənt] *n.* Herabsetzung, *die;* **speak with ~ of sth./sb.** sich verächtlich über etw./jmdn. äußern
disparaging [dɪ'spærɪdʒɪŋ] *adj.* abschätzig
disparagingly [dɪ'spærɪdʒɪŋlɪ] *adv.* abschätzig
disparate ['dɪspərət] *adj.* [völlig] verschieden; disparat *(geh.)*
disparity [dɪ'spærɪtɪ] *n.* Disparität, *die (geh.); (difference also)* Unterschied, *der; (lack of parity)* Ungleichheit, *die*
dispassionate [dɪ'spæʃənət] *adj.* leidenschaftslos; *(impartial)* unvoreingenommen
dispassionately [dɪ'spæʃənətlɪ] *adv.* leidenschaftslos; *(impartially)* unvoreingenommen
dispatch [dɪ'spætʃ] 1. *v.t.* **a)** *(send off)* schicken; **~ sb. [to do sth.]** jmdn. entsenden *(geh.)* [um etw. zu tun]; **b)** *(get through)* erledigen; abschließen ‹*Geschäft*›; erfüllen ‹*Pflicht*›; **c)** *(kill)* töten; **d)** *(eat)* verschlingen; verputzen *(ugs.).* 2. *n.* **a)** *(official report, Journ.)* Bericht, *der;* Depesche, *die (veralt.);* **they were mentioned in ~es** *(Mil.)* ≈ ihnen wurde förmliche Anerkennung ausgesprochen; **b)** *(sending off)* Absenden, *das; (of troops, messenger, delegation)* Entsendung, *die (geh.);* **c)** *(killing)* Tötung, *die;* **d)** *(prompt execution)* Erledigung, *die;* **e)** *(prompt efficiency)* **act with ~:** prompt handeln
dispatch: ~-box, ~-case *ns.* Aktenkoffer, *der*
dispatcher [dɪ'spætʃə(r)] *n.* Verkehrsbetriebsregler, *der*
dispatch: ~ note *n.* Versandanzeige, *die;* **~-rider** *n.* Bote, *der; (Mil.)* Meldefahrer, *der*
dispel [dɪ'spel] *v.t.,* **-ll-** vertreiben; zerstreuen ‹*Besorgnis, Befürchtung*›; verdrängen, unterdrücken ‹*Gefühl, Erinnerung, Vorahnung*›
dispensable [dɪ'spensəbl] *adj.* entbehrlich
dispensary [dɪ'spensərɪ] *n.* *(Pharm.)* Apotheke, *die; (in hospital)* [Krankenhaus]apotheke, *die*
dispensation [dɪspen'seɪʃn] *n.* **a)** *(distribution)* Verteilung, *die* (**to** an + *Akk.*); *(of grace)* Zuteilwerdenlassen, *das; (of favours)* Gewährung, *die;* **~ of justice** Rechtsprechung, *die;* **b)** *(management)* Verfügung, *die; (Theol.: by Providence)* **divine ~:** göttliche Fügung; **c)** *(exemption)* Sonderregelung, *die;* **~ from the examination** Erlaß der Prüfung; **d)** *(Eccl.)* Dispens, *die*
dispense [dɪ'spens] 1. *v.i.* **~ with** verzichten auf (+ *Akk.*); *(set aside)* außer acht lassen; *(do away with)* überflüssig machen. 2. *v.t.* **a)** *(distribute, administer)* verteilen (**to** an + *Akk.*); gewähren ‹*Gastfreundschaft*›; zuteil werden lassen ‹*Gnade*›; spenden ‹*Sakrament*›; **~ justice** Recht sprechen; **the machine ~s hot drinks** der Automat gibt heiße Getränke aus; **the device ~s liquid soap/toilet-paper** aus der Vorrichtung kommt flüssige Seife/Toilettenpapier; **b)** *(Pharm.)* dispensieren *(fachspr.);* bereiten und abgeben
dispenser [dɪ'spensə(r)] *n.* **a)** *(Pharm.)* Apotheker, *der*/Apothekerin, *die;* **b)** *(vending-machine)* Automat, *der; (container)* Spender, *der*
dispensing 'chemist *n.* Apotheker, *der*/Apothekerin, *die*
dispersal [dɪ'spɜ:sl] *n.* **a)** *(scattering)* Zerstreuung, *die; (diffusion)* Ausbreitung, *die; (of mist, oil slick)* Auflösung, *die; (Mil.)* Auseinanderziehen, *das;* **b)** *(Bot., Zool.)* Verbreitung, *die;* **c)** *(Phys.)* Dispersion, *die*
disperse [dɪ'spɜ:s] 1. *v.t.* **a)** *(scatter)* zerstreuen; *(dispel)* auflösen ‹*Dunst, Öl*›; vertreiben ‹*Wolken, Gase*›; *(Mil.)* auseinanderziehen; **b)** *(Phys.)* dispergieren *(fachspr.);* verteilen; zerlegen ‹*Lichtstrahl*›. 2. *v.i.* sich zerstreuen; *(Phys.)* sich verteilen
dispersion [dɪ'spɜ:ʃn] *n.* **a)** *(scattering)* Zerstreuung, *die; (diffusion)* Ausbreitung, *die; (Mil.)* Auseinanderziehen, *das;* **b)** **D~** *(Jewish Hist.) see* **Diaspora**; **c)** *(Phys.)* Dispersion, *die; (system)* Dispersoid, *das;* **d)** *(Statistics)* Streuung, *die;* Dispersion, *die (fachspr.)*
dispirit [dɪ'spɪrɪt] *v.t.* entmutigen
dispirited [dɪ'spɪrɪtɪd] *adj.* entmutigt; mutlos ‹*Gesichtsausdruck*›; halbherzig ‹*Versuch*›
dispiritedly [dɪ'spɪrɪtɪdlɪ] *adv.* entmutigt
dispiriting [dɪ'spɪrɪtɪŋ] *adj.* entmutigend
displace [dɪs'pleɪs] *v.t.* **a)** *(move from place)* verschieben; *(force to flee)* vertreiben; *(remove from office)* entlassen; **b)** *(supplant)* ersetzen; *(crowd out)* verdrängen; **c)** *(Phys.: take the place of)* verdrängen
displaced 'person *n.* Vertriebene, *der/die*
displacement [dɪs'pleɪsmənt] *n.* **a)** *(moving)* Verschiebung, *die; (removal from office)* Entlassung, *die;* **b)** *(supplanting)* Ersetzung, *die;* **c)** *(Phys.: [amount] taking the place of sth.)* Verdrängung, *die;* **d)** *(Naut.: weight displaced)* [Wasser]verdrängung, *die;* **e)** *(Psych.)* Verschiebung, *die;* **f)** *(Motor Veh.)* Hubraum, *der*
display [dɪ'spleɪ] 1. *v.t.* **a)** tragen ‹*Abzeichen*›; vorzeigen ‹*Fahrkarte, Einladung*›; aufstellen ‹*Trophäe*›; *(to public view)* ausstellen; *(on notice-board)* aushängen; *(standing)* aufstellen ‹*Schild*›; *(attached)* aufhängen ‹*Schild, Fahne*›; *(make manifest)* zeigen; *(depict)* zeigen, darstellen; **b)** *(flaunt)* zur Schau stellen; **c)** *(Commerc.)* ausstellen; **d)** *(reveal involuntarily)* zeigen; **e)** *(Printing)* hervorheben. 2. *n.* **a)** Aufstellung, *die; (to public view)* Ausstellung, *die; (manifestation)* Demonstration, *die;* **a ~ of ill-will/courage** eine Demonstration von jmds. Übelwollen/Mut; **b)** *(exhibition)* Ausstellung, *die; (Commerc.)* Auslage, *die;* Display, *das (Werbespr.);* **a military ~:** eine öffentliche militärische Veranstaltung; **a fashion ~:** eine Modenschau; **a ~ of flowers** ein Blumenarrangement; **an air ~:** eine Flugschau; **be on ~:** ausgestellt werden; **[be] for ~:** zur Ansicht [sein]; **put a house on ~:** ein Haus als Musterhaus herrichten; **c)** *(ostentatious show)* Zurschaustellung, *die;* **make a ~ of one's knowledge/affection** sein Wissen/seine Gefühle zur Schau stellen; **d)** *(Communications)* optische Darstellung; *(on radar screen)* Schirmbilddarstellung, *die; (device)* Display, *das;* **e)** *(Printing)* Hervorhebung, *die;* **~ advertising** [größere] Zeitungsanzeige; **f)** *(Ornith.)* Imponiergehabe, *das; (courtship ~)* Balzverhalten, *das*
display: ~ cabinet, ~ case *see* ²**case 1 d**; **~ window** *n.* Schaufenster, *das*
displease [dɪs'pli:z] *v.t.* **a)** *(earn disapproval of)* **~ sb./the authorities** jmds. Mißfallen/das Mißfallen der Behörden erregen; **b)** *(annoy)* verärgern; **be ~d [with sb./at sth.]** [über jmdn./etw.] verärgert sein; **she was most ~d to see that ...:** sie war sehr ärgerlich, als sie sah, daß ...
displeasing [dɪs'pli:zɪŋ] *adj.* unangenehm; unerfreulich ‹*Anblick, Aussicht*›; unschön ‹*Akzent*›; **be ~ to sb./to the eye/ear** jmdm. mißfallen/keine Freude für das Auge/das Ohr sein
displeasure [dɪs'pleʒə(r)] *n., no pl.* Mißfallen, *das* (**at** über + *Akk.*); **arouse/cause ~:** Mißfallen erregen
disport [dɪ'spɔ:t] *v. refl. & i. (literary)* sich vergnügen
disposable [dɪ'spəʊzəbl] 1. *adj.* **a)** *(to be thrown away after use)* Wegwerf-; **~ bottle/container/syringe** Einwegflasche/-behälter/-spritze; **be ~:** nach Gebrauch weggeworfen werden; **b)** *(available)* verfügbar; *(Finance also)* disponibel *(fachspr.).* 2. *n.* Wegwerfartikel, *der*
disposable: ~ 'assets *n. pl. (Finance)* frei verfügbares *od.* disponibles Vermögen; **~ 'income** *n. (Finance)* verfügbares Einkommen
disposal [dɪ'spəʊzl] *n.* **a)** *(getting rid of, kill-*

ing) Beseitigung, *die; (of waste)* Entsorgung, *die;* ~ **of sewage** Abwasserbeseitigung, *die;* **b)** *(putting away)* Forträumen, *das;* **c)** *(eating up)* Aufessen, *das;* **d)** *(settling)* Erledigung, *die; (of argument)* Beilegung, *die;* **e)** *(treating)* Abhandlung, *die;* **f)** *(bestowal)* Übertragung, *die* **(to** auf + *Akk.*); **g)** *(sale)* Veräußerung, *die;* **h)** *(control)* Verfügung, *die;* **place** *or* **put sth./sb. at sb.'s [complete]** ~: jmdm. etw./jmdn. [ganz] zur Verfügung stellen; **have sth./sb. at one's** ~: etw./jmdn. zur Verfügung haben; **be at sb.'s** ~: jmdm. zur Verfügung *od.* zu jmds. Verfügung stehen; **i)** *see* **disposition a**

dispose [dɪ'spəʊz] **1.** *v. t.* **a)** *(make inclined)* ~ **sb. to sth.** jmdn. zu etw. veranlassen; ~ **sb. to do sth.** jmdn. dazu veranlassen, etw. zu tun; **b)** *(arrange)* anordnen; *(Mil.)* aufstellen ⟨*Truppen*⟩. **2.** *v. i.* *(determine course of events)* entscheiden; Entscheidungen treffen; **man proposes, God ~s** *(prov.)* der Mensch denkt, Gott lenkt *(Spr.)*

~ **of** *v. t.* **a)** *(do as one wishes with)* ~ **of sth./sb.** über etw./jmdn. frei verfügen; **b)** *(kill, get rid of)* beseitigen ⟨*Rivalen, Leiche, Abfall*⟩; erlegen, töten ⟨*Gegner, Drachen*⟩; **she ~d of the tea-leaves down the sink** sie hat die Teeblätter in den Ausguß getan *od.* den Ausguß hinuntergespült; **c)** *(put away)* wegräumen; **d)** *(eat up)* aufessen; verputzen *(ugs.)*; **e)** *(settle, finish)* erledigen; ~ **of the business** das Geschäftliche erledigen *od.* regeln; **f)** *(disprove)* widerlegen

disposed [dɪ'spəʊzd] *adj.* **be ~ to sth.** zu etw. neigen; **be ~ to do sth.** dazu neigen, etw. zu tun; **be ~ to anger** leicht zornig werden; **I'm not ~/don't feel ~ to help that lazy fellow** ich bin nicht geneigt/fühle mich nicht veranlaßt, diesem Faulpelz zu helfen; **feel ~ to make a complaint** meinen, daß man sich beschweren muß; **be well/ill ~ towards sb.** jmdm. wohl/übel gesinnt sein; **be well/ill ~ towards sth.** einer Sache *(Dat.)* positiv/ablehnend gegenüberstehen

disposition [dɪspə'zɪʃn] *n.* **a)** *(arrangement; also Mil.: attack plan)* Aufstellung, *die; (of guards etc.)* Aufstellung, *die;* Postierung, *die; (of seating, figures)* Anordnung, *die;* ~ **of troops** Truppenaufstellung, *die;* **b)** *in pl. (preparations; also Mil.)* Vorbereitungen *Pl.;* **c)** *(ordinance of Providence, fate, or God)* Fügung, *die;* **d)** *(temperament)* Veranlagung, *die;* Disposition, *die;* **his boastful** ~: seine prahlerische Art; **she has a/is of a rather irritable** ~: sie ist ziemlich reizbar; **e)** *(inclination)* Hang, *der;* Neigung, *die* **(towards** zu); **have a ~ to do sth./to[wards] sth.** dazu neigen, etw. zu tun/zu etw. neigen

dispossess [dɪspə'zes] *v. t.* **a)** *(oust)* verdrängen; entthronen ⟨*Monarchen*⟩; stürzen ⟨*Diktator*⟩; enterben ⟨*Kind*⟩; **b)** *(deprive)* ~ **sb. of sth.** jmdm. etw. entziehen; *(fig.)* jmdm. etw. rauben

disproportion [dɪsprə'pɔːʃn] *n.* Mißverhältnis, *das*

disproportionate [dɪsprə'pɔːʃənət] *adj.* **a)** *(relatively too large/small)* vom Normalen abweichend; unangemessen; **be [totally] ~ to sth.** in einem [völligen] Mißverhältnis *od.* in [gar] keinem Verhältnis zu etw. stehen; **b)** *(lacking proportion)* unproportioniert

disproportionately [dɪsprə'pɔːʃənətlɪ] *adv.* unverhältnismäßig

disprove [dɪs'pruːv] *v. t.* widerlegen; ~ **sb.'s innocence** jmds. Schuld beweisen

disputable [dɪ'spjuːtəbl, 'dɪspjʊtəbl] *adj.* strittig; disputabel *(geh.)*

disputant [dɪ'spjuːtənt] *n.* Disputant, *der/*Disputantin, *die*

disputation [dɪspjʊ'teɪʃn] *n.* **a)** *no pl. (argument)* Meinungsverschiedenheiten *Pl.;* Streit, *der;* **b)** *(arch.: academic debate)* Disputation, *die*

disputatious [dɪspjʊ'teɪʃəs] *adj.* streitlustig; streitbar

dispute [dɪ'spjuːt] **1.** *n.* **a)** *no pl. (controversy)* Streit, *der;* **there has been some ~ as to what ...:** es hat Streit darüber gegeben, was ...; **be a matter/subject of much ~:** eine sehr umstrittene Frage/ein sehr umstrittenes Thema sein; **it is a matter of ~ whether ...:** man kann darüber streiten, ob ...; **that is [not] in ~:** darüber wird [nicht] gestritten; **be beyond ~:** außer Frage stehen; **b)** *(argument)* Streit, *der* **(over** um); **a ~ arose as to whether ...:** wegen der Frage, ob ..., kam es zum *od.* zu einem Streit; *see also* **demarcation dispute; industrial dispute. 2.** *v. t.* **a)** *(discuss)* sich streiten über (+ *Akk.*); ~ **whether .../how ...:** sich darüber streiten, ob .../wie ...; **b)** *(oppose)* bestreiten; anfechten ⟨*Rechtsanspruch*⟩; angreifen ⟨*Entscheidung*⟩; **c)** *(resist)* [an]kämpfen gegen; **d)** *(contend for)* streiten um; **they are disputing the leadership of the party** sie machen sich *(Dat.)* gegenseitig die Parteiführung streitig. **3.** *v. i. (argue)* streiten; ~ **with sb. on** *or* **about sth.** mit jmdm. über etw. *(Akk.)* diskutieren

disqualification [dɪskwɒlɪfɪ'keɪʃn] *n.* **a)** *(disqualifying)* Ausschluß, *der* **(from** von); *(Sport)* Disqualifikation, *die;* **b)** *(thing that disqualifies)* Grund zum Ausschluß

disqualify [dɪs'kwɒlɪfaɪ] *v. t.* **a)** *(debar)* ausschließen **(from** von); *(Sport)* disqualifizieren; **b)** *(make unfit)* ungeeignet machen; ~ **sb./sth. for sth.** jmdn./etw. für etw. ungeeignet machen; **c)** *(incapacitate)* verbieten (+ *Dat.*)

disquiet [dɪs'kwaɪət] *n.* Unruhe, *die*

disquisition [dɪskwɪ'zɪʃn] *n.* Abhandlung, *die; (long speech)* Vortrag, *der;* Sermon, *der (abwertend)*

disregard [dɪsrɪ'gɑːd] **1.** *v.t.* ignorieren; nicht berücksichtigen ⟨*Tatsache*⟩; ~ **a request** einer Bitte *(Dat.)* nicht nachkommen. **2.** *n.* Mißachtung, *die* **(of, for** *Gen.*); *(of wishes, feelings)* Gleichgültigkeit, *die* **(for, of** gegenüber); **he shows a total ~ of** *or* **for other people/others' feelings/wishes** ihm sind andere/die Gefühle anderer/die Wünsche anderer völlig gleichgültig

disrepair [dɪsrɪ'peə(r)] *n.* *(of building)* schlechter [baulicher] Zustand; Baufälligkeit, *die; (of furniture etc.)* schlechter Zustand; **the house is in a state of/has fallen into ~:** das Haus ist baufällig

disreputable [dɪs'repjʊtəbl] *adj.* zwielichtig; übelbeleumdet ⟨*Person*⟩; verrufen ⟨*Etablissement, Gegend*⟩; schäbig ⟨*Aussehen, Kleidung*⟩

disrepute [dɪsrɪ'pjuːt] *n.* Verruf, *der; (of area)* Verrufenheit, *die;* **bring sb./sth. into ~:** jmdn./etw. in Verruf bringen; **fall into ~:** in Verruf kommen *od.* geraten

disrespect [dɪsrɪ'spekt] *n.* Mißachtung, *die;* **show [only] ~ for sb./sth.** [überhaupt] keine Achtung *od.* keinen Respekt vor jmdm./etw. haben; **I meant no ~ [to you]** ich wollte [Ihnen gegenüber] nicht respektlos sein

disrespectful [dɪsrɪ'spektfl] *adj.* respektlos; **be ~ towards sb.** vor jmdm. keinen Respekt *od.* keine Achtung haben

disrespectfully [dɪsrɪ'spektfəlɪ] *adv.* respektlos

disrobe [dɪs'rəʊb] *(formal)* **1.** *v. t.* **a)** *(divest of robe)* das Gewand abnehmen (+ *Dat.*); **b)** *(undress)* ausziehen; entkleiden *(geh.)*. **2.** *v. i.* **a)** *(divest oneself of robe, coat, etc.)* ablegen; **b)** *(undress)* sich ausziehen; sich entkleiden *(geh.)*

disrupt [dɪs'rʌpt] *v. t.* **a)** *(break up)* zerschlagen ⟨*Regierung, Partei, System*⟩; **b)** *(interrupt)* unterbrechen; stören ⟨*Klasse, Sitzung*⟩

disruption [dɪs'rʌpʃn] *n.* **a)** *(break-up)* Zerschlagung, *die;* **b)** *(interruption)* Unterbrechung; *(of class, meeting)* Störung, *die*

disruptive [dɪs'rʌptɪv] *adj.* **a)** *(breaking up)* zerstörerisch; **b)** *(violently interrupting)* störend

dissatisfaction [dɪsætɪs'fækʃn] *n., no pl.* Unzufriedenheit, *die* **(with, at** mit)

dissatisfied [dɪ'sætɪsfaɪd] *adj.* **be ~ with sb./ with** *or* **at sth.** mit jmdm./etw. unzufrieden sein

dissect [dɪ'sekt] *v. t.* **a)** *(cut into pieces)* zerschneiden, zerlegen **(into** in + *Akk.*); **b)** *(Med., Biol.)* präparieren; sezieren, präparieren ⟨*Leiche*⟩; **c)** *(analyse)* zergliedern; sezieren

dissection [dɪ'sekʃn] *n.* **a)** *(cutting into pieces)* Zerlegung, *die;* **b)** *(Med., Biol.)* Präparation, *die; (of body)* Sektion, *die;* Präparation, *die;* **c)** *(Med.: thing cut up)* Präparat, *das;* **d)** *(analysis)* Zergliederung, *die;* Sezierung, *die*

dissemble [dɪ'sembl] **1.** *v. t.* *(disguise)* verbergen ⟨*Gefühle, Absichten*⟩; verheimlichen ⟨*Liebe*⟩. **2.** *v. i.* **a)** *(conceal one's motives)* sich verstellen; **b)** *(talk or act hypocritically)* heucheln

disseminate [dɪ'semɪneɪt] *v. t.* *(lit. or fig.)* verbreiten; verstreuen ⟨*Samen, Truppen, Flüchtlinge*⟩; *see also* **sclerosis a**

dissemination [dɪsemɪ'neɪʃn] *n.* Verbreitung, *die*

dissension [dɪ'senʃn] *n.* Dissens, *der;* Streit, *der* **(on** über + *Akk.*); **~s** Streitigkeiten; Meinungsverschiedenheiten

dissent [dɪ'sent] **1.** *v. i.* **a)** *(refuse to assent)* nicht zustimmen; ~ **from sth.** mit etw. nicht übereinstimmen; **b)** *(disagree)* ~ **from sth.** von etw. abweichen. **2.** *n.* **a)** *(difference of opinion)* Ablehnung, *die; (from majority)* Abweichung, *die;* **b)** *(refusal to accept)* Ablehnung, *die*

dissenter [dɪ'sentə(r)] *n.* Andersdenkende, *der/die;* **be a ~ from sth.** etw. ablehnen

dissentient [dɪ'senʃɪənt, dɪ'senʃənt] **1.** *adj.* andersdenkend ⟨*Person, Minderheit*⟩; abweichend ⟨*Meinung, Vorstellung, Standpunkt*⟩. **2.** *n.* Andersdenkende, *der/die*

dissertation [dɪsə'teɪʃn] *n.* *(spoken)* Vortrag, *der; (written)* Abhandlung, *die; (for bachelor's degree)* Diplomarbeit, *die; (for master's degree)* Magisterarbeit, *die; (for Ph. D.)* Dissertation, *die*

disservice [dɪ'sɜːvɪs] *n.* **do sb. a ~:** jmdm. einen schlechten Dienst erweisen

dissidence ['dɪsɪdəns] *n., no pl.* Uneinigkeit, *die;* Meinungsverschiedenheit, *die*

dissident ['dɪsɪdənt] **1.** *adj.* **a)** *(disagreeing)* andersdenkend; **a ~ person** ein Andersdenkender; **a ~ group/faction** eine Dissidentengruppe; **b)** *(dissentient)* **hold a ~ view** *or* **opinion** eine abweichende Meinung vertreten. **2.** *n.* Dissident, *der/*Dissidentin, *die;* Regimekritiker, *der/*-kritikerin, *die*

dissimilar [dɪ'sɪmɪlə(r)] *adj.* unähnlich; unterschiedlich, verschieden ⟨*Ideen, Ansichten, Geschmäcker*⟩; **be [highly] ~ to sth./sb.** [ganz] anders als etw./jmd. sein

dissimilarity [dɪsɪmɪ'lærɪtɪ] *n.* Unähnlichkeit, *die*

dissimulate [dɪ'sɪmjʊleɪt] *v. t.* verbergen ⟨*Gefühle*⟩; verheimlichen ⟨*Tatsache, Wahrheit, Ideale*⟩; verleugnen ⟨*Identität*⟩.

dissipate ['dɪsɪpeɪt] **1.** *v. t.* **a)** *(dispel)* auflösen ⟨*Nebel, Dunst*⟩; vertreiben ⟨*Angst, Sorgen, Wolken*⟩; zerstreuen ⟨*Befürchtungen, Zweifel*⟩; zunichte machen ⟨*Begeisterung, Illusion*⟩; aufhellen, heben ⟨*düstere Stimmung*⟩; **b)** *(bring to nothing)* zerstören; **c)** *(break up)* auseinandertreiben ⟨*Gruppe, Truppen, Menge*⟩; auseinanderbrechen lassen ⟨*Familie, Gemeinde, Volk*⟩; **d)** *(fritter away)* vergeuden; *(squander)* durchbringen ⟨*Vermögen, Erbschaft*⟩; verschwenden ⟨*Geld*⟩; ~ **sb.'s energy** jmdn. entkräften; jmds. Energien aufzehren. **2.** *v.i.* ⟨*Nebel, Dunst:*⟩ sich auflösen

dissipated ['dɪsɪpeɪtɪd] *adj.* ausschweifend; zügellos; ~ **morals** lockere Moral

dissipation [dɪsɪ'peɪʃn] *n.* **a)** *(scattering)* Auflösung, *die;* **b)** *(intemperate living)* Ausschweifung, *die;* **c)** *(wasteful expenditure)* Verschwendung, *die; (of fortune, inheritance)* Vergeudung, *die;* ~ **of money/energy** Geld-/Energieverschwendung, *die;* **d)** *(frivolous amusement)* Amüsement, *das*

dissociate [dɪ'səʊʃɪeɪt, dɪ'səʊsɪeɪt] *v.t.* **a)** *(disconnect)* trennen; ~ **oneself from sth./sb.** sich von etw./jmdm. distanzieren; ~ **oneself from all responsibility** alle Verantwortung ablehnen; **b)** *(Chem.)* dissoziieren

dissociation [dɪsəʊsɪ'eɪʃn] *n.* **a)** Distanzierung, *die* **(of** von); *(of ideas)* Abgrenzung, *die;* **b)** *(Chem.)* Dissoziation, *die*

dissolute ['dɪsəlu:t, 'dɪsəlju:t] *adj.* *(licentious)* ausschweifend; *(against morality)* lasterhaft; freizügig ⟨*Mode*⟩; zügellos ⟨*Benehmen*⟩

dissolutely ['dɪsəlu:tlɪ, 'dɪsəlju:tlɪ] *adv.* lasterhaft ⟨*leben*⟩; zügellos ⟨*sich benehmen*⟩

dissolution [dɪsə'lu:ʃn, dɪsə'lju:ʃn] *n.* **a)** *(disintegration)* Zersetzung, *die;* **b)** *(undoing, dispersal)* Auflösung, *die;* ~ **of a bond** Lösung einer Bindung

dissolve [dɪ'zɒlv] **1.** *v.t.* auflösen; abbrechen ⟨*Freundschaft*⟩; **acid ~s protein** Säure zersetzt Eiweiß. **2.** *v.i.* **a)** sich auflösen; *(in acid)* sich zersetzen; ⟨*Vorstellung:*⟩ vorbeigehen; ~ **into tears/laughter** in Tränen/Gelächter ausbrechen; ~ **into thin air** sich in Luft auflösen; **b)** *(Cinemat.)* überblenden. **3.** *n. (Cinemat.)* Überblendung, *die*

dissonance ['dɪsənəns] *n.* *(Mus.)* Dissonanz, *die; (fig.)* Disharmonie, *die*

dissonant ['dɪsənənt] *adj.* *(Mus.)* dissonant; *(fig.)* disharmonisch; voneinander abweichend ⟨*Meinungen*⟩

dissuade [dɪ'sweɪd] *v.t.* ~ **sb. from sth.** jmdn. von etw. abbringen; ~ **sb. from doing sth.** jmdn. davon abbringen, etw. zu tun

dissuasion [dɪ'sweɪʒn] *n.* Abbringen, *das*

distance ['dɪstəns] **1.** *n.* **a)** Entfernung, *die* **(from** zu); **their ~ from each other** die räumliche Entfernung zwischen ihnen; **keep [at] a [safe] ~ [from sb./sth.]** jmdm./einer Sache nicht zu nahe kommen; **maintain a safe ~ from the car in front** einen Sicherheitsabstand zum Vordermann einhalten; **b)** *(fig.: aloofness)* Abstand, *der;* **keep one's ~** *or* **at a ~ [from sb./sth.]** Abstand [zu jmdm./etw.] wahren; **c)** *(way to cover)* Strecke, *die;* Weg, *der; (gap)* Abstand, *der;* **accompany sb. for part of the ~:** jmdn. einen Teil des Weges *od.* ein Stück begleiten; **from this ~:** aus dieser Entfernung; von hier aus; **at a ~ of ... [from sb./sth.]** in einer Entfernung von ... [von jmdm./etw.]; **a short ~ away** ganz in der Nähe; **fall a ~ of one metre** einen Meter tief fallen; **that's no [great] ~:** das ist nicht weit; das ist keine Entfernung; **d)** *(remoter field of vision)* Ferne, *die;* **in/into the ~:** in der/die Ferne; **run off into the ~:** weit weglaufen; **the car vanished into the ~:** das Auto verschwand in der Ferne; **middle ~** *(Art)* Mittelgrund, *der;* **e)** *(distant point)* Entfernung, *die;* **at a ~/[viewed] from a ~:** von weitem; *(fig.)* oberflächlich betrachtet; **they remained at a ~:** sie blieben in einiger Entfernung stehen; **f)** *(space of time)* Abstand, *der;* **at a ~ of 20 years** aus einem Abstand von 20 Jahren; nach [einem Zeitraum von] 20 Jahren; **g)** *(Racing, Boxing)* Distanz, *die;* **go** *or* **stay the ~:** über die volle Distanz gehen; *(fig.)* [bis zum Schluß] durchhalten. *See also* **²hail 1 a; striking-distance. 2.** *v.t.* **a)** *(leave behind in race)* hinter sich *(Dat.)* lassen; **b)** *(fig.)* entfremden; ~ **oneself from sb./sth.** sich von jmdm./etw. distanzieren

distance: ~ **learning** *n.* Fernstudium, *das;* ~ **runner** *n.* Langstreckenläufer, *der*/-läuferin, *die*

distant ['dɪstənt] *adj.* **a)** *(far)* fern; **from nearby and ~ parts** von *od.* aus nah und fern; **be ~ [from sb.]** weit [von jmdm.] weg sein; **about three miles ~ from here** ungefähr drei Meilen von hier [entfernt]; **b)** *(fig.: remote)* entfernt ⟨*Ähnlichkeit, Verwandtschaft, Verwandte, Beziehung*⟩; **it's a ~ prospect/possibility** das ist Zukunftsmusik; ~ **memories/recollections** weit zurückreichende Erinnerungen; **have a ~ memory of sth.** sich an etw. *(Akk.)* vage erinnern; **c)** *(in time)* fern; **in the ~ past/future** in ferner Vergangenheit/Zukunft; **in some ~ era** in fernen Zeiten; **d)** *(cool)* reserviert, distanziert ⟨*Mensch, Haltung*⟩; **be ~ with sb.** jmdm. gegenüber reserviert sein

distantly ['dɪstəntlɪ] *adv.* **a)** *(far)* fern; **b)** *(fig.: remotely)* entfernt; ~ **resemble each other** eine entfernte Ähnlichkeit aufweisen; **c)** *(coolly)* reserviert

distaste [dɪs'teɪst] *n.* Abneigung, *die;* **[have] a ~ for sb./sth.** eine Abneigung gegen jmdn./etw. [haben]; **in ~:** aus Abneigung; **turn away in ~:** sich angewidert abwenden

distasteful [dɪs'teɪstfl] *adj.* unangenehm; **be ~ to sb.** jmdm. zuwider sein

distastefully [dɪs'teɪstfəlɪ] *adv.* geschmacklos; **look ~ at sth.** etw. angewidert betrachten

distastefulness [dɪs'teɪstflnɪs] *n., no pl.* Widerwärtigkeit, *die*

¹distemper [dɪ'stempə(r)] **1.** *n.* **a)** *(paint)* Temperafarbe, *die;* **b)** *(method)* Temperamalerei, *die.* **2.** *v.t.* mit Temperafarbe bemalen

²distemper *n. (animal disease)* Staupe, *die*

distend [dɪ'stend] *v.t.* aufblähen, auftreiben ⟨*Leib, Bauch*⟩; blähen ⟨*Nüstern*⟩; aufblasen ⟨*Backen, Ballon*⟩; erweitern ⟨*Gefäße, Darm, Ader*⟩; aufschwellen ⟨*Euter*⟩

distension [dɪ'stenʃn] *n.* Aufblähung, *die;* Auftreiben, *das; (of blood-vessel, intestine)* Erweiterung, *die*

distich ['dɪstɪk] *n. (Pros.)* Distichon, *das*

distil, *(Amer.)* **distill** [dɪ'stɪl] *v.t.,* **-ll-** *(lit. or fig.)* destillieren; brennen ⟨*Branntwein*⟩; ~ **sth. from sth.** *(fig.)* etw. aus etw. [heraus]destillieren

distillate ['dɪstɪleɪt] *n.* Destillat, *das*

distillation [dɪstɪ'leɪʃn] *n.* Destillation, *die; (fig.)* Herausdestillieren, *das; (result)* Destillat, *das*

distiller [dɪ'stɪlə(r)] *n.* Destillateur, *der;* Branntweinbrenner, *der*

distillery [dɪ'stɪlərɪ] *n.* [Branntwein]brennerei, -destillation, *die;* Destille, *die*

distinct [dɪ'stɪŋkt] *adj.* **a)** *(different)* verschieden; **keep two things ~:** zwei Dinge auseinanderhalten; **as ~ from** im Unterschied zu; **b)** *(clearly perceptible, decided)* deutlich; klar ⟨*Stimme, Sicht*⟩; ausgeprägt ⟨*Falten, Charme*⟩; **c)** *(separate)* unterschiedlich; **d)** *(particular)* bestimmt ⟨*Gegend, Gebiet*⟩

distinction [dɪ'stɪŋkʃn] *n.* **a)** *(making a difference)* Unterscheidung, *die;* **by way of ~, for ~:** zur Unterscheidung; **b)** *(difference)* Unterschied, *der;* **there is a clear ~ between A and B** es besteht ein deutlicher Unterschied zwischen A und B; **make** *or* **draw a ~ between A and B** einen Unterschied zwischen A und B machen; **draw a sharp/clear ~ between A and B** streng/klar zwischen A und B trennen; **a ~ without a difference** ein nomineller Unterschied; **c)** *(being different)* Andersartigkeit, *die;* **d)** *(distinctive feature)* besonderes Merkmal; **have the ~ of being ...:** sich dadurch auszeichnen, daß man ... ist; **e)** *(showing of special consideration)* Ehrung, *die;* **be mentioned with special ~:** besonders lobend erwähnt werden; **a mark of ~:** eine Ehre *od.* Auszeichnung; **f)** *(mark of honour)* Auszeichnung, das, *die;* **gain** *or* **get a ~ in one's examination** das Examen mit Auszeichnung bestehen; **g)** *(excellence)* hoher Rang; **a scientist of ~:** ein Wissenschaftler von Rang [und Namen]

distinctive [dɪ'stɪŋktɪv] *adj.* unverwechselbar; **be ~ of sth.** für etw. typisch *od.* charakteristisch sein

distinctively [dɪ'stɪŋktɪvlɪ] *adv.* unverwechselbar

distinctly [dɪ'stɪŋktlɪ] *adv.* **a)** *(clearly)* deutlich; **we couldn't see ~ in the mist** in dem Nebel konnten wir nichts deutlich erkennen; **b)** *(decidedly)* merklich; **be ~ aware of sth.** etw. deutlich spüren; **c)** *(markedly)* ausgeprägt

distinctness [dɪ'stɪŋktnɪs] *n., no pl.* **a)** *(difference)* Verschiedenheit, *die;* **b)** *(separateness)* Getrenntheit, *die*

distinguish [dɪ'stɪŋgwɪʃ] **1.** *v.t.* **a)** *(make out)* erkennen; *(hear)* verstehen; *(read)* lesen; entziffern; **b)** *(differentiate)* unterscheiden; *(characterize)* kennzeichnen; ~ **sth./sb. from sth./sb.** etw./jmdn. von etw./jmdm. unterscheiden; **c)** *(divide)* einteilen; ~ **things/persons into ...:** Dinge/Personen einteilen in (+ *Akk.*); **d)** *(make prominent)* ~ **oneself [by sth.]** sich [durch etw.] hervortun; ~ **oneself by doing sth.** sich dadurch hervortun, daß man etw. tut; ~ **oneself in an exam** in einem Examen glänzen *(ugs.)*; **you've really ~ed yourself, haven't you?** *(iron.)* na, da hast du vielleicht 'ne Glanzleistung vollbracht! **2.** *v.i.* unterscheiden; ~ **between persons/things** Personen/Dinge auseinanderhalten *od.* voneinander unterscheiden; **one can barely ~ between the original and the copy** man kann das Original kaum von der Kopie unterscheiden

distinguishable [dɪ'stɪŋgwɪʃəbl] *adj.* **a)** *(able to be made out)* erkennbar; *(audible)* hörbar; *(readable)* lesbar; *(decipherable)* entzifferbar; **b)** *(able to be differentiated)* erkennbar; unterscheidbar; **c)** *(able to be divided)* einteilbar

distinguished [dɪ'stɪŋgwɪʃt] *adj.* **a)** *(eminent)* namhaft, angesehen ⟨*Persönlichkeit, Schule, Firma*⟩; glänzend ⟨*Laufbahn*⟩; hervorragend ⟨*Qualität*⟩; **a ~ politician** ein Politiker von Rang [und Namen]; **b)** *(looking eminent)* vornehm, *(geh.)* distinguiert ⟨*Aussehen, Mensch*⟩; **c)** *(remarkable)* ~ **[for/by sth.]** sich [durch etw.] auszeichnend *attr.*

distort [dɪ'stɔ:t] *v.t.* **a)** verzerren ⟨*Gesicht, Stimme, Musik*⟩; verformen ⟨*Gegenstand*⟩; ⟨*Schmerz, Krankheit:*⟩ entstellen; **b)** *(misrepresent)* entstellt *od.* verzerrt wiedergeben; verdrehen ⟨*Worte, Wahrheit*⟩

distortion [dɪ'stɔ:ʃn] *n.* **a)** Verzerrung, *die; (by disease)* Entstellung, *die;* **b)** *(misrepresentation)* Entstellung, *die; (of words, truth)* Verdrehung, *die*

distract [dɪ'strækt] *v.t.* **a)** *(divert)* ablenken; ~ **sb.['s attention/concentration/mind from sth.]** jmdn. [von etw.] ablenken; **b)** *usu. in pass. (make mad or angry)* wahnsinnig machen; **grow ~ed** außer sich geraten; **~ed with joy/worry** außer sich vor Freude/Sorge; **c)** *(bewilder)* irritieren

distracted [dɪ'stræktɪd] *adj.* **a)** *(mad)* von Sinnen *nachgestellt;* außer sich *nachgestellt; (worried)* besorgt; beunruhigt; **run round like one ~:** wie von Sinnen umherlaufen; **b)** *(mentally far away)* abwesend

distraction [dɪ'strækʃn] *n.* **a)** *(frenzy)* Wahnsinn, *der;* **love sb. to ~:** jmdn. wahnsinnig *od.* bis zur Raserei lieben; **drive sb. to ~:** jmdn. wahnsinnig machen *od.* zum Wahnsinn treiben; **be worried to ~ by sth.** sich *(Dat.)* wegen etw. wahnsinnige *(ugs.)* Sorgen machen; **b)** *(confusion)* Unruhe, *die;* **c)** *(diversion)* Ablenkung, *die;* **d)** *(interruption)* Störung, *die;* **I don't want any ~s** ich möchte nicht gestört werden; **be a ~:** ein Störfaktor sein; **e)** *(amusement)* Zerstreuung, *die; (pastime)* Zeitvertreib, *der*

distrain [dɪ'streɪn] *v.i. (Law)* ~ **[upon sb./sth.]** [jmdn. *od.* bei jmdm./etw.] pfänden

distraint [dɪ'streɪnt] *n. (Law)* Pfändung, *die*

distraught [dɪ'strɔ:t] *adj.* aufgelöst (**with** vor + *Dat.*); verstört ‹*Blick, Gesichtsausdruck*›; **tearful and ~**: in Tränen aufgelöst

distress [dɪ'stres] **1.** *n.* **a)** *(anguish)* Kummer, *der* (**at** über + *Akk.*); **suffer ~**: Leid erdulden; Kummer ertragen; **be in [a state of] ~**: in Sorge sein; **cause sb. much ~**: jmdm. viel Kummer zufügen *od.* bereiten; **b)** *(suffering caused by want)* Not, *die;* Elend, *das;* **c)** *(danger)* Not, *die;* Gefahr, *die;* **an aircraft/a ship in ~**: ein Flugzeug in Not/ein Schiff in Seenot; **d)** *(exhaustion)* Erschöpfung, *die;* **e)** *(misfortune)* Unglück, *das;* Schicksalsschlag, *der;* **f)** *(Law) see* **distraint. 2.** *v. t.* **a)** *(worry)* bedrücken; bekümmern; *(cause anguish to)* ängstigen; *(upset)* nahegehen (+ *Dat.*); mitnehmen; **don't ~ yourself/try not to ~ yourself** ängstigen Sie sich nicht; **we were most ~ed** wir waren zutiefst betroffen *od.* bestürzt; **b)** *(exhaust)* erschöpfen; **c)** *(afflict)* plagen; heimsuchen

distressed [dɪ'strest] *adj.* **a)** *(anguished)* leidvoll; betrübt; *(desperate)* gequält; verzweifelt; **b)** *(impoverished)* notleidend ‹*Volkswirtschaft, Dritte Welt*›; verarmt ‹*Adel*›; armselig ‹*Verhältnisse*›

distressed 'area *n. (Brit.)* Notstandsgebiet *(mit hoher Arbeitslosigkeit)*

distressing [dɪ'stresɪŋ] *adj.* **a)** *(upsetting)* erschütternd; **be ~ to sb.** jmdn. sehr belasten; **b)** *(regrettable)* beklagenswert

di'stress signal *n.* Notsignal, *das*

distribute [dɪ'strɪbju:t] *v. t.* **a)** verteilen (**to** an + *Akk.*, **among** unter + *Akk.*); austeilen ‹*Sakramente*›; **b)** *(divide, classify)* aufteilen; **~ sth. into parts/categories/groups** etw. in Absätze/Kategorien unterteilen/in Gruppen aufteilen; **c)** *(Printing)* ablegen

distribution [dɪstrɪ'bju:ʃn] *n.* **a)** Verteilung, *die* (**to** an + *Akk.*, **among** unter + *Akk.*); *(of seeds)* [Aus]streuen, *das; (Econ.: of goods)* Distribution, *die (fachspr.);* Vertrieb, *der; (of films)* Verleih, *der;* **~ of weight** Gewichtverteilung, *die;* **the ~ of wealth** die Vermögensverteilung; **b)** *(division)* Aufteilung, *die; (classification)* Einteilung, *die*

distributive [dɪ'strɪbjʊtɪv] *(Ling.)* **1.** *n.* Distributivum, *das.* **2.** *adj. see* **pronoun**

distributor [dɪ'strɪbjʊtə(r)] *n.* **a)** Verteiler, *der*/Verteilerin, *die; (Econ.)* Vertreiber, *der; (firm)* Vertrieb, *der; (of films)* Verleih[er], *der;* **b)** *(Motor Veh.)* [Zünd]verteiler, *der*

district ['dɪstrɪkt] *n.* **a)** *(administrative area)* Bezirk, *der;* **b)** *(Brit.: part of county)* Distrikt, *der;* **c)** *(Amer.: political division)* Wahlkreis, *der;* **d)** *(tract of country, area)* Gegend, *die;* **residential ~**: Wohngebiet, *das*

district: ~ at'torney *n. (Amer. Law)* [Bezirks]staatsanwalt, *der*/-anwältin, *die;* **~ 'court** *n. (Amer. Law)* [Bundes]bezirksgericht, *das;* **~ 'heating** *n.* Fernheizung, *die;* **~ 'nurse** *n. (Brit.)* Gemeindeschwester, *die*

distrust [dɪs'trʌst] **1.** *n.* Mißtrauen, *das* (**of** gegen); **show ~ of sb.** jmdm. Mißtrauen entgegenbringen. **2.** *v. t.* mißtrauen (+ *Dat.*); *(because of bad experiences)* mit Argwohn *od.* Mißtrauen begegnen (+ *Dat.*); **I rather ~ his driving ability/his motives** ich traue seinen Fahrkünsten nicht so recht/ich bezweifle seine Motive

distrustful [dɪs'trʌstfl] *adj.* mißtrauisch; **be ~ of sb./sth.** jmdm./einer Sache nicht trauen

disturb [dɪ'stɜ:b] *v. t.* **a)** *(break calm of)* stören; aufscheuchen ‹*Vögel*›; aufhalten, behindern ‹*Fortschritt*›; **'do not ~!'** „bitte nicht stören!"; **~ing the peace** Ruhestörung, *die;* **sorry to ~ you at this late hour** entschuldigen Sie bitte die späte Störung; **if you find that the noise ~s you** wenn Sie sich durch den Lärm gestört fühlen; **~ sb.'s sleep** jmdn. im Schlaf stören; **don't let us ~ you** lassen Sie sich [durch uns] nicht stören; **they hoped they would not be ~ed** sie hofften, ungestört zu sein; **b)** *(move from settled position)* durcheinanderbringen; bewegen ‹*Blätter*›; **could I ~ you for a minute?** dürfte ich Sie einen Augenblick stören?; **c)** *(worry)* beunruhigen; *(agitate)* nervös machen; **be greatly ~ed by the fact that ...**: sehr darüber beunruhigt sein, daß ...; **don't be ~ed** beunruhigen Sie sich nicht

disturbance [dɪ'stɜ:bəns] *n.* **a)** *(interruption)* Störung, *die; (nuisance)* Belästigung, *die;* **be a ~ to sth.** etw. stören; **I don't want any ~s** ich möchte nicht gestört werden; **b)** *(agitation, tumult)* Unruhe, *die;* **social/political ~s** soziale/politische Unruhen; **racial ~[s]** Rassenunruhen

disturbed [dɪ'stɜ:bd] *adj.* **a)** *(worried)* besorgt ‹*Eindruck, Ausdruck*›; *(restless)* unruhig ‹*Nacht*›; **b)** *(Psych.)* **be [mentally] ~**: geistig gestört sein; **a ~ person** ein Geistesgestörter/eine Geistesgestörte

disunity [dɪs'ju:nɪtɪ] *n.* Uneinigkeit, *die*

disuse [dɪs'ju:s] *n.* **a)** *(discontinuance)* Außer-Gebrauch-Kommen, *das; (disappearance)* Verschwinden, *das; (abolition)* Abschaffung, *die;* **the bicycle was rusty from ~**: das Fahrrad war rostig, weil es nicht benutzt wurde; **b)** *(disused state)* **fall into ~**: außer Gebrauch kommen

disused [dɪs'ju:zd] *adj.* stillgelegt ‹*Bergwerk, Eisenbahnlinie*›; leerstehend ‹*Gebäude*›; ausrangiert *(ugs.)* ‹*Fahrzeug, Möbel*›

disyllabic [dɪsɪ'læbɪk, daɪsɪ'læbɪk] *adj. (Ling.)* zweisilbig

ditch [dɪtʃ] **1.** *n.* Graben, *der; (at side of road)* Straßengraben, *der;* **be driven to the last ~** *(fig.)* in die Enge getrieben werden; **die in a ~** *(lit. or fig.)* im Straßengraben sterben. **2.** *v. t. (sl.)* **a)** *(abandon)* sitzenlassen ‹*Familie, Freunde*›; sausenlassen *(ugs.)* ‹*Plan*›; **b)** *(make forced sea-landing with)* im Bach landen mit *(salopp)*

'ditchwater *n.* stehendes, fauliges Wasser; **[as] dull as ~**: sterbenslangweilig

dither ['dɪðə(r)] **1.** *v. i.* schwanken; **I'm ~ing** ich bin noch am Schwanken; **~ about doing sth.** lange hin und her überlegen, ob man etw. tun soll [oder nicht]. **2.** *n. (coll.)* **be all of a ~** *or* **in a ~**: am Rotieren *(ugs.)* sein

dithery ['dɪðərɪ] *adj.* unentschlossen

ditto ['dɪtəʊ] *n., pl.* **~s: p. 5 is missing, p. 19 ~**: S. 5 fehlt, ebenso S. 19; **~ marks** Unterführungszeichen, *das;* **I'm hungry. – D~**: Ich habe Hunger. – Ich auch

ditty ['dɪtɪ] *n.* Weise, *die*

'ditty bag *n. (Naut.) Segeltuchtasche für Werkzeug, Nähzeug, Rasierzeug usw. des Seemanns*

diuretic [daɪjʊə'retɪk] *(Med.)* **1.** *adj.* diuretisch *(fachspr.);* harntreibend; **~ drug/substance/remedy** *see* **2. 2.** *n.* Diuretikum, *das (fachspr.);* harntreibendes Mittel

diurnal [daɪ'ɜ:nl] *adj.* **a)** *(of the day)* Tages-; **b)** *(daily)* täglich

diva ['di:və] *n.* Primadonna, *die;* Göttin, *die (fig. geh.)*

divan [dɪ'væn] *n.* **a)** *(couch, bed)* [Polster]liege, *die;* **b)** *(long seat)* Chaiselongue, *die*

di'van bed *see* **divan a**

dive [daɪv] **1.** *v. i.,* **~d** *or (Amer.)* **dove** [dəʊv] **a)** *(plunge into water)* tauchen; *(from diving-board, rock, etc.)* einen Kopfsprung machen; **b)** *(plunge downwards)* ‹*Vogel, Flugzeug usw.:*› einen Sturzflug machen; ‹*Unterseeboot usw.:*› abtauchen *(Seemannsspr.),* tauchen; ‹*Achterbahn usw.:*› hinunterschießen; **c)** *(dart down)* sich hinwerfen; **~ under the table for protection** schnell unter dem Tisch Schutz suchen; **d)** *(dart)* **~ [out of sight]** sich schnell verstecken; *(when frightened)* sich flüchten *od.* verkriechen; sich schnell verstecken; **e)** *(rush)* hechten; springen; **~ into the nearest pub** gleich in die nächste Kneipe stürzen; **~ into bed** ins Bett springen; **f)** *(plunge with hand)* **~ into sth.** in etw. *(Akk.)* mit der Hand greifen *od.* fassen; *(fig.: begin to eat)* über etw. *(Akk.)* herfallen; **g)** *(begin to work)* **~ into a job** sich auf eine Arbeit stürzen. **2.** *n.* **a)** *(plunge)* Kopfsprung, *der; (of bird, aircraft, etc.)* Sturzflug, *der* (**towards** auf + *Akk.*); *(of submarine etc.)* [Unter]tauchen; **b)** *(sudden darting movement)* Sprung, *der;* Satz, *der;* **make a ~ for cover** schnell in Deckung gehen; **c)** *(coll.: disreputable place)* Spelunke, *die (abwertend)*

~ 'in *v. i.* [mit dem Kopf voraus] hineinspringen; *(fig.: help oneself)* zulangen

dive: ~-bomb *v. t. (Mil.)* im Sturzflug bombardieren; **~-bomber** *n. (Mil.)* Sturzkampfflugzeug, *das*

diver ['daɪvə(r)] *n.* **a)** *(Sport)* Kunstspringer, *der*/-springerin, *die;* **b)** *(as profession)* Taucher, *der*/Taucherin, *die;* **c)** *(diving bird)* Taucher, *der*

diverge [daɪ'vɜ:dʒ, dɪ'vɜ:dʒ] *v. i.* **a)** auseinandergehen; **here the road ~s from the river** hier entfernt die Straße sich vom Fluß; **b)** *(fig.)* ‹*Berufswege, Pfade:*› sich trennen; *(from norm etc.)* abweichen; **c)** *(differ)* ‹*Meinungen, Ansichten:*› voneinander abweichen, *(geh.)* divergieren

divergence [daɪ'vɜ:dʒəns, dɪ'vɜ:dʒəns] *n.* **a)** Divergenz, *die (fachspr.);* Auseinandergehen, *das;* **b)** *(fig.)* Abweichung, *die; (of careers, life-styles)* Auseinanderstreben, *das;* **~ of opinions/views** Meinungsverschiedenheit, *die* (**over** über + *Akk.*)

divergent [daɪ'vɜ:dʒənt, dɪ'vɜ:dʒənt] *adj.* **a)** divergent *(fachspr.);* auseinandergehend, -laufend ‹*Routen, Wege*›; *(fig.)* auseinanderstrebend ‹*Berufswege*›; **~ lens** *(Optics)* Zerstreuungslinse, *die;* **b)** *(differing)* unterschiedlich, voneinander abweichend ‹*Ansichten, Methoden*›

diverse [daɪ'vɜ:s, dɪ'vɜ:s] *adj.* **a)** *(unlike)* verschieden[artig]; unterschiedlich; **be [very] ~ from sth.** [ganz] anders sein als etw.; **b)** *(varied)* vielseitig, breit gefächert ‹*[Aus]bildung, Interessen, Kenntnisse*›; umfassend ‹*Wissen*›; vielfältig ‹*Arbeitsgebiet*›; bunt [gewürfelt] ‹*Mischung*›

diversification [daɪvɜ:sɪfɪ'keɪʃn, dɪvɜ:sɪfɪ'keɪʃn] *n.* **a)** *(varying)* [Auf]fächerung, *die;* breite Fächerung; **b)** *(Econ.)* Streuung, *die;* **~ [of production]** Diversifikation, *die*

diversify [daɪ'vɜ:sɪfaɪ, dɪ'vɜ:sɪfaɪ] **1.** *v. t.* **a)** *(vary)* abwechslungsreich[er] gestalten; Abwechslung bringen in (+ *Akk.*); **b)** *(Econ.)* diversifizieren *(fachspr.).* **2.** *v. i.* sich auf neue Produktions-/Produktbereiche umstellen

diversion [daɪ'vɜ:ʃn, dɪ'vɜ:ʃn] *n.* **a)** *(diverting of attention)* Ablenkung, *die;* **b)** *(feint)* Ablenkungsmanöver, *das;* **create a ~**: ein Ablenkungsmanöver durchführen; **c)** *no pl. (recreation)* Unterhaltung, *die; (distraction)* Zerstreuung, *die;* Abwechslung, *die;* **d)** *(amusement)* [Möglichkeit der] Freizeitbeschäftigung; **the ~s of the big city** das Unterhaltungsangebot der Großstadt; **e)** *(deviating) (of river, traffic)* Ableitung, *die;* **f)** *(Brit.: alternative route)* Umleitung, *die;* **there is a traffic ~ on the road** der Verkehr auf der Straße wird umgeleitet

diversionary [daɪ'vɜ:ʃənərɪ, dɪ'vɜ:ʃənərɪ] *adj.* Ablenkungs‹*angriff, -bombardement, -manöver*›

diversity [daɪ'vɜ:sɪtɪ, dɪ'vɜ:sɪtɪ] *n.* Vielfalt, *die;* **~ of opinion, ~ in opinions** *or* **views** Meinungsvielfalt, *die*

divert [daɪ'vɜ:t, dɪ'vɜ:t] *v. t.* **a)** umleiten ‹*Verkehr, Fluß, Fahrzeug*›; ablenken ‹*Aufmerksamkeit, Gedankengang, Blick*›; ableiten ‹*Lavastrom, Blitz*›; lenken ‹*Energien, Aggressionen*›; **~ sb.'s attention/gaze from sth. to sth. else** jmds. Aufmerksamkeit/Blick von etw. auf etw. anderes lenken; **b)** *(distract)* ablenken; **c)** *(entertain)* unterhalten

diverting [daɪ'vɜ:tɪŋ, dɪ'vɜ:tɪŋ] *adj. (entertaining)* unterhaltsam

divest [daɪ'vest, dɪ'vest] *v.t.* **a)** *(formal: unclothe)* entkleiden *(geh.)*; ~ **sb. of sth.** jmdm. etw. abnehmen; ~ **sth. of sth.** etw. einer Sache *(Gen.)* entkleiden; ~ **oneself of one's clothing/jewellery** seine Kleidung/seinen Schmuck ablegen; **b)** ~ **sb./sth. of sth.** *(deprive)* jmdn./etw. einer Sache *(Gen.)* berauben; *(rid)* jmdn./etw. von einer Sache befreien; ~ **sb. of a responsibility** jmdn. einer Verantwortung *(Gen.)* entheben; ~ **oneself of sth.** sich einer Sache *(Gen.)* entledigen

divide [dɪ'vaɪd] **1.** *v.t.* **a)** teilen; *(subdivide)* aufteilen; *(with precision)* einteilen; *(into separated pieces)* zerteilen; ~ **sth. in[to] parts** *(separate)* etw. [in Stücke *(Akk.)*] aufteilen; ~ **sth. into halves/quarters** etw. halbieren/vierteln; ~ **sth. in two** etw. [in zwei Teile] zerteilen; **b)** *(by marking out)* ~ **sth. into sth.** etw. in etw. *(Akk.)* unterteilen; **c)** *(part by marking)* trennen; ~ **sth./sb. from** *or* **and sth./sb.** etw./jmdn. von etw./jmdm. trennen; **d)** *(mark off)* ~ **sth. from sth. else** etw. von etw. anderem abgrenzen; **dividing line** Trennungslinie, *die*; **e)** *(distinguish)* unterscheiden; **f)** *(classify)* einteilen ‹*Lebewesen, Gegenstände, Gesellschaft*›; **g)** *(cause to disagree)* entzweien; **be ~d over an issue** in einer Angelegenheit nicht einig sein; **opinion is ~d** die Meinungen sind geteilt; **be ~d against itself** zerstritten sein; **h)** *(distribute)* aufteilen; ~ **sth. among/between persons/groups** etw. unter Personen/Gruppen *(Akk. od. Dat.)* aufteilen; **i)** *(share)* teilen; **j)** *(Math.)* dividieren *(fachspr.)*, teilen (by durch); ~ **three into nine** neun durch drei dividieren *od.* teilen; **k)** *(part for voting)* [durch Hammelsprung] abstimmen lassen. **2.** *v.i.* **a)** *(separate)* ~ **[in** *or* **into parts]** sich [in Teile] teilen; ‹*Buch, Urkunde usw.*:› sich [in Teile] gliedern *od.* [in Teile] gegliedert sein; **we ~d into groups for discussion** wir bildeten Diskussionsgruppen; ~ **into two** sich in zwei Teile teilen; **b)** ~ **[from sth.]** von etw. abzweigen; **c)** *(Math.)* ~ **[by a number/amount]** sich [durch eine Zahl/einen Betrag] dividieren *(fachspr.) od.* teilen lassen; **3 ~s into 36 to give 12** 3 geht zwölfmal in 36; **d)** *(be parted in voting)* **the council ~d and a vote was taken** der Rat stimmte [durch Hammelsprung] ab. **3.** *n.* **a)** *(Geog.)* Wasserscheide, *die*; **b)** *(fig.)* *(line)* Grenze, *die*; *(gulf)* Kluft, *die*; *(rift)* Riß, *der*; **the Great D~:** die Scheidelinie; *(euphem.)* die Schwelle des Todes *(geh.)*

~ **'off 1.** *v.t.* trennen; ~ **off an area** einen Bereich abtrennen *od.* abteilen. **2.** *v.i.* ~ **off from sth.** sich von etw. trennen

~ **'out** *v.t.* ~ **sth. out [among/between persons]** etw. unter Personen *(Akk. od. Dat.)* aufteilen; *(distribute)* etw. an Personen *(Akk.)* verteilen

~ **'up 1.** *v.t.* aufteilen; ~ **persons up into groups** Personen in Gruppen einteilen. **2.** *v.i.* ~ **up into sth.** sich in etw. *(Akk.)* aufteilen lassen

divided [dɪ'vaɪdɪd]: ~ **'highway** *n.* *(Amer.)* *see* **dual carriageway**; ~ **'skirt** *n.* Hosenrock, *der*

dividend ['dɪvɪdend] *n.* **a)** *(Commerc., Finance)* Dividende, *die*; **b)** *in pl.* *(fig.: benefit)* Vorteil, *der*; **your studying will pay ~s** Ihr Studium wird sich auszahlen *od.* rentieren; **reap the ~s** die Früchte ernten *od.* den Nutzen daraus ziehen

dividend: ~ **stripping** *n.* *(Finance)* Rosinenpickerei, *die (abwertend)*; **~-warrant** *n.* *(Brit. Finance)* Dividendenschein, *der*

divider [dɪ'vaɪdə(r)] *n.* **a)** *(screen)* Trennwand, *die*; *(other means)* Abgrenzung, *die*; **b)** ~**s** *pl.* Stechzirkel, *der*

divination [dɪvɪ'neɪʃn] *n.* **a)** *(foreseeing)* Ahnung, *die*; **powers of ~:** Gabe der Weissagung; **b)** *(discovering)* Deutung, *die*

divine [dɪ'vaɪn] **1.** *adj.*, **~r** [dɪ'vaɪnə(r)], **~st** [dɪ'vaɪnɪst] **a)** göttlich; *(devoted to God)* gottgeweiht; ~ **service** Gottesdienst, *der*; **the ~ right of kings** das Gottesgnadentum; **have no ~ right to do sth.** kein gottgewolltes Recht haben, etw. zu tun; **b)** *(superhumanly excellent)* überragend ‹*Begabung*›; göttlich ‹*Schönheit, Musik*›; *(superhumanly gifted)* gottbegnadet; **c)** *(coll.: delightful)* traumhaft. **2.** *n.* Geistliche, *der/die*. **3.** *v.t.* **a)** *(discover)* deuten; *(guess)* erraten; ~ **what sb. is thinking** *or* **sb.'s thoughts** jmds. Gedanken lesen; **b)** *(locate)* aufspüren; **c)** *(foresee)* vorhersehen; *(foretell)* weissagen; ~ **the future** in die Zukunft sehen

divinely [dɪ'vaɪnlɪ] *adv.* **a)** *(by God/a god)* von Gott/von einem Gott; **b)** *(with superhuman excellence)* genial; virtuos; *(with superhuman giftedness)* gottbegnadet; **c)** *(coll.: excellently, extremely well)* traumhaft

diving ['daɪvɪŋ] *n.* *(Sport)* Kunstspringen, *das*

diving: **~-bell** *n.* Taucherglocke, *die*; **~-board** *n.* Sprungbrett, *das*; **~-suit** *n.* Taucheranzug, *der*

divining-rod [dɪ'vaɪnɪŋrɒd] *see* **dowsing-rod**

divinity [dɪ'vɪnɪtɪ] *n.* **a)** *(god)* Gottheit, *die*; **b)** *no pl.* *(being a god)* Göttlichkeit, *die*; **c)** *no pl.* *(theology)* Theologie, *die*

divisible [dɪ'vɪzɪbl] *adj.* **a)** *(separable)* aufteilbar; *(capable of being marked out)* [unter-, ein]teilbar; **be ~ into ...:** sich in ... aufteilen lassen; **b)** *(Math.)* **be ~ [by a number/an amount]** [durch eine Zahl/einen Betrag] teilbar sein

division [dɪ'vɪʒn] *n.* **a)** *see* **divide 1 a:** Teilung/Auf-/Ein-/Zerteilung, *die*; **b)** *(parting)* *(of things)* Abtrennung, *die*; *(of persons)* Trennung, *die*; *(marking off)* Abgrenzung, *die*; **c)** *(distinguishing)* Unterscheidung, *die*; Abgrenzung, *die* **(from** gegenüber); **d)** *(classifying)* Einteilung, *die*; **e)** *(distributing)* Verteilung, *die* **(between/among** an + *Akk.*); *(sharing)* Teilen, *das*; ~ **of labour** Arbeitsteilung, *die*; **f)** *(disagreement)* Unstimmigkeit, *die*; **g)** *(Math.)* Teilen, *das*; Dividieren, *das*; Division, *die (fachspr.)*; **do ~:** dividieren; **long ~:** ausführliche Division *(mit Aufschreiben der Zwischenprodukte)*; **short ~:** verkürzte Division *(ohne Aufschreiben der Zwischenprodukte)*; **h)** *(separation in voting)* Abstimmung [durch Hammelsprung]; **i)** *(dividing line)* Trennungslinie, *die*; *(between states)* Grenze, *die*; *(partition)* Trennwand, *die*; **j)** *(part)* Unterteilung, *die*; Abschnitt, *der*; *(of drawer)* Fach, *das*; **k)** *(section)* Abteilung, *die*; **l)** *(group)* Gruppe, *die*; **m)** *(Mil. etc.)* Division, *die*; *(of police)* Einheit, *die*; **n)** *(of High Court)* Kammer, *die*; **o)** *(Footb. etc.)* Liga, *die*; Spielklasse, *die*; *(in British football)* Division, *die*; **p)** *(administrative district)* [Verwaltungs]bezirk, *der*

divisional [dɪ'vɪʒənl] *adj.* *(of section)* Abteilungs-

division: **~-bell** *n.* *(Parl.)* Abstimmungsklingel, *die*; ~ **sign** *n.* Divisionszeichen, *das*

divisive [dɪ'vaɪsɪv] *adj.* **a)** *(dividing in opinion etc.)* strittig; umstritten ‹*Vorschlag*›; **b)** *(dividing)* spalterisch; **have a ~ effect on sth.** etw. spalten

divisor [dɪ'vaɪzə(r)] *n.* *(Math.)* Divisor, *der*; Teiler, *der*

divorce [dɪ'vɔːs] **1.** *n.* **a)** [Ehe]scheidung, *die*; *attrib.* ~ **court** Scheidungsgericht, *das*; ~ **proceedings** [Ehe]scheidungsverfahren, *das*; **want a ~:** sich scheiden lassen wollen; **get** *or* **obtain a ~:** sich scheiden lassen; geschieden werden; **grounds for ~:** Scheidungsgründe; **b)** *(fig.)* Trennung, *die*. **2.** *v.t.* **a)** *(dissolve marriage of)* scheiden ‹*Ehepartner*›; **they were ~d last year** sie wurden letztes Jahr geschieden *od.* ließen sich letztes Jahr scheiden; **b)** ~ **one's husband/wife** sich von seinem Mann/seiner Frau scheiden lassen; **her husband refused to ~ her** ihr Mann willigte nicht in die Scheidung ein; **c)** *(fig.)* ~ **sth./sb. from sth.** etw./jmdn. von etw. loslösen; **keep sth. ~d from sth.** etw. von etw. getrennt halten

divorcee [dɪvɔː'siː] *n.* Geschiedene, *der/die*; **be a ~:** geschieden sein

divot ['dɪvət] *n.* *(Golf)* ausgehacktes Rasenstück

divulge [daɪ'vʌldʒ, dɪ'vʌldʒ] *v.t.* preisgeben; enthüllen ‹*Identität*›; bekanntgeben ‹*Nachrichten*›; lüften ‹*Geheimnis*›; verraten ‹*Alter*›

divvy ['dɪvɪ] *(coll.)* **1.** *n.* **a)** *(share)* Anteil, *der*; **b)** *(distribution)* Verteilung, *die*

Dixie ['dɪksɪ] *n.* **a)** die Südstaaten [der USA]; **b)** *(Mus.)* Dixie, *der*

dixie *n.* *(Brit.)* Kochkessel, *der*

'Dixieland *n.* **a)** *(Mus.)* Dixie[land], *der*; **b)** *see* **Dixie a**

DIY *abbr.* **do-it-yourself**

dizzily ['dɪzɪlɪ] *adv.* **a)** *(giddily)* taumelnd; schwankend; *(fig.)* benommen; **b)** *(so as to cause giddiness)* auf schwindelerregende Weise

dizziness ['dɪzɪnɪs] *n.*, *no pl.* Schwindelgefühl, *das*

dizzy ['dɪzɪ] *adj.* **a)** *(giddy)* schwind[e]lig; **I feel ~:** mir ist schwindlig; **he felt ~:** ihm wurde schwindlig; **b)** *(making giddy)* schwindelerregend; **the ~ heights of fame** die schwindelerregenden Höhen des Ruhms

DJ [diː'dʒeɪ] *abbr.* **a)** *(disc jockey)* Diskjockey, *der*; **b)** *(Brit.: dinner-jacket)* Smokingjacke, *die*

D. Litt. [diː 'lɪt] *abbr.* **Doctor of Letters** ≈ Dr. habil.; *see also* **B. Sc.**

DM, D-mark ['diːmɑːk] *abbr.* **Deutschmark** DM; D-Mark, *die*

D. Mus. [diː 'mʌz] *abbr.* **Doctor of Music** Doktor der Musikwissenschaften; *see also* **B.Sc.**

DNA *abbr.* **deoxyribonucleic acid** DNS

D-notice ['diː nəʊtɪs] *n.* *(Brit.)* **the government had issued a ~ to the media** die Regierung hatte den Medien die Veröffentlichung [aus Sicherheitsgründen] untersagt

¹do [də, *stressed* duː] **1.** *v.t.*, *neg. coll.* **don't** [dəʊnt], *pres. t.* **he does** [dʌz], *neg.* *(coll.)* **doesn't** ['dʌznt], *p.t.* **did** [dɪd], *neg.* *(coll.)* **didn't** ['dɪdnt], *pres. p.* **doing** ['duːɪŋ], *p.p.* **done** [dʌn] **a)** *(impart)* tun; **do sb. a favour** jmdm. einen Gefallen tun; **b)** *(perform)* machen ‹*Hausaufgaben, Hausarbeit, Examen, Striptease, Handstand*›; vollbringen ‹*Tat*›; tun, erfüllen ‹*Pflicht*›; tun, verrichten ‹*Arbeit*›; ausführen ‹*Malerarbeiten*›; vorführen ‹*Trick, Nummer, Tanz*›; durchführen ‹*Test*›; aufführen ‹*Stück*›; singen ‹*Lied*›; mitmachen ‹*Rennen, Wettbewerb*›; spielen ‹*Musikstück, Rolle*›; tun ‹*Buße*›; **do the shopping / washing-up / cleaning / gardening** einkaufen [gehen]/abwaschen/saubermachen/die Gartenarbeit erledigen; **do a test on sb.** jmdn. einem Test unterziehen; **do a lot of reading/walking** *etc.* viel lesen/spazierengehen *usw.*; **do a dance/the foxtrot** tanzen/Foxtrott tanzen; **do one's round** seine Runde machen; **is there anything we can do to help?** können wir [Ihnen] irgendwie helfen *od.* behilflich sein?; **have nothing to do** nichts zu tun haben; **what are you going/planning to do?** was hast du vor?; **what does he do for a living?** was macht er beruflich?; **what is 'he/'that doing here?** was hat er/das hier zu suchen?; **Don't just sit there! Do something!** Sitz nicht so tatenlos herum! Tu *od.* Unternimm doch etwas!; **have sth. [already] done** etw. fertig haben *od.* mit etw. fertig sein; **what are you doing this evening?** was machst du heute abend?; **what am I going to do?** *(baffled)* was mach' ich bloß?; **do sth. to sth./sb.** etw. mit etw./jmdm. machen; **what have you done to yourself/the**

cake? was hast du bloß mit dir/dem Kuchen gemacht?; **do one or two things to the car** noch ein oder zwei Dinge am Wagen in Ordnung bringen; **how could you do this to me?** wie konntest du mir das nur antun!; **he/it does something** *or* **things to me** *(fig. coll.)* er/das macht mich an *(salopp)*; **do sth. for sb./sth.** etw. für jmdn./etw. tun; **what can I do for you?** was kann ich für Sie tun?; *(in shop)* was darf's sein?; **this dress does something/nothing for you** *(coll.)* dieses Kleid steht dir gut/nicht [gut]; **do sth. about sth./sb.** etw. gegen etw./jmdn. unternehmen; **there's nothing we can do about the noise** wir können nichts gegen den Lärm tun *od.* machen; **why don't you do something about your hair?** tu doch mal was für dein Haar!; **what are you going to do about money while you're on holiday?** wie machst du das mit dem Geld, wenn du im Urlaub bist?; **what shall we do for food?** was machen wir mit dem Essen?; **can you do anything with these apples?** kannst du etwas mit diesen Äpfeln anfangen?; **what's to do?** was ist zu tun?; **not know what to do with oneself** nicht wissen, was man machen soll; **that does it** jetzt reicht's *(ugs.)*; **that's done it** das war der ausschlaggebende Faktor; *(caused a change for the worse)* das hat das Faß zum Überlaufen gebracht; *(caused a change for the better)* das hätten wir; **that will/should do it** so müßte es gehen; *(is enough)* das müßte genügen; **he's [really] done it** *(ruined things)* er hat es [wahrlich] geschafft; *(achieved something)* er hat es [wirklich] geschafft; **do a Garbo** *(coll.)* es der Garbo *(Dat.)* gleichtun; **how many miles has this car done?** wie viele Kilometer hat der Wagen gefahren?; **the car does** *or* **can do/was doing about 100 m.p.h./does 45 miles to the gallon** das Auto schafft/fuhr mit ungefähr 160 Stundenkilometer/frißt *(ugs.) od.* braucht sechs Liter pro 100 Kilometer; **c)** *(spend)* **do a spell in the armed forces** eine Zeitlang bei der Armee sein; **how much longer have you to do at college?** wie lange mußt du noch aufs College gehen?; **d)** *(produce)* machen ‹*Übersetzung, Kopie*›; schreiben ‹*Gedicht, Roman, Brief*›; anfertigen ‹*Bild, Skulptur*›; herstellen ‹*Artikel, Produkte*›; schaffen ‹*Pensum*›; **e)** *(provide)* haben ‹*Vollpension, Mittagstisch*›; *(coll.: offer for sale)* führen; *(effect)* erreichen; **f)** *(deal with)* *(prepare)* machen ‹*Bett, Frühstück*›; *(work on)* machen *(ugs.)*, fertig machen ‹*Garten, Hecke*›; *(clean)* saubermachen; putzen ‹*Schuhe, Fenster*›; machen *(ugs.)* ‹*Treppe*›; *(arrange)* [zurecht]machen ‹*Haare*›; fertig machen ‹*Korrespondenz, Akten, Zimmer*›; *(make up)* schminken ‹*Lippen, Augen, Gesicht*›; machen *(ugs.)* ‹*Nägel*›; *(cut)* schneiden ‹*Nägel*›; schneiden ‹*Gras, Hecke, Blumen*›; *(paint)* machen *(ugs.)* ‹*Zimmer*›; streichen ‹*Haus, Möbel*›; *(attend to)* sich kümmern um ‹*Bücher, Rechnungen, Korrespondenz*›; abfertigen ‹*Patienten*›; *(repair)* in Ordnung bringen; machen ‹*Garten*›; *(wash)* abwaschen ‹*Geschirr*›; **a living-room done in blue** ein blau gestrichenes Wohnzimmer; **g)** *(cook)* braten; **how do you like your meat done?** wie hätten Sie gern das Fleisch?; **well done** durch[gebraten]; **the meat isn't/the potatoes aren't done [enough] yet** das Fleisch ist/die Kartoffeln sind noch nicht richtig durch *od.* gar; **h)** *(solve)* lösen ‹*Problem, Rätsel*›; machen ‹*Puzzle, Kreuzworträtsel*›; **i)** *(translate)* übersetzen; **j)** *(study, work at)* machen; haben ‹*Abiturfach*›; durchnehmen ‹*Wissensgebiet*›; **do history at university** Geschichte studieren; **k)** *(play the part of)* spielen; *(impersonate)* imitieren; nachmachen; *(act like)* spielen; mimen *(ugs.)*; **l)** *(sl.: rob)* einsteigen in (+ *Akk.*) ‹*Haus*› *(ugs.)*; **m)** *(sl.: prosecute)* **do sb. [for sth.]** jmdn. wegen etw. rankriegen *(ugs.)*; **n)** *(sl.: with sexual intercourse)* **do sb.** jmdn. bumsen *(salopp)*; **do it [with sb.]** es [mit jmdm.] machen *(salopp)*; **o)** *(sl.: swindle)* reinlegen *(ugs.)*; **do sb. out of sth.** jmdn. um etw. bringen; **p)** *(sl.)* *(defeat, kill)* fertigmachen *(ugs.)*; *(ruin)* erledigen *(ugs.)*; **q)** *(coll.: exhaust)* schaffen *(ugs.)*; fertigmachen *(ugs.)*; **we were completely done [in** *or* **up]** wir waren total geschafft *(ugs.) od.* fix und fertig *(ugs.)*; **r)** *(traverse)* schaffen ‹*Entfernung*›; **s)** *(sl.: undergo)* absitzen, *(salopp)* abreißen ‹*Strafe*›; **t)** *(coll.: visit)* besuchen; **do Europe in three weeks** Europa in drei Wochen absolvieren *od.* abhaken *(ugs.)*; **u)** *(Brit. coll.: provide sth. for)* versorgen; **do oneself well** es sich *(Dat.)* gutgehen lassen; **v)** *(satisfy)* zusagen (+ *Dat.*); *(suffice for, last)* reichen (+ *Dat.*); **do sb. very nicely/better** jmdm. voll und ganz/mehr zusagen; **we've got enough food here to do us for a week** wir haben genug Essen für eine Woche hier. **2.** *v. i., forms as* **1: a)** *(act)* tun; *(perform)* spielen; **you can do just as you like** du kannst machen, was du willst; **do as they do** mach es wie sie; **b)** *(perform deeds)* **do or die** kämpfen oder untergehen; **do-or-die** verzweifelt ‹*Versuch, Angriff*›; wild entschlossen ‹*Gesichtsausdruck*›; **c)** *(fare)* **how are you doing?** wie geht's dir?; **d)** *(get on)* vorankommen; *(in exams)* abschneiden; **how are you doing at school?** wie geht es in der Schule?; was macht die Schule?; **do well/badly at school** gut/schlecht in der Schule sein; **e) how do you do?** *(formal)* guten Tag/Morgen/Abend!; **f)** *(coll.: manage)* **how are we doing for time** *or* **as regards time?** wie steht es mit der Zeit *od.* *(ugs.)* sieht es mit der Zeit aus?; **g)** *(finish)* **have done with** *see* **done e; h)** *(serve purpose)* es tun; *(suffice)* [aus]reichen; *(be suitable)* gehen; **would that do?** tut's das [auch]?; **that won't do** das geht nicht; **that will never do** das geht einfach nicht; **you won't do, Peter** du bist nicht gut genug, Peter; **nothing but the best will do for her** das Beste ist gerade gut genug für sie; **that will do!** jetzt aber genug!; **it doesn't/wouldn't do to tell lies/be late for work/believe all that one is told** es ist/wäre nicht gut zu lügen/zu spät zur Arbeit zu kommen/alles zu glauben, was einem gesagt wird; **i)** *(be usable)* **do for** *or* **as sth.** als etw. benutzt werden können; **make do** *see* **make 1 t; j)** *(happen)* **what's doing?** was ist los?; **what's doing at your place?** was ist bei euch los?; was läuft bei euch? *(ugs.)*; **there's nothing doing on the job market** es tut sich nichts auf dem Arbeitsmarkt *(ugs.)*; **Nothing doing. He's not interested** Nichts zu machen *(ugs.)*. Er ist nicht interessiert; **what's to do?** was ist los? *See also* **doing; done. 3.** *v. substitute, forms as* **1: a)** *replacing v.: usually not translated;* **you mustn't act as he does** du darfst nicht so wie er handeln; **if you drank as much water as you do coffee** wenn du soviel Wasser trinken würdest, wie du Kaffee trinkst; **b)** *replacing v. and obj. etc.* **he read the Bible every day as his father did before him** er las täglich in der Bibel, wie es schon sein Vater vor ihm getan hatte *od.* wie schon vor ihm sein Vater; **as they did in the Middle Ages** wie sie es im Mittelalter taten; wie im Mittelalter; **if I ate as much chocolate as you do** wenn ich soviel Schokolade äße wie du; **you might not want to ..., but if you do, ...:** du willst vielleicht nicht ..., falls aber doch, ...; **c)** *as ellipt. aux.* **You went to Paris, didn't you? – Yes, I did** Du warst doch in Paris, oder *od.* nicht wahr? – Ja[, stimmt *od.* war ich]; **d)** *with 'so', 'it', 'which', etc.* **I knew John Lennon. – So did I** Ich kannte John Lennon. – Ich auch; **if you want to go abroad then do so** wenn du ins Ausland reisen willst, tu es [ruhig]; **go ahead and do it** nur zu; **then please do so within 10 days** dann [tun Sie das] bitte innerhalb von 10 Tagen; **e)** *in emphatic repetition* **come in, do!** komm doch herein!; **take a seat, do!** nehmen Sie doch Platz!; **f)** *in tag questions* **I know you from somewhere, don't I?** wir kennen uns doch irgendwoher, nicht?; **he doesn't by any chance play the guitar, does he?** er spielt nicht zufällig Gitarre, oder?; **so you enjoyed yourself in Spain, did you?** es hat Ihnen also in Spanien gefallen, ja?. **4.** *v. aux.* + *inf. as pres. or past, forms as* **1: a)** *for special emphasis* **I do love Greece** Griechenland gefällt mir wirklich gut; ich liebe Griechenland ganz einfach; **I do apologize** es tut mit wirklich leid; **you do look glum** du siehst ja so bedrückt aus; **you do smoke a lot** du rauchst ja wirklich viel; **so we did go after all** also gingen wir schließlich doch; **but I tell you, I did see him** aber ich sage dir doch, daß ich ihn gesehen habe; **b)** *for inversion* **little did he know that ...:** er hatte keine Ahnung, daß ...; **rarely do such things happen** so etwas passiert nur selten; **did he but realize it** wenn ihm das bloß klar wäre!; **c)** *in questions* **do you know him?** kennst du ihn?; **what does he want?** was will er?; **doesn't/didn't he want** *or* **does/did he not want to accompany us?** will/wollte er uns nicht begleiten?; **didn't they look wonderful?** haben sie nicht wunderhübsch ausgesehen?; **d)** *in negation* **I don't** *or* **do not wish to take part** ich möchte nicht teilnehmen; **e)** *in neg. commands* **don't** *or* **do not expect to find him in a good mood** erwarten Sie nicht, daß Sie ihn in guter Stimmung antreffen; **children, do not forget ...:** Kinder, vergeßt [ja] nicht ...; **don't be so noisy!** seid [doch] nicht so laut!; **don't worry yourselves** macht euch keine Sorgen; **don't!** tu's/tut's/tun Sie's nicht!; **f)** + *inf. as imper. for emphasis etc.* **do sit down, won't you?** bitte setzen Sie sich doch!; wollen Sie sich nicht setzen?; **do let us know how you ...:** sag uns aber Bescheid, wie du ...; **do be quiet, Paul!** Paul, sei doch mal ruhig!; **do look here** schau doch mal her!; **do hurry up** beeil dich doch!; **do cheer up!** Kopf hoch!

do a'way with *v. t.* abschaffen

'do by *v. t.* **do well by sb.** jmdn. gut behandeln; **he felt hard done by** er fühlte sich zurückgesetzt *od.* schlecht behandelt; **do as you would be done by** handle so, wie du behandelt werden möchtest

do 'down *v. t.* *(coll.)* **a)** *(get the better of)* ausstechen; **b)** *(speak ill of)* schlechtmachen; heruntermachen *(ugs.)*

'do for *v. t.* **a)** *see* **¹do 2 i; b)** *(coll.: destroy)* **do for sb.** jmdn. fertigmachen *od.* schaffen *(ugs.)*; **do for sth.** etw. kaputtmachen *(ugs.)*; **be done for** *(exhausted)* fix und fertig *(ugs.) od.* ganz geschafft *(ugs.)* sein; **if we don't do better next time we're done for** wenn wir das nächste Mal nicht besser sind, sind wir erledigt; **c)** *(Brit. coll.: keep house for)* **do for sb.** für jmdn. sorgen; ‹*Putzfrau:*› für *od.* bei jmdm. putzen

do 'in *v. t.* *(sl.)* kaltmachen *(salopp)*; alle machen *(derb)*; *see also* **¹do 1 q**

do 'out *v. t.* *(clean)* saubermachen; *(redecorate)* streichen; *(in wallpaper)* tapezieren; *(decorate, furnish)* herrichten

do 'over *v. t.* **a)** *(sl.: beat)* zusammenschlagen; **b)** *(Amer. coll.: do again)* noch einmal machen

do 'up 1. *v. t.* **a)** *(fasten)* zumachen; binden ‹*Schnürsenkel, Fliege*›; **b)** *(wrap)* einpacken; verpacken; *(arrange)* zurechtmachen; **she did her hair up in a bun** sie machte sich *(Dat.)* einen Knoten; **c)** *(adorn)* zurechtmachen ‹*Menschen*›; schmücken ‹*Kutsche, Pferd, Haus*›; dekorieren ‹*Haus*›. **2.** *v. i.* ‹*Kleid, Reißverschluß, Knopf usw.:*› zugehen

'do with *v. t.* **a)** *(get by with)* auskommen

mit; *(get benefit from)* **I could do with a glass of orange-juice** ich könnte ein Glas Orangensaft vertragen *(ugs.)*; **he could do with a good hiding** eine Tracht Prügel würde ihm nicht schaden; **b) have to do with** zu tun haben mit; **have something/nothing/little to do with sth./sb.** etwas/nichts/wenig mit etw./jmdm. zu tun haben; **it's to do with that job I applied for** es geht um die Stelle, für die ich mich beworben habe

'do without *v. t.* **do without sth.** ohne etw. auskommen; auf etw. *(Akk.)* verzichten; **he could not do without her** er konnte nicht ohne sie leben; **he can't do without drink** er kann das Trinken nicht lassen; *abs.* **you've never had to do with'out** du hast nie auf etwas verzichten müssen

[2]do [du:] *n., pl.* **dos** *or* **do's** [du:z] **a)** *(sl.: swindle)* Schwindel, *der;* krumme Sache *(ugs.)*; **b)** *(Brit. coll.: festivity)* Feier, *die;* Fete, *die (ugs.)*; **c)** *in pl.* **the dos and don'ts** die Ge- und Verbote (**of** *Gen.*); **the dos and don'ts of bringing up children** was man bei der Kindererziehung tun und lassen sollte; **d)** *in pl. (Brit. coll.)* **fair dos!** gleiches Recht für alle

[3]do *see* **doh**

do. *abbr.* **ditto** do.; dto.

doc [dɒk] *n. (coll.)* Doktor, *der (ugs.)*; *as address* Herr/Frau Doktor

docile ['dəʊsaɪl] *adj.* sanft; *(submissive)* unterwürfig

docilely ['dəʊsaɪllɪ] *adv.* unterwürfig ‹*sich verhalten*›

docility [də'sɪlɪtɪ] *n., no pl.* Sanftmut, *die;* *(submissiveness)* Unterwürfigkeit, *die*

[1]dock [dɒk] **1.** *n.* **a)** Dock, *das;* **the ship came into ~:** das Schiff ging in[s] Dock; **be in ~:** im Dock liegen; *(coll.: in hospital)* im Krankenhaus liegen; **b)** *usu. in pl. (area)* Hafen, *der;* **at the ~s in Hull** im Hafen von Hull; **down by the ~[s]** unten im Hafen; **c)** *(Amer.)* *(ship's berth)* Kai, *der;* *(for trucks etc.)* Laderampe, *die.* **2.** *v. t.* **a)** *(bring into ~)* [ein]docken; **b)** *(Astronaut.)* docken. **3.** *v. i.* **a)** *(come into ~)* anlegen; **b)** *(Astronaut.)* docken

[2]dock *n. (in lawcourt)* Anklagebank, *die;* **stand/be in the ~** *(lit. or fig.)* ≈ auf der Anklagebank sitzen; **put sb. in the ~** *(lit. or fig.)* ≈ jmdn. auf die Anklagebank bringen

[3]dock *n. (Bot.)* Ampfer, *der*

[4]dock *v. t.* **a)** *(cut short)* kupieren ‹*Hund, Pferd, Schwanz*›; **b)** *(lessen)* kürzen ‹*Lohn, Stipendium usw.*›; **he had his pay ~ed by £14, he had £14 ~ed from his pay** sein Lohn wurde um 14 Pfund gekürzt

docker ['dɒkə(r)] *n.* Hafenarbeiter, *der;* Schauermann, *der;* Docker, *der*

docket ['dɒkɪt] **1.** *n.* **a)** *(Brit. Commerc.: list)* Liste, *die;* **b)** *(Brit.: custom-house warrant)* Zollquittung, *die;* **c)** *(voucher)* Bestellschein, *der;* *(delivery note)* Lieferschein, *der;* **d)** *(endorsement on documents etc.)* [Register mit] Inhaltsangabe. **2.** *v. t.* *(endorse)* mit Inhaltsangabe versehen; *(label)* etikettieren

dock: ~-land *n.* das Hafenviertel; **~-yard** *n.* Schiffswerft, *die*

doctor ['dɒktə(r)] **1.** *n.* **a)** *(physician)* Arzt, *der*/Ärztin, *die;* Doktor, *der (ugs.)*; *as title* Doktor, *der;* *as address* Herr/Frau Doktor; **~'s orders** ärztliche Anweisung; **just what the ~ ordered** [ganz] genau das richtige!; **an apple a day keeps the ~ away** *(prov.)* [iß] täglich einen Apfel, und du bleibst gesund; **you're the ~** *(coll.)* Sie sind der Fachmann; **works ~:** Werksarzt, *der;* **b)** *(Amer.: dentist)* Zahnarzt, *der*/-ärztin, *die;* **c)** *(Amer.: veterinary surgeon)* Tierarzt, *der*/-ärztin, *die;* **d)** *(holder of degree)* Doktor, *der;* **D~ of Medicine/Divinity** Doktor der Medizin/Theologie; **graduate as ~, do one's ~'s degree** promovieren; seinen Doktor machen *(ugs.)*. **2.** *v. t. (coll.)* **a)** *(falsify)* verfälschen ‹*Dokumente, Tonbänder*›; frisieren *(ugs.)* ‹*Bilanzen, Bücher*›; *(adulterate)* panschen *(ugs.)* ‹*Wein*›; verwürzen ‹*Gericht*›; *(improve by altering)* verfeinern ‹*Gericht*›; verschönern ‹*Aussehen*›; **her punch had been ~ed with something** ihrem Punsch war etwas beigemischt worden; **b)** *(treat)* behandeln ‹*Patienten*›; **~ oneself** sein eigener Arzt sein; **c)** *(patch up)* zusammenflicken *(ugs.)*; **d)** *(sterilize)* sterilisieren ‹*Tier*›

doctoral ['dɒktərl] *adj.* Doktor-; **~ thesis** Dissertation, *die;* Doktorarbeit, *die*

doctorate ['dɒktərət] *n.* Doktorwürde, *die;* **do a ~:** seinen Doktor machen *(ugs.)*; promovieren

doctrinaire [dɒktrɪ'neə(r)] *adj.* doktrinär

doctrinal [dɒk'traɪnl, 'dɒktrɪnl] *adj.*, **doctrinally** [dɒk'traɪnəlɪ, 'dɒktrɪnəlɪ] *adv.* doktrinell

doctrine ['dɒktrɪn] *n.* **a)** *(principle)* Lehre, *die;* **the ~ of free speech/equality** der Grundsatz der Redefreiheit/der Gleichheitsgrundsatz; **educational ~s** pädagogische Grundsätze; **b)** *(body of instruction)* Doktrin, *die;* Lehrmeinung, *die*

document 1. ['dɒkjʊmənt] *n.* Dokument, *das;* Urkunde, *die;* **all the necessary ~s** alle erforderlichen Unterlagen. **2.** ['dɒkjʊment] *v. t.* **a)** *(prove by document[s])* dokumentieren; [mit Dokumenten] belegen; **b)** *(furnish with document[s])* **be well ~ed** ‹*Leben, Zeit usw.:*› gut belegt sein

documentary [dɒkjʊ'mentərɪ] **1.** *adj.* **a)** *(pertaining to documents)* dokumentarisch, urkundlich ‹*Beweis*›; **b)** *(factual)* dokumentarisch; **~ film** Dokumentarfilm, *der.* **2.** *n.* *(film)* Dokumentarfilm, *der*

documentation [dɒkjʊmen'teɪʃn] *n.* **a)** *(documenting)* Dokumentation, *die;* **b)** *(material)* Dokument, *das;* Beweisstücke

dodder ['dɒdə(r)] *v. i.* **a)** *(totter)* wacklig gehen; **b)** *(tremble)* zittern

dodderer ['dɒdərə(r)] *n.* Tattergreis, *der (ugs.)*

doddery ['dɒdərɪ] *adj.* tatterig *(ugs.)* ‹*alter Mann*›; zittrig ‹*Beine, Bewegungen*›

doddle ['dɒdl] *n. (Brit. coll.)* Kinderspiel, *das (fig.)*

dodecaphonic [dəʊdekə'fɒnɪk] *adj. (Mus.)* Zwölfton-

dodge [dɒdʒ] **1.** *v. i.* **a)** *(move quickly)* ausweichen; **~ [out of sight]** schnell verschwinden; **~ behind the hedge/the trees** hinter die Hecke/die Bäume springen *od.* schlüpfen; **~ out of the way/to the side** zur Seite springen; **b)** *(move to and fro)* ständig in Bewegung sein; **~ through the traffic** sich durch den Verkehr schlängeln. **2.** *v. t.* *(elude by movement)* ausweichen (+ *Dat.*) ‹*Schlag, Hindernis usw.*›; entkommen (+ *Dat.*) ‹*Polizei, Verfolger*›; *(avoid)* sich drücken vor (+ *Dat.*) ‹*Wehrdienst*›; umgehen ‹*Steuer*›; aus dem Weg gehen (+ *Dat.*) ‹*Frage, Problem*›; *(evade by trickery)* austricksen *(ugs.)*; **~ doing sth.** es umgehen, etw. zu tun; sich davor drücken, etw. zu tun; *see also* **column. 3.** *n.* **a)** *(move)* Sprung zur Seite; **b)** *(trick)* Trick, *der;* **he's up to all the ~s** er ist mit allen Wassern gewaschen

dodgem ['dɒdʒəm] *n.* [Auto]skooter, *der;* *in pl.* [Auto]skooterbahn, *die;* **have a ride/go on the ~s** Autoskooter fahren

dodger ['dɒdʒə(r)] *n.* Drückeberger, *der (ugs. abwertend)*

dodgy ['dɒdʒɪ] *adj.* **a)** *(cunning)* gerissen *(ugs.)*; ausgekocht *(ugs.)*; **b)** *(Brit. coll.)* *(unreliable)* unsicher; schwach ‹*Knie, Herz usw.*›; *(awkward)* verzwickt; vertrackt; *(tricky)* knifflig; *(risky)* gewagt; heikel; **the car's a bit ~ sometimes** das Auto hat hin und wieder seine Mucken *(ugs.)*

dodo ['dəʊdəʊ] *n., pl.* **~s** *or* **~es** Dodo, *der;* Dronte, *die;* **[as] dead as the** *or* **a ~:** völlig ausgestorben

doe [dəʊ] *n. (Zool.)* **a)** *(deer)* Damtier, *das;* Damgeiß, *die;* **b)** *(hare)* Häsin, *die;* **c)** *(rabbit)* [Kaninchen]weibchen, *das*

DOE *abbr. (Brit.)* **Department of the Environment** Umweltministerium, *das*

does [dʌz] *see* **[1]do**

'doe-skin *n.* **a)** Rehfell, *das;* **b)** *(leather)* Rehleder, *das;* **c)** *(fine cloth)* Doeskin, *der*

doesn't ['dʌznt] *(coll.)* = **does not;** *see* **[1]do**

doff [dɒf] *v. t.* sich entledigen (+ *Gen.*) ‹*Kleidung*›; abnehmen ‹*Hut*›

dog [dɒg] **1.** *n.* **a)** Hund, *der;* **not [stand** *or* **have] a ~'s chance** nicht die geringste Chance [haben]; **I was as sick as a ~:** mir war hundeelend; *(fig.)* ich hätte heulen können; **it shouldn't happen to a ~:** das würde man seinem ärgsten Feind nicht wünschen; **dressed up/done up like a ~'s dinner** *(coll.)* aufgeputzt wie ein Pfau *(ugs.)*; ‹*Frau:*› aufgetakelt wie eine Fregatte *(ugs.)*; **a hair of the ~ [that bit one]** ein Schluck gegen den Kater; **give a ~ a bad name [and hang him]** einmal in Verruf gekommen, bleibt man immer verdächtig; **go to the ~s** vor die Hunde gehen *(ugs.)*; **help a lame ~ over a stile** einem Bedürftigen unter die Arme greifen; **love me, love my ~:** man muß mich so nehmen, wie ich bin; **a ~ in the manger** ein Biest, das keinem was gönnt; **~-in-the-manger** mißgünstig ‹*Benehmen*›; **put on ~** *(coll.)* angeben *(ugs.)*; **be like a ~ with two tails** sich freuen wie ein Schneekönig *(ugs.)*; **see a man about a ~:** etwas erledigen; *(visit lavatory)* hingehen, wo auch der Kaiser zu Fuß hingeht *(scherzh.)*; **there's life in the old ~ yet** er ist noch ganz schön fit für sein Alter *(ugs.)*; er gehört noch nicht zum alten Eisen *(ugs.)*; **you can't teach an old ~ new tricks** alte Menschen können sich nicht mehr umstellen; **the ~s** *(Brit. coll.: greyhound-racing)* das Windhundrennen; **try it on the ~:** ihn/sie *usw.* als Versuchskaninchen benutzen; *see also* **cat a; day e; hot; sleeping; b)** *(Hunting)* [Jagd]hund, *der;* **[you must] let the ~ see the rabbit** *(fig.)* laß mich mal ran *(ugs.)*; *(sb. must be given a fair chance)* du mußt ihn *usw.* ranlassen; **c)** *(male ~)* Rüde, *der;* **d)** *(despicable person; coll.: fellow)* Hund, *der (derb)*; **you ~!** du Hund[esohn]! *(derb)*; **wise old ~/clever old ~/sly ~/cunning ~:** schlauer Fuchs *(ugs.)*. **2.** *v. t.*, **-gg-** *(follow)* verfolgen; *(fig.)* heimsuchen; verfolgen; **~ sb.'s steps** jmdm. hart auf den Fersen bleiben

dog: ~-biscuit *n.* Hundekuchen, *der;* **~-breeder** *see* **breeder; ~cart** *n.* Dogcart, *der;* **~-collar** *n.* **a)** [Hunde]halsband, *das;* **b)** *(joc.: clerical collar)* Kollar, *das;* **~ days** *n. pl.* Hundstage *Pl.*; **~-dirt** *n. (coll.)* Hundedreck, *der (ugs.)*

doge [dəʊdʒ] *n. (Hist.)* Doge, *der*

dog: ~-eared *adj.* **a ~-eared book** ein Buch mit Eselsohren; **~-eat-'~** *adj.* gnadenlos; **~-end** *n. (sl.)* Kippe, *die (ugs.)*; **~fight** *n.* **a)** Hundekampf, *der;* *(fig.)* Handgemenge, *das;* **b)** *(between aircraft)* Luftkampf, *der;* **~fish** *n.* **[spotted/spiny] ~:** Katzen-/Dornhai, *der*

dogged ['dɒgɪd] *adj.* hartnäckig ‹*Weigerung, Verurteilung*›; zäh ‹*Durchhaltevermögen, Ausdauer*›; beharrlich ‹*Haltung, Kritik*›

doggedly ['dɒgɪdlɪ] *adv. see* **dogged:** hartnäckig; zäh; beharrlich

doggerel ['dɒgərəl] **1.** *adj.* holp[e]rig, unbeholfen ‹*Übersetzung, Geschreibsel*›; **~ verse** *or* **rhyme** Knittelvers, *der.* **2.** *n.* Knittelvers, *der*

doggie ['dɒgɪ] *n. (coll.)* Hündchen, *das*

'doggie-bag *n. (coll.)* *Tüte, in der man Essensreste [bes. von einer Mahlzeit im Restaurant] mit nach Hause nimmt*

doggo ['dɒgəʊ] *adv. (sl.)* **lie ~:** sich nicht mucksen *(ugs.)* *od.* rühren

doggone ['dɒgɒn] *adj., adv. (Amer. sl.)* verdammt

doggy *see* **doggie**
dog: **~house** *n.* **a)** *(Amer.)* Hundehütte, *die;* **b) be in the ~house** *(sl.: in disgrace)* in Ungnade sein; verschissen haben *(derb);* **he is in the ~house** *(in family life)* bei ihm hängt der Haussegen schief; **~-leg** *n.* Knick, *der;* ~ **licence** *n.* Hundesteuerbescheinigung, *die;* **~like** *adj.* hundeähnlich ⟨*Aussehen*⟩; hündisch ⟨*Ergebenheit*⟩
dogma ['dɒgmə] *n.* Dogma, *das*
dogmatic [dɒg'mætɪk] *adj.* dogmatisch; ~ **theology** Dogmatik, *die;* **be ~ about sth.** in etw. *(Dat.)* dogmatisch sein
dogmatically [dɒg'mætɪkəlɪ] *adv.* dogmatisch
dogmatism ['dɒgmətɪzm] *n.* Dogmatismus, *der*
do-gooder [du:'gʊdə(r)] *n.* Wohltäter, *der (iron.); (reformer)* Weltverbesserer, *der (iron.)*
dog: **~-paddle** *v.i.* Hundepaddeln machen; **~rose** *n. (Bot.)* Hundsrose, *die;* **~sbody** *n. (Brit. coll.)* Mädchen für alles; **~'s 'breakfast** *n. (sl.)* Bockmist, *der (salopp);* **make a ~'s breakfast of sth.** etw. verbocken *(ugs.);* **~'s life** *n.* **a ~'s life** ein Hundeleben; **give** *or* **lead sb. a ~'s life** jmdn. schäbig behandeln; **~-star** *n.* Sirius, *der;* Hundsstern, *der;* **~-tag** *n. (lit. or fig.)* Hundemarke, *die;* **~-'tired** *adj.* hundemüde; **~-tooth** *n. (Archit.)* Hundszahnornament, *das;* **~-trot** *n.* gemächlicher Trott; **~-violet** *n. (Bot.)* Hundsveilchen, *das;* **~-watch** *n. (Naut.) (from 4 p.m. to 6 p.m./ from 6 p.m. to 8 p.m.)* 1./2. Plattfuß, *der (Seemannsspr.);* **~wood** *n. (Bot.)* Hartriegel, *der;* Hornstrauch, *der*
doh [dəʊ] *n. (Mus.)* do
doily ['dɔɪlɪ] *n.* [Spitzen-, Zier]deckchen, *das*
doing ['du:ɪŋ] **1.** *pres. p. of* [1]**do. 2.** *n.* **a)** *vbl. n. of* [1]**do; b)** *no pl.* Tun, *das;* **be [of] sb.'s ~:** jmds. Werk sein; **it was not [of]** *or* **none of his ~:** er hatte nichts damit zu tun; **that takes a lot of/some ~:** da gehört sehr viel/ schon etwas dazu; **c)** *in pl.* **sb.'s ~s** *(actions)* jmds. Tun und Treiben; **the ~s** *(sl.)* die Dinger *(ugs.); (thing with unknown name)* das Dings *(ugs.)*
do-it-yourself [du:ɪtjə'self] **1.** *adj.* Do-it-yourself-; ~ **equipment** Heimwerkerausrüstung, *die.* **2.** *n.* Heimwerken, *das;* Do-it-yourself, *das*
doldrums ['dɒldrəmz] *n. pl.* **a)** *(low spirits)* Niedergeschlagenheit, *die;* Trübsinn, *der;* **in the ~:** niedergeschlagen; **b)** *(Naut.)* **in the ~:** ohne Wind; *(fig.)* in einer Flaute
dole [dəʊl] **1.** *n. (coll.)* **the ~:** Stempelgeld, *das (ugs.);* Stütze, *die (ugs.);* **draw the ~:** Stempelgeld *od.* Stütze kriegen; **be/go on the ~:** stempeln gehen *(ugs.).* **2.** *v.t.* ~ **out** [in kleinen Mengen] verteilen; [sparsam] austeilen
doleful ['dəʊlfl] *adj.* traurig ⟨*Augen, Blick, Gesichtsausdruck*⟩
dolefully ['dəʊlfəlɪ] *adv. (sadly)* traurig; trübselig
doll [dɒl] **1.** *n.* **a)** *(small model of person, dummy)* Puppe, *die;* **b)** *(pretty but silly woman)* Dummchen, *das (ugs.);* Püppchen, *das (ugs.); (sl.: young woman)* Mieze, *die (ugs.).* **2.** *v.t.* ~ **up** herausputzen; herausstaffieren *(abwertend);* auftakeln ⟨*Frau*⟩ *(abwertend);* **she was all ~ed up** sie war so richtig aufgedonnert *(abwertend)*
dollar ['dɒlə(r)] *n.* Dollar, *der;* **feel/look like a million ~s** *(coll.)* sich pudelwohl fühlen *(ugs.)*/tipptopp aussehen *(ugs.);* **sixty-four [thousand] ~ question** *(lit. or fig.)* Preisfrage, *die; see also* **bottom 2 b**
dollar: ~ **'bill** *n.* Dollarnote, *die;* Dollarschein, *der;* ~ **sign** *n.* Dollarzeichen, *das*
'dollhouse *(Amer.) see* **doll's house**
dollop ['dɒləp] **1.** *n. (coll.)* Klacks, *der (ugs.).* **2.** *v.t. (coll.)* klatschen *(ugs.)*
doll's house *n.* Puppenhaus, *das*
dolly ['dɒlɪ] *n.* **a)** Puppe, *die;* Püppchen, *das; (child language)* Püppi, *die (Kinderspr.);* **b)** *see* **dolly-bird**
'dolly-bird *n. (coll.)* Mieze, *die (ugs.)*
dolmen ['dɒlmən] *n. (Archaeol.)* Dolmen, *der*
Dolomites ['dɒləmaɪts] *pr. n. pl.* **the ~:** die Dolomiten
dolorous ['dɒlərəs] *adj. (literary/dated)* **a)** *(dismal)* düster; trist; schwermütig ⟨*Klang*⟩; *(distressing)* bedrückend ⟨*Nachricht, Vorstellung*⟩; **b)** *(distressed)* gequält ⟨*Blick, Ausdruck, Seufzer*⟩
dolphin ['dɒlfɪn] *n. (Zool., Her., Sculpture)* Delphin, *der*
dolt [dəʊlt] *n.* Tölpel, *der;* Tolpatsch, *der*
domain [də'meɪn] *n.* **a)** *(estate)* Gut, *das;* Ländereien *Pl.; (of the State; also fig.)* Domäne, *die; see also* **public domain; b)** *(field)* Domäne, *die (geh.);* [Arbeits-, Wissens-, Aufgaben]gebiet, *das*
dome [dəʊm] *n.* Kuppel, *die; (fig.)* Gewölbe, *das*
Domesday [Book] ['du:mzdeɪ (bʊk)] *n. das Reichsgrundbuch Englands aus dem Jahre 1086*
domestic [də'mestɪk] **1.** *adj.* **a)** *(household)* häuslich ⟨*Verhältnisse, Umstände*⟩; *(family)* familiär ⟨*Atmosphäre, Angelegenheit, Reibereien*⟩; ⟨*Wasserversorgung, Ölverbrauch*⟩ der privaten Haushalte; ~ **servant** Hausgehilfe, *der*/-gehilfin, *die;* ~ **help** Haushaltshilfe, *die;* ~ **waste** Hausmüll, *der;* ~ **life** Familienleben, *das;* **b)** *(of one's own country)* inländisch; einheimisch ⟨*Produkt, Tier-/ Pflanzenart*⟩; innenpolitisch ⟨*Problem, Auseinandersetzungen*⟩; *(home-produced)* im Inland hergestellt; ~ **economy/trade** Binnenwirtschaft, *die*/Binnenhandel, *der;* **c)** *(kept by man)* ~ **animal** Haustier, *das;* ~ **rabbit/cat** Hauskaninchen, *das*/Hauskatze, *die;* **d)** *(fond of home life)* häuslich [veranlagt]. **2.** *n.* Domestik, *der (veralt.);* Hausangestellte, *der/die*
domesticate [də'mestɪkeɪt] *v.t.* **a)** *(make fond of home life or work)* fürs häusliche Leben begeistern; *(accustom to home life or work)* an häusliches Leben gewöhnen; **b)** *(naturalize)* einbürgern ⟨*Tier, Pflanze*⟩; **c)** *(tame)* zähmen; domestizieren *(fachspr.)*
domesticated [də'mestɪkeɪtɪd] *adj.* **a)** *(fond of home life or work)* häuslich; **b)** *(naturalized)* eingebürgert; **c)** *(tamed)* domestiziert *(fachspr.);* gezähmt
domesticity [dəʊmes'tɪsɪtɪ, dɒmes'tɪsɪtɪ] *n., no pl. (being domestic)* Häuslichkeit, *die*
domestic 'science *n., no pl.* Hauswirtschaftslehre, *die*
domicile ['dɒmɪsaɪl, 'dɒmɪsɪl] **(domicil** ['dɒmɪsɪl]) **1.** *n.* **a)** *(home)* Heimat, *die;* **b)** *(Law) (place of residence)* [ständiger] Wohnsitz; *(fact of residing)* Aufenthalt, *der.* **2.** *v.t.* ansiedeln
dominance ['dɒmɪnəns] *n., no pl.* Dominanz, *die;* Vorherrschaft, *die* **(over** über + *Akk.*); *(of colours etc.)* Vorherrschen, *das*
dominant ['dɒmɪnənt] **1.** *adj.* **a)** dominierend *(geh.);* beherrschend; hervorstechend, herausragend ⟨*[Wesens]merkmal, Eigenschaft*⟩; vorherrschend ⟨*Kultur, Farbe, Geschmack*⟩; **have a ~ position** eine beherrschende Stellung einnehmen; **be ~ over** dominieren über (+ *Akk.*); **b)** *(imposing)* beherrschend ⟨*Gebäude, Berg usw.*⟩; **c)** *(Mus.)* dominant; ~ **seventh** Dominantseptakkord, *der;* **d)** *(Genetics)* dominant. **2.** *n. (Mus.)* Dominante, *die*
dominate ['dɒmɪneɪt] **1.** *v.t.* beherrschen. **2.** *v.i.* **a)** ~ **over sb./sth.** jmdn./etw. beherrschen; ⟨*großer Mensch, Turm:*⟩ jmdn./etw. überragen; **b)** *(be the most influential)* dominieren
domination [dɒmɪ'neɪʃn] *n., no pl.* [Vor]herrschaft, *die* **(over** über + *Akk.*); **under Roman ~:** unter römischer Herrschaft; **X's ~ of the car market** die Vorherrschaft von X auf dem Automarkt
domineer [dɒmɪ'nɪə(r)] *v.i.* despotisch herrschen; ~ **over sb./sth.** jmdn./etw. tyrannisieren
domineering [dɒmɪ'nɪərɪŋ] *adj.* herrisch, herrschsüchtig ⟨*Person*⟩
Dominican [də'mɪnɪkən] **1.** *adj.* dominikanisch. **2.** *n.* Dominikaner[mönch], *der*
Dominican Re'public *pr. n.* **the ~:** die Dominikanische Republik
dominion [də'mɪnjən] *n.* **a)** *(control)* Herrschaft, *die* **(over** über + *Akk.*); **[be] under Roman ~:** unter römischer Herrschaft [stehen]; **have ~ over sb./a country** Macht über jmdn. haben/ein Land beherrschen; **b)** *usu. in pl. (feudal domains)* Ländereien *Pl.; (territory of sovereign or government)* Reich, *das;* **c)** *(Commonwealth Hist.)* Dominion, *das;* **the D~ of Canada** das Dominion Kanada
domino ['dɒmɪnəʊ] *n., pl.* **~es a)** *(piece for game)* Domino[stein], *der;* **b) ~es** *sing. (game)* Domino[spiel], *das;* **play ~es** Domino spielen; **c)** *(cloak)* Domino, *der*
'domino effect *n.* Dominoeffekt, *der*
[1]**don** [dɒn] *n.* **a) Don** *(Spanish title)* Don; **b)** *(Spanish gentleman)* spanischer Edelmann; **c)** *(Univ.)* [Universitäts]dozent, *der (bes. in Oxford und Cambridge)*
[2]**don** *v.t.,* **-nn-** anlegen *(geh.);* anziehen ⟨*Mantel usw.*⟩; aufsetzen ⟨*Hut*⟩
donate [də'neɪt] *v.t.* spenden ⟨*Organe*⟩; stiften, spenden ⟨*Geld, Kleidung*⟩; stiften ⟨*Land*⟩; ~ **money to charity** Geld für wohltätige Zwecke stiften; **he ~d his body to science** er stellte seinen Körper der Wissenschaft zur Verfügung
donation [də'neɪʃn] *n.* Spende, *die* **(to[wards]** für); Schenkung, *die (Rechtsspr.); (large-scale)* Stiftung, *die;* **a ~ of money/ clothes** eine Geld-/Kleiderspende; **make a ~ of £1,000 [to charity]** 1000 Pfund [für wohltätige Zwecke] spenden *od.* stiften
done [dʌn] *adj.* **a)** *p.p. of* [1]**do; what's ~ is ~:** geschehen ist geschehen; **well ~!** großartig!; **b)** *(coll.: acceptable)* **it's not ~ [in this country]** das macht man [hierzulande] nicht; **it's [not] the ~ thing** es ist [nicht] üblich; **c)** *as int. (accepted)* abgemacht!; einverstanden!; **d)** *(finished)* **be ~:** vorbei sein; **be ~ with sth.** mit etw. fertig sein; *(fed up)* etw. satt haben; **she's ~ with him** sie ist fertig mit ihm *(ugs.);* **be ~ with alcohol/cigarettes** das Trinken/Zigarettenrauchen aufgegeben haben; **is your plate ~ with?** brauchen Sie Ihren Teller noch?; **when the operation was ~ with** als die Operation vorbei *od.* beendet war; **e) have ~ [doing sth.]** aufgehört haben, etw. zu tun; **have ~ with sth./ doing sth.** mit etw. aufhören/aufhören, etw. zu tun
donjon ['dɒndʒən, 'dʌndʒən] *n.* Hauptturm, *der;* Wachtturm, *der*
donkey ['dɒŋkɪ] *n. (lit. or fig.)* Esel, *der;* **she could talk the hind leg[s] off a ~!** *(fig.)* die kann einem die Ohren abreden! *(ugs.)*
donkey: ~ **jacket** *n.* dicke, wasserundurchlässige Jacke; **~'s years** *n. pl. (coll.)* eine Ewigkeit *(ugs.);* **for** *or* **in ~'s years** eine Ewigkeit *(ugs.);* **~-work** *n.* Schwerarbeit, *die*
donnish ['dɒnɪʃ] *adj.* **a)** *(of college don)* akademisch; professoral *(oft abwertend);* **b)** *(pedantic)* oberlehrerhaft *(abwertend);* professoral *(abwertend)*
donor ['dəʊnə(r)] *n.* **a)** *(of gift)* Schenker, *der*/Schenkerin, *die; (to institution etc.)* Stifter, *der*/Stifterin, *die;* **b)** *(of blood, organ, etc.)* Spender, *der*/Spenderin, *die;* **be a ~ of sth.** etw. spenden; **blood ~:** Blutspender, *der*/-spenderin, *die*
Don Quixote [dɒn 'kwɪksət] *pr. n.* Don Quichotte
don't [dəʊnt] **1.** *v.i. (coll.)* = **do not;** *see* [1]**do.**

2. *n.* Nein, *das;* Verbot, *das;* **dos and ~s** *see* ²**do** c

don't: **~-'care** *n.* Gleichgültige, *der/die;* **~-'know** *n.* jmd., der keine Meinung hat; **be a ~-know** zu etw. unentschieden sein

doodad ['du:dæd] *n. (Amer.)* **a)** *(fancy article, trivial ornament)* Spielerei, *die; in pl.* Kinkerlitzchen *Pl. (ugs.);* Firlefanz, *der (ugs.);* **b)** *(gadget)* Dingsbums, *das (ugs.);* Apparillo, *der (ugs.)*

doodah ['du:dɑ:] *n. (sl.)* **a)** *(gadget) see* **doodad b; b)** *(thingamy) (thing)* Dings, *das (ugs.);* Dingsbums, *das (ugs.); (person)* Dingsbums, *der/die;* Dingsda, *der/die;* **c) be all of a ~:** ganz aus dem Häuschen sein *(ugs.)*

doodle ['du:dl] **1.** *v.i.* ≈ Männchen malen; [herum]kritzeln; doodeln. **2.** *n.* Kritzelei, *die; in pl.* Gekritzel, *das;* Kritzeleien *Pl.*

'doodle-bug *n.* **a)** *(Amer. Zool.) (tigerbeetle)* Ameisenjungfer, *die; (larva)* Ameisenlöwe, *der;* **b)** *(Hist. coll.: flying bomb)* V1-Rakete, *die*

doom [du:m] **1.** *n.* **a)** *(fate)* Schicksal, *das; (ruin)* Verhängnis, *das;* **meet one's ~:** vom Schicksal heimgesucht *od. (geh.)* ereilt werden; **b)** *no pl., no art. (Last Judgement)* das Jüngste Gericht; *see also* **crack. 2.** *v.t.* verurteilen; verdammen; **~ sb./sth. to sth.** jmdn./eine Sache zu etw. verdammen *od.* verurteilen; **~ sb. to die** jmdn. dem Tode weihen *(geh.);* **be ~ed to fail** *or* **failure** zum Scheitern verurteilt sein; **be ~ed to exile** ins Exil verbannt werden; **be ~ed** verloren sein

doomsday ['du:mzdeɪ] *n.* der Jüngste Tag; **till ~** *(fig.)* bis zum Jüngsten Tag; noch Ewigkeiten

door [dɔ:(r)] *n.* **a)** Tür, *die; (of castle, barn)* Tor, *das; (of car, coach)* Tür, *die;* [Wagen]schlag, *der;* **'~s open at 7'** „Einlaß ab 7 Uhr"; **he popped** *(coll.) or* **put his head round the ~:** er streckte den Kopf durch die Tür; **just pop a note through the ~** *(coll.)* wirf einfach einen Zettel durch den Briefschlitz; **walk sb. right to the ~:** jmdn. bis vor die *od.* bis zur Haustür begleiten; **I'll drop you at the ~:** ich bringe dich vorbei; **milk is delivered to the ~:** Milch wird an die Haustür geliefert; **lay sth. at sb.'s ~** *(fig.)* jmdm. etw. anlasten *od.* zur Last legen; **next ~:** nebenan; **the boy/girl next ~:** der Junge/das Mädchen von nebenan; **two/three ~s away [from ...]** zwei/drei Türen *od.* Häuser entfernt [von ...]; **live next ~ to sb.** neben jmdm. *od.* nebenan wohnen; **next ~ to** *(fig.) (beside)* neben (+ *Dat.*); *(almost)* fast; beinahe; **from ~ to ~:** von Haus zu Haus; von Tür zu Tür; **go from ~ to ~:** von Tür zu Tür gehen; Klinken putzen *(ugs. abwertend);* **b)** *(fig.: entrance)* Zugang, *der* **(to** zu); **all ~s are open/closed to him** ihm stehen alle Türen offen/sind alle Türen verschlossen; **close the ~ to sth.** etw. unmöglich machen; **have/get one's foot/keep a foot in the ~:** mit einem Fuß *od.* Bein drin sein/hineinkommen/drinbleiben; **leave the ~ open for sth.** die Tür für *od.* zu etw. offenhalten; **leave the ~ open for sb. to do sth.** jmdm. die Tür offenhalten, etw. zu tun; **open the ~ to** *or* **for sth.** etw. möglich machen; **packed to the ~s** voll [besetzt]; gerammelt voll *(ugs.);* **show sb. the ~:** jmdm. die Tür weisen; jmdn. vor die Tür setzen *(ugs.);* **c)** *(~way)* [Tür]eingang, *der;* **walk through the ~:** zur Tür hineingehen/hereinkommen; **shop ~:** Geschäftseingang, *der;* **d) out of ~s** im Freien; draußen; **go out of ~s** nach draußen gehen; ins Freie gehen. *See also* **darken 1 b; indoors**

door: **~bell** *n.* Türklingel, *die;* **~ chimes** *n. pl.* Türglocke, *die;* **~-handle** *n.* Türklinke, *die;* **~-keeper** *n.* Pförtner, *der;* Portier, *der;* **~knob** *n.* Türknopf, -knauf, *der;* **~-knocker** *see* **knocker a; ~man** *n.* Portier, *der;* **~mat** *n.* Fußmatte, *die; (fig.)* Fußabtreter, *der;* Putzlappen, *der;* **~nail** *n.* Türnagel, *der;* Tornagel, *der; see also* **dead 1 a; ~post** *n.* Türpfosten, *der;* **~step** *n.* Eingangsstufe, *die;* Türstufe, *die; (sl.: slice)* dicke Scheibe Brot; **on one's/the ~step** *(fig.)* vor jmds./der Tür; **have sth. right on the ~step** *(fig.)* etw. direkt vor der [Haus]tür haben; **~stop** *n.* Türanschlag, *der; (stone, wedge, etc.)* Türstopper, *der;* **~-to-~** *adj.* **~-to-~ collection** Haussammlung, *die;* **~-to-~ journey** Fahrt von Haus zu Haus; **~-to-~ selling** Hausverkauf, *der;* **~-to-~ salesman** Vertreter, *der;* Hausierer, *der (abwertend);* **~way** *n.* Eingang, *der;* **~yard** *n. (Amer.) (garden-patch)* Vorgarten, *der; (yard)* Vorhof, *der*

dope [dəʊp] **1.** *n.* **a)** *(stimulant)* Aufputschmittel, *das; (sl.: narcotic)* Stoff, *der (salopp);* **~ test** Dopingkontrolle, *die;* **b)** *(sl.) (information)* Informationen *Pl.; (misleading information)* Märchen *Pl. (ugs.);* **c)** *(coll.: fool)* Dussel, *der (ugs.);* **I felt such a ~:** ich kam mir ziemlich dußlig vor *(ugs.).* **2.** *v.t. (administer stimulant to)* dopen ⟨*Pferd, Athleten*⟩; *(administer narcotic to)* Rauschgift verabreichen (+ *Dat.*); *(stupefy)* betäuben. **3.** *v.i.* Rauschgift *od.* Drogen nehmen

~ 'out *v.t. (sl.)* rauskriegen *(ugs.)*

dopey ['dəʊpɪ] *adj. (sl.)* **a)** benebelt *(ugs.);* **b)** *(stupid)* blöd; dämlich; bekloppt

dorm [dɔ:m] *n. (coll.) see* **dormitory a, c**

dormant ['dɔ:mənt] *adj.* untätig ⟨*Vulkan*⟩; ruhend ⟨*Tier, Pflanze*⟩; verborgen, schlummernd ⟨*Talent, Fähigkeiten*⟩; **lie ~** ⟨*Tier:*⟩ schlafen; ⟨*Pflanze, Ei:*⟩ ruhen; ⟨*Talent, Fähigkeiten:*⟩ schlummern; **be** *or* **lie ~:** ⟨*Regel, Gesetz, Anspruch:*⟩ ruhen

dormer ['dɔ:mə(r)]: **~ [window]** *n.* Mansardenfenster, *das*

dormitory ['dɔ:mɪtərɪ] *n.* **a)** Schlafsaal, *der;* **b)** *(commuter area)* **~ suburb** *or* **town** Schlafstadt, *die;* **c)** *(Amer.: student hostel)* Studentenwohnheim, *das*

dormouse ['dɔ:maʊs] *n., pl.* **dormice** ['dɔ:maɪs] Haselmaus, *die*

dorsal ['dɔ:səl] *adj. (Anat., Zool., Bot.)* dorsal *(fachspr.);* Rücken-

dory *n. (Naut.)* Dory, *das (fachspr.)*

dos *pl. of* ²**do**

dosage ['dəʊsɪdʒ] *n.* **a)** *(giving of medicine)* Dosierung, *die;* **b)** *(size of dose)* Dosis, *die*

dose [dəʊs] **1.** *n.* **a)** *(amount of medicine)* Dosis, *die; (fig.)* Dosis, *die;* Quantum, *das;* **take a ~ of medicine** Medizin [ein]nehmen; **in small ~s** *(fig.)* in kleinen Mengen; **like a ~ of salts** *(sl.)* in Null Komma nichts *(ugs.);* **b)** *(amount of radiation)* Strahlen-, Bestrahlungsdosis, *die;* **c)** *(sl.: venereal infection)* Tripper, *der.* **2.** *v.t. (give medicine to)* Arznei geben (+ *Dat.*); **~ sb. with sth.** jmdm. etw. geben *od.* verabreichen

doss [dɒs] *(Brit. sl.)* **1.** *n. (bed)* was zum Pennen *(salopp); (of down-and-out)* Platte, *die (salopp).* **2.** *v.i.* **a)** pennen *(salopp);* **b) ~ down** sich hinhauen *(salopp)*

doss-house *n. (Brit. sl.)* Nachtasyl, *das*

dossier ['dɒsɪə(r), 'dɒsjeɪ] *n.* Akte, *die; (bundle of papers)* Dossier, *das;* **compile a ~ of information** ein Dossier anlegen

dot [dɒt] **1.** *n.* **a)** Punkt, *der; (smaller)* Pünktchen, *das;* **b) on the ~:** auf den Punkt genau; **at 5 on the ~, on the ~ of 5** Punkt 5 Uhr; **[in] the year ~** *(Brit. coll.)* Anno dunnemals *(ugs. scherzh.).* **2.** *v.t.,* **-tt-: a)** *(mark with ~)* mit Punkten/einem Punkt markieren; **~ted with white** weiß gepunktet; **b)** *(place [diacritical] ~ over)* **~ one's i's/j's** i-/j-Punkte machen; **dot the i's and cross the t's** *(fig.)* peinlich genau sein; **c)** *(Mus.)* punktieren; **d)** *(mark as with ~s)* [be]sprenkeln; **the sky was ~ted with stars** der Himmel war von Sternen übersät; **e)** *(scatter)* verteilen; **be ~ted about the place** über den ganzen Ort verstreut sein

dotage ['dəʊtɪdʒ] *n.* Senilität, *die (abwertend);* Altersblödsinn, *der (fachspr.);* **be in one's ~:** senil sein

dotard ['dəʊtəd] *n.* seniler Mensch *(abwertend);* **that old ~:** der/die senile Alte

dote [dəʊt] *v.i.* **[absolutely] ~ on sb./sth.** jmdn./etw. abgöttisch lieben

doting ['dəʊtɪŋ] *adj.* vernarrt; **her ~ father/husband** ihr in sie vernarrter Vater/Mann

'dot matrix *n. (Computing)* Punktmatrix, *die;* **~ printer** Nadeldrucker, *der*

dotted ['dɒtɪd] *adj.* gepunktet ⟨*Kleid, Linie*⟩; *(Mus.)* punktiert ⟨*Note usw.*⟩; **sign on the ~ line** *(fig.)* unterschreiben

dotty ['dɒtɪ] *adj. (coll.)* **a)** *(silly)* dümmlich; **a ~ female** ein Dumm[er]chen *(ugs.);* **be ~ over** *or* **about sb./sth.** in jmdn./etw. vernarrt sein; **go ~ over** *or* **about sb./sth.** für jmdn./etw. schwärmen; **b)** *(feeble-minded)* schrullig *(ugs. abwertend);* vertrottelt *(ugs. abwertend);* **go ~:** vertrotteln; **c)** *(absurd)* blödsinnig *(ugs.);* verrückt ⟨*Idee*⟩; **that was a ~ thing to do** das war Blödsinn *(ugs.)*

double ['dʌbl] **1.** *adj.* **a)** *(consisting of two parts etc.)* doppelt ⟨*Anstrich, Stofflage, Sohle*⟩; **~ wall** Doppelwand, *die;* **b)** *(twofold)* doppelt ⟨*Sandwich, Futter, Fenster, Boden*⟩; **win a ~ gold** zwei Goldmedaillen gewinnen; **give a ~ ring on the phone** das Telefon zweimal klingeln lassen; **underline sth. with a ~ line** etw. doppelt unterstreichen; **~ sink** Doppelspüle, *die;* **sleep with a ~ layer of blankets** unter zwei Bettdecken schlafen; **c)** *(with pl.: two)* zwei ⟨*Punkte, Klingen*⟩; **d)** *(for two persons)* Doppel-; **~ seat** Doppelsitz, *der;* **~ bed/room/cabin** Doppelbett, *das*/-zimmer, *das*/-kabine, *die;* **e) folded ~:** einmal *od.* einfach gefaltet; **be bent ~ with pain** sich vor Schmerzen krümmen; **f)** *(having some part ~)* Doppel-⟨*adler, -heft, -stecker*⟩; **~ flower** *(Bot.)* gefüllte *od.* doppelte Blüte; **~ domino/six** Pasch/Sechserpasch, *der;* **g)** *(dual)* doppelt ⟨*Sinn, [Verwendungs]zweck*⟩; **have a ~ meaning** einen doppelten Sinn haben; doppeldeutig sein; **h)** *(twice as much)* doppelt ⟨*Anzahl*⟩; **a room ~ the size of this** ein doppelt so großes Zimmer wie dieses; **that's ~ what I usually eat** das ist doppelt soviel, wie ich sonst esse; **be ~ the height/width/length/area/time** doppelt so hoch/breit/lang/groß/lang sein; **be ~ the breadth/weight/cost** doppelt so breit/schwer/teuer sein; **~ the heat/strength** doppelt so heiß/stark; **at ~ the cost** zum doppelten Preis; **have ~ the responsibility** doppelt so große Verantwortung haben; **i)** *(twice as many)* doppelt so viele wie; **j)** *(of twofold size etc.)* doppelt ⟨*Portion, Lautstärke, Kognak, Whisky*⟩; **k)** *(of extra size etc.)* doppelt so groß ⟨*Anstrengung, Mühe, Schwierigkeit, Problem, Anreiz*⟩; **l)** *(deceitful)* falsch ⟨*Spiel*⟩. **2.** *adv. (to twice the amount)* doppelt. **3.** *n.* **a)** *(~ quantity)* Doppelte, *das;* **b)** *(~ measure of whisky etc.)* Doppelte, *der;* *(~ room)* Doppelzimmer, *das;* **c)** *(twice as much)* das Doppelte; doppelt soviel; *(twice as many)* doppelt so viele; **~ or quits** doppelt oder nichts; **d)** *(duplicate person)* Doppelgänger, *der*/-gängerin, *die;* **I saw somebody today who was your ~:** ich habe heute jemanden gesehen, der Ihnen zum Verwechseln ähnlich sah; **e)** *(duplicate thing)* Gegenstück, *das* **(of zu)**; **f) at the ~:** unverzüglich; *(Mil.)* aufs schnellste; **g)** *(pair of victories)* Doppelerfolg, *der;* **h)** *(pair of championships)* Double, *das;* Doppel, *das;* **i)** *(Bridge)* Verdoppelung, *die;* **j)** *in pl. (Tennis etc.)* Doppel, *das;* **women's** *or* **ladies'/men's/mixed ~s** Damen-/Herrendoppel, *das*/gemischtes Doppel; **k)** *(Darts) Wurf mit doppeltem Punktwert;* **l)** *(Racing)* Doppelwette, *die.* **4.** *v.t.* **a)** verdoppeln; *(make ~)* doppelt nehmen ⟨*Decke*⟩; **b)** *(Bridge, Mus.)* verdoppeln; **c)** *(Naut.)* umschiffen ⟨*Kap usw.*⟩; **d)** *(clench)* ballen

⟨*Faust*⟩; **e)** *(bend over upon itself)* ~ **[over]** doppelt nehmen. **5.** *v. i.* **a)** sich verdoppeln; **b)** *(run)* laufen; *(turn sharply)* einen Haken schlagen; **c)** *(have two functions)* doppelt verwendbar sein; **the sofa ~s as a bed** man kann das Sofa auch als Bett benutzen

~ **'back** *v. i.* kehrtmachen *(ugs.)*

~ **'up 1.** *v. i.* **a)** sich krümmen; ~ **up with pain** sich vor Schmerzen *(Dat.)* krümmen; **b)** *(fig.)* ~ **up with laughter/mirth** sich vor Lachen/Heiterkeit krümmen; **c)** *(share quarters)* sich *(Dat.)* eine Unterkunft teilen; *(in hotel etc.)* sich *(Dat.)* ein Zimmer teilen. **2.** *v. t.* **a)** in die Knie zwingen; *(fig.)* **the sight ~d us up with laughter/mirth** bei dem Anblick krümmten wir uns vor Lachen/Heiterkeit; **be ~d up with laughter/pain** *etc.* sich vor Lachen/Schmerzen *usw.* krümmen; **b)** *(fold)* einmal falten

double: ~-'acting *adj.* doppelt wirkend; ~ **'agent** *n.* Doppelagent, *der*/-agentin, *die;* **~-barrelled** (*Amer.:* **~-barreled**) ['dʌblbærəld] *adj.* **a)** doppelläufig; **~-barrelled [shot]gun/rifle** Doppelflinte/-büchse, *die;* **b)** *(fig.: twofold)* doppelt; Doppel-; zweifach; **c)** *(fig.: with two parts)* Doppel-; **~-barrelled surname** *(Brit.)* Doppelname, *der;* **~-bass** [dʌbl'beɪs] *n. (Mus.)* Kontrabaß, *der;* **~-bedded** [dʌbl'bedɪd] *adj.* ⟨*Zimmer*⟩ mit Doppelbett/mit zwei Einzelbetten; ~ **'bend** *n.* S-Kurve, *die;* ~ **'bill** *n.* Doppelprogramm, *das;* ~ **'bind** *n.* Zwickmühle, *die;* **be in a ~ bind** in einer Zwickmühle stecken; **~-'blind** *(Med., Psych.)* **1.** *adj.* Doppelblind-; **2.** *n.* Doppelblindversuch, *der;* ~ **'boiler** *n. (Cookery)* Wasserbadtopf, *der;* **~-'book** *v. t.* doppelt reservieren; *(fig.)* sich zweierlei vornehmen für; **~-breasted** [dʌbl'brestɪd] *adj. (Tailoring)* zwei- *od.* doppelreihig; **~-breasted jacket** Zweireiher, *der;* **~-'check** *v. t.* **a)** *(verify twice)* zweimal kontrollieren; **~-check sb.'s statements** jmds. Aussagen zweimal überprüfen; **b)** *(verify in two ways)* zweifach überprüfen; ~ **'chin** *n.* Doppelkinn, *das;* ~ **'cream** *n.* Sahne mit hohem Fettgehalt; **~-'cross 1.** *n.* Doppelspiel, *das;* **2.** *v. t.* ein Doppelspiel treiben mit; reinlegen *(ugs.);* **~-'dealer** *n.* Betrüger, *der;* **~-dealing 1.** [--'--] *n.* Betrügerei, *die;* **2.** ['----] *adj.* betrügerisch; **~-decker** [dʌbldekə(r)] **1.** ['----] *adj.* Doppeldecker-; Doppelstock- *(Amtsspr.);* **~-decker bus** Doppeldeckerbus, *der;* Doppelstockomnibus, *der (Amtsspr.);* **~-decker train** Doppelstockzug, *der;* **a ~-decker sandwich** ein doppelter Sandwich; ein Doppeldecker *(ugs.);* **2.** [--'--] *n.* Doppeldecker, *der; (train)* Doppelstockzug, *der;* **~-de'clutch** *see* **declutch;** ~ **'door** *n. (door with two parts)* Flügeltür, *die; (twofold door)* Doppeltür, *die;* ~ **'Dutch** *see* **Dutch 2c; ~-dyed** *adj. (Textiles)* doppelt gefärbt; *(fig.)* Erz⟨*schurke, -ganove*⟩; unverbesserlich ⟨*Heuchler*⟩; **~-edged** *adj. (lit. or fig.)* zweischneidig

double entendre [du:bl ɑ̃'tɑ̃dr] *n.* Zweideutigkeit, *die*

double: ~ **'entry** *see* **entry h;** ~ **ex'posure** *n. (Photog.)* Doppelbelichtung, *die; (result)* doppelt belichtetes Foto; ~ **'fault** *see* **fault 1d;** ~ **'feature** *n.* Doppelprogramm, *das;* ~ **'figures** *see* **figure 1l; ~-'glazed** *adj.* Doppel⟨*fenster*⟩; ~ **'glazing** *n.* Doppelverglasung, *die;* ~ **'harness** *n.* **a)** *(fig.: matrimony)* Ehe, *die;* **b)** *(fig.: close partnership)* enge Zusammenarbeit; ~ **'header** *n. (Amer.) zwei Spiele zwischen denselben Gegnern an einem Tag;* **~-'jointed** *adj.* sehr gelenkig; ~ **'life** *n.* Doppelleben, *das;* **~-'lock** *v. t.* zweimal abschließen; ~ **'meaning** *see* **double entendre;** ~ **'negative** *n.* doppelte Verneinung; **~-page 'spread** *see* **spread 3k; ~-park** *v. t. & i.* in der zweiten Reihe parken; **~-'parking** *n.* Parken in der zweiten Reihe; ~ **'play** *n. (Baseball)* doppeltes Ausmachen; **~-quick 1.** ['---] *adj.* **a) in ~-quick time/at a ~-quick pace** im Laufschritt; **b)** *(fig.)* ganz schnell; **2.** [--'-] *adv. (Mil.)* im Laufschritt; *(fig.)* ganz schnell; ~ **'room** *n.* Doppelzimmer, *das;* ~ **'saucepan** *see* ~ **boiler; ~-'spaced** *adj.* mit doppeltem Zeilenabstand *nachgestellt;* ~ **'spread** *see* **spread 3k;** ~ **'standard** *n. (rule)* Doppelmoral, *die;* ~ **star** *n. (Astron.)* Doppelstern, *der;* **~-stop** *v. i. (Mus.)* mit Doppelgriff spielen

doublet ['dʌblɪt] *n.* **a)** *(Hist.: garment)* Wams, *das;* **b)** *(one of pair)* Dublette, *die*

double: ~ 'take *n.* **he did a ~ take a moment after he saw her walk by** nachdem sie vorbeigegangen war, stutzte er und sah er ihr nach; **~-talk** *n.* Doppeldeutigkeiten; **~-think** *n.* zwiespältiges Denken; ~ **'time** *n.* **a)** *(Econ.)* doppelter Stundenlohn; **be on ~ time** 100% Zuschlag bekommen; **b)** *(Mil.: running pace)* Laufschritt, *der;* ~ **'track** *see* **track 1e;** ~ **'vision** *n. (Med.)* Doppeltsehen, *das;* ~ **'wedding** *n.* Doppelhochzeit, *die*

doubloon [dʌ'blu:n, də:blu:n] *n. (Hist.)* Dublone, *die*

doubly ['dʌblɪ] *adv.* doppelt; **make ~ sure that ...:** [ganz] besonders darauf achten, daß ...; **this response made him ~ angry/upset** diese Antwort hat ihn sehr *od.* besonders geärgert/bestürzt

doubt [daʊt] **1.** *n.* **a)** Zweifel, *der;* **~[s] [about** *or* **as to sth./as to whether ...]** *(as to future)* Ungewißheit, *(as to fact)* Unsicherheit [über etw. *(Akk.)*/darüber, ob ...]; **there was no ~** *or* **there were no ~s in our minds about** *or* **as to ...:** uns war ... klar; wir waren uns über ... *(Akk.)* im klaren; **~[s] about** *or* **as to sth.,** ~ **of sth.** *(inclination to disbelieve)* Zweifel an etw. *(Dat.);* **there's no ~ that ...:** es besteht kein Zweifel daran, daß ...; **~[s]** *(hesitations)* Bedenken *Pl.;* **have ~ about doing sth., have [one's] ~s about doing sth.** [seine] Bedenken haben, ob man etw. tun soll [oder nicht]; **he's now having ~s [about whether ...]** ihm kommen jetzt Bedenken[, ob ...]; **have one's ~s [about sb./sth.]** seine Bedenken [gegen jmdn./etw.] haben; **have one's ~s about whether ...:** bezweifeln *od.* daran zweifeln, daß ...; **be in ~ about** *or* **as to sth.** *(disbelieve)* über etw. *(Akk.)* im Zweifel sein; **be in no ~ about** *or* **as to sth.** nicht an etw. *(Dat.)* zweifeln; **be in ~ about** *or* **as to whether to do sth.** *(have reservations)* Bedenken haben, ob man etw. tun soll; **when** *or* **if in ~:** im Zweifelsfall; **no ~** *(certainly)* gewiß; *(probably)* sicherlich; *(admittedly)* wohl; **there's no ~ about it** daran besteht kein Zweifel; das steht fest; **cast ~ on sth.** etw. in Zweifel ziehen; **b)** *no pl. (uncertain state of things)* Ungewißheit, *die;* **be in ~:** ungewiß sein; **beyond [all] ~, without [a] ~:** ohne [jeden] Zweifel; **it is beyond [all] ~ that ...:** es steht [völlig] außer Zweifel, daß ...; **without a shadow of [a] ~:** ohne den geringsten Zweifel. **2.** *v. i.* zweifeln; ~ **of sth./sb.** an etw./jmdm. zweifeln. **3.** *v. t.* anzweifeln; zweifeln an (+ *Dat.*); **she ~ed him** sie zweifelte an ihm; **I don't ~ that** *or* **it** ich zweifle nicht daran; ich bezweifle das nicht; **I ~ whether** *or* **if** *or* **that ...:** ich bezweifle, daß ...; ich zweifle daran, daß ...; **not ~ that** *or* **but that** *or* **but** nicht daran zweifeln, daß ...; nicht bezweifeln, daß ...

doubter ['daʊtə(r)] *n.* Zweifler, *der*/Zweiflerin, *die*

doubtful ['daʊtfl] *adj.* **a)** *(sceptical)* skeptisch ⟨*Mensch, Wesen*⟩; **a ~ person** ein Skeptiker/eine Skeptikerin; **b)** *(showing doubt)* ungläubig ⟨*Gesicht, Blick, Stirnrunzeln*⟩; **c)** *(uncertain)* zweifelnd; **be ~ as to** *or* **about sth.** an etw. *(Dat.)* zweifeln; **be ~ whether ...:** daran zweifeln, daß ...; *(be unsure)* sich *(Dat.)* nicht sicher sein, ob ...; **be ~ about sth.** hinsichtlich einer Sache unsicher sein; **d)** *(causing doubt)* fraglich; **the situation looks ~:** die Lage ist unsicher; **e)** *(uncertain in meaning etc.)* ungewiß ⟨*Ergebnis, Ausgang, Herkunft, Aussicht*⟩; *(questionable)* zweifelhaft ⟨*Ruf, Charakter, Organisation, Wert, Tugend, Autorität, Kräfte, Potential*⟩; *(ambiguous)* unklar ⟨*Bedeutung*⟩; *(unsettled)* unsicher ⟨*Lage*⟩; **f)** *(unreliable)* zweifelhaft ⟨*Person, Maßstab, Stütze*⟩; **g)** *(giving reason to suspect evil)* bedenklich ⟨*Gewohnheit, Spiel, Botschaft*⟩

doubtfully ['daʊtfəlɪ] *adv.* **a)** *(with doubt)* skeptisch; **b)** *(ambiguously)* mißverständlich

doubting Thomas [daʊtɪŋ 'tɒməs] *n.* ungläubiger Thomas

doubtless ['daʊtlɪs] *adv.* **a)** *(certainly)* gewiß; **b)** *(probably)* sicherlich; **c)** *(admittedly)* wohl

douche [du:ʃ] *n.* **a)** *(jet)* Dusche, *die; (Med.)* Spülung, *die;* **b)** *(device)* Dusche, *die; (Med.)* Spülapparat, *der*

dough [dəʊ] *n.* **a)** Teig, *der;* **yeast ~:** Hefeteig, *der;* **b)** *(sl.: money)* Knete, *die (salopp)*

'doughnut *n.* [Berliner] Pfannkuchen, *der;* Berliner, *der (landsch.)*

doughtily ['daʊtɪlɪ] *adv.,* **doughty** ['daʊtɪ] *adj. (arch./joc.)* kühn; wacker *(veralt./scherzh.)*

doughy ['dəʊɪ] *adj.* teigig ⟨*Konsistenz, Finger, Schüssel, Masse*⟩

dour [dʊə(r)] *adj.* hartnäckig ⟨*Person, Charakter, Arbeiten*⟩; düster ⟨*Blick, Gesicht*⟩; finster ⟨*Miene, Stirnrunzeln*⟩

douse [daʊs] *v. t.* **a)** *(extinguish)* ausmachen ⟨*Licht, Laterne, Kerze, Feuer*⟩; **b)** *(throw water on)* übergießen ⟨*Feuer, Flamme, Menschen*⟩; ~ **sth. with water** etw. mit Wasser übergießen

[1]**dove** [dʌv] *n. (Ornith., Polit., Relig.)* Taube, *die*

[2]**dove** [dəʊv] *see* **dive 1**

dove: ~-coloured *adj.* taubengrau; **~cot, ~-cote** *n.* Taubenschlag, *der;* **flutter the ~cots** *(fig.)* für einige Aufregung sorgen; **~-grey** *see* **~-coloured; ~tail 1.** *n. (Carpentry)* **a)** *(joint)* Schwalbenschwanzverbindung, *die;* **b)** *(tenon)* Schwalbenschwanz, *der;* **2.** *v. t.* **a)** *(fig.: fit together)* aufeinander abstimmen ⟨*Pläne, Verabredungen, Termine*⟩; **b)** *(put together with ~tails)* verschwalben **(into, with** mit); **3.** *v. i. (fig.: fit together)* ⟨*Vorbereitungen, Zeitpläne:*⟩ aufeinander abgestimmt sein

dovish ['dʌvɪʃ] *adj.* gemäßigt; kompromißbereit

dowager ['daʊədʒə(r)] *n.* **a)** *(widow with title or property)* Witwe von Stand; **Queen ~/~ duchess** Königin-/Herzoginwitwe, *die;* **b)** *(coll.: dignified elderly lady)* Matrone, *die*

dowdily ['daʊdɪlɪ] *adv.* schäbig

dowdiness ['daʊdɪnɪs] *n.* Unansehnlichkeit, *die; (shabbiness)* Schäbigkeit, *die*

dowdy ['daʊdɪ] *adj.* *(unattractively dull)* unansehnlich; *(shabby)* schäbig

dowel ['daʊəl] *(Carpentry)* **1.** *n.* [Holz]dübel, *der.* **2.** *v. t., (Brit.)* **-ll-:** ~ **[together]** zusammendübeln

doweling, *(Brit.)* **dowelling** ['daʊəlɪŋ] *n.* Verdübelung, *die*

'dower house *n. (Brit.)* Haus einer Witwe *(Teil des Wittums)*

Dow-Jones index [daʊ'dʒəʊnz ɪndeks] *n. (Econ.)* Dow-Jones-[Aktien]index, *der*

[1]**down** [daʊn] *n. (Geog.)* [baumloser] Höhenzug; *in pl.* Downs *Pl. (an der Süd- und Südostküste Englands);* **the North/South D~s** die North/South Downs

[2]**down** *n.* **a)** *(of bird)* Daunen *Pl.;* Flaum, *der;* **chicks covered in ~:** Vogeljunge im Daunenkleid; **b)** *(hair)* Flaum, *der;* **have a covering of ~:** mit Flaum bedeckt sein; **c)** *(fluffy substance)* Flausch, *der; (of thistle, dandelion)* Flaum, *der*

[3]**down 1.** *adv.* **a)** *(to lower place)* runter *(bes.*

ugs.); herunter/hinunter *(bes. schriftsprachlich)*; *(in lift)* abwärts; *(in crossword puzzle)* senkrecht; **[right] ~ to sth.** [ganz] bis zu etw. her-/hinunter; **come on ~!** komm [hier/weiter] herunter!; **b)** *(to ~stairs)* runter *(bes. ugs.)*; herunter/hinunter *(bes. schriftsprachlich)*; **c)** *(of money: at once)* sofort; **pay ~ for sth., pay for sth. cash ~**: etw. [in] bar bezahlen; **d)** *(into prostration)* nieder‹*fallen, -geschlagen werden*›; **shout the place/house ~** *(fig.)* schreien, daß die Wände zittern; **e)** *(on to paper)* **copy sth. ~ from the board** etw. von der Tafel abschreiben; **f)** *(on programme)* **put a meeting ~ for 2 p.m.** ein Treffen für *od.* auf 14 Uhr ansetzen; **put oneself ~ for a dental appointment** sich *(Dat.)* einen Termin beim *od.* vom Zahnarzt geben lassen; **g)** *(to place regarded as lower)* runter *(bes. ugs.)*; herunter/hinunter *(bes. schriftsprachlich)*; **go ~ to the shops/the end of the road** zu den Läden/zum Ende der Straße hinuntergehen; **h)** *(with current)* stromab[wärts]; *(with wind)* mit/vor dem Wind; **brought ~ by river** flußabwärts befördert; **i)** *(to place regarded as less important)* **go ~ to one's cottage in the country for the weekend** zum Wochenende in sein Ferienhaus auf dem Land *od. (DDR)* seine Datsche fahren; **j)** *(southwards)* runter *(bes. ugs.)*; herunter/hinunter *(bes. schriftsprachlich)*; **come ~ from Edinburgh to London** von Edinburgh nach London [he]runterkommen; **k)** *(Brit.: from capital)* raus *(bes. ugs.)*; heraus/hinaus *(bes. schriftsprachlich)*; **get ~ to Reading from London** von London nach Reading raus-/hinausfahren; **l)** *(Brit.: from university)* **come ~ [from Oxford]** das Studium [in Oxford] abschließen; **m)** *(Naut.: with rudder to windward)* in Lee; **put the helm ~**: das Ruder in Lee legen; **n)** *as int.* runter! *(bes. ugs.)*; *(to dog)* leg dich!; nieder!; *(Mil.)* hinlegen!; **~ with imperialism/the president!** nieder mit dem Imperialismus/dem Präsidenten!; **o)** *(in lower place)* unten; **~ on the floor** auf dem Fußboden; **low/lower ~**: tief/tiefer unten; **~ at the bottom of the hill** [unten] am Fuß des Berges; **~ under the table** unter dem Tisch; **wear one's hair ~**: sein Haar offen tragen; **~ below the horizon** hinter *od.* unter dem Horizont; **~ at the bottom of the sea/pool** [tief] auf dem Meeresgrund/Grund des Schwimmbeckens; **~ there/here** da/hier unten; **X metres ~**: X Meter tief; **his flat is on the next floor ~**: seine Wohnung ist ein Stockwerk tiefer; **p)** *(facing ~wards, bowed)* zu Boden; **keep one's eyes ~**: zu Boden sehen; **q)** *(~stairs)* unten; **r)** *(in fallen position)* unten; **~ [on the floor]** *(Boxing)* am Boden; auf den Brettern; **~ and out** *(Boxing)* k.o.; *(fig.)* fertig *(ugs.)*; *see also* **down-and-out**; **s)** *(prostrate)* auf dem Fußboden/der Erde; **be ~ with an illness** eine Krankheit haben; **t)** ausgefallen ‹*Computer*›; **u)** *(on paper)* nieder-; **be ~ in writing/on paper/in print** niedergeschrieben/zu Papier gebracht/gedruckt sein; **v)** *(on programme)* angesetzt ‹*Termin, Treffen*›; **be ~ for an appointment** einen Termin haben; **be ~ to speak** als Redner vorgesehen sein; **be ~ to run in a race** für ein Rennen gemeldet sein; **w)** *(in place regarded as lower)* unten; **~ at the bottom of the garden** am unteren Ende des Gartens; **~ at the doctor's/social security office** beim Arzt/Sozialamt; **x)** *(brought to the ground)* **be ~**: am Boden liegen; **y)** *(in place regarded as less important)* **~ in Wales/in the country** weit weg in Wales/draußen auf dem Lande; **~ on the farm** auf dem Bauernhof; **z)** **~ [south]** unten [im Süden] *(ugs.)*; **aa)** *(Brit.: not in capital)* draußen; **bb)** *(Brit.: not in university)* nicht mehr im Studium; *(for vacation)* nicht an der Universität; **how long have you been ~ from Oxford?** seit wann sind Sie nicht mehr an der Universität Oxford?; **cc)** *(Amer.)* **~ south/east** in den Südstaaten/im Osten; **dd)** *(in depression)* **~ [in the mouth]** niedergeschlagen; **are you [feeling] ~ about something?** bedrückt Sie etwas?; **ee)** **be ~ on sb./sth.** *(dislike)* etwas gegen jmdn./etw. haben; **be very ~ on sb./sth.** jmdm./einer Sache gegenüber sehr kritisch eingestellt sein; **ff)** **~ to the ground** *see* [1]**ground 1 b**; **gg)** *(now cheaper)* [jetzt] billiger; **prices have gone/are ~**: die Preise sind gesunken; **hh)** **be ~ to ...** *(have only ... left)* nichts mehr haben außer ...; **we're ~ to our last £100** wir haben nur noch 100 Pfund; **strip off ~ to one's underwear** sich bis auf die Unterwäsche ausziehen; **be [left] ~ to sb.** an jmdm. hängenbleiben; **now it's ~ to him to do something** nun liegt es bei *od.* an ihm, etwas zu tun; **ii)** *(to reduced consistency or size)* **thin gravy ~**: Soße verdünnen; **the water had boiled right ~**: das Wasser war fast verdampft; **wear the soles ~**: die Sohlen ablaufen; **jj)** *(to smoother state)* **sand sth. ~**: etw. abschmirgeln; **kk)** *(including lower limit)* **from ... ~ to ...**: von ... bis zu ... hinunter; **ll)** *(from earlier time)* weiter-; **last ~ to the present day/our time** bis zum heutigen Tag/ bis in unsere Zeit weitergegeben werden; **mm)** *(more quietly)* leiser; **put the sound/TV ~**: den Ton/Fernseher leiser stellen; **nn)** *(in position of lagging or loss)* weniger; **be three points/games ~**: mit drei Punkten/Spielen zurückliegen; **start the second half 1-0 ~**: mit einem 1:0-Rückstand in die zweite Halbzeit gehen; **we're £3,000 ~ on last year, in terms of profit** was unseren Gewinn angeht, so liegt er um 3000 Pfund unter dem des letzten Jahres; **be ~ on one's earnings of the previous year** weniger verdienen als im Vorjahr; **be ~ on one's luck** eine Pechsträhne haben. *See also* [1]**heel 1 b**; **up 1 aa**. **2.** *prep.* **a)** *(~wards along)* runter *(bes. ugs.)*; herunter/hinunter *(bes. schriftsprachlich)*; **lower ~ the river** weiter unten am Fluß; **fall ~ the stairs/steps** die Treppe/Stufen herunterstürzen; **fall ~ the ladder** die Leiter runter-/herunterrutschen; **walk ~ the hill/road** den Hügel/die Straße heruntergehen; **lower sb. ~ a cliff** jmdn. an einem Felsen herunterlassen; **b)** *(~wards through)* durch; **c)** *(~wards into)* rein in (+ *Akk.*) *(bes. ugs.)*; hinein in (+ *Akk.*) *(bes. schriftsprachlich)*; **fall ~ a hole/well/ditch** in ein Loch/ einen Brunnen/einen Graben fallen; **trickle ~ the plug-hole** ins Abflußloch tröpfeln; **d)** *(~wards over)* über (+ *Akk.*); **ivy grew ~ the wall** Efeu wuchs an der Mauer herunter; **spill water all ~ one's skirt** sich *(Dat.)* Wasser über den Rock gießen; **condensation running ~ the windows** an den Fenstern herunterlaufendes Kondenswasser; **e)** *(from top to bottom of)* runter *(bes. ugs.)*; herunter/hinunter *(bes. schriftsprachlich)*; **his eye travelled ~ the list** sein Auge wanderte über die Liste; **draw a line ~ the page** eine Linie längs über die Seite ziehen; **f)** *(~wards in time)* weiter-; **the tradition has continued ~ the ages** die Tradition ist von Generation zu Generation weitergegeben worden; **g)** *(along)* **go ~ the road/corridor/track** die Straße/den Korridor/den Weg hinunter- *od.* entlang- *od. (ugs.)* langgehen; **come ~ the street** die Straße herunter- *od.* entlangkommen; **turn ~ a side-street** in eine Seitenstraße einbiegen; **part one's hair ~ the middle** einen Mittelscheitel tragen; **h)** *(Brit. sl.: to)* **go ~ the pub/disco** in die Kneipe/Disko gehen; **i)** *(at or in a lower position in or on)* [weiter] unten; **further ~ the ladder/coast** weiter unten auf der Leiter/an der Küste; **live in a hut ~ the mountain/hill** in einer Hütte weiter unten am Berg wohnen; **live just ~ the road** ein Stück weiter unten in der Straße wohnen; **a place just ~ the river** eine Stelle etwas weiter flußabwärts; *see also* **downtown**; **j)** *(from top to bottom along)* an (+ *Dat.*); **~ the stem of a plant/the side of a house** am Stiel einer Pflanze/an der Seite eines Hauses; **the lines ~ the page** die senkrechten Linien auf der Seite; **the buttons ~ the back of the dress** die senkrechte Knopfreihe auf dem Rücken des Kleides; **there were festivities ~ every road** auf allen Straßen wurde gefeiert; **k)** *(all over)* überall auf (+ *Dat.*); **I've got coffee [all] ~ my skirt** mein ganzer Rock ist voll Kaffee; **leave marks ~ sb.'s face** in jmds. ganzem Gesicht Spuren hinterlassen; **l)** *(Brit. sl.: in, at)* **~ the pub/café/town** in der Kneipe/im Café/in der Stadt; **be ~ the shops** einkaufen sein *(ugs.)*. *See also* **stage 1 a**; **up 2 d**. **3.** *adj.* *(directed ~wards)* nach unten führend ‹*Rohr, Kabel*›; ‹*Rolltreppe*› nach unten; nach unten gerichtet ‹*Kolbenhub, Sog*›; **~ train/line/journey** *(Railw.)* Zug/Gleis/Fahrt Richtung Stadt. **4.** *v.t.* *(coll.)* **a)** *(knock ~)* auf die Bretter schicken ‹*Boxer*›; **b)** *(fig.: defeat)* fertigmachen *(ugs.)* ‹*Gegner*›; **c)** *(drink ~)* leer machen *(ugs.)* ‹*Flasche, Glas*›; schlucken *(ugs.)* ‹*Getränk*›; **d)** *(throw ~)* ‹*Tier:*› abschmeißen *(ugs.)* ‹*Reiter, Last*›; **~ tools** *(cease work)* zu arbeiten aufhören; *(make a break)* die Arbeit unterbrechen; *(finish work)* Feierabend machen; *(go on strike)* die Arbeit niederlegen; **e)** *(shoot ~)* abschießen, runterholen *(ugs.)* ‹*Flugzeug*›; **f)** *(stop by shot etc.)* zusammenschießen *(ugs.)*; **g)** *(Footb.)* legen *(Sportjargon)* ‹*Gegenspieler*›. **5.** *n.* **a)** *(Wrestling)* Wurf, *der*; **b)** *(Amer. and Can. Footb.)* Versuch, *der*; **c)** **ups and ~s** *see* **up 4**; **d)** *(coll.)* **have a ~ on sb./sth.** jmdn./etw. auf dem Kieker haben *(ugs.)*

down: **~-and-out** *n.* Stadtstreicher, *der*/Stadtstreicherin, *die*; Penner, *der*/Pennerin, *die (ugs.)*; **~beat 1.** *n.* *(Mus.)* erster/ betonter Takteil; **2.** *adj.* *(coll.)* **a)** *(relaxed)* ungezwungen; **b)** *(pessimistic)* düster ‹*Film usw.*›; **~cast** *adj.* **a)** *(dejected)* niedergeschlagen ‹*Blick, Gesicht*›; **b)** *(directed ~wards)* gesenkt ‹*Blick, Kopf*›; **with one's head ~cast** mit gesenktem Kopf; **~draught** *n.* [Luft]zug von oben; **~fall** *n.* *(ruin)* Untergang, *der*; **be** *or* **mean sb.'s ~fall** jmds. Untergang *od.* Ruin sein; **~grade** *n.* Gefällstrecke, *die*; **he was on the ~ grade** es ging bergab mit ihm; **~grade** *v.t.* niedriger einstufen; **~-'hearted** *adj.* niedergeschlagen ‹*Blick, Gesicht*›; **~hill 1.** ['--] *adj.* bergab führend ‹*Fahrt*›; ‹*Strecke, Weg*› bergab; **the journey was ~hill** die Reise führte bergab; **he's on the ~hill path** *(fig.)* es geht bergab mit ihm; **a ~hill trend** *(fig.)* ein Abwärtstrend; **the ~hill course of the economy** *(fig.)* die Talfahrt der Wirtschaft; **be ~hill all the way** *(fig.)* ganz einfach sein; **2.** [-'-] *adv.* bergab; **come ~hill** den Berg herunterkommen; **sb./sth. is going ~hill** *(fig.)* es geht bergab mit jmdm./etw.; **3.** ['--] *n.* **a)** *(~ward slope)* Gefällstrecke, *die*; **b)** *(Skiing)* Abfahrtslauf, *der*; **~land** *n.* [baumloses] Hügelland; **~-market** *adj.* weniger anspruchsvoll; **~ payment** *n.* Anzahlung, *die*; **~pipe** *n.* [Regenab]fallrohr, *das*; **~pour** *n.* Regenguß, *der*; **~right 1.** *adj.* **a)** *(utter)* ausgemacht ‹*Frechheit, Dummheit, Idiot, Lügner*›; glatt ‹*Lüge*›; **b)** *(straightforward)* ehrlich ‹*Rat, Darstellung, Person*›; offen ‹*Wort*›; **2.** *adv.* geradezu; ausgesprochen; **it would be ~right stupid to do that** es wäre eine ausgemachte Dummheit, das zu versuchen; **~stage** *(Theatre)* **1.** *adv.* im Vordergrund der Bühne; **move ~stage** sich zum Vordergrund der Bühne bewegen; **2.** *adj.* **a ~stage door/entrance** eine Vordertür/ein Vordereingang zur Bühne; **~stairs 1.** [-'-] *adv.* die Treppe hinunter ‹*gehen, fallen, kommen*›; unten ‹*wohnen, sein*›; **2.** ['--] *adj.* im Parterre *od.* Erdgeschoß *nachgestellt;* Parterre‹*wohnung*›; **3.** [-'-] *n.* Untergeschoß, *das;* **~stream 1.** [-'-] *adv.* flußabwärts; **2.** ['--] *adj.* flußabwärts gelegen ‹*Ort*›; **the ~stream voyage** die Reise flußabwärts; **~-stroke** *n.* **a)** *(in writing)* Abstrich, *der;* **b)** *(Mech.: of piston)* Abwärtshub, *der;* **~-swing** *n. (Golf, Commerc.)* Abschwung, *der;* **~ time** *n. (Computing)* Ausfallzeit, *die;* **~-to-earth** *adj.* praktisch, nüchtern ‹*Person*›; realistisch ‹*Plan, Vorschlag*›; sachlich ‹*Bemerkung, Antwort*›; **~town** *(Amer.)* **1.** *adj.* im Stadtzentrum *nachgestellt;* in der Innenstadt *nachgestellt;* **~town Manhattan** das Stadtzentrum Manhattan; **2.** *adv.* ins Stadtzentrum, in die Innenstadt ‹*gehen, fahren*›; im Stadtzentrum, in der Innenstadt ‹*leben, liegen, sein*›; **3.** *n.* Stadtzentrum, *das;* Innenstadt, *die;* **~trodden** *adj.* geknechtet; unterdrückt; **~turn** *n. (Econ., Commerc.)* Abschwung, *der;* **~ 'under** *(coll.)* **1.** *adv.* in/*(to)* nach Australien/Neuseeland; **2.** *n. (Australia)* Australien *(das); (New Zealand)* Neuseeland *(das)*

downward ['daʊnwəd] **1.** *adj.* nach unten *nachgestellt;* nach unten gerichtet; **~ movement/trend** *(lit. or fig.)* Abwärtsbewegung, *die*/-trend, *der;* **~ gradient** *or* **slope** Gefälle, *das;* **move in a ~ direction** sich abwärts *od.* nach unten bewegen; **he was on a/the ~ path** *(fig.)* mit ihm ging es bergab. **2.** *adv.* abwärts ‹*sich bewegen*›; nach unten ‹*sehen, gehen*›; *see also* **face down[ward]**

downwards ['daʊnwədz] *see* **downward 2**

'downwind 1. *adv.* mit dem Wind; vor dem Wind ‹*segeln*›; **be ~ of sb./sth.** in jmds. Windschatten/im Windschatten einer Sache *(Gen.)* sein. **2.** *adj.* in Windrichtung liegend; **the ~ side** die windabgewandte Seite

downy ['daʊnɪ] *adj.* flaumig; flaumweich ‹*Haar, Haut*›; Flaum‹*haar, -bart*›

dowry ['daʊrɪ] *n.* Mitgift, *die (veralt.);* Aussteuer, *die*

¹dowse *see* **douse**

²dowse [daʊz] *v.i.* mit der Wünschelrute suchen **(for** nach)

dowser ['daʊzə(r)] *n. (person)* Wünschelrutengänger, *der*/-gängerin, *die*

dowsing-rod ['daʊzɪŋrɒd] *n.* Wünschelrute, *die*

doxology [dɒk'sɒlədʒɪ] *n. (Eccl.)* Doxologie, *die*

doyen ['dɔɪən, 'dwɑ:jæ̃] *n.* Doyen, *der*

doyenne [dɔɪ'en, dwɑ:jen] *n.* Doyenne, *die*

doyley *see* **doily**

doz. *abbr.* **dozen** Dtzd.

doze [dəʊz] **1.** *v.i.* dösen *(ugs.);* [nicht tief] schlafen; **lie dozing** im Halbschlaf liegen. **2.** *n.* Nickerchen, *das (ugs.);* **fall into a ~:** eindösen *(ugs.)*

~ **'off** *v.i.* eindösen *(ugs.)*

dozen [dʌzn] *n.* **a)** *pl. same (twelve)* Dutzend, *das;* **six ~ bottles of wine** sechsmal zwölf Flaschen Wein; **there were several/a few ~ [people] there** Dutzende von Leuten/ein paar Dutzend Leute waren da; **a ~ times/reasons** *(fig. coll.: many)* dutzendmal/Dutzende von Gründen; **half a ~:** sechs; ein halbes Dutzend *(veralt.);* **b)** *pl.* **~s** *(set of twelve)* Dutzend, *das;* **by the ~** *(in twelves)* im Dutzend; *(fig. coll.: in great numbers)* in großen Scharen; **do one's daily ~** *(coll.)* Frühsport machen; **c)** *in pl. (coll.: many)* Dutzende *Pl.;* **in [their] ~s** *(in great numbers)* in großen Scharen; **~s of times** dutzendmal

dozy ['dəʊzɪ] *adj. (drowsy)* dösig *(ugs.);* schläfrig

D. Phil. [di:'fɪl] *abbr.* **Doctor of Philosophy** Dr. phil.; *see also* **B. Sc.**

DPP *abbr. (Brit.)* **Director of Public Prosecutions** ≈ Generalstaatsanwalt, *der*

Dr *abbr.* **a) doctor** *(as prefix to name)* Dr.; **b) debtor** Sch.

drab [dræb] *adj.* **a)** *(dull brown)* gelblich braun; sandfarben; *(dull-coloured)* matt; **b)** *(dull, monotonous)* langweilig ‹*Ort, Gebäude*›; trostlos, öde ‹*Landschaft, Umgebung*›; grau, trist ‹*Stadt*›; farblos ‹*Person*›; **c)** *(fig.)* eintönig, trist ‹*Leben*›

drabness ['dræbnɪs] *n., no pl.* **a)** *(of surroundings)* Trostlosigkeit, *die;* Ödheit, *die;* **b)** *(fig.: of life, existence)* Eintönigkeit, *die*

drachma ['drækmə] *n. pl.* **~s** *or* **drachmae** ['drækmi:] Drachme, *die*

Draconian [drə'kəʊnɪən] *adj.* drakonisch

draft [drɑ:ft] **1.** *n.* **a)** *(rough copy) (of speech)* Konzept, *das; (of treaty, parliamentary bill)* Entwurf, *der;* **~ copy/version** Konzept, *das;* **~ letter** Entwurf eines Briefes; **b)** *(plan of work)* Skizze, *die;* [Bau-, Riß-]zeichnung, *die;* **c)** *(Mil.: detaching for special duty)* Sonderkommando, *das; (Brit.: those detached)* Abkommandierte *Pl.;* Sonderkommando, *das;* **d)** *(Amer. Mil.: conscription)* Einberufung, *die; (those conscripted)* Wehrpflichtige *Pl.;* Einberufene *Pl.;* **e)** *(Commerc.)* Abhebung, *die;* Abheben, *das; (cheque drawn)* Wechsel, *der;* Tratte, *die;* **f)** *(Amer.) see* **draught. 2.** *v.t.* **a)** *(make rough copy of)* entwerfen; **b)** *(Mil.)* abkommandieren; **c)** *(Amer. Mil.: conscript)* einberufen; **be ~ed** eingezogen *od.* einberufen werden; **d)** *(fig.) (call upon)* berufen; *(select)* auswählen

'draft-dodger *n. (Amer. Mil.) jmd., der sich dem Wehrdienst entzieht*

draftee [drɑ:f'ti:] *n. (Amer. Mil.)* Wehrpflichtige, *der*

draftsman ['drɑ:ftsmən] *n., pl.* **draftsmen** ['drɑ:ftsmən] **a)** *jemand, der Gesetzesvorlagen usw. verfaßt;* ≈ Schreiber, *der;* **b)** *see* **draughtsman**

drafty *(Amer.) see* **draughty**

drag [dræg] **1.** *n.* **a)** *(dredging apparatus)* Suchanker, *der;* **b)** *see* **drag-net; c)** *(Hunting) (artificial scent)* Fuchs, *der; (club)* Schleppjagd, *die;* Reitjagd, *die;* **d)** *(difficult progress)* **it was a long ~ up the hill** der Aufstieg auf den Hügel war ein ganz schöner Schlauch *(ugs.);* **e)** *(Aeronaut.)* Strömungswiderstand, *der;* **~ coefficient** *or* **factor** [Luft]widerstandszahl, *die;* **f)** *(obstruction)* Hindernis, *das* **(on** für); Hemmnis, *das* **(on** für); **be a ~ on sb./sth.** jmdm./für etw. eine Last sein; **g)** *(boring thing)* langweilige Sache *od.* Angelegenheit; **be a ~:** langweilig sein; **h)** *(sl.: at cigarette)* Zug, *der;* **i)** *no pl. (sl.: women's dress worn by men)* Frauenkleider *Pl.;* **j)** *(Amer. sl.: road)* **the main ~:** die Hauptstraße; **k)** *(Amer. sl.: influence)* Einfluß, *der.* **2.** *v.t.,* **-gg-: a)** [herum]schleppen; **~ one's feet** *or* **heels** *(fig.)* sich *(Dat.)* Zeit lassen **(over, in** mit); **b)** *(move with effort)* **~ oneself** sich schleppen; **~ one's feet** [mit den Füßen] schlurfen; **I could scarcely ~ myself out of bed** ich konnte mich kaum aufraffen aufzustehen; **c)** *(fig. coll.: take despite resistance)* **he ~ged me to a dance** er schleifte mich *(ugs.)* zu einer Tanzveranstaltung; **~ the children away from the television** die Kinder [mit Gewalt] vom Fernsehen losreißen; **he ~s her about with him everywhere** er schleppt sie überall mit sich herum; **~ sb. into sth.** jmdn. in etw. *(Akk.)* hineinziehen; **~ sb. into doing sth.** jmdn. dazu drängen, etw. zu tun; **d)** *(search)* [mit einem Schleppnetz] absuchen ‹*Fluß-, Seegrund*›; **e)** *(Naut.)* **the ship ~s her anchor** das Schiff treibt vor Anker. **3.** *v.i.,* **-gg-: a)** schleifen; **~ on** *or* **at a cigarette** *(coll.)* an einer Zigarette ziehen; **b)** *(fig.: pass slowly)* sich [hin]schleppen

~ **'down** *v.t.* nach unten ziehen; **~ sb. down to one's own level** *(fig.)* jmdn. auf sein Niveau herabziehen

~ **'in** *v.t.* hineinziehen

~ **'on** *v.i. (continue)* sich [da]hinschleppen; **time ~ged on** die Zeit verstrich; **~ on for months** sich über Monate hinziehen

~ **'out** *v.t. (protract unduly)* hinausziehen; in die Länge ziehen; **~ out [one's days/existence]** [sein Leben/Dasein] fristen

~ **'up** *v.t. (coll.)* wieder ausgraben ‹*alte Geschichte, Skandal*›

drag: ~-hounds *n. pl.* Hunde für die Schleppjagd; **~-net** *n. (lit. or fig.)* Schleppnetz, *das; (fig.)* Netz, *das*

dragon ['drægn] *n.* Drache, *der; (fig.: fearsome person)* Drachen, *der*

'dragon-fly *n. (Zool.)* Libelle, *die*

dragoon [drə'gu:n] **1.** *n. (Mil.)* Dragoner, *der.* **2.** *v.t.* zwingen; **~ sb. into doing sth.** jmdn. zwingen, etw. zu tun

'drag racing *n.* Beschleunigungsrennen *Pl.*

dragster ['drægstə(r)] *n.* Dragster, *der; für Beschleunigungsrennen gebautes Fahrzeug*

drain [dreɪn] **1.** *n.* **a)** Abflußrohr, *das; (underground)* Kanalisationsrohr, *das; (grating at roadside)* Gully, *der;* **open ~:** Abflußrinne, *die;* **down the ~** *(fig. coll.)* für die Katz *(ugs.);* **go down the ~** *(fig. coll.)* umsonst *od.* vergeblich *od. (ugs.)* für die Katz sein; **that was money [thrown] down the ~** *(fig. coll.)* das Geld war zum Teufel *(salopp) od.* zum Fenster hinausgeworfen *(ugs.);* **be going down the ~:** vor die Hunde gehen *(geh.);* **laugh like a ~** *(fig. coll.)* schallend lachen; sich vor Lachen ausschütten wollen; **b)** *(fig.: constant demand)* Belastung, *die* **(on** *Gen.***); be a ~ on sb.'s strength** an jmds. Kräften zehren. **2.** *v.t.* **a)** trockenlegen ‹*Teich*›; entwässern ‹*Land*›; ableiten ‹*Wasser*›; **b)** *(Cookery)* abgießen ‹*Wasser, Kartoffeln, Gemüse*›; **c)** *(Geog.)* **the river ~s the valley** der Fluß nimmt das Wasser des ganzen Tales auf; **d)** *(drink all contents of)* austrinken; **e)** *(fig.: deprive)* **~ a country of its manpower/wealth** *or* **resources** ein Land ausbluten/auslaugen; **~ sb. of his energy** jmdn. auslaugen. **3.** *v.i.* **a)** ‹*Geschirr, Gemüse:*› abtropfen; ‹*Flüssigkeit:*› ablaufen; **b) the colour ~ed from her face** *(fig.)* die Farbe wich aus ihrem Gesicht

drainage ['dreɪnɪdʒ] *n.* **a)** *(draining)* Entwässerung, *die;* Trockenlegung, *die; (fig.)* Ausbeutung, *die;* **b)** *(Geog.: natural ~)* [natürliche] Entwässerung; *(artificial ~ of fields etc.)* Entwässerung, *die;* Dränung *od.* Dränage, *die (fachspr.); (system)* Entwässerungssystem, *das; (of city, house, etc.)* Kanalisation, *die*

draining-board ['dreɪnɪŋ bɔ:d] *(Brit.; Amer.:* **'drainboard)** *n.* Abtropfbrett, *das*

drain: ~-pipe *n.* **a)** *(to carry off rain-water)* Regen[abfall]rohr, *das;* **b)** *(to carry off sewage)* Abwasserleitung, *die; (underground)* Kanalisationsleitung, *die;* **~-pipes, ~-pipe 'trousers** *ns. pl. (Fashion)* Röhrenhosen

drake [dreɪk] *n.* Enterich, *der;* Erpel, *der; see also* **¹duck 1 a**

dram [dræm] *n.* **a)** *(Pharm.) (weight)* Drachme, *die;* **fluid ~** *(Brit.)* 3,5515 cm³; *(Amer.)* 3,6967 cm³; **b)** *(small drink)* Schlückchen, *das (ugs.)*

drama ['drɑ:mə] *n.* **a)** *(play, lit. or fig.)* Drama, *das;* **b)** *no pl. (genre)* Drama, *das; (dramatic art)* Schauspielkunst, *die;* Dramatik, *die; (fig.: episode as in play)* Schauspiel, *das; attrib.* **~ critic** Theaterkritiker, *der;* **~ school** Schauspielschule, *die*

dramatic [drə'mætɪk] *adj.* **a)** *(Theatre)* dramatisch; **~ art** Dramatik, *die;* **a ~ critic** ein Theaterkritiker; **b)** *(fig.)* dramatisch; *(exaggerated)* theatralisch; bühnenreif

dramatically [drə'mætɪkəlɪ] *adv.* dramatisch; *(in exaggerated way)* theatralisch

dramatic 'irony *n.* tragische Ironie *(Literaturwiss.)*

dramatics [drə'mætɪks] *n., no pl.* **a)** Theater[spiel], *das;* **amateur ~:** Laientheater, *das;* **b)** *(fig. derog.)* Theatralik, *die (geh. abwertend)*

dramatisation, dramatise *see* **dramatiz-**

dramatis personae [dræmətɪs pə'səʊni:,

dræmətɪs pə'səʊnaɪ] *n. pl., often constr. as sing.* dramatis personae; die Personen; *(fig.)* Hauptpersonen *Pl.*

dramatist ['dræmətɪst] *n.* Dramatiker, *der*/Dramatikerin, *die*

dramatization [dræmətaɪ'zeɪʃn] *n.* **a)** Dramatisierung, *die;* **a television/stage ~:** eine Fernseh-/Bühnenbearbeitung; **b)** *(fig.)* Dramatisieren, *das*

dramatize ['dræmətaɪz] *v.t.* **a)** dramatisieren; [für die Bühne/das Fernsehen *usw.*] bearbeiten; **b)** *(fig.)* dramatisieren; [künstlich] hochspielen; *(emphasize)* betonen

drank *see* **drink 2, 3**

drape [dreɪp] **1.** *v.t.* **a)** *(cover, adorn)* **~ oneself/sb. in sth.** sich/jmdn. in etw. *(Akk.)* hüllen; **~ an altar/walls with sth.** einen Altar/Wände mit etw. behängen; **b)** *(put loosely)* **~ sth. over/round sth.** etw. über etw. *(Akk.)*/um etw. legen *od.* drapieren; **c)** *(rest casually)* legen; hängen. **2.** *n.* **a)** *(cloth)* Tuch, *das;* **b)** *usu. in pl. (Amer.: curtain)* Vorhang, *der*

draper ['dreɪpə(r)] *n. (Brit.)* Textilkaufmann, *der;* **the ~'s [shop]** das Textilgeschäft; *see also* **baker**

drapery ['dreɪpərɪ] *n.* **a)** *(Brit.: cloth)* Stoffe; Textilien *Pl.;* **b)** *(Brit.: trade)* Textilgewerbe, *das;* **~ shop** Textilgeschäft, *das;* **c)** *(arrangement of cloth)* Draperie, *die;* **d)** *(cloth artistically arranged)* Faltenwurf, *der;* **e)** *usu. in pl. (Amer.: curtain)* Vorhang, *der*

drastic ['dræstɪk, 'drɑ:stɪk] *adj.* drastisch; erheblich ⟨*Wandel, Verbesserung*⟩; durchgreifend, rigoros ⟨*Mittel*⟩; dringend ⟨*Bedarf*⟩; einschneidend ⟨*Veränderung*⟩; erschreckend ⟨*Mangel*⟩; bedrohlich ⟨*Lage*⟩; **something ~ will have to be done** drastische Maßnahmen müssen ergriffen werden

drastically ['dræstɪkəlɪ, 'drɑ:stɪkəlɪ] *adv.* drastisch; erheblich; rigoros, hart ⟨*durchgreifen*⟩; **be ~ in need of sth.** dringenden Bedarf an etw. *(Dat.)* haben

drat [dræt] *v.t. (coll.)* **~ [it]/him/the weather!** verflucht!/verfluchter Kerl!/verfluchtes Wetter! *(salopp)*

dratted ['drætɪd] *adj. (coll.)* verflucht

draught [drɑ:ft] *n.* **a)** *(of air)* [Luft]zug, *der;* **where is the ~ coming from?** woher zieht es?; **be [sitting] in a ~:** im Zug sitzen; **there's a ~ [in here]** es zieht [hier]; **feel the ~** *(fig. sl.)* [finanziell] in der Klemme sitzen *(ugs.);* **b) [beer] on ~:** [Bier] vom Faß; **c)** *(swallowing) (act)* Zug, *der; (amount)* Schluck, *der;* **d)** *(Naut.)* Tiefgang, *der*

draught: ~ animal *n.* Zugtier, *das;* **~ 'beer** *n.* Faßbier, *das;* **~-board** *n. (Brit.)* Damebrett, *das;* **~-excluder** *n.* Abdichtvorrichtung, *die;* Zugluft-Verhinderer, *der;* **~horse** *n.* Zugpferd, *das;* **~-proof 1.** *adj.* winddicht; **2.** *v.t.* winddicht machen

draughts [drɑ:fts] *n., no pl. (Brit.)* Damespiel, *das;* **have a game of ~:** eine Partie Dame spielen; **play ~:** Dame spielen

draughtsman ['drɑ:ftsmən] *n., pl.* **draughtsmen** ['drɑ:ftsmən] *(Brit.)* **a)** Zeichner, *der*/Zeichnerin, *die;* **b)** *(in game)* Damestein, *der*

draughtsmanship ['drɑ:ftsmənʃɪp] *n. (art and practice)* Zeichenkunst, *die; (skill)* zeichnerisches Können

draughty ['drɑ:ftɪ] *adj.* zugig

Dravidian [drə'vɪdɪən] *(Ethnol.)* **1.** *adj.* drawidisch. **2.** *n.* **a)** *(person)* Drawide, *der*/Drawidin, *die;* **b)** *(language)* Drawidisch, *das*

draw [drɔ:] **1.** *v.t.,* **drew** [dru:], **drawn** [drɔ:n] **a)** *(pull)* ziehen; einholen ⟨*Fangnetz*⟩; spannen ⟨*Bogen*⟩; **~ the curtains/blinds** *(open)* die Vorhänge aufziehen/die Jalousien hochziehen; *(close)* die Vorhänge zuziehen/die Jalousien herunterlassen; **~ the bolt** *(fasten)* den Riegel vorschieben; *(unfasten)* den Riegel zurückschieben; **~ sth. towards one** etw. zu sich heran- *od.* hinziehen; **b)** *(attract, take in)* anlocken ⟨*Publikum, Menge, Kunden*⟩; **all eyes were ~n to him** alle Blicke waren auf ihn gerichtet; **~ the fresh air into one's lungs** die frische Luft tief einatmen; **~ criticism upon oneself** Kritik auf sich *(Akk.)* ziehen; **be ~n to sb.** von jmdm. angezogen werden; **feel ~n to sb.** sich von jmdm. angezogen *od.* zu jmdm. hingezogen fühlen; **~ sb. into sth.** jmdn. in etw. *(Akk.)* mit hineinziehen; **he refused to be ~n** *(be provoked)* er ließ sich nichts entlocken; **~ sb. out of himself** jmdn. aus sich herauslocken; **~ the enemy's/***(fig.)* **sb.'s fire** das feindliche Feuer/jmds. Kritik auf sich ziehen; *see also* **breath a, b; c)** *(take out)* herausziehen; ziehen **(from** aus); aufstöbern, aufjagen ⟨*Fuchs, Dachs*⟩ **(from** aus); **~ money from the bank/one's account** Geld bei der Bank holen/von seinem Konto abheben; **~ a pistol on sb.** eine Pistole auf jmdn. richten; **~ the cork from the bottle** die Flasche entkorken; **~ water from a well** Wasser an einem Brunnen holen *od.* schöpfen; **~ beer from a barrel** Bier vom Faß zapfen; *see also* **blood 1a; ~ trumps** Trümpfe ziehen; **~ cards from a pack** Karten von einem Haufen abheben; **d)** *(derive, elicit)* finden; **~ an example from a book** ein Beispiel einem Buch entnehmen; **~ a response from sb.** von jmdm. eine Antwort bekommen; *(interested)* Echo bei jmdm. finden; **~ comfort/sustenance from sth.** Trost/Halt in etw. *(Dat.)* finden; **~ reassurance/encouragement from sth.** Zuversicht/Mut aus etw. schöpfen; **~ inspiration from sth.** sich von etw. inspirieren lassen; Anregungen bei *od.* in etw. *(Dat.)* finden; **~ applause/a smile [from sb.]** Applaus/ein Lächeln [bei jmdm.] hervorrufen; *see also* **conclusion d; e)** *(get as one's due)* erhalten; bekommen; beziehen ⟨*Gehalt, Rente, Arbeitslosenunterstützung*⟩; **f)** *(select at random)* **~ [straws]** [Lose] ziehen; losen; **~ [for partners]** [die Partner] auslosen; **Italy has been ~n against Spain in the World Cup** Italien ist als Gegner für Spanien im Weltmeisterschaftsspiel ausgelost worden; **~ a winner** ein Gewinnlos ziehen; **g)** *(trace)* ziehen ⟨*Strich*⟩; zeichnen ⟨*geometrische Figur, Bild*⟩; *(fig.: represent in words)* darstellen; **do you ~?** kannst du zeichnen?; **~ the line at sth.** *(fig.)* bei etw. nicht mehr mitmachen; **the line has to be ~n somewhere** *or* **at some point** *(fig.)* irgendwo muß Schluß sein; **it's difficult to ~ the line** *(fig.)* es ist schwierig, die Grenze zu ziehen; **h)** *(Commerc.: write out)* ziehen ⟨*Wechsel*⟩ **(on** auf + *Akk.***)**; **~ a cheque on one's bank for £100** einen Scheck über 100 Pfund auf seine Bank ausstellen; **i)** *(formulate)* ziehen ⟨*Parallele, Vergleich*⟩; herstellen ⟨*Analogie*⟩; herausstellen ⟨*Unterschied*⟩; *see also* **distinction b; j)** *(end with neither side winner)* unentschieden beenden ⟨*Spiel*⟩; **the match was ~n** das Spiel ging unentschieden aus; *abs.* **they drew three-all** sie spielten 3 : 3 unentschieden; **k)** *(disembowel)* ausnehmen ⟨*Geflügel, Fisch*⟩; ausweiden ⟨*Wild*⟩; **l)** *(extend)* [aus]dehnen; ziehen ⟨*Draht*⟩; **long ~n death agony** lang dauernder Todeskampf; **m)** *(Naut.)* **~ 3m. [of water]** 3 m Tiefgang haben; **n)** *(Hunting)* **~ a covert** [ein Tier aus seinem Versteck] aufjagen. *See also* **blank 2c; hang 1f; lot g. 2.** *v.i.,* **drew, drawn a)** *(make one's way, move)* ⟨*Person:*⟩ gehen; ⟨*Fahrzeug:*⟩ fahren; ⟨*Flugzeug:*⟩ fliegen; **~ into sth.** ⟨*Zug:*⟩ in etw. *(Akk.)* einfahren; ⟨*Schiff:*⟩ in etw. *(Akk.)* einlaufen; **~ towards sth.** sich einer Sache *(Dat.)* nähern; **~ together** zusammenkommen; **~ closer together** enger zusammenrücken; **~ to an end** zu Ende gehen; **b)** *(allow draught)* ⟨*Kamin, Zigarette:*⟩ ziehen; **~ well/badly** einen guten/schlechten Zug haben; **c)** *(infuse)* ⟨*Tee:*⟩ ziehen. **3.** *n.* **a)** *(raffle)* Tombola, *die; (for matches, contests)* Auslosung, *die;* **be the luck of the ~** *(fig.)* Glück[s]sache sein; **b)** *([result of] drawn game)* Unentschieden, *das; (Chess)* Remis, *das;* **end in a ~:** mit einem Unentschieden enden; **c)** Attraktion, *die; (film, play)* Publikumserfolg, *der;* **d) be quick/slow on the ~:** den Finger schnell/zu langsam am Abzug haben; *(fig.)* sich geistesgegenwärtig zeigen/nicht geistesgegenwärtig genug sein; ⟨*Quizteilnehmer:*⟩ schlagfertig sein/nicht schlagfertig genug sein; **e)** *(Amer.: in smoking)* Zug, *der*

~ a'side *v.t.* zur Seite ziehen; **~ sb. aside** jmdn. beiseite nehmen

~ a'way 1. *v.i.* **a)** *(move ahead)* **~ away from sth./sb.** sich von etw. entfernen/jmdm. davonziehen; **b)** *(set off)* losfahren; **c)** *(recoil)* zurückweichen **(from** vor + *Dat.***)**. **2.** *v.t.* wegnehmen; wegziehen; weglocken ⟨*Person*⟩

~ 'back 1. *v.t.* zurückziehen; aufziehen ⟨*Vorhang*⟩. **2.** *v.i.* zurückweichen; *(fig.)* sich zurückziehen

~ 'in 1. *v.i.* **a)** *(move in and stop)* einfahren; **the car drew in to the side of the road** das Auto fuhr an den Straßenrand heran; **b)** ⟨*Tage:*⟩ kürzer werden; ⟨*Abende, Nächte:*⟩ länger werden. **2.** *v.t. (fig.)* hineinziehen ⟨*Person*⟩; zum Mitmachen überreden; **I refuse to be ~n in** ich will nicht mit hineingezogen werden

~ 'off *v.t.* ausziehen ⟨*Kleidung*⟩; ablassen ⟨*Flüssigkeit*⟩

~ on 1. [-'-] *v.i.* ⟨*Zeit:*⟩ vergehen, *(geh.)* fortschreiten; *(approach)* ⟨*Winter, Nacht:*⟩ nahen. **2.** *v.t.* **a)** ['--] anziehen ⟨*Kleidung*⟩; **b)** [-'-] *(induce)* anziehen *(fig.)* ⟨*Person*⟩; **c)** ['--] **~ on sth.** von etw. zehren; **you may ~ on my account** du kannst von meinem Konto abheben

~ 'out 1. *v.t. (extend)* ausdehnen; in die Länge ziehen; **long ~n out** ausgedehnt; in die Länge gezogen. **2.** *v.i.* **a)** abfahren; **the train/bus drew out of the station** der Zug fuhr aus dem Bahnhof aus/der Bus verließ den Busbahnhof; **b)** ⟨*Tage:*⟩ länger werden; ⟨*Abende:*⟩ kürzer werden

~ 'up 1. *v.t.* **a)** *(formulate)* abfassen; aufsetzen ⟨*Vertrag*⟩; aufstellen ⟨*Liste*⟩; entwerfen ⟨*Plan, Budget*⟩; **b)** heranziehen; **~ up a chair!** holen Sie sich doch einen Stuhl!; **c) ~ oneself up [to one's full height]** sich [zu seiner vollen Größe] aufrichten; **d)** aufstellen ⟨*Truppen, Fahrzeuge*⟩. **2.** *v.i.* [an]halten

~ upon *see* **~ on 2c**

draw: ~back *n. (snag)* Nachteil, *der;* **~bridge** *n.* Zugbrücke, *die*

drawee [drɔ:'i:] *n. (Commerc.)* Bezogene, *der;* Trassat, *der (fachspr.)*

drawer *n.* **a)** [drɔ:(r), 'drɔ:ə(r)] *(in furniture)* Schublade, *die;* **b)** ['drɔ:ə(r)] *(maker of drawings)* Zeichner, *der*/Zeichnerin, *die;* **c)** *(Commerc.)* Aussteller, *der;* Trassant, *der (fachspr.);* **d)** *in pl.* [drɔ:z, 'drɔ:əz] *(dated/joc.: underpants)* Unterhosen *Pl.; (for women)* Schlüpfer *Pl.*

drawing ['drɔ:ɪŋ] *n.* **a)** *(activity)* Zeichnen, *das;* **be good at ~:** gut zeichnen können; **b)** *(sketch)* Zeichnung, *die*

drawing: ~-board *n.* Zeichenbrett, *das;* **so it's back to the ~-board, I'm afraid** dann müssen wir wohl wieder von vorne beginnen, fürchte ich; **~-office** *n.* Konstruktionsbüro, *das;* **~-paper** *n.* Zeichenpapier, *das;* **~-pin** *n. (Brit.)* Reißzwecke, *die;* **~-room** *n.* Salon, *der*

'drawknife *n.* Zugmesser, *das*

drawl [drɔ:l] **1.** *v.i.* gedehnt *od. (ugs.)* breit sprechen. **2.** *v.t.* dehnen; gedehnt *od. (ugs.)* breit aussprechen. **3.** *n.* gedehntes *od. (ugs.)* breites Sprechen; **speak with a ~:** gedehnt sprechen

drawn [drɔ:n] **1.** *p.p. of* **draw. 2.** *adj.* verzogen ⟨*Gesicht*⟩; **look ~:** *(from tiredness)* abgespannt aussehen; *(from worries)* abgehärmt aussehen; c) (Sport) unentschieden; ~ game Unentschieden, das; (Chess) Remis, das

'draw-string n. Durchziehband, das

dray [dreɪ] n. Tafelwagen, der; Rollwagen, der

dread [dred] 1. v. t. sich sehr fürchten vor (+ Dat.); große Angst haben vor (+ Dat.); the ~ed day/moment der gefürchtete od. mit Schrecken erwartete Tag/Augenblick; I ~ the moment when ...: ich fürchte mich vor dem Augenblick, wenn ...; I ~ to think [what may have happened] ich mag gar nicht daran denken[, was passiert sein könnte]; I ~ the thought of ...: mich schreckt der Gedanke an (+ Akk.) ... 2. n., no pl. (terror) Angst, die; be or live or stand in ~ of sth./sb. in [ständiger] Furcht vor etw./jmdm. leben. 3. adj. (literary) fürchterlich

dreadful ['dredfl] adj. schrecklich; furchtbar; (coll.: very bad) fürchterlich; I feel ~ (unwell) ich fühle mich scheußlich (ugs.); (embarrassed) es ist mir furchtbar peinlich

dreadfully ['dredfəlɪ] adv. a) schrecklich; entsetzlich, furchtbar ⟨leiden⟩; (coll.: very badly) grauenhaft, fürchterlich; b) (coll.: extremely) schrecklich; furchtbar

dream [dri:m] 1. n. a) Traum, der; sweet ~s! träume süß!; have a ~ about sb./sth. von jmdm./etw. träumen; I had a bad ~ last night letzte Nacht habe ich schlecht geträumt; it was all a bad ~: das ganze war wie ein böser Traum; in a ~: im Traum; go/work like a ~ (coll.) wie eine Eins fahren/funktionieren (ugs.); b) (fig.: reverie) go or walk around/be/live in a [complete] ~: in einer [perfekten] Traumwelt leben; c) (ambition, vision) Traum, der; have ~s of doing sth. davon träumen, etw. zu tun; never in one's wildest ~s nicht in seinen kühnsten Träumen; d) (perfect person) ~ [man/woman] Traummann, der/-frau, die; (perfect thing) Traum, der; attrib. traumhaft; Traum⟨haus, -auto, -urlaub⟩. See also wet dream. 2. v. i., ~t [dremt] or ~ed träumen; (while awake) vor sich (Akk.) hin träumen; ~ about or of sb./sth. von jmdm./etw. träumen; ~ of doing sth. (fig.) davon träumen, etw. zu tun; he wouldn't ~ of doing it (fig.) er würde nicht im Traum daran denken od. es würde ihm nicht im Traum einfallen, das zu tun. 3. v. t., ~t or ~ed träumen; she never or little ~t that she'd win sie hätte sich (Dat.) nie träumen lassen, daß sie gewinnen würde

~ **'up** v. t. sich (Dat.) ausdenken; sich (Dat.) einfallen lassen

dreamer ['dri:mə(r)] n. (in sleep) Träumende, der/die; (day-dreamer) Träumer, der/Träumerin, die

dreamily ['dri:mɪlɪ] adv. verträumt

'dream-land n. Traumland, das; Reich der Träume, das

dreamless ['dri:mlɪs] adj. traumlos

dreamlike ['dri:mlaɪk] adj. traumhaft

dreamt see dream 2, 3

dreamy ['dri:mɪ] adj. a) verträumt ⟨Person, Blick⟩; träumerisch ⟨Stimmung⟩; b) (dreamlike) traumähnlich; c) (coll.: delightful) traumhaft [schön]

'dreamy-eyed adj. ⟨Verliebte, Mädchen, Kind⟩ mit verträumten Augen

drearily ['drɪərɪlɪ] adv. see dreary: monoton; düster

dreary ['drɪərɪ] adj. trostlos; monoton ⟨Musik⟩; langweilig ⟨Unterricht, Lehrbuch⟩; düster ⟨Gemüt, Gedanken⟩

dredge [dredʒ] v. t. ausbaggern; (fig.) ausgraben; ~ up (fig.) ausgraben

dredger ['dredʒə(r)] n. Bagger, der; (boat) Schwimmbagger, der; Naßbagger, der

dregs [dregz] n. pl. a) [Boden]satz, der; drain one's glass to the ~: sein Glas bis zur Neige od. bis zum letzten Tropfen leeren; b) (fig.) Abschaum, der

drench [drenʃ] v. t. durchnässen; get completely ~ed, get ~ed to the skin naß bis auf die Haut werden

drenching ['drenʃɪŋ] 1. n. get a ~: bis auf die Haut naß werden. 2. adj. ~ rain strömender Regen

Dresden ['drezdn] pr. n. Dresden (das); ~ china or porcelain Meißner Porzellan

dress [dres] 1. n. a) (woman's or girl's frock) Kleid, das; b) no pl. (clothing) Kleidung, die; be in native/formal ~: nach Art der Einheimischen/formell gekleidet sein; articles of ~: Kleidungsstücke; c) no pl. (manner of dressing) Kleidung, die; she's rather slovenly in her ~: sie kleidet sich sehr nachlässig; d) (external covering) Kleid, das. See also evening dress; full dress; morning dress. 2. v. t. a) (clothe) anziehen; be ~ed angezogen sein; be well ~ed gut gekleidet sein; the bride was ~ed in white die Braut trug Weiß; get ~ed sich anziehen; b) (provide clothes for) einkleiden ⟨Familie⟩; c) (deck, adorn) schmücken; beflaggen ⟨Schiff⟩; dekorieren ⟨Schaufenster⟩; d) (arrange) frisieren ⟨Haare⟩; e) (Med.) verbinden, versorgen ⟨Wunde⟩; f) (Cookery) zubereiten; g) (treat, prepare) hobeln ⟨Holz⟩; gerben ⟨tierische Häute, Felle⟩; schleifen ⟨Tontöpfe, Metall, Stein⟩; (put finish on) appretieren ⟨Gewebe, Holz, Leder⟩; polieren ⟨Tontöpfe, Metall, Stein⟩; h) (Mil.) ~ ranks die Front ausrichten; i) (Agric.: manure) düngen. 3. v. i. (wear clothes) sich anziehen; sich kleiden; (get ~ed) sich anziehen; sich ankleiden (geh.); I like to ~ in dark colours ich trage gerne dunkle Farben; ~ for dinner sich zum Abendessen umziehen

~ **'down** v. t. (fig.) zurechtweisen

~ **'up** 1. v. t. a) (in formal clothes) feinmachen; fein anziehen; sb. is all ~ed up and nowhere to go (fig.) jmds. ganzer Aufwand ist umsonst (ugs.); b) (disguise) verkleiden; (elaborately as a game) herausputzen; c) (smarten) verschönern. 2. v. i. a) (wear formal clothes) sich feinmachen; b) (disguise oneself) sich verkleiden; (elaborately as a game) sich herausputzen

dressage ['dresɑ:ʒ] n. Dressurreiten, das

dress: ~ **circle** n. (Theatre) erster Rang; ~ **coat** n. Frack, der; ~**-conscious** adj. modebewußt; ~**-designer** n. Modeschöpfer, der/-schöpferin, die; Modedesigner, der/-designerin, die

[1]dresser ['dresə(r)] n. a) (sideboard) Anrichte, die; Büfett, das; b) (Amer.) see dressing-table

[2]dresser n. a) he's a careless/elegant/tasteful ~: er kleidet sich nachlässig/elegant/geschmackvoll; b) (Theatre) Garderobier, der/Garderobiere, die; c) (Med.) Operationsassistent, der/-assistentin, die

dressing ['dresɪŋ] n. a) no pl. Anziehen, das; Ankleiden, das (geh.); b) (Cookery) Dressing, das; c) (Med.) Verband, der; d) (Agric.) Dünger, der

dressing: ~**-case** n. Kosmetikkoffer, der; ~ **'down** n. give sb. a ~ down jmdm. einen Rüffel verpassen od. eine Standpauke halten (ugs.); get a ~ down zurechtgewiesen od. (ugs.) heruntergemacht werden; eins auf den Deckel kriegen (ugs.); ~**-gown** n. Bademantel, der; ~**-room** n. a) (of actor or actress) [Schauspieler]garderobe, die; [Künstler]garderobe, die; b) (for games-players) Umkleidekabine, die; c) (in house) Ankleideraum, der; Ankleidezimmer, das; ~**-table** n. Frisierkommode, die; (with knee-hole) Frisiertoilette, die

dress: ~ **length** n. Stoffstück, das für ein Kleid ausreicht; ~**maker** n. Damenschneider, der/-schneiderin, die; ~**making** n. Damenschneiderei, die; ~ **rehearsal** n. (lit. or fig.) Generalprobe, die; ~ **sense** n. she hasn't much ~ sense sie hat nicht viel Sinn für Mode; ~ **'shirt** n. Smokinghemd, das; ~**-shop** n. Geschäft für Damenbekleidung; Kleiderladen, der (ugs.); ~ **'suit** n. Abendanzug, der; ~**-uniform** n. (Mil.) Paradeuniform, die

dressy ['dresɪ] adj. a) be ~ ⟨Person:⟩ immer schick angezogen sein; b) (smart) fein, elegant ⟨Kleidung⟩; c) (grand, formal) vornehm ⟨Veranstaltung⟩

drew see draw 1, 2

dribble ['drɪbl] 1. v. i. a) (trickle) tropfen; b) (slobber) ⟨Baby:⟩ sabbern; c) (Sport) dribbeln. 2. v. t. a) ⟨Baby:⟩ kleckern; b) (Sport) dribbeln mit ⟨Ball⟩. 3. n. (trickle) Tröpfeln, das

driblet ['drɪblɪt] n. Tropfen, der; in or by ~s in kleinen Mengen; kleckerweise (ugs.)

dribs n. pl. ~ and drabs [drɪbz n 'dræbz] kleine Mengen; in ~ and drabs kleckerweise (ugs.)

dried [draɪd] adj. getrocknet; ~ fruit[s] Dörr- od. Backobst, das; ~ milk/egg/meat Trockenmilch, die od. Milchpulver, das/Trockenei od. Eipulver, das/Trockenfleisch, das

[1]drier see dry 1

[2]drier ['draɪə(r)] n. (for hair) Trockenhaube, die; (hand-held) Fön ®, der; Haartrockner, der; (for laundry) [Wäsche]trockner, der

driest see dry 1

drift [drɪft] 1. n. a) (flow, steady movement) Wanderung, die; b) (fig.: trend, shift, tendency) Tendenz, die; c) (flow of air or water) Strömung, die; the North Atlantic D~: der Nordatlantische Strom; d) (Naut., Aeronaut.: deviation from course) Abdrift, die (fachspr.); Abweichung vom Sollkurs; e) (Motor Veh.: controlled slide) Driften, das; f) (wind-propelled mass) (of snow or sand) Verwehung, die; (of leaves) zusammengewehter Haufen; g) (fig.: gist, import) das Wesentliche; get or catch the ~ of sth. etw. im wesentlichen verstehen; I don't get your ~: ich kann Ihnen nicht ganz folgen od. verstehe nicht ganz, worauf Sie hinauswollen; h) (Geol.: deposits) Geschiebe, das; glacial ~: [Glazial]geschiebe, das. 2. v. i. a) (be borne by current; fig.: move passively or aimlessly) treiben; ⟨Wolke:⟩ ziehen; ~ out to sea aufs Meer hinaustreiben; ~ off course abtreiben; vom Kurs abgelenkt werden; come ~ing along angetrieben kommen; the mist ~ed away der Nebel verwehte; the smoke ~ed to the east der Rauch zog nach Osten ab; his thoughts ~ed er schweifte mit seinen Gedanken ab; let things ~: die Dinge treiben lassen; den Dingen ihren Lauf lassen; ~ along (fig.) sich treiben lassen; ~ into crime in die Kriminalität [ab]driften; ~ into unconsciousness in Bewußtlosigkeit versinken; months ~ed by die Monate vergingen; b) (coll.: come or go casually) ~ in hereinschneien (ugs.); ~ out abziehen (ugs.); ~ in at 1 a. m. um ein Uhr nachts eintrudeln (ugs.); c) (form ~s) zusammengeweht werden; ~ing sand Treibsand, der

~ **a'part** v. i. sich (Dat.) fremd werden; (in marriage) sich auseinanderleben

drifter ['drɪftə(r)] n. a) (Naut.) Drifter, der; b) (person) jmd., der sich treiben läßt; (vagrant) Gammler, der (ugs.); be a ~: sich treiben lassen

drift: ~**-ice** n. Treibeis, das; ~**-net** n. Treibnetz, das; ~**wood** n. Treibholz, das

[1]drill [drɪl] 1. n. a) (tool) Bohrer, der; (Dent.) Bohrinstrument, das; (Metalw.) Drillbohrer, der; (Carpentry, Building) Bohrmaschine, die; b) (Mil.: training) Drill, der; c) (Educ.; also fig.) Übung, die; lifeboat ~: Rettungsbootübung, die; d) (Brit. coll.: agreed procedure) Prozedur, die; know the ~: wissen, wie es gemacht wird; what's the ~? wie wird das gemacht? 2. v. t. a) (bore) bohren ⟨Loch, Brunnen⟩; an-, ausbohren ⟨Zahn⟩; ~ sth. (right through) etw. durchbohren; **b)** *(Mil.: instruct)* drillen; **c)** *(Educ.; also fig.)* ~ **sb. in sth.,** ~ **sth. into sb.** mit jmdm. etw. systematisch einüben; jmdm. etw. eindrillen *(ugs.) od. (abwertend)* einpauken. **3.** *v. i.* **a)** *(bore)* bohren **(for** nach); ~ **deep/50 ft. into the ground** tief/15 m tief bohren; **finish ~ing** die Bohrung/Bohrungen beenden; ~ **down a long way** tief bohren; ~ **through sth.** etw. durchbohren; **b)** *(Mil.)* exerzieren

²drill *n. (Agric.)* **a)** *(furrow)* Saatrille, *die;* **b)** *(machine)* Drillmaschine, *die*

³drill *n. (Textiles)* Drillich, *der*

drill: ~-bit *n.* Bohrer, *der;* **~-chuck** *n.* Bohrfutter, *das*

drilling ['drɪlɪŋ]: ~ **platform** *n.* Bohrturmplattform, *die;* ~ **rig** *n.* Bohrturm, *der; (in offshore ~)* Bohrinsel, *die*

drily *see* **dryly**

drink [drɪŋk] **1.** *n.* **a)** *(type of liquid)* Getränk; *das; (class of liquids)* Getränke *Pl.;* **many different sorts of ~s** viele verschiedene Getränke; **b)** *(quantity of liquid)* Getränk, *das;* **have a ~:** [etwas] trinken; **would you like a ~ of milk?** möchten Sie etwas Milch [trinken]?; **take a long ~ from sth.** einen großen Schluck aus etwas nehmen; **give sb. a ~ [of fruit-juice]** jmdm. etwas [Fruchtsaft] zu trinken geben; **c)** *(glass of alcoholic liquor)* Glas, *das; (not with food)* Drink, *der;* Glas, *das;* Gläschen, *das;* **have a ~:** ein Glas trinken; **let's have a ~!** trinken wir einen!; **she likes a ~ now and then** hin und wieder trinkt sie ganz gern einen *od.* ein Glas; **I think we all need a ~!** ich glaube, wir können alle einen vertragen *(ugs.);* **he has had a few ~s** er hat einige getrunken *(ugs.);* **d)** *no pl., no art. (intoxicating liquor)* Alkohol, *der;* **[strong] ~:** scharfe *od.* hochprozentige Getränke; **in ~, the worse for ~:** betrunken; **take to ~:** zu trinken anfangen; **~ was his ruin** der Alkohol war sein Verderben; **the ~ problem** der Alkoholismus *od.* Alkoholmißbrauch; **have a ~ problem** Probleme mit [dem] Alkohol haben; **drive sb. to ~:** jmdn. zum Trinker werden lassen; **e)** *(coll.: sea)* **the ~:** der große Bach *(Flieger-, Seemannsspr.).* **2.** *v. t.,* **drank** [dræŋk], **drunk** [drʌŋk] **a)** trinken ‹*Kaffee, Glas Milch, Flasche Whisky*›; **~ down** *or* **off [in one gulp]** [in einem *od.* auf einen Zug] austrinken; **b)** *(absorb)* ‹*Pflanze, poröses Material:*› aufsaugen; **the car ~s petrol** *(fig.)* das Auto schluckt viel Benzin; **c)** ~ **oneself to death** sich zu Tode trinken; ~ **sb. under the table** jmdn. unter den Tisch trinken. **3.** *v. i.,* **drank, drunk** trinken; ~ **from a bottle** aus einer Flasche trinken; ~ **of sth.** *(literary)* von etw. trinken; **~[ing and] driving** Alkohol am Steuer; ~ **and drive** unter Alkoholeinfluß fahren; ~ **to sb./sth.** auf jmdn./etw. trinken; **I'll ~ to that** *(coll.)* dem kann ich nur zustimmen; *see also* **fish 1 a**

~ **'in** *v. t.* **a)** *(readily take in)* einsaugen ‹*Luft; fig.: Schönheit*›; ‹*Pflanze:*› aufsaugen ‹*Wasser*›; **b)** *(absorb eagerly)* begierig aufnehmen ‹*Worte, Geschichten*›

~ **'up** *v. t. & i.* austrinken; ‹*Pflanze:*› aufsaugen

drinkable ['drɪŋkəbl] *adj.* **a)** *(suitable for drinking)* trinkbar ‹*Wasser*›; **b)** *(pleasant to drink)* trinkbar *(ugs.)* ‹*Wein*›

drinker ['drɪŋkə(r)] *n.* Trinker, *der*/Trinkerin, *die*

drinkie ['drɪŋkɪ] *n. (coll.)* was zu trinken *(ugs.);* **have ~s** trinken

drinking ['drɪŋkɪŋ]: **~-bout** *n.* Trinkgelage, *das;* ~ **fountain** *n.* Trinkbrunnen, *der;* **~-glass** *n.* Glas, *das;* **~-song** *n.* Trinklied, *das;* **~-'up time** *n. (Brit.) Zeit zwischen Ende des Ausschanks und der Schließung der Gaststätte (meist 10 Minuten);* **~-vessel** *see* **vessel a;** **~-water** *n.* Trinkwasser, *das*

drip [drɪp] **1.** *v. i.,* **-pp-: a)** tropfen; *(overflow in drops)* triefen; **be ~ping with water/moisture** triefend naß sein; **the windows were ~ping with condensation** an den Fenstern lief Kondenswasser herunter; ~ **off/down sth.** von etw. [herunter]tropfen; **b)** *(fig.)* **be ~ping with** überladen sein mit ‹*Schmuck*›; überlaufen vor (+ *Dat.*) ‹*Gefühlen*›; triefen von *od.* vor ‹*Ironie, Sentimentalität usw.*›. **2.** *v. t.,* **-pp-** tropfen lassen. **3.** *n.* **a)** *(act)* Tropfen, *das;* **b)** *(liquid)* Tropfen, *der;* **c)** *(Med.)* Tropfinfusion, *die;* **the patient was on a ~:** der Patient hing am Tropf; **d)** *(coll.: feeble, spineless person)* Schlappschwanz, *der (salopp abwertend)*

drip: ~-dry *(Textiles)* **1.** ['-'] *v. i.* knitterfrei trocknen; **2.** ['--] *adj.* bügelfrei; schnelltrocknend; **~-feed** *v. t. (Med.)* durch parenterale Tropfinfusion ernähren

dripping ['drɪpɪŋ] **1.** *adj.* tropfend ‹*Wasserhahn*›; ~ **bathing-costumes** tropfnasse Badeanzüge. **2.** *adv.* ~ **wet** tropf- *od. (ugs.)* patsch- *od. (ugs.)* klitschnaß. **3.** *n.* **a)** Tropfen, *das;* **b)** *(Cookery)* Schmalz, *das;* **bread and ~:** Schmalzbrot, *das*

drive [draɪv] **1.** *n.* **a)** *(trip)* Fahrt, *die;* **take sb. for a ~:** jmdn. *od.* mit jmdm. spazierenfahren; **b)** *(distance travelled)* [Auto]fahrt, *die;* **a ~ of 40 kilometres, a 40-kilometre ~:** eine [Auto]fahrt von 40 Kilometern; **a nine-hour ~, a ~ of nine hours** eine neunstündige Autofahrt; **within an hour's ~ of sth.** keine Autostunde von etw. entfernt; **be an hour's ~ from sth.** eine Autostunde von etw. entfernt sein; **have a long ~ to work** eine lange Anfahrt zur Arbeit haben; **c)** *(street)* Straße, *die;* **d)** *(private road)* Zufahrt, *die; (entrance) (to small building)* Einfahrt, *die; (to large building)* Auffahrt, *die;* **e)** *(energy to achieve)* Tatkraft, *die;* **a salesman with ~:** ein dynamischer Vertreter; **f)** *(Commerc., Polit., etc.: vigorous campaign)* Aktion, *die;* Kampagne, *die;* **export/sales/recruiting/charity ~:** Export-/Verkaufs-/Anwerbe-/Wohltätigkeitskampagne, *die;* **g)** *(Mil.: offensive)* Vorstoß, *der;* **h)** *(Psych.)* Trieb, *der;* **i)** *(Motor Veh.: position of steering-wheel)* **left-hand/right-hand ~:** Links-/Rechtssteuerung *od.* -lenkung, *die;* **be left-hand ~:** Linkssteuerung haben; ein Linkslenker sein *(Kfz-W.);* **j)** *(Motor Veh., Mech. Engin.: transmission of power)* Antrieb, *der;* **belt/front-wheel/rear-wheel ~:** Riemen-/Front-/Heckantrieb, *der;* **fluid ~:** hydraulische Kupplung; **k)** *(Cards etc.)* **whist/bridge ~:** Whist-/Bridge-Runde mit vielen Teilnehmern; **l)** *(Sport)* Drive, *der (fachspr.);* Treibschlag, *der.* **2.** *v. t.,* **drove** [drəʊv], **driven** ['drɪvn] **a)** fahren ‹*Auto, Lkw, Route, Strecke, Fahrgast*›; lenken ‹*Kutsche, Streitwagen*›; treiben ‹*Tier*›; führen ‹*Pflug*›; **this is a nice car to ~/this car is easy to ~:** dieses Auto fährt sich gut/leicht; **~ a carriage** *or* **coach and four through** *(fig.)* zerfetzen *(fig.);* zunichte machen ‹*Argumentation*›; **b)** *(as job)* ~ **a lorry/train** Lkw-Fahrer/Lokomotivführer sein; **c)** *(compel to move)* vertreiben; ~ **sb. out of** *or* **from a place/country** jmdn. von einem Ort/aus einem Land vertreiben; ~ **sb. out of** *or* **from the house** jmdn. aus dem Haus jagen; **d)** *(chase, urge on)* treiben ‹*Vieh, Wild*›; **e)** *(fig.)* ~ **sb. to sth.** jmdn. zu etw. treiben; ~ **sb. to do sth.** *or* **into doing sth.** jmdn. dazu treiben, etw. zu tun; ~ **sb. to suicide** jmdn. zum *od.* in den Selbstmord treiben; ~ **sb. out of his mind** *or* **wits** jmdn. in den Wahnsinn treiben *od.* um den Verstand bringen; **f)** ‹*Wind, Wasser:*› treiben; **be ~n off course** abgetrieben werden; **g)** *(cause to penetrate)* ~ **sth. into sth.** etw. in etw. *(Akk.)* treiben; ~ **sth. into sb.'s head** *(fig.)* jmdm. etw. einbleuen *od.* einhämmern *(ugs.);* **h)** *(power)* antreiben ‹*Mühle, Maschine*›; **be steam-~n** *or* **~n by steam** dampfgetrieben sein; **be ~n by electricity** [einen] Elektroantrieb haben; **i)** *(incite to action)* antreiben; **he was hard ~n** er wurde hart herangenommen; **be ~n by ambition** von Ehrgeiz getrieben werden; **j)** *(overwork)* ~ **oneself [too] hard** sich [zu sehr] schinden; **k)** *(transact)* ~ **a good bargain** ein gutes Geschäft machen; *see also* **hard 1 a. 3.** *v. i.,* **drove, driven a)** *(conduct motor vehicle)* fahren; **in Great Britain we ~ on the left** bei uns in Großbritannien ist Linksverkehr; **he ~s to see her every weekend** er besucht sie jedes Wochenende mit dem Auto; ~ **at 30 m.p.h.** mit 50 km/h fahren; **learn to ~:** [Auto]fahren lernen; den Führerschein machen *(ugs.);* **can you ~?** kannst du Auto fahren?; ~ **past** vorbeifahren; ~ **into a bollard/the back of a lorry** gegen einen Poller fahren/auf einen Lastwagen fahren; **b)** *(travel)* mit dem [eigenen] Auto fahren; **c)** *(rush, dash violently)* ‹*Hagelkörner, Wellen:*› schlagen; **clouds were driving across the sky** Wolken jagten über den Himmel

~ **at** *v. t.* hinauswollen auf (+ *Akk.*); **what are you driving at?** worauf wollen Sie hinaus?

~ **a'way 1.** *v. i.* wegfahren. **2.** *v. t.* **a)** wegfahren, wegbringen ‹*Ladung, Fahrzeug*›; *(chase away)* wegjagen; **b)** *(fig.)* zerstreuen ‹*Bedenken, Befürchtungen, Verdacht*›

~ **'back** *v. t. (force to retreat)* zurückschlagen ‹*Eindringlinge*›; **be ~n back on doing sth.** *(fig.)* keine andere Wahl haben, als etw. zu tun

~ **'off 1.** *v. i.* **a)** wegfahren; **b)** *(Golf)* abschlagen. **2.** *v. t. (repel)* zurückschlagen ‹*Angreifer*›

~ **'on 1.** *v. i.* weiterfahren. **2.** *v. t. (impel)* treiben **(to** zu)

~ **'out** *v. t.* **a)** hinauswerfen ‹*Person*›; hinausjagen ‹*Hund*›; hinausblasen ‹*Luft*›; **b)** *(fig.)* vertreiben ‹*Sorgen*›; austreiben ‹*bösen Geist*›

~ **'up 1.** *v. i.* vorfahren **(to** vor + *Dat.*); **she drove up to the starting line** sie fuhr an die Startlinie heran. **2.** *v. t.* hochtreiben ‹*Kosten*›

drive: ~-belt *n. (Mech. Engin.)* Treibriemen, *der;* **~-in** *adj.* Drive-in-; **~-in bank** Bank mit Autoschalter; **~-in cinema** *or (Amer.)* **movie [theater]** Autokino, *das*

drivel ['drɪvl] **1.** *n.* Gefasel, *das (ugs. abwertend);* **talk ~:** faseln *(ugs. abwertend).* **2.** *v. i., (Brit.)* **-ll-: a)** *(talk stupidly)* faseln *(ugs. abwertend);* **b)** *(slaver)* geifern

driven *see* **drive 2, 3**

'drive-on *adj.* ~ **car ferry** Autofährschiff, *das*

driver ['draɪvə(r)] *n.* **a)** Fahrer, *der*/Fahrerin, *die;* Führer, *der (Amtsspr.); (of locomotive)* Führer, *der*/Führerin, *die; (of horse-drawn carriage)* Kutscher, *der*/Kutscherin, *die;* **be in the ~'s seat** *(fig.)* das Steuer *od.* die Zügel in der Hand haben *(fig.);* **b)** *(Golf)* Driver, *der (fachspr.);* Holz 1, *das*

driverless ['draɪvəlɪs] *adj.* führerlos

'driver's license *(Amer.) see* **driving-licence**

drive: ~-shaft *n.* Antriebswelle, *die;* **~way** *n. see* **drive 1 d**

driving ['draɪvɪŋ] **1.** *n., no pl.* Fahren, *das;* **his ~ is awful** er fährt furchtbar. **2.** *adj.* **a)** ~ **rain** peitschender Regen; **b)** *(fig.)* treibend; ~ **ambition** brennender Ehrgeiz

driving: ~-gloves *n. pl.* Autohandschuhe; **~-instructor** *n.* Fahrlehrer, *der*/-lehrerin, *die;* **~-lesson** *n.* Fahrstunde, *die;* **[take] ~-lessons** Fahrunterricht [nehmen]; **~-licence** *n.* Führerschein, *der;* **~-mirror** *n.* Rückspiegel, *der;* **~-range** *n. (Golf)* Drivingrange, *das;* **~-school** *n.* Fahrschule, *die;* **~-seat** *n.* **a)** Fahrersitz, *der;* **b) be in the ~-seat = be in the driver's seat** *see* **driver a;** **~-test** *n.* Fahrprüfung, *die;* **take/pass/fail one's ~-test** die Fahrprüfung ablegen/bestehen/nicht bestehen; **~-wheel** *n.* Treibrad, *das*

drizzle [ˈdrɪzl] **1.** *n.* Sprühregen, *der;* Nieseln, *das;* **there was light ~:** es hat leicht genieselt. **2.** *v. i.* **it's drizzling** es nieselt; **drizzling rain** Nieselregen, *der*

droll [drəʊl] *adj.* **a)** *(amusing)* drollig; **b)** *(odd)* komisch

dromedary [ˈdrɒmɪdərɪ, ˈdrʌmɪdərɪ] *n.* *(Zool.)* Dromedar, *das*

drone [drəʊn] **1.** *n.* **a)** *(of bees, flies)* Summen, *das;* *(of machine)* Brummen, *das;* **b)** *(derog.: monotonous tone of speech)* Geleier, *das;* **c)** *(Zool.: bee; Aeronaut.)* Drohne, *die;* *(fig.: idler)* Müßiggänger, *der;* **d)** *(of bagpipe)* Bordunpfeife, *die.* **2.** *v. i.* **a)** *(buzz, hum)* ⟨*Biene:*⟩ summen; ⟨*Maschine:*⟩ brummen; **b)** *(derog.: monotonously)* ⟨*Rezitator:*⟩ leiern; ⟨*Rede, Predigt:*⟩ in einförmigem Tonfall vorgetragen werden. **3.** *v. t.* leiern

drool [druːl] *v. i.* **a)** *(show excessive delight)* **~ over sb./sth.** über jmdn./etw. in Verzückung geraten; **b)** *(slaver)* geifern

droop [druːp] **1.** *v. i.* **a)** herunterhängen; ⟨*Blume:*⟩ den Kopf hängen lassen; ⟨*Stiel:*⟩ sich beugen, sich biegen; **his shoulders ~:** seine Schultern hängen; **her head ~ed forwards** ihr Kopf sank nach vorn; **his eyelids were ~ing** ihm fielen die Augen zu; **the dog's tail ~ed** der Hund ließ den Schwanz hängen; **b)** *(fig.: flag)* ⟨*Mut, Moral:*⟩ sinken; ⟨*Mensch:*⟩ ermatten. **2.** *v. t.* [herunter]hängen lassen

drop [drɒp] **1.** *n.* **a)** *(of liquid)* Tropfen, *der;* **~s of rain/dew/blood/sweat** Regen-/Tau-/Bluts-/Schweißtropfen; **~ by ~, in ~s** tropfenweise; **be a ~ in the ocean** *or* **in the** *or* **a bucket** *(fig.)* ein Tropfen auf einen heißen Stein sein; **b)** *(fig.: small amount)* **[just] a ~:** [nur] ein kleiner Tropfen; **a ~ too much** *(of flavouring etc.)* eine Idee zuviel; **c)** *(fig. coll.: of alcohol)* Gläschen, *das;* **have had a ~ too much** ein Glas über den Durst getrunken haben *(ugs.);* **take a ~:** sich *(Dat.)* einen genehmigen *(ugs.);* **that's a nice ~ of beer/wine** das ist ein feines Bierchen/Weinchen *(ugs.);* **d)** *in pl. (Med.)* Tropfen *Pl.;* **e)** *(sweet)* Drops, *der;* **f)** *(vertical distance)* **there was a ~ of 50 metres from the roof to the ground below** vom Dach bis zum Boden waren es 50 Meter; **g)** *(abrupt descent of land)* plötzlicher Abfall; Absturz, *der;* **there was a sheer** *or* **steep ~ of some 500 ft.** das Gelände fiel etwa 150 m steil ab; **h)** *(Aeronaut.) (of men)* Absetzen, *das;* *(of supplies)* Abwurf, *der;* **i)** *(fig.: decrease)* Rückgang, *der;* **~ in temperature/prices/outgoings** Temperatur- / Preis- / Ausgabenrückgang, *der;* **a ~ in the price of coffee/in house prices** ein Preisrückgang bei Kaffee/bei Häusern; **a ~ in the cost of living** ein Sinken der Lebenshaltungskosten; **a ~ in salary/wages/income** eine Gehalts-/Lohn-/Einkommensminderung; **a ~ in value** eine Wertminderung; ein Wertverlust; **a ~ in atmospheric pressure/the voltage/power output** *(Phys.)* ein Druck-/Spannungs-/Leistungsabfall; **a ~ in crime** ein Rückgang der Kriminalität; **a ~ in turnover/sales/production** ein Umsatz-/Absatz-/Produktionsrückgang; **j)** *(coll.: advantage)* **get** *or* **have the ~ on sb.** jmdm. zuvorkommen; **k)** *(pendant, hanging ornament)* Gehänge, *das;* *(of ear-ring)* Ohrgehänge, *das;* **l)** *(underworld sl.: hiding-place)* Versteck, *das. See also* **hat b. 2.** *v. i.,* **-pp- a)** *(fall) (accidentally)* [herunter]fallen; *(deliberately)* sich [hinunter]fallen lassen; *(have abrupt descent)* abstürzen **(to** zu); **~ out of** *or* **from sb.'s hand** jmdm. aus der Hand fallen; **let sth. ~:** etw. fallen lassen; **b)** *(sink to ground)* ⟨*Mensch:*⟩ fallen; **~ to the ground** umfallen; zu Boden fallen; **~ like flies** wie die Fliegen umfallen; **~ [down] dead** tot umfallen; **~ dead!** *(sl.)* scher dich zum Teufel!; **~ into bed/an armchair** ins Bett/in einen Sessel sinken; **be fit** *or* **ready to ~** *(coll.)* zum Umfallen *od.* Umsinken müde sein; **~ on** *or* **to one's knees** auf die Knie fallen; **c)** *(in amount etc.)* sinken; ⟨*[An]zahl:*⟩ abnehmen, sinken; ⟨*Preis, Wert, Verkaufsziffern:*⟩ sinken, fallen; ⟨*Wind:*⟩ abflauen, sich legen; ⟨*Stimme:*⟩ sich senken; ⟨*Kinnlade:*⟩ herunterfallen *od.* -klappen; **the record has ~ped a place/to third place** die Schallplatte ist um einen Platz/auf Platz drei gefallen; **d)** *(move, go)* **~ down stream** [sich] stromabwärts treiben [lassen]; **~ back** *(Sport)* zurückfallen; **~ behind in one's work** mit seiner Arbeit in Rückstand geraten; **~ behind schedule** hinter dem Zeitplan zurückbleiben; **~ astern** *(Naut.)* achteraus sacken; **e)** *(fall in drops)* ⟨*Flüssigkeit:*⟩ tropfen **(from** aus); **f)** *(pass into some condition)* **~ [back] into one's old routine** in den alten Trott verfallen *od.* zurückfallen; **~ into the habit** *or* **way of doing sth.** die Gewohnheit annehmen *od.* sich *(Dat.)* angewöhnen, etw. zu tun; **~ into a dialect** in einen Dialekt fallen; **g)** *(cease)* **the affair was allowed to ~:** man ließ die Angelegenheit auf sich *(Dat.)* beruhen; **and there the matter ~ped** und dabei blieb es; **h) let ~:** beiläufig erwähnen ⟨*Termin, Tatsache, Absicht*⟩; fallenlassen ⟨*Bemerkung*⟩; **let [it] ~ that/when ...:** beiläufig erwähnen, daß/wann ... *See also* **pin 1 a. 3.** *v. t.,* **-pp-: a)** *(let fall)* fallen lassen; abwerfen ⟨*Bomben, Flugblätter, Nachschub*⟩; absetzen ⟨*Fallschirmjäger, Truppen*⟩; **~ a letter in the letter-box** einen Brief einwerfen *od.* in den Briefkasten stecken; **~ the curtain** *(Theatre)* den Vorhang herablassen; **~ the latch on the door** den Türriegel vorlegen; **b)** *(by mistake)* fallen lassen; **she ~ped crumbs on the floor/juice on the table** ihr fielen Krümel auf den Boden/tropfte Saft auf den Tisch; **he ~ped the glass/ball** ihm fiel das Glas/der Ball herunter; **c)** *(let fall in ~s)* tropfen; **d)** *(utter casually)* fallenlassen ⟨*Namen*⟩; **~ a hint** eine Anspielung machen; **~ a word in sb.'s ear [about sth.]** einmal mit jmdm. [über etw.] sprechen; **e)** *(send casually)* **~ sb. a note** *or* **line** jmdm. [ein paar Zeilen] schreiben; **~ sb. a postcard** jmdm. eine Karte schreiben; **f)** *(set down, unload from car)* absetzen ⟨*Mitfahrer, Fahrgast*⟩; *(from ship)* an Land gehen lassen; *(from aircraft)* von Bord gehen lassen; **g)** *(omit) (in writing)* auslassen; *(in speech)* nicht aussprechen; **~ one's h's** das h [im Anlaut] nicht aussprechen; **~ a subject from the syllabus/a name from a list** ein Fach aus dem Lehrplan/einen Namen von einer Liste streichen; **h)** *(discontinue, abandon)* fallenlassen ⟨*Plan, Thema, Schlagzeile, Anklage*⟩; einstellen ⟨*Untersuchung, Ermittlungen*⟩; ablegen ⟨*Titel*⟩; absetzen ⟨*Fernsehsendung*⟩; beiseite lassen ⟨*Formalitäten*⟩; aufgeben, Schluß machen mit ⟨*Verstellung, Heuchelei*⟩; **~ it!** laß das!; **~ everything!, ~ whatever you're doing!** laß alles stehen und liegen!; **shall we ~ the subject?** lassen Sie uns [lieber] das Thema wechseln; **~ a case** *(Law)* einen Fall zu den Akten legen; **i)** *(stop associating with)* fallenlassen ⟨*Freund, Freundin*⟩; *(exclude)* **~ sb. from a team** jmdn. aus einer Mannschaft nehmen; **~ sb. from a committee** jmdn. aus einem Ausschuß entlassen; **j) ~ one's voice** die Stimme senken; **k)** *(lower)* tiefer hängen ⟨*Lampe*⟩; auslassen ⟨*Rocksaum*⟩; **~ped handlebars** Rennlenker, *der;* **l)** *(knock down, fell)* zu Boden strecken; **m)** *(lose by gambling or in business)* verlieren. *See also* **brick 1 a; clanger; curtsy 1**

~ aˈway *v. i.* ⟨*Mitgliedschaft, Einnahmen:*⟩ sinken; ⟨*Gelände:*⟩ abfallen

~ by 1. [ˈ-ˈ] *v. i.* vorbeikommen. **2.** [ˈ--] *v. t.* **~ by sb.'s house** bei jmdm. vorbeigehen *od.* hereinschauen

~ ˈin 1. *v. t. (deliver)* vorbeibringen. **2.** *v. i.* **a)** hineinfallen; **b)** *(visit)* hereinschauen; vorbeikommen; **~ in on sb.** *or* **at sb.'s house** bei jmdm. hereinschauen; **~ in for a pint** auf ein Bier vorbeikommen

~ ˈoff 1. *v. i.* **a)** *(fall off)* abfallen; *(become detached)* abgehen; **b)** *(fall asleep)* einnicken; **c)** *(decrease)* ⟨*Teilnahme, Geschäft:*⟩ zurückgehen; ⟨*Unterstützung, Interesse:*⟩ nachlassen; ⟨*Absatz:*⟩ rückläufig sein. **2.** *v. t.* **a)** *(fall off)* abfallen von; **~ off a truck** von einem Lkw herunterfallen; **b)** *(set down)* absetzen ⟨*Fahrgast*⟩; **the ship ~ped off the cargo** das Schiff hat seine Ladung gelöscht; **~ a package/the shopping off at sb.'s house** ein Paket/die Einkäufe bei jmdm. vorbeibringen

~ ˈout *v. i.* **a)** *(fall out)* herausfallen **(of** aus); **your teeth will ~ out** Ihnen werden die Zähne ausfallen; **b)** *(withdraw beforehand)* seine Teilnahme absagen; *(withdraw while in progress)* aussteigen *(ugs.)* **(of** aus); *(abandon sth.)* ausscheiden **(of** aus); *(disappear from one's place in a series or group)* ausfallen; **~ out of the bidding** aussteigen *(ugs.);* nicht mehr mitbieten; **c)** *(cease to take part)* aussteigen *(ugs.)* **(of** aus); ⟨*Student:*⟩ das Studium abbrechen *od.* aufgeben; **~ out of university/the course** das Studium abbrechen *od.* aufgeben; **~ out [of society]** aussteigen *(ugs.);* **d)** *(be omitted)* aus-, weggelassen werden **(of** aus). *See also* **drop-out**

~ ˈround *v. i.* vorbeikommen

drop: ~-forging *n. (Metalw.)* Gesenkschmieden, *das;* **~-head** *n. (Brit. Motor Veh.)* Klappverdeck, *das;* *(vehicle)* Kabriolett, *das;* **~-kick** *n. (Football)* Dropkick, *der;* *(Rugby)* Sprungtritt, *der;* **~-leaf table** *n.* Klapptisch, *der*

droplet [ˈdrɒplɪt] *n.* Tröpfchen, *das*

ˈdrop-out *n. (coll.)* **a)** *(act of withdrawing)* Aussteigen, *das (ugs.);* *(from expedition or trip)* Ausfall, *der;* Rücktritt, *der;* **the ~ rate** die Aussteigerquote; *(among students or trainees)* die Zahl der Abbrecher; **b)** *(person) (from college etc.)* Abbrecher, *der*/Abbrecherin, *die;* *(from society)* Aussteiger, *der*/Aussteigerin, *die (ugs.)*

dropper [ˈdrɒpə(r)] *n. (esp. Med.)* Tropfer, *der;* Guttiole, *die (fachspr.)*

droppings [ˈdrɒpɪŋz] *n. pl.* Mist, *der;* *(of horse)* Pferdeäpfel *Pl.;* *(of cattle)* Kuhfladen *Pl.*

ˈdrop-shot *n. (Tennis etc.)* Stoppball, *der*

dropsy [ˈdrɒpsɪ] *n.* Wassersucht, *die*

dross [drɒs] *n.* **a)** Abfall, *der;* **b)** *(Metallurgy)* Gekrätz, *das;* **c)** *(fig.)* Tand, *der (geh. veralt.);* **human ~** *(derog.)* Abschaum, *der (abwertend)*

drought [draʊt] *(Amer., Scot., Ir./poet.:* **drouth** [draʊθ]) *n.* **a)** Dürre, *die;* **a period of ~:** eine Dürreperiode; **b)** *(fig.: shortage)* Mangel, *der* **(of an** + *Dat.)*

¹drove *see* **drive 2, 3**

²drove [drəʊv] *n.* **a)** *(herd)* Herde, *die;* **b)** *usu. in pl. (fig.: of people)* Schar, *die;* **in ~s** scharenweise; in Scharen

drover [ˈdrəʊvə(r)] *n.* Viehtreiber, *der*

drown [draʊn] **1.** *v. i.* ertrinken. **2.** *v. t.* **a)** ertränken; **be ~ed** ertrinken; **b)** *(fig.)* **~ one's sorrows [in liquor]** seine Sorgen [im Alkohol] ertränken; **c)** *(submerge, flood)* überfluten; überschwemmen; verwässern ⟨*Whisky, Brandy*⟩; **~ed valley** *(Geog.)* überflutetes Tal; Ria[s]tal, *das;* **d)** *(make inaudible)* übertönen ⟨*Geräusch, Musik*⟩. *See also* **rat 1 a**

~ ˈout *v. t. (make inaudible)* übertönen; niederschreien ⟨*Redner*⟩

drowse [draʊz] *v. i.* [vor sich hin]dösen; **~ off** eindösen; einnicken

drowsily [ˈdraʊzɪlɪ] *adv.* *(while falling asleep)* schläfrig; *(on just waking)* verschlafen

drowsiness [ˈdraʊzɪnɪs] *n., no pl.* Schläfrigkeit, *die;* **cause ~:** müde *od.* schläfrig machen

drowsy [ˈdraʊzɪ] *adj.* **a)** *(half asleep)* schläfrig; *(on just waking)* verschlafen; **feel ~:** sich schläfrig fühlen; **b)** *(soporific)* einschläfernd

drub [drʌb] *v. t.*, **-bb-** *(thrash)* verprügeln; verdreschen *(ugs.)*; *(beat in fight)* schlagen

drubbing ['drʌbɪŋ] *n.* **a)** *(thrashing)* Tracht Prügel, *die;* **b)** *(fig.)* Niederlage, *die*

drudge [drʌdʒ] **1.** *n.* Schwerarbeiter, *der (fig.)*; Kuli, *der (ugs. abwertend)*. **2.** *v. i.* schuften; sich abplacken

drudgery ['drʌdʒərɪ] *n.* Schufterei, *die;* Plackerei, *die*

drug [drʌg] **1.** *n.* **a)** *(Med., Pharm.)* Medikament, *das;* [Arznei]mittel, *das; (as ingredient)* Mittel, *das;* **this patient is on ~s** dieser Patient muß Medikamente nehmen; **b)** *(narcotic, opiate, etc.)* Droge, *die;* Rauschgift, *das;* **take ~s** Drogen *od.* Rauschgift nehmen; **be on ~s** [regelmäßig] Drogen *od.* Rauschgift nehmen; **c)** *(Commerc. fig.)* **a ~ on the market** unverkäufliche Ware; ein Ladenhüter *(ugs.)*. **2.** *v. t.*, **-gg- a)** *(administer ~ to)* **he was ~ged and kidnapped** er wurde betäubt und entführt; **b)** *(add ~ to)* **~ sb.'s food/drink** jmds. Essen/Getränk *(Dat.)* ein Betäubungsmittel beimischen

drug: ~ addict *n.* Drogen- *od.* Rauschgiftsüchtige, *der/die;* **~ addiction** *n.;* Drogen- *od.* Rauschgiftsucht, *die*

druggist ['drʌgɪst] *n.* Drogist, *der*/Drogistin, *die*

drug: ~-peddler *n.* Dealer, *der (Drogenszene);* Drogen- *od.* Rauschgifthändler, *der;* **~-pusher** Pusher, *der (Drogenszene);* Drogen- *od.* Rauschgifthändler, *der;* **~store** *n. (Amer.)* Drugstore, *der;* **~-taking** *n., no pl.* Drogeneinnahme, *die*

Druid ['dru:ɪd] *n.* Druide, *der*

drum [drʌm] **1.** *n.* **a)** Trommel, *die;* **b)** *in pl. (in jazz or pop)* Schlagzeug, *das; (section of band etc.)* Trommeln *Pl.;* **c)** *(sound)* Trommeln, *das;* **d)** *(Anat.) see* **ear-drum; e)** *(container for oil etc.)* Faß, *das;* **~ of paint** Farbenhobbock, *der.* **2.** *v. i.*, **-mm-** trommeln. **3.** *v. t.*, **-mm-: ~ one's fingers on the desk** mit den Fingern auf den Tisch trommeln

~ into *v. t.* **~ sth. into sb.** jmdm. etw. einhämmern *(ugs.) od.* einbleuen *(ugs.)*

~ 'out *v. t. (Mil.)* **~ sb. out** jmdn. austrommeln *(veralt.); (fig.)* jmdn. [mit Schimpf und Schande] ausstoßen; **he was ~med out of town** er wurde aus der Stadt gejagt

~ 'up *v. t. (Mil.)* zusammentrommeln; *(fig.)* auftreiben ‹*Kunden, Unterstützung*›; erwecken ‹*Enthusiasmus*›; zusammentrommeln *(ugs.)* ‹*Helfer, Anhänger*›; anbahnen ‹*Geschäfte*›

drum: ~-beat *n.* Trommelschlag, *der;* **~ brake** *n.* Trommelbremse, *die;* **~fire** *n. (Mil.; also fig.)* Trommelfeuer, *das;* **~head** *n.* **a)** *(Mus.)* [Trommel]fell, *das;* **b)** *attrib.* **~head court martial** Standgericht, *das*

drumlin ['drʌmlɪn] *n. (Geol.)* Drumlin, *der*

drum: ~ 'major *n. (Mil.)* Tambourmajor, *der;* **~ majo'rette** *n.* Tambourmajorette, *die*

drummer ['drʌmə(r)] *n.* **a)** Schlagzeuger, *der;* **b)** *(Amer.: representative)* Vertreter, *der*/Vertreterin, *die*

'drumstick *n.* **a)** *(Mus.)* Trommelschlegel, *der;* **b)** *(of fowl)* Keule, *die;* Schlegel, *der (südd., österr., schweiz.)*

drunk [drʌŋk] **1.** *adj.* **be ~:** betrunken sein; **be half ~:** angetrunken sein; **get ~ [on gin]** [von Gin] betrunken werden; *(intentionally)* sich [mit Gin] betrinken; **get sb. ~:** jmdn. betrunken machen; **be ~ as a lord** *(coll.)* voll wie eine Haubitze sein *(ugs.)*; **~ in charge [of a vehicle]** betrunken am Steuer. **2.** *n.* Betrunkene, *der/die*

drunkard ['drʌŋkəd] *n.* Trinker, *der*/Trinkerin, *die;* Säufer, *der*/Säuferin, *die (derb abwertend)*

drunken ['drʌŋkn] *attrib. adj.* **a)** betrunken; besoffen *(derb)*; *(habitually drunk)* versoffen *(derb)*; **b) a ~ brawl** *or* **fight** eine Schlägerei zwischen Betrunkenen; **in a ~ stupor** im Vollrausch; **~ driving** Trunkenheit am Steuer

drunkenness ['drʌŋknnɪs] *n., no pl.* **a)** *(temporary)* Betrunkenheit, *die;* **b)** *(habitual)* Trunksucht, *die*

drupe [dru:p] *n. (Bot.)* Steinfrucht, *die*

Druze [dru:z] *n.* Druse, *der*/Drusin, *die*

dry [draɪ] **1.** *adj.*, **drier** ['draɪə(r)], **driest** ['draɪɪst] **a)** trocken; trocken, *(very ~)* herb ‹*Wein*›; ausgetrocknet ‹*Fluß, Flußbett*›; **get** *or* **become ~:** trocken werden; trocknen; **~ bread** trocken[es] Brot; **go ~:** austrocknen; **my throat is** *or* **feels ~:** meine Kehle ist wie ausgetrocknet; **~ work** Arbeit, die durstig macht; **as ~ as a bone** völlig trocken; **there wasn't a ~ eye in the house** da blieb kein Auge trocken; **store sth. in a ~ place** etw. trocken lagern; **b)** *(not using liquid)* Trocken-; **~ shave/shampoo** Trockenrasur, *die*/-shampoo, *das;* **c)** *(not rainy)* trocken ‹*Wetter, Klima*›; **d)** *(coll.: thirsty)* durstig; **I'm a bit ~:** ich habe eine trockene Kehle; **e) go ~:** ‹*Flüssigkeit:*› verdunsten; ‹*Suppe usw.:*› verkochen; **f)** *(not yielding)* ausgetrocknet, versiegt ‹*Brunnen*›; **g)** *(teetotal)* **go ~:** das Alkoholverbot *od.* die Prohibition einführen; **h)** *(fig.)* trocken ‹*Humor*›; *(impassive, cold)* kühl ‹*Art, Bemerkung usw.*›; **i)** *(fig.: meagre, bare)* nüchtern ‹*Fakten, Dankesworte*›; nackt ‹*Tatsachen*›; *(dull)* trocken ‹*Stoff, Bericht, Vorlesung*›; **be as ~ as dust** sterbenslangweilig *od. (ugs.)* stinklangweilig sein. **2.** *n. (coll.)* **a) give it a good ~:** trockne es gut ab; **b)** *(place)* **in the ~:** im Trock[e]nen. **3.** *v. t.* **a)** trocknen ‹*Haare, Wäsche*›; abtrocknen ‹*Geschirr, Baby*›; **~ oneself** sich abtrocknen; **~ one's eyes** *or* **tears/hands** sich *(Dat.)* die Tränen abwischen/die Hände abtrocknen; **b)** *(preserve)* trocknen ‹*Kräuter, Holz, Blumen*›; dörren ‹*Obst, Fleisch*›. **4.** *v. i.* trocknen; trocken werden; **~ hard on sth.** ‹*Schlamm:*› an etw. *(Dat.)* an- *od.* festtrocknen

~ 'out 1. *v. t.* **a)** trocknen; **b)** einer Entziehungskur unterziehen ‹*Alkoholiker, Drogenabhängigen*›; trockenlegen *(ugs.)* ‹*Alkoholiker*›; ausnüchtern ‹*Betrunkenen*›. **2.** *v. i.* **a)** trocknen; **b)** ‹*Alkoholiker, Drogenabhängiger:*› eine Entziehung[skur] machen; ‹*Alkoholiker:*› trocken werden *(ugs.)*; ‹*Betrunkener:*› ausnüchtern

~ 'up 1. *v. t.* **a)** abtrocknen ‹*Geschirr*›; **b)** austrocknen ‹*Fluß, Teich*›; versiegen lassen ‹*Brunnen*›. **2.** *v. i.* **a)** *(~ the dishes)* abtrocknen; *see also* **drying-up; b)** ‹*Brunnen, Quelle:*› versiegen; ‹*Fluß, Teich:*› austrocknen; **a dried-up person** ein vertrockneter Typ; **c)** *(fig.)* ‹*Initiative, Ideen, Erfindergeist:*› versiegen; ‹*Renten, Ersparnisse:*› schrumpfen; **d)** *(be unable to continue)* steckenbleiben; **e)** *(coll.: stop talking)* **~ up!** halt die Klappe! *(ugs.)*; hör auf zu sülzen! *(salopp)*

dryad ['draɪæd] *n. (Mythol.)* Dryade, *die*

dry: ~ 'battery *n. (Electr.)* Trockenbatterie, *die;* **~ 'cell** *n. (Electr.)* Trockenelement, *das;* **~-'clean** *v. t.* chemisch reinigen; **have sth. ~-cleaned** etw. in die Reinigung geben; **'~-clean only'** „chemisch reinigen"; **~-'cleaners** *n. pl.* chemische Reinigung; **~-'cleaning** *n.* chemische Reinigung; **~ 'dock** *n.* Trockendock, *das*

dryer *see* [2]**drier**

dry: ~-eyed *adj.* ohne Rührung; **~ goods** *n. pl. (Commerc.)* Textilwaren *Pl.;* Kurzwaren *Pl.;* **~ 'ice** *n.* Trockeneis, *das*

drying ['draɪɪŋ]: **~-cupboard** *n.* Wäschetrockenschrank, *der;* **~-'up** *n.* Abtrocknen, *das;* **do the ~-up** abtrocknen

dry 'land *n.* Festland, *das;* **be back on ~** wieder festen Boden unter den Füßen haben

dryly ['draɪlɪ] *adv. (fig.)* **a)** *(coldly)* kühl; **b)** *(with dry humour)* trocken; **sb. is ~ humorous** jmd. hat einen trockenen Humor

'dry measure *n.* Trocken[hohl]maß, *das*

dryness ['draɪnɪs] *n., no pl.* **a)** Trockenheit, *die;* **b)** *(fig.: coldness)* Kühle, *die;* **c)** *(fig.: of humour)* Trockenheit, *die;* **d)** *(fig.: dullness)* Trockenheit, *die;* Langweiligkeit, *die*

dry: ~ 'rot *n.* **a)** Trockenfäule, *die;* **b)** *(fungi)* Polyparus, *der (fachspr.)*; Hausschwamm, *der;* Holzschwamm, *der;* **~ 'run** *n. (coll.)* Probelauf, *der;* **~stone** *adj.* **~stone wall** Trockensteinmauer, *die*

D. Sc. [di:es'si:] *abbr.* **Doctor of Science** Dr. rer. nat.; *see also* **B.Sc.**

DSS *abbr. (Brit.)* **Department of Social Security** Amt für Sozialwesen

DTs [di: 'ti:z] *n. pl. (coll.)* Delirium, *das;* **have the ~:** [vom Trinken] das Zittern haben *(ugs.)*

dual ['dju:əl] *adj.* **a)** doppelt; Doppel-; **~ status/role/function** Doppelstatus, *der*/-rolle, *die*/-funktion, *die;* **b)** *(Psych.)* **~ personality** gespaltene Persönlichkeit

dual: ~ 'carriageway *n. (Brit.)* zweispurige Straße; **~ con'trol** *n. (Aeronaut.)* Doppelsteuerung, *die; (Motor Veh.)* doppelte Bedienungselemente

dualism ['dju:əlɪzm] *n. (Philos., Theol.)* Dualismus, *der*

duality [dju:'ælɪtɪ] *n.* Dualität, *die*

dual-'purpose *adj.* zweifach verwendbar

[1]**dub** [dʌb] *v. t.*, **-bb-** *(Cinemat.)* synchronisieren

[2]**dub** *v. t.*, **-bb-: a) ~ sb. [a] knight** jmdn. zum Ritter schlagen; **b)** *(call, nickname)* titulieren

[3]**dub** *n. (sl.: novice)* Flasche, *die (ugs.)*

dubbin ['dʌbɪn] *n.* Lederfett, *das*

dubious ['dju:bɪəs] *adj.* **a)** *(doubting)* unschlüssig; **feel ~ of sb.'s honesty** an jmds. Ehrlichkeit *(Dat.)* zweifeln; **I'm ~ about accepting the invitation** ich weiß nicht recht, ob ich die Einladung annehmen soll; **b)** *(suspicious)* dubios; zweifelhaft; **c)** *(questionable)* zweifelhaft; fragwürdig; **d)** *(of doubtful result)* ungewiß; **e)** *(unreliable)* zweifelhaft

dubiously ['dju:bɪəslɪ] *adv.* **a)** *(doubtingly)* unschlüssig; **b)** *(suspiciously)* dubios

ducal ['dju:kl] *adj.* herzoglich; Herzogs‹*titel, -krone*›

duchess ['dʌtʃɪs] *n.* Herzogin, *die*

duchy ['dʌtʃɪ] *n.* Herzogtum, *das*

[1]**duck** [dʌk] **1.** *n.* **a)** *pl.* **~s** *or (collect.) same (Ornith.; as food)* Ente, *die;* **wild ~:** Wildente, *die;* **toy ~:** Schwimmente, *die;* Spielzeugente, *die;* **can a ~ swim?** *(iron.)* und ob!; **it was [like] water off a ~'s back** *(fig.)* das lief alles an ihm/ihr *usw.* ab; **take to sth. like a ~ to water** bei etw. gleich in seinem Element sein; **fine weather for ~s** *(joc./iron.)* bei dem Wetter könnte man Flossen gebrauchen *(scherzh.)*; **play [at] ~s and drakes** [flache] Steine über die Wasseroberfläche springen lassen; titschern; **play ~s and drakes with, make ~s and drakes of** *(fig.)* verschwenden; durchbringen ‹*Ersparnisse, Vermögen*›; zum Fenster hinauswerfen ‹*Geld*›; **b)** *(Brit. coll.: dear)* **[my] ~:** Schätzchen; **c)** *(Cricket)* **be out for a ~:** ohne einen Punkt zu machen aus sein; **break one's ~:** den ersten Punkt holen. *See also* **dead duck; lame duck. 2.** *v. i.* **a)** *(bend down)* sich [schnell] ducken; **~ [down] [out of sight]** sich ducken, um nicht gesehen zu werden; **b)** *(under water)* tauchen; **c)** *(coll.: move hastily)* türmen *(ugs.)*. **3.** *v. t.* **a) ~ sb. [in water]** jmdn. untertauchen; jmdn. tunken *(landsch.)*; **b) ~ one's head** den Kopf einziehen; **c)** *(fig. coll.: evade)* ausweichen ‹*einer Frage, einem Problem*›

~ 'out *v. i. (coll.)* **~ out [of sth.]** sich [vor etw. *(Dat.)*] drücken *(ugs.)*; [vor etw. *(Dat.)*] kneifen *(ugs. abwertend)*

[2]duck *n. (Textiles)* Segeltuch, *das*

duck: **~-bill, ~-billed 'platypus** *see* **platypus; ~-boards** *n. pl.* Lattenrost, *der;* **~-egg** *n.* Entenei, *das;* **~-egg 'blue** *n.* zartes Blaugrau

duckie ['dʌkɪ] *see* **[1]duck 1 b**

ducking ['dʌkɪŋ] *n. (immersion)* [Ein-, Unter]tauchen, *das;* **give sb. a ~:** jmdn. untertauchen; jmdn. tunken *(landsch.)*

'ducking-stool *n. (Hist.)* Tauchstuhl, *der*

duckling ['dʌklɪŋ] *n.* Entenküken, *das; (as food)* junge Ente; *see also* **ugly a**

'duck-pond *n.* Ententeich, *der*

ducks [dʌks] *see* **[1]duck 1 b**

'duckweed *n. (Bot.)* Wasserlinse, *die;* Entengrütze, *die*

duct [dʌkt] **1.** *n.* **a)** *(for fluid, gas, cable)* [Rohr]leitung, *die;* Rohr, *das; (for air)* Ventil, *das;* **b)** *(Anat.)* Gang, *der;* **hepatic/cystic/acoustic ~:** Leber-/Gallenblasen-/Gehörgang, *der;* **spermatic ~:** Samenleiter, *der;* **tear-~:** Tränenkanal, *der;* **c)** *(Bot.)* Gang, *der;* Kanal, *der.* **2.** *v. t.* leiten

ductile ['dʌktaɪl] *adj.* dehnbar, *(fachspr.)* duktil ⟨*Metall*⟩

ducting ['dʌktɪŋ] *n.* Leitungssystem, *das*

dud [dʌd] *(coll.)* **1.** *n.* **a)** *(useless thing)* Niete, *die (ugs.); (counterfeit)* Fälschung, *die; (banknote)* Blüte, *die (ugs.); (failure)* Reinfall, *der (ugs.); (Cards)* Lusche, *die (ugs.);* **this battery/light-bulb/watch/ball-point is a ~:** diese Batterie/Glühlampe/Uhr/dieser Kugelschreiber taugt nichts; **that cheque was a ~:** der Scheck war faul *(ugs.);* **b)** *(bomb etc.)* Blindgänger, *der;* **c)** *(ineffectual person)* Niete, *die (ugs.);* Versager, *der.* **2.** *adj.* **a)** mies *(ugs.);* schlecht; *(fake)* gefälscht; geplatzt ⟨*Scheck*⟩; **a ~ banknote** eine Blüte *(ugs.);* **b) a ~ bullet/shell/bomb** ein Blindgänger

dude [dju:d, du:d] *n. (Amer. sl.)* feiner Pinkel aus der Stadt *(ugs.)*

'dude ranch *n. (Amer.)* Ferienranch, *die*

dudgeon ['dʌdʒn] *n.* **in high ~:** äußerst empört

due [dju:] **1.** *adj.* **a)** *(owed)* geschuldet; zustehend ⟨*Eigentum, Recht usw.*⟩; **the share/reward ~ to him** der ihm zustehende Anteil/die ihm zustehende Belohnung; der Anteil, der/die Belohnung, die ihm zusteht; **the amount ~:** der zu zahlende Betrag; **there's sth. ~ to me, I've got sth. ~, I'm ~ for sth.** mir steht etw. zu; **b)** *(immediately payable, lit. or fig.)* fällig; **be more than ~** *(fig.)* überfällig sein; **c)** *(that it is proper to give)* gebührend, geziemend *(geh.);* erforderlich ⟨*Hilfe*⟩; entsprechend ⟨*Ermutigung*⟩; angemessen ⟨*Belohnung*⟩; **be ~ to sb.** jmdm. gebühren; **recognition ~ to sb.** Anerkennung, die jmdm. gebührt; **respect ~ from sb. to sb.** Respekt, den jmd. jmdm. schuldet; **with all ~ respect, madam** bei allem gebotenen Respekt, meine Dame; **with ~ allowance** *or* **regard** unter gebührender Berücksichtigung **(for** *Gen.*); **d)** *(that it is proper to use)* gebührend, geziemend *(geh.);* nötig; reiflich ⟨*Überlegung*⟩; **with ~ caution/care** mit der nötigen Vorsicht/Sorgfalt; **they were given ~ warning** sie wurden hinreichend gewarnt; **in ~ time** rechtzeitig; **~ process of law** ordentliches Gerichtsverfahren; **e)** *(attributable)* **~ to negligence** auf Grund von Nachlässigkeit; **the mistake was ~ to negligence** der Fehler war durch Nachlässigkeit verursacht; **the discovery is ~ to Newton** die Entdeckung ist Newton *(Dat.)* zu verdanken; **it's ~ to her that we missed the train** ihretwegen verpaßten wir den Zug; es lag an ihr, daß wir den Zug verpaßten; **his death was ~ to a heart attack** Ursache seines Todes war ein Herzanfall; **the difficulty is ~ to our ignorance** die Schwierigkeit ergibt sich aus unserer Unwissenheit; **be ~ to the fact that ...:** darauf zurückzuführen sein, daß ...; **f)** *(scheduled, expected, under engagement or instructions)* **be ~ to do sth.** etw. tun sollen; **I'm ~** *(my plan is)* **to leave tomorrow** ich werde morgen abfahren; **be ~ [to arrive]** ankommen sollen; **the train is now ~:** der Zug müßte jetzt planmäßig ankommen; **when are we ~ to land/dock?** wann landen wir/laufen wir ein?; **I'm ~ in Paris tonight** ich muß heute abend in Paris sein; **the baby is ~ in two weeks' time** das Baby kommt in zwei Wochen; **g)** *(likely to get, deserving)* **be ~ for sth.** etw. verdienen; **he is ~ for promotion** seine Beförderung ist fällig. *See also* **course 1 c. 2.** *adv.* **a) ~ north** genau nach Norden; **~ north wind** Wind direkt von Norden; **the town is ~ north of us** die Stadt liegt genau nördlich von uns; **b) ~ to** auf Grund (+ *Gen.*); aufgrund (+ *Gen.*). **3.** *n.* **a)** *in pl. (debt)* Schulden *Pl.;* **pay one's ~s** seine Schulden bezahlen; **b)** *no pl. (fig.: just deserts, reward)* **sb.'s ~:** das, was jmdm. zusteht; das, was jmdm. gebührt *(geh.);* **that was no more than his ~:** das hatte er auch verdient; das stand ihm auch zu; **give sb. his ~:** jmdm. Gerechtigkeit widerfahren lassen; **but to give him** *or* **the Devil his ~ he ...:** aber das muß man ihm lassen, er ...; **c)** *usu. in pl. (fee)* Gebühr, *die; (toll)* Zoll, *der;* **membership ~s** Mitgliedsbeiträge *Pl.*

duel ['dju:əl] **1.** *n.* **a)** Duell, *das; (Univ.)* Mensur, *die;* **fight a ~:** ein Duell/eine Mensur austragen; **b)** *(fig.: contest)* Kampf, *der;* **~ of wits** geistiger Wettstreit; **~ of words** Wortgefecht, *das;* Rededuell, *das;* **propaganda ~:** Propagandagefecht, *das.* **2.** *v. i., (Brit.)* **-ll-** sich duellieren; *(Univ.)* eine Mensur austragen *od.* schlagen

duet [dju:'et] *n. (Mus.) (for voices)* Duett, *das; (instrumental)* Duo, *das*

duettist [dju:'etɪst] *n.* [Duett]partner, *der*/[Duett]partnerin, *die*

duff [dʌf] *adj. (Brit. sl.)* mies *(ugs.)*

duffel bag, duffel coat *see* **duffle bag, duffle coat**

duffer ['dʌfə(r)] *n.* Trottel, *der (ugs. abwertend);* **be a ~ at football/school** im Fußball/in der Schule eine Niete sein *(ugs.)*

duffle ['dʌfl]: **~ bag** *n.* Matchbeutel, *der; (waterproof, also)* Seesack, *der;* **~ coat** *n.* Dufflecoat, *der*

dug *see* **dig 1, 2**

'dug-out *n.* **a)** *(canoe)* Einbaum, *der;* **b)** *(Mil.: shelter)* Unterstand, *der*

duke [dju:k] *n.* **a)** Herzog, *der;* **royal ~:** Herzog und Mitglied des Königshauses; **b)** *in pl. (sl.: fists)* Flossen *Pl. (salopp);* **put up your ~s** Fäuste hoch! *(salopp)*

dukedom ['dju:kdəm] *n.* **a)** *(territory)* Herzogtum, *das;* **b)** *(rank)* Herzogswürde, *die*

dulcet ['dʌlsɪt] *adj.* lieblich; **sb.'s ~ tones** *(iron.)* jmds. zarte Stimme *(iron.)*

dulcimer ['dʌlsɪmə(r)] *n. (Mus.)* Hackbrett, *das;* Zimbal, Zymbal, *das*

dull [dʌl] **1.** *adj.* **a)** *(stupid)* beschränkt; *(slow to understand)* begriffsstutzig *(abwertend);* **b)** *(boring)* langweilig; stumpfsinnig ⟨*Arbeit, Routine*⟩; nichtssagend ⟨*Eindruck*⟩; **c)** *(gloomy)* trübe ⟨*Wetter, Tag*⟩; **d)** *(not bright)* matt, stumpf ⟨*Farbe, Glanz, Licht, Metall*⟩; trübe ⟨*Augen*⟩; blind ⟨*Spiegel*⟩; *(not sharp)* dumpf ⟨*Geräusch, Aufprall, Schmerz, Gefühl*⟩; **e)** *(not keen)* unscharf; schwach ⟨*Augen, Gehör*⟩; **grow ~** ⟨*Geisteskräfte:*⟩ nachlassen; **f)** *(sluggish)* träge; **g)** *(listless)* lustlos; *(dejected)* niedergeschlagen; bedrückt; **h)** *(blunt)* stumpf; **i)** *(Commerc.)* flau. *See also* **ditchwater. 2.** *v. t.* **a)** *(make less acute)* schwächen; trüben; betäuben ⟨*Schmerz*⟩; **b)** *(make less bright or sharp)* stumpf werden lassen; verblassen lassen ⟨*Farbe*⟩; **c)** *(blunt)* stumpf machen; **d)** *(fig.)* dämpfen ⟨*Freude, Enthusiasmus*⟩; abstumpfen ⟨*Geist, Sinne, Verstand, Vorstellungskraft*⟩; lindern ⟨*Kummer, Haß*⟩; **~ the edge of sth.** *(fig.)* einer Sache *(Dat.)* ihren Reiz nehmen

dullard ['dʌləd] *n.* Dummkopf, *der (ugs.)*

dullness ['dʌlnɪs] *n., no pl.* **a)** *(stupidity)* Beschränktheit, *die; (slow-wittedness)* Begriffsstutzigkeit, *die (abwertend);* [geistige] Trägheit; **b)** *(boringness)* Langweiligkeit, *die; (of work, life, routine)* Stumpfsinn, *der;* **c)** *(of weather)* Trübheit, *die;* **d)** *(of colour, light, metal)* Stumpfheit, *die;* Mattheit, *die;* **e)** *(of sight, hearing etc.)* Schwächung, *die; (of sight, mind, senses)* Trübung, *die;* **f)** *(sluggishness)* Trägheit, *die*

dull-witted [dʌl'wɪtɪd] *see* **dull 1 a**

dully ['dʌllɪ] *adv.* **a)** *(dimly, indistinctly)* trübe ⟨*scheinen*⟩; dumpf ⟨*fühlen, aufprallen, tönen, schmerzen*⟩; **his arm was aching ~:** er spürte einen dumpfen Schmerz im Arm; **b)** *(sluggishly)* träge; **c)** *(listlessly)* lustlos; *(dejectedly)* niedergeschlagen; bedrückt

duly ['dju:lɪ] *adv.* **a)** *(rightly, properly)* ordnungsgemäß; **b)** *(sufficiently)* ausreichend; hinreichend; **he was ~ punished** er wurde gehörig bestraft; **c)** *(punctually)* pünktlich

dumb [dʌm] **1.** *adj.,* **~er** ['dʌmə(r)], **~est** ['dʌmɪst] **a)** stumm; **a ~ person** ein Stummer/eine Stumme; **~ animals** *or* **creatures** die Tiere; die stumme Kreatur *(dichter.);* **~ friend** vierbeiniger Freund; **b)** *(temporarily speechless)* stumm; **he was [struck] ~ with fright/amazement** vor Furcht/Staunen verschlug es ihm die Sprache; **c)** *(inarticulate)* sprachlos ⟨*Massen, Millionen*⟩; *(saying nothing)* stumm, schweigend; **d)** *(coll.: stupid)* doof *(ugs.);* **act ~:** sich dumm stellen *(ugs.);* **a ~ blonde** eine dümmliche Blondine *(ugs.).* **2.** *n. pl.* **the ~:** die Stummen; **the deaf and ~:** die Taubstummen

'dumb-bell *n.* **a)** Hantel, *die;* **b)** *(sl.: stupid person)* Dummkopf, *der (ugs.);* Dümmling, *der (ugs.)*

dumbfound [dʌm'faʊnd] *v. t.* sprachlos machen; verblüffen

dumbfounded [dʌm'faʊndɪd] *adj.* sprachlos; verblüfft; **be ~:** sprachlos sein

dumbly ['dʌmlɪ] *adv.* stumm

dumb: **~ show** *n.* **in ~ show** durch Mimik; **~ 'waiter** *n.* **a)** *(trolley)* stummer Diener; **b)** *(lift)* Speisenaufzug, *der*

dumdum ['dʌmdʌm] *n.* **~ [bullet]** Dumdum[geschoß], *das*

dummy ['dʌmɪ] **1.** *n.* **a)** *(of tailor)* Schneiderpuppe, *die; (in shop)* Modepuppe, *die;* Schaufensterpuppe, *die; (of ventriloquist)* Puppe, *die; (figurehead, person acting for another)* Strohmann, *der; (stupid person)* Dummkopf, *der (ugs.);* Doofi, *der (ugs.);* **like a stuffed ~:** wie ein Olgötze *(ugs.);* **b)** *(imitation)* Attrappe, *die;* Dummy, *der; (Commerc.)* Schaupackung, *die;* **c)** *(esp. Brit.: for baby)* Schnuller, *der;* **d)** *(Bridge etc.) (person)* Strohmann, *der; (hand)* Tisch, *der;* **e)** *(Rugby coll.)* **sell sb. the** *or* **a ~:** jmdn. antäuschen. **2.** *attrib. adj.* unecht; blind ⟨*Tür, Fenster*⟩; Übungs- *(Mil.);* **~ gun** Gewehrattrappe, *die;* **~ run** Probelauf, *der*

dump [dʌmp] **1.** *n.* **a)** *(place)* Müllkippe, *die; (heap)* Müllhaufen, *der; (permanent)* Müllhalde, *die;* **b)** *(Mil.)* Depot, *das;* Lager, *das;* **c)** *(coll. derog.: unpleasant place)* Schweinestall, *der (derb abwertend);* Dreckloch, *das (salopp abwertend); (boring town)* Kaff, *das (ugs. abwertend);* Nest, *das (ugs. abwertend).* **2.** *v. t.* **a)** *(dispose of)* werfen; *(deposit)* abladen, kippen ⟨*Sand, Müll usw.*⟩; *(leave)* lassen; *(place)* abstellen; **b)** *(Commerc.: send abroad)* zu Dumpingpreisen verkaufen; **c)** *(fig. coll.: abandon)* abladen *(ugs.)*

dumper ['dʌmpə(r)] *n.* Kipper, *der*

dumping ['dʌmpɪŋ] *n.* **a)** [Schutt]abladen, *das;* **'no ~ [of refuse]'** „Schuttabladen verboten"; **b)** *(Commerc.: sending abroad)* Dumping, *das*

'dumping-ground *n.* Müllkippe, *die;* Schuttabladeplatz, *der; (fig.)* Abstellplatz, *der*

dumpling ['dʌmplɪŋ] *n.* **a)** *(Gastr.)* Kloß, *der;* **apple ~:** Apfel im Schlafrock; **b)** *(coll.: short, plump person)* Tönnchen, *das (ugs.)*
dumps [dʌmps] *n. pl. (coll.)* **be** *or* **feel [down] in the ~:** ganz down sein *(ugs.)*
'**dump truck** *n.* Kipper, *der*
dumpy ['dʌmpɪ] *adj.* pummelig *(ugs.)*
[1]**dun** [dʌn] **1.** *adj.* graubraun. **2.** *n.* Graubraun, *das*
[2]**dun** *v. t.,* **-nn-** *(demand money due from)* [Geld] anmahnen bei; **~ sb. for sth.** bei jmdm. etw. anmahnen
dunce [dʌns] *n.* Null, *die (ugs. abwertend);* Niete, *die (ugs. abwertend);* **the ~ of the class** das Schlußlicht der Klasse *(ugs.);* **~'s cap** *(Hist.)* Spotthut, *der (für schlechte Schüler)*
dunderhead ['dʌndəhed] *n.* Schwachkopf, *der (ugs. abwertend)*
dune [dju:n] *n.* Düne, *die*
dung [dʌŋ] **1.** *n.* Dung, *der;* Mist, *der.* **2.** *v. t.* mit Mist düngen
dungaree [dʌŋgə'ri:] *n.* **a)** *(fabric)* grober Kattun; **b)** *in pl. (garment)* Latzhose, *die;* **a pair of ~s** eine Latzhose
'**dung-beetle** *n.* Mistkäfer, *der*
dungeon ['dʌndʒn] *n.* Kerker, *der;* Verlies, *das*
'**dunghill** *n.* Misthaufen, *der*
dunk [dʌŋk] *v. t.* **a)** tunken; stippen *(bes. nordd.);* **b)** *(immerse)* tauchen
Dunkirk [dʌn'kɜ:k] *pr. n.* Dünkirchen *(das);* **~ spirit** Durchhaltevermögen, *das*
dunlin ['dʌnlɪn] *n. (Ornith.)* Alpenstrandläufer, *der*
duo ['dju:əʊ] *n., pl.* **~s a)** *(Theatre)* Paar, *das;* **comedy ~:** Komikerpaar, *das;* **b)** *(Mus.)* Duo, *das;* **c)** *(coll.: couple)* Duo, *das (oft iron.);* **an odd ~:** ein komisches Gespann *(ugs.)*
duodenal [dju:ə'di:nl] *adj. (Anat.)* duodenal *(fachspr.);* Zwölffingerdarm-
duodenal '**ulcer** *n. (Med.)* Zwölffingerdarmgeschwür, *das*
duodenum [dju:ə'di:nəm] *n. (Anat.)* Duodenum, *das (fachspr.);* Zwölffingerdarm, *der*
dupe [dju:p] **1.** *v. t.* düpieren *(geh.);* übertölpeln; **be ~d [into doing sth.]** sich übertölpeln lassen [und etw. tun]; **be ~d into believing sth.** auf etw. *(Akk.)* hereinfallen. **2.** *n.* Düpierte, *der/die (geh.);* Dumme, *der/die;* Gelackmeierte, *der/die (salopp scherzh.)*
duple ['dju:pl] *adj.* **~ time** *(Mus.)* gerader Takt
duplex ['dju:pleks] **1.** *adj.* **a)** *(twofold)* doppelt; zweifach; **b)** *(esp. Amer.: two-storey)* zweistöckig ‹*Wohnung*›; **c)** *(esp. Amer.: two-family)* Zweifamilien‹*haus*›. **2.** *n. (esp. Amer.)* zweistöckige Wohnung
duplicate 1. ['dju:plɪkət] *adj.* **a)** *(identical)* Zweit-; **~ key** Nach- *od.* Zweitschlüssel, *der;* **~ copy** Zweit- *od.* Abschrift, *die;* Doppel, *das;* **b)** *(twofold)* doppelt; **c)** *(Cards)* **~ bridge/whist** *Form des Bridge/Whists, bei der das Spiel mit derselben Verteilung der Karten, aber mit anderen Spielern wiederholt wird.* **2.** *n.* **a)** Kopie, *die; (second copy of letter/document/key)* Duplikat, *das;* **b) prepare/complete sth. in ~:** etw. in doppelter Ausfertigung machen/ausfüllen; **make sth. in ~:** etw. doppelt anfertigen; **c)** *(Cards)* = **~ bridge** *etc.; see* **1c. 3.** ['dju:plɪkeɪt] *v. t.* **a)** *(make a copy of, make in duplicate)* **~ sth.** eine zweite Anfertigung von etw. machen; etw. nachmachen *(ugs.);* **they have tried to ~ his results** sie haben versucht, zu denselben Ergebnissen wie er zu kommen; **b)** *(be exact copy of)* genau gleichen (+ *Dat.*); **c)** *(on machine)* vervielfältigen; **d)** *(unnecessarily)* [unnötigerweise] noch einmal tun
duplicating ['dju:plɪkeɪtɪŋ]: **~ machine** *see* **duplicator; ~ paper** *n. (Printing)* Vervielfältigungspapier, *das*
duplication [dju:plɪ'keɪʃn] *n.* **a)** Wiederholung, *die;* **b)** *(on machine)* Vervielfältigung, *die;* **c)** *(unnecessary)* [unnötige] Wiederholung; **avoid unnecessary ~!** vermeiden Sie unnötige Wiederholungen!; **~ of effort** doppelte Arbeit
duplicator ['dju:plɪkeɪtə(r)] *n. (Printing)* Vervielfältigungsgerät, *das*
duplicity [dju:'plɪsɪtɪ] *n.* Falschheit, *die*
durability [djʊərə'bɪlɪtɪ] *n., no pl.* **a)** *(permanence) (of friendship, peace, etc.)* Dauerhaftigkeit, *die; (of person)* Unverwüstlichkeit, *die;* **b)** *(resistance to wear or decay) (of garment, material)* Haltbarkeit, die; Strapazierfähigkeit, *die; (of metal, rock, component)* Widerstandsfähigkeit, *die*
durable ['djʊərəbl] **1.** *adj.* **a)** *(lasting)* dauerhaft ‹*Friede, Freundschaft usw.*›; **b)** *(resisting wear or decay)* solide; strapazierfähig, haltbar ‹*Kleidung, Stoff*›; widerstandsfähig ‹*Metall, Fels, Bauelement*›; **~ goods** *see* **2. 2.** *n. in pl. (Econ.)* **consumer ~s** langlebige *od.* dauerhafte Konsumgüter
duration [djʊə'reɪʃn] *n.* Dauer, *die;* **be of short/long ~:** von kurzer/langer Dauer sein; **the courses are of three years' ~:** die Kurse dauern drei Jahre; **for the ~ of sth.** für die Dauer *od.* während [der Dauer] einer Sache *(Gen.);* **for the ~** *(of war)* auf Kriegsdauer; **I'm afraid we're here for the ~** *(fig. coll.)* wir werden wohl bis zum Ende ausharren müssen, fürchte ich
duress [djʊə'res, 'djʊəres] *n., no pl.* Zwang, *der;* **under ~:** unter Zwang
during ['djʊərɪŋ] *prep.* während; *(at a point in)* in (+ *Dat.*); **~ the rehearsal/wedding ceremony** während *od.* bei der Probe/Trauung; **~ the night** während *od.* in der Nacht; **~ the journey** während *od.* auf der Reise
dusk [dʌsk] *n. (twilight)* [Abend]dämmerung, *die;* Einbruch der Dunkelheit; **at/after/until ~:** bei/nach/bis zum Einbruch der Dunkelheit
dusky ['dʌskɪ] *adj. (dark-coloured)* dunkel; dunkelhäutig ‹*Person, Schönheit*›; **a ~ blue/red** ein dunkles Blau/Rot
dust [dʌst] **1.** *n., no pl.* **a)** Staub, *der; (pollen)* Blütenstaub, *der;* **be covered in ~:** ‹*Erde:*› staubbedeckt sein; ‹*Gegenstände:*› eingestaubt *od.* verstaubt sein; **the ~ of ages** der Staub der Jahrhunderte; **make a great deal of ~:** sehr stauben; **throw ~ in sb.'s eyes** *(fig.)* jmdm. Sand in die Augen streuen; **shake the ~ off one's feet** *(fig.)* den Staub von den Füßen schütteln *(geh.);* **turn to ~ and ashes** Staub werden; *(fig.)* zunichte werden; **wait till the ~ has settled** *(fig.)* warten, bis sich die Wogen geglättet haben; **you couldn't see him for ~** *(fig.)* man konnte nur noch seine Staubwolke sehen; **b)** *(coll.:* **~ing)** Staubwischen, *das;* **give sth. a ~:**den Staub von etw. abwischen; etw. abstauben. *See also* **bite 1; raise 1b. 2.** *v. t.* **a)** *(clear of ~)* abstauben ‹*Möbel*›; **~ a room/house** in einem Zimmer/Haus Staub wischen; **the house/the furniture needs ~ing** *or* **to be ~ed** in dem Haus muß Staub gewischt werden/die Möbel müssen abgestaubt werden; **b)** *(sprinkle; also Cookery)* **~ sth. with sth.** etw. mit etw. bestäuben; *(with talc etc.)* etw. mit etw. pudern; *(with grated material)* etw. mit etw. bestreuen; **~ sth. over** *or* **on [to] sth.** *(using powder)* etw. auf etw. *(Akk.)* stäuben; *(using grated material)* etw. auf etw. *(Akk.)* streuen. **3.** *v. i.* Staub wischen
~ '**off** *v. t.* abstauben; *(fig. derog.)* aus der Mottenkiste hervorholen
dust: ~bin *n. (Brit.)* Mülltonne, *die;* Abfalltonne, *die;* **relegate sth. to the ~bin** *(fig.)* etw. in *od.* auf den Müll wandern lassen *(ugs.);* **~ bowl** *n. (Geog.)* Trockengebiet, *das (mit häufigen Staubstürmen);* **~-cart** *n. (Brit.)* Müllwagen, *der;* **~-cloth** *n.* Schonbezug, *der; (duster)* Staubtuch, *das;* **~-coat** *n. (Brit.)* Staubmantel, *der;* **~-cover** *n. (on record-player)* Abdeckhaube, *die; (for clothes)* Staubschutz, *der; (on book) see* **~-jacket; ~ devil** *see* **devil 1i**
duster ['dʌstə(r)] *n.* **a)** *(cloth)* Staubtuch, *das;* **b)** *(coat)* Staubmantel, *der*
dusting ['dʌstɪŋ] *n.* **a)** *(removal of dust) see* **dust 2a:** Abstauben, *das;* Staubwischen, *das;* **give a room a ~:** in einem Zimmer Staub wischen; **b)** *(sprinkling)* Bestreuen, *das; see also* **crop-dusting**
dust: ~-jacket *n.* Schutzumschlag, *der;* **~man** ['dʌstmən] *n., pl.* **~men** ['dʌstmən] *(Brit.)* Müllwerker, *der (Berufsbez.);* Müllmann, *der;* **~pan** *n.* Kehrschaufel, *die;* **~-proof** *adj.* staubdicht; **~-sheet** *n.* Staubdecke, *die;* **~ storm** *n.* Staubsturm, *der;* **~-trap** *n.* Staubfänger, *der (abwertend);* **~-up** *n. (coll.)* Krach, *der (ugs.);* **~-wrapper** *see* **~-jacket**
dusty ['dʌstɪ] *adj.* **a)** staubig ‹*Straße, Stadt, Zimmer*›; verstaubt ‹*Bücher, Möbel*›; **the house is/has got very ~:** das Haus ist sehr verstaubt; im Haus hat sich viel Staub angesammelt; **b)** *(dull)* schmutzig ‹*Rosa, Blau, Grün*›; **c)** *(vague)* vage; **d)** *(bad-tempered)* schroff ‹*Antwort*›; **e) not so ~** *(Brit. dated sl.)* gar nicht so übel *(ugs.)*
Dutch [dʌtʃ] **1.** *adj.* **a)** holländisch; niederländisch; **b)** *(coll.)* **go ~ [with sb.] [on sth.]** getrennte Kasse [mit jmdm.] [bei etw.] machen; **talk to sb. like a ~ uncle** jmdm. ernstlich ins Gewissen reden. *See also* **English 1. 2.** *n.* **a)** *constr. as pl.* **the ~:** die Holländer *od.* Niederländer; **b)** *(language)* Holländisch, *das;* Niederländisch, *das;* **[Cape] ~:** Kapholländisch, *das;* **c) it was all double ~ to him** das waren alles böhmische Dörfer für ihn. *See also* **English 2a**
dutch *n. (Brit. sl.)* **my old ~:** meine gute Alte
Dutch: ~ 'auction *see* **auction 1a; ~ 'barn** *n.* offene Scheune; **~ 'courage** *n.* angetrunkener Mut; **give oneself** *or* **get ~ courage** sich *(Dat.)* Mut antrinken; **~ 'doll** *n.* holländische Gliederpuppe; **~ 'door** *n. (Amer.)* quergeteilte Tür; **~ 'elm disease** *n. (Bot.)* Ulmensterben, *das;* **~ 'hoe** *n. (Agric.)* Schuffel, *die;* **~man** ['dʌtʃmən] *n., pl.* **~men** ['dʌtʃmən] **a)** Holländer, *der;* Niederländer, *der;* **b)** *(fig. coll.)* **or I'm a ~man** oder ich will Emil heißen; **c)** *(ship)* holländisches Schiff; **The Flying ~man** Der Fliegende Holländer; **~ 'oven** *n. (Cookery)* **a)** *(box) Backgefäß mit mehreren Fächern;* **b)** *(pot)* Schmortopf, *der;* **~ 'treat** *n. gemeinsames Vergnügen, bei dem jeder für sich selbst bezahlt;* **~woman** *n.* Holländerin, *die;* Niederländerin, *die*
dutiable ['dju:tɪəbl] *adj. (Customs)* zollpflichtig; abgabenpflichtig
dutiful ['dju:tɪfl] *adj.* pflichtbewußt ‹*Ehefrau, Arbeiter, Bürger*›; gehorsam ‹*Tochter, Sklave*›; ehrerbietig ‹*Antwort*›
dutifully ['dju:tɪfəlɪ] *adv.* pflichtbewußt ‹*handeln*›; treu ‹*dienen*›
duty ['dju:tɪ] *n.* **a)** *no pl. (moral or legal obligation)* Pflicht, *die;* Verpflichtung, *die;* **~ calls** die Pflicht ruft; **have a ~ to do sth.** die Pflicht haben, etw. zu tun; **have a ~ to sb.** jmdm. gegenüber eine Verpflichtung haben; **one's ~ to** *or* **towards sb./sth.** seine Pflicht gegenüber jmdm./einer Sache; **do one's ~ [by sb.]** [jmdm. gegenüber] seine Pflicht [und Schuldigkeit] tun; **make it one's ~ to do sth.** es sich *(Dat.)* zur Pflicht machen, etw. zu tun; **be/feel in ~ bound to do sth.** verpflichtet sein/sich verpflichtet fühlen, etw. zu tun; **in ~ bound** pflichtschuldigst; **b)** *(specific task, esp. professional)* Aufgabe, *die;* Pflicht, *die;* **do one's ~:** seine Pflicht tun; **take up one's duties** seinen Dienst antreten; **your duties will consist of ...:** zu Ihren Aufgaben gehören ...; **[purely] in [the] line of ~:** [rein] dienstlich; **the ~-nurse/~-porter** die diensthabende Schwester/der diensthabende Pförtner; **on**

~: im Dienst; **be on ~:** Dienst haben; **while on ~:** während des Dienstes; im Dienst; **go/come on ~ at seven p.m.** um 19 Uhr seinen Dienst antreten; **off ~:** nicht im Dienst; **be off ~:** keinen Dienst haben; ‹*ab ... Uhr*› dienstfrei sein; **go/come off ~ at eight a.m.** seinen Dienst um acht Uhr beenden; **Dr Smith is off ~ tomorrow** Dr. Smith hat morgen dienstfrei; *see also* **off-duty; c)** *(Econ.: tax)* Zoll, *der;* **pay ~ on sth.** Zoll für etw. bezahlen; etw. verzollen; **be liable to ~:** zollpflichtig sein; **~ on alcohol** Branntweinsteuer, *die;* **free of ~:** zollfrei ‹*Ware, Preis*›; **d) do ~ as/for sth.** *(serve as)* als/zu etw. dienen; **e)** *(arch.: respect, respectful conduct)* Ehrerbietung, *die (geh.)*

duty: ~-bound *adj.* **be/feel [oneself] ~-bound to do sth.** verpflichtet sein/sich verpflichtet fühlen, etw. zu tun; *see also* **duty a; ~-free** *adj.* zollfrei ‹*Ware, Preis*›; **~-frees** *n. pl. (coll.)* zollfreie Waren; **~-free 'shop** *n.* Duty-free-Shop, *der;* **~ officer** *n. (Mil.)* Offizier vom Dienst; **~-paid** *adj. (Econ.)* verzollt ‹*Ware*›; **~ visit** *n.* Pflichtbesuch, *der*

duvet ['du:veɪ] *n.* Federbett, *das*

dwarf [dwɔ:f] **1.** *n., pl.* **~s** *or* **dwarves** [dwɔ:vz] **a)** *(person)* Liliputaner, *der*/Liliputanerin, *die;* Zwerg, *der*/Zwergin, *die (auch abwertend);* **b)** *(tree)* Zwergbaum, *der; (plant)* Zwergpflanze, *die; (animal)* Zwergtier, *das;* **c)** *(Mythol.)* Zwerg, *der*/Zwergin, *die;* **d)** *(Astron.)* Zwerg[stern], *der.* **2.** *adj.* **a)** Zwerg‹*baum, -stern*›; **b)** *(stunted)* winzig. **3.** *v. t.* **a)** *(stunt in growth)* verkümmern lassen; **b)** *(cause to look small)* klein erscheinen lassen; verzwergen *(geh.);* **c)** *(fig.)* in den Schatten stellen; verzwergen *(geh.)*

dwarfish ['dwɔ:fɪʃ] *adj.* zwergenhaft ‹*Gestalt*›; sehr klein ‹*Tier, Pflanze*›

dwell [dwel] *v. i.,* **dwelt** [dwelt] *(literary; lit. or fig.)* wohnen; weilen *(geh.)*

~ [up]on *v. t.* **a)** *(in discussion)* sich länger *od.* ausführlich befassen mit; *(in thought)* in Gedanken verweilen bei; **don't ~ upon the past** halten Sie sich nicht bei *od.* mit der Vergangenheit auf; **b)** *(prolong)* gedehnt aussprechen ‹*Wort, Silbe*›; *(Mus.)* [aus]halten ‹*Note*›

dweller ['dwelə(r)] *n., esp. in comb.* Bewohner, *der*/Bewohnerin, *die;* **city-~s** Großstädter *Pl.;* **caravan-~s** [ständige] Caravaner *Pl.*

dwelling ['dwelɪŋ] *n. (Admin. lang./literary)* Wohnung, *die;* **council ~:** Sozialwohnung, *die*

dwelling: ~-house *n.* Wohnhaus, *das;* **~-place** *n.* Wohnsitz, *der*

dwelt *see* **dwell**

dwindle ['dwɪndl] *v.i.* **a) ~ [away]** abnehmen; ‹*Unterstützung, Interesse:*› nachlassen; ‹*Güter, Vermögen:*› zusammenschrumpfen; ‹*Vorräte, Handel, Hoheitsgebiet:*› schrumpfen; ‹*Macht, Einfluß, Tageslicht:*› schwinden *(geh.);* ‹*Gewinn, Umsatz:*› rückläufig sein; ‹*Bodenschätze:*› zur Neige gehen *(geh.);* ‹*Ruhm:*› verblassen *(geh.);* **~ in importance** an Bedeutung abnehmen *od.* verlieren; **~ away to nothing** dahinschwinden; **b)** *(fig.: degenerate)* herunterkommen **(into** zu)

dye [daɪ] **1.** *n.* **a)** *(substance)* Färbemittel, *das;* **eyelash ~:** Wimperntusche, *die;* **b)** *(colour)* Farbe, *die.* **2.** *v. t.,* **~ing** ['daɪɪŋ] färben; **~d blond hair** blondgefärbtes Haar; **~d-in-the-wool** *(fig.)* eingefleischt, *(ugs.)* in der Wolle gefärbt ‹*Konservativer, Gewerkschaftler, Reaktionär*›. **3.** *v. i.,* **~ing** sich färben lassen

dyer ['daɪə(r)] *n.* Färber, *der*/Färberin, *die*

'dyestuff *see* **dye 1 a**

dying ['daɪɪŋ] **1.** *adj.* **a)** sterbend ‹*Person, Tier*›; eingehend ‹*Pflanze*›; absterbend ‹*Baum*›; verendend ‹*Tier*›; aussterbend ‹*Kunst, Kultur, Tradition, [Tier]art, Menschenschlag*›; zuendegehend ‹*Jahr*›; erlöschend ‹*Glut, Leidenschaft*›; **he's a ~ man** *(will not recover)* er lebt nicht mehr lange; **b)** *(related to time of death)* letzt...; **to my ~ day** bis an mein Lebensende. **2.** *n. pl.* **the ~:** die Sterbenden. *See also* **[1]die**

dyke *see* **dike**

dynamic [daɪ'næmɪk] *adj.,* **dynamically** [daɪ'næmɪkəlɪ] *adv. (lit. or fig.; also Mus.)* dynamisch

dynamics [daɪ'næmɪks] *n., no pl.* **a)** *(Mech.)* Dynamik, *die (fachspr.);* Kräftelehre, *die;* **b)** *(in other sciences)* -dynamik, *die*

dynamism ['daɪnəmɪzm] *n.* Dynamik, *die*

dynamite ['daɪnəmaɪt] **1.** *n.* **a)** *(explosive)* Dynamit, *das;* **b)** *(fig.: politically dangerous person or thing)* Sprengstoff, *der;* **these revelations are ~:** diese Enthüllungen sind [politisch] brisant; **c)** *(fig.: sensational person or thing)* **be ~** ‹*Person:*› eine Wucht sein *(salopp);* ‹*Sache:*› eine Sensation sein. **2.** *v. t.* mit Dynamit sprengen

dynamo ['daɪnəməʊ] *n., pl.* **~s a)** Dynamomaschine, *die; (of car)* Lichtmaschine, *die; (of bicycle)* Dynamo, *der;* **b)** *(fig.)* **[human] ~:** Energiebündel, *das (ugs.)*

dynastic [dɪ'næstɪk] *adj.* dynastisch; ‹*Regierung, Herrschaft, Diktatur*› einer Dynastie; **~ families** Familiendynastien *Pl.*

dynasty ['dɪnəstɪ] *n. (lit. or fig.)* Dynastie, *die*

dyne [daɪn] *n. (Phys.)* Dyn, *das*

dysentery ['dɪsəntərɪ] *n. (Med.)* Ruhr, *die;* Dysenterie, *die (fachspr.)*

dyslexia [dɪs'leksɪə] *n. (Med., Psych.)* Dyslexie, *die (fachspr.);* Lesestörung, *die*

dyslexic [dɪs'leksɪk] *(Med., Psych.)* **1.** *adj.* dyslektisch *(fachspr.);* **a ~ child** ein Kind mit einer Lesestörung. **2.** *n.* Dyslektiker, *der*/Dyslektikerin, *die (fachspr.);* Mensch mit einer Lesestörung

dyspepsia [dɪs'pepsɪə] *n. (Med.)* Dyspepsie, *die (fachspr.);* Verdauungsstörung, *die*

dystrophy ['dɪstrəfɪ] *n. (Med.)* Dystrophie, *die (fachspr.);* Ernährungsstörung, *die;* **muscular ~:** Muskeldystrophie, *die; (fortschreitender)* Muskelschwund

E

E, e [i:] *n., pl.* **Es** *or* **E's a)** *(letter)* E, e, *das;* **b) E** *(Mus.)* E, e, *das;* **E flat** es, Es, *das;* **c) E** *(Sch., Univ.: mark)* Fünf, *die;* **he got an E** er bekam „mangelhaft" *od.* eine Fünf

E. *abbr.* **a)** east O; **b)** eastern ö.

each [i:tʃ] **1.** *adj.* jeder/jede/jedes; **there's cream between ~ layer** zwischen den einzelnen Schichten ist Sahne; **we have two votes ~, we ~ have two votes** jeder von uns hat zwei Stimmen; **they cost** *or* **are a pound ~:** sie kosten ein Pfund pro Stück *od.* je[weils] ein Pfund; **they ~ have ...:** sie haben jeder ...; jeder von ihnen hat ...; **books at £1 ~:** Bücher zu je einem Pfund *od.* für je ein Pfund; **two teams with 10 players ~:** zwei Mannschaften mit je 10 Spielern; **I gave them a book ~** *or* **~ a book** ich habe jedem von ihnen ein Buch *od.* ihnen je ein Buch gegeben; **~ one of them** jeder/jede/jedes einzelne von ihnen; **~ and every employee** jeder einzelne Mitarbeiter; **I travelled 10 miles ~ way every day** ich habe jeden Tag 16 km pro Weg zurückgelegt; **back a horse ~ way** *(Brit. Racing)* auf Sieg oder Platz eines Pferdes wetten; **the houses ~ have their own garage[s]** die Häuser haben alle ihre eigene Garage. **2.** *pron.* **a)** jeder/jede/jedes; **they are ~ of them ...** jeder *usw.* von ihnen ist ...; **~ despises the other** jeder verachtet den anderen; sie verachten sich [gegenseitig]; **have some of ~:** von jedem etwas nehmen/haben *usw.;* **b) ~ other** sich [gegenseitig]; einander *(meist geh.);* **they are cross with ~ other** sie sind böse aufeinander; **we have not seen ~ other in years** wir haben uns jahrelang nicht gesehen; **they wore ~ other's hats** jeder trug den Hut des anderen; **be in love with ~ other** ineinander verliebt sein; **live next door to ~ other** Tür an Tür wohnen

eager ['i:gə(r)] *adj.* eifrig ‹*Person, Arbeiter, Art*›; rege, lebhaft ‹*Interesse*›; brennend, sehnlich ‹*Wunsch*›; erwartungsvoll ‹*Ton, Gesichtsausdruck, Lächeln*›; begeistert ‹*Anhänger einer Partei*›; **be ~ to do sth.** etw. unbedingt tun wollen; **be ~ to make a good impression** eifrig bemüht sein, einen guten Eindruck zu machen; **be ~ to learn** lernbegierig *od.* -eifrig sein; **be ~ for sth.** etw. unbedingt haben wollen; *see also* **beaver 1 a**

eagerly ['i:gəlɪ] *adv.* eifrig ‹*ja sagen, zustimmen*›; bereitwillig ‹*Auskunft geben*›; gespannt, ungeduldig ‹*warten, Ausschau halten, aufblicken*›; erwartungsvoll ‹*lächeln*›; begierig ‹*ergreifen*›; **look forward ~ to sth.** sich sehr auf etw. *(Akk.)* freuen; **~ seize an opportunity** eine Gelegenheit beim Schopf ergreifen

eagerness ['i:gənɪs] *n., no pl.* Eifer, *der;* **~ to learn** Lerneifer, *der;* Lernbegier[de], *die;* **~ to succeed** Erfolgshunger, *der;* **~ to assist** Hilfsbereitschaft, *die*

eagle ['i:gl] *n.* **a)** Adler, *der;* **b)** *(Golf)* Eagle, *das*

eagle: ~ 'eye *n.* Falkenauge, *das (geh.);* **have/keep/fix one's ~ eye on sb./sth.** ein wachsames Auge *od.* einen wachsamen Blick auf jmdn./etw. haben; **~-eyed** *adj.* adleräugig

eaglet ['i:glɪt] *n. (Ornith.)* Adlerjunge, *das*

[1]ear [ɪə(r)] *n.* **a)** Ohr, *das; (of red deer)* Lauscher, *der; (of red fox)* Gehör, *das; (of rabbit, hare)* Löffel, *der; (of hound)* Behang, *der (Jägerspr.);* **his good/bad ~:** sein besseres/schlechteres Ohr; **~, nose, and throat hospital/specialist** Hals-Nasen-Ohren-Klinik, *die*/-Arzt, *der*/-Ärztin, *die;* **smile from ~ to ~:** von einem Ohr zum anderen strahlen *(ugs.);* **have nothing between one's ~s** *(fig. coll.)* nichts im Kopf haben *(ugs.);* **be out on one's ~** *(fig. coll.)* auf der Straße stehen *(ugs.);* **this brought a storm of criticism about his ~s** das setzte ihn einem Sturm der Kritik aus; **sb. would give his/her ~s to do sth.** jmd. würde alles darum geben, etw. zu tun; **over head and ~s, head over ~s** *(fig. coll.)* bis über die *od.* beide Ohren; **up to one's ~s in work/debt** bis zum Hals in Arbeit/Schulden; **be pleasing to the ~[s]** sich angenehm anhören; **come to** *or* **reach sb.'s ~s** jmdm. zu Ohren kommen; **have a word in sb.'s ~:** jmdm. ein Wort im Vertrauen sagen; **listen with half an ~:** [nur] mit halbem Ohr zuhören; **keep one's ~s open** *(fig.)* die Ohren offenhalten; **have/keep an ~ to the ground** sein Ohr ständig am Puls der Masse haben *(ugs. scherzh.);* **be[come] all ~s** [plötzlich] ganz Ohr sein; **go in [at] one ~ and out [at] the other** *(coll.)* zum einen Ohr herein, zum anderen wieder hinausgehen; **lend an ~ to sb.** jmdm. Gehör schenken; **give ~ to** ein geneigtes Ohr haben für *(geh.);* **have**

sb.'s ~/get *or* **win the ~ of sb.** bei jmdm. Gehör *od.* ein offenes Ohr finden; **b)** *no pl.* *(faculty of discriminating sound)* Gehör, *das;* **have an ~** *or* **a good ~/no ~ for music** ein [gutes]/kein Gehör für Musik haben; **play by ~** *(Mus.)* nach dem Gehör spielen; **play it by ~** *(fig.)* es auf sich *(Akk.)* zukommen lassen *(und dementsprechend reagieren)*

[2]**ear** *n. (Bot.)* Ähre, *die;* **~ of corn** Kornähre, *die*

ear: ~ache *n. (Med.)* Ohrenschmerzen *Pl.;* **~-clip** *n.* Ohr[en]klipp, *der;* **~-drops** *n. pl.* **a)** *(Med.)* Ohrentropfen *Pl.;* **b)** *(earrings)* Ohrgehänge, *das;* **~-drum** *n. (Anat.)* Trommelfell, *das*

-eared [ɪəd] *adj. in comb.* **long-/short-~** lang-/kurzohrig

'**ear-flap** *n.* Ohrenklappe, *die*

earful ['ɪəfʊl] *n. (coll.)* **get an ~:** ordentlich was zu hören bekommen *(ugs.);* **give sb. an ~ about sth.** jmdm. ein paar Takte [über etw.] erzählen *(ugs.)*

earl [ɜ:l] *n.* Graf, *der*

earldom ['ɜ:ldəm] *n.* **a)** *(territory)* Grafschaft, *die;* **b)** *(rank)* Grafenwürde, *die*

'**ear-lobe** *n.* Ohrläppchen, *das*

early ['ɜ:lɪ] **1.** *adj.* **a)** früh; **they had an ~ lunch** sie aßen früh zu Mittag; **I am a bit ~:** ich bin etwas zu früh gekommen *od. (ugs.)* dran; **the train was 10 minutes ~:** der Zug kam 10 Minuten zu früh; **an ~ train** *(earlier than one usually takes)* ein früherer Zug; **have an ~ night** früh ins Bett gehen; **~ riser** Frühaufsteher, *der*/-aufsteherin, *die;* **~ to bed, ~ to rise [makes a man healthy, wealthy, and wise]** *(prov.)* früh zu Bette und auf zu früher Stund', macht den Menschen glücklich, reich, gesund *(Spr.);* **an ~ reply** eine baldige Antwort; **at the earliest** frühestens; **the ~ part of** der Anfang (+ *Gen.*); **in the ~ afternoon/evening** am frühen Nachmittag/Abend; **into the ~ hours** bis in die frühen Morgenstunden; **at/from an ~ age** in jungen Jahren/von klein auf; **from one's earliest years** von frühester Kindheit an; **at an ~ stage, in its ~ stages** im Frühstadium; **~ Gothic** Frühgotik, *die;* **an ~ work/the ~ writings of an author** ein Frühwerk/die Frühschriften eines Autors; **~ Christian times** die frühchristliche Zeit; **b)** *(of the distant past)* vorgeschichtlich ⟨*Fund, Fossilien*⟩; *(prehistoric)* frühgeschichtlich ⟨*Fund, Fossilien*⟩; **the earliest records of a civilization** die frühesten Spuren einer Zivilisation; **at a very ~ date** schon sehr früh; **c)** *(forward in flowering, ripening, etc.)* frühblühend ⟨*Pflanze*⟩; Früh⟨*gemüse, -obst*⟩. **2.** *adv.* früh; **~ next week** Anfang der nächsten Woche; **~ next Wednesday** nächsten Mittwoch früh; **~ in June** Anfang Juni; **the earliest I can come is Friday** ich kann frühestens Freitag kommen; **I cannot come earlier than Thursday** ich kann nicht vor Donnerstag kommen; **from ~ in the morning till late at night** von früh [morgens] bis spät [nachts]; **~ on** schon früh; **earlier on this week/year** früher in der Woche/im Jahr

early: ~ bird *n. (joc.) jmd., der etw. frühzeitig tut; (getting up)* Frühaufsteher, *der*/-aufsteherin, *die;* **the ~ bird catches the worm** *(prov.)* Morgenstunde hat Gold im Munde *(Spr.);* **~ 'closing** *n.* **it is ~ closing** die Geschäfte haben nachmittags geschlossen; **~-'closing day** *n. Tag, an dem die Geschäfte nachmittags geschlossen haben;* **~ 'days** *n. pl.* **in the ~ days** am Anfang (of *Gen.*); **it is ~ days [yet]** es ist noch zu früh; **~-'warning** *attrib. adj.* Frühwarn-

ear: ~mark 1. *n.* Ohrmarke, *die; (fig.)* Kennzeichen, *das;* **2.** *v. t.* **a)** *(mark, lit. or fig.)* [kenn]zeichnen; **b)** *(assign to definite purpose)* bestimmen; vorsehen; **~-muffs** *n. pl.* Ohrenschützer *Pl.*

earn [ɜ:n] *v. t.* **a)** ⟨*Person, Tat, Benehmen:*⟩ verdienen; **~ed income** Einkommen aus Arbeit; **it ~ed him much respect** es trug ihm viel Respekt ein; **b)** *(bring in as income or interest)* einbringen; **c)** *(incur)* eintragen; einbringen; **he ~ed nothing but ingratitude** er erntete nur Undank

earner ['ɜ:nə(r)] *n.* **be a nice little ~** *(coll.)* ganz schön was einbringen *(ugs.)*

[1]**earnest** ['ɜ:nɪst] **1.** *adj.* **a)** *(serious, zealous)* ernsthaft; **be ~ in one's endeavour to do sth.** sich ernsthaft bemühen, etw. zu tun; **b)** *(ardent)* innig ⟨*Wunsch, Gebet, Hoffnung*⟩; leidenschaftlich ⟨*Appell*⟩. **2.** *n.* **in ~:** mit vollem Ernst; **this time I'm in ~ [about it]** diesmal ist es mir Ernst *od.* meine ich es ernst [damit]; **it's raining in ~ now** jetzt regnet es richtig

[2]**earnest** *n.* **a)** *(money)* Handgeld, *das;* **b)** *(foretaste)* Vorgeschmack, *der* (**of** von)

earnestly ['ɜ:nɪstlɪ] *adv.* ernsthaft

earning ['ɜ:nɪŋ] *n.* **a)** Erreichen, *das; (of money)* Verdienen, *das;* **b)** *in pl. (money earned)* Verdienst, *der; (of business etc.)* Ertrag, *der*

ear: ~phone *n.* Kopfhörer, *der;* **~-piece** *n.* Hörmuschel, *die;* **~-piercing 1.** *adj.* durch Mark und Bein gehend ⟨*Lärm*⟩; **2.** *n.* Durchstechen der Ohrläppchen; **~-plug** *n.* Ohropax, *das* Ⓦⓩ; **~-ring** *n.* Ohrring, *der;* **~shot** *n.* **out of/within ~shot** außer/in Hörweite; **~-splitting** *adj.* ohrenbetäubend

earth [ɜ:θ] **1.** *n.* **a)** *(land, soil)* Erde, *die; (ground)* Boden, *der;* **be brought/come down** *or* **back to ~ [with a bump]** *(fig.)* [schnell] wieder auf den Boden der Tatsachen zurückgeholt werden/zurückkommen; **b)** *or* **E~** *(planet)* Erde, *die;* **c)** *(abode of man)* Erde, *die;* **on ~** *(existing anywhere)* auf der Welt; auf Erden *(geh.);* **nothing on ~ will stop me** keine Macht der Welt kann mich aufhalten; **how/what** *etc.* **on ~ ...?** wie/was *usw.* in aller Welt ...?; **who on ~ is that?** wer ist das bloß?; **what on ~ do you mean?** was meinst du denn nur?; **where on ~ has she got to?** wo ist sie denn bloß hingegangen?; **look like nothing on ~:** *(be unrecognizable)* nicht zu erkennen sein; *(look repellent)* furchtbar aussehen; **be like nothing on ~:** unvergleichlich sein; **feel like nothing on ~:** sich ganz mies fühlen *(ugs.);* **on ~** *(Relig.)* auf Erden; **d)** *(land and sea together)* Erde, *die;* Welt, *die;* **e)** *(of animal)* Bau, *der;* **run to ~:** in seinen Unterschlupf hetzen ⟨*Tier*⟩; **have gone to ~** *(fig.)* untergetaucht sein; **f)** *(coll.)* **charge/cost/pay the ~:** ein Vermögen *od. (ugs.)* eine ganze Stange Geld verlangen/kosten/bezahlen; **it won't cost the ~:** das kostet nicht die Welt *(ugs.);* **promise sb. the ~:** jmdm. das Blaue vom Himmel versprechen *(ugs.);* **g)** *(Chem.)* Erde, *die;* **h)** *(Brit. Electr.)* Erde, *die;* Erdung, *die.* **2.** *v. t.* *(Brit. Electr.)* erden

~ '**up** *v.t.* mit Erde bedecken

'**earth-closet** *n. (Brit.)* Humustoilette, *die*

earthen ['ɜ:θn] *adj. (made of clay)* irden; Ton-

earthenware ['ɜ:θnweə(r)] **1.** *n., no pl.* **a)** *(vessels etc.)* Tonwaren *Pl.;* Irdenware, *die (selten);* **b)** *(clay)* Ton, *der.* **2.** *adj.* Ton-; tönern

earthiness ['ɜ:θɪnɪs] *n., no pl.* **a)** Erdigkeit, *die;* **b)** *(of person)* Derbheit, *die*

earthly ['ɜ:θlɪ] *adj.* irdisch; **no ~ use** *etc.* *(coll.)* nicht der geringste Nutzen *usw.;* **this is no ~ use to me** *(coll.)* das nützt mir nicht im geringsten *od.* überhaupt nicht; **not an ~** *(sl.)* nicht die geringste Chance

earth: ~-moving 1. *n.* Erdarbeiten *Pl.;* **2.** *adj.* **~-moving vehicle** Fahrzeug für Erdarbeiten; **~quake** *n.* Erdbeben, *das;* **~ sciences** *n. pl.* Geowissenschaften *Pl.;* **~-shaking, ~-shattering** *adjs. (fig.)* weltbewegend; **not of ~-shattering importance** nicht weltbewegend; **~ tremor** *n.* Erdstoß, *der;* leichtes Erdbeben; **~work** *n.* **a)** *(bank)* Wall, *der;* **b)** *(raising of bank)* Erdarbeiten *Pl.;* **~worm** *n.* Regenwurm, *der*

earthy ['ɜ:θɪ] *adj.* **a)** erdig; **b)** derb ⟨*Person*⟩

ear: ~-trumpet *n.* Hörrohr, *das;* **~-wax** *n.* Ohrenschmalz, *das*

earwig ['ɪəwɪg] *n.* Ohrwurm, *der*

ease [i:z] **1.** *n.* **a)** *(freedom from pain or trouble)* Ruhe, *die;* **set sb. at ~:** jmdn. beruhigen; **b)** *(leisure)* Muße, *die; (idleness)* Müßiggang, *der;* **a life of ~:** ein Leben der Muße; **c)** *(freedom from constraint)* Entspanntheit, *die;* **at [one's] ~:** entspannt; behaglich; **she sat there taking her ~:** sie machte es sich gemütlich *od.* behaglich; **be** *or* **feel at [one's] ~:** sich wohl fühlen; **put** *or* **set sb. at his ~:** jmdm. die Befangenheit nehmen; **he is always at his ~** *(never embarrassed)* er ist immer unbefangen *od.* ungezwungen; **d) with ~** *(without difficulty)* mit Leichtigkeit; **e)** *(relief from pain)* Linderung, *die;* **f)** *(Mil.)* **[stand] at ~!** rührt euch! *See also* **ill 3 c. 2.** *v. t.* **a)** *(relieve)* lindern ⟨*Schmerz, Kummer*⟩; *(make lighter, easier)* erleichtern ⟨*Last, Arbeit*⟩; entspannen ⟨*Lage, Person*⟩; verringern ⟨*Belastung, Druck*⟩; **~ sb. of a burden** jmdm. eine Last abnehmen; **b)** *(give mental ~ to)* erleichtern; **~ sb.'s mind** jmdn. beruhigen; **c)** *(relax, adjust)* lockern ⟨*Griff, Knoten*⟩; verringern ⟨*Druck, Spannung, Geschwindigkeit*⟩; beruhigen ⟨*Verkehr*⟩; **d)** *(joc.: rob)* erleichtern *(ugs. scherzh.);* **~ sb. of sth.** jmdn. um etw. erleichtern; **e)** *(cause to move)* behutsam bewegen; **~ the clutch in** die Kupplung langsam kommen lassen; **~ the cap off a bottle** eine Flasche vorsichtig öffnen. **3.** *v. i.* **a)** ⟨*Belastung, Druck, Wind, Sturm:*⟩ nachlassen; **b) ~ off** *or* **up** *(begin to take it easy)* sich entspannen; **~ off, you're going much too fast** fahre ein bißchen langsamer, du bist viel zu schnell; **c)** ⟨*Aktien usw.:*⟩ nachgeben

easel ['i:zl] *n.* Staffelei, *die*

easily ['i:zɪlɪ] *adv.* **a)** *(without difficulty)* leicht; **more ~ said than done** leichter gesagt als getan; **b)** *(without doubt)* zweifelsohne; **it is ~ a hundred metres deep** es ist gut und gerne 100 m tief; **c)** *(quite possibly)* leicht; **that may ~ be** das kann gut sein

easiness ['i:zɪnɪs] *n.* Leichtigkeit, *die*

east [i:st] **1.** *n.* **a)** Osten, *der;* **the ~** Ost *(Met., Seew.);* **in/to[wards]/from the ~:** im/nach *od. (geh.)* gen/von Osten; **to the ~ of** östlich von; östlich (+ *Gen.*); **~, west, home's best** *(prov.)* ob Osten oder Westen, zu Hause ist's zum besten; **b)** *usu.* **E~** *(part lying to the ~)* Osten, *der; (Geog., Polit.: world lying ~ of Europe)* Osten, *der;* Orient, *der;* Morgenland, *das (dichter.);* **from the E~:** aus dem Osten; **the E~** *(Amer.: NE part of US)* der Osten; *see also* **Far East; Middle East; Near East; c)** *(Cards)* Ost. **2.** *adj.* östlich; Ost⟨*küste, -wind, -grenze, -tor*⟩. **3.** *adv.* ostwärts; nach Osten; **~ of** östlich von; östlich (+ *Gen.*); **~ and west** nach Osten und Westen ⟨*verlaufen, sich erstrecken*⟩; **~ by north/south** *see* [1]**by 1 d**

east: E~ 'Africa *pr. n.* Ostafrika *(das);* **E~ Anglia** [i:st 'æŋglɪə] *pr. n. die beiden englischen Grafschaften Norfolk und Suffolk;* **E~ Ber'lin** *pr. n. (Hist.)* Ost-Berlin *(das);* **~bound** *adj.* ⟨*Zug, Verkehr usw.*⟩ in Richtung Osten; **E~ End** *n. (Brit.)* Londoner Osten; **E~-Ender** [i:st'endə(r)] *n. (Brit.)* Bewohner/Bewohnerin des Londoner Ostens

Easter ['i:stə(r)] *n.* Ostern, *das od. Pl.;* **at ~:** [zu *od.* an] Ostern; **next/last ~:** nächste/letzte Ostern

Easter: ~ 'Day *n.* Ostersonntag, *der;* **~ egg** *n.* Osterei, *das*

easterly ['i:stəlɪ] **1.** *adj.* **a)** *(in position or direction)* östlich; **in an ~ direction** nach Osten; **b)** *(from the east)* ⟨*Wind*⟩ aus östlichen Richtungen; **the wind was ~:** der Wind

kam aus östlichen Richtungen. **2.** *adv.* **a)** *(in position)* östlich; *(in direction)* ostwärts; **b)** *(from the east)* aus *od.* von Ost[en]. **3.** *n.* Ost[wind], *der*
eastern ['i:stən] *adj.* östlich; Ost⟨*grenze, -hälfte, -seite, -fenster, -wind*⟩; ~ **Germany** Ostdeutschland; *see also* **bloc; Far Eastern; Middle Eastern; Near Eastern**
Eastern: ~ **'Europe** *pr. n.* Osteuropa *(das);* ~ **Euro'pean 1.** *adj.* osteuropäisch; **2.** *n.* Osteuropäer, *der*/-europäerin, *die*
easternmost ['i:stənməʊst] *adj.* östlichst...
Easter: ~ **'Sunday** *see* ~ **Day;** ~ **term** *n. (Brit.)* **a)** *(Univ.) see* **Trinity term; b)** *(Law)* Sitzungsperiode von Ostern bis Pfingsten; **~tide** *n. (arch.)* [Tage *Pl.* nach] Ostern; ~ **week** *n.* Osterwoche, *die*
east: E~ 'German *(Hist.)* **1.** *adj.* ostdeutsch; **2.** *n.* Ostdeutsche, *der/die;* **E~ 'Germany** *pr. n. (Hist.)* Ostdeutschland *(das);* **E~ 'Indies** *see* **Indies b; ~-north-'~: 1.** *n.* Ostnordost[en], *der;* **2.** *adj.* ostnordöstlich; **3.** *adv.* nach Ostnordost[en]; **E~ 'Prussia** *pr. n.* Ostpreußen *(das);* **E~ Side** *n. (Amer.) Ostteil von Manhattan;* **~-south-'~: 1.** *n.* Ostsüdost[en], *der;* **2.** *adj.* ostsüdöstlich; **3.** *adv.* nach Ostsüdost[en]
eastward ['i:stwəd] **1.** *adj.* nach Osten gerichtet; *(situated towards the east)* östlich; **in an ~ direction** nach Osten; [in] Richtung Osten. **2.** *adv.* ostwärts; **they are ~ bound** sie fahren nach *od.* [in] Richtung Osten. **3.** *n.* Osten, *der*
eastwards ['i:stwədz] *see* **eastward 2**
easy ['i:zɪ] **1.** *adj.* **a)** *(not difficult)* leicht; ~ **to clean/learn/see** *etc.* leicht zu reinigen/lernen/sehen *usw.;* **it is ~ to see that ...:** es ist offensichtlich, daß ...; man sieht sofort, daß ...; **it's as ~ as falling off a log** *or* **as ~ as pie** *or* **as ~ as anything** *(coll.)* es ist kinderleicht; **be an ~ winner** mit Leichtigkeit siegen; **the ~ fit of a coat** *etc.* der bequeme Sitz eines Mantels *usw.;* **it is ~ for him to talk** er hat leicht *od.* gut reden; **it's ~ for him to complain** er kann sich gut beklagen; **on ~ terms** auf Raten ⟨*kaufen*⟩; **b)** *(free from pain, anxiety, etc.)* sorglos, angenehm ⟨*Leben, Zeit*⟩; **make life ~ for oneself** sich *(Dat.)* das Leben leichtmachen; **make it** *or* **things ~ for sb.** es jmdm. leichtmachen; **[not] ~ in one's mind** be[un]ruhigt; **I do not feel altogether ~ about it/her** ich mache mir deswegen/ihretwegen doch Sorgen; ~ **circumstances** *(coll.)* Wohlstand, *der; see also* **conscience; c)** *(free from constraint, strictness, etc.)* ungezwungen; unbefangen ⟨*Art*⟩; **at an ~ pace** in einem gemütlichen *od.* gemächlichen Tempo; **he is an ~ person** *or* **is ~ to get on with/work with** mit ihm kann man gut auskommen/zusammenarbeiten; **I'm ~** *(coll.)* es ist mir egal; **be ~ on the eye** *(coll.)* ansprechend aussehen; **woman** *or* **lady of ~ virtue** *(euphem.)* Freudenmädchen, *das (verhüll.).* **2.** *adv.* leicht; **easier said than done** leichter gesagt als getan; ~ **come ~ go** *(coll.)* wie gewonnen, so zerronnen *(Spr.);* ~ **does it** immer langsam *od.* sachte; **go ~:** vorsichtig sein; **go ~ on** *or* **with** sparsam sein *od.* umgehen mit; **be** *or* **go ~ on** *or* **with sb.** mit jmdm. nachsichtig sein; **take it ~!** beruhige dich!; **take it** *or* **things** *or* **life ~:** sich nicht übernehmen; **stand ~!** *(Brit. Mil.)* rührt euch!
easy: ~-care *attrib. adj.* pflegeleicht; ~ **'chair** *n.* Sessel, *der;* **~-going** *adj. (calm, placid)* gelassen; *(casually pleasant)* gemütlich; *(informal)* ungezwungen; *(lax)* nachlässig; *(careless)* unbekümmert; ~ **'meat** *n. (coll.)* leichte Beute; **sth./sb. is ~ meat** man hat [ein] leichtes Spiel mit etw./jmdm.; ~ **'money** *n.* leicht verdientes Geld; ~ **'option** *n.* leichter Weg; **E~ Street** *n.* **be on** E ~ Street im Wohlstand leben
eat [i:t] **1.** *v. t.,* **ate** [et, eɪt], **eaten** ['i:tn] **a)** ⟨*Mensch:*⟩ essen; ⟨*Tier:*⟩ fressen; **I've had enough to ~:** ich habe genug gegessen; ich bin satt *od.* gesättigt; **I could ~ a horse!** ich habe einen Bärenhunger! *(ugs.);* **you should ~ regular meals** du solltest regelmäßig essen; **don't be afraid – he won't ~ you!** *(fig.)* keine Angst, er wird dich schon nicht fressen *(ugs.);* **I could ~ you** du siehst zum Fressen aus *(ugs.);* **she looks nice enough to ~:** sie sieht zum Anbeißen aus *(ugs.);* ~ **sb. out of house and home** jmdn. arm essen; jmdm. die Haare vom Kopf fressen *(ugs.);* **what's ~ing you?** *(coll.)* was hast du denn?; ~ **one's words** seine Worte zurücknehmen; **b)** *(destroy, consume, make hole in)* fressen; ~ **its way into/through sth.** sich in etw./durch etw. hindurchfressen. *See also* **bread 1 b; dirt a; hat b; heart 1 a; humble 1 a. 2.** *v. i.,* **ate, eaten a)** ⟨*Person:*⟩ essen; ⟨*Tier:*⟩ fressen; ~ **out of sb.'s hand** *(lit. or fig.)* jmdm. aus der Hand fressen *(ugs.);* **b)** *(make a way by gnawing or corrosion)* ~ **into** sich hineinfressen in (+ *Akk.*); ~ **through sth.** sich durch etw. durchfressen
~ **'out** *v. i.* essen gehen
~ **'up 1.** *v. t.* **a)** *(consume)* ⟨*Person:*⟩ aufessen; ⟨*Tier:*⟩ auffressen; **the chickens were ~en up by the fox** die Hühner wurden vom Fuchs gefressen; **the car ~s up a lot of petrol** das Auto verbraucht *od. (ugs.)* frißt viel Benzin; **be ~en up by sth.** *(fig.)* vor etw. [fast] vergehen; **b)** *(traverse rapidly)* **our car ~s up the miles** unser Auto frißt die Meilen nur so *(ugs.).* **2.** *v. i.* aufessen
eatable ['i:təbl] **1.** *adj.* genießbar; eßbar. **2.** *n. in pl.* Lebensmittel *Pl.;* **have no ~s with one** nichts zu essen dabeihaben
'eat-by date *n.* Verfallsdatum, *das*
eaten *see* **eat**
eater ['i:tə(r)] *n.* **a)** *(person)* Esser, *der*/Esserin, *die;* **a big ~:** ein guter Esser; **b)** *(apple)* Eßapfel, *der*
eating ['i:tɪŋ] *n.* Essen, *das;* **make good ~:** ein gutes Essen sein; **not for ~:** nicht zum Essen [geeignet]
eating: ~ apple *n.* Eßapfel, *der;* **~-house** *n.* Restaurant, *das;* Speisehaus, *das;* **~-place** *n.* Eßgelegenheit, *die*
eats [i:ts] *n. pl. (coll.)* Fressalien *Pl. (ugs.);* **what's for ~?** was gibt's zu essen? *(ugs.)*
eau-de-Cologne [əʊdəkə'ləʊn] *n.* Eau de Cologne, *das;* Kölnisch Wasser, *das*
eaves [i:vz] *n. pl.* Dachgesims, *das*
eaves: ~drop *v. i.* lauschen; **~drop on sth./sb.** etw./jmdn. belauschen; **~dropper** *n.* Lauscher, *der*/Lauscherin, *die*
ebb [eb] **1.** *n.* **a)** *(of tide)* Ebbe, *die;* **the tide is on the ~:** es ist Ebbe; **b)** *(decline, decay)* Niedergang, *der;* **their morale was at its lowest ~:** ihre Moral war auf dem Tiefpunkt angelangt; **my funds are at a low ~:** in meinem Geldbeutel ist Ebbe *(ugs.);* **the ~ and flow** das Auf und Ab; **the ~ and flow of life** die Höhen und Tiefen des Lebens. **2.** *v. i.* **a)** *(flow back)* zurückgehen; **b)** *(recede, decline)* schwinden; ~ **away** dahinschwinden; **his life is ~ing out** mit ihm geht es zu Ende
'ebb-tide *n.* Ebbe, *die*
ebony ['ebənɪ] **1.** *n.* Ebenholz, *das.* **2.** *adj.* Ebenholz⟨*baum*⟩; ebenholzfarben ⟨*Haar, Haut*⟩; ~ **box** *etc.* Kiste *usw.* aus Ebenholz
ebullience [ɪ'bʌlɪəns, ɪ'bʊlɪəns] *n.* Überschwenglichkeit, *die;* ~ **of youth** jugendlicher Überschwang
ebullient [ɪ'bʌlɪənt, ɪ'bʊlɪənt] *adj. (exuberant)* überschwenglich; übersprudelnd, überschäumend ⟨*Temperament, Laune*⟩
EC *abbr.* **European Community** EG
eccentric [ɪk'sentrɪk] **1.** *adj.* **a)** *(odd, whimsical)* exzentrisch ⟨*Person*⟩; *(differing from the usual)* ausgefallen, ungewöhnlich ⟨*Person*⟩; **b)** *(not placed centrally, irregular)* exzentrisch; einseitig ⟨*Belastung*⟩. **2.** *n.* Exzentriker, *der*/Exzentrikerin, *die*
eccentrically [ɪk'sentrɪkəlɪ] *adv.* exzentrisch
eccentricity [eksən'trɪsɪtɪ] *n.* Exzentrizität, *die*
Eccles cake ['eklz keɪk] *n. (Brit.) rundes Rosinengebäck*
Ecclesiastes [ɪkli:zɪ'æsti:z] *n. (Bibl.)* Ekklesiastes, *der;* Prediger Salomo
ecclesiastic [ɪkli:zɪ'æstɪk] *n.* Kleriker, *der*/Klerikerin, *die;* Geistliche, *der/die*
ecclesiastical [ɪkli:zɪ'æstɪkl] *adj.* kirchlich; Kirchen⟨*recht, -gebäude, -amt, -jahr*⟩; ~ **music** geistliche Musik; Kirchenmusik, *die*
ECG *abbr.* **electrocardiogram** EKG
echelon ['eʃəlɒn, 'eɪʃəlɒn] *n.* **a)** *(of troops)* Echelon, *der;* Staffelstellung, *die* **in ~:** in Staffelstellung; **b)** *(of ships, aircraft, etc.)* Staffel, *die;* **in ~:** in staffelförmiger Formation; **c)** *(group in an organization)* Stab, *der;* **the lower ~s** die niedrigeren Ränge
echinoderm [ɪ'kaɪnədɜ:m, 'ekɪnədɜ:m] *n. (Zool.)* Echinoderme, *der (fachspr.);* Stachelhäuter, *der*
echo ['ekəʊ] **1.** *n., pl.* **~es a)** Echo, *das;* **cheer sb. to the ~:** jmdn. begeistert *od.* stürmisch feiern; **b)** *(fig.)* Anklang, *der* **(of** an + *Akk.*). **2.** *v. i.* **a)** ⟨*Ort:*⟩ hallen **(with** von); **it ~es in here** hier gibt es ein Echo; **b)** *(Geräusch:)* widerhallen. **3.** *v. t.* **a)** *(repeat)* zurückwerfen; **b)** *(repeat words of)* echoen; wiederholen; *(imitate words or opinions of)* widerspiegeln
éclair ['eɪkleə(r), eɪ'kleə(r)] *n.* Eclair, *das*
eclectic [ɪ'klektɪk] **1.** *adj.* eklektisch. **2.** *n.* Eklektiker, *der*
eclipse [ɪ'klɪps] **1.** *n.* **a)** *(Astron.)* Eklipse, *die (fachspr.);* Finsternis, *die;* ~ **of the sun, solar ~:** Sonnenfinsternis, *die;* ~ **of the moon, lunar ~:** Mondfinsternis, *die;* **in ~:** verfinstert; **b)** *(deprivation of light)* Dunkelheit, *die;* Finsternis, *die;* **c)** *(fig.)* Niedergang, *der;* **his fame suffered a total ~:** sein Ruhm verblaßte völlig; **in ~:** im Dunkel. **2.** *v. t.* **a)** verfinstern ⟨*Sonne, Mond*⟩; **b)** *(fig.: outshine, surpass)* in den Schatten stellen
ecliptic [ɪ'klɪptɪk] *n. (Astron.)* Ekliptik, *die*
eco- ['i:kə] *in comb.* öko-/Öko-
ecological [i:kə'lɒdʒɪkl] *adj.* ökologisch
ecologist [i:'kɒlədʒɪst] *n.* Ökologe, *der*/Ökologin, *die*
ecology [i:'kɒlədʒɪ] *n.* Ökologie, *die*
economic [i:kə'nɒmɪk, ekə'nɒmɪk] *adj.* **a)** *(of economics)* Wirtschafts⟨*politik, -abkommen, -system, -modell*⟩; ökonomisch, wirtschaftlich ⟨*Entwicklung, Zusammenbruch*⟩; ~ **cycle** Konjunkturzyklus, *der;* Konjunkturablauf, *der;* **b)** *(giving adequate return)* wirtschaftlich ⟨*Miete*⟩; **c)** *(maintained for profit)* wirtschaftlich; gewinnbringend
economical [i:kə'nɒmɪkl, ekə'nɒmɪkl] *adj.* wirtschaftlich; ökonomisch; sparsam ⟨*Person*⟩; **be ~ with sth.** mit etw. haushalten; **the car is ~ to run** das Auto ist wirtschaftlich; ~ **use of words** knappe *od.* kurzgefaßte Ausdrucksweise
economically [i:kə'nɒmɪkəlɪ, ekə'nɒmɪkəlɪ] *adv.* **a)** *(with reference to economics)* wirtschaftlich; **b)** *(in a saving manner)* sparsam; **be ~ minded** wirtschaftlich denken
economics [i:kə'nɒmɪks, ekə'nɒmɪks] *n., no pl.* **a)** Wirtschaftswissenschaft, *die (meist Pl.);* [politische] Ökonomie; **b)** *(application of the science)* wirtschaftlicher Aspekt; **the ~ of the situation** die wirtschaftliche *od.* finanzielle Seite der Situation; **c)** *(condition of a country)* Wirtschaft, *die*
economise *see* **economize**
economist [ɪ'kɒnəmɪst] *n.* Wirtschaftswissenschaftler, *der*/-wissenschaftlerin, *die;* **political ~:** Wirtschaftspolitiker, *der*/-politikerin, *die*
economize [ɪ'kɒnəmaɪz] *v. i.* sparen; ~ **on sth.** etw. sparen
economy [ɪ'kɒnəmɪ] *n.* **a)** *(frugality)* Sparsamkeit, *die; (of effort, motion)* Wirtschaftlichkeit, *die; (of style)* Kürze, *die;* Knapp-

heit, *die;* **b)** *(instance)* Einsparung, *die;* **make economies** zu Sparmaßnahmen greifen; **c)** *(of country etc.)* Wirtschaft, *die*
economy: ~ **class** *n.* Touristenklasse, *die;* Economyklasse, *die;* ~ **size** *n.* Haushaltspackung, *die;* Sparpackung, *die;* **an ~-size packet of salt** eine Haushaltspackung Salz
ecstasy ['ekstəsɪ] *n.* Ekstase, *die;* Verzückung, *die;* **be in/go into ecstasies [over sth.]** in Ekstase [über etw. *(Akk.)*] sein/geraten
ecstatic [ɪk'stætɪk] *adj.*, **ecstatically** [ɪk'stætɪkəlɪ] *adv.* ekstatisch; verzückt
ECT *abbr.* **electroconvulsive therapy** EKT
ECU, ecu ['eɪkju:] *abbr.* **European currency unit** Ecu, *der od. die*
Ecuador [ekwa'dɔ:(r)] *pr. n.* Ekuador *(das)*
Ecuadorean [ekwə'dɔ:rɪən] **1.** *adj.* ecuadorianisch; ekuadorianisch; **sb. is ~:** jmd. ist Ekuadorianer/Ekuadorianerin. **2.** *n.* Ekuadorianer, *der*/Ekuadorianerin, *die*
ecumenical [i:kjʊ'menɪkl, ekjʊ'menɪkl] *adj.* **a)** *(Relig.)* ökumenisch; **E~ Council** Ökumenisches Konzil; **b)** *(world-wide)* [welt]umfassend; [welt]umspannend
ecumenicalism [i:kjʊ'menɪkəlɪzm, ekjʊ'menɪkəlɪzm] *n.* *(Relig.)* ökumenische Bewegung; Ökumenismus, *der (kath. Kirche)*
ecumenism [i:'kju:mənɪzm] *n.* *(Relig.)* Ökumene, *die;* ökumenische Bewegung
eczema ['ekzɪmə, 'eksɪmə] *n.* *(Med.)* Ekzem, *das (fachspr.);* Hautausschlag, *der*
ed. *abbr.* **a) edited [by]** hg.; hrsg.; **b) edition** Ausg.; **c) editor** Hrsg.; **d) editor's note** Anm. d. Hrsg.; *(in newspaper)* Anm. d. Red.
Edam ['i:dæm] *n.* Edamer [Käse], *der*
eddy ['edɪ] **1.** *n.* **a)** *(whirlpool)* Strudel, *der;* **b)** *(of wind, fog, smoke)* Wirbel, *der;* **eddies of dust** Staubwirbel *Pl.* **2.** *v. i.* ⟨*Blätter:*⟩ wirbeln; ⟨*Wasser:*⟩ sprudeln
edelweiss ['eɪdlvaɪs] *n.* Edelweiß, *das*
edema *(Amer.) see* **oedema**
Eden ['i:dn] *n.* Eden *(das); (fig.)* Paradies, *das;* **the Garden of ~** der Garten Eden
edge [edʒ] **1.** *n.* **a)** *(of knife, razor, weapon)* Schneide, *die; (sharpness)* Schärfe, *die; (fig.: effectiveness)* Schärfe, *die;* Beißende, *das;* Schneidende, *das;* **the knife has lost its ~/has no ~:** das Messer ist stumpf geworden *od.* ist nicht mehr scharf/ist stumpf *od.* schneidet nicht; **take the ~ off sth.** etw. stumpf machen; *(fig.)* etw. abschwächen; **that took the ~ off our hunger** das nahm uns erst einmal den Hunger; **be on ~ [about sth.]** [wegen etw.] nervös *od.* gereizt sein; **her nerves have been all on ~ lately** in letzter Zeit ist sie schrecklich nervös; **set sb.'s teeth on ~:** jmdn. nervös machen; **give sb. the rough** *or* **sharp ~ of one's tongue** jmdm. gehörig Bescheid sagen *(ugs.);* **have/get the ~ [on sb./sth.]** *(coll.)* jmdm./einer Sache überlegen *od.* *(ugs.)* über sein/jmdn./etw. übertreffen; **b)** *(of solid, bed, brick, record, piece of cloth)* Kante, *die; (of dress)* Saum, *der;* **~ of a table** Tischkante, *die;* **roll off the ~ of the table** vom Tisch hinunterrollen; **a book with gilt ~s** ein Buch mit Goldschnitt; **c)** *(boundary) (of sheet of paper, road, forest, desert, cliff)* Rand, *der; (of sea, lake, river)* Ufer, *das; (of estate)* Grenze, *die;* **~ of the paper/of a road** Papierrand, *der*/Straßenrand, *der;* **platform ~:** Bahnsteigkante, *die;* **the ~ of the kerb** die Bordsteinkante; **at the ~ of a precipice** am Rande eines Abgrundes; **fall off the ~ of the cliff** die Klippe hinunterfallen; **on the ~ of sth.** *(fig.)* am Rande einer Sache *(Gen.);* **be on the ~ of disaster/bankruptcy** am Rande des Untergangs/Bankrotts stehen; **go over the ~** *(fig. coll.)* verrückt werden *(salopp).* **2.** *v. i.* *(move cautiously)* sich schieben; **~ along sth.** sich an etw. *(Dat.)* entlangschieben; **~ away** sich davonstehlen; sich wegschleichen; **~ away from sb./sth.** sich allmählich von jmdm./etw. entfernen; **~ up to sb.** sich an jmdn. heranmachen *(ugs.);* **~ out of the room** sich aus dem Zimmer stehlen. **3.** *v. t.* **a)** *(furnish with border)* säumen ⟨*Straße, Platz*⟩; besetzen ⟨*Kleid, Hut*⟩; einfassen ⟨*Garten, Straße*⟩; **~ with fur** mit Pelz verbrämen ⟨*Kragen*⟩; **b)** *(push gradually)* [langsam] schieben; **~ oneself** *or* **one's way through a crowd** sich [langsam] durch eine Menschenmenge schieben *od.* drängen; **he ~d his chair nearer to the fire** er rückte mit seinem Stuhl etwas näher ans Feuer; **c)** *(Cricket)* mit der Kante des Schlägers schlagen ⟨*Ball*⟩
edged [edʒd] *adj.* mit einer Schneide versehen; **an ~ blade/tool** eine scharfe Klinge/ein Werkzeug mit einer Schneide; **double-** *or* **two-~ blade** zweischneidige Klinge; **sharp-/dull-~:** scharf/stumpf; **black-/rough-~:** schwarzrandig/mit einem unebenen Rand
edgeways ['edʒweɪz], **edgewise** ['edʒwaɪz] *adv.* **a)** *(with edge uppermost or foremost)* mit der Schmalseite voran; **stand sth. ~:** etw. hochkant stellen; **b)** *(edge to edge)* Kante an Kante; **c)** *(fig.)* **I can't get a word in ~!** ich komme überhaupt nicht zu Wort!
edging ['edʒɪŋ] *n.* *(border, fringe) (of dress)* Borte, *die; (of lawn, garden, flower-bed)* Einfassung, *die; (lace, ribbon)* Paspel, *die;* **fur ~:** Pelzbesatz, *der*
'edging-shears *n. pl.* Kantenschneider, *der*
edgy ['edʒɪ] *adj.* nervös
edible ['edɪbl] **1.** *adj.* eßbar; genießbar. **2.** *n. in pl.* Nahrungsmittel *Pl.;* Lebensmittel *Pl.*
edict ['i:dɪkt] *n.* Erlaß, *der;* Edikt, *das (hist.)*
edification [edɪfɪ'keɪʃn] *n.* Erbauung, *die;* **for the ~ of ...:** zur Erbauung (+ *Gen.*)
edifice ['edɪfɪs] *n.* Gebäude, *das; (fig.)* Gefüge, *das;* Gebäude, *das*
edifying ['edɪfaɪɪŋ] *adj.* erbaulich
edit ['edɪt] *v. t.* **a)** *(act as editor of)* herausgeben ⟨*Zeitung*⟩; **b)** *(set in order for publication)* redigieren ⟨*Buch, Artikel, Manuskript*⟩; **c)** *(prepare an edition of)* bearbeiten; **~ the works of Homer** die Werke Homers neu herausgeben; **d)** *(take extracts from and collate)* schneiden, cutten, montieren ⟨*Film, Bandaufnahme*⟩; **e) ~ sth. out** etw. weglassen
edition [ɪ'dɪʃn] *n.* **a)** *(form of work, one copy; also fig.)* Ausgabe, *die;* **paperback ~:** Taschenbuchausgabe, *die;* **first ~:** Erstausgabe, *die;* **he is a second ~ of his father** er gleicht seinem Vater aufs Haar; **b)** *(from same types or at one time)* Auflage, *die;* **the book is in its fourth ~:** das Buch erscheint in seiner vierten Auflage; **the work has already gone through six ~s** die Arbeit erscheint schon in der sechsten Auflage; **morning/evening ~ of a newspaper** Morgen-/Abendausgabe einer Zeitung
editor ['edɪtə(r)] *n.* **a)** *(who prepares the work of others)* Redakteur, *der*/Redakteurin, *die; (of particular work)* Bearbeiter, *der*/Bearbeiterin, *die; (scholarly)* Herausgeber, *der*/-geberin, *die;* **b)** *(who conducts a newspaper or periodical)* Herausgeber, *der*/-geberin, *die;* **chief/sports/business ~:** Chef-/Sport-/Wirtschaftsredakteur, *der;* **c)** *(of films etc.)* Cutter, *der*/Cutterin, *die*
editorial [edɪ'tɔ:rɪəl] **1.** *n.* Leitartikel, *der.* **2.** *adj.* *(of an editor)* redaktionell; Redaktions⟨*assistent*⟩; **~ staff** Redaktion[sangestellte *Pl.*], *die;* **~ department** Redaktion, *die;* **~ job/work** Lektorenstelle, *die*/Lektorentätigkeit, *die;* **~ article** Leitartikel, *der*
editorship ['edɪtəʃɪp] *n.* Chefredaktion, *die;* Schriftleitung, *die;* **under the [general] ~ of Mr X** unter Herrn X als Herausgeber
EDP *abbr.* **electronic data processing** EDV
EDT *abbr.* *(Amer.)* **Eastern Daylight Time** östliche Sommerzeit
educable ['edjʊkəbl] *adj.* erziehbar
educate ['edjʊkeɪt] *v. t.* **a)** *(bring up)* erziehen; **~ sb. in sth.** jmdm. etw. beibringen; **b)** *(provide schooling for)* **he was ~d at Eton and Cambridge** er hat seine Ausbildung in Eton und Cambridge erhalten; **c)** *(give intellectual and moral training to)* bilden; **~ oneself** sich [weiter]bilden; **the public must be ~d how to save energy** die Öffentlichkeit muß aufgeklärt werden, wie man Energie spart; **d)** *(train)* schulen ⟨*Geist, Körper*⟩; [aus]bilden ⟨*Geschmack*⟩; dressieren, abrichten ⟨*Tier*⟩; **~ oneself to do sth.** sich dazu erziehen, etw. zu tun
educated ['edjʊkeɪtɪd] *adj.* gebildet; **make an ~ guess** eine wohlbegründete *od.* fundierte Vermutung anstellen
education [edjʊ'keɪʃn] *n.* **a)** *(instruction)* Erziehung, *die; (course of instruction)* Ausbildung, *die; (system)* Erziehungs[- und Ausbildungs]wesen, *das; (science)* Erziehungswissenschaften *Pl.;* Pädagogik, *die;* **~ is free** die Schulausbildung ist kostenlos; **Ministry of E~:** Ministerium für Erziehung und Unterricht; Kultusministerium, *das;* **be a man of ~:** ein gebildeter Mensch sein; **receive a good ~:** eine gute Ausbildung genießen; **sb. with school/a higher/university ~:** jmd. mit Schulbildung/mit einer höheren Schulbildung/Universitätsausbildung; **literary/scientific ~:** literarische/naturwissenschaftliche Bildung; **lecturer in ~:** Dozent/Dozentin für Pädagogik; **science/methods of ~:** Erziehungswissenschaften *Pl.*/-methoden *Pl.;* **b)** *(development of character or mental powers)* Schulung, *die. See also* **College of Education**
educational [edjʊ'keɪʃənl] *adj.* pädagogisch; erzieherisch; Lehr⟨*film, -spiele, -anstalt*⟩; Erziehungs⟨*methoden, -arbeit*⟩; **~ equipment** Unterrichtsmittel *Pl.;* **for ~ purposes** zu Lehr- *od.* Unterrichtszwecken
educationalist [edjʊ'keɪʃənəlɪst] *n.* Pädagoge, *der*/Pädagogin, *die;* Erziehungswissenschaftler, *der*/-wissenschaftlerin, *die*
educationally [edjʊ'keɪʃənəlɪ] *adv.* pädagogisch; **~ subnormal** lernbehindert; **be ~ backward** ein niedriges Bildungsniveau haben
educationist [edjʊ'keɪʃənɪst] *see* **educationalist**
educative ['edjʊkətɪv] *adj.* *(educational)* erzieherisch, pädagogisch ⟨*Fragen, Gründe*⟩; *(instructive)* erzieherisch; Erziehungs-; lehrreich ⟨*Film, Buch*⟩
educator ['edjʊkeɪtə(r)] *n.* Pädagoge, *der*/Pädagogin, *die;* Erzieher, *der*/Erzieherin, *die; (fig.)* Erzieher, *der*
Edward ['edwəd] *pr. n.* *(Hist., as name of ruler etc.)* Eduard *(der)*
Edwardian [ed'wɔ:dɪən] **1.** *adj.* Edwardianisch. **2.** *n.* Edwardianer, *der*
EEC *abbr.* **European Economic Community** EWG
eel [i:l] *n.* Aal, *der;* **be as slippery as an ~:** aalglatt sein
e'en [i:n] *(arch./poet.) see* [1,2]**even**
e'er [eə(r)] *(poet.) see* **ever**
eerie ['ɪərɪ] *adj.* unheimlich ⟨*Ort, Gebäude, Form*⟩; schaurig ⟨*Klang*⟩; schauerlich ⟨*Schrei*⟩; **give sb. an ~ feeling** jmdn. schaudern lassen
eerily ['ɪərɪlɪ] *adv. see* **eerie:** unheimlich; schaurig
eff [ef] *v. i.* *(sl.)* **~ and blind** fluchen
efface [ɪ'feɪs] **1.** *v. t.* **a)** *(rub out)* beseitigen ⟨*Inschrift*⟩; **b)** *(fig.: obliterate)* auslöschen; tilgen *(geh.).* **2.** *v. refl.* sich im Hintergrund halten
effect [ɪ'fekt] **1.** *n.* **a)** *(result)* Wirkung, *die* (on auf + *Akk.*); **her words had little ~ on him** ihre Worte erzielten bei ihm nur eine geringe Wirkung; **the ~s of sth. on sth.** die Auswirkungen einer Sache *(Gen.)* auf etw. *(Akk.);* die Folgen einer Sache *(Gen.)* für etw.; **the ~ of this was that ...:** das hatte zur Folge, daß ...; **be of no** *or* **to no ~:** erfolglos

od. ergebnislos sein; **with the ~ that ...:** mit der Folge *od.* dem Resultat, daß ...; **take ~:** wirken; die erwünschte Wirkung erzielen; **in ~:** in Wirklichkeit; praktisch; **b)** *no art. (impression)* Wirkung, *die;* Effekt, *der;* **solely** *or* **only for ~:** nur des Effekts wegen; aus reiner Effekthascherei *(abwertend);* **c)** *(meaning)* Inhalt, *der;* Sinn, *der;* **or words to that ~:** oder etwas in diesem Sinne; **a letter to the following ~:** ein Brief folgenden Inhalts; **we received a letter to the ~ that ...:** wir erhielten ein Schreiben des Inhalts, daß ...; **all families received instructions to that ~:** alle Familien bekamen entsprechende Anweisungen; **to the same ~:** desselben Inhalts; **d)** *(operativeness)* Kraft, *die;* Gültigkeit, *die;* **be in ~:** gültig *od.* in Kraft sein; **come into ~:** gültig *od.* wirksam werden; ⟨*bes. Gesetz:*⟩ in Kraft treten; **bring** *or* **carry** *or* **put into ~:** in Kraft setzen ⟨*Gesetz*⟩; verwirklichen ⟨*Plan*⟩; verwerten ⟨*Erfahrung, Kenntnisse*⟩; **give ~ to sth.** etw. in Kraft treten lassen; **take ~:** in Kraft treten; **with ~ from 2 November/Monday** mit Wirkung vom 2. November/von Montag; **e)** *in pl. (in play, film, broadcast)* **light ~s** Lichteffekte *Pl.;* **f)** *in pl. (property)* Vermögenswerte *Pl.;* Eigentum, *das;* **personal ~s:** persönliches Eigentum; Privateigentum, *das;* **household ~s:** Hausrat, *der.* **2.** *v. t.* durchführen; herbeiführen ⟨*Einigung*⟩; erzielen ⟨*Übereinstimmung, Übereinkommen*⟩; tätigen ⟨*Umsatz, Kauf*⟩; abschließen ⟨*Versicherung*⟩; leisten ⟨*Zahlung*⟩; **~ one's purpose** *or* **intention/desire** seine Absicht verwirklichen *od.* in die Tat umsetzen/sich *(Dat.)* einen Wunsch erfüllen; **payment was ~ed in dollars** die Zahlung erfolgte in Dollar

effective [ɪ'fektɪv] *adj.* **a)** *(having an effect)* wirksam ⟨*Mittel*⟩; effektiv ⟨*Maßnahmen*⟩; gleichwertig ⟨*Ersatz*⟩; **the measures have not been ~:** die Maßnahmen blieben ohne Wirkung *od.* waren wirkungslos; **be ~** ⟨*Arzneimittel:*⟩ wirken; **b)** *(having come into operation)* gültig; **~ from/as of** mit Wirkung vom; **the law is no longer ~/is ~ as from 1 September** das Gesetz hat keine Gültigkeit mehr *od.* ist außer Kraft/tritt ab 1. September in Kraft *od.* wird ab 1. September wirksam; **c)** *(powerful in effect)* überzeugend ⟨*Rede, Redner, Worte*⟩; kraftvoll ⟨*Stimme*⟩; **d)** *(striking)* wirkungsvoll; effektvoll; **e)** *(existing)* wirklich, tatsächlich ⟨*Hilfe*⟩; effektiv ⟨*Gewinn, Umsatz*⟩; **the ~ strength of the army** die Ist-Stärke der Armee

effectively [ɪ'fektɪvlɪ] *adv. (in fact)* effektiv; *(with effect)* wirkungsvoll; effektvoll; **they are ~ the same** effektiv sind sie gleich

effectiveness [ɪ'fektɪvnɪs] *n., no pl.* Wirksamkeit, *die;* Effektivität, *die*

effectual [ɪ'fektjʊəl] *adj.* **a)** *(sufficient)* wirksam ⟨*Mittel, Maßnahmen*⟩; **b)** *(valid)* [rechts]gültig, bindend ⟨*Vertrag, Dokument*⟩

effectually [ɪ'fektjʊəlɪ] *adv.* erfolgreich

effectuate [ɪ'fektjʊeɪt] *v. t.* bewirken; herbeiführen ⟨*Änderung*⟩; erzielen ⟨*Übereinstimmung*⟩

effeminate [ɪ'femɪnət] *adj.* unmännlich, *(geh.)* effeminiert ⟨*Mann*⟩

effervesce [efə'ves] *v. i.* sprudeln; efferveszieren *(fachspr.); (fig.)* übersprudeln; überschäumen; **be effervescing with sth.** vor etw. übersprudeln *od.* überschäumen

effervescence [efə'vesəns] *n., no pl.* Sprudeln, *das; (fig.)* Übersprudeln, *das;* Überschäumen, *das*

effervescent [efə'vesənt] *adj.* sprudelnd; *(fig.)* übersprudelnd, überschäumend ⟨*Freude, Verhalten*⟩; überschwenglich ⟨*Stimme*⟩; **~ tablets** Brausetabletten

effete [e'fi:t] *adj. (exhausted, worn out)* verbraucht; saft- und kraftlos ⟨*Person*⟩; überlebt ⟨*System*⟩; *(soft, decadent)* verweichlicht

efficacious [efɪ'keɪʃəs] *adj.* wirksam ⟨*Methode, Mittel, Medizin*⟩

efficaciousness [efɪ'keɪʃəsnɪs], **efficacy** ['efɪkəsɪ] *ns., no pl.* Wirksamkeit, *die*

efficiency [ɪ'fɪʃənsɪ] *n.* **a)** *(of person)* Fähigkeit, *die;* Tüchtigkeit, *die; (of machine, factory, engine)* Leistungsfähigkeit, *die; (of organization, method)* Rationalität, *die;* Effizienz, *die (geh.);* **b)** *(Mech., Phys.)* Wirkungsgrad, *der*

efficient [ɪ'fɪʃənt] *adj.* effizient *(geh.);* fähig ⟨*Person*⟩; tüchtig ⟨*Arbeiter, Sekretärin*⟩; leistungsfähig ⟨*Maschine, Abteilung, Fabrik*⟩; rationell ⟨*Methode, Organisation*⟩

efficiently [ɪ'fɪʃəntlɪ] *adv.* einwandfrei; gut; effizient *(geh.)*

effigy ['efɪdʒɪ] *n.* Bildnis, *das;* **hang/burn sb. in ~:** jmdn. in effigie hängen/verbrennen *(geh.)*

effing ['efɪŋ] *adj. (sl.)* Scheiß- *(salopp)*

effluent ['eflʊənt] **1.** *adj.* abfließend ⟨*Fluß, Wasser*⟩; **~ drain** Abfluß, *der.* **2.** *n.* **a)** *(stream)* Abfluß, *der;* **b)** *(outflow from sewage tank, waste etc.)* Abwässer *Pl.*

effluvium [e'flu:vɪəm] *n., pl.* **effluvia** [e'flu:vɪə] Ausdünstung, *die*

effort ['efət] *n.* **a)** *(exertion)* Anstrengung, *die;* Mühe, *die;* **make an/every ~** *(physically)* sich anstrengen; *(mentally)* sich bemühen; **without [any]/only with the greatest ~:** ohne Anstrengung *od.* mühelos/nur mit äußerster Anstrengung *od.* größter Mühe; **for all his ~s** trotz all seiner Bemühungen; **vain ~s** vergebliche Bemühungen; **it is an ~ [for me] to get up in the mornings** es kostet [mich] einige Mühe *od.* Anstrengung, morgens aufzustehen; **[a] waste of time and ~:** verlorene *od.* vergebliche Liebesmüh; **make every possible ~ to do sth.** jede nur mögliche Anstrengung unternehmen *od.* machen, etw. zu tun; **he makes no ~ at all** er bemüht sich überhaupt nicht; er gibt sich überhaupt keine Mühe; **b)** *(attempt)* Versuch, *der;* **in an ~ to do sth.** beim Versuch, etw. zu tun; **make no ~ to be polite** sich *(Dat.)* nicht die Mühe machen, höflich zu sein; **make one last ~:** einen letzten Versuch unternehmen; **~s are being made to do sth.** es sind Bestrebungen im Gange, etw. zu tun; **c)** *(activity)* **research ~[s]** Einsatz in der Forschungsarbeit; **business ~s** geschäftliche Unternehmungen; **d)** *(coll.: result)* Leistung, *die;* **he made a pretty poor ~ of the job** er hat ziemlich nachlässige Arbeit geleistet; **the book was one of his first ~s** das Buch war einer seiner ersten Versuche

effortless ['efətlɪs] *adj.* mühelos; leicht; flüssig, leicht ⟨*Stil*⟩

effortlessly ['efətlɪslɪ] *adv.* mühelos; ohne Anstrengung; flüssig ⟨*schreiben*⟩

effrontery [ɪ'frʌntərɪ] *n.* Dreistigkeit, *die;* **have the ~ to do sth.** die Frechheit *od. (geh.)* Stirn besitzen, etw. zu tun

effusion [ɪ'fju:ʒn] *n.* **a)** *(pouring forth) (of light, sound)* Ausströmen, *das;* Entströmen, *das; (of the Holy Spirit)* Ausgießung, *die;* **b)** *(utterance)* Überschwang, *der;* **literary/romantic ~s** literarische/romantische Ergüsse

effusive [ɪ'fju:sɪv] *adj.* überschwenglich; exaltiert *(geh.)* ⟨*Mensch, Stil, Charakter*⟩

effusively [ɪ'fju:sɪvlɪ] *adv. see* **effusive:** überschwenglich; exaltiert *(geh.)*

effusiveness [ɪ'fju:sɪvnɪs] *n., no pl. (of speech, action, greeting)* Überschwenglichkeit, *die; (of style)* Exaltiertheit, *die (geh.)*

Efta ['eftə], **EFTA** *n. abbr.* **European Free Trade Association** EFTA

e.g. [i:'dʒi:] *abbr.* **for example** z. B.

egalitarian [ɪgælɪ'teərɪən] **1.** *adj.* egalitär *(geh.)* ⟨*Person, Einstellung, Gruppe*⟩; Gleichheits⟨*prinzipien*⟩. **2.** *n.* Verfechter/Verfechterin des Egalitarismus

¹egg [eg] *n.* Ei, *das;* **a bad ~** *(fig. coll.) (person)* eine üble Person; **a good/tough ~** *(sl.) (person)* ein feiner *od. (veralt.)* famoser/harter Kerl *(ugs.);* **good ~!** *(dated coll.)* famos! *(veralt.);* **have** *or* **put all one's ~s in one basket** *(fig. coll.)* alles auf eine Karte setzen; **it's like teaching your grandmother to suck ~s** da will das Ei wieder klüger sein als die Henne; **as sure as ~s is** *or* **are ~s** *(coll.)* so sicher wie das Amen in der Kirche *(ugs.)*

²egg *v. t.* anstacheln (to zu); **~ sb. on [to do sth.]** jmdn. anstacheln *od.* aufhetzen[, etw. zu tun]

egg: **~-and-'spoon race** Eierlaufen, *das;* **~-beater** *n.* **a)** *(device)* Rührbesen, *der;* **b)** *(Amer. sl.: helicopter)* Hubschrauber, *der;* **~-cosy** *n. (Brit.)* Eierwärmer, *der;* **~-cup** *n.* Eierbecher, *der;* **~ 'custard** *n.* Eierkrem, *die;* **~ 'flip** *n.* Eierlikör, *der;* **~head** *n. (coll.)* Eierkopf, *der (abwertend);* Egghead, *der (geh. oft scherzhaft od. abwertend);* **~-'nog** *see* **~-flip;** **~-plant** *n.* Aubergine, *die; (fruit also)* Eierfrucht, *die; (plant also)* Eierpflanze, *die;* **~ powder** *n.* Eipulver, *das;* **~-shaped** *adj.* eiförmig; **~shell** *n.* **a)** Eierschale, *die;* **b)** *attrib. (fragile)* **~shell china** Eierschalenporzellan, *das;* **~shell glaze** Mittelglanzglasur, *die;* **~-slice** *n.* ≈ Wender, *der;* **~-spoon** *n.* Eierlöffel, *der;* **~-timer** *n.* Eieruhr, *die;* **~-whisk** *n.* Schneebesen, *der;* **~-white** *n.* Eiweiß, *das;* **~ yolk** *n.* Eigelb, *das;* Eidotter, *der od. das*

ego ['egəʊ, 'i:gəʊ] *n., pl.* **~s** **a)** *(Psych.)* Ego, *das; (Metaphys.)* Ich, *das;* **b)** *(self-esteem)* Selbstbewußtsein, *das;* **inflated ~:** übersteigertes Selbstbewußtsein; **boost sb.'s ~:** jmds. Selbstbewußtsein stärken; jmdm. Auftrieb geben

egocentric [egəʊ'sentrɪk] *adj.* egozentrisch; ichbezogen

egoism ['egəʊɪzm] *n., no pl.* **a)** *(systematic selfishness)* Egoismus, *der;* Selbstsucht, *die (abwertend);* **b)** *(self-opinionatedness)* Selbstherrlichkeit, *die;* **c)** *see* **egotism a**

egoist ['egəʊɪst] *n.* Egoist, *der*/Egoistin, *die*

egoistic [egəʊ'ɪstɪk], **egoistical** [egəʊ'ɪstɪkl] *adj.* **a)** *(self-regarding, selfish)* egoistisch; selbstsüchtig; eigennützig; **b)** *see* **egotistic a**

egotism ['egətɪzm] *n., no pl.* **a)** Egotismus, *der (fachspr.);* Ichbezogenheit, *die;* **b)** *(self-conceit)* Egotismus, *der;* Selbstgefälligkeit, *die;* **c)** *see* **egoism a**

egotist ['egətɪst] *n.* Egotist, *der*/Egotistin, *die (fachspr.); (one who thinks or talks too much of himself/herself)* Egozentriker, *der*/Egozentrikerin, *die*

egotistic [egə'tɪstɪk], **egotistical** [egə'tɪstɪkl] *adj.* **a)** ichbezogen ⟨*Rede, Gespräch*⟩; **b)** selbstsüchtig, selbstgefällig *(abwertend)* ⟨*Person*⟩

egregious [ɪ'gri:dʒəs] *adj.* ungeheuer[lich]; ausgemacht ⟨*Trottel*⟩

egress ['i:gres] *n. (formal)* Ausgang, *der* (to, into zu)

egret ['i:grɪt, 'egrɪt] *n. (Ornith.)* Reiher, *der*

Egypt ['i:dʒɪpt] *pr. n.* Ägypten *(das)*

Egyptian [ɪ'dʒɪpʃn] **1.** *adj.* ägyptisch; **sb. is ~:** jmd. ist Ägypter/Ägypterin; *see also* **English 1. 2.** *n.* **a)** *(person)* Ägypter, *der*/Ägypterin, *die;* **b)** *(language)* Ägyptisch, *das; see also* **English 2 a**

Egyptologist [i:dʒɪp'tɒlədʒɪst] *n.* Ägyptologe, *der*/Ägyptologin, *die*

Egyptology [i:dʒɪp'tɒlədʒɪ] *n., no pl.* Ägyptologie, *die*

eh [eɪ] *int. (coll.) expr. inquiry or surprise* wie?; wie bitte?; *inviting assent* nicht [wahr]?; *asking for sth. to be repeated or explained* was?; hä? *(salopp);* **wasn't that good, eh?** war das nicht gut?; **let's not have any more fuss, eh?** Schluß mit dem Theater, ja? *(ugs.)*

eider ['aɪdə(r)]: **~ [duck]** *n.* Eiderente, *die;* **~[-down]** *n.* [Eider]daunen *Pl.;* Flaumfedern *Pl.*

eiderdown ['aɪdədaʊn] *n.* Daunenbett, *das;* Federbett, *das*

eight [eɪt] **1.** *adj.* acht; **at ~:** um acht; **it's ~ [o'clock]** es ist acht [Uhr]; **half past ~:** halb neun; **~ thirty** acht Uhr dreißig; **~ ten/fifty** zehn nach acht/vor neun; *(esp. in timetable)* acht Uhr zehn/fünfzig; **around** *or* **at about ~:** gegen acht [Uhr]; **half ~** *(coll.)* halb neun; **girl of ~:** Mädchen von acht Jahren; **~-year-old boy** achtjähriger Junge; **an ~-year-old** ein Achtjähriger/eine Achtjährige; **be ~ [years old]** acht [Jahre alt] sein; **at [the age of] ~, aged ~:** mit acht Jahren; im Alter von acht Jahren; **he won ~-six** er hat acht zu sechs gewonnen; **Book/Volume/Part/Chapter E~:** Buch/Band/Teil/Kapitel acht; achtes Buch/achter Band/achter Teil/achtes Kapitel; **~-figure number** achtstellige Zahl; **~-page** achtseitig; **~-storey[ed] building** achtstöckiges *od.* achtgeschossiges Gebäude; **~-sided polygon** achtseitiges Vieleck; **bet at ~ to one** acht zu eins wetten; **~ times** achtmal. **2.** *n.* **a)** *(number, symbol)* Acht, *die;* **the first/last ~:** die ersten/letzten acht; **there were ~ of us present** wir waren [zu] acht; **~ of us attended the lecture** wir waren [zu] acht bei der Vorlesung; **come ~ at a time/in ~s** acht auf einmal kommen/zu je acht kommen; **arabic/Roman ~:** arabische/römische Acht; **stack the boxes in ~s** die Kisten zu achten stapeln; **the [number] ~ [bus]** die Buslinie Nr. 8; der Achter *(ugs.);* **two-~ time** *(Mus.)* Zweiachteltakt, *der;* **behind the ~ ball** *(Amer.) (at a disadvantage)* im Nachteil; *(in a baffling situation)* in einer mißlichen Lage; **b)** *(8-shaped figure)* **[figure of] ~:** Achter, *der (ugs.);* Acht, *die;* **c)** *(Cards)* **~ of hearts/trumps** Herz-/Trumpfacht, *die;* **d)** *(size)* **a size ~ dress** ein Kleid [in] Größe 8; **wear size ~ shoes** [Schuh]größe 8 haben *od.* tragen; **wear an ~, be size ~:** Größe 8 tragen *od.* haben; **e)** *(Rowing) (crew)* Achtermannschaft, *die; (boat)* Achter, *der;* **the E~s** *(boat-races)* Achterrennen, *das;* **f) have had one over the ~** *(sl.)* einen über den Durst getrunken haben *(ugs.)*

eighteen [eɪ'ti:n] **1.** *adj.* achtzehn; *see also* **eight 1. 2.** *n.* Achtzehn, *die;* **in the ~ seventies** in den siebziger Jahren des neunzehnten Jahrhunderts; **~ hundred hours** *see* **hundred 1 a;** *see also* **eight 2 a, d**

eighteenth [eɪ'ti:nθ] **1.** *adj.* achtzehnt...; *see also* **eighth 1. 2.** *n. (fraction)* Achtzehntel, *das; see also* **eighth 2**

eightfold ['eɪtfəʊld] **1.** *adj.* achtfach; **an ~ increase** ein Anstieg um das Achtfache. **2.** *adv.* achtfach; **multiply ~:** sich verachtfachen; **increase ~:** sich auf das Achtfache erhöhen

eighth [eɪtθ] **1.** *adj.* acht...; **be/come ~:** achter sein/als achter ankommen; **an ~ part/share** ein Achtel; **~ largest** achtgrößt... **2.** *n. (in sequence)* achte, *der/die/das; (in rank)* Achte, *der/die/das; (fraction)* Achtel, *das;* **be the ~ to do sth.** der/die/das achte sein, der/die/das etw. tut; *(day)* **the ~ of May** der achte Mai; **the ~ [of the month]** der Achte [des Monats]

'eighth-note *n. (Amer. Mus.)* Achtel, *das;* Achtelnote, *die*

eightieth ['eɪtɪɪθ] **1.** *adj.* achtzigst...; *see also* **eighth 1. 2.** *n. (fraction)* Achtzigstel, *das; see also* **eighth 2**

eighty ['eɪtɪ] **1.** *adj.* achtzig; **one-and-~** *(arch.) see* **~-one 1;** *see also* **eight 1. 2.** *n.* Achtzig, *die;* **be in one's eighties** in den Achtzigern sein; **be in one's early/late eighties** Anfang/Ende Achtzig sein; **the eighties** *(years)* die achtziger Jahre; **the temperature will be rising [well] into the eighties** die Temperatur steigt auf [gut] über 80 Grad Fahrenheit; **one-and-~** *(arch.) see* **~-one 2;** *see also* **eight 2 a**

eighty: ~-'first *etc. adj.* einundachtzigst... *usw.; see also* **eighth 1; ~-'one** *etc.* **1.** *adj.* einundachtzig *usw.; see also* **eight 1; 2.** *n.* Einundachtzig *usw., die; see also* **eight 2 a**

Eire ['eərə] *pr. n.* Irland *(das);* Eire *(das)*

eisteddfod [aɪ'steðvəd] *n., pl.* **~s** *or* **~au** [aɪ'steðvədaɪ] **a)** *(of Welsh bards)* Eisteddfod, *das;* **b)** *(gathering for competitions)* Dichter- und Sängerfest, *das*

either ['aɪðə(r), 'i:ðə(r)] **1.** *adj.* **a)** *(each)* **at ~ end of the table** an beiden Enden des Tisches; **on ~ side of the road** auf beiden Seiten der Straße; **~ way** *see* **way 1 c; b)** *(one or other)* [irgend]ein ... [von beiden]; **take ~ one** nimm einen/eine/eins von [den] beiden. **2.** *pron.* **a)** *(each)* beide *Pl.;* **~ is possible** beides ist möglich; **I can't cope with ~:** ich kann mit keinem von beiden fertig werden; **I don't like ~ [of them** *or* **of the two]** ich mag beide nicht *od.* keinen von beiden; **b)** *(one or other)* einer/eine/ein[e]s [von beiden]; **~ of the buses** jeder der beiden Busse; beide Busse. **3.** *adv.* **a)** *(any more than the other)* auch [nicht]; **'I don't like that ~:** ich mag es auch nicht; **I don't like 'that ~:** auch das mag ich nicht; **she plays the piano badly and she can't sing ~:** sie spielt schlecht Klavier, und singen kann sie auch nicht; **b)** *(moreover, furthermore)* noch nicht einmal; **there was a time, and not so long ago ~:** früher, noch gar nicht einmal so lange her. **4.** *conj.* **~ ... or ...:** entweder ... oder ...; *(after negation)* weder ... noch ...; **I've never been to ~ Berlin or Munich** ich bin weder in Berlin noch in München gewesen

'either-or 1. *adj.* Entweder-Oder-⟨*Problem*⟩. **2.** *n.* Entweder-Oder, *das*

ejaculate [ɪ'dʒækjʊleɪt] **1.** *v. t.* **a)** *(utter suddenly)* ausstoßen ⟨*Fluch, Gebet*⟩; **b)** *(eject)* ausstoßen; ejakulieren ⟨*Samen*⟩. **2.** *v. i. (eject semen)* ejakulieren

ejaculation [ɪdʒækjʊ'leɪʃn] *n.* **a)** *(utterance)* Ausbruch, *der; (cry)* Ausruf, *der;* **b)** *(ejection)* Ausstoß, *der; (of semen)* Ejakulation, *die;* Samenerguß, *der*

eject [ɪ'dʒekt] **1.** *v. t.* **a)** *(expel) (from committee, hall, meeting)* hinauswerfen (**from** aus); *(from machine-gun)* auswerfen; *(from aircraft)* hinausschleudern; **b)** *(dispossess)* hinauswerfen; exmittieren *(Amtsspr.).* **2.** *v. i.* sich hinauskatapultieren

ejection [ɪ'dʒekʃn] *n. (of intruder etc.)* Vertreibung, *die; (of heckler, troublesome drunk)* Hinauswurf, *der; (of empty cartridge)* Ausstoß, *der;* Auswerfen, *das; (of pilot)* Hinausschleudern, *das*

ejector [ɪ'dʒektə(r)] *n. (of firearm)* Auswerfer, *der*

e'jector seat *n.* Schleudersitz, *der*

eke [i:k] *v. t.* **~ out** strecken ⟨*Vorräte, Essen, Einkommen*⟩; **~ out a living** *or* **an existence** sich *(Dat.)* seinen Lebensunterhalt [notdürftig *od.* mühsam] verdienen

elaborate 1. [ɪ'læbərət] *adj.* kompliziert; ausgefeilt ⟨*Stil*⟩; durchorganisiert ⟨*Studium, Forschung*⟩; kunstvoll [gearbeitet] ⟨*Arrangement, Stickerei, Verzierung, Kleidungsstück*⟩; üppig, umfangreich ⟨*Menü*⟩. **2.** [ɪ'læbəreɪt] *v. t.* weiter ausarbeiten; weiter ausführen ⟨*Arbeit, Plan, Thema*⟩. **3.** *v. i.* mehr ins Detail gehen; **could you ~?** könnten Sie das näher ausführen?; **~ on sth.** etw. ausführlicher erklären *od.* näher ausführen

elaborately [ɪ'læbərətlɪ] *adv.* anspruchsvoll ⟨*sich kleiden*⟩; kompliziert ⟨*ausarbeiten, planen*⟩; kunstvoll ⟨*entwerfen, verzieren*⟩; umfangreich ⟨*vorbereiten*⟩

elaboration [ɪlæbə'reɪʃn] *n. (of plan, theory, etc.)* Ausarbeitung, *die (meist Pl.); (of style)* Ausfeilung, *die; (that which elaborates)* Elaborat, *das (abwertend)*

élan ['eɪlɑ̃] *n., no pl.* Energie, *die;* Schwung, *der*

eland ['i:lənd] *n. (Zool.)* Eleantilope, *die*

elapse [ɪ'læps] *v. i.* ⟨*Zeit:*⟩ vergehen, ins Land gehen

elastic [ɪ'læstɪk, ɪ'lɑ:stɪk] **1.** *adj.* **a)** elastisch; **b)** *(springy)* geschmeidig ⟨*Bewegung*⟩; federnd ⟨*Gang*⟩; elastisch ⟨*Muskel*⟩; **c)** *(fig.: flexible)* flexibel; weit ⟨*Gewissen*⟩; weit auslegbar ⟨*Klausel, Bestimmung*⟩; Gummi⟨*begriff, -paragraph*⟩ *(ugs.).* **2.** *n.* (**~ band**) Gummiband, *das; (fabric)* elastisches Material

elasticated [ɪ'læstɪkeɪtɪd, ɪ'lɑ:stɪkeɪtɪd] *adj.* elastisch

elastic 'band *n.* Gummiband, *das*

elasticity [elæs'tɪsɪtɪ, i:læs'tɪsɪtɪ] *n., no pl.* **a)** *(of material etc.)* Elastizität, *die;* **b)** *(springiness)* Geschmeidigkeit, *die;* **c)** *(fig.: flexibility)* Flexibilität, *die; (of rules, laws)* [weite] Auslegbarkeit; **d)** *(Econ.)* Anpassungsfähigkeit, *die*

elastic 'stocking *n.* Gummistrumpf, *der*

elate [ɪ'leɪt] *v. t.* erfreuen; erbauen *(geh.);* **be ~d by/over sth.** aufgrund einer Sache *(Gen.)*/über etw. *(Akk.)* hocherfreut *od.* in Hochstimmung sein

elated [ɪ'leɪtɪd] *adj.* freudig erregt; **~ mood** *or* **state of mind** Hochstimmung, *die;* **be** *or* **feel ~:** in Hochstimmung sein

elation [ɪ'leɪʃn] *n., no pl.* freudige Erregung; **feel ~ at one's success** über seinen Erfolg hocherfreut sein

elbow ['elbəʊ] **1.** *n.* **a)** Ell[en]bogen, *der;* **b)** *(of piping)* Knie, *das;* **c)** *(bend, corner)* Knick, *der; (of river)* Biegung, *die;* Knie, *das; (of road)* Biegung, *die;* **d)** *(of garment)* Ellbogen, *der;* **e) at one's ~:** bei sich; in Reichweite; **sth./sb. is at sb.'s ~:** etw. ist in Reichweite/jmd. ist in jmds. Nähe; **bend** *or* **lift one's ~** *(coll.: drink)* einen heben *(ugs.);* **give sb. the ~** *(coll.)* jmdm. den Laufpaß geben *(ugs.);* **out at ~s** an den Ellbogen abgetragen *od.* durchgewetzt ⟨*Mantel*⟩; heruntergekommen ⟨*Person*⟩; **be up to one's** *or* **the ~s in sth./work** mit etw. alle Hände voll zu tun haben/bis über die Ohren in Arbeit stecken. **2.** *v. t.* **~ one's way** sich mit den Ellenbogen einen Weg bahnen; sich drängeln *(ugs.);* **~ sb. aside** jmdn. mit den Ellenbogen zur Seite stoßen; **~ sb. out** *(fig.)* jmdn. hinausdrängeln

elbow: ~-grease *n., no pl. (joc.)* Muskelkraft, *die;* **~ patch** *n.* [Ellbogen]flicken, *der;* Ellbogenverstärkung, *die (Textilw.);* **~-room** *n. (lit. or fig.)* Ell[en]bogenfreiheit, *die; (fig.)* Spielraum, *der*

¹elder ['eldə(r)] **1.** *attrib. adj.* älter...; **Pliny the E~, the ~ Pliny** Plinius der Ältere. **2.** *n.* **a)** *(senior)* Ältere, *der/die;* **he is my ~ by several years** er ist mehrere Jahre älter als ich; **b)** *in pl.* Alten *Pl.;* **our ~s and betters** die Älteren mit mehr Lebenserfahrung; **the village ~s** die Dorfältesten; **the ~s of the tribe** die Stammesältesten; **c)** *(official in Church)* [Kirchen]älteste, *der/die*

²elder *n. (Bot.)* Holunder, *der*

elder: ~berry *n.* Holunderbeere, *die;* **~berry 'wine** *n.* Holunderbeerwein, *der;* **~flower** *n.* Holunderblüte, *die;* **~flower 'wine** *n.* Holunderblütenwein, *der*

elderly ['eldəlɪ] **1.** *adj.* älter. **2.** *n. pl.* **the ~:** ältere Menschen

elder: ~ 'statesman *n.* Elder statesman, *der (Politik);* **~ 'wine** *see* **elderberry wine**

eldest ['eldɪst] *adj.* ältest...

eldorado [eldə'rɑ:dəʊ] *n., pl.* **~s** Eldorado, *das*

elect [ɪ'lekt] **1.** *adj.* **a)** *postpos. (chosen but not installed)* gewählt; **the President ~:** der gewählte *od.* designierte Präsident; **b)** *(choice)* auserlesen, exklusiv ⟨*Gruppe*⟩; *(chosen)* [aus]erwählt. **2.** *v. t.* **a)** *(choose by vote)* wählen; **~ sb. chairman/MP** *etc.* jmdn. zum Vorsitzenden/Abgeordneten *usw.* wählen; **~ sb. to the chair/to the Senate** jmdn. zum Vorsitzenden/in den Senat wählen; **b)** *(choose)* **~ to do sth.** sich dafür entscheiden, etw. zu tun

election [ɪ'lekʃn] *n.* Wahl, *die;* **presidential ~s** *(Amer.)* Präsidentschaftswahlen *Pl.;* **general/local ~:** allgemeine/kommunale Wahlen; **~ as chairman** Wahl zum Vorsitzenden; ~ **results** Wahlergebnisse *Pl.*; ~ **day** Wahltag, *der; see also* **by-election**

e'lection campaign *n.* Wahlkampf, *der; (in US presidential election)* Wahlkampagne, *die*

electioneer [ɪlekʃə'nɪə(r)] *v.i.* **be/go ~ing** Wahlkampf machen

electioneering [ɪlekʃə'nɪərɪŋ] *n.* Agitation, *die* (**for/against** für/gegen)

elective [ɪ'lektɪv] *adj.* **a)** *(chosen or filled by election)* gewählt; **an ~ office** ein Amt, das durch Wahl besetzt wird/wurde; **b)** *(having the power to elect)* wahlberechtigt; **c)** *(optional)* wahlfrei, fakultativ ⟨*Kursus, Fach*⟩

elector [ɪ'lektə(r)] *n.* **a)** Wähler, *der*/Wählerin, *die;* Wahlberechtigte, *der/die;* **b)** **E~** *(Hist.: prince)* Kurfürst, *der*

electoral [ɪ'lektərl] *adj.* Wahl⟨*liste, -zettel, -system, -bezirk, -berechtigung*⟩; Wähler⟨*liste, -verzeichnis, -wille, -gruppe*⟩

electoral 'college *n.* Wahlmännergremium, *das;* Wahlausschuß, *der*

electorate [ɪ'lektərət] *n.* Wähler *Pl.*; Wählerschaft, *die*

electric [ɪ'lektrɪk] **1.** *adj.* elektrisch ⟨*Strom, Feld, Licht, Orgel usw.*⟩; Elektro⟨*kabel, -motor, -karren, -herd, -kessel*⟩; Elektrizitäts⟨*lehre, -erzeuger, -werk*⟩; Strom⟨*versorgung*⟩; *(fig.)* spannungsgeladen ⟨*Atmosphäre*⟩; elektrisierend ⟨*Wirkung*⟩. **2.** *n. in pl.* elektrische Geräte; Elektrogeräte *Pl.*; *(whole system)* Elektrik, *die*

electrical [ɪ'lektrɪkl] *adj.* elektrisch ⟨*Defekt, Kontakt*⟩; Elektro⟨*abteilung, -handel, -geräte*⟩

electrical: ~ engi'neer *n.* Elektroingenieur, *der*/-ingenieurin, *die;* **~ engi'neering** *n.* Elektrotechnik, *die*

electrically [ɪ'lektrɪkəlɪ] *adv.* elektrisch; *(fig.)* [wie] elektrisiert

electric: ~ 'blanket *n.* Heizdecke, *die;* **~ 'blue** *n.* Stahlblau, *das;* **~ 'chair** *n.* elektrischer Stuhl; **~ cooker** *n.* Elektroherd, *der;* **~ 'eel** *n.* Zitteraal, *der;* **~ 'eye** *n.* Photozelle, *die;* **~ 'fan** *n.* Ventilator, *der;* **~ 'fence** *n.* elektrischer Zaun; Elektrozaun, *der;* **~ 'fire** *n.* [elektrischer] Heizofen; Heizstrahler, *der;* **~ gui'tar** *n.* elektrische Gitarre; E-Gitarre, *die*

electrician [ɪlek'trɪʃn, elek'trɪʃn] *n.* Elektriker, *der*/Elektrikerin, *die; (who sets up electrical apparatus)* Elektromechaniker, *der*/-mechanikerin, *die*

electricity [ɪlek'trɪsɪtɪ, elek'trɪsɪtɪ] *n., no pl.* **a)** Elektrizität, *die;* **b)** *(supply)* Strom, *der;* **install ~:** Stromanschlüsse legen; **c)** *(fig.)* Spannung, *die*

electricity: ~ bill *n.* Stromrechnung, *die;* **~ man** *n. (fitter)* Elektroinstallateur, *der; (meter-reader, collector)* Stromableser, *der;* Strommann, *der (ugs.);* **~ meter** *n.* Stromzähler, *der*

electric: ~ 'shock *n.* Stromschlag, *der;* [elektrischer] Schlag; *(Med.)* Elektroschock, *der;* **~ 'storm** *n.* Gewitter, *das;* Gewittersturm, *der*

electrification [ɪlektrɪfɪ'keɪʃn] *n.* **a)** *(charging)* Unter-Strom-Setzen, *das;* **b)** *(conversion)* Elektrifizierung, *die;* **c)** *(fig.)* Elektrisierung, *die*

electrify [ɪ'lektrɪfaɪ] *v.t.* **a)** *(charge)* an das Stromnetz anschließen ⟨*Maschine*⟩; unter Strom setzen ⟨*Kabel, Leiter*⟩; **b)** *(convert)* elektrifizieren ⟨*Eisenbahnstrecke*⟩; **c)** *(fig.)* elektrisieren

electro- [ɪlektrəʊ] *in comb.* elektro-/Elektro-

electro'cardiogram *n.* Elektrokardiogramm, *das*

electro'chemical *adj.* elektrochemisch

electrocon'vulsive *adj.* Elektrokrampf-; **~ shock/treatment** *or* **therapy** Elektroschock, *der*/Elektroschockbehandlung, *die*

electrocute [ɪ'lektrəkju:t] *v.t.* durch Stromschlag töten

electrocution [ɪlektrə'kju:ʃn] *n.* **a)** *(execution)* Hinrichtung auf dem elektrischen Stuhl; **b)** *(death)* Tod durch Stromschlag

electrode [ɪ'lektrəʊd] *n.* Elektrode, *die*

electrolyse [ɪ'lektrəlaɪz] *v.t.* **a)** *(Chem.)* elektrolysieren; **b)** *(Med.)* elektroresezieren

electrolysis [ɪlek'trɒlɪsɪs, elek'trɒlɪsɪs] *n., pl.* **electrolyses** [ɪlek'trɒlɪsi:z, elek'trɒlɪsi:z] **a)** *(Chem.)* Elektrolyse, *die;* **b)** *(Med.)* Elektroresektion, *die*

electrolyte [ɪ'lektrəlaɪt] *n.* Elektrolyt, *der*

electrolytic [ɪlektrə'lɪtɪk] *adj. (Chem.)* elektrolytisch

electrolyze *(Amer.) see* **electrolyse**

electro'magnet *n.* Elektromagnet, *der*

electromag'netic *adj.* elektromagnetisch

electro'magnetism *n.* Elektromagnetismus, *der*

electron [ɪ'lektrɒn] *n.* Elektron, *das*

electron: ~ 'beam *n.* Elektronenstrahl, *der;* **~ 'gun** *n.* Elektronenkanone, *die*

electronic [ɪlek'trɒnɪk, elek'trɒnɪk] *adj.* elektronisch; Elektronen⟨*uhr, -orgel*⟩

electronic: ~ 'brain *n. (coll.)* Elektronen[ge]hirn, *das (ugs.);* **~ com'puter** *n.* Computer, *der;* Elektronenrechner, *der;* **~ 'flash** *n.* Elektronenblitz, *der;* **~ mail** *n.* elektronische Post

electronics [ɪlek'trɒnɪks, elek'trɒnɪks] *n., no pl.* Elektronik, *die*

electron: ~ 'microscope *n.* Elektronenmikroskop, *das;* **~ 'optics** *n.* Elektronenoptik, *die*

e'lectroplate *v.t.* galvanisieren

electro'static *adj.* elektrostatisch

elegance ['elɪgəns] *n., no pl.* Eleganz, *die; (of life-style)* Kultiviertheit, *die*

elegant ['elɪgənt] *adj.* elegant; kultiviert ⟨*Lebensstil*⟩

elegantly ['elɪgəntlɪ] *adv.* elegant

elegiac [elɪ'dʒaɪək] **1.** *adj.* elegisch. **2.** *n. in pl.* elegische Verse

elegy ['elɪdʒɪ] *n.* Elegie, *die*

element ['elɪmənt] *n.* **a)** *(component part)* Element, *das;* **a novel with a strong ~ of religion** ein Roman mit einem stark religiösen Element; **have all the ~s of a real scandal** alle Voraussetzungen für einen richtigen Skandal tragen; **an ~ of truth** ein Körnchen Wahrheit; **an ~ of chance/danger in sth.** eine gewisse Zufälligkeit/Gefahr bei etw.; **when reduced to its ~s** im Grunde [genommen]; **b)** *(Chem.)* Element, *das;* Grundstoff, *der;* **c)** *in pl. (atmospheric agencies)* Elemente *Pl.*; **d)** *(Philos.)* **the four ~s** die vier Elemente; **be in one's ~** *(fig.)* in seinem Element sein; **be out of one's ~** *(fig.)* sich fehl am Platz fühlen; **e)** *(Electr.) (wire)* Heizelement, *das; (electrode)* Elektrode, *die;* **f)** *in pl. (rudiments of learning)* Grundlagen *Pl.*; Elemente *Pl.*; **g)** *in pl. (Relig.)* Brot und Wein; **h)** *(Math., Logic)* Element, *das*

elemental [elɪ'mentl] *adj.* **a)** *(of the four elements)* urgewaltig; elementar; **b)** Natur⟨*gottheit, -religion*⟩; Elementar⟨*geist*⟩; **c)** *(fig.)* elementar; natürlich ⟨*Größe*⟩; urwüchsig, ursprünglich ⟨*Leben, Phantasie*⟩; **d)** *(essential)* grundlegend

elementary [elɪ'mentərɪ] *adj.* **a)** elementar; grundlegend ⟨*Fakten, Wissen*⟩; schlicht ⟨*Fabel, Stil*⟩; Grundschul⟨*lehrer, -bildung*⟩; Grund⟨*stufe, -kurs, -ausbildung, -rechnen, -kenntnisse*⟩; Ausgangs⟨*text, -thema*⟩; Anfangs⟨*stadium*⟩; **course in ~ German** Grundkurs in Deutsch; **my knowledge is ~:** ich habe nur Anfängerkenntnisse; **be still in its ~ stages** noch in den Anfängen stecken; **an ~ mistake** ein grober Fehler; **b)** *(Chem.)* elementar; Elementar-

elementary: ~ 'particle *n. (Phys.)* Elementarteilchen, *das;* **~ school** *n.* Grundschule, *die*

elephant ['elɪfənt] *n.* Elefant, *der;* **see pink ~s** weiße Mäuse sehen; **white ~** *(fig.)* nutzloser Besitz; *(costly thing)* ≈ Faß ohne Boden *(fig.)*; **a white ~ stall** *eine Bude, an der Sachen angeboten werden, die deren ehemalige Besitzer gern loswerden wollen*

elephantine [elɪ'fæntaɪn] *adj.* **a)** *(of elephants)* Elefanten-; **b)** *(huge)* massig ⟨*Körper, Mensch, Ringer, Boxer*⟩; gigantisch ⟨*Masse*⟩; **c)** *(clumsy)* schwerfällig

elevate ['elɪveɪt] *v.t.* **a)** *(bring higher)* erhöhen ⟨*Temperatur*⟩; aufschütten ⟨*Boden*⟩; [empor]heben ⟨*Gerät, Gegenstand*⟩; *(fig.)* aufwerten ⟨*Stellung*⟩ (**into** zu); **b)** *(Eccl.)* emporheben, zeigen ⟨*Hostie*⟩; **c)** *(raise)* heben ⟨*Stimme, Blick*⟩; aufrichten ⟨*Blick, Geschützrohr*⟩; auf einer Hochtrasse führen ⟨*Bahn*⟩; **d)** *(in rank)* befördern; **~ sb. to top management/a professorship/the peerage** jmdn. in die Unternehmensspitze berufen/auf einen Lehrstuhl berufen/in den Adelsstand erheben; **e)** *(morally, intellectually)* erbauen ⟨*Geist, Person*⟩; aufrichten ⟨*Mut*⟩; erheben ⟨*Seele, Gemüt*⟩

elevated ['elɪveɪtɪd] *adj.* **a)** *(raised)* gehoben ⟨*Stellung*⟩; erhöht ⟨*Lage, Plazierung*⟩; hochgelegen ⟨*Land*⟩; aufgeschüttet ⟨*Damm, Straße*⟩; erhoben ⟨*Stimme, Blick, Bein, Arm*⟩; **keep one's arm in an ~ position** den Arm erhoben halten; **b)** *(above ground level)* Hoch⟨*bahn, -straße*⟩; **c)** *(noble, refined)* erhaben; edel; **feel ~:** sich aufgerichtet fühlen; **d)** *(formal, dignified)* gehoben ⟨*Stil, Rede, Wortwahl*⟩

elevation [elɪ'veɪʃn] *n.* **a)** *(position of house, building, land)* erhöhte Lage; **b)** *(Eccl.: of the Host)* Elevation, *die;* **c)** *(of temperature)* Ansteigen, *das;* Anstieg, *der;* **d)** *(of voice)* Heben, *das;* Hebung, *die;* **e)** *(in rank)* Beförderung, *die; (to the peerage)* Erhebung, *die; (to top management, professorship)* Berufung, *die;* **f)** *(of mind, thought)* Erhebung, *die; (state)* Erhabenheit, *die;* **the ~ of his style** sein gehobener Stil; **g)** *(height)* Höhe, *die;* **~ of the ground** Bodenerhebung *od.* Anhöhe *die;* **h)** *(angle)* Elevation, *die;* **angle of ~:** Elevationswinkel, *der;* Erhöhungswinkel, *der;* **i)** *(drawing, diagram)* Aufriß, *der*

elevator ['elɪveɪtə(r)] *n.* **a)** *(machine)* Förderwerk, *das;* Elevator, *der;* **b)** *(storehouse)* Getreidesilo, *der od. das;* **c)** *(Amer.) see* **lift 3b**; **d)** *(Aeron.)* Höhenruder, *das*

eleven [ɪ'levn] **1.** *adj.* elf; *see also* **eight 1. 2.** *n. (number, symbol; also Sport)* Elf, *die; see also* **eight 2a, d**

eleven-'plus *n. (Brit. Educ. Hist.)* ~ [**examination**] *Prüfung der elf- bis zwölfjährigen Schüler [vor Fortsetzung der schulischen Laufbahn an höherer Schule]*

elevens [ɪ'levnz], **elevenses** [ɪ'levnzɪz] *n. sing. or pl. (Brit. coll.)* ≈ zweites Frühstück [gegen elf Uhr]

eleventh [ɪ'levnθ] **1.** *adj.* elft...; **at the ~ hour** im letzten Augenblick; in letzter Minute; **an ~-hour change of plan** eine Planungsänderung in letzter Minute; *see also* **eighth 1. 2.** *n. (fraction)* Elftel, *das; see also* **eighth 2**

elf [elf] *n., pl.* **elves** [elvz] **a)** *(Mythol.)* Elf, *der*/Elfe, *die;* **b)** *(mischievous creature)* [boshafter] Schelm; Kobold, *der*

elfin ['elfɪn] *adj.* elfenhaft

elfish ['elfɪʃ] *adj.* elfenhaft; *(mischievous)* schalkhaft; koboldhaft

elicit [ɪ'lɪsɪt] *v.t.* entlocken ⟨*Antwort, Auskunft, Wahrheit, Geheimnis*⟩ (**from** *Dat.*); hervorrufen ⟨*Begeisterung, Zustimmung*⟩; gewinnen ⟨*Unterstützung*⟩ (**amongst** bei); **the discussion has ~ed some important facts** die Diskussion brachte einige interessante Einzelheiten ans Tageslicht

elide [ɪ'laɪd] *v.t. (Ling.)* elidieren *(fachspr.)*; auslassen

eligibility [elɪdʒɪ'bɪlɪtɪ] *n., no pl. (fitness)* Qualifikation, *die; (for a job)* Eignung, *die; (entitlement)* Berechtigung, *die* (**for** zu)

eligible ['elɪdʒɪbl] *adj.* **a) be ~ for sth.** *(fit)* für etw. qualifiziert *od.* geeignet sein; *(entitled)* zu etw. berechtigt sein; **be ~ for membership/a pension/an office** mitglieds-/pensionsberechtigt sein/für ein Amt in Frage kommen; **be ~ to do sth.** etw. tun dürfen; **become ~ to vote** das Wahlrecht erhalten; **b)** *(marriageable)* begehrt ‹*Junggeselle*›
eliminate [ɪ'lɪmɪneɪt] *v. t.* **a)** *(remove)* beseitigen ‹*Zweifel, Fehler*›; ausschließen ‹*Möglichkeit*›; eliminieren, beseitigen ‹*Gegner*›; **b)** *(exclude)* ausschließen; *(Sport)* aus dem Wettbewerb werfen; **the team was ~d at the end of the third round** die Mannschaft schied nach der dritten Runde aus; **c)** *(Physiol.)* ausscheiden
elimination [ɪlɪmɪ'neɪʃn] *n.* **a)** *(removal) (of doubt, error)* Beseitigung, *die; (of opponent)* Eliminierung, *die;* Beseitigung, *die;* **process of ~:** Ausleseverfahren, *das;* **b)** *(exclusion)* Ausschluß, *der; (Sport)* Ausscheiden, *das;* **c)** *(Physiol.)* Ausscheidung, *die*
elision [ɪ'lɪʒn] *n. (Ling.)* Elision, *die (fachspr.);* Auslassung, *die*
élite [eɪ'li:t] *n. (the best)* Elite, *die; (of society, club)* Spitze, *die;* Crème, *die; (group, class)* Elite, *die;* **the ~** *(high society)* die oberen Zehntausend *(ugs.)*
élitism [eɪ'li:tɪzm] *n.* Elitedenken, *das*
élitist [eɪ'li:tɪst] **1.** *adj.* elitär; Elite‹*denken*›. **2.** *n.* Anhänger/Anhängerin des Elitedenkens; elitär Denkender/Denkende
elixir [ɪ'lɪksə(r)] *n.* Heilmittel, *das;* **~ [of life]** [Lebens]elixier, *das*
Elizabeth [ɪ'lɪzəbəθ] *pr. n. (Hist., as name of ruler etc.)* Elisabeth
Elizabethan [ɪlɪzə'bi:θn] **1.** *adj.* elisabethanisch. **2.** *n.* elisabethanischer Zeitgenosse
elk [elk] *n., pl.* **~s** *or same* **a)** *(deer)* Elch, *der;* **b)** *(moose)* Riesenelch, *der*
'elk-hound *n.* Jämthund, *der*
¹ellipse [ɪ'lɪps] *n. (Math.)* Ellipse, *die*
ellipsis [ɪ'lɪpsɪs] **(²ellipse)** *n., pl.* **ellipses** [ɪ'lɪpsi:z] **a)** *(Ling., Lit.)* Ellipse, *die;* **b)** *(set of dots etc.)* Auslassungszeichen *Pl.*
elliptic [ɪ'lɪptɪk], **elliptical** [ɪ'lɪptɪkl] *adj.* **a)** *(of ellipses; also Ling.)* elliptisch; Ellipsen‹*bogen, -bahn*›; **b)** *(Lit.)* kryptisch *(geh.);* **c)** *(brief, concise)* komprimiert; knapp
elliptically [ɪ'lɪptɪkəlɪ] *adv. (Ling., Lit.)* in elliptischen Sätzen
elm [elm] *n.* Ulme, *die*
'elmwood *n.* Ulmen- *od.* Rüsternholz, *das*
elocution [elə'kju:ʃn] *n.* **a)** *no pl. (art)* Sprechkunst, *die;* Vortragskunst, *die;* **teacher of ~:** Sprecherzieher, *der*/-erzieherin, *die;* **give lessons in ~** Sprechunterricht geben; **b)** *(style of speaking)* Redeweise, *die;* Diktion, *die*
elocutionary [elə'kju:ʃənərɪ] *adj.* deklamatorisch ‹*Sprechweise, Fertigkeit, Effekt*›
elocutionist [elə'kju:ʃənɪst] *n.* Vortragskünstler, *der*/-künstlerin, *die*
elongate ['i:lɒŋgeɪt] *v. t.* länger werden lassen ‹*Schatten*›; strecken ‹*Körper*›; recken ‹*Hals*›
elongated ['i:lɒŋgeɪtɪd] *adj.* langgestreckt ‹*Gestalt, Gliedmaße*›; langgereckt ‹*Hals*›
elongation [i:lɒŋ'geɪʃn] *n.* Verlängerung, *die; (of limbs, neck)* [Aus]recken, *das; (of forms, shapes)* Strecken, *das*
elope [ɪ'ləʊp] *v. i.* weglaufen; durchbrennen *(ugs.)*
elopement [ɪ'ləʊpmənt] *n.* Weglaufen, *das;* Durchbrennen, *das (ugs.)*
eloquence ['eləkwəns] *n.* Beredtheit, *die;* Eloquenz, *die (geh.);* **he is a man of great ~:** er ist ein sehr beredter Mann
eloquent ['eləkwənt] *adj.* **a)** eloquent *(geh.);* gewandt ‹*Sprechweise, Ausdruck, Stil, Redner*›; beredt ‹*Person*›; **b)** *(fig.)* beredt ‹*Blick, Schweigen*›
eloquently ['eləkwəntlɪ] *adv.* **a)** gewandt ‹*sprechen, schreiben, sich ausdrücken, formulieren*›; **b)** *(fig.)* beredt ‹*schauen*›
else [els] *adv.* **a)** *(besides, in addition)* sonst [noch]; **anybody/anything ~?** sonst noch jemand/etwas?; **don't mention it to anybody ~:** erwähnen Sie es gegenüber niemandem sonst; **somebody/something ~:** [noch] jemand anders/noch etwas; **everybody/everything ~:** alle anderen/alles andere; **nobody ~:** niemand sonst; sonst niemand; **nothing ~:** sonst *od.* weiter nichts; **will there be anything ~, sir?** *(asked by salesperson)* darf es sonst noch etwas sein[, der Herr]?; *(asked by butler)* haben Sie sonst noch einen Wunsch, Herr ...?; **nothing ~, thank you** das ist alles, danke; **that is something ~ again** das ist wieder etwas anderes; **be something ~** *(Amer. coll.: very good)* schon was besonderes sein *(ugs.);* **anywhere ~?** anderswo? *(ugs.);* woanders?; **not anywhere ~:** sonst nirgendwo; **somewhere ~:** anderswo *(ugs.);* woanders; **go somewhere ~:** anderswohin *(ugs.) od.* woandershin gehen; **everywhere ~:** auch sonst überall; **go everywhere ~:** sonst überallhin gehen; **nowhere ~:** sonst nirgendwo; **go nowhere ~:** sonst nirgendwohin gehen; **little ~:** kaum noch etwas; nur noch wenig; **much ~:** [noch] vieles andere *od.* mehr; **not much ~:** nicht mehr viel; nur noch wenig; **who/what/when/how ~?** wer/was/wann/wie sonst noch?; **where ~?** wo/wohin sonst noch?; **why ~?** warum sonst?; **b)** *(instead)* ander...; **sb. ~'s hat** der Hut von jmd. anders *od.* jmd. anderem *(ugs.);* **anybody/anything ~?** [irgend] jemand anders/etwas anderes?; **anyone ~ but Joe would have realized that** jeder [andere] außer Joe hätte das bemerkt; **somebody/something ~:** jemand anders/etwas anderes; **everybody/everything ~:** alle anderen/alles andere; **nobody/nothing ~:** niemand anders/nichts anderes; **no one ~ but he** nur er; niemand außer ihm; **nothing ~ but the best** nur das Beste; **there's nothing ~ for it** es hilft nichts; **anywhere ~?** anderswo? *(ugs.);* woanders?; **somewhere ~:** anderswo *(ugs.);* woanders; **go somewhere ~:** woandershin gehen; **his mind was/his thoughts were somewhere ~:** im Geist/mit seinen Gedanken war er woanders; **everywhere ~:** überall anders; überall sonst; **nowhere ~** nirgendwo sonst; **go nowhere ~:** nirgendwo sonst hingehen; **there's not much ~ we can do but ...:** wir können kaum etwas anderes tun, als ...; **who ~ [but]?** wer anders [als]?; **it was John – who ~?** es war John – wer [denn] sonst? **what ~ can I do?** was kann ich anderes machen?; **why ~ would I have done it?** warum hätte ich es sonst getan?; **when/where ~ can we meet?** wann/wo können wir uns statt dessen treffen?; **where ~ could we go?** wohin könnten wir statt dessen gehen?; **how ~ would you do it?** wie würden Sie es anders *od.* sonst machen?; **c)** *(otherwise)* sonst; anderenfalls; **or ~:** oder aber; **do it or ~ ...!** tun Sie es, sonst ...!; **do it or ~!** *(coll.)* tu es gefälligst!
'elsewhere *adv.* woanders; **go ~** woandershin gehen; **his mind was/his thoughts were ~:** im Geist/mit seinen Gedanken war er woanders
elucidate [ɪ'lju:sɪdeɪt, ɪ'lu:sɪdeɪt] *v. t.* erläutern; aufklären ‹*Geheimnis*›
elucidation [ɪlju:sɪ'deɪʃn, ɪlu:sɪ'deɪʃn] *n.* Erläuterung, *die; (of mystery)* Aufklärung, *die*
elude [ɪ'lju:d, ɪ'lu:d] *v. t.* sich entziehen (+ *Dat.*); mißachten ‹*Befehl, Gesetz, Forderung*›; umgehen ‹*Verpflichtung*›; *(avoid)* ausweichen (+ *Dat.*) ‹*Person, Schlag, Angriff, Blick, Frage, Gefahr*›; *(escape from)* entkommen (+ *Dat.*); **the causes of this disease have so far ~d medical science** die Mediziner konnten die Ursachen dieser Krankheit noch nicht herausfinden; **~ the police** sich dem Zugriff der Polizei entziehen; **sleep ~s me** der Schlaf flieht mich *(veralt. geh.);* ich kann keinen Schlaf finden; **the name ~s me at the moment** der Name ist mir im Moment entfallen *od.* fällt mir im Moment nicht ein; **the significance of his remark ~s me** die Bedeutung seiner Bemerkung ist mir nicht klar
elusive [ɪ'lju:sɪv, ɪ'lu:sɪv] *adj.* **a)** *(avoiding grasp or pursuit)* schwer zu erreichen ‹*Person*›; schwer zu fassen ‹*Straftäter*›; scheu ‹*Fuchs, Waldbewohner*›; **I have phoned every day but she has been very ~:** ich habe jeden Tag angerufen, aber sie ist sehr schwer zu erreichen; **b)** *(incapable of being prolonged)* flüchtig ‹*Freude, Glück*›; **c)** *(tending to escape from memory)* schwer zu behaltend; *(präd.)* schwer zu behalten ‹*Gedanke, Wort*›; **~ memory** schwache Erinnerung; **d)** *(avoiding definition)* schwer definierbar ‹*Begriff, Sinn*›; **e)** *(hard to pin down or identify)* schwer zu bestimmend, *(präd.)* schwer zu bestimmen ‹*Geruch*›; schwer durchschaubar ‹*Mensch*›; **f)** *(evasive)* ausweichend ‹*Antwort*›
elver ['elvə(r)] *n. (Zool.)* Glasaal, *der*
elves *pl. of* **elf**
elvish ['elvɪʃ] *see* **elfish**
Elysium [ɪ'lɪzɪəm] *n.* **a)** *(Greek Mythol.)* Elysium, *das;* **b)** *(fig.: place of ideal happiness)* Paradies, *das;* Elysium, *das (dichter.)*
em [em] *n. (Printing)* Cicero, *das*
'em [əm] *pron. (coll.)* se *(Akk.) (ugs.);* ihnen *(Dat.)*
emaciated [ɪ'meɪsɪeɪtɪd, ɪ'meɪʃɪeɪtɪd] *adj.* ausgemergelt; abgezehrt; **become ~:** abmagern
emaciation [ɪmeɪsɪ'eɪʃn] *n., no pl.* Ausmergelung, *die;* Abzehrung, *die*
e-mail *abbr.* **electronic mail**
emanate ['eməneɪt] *v. i.* **a)** *(originate)* ausgehen **(from** von); **b)** *(proceed, issue)* ausgestrahlt werden **(from** von); ausstrahlen; **c)** *(formal: be sent out)* ‹*Befehle:*› erteilt *od.* erlassen werden; ‹*Briefe, Urkunden:*› ausgestellt *od.* ausgefertigt werden
emanation [emə'neɪʃn] *n.* **a)** *(Theol.)* Emanation, *die* **(from** aus); **b)** *no pl. (issuing)* Ausstrahlen, *das;* **c)** *(sth. proceeding from source)* Ausströmung, *die;* **d)** *(fig.)* Ausfluß, *der;* **be an ~ of** *or* **from sth.** von etw. ausgehen; **~ of grace/love from God** Ausgehen von Gnade/Liebe von Gott
emancipate [ɪ'mænsɪpeɪt] *v. t.* emanzipieren; unabhängig machen; **~ sb. from slavery** jmdn. aus der Sklaverei befreien; **~ oneself from sth./sb.** sich von etw. emanzipieren *od.* frei machen/sich von jmdm. frei machen
emancipated [ɪ'mænsɪpeɪtɪd] *adj.* emanzipiert ‹*Frau, Vorstellung, Einstellung*›; **become ~:** sich emanzipieren; **~ slave** freigelassener Sklave
emancipation [ɪmænsɪ'peɪʃn] *n.* Emanzipation, *die; (of slave)* Freilassung, *die;* **~ from servitude/superstition** Befreiung aus der Knechtschaft/vom Aberglauben
emasculate [ɪ'mæskjʊleɪt] *v. t.* **a)** *(Med.: castrate)* entmannen; emaskulieren *(fachspr.);* kastrieren ‹*Tier*›; **b)** *(weaken)* schwächen; kastrieren *(ugs. scherzh.);* verwässern ‹*Plan, Vorschlag, Gesetzentwurf*›
emasculation [ɪmæskjʊ'leɪʃn] *n.* **a)** *(Med.: castration)* Entmannung, *die;* Emaskulation, *die (fachspr.); (of animal)* Kastration, *die;* **b)** *(weakening)* Schwächung, *die;* Kastration, *die; (of plan, proposal)* Verwässerung, *die*
embalm [ɪm'bɑ:m] *v. t.* einbalsamieren
embankment [ɪm'bæŋkmənt] *n.* Damm, *der;* **~ of a river** Uferdamm, *der;* **~ of earth/stone** Erd-/Steindamm, *der;* **~ of a road** Straßendamm, *der;* Böschung, *die;* **~ of a track/railway** Bahndamm, *der;* **the Thames E~** die Themse-Uferstraße *(in London)*
embargo [em'bɑ:gəʊ, ɪm'bɑ:gəʊ] **1.** *n., pl.* **~es a)** Embargo, *das;* **be under an ~:** mit

einem Embargo belegt sein; **put** *or* **lay an ~ on sth., place** *or* **lay sth. under an ~:** etw. mit einem Embargo belegen; **lift** *or* **raise** *or* **remove an ~ [from sth.]** ein Embargo [für etw.] aufheben; **b)** *(impediment)* Stopp, *der;* **~ on new appointments** Einstellungsstopp, *der;* Einstellungssperre, *die;* **~ on further spending** Ausgabenstopp, *der.* **2.** *v. t.* mit einem Embargo belegen

embark [ɪm'bɑ:k] **1.** *v. t.* einschiffen ‹*Passagiere, Waren*›. **2.** *v. i.* **a)** sich einschiffen (**for** nach); **the troops ~ed at night** die Truppen wurden nachts eingeschifft; **b)** *(engage)* **~ [up]on sth.** etw. in Angriff nehmen; **~ [up]on a war** einen Krieg anfangen *od.* beginnen

embarkation [embɑ:'keɪʃn] *n.* Einschiffung, *die;* **port of ~:** Einschiffungshafen, *der;* **~ leave** Einschiffungsurlaub, *der*

embarrass [ɪm'bærəs] *v. t.* **a)** *(make feel awkward)* in Verlegenheit bringen; **become seriously ~ed** in ernste Verlegenheit kommen; **be ~ed by lack of money** in Geldverlegenheit sein; **b)** *(arch.: encumber)* behindern

embarrassed [ɪm'bærəst] *adj.* verlegen ‹*Person, Blick, Lächeln, Benehmen, Schweigen*›; **be** *or* **feel/look/get ~:** verlegen sein/aussehen/werden; **now don't be ~!** geniere dich nicht!; **make sb. feel ~:** jmdn. verlegen machen

embarrassing [ɪm'bærəsɪŋ] *adj.* peinlich ‹*Benehmen, Schweigen, Situation, Augenblick, Frage, Thema*›; beschämend ‹*Großzügigkeit*›; verwirrend ‹*Auswahl*›; **~ person** jmd., der andere blamiert; **I find it very ~ to have to say this, but ...:** es ist mir sehr peinlich, so etwas sagen zu müssen, aber ...

embarrassingly [ɪm'bærəsɪŋlɪ] *adv.* peinlich; irritierend ‹*freimütig*›; unerhört ‹*grob*›; beschämend ‹*großzügig*›

embarrassment [ɪm'bærəsmənt] *n.* Verlegenheit, *die;* *(instance)* Peinlichkeit, *die;* **much to his ~:** zu seiner großen Verlegenheit; **cause sb. ~:** jmdn. verlegen machen; **cause sb. a great deal of ~:** jmdn. in große Verlegenheit bringen; **he was a source of ~ to his family** seine Familie mußte sich seinetwegen schämen; **financial ~[s]** Geldverlegenheit, *die;* **~ of riches** verwirrende [Über]fülle

embassy ['embəsɪ] *n.* Botschaft, *die*

embattled [ɪm'bætld] *adj.* kampfbereit ‹*Armee*›; befestigt ‹*Turm, Wall, Gebäude*›

embed [ɪm'bed] *v. t.*, **-dd- a)** *(fix)* einlassen; **stones ~ded in rock** in Fels eingelagerte Steine; **a brick firmly ~ded in mortar** ein fest in Mörtel gefügter Ziegelstein; **~ sth. in cement/concrete** etw. einzementieren/einbetonieren; **the bullet ~ded itself in the ground** die Kugel bohrte sich in den Boden; **~ded in the mud** im Schlamm versunken; **~ded sentences** *(Ling.)* eingeschobene Sätze; **b)** *(fig.)* **be firmly ~ded in sth.** fest in etw. *(Dat.)* verankert sein

embellish [ɪm'belɪʃ] *v. t.* **a)** *(beautify)* schmücken; beschönigen ‹*Wahrheit*›; **b)** ausschmücken ‹*Geschichte, Bericht*›

embellishment [ɪm'belɪʃmənt] *n.* **a)** *no pl.* *(ornamentation) (of church, room)* Verschönerung, *die; (of story)* Ausschmückung, *die; (of truth)* Beschönigung, *die;* **b)** *(sth. that embellishes)* Verzierung, *die; (in narrative)* Mittel der Ausschmückung; **c)** *(Mus.)* Verzierung, *die;* Ornament, *das (fachspr.)*

ember ['embə(r)] *n., usu. in pl. (lit. or fig.)* Glut, *die;* **dying ~s** verlöschende Glut; *see also* **'fan 2**

'ember day *n. (Eccl.)* Quatember, *der*

embezzle [ɪm'bezl] *v. t.* unterschlagen; veruntreuen

embezzlement [ɪm'bezlmənt] *n.* Unterschlagung, *die;* Veruntreuung, *die*

embitter [ɪm'bɪtə(r)] *v. t.* verschlimmern; verschärfen ‹*Kampf*›; verschlechtern, trüben ‹*Beziehungen*›; verbittern ‹*Person*›

emblazon [ɪm'bleɪzn] *v. t.* **a)** *(Her.)* verzieren; blasonieren *(fachspr.);* **b)** *(mark boldly)* **the book-covers were ~ed with his name** sein Name prangte auf den Umschlägen

emblem ['embləm] *n.* **a)** *(Her.)* Wappenbild, *das;* **b)** *(symbol)* Emblem, *das;* Wahrzeichen, *das; (on national flag etc.)* Hoheitszeichen, *das;* **~ of peace** Friedenssymbol, *das*

emblematic [emblɪ'mætɪk], **emblematical** [emblɪ'mætɪkl] *adj.* emblematisch; sinnbildlich; **be ~ of sth.** das Sinnbild einer Sache *(Gen.)* sein

embodiment [ɪm'bɒdɪmənt] *n.* **a)** *(act, state)* Verkörperung, *die;* **b)** *(incarnation)* Inbegriff, *der;* **c)** *(incorporation)* Eingliederung, *die;* Integration, *die (geh.)*

embody [ɪm'bɒdɪ] *v. t.* **a)** *(express tangibly)* Ausdruck verleihen (+ *Dat.*); **his ideas are embodied in this letter** seine Vorstellungen kommen in diesem Brief zum Ausdruck *od.* erhalten in diesem Brief Form und Gestalt; **b)** *(give concrete form to)* verkörpern ‹*Vorstellungen, Gefühle, Ideale*›; **c)** *(be incarnation of)* personifizieren; verkörpern; der Inbegriff (+ *Gen.*) sein; **d)** *(include)* enthalten

embolden [ɪm'bəʊldn] *v. t.* ermutigen; **~ sb. to do sth.** jmdn. [dazu] ermutigen, etw. zu tun

embolism ['embəlɪzm] *n. (Med.)* Embolie, *die*

emboss [ɪm'bɒs] *v. t.* prägen ‹*Metall, Papier, Leder usw.*›; *(with heat)* gaufrieren ‹*Papier, Gewebe usw.*›; **an ~ed design** ein erhabenes Muster; **~ed notepaper** geprägtes Briefpapier; **~ed stamp** im Prägedruck hergestellte Brief-/Wertmarke

embrace [ɪm'breɪs] **1.** *v. t.* **a)** *(hold in arms)* umarmen; **they ~d [each other]** sie umarmten sich *od.* *(geh.)* einander; **b)** *(fig.: surround)* umgeben; **c)** *(accept)* wahrnehmen, ergreifen ‹*Gelegenheit*›; annehmen ‹*Angebot*›; **d)** *(adopt)* annehmen; **~ a cause** eine Sache zu seiner eigenen machen; **~ Catholicism** sich zum Katholizismus bekennen; **e)** *(include)* umfassen. **2.** *n.* Umarmung, *die;* **he held her to him in a close ~:** er hielt sie eng umschlungen

embrasure [ɪm'breɪʒə(r)] *n.* **a)** *(of door, window)* [abgeschrägte] Laibung; **b)** *(in parapet)* Schießscharte, *die*

embrocation [embrə'keɪʃn] *n.* Einreibemittel, *das;* Liniment, *das (fachspr.)*

embroider [ɪm'brɔɪdə(r)] *v. t.* sticken ‹*Blumen, Muster*›; besticken ‹*Tuch, Kleid*›; *(fig.)* ausschmücken ‹*Erzählung, Wahrheit*›

embroiderer [ɪm'brɔɪdərə(r)] *n.* Sticker, *der*/Stickerin, *die*

embroidery [ɪm'brɔɪdərɪ] *n.* **a)** Stickerei, *die;* **b)** *no pl. (embroidering)* Sticken, *das;* **c)** *(fig.: ornament)* Ausschmückungen *Pl.;* schmückendes Beiwerk

embroil [ɪm'brɔɪl] *v. t.* **~ sb. in sth.** jmdn. in etw. *(Akk.)* hineinziehen; **become/be ~ed in a war** in einen Krieg verwickelt werden/sein; **~ oneself in a dispute** sich in einen Streit einmischen

embryo ['embrɪəʊ] *n., pl.* **~s** Embryo, *der;* **in ~** *(fig.)* im Keim; in nuce *(geh.);* **the plans are as yet in ~:** die Planungen befinden sich erst im Anfangsstadium

embryology [embrɪ'ɒlədʒɪ] *n. (Biol.)* Embryologie, *die*

embryonic [embrɪ'ɒnɪk] *adj. (Biol., fig.)* Embryonal‹*entwicklung, -struktur, -zustand, -stadium*›; unausgereift ‹*Vorstellung*›; **~ membrane** Eihülle, *die;* **~ plant** Pflanzenembryo, *der;* **~ plan** Plan im Embryonalstadium

'em dash *n. (Printing)* Geviertstrich, *der*

emend [ɪ'mend] *v. t.* *(Lit.)* emendieren *(fachspr.);* berichtigen

emendation [i:men'deɪʃn] *n. (Lit.)* Emendation, *die (fachspr.);* Berichtigung, *die*

emerald ['emərəld] **1.** *n.* **a)** Smaragd, *der;* **b)** *see* **emerald green. 2.** *adj.* **a)** smaragdgrün; **b) ~ ring** Smaragdring, *der;* **c) the E~ Isle** die Grüne Insel

emerald 'green *n.* Smaragdgrün, *das*

emerge [ɪ'mɜ:dʒ] *v. i.* **a)** *(come up out of liquid, come into view, crop up)* auftauchen (**from** aus, **from behind** hinter + *Dat.*, **from beneath** *or* **under** unter + *Dat.* hervor); **the sun ~d from behind the clouds** die Sonne trat hinter den Wolken hervor; **~ from the shadow into bright daylight** aus dem Schatten ans helle Tageslicht treten *od.* kommen; **the river ~s from the mountains** der Fluß tritt aus dem Gebirge heraus; **the caterpillar ~d from the egg/as a beautiful butterfly** die Raupe schlüpfte aus dem Ei/wurde zu einem wunderschönen Schmetterling; **difficulties may ~ in this venture** bei diesem Unterfangen können sich Schwierigkeiten einstellen; **b)** *(come out, become known, arise by evolution)* hervorgehen (**from** aus); ‹*Leben:*› entstammen (**from** + *Dat.*); ‹*Wahrheit:*› an den Tag kommen; ‹*Virus usw.:*› entstehen; **it ~s that ...:** es zeigt sich *od.* stellt sich heraus, daß ...; **it ~s from this that ...:** hieraus geht hervor, daß ...; **two essential points ~d from the discussion** aus der Diskussion haben sich zwei wesentliche Punkte ergeben

emergence [ɪ'mɜ:dʒəns] *n.* **a)** *(rising out of liquid)* Auftauchen, *das;* **b)** *(coming forth)* Hervortreten, *das; (of mode, school of thought, new ideas)* Aufkommen, *das*

emergency [ɪ'mɜ:dʒənsɪ] **1.** *n.* **a)** *(serious happening)* Notfall, *der;* **in an** *or* **in case of ~:** im Notfall; **be prepared for any ~:** auf den Notfall vorbereitet sein; **[case of] ~:** *(Med.)* Notfall, *der;* **be called out on an ~:** zu einem Notfall gerufen werden; **b)** *(Polit.)* Ausnahmezustand, *der;* **declare a state of ~:** den Ausnahmezustand ausrufen *od.* erklären. **2.** *adj.* Not‹*bremse, -ruf, -ausgang, -landung*›; **~ ward** Unfallstation, *die*

emergent [ɪ'mɜ:dʒənt] *adj.* **a)** *(rising out)* aufragend ‹*Insel, Felsen, Baum*› (**from** aus); jung, sprießend ‹*Vegetation*›; **b)** jung, aufstrebend ‹*Volk*›

emeritus [ɪ'merɪtəs] *adj.* emeritiert ‹*Professor*›; **professor ~:** Professor emeritus

emery ['emərɪ] *n.* Schmirgel, *der*

emery: ~-board *n.* Schleifbrett, *das; (strip for finger-nails)* Sandblattfeile, *die;* **~-paper** *n.* Schmirgelpapier, *das*

emetic [ɪ'metɪk] *(Med.)* **1.** *adj.* emetisch *(fachspr.);* Brechreiz erregend; **be ~:** Brechreiz erregen. **2.** *n.* Emetikum, *das (fachspr.);* Brechmittel, *das*

EMF *abbr.* **electromotive force** EMK

emigrant ['emɪgrənt] **1.** *adj.* auswandernd; emigrierend; **~ birds** Zugvögel *Pl;* **the ~ population in the USA** die Einwanderer in den USA. **2.** *n.* *(person)* Auswanderer, *der*/Auswanderin, *die;* Emigrant, *der*/Emigrantin, *die; (plant)* Wanderpflanze, *die*

emigrate ['emɪgreɪt] *v. i.* auswandern, emigrieren (**to** nach, **from** aus)

emigration [emɪ'greɪʃn] *n.* Auswanderung, Emigration, *die* (**to** nach, **from** aus)

émigré ['emɪgreɪ] *n.* Emigrant, *der*/Emigrantin, *die*

eminence ['emɪnəns] *n.* **a)** *no pl. (distinguished superiority)* hohes Ansehen; **person of great ~:** bedeutender *od.* hochangesehener Mensch; **win/reach/attain ~:** hohes Ansehen erwerben/erreichen/erlangen; **rise to** *or* **reach ~:** zu hohem Ansehen gelangen; **b)** *(person)* angesehener Mensch; **c)** *(rising ground)* Erhebung, *die;* **d) E~** *(Eccl.)* Eminenz, *die*

éminence grise [eɪmi:nɑ̃s 'gri:z] *n.* graue Eminenz

eminent ['emɪnənt] *adj.* **a)** *(exalted, distinguished)* bedeutend, hochangesehen ‹*Redner, Gelehrter, Künstler*›; **~ guest** hoher

Gast; **the most ~ citizens** die angesehensten Bürger; **be ~ in one's field** eine Koryphäe auf seinem Gebiet sein; **b)** *(remarkable)* ausnehmend ⟨*Eigenschaft*⟩
eminently ['emɪnəntlɪ] *adv.* ausnehmend; vorzüglich ⟨*geeignet*⟩; überaus ⟨*erfolgreich*⟩; **~ respectable** hochangesehen
emir [e'mɪə(r)] *n.* Emir, *der*
emirate ['emɪərət] *n.* Emirat, *das*
emissary ['emɪsərɪ] *n.* Emissär, *der*/Emissärin, *die;* Abgesandte, *der/die;* **special ~:** Sonderbotschafter, *der*/-botschafterin, *die*
emission [ɪ'mɪʃn] *n.* **a)** *(giving off or out)* Aussendung, *die; (of vapour)* Ablassen, *das; (of liquid)* Ausscheidung, *die; (of sparks)* Versprühen, *das;* **~ of light/heat** Licht-/Wärmeausstrahlung, *die;* **~ of fumes** Abgasemission, *die;* **~ of smell/gas** Geruchs-/Gasausströmung, *die;* **~ of rays** Strahlenaussendung, *die;* **~ of sound** Geräuschabgabe, *die;* **~ of smoke/lava** Rauch-/Lavaausstoß, *der;* **b)** *(thing given off)* Abstrahlung, *die; (effluvium)* Ausdünstung, *die; (of semen)* Samenerguß, *der*
emit [ɪ'mɪt] *v. t.*, **-tt-** aussenden ⟨*Strahlen*⟩; ausstrahlen ⟨*Wärme, Licht*⟩; ausstoßen ⟨*Lava, Asche, Rauch, Schrei*⟩; ausscheiden ⟨*Flüssigkeit*⟩; abgeben ⟨*Geräusch*⟩; versprühen ⟨*Funken*⟩; ausströmen ⟨*Geruch, Gas*⟩; ablassen ⟨*Dampf*⟩
emolument [ɪ'mɒljʊmənt] *n., usu. in pl.* Vergütung, *die;* Bezüge *Pl.*
emotion [ɪ'məʊʃn] *n.* **a)** *(state)* Ergriffenheit, *die;* Bewegtheit, *die;* **speak with deep ~:** tief ergriffen *od.* bewegt sprechen; **charged with ~:** gefühlsgeladen; **be overcome with ~:** von Gefühl übermannt sein; **be touched with/full of ~:** ergriffen/bewegt sein; **show no ~:** keine Gefühlsregung *od.* Emotionen zeigen; **b)** *(feeling)* Gefühl, *das;* **conflicting ~s** widerstrebende Gefühle
emotional [ɪ'məʊʃənl] *adj.* **a)** *(of emotions)* emotional; Gefühls⟨*ausdruck, -leben, -erlebnis, -reaktion*⟩; Gemüts⟨*zustand, -störung*⟩; seelisch ⟨*Belastung*⟩; psychologisch ⟨*Erpressung*⟩; gefühlsgeladen ⟨*Worte, Musik, Geschichte, Film*⟩; gefühlsbetont, emotional ⟨*Verhalten*⟩; gefühlsmäßig ⟨*Einschätzung, Entscheidung*⟩; gefühlvoll ⟨*Stimme, Ton*⟩; **~ appeal** Appell an die Gefühle *od.* Emotionen; **b)** *(liable to excessive emotion)* emotiv *(geh.)*; leicht erregbar ⟨*Person*⟩; **~ character** *or* **nature** *or* **disposition** leichte Erregbarkeit; **get ~ over sth.** sich über etw. *(Akk.)* erregen
emotionalism [ɪ'məʊʃənəlɪzm] *n., no pl.* Gefühlsbetontheit, *die;* Rührseligkeit, *die (abwertend)*
emotionally [ɪ'məʊʃənəlɪ] *adv.* emotional; gefühlvoll ⟨*sprechen, sich verhalten*⟩; gefühlsmäßig, emotional ⟨*reagieren*⟩; gefühlsbetont ⟨*denken*⟩; **thank sb. ~:** [sich bei] jmdm. von Herzen [be]danken; **be ~ exhausted/worn out/disturbed** seelisch erschöpft/ausgelaugt/gestört sein; **get ~ involved with sb.** eine gefühlsmäßige Bindung mit jmdm. eingehen
emotionless [ɪ'məʊʃnlɪs] *adj.* emotionslos; emotionsfrei; gefühllos; ausdruckslos ⟨*Gesicht*⟩; gleichgültig ⟨*Stimme*⟩
emotive [ɪ'məʊtɪv] *adj.* emotional; gefühlsbetont; emotiv *(Psych., Sprachw.)*
empathy ['empəθɪ] *n.* Empathie, *die (Psych.);* Einfühlung, *die*
emperor ['empərə(r)] *n.* Kaiser, *der;* **~ penguin** Kaiserpinguin, *der*
emphasis ['emfəsɪs] *n., pl.* **emphases** ['emfəsi:z] **a)** *(in speech etc.)* Betonung, *die;* **the ~ is on ...:** die Betonung liegt auf ...; **lay** *or* **place** *or* **put ~ on sth.** etw. betonen; **b)** *(intensity)* Nachdruck, *der;* **do sth. with ~:** etw. nachdrücklich tun; **c)** *(importance attached)* Gewicht, *das;* **lay** *or* **place** *or* **put [considerable] ~ on sth.** [großes] Gewicht auf etw. *(Akk.)* legen; **the school's ~ is on languages** die Schule legt das Schwergewicht auf die [Fremd]sprachen; **the ~ has shifted** der Akzent hat sich verlagert; **with particular** *or* **special ~ on sth.** unter besonderer Berücksichtigung einer Sache *(Gen.)*
emphasize (emphasise) ['emfəsaɪz] *v. t. (lit. or fig.)* betonen; *(attach importance to)* Gewicht auf etw. *(Akk.)* legen; **sth. cannot be too strongly ~d** etw. kann nicht genug betont werden
emphatic [ɪm'fætɪk] *adj.* nachdrücklich; emphatisch *(geh.)*; eindringlich, emphatisch *(geh.)* ⟨*Redner*⟩; *(forcible)* demonstrativ ⟨*Rückzug, Ablehnung*⟩; eindringlich ⟨*Demonstration*⟩; **make sth. more ~:** einer Sache *(Dat.)* Nachdruck verleihen; **be quite ~ that ...:** durchaus darauf bestehen, daß ...
emphatically [ɪm'fætɪkəlɪ] *adv.* nachdrücklich; emphatisch *(geh.)*; eindringlich ⟨*sprechen*⟩; *(decisively)* entschieden ⟨*bestreiten usw.*⟩
emphysema [emfɪ'si:mə] *n. (Med.)* Emphysem, *das*
empire ['empaɪə(r)] **1.** *n.* **a)** Reich, *das;* **the E~** *(Hist.) (British)* das Empire; das britische Weltreich; *(Holy Roman)* das Heilige Römische Reich; **b)** *(commercial organization)* Imperium, *das (fig.)*
empire: ~-builder *n. (fig.)* **be an ~-builder** seinen Einflußbereich ausweiten wollen; **~-building** *n. (fig.)* **it is just ~-building** es geht dabei nur um den Aufbau eines kleinen Imperiums
empirical [ɪm'pɪrɪkl] *adj.* empirisch; empirisch begründet ⟨*Entscheidung, Argument, Wissen, Schlußfolgerung*⟩
empirically [ɪm'pɪrɪkəlɪ] *adv.* empirisch
empiricism [ɪm'pɪrɪsɪzm] *n., no pl.* **a)** *(method)* Empirie, *die;* **b)** *(Philos.)* Empirismus, *der*
emplacement [ɪm'pleɪsmənt] *n. (Mil.)* Geschützstand, *der*
employ [ɪm'plɔɪ] **1.** *v. t.* **a)** *(take into one's service)* einstellen; *(keep in one's service)* beschäftigen; **are you ~ed in London/as a teacher?** arbeiten Sie in London/als Lehrer?; **be ~ed by** *or* **with a company** bei einer Firma arbeiten; **b)** *(use services of)* **~ sb. in** *or* **on sth.** jmdn. für etw. einsetzen; **~ sb. in** *or* **on doing sth., ~ sb. to do sth.** jmdn. dafür einsetzen, etw. zu tun; **c)** *(use)* einsetzen **(for, in, on** für); unternehmen ⟨*Anstrengungen*⟩; anwenden ⟨*Methode, List*⟩ **(for, in, on** bei); **~ sth. to do sth.** etw. anwenden, um etwas zu tun; **~ [one's] time on sth./ [on] doing sth.** [seine] Zeit mit etw. verbringen/damit verbringen, etw. zu tun; **d)** *(busy)* **~ oneself/ sb. doing sth./in sth.** sich/jmdn. damit beschäftigen, etw. zu tun/mit etw. beschäftigen. **2.** *n., no pl., no indef. art.* Arbeit, *die;* Beschäftigung, *die;* **be in the ~ of sb.** bei jmdm. beschäftigt sein; in jmds. Diensten stehen *(veralt.)*; **the firm has 500 people in its ~:** bei der Firma sind 500 Leute beschäftigt
employable [ɪm'plɔɪəbl] *adj.* **a)** *(fit to be taken into service)* **be ~:** zu beschäftigen sein; **b)** *(usable)* verwendbar; **be ~ as/for sth.** als/für etw. verwendet werden können
employee *(Amer.:* **employe)** [emplɔɪ'i:, em'plɔɪi:] *n.* Angestellte, *der/die; (in contrast to employer)* Arbeitnehmer, *der*/-nehmerin, *die;* **the firm's ~s** die Belegschaft der Firma
employer [ɪm'plɔɪə(r)] *n.* Arbeitgeber, *der*/-geberin, *die;* **the firm is only a small ~:** die Firma hat nur wenige Beschäftigte
employment [ɪm'plɔɪmənt] *n., no pl.* **a)** *(work)* Arbeit, *die;* **there's no ~ available** es gibt keine freien Stellen *od.* keine Arbeit; **be in gainful ~:** erwerbstätig sein; **be in ~ with sb.** bei jmdm. arbeiten; **be in/without regular ~:** eine/keine feste Anstellung haben; **b)** *(regular trade or profession)* Beschäftigung, *die;* **what is your ~?** welchen Beruf üben Sie aus?; **c)** *no art. (amount of work available)* **full ~:** Vollbeschäftigung, *die;* **d) Secretary for E~** *(Brit.)* Arbeitsminister, *der*/ministerin, *die*
employment: ~ agency *n.* Stellenvermittlung, *die;* **~ exchange, ~ office** *ns. (Brit.)* Arbeitsamt, *das*
emporium [em'pɔ:rɪəm] *n., pl.* **~s** *or* **emporia** [em'pɔ:rɪə] **a)** *(market)* Handelszentrum, *das;* **b)** *(shop)* Kaufhaus, *das*
empower [ɪm'paʊə(r)] *v. t. (authorize)* ermächtigen; *(enable)* befähigen
empress ['emprɪs] *n.* Kaiserin, *die*
emptiness ['emptɪnɪs] *n., no pl. (lit. or fig.)* Leere, *die*
empty ['emptɪ] **1.** *adj.* **a)** leer; **find an ~ seat/parking-place** einen freien Sitz-/Parkplatz finden; **~ of sth.** ohne etw.; **~ of people** menschenleer; **the street is ~ of traffic** in der Straße herrscht kein Verkehr; *see also* **stomach 1 a; b)** *(coll.: hungry)* **I feel a bit ~:** ich bin ein bißchen hungrig; **an hour later you feel quite ~:** eine Stunde später hat man schon wieder Hunger; **c)** *(fig.) (foolish)* dumm; hohl ⟨*Kopf*⟩; *(meaningless)* leer. **2.** *n. (vehicle)* Leerfahrzeug, *das; (bottle)* leere Flasche; *(container)* leerer Behälter. **3.** *v. t.* **a)** *(remove contents of)* leeren; [aus]leeren ⟨*Tasche*⟩; *(finish using contents of)* aufbrauchen; *(remove people from)* räumen; *(eat/drink whole contents of)* leer essen/leeren; **~ one's bladder/bowels** die Blase/den Darm entleeren; **b)** *(transfer)* umfüllen **(into** in + *Akk.*); *(pour)* schütten **(over** über + *Akk.*); **~ sth. into/down the sink** etw. in den Ausguß schütten. **4.** *v. i.* **a)** *(become ~)* sich leeren; **b)** *(discharge)* **~ into** ⟨*Fluß, Abwasserkanal:*⟩ münden in (+ *Akk.*)
empty: ~-'handed *pred. adj.* mit leeren Händen; **~-headed** *adj.* hohlköpfig *(abwertend)*
EMS *abbr.* **European Monetary System** EWS
emu ['i:mju:] *n. (Ornith.)* Emu, *der*
emulate ['emjʊleɪt] *v. t.* **a)** *(try to equal or excel)* nacheifern (+ *Dat.*); **b)** *(imitate zealously)* nachahmen
emulation [emjʊ'leɪʃn] *n.* **a)** *(attempt at equalling or excelling)* **~ of sb.** Bestreben, es jmdm. gleichzutun; **b)** *(zealous imitation)* Nachahmung, *die*
emulsifier [ɪ'mʌlsɪfaɪə(r)] *n.* Emulgator, *der*
emulsify [ɪ'mʌlsɪfaɪ] *v. t.* emulgieren
emulsion [ɪ'mʌlʃn] *n.* **a)** Emulsion, *die;* **b)** *see* **emulsion paint**
e'mulsion paint *n.* Dispersionsfarbe, *die*
en [en] *n. (Printing)* Halbgeviert, *das*
enable [ɪ'neɪbl] *v. t.* **~ sb. to do sth.** es jmdm. ermöglichen, etw. zu tun; **~ sth. [to be done]** etw. ermöglichen; **~ an investigation to be made** eine Untersuchung ermöglichen; **enabling act** *(Law)* Ermächtigungsgesetz, *das; (Amer. Law: legalizing)* gesetzliche Sonderregelung
enact [ɪ'nækt] *v. t.* **a)** *(ordain, make law)* erlassen; **~ that ...:** verfügen, daß ...; **b)** *(act out)* aufführen ⟨*Theaterstück*⟩; spielen ⟨*Rolle*⟩; mitwirken bei ⟨*Feier*⟩; **be ~ed** ⟨*Geschehen, Szene:*⟩ sich abspielen
enamel [ɪ'næml] **1.** *n.* **a)** Emaille, *die;* Email, *das; (paint)* Lack, *der; (on pottery)* Glasur, *die;* **b)** *(~ painting)* Email[le]malerei, *die;* **c)** *(Anat.)* [Zahn]schmelz, *der.* **2.** *attrib. adj.* **a)** *(containing ~)* Email[le]-; **b)** *(with ~ coating and/or design)* emailliert; Email[le]⟨*geschirr*⟩. **3.** *v. t., (Brit.)* **-ll-:** emaillieren; glasieren ⟨*Ton, Steinzeug*⟩
enamoured *(Brit.; Amer.:* **enamored)** [ɪ'næməd] *adj.* **~ of sb.** *(in love with)* in jmdn. verliebt; *(liking)* von jmdm. angetan; **[not exactly** *or* **particularly] ~ of sth.** von etw. [nicht gerade] begeistert
en bloc [ɑ̃ 'blɒk] *adv.* en bloc
encamp [ɪn'kæmp] *(Mil.)* **1.** *v. t.* **the troops**

were ~ed near the border die Truppen bezogen ein Lager nahe der Grenze. **2.** *v.i.* ein Lager aufschlagen
encampment [ɪn'kæmpmənt] *n.* **a)** *no pl.* Lagern, *das;* **b)** *(place)* Lager, *das*
encapsulate [ɪn'kæpsjʊleɪt] *v.t.* **a)** *(in capsule)* einkapseln ‹*Medikament*›; in eine[r] Kapsel einschließen; *(as in capsule)* einschließen; **b)** *(fig.)* festhalten; einfangen *(geh.)*
encase [ɪn'keɪs] *v.t.* einschließen; fassen ‹*Edelstein*›; **the watch was ~d in metal** die Armbanduhr hatte ein Metallgehäuse; **~ in plaster** eingipsen ‹*Bein, Arm*›
encash [ɪn'kæʃ] *v.t.* *(Brit.)* *(realize)* [in bar] einnehmen; sich *(Dat.)* [bar] auszahlen lassen ‹*Gewinn*›; *(convert into cash)* [bar] einlösen
encephalitis [ensefə'laɪtɪs] *n.* *(Med.)* Enzephalitis, *die (fachspr.);* Gehirnentzündung, *die*
enchant [ɪn'tʃɑ:nt] *v.t.* **a)** *(bewitch)* verzaubern; **she ~s men with her beauty** *(fig.)* sie bezaubert die Männer mit ihrer Schönheit; **b)** *(delight)* entzücken; **be ~ed by sth.** von etw. entzückt sein; **we were ~ed by the place** wir waren von dem Ort bezaubert
enchanted [ɪn'tʃɑ:ntɪd] *adj.* **a)** *(bewitched)* verzaubert; **~ forest** Zauberwald, *der;* **~ evening** *(fig.)* zauberischer Abend *(geh.);* **b)** *(delighted)* entzückt
enchanting [ɪn'tʃɑ:ntɪŋ] *adj.* **a)** zauberisch *(veralt.);* **~ power** Zauberkraft, *die;* **b)** *(delightful)* entzückend; bezaubernd
enchantingly [ɪn'tʃɑ:ntɪŋlɪ] *adv.* bezaubernd
enchantment [ɪn'tʃɑ:ntmənt] *n.* **a)** Verzauberung, *die; (fig.)* Zauber, *der;* **world of ~:** Zauberwelt, *die;* **b)** *(delight)* Entzücken, *das* **(with** über + *Akk.***)**
enchantress [ɪn'tʃɑ:ntrɪs] *n.* *(lit. or fig.)* Zauberin, *die*
encipher [ɪn'saɪfə(r)] *v.t.* verschlüsseln; chiffrieren
encircle [ɪn'sɜ:kl] *v.t.* **a)** umgeben; **the enemy ~d us** der Feind kreiste uns ein *od.* umstellte uns; **~d with** *or* **by bodyguards** von Leibwächtern umringt; **his arms ~d her waist** seine Arme umschlangen ihre Taille; **b)** *(mark with circle)* einkreisen ‹*Buchstabe, Antwort*›
encirclement [ɪn'sɜ:klmənt] *n.* *(Mil.)* Einkreisung, *die*
encl. *abbr.* enclosed a, enclosure[s] Anl.
enclave ['enkleɪv] *n.* *(lit. or fig.)* Enklave, *die*
enclitic [en'klɪtɪk] *(Ling.)* **1.** *adj.* enklitisch. **2.** *n.* Enklitikon, *das*
enclose [ɪn'kləʊz] *v.t.* **a)** *(surround)* umgeben; *(shut up or in)* einschließen; **be ~d in a cell/tomb/coffin** in einer Zelle/einem Grab/Sarg eingeschlossen sein; **~d in this casing is ...:** in diesem Gehäuse befindet sich ...; **~ land in** *or* **with barbed wire** Land mit Stacheldraht einzäunen; **b)** *(put in envelope with letter)* beilegen **(with, in** *Dat.***)**; **I [herewith] ~ the completed application form** anbei der ausgefüllte Bewerbungsbogen; **your passport is ~d herewith** Ihr Paß liegt als Anlage bei; **please find ~d, ~d please find** als Anlage übersenden wir Ihnen; anbei erhalten Sie; **a cheque for £10 is ~d** beiliegend finden Sie einen Scheck über 10 Pfund; **c)** *(Math.)* einschließen; **d)** *(Hist.: make private)* zur privaten Nutzung einfrieden
enclosed [ɪn'kləʊzd] *adj.* **a)** *(in a container)* darin enthalten; *(included with letter)* beigelegt; beigefügt; **from the ~ you will see that ...:** aus der Anlage werden Sie ersehen, daß ...; **b)** *(closed off)* eingefriedet; *(by fence)* eingezäunt
enclosure [ɪn'kləʊʒə(r)] *n.* **a)** *(action)* Einfriedung, *die; (with fence)* Einzäunung, *die;* **b)** *(place)* eingefriedeter/eingezäunter Bereich; *(in zoo)* Gehege, *das; (paddock)* Koppel, *die;* **c)** *(fence)* Umzäunung, *die; (wall etc.)* Einfriedung, *die;* **d)** *(with letter in envelope)* Anlage, *die*
encode [ɪn'kəʊd] *v.t.* verschlüsseln; chiffrieren
encomium [en'kəʊmɪəm] *n., pl.* **~s** *or* **encomia** [en'kəʊmɪə] Lobpreisung, *die (geh.);* **give sb. an ~:** jmdn. lobpreisen *(geh.)*
encompass [ɪn'kʌmpəs] *v.t.* **a)** *(encircle)* umgeben; *(surround)* umringen; **b)** *(take in)* umfassen; **c)** *(contain)* einhüllen
encore [ɒŋ'kɔ:(r), 'ɒŋkɔ:(r)] **1.** *int.* Zugabe! **2.** *n.* Zugabe, *die;* **receive three ~s** drei Zugaben geben müssen; **give an ~** ‹*Band, Orchester:*› eine Zugabe spielen. **3.** *v.t.* als Zugabe verlangen ‹*Lied, Tanz usw.*›; um eine Zugabe bitten ‹*Sänger, Tänzer, Künstler*›
encounter [ɪn'kaʊntə(r)] **1.** *v.t.* **a)** *(as adversary)* treffen auf (+ *Akk.*); **b)** *(by chance)* begegnen (+ *Dat.*); **c)** *(meet with, come across)* stoßen auf (+ *Akk.*) ‹*Problem, Schwierigkeit, Kritik, Widerstand usw.*›. **2.** *n.* **a)** *(in combat)* Zusammenstoß, *der;* **have an ~ with the authorities over a matter** mit den Behörden wegen einer Angelegenheit aneinandergeraten; **I had a slight ~ with another car yesterday** *(coll. iron.)* ich hatte gestern eine etwas heftige Begegnung mit einem anderen Auto *(iron.);* **verbal ~:** Wortgefecht, *das;* **this was not his first ~ with the law** das war nicht das erste Mal, daß er mit dem Gesetz in Konflikt kam; **b)** *(chance meeting, introduction)* Begegnung, *die;* **have a chance ~ with sb.** jmdm. zufällig begegnen
en'counter group *n.* Encountergruppe, *die (Psych.)*
encourage [ɪn'kʌrɪdʒ] *v.t.* **a)** *(stimulate, incite)* ermutigen; **bread ~s rats and mice** Brot lockt Ratten und Mäuse an; **b)** *(promote)* fördern; beleben ‹*Verkauf*›; **~ a smile/a response from sb.** jmdm. ein Lächeln/eine Reaktion entlocken; **~ bad habits** schlechte Angewohnheiten unterstützen; **we do not ~ smoking in this office** wir unterstützen es nicht, daß in diesem Büro geraucht wird; **c)** *(urge)* **~ sb. to do sth.** jmdn. dazu ermuntern, etw. zu tun; **d)** *(cheer)* **be [much] ~d by sth.** durch etw. neuen Mut schöpfen; **we were ~d to hear** *or* **felt ~d when we heard ...:** wir schöpften neuen Mut, als wir hörten ...
encouragement [ɪn'kʌrɪdʒmənt] *n.* **a)** *(support, incitement)* Ermutigung, *die* **(from** durch); **give sb. ~:** jmdn. ermutigen; **get** *or* **receive ~ from sth.** durch etw. ermutigt werden; **b)** *(urging)* Ermunterung, *die;* **c)** *(stimulus)* Ansporn, *der;* **be an ~ to rats/moths** *etc.* Ratten/Motten *usw.* anlocken
encouraging [ɪn'kʌrɪdʒɪŋ] *adj.* ermutigend; **the teacher is very ~** *(by nature)* der Lehrer hat eine sehr ermutigende Art
encouragingly [ɪn'kʌrɪdʒɪŋlɪ] *adv.* ermutigend
encroach [ɪn'krəʊtʃ] *v.i.* *(lit. or fig.)* **~ [on sth.]** [in etw. *(Akk.)*] eindringen; **the shadows began ~ing on the lawn** die Schatten drangen allmählich auf den Rasen vor; **the sea is ~ing [on the land]** das Meer dringt vor; **~ on sb.'s time** jmds. Zeit immer mehr in Anspruch nehmen
encroachment [ɪn'krəʊtʃmənt] *n.* *(lit. or fig.)* Eindringen, *das* **(on in** + *Akk.***)**; **make ~s on sb.'s time** jmds. Zeit immer mehr in Anspruch nehmen
encrust [ɪn'krʌst] *v.t.* überkrusten; **be ~ed with diamonds/beads/gold** über und über mit Diamanten/Perlen besetzt/mit Gold überzogen sein
encumber [ɪn'kʌmbə(r)] *v.t.* **a)** *(hamper)* behindern; **~ oneself/sb. with sth.** sich/jmdn. mit etw. belasten; **b)** *(burden)* **~ sb. with debt** jmdn. mit Schulden belasten
encumbrance [ɪn'kʌmbrəns] *n.* **a)** *(burden)* Last, *die; (nuisance)* Belastung, *die;* **b)** *(impediment)* Hindernis, *das* **(to** für); **be without ~** *(without family)* ohne Anhang sein; **c)** *(on property)* Belastung, *die*
encyclic [en'sɪklɪk], **encyclical** [en'sɪklɪkl] **1.** *adj.* **~ letter** Enzyklika, *die.* **2.** *n.* Enzyklika, *die*
encyclopaedia [ensaɪklə'pi:dɪə, ɪnsaɪklə'pi:dɪə] *n.* **a)** Lexikon, *das;* Enzyklopädie, *die;* **b)** *(Hist.)* **the E~:** die Enzyklopädie. *See also* **walking 1**
encyclopaedic [ensaɪklə'pi:dɪk, ɪnsaɪklə'pi:dɪk] *adj.* enzyklopädisch
encyclopedia *etc. see* **encyclopaedia** *etc.*
end [end] **1.** *n.* **a)** *(extremity, farthest point, limit)* Ende, *das; (of nose, hair, tail, branch, finger)* Spitze, *die;* **go to the ~s of the earth** bis ans Ende der Welt gehen; **that was the ~** *(coll.) (no longer tolerable)* da war Schluß *(ugs.); (very bad)* das war das Letzte *(ugs.);* **you are the ~** *(coll.)* du bist [einfach] unmöglich; **he beat him all ~s up** er hat ihn vernichtend geschlagen; **at an ~:** zu Ende; **come to an ~:** enden *(see also* **1 g**); **my patience has come to** *or* **is now at an ~:** meine Geduld ist jetzt am Ende; **our supplies have come to an ~:** unsere Vorräte sind erschöpft; **come to/be coming to the ~ of sth.** etw. aufbrauchen/fast aufgebraucht haben; **turn sth. ~ for ~:** etw. umdrehen; **look at a building/a pencil ~ on** ein Gebäude von der Schmalseite/einen Bleistift von der Spitze her betrachten; **~ on against** *or* **to sth.** mit dem Ende gegen etw.; **from ~ to ~:** von einem Ende zum anderen; **~ to ~:** längs hintereinander; **lay ~ to ~:** aneinanderreihen; **keep one's ~ up** *(fig.)* seinen Mann stehen; **make an ~ of sth.** etw. abschaffen; **make [both] ~s meet** *(fig.)* [mit seinem Geld] zurechtkommen; **no ~** *(coll.)* unendlich viel; **it's been criticized no ~:** es ist über die Maßen kritisiert worden; **have no ~ of trouble/a surprise** nichts als Ärger haben/maßlos überrascht sein; **no ~ of a fuss** ein wahnsinniges Theater *(ugs.);* **there is no ~ to sth.** *(coll.)* etw. nimmt kein Ende; **there's no ~ to what you can achieve/learn** du kannst unendlich viel erreichen/lernen; **put an ~ to sth.** einer Sache *(Dat.)* ein Ende machen; **not know** *or* **not be able to tell one ~ of sth. from the other** bei etw. nicht wissen, wo hinten und vorne ist *(ugs.);* **b)** *(of box, packet, tube, etc.)* Schmalseite, *die; (top/bottom surface)* Ober-/Unterseite, *die;* **on ~** *(upright)* hochkant; **sb.'s hair stands on ~** *(fig.)* jmdm. stehen die Haare zu Berge *(ugs.); see also* **g**; **c)** *(remnant)* Rest, *der; (of cigarette, candle)* Stummel, *der;* **tie up the/a few [loose] ~s** *(fig.)* die/ein paar Einzelheiten erledigen; **d)** *(side)* Seite, *die;* **how are things at the business/social/at your ~?** wie sieht es geschäftlich/mit den sozialen Kontakten/bei dir aus?; **be on the receiving ~ of sth.** etw. abbekommen *od.* einstecken müssen; **he was on the receiving ~ in the fight** er mußte in dem Kampf einiges einstecken; **e)** *(half of sports pitch or court)* Spielfeldhälfte, *die;* **change ~s** die Seiten wechseln; **choice of ~s** Seitenwahl, *die;* **f)** *(of swimming-pool)* **deep/shallow ~ [of the pool]** tiefer/flacher Teil [des Schwimmbeckens]; **go in/be thrown in at the deep ~** *(fig.)* ins kalte Wasser springen/geworfen werden; **go [in] off the deep ~** *(fig. coll.)* aus der Haut fahren *(ugs.);* **g)** *(conclusion, lit. or fig.)* Ende, *das; (of lesson, speech, story, discussion, meeting, argument, play, film, book, sentence)* Schluß, *der;* Ende, *das;* **the ~ is not yet** ein Ende ist noch nicht abzusehen; *(there is still hope)* es ist noch nicht aller Tage Abend; **by the ~ of the hour/day/week** *etc.* **we were exhausted** als die Stunde/der Tag/die Woche *usw.* herum war, waren wir erschöpft; **at the ~ of 1987/March** Ende 1987/März; **by the ~ of the meeting** als die Versammlung zu Ende war; **until** *or* **till the ~ of time** bis

ans Ende aller Tage; **read to the ~ of the page** die Seite zu Ende lesen; **leave before the ~ of the film** gehen, ehe der Film zu Ende ist; **that's the ~ of sth.** *(coll.: sth. is used up)* etw. ist alle *(ugs.)*; **that's the ~ of 'that** *(fig.)* damit ist die Sache erledigt; **will there never be an ~ to all this?** wird das alles nie ein Ende nehmen?; **want [to see] an ~ to sth.** das Ende einer Sache *(Gen.)* wollen; **I shall never hear the ~ of it** *(joc.)* das werde ich noch lange zu hören bekommen; **I wonder if there's an ~ to it all** ich frage mich, ob das denn gar kein Ende nimmt; **be at an ~:** zu Ende sein; **bring a meeting/discussion/lesson to an ~:** eine Versammlung/Diskussion/Unterrichtsstunde beenden; **his education/journey was brought to an abrupt ~:** seine Ausbildung/Reise fand ein plötzliches Ende; **come to an ~:** ein Ende nehmen *(see also* **1 a**); **have come to the ~ of sth.** mit etw. fertig sein; **be coming to the ~ of sth.** mit etw. fast fertig sein; **when you come to the ~ of the page** wenn Sie mit der Seite fertig sind; **in the ~:** schließlich; **on ~:** ununterbrochen; *see also* **b; h)** *(downfall, destruction)* Ende, *das; (death)* Ende, *das (geh. verhüll.)*; **meet one's ~:** den Tod finden *(geh.)*; **meet its ~** ⟨*Sache:*⟩ sein Ende finden *(fig.)*; **sb. is nearing his ~:** mit jmdm. geht es zu Ende *(verhüll.)*; **this will be the ~ of him** das bedeutet das Ende für ihn; **drink will be the ~ of him** der Alkohol wird ihn noch ins Grab bringen; **sb. comes to a bad** *or* **sticky ~:** es nimmt ein böses *od.* schlimmes Ende mit jmdm.; **i)** *(purpose, object)* Ziel, *das;* Zweck, *der;* **~ in itself** Selbstzweck, *der;* **be an ~ in itself** *(likewise a purpose)* auch ein lohnendes Ziel sein; *(the only purpose)* das eigentliche Ziel sein; **the ~ justifies the means** der Zweck heiligt die Mittel; **with this ~ in view** mit diesem Ziel vor Augen; **as a means to an ~:** als Mittel zum Zweck; **for material ~s** aus materiellen Gründen; **gain** *or* **win** *or* **achieve one's ~s** seine Ziele erreichen; **to** *or* **for this ~:** zu diesem Zweck *od. (veralt.)* Ende; **to** *or* **for what ~[s]** zu welchem Zweck *od. (veralt.)* Ende; **to no ~:** vergebens; ohne Erfolg. *See also* **bitter 1 b; East End; tether 1 b; West End; without 1 a; world a. 2.** *v. t.* **a)** *(bring to an ~)* beenden; kündigen ⟨*Abonnement*⟩; **~ one's life/days** *(spend last part of life)* sein Leben/seine Tage beschließen; **b)** *(put an ~ to, destroy)* ein Ende setzen (+ *Dat.*); **~ it [all]** *(coll.: kill oneself)* [mit dem Leben] Schluß machen *(ugs.)*; **c)** *(stand as supreme example of)* **a car/feast/race** *etc.* **to ~ all cars/feasts/races** *etc.* ein Auto/Fest/Rennen *usw.*, das alles [bisher Dagewesene] in den Schatten stellt. **3.** *v. i.* enden; **where does it all ~?** wo soll das noch hinführen?; **~ by doing sth.** schließlich etw. tun; **the project ~ed in chaos/disaster** das Vorhaben endete im Chaos/in einer Katastrophe; **the discussion ~ed in a quarrel** die Diskussion endete mit einem Streit; **the match ~ed in a draw** das Spiel ging unentschieden aus

~ 'up *v. i.* enden; **we ~ed up in a ditch** *(coll.)* wir landeten in einem Graben *(ugs.)*; **he'll ~ up in prison** *(coll.)* er wird im Gefängnis landen *(ugs.)*; **we ~ed up at his place** *(coll.)* wir landeten schließlich bei ihm zu Hause *(ugs.)*; **~ up [as] a teacher/an alcoholic** *(coll.)* schließlich Lehrer/zum Alkoholiker werden; **I always ~ up doing all the work** *(coll.)* am Ende bleibt die ganze Arbeit immer an mir hängen

'end-all *see* **be 4**

endanger [ɪn'deɪndʒə(r)] *v. t.* gefährden

endangered [ɪn'deɪndʒəd] *adj.* gefährdet; **an ~ species** eine vom Aussterben bedrohte Art

'en dash *n. (Printing)* Halbgeviertstrich, *der*

endear [ɪn'dɪə(r)] *v. t.* **~ sb./sth./oneself to sb.** jmdn./etw./sich bei jmdm. beliebt machen

endearing [ɪn'dɪərɪŋ] *adj.* reizend; gewinnend ⟨*Lächeln, Art*⟩

endearingly [ɪn'dɪərɪŋlɪ] *adv.* reizend; gewinnend ⟨*lächeln*⟩

endearment [ɪn'dɪəmənt] *n.* Zärtlichkeit, *die;* **term of ~:** Kosename, *der*

endeavour (*Brit.; Amer.:* **endeavor**) [ɪn'devə(r)] **1.** *v. i.* **~ to do sth.** sich bemühen, etw. zu tun. **2.** *n.* Bemühung, *die; (attempt)* Versuch, *der;* **~ to do sth.** Bemühen, etw. zu tun *(geh.)*; **make every ~ to do sth.** alle Anstrengungen unternehmen, um etw. zu tun; **make an ~** *or* **make ~s to do sth.** *or* **at doing sth.** sich bemühen, etw. zu tun; **despite his best ~s** obwohl er sich nach Kräften bemühte; **human ~:** das Streben des Menschen

endemic [en'demɪk] *adj. (Biol., Med.)* endemisch; einheimisch ⟨*Pflanze, Tier*⟩; örtlich begrenzt auftretend ⟨*Infektionskrankheit*⟩; *(regularly found)* verbreitet ⟨*Krankheit*⟩; [allgemein] verbreitet ⟨*Gewalt, Alkoholismus, Rastlosigkeit*⟩

endemically [en'demɪkəlɪ] *adv.* endemisch

'end-game *n.* Endspiel, *das*

ending ['endɪŋ] *n.* Schluß, *der; (of word)* Endung, *die; see also* **happy ending**

endive ['endɪv] *n.* **a)** Endivie, *die;* **b)** *(Amer.: chicory crown)* Brüsseler Endivie; Chicorée, *der od. die*

endless ['endlɪs] *adj.* **a)** endlos; *(coll.: innumerable)* unzählig; *(eternal)* unendlich; **have an ~ wait, wait an ~ time** endlos lange warten; **the journey seemed ~:** die Reise schien kein Ende zu nehmen; **b)** *(infinite)* unendlich; endlos ⟨*Straße*⟩; unbegrenzt ⟨*Auswahl*⟩; unendlich lang ⟨*Straße, Liste*⟩

endless 'cable *n.* Umlaufseil, *das*

endlessly ['endlɪslɪ] *adv.* **a)** *(incessantly)* unaufhörlich ⟨*streiten, schwatzen*⟩; *(interminably)* endlos lange ⟨*warten*⟩; **b)** *(infinitely)* endlos ⟨*sich erstrecken, lang*⟩

endmost ['endməʊst] *adj.* letzt...; **the ~ leaves on the branches** die Blätter an den Spitzen der Zweige/Äste

endocrine ['endəʊkrɪn] *adj. (Physiol.)* endokrin

endorse [ɪn'dɔ:s] *v. t.* **a)** *(write on back of)* auf der Rückseite beschriften; **~ sth. with one's signature** etw. auf der Rückseite signieren; **~ sth. on the [back of the] document** etw. auf die Rückseite des Dokuments schreiben; **b)** *(sign one's name on back of)* indossieren ⟨*Scheck, Wechsel*⟩; **~ a cheque** *etc.* **[over] to sb.** einen Scheck *usw.* durch Indossament auf jmdn. übertragen; **c)** *(support, declare approval of)* beipflichten (+ *Dat.*) ⟨*Meinung, Aussage*⟩; billigen, gutheißen ⟨*Entscheidung, Handlung, Einstellung*⟩; unterstützen ⟨*Antrag, Vorschlag, Kandidaten, Kandidatur*⟩; **d)** *(Brit.: make entry regarding offence on)* einen Strafvermerk machen auf (+ *Akk. od. Dat.*)

endorsement [ɪn'dɔ:smənt] *n.* **a)** *(writing on back)* Beschriftung auf der Rückseite; **the ~ of a document with one's signature** das Unterzeichnen eines Dokuments auf der Rückseite; **b)** *(of cheque)* Indossament, *das;* **~ to sb.** Übertragung durch Indossament auf jmdn.; **c)** *(support, declaration of approval)* Billigung, *die; (of proposal, move, candidate)* Unterstützung, *die;* **d)** *(Brit.: entry regarding offence)* Strafvermerk, *der* **(of** auf + *Akk. od. Dat.*)

endow [ɪn'daʊ] *v. t.* **a)** *(give permanent income to)* [über Stiftungen/eine Stiftung] finanzieren ⟨*Einrichtung, Krankenhaus usw.*⟩; mit Geld ausstatten ⟨*Person*⟩; stiften ⟨*Preis, Lehrstuhl*⟩; **~ed school** durch Stiftungen finanzierte Schule; **b)** *(fig.)* **nature has ~ed her with great beauty** die Natur hat sie mit großer Schönheit ausgestattet; **be ~ed with charm/a talent for music** *etc.* Charme/musikalisches Talent *usw.* besitzen; **be well ~ed** ⟨*Frau:*⟩ Holz vor der Hütte haben *(ugs.)*; ⟨*Mann:*⟩ stark gebaut sein *(verhüll.)*

endowment [ɪn'daʊmənt] *n.* **a)** *(endowing, property, fund, etc.)* Stiftung, *die;* **b)** *(talent etc.)* Begabung, *die*

endowment: ~ assurance *n.* abgekürzte *od.* gemischte Lebensversicherung; **~ mortgage** *n.* ≈ Tilgungslebensversicherung, *die;* **~ policy** *see* **~ assurance**

end: ~-paper *n.* Vorsatz, *der;* Vorsatzblatt, *das;* **~-point** *n.* **a)** *(Chem.)* Umschlagspunkt, *der;* **b)** *(fig.)* Endpunkt, *der;* **~-product** *n. (lit. or fig.; also Chem.)* Endprodukt, *das; (fig.)* Resultat, *das*

endue [ɪn'dju:] *v. t. (literary)* **a)** *(clothe)* bekleiden **(with** mit); **b)** *(furnish) see* **endow b**

endurable [ɪn'djʊərəbl] *adj.* erträglich

endurance [ɪn'djʊərəns] *n.* **a)** Widerstandskraft, *die* **(of** gegen); *(ability to withstand strain)* Ausdauer, *die; (patience)* Geduld, *die;* **the material's ~ [of wear and tear]** die Strapazierfähigkeit des Materials; **past** *or* **beyond ~:** unerträglich; **b)** *(lastingness)* Dauerhaftigkeit, *die*

en'durance test *n.* Belastungsprobe, *die*

endure [ɪn'djʊə(r)] **1.** *v. t. (undergo, tolerate)* ertragen; *(submit to)* über sich ergehen lassen; *(suffer)* erleiden ⟨*Verlust, Unrecht*⟩; **~ to do sth.** es ertragen, etw. zu tun; **I can't ~ the thought of** *or* **to think of him alone there** der Gedanke, daß er allein dort ist, ist mir unerträglich. **2.** *v. i.* fortdauern; **Shakespeare is a name which will ~:** der Name Shakespeares wird die Zeit überdauern

enduring [ɪn'djʊərɪŋ] *adj. (lasting)* dauerhaft; beständig ⟨*Glaube, Tradition*⟩

'end user *n. (Econ.)* Endverbraucher, *der*

endways ['endweɪz], **endwise** ['endwaɪz] *advs.* **a)** *(with end towards spectator)* **turn sth. ~ towards sb.** jmdm. die Schmalseite einer Sache *(Gen.)* zuwenden; **b)** *(with end foremost)* **~ [on]** längs; **let's have the bed facing that wall ~ [on]** laß uns das Bett mit der Schmalseite zu der Wand aufstellen!; **c)** *(with end uppermost)* **~ [on]** hochkant; **d)** *(end to end)* der Länge nach hintereinander; längs hintereinander

ENE [i:stnɔ:θ'i:st] *abbr.* **east-north-east** ONO

enema ['enɪmə] *n., pl.* **~s** *or* **enemata** [enɪ'mɑ:tə] *(Med.)* **a)** *(injection, substance)* Einlauf, *der;* Klistier, *das (Med.)*; **b)** *(syringe)* Klistierspritze, *die (Med.)*

enemy ['enəmɪ] **1.** *n.* **a)** *(lit. or fig.)* Feind, *der* **(of, to** *Gen.*); **make enemies** sich *(Dat.)* Feinde machen *od.* schaffen; **make an ~ of sb.** sich *(Dat.)* jmdn. zum Feind machen; **~ of the people/state** Volks-/Staatsfeind, *der;* **the ~ at the gate/within** der Feind vor den Toren/in den eigenen Reihen; **the E~:** der böse Feind *(verhüll.)*; **how goes the ~?** *(dated fig. coll.: the time)* wie spät ist es?; **be one's own worst ~, be nobody's ~ but one's own** niemandem schaden als sich *(Dat.)* selbst; **b)** *(member of hostile army or nation, hostile force)* Feind, *der; (ship)* feindliches Schiff. **2.** *adj.* feindlich; **destroyed by ~ action** durch Feindeinwirkung zerstört

energetic [enə'dʒetɪk] *adj.* **a)** *(strenuously active)* energiegeladen; schwungvoll ⟨*Redner*⟩; tatkräftig ⟨*Mitarbeiter*⟩; lebhaft ⟨*Kind*⟩; **be an ~ person** sehr tatkräftig sein; **I don't feel ~ enough** ich habe nicht genug Energie; **b)** *(vigorous)* schwungvoll; entschieden, energisch ⟨*Zustimmung, Ablehnung*⟩; kräftig ⟨*Rühren, Schlag, Beifall*⟩

energetically [enə'dʒetɪkəlɪ] *adv.* schwungvoll; entschieden ⟨*sich äußern*⟩

energize (energise) ['enədʒaɪz] *v. t.* **a)** *(infuse energy into)* in Schwung bringen *(ugs.)*; **b)** *(Electr.)* mit Strom versorgen

energy ['enədʒɪ] *n.* **a)** *(vigour)* Energie, *die; (active operation)* Kraft, *die;* **save your ~:** schone deine Kräfte!; **I've no ~ left** ich habe keine Energie mehr; **build up one's ~:** Kräfte sammeln; **b)** *in pl. (individual's powers)* Kraft, *die;* **c)** *(Phys.)* Energie, *die;* **sources of ~:** Energiequellen; *see also* **conservation b; potential 1**

energy: ~ crisis *n.* Energiekrise, *die;* **~-giving** *adj.* energiespendend; **~ value** *n.* Nährwert, *der*

enervate ['enəveɪt] *v. t.* schwächen

enervation [enə'veɪʃn] *n.* Schwächung, *die; (state)* Schwäche, *die*

enfant terrible [ɑ̃fɑ̃ te'ri:bl] *n., pl.* **enfants terribles** [ɑ̃fɑ̃ te'ri:bl] Enfant terrible, *das*

enfeeble [ɪn'fi:bl] *v. t.* schwächen

enfeeblement [ɪn'fi:blmənt] *n.* Schwächung, *die; (state)* Schwäche, *die*

enfold [ɪn'fəʊld] *v. t.* **a)** *(wrap up)* **~ sb. in** *or* **with sth.** jmdn. in etw. *(Akk.)* einhüllen *od.* mit etw. umhüllen; **b)** *(clasp)* umschließen; **he ~ed her in his arms** er schloß sie in seine Arme

enforce [ɪn'fɔ:s] *v. t.* **a)** erzwingen; **~ sth. [up]on sb.** jmdm. etw. aufzwingen; **~ the law** dem Gesetz Geltung verschaffen; das Gesetz durchsetzen; **b)** *(give more force to)* Nachdruck verleihen (+ *Dat.*)

enforceable [ɪn'fɔ:səbl] *adj.* durchsetzbar

enforcement [ɪn'fɔ:smənt] *n.* Erzwingung, *die; (of law)* Durchsetzung, *die*

enfranchise [ɪn'fræntʃaɪz] *v. t.* **a)** *(invest with municipal rights)* einen Parlamentssitz verleihen (+ *Dat.*); **b)** *(give vote to)* das Wahlrecht verleihen (+ *Dat.*); **be ~d** das Wahlrecht erhalten

enfranchisement [ɪn'fræntʃɪzmənt] *n.* **a)** *(investing with municipal rights)* Verleihung eines Parlamentssitzes (**of** an + *Akk.*); **b)** *(giving of vote to)* Verleihung des Wahlrechts (**of** an + *Akk.*)

ENG *abbr.* **electronic news-gathering** elektronische Berichterstattung; EB

Engadine ['eŋgədi:n] *pr. n.* **the ~:** das Engadin

engage [ɪn'geɪdʒ] **1.** *v. t.* **a)** engagieren; **a singer was ~d to sing at the wedding** ein Sänger/eine Sängerin wurde engagiert *od.* verpflichtet, der/die bei der Hochzeit singen sollte; **b)** *(hire)* einstellen; **we have ~d his services** er arbeitet für uns; wir nehmen seine Dienste in Anspruch; **c)** *(employ busily)* beschäftigen (**in** mit); *(involve)* verwickeln (**in** in + *Akk.*); **~ oneself in sth.** sich mit etw. befassen *od.* beschäftigen; **~ sb. in conversation** jmdn. ins Gespräch ziehen; *(more absorbingly)* jmdn. in ein Gespräch verwickeln; **d)** *(attract and hold fast)* wecken [und wachhalten] ⟨*Interesse*⟩; auf sich *(Akk.)* ziehen ⟨*Aufmerksamkeit*⟩; fesseln ⟨*Person*⟩; in Anspruch nehmen ⟨*Konzentration*⟩; gewinnen ⟨*Sympathie, Unterstützung*⟩; **e)** *(arrange to occupy)* mieten; **f)** *(enter into conflict with)* angreifen; *(bring into conflict)* **~ sb. in a duel** jmdn. in einen Zweikampf verwickeln; **g)** *(Mech.)* **~ one cog with another** die Zahnräder ineinandergreifen lassen; **~ the clutch/gears** einkuppeln/einen Gang einlegen; **h)** *(Fencing)* **~ [foils]** [die Klingen] kreuzen. **2.** *v. i.* **a)** **~ in sth.** sich an etw. *(Dat.)* beteiligen; **~ in politics** sich politisch engagieren; **~ in various sports** verschiedene Sportarten betreiben; **b)** *(pledge)* **~ to do sth.** sich verpflichten, etw. zu tun; *(vow)* geloben, etw. zu tun; **~ that ...:** versprechen, daß ...; **c)** *(Mech.)* ineinandergreifen; **the clutch would not ~:** die Kupplung ließ sich nicht einrücken *od.* faßte nicht; **d)** *(come into conflict)* **~ with the enemy** den Feind angreifen

engaged [ɪn'geɪdʒd] *adj.* **a)** *(to be married)* verlobt; **be ~ [to be married] [to sb.]** [mit jmdm.] verlobt sein; **become** *or* **get ~ [to be married] [to sb.]** sich [mit jmdm.] verloben; **b)** *(bound by promise)* verabredet; **be otherwise ~:** etwas anderes vorhaben; **are you ~ this evening?** bist du für heute abend verabredet?; hast du [für] heute abend etwas vor?; **c)** *(occupied with business)* beschäftigt; **be** *or* **have become ~ in sth./in doing sth.** mit etw. befaßt *od.* beschäftigt sein/damit befaßt *od.* beschäftigt sein, etw. zu tun; **d)** *(occupied or used by person)* besetzt ⟨*Toilette, Taxi*⟩; **the telephone [line]/number is ~** der [Telefon]anschluß/die Nummer ist besetzt; **you're always ~:** bei dir ist immer besetzt; **~ signal** *or* **tone** *(Brit. Teleph.)* Besetztzeichen, *das*

engagement [ɪn'geɪdʒmənt] *n.* **a)** *(to be married)* Verlobung, *die* (**to** mit); **have a long ~:** lange verlobt sein; **b)** *(appointment made with another)* Verabredung, *die;* **have a previous** *or* **prior ~:** schon anderweitig festgelegt sein; **social ~** gesellschaftliche Verpflichtung; **lunch/dinner ~** Verabredung zum Mittag-/Abendessen; **c)** *(booked appearance)* Engagement, *das;* **d)** *(hiring, appointment)* Einstellung, *die;* **e)** *(Mil.)* Kampfhandlung, *die*

en'gagement ring *n.* Verlobungsring, *der*

engaging [ɪn'geɪdʒɪŋ] *adj.* bezaubernd; gewinnend ⟨*Lächeln*⟩; einnehmend ⟨*Persönlichkeit, Art*⟩

engagingly [ɪn'geɪdʒɪŋlɪ] *adv.* gewinnend ⟨*lächeln*⟩

engender [ɪn'dʒendə(r)] *v. t.* zur Folge haben; erzeugen; ⟨*Person:*⟩ hervorrufen

engine ['endʒɪn] *n.* **a)** *(mechanical contrivance)* Motor, *der; (of spacecraft, jet aircraft)* Triebwerk, *das;* **b)** *(locomotive)* Lok[omotive], *die*

'engine-driver *n. (Brit.)* Lok[omotiv]führer, *der*

engineer [endʒɪ'nɪə(r)] **1.** *n.* **a)** Ingenieur, *der*/Ingenieurin, *die; (service ~, installation ~)* Techniker, *der*/Technikerin, *die; see also* **chemical engineer; civil engineer; electrical engineer; mechanical engineer; sound engineer; b)** *(maker or designer of engines)* Maschinenbauingenieur, *der;* **c)** **[ship's] ~:** Maschinist, *der;* **d)** *(Amer.: engine-driver)* Lok[omotiv]führer, *der;* **e)** *(Mil.) (designer and constructor of military works)* technischer Offizier; *(soldier)* Pionier, *der; see also* **Royal Engineers. 2.** *v. t.* **a)** *(coll.: contrive)* arrangieren; entwickeln ⟨*Plan*⟩; **b)** *(manage construction of)* konstruieren

engineering [endʒɪ'nɪərɪŋ] *n., no pl.* **a)** Technik, *die;* **career in ~:** Ingenieurlaufbahn, *die;* **b)** *attrib.* technisch ⟨*Arbeiten, Fähigkeiten*⟩; **~ science** Ingenieurwesen, *das;* **~ company** *or* **firm** Maschinenbaufirma, *die*

'engine-room *n.* Maschinenhaus, *das;* Maschinenraum, *der*

England ['ɪŋglənd] *pr. n.* England *(das)*

Englander ['ɪŋgləndə(r)] *n. (Hist.)* **Little ~:** *Gegner der imperialistischen Politik Englands*

English ['ɪŋglɪʃ] **1.** *adj.* englisch; **he/she is ~:** er ist Engländer/sie ist Engländerin; *see also* **bond 1 h. 2.** *n.* **a)** *(language)* Englisch, *das;* **grammar of ~:** englische Grammatik; Grammatik der englischen Sprache; **say sth. in ~:** etw. auf englisch sagen; **speak ~:** Englisch sprechen; **be speaking ~:** englisch sprechen; **I [can] speak/read ~:** ich spreche Englisch/kann Englisch lesen; **I cannot** *or* **do not speak/read ~:** ich spreche kein Englisch/kann Englisch nicht lesen; **translate into/from [the] ~:** ins Englische/aus dem Englischen übersetzen; **speak a very pure [form of] ~:** ein sehr reines Englisch sprechen; **write sth. in ~:** etw. [auf *od.* in] englisch schreiben; **is that [good** *or* **correct] ~?** ist das gutes Englisch?; **what you've written is just not ~!** was du da geschrieben hast, ist einfach kein Englisch!; **her ~ is very good** sie schreibt/spricht ein sehr gutes Englisch; **the King's/Queen's ~:** die englische Hochsprache; **British/American ~:** britisches/amerikanisches Englisch; **Northern/Southern ~:** in Nordengland/Südengland gesprochenes Englisch; **Middle ~:** Mittelenglisch, *das;* **Old ~:** Altenglisch, *das;* **in plain ~:** in einfachen Worten; **say sth. in plain ~:** etw. frei heraussagen; **now put it into plain ~:** ≈ nun sag es noch mal auf deutsch; **b)** *pl.* **the ~:** die Engländer; **c)** *(Amer. Billiards) see* **side 1 k.** *See also* **pidgin English**

English: ~ 'breakfast *n.* englisches Frühstück; **~ 'Channel** *pr. n.* **the ~ Channel** der [Ärmel]kanal; **~ 'horn** *n. (Mus.)* Englischhorn, *das;* Englisch Horn, *das (fachspr.);* **~man** ['ɪŋglɪʃmən] *n., pl.* **~men** ['ɪŋglɪʃmən] Engländer, *der; see also* **castle 1 a**

Englishness ['ɪŋglɪʃnɪs] *n., no pl.* englische Eigenart

'Englishwoman *n.* Engländerin, *die*

engrave [ɪn'greɪv] *v. t.* **a)** gravieren ⟨*Platte, Porträt, Illustration*⟩; **the brass plate had been ~d with his name** sein Name war in die Messingplatte eingraviert worden; **b)** *(carve)* **~ figures** *etc.* **[up]on a surface** Figuren *usw.* in eine Oberfläche eingravieren; **~ sth. [up]on a stone** etw. in einen Stein meißeln; **~ one's name on a tree** seinen Namen in einen Baum schnitzen; **the memory of that day has been** *or* **is ~d indelibly on my mind** *(fig.)* die Erinnerung an diesen Tag hat sich mir unauslöschlich eingeprägt *od.* eingegraben

engraver [ɪn'greɪvə(r)] *n. (of metal)* Graveur, *der;* Stecher, *der; (of wood)* Holzschneider, *der; (of stone)* Steinschneider, *der;* Graveur, *der*

engraving [ɪn'greɪvɪŋ] *n.* **a)** *(action)* Gravieren, *das;* **b)** *(design, marks)* Gravur, *die;* Gravierung, *die;* **c)** *(Art) (form)* Gravierkunst, *die;* Kupferstich, *der; (print)* Stich, *der; (print from wood)* Holzschnitt, *der*

engross [ɪn'grəʊs] *v. t. (fully occupy)* fesseln; völlig in Anspruch nehmen ⟨*Zeit, Kraft usw.*⟩; **be ~ed in sth.** in etw. *(Akk.)* vertieft sein; **become** *or* **get ~ed in sth.** sich in etw. *(Akk.)* vertiefen

engrossing [ɪn'grəʊsɪŋ] *adj.* fesselnd

engulf [ɪn'gʌlf] *v. t.* verschlingen *(auch fig.); (wrap up)* einhüllen; **the house was ~ed in flames** das Haus stand in hellen Flammen

enhance [ɪn'hɑ:ns] *v. t.* erhöhen ⟨*Wert, [An]reiz, Macht, Aussichten, Schönheit*⟩; verstärken ⟨*Wirkung*⟩; steigern ⟨*Qualität, Wirkung*⟩; heben ⟨*Stimmung, Aussehen*⟩; betonen ⟨*Augen*⟩

enhancement [ɪn'hɑ:nsmənt] *n. see* **enhance:** Erhöhung, *die;* Verstärkung, *die;* Steigerung, *die;* Hebung, *die;* Betonung, *die*

enigma [ɪ'nɪgmə] *n.* Rätsel, *das*

enigmatic [enɪg'mætɪk], **enigmatical** [enɪg'mætɪkl] *adj.* rätselhaft

enjambment (enjambement) [en'dʒæmmənt] *n. (Pros.)* Enjambement, *das*

enjoin [ɪn'dʒɔɪn] *v. t.* **~ a duty/restriction on sb.** jmdm. eine Pflicht/Einschränkung auferlegen; **~ silence/obedience [on sb.]** [jmdn.] zum Schweigen ermahnen/Gehorsam [von jmdm.] fordern; **notices on the wall ~ed silence** Schilder an der Wand mahnten zur Ruhe; **~ caution on sb.** jmdn. zur Vorsicht ermahnen; **~ sb. [not] to do sth.** jmdn. eindringlich ermahnen, etw. [nicht] zu tun; **~ that sth. should be done** nachdrücklich fordern, daß etw. getan wird

enjoy [ɪn'dʒɔɪ] **1.** *v. t.* **a)** **I ~ed the book/film/work** das Buch/der Film/die Arbeit hat mir gefallen; **are you ~ing your meal?** schmeckt dir das Essen?; **he ~s reading/travelling** er liest/reist gern; **he ~s music and drama** er mag Musik und Theater; **we really ~ed seeing you again** wir haben uns wirklich gefreut, euch wiederzusehen; **as a rule, people don't actually ~ going to the dentist** im allgemeinen geht man nicht gerade gern zum Zahnarzt; **b)** *(have use of)* genießen ⟨*Rechte, Privilegien, Vorteile*⟩; sich erfreuen (+ *Gen.*) ⟨*hohen Einkommens*⟩; **~ the right**

to vote das Wahlrecht ausüben können; **c)** *(experience)* sich erfreuen (+ *Gen.*) ‹*Respekts, guter Gesundheit*›; genießen ‹*Achtung*›. **2.** *v. refl.* sich amüsieren; **you look as if you're ~ing yourself** du siehst ganz vergnügt aus; **we thoroughly ~ed ourselves in Spain** wir hatten viel Spaß in Spanien; **~ yourself at the theatre** viel Spaß im Theater!; **the children ~ed themselves making sandcastles** die Kinder vergnügten sich damit, Sandburgen zu bauen

enjoyable [ɪn'dʒɔɪəbl] *adj.* schön; angenehm ‹*Empfindung, Unterhaltung, Arbeit*›; unterhaltsam ‹*Buch, Film, Stück*›

enjoyably [ɪn'dʒɔɪəblɪ] *adv.* angenehm

enjoyment [ɪn'dʒɔɪmənt] *n.* *(delight)* Vergnügen, *das* (**of** an + *Dat.*); **don't spoil other people's ~:** verdirb anderen nicht die Freude

enlarge [ɪn'lɑ:dʒ] **1.** *v.t.* vergrößern; *(widen)* verbreitern ‹*Straße, Durchgang*›; weiter machen ‹*Kleidungsstück*›; erweitern ‹*Wissen*›; **the tumour had become ~d** der Tumor war größer geworden. **2.** *v.i.* **a)** sich vergrößern; größer werden; *(widen)* sich verbreitern; **b) ~ [up]on sth.** etw. weiter ausführen

enlargement [ɪn'lɑ:dʒmənt] *n.* **a)** Vergrößerung, *die; (making or becoming wider)* Verbreiterung, *die;* **b)** *(further explanation)* weitere Ausführung

enlarger [ɪn'lɑ:dʒə(r)] *n.* *(Photog.)* Vergrößerungsapparat, *der*

enlighten [ɪn'laɪtn] *v.t.* aufklären (**on, as to** über + *Akk.*); **let me ~ you on the matter** laß mich dir die Sache erklären; **be ~ing** erhellend sein

enlightened [ɪn'laɪtnd] *adj.* aufgeklärt

enlightenment [ɪn'laɪtnmənt] *n., no pl.* Aufklärung, *die;* **[spiritual] ~:** [geistige] Erleuchtung; **the E~** *(Hist.)* die Aufklärung; **the Age of E~:** das Zeitalter der Aufklärung

enlist [ɪn'lɪst] **1.** *v.t.* **a)** *(Mil.)* anwerben; **~ed person** *(Amer.) (soldier)* Soldat, *der; (sailor)* Matrose, *der;* **b)** *(secure as means of help)* gewinnen. **2.** *v.i.* **~ [for the army/navy]** in die Armee/Marine eintreten; **~ [as a soldier]** Soldat werden

enlistment [ɪn'lɪstmənt] *n.* **a)** *(Mil.)* Anwerbung, *die;* **b)** *(securing as means of help)* Gewinnung, *die*

enliven [ɪn'laɪvn] *v.t.* beleben; anregen ‹*Phantasie*›; in Schwung bringen *(ugs.)* ‹*Person, Schulklasse usw.*›; lebhafter gestalten ‹*Tanz, Unterricht*›

en masse [ɑ̃ 'mæs] *adv.* **a)** *(all together)* alle zusammen; **taken ~:** alles in allem; **b)** *(in a crowd)* in Massen

enmesh [ɪn'meʃ] *v.t.* **~ sb./sth. [in sth.]** jmdn./etw. [mit etw.] fangen; *(fig.)* jmdn./etw. [in etw. *(Akk.)*] verstricken; **a fly had become ~ed in the spider's web** eine Fliege hatte sich in dem Spinnennetz verfangen

enmity ['enmɪtɪ] *n.* Feindschaft, *die*

ennoble [ɪ'nəʊbl] *v.t.* **a)** adeln; **b)** *(elevate)* erheben

ennui ['ɒnwi:] *n.* Ennui, *der (geh.)*

enormity [ɪ'nɔ:mɪtɪ] *n.* **a)** *(atrocity)* Ungeheuerlichkeit, *die (abwertend);* **b)** *see* **enormousness**

enormous [ɪ'nɔ:məs] *adj.* enorm; riesig, gewaltig ‹*Figur, Tier, Meer, Kathedrale, Fluß, Wüste, Menge*›; gewaltig, enorm ‹*Veränderung, Unterschied, Liebe, Haß, Widerspruch, Größe, Ausgabe, Kraft*›; ungeheuer ‹*Mut, Charme, Schmerz, Problem, Gefahr*›; **b)** *(fat)* ungeheuer dick

enormously [ɪ'nɔ:məslɪ] *adv.* ungeheuer; enorm, ungeheuer ‹*groß, hoch, sich ändern, wachsen, sich bessern*›

enormousness [ɪ'nɔ:məsnɪs] *n., no pl.* ungeheure Größe; Riesenhaftigkeit, *die; (of size, length, height)* ungeheures Ausmaß

enough [ɪ'nʌf] **1.** *adj.* genug; genügend; **that's ~ arguing for one evening** für heute [abend] haben wir uns genug gestritten; **there's ~ room** *or* **room ~:** es ist Platz genug *od.* genügend Platz; **be man/fool/miser** *etc.* **~ to do sth.** Manns/dumm/geizig *usw.* genug sein, etw. zu tun; **he made ~ fuss about getting it/having got it** *(iron.)* er hat so einen Wirbel darum gemacht, daß er es haben wollte/er hat großen Wirbel darum gemacht, daß er es bekommen hatte; **more than ~:** mehr als genug; **~ noise to wake the dead** ein Lärm, um Tote aufzuwecken. **2.** *n., no pl., no art.* genug; **be ~ to do sth.** genügen, etw. zu tun; **she says she's not getting ~ out of her marriage** sie sagt, ihre Ehe gebe ihr nicht genug *od.* fülle sie nicht aus; **are there ~ of us to lift this heavy weight?** sind wir genug [Leute], um diese schwere Last zu heben?; **four people are quite ~:** vier Leute genügen völlig; **he's had quite ~** *(is drunk)* er hat genug; **that [amount] will be ~ to go round** das reicht für alle; **you [already] have ~ to do looking after the baby** du hast schon genug damit zu tun, auf das Baby aufzupassen; **~ of ...:** genug von ...; **have you had ~ of the meat dish?** hast du genug Fleisch gehabt?; **I've seen ~ of Bergman's films** ich habe genug Bergman-Filme gesehen; **are there ~ of these books to go round?** reichen diese Bücher für alle?; **~ of that!** genug davon!; **[that's] ~ [of that]!** [jetzt ist es] genug!; **~ of your nonsense!** Schluß mit dem Unsinn!; **have had ~ [of sb./sth.]** genug [von jmdm./etw.] haben; **I've had ~:** jetzt reicht's mir aber!; jetzt habe ich aber genug!; **haven't you had ~ of travelling?** hast du nicht langsam genug vom Reisen?; **more than ~, ~ and to spare** mehr als genug; **[that's] ~ about ...:** genug über ... *(Akk.)* geredet; **but ~ about politics** aber Schluß mit der Politik; **~ about that** genug davon!; Schluß damit!; **~ said** mehr braucht man dazu nicht zu sagen; **~ is ~:** mal muß es auch genug sein *(ugs.)*; **it's ~ to make you weep** es ist zum Weinen; **it's ~ to make you sick** da wird einem ganz schlecht; **~ is as good as a feast** allzuviel ist ungesund *(Spr.)*; **cry '~'** *(fig.)* aufgeben; **as if that were not ~:** als ob das noch nicht genügte; **be ~ of a man/fool/miser** *etc.* **to do sth.** Manns/dumm/geizig *usw.* genug sein, etw. zu tun. **3.** *adv.* genug; **the meat is not cooked ~:** das Fleisch ist nicht genügend durch; **you don't express your views ~:** du sagst zu wenig über deine Ansichten; **he is not trying hard ~:** er gibt sich nicht genug *od.* genügend Mühe; **they were friendly ~ towards us** sie waren soweit recht nett zu uns; **she's a pretty ~ girl** sie ist doch ein recht hübsches Mädchen; **you know well ~ what we're referring to** ihr wißt recht gut, was wir meinen; **oddly/strangely/funnily ~:** merkwürdiger-/seltsamer-/*(ugs.)* komischerweise; **sure ~:** natürlich; **be good/kind ~ to do sth.** so gut sein, etw. zu tun; *see also* **²fair 1 a; right 1 b; true 1 a**

en passant [ɑ̃ 'pæsɑ̃] *adv.* en passant *(geh.)*; beiläufig; **just ~:** ganz nebenbei

enquire *etc. see* **inquir-**

enrage [ɪn'reɪdʒ] *v.t.* wütend machen; reizen ‹*wildes Tier*›; **be ~d by sth.** über etw. *(Akk.)* wütend werden/von etw. gereizt werden; **be ~d at** *or* **with sb./sth.** auf jmdn./etw. wütend sein; **become** *or* **get ~d** wütend werden (**at, with** über, auf + *Akk.*); **I was ~d to hear that ...:** ich war wütend, als ich erfuhr, daß ...

enrapture [ɪn'ræptʃə(r)] *v.t.* entzücken; ‹*Gesang, Musik:*› bezaubern; **be ~d by sth./sb.** von etw./jmdm. entzückt sein

enraptured [ɪn'ræptʃəd] *adj.* entzückt; verzückt

enrich [ɪn'rɪtʃ] *v.t.* **a)** *(make wealthy)* reich machen; bereichern *(veralt.)*; **b)** *(fig.)* bereichern; anreichern ‹*Nahrungsmittel, Boden, Uran*›; verbessern ‹*Haut, Qualität, Gewebe*›; erweitern ‹*Kenntnisse*›; **we were greatly ~ed by the experience** diese Erfahrung hat uns sehr bereichert

enrichment [ɪn'rɪtʃmənt] *n.* *(lit. or fig.)* Bereicherung, *die; (of soil, food, uranium)* Anreicherung, *die*

enrol (*Amer.:* **enroll**) [ɪn'rəʊl] **1.** *v.i.*, **-ll-** sich anmelden; sich einschreiben *od.* eintragen [lassen]; *(Univ.)* sich einschreiben; sich immatrikulieren; **~ in sth.** in etw. *(Akk.)* eintreten; **~ for a course/test** sich zu einem Kurs/einer Prüfung anmelden. **2.** *v.t.*, **-ll-** einschreiben ‹*Studenten, Kursteilnehmer*›; anwerben ‹*Rekruten*›; aufnehmen ‹*Schüler, Mitglied, Rekrut*›; **~ sb. in sth.** jmdn. in etw. *(Akk.)* aufnehmen; **~ sb. for a course/the army** jmdn. für einen Kurs annehmen/in die Armee aufnehmen; **State E~led Nurse** *(Brit.)* ≈ Krankenpflegehelfer, *der*/-helferin, *die*

enrolment (*Amer.:* **enrollment**) [ɪn'rəʊlmənt] *n.* **a)** Anmeldung, *die; (Univ.)* Immatrikulation, *die;* Einschreibung, *die; (in army)* Eintritt, *der;* **b)** *(Amer.: number of students)* Studentenzahl, *die*

en route [ɑ̃ 'ru:t] *adv.* unterwegs; auf dem Weg; **~ to Scotland/for Edinburgh** unterwegs *od.* auf dem Weg nach Schottland/Edinburgh; **~ [for] home/to school** auf dem Heim-/Schulweg

ensconce [ɪn'skɒns] *v.t.* **~ oneself in sth.** sich in etw. *(Dat.)* niederlassen; *(hide)* sich in etw. *(Dat.)* verbergen; **be ~d in/behind sth.** sich in/hinter etw. *(Dat.)* niedergelassen haben

ensemble [ɑ̃'sɑ̃bl] *n.* Ensemble, *das*

enshrine [ɪn'ʃraɪn] *v.t.* *(lit. or fig.)* bewahren

ensign ['ensaɪn, 'ensn] *n.* **a)** *(banner)* Hoheitszeichen, *das;* **b)** *(Brit.)* **blue/red/white ~:** Flagge der britischen Marinereserve/britischen Handelsschiffe/britischen Marine; **c)** *(standard-bearer)* Fähnrich, *der; (Hist.: infantry officer)* Fahnenjunker, *der;* **d)** *(Amer.: naval officer)* Fähnrich zur See

enslave [ɪn'sleɪv] *v.t.* **a)** versklaven; **b)** *(fig.)* **marriage had ~d her to the kitchen sink** die Ehe hatte sie an den Spülstein gekettet; **become ~d to a habit** zum Sklaven einer Gewohnheit werden

ensnare [ɪn'sneə(r)] *v.t.* *(lit. or fig.)* fangen; **the questions were designed to ~ him** *(fig.)* die Fragen waren als Falle für ihn gedacht

ensue [ɪn'sju:] *v.i.* folgen (**from, on** aus); **the discussion which ~d** die anschließende *od.* folgende Diskussion; **points/problems ensuing from this** Punkte/Probleme, die sich hieraus ergeben

ensuing [ɪn'sju:ɪŋ] *adj.* darauffolgend

en suite [ɑ̃ 'swi:t] *adv.* daran anschließend; **rooms arranged ~:** miteinander verbundene Zimmer; **with ... ~:** mit sich [daran] anschließendem / anschließender / anschließenden ...

ensure [ɪn'ʃʊə(r)] *v.t.* **a) ~ that ...** *(satisfy oneself that)* sich vergewissern, daß ...; *(see to it that)* gewährleisten, daß ...; **b)** *(secure)* **~ sth.** etw. gewährleisten; **this will ~ victory for the Labour Party** dies wird der Labour Party den Sieg sichern; **I cannot ~ you a good seat** ich kann nicht dafür garantieren, daß Sie einen guten Platz bekommen; **c)** *(make safe)* **~ sb./sth. against sth.** jmdn./etw. vor etw. *(Dat.)* *od.* gegen etw. schützen; **they ~d themselves against possible disappointment/criticism/hostility** sie sicherten sich gegen eine eventuelle Enttäuschung/Kritik/Anfeindung ab; *abs.* **proper insulation will ~ against loss of heat** sorgfältige Isolierung schützt gegen Wärmeverlust

ENT *abbr.* *(Med.)* **ear, nose, and throat** HNO

entablature [ɪn'tæblətʃə(r)] *n.* *(Archit.)* Gebälk, *das*

entail [ɪn'teɪl] **1.** *v. t.* **a)** *(involve)* mit sich bringen; **what exactly does your job ~?** worin besteht Ihre Arbeit ganz genau?; **sth. ~s doing sth.** etw. bedeutet, daß man etw. tun muß; **b)** *(impose)* **~ sth. [on sb.]** etw. [für jmdn.] mit sich bringen; ⟨*Person:*⟩ [jmdm.] etw. aufbürden; **~ disgrace on sb./one's family** jmdm./seiner Familie Schande machen; **c)** *(Law)* in ein Fideikommiß umwandeln; *(leave)* als Fideikommiß vererben. **2.** *n. (Law)* Fideikommiß, *das*
entailment [ɪn'teɪlmənt] *n. (Law)* Umwandlung in ein Fideikommiß
entangle [ɪn'tæŋgl] *v. t.* **a)** *(catch)* einfangen; sich verfangen lassen; **he got bits of straw ~d in his hair** Strohhalme verfingen sich in seinem Haar; **he got his trouser-leg ~d in his bicycle chain** sein Hosenbein hat sich in der Fahrradkette verfangen; **get [oneself]** *or* **become ~d in** *or* **with sth.** sich in etw. *(Dat.)* verfangen; **get [oneself]** *or* **become ~d in a mass of details** *(fig.)* sich in einer Unmenge von Einzelheiten verlieren; **be ~d in sth.** sich in etw. *(Dat.)* verfangen haben; **b)** *(fig.: involve)* verwickeln; **don't ~ yourself in obligations you cannot meet** laß dich nicht auf Verpflichtungen *(Akk.)* ein, die du nicht erfüllen kannst; **get [oneself] ~d in sth.** sich in etw. *(Akk.)* verwickeln lassen; **be/become ~d in sth.** in etw. *(Akk.)* verwickelt sein/werden; **get [oneself]/be ~d with** sich einlassen/eingelassen haben auf (+ *Akk.*) ⟨*Probleme*⟩; in Konflikt geraten/sein mit ⟨*Gesetz*⟩; sich einlassen/eingelassen haben mit ⟨*Frau, Mann, politischer Gruppe*⟩; **c)** *(make tangled)* völlig durcheinanderbringen; **get sth. ~d [with sth.]** etw. [mit etw.] durcheinanderbringen; **the threads have become** *or* **are ~d [with each other]** die Fäden haben sich verwirrt
entanglement [ɪn'tæŋglmənt] *n.* **a)** Verwicklung, *die;* Verfangen, *das;* **b)** *(fig.: involvement)* **his ~ in a divorce case** seine Verwicklung in eine Scheidungsaffäre; **get oneself into an ~ with sb.** sich mit jmdm. einlassen; **c)** *(thing that entangles)* Verwicklung, *die; (entangled things)* Durcheinander, *das; (Mil.)* [Draht]verhau, *der*
entente [ɑ̃'tɑ̃t] *n.* Entente, *die;* **~ cordiale** [ɑ̃tɑ̃t kɔ:dɪ'ɑ:l] *(Hist.)* Entente cordiale, *die*
enter ['entə(r)] **1.** *v. i.* **a)** *(go in)* hineingehen; ⟨*Fahrzeug:*⟩ hineinfahren; *(come in)* hereinkommen; *(walk into room)* eintreten; *(cross border into country)* einreisen; *(drive into tunnel etc.)* hineinfahren; *(come on stage)* auftreten; **~ Macbeth** *(Theatre)* Auftritt Macbeth; **~ into a building/another world** ein Gebäude/eine andere Welt betreten; **~ into the world of entertainment** in die Unterhaltungsbranche einsteigen *(ugs.);* **someone called 'E~!'** jemand rief: „Herein!"; **only a small amount of light ~ed through the windows** durch die Fenster fiel *od.* kam nur wenig Licht; **b)** *(penetrate)* eindringen; **c)** *(announce oneself as competitor in race etc.)* sich zur Teilnahme anmelden (**for** an + *Dat.*). **2.** *v. t.* **a)** *(go into)* [hinein]gehen in (+ *Akk.*); ⟨*Fahrzeug:*⟩ [hinein]fahren in (+ *Akk.*); ⟨*Flugzeug:*⟩ [hinein]fliegen in (+ *Akk.*); betreten ⟨*Gebäude, Zimmer*⟩; eintreten in (+ *Akk.*) ⟨*Zimmer*⟩; einlaufen in (+ *Akk.*) ⟨*Hafen*⟩; einreisen in (+ *Akk.*) ⟨*Land*⟩; *(drive into)* hineinfahren in (+ *Akk.*); *(come into)* [herein]kommen in (+ *Akk.*); **~ a bus/train** in einen Bus/Zug [ein]steigen; **~ the ship/plane** *(go/come into)* an Bord [des Schiffes/Flugzeugs] gehen/kommen; **a small amount of light ~ed the room** in den Raum fiel *od.* kam wenig Licht; **the poison ~ed the blood** das Gift gelangte ins Blut; **it would never ~ his mind** *or* **head to cheat you** es käme ihm nie in den Sinn, dich zu betrügen; **has it ever ~ed your mind** *or* **head that ...?** ist dir nie der Gedanke gekommen, daß ...?; **~ sb.'s heart/soul** von jmdm. Besitz ergreifen *(geh.);* **b)** *(penetrate)* eindringen in (+ *Akk.*); **c)** *(become a member of)* beitreten (+ *Dat.*) ⟨*Verein, Klub, Organisation, Partei*⟩; eintreten in (+ *Akk.*) ⟨*Kirche*⟩; ergreifen ⟨*Beruf*⟩; **~ the army/[the] university** zum Militär/auf die *od.* zur Universität gehen; **~ school** in die *od.* zur Schule kommen; **~ the legal profession/the medical profession/teaching** die juristische Laufbahn einschlagen/den Arztberuf ergreifen/den Lehrberuf ergreifen; Jurist/Arzt/Lehrer werden; **~ a monastery/nunnery** Mönch/Nonne werden; in ein Kloster eintreten; **~ the House of Commons** Mitglied *od.* Abgeordneter des Unterhauses werden; **d)** *(participate in)* sich beteiligen an (+ *Dat.*) ⟨*Diskussion, Unterhaltung*⟩; teilnehmen an (+ *Dat.*) ⟨*Rennen, Wettbewerb*⟩; **e)** *(procure admission for)* **be ~ed in a school** an einer Schule zugelassen werden; **f)** *(write)* **~ sth. in a book/register** *etc.* etw. in ein Buch/Register *usw.* eintragen; **~ a name in** *or* **on a list** einen Namen in eine Liste eintragen *od.* auf eine Liste setzen; **~ sth. in a dictionary/an index** etw. in ein Wörterbuch/ein Register aufnehmen; **g)** *(record)* **~ an action against sb.** gegen jmdn. Klage einreichen *od.* erheben; **~ a caveat** Einspruch einlegen *od.* erheben; **~ a judgement** ein Urteil fällen; **~ one's protest** Protest *od.* Widerspruch erheben; **~ a bid** ein Gebot abgeben; **h)** **~ sb./sth. for** jmdn./etw. anmelden für ⟨*Rennen, Wettbewerb, Prüfung*⟩; **~ one's name for** sich anmelden für ⟨*Rennen, Wettbewerb, Prüfung*⟩
~ into *v. t.* **a)** *(engage in)* anknüpfen ⟨*Gespräch*⟩; sich beteiligen an (+ *Dat.*) ⟨*Diskussion, Debatte, Wettbewerb*⟩; aufnehmen ⟨*Beziehung, Verhandlungen*⟩; *(bind oneself by)* eingehen ⟨*Verpflichtung, Ehe, Beziehung*⟩; schließen ⟨*Vertrag*⟩; **~ into details/long-drawn-out explanations** ins Detail gehen/sich in langatmigen Erklärungen ergehen; **it's not worth ~ing into a discussion about it** es lohnt sich nicht, eine Diskussion darüber anzufangen; **~ into an understanding with sb.** mit jmdm. eine Vereinbarung treffen *od.* eingehen; **~ into the pros and cons** auf das Für und Wider eingehen; **b)** *(sympathize with)* nachempfinden ⟨*jmds. Gefühle*⟩; nachvollziehen ⟨*jmds. Gedanken*⟩; sich hineinversetzen, einfühlen in (+ *Akk.*) ⟨*Person, Rolle, Stimmung*⟩; **~ into the spirit of Christmas** in Weihnachtsstimmung kommen; **she really ~s into anything she does** sie ist bei allem, was sie tut, ganz bei der Sache; **c)** *(form part of)* Bestandteil sein von; **~ into sb.'s considerations** bei jmds. Überlegungen eine Rolle spielen; **having children doesn't ~ into our plans** Kinder sind [bei uns] nicht geplant; **that doesn't ~ into it at all** das hat damit gar nichts zu tun
~ on *v. t.* **a)** *(Law: assume possession of)* in Besitz nehmen; **b)** *(begin)* beginnen ⟨*Karriere, Laufbahn, Amtsperiode*⟩; aufnehmen ⟨*Studium*⟩; in Angriff nehmen ⟨*Aufgabe, Projekt*⟩
~ 'up *v. t.* eintragen; **~ up the books** die Bücher auf den letzten Stand bringen
~ upon *see* **~ on**
enteric [en'terɪk] *adj.* **a)** *(Anat.)* Darm-; **b)** **~ fever** *(Med.)* Typhus, *der;* Typhus abdominalis, *der (fachspr.)*
enteritis [entə'raɪtɪs] *n. (Med.)* Enteritis, *die (fachspr.);* Dünndarmentzündung, *die*
enterprise ['entəpraɪz] *n.* **a)** *(undertaking)* Unternehmen, *das;* **commercial ~:** Handelsunternehmen, *das;* **free/private ~:** freies/privates Unternehmertum; **b)** *no indef. art. (readiness to undertake new ventures)* Unternehmungsgeist, *der*
enterprising ['entəpraɪzɪŋ] *adj.* unternehmungslustig; rührig ⟨*Geschäftsmann*⟩; kühn ⟨*Reise, Gedanke, Idee*⟩
entertain [entə'teɪn] *v. t.* **a)** *(amuse)* unterhalten; **we were greatly ~ed by ...:** wir haben uns köstlich über ... *(Akk.)* amüsiert; **b)** *(receive with hospitality)* bewirten; **they enjoy ~ing** sie haben gern Gäste; **do some** *or* **a bit of/a lot of ~ing** manchmal/sehr oft Gäste einladen; **~ sb. to lunch/dinner** *(Brit.)* jmdn. zum Mittag-/Abendessen einladen; **c)** *(have in the mind)* haben ⟨*Meinung, Vorstellung*⟩; hegen *(geh.)* ⟨*Gefühl, Vorurteil, Verdacht, Zweifel, Groll*⟩; *(consider)* in Erwägung ziehen; **he would never ~ the idea of doing that** er würde es nie ernstlich erwägen, das zu tun; **~ ambitions/ideas** *or* **thoughts of doing sth.** den Ehrgeiz haben/sich mit dem Gedanken tragen, etw. zu tun; **~ hopes of achieving sth.** sich *(Dat.)* Hoffnungen machen, etw. zu erreichen
entertainer [entə'teɪnə(r)] *n.* Entertainer, *der*/Entertainerin, *die;* Unterhalter, *der*/Unterhalterin, *die*
entertaining [entə'teɪnɪŋ] **1.** *adj.* unterhaltsam. **2.** *n., no pl., no indef. art.* **she does a lot of ~:** sie bewirtet häufig Gäste; **she's not very good at ~:** sie ist keine sehr gute Gastgeberin
entertainment [entə'teɪnmənt] *n.* **a)** *(amusement)* Unterhaltung, *die;* **much to our ~, to our great ~:** zu unserem großen Vergnügen; **get ~ from sth.** etw. unterhaltsam finden; **the world of ~:** die Welt des Showbusineß; **~ value** Unterhaltungswert, *der;* **have [great] ~ value** [sehr] unterhaltsam sein; **provide ~ for the children** für die Unterhaltung der Kinder sorgen; **b)** *(public performance, show)* Veranstaltung, *die*
enthral (*Amer.:* **enthrall**) [ɪn'θrɔ:l] *v. t.*, **-ll-: a)** *(captivate)* gefangennehmen *(fig.);* **b)** *(delight)* begeistern; entzücken
enthrone [ɪn'θrəʊn] *v. t.* inthronisieren; **he was ~d [as] King** er bestieg den Königsthron
enthronement [ɪn'θrəʊnmənt] *n.* Inthronisation, *die;* Thronbesteigung, *die*
enthuse [ɪn'θju:z, ɪn'θu:z] *(coll.)* **1.** *v. i.* **~ [about** *or* **over sth./sb.]** [über etw./jmdn.] in Begeisterung ausbrechen. **2.** *v. t.* begeistern
enthusiasm [ɪn'θju:zɪæzəm, ɪn'θu:zɪæzəm] *n.* **a)** *no pl.* Begeisterung, *die;* Enthusiasmus, *der;* **~ for** *or* **about sth.** Begeisterung für *od.* über etw. *(Akk.);* **for this job we want someone with ~:** wir brauchen einen begeisterungsfähigen Menschen für diese Arbeit; **I've no ~ about going out shopping** ich habe keine Lust, einkaufen zu gehen; **b)** *(object)* Leidenschaft, *die*
enthusiast [ɪn'θju:zɪæst, ɪn'θu:zɪæst] *n.* Enthusiast, *der; (for sports, pop music)* Fan, *der;* **a great DIY/cookery ~:** ein begeisterter Heimwerker/Koch; **be a great ~ for sth.** sich sehr für etw. begeistern
enthusiastic [ɪnθju:zɪ'æstɪk, ɪnθu:zɪ'æstɪk] *adj.* begeistert; enthusiastisch, begeistert ⟨*Applaus, Empfang, Lob*⟩; **be ~ about sth.** von etw. begeistert sein; **not be very ~ about doing sth.** keine große Lust haben, etw. zu tun; **become ~ about sth.** sich für etw. begeistern
enthusiastically [ɪnθju:zɪ'æstɪkəlɪ, ɪnθu:zɪ'æstɪkəlɪ] *adv.* begeistert; enthusiastisch, begeistert ⟨*empfangen, applaudieren, loben*⟩
entice [ɪn'taɪs] *v. t.* locken (**into** in + *Akk.*); **~ sb./sth. [away] from sb./sth.** jmdn./etw. von jmdm./etw. fortlocken; **~ mice from their holes** Mäuse aus ihren Mauselöchern [heraus]locken; **~ sb. into doing** *or* **to do sth.** jmdn. dazu verleiten, etw. zu tun
enticement [ɪn'taɪsmənt] *n.* **a)** *no pl.* Lockung, *die; (into depravity, immorality)* Verleitung, *die* (**into** zu); **~ from sth.** Fortlockung von etw.; **b)** *(thing)* Lockmittel, *das*
enticing [ɪn'taɪsɪŋ] *adj.*, **enticingly** [ɪn'taɪsɪŋlɪ] *adv.* verlockend
entire [ɪn'taɪə(r)] *adj.* **a)** *(whole)* ganz; **take an ~ fortnight for one's holiday** volle vier-

zehn Tage Urlaub machen; **b)** *(intact)* vollständig ⟨*Buch, Manuskript, Service, Ausgabe*⟩; **remain ~:** unversehrt bleiben

entirely [ɪn'taɪəlɪ] *adv.* **a)** *(wholly)* völlig; ganz ⟨*wach*⟩; **not ~ suitable for the occasion** dem Anlaß nicht ganz angemessen; **b)** *(solely)* ganz ⟨*für sich behalten*⟩; allein, voll ⟨*verantwortlich sein*⟩; **it's up to you ~:** es liegt ganz bei dir; **it's your responsibility ~:** du allein hast die Verantwortung

entirety [ɪn'taɪərətɪ] *n., no pl. (completeness)* Uneingeschränktheit, *die;* **in its ~:** als Ganzes; in seiner Gesamtheit

entitle [ɪn'taɪtl] *v. t.* **a)** *(give title of)* **~ a book/film ...:** einem Buch/Film den Titel ... geben; **b)** *(give rightful claim)* berechtigen **(to** zu); **~ sb. to do sth.** jmdn. berechtigen *od.* jmdm. das Recht geben, etw. zu tun; **your degree does not ~ you to more pay** auf Grund Ihres akademischen Grades haben Sie noch keinen Anspruch auf höhere Bezahlung; **she is ~d to a bit of respect from you** sie kann ein wenig Respekt von dir verlangen; **be ~d to [claim] sth.** Anspruch auf etw. *(Akk.)* haben; **be ~d to do sth.** das Recht haben, etw. zu tun

entitlement [ɪn'taɪtlmənt] *n.* *(rightful claim)* Anspruch, *der* **(to** auf + *Akk.*); **your leave ~ is four weeks** Sie haben Anspruch auf vier Wochen Urlaub

entity ['entɪtɪ] *n.* **a)** *no pl. (existence)* Entität, *die (Philos.);* Existenz, *die; (independence)* Eigenständigkeit, *die;* **b)** *(thing that exists)* **[separate] ~:** eigenständiges Gebilde

entomb [ɪn'tu:m] *v. t. (place in tomb)* beisetzen *(geh.); (fig.)* einkerkern

entombment [ɪn'tu:mmənt] *n.* Beisetzung, *die (geh.); (fig.)* Einkerkerung, *die*

entomological [entəmə'lɒdʒɪkl] *adj.* entomologisch

entomologist [entə'mɒlədʒɪst] *n.* Entomologe, *der*/Entomologin, *die*

entomology [entə'mɒlədʒɪ] *n.* Entomologie, *die;* Insektenkunde, *die*

entourage [ɒntʊ'rɑ:ʒ] *n.* Gefolge, *das;* **have a permanent ~ of beautiful women** ständig von schönen Frauen umgeben sein

entr'acte ['ɒntrækt] *n. (Theatre)* **a)** *(interval)* Zwischenakt, *der;* **b)** *(performance in interval)* Entreakt, *der*

entrails ['entreɪlz] *n. pl.* Eingeweide; Gedärm, *das; (fig.)* Innere, *das;* **read the ~** *(fig.)* die Zukunft deuten

¹entrain [ɪn'treɪn] *v. t.* **a)** *(result in)* nach sich ziehen; **b)** *(carry along in flow)* mitführen ⟨*Tröpfchen, Dampf*⟩

²entrain **1.** *v. t.* [in einen/den Zug] verladen. **2.** *v. i.* [in einen/den Zug] einsteigen; **~ for London** in den Zug nach London einsteigen

¹entrance ['entrəns] *n.* **a)** *(entering)* Eintritt, *der* **(into** in + *Akk.*); *(of troops)* Einzug, *der; (of vehicle)* Einfahrt, *die; (into office, position)* Antritt, *der* **(into, upon** *Gen.*); **before his ~ into the room** bevor er das Zimmer betrat *od.* ins Zimmer trat; **[ceremonial] ~:** [feierlicher] Einzug; **b)** *(on to stage, lit. or fig.)* Auftritt, *der;* **make an** *or* **one's ~:** seinen Auftritt haben; **she likes to make a dramatic ~** *(fig.)* sie setzt sich gern in Szene; **c)** *(way in)* Eingang, *der* **(to** *Gen. od.* zu); *(for vehicle)* Einfahrt, *die;* **factory ~:** Fabrik- *od.* Werk[s]tor, *das;* **the ~ to the cellar/city is through a trapdoor/large gates** man gelangt durch eine Falltür/große Tore in den Keller/die Stadt; **d)** *no pl., no art. (right of admission)* Aufnahme, *die* **(to** in + *Akk.*); **gain ~ to/apply for ~ at a school/university** an einer Schule/Universität aufgenommen werden/sich um die Aufnahme an einer Schule/Universität bewerben; **~ to the concert is by ticket only** man kommt nur mit einer Eintrittskarte in das Konzert; *see also* **common entrance; e)** *(fee)* Eintritt, *der*

²entrance [ɪn'trɑ:ns] *v. t.* **a)** *(throw into trance)* in Trance versetzen; **b)** *(carry away as in trance)* hinreißen; bezaubern; **become ~d** verzaubert werden; **be ~d by** *or* **with sth.** von etw. hingerissen *od.* bezaubert sein

entrance ['entrəns]: **~ examination** *n.* Aufnahmeprüfung, *die;* **~ fee** *n.* Eintrittsgeld, *das; (for competition)* Teilnahmegebühr, *die; (on joining club)* Aufnahmegebühr, *die;* **~ hall** *n.* Eingangshalle, *die;* **~ money** *see* **~ fee; ~ requirement** *n.* Aufnahmebedingung, *die*

entrancing [ɪn'trɑ:nsɪŋ] *adj.* bezaubernd; hinreißend

entrant ['entrənt] *n.* **a)** Eintretende, *der/die; (into country)* Einreisende, *der/die;* **b)** *(immigrant)* Einwanderer, *der;* **illegal ~s into the country** illegale Einwanderer; **c)** *(into a profession etc.)* Anfänger, *der*/Anfängerin, *die;* **d)** *(for competition, race, etc.)* Teilnehmer, *der*/Teilnehmerin, *die* **(for** *Gen.*, an + *Dat.*)

entrap [ɪn'træp] *v. t.,* **-pp-: a)** *(catch in trap)* fangen; **be ~ped** gefangen sein; in der Falle sitzen; **b)** *(enclose and retain)* einschließen; **c)** *(beguile)* locken **(to** in + *Akk.*); **~ sb. into doing sth./into sth.** jmdn. verlocken *(geh.) od.* verleiten, etw. zu tun/jmdn. zu etw. verlocken *(geh.) od.* verleiten

entreat [ɪn'tri:t] *v. t. (ask)* inständig bitten; *(beseech)* anflehen; **~ sb. to do sth.** jmdn. inständig bitten/jmdn. anflehen, etw. zu tun

entreating [ɪn'tri:tɪŋ] *adj.*, **entreatingly** [ɪn'tri:tɪŋlɪ] *adv.* flehentlich

entreaty [ɪn'tri:tɪ] *n. see* **entreat:** inständige/flehentliche Bitte; **make an ~ to sb. to do sth.** jmdn. inständig/flehentlich bitten, etw. zu tun

entrecôte ['ɒntrəkəʊt] *n. (Gastr.)* **~ [steak]** Entrecote, *das*

entrée ['ɒntreɪ, 'ɑ̃treɪ] *n.* **a)** *(right of admission)* Zutritt, *der* **(of, to, into** zu); **give sb. an/the ~ to sth.** jmdm. Zutritt zu etw. verschaffen; **b)** *(Gastr.) (Brit.)* Entree, *das;* Zwischengericht, *das; (Amer.: main dish)* Hauptgericht, *das*

entrench [ɪn'trenʃ] *v. t.* **a)** in Sicherheit bringen ⟨*Person, Besitz*⟩; **~ oneself in/behind sth.** *(lit. or fig.)* sich in/hinter etw. *(Dat.)* verschanzen; **become ~ed** *(fig.)* ⟨*Vorurteil, Gedanke:*⟩ sich festsetzen; ⟨*Tradition:*⟩ sich verwurzeln; **b)** *(apply extra safeguards to)* verankern ⟨*Rechte, Privilegien*⟩

entrenchment [ɪn'trenʃmənt] *n. (lit. or fig.)* Verschanzung, *die*

entre nous [ɒntrə 'nu:] *adv.* unter uns; **well, ~, what really happened was ...:** nun, unter uns gesagt, was wirklich geschah, war ...

entrepôt ['ɒntrəpəʊ] *n.* **a)** *(commercial centre)* Umschlagplatz, *der;* **b)** *(storehouse)* Speicher, *der*

entrepreneur [ɒntrəprə'nɜ:(r)] *n.* **a)** Unternehmer, *der*/Unternehmerin, *die;* **b)** *(middleman)* Vermittler, *der*

entrepreneurial [ɒntrəprə'nɜ:rɪəl] *adj.* unternehmerisch

entropy ['entrəpɪ] *n. (Phys.)* Entropie, *die*

entrust [ɪn'trʌst] *v. t.* **~ sb. with sth.** jmdm. etw. anvertrauen; **he could not be ~ed with such responsibility** man konnte ihm keine solche Verantwortung übertragen; **~ sb./sth. to sb./sth.** jmdn./etw. jmdm./einer Sache anvertrauen; **~ a task to sb.** jmdn. mit einer Aufgabe betrauen; **~ sth. to sb.'s safe keeping** jmdm. etw. zur Aufbewahrung anvertrauen

entry ['entrɪ] *n.* **a)** Eintritt, *der* **(into** in + *Akk.*); *(of troops)* Einzug, *der; (of foreign matter into wound etc.)* Eindringen, *das; (into organization, cartel)* Beitritt, *der* **(into** zu); *(into country)* Einreise, *die; (ceremonial entrance)* [feierlicher] Einzug; **upon ~ into Britain** bei der Einreise nach Großbritannien; **gain ~ to the house** ins Haus gelangen; **gain ~ to the EEC** der EG beitreten; **force an ~:** sich *(Dat.)* [gewaltsam] Zutritt *od.* Zugang verschaffen; *see also* **¹port 1 a; b)** *(on to stage)* Auftritt, *der;* **c)** *no pl., no art. (liberty to enter) (into car-park)* Einfahrt, *die* **(into** in + *Akk.*); *(into building)* Zutritt, *der* **(into** zu); *(into country)* Einreise, *die* **(to** in + *Akk.*); *see also* **'no entry'; d)** *(Law: taking possession)* Inbesitznahme, *die;* **make ~ of** *or* **on** in Besitz nehmen; **e)** *(way in)* Eingang, *der; (for vehicle)* Einfahrt, *die;* **f)** *(passage between buildings)* Durchgang, *der;* **g)** *(Mus.)* Einsatz, *der;* **h)** *(registration, item registered)* Eintragung, *die* **(in, into** in + *Akk. od. Dat.*); *(in dictionary, encyclopaedia, yearbook, index)* Eintrag, *der;* **make an ~:** eine Eintragung vornehmen; **double/single ~** *(Bookk.)* doppelte/einfache Buchführung; **i)** *(body of entrants) (for race etc.)* Teilnehmerfeld, *das; (for university/school)* [Zahl der] Studienanfänger/Schulanfänger; **j)** *(person or thing in competition)* Nennung, *die; (set of answers etc.)* Lösung, *die;* **latest date for entries** Einsendeschluß, *der; (for sporting event)* Meldeschluß, *der*

entry: ~ fee *see* **entrance fee; ~ form** *n.* Anmeldeformular, *das; (for competition)* Teilnahmeschein, *der;* **~ permit** *n.* Einreiseerlaubnis, *die;* Einreisegenehmigung, *die;* **E~phone, (P)** *n.* Sprechanlage, *die;* **~ visa** *n.* Einreisevisum, *das*

entwine [ɪn'twaɪn] *v. t.* **a)** *(interweave, lit. or fig.)* verflechten **(with** mit); **~ one's hair with ribbons** sich *(Dat.)* Bänder ins Haar flechten; **b)** *(wreathe)* **~ sth. about** *or* **round sb./sth.** etw. um jmdn./etw. schlingen *od. (geh.)* winden; **~ sth. with sth.** etw. mit etw. umschlingen *od. (geh.)* umwinden

enumerable [ɪ'nju:mərəbl] *adj.* zählbar

'E number *n. (Commerc.)* E-Nummer, *die*

enumerate [ɪ'nju:məreɪt] *v. t.* **a)** *(count)* zählen; **b)** *(mention one by one)* [einzeln] aufzählen *od.* aufführen

enumeration [ɪnju:mə'reɪʃn] *n.* **a)** *(counting)* Zählung, *die;* **b)** *(mentioning one by one)* Aufzählung, *die;* Auflistung, *die;* **c)** *(list)* Auflistung, *die*

enunciate [ɪ'nʌnsɪeɪt] *v. t.* **a)** *(pronounce)* artikulieren; **b)** *(express)* formulieren ⟨*Idee, Theorie*⟩; zum Ausdruck bringen ⟨*Überzeugung, Wahrheit*⟩

enunciation [ɪnʌnsɪ'eɪʃn] *n.* **a)** *(pronunciation)* Artikulation, *die;* [deutliche] Aussprache; **b)** *(expression)* Formulierung, *die*

enure *see* **inure**

envelop [ɪn'veləp] *v. t.* [ein]hüllen **(in** in + *Akk.*); **we were ~ed in mist** Nebel hüllte uns ein; **be ~ed in flames** ganz von Flammen umgeben sein; **he ~ed her in his arms** er schloß sie in die Arme

envelope ['envələʊp, 'ɒnvələʊp] *n.* **a)** *(for letter)* [Brief]umschlag, *der;* **b)** *(Aeronaut.: gas-container)* Hülle, *die*

enviable ['envɪəbl] *adj.* beneidenswert; **be ~ for sth.** um etw. zu beneiden sein

envious ['envɪəs] *adj.* neidisch **(of** auf + *Akk.*); **speak in ~ tones** in neiderfülltem Ton sprechen; **I'm so ~ of you!** wie ich dich beneide!

enviously ['envɪəslɪ] *adv.* neidisch; neiderfüllt

environment [ɪn'vaɪərənmənt] *n.* **a)** *(natural surroundings)* **the ~:** die Umwelt; **the Department of the E~** *(Brit.)* das Umweltministerium; **b)** *(surrounding objects, region)* Umgebung, *die; (surrounding circumstances)* Umwelt, *die;* Umfeld, *das (bes. Psych., Soziol.); (social surroundings)* Milieu, *das;* **physical/working/metropolitan ~:** Umwelt, *die*/Arbeitswelt, *die*/Großstadtmilieu, *das;* **home/family ~:** häusliches Milieu/Familienverhältnisse *Pl.*

environmental [ɪnvaɪərən'mentl] *adj.* Umwelt⟨*verschmutzung, -schutz, -einflüsse*⟩; **for ~ reasons** aus Gründen des Umweltschutzes; **~ group** Umweltschutzorganisation, *die*

environmentalist [ɪnvaɪərən'mentəlɪst] *n.* Umweltschützer, *der*/-schützerin, *die*
environs [ɪn'vaɪərənz, 'envɪrənz] *n. pl.* Umgebung, *die;* **Oxford and its ~:** Oxford und Umgebung
envisage [ɪn'vɪzɪdʒ], **envision** [ɪn'vɪʒn] *v. t. (imagine, contemplate)* sich *(Dat.)* vorstellen; **what do you ~ for the future of the department?** wie siehst du die Zukunft der Abteilung?; **what do you ~ doing [about it]?** was gedenkst du [in der Sache] zu tun?; **she doesn't ~ staying in London for much longer** sie hat nicht vor, noch länger in London zu bleiben
envoy ['envɔɪ] *n.* Bote, *der*/ Botin, *die; (Diplom. etc.)* Gesandte, *der*/ Gesandtin, *die*
envy ['envɪ] **1.** *n.* **a)** Neid, *der;* **feelings of ~:** Neidgefühle; **they could not conceal their ~ of her** sie konnten nicht verbergen, daß sie neidisch auf sie waren; **b)** *(object)* **his new sports car was the ~ of all his friends** alle seine Freunde beneideten ihn um seinen neuen Sportwagen; **you'll be the ~ of all your friends** alle deine Freunde werden dich beneiden. **2.** *v. t.* beneiden; **~ sb. sth.** jmdn. um etw. beneiden; **I don't ~ you** dich kann ich nicht beneiden; **I don't ~ you your job** ich beneide dich nicht um deine Tätigkeit
enwrap [ɪn'ræp] *v. t.,* **-pp- ~ sb./sth. in sth.** jmdn./etw. in etw. *(Akk.)* [ein]hüllen *od.* [ein]wickeln
enzyme ['enzaɪm] *n. (Chem.)* Enzym, *das*
Eocene ['i:əsi:n] *(Geol.)* **1.** *adj.* eozän; Eozän-. **2.** *n.* Eozän, *das*
eon *see* **aeon**
EP *abbr.* **extended-play [record]** EP
epaulette *(Amer.:* **epaulet)** ['epɔ:let, 'epəʊlet, epə'let] *n.* **a)** Epaulette, *die;* **b)** *(shoulder-strap)* Schulterklappe, *die*
épée ['epeɪ] *n.* [Fecht]degen, *der*
ephemeral [ɪ'fi:mərl, ɪ'femərl] *adj.* **a)** *(short-lived)* ephemer[isch] *(geh.);* kurzlebig; **b)** *(lasting only a day)* eintägig
epic ['epɪk] **1.** *adj.* **a)** episch; **~ poet** epischer Dichter; Epiker, *der;* **~ subject** Stoff für ein Epos; **b)** *(of heroic type or scale, lit. or fig.)* monumental; **~ film** Filmepos, *das;* **~ book** monumentaler Roman; Epos, *das (fig.);* **an ~ voyage** eine waghalsige Reise. **2.** *n.* Epos, *das; (film)* [Film]epos, *das; (book)* monumentaler Roman; Epos, *das (fig.);* **folk/national ~:** Volks-/Nationalepos, *das*
epicentre *(Brit.; Amer.:* **epicenter)** ['epɪsentə(r)] *n.* Epizentrum, *das*
epicure ['epɪkjʊə(r)] *n.* Feinschmecker, *der;* Gourmet, *der*
epicurean [epɪkjʊə'ri:ən] **1.** *adj. (devoted to pleasure)* epikureisch *(geh.);* **~ person** *see* **2. 2.** *n. (person devoted to pleasure)* Epikureer, *der (geh.);* Genußmensch, *der*
epidemic [epɪ'demɪk] *(Med.; also fig.)* **1.** *adj.* epidemisch. **2.** *n.* Epidemie, *die*
epidermal [epɪ'dɜ:ml] *adj. (Anat., Biol.)* epidermal
epidermis [epɪ'dɜ:mɪs] *n. (Anat., Biol.)* Epidermis, *die (fachspr.);* Oberhaut, *die*
epidiascope [epɪ'daɪəskəʊp] *n.* Epidiaskop, *das*
epidural [epɪ'djʊərəl] *n. (Med.)* Epiduralanästhesie, *die*
epiglottis [epɪ'glɒtɪs] *n. (Anat.)* Epiglottis, *die (fachspr.);* Kehldeckel, *der*
epigram ['epɪgræm] *n. (Lit.)* **a)** *(short poem)* Epigramm, *das;* Sinngedicht, *das;* **b)** *(pointed saying)* Sinnspruch, *der;* **c)** *(mode of expression)* epigrammatischer Ausdruck
epigrammatic [epɪgrə'mætɪk] *adj. (Lit.)* epigrammatisch
epigraph ['epɪgrɑ:f] *n.* **a)** *(inscription)* Epigraph, *das;* **b)** *(motto)* Motto, *das*
epilepsy ['epɪlepsɪ] *n. (Med.)* Epilepsie, *die*
epileptic [epɪ'leptɪk] *(Med.)* **1.** *adj.* epileptisch; *see also* **¹fit a. 2.** *n.* Epileptiker, *der*/Epileptikerin, *die*
epilogue *(Amer.:* **epilog)** ['epɪlɒg] *n. (Lit.)* Epilog, *der; (concluding part of literary work also)* Nachwort, *das*
Epiphany [ɪ'pɪfənɪ] *n. (Relig.)* Epiphanie, die; **[Feast of the] ~:** Epiphanias, *das;* Dreikönigsfest, *das;* **at ~:** am Dreikönigstag
episcopal [ɪ'pɪskəpl] *adj.* episkopal; bischöflich; Episkopal‹*system, -kirche*›; Bischofs‹*ornat, -mütze*›
episcopalian [ɪpɪskə'peɪlɪən] **1.** *adj. (of episcopal church)* der Episkopalkirche *nachgestellt.* **2.** *n.* **a)** *(member of episcopal church)* Episkopale, *der/die;* **b)** *(adherent of episcopacy)* Episkopalist, *der*/Episkopalistin, *die*
episcopate [ɪ'pɪskəpət] *n. see* **bishopric a**
episode ['epɪsəʊd] *n.* **a)** *(also Mus.)* Episode, *die;* **b)** *(instalment of serial)* Folge, *die;* **read next week's exciting ~:** lesen Sie die spannende Fortsetzung in der nächsten Woche!
episodic [epɪ'sɒdɪk], **episodical** [epɪ'sɒdɪkl] *adj.* episodisch; episodenhaft ‹*Szene, Ereignis*›
epistemology [epɪstɪ'mɒlədʒɪ] *n. (Philos.)* Epistemologie, *die (fachspr.);* Erkenntnislehre, *die*
epistle [ɪ'pɪsl] *n. (Bibl., Lit., or usu. joc.: letter)* Epistel, *die*
epistolary [ɪ'pɪstələrɪ] *adj.* epistolarisch *(veralt.);* **~ style** Briefstil, *der*
epitaph ['epɪtɑ:f] *n.* Epitaph, *das;* Grab[in]schrift, *die*
epithet ['epɪθet] *n.* **a)** *(expressing quality or characteristic)* Beiname, *der; (as term of abuse)* Schimpfname, *der;* **b)** *(Ling.)* Epitheton, *das (fachspr.);* Beiwort, *das*
epitome [ɪ'pɪtəmɪ] *n.* **a)** *(of quality, type, etc.)* Inbegriff, *der;* **b)** *(thing representing another in miniature)* Widerspiegelung im kleinen; **be the ~ of sth.** etw. im kleinen widerspiegeln
epitomize [ɪ'pɪtəmaɪz] *v. t.* **a)** *(fig.: represent in miniature)* im kleinen widerspiegeln; **b)** *(fig.: embody)* **~ sth.** der Inbegriff einer Sache *(Gen.)* sein
epoch ['i:pɒk, 'epɒk] *n. (also Geol.)* Epoche, *die;* **a new ~ in British politics** eine neue Ära in der britischen Politik
epochal ['i:pɒkl, 'epɒkl] *adj.* **a)** *(of epoch[s])* der Epoche[n] *nachgestellt;* **b)** *see* **epoch-making**
'epoch-making *adj.* epochal ‹*Bedeutung*›; epochemachend ‹*Entdeckung*›
eponymous [ɪ'pɒnɪməs] *adj.* namengebend
epoxy [ɪ'pɒksɪ] *(Chem.)* **1.** *adj.* Epoxyd-; Epoxid- *(fachspr.);* **~ resin** *see* **2. 2.** *n.* Epoxydharz, *das;* Epoxidharz, *das (fachspr.)*
epsilon [ep'saɪlən] *n.* Epsilon, *das*
Epsom salt [epsəm 'sɔ:lt, epsəm 'sɒlt] *n.* **~[s]** *(Med.)* Bittersalz, *das*
equable ['ekwəbl] *adj.* **a)** *(uniform)* gleichförmig ‹*Stil*›; **b)** *(balanced)* ausgeglichen ‹*Wesen, Person, Klima*›; **c)** *(equally proportioned)* ausgewogen ‹*Maße, System, Proportionen*›; **d)** *(fair-minded)* sachlich ‹*Einstellung, Art*›
equably ['ekwəblɪ] *adv.* **a)** *(in uniform style)* gleichförmig; **b)** *(in balanced manner)* **~ [disposed** *or* **tempered]** ausgeglichen; **c)** *(in equal proportions)* gleichmäßig; **d)** *(in fair-minded manner)* sachlich
equal ['i:kwl] **1.** *adj.* **a)** gleich; **~ in** *or* **of ~ height/weight/size/importance/strength** *etc.* gleich hoch/schwer/groß/wichtig/stark *usw.;* **add flour and cornflour in ~ measure** *or* **amounts** gleich viel Mehl und Stärkemehl hinzufügen; **marry sb. of ~ rank** standesgemäß heiraten; **not ~ in length** verschieden lang; **~ rights** gleiche Rechte; Gleichberechtigung, *die;* **divide a cake into ~ parts/portions** einen Kuchen in gleich große Stücke/Portionen aufteilen; **~ amounts of milk and water** gleich viel Milch und Wasser; **she had ~ success with her second novel** mit ihrem zweiten Roman hatte sie ebenso großen Erfolg; **she does both jobs with ~ pleasure/enjoyment** beide Tätigkeiten machen ihr gleich viel Spaß; **all men were created ~:** alle Menschen sind gleich geschaffen; **some are more ~ than others** *(joc.)* einige sind gleicher; **his salary is ~ to mine** er verdient genausoviel wie ich; **be ~ in size to sth.** ebenso groß wie etw. sein; **three times four is ~ to twelve** drei mal vier ist [gleich] zwölf; **none was ~ to her in beauty/elegance** keine kam ihr an Schönheit/Eleganz gleich; **Britain is now ~ with France in terms of medals won** Großbritannien ist *od.* liegt jetzt im Medaillenspiegel gleichauf mit Frankreich; **Michael came ~ third** *or* **third ~ with Richard in the class exams** bei den Klassenprüfungen kam Michael zusammen mit Richard auf den dritten Platz; **~ pay [for ~ work]** gleicher Lohn für gleiche Arbeit; **have ~ standing [with sb.]** [jmdm.] gleichgestellt sein; **be on ~ terms [with sb.]** [mit jmdm.] gleichgestellt sein; **meet each other/discuss matters on ~ terms** als Gleichgestellte zusammenkommen/ Angelegenheiten als Gleichgestellte erörtern; **all/other things being ~:** wenn nichts dazwischen kommt; *see also* **equal opportunity; b) ~ to** *(adequate for):* **be ~ to sth./sb.** *(strong, clever, etc. enough)* einer Sache/ jmdm. gewachsen sein; **a job ~ to sb.'s abilities** eine Arbeit, die jmds. Fähigkeiten entspricht; **be ~ to doing sth.** imstande sein, etw. zu tun; **c)** *(impartial)* gerecht; **they were all given ~ treatment** sie wurden alle gleich behandelt; **d)** *(evenly balanced)* ausgeglichen; **the battle was not ~:** es war ein ungleicher Kampf. **2.** *n.* Gleichgestellte, *der/ die;* **be among [one's] ~s** unter seinesgleichen sein; **talk to sb. as [if he were] one's ~:** mit jmdm. wie mit seinesgleichen sprechen; **be sb.'s/sth.'s ~:** jmdm. ebenbürtig sein/einer Sache *(Dat.)* gleichkommen; **he/ she/it has no** *or* **is without ~:** er/sie/es hat nicht seines-/ihresgleichen; **he has met an** *or* **his ~ in her** in ihr hat er jemanden gefunden, der ihm ebenbürtig ist. **3.** *v. t., (Brit.)* **-ll- a)** *(be equal to)* **~ sb./sth. [in sth.]** jmdm./ einer Sache [in etw. *(Dat.)*] entsprechen; **three times four ~s twelve** drei mal vier ist [gleich] zwölf; **she easily ~s him in intelligence** so intelligent wie er ist sie allemal; **the square on the hypotenuse ~s the sum of the squares on the other two sides** das Quadrat über der Hypotenuse ist gleich der Summe der Quadrate über den Katheten; **no pop group has ~led the Beatles in terms of success** keine Popgruppe ist je an den Erfolg der Beatles herangekommen; **b)** *(do sth. equal to)* **~ sb.** es jmdm. gleichtun; **I don't know if I could ever ~ such a high score/your success/such an achievement** ich weiß nicht, ob ich je eine so hohe Punktzahl erreichen könnte/so erfolgreich sein könnte wie Sie/eine solche Leistung vollbringen könnte
equalisation, equalise, equaliser *see* **equaliz-**
equality [ɪ'kwɒlɪtɪ] *n.* Gleichheit, *die; (equal rights)* Gleichberechtigung, *die;* **~ between the races/the religions, racial/religious ~:** Gleichberechtigung der Rassen/Konfessionen; **~ between the sexes** Gleichheit von Mann und Frau; **women are campaigning for ~ with men** die Frauen kämpfen für ihre Gleichstellung den Männern gegenüber
equalization [i:kwəlaɪ'zeɪʃn] *n.* Angleichung, *die* **(to, with** an + *Akk.)*
equalize ['i:kwəlaɪz] **1.** *v. t.* ausgleichen ‹*Druck, Temperatur*›, angleichen ‹*Maßstäbe, Einkommen, Chancen*› **(with** *Dat.*); gleichstellen ‹*Personen, gesellschaftliche Gruppen*› **(to, with** *Dat. od.* mit). **2.** *v. i.* **a)** *(become equal)* sich ausgleichen; **~ with sth.** sich einer Sache *(Dat.)* angleichen; **b)** *Footb. etc.)* den Ausgleich[streffer] erzielen

equalizer ['i:kwəlaɪzə(r)] *n. (Footb. etc.)* Ausgleich[streffer], *der*
equally ['i:kwəlɪ] *adv.* **a)** ebenso; **rank ~ [with one another]** den gleichen Rang einnehmen; **be ~ close to a and b** von a und b gleich weit entfernt sein; **the two are ~ gifted** die beiden sind gleich begabt; **b)** *(in equal shares)* in gleiche Teile ⟨*aufteilen*⟩; gleichmäßig ⟨*verteilen*⟩; **consist ~ of A and B** zu gleichen Teilen aus A und B bestehen; **c)** *(according to the same rule and measurement)* in gleicher Weise; gleich ⟨*behandeln*⟩
equal opportunity *n.* Chancengleichheit, *die;* **an ~** *or* **equal opportunities employer** ein Arbeitgeber, der jedem die gleiche Chance gibt *(unabhängig von Geschlecht, Rasse usw.)*
'equals sign *n. (Math.)* Gleichheitszeichen, *das*
equanimity [ekwə'nɪmɪtɪ, i:kwə'nɪmɪtɪ] *n., no pl.* **a)** *(composure, resignation)* Gelassenheit, *die;* **b)** *(evenness of mind, temper)* Gleichmut, *der*
equate [ɪ'kweɪt] *v. t.* **~ sth. [to** *or* **with sth.]** etw. [einer Sache *(Dat.)* od. mit etw.] gleichsetzen
equation [ɪ'kweɪʒn] *n.* **a)** *(Math.)* Gleichung, *die;* **b)** *(Chem.)* [chemische] Gleichung; [Reaktions]gleichung, *die*
equator [ɪ'kweɪtə(r)] *n. (Geog., Astron.)* Äquator, *der*
equatorial [ekwə'tɔ:rɪəl, i:kwə'tɔ:rɪəl] *adj. (Geog., Astron.)* äquatorial ⟨*Hitze, Klima*⟩; Äquatorial⟨*gegend, -strom*⟩; Äquator⟨*linie, -durchmesser, -gürtel, -sonne*⟩; **~ telescope** *(Astron.)* Äquatoreal, *das*
equerry ['ekwərɪ] *n.* **a)** *(in charge of horses)* königlicher Stallmeister; **b)** *(of royal household)* Kammerherr, *der*
equestrian [ɪ'kwestrɪən] **1.** *adj.* **a)** *(of horseriding)* reiterlich; Reit⟨*turnier, -talent*⟩; **b)** *(on horseback)* Reiter⟨*standbild, -bildnis*⟩; **c)** *(of knights)* Ritter-. **2.** *n.* Reiter, *der*/Reiterin, *die;* **circus ~s** Zirkusreiter
equestrianism [ɪ'kwestrɪənɪzm] *see* **horsemanship**
equidistant [i:kwɪ'dɪstənt] *adj.* gleich weit entfernt **(from** von)
equilateral [i:kwɪ'lætərl] *adj. (Math.)* gleichseitig ⟨*Dreieck, Rechteck, Hyperbel*⟩
equilibrium [i:kwɪ'lɪbrɪəm] *n., pl.* **equilibria** [i:kwɪ'lɪbrɪə] *or* **~s** Gleichgewicht, *das; (sense of balance)* Gleichgewichtssinn, *der;* **lose/keep one's ~** das Gleichgewicht verlieren/nicht verlieren; **mental/emotional ~:** geistige/emotionale Ausgeglichenheit; **in ~:** im Gleichgewicht; **maintain/restore ~:** das Gleichgewicht halten/wiederfinden; **~ of power** *(fig.)* Gleichgewicht der Kräfte; **stable/unstable/neutral ~** *(Phys.)* stabiles/labiles/indifferentes Gleichgewicht
equine ['ekwaɪn, 'i:kwaɪn] *adj.* **a)** *(of horse)* Pferde⟨*körper*⟩; **b)** *(like horse)* pferdeähnlich ⟨*Gang, Haltung, Gesichtszüge, Augen*⟩
equinoctial [i:kwɪ'nɒkʃl, ekwɪ'nɒkʃl] *adj. (Astron., Geog.)* Äquinoktial⟨*punkt, -kreis, -stürme*⟩; **~ line** Himmelsäquator, *der*
equinox ['i:kwɪnɒks, 'ekwɪnɒks] *n.* **a)** Tagundnachtgleiche, *die;* Äquinoktium, *das (fachspr.);* **spring** *or* **vernal ~:** Frühjahrs-Tagundnachtgleiche, *die;* **autumn** *or* **autumnal ~:** Herbst-Tagundnachtgleiche, *die;* **b)** *(Astron.: equinoctial point)* Äquinoktialpunkt, *der;* see also **precession**
equip [ɪ'kwɪp] *v. t.,* **-pp-** ausrüsten ⟨*Fahrzeug, Armee*⟩; ausstatten ⟨*Zimmer, Küche*⟩; **fully ~ped** komplett ausgerüstet/ausgestattet; **~ sb./oneself [with sth.] [for a journey** *etc.*] jmdn./sich [für eine Reise *usw.*] [mit etw.] ausrüsten; **be ~ped with sth.** *(fig.)* über etw. *(Akk.)* verfügen; **he is well ~ped for the job** *(fig.)* er bringt gute Voraussetzungen für den Job mit
equipment [ɪ'kwɪpmənt] *n.* **a)** Ausrüstung, *die; (of kitchen, laboratory, etc.)* Ausstattung, *die; (sth. needed for activity)* Geräte; **breathing ~:** Sauerstoffgerät, *das;* **climbing/diving ~:** Bergsteiger-/Taucherausrüstung, *die;* **fighting/skiing ~:** Kampf-/Skiausrüstung, *die;* **gardening/gymnastics/recording ~:** Garten-/Turn-/Aufnahmegeräte; **mining ~:** Bergbauausrüstung, *die;* **playground ~:** Spielgeräte *(auf einem Spielplatz);* **riding ~:** Reitzeug, *das (ugs.);* **writing ~:** Schreibutensilien; **b)** *(fig.: intellectual resources)* **mental/intellectual ~:** geistiges Rüstzeug
equitable ['ekwɪtəbl] *adj.* **a)** *(fair)* gerecht; **in an ~ manner** gerecht; **b)** *(valid)* billig; **~ jurisdiction** Rechtsprechung nach dem Billigkeitsrecht
equitably ['ekwɪtəblɪ] *adv.* gerecht
equity ['ekwɪtɪ] *n.* **a)** *(Law)* billiges *od.* natürliches Recht; **in ~:** billigermaßen; **acknowledge a claim in ~:** einen Anspruch billigerweise anerkennen; **b)** *(fairness)* Gerechtigkeit, *die;* **with ~:** gerecht; **c)** *(use of justice as well as law)* Billigkeit, *die;* **on the basis of ~:** auf der Grundlage der Billigkeit; **d) E~** *(Brit. Theatre) britische Schauspielergewerkschaft;* **e)** *in pl. (stocks and shares without fixed interest)* [Stamm]aktien; **f)** *(value of shares)* Eigenkapital, *das;* **g)** *(net value of mortgaged property) Wert eines Besitzes nach Abzug der Belastungen*
equivalence [ɪ'kwɪvələns], **equivalency** [ɪ'kwɪvələnsɪ] *n.* **a)** *(being equivalent)* **~ [of value]** Gleichwertigkeit, *die;* *(of two amounts)* Wertgleichheit, *die;* **b)** *(having equivalent meaning)* **~ [in meaning]** Äquivalenz, *die (bes. Logik);* Bedeutungsgleichheit, *die;* **c)** *(correspondence)* Entsprechung, *die;* **d)** *(Chem.)* Äquivalenz, *die*
equivalent [ɪ'kwɪvələnt] **1.** *adj.* **a)** *(equal, having same result)* gleichwertig; **be ~ to sth.** einer Sache *(Dat.)* entsprechen; **be ~ to doing sth.** dasselbe sein, wie wenn man etw. tut; **something of ~ value** etwas Gleichwertiges; **an ~ amount [of money]** ein entsprechender *od.* gleich hoher Betrag; **an ~ amount of flour** gleich viel Mehl; **b)** *(meaning the same)* äquivalent *(Sprachw.);* entsprechend; **these two words are [not] ~ in meaning** diese beiden Wörter sind [nicht] bedeutungsgleich; **c)** *(corresponding)* entsprechend; **be ~ to sth.** einer Sache *(Dat.)* entsprechen; **d)** *(Chem.)* äquivalent. **2.** *n.* **a)** *(equivalent or corresponding thing or person)* Pendant, *das;* Gegenstück, *das;* **be the ~ of sb./sth.** das Pendant *od.* Gegenstück zu jmdm./einer Sache sein; **b)** *(word etc. having same meaning)* Entsprechung, *die* **(of** zu); Äquivalent, *das* **(of** für); **c)** *(thing having same result)* **be the ~ of sth.** einer Sache *(Dat.)* entsprechen; **d)** *(Chem.)* Äquivalent, *das*
equivocal [ɪ'kwɪvəkl] *adj.* **a)** *(ambiguous)* zweideutig; **~ meaning** Zweideutigkeit, *die;* **b)** *(questionable)* zweifelhaft ⟨*Person, Erfolg, Glück, Ruf*⟩
equivocally [ɪ'kwɪvəkəlɪ] *adv. (ambiguously)* zweideutig
equivocate [ɪ'kwɪvəkeɪt] *v. i.* zweideutige Aussagen machen; ausweichen
equivocation [ɪkwɪvə'keɪʃn] *n.* zweideutige Formulierungen
ER *abbr.* **King Edward/Queen Elizabeth**
er [ɜ:(r)] *int.* äh
era ['ɪərə] *n.* **a)** *(system of chronology)* Ära, *die;* **b)** *(period)* Zeit; **the Adenauer ~:** die Ära Adenauer; **Byzantine/computer ~:** byzantinische Zeit/*(ugs.)* Computerzeitalter, *das;* **the Renaissance/Beatles ~:** die Zeit der Renaissance/Beatles; **Roman/Viking ~:** Römer-/Wikingerzeit, *die;* **a new ~ in fashion began** in der Mode begann eine neue Ära; **c)** *(Geol.)* Ära, *die (fachspr.);* Erdzeitalter, *das*
eradicate [ɪ'rædɪkeɪt] *v. t. (remove)* ausrotten; gründlich beseitigen ⟨*Ursache*⟩
eradication [ɪrædɪ'keɪʃn] *n.* Ausrottung, *die*
eradicator [ɪ'rædɪkeɪtə(r)] *n.* Tintenentferner, *der*
erase [ɪ'reɪz] *v. t.* **a)** *(rub out)* auslöschen; *(with rubber, knife)* ausradieren; **b)** *(obliterate)* tilgen *(geh.)* **(from** aus); **c)** *(remove recorded signal from; also Computing)* löschen
eraser [ɪ'reɪzə(r)] *n.* **[pencil] ~:** Radiergummi, *der;* **[blackboard] ~:** *Block mit Filzbelag o. ä. zum Löschen von Kreideschrift; (sponge)* Tafelschwamm, *der*
erasure [ɪ'reɪʒə(r)] *n.* **a)** *(rubbing out)* Auslöschen, *das; (with rubber)* Ausradieren, *das;* **b)** *(obliteration)* Tilgung, *die* **(from** aus); **c)** *(removal of recorded signal)* Löschen, *das; (place)* gelöschte Stelle
ere [eə(r)] *(poet./arch.)* **1.** *prep.* vor (+ *Dat.*) **~ long** binnen kurzem; **~ now** bereits; **~ then** bis dann. **2.** *conj.* ehe
erect [ɪ'rekt] **1.** *adj.* **a)** *(upright, vertical; also fig.)* aufrecht; gerade ⟨*Rücken, Wuchs*⟩; **stand ~:** ⟨*Soldat:*⟩ strammstehen; **with head ~:** mit hocherhobenem Kopf; **b)** *(Physiol.: enlarged and rigid)* erigiert; **c)** *(raised)* aufgestellt ⟨*Ohren*⟩. **2.** *v. t.* **a)** *(build)* errichten; aufbauen ⟨*Gerüst*⟩; aufstellen ⟨*Standbild, Mast, Verkehrsschild*⟩; aufschlagen, aufstellen ⟨*Zelt*⟩; konstruieren ⟨*Theorie*⟩; **b)** *(raise)* aufrichten ⟨*Körper, Ohren, Stacheln*⟩
erectile [ɪ'rektaɪl] *adj. (Physiol.)* schwellfähig; erektil *(fachspr.)*
erection [ɪ'rekʃn] *n.* **a)** *(building) see* **erect 2 a:** Errichtung, *die;* Aufbau, *der;* Aufstellen, *das;* Aufschlagen, *das;* Konstruieren, *das;* **b)** *(structure)* Bauwerk, *das; (other than a building)* Konstruktion, *die;* **c)** *(raising)* Aufstellen, *das;* **d)** *(Physiol.)* Anschwellen, *das; (of penis)* Erektion, *die*
erectly [ɪ'rektlɪ] *adv. (in upright manner, vertically; also fig.)* aufrecht
erectness [ɪ'rektnɪs] *n., no pl. (uprightness)* **~ [of stance** *or* **bearing** *or* **posture]** aufrechte Haltung
erg [ɜ:g] *n. (Phys.)* Erg, *das*
ergo ['ɜ:gəʊ] *adv. (literary)* ergo
ergonomic [ɜ:gə'nɒmɪk] *adj.* ergonomisch
ergonomics [ɜ:gə'nɒmɪks] *n., no pl.* Ergonomie, *die;* Ergonomik, *die*
ergot ['ɜ:gət] *n.* **a)** *(disease)* Mutterkornbefall, *der;* **b)** *(fungus)* Mutterkornpilz, *der;* **c)** *(dried mycelium)* Mutterkorn, *das*
erica ['erɪkə, ɪ'ri:kə] *n. (Bot.)* Erika, *die*
ermine ['ɜ:mɪn] *n.* **a)** *(fur; also Her.)* Hermelin, *der;* **b)** *(Zool.)* Hermelin, *das*
Ernie ['ɜ:nɪ] *n. (Brit. coll.; abbr. of Electronic Random Number Indicator Equipment) Gerät zur Ziehung der Gewinnzahlen für Prämienanleihen;* **have you ever won anything on ~?** haben Sie je etwas mit Prämienanleihen gewonnen?
erode [ɪ'rəʊd] **1.** *v. t.* **a)** ⟨*Säure, Rost:*⟩ angreifen; ⟨*Wasser, Regen, Meer:*⟩ auswaschen; ⟨*Wind:*⟩ verwittern lassen; ⟨*Wasser, Regen, Meer, Wind:*⟩ erodieren *(Geol.);* **b)** *(fig.)* unterminieren ⟨*Grundlage, Fundament, Beziehung*⟩. **2.** *v. i.* **a)** verwittern; **b)** *(fig.)* unterminiert werden
erogenous [ɪ'rɒdʒɪnəs] *adj.* erogen ⟨*Zone*⟩; **~ stimulation** sexuelle Stimulation
erosion [ɪ'rəʊʒn] *n.* **a)** *see* **erode 1 a:** Angreifen, *das;* Auswaschung, *die;* Verwitterung, *die;* Erosion, *die (Geol.);* **b)** *(fig.)* Unterminierung, *die*
erosive [ɪ'rəʊsɪv] *adj. (Geol.)* erodierend
erotic [ɪ'rɒtɪk] *adj.* erotisch
erotica [ɪ'rɒtɪkə] *n. pl.* Erotika
erotically [ɪ'rɒtɪkəlɪ] *adv.* erotisch
eroticism [ɪ'rɒtɪsɪzm] *n.* Erotik, *die*
err [ɜ:(r)] *v.i.* sich irren; **to ~ is human** *(prov.)* Irren ist menschlich; **you ~ in your opinion of him** Sie schätzen ihn falsch ein; **let's ~ on the right** *or* **safe side and ...:** um sicher zu gehen, wollen wir ...

errand ['erənd] *n.* **a)** Botengang, *der; (shopping)* Besorgung, *die;* **go on** *or* **run an ~:** einen Botengang/eine Besorgung machen; **go** *or* **run ~s** Botengänge/Besorgungen machen; **send sb. on an ~:** jmdn. auf einen Botengang schicken/jmdn. etwas besorgen lassen; **go on an ~ of mercy [for sb.]** Hilfe für jmdn. holen; **send sb. on an ~ of mercy** jmdn. auf eine Rettungsmission entsenden; *see also* **fool's errand; b)** *(object of journey)* Auftrag, *der;* **c)** *(purpose)* Zweck, *der*

errand: ~-boy *n.* Laufbursche, *der;* Bote[njunge], *der;* **~-girl** *n.* Laufmädchen, *das;* Botin, *die*

errant ['erənt] *adj.* irrig, falsch ‹*Prinzip, Maßstab, Meinung, Vorstellung*›; fehlgeleitet ‹*Person, Verhalten*›; untreu ‹*Ehemann, Ehefrau*›; *see also* **knight errant**

errata *pl. of* **erratum**

erratic [ɪ'rætɪk] **1.** *adj.* unregelmäßig; sprunghaft ‹*Wesen, Person, Art*›; unbeständig ‹*Charakter, Leistung, Wetter*›; launenhaft ‹*Verhalten*›; ungleichmäßig ‹*Bewegung, Verlauf*›; **the ~ moods of the weather** die wechselnden Launen des Wetters; **he is rather ~ in the standard of work he produces** das Niveau seiner Arbeiten ist recht unterschiedlich. **2.** *n. see* **erratic block**

erratically [ɪ'rætɪkəlɪ] *adv.* unregelmäßig; launenhaft ‹*sich verhalten*›; ungleichmäßig ‹*sich bewegen, verlaufen*›

erratic 'block *n. (Geol.)* erratischer Block *(fachspr.);* Findling, *der*

erratum [e'reɪtəm, e'rɑ:təm] *n., pl.* **errata** [e'reɪtə, e'rɑ:tə] *(Bibliog., Printing)* Erratum, *das (fachspr.);* Druckfehler, *der*

erroneous [ɪ'rəʊnɪəs] *adj.* falsch; irrig ‹*Schlußfolgerung, Eindruck, Ansicht, Auffassung, Annahme*›

erroneously [ɪ'rəʊnɪəslɪ] *adv.* fälschlich; irrigerweise

error ['erə(r)] *n.* **a)** *(mistake)* Fehler, *der;* **gross ~ of judgement** grobe Fehleinschätzung; **printing/typographical ~:** Druck-/Setzfehler, *der;* **b)** *(wrong opinion)* Irrtum, *der;* **lead sb. into ~:** jmdn. irreleiten; **realize the ~ of one's ways** seine Fehler einsehen; **in ~:** irrtümlich[erweise]; **be in ~ in one's calculations** sich verrechnen; **c)** *(Math. etc.)* Abweichung, *die*

erstwhile ['ɜ:stwaɪl] *adj.* einstig; einstmalig *(veralt.)*

erudite ['erʊdaɪt] *adj.* gelehrt ‹*Abhandlung, Vortrag*›; gebildet, gelehrt ‹*Person*›

erudition [erʊ'dɪʃn] *n., no pl.* Gelehrsamkeit, *die (geh.)*

erupt [ɪ'rʌpt] *v. i.* **a)** ‹*Vulkan, Geysir:*› ausbrechen; **ashes and lava ~ed from the volcano** Asche und Lava wurden aus dem Vulkan geschleudert; **~ with anger/into a fit of rage** *(fig.)* einen Wutanfall bekommen; **b)** *(appear)* ‹*Hautausschlag:*› ausbrechen

eruption [ɪ'rʌpʃn] *n.* **a)** *(of volcano, geyser)* Ausbruch, *der;* Eruption, *die (Geol.);* **b)** *(rash)* Eruption, *die (Med.);* Hautausschlag, *der;* **c)** *(fig.)* Ausbruch, *der*

eruptive [ɪ'rʌptɪv] *adj.* eruptiv; **~ rocks** *(Geol.)* Eruptivgestein, *das*

erythema [erɪ'θi:mə] *n. (Med.)* Erythem, *das (fachspr.);* Hautrötung, *die*

erythrocyte [ɪ'rɪθrəsaɪt] *n. (Anat.)* Erythrozyt, *der (fachspr.);* rotes Blutkörperchen

escalate ['eskəleɪt] **1.** *v. i.* sich ausweiten **(into** zu); eskalieren *(geh.)* **(into** zu); ‹*Löhne, Preise, Kosten:*› [ständig] steigen. **2.** *v. t.* ausweiten **(into** zu); eskalieren *(geh.)* **(into** zu); beschleunigen ‹*Anstieg*›

escalation [eskə'leɪʃn] *n. (of rioting, war)* Ausweitung, *die;* Eskalation, *die (geh.); (of wages, prices, costs)* Anstieg, *der*

escalator ['eskəleɪtə(r)] *n.* **a)** Rolltreppe, *die;* **b)** *(Commerc.)* **~ clause** Gleitklausel, *die*

escalope ['eskələʊp] *n. (Gastr.)* Schnitzel, *das*

escapade [eskə'peɪd] *n.* Eskapade, *die (geh.)*

escape [ɪ'skeɪp] **1.** *n.* **a)** *(lit. or fig.)* Flucht, *die* **(from** aus); *(from prison or mental hospital also)* Ausbruch, *der* **(from** aus); *(of large wild animal)* Ausbruch, *der; (of small animal)* Entlaufen, *das; (of bird)* Entfliegen, *das;* **there is no ~** *(lit. or fig.)* es gibt kein Entkommen; **~ vehicle** Fluchtfahrzeug, *das;* **~ route** *(lit. or fig.)* Fluchtweg, *der;* **make one's ~ [from sth.]** [aus etw.] entkommen; **have a narrow/miraculous ~:** gerade noch einmal/wie durch ein Wunder davonkommen; **have a lucky ~:** glücklich davonkommen; noch einmal Glück haben; **that was a narrow ~** *(joc.)* gerade noch mal davongekommen; **you had a lucky ~** *(joc.)* da haben Sie aber noch mal Glück gehabt; **~ from reality** Flucht vor der Realität; **b)** *(leakage of gas etc.)* Austritt, *der;* Entweichen, *das;* **c)** *(plant)* verwilderte Pflanze. *See also* **fire-escape. 2.** *v. i.* **a)** *(lit. or fig.)* fliehen **(from** aus); entfliehen *(geh.)* **(from** *Dat.*); *(successfully)* entkommen **(from** *Dat.*); *(from prison or mental hospital also)* ausbrechen **(from** aus); ‹*Großtier:*› ausbrechen; ‹*Kleintier:*› entlaufen **(from** *Dat.*); ‹*Vogel:*› entfliegen **(from** *Dat.*); **~ to freedom** in die Freiheit entkommen; **while trying to ~:** auf der Flucht; **~d prisoner/convict** entflohener Gefangener/Sträfling; **~ to one's room** sich in sein Zimmer zurückziehen; **~ into a dream world** *(fig.)* in eine Traumwelt flüchten; **b)** *(leak)* ‹*Gas:*› ausströmen; ‹*Flüssigkeit:*› auslaufen; **c)** *(avoid harm)* davonkommen; **~ alive** mit dem Leben davonkommen; **he ~d, but she was killed** er überlebte, während sie getötet wurde. **3.** *v. t.* **a)** entkommen (+ *Dat.*) ‹*Verfolger, Angreifer, Feind*›; entgehen (+ *Dat.*) ‹*Bestrafung, Gefangennahme, Tod, Entdeckung, Schicksal*›; verschont bleiben von ‹*Katastrophe, Krankheit, Zerstörung, Reduzierung, Auswirkungen*›; **~ observation/a duty** sich der Beobachtung/einer Pflicht entziehen; **he ~d the consequences** ihm blieben die Konsequenzen erspart; **~ being seen** nicht gesehen werden; **she narrowly ~d being killed** sie wäre fast getötet worden; **the car ~d damage** der Wagen blieb unbeschädigt; **one can't ~ the fact that ...:** es läßt sich nicht leugnen, daß ...; **b)** *(not be remembered by)* entfallen sein (+ *Dat.*); **c) ~ sb.['s notice]** *(not be seen)* jmdm. entgehen; **~ notice** nicht bemerkt werden; **~ sb.'s attention** jmds. Aufmerksamkeit *(Dat.)* entgehen; *see also* **memory b; d)** *(not be understood by)* **~ sb.** sich jmds. Verständnis *(Dat.)* entziehen; **e)** *(be uttered involuntarily by)* entfahren (+ *Dat.*)

escape: ~ artist *see* **escapologist; ~ clause** *n. (Law)* Ausweichklausel, *die*

escapee [ɪskeɪ'pi:, e'skeɪpi:] *n.* Entflohene, *der/die*

escape: ~-hatch *n. (Naut., Aeronaut.)* Notausstieg, *der; (fig.)* Rettungsanker, *der;* **~ mechanism** *n. (Psych.)* Abwehrmechanismus, *der*

escapement [ɪ'skeɪpmənt] *n. (Horol.)* Hemmung, *die*

e'scape-proof *adj.* ausbruchsicher

escaper [ɪ'skeɪpə(r)] *n.* Entflohene, *der/die*

escape: ~ road *n.* Auslaufstrecke, *die;* **~ route** *n.* Fluchtweg, *der;* **~ valve** *n.* Sicherheitsventil, *das*

escapism [ɪ'skeɪpɪzm] *n. (Psych.)* Eskapismus, *der (fachspr.);* Realitätsflucht, *die*

escapist [ɪ'skeɪpɪst] *(Psych.)* **1.** *n.* Eskapist, *der (fachspr.);* Aussteiger, *der*/Aussteigerin, *die (ugs.).* **2.** *adj.* eskapistisch *(fachspr.);* Aussteiger- *(ugs.)*

escapologist [eskə'pɒlədʒɪst] *n. (Brit.)* Entfesselungskünstler, *der*

escarpment [ɪ'skɑ:pmənt] *n. (Geog.)* Steilhang, *der*

eschatology [eskə'tɒlədʒɪ] *n. (Theol.)* Eschatologie, *die*

eschew [ɪs'tʃu:] *v. t. (literary)* meiden *(geh.)*

escort 1. ['eskɔ:t] *n.* **a)** *(armed guard)* Eskorte, *die;* Geleitschutz, *der (Milit.);* **police ~:** Polizeieskorte, *die;* **with an ~, under ~:** mit einer Eskorte; **fighter ~:** Jagdschutz, *der;* **b)** *(person[s] protecting or guiding)* Begleitung, *die;* **be sb.'s ~:** jmdn. begleiten; **c)** *(man accompanying woman socially)* Begleiter, *der;* **d)** *(hired companion)* Begleiter, *der*/Begleiterin, *die; (woman also)* ≈ Hostess, *die.* **2.** [ɪ'skɔ:t] *v. t.* **a)** begleiten; *(lead)* führen; geleiten *(geh.); (as guard of honour; also Mil.)* eskortieren; **~ sb. to safety** jmdn. in Sicherheit bringen; **b)** *(take forcibly)* bringen

escort ['eskɔ:t]: **~ agency** *n. Agentur für Begleiter/Begleiterinnen;* **~ carrier** *n. (Navy)* Geleitflugzeugträger, *der;* **~ duty** *n.* **be on ~ duty** als Geleitschutz eingesetzt sein; **~ vessel** *n. (Navy)* Geleitschiff, *das*

escritoire [eskrɪ'twɑ:(r)] *n.* Sekretär, *der*

escutcheon [ɪ'skʌtʃn] *n. (Her.)* Schild, *der;* **be a blot on sb.'s ~** *(fig.)* jmds. Ehre beflecken

ESE [i:stsaʊθ'i:st] *abbr.* **east-south-east** OSO

Eskimo ['eskɪməʊ] **1.** *adj.* Eskimo-; *see also* **English 1. 2.** *n.* **a)** *no pl. (language)* Eskimoisch, *das; see also* **English 2 a; b)** *pl.* **~s** *or same* Eskimo, *der*/Eskimofrau, *die;* **the ~[s]** die Eskimos

'Eskimo dog *n.* Eskimohund, *der*

ESN *abbr.* **educationally subnormal**

esophagus *(Amer.) see* **oesophagus**

esoteric [esə'terɪk, i:sə'terɪk] *adj.* esoterisch *(geh.)*

ESP *abbr. (Psych.)* **extra-sensory perception** ASW

espalier [ɪ'spælɪə(r)] *n.* **a)** *(trellis)* Spalier, *das;* **b)** *(tree)* Spalierbaum, *der*

esparto [ɪ'spɑ:təʊ] *n.* **~ [grass]** *(Bot.)* Esparto, *der;* Espartogras, *das*

especial [ɪ'speʃl] *attrib. adj.* [ganz] besonder...; **have ~ talent** besonders begabt sein; **for your ~ benefit** gerade um deinetwillen

especially [ɪ'speʃəlɪ] *adv.* besonders; **more ~ because ...:** um so eher, als ...; **what ~ do you want to see?** was möchten Sie insbesondere sehen?; **~ as** zumal; **more ~:** ganz besonders

Esperanto [espə'ræntəʊ] *n., no pl.* Esperanto, *das; see also* **English 2 a**

espionage ['espɪənɪdʒ, 'espɪənɑ:ʒ] *n.* Spionage, *die;* **carry out ~ for sb.** für jmdn. spionieren; *see also* **industrial espionage**

esplanade [esplə'neɪd, esplə'nɑ:d] *n.* Esplanade, *die (geh.)*

espousal [ɪ'spaʊzl] *n.* Eintreten, *das* **(of** für)

espouse [ɪ'spaʊz] *v. t.* **a)** eintreten für; **b)** *(arch.) (marry)* ehelichen *(veralt.); (give in marriage)* vermählen *(veralt.)* **(to** mit)

espresso [e'spresəʊ] *n., pl.* **~s** *(coffee)* Espresso, *der*

e'spresso bar *n.* Espressobar, *die;* Espresso, *das*

esprit de corps [espri: də 'kɔ:] *n.* Korpsgeist, *der (geh.);* Gemeinschaftsgeist, *der*

espy [ɪ'spaɪ] *v. t. (dated/joc.)* entdecken

Esq. *abbr.* **Esquire** ≈ Hr.; *(on letter)* ≈ Hrn.; **Jim Smith, ~:** Hr./Hrn. Jim Smith

essay 1. ['eseɪ] *n.* Essay, *der;* Aufsatz, *der (bes. Schulw.).* **2.** [ɪ'seɪ] *v. t.* sich versuchen an (+ *Dat.*); **~ to do sth.** sich bemühen, etw. zu tun

essayist ['eseɪɪst] *n.* Essayist, *der*/Essayistin, *die*

essence ['esəns] *n.* **a)** Wesen, *das; (gist)* Wesentliche, *das; (of problem, message, teaching)* Kern, *der;* **she is the [very] ~ of grace/kindness** sie ist der Inbegriff der Anmut/der Liebenswürdigkeit; **in ~:** im wesentlichen; **be of the ~:** von entscheidender Bedeutung sein; **b)** *(Cookery)* Essenz, *die*

essential [ɪ'senʃl] **1.** *adj.* **a)** *(fundamental)* wesentlich ⟨*Unterschied, Merkmal, Aspekt*⟩; entscheidend ⟨*Frage*⟩; zentral ⟨*Thema*⟩; **b)** *(indispensable)* unentbehrlich; lebenswichtig ⟨*Versorgungseinrichtungen, Nahrungsmittel, Güter, Organe*⟩; unabdingbar ⟨*Erfordernis, Qualifikation, Voraussetzung*⟩; unbedingt notwendig ⟨*Bestandteile, Maßnahmen, Ausrüstung*⟩; wesentlich, entscheidend ⟨*Rolle*⟩; **the ~ thing is for her to be happy** die Hauptsache ist, daß sie glücklich ist; **~ to life** lebensnotwendig *od.* -wichtig; **it is [absolutely** *or* **most] ~ that ...:** es ist unbedingt notwendig, daß ...; **these measures are ~:** diese Maßnahmen sind unbedingt erforderlich; **~ oil** *see* **ethereal oil. 2.** *n., esp. in pl.* **a)** *(indispensable element)* Notwendigste, *das;* **be an ~ for sth.** für etw. unentbehrlich sein; **the ~s of life** die lebensnotwendigsten Güter; **the bare ~s** das Allernotwendigste; **b)** *(fundamental element)* Wesentliche, *das;* **confine oneself to the ~:** sich auf das Wesentliche beschränken; **the ~s of French grammar** die Grundzüge der französischen Grammatik

essentially [ɪ'senʃəlɪ] *adv.* im Grunde; **my opinion does not ~ differ from yours** ich bin nicht grundsätzlich anderer Meinung als Sie

establish [ɪ'stæblɪʃ] **1.** *v. t.* **a)** *(set up, create, found)* schaffen ⟨*Einrichtung, Frieden, Präzedenzfall, Ministerposten*⟩; gründen ⟨*Organisation, Institut*⟩; stiften ⟨*Krankenhaus, Frieden*⟩; errichten ⟨*Reich, Geschäft, Lehrstuhl, System*⟩; einsetzen, bilden ⟨*Regierung, Ausschuß*⟩; einsetzen ⟨*Sakrament*⟩; herstellen ⟨*Kontakt, Beziehungen*⟩ **(with** zu); aufschlagen ⟨*Hauptquartier*⟩; aufstellen ⟨*Rekord*⟩; erlassen ⟨*Gesetz*⟩; einführen ⟨*Mode, Steuer, neue Methoden*⟩; ins Leben rufen, begründen ⟨*Bewegung*⟩; **~ a routine** Routine entwickeln; **~ one's authority** sich *(Dat.)* Autorität verschaffen; **~ law and order** Recht und Ordnung herstellen; **b)** *(settle, place)* unterbringen; **be ~ed in one's new home** sich in seinem neuen Heim eingerichtet haben; **~ sb. in business** jmdm. zum Start im Geschäftsleben verhelfen; **~ sb. in a business of his/her own** jmdm. zur Gründung eines eigenen Geschäfts verhelfen; **c)** *(appoint)* einsetzen; **d)** *(secure acceptance for)* etablieren; **become ~ed** sich einbürgern; **be firmly ~ed** einen festen Platz haben; **~ one's reputation** sich einen Namen machen; **e)** *(prove)* beweisen ⟨*Schuld, Unschuld, Tatsache*⟩; unter Beweis stellen ⟨*Können*⟩; nachweisen ⟨*Anspruch*⟩; **an inspection ~ed that ...:** eine Prüfung ergab, daß ...; **f)** *(discover)* feststellen; ermitteln ⟨*Umstände, Aufenthaltsort*⟩. **2.** *v. refl. (take up one's quarters)* **~ oneself [at** *or* **in a place]** sich [an einem Ort] niederlassen; **the practice has ~ed itself** der Brauch hat sich eingebürgert; **~ oneself as a carpenter** sich *(Dat.)* als Tischler einen festen Kundenkreis gewinnen

established [ɪ'stæblɪʃt] *adj.* **a)** *(entrenched)* eingeführt ⟨*Geschäft usw.*⟩; bestehend ⟨*Ordnung*⟩; etabliert ⟨*Schriftsteller*⟩; **long-~ company** alteingeführte *od.* -eingesessene Firma; **this firm has an ~ reputation** diese Firma ist sehr renommiert; **~ civil servant** ≈ Beamter auf Lebenszeit; **b)** *(accepted)* üblich; etabliert ⟨*Stilrichtung, Gesellschaftsordnung*⟩; geltend ⟨*Norm*⟩; fest ⟨*Brauch*⟩; feststehend ⟨*Tatsache*⟩; überkommen ⟨*Glaube*⟩; **become ~:** sich durchsetzen; **c)** *(Eccl.)* **~ church/religion** Staatskirche/-religion, *die*

establishment [ɪ'stæblɪʃmənt] *n.* **a)** *(setting up, creation, foundation)* Gründung, *die; (of government, committee)* Einsetzung, *die; (of democracy, empire)* Errichtung, *die; (of movement)* Begründung, *die; (of peace, relations)* Schaffung, *die;* **b)** *(settlement, placement)* Unterbringung, *die;* **c)** *(appointment)* Einsetzung, *die;* **d)** *(proving)* Nachweis, *der;* **e)** *(institution)* **[business] ~:** Unternehmen, *das;* **commercial/industrial ~:** Handels-/Industrieunternehmen, *das;* **educational ~:** Schule, *die;* **f)** *(household, residence)* Haus, *das;* **g)** *(organized body)* Truppe, *die; (quota)* Personalbestand, *der;* **peace[-time]/war ~** *(Mil.)* Friedens-/Kriegsstärke, *die;* **h)** *(Brit.)* **the E~** *(social group)* das Establishment

estate [ɪ'steɪt] *n.* **a)** *(landed property)* Gut, *das;* **family/private ~:** Familien-/Privatbesitz, *der;* **~ in the country** Landgut, *das;* **b)** *(Brit.: area with buildings) (housing ~)* [Wohn]siedlung, *die; (industrial ~)* Industriegebiet, *das; (trading ~)* Gewerbegebiet, *das;* **live on an ~:** in einer Wohnsiedlung leben; **on the industrial/trading ~:** im Industrie-/Gewerbegebiet; **c)** *(plantation)* Plantage, *die;* **d)** *(total assets) (of deceased person)* Erbmasse, *die (Rechtsspr.);* Nachlaß, *der; (of bankrupt)* Konkursmasse, *die (Wirtsch., Rechtsspr.);* **e)** *(Law: person's interest in landed property)* Eigentumsrecht, *das; see also* **personal estate; real estate; f)** *(political class)* Stand, *der;* **the Three E~s [of the Realm]** die drei [Reichs]stände; **the fourth ~** *(joc.)* die Zunft der Journalisten *(scherzh.);* **g)** *(arch.: condition)* Stand, *der;* **reach man's ~:** in den Mannesstand treten *(veralt.);* **the [holy] ~ of matrimony** der heilige Stand der Ehe *(geh.);* **h)** *(Brit.) see* **estate car**

estate: ~ agent *n. (Brit.)* **a)** Grundstücksmakler, *der;* Immobilienmakler, *der;* **b)** *(steward)* Gutsverwalter, *der;* **~ car** *n. (Brit.)* Kombiwagen, *der;* **~ duty** *(Brit.),* **~ tax** *(Amer.) ns.* Erbschaftssteuer, *die*

esteem [ɪ'sti:m] **1.** *n., no pl.* Achtung, *die* **(for** vor + *Dat.*); Wertschätzung, *die (geh.)* **(for** *Gen.,* für); **hold sb./sth. in [high** *or* **great] ~:** [hohe *od.* große] Achtung vor jmdm./etw. haben; **go up** *or* **rise/go down** *or* **sink in sb.'s ~:** in jmds. Achtung steigen/sinken; **[as a] token** *or* **mark of my ~:** [als] Zeichen meiner Hochachtung *od. (geh.)* Wertschätzung. **2.** *v. t.* **a)** *(think favourably of)* schätzen; **highly** *or* **much** *or* **greatly ~ed** hochgeschätzt *(geh.);* sehr geschätzt; **b)** *(consider)* **~ [as]** erachten für *(geh.);* ansehen als; **~ sth. an honour** sich *(Dat.)* etw. zur Ehre anrechnen *(geh.)*

ester ['estə(r)] *n. (Chem.)* Ester, *der*

esthetic *etc. (Amer.) see* **aesthetic** *etc.*

estimable ['estɪməbl] *adj.* schätzenswert

estimate 1. ['estɪmət] *n.* **a)** *(of number, amount, etc.)* Schätzung, *die;* **at a rough ~:** grob geschätzt; **b)** *(of character, qualities, etc.)* Einschätzung, *die;* **form an ~ of sb.'s abilities** jmds. Fähigkeiten beurteilen; **c)** *(Commerc.)* Kostenvoranschlag, *der;* **give an ~ of £50** die Kosten auf 50 Pfund veranschlagen; **d)** *(Brit. Parl.)* **the E~s** der Etat. **2.** ['estɪmeɪt] *v. t.* schätzen ⟨*Größe, Entfernung, Zahl, Umsatz*⟩ **(at** auf + *Akk.*); einschätzen ⟨*Fähigkeiten, Durchführbarkeit, Aussichten*⟩; **how far would you ~ the distance to be?** wie groß ist nach Ihrer Schätzung die Entfernung

estimation [estɪ'meɪʃn] *n.* Schätzung, *die; (of situation etc.)* Einschätzung, *die;* Beurteilung, *die; (esteem)* Wertschätzung, *die (geh.);* **in sb.'s ~:** nach jmds. Schätzung; **go up/down in sb.'s ~:** in jmds. Achtung steigen/sinken

estimator ['estɪmeɪtə(r)] *n.* Kalkulator, *der*

Estonia [e'stəʊnɪə] *pr. n.* Estland *(das)*

Estonian [e'stəʊnɪən] **1.** *adj.* estländisch; estnisch; *see also* **English 1. 2.** *n.* **a)** *(language)* Estnisch[e], *das;* Estländisch[e], *das; see also* **English 2 a; b)** *(person)* Este, *der*/Estin, *die;* Estländer, *der*/Estländerin, *die*

estrange [ɪ'streɪndʒ] *v. t.* entfremden **(from** *Dat.*); **be/become ~d from sb.** jmdm. entfremdet sein/sich jmdm. entfremden; **they are ~d** sie sind einander fremd geworden; *(married couple also)* sie haben sich auseinandergelebt; **her ~d husband/his ~d wife** ihr fremd gewordener Mann/seine ihm fremd gewordene Frau; **the ~d couple** die einander fremd gewordenen Ehepartner

estrangement [ɪ'streɪndʒmənt] *n.* Entfremdung, *die* **(from** von); **since their ~:** seit sie sich fremd geworden sind; *(of married couple also)* seit sie sich auseinandergelebt haben

estrogen *(Amer.) see* **oestrogen**

estuary ['estjʊərɪ] *n. (Geog.)* Ästuar, *das (fachspr.);* [Trichter]mündung, *die;* **the Thames ~:** die Mündung der Themse

ETA *abbr.* **estimated time of arrival** voraussichtliche Ankunftszeit

et al. [et 'æl] *abbr.* **and others** et al.

etc. *abbr.* **et cetera** usw.

et cetera, etcetera [et'setərə, ɪt'setərə] und so weiter; et cetera

etch [etʃ] **1.** *v. t.* **a)** ätzen **(on** auf *od.* in + *Akk.*); *(on metal also)* ⟨*bes. Künstler:*⟩ radieren; **b)** *(fig.)* einprägen **(in, on** *Dat.*); **be ~ed in** *or* **on sb.'s mind/memory** sich jmdm. eingeprägt haben/ins Gedächtnis eingegraben haben. **2.** *v. i.* ätzen; *(on metal also)* ⟨*bes. Künstler:*⟩ radieren

etching ['etʃɪŋ] *n.* Ätzung, *die; (piece of art)* Radierung, *die;* **come up and see my ~s** *(joc.)* komm mit rauf, ich zeig' dir meine Briefmarkensammlung *(ugs. scherzh.)*

eternal [ɪ'tɜ:nl, i:'tɜ:nl] *adj.* **a)** ewig; **be called to one's ~ rest** in die Ewigkeit abberufen werden *(geh. verhüll.);* **life ~:** das ewige Leben; **~ triangle** Dreiecksverhältnis, *das;* **b)** *(coll.: unceasing)* ewig *(ugs.);* **you'll have my ~ thanks** *or* **gratitude** ich werde Ihnen ewig dankbar sein

eternally [ɪ'tɜ:nəlɪ, i:'tɜ:nəlɪ] *adv.* **a)** ewig; **be ~ damned** auf ewig verdammt sein; **b)** *(coll.: unceasingly)* ewig *(ugs.)*

eternity [ɪ'tɜ:nɪtɪ, i:'tɜ:nɪtɪ] *n.* **a)** Ewigkeit, *die;* **for** *or* **in all** *or* **throughout ~, from here to ~:** [bis] in alle Ewigkeit; **b)** *(coll.: long time)* Ewigkeit, *die (ugs.);* **wait for [what seemed] an ~:** [scheinbar] eine Ewigkeit warten

ether ['i:θə(r)] *n.* **a)** *(Chem.)* Äther, *der;* **b)** *(Phys.; also fig.)* Äther, *der*

ethereal [ɪ'θɪərɪəl] *adj.* **a)** *(delicate, light, airy; also Phys., Chem.)* ätherisch; **b)** *(poet.: heavenly)* ätherisch *(veralt.);* himmlisch

ethereal 'oil *n. (Chem.)* ätherisches Öl

ethic ['eθɪk] **1.** *n.* Ethik, *die (geh.);* Ethos, *das (geh.).* **2.** *adj. see* **ethical a, b, d**

ethical ['eθɪkl] *adj.* **a)** *(relating to morals)* ethisch; **~ philosophy** Ethik, *die;* **~ philosopher** Ethiker, *der*/Ethikerin, *die;* **b)** *(morally correct)* moralisch einwandfrei; **it is not ~ for a doctor ...:** es entspricht nicht dem Berufsethos eines Arztes ...; **c)** *(Med.)* verschreibungspflichtig ⟨*Medikament*⟩; **d)** *(Ling.)* **~ dative** Dativus ethicus, *der*

ethicality [eθɪ'kælɪtɪ] *n., no pl. (moral correctness)* Sittlichkeit, *die*

ethically ['eθɪkəlɪ] *adv.* **a)** *(according to ethical rules)* ethisch; **be ~ obliged** *or* **bound to do sth.** die moralische Verpflichtung haben, etw. zu tun; **b)** *(in a morally correct way)* moralisch einwandfrei

ethics ['eθɪks] *n., no pl.* **a)** Moral, *die; (moral philosophy)* Ethik, *die;* **b)** *usu. constr. as pl. (moral code of person, group, etc.)* Ethik, *die (geh.);* Ethos, *das (geh.);* **medical ~:** ärztliche Ethik; **professional ~:** Berufsethos, *das;* **legal ~:** Standespflichten der Juristen; **c)** *constr. as pl. (moral correctness)* ethische Berechtigung

Ethiopia [i:θɪ'əʊpɪə] *pr. n.* Äthiopien *(das)*

Ethiopian [i:θɪ'əʊpɪən] **1.** *adj.* äthiopisch; **sb. is ~:** jmd. ist Äthiopier/Äthiopierin. **2.** *n.* Äthiopier, *der*/Äthiopierin, *die*

ethnic ['eθnɪk] *adj.* **a)** *(ethnological)* ethnisch; Volks‹*gruppe, -musik, -tanz*›; ~ **mix** Völkergemishc, *das;* ~ **minority** ethnische Minderheit; **b)** *(from specified group)* Volks‹*chinesen, -deutsche*›
ethnic 'cleansing *n.* ethnische Säuberung
ethnology [eθ'nɒlədʒɪ] *n.* Ethnologie, *die;* vergleichende Völkerkunde
ethology [i:'θɒlədʒɪ] *n.* **a)** *(science of animal behaviour)* Verhaltensforschung, *die;* Ethologie, *die;* **b)** *(science of character-formation)* Charakterkunde, *die;* Charakterologie, *die*
ethos ['i:θɒs] *n. (guiding beliefs)* Gesinnung, *die; (fundamental values)* Ethos, *das (geh.); (characteristic spirit)* Geist, *der*
ethyl ['eθɪl, 'i:θaɪl] *n. (Chem.)* Äthyl, *das*
ethyl 'alcohol *n. (Chem.)* Äthylalkohol, *der*
ethylene ['eθɪli:n] *n. (Chem.)* Äthylen, *das;* ~ **'glycol** Äthylenglykol, *das*
etiology *(Amer.) see* **aetiology**
etiquette [etɪ'ket, 'etɪket] *n.* **a)** *(social convention, court ceremonial)* Etikette, *die;* **breach of** ~: Verstoß gegen die Etikette; **book of** ~: Buch mit Verhaltensregeln; **that's** ~: das gehört sich so; **it's not** ~: das gehört sich nicht; **b)** *(professional code)* **professional** ~ **[of the law]** Berufspraxis [der Juristen]; **medical/legal** ~: Berufspraxis der Ärzte/Juristen
Etna ['etnə] *pr. n.* **[Mount]** ~: der Ätna
Etonian [i:'təʊnɪən] *n.* Etonschüler, *der*
Etruscan [ɪ'trʌskn] *(Ethnol.)* **1.** *adj.* etruskisch. **2.** *n.* **a)** *(language)* Etruskisch, *das;* **b)** *(person)* Etrusker, *der*/Etruskerin, *die*
étude ['eɪtju:d, eɪ'tju:d] *n. (Mus.)* Etüde, *die*
etymological [etɪmə'lɒdʒɪkl] *adj.*, **etymologically** [etɪmə'lɒdʒɪkəlɪ] *adv. (Ling.)* etymologisch
etymologist [etɪ'mɒlədʒɪst] *n. (Ling.)* Etymologe, *der*/Etymologin, *die*
etymology [etɪ'mɒlədʒɪ] *n. (Ling.)* Etymologie, *die; see also* **folk etymology**
EU *abbr.* **European Union**
eucalypt ['ju:kəlɪpt], **eucalyptus** [ju:kə'lɪptəs] *n.* **a)** ~ **[oil]** *(Pharm.)* Eukalyptusöl, *das;* **b)** *(Bot.)* Eukalyptus[baum], *der*
Eucharist ['ju:kərɪst] *n.* Eurcharistie, *die*
eugenics [ju:'dʒenɪks] *n., no pl.* Eugenik, *die (fachspr.);* Erbgesundheitslehre, *die*
eulogise *see* **eulogize**
eulogistic [ju:lə'dʒɪstɪk] *adj.* lobrednerisch
eulogize ['ju:lədʒaɪz] *v.t.* preisen *(geh.);* rühmen
eulogy ['ju:lədʒɪ] *n.* **a)** *(speech, writing)* Lobrede, *die;* Eloge, *die (geh.); (Amer.: funeral oration)* Grabrede, *die;* **b)** *(praise)* Lobspruch, *der*
eunuch ['ju:nək] *n.* Eunuch, *der; (fig. derog.)* Schwächling, *der (abwertend)*
euonymus [ju:'ɒnɪməs] *n. (Bot.)* Spindelstrauch, *der;* Evonymus, *der od. die; (Euonymus europaeus)* Pfaffenhütchen, *das*
euphemism ['ju:fəmɪzm] *n.* Euphemismus, *der (bes. Sprachw.);* verhüllende Umschreibung; **resort to** ~: zu Euphemismen greifen
euphemistic [ju:fə'mɪstɪk] *adj.*, **euphemistically** [ju:fə'mɪstɪkəlɪ] *adv.* euphemistisch *(bes. Sprachw.);* verhüllend
euphonious [ju:'fəʊnɪəs] *adj.* **a)** *(pleasant-sounding)* wohlklingend *(geh.);* **b)** *(Ling., Phonet.)* euphonisch
euphonium [ju:'fəʊnɪəm] *n. (Mus.)* Euphonium, *das*
euphony ['ju:fənɪ] *n.* **a)** *(pleasing sound)* Wohlklang, *der (geh.);* **b)** *(Ling., Phonet.)* Euphonie, *die*
euphoria [ju:'fɔ:rɪə] *n., no pl.* Euphorie, *die (geh.); (elation also)* Hochstimmung, *die*
euphoric [ju:'fɔ:rɪk] *adj.* euphorisch *(geh.)*
Euphrates [ju:'freɪti:z] *pr. n.* Euphrat, *der*
Eurasia [jʊə'reɪʒə] *pr. n.* Eurasien *(das)*
Eurasian [jʊə'reɪʒn] **1.** *adj.* eurasisch. **2.** *n.* Eurasier, *der*/Eurasierin, *die*
eureka [jʊə'ri:kə] *int.* heureka *(geh.);* ich hab's *(ugs.)*
Euro- ['jʊərəʊ] *in comb.* euro-/Euro-
Eurocrat ['jʊərəkræt] *n.* Eurokrat, *der*/Eurokratin, *die*
'Eurodollar *n. (Econ.)* Eurodollar, *der*
Europe ['jʊərəp] *pr. n.* **a)** Europa *(das);* **the continent of** ~: der europäische Kontinent; **b)** *(Brit. coll.: EC)* EG, *die;* **go into** ~: der EG beitreten; **c)** *(Brit. coll.: mainland* ~*)* Kontinent, *der*
European [jʊərə'pi:ən] **1.** *adj.* europäisch; **sb. is** ~: jmd. ist Europäer/Europäerin; **win** ~ **recognition** in ganz Europa Anerkennung finden. **2.** *n.* Europäer, *der*/Europäerin, *die*
European: ~ **'Cup** *n. (Footb.)* Europacup, *der;* Europapokal, *der;* ~ **Eco'nomic Community** *n.* Europäische Wirtschaftsgemeinschaft; ~ **Free Trade Association** *n.* Europäische Freihandelsassoziation
Europeanise *see* **Europeanize**
Europeanism [jʊərə'pi:ənɪzm] *n.* Europäertum, *das; (ideal of the unification of Europe)* europäischer Gedanke
Europeanize [jʊərə'pi:ənaɪz] *v.t.* europäisieren
European: ~ **'Monetary System** *n.* Europäisches Währungssystem; ~ **Parliament** *n.* Europäisches Parlament; ~ **plan** *n. (Amer. Hotel Managem.)* Unterkunft ohne Verpflegung; ~ **'Union** *n.* Europäische Union
'Eurovision *n. (Telev.)* Eurovision, *die*
Eustachian tube [ju:s'teɪʃn tju:b] *n. (Anat.)* Eustachische Röhre
euthanasia [ju:θə'neɪzɪə] *n.* Euthanasie, *die;* Sterbehilfe, *die*
evacuate [ɪ'vækjʊeɪt] *v.t.* **a)** *(remove from danger, clear of occupants)* evakuieren **(from** aus); **b)** *(esp. Mil.: cease to occupy)* räumen; **c)** *(Physiol.)* entleeren ‹*Darm*›
evacuation [ɪvækjʊ'eɪʃn] *n.* **a)** *(removal of people or things, clearance of place)* Evakuierung, *die* **(from** aus); **b)** *(esp. Mil.: withdrawal from occupation)* **the** ~ **of a territory** die Räumung eines Gebietes; **the** ~ **of the army** der Abzug der Armee; **c)** *(Physiol.)* Entleerung, *die*
evacuee [ɪvækjʊ'i:] *n.* Evakuierte, *der/die; attrib.* ~ **children** evakuierte Kinder
evade [ɪ'veɪd] *v.t.* **a)** ausweichen (+ *Dat.*) ‹*Angriff, Angreifer, Schlag, Blick, Problem, Schwierigkeit, Tatsache, Frage, Hindernis, Thema*›; sich entziehen (+ *Dat.*) ‹*Verhaftung, Ergreifung, Wehrdienst, Einberufung, Gerechtigkeit, Pflicht, Verantwortung, Liebkosung*›; entkommen (+ *Dat.*) ‹*Polizei, Verfolger, Verfolgung, Gegner*›; hinterziehen ‹*Steuern, Zölle*›; umgehen ‹*Zahlungsverpflichtung*›; ~ **recognition** nicht erkannt werden; ~ **doing sth.** vermeiden, etw. zu tun; ~ **giving an answer** der Beantwortung einer Frage ausweichen; **b)** *(circumvent)* umgehen ‹*Gesetz, Vorschrift*›; **c)** *(elude)* **the significance of his remark** ~**s me** die Bedeutung seiner Bemerkung ist mir nicht klar; ~ **definition** sich einer Definition entziehen
evaluate [ɪ'væljʊeɪt] *v.t.* **a)** *(value)* schätzen ‹*Wert, Preis, Schaden, Kosten*›; **b)** *(quantify, express numerically)* in Zahlen ausdrücken; quantifizieren; **c)** *(appraise)* einschätzen; *(judge)* beurteilen
evaluation [ɪvæljʊ'eɪʃn] *n.* **a)** Schätzung, *die; (quantification)* Berechnung, *die;* Quantifizierung, *die;* **b)** *(appraisal)* Einschätzung, *die; (of data)* Auswertung, *die*
evanescent [i:və'nesənt, evə'nesənt] *adj.* flüchtig ‹*Erscheinung, Vision, Glück*›; vergänglich ‹*Reiz*›
evangelical [i:væn'dʒelɪkl] *adj.* **a)** *(of the Gospels)* ~ **texts/preaching** Texte/Verkündigung des Evangeliums; **b)** *(Protestant)* evangelikal; **c)** *(evangelizing, crusading)* missionarisch *(fig.)*
evangelicalism [i:væn'dʒelɪkəlɪzm] *n., no pl.* evangelikale Lehre
evangelise *see* **evangelize**
evangelism [ɪ'vændʒəlɪzm] *n.* **a)** *(preaching the Gospel)* Evangelisation, *die;* **b)** *(evangelicalism)* evangelikale Lehre; **c)** *(crusading zeal)* Bekehrungseifer, *der*
evangelist [ɪ'vændʒəlɪst] *n.* **a)** *(Gospel-writer)* Evangelist, *der;* **b)** *(Gospel-preacher)* Evangelist, *der;* Prediger, *der; (itinerant preacher)* Wanderprediger, *der*
evangelize [ɪ'vændʒəlaɪz] *v.t.* evangelisieren
evaporate [ɪ'væpəreɪt] **1.** *v.i.* **a)** *(become vapour)* verdunsten; **b)** *(lose liquid)* eindicken; *(completely)* eintrocknen; **c)** *(fig.)* sich in Luft auflösen; dahinschwinden *(geh.);* ‹*Furcht, Begeisterung:*› verfliegen. **2.** *v.t.* **a)** *(turn into vapour)* verdunsten lassen; **b)** *(cause to lose liquid)* evaporieren *(Chem.);* eindampfen *(Chem.)*
evaporated 'milk *n.* Kondensmilch, *die*
evaporation [ɪvæpə'reɪʃn] *n.* **a)** *(changing into vapour)* Verdunstung, *die;* **b)** *(losing liquid)* Eindickung, *die; (completely)* Eintrocknung, *die*
evasion [ɪ'veɪʒn] *n.* **a)** *(avoidance)* Umgehung, *die; (of duty)* Vernachlässigung, *die; (of responsibility, question)* Ausweichen, *das* **(of** vor + *Dat.*); **tax** ~: Steuerhinterziehung, *die;* **b)** *(evasive statement)* Ausrede, *die;* ~**s** Ausflüchte *Pl.;* **c)** *(prevarication)* Ausflüchte *Pl.*
evasive [ɪ'veɪsɪv] *adj.* **a) be/become [very]** ~: [ständig] ausweichen; **be** ~ **about sth.** um etw. herumreden; **b)** *(aimed at evasion)* ausweichend ‹*Antwort*›; **take** ~ **action** ein Ausweichmanöver machen
evasively [ɪ'veɪsɪvlɪ] *adv.* ausweichend
Eve [i:v] *pr. n. (Bibl.)* Eva *(die)*
eve *n.* **a)** Vorabend, *der; (day)* Vortag, *der;* **the** ~ **of** der Abend/Tag vor (+ *Dat.*); der Vorabend/Vortag (+ *Gen.*); *see also* **Christmas Eve; New Year's Eve; b)** *(fig.)* **[be] on the** ~ **of sth.** kurz vor etw. *(Dat.)* [stehen]; **c)** *(arch.: evening)* Abend, *der*
'even ['i:vn] **1.** *adj.*, ~**er** ['i:vənə(r)], ~**est** ['i:vənɪst] **a)** *(smooth, flat)* eben ‹*Boden, Fläche*›; glatt ‹*Faser, Gewebe*›; **make sth.** ~: etw. ebnen/glätten; **b)** *(level)* gleich hoch ‹*Stapel, Stuhl-, Tischbein*›; gleich lang ‹*Vorhang, Stuhl-, Tischbein usw.*›; **be of** ~ **height/length** gleich hoch/lang sein; ~ **with** genauso hoch/lang wie; **on an** ~ **keel** *(Naut., Aeronaut.)* auf ebenem Kiel *(Seemannsspr.);* ≈ ausgetrimmt *(Seemannsspr., Fliegerspr.); (fig.)* ausgeglichen; **keep the firm on an** ~ **keel** die Firma über Wasser halten; **c)** *(straight)* gerade ‹*Saum, Kante*›; **d)** *(parallel)* parallel **(with** zu); **e)** *(regular)* regelmäßig ‹*Zähne*›; ebenmäßig ‹*Gesichtszüge*›; *(steady)* gleichmäßig ‹*Schrift, Rhythmus, Atmen, Schlagen*›; stetig ‹*Fortschritt*›; **f)** *(equal)* gleich [groß] ‹*Menge, Abstand*›; ausgewogen ‹*Kräfteverhältnis*›; gleichmäßig ‹*Verteilung, Aufteilung*›; ausgeglichen ‹*Punktestand*›; **start out** ~: mit den gleichen Voraussetzungen beginnen; **the teams are/the score is** ~: die Mannschaften sind punktgleich/die Punktzahl ist dieselbe *od.* gleich; **we need another goal to make it** ~: wir brauchen noch ein Tor zum Ausgleich; **the match is still** ~: die Begegnung steht noch unentschieden; ~**s** *(Brit.),* ~ **money** *(Betting)* eins zu eins; **an** ~**s** *or* ~ **money favourite [to win]** ein 1 : 1-Favorit; **I have an** ~ **chance of getting there on time** meine Chancen, pünktlich anzukommen, stehen fünfzig zu fünfzig *od. (ugs.)* fifty-fifty; **the odds are** ~, **it's** ~ **odds** *or* **an** ~ **bet** die Chancen stehen fünfzig zu fünfzig *od. (ugs.)* fifty-fifty; ~ **Stephen** [i:vn 'sti:vn] *(coll.)* ≈ fifty-fifty *(ugs.);* **g)** *(balanced)* im Gleichgewicht; **with an** ~ **hand** *(fig.)* gerecht; **h)** *(quits, fully revenged)* **be** *or* **get** ~ **with sb.**

es jmdm. heimzahlen; **i)** *(uniform)* gleichmäßig; **j)** *(calm)* ausgeglichen; **have an ~ temper** ausgeglichen sein; **k)** *(divisible by two, so numbered)* gerade ‹*Zahl, Seite, Hausnummer*›; **the ~ syllables** die zweite, vierte usw. Silbe; **l)** *(exact)* **an ~ dozen** ein rundes Dutzend *(ugs.)*; **let's make it an ~ ten** sagen wir rund zehn *(ugs.)*. *See also* **break even. 2.** *adv.* **a)** sogar; selbst; **~ perhaps ...:** vielleicht sogar ...; **hard, unbearable ~:** hart, sogar *od.* wenn nicht gar unerträglich; **does he ~ suspect the danger?** ahnt er überhaupt die Gefahr?; **do sth. ~ without being told** etw. auch ohne Aufforderung tun; **~ afterwards** selbst *od.* sogar danach; **~ before[hand]** auch schon vorher; **~ today** selbst *od.* sogar heute noch; **b)** *with negative* **not** *or* **never ~ ...:** [noch] nicht einmal ...; **without ~ saying goodbye** ohne wenigstens auf Wiedersehen zu sagen; **c)** *with compar. adj. or adv.* sogar noch ‹*komplizierter, weniger, schlimmer usw.*›; **d) ~ if** *or* **though Arsenal win** selbst wenn Arsenal gewinnt; **~ if Arsenal won** selbst wenn Arsenal gewinnen würde; *(fact)* obgleich Arsenal gewann; **~ supposing we had been present** selbst wenn wir dabeigewesen wären; **~ were she to appear** selbst wenn sie auftauchen sollte; **~ as** *(just when)* gerade als; *(in just the way that)* geradeso wie; *(during the period that)* während ... noch; **~ so** [aber] trotzdem *od.* dennoch; *(arch.: that is correct)* so ist es; **~ now/then** *(as well as previously)* selbst *od.* sogar jetzt/dann; *(at this/that very moment)* gerade in diesem Augenblick. **3.** *v. t.* ebnen; *(smooth)* glätten

~ 'out 1. *v. t.* **a)** *(make smooth)* glätten; **b)** *(distribute more equally)* gleich verteilen; ausgleichen ‹*Unterschiede*›. **2.** *v. i.* **a)** *(become smooth)* ‹*Boden:*› sich einebnen; **b)** *(become more equal)* sich ausgleichen

~ 'up 1. *v. t.* ausgleichen; **so as to ~ things up** zum Ausgleich. **2.** *v. i.* *(settle debt, get revenge)* abrechnen

²even *n. (poet.)* Abend, *der*

even-'handed *adj.* gerecht

evening ['i:vnɪŋ] *n.* **a)** Abend, *der; attrib.* Abend‹*vorstellung, -ausgabe, -messe*›; **this/tomorrow ~:** heute/morgen abend; **during the ~:** am Abend; **[early/late] in the ~:** am [frühen/späten] Abend; *(regularly)* [früh/spät] abends; **at eight in the ~:** um acht Uhr abends; **on the ~ of 2 May** am Abend des 2. Mai; **on Wednesday ~s/~:** Mittwoch abends/am Mittwoch abend; **one ~:** eines Abends; **every ~:** jeden Abend; **~ came** es wurde Abend; **~s, of an ~:** abends; **two ~s ago** vorgestern abend; **the other ~:** neulich abends; **a good ~'s viewing** ein gutes Abendprogramm [im Fernsehen]; **the cool of the ~** die Abendkühle; **an ~ of cards** ein Abend beim Kartenspiel; *see also* **good 1 m; b)** *(coll: greeting)* 'n Abend! *(ugs.)*; **c)** *(soirée)* Abend, *der;* **discussion ~:** Diskussionsabend, *der;* **d)** *(fig.)* Abend, *der (geh.)*; *(of life)* Lebensabend, *der (geh.)*

evening: ~ class *n.* Abendkurs, *der;* **take** *or* **do ~ classes in pottery** *etc.* Abendkurse im Töpfern *usw.* besuchen; **~ 'dress** *n.* Abendkleidung, *die;* **in [full] ~ dress** in Abendkleidung; **~ dress, ~ gown** *ns.* Abendkleid, *das;* **~ 'meal** *n.* Abendessen, *das;* **~ 'paper** *n.* Abendzeitung, *die;* **~ 'primrose** *n.* Nachtkerze, *die;* **~ school** *n.* Abendschule, *die;* **~ 'service** *n. (Eccl.)* Abendandacht, *die; (mass)* Abendgottesdienst, *der;* **~ 'star** *n.* Abendstern, *der*

evenly ['i:vnlɪ] *adv.* gleichmäßig; **say sth. ~:** etw. in ruhigem Ton sagen; **be ~ spaced** den gleichen Abstand voneinander haben; **the runners are ~ matched** die Läufer sind einander ebenbürtig

even-numbered ['i:vnnʌmbəd] *adj.* gerade; **the houses are ~:** die Häuser haben gerade Hausnummern

'evensong *n. (Eccl.)* Abendandacht, *die*

event [ɪ'vent] *n.* **a) in the ~ of his dying** *or* **death** im Falle seines Todes; falls er stirbt; **in the ~ of rain** bei Regenwetter; **in the ~ of sickness/war** im Falle einer Krankheit/im Kriegsfalle; **in that ~:** in dem Falle; **in such an ~:** in solch einem Falle; **in the unlikely ~ of sb. doing sth.** falls, was nicht sehr wahrscheinlich ist, jmd. etw. tut; **in the ~ that** *(Amer.)* im Falle, daß; **b)** *(outcome)* **in any/either ~ = in any case** *see* **¹case a; at all ~s** auf jeden Fall; **in the ~:** letzten Endes; **c)** *(occurrence)* Ereignis, *das;* **~s have proved ...:** die Ereignisse haben gezeigt ...; **the dramatic ~s in Rome** das dramatische Geschehen in Rom; **~s are taking place in Argentina which ...:** es geschehen Dinge in Argentinien, die ...; **sth. is [quite] an ~:** etw. ist schon ein Ereignis; *see also* **course 1 a; wise; d)** *(Sport)* Wettkampf, *der;* **show-jumping ~:** Jagdspringen, *das;* Springprüfung, *die;* **three-day ~:** Military, *die;* Vielseitigkeitsprüfung, *die*

even-'tempered *adj.* ausgeglichen

eventful [ɪ'ventfl] *adj.* ereignisreich ‹*Tag, Zeiten*›; bewegt ‹*Leben, Jugend, Zeiten*›

'eventide *n. (arch.)* Abendzeit, *die (geh.)*

eventual [ɪ'ventjʊəl] *adj.* **predict sb.'s ~ downfall** vorhersagen, daß jmd. schließlich zu Fall kommen wird; **lead to sb.'s ~ downfall** schließlich zu jmds. Sturz führen; **the career of Napoleon and his ~ defeat** der Aufstieg Napoleons und schließlich seine Niederlage; **we are heading towards ~ destruction** wir steuern letztlich auf den Untergang zu

eventuality [ɪventjʊ'ælɪtɪ] *n.* Eventualität, *die;* **the ~ of war** der mögliche Kriegsfall; **in certain eventualities** in bestimmten [möglichen] Fällen; **be ready for all eventualities** auf alle Eventualitäten gefaßt sein

eventually [ɪ'ventjʊəlɪ] *adv.* schließlich; **she'll ~ get married** sie wird irgendwann *od.* eines Tages heiraten; **I'll do that ~:** ich mache das irgendwann [noch]

eve-of-'poll *adj.* **~ [survey]** [Umfrage] kurz vor der Wahl

ever ['evə(r)] *adv.* **a)** *(always, at all times)* immer; stets; **for ~:** für immer ‹*weggehen, gelten*›; ewig ‹*lieben, dasein, leben*›; auf ewig *(dichter.)* ‹*unerreichbar*›; **go on for ~:** immer so bleiben; *(derog.)* ewig dauern; **it is for ~ changing** es ändert sich dauernd; **the traffic-lights took for ~ to change** *(coll.)* die Ampeln schalteten erst nach einer Ewigkeit um; **Arsenal for ~!** es lebe Arsenal!; **for ~ and ~:** immer und ewig; *(in the Lord's Prayer)* in Ewigkeit; **for ~ and a day** eine Ewigkeit; **~ since [then]** seit [dieser Zeit]; **~ after[wards]** seitdem; **I've been frightened of dogs ~ 'since** *or* **'after** seitdem *od.* seit diesem Tag habe ich Angst vor Hunden; **~ since he inherited it** von dem Tag an, an dem er das geerbt hat; **~ since I've known her** solange ich sie kenne; **~ since I can remember** soweit ich zurückdenken kann; **~ since she was a child** von Kindheit an; **~ yours** *or* **yours ~, Ethel** Deine/Eure Ethel; immer die Deine/Eure, Ethel *(veralt.)*; **b)** *in comb. with compar. adj. or adv.* noch; immer; **get ~ deeper into debt** sich noch *od.* immer mehr verschulden; **~ further** noch immer weiter; **c)** *in comb. with participles etc.* **~-increasing** ständig zunehmend; **~-recurring** immer wiederkehrend; **~-present** allgegenwärtig; **~-youthful** ewig jugendlich; **~-changing rules** sich ständig ändernde Vorschriften; **an ~-patient mother** eine Mutter, die nie die Geduld verliert; **go round in ~-decreasing circles** *(fig. coll.)* [mit immer größeren Anstrengungen] immer weniger erreichen; **d)** *(at any time)* je[mals]; **not ~:** noch nie; **~ before** je zuvor; **never ~:** nie im Leben; **never ~ before** noch nie zuvor; **nothing ~ happens** es passiert nie etwas; **his best performance ~:** seine beste Vorstellung überhaupt; **it hardly ~ rains** es regnet so gut wie nie; **don't you ~ do that again!** mach das bloß nicht noch mal!; **did you ~?** *(coll.)* hast du Töne? *(salopp)*; **he's a devil if ~ there was one** *(coll.)* er ist ein Teufel, alles, was recht ist *(ugs.)*; **better than ~:** besser denn je; **more frequently than ~:** häufiger als je zuvor; **the same as ~** *or* **as it ~ was** das gleiche wie immer; **as ~:** wie gewöhnlich; *(iron.)* wie gehabt; **yours as ~, Bob** *(in letter)* wie immer, Dein Bob; **as ... as ~:** unverändert ...; **I'm as stupid as ~:** ich bin immer noch nicht schlauer; **he's as kind a man as ~ lived** er ist der freundlichste Mensch, den es je gegeben hat; **if I ~ catch you doing that again** wenn ich dich dabei noch einmal erwische; **seldom, if ~,** *(coll.)* **seldom ~:** so gut wie nie; **as if I ~ would!** ich doch nicht!; **a fool if ~ there was one** der größte Narr, den man sich *(Dat.)* vorstellen kann; **is he ~ conceited** *(Amer. coll.)* ist der vielleicht eingebildet! *(ugs.)*; **the first men ~** *or* **the first ~ men to reach the moon** die ersten, die je auf dem Mond waren; **you're the first ~:** du bist der/die allererste; **the greatest tennis-player ~:** der größte Tennisspieler, den es je gegeben hat; **the hottest day ~:** der heißeste Tag seit Menschengedenken; **e)** *(coll.) emphasizing question* **what ~ does he want?** was will er nur?; **who/which ~ could it be?** wer/welcher könnte das nur sein?; **how ~ did I drop it?/could I have dropped it?** wie konnte ich es nur fallen lassen?; **when ~ did he do it?** wann hat er es nur getan?; **where ~ in the world have you been?** wo in aller Welt hast du bloß gesteckt?; **why ~ not?** warum denn nicht?; **f)** *intensifier* **before ~ he opened his mouth** noch bevor er seinen Mund aufmachte; **as soon as ~ I can** so bald wie irgend möglich; **I'm ~ so sorry** *(coll.)* mir tut es ja so leid; **~ so nice** *(coll.)* so ungemein schön; **~ so slightly drunk** *(coll.)* ein ganz klein wenig betrunken; **thanks ~ so [much]** *(coll.)* vielen herzlichen Dank; **he liked her ~ so** *(coll.)* er mochte sie so sehr; **it was ~ such a shame** *(coll.)* es war so schade; **g)** *(arch.: always)* all[e]zeit *(veralt.)*; **it was ~ thus** so ist es immer; **h) ~ and again** *or (literary)* **anon** dann und wann

'everglade *n. (Amer. Geog.)* Sumpfgebiet, *das;* **the E~s** die Everglades

'evergreen 1. *adj.* **a)** immergrün ‹*Baum, Strauch, Landschaft*›; **b)** *(fig.)* immer wieder aktuell ‹*Problem, Thema*›; immer wieder gern gehört ‹*Lied, Schlager, Sänger*›; **~ song** Evergreen, *der.* **2.** *n.* immergrüne Pflanze/immergrüner Baum

ever'lasting *adj.* **a)** *(eternal)* immerwährend; ewig ‹*Leben, Gesetz, Höllenqualen, Gott, Gedenken, Berge, Fels*›; unvergänglich ‹*Ruhm, Ehre*›; **b)** *(incessant)* ewig *(ugs.)*; endlos

everlastingly [evə'lɑ:stɪŋlɪ] *adv.* **a)** *(eternally)* ewig ‹*leben, leiden*›; **b)** *(incessantly)* ewig *(ugs.)*; ständig

'ever-loving *adj.* **your ~ wife/husband** *(in letter)* Deine Dich ewig liebende Frau/Dein Dich ewig liebender Mann

ever'more *adv.* auf ewig; **for ~:** in [alle] Ewigkeit

every ['evrɪ] *adj.* **a)** *(each single)* jeder/jede/jedes; **~ man will do his duty** jeder [einzelne] wird seine Pflicht tun; **have ~ reason** allen Grund haben; **~ [single] time/on ~ [single] occasion** [aber auch] jedesmal; **~ [single] time we ...:** [aber auch] jedesmal, wenn wir ...; **there was one man for ~ three women** auf einen Mann kamen drei Frauen; **he ate ~ last** *or* **single biscuit** *(coll.)* er hat die ganzen Kekse aufgegessen *(ugs.)*; **she's spent ~ last penny** *(coll.)* sie hat das ganze Geld ausgegeben; **~ one** jeder/jede/jedes [einzelne]; **~ time** *(coll.: without any hesita-*

tion) jederzeit; **give me** *or* **I prefer Switzerland ~ time** *(coll.)* es geht doch nichts über die Schweiz; **~ which way** *(Amer.)* in alle Richtungen; **b)** *after possessive adj.* **your ~ wish** all[e] deine Wünsche; **his ~ thought** all[e] seine Gedanken; **c)** *(indicating recurrence)* **she comes [once] ~ day** sie kommt jeden Tag [einmal]; **~ three/few days** alle drei/paar Tage; **~ third day** jeder dritte/jeden dritten Tag; **~ other** *(every second, or fig.: almost every)* jeder/jede/jedes zweite; **~ now and then** *or* **again, ~ so often, ~ once in a while** hin und wieder; **d)** *(the greatest possible)* unbedingt, uneingeschränkt ‹*Vertrauen*›; voll ‹*Beachtung*›; all ‹*Respekt, Aussicht*›; **there's ~ prospect of a victory for England** alles deutet auf einen Sieg Englands hin; **I wish you ~ happiness/success** ich wünsche dir alles Gute/viel Erfolg; **there's ~ likelihood of their coming** aller Wahrscheinlichkeit nach kommen sie

'everybody *n. & pron.* jeder; **has ~ seen it?** haben es alle *od.* hat es jeder gesehen?; **~ else** alle anderen; **~ knows ~ else round here** hier kennt jeder jeden; **he asked ~ to be quiet** er bat alle um Ruhe; **hello, ~!** *(coll.)* Tag, zusammen! *(ugs.)*; **would ~ be quiet please?** würden Sie bitte alle ruhig sein?; **it's not ~ who can ...**: nicht jeder kann ...; **it's ~'s duty** es ist jedermanns Pflicht; jeder[mann] ist verpflichtet; **opera isn't [to] ~'s taste** Oper ist nicht jedermanns Sache; **holidays to suit ~'s purse** Urlaub für jeden Geldbeutel; *see also* **anybody c**

'everyday *attrib. adj.* alltäglich; Alltags‹*kleidung, -sprache*›; routinemäßig ‹*Geschäftsführung*›; **in ~ life** im Alltag; im täglichen Leben; **an ~ story of country folk** eine Geschichte über den Alltag der Leute vom Lande; **~ reality** Alltag, *der;* **~ expressions** Ausdrücke der Alltagssprache; **it is a matter of ~ knowledge that ...** jedermann weiß, daß ...

'Everyman *n., no pl.* der Durchschnittsbürger; [Herr] Jedermann *(veralt.)*

everyone ['evrɪwʌn, 'evrɪwən] *see* **everybody**

'everyplace *(Amer.) see* **everywhere**

'everything *n. & pron.* **a)** alles; **~ [that] you have** alles, was du hast; **~ else** alles andere; **some pupils are good at ~**: manche Schüler sind in allen Fächern gut; **~ comes to him who waits** *(prov.)* mit Geduld und Spucke fängt man eine Mucke *(ugs.)*; **the man who has ~**: der Mann, der schon alles hat; **~ interesting/valuable** alles Interessante/Wertvolle; **there's a [right] time for ~**: alles zu seiner Zeit; **they bought the house and ~ in it** sie kauften das Haus mit allem Inventar; **he is ~ a man should be** er hat alle Qualitäten, die ein Mann besitzen sollte; **b)** *(coll.: all that matters)* alles; **looks aren't ~**: das Aussehen [allein] ist nicht alles; **her child is ~ to her** das Kind ist ihr ein und alles; **have ~**: [einfach] alles haben

'everyway *adv.* in jeder Beziehung

'everywhere 1. *adv.* **a)** *(in every place)* überall; **b)** *(to every place)* **go ~**: überall hingehen/-fahren; **~ you go/look** wohin man auch geht/sieht. **2.** *n.* **from ~**: überallher; von überall [her]; **~ is quiet in Holland on a Sunday** überall in Holland ist es sonntags ruhig

evict [ɪ'vɪkt] *v.t.* exmittieren *(Rechtsspr.)*; **~ a family [from the house]** eine Familie zur Räumung [des Hauses] zwingen

eviction [ɪ'vɪkʃn] *n.* Zwangsräumung, *die;* Exmission, *die (Rechtsspr.)*; **the ~ of the tenant** die zwangsweise Vertreibung des Mieters [aus seiner Wohnung]; **action for ~** *(Law)* Räumungsklage, *die;* **~ order** *(Law)* Räumungsbefehl, *der*

evidence ['evɪdəns] **1.** *n.* **a)** Beweis, *der; (indication)* Anzeichen, *das;* Beweis, *der;* **be ~ of sth.** etw. beweisen; **provide ~ of sth.** den Beweis *od.* Beweise für etw. liefern; **as ~ of sth.** als *od.* zum Beweis für etw.; **we do not have any ~ for this** wir haben nicht einen einzigen Beweis *od.* keinerlei Anhaltspunkte dafür; **there was no ~ of a fight** nichts deutete auf einen Kampf hin; **give ~ of having been damaged** offensichtlich beschädigt worden sein; **hard ~**: durchschlagende Beweise; *see also* **external 1f; internal evidence; b)** *(Law)* Beweismaterial, *das; (object)* Beweisstück, *das; (testimony)* [Zeugen]aussage, *die;* **give ~**: [als Zeuge] aussagen; **give ~ under oath/for sb./against sb.** unter Eid/für jmdn./gegen jmdn. aussagen; **refuse to give ~**: die Aussage verweigern; **hear** *or* **take ~**: Zeugen vernehmen; **hearing** *or* **taking of ~**: Beweisaufnahme, *die;* **because of insufficient ~**: aus Mangel an Beweisen; mangels Beweise *(Amtsspr.)*; **piece of ~**: Beweisstück, *das; (statement)* Beweis, *der;* **incriminating ~**: Belastungsmaterial, *das;* **[turn] King's/Queen's ~** *(Brit.) or (Amer.)* **State's ~**: [als] Kronzeuge [auftreten]; **the witness said in ~ that ...**: der Zeuge sagte aus, daß ...; **call sb. in ~**: jmdn. als Zeugen benennen *od.* anrufen; **submit sth. in ~**: etw. als Beweis vorlegen; *see also* **circumstantial a; presumptive; c) be [much] in ~**: [stark] in Erscheinung treten; **he was nowhere in ~**: er war nirgends zu sehen; **sth. is very much in ~**: überall sieht man etw. **2.** *v.t.* zeugen von

evident ['evɪdənt] *adj.* offensichtlich; deutlich ‹*Verbesserung*›; **the effect is still ~**: die Wirkung ist [immer] noch deutlich sichtbar; **be ~ to sb.** jmdm. klar sein; **it soon became ~ that ...**: es stellte sich bald heraus, daß ...

evidently ['evɪdəntlɪ] *adv.* offensichtlich

evil ['i:vl, 'i:vɪl] **1.** *adj.* **a)** böse; schlecht ‹*Charakter, Beispiel, Einfluß, System*›; übel, verwerflich ‹*Praktiken*›; **with ~ intent** in *od.* aus böser Absicht; **the E~ One** der Böse; **~ doings** Missetaten *Pl.;* **~ tongue** böse Zunge; Lästerzunge, *die (abwertend);* **the ~ eye** der böse Blick; **b)** *(unlucky)* verhängnisvoll, unglückselig ‹*Tag, Stunde*›; böse, schlecht ‹*Zeichen*›; schwer, schlimm ‹*Schicksal*›; **~ days** *or* **times** schlechte *od.* schlimme Zeiten; **fall on ~ days** ins Unglück geraten; **c)** *(disagreeable)* übel ‹*Geruch, Geschmack*›; *(coll.: unattractive)* mies *(ugs.)*‹*Kneipe, Wetter*›. **2.** *n.* **a)** *no pl. (literary)* Böse, *das;* **the root of all ~**: die Wurzel allen Übels; **deliver us from ~** *(Relig.)* erlöse uns von dem Übel *(bibl.)*; **he saw the ~ of his ways** er erkannte, daß er auf dem Pfad der Sünde wandelte *(geh.)*; **speak ~ of sb.** schlecht über jmdn. reden; **do ~**: Böses tun; sündigen; **b)** *(bad thing)* Übel, *das;* **necessary** *or* **inescapable ~**: notwendiges Übel; **social ~s** soziale Mißstände; **the lesser ~**: das kleinere Übel; **choose the lesser of two ~s** von zwei Übeln das kleinere wählen

evil: ~-doer ['i:vldu:ə(r)] *n.* Übeltäter, *der*/-täterin, *die;* **~-'minded** *adj.* bösartig; böswillig; **~-smelling** *adj.* übelriechend; **~-tasting** *adj.* widerlich schmeckend

evince [ɪ'vɪns] *v.t.* ‹*Person:*› an den Tag legen; ‹*Äußerung, Handlung:*› zeugen von

eviscerate [ɪ'vɪsəreɪt] *v.t.* ausweiden ‹*Wild*›; ausnehmen ‹*Geflügel, Fisch*›; *(fig.)* der Substanz berauben

evocation [evə'keɪʃn] *n.* Heraufbeschwören, *das;* Evokation, *die (geh.)*; **the film is an ~ of Edwardian England** in dem Film lebt das England unter Edward VII noch einmal auf

evocative [ɪ'vɒkətɪv] *adj.* evokativ *(geh.)*; *(thought-provoking)* aufrüttelnd *(fig.)*; **be ~ of sth.** an etw. *(Akk.)* erinnern; etw. heraufbeschwören; **an ~ scent** ein Duft, der Erinnerungen weckt

evoke [ɪ'vəʊk] *v.t.* **a)** evozieren *(geh.)*; heraufbeschwören; **b)** *(elicit, provoke)* hervorrufen ‹*Bewunderung, Überraschung, Wirkung*›; erregen ‹*Interesse*›

evolution [i:və'lu:ʃn, evə'lu:ʃn] *n.* **a)** *(development)* Entwicklung, *die;* **b)** *(Biol.: of species etc.)* Evolution, *die;* **theory of ~**: Evolutionstheorie, *die;* **c)** *(Mil., Naut.)* Formierung, *die;* Evolution, *die (veralt.)*; *(Dancing etc.)* Figur, *die;* Evolution, *die (veralt.)*; **d)** *(of heat, gas, etc.)* Entstehung, *die*

evolutionary [i:və'lu:ʃənərɪ, evə'lu:ʃənərɪ] *adj.* **a)** evolutionär; sich [langsam] entwickelnd; **the ~ process** der Entwicklungsprozeß; **b)** *(Biol.)* evolutionär; **~ theory** Evolutionstheorie, *die*

evolutionism [i:və'lu:ʃənɪzm, evə'lu:ʃənɪzm] *n., no pl.* Evolutionismus, *der*

evolutionist [i:və'lu:ʃənɪst, evə'lu:ʃənɪst] *n.* Evolutionist, *der*/Evolutionistin, *die*

evolve [ɪ'vɒlv] **1.** *v.i.* **a)** *(develop)* sich entwickeln **(from** aus); **b)** *(Biol.)* sich entwickeln **(into** zu); **~ out of** entstehen aus; sich entwickeln aus. **2.** *v.t.* **a)** entwickeln; **b)** *(Biol.)* entwickeln ‹*Art usw.*› **(from** aus)

ewe [ju:] *n.* Mutterschaf, *das*

ewer ['ju:ə(r)] *n.* [Wasch]krug, *der*

¹ex [eks] *n. (coll.)* Verflossene, *der/die (ugs.)*

²ex *prep.* **a)** *(Commerc.)* **ex works/store** ‹*Güter*› ab Werk/Lager; **b)** *(Finance)* ohne

ex- *pref.* Ex-‹*Freundin, Präsident, Champion*›; Alt‹*[bundes]kanzler, -bundespräsident, -bürgermeister*›; ehemalig

exacerbate [ek'sæsəbeɪt] *v.t.* verschlimmern ‹*Schmerz, Krankheit, Wut*›; steigern ‹*Unzufriedenheit, Feindschaft*›; verschlechtern ‹*Zustand*›; verschärfen ‹*Lage*›

exact [ɪg'zækt] **1.** *adj.* **a)** genau; exakt, genau ‹*Daten, Berechnung*›; **those were his ~ words** das waren genau seine Worte; **an ~ copy of the painting/inscription** eine perfekte Kopie des Gemäldes/eine wortgetreue Wiedergabe der Inschrift; **on the ~ spot where ...**: genau an der Stelle, wo ...; **could you give me the ~ money?** könnten Sie mir das Geld passend geben?; **11 to be ~**: 11, um genau zu sein; **be ~ in one's work** es mit der Arbeit genau nehmen; **b)** *(rigorous)* streng; **c) ~ science** exakte Wissenschaft. **2.** *v.t.* **a)** fordern, verlangen; erheben ‹*Gebühr, Zoll*›; **~ from sb. a promise of sth.** von jmdm. verlangen, daß er etw. verspricht; **b)** *(call for)* ‹*Sache:*› erfordern, verlangen

exacting [ɪg'zæktɪŋ] *adj.* anspruchsvoll; streng ‹*Prüfer, Lehrer, Maßstab*›; hoch ‹*Anforderung, Maßstab*›; **be very ~ about punctuality** großen Wert auf Pünktlichkeit legen

exaction [ɪg'zækʃn] *n.* Forderung, *die* **(of** nach)

exactitude [ɪg'zæktɪtju:d] *n., no pl.* Genauigkeit, *die;* **with complete ~**: mit letzter Genauigkeit

exactly [ɪg'zæktlɪ] *adv.* **a)** genau; **when ~** *or* **~ when did he leave?** wann genau ging er?; wann ging er genau?; **~ what happened we'll never know** was genau geschehen ist, werden wir nie erfahren; **at ~ the right moment** genau im richtigen Moment; **~!** genau!; **~ a year ago today** heute vor genau einem Jahr; **I'm not ~ sure** ich bin nicht ganz sicher; **at four o'clock ~**: Punkt vier Uhr; **~ as** genau[so] wie; **~ as you wish** ganz wie du willst; **not ~** *(coll. iron.)* nicht gerade; **I'll tell her ~ what I think of her** ich werde ihr ganz genau sagen, was ich von ihr halte; **b)** *(with perfect accuracy)* [ganz] genau; **so ~**: mit solcher Genauigkeit

exactness [ɪg'zæktnɪs] *n., no pl.* Genauigkeit, *die;* **doubt the ~ of the figure** bezweifeln, daß die Zahl genau stimmt

exaggerate [ɪg'zædʒəreɪt] *v.t.* **a)** übertreiben; **you are exaggerating his importance/its worth** du machst ihn wichtiger, als er ist/so wertvoll ist/war es nun auch wieder nicht; **the story had been grossly ~d** die Sache war gewaltig aufgebauscht worden *(ab-*

wertend); **you always ~:** du mußt immer übertreiben; **b)** *(accentuate)* unterstreichen; betonen

exaggerated [ɪg'zædʒəreɪtɪd] *adj.* übertrieben; **grossly** *or* **highly ~:** stark übertrieben; **he has an ~ opinion of himself** er hat eine übertrieben hohe Meinung von sich selbst

exaggeratedly [ɪg'zædʒəreɪtɪdlɪ] *adv.* übertrieben

exaggeration [ɪgzædʒə'reɪʃn] *n.* Übertreibung, *die;* **it is a wild/is no ~ to say that ...:** es ist stark/nicht übertrieben, wenn man sagt, daß ...; **no ~!** ohne Übertreibung!; **he's prone to ~:** er übertreibt gern; **that, of course, is an ~:** das ist natürlich übertrieben; **that's a bit of an** *or* **a slight ~:** das ist leicht übertrieben

exalt [ɪg'zɔ:lt] *v. t.* **a)** *(praise)* [lob]preisen; **~ sb. to the skies** jmdn. in den Himmel heben *(ugs.);* **b)** *(raise in rank or power)* erheben; *(raise in estimation)* hochachten

exaltation [egzɔ:l'teɪʃn, eksɔ:l'teɪʃn] *n.* **a)** *(fig.: elevation)* Erhebung, *die;* **b)** *(elation)* Begeisterung, *die*

exalted [ɪg'zɔ:ltɪd] *adj.* **a)** *(high-ranking)* hoch; **those in ~ positions** hochgestellte Persönlichkeiten; **b)** *(lofty, sublime)* hoch ‹*Ideal*›; erhaben ‹*Thema, Stil, Stimmung, Gedanke*›

exam [ɪg'zæm] *(coll.) see* **examination c**

examination [ɪgzæmɪ'neɪʃn] *n.* **a)** *(inspection)* Untersuchung, *die; (of accounts)* [Über]prüfung, *die;* **on ~ it was found to contain drugs** die Untersuchung ergab, daß es Drogen enthielt; **on closer** *or* **further ~:** bei genauerer *od.* näherer Untersuchung *od.* Überprüfung; **be under ~:** untersucht *od.* überprüft werden; **give sth. a thorough ~:** etw. gründlich untersuchen *od.* überprüfen; **carry out an ~ of sth./into sth.** etw. untersuchen *od.* überprüfen/eine Untersuchung über etw. *(Akk.)* anstellen *od.* durchführen; **b)** *(Med.)* Untersuchung, *die;* **give sb. a thorough ~:** jmdn. gründlich untersuchen; **undergo an ~:** sich untersuchen lassen; **c)** *(test of knowledge or ability)* Prüfung, *die; (final ~ at university)* Examen, *das; attrib.* Prüfungs-/Examens-; **~ nerves** Prüfungsangst, *die;* **d)** *(Law) (of witness, accused)* Verhör, *das;* Vernehmung, *die; (of case)* Untersuchung, *die;* **he is still under ~:** er wird noch verhört *od.* vernommen; **be subjected to ~:** einem Verhör *od.* einer Vernehmung unterzogen werden

exami'nation-paper *n.* **a)** ~[s] schriftliche Prüfungsaufgaben; **b)** *(with candidate's answers)* ≈ Klausurarbeit, *die*

examine [ɪg'zæmɪn] *v. t.* **a)** *(inspect)* untersuchen (**for** auf + *Akk.*); prüfen ‹*Dokument, Gewissen, Gefühle, Geschäftsbücher*›; kontrollieren ‹*Ausweis, Gepäck*›; **b)** *(Med.)* untersuchen; **c)** *(test knowledge or ability of)* prüfen (**in** in + *Dat.*); **~ sb. on his knowledge of French** jmds. Französischkenntnisse prüfen; **d)** *(Law)* verhören; vernehmen

examinee [ɪgzæmɪ'ni:] *n.* Prüfungskandidat, *der*/-kandidatin, *die;* Prüfling, *der; (Univ. also)* Examenskandidat, *der*/-kandidatin, *die; (to qualify for higher education also)* Abiturient, *der*/Abiturientin, *die*

examiner [ɪg'zæmɪnə(r)] *n.* Prüfer, *der*/Prüferin, *die;* **board of ~s** Prüfungsausschuß, *der*

examining body [ɪg'zæmɪnɪŋ bɒdɪ] *n.* ≈ Prüfungsamt, *das*

example [ɪg'zɑ:mpl] *n.* **a)** Beispiel, *das;* **by way of [an] ~:** als Beispiel; **she is a perfect ~ of how ...:** sie ist das beste Beispiel dafür, wie ...; **take sth. as an ~:** etw. zum Beispiel nehmen; **just to give [you] an** *or* **one ~:** um [dir] nur ein Beispiel zu nennen; **for ~:** zum Beispiel; **she's an ~ to us all** sie gibt uns *(Dat.)* allen ein Beispiel; **set an ~** *or* **a good ~ to sb.** jmdm. ein Beispiel geben; **follow sb.'s ~ [in doing sth.]** sich *(Dat.)* an jmdm. ein Beispiel nehmen [und etw. tun]; *(in a particular action)* jmds. Beispiel folgen; **b)** *(as warning)* [abschreckendes] Beispiel; **make an ~ of sb.** ein Exempel an jmdm. statuieren; **punish sb. as an ~ to others** jmdn. exemplarisch bestrafen; **let that be an ~ to you** laß dir das eine Lehre sein

exasperate [ɪg'zæspəreɪt, ɪg'zɑ:spəreɪt] *v. t. (irritate)* verärgern; *(infuriate)* zur Verzweiflung bringen; **be ~d at** *or* **by sb./sth.** über jmdn./etw. verärgert/verzweifelt sein; **feel ~d** verärgert/verzweifelt sein; **become** *or* **get ~d [with sb.]** sich [über jmdn.] ärgern

exasperating [ɪg'zæspəreɪtɪŋ, ɪg'zɑ:spəreɪtɪŋ] *adj.* ärgerlich; ‹*Aufgabe*› die einen zur Verzweiflung bringt; **be ~:** einen zur Verzweiflung bringen

exasperatingly [ɪg'zæspəreɪtɪŋlɪ, ɪg'zɑ:spəreɪtɪŋlɪ] *adv.* zum Verzweifeln

exasperation [ɪgzæspə'reɪʃn, ɪgzɑ:spə'reɪʃn] *n. see* **exasperate:** Ärger, *der*/Verzweiflung, *die* (**with** über + *Akk.*); **in ~:** verärgert/verzweifelt

excavate ['ekskəveɪt] *v. t.* **a)** ausschachten; *(with machine)* ausbaggern; fördern, abbauen ‹*Erz, Metall*›; **b)** *(Archaeol.)* ausgraben; *abs.* Ausgrabungen vornehmen

excavation [ekskə'veɪʃn] *n.* **a)** Ausschachtung, *die; (with machine)* Ausbaggerung, *die; (of ore, metals)* Förderung, *die;* Abbau, *der;* **b)** *(Archaeol.)* Ausgrabung, *die;* **~ work** Ausgrabungsarbeiten *Pl.;* **c)** *(place)* [Bau]grube, *die; (Archaeol.)* Ausgrabungsstätte, *die*

excavator ['ekskəveɪtə(r)] *n.* **a)** *(machine)* Bagger, *der;* **b)** *(Archaeol.: person)* Ausgräber, *der*/Ausgräberin, *die*

exceed [ɪk'si:d] *v. t.* **a)** *(be greater than)* übertreffen (**in** an + *Dat.*); ‹*Kosten, Summe, Anzahl:*› übersteigen (**by** um); **not ~ing** bis zu; **b)** *(go beyond)* überschreiten; hinausgehen über (+ *Akk.*) ‹*Auftrag, Befehl*›; *(surpass)* übertreffen (**in** an + *Dat.*)

exceedingly [ɪk'si:dɪŋlɪ] *adv.* äußerst; ausgesprochen ‹*häßlich, dumm*›; **fit ~ well** ausgezeichnet passen; **a joke in ~ bad taste** ein ausgesprochen geschmackloser Witz; **it was ~ obvious that she was pregnant** es war überdeutlich zu sehen, daß sie schwanger war

excel [ɪk'sel] **1.** *v. t.,* **-ll-** übertreffen; **~ oneself** *(lit. or iron.)* sich selbst übertreffen. **2.** *v. i.,* **-ll-** sich hervortun (**at, in** in + *Dat.*); **~ as an orator** ein hervorragender Redner sein; **she ~s at cookery** sie ist eine glänzende Köchin

excellence ['eksələns] *n.* hervorragende Qualität; *(merit)* hervorragende Leistung; **an unusual degree of ~:** eine außergewöhnlich hohe Qualitätsstufe/ein außergewöhnlich hohes Leistungsniveau; **moral/academic ~:** höchster moralischer/wissenschaftlicher Rang; **this school is known for its standards of ~:** diese Schule ist für ihr außerordentliches Niveau bekannt

excellency ['eksələnsɪ] *n.* Exzellenz, *die*

excellent ['eksələnt] *adj.* ausgezeichnet; hervorragend; exzellent *(geh.);* vorzüglich ‹*Wein, Koch, Speise*›; **be in an ~ mood** bester Laune sein; **he's an ~ chap** er ist ein Prachtkerl *(ugs.)*

excellently ['eksələntlɪ] *adv.* ausgezeichnet; hervorragend; exzellent *(geh.)*

except [ɪk'sept] **1.** *prep.* **~ [***(coll.)* **for]** außer (+ *Dat.*); **~ for** *(in all respects other than)* bis auf (+ *Akk.*); abgesehen von; **~ [for the fact] that ...,** *(coll.)* **~ ...:** abgesehen davon, daß ...; **I know little of her ~ that she ...** *or (coll.)* **~ she ...:** ich weiß wenig über sie, nur daß sie ...; **I should buy a new car ~ that** *or (coll.)* **~ I've no money** ich würde mir ein neues Auto kaufen, ich habe nur kein Geld; **I'd come, ~ that** *or (coll.)* **~ I have no time** ich würde kommen, doch ich habe keine Zeit; **there was nothing to be done ~ [to] stay there** man konnte nichts anderes tun als dableiben; **where could he be ~ in the house?** wo könnte er [denn] sonst sein, wenn nicht im Haus?; **she's everywhere ~ where she ought to be** sie ist überall, nur nicht da, wo sie sein soll. **2.** *v. t.* ausnehmen (**from** bei); **~ed** ausgenommen; **nobody ~ed** alle ohne Ausnahme; **errors ~ed** Irrtümer vorbehalten; **present company ~ed** Anwesende ausgenommen

excepting [ɪk'septɪŋ] *prep.* außer (+ *Dat.*); **not ~ Peter** Peter nicht ausgenommen; **~ that ...,** *(coll.)* **~ ...:** abgesehen davon, daß ...

exception [ɪk'sepʃn] *n.* **a)** Ausnahme, *die;* **with the ~ of** mit Ausnahme (+ *Gen.*); **with the ~ of her/myself** mit Ausnahme von ihr/mir; **the ~ proves the rule** *(prov.)* Ausnahmen bestätigen die Regel; **this case is an ~ to the rule** dieser Fall ist die Ausnahme von der Regel; **be no ~ [to the rule]** durchaus keine Ausnahme sein; **there's an ~ to every rule** keine Regel ohne Ausnahme; **make an ~ [of/for sb.]** [bei jmdm.] eine Ausnahme machen; **by way of an ~:** ausnahmsweise; **b)** *no pl., no art.* **take ~ to sth.** *(be offended by sth., object to sth.)* an etw. *(Dat.)* Anstoß nehmen; **great ~ is taken to sth.** etw. erregt großen Unwillen

exceptional [ɪk'sepʃənl] *adj.* außergewöhnlich; **in ~ cases** in Ausnahmefällen

exceptionally [ɪk'sepʃənəlɪ] *adv.* **a)** *(as an exception)* ausnahmsweise; **b)** *(remarkably)* ungewöhnlich; außergewöhnlich

excerpt 1. ['eksɜ:pt] *n.* Auszug, *der* (**from, of** aus); *(from book also)* Exzerpt, *das (geh.); (from film, speech)* Ausschnitt, *der; (from record)* Stück, *das.* **2.** [ɪk'sɜ:pt] *v. t.* exzerpieren *(geh.)* (**from** aus)

excess [ɪk'ses] *n.* **a)** *(inordinate degree or amount)* Übermaß, *das* (**of** an + *Dat.*); **produce an ~ of sth.** einen Überschuß an etw. *(Dat.)* produzieren; **such ~ of detail** ein solches Übermaß an Details; **eat/drink/be generous to ~:** übermäßig essen/trinken/großzügig sein; **don't do anything to ~:** man soll nichts übertreiben; **carry sth. to ~:** etw. bis zum Exzeß treiben; **in ~:** im Übermaß; **b)** *esp. in pl. (act of immoderation, overindulgence)* Exzeß, *der; (sexual or gluttonous also)* Ausschweifung, *die; (savage also)* Ausschreitung, *die;* **c) be in ~ of sth.** etw. übersteigen; **a figure in ~ of a million** eine Zahl von über einer Million; **a speed in ~ of ...:** eine Geschwindigkeit von mehr als ...; **d)** *(surplus)* Überschuß, *der;* **~ weight** Übergewicht, *das;* **e)** *(esp. Brit. Insurance)* Selbstbeteiligung, *die;* Selbstbehalt, *der (fachspr.)*

excess ['ekses]: **~ 'baggage** *n.* Mehrgepäck, *das;* **~ 'fare** *n.* Zuschlag, *der*

excessive [ɪk'sesɪv] *adj.* übermäßig; exzessiv; übertrieben ‹*Forderung, Lob, Ansprüche*›; zu stark ‹*Schmerz, Belastung*›; unmäßig ‹*Esser, Trinker*›; **~ drinking of alcohol** übermäßiger Alkoholgenuß; **an ~ talker/eater** ein Schwätzer *(abwertend)*/Vielfraß *(ugs.);* **sb. is being rather ~:** jmd. ist ziemlich extrem

excessively [ɪk'sesɪvlɪ] *adv.* **a)** *(immoderately)* übertrieben; exzessiv; unmäßig ‹*trinken, essen*›; **~ cautious** übervorsichtig; **talk/spend ~:** [all]zuviel reden/ausgeben; **b)** *(exceedingly)* ausgesprochen

excess ['ekses]: **~ 'luggage** *see* **~ baggage; ~ 'postage** *n.* Nachgebühr, *die*

exchange [ɪks'tʃeɪndʒ] **1.** *v. t.* **a)** tauschen ‹*Plätze, Zimmer, Ringe, Küsse*›; umtauschen, wechseln ‹*Geld*›; austauschen ‹*Adressen, [Kriegs]gefangene, Erinnerungen, Gedanken, Erfahrungen*›; wechseln ‹*Blicke, Worte, Ringe*›; **[no] shots were ~d** es fand [k]ein Schußwechsel statt; **the two men ~d letters** die beiden Männer führten einen Briefwechsel; **~ blows/insults** sich schlagen/sich gegenseitig beleidigen; **b)** *(give in place of another)* eintauschen (**for** für, gegen); umtauschen ‹*[gekaufte] Ware*› (**for** gegen); austauschen ‹*Spion*› (**for** gegen); *(interchange)* austauschen (**for** gegen). **2.** *v. i.* tauschen. **3.** *n.* **a)** Tausch, *der; (of prisoners, spies, compliments, greetings, insults)* Austausch, *der;* **an ~ of ideas/blows** ein Meinungsaustausch/Handgreiflichkeiten *Pl.;* **in ~:** dafür; **in ~ for sth.** für etw.; **fair ~ is no robbery** *(prov.; joc./iron.)* so kann jeder zufrieden sein *(scherzh./iron.);* **b)** *(Educ.)* Austausch, *der;* **an ~ of pupils** ein Schüleraustausch; **an ~ student** ein Austauschstudent/eine Austauschstudentin; **the pupils are going on [an] ~ to Paris** die Schüler fahren im Rahmen eines Austauschprogramms nach Paris; **c)** *(quarrel)* Wortwechsel, *der;* **d)** *(of money)* Umtausch, *der;* **bill of ~:** Wechsel, *der;* Tratte, *die (Bankw.);* **~ [rate], rate of ~:** Wechsel- *od.* Umrechnungskurs, *der;* **e)** *see* **telephone exchange; f)** *(Commerc.: building)* Börse, *die. See also* **employment exchange; foreign exchange; Labour Exchange; stock exchange**

exchangeable [ɪks'tʃeɪndʒəbl] *adj.* austauschbar (**for** gegen); **these goods are not ~:** diese Waren sind vom Umtausch ausgeschlossen

exchequer [ɪks'tʃekə(r)] *n.* **a)** *(Brit.)* Schatzamt, *das;* Finanzministerium, *das; see also* **chancellor a; b)** *(royal or national treasury)* Staatsschatz, *der*

¹excise ['eksaɪz] *n.* Verbrauchsteuer, *die;* **Customs and E~ Department** *(Brit.) Amt für Zölle und Verbrauchsteuern*

²excise [ɪk'saɪz] *v. t.* **a)** *(from book, article)* entfernen (**from** aus); *(from film also)* herausschneiden (**from** aus); **b)** *(Med.)* entfernen; exzidieren *(fachspr.)*

excision [ɪk'sɪʒn] *n.* **a)** Entfernung, *die* (**from** aus); **b)** *(Med.)* Entfernung, *die;* Exzision, *die (fachspr.)*

excitable [ɪk'saɪtəbl] *adj.* leicht erregbar; **have an ~ temper** reizbar sein

excite [ɪk'saɪt] *v. t.* **a)** *(thrill)* begeistern; **she was/became ~d by the idea** die Idee begeisterte sie; **it greatly ~d the children** es machte die Kinder ganz aufgeregt; **b)** *(agitate)* aufregen; **be/become ~d by sth.** sich über etw. *(Akk.)* aufregen *od.* erregen; **c)** *(elicit)* erregen; **d)** *(stimulate; also Physiol.)* anregen; *(sexually)* erregen; **e)** *(provoke)* aufstacheln (**to** zu)

excited [ɪk'saɪtɪd] *adj.* **a)** *(pleasurably)* aufgeregt (**at** über + *Akk.*); **you don't seem very ~ [about it]** du scheinst [davon] nicht sehr begeistert zu sein; **I'm ~ to see what happens next** ich bin gespannt, was als nächstes geschieht; **it's nothing to get ~ about** es ist nichts Besonderes; **don't get ~:** sei nicht gleich so aufgeregt; **b)** *(agitated)* erregt; aufgeregt; **it's nothing to get ~ about** es besteht kein Grund zur Aufregung; **don't get ~, it's only Tom** keine Aufregung, es ist nur Tom; **don't get so ~:** reg dich nicht so auf; **get all ~** *(coll.)* sich furchtbar aufregen *(ugs.);* **c)** *(Physiol.)* angeregt; *(sexually)* erregt

excitedly [ɪk'saɪtɪdlɪ] *adv.* aufgeregt; gespannt ‹*warten*›; **look forward ~ to the holidays** den Ferien entgegenfiebern

excitement [ɪk'saɪtmənt] *n.* **a)** *no pl.* Aufregung, *die; (enthusiasm)* Begeisterung, *die; (suspense)* Spannung, *die;* **in [a state of] ~:** aufgeregt; **in all the ~/in his ~ he forgot to say thank you** in der Aufregung vergaß er, sich zu bedanken; **full of ~:** ganz aufgeregt; **wild with ~:** wie toll vor Aufregung *od.* Erregung; **b)** *(incident)* Aufregung, *die;* **c)** *(Physiol.: sexual)* Erregung, *die*

exciting [ɪk'saɪtɪŋ] *adj.* aufregend; *(full of suspense)* spannend; **it isn't exactly ~:** es ist nicht gerade berauschend *(ugs.)*

exclaim [ɪk'skleɪm] **1.** *v. t.* ausrufen; **~ that ...:** rufen, daß ... **2.** *v. i.* aufschreien; **~ in delight** vor Freude aufschreien

exclamation [eksklə'meɪʃn] *n.* Ausruf, *der;* **utter an ~ of pain/delight** vor Schmerz aufschreien/einen Freudenschrei ausstoßen

exclamation: ~ mark, *(Amer.)* **~ point** *ns.* Ausrufezeichen, *das*

exclude [ɪk'sklu:d] *v. t.* **a)** *(keep out, debar)* ausschließen (**from** von); **sb. is ~d from a profession/the Church/a room** jmdm. ist die Ausübung eines Berufes/die Zugehörigkeit zur Kirche/der Zutritt zu einem Raum verwehrt; **the public were ~d from the courtroom** die Verhandlung fand unter Ausschluß der Öffentlichkeit statt; **~ noise/draughts from a room** Lärm von einem Zimmer fernhalten/ein Zimmer gegen Zugluft abdichten; **~ sb. from one's will/the Party** jmdn. im Testament nicht bedenken/aus der Partei ausschließen; **b)** *(make impossible, preclude)* ausschließen; **this ~s any [further] question of sth.** damit ist etw. völlig ausgeschlossen; **c)** *(leave out of account)* nicht berücksichtigen (**from** bei)

excluding [ɪk'sklu:dɪŋ] *prep.* **~ drinks/VAT** Getränke ausgenommen/ohne Mehrwertsteuer

exclusion [ɪk'sklu:ʒn] *n.* Ausschluß, *der;* **[talk about sth.] to the ~ of everything else** ausschließlich [über etw. *(Akk.)* sprechen]

exclusive [ɪk'sklu:sɪv] **1.** *adj.* **a)** *(not shared)* alleinig ‹*Besitzer, Kontrolle*›; ungeteilt ‹*Aufmerksamkeit*›; einzig ‹*Beschäftigung*›; Allein‹*eigentum*›; *(Journ.)* Exklusiv‹*bericht, -interview*›; *(Fashion)* Modell‹*kleid usw.*›; **~ right** Alleinrecht, *das; (Journ.)* Exklusivrecht, *das;* **have ~ rights** die Alleinrechte/Exklusivrechte haben; **b)** *(select, privileged)* exklusiv; *(unwilling to mix)* unnahbar; distanziert; **c)** *(excluding)* ausschließlich; **~ of** ohne; **~ of drinks** Getränke ausgenommen; **the price is ~ of postage** Versandkosten sind im Preis nicht inbegriffen; **be mutually ~:** sich gegenseitig ausschließen. **2.** *n. (Journ.)* Exklusivbericht, *der*

exclusively [ɪk'sklu:sɪvlɪ] *adv.* ausschließlich; *(Journ.)* exklusiv

exclusiveness [ɪk'sklu:sɪvnɪs] *n., no pl.* Exklusivität, *die*

excommunicate [ekskə'mju:nɪkeɪt] *v. t. (Eccl.)* exkommunizieren

excommunication [ekskəmju:nɪ'keɪʃn] *n. (Eccl.)* Exkommunikation, *die*

excoriate [eks'kɔ:rɪeɪt] *v. t. (fig.: censure)* vernichtend kritisieren

excrement ['ekskrɪmənt] *n. in sing. or pl.* Exkremente *Pl. (bes. Med.);* Kot, *der (geh.)*

excrescence [ɪk'skresəns] *n.* **a)** Auswuchs, *der;* Wucherung, *die;* Exkreszenz, *die (fachspr.);* **b)** *(fig.)* Auswuchs, *der*

excreta [ɪk'skri:tə] *n. pl.* Ausscheidungen *Pl.*

excrete [ɪk'skri:t] *v. t.* ausscheiden

excretion [ɪk'skri:ʃn] *n.* Ausscheidung, *die*

excretory [ɪk'skri:tərɪ] *adj.* Ausscheidungs-

excruciating [ɪk'skru:ʃɪeɪtɪŋ] *adj.* unerträglich; qualvoll ‹*Tod*›; quälend ‹*Frage*›; **it is ~:** es ist unerträglich *od.* nicht auszuhalten; **be in ~ pain** unerträgliche Schmerzen haben; **an ~ pun** ≈ ein schlimmer Kalauer

excruciatingly [ɪk'skru:ʃɪeɪtɪŋlɪ] *adv.* entsetzlich; furchtbar; wahnsinnig ‹*lustig*›

exculpate ['ekskəlpeɪt] *v. t.* freisprechen; **he was ~d** seine Unschuld wurde festgestellt; **~ oneself** sich rechtfertigen (**from** gegenüber)

exculpation [ekskəl'peɪʃn] *n., no pl.* Entlastung, *die; (vindication)* Rechtfertigung, *die*

excursion [ɪk'skɜ:ʃn] *n.* **a)** Ausflug, *der;* **day ~:** Tagesausflug, *der;* **go on/make an ~:** einen Ausflug machen; **~ rates/fares** Sonderpreis [für Ausflüge]; **b)** *(fig.: digression)* Ausflug, *der;* Exkurs, *der (geh.)*

excursionist [ɪk'skɜ:ʃənɪst] *n.* Ausflügler, *der*/Ausflüglerin, *die*

excursion: ~ ticket *n.* Ausflugskarte, *die;* **~ train** *n. (Amer.)* Sonderzug, *der*

excusable [ɪk'skju:zəbl] *adj.* entschuldbar; verzeihlich

excusably [ɪk'sku:zəblɪ] *adv.* verständlicherweise

excuse 1. [ɪk'skju:z] *v. t.* **a)** *(forgive, exonerate)* entschuldigen; **~ oneself** *(apologize)* sich entschuldigen; **~ me** Entschuldigung; Verzeihung; **please ~ me** bitte entschuldigen Sie; **~ me[, what did you say]?** *(Amer.)* Verzeihung[, was haben Sie gesagt]?; **~ me if I don't get up** entschuldigen Sie, wenn ich nicht aufstehe; **~ sth. in sb., ~ sb. sth.** etw. bei jmdm. entschuldigen; **I can be ~d for confusing them** es ist verzeihlich, daß ich sie verwechselt habe; **sb. can be ~d for that** das ist verzeihlich; **acts which nothing can ~:** Taten, die durch nichts zu entschuldigen sind; **b)** *(release, exempt)* befreien; **~ sb. [from] sth.** jmdn. von etw. befreien; **they were ~d payment of all taxes** ihnen wurden alle Steuern erlassen; **~ oneself from doing sth.** sich erlauben, etw. nicht zu tun; **c)** *(allow to leave)* entschuldigen; **~ oneself** sich entschuldigen; **and now, if I may be ~d** *or* **if you will ~ me** wenn Sie mich jetzt bitte entschuldigen wollen; **you are ~d** ihr könnt gehen; **may I be ~d?** *(wishing to leave the table)* darf ich aufstehen?; *(euphem.: wishing to go to the toilet)* darf ich mal verschwinden *od.* austreten? **2.** [ɪk'skju:s] *n.* **a)** Entschuldigung, *die;* **give** *or* **offer an ~ for sth.** sich für etw. entschuldigen; **there is no ~ for what I did** was ich getan habe, ist nicht zu entschuldigen; **what did he give as his ~ this time?** welche Entschuldigung hatte er diesmal?; **I'm not trying to make ~s, but ...:** das soll keine Entschuldigung sein, aber ...; **make one's/sb.'s ~s to sb.** sich/jmdn. bei jmdm. entschuldigen; **any ~ for a drink!** zum Trinken gibt es immer einen Grund; **be as good an ~ as any** ein willkommener Anlaß sein; **b)** *(evasive statement)* Ausrede, *die;* **make ~s** sich herausreden; **c)** *(pathetic specimen)* **this is an ~ for a pencil/letter** *etc.*, **isn't it!** das kann man wohl kaum als Bleistift/Brief *usw.* bezeichnen

ex-di'rectory *adj. (Brit. Teleph.)* Geheim‹*nummer, -anschluß*›; **famous people are usually ~:** berühmte Leute stehen gewöhnlich nicht im Telefonbuch

ex 'dividend *(Finance) adv.* abzüglich Dividende

execrable ['eksɪkrəbl] *adj.*, **execrably** ['eksɪkrəblɪ] *adv.* abscheulich

execration [eksɪ'kreɪʃn] *n.* **a)** *(act)* Fluchen, *das;* **b)** *(curse)* Fluch, *der;* Verwünschung, *die;* **c)** *no pl. (abhorrence)* Abscheu, *der;* **hold sth. in ~:** etw. verabscheuen

execute ['eksɪkju:t] *v. t.* **a)** *(kill)* hinrichten; exekutieren *(Milit.);* **b)** *(put into effect, perform)* ausführen; durchführen ‹*Vorschrift, Gesetz*›; **c)** *(Law: give effect to)* vollstrecken; *(make legally valid)* rechtsgültig machen; unterzeichnen ‹*Urkunde*›

execution [eksɪ'kju:ʃn] *n.* **a)** *(killing)* Hinrichtung, *die;* Exekution, *die (Milit.);* **b)** *(putting into effect, performance)* Ausführung, *die;* Durchführung, *die; (of will, verdict)* Vollstreckung, *die;* **put sth. into ~:** etw. aus- *od.* durchführen/vollstrecken; **in the ~ of one's duty/duties** bei Erfüllung seiner Pflicht; in [treuer] Pflichterfüllung; **c)** *(Mus.)* Vortrag, *der;* **d)** *(Law: seizure of property, carrying out)* Vollstreckung, *die; (rendering legally valid)* [rechtsgültige] Unterzeichnung

executioner [eksɪ'kju:ʃənə(r)] *n.* Scharfrichter, *der*

executive [ɪg'zekjʊtɪv] **1.** *n.* **a)** *(person)* leitender Angestellter/leitende Angestellte; **b)** *(administrative body)* **the ~** *(of government)* die Exekutive; *(of political organization, trade union)* der Vorstand. **2.** *adj.* **a)** *(Commerc.)* leitend ‹*Stellung, Funktion*›; geschäftsführend ‹*Vorsitzende[r]*›; **~ powers**

Vollmacht, *die; (Commerc. Law)* Prokura, *die;* ~ **ability** Führungsqualitäten *Pl.;* **b)** *(relating to government)* exekutiv; ~ **powers** Exekutivgewalt, *die*

executive: ~ **com'mittee** *n.* [geschäftsführender] Vorstand; ~ **'council** *n.* Ministerrat, *der*

executor [ɪg'zekjʊtə(r)] *n. (Law)* Testamentsvollstrecker, *der;* **the ~ of his will** sein Testamentsvollstrecker; **literary ~:** Verwalter/Verwalterin des literarischen Nachlasses

exegesis [eksɪ'dʒiːsɪs] *n., pl.* **exegeses** [eksɪ'dʒiːsiːz] Auslegung, *die;* Exegese, *die (auch Theol.)*

exemplary [ɪg'zemplərɪ] *adj.* **a)** *(model)* vorbildlich; **b)** *(deterrent)* exemplarisch; ~ **damages** *(Law)* Buße, *die;* **c)** *(illustrative)* beispielhaft; exemplarisch

exemplification [ɪgzemplɪfɪ'keɪʃn] *n.* Veranschaulichung, *die;* Exemplifikation, *die (geh.)*

exemplify [ɪg'zemplɪfaɪ] *v. t.* veranschaulichen; exemplifizieren *(geh.); (serve as example of)* als Beispiel dienen für

exempt [ɪg'zempt] **1.** *adj.* **[be] ~ [from sth.]** [von etw.] befreit [sein]; **make sb. ~ from sth.** jmdn. von etw. befreien. **2.** *v. t.* befreien; **be ~ed from sth.** von etw. befreit werden

exemption [ɪg'zempʃn] *n.* Befreiung, *die;* ~ **from payment of a fine** Erlaß einer Geldstrafe

exercise ['eksəsaɪz] **1.** *n.* **a)** *no pl., no indef. art. (physical exertion)* Bewegung, *die; (of dog also)* Auslauf, *der; (fig.)* Training, *das;* **get ~:** Bewegung haben; **take ~:** sich *(Dat.)* Bewegung verschaffen; **provide ~ for sth.** etw. trainieren; eine gute Übung für etw. sein; **b)** *(task set, activity; also Mus., Sch.)* Übung, *die;* **the object of the ~:** der Sinn der Übung; **c)** *(to improve fitness)* [Gymnastik]übung, *die;* **morning ~s** Morgengymnastik, *die;* **d)** *no pl. (employment, application)* Ausübung, *die;* **the ~ of tolerance is essential** Toleranz zu üben ist sehr wichtig; **e)** *usu. in pl. (Mil.)* Übung, *die;* **go on ~s** eine Übung machen; **f)** *in pl. (Amer.: ceremony)* Feierlichkeiten *Pl.*. **2.** *v. t.* **a)** ausüben ⟨*Recht, Macht, Einfluß*⟩; walten lassen ⟨*Vorsicht*⟩; ~ **restraint/discretion/patience** sich in Zurückhaltung/Diskretion/Geduld üben; ~ **one's right of veto** von seinem Vetorecht Gebrauch machen; ~ **tact** taktvoll sein; ~ **great care** sehr vorsichtig sein; **b)** *(tax the powers of)* in Anspruch nehmen; *(perplex, worry)* beschäftigen; ~ **the mind** die geistigen Fähigkeiten herausfordern; **c)** *(physically)* trainieren; **d)** *(Mil.)* drillen. **3.** *v. i.* sich *(Dat.)* Bewegung verschaffen

'exercise book *n.* [Schul]heft, *das*

exerciser ['eksəsaɪzə(r)] *n. (device)* Trainingsgerät, *das*

exert [ɪg'zɜːt] **1.** *v. t.* aufbieten ⟨*Kraft, Beredsamkeit*⟩; ausüben ⟨*Einfluß, Druck, Macht*⟩; ~ **all one's force on the door** sich mit aller Kraft gegen die Tür stemmen. **2.** *v. refl.* sich anstrengen; **don't ~ yourself** *(iron.)* überanstrenge dich nur nicht

exertion [ɪg'zɜːʃn] *n.* **a)** *no pl. (exerting) (of strength, force)* Aufwendung, *die; (of influence, pressure, force)* Ausübung, *die;* **by the ~ of all sb.'s strength** unter Aufbietung aller Kräfte; **b)** *(effort)* Anstrengung, *die;* **by her own ~s she managed ...:** durch eigene Anstrengung gelang es ihr, ...

exeunt ['eksɪʌnt] *v. i. (Theatre: as stage direction)* ab; ~ **omnes** [eksɪʌnt 'ɒmniːz] alle ab

ex gratia [eks 'greɪʃə] *adj.* freiwillig; ohne Anerkennung einer Rechtspflicht

exhalation [ekshə'leɪʃn] *n.* **a)** *(breathing out)* Ausatmung, *die; (of smoke, gas; also Med.)* Exhalation, *die;* **b)** *(puff of breath)* Atemzug, *der;* **c)** *(gas etc. emitted)* exhalierte Dämpfe/Gase

exhale [eks'heɪl] **1.** *v. t.* **a)** *(from lungs)* ausatmen; exhalieren *(Med.);* **b)** *(emit)* verströmen ⟨*Duft*⟩; ausstoßen ⟨*Rauch, Gas*⟩. **2.** *v. i.* ausatmen; exhalieren *(Med.)*

exhaust [ɪg'zɔːst] **1.** *v. t.* **a)** *(use up)* erschöpfen; erschöpfend behandeln ⟨*Thema*⟩; *(try out fully)* ausschöpfen; **she ~ed her ideas in her first novel** sie hat den Vorrat ihrer Ideen bereits in ihrem ersten Roman erschöpft; **b)** *(drain of strength, resources, etc.)* erschöpfen; **have been ~ed by sth./have ~ed oneself** von etw. erschöpft sein/sich völlig verausgabt haben; **this work is ~ing me** diese Arbeit strengt mich sehr an; **c)** *(draw off)* herauspumpen; ~ **sth. from sth.** etw. aus etw. [heraus]pumpen; **d)** *(empty)* auspumpen. **2.** *n.* **a)** ~ **[system]** Abgasrohr, *das; (Motor Veh.)* Auspuff, *der; (of train)* Abgasleitung, *die;* **b)** *(what is expelled)* Abgase *Pl.; (of car)* Auspuffgase *Pl.*

exhausted [ɪg'zɔːstɪd] *adj.* erschöpft

exhausting [ɪg'zɔːstɪŋ] *adj.* anstrengend; beschwerlich ⟨*Husten*⟩; ermüdend ⟨*Wetter*⟩; **he is ~ company** *or* ~ **to be with** er ist sehr anstrengend

exhaustion [ɪg'zɔːstʃn] *n., no pl.* Erschöpfung, *die*

exhaustive [ɪg'zɔːstɪv] *adj.* umfassend

exhaustively [ɪg'zɔːstɪvlɪ] *adv.* umfassend; **treat a subject ~:** ein Thema erschöpfend *od.* umfassend behandeln

ex'haust-pipe *n.* Abzugsrohr, *das; (of car)* Auspuffrohr, *das*

exhibit [ɪg'zɪbɪt] **1.** *v. t.* **a)** *(display)* vorzeigen; *(show publicly)* ausstellen; **he has ~ed in London** er hat in London ausgestellt; ~ **in court** *(Law)* dem Gericht vorlegen; **b)** *(manifest)* zeigen ⟨*Mut, Verachtung, Symptome, Neigung, Angst*⟩; beweisen ⟨*Mut, Können*⟩. **2.** *n.* **a)** Ausstellungsstück, *das;* **b)** *(Law: in court; also fig.)* Beweisstück, *das*

exhibition [eksɪ'bɪʃn] *n.* **a)** *(public display)* Ausstellung, *die;* ~ **catalogue** Ausstellungskatalog, *der;* **b)** *(act)* Vorführung, *die; (manifestation)* **give an ~ of one's skills** sein Können demonstrieren; **her ~ of grief** die Zurschaustellung ihrer Trauer; **c)** *(derog.)* **make an ~ of oneself** sich unmöglich aufführen; **what an ~!** ein unmögliches Benehmen!; **d)** *(Brit. Univ.: scholarship)* Stipendium, *das*

exhibitioner [eksɪ'bɪʃənə(r)] *n. (Brit. Univ.)* Stipendiat, *der*

exhibitionism [eksɪ'bɪʃənɪzm] *n.* Exhibitionismus, *der*

exhibitionist [eksɪ'bɪʃənɪst] *n.* Exhibitionist, *der*/Exhibitionistin, *die*

exhibitor [ɪg'zɪbɪtə(r)] *n.* Aussteller, *der*/ Ausstellerin, *die*

exhilarate [ɪg'zɪləreɪt] *v. t.* erfrischen, beleben; *(gladden)* fröhlich stimmen; *(stimulate)* anregen

exhilarated [ɪg'zɪləreɪtɪd] *adj.* erfrischt; belebt; *(gladdened)* fröhlich gestimmt; *(stimulated)* angeregt; **feel ~:** sich erfrischt/angeregt fühlen/fröhlich gestimmt sein

exhilarating [ɪg'zɪləreɪtɪŋ] *adj.* belebend; fröhlich stimmend ⟨*Nachricht, Musik, Anblick*⟩; ~ **feeling** erhebendes Gefühl

exhilaration [ɪgzɪlə'reɪʃn] *n.* **[feeling of] ~:** Hochgefühl, *das;* **the ~ of hang-gliding** das Hochgefühl beim Drachenfliegen

exhort [ɪg'zɔːt] *v. t.* ~ **sb. to do sth.** jmdn. [ernsthaft] ermahnen, etw. zu tun

exhortation [eksɔː'teɪʃn] *n.* **a)** *(exhorting)* Ermahnung, *die;* **b)** *(formal address)* Appell, *der;* Exhortation, *die (kath. Rel.)*

exhumation [eksjʊ'meɪʃn] *n.* Exhumierung, *die*

exhume [ɪg'zjuːm] *v. t.* exhumieren; *(fig.)* ausgraben

exigence ['eksɪdʒəns], **exigency** ['eksɪdʒənsɪ] *n.* **a)** *usu. in pl. (urgent demand)* Erfordernis, *das;* **b)** *(emergency)* Notlage, *die; (Polit. also)* Krisensituation, *die;* **c)** *(urgency)* Dringlichkeit, *die*

exigent ['eksɪdʒənt] *adj.* **a)** *(exacting)* anspruchsvoll; **b)** *(urgent)* dringend ⟨*Fall, Lage*⟩; zwingend ⟨*Grund, Notwendigkeit, Umstand*⟩

exiguous [eg'zɪgjʊəs] *adj.* gering; schmal *(geh.)* ⟨*Gehalt, Budget*⟩; dürftig ⟨*Kost*⟩

exile ['eksaɪl, 'egzaɪl] **1.** *n.* **a)** Exil, *das; (forcible also)* Verbannung, *die* **(from** aus); **order sb.'s ~:** jmdn. ins Exil schicken; **live/be in ~:** im Exil leben/sein; **go into ~:** ins Exil gehen; **internal ~:** Verbannung, *die (an einen Ort innerhalb des eigenen Landes);* **the E~** *(Jewish Hist.)* die Babylonische Gefangenschaft; **b)** *(exiled person, lit. or fig.)* Verbannte, *der/die;* Exilierte, *der/die (geh.).* **2.** *v. t.* verbannen; exilieren *(geh.);* **~d Russian** Exilrusse, *der*/-russin, *die*

exist [ɪg'zɪst] *v. i.* **a)** *(be in existence)* existieren; ⟨*Zweifel, Gefahr, Problem, Zusammenarbeit, Brauch, Einrichtung:*⟩ bestehen; **ever since records have ~ed ...:** seit es Aufzeichnungen gibt, ...; **fairies do ~:** es gibt Feen; **the biggest book that has ever ~ed** das größte Buch aller Zeiten; **the conditions that ~ in the Third World** die Bedingungen, die man in der dritten Welt vorfindet; **does life ~ on Venus?** gibt es Leben auf der Venus?; **b)** *(survive)* existieren; überleben; ~ **on sth.** von etw. leben; **c)** *(be found)* **sth. ~s only in Europe** es gibt etw. nur in Europa

existence [ɪg'zɪstəns] *n.* **a)** *(existing)* Existenz, *die;* **doubt sb.'s ~/the ~ of sth.** bezweifeln, daß es jmdn./etw. gibt; **the continued ~ of this tradition** das Fortbestehen dieser Tradition; **be in ~:** existieren; **the only such plant [which is] in ~:** die einzige Pflanze dieser Art, die es gibt; **come into ~:** entstehen; **bring sth. into ~:** etw. einführen; **go out of ~:** verschwinden; **b)** *(mode of living)* Dasein, *das; (survival)* Existenz, *die;* **struggle for ~:** Existenzkampf, *der;* **means of ~:** Existenzgrundlage, *die*

existent [ɪg'zɪstənt] *see* **existing**

existential [egzɪ'stenʃl] *adj.* existentiell

existentialism [egzɪ'stenʃəlɪzm] *n., no pl. (Philos.)* Existentialismus, *der*

existentialist [egzɪ'stenʃəlɪst] *n. (Philos.)* Existentialist, *der*/Existentialistin, *die; attrib.* existentialistisch

existing [ɪg'zɪstɪŋ] *adj.* existierend; *(present)* bestehend ⟨*Ordnung, Schwierigkeiten*⟩; gegenwärtig ⟨*Lage, Führung, Stand der Dinge*⟩

exit ['eksɪt] **1.** *n.* **a)** *(way out)* Ausgang, *der* **(from** aus); *(from drive, motorway)* Ausfahrt, *die;* **b)** *(from stage)* Abgang, *der;* **make one's ~:** abgehen; **c)** *(from room)* Hinausgehen, *das; (from group)* Weggehen, *das;* **make a speedy ~:** schnell hinausgehen/weggehen; **she made a dramatic ~:** ihr Abgang war dramatisch; **d)** *(departure)* **right of ~ from a country** Recht, ein Land zu verlassen. **2.** *v. i.* **a)** *(make one's ~)* hinausgehen **(from** aus); *(from stage)* abgehen **(from** von); **b)** *(Theatre: as stage direction)* ab: ~ **Hamlet** Hamlet ab

exit: ~ **permit** *n.* Ausreiseerlaubnis, *die;* ~ **poll** *n. Befragung der ein Wahllokal verlassenden Wähler;* ~ **visa** *n.* Ausreisevisum, *das*

exodus ['eksədəs] *n.* Auszug, *der;* Exodus, *der (geh.);* **general ~:** allgemeiner Aufbruch; **[the Book of] E~:** das zweite Buch Mose

ex officio [eks ə'fɪʃɪəʊ] **1.** *adv.* ex officio *(geh.);* von Amts wegen. **2.** *adj.* ~ **chairman** Vorsitzender von Amts wegen *od.* ex officio *(geh.);* **be an ~ member** kraft seines Amtes Mitglied sein

exonerate [ɪg'zɒnəreɪt] *v. t.* entlasten; ~ **sb. from a duty/task** jmdn. von einer Pflicht/ Aufgabe befreien; ~ **sb. from blame** jmdn. von der Schuld freisprechen

exoneration [ɪgzɒnə'reɪʃn] *n.* Entlastung, *die; (from task, obligation)* Befreiung, *die*

exorbitance [ɪg'zɔ:bɪtəns] *n., no pl.* Maßlosigkeit, *die;* Exorbitanz, *die (geh.)*

exorbitant [ɪg'zɔ:bɪtənt] *adj.* [maßlos] überhöht ‹*Preis, Miete, Gewinn, Anforderung, Rechnung*›; maßlos ‹*Ehrgeiz, Forderung*›; exorbitant *(geh.);* **£10 – that's ~!** 10 Pfund – das ist unverschämt viel! *(ugs.);* **be ~ in one's demands** [maßlos] überhöhte Ansprüche stellen

exorcise *see* **exorcize**

exorcism ['eksɔ:sɪzm] *n.* Exorzismus, *der;* Teufelsaustreibung, *die*

exorcist ['eksɔ:sɪst] *n.* Exorzist, *der*

exorcize ['eksɔ:saɪz] *v.t.* austreiben; exorzieren; **be ~d from** *or* **out of sb./sth.** jmdm./einer Sache ausgetrieben werden

exotic [ɪg'zɒtɪk] **1.** *adj.* exotisch. **2.** *n.* Exot[e], *der*/Exotin, *die*

exotica [ɪg'zɒtɪkə] *n. pl.* Exotika *Pl.*

exotically [ɪg'zɒtɪkəlɪ] *adv.* exotisch; **~ named ...:** mit dem exotischen Namen ...

expand [ɪk'spænd] **1.** *v.i.* **a)** *(get bigger)* sich ausdehnen; ‹*Unternehmen, Stadt, Staat:*› expandieren; ‹*Verkehrsaufkommen, Wissen:*› zunehmen; ‹*Institution:*› erweitert werden; ‹*geistiger Horizont:*› sich erweitern; **~ into sth.** zu etw. anwachsen; **~ing watch-strap** elastisches Gliederband; **b)** *(Commerc.)* expandieren; **~ into a large organization** zu einer großen Organisation heranwachsen; **~ into other areas of production** die Produktion um andere Sektoren erweitern; **c) ~ on a subject** ein Thema weiter ausführen; **d)** *(spread out)* sich öffnen; **e)** *(become genial)* freundlich werden. **2.** *v.t.* **a)** *(enlarge)* ausdehnen; erweitern ‹*Horizont, Wissen*›; dehnen ‹*Körper*›; aufblasen ‹*Ballon*›; aufpumpen ‹*Reifen*›; **~ sth. into sth.** etw. zu etw. erweitern; **~ed metal** Streckmetall, *das (Bauw.);* **b)** *(Commerc.: develop)* erweitern; **~ the economy** das Wirtschaftswachstum fördern; **c)** *(amplify)* weiter ausführen ‹*Gedanken, Notiz, Idee*›

expandable [ɪk'spændəbl] *adj.* [aus]dehnbar; *(Commerc.)* entwicklungsfähig

expanse [ɪk'spæns] *n.* [weite] Fläche; **~ of water** Wasserfläche, *die;* **surrounded by a huge ~ of desert** umgeben von einer sich weithin erstreckenden Wüste; **she was swathed in an ~ of red silk** sie war in weite Bahnen roter Seide gehüllt

expansion [ɪk'spænʃn] *n.* **a)** Ausdehnung, *die; (of territorial rule also)* Expansion, *die; (of sphere of influence)* Ausweitung, *die; (of knowledge, building)* Erweiterung, *die;* **the ~ of the volume of traffic on the roads** die zunehmende Verkehrsdichte auf den Straßen; **b)** *(Commerc.)* Expansion, *die;* **the ~ of this small business into a huge organization** die Erweiterung dieses kleinen Betriebes zu einer großen Firma; **c)** *(amplification)* Erweiterung, *die;* **further ~ of the ideas** weitere Ausführung der Ideen

expansionary [ɪk'spænʃənərɪ] *adj. (also Commerc.)* expansionistisch

ex'pansion joint *n.* Dehnungsfuge, *die*

expansive [ɪk'spænsɪv] *adj. (effusive)* offen; *(responsive)* zugänglich; **be ~:** aus sich herausgehen

expatiate [ɪk'speɪʃɪeɪt] *v.i.* **~ [up]on sth.** etw. ausführlich erörtern; sich über etw. *(Akk.)* verbreiten *(oft abwertend)*

expatiation [ɪkspeɪʃɪ'eɪʃn] *n.* [ausführliche] Erörterung ([**up**]**on** *Gen.*)

expatriate 1. [eks'pætrɪeɪt, eks'peɪtrɪeɪt] *v.t. (exile)* ausbürgern; expatriieren. **2.** [eks'pætrɪət, eks'peɪtrɪət] *adj.* im Ausland lebend; **~ community** Kolonie, *die.* **3.** *n. (exile)* Exilant, *der*/Exilantin, *die; (foreigner)* Ausländer, *der*/Ausländerin, *die; (emigrant)* Auswanderer, *der*/Auswanderin, *die*

expatriation [ekspætrɪ'eɪʃn, ekspeɪtrɪ'eɪʃn] *n. (forcible)* Ausbürgerung, *die;* Expatriation, *die; (voluntary)* [freiwilliges] Exil

expect [ɪk'spekt] *v.t.* **a)** *(regard as likely, anticipate)* erwarten; **~ to do sth.** damit rechnen, etw. zu tun; **~ sth. from sb.** etw. von jmdm. erwarten; **~ sb. to do sth.** damit rechnen, daß jmd. etw. tut; **I ~ you'd like something to eat** ich nehme an, daß du gern etwas essen möchtest ; **don't ~ me to help you out** von mir hast du keine Hilfe zu erwarten; **it is ~ed that ...:** man erwartet, daß ...; **that was [not] to be ~ed** das war [auch nicht] zu erwarten; **I ~ed as much** das habe ich erwartet; **it is everything one ~s** es erfüllt alle Erwartungen; **it is all one can ~:** mehr kann man [auch] nicht erwarten; **~ the worst** mit dem Schlimmsten rechnen; **be ~ing a baby/child** ein Baby/Kind erwarten; **be ~ing** *abs.* schwanger sein; **is he/she ~ing you?** werden Sie erwartet?; **I/we shall not ~ you till I/we see you** wenn du kommst, bist du da *(ugs.);* **~ me when you see me** *(coll.)* wenn ich komme, bin ich da *(ugs.);* **b)** *(require)* erwarten; **~ sb. to do sth.** von jmdm. erwarten, daß er etw. tut; **~ sth. from** *or* **of sb.** etw. von jmdm. erwarten; **they are ~ed to be present** man erwartet [von ihnen], daß sie da sind; **c)** *(coll.: think, suppose)* glauben; **I ~ so** ich glaube schon; **I rather ~ not** ich glaube kaum; **I don't ~ so** ich glaube nicht; **I ~ it was/he did** *etc.* das glaube ich gern

expectancy [ɪk'spektənsɪ] *n.* **a)** *no pl.* Erwartung, *die;* **with an air** *or* **a look of ~:** mit erwartungsvoller Miene; **mood of ~:** erwartungsvolle Stimmung; **b)** *(prospective chance)* **an ~ of another 28 years of life** eine Lebenserwartung von noch 28 Jahren; *see also* **life expectancy**

expectant [ɪk'spektənt] *adj.* **a)** erwartungsvoll; **b) ~ mother** werdende Mutter

expectantly [ɪk'spektəntlɪ] *adv.* erwartungsvoll; gespannt ‹*warten*›

expectation [ekspek'teɪʃn] *n.* **a)** *no pl. (expecting)* Erwartung, *die;* **in the ~ of sth.** in Erwartung einer Sache *(Gen.);* **b)** *usu. in pl. (thing expected)* Erwartung, *die;* **have great ~s for sb./sth.** große Erwartungen in jmdn./etw. setzen; **come up to ~[s]/sb.'s ~s** den/jmds. Erwartungen entsprechen; **contrary to ~** *or* **to all ~s** wider Erwarten; **be a success beyond all ~s** über alles Erwarten erfolgreich sein; **c) ~ of life** *see* **life e; d)** *in pl. (prospects of inheritance)* **have great ~s** ein großes Erbe in Aussicht haben

expectorate [ɪk'spektəreɪt] *v.t. & i.* aushusten; *(spit)* [aus]spucken

expedience [ɪk'spi:dɪəns], **expediency** [ɪk'spi:dɪənsɪ] *n.* Zweckmäßigkeit, *die;* **he has sacrificed his integrity for ~:** er hat seine Integrität den sogenannten Sachzwängen geopfert

expedient [ɪk'spi:dɪənt] **1.** *adj., usu. pred.* **a)** *(appropriate, advantageous)* angebracht; **b)** *(politic)* zweckmäßig. **2.** *n.* Mittel, *das*

expediently [ɪk'spi:dɪəntlɪ] *adv.* zweckmäßigerweise; **act ~:** handeln, wie man es für zweckmäßig hält

expedite ['ekspɪdaɪt] *v.t. (hasten)* beschleunigen; vorantreiben; *(execute promptly)* umgehend ausführen

expedition [ekspɪ'dɪʃn] *n.* **a)** Expedition, *die;* **b)** *(Mil.)* Feldzug, *der;* Expedition, *die (veralt.);* **send an ~ to Egypt** Truppen nach Ägypten schicken; **c)** *(excursion)* Ausflug, *der;* **go on a hunting/shopping ~:** einen Jagdausflug/eine Einkaufstour machen; **d)** *no pl. (speed)* Eile, *die*

expeditionary [ekspɪ'dɪʃənərɪ] *adj.* **~ force** *(Mil.)* Expeditionskorps, *das*

expeditious [ekspɪ'dɪʃəs] *adj. (doing or done speedily)* schnell; *(suited for speedy performance)* schnell durchführbar

expeditiously [ekspɪ'dɪʃəslɪ] *adv.* schnell

expel [ɪk'spel] *v.t.,* **-ll-: a)** ausweisen; **~ sb. from school [for misconduct]** jmdn. [wegen schlechten Betragens] von der Schule verweisen; **~ sb. from a country** jmdn. aus einem Land ausweisen; **~ from a club** aus einem Verein ausschließen; **b)** *(with force)* vertreiben **(from** aus); auswerfen ‹*Patrone*›; absaugen ‹*Küchendunst*›; **c)** *(from substance; also Med.)* austreiben ‹*Gas, Wasser usw.*›

expend [ɪk'spend] *v.t.* **a)** aufwenden ([**up**]**on** für); **~ much care in doing sth.** etw. mit viel Sorgfalt tun; **b)** *(use up)* aufbrauchen ([**up**]**on** für)

expendable [ɪk'spendəbl] *adj.* **a)** *(inessential)* entbehrlich; **be ~** *(Mil.; also fig.)* geopfert werden können; **b)** *(used up in service)* zum Verbrauch bestimmt

expenditure [ɪk'spendɪtʃə(r)] *n.* **a)** *(amount spent)* Ausgaben *Pl.* **(on** für); *(of fuel, effort, etc.)* Aufwand, *der;* **b)** *(spending)* Ausgabe, *die; (using up of fuel or effort)* Aufwand, *der* **(of** an + *Akk.*); **~ of money/time** Geldausgabe, *die*/Zeitaufwand, *der*

expense [ɪk'spens] *n.* **a)** Kosten *Pl.*; **regardless of ~:** ungeachtet der Kosten; **those who can afford the ~:** diejenigen, die es sich leisten können; **at little ~:** preiswert; **at great ~ to sb./sth.** unter großen Kosten für jmdn./etw.; **living ~s** Lebenshaltungskosten *Pl.;* **at sb.'s ~:** auf jmds. Kosten *(Akk.);* **at one's own ~:** auf eigene Kosten; **go to the ~ of travelling first-class** sogar noch das Geld für die erste Klasse ausgeben; **go to some/great ~:** sich in Unkosten/große Unkosten stürzen; **put sb. to the ~ of sth./of doing sth.** jmdm. die Kosten für etw. zumuten/dafür zumuten, etw. zu tun; **b)** *(expensive item)* teure Angelegenheit; **be** *or* **prove a great** *or* **big ~:** mit großen Ausgaben verbunden sein; **c)** *usu. in pl. (Commerc. etc.: amount spent [and repaid])* Spesen *Pl.;* **with [all] ~s paid** auf Spesen; **the ~s incurred** die anfallenden Spesen; **he is able to claim ~s** er kann sich *(Dat.)* seine Spesen erstatten lassen; **put sth. on ~s** etw. auf die Spesenabrechnung setzen; **it all goes on to ~s** das geht alles auf Spesen; **d)** *(fig.)* Preis, *der;* **[be] at the ~ of sth.** auf Kosten von etw. [gehen]; **at considerable ~ in terms of human lives** unter großem Verlust an Menschenleben; **he achieved it, but at the ~ of his life** er erreichte es, aber es kostete ihn das Leben; **at sb.'s ~:** auf jmds. Kosten *(Akk.)*

ex'pense account *n.* Spesenabrechnung, *die; attrib.* ‹*Essen, Leben*› auf Spesen

expensive [ɪk'spensɪv] *adj.* teuer; **prove ~ to sb.** jmdn. teuer zu stehen kommen

expensively [ɪk'spensɪvlɪ] *adv.* teuer; **~ priced** teuer

experience [ɪk'spɪərɪəns] **1.** *n.* **a)** *no pl., no indef. art.* Erfahrung, *die;* **have ~ of sth./sb.** Erfahrung in etw. *(Dat.)* /mit jmdm. haben; **have ~ of doing sth.** Erfahrung darin haben, etw. zu tun; **several years' ~:** mehrjährige Erfahrung; **learn by** *or* **through** *or* **from ~:** durch eigene *od.* aus eigener Erfahrung lernen; **he learnt through** *or* **by ~ that ...:** die Erfahrung hat ihn gelehrt, daß ...; **his first ~ of war/freedom** seine erste Begegnung mit dem Krieg/der Freiheit; **a man of your ~:** ein Mann mit deiner Erfahrung; **in/from my [own] [previous] ~:** nach meiner/aus eigener Erfahrung; **know from** *or* **by ~ that ...:** aus Erfahrung wissen, daß ...; **~ has shown that ...:** die Erfahrung hat gezeigt, daß ...; **chalk** *or* **charge it up** *or* **put it down to ~:** durch Schaden wird man klug; **~ of life** Lebenserfahrung, *die;* Erlebnis, *das;* **b)** *(incident)* Erfahrung, *die;* Erlebnis, *das;* **have an [unpleasant/odd] ~:** eine [unangenehme/merkwürdige] Erfahrung machen; **he went through some terrible wartime ~s** er hat im Krieg Schreckliches mitgemacht; **it's quite an ~!** das ist [schon] ein Erlebnis!; **c) the American ~ shows how ...:** das Beispiel Amerika zeigt, wie ... **2.** *v.t.* erleben; stoßen auf (+ *Akk.*), haben ⟨*Schwierigkeiten*⟩; kennenlernen ⟨*Lebensweise*⟩; verspüren, empfinden ⟨*Hunger, Kälte, Schmerz, Freude, Trauer, Gefühl*⟩; **he is unable to ~ things deeply** er ist nicht fähig, etwas tief zu empfinden; **only he who has himself ~d poverty** nur wer Armut selbst erfahren hat

experienced [ɪk'spɪərɪənst] *adj.* erfahren; **be ~ in sth.** in etw. *(Dat.)* erfahren sein; mit etw. Erfahrung haben; **an ~ eye** ein geschulter Blick

experiment 1. [ɪk'sperɪmənt] *n.* **a)** Experiment, *das* (**on** an + *Dat.*); Versuch, *der* (**on** an + *Dat.*); **do an ~:** ein Experiment machen; **series of ~s** Versuchsreihe, *die;* **b)** *(fig.)* Experiment, *das;* **by ~:** experimentell; **as an ~:** versuchsweise. **2.** [ɪk'sperɪment] *v.i.* experimentieren; Versuche anstellen; **~ on sb./sth.** an jmdm./etw. experimentieren *od.* Versuche anstellen; **~ with sth.** mit etw. experimentieren

experimental [ɪksperɪ'mentl] *adj.* **a)** experimentell; *(based on experiment)* Experimental⟨*physik, -psychologie*⟩; *(used for experiments)* Experimentier⟨*theater, -kino*⟩; Versuchs⟨*labor, -bedingungen*⟩; *(used in experiment)* Versuchs⟨*tier*⟩; **at the/an ~ stage** im Versuchsstadium; im Experimentierstadium; **b)** *(fig.: tentative)* vorläufig; **~ drilling/flight** Probebohrung, *die*/-flug, *der;* **on an ~ basis** versuchsweise

experimentalist [ɪksperɪ'mentəlɪst] *n.* Experimentator, *der*

experimentally [ɪksperɪ'mentəlɪ] *adv.* **a)** *(as an experiment)* versuchsweise; **b)** *(by experiment)* experimentell

experimentation [ɪksperɪmen'teɪʃn] *n.* Experimentieren, *das*

experimenter [ɪk'sperɪmentə(r)] *n.* Experimentator, *der*

expert ['ekspɜ:t] **1.** *adj.* **a)** ausgezeichnet; **be ~ in** *or* **at sth.** Fachmann *od.* Experte in etw. *(Dat.)* sein; sich in etw. *(Dat.)* sehr gut auskennen; **be ~ in** *or* **at doing sth.** etw. ausgezeichnet können; **b)** *(of an ~)* fachmännisch; **~ witness** sachverständiger Zeuge; **an ~ opinion** die Meinung eines Fachmanns; **~ knowledge** Fachkenntnis, *die;* **cast one's ~ eye over sth.** etw. fachmännisch begutachten; **do an ~ job** fachmännisch arbeiten. **2.** *n.* Fachmann, *der;* Experte, *der*/Expertin, *die; (Law)* Sachverständige, *der/die;* **among ~s** unter Fachleuten; in Fachkreisen; **be an ~ in** *or* **at/on sth.** Fachmann *od.* Experte in etw. *(Dat.)*/für etw. sein; **an ~ on the subject** ein Fachmann *od.* Experte auf dem Gebiet; **she's an ~ at solving riddles** sie ist eine Expertin im Rätsellösen; **forensic/mining ~:** Gerichts-/Bergbausachverständige, *der/die*

expertise [ekspɜ:'ti:z] *n.* Fachkenntnisse; *(skill)* Können, *das;* **area of ~:** Fachgebiet, *das*

expertly ['ekspɜ:tlɪ] *adv.* meisterhaft; fachmännisch ⟨*reparieren, beraten, beurteilen*⟩

expiate ['ekspɪeɪt] *v.t.* sühnen *(geh.)*

expiation [ekspɪ'eɪʃn] *n.* Sühne, *die (geh.);* Buße, *die;* **in ~ of** zur *od.* als Buße für

expiatory ['ekspɪeɪtərɪ] *adj.* **an ~ act** ein Akt der Sühne; **~ sacrifice** Sühneopfer, *das*

expiration [ekspɪ'reɪʃn] *n.* **a)** *see* **expiry; b)** *(of air)* Ausatmung, *die*

expire [ɪk'spaɪə(r)] **1.** *v.i.* **a)** *(become invalid)* ablaufen; ⟨*Patent, Titel:*⟩ erlöschen; ⟨*Gesetz, Statut:*⟩ außer Kraft treten; ⟨*Gutschein:*⟩ verfallen; ⟨*Vertrag, Amtszeit:*⟩ auslaufen; **b)** *(literary: die)* versterben *(geh.).* **2.** *v.t. (exhale)* ausatmen

expiry [ɪk'spaɪərɪ] *n. see* **expire 1 a:** Ablauf, *der;* Erlöschen, *das;* Außerkrafttreten, *das;* Verfall, *der;* **before/at** *or* **on the ~ of sth.** vor/nach Ablauf einer Sache *(Gen.);* **the ~ date** *or* **date of ~ is the ...:** der Vertrag/die Pacht *usw.* läuft am ... ab *usw.*

explain [ɪk'spleɪn] **1.** *v.t., also abs.* erklären; erläutern ⟨*Grund, Motiv, Gedanken*⟩; darlegen ⟨*Absicht, Beweggrund*⟩; aufklären ⟨*Geheimnis*⟩; **I need to have it ~ed [to me]** ich brauche eine Erklärung; **be good at ~ing [things]** gut erklären können; **how do you ~ that?** wie erklären Sie sich *(Dat.)* das? **2.** *v. refl.* **a)** *often abs. (justify one's conduct)* **please ~ [yourself]** bitte erklären Sie mir das; **he refused to ~:** er wollte mir keine Erklärung dafür geben; **let me ~ [myself]** lassen Sie mich Ihnen das erklären; **I'd better ~ [myself]** ich sollte Ihnen das erklären; **you've got some ~ing to do** Sie müssen mir da einiges erklären; **b)** *(make one's meaning clear)* **please ~ yourself** bitte erklären Sie das [näher]

~ a'way *v.t.* eine [plausible] Erklärung finden für

explainable [ɪk'spleɪnəbl] *adj.* zu erklärend *nicht präd.;* **be ~:** sich erklären lassen

explanation [eksplə'neɪʃn] *n.* Erklärung, *die;* **need ~:** einer Erklärung bedürfen; **in ~ [of sth.]** zur Erklärung [einer Sache *(Gen.)*]; **what is the ~ of this?** wie soll ich mir das erklären?; **some ~ is called for** es bedarf einer Erklärung *(Gen.)*

explanatory [ɪk'splænətərɪ] *adj.* erklärend; erläuternd ⟨*Bemerkung*⟩

expletive [ɪk'spli:tɪv, ek'spli:tɪv] **1.** *n.* **a)** *(oath)* Kraftausdruck, *der;* **b)** *(Ling.)* Füllwort, *das;* Expletiv, *das (fachspr.).* **2.** *adj. (Ling.)* füllend; **~ word** Füllwort, *das*

explicable [ɪk'splɪkəbl] *adj.* erklärbar

explicate ['eksplɪkeɪt] *v.t.* **a)** *(explain)* erläutern; explizieren *(geh.);* aufklären ⟨*Geheimnis*⟩; **b)** *(develop meaning of)* ausführen

explicit [ɪk'splɪsɪt] *adj.* **a)** *(stated in detail)* ausführlich; *(openly expressed)* offen; unverhüllt; *(definite)* klar; ausdrücklich ⟨*Zustimmung, Erwähnung*⟩; **please would you be more ~:** bitte drücken Sie sich etwas deutlicher aus; **he did not make his meaning very ~:** er wurde nicht sehr deutlich; **make ~ mention of sth.** etw. ausdrücklich erwähnen; **b)** *(Theol.)* **~ faith** Fides explicita, *die*

explicitly [ɪk'splɪsɪtlɪ] *adv.* ausdrücklich; deutlich ⟨*beschreiben, ausdrücken*⟩; *(in openly expressed manner)* unverhüllt

explicitness [ɪk'splɪsɪtnɪs] *n., no pl.* Deutlichkeit, *die; (open expression)* **with less ~:** weniger deutlich

explode [ɪk'spləʊd] **1.** *v.i.* **a)** explodieren; **b)** *(fig.)* explodieren; ⟨*Bevölkerung:*⟩ rapide zunehmen; **~ with laughter** in Gelächter ausbrechen. **2.** *v.t.* **a)** zur Explosion bringen; **b)** *(fig.)* widerlegen ⟨*Vorstellung, Doktrin, Theorie*⟩

exploded 'view *n.* Explosionsdarstellung, *die;* auseinandergezogene Darstellung

exploit 1. ['eksplɔɪt] *n. (feat; also joc.: deed)* Heldentat, *die.* **2.** [ɪk'splɔɪt] *v.t.* **a)** *(derog.)* ausbeuten ⟨*Arbeiter, Kolonie usw.*⟩; ausnutzen ⟨*Gutmütigkeit, Freund, Unwissenheit*⟩; **b)** *(utilize)* nutzen; nützen; ausnutzen ⟨*Gelegenheit, Situation*⟩; ausbeuten ⟨*Grube*⟩

exploitation [eksplɔɪ'teɪʃn] *n.* **a)** *(derog.) (of the working classes)* Ausbeutung, *die; (of genius, good nature)* Ausnutzung, *die;* **b)** *(utilization)* Nutzung, *die*

exploitative [ɪk'splɔɪtətɪv], **exploitive** [ɪk'splɔɪtɪv] *adj. (derog.)* ausbeuterisch

exploration [eksplə'reɪʃn] *n.* **a)** Erforschung, *die; (of town, house)* Erkundung, *die;* **in the course of his ~s** im Verlauf seiner Erforschung/Erkundung; **voyage of ~:** Entdeckungsreise, *die;* **b)** *(fig.)* Untersuchung, *die;* **c)** *(Med.)* Untersuchung, *die;* Exploration, *die (fachspr.)*

explorative [ɪk'splɒrətɪv], **exploratory** [ɪk'splɒrətərɪ] *adjs.* Forschungs-; **~ talks** Sondierungsgespräche; **~ drilling** Suchbohrung, *die;* **~ operation** *(Med.)* explorative Operation; Operation zu diagnostischen Zwecken

explore [ɪk'splɔ:(r)] *v.t.* **a)** erforschen; erkunden ⟨*Stadt, Haus*⟩; **go exploring/out to ~:** auf Entdeckungsreise gehen; **b)** *(fig.)* untersuchen; **~ every avenue** alle möglichen Wege prüfen; **~ how the land lies** das Terrain sondieren

explorer [ɪk'splɔ:rə(r)] *n.* **a)** Entdeckungsreisende, *der/die;* **Arctic ~:** Arktisforscher, *der*/-forscherin, *die;* **~s of the Nile** Erforscher des Nils; **b)** *(Amer.: Scout)* Pfadfinder, *der*

explosion [ɪk'spləʊʒn] *n.* **a)** Explosion, *die; (noise)* [Explosions]knall, *der;* **b)** *(fig.: of anger etc.)* Ausbruch, *der;* **if the boss gets to hear of this there will be an ~:** wenn das der Chef erfährt, explodiert er; **c)** *(rapid increase)* Explosion, *die;* explosionsartiger Anstieg; **~ of population** Bevölkerungsexplosion, *die*

explosive [ɪk'spləʊsɪv, ɪk'spləʊzɪv] **1.** *adj.* **a)** explosiv; **highly ~:** hochexplosiv; **~ substance** Explosivstoff, *der;* **~ device** Sprengkörper, *der;* **b)** *(fig.)* explosiv; brisant ⟨*Thema*⟩. **2.** *n.* Sprengstoff, *der;* **high ~:** hochexplosiver Stoff; **~s expert** Sprengstoffexperte, *der*/-expertin, *die*

explosively [ɪk'spləʊsɪvlɪ, ɪk'spləʊzɪvlɪ] *adv. (lit. or fig.)* explosionsartig

exponent [ɪk'spəʊnənt] *n.* **a)** *(of doctrine)* Vertreter, *der*/Vertreterin, *die; (representative also)* Exponent, *der*/Exponentin, *die; (of cause)* Verfechter, *der*/Verfechterin, *die;* **b)** *(Math.)* Exponent, *der;* Hochzahl, *die;* **c)** *(Mus.)* Interpret, *der*/Interpretin, *die*

exponential [ekspə'nenʃl] *adj.* exponentiell; Exponential-; **~ function** *(Math.)* Exponentialfunktion, *die*

exponentially [ekspə'nenʃəlɪ] *adv.* exponentiell

export 1. [ɪk'spɔ:t, 'ekspɔ:t] *v.t.* exportieren; ausführen; **~ing country** Ausfuhrland, *das;* **~ to other nations/to South Africa** in andere Länder/nach Südafrika exportieren; **oil-~ing countries** [erd]ölexportierende Länder. **2.** ['ekspɔ:t] *n.* **a)** *(process, amount exported)* Export, *der;* Ausfuhr, *die; (exported articles)* Exportgut, *das;* Ausfuhrgut, *das;* **boost ~s** den Export *od.* die Ausfuhr ankurbeln; **ban on the ~ of grain** Ausfuhrverbot für Getreide; **~s of sugar** Zuckerexporte *od.* -ausfuhren; **b)** *attrib.* Export⟨*leiter, -handel, -markt, -kaufmann*⟩

exportation [ekspɔ:'teɪʃn] *n.* Export, *der;* Ausfuhr, *die*

export ['ekspɔ:t]: **~ drive** *n.* Exportkampagne, *die;* **~ duty** *n.* Exportzoll, *der;* Ausfuhrzoll, *der*

exporter [ɪk'spɔ:tə(r), 'ekspɔ:tə(r)] *n.* Exporteur, *der; (person also)* Exporthändler, *der; (firm also)* Exportfirma, *die; (country)* **be an ~ of coal** Kohle exportieren

export ['ekspɔ:t]: **~ licence** *n.* Ausfuhrlizenz, *die;* **~ permit** *n.* Exporterlaubnis, *die;* Ausfuhrerlaubnis, *die;* **~ 'reject** *n.* [wegen ungenügender Qualität] nicht exportfähige Ware; **~ surplus** *n.* Exportüberschuß, *der*

expose [ɪk'spəʊz] **1.** *v.t.* **a)** *(uncover)* freilegen; bloßlegen ⟨*Draht, Nerv*⟩; entblößen ⟨*Haut, Körper, Knie*⟩; **~ to view** freilegen; sichtbar machen; **b)** *(make known)* offenbaren ⟨*Schwäche, Tatsache, Geheimnis, Plan*⟩; aufdecken ⟨*Irrtum, Mißstände, Verbrechen, Verrat*⟩; entlarven ⟨*Täter, Verräter, Spion*⟩; **c)** *(subject)* **~ to sth.** einer Sache *(Dat.)* aussetzen; *(acquaint with sth.)* mit etw. vertraut machen; **~ to ridicule** der Lächerlichkeit *(Dat.)* preisgeben; **d)** *(Photog.)* belichten; **e)** *(leave out of doors to die)* aussetzen. **2.** *v. refl.* sich [unsittlich] entblößen

exposé [ek'spəʊzeɪ] *n.* **a)** *(of facts)* Exposé, *das;* **b)** *(of sth. discreditable)* Enthüllung, *die; (of crime)* Aufdeckung, *die*

exposed [ɪk'spəʊzd] *adj.* **a)** *(unprotected)* ungeschützt; **~ to the wind/elements** dem

Wind/den Elementen ausgesetzt; ~ **position** *(lit. or fig.)* exponierte Stellung; **b)** *(visible)* freigelegt; sichtbar ⟨*Körperteil*⟩; **c)** *(Photog.)* belichtet

exposition [ekspə'zɪʃn] *n.* **a)** *(statement, presentation)* Darstellung, *die; (commentary)* Kommentar, *der* **(of** zu); *(explanation)* Erläuterung, *die* **(of** zu); *(act of expounding)* ~ **of heretical views** Verbreitung ketzerischer Ansichten; **b)** *(Mus., Lit.: of principal themes)* Exposition, *die;* **c)** *(exhibition)* Ausstellung, *die*

expostulate [ɪk'spɒstjʊleɪt] *v.i.* protestieren; ~ **with sb. about** *or* **on sth.** mit jmdm. über etw. *(Akk.)* debattieren

expostulation [ɪkspɒstjʊ'leɪʃn] *n.* Protest, *der*

exposure [ɪk'spəʊʒə(r)] *n.* **a)** *(to air, cold, etc.) (being exposed)* Ausgesetztsein, *das; (exposing)* Aussetzen, *das; (of goods etc.)* Ausstellung, *die; (of children)* Aussetzung, *die;* **die of/suffer from ~ [to cold]** an Unterkühlung *(Dat.)* sterben/leiden; ~ **to infection** Kontakt mit Krankheitserregern; **indecent ~:** Entblößung in schamverletzender Weise; **media ~:** Publicity, *die;* **b)** *(unmasking) (of fraud etc.)* Enthüllung, *die; (of criminal)* Entlarvung, *die; (of hypocrite or hypocrisy)* Bloßstellung, *die;* **c)** *(Photog.) (exposing time)* Belichtung, *die; (picture)* Aufnahme, *die*

ex'posure meter *n. (Photog.)* Belichtungsmesser, *der*

expound [ɪk'spaʊnd] *v.t.* **a)** darlegen ⟨*These, Theorie, Doktrin*⟩ **(to** *Dat.*); **b)** *(explain)* auslegen ⟨*Schriften, Gesetz*⟩ **(to** *Dat.*)

express [ɪk'spres] **1.** *v.t.* **a)** *(indicate)* ausdrücken; **b)** *(put into words)* äußern, zum Ausdruck bringen ⟨*Meinung, Wunsch, Dank, Bedauern, Liebe*⟩; ~ **sth. in another language** etw. in einer anderen Sprache ausdrücken; ~ **oneself** sich ausdrücken; **he ~ed himself strongly on that subject** er äußerte sich sehr entschieden zu diesem Thema; ~ **one's willingness** *or* **readiness to do sth.** sich bereit erklären, etw. zu tun; **c)** *(represent by symbols)* ausdrücken ⟨*Zahl, Wert*⟩; **d)** *(squeeze)* [heraus]drücken; [heraus]pressen; **e)** *(send by ~ delivery)* als Schnellsendung schicken. **2.** *attrib. adj.* **a)** Eil⟨*brief, -bote usw.*⟩; Schnell⟨*paket, -sendung*⟩; *see also* ~ **train; b)** *(particular)* besonder...; bestimmt; ausdrücklich ⟨*Absicht*⟩; **c)** *(stated)* ausdrücklich ⟨*Wunsch, Befehl usw.*⟩. **3.** *adv.* als Eilsache ⟨*senden*⟩. **4.** *n.* **a)** *(train)* Schnellzug, *der;* D-Zug, *der; (messenger)* Eilbote, *der;* **by ~:** durch Eilboten; **b)** *(Amer.: company)* Transportunternehmen, *das*

express: ~ company *n. (Amer.)* Transportunternehmen, *das;* ~ **de'livery** *n.* Eilzustellung, *die*

expression [ɪk'spreʃn] *n.* **a)** Ausdruck, *der;* **find ~ in sth.** in etw. *(Dat.)* Ausdruck finden *od.* zum Ausdruck kommen; **give ~ to one's gratitude** seine Dankbarkeit zum Ausdruck bringen; seiner Dankbarkeit *(Dat.)* Ausdruck verleihen *(geh.);* **manner** *or* **mode of ~:** Ausdrucksweise, *die;* **profuse ~s of gratitude** überschwengliche Dankesbezeugungen; **the ~ on his face** *or* **his facial ~ was one of deepest hatred** sein Gesichtsausdruck zeugte von tiefstem Haß; tiefster Haß stand ihm im Gesicht geschrieben; **full of/without ~:** ausdrucksvoll/-los; **devoid of all ~:** völlig ausdruckslos; **she put a martyred ~ on her face** sie setzte ihre Duldermiene auf; **b)** *(Art, Mus., Math.)* Ausdruck, *der;* **play/sing with ~:** ausdrucksvoll *od.* -stark spielen/singen

expressionism [ɪk'spreʃənɪzm] *n., no pl.* Expressionismus, *der*

expressionist [ɪk'spreʃənɪst] *n.* Expressionist, *der*/Expressionistin, *die; attrib.* expressionistisch ⟨*Kunst usw.*⟩

expressionistic [ɪkspreʃə'nɪstɪk] *adj.* expressionistisch

expressionless [ɪk'spreʃnlɪs] *adj.* ausdruckslos

ex'pression-mark *n. (Mus.)* Vortragsbezeichnung, *die*

expressive [ɪk'spresɪv] *adj.* **a) be ~ of sth.** etw. ausdrücken; **b)** *(significant)* ausdrucksvoll; vielsagend ⟨*Schweigen*⟩; expressiv *(geh.),* ausdrucksvoll ⟨*Geste*⟩

expressively [ɪk'spresɪvlɪ] *adv.* ausdrucksvoll

express: ~ 'letter *n.* Eilbrief, *der;* ~ **'lift** *n.* Schnellaufzug, *der*

expressly [ɪk'spreslɪ] *adv.* **a)** *(particularly)* ausdrücklich; **b)** *(definitely)* eindeutig; ausdrücklich

express: ~ 'train *n.* Schnellzug, *der;* D-Zug, *der;* ~**way** *n. (Amer.)* Schnell[verkehrs]straße, *die*

expropriate [eks'prəʊprɪeɪt] *v.t.* enteignen; ⟨*Staat usw.:*⟩ verstaatlichen

expropriation [eksprəʊprɪ'eɪʃn] *n.* Enteignung, *die;* Expropriation, *die (veralt.); (esp. by State)* Verstaatlichung, *die*

expulsion [ɪk'spʌlʃn] *n. (from school, college)* Verweisung, *die* **(from** von); Relegation, *die* **(from** von); *(from home)* Vertreibung, *die* **(from** aus); *(from country)* Ausweisung, *die* **(from** aus); *(from club)* Ausschluß, *der* **(from** aus); *(Med.: from the body)* Austreibung, *die* **(from** aus); *(of gas, water, etc. from substance)* Austreiben, *das* **(from** aus)

expunge [ɪk'spʌndʒ] *v.t.* [aus]streichen **(from** aus); *(fig.)* tilgen **(from** aus)

expurgate ['ekspəgeɪt] *v.t. (purify)* zensieren, *(verhüll.)* säubern ⟨*Text, Buch, Theaterstück*⟩; **~d version/edition** zensierte *od. (verhüll.)* bereinigte Fassung/Ausgabe

exquisite ['ekskwɪzɪt, ɪk'skwɪzɪt] *adj.* **a)** erlesen; exquisit, bezaubernd ⟨*Aussicht, Landschaft, Muster, Melodie, Frau, Anmut*⟩; ausgesucht ⟨*Höflichkeit*⟩; **b)** *(acute)* heftig ⟨*Schmerz, Freude*⟩; riesig ⟨*Triumph*⟩; unerträglich ⟨*Leiden, Schmerzen*⟩

exquisitely ['ekskwɪzɪtlɪ, ɪk'skwɪzɪtlɪ] *adv.* **a)** *(excellently, beautifully)* vorzüglich; kunstvoll ⟨*verziert, geschnitzt*⟩; **b)** *(acutely)* äußerst; außerordentlich

ex-'service *adj. (Brit.)* Veteranen-; **~man** ehemaliger Soldat

ext. *abbr.* **a) exterior; b) external; c) [telephone] extension** App.

extant [ek'stænt, 'ekstənt] *adj.* [noch] vorhanden *od.* existent

extemporaneous [ɪkstempə'reɪnɪəs] *adj.* improvisiert; ~ **translation** Stegreifübersetzung, *die*

extempore [ɪk'stempərɪ] **1.** *adv.* aus dem Stegreif; ex tempore *(Theater, geh.);* **speak ~:** frei sprechen; extemporieren. **2.** *adj.* improvisiert ⟨*Gedicht, Lied*⟩; **give an ~ speech** eine Rede aus dem Stegreif *od.* eine Stegreifrede halten

extemporisation, extemporise *see* **extemporiz-**

extemporization [ɪkstempəraɪ'zeɪʃn] *n.* Improvisation, *die;* Extempore, *das*

extemporize [ɪk'stempəraɪz] *v.t. & i.* improvisieren; extemporieren

extend [ɪk'stend] **1.** *v.t.* **a)** *(stretch out)* ausstrecken ⟨*Arm, Bein, Hand*⟩; ausziehen ⟨*Leiter, Teleskop*⟩; spannen ⟨*Seil*⟩; ausbreiten ⟨*Flügel*⟩; ~ **one's hand to sb.** jmdm. die Hand reichen *od.* entgegenstrecken; **the table can be ~ed** der Tisch ist ausziehbar; **b)** *(make longer) (in space)* verlängern; ausdehnen ⟨*Grenze*⟩; ausbauen ⟨*Bahnlinie, Straße*⟩; *(in time)* verlängern; verlängern lassen ⟨*Leihbuch, Visum*⟩; ~ **a credit** Kreditverlängerung gewähren; ~ **the time limit** den Termin hinausschieben; **c)** *(enlarge)* ausdehnen ⟨*Einfluß, Macht, Forschung[sgebiet]*⟩; erweitern ⟨*Wissen, Wortschatz, Bedeutung, Freundeskreis, Besitz, Geschäft*⟩; verlängern ⟨*Aufsatz, Referat*⟩; ausbauen, vergrößern ⟨*Haus, Geschäft, Fabrik, Unternehmen*⟩; **d)** *(offer)* gewähren, zuteil werden lassen ⟨*[Gast]freundschaft, Schutz, Gunst, Hilfe, Kredit*⟩ **(to** *Dat.*); erweisen ⟨*Freundlichkeit, Gefallen*⟩ **(to** *Dat.*); *(accord)* aussprechen ⟨*Dank, Einladung, Glückwunsch*⟩ **(to** *Dat.*); ausrichten ⟨*Gruß*⟩ **(to** *Dat.*); ~ **a welcome to sb.** jmdn. willkommen heißen; **e)** *(tax)* fordern; ~ **oneself** sich verausgaben. **2.** *v.i.* sich erstrecken; **the wall ~s for miles** die Mauer zieht sich meilenweit hin; **the bridge ~s over the river** die Brücke führt über den Fluß; **the road ~s from X to Y** die Straße führt von X nach Y; **the winter season ~s from November to March** die Wintersaison währt von November bis März; **negotiations ~ed over weeks** die Verhandlungen zogen sich über Wochen *od.* wochenlang hin; **the problem ~s to other fields as well** das Problem berührt auch andere Bereiche

extended [ɪk'stendɪd]: ~ **'family** *n.* Großfamilie, *die;* **~-play** *adj.* EP-⟨*Platte, Band*⟩

extendible [ɪk'stendɪbl], **extensible** [ɪk'stensɪbl] *adjs.* [aus]dehnbar ⟨*Stoff*⟩; ausziehbar ⟨*Fernrohr, Leiter*⟩; erweiterungsfähig ⟨*Gebäude, Gewerbe, Firma, Industrie*⟩

extension [ɪk'stenʃn] *n.* **a)** *(stretching out) (of arm, leg, hand)* [Aus]strecken, *das; (of wings)* Ausbreiten, *das; (of muscle)* Streckung, *die;* **b)** *(extent)* Umfang, *der; (range)* Reichweite, *die;* **c)** *(prolonging)* Verlängerung, *die; (of road, railway)* Ausbau, *der;* ~ **of time** Fristverlängerung, *die;* **ask for an ~:** um Verlängerung bitten; Verlängerung beantragen; **be granted** *or* **get an ~:** Verlängerung bekommen; **d)** *(enlargement) (of power, influence, research, frontier)* Ausdehnung, *die; (of enterprise, trade, knowledge)* Erweiterung, *die; (of house, estate)* Ausbau, *der;* **e)** *(additional part) (of house)* Anbau, *der; (of office, university, hospital, etc.)* Erweiterungsbau, *der;* **build an ~ to a hospital** einen Erweiterungsbau zu einem Krankenhaus errichten; ein Krankenhaus ausbauen; **two ~s** zwei Anbauten; **f)** *(telephone)* Nebenanschluß, *der;* Fernsprechnebenstelle, *die (fachspr.); (number)* Apparat, *der;* **g)** ~ **course** *(correspondence course)* Fernstudium, *das*

extension: ~ cord *(Amer.) see* ~ **lead;** ~ **ladder** *n.* Ausziehleiter, *die;* ~ **lead** *n. (Brit.)* Verlängerungsschnur, *die*

extensive [ɪk'stensɪv] *adj.* ausgedehnt ⟨*Ländereien, Reisen, Stadt, Wald, Besitz[tümer], Handel, Forschungen*⟩; extensiv ⟨*Wirtschaft*⟩; weit ⟨*Land[strich], Meer[esfläche], Blick*⟩; umfangreich ⟨*Reparatur, Investitionen, Wissen, Nachforschungen, Studien, Auswahl, Angebot, Sammlung*⟩; beträchtlich ⟨*Schäden, Geldmittel, Anstrengungen*⟩; weitreichend ⟨*Änderungen, Reformen, Einfluß, Machtbefugnis, Unterstützung*⟩; langwierig ⟨*Operation, Unternehmung, Suche*⟩; ausführlich ⟨*Bericht, Einleitung*⟩; **make ~ use of sth.** von etw. ausgiebig Gebrauch machen

extensively [ɪk'stensɪvlɪ] *adv.* beträchtlich ⟨*ändern, beschädigen*⟩; gründlich ⟨*reparieren*⟩; ausführlich ⟨*berichten, schreiben*⟩; **they used these rooms ~:** sie machten ausgiebig von diesen Räumen Gebrauch

extent [ɪk'stent] *n.* **a)** *(space over which sth. extends)* Ausdehnung, *die; (of wings)* Spannweite, *die;* **b)** *(scope) (of damage, debt, knowledge, power, authority)* Umfang, *der; (of influence, genius)* Größe, *die; (of damage, loss, disaster, power, authority)* Ausmaß, *das;* **losses to the ~ of £100** Verluste in Höhe von 100 Pfund; **to what ~?** inwieweit?; in welchem Maße?; **the full ~ of his power** seine ganze Machtfülle; **to a great**

or **large/small** *or* **slight ~:** in hohem/geringem Maße; **to some** *or* **a certain ~:** in gewissem Maße; **to the same ~ as ...:** im selben Maße wie ...; **to a greater/lesser ~:** in höherem/geringerem Maße; **to a greater or lesser ~:** mehr oder weniger; **to such an ~ that ...:** in solchem Maße, daß ...; **her condition has not improved to any [great] ~:** ihr Zustand hat sich [fast] überhaupt nicht gebessert; **c)** *(area of sea, land)* Weite, *die;* **you can see the whole ~ of the park** man kann den Park in seiner ganzen Ausdehnung sehen

extenuate [ɪk'stenjʊeɪt] *v.t.* verharmlosen, beschönigen ‹*Vergehen, Verbrechen, Fehler, Schuld*›; entschuldigen ‹*Benehmen*›; **extenuating circumstances** mildernde Umstände

extenuation [ɪkstenjʊ'eɪʃn] *n. (of crime, offence, fault, guilt)* Verharmlosung, *die;* Beschönigung, *die;* **in ~ of sth./sb.** als Entschuldigung für etw./jmdn.

exterior [ɪk'stɪərɪə(r)] **1.** *adj.* **a)** äußer...; Außen‹*fläche, -wand, -anstrich*›; **~ varnish** Lack für Außenanstriche; **b)** *([coming from] outside)* äußer...; außerhalb gelegen; **c)** *(Cinemat.)* **~ scene** Außenaufnahme, *die.* **2.** *n.* **a)** Äußere, *das; (of house)* Außenwände *Pl.;* **b)** *(appearance)* Äußere, *das;* **a man with a pleasant/rough ~:** ein Mann von angenehmem/ungeschlachtem Äußerem; **judge people by their ~:** Menschen nach ihrem Äußeren beurteilen; **c)** *(Cinemat.)* Außenaufnahme, *die*

exterminate [ɪk'stɜ:mɪneɪt] *v.t.* ausrotten; vertilgen, vernichten ‹*Ungeziefer*›

extermination [ɪkstɜ:mɪ'neɪʃn] *n.* Ausrottung, *die; (of pests)* Vertilgung, *die;* Vernichtung, *die*

external [ɪk'stɜ:nl] **1.** *adj.* **a)** äußer...; Außen‹*fläche, -wirkung, -druck, -winkel, -durchmesser, -abmessungen*›; **give the ~ appearance of ease** äußerlich einen ungezwungenen Eindruck machen; **purely ~:** nur *od.* rein äußerlich; **b)** *(applied to outside)* äußerlich ‹*Heilmittel*›; **for ~ use only** nur äußerlich anzuwenden; nur zur äußerlichen Anwendung; **c)** *(of foreign affairs)* Außen‹*minister, -handel, -wirtschaft, -politik*›; **Ministry of E~ Affairs** Außenministerium, *das;* Ministerium für auswärtige Angelegenheiten *od.* des Auswärtigen; **d)** *(Univ.)* extern; **~ student** Externe, *der/die;* **do ~ studies/an ~ degree** ein Fernstudium absolvieren; **e)** *(of world of phenomena)* äußer...; **the ~ world** die Welt der Erscheinungen; **f) ~ evidence** sich auf äußere Umstände gründender Beweis. **2.** *n. in pl.* Äußerlichkeiten *Pl.*

externalize (externalise) [ɪk'stɜ:nəlaɪz] *v.t.* nach außen projizieren; *(Philos.)* veräußerlichen; *(Psych.)* externalisieren

externally [ɪk'stɜ:nəlɪ] *adv.* äußerlich; **the medicine is only to be used ~:** die Medizin ist nur zur äußerlichen Anwendung [bestimmt]; **be ~ calm** äußerlich *od.* nach außen hin ruhig sein; **the work is done ~:** die Arbeit wird außer Haus[e] erledigt

extinct [ɪk'stɪŋkt] *adj.* erloschen ‹*Vulkan, Feuer, Leidenschaft, Liebe, Hoffnung*›; ausgestorben ‹*Art, Rasse, Volk, Gattung, Leben*›; untergegangen ‹*Volk, Dynastie, Reich, Kultur, Sitte, Brauch*›; abgeschafft ‹*Einrichtung, Amt, Posten, System, Gesetz*›; tot ‹*Sprache*›; **become ~** ‹*Art, Rasse, Volk, Gattung:*› aussterben; ‹*Vulkan, Hoffnung, Adelstitel:*› erlöschen

extinction [ɪk'stɪŋkʃn] *n., no pl. (of fire, light) (extinguishing)* Löschen, *das; (being extinguished)* Erlöschen, *das;* Verlöschen, *das; (abolition) (of religion, system, institution, law, custom)* Abschaffung, *die; (of debt)* Tilgung, *die; (of independence etc.)* Aufhebung, *die;* **threatened with ~:** vom Aussterben bedroht

extinguish [ɪk'stɪŋgwɪʃ] *v.t.* **a)** löschen; erlöschen lassen ‹*Leidenschaft, Hoffnung*›; auslöschen ‹*Leben*›; **b)** *(destroy)* beseitigen

extinguisher [ɪk'stɪŋgwɪʃə(r)] *n.* **a)** *(for fire)* Feuerlöscher, *der;* **b)** *(for candle)* Löschhütchen, *das*

extirpate ['ekstɜ:peɪt] *v.t.* [mit der Wurzel] ausreißen ‹*Pflanze, Haare*›; entfernen ‹*Tumor*›; ausrotten ‹*Rasse, Volk, Sekte, Gattung*›; aufräumen mit, ausmerzen ‹*Ketzerei, Unsitten, Vorurteil*›

extol [ɪk'stəʊl, ɪk'stɒl] *v.t.,* **-ll-** rühmen; preisen

extort [ɪk'stɔ:t] *v.t.* erpressen **(out of, from** von); **~ a secret/confession from sb.** ein Geheimnis/Geständnis aus jmdm. herauspressen

extortion [ɪk'stɔ:ʃn] *n.* **a)** *(of money, taxes)* Erpressung, *die;* **£50? This is sheer ~!** 50 Pfund? Das ist ja Wucher!; **b)** *(illegal exaction)* Erpressung im Amt

extortionate [ɪk'stɔ:ʃənət] *adj.* **a)** *(excessive, exorbitant)* Wucher‹*preis, -zinsen usw.*›; horrend ‹*Gebühr, Steuer*›; maßlos überzogen ‹*Forderung*›; **b)** *(using extortion)* erpresserisch ‹*Methode*›

extortioner [ɪk'stɔ:ʃənə(r)] *n.* Erpresser, *der*/Erpresserin, *die*

extra ['ekstrə] **1.** *adj.* **a)** *(additional)* zusätzlich; Mehr‹*arbeit, -kosten, -ausgaben, -aufwendungen*›; Sonder‹*bus, -zug*›; **~ hours of work** Überstunden; **all we need is an ~ hour/three pounds** wir brauchen nur noch eine Stunde/drei Pfund [zusätzlich]; **without any ~ charge** ohne Aufschlag; **drinks are ~:** Getränke werden extra bezahlt *od. (ugs.)* gehen extra; **make an ~ effort** sich besonders anstrengen; **take ~ care** besonders vorsichtig sein; **for ~ safety** als zusätzliche *od.* besondere Sicherheitsvorkehrung; **can I have an ~ helping?** kann ich noch eine Portion haben?; **b)** *(more than is necessary)* überzählig ‹*Exemplar, Portion*›; **an ~ pair of gloves** noch ein *od.* ein zweites Paar Handschuhe; **have an ~ bed** noch ein Bett frei *od.* ein unbenutztes Bett haben; **we have an ~ ten minutes to kill** wir müssen noch zehn Minuten mehr totschlagen. **2.** *adv.* **a)** *(more than usually)* besonders; extra ‹*lang, stark, fein*›; überaus ‹*froh*›; **an ~ large blouse** eine Bluse in Übergröße; **an ~ special occasion** eine ganz besondere Gelegenheit; **b)** *(additionally)* extra; **packing and postage ~:** zuzüglich Verpackung und Porto. **3.** *n.* **a)** *(added to services, salary, etc.)* zusätzliche Leistung; *(on car etc. offered for sale)* Extra, *das; (adornment on dress etc.)* besondere Note; *(outside normal school curriculum)* zusätzliches Angebot; **b)** *(sth. with ~ charge)* **be an ~:** zusätzlich berechnet werden; **c)** *(in play, film, etc.)* Statist, *der*/Statistin, *die;* Komparse, *der*/Komparsin, *die;* **d)** *(Cricket) Lauf, der nicht durch Schlag erzielt wird*

extra- [ekstrə] *pref.* außer-; extra- *(mit Fremdwörtern lateinischen Ursprungs)*

extract 1. ['ekstrækt] *n.* **a)** Extrakt, *der (fachspr. auch: das);* **an ~ of certain plants** ein Auszug *od.* Extrakt aus bestimmten Pflanzen; **b)** *(from book, music, etc.)* Auszug, *der;* Extrakt, *der (geh.);* **in ~s** auszugsweise; im Extrakt *(geh.).* **2.** [ɪk'strækt] *v.t.* **a)** ziehen, *(fachspr.)* extrahieren ‹*Zahn*›; herausziehen ‹*Dorn, Splitter usw.*›; **~ a bullet from a wound** eine Kugel aus einer Wunde entfernen; **she ~ed herself from his embrace** sie befreite *od.* löste sich aus seiner Umarmung; **~ sth. from sb.** *(fig.)* etw. aus jmdm. herausholen; **~ a promise from sb.** jmdm. ein Versprechen abnötigen; **b)** *(obtain)* extrahieren; **~ the juice of apples** Äpfel entsaften; **~ sugar from beet** aus Rüben Zucker gewinnen; **~ oil from the earth** Erdöl fördern; **~ metal from ore/honey from the honeycomb** Metall aus Erz/Honig aus der Wabe gewinnen; **~ papers from a folder** einem Aktenordner Unterlagen entnehmen; **c)** *(derive)* erfassen ‹*Bedeutung, Hauptpunkte*›; **~ happiness/pleasure/comfort from sth.** Fröhlichkeit/Freude/Trost aus etw. schöpfen; **~ much pleasure from life** dem Leben viel Freude abgewinnen; **d)** *(Math.)* ziehen ‹*Wurzel*›

extraction [ɪk'strækʃn] *n.* **a)** *(of tooth; also Chem.)* Extraktion, *die; (of thorn, splinter, etc.)* Herausziehen, *das; (of bullet)* Entfernen, *das; (of juice, honey, metal)* Gewinnung, *die; (of oil)* Förderung, *die;* **b)** *(descent)* Abstammung, *die;* Herkunft, *die;* **be of German ~:** deutscher Abstammung *od.* Herkunft sein

extractive [ɪk'stræktɪv] *adj.* **~ industries** Rohstoffindustrie, *die;* **~ processes** Extraktionsverfahren *Pl.*

extractor [ɪk'stræktə(r)] *n. (for extracting juice)* Entsafter, *der*

ex'tractor fan *n.* Entlüfter, *der;* Exhaustor, *der*

extra-curricular [ekstrəkə'rɪkjʊlə(r)] *adj.* extracurricular *(fachspr.);* ‹*Aktivität*› außerhalb des Lehrplans

extraditable [ekstrə'daɪtəbl] *adj.* **this is an ~ offence** für dieses Vergehen kann man ausgeliefert werden

extradite ['ekstrədaɪt] *v.t.* **a)** ausliefern ‹*Verbrecher*›; **b)** *(obtain extradition of)* **~ sb.** jmds. Auslieferung erwirken

extradition [ekstrə'dɪʃn] *n.* Auslieferung, *die;* **~ treaty** Auslieferungsvertrag, *der*

extra-'marital *adj.* außerehelich

extra'mural *adj. (Univ.)* außerhalb der Universität *nachgestellt;* außeruniversitär; **~ courses** *or* **classes** Hochschulkurse außerhalb der Universität; Fernkurse

extraneous [ɪk'streɪnɪəs] *adj.* **a)** *(from outside)* von außen; *(Med.)* körperfremd; **free from ~ matter** frei von Fremdstoffen; **b)** *(irrelevant)* belanglos; **be ~ to sth.** für etw. ohne Belang sein

extraordinarily [ɪk'strɔ:dɪnərɪlɪ, ekstrə'ɔ:dɪnərəlɪ] *adv.* außergewöhnlich; überaus, ungemein ‹*merkwürdig*›

extraordinary [ɪk'strɔ:dɪnərɪ, ekstrə'ɔ:dɪnərɪ] *adj.* **a)** *(exceptional)* außergewöhnlich; *(unusual, peculiar)* ungewöhnlich ‹*Gabe*›; merkwürdig, eigenartig ‹*Zeichen, Benehmen, Angewohnheit*›; außerordentlich ‹*Verdienste, Einfluß*›; *(additional)* außerordentlich ‹*Versammlung*›; **how ~!** wie seltsam!; **b)** *(more than ordinary)* ungewöhnlich; **~ powers** außerordentliche Vollmachten; **c)** *(specially employed)* außerordentlich ‹*Gesandte[r], Professor[in]*›; **ambassador ~:** Sonderbotschafter, *der*

extrapolate [ɪk'stræpəleɪt] *(Math. etc.)* **1.** *v.t.* extrapolieren **(to** auf + *Akk.,* **from** aus); *(fig.)* ableiten; extrapolieren *(geh.).* **2.** *v.i.* extrapolieren

extra: ~-'sensory *adj.* außersinnlich; **~-sensory perception** außersinnliche Wahrnehmung; **~ter'restrial** *adj.* außerirdisch; ex[tra]terrestrisch *(fachspr.);* **~terri'torial** *adj.* exterritorial

extra 'time *n. (Sport)* **after ~:** nach einer Verlängerung; **the match went to ~:** das Spiel wurde verlängert; **play ~:** in die Verlängerung gehen

extravagance [ɪk'strævəgəns] *n.* **a)** *no pl. (being extravagant)* Extravaganz, *die; (of claim, wish, order, demand)* Übertriebenheit, *die; (of words, thoughts, ideas, etc.)* Verstiegenheit, *die; (with money)* Verschwendungssucht, *die;* **the ~ of her tastes** ihr teurer Geschmack; **b)** *(extravagant thing)* Luxus, *der*

extravagancy [ɪk'strævəgənsɪ] *see* **extravagance a**

extravagant [ɪk'strævəgənt] *adj.* **a)** *(wasteful)* verschwenderisch; aufwendig ‹*Lebensstil*›; teuer ‹*Geschmack*›; **b)** *(immoderate)* übertrieben ‹*Benehmen, Lob, Eifer, Begeisterung usw.*›; maßlos ‹*Gebrauch, Begeisterung*›; c) *(beyond bounds of reason)* abwegig ‹*Theorie, Frage, Einfall*›; it is not ~ to suppose that ...: die Vermutung liegt nahe, daß ...; d) *(exorbitant)* überhöht ‹*Preis*›

extravagantly [ɪk'strævəgəntlɪ] *adv.* extravagant ‹*einrichten, ausstatten, sich kleiden*›; verschwenderisch ‹*benutzen, verbrauchen*›; luxuriös, aufwendig ‹*leben*›; außergewöhnlich ‹*sich benehmen*›; überschwenglich ‹*loben*›; spend money ~: mit vollen Händen Geld ausgeben

extravaganza [ɪkstrævə'gænzə] *n.* *(composition) (Lit.)* phantastische Dichtung; *(Mus.)* phantastische Komposition; *(Theatre)* Ausstattungsstück, *das*

extreme [ɪk'stri:m] 1. *adj.* a) *(outermost, utmost)* äußerst... ‹*Spitze, Rand, Ende*›; extrem, kraß ‹*Gegensätze*›; the ~ end of the finger die Fingerspitze *od.* -kuppe; the ~ points of a line/scale die Endpunkte einer Linie/Skala; at the ~ edge/left ganz am Rand/ganz links; in the ~ North im äußersten Norden; b) *(reaching high degree)* extrem; gewaltig ‹*Entfernung, Unterschied*›; höchst... ‹*Gefahr*›; äußerst... ‹*Notfall, Grenzen, Höflichkeit, Bescheidenheit*›; stärkst... ‹*Schmerzen*›; heftigst... ‹*Zorn*›; tiefst... ‹*Haß, Dankbarkeit*›; größt... ‹*Überraschung, Wichtigkeit, Wunsch*›; stürmisch ‹*Begeisterung*›; c) *(not moderate)* extrem ‹*Person, Einstellung, Gesinnung, Forderungen, Ideen, Tendenzen, Kritik*›; ~ right-wing views rechtsextreme Ansichten; d) *(RC & Orthodox Ch.)* ~ unction die Letzte Ölung; e) *(severe)* drastisch ‹*Maßnahme*›; take ~ action against sb. rigoros gegen jmdn. vorgehen. 2. *n.* Extrem, *das;* [krasser] Gegensatz; ~s of heat and cold extreme Hitze und Kälte; the ~s of wealth and poverty größter Reichtum und äußerste Armut; ~s of passion extreme Pole der Leidenschaft; ~s of temperature extreme Temperaturunterschiede; go to the ~ of doing sth. bis zum Äußersten gehen und etw. tun; go to ~s *or* to any ~ *or* to the last ~: vor nichts zurückschrecken; go to the other ~: ins andere Extrem verfallen; go from one ~ to another von *od.* aus einem Extrem ins andere fallen; annoying/monotonous in the ~: äußerst unangenehm/extrem *od.* äußerst eintönig; run to ~s einen Hang zum Extremen haben; *see also* carry 1 g

extremely [ɪk'stri:mlɪ] *adv.* äußerst; Did you enjoy the party? – Yes, ~: Hat dir die Party gefallen? – Ja, sehr sogar!

extremeness [ɪk'stri:mnɪs] *n., no pl.* *(of views, actions, policies)* Extremität, *die;* *(of measures)* Härte, *die*

extremism [ɪk'stri:mɪzm] *n., no pl.* Extremismus, *der*

extremist [ɪk'stri:mɪst] *n.* a) Extremist, *der*/Extremistin, *die;* right-wing ~: Rechtsextremist, *der*/-extremistin, *die;* b) *attrib.* extremistisch

extremity [ɪk'stremɪtɪ] *n.* a) *(of branch, path, road)* äußerstes Ende; *(of region)* Rand, *der;* the southernmost ~ of a continent die Südspitze eines Kontinents; b) *in pl.* *(hands and feet)* Extremitäten *Pl.;* c) *(adversity)* äußerste *od.* höchste Not; *(intensity)* Heftigkeit, *die;* be reduced to ~: in eine Notlage geraten

extricate ['ekstrɪkeɪt] *v.t.* ~ sth. from sth. etw. aus etw. herausziehen; ~ oneself/sb. from sth. sich/jmdn. aus etw. befreien

extrinsic [ek'strɪnsɪk] *adj.* a) äußer...; äußerlich ‹*Wert*›; extrinsisch *(Philos.);* be ~ to sth. einer Sache *(Dat.)* fremd sein; b) *(not essential)* irrelevant (to für)

extrovert ['ekstrəvɜ:t] 1. *n.* extravertierter Mensch; Extravertierte, *der/die;* be an ~: extravertiert sein. 2. *adj.* extravertiert; have ~ tendencies zur Extravertiertheit neigen

extroverted ['ekstrəvɜ:tɪd] *adj.* extravertiert

extrude [ɪk'stru:d] *v.t.* ausstoßen; ausstrecken ‹*Fühler*›; extrudieren *(fachspr.)* ‹*Metall, Kunststoff*›; *(Geol.)* auswerfen ‹*Gestein*›; *(fig.: expel)* ausschließen (from aus)

extrusion [ɪk'stru:ʒn] *n.* *(of metal, plastic, etc.)* Extrudieren, *das (fachspr.);* *(article extruded)* Formstück, *das*

exuberance [ɪg'zju:bərəns] *n.* a) *(vigour)* Überschwang, *der;* *(of health)* Robustheit, *die;* ~ of joy/spirits überschwengliche Freude/Stimmung; ~ of youth jugendlicher Überschwang; b) *(of language, style)* Lebendigkeit, *die*

exuberant [ɪg'zju:bərənt] *adj.* a) *(overflowing, abounding)* strotzend ‹*Gesundheit*›; überschäumend ‹*Kraft, Freude, Eifer, Heiterkeit*›; b) *(effusive)* überschwenglich; sehr lebhaft ‹*Farbe*›; he was ~ when ...: er freute sich überschwenglich, als ...

exuberantly [ɪg'zju:bərəntlɪ] *adv.* überschwenglich ‹*begrüßen, beschreiben*›; ~ happy überglücklich

exude [ɪg'zju:d] 1. *v.i.* abgesondert werden (from aus); ‹*Blut:*› fließen (from aus); *(fig.)* ausgehen (from von). 2. *v.t.* absondern ‹*Flüssigkeit, Harz*›; ausströmen ‹*Geruch*›; *(fig.)* ausstrahlen ‹*Charme, Zuversicht*›

exult [ɪg'zʌlt] *v.i.* a) *(literary: rejoice)* jubeln; frohlocken *(geh.)* (in, at, over über + *Akk.*); ~ to find that ...: darüber frohlocken, daß ...; ~ with joy vor Freude jubeln; b) *(triumph)* triumphieren (over über + *Akk.*)

exultant [ɪg'zʌltənt] *adj.* a) *(literary: exulting)* jubelnd ‹*Person, Menge, Lachen*›; unbändig ‹*Freude*›; be ~: jubeln; be in an ~ mood in Hochstimmung sein; b) *(triumphant)* triumphierend ‹*Sieger*›

exultantly [ɪg'zʌltəntlɪ] *adv.* überglücklich

exultation [egzʌl'teɪʃn] *n.* Jubel, *der*

eye [aɪ] 1. *n.* a) Auge, *das;* as far as the ~ can see soweit das Auge reicht; ~s *(look, glance, gaze)* Blick, *der;* a pair of blue ~s zwei blaue Augen; close *or* shut/open one's ~s die Augen schließen/öffnen; that will make him open his ~s *(fig.)* da wird er Augen machen; open sb.'s ~s to sth. *(fig.)* jmdm. die Augen über etw. *(Akk.)* öffnen; shut *or* close one's ~s to sth. *(fig.)* die Augen vor etw. *(Dat.)* verschließen; the sun/light is [shining] in my ~s die Sonne/das Licht blendet mich; I've got the sun in my ~s die Sonne blendet mich; out of the corner of one's ~: aus den Augenwinkeln; lift up one's ~s die Augen erheben; aufblicken; drop *or* lower one's ~s die Augen niederschlagen; den Blick senken; with one's own *or* very ~s mit eigenen Augen; under/before sb.'s very ~s unter/vor jmds. Augen *(Dat.);* measure a distance by ~ *or* with one's ~[s] einen Abstand nach Augenmaß schätzen; judge sth. by ~: etw. nach dem Augenschein beurteilen *(geh.);* paint/draw sth. by ~: etw. nach der Natur malen/zeichnen; with the ~ of an artist, with an artist's ~: mit den Augen eines Künstlers; look sb. in the ~: jmdm. gerade in die Augen sehen; not be able to look sb. in the ~: jmdm. nicht ins Gesicht sehen können; have ~s [only] for sb. sich [nur] für jmdn. interessieren; be unable to take one's ~s off sb./sth. die Augen *od.* den Blick nicht von jmdm./etw. abwenden können; make [sheep's] ~s at sb. jmdm. [schöne] Augen machen; keep an ~ on sb./sth. auf jmdn./etw. aufpassen; ein Auge auf jmdn./etw. haben; keep a sharp *or* close *or* strict ~ on sb./sth. scharf auf jmdn./etw. aufpassen; streng auf jmdn./etw. achten; keep one's ~[s] on sb./sth. jmdn./etw. im Auge behalten; have [got] an *or* one's ~[s] on sb./sth. ein Auge auf jmdn./etw. geworfen haben; I've got my ~ on you! ich lasse dich nicht aus den Augen!; keep an ~ open *or* out [for sb./sth.] [nach jmdm./etw.] Ausschau halten; keep one's ~s open die Augen offenhalten; keep one's ~s skinned *or* peeled *(coll.)* wie ein Schießhund aufpassen *(ugs.);* keep one's ~s open *or* *(coll.)* peeled *or* *(coll.)* skinned for sth. nach etw. Ausschau halten; keep one's ~s and ears open Augen und Ohren offenhalten; with one's ~s open *(fig.)* mit offenen Augen; bewußt; with one's ~s shut *(fig.)* *(without full awareness)* blind; *(with great ease)* im Schlaf; with a friendly/jealous/eager/critical ~: freundlich / eifersüchtig / erwartungsvoll / kritisch; have you no ~s in your head? hast du keine Augen im Kopf? *(ugs.);* bist du blind?; where are your ~s?, use your ~s! wo hast du deine Augen?; I haven't [got] ~s at *or* in the back of my head ich habe hinten keine Augen; in the ~s of God/the law vor Gott/nach dem Gesetz; in sb.'s ~s in jmds. Augen *(Dat.);* see sb./sth. through sb.'s ~s jmdn./etw. mit jmds. Augen sehen; look at sth. through the ~s of sb. etw. mit jmds. Augen betrachten; pore one's ~s out over a book über einem Buch sitzen, bis die Augen ermüden; tire one's ~s out seine Augen ermüden; be all ~s gespannt zusehen; [all] my ~ *(sl.)* [alles] Schnickschnack *(ugs. abwertend);* do sb. in the ~ *(coll.)* jmdn. übers Ohr hauen *(ugs.);* [an] ~ for [an] ~: Auge um Auge; ~s front!/right!/left! *(Mil.)* Augen geradeaus/rechts/links!; have an ~ to sth./doing sth. auf etw. *(Akk.)* bedacht sein/darauf bedacht sein, etw. zu tun; with an ~ to sth. im Hinblick auf etw. *(Akk.);* with an ~ to doing sth. mit dem Gedanken, etw. zu tun; hit sb. in the ~ *(fig.)* jmdm. ins Auge springen *od.* fallen; that was one in the ~ for him *(coll.)* das war ein Schlag ins Kontor *(ugs.)* für ihn; see ~ to ~ [on sth. with sb.] [mit jmdm.] einer Meinung [über etw. *(Akk.)*] sein; not see ~ to ~ with sb. on sth. über etw. *(Akk.)* anderer Meinung als jmd. sein; be up to one's ~s *(fig.)* bis über beide Ohren drinstecken *(ugs.);* be up to one's ~s in work/debt bis über beide Ohren in der Arbeit/in Schulden stecken *(ugs.);* have an ~ for sth. ein Auge *od.* einen Blick für etw. haben; have an ~ for sb. jmdn. gern haben; a man with an ~ for the ladies ein Mann, der die Frauen gern hat; have a keen/good ~ for sth. einen geschärften/einen sicheren *od.* den richtigen Blick für etw. haben; see with half an ~ that ...: auf den ersten Blick sehen, daß ...; get one's ~ in at shooting/tennis sich einschießen/sich einspielen; b) *(sth. like an ~)* Auge, *das;* *(of peacock's tail)* Pfauenauge, *das;* *(on butterfly's wing)* Augenfleck, *der;* *(of needle, fish-hook)* Öhr, *das;* *(metal loop)* Öse, *die.* 2. *v.t.,* ~ing *or* eying ['aɪɪŋ] beäugen; ~ sb. up and down/from head to foot jmdn. von oben bis unten/von Kopf bis Fuß mustern

eye: ~**ball** *n.* Augapfel, *der;* ~ball to ~ball *(coll.)* hautnah ‹*Konfrontation*›; be *or* meet ~ball to ~ball sich *(Dat.)* Auge in Auge gegenüberstehen; ~**-bath** *n.* Augenbadewanne, *die;* ~**black** *n.* *(dated)* schwarze Wimperntusche; ~**bright** *n.* *(Bot.)* Augentrost, *der;* ~**brow** *n.* Augenbraue, *die;* raise *or* lift an ~brow *or* one's ~brows [at sth.] die [Augen]brauen [wegen etw.] hochziehen; *(fig.)* *(in surprise)* die Stirn runzeln (at über + *Akk.*); *(superciliously)* die Nase rümpfen (at über + *Akk.*); it will raise a few ~brows das wird einiges Stirnrunzeln hervorrufen; up to the *or* one's ~brows [in sth.] bis über beide Ohren [in etw. *(Dat.)*]; ~brow pencil Augenbrauenstift, *der;* ~**-catching** *adj.* ins Auge springend *od.* fallend ‹*Inserat, Plakat, Buchhülle usw.*›; be [very] ~-catching ein [wirkungsvoller] Blickfang sein; she is very ~-catching sie zieht die Augen aller auf sich *(Akk.);* ~**-contact** *n.* Blickkontakt, *der*

-eyed [aɪd] *adj. in comb.* -äugig; **big-~/bright-~:** groß-/helläugig; **fierce-~/sad-~:** mit grimmigen/traurigen Augen *od.* grimmigem/traurigem Blick *nachgestellt;* **be sad-~:** traurige Augen haben

eye: ~-dropper *n. (Med.)* Augentropfer, *der;* **~-drops** *n. pl. (Med.)* Augentropfen *Pl.*

eyeful ['aɪfʊl] *n. (coll.) (woman)* Klassefrau, *die (ugs.); (sight)* **get an ~ [of sth.]** einiges [von etw.] zu sehen bekommen

eye: ~glass *n. (dated)* Augenglas, *das (veralt.);* **~ hospital** *n.* Augenklinik, *die;* **~lash** *n.* Augenwimper, *die; see also* **flutter 2 a**

eyeless ['aɪlɪs] *adj.* blind ‹*Person, Tier*›

eyelet ['aɪlɪt] *n.* **a)** Öse, *die; (Naut.)* Auge, *das;* **b)** *(to look through)* Guckloch, *das*

eye: ~-level *n.* Augenhöhe, *die; attrib.* in Augenhöhe *nachgestellt;* **~lid** *n.* Augenlid, *das;* **~-liner** *n.* Eyeliner, *der;* Lidstrich, *der;* **~-opener** *n. (surprise, revelation)* Überraschung, *die;* **the book was an ~-opener to the public** das Buch hat der Öffentlichkeit die Augen geöffnet; **~-patch** *n.* Augenklappe, *die;* **~piece** *n. (Optics)* Okular, *das;* **~-shade** *n.* Augenschirm, *der;* **~-shadow** *n.* Lidschatten, *der;* **~sight** *n.* Sehkraft, *die;* **have good ~sight** gute Augen haben; gut sehen können; **his ~sight is poor** er hat schlechte Augen; **~sore** *n.* Schandfleck, *der (abwertend);* **the building is an ~sore** das Gebäude beleidigt das Auge; **~-strain** *n.* Überanstrengung der Augen; **be a cause of ~-strain** die Augen überanstrengen; **~ test** *n.* Sehtest, *der;* **~-tooth** *n.* Eckzahn, *der;* **cut one's ~-teeth** *(fig.)* Erfahrungen sammeln; **she would give her ~-teeth for it/to do it** sie würde alles dafür geben/darum geben, es zu tun; **~wash** *n.* **a)** *(Med.: lotion)* Augenwasser, *das;* **b)** *(coll.) (nonsense)* Gewäsch, *das (ugs. abwertend); (concealment)* Augen[aus]wischerei, *die (ugs.);* **~witness** *n.* Augenzeuge, *der*/-zeugin, *die;* **~witness account** *or* **report** Augenzeugenbericht, *der;* **be an ~witness of sth.** Augenzeuge einer Sache *(Gen.)* sein

eyrie ['ɪərɪ] *n. (nest)* Horst, *der*

F

F, f [ef] *n., pl.* **Fs** *or* **F's a)** *(letter)* F, f, *das;* **b)** F *(Mus.)* F, f, *das;* **F sharp** fis, Fis, *das;* **c)** F *(Sch., Univ.: mark)* Sechs, *die;* **he got an F** er bekam „ungenügend" *od.* eine Sechs

F. *abbr.* **a) Fahrenheit** F; **b) Fellow; c)** *(on pencil)* **firm** F; **d) franc** F; **e)** *(Phys.)* **farad[s]** F

f. *abbr.* **a) female** weibl.; **b) feminine** f.; **c) focal length** f; **f/8** *(Photog.)* Blende 8; **d) following [page]** f.; **e) forte** f; **f) folio** F.

FA *abbr. (Brit.)* **Football Association** *(Britischer Fußballverband)*

fa *see* **fah**

fab [fæb] *adj. (Brit. coll.)* fabelhaft *(ugs.);* dufte, toll *(salopp)*

Fabian ['feɪbɪən] *adj.* Hinhalte-; Verzögerungs‹*taktik, -manöver*›

fable ['feɪbl] *n.* **a)** *(story of the supernatural, myth, lie)* Märchen, *das;* **land of ~:** Märchen- *od.* Fabelland, *das;* **separate fact from ~:** Dichtung und Wahrheit unterscheiden; **b)** *(thing that does not really exist, brief story)* Fabel, *die*

fabled ['feɪbld] *adj.* **a)** *(told as in fable)* **it is ~ that ...:** es heißt, daß ...; **b)** *(mythical)* Fabel‹*land, -wesen, -tier*›; **c)** *(celebrated)* berühmt **(for** für)

fabric ['fæbrɪk] *n.* **a)** *(material, construction, texture)* Gewebe, *das;* **woven/knitted/ribbed/coarse/mixed ~:** Web-/Strickware, *die*/Rips, *der*/Grob-/Mischgewebe, *das;* **b)** *(thing put together)* Gebilde, *das;* **c)** *(fig.: frame)* Gefüge, *das;* **destroy the ~ of sb.'s life** jmds. Welt zerstören; **d)** *(of building)* bauliche Substanz; Bausubstanz, *die*

fabricate ['fæbrɪkeɪt] *v. t.* **a)** *(invent)* erfinden; *(forge)* fälschen; **b)** *(construct, manufacture)* herstellen

fabrication [fæbrɪ'keɪʃn] *n.* **a)** *(of story etc., falsehood)* Erfindung, *die;* **the story is [a] pure ~:** die Geschichte ist frei erfunden; **b)** *(construction, manufacture)* Herstellung, *die*

fabulous ['fæbjʊləs] *adj.* **a)** *(unhistorical, legendary, celebrated)* sagenhaft; **~ animal/creature** *or* **being** Fabeltier/-wesen, *das;* **b)** *(exaggerated)* phantastisch ‹*Geschichte*›; **c)** *(coll.: marvellous)* fabelhaft *(ugs.)*

façade [fə'sɑːd] *n. (lit. or fig.)* Fassade, *die;* **that's just a ~** *(fig.)* das ist alles nur Fassade

face [feɪs] **1.** *n.* **a)** Gesicht, *das;* **wash one's ~:** sich *(Dat.)* das Gesicht waschen; **blush/be smiling all over one's ~:** bis über die Ohren rot werden/über das ganze Gesicht strahlen; **go purple** *or* **black in the ~** *(with strangulation),* **go blue in the ~** *(with cold)* blau im Gesicht werden; **go red** *or* **purple in the ~** *(with exertion or passion or shame)* rot im Gesicht werden; **the stone struck me on my ~** *or* **in the ~:** der Stein traf mich ins Gesicht; **the ~ of an angel/a devil/a criminal** ein Engels-/Teufels-/Verbrechergesicht; **bring A and B ~ to ~:** A und B einander *(Dat.)* gegenüberstellen; **stand ~ to ~:** sich *(Dat.)* gegenüberstehen; **meet sb. ~ to ~:** jmdn. persönlich kennenlernen; **come** *or* **be brought ~ to ~ with sb.** mit jmdm. konfrontiert werden; **come ~ to ~ with the fact that ...:** vor der Tatsache stehen, daß ...; **fly in the ~ of sb./sth.** jmdn. mit Verachtung strafen/sich über etw. *(Akk.)* hinwegsetzen; **in [the] ~ of sth.** *(despite)* trotz; *(confronted with)* vor (+ *Dat.*); **cowardice in the ~ of the enemy** Feigheit vor dem Feind; **slam the door in sb.'s ~:** jmdm. die Tür vor der Nase zuknallen *(ugs.);* **shine in sb.'s ~:** jmdm. ins Gesicht scheinen; **fall [flat] on one's ~** *(lit. or fig.)* auf die Nase fallen *(ugs.);* **look sb./sth. in the ~:** jmdm./einer Sache ins Gesicht sehen; **put one's ~ on** *(coll.)* sich anmalen *(ugs.);* **set one's ~ against sb./sth.** sich jmdm./einer Sache entgegenstellen; **show one's ~:** sich sehen *od.* blicken lassen; **tell sb. to his ~ what ...:** jmdm. [offen] ins Gesicht sagen, was ...; **use sb.'s nickname to his ~:** jmds. Spitznamen in seiner Gegenwart benutzen; **talk/scream/complain** *etc.* **till one is blue in the ~:** reden/schreien/klagen *usw.* bis man verrückt wird *(ugs.);* **shut one's ~** *(sl.)* die *od.* seine Klappe halten *(salopp);* **have the ~ to do sth.** die Stirn haben, etw. zu tun; **save one's ~:** das Gesicht wahren *od.* retten; **lose ~ [with sb.] [over sth.]** das Gesicht [vor jmdm.] [wegen etw.] verlieren; **sth. makes sb. lose ~:** etw. kostet jmdn. das Gesicht *od.* Ansehen; **see by sb.'s ~ that ...:** es jmdm. [am Gesicht] *od.* es jmds. Gesicht *(Dat.)* ansehen, daß ...; **make** *or* **pull a ~/~s [at sb.]** *(to show dislike)* ein Gesicht/Gesichter machen *od.* ziehen; *(to amuse or frighten)* eine Grimasse/Grimassen schneiden; **don't make a ~!** mach nicht so ein Gesicht!; **with a ~ like thunder** *or* **as black as thunder** schwarz vor Ärger; **on the ~ of it** dem Anschein nach; **change the ~ of sth.** einer Sache *(Dat.)* ein neues Gesicht geben; **put a brave** *or* **good** *or* **bold ~ on it/the matter/the affair** *etc.* gute Miene zum bösen Spiel machen; **b)** *(front) (of mountain, cliff)* Wand, *die; (of building)* Stirnseite, *die; (of clock, watch)* Zifferblatt, *das; (of dice)* Seite, *die; (of coin, medal, banknote, playing-card)* Vorderseite, *die; (of tool)* Bahn, *die; (of golf-club, cricket-bat, hockey-stick, tennis-racket)* Schlagfläche, *die;* **c)** *(surface)* **the ~ of the earth** die Erde; **disappear off** *or* **from the ~ of the earth** spurlos verschwinden; **be wiped off the ~ of the earth** ausradiert werden; **d)** *(Geom.; also of crystal, gem)* Fläche, *die;* **e)** *see* **type-face; f)** *see* **coal-face.** *See also* **face down[ward]; face up[ward]; fall 2 n; laugh 2; [1]long 1 b; [2]smack 1 b; straight face. 2.** *v. t.* **a)** *(look towards)* sich wenden zu; **sb. ~s the front** jmd. sieht nach vorne; **[stand] facing one another** sich *(Dat.) od. (meist geh.)* einander gegenüber [stehen]; **the house facing the church** das Haus gegenüber der Kirche; **the window ~s the garden/front** das Fenster geht zum Garten/zur Straße hinaus *od.* liegt zum Garten/zur Straße; **travel/sit facing the engine** mit dem Gesicht in Fahrtrichtung fahren/in Fahrtrichtung sitzen; **sit facing the stage** vor der Bühne *od.* mit dem Gesicht zur Bühne sitzen; **b)** *(fig.: have to deal with)* ins Auge sehen (+ *Dat.*) ‹*Tod, Vorstellung*›; gegenübertreten (+ *Dat.*) ‹*Kläger*›; sich stellen (+ *Dat.*) ‹*Anschuldigung, Kritik*›; stehen vor (+ *Dat.*) ‹*Ruin, Entscheidung*›; eingehen ‹*Risiko*›; **~ trial for murder, ~ a charge of murder** sich wegen Mordes vor Gericht verantworten müssen; **c)** *(not shrink from)* ins Auge sehen (+ *Dat.*) ‹*Tatsache, Wahrheit*›; mit Fassung gegenübertreten (+ *Dat.*) ‹*Kläger*›; **~ sth. out** etw. durchstehen; **~ sb. down** jmdn. demoralisieren *od. (ugs.)* kleinkriegen; **refuse to be ~d down by threats** sich von Drohungen nicht kleinkriegen lassen *(ugs.);* **~ the music** *(fig.)* die Suppe auslöffeln *(ugs.);* **let's ~ it** *(coll.)* machen wir uns *(Dat.)* doch nichts vor *(ugs.);* **d) ~d with these facts** mit diesen Sachen konfrontiert; **be ~d with sth.** sich einer Sache *(Dat.)* gegenübersehen; **he was ~d with the possibility** für ihn ergab sich die Möglichkeit; **he is ~d with a lawsuit** gegen ihn wird ein Prozeß eingeleitet; **the problems/questions that we are ~d with** die Probleme/Fragen, vor denen wir stehen; **e)** *(coll.: bear)* verkraften; abkönnen *(nordd. salopp, meist verneint);* **f)** *(dress, trim)* besetzen ‹*Kleidungsstück*›; verkleiden, verblenden ‹*Wand*›; **a cloak ~d with white** ein Umhang mit weißem Besatz. **3.** *v. i.* **a)** *(look)* **~ forwards/backwards** ‹*Person/Bank, Sitz:*› in/entgegen Fahrtrichtung sitzen/aufgestellt sein; **in which direction was he facing?** in welche Richtung blickte er?; **~ away [from sb.]** das Gesicht [von jmdm.] abwenden; **stand facing away from sb.** mit dem Rücken zu jmdm. stehen; **~ away from/on to the road/east[wards]** *or* **to[wards] the east** ‹*Fenster, Zimmer:*› nach hinten/vorn/Osten liegen; **one side of the house ~s to[wards] the sea** eine Seite des Hauses liegt zum Meer; **b)** *(Amer. Mil.)* eine Wendung machen; **~ about/to the right/left** eine Kehrt-/Rechts-/Linkswendung machen; **left/right ~!** ganze Abteilung links/rechts um!

~ 'up to *v. t.* ins Auge sehen (+ *Dat.*); sich abfinden mit ‹*Möglichkeit*›; auf sich nehmen ‹*Verantwortung*›

face: ~ card *see* **court card; ~-cloth** *n. (cloth for ~)* Waschlappen [für das Gesicht]; **~-cream** *n.* Gesichtscreme, *die*

-faced [feɪst] *adj. in comb.* -gesichtig

face: ~ 'down[ward] *adv.* mit der Vorderseite nach unten; **put one's cards ~ down on the table** seine Karten verdeckt auf den Tisch legen; **lie ~ down[ward]** ⟨*Person:*⟩ auf dem Bauch liegen; ⟨*Buch:*⟩ auf dem Gesicht liegen; *see also* **face 2c**; **~-flannel** *(Brit.) see* **~-cloth**

faceless ['feɪslɪs] *adj.* **a)** *(without face)* gesichtslos; **b)** *(anonymous)* anonym *(fig.)*

face: ~-lift *n.* **a)** Facelifting, *das;* **have** *or* **get a ~-lift** sich *(Dat.)* die Gesichtshaut liften *od.* straffen lassen; **b)** *(fig.: improvement in appearance)* Verschönerung, *die;* **~-off** *n. (Ice Hockey)* Bully, *das;* **~-powder** *n.* Gesichtspuder, *das;* **~-saving 1.** *adj.* zur Wahrung des Gesichts *nachgestellt;* **as a ~-saving gesture** um das Gesicht zu retten *od.* zu wahren; **2.** *n.* Wahrung des Gesichts

facet ['fæsɪt] *n.* **a)** *(of many-sided body, esp. of cut stone)* Facette, *die;* **b)** *(aspect)* Seite, *die;* **every ~:** alle Seiten *od. (geh.)* Facetten

faceted ['fæsɪtɪd] *adj.* facettiert ⟨*Edelstein, Diamant, Linse*⟩

facetious [fə'si:ʃəs] *adj.* [gewollt] witzig; *(impudently)* frech; **[not] be ~ [about sth.]** [keine] Witze [über etw. *(Akk.)*] machen *(ugs.)*

facetiously [fə'si:ʃəslɪ] *adv.* [gewollt] witzig

face: ~-to-face *adj.* unmittelbar ⟨*Gegenüberstellung*⟩; **~ 'up[ward]** *adv.* mit der Vorderseite nach oben; **lie ~ up[ward]** ⟨*Karte:*⟩ offen *od.* aufgedeckt liegen; ⟨*Person:*⟩ auf dem Rücken liegen; *(open)* ⟨*Buch:*⟩ aufgeschlagen liegen; **~ value** *n. (Finance)* Nominalwert, *der (fachspr.);* Nennwert, *der;* **accept sth. at [its] ~ value** *(fig.)* etw. für bare Münze nehmen; **take sb. at [his/her] ~ value** *(fig.)* jmdn. nach seinem Äußeren beurteilen; **~-worker** *n. (Mining)* Untertagearbeiter, *der*

facia ['feɪʃə] *n.* **a)** *(plate)* **~ [board]** Firmenschild, *das;* **b)** *(Motor Veh.)* **~ [board or panel]** Armaturenbrett, *das*

facial ['feɪʃl] **1.** *adj.* Gesichts-. **2.** *n.* Gesichtsmassage, *die;* **have a ~:** sich *(Dat.)* das Gesicht massieren lassen

facile ['fæsaɪl, 'fæsɪl] *adj. (often derog.)* leicht ⟨*Sieg, Arbeit, Aufgabe*⟩; einfach ⟨*Art, Methode, Technik*⟩; gewandt ⟨*Lügner, Schriftsteller*⟩; nichtssagend, banal ⟨*Bemerkung*⟩; oberflächlich, *(abwertend)* flach ⟨*Person, Einstellung*⟩

facilitate [fə'sɪlɪteɪt] *v. t.* erleichtern

facility [fə'sɪlɪtɪ] *n.* **a)** *esp. in pl.* Einrichtung, *die;* **cooking/washing facilities** Koch-/Waschgelegenheit, *die;* **sports facilities** Sportanlagen; **drying facilities** *(indoor)* Trockenraum, *der; (outdoor)* Trockenplatz, *der;* **postal facilities** Postdienste; **shopping facilities** Einkaufsmöglichkeiten; **banking facilities** Banken; **travel facilities** Verkehrsmittel; **b)** *(unimpeded opportunity)* Möglichkeit, *die;* **c)** *(ease, aptitude, freedom from difficulty)* Leichtigkeit, *die; (dexterity)* Gewandtheit, *die;* **~ in speech/writing** Rede-/Schreibgewandtheit, *die*

facing ['feɪsɪŋ] *n.* **a)** *(on garment)* Aufschlag, *der;* Besatz, *der;* **b)** *in pl. (cuffs, collar, etc. of jacket)* [Uniform]aufschläge *Pl.;* **c)** *(covering)* Verblendung, *die;* Verkleidung, *die*

facsimile [fæk'sɪmɪlɪ] *n.* **a)** Faksimile, *das;* **b)** *(system)* Bildfunk, *der*

fact [fækt] *n.* **a)** *(true thing)* Tatsache, *die;* **~s and figures** Fakten und Zahlen; **the ~ remains that ...:** Tatsache bleibt: ...; **the true ~s of the case** *or* **matter** der wahre Sachverhalt; **know for a ~ that ...:** genau *od.* sicher wissen, daß ...; **is that a ~?** *(coll.)* Tatsache? *(ugs.);* **and that's a ~:** und daran gibt's nichts zu zweifeln *(ugs.);* **the value/reason lies in the ~ that ...:** der Nutzen/Grund besteht darin, daß ...; **look the ~s in the face, face [the] ~s** den Tatsachen ins Gesicht sehen; **it is a proven/an established/an undisputed/an accepted ~ that ...:** es ist erwiesen/steht fest/ist unbestritten/man geht davon aus, daß ...; **the ~ [of the matter] is that ...:** die Sache ist die, daß ...; **[it is a] ~ of life** [das ist die] harte *od.* rauhe Wirklichkeit; **tell** *or* **teach sb. the ~s of life** *(coll. euphem.)* jmdn. [sexuell] aufklären; **b)** *(reality)* Wahrheit, *die;* Tatsachen *Pl.;* **distinguish ~ from fiction** Fakten und Fiktion *(geh.) od.* Dichtung und Wahrheit unterscheiden; **in ~:** tatsächlich; **I don't suppose you did/would do it? – In ~, I did/would** Ich nehme an, Sie haben es nicht getan/würden es nicht tun. – Doch[, ich habe es tatsächlich getan/würde es tatsächlich tun]; **I was planning to go to your party and had in ~ bought a bottle of wine** ich wollte zu deiner Party kommen und hatte sogar *od.* auch schon eine Flasche Wein gekauft; **he was supposed to arrive before eight, but he didn't in ~ get here till after twelve** er sollte vor acht Uhr ankommen, ist dann aber doch erst nach 12 Uhr hier eingetroffen; **he has left us; in ~ he is not coming back** er hat uns verlassen, und er kommt auch nicht mehr zurück; **I don't think he'll come back; in ~ I know he won't** ich glaube nicht, daß er zurückkommt, ich weiß es sogar; **c)** *(thing assumed to be ~)* Faktum, *das;* **deny the ~ that ...:** [die Tatsache] abstreiten, daß ...; **d)** *(Law: crime)* [Straf]tat, *die;* **be an accessory before/after the ~:** jmdm. Beihilfe leisten/Begünstigung gewähren. *See also* **matter 1d**

'fact-finding *adj.* Erkundungs⟨*fahrt, -flug, -trupp*⟩; **~ committee/trip/study** Untersuchungsausschuß, *der*/Informationsreise, *die*/Ermittlungsarbeit, *die*

faction ['fækʃn] *n.* **a)** *(party or group)* Splittergruppe, *die;* Faktion, *die (veralt.);* **b)** *no pl. (party strife)* Parteihader, *der*

factional ['fækʃənl] *adj.* parteiintern ⟨*Konflikt, Uneinigkeit, Streit*⟩; **a ~ group/splinter group** eine Gruppierung/Splittergruppe

factious ['fækʃəs] *adj.* faktiös; parteisüchtig ⟨*Absicht*⟩

factitious [fæk'tɪʃəs] *adj.*, **factitiously** [fæk'tɪʃəslɪ] *adv.* künstlich

factor ['fæktə(r)] **1.** *n.* **a)** *(Math.; also fact, circumstance)* Faktor, *der;* **b)** *(Biol.)* Erbfaktor, *der;* **c)** *(merchant)* Kommissionär, *der;* **d)** *(Scot.: land-agent, steward)* Gutsverwalter, *der;* **e)** *(agent, deputy)* Vertreter, *der. See also* **common factor. 2.** *v. t.* **a)** *(Math.)* in Faktoren zerlegen; **b)** *(resolve into components)* zerlegen

factoring ['fæktərɪŋ] *n. (Commerc.)* Factoring, *das*

factorize (factorise) ['fæktəraɪz] *(Math.)* **1.** *v. t.* in Faktoren zerlegen. **2.** *v. i.* sich in Faktoren zerlegen lassen

factory ['fæktərɪ] *n.* Fabrik, *die;* Werk, *das;* **a ~ for assembling cars/machines** ein Kraftfahrzeug[montage]werk/eine Maschinenfabrik

factory: ~ farm *n. (Agric.)* [voll]automatisierter landwirtschaftlicher Betrieb; **~-made** *adj.* fabrik- *od.* serienmäßig hergestellt; **~-made clothes/furniture** Konfektion[skleidung], *die*/Serienmöbel *Pl.;* **~ ship** *n.* Fabrikschiff, *das;* **~ work** *n.* Fabrikarbeit, *die;* **~ worker** *n.* Fabrikarbeiter, *der*/-arbeiterin, *die*

factotum [fæk'təʊtəm] *n.* Faktotum, *das*

factual ['fæktʃʊəl] *adj.* sachlich ⟨*Bericht, Darlegung, Stil*⟩; auf Tatsachen beruhend ⟨*Aspekt, Punkt, Beweis*⟩; wahr ⟨*Geschichte*⟩; **~ error** Sachfehler, *der*

factually ['fæktʃʊəlɪ] *adv.* sachlich; mit Tatsachen *od.* Fakten ⟨*beweisen*⟩

faculty ['fækəltɪ] *n.* **a)** *(physical capability)* Fähigkeit, *die;* Vermögen, *das;* **~ of sight/speech/hearing/thought** Seh-/Sprach-/Hör-/Denkvermögen, *das;* **b)** *(mental power)* **mental ~, ~ of the mind** geistige Kraft; Geisteskraft, *die;* **in [full] possession of [all] one's faculties** im [Voll]besitz [all] seiner [geistigen] Kräfte; **all one's creative faculties** seine ganze Kreativität *od.* schöpferische Kraft; **c)** *(aptitude)* Begabung, *die;* Fähigkeit, *die;* **have a ~ for doing sth.** die Fähigkeit *od.* das Talent haben, etw. zu tun; **d)** *(Univ.: department)* Fakultät, *die;* Fachbereich, *der;* **~ of arts/sciences/medicine** philosophische/naturwissenschaftliche/medizinische Fakultät; **e)** *(Amer. Sch., Univ.: staff)* Lehrkörper, *der;* **f)** *(members of particular profession)* Berufsstand, *der;* **the [medical] ~:** die Ärzteschaft; der Ärztestand

fad [fæd] *n.* Marotte, *die;* Spleen, *der (ugs.);* **the latest fashion ~:** die neueste Modetorheit; **a ~ for doing sth.** die Marotte *od.* der Spleen, etw. zu tun

faddish ['fædɪʃ], **faddy** ['fædɪ] *adjs.* heikel ⟨*Person, Geschmack*⟩

fade [feɪd] **1.** *v. i.* **a)** *(droop, wither)* ⟨*Blätter, Blumen, Kränze:*⟩ [ver]welken, welk werden; **b)** *(lose freshness, vigour)* verblassen; [v]erlöschen; ⟨*Läufer:*⟩ langsamer werden; ⟨*Frau, Schönheit:*⟩ verblühen; **c)** *(lose colour)* bleichen; **~ [in colour]** [ver]bleichen; verschießen; **guaranteed not to ~:** garantiert farbecht; **d)** *(grow pale, dim)* **the light ~d [into darkness]** es dunkelte; **the fading light of evening** das dämmrige Abendlicht *(dichter.);* die Abenddämmerung; **e)** *(fig.: lose strength)* ⟨*Erinnerung:*⟩ verblassen; ⟨*Eingebung, Kreativität, Optimismus:*⟩ nachlassen; ⟨*Freude, Lust, Liebe:*⟩ erlöschen; ⟨*Ruhm:*⟩ verblassen; ⟨*Traum, Hoffnung:*⟩ zerrinnen; schwinden; **~ from sb.'s mind** jmds. Gedächtnis *(Dat.)* entfallen; **f)** *(disappear, depart, leave)* weichen; ⟨*Metapher, Bedeutung, Stern:*⟩ verschwinden; *(blend)* übergehen **(into** in + *Akk.*); *(grow faint)* ⟨*Laut:*⟩ verklingen; **~ into the distance** in der Ferne entschwinden; ⟨*Laut, Stimme:*⟩ in der Ferne verklingen; **~ from sight** *or* **sb.'s eyes** dem Blick entschwinden *(geh.);* **his smile ~d from his face** das Lächeln schwand aus seinem Gesicht; **g)** *(lose power)* ⟨*Bremskraft, Bremse:*⟩ nachlassen; **h)** *(Radio, Telev., Cinemat.)* **~ [down]** ausgeblendet werden; **~ up** eingeblendet werden; **i)** *(deviate)* ⟨*Golfball usw.:*⟩ einen Bogen beschreiben. **2.** *v. t.* **a)** *(cause to ~)* ausbleichen ⟨*Vorhang, Gobelin, Teppich, Farbe*⟩; **b)** *(Radio, Telev., Cinemat.)* einblenden **(into** in + *Akk.*); **~ one scene into another** eine Szene in eine andere überblenden; **~ a sound down/up** ein Geräusch aus-/einblenden. **3.** *n. (Radio, Telev., Cinemat., Motor Veh.)* Fading, *das (fachspr.)*

~ a'way *v. i.* **a)** schwinden; ⟨*Farbe:*⟩ verblassen; ⟨*Laut:*⟩ verklingen **(into** in + *Dat.*); ⟨*Erinnerung, Augenlicht, Kraft:*⟩ nachlassen; ⟨*Kranke[r]:*⟩ immer schwächer werden; ⟨*Interesse, Hoffnung:*⟩ erlöschen; *(joc.)* ⟨*dünne Person:*⟩ immer weniger werden *(scherzh.);* **the daylight ~d away** es dämmerte; **b)** *(depart, leave)* gehen

~ 'in *(Radio, Telev., Cinemat.)* **1.** *v. i.* eingeblendet werden. **2.** *v. t.* einblenden. *See also* **fade-in**

~ 'out 1. *v. i.* **a)** *(Radio, Telev., Cinemat.)* ausgeblendet werden; **b)** *(disappear, depart)* **~ out of sb.'s life/mind** aus jmds. Leben/Bewußtsein verschwinden. **2.** *v. t. (Radio, Telev., Cinemat.)* ausblenden. *See also* **fade-out**

faded ['feɪdɪd] *adj.* welk ⟨*Blume, Blatt, Laub*⟩; verblichen ⟨*Stoff, Jeans, Farbe, Gemälde, Ruhm, Teppich*⟩; verblüht ⟨*Schönheit*⟩; verblaßt ⟨*Erinnerung*⟩

'fade-in *n. (Radio, Telev., Cinemat.)* Einblendung, *die*

fadeless ['feɪdlɪs] *adj.* farbecht ⟨*Stoff*⟩; echt ⟨*Farbe*⟩

'fade-out *n.* **a)** *(Radio, Telev., Cinemat.)* Ausblendung, *die;* **b)** *(Radio: by ionospheric* *disturbances)* Fading, *das (fachspr.);* Schwund, *der;* **c)** *(fig.: disappearance)* Niedergang, *der*

fading ['feɪdɪŋ] *n. (Radio)* Fading, *das (fachspr.);* Schwund, *der*

faecal ['fi:kl] *adj. (Physiol.)* Kot-; kotig; fäkal *(fachspr.)*

faeces ['fi:si:z] *n. pl.* Fäkalien *Pl.*

faff about [fæf ə'baʊt] *v. i. (Brit. coll.)* herummachen *(ugs.);* **stop faffing about!** reg dich ab! *(ugs.)*

[1]**fag** [fæg] **1.** *v. i.,* **-gg- a)** *(toil)* sich [ab]schinden *(ugs.),* sich abrackern *(salopp)* (**[away] at** mit); **b)** *(Brit. Sch.)* **~ for a senior** einen älteren Schüler bedienen. **2.** *v. t.,* **-gg-: ~ sb. [out]** jmdn. schlauchen *(ugs.);* **~ oneself out** sich [ab]schinden *(ugs.);* **be ~ged out** geschlaucht sein *(ugs.).* **3.** *n.* **a)** *(Brit. coll.)* Schinderei, *die (ugs. abwertend);* **b)** *(Brit. Sch.)* Diener, *der; Internatsschüler, der einem älteren bestimmte Dienste leistet;* **c)** *(sl.: cigarette)* Glimmstengel, *der (ugs. scherzh.)*

[2]**fag** *n. (sl.: homosexual)* Schwule, *der (ugs.)*

'**fag-end** *n.* **a)** *(remnant)* Schluß, *der;* Ende, *das;* **b)** *(sl.: cigarette-end)* Kippe, *die (ugs.)*

faggot (*Amer.:* **fagot**) ['fægət] *n.* **a)** *(sticks, twigs)* Reisigbündel, *das;* **b)** *usu. in pl. (Gastr.)* Leberknödel, *der;* **c)** *(woman)* Weib, *das (abwertend);* **d)** *(sl.: homosexual)* Schwule, *der*

fah [fɑ:] *n. (Mus.)* fa

Fahr. *abbr.* **Fahrenheit** F

Fahrenheit ['færənhaɪt] *adj.* Fahrenheit; **~ scale** Fahrenheitskala, *die*

fail [feɪl] **1.** *v. i.* **a)** *(not succeed)* scheitern; **~ in sth.** mit etw. scheitern; **he ~ed in doing it** es gelang ihm nicht, es zu tun; **~ in one's duty** seine Pflicht versäumen; **~ as a human being/a doctor** als Mensch/Arzt versagen; **he ~ed in his attempts to escape** seine Fluchtversuche schlugen fehl *od.* mißlangen; **b)** *(miscarry, come to nothing)* scheitern; fehlschlagen; **if all else ~s** wenn alle Stricke *od.* Stränge reißen *(ugs.);* **c)** *(become bankrupt)* Bankrott machen; bankrott gehen; **d)** *(in examination)* nicht bestehen (**in** in + *Dat.*); durchfallen *(ugs.)* (**in** in + *Dat.*); **e)** *(be rejected)* ⟨*Bewerber, Kandidat, Bewerbung:*⟩ abgelehnt werden; **f)** *(become weaker)* ⟨*Augenlicht, Gehör, Gedächtnis, Stärke, Eifer, Entschlossenheit:*⟩ nachlassen; ⟨*Atem:*⟩ schwächer werden; ⟨*Mut:*⟩ sinken; **his voice ~ed** ihm versagte die Stimme; **he** *or* **his health is ~ing** sein Gesundheitszustand verschlechtert sich; **the light was ~ing** *(fig. literary)* es dämmerte; **g)** *(break down, stop)* ⟨*Versorgung:*⟩ zusammenbrechen; ⟨*Motor, Radio:*⟩ aussetzen; ⟨*Generator, Batterie, Pumpe:*⟩ ausfallen; ⟨*Bremse, Herz:*⟩ versagen; **h)** *(prove misleading)* ⟨*Prophezeiung, Vorhersage:*⟩ sich nicht bewahrheiten; **i)** *(be insufficient)* ⟨*Ernte:*⟩ schlecht ausfallen; **j)** *(formal: fall short)* **sth. ~s of its intended effect** etw. erreicht die beabsichtigte Wirkung nicht. **2.** *v. t.* **a) ~ to do sth.** *(not succeed in doing)* etw. nicht tun [können]; **~ to reach a decision** zu keinem Entschluß kommen; **~ to achieve one's purpose/aim** seine Absicht/sein Ziel verfehlen; **~ to pass an exam** eine Prüfung nicht bestehen; in einer Prüfung durchfallen *(ugs.);* **~ to remember sth.** etw. vergessen; **his hopes ~ed to materialize** seine Hoffnungen haben sich nicht verwirklicht; **the letter ~ed to reach its destination** der Brief ist nicht an seinem Bestimmungsort eingetroffen; **b)** *(be unsuccessful in)* nicht bestehen ⟨*Prüfung*⟩; durchfallen in (+ *Dat.*) *(ugs.)* ⟨*Prüfung*⟩; **c)** *(reject)* durchfallen lassen *(ugs.)* ⟨*Prüfling*⟩; **d) ~ to do sth.** *(not do)* etw. nicht tun; *(neglect to do)* [es] versäumen, etw. zu tun; **not ~ to do sth.** etw. tun; **he never ~s to send me a card** er schreibt mir immer eine Karte *od.* versäumt es nie, mir eine Karte zu schreiben; **I ~ to see the reason why ...:** ich sehe nicht ein, warum ...; **e)** *(not suffice for)* im Stich lassen; **his legs ~ed him** seine Beine ließen ihn im Stich *od. (geh.)* versagten ihm den Dienst; **his heart** *or* **courage ~ed him** ihn verließ der Mut; **words ~ sb.** jmdm. fehlen die Worte; jmd. findet keine Worte; **f) the wind ~ed us** *(did not blow)* wir hatten keinen Wind; *(was blowing the wrong way)* die Windrichtung war ungünstig. **3.** *n.* **without ~:** auf jeden Fall; garantiert

failed [feɪld] *attrib. adj.* nicht bestanden ⟨*Prüfung*⟩; durchgefallen *(ugs.)* ⟨*Prüfling*⟩; gescheitert ⟨*Person, Geschäft, Ehe, Versuch*⟩

failing ['feɪlɪŋ] **1.** *n.* Schwäche, *die.* **2.** *prep.* **~ that** *or* **this** andernfalls; wenn nicht; **~ which** widrigenfalls *(Papierdt.);* **..., ~ which you can ...:** ..., ansonsten können Sie ... **3.** *adj.* sich verschlechternd ⟨*Gesundheitszustand*⟩; nachlassend ⟨*Kraft*⟩; sinkend ⟨*Mut*⟩; dämmrig ⟨*Licht*⟩

'**fail-safe** *adj.* ausfallsicher; abgesichert ⟨*Methode*⟩; Failsafe-⟨*Vorkehrung, Prinzip*⟩ *(fachspr.)*

failure ['feɪljə(r)] *n.* **a)** *(omission, neglect)* Versäumnis, *das;* **~ to do sth.** das Versäumnis, etw. zu tun; **~ to observe** *or* **follow the rule** Nichtbeachtung *od.* Übertretung der Regel; **~ to appear in court** Nichterscheinen *(Amtsspr.)* vor Gericht; **~ to deliver goods** Nichtlieferung von Waren; **~ to pass an exam** Nichtbestehen einer *od. (ugs.)* Durchfall bei einer Prüfung; **b)** *(lack of success)* Scheitern, *das; (of an application)* Ablehnung, *die;* **be doomed to ~, be bound to end in ~:** zum Scheitern verurteilt sein; **end in ~:** scheitern; **c)** *(unsuccessful person or thing)* Versager, *der;* **the party/play/film was a ~:** das Fest/Stück/der Film war ein Mißerfolg; **our plan/attempt was a ~:** unser Plan/Versuch war fehlgeschlagen; **the cake/dish turned out a ~:** der Kuchen/das Gericht mißlang; **be a ~ as a doctor/teacher** als Arzt/Lehrer versagen; **be a ~ at doing sth.** keine glückliche Hand bei etw. haben; **d)** *(non-occurrence of a process)* **the ~ of the medicine to have the desired effect** das Ausbleiben der Wirkung der Arznei; **my ~ to understand his motives** mein fehlendes Verständnis für seine Motive; **his ~ to keep in touch/to contact us was ...:** daß er es unterlassen hat, von sich hören zu lassen/mit uns Kontakt aufzunehmen, war ...; **e)** *(running short, breaking down) (of supply)* Zusammenbruch, *der; (of engine, generator)* Ausfall, *der;* **signal/pump/engine/generator ~:** Ausfall des Signals/der Pumpe/des Motors/des Generators; **power** *or* **electricity ~:** Stromausfall, *der;* **brake ~:** Versagen der Bremsen; **crop ~, ~ of crops** Mißernte, *die;* **f)** *(Med.)* Versagen, *das;* Insuffizienz, *die (fachspr.);* **g)** *(deterioration, weakening) (of health)* Verschlechterung, *die; (of hearing, eyesight, strength)* Nachlassen, *das; (of energy)* Erlahmen, *das; (of courage)* Sinken, *das;* **h)** *(absence, non-existence)* Fehlen, *das;* **~ of justice** Versagen der Justiz; **i)** *(bankruptcy)* Zusammenbruch, *der;* **a bank ~:** der Zusammenbruch einer Bank

fain [feɪn] *(arch.)* **1.** *adv.* [zu] gern. **2.** *pred. adj.* bereit; geneigt; **be ~ to do** *or* **of doing sth.** geneigt sein, etw. zu tun

faint [feɪnt] **1.** *adj.* **a)** *(dim, indistinct, pale)* matt ⟨*Licht, Farbe, Stimme, Lächeln*⟩; schwach ⟨*Geruch, Duft*⟩; leise ⟨*Flüstern, Geräusch, Stimme, Ton, Ruf, Schritt*⟩; entfernt ⟨*Ähnlichkeit*⟩; undeutlich ⟨*Umriß, Linie, Gestalt, Spur, Stimme, Fotokopie*⟩; **b)** *(weak, vague)* leise ⟨*Wunsch, Hoffnung, Verdacht, Ahnung*⟩; gering ⟨*Chance*⟩; **not have the ~est idea** *or* **notion** nicht die geringste *od.* blasseste Ahnung haben; **Where is he? – I haven't the ~est idea** *or (coll.)* **~est** Wo ist er? – Keine Ahnung! *(ugs.);* **c)** *(giddy, weak)* matt; schwach; **she felt/looked ~:** sie fühlte sich/schien einer Ohnmacht nahe; ihr war schwindelig/ihr schien schwindelig zu sein; **be ~ with** *or* **feel ~ from hunger** *etc.* vor Hunger *usw.* matt *od.* schwach sein; **his breathing grew ~:** sein Atem wurde schwächer; **d)** *(timid)* gering, schwach ⟨*Mut*⟩; **~ heart never won fair lady** *(prov.)* wer nicht wagt, der nicht gewinnt *(Spr.);* **e)** *(feeble)* schwach ⟨*Lob, Widerstand*⟩; zaghaft ⟨*Versuch, Bemühung*⟩; *see also* **damn 1 a; f)** *see* [2]**feint. 2.** *v. i.* ohnmächtig werden, in Ohnmacht fallen (**from** vor + *Dat.*). **3.** *n.* Ohnmacht, *die;* **in a [dead] ~:** ohnmächtig; **go off in** *or* **fall into a ~:** ohnmächtig werden; in Ohnmacht fallen

faint: ~-heart *n.* Hasenherz, *das (abwertend);* **~-hearted** *adj.* hasenherzig *(abwertend);* zaghaft ⟨*Versuch*⟩; **~-heartedly** hasenherzig *(abwertend)*

faintly ['feɪntlɪ] *adv.* **a)** *(indistinctly)* undeutlich ⟨*markieren, hören*⟩; kaum ⟨*sichtbar*⟩; schwach ⟨*riechen, scheinen*⟩; entfernt ⟨*sich ähneln*⟩; **b)** *(slightly)* leise ⟨*hoffen, verdächtigen*⟩; wenig ⟨*interessieren*⟩; leicht ⟨*enttäuschen, herablassend*⟩; **c)** *(feebly)* zaghaft ⟨*versuchen, lächeln*⟩

faintness ['feɪntnɪs] *n., no pl.* **a)** *(dimness, feebleness) (of marking, outline, voice)* Undeutlichkeit, *die; (of resemblance)* Entferntheit, *die; (of colour)* Mattheit, *die; (of old photograph)* Verblaßtheit, *die;* **the ~ of the smell/light** der schwache Geruch/das schwache Licht; **the ~ of his smile/recollection** sein schwaches Lächeln/seine schwache Erinnerung; **b)** *(dizziness)* Schwäche, *die;* Mattigkeit, *die;* **feeling of ~:** Schwächegefühl, *das;* **c)** *(cowardice)* **~ of spirits** Verzagtheit, *die;* **~ of heart** *(literary)* Zagheit, *die (geh.)*

[1]**fair** [feə(r)] *n.* **a)** *(gathering)* Markt, *der; (with shows, merry-go-rounds)* Jahrmarkt, *der;* **village/cattle ~:** Dorf-/Viehmarkt, *der;* **a day after the ~** *(fig.)* zu spät; **b)** *see* **fun-fair; c)** *(exhibition)* Ausstellung, *die;* Messe, *die;* **agricultural/world/industries ~:** Landwirtschafts-/Welt-/Industrieausstellung, *die;* **book/antiques/trade ~:** Buch-/Antiquitäten-/Handelsmesse, *die*

[2]**fair 1.** *adj.* **a)** *(just)* gerecht; begründet ⟨*Beschwerde, Annahme*⟩; berechtigt ⟨*Frage*⟩; fair ⟨*Spiel, Kampf, Prozeß, Preis, Beurteilung, Handel*⟩; *(representative, typical)* typisch, markant ⟨*Beispiel, Kostprobe*⟩; **be ~ with** *or* **to sb.** gerecht gegen jmdn. *od.* zu jmdm. sein; **it's only ~ to do sth./for sb. to do sth.** es ist nur recht und billig, etw. zu tun/daß jmd. etw. tut; **strict but ~:** streng, aber gerecht; **a ~ day's wages for a ~ day's work** anständiger Lohn für anständige Arbeit; **that's not ~, you're not ~:** das ist ungerecht *od.* unfair; **[well, that's] ~ enough!** *(coll.)* dagegen ist nichts einzuwenden; *(OK)* na gut; **by ~ means or foul** egal wie *(ugs.);* auf ehrliche oder unehrliche Weise; **all's ~ in love and war** in der Liebe und im Krieg ist alles erlaubt; **~ play** Fairneß, *die;* Fair play, *das;* **~ play in business** anständiges Geschäftsgebaren; **~ and square** ehrlich; *see also* **crack 1 a;** [1]**deal 3 a;** [2]**do d; field 1 e;** [1]**game 1 g; share 1 a; b)** *(not bad, pretty good)* ganz gut ⟨*Bilanz, Vorstellung, Anzahl, Menge, Kenntnisse, Chance*⟩; ziemlich ⟨*Maß, Geschwindigkeit*⟩; **a ~ amount of work** ein schönes Stück Arbeit; **she has a ~ amount of sense** sie ist ganz vernünftig; **not all, but a ~ number** nicht alle, aber doch recht viele; **be a ~ judge of character** ein recht guter Menschenkenner sein; *see also* **middling 1 b; c)** *(favourable)* schön ⟨*Wetter, Tag, Abend*⟩; günstig ⟨*Wetterlage, Wind*⟩; heiter ⟨*Wetter, Tag, Himmel, Morgen*⟩; **the barometer/weather is set ~:** das Barometer steht auf Schönwetter/das schöne Wetter hält an; **be in a ~ way to doing sth.** gute Aus-

sichten haben, etw. zu tun; **be in a ~ way to succeed/winning** gute Erfolgs-/Gewinnchancen haben; **d)** *(considerable, satisfactory)* ansehnlich ‹*Erbe, Vermögen*›; **e)** *(specious)* groß ‹*Rede, Worte, Versprechung*›; schön ‹*Geschichte*›; **f)** *(complimentary)* schön ‹*Rede, Worte*›; **g)** *(blond)* blond ‹*Haar, Person*›; *(not dark)* hell ‹*Teint, Haut*›; hellhäutig ‹*Person*›; **very ~:** hellblond; **a ~ head** ein Blondkopf; **h)** *(poet. or literary: beautiful)* hold *(dichter. veralt.)* ‹*Kind, Mädchen, Maid, Prinz, Gesicht*›; schön ‹*Stadt*›; *(pure, unsullied)* gut, unbescholten ‹*Name, Ruf*›; **the ~ sex** das schöne Geschlecht; **with her own ~ hands** *(iron.)* mit ihren zarten Händen; **i)** *(clean, clear)* rein *(meist geh.)* ‹*Wasser*›; sauber ‹*Handschrift*›; **~ copy** Reinschrift, *die;* **make a ~ copy of sth.** etw. ins reine schreiben. **2.** *adv.* **a)** *(in a fair manner)* fair ‹*kämpfen, spielen*›; gerecht ‹*behandeln*›; **b)** *(coll.: completely)* völlig; **the sight ~ took my breath away** der Anblick hat mir glatt *(ugs.)* den Atem verschlagen; **c) ~ and square** *(honestly)* offen und ehrlich; *(accurately)* voll, genau ‹*schlagen, treffen*›. *See also* **bid 2a; dinkum; play 2a. 3.** *n.* **~'s ~** *(coll.)* Gerechtigkeit muß sein

fair: ~-faced *adj. (having light complexion)* hellhäutig; **~ground** *n.* Festplatz, *der;* **~-haired** *adj.* blond; **~-haired boy** *(Amer. fig.)* Liebling, *der;* Favorit, *der*

fairing *n. (structure)* Verkleidung, *die*

fairish ['feərɪʃ] *adj.* passabel

'**Fair Isle** *attrib. adj. (Textiles) für die Insel Fair Isle typisch;* ≈ Shetland‹*pullover, -muster*›

fairly ['feəlɪ] *adv.* **a)** fair ‹*kämpfen, spielen*›; gerecht ‹*bestrafen, beurteilen, behandeln*›; **come by sth. ~:** auf ehrliche Weise zu etw. kommen; **b)** *(tolerably)* ziemlich; **c)** *(completely)* völlig; heftig, sehr ‹*bestürmen, bedrängen*›; **it ~ took my breath away** es hat mir glatt *(ugs.)* den Atem verschlagen; **d)** *(actually)* richtig; **I ~ jumped for joy** ich habe einen regelrechten Freudensprung gemacht; **e) ~ and squarely** *(honestly)* offen und ehrlich; *(accurately)* voll, genau ‹*schlagen, treffen*›; **look at a situation ~ and squarely** eine Lage nüchtern betrachten; **beat sb. ~ and squarely** jmdn. nach allen Regeln der Kunst *(ugs.)* besiegen

'**fair-minded** *adj.* unvoreingenommen

fairness ['feənɪs] *n., no pl.* Gerechtigkeit, *die;* **sense of ~:** Gerechtigkeitsgefühl, *das;* **in all ~ [to sb.]** fairerweise; um fair [gegen jmdn.] zu sein

fair: ~way *n.* **a)** *(channel)* Fahrrinne, *die;* **b)** *(Golf)* Fairway, *das;* **~-weather friend** *n.* Freund, der/Freundin, die nur in guten Zeiten treu ist

fairy ['feərɪ] **1.** *n.* **a)** *(Mythol.)* Fee, *die; (in a household)* Kobold, *der;* **b)** *(sl.: homosexual)* Tunte, *die (salopp);* Warme, *der (salopp).* **2.** *attrib. adj.* feenhaft ‹*Stimme, Wesen*›; Feen‹*reigen, -reich*›

fairy: ~ 'godmother *n. (lit. or fig.)* gute Fee; **F~land** *n. (land of fairies)* Feenland, *das; (enchanted region)* Märchenland, *das;* **winter ~land** winterliche Märchenlandschaft; **~ lights** *n. pl.* kleine farbige Lichter; **~ 'ring** *n. (Bot.)* Hexenring, *der;* **~ story** *see* **~-tale 1; ~-tale 1.** *n. (lit. or fig.)* Märchen, *das;* **2.** *adj.* Märchen‹*landschaft*›; märchenhaft schön ‹*Szene, Wirkung, Kleid, Ball*›; märchenhaft ‹*Schönheit*›

fait accompli [feɪt ə'kɒmplɪ] *n., pl.* **faits accomplis** [feɪt ə'kɒmplɪ] vollendete Tatsache; Fait accompli, *das (geh.)*

faith [feɪθ] *n.* **a)** *(reliance, trust)* Vertrauen, *das;* **have ~ in sb./sth.** Vertrauen zu jmdm./etw. haben; auf jmdn./etw. vertrauen; **have ~ in oneself** Selbstvertrauen haben; **lose ~ in sb./sth.** das Vertrauen zu jmdm./etw. verlieren; **pin one's ~ on** *or* **put one's ~ in sb./sth.** sein Vertrauen auf *od.* in jmdn./etw. setzen; **b)** *(belief)* Glaube, *der;* **on ~:** in gutem Glauben; **c)** *(religious belief)* Glaube, *der;* **the ~:** der [christliche] Glaube; **different Christian ~s** verschiedene christliche Glaubensrichtungen; **a matter of ~:** eine Glaubenssache; **d)** *(promise)* [Ehren]wort, *das; (pledge of fidelity)* Treue, *die;* **pledge one's ~ to sb.** jmdm. Treue geloben; **to do that would be breaking ~:** das zu tun, wäre [ein] Wortbruch; **break ~ with an ally** an einem Verbündeten treubrüchig werden; **keep ~ with sb.** jmdm. treu bleiben *od.* die Treue halten; **e)** *(loyalty)* Redlichkeit, *die;* **good/bad ~:** Vertrauen/Mißtrauen, *das;* **in good ~:** ohne Hintergedanken; *(unsuspectingly)* in gutem Glauben; guten Glaubens; **in all good ~:** auf Treu und Glauben; **in bad ~:** in böser Absicht

faithful ['feɪθfl] **1.** *adj.* **a)** *(showing faith, loyal)* treu; **remain ~ to sb./sth.** jmdm./einer Sache treu bleiben; **remain ~ to one's promise** [sein] Wort halten; sein Versprechen halten; **b)** *(conscientious)* pflichttreu; treu ‹*Briefschreiber*›; [ge]treu ‹*Diener*›; **c)** *(accurate)* [wahrheits]getreu; originalgetreu ‹*Wiedergabe, Kopie*›. **2.** *n. pl.* **the ~:** die Gläubigen; **the party ~:** treue Anhänger der Partei

faithfully ['feɪθfəlɪ] *adv.* **a)** *(loyally)* treu ‹*dienen*›; pflichttreu ‹*überbringen, zustellen*›; gewissenhaft ‹*hüten, halten*›; hoch und heilig, fest ‹*versprechen*›; **promise [me] ~ that ...** *(coll.: emphatically)* versprich mir ganz fest, daß ...; **b)** *(accurately)* wahrheitsgetreu ‹*erzählen*›; originalgetreu ‹*wiedergeben*›; genau ‹*befolgen*›; **c) yours ~** *(in letter)* mit freundlichen Grüßen; *(more formally)* hochachtungsvoll

faith: ~-healer *n.* Gesundbeter, *der/*-beterin, *die;* **~-healing** *n.* Gesundbeten, *das*

faithless ['feɪθlɪs] *adj.* **a)** *(perfidious, unreliable)* untreu ‹*Geliebte[r], Mann, Frau*›; treulos ‹*Untertan, Diener, Freund, Handeln, Verhalten*›; **be ~ to sb./sth.** jmdm./einer Sache untreu sein; **b)** *(unbelieving)* ungläubig

fake [feɪk] **1.** *adj.* unecht; gefälscht ‹*Dokument, Banknote, Münze*›; **~ money** Falschgeld, *das.* **2.** *n.* **a)** *(thing ~d up)* Imitation, *die; (painting)* Fälschung, *die;* **b)** *(trick)* Finte, *die; (fig.)* Schwindel, *der (abwertend);* **c)** *(spurious person)* Schwindler, *der/*Schwindlerin, *die.* **3.** *v. t.* **a)** *(feign, contrive)* nachahmen ‹*Akzent*›; fälschen ‹*Unterschrift*›; vortäuschen ‹*Krankheit, Einbruch, Unfall*›; **b)** *(make plausible)* **~ [up]** imitieren ‹*Diamanten*›; fälschen ‹*Gemälde*›; erfinden ‹*Geschichte*›; **c)** *(alter so as to deceive)* frisieren *(ugs.);* verfälschen. **4.** *v. i.* simulieren

faker ['feɪkə(r)] *n. (swindler)* Schwindler, *der/*Schwindlerin, *die; (pretender)* Heuchler, *der/*Heuchlerin, *die*

fakir ['feɪkɪə(r), fə'kɪə(r)] *n.* Fakir, *der*

falcon ['fɔ:lkn, 'fɔ:kn] *n. (Ornith.)* Falke, *der*

falconer ['fɔ:lkənə(r), 'fɔ:kənə(r)] *n. (Hunting)* Falkner, *der/*Falknerin, *die*

falconry ['fɔ:lknrɪ, 'fɔ:knrɪ] *n., no pl., no indef. art.* Falknerei, *die*

fall [fɔ:l] **1.** *n.* **a)** *(act or manner of falling)* Fallen, *das; (of person)* Sturz, *der;* **~ of leaves/snow/rain** Blatt- *od.* Laub-/Schnee-/Regenfall, *der;* **in a ~:** bei einem Sturz; **have a ~:** stürzen; **a ten-inch ~ of rain/snow** eine Niederschlagsmenge von 254 mm/25 cm Schnee[fall]; **b)** *(collapse, defeat)* Fall, *der; (of culture, dynasty, empire)* Untergang, *der; (of government)* Sturz, *der;* **~ from power** Entmachtung, *die;* **c)** *(lapse into sin)* [Sünden]fall, *der;* **the F~ [of man]** *(Theol.)* der Sündenfall; **d)** *(slope)* Abfall, *der* **(to** zu, **nach)**; **e)** *usu. in pl. (waterfall)* [Wasser]fall, *der;* **Niagara F~s** Niagarafälle; der Niagarafall; **f)** *(fig.: decrease) see* **drop 1 i; g)** *(of night etc.)* Einbruch, *der;* **h)** *(Amer.: autumn)* Herbst, *der;* **i)** *(Wrestling) (throw)* Schulterwurf, *der; (wrestling-bout)* Ringkampf, *der; (fig.)* **try a** *or* **one's ~ with sb.** es auf eine Kraftprobe mit jmdm. ankommen lassen. *See also* **ride 2c. 2.** *v. i.*, **fell** [fel], **~en** ['fɔ:ln] **a)** *(drop)* fallen; **~ off sth., ~ down from sth.** von etw. [herunter]fallen; **~ down [into] sth.** in etw. *(Akk.)* [hinein]fallen; **~ out of sth.** aus etw. [heraus]fallen; **~ to the ground** zu Boden *od.* auf den Boden fallen; **she let sth. ~ [from her hand]** *(deliberately)* sie hat etw. [aus der Hand] fallen lassen; *(by mistake)* ihr ist etw. aus der Hand gefallen; **~ down dead** tot umfallen; **~ down the stairs** *or* **downstairs** die Treppe herunter-/hinunterfallen; **~ into the trap** in die Falle gehen; **always ~ on one's feet** *(fig.)* immer [wieder] auf die Beine *(ugs.) od.* Füße fallen; **nearly** *or* **almost ~ off one's chair** *(lit. or fig.)* fast vom Stuhl fallen *(ugs.);* **~ to earth** auf die Erde *od.* zur Erde fallen; **the blossom ~s** die Blüte fällt ab; **the land ~s to sea level** das Gelände fällt auf Meeresspiegelhöhe ab; **~ from a great height** aus großer Höhe abstürzen; **~ing star** *(Astron.)* Sternschnuppe, *die;* **rain/snow is ~ing** es regnet/schneit; **b)** *(fig.)* ‹*Nacht, Dunkelheit:*› hereinbrechen; ‹*Abend:*› anbrechen; ‹*Stille:*› eintreten; **night began to ~:** die Nacht brach herein; **c)** *(fig.: swoop)* **~ upon** ‹*Katastrophe, Unglück, Seuche:*› hereinbrechen über (+ *Akk.*) *(geh.);* ‹*Rache:*› treffen; ‹*Furcht:*› befallen; **d)** *(fig.: be uttered)* ‹*Worte, Bemerkungen:*› fallen; **~ from sb.'s lips** *or* **mouth** über jmds. Lippen *(Akk.)* kommen; **let ~ a remark** eine Bemerkung fallenlassen; **e)** *(lose high position)* fallen; **~ from power** entmachtet werden; **~ from one's high estate** seinen hohen Rang einbüßen; **~en angel** gefallener Engel; **~en arch** *(Med.)* Senkfuß, *der;* **f)** *(lose chastity)* fallen; *(become pregnant)* **~ [with child]** schwanger werden; **a ~en woman** ein gefallenes Mädchen; **g)** *(become detached)* ‹*Blätter:*› [ab]fallen; **~ out** ‹*Haare, Federn:*› ausfallen; **h)** *(hang down)* fallen; **a lock fell over her face** eine Locke fiel *od.* hing ihr ins Gesicht; **i)** *(be born)* ‹*Lamm, Kalb usw.:*› geworfen werden; **j)** *(sink to lower level)* sinken; ‹*Barometer:*› fallen; ‹*Absatz, Verkauf:*› zurückgehen; *(in pitch)* ‹*Musik:*› [in der Tonhöhe] fallen; **~ by 10 per cent/from 10[°C] to 0[°C]** um 10%/von 10[°C] auf 0[°C] sinken; **[make sb.] ~ in sb.'s esteem** *or* **estimation/eyes** *(fig.)* [jmdn.] in jmds. Achtung/Augen *(Dat.)* sinken [lassen]; **~ into error/sin/temptation** einen Fehler/eine Sünde begehen/der Versuchung er- *od.* unterliegen; **k)** *see* **~ away b; l)** *(issue)* ‹*Fluß:*› münden **(into** in + *Akk.*); **m)** *(subside)* ‹*Wasserspiegel, Gezeitenhöhe:*› fallen; ‹*Wind, Sturm:*› sich legen; **n)** *(show dismay)* **his/her face** *or* **countenance fell** er/sie machte ein langes Gesicht *(ugs.);* **o)** *(look down)* **his/her glance/eyes fell** er/sie senkte den Blick/die Augen; **p)** *(no longer stand)* fallen; ‹*Baum:*› umstürzen; ‹*Pferd:*› stürzen; **~ to the ground** zu Boden fallen; *(fig.)* ‹*Plan, Verabredung usw.:*› ins Wasser fallen; ‹*Argument, These:*› in sich zusammenfallen; **~ into one another's arms** einander in die Arme fallen *od.* sinken; **~ on one's knees** auf die Knie fallen; sich auf die Knie werfen; **~ at sb.'s feet** *or* **down before sb.** jmdm. zu Füßen fallen; **~ [flat] on one's face** *(lit. or fig.)* auf die Nase fallen *(ugs.);* **q)** *(be defeated)* ‹*Festung, Stadt:*› fallen; ‹*Monarchie, Regierung:*› gestürzt werden; ‹*Reich:*› untergehen; **the fortress fell to the enemy** die Festung fiel dem Feind in die Hände; **r)** *(fail)* untergehen; **united we stand, divided we ~:** Einigkeit macht stark *(Spr.);* **s)** *(perish)* ‹*Soldat:*› fallen; **the ~en [soldiers]** die Gefallenen; **t)** *(collapse, break)* einstürzen;

cause a building to ~: ein Gebäude zum Einsturz bringen; ~ **to pieces**, ~ **apart** ⟨*Buch, Wagen:*⟩ auseinanderfallen; *(fig.)* ⟨*Unternehmen, jmds. Welt:*⟩ zusammenbrechen; ~ **in two** entzweigehen; ~ **apart at the seams** an den Nähten aufplatzen; *(fig.)* ⟨*Plan:*⟩ ins Wasser fallen *(ugs.)*; **u)** *(Cricket)* **a wicket** ~**s** ein Schlagmann wird ausgeschlagen; **v)** *(come by chance, duty, etc.)* fallen (**to** an + *Akk.*); **it fell to me** *or* **to my lot to do it** das Los, es tun zu müssen, hat mich getroffen; ~ **[in] sb.'s way** jmdm. zufallen; ~ **among thieves** unter die Räuber fallen; ~ **into an ambush** in einen Hinterhalt fallen; **he has** ~**en into the role of a mere spectator** er ist in die Rolle des Zuschauers gedrängt worden; ~ **into bad company** in schlechte Gesellschaft geraten; ~ **into conversation with sb.** mit jmdm. ins Gespräch kommen; ~ **into decay** ⟨*Gebäude:*⟩ verfallen; *(fig.)* ⟨*Monarchie, Reich, Institution:*⟩ zerfallen; ⟨*Gesetz:*⟩ seine Bedeutung verlieren; ~ **into parts/sections** in Teile/Abschnitte zerfallen; ⟨*Roman:*⟩ sich in Teile/Abschnitte gliedern; ~ **into different categories** in *od.* unter verschiedene Kategorien fallen; ~ **to doing sth.** anfangen *od.* beginnen, etw. zu tun; **they fell to fighting among themselves** es kam zu einer Schlägerei zwischen ihnen; *abs.* ~ to beginnen, drauflos zu essen/arbeiten *usw.*; *see also* ~ **on**; **w)** *(take specified direction)* ⟨*Auge, Strahl, Licht, Schatten:*⟩ fallen (**upon** auf + *Akk.*); **x)** *(have specified place)* liegen (**on, to** auf + *Dat.*, **within** in + *Dat.*); ~ **into** *or* **under a category** in *od.* unter eine Kategorie fallen; **y)** *(pass into specified state)* ~ **into a rage** einen Wutanfall bekommen; ~ **into despair** verzweifeln; ~ **into a deep sleep** in tiefen Schlaf fallen *od. (geh.)* versinken; ~ **ill** krank werden; ~ **into a swoon** *or* **faint** in Ohnmacht fallen; **z)** *(occur)* fallen (**on** auf + *Akk.*) ⟨*Datum*⟩; **Easter** ~**s late this year** Ostern fällt dieses Jahr spät. *See also* **asleep a**; **astern**; **²flat 1 a, b**; **foul 1 f**; **grace 1 e**; **hand 1 c**; **¹line 1 f**; **love 1 a**; **place 1 j**; **prey 1 b**; **push 1 a**; **short 2 c**; **silent a**; **victim a**; **wayside**

~ **a'bout** *v. i.* ~ **about [laughing** *or* **with laughter]** sich [vor Lachen] kringeln *(ugs.)*

~ **a'way** *v. i.* **a)** abfallen (**from** von); *(from allegiance)* sich lösen (**from** aus); ⟨*Mitgliedschaft, Einnahmen:*⟩ sinken; *(from friend, truth)* sich abwenden (**from** von); **b)** *(have slope)* abfallen (**to** zu)

~ **'back** *v. i.* zurückweichen; ⟨*Armee:*⟩ sich zurückziehen; *(lag)* zurückbleiben; *see also* **fall-back**

~ **'back on** *v. t.* zurückgreifen auf (+ *Akk.*)

~ **behind 1.** ['---] *v. t.* zurückfallen hinter (+ *Akk.*). **2.** [--'-] *v. i.* zurückbleiben; ~ **behind with sth.** mit etw. in Rückstand *(Akk.)* geraten

~ **'down** *v. i.* **a)** *see* ~ **2 a**; **b)** *(collapse)* ⟨*Brücke, Gebäude:*⟩ einstürzen; ⟨*Person:*⟩ hinfallen; ~ **down [on sth.]** *(fig. coll.)* [bei etw.] versagen; **the argument** ~**s down on one point** das Argument sticht in einem Punkt nicht; **the theory fell down for** *or* **on lack of evidence** die Theorie war nicht haltbar, weil es an Beweisen fehlte; ~ **down on a job** einer Aufgabe nicht gewachsen sein

~ **for** *v. t. (coll.)* **a)** *(~ in love with)* sich verknallen in *(ugs.)*; **b)** *(be persuaded by)* hereinfallen auf (+ *Akk.*) *(ugs.)*

~ **'in** *v. i.* **a)** hineinfallen; **b)** *(Mil.)* antreten (**for** zu); ~ **in!** angetreten!; **c)** *(collapse)* ⟨*Gebäude, Wand usw.:*⟩ einstürzen

~ **'in with** *v. t.* **a)** *(meet and join)* stoßen zu; **b)** *(agree)* beipflichten (+ *Dat.*) ⟨*Person, Meinung, Vorschlag usw.*⟩; eingehen auf (+ *Akk.*) ⟨*Plan, Person, Bitte, Forderung*⟩; entsprechen (+ *Dat.*) ⟨*Forderung, Bitte*⟩; einstimmen in (+ *Akk.*) ⟨*Ton*⟩

~ **'off** *v. i.* **a)** *see* ~ **2 a**; **b)** ⟨*Nachfrage, Produktion, Aufträge, Anzahl:*⟩ zurückgehen; **c)** ⟨*Mut, Niveau:*⟩ sinken; ⟨*Dienstleistungen, Gesundheit, Geschäft:*⟩ sich verschlechtern; ⟨*Begeisterung, Eifer, Interesse:*⟩ nachlassen. *See also* **fall-off**

~ **on** *v. t.* **a)** *(lit., or fig.: attack)* herfallen über; **b)** *(be borne by)* ~ **on sb.** jmdm. zufallen; ⟨*Verdacht, Schuld, Los:*⟩ auf jmdn. fallen

~ **'out** *v. i.* **a)** herausfallen; **b)** *see* ~ **2 g**; **c)** *(quarrel)* ~ **out [with sb. over sth.]** sich [mit jmdm. über etw. *(Akk.)*] [zer]streiten; **d)** *(come to happen)* vonstatten gehen; **see how things** ~ **out** abwarten, wie sich die Dinge entwickeln; **it [so] fell out that ...** *(literary)* es begab sich *(geh.)*, daß ...; **e)** *(Mil.)* wegtreten; ~ **out!** weggetreten! *See also* **fall-out**

~ **over 1.** ['---] *v. t.* **a)** *(stumble over)* fallen über (+ *Akk.*); **they were** ~**ing over each other to get the sweets** sie drängelten sich, um die Süßigkeiten zu bekommen; ~ **over oneself** *or* **one's own feet** über seine eigenen Füße stolpern; **b)** ~ **over oneself to do sth.** *(fig. coll.)* sich vor Eifer überschlagen, um etw. zu tun *(ugs.)*. **2.** [-'--] *v. i.* umfallen; *(in faint)* hinfallen; ~ **over on to sth.** auf etw. *(Akk.)* fallen; *see also* **backwards a**

~ **'through** *v. i. (fig.)* ins Wasser fallen *(ugs.)*; ⟨*Einigungsversuch:*⟩ fehlschlagen

~ **upon a)** *see* ~ **on**; **b)** *see* ~ **2 c, w**

fallacious [fə'leɪʃəs] *adj.* **a)** *(containing a fallacy)* irrig; ~ **conclusion/syllogism** Fehl- *od.* Trugschluß, *der*; **b)** *(deceptive, delusive)* irreführend ⟨*Methode, Bericht*⟩; trügerisch ⟨*Hoffnung, Friede*⟩

fallacy ['fæləsɪ] *n.* **a)** *(delusion, error)* Irrtum, *der*; **b)** *(unsoundness, delusiveness)* Irrigkeit, *die*; **c)** *(Logic)* Trugschluß, *der*

'fall-back *adj.* ~ **pay** Überbrückungsgeld, *das*; ~ **job** *(for seasonal worker)* Nebenerwerb, *der (zur Überbrückung außerhalb der Saison)*

fallen *see* **fall 2**

'fall guy *n. (sl.)* **a)** *(victim)* Lackierte, *der/die (salopp)*; **b)** *(scapegoat)* Prügelknabe, *der (ugs.)*; **be the** ~ **for sb.** den Prügelknaben für jmdn. abgeben

fallibility [fælɪ'bɪlɪtɪ] *n., no pl.* Fehlbarkeit, *die*

fallible ['fælɪbl] *adj.* **a)** *(liable to err)* fehlbar ⟨*Person*⟩; ~ **human nature** die Fehlbarkeit des Menschen; **b)** *(liable to be erroneous)* nicht unfehlbar

'fall-off *n. (in quality)* [Ver]minderung, *die* (**in** *Gen.*); *(in quantity)* Rückgang, *der* (**in** *Gen.*); ~ **in quality/exports** Qualitäts[ver]minderung, *die*/Exportrückgang, *der*

Fallopian tube [fə'ləʊpɪən tju:b] *n. (Anat.)* Eileiter, *der*

'fall-out *n.* radioaktiver Niederschlag; *(fig.: side-effects)* Abfallprodukte; ~ **shelter** Atombunker, *der*

¹fallow ['fæləʊ] **1.** *n. (Agric.)* Brache, *die*. **2.** *adj. (lit. or fig.)* brachliegend; ~ **ground** *or* **field/land** Brache, *die*/Brachland, *das*; **lie** ~ *(lit. or fig.)* brachliegen

²fallow *adj. (in colour)* rotbraun

'fallow deer *n.* Damhirsch, *der*

false [fɔ:ls, fɒls] **1.** *adj.* **a)** falsch; Fehl⟨*deutung, -urteil*⟩; Falsch⟨*meldung, -eid, -aussage, -geld*⟩; treulos ⟨*Geliebte[r]*⟩; gefälscht ⟨*Urkunde, Dokument*⟩; ~ **doctrine** Irrlehre, *die*; **be** ~ **to one's wife** seine Frau betrügen; seiner Frau *(Dat.)* untreu sein; **b)** *(sham)* falsch ⟨*Scham, Bescheidenheit, Stolz*⟩; künstlich ⟨*Wimpern, Auge*⟩; *(deliberate)* geheuchelt ⟨*Bescheidenheit*⟩; gekünstelt ⟨*Tränen, Lächeln*⟩; **distinguish the real from the** ~: zwischen Richtigem und Falschem *od.* Echtem und Unechtem unterscheiden; **under a** ~ **name** unter falschem Namen; **c)** *(deceptive)* falsch ⟨*Hoffnung, Sparsamkeit*⟩; unberechtigt ⟨*Furcht*⟩; trügerisch ⟨*Wärme, Licht*⟩. **2.** *adv.* unehrlich; **play sb.** ~: mit jmdm. ein falsches Spiel treiben

false: ~ **a'larm** *n.* blinder Alarm; ~ **'bottom** *n.* doppelter Boden; ~ **'card** *n. zwecks Irreführung des Gegners gespielte Karte*; ~ **'colours** *n. pl.* **sail under** ~ **colours** *(fig.)* unter falscher Flagge segeln; ~ **'dawn** *n. (Astron.)* ≈ Zodiakallicht, *das*; *(fig.)* Täuschung, *die*; ~ **'hair** *n.* falsches Haar

falsehood ['fɔ:lshʊd, 'fɒlshʊd] *n.* **a)** *no pl. (falseness)* Unrichtigkeit, *die*; **b)** *(untrue thing)* Unwahrheit, *die*; **tell a** ~: die Unwahrheit sagen

false 'keel *n. (Naut.)* Schutzkiel, *der*

falsely ['fɔ:lslɪ, 'fɒlslɪ] *adv.* **a)** *(dishonestly)* unaufrichtig ⟨*sprechen*⟩; falsch ⟨*schwören*⟩; **b)** *(incorrectly, unjustly)* falsch ⟨*auslegen, verstehen*⟩; fälschlich[erweise] ⟨*annehmen, glauben, behaupten, anklagen, beschuldigen, verurteilen*⟩; **c)** *(insincerely)* gekünstelt ⟨*lächeln*⟩

false 'move *see* **false step**

falseness ['fɔ:lsnɪs, 'fɒlsnɪs] *n., no pl.* **a)** *(incorrectness)* Unrichtigkeit, *die*; Falschheit, *die*; **b)** *(faithlessness)* Treulosigkeit, *die* (**to** gegenüber); **c)** *(insincerity)* Unaufrichtigkeit, *die*

false: ~ **po'sition** *n. Lage, in der man scheinbar entgegen seinen Prinzipien handeln muß*; **he was put in a** ~ **position** er wurde in ein schiefes Licht gerückt; ~ **pre'tences** *n. pl.* Vorspiegelung falscher Tatsachen; ~ **'start** *n. (Sport; also fig.)* Fehlstart, *der*; ~ **'step** *n. (lit. or fig.)* falscher Schritt; **make a** ~ **step** einen falschen Schritt tun; ~ **'teeth** *n. pl.* [künstliches] Gebiß; Prothese, *die*

falsetto [fɔ:l'setəʊ, fɒl'setəʊ] *n., pl.* ~**s** *(voice)* Kopfstimme, *die*; *(Mus.: of man)* Falsett, *das*; Fistelstimme, *die*

falsies ['fɔ:lsɪz, 'fɒlsɪz] *n. pl. (coll.)* Gummibusen, *der (salopp)*

falsification [fɔ:lsɪfɪ'keɪʃn, fɒlsɪfɪ'keɪʃn] *n.* **a)** *(alteration)* Fälschung, *die*; *(of fact, event, truth, history)* Verfälschung, *die*; **lies and** ~**s** Lügen und Unwahrheiten; **b)** *(showing that sth. is false)* Widerlegung, *die*

falsify ['fɔ:lsɪfaɪ, 'fɒlsɪfaɪ] *v. t.* **a)** *(alter)* fälschen; *(misrepresent)* verfälschen ⟨*Tatsache, Geschichte, Ereignis, Wahrheit*⟩; **b)** *(show to be false)* widerlegen; falsifizieren *(geh.)*

falsity ['fɔ:lsɪtɪ, 'fɒlsɪtɪ] *n., no pl.* **a)** *(incorrectness)* Falschheit, *die*; **b)** *(falsehood)* Unwahrheit, *die*; *(error)* Unrichtigkeit, *die*; **c)** *(deceitfulness, unfaithfulness)* Treulosigkeit, *die*; **d)** *(artificiality)* Unnatürlichkeit, *die*

falter ['fɔ:ltə(r), 'fɒltə(r)] **1.** *v. i.* **a)** *(waver)* stocken; ⟨*Mut, Hoffnung:*⟩ sinken; ~ **in one's resolve/desire/determination** in seinem Entschluß/Wunsch/seiner Entschlossenheit schwankend werden; **their courage/hopes did not** ~: sie verloren nicht den Mut/die Hoffnung; **b)** *(stumble, stagger)* wanken; **with** ~**ing steps** mit [sch]wankenden Schritten. **2.** *v. t.* ~ **[out] sth.** etw. stammeln

fame [feɪm] *n., no pl.* Ruhm, *der*; **rise to** ~: zu Ruhm kommen *od.* gelangen; **win** ~ **for oneself** Ruhm gewinnen; **a man of [great] literary/political** ~: ein [sehr] berühmter Literat/Politiker; **is that Erich Segal of 'Love Story'** ~**?** ist das der Erich Segal, der mit „Love Story" berühmt geworden ist?; **ill** ~: schlechter Ruf; *see also* **house 1 e**

famed [feɪmd] *adj.* berühmt (**for** für, wegen); *see also* **far-famed**

familiar [fə'mɪljə(r)] **1.** *adj.* **a)** *(well acquainted)* bekannt; **be** ~ **with sb.** jmdn. näher kennen; **we never really got** ~: wir lernten uns *(Akk.)* nie richtig kennen *od. (ugs.)* wurden nie so richtig warm miteinander; **b)** *(having knowledge)* vertraut; **are you** ~ **with Ancient Greek?** können Sie Altgriechisch?; **c)** *(well known)* vertraut; bekannt ⟨*Gesicht, Name, Lied*⟩; gewohnt ⟨*Geruch*⟩; *(common, usual)* geläufig ⟨*Ausdruck*⟩; gängig ⟨*Vorstellung*⟩; **be on** ~ **ground** *(fig.)* Bescheid wissen; **he looks** ~: er kommt mir bekannt vor;

his name seems ~ [to me] sein Name kommt mir bekannt vor; **the word is ~ to me** das Wort ist mir geläufig; **d)** *(informal)* familiär, freundschaftlich ‹*Ton, Begrüßung*›; ungezwungen ‹*Sprache, Art, Stil*›; **are you on ~ terms with him?** kennt ihr euch gut?; **a ~ term of address** eine vertrauliche Anrede; **e)** *(presumptuous)* plump-vertraulich *(abwertend)*; **f)** *(intimate)* intim; **make oneself** *or* **become** *or* **get too ~ with sb.** mit jmdm. zu vertraulich werden; **be on ~ terms with sb.** enge Beziehungen zu jmdm. unterhalten. **2.** *n. (literary: friend, associate)* Vertraute, *der/die (geh.)*

familiarity [fəmɪlɪ'ærɪtɪ] *n.* **a)** *no pl. (acquaintance)* Vertrautheit, *die;* **b)** *no pl. (relationship)* ungezwungenes Verhältnis; familiäres Verhältnis; **c)** *(of action, behaviour)* Vertraulichkeit, *die;* **the ~ of their greeting** ihre freundschaftliche Begrüßung; **~ breeds contempt** *(prov.)* zu große Vertraulichkeit erzeugt Verachtung; **d)** *no pl. (sexual intimacy)* Intimität, *die;* Vertraulichkeiten *Pl.;* **attempts at ~:** plumpe Annäherungsversuche; **e)** *in pl. (caresses)* Intimitäten *Pl.;* Vertraulichkeiten *Pl.*

familiarize (familiarise) [fə'mɪljəraɪz] *v. t.* vertraut machen; einweisen ‹*neuen Mitarbeiter*›; **~ oneself with a/one's new job** sich einarbeiten

familiarly [fə'mɪljəlɪ] *adv.* **a)** *(informally)* ungezwungen; **b)** *(intimately)* näher ‹*kennen*›; **c)** *(presumptuously)* plump-vertraulich *(abwertend)*; **d)** *(commonly)* **~ known as ...:** allgemein ... genannt; **more ~ known as** besser bekannt als

family ['fæməlɪ] *n.* **a)** Familie, *die;* **be one of the ~:** zur Familie gehören; **with just the immediate ~:** im engsten Familienkreis; **start a ~:** eine Familie gründen; **give my regards to Mr and Mrs Brown and ~:** grüßen Sie Familie Brown von mir; **run in the ~:** in der Familie liegen; **be in the** *or* **a ~ way** *(coll.)* in anderen Umständen sein *(verhüll.)*; **b)** *(ancestry)* **of [good] ~:** aus guter Familie; **c)** *(group, race)* Geschlecht, *das;* **the ~ of human beings** das Menschengeschlecht; **d)** *(brotherhood)* [große] Familie; **the ~ of Christians/of man** die Christenheit/die Menschheit; **the ~ of nations** die Völkerfamilie *(geh.)*; **e)** *(group of things; also Biol.)* Familie, *die; (Ling.)* [Sprach]familie, *die;* **f)** *attrib.* Familien-; familiär ‹*Hintergrund*›; **in the ~ circle** im Kreis der Familie; *see also* **council a**

family: ~ al'lowance *n.* Kindergeld, *das;* **~ 'Bible** *n.* Familienbibel, *die;* **F~ Division** *n. (Brit. Law) Abteilung für Familienrecht im obersten Gericht;* **~ 'doctor** *n.* Hausarzt, *der;* **~ 'income supplement** *n. (Brit.)* ≈ Familienzulage, *die;* **~ man** *n.* Familienvater, *der; (home-loving man)* häuslich veranlagter Mann; **~ name** *n.* Familienname, *der;* Nachname, *der;* **~ 'planning** *n.* Familienplanung, *die;* **~ 'planning clinic** *n.* ≈ Familienberatung[sstelle], *die;* **~ 'tree** *n.* Stammbaum, *der*

famine ['fæmɪn] *n.* **a)** Hungersnot, *die;* **b)** *(shortage)* Knappheit, *die;* **~-stricken** von Hunger betroffen

famish ['fæmɪʃ] *v. i.* hungern; **I'm ~ing!** *(coll.)* ich sterbe vor Hunger *(ugs.)*

famished ['fæmɪʃt] *adj.* ausgehungert; halb verhungert; **I'm absolutely ~** *(coll.)* ich sterbe vor Hunger *(ugs.)*

famous ['feɪməs] *adj.* **a)** *(well-known)* berühmt; **a ~ victory** ein rühmlicher Sieg; **b)** *(coll.: excellent)* prima *(ugs.)*; famos *(ugs. veralt.)*

famously ['feɪməslɪ] *adv. (coll.)* prima *(ugs.)*; famos *(ugs. veralt.)*

[1]**fan** [fæn] **1.** *n.* **a)** Fächer, *der;* **b)** *(sth. spread out)* Fächer, *der; (of peacock)* Rad, *das;* **c)** *(apparatus)* Ventilator, *der.* **2.** *v. t.*, **-nn-:** fächeln ‹*Gesicht*›; anfachen ‹*Feuer*›; **~ oneself/sb.** sich/jmdm. Luft zufächeln; **~ one's face** sich *(Dat.)* das Gesicht fächeln; **~ the fire into a brisk blaze** das Feuer anfachen, bis es hell lodert; **~ the flame[s]** *or* **embers** *(fig.)* das Feuer schüren; Öl ins Feuer gießen; **~ dissatisfaction/hate** Unzufriedenheit/Haß schüren

~ 'out 1. *v. t.* fächern; auffächern ‹*Spielkarten*›. **2.** *v. i.* fächern; ‹*Soldaten:*› ausfächern

[2]**fan** *n. (devotee)* Fan, *der;* **she is a Garbo ~:** sie ist ein Garbo-Fan; **I'm quite a ~ of yours!** ich bewundere Sie!

fanatic [fə'nætɪk] **1.** *adj.* fanatisch. **2.** *n.* Fanatiker, *der*/Fanatikerin, *die*

fanatical [fə'nætɪkl] *see* **fanatic 1**

fanatically [fə'nætɪkəlɪ] *adv.* fanatisch

fanaticism [fə'nætɪsɪzm] *n.* Fanatismus, *der*

'fan belt *n. (Motor Veh.)* Keilriemen, *der*

fancier ['fænsɪə(r)] *n.* Liebhaber, *der*/Liebhaberin, *die;* **be a rose-/pigeon-~:** Rosen/Tauben züchten

fanciful ['fænsɪfl] *adj.* **a)** *(whimsical)* versponnen ‹*Person*›; abstrus, überspannt ‹*Vorstellung, Gedanke*›; **b)** *(fantastically designed)* phantastisch ‹*Gemälde, Design*›; reich verziert ‹*Kleid, Kostüm*›

fancifully ['fænsɪfəlɪ] *adv.* phantasievoll ‹*erzählen*›; phantastisch ‹*[aus]geschmückt*›

fan: ~ club *n.* Fanklub, *der;* **~-cooled** *adj.* gebläsegekühlt

fancy ['fænsɪ] **1.** *n.* **a)** *(taste, inclination)* **have a ~ for sth.** eine augenblickliche Schwäche für etw. haben; **have a ~ for a drink/some ice cream** Lust auf einen Drink/ein Eis haben; **he has taken a ~ to our plan/a new car/her** unser Plan/ein neues Auto/sie hat es ihm angetan; **take** *or* **catch sb.'s ~:** jmdm. gefallen; jmdn. ansprechen; **b)** *(whim)* Laune, *die;* **I just go where the ~ takes me** ich fahre einfach drauf los *od.* ins Blaue; **just as the ~ takes me** ganz nach Lust und Laune; **he only paints when the ~ takes him** er malt nur, wenn ihm [gerade] danach ist; **a passing ~:** eine [vorübergehende] Laune; nur so eine Laune; **tickle sb.'s ~:** jmdn. reizen; **c)** *(notion)* merkwürdiges Gefühl; *(delusion, belief)* Vorstellung, *die;* **a mere ~:** bloße Einbildung; **have a ~ that something is wrong** so ein Gefühl haben, daß etwas nicht stimmt; **d)** *(faculty of imagining)* Phantasie, *die;* **let one's ~ roam** seine Phantasie schweifen lassen *(geh.)*; seiner Phantasie *(Dat.)* freien Lauf lassen; **in ~ he saw himself as ...:** in Gedanken sah er sich als ...; **e)** *(mental image)* Phantasievorstellung, *die;* **just a ~:** nur Einbildung; **f)** *(cake)* fein[st]es Gebäck; **g)** *constr. as pl. (fanciers)* Liebhaber *Pl.;* Kreis der Kenner. **2.** *attrib. adj.* **a)** *(ornamental)* kunstvoll ‹*Arbeit, Muster, Dribbling*›; ausgefallen ‹*Artikel, Design*›; schick ‹*Auto, Laden*›; raffiniert ‹*Gerät*›; fein[st] ‹*Kuchen, Spitzen*›; **~ jewellery** Modeschmuck, *der;* **nothing ~:** etwas ganz Schlichtes; **the meal will be nothing ~:** es gibt nichts Besonderes *od.* nur etwas ganz Einfaches zu essen; **b)** *(whimsical)* überspannt; **c)** *(extravagant)* stolz *(ugs.)*; **~ prices** Phantasiepreise *(ugs.)*; gepfefferte Preise *(ugs.)*; **d)** *(based on imagination)* phantasievoll; **e)** *(specially bred)* speziell gezüchtet ‹*Tier*›; **f)** *(Amer.: high-quality)* feinst... ‹*Lebensmittel*›; Delikateß‹*gurke, -senf*›. **3.** *v. t.* **a)** *(imagine)* sich *(Dat.)* einbilden; **~ oneself [to be] clever** sich einbilden, klug zu sein; sich für klug halten; **a fancied resemblance** eine eingebildete Ähnlichkeit; **b)** *(coll.) in imper. as excl. of surprise* **~ meeting you here!** na, so etwas, Sie hier zu treffen!; **~ his still being so naïve** nicht zu fassen, daß er noch immer so naiv ist; **~ that!** sieh mal einer an!; also so etwas!; **just ~, she's run off with ...:** stell dir vor, sie ist mit ... durchgebrannt!; **c)** *(suppose)* glauben; denken; **..., I ~:** ..., möchte ich meinen; **d)** *(wish to have)* mögen; **what do you ~ for dinner?** was hättest du gern zum Abendessen?; **I don't ~ this house at all** mir gefällt dieses Haus überhaupt nicht; **he fancies [the idea of] doing sth.** er würde gern etw. tun; er hätte Lust, etw. zu tun; **I don't ~ a secretarial job** eine Sekretärinnenstelle reizt mich überhaupt nicht; **~ a walk?** hast du Lust zu einem Spaziergang?; **do you think she fancies him?** glaubst du, sie mag ihn?; **e)** *(coll.: have high opinion of)* **~ oneself** von sich eingenommen sein; **~ oneself as a singer** sich für einen [großen] Sänger halten; **~ one's/sb.'s chances** seine/jmds. Chancen hoch einschätzen; **he fancies his chances with her** er glaubt, bei ihr landen zu können *(ugs.)*

fancy: ~ 'dress *n.* [Masken]kostüm, *das;* **in ~ dress** kostümiert; **~-dress party** Kostümfest, *das;* **~-dress ball** *or* **dance** Maskenball, *der;* **~-'free** *adj.* frei und ungebunden; *see also* **footloose; ~ goods** *n. pl.* Geschenkartikel; **~ man** *n. (sl. derog.)* **a)** *(woman's lover)* Liebhaber, *der;* **b)** *(pimp)* Zuhälter, *der;* **~ woman** *n. (sl. derog.)* Geliebte, *die;* **~-work** *n.* feine Handarbeit

fanfare ['fænfeə(r)] *n.* Fanfare, *die;* **a ~ of trumpets** Trompetenstöße *Pl.*

fang [fæŋ] *n.* **a)** *(canine tooth)* Reißzahn, *der;* Fang[zahn], *der; (of boar; joc.: of person)* Hauer, *der; (of vampire)* Vampirzahn, *der;* **draw sb.'s/sth.'s ~s** *(fig.)* jmdn./etw. unschädlich machen; **b)** *(of snake)* Giftzahn, *der;* **c)** *(root of tooth)* Zahnwurzel, *die*

fan: ~ heater *n.* Heizlüfter, *der;* **~light** *n.* Oberlicht, *das; (fan-shaped)* Fächerfenster, *das (Archit.)*; **~ mail** *n.* Fanpost, *die;* Verehrerpost, *die*

fanny ['fænɪ] *n.* **a)** *(Amer. sl.: buttocks)* Po, *der (fam.)*; **b)** *(Brit. coarse: vulva)* Möse, *die (vulg.)*

fan: ~ palm *n.* Fächerpalme, *die;* **~-shaped** *adj.* fächerförmig; **~tail** *n.* Fächerschwanz, *der; (pigeon)* Pfautaube, *die*

fantasia [fæn'teɪzɪə, fæntə'zi:ə] *n. (Mus.)* Fantasia, *die (fachspr.)*; Fantasie, *die*

fantastic [fæn'tæstɪk] *adj.* **a)** *(grotesque, quaint)* bizarr; skurril; *(fanciful)* phantastisch; *(eccentric)* absurd ‹*Gerücht, Plan, Geschichte*›; **b)** *(coll.: magnificent, excellent, extraordinary)* phantastisch *(ugs.)*

fantastically [fæn'tæstɪkəlɪ] *adv.* **a)** phantastisch; **b)** *(coll.: excellently, extraordinarily)* phantastisch *(ugs.)*

fantasy ['fæntəzɪ] *n.* **a)** Phantasie, *die; (mental image, day-dream)* Phantasiegebilde, *das;* **b)** *(Lit.)* Fantasie, *die;* **c)** *(Mus.) see* **fantasia**

fan: ~ 'tracery *n. (Archit.)* fächerförmiges Maßwerk; **~ 'vaulting** *n. (Archit.)* Fächergewölbe, *das*

far [fɑ:(r)] **1.** *adv.*, **farther, further; farthest, furthest a)** *(in space)* weit; **~ away** weit entfernt *(see also* **d)**; **~ [away] from** weit entfernt von *(see also* **d)**; **see sth. from ~ away** etw. aus der Ferne sehen; **have you come [from] ~** *or* **from ~ off** *or* **away?** hatten Sie einen weiten Weg?; kommen Sie von weither?; **how ~ have you come?** wieviel Kilometer mußten Sie zurücklegen?; **he travelled ~ into Russia/the desert/the jungle** er reiste bis tief ins Innere Rußlands/in die Wüste/in den Dschungel; **I won't be ~ off** *or* **away** ich werde ganz in der Nähe sein; **~ above/below** hoch über/tief unter (+ *Dat.*); *adv.* hoch oben/tief unten; **so ~:** bis hierher *(see also* **d)**; **fly as ~ as Munich** bis [nach] München fliegen; **~ and near** fern und nah; **~ and wide** weit und breit; **from ~ and near** *or* **wide** von fern und nah; **b)** *(in time)* weit; **~ into the night** bis spät *od.* tief in die Nacht; **the day** *or* **time is not ~ off** *or* **distant when ...:** es dauert nicht mehr lange, bis ...;

as ~ **back as I can remember** soweit ich zurückdenken kann; **c)** *(by much)* weit; ~ **too** viel zu; ~ **different from** ganz *od.* völlig anders als; ~ **longer/better** weit[aus] länger/besser; **the rent is ~ beyond what I can afford to pay** die Miete übersteigt bei weitem meine Mittel; **they were not ~ wrong** sie hatten gar nicht so unrecht; **you were/I was not ~ out** du lagst/ich lag gar nicht so falsch *(ugs.)*; **your guess wasn't ~ out** deine Vermutung war gar nicht so abwegig; **your shot/guess wasn't ~ off** du hast fast getroffen/richtig vermutet; **d)** *(fig.)* **as ~ as** *(to whatever extent, to the extent of)* so weit [wie]; **I haven't got as ~ as phoning her** ich bin noch nicht dazu gekommen, sie anzurufen; **not as ~ as I know** nicht, daß ich wüßte; **your plans are all right as ~ as they go** Ihre Pläne sind soweit gut; **as ~ as I remember/know** soweit ich mich erinnere/weiß; **go so ~ as to do sth.** so weit gehen und etw. tun; **he's gone so ~ as to collect the material** er sammelt immerhin schon Material; **in so ~ as** insofern *od.* insoweit als; **so ~** *(until now)* bisher; bis jetzt; **so ~ so good** so weit, so gut; ~ **away** *(in thought)* weit weg; ~ **and away** bei weitem; weitaus; **by ~:** bei weitem; **better by ~:** weitaus besser; **by ~ the best** der/die/das weitaus beste/*(in rank)* Beste; ~ **from easy/good** alles andere als leicht/gut; ~ **from admiring his paintings, I dislike them intensely** nicht nur, daß ich seine Gemälde nicht bewundere, sie gefallen mir ganz und gar nicht; ~ **from it!** ganz im Gegenteil!; ~ **be it from me/us** *etc.* **to do that** es liegt mir/uns *usw.* fern, das zu tun; **go ~:** weit kommen; **I am ~ from doing sth.** ich bin weit davon entfernt, etw. zu tun; **he will go ~ in life** er wird es im Leben weit bringen; **go ~ to** *or* **towards sth./doing sth.** viel zu etw. beitragen/dazu beitragen, etw. zu tun; **not go ~:** nicht weit *od.* lange reichen; **one pound won't go ~:** ein Pfund ist schnell alle *od. (ugs.)* weg; **go too ~:** zu weit gehen; **this has gone ~ enough** damit ist jetzt Schluß; **carry** *or* **take sth. too ~:** etw. zu weit treiben; **that's carrying the joke too ~:** da hört der Spaß auf; **you are carrying things too ~ by saying that ...:** du übertreibst, wenn du sagst, daß ...; **how ~ [can she be trusted]?** inwieweit [kann man ihr trauen]?; **he's too ~ gone** er ist nicht mehr in der Lage, etw. zu tun; *(drunk)* er hat zuviel intus *(ugs.)*; *(delirious)* er ist nicht mehr ganz bei Sinnen *od.* klar im Kopf. *See also* **few 1a; further 2; furthest 2. 2.** *adj.*, **farther, further; farthest, furthest a)** *(remote)* weit entfernt; *(remote in time)* fern; **in the ~ distance** in weiter Ferne; **b)** *(more remote)* weiter entfernt; **the ~ bank of the river/side of the road** das andere Flußufer/die andere Straßenseite; **the ~ door/wall** *etc.* die hintere Tür/Wand *usw. See also* **cry 1a; further 1; furthest 1**

'far-away *attrib. adj.* **a)** *(remote in space)* entlegen; abgelegen; *(remote in time)* fern; **b)** *(dreamy)* verträumt ⟨*Stimme, Blick, Augen*⟩

farce [fɑːs] *n.* **a)** Farce, *die;* **become nothing but a ~:** zur reinen Farce werden; **b)** *(Theatre)* Posse, *die;* Farce, *die*

farcical ['fɑːsɪkl] *adj.* **a)** *(absurd)* farcenhaft; absurd; **b)** *(Theatre)* possenhaft ⟨*Stück, Element*⟩

farcically ['fɑːsɪkəlɪ] *adv.* *(absurdly)* absurd

fare [feə(r)] **1.** *n.* **a)** *(price)* Fahrpreis, *der;* *(money)* Fahrgeld, *das;* **train/boat ~:** Bahnpreis/Preis für die Überfahrt; **what** *or* **how much is the ~?** was kostet die Fahrt/*(by air)* der Flug/*(by boat)* die Überfahrt?; **have the exact ~:** das Fahrgeld passend haben; **have one's ~ ready** das Fahrgeld bereithalten; **[all] ~s, please, any more ~s?** noch jemand zugestiegen? noch jemand ohne [Fahrschein]?; **b)** *(passenger)* Fahrgast, *der;* **c)** *(food)* Kost, *die; see also* **[3]bill 1d. 2.** *v.i.* *(get on)* **I don't know how he is faring/how he ~d on his travels** ich weiß nicht, wie es ihm geht/wie es ihm auf seinen Reisen ergangen ist; ~ **thee well** *(arch.)* leb[e] wohl *(veralt.)*

Far: ~ **'East** *n.* **the ~ East** der Ferne Osten; Fernost *o. Art.*; ~ **'Eastern** *adj.* fernöstlich; des Fernen Ostens *nachgestellt;* ⟨*Person*⟩ aus dem Fernen Osten

'fare-stage *n.* Teilstrecke, *die;* *(end of section)* Zahlgrenze, *die (Verkehrsw.)*

farewell [feə'wel] **1.** *int.* leb[e] wohl *(veralt.)*; **say ~ to sth.** von etw. Abschied nehmen. **2.** *n.* **a) a few words of ~:** ein paar Worte des Abschieds *od. (veralt.)* Lebewohls; **make one's ~s** sich verabschieden; *(by visiting)* Abschiedsbesuche machen; *see also* **bid 1e; b)** *attrib.* ~ **speech/gift** *etc.* Abschiedsrede, *die*/-geschenk, *das usw.*

far: **~-famed** *adj.* weithin berühmt; **~-fetched** *adj.* weit hergeholt; an *od.* bei den Haaren herbeigezogen *(ugs.)*; **~-flung** *adj.* *(widely spread)* weit ausgedehnt; *(distant)* weit entfernt; abgelegen

farm [fɑːm] **1.** *n.* **a)** [Bauern]hof, *der;* [Land]wirtschaft, *die;* *(larger)* Gut, *das;* Gutshof, *der;* *(in English-speaking countries outside Europe)* Farm, *die;* **poultry/chicken ~:** Geflügel-/Hühnerfarm, *die;* ~ **bread/eggs** Landbrot, *das*/Landeier *Pl.*; ~ **animals** Nutzvieh, *das; see also* **dairy farm; b)** *see* **farmhouse; c)** *(place for breeding animals)* Zucht, *die;* **trout ~:** Forellenzucht, *die.* **2.** *v.t.* **a)** bebauen, bewirtschaften ⟨*Land*⟩; züchten ⟨*Lachs, Forellen*⟩; **be engaged in sheep-~ing** Schafzucht betreiben; **b)** *(take proceeds of)* pachten; **c)** *see* ~ **out. 3.** *v.i.* Landwirtschaft betreiben; **he ~s in Africa** er ist Landwirt in Afrika; er hat eine Farm in Afrika

~ **'out** *v.t.* **a)** verpachten ⟨*Land*⟩; **b)** vergeben ⟨*Arbeit*⟩ **(to** an + *Akk.*); **c)** *(hire out)* verdingen *(veralt.)* ⟨*Arbeitskräfte*⟩; in Lohnarbeit geben ⟨*Arbeitskräfte*⟩; **d)** in Pflege geben ⟨*Kinder*⟩ **(to** *Dat.*, bei)

farmer ['fɑːmə(r)] *n.* Landwirt, *der*/-wirtin, *die;* Bauer, *der*/Bäuerin, *die;* **poultry ~:** Geflügelzüchter, *der*/-züchterin, *die*

farm: **~-hand** *n.* Landarbeiter, *der*/-arbeiterin, *die;* *(on a small farm)* Knecht, *der*/Magd, *die (veralt.)*; **~house** *n.* Bauernhaus, *das;* *(larger)* Gutshaus, *das*

farming ['fɑːmɪŋ] *n, no pl., no indef. art.* Landwirtschaft, *die;* ~ **of crops** Ackerbau, *der;* ~ **of animals** Viehzucht, *die;* ~ **community** Landwirtschaft betreibende Gemeinde; ~ **implement** Ackergerät, *das;* landwirtschaftliches Gerät; **go into ~:** Landwirt *od.* Bauer werden

farm: **~stead** *n.* Bauernhof, *der;* Gehöft, *das;* **~-worker** *n.* Landarbeiter, *der*/-arbeiterin, *die;* **~yard** *n.* Hof, *der*

Faroes ['feərəʊz] *pr. n. pl.* Färöer *Pl.*

'far-off *adj.* *(in space)* [weit] entfernt; *(in time)* fern

'far-out *adj.* **a)** *(distant)* [weit] entfernt; **b)** *(fig. coll.: excellent)* toll *(ugs.)*; super *(ugs.)*

farrago [fə'rɑːgəʊ] *n., pl.* **~s** *(Amer.:* **~es)** *(mixture)* Gemisch, *das;* *(disordered assemblage)* Allerlei, *das*

'far-reaching *adj.* ausgedehnt ⟨*Wälder, Felder*⟩; weitreichend ⟨*Konsequenzen, Bedeutung, Wirkung*⟩

farrier ['færɪə(r)] *n.* *(Brit.: smith)* Hufschmied, *der*

farrow ['færəʊ] **1.** *n.* Wurf, *der (von Ferkeln, Frischlingen).* **2.** *v.t.* werfen ⟨*Ferkel, Frischling*⟩. **3.** *v.i.* ⟨*Sau:*⟩ ferkeln; ⟨*Bache:*⟩ frischen

far: **~-seeing** *adj.* weitblickend; **~-sighted** *adj.* **a)** *(able to see a great distance)* scharfsichtig; **b)** *(having foresight)* weitblickend

fart [fɑːt] *(coarse)* **1.** *v.i.* **a)** furzen *(derb)*; **b)** *(fool)* ~ **about** *or* **around** sich mit jedem Scheißdreck aufhalten *(derb).* **2.** *n.* **a)** Furz, *der (derb)*; **b)** *(person)* Scheißer, *der (derb)*

farther ['fɑːðə(r)] *see* **further 1a, 2a**

farthermost ['fɑːðəməʊst] *see* **furthermost**

farthest ['fɑːðɪst] *see* **furthest**

farthing ['fɑːðɪŋ] *n.* **a)** *(Brit. Hist.)* Farthing, *der;* **that old bike isn't worth a ~:** das alte Fahrrad ist keinen [roten] Heller wert; **to the last ~:** auf Heller und Pfennig; **b)** *(fig.)* **it doesn't matter a ~:** es macht nicht das geringste *od. (ugs.)* nicht die Bohne was aus; **he doesn't care a ~ for her** er kümmert sich keinen Deut um sie; sie ist ihm völlig schnuppe *(ugs. abwertend)*; *see also* **brass farthing**

Far 'West *n.* *(Amer.)* **the ~:** der Westen der USA

fascia ['feɪʃɪə, 'feɪʃə] *n.* **a)** *(Archit.)* Faszie, *die;* **b)** *see* **facia**

fascicle ['fæsɪkl] *n.* Lieferung, *die;* Faszikel, *der (Buchw.)*

fascinate ['fæsɪneɪt] *v.t.* **a)** fesseln; bezaubern; faszinieren *(geh.)*; **it ~s me how ...:** ich finde es erstaunlich *od.* faszinierend, wie ...; **b)** *(deprive of power)* hypnotisieren ⟨*Beute*⟩

fascinated ['fæsɪneɪtɪd] *adj.* *(enchanted)* fasziniert; **the audience watched ~:** das Publikum sah gebannt zu

fascinating ['fæsɪneɪtɪŋ] *adj.* faszinierend *(geh.)*; bezaubernd; hochinteressant ⟨*Thema, Faktum, Meinung*⟩; spannend, fesselnd ⟨*Buch*⟩; **there is something ~ about her** sie hat etwas Faszinierendes [an sich *(Dat.)*]

fascinatingly ['fæsɪneɪtɪŋlɪ] *adv.* faszinierend *(geh.)*; hochinteressant, fesselnd ⟨*erzählen, beschreiben*⟩; berauschend, hinreißend ⟨*schön*⟩

fascination [fæsɪ'neɪʃn] *n., no pl.* Faszination, *die (geh.)*; *(quality of fascinating)* Zauber, *der;* Reiz, *der;* **find a certain ~ in sth.** einen gewissen Reiz an einer Sache verspüren; **have a ~ for sb.** einen besonderen Reiz auf jmdn. ausüben

Fascism ['fæʃɪzm] *n.* Faschismus, *der;* **Italian ~:** der italienische Faschismus

Fascist ['fæʃɪst] **1.** *n.* Faschist, *der*/Faschistin, *die.* **2.** *adj.* faschistisch

fashion ['fæʃn] **1.** *n.* **a)** Art [und Weise]; **talk/behave in a peculiar ~:** merkwürdig sprechen/sich merkwürdig verhalten; **dress in a similar ~:** sich ähnlich kleiden; **she will do it in her own ~:** sie wird es auf ihre [eigene] Art [und Weise] tun; **in the Japanese ~:** im japanischen Stil; **in the usual ~:** in der üblichen Art; *as sentence-modifier* wie üblich; **in this ~:** auf diese Weise; so; **he expresses himself in a striking ~:** er hat eine bemerkenswerte Ausdrucksweise *od.* einen bemerkenswerten Ausdruck; **walk crab-~/in a zigzag ~:** im Krebsgang/Zickzack gehen; **German-~** nach deutscher Sitte; nach Art der Deutschen; **after** *or* **in the ~ of** im Stil *od.* nach Art von; **in best British ~:** nach guter, alter britischer Art; **after** *or* **in a ~:** schlecht und recht; einigermaßen; **after** *or* **in one's/its ~:** auf seine/ihre Art; **Were you successful? – Well yes, after** *or* **in a ~:** Hast du Erfolg gehabt? – Na ja, so einigermaßen *od.* es geht *(ugs.)*; **b)** *(custom, esp. in dress)* Mode, *die;* **be dressed in the height of** *or* **the latest ~:** hochmodern *od.* nach der neuesten Mode gekleidet sein; **the latest summer/autumn ~s** die neusten Sommer-/Wintermodelle; **~s for men's clothes/women's clothes** die Herrenmode/Damenmode; **the Paris ~s** die Pariser Mode; **it is the ~:** es ist Mode *od.* modern; **hats are the ~ this summer** in diesem Sommer sind Hüte in Mode; **be all the ~:** große Mode *od.* groß in Mode sein; **in ~:** in Mode; modern; **she always follows the/every ~:** sie geht immer nach *od.* mit der Mode/sie macht immer jede Mode mit; **be out of ~:** nicht mehr modern *od.* in Mode sein; **come into/go out of ~:** in Mode/aus der Mode kommen; **bring sth. into ~:** etw. in Mode bringen; **lead** *or* **set the ~:** die Mode vorschreiben; **the ~s in literature/music/art** die Richtungen in der Literatur/Musik-/Kunstrichtungen; **c)** *(usages of society)* Sitte, *die;* Brauch, *der;* **it was the ~ in those days** das war damals Sitte *od.* Brauch; **men/women of ~:** Herren/Damen der Gesellschaft. *See also* **old-fashioned. 2.** *v.t.* **a)** formen, gestalten **(after, according to** nach; **out of, from** aus; **[in]to** zu); **~ sth. after sth.** etw. einer Sache *(Dat.)* nachbilden; **b)** *(shape to leg)* in Paßform bringen ‹*Strümpfe*›

fashionable ['fæʃənəbl] *adj.* modisch ‹*Kleider, Person, Design*›; modern ‹*Sitte*›; vornehm ‹*Gegend, Hotel, Restaurant*›; zur Zeit bevorzugt ‹*Tätigkeit*›; Mode‹*farbe, -krankheit, -wort, -autor*›; **it isn't ~ any more** es ist nicht mehr modern *od.* in Mode; **all the ~ people** die Schickeria

fashionably ['fæʃənəblɪ] *adv.* modisch ‹*sich kleiden*›; modern ‹*leben*›

fashion: ~-conscious *adj.* modebewußt; **~ designer** *n.* Modeschöpfer, *der*/-schöpferin, *die;* **~ magazine** *n.* Modezeitschrift, *die;* Modemagazin, *das;* **~ parade** *n.* Mode[n]schau, *die;* **~-plate** *n.* **a)** *(picture)* Modezeichnung, *die;* **b)** *(fig.: man/woman)* Modegeck, *der*/-puppe, *die (abwertend);* **~ show** *n.* Mode[n]schau, *die*

¹fast [fɑ:st] **1.** *v.i.* fasten; **a day of ~ing** ein Fast[en]tag. **2.** *n. (going without food)* Fasten, *das; (hunger-strike)* Hungerstreik, *der; (day)* Fast[en]tag, *der; (season)* Fastenzeit, *die;* **break one's ~:** das Fasten brechen; **a 40-day ~:** eine Fastenzeit von 40 Tagen

²fast 1. *adj.* **a)** *(fixed, attached)* fest; **the rope is ~:** das Tau ist fest[gemacht]; **make [the boat] ~:** das Boot festmachen *od.* vertäuen; **hard and ~:** fest; bindend, verbindlich ‹*Regeln*›; klar ‹*Entscheidung*›; **b)** *(steady, close)* fest ‹*Freundschaft*›; unzertrennlich, treu ‹*Freunde*›; **c)** *(not fading)* farbecht ‹*Stoff*›; echt, beständig ‹*Farbe*›; *(against light)* lichtecht; *(against washing)* waschecht; **d)** *(rapid)* schnell; tempogeladen, aktionsreich ‹*Krimi, Film*›; **~ train** Schnellzug, *der;* D-Zug, *der;* **~ speed** hohe Geschwindigkeit; **he is a ~ worker** *(lit. or fig.)* er arbeitet schnell; *(in amorous activities)* er geht mächtig ran *(ugs.);* **I say, that was ~ work** na, das ging ja sehr schnell; **pull a ~ one [on sb.]** *(sl.)* jmdn. übers Ohr hauen *od.* reinlegen *(ugs.);* **e) be ~ [by ten minutes], be [ten minutes] ~** ‹*Uhr:*› [zehn Minuten] vorgehen; **f)** schnell ‹*Tennisplatz, Billardtisch usw.*›; **~ road** Straße, auf der man schnell vorankommt; **~ line** *(Railw.)* Schnellverkehrsgleis, *das;* **g)** *(immoral)* flott ‹*Person, Leben*›; locker ‹*Lebenswandel*›; leichtlebig ‹*Frau*›; **h)** *(Photog.)* hochempfindlich ‹*Film*›; lichtstark ‹*Objektiv*›. *See also* **furious. 2.** *adv.* **a)** *(lit. or fig.)* fest; **the wall stood ~:** die Mauer blieb stehen; **hold ~ to sth.** sich an etw. *(Dat.)* festhalten; *(fig.)* an etw. *(Dat.)* festhalten; **stand ~ in one's belief** an seiner Meinung festhalten; **stand ~ by sth./sb.** zu etw./jmdm. stehen; **b)** *(soundly)* **be ~ asleep** fest schlafen; *(when one should be awake)* fest eingeschlafen sein; **c)** *(quickly)* schnell; **not so ~!** nicht so hastig!; **d)** *(ahead)* **that clock is running ~:** diese Uhr geht vor; **play ~ and loose with sb.** mit jmdm. ein falsches *od.* doppeltes Spiel treiben

fast: ~back *n. (back of car)* Fließheck, *das;* Fastback, *das; (car)* Wagen mit Fließheck; Fastback, *das;* **~ 'bowler** *n. (Cricket)* schneller Werfer; **~ 'breeder [reactor]** *n.* schneller Brüter; **~ 'buck** *see* **⁴buck; ~ day** *n.* Fast[en]tag, *der*

fasten ['fɑ:sn] **1.** *v.t.* **a)** festmachen, befestigen **(on, to** an + *Dat.*); festmachen, vertäuen **(to** an + *Dat.*) ‹*Boot*›; festziehen, anziehen ‹*Schraube*›; zumachen ‹*Kleid, Spange, Knöpfe, Jacke*›; [ab]schließen, [ver]schließen ‹*Tür*›; schließen ‹*Fenster*›; anstecken ‹*Brosche*› **(to** an + *Akk.*); **~ sth. together with a clip** etw. zusammenheften; **~ the rope to a post** das Tau an einem Pfosten anbinden *od.* festmachen; **~ sth. up with string** etw. zu- *od.* verschnüren; **~ one's safety-belt** sich anschnallen; seinen Sicherheitsgurt anlegen; **~ up one's shoes** seine Schuhe binden *od.* schnüren; **she ~ed her hair back** sie band ihre Haare zurück; **~ off a thread** einen Fadens vernähen; **b)** heften ‹*Blick*› **([up]on** auf + *Akk.*); richten ‹*Aufmerksamkeit, Gedanken*› **([up]on** auf + *Akk.*); setzen ‹*Erwartungen, Hoffnungen*› **([up]on** auf + *Akk.*); **~ one's attention/affections on sb.** jmdm. seine Aufmerksamkeit zuwenden/Zuneigung schenken; **c)** *(assign)* anhängen, beilegen ‹*Spottnamen*› **([up]on** + *Dat.*); **~ the blame/charge [up]on sb.** die Schuld auf jmdn. schieben; jmdm. die Schuld in die Schuhe schieben *(ugs.).* **2.** *v.i.* **a)** sich schließen lassen; **the skirt ~s at the back** der Rock wird hinten zugemacht; **the hook and the eye ~ together** der Haken und die Öse werden miteinander verbunden; **b) ~ [up]on sth.** *(lay hold of)* festhalten ‹*Person*›; *(fig.) (single out)* etw. herausgreifen; *(seize upon)* etw. aufs Korn nehmen *(ugs.)*

fastener ['fɑ:snə(r)] *n.* Verschluß, *der*

fastening ['fɑ:snɪŋ] *n. (device)* Verschluß, *der*

'fast food *n. im Schnellrestaurant angebotenes Essen;* Fast food, *das;* **~ restaurant** Schnellrestaurant, *das*

fastidious [fæ'stɪdɪəs] *adj. (hard to please)* heikel, *(ugs.)* pingelig **(about** in bezug auf + *Akk.*); *(carefully selective)* wählerisch **(about** in bezug auf + *Akk.*)

fastidiously [fæ'stɪdɪəslɪ] *adv.* **behave ~:** pingelig *(ugs.)*/wählerisch sein; **dress ~:** in seiner/ihrer Kleidung untadelig sein; **~ clean** peinlich sauber

fast: ~ lane *n.* Überholspur, *die;* **life in the ~ lane** *(fig.)* schnelles, lockeres Leben; Leben auf vollen Touren *(ugs.);* **~-moving** *adj.* schnell; spannend, tempogeladen ‹*Film, Drama*›; **a ~-moving train** ein schnell fahrender Zug

fastness ['fɑ:stnɪs] *n.* **a)** *no pl. (of colour, dye)* [Farb]echtheit, *die; (against light)* Lichtechtheit, *die; (against washing)* Waschechtheit, *die;* **b)** *no pl. (of vehicle, person, etc.)* Schnelligkeit, *die;* **c)** *(stronghold)* Feste, *die*

fat [fæt] **1.** *adj.* **a)** dick; fett *(abwertend);* rund ‹*Wangen, Gesicht*›; fett ‹*Schwein*›; **grow** *or* **get ~:** dick werden; **grow ~** *(fig.)* reich werden; **you won't get ~ on that** *(fig. coll.)* das wird dir nicht viel einbringen; **b) ~ cattle** Mast- *od.* Schlachtvieh, *das;* **c)** *(containing much ~)* fett ‹*Essen, Fleisch, Brühe*›; **d)** *(fig.)* dick ‹*Bündel, Buch, Brieftasche, Zigarre*›; umfangreich ‹*Filmrolle, Band*›; üppig, fett ‹*Gewinn, Gehalt, Bankkonto, Scheck*›; **e)** *(sl. iron.)* **~ lot of good 'you are** du bist mir 'ne schöne Hilfe *(iron.);* **a ~ lot [of good it would do me]** [das würde mir] herzlich wenig [helfen]; **~ lot he knows** was der nicht alles weiß *(iron.);* **a ~ chance** herzlich wenig Aussicht; **~ chance 'he's got** da hat er ja Mordschancen *(iron.).* **2.** *n.* Fett, *das;* **low in ~:** fettarm ‹*Nahrungsmittel*›; **put on ~:** Fett ansetzen; **lose ~:** abnehmen; **the ~ is in the fire** *(fig.)* der Teufel ist los *(ugs.);* **live off** *or* **on the ~ of the land** *(fig.)* wie die Made im Speck leben *(ugs.). See also* **chew 1. 3.** *v.t.,* **-tt-** mästen; herausfüttern; **~ted cattle** Schlacht- *od.* Mastvieh, *das;* **kill the ~ted calf [for sb.]** [jmdm.] ein Festessen zum Empfang geben

fatal ['feɪtl] *adj.* **a)** *(ruinous, disastrous)* verheerend (to für); fatal; schicksalsschwer ‹*Tag, Moment*›; **it would be ~:** das wäre das Ende; **it is ~ to assume that ...:** es ist ein verhängnisvoller Irrtum anzunehmen, daß ...; **b)** *(deadly)* tödlich ‹*Unfall, Verletzung*›; **that sort of thing in her present state would be ~:** das würde in ihrem augenblicklichen Zustand den sicheren Tod für sie bedeuten; **deal sb. a ~ blow** jmdm. einen vernichtenden Schlag versetzen; **be** *or* **come as a ~ blow to sb.** *(fig.)* ein schwerer Schlag für jmdn. sein; **c)** *(inevitable)* unabwendbar; unvermeidlich; schicksalhaft ‹*Tag*›; **d)** *(of destiny)* schicksalhaft; Schicksals-

fatalism ['feɪtəlɪzm] *n., no pl.* Fatalismus, *der (geh.);* Schicksalsergebenheit, *die*

fatalist ['feɪtəlɪst] *n.* Fatalist, *der*/Fatalistin, *die*

fatalistic [feɪtə'lɪstɪk] *adj.* fatalistisch; schicksalsergeben ‹*Person*›

fatality [fə'tælɪtɪ] *n. (death)* Todesfall, *der; (in car crash, war, etc.)* [Todes]opfer, *das*

fatally ['feɪtəlɪ] *adv.* tödlich ‹*verwunden, enden*›; *(disastrously)* verhängnisvoll; auf verhängnisvolle Weise ‹*beeinflußt*›; unwiderstehlich ‹*attraktiv*›; **be ~ wrong** *or* **mistaken** einem verhängnisvollen Irrtum unterliegen; **be ~ ill** todkrank sein

'fat cat *n. (Amer. sl.)* Geldsack, *der (ugs.) (mit politischem Einfluß)*

fate [feɪt] *n.* **a)** Schicksal, *das;* **an accident** *or* **stroke of ~:** eine Fügung des Schicksals; **~ decided otherwise** das Schicksal hat es anders bestimmt *od.* wollte es anders; **as sure as ~:** todsicher; **b)** *(Mythol.)* **the F~s** die Parzen. *See also* **death a**

fated ['feɪtɪd] *adj. (doomed)* zum Scheitern verurteilt ‹*Plan, Projekt*›; **be ~ to fail** *or* **to be unsuccessful** zum Scheitern verurteilt sein; **it was ~ that we should never meet again** es war uns *(Dat.)* bestimmt, uns nie wiederzusehen; **be ~:** unter einem ungünstigen Stern stehen

fateful ['feɪtfl] *adj.* **a)** *(important, decisive)* schicksalsschwer ‹*Tag, Stunde, Entscheidung*›; entscheidend ‹*Worte*›; **b)** *(controlled by fate)* schicksalhaft ‹*Begegnung, Treffen, Ereignis*›; **c)** *(prophetic)* schicksalverkündend; *(of misfortune)* unheilverkündend; prophetisch ‹*Worte, Äußerung*›

fat: ~-head *n.* Dummkopf, *der (ugs.);* Schafskopf, *der (ugs. abwertend);* **~-headed** *adj.* dumm; blöd *(ugs.)*

father ['fɑ:ðə(r)] **1.** *n.* **a)** Vater, *der;* **become a ~:** Vater werden; **he is a** *or* **the ~ of six** er hat sechs Kinder; **be ~ to sb.** jmds. Vater sein; **be [like] a ~ to sb.** wie ein Vater zu jmdm. sein; **he is his ~'s son** er ist ganz der Vater; **like ~ like son** der Apfel fällt nicht weit vom Stamm *(ugs. scherzhaft, Spr.);* **the wish is ~ to the thought** der Wunsch ist der Vater des Gedankens; **the ~ and mother of a row/beating** *(coll.)* ein furchtbarer Krach/eine furchtbare Tracht Prügel *(ugs.); see also* **child; b)** *in pl. (forefathers)* Väter *Pl.;* **c)** *(originator)* Vater, *der;* Urheber, *der;* **F~s [of the Church]** Kirchenväter *Pl.;* **d)** *(revered person)* Vater, *der;* **the ~ of his country** der Landesvater; **e)** *(God)* **[our heavenly] F~:** [unser himmlischer] Vater; **God the F~, the Son, and the Holy Ghost** der Vater, der Sohn und der Heilige Geist; **the Our F~:** das Vaterunser; **f)** *(confessor)* Beichtvater, *der; (priest)* Pfarrer, *der; (monk)* Pater, *der;* **F~** *(as title: priest)* Herr Pfarrer; *(as title: monk)* Pater; **the Holy F~:** der Heilige Vater; **Right/Most Reverend F~ [in God]** Ehrwürdiger Vater; **F~ Superior** Prior, *der;* **g) F~** *(venerable person, god)* Vater, *der;* **F~ Thames** die Themse; **[Old] F~ Time** der Chronos *(geh.);* **h)** *(oldest member)* [Dienst]älteste, *der;* **F~ of the House of Commons** *(Brit. Polit.)* der Alterspräsident des Unterhauses. *See also* **city fathers; Pil-**

grim Fathers. **2.** *v. t.* **a)** *(beget)* zeugen; **b)** *(originate)* ins Leben rufen

father: F~ 'Christmas *n.* der Weihnachtsmann; **~-figure** *n.* Vaterfigur, *die*

fatherhood ['fɑːðəhʊd] *n., no pl.* Vaterschaft, *die*

father: ~-in-law *n., pl.* **~s-in-law** Schwiegervater, *der;* **~land** *n.* Vaterland, *das*

fatherless ['fɑːðəlɪs] *adj.* vaterlos; **be ~:** keinen Vater haben

fatherly ['fɑːðəlɪ] **1.** *adj.* väterlich; **~ responsibilities** Vaterpflichten *Pl.;* **~ words of advice** väterliche Ratschläge. **2.** *adv.* wie ein Vater; väterlich ‹*belehren*›

'Father's Day *n.* Vatertag, *der*

fathom ['fæðəm] **1.** *n.* *(Naut.)* Fathom, *das (geh.);* Faden, *der.* **2.** *v. t.* **a)** *(measure)* mit dem Lot messen; **b)** *(fig.: comprehend)* verstehen; **~ sb./sth. out** jmdn./etw. ergründen; **I just cannot ~ him out** er ist mir ein Rätsel

fathomless ['fæðəmlɪs] *adj.* *(immeasurable)* unermeßlich; grenzenlos, unendlich ‹*Liebe Gottes*›; bodenlos ‹*Abgrund*›

fatigue [fə'tiːg] **1.** *n.* **a)** Ermüdung, *die;* Erschöpfung, *die;* **fight against ~:** gegen die Müdigkeit ankämpfen; **extreme ~:** Übermüdung, *die;* **b)** *(of metal etc.)* Ermüdung, *die;* **c)** *(of muscle, organ, etc.)* Übermüdung, *die;* Überanstrengung, *die;* **d)** *(task)* mühselige Arbeit; Mühsal, *die (geh.);* **e)** *(Mil.)* Arbeitsdienst, *der;* **be put on ~ duty** zum Arbeitsdienst eingeteilt werden; **~s** *see* **fatigue-dress. 2.** *v. t.* ermüden; **with a ~d look** mit müdem Blick; **feel ~d** sich müde *od.* abgespannt fühlen; **look ~d** erschöpft aussehen; **too ~d to do sth.** zu erschöpft, etw. zu tun

fatigue: ~-dress *n.* *(Mil.)* Arbeitsanzug, *der;* **~-party** *n.* *(Mil.)* Arbeitskommando, *das*

fatless ['fætlɪs] *adj.* ohne Fett *nachgestellt;* mager ‹*Fleisch*›

fatness ['fætnɪs] *n., no pl.* *(corpulence)* Dicke, *die;* Beleibtheit, *die (verhüll.);* Fettheit, *die (abwertend)*

'fatstock *n., no pl.* Mastvieh, *das*

fatted ['fætɪd] *adj. see* **fat 3**

fatten ['fætn] **1.** *v. t.* herausfüttern ‹*Person*›; mästen ‹*Tier*›; **~ oneself on sth.** *(fig.)* sich an etw. *(Akk.)* bereichern. **2.** *v. i.* ‹*Tier:*› fett werden; ‹*Person:*› dick werden; fett werden *(abwertend);* **~ on sth.** sich mästen mit etw.; *(fig.)* profitieren von etw.; Nutzen ziehen aus etw.

fattening ['fætnɪŋ] *adj.* dick machend ‹*Nahrungsmittel*›; **~ foods** Dickmacher *Pl. (ugs.);* **be ~:** dick machen

fatty ['fætɪ] **1.** *adj.* **a)** fett ‹*Fleisch, Soße*›; fetthaltig ‹*Speise, Nahrungsmittel*›; fettig ‹*Substanz*›; **b)** *(consisting of fat)* Fett-; **~ tissue/tumour** Fettgewebe, *das*/Fettgeschwulst, *die.* **2.** *n.* *(coll.)* Dicke, *der/die;* Dickerchen, *das (scherzh.)*

fatty 'acid *n.* *(Chem.)* Fettsäure, *die*

fatuous ['fætjʊəs] *adj.* albern; töricht; einfältig ‹*Grinsen*›

fatuously ['fætjʊəslɪ] *adv.* albern; töricht ‹*handeln*›; einfältig ‹*bewundern*›

faucet ['fɔːsɪt] *n.* **a)** *(for barrel)* Faßzapfen, *der;* **b)** *(Amer.: tap)* Wasserhahn, *der*

fault [fɔːlt, fɒlt] **1.** *n.* **a)** *(defect)* Fehler, *der;* **we all have our little ~s** wir alle haben unsere Schwächen; **confess one's ~s** seine Sünden bekennen; **to a ~:** allzu übertrieben; übermäßig; **meticulous to a ~:** peinlich genau; **find ~ [with sb./sth.]** etw. [an jmdm./etw.] auszusetzen haben; **find ~ with goods** Mängel an Waren feststellen; **[sold] with all ~s** ohne Mängelgewähr [verkauft]; **free from** *or* **without ~:** mangelfrei; **b)** *(responsibility)* Schuld, *die;* Verschulden, *das;* **whose ~ was it?** wer war schuld [daran]?; **it's all your own ~!** das ist deine eigene Schuld!; du bist selbst schuld!; **it isn't my ~:** ich habe keine Schuld; es ist nicht meine Schuld; **not through any ~ of mine** nicht durch meine Schuld; **the ~ lies with him** die Schuld liegt bei ihm; **be at ~:** im Unrecht sein *(see also* **g)**; **my memory was at ~:** mein Gedächtnis hat mich getrogen *(geh.);* **it is difficult to determine who is at ~:** es ist schwierig zu sagen, wer die Schuld daran trägt *od.* wer dafür verantwortlich ist; **c)** *(thing wrongly done)* Fehler, *der;* **commit a ~:** einen Fehler begehen; **d)** *(Tennis etc.)* Fehler, *der;* **double ~:** Doppelfehler, *der;* **e)** *(in gas or water supply; also Electr.)* Defekt, *der;* **f)** *(Geol.)* Verwerfung, *die;* **g)** *(Hunting)* Verlieren der Fährte; **be at ~:** die Fährte verloren haben; *(fig.)* vor einem Rätsel stehen; nicht mehr weiter wissen *(see also* **b). 2.** *v. t.* **a)** Fehler finden an (+ *Dat.*); etwas auszusetzen haben an (+ *Dat.*); **he/his argument had been ~ed** er/seine Argumentation war bemängelt *od.* kritisiert worden; **b)** *(declare faulty)* bemängeln

fault: ~finder *n.* Krittler, *der*/Krittlerin, *die (abwertend);* **~finding 1.** *n.* Krittelei, *die (abwertend);* **2.** *adj.* krittelig *(abwertend);* **~finding critic/criticism** Krittler, *der*/Krittelei, *die*

faultily ['fɔːltɪlɪ, 'fɒltɪlɪ] *adv.* fehlerhaft; mangelhaft

faultless ['fɔːltlɪs, 'fɒltlɪs] *adj.* einwandfrei; tadellos ‹*Erscheinung*›; fehlerlos, fehlerfrei ‹*Übersetzung, Englisch*›; untadelig ‹*Betragen*›; ausgezeichnet ‹*Ruf*›

faultlessly ['fɔːltlɪslɪ, 'fɒltlɪslɪ] *adv.* fehlerfrei; fehlerlos; makellos ‹*schön*›; **the dress fits ~:** das Kleid hat einen tadellosen Sitz

faulty ['fɔːltɪ, 'fɒltɪ] *adj.* fehlerhaft; unzutreffend ‹*Argument*›; defekt ‹*Gerät usw.*›; **~ design/calculation** Fehlkonstruktion, *die*/Fehlkalkulation, *die*

faun [fɔːn] *n.* *(Mythol.)* Faun, *der*

fauna ['fɔːnə] *n., pl.* **~e** ['fɔːniː] *or* **~s** *(Zool.)* Fauna, *die*

faute de mieux [fəʊt də 'mjɜː] *adv.* faute de mieux *(geh.);* in Ermangelung eines Besseren; im Notfall

faux pas [fəʊ 'pɑː] *n., pl. same* [fəʊ 'pɑːz] Fauxpas, *der*

favor *etc.* *(Amer.) see* **favour** *etc.*

favour ['feɪvə(r)] *(Brit.)* **1.** *n.* **a)** Gunst, *die;* Wohlwollen, *das;* **look with ~ on** mit Wohlwollen betrachten; wohlwollend gegenüberstehen (+ *Dat.*) ‹*Person, Plan, Idee usw.*›; **find ~ in the eyes of sb.** *or* **in sb.'s eyes** *(literary)* vor jmds. Augen *(Dat.)* Gnade finden; **find/lose ~ with sb.** ‹*Sache:*› bei jmdm. Anklang finden/jmdm. nicht mehr gefallen; ‹*Person:*› jmds. Wohlwollen gewinnen/verlieren; **as a mark of her ~:** als *od.* zum Zeichen ihrer Wertschätzung *od.* Anerkennung; **be in ~ [with sb.]** [bei jmdm.] beliebt *od. (ugs.)* gut angeschrieben sein; ‹*Idee, Kleidung usw.:*› [bei jmdm.] in Mode sein; **be out of ~ [with sb.]** [bei jmdm.] unbeliebt *od. (ugs.)* schlecht angeschrieben sein; [bei jmdm.] in Ungnade sein *(oft spött.);* ‹*Idee, Kleidung usw.:*› [bei jmdm.] nicht mehr in Mode sein; **get back in[to] sb.'s ~:** jmds. Gunst *od.* Wohlwollen wiedergewinnen; **b)** *(kindness)* Gefallen, *der;* Gefälligkeit, *die;* **sb. requests the ~ of your company** *(formal)* jmd. gibt sich *(Dat.)* die Ehre, Sie einzuladen; **ask a ~ of sb.** jmdn. um einen Gefallen bitten; **do sb. a ~, do a ~ for sb.** jmdm. einen Gefallen tun; **do me the ~ of shutting up** *(iron.)* tu mir den Gefallen und halt den Mund; **as a ~:** aus Gefälligkeit; **as a ~ to sb.** jmdm. zuliebe; **get special ~s** besondere Vergünstigungen genießen; **c)** *(aid, support)* **be in ~ of sth.** für etw. sein; **in ~ of** zugunsten (+ *Gen.*); **all those in ~:** alle, die dafür sind; **in sb.'s ~:** zu jmds. Gunsten; **the exchange rate is in our ~:** der Wechselkurs steht *od.* ist günstig für uns; **d)** *(partiality)* Begünstigung, *die;* **show ~ to[wards] sb.** jmdn. begünstigen; **e)** *(ornament, badge)* Andenken, *das; (ribbon, cockade)* Schleife, *die;* Kokarde, *die; (party-badge)* Abzeichen, *das;* Plakette, *die. See also* **fear 1 a. 2.** *v. t.* **a)** *(approve)* für gut halten, gutheißen ‹*Plan, Idee, Vorschlag*›; *(think preferable)* bevorzugen; **I ~ the first proposal** ich bin für den ersten Vorschlag; **b) ~ sb.** *(treat sb. kindly)* jmdm. günstig gesinnt sein; jmdm. wohlwollen; *(encourage or sponsor sb.)* jmdn. unterstützen; jmdn. fördern; **c)** *(oblige)* beehren **(with** mit) *(geh.);* **~ sb. with a smile/glance/an interview** jmdm. ein Lächeln/einen Blick schenken/ein Interview gewähren *(geh.);* **he ~ed me with a visit** *(iron.)* er beglückte mich mit einem Besuch; **d)** *(treat with partiality)* bevorzugen; **e)** *(aid, support)* helfen (+ *Dat.*); **f)** *(confirm)* bekräftigen, bestätigen ‹*Ansicht, Meinung, Theorie*›; **g)** *(prove advantageous to)* begünstigen; **the weather ~ed our journey** das Wetter trug zum Gelingen unserer Reise [wesentlich] bei

favourable ['feɪvərəbl] *adj.* *(Brit.)* **a)** günstig ‹*Eindruck, Licht*›; gewogen ‹*Haltung, Einstellung*›; wohlmeinend ‹*Blick, Urteil*›; **~ attitude towards sth.** positive Einstellung einer Sache gegenüber; **be ~ to[wards] sth.** einer Sache *(Dat.)* positiv gegenüberstehen; **b)** *(praising)* freundlich ‹*Erwähnung, Empfehlung*›; positiv, günstig ‹*Bericht[erstattung], Bemerkung*›; **c)** *(promising)* vielversprechend; gut ‹*Omen, Zeichen*›; **d)** *(helpful)* günstig **(to** für) ‹*Wetter, Wind, Umstand*›; **be ~ for doing sth.** günstig sein, um etw. zu tun; **e)** *(giving consent)* zustimmend; **give sb. a ~ answer** jmdm. eine Zusage geben

favourably ['feɪvərəblɪ] *adv.* *(Brit.)* **a)** wohlwollend ‹*ansehen, anhören, denken, urteilen*›; günstig ‹*stimmen*›; **be ~ impressed with sb./sb.'s ideas** von jmdm./jmds. Ideen sehr angetan sein; **be ~ disposed towards sb./sth.** jmdm./einer Sache positiv gegenüberstehen; **b)** *(in praising manner)* lobend ‹*erwähnen*›; positiv ‹*vermerken*›; **c)** *(promisingly)* vielversprechend; **d)** *(helpfully)* günstig; **e)** *(with consent)* **answer ~:** eine positive Antwort geben

favoured ['feɪvəd] *adj.* *(Brit.)* *(privileged)* bevorzugt; *(well-liked)* Lieblings‹*platz, -buch, -gericht*›; **the ~ few** die kleine Gruppe der Auserwählten *(iron.);* **most-~ nation** meistbegünstigter Staat; **most-~-nation treatment** Meistbegünstigung, *die (Wirtsch.)*

favourite ['feɪvərɪt] *(Brit.)* **1.** *adj.* Lieblings-; **~ son** *(Amer. Polit.)* Favorit, *der;* Spitzenkandidat, *der;* **sb.'s ~ person** jmds. Liebling. **2.** *n.* **a)** *(film/food/country/pupil etc.)* Lieblingsfilm, *der*/-essen, *das*/-land, *das*/-schüler, *der usw.; (person in general)* Liebling, *der;* **this/he is my ~:** das/ihn mag ich am liebsten; **she's a great ~ with the children** sie wird von den Kindern sehr geliebt; **b)** *(Sport)* Favorit, *der*/Favoritin, *die;* **start ~:** als Favorit an den Start gehen; **c)** *(unduly favoured intimate)* Günstling, *der*

favouritism ['feɪvərɪtɪzm] *n., no pl.* *(Brit.)* Begünstigung, *die; (when selecting sb. for a post etc.)* Günstlingswirtschaft, *die*

[1]fawn [fɔːn] **1.** *n.* **a)** *(fallow deer)* [Dam]kitz, *das; (buck)* Bockkitz, *das; (doe)* Geißkitz, *das;* **b)** *(colour)* Rehbraun, *das.* **2.** *adj.* rehfarben; **~ colour** Rehbraun, *das*

[2]fawn *v. i.* **a)** *(show affection)* seine Freude zeigen; ‹*Hund:*› [bellen und] mit dem Schwanz wedeln; **~ [up]on sb.** um jmdn. herumstreichen; **b)** *(cringe)* **~ [on** *or* **upon sb.]** sich [bei jmdm.] einschmeicheln; [vor jmdm.] katzbuckeln *(abwertend)*

'fawn-coloured *adj.* rehfarben

fawning ['fɔːnɪŋ] *adj.* *(showing affection)* schwanzwedelnd [und bellend] ‹*Hund*›; *(cringing)* sich einschmeichelnd; katzbuckelnd *(abwertend)*

fax [fæks] **1.** *n.* Fax, *das;* Fernkopie, *die.* **2.** *v.t.* faxen; fernkopieren

'fax machine *n.* Fernkopierer, *der*

FBI *abbr. (Amer.)* **Federal Bureau of Investigation** FBI, *das*

FC *abbr.* **Football Club** FC, *der*

FCO *abbr. (Brit.)* **Foreign and Commonwealth Office** [Britisches] Außen- und Commonwealthministerium; ≈ AA

fealty ['fi:əltɪ] *n. (Hist.)* Lehnstreue, *die; (fig.)* Treue, *die*

fear [fɪər] **1.** *n.* **a)** Furcht, Angst, *die* (**of** vor + *Dat.*); *(instance)* Befürchtung, *die;* **out of ~:** aus Angst; **~ of death** *or* **dying/heights/open spaces** Todes-/Höhen-/Platzangst, *die;* **~ of flying** Flugangst, *die;* Angst vorm Fliegen *(ugs.);* **~ of doing sth.** Angst *od.* Furcht davor, etw. zu tun; **have a [terrible] ~ of sth./sb.** [furchtbare] Angst vor etw./jmdm. haben; **have a ~** *or* **have ~s of doing sth.** Angst davor haben, etw. zu tun; **in ~:** angstvoll; angsterfüllt; **be in ~:** Angst haben; **in ~ of being caught** in der Angst, gefaßt zu werden; **in ~ and trembling** zitternd und zagend *(geh.);* mit schlotternden Knien *(ugs.);* **for ~ of waking** *or* **[that] we should wake** *or* **lest we [should] wake the others** aus Angst [davor], die anderen zu wecken *od.* daß wir die anderen wecken könnten; **without ~ or favour** völlig unparteiisch *od.* unvoreingenommen; **b)** *(object of ~)* Furcht, *die; in pl.* Befürchtungen *Pl.;* **what are your main ~s?** wovor haben Sie am meisten Angst?; **c)** *(dread and reverence)* [Ehr]furcht, *die* (**of** vor + *Dat.*); **put the ~ of God into sb.** *(fig.)* jmdn. fürchterlich erschrecken; jmdm. gehörig Angst einjagen; **d)** *(anxiety for sb.'s/sth.'s safety)* Sorge, *die* (**for** um); **go** *or* **be in ~ of one's life** Angst um sein Leben haben; in Todesangst sein; **e)** *(coll.: risk)* Gefahr, *die;* **no** *or* **not any ~ of sth./'that happening** keine Gefahr, daß etw./dies geschieht; **there's no ~ of 'that [ever happening]!** *(iron.)* die Gefahr besteht bestimmt nicht! *(iron.);* **no ~!** *(coll.)* keine Bange! *(ugs.).* **2.** *v.t.* **a)** *(be afraid of)* **~ sb./sth.** vor jmdm./etw. Angst haben; sich vor jmdm./etw. fürchten; **~ to do** *or* **doing sth.** Angst haben *od.* sich fürchten, etw. zu tun; **you have nothing to ~:** Sie haben nichts zu befürchten; **~ the worst** das Schlimmste befürchten; **b)** *(be worried about)* befürchten; **~ [that ...]** fürchten[, daß ...]; **it is to be ~ed that ...:** es steht zu befürchten, daß ...; **we need not ~ that/but [that] he will come** wir brauchen uns keine Sorgen zu machen, daß er kommt/nicht kommt. **3.** *v.i.* sich fürchten; **~ for sb./sth.** um jmdn./etw. bangen *(geh.) od.* fürchten; **never ~** *(also joc. iron.)* keine Bange *(ugs.)*

fearful ['fɪəfl] *adj.* **a)** *(terrible)* furchtbar; grauenhaft ‹*Erfahrung, Anblick, Tod, Untier*›; *(coll.: extreme)* fürchterlich; scheußlich ‹*Farbe, Wetter*›; **we had a ~ wait** wir mußten furchtbar lange warten; **b)** *(frightened)* ängstlich; *(apprehensive)* **~ of sth./sb.** erfüllt von Angst vor etw./jmdm.; **be ~ of sth./sb.** vor etw./jmdm. Angst haben; **be ~ of doing sth.** Angst [davor] haben, etw. zu tun; **be ~ [that** *or* **lest] ...:** Angst haben, daß ...

fearfully ['fɪəfəlɪ] *adv.* **a)** *(terribly)* furchtbar; *(coll.: extremely)* fürchterlich; schrecklich; furchtbar ‹*nett, gut, laut, heiß*›; **b)** *(in frightened manner)* ängstlich

fearless ['fɪəlɪs] *adj.* furchtlos; *(through skill)* kühn; **be ~ [of sth./sb.]** keine Angst [vor etw./jmdm.] haben *od.* kennen

fearlessly ['fɪəlɪslɪ] *adv.* furchtlos; ohne Angst

fearsome ['fɪəsəm] *adj.* furchteinflößend; furchterregend; gräßlich ‹*Anblick*›; **he/it is a ~-looking man/weapon** er/die Waffe sieht furchterregend aus

feasibility [fi:zɪ'bɪlɪtɪ] *n., no pl.* **a)** *(practicability)* Durchführbarkeit, *die; (of method)* Tauglichkeit, *die;* Anwendbarkeit, *die; (possibility)* Möglichkeit, *die;* **b)** *(coll.) (manageability)* Machbarkeit, *die; (convenience)* Annehmlichkeit, *die*

feasi'bility study *n.* Tauglichkeitsstudie, *die;* Eignungsstudie, *die*

feasible ['fi:zɪbl] *adj.* **a)** *(practicable)* durchführbar ‹*Plan, Vorschlag*›; anwendbar ‹*Methode*›; erreichbar ‹*Ziel*›; gangbar ‹*Weg, Lösung*›; *(possible)* möglich; **b)** *(coll.) (manageable)* machbar; *(convenient)* möglich

feast [fi:st] **1.** *n.* **a)** *(Relig.)* Fest, *das;* **the ~ of Christmas/Easter/Epiphany** das Weihnachts-/Oster-/Erscheinungsfest; **movable/immovable ~:** beweglicher/unbeweglicher Feiertag; **breakfast is a movable ~ in our family** *(joc.)* wir frühstücken nicht zu festen Zeiten; **b)** *(banquet)* Festessen, *das;* Bankett, *das (geh.); (fig.)* Labsal, *das (geh.);* **a ~ for the eyes/ears** eine Augenweide/ein Ohrenschmaus; *see also* **enough 2. 2.** *v.i.* **a)** schlemmen; schwelgen; **~ on sth.** sich an etw. *(Dat.)* gütlich tun; *(fig.)* sich an etw. *(Dat.)* laben *(geh.);* sich an etw. *(Dat.)* weiden *(geh.);* **b)** *(celebrate with festivities)* Feste/ein Fest begehen; feiern. **3.** *v.t.* festlich bewirten; **he ~ed his eyes on her beauty** seine Augen labten *od.* weideten sich an ihrer Schönheit *(geh.)*

'feast-day *n.* [kirchlicher] Feiertag

feat [fi:t] *n. (action)* Meisterleistung, *die;* Bravourleistung, *die; (thing)* Meisterwerk, *das;* **a ~ of intellect/strength** eine intellektuelle/physische Meisterleistung; **no mean** *or* **small ~:** eine beachtliche Leistung

feather ['feðə(r)] **1.** *n.* **a)** Feder, *die; (on arrow)* [Pfeil]feder, *die; (for hat)* [Hut]feder, *die;* **as light as a ~:** federleicht; herrlich locker ‹*Kuchen*›; **show the white ~** *(fig.)* es mit der Angst [zu tun] kriegen *(ugs.);* kneifen *(ugs.);* **fine ~s make fine birds** *(prov.)* Kleider machen Leute *(Spr.);* **a ~ in sb.'s cap** *(fig. coll.)* ein Grund für jmdn., stolz zu sein; **ruffle sb.'s ~s** jmdn. reizen *od.* aufregen; **you could have knocked me down with a ~:** ich war völlig von den Socken *(ugs.);* **make the ~s fly = make the fur fly** *see* **fur 1 a; b)** *collect. (plumage)* Gefieder, *das;* Federkleid, *das (geh.);* **in high** *or* **full** *or* **fine ~** *(fig.)* in guter Form. *See also* **bird a. 2.** *v.t.* **a)** *(furnish with ~s)* mit Federn versehen; befiedern; **~ one's nest** *(fig.)* auf seinen finanziellen Vorteil bedacht sein; **b)** *(turn edgeways)* aufdrehen ‹*Paddel, Ruder*›. *See also* **'tar 2**

feather: ~ 'bed *n.* mit Federn gefüllte Matratze; **~-bed** *v.t.* [ver]hätscheln; **~ 'boa** *n.* Federboa, *die;* **~-brain** *n.* Schwachkopf, *der (ugs.);* **~-brained** ['feðəbreɪnd] *adj.* schwachköpfig *(ugs.);* **~ 'duster** *n.* Flederwisch, *der*

feathered ['feðəd] *adj.* gefiedert

feather: ~-stitch *n.* Federstich, *der;* **~weight** *n.* **a)** *(very light thing/person)* Fliegengewicht, *das;* **be a ~weight** federleicht sein; **b)** *(Boxing etc.)* Federgewicht, *das; (person also)* Federgewichtler, *der*

feathery ['feðərɪ] *adj.* **a)** *(covered with feathers)* befiedert; gefiedert; **b)** *(adorned with feathers)* federngeschmückt; Feder‹*hut, -schmuck*›; **c)** *(feather-like) (in quality)* federnartig; gefiedert ‹*Blatt*›; *(in weight)* federleicht; locker ‹*Kuchenteig*›

feature ['fi:tʃə(r)] **1.** *n.* **a)** *usu. in pl. (part of face)* Gesichtszug, *der;* **facial ~s** Gesichtszüge; **b)** *(distinctive characteristic)* Charakteristische, *das;* [charakteristisches] Merkmal; Charakteristikum, *das;* **be a ~ of sth.** charakteristisch für etw. sein; **which ~s of city life attract you most?** was zieht dich am Stadtleben besonders an?; **a/one particular ~:** ein besonderes Merkmal; **make a ~ of sth.** etw. [sehr] betonen *od.* herausstellen; **c)** *(Journ. etc.)* Reportage, *die;* Dokumentarbericht, *der;* Feature, *das;* **d)** *(Cinemat.)* **~ [film]** Hauptfilm, *der;* Spielfilm *der;* **e)** *(Radio, Telev.)* **~ [programme]** Feature, *das.* **2.** *v.t. (make attraction of)* vorrangig vorstellen; den Vorrang geben (+ *Dat.*); *(give special prominence to) (in film)* in der Hauptrolle zeigen; *(in show)* als Stargast präsentieren. **3.** *v.i.* **a)** *(be ~)* vorkommen; **b)** *(be [important] participant)* **~ in sth.** eine [bedeutende] Rolle bei etw. spielen; **~ in a film** die Hauptrolle in einem Film spielen

featureless ['fi:tʃəlɪs] *adj.* eintönig; ereignislos ‹*Zeit*›

Feb. *abbr.* **February** Febr.

febrile ['fi:braɪl] *adj.* fiebrig; Fieber‹*schweiß, -schlaf, -zustand*›

February ['februərɪ] *n.* Februar, *der; see also* **August**

feces *(Amer.) see* **faeces**

feckless ['feklɪs] *adj. (feeble)* schwächlich ‹*Person*›; *(futile)* vergeblich ‹*Versuch, Anstrengung*›; nutzlos, vertan ‹*Leben*›; *(inefficient)* untauglich; *(aimless)* ziellos

fecund ['fi:kənd, 'fekənd] *adj. (fertile, fertilizing, lit. or fig.)* fruchtbar

fecundity [fɪ'kʌndɪtɪ] *n., no pl. (fertility, fertilizing power, lit. or fig.)* Fruchtbarkeit, *die*

fed [fed] **1.** *see* **feed 1, 2. 2.** *pred. adj. (sl.)* **be/get ~ up with sb./sth.** jmdn./etw. satt haben *(ugs.);* **you're looking rather ~ up** du siehst aus, als hättest du die Nase voll *(ugs.);* **be/get ~ up with doing sth.** es satt haben, etw. zu tun *(ugs.);* **be/get ~ up to the [back] teeth with sb./sth.** jmdn./etw. zum Kotzen finden *(derb)*

federal ['fedərl] *adj.* **a)** Bundes-; föderativ ‹*System*›; bundesweit ‹*Feiertag*›; bundeseigen ‹*Betrieb*›; **~ district/territory** *etc.* Bundesdistrikt, *der*/-territorium, *das usw.;* **~ legislation/representative** Gesetzgebung/Abgeordneter des Bundes; **b)** *(relating to or favouring the central government)* föderalistisch ‹*Partei usw.*›; **~ supporter/tendency** Anhänger des/Neigung zum Föderalismus; **c) F~** *(Amer. Hist.: of Northern States in Civil War)* der Unionisten *nachgestellt;* **d)** *(having largely independent units)* föderiert

federate ['fedəreɪt] **1.** *v.t.* **a)** *(organize on federal basis)* föderalistisch organisieren; föderalisieren; **b)** *(band together in league)* zu einem Bund zusammenschließen; föderieren. **2.** *v.i.* sich [zu einem Bund] zusammenschließen

federation [fedə'reɪʃn] *n.* **a)** *(federating)* Zusammenschluß, *der;* **b)** *(group of states)* Bündnis, *das;* Föderation, *die; (society)* Bund, *der;* Verband, *der*

fee [fi:] *n.* **a)** Gebühr, *die;* **b)** *(of doctor, lawyer, etc.)* Honorar, *das; (of performer)* Gage, *die;* **what ~ do you charge?** was verlangen Sie als Honorar/Gage?; **c)** *in pl. (of company director etc.)* Bezüge *Pl.;* **d)** *see* **transfer fee; e)** *(entrance money)* Gebühr, *die;* **matriculation/registration ~:** Einschreibe-/Aufnahmegebühr, *die;* **f)** *(administrative charge)* Bearbeitungsgebühr, *die;* **g)** *in pl. (regular payment for instruction)* **school ~s** Schulgeld, *das;* **tuition ~s** *see* **tuition b**

feeble ['fi:bl] *adj.* **a)** *(weak)* schwach; **b)** *(deficient)* schwächlich; *(in resolve, argument, commitment)* halbherzig; **c)** *(lacking energy)* schwach ‹*Leistung, Kampf, Stimme, Applaus*›; wenig überzeugend ‹*Argument, Entschuldigung, Erklärung, Vorstellung*›; zaghaft, kläglich ‹*Versuch, Bemühung*›; kraftlos ‹*Drohung*›; lahm *(ugs.)* ‹*Witz*›; **d)** *(indistinct)* schwach ‹*[Licht]schein, Herzschlag*›

'feeble-minded *adj.* **a)** töricht; **b)** *(Psych.)* geistesschwach; **~ person** Schwachsinnige, *der/die*

feebly ['fi:blɪ] *adv.* **a)** *(weakly)* mühsam ‹*gehen, sich bewegen*›; **b)** *(deficiently)* schwach; kaum ‹*reagieren*›; **c)** *(without* *energy)* schwach ⟨*widerstehen, unterstützen, applaudieren*⟩; zaghaft ⟨*versuchen, ablehnen, widersprechen, behaupten*⟩

feed [fi:d] **1.** *v. t.*, **fed** [fed] **a)** *(give food to)* füttern; ~ **sb./an animal with sth.** jmdm. etw. zu essen/einem Tier [etw.] zu fressen geben; ~ **a baby/an animal/an invalid on** *or* **with sth.** ein Baby/Tier/einen Invaliden mit etw. füttern; **the dog is fed every evening at 6 o'clock** der Hund bekommt jeden Abend um 6 Uhr sein Fressen; ~ **intravenously** intravenös ernähren; ~ **[at the breast]** stillen; **b)** *(provide food for)* ernähren; satt machen; ~ **sb./an animal on** *or* **with sth.** jmdn./ein Tier mit etw. ernähren; **c)** *(put food into mouth of)* füttern; ~ **oneself** allein *od.* ohne Hilfe essen; **can the child** ~ **herself with a spoon yet?** kann das Kind schon mit dem Löffel essen?; **be ~ing one's face** *(coll. derog.)* fressen *(abwertend)*; **d)** *(graze)* weiden lassen; weiden; **e)** *(produce food for)* ~ **sb. [with sth.]** jmdn. [mit etw.] versorgen; **f)** *(nourish)* mit Nährstoffen versorgen; *(fig.)* verstärken; **g)** *see* ~ **up**; **h)** *(give out)* verfüttern ⟨*Viehfutter*⟩; **i)** *(keep supplied)* speisen ⟨*Wasserreservoir*⟩; unterhalten ⟨*Feuer*⟩; am Brennen halten ⟨*Ofen*⟩; *(supply with material)* versorgen; *(supply)* ~ **a film into the projector** einen Film in das Vorführgerät einlegen; ~ **data into the computer** Daten in den Computer eingeben; den Computer mit Daten füttern; ~ **sth. to sb.**, ~ **sb. sth.** *(fig.)* jmdn. mit etw. füttern; ~ **sth. to the flames** etw. den Flammen übergeben; *see also* **'meter 1 b**; **j)** *(lead)* ~ **sth. through sth.** etw. durch etw. hindurchführen; **k)** *(Theatre sl.)* ~ **the actor [with] his cues** *or* **the cues to the actor** dem Schauspieler das Stichwort geben; **l)** *(Football etc.)* zuspielen **(to** *Dat.***)**. *See also* **fed 2. 2.** *v. i.*, **fed** ⟨*Tier:*⟩ fressen **(from** aus); ⟨*Person:*⟩ essen **(off** von); ~ **on sth.** ⟨*Tier:*⟩ etw. fressen, mit etw. gefüttert werden; ⟨*Person:*⟩ sich von etw. [er]nähren, etw. essen, etw. futtern *(ugs.)*; *(fig.)* von etw. leben; ~ **off sth.** sich von etw. ernähren; *(fig.)* von etw. leben. **3.** *n.* **a)** *(instance of eating)* *(of animals)* Fressen, *das;* *(of baby)* Mahlzeit, *die;* **when is the baby's next** ~ **due?** wann muß das Baby wieder gefüttert werden?; **on the** ~ *(feeding)* am *od.* beim Fressen; bei der Nahrungsaufnahme; *(looking out for food)* auf Nahrungssuche; **b)** *(pasture)* Viehfutter, *das;* **out at** ~: auf der Weide; **c)** *(horse's oats etc.)* [Futter]ration, *die;* *(fodder)* **[cattle/sheep/pig]** ~: [Vieh-/Schaf-/Schweine]futter, *das;* **be off its** ~ ⟨*Tier:*⟩ schlecht fressen; **be off one's** ~ ⟨*Person:*⟩ schlecht essen; keinen Appetit haben; **d)** *(coll.)* *(meal)* Mahlzeit, *die;* *(feast)* Mahl, *das;* **have [quite] a** ~: [ordentlich] futtern *(ugs.)*; [kräftig] zulangen; **e)** *(of machine)* Versorgung, *die;* *(of furnace)* Begichtung, *die;* *(supplying of material)* Einspeisung, *die;* **f)** *(material supplied to machine)* Nachschub, *der;* *(amount supplied)* Nachschub, *der;* Nachfüllmenge, *die;* *(into computer)* Einspeisung, *die;* **g)** *(hopper)* Trichter, *der*

~ **'back 1.** *v. t.* **a)** zurückleiten; weiterleiten, -geben ⟨*Informationen*⟩; **be fed back** zurückfließen; **b)** *(Electr.)* rückkoppeln. **2.** *v. i.* ~ **back into sth.** in etw. *(Akk.)* zurückfließen; ~ **back to sth./sb.** an etw./jmdn. weitergeleitet werden. *See also* **feedback**

~ **'up** *v. t.* *(fatten)* mästen; *(fill up with food)* vollstopfen *(ugs.)*; *see also* **fed 2**

'feedback *n.* **a)** *(information about result, response)* Reaktion, *die;* Feedback, *das* *(fachspr.)*; **b)** *(Electr.)* **[positive/negative]** ~: [positive/negative] Rückkopplung; **c)** *(Biol., Psych., etc.)* Reafferenz, *die* *(fachspr.)*; Rückkopplung, *die*

feeding ['fi:dıŋ]: **~-bottle** *n.* [Saug]flasche, *die;* **~-time** *n.* **a)** Fütterungszeit, *die;* **b)** *(fig. joc.)* Essenszeit, *die;* **~-time!** Essen!

feed: ~lot *n.* Weide, *die;* **~-pipe** *n.* Zuleitungsrohr, *das;* Füllrohr, *das;* **~stock** *n.* Einsatz- *od.* Ausgangsmaterial, *das*

feel [fi:l] **1.** *v. t.*, **felt** [felt] **a)** *(explore by touch)* befühlen; ~ **sb.'s pulse** jmdm. den Puls fühlen; *(fig.)* bei jmdm. vorfühlen; jmdm. auf den Zahn fühlen *(ugs.)* **(on, about** hinsichtlich); ~ **one's way** sich *(Dat.)* seinen Weg ertasten; *(fig.: try sth. out)* vorsichtig vorgehen; sich vorsichtig vor[an]tasten; **be ~ing one's way** versuchen, sich zurechtzufinden; ~ **one's way along the corridor/towards the door** sich den Flur entlangtasten/sich zur Tür tasten; **b)** *(perceive by touch)* fühlen; *(become aware of)* bemerken; *(be aware of)* merken; *(have sensation of)* spüren; ~ **sb.'s temperature** fühlen, ob jmd. Fieber hat; **c)** *see* ~ **up**; **d)** *(be conscious of)* empfinden ⟨*Mitleid, Dank, Eifersucht*⟩; verspüren ⟨*Drang, Wunsch*⟩; spüren ⟨*Gefühle anderer*⟩; ~ **the cold/heat** unter der Kälte/Hitze leiden; ~ **one's age** sein Alter spüren; ~ **pride in sb./sth.** stolz auf jmdn./etw. sein; ~ **bitterness/amazement** verbittert/erstaunt sein; ~ **the temptation** sich versucht fühlen; **make itself felt** zu spüren sein; *(have effect)* sich bemerkbar machen; **make one's presence felt** sich bemerkbar machen; **e)** *(experience)* empfinden; *(be affected by)* zu spüren bekommen; **f)** *(be emotionally affected by)* leiden unter (+ *Dat.*); **he felt it terribly when his dog died** er litt ganz furchtbar, als sein Hund starb; **g)** *(have vague or emotional conviction)* ~ **[that] ...:** das Gefühl haben, daß ...; **h)** *(think)* **if that's what you** ~ **about the matter** wenn du so darüber denkst; ~ **it to be one's duty to ...:** es für seine Pflicht halten, zu ...; ~ **oneself hard done by** sich schlecht behandelt fühlen; ~ **[that] ...:** glauben, daß ...; **if you** ~ **[that] you would like to know more** wenn Sie gern mehr wissen möchten. *See also* **bone 1 a**; **draught a. 2.** *v. i.*, **felt a)** *(search with hand etc.)* ~ **[about] in sth. [for sth.]** in etw. *(Dat.)* [nach etw.] [herum]suchen; ~ **[about] in one's bag/pocket [to see whether ...]** in seiner Tasche [herum]kramen[, um festzustellen, ob ...] *(ugs.)*; ~ **[about] [after** *or* **for sth.] with sth.** mit etw. [nach etw.] [umher]tasten; **b)** *(have sense of touch)* fühlen; **c)** *(be conscious that one is)* sich ... fühlen; ~ **angry/enthusiastic/sure/delighted/disappointed** böse/begeistert/sicher/froh/enttäuscht sein; **she felt quite sick/horrified at the idea** der Gedanke machte sie ganz krank/widerte sie an; **I felt such a fool** ich kam mir wie ein Idiot vor; ~ **[the] better for sth.** *(in mind)* sich erleichtert fühlen; *(in body)* sich besser fühlen; ~ **inclined to do sth.** dazu neigen, etw. zu tun; ~ **committed to sth.** sich einer Sache *(Dat.)* verschrieben haben; **the child did not** ~ **loved/wanted/needed** das Kind hatte das Gefühl, ungeliebt/unerwünscht/überflüssig zu sein; **I** ~ **dubious about doing that** ich weiß nicht recht, ob ich das machen soll; ~ **quite hopeful** guter Hoffnung sein; **I felt sorry for him** er tat mir leid; ~ **hard done by** sich schlecht behandelt fühlen; ~ **like sth.** sich *(Dat.)* vorkommen wie etw.; **he makes you** ~ **like a fool/lady** bei ihm kommt man sich *(Dat.)* wie ein Idiot vor/er gibt einem das Gefühl, eine Dame zu sein; ~ **like a new man/woman** sich wie neugeboren fühlen; **what do you** ~ **like** *or* **how do you** ~ **today?** wie fühlst du dich *od.* wie geht es dir heute?; **what would you** ~ **like** *or* **how would you** ~ **if someone said such a thing to you?** was würdest du empfinden *od.* denken, wenn jemand so etwas zu dir sagte?; **let's see what we** ~ **like** *or* **how we** ~ **when ...:** warten wir ab, in welcher Verfassung wir sind *od.* *(what we should like to do)* wie uns der Sinn steht, wenn ...; ~ **like sth./doing sth.** *(coll.: wish to have/do)* auf etw. *(Akk.)* Lust haben/Lust haben, etw. zu tun; **do you** ~ **like a cup of tea?** möchtest du eine Tasse Tee?; **I** ~ **like a new hairdo** ich könnte eine neue Frisur gebrauchen; **we** ~ **as if** *or* **as though ...:** es kommt uns vor, als ob ...; *(have the impression that)* wir haben das Gefühl, daß ...; **how do you** ~ **about him now/the idea?** was empfindest du jetzt für ihn/was hältst du von der Idee?; **if that's how** *or* **the way you** ~ **about it** wenn du so darüber denkst; **she just didn't** ~ **that way about him** sie hatte nun einmal nicht solche Gefühle für ihn; ~ **the same [way] about each other** für einander das gleiche empfinden; ~ **[quite] one'self** sich wohl fühlen; **d)** *(be emotionally affected)* ~ **passionately/bitterly about sth.** sich für etw. begeistern/über etw. *(Akk.)* verbittert sein; ~ **kindly towards sb.** jmdm. wohlgesonnen sein; **e)** *(be consciously perceived as)* sich ... anfühlen; ~ **like sth.** sich wie etw. anfühlen; **it ~s funny/strange/nice/uncomfortable** es ist ein komisches / seltsames / angenehmes / unangenehmes Gefühl; **it ~s so good to be away from the hustle** es tut gut, der Hetze entronnen zu sein; **it all ~s so strange here** es kommt einem hier alles so seltsam vor. *See also* **cheap 1 c. 3.** *n.* **a)** *(sense of touch)* [Be]tasten, *das;* **be dry/soft** *etc.* **to the** ~: sich trocken/weich *usw.* anfühlen; **b)** *(act of feeling)* Abtasten, *das;* **c)** *(sensation when touched)* Gefühl, *das;* **d)** *(sensation characterizing a situation, place, etc.)* Atmosphäre, *die;* **there is a mysterious/ghostly** ~ **about the place** der Ort hat etwas Mysteriöses/Gespenstisches [an sich]; **get a [real]/the** ~ **of sth.** ein [wirkliches] Gespür für etw. bekommen; **get the** ~ **of things in a firm/of a new job** sich in einer Firma zurechtfinden/sich in eine neue Arbeit hineinfinden; **have a** ~ **for sth.** *(fig.)* ein Gespür *od.* einen Blick für etw. haben; *(talent)* eine Ader für etw. haben

~ **for** *v. t.* ~ **for sb.** mit jmdm. Mitleid haben

~ **'out** *v. t.* **a)** *(sound out)* ~ **sb. out** jmds. Ansichten feststellen; **b)** *(test practicability of)* zur Diskussion stellen; austesten

~ **'up** *v. t.* *(sl.)* befummeln *(salopp)*

~ **with** *v. t.* Mitgefühl haben mit; mitfühlen; **I** ~ **with you** Sie haben mein Mitgefühl

feeler ['fi:lə(r)] *n.* Fühler, *der;* **put out ~s** *(fig.)* seine Fühler ausstrecken

feeling ['fi:lıŋ] **1.** *n.* **a)** *(sense of touch)* **[sense of]** ~: Tastsinn, *der;* **have no** ~ **in one's legs** kein Gefühl in den Beinen haben; **b)** *(physical sensation)* Gefühl, *das;* **you'll have a painful** ~: es wird weh tun; **c)** *(emotion)* Gefühl, *das;* **what are your ~s for each other?** was empfindet ihr füreinander?; **say sth. with** ~: etw. mit Nachdruck sagen; **~s were running high** Emotionen wurden geweckt; **there were strong ~s about it** es gab sehr entschiedene Ansichten darüber; **bad** ~ *(jealousy)* Neid, *der;* *(annoyance)* Verstimmung, *die;* **d)** *in pl.* *(sensibilities)* Gefühle; **hurt sb.'s ~s** jmdn. verletzen; **e)** *(sympathy)* Mitgefühl, *das;* Einfühlungsvermögen, *das;* **f)** *(consciousness)* **a** ~ **of hopelessness/harmony** *etc.* ein Gefühl der Hoffnungslosigkeit/Harmonie *usw.;* **there was a** ~ **of mystery/peace about the place** der Ort hatte etwas Mysteriöses/Friedvolles [an sich *(Dat.)*] *od.* mutete mysteriös/friedvoll an; **I have a funny** ~ **that ...:** ich habe das komische Gefühl, daß ... *(ugs.)*; **g)** *(belief)* Gefühl, *das;* **have a/the** ~ **[that] ...:** das Gefühl haben, daß ...; **h)** *(sentiment)* Ansicht, *die;* **air one's ~s** seinem Herzen Luft machen; seine Ansicht äußern; **the general** ~ **was that ...:** man war allgemein der Ansicht, daß ...; *see also* **mixed a**; **i)** *(general emotional effect)* Eindruck, *der.* **2.** *adj.* **a)** *(sensitive)* empfindlich; **b)** *(sympathetic)* einfühlsam; **be** ~ **about other people** sich in andere Leute einfühlen können; **c)** *(showing emotion)* gefühlvoll

feelingly ['fi:lɪŋlɪ] *adv.* **a)** *(sympathetically)* mitfühlend ⟨*reagieren*⟩; **b)** *(in manner showing emotion)* gefühlvoll; **say sth. ~:** etw. mit Nachdruck sagen

feet *pl. of* **foot**

feign [feɪn] *v. t.* vorspiegeln; vortäuschen; **~ ignorance** sich dumm stellen; **~ that one is ...:** vorgeben, ... zu sein; **~ to do sth.** vorgeben, etw. zu tun

[1]**feint** [feɪnt] **1.** *n.* **a)** *(Boxing, Fencing)* Finte, *die;* **make a ~:** eine Finte ausführen; fintieren; **b)** *(Mil.)* Scheinangriff, *der;* **make a ~ [at** *or* **of attacking sb./sth.]** einen Scheinangriff [auf jmdn./etw.] ausführen. **2.** *v. i.* **a)** *(Boxing, Fencing)* **~ at sb./sth.** eine Finte gegen jmdn./etw. ausführen; **b)** *(Mil.)* **~ at** *or* **[up]on sb./sth.** einen Scheinangriff auf jmdn./etw. durchführen

[2]**feint** *adj. (Commerc.)* **~ lines** feine Linierung; **ruled ~:** fein liniert

feldspar ['feldspɑ:(r)] *see* **felspar**

felicitate [fɪ'lɪsɪteɪt] *v. t. (literary)* **~ sb. [on sth.]** jmdn. [zu etw.] beglückwünschen

felicitation [fɪlɪsɪ'teɪʃn] *n.* Glückwunsch, *der;* Gratulation, *die;* **give sb. one's ~s on sth.** jmdn. zu etw. beglückwünschen; jmdm. zu etw. gratulieren

felicitous [fɪ'lɪsɪtəs] *adj.* glücklich ⟨*Zufall, Nachricht, Umstand, Wahl*⟩; nett ⟨*Bemerkung, Art*⟩; gelungen ⟨*Formulierung, Kommentar, Anspielung*⟩; geeignet, passend ⟨*Worte*⟩

felicitously [fɪ'lɪsɪtəslɪ] *adv.* glücklich

felicity [fɪ'lɪsɪtɪ] *n.* **a)** *no pl. (happiness)* Glück, *das;* **b)** *(thing or person causing happiness)* Glück, *das;* **c)** *(fortunate trait)* glückliche Gabe; **d)** *(in choice of words)* Formulierungskunst, *die;* **~ of expression** glückliche Wahl des Ausdrucks

feline ['fi:laɪn] **1.** *adj. (of cat[s])* Katzen-; *(catlike)* katzenartig; katzenhaft. **2.** *n.* Katze, *die;* **the ~s** die Katzen *od. (fachspr.)* Feliden

[1]**fell** *see* **fall 2**

[2]**fell** [fel] *v. t.* **a)** *(cut down)* fällen ⟨*Baum*⟩; **b)** *(strike down)* niederstrecken ⟨*Gegner*⟩

[3]**fell** *n. (Brit.)* **a)** *(in names: hill)* Berg, *der;* **b)** *(stretch of high moorland)* Hochmoor, *das*

[4]**fell** *adj.* **a) at** *or* **in one ~ swoop** auf einen Schlag; **b)** *(poet./rhet.) (fierce)* wild; grimmig ⟨*Drohung, Feind*⟩; *(destructive)* vernichtend

fellatio [fə'lɑ:tɪəʊ] *n.* Fellatio, *die*

fellow ['feləʊ] **1.** *n.* **a)** *usu. in pl. (comrade)* Kamerad, *der;* **~s at school/work** Schulkameraden/Arbeitskollegen; **a good ~:** ein guter Kumpel *(ugs.);* **b)** *usu. in pl. (equal)* Gleichgestellte, *der/die;* **be among one's ~s** unter seinesgleichen sein; **c)** *(contemporary)* Zeitgenosse, *der*/-genossin, *die;* **d)** *(counterpart)* Gegenstück, *das;* **e)** *(Brit. Univ.)* Fellow, *der; (elected graduate)* graduierter Stipendiat/graduierte Stipendiatin; *(member of governing body)* Mitglied des Verwaltungsrats; **f)** *(member of academy or society)* Fellow, *der;* Mitglied, *das;* **g)** *(coll.: man, boy)* Bursche, *der (ugs.);* Kerl, *der (ugs.); (boy-friend)* Freund, *der;* **the ~s** die Jungs *(ugs.);* **well, young ~:** nun, junger Mann; **old** *or* **dear ~:** alter Junge *od.* Knabe *(ugs.);* **a ~** *(anyone)* ein Mann; **young ~-my-lad** junger Mann; **I'm not the sort of ~ who ...:** ich bin nicht der Typ, der ...; **a devil of a ~:** ein Teufelskerl; **the other ~** *(fig.)* der andere; **h)** *(derog.: despised person)* Kerl, *der (abwertend). See also* [2]**hail 4; stout 1 c. 2.** *attrib. adj.* Mit-; **~ lodger/worker** Mitbewohner/Kollege, *der*/Mitbewohnerin/Kollegin, *die;* **~ man** *or* **human being** Mitmensch, *der;* **~ sufferer** Leidensgenosse, *der*/-genossin, *die;* **my ~ teachers/workers** *etc.* meine Lehrer-/Arbeitskollegen *usw.;* **~ member of the party** Parteigenosse, *der*/-genossin, *die;* **~ member of the club** Klubkamerad, *der*/-kameradin, *die;* **~ student** Kommilitone, *der*/Kommilitonin, *die*

fellow: ~ 'countryman *see* **countryman a; ~-'feeling** *n.* **a)** *(sympathy)* Mitgefühl, *das;* **have a ~-feeling for sb.** mit jmdm. fühlen; **b)** *(mutual understanding)* Zusammengehörigkeitsgefühl, *das*

fellowship ['feləʊʃɪp] *n.* **a)** *no pl. (companionship)* Gesellschaft, *die;* **in a spirit of good ~:** von Gemeinschaftsgeist erfüllt; **b)** *no pl. (community of interest)* Zusammengehörigkeit, *die;* **c)** *(association)* Verbundenheit, *die;* **d)** *(brotherhood)* [Glaubens]gemeinschaft, *die;* **e)** *(Univ. etc.)* Status eines Fellows; Fellowship, *die*

fellow-'traveller *n.* **a)** *(who travels with another)* Mitreisende, *der/die;* **b)** *(with Communist sympathies)* Sympathisant, *der*/Sympathisantin, *die*

felonious [fə'ləʊnɪəs] *adj.* verbrecherisch

felony ['felənɪ] *n.* Kapitalverbrechen, *das*

felspar ['felspɑ:(r)] *n. (Min.)* Feldspat, *der*

[1]**felt** [felt] *n. (cloth)* Filz, *der;* **~ hat/slippers/mat** Filzhut, *der*/-pantoffeln *Pl.* /-matte, *die*

[2]**felt** *see* **feel 1, 2**

felt[-tipped] 'pen *n.* Filzstift, *der*

female ['fi:meɪl] **1.** *adj.* **a)** weiblich; Frauen⟨*stimme, -station, -chor, -verein*⟩; **~ animal/bird/fish/insect** Weibchen, *das;* **~ child/doctor** Mädchen, *das*/Ärztin, *die;* **~ elephant/whale** [Elefanten-/Wal]kuh, *die;* **a ~ engineer/student/slave** eine Ingenieurin/Studentin/Sklavin; **~ impersonator** Frauendarsteller, *der;* **b) ~ screw/thread** [Schrauben]mutter, *die*/Innengewinde, *das.* **2.** *n.* **a)** *(person)* Frau, *die; (foetus, child)* Mädchen, *das; (animal)* Weibchen, *das;* **b)** *(derog.: woman)* Weib[sbild], *das (ugs. abwertend)*

feminine ['femɪnɪn] **1.** *adj.* **a)** *(of women)* weiblich; Frauen⟨*angelegenheit, -problem, -leiden*⟩; Damen⟨*mode*⟩; *(womanly)* fraulich; feminin; feminin, *(abwertend)* weibisch ⟨*Mann*⟩; **she is so very ~ [in her ways]** sie gibt sich so betont fraulich; **b)** *(Ling.)* weiblich; feminin *(fachspr.).* **2.** *n. (Ling.)* Femininum, *das*

feminine 'rhyme *n. (Pros.)* weiblicher Reim

femininity [femɪ'nɪnɪtɪ] *n., no pl.* Weiblichkeit, *die; (more mature)* Fraulichkeit, *die*

feminism ['femɪnɪzm] *n., no pl.* Feminismus, *der*

feminist ['femɪnɪst] **1.** *n.* Feministin, *die*/Feminist, *der;* Frauenrechtlerin, *die*/-rechtler, *der.* **2.** *adj.* feministisch; Feministen⟨*bewegung, -blatt, -gruppe*⟩

femme fatale [fæm fæ'tɑl] *n.* Femme fatale, *die (geh.)*

femoral ['femərl] *adj. (Anat.)* femoral *(fachspr.);* Oberschenkel[knochen]-

femur ['fi:mə(r)] *n., pl.* **~s** *or* **femora** ['femərə] **a)** *(Anat.)* Oberschenkelknochen, *der;* Femur, *der (fachspr.);* **b)** *(Zool.)* Femur, *der*

fen [fen] *n.* Sumpfland, *das;* Fenn, *das;* Fehn, *das (nordd.);* **the Fens** die Fens

fence [fens] **1.** *n.* **a)** Zaun, *der;* **sunk ~:** Sicherungsgraben, *der;* **mend one's ~s** *(fig.)* das Kriegsbeil begraben *(ugs.);* **sit on the ~** *(fig.)* sich nicht einmischen; sich neutral verhalten; **b)** *(for horses to jump)* Hindernis, *das;* **c)** *(sl.: receiver)* Hehler, *der*/Hehlerin, *die.* **2.** *v. i. (Sport)* fechten. **3.** *v. t. (surround with fence)* einzäunen; *(surround)* umgeben; *(fig.)* absichern **(with** durch)

~ 'in *v. t.* einzäunen; *(fig.)* einengen **(with** durch)

~ 'off *v. t.* abzäunen; *(fig.)* absperren

fencer ['fensə(r)] *n.* Fechter, *der*/Fechterin, *die*

fencing ['fensɪŋ] *n., no pl.* **a)** Einzäunen, *das;* **b)** *(Sport/Hist.)* Fechten, *das; attrib.* Fecht-; **c)** *(enclosure)* Zaun, *der;* Einzäunung, *die;* **d)** *(fences)* Zäune *Pl.;* Umfriedung, *die (geh.);* **e)** *(material for fences)* Zaun, *der*

fend [fend] *v. i.* **~ for sb.** für jmdn. sorgen; **~ for oneself** für sich selbst sorgen; *(in hostile surroundings)* sich allein durchschlagen

~ 'off *v. t.* abwehren; von sich fernhalten; **~ off these criticisms/the flies/fans** sich gegen diese Kritik wehren/sich *(Dat.)* die Fliegen/Fans vom Leib halten

fender ['fendə(r)] *n.* **a)** Schutz, *der, o. Pl.;* Schutzvorrichtung, *die;* **b)** *(for fire)* Kaminschutz, *der;* **c)** *(for dock-wall etc.)* Fender, *der;* Dalbe, *die (Seemannsspr.);* **d)** *(on ship)* Fender, *der;* **e)** *(Brit.: car bumper)* Stoßstange, *die;* **f)** *(Amer.) (train bumper)* Rammbohle, *die; (car mudguard or wing)* Kotflügel, *der; (bicycle mudguard)* Schutzblech, *das*

fenland ['fenlənd] *n.* Marschland, *das*

fennel ['fenl] *n. (Bot.)* Fenchel, *der*

fenugreek ['fenjʊgri:k] *n. (Bot.)* Griechisch-Heu, *das;* Bockshornklee, *der*

feral ['fɪərl, 'ferl] *adj.* **a)** *(wild)* wild; wildwachsend ⟨*Pflanze*⟩; **b)** *(after escape)* verwildert; **become ~:** verwildern

ferment 1. [fə'ment] *v. i.* **a)** *(undergo fermentation)* gären; **cause to ~:** in *od.* zur Gärung bringen; **begin to ~:** in Gärung übergehen; **b)** *(be in state of agitation)* gären; ⟨*Plan, Idee:*⟩ reifen; ⟨*Wut, Frustration:*⟩ rumoren, brodeln. **2.** *v. t.* **a)** *(subject to fermentation)* zur Gärung bringen; **b)** *(excite)* heraufbeschwören ⟨*Gewalt, Unzufriedenheit, Unruhe*⟩. **3.** ['fɜ:ment] *n.* **a)** *(fermenting agent)* Enzym, *das;* **b)** *(fermentation)* Gärung, *die;* Fermentation, *die (fachspr.);* **c)** *(agitation)* Unruhe, *die;* Aufruhr, *der;* **in [a] ~:** in Unruhe *od.* Aufruhr

fermentation [fɜ:men'teɪʃn] *n.* **a)** Gärung, *die;* Fermentation, *die (fachspr.);* **be under** *or* **undergo ~:** gären; sich in Gärung befinden; **b)** *(agitation) (political)* Unruhe, *die; (of ideas)* Reifen, *das*

fern [fɜ:n] *n.* Farnkraut, *das; collect.* Farn, *der*

ferocious [fə'rəʊʃəs] *adj.* wild ⟨*Tier, Person, Aussehen, Blick, Lachen*⟩; grimmig ⟨*Stimme*⟩; heftig ⟨*Schlag, Kampf, Stoß*⟩; *(fig.)* scharf ⟨*Kritik, Angriff*⟩; heftig ⟨*Bemerkung, Äußerung, Streit, Auseinandersetzung*⟩; **~-looking** furchterregend

ferociously [fə'rəʊʃəslɪ] *adv.* wütend ⟨*bellen, knurren*⟩; grimmig ⟨*blicken, lachen, sagen*⟩; heftig ⟨*kämpfen, streiten*⟩; *(fig.)* scharf, heftig ⟨*angreifen, kritisieren*⟩

ferociousness [fə'rəʊʃəsnɪs], **ferocity** [fə'rɒsɪtɪ] *ns., no pl. see* **ferocious:** Wildheit, *die;* Grimmigkeit, *die;* Heftigkeit, *die;* Schärfe, *die*

ferrel ['ferl] *see* **ferrule**

ferret ['ferɪt] **1.** *n.* Frettchen, *das.* **2.** *v. i.* **~ [about** *or* **around]** herumstöbern *(ugs.);* herumschnüffeln *(abwertend);* **~ for sth.** nach etw. stöbern *(ugs.) od. (abwertend)* schnüffeln

~ 'out *v. t.* aufspüren; aufstöbern *(ugs.)*

Ferris wheel ['ferɪs wi:l] *n.* Riesenrad, *das*

ferro- [ferəʊ] *in comb.* Ferro-

ferro'concrete *n.* Stahlbeton, *der*

ferrous ['ferəs] *adj. (containing iron)* eisenhaltig; Eisen-

ferrule ['feru:l, 'ferl] *n.* Zwinge, *die*

ferry ['ferɪ] **1.** *n.* **a)** Fähre, *die;* **b)** *(service)* Fährverbindung, *die;* Fähre, *die (ugs.).* **2.** *v. t.* **a)** *(convey in boat)* **~ [across** *or* **over]** übersetzen; **b)** *(transport)* befördern, bringen ⟨*Güter, Personen*⟩; **~ the children back and forth to school** die Kinder zur Schule und wieder nach Hause fahren

ferry: ~-boat *n.* Fährboot, *das; (punt)* Stakfähre, *die;* Kahnfähre, *die;* **~man** ['ferɪmən] *n., pl.* **~men** ['ferɪmən] Fährmann, *der;* **~ service** *n.* **a)** Fährverbindung, *die;* **b)** *(business)* Fährbetrieb, *der*

fertile ['fɜ:taɪl] *adj.* **a)** *(fruitful)* fruchtbar **(in** an + *Dat.*); *(fig.)* produktiv; schöpferisch; **have a ~ imagination** viel Phantasie haben;

b) *(capable of developing)* befruchtet; c) *(able to become parent)* fortpflanzungsfähig
fertilisation, fertilise, fertiliser *see* **fertiliz-**
fertility [fɜːˈtɪlɪtɪ] *n., no pl.* a) Fruchtbarkeit, *die (auch fig.);* Fertilität, *die;* b) *(ability to become parent)* Fortpflanzungsfähigkeit, *die*
fertility: ~ drug *n. (Med.)* Hormonpräparat, *das (zur Steigerung der Fruchtbarkeit);* **~ symbol** *n. (Anthrop.)* Fruchtbarkeitssymbol, *das*
fertilization [fɜːtɪlaɪˈzeɪʃn] *n.* a) *(Biol.)* Befruchtung, *die;* b) *(Agric.)* Düngung, *die*
fertilize [ˈfɜːtɪlaɪz] *v. t.* a) *(Biol.)* befruchten; b) *(Agric.)* düngen
fertilizer [ˈfɜːtɪlaɪzə(r)] *n.* Dünger, *der*
fervency [ˈfɜːvənsɪ] *n., no pl. see* **fervent:** Leidenschaftlichkeit, *die;* Inbrunst, *die;* Glut, *die*
fervent [ˈfɜːvənt] *adj.* leidenschaftlich; inbrünstig ‹*Gebet, Wunsch, Hoffnung*›; glühend ‹*Leidenschaft, Verehrer, Liebe, Haß*›
fervently [ˈfɜːvəntlɪ] *adv. see* **fervent:** leidenschaftlich; inbrünstig; glühend
fervour (*Brit.; Amer.:* **fervor**) [ˈfɜːvə(r)] *n. (of discussion, feeling, person, campaign)* Leidenschaftlichkeit, *die; (of love, belief)* Inbrunst, *die; (of passion)* Glut, *die*
fess[e] [fes] *n. (Her.)* Balken, *der*
fest [fest] *n. (Amer.)* Fest, *das*
fester [ˈfestə(r)] *v. i.* a) *(lit. or fig.)* eitern; schwären *(geh.);* b) *(putrefy)* verfaulen
festival [ˈfestɪvl] 1. *n.* a) *(feast day)* Fest, *das;* **the ~ of Christmas/Easter** das Weihnachts-/Osterfest; b) *(special performance)* Festival, *das;* Festspiele *Pl.;* **the Bayreuth F~:** die Bayreuther Festspiele; **the Edinburgh F~:** das Edinburgh-Festival. 2. *attrib. adj.* Fest-
festive [ˈfestɪv] *adj.* a) *(joyous)* festlich; fröhlich; b) *(of a feast)* Fest-; **the ~ season** die Weihnachtszeit; c) *(convivial)* gesellig
festivity [feˈstɪvɪtɪ] *n.* a) *no pl. (gaiety)* Feststimmung, *die;* b) *(festive celebration)* Feier, *die;* **festivities** Feierlichkeiten *Pl.*
festoon [feˈstuːn] 1. *n.* a) *(chain of flowers)* Girlande, *die;* b) *(carved ornament)* Feston, *das.* 2. *v. t.* schmücken (**with** mit)
fetal *(Amer.) see* **foetal**
fetch [fetʃ] 1. *v. t.* a) holen; *(collect)* abholen (**from** von); **~ sb. sth., ~ sth. for sb.** jmdm. etw. holen; b) *(be sold for)* erzielen ‹*Preis*›; **my car ~ed £500** ich habe für den Wagen 500 Pfund bekommen; c) **~ a sigh** aufseufzen; **~ a deep breath** tief Atem *od.* Luft holen; **just give me time to ~ my breath** laß mich erst mal wieder zu Atem kommen; d) *(deal)* **~ sb. a blow/punch** jmdm. einen Schlag versetzen; e) *(draw forth)* erregen ‹*Bewunderung, Ärger*›; entlocken ‹*Tränen, Lachen*› (**from** + *Dat.*). 2. *v. i.* **~ and carry [for sb.]** [bei jmdm.] Mädchen für alles sein *(ugs.);* **he is always there to ~ and carry for her** *(does every little thing)* er bedient sie vorn und hinten *(ugs.)*
~ ˈup *(coll.)* 1. *v. t.* erbrechen; wieder von sich geben; *(fig.)* speien. 2. *v. i.* landen *(ugs.)*
fetching [ˈfetʃɪŋ] *adj.* einnehmend, gewinnend ‹*Lächeln, Stimme, Wesen, Benehmen*›; schick ‹*Kleidung*›; **that suit looks very ~ on you** das Kostüm steht dir ausgezeichnet
fetchingly [ˈfetʃɪŋlɪ] *adv.* einnehmend ‹*lächeln, sich benehmen*›; ausgesprochen ‹*hübsch*›; schick, geschmackvoll ‹*gekleidet, eingerichtet*›
fête [feɪt] 1. *n.* a) [Wohltätigkeits]basar, *der;* b) *(festival)* Fest, *das;* Feier, *die.* 2. *v. t.* feiern
fetid [ˈfetɪd] *adj.* stinkend; übelriechend; **~ smell/odour/stench** Gestank, *der*
fetish [ˈfetɪʃ] *n.* a) Manie, *die (geh.);* Fetisch, *der (geh.);* Fimmel, *der (ugs.);* **she makes something of a ~ of** *or* **has a ~ about tidiness** Sauberkeit ist bei ihr zur Manie geworden; sie hat einen richtigen Sauberkeitsfimmel *(ugs.);* b) *(inanimate object of worship; also Psych.)* Fetisch, *der*
fetishism [ˈfetɪʃɪzm] *n.* Fetischismus, *der*
fetishist [ˈfetɪʃɪst] *n.* Fetischist, *der/*Fetischistin, *die*
fetlock [ˈfetlɒk] *n.* Köte, *die*
fetter [ˈfetə(r)] 1. *n.* a) *(shackle)* Fußfessel, *die;* b) *usu. in pl. (bond)* Fesseln *Pl.; in pl. (fig.: captivity)* Gefangenschaft, *die;* Fesseln *Pl.;* c) *in pl. (restraint)* Fesseln *Pl..* 2. *v. t.* a) *(bind [as] with ~s)* fesseln; **be ~ed to sth./sb.** *(fig.)* an etw./jmdn. gekettet sein; b) *(impede)* einengen ‹*Freiheit, Rechte, Souveränität, Personen*›; hemmen ‹*Fortschritt, Entwicklung, Wachstum, Entfaltung*›; lähmen ‹*Phantasie*›
fettle [ˈfetl] *n.* **be in good** *or* **fine/poor ~:** sich in guter/schlechter Verfassung befinden; ‹*Sache:*› sich in gutem/schlechtem Zustand befinden
fetus *(Amer.) see* **foetus**
feud [fjuːd] 1. *n.* Zwist, *der;* Zwistigkeiten *Pl.; (Hist./fig.)* Fehde, *die;* **carry on a ~ with sb.** eine Fehde mit jmdm. ausfechten *od.* austragen. 2. *v. i.* **~ [with sb./each other]** [mit jmdm./miteinander] im Streit liegen
feudal [ˈfjuːdl] *adj.* a) *(of [holding of] fief)* Leh[e]ns-; b) *(of or according to feudal system)* Feudal-; feudalistisch; **~ overlord** Feudal- *od.* Lehnsherr, *der;* **~ rights** Lehensherrlichkeit, *die;* **in ~ Britain** im feudalistischen England
feudalism [ˈfjuːdəlɪzm] *n., no pl.* Feudalismus, *der*
ˈfeudal system *n. (Hist.)* Feudalsystem, *das*
fever [ˈfiːvə(r)] *n.* a) *no pl. (Med.: high temperature)* Fieber, *das;* **have a** *or* **suffer from a [high] ~:** [hohes] Fieber haben; **a ~ of 105 °F** 40,5 °C Fieber; b) *(Med.: disease)* Fieberkrankheit, *die;* c) *(nervous excitement)* Erregung, *die;* Aufregung, *die;* **the crowd was in a ~ of excitement** die Menge befand sich in heller Aufregung; **in a ~ of anticipation** im Fieber der Erwartung
fevered [ˈfiːvəd] *adj.* fiebrig ‹*Stirn, Gesicht, Haut usw.*›
fever: ~ heat *n.* a) *(high temperature)* Fieberhitze, *die;* b) *(fig.) see* **fever pitch; ~ hospital** *n.* Seuchenkrankenhaus, *das*
feverish [ˈfiːvərɪʃ] *adj.* a) *(Med.: having symptoms of fever)* fiebrig; Fieber‹*zustand, -schweiß, -traum*›; **be ~:** fiebern; Fieber haben; **spend a ~ night** eine Nacht im Fieber verbringen; b) *(excited)* erregt, aufgeregt ‹*Geschrei, Lachen*›; fiebrig ‹*Erwartung, Nervosität*›; heftig ‹*Andrang*›; fieberhaft ‹*Aufregung, Eifer, Kampf, Eile*›; **make ~ attempts to do sth.** fieberhaft versuchen, etw. zu tun
feverishly [ˈfiːvərɪʃlɪ] *adv.* a) *(Med.)* im Fieber; **toss and turn ~:** sich im Fieber hin und her wälzen; b) *(excitedly)* fieberhaft ‹*kämpfen, gestikulieren*›
ˈfever pitch *n.* Siedepunkt, *der (fig.);* **reach ~:** auf dem Siedepunkt angelangt sein; **at ~:** auf dem Siedepunkt
few [fjuː] 1. *adj.* a) *(not many)* wenige; *abs.* nur wenige; **~ people** [nur] wenige [Leute]; **these ~ marks** die paar Mark; **openings for sociologists are ~:** freie Stellen für Soziologen sind knapp *od.* rar; **trees were ~ in that barren region** es gab nur wenige Bäume in dieser kargen Gegend; **the responsibility of these ~ men** die Verantwortung dieser wenigen; **with very ~ exceptions** mit ganz wenigen Ausnahmen; **very ~ housewives know that** das wissen die wenigsten Hausfrauen; **his ~ belongings** seine paar Habseligkeiten; seine wenige Habe; **how could those ~ people have achieved such a thing?** wie konnten so wenige [Leute] das nur erreicht haben?; **[all] too ~ people** [viel] zu wenig Leute; **~ and far between** rar; **they were ~ in number** sie waren nur sehr wenige *od.* nur ein kleines Häuflein; **these stamps are ~ in number** diese Briefmarken sind selten; **a ~ ...:** wenige ...; **not a ~ ...:** eine ganze Reihe ...; **they made not a ~ criticisms of the idea** sie übten nicht wenig Kritik an der Idee; **[just** *or* **only] a ~ trouble-makers** einige [wenige] Störenfriede; **just a ~ words from you** nur ein paar Worte von dir; b) *(some)* wenige; **he said his ~ words** er sagte nur seine paar Worte; **a ~ ...:** einige *od.* ein paar ...; **a very ~:** nur wenige; **a ~ more ...:** noch einige *od.* ein paar ...; **some ~ [...]** einige wenige [...]; **every ~ minutes** alle paar Minuten; **a good ~ [...]/quite a ~ [...]** *(coll.)* eine ganze Menge [...]/ziemlich viele [...]; **there are a ~ which ...:** es gibt welche *od.* ein paar, die ... 2. *n.* a) *(not many)* wenige; **these are the beliefs of ~:** das glauben nur wenige; **a ~:** wenige; **the ~:** die wenigen; **the wealthy ~:** die wenigen Reichen; **~ of us/them** nur wenige von uns/nur wenige [von ihnen]; **~ of the people** nur wenige [Leute]; **~ of the words meant anything to him** er konnte mit nur wenigen Wörtern etwas anfangen; **they are among** *or* **some of the very ~ who ...:** sie gehören zu den wenigen, die ...; **only a ~ of them/the applicants** nur wenige [von ihnen]/[der] Bewerber; **just a ~ of you/her friends** nur ein paar von euch/ihrer Freunde; **the privilege of [only] a ~:** das Vorrecht von nur wenigen *od.* einiger weniger; **not a ~ of them** eine ganze Reihe von ihnen; **not a ~:** nicht wenige; ziemlich viele; b) *(some)* **the/these/those ~ who** diejenigen, die; **there were a ~ of us who ...:** es gab einige unter uns, die ...; **with a ~ of our friends** mit einigen *od.* ein paar unserer Freunde; **a ~ [more] of these biscuits** [noch] ein paar von diesen Keksen; **a ~ [who]** einige[, die]; **some ~:** einige wenige [Leute]; **some ~ of us/the members** einige wenige von uns/[der] Mitglieder; **a good ~/quite a ~** *(coll.)* eine ganze Menge/ziemlich viele [Leute]; **a good ~ of us/quite a ~ of us** *(coll.)* eine ganze Menge von uns/ziemlich viele von uns; **have had a ~** *(coll.: be drunk)* einen sitzen haben *(salopp). See also* **fewer; fewest**
fewer [ˈfjuːə(r)] 1. *adj.* weniger; **become ~ and ~:** immer weniger werden; **smokers are ~ in number than twenty years ago** es gibt weniger Raucher als vor zwanzig Jahren. 2. *n.* **~ of the apples/of us** weniger Äpfel/von uns
fewest [ˈfjuːɪst] 1. *adj.* **[the] ~ [...]** die wenigsten [...]. 2. *n.* **the ~ [of us/them]** die wenigsten [von uns/ihnen]; **at [the] ~:** mindestens
fey [feɪ] *adj.* a) *(disordered in mind)* versponnen; b) *(clairvoyant)* hellseherisch; *(otherworldly)* entrückt
fez [fez] *n., pl.* **~zes** Fes, *der*
ff *abbr.* **fortissimo** ff
ff. *abbr.* a) **and following pages** ff.; b) **folios** Bl.
fiancé [fɪˈɑ̃seɪ] *n.* Verlobte, *der*
fiancée [fɪˈɑ̃seɪ] *n.* Verlobte, *die*
fiasco [fɪˈæskəʊ] *n., pl.* **~s** Fiasko, *das*
fiat [ˈfiːæt, ˈfiːət] *n.* a) *(authorization)* Genehmigung, *die;* b) *(decree)* Anordnung, *die*
fib [fɪb] 1. *n.* Flunkerei, *die (ugs.);* **tell ~s** flunkern *(ugs.);* schwindeln; **that was a ~:** das war geschwindelt. 2. *v. i.,* **-bb-** schwindeln; flunkern *(ugs.).* 3. *v. t.,* **-bb-: ~ one's way out [of sth.]** sich [aus etw.] herausschwindeln
fibber [ˈfɪbə(r)] *n.* Flunkerer, *der (ugs.);* Schwindler, *der/*Schwindlerin, *die*
fibre (*Brit.; Amer.:* **fiber**) [ˈfaɪbə(r)] *n.* a) Faser, *die;* **with every ~ of his being** *(fig.)* mit jeder Faser seines Herzens; b) *(substance consisting of fibres)* [Faser]gewebe, *das;* c) *(substance that can be felted)* Faserstoff, *der;* d) *(roughage)* Ballaststoffe

Pl.; **e)** *(fibrous structure)* Fasergefüge, *das;* Faserstruktur, *die;* **f)** *(character)* Wesensart, *die; (strength)* Festigkeit, *die; (essence)* Grundstruktur, *die;* **moral ~:** Charakterstärke, *die. See also* **optical fibre**

fibre: ~board *n.* Holzfaserplatte, *die;* **~glass** (*Amer.:* **fiber glass**) *n. (fibrous glass)* Glasfaser, *die; (plastic)* glasfaserverstärkter Kunststoff; **~glass boat** Kunststoffboot, *das;* **~'optics** *n.* Faseroptik, *die*

fibrillation [fɪbrɪ'leɪʃn] *n. (Med.)* Zucken, *das; (esp. of heart-muscle)* Flimmern, *das*

fibrin ['faɪbrɪn] *n. (Med.)* Fibrin, *das*

fibrositis [faɪbrə'saɪtɪs] *n. (Med.)* Rheumatismus der Weichteile; Fibrositis, *die (fachspr.)*

fibrous ['faɪbrəs] *adj.* faserig ‹*Aufbau, Beschaffenheit, Eigenschaft*›; Faser‹*gewebe, -holz, -stoff*›

fibula ['fɪbjʊlə] *n., pl.* **~e** ['fɪbjʊli:] *or* **~s a)** *(Anat.)* Wadenbein, *das;* **b)** *(Hist.: brooch)* Fibel, *die*

fiche [fi:ʃ] *n., pl. same or* **~s** *see* **microfiche**

fickle ['fɪkl] *adj.* unberechenbar, launisch ‹*Glück, Schicksal, Person*›

fiction ['fɪkʃn] *n.* **a)** *(literature)* erzählende Literatur; **b)** *(thing feigned or imagined)* **a ~/~s** eine Erfindung; **be pure ~** *or* **a mere ~:** [eine] reine Erfindung sein; *(conventionally accepted falsehood)* kleine Unaufrichtigkeit. *See also* **fact b; legal fiction**

fictional ['fɪkʃənl] *adj.* belletristisch; fiktional *(fachspr.);* erfunden ‹*Inhalt, Geschichte*›; **~ literature** erzählende Literatur; Belletristik, *die (ohne Lyrik);* **~ characters** fiktive Figuren

fictionalize ['fɪkʃənəlaɪz] *v.t.* als Fiktion darstellen

'fiction-writer *n.* Belletrist, *der*/Belletristin, *die*

fictitious [fɪk'tɪʃəs] *adj.* **a)** *(counterfeit)* fingiert; vorgetäuscht ‹*Ohnmacht, Verletzung*›; Schein‹*schwangerschaft*›; unwahr ‹*Behauptung, Darstellung*›; **b)** *(assumed)* falsch ‹*Name, Identität*›; angenommen ‹*Rolle*›; **c)** *(imaginary)* [frei] erfunden ‹*Person, Figur, Geschichte*›; **d)** *(regarded as what it is called by legal or conventional fiction)* Schein-; fiktiv; **~ character** *or* **person** erfundene *od.* fiktive Person; **~ person** *(legal entity)* juristische Person; **e)** *(of or in novels)* fiktiv

fiddle ['fɪdl] **1.** *n.* **a)** *(Mus.) (coll./derog.)* Fidel, *die; (violin for traditional or folk music)* Geige, *die;* Fidel, *die;* **[as] fit as a ~:** kerngesund; **a face as long as a ~** *(fig.)* ein Gesicht wie drei *od.* sieben Tage Regenwetter *(ugs.);* **play first/second ~** *(fig.)* die erste/zweite Geige spielen *(ugs.);* **play second ~ to sb.** in jmds. Schatten *(Dat.)* stehen; **b)** *(sl.: swindle)* Gaunerei, *die;* **it's some sort of ~:** an der Sache ist was faul *(ugs.);* **it's all a ~:** das ist alles Schiebung *(ugs.);* **get sth. by a ~:** sich *(Dat.)* etw. ergaunern; **be on the ~:** krumme Dinger machen *(ugs.).* **2.** *v. i.* **a)** *(coll.: play the ~)* Geige spielen; **b) ~ about** *(coll.: waste time)* herumtrödeln *(ugs.); (be frivolous)* [herum]schludern *(ugs.);* **~ about with** *or* **away at sth.** *(work on to adjust etc.)* an etw. *(Dat.)* herumfummeln *(ugs.); (tinker with)* an etw. *(Dat.)* herumbasteln *(ugs.);* **~ at sth.** an etw. *(Dat.)* herumspielen *od.* herumfingern; **~ with sth.** *(play with)* mit etw. herumspielen; **c)** *(sl.: deceive)* krumme Dinger drehen *(ugs.);* **he ~d, lied, and cheated** er hat geschoben, gelogen und betrogen. **3.** *v. t. (sl.) (falsify)* frisieren *(ugs.)* ‹*Bücher, Rechnungen*›; *(get by cheating)* [sich *(Dat.)*] ergaunern *(ugs.);* **~ one's way into sth. [by lying/cheating]** sich [mit Lügen/Betrügereien] in etw. *(Akk.)* einschleichen

fiddle-de-dee [fɪdldɪ'di:] **1.** *int.* Schnickschnack. **2.** *n.* Schnickschnack, *der (ugs.)*

fiddle-faddle ['fɪdlfædl] *n.* Unsinn, *der;* Unfug, *der*

fiddler ['fɪdlə(r)] *n.* **a)** *(player)* Geiger, *der*/Geigerin, *die;* **b)** *(sl.: swindler etc.)* Gauner, *der*/Gaunerin, *die (abwertend)*

'fiddler crab *n.* Winkerkrabbe, *die*

'fiddlestick *(coll.)* **1.** *n.* Geigenbogen, *der.* **2.** *int.* **~s** dummes Zeug *(ugs.);* Schnickschnack *(ugs.)*

fiddling ['fɪdlɪŋ] *adj.* **a)** *(petty)* belanglos; **b)** *(coll.) see* **fiddly**

fiddly ['fɪdlɪ] *adj. (coll.)* **a)** *(awkward to do)* knifflig; **b)** *(awkward to use)* umständlich

fidelity [fɪ'delɪtɪ] *n.* **a)** *(faithfulness)* Treue, *die* **(to** zu); **oath of ~:** Treueid, *der;* **breach of ~:** Treubruch, *der;* **b)** *(conformity to truth or fact)* Glaubwürdigkeit, *die;* **c)** *(exact correspondence to the original) (of photograph, imitation)* Naturtreue, *die; (of translation)* [Wort]treue, *die;* **d)** *(Radio, Telev., etc.)* Wiedergabetreue, *die;* [original]getreue Wiedergabe; *(of sound)* Klangtreue, *die; (of picture)* Bildtreue, *die*

fidget ['fɪdʒɪt] **1.** *n.* **a) [be] in a [terrible] ~:** [ganz] zappelig [sein] *(ugs.);* **put sb. in a ~:** jmdn. unruhig machen; **have/get the ~s** zappelig sein/werden *(ugs.);* **give sb. the ~s** jmdn. zappelig *od.* kribbelig machen *(ugs.);* **b)** *(restless mood)* Unrast, *die;* **be [all] in a ~:** [sehr] unruhig sein; **have/get the ~s** ruhelos sein/werden; **c)** *(person)* Zappelphilipp, *der (ugs.).* **2.** *v. i.* **a) ~ [about]** [herum]zappeln *(ugs.);* herumrutschen; **b)** *(be uneasy)* nervös sein; **make sb. ~:** jmdn. unruhig machen

fidgety ['fɪdʒɪtɪ] *adj.* unruhig ‹*Person, Pferd, Stimmung*›; nervös ‹*Bewegungen, Zuckungen*›

fiduciary [fɪ'dju:ʃərɪ] *adj.* **a)** treuhänderisch; **~ money** Giralgeld, *das;* **b)** *(Finance: depending on public confidence or securities)* ungedeckt ‹*Papiergeld*›

fief [fi:f] *n.* **a)** *(feudal benefice)* Lehen, *das;* **b)** *(sphere of control)* Machtbereich, *der*

field [fi:ld] **1.** *n.* **a)** *(cultivated)* Feld, *das;* Acker, *der; (for grazing)* Weide, *die; (meadow)* Wiese, *die;* **wheat/tobacco/poppy ~:** Weizen-/Tabak-/Mohnfeld, *das;* **work in the ~s** auf dem Feld arbeiten; **~s of rye** Roggenfelder; **b)** *(area rich in minerals etc.)* Lagerstätte, *die;* **gas-~:** Gasfeld, *das;* **c)** *(battlefield)* Schlachtfeld, *das; (fig.)* Feld, *das;* **leave sb. a clear** *or* **the ~** *(fig.)* jmdm. das Feld überlassen; **hold the ~:** das Feld beherrschen; **d)** *(scene of campaign)* [Kriegs]schauplatz, *der;* **enter the ~** *(fig.)* eingreifen; auf der Bildfläche erscheinen *(ugs.);* **in the ~:** im Feld; an der Front; *(fig.)* ‹*Vertreter*› im Außendienst; ‹*Student*› in der Praxis; **be sent out into the ~:** [hin]ausgeschickt werden; **keep the ~:** weiterkämpfen; **take the ~:** in den Kampf ziehen (*see also* **f**); **e)** *(battle)* **a hard-fought/hard-won ~:** eine erbitterte Schlacht/ein schwer erkämpfter Sieg; **win/lose the ~:** siegreich sein/die Schlacht verlieren; **f)** *(playing ~)* Sportplatz, *der; (ground marked out for game)* Platz, *der;* [Spiel]feld, *das;* **send sb. off the ~:** jmdn. vom Platz schicken; **take the ~:** das Spielfeld betreten (*see also* **d**); **g)** *(Sport: area for defence or attack)* [Spiel]feld, *das;* **h)** *(competitors in sports event)* Feld, *das; (fig.)* Teilnehmerkreis, *der;* **play the ~** *(fig. coll.)* sich nicht festlegen [wollen]; alles nehmen, wie es kommt; *(take advantage of all chances offered)* alle gebotenen Chancen wahrnehmen; **i)** *(Hunting)* Feld, *das;* Gruppe, *die;* **lead the ~** *(lit. or fig.)* das Feld anführen; **j)** *(airfield)* Flugplatz, *der;* Flugfeld, *das (veralt.);* **k)** *(expanse)* Fläche, *die; (fig.)* Gebiet, *das;* **l)** *(Her.)* Feld, *das;* Grund, *der;* **m)** *(of picture etc.)* Grund, *der;* **n)** *(area of operation, subject areas, etc.)* Fach, *das;* [Fach]gebiet, *das; (range of vision or view)* Sichtfeld, *das;* **his researches range over a wide ~:** seine Forschungen, die sich über ein großes Gebiet erstrecken; **in the ~ of medicine** auf dem Gebiet der Medizin; **workers in the ~:** die Leute vom Fach; **he's working in his own ~:** er arbeitet in seinem [erlernten] Beruf; **that is outside my ~:** das fällt nicht in mein Fach; **~ of vision** *or* **view** Blickfeld, *das;* **o)** *(Phys.)* **magnetic/gravitational ~:** Magnet-/Gravitationsfeld, *das;* **p)** *attrib. (found in open country)* Feld-; **~-marigold** [Saat]wucherblume, *die;* **~-mushroom** Wiesenchampignon, *der;* **~-poppy** Klatschmohn, *der;* **q)** *attrib. (carried out in natural environment; light and mobile)* Feld‹*studie, -forschung, -artillerie, -ausrüstung*›. *See also* **airfield; coalfield; gold-field; minefield; oilfield. 2.** *v. i. (Cricket, Baseball, etc.)* als Fänger spielen; **he ~s well** er ist ein guter Fänger. **3.** *v. t.* **a)** *(Cricket, Baseball, etc.) (stop)* fangen ‹*Ball*›; *(stop and return)* auffangen und zurückwerfen; **b)** *(put into ~)* aufstellen, aufs Feld schicken ‹*Mannschaft, Spieler*›; **c)** *(fig.: deal with)* fertig werden mit; parieren ‹*Fragen*›

'field-day *n.* **a)** *(Mil.)* Feldübung, *die;* Manöver, *das;* **b)** *(fig.)* großer Tag; **have a ~-day** seinen großen Tag haben

fielder ['fi:ldə(r)] *n. (Cricket, Baseball, etc.)* Feldspieler, *der*

'field events *n. pl. (Sport)* technische Disziplinen

fieldfare ['fi:ldfeə(r)] *n. (Ornith.)* Wacholderdrossel, *die*

field: ~-glasses *n. pl.* Feldstecher, *der;* **~ hockey** *(Amer.) see* **hockey a; ~ hospital** *n. (Mil.)* Feldlazarett, *das;* **F~ 'Marshal** *n. (Brit. Mil.)* Feldmarschall, *der;* **~ mouse** *n.* Brandmaus, *die;* **~ officer** *n. (Mil.)* Stabsoffizier, *der;* **~sman** ['fi:ldzmən] *n., pl.* **~smen** ['fi:ldzmən] *see* **fielder; ~ sports** *n. pl.* Sport im Freien *(bes. Jagen und Fischen);* **~-test 1.** *n. see* **~-trial; 2.** *v. t.* in der Praxis erproben; **~-trial** *n.* Feldversuch, *der;* **~-trip** *n.* Exkursion, *die;* **~-work** *n.* **a)** *(Mil.: temporary fortification)* Feldbefestigung, *die;* **b)** *(outdoor work) (of surveyor etc.)* Arbeit im Gelände; *(of sociologist, collector of scientific data, etc.)* Feldforschung, *die;* **~-worker** *n.* Feldforscher, *der*/-forscherin, *die*

fiend [fi:nd] *n.* **a)** *(very wicked person)* Scheusal, *das;* Unmensch, *der;* **b) the F~:** der Teufel *od.* Satan; **c)** *(evil spirit)* böser Geist; **d)** *(coll.) (mischievous or tiresome person)* Plagegeist, *der; (artful person)* Schlaufuchs, *der;* **e)** *(devotee)* Fan, *der;* **travel/theatre ~:** Reise-/Theaternarr, *der*/-närrin, *die;* **motor-bike/health-food ~:** Motorrad-/Naturkostfreak, *der;* **fresh-air ~:** Frischluftfanatiker, *der*/-fanatikerin, *die*

fiendish ['fi:ndɪʃ] *adj.* **a)** *(deviously treacherous)* niederträchtig; **b)** *(coll.: artful)* gerissen *(ugs.);* ausgefuchst *(ugs.);* **c)** *(extremely awkward)* höllisch; **d)** *(fiendlike)* teuflisch

fiendishly ['fi:ndɪʃlɪ] *adv.* **a)** *(in deviously treacherous manner)* niederträchtig; auf niederträchtige Weise; **b)** *(coll.: artfully)* auf gerissene Weise; **~ clever** gerissen und schlau; **c)** *(extremely awkwardly)* höllisch; **d)** *(in fiendlike manner)* teuflisch

fierce [fɪəs] *adj.* **a)** *(violently hostile)* wild; erbittert ‹*Widerstand, Kampf*›; wuchtig ‹*Schlag*›; heftig ‹*[Bomben]angriff*›; feindselig ‹*Benehmen*›; **b)** *(raging)* wütend; tobend ‹*Wind*›; grimmig ‹*Haß, Wut*›; grausam ‹*Krankheit, Tyrannei*›; scharf ‹*Kritik, Verurteilung*›; wild ‹*Tier*›; **c)** *(ardent)* ungestüm ‹*Leidenschaft, Verlangen*›; heftig ‹*Andrang, Streit*›; heiß ‹*Wettbewerb*›; hitzig ‹*Kampagne*›; leidenschaftlich ‹*Ehrgeiz, Stolz, Wille*›; wild ‹*Entschlossenheit, Jagd*›; **d)** *(unpleasantly strong or intense)* unerträglich; **the heat is a bit ~:** die Hitze ist ein bißchen zu stark; **e)** *(violent in action)* hart ‹*Bremsen, Ruck*›

fiercely ['fɪəslɪ] *adv.* **a)** *(with violent hos-*

tility) heftig ‹*angreifen, Widerstand leisten*›; wütend, grimmig ‹*brüllen*›; **b)** *(with raging force)* wütend ‹*toben*›; aufs heftigste ‹*kritisieren, bekämpfen*›; **the fire burnt ~ for several hours** der Brand wütete mehrere Stunden; **c)** *(ardently)* äußerst ‹*stolz, unabhängig sein*›; wild ‹*entschlossen, kämpfen*›; **d)** *(with unpleasant strength or intensity)* unerträglich; **e)** *(with violent action)* heftig; scharf ‹*bremsen*›

fiery ['faɪərɪ] *adj.* **a)** *(consisting of or flaming with fire)* glühend; feurig ‹*Atem*›; **b)** *(looking like fire)* feurig; *(blazing red)* feuerrot; glutrot; **c)** *(hot as fire)* glühendheiß; **~ temperature** Gluthitze, *die;* **d)** *(producing burning sensation)* brennend, juckend ‹*Ausschlag*›; feurig ‹*Geschmack, Gewürz*›; scharf ‹*Getränk*›; **e)** *(fervent, full of spirit)* feurig ‹*Liebhaber, Pferd*›; *(irascible, impassioned)* hitzig ‹*Temperament, Debatte*›; feurig ‹*Rede, Redner*›; **~ zeal** Feuereifer, *der;* **have a ~ temper** ein Hitzkopf sein

⋆ **fiery 'cross** *n.* **a)** *(Hist.: rallying-signal of Scottish Highlanders)* Feuerkreuz, *das;* **b)** *(Amer.: of Ku Klux Klan)* Flammenkreuz, *das*

fiesta [fiː'estə] *n.* Fest, *das*

FIFA ['fiːfə] *abbr.* **International Football Federation** FIFA, *die;* Fifa, *die*

fife [faɪf] *n.* Pfeife, *die*

fifteen [fɪf'tiːn] **1.** *adj.* fünfzehn; *see also* **eight 1. 2.** *n.* **a)** Fünfzehn, *die; see also* **eight 2a, d; eighteen 2; b)** *(Rugby Football)* [Rugby]mannschaft, *die*

fifteenth [fɪf'tiːnθ] **1.** *adj.* fünfzehnt...; *see also* **eighth 1. 2.** *n. (fraction)* Fünfzehntel, *das; see also* **eighth 2**

fifth [fɪfθ] **1.** *adj.* fünft...; *see also* **eighth 1. 2.** *n.* **a)** *(in sequence)* fünfte, *der/die/das; (in rank)* Fünfte, *der/die/das; (fraction)* Fünftel, *das;* **b)** *(~ form)* fünfte [Schul]klasse; Fünfte, *die (Schuljargon);* **c)** *(Mus.)* Quinte, *die;* **d)** *(day)* **the ~ of May** der fünfte Mai; **the ~ [of the month]** der Fünfte [des Monats]; **e)** *(Amer. coll.) (bottle)* ≈ Dreiviertelliterflasche, *die; (of a gallon) ca. dreiviertel Liter. See also* **eighth 2**

fifth: ~ 'column *n.* fünfte Kolonne; **~-'columnist** *n.* Mitglied der fünften Kolonne; **~ form** *see* **form 1d**

fiftieth ['fɪftɪɪθ] **1.** *adj.* fünfzigst...; *see also* **eighth 1. 2.** *n. (fraction)* Fünfzigstel, *das; see also* **eighth 2**

fifty ['fɪftɪ] **1.** *adj.* **a)** fünfzig; **one-and-~** *(arch.) see* **fifty-one 1; b)** *(large indefinite number)* **~ times** hundertmal; zigmal *(ugs.). See also* **eight 1. 2.** *n.* Fünfzig, *die;* **one-and-~** *(arch.) see* **fifty-one 2;** *see also* **eight 2a; eighty 2**

fifty: ~-~ *adv., adj.* fifty-fifty *(ugs.);* halbehalbe *(ugs.);* **go ~-~:** fifty-fifty *od.* halbpart machen; **on a ~-~ basis** auf der Basis, daß fifty-fifty geteilt wird; **~-'first** *etc. adj.* einundfünfzigst... *usw.; see also* **eighth 1; ~fold** ['fɪftɪfəʊld] *adj., adv.* fünfzigfach; *see also* **eightfold; ~-'one** *etc.* **1.** *adj.* einundfünfzig *usw.; see also* **eight 1; 2.** *n.* Einundfünfzig *usw., die; see also* **eight 2a**

¹fig [fɪg] *n.* **a)** Feige, *die;* **b)** *(valueless thing)* **it's not worth a ~:** das ist keinen Pfifferling *od.* keine müde Mark wert *(ugs.);* **not care** *or* **give a ~ about** *or* **for sth.** sich nicht die Bohne *(ugs.) od.* keinen Deut für etw. interessieren

²fig *n. (attire)* Staat, *der; (legal, academic, etc.)* Ornat, *der;* **in full ~:** in vollem Staat

fig. *abbr.* **figure** Abb.

fight [faɪt] **1.** *v.i.,* **fought** [fɔːt] **a)** *(lit. or fig.)* kämpfen; *(with fists)* sich schlagen; **~ to do sth.** kämpfen, um etw. zu tun; **~ to save sb.'s life** um jmds. Leben kämpfen; **watch animals/people ~ing** Tieren/Menschen beim Kampf zusehen; **~ shy of sb./sth.** jmdm./einer Sache aus dem Weg gehen; **~ shy of doing sth.** sich davor drücken, etw. zu tun *(ugs.);* es vermeiden, etw. zu tun; **b)** *(squabble)* [sich] streiten, [sich] zanken **(about** wegen). *See also* **cat a; ¹cock 1a; hand 1a; tooth a. 2.** *v.t.,* **fought a)** *(in battle)* **~ sb./sth.** gegen jmdn./etw. kämpfen; *(using fists)* **~ sb.** sich mit jmdm. schlagen; ‹*Boxer:*› gegen jmdn. boxen; **b)** *(seek to overcome)* bekämpfen; *(resist)* **~ sb./sth.** gegen jmdn./etw. ankämpfen; **c)** *(contend in)* durchfechten; durchkämpfen; **~ a battle** einen Kampf austragen; **be ~ing a losing battle** *(fig.)* auf verlorenem Posten stehen *od.* kämpfen; **~ sb.'s battles for him** *(fig.)* jmdm. alle Schwierigkeiten aus dem Weg räumen; **~ the good fight** *(fig.)* für die gute *od.* gerechte Sache kämpfen; **d)** ausfechten ‹*Problem*›; führen ‹*Kampagne*›; kandidieren bei ‹*Wahl*›; **e) ~ one's way** sich *(Dat.)* den Weg freikämpfen; *(fig.)* sich *(Dat.)* seinen Weg bahnen; **~ one's way to the top** *(fig.)* sich an die Spitze kämpfen; **~ one's way up** *(fig.)* sich nach oben kämpfen; sich hochkämpfen. **3.** *n.* **a)** *(combat, campaign, boxing-match)* Kampf, *der* **(for** um); *(brawl)* Schlägerei, *die; (literary: battle)* Schlacht, *die;* **their ~ for freedom** ihr Freiheitskampf; **make a ~ of it, put up a ~:** sich wehren; *(fig.)* sich zur Wehr setzen; **give in without a ~** *(fig.)* klein beigeben; **aren't you going to make a ~ of it?** *(fig.)* willst du dir das etwa gefallen lassen?; **world championship title ~:** Titelkampf um die Weltmeisterschaft; **b)** *(squabble)* Streit, *der;* **they are always having ~s** zwischen ihnen gibt es dauernd Streit; **he likes a good ~:** er hat nichts gegen einen guten Streit; **c)** *(ability to ~)* Kampffähigkeit, *die; (appetite for ~ing)* Kampfgeist, *der;* **have no ~ left in one** nicht mehr zum Kampf fähig sein; *(fig.)* erledigt *od.* fertig sein; **all the ~ had gone out of him** *(fig.)* sein Kampfgeist war erloschen; **show ~** *(lit. or fig.)* Stärke demonstrieren

~ against *v.t.* **a)** *(in war)* kämpfen gegen; *(in boxing-match)* antreten gegen; **b)** *(resist)* kämpfen gegen; ankämpfen gegen ‹*Wellen, Wind, Gefühle*›; bekämpfen ‹*Krankheit, Analphabetentum*›

~ 'back 1. *v.i.* zurückschlagen; sich zur Wehr setzen. **2.** *v.t.* **a)** *(suppress)* zurückhalten; **b)** *(resist)* zurückdrängen; aufhalten ‹*Vormarsch*›

~ 'down *v.t.* zurückhalten

~ for *v.t. (lit. or fig.)* kämpfen für; **~ for one's life** um sein Leben kämpfen

~ 'off *v.t. (lit. or fig.)* abwehren; abwimmeln *(ugs.)* ‹*Reporter, Fans, Bewunderer*›; widerstehen (+ *Dat.*) ‹*Versuchung*›; bekämpfen ‹*Erkältung*›; **~ off the desire** dem Wunsch widerstehen

~ 'out *v.t. (lit. or fig.)* ausfechten; **~ it out amongst yourselves** macht das unter euch *(Dat.)* aus

~ over *v.t.* **a)** *(~ with regard to)* [sich] streiten über (+ *Akk.*); **b)** *(~ to gain possession of)* kämpfen um; *(squabble to gain possession of)* [sich] streiten um; [sich] zanken um

~ with *v.t.* **a)** kämpfen mit; **b)** *(squabble with)* [sich] streiten mit; [sich] zanken mit; **c)** *(~ on the side of)* kämpfen [zusammen] mit

fighter ['faɪtə(r)] *n.* **a)** Kämpfer, *der*/Kämpferin, *die; (warrior)* Krieger, *der; (boxer)* Fighter, *der;* **b)** *(aircraft)* Kampfflugzeug, *das;* **~ pilot** Jagdflieger, *der*

fighting ['faɪtɪŋ] **1.** *adj.* Kampf‹*truppen, -schiff, -flugzeug*›; *see also* **¹cock 1a. 2.** *n.* Kämpfe; **be in a ~ mood** kämpferisch gestimmt sein

fighting: ~ 'chance *n.* **have a ~ chance of succeeding/of doing sth.** Aussicht auf Erfolg haben/gute Chancen haben, etw. zu tun; **~ 'drunk** *adj. (coll.)* betrunken und streitsüchtig; **~ fish** *n.* Kampffisch, *der;* **~ 'fit** *adj.* topfit *(ugs.);* **~ fund** *n. Geldmittel [aus einer Spendenaktion] zur Durchführung einer Kampagne;* **raise a ~ fund** eine Spendenaktion durchführen; **~ 'mad** *adj.* [vor Wut] rasend; **~ 'words** *n. pl. (coll.)* Kampfparolen

'fig-leaf *n. (lit. or fig.)* Feigenblatt, *das*

figment ['fɪgmənt] *n. (imagined thing)* Hirngespinst, *das;* **a ~ of one's** *or* **the imagination** pure Einbildung

'fig-tree *n.* Feigenbaum, *der*

figurative ['fɪgjʊrətɪv, 'fɪgərətɪv] *adj.* **a)** *(metaphorical)* bildlich; übertragen; figurativ *(Sprachw.);* **b)** *(metaphorically so called)* im übertragenen Sinne; **c)** *(with many figures of speech)* bilderreich; **d)** *(emblematic)* symbolisch; **be ~ of sth.** symbolisch für etw. stehen

figuratively ['fɪgjʊrətɪvlɪ, 'fɪgərətɪvlɪ] *adv.* **a)** *(metaphorically)* bildlich; [im] übertragenen [Sinne]; figurativ *(Sprachw.);* **b)** *(with many figures of speech)* bilderreich; **c)** *(emblematically)* symbolisch

figure ['fɪgə(r)] **1.** *n.* **a)** *(shape)* Form, *die;* **b)** *(Geom.)* Figur, *die;* **c)** *(one's bodily shape)* Figur, *die;* **have to worry about one's ~:** auf seine Figur achten müssen; **keep one's ~:** sich *(Dat.)* seine Figur bewahren; schlank bleiben; **lose one's ~:** dick werden; **d)** *(person as seen)* Gestalt, *die; (literary ~)* Figur, *die; (historical etc. ~)* Persönlichkeit, *die;* **a fine ~ of a man/woman** eine stattliche Erscheinung; **a ~ of fun** eine Spottfigur; **make** *or* **cut a brilliant/poor** *etc.* **~:** eine glänzende/erbärmliche *usw.* Figur machen *od.* abgeben; **e)** *(image)* Bild, *das;* **she looked a ~ of misery** sie bot ein Bild des Jammers; **f)** *(three-dimensional representation)* Figur, *die; (two-dimensional representation)* Gestalt, *die;* **g)** *(emblem)* Symbol, *das;* **a ~ of peace** ein Friedenssymbol; **h)** *(simile etc.)* **~ [of speech]** Redewendung, *die; (Rhet.)* Redefigur, *die;* **it's just a ~ of speech** das habe ich nicht wirklich gemeint; **i)** *(illustration)* Abbildung, *die;* **j)** *(decorative pattern)* Muster, *das;* **k)** *(Dancing, Skating)* Figur, *die;* **l)** *(numerical symbol)* Ziffer, *die; (number so expressed)* Zahl, *die; (amount of money)* Betrag, *der; (amount paid for sth.)* Erlös, *der; (value)* [Zahlen]wert, *der;* **double ~s** zweistellige Zahlen; **membership is in double ~s** die Mitgliederzahl ist zweistellig; **three/four** *etc.* **~s** drei-/vierstellige *usw.* Zahlen; **go** *or* **run into three ~s** sich auf dreistellige Zahlen belaufen; **three-/four-** *etc.* **~:** drei-/vierstellig *usw.;* **m)** *in pl. (arithmetical calculations)* Rechnen, *das; (accounts, result of calculations)* Zahlen *Pl.;* **can you check my ~s?** kannst du mal nachrechnen?; **do the ~s** den [Jahres-, Rechnungs]abschluß durchführen; **last month's ~s** die Zahlen/Werte des Vormonats; **he is good at ~s** er kann gut rechnen; *see also* **head 1b; n)** *(Ling.)* [grammatische] Figur. *See also* **eight 2b; father-figure. 2.** *v.t.* **a)** *(represent pictorially)* darstellen; **b)** *(picture mentally)* sich *(Dat.)* vorstellen; **~ oneself as sth.** sich selbst als etw. [an]sehen; **c)** *(be symbol of)* versinnbildlichen; **d)** *(embellish)* verzieren; **e)** *(Mus.)* beziffern; **f)** *(mark with number[s])* mit einer Zahl versehen; **g)** *(calculate)* schätzen; sagen; **h)** *(Amer.: understand)* verstehen; **i)** *(Amer.: ascertain)* herausfinden. *See also* **³bass 2c. 3.** *v.i.* **a)** *(make appearance)* vorkommen; erscheinen; *(in play)* auftreten; **children don't ~ in her plans for the future** Kinder spielen in ihren Zukunftsplänen keine Rolle; **this image often ~d in her dreams** dieses Bild tauchte in ihren Träumen häufig auf; **~ prominently on the music scene/in world politics** in der Musikszene/Weltpolitik eine bedeutende Rolle spielen; **b)** *(do arithmetic)* rechnen; **c)** *(coll.: be likely, understandable)* **it ~s that ...:** es kann gut sein, daß ...; **that ~s** das kann gut sein *od.* stimmt sicher

~ **on** *v. t.* rechnen mit; ~ **on doing sth.** damit rechnen, etw. zu tun

~ **'out** *v. t.* **a)** *(work out by arithmetic)* ausrechnen; **b)** *(Amer.: estimate)* ~ **out that ...:** damit rechnen, daß ...; **c)** *(understand)* verstehen; **I can't** ~ **him out** ich werde nicht schlau aus ihm; **d)** *(ascertain)* herausfinden; **it's difficult to** ~ **out whether ...:** es ist schwer zu sagen, ob ...; **I can't** ~ **out where we've met before** ich weiß nicht, wo wir uns schon gesehen haben

figure: **~-head** *n. (lit. or fig.)* Galionsfigur, *die;* **~-skating** *n.* Eiskunstlauf, *der;* **~-work** *n., no pl.* **do some ~-work** ein paar Berechnungen anstellen

Fiji ['fi:dʒi:] *pr. n.* Fidschi *(das);* Fidschiinseln *Pl.*

filament ['fɪləmənt] *n.* **a)** Faden, *der; (Chem.)* Filament, *das (fachspr.);* Faser, *die;* **b)** *(conducting wire or thread)* Glühfaden, *der;* **c)** *(Bot.)* Staubfaden, *der;* Filament, *das (fachspr.)*

filbert ['fɪlbət] *n.* **a)** *(cultivated hazel)* Haselnußstrauch, *der;* **b)** *(nut)* Haselnuß, *die*

filch [fɪltʃ] *v. t.* stibitzen *(ugs.)*

¹file [faɪl] **1.** *n.* Feile, *die; (nail-~)* [Nagel]feile, *die.* **2.** *v. t.* feilen ‹*Fingernägel*›; mit der Feile bearbeiten ‹*Holz, Eisen*›; ~ **sth. to make it smooth** etw. glatt feilen

~ **a'way** *v. t.* abfeilen

~ **'down** *v. t.* abfeilen

²file **1.** *n.* **a)** *(holder)* Ordner, *der; (box)* Kassette, *die;* [Dokumenten]schachtel, *die;* **on ~:** in der Kartei/in *od.* bei den Akten; **on** *or* **in sb.'s ~s** in jmds. Kartei/in *od.* bei jmds. Akten; **put sth. on ~:** etw. in die Akten/Kartei aufnehmen; **b)** *(set of papers)* Ablage, *die; (as cards)* Kartei, *die;* **open/keep a ~ on sb./sth.** eine Akte über jmdn./etw. anlegen/führen; **c)** *(series of issues of newspaper etc.)* [Zeitungs]bündel, *das (von aufeinanderfolgenden Nummern);* **d)** *(Computing)* Datei, *die;* **e)** *(stiff wire)* Zettelspieß, *der;* **f)** *(Law)* Akten *Pl.;* **reopen/close the ~ on a case** einen Fall wiederaufnehmen/abschließen. **2.** *v. t.* **a)** *(place on a ~)* [in die Kartei] einordnen/[in die Akten] aufnehmen; ablegen *(Bürow.); (place among public records)* archivieren; ~ **sth. in drawers** etw. [geordnet] in Schubladen aufbewahren; **b)** *(submit)* einreichen ‹*Antrag*›; **c)** ‹*Journalist:*› einsenden ‹*Bericht*›

~ **a'way** *v. t.* ablegen *(Bürow.)*

³file **1.** *n.* **a)** *(Mil. etc.)* Reihe, *die;* **stand in ~:** in Reih und Glied stehen; **[in] single** *or* **Indian ~:** [im] Gänsemarsch; **b)** *(row of persons or things)* Reihe, *die.* **2.** *v. i.* in einer Reihe gehen; nacheinander gehen

~ **a'way** *v. i.* [einer nach dem anderen] weggehen; [nacheinander] fortgehen

~ **'off** *see* ~ **away**

file: ~ **card** *n.* Karteikarte, *die;* ~ **copy** *n.* Belegexemplar, *das; (of letter)* Kopie für die Akten

filet ['fɪleɪ] *n. (Gastr.)* Filet, *das*

filial ['fɪlɪəl] *adj.* **a)** *(of or due from son or daughter)* kindlich ‹*Gehorsam, Achtung, Treue*›; Kindes-, Sohnes-/Tochter‹*liebe, -pflicht*›; **b)** *(Biol.)* ~ **generation** Filialgeneration, *die*

filibuster ['fɪlɪbʌstə(r)] **1.** *n. (obstructionist)* Verschleppungstaktiker, *der; (obstruction)* Verschleppungstaktik, *die;* Filibuster, *das.* **2.** *v. i.* obstruieren; Dauerreden halten

filigree ['fɪlɪgri:] *n. (lit. or fig.)* Filigran, *das*

¹filing ['faɪlɪŋ] *n.* **~s** *(particles)* Späne; **iron ~s** Eisen[feil]späne

²filing *n.* (*action of* **²file 2 a**) Ablage, *die*

filing: ~ **cabinet** *n.* Aktenschrank, *der;* ~ **clerk** *n.* Archivkraft, *die;* ~ **system** *n.* Ablagesystem, *das*

Filipino [fɪlɪ'pi:nəʊ] **1.** *adj.* philippinisch. **2.** *n., pl.* **~s** Filipino, *der*/Filipina, *die*

fill [fɪl] **1.** *v. t.* **a)** *(make full)* ~ **sth. [with sth.]** etw. [mit etw.] füllen; **the room was ~ed** *(with people)* der Raum war fast voll besetzt; ~ **the walls with photos** die Wände mit Fotos vollhängen; ~ **sb./sb.'s heart with fear** jmdm. Furcht einflößen; **~ed with** voller ‹*Reue, Bewunderung, Neid, Verzweiflung*› (at über + *Akk.*); **be ~ed with envy at sb.'s success** auf jmds. Erfolg *(Akk.)* neidisch sein; **b)** *(distend)* blähen ‹*Segel*›; **c)** *(stock abundantly)* füllen; *(fig.)* anfüllen; **be ~ed with people/flowers/fish** *etc.* voller Menschen/Blumen/Fische *usw.* sein; **the journey had ~ed his mind with new ideas** die Reise hatte ihm zahlreiche neue Anregungen gegeben; **d)** *(occupy whole capacity of, spread over)* füllen; besetzen ‹*Sitzplätze*›; *(fig.)* ausfüllen ‹*Gedanken, Zeit*›; **the room was ~ed to capacity** der Raum war voll besetzt *od. (ugs.)* [proppen]voll; **tears suddenly ~ed her eyes** plötzlich standen ihr Tränen in den Augen; **when you've ~ed this notebook ...:** wenn dein Heft voll ist ...; **the fat lady ~ed two seats** die dicke Dame brauchte zwei Plätze; **enough cake to ~ three large plates** genug Kuchen für drei große Teller; ~ **the bill** *(fig.)* den Erwartungen entsprechen; *(be appropriate)* angemessen sein; **e)** *(pervade)* erfüllen; **light/silence ~ed the room** Licht strömte in das Zimmer/Schweigen breitete sich im Zimmer aus; **f)** *(block up)* füllen ‹*Lücke*›; füllen, *(veralt.)* plombieren ‹*Zahn*›; **g)** *(Cookery) (stuff)* füllen; *(put layer of sth. solid in)* belegen; *(put layer of sth. spreadable in)* bestreichen; **h)** *(satisfy)* sättigen; satt machen; **i)** *(hold)* innehaben ‹*Posten*›; versehen ‹*Amt*›; *(take up)* ausfüllen ‹*Position*›; **j)** *(execute)* ausführen ‹*Auftrag*›; **k)** *(appoint sb. to)* besetzen ‹*Posten, Lehrstuhl*›. **2.** *v. i.* **a)** *(become full)* ~ **[with sth.]** sich [mit etw.] füllen; *(fig.)* sich [mit etw.] erfüllen; **b)** *(be distended by wind)* sich blähen. **3.** *n.* **a)** *(as much as one wants)* **eat/drink one's ~:** sich satt essen/trinken; **have had one's ~ [of food and drink]** seinen Hunger und Durst gestillt haben; **weep one's ~:** sich ausweinen; **have had one's ~ of sth./doing sth.** genug von etw. haben/etw. zur Genüge getan haben; **b)** *(enough to ~ sth.)* **he needs a ~ of tobacco for his pipe/of petrol/of ink** er muß seine Pfeife stopfen/tanken/Tinte nachfüllen

~ **'in** **1.** *v. t.* **a)** füllen; zuschütten, auffüllen ‹*Erdloch*›; **b)** *(complete)* ausfüllen; ergänzen ‹*Auslassungen*›; **c)** *(insert)* einsetzen; **d)** *(find occupation during)* überbrücken ‹*Zeit*›; **how did you ~ in your evenings?** was hast du abends unternommen?; **e)** *(coll.: inform)* ~ **sb. in [on sth.]** jmdn. [über etw. *(Akk.)*] unterrichten *od.* ins Bild setzen. **2.** *v. i.* ~ **in for sb.** für jmdn. einspringen

~ **'out** **1.** *v. t.* **a)** *(enlarge to proper size or extent)* ausfüllen; vervollständigen ‹*Essay, Aufsatz*›; **b)** *(Amer.: complete)* ausfüllen ‹*Formular usw.*›. **2.** *v. i.* **a)** *(become enlarged)* sich ausdehnen; **b)** *(become plumper)* [Fett] ansetzen; voller werden

~ **'up** **1.** *v. t.* **a)** *(make full)* ~ **sth. up [with sth.]** etw. [mit etw.] füllen; **put a little milk into the cup and then ~ it up with water** gießen Sie etwas Milch in die Tasse und füllen Sie mit Wasser auf; ~ **oneself/sb. up [with sth.]** sich/jmdn. [mit etw.] vollstopfen; **their mother tried to ~ them up** ihre Mutter versuchte, sie satt zu kriegen; **that will ~ you up!** davon wirst du satt!; **b)** *(put petrol into)* ~ **up [the tank]** tanken; ~ **her up!** *(coll.)* voll[tanken]!; **c)** auffüllen ‹*Loch*›; zuschmieren ‹*Riß*›; **d)** *(complete)* ausfüllen ‹*Formular usw.*›. **2.** *v. i.* ‹*Theater, Zimmer, Zug usw.:*› sich füllen; ‹*Becken, Spülkasten:*› vollaufen

filled [fɪld] *adj.* gefüllt; **a cream-~ cake** ein Kuchen mit Cremefüllung

filler ['fɪlə(r)] *n.* **a)** *(to fill cavity)* Füllmasse, *die;* Spachtelmasse, *die;* **b)** *(to increase bulk)* Sattmacher, *der*

'filler cap *n.* Tankverschluß, *der*

fillet ['fɪlɪt] **1.** *n.* **a)** *(Gastr.)* Filet, *das;* ~ **[steak]** *(slice)* Filetsteak, *das; (cut)* Filet, *das;* ~ **of pork/beef/cod/halibut** Schweine-/Rinder-/Kabeljau-/Heilbuttfilet, *das;* **b)** *(Archit.) (narrow flat band)* Leiste, *die; (between flutes of column)* Kannelüre, *die;* **c)** *(headband)* Haarband, *das.* **2.** *v. t.* **a)** *(divide into fillets)* filetieren; **b)** *(remove bones from)* entgräten ‹*Fisch*›; ausbeinen ‹*Fleisch*›

filling ['fɪlɪŋ] **1.** *n.* **a)** *(for teeth)* Füllung, *die;* Plombe, *die (veralt.);* **b)** *(for pancakes etc.)* Füllung, *die; (for sandwiches etc.)* Belag, *der; (for spreading)* Aufstrich, *der.* **2.** *adj.* sättigend

'filling station *n.* Tankstelle, *die*

fillip ['fɪlɪp] *n.* Anreiz, *der;* Ansporn, *der;* **give sb. a ~:** jmdn. anspornen; **give** *or* **be a ~ to the economy** die Wirtschaft beleben

filly ['fɪlɪ] *n.* **a)** junge Stute; Stutfohlen, *das;* **b)** *(sl.: young woman)* Käfer, *der (ugs. veralt.);* Biene, *die (ugs. veralt.)*

film [fɪlm] **1.** *n.* **a)** *(thin layer)* Schicht, *die;* ~ **[of varnish/dust]** [Lack-/Staub]schicht, *die;* ~ **[of oil/slime]** [Öl-/Schmier]film, *der;* **b)** *(Photog.)* Film, *der;* **put sth. on ~:** etw. ablichten; **the events are all on ~:** die Vorgänge sind alle gefilmt worden; **c)** *(Cinemat.: story etc.)* Film, *der;* Streifen, *der (ugs.);* **make/direct a ~:** einen Film drehen/bei einem Film Regie führen; **d)** *in pl. (cinema industry)* Kino, *das;* Film, *der;* **go into ~s** zum Kino *od.* Film gehen; **she is in ~s** sie ist beim Film; **e)** *no pl. (as art-form)* der Film; **are you interested in ~?** interessieren Sie sich für [den] Film? **2.** *v. t. (Cinemat. etc.)* **a)** *(record on motion ~)* filmen; *(for motion picture)* drehen ‹*Kinofilm, Szene*›; **b)** *(make cinema etc. ~ of)* verfilmen ‹*Buch usw.*›. **3.** *v. i.* ‹*Szene:*› sich filmen lassen; ‹*Buch, Geschichte:*› sich verfilmen lassen

~ **'over** *v. i.* ‹*Spiegel, Glas:*› anlaufen; **her eyes ~ed over with tears** Tränen traten ihr in die Augen

film: ~ **clip** *see* **²clip 2 b;** ~ **crew** *n.* Kamerateam, *das;* ~ **director** *n.* Filmregisseur, *der*/-regisseurin, *die;* ~ **editor** *n.* Cutter, *der*/Cutterin, *die;* **~-goer** *n.* Kinogänger, *der*/-gängerin, *die;* ~ **library** *n.* Filmarchiv, *das;* ~ **projector** *n.* Projektor, *der;* ~ **script** *n.* Drehbuch, *das;* ~ **set** *n.* Dekoration, *die;* **~setting** *n. (Printing)* Lichtsatz, *der;* ~ **show** *n.* Filmvorführung, *die;* ~ **star** *n.* Filmstar, *der;* **~-strip** *n.* Filmstreifen, *der*

filmy ['fɪlmɪ] *adj.* hauchdünn

Filofax, (P) ['faɪləʊfæks] *n.* ≈ Terminplaner, *der*

filter ['fɪltə(r)] **1.** *n.* **a)** Filter, *der;* **b)** *(Brit.) (route)* Abbiegespur, *die; (light)* grünes Licht für Abbieger. **2.** *v. t.* filtern. **3.** *v. i.* **a)** *(flow through filter)* ‹*Flüssigkeiten:*› sickern; ‹*Luft usw.:*› durch einen Filter strömen; **b)** *(make way gradually)* ~ **through/into/down sth.** durch etw. hindurch-/in etw. *(Akk.)* hinein-/etw. hinuntersickern; **c)** *(at road junction)* sich einfädeln; ~ **off** sich ausfädeln

~ **'out** **1.** *v. t. (lit. or fig.)* herausfiltern. **2.** *v. i.* durchsickern

~ **'through** *see* ~ **out 2**

filter: **~-bed** *n.* Filterkies, *der;* Filtersand, *der;* ~ **coffee** *n.* Filterkaffee, *der;* ~ **lane** *n. (Brit.)* Abbiegespur, *die;* ~ **paper** *n.* Filterpapier, *das;* **~-tip** *n.* **a)** Filter, *der;* **b)** **~-tip [cigarette]** Filterzigarette, *die*

filth [fɪlθ] *n., no pl.* **a)** *(disgusting dirt)* Dreck, *der; (pollution)* Schmutzigkeit, *die;* **b)** *(moral corruption)* Verderbtheit, *die; (vileness)* Abscheulichkeit, *die;* **c)** *(obscenity)* Schmutz [und Schund]; **d)** *(foul language)* unflätige Sprache; Schweinereien *(ugs.)*

filthiness ['fɪlθɪnɪs] *n., no pl.* **a)** Schmutzigkeit, *die;* Verdrecktheit, *die (ugs.);* **b)** *(obscenity)* Unzüchtigkeit, *die*

filthy [ˈfɪlθɪ] **1.** *adj.* **a)** *(disgustingly dirty)* dreckig *(ugs.);* schmutzig; *(fig.)* widerlich ⟨*Angewohnheit*⟩; *(fond of filth)* im Dreck lebend ⟨*Tiere*⟩; **b)** *(vile)* widerlich; gemein ⟨*Lügner, Trick*⟩; schmutzig ⟨*Phantasie, Gedanken*⟩; ~ **lucre** schnöder Mammon *(abwertend, auch scherzh.);* **c)** *(very unpleasant)* ekelhaft; scheußlich; ~ **weather** scheußliches Wetter; Dreckwetter, *das (ugs.);* **d)** *(obscene)* schweinisch *(ugs.);* obszön, unflätig ⟨*Sprache*⟩; **he is ~, he is a ~ devil** er ist ein Schweinigel *(ugs.);* **a ~-minded person** ein Mensch mit einer schmutzigen Phantasie. **2.** *adv.* ~ **dirty** völlig verdreckt *(ugs.);* ~ **rich** *(coll.)* stinkreich *(ugs.)*

filtrate [ˈfɪltreɪt] *n.* Filtrat, *das*

filtration [fɪlˈtreɪʃn] *n.* Filtrierung, *die; (percolation)* Durchsickern, *das*

fin [fɪn] *n.* **a)** *(Zool.; on boat)* Flosse, *die; (flipper)* [Schwimm]flosse, *die; (on car)* Heckflosse, *die;* **b)** *(in internal-combustion engine)* Kühlrippe, *die; (on radiator etc.)* Rippe, *die. See also* **tail-fin**

final [ˈfaɪnl] **1.** *adj.* **a)** *(ultimate)* letzt...; End⟨*spiel, -stadium, -stufe, -ergebnis*⟩; Schluß⟨*bericht, -szene, -etappe, -phase*⟩; ~ **examination** Abschlußprüfung, *die;* **have a ~ swim** ein letztes Mal schwimmen gehen; **give a ~ wave** noch einmal *od.* ein letztes Mal winken; **what will be the ~ outcome of this crisis?** wie wird diese Krise letztendlich ausgehen?; **b)** *(conclusive)* endgültig ⟨*Urteil, Entscheidung*⟩; **have the ~ word** das letzte Wort haben; **is this your ~ decision/word/verdict?** ist das Ihr letztes Wort?; **the ~ solution** *(euphem.)* die Endlösung; **I'm not coming with you, and that's ~!** ich komme nicht mit, und damit basta! *(ugs.);* **c)** *(concerned with goal)* ~ **cause** Endziel, *das;* ~ **clause** *(Ling.)* Finalsatz, *der.* **2.** *n.* **a)** *(Sport etc.)* Finale, *das; (of ball game also)* Endspiel, *das; (of quiz game)* Endrunde, *die;* **b)** *in sing. or pl. (examination)* Abschlußprüfung, *die; (at university)* Examen, *das;* **c)** *(newspaper)* Spätausgabe, *die*

final 'drive *n. (Motor Veh.)* Achsantrieb [mit Gelenkwelle]

finale [fɪˈnɑːlɪ] *n.* **a)** *(Mus.)* Finale, *das;* **b)** *(close of drama)* Schlußszene, *die;* **c)** *(conclusion)* Abschluß, *der*

finalise *see* **finalize**

finalist [ˈfaɪnəlɪst] *n.* Teilnehmer/Teilnehmerin in der Endausscheidung; *(Sport)* Finalist, *der*/Finalistin, *die*

finality [faɪˈnælɪtɪ] *n., no pl.* Endgültigkeit, *die; (of tone of voice)* Entschiedenheit, *die*

finalize [ˈfaɪnəlaɪz] *v. t.* [endgültig] beschließen; unter Dach und Fach bringen ⟨*Geschäft, Vertrag*⟩; *(complete)* zum Abschluß bringen; ~ **sth. with sb.** etw. mit jmdm. [endgültig] absprechen

finally [ˈfaɪnəlɪ] *adv.* **a)** *(in the end)* schließlich; *(expressing impatience etc.)* endlich; **b)** *(in conclusion)* abschließend; zum Schluß; **c)** *(conclusively)* bestimmt, entschieden ⟨*sagen*⟩; *(once for all)* ein für allemal

finance [faɪˈnæns, fɪˈnæns, ˈfaɪnæns] **1.** *n.* **a)** *in pl. (resources)* Finanzen *Pl.;* **b)** *(management of money)* Geldwesen, *das;* **high ~:** Hochfinanz, *die;* **be in ~:** im Finanz- und Geldwesen tätig sein; **c)** *(support)* Gelder *Pl. (ugs.);* Geldmittel *Pl.* **2.** *v. t.* finanzieren; finanziell unterstützen ⟨*Person*⟩; **how are you going to ~ yourself at university?** wie willst du dein Studium finanzieren?

finance: ~ **company** *n.* Finanzierungsgesellschaft, *die;* ~ **director** *n.* Leiter der Finanzabteilung; ~ **house** *see* ~ **company**

financial [faɪˈnænʃl, fɪˈnænʃl] *adj.* finanziell; Finanz⟨*mittel, -quelle, -experte, -lage*⟩; Geld⟨*mittel, -geber, -sorgen*⟩; Finanzierungs⟨*last, -geschäft*⟩; Wirtschafts⟨*nachrichten, -bericht*⟩

financially [faɪˈnænʃəlɪ, fɪˈnænʃəlɪ] *adv.* finanziell; **be ~ rewarded for sth.** für etw. mit Geld entlohnt werden

financial 'year *n.* Geschäftsjahr, *das; (im öffentlichen Haushalt)* Rechnungsjahr, *das*

financier [faɪˈnænsɪə(r), fɪˈnænsɪə(r)] *n.* **a)** *(expert)* Finanzexperte, *der*/-expertin, *die;* **b)** *(capitalist)* Finanzier, *der*

fin-back 'whale *see* **rorqual**

finch [fɪnʃ] *n. (Ornith.)* Fink[envogel], *der*

find [faɪnd] **1.** *v. t.,* **found** [faʊnd] **a)** *(get possession of by chance)* finden; *(come across unexpectedly)* entdecken; ~ **that ...:** herausfinden *od.* entdecken, daß ...; **hope this letter ~s you well** [ich] hoffe, daß dieser Brief Dich gesund antreffen wird; **he was found dead/injured** er wurde tot/verletzt aufgefunden; **b)** *(obtain)* finden ⟨*Zustimmung, Erleichterung, Rückendeckung, Trost, Gegenliebe*⟩; stoßen auf (+ *Akk.*) ⟨*Kritik, Ablehnung*⟩; erlangen ⟨*Popularität*⟩; **have found one's feet** *(be able to walk)* laufen können; *(be able to act by oneself)* selbständig sein; auf eigenen Füßen stehen; **c)** *(recognize as present)* sehen ⟨*Veranlassung, Schwierigkeit*⟩; feststellen ⟨*Züge, Ähnlichkeit*⟩; *(acknowledge or discover to be)* finden; ~ **no difficulty in doing sth.** etw. nicht schwierig finden; **these plants are found nowhere else** diese Pflanzen findet man sonst nirgendwo; **you don't ~ many flowers here** es gibt hier nicht viele Blumen; ~ **sb. in/out** jmdn. antreffen/nicht antreffen; ~ **sb./sth. to be ...:** feststellen, daß jmd./etw. ... ist/war; ~ **oneself somewhere** sich irgendwo wiederfinden; **when I came in, I found him opening his/my letters** als ich hineinkam, war er gerade dabei, seine Briefe zu öffnen/ertappte ich ihn dabei, wie er meine Briefe öffnete; ~ **oneself doing sth.** sich dabei ertappen, wie man etw. tut; **you must** *or* **will have to take us as you ~ us** du darfst dich nicht daran stören, wie es bei uns aussieht/zugeht *usw.;* **you won't ~ me doing 'that** das wirst du nicht erleben, daß ich das tue; **d)** *(discover by trial or experience to be or do)* für ... halten; **do you ~ him easy to get on with?** finden Sie, daß sich gut mit ihm auskommen läßt?; **she ~s it hard to come to terms with his death** es fällt ihr schwer, sich mit seinem Tod abzufinden; **she ~s it impossible to discuss the subject** es ist ihr unmöglich, das Thema zu erörtern; ~ **sth. necessary** etw. für nötig befinden *od.* erachten; ~ **sth./sb. to be ...:** herausfinden, daß etw./jmd. ... ist/war; **sth. has been found to be ...:** man hat herausgefunden, daß etw. ... ist; **I found that it was already noon** ich stellte fest, daß es schon mittag war; **we ~ [that] we are struggling all the time** wir sehen, wie wir uns die ganze Zeit abmühen; **you will ~ [that] ...:** Sie werden sehen *od.* feststellen, daß ...; **e)** *(discover by search)* finden; **want to ~ sth.** etw. suchen; ~ **[again]** wiederfinden; **f)** *(Hunting)* aufstöbern; *abs.* Wild aufstöbern; **g)** *(reach by natural or normal process)* [heraus]finden; ~ **one's place in society** seinen Platz in der Gesellschaft finden; **h)** *(succeed in obtaining)* finden ⟨*Zeit, Mittel und Wege, Worte*⟩; auftreiben ⟨*Geld, Gegenstand*⟩; aufbringen ⟨*Kraft, Energie*⟩; **when I ~ the opportunity** bei passender Gelegenheit; ~ **it in oneself** *or* **one's heart to do sth.** es über sich *od.* übers Herz bringen, etw. zu tun; ~ **its mark** sein Ziel finden *od.* treffen; **i)** *(ascertain by study or calculation or inquiry)* finden; **love will ~ a way** der Liebe ist kein Ding unmöglich *(veralt.);* ~ **what time the train leaves** herausfinden, wann der Zug [ab]fährt; ~ **one's way [to/into sth.]** [zu etw.] hinfinden/[in etw. *(Akk.)*] hineinfinden; *(accidentally)* [zu etw.] hingelangen/[in etw. *(Akk.)*] hineingeraten; ~ **one's way home** nach Hause zurückfinden; ~ **one's way into journalism/films** zum Journalismus/Film kommen; **she found her way into teaching quite by accident** eher zufällig war sie Lehrerin geworden; ~ **its way [into sth.]** [in etw. *(Akk.)*] gelangen; **the disease found its way into other organs** die Krankheit griff auf andere Organe über; **j)** *(Law)* ~ **sb. guilty/not guilty** jmdn. schuldig sprechen/freisprechen; ~ **a verdict of guilty/innocent** [im Urteil] auf schuldig/nicht schuldig erkennen; **the jury found him not guilty of murder** die Geschworenen entschieden, daß er des Mordes nicht schuldig war; **k)** *(supply)* besorgen; ~ **sb. sth.** *or* **sth. for sb.** jmdn. mit etw. versorgen; ~ **sb. in sth.** jmdn. mit etw. versehen; jmdm. etw. verschaffen; **all found** bei freier Kost und Logis; bei freier Station *(veralt.).* **2.** *v. refl.,* **found a)** *(provide for one's own needs)* ~ **oneself [in sth.]** sich selbst [mit etw.] versorgen; **b)** *(discover one's vocation)* zu sich selbst finden; seine wahre Bestimmung finden. **3.** *n.* **a)** Fund, *der;* **make a ~/two ~s** fündig/zweimal fündig werden; **b)** *(person)* Entdeckung, *die*

~ **for** *v. t. (Law)* ~ **for the defendant/plaintiff** zugunsten der Verteidigung/des Klägers entscheiden; ~ **for the accused** auf Freispruch erkennen

~ **'out** *v. t.* **a)** *(discover, devise)* herausfinden; bekommen ⟨*Informationen*⟩; ~ **out new ways** einen neuen Weg finden; **manage to ~ out how ...:** herausbekommen, wie ...; ~ **out about** *(get information on)* sich informieren über (+ *Akk.*); *(learn of)* erfahren von; **b)** *(detect in offence, act of deceit, etc.)* erwischen, ertappen ⟨*Dieb usw.*⟩; ~ **out a liar** einem Lügner auf die Schliche kommen; einen Lügner durchschauen; **your sins will ~ you out** deine Sünden werden an den Tag kommen

findable [ˈfaɪndəbl] *pred. adj.* **be [easily] ~:** [leicht] zu finden sein

finder [ˈfaɪndə(r)] *n.* **a)** *(of sth. lost)* Finder, *der*/Finderin, *die; (of sth. unknown)* Entdecker, *der*/Entdeckerin, *die;* **~s keepers** *(coll.)* wer's findet, dem gehört's *(ugs.);* **b)** *(Photog.)* Sucher, *der*

fin de siècle [fæ̃ də ˈsjekl] *adj.* Fin-de-siècle-⟨*Architektur, Atmosphäre usw.*⟩

finding [ˈfaɪndɪŋ] *n.* **a)** Finden, *das;* ~ **is keeping** wer's findet, dem gehört's *(ugs.);* **b)** *usu. in pl. (conclusion[s])* Ergebnis, *das; (verdict)* Urteil, *das;* **what were the ~s of the investigations?** was haben die Ermittlungen ergeben?; **c)** *in pl. (Amer.) (small parts or tools)* Handwerkszeug, *das; (sewing essentials)* Nähzeug, *das*

¹fine [faɪn] **1.** *n.* **a)** Geldstrafe, *die; (for minor offence)* Bußgeld, *das;* **b)** *(literary)* **in ~** *(finally)* zu guter Letzt; *(to sum up)* kurzum; *(in short)* kurz und gut. **2.** *v. t.* mit einer Geldstrafe belegen; **we were ~d £10** wir mußten ein Bußgeld von 10 Pfund bezahlen; **be ~d for speeding** ein Bußgeld wegen überhöhter Geschwindigkeit zahlen müssen

²fine 1. *adj.* **a)** *(of high quality)* gut; hochwertig ⟨*Qualität, Lebensmittel*⟩; fein ⟨*Besteck, Gewebe, Spitze*⟩; edel ⟨*Pferd, Holz, Wein*⟩; **b)** *(pure)* rein ⟨*Öl, Metall, Wein*⟩; **c)** *(containing specified proportion of pure metal)* fein; **gold 18 carats ~:** 18karätiges Gold; **d)** *(delicately beautiful)* zart ⟨*Porzellan, Spitze*⟩; ansprechend ⟨*Beleuchtung, Manuskript*⟩; fein ⟨*Muster, Kristall, Stickerei, Gesichtszüge*⟩; **e)** *(refined)* edel ⟨*Empfindungen*⟩; fein ⟨*Taktgefühl, Geschmack*⟩; **a man of ~ feelings** ein Mann mit viel Feingefühl; **sb.'s ~r feelings** das Gute in jmdm.; **f)** *(delicate in structure or texture)* fein; **g)** *(thin)* fein; hauchdünn; **cut** *or* **run it ~:** knapp kalkulieren; **we'd be cutting it ~ if there are only three minutes to spare** es wird etwas knapp werden, wenn wir nur drei Minuten Zeit haben; **h)** *([in] small particles)* [hauch]fein ⟨*Sand, Staub*⟩; ~ **rain** Nieselregen, *der;* **i)** *(sharp, narrow-pointed)* scharf ⟨*Spitze, Klinge*⟩; spitz ⟨*Nadel, Schreibfeder*⟩; **j)** ~ **print** *see* **small print; k)** *(capable of delicate perception, discrimination)* fein ⟨*Gehör*⟩; scharf ⟨*Auge*⟩; genau ⟨*Waage, Werkzeug*⟩; empfindlich ⟨*Meßgerät*⟩; **l)** *(perceptible only with difficulty)* fein ⟨*Unterschied, Nuancen*⟩; *(precise)* klein ⟨*Detail*⟩; **the ~r points** die Feinheiten; **m)** *(excellent)* schön; gut ⟨*Ruf, Charakter, Stimmung, Hotel*⟩; edel ⟨*Gesinnung*⟩; ausgezeichnet ⟨*Sänger, Schauspieler*⟩; nett ⟨*Person*⟩; **a ~ time to do sth.** *(iron.)* ein passender Zeitpunkt, etw. zu tun *(iron.)*; **well, that's a ~ thing to say** *(iron.)* das ist wirklich nett *od.* reizend, so was zu sagen *(iron.)*; **that's a ~ excuse/way to treat your father** *(iron.)* das ist ja eine schöne Entschuldigung/feine Art, seinen Vater zu behandeln *(iron.)*; **you are a ~ one!** *(iron.)* du bist mir vielleicht einer! *(ugs.)*; **[this/that is] all very ~, but ...:** [das ist ja] alles schön und gut, aber ...; **n)** *(satisfactory)* schön; gut; **that's ~ with** *or* **by me** ja, ist mir recht; **everything is ~:** es ist alles in Ordnung; **o)** *(well conceived or expressed)* schön ⟨*Worte, Ausdruck usw.*⟩; gelungen ⟨*Rede, Übersetzung usw.*⟩; **p)** *(of handsome appearance or size)* schön; stattlich ⟨*Mann, Baum, Tier*⟩; **~-looking** gutaussehend; **a ~ body of men** eine vortreffliche Gruppe; **q)** *(in good health or state)* gut; **feel ~:** sich wohl fühlen; **she is ~ there now** sie fühlt sich jetzt wohl dort; **they had a few problems, but they're ~ now** es gab Probleme zwischen ihnen, aber jetzt kommen sie klar; **How are you? – F~, thanks. And you?** Wie geht es Ihnen? – Gut, danke. Und Ihnen?; **the car is ~ now** das Auto ist jetzt wieder in Ordnung *od.* läuft wieder; **r)** *(bright and clear)* schön ⟨*Wetter, Sommerabend*⟩; **~ and sunny** heiter und sonnig; **one ~ day ...:** eines schönen Tages ...; **one of these ~ days ...:** eines [schönen] Tages; **s)** *(ornate)* prächtig ⟨*Kleidung*⟩; **~ feathers** prächtiges Gefieder; *(fig.)* prächtige Gewänder; *see also* **feather 1 a; t)** *(fastidious)* vornehm, fein ⟨*Dame, Herr, Art, Manieren*⟩; *(affectedly ornate)* geziert; schönklingend ⟨*Worte*⟩; gewählt ⟨*Ausdrucksweise*⟩; **his ~ sensibilities** sein Feingefühl; **she's too ~ to associate with us** sie ist sich *(Dat.)* zu fein für uns. *See also* **dandy 2; point 1 b. 2.** *n. (fine weather)* schönes Wetter; **in rain or ~:** bei Regen oder Sonnenschein; **in the ~:** bei schönem Wetter. **3.** *adv.* **a)** *(in small particles)* fein ⟨*mahlen, raspeln, hacken*⟩; **b)** *(elegantly)* gewählt ⟨*sich ausdrücken*⟩; **c)** *(delicately)* fein ⟨*gewebt, gesponnen usw.*⟩; **d)** *(coll.: well)* gut

fine: ~ 'art *n.* **a)** *(subject)* bildende Kunst; **b)** *(skill)* **get** *or* **have [got] sth. [down] to a ~ art** etw. zu einer richtigen Kunst entwickeln; etw. aus dem Effeff beherrschen *(ugs.)*; **c) the ~ arts** die Schönen Künste; **~-drawn** *adj.* sehnig, hager ⟨*Gestalt*⟩; fein geschnitten ⟨*Gesichtszüge*⟩; *(subtle)* feinsinnig; **~-grained** *adj.* fein gekörnt ⟨*Sand, Salz, Papier*⟩; fein genarbt ⟨*Leder*⟩; fein gemasert ⟨*Holz*⟩

finely ['faɪnlɪ] *adv.* **a)** *(exquisitely)* **~ executed** *or* **crafted jewellery** fein gearbeiteter Schmuck; **b)** *(delicately)* fein ⟨*gewebt, gehäkelt usw.*⟩; genau ⟨*ausbalanciert*⟩; **c)** *(to a fine point or edge)* **a ~-sharpened blade** eine sorgfältig geschärfte Klinge; **a ~-pointed needle** eine feinspitzige Nadel; eine Nadel mit feiner Spitze; **a ~-drawn line** eine fein *od.* dünn [aus]gezogene Linie; **d)** *(into small particles)* fein ⟨*mahlen*⟩; **e)** *(subtly)* fein[sinnig]

fine 'print *see* **small print**

finery ['faɪnərɪ] *n., no pl.* Pracht, *die; (garments etc.)* Staat, *der;* **in all her wedding ~:** in ihrem Hochzeitsstaat

finesse [fɪ'nes] **1.** *n.* **a)** *(refinement)* Feinheit, *die; (of diplomat)* Gewandtheit, *die; (delicate manipulation)* Finesse, *die;* **b)** *(artfulness)* Raffinesse, *die;* **the ~ of the negotiators** das Geschick der Verhandlungspartner; **c)** *(Cards)* Schneiden, *das.* **2.** *v. i.* **a)** mit aller Raffinesse vorgehen; **b)** *(Cards)* schneiden. **3.** *v. t. (Cards)* schneiden mit

fine-tooth 'comb *n.* feingezähnter Kamm; **go through a manuscript** *etc.***/house** *etc.* **with a ~** *(fig.)* ein Manuskript *usw.* Punkt für Punkt durchgehen/ein Haus *usw.* durchkämmen

finger ['fɪŋgə(r)] **1.** *n.* **a)** Finger, *der;* **sb.'s ~s itch [to do sth.]** es juckt jmdm. in den Fingern[, etw. zu tun] *(ugs.)*; **lay a ~ on sb.** *(fig.)* jmdm. ein Härchen krümmen *(ugs.)*; **they never lift** *or* **move** *or* **raise a ~ to help her** *(fig.)* sie rühren keinen Finger, um ihr zu helfen; **they didn't lift** *or* **move** *or* **raise a ~** *(fig.)* sie haben keinen Finger krumm gemacht; **get** *or* **pull** *or* **take one's ~ out** *(fig. sl.)* Dampf dahinter machen *(ugs.)*; **point a** *or* **one's ~ at sb./sth.** mit dem Finger/*(fig. ugs.)* mit Fingern auf jmdn./etw. zeigen; **put the ~ on sb.** *(fig. sl.)* jmdn. verpfeifen *(ugs. abwertend)*; **have a ~ in sth.** *(fig.)* die Finger in etw. *(Dat.)* haben; **put** *or* **lay one's ~ on sth.** *(fig.)* etw. genau ausmachen; **I can't put my ~ on it** *(fig.)* ich kann es nicht genau ausmachen; **sth. slips through sb.'s ~s** etw. gleitet jmdm. durch die Finger; *(fig.)* etw. geht jmdm. durch die Lappen *(ugs.)*; **let sth. slip through one's ~s** *(fig.)* sich *(Dat.)* etw. entgehen *od. (ugs.)* durch die Lappen gehen lassen; **his ~s are [all] thumbs, he is all ~s and thumbs** er hat zwei linke Hände *(ugs.)*; **count the things/people on the ~s of one hand** die Dinge/Menschen an einer Hand abzählen; **b)** *(of glove etc.)* Finger, *der;* **c)** *(finger-like object)* **chocolate ~:** Löffelbiskuit mit Schokoladeüberzug; **a ~ of toast** ein Streifen Toast; **sponge ~s** schmale Stücke Rührkuchen; **d)** *(sl.: amount of liquor)* Fingerbreit, *der;* **a ~ of whisky** ein Fingerbreit Whisky. *See also* **bone 1 a; ¹burn 2 c; cross 2 a; fish finger; forefinger; green 1 a; index finger; little finger; middle finger; pie; ring-finger. 2.** *v. t.* **a)** *(touch with ~s)* berühren ⟨*Ware*⟩; greifen ⟨*Akkord*⟩; *(turn about with ~s)* anfassen; *(toy or meddle with)* befingern; herumfingern an (+ *Dat.*); **b)** *(Amer. sl.: indicate)* **~ sb./sth. to the police** jmdn. bei der Polizei verpfeifen/etw. der Polizei stecken *(ugs. abwertend)*

finger: ~-board *n.* Griffbrett, *das;* **~-bowl** *n.* Fingerschale, *die;* **~-end** Fingerspitze, *die;* **~-glass** *see* **~-bowl**

fingering ['fɪŋgərɪŋ] *n. (Mus.)* Fingersatz, *der; (proper method)* Fingertechnik, *die*

finger: ~-mark *n.* Fingerabdruck, *der;* **~-nail** *n.* Fingernagel, *der;* **~-paint** *n.* Fingerfarbe, *die;* **~-post** *n.* Wegweiser, *der;* **~print 1.** *n.* Fingerabdruck, *der;* **leave one's ~prints** *(fig.)* seine Fingerabdrücke hinterlassen; *see also* **take 1 i; 2.** *v. t.* einen Fingerabdruck nehmen von; **~print sb.** jmdm. die Fingerabdrücke abnehmen; **~-stall** *n.* Fingerling, *der;* **~tip** *n.* Fingerspitze, *die;* **have sth. at one's ~tips** *(fig.)* etw. aus dem Effeff können *od.* im kleinen Finger haben *(ugs.)*; **to the ~tips** *(fig.)* durch und durch; **he's a Spaniard to the very ~tips** er ist durch und durch Spanier

finial ['fɪnɪəl] *n. (Archit.)* Kreuzblume, *die*

finical ['fɪnɪkl], **finicking** ['fɪnɪkɪŋ] *adjs.* heikel; **she's so ~ about her appearance** sie ist so heikel, wenn es um ihr Äußeres geht; **she's so ~ about what she eats** in puncto Essen ist sie sehr wählerisch

finicky ['fɪnɪkɪ] *adj.* **a)** *see* **finical; b)** *(needing much attention to detail)* kniff[e]lig ⟨*Arbeit, Stickerei*⟩

finish ['fɪnɪʃ] **1.** *v. t.* **a)** *(bring to an end)* beenden ⟨*Unterhaltung*⟩; erledigen ⟨*Arbeit*⟩; abschließen ⟨*Kurs, Ausbildung*⟩; **have you ~ed the letter/book?** hast du den Brief/das Buch fertig[geschrieben]?; **have ~ed sth.** etw. fertig haben; mit etw. fertig sein; **have ~ed doing one's homework** seine Hausaufgaben fertig haben; mit seinen Hausaufgaben fertig sein; **~ writing/reading sth.** etw. zu Ende schreiben/lesen; **haven't you ~ed eating yet?** hast du noch nicht zu Ende gegessen *od.* fertiggegessen?; *abs.* **please let me ~ [speaking]** bitte lassen Sie mich ausreden; **have you quite ~ed?** sind Sie fertig?; *(iron.)* nun, bist du jetzt endlich fertig?; **b)** *(get through)* aufessen ⟨*Mahlzeit*⟩; auslesen ⟨*Buch, Zeitung*⟩; austrinken ⟨*Flasche, Glas*⟩; **I should ~ the book by this evening** ich müßte das Buch bis heute abend durchhaben *(ugs.)*; **c)** *(kill)* umbringen; *(destroy)* vernichten ⟨*Ernte*⟩; *(coll.: overcome)* schaffen *(ugs.)*; *(overcome completely)* bezwingen ⟨*Feind*⟩; *(ruin)* zugrunde richten; **any more stress would ~ him** noch mehr Streß würde ihn kaputtmachen *(ugs.)*; **a cold would ~ her** eine Erkältung würde das Ende für sie bedeuten; **it almost ~ed me!** das hat mich fast geschafft! *(ugs.)*; **this scandal ~ed her as an actress** dieser Skandal bedeutete das Ende ihrer Schauspielerkarriere; **d)** *(perfect)* vervollkommnen; den letzten Schliff geben (+ *Dat.*); **~ a seam** einen Saum vernähen; **e)** *(complete education of)* ausbilden; *(make highly accomplished)* mit allen Fertigkeiten ausstatten; *(make polished)* verfeinern ⟨*Umgangsformen*⟩; ausfeilen ⟨*Sprechweise*⟩; **f)** *(complete manufacture of by surface treatment)* eine schöne Oberfläche geben (+ *Dat.*); glätten ⟨*Papier, Holz*⟩; appretieren ⟨*Gewebe, Leder*⟩; glasieren ⟨*Tonwaren*⟩; polieren ⟨*Metall*⟩; verputzen ⟨*Mauerwerk*⟩; **~ sth. with a coat of varnish/waterproof coating/by polishing it** etw. zum Schluß lackieren/imprägnieren/polieren; **the ~ed article** *or* **product** das fertige Produkt. **2.** *v. i.* **a)** *(reach the end)* aufhören; ⟨*Geschichte, Episode:*⟩ enden; ⟨*Sturm, Unwetter:*⟩ sich legen; **when does the concert ~?** wann ist das Konzert aus?; **coffee to ~:** Kaffee zum Abschluß; **b)** *(come to end of race)* das Ziel erreichen; **~ first** als erster durchs Ziel gehen; erster werden; **~ badly/well** nicht durchhalten/einen guten Endspurt haben; **c) ~ in sth.** mit etw. enden; **~ by doing sth.** zum Schluß etw. tun. **3.** *n.* **a)** *(termination, cause of ruin)* Ende, *das;* **fight to a ~:** bis zur Entscheidung kämpfen; **it would be the ~ of him as a politician** das würde das Ende seiner Karriere als Politiker bedeuten; **b)** *(Hunting)* Ende der Jagd; **be in at the ~:** beim Halali dabeisein; *(fig.)* das Ende *od.* den Schluß miterleben; **c)** *(point at which race etc. ends)* Ziel, *das;* **arrive at the ~:** das Ziel erreichen; durchs Ziel gehen; **d)** *(what serves to give completeness)* letzter Schliff; **a ~ to sth.** die Vervollkommnung *od.* Vollendung einer Sache; **form a perfect ~ to a memorable evening** einen krönenden Abschluß eines unvergeßlichen Abends bilden; **e)** *(accomplished or completed state)* Schliff, *der;* **have ~:** Schliff haben; **f)** *(mode of finishing)* [technische] Ausführung; Finish, *das; (of paper)* Oberflächenfinish, *das; (of material, fabric)* Appretur, *die; (of metal)* Politur, *die;* **paintwork with a matt/gloss ~:** Matt-/Hochglanzlack, *der;* **kitchen furniture with a vinyl ~:** vinylbeschichtete Küchenmöbel

~ 'off *v. t.* **a)** *see* **~ 1 c, d; b)** *(provide with ending)* abschließen; beenden; **~ off a story** eine Geschichte zu Ende schreiben/erzählen; **c)** *(finish or trim neatly)* sauber verarbeiten

~ 'up *v. i.* **a)** *see* **~ 2 c; b) = end up; c)** *(complete all outstanding work)* alles erledigen

~ **with** *v. t.* **a)** *(complete one's use of)* **have you ~ed with the sugar?** brauchen Sie den Zucker noch?; **have ~ed with a book** ein Buch aus- *od.* fertiggelesen *od.* zu Ende gelesen haben; **are you ~ed with your plate?** hast du deinen Teller leergegessen?; **if these clothes are ~ed with, then throw them away** wenn du diese Sachen nicht mehr brauchst, wirf sie weg; **b)** *(end association with)* brechen mit; **she ~ed with her boyfriend** sie hat mit ihrem Freund Schluß gemacht; **c) have ~ed with doing sth.** es aufgegeben haben, etw. zu tun

finisher ['fɪnɪʃə(r)] *n.* **a)** *(person)* Fertigbearbeiter, *der*/-bearbeiterin, *die;* **metal-~:** Polierer, *der*/Poliererin, *die;* **cloth-~:** Appretierer, *der*/Appretiererin, *die;* **b)** *(coll.) (crushing blow)* vernichtender Schlag; **be a ~ to sb.** jmdn. schaffen *od.* jmdm. den Rest geben *(ugs.)*

finishing: **~-post** *n.* Zielpfosten, *der;* **~-school** *n.* Mädchenpensionat, *das (veralt.) (besonders zur Vorbereitung auf das gesellschaftliche Leben);* ~ **'touch** *n.* **as a ~ touch to sth.** zur Vollendung *od.* Vervollkommnung einer Sache; um eine Sache abzurunden; **put the ~ touches to sth.** einer Sache *(Dat.)* den letzten Schliff geben

finite ['faɪnaɪt] **a)** *(bounded)* begrenzt; ~ **number** *(Math.)* endliche Zahl; **b)** *(Ling.)* finit

Finland ['fɪnlənd] *pr. n.* Finnland *(das)*

Finn [fɪn] *n.* Finne, *der*/Finnin, *die*

Finnish ['fɪnɪʃ] **1.** *adj.* finnisch; **sb. is ~:** jmd. ist Finne/Finnin; **the ~ language** das Finnische; *see also* **English 1. 2.** *n.* Finnisch, *das; see also* **English 2a**

'fin whale *see* **rorqual**

fiord [fjɔ:d] *n.* Fjord, *der*

fir [fɜ:(r)] *n.* **a)** *(tree)* Tanne, *die;* **b)** *(wood)* Tanne, *die;* Tannenholz, *das. See also* **Scotch fir; silver fir**

'fir-cone *n.* Tannenzapfen, *der*

fire ['faɪə(r)] **1.** *n.* **a)** Feuer, *das; (flame)* Flamme, *die;* **set ~ to sth.** ⟨*Person:*⟩ etw. anzünden; **set ~ to oneself** sich anzünden; **strike ~ from sth.** Funken aus etw. schlagen; **be on ~:** brennen *(auch fig.);* in Flammen stehen; **catch** *or* **take ~,** *(Scot., Ir.)* **go on ~** *(lit. or fig.)* Feuer fangen; ⟨*Wald, Gebäude:*⟩ in Brand geraten; **set sth. on ~:** etw. anzünden; *(in order to destroy)* etw. in Brand stecken; *(deliberately)* Feuer an etw. *(Akk.)* legen; **he won't/it's not going to set the Thames** *(Brit.) or (Amer.)* **the world on ~:** er hat das Pulver nicht erfunden *(ugs.)*/es ist nichts Weltbewegendes *od.* Welterschütterndes; **b)** *(in grate)* [offenes] Feuer; *(electric or gas ~)* Heizofen, *der; (in the open air)* Lagerfeuer, *das;* **open ~:** Kaminfeuer, *das;* **round** *or* **by the ~:** am warmen Ofen; **over a low ~:** auf kleinem Feuer; **make up the ~:** nachlegen; **turn up the ~** *(electric)* die Heizung/*(gas)* das Gas höher drehen *od.* aufdrehen; **switch on another bar of the ~:** einen weiteren Heizstab einschalten; **have ~ in one's belly** *(ambition)* Ehrgeiz haben; *(enthusiasm)* begeisterungsfähig sein; **play with ~** *(lit. or fig.)* mit dem Feuer spielen; **light the ~:** den Ofen anstecken; *(in grate)* das [Kamin]feuer anmachen; **lay a ~:** ein Feuer anlegen; **make a ~:** ein Feuer [an]machen; **c)** *(destructive burning)* Brand, *der;* **in case of ~, follow these instructions** bei Feuer *od.* im Brandfall ist diesen Anweisungen Folge zu leisten; **insure sth. against ~:** etw. gegen Feuer versichern; **where's the ~?** *(coll. iron.)* wo brennt's denn? *(ugs.);* **F~!** Feuer!; es brennt!; **go through ~ and water [to help sb.]** *(fig.)* [für jmdn.] durchs Feuer gehen; **d)** *(fervour)* Feuer, *das;* **the ~ with which he speaks** die Leidenschaft, mit der er spricht; **his speech was full of ~:** er hielt eine glühende *od.* feurige *od. (geh.)* flammende Rede; **e)** *(firing of guns)* Schießen, *das;* Schießerei, *die;* **pistol ~:** [Pistolen]schüsse; **cannon ~:** Kanonenfeuer, *das;* **be exposed to the ~ of critics** *(fig.)* im Kreuzfeuer der Kritik stehen; von den Kritikern unter Beschuß genommen werden; **line of ~** *(lit. or fig.)* Schußlinie, *die;* **running ~** *(lit. or fig.)* Trommelfeuer, *das;* **between two ~s** *(lit. or fig.)* zwischen zwei Feuern; **be/come under ~:** beschossen werden/unter Beschuß geraten; *(fig.)* heftig angegriffen werden/unter Beschuß geraten. *See also* **cease 2b; coal b; draw 1b; fat 2; frying-pan; fuel 1; hang 1i; hold 1t; iron 1b; open 3c; smoke 1a. 2.** *v. t.* **a)** *(set fire to)* anzünden; in Brand stecken; **b)** *(kindle)* zünden ⟨*Sprengladung*⟩; **c)** *(fig.: stimulate)* beflügeln ⟨*Phantasie*⟩; anregen ⟨*Ehrgeiz*⟩; erregen ⟨*Interesse*⟩; inspirieren, anregen ⟨*Person*⟩; *(fill with enthusiasm)* begeistern, in Begeisterung versetzen ⟨*Person*⟩; **d)** *(bake)* brennen ⟨*Tonwaren, Ziegel*⟩; **e)** *(supply with fuel)* befeuern ⟨*Ofen*⟩; [be]heizen ⟨*Lokomotive*⟩; **f)** *(cause to explode)* zünden ⟨*Sprengladung*⟩; [in die Luft] sprengen ⟨*Mine*⟩; **g)** *(discharge)* abschießen ⟨*Gewehr*⟩; abfeuern ⟨*Kanone*⟩; **~ one's gun/pistol/rifle at sb.** auf jmdn. schießen; **h)** *(produce with guns)* ~ **a 21-gun salute** 21 Salutschüsse abgeben; **i)** *(propel from gun etc.)* abgeben, abfeuern ⟨*Schuß*⟩; *(fig.)* vom Stapel lassen *(ugs.)*⟨*Kritik, Bemerkungen*⟩; ~ **a bullet/cartridge** einen Schuß abgeben; ~ **blank cartridges** mit Platzpatronen schießen; **two shots were ~d/~d by sb.** es fielen zwei Schüsse/zwei Schüsse wurden von jmdm. abgegeben; ~ **questions at sb.** jmdn. mit Fragen bombardieren; Fragen auf jmdn. abfeuern; **j)** *(coll.: dismiss)* feuern *(ugs.)*⟨*Angestellten*⟩. **3.** *v. i.* **a)** *(shoot)* schießen; feuern; **~!** [gebt] Feuer!; **be the first to ~:** das Feuer eröffnen; **~ at/on sth./sb.** auf etw./jmdn. schießen; ~ **into the air/at the ground/into the crowd** in die Luft/in den Boden/in die Menge schießen; ~ **on sth. from above** etw. aus der Luft beschießen; **b)** ⟨*Motor:*⟩ zünden; **the engine is not firing properly** der Motor läuft nicht richtig

~ **a'way** *v. i. (fig. coll.)* losschießen *(fig. ugs.);* **~ away!** schieß los!; fang an!

~ **'out** *(Amer.) see* ~ **2j**

fire: **~-alarm** *n.* Feuermelder, *der;* **~arm** *n.* Schußwaffe, *die;* **~-axe** *n.* Feuerwehraxt, *die;* **~-ball** *n.* **a)** *(large meteor)* Feuerkugel, *die;* **b)** *(ball of flame)* Feuerball, *der;* **c)** *(globular lightning)* Kugelblitz, *der;* **d)** *(energetic person)* Energiebündel, *das (ugs.);* **~-bell** *n.* Feuerglocke, *die;* **~brand** *n.* Brandfackel, *die; (fig.)* Unruhestifter, *der*/-stifterin, *die;* Aufwiegler, *der*/Aufwieglerin, *die;* **~-break** *n.* Brandschneise, *die;* **~-breathing** *adj.* feuerspeiend; **~-brick** *n.* Schamottestein, *der;* ~ **brigade** *n. (Brit.)* Feuerwehr, *die;* **~-bucket** *n.* Löscheimer, *der;* ~ **chief** *n. (Amer.)* Branddirektor, *der;* **~-clay** *n.* Schamotte, *die;* **~-damaged** *adj.* durch Brand beschädigt; **~-damp** *n.* Grubengas, *das;* ~ **department** *(Amer.) see* ~ **brigade;** ~ **door** *n.* Feuerschutztür, *die;* **~-drill** *n. (for firemen)* Feuerwehrübung, *die; (for others)* Probe[feuer]alarm, *der;* **~-eater** *n.* **a)** *(conjurer)* Feuerschlucker, *der;* **b)** *(fond of fighting)* Kampfhahn, *der (ugs.); (fond of quarrelling)* Streithahn, *der (ugs.);* **~-engine** *n.* Löschfahrzeug, *das;* **~-escape** *n. (staircase)* Feuertreppe, *die; (ladder)* Feuerleiter, *die;* ~ **extinguisher** *n.* Feuerlöscher, *der;* **portable ~ extinguisher** Handfeuerlöscher, *der;* **~-fighter** *n.* Feuerwehrmann, *der*/-frau, *die;* **~-fighting** *n.* Feuerbekämpfung, *die;* Brandbekämpfung, *die;* **~-fighting equipment** Feuerlöscheinrichtung, *die;* **~fly** *n.* Leuchtkäfer, *der;* Glühwürmchen, *das (ugs.);* **~-guard** *n.* Schutzgitter, *das;* Kamingitter, *das;* ~ **hazard** *n.* Brandrisiko, *das;* **~-hose** *n.* Feuerwehrschlauch, *der;* ~ **insurance** *n.* Feuerversicherung, *die;* Brandversicherung, *die;* **~-irons** *n. pl.* Kaminbesteck, *das;* **~light** *n.* Schein des Feuers; Schein der Flammen; **~-lighter** *n. (Brit.)* Feueranzünder, *der;* **~man** ['faɪəmən] *n., pl.* **~men** ['faɪəmən] **a)** *(member of fire brigade)* Feuerwehrmann, *der;* **~man's lift** Feuerwehrgriff, *der;* **b)** *(Railw.)* Heizer, *der;* **~place** *n.* Kamin, *der;* **~-power** *n.* Feuerkraft, *die;* **~-practice** *see* **~-drill;** ~ **precautions** *n. pl.* Feuerschutz, *der;* **~proof 1.** *adj.* feuerfest; **2.** *v. t.* feuerfest machen; **~-raiser** *n. (Brit.)* Brandstifter, *der*/-stifterin, *die;* **~-raising** *n. (Brit.)* Brandstiftung, *die;* **~-resistant** *adj.* feuerbeständig; ~ **risk** *see* ~ **hazard;** **~-screen** *n.* Ofenschirm, *der;* **F~ Service** *n.* Feuerwehr, *die;* **~side** *n.* Kaminecke, *die;* **at** *or* **by the ~side** am Kamin; **at** *or* **by one's own ~side** am heimischen Herde; **~side chat** Plauderei am Kamin; ~ **station** *n.* Feuerwache, *die;* **~-tender** *n.* Gerätewagen *(der Feuerwehr);* **~-tongs** *n. pl.* Feuerzange, *die;* **a pair of ~-tongs** eine Feuerzange; **~-trap** *n.* Feuerfalle, *die;* **~-walker** *n. jmd., der barfüßig über glühende Steine läuft;* Feuerläufer, *der*/-läuferin, *die;* **~-watcher** *n.* Feuerposten, *der;* Brandwart, *der; (in war)* Luftschutzwart, *der;* **~-water** *n. (coll.)* Feuerwasser, *das (ugs.);* **~wood** *n.* Brennholz, *das;* **~work** *n.* **a)** Feuerwerkskörper, *der;* **~work display** Feuerwerk, *das;* **b)** *in pl. (display)* Feuerwerk, *das; (fig.: display of wit)* Feuerwerk des Geistes; **intellectual ~-works** ein geistiges *od.* intellektuelles Feuerwerk; **there were** *or* **it caused ~works** *(fig.)* da war was los *od.* flogen die Funken *(ugs.)*

firing ['faɪərɪŋ] *n.* **a)** *(of houses)* Anzünden, *das; (of pottery)* Brennen, *das;* **b)** *(fuel)* Feuerung, *die;* **the ~ for these furnaces was coal** diese Öfen wurden mit Kohle befeuert; **c)** *no pl. (of guns)* Abfeuern, *das;* **we could hear ~ in the distance** in der Ferne konnten wir Schüsse hören; **the ~ in the streets** die Schießerei in den Straßen

firing: **~-line** *n. (lit. or fig.)* Feuerlinie, *die;* **~-party, ~-squad** *ns. (at military funeral)* Ehrensalutkommando, *das; (at military execution)* Exekutionskommando, *das*

¹firm [fɜ:m] *n.* **a)** *(carrying on a business)* Firma, *die;* ~ **of architects/decorators** Architektenbüro, *das*/Malerbetrieb, *der;* **b)** *(group working together)* Team, *das;* Arbeitsgemeinschaft, *die*

²firm 1. *adj.* **a)** fest; stabil ⟨*Verhältnis, Konstruktion, Stuhl*⟩; straff ⟨*Busen*⟩; stramm ⟨*Bäckchen*⟩; verbindlich ⟨*Angebot*⟩; **be on ~ ground again** *(lit. or fig.)* wieder festen Boden unter den Füßen haben; **do sth. to make a chair/bench ~:** etw. tun, damit ein Stuhl/eine Bank feststeht; **as ~ as a rock** felsenfest; **they are ~ friends** sie sind gut befreundet; **have a ~ grip on sth.** etw. fest in der Hand haben; **the chair is not ~:** der Stuhl wackelt *od.* ist wacklig; **make a ~ date** eine feste Zeit vereinbaren; **b)** *(resolute)* entschlossen ⟨*Blick*⟩; bestimmt, entschieden ⟨*Ton*⟩; stark ⟨*Widerstand*⟩; **in ~ pursuit of his goal** in energischer *od.* entschiedener Verfolgung seines Ziels; **be a ~ believer in sth.** fest an etw. *(Akk.)* glauben; **be ~ when you speak to him** sei bestimmt, wenn du mit ihm sprichst; **be ~ in one's beliefs** fest auf seiner Überzeugung beharren; an seiner Überzeugung festhalten; ~ **insistence** Beharrlichkeit, *die;* **she has a ~ character** sie besitzt Charakterstärke; **c)** *(insisting on obedience etc.)* bestimmt; **be ~ with sb.** jmdm. gegenüber bestimmt auftreten; **a ~ hand** eine feste Hand; **with a ~ hand** mit fester *od.* starker Hand; **d)** *(Commerc.)* fest; stabil ⟨*Markt*⟩; **oil is not ~:** der Ölmarkt ist nicht stabil. **2.** *adv.* **stand ~!** *(fig.)* sei standhaft!; laß dich nicht davon abbringen!; **stand ~ in sth.** *(fig.)* fest *od.* unerschütterlich bei etw. bleiben; **hold ~ to sth.** *(fig.)* an einer Sache festhalten. **3.** *v. t.* **a)** *(make firm or solid)* fest werden lassen; festigen, straffen ‹*Muskulatur, Körper*›; **b)** fest [ein]pflanzen ‹*Pflanzen*›

~ 'up 1. *v. t.* konkretisieren ‹*Plan, Geschäft, Vereinbarung*›. **2.** *v. i.* ‹*Plan, Geschäft, Vereinbarung:*› sich konkretisieren

firmament ['fɜːməmənt] *n. (literary)* Firmament, *das*

firmly ['fɜːmlɪ] *adv.* **a)** fest; **the jelly has set ~:** der Gelee ist fest geworden; **a ~-built structure** eine stabile Konstruktion; **sth. is ~ under lock and key** etw. ist sicher weggeschlossen; **b)** *(resolutely)* beharrlich ‹*unterstützen, sich widersetzen*›; bestimmt, energisch ‹*reden*›; **deal with** *or* **treat sb. ~:** jmdm. gegenüber bestimmt auftreten

firmness ['fɜːmnɪs] *n., no pl.* **a)** *(solidity)* Festigkeit, *die; (of foundations, building)* Stabilität, *die; (of offer)* Verbindlichkeit, *die;* **b)** *(resoluteness)* Entschlossenheit, *die; (of voice)* Bestimmtheit, *die; (of support, belief)* Beständigkeit, *die;* Beharrlichkeit, *die;* **the ~ of his resolve** seine feste Entschlossenheit; **c)** *(insistence on obedience etc.)* Bestimmtheit, *die;* **use ~ with sb., treat sb. with ~:** jmdm. gegenüber bestimmt auftreten

first [fɜːst] **1.** *adj.* erst...; *(for the ~ time ever)* Erst‹*aufführung, -besteigung*›; *(of an artist's ~ achievement)* Erstlings‹*film, -roman, -stück, -werk*›; **he was ~ to arrive** er kam als erster an; **who was ~?** wer war erster?; **for the [very] ~ time** zum [aller]ersten Mal; **there's always a ~ time** *(coll.)* irgendwann passiert's dann eben doch *(ugs.);* **~ thing you know** *(coll.)* ehe du dich's versiehst; **just buy the ~ thing one sees** das erste beste kaufen; **I'll do it at the ~ opportunity** ich tue es bei der erstbesten Gelegenheit; **say the ~ thing that comes into one's head** das sagen, was einem zuerst einfällt; **the ~ two** die ersten beiden *od.* zwei; **come in ~** *(win race)* [das Rennen] gewinnen; **head/feet ~:** mit dem Kopf/den Füßen zuerst *od.* voran; **~ thing after breakfast** *(coll.)* gleich nach dem Frühstück; **~ thing in the morning** gleich frühmorgens; *(coll.: tomorrow)* gleich morgen früh; **~ thing on arrival** *(coll.)* gleich nach der Ankunft; **the ~ thing [to do]** *(coll.)* das erste [, was man tun muß]; **~ things ~** *(coll.)* eins nach dem anderen; immer [hübsch] der Reihe nach; **have [the] ~ claim to sth.** eine Option auf etw. *(Akk.)* haben; **she is ~ in the class** sie ist Klassenbeste *od.* die Beste in der Klasse; **he's always [the] ~ to help** er ist immer als erster zur Stelle, wenn Hilfe benötigt wird; **not know the ~ thing about a matter** von einer Sache nicht das geringste verstehen; **~ soprano/cello** *(Mus.)* erster Sopran/Cellist; *see also* **eighth 1. 2.** *adv.* **a)** *(before anyone else)* zuerst; als erster/erste ‹*sprechen, ankommen*›; *(before anything else)* an erster Stelle ‹*stehen, kommen*›; *(when listing: firstly)* zuerst; als erstes; **women and children ~!** Frauen und Kinder zuerst; **ladies ~!** Ladies first!; den Damen der Vortritt!; **you [go] ~** *(as invitation)* Sie haben den Vortritt; bitte nach Ihnen; **~ come ~ served** wer zuerst kommt, mahlt zuerst *(Spr.);* **we must put our children's education ~:** die Schulbildung unserer Kinder muß für uns an erster Stelle stehen; **this matter is** *or* **comes ~ on the agenda** diese Angelegenheit ist der erste Punkt unserer Tagesordnung; **come ~ with sb.** *(fig.)* bei jmdm. zuerst kommen; **say ~ one thing and then another** erst so und dann wieder so sagen *(ugs.);* **b)** *(beforehand)* vorher; **... but ~ we must ...:** ... aber zuerst *od.* erst müssen wir ...; **c)** *(for the ~ time)* zum ersten Mal; das erste Mal; erstmals ‹*bekanntgeben, sich durchsetzen*›; **d)** *(in preference)* eher; lieber; **I'd [rather] die ~:** eher *od.* lieber würde ich sterben; **I wouldn't give him a penny. I'd see him damned ~:** ich würde ihm keinen Pfennig geben, soll er zum Teufel gehen! *(ugs.);* **e) ~ of all** zuerst; *(in importance)* vor allem; **~ of all let me express my gratitude to you** zu [aller]erst *od.* als erstes möchte ich Ihnen meinen Dank aussprechen; **~ and foremost** *(basically)* zunächst einmal; *(in importance)* vor allem; **~ and last** *(almost entirely)* in erster Linie; *(reckoned altogether)* im ganzen; insgesamt; **f)** *(~-class)* **travel ~:** erster Klasse reisen. **3.** *n.* **a) the ~** *(in sequence)* der/die/das erste; *(in rank)* der/die/das Erste; **the ~ shall be last** *(Bibl.)* die Ersten werden die Letzten sein; **be the ~ to arrive** als erster/erste ankommen; **she is the ~ in the class** sie ist Klassenbeste *od.* die Beste in der Klasse; **~ among equals** Primus inter pares *(geh.);* **this is the ~ I've heard of it** das höre ich zum ersten Mal; **b) at ~:** zuerst; anfangs; **from the ~:** von Anfang an; **from ~ to last** von Anfang bis Ende; **I've always said from ~ to last that ...:** ich habe schon immer gesagt, daß ...; **it took five years, from ~ to last** es hat alles in allem fünf Jahre gedauert; **c)** *(day)* **the ~ of May** der erste Mai; **the ~ [of the month]** der Erste [des Monats]; **d)** *(Brit. Univ.)* Eins, *die; (person)* **he's a ~ [in History]** er hat eine Eins [in Geschichte] bekommen; **get** *or* **take** *or* **be awarded a ~ in one's finals** sein Examen mit [der Note] Eins bestehen; **e)** *(~ form)* erste [Schul]klasse; Erste, *die (Schuljargon);* **f)** *(Motor Veh.)* erster Gang; **in ~:** im ersten [Gang]; **change down to ~:** in den ersten [Gang] runterschalten; **g)** *(pioneering feat)* Pioniertat, *die;* **h)** *in pl. (best-quality goods)* erstklassige Ware; Ware von erster *od.* bester Qualität. *See also* **eighth 2**

first: ~ 'aid *n.* Erste Hilfe; **give [sb.] ~ aid** [jmdm.] Erste Hilfe leisten; **~-aid tent/post** *or* **station** Sanitätszelt, *das*/-wache, *die;* **~-aid box/kit** Verbandskasten, *der*/Erste-Hilfe-Ausrüstung, *die;* **~ 'base** *see* **'base 1 c; ~ 'blood** *see* **blood 1 a; ~-born 1.** *adj.* erstgeboren; **2.** *n.* Erstgeborene, *der/die;* **~ 'class** *n.* **a)** erste Kategorie; *(for produce)* Klasse A; **b)** *(Transport)* erste Klasse; **travel in the ~ class** erster Klasse reisen; **c)** *(Brit. Univ.) see* **first 3 d; d)** *(Post) bevorzugt beförderte Post;* **~-class 1.** ['--] *adj.* **a)** *(of the ~ class)* **~-class carriage** Erste[r]-Klasse-Wagen, *der;* **~-class ticket** Fahrkarte erster Klasse; **~-class compartment** Erste[r]-Klasse-Abteil, *das;* Abteil erster Klasse; **~-class honours degree** *(Brit. Univ.)* Prädikatsexamen, *das;* **~-class mail** *or* **post** *bevorzugt beförderte Post;* **~-class stamp** *Briefmarke für bevorzugt beförderte Post;* **b)** *(excellent)* erstklassig; **a ~-class idiot** *(iron.)* ein Vollidiot; **2.** [-'-] *adv.* **a)** *(by the ~ class)* erster Klasse ‹*reisen*›; **send a letter ~-class** *einen Brief bevorzugt befördern lassen;* **b)** *(coll.: excellently)* prima *(ugs.);* großartig; **~ 'coat** *n. (of paint)* erster Anstrich; **~ 'cousin** *see* **cousin; ~ e'dition** *n.* Erstausgabe, *die;* **~ 'floor** *see* **floor 1 b; ~ form** *see* **form 1 d; ~-'fruits** *n. pl.* Erstlinge; *(fig.)* erste Ergebnisse; **~ 'gear** *n., no pl. (Motor Veh.)* erster Gang; *see also* **gear 1 a; ~hand** *adj.* aus erster Hand *nachgestellt;* **from ~hand experience** aus eigener Erfahrung; **have ~hand knowledge of sth.** etw. aus erster Hand wissen; **have ~hand acquaintance with suffering** viel Leid erfahren haben; *see also* **hand 1 j; F~ 'Lady** *n.* First Lady, *die;* **~ lieu'tenant** *see* **lieutenant a; ~ 'light** *n.* **at ~ light** im *od.* beim Morgengrauen

firstly ['fɜːstlɪ] *adv.* zunächst [einmal]; *(followed by 'secondly')* erstens

first: ~ name *n.* Vorname, *der;* **be on ~-name terms with sb.** jmdn. mit Vornamen anreden; **~-named** *attrib. adj.* erstgenannt...; **~ 'night** *n. (Theatre)* Premiere, *die;* **~-night nerves/audience** Premierenfieber, *das*/-publikum, *das;* **~ off** *adv. (coll.)* zuerst; **~ of'fender** *n.* Ersttäter, *der;* **~ 'officer** *n. (Naut.)* Erster Offizier; **~ 'person** *see* **person d; ~ 'proof** *see* **proof 1 f; ~-rate 1.** ['--] *adj.* **a)** *(excellent)* erstklassig; **b)** *(coll.)* **feel a ~-rate fool** *(iron.)* sich *(Dat.)* wie ein Dummkopf ersten Ranges vorkommen; **2.** [-'-] *adv. (coll.)* prima *(ugs.);* großartig; **~ 'reading** *see* **reading g; ~ refusal** *see* **refusal; ~ school** *n. (Brit.)* ≈ Grundschule, *die;* **F~ 'Secretary** *n.* Erster Sekretär; **~ 'strike** *n. (Mil.)* Erstschlag, *der;* Präventivschlag, *der;* **~-strike capability** Präventivschlagkapazität, *die;* **~ 'string** *see* **string 1 b; ~-time** *attrib. adj.* **~-time voter** Erstwähler, *der;* **~-time buyer** *jmd., der zum ersten Mal ein eigenes Haus/eine Eigentumswohnung kauft;* **~ 'water** *see* **water 1 d**

firth [fɜːθ] *n.* Förde, *die*

'fir tree *see* **fir a**

fiscal ['fɪskl] *adj.* fiskalisch; finanzpolitisch; **~ policy** Fiskal- *od.* Finanzpolitik, *die;* **~ year** *(Brit.)* Geschäftsjahr, *das;* Rechnungsjahr, *das; (Amer.)* Finanzjahr, *das;* Etatjahr, *das;* **~ autonomy** Finanzhoheit, *die*

fiscally ['fɪskəlɪ] *adv.* fiskalisch; finanzpolitisch

fish [fɪʃ] **1.** *n., pl. same or (esp. child lang./poet.)* **~es a)** Fisch, *der;* **~ and chips** Fisch mit Pommes frites; **~ and chip shop** ≈ Fischbraterei, *die;* **a big ~ in a little pond** *(fig.)* ein Großer bei den Kleinen; **a little ~ in a big pond** *(fig.)* nur einer von vielen; **[be] like a ~ out of water** [sich] wie ein Fisch auf dem Trockenen [fühlen]; **drink like a ~** *(coll.)* wie ein Loch saufen *(derb);* **have other ~ to fry** *(fig. coll.)* Wichtigeres zu tun haben; **neither ~ nor fowl** *(fig.)* weder Fisch noch Fleisch *(ugs.);* **there are plenty more ~ in the sea** *(fig. coll.)* es gibt noch andere auf der Welt; **b)** *(Astrol.)* **the F~[es]** die Fische; *see also* **archer b; c)** *(coll.: person)* **queer ~:** komischer Kauz; **big ~:** großes Tier; großer *od.* dicker Fisch *(ugs., scherzh.);* **cold ~:** kalter Fisch *(ugs.);* **the poor ~!** der arme Tropf! **2.** *v. i.* **a)** fischen; *(with rod)* angeln; **go ~ing** fischen/angeln gehen; **go trout-~ing** auf Forellenfang gehen; **~ in troubled waters** *(fig.)* im trüben fischen; **b)** *(fig. coll.) (try to get information)* auf Informationen aussein; *(delve)* **~ around in one's bag** in der Tasche herumsuchen. **3.** *v. t.* **a)** fischen; fangen ‹*Fisch*›; *(with rod)* angeln; **~ a river/lake** in einem Fluß/See fischen/angeln; **b)** *(fig.: take, pull)* [heraus]fischen *(ugs.)* **(out** of aus)

~ for *v. t.* **a)** fischen/angeln; fischen/angeln auf (+ *Akk.*) *(Anglerjargon);* **b)** *(fig. coll.)* suchen nach; **be ~ing for sth.** auf etw. *(Akk.)* aussein *(ugs.)*

~ 'out *v. t. (fig. coll.)* herausfischen *(ugs.);* **~ sb./a dead body out of the river** jmdn./eine Leiche aus dem Fluß fischen *(ugs.)*

~ 'up *v. t.* herausfischen

fish: ~-bone *n.* [Fisch]gräte, *die;* **~-bowl** *n.* Fischglas, *das;* **~ cake** *n. (Cookery)* Fischfrikadelle, *die;* **~ course** *n.* Fischgang, *der*

fisherman ['fɪʃəmən] *n., pl.* **fishermen** ['fɪʃəmən] Fischer, *der; (angler)* Angler, *der;* **~'s story** Seemannsgarn, *das*

fishery ['fɪʃərɪ] *n.* **a)** *no pl., no indef. art. (fishing)* Fischfang, *der;* Fischerei, *die;* **b)** *(fishing-grounds)* Fischfanggebiet, *das;* Fischereigewässer, *das;* **in-shore fisheries** Küstenfischerei, *die;* **deep-sea fisheries** Hochseefischerei, *die*

fishery pro'tection vessel *n. (Naut.)* Fischereischutzboot, *das*

fish: ~-eye lens *n. (Photog.)* Fischaugenobjektiv, *das;* **~-farm** *n.* Fischzucht[anlage], *die;* ~**-farming** *n.* Fischzucht, *die;* ~ '**finger** *n.* Fischstäbchen, *das;* ~**-fork** *n.* Fischgabel, *die;* ~**-glue** *n.* Fischleim, *der;* ~**-hook** *n.* Angelhaken, *der*

fishing ['fɪʃɪŋ] *n. (occupation)* Fischen, *das; (with rod)* Angeln, *das; attrib.* Fischerei-; **freshwater** ~: Süßwasserfischerei, *die;* ~ **craft** *pl.* Fischereifahrzeuge

fishing: ~ **boat** *n.* Fischerboot, *das;* ~ **expedition** *n.* **a)** Fangfahrt, *die;* **go on a** ~ **expedition** auf Fischfang gehen; **b)** *(fig.)* Schnüffeltour, *die (ugs.);* ~ **fleet** *n.* Fischereiflotte, *die;* ~**-grounds** *n. pl.* Fischgründe *Pl.;* ~ **limits** *n. pl.* Fischereigrenze, *die;* ~**-line** *n.* Angelschnur, *die;* ~**-net** *n.* Fischernetz, *das;* ~ **rights** *n. pl.* Fischereirecht, *das;* ~**-rod** *n.* Angelrute, *die;* ~**-smack** *n.* Fischkutter, *der;* ~ **story** *n.* Seemannsgarn, *das;* ~**-tackle** *n.* Angelgeräte; ~**-vessel** *n.* Fischereifahrzeug, *das;* ~ **village** *n.* Fischerdorf, *das*

fish: ~**-kettle** *n.* Fischkessel, *der;* ~**-knife** *n.* Fischmesser, *das;* ~**-knife and -fork** Fischbesteck, *das;* ~**-ladder** *n.* Fischleiter, *die;* Fischpaß, *der;* ~**like** *adj.* fischartig; ~**-meal** *n.* Fischmehl, *das;* ~**monger** ['fɪʃmʌŋgə(r)] *n. (Brit.)* Fischhändler, *der*/-händlerin, *die;* **a** ~**monger's** ein Fischgeschäft; *see also* **baker;** ~**-net** *n.* Fischnetz, *das;* ~**-net stockings** Netzstrümpfe; ~ **paste** *n.* Fischpaste, *die;* ~**-pond** *n.* Fischteich, *der;* ~ **shop** *n.* Fischgeschäft, *das;* ~**-slice** *n.* Wender, *der; (carving-knife)* Fischvorlegemesser, *das;* ~**-tank** *n.* Fischkasten, *der;* Fischbehälter, *der;* ~**wife** *n. (derog.)* Fischweib, *das (veralt.)*

fishy ['fɪʃɪ] *adj.* **a)** fischartig; ~ **smell/taste** Fischgeruch/-geschmack, *der;* **b)** *(coll.: questionable)* verdächtig; zweifelhaft, fragwürdig ⟨*Umstände*⟩; nicht ganz astrein *(ugs.)* ⟨*Sache*⟩; **there's something** ~ **about this whole business** an der ganzen Sache ist was faul *(ugs.)*

fissile ['fɪsaɪl] *adj. (Nucl. Phys.)* fissil *(fachspr.);* spaltbar

fission ['fɪʃn] **1.** *n.* **a)** *(Nucl. Phys.)* [Kern]spaltung, *die;* Fission, *die (fachspr.);* **b)** *(Biol.)* [Zell]teilung, *die;* Fission, *die (fachspr.)*

fissionable ['fɪʃənəbl] *adj. (Nucl. Phys.)* spaltbar; fissil *(fachspr.)*

fissure ['fɪʃə(r)] *n.* Riß, *der; (Geol.)* Erdspalte, *die;* Bodenriß, *der*

fist [fɪst] *n.* **a)** Faust, *die;* **b)** *(coll.: hand)* Hand, *die;* Pfote, *die (salopp); (joc.: handwriting)* Handschrift, *die;* Klaue, *die (ugs. abwertend)*

'**fist-fight** *n.* Schlägerei, *die*

fistful ['fɪstfʊl] *n.* Handvoll, *die;* **a** ~ **of coins** eine Handvoll Münzen

fisticuffs ['fɪstɪkʌfs] *n. pl.* Handgreiflichkeiten *Pl.;* **the quarrel ended in** ~: der Streit endete mit einer Schlägerei

fistula ['fɪstjʊlə] *n. (Med., Zool.)* Fistel, *die*

¹fit [fɪt] *n.* **a)** Anfall, *der;* ~ **of coughing** Hustenanfall, *der;* **fainting** ~: Ohnmachtsanfall, *der;* **collapse in a** ~: einen Kollaps *od.* Anfall erleiden; zusammenbrechen; **epileptic** ~: epileptischer Anfall; **b)** *(fig.)* [plötzliche] Anwandlung; **give sb. a** ~ *(startle sb.)* jmdm. einen Schrecken einjagen; *(outrage sb.)* jmdn. aus der Haut fahren lassen *(ugs.);* **[almost] have** *or* **throw a** ~: [fast] Zustände kriegen *(ugs.);* **she'll have a** ~ **when she hears that** *(fig. coll.)* sie kriegt einen Anfall, wenn sie das erfährt *(ugs.);* **have forty** ~**s** *(coll.)* Zustände kriegen *(ugs.);* einen Anfall bekommen *(ugs.);* **be in** ~**s of laughter** sich vor Lachen biegen; **sb./sth. has sb. in** ~**s [of laughter]** jmd. ruft dröhnendes Gelächter bei jmdm. hervor/etw. löst dröhnendes Gelächter bei jmdm. aus; **in a** ~ **of ...:** in einem Anfall *od.* einer Anwandlung von ...; **in** *or* **by** ~**s [and starts]** mit [häufigen] Unterbrechungen

²fit 1. *adj.* **a)** *(suitable)* geeignet; ~ **to eat** *or* **to be eaten/for human consumption** eßbar/zum Verzehr geeignet; **be** ~ **to be seen** sich sehen lassen können; *see also* **survival a; b)** *(worthy)* würdig; wert; **a man not** ~ **to hold high office** ein Mann, der eines hohen Amtes nicht würdig ist; *see also* **candle 1 a; c)** *(right and proper)* richtig; **as is only** ~ **[and proper]** wie es sich gehört *od. (geh.)* gebührt; **see** *or* **think** ~ **[to do sth.]** es für richtig *od.* angebracht halten[, etw. zu tun]; **do as you see** *or* **think** ~: tu, was du für richtig hältst; **d)** *(ready)* **be** ~ **to drop** zum Umfallen müde sein; **e)** *(healthy)* gesund; fit *(ugs.);* in Form *(ugs.);* **keep** *or* **stay** ~: sich fit halten; fit bleiben; **get** ~ **again after an illness** nach einer Krankheit wieder zu Kräften kommen; **be** ~ **and well** in guter körperlicher Verfassung sein; ~ **for duty** *or* **service** dienstfähig *od.* -tauglich; ~ **for work/travel** arbeits-/reisefähig; *see also* **fiddle 1 a. 2.** *n.* Paßform, *die;* **it is a good/bad** ~: es sitzt *od.* paßt gut/nicht gut; **be an excellent** ~: einen tadellosen Sitz haben; wie angegossen sitzen *od.* passen; **the coat is a tight** ~: das Jackett sitzt stramm *od.* ist eng; **three in the back seat is a tight** ~: drei auf dem Rücksitz ist sehr eng; **I can just get it in the suitcase, but it's a tight** ~ *(fig.)* ich kriege es noch in den Koffer, aber nur gerade so *(ugs.).* **3.** *v. t.,* **-tt-: a)** ⟨*Kleider:*⟩ passen (+ *Dat.*); ⟨*Schlüssel:*⟩ passen in (+ *Akk.*); ⟨*Deckel, Bezug:*⟩ passen auf (+ *Akk.*); **the suit** ~**s him properly** der Anzug paßt ihm gut *od.* sitzt gut; **make sth. to** ~: etw. passend machen; **b)** *(Dressm. etc.)* anpassen ⟨*Kleidungsstück, Brille*⟩; **when may I come to be** ~**ted?** wann kann ich zur Anprobe kommen?; **c)** *(correspond to, suit)* entsprechen (+ *Dat.*); *(make correspond)* abstimmen **(to** auf + *Akk.*); anpassen **(to an** + *Akk.*); **the description** ~**s this man** die Beschreibung paßt auf diesen Mann *od.* trifft auf diesen Mann zu; **the translation** ~**s the context** die Übersetzung wird dem Kontext gerecht; ~ **the bill = fill the bill** *see* **fill 1 d; d)** *(put into place)* anbringen **(to** an + *Dat. od. Akk.*); einbauen ⟨*Motor, Ersatzteil*⟩; einsetzen ⟨*Scheibe, Tür, Schloß*⟩; *(equip)* ausstatten; **e)** *(make competent)* befähigen **(for** zu); **the experience helped to** ~ **her for the task** die Erfahrung trug dazu bei, daß sie für die Aufgabe gerüstet war. **4.** *v. i.,* **-tt-** passen; *(agree)* zusammenpassen; übereinstimmen; ~ **well** ⟨*Kleidungsstück:*⟩ gut sitzen; **the two pieces** ~ **together to form a screwdriver** die beiden Teile zusammen ergeben einen Schraubenzieher; **we must find a lid that** ~**s** wir müssen einen passenden Deckel finden; *see also* **cap 1 a; glove a**

~ '**in 1.** *v. t.* **a)** unterbringen; **b)** *(install)* einbauen; **c)** *(to a schedule)* einen Termin geben (+ *Dat.*); unterbringen, einschieben ⟨*Treffen, Besuch, Sitzung*⟩; **I could** ~ **you in just before lunch** so kurz vor Mittag hätte ich Zeit für Sie; **the hairdresser usually manages to** ~ **me in** gewöhnlich kann mich der Friseur zwischendurch drannehmen *(ugs.);* ~ **sth. in with sth.** etw. mit etw. abstimmen. **2.** *v. i.* **a)** hineinpassen; **b)** *(be in accordance)* ~ **in with sth.** mit etw. übereinstimmen; ~ **in with sb.'s plan/ideas** in jmds. Plan/Konzept *(Akk.)* passen; **how does that** ~ **in?** wie paßt das dazu *od.* ins Ganze?; **it didn't** ~ **in with our plans** es ließ sich nicht mit unseren Plänen vereinbaren; **I'll just** ~ **in with you/your arrangements** ich richte mich ganz nach dir/deinen Plänen; **c)** *(settle harmoniously)* ⟨*Person:*⟩ sich anpassen **(with** an + *Akk.*); ~ **in easily with a group** sich leicht in eine Gruppe einfügen; **he** ~**s in well here/with the others** er paßt gut hierher/mit den anderen zusammen

~ '**out** *v. t.* ausstatten; *(for expedition etc.)* ausrüsten

~ '**up** *v. t. (fix)* anbringen ⟨*Lampe, Waschbecken*⟩; *(install, mount)* aufstellen ⟨*Arbeitsbank usw.*⟩; ~ **sb./sth. up with sth.** jmdn./etw. mit einer Sache versehen *od.* ausstatten; ~ **a room up as an office** ein Zimmer als Büro einrichten

fitful ['fɪtfl] *adj.* unbeständig; unruhig ⟨*Schlaf*⟩; vereinzelt ⟨*Schüsse*⟩; ungleichmäßig ⟨*Fortgang, Arbeitsweise*⟩; launisch ⟨*Brise*⟩

fitfully ['fɪtfəlɪ] *adv.* unregelmäßig; sporadisch ⟨*arbeiten*⟩; unruhig ⟨*schlafen*⟩; **the sun shone** ~: die Sonne kam vereinzelt durch

fitfulness ['fɪtflnɪs] *n., no pl.* Unbeständigkeit, *die; (of sleep)* Unregelmäßigkeit, *die*

fitment ['fɪtmənt] *n. (piece of furniture)* Einrichtungsgegenstand, *der; (piece of equipment)* Zubehörteil, *das;* ~**s** Ausstattung, *die*

fitness ['fɪtnɪs] *n., no pl.* **a)** *(physical)* Fitneß, *die;* ~ **for active service** *(Mil.)* Wehrdiensttauglichkeit, *die;* **b)** *(suitability)* Eignung, *die; (appropriateness)* Angemessenheit, *die;* **have a sense of the** ~ **of things** ein Gefühl dafür haben, was angebracht *od.* angemessen ist

fitted ['fɪtɪd] *adj.* **a)** *(suited)* geeignet **(for** für, zu); **b)** *(shaped)* tailliert, auf Taille gearbeitet ⟨*Kleider*⟩; ~ **carpet** Teppichboden, *der;* ~ **sheet** Spannbettuch, *das;* ~ **kitchen/cupboards** Einbauküche, *die*/Einbauschränke

fitter ['fɪtə(r)] *n.* **a)** Monteur, *der; (of pipes)* Installateur, *der; (of machines)* Maschinenschlosser, *der;* **electrical** ~: Elektriker, *der;* Elektroinstallateur, *der;* **b)** *(of clothes)* Schneider, *der*/Schneiderin, *die (als Zuschneider u. für Änderungen)*

fitting ['fɪtɪŋ] **1.** *adj. (appropriate)* passend; angemessen; geeignet ⟨*Moment, Zeitpunkt*⟩; günstig, passend ⟨*Gelegenheit*⟩; *(becoming)* schicklich *(geh.)* ⟨*Benehmen*⟩; **I thought it** ~ **to inform him** ich hielt es für angebracht, ihn zu informieren; **it is not** ~ **for a young woman ...:** es schickt sich nicht für eine junge Dame, ... **2.** *n.* **a)** *usu. in pl. (fixture)* Anschluß, *der; (connecting piece used for installations)* Fitting, *das (Technik);* ~**s** *(furniture)* Ausstattung, *die;* **a car with luxurious** ~**s** ein Wagen mit Luxusausstattung; **electrical** ~**s** Elektroinstallationen; *see also* **fixture a; b)** *(of clothes)* Anprobe, *die;* **go to the tailor's for a** ~: zur Anprobe gehen; **c)** *(Brit.: size)* Größe, *die;* **shoes of a wide/narrow** ~: weite/enge Schuhe

fittingly ['fɪtɪŋlɪ] *adv.* passend ⟨*sich kleiden*⟩; angemessen ⟨*enden*⟩; schicklich ⟨*sich benehmen*⟩

fitting: ~**-room** *n.* Anprobe, *die;* ~**-shop** *n.* Montagehalle, *die*

five [faɪv] **1.** *adj.* **a)** fünf; *see also* **eight 1; b)** ~**-finger exercise** *(Mus.: also fig.)* Fingerübung, *die;* ~ **o'clock shadow** [nachmittäglicher] Stoppelbart *(ugs.); see also* **week. 2.** *n. (number, symbol)* Fünf, *die; see also* **eight 2 a, c, d**

five-and-'ten *n. (Amer.)* Billigkaufhaus, *das*

fivefold ['faɪvfəʊld] *adj., adv.* fünffach; *see also* **eightfold**

fiver ['faɪvə(r)] *n. (coll.) (Brit.)* Fünfpfundschein, *der; (Amer.)* Fünfdollarschein, *der*

fives [faɪvz] *n. sing.: ein Wandballspiel;* **Eton** ['i:tn] ~: *Wandballspiel mit drei Wänden;* **Rugby** ~: *Wandballspiel mit vier Wänden*

five: ~**-star** *adj.* Fünf-Sterne-⟨*Hotel, General*⟩; *(fig.)* ausgezeichnet; ~**-'year plan** *n.* Fünfjahresplan, *der*

fix [fɪks] **1.** *v. t.* **a)** *(place firmly, attach, prevent from moving)* befestigen; festmachen; *(fig.: imprint)* einprägen; ~ **a post in[to] the ground** einen Pfosten im Boden verankern; ~ **a stone firmly into position** einen Stein an der vorgesehenen Stelle einsetzen; ~ **sth. to/on sth.** etw. an/auf etw. *(Dat.)* befestigen *od.* festmachen; ~ **shelves to the wall/a**

handle on the door Regale an der Wand/eine Klinke an der Tür anbringen; **~ bayonets** Bajonette aufpflanzen; **~ sth. in one's mind** sich *(Dat.)* etw. fest einprägen; **b)** *(direct steadily)* richten ‹*Blick, Gedanken, Augen*› (**[up]on** auf + *Akk.*); setzen ‹*Hoffnung*› (**[up]on** auf + *Akk.*); **her mind was [firmly] ~ed on her work** sie war ganz auf ihre Arbeit fixiert; **his thoughts were ~ed elsewhere** er war mit seinen Gedanken [ganz] woanders; **c)** *(decide, specify)* festsetzen, festlegen ‹*Termin, Preis, Strafe, Grenze*›; *(settle, agree on)* ausmachen; *(allocate)* übertragen ‹*Verantwortung*›; zuschieben ‹*Schuld*› (**[up]on** + *Dat.*); **~ the price at £50** den Preis auf 50 Pfund festsetzen; **nothing's been ~ed yet** es ist noch nichts fest [ausgemacht *od.* beschlossen]; **it was ~ed that ...:** es wurde beschlossen *od.* vereinbart, daß ...; **d)** *(repair)* in Ordnung bringen; reparieren; **need ~ing** repariert werden müssen; **e)** *(arrange)* arrangieren; **~ a rehearsal for Friday** eine Probe für *od.* auf Freitag *(Akk.)* ansetzen; **they tried to ~ things so that ...:** sie versuchten es so zu arrangieren, daß ...; **have you anything ~ed for Saturday evening?** hast du [für] Samstagabend schon etwas vor?; **nothing definite has been ~ed yet** es ist noch nichts Endgültiges vereinbart *od.* ausgemacht; **f)** *(manipulate fraudulently)* manipulieren ‹*Rennen, Kampf*›; bestechen ‹*Zeugen*›; **the whole thing was ~ed** das war eine abgekartete Sache; **g)** *(Amer. coll.: prepare)* machen ‹*Essen, Kaffee, Drink*›; **~ one's hair** sich frisieren; **~ one's face** sich schminken; **h)** *(sl.: deal with)* in Ordnung bringen; regeln; **~ sb.** *(get even with)* es jmdm. heimzahlen; *(kill)* jmdn. kaltmachen *(salopp)*; **Don't bother about that. I'll ~ things with her** Mach dir deswegen keine Sorgen. Ich regle das mit ihr *od.* bringe das mit ihr in Ordnung; **I'll soon ~ that** *(prevent)* das werd' ich zu verhindern wissen; **that'll ~ her** dann kann sie nichts mehr machen; **i)** *(make permanent)* fixieren ‹*Farben, Photo, Gewebe*›; **j)** *(coll.: castrate)* kastrieren; **k)** *(Bot.: assimilate)* ‹*Pflanze:*› binden. **2.** *v.i.* **a)** *(coll.: arrange)* **~ for sb. to do sth.** es arrangieren, daß jmd. etw. tun kann; **b)** *(Amer. coll.: intend)* vorhaben; **be ~ing to do sth.** vorhaben, etw. zu tun; **c)** *(sl.: inject narcotics)* fixen *(Drogenjargon)*. **3.** *v. refl. see* **2c. 4.** *n.* **a)** *(predicament)* Patsche, *die (ugs.)*; Klemme, *die (ugs.)*; **be in a ~:** in der Klemme sein *(ugs.)*; **get oneself in[to] a ~:** sich *(Dat.)* eine schöne Suppe einbrocken *(ugs.)*; **b)** *(Naut.)* Standort, *der;* Position, *die;* **radio ~:** Funkortung, *die;* **c)** *(sl.: of narcotics)* Fix, *der (Drogenjargon)*; **d)** *(Amer. sl.: bribery)* Bestechung, *die; (illicit arrangement)* abgekartete Sache *(ugs.)*

~ on *v.t.* **a)** [-'-] anbringen; **b)** ['--] *(decide on)* sich entscheiden für; *(determine)* festsetzen, festlegen ‹*Termin*›; **~ on doing sth.** beschließen, etw. zu tun

~ 'up *v.t.* **a)** *(arrange)* arrangieren; festsetzen, ausmachen ‹*Termin, Treffpunkt*›; **we've nothing ~ed up for tonight** wir haben noch nichts vor [für] heute abend; **let's ~ up when and where we'll next meet** machen wir aus, wann und wo wir uns das nächste Mal treffen; **we ~ed up that ...:** wir vereinbarten, daß ...; **I'll ~ up for you to accompany me** ich werde es arrangieren, daß du mich begleiten kannst; **b)** *(provide)* versorgen; *(provide with accommodation)* unterbringen; **~ sb. up with sth.** jmdm. etw. verschaffen *od.* besorgen; **~ sb. up [with a bed] for the night** jmdn. für die Nacht unterbringen; **c)** *(establish)* **get oneself ~ed up** sich etablieren; **you can stay with us until you get yourself ~ed up** du kannst bei uns wohnen, bis du ein Zimmer/eine Wohnung *usw.* hast; **~ sb. up in the spare room** jmdn. im Gästezimmer unterbringen; **d)** *(furnish)* einrichten

fixate [fɪk'seɪt] *v.t. (Psych.)* fixieren (**upon** auf + *Akk.*)

fixation [fɪk'seɪʃn] *n. (fixing, being fixed, obsession, Psych.)* Fixierung, *die;* **he has a ~ about his mother** er ist zu stark auf seine Mutter fixiert

fixed [fɪkst] *adj.* **a)** *pred. (coll.: placed)* **how are you/is he** *etc.* **~ for cash/fuel?** wie sieht's bei dir/ihm *usw.* mit dem Geld/Treibstoff aus? *(ugs.)*; **they are better ~ financially than we are** sie stehen finanziell besser da als wir; **how are you ~ for this evening?** was hast du [für] heute abend vor?; **b)** *(not variable)* fest; starr ‹*Lächeln, Gesichtsausdruck*›; **~ assets** Anlagevermögen, *das;* **~ cost** Fixkosten *Pl.*; **~ price** Festpreis, *der;* **~-interest stocks** festverzinsliche Wertpapiere; **~ capital** Anlagekapital, *das;* **~ focus** *(Photog.)* Fixfokus, *der;* **~ idea** fixe Idee; **have no ~ ideas on sth.** keine feste Vorstellung von etw. haben; **~ income** festes Einkommen; **~-income investments** Festgeldanlagen; **~ odds** feste *od.* gleichbleibende Gewinnchancen; **~ salary** Fixum, *das;* **~ star** Fixstern, *der;* **~-wing aircraft** Starrflügelflugzeug, *das;* Starrflügler, *der; see also* [1]**abode; address 2a; c)** *(firm, resolute)* fest ‹*Absicht*›; **be ~ in one's determination** fest entschlossen sein; **with the ~ intention of doing sth.** in *od.* mit der festen Absicht, etw. zu tun

fixedly ['fɪksɪdlɪ] *adv.* starr, unverwandt ‹*blicken, lächeln*›; **stare ~ out of the window** aus dem Fenster starren

fixed 'point *n.* **a)** *(Phys.)* Fixpunkt, *der;* Festpunkt, *der;* **b)** *(Computing)* Festkomma, *das*

fixer ['fɪksə(r)] *n.* **a)** *(Photog.)* Fixiermittel, *das;* **b)** *(coll.: person)* Organisator, *der; (derog.) Mittelsmann, der durch Schmiergeldzahlungen unlautere geschäftliche Transaktionen ermöglicht*

fixings ['fɪksɪŋz] *n. pl. (Amer. Cookery: trimmings)* Beilagen *Pl.*

fixity ['fɪksɪtɪ] *n., no pl.* Beständigkeit, *die;* **~ of purpose** Zielstrebigkeit, *die*

fixture ['fɪkstʃə(r)] *n.* **a)** *(furnishing)* eingebautes Teil; *(pipe etc.)* fest verlegtes Rohr *usw.*; *(accessory)* festes Zubehörteil; **~s** *(Law)* unbewegliches Inventar; **~s and fittings** Ausstattung und Installationen; **lighting ~s** Beleuchtungskörper; **b)** *(Sport)* Veranstaltung, *die;* **the Derby is an annual ~:** das Derby findet jedes Jahr statt; **~ list** Spielplan, *der;* **c)** *(fig. joc.: established person or thing)* [lebendes] Inventar *(scherzh.)*; **be a ~:** zum Inventar gehören *(scherzh.)*

fizz [fɪz] **1.** *v.i.* [zischend] sprudeln. **2.** *n.* **a)** *(effervescence)* Sprudeln, *das;* **the lemonade has lost its ~:** die Limonade sprudelt nicht mehr; **b)** *(coll.: effervescent drink)* Sprudel, *der; (flavoured)* Brause[limonade], *die (ugs.)*; **gin ~:** Gin-Fizz, *der*

fizzle ['fɪzl] *v.i.* zischen

~ 'out *v.i.* ‹*Feuerwerk:*› zischend verlöschen; ‹*Begeisterung:*› sich legen; ‹*Kampagne:*› im Sande verlaufen

fizzy ['fɪzɪ] *adj.* sprudelnd; **~ lemonade** Brause[limonade], *die;* **~ drinks** kohlensäurehaltige Getränke; **be ~:** sprudeln

fjord see **fiord**

fl. *abbr.* **a) floor** OG; **b) fluid** fl.

flab [flæb] *n. (coll.)* Fett, *das;* Speck, *der (ugs.)*

flabbergast ['flæbəgɑ:st] *v.t.* verblüffen; umhauen *(ugs.)*; **I was [absolutely] ~ed** ich war [völlig] verblüfft; es hat mich [einfach] umgehauen *(ugs.)*; **she looked at them, ~ed** sie sah sie völlig verblüfft an

flabby ['flæbɪ] *adj.* schlaff ‹*Muskeln, Bauch, Fleisch, Hände, Wangen, Brüste*›; wabbelig *(ugs.)*, schwammig ‹*Bauch, Fleisch*›; *(fig.)* schwammig; schwach ‹*Willenskraft*›

flaccid ['flæksɪd] *adj.* schlaff; *(fig.)* lasch

[1]**flag** [flæg] **1.** *n.* Fahne, *die; (small paper etc. device)* Fähnchen, *das; (national ~, ~ on ship)* Flagge, *die;* **red/white ~:** rote/weiße Fahne; **yellow ~:** Quarantäneflagge, *die;* **~ of convenience** billige Flagge *(Seew.)*; **~ of truce** Parlamentärflagge, *die;* **keep the ~ flying** *(fig.)* die Fahne hochhalten; **show the ~** *(fig.)* seiner Repräsentationspflicht nachkommen; **put the ~[s] out** *(fig. coll.)* drei Kreuze machen *(ugs.)*. **2.** *v.t.*, **-gg-: a)** beflaggen ‹*Gebäude*›; *(mark with ~s)* [mit Fähnchen] markieren; *(Computing)* markieren; kennzeichnen; **b)** *(communicate by ~-signals)* [mit Fahne *od.* Fähnchen] signalisieren; **c)** *see* **~ down**

~ 'down *v.t.* [durch Winken] anhalten

[2]**flag** *v.i.*, **-gg-: a)** *(lose vigour)* erlahmen; **business is ~ging** die Geschäfte lassen nach; **b)** ‹*Blume:*› den Kopf hängen lassen; ‹*Pflanze:*› schlappen *(ugs.)*, die Blätter hängen lassen

[3]**flag 1.** *n. see* **flagstone. 2.** *v.t.*, **-gg-** mit Fliesen/Steinplatten belegen; fliesen ‹*Fußboden*›

flag: ~-captain *n. (Navy)* Kommandant des Flaggschiffs; **~-day** *n.* **a)** *(Brit.) Tag der Straßensammlung für wohltätige Zwecke;* **b) F~ Day** *(Amer.) 14. Juni als Gedenktag der Einführung der amerikanischen Nationalflagge*

flagella *pl. of* **flagellum**

[1]**flagellate** ['flædʒəleɪt] *v.t.* geißeln

[2]**flagellate** ['flædʒələt] *(Zool.)* **1.** *adj.* geißelförmig; **~ organism** *see* **2. 2.** *n.* Flagellat, *der (fachspr.)*; Geißeltierchen, *das*

flagellation [flædʒə'leɪʃn] *n.* Flagellation, *die;* Geißelung, *die*

flagellum [flə'dʒeləm] *n., pl.* **flagella** [flə'dʒelə] **a)** *(Bot.: runner)* Ausläufer, *der;* **b)** *(Biol.)* Flagellum, *das;* Geißel, *die*

flageolet [flædʒə'let, 'flædʒəlet] *n. (Mus.)* Flageolett, *das*

flag: ~-lieutenant *n. (Navy)* Flaggleutnant, *der;* **~-officer** *n. (Navy)* Flaggoffizier, *der*

flagon ['flægən] *n.* **a)** *(with handle and spout; for Eucharist)* Kanne, *die;* **b)** *(big bottle)* [bauchige] Weinflasche *(in Bocksbeutelform)*

'flag-pole *see* **flagstaff**

flagrancy ['fleɪgrənsɪ] *n., no pl.* Schändlichkeit, *die; (of disregard, defiance)* Schamlosigkeit, *die*

'flag-rank *n. (Navy)* Rang eines Flaggoffiziers; ≈ Admiralsrang, *der*

flagrant ['fleɪgrənt] *adj.* eklatant; flagrant ‹*Verstoß*›; *(scandalous)* ungeheuerlich; himmelschreiend ‹*Unrecht*›; schamlos ‹*Verbrecher, Sünder*›

flagrante delicto *see* **in flagrante [delicto]**

flagrantly ['fleɪgrəntlɪ] *adv.* eklatant; flagrant ‹*verstoßen*›; unverhohlen ‹*beleidigen*›; **a ~ criminal act** ein ungeheuerliches Verbrechen

flag: ~ship *n. (Navy)* Flaggschiff, *das; (fig. attrib.)* führend...; **~staff** *n.* Flaggenmast, *der;* Fahnenmast, *der; (horizontal)* Fahnenstange, *die; (on ship)* Flaggenstock, *der (Seemannsspr.)*; **~stone** *n.* Steinplatte, *die; (for floor)* Fliese, *die; in pl. (pavement)* Straßenpflaster, *das;* **~ stop** *(Amer.) see* **request stop**

flail [fleɪl] **1.** *v.i.* [wild] um sich schlagen; ‹*Propeller:*› sich rasend drehen; **with arms ~ing he tried to keep his balance** mit den Armen fuchtelnd, versuchte er, das Gleichgewicht zu halten. **2.** *v.t. (strike with ~)* dreschen; *(strike as if with ~)* [wild] einschlagen auf (+ *Akk.*). **3.** *n.* Dreschflegel, *der*

flair [fleə(r)] *n.* Gespür, *das; (special ability)* Talent, *das;* [natürliche] Begabung; **have ~** *(talent)* Talent haben; talentiert sein; *(for dress)* Stil *od.* Geschmack haben; **have a ~ for sth.** *(talent)* ein Talent *od.* eine Begabung für etw. haben; *(instinct)* ein [feines] Gespür für etw. haben; **have [quite] a ~ for**

writing/[learning] languages schriftstellerisch [recht] begabt sein/[recht] sprachbegabt sein; **he has a ~ for making money** er weiß, wie man zu Geld kommt

flak [flæk] *n.* Flakfeuer, *das (Milit.); (gun)* Flak, *die (Milit.);* **get a lot of ~ for sth.** *(fig.)* wegen etw. [schwer] unter Beschuß geraten; **give sb. a lot of ~ for sth.** *(fig.)* jmdn. wegen etw. [schwer] unter Beschuß nehmen

flake [fleɪk] **1.** *n.* **a)** *(of snow, soap, cereals)* Flocke, *die; (of dry skin)* Schuppe, *die; (of plaster)* ≈ Bröckchen, *das; (of metal)* ≈ Span, *der; (of enamel, paint)* ≈ Splitter, *der; (of pastry, rust)* ≈ Krümel, *der; (of chocolate, coconut)* Raspel, *die;* **b)** *(of fish's flesh)* ≈ Stück, *das;* **c)** *(shark as food)* Seeaal, *der.* **2.** *v. i.* ‹*Stuck, Verputz, Stein:*› abbröckeln; ‹*Farbe, Rost, Emaille:*› abblättern; ‹*Haut:*› sich schuppen

~ 'off *v. i.* ‹*Farbe, Rost, Emaille:*› abblättern; ‹*Stuck, Verputz, Stein:*› abbröckeln

~ 'out *v. i. (coll.)* umkippen *(ugs.);* **be ~d out** total erschöpft sein

'flak jacket *n.* kugelsichere Weste

flaky ['fleɪkɪ] *adj.* bröcklig ‹*Farbe, Gips, Rost*›; blättrig ‹*Kruste*›; schuppig ‹*Haut*›; **~ pastry** Blätterteig, *der*

flambé ['flɑ̃beɪ] *(Cookery)* **1.** *adj.* flambiert. **2.** *v. t.* flambieren

flamboyance [flæm'bɔɪəns], **flamboyancy** [flæm'bɔɪənsɪ] *n.* Extravaganz, *die; (of plumage)* Pracht, *die; (of clothes, lifestyle)* Pracht, *die;* Pomp, *der (abwertend)*

flamboyant [flæm'bɔɪənt] *adj.* **a)** extravagant; prächtig ‹*Farben, Federkleid*›; *(derog.)* großspurig ‹*Wesen, Verhalten, Geste*›; **b)** *(Archit.)* **~ style** Flamboyantstil, *der*

flamboyantly [flæm'bɔɪəntlɪ] *adv.* extravagant; prächtig, extravagant ‹*schmücken, kleiden*›

flame [fleɪm] **1.** *n.* **a)** Flamme, *die;* **be in ~s** in Flammen stehen; **burst into ~:** in Brand geraten; **go up in ~s** in Flammen aufgehen; **b)** *(colour)* ≈ Rotorange, *das;* **c)** *(joc.: sweetheart)* Flamme, *die (ugs.);* **old ~:** alte Flamme *(ugs. veralt.). See also* **[1]fan 2; feed 1 i. 2.** *v. i.* **a)** brennen; **b)** *(glow)* glühen

~ 'up *v. i. (lit. or fig.)* aufflammen; ‹*Fett:*› anfangen zu brennen

flame: ~-coloured *adj.* feuerfarben; **~ gun** *n.* Flämmgerät, *das*

flameless ['fleɪmlɪs] *adj.* ohne offene Flamme *nachgestellt*

flamenco [flə'meŋkəʊ] *n., pl.* **~s** Flamenco, *der*

flame: ~-proof *see* **proof 2 b, 3 c; ~-thrower** *n.* Flammenwerfer, *der*

flaming ['fleɪmɪŋ] **1.** *adj.* **a)** *(bright-coloured)* feuerrot; flammend ‹*Rot, Abendhimmel*›; hochrot ‹*Wangen*›; **b)** *(very hot)* glühend heiß; *(coll.: passionate)* heftig, leidenschaftlich ‹*Auseinandersetzung*›; **be in a ~ temper** *(coll.)* geladen sein *(salopp);* kochen *(ugs.);* **~ June** der heiße Juni; **c)** *(coll.: damned)* verdammt. **2.** *adv.* **a)** **~ red** feuerrot; **b)** *(coll.: damned)* **he is too ~ idle** *or* **lazy** er ist, verdammt noch mal, einfach zu faul *(ugs.);* **who does he ~ well think he is?** verdammt noch mal, für wen hält der sich eigentlich? *(ugs.)*

flamingo [flə'mɪŋgəʊ] *n., pl.* **~s** *or* **~es** *(Ornith.)* Flamingo, *der*

flammability [flæmə'bɪlɪtɪ] *see* **inflammability**

flammable ['flæməbl] *see* **inflammable a**

flan [flæn] *n.* **[fruit] ~:** [Obst]torte, *die;* **[cheese] ~:** *flache Pastete mit [Käse]füllung oder -belag*

'flan case *n.* Tortenboden, *der*

Flanders ['flɑːndəz] *pr. n.* Flandern *(das)*

flange [flændʒ] *n.* Flansch, *der; (of wheel)* Spurkranz, *der*

flanged [flændʒd] *adj.* mit Flansch/Spurkranz versehen

flank [flæŋk] **1.** *n. (of person)* Seite, *die; (of animal; also Mil.)* Flanke, *die; (of mountain, building)* Seite, *die;* Flanke, *die (selten); (of beef)* Dünnung, *die;* **attack sb.'s ~** *(Mil.)* jmdn. von der Flanke her angreifen; **~ forward** *(Rugby)* Außenstürmer, *der.* **2.** *v. t.* **a)** flankieren; **a road ~ed by** *or* **with trees** eine von Bäumen flankierte Straße; **b)** **~ing movement** Flankenangriff, *der*

flannel ['flænl] **1.** *n.* **a)** *(fabric)* Flanell, *der;* **b)** *in pl. (trousers)* Flanellhose, *die; (garments)* Flanellsachen *Pl.;* **cricketing ~s** Kricketkleidung [aus Flanell]; **c)** *(Brit.) (for washing oneself)* Waschlappen, *der; (for washing the floor)* Aufwischlappen, *der;* **d)** *(Brit. sl.) (verbose nonsense)* Geschwafel, *das (ugs. abwertend); (flattery)* Schmeicheleien. **2.** *attrib. adj.* Flanell-

flannelette [flænə'let] *n.* [Baumwoll]flanell, *der*

flap [flæp] **1.** *v. t.,* **-pp-** schlagen; **~ its wings** mit den Flügeln schlagen; *(at short intervals)* [mit den Flügeln] flattern. **2.** *v. i.,* **-pp-** **a)** ‹*Flügel:*› schlagen; ‹*Segel, Fahne, Vorhang:*› flattern; **b)** **sb.'s ears were ~ping** *(fig. coll.)* jmd. hat mitgehört; *(was very interested)* jmd. spitzte die Ohren; **c)** *(fig. coll.: panic)* die Nerven verlieren; **stop ~ping** reg dich ab *(ugs.).* **3.** *n.* **a)** Klappe, *die; (of leather shorts)* Hosenlatz, *der; (of saddle)* Seitenblatt, *das; (envelope-seal, tongue of shoe)* Lasche, *die; (of table)* klappbarer Teil; **b)** *(fig. coll.: panic)* **be in a ~:** furchtbar aufgeregt sein; **get [oneself] in[to] a ~:** sich furchtbar aufregen; durchdrehen *(ugs.);* **there's a ~ on** es herrscht große Aufregung

flapjack ['flæpdʒæk] *n.* **a)** *(oatcake)* süßer Haferkeks; **b)** *(pancake)* Pfannkuchen, *der*

flare [fleə(r)] **1.** *v. i.* **a)** *(blaze)* flackern; *(fig.)* ausbrechen; **tempers ~d** die Gemüter erhitzten sich; **b)** *(widen)* sich erweitern; *(Dressm., Tailoring)* ausgestellt sein; **c)** *(billow)* sich bauschen. **2.** *n.* **a)** *(as signal; also Naut.)* Leuchtsignal, *das; (from pistol)* Leuchtkugel, *die; (Aeronaut.: to illuminate target)* Leuchtbombe, *die;* **b)** *(blaze of light)* Lichtschein, *der;* **c)** *(widening)* **skirt/trousers with ~s** ausgestellter Rock/ausgestellte Hose; **d)** *in pl. (trousers)* ausgestellte Hose

~ 'up *v. i.* **a)** *(burn more fiercely)* aufflackern; auflodern; **b)** *(break out)* [wieder] ausbrechen; **~ up again** ‹*Kampf, Streit:*› wieder aufflackern; **c)** *(become angry)* aufbrausen; aus der Haut fahren *(ugs.). See also* **flare-up**

flared [fleəd] *adj. (Dressm., Tailoring)* ausgestellt

flare: ~-path *n. (Aeronaut.)* Anflugbefeuerung, *die;* **~-up** *n.* **a)** *(of fire)* Aufflackern, *das;* Auflodern, *das;* **b)** *(of violence, rioting)* Ausbruch, *der;* **a new ~-up** ein erneutes Aufflackern; **c)** *(of rage)* Aufregung, *die*

flash [flæʃ] **1.** *n.* **a)** *(of light)* Aufleuchten, *das;* Aufblinken, *das; (as signal)* Lichtsignal, *das;* Blinkzeichen, *das;* **~es from a gun** Mündungsfeuer eines Gewehrs; **did you see the ~?** hast du es aufblitzen *od.* aufleuchten sehen?; **~ of lightning** Blitz, *der;* **[as] quick as a ~** *(coll.)* schnell wie ein Blitz *(ugs.);* **reply as quick as a ~** *(coll.)* wie aus der Pistole geschossen antworten *(ugs.);* **give a ~ of the headlamps** *(Motor Veh.)* aufblenden; die Lichthupe betätigen; **~ in the pan** *(fig. coll.)* Zufallstreffer, *der;* **b)** *(Photog.)* Blitzlicht, *das;* **use [a] ~:** mit Blitzlicht fotografieren; **~ photo** Blitzlichtaufnahme, *die;* **c)** *(fig.)* **~ of genius** *or* **inspiration** *or* **brilliance** Geistesblitz, *der;* **~ of wit** geistreicher Einfall; **~ of insight** *or* **intuition** Eingebung, *die;* **~ of temper** *or* **anger** Wutausbruch, *der;* **d)** *(instant)* **be over in a ~:** gleich *od.* im Nu vorbei sein; **the answer came to me in a ~:** blitzartig kam mir die Antwort; **it all happened in a ~:** es geschah alles blitzschnell; **e)** *(Radio, Telev.) see* **news flash; f)** *(Cinemat.)* [kurze] Einblendung; **g)** *(Brit. Mil.: insignia)* Abzeichen, *das.* **2.** *v. t.* **a)** aufleuchten lassen; **~ a torch in sb.'s face** jmdm. mit einer Taschenlampe ins Gesicht leuchten; **~ a signal/warning** blinken/zur Warnung blinken; **~ a message** eine Botschaft blinken; **~ the/one's headlights** aufblenden; die Lichthupe betätigen; **~ sb. with one's headlamps** jmdn. anblinken *od.* mit der Lichthupe anblenden; **b)** *(fig.)* **her eyes ~ed fire** ihre Augen sprühten Feuer *od.* funkelten böse; **her eyes ~ed back defiance** ihre Augen funkelten trotzig; **c)** *(give briefly and suddenly)* **~ sb. a smile/glance** jmdm. ein Lächeln/einen Blick zuwerfen; **d)** *(display briefly)* kurz zeigen; *(flaunt)* zur Schau tragen ‹*Reichtum*›; funkeln lassen ‹*Diamanten*›; **~ one's money about** *or* **around** mit [dem] Geld um sich werfen *(ugs.);* **e)** *(Communications)* durchgeben; **~ news across the world** Nachrichten in die ganze Welt ausstrahlen. **3.** *v. i.* **a)** aufleuchten; **the lightning ~ed** es blitzte; **a signal was ~ing** ein Lichtsignal blitzte; **the lighthouse ~es once a minute** der Leuchtturm gibt einmal in der Minute ein Signal; **~ing light** Blinklicht, *das; (device) (Naut.)* Blinkfeuer, *das; (Motor Veh.)* Blinkleuchte, *die;* **~ at sb. with one's headlamps** jmdn. anblinken *od.* mit der Lichthupe anblenden; **b)** *(fig.)* **her eyes ~ed in anger** ihre Augen blitzten vor Zorn; **c)** *(move swiftly)* **~ by** *or* **past** vorbeiflitzen *(ugs.); (fig.)* ‹*Zeit, Ferien:*› wie im Fluge vergehen; **d)** *(burst suddenly into perception)* **sth. ~ed through my mind** etw. schoß mir durch den Kopf; **the truth ~ed upon me** die Wahrheit kam über mich; **his whole life ~ed before his eyes** sein ganzes Leben rollte noch einmal vor seinen Augen ab; **e)** *(Brit. sl.: expose oneself)* sich [unsittlich] entblößen. **4.** *adj. (coll.)* protzig *(ugs. abwertend);* **~ Harry** *(Brit.)* Stenz, *der (ugs. abwertend)*

~ 'over *v. i. (Electr.)* überspringen

flash: ~back *n. (Cinemat. etc.)* Rückblende, *die* **(to** auf + *Akk.*); **~ bulb** *n. (Photog.)* Blitzbirnchen, *das;* **~ card** *n. als Lernhilfe verwendete Karte, mit der dem Schüler ein Wort, Buchstabe oder sonstiges Zeichen kurz gezeigt wird;* **~-cube** *n. (Photog.)* Blitzwürfel, *der;* Würfelblitz, *der*

flasher ['flæʃə(r)] *n.* **a)** *(in advertising)* blinkende Leuchtreklame; *(Motor Veh.)* Blinker, *der;* **headlamp ~:** Lichthupe, *die;* **b)** *(Brit. sl.: who exposes himself)* Exhibitionist, *der*

flash: ~-flood *n.* Überschwemmung, *die (durch heftige Regenfälle);* **~-gun** *n. (Photog.)* Blitz[licht]gerät, *das*

flashily ['flæʃɪlɪ] *adv.* auffällig; protzig *(ugs. abwertend)*

flashing ['flæʃɪŋ] *n. (Building)* Dichtungsblech, *das*

flash: ~-lamp *n.* Blinklampe, *die;* **~light** *n.* **a)** *(for signals)* Blinklicht, *das; (in lighthouse)* Leuchtfeuer, *das;* **b)** *(Photog.)* Blitzlicht, *das;* **c)** *(Amer.)* Taschenlampe, *die;* **~-point** *n.* Flammpunkt, *der; (fig.)* Siedepunkt, *der*

flashy ['flæʃɪ] *adj.* auffällig; protzig *(ugs. abwertend);* **he's a ~ dresser** er kleidet sich [sehr] auffällig; **~ young men** großspurige junge Männer

flask [flɑːsk] *n.* **a)** *see* **Thermos; vacuum flask; b)** *(for wine, oil)* [bauchige] Flasche; *(Chem.)* Kolben, *der;* **c)** *(hip-flask)* Taschenflasche, *die;* Flachmann, *der (ugs. scherzh.)*

[1]flat [flæt] *n. (Brit.: dwelling)* Wohnung, *die*

[2]flat 1. *adj.* **a)** flach; eben ‹*Fläche*›; platt ‹*Nase, Reifen*›; *(uniform)* gleichmäßig ‹*Tönung, Farbton*›; **knock sb. ~:** jmdn. niederstrecken; **the rug is not ~:** der Teppich liegt nicht glatt; **spread the blanket ~ on the**

ground die Decke glatt auf dem Boden ausbreiten; **fall ~ on the ground** der Länge nach hinfallen; **fall ~ on one's back** auf den Rücken fallen; **lie ~ on one's stomach** flach auf dem Bauch liegen; **b)** *(fig.)* *(monotonous)* eintönig; *(dull)* lahm *(ugs.)*; fade; *(stale)* schal, abgestanden ⟨*Bier, Sekt*⟩; *(Electr.)* leer ⟨*Batterie*⟩; *(Commerc.: inactive)* flau; **fall ~**: nicht ankommen *(ugs.)*; seine Wirkung verfehlen; **go ~**: schal werden; **feel ~**: erschöpft sein; **c)** *(downright)* glatt *(ugs.)* ⟨*Absage, Weigerung, Widerspruch*⟩; **[and] that's ~**: und damit basta *(ugs.)*; **d)** *(Mus.)* [um einen Halbton] erniedrigt ⟨*Note*⟩; **e)** *(Phonet.)* kurz und offen ⟨*Vokal*⟩. **2.** *adv.* **a)** flach; **b)** *(outright)* rundweg; glattweg *(ugs.)*; **c)** *(Mus.)* zu tief ⟨*spielen, singen*⟩; **d)** *(coll.: completely)* **~ broke** total pleite; **e)** *(coll.: exactly)* **in two hours ~**: in genau zwei Stunden; **in no time ~**: in Null Komma nichts *(ugs.)*. **3.** *n.* **a)** flache Seite; **~ of the hand** Handfläche, *die;* **b)** *(level ground)* Ebene, *die;* *(shoal)* Untiefe, *die;* **walk on the ~**: auf ebener Strecke gehen; **c)** *(Mus.)* erniedrigter Ton; *(symbol)* Erniedrigungszeichen, *das;* **d)** *(Horse-racing)* **the ~**: das Flachrennen; *(season)* die Saison für Flachrennen; **on the ~**: bei Flachrennen; **e)** *(coll.: flat tyre)* Platte, *der (ugs.)*; Plattfuß, *der (ugs.)*; **f)** *(Theatre)* Kulisse, *die*

flat: ~-bottomed ['flætbɒtəmd] *adj.* flach; **~car** *n.* *(Amer. Railw.)* Flachwagen, *der;* **~-chested** [flæt'tʃestɪd] *adj.* flachbrüstig; flachbusig; **~ 'feet** *n. pl.* Plattfüße; **~-fish** *n.* Plattfisch, *der;* **~-footed** [flæt'fʊtɪd] *adj.* plattfüßig; *(fig. coll.)* *(uninspired)* phantasielos; platt *(abwertend)*; *(unprepared)* unvorbereitet; **~-heeled** *adj.* ⟨*Schuh*⟩ mit flachem Absatz; flach ⟨*Schuh*⟩; **~-hunting** *n.* *(Brit.)* Wohnungssuche, *die;* **~-iron** *n.* Bügeleisen, *das;* Plätteisen, *das*

flatlet ['flætlɪt] *n.* *(Brit.)* Appartement, *das*

flatly ['flætlɪ] *adv.* rundweg; glatt *(ugs.)*

'flat-mate *n.* *(Brit.)* Mitbewohner, *der*/Mitbewohnerin, *die;* **they were ~s** sie haben zusammengewohnt

flatness ['flætnɪs] *n., no pl.* **a)** Flachheit, *die;* *(of nose)* Plattheit, *die;* **b)** *(uniformity)* Gleichmäßigkeit, *die;* **c)** *(fig.: monotony)* Eintönigkeit, *die;* *(dullness)* Fadheit, *die*

flat: ~ 'out *adv.* **a)** *(at top speed)* **he ran/worked ~ out** er rannte/arbeitete, so schnell er konnte; **drive ~ out** mit Vollgas fahren; **go ~ out** ⟨*Fahrzeug:*⟩ mit Höchstgeschwindigkeit fahren; **b)** *(exhausted)* total erledigt; total erschöpft; **~-pack** *adj.* ⟨*Möbel*⟩ zum Selbstbauen; **~ race** *n.* Flachrennen, *das;* **~ racing** *n., no pl., no indef. art.* Flachrennen, *das;* **~ rate** *n.* Einheitstarif, *der;* **~ 'spin** *n.* *(Aeronaut.)* Flachtrudeln, *das;* **go into a ~ spin** ins Flachtrudeln kommen; *(fig. coll.)* durchdrehen *(ugs.)*

flatten ['flætn] **1.** *v.t.* **a)** flach *od.* platt drücken ⟨*Schachtel*⟩; dem Erdboden gleichmachen ⟨*Stadt, Gebäude*⟩; umknicken ⟨*Bäume, Kornähren*⟩; **~ed against the door** flach *od.* platt gegen die Tür gedrückt; **b)** *(humiliate)* **feel ~ed** sich niedergedrückt *od.* niedergeschlagen fühlen; **c)** *(Mus.)* erniedrigen. **2.** *v. refl.* **~ oneself against sth.** sich flach *od.* platt gegen etw. drücken

~ 'out 1. *v.i.* **a)** flacher werden; **b)** *(Aeronaut.)* in die Waagerechte gehen. **2.** *v.t.* ganz flach drücken

flatter ['flætə(r)] **1.** *v.t.* **a)** schmeicheln (+ *Dat.*); **I'm not just ~ing [you]** das ist keine bloße Schmeichelei; **feel ~ed** sich geschmeichelt fühlen; **be ~ed [by sth.]** sich [durch etw.] geschmeichelt fühlen; **the portrait ~s her/him** das Porträt ist geschmeichelt; **b)** *(falsely encourage)* **sth. ~s sb. into doing sth.** etw. verleitet jmdn. dazu, etw. zu tun. **2.** *v. refl.* **~ oneself [on being/having sth.]** sich *(Dat.)* einbilden[, etw. zu sein/haben]

flatterer ['flætərə(r)] *n.* Schmeichler, *der*/Schmeichlerin, *die*

flattering ['flætərɪŋ] *adj.* schmeichelhaft; schmeichelnd, schmeichlerisch ⟨*Person*⟩; vorteilhaft ⟨*Kleid, Licht, Frisur*⟩

flattery ['flætərɪ] *n.* Schmeichelei, *die;* **~ will get you nowhere** mit Schmeicheleien erreichst du gar nichts

flat 'tyre *n.* Reifenpanne, *die;* *(the tyre itself)* platter Reifen

flatulence ['flætjʊləns] *n.* Blähungen; Flatulenz, *die (Med.)*; **suffer from ~**: Blähungen haben

flat: ~ware *n., no pl.* *(dishes)* Geschirr, *das;* *(Amer.: cutlery)* Besteck, *das;* **~worm** *n.* Plattwurm, *der*

flaunt [flɔ:nt] **1.** *v.t.* zur Schau stellen. **2.** *v.i.* ⟨*Fahne:*⟩ [stolz] flattern; ⟨*Blume:*⟩ sich wiegen, prangen

flautist ['flɔ:tɪst] *n.* Flötist, *der*/Flötistin, *die*

flavor *etc.* *(Amer.)* *see* **flavour** *etc.*

flavour ['fleɪvə(r)] *(Brit.)* **1.** *n.* **a)** Aroma, *das;* *(taste)* Geschmack, *der;* **the dish lacks ~**: das Gericht schmeckt fade; **add ~ to sth.** einer Sache *(Dat.)* Geschmack geben; **different ~s** verschiedene Geschmacksrichtungen; **b)** *(fig.)* Touch, *der (ugs.)*; Anflug, *der;* **nostalgic ~**: nostalgischer Touch; Anflug von Nostalgie. **2.** *v.t.* **a)** abschmecken; würzen; **orange-~ed sweets** Bonbons mit Orangengeschmack; **b)** *(fig.)* Würze verleihen (+ *Dat.*)

flavouring ['fleɪvərɪŋ] *n.* *(Brit.)* Aroma, *das;* **add [more] ~ to sth.** etw. [stärker] würzen

flavourless ['fleɪvəlɪs] *adj.* *(Brit.)* fade

flavoursome ['fleɪvəsəm] *adj.* *(Brit.)* schmackhaft

flaw [flɔ:] **1.** *n.* **a)** *(imperfection)* Makel, *der;* *(in plan, argument, character, or logic; crack in china, glass, or jewel)* Fehler, *der;* *(in workmanship, or goods)* Mangel, *der;* **b)** *(Law)* Formfehler, *der.* **2.** *v.t.* entstellen ⟨*Gesicht, Schönheit*⟩; beschädigen ⟨*Porzellan, Glas*⟩

flawed [flɔ:d] *adj.* fehlerhaft

flawless ['flɔ:lɪs] *adj.* **a)** makellos ⟨*Schönheit*⟩; untadelig ⟨*Verhalten*⟩; einwandfrei, fehlerlos ⟨*Aussprache, Verarbeitung*⟩; **b)** *(masterly)* vollendet ⟨*Aufführung, Wiedergabe*⟩; **c)** lupenrein ⟨*Edelstein*⟩

flawlessly ['flɔ:lɪslɪ] *adv. see* **flawless a, b**: makellos; untadelig; einwandfrei; fehlerlos; vollendet

flax [flæks] *n.* **a)** *(Bot.)* Flachs, *der;* **b)** *(Textiles: fibre)* Flachsfaser, *die;* Flachs, *der*

flaxen ['flæksn] *adj.* flachsfarben; *(made of flax)* flächsern; **she's a ~ blonde** sie ist flachsblond

'flaxen-haired *adj.* flachsblond

flay [fleɪ] *v.t.* **a)** häuten; abziehen ⟨*Haut*⟩; abschälen ⟨*Rinde*⟩; **~ sb. alive** jmdm. bei lebendigem Leibe die Haut abziehen; *(fig. coll.)* jmdm. das Fell gerben *(salopp)*; **b)** *(fig.: criticize)* heruntermachen *(ugs.)*; **he was ~ed by them** sie ließen kein gutes Haar an ihm *(ugs.)*

flea [fli:] *n.* Floh, *der;* **send sb. away** *or* **off with a ~ in his/her ear** *(fig. coll.)* jmdn. abblitzen lassen *(ugs.)*; **as fit as a ~** *(coll.)* kerngesund

flea: ~-bite *n.* Flohbiß, *der;* **it's just a ~-bite** *(fig.)* es ist nur eine Kleinigkeit *od.* *(ugs.)* ein Klacks; **~-circus** *n.* Flohzirkus, *der;* **~ market** *n.* *(coll. joc.)* Flohmarkt, *der;* **~-pit** *n.* *(Brit. sl. derog.)* Flohkino, *das (ugs.)*

fleck [flek] **1.** *n.* **a)** Tupfen, *der;* *(small)* Punkt, *der;* *(blemish on skin)* Fleck, *der;* **b)** *(speck)* Flocke, *die.* **2.** *v.t.* sprenkeln; **the sky is ~ed with wispy clouds** der Himmel ist mit Wölkchen übersät; **green eyes ~ed with brown** braungesprenkelte grüne Augen

fled *see* **flee**

fledg[e]ling ['fledʒlɪŋ] *n.* Jungvogel, *der;* *(fig.)* Anfänger, *der;* Grünschnabel, *der (abwertend)*; **~ writer** Jungautor, *der*/-autorin, *die;* **~ actor** Nachwuchsschauspieler, *der*/-schauspielerin, *die*

flee [fli:] **1.** *v.i.*, **fled** [fled] **a)** fliehen; **~ from sth./sb.** aus etw./vor jmdm. flüchten *od.* fliehen; **~ abroad** [sich] ins Ausland flüchten; **~ before** *or* **from the storm** vor dem Sturm flüchten *od.* fliehen; **~ from sth.** *(fig.)* einer Sache *(Dat.)* entfliehen; **the police arrived and the thieves fled** als die Polizei kam, ergriffen die Diebe die Flucht; **be ~ing from justice** auf der Flucht vor den Richtern sein; **b)** *(vanish)* sich verflüchtigen; ⟨*Jugend, Zeit:*⟩ vergehen. **2.** *v.t.*, **fled a)** fliehen aus; **~ the country** aus dem Land fliehen *od.* flüchten; **b)** *(avoid, shun)* sich entziehen (+ *Dat.*); fliehen *(geh.)* ⟨*Gesellschaft, Personen*⟩

fleece [fli:s] **1.** *n.* Vlies, *das;* [Schaf]fell, *das;* *(quantity shorn)* Schur, *die;* *(woollen fabric)* Flausch, *der;* *(artificial fabric)* Webpelz, *der; see also* **Golden Fleece. 2.** *v.t.* *(fig.)* ausplündern; *(charge excessively)* neppen *(ugs. abwertend)*; **be ~d of one's money** um sein Geld gebracht werden

fleecy ['fli:sɪ] *adj.* flauschig; **~ cloud** Schäfchenwolke, *die*

[1]fleet [fli:t] *n.* **a)** *(Navy)* Flotte, *die;* **the F~**: die Marine; *see also* **admiral a**; **b)** *(in operation together)* *(vessels)* Flotte, *die;* *(aircraft)* Geschwader, *das;* *(vehicles)* ≈ Kolonne, *die;* **a fishing ~**: eine Fischfangflotte; *see also* **merchant fleet**; **c)** *(under same ownership)* Flotte, *die (fig.)*; **he owns a ~ of cars** ihm gehört ein ganzer Wagenpark

[2]fleet *adj.* *(poet./literary)* flink; **~ of foot, ~-footed** leichtfüßig; schnellfüßig

fleeting ['fli:tɪŋ] *adj.* flüchtig; vergänglich ⟨*Natur, Schönheit*⟩; **~ visit** Stippvisite, *die (ugs.)*

fleetingly ['fli:tɪŋlɪ] *adv.* flüchtig; **she was here ~**: sie war kurz hier

'Fleet Street *pr. n.* *(Brit. fig.)* die [überregionale britische] Presse

Fleming ['flemɪŋ] *n.* Flame, *der*/Flämin, *die*

Flemish ['flemɪʃ] **1.** *adj.* flämisch; *see also* **English 1. 2.** *n.* Flämisch, *das; see also* **English 2 a**

flesh [fleʃ] *n., no pl., no indef. art.* **1. a)** Fleisch, *das;* **he's got no ~ on him** er hat kein Fleisch auf den Rippen; **~ and blood** Fleisch und Blut; **it's more than ~ and blood can stand** das ist mehr, als ein Mensch ertragen kann; **one's own ~ and blood** sein eigen[es] Fleisch und Blut *(geh.)*; *see also* **creep 1 b**; **b)** *(of fruit, plant)* [Frucht]fleisch, *das;* **c)** *(fig.: body)* Fleisch, *das (geh.)*; **and the Word was made ~** *(Bibl.)* und das Wort ist Fleisch geworden; **go the way of all ~**: den Weg allen Fleisches gehen *(geh.)*; **in the ~**: in natura; **one ~**: ein Leib und eine Seele; **sins of the ~**: fleischliche Sünden; *see also* **spirit 1 d**; **d)** *(as food)* Fleisch, *das;* **human ~**: Menschenfleisch, *das.* **2.** *v.t.* **~ out** ausstatten; untermauern ⟨*Plan*⟩. **3.** *v.i.* **~ out** Fleisch ansetzen

flesh: ~-colour *n.* Fleischfarbe, *die;* **~-coloured** *adj.* fleischfarben; **~-eating** *adj.* fleischfressend

fleshly ['fleʃlɪ] *adj.* *(carnal)* fleischlich; *(mortal, worldly)* irdisch

flesh: ~-pots *n. pl.* **a)** *(high living)* **wallow in the ~-pots** wie die Made im Speck leben; **b)** *(strip-tease clubs etc.)* einschlägige Lokale; **~ tints** *n. pl.* *(Art)* Fleischtöne; **~-wound** *n.* Fleischwunde, *die*

fleshy ['fleʃɪ] *adj.* **a)** *(fat, boneless)* fett; fleischig ⟨*Hände*⟩; **the ~ parts of a fish** die grätenlosen Stücke eines Fisches; **b)** *(Bot.)* fleischig; **c)** *(like flesh)* fleischartig

fleur-de-lis [flɜ:də'li:] *n., pl.* **fleurs-de-lis** [flɜ:də'li:] **a)** *(Her.)* Lilie, *die;* **b)** *in sing. or*

pl. (Hist.: arms of France) bourbonische Lilie; **c)** *(Bot.)* Lilie, *die*
flew *see* ²**fly 1, 2**
¹**flex** [fleks] *n. (Brit. Electr.)* Kabel, *das*
²**flex** *v. t.* **a)** *(Anat.)* beugen ‹*Arm, Knie*›; **b)** ~ **one's muscles** *(lit. or fig.)* seine Muskeln spielen lassen
flexibility [fleksɪ'bɪlɪtɪ] *n., no pl.* **a)** Biegsamkeit, *die;* Elastizität, *die;* **b)** *(fig.)* Flexibilität, *die*
flexible ['fleksɪbl] *adj.* **a)** biegsam; elastisch; **b)** *(fig.)* flexibel; dehnbar ‹*Vorschriften*›; schwach ‹*Wille*›; ~ **working hours** *or* **time** gleitende Arbeitszeit
flexibly ['fleksɪblɪ] *adv.* **a)** elastisch; **b)** *(fig.)* flexibel
flexitime ['fleksɪtaɪm] *(Brit.),* **flextime** ['flekstaɪm] *(Amer.) ns. (Office Managem.)* Gleitzeit, *die;* **be on** *or* **work** ~: gleitende Arbeitszeit haben
flibbertigibbet [flɪbətɪ'dʒɪbɪt] *n.* Leichtfuß, *der (ugs.); (gossipy person)* Klatschbase, *die (ugs.)*
flick [flɪk] **1.** *n.* **a)** ~ **of the wrist** kurze, schnelle Drehung des Handgelenks; **a ~ of the switch** ein einfaches Klicken des Schalters; **a ~ with the whip** ein Schnalzen mit der Peitsche; **with a ~ of its tongue/tail** mit vorschnellender Zunge/mit einem Schlag des Schwanzes; **he removed the piece of dirt with a ~ of his finger[s]** er schnippte den Schmutz mit den Fingern weg; **give the room a quick ~ with the duster** *(coll.)* kurz mit dem Staubtuch durchs Zimmer gehen; **b)** *(sound) (of switch)* Klicken, *das; (of whip)* Schnalzen, *das; (of fingers)* Schnipsen, *das. See also* **flicks. 2.** *v. t.* schnippen; anknipsen ‹*Schalter*›; verspritzen ‹*Tinte*›; ~ **one's fingers/whip** mit den Fingern schnipsen/mit der Peitsche schnalzen; ~ **sth. from** *or* **off sth.** *(with fingers)* etw. von etw. schnippen; *(with duster)* etw. von etw. wischen; **the cow ~ed her tail** die Kuh schlug mit dem Schwanz; **would you just ~ the duster round the room?** *(coll.)* würdest du bitte eben mit dem Staubtuch durchs Zimmer gehen? *(ugs.).* **3.** *v. i.* **the lizard's tongue ~ed out** die Eidechse ließ die Zunge hervorschnellen
~ **through** *v. t.* durchblättern
flicker ['flɪkə(r)] **1.** *v. i.* **a)** flackern; ‹*Fernsehapparat:*› flimmern; **shadows ~ed on the wall** Schatten huschten über die Wand; **a smile ~ed round her lips** ein Lächeln spielte um ihre Lippen; **b)** *(quiver)* ‹*Zunge:*› züngeln; ‹*Fahne, Lid:*› flattern; ‹*Blatt:*› zittern. **2.** *n.* **a)** Flackern, *das; (of TV)* Flimmern, *das; (of shadow)* Huschen, *das; (fig.)* Aufflackern, *das; (of smile)* Anflug, *der; (of hope, life)* Funke, *der;* **b)** *(of bird's tail)* Wippen, *das; (of eyelid)* Flattern, *das*
~ **'out** *v. i. (lit. or fig.)* verlöschen
'flick-knife *n. (Brit.)* Schnappmesser, *das*
flicks [flɪks] *n. pl. (coll.)* **the** ~ das Kino; **what's on at the ~?** was gibt's im Kino?
flier *see* **flyer**
¹**flight** [flaɪt] **1.** *n.* **a)** *(flying)* Flug, *der;* **in** ~: im Flug; **whilst in** ~: während des Fluges; **b)** *(journey, passage)* Flug, *der; (migration of birds)* Zug, *der;* **the six o'clock ~ to ...:** die 6-Uhr-Maschine nach ...; **on [board] a ~ to ...:** an Bord eines Flugzeugs nach ...; **the ~ from Paris to Rome takes about two hours** die Flugzeit von Paris nach Rom beträgt etwa zwei Stunden; **c)** *(fig.: of thought)* Höhenflug, *der;* **d)** *(set of stairs)* ~ **[of stairs** *or* **steps]** Treppe, *die;* **live two ~s up** zwei Treppen hoch wohnen; **e)** *(flock of birds)* Schwarm, *der;* Flug, *der (Jägerspr.); (volley of arrows)* [Pfeil]hagel, *der; (Air Force)* ≈ Staffel, *die;* **in the first** *or* **top ~** *(fig.)* in der Spitzengruppe; **the first** *or* **top ~ of actors** die besten Schauspieler; die Spitzenschauspieler; **f)** *(tail of dart)* Befiederung, *die.* **2.** *v. t. (Cricket etc.)* ~ **the ball** den Ball mit unberechenbarer Flugbahn werfen

²**flight** *n.* **a)** *(fleeing)* Flucht, *die;* **take [to] ~:** die Flucht ergreifen; **put to ~:** in die Flucht schlagen; **b)** *(Econ.)* **the ~ from the dollar** die Flucht aus dem Dollar
flight: ~ **attendant** *n.* Flugbegleiter, *der*/-begleiterin, *die;* ~ **bag** *n.* ≈ Reisetasche, *die;* ~ **control** *n.* **a)** *(Aeronaut.)* ≈ Flugsicherung, *die;* **b)** *(system of levers, cables, etc.)* Steuerung, *die;* ~ **controller** *n. (Aeronaut.)* Fluglotse, *der;* ~**-deck** *n.* **a)** *(of aircraft-carrier)* Flugdeck, *das;* **b)** *(of aircraft)* Cockpit, *das;* ~ **engineer** *n.* Flugingenieur, *der*
flightless ['flaɪtlɪs] *adj.* flugunfähig
flight: ~ **lieutenant** *n. (Air Force)* Hauptmann [der Luftwaffe]; ~ **mechanic** *n.* Bordmechaniker, *der;* Bordwart, *der;* ~ **number** *n.* Flugnummer, *die;* ~ **officer** *n.* **a)** *(Brit. Air Force)* [weiblicher] Hauptmann; **b)** *(Amer. Air Force)* Stabsfeldwebel, *der;* ~ **path** *n. (Aeronaut.)* Flugweg, *der; (Astronaut.)* Flugbahn, *die;* ~ **plan** *n.* Flugplan, *der;* ~**-recorder** *n.* Flugschreiber, *der;* ~ **simulator** *n.* Flugsimulator, *der;* ~**-test** *v. t.* [im Flug] testen
flighty ['flaɪtɪ] *adj.* **a)** *(fickle)* flatterhaft; **b)** *(capricious)* kapriziös
flimsily ['flɪmzɪlɪ] *adv.* dünn; hastig ‹*errichtet*›; schlecht ‹*gebunden, verpackt*›; **a ~ built** *or* **constructed raft** ein flüchtig zusammengezimmertes Floß
flimsy ['flɪmzɪ] **1.** *adj.* **a)** dünn; *(very thin)* hauchdünn ‹*Seide, Papier*›; fadenscheinig ‹*Kleidung, Vorhang*›; *(of inadequate material or workmanship)* nicht [sehr] haltbar ‹*Verpackung*›; nicht [sehr] stabil ‹*Konstruktion, Haus, Schiff*›; **b)** *(fig.)* fadenscheinig *(abwertend)* ‹*Entschuldigung, Argument*›; dürftig *(abwertend)* ‹*Entwurf, Handlung*›. **2.** *n. (thin paper)* Durchschlagpapier, *das; (document)* Durchschlag, *der*
flinch [flɪnʃ] *v.i.* **a)** zurückschrecken; ~ **from sth./doing sth.** vor einer Sache zurückschrecken/davor zurückschrecken, etw. zu tun; ~ **from one's responsibilities** sich seinen Pflichten entziehen; **don't ~ from the facts** man muß den Tatsachen ins Auge sehen; **b)** *(wince)* zusammenzucken
fling [flɪŋ] **1.** *n.* **a)** *(throw)* **give sth. a ~:** etw. werfen; **b)** *(fig.: attempt)* **have a ~ at sth., give sth. a ~:** es mit etw. versuchen; **have a ~ at doing sth.** es damit versuchen, etw. zu tun; **c)** *(fig.: indulgence)* **have one's ~:** sich ausleben; **youth must have its ~:** die Jugend muß sich austoben [können]; **have one last ~:** sein Leben noch einmal richtig genießen; *(by going on a drinking spree)* noch einmal einen draufmachen *(ugs.).* **2.** *v. t.,* **flung** [flʌŋ] **a)** werfen; ~ **open/shut** aufreißen/zuwerfen; ~ **back one's head** den Kopf zurückwerfen; ~ **one's arms round sb.'s neck** jmdm. die Arme um den Hals werfen; ~ **sth. away** *(lit. or fig.)* etw. fortwerfen; ~ **down the money** das Geld hinschmeißen *(ugs.);* ~ **off one's attacker** seinen Angreifer wegstoßen; ~ **off one's clothes** die Kleider von sich werfen; ~ **on one's jacket** [sich *(Dat.)*] die Jacke überwerfen; **the horse flung him off** das Pferd warf ihn ab; **b)** *(fig.)* ~ **sb. into jail** jmdn. ins Gefängnis werfen; ~ **sb. into confusion** jmdn. in Verwirrung stürzen; ~ **sb. a despairing look** jmdm. einen verzweifelten Blick zuwerfen; ~ **down a challenge to sb.** jmdn. herausfordern; ~ **caution/prudence to the winds/~ aside one's scruples** alle Vorsicht/alle Umsicht/seine Skrupel über Bord werfen; ~ **off restraints** Fesseln abwerfen. **3.** *v. refl.,* **flung a)** ~ **oneself at sb.** sich auf jmdn. stürzen; ~ **oneself in front of/upon** *or* **on to sth.** sich vor/auf etw. *(Akk.)* werfen; ~ **oneself at sb.'s feet** sich jmdm. zu Füßen werfen; ~ **oneself into a chair** sich in einen Sessel fallen lassen *od.* werfen; ~ **oneself into sb.'s arms** in jmds. Arme stürzen; **b)** *(fig.)* ~ **oneself into sth.** sich in etw. *(Akk.)* stürzen; ~ **oneself at sb.** sich jmdm. an den Hals werfen *(ugs.)*
flint [flɪnt] *n.* Feuerstein, *der;* Flint, *der (veralt.);* **as hard as ~:** hart wie Stein
flint: ~ **glass** *n.* Flintglas, *das;* ~**lock** *n. (Hist.)* Steinschloßgewehr, *das*
flinty ['flɪntɪ] *adj.* **a)** *(containing flint)* feuersteinhaltig; *(resembling flint)* feuersteinartig; **b)** *(fig.)* unbeugsam; **have a ~ heart** ein Herz aus Stein haben
¹**flip** [flɪp] **1.** *n.* **a)** Schnipsen, *das;* **give sth. a ~:** etw. hochschnipsen; **b)** *(coll.: outing)* [kurzer] Ausflug. **2.** *adj. (coll.)* schnodderig *(ugs.).* **3.** *v. t.,* **-pp-** schnipsen; ~ **[over]** *(turn over)* umdrehen; ~ **one's lid** *(fig. sl.)* ausflippen *(ugs.).* **4.** *v. i.,* **-pp-: a)** *(sl.)* ausflippen; **b)** *(turn over)* **the plane ~ped [over] on to its back** das Flugzeug drehte sich auf den Rücken
~ **through** *see* **flick through**
²**flip** *n. (drink)* Flip, *der; see also* **egg-flip**
'flip chart *n.* Flip-chart, *die*
'flip-flops *n. pl.* [Plastik-/Gummi]sandalen
flippancy ['flɪpənsɪ] *n., no pl.* Unernst, *der;* Leichtfertigkeit, *die*
flippant ['flɪpənt] *adj.,* **flippantly** ['flɪpəntlɪ] *adv.* unernst; leichtfertig
flipper ['flɪpə(r)] *n.* **a)** *(Zool.)* Flosse, *die;* **b)** *(of swimmer)* [Schwimm]flosse, *die*
flipping ['flɪpɪŋ] *(Brit. sl.)* **1.** *adj.* **it's a ~ nuisance/waste of time** das ist schon verflixt ärgerlich/eine blöde Zeitvergeudung *(ugs.);* **you're a ~ idiot** du bist wirklich ein Idiot!; ~ **heck!** Scheibe! *(ugs. verhüll.).* **2.** *adv.* verflixt *(ugs.)* ‹*lästig, ärgerlich, kalt*›; ganz schön *(ugs.)* ‹*schlimm, wütend*›
'flip side *n.* B-Seite, *die*
flirt [flɜ:t] **1.** *n.* **he/she is just a ~:** er/sie will nur flirten; **she looks a bit of a ~:** sie scheint einem Flirt nicht abgeneigt zu sein. **2.** *v. i.* **a)** ~ **[with sb.]** [mit jmdm.] flirten; **b)** *(fig.)* ~ **with sth.** mit etw. liebäugeln; ~ **with the idea of doing sth.** mit dem Gedanken spielen *od.* liebäugeln, etw. zu tun; ~ **with danger/death** die Gefahr [leichtfertig] herausfordern/mit dem Leben spielen
flirtation [flɜ:'teɪʃn] *n.* Flirt, *der;* **there's a lot of ~ between the two of them** die beiden flirten ganz schön miteinander; **it was merely innocent ~:** es war nur ein unschuldiger Flirt
flirtatious [flɜ:'teɪʃəs] *adj.* kokett ‹*Blick, Art*›; **their ~ involvement** ihr Flirt; **she's a ~ woman** sie flirtet gern
flirtatiousness [flɜ:'teɪʃəsnɪs] *n., no pl.* Koketterie, *die*
flit [flɪt] **1.** *v. i.,* **-tt-: a)** huschen; **thoughts/recollections ~ted through his mind** Gedanken/Erinnerungen schossen ihm durch den Kopf; **his mind ~ted from one thing to another** seine Gedanken eilten von einem Thema zum anderen; **b)** *(depart)* ~ **northward** nach Norden ziehen; ~ **away** verschwinden; **c)** *(esp. Scot., N. Engl.: move house)* umziehen. **2.** *n.* **do a ~** *(coll.)* sich absetzen *(ugs.); see also* **moonlight 2**
flitch [flɪtʃ] *n.* ~ **[of bacon]** Speckseite, *die*
float [fləʊt] **1.** *v. i.* **a)** *(on water)* treiben; ‹*gestrandetes Schiff:*› flott werden; ~ **away** wegtreiben; **she just ~ed for some time** sie ließ sich eine Weile treiben; ~ **to the surface** an die Oberfläche treiben; **b)** *(through air)* schweben; ~ **across sth.** ‹*Wolke, Nebel:*› über etw. *(Akk.)* ziehen; ~ **away** fortschweben; **c)** *(fig.)* ~ **about** *or* **[a]round** umgehen; im Umlauf sein; **thoughts ~ through my mind** Gedanken gehen mir durch den Kopf; **d)** *(sl.: move casually)* ~ **[around** *or* **about]** herumziehen *(ugs.);* ~ **in and out** rein- und rausgehen *(ugs.);* ~ **about the area** sich in der Gegend herumtreiben; **e)** *(Finance)* floaten. **2.** *v. t.* **a)** *(convey by water, on rafts)* flößen; *(set afloat)* flott machen ‹*Schiff*›; *(through air)* schweben lassen; **the ship was ~ed by the tide** das Schiff kam bei

Flut wieder flott; ~ **the cream on top of the soup** die Sahne [vorsichtig] auf die Suppe geben; **b)** *(fig.: circulate)* in Umlauf bringen; **c)** *(Finance)* floaten lassen; freigeben; **d)** *(Commerc.)* ausgeben, auf den Markt bringen ‹*Aktien*›; gründen ‹*Unternehmen*›; lancieren ‹*Plan, Idee*›; lancieren, auflegen ‹*Anleihe*›. **3.** *n.* **a)** *(for carnival)* Festwagen, *der; (Brit.: delivery cart)* Wagen, *der; see also* **milk-float; b)** *(petty cash)* Bargeld, *das; (to provide change)* Wechselgeld, *das;* **c)** *(Angling)* Floß, *das (fachspr.);* Schwimmer, *der; (on net)* Schwimmkörper, *der;* **d)** *(in cistern, carburettor; also Aeronaut.)* Schwimmer, *der;* **e)** *(of fish)* Schwimmblase, *die;* **f)** *in sing. or pl. (Theatre: footlights)* Rampenlicht, *das;* **g)** *(of plasterer)* Reibebrett, *das*

floating ['fləʊtɪŋ] *adj.* treibend; schwimmend ‹*Hotel*›; **the ~ population** *(fig.)* die mobile Bevölkerung

floating: ~ **'bridge** *n. (bridge)* Pontonbrücke, *die; (ferry)* Kettenfähre, *die;* ~ **'capital** *n.* frei verfügbares Kapital; ~ **'debt** *n. (Finance)* schwebende Schuld; ~ **'dock** *n.* Schwimmdock, *das;* ~ **'kidney** *n. (Med.)* Wanderniere, *die;* ~ **'point** *n. (Computing)* Fließkomma, *das;* ~ **'rib** *n. (Anat.)* freie Rippe; ~ **'voter** *n.* Wechselwähler, *der/*-wählerin, *die*

¹flock [flɒk] **1.** *n.* **a)** *(of sheep, goats; also Eccl.)* Herde, *die; (of birds)* Schwarm, *der;* **b)** *(of people)* Schar, *die;* **in ~s** in [großen *od.* hellen] Scharen; scharenweise; **c)** *(of things)* Reihe, *die.* **2.** *v.i.* strömen; **~ round sb.** sich um jmdn. scharen; ~ **in/out/together** [in Scharen] hinein-/heraus-/zusammenströmen; ~ **to Mecca/the seaside** [in Scharen] nach Mekka/ans Meer strömen; **~/come ~ing to hear sb. speak** herbeiströmen/herbeigeströmt kommen, um jmdn. reden zu hören

²flock *n.* **a)** *(of wool, cotton, etc.)* Flocke, *die;* **b)** *in pl. (material)* Reißwolle, *die*

flock: ~-mattress *n. mit Reißwolle gefüllte Matratze;* ~ **'wallpaper** *n.* Velourstapete, *die;* Flocktapete, *die (fachspr.)*

floe [fləʊ] *n.* Eisscholle, *die*

flog [flɒg] *v.t.*, **-gg-: a)** *(beat as punishment)* auspeitschen; *(urge on)* [mit der Peitsche] antreiben; ~ **a dead horse** *(fig.)* seine Kraft und Zeit verschwenden; ~ **sth. to death** *(fig.)* etw. zu Tode reiten; ~ **oneself to death** *(fig.)* sich fast zu Tode arbeiten; **b)** *(Brit. sl.: sell)* verscheuern *(salopp)*

flood [flʌd] **1.** *n.* **a)** Überschwemmung, *die;* **the river is in ~:** der Fluß führt Hochwasser; **the F~** *(Bibl.)* die Sintflut; *attrib.* ~ **area** Überschwemmungsgebiet, *das;* **b)** *(fig.)* Flut, *die;* **in full ~:** in voller Stärke; **in ~s of tears** tränenüberströmt; **c)** *(Theatre coll.) see* **floodlight 1; d)** *(of tide)* Flut, *die; (poet.: river)* Strom, *der;* ~ **and field** *(literary)* Wasser und Land; **the tide is at the ~:** es ist Flut. **2.** *v.i.* **a)** ‹*Fluß:*› über die Ufer treten; **there's danger of ~ing** es besteht Überschwemmungsgefahr; **there's been a lot of ~ing in the area** es ist in dem Gebiet schon zu zahlreichen Überschwemmungen gekommen; **b)** *(fig.)* strömen; ~ **through sb.** jmdn. durchströmen *od.* -fluten; **light ~ed into the room** Licht flutete ins Zimmer; **applications for the job ~ed in** eine Flut von Bewerbungen ging ein. **3.** *v.t.* **a)** überschwemmen; *(with moving liquid)* überfluten; *(deluge, irrigate)* unter Wasser setzen; **the cellar was ~ed** der Keller stand unter Wasser; **be ~ed out** durch eine Überschwemmung obdachlos werden; **b)** *(fig.)* überschwemmen; **~ed with light** lichtdurchflutet

flood: ~ **control** *n.* Hochwasserschutz, *der;* **~gate** *n. (Hydraulic Engin.)* Schütze, *die;* **open the ~gates to sth.** *(fig.)* einer Sache *(Dat.)* Tür und Tor öffnen; **~light 1.** *n.* Scheinwerfer, *der; (illumination in a broad beam)* Flutlicht, *das;* **2.** *v.t.*, **~lit** ['flʌdlɪt] anstrahlen ‹*Bauwerk*›; beleuchten ‹*Weg, Straße*›; mit Flutlicht erhellen ‹*Stadion*›; **~lighting** *n., no indef. art. (lights)* Flutlichtanlage, *die;* **~-tide** *n.* Flut, *die;* ~ **warning** *n.* Hochwasserwarnung, *die; (at the seaside)* Flutwarnung, *die;* ~ **water** *n.* Hochwasser, *das; (in motion)* anflutendes Wasser

floor [flɔ:(r)] **1.** *n.* **a)** Boden, *der; (of room)* [Fuß]boden, *der;* **built-in ~-to-ceiling cupboards** raumhohe Einbauschränke; **wipe the ~ with sb.** *(fig. sl.)* jmdn. auseinandernehmen *(salopp);* **take the ~** *(dance)* sich aufs Parkett begeben; *see also* **c; b)** *(storey)* Stockwerk, *das;* **first ~** *(Amer.)* Erdgeschoß, *das;* **first ~** *(Brit.),* **second ~** *(Amer.)* erster Stock; **on the top ~:** im obersten Stock; **ground ~:** Erdgeschoß, *das;* Parterre, *das;* **get in on the ground ~ [of sth.]** *(fig. coll.)* [bei etw.] von Anfang an dabeisein; **c)** *(in debate, meeting)* Sitzungssaal, *der; (Parl.)* Plenarsaal, *der;* **cross the ~** *(Brit.)* mit der Gegenpartei stimmen; **from the ~:** seitens der Anwesenden; *(Parl.)* seitens des Plenums; **be given** *or* **have the ~:** das Wort haben; **take the ~** *(Amer.: speak)* das Wort ergreifen; *see also* **a; ²hold 1 n; d)** *(fig.: of prices/wages)* Mindestpreis/-lohn, *der.* **2.** *v.t.* **a)** *(confound)* überfordern; *(overcome, defeat)* besiegen; **her rejoinder ~ed him completely** mit ihrer Antwort hat sie es ihm ganz schön gegeben *(ugs.);* **b)** *(knock down)* zu Boden schlagen *od.* strecken; **c)** *(pave)* ~ **[with sth.]** mit einem Boden [aus etw.] versehen

floor: ~ **area** *n.* Grundfläche, *die;* **~board** *n.* Dielenbrett, *das;* **~-cloth** *n. (Brit.)* Scheuertuch, *das;* **~-covering** *n.* Fußbodenbelag, *der*

flooring ['flɔ:rɪŋ] *n.* Fußboden[belag], *der;* **parquet ~:** Parkettfußboden, *der*

floor: ~ **lamp** *n. (Amer.)* Stehlampe, *die;* ~ **manager** *n.* **a)** *(Telev.)* Aufnahmeleiter, *der;* **b)** *(in shop)* ≈ Abteilungsleiter, *der;* ~ **plan** *n.* Grundriß eines/des Stockwerks; **~-polish** *n.* Bohnerwachs, *das;* **~-polisher** *n.* Bohnermaschine, *die;* Bohner, *der (DDR);* ~ **show** *n.* ≈ Unterhaltungsprogramm, *das;* ~ **space** *n.* Grundfläche, *die;* **~-tile** *n.* Fliese, *die;* **~-walker** *n. (Amer.)* ≈ Abteilungsleiter, *der*

floozie (floosie) ['flu:zɪ] *n. (coll.)* Flittchen, *das (ugs. abwertend)*

flop [flɒp] **1.** *v.i.*, **-pp-: a)** plumpsen; *(flap)* flattern; **she ~ped into a chair** sie ließ sich in einen Sessel plumpsen; **the fish ~ped about in the boat** der Fisch zappelte im Boot; **he ~ped down on his knees** er ließ sich auf die Knie fallen; **b)** *(coll.: fail)* fehlschlagen; ein Reinfall sein *(ugs.);* ‹*Theaterstück, Show:*› durchfallen. **2.** *n.* **a)** *(coll.: failure)* Reinfall, *der (ugs.);* Flop, *der (ugs.);* **b)** *(motion, sound)* Plumps, *der*

floppy ['flɒpɪ] *adj.* weich und biegsam; ~ **disc** *see* **disc c;** ~ **ears/hat** Schlappohren/Schlapphut, *der*

flora ['flɔ:rə] *n., pl.* **~e** ['flɔ:ri:] *or* **~s** Flora, *die; (list, treatise)* **a ~ of North America** eine Übersicht/Abhandlung über die Flora Nordamerikas

floral ['flɔ:rl, 'flɒrl] *adj.* geblümt ‹*Kleid, Stoff, Tapete*›; Blumen‹*gesteck, -arrangement, -muster*›; ~ **perfumes** nach Blumen duftende Parfüms; **a ~ tribute to sb.** ein Blumengruß für jmdn.

Florence ['flɒrəns] *pr. n.* Florenz *(das)*

Florentine ['flɒrəntaɪn] **1.** *adj.* florentinisch. **2.** *n.* Florentiner, *der/*Florentinerin, *die*

floret ['flɔ:rɪt] *n. (Bot.) Einzelblüte eines Blütenstandes*

florid ['flɒrɪd] *adj.* **a)** *(over-ornate)* schwülstig *(abwertend);* blumig ‹*Stil, Redeweise*›; überladen ‹*Architektur, Stil, Ornament*›; **b)** *(high-coloured)* gerötet ‹*Teint*›

florist ['flɒrɪst] *n.* Florist, *der/*Floristin, *die; (grower of flowers)* ≈ Gärtner, *der/*Gärtnerin, *die;* **~'s [shop]** Blumenladen, *der*

floss [flɒs] *n.* **a)** *(silk, thread)* Rohseide, *die; (loosely twisted, of silk or cotton)* ≈ Sticktwist, *der;* **b)** *(on cocoon)* Flockseide, *die. See also* **candy-floss; dental floss**

flotation [fləʊ'teɪʃn] *n.* **a)** *(Phys.)* Auftrieb, *der;* **b)** *(Metall.)* Schwimmaufbereitung, *die;* Flotation, *die;* **c)** *(Commerc.) see* **float 2 d:** Ausgabe, *die;* Gründung, *die;* Lancierung, *die*

flotilla [flə'tɪlə] *n.* Flottille, *die*

flotsam ['flɒtsəm] *n.* ~ **[and jetsam]** Treibgut, *das;* ~ **and jetsam** *(fig.: of society)* menschliches Treibgut

¹flounce [flaʊns] *v.i.* stolzieren

²flounce *(Dressm.)* **1.** *n.* Volant, *der.* **2.** *v.t.* mit einem Volant besetzen

¹flounder ['flaʊndə(r)] *v.i.* taumeln; *(stumble, lit. or fig.)* stolpern; *(struggle)* sich quälen; ~ **through a speech** eine Rede zusammenstottern

²flounder *n. (Zool.)* Flunder, *die*

flour [flaʊə(r)] **1.** *n.* Mehl, *das; see also* **cornflour. 2.** *v.t. (Cookery)* mit Mehl bestäuben; bemehlen *(fachspr.)*

flourish ['flʌrɪʃ] **1.** *v.i.* **a)** gedeihen; ‹*Handel, Geschäft:*› florieren, gutgehen; ‹*Kunst, Musik, Kirche:*› eine Blütezeit erleben *od.* haben; ‹*Zeitung, Firma:*› sich gut entwickeln; **b)** *(be active)* seine Blütezeit erleben *od.* haben; ‹*Künstler:*› seine beste Schaffensperiode haben. **2.** *v.t.* schwingen; ~ **one's cane at sb.** vor jmdm. mit dem Stock herumfuchteln *(ugs.).* **3.** *n.* **a) do sth. with a ~:** etw. schwungvoll *od.* mit einer schwungvollen Bewegung tun; **with a ~ of his stick/hand** seinen Stock schwenkend/mit einer schwungvollen Handbewegung; **b)** *(in writing)* Schnörkel, *der;* **c)** *(ornate language)* Ausschmückung, *die;* **a ~ of fine words** ein Feuerwerk von schönen Worten; **d)** *(Mus.: fanfare)* Fanfare, *die; (florid passage)* Verzierung, *die;* ~ **of trumpets** Fanfarenstoß, *der*

floury ['flaʊərɪ] *adj.* mehlig

flout [flaʊt] *v.t.* mißachten; sich hinwegsetzen über (+ *Akk.*) ‹*Ratschlag, Wunsch, öffentliche Meinung*›

flow [fləʊ] **1.** *v.i.* **a)** fließen; ‹*Körner, Sand:*› rinnen, rieseln; ‹*Gas:*› strömen; **two rivers ~ into each other/into the sea** zwei Flüsse fließen zusammen/münden ins Meer; **the river ~ed over its banks** der Fluß trat über die Ufer; **the oil has ~ed out** das Öl ist ausgelaufen; **lava ~ed across the valley** Lava ergoß sich *od.* strömte ins Tal; **blood will ~** *(fig.)* es wird Blut fließen; **b)** *(fig.)* fließen; ‹*Personen:*› strömen; **keep the traffic ~ing smoothly** den Verkehr fließend halten; **keep the conversation ~ing** das Gespräch in Fluß halten; **the writing does not ~:** der Text ist nicht flüssig geschrieben; **talk ~ed freely** das Gespräch war sehr lebhaft; **is the work ~ing smoothly?** geht die Arbeit gut von der Hand?; **c)** *(abound)* ~ **freely** *or* **like water** reichlich *od.* in Strömen fließen; **d) ~ from** *(be derived from)* sich ergeben aus; *(be produced from)* fließen aus ‹*Feder*›; fließen von ‹*Lippen*›; **e)** *(rise)* ‹*Flut, Wasser:*› steigen; **the tide ~s twice a day** die Flut kommt zweimal am Tag. **2.** *n.* **a)** Fließen, *das; (progress)* Fluß, *der; (volume)* Durchflußmenge, *die;* ~ **of water/blood/air/gas/lava/money/people** Wasser-/Blut-/Luft-/Gas-/Lava-/Geld-/Menschenstrom, *der;* ~ **of electricity/traffic/capital/conversation** Strom-/Verkehrs-/Kapital-/Gesprächsfluß, *der;* ~ **of information/news/ideas/thoughts/words** Informations-/Nachrichten-/Ideen-/Gedanken-/Redefluß, *der;* **the elegant ~ of**

his prose der elegante Fluß seiner Prosa; **improve the work** ~: den Arbeitsablauf verbessern; *see also* **cash-flow; b)** *(of tide, river)* Flut, *die;* **the tide is on the** ~: die Flut kommt; es ist Flut; **c)** *(Phys.: of solid)* Fließen, *das*

~ **a'way** *v. i.* abfließen

'flow chart *n.* Flußdiagramm, *das*

flower [flaʊə(r)] **1.** *n.* **a)** *(blossom)* Blüte, *die; (plant)* Blume, *die;* **send sb. ~s** jmdm. Blumen schicken; **'no ~s [by request]'** „es wird gebeten, von Blumenspenden abzusehen"; **say it with ~s** es mit Blumen sagen; Blumen sprechen lassen; **[be] in [full]** ~: in [voller] Blüte [stehen]; **come into** ~: zu blühen beginnen; **b)** *no pl. (fig.: best part)* Zierde, *die; (prime)* Blüte, *die;* **in the ~ of youth/her age** in der Blüte der Jugend/ihrer Jahre. **2.** *v. i.* blühen; *(fig.)* erblühen **(into** zu)

flower: ~ **arrangement** *n.* **a)** *see* **flower-arranging; b)** *(result)* Blumenarrangement, *das; (smaller also)* Gesteck, *das;* **~-arranging** *n.* Blumenstecken, *das;* **~-bed** *n.* Blumenbeet, *das*

flowered [flaʊəd] *adj.* geblümt ⟨*Stoff, Teppich, Tapete*⟩; **purple-~** purpurblühend ⟨*Pflanze*⟩

flower: **~-garden** *n.* Blumengarten, *der;* **~-girl** *n.* Blumenverkäuferin, *die;* **~-head** *n.* Köpfchen, *das (Bot.); (of composite)* Körbchen, *das (Bot.)*

flowering ['flaʊərɪŋ] *adj.* ~ **cherry/shrub/currant** Zierkirsche, *die*/Blütenstrauch, *der*/Goldjohannisbeere, *die*

flowerless ['flaʊəlɪs] *adj.* blütenlos ⟨*Pflanze*⟩; ~ **gardens** Gärten ohne Blumen

flower: ~ **people** *n. pl.* Blumenkinder; **~pot** *n.* Blumentopf, *der;* **~-shop** *n.* Blumenladen, *der;* **~-show** *n.* Blumenschau, *die*

flowery ['flaʊərɪ] *adj.* ⟨*Wiese*⟩ voller Blumen; ⟨*Garten*⟩ voller Blumen/Blüten; geblümt ⟨*Stoff, Muster*⟩; blumig ⟨*Duft, Wein*⟩; *(fig.)* blumig ⟨*Sprache, Ausdruck*⟩

flowing ['fləʊɪŋ] *adj.* fließend; wallend ⟨*Haar, Bart, Gewand*⟩; flüssig ⟨*Handschrift*⟩

'flow-meter *n.* Durchflußmeßgerät, *das*

flown *see* **[2]fly 1, 2**

flow: ~ **rate** *n.* Durchflußmenge, *die;* **~-sheet** *see* **flow chart**

flu [flu:] *n. (coll.)* Grippe, *die;* **get** *or* **catch [the]** ~: Grippe bekommen

fluctuate ['flʌktjʊeɪt] *v. i.* schwanken; fluktuieren *(bes. Wirtsch., Soziol.);* **the level of attendance ~s** die Teilnehmerzahl schwankt *od.* ist schwankend

fluctuation [flʌktjʊ'eɪʃn] *n.* Schwankung, *die;* Fluktuation, *die (bes. Wirtsch., Soziol.)*

flue [flu:] *n.* **a)** *(in chimney)* Rauchabzug, *der;* Feuerzug, *der (Technik);* **b)** *(for passage of hot air)* Luftkanal, *der;* **c)** *(in boiler)* Flammrohr, *das (Technik)*

fluency ['flu:ənsɪ] *n.* Gewandtheit, *die; (in speaking)* Redegewandtheit, *die;* **I was complimented on the ~ of my Greek** mein flüssiges *od.* gutes Griechisch wurde gelobt

fluent ['flu:ənt] *adj.* gewandt ⟨*Stil, Redeweise, Redner, Schreiber, Erzähler*⟩; **be ~ in Russian, speak ~ Russian, be a ~ speaker of Russian** fließend Russisch sprechen; **you'll soon become** ~: du wirst bald fließend sprechen [können]; **my Arabic is** ~: ich spreche fließend Arabisch

fluently ['flu:əntlɪ] *adv.* fließend ⟨*sprechen, lesen*⟩; flüssig ⟨*schreiben*⟩; gewandt ⟨*sich ausdrücken*⟩; ununterbrochen ⟨*fluchen*⟩

fluff [flʌf] **1.** *n.* **a)** Flusen; Fusseln; *(on birds, rabbits, etc.)* Flaum, *der;* **there are pieces of ~ all over my trousers** meine Hose ist voller Fusseln; **the carpet is covered in** ~: der Teppich ist mit Flusen bedeckt; **bit of** ~ *(coll.: young woman)* Mieze, *die (ugs.);* **b)** *(sl.: mistake)* Patzer, *der (ugs.).* **2.** *v. t.* **a)** ~ **out** *or* **up** aufschütteln ⟨*Kissen*⟩; **the bird ~ed itself/its feathers** der Vogel plusterte sich/seine Federn auf; **b)** *(sl.: bungle)* verpatzen *(ugs.);* ~ **one's lines** seinen Text verpatzen

fluffy ['flʌfɪ] *adj.* [flaum]weich ⟨*Kissen, Küken, Haar*⟩; flauschig ⟨*Spielzeug, Stoff, Decke*⟩; locker ⟨*Haar, Omelett, Brot*⟩; flockig ⟨*Schnee*⟩; schaumig ⟨*Eiweiß*⟩

flugelhorn ['flu:glhɔ:n] *n. (Mus.)* Flügelhorn, *das*

fluid ['flu:ɪd] **1.** *n.* **a)** *(liquid)* Flüssigkeit, *die;* **b)** *(liquid or gas)* Fluid, *das (Technik, Chemie).* **2.** *adj.* **a)** *(liquid)* flüssig; *see also* **dram a; b)** *(liquid or gaseous)* fluid *(Technik, Chemie);* **c)** *(flowing)* flüssig ⟨*Stil*⟩; fließend ⟨*Linie, Form*⟩; **d)** *(fig.)* ungewiß, unklar ⟨*Lage*⟩; [noch] nicht fest umrissen ⟨*Plan*⟩

fluid: ~ **'clutch** *n. (Motor Veh.),* ~ **'coupling** *n. (Mech. Engin.)* hydraulische Kupplung; Flüssigkeitskupplung, *die*

fluidity [flu:'ɪdɪtɪ] *n., no pl.* Flüssigkeit, *die;* Fluidität, *die (Technik, Chemie)*

fluid: ~ **'ounce** *n. (Brit.)* 28,41 cm³; **~'ounce** *n. (Amer.)* 29,57 cm³; ~ **pressure** *n.* hydrostatischer Druck *(Physik)*

[1]fluke [flu:k] *n. (piece of luck)* Glücksfall, *der;* **by a** *or* **some [pure]** ~: [nur] durch einen glücklichen Zufall; **by some extraordinary** ~: durch außergewöhnliches Glück; **it was a bit of a** ~: es war ein bißchen Glück dabei

[2]fluke *n.* **a)** *(Vet. Med.: flatworm)* Saugwurm, *der;* Trematode, *die (fachspr.);* **liver** ~: Leberegel, *der;* **b)** *(fish)* Flunder, *die*

[3]fluke *n.* **a)** *(of whale's tail)* Fluke, *die (Zool.);* Schwanzflosse, *die;* **b)** *(of anchor)* Flunke, *die (Seemannsspr.);* Ankerarm, *der;* **c)** *(of lance, harpoon, etc.)* Widerhaken, *der*

fluky ['flu:kɪ] *adj.* glücklich ⟨*Zufall, Zusammentreffen, Sieg*⟩; zufällig ⟨*Ergebnis, Relikt*⟩; Zufalls⟨*treffer, -ergebnis*⟩

flummox ['flʌməks] *v. t. (coll.)* aus der Fassung bringen; durcheinanderbringen; **be ~ed by sth.** durch etw. verwirrt sein

flung *see* **fling 2, 3**

flunk [flʌŋk] *(Amer. coll.)* **1.** *v. i.* durchfallen *(ugs.).* **2.** *v. t.* verhauen *(ugs.)* ⟨*Prüfung, Examen*⟩; durchfallen lassen *(ugs.)* ⟨*Kandidaten*⟩; ~ **the exam** im Examen *od.* bei der Prüfung durchfallen *(ugs.);* **get ~ed** durchfallen *(ugs.)*

~ **'out** *v. i.* rausfliegen *(salopp);* [hinaus]fliegen *(ugs.);* ~ **out of school** von der Schule fliegen *(ugs.)*

funkey, flunky ['flʌŋkɪ] *n. (usu. derog.)* Lakai, *der (abwertend)*

fluoresce [flu:ə'res] *v. i.* fluoreszieren

fluorescence [flu:ə'resəns] *n.* Fluoreszenz, *die*

fluorescent [flu:ə'resənt] *adj.* fluoreszierend; ~ **material** Leuchtstoff, *der;* ~ **display** Leuchtanzeige, *die*

fluorescent: ~ **'lamp,** ~ **'light** *ns.* Leuchtstofflampe, *die (Elektrot.);* ≈ Neonlampe, *die;* ~ **'lighting** *n.* Neonbeleuchtung, *die;* Neonlicht, *das;* ~ **'screen** *n.* Leuchtschirm, *der;* ~ **'tube** *n.* Leucht[stoff]röhre, *die*

fluoridate ['flu:ərɪdeɪt] *v. t.* fluori[si]eren

fluoridation [flu:ərɪ'deɪʃn] *n.* Fluori[si]erung, *die*

fluoride ['flu:əraɪd] *n.* Fluorid, *das;* ~ **toothpaste** fluorhaltige Zahnpasta

fluorine ['flu:əri:n] *n. (Chem.)* Fluor, *das*

fluorspar ['flu:əspɑ:(r)] *n. (Min.)* Flußspat, *der;* Fluorit, *der*

flurried ['flʌrɪd] *adj.* nervös

flurry ['flʌrɪ] **1.** *n.* **a)** Aufregung, *die;* **there was a sudden ~ of activity** es herrschte plötzlich rege Betriebsamkeit; **a ~ of excitement** helle *od.* große Aufregung; **b)** *(of rain/snow)* [Regen-/Schnee]schauer, *der;* ~ **[of wind]** Windstoß, *der.* **2.** *v. t.* durcheinanderbringen; **don't let yourself be flurried** laß dich nicht nervös *od. (ugs.)* verrückt machen

[1]flush [flʌʃ] **1.** *v. i. (blush)* rot werden; erröten **(with** vor + *Dat.*); ~ **hotly/bright red** puter-/knallrot anlaufen *od.* werden. **2.** *v. t.* ausspülen ⟨*Becken*⟩; durch-, ausspülen ⟨*Rohr*⟩; ~ **the toilet** *or* **lavatory** spülen; ~ **sth. down the toilet** etw. die Toilette hinunterspülen. **3.** *n.* **a)** *(blush)* Erröten, *das; (in fever, menopause)* Flush, *der (Med.);* fliegende Hitze; *(glow of light or colour)* Glühen, *das;* **hot ~es** Hitzewallungen; **b)** *(elation)* **in the [first]** ~ **of victory** *or* **conquest** im [ersten] Siegestaumel; ~ **of excitement** Woge der Begeisterung; ~ **of enthusiasm** Begeisterungstaumel, *der;* **c)** *(bloom, vigour)* Blüte, *die (geh.);* **in the first ~ of youth/romance** in der ersten Blüte der Jugend/in der ersten Liebesglut; **d)** *(of lavatory, drain, etc.)* Spülung, *die;* **e)** *(sudden abundance)* Flut, *die*

[2]flush *adj.* **a)** *(level)* bündig; **be ~ with sth.** mit etw. bündig abschließen; *(horizontally)* auf gleicher Ebene mit etw. liegen; **b)** *usu. pred. (plentiful)* reichlich vorhanden *od.* im Umlauf ⟨*Geld*⟩; **be ~ [with money]** gut bei Kasse sein *(ugs.)*

[3]flush *v. t.* aufscheuchen ⟨*Vögel, Wild*⟩

~ **'out** *v. t.* aufscheuchen *(fig.)* ⟨*Spion, Verbrecher*⟩

[4]flush *n. (Cards) Karten derselben Farbe; (Poker)* Flush, *der;* **straight** ~: Straight Flush, *der;* Farbsequenz, *die;* **royal** ~: Royal Flush, *der;* höchste Farbsequenz

flushed [flʌʃt] *adj.* gerötet ⟨*Wangen, Gesicht*⟩; **you're extremely** ~: du bist ganz rot [im Gesicht]; ~ **with pride** vor Stolz glühend

flush 'toilet *n.* Toilette mit Wasserspülung

fluster ['flʌstə(r)] **1.** *v. t.* aus der Fassung bringen; **she is not easily ~ed** sie ist nicht leicht aus der Fassung zu bringen. **2.** *n.* **be [all] in a** ~: [völlig] durcheinander *od.* verstört sein

flustered ['flʌstəd] *adj.* **be/become** ~: nervös sein/werden

flute [flu:t] *n.* **a)** *(Mus.)* Flöte, *die;* **b)** *(Archit.)* Kannelüre, *die;* **~s** Kannelierung, *die;* **c)** *(wineglass)* [Sekt]flöte, *die*

fluted ['flu:tɪd] *adj.* gerüscht ⟨*Stoff, Manschette*⟩; gerillt ⟨*Griff, Tischbein, Stiel*⟩; *(Archit.)* kanneliert

flutist ['flu:tɪst] *see* **flautist**

flutter ['flʌtə(r)] **1.** *v. i.* **a)** ⟨*Vogel, Motte, Papier usw.*:⟩ flattern; ~ **down** hinunter-/herunterflattern; **a leaf ~ed down** ein Blatt taumelte zur Erde; ~ **about** umherflattern; **she was ~ing about** *(fig.)* sie lief unruhig hin und her; **b)** *(flap)* ⟨*Vorhang, Fahne, Segel, Drachen, Flügel*:⟩ flattern; ⟨*Blumen, Gräser usw.*:⟩ schaukeln; **c)** *(beat abnormally)* ⟨*Herz*:⟩ schneller *od.* höher schlagen; *(Med.)* ⟨*Puls, Herz*:⟩ flattern. **2.** *v. t.* **a)** flattern mit ⟨*Flügel*⟩; ~ **one's eyelashes** mit den Wimpern klimpern; ~ **one's eyelashes at sb.** jmdm. mit den Wimpern zuklimpern; **b)** *(agitate)* erregen; *see also* **dovecot. 3.** *n.* **a)** Flattern, *das;* **b)** *(fig.) (stir)* [leichte] Unruhe; *(nervous state)* Aufregung, *die;* **put sb. in a** ~: jmdn. in Aufregung versetzen; **be in a [great]** ~: ganz aufgelöst sein; **be all of a** ~: vor Aufregung fast vergehen; **c)** *(Brit. sl.: bet)* Wette, *die; (small speculative venture)* kleine Spekulation; **have a** ~: ein paar Scheinchen riskieren *(ugs.);* **I enjoy an occasional** ~: hin und wieder riskiere ich ganz gern ein paar Scheinchen *(ugs.);* **d)** *(Med.)* **heart/ventricular** ~: Herz-/Kammerflattern, *das;* **e)** *(Mus.)* Flatterzunge, *die;* **f)** *(Electronics) (in pitch)* rasches Schwanken der Tonhöhe; *(in loudness)* rasches Schwanken der Tonstärke

flux [flʌks] *n.* **a)** *(change)* **be in a state of** ~: im Fluß sein; sich verändern; **b)** *(Metalw.)* Flußmittel, *das;* **c)** *(Phys.)* Fluß, *der; (amount of radiation or particles)* Fluß, *der;* Flux, *der*

[1]fly [flaɪ] *n.* **a)** *(Zool.)* Fliege, *die;* **the only ~ in the ointment** *(fig.)* der einzige Haken [bei der Sache] *(ugs.)*; **he wouldn't hurt a ~** *(fig.)* er kann keiner Fliege etwas zuleide tun; **[die** *or* **drop** *or* **fall] like flies** *(fig.)* [sterben *od.* umfallen] wie die Fliegen; **I'd like to be a ~ on the wall of his classroom** in seiner Klasse möchte ich gern Mäuschen sein *od.* spielen *(ugs.)*; **[there are] no flies on him** *(fig. sl.)* ihm kann man nichts vormachen *(ugs.)*; *see also* **breed 2 a**; **b)** *(Angling)* Fliege, *die*

[2]**fly 1.** *v. i.*, **flew** [flu:], **flown** [fləʊn] **a)** fliegen; **~ about/away** *or* **off** umher-/weg- *od.* davonfliegen; **~ high** *(fig.) (be ambitious)* hoch hinauswollen; *(prosper)* Karriere machen; *see also* **crow 1 a**; **high-flown**; **b)** *(as or in aircraft or spacecraft)* fliegen; *(in balloon)* fliegen; fahren; **~ into Heathrow** in Heathrow landen; **~ under a bridge** unter einer Brücke hindurchfliegen; **~ past [sth.]** [an etw. *(Dat.)*] vorbeifliegen; **c)** *(float, flutter)* fliegen; **rumours are ~ing about** *(fig.)* es gehen Gerüchte um; **d)** *(move quickly)* fliegen; **glass was ~ing everywhere** überall flogen Glassplitter herum; **come ~ing towards sb.** jmdm. entgegengeflogen kommen; **~ to sb.'s assistance** jmdm. zu Hilfe eilen; **~ open** auffliegen; *(be opened)* aufgerissen werden; **knock** *or* **send sb./sth. ~ing** jmdn./etw. umstoßen; **send sth. ~ing to the other side of the room** etw. quer durchs Zimmer schleudern; **~ to arms** *(arch.)* zu den Waffen eilen; **e)** *(fig.)* **~ [by** *or* **past]** wie im Fluge vergehen; dahinfliegen *(dichter.)*; **how time flies!, doesn't time ~!** wie die Zeit vergeht!; **f)** *(wave in the air)* ‹*Fahne:*› gehißt sein; *see also* [1]**flag 1**; **g)** *(attack angrily, react violently)* **~ at sb.** *(lit. or fig.)* über jmdn. herfallen; **let ~:** zuschlagen; *(fig.: become angry)* außer sich geraten; *(fig.: use strong language)* losschimpfen; **let ~ with** abschießen ‹*Pfeil, Rakete, Gewehr*›; werfen ‹*Stein*›; **let ~ at sb. with a gun/hammer** auf jmdn. schießen/mit einem Hammer auf jmdn. losgehen; **~ into a temper** *or* **rage** *or* **tantrum** einen Wutanfall bekommen; *see also* **face 1 a**; **handle 1 a**; **h)** *(flee)* fliehen; *(coll.: depart hastily)* eilig aufbrechen; **~ for one's life** um sein Leben rennen/fahren *usw.*; **I really must ~** *(coll.)* jetzt muß ich aber schnell los. **2.** *v. t.*, **flew, flown a)** *(operate, transport or perform by ~ing)* fliegen ‹*Flugzeug, Fracht, Einsatz*›; fliegen über (+ *Akk.*) ‹*Strecke*›; *(travel over)* überfliegen; überqueren; **~ sb./sth. to and from Berlin** jmdn./etw. nach Berlin fliegen und aus Berlin ausfliegen; **~ sth. into Gatwick** etw. nach Gatwick fliegen; **~ Concorde/Lufthansa** mit der Concorde/Lufthansa fliegen; **b)** *(cause to ~)* gehißt haben, *(as mark of nationality etc.)* führen ‹*Flagge*›; fliegen lassen ‹*Taube, Falke*›; **~ a kite** einen Drachen steigen lassen; *(fig.)* einen Versuchsballon steigen lassen; **go ~ a kite!** *(sl.)* hau ab! *(salopp)*; **c)** *(flee)* **~ the country** aus dem Land fliehen; **~ one's pursuers** vor seinen Verfolgern fliehen; **the bird has flown its cage** der Vogel ist aus seinem Käfig entflogen; **~ the coop** *(Amer. fig. coll.)* sich aus dem Staube machen *(ugs.)*; *(leave home)* durchbrennen *(ugs.)*. **3.** *n.* **a)** *in sing. or pl. (on trousers)* Hosenschlitz, *der*; **b)** *(of flag)* Flugseite, *die*; fliegendes Ende; **c)** *in pl. (Theatre)* Schnürboden, *der*

~ 'in 1. *v. i. (arrive in aircraft)* [mit dem Flugzeug] eintreffen (**from** aus); *(come in to land)* landen. **2.** *v. t. (cause to land)* landen; *(bring by aircraft)* einfliegen

~ 'off *v. i.* **a)** abfliegen; **b)** *(become detached)* abgehen; ‹*Hut:*› wegfliegen

~ 'out 1. *v. i.* abfliegen (**of** von); **~ out there** dort hinfliegen. **2.** *v. t.* ausfliegen; **~ troops out to the disaster area** Truppen in das Katastrophengebiet fliegen

[3]**fly** *adj. (esp. Brit. sl.)* clever

fly: ~ 'agaric *n.* Fliegenpilz, *der*; **~-away** *adj.* widerspenstig ‹*Haar*›; **~-blown** *adj.* *(infested with flies' eggs)* ≈ von Fliegenlarven befallen; *(fig.)* befleckt; **~-by** *n. (Astronaut.)* Vorbeiflug, *der*; **~-by-night 1.** *adj.* zwielichtig; **2.** *n. jmd., der sich nachts heimlich aus dem Staub macht*; **~-by-wire** *n. (Aeronaut.)* elektronische Flugsteuerung; *attrib.* **a ~-by-wire aircraft** ein Flugzeug mit elektronischer Flugsteuerung; **~catcher** *n. (Ornith.)* Schnäpper, *der*

flyer ['flaɪə(r)] *n.* **a)** *(bird)* Flieger, *der*; **b)** *(pilot)* Flieger, *der*/Fliegerin, *die*; **c)** *(fast-moving vehicle or animal)* Flitzer, *der (ugs.)*; *(train)* Expreß, *der*; **the horse is a ~:** das Pferd ist pfeilschnell; **d)** *see* **high-flyer**; **e)** *(handbill)* Handzettel, *der*; *(Police)* Steckbrief, *der*; **f)** *(Amer.: investment)* Spekulation, *die*; **take a ~:** spekulieren

fly: ~-fish *v. i.* mit [künstlichen] Fliegen fischen; **~-fishing** *n.* Fliegenfischerei, *die*; **~-'half** *n. (Rugby)* Halbspieler, *der*

flying ['flaɪɪŋ] **1.** *adj.* Kurz-; *(designed for rapid action)* fliegend ‹*Verband, Kolonne, Ambulanz*›; **~ visit** Stippvisite, *die (ugs.)*. **2.** *n.* Fliegen, *das*; *attrib.* Flug‹*wetter, -zeit, -geschwindigkeit, -erfahrung*›; **an hour's ~ time** eine Flugstunde; **be frightened of ~:** Angst vor dem Fliegen haben

flying: ~ 'bomb *n.* V-Waffe, *die*; **~ 'buttress** *n. (Archit.)* Strebebogen, *der*; Schwibbogen, *der*; **~ 'doctor** *n. Arzt, der seine Patienten mit dem Flugzeug besucht*; **F~ Dutchman** *see* **Dutchman c**; **~ field** *n.* Flugfeld, *das*; **~ 'fish** *n.* fliegender Fisch; **~ 'fox** *n. (Zool.)* Flugfuchs, *der*; Fliegender Hund; **~ instructor** *n.* Fluglehrer, *der*; **~ 'jump, ~ 'leap** *ns.* Sprung mit Anlauf; großer Satz *(ugs.)*; **take a ~ jump** *or* **leap** Anlauf nehmen; **~ machine** *n.* Luftfahrzeug, *das*; Flugmaschine, *die (veralt.)*; **~ 'mare** *n. (Wrestling)* Schulterschwung, *der*; **~ officer** *n. (Brit. Air Force)* Oberleutnant, *der*; **~ 'picket** *n.* mobiler Streikposten; **~ 'saucer** *n.* fliegende Untertasse; **~ school** *n.* Fliegerschule, *die*; **~ squad** *n. (Police)* Überfallkommando, *das*; **~ 'start** *n. (Sport)* fliegender Start; **get off to** *or* **have a ~ start** *(fig.) (begin successfully)* einen glänzenden Start haben; *(have an advantage)* die besten Voraussetzungen haben *(fig.)*; **have got a ~ start over others** anderen gegenüber im Vorteil sein; **~-suit** *n.* Fliegerkombination, *die*; **~ 'tackle** *n. (Rugby, Amer. Footb.)* Fassen, *das (im Lauf oder Sprung)*

fly: ~leaf *n.* Vorsatzblatt, *das*; Vorsatz, *der*; **~over** *n. (Brit.)* [Straßen]überführung, *die*; Fly-over, *der*; **~-paper** *n.* Fliegenfänger, *der*; **~-past** *n.* Luftparade, *die*; **~-post 1.** *v. t.* illegal Plakate kleben für; **2.** *v. i.* illegal Plakate kleben; **~-screen** *n.* Fliegengitter, *das*; **~sheet** *n.* Prospekt, *der*; **~-spray** *n.* Insektenspray, *der od. das*; **~-swatter** *n.* Fliegenklappe, *die*; Fliegenklatsche, *die*; **~-tipping** *n., no pl., no indef. art.* illegales Deponieren von Bauschutt; **~-trap** *n. (trap)* Fliegenfänger, *der*; *(plant)* [Venus]fliegenfalle, *die*; **~weight** *n. (Boxing etc.)* Fliegengewicht, *das*; *(person also)* Fliegengewichtler, *der*; **~wheel** *n.* Schwungrad, *das*; **fluid ~wheel** *(Motor Veh.)* Flüssigkeitskupplung, *die*; **~-whisk** *n.* Fliegenwedel, *der*

FM *abbr.* **a) Field Marshal** FM; **b) frequency modulation** FM

f-number ['efnʌmbə(r)] *n. (Photog.)* Blende[nzahl], *die*

FO *abbr. (Brit. Hist.)* **Foreign Office** ≈ AA

foal [fəʊl] **1.** *n.* Fohlen, *das*; **in** *or* **with ~:** trächtig. **2.** *v. i.* fohlen

foam [fəʊm] **1.** *n.* **a)** Schaum, *der*; **b)** *see* **foam plastic**; **c)** *see* **foam rubber**. **2.** *v. i. (lit. or fig.)* schäumen (**with** *or* **vor** + *Dat.*); **~ at the mouth** Schaum vorm Mund haben; *(fig. coll.)* [vor Wut] schäumen

foam: ~-backed *adj.* schaumstoffverstärkt; **~ bath** *n.* Schaumbad, *das*; **~ extinguisher** *n.* Schaumlöscher, *der*; Schaumlöschgerät, *das*; **~ 'mattress** *n.* Schaumgummimatratze, *die*; **~ 'plastic** *n.* Schaumstoff, *der*; **~ 'rubber** *n.* Schaumgummi, *der*

foamy ['fəʊmɪ] *adj.* schaumig; schäumend ‹*Brandung*›

[1]**fob** [fɒb] *v. t.*, **-bb-: ~ sb. off with sth.** jmdn. mit etw. abspeisen *(ugs.)*; **~ sth. off on [to] sb.** jmdm. etw. andrehen *(ugs.)*

[2]**fob** *n.* Uhrtasche, *die*

f. o. b. *abbr.* **free on board** fob

focal ['fəʊkl]: **~ 'distance, ~ 'length** *ns.* Brennweite, *die*; **~ plane** *n.* Brennebene, *die*; **~ point** *n.* Brennpunkt, *der (auch fig.)*; Fokus, *der*; **become the ~ point of interest** *or* **attention** in den Brennpunkt des Interesses rücken

foc's'le ['fəʊksl] *see* **forecastle**

focus ['fəʊkəs] **1.** *n., pl.* **~es** *or* **foci** ['fəʊsaɪ] **a)** *(Optics, Photog.)* Brennpunkt, *der*; *(focal length)* Brennweite, *die*; *(adjustment of eye or lens)* Scharfeinstellung, *die*; **depth of ~:** *(adjustment)* Schärfentiefe, *die*; *(focal length)* Brennweite, *die*; **out of/in ~:** unscharf/scharf eingestellt ‹*Kamera, Teleskop*›; unscharf/scharf ‹*Foto, Film, Vordergrund usw.*›; *(fig.)* unklar *od.* verschwommen/klar; **see things in ~** *(fig.)* die Gegebenheiten klar erkennen; **get sth. in ~** *(fig.)* etw. klarer erkennen; **bring into ~:** scharf einstellen; *(fig.)* deutlich machen; **come into ~:** scharf werden; *(fig.)* sich herauskristallisieren; **b)** *(fig.: centre, central object)* Mittelpunkt, *der*; *(of storm)* Zentrum, *das*; *(of earthquake)* Herd, *der*; Hypozentrum, *das (Geol.)*; *(Med.: of disease)* Herd, *der*; **be the ~ of attention** im Brennpunkt des Interesses stehen; **the principal ~ of research is ...:** im Mittelpunkt der Forschung steht...; **c)** *(Geom.)* Brennpunkt, *der*. **2.** *v. t.*, **-s-** *or* **-ss-: a)** *(Optics, Photog.)* einstellen (**on** auf + *Akk.*); fokussieren *(fachspr.)*; **~ a camera properly** *or* **correctly** eine Kamera auf die richtige Entfernung einstellen; **badly ~ed picture** unscharfes Bild; **~ one's eyes on sth./sb.** die Augen auf etw./jmdn. richten; **b)** *(concentrate)* bündeln ‹*Licht, Strahlen*›; *(fig.)* konzentrieren (**on** auf + *Akk.*). **3.** *v. i.*, **-s-** *or* **-ss-: a) the camera ~es automatically** die Kamera hat automatische Scharfeinstellung; **he can't** *or* **his eyes don't ~ properly** er sieht nicht klar *od.* nur verschwommen; **I can't ~ on print at that distance** ich kann Gedrucktes auf diese Entfernung nicht klar erkennen; **his eyes ~ed [up]on the window** sein Blick war auf das Fenster gerichtet; **b)** ‹*Licht, Strahlen:*› sich bündeln; *(fig.)* sich konzentrieren (**on** auf + *Akk.*)

fodder ['fɒdə(r)] *n.* [Vieh]futter, *das*; *(fig.)* Futter, *das*; **~ plant** Futterpflanze, *die*; *see also* **cannon-fodder**

foe [fəʊ] *n. (poet./rhet.)* Feind, *der*

'foeman ['fəʊmən] *n., pl.* **~men** ['fəʊmən] *(arch./literary)* Widersacher, *der (geh.)*

foetal ['fi:tl] *adj.* fötal; fetal; **the ~ position** die Fötuslage

foetid ['fi:tɪd] *see* **fetid**

foetus ['fi:təs] *n.* Fötus, *der*; Fetus, *der*

fog [fɒg] **1.** *n.* **a)** Nebel, *der*; **there are ~s in winter** es herrscht oft dichter Nebel im Winter; **drive in ~:** bei *od.* im Nebel fahren; **London was blanketed in ~:** über London lag eine Nebeldecke; **be in a [complete] ~** *(fig.)* [völlig] verunsichert sein; **be in a ~ about sth./as to what to do** sich *(Dat.)* im unklaren über etw. *(Akk.)* sein/darüber sein, was zu tun ist; **b)** *(Photog.)* Schleier, *der*. **2.** *v. t.*, **-gg-: a)** in Nebel hüllen; *(bewilder)* verwirren; **~ [up]** *(obscure as if with ~, make confusing)* vernebeln ‹*Aussicht, Straße, Sachverhalt*›; **b)** *(Photog.)* **the negative is ~ged** das Negativ hat einen

Schleier. **3.** *v. i.*, **-gg-: a)** ~ **[up]** *(become blurred)* beschlagen; **b)** *(Photog.)* einen Schleier bekommen
fog: ~-bank *n.* Nebelbank, *die;* **~-bound** *adj.* **a)** *(surrounded)* in Nebel gehüllt; **b)** *(immobilized)* durch Nebel festgehalten
fogey *see* **fogy;** *see also* **young fogey**
foggy ['fɒgɪ] *adj.* **a)** neblig; **b)** *(fig.)* nebelhaft ⟨*Vorstellung, Sprache, Bewußtsein*⟩; **[I] haven't the foggiest [idea** *or* **notion]** *(coll.)* [ich] hab' keinen blassen Schimmer *(ugs.)*
fog: ~-horn *n. (Naut.)* Nebelhorn, *das;* **a voice like a ~-horn** *(fig.)* eine dröhnende *od.* durchdringende Stimme; **~-lamp, ~-light** *ns. (Motor Veh.)* Nebelscheinwerfer, *der;* **~-signal** *n.* **a)** *(Railw.)* Knallsignal, *das;* **b)** *(Naut.)* Nebelsignal, *das*
fogy ['fəʊgɪ] *n.* **[old]** ~: [alter *od.* rückständiger] Opa *(salopp)*/[alte *od.* rückständige] Oma *(salopp)*
föhn [fɜ:n] *n. (Meteorol.)* Föhn, *der*
foible ['fɔɪbl] *n.* **a)** Eigenheit, *die;* **b)** *(Fencing)* ≈ Klingenschwäche, *die*
[1]**foil** [fɔɪl] *n.* **a)** *(metal as thin sheet)* Folie, *die;* **tin ~:** Stanniol[papier], *das;* **aluminium ~:** Alu[minium]folie, *die;* **b)** *(to wrap or cover food etc.)* Folie, *die;* **c)** *(behind mirror-glass)* Spiegelbelag, *der (Technik);* **d)** *(sb./sth. contrasting)* ≈ Kontrast, *der*
[2]**foil** *v. t.* **a)** *(frustrate)* vereiteln ⟨*Versuch, Plan, Flucht*⟩; durchkreuzen ⟨*Vorhaben, Plan*⟩; **they were ~ed in their attempts to escape** ihre Fluchtversuche wurden zunichte gemacht *od.* vereitelt; **[I've been] ~ed again** es war wieder nichts; **b)** *(parry)* parieren *(auch fig.);* abwehren
[3]**foil** *n. (sword)* Florett, *das*
[4]**foil** *n. (hydrofoil)* Tragflächenboot, *das;* Gleitboot, *das*
foist [fɔɪst] *v. t.* **a)** *(introduce surreptitiously)* ~ **sth./sb. into sth.** etw./jmdn. in etw. *(Akk.)* einschmuggeln; **b)** *(palm)* ~ **[off] on to** *or* **[up]on sb.** jmdm. andrehen *(ugs.)* ⟨*schlechte Waren*⟩; jmdm. zuschieben ⟨*Schuld, Verantwortung*⟩; auf jmdn. abwälzen ⟨*Probleme, Verantwortung*⟩; ~ **oneself on [to] sb.** sich jmdm. aufdrängen
[1]**fold** [fəʊld] **1.** *v. t.* **a)** *(double over on itself)* [zusammen]falten; zusammenlegen ⟨*Laken, Wäsche*⟩; **b)** *(collapse)* zusammenklappen; **c)** *(embrace)* ~ **sb. in one's arms** jmdn. in die Arme schließen; **d)** *(wind)* ~ **one's arms about** *or* **[a]round sb.** die Arme um jmdn. schlingen *od.* legen; **e)** ~ **one's arms** die Arme verschränken; ~ **one's hands** die Hände falten; **the crow ~ed its wings** die Krähe legte die Flügel an; **f)** *(envelop)* ~ **sth./sb. in sth.** etw./jmdn. in etw. *(Akk.)* einhüllen; **~ed in a handkerchief** in ein Taschentuch eingewickelt. **2.** *v. i.* **a)** *(become ~ed)* sich zusammenlegen; sich zusammenfalten; **b)** *(collapse)* zusammenklappen; *(fig.)* *(cease to function)* eingehen *(ugs.); (go bankrupt)* Konkurs *od.* Bankrott machen; **c)** *(be able to be ~ed)* sich falten lassen; **it ~s easily** es ist leicht zu falten; es läßt sich leicht falten; **d)** *(be collapsible)* sich zusammenklappen lassen. **3.** *n.* **a)** *(doubling)* Falte, *die;* **the baggy ~s of skin under his eyes** die Tränensäcke unter seinen Augen; **~s of flesh** Fettwülste; **b)** *(hollow, nook in mountain, etc.)* Falte, *die (Geol.);* [Tal]mulde, *die;* **c)** *(coil of serpent, string, etc.)* Windung, *die;* **d)** *(act of ~ing)* Faltung, *die;* **e)** *(line made by ~ing)* Kniff, *der;* **f)** *(Geol.)* [Gebirgs]faltung, *die*
~ **a'way 1.** *v. t.* zusammenklappen. **2.** *v. i.* zusammenklappbar sein; sich zusammenklappen lassen. *See also* **foldaway**
~ **'back 1.** *v. t.* zurückschlagen, aufschlagen ⟨*Laken*⟩; zurückklappen ⟨*Rücksitz*⟩; umknicken ⟨*Papier*⟩. **2.** *v. i.* sich zurückschlagen lassen
~ **'down 1.** *v. t.* **a)** *(make more compact)* zusammenklappen; **b)** *(bend back part of)* *see* ~ **back 1; c)** *(open out)* ausklappen. **2.** *v. i.* *see* **1:** sich zusammenklappen lassen; sich zurückschlagen lassen
~ **'in** *v. t.* **a)** *(double over and inwards)* nach innen umlegen; **b)** *(Cookery)* unterrühren; unterheben, unterziehen ⟨*Eischnee*⟩
~ **into** *v. t. (Cookery)* unterrühren unter (+ *Akk.*); unterheben unter (+ *Akk.*), unterziehen ⟨*Eischnee*⟩ unter (+ *Akk.*)
~ **'out** *v. i.* ⟨*Landkarte:*⟩ sich auseinanderfalten lassen; ⟨*Tisch:*⟩ sich hochklappen lassen; **the settee ~s out to become a double bed** das Sofa läßt sich zu einem Doppelbett ausklappen; *see also* **fold-out**
~ **'over** *v. t.* umlegen ⟨*Saum*⟩; umknicken ⟨*Seiten*⟩
~ **'up 1.** *v. t.* **a)** *(make more compact by ~ing)* zusammenfalten; zusammenlegen ⟨*Laken, Wäsche*⟩; **b)** *(collapse)* zusammenklappen. **2.** *v. i.* **a)** *(be able to be ~ed up)* sich zusammenfalten lassen; **b)** *(collapse)* sich zusammenklappen lassen; **how does this table ~ up?** wie wird dieser Tisch zusammengeklappt?; *(fig.)* *see* [1]**fold 2 b** *(fig.)*
[2]**fold** *n.* **a)** *see* **sheep-fold; b)** *(fig.: body of believers)* Gemeinde, *die;* Herde, *die (geh.);* **he has left the ~:** er hat den Schoß der Kirche verlassen *(geh.)*
-fold 1. *adj. in comb.* **a)** *(times)* -fach; **b)** *(having so many parts etc.)* -fältig. **2.** *adv. in comb.* -fach
'foldaway *adj.* zusammenklappbar; Klapp⟨*tisch, -stuhl, -fahrrad, -bett*⟩
folder ['fəʊldə(r)] *n.* **a)** *(cover, holder for loose papers)* Mappe, *die;* **b)** *(folded circular etc.)* Faltblatt, *das; (map also)* Faltkarte, *die*
folding ['fəʊldɪŋ] *adj. see* **foldaway**
folding: ~ **'door** *n.* Falttür, *die;* ~ **'doors** *n. pl.* Falttür, *die; (of hangar, barn, etc.)* Falttor, *das*
'fold-out *n.* ausfaltbare Seite
foliage ['fəʊlɪɪdʒ] *n., no pl.* **a)** *(leaves)* Blätter *Pl.; (of tree also)* Laub, *das;* **b)** *(Art)* Laubwerk, *das*
foliage: ~ **leaf** *n.* [Laub]blatt, *das;* ~ **plant** *n.* Blattpflanze, *die*
folio ['fəʊlɪəʊ] **1.** *n., pl.* **~s a)** *(leaf of paper etc.)* [nur auf der Vorderseite numeriertes] Blatt; **b)** *(leaf- or page-number of printed book)* Seitenzahl, *die;* **c)** *(sheet folded once)* Doppelbogen, *der;* **in ~:** in Folio; im Folioformat; **d)** *(book)* Foliant, *der;* **First F~:** erste Folioausgabe. **2.** *adj.* Folio-
folk [fəʊk] *n., pl. same or* **~s a)** *(a people)* Volk, *das;* **b)** *in pl.* **~[s]** *(people)* Leute *Pl.; (people in general)* die Leute; **some ~[s]** manche [Leute]; **c)** *in pl.* **~s** *(coll., as address: people, friends)* Leute *Pl. (ugs.);* **d)** *in pl. (people of a particular class)* **[the] rich/poor ~:** die Reichen/Armen; **old ~[s]** alte Leute; **e)** *in pl.* **~s** *(coll.) (one's relatives)* Verwandte *Pl.;* Leute *Pl. (ugs.); (one's parents)* Alte Herrschaften *(ugs.);* **f)** *see* **folk-music; g)** *attrib. (of the people, traditional)* Volks-; ~ **handicrafts** Volkskunst, *die;* ~ **museum** Heimatmuseum, *das*
folk: ~-dance *n.* Volkstanz, *der;* **~-dancing** *n.* Volkstanz, *der;* ~ **etymology** *n.* Volksetymologie, *die;* **~-hero** *n.* Volksheld, *der;* **~lore** *n.* **a)** *(traditional beliefs)* [volkstümliche] Überlieferung; Folklore, *die;* **b)** *(study)* Volkskunde, *die;* Folklore, *die;* **~-memory** *n.* mündliche Überlieferung, *die;* **~-music** *n.* Volksmusik, *die;* **~-singer** *n.* Sänger/Sängerin von Volksliedern; *(modern)* Folksänger, *der*/-sängerin, *die;* **~-singing** *n.* Singen von Volksliedern *od. (modern)* Folksongs; **~-song** *n.* Volkslied, *das; (modern)* Folksong, *der*
folksy ['fəʊksɪ] *adj.* **a)** *(sociable, informal)* gesellig; **b)** *(having characteristics of folk art)* volkstümlich
folk: ~-tale *n.* Volksmärchen, *das;* **~ways** *n. pl.* traditionelle Lebensweise; **~weave** *n.* grobgewebter Stoff
folky ['fəʊkɪ] *see* **folksy b**
follicle ['fɒlɪkl] *n.* Follikel, *der (Biol., Med.)*
follow ['fɒləʊ] **1.** *v. t.* **a)** folgen (+ *Dat.*); **you're being ~ed** Sie werden verfolgt; **b)** *(go along)* folgen (+ *Dat.*); entlanggehen/-fahren ⟨*Straße usw.*⟩; **c)** *(come after in order or time)* folgen (+ *Dat.*); folgen auf (+ *Akk.*); **A is ~ed by B** auf A folgt B; **d)** *(accompany)* [nach]folgen (+ *Dat.*); **e)** *(provide with sequel)* ~ **sth. with sth.** einer Sache *(Dat.)* etw. folgen lassen; ~ **your meal with a brandy** schließen Sie Ihr Essen mit einem Kognak ab; **his first novel was ~ed by a string of best-sellers** auf seinen ersten Roman folgte eine ganze Reihe von Bestsellern; **that's a hard act to ~** *(fig.)* das macht ihm/ihr keiner so leicht nach; ~ **that!** *(coll.)* das mach mir erst mal nach!; **f)** *(go after as admirer or suitor)* verehren; anhängen *(geh.)* (+ *Dat.*); **g)** *(result from)* die Folge sein von; hervorgehen aus; **a stroke is often ~ed by permanent paralysis** die Folge eines Schlaganfalls ist oft eine dauernde Lähmung; **h)** *(treat or take as guide or leader)* folgen (+ *Dat.*); sich orientieren an (+ *Dat.*); *(adhere to)* anhängen (+ *Dat.*); sich bekennen zu; **i)** *(act according to)* folgen (+ *Dat.*) ⟨*Prinzip, Instinkt, Trend*⟩; verfolgen ⟨*Politik*⟩; befolgen ⟨*Vorschrift, Regel, Anweisung, Rat, Warnung*⟩; handeln nach ⟨*Gefühl, Wunsch*⟩; sich halten an (+ *Akk.*) ⟨*Konventionen, Diät, Maßstab*⟩; ~ **one's heart** der Stimme des Herzens folgen; *see also* **example a; fashion 1 b;** [2]**lead 3 a; nose 1 a; j)** *(practise)* ausüben ⟨*Beruf, Handwerk, eine Kunst*⟩; ~ **the teaching/medical profession/the arts** Lehrer/Arzt/Künstler sein; **k)** *(keep up with mentally, grasp meaning of)* folgen (+ *Dat.*); **I can't ~ what he says** ich kann ihm nicht folgen; **do you ~ me?, are you ~ing me?** verstehst du, was ich meine?; **I don't ~ you/your meaning** ich verstehe Sie nicht/verstehe nicht, was Sie meinen; ~ **the music from the score** die Partitur mitlesen; **l)** *(be aware of the present state or progress of)* verfolgen ⟨*Ereignisse, Nachrichten, Prozeß*⟩; ~ **a TV serial** eine Fernsehserie regelmäßig sehen. **2.** *v. i.* **a)** *(go, come)* ~ **after sb./sth.** jmdm./einer Sache folgen; **b)** *(go or come after person or thing)* folgen; **you go ahead in the car and I'll ~ on my bike** du fährst mit dem Auto voraus, und ich komme mit dem Fahrrad nach; ~ **in the wake of sth.** etw. ablösen; auf etw. *(Akk.)* folgen; **c)** *(come next in order or time)* folgen; **in the years that ~ed** in den darauffolgenden Jahren; **as ~s** wie folgt; **the details are as ~s** die Einzelheiten lauten folgendermaßen; **there are two options, as ~s: ...:** es gibt zwei Möglichkeiten, und zwar folgende: ...; **would you like coffee to ~?** hätten Sie danach *od.* anschließend gerne [einen] Kaffee?; **what ~s next?** was kommt danach? ; **d)** *(ensue)* folgen; **e)** ~ **from sth.** *(result)* die Folge von etw. sein; *(be deducible)* aus etw. folgen; **it ~s [from this] that ...:** daraus folgt, daß ...; das heißt, daß ...
~ **'on** *v. i.* **a)** *(continue)* ~ **on from sth.** die Fortsetzung von etw. sein; **b)** *(Cricket)* sofort zum zweiten Mal schlagen; *see also* **follow-on**
~ **'out** *v. t.* **a)** *(pursue to the end)* durchführen ⟨*Plan, Projekt*⟩; sich *(Dat.)* erfüllen ⟨*Wunsch*⟩; zu Ende verfolgen ⟨*Ziel, Politik, Idee*⟩; **b)** *(carry out)* [genau] befolgen ⟨*Regel, Anweisung*⟩
~ **'through 1.** *v. t.* zu Ende verfolgen; durchziehen *(ugs.).* **2.** *v. i. (Sport)* durchschwingen; *see also* **follow-through**
~ **'up** *v. t.* **a)** *(pursue steadily)* stetig verfolgen; **b)** *(add further action etc. to)* ausbauen ⟨*Erfolg, Sieg*⟩; **c)** *(investigate further)* nachgehen (+ *Dat.*) ⟨*Hinweis*⟩; *(consider further)* berücksichtigen ⟨*Bitte, Angebot*⟩. *See also* **follow-up**

follower ['fɒləʊə(r)] *n.* Anhänger, *der*/Anhängerin, *die;* **be a dedicated ~ of fashion** immer mit der Mode gehen

following ['fɒləʊɪŋ] **1.** *adj.* **a)** *pres. p. of* **follow; on the ~ day** am Tag danach *od.* darauf; **on the ~ Monday** am nächsten Montag; **b)** *(now to be mentioned)* folgend; **the ~ items** folgende Gegenstände; **in the ~ way** folgendermaßen; **for the ~ reasons** aus folgenden Gründen; **the ~:** folgendes; *(persons)* folgende; **c)** *(blowing in one's direction of travel)* **~ wind** Rückenwind, *der.* **2.** *prep.* nach. **3.** *n.* Anhängerschaft, *die*

follow: ~-my-'leader *(Amer.:* **~-the-'leader)** *n. Spiel, bei dem alle Mitspieler das nachmachen, was einer vormacht;* **~-on** *n. (Cricket)* ≈ sofortiger zweiter Durchgang *(nachdem man im ersten nicht nahe genug an die Punktzahl des Gegners herangekommen ist);* **~-through** *n. (Sport)* Durchschwung, *der;* **~-up** *n.* Fortsetzung, *die; (Med.)* Nachuntersuchung, *die;* **there's never any ~-up to his promises** er erfüllt *od.* hält seine Versprechen nie; **as a ~-up** im Anschluß **(to** an + *Akk.*); **~-up letter/visit** Nachfaßbrief, *der*/-besuch, *der (Werbespr.)*

folly ['fɒlɪ] *n.* **a)** Torheit, *die (geh.);* **it would be [sheer] ~:** es wäre [äußerst] töricht *(geh.);* **an act of ~:** eine Torheit *(geh.);* **b)** *(costly structure considered useless)* nutzloser Prunkbau; **c)** *in pl. (Theatre)* Revue mit Glamourgirls

foment [fə'ment, fəʊ'ment] *v. t.* **a)** *(foster)* schüren; **b)** *(bathe)* mit feuchter Wärme behandeln

fomentation [fəʊmen'teɪʃn] *n.* **a)** *(fostering)* Schüren, *das;* **b)** *(warm cloth[s])* heißer Umschlag; **c)** *(application of warm cloth[s])* Behandlung mit feuchter Wärme *od.* mit heißen Umschlägen

fond [fɒnd] *adj.* **a)** *(tender)* zärtlich; *(affectionate)* liebevoll ‹*Blick*›; lieb ‹*Erinnerung*›; *(in letters)* **~[est] love** mit lieben Grüßen; alles Liebe; **say a ~ farewell** sich überschwenglich verabschieden; **be ~ of sb.** jmdn. mögen *od.* gern haben; **be ~ of sth.** etw. mögen; **be ~ of doing sth.** etw. gern tun; **she's very ~ of Greece/the theatre** sie liebt Griechenland/das Theater; **I'm not very ~ of sweets** ich mache mir nicht viel aus Süßigkeiten; **he's become very ~ of living in Spain** er lebt mittlerweile sehr gern in Spanien; **b)** *(foolishly credulous or hopeful)* kühn ‹*Hoffnung, Traum*›; gutgläubig ‹*Person*›; allzu zuversichtlich ‹*Glaube*›; voreingenommen ‹*Eltern*›; **he had ~ hopes of becoming an ambassador one day** er glaubte allen Ernstes daran, einmal Botschafter zu werden; **c)** *(over-affectionate)* übertrieben liebevoll

fondant ['fɒndənt] *n.* Fondant, *der od. das*

fondle ['fɒndl] *v. t.* streicheln

fondly ['fɒndlɪ] *adv.* **a)** *(tenderly)* zärtlich; *(with affection)* liebevoll; **he looks ~ back upon his days at university** er erinnert sich gern an seine Studentenzeit; **b)** *(with foolish credulousness or hopefulness)* allzu zuversichtlich

fondness ['fɒndnɪs] *n., no pl.* **a)** *(tenderness)* Zärtlichkeit, *die; (affection)* Liebe, *die;* **look back with great ~ on sth.** sich sehr gern an etw. *(Akk.)* erinnern; **~ for sth./doing sth.** *(special liking)* Vorliebe für etw./dafür, etw. zu tun; **~ for sb./art/the sea** Liebe zu jmdm./zur Kunst/zum Meer; **b)** *(foolish credulousness or hopefulness)* allzu große Gutgläubigkeit; törichte Zuversicht

fondue ['fɒndju:, 'fɒndu:] *n. (Gastr.)* Fondue, *das od. die*

¹font [fɒnt] *n.* Taufstein, *der*

²font *(Amer.) see* **²fount**

food [fu:d] *n.* **a)** *no pl., no art.* Nahrung, *die; (for animals)* Futter, *das;* **take ~:** Nahrung zu sich nehmen; **lack of ~:** Nahrungsmangel, *der;* **nutritious ~:** nahrhafte Kost; **be ~ for [the] worms** tot sein; **b)** *no pl., no art. (as commodity)* Lebensmittel *Pl.;* **one's week's shopping for ~** *or* **~ shopping** der wöchentliche Lebensmitteleinkauf; **c)** *no pl. (in solid form)* Essen, *das;* **some ~:** etwas zu essen; **there was plenty of ~ and drink** es gab reichlich zu essen und zu trinken; **she had prepared some delicious ~ for the party** für die Party hatte sie einige leckere Sachen vorbereitet; **he likes his ~ too much for that!** dazu ißt er viel zu gern!; **he's very keen on Italian ~:** er mag die italienische Küche; er ißt gern italienisch; **d)** *(particular kind)* Nahrungsmittel, *das;* Kost, *die; (for animals)* Futter, *das;* **nuts are a very nutritious ~:** Nüsse sind sehr nahrhaft; **canned ~s** Konserven *Pl.;* **preserved/imported ~s** eingemachte/importierte Nahrungsmittel; **e)** *(nutriment)* Nahrung, *die;* **f)** *(fig.: material for mental work)* Stoff, *der;* **~ for thought** Stoff zum Nachdenken; **~ for discussion** Diskussionsstoff, *der*

food: ~-chain *n. (Ecol.)* Nahrungskette, *die;* **~ fish** *n.* Speisefisch, *der*

foodie ['fu:dɪ] *n. (Brit. coll.)* ≈ Feinschmecker, *der*/-schmeckerin, *die*

food: ~ parcel *n.* Lebensmittelpaket, *das;* **~ poisoning** *n.* Lebensmittelvergiftung, *die;* **~-processor** *n.* Küchenmaschine, *die;* **~ rationing** *n.* Rationierung [von Lebensmitteln]; **~ shop** *see* **~ store; ~ stamps** *n. pl. (Amer.)* Lebensmittelgutscheine; **~ store** *n.* Lebensmittelgeschäft, *das;* **~stuff** *n.* Nahrungsmittel, *das;* **perishable ~stuffs** leicht verderbliche Lebensmittel; **~ supplies** *n. pl.* Vorräte; **~ value** *n.* Nährwert, *der*

¹fool [fu:l] **1.** *n.* **a)** Dummkopf, *der (ugs.);* **look a ~:** unmöglich *(ugs.)* aussehen; *(as regards behaviour)* dumm dastehen *(ugs.);* **he's a ~ to believe stories like that** er ist ein Narr *od. (ugs.)* er ist schön dumm, wenn er solche Geschichten glaubt; **what a ~ I am!** wie dumm von mir!; **oh, you 'are a ~!** wie kannst du nur so dumm sein!; **he makes you feel like a ~:** bei ihm kommt man sich *(Dat.)* wie ein Narr vor; **be no** *or* **nobody's ~:** nicht dumm *od. (ugs.)* nicht auf den Kopf gefallen sein; **I would never be such a ~:** so dumm wäre ich nie; **be ~ enough to do sth.** so dumm *od. (ugs.)* so blöd sein *od.* dumm genug sein, etw. zu tun; **make a ~ of oneself** sich lächerlich machen; **there's no ~ like an old ~:** Alter schützt vor Torheit nicht[, ganz im Gegenteil]; **a ~ and his money are soon parted** ein Dummkopf ist sein Geld bald wieder los; **a ~'s bolt is soon shot** ein Dummkopf hat sein Pulver bald verschossen *(ugs.);* **not suffer ~s gladly** Dummheit nicht ertragen können; **~s rush in where angels fear to tread** blinder Eifer schadet nur *(Spr.);* **b)** *(Hist.: jester, clown)* Narr, *der;* **act** *or* **play the ~:** herumalbern *(ugs.);* den Clown spielen *(abwertend);* **c)** *(dupe)* **make a ~ of sb.** jmdn. blamieren. *See also* **all 1b; April. 2.** *v. i.* herumalbern *(ugs.);* **you're ~ing!** mach keine Witze! *(ugs.).* **3.** *v. t.* **a)** *(cheat)* **~ sb. out of sth.** jmdn. um etw. betrügen; **~ sb. into doing sth.** jmdn. [durch Tricks] dazu bringen, etw. zu tun; **b)** *(dupe)* täuschen; hereinlegen *(ugs.); (play tricks on)* foppen; **don't be ~ed by him** laß dich von ihm nicht täuschen *od. (ugs.)* hereinlegen; **you could have ~ed me** *(iron.)* ach, was du nicht sagst!

~ a'bout, ~ a'round *v. i. (play the ~)* herumalbern *(ugs.);* Unsinn machen; *(idle)* herumtrödeln *(ugs.); (trifle)* Zeit vergeuden; **~ about** *or* **around with sth./sb.** mit etw./jmdm. herumspielen

~ a'way *v. t.* verschwenden; vergeuden

~ with *v. t.* [herum]spielen mit

²fool *n. (Gastr.) Süßspeise aus Kompott, das mit Sahne o. ä. verrührt ist*

foolery ['fu:lərɪ] *n., no pl.* Alberei, *die*

foolhardy ['fu:lhɑ:dɪ] *adj.* tollkühn ‹*Handlung, Behauptung, Person*›; draufgängerisch ‹*Person*›; **that was a ~ thing to say** es war sehr riskant, das zu sagen

foolish ['fu:lɪʃ] *adj.* **a)** töricht; verrückt *(ugs.)* ‹*Idee, Vorschlag*›; **we were ~ to expect miracles** es war töricht von uns, Wunder zu erwarten; **~ minds** Dummköpfe *(ugs.);* **don't do anything ~:** mach keinen Unsinn; **what a ~ thing to do/say** wie kann man nur so etwas Dummes tun/sagen; **b)** *(ridiculous)* albern *(ugs.)* ‹*Verhalten*›; blöd, dumm *(ugs.)* ‹*Grinsen, Bemerkung*›; lächerlich ‹*Aussehen*›

foolishly ['fu:lɪʃlɪ] *adv.* **a)** *(in foolish manner)* törichterweise; **b)** *(in ridiculous manner)* lächerlich ‹*sich benehmen*›; blöd, dumm *(ugs.)* ‹*grinsen*›

fool: ~proof *adj. (not open to misuse)* wasserdicht *(fig.); (not open to misinterpretation)* unmißverständlich; *(infallible)* absolut sicher; *(that cannot break down)* narrensicher *(ugs.);* **~scap** ['fu:lskæp, 'fu:lzkæp] *n.* **a)** *(size of paper)* Kanzleiformat, *das;* **b)** *(paper of this size)* Kanzleipapier, *das;* **~'s 'errand** *n.* nutzloses Unternehmen; **go on a ~'s errand** sich vergeblich bemühen; **I was sent on a ~'s errand** man hat mich völlig umsonst losgeschickt; **~'s 'paradise** *n.* Traumwelt, *die;* **be** *or* **live in a ~'s paradise** in einer Traumwelt leben; sich *(Dat.)* Illusionen machen; **~'s 'parsley** *n. (Bot.)* Hundspetersilie, *die*

foot [fʊt] **1.** *n., pl.* **feet** [fi:t] **a)** Fuß, *der;* **at sb.'s feet** zu jmds. Füßen; **be at sb.'s feet** *(fig.)* jmdm. zu Füßen liegen *(geh.);* **fall/sit at sb.'s feet** jmdm. zu Füßen fallen/sitzen; **sit at sb.'s feet** *(fig.)* jmds. Jünger sein; **lay the blame for sth. at sb.'s feet** jmdm. etw. anlasten *od.* zur Last legen; **put one's best ~ forward** *(fig.)* sein Bestes tun; **please wipe your feet** bitte Schuhe abtreten; **do sth. with both feet** *(fig.)* sich voll in etw. *(Akk.)* reinknien *(ugs.);* **feet of clay** *(fig.)* eine Schwachstelle; **feet first** mit den Füßen zuerst *od.* voran; **go into sth. feet first** *(fig.)* sich Hals über Kopf *(ugs.)* in etw. hineinstürzen; **have one ~ in the grave** *(fig.)* mit einem Fuß im Grabe stehen; **have both [one's] feet on the ground** *(fig.)* mit beiden Beinen [fest] auf der Erde stehen; **keep one's feet** *(fig.)* nicht hinfallen; **have a ~ in both camps** *(fig.)* auf beiden Schultern Wasser tragen; **my ~!** *(coll.)* beileibe nicht!; **on ~:** zu Fuß; **set sth. on ~:** etw. in Gang bringen *od.* setzen; **on one's/its feet** *(lit. or fig.)* auf den Beinen; **you'll be back on your feet again before long** *(fig.)* bald wirst du wieder auf die Beine kommen; **put** *or* **get sb. [back] on his feet** *(fig.)* jmdn. auf die Beine bringen; **put** *or* **get** *or* **set sth. [back] on its feet** *(fig.)* etw. [wieder] auf die Beine bringen *od.* stellen; **get on one's feet** sich erheben; aufstehen; **put one's ~ down** *(fig.) (be firmly insistent or repressive)* energisch werden; *(accelerate motor vehicle)* [Voll]gas geben; **put one's ~ in it** *(fig. coll.)* ins Fettnäpfchen treten *(ugs.);* einen Fauxpas begehen; **put one's feet up** die Beine hochlegen; **start [off]** *or* **get off** *or* **begin on the right/wrong ~** *(fig.)* einen guten/schlechten Start haben; **set ~ in/on sth.** etw. betreten; **go away and never set ~ in here** *or* **in this place again** geh fort und setze keinen Fuß mehr über diese Schwelle; **he had never set ~ in Britain/outside London** er hatte noch nie einen Fuß auf britischen Boden gesetzt/er war noch nie aus London herausgekommen; **be rushed off one's feet** *(fig.)* in Trab gehalten werden *(ugs.);* **stand on one's own [two] feet** *(fig.)* auf eigenen Füßen stehen; **sweep sb. off his/her feet** *(fig.)* jmdn. *od.* jmds. Herz im Sturm erobern; **rise** *or* **get to one's feet** sich erheben; aufstehen; **help sb. to his feet** jmdm. aufhelfen; **it's a bit muddy under ~:** der Boden ist ein bißchen matschig; **tread sth./sb. under ~:** auf etw./jmdn. treten; *(fig.)* etw./jmdn. unterdrücken; **get under sb.'s feet** *(fig.)* jmdm. vor die Füße laufen; **with four children under her feet** mit vier Kindern, die ihr vor den Füßen herumlaufen; **get one's feet wet** *(fig.)* sich hineinfinden; **never put a ~ wrong** *(fig.)* nie etwas falsch machen; **b)** *(step)* **swift/light of ~:** schnell-/leichtfüßig; **c)** *pl. same (Brit. Hist.)* Infanterie, *die (Milit.)*; **five hundred ~:** fünfhundert Infanteristen *(Milit.) od.* Fußsoldaten; **d)** *(far end)* unteres Ende; *(of bed)* Fußende, *das; (lowest part)* Fuß, *der; (of sail)* Unterliek, *das*; **at the ~ of the list/page** unten auf der Liste/Seite; **the compost heap is at the ~ of the garden** der Komposthaufen ist im hinteren Teil des Gartens; **e)** *(of stocking etc.)* Fuß, *der;* Füßling, *der;* **f)** *(Pros.: metrical unit)* [Vers]fuß, *der;* **g)** *(Phonet.: unit of speech)* ≈ Akzentgruppe, *die;* **h)** *pl.* **feet** *or* **same** *(linear measure)* Fuß, *der (30,48 cm)*; **7 ~** *or* **feet** 7 Fuß; **i)** *(base)* Fuß, *der; (of statue, pillar)* Sockel, *der;* Basis, *die;* **j)** *(Zool.: of invertebrate)* Fuß, *der;* **k)** *(Bot.)* Ansatzstelle, *die. See also* **¹ball 1 b; cold feet; cubic b; door b; drag 2 a; fall 2 a, p; find 1 b; hand 1 a; square 2 b; walk 2 b. 2.** *v. t.* **a) ~ it** *(dance)* tanzen; *(walk)* zu Fuß gehen; **b)** *(pay)* **~ the bill** die Rechnung bezahlen

footage ['fʊtɪdʒ] *n.* Filmmaterial, *das*

foot-and-'mouth [disease] *n.* Maul- und Klauenseuche, *die*

football ['fʊtbɔ:l] *n.* **a)** Fußball, *der; (elongated)* [ovaler] Ball; *(fig.)* Spielball, *der;* **b)** *(Brit.: soccer)* Fußball, *der; (Amer.: American ~)* Football, *der. See also* **American football; Rugby football**

'football boot *n.* Fußballschuh, *der*

footballer ['fʊtbɔ:lə(r)] *n.* **a)** *(Brit.: soccer player)* Fußballspieler, *der;* Fußballer, *der (ugs.);* **b)** *(Amer.: American football player)* Footballspieler, *der*

football: ~ pitch *n.* Fußballplatz, *der;* **~ pools** *n. pl.* **the ~ pools** das Fußballtoto; *see also* **²pool 1 a**

foot: ~-bath *n.* **a)** *(washing of feet)* Fußbad, *das;* **b)** *(small bath)* Fußwanne, *die;* **~-brake** *n.* Fußbremse, *die;* **~-bridge** *n.* Steg, *der; (across road, railway, etc.)* Fußgängerbrücke, *die*

-footed ['fʊtɪd] *adj. in comb.* -füßig; **nimble-~:** leichtfüßig; **large-/small-~:** mit großen/kleinen Füßen *nachgestellt*

footer ['fʊtə(r)] *(Brit. sl.) see* **football 1 b**

-footer ['fʊtə(r)] *n. in comb.* **she is a six-~:** sie ist sechs Fuß groß; **the boat was a nine-~:** das Boot war neun Fuß lang

foot: ~fall *n.* Schritt, *der;* **~-fault** *(Lawn Tennis)* **1.** *n.* Fußfehler, *der;* **2.** *v. i.* einen Fußfehler machen; **~hill** *n., usu. pl.* [Gebirgs]ausläufer, *der;* **~hold** *n.* Halt, *der; (fig.)* Stützpunkt, *der;* **get a ~hold** *(fig.)* Fuß fassen

footing ['fʊtɪŋ] *n.* **a)** *(fig.: status)* Stellung, *die;* **be on an equal ~ [with sb.]** [jmdm.] gleichgestellt sein; **put A on an equal ~ with B** A mit B auf die gleiche Stufe stellen; **place sth. on a firm ~:** etw. auf eine feste Basis stellen; **be on a friendly ~ with sb.** ein freundschaftliches Verhältnis zu jmdm. haben; **be on a war ~:** sich im Kriegszustand befinden; **b)** *(foothold)* Halt, *der;* **lose/miss/keep one's ~:** den Halt verlieren/keinen Halt finden/sich halten; **c)** *(surface for standing on)* Grund, *der; (fig.)* Stellung, *die;* **gain a ~ as a journalist** sich *(Dat.)* eine Position als Journalist schaffen; als Journalist Fuß fassen; **d)** *(Building)* Bankett, *das*

footle ['fu:tl] *v. i. (sl.)* **~ about** *(trifle)* herumtrödeln *(ugs.); (play the fool)* Unfug treiben

'footlights *n. pl. (Theatre)* Rampenlicht, *das*

footling ['fu:tlɪŋ] *adj.* läppisch *(abwertend);* albern *(ugs.)*

foot: ~loose *adj.* ungebunden; **~loose and fancy-free** frei und ledig; **~man** ['fʊtmən] *n., pl.* **~men** ['fʊtmən] *(servant)* Lakai, *der;* Diener, *der;* **~mark** *see* **~print; ~-muff** *n.* Fußsack, *der;* **~note** *n.* Fußnote, *die;* **~path** *n. (path)* Fußweg, *der; (Brit.: pavement)* Gehsteig, *der;* Bürgersteig, *der;* **~plate** *n. (Brit. Railw.)* Führerstand, *der;* **~plate workers** Lokomotivführer und Heizer; **~print** *n.* Fußabdruck, *der;* **~prints in the snow** Fußspuren im Schnee; **~-race** *n.* Wettlauf, *der;* Wettrennen, *das;* **~-rest** *n.* Fußstütze, *die; (on bicycle or motor cycle)* Fußraste, *die;* **~-rot** *n. (Vet. Med.)* Stoppellähme, *die;* **~-rule** *n.* [einen Fuß langes] Lineal; **~-scraper** *n.* Fußabstreifer, *der;* Abtreter, *der*

footsie ['fʊtsɪ] *n. (coll.)* **play ~ [with sb.]** [mit jmdm.] füßeln

foot: ~-slog *(coll.)* **1.** *v. i.* latschen *(salopp);* **2.** *n.* Gelaufe, *das;* **~-soldier** *n.* Infanterist, *der (Milit.);* Fußsoldat, *der;* **~sore** *pred. adj.* **be ~sore** wunde Füße haben; **~step** *n.* Schritt, *der;* **follow** *or* **tread in sb.'s ~steps** *(fig.)* in jmds. Fußstapfen *(Akk.)* treten; **~stool** *n.* Fußbank, *die;* Fußschemel, *der;* **~way** *n.* Fußweg, *der;* **~wear** *n., no pl.* Schuhe *Pl.;* Schuhwerk, *das;* Fußbekleidung, *die (Kaufmannsspr.);* **~work** *n., no pl. (Sport, Dancing)* Beinarbeit, *die*

foppish ['fɒpɪʃ] *adj.* dandyhaft *(geh.);* geckenhaft *(abwertend)*

for [fə(r), *stressed* fɔ:(r)] **1.** *prep.* **a)** *(representing, on behalf of, in exchange against)* für; *(in place of)* für; anstelle von; **what is the German ~ 'buzz'?** wie heißt „buzz" auf Deutsch?; **I. Smith ~ B. Jones** *(as signature)* B. Jones, i. A. I. Smith; *see also* **eye 1 a; b)** *(in defence, support, or favour of)* für; **be ~ doing sth.** dafür sein, etw. zu tun; **the voting was 5 ~ and 10 against** es stimmten 5 dafür und 10 dagegen; **it's each [man]** *or* **every man ~ himself** jeder ist auf sich selbst gestellt; **c)** *(to the benefit of)* für; **do sth. ~ sb.** für jmdn. etw. tun; **die ~ one's country** für sein Land sterben; **d)** *(with a view to)* für; *(conducive[ly] to)* zu; **they invited me ~ Christmas/Monday/supper** sie haben mich zu Weihnachten/für Montag/zum Abendessen eingeladen; **meet ~ a discussion** sich zu einer Besprechung treffen; **what is it ~?** wofür/wozu ist das? **that's what I'm there ~:** dafür/dazu bin ich ja da; **be saving up ~ sth.** auf etw. *(Akk.)* sparen; **he did everything ~ his family's well-being** er tat alles für das Wohlergehen der Familie; **e)** *(being the motive of)* für; *(having as purpose)* zu; **reason ~ living** Grund zu leben; **a dish ~ holding nuts** eine Schale für Nüsse; **f)** *(to obtain, win, save)* **a request ~ help** eine Bitte um Hilfe; **study ~ a university degree** auf einen Hochschulabschluß hin studieren; **go/run ~ a doctor** gehen/laufen, um einen Arzt zu holen; **phone ~ a doctor** nach einem Arzt telefonieren; **take sb. ~ a ride in the car/a walk** jmdn. im Auto spazierenfahren/mit jmdm. einen Spaziergang machen; **work ~ a living** für den Lebensunterhalt arbeiten; **draw on sb. ~ money** jmdn. um Geld angehen; **oh ~ a few minutes' peace!** wäre hier doch *od.* hätte ich doch einmal ein paar Minuten Ruhe!; **run/jump** *etc.* **~ it** loslaufen/-springen *usw.*; *see also* **life a; g)** *(to reach)* nach; **set out ~ England/the north/an island** nach England/Norden/zu einer Insel aufbrechen; **7.30 ~ 8** zwischen halb acht und acht; **h)** *(to be received by)* für; **there's** *or* **that's gratitude** *etc.* **~ you!** *(iron.)* und so was nennt sich Dankbarkeit *usw.!*; **that's Jim ~ you** das sieht Jim mal wieder ähnlich; **i)** *(as regards)* **checked ~ accuracy** auf Richtigkeit geprüft; **be dressed/ready ~ dinner** zum Dinner angezogen/fertig sein; **open ~ business** eröffnet; **open ~ lunch [from ... to ...]** Mittagstisch [von ... bis ...]; **have sth. ~ breakfast/pudding** etw. zum Frühstück/Nachtisch haben; **whether you should do it is not ~ me to say** ob du es tun sollst, kann ich dir nicht sagen; **enough ... ~:** genug ... für; **that's quite enough ~ me** das reicht mir völlig; **too ... ~:** zu ... für; **sb. is not long ~ this world** jmd. wird nicht mehr lange unter uns *(Dat.)* weilen; **there is nothing ~ it but to do sth.** es gibt keine andere Möglichkeit, als etw. zu tun; **be '~ it** *(sl.: face trouble)* dran sein *(ugs.);* **j)** *(Cricket)* **be out ~ a duck/59** ohne Punktgewinn/mit 59 Punkten aus sein; **65 ~ 3 [wickets]** 65 Punkte mit drei Schlägern ausgeschlagen; **k)** *(to the amount of)* **cheque/bill ~ £5** Scheck/Rechnung über *od.* in Höhe von 5 Pfund; **the voucher is good ~ 50p** der Gutschein ist 50 p wert; **l)** *(to affect, as if affecting)* für; **things don't look very promising ~ the business** was die Geschäfte angeht, sieht das alles nicht sehr vielversprechend aus; **learn to do things ~ oneself** lernen, die Dinge selbständig zu erledigen; **I think it would work out ~ us to meet some time** ich glaube, es läßt sich machen, daß wir uns einmal treffen; **it is wise/advisable ~ sb. to do sth.** es ist vernünftig/ratsam, daß jmd. etw. tut; **it's always nice ~ us to know that you're well** wir hören immer wieder gern, daß es dir gutgeht; **it's hopeless ~ me to try and explain the system** es ist sinnlos, dir das System erklären zu wollen; **m)** *(as being)* für; **what do you take me ~?** wofür hältst du mich?; **I/you** *etc.* **~ one** ich/du *usw.* für mein[en]/dein[en] *usw.* Teil; **see sb. ~ what he really is** jmdn. als das erkennen, was er wirklich ist *od.* so sehen, wie er wirklich ist; **n)** *(on account of, as penalty of)* wegen; **famous/well-known ~ sth.** berühmt/bekannt wegen *od.* für etw.; **live ~ one's work** für seine *od.* die Arbeit leben; **~ love of his wife** aus Liebe zu seiner Frau; **jump/shout ~ joy** vor Freude in die Luft springen/schreien; **this is ~ being good** das kriegst du, weil du so artig warst; **had it not been ~ him** wäre er nicht gewesen; **but ~ you/your kindness we might not be here today** nur deinetwegen/nur dank deiner Güte sind wir heute hier; **were it not ~ you/your help, I should not be able to do it** ohne dich/deine Hilfe wäre ich nicht dazu in der Lage; **o)** *(on the occasion of)* **~ the first time** zum ersten Mal; **why can't you help ~ once?** warum kannst du nicht einmal helfen?; **you are mistaken ~ once** nun hast du dich aber mal geirrt; **what shall I give him ~ his birthday?** was soll ich ihm zum Geburtstag schenken?; **p)** *(in spite of)* **~ all ...:** trotz ...; **~ all that, ...:** trotzdem ...; **~ all that he ...:** obwohl er ...; **q)** *(on account of the hindrance of)* vor (+ *Dat.*); **~ fear of ...:** aus Angst vor (+ *Dat.*); **he couldn't see the ring ~ looking at it** *(iron.)* er sah den Ring einfach nicht, obwohl er doch gerade auf ihn blickte; **but ~ ..., except ~ ...:** wenn nicht ... gewesen wäre, [dann] ...; **but ~ the captain's carelessness** wenn der Kapitän nicht so leichtfertig gewesen wäre; **were it not ~ the children** wenn die Kinder nicht wären; *see also* **wood a; r)** *(corresponding to)* für; **~ every cigarette you smoke you are reducing your life expectancy by one day** jede Zigarette, die du rauchst, verkürzt deine Lebenserwartung um einen Tag; **~ fifty fish eggs that die, a hundred survive** auf fünfzig Fischeier, die absterben, kommen hundert, die sich weiterentwickeln; **man ~ man** Mann für Mann; **s)** *(so far as concerns)* **~ all I know/care ...:** möglicherweise/was mich betrifft, ...; **~ my part** *or* **~ myself, I ...:** ich für mein[en] Teil ...; **~ one thing, ...:** zunächst einmal ...; **t)** *(considering the usual* *nature of)* für; **not bad ~ a first attempt** nicht schlecht für den ersten Versuch; **very active ~ a man of eighty** sehr rege für einen Achtziger; **u)** *(during)* seit; **we've/we haven't been here ~ three years** wir sind seit drei Jahren hier/nicht mehr hier gewesen; **we waited ~ hours/three hours** wir warteten stundenlang/drei Stunden lang; **we have been waiting ~ hours [on end]** wir warten schon seit Stunden; **how long are you here ~?** *(coll.)* wie lange bleiben Sie hier?; **stay here ~ a week/some time** eine Woche/einige Zeit hier bleiben; **sit here ~ now** *or* **~ the moment** *or* **~ the present** bleiben Sie im Augenblick hier sitzen; *see also* **ever a**; **v)** *(to the extent of)* **walk ~ 20 miles/~ another 20 miles** 20 Meilen [weit] gehen/weiter gehen. **2.** *conj. (since, as proof)* denn

forage ['fɒrɪdʒ] **1.** *n.* **a)** *(food for horses or cattle)* Futter, *das;* **b)** *(search for ~)* Nahrungssuche, *die;* Futtersuche, *die;* **on the ~:** auf Nahrungssuche; **c)** *(fig.: search for thing)* **on the ~ for sth.** auf der Jagd nach etw. *(ugs.)*. **2.** *v. i.* auf Nahrungssuche sein; **~ for sth.** auf der Suche nach etw. sein; *(fig.: rummage)* nach etw. stöbern; **~ in sb.'s suitcase/among sb.'s papers** jmds. Koffer/Papiere durchstöbern *od.* -wühlen

'forage cap *n.* Käppi, *das*

forasmuch [fɒrəz'mʌtʃ] *adv. (Law/arch.)* **~ as** insofern [als]

foray ['fɒreɪ] **1.** *n.* Streifzug, *der; (Mil.)* Ausfall, *der; (brief trip)* kurzer Besuch *(iron.)* (to bei); *(fig.: venture)* Ausflug, *der (scherzh.)*; **go on** *or* **make a ~:** einen Streifzug unternehmen; *(Mil.)* einen Ausfall machen. **2.** *v. i.* plündernd einfallen

forbad, forbade *see* **forbid**

¹forbear ['fɔ:beə(r)] *n., usu. in pl.* Vorfahr, *der*

²forbear [fɔ:'beə(r)] **1.** *v. i.,* **forbore** [fɔ:'bɔ:(r)], **forborne** [fɔ:'bɔ:n] **a)** *(refrain)* **~ from doing sth.** davon Abstand nehmen, etw. zu tun; **b)** *(be patient)* sich gedulden; **~ with sth.** etw. geduldig ertragen; **be ~ing** Geduld haben. **2.** *v. t.,* **forbore, forborne: ~ sth./to do** *or* **doing sth.** auf etw. *(Akk.)* verzichten/darauf verzichten, etw. zu tun

forbearance [fɔ:'beərəns] *n., no pl.* Nachsicht, *die; (forbearing nature)* Nachsichtigkeit, *die;* **show ~:** sich nachsichtig zeigen; Nachsicht üben

forbid [fə'bɪd] *v. t.,* **-dd-, forbad** [fə'bæd] *or* **forbade** [fə'bæd, fə'beɪd], **forbidden** [fə'bɪdn] **a) ~ sb. to do sth.** jmdm. verbieten, etw. zu tun; **~ [sb.] sth.** [jmdm.] etw. verbieten; **it is ~den [to do sth.]** es ist verboten *od.* nicht gestattet[, etw. zu tun]; **'the taking of photographs is ~den'** „Fotografieren nicht gestattet"; **b)** *(make impossible)* nicht zulassen; nicht erlauben; **I'd like to do it but time ~s** ich würde es gern tun, finde aber nicht die Zeit dazu; **but decency ~s** aber das verbietet [mir] der Anstand; **God/Heaven ~ [that ...]!** Gott/der Himmel bewahre[, daß ...]!; *(future)* der Himmel verhüte[, daß ...]

forbidden [fə'bɪdn] **1.** *see* **forbid. 2.** *adj.* verboten; **~ fruit** *(fig.)* verbotene Früchte; **~ ground** Gebiet, das nicht betreten werden darf; *(fig.)* **be ~ ground** tabu sein; *see also* **degree e**

forbidding [fə'bɪdɪŋ] *adj.* furchteinflößend ⟨*Aussehen, Stimme*⟩; unwirtlich ⟨*Landschaft*⟩; *(fig.)* düster ⟨*Aussicht*⟩

forbiddingly [fə'bɪdɪŋlɪ] *adv.* drohend ⟨*sich abzeichnen*⟩; entmutigend ⟨*lang, steil, teuer, schwer*⟩

forbore, forborne *see* **²forbear**

¹force [fɔ:s] **1.** *n.* **a)** *no pl. (strength, power)* Stärke, *die; (of bomb, explosion, attack, storm)* Wucht, *die; (physical strength)* Kraft, *die;* **[a wind of] ~ 12** *(Meteorol.)* Windstärke 12; **destructive ~ of a bomb** Zerstörungskraft einer Bombe; **achieve sth. by brute ~:** etw. mit roher Gewalt erreichen; **in ~/in great ~** *(in large numbers)* zahlreich/in großer Zahl; *see also* **b**; **b)** *no pl. (fig.: power, validity)* Kraft, *die; (power to convince)* Überzeugungskraft, *die;* **by ~ of** auf Grund (+ *Gen.*); kraft (+ *Gen.*) *(Papierdt.)*; **achieve a victory by ~ of numbers** einen Sieg durch zahlenmäßige Überlegenheit erringen; **~ of conviction/will** Überzeugungs-/Willenskraft, *die;* **~ of arms** Waffengewalt, *die;* **~ of character** Charakterstärke, *die;* **~ of evidence** Beweiskraft, *die;* **have the ~ of law** Gesetzeskraft haben; **argue with much ~:** sehr überzeugend argumentieren; **his dramatic sense comes out with great ~:** seine dramatische Begabung zeigt sich [hier] in voller Stärke; **in ~** *(in effect)* in Kraft; **come into ~** ⟨*Gesetz usw.:*⟩ in Kraft treten; **put in[to] ~:** in Kraft setzen; **the methods currently in ~:** die zur Zeit gängigen Methoden; *see also* **a**; **c)** *(coercion, violence)* Gewalt, *die;* **use** *or* **employ ~ [against sb.]** Gewalt [gegen jmdn.] anwenden; **use of ~:** Gewaltanwendung, *die;* **by ~:** gewaltsam; mit Gewalt; **resort to ~:** zur Gewalt greifen; **with the threat of ~:** unter Androhung von Gewalt; **d)** *(organized group) (of workers)* Kolonne, *die;* Trupp, *der; (of police)* Einheit, *die; (Mil.)* Armee, *die;* Streitmacht, *die (veralt.)*; **the ~s** die Armee; **be in the ~s** beim Militär sein; **the ~** *(Police)* die Polizei; **a large ~ of infantry/naval ~:** starke Infanterie-/Marineverbände; **join ~s [with sb.]** *(fig.)* sich [mit jmdm.] zusammentun; *see also* **armed; labour force; police force; sales force; task force; work-force**; **e)** *(forceful agency or person)* Kraft, *die;* Macht, *die;* **a ~ for evil** ein Handlanger *od.* Werkzeug des Bösen; **the ~s of destiny/evil** die Macht des Schicksals/Bösen; **there are ~s in action/at work here ...:** hier walten Kräfte/sind Kräfte am Werk ...; **he is a ~ in the land** *(fig.)*/**a ~ to be reckoned with** er ist ein einflußreicher Mann im Land/eine Macht, die nicht zu unterschätzen ist; *see also* **life force; spent b**; **f)** *(meaning)* Bedeutung, *die;* **g)** *(Phys.)* Kraft, *die.* **2.** *v. t.* **a)** *(coerce by violent means)* **~ sb. to do sth.** jmdn. zwingen, etw. zu tun; **~ sb. into marriage/compliance** jmdn. zur Heirat zwingen/jmds. Einverständnis erzwingen; **be ~d into war** sich zum Krieg gezwungen sehen; **be ~d to do sth.** gezwungen sein *od.* sich gezwungen sehen, etw. zu tun; **~ sb. out of the room [at gunpoint]** jmdn. [mit vorgehaltener Waffe] zwingen, das Zimmer zu verlassen; **b)** *(compel by non-violent means)* **~ sb./oneself [to do sth.]** jmdn./sich zwingen[, etw. zu tun]; **~ sb./oneself into sth.** *(fig.)* jmdn./sich zu etw. zwingen; **I was ~d to accept/into accepting the offer** ich fühlte mich verpflichtet/ich war *od.* sah mich gezwungen, das Angebot anzunehmen; **I was ~d to the conclusion** *or* **to conclude that ...** *(fig.)* ich mußte zu dem Schluß gelangen, daß ...; **~ sb.'s hand** *(fig.)* jmdn. zwingen zu handeln; *see also* **issue 1 f**; **c)** *(take by ~)* **~ sth. from sb.** jmdm. etw. entreißen; **he ~d it out of her hands** er riß es ihr aus der Hand; **~ a promise out of sb.** *(fig.)* jmdm. ein Versprechen abringen; **~ a confession from sb.** *(fig.)* jmdn. zu einem Geständnis zwingen; **~ a smile from sb.** *(fig.)* jmdm. ein Lächeln entlocken; **d)** *(push)* **~ sth. into sth.** etw. in etw. *(Akk.)* [hinein]zwängen; **~ sth. [up] through an opening** etw. [nach oben und] durch eine Öffnung pressen; **~ one's way** sich *(Dat.)* [gewaltsam] einen Weg bahnen; **e)** *(impose, inflict)* **~ sth. [up]on sb.** jmdm. etw. aufzwingen *od.* aufnötigen; **he ~d his attentions on her** er drängte sich ihr mit seinen Aufmerksamkeiten auf; **f)** *(break open)* **~ [open]** aufbrechen; **g)** *(storm)* stürmen ⟨*Festung*⟩; **h)** *(effect by violent means)* sich *(Dat.)* erzwingen ⟨*Zutritt*⟩; **~ one's way in[to a building]** sich *(Dat.)* mit Gewalt Zutritt [zu einem Gebäude] verschaffen; **I had to ~ my way out** ich mußte Gewalt anwenden, um herauszukommen; **i) ~ the pace** *(lit. or fig.)* das Tempo forcieren; **~ the bidding** das Gebot in die Höhe treiben; **j)** *(produce with effort)* sich zwingen zu; **~ a smile** sich zu einem Lächeln zwingen; **k)** *(put strained sense upon)* Gewalt antun (+ *Dat.*); vergewaltigen ⟨*Sprache*⟩; überstrapazieren ⟨*Vergleich*⟩; **l)** treiben ⟨*Pflanzen*⟩; **m)** *(rape)* **~ a woman** einer Frau *(Dat.)* Gewalt antun *(veralt.)*

~ 'down *v. t.* **a)** drücken ⟨*Preis*⟩; **b)** *(compel to land)* zur Landung zwingen ⟨*Flugzeug*⟩; **c)** *(make oneself eat)* herunterwürgen *(ugs.)* ⟨*Nahrung*⟩

~ 'up *v. t.* hochtreiben ⟨*Preis*⟩

²force *n. (N. Engl.)* Wasserfall, *der*

forced [fɔ:st] *adj.* **a)** *(contrived, unnatural)* gezwungen; gewollt ⟨*Geste, Vergleich, Metapher*⟩; gekünstelt ⟨*Benehmen*⟩; **b)** *(compelled by force)* erzwungen; Zwangs⟨*arbeit, -anleihe*⟩; **~-labour camp** Arbeitslager, *das;* **c)** *(produced artificially)* **~ vibration** *(Phys.)* unfreie *od.* erzwungene Schwingung; **~-air ventilation** Zwangslüftung, *die (Technik)*

forced: ~ 'landing *n.* Notlandung, *die;* **~ 'march** *n. (Mil.)* Gewaltmarsch, *der;* **~ 'marriage** *n.* erzwungene Ehe

'force-feed *v. t.* zwangsernähren; *(fig.)* vollstopfen (**on** mit)

forceful ['fɔ:sfl] *adj.* stark ⟨*Persönlichkeit, Charakter*⟩; energisch ⟨*Person, Art, Stimme, Maßnahme*⟩; überzeugend ⟨*Darlegung*⟩; schwungvoll ⟨*Rede-, Schreibweise*⟩; eindrucksvoll ⟨*Sprache*⟩; eindringlich ⟨*Worte*⟩

forcefully ['fɔ:sfəlɪ] *adv.* eindringlich ⟨*reden, darlegen*⟩; energisch ⟨*verfolgen, umgehen*⟩; nachdrücklich ⟨*erinnern*⟩

force majeure [fɔ:s mɑ'ʒɜ:(r)] *n.* höhere Gewalt

'forcemeat *n. (Cookery)* Farce, *die*

forceps ['fɔ:seps] *n., pl. same* **[pair of] ~:** Zange, *die;* **obstetrical ~:** Geburtszange, *die;* **~ baby/delivery** Zangengeburt, *die*

forcible ['fɔ:sɪbl] *adj.* **a)** *(done by force)* gewaltsam; **b)** *see* **forceful**

forcibly ['fɔ:sɪblɪ] *adv.* **a)** *(by force)* gewaltsam; mit Gewalt; **b)** *see* **forcefully**

forcing-house ['fɔ:sɪŋhaʊs] *n. (lit. or fig.)* Treibhaus, *das*

ford [fɔ:d] **1.** *n.* Furt, *die.* **2.** *v. t.* durchqueren; *(wade through)* durchwaten

fore [fɔ:(r)] **1.** *adj., esp. in comb.* vorder...; Vorder⟨*teil, -front usw.*⟩. **2.** *n.* **[be/come] to the ~:** im Vordergrund [stehen]/in den Vordergrund [rücken]. **3.** *int. (Golf)* Achtung. **4.** *adv. (Naut.)* vorn; **~ and aft** längs[schiffs]

fore-and-'aft *(Naut.)* **1.** *adj.* Längs-; **~ sail** Schratsegel, *das.* **2.** *adv.* längs[schiffs]; **~ rigged** längsschiffs getakelt

¹'forearm *n.* Unterarm, *der*

²fore'arm *v. t.* rüsten; *(fig.)* **be ~ed** gerüstet *od.* vorbereitet sein; *see also* **forewarn**

forebear *see* **¹forbear**

fore'bode *v. t. (portend)* ankündigen; **these clouds ~ a storm** die Wolken bedeuten *od.* deuten auf Sturm

foreboding [fɔ:'bəʊdɪŋ] *n.* Vorahnung, *die; (unease caused by premonition)* ungutes Gefühl; *(omen)* Vorzeichen, *das;* Omen, *das*

'forecast 1. *v. t.,* **~** *or* **~ed** vorhersagen. **2.** *n.* Voraussage, *die;* Prognose, *die; (Meteorol.)* [Wetter]vorhersage, *die;* Wetterbericht, *der;* **the ~ is for rain** laut Wettervorhersage wird es regnen

'forecaster *n.* Meteorologe, *der*/Meteorologin, *die*

forecastle ['fəʊksl] *n. (Naut.)* Back, *die; (Hist.: deck)* [Vorder]kastell, *das*

foreclose [fɔ:'kləʊz] *(Law)* **1.** *v. t.* kündigen; **~ a mortgage** eine Hypothekenforderung geltend machen. **2.** *v. i.* **~ on sb./a mortgage** eine Hypothekenforderung gegenüber jmdm./eine Hypothekenforderung geltend machen

'forecourt *n.* Vorhof, *der;* ~ **attendant** ≈ Tankwart, *der;* ~ **service** Service an der Tankstelle
'foredeck *n. (Naut.)* Vordeck, *das*
fore'doom *v.t.* vorherbestimmen; **be ~ed to failure** zum Scheitern verurteilt sein
'forefather *n., usu. in pl.* Vorfahr, *der;* **our ~s** unsere Vorväter
'forefinger *n.* Zeigefinger, *der*
'forefoot *n.* Vorderfuß, *der*
'forefront *n.* **[be] in the ~ of** in vorderster Linie (+ *Gen.*) [stehen]
foregather *see* **forgather**
forego *see* **forgo**
foregoing ['fɔ:gəʊɪŋ, fɔ:'gəʊɪŋ] *adj.* vorhergehend
'foregone *adj.* **be a ~ conclusion** *(be predetermined)* von vornherein feststehen; *(be certain)* so gut wie sicher sein
'foreground *n.* Vordergrund, *der*
'forehand *(Tennis etc.)* **1.** *adj.* Vorhand-. **2.** *n. (also part of horse)* Vorhand, *die*
forehead ['fɒrɪd, 'fɔ:hed] *n.* Stirn, *die*
foreign ['fɒrɪn] *adj.* **a)** *(from abroad)* ausländisch; Fremd⟨*herrschaft, -kapital, -sprache*⟩; fremdartig ⟨*Gebräuche*⟩; fremdländisch ⟨*Aussehen*⟩; ~ **word** fremdsprachliches Wort; *(used in English)* Fremdwort, *das;* **talk ~** *(coll.)* auswärts reden *od.* sprechen *(ugs. scherzh.);* ~ **worker** Gastarbeiter, *der*/-arbeiterin, *die;* **he is ~:** er ist Ausländer; **b)** *(abroad)* fremd; Auslands⟨*reise, -niederlassung, -markt*⟩; ~ **country** Ausland, *das;* **from a ~ country** aus einem anderen Land; aus dem Ausland; ~ **travel** Reisen ins Ausland; *see also* **part 1 g; c)** *(related to countries abroad)* außenpolitisch; Außen⟨*politik, -handel*⟩; ~ **affairs** auswärtige Angelegenheiten; **spokesman on ~ affairs** außenpolitischer Sprecher; ~ **news** Nachrichten aus dem Ausland; **d)** *(from outside)* fremd; ~ **body** *or* **substance** Fremdkörper, *der;* **e)** *(alien, unfamiliar)* fremd; **be ~ to sb./sb.'s nature** jmdm. fremd sein/nicht jmds. Art sein; **be ~ to sth.** *(unrelated)* in keiner Beziehung zu etw. stehen
foreign: ~ **'aid** *n.* Entwicklungshilfe, *die;* **F~ and 'Commonwealth Office** *n. (Brit.)* Außenministerium, *das;* ~ **corre'spondent** *n. (Journ.)* Auslandskorrespondent, *der*/-korrespondentin, *die*
foreigner ['fɒrɪnə(r)] *n.* Ausländer, *der*/Ausländerin, *die*
foreign: ~ **ex'change** *n. (dealings)* Devisenhandel, *der; (currency)* fremde Währung; Devisen *Pl.;* ~ **exchange market** Devisenmarkt, *der;* ~ **'language** *n.* Fremdsprache, *die; attrib.* **~-language newspaper/broadcast** fremdsprachige Zeitung/Rundfunksendung; **~-language teaching** Fremdsprachenunterricht, *der;* ~ **'legion** *n.* Fremdenlegion, *die;* **F~ 'Minister** *n.* Außenminister, *der;* **F~ 'Ministry** *n.* Außenministerium, *das;* **F~ Office** *n. (Brit. Hist./coll.)* Außenministerium, *das;* Auswärtiges Amt; **~-owned** *adj.* **~-owned subsidiaries** Tochtergesellschaften in ausländischem Besitz; **F~ 'Secretary** *n. (Brit.)* Außenminister, *der;* ~ **service** *see* **diplomatic service**
fore'knowledge *n.* vorherige Kenntnis; **with the ~ that ...:** im Wissen, daß ...
forelady *(Amer.) see* **forewoman a**
foreland ['fɔ:lənd] *n. (Geog.)* Kap, *das*
'foreleg *n.* Vorderbein, *das;* Vorderlauf, *der (Jägerspr.)*
'forelimb *n.* Vordergliedmaße, *die*
'forelock *n.* Stirnlocke, *die;* **take time** *etc.* **by the ~** *(fig.)* die Gelegenheit beim Schopf ergreifen; **touch one's ~** *(coll. joc.)* einen Diener machen *(iron.)*
foreman ['fɔ:mən] *n., pl.* **foremen** ['fɔ:mən] **a)** *(chief workman)* Vorarbeiter, *der;* Werkmeister, *der;* **b)** *(Law)* Sprecher [der Geschworenen/*(in Germany)* der Schöffen]
'foremast *n. (Naut.)* Fockmast, *der*
foremost ['fɔ:məʊst, 'fɔ:məst] **1.** *adj.* **a)** vorderst...; **the two ~ runners** die beiden Läufer an der Spitze; **fall downstairs head ~:** mit dem Kopf zuerst die Treppe hinunterfallen; **b)** *(fig.)* führend; **be in the ~ rank** zur Spitze zählen. **2.** *adv. see* **first 2 e**
'forename *n.* Vorname, *der*
'forenoon *n. (Naut., Law/arch.)* Vormittag, *der;* **in the ~:** am Vormittag
forensic [fə'rensɪk] *adj.* gerichtlich; forensisch *(fachspr.);* ~ **medicine** Gerichtsmedizin, *die;* ~ **science** Kriminaltechnik, *die;* ~ **laboratory** kriminaltechnisches Labor
'fore-paw *n.* Vorderpfote, *die*
'foreplay *n.* Vorspiel, *das*
'forerunner *n.* **a)** *(predecessor)* Vorläufer, *der*/Vorläuferin, *die;* **b)** *(harbinger, sign)* Vorbote, *der*
foresail ['fɔ:seɪl, 'fɔ:sl] *n. (Naut.)* Focksegel, *das*
foresaw *see* **foresee**
foresee [fɔ:'si:] *v.t., forms as* **'see** voraussehen; **trouble which had not been ~n** unvorhergesehener Ärger; **as far as one can ~** *or* **as can be ~n** aller Voraussicht nach
foreseeable [fɔ:'si:əbl] *adj.* **a)** vorhersehbar; **b) in the ~ future** in nächster Zukunft; in absehbarer Zeit
foreseen *see* **foresee**
fore'shadow *v.t.* vorausahnen lassen; vorausdeuten auf (+ *Akk.*)
'foreshore *n.* Vorland, *das; (between high-water and low-water marks)* ≈ Strand, *der*
fore'shorten *v.t.* **a)** *(Art, Photog.)* [perspektivisch] verkürzen; **b)** *(shorten, condense)* verkürzen; verdichten *(fig.)* ⟨*Ereignisse*⟩
'foresight *n., no pl.* Weitblick, *der;* Voraussicht, *die;* **act with ~:** vorausschauend handeln; **use ~:** vorausschauend sein; Weitblick zeigen; **have the ~ to do sth.** so vorausschauend sein, etw. zu tun
'foreskin *n. (Anat.)* Vorhaut, *die*
forest ['fɒrɪst] *n.* **a)** Wald, *der; (commercially exploited)* Forst, *der; attrib.* Wald⟨*brand, -land*⟩; **covered in ~s** bewaldet; ~ **law** Forstrecht, *das;* ~ **warden** *or (Amer.)* **ranger** Förster, *der; see also* **deer-forest; b)** *(fig.)* Wald, *der* **(of** von); *(of ideas etc.)* Gewirr, *das;* Wust, *der (abwertend)*
fore'stall *v.t.* zuvorkommen (+ *Dat.*); *(prevent by prior action)* vermeiden; *(anticipate)* vorhersehen
'forestay *n. (Naut.)* Vorstag, *das*
forested ['fɒrɪstɪd] *adj.* bewaldet
forester ['fɒrɪstə(r)] *n.* **a)** *(warden)* Förster, *der;* **b)** *(dweller)* Waldbewohner, *der*
forestry ['fɒrɪstrɪ] *n.* Forstwirtschaft, *die; (science)* Forstwissenschaft, *die;* **F~ Commission** *(Brit.) britische Forstbehörde*
'forest-tree *n.* Waldbaum, *der;* Forstbaum, *der*
'foretaste *n.* Vorgeschmack, *der;* **have a ~ of sth.** einen Vorgeschmack von etw. bekommen
fore'tell *v.t.,* **foretold** vorhersagen; voraussagen
'forethought *n. (prior deliberation)* [vorherige] Überlegung; *(care for the future)* Vorausdenken, *das; (premeditation)* Vorausplanung, *die*
foretold *see* **foretell**
forever [fə'revə(r)] *(Amer.)* = **for ever;** *see* **ever a**
fore'warn *v.t.* vorwarnen; **we were ~ed of the difficulties** man hatte uns vor den Schwierigkeiten gewarnt; **~ed is forearmed** *(prov.)* wer gewarnt ist, ist gewappnet
fore'warning *n.* Vorwarnung, *die;* **be given adequate ~:** hinreichend vorgewarnt sein
'forewoman *n.* **a)** *(chief workwoman)* Vorarbeiterin, *die;* **b)** *(Law)* Sprecherin [der Geschworenen/*(in Germany)* der Schöffen]
'foreword *n.* Vorwort, *das*
forfeit ['fɔ:fɪt] **1.** *v.t.* verlieren *(auch fig.);* einbüßen *(geh., auch fig.);* verlustig gehen (+ *Gen.*) *(Amtsspr.);* verwirken *(geh.)* ⟨*Recht, jmds. Gunst*⟩; **he ~ed the good opinion of his friends** er verscherzte sich *(Dat.)* die Sympathien seiner Freunde. **2.** *n.* **a)** *(penalty)* Strafe, *die; (fig.)* Preis, *der;* **b)** *(Games)* Pfand, *das;* **pay/redeem a ~:** ein Pfand geben/einlösen; **c)** *(~ing)* Verlust, *der;* Einbuße, *die.* **3.** *adj.* **be ~:** verfallen **(to** *Dat.*); ⟨*Leben, Recht:*⟩ verwirkt sein *(geh.)*
forfeiture ['fɔ:fɪtʃə(r)] *n.* Verlust, *der;* Einbuße, *die*
forgather [fɔ:'gæðə(r)] *v.i.* sich treffen; zusammenkommen
forgave *see* **forgive**
¹forge [fɔ:dʒ] **1.** *n.* **a)** *(workshop)* Schmiede, *die;* **b)** *(blacksmith's hearth)* Esse, *die; (furnace for melting or refining metal)* Schmiedeofen, *der.* **2.** *v.t.* **a)** schmieden **(into** zu); **b)** *(fig.)* schmieden ⟨*Plan, Verbindung*⟩; schließen ⟨*Vereinbarung, Freundschaft, Frieden*⟩; prägen ⟨*Charakter*⟩; *(fabricate)* erfinden; sich *(Dat.)* ausdenken; **c)** *(counterfeit)* fälschen; **~d money** Falschgeld, *das*
²forge *v.i.* **a)** *(advance rapidly)* ~ **into the lead** die Führung übernehmen; in Führung gehen; ~ **ahead** [das Tempo] beschleunigen; ⟨*Wettläufer:*⟩ vorstoßen; *(fig.)* vorankommen; Fortschritte machen; *(take lead)* sich an die Spitze setzen; die Führung übernehmen; **b)** *(progress steadily)* ~ **on** *(lit. or fig.)* [stetig] vorankommen
forger ['fɔ:dʒə(r)] *n.* Fälscher, *der*/Fälscherin, *die*
forgery ['fɔ:dʒərɪ] *n.* Fälschung, *die;* **commit an act of ~:** eine Fälschung begehen
forget [fə'get] **1.** *v.t.,* **-tt-, forgot** [fə'gɒt], **forgotten** [fə'gɒtn] *or (Amer./arch./poet.)* **forgot a)** vergessen; *(~ learned ability)* verlernen; vergessen; **these names are easy to ~** *or* **easily forgotten** diese Namen vergißt man leicht; **gone but not forgotten** in bleibender Erinnerung; *(iron.)* aus den Augen, aber schwerlich aus dem Sinn; **never-to-be-forgotten** unvergeßlich; **I was quite ~ting you know her** ich habe ganz vergessen, daß du sie ja kennst; **I ~ his name** *(have forgotten)* ich habe seinen Namen vergessen; ~ **doing sth./having done sth.** vergessen, daß man etw. getan hat; ~ **to do sth.** vergessen, etw. zu tun; **don't ~ that ...:** vergiß nicht *od.* denk[e] daran, daß ...; ~ **how to dance** das Tanzen verlernen; **a thrashing he won't ~ in a hurry** eine Tracht Prügel, die er nicht so schnell vergessen wird; **b)** *(leave)* vergessen; **c) and don't you ~ it** *(coll.)* vergiß das ja nicht; ~ **sth.** *(decide to ignore)* etw. beiseite lassen; **~ it!** *(coll.)* schon gut!; vergiß es! **2.** *v.i.,* **-tt-, forgot, forgotten** es vergessen; **I almost forgot** fast hätte ich es vergessen; **I quite forgot** ich habe es ganz vergessen; ~ **about sth.** etw. vergessen; **~ about it!** *(coll.)* schon gut!; **I had forgotten all about his** *or* **him coming today** ich hatte ganz vergessen, daß er heute kommt; **I forgot about Joe** ich habe gar nicht an Joe gedacht. **3.** *v. refl.,* **-tt-, forgot, forgotten a)** *(act unbecomingly or unworthily)* sich vergessen; **b)** *(neglect one's own interests)* sich selbst vergessen; nicht an sich *(Akk.)* denken
forgetful [fə'getfl] *adj.* **a)** *(absent-minded)* vergeßlich; **b) ~ of sth.** ohne an etw. *(Akk.)* zu denken; **be ~ of sth.** etw. vergessen; **be ~ of one's duty** seine Pflicht vernachlässigen
forgetfully [fə'getfəlɪ] *adv.* in Gedanken
forgetfulness [fə'getflnɪs] *n., no pl.* Vergeßlichkeit, *die;* Zerstreutheit, *die;* **in a moment of ~:** in einem Moment von Geistesabwesenheit
for'get-me-not *n. (Bot.)* Vergißmeinnicht, *das; attrib.* ~ **blue** vergißmeinnichtblau
forgettable [fə'getəbl] *adj.* **easily ~:** leicht zu vergessen

forging ['fɔːdʒɪŋ] *n. (object)* Schmiedestück, *das*

forgivable [fə'gɪvəbl] *adj.* verständlich; verzeihlich

forgivably [fə'gɪvəblɪ] *adv.* verständlicherweise

forgive [fə'gɪv] *v.t.*, **forgave** [fə'geɪv], **forgiven** [fə'gɪvn] **a)** vergeben ⟨*Sünden*⟩; verzeihen ⟨*Unrecht*⟩; entschuldigen, verzeihen ⟨*Unterbrechung, Neugier, Ausdrucksweise*⟩; **~ sb. [sth.** *or* **for sth.]** jmdm. [etw.] verzeihen *od.* *(geh.)* vergeben; **~ sb. for doing sth.** jmdm. verzeihen, daß er/sie etw. getan hat; **God ~ me** möge Gott mir vergeben; **am I ~n?** verzeihst du mir?; **you are ~n** ich verzeihe dir; **~ us [for] our sins** vergib uns unsere Sünden; **I'll never ~ myself for not having offered to help** ich werde es mir nie verzeihen, nicht wenigstens meine Hilfe angeboten zu haben; **~ me for saying so, but ...:** entschuldigen *od.* verzeihen Sie[, daß ich es sage], [aber] ...; **she doesn't ~ easily** es fällt ihr schwer zu verzeihen; **~ and forget** vergeben und vergessen; **b)** *(remit, let off)* erlassen; **~ sb. a debt** jmdm. eine Schuld erlassen

forgiveness [fə'gɪvnɪs] *n., no pl.* Verzeihung, *die; (esp. of sins)* Vergebung, *die (geh.)*; **ask/beg [sb.'s] ~:** [jmdn.] um Verzeihung/*(geh.)* Vergebung bitten; **grant sb. [one's] ~:** jmdm. verzeihen; **~ of sins** Vergebung der Sünden; Sündenvergebung, *die*

forgiving [fə'gɪvɪŋ] *adj.*, **forgivingly** [fə'gɪvɪŋlɪ] *adv.* versöhnlich

forgo [fɔː'gəʊ] *v.t., forms as* ¹**go** verzichten auf (+ *Akk.*)

forgone *see* **forgo**

forgot, forgotten *see* **forget**

fork [fɔːk] **1.** *n.* **a)** *(for eating with)* Gabel, *die*; **knife and ~:** Messer und Gabel; Besteck, *das*; **the knives and ~s** das Besteck; **~ lunch** Gabelfrühstück, *das (veralt.)*; ≈ kaltes Büfett; **~ supper** ≈ kaltes Büfett; **b)** *(Agric.)* Gabel, *die*; Forke, *die (bes. nordd.)*; **c)** *in sing. or pl. (on bicycle)* Gabel, *die*; **d)** *([point of] division into branches)* Gabelung, *die; (one branch)* Abzweigung, *die; (of tree)* Astgabel, *die.* **2.** *v.i.* **a)** *(divide)* sich gabeln; **b)** *(turn)* abbiegen; **~ [to the] left [for]** [nach] links abbiegen [nach]. **3.** *v.t.* gabeln; **~ in manure** Mist [mit einer Gabel] untergraben

~ 'out *(sl.)* **1.** *v.t.* lockermachen *(ugs.)*; **~ out money** blechen *(ugs.)*. **2.** *v.i.* **~ out [for sth.]** [für etw.] blechen *(ugs.)*

~ 'over *v.t.* lockern ⟨*Boden*⟩

~ 'up *see* **~ out**

forked [fɔːkt] *adj.* gegabelt; **speak with ~ tongue** *(fig.)* mit gespaltener *od.* doppelter Zunge sprechen *(geh.)*

forked 'lightning *n., no pl., no indef. art.* Linienblitz, *der*

'fork-lift truck *n.* Gabelstapler, *der*

forlorn [fə'lɔːn] *adj.* **a)** *(desperate)* verzweifelt; **~ hope** *(faint hope)* verzweifelte Hoffnung; *(desperate enterprise)* aussichtsloses Unterfangen; **b)** *(forsaken)* [einsam und] verlassen; *(wretched)* erbärmlich *(auch fig.)*; desolat ⟨*Anblick, Zustand*⟩

form [fɔːm] **1.** *n.* **a)** *(type, guise, style)* Form, *die*; **~ of address** [Form der] Anrede; **~ of life/government** Lebens-/Regierungsform, *die*; **the reward will take the ~ of a holiday** die Belohnung wird eine Urlaubsreise sein; **malaria takes various ~s** Malaria äußert sich in verschiedenen Formen; **in human ~:** in menschlicher Gestalt; in Menschengestalt; **in the ~ of** in Form von *od.* + *Gen.*; **in book ~:** in Buchform; als Buch; **b)** *no pl. (shape, visible aspect)* Form, *die*; Gestalt, *die; (Lit., Mus., Art)* Form, *die*; **~ without substance** Form ohne Inhalt; **take ~** *(lit. or fig.)* Gestalt annehmen *od.* gewinnen; **give ~ to sth.** einer Sache *(Dat.)* Gestalt geben *od.* verleihen; **the ~ and content of a novel** Form und Inhalt eines Romans; **c)** *(printed sheet)* Formular, *das*; **d)** *(Brit. Sch.)* Klasse, *die*; **first/second** *etc.* **~:** erste/zweite *usw.* Klasse *(an einer weiterführenden Schule)*; *see also* **sixth form**; **e)** *(bench)* Bank, *die*; **f)** *no pl., no indef. art. (Sport: physical condition)* Form, *die*; **peak ~:** Bestform, *die*; **improvement in ~:** Formanstieg, *der*; **out of ~:** außer Form; nicht in Form; **in [good] ~** *(lit. or fig.)* [gut] in Form; **in top ~/at the top of his** *etc.* **~** *(lit. or fig.)* in Höchstform; **she was in great ~ at the party** *(fig.)* bei der Party war sie groß in Form; **on/off ~** *(lit. or fig.)* in/nicht in Form; **be slightly off ~:** nicht ganz in Form sein; **g)** *(Sport: previous record)* bisherige Leistungen; **on/judging by [past/present] ~** *(fig.)* nach der Papierform; **true to ~** *(fig.)* wie üblich *od.* zu erwarten; **h)** *(set procedure)* **in due/proper ~:** in angemessener/richtiger Form; **matter of ~:** Routineangelegenheit *od.* -sache, *die*; **as a matter of ~:** der Form halber; **common ~:** übliches Verfahren; **what's the ~?** was ist das übliche Verfahren?; **tell me the ~:** wie wird üblicherweise verfahren?; **i)** *(etiquette)* **for the sake of ~:** der Form halber; um der Form zu genügen; **good/bad ~:** gutes/schlechtes Benehmen; **it's bad** *or* **not good ~ to do this** so etwas gehört sich nicht; **j)** *(figure)* Gestalt, *die*; **k)** *(Ling.)* Form, *die*; **plural ~:** Pluralform, *die*; Plural, *der*; **feminine ~:** Femininum, *das*; **negative ~:** Verneinung, *die*; Negation, *die*; **l)** *(Philos.)* Form, *die*; **m)** *no pl. (sl.: criminal record)* Vorstrafe, *die*; **have ~:** vorbestraft sein; **n)** *(hare's lair)* Lager, *das*; Sasse, *die (Jägerspr.)*; **o)** *see* **formwork. 2.** *v.t.* **a)** *(make; also Ling.)* bilden; **be ~ed from sth.** aus etw. entstehen; **b)** *(shape, mould)* formen, gestalten **(into** zu); *(fig.)* formen ⟨*Charakter usw.*⟩; **c)** *(construct in the mind)* sich *(Dat.)* bilden ⟨*Meinung, Urteil*⟩; gewinnen ⟨*Eindruck*⟩; fassen ⟨*Entschluß, Plan*⟩; kommen zu ⟨*Schluß*⟩; vornehmen ⟨*Schätzung*⟩; *(acquire, develop)* entwickeln ⟨*Vorliebe, Gewohnheit, Wunsch*⟩; schließen ⟨*Freundschaft*⟩; **d)** *(constitute, compose, be, become)* bilden; **Schleswig once ~ed [a] part of Denmark** Schleswig war einmal ein Teil von Dänemark; **Joe ~ed one of our party** Joe war einer von uns; **young people ~ed the bulk of the protesters** das Gros der Protestierenden bestand aus jungen Leuten; **e)** *(establish, set up)* bilden ⟨*Regierung*⟩; gründen ⟨*Bund, Verein, Firma, Partei, Gruppe*⟩; **the men ~ed themselves into a committee** die Männer gründeten ein Komitee; **f)** *(take formation as)* bilden; **the dancers ~ed [themselves into] a circle** die Tänzer bildeten einen Kreis. **3.** *v.i.* **a)** *(come into being)* sich bilden; ⟨*Idee:*⟩ sich formen, Gestalt annehmen; **b)** *(fully develop)* sich ausformen; **c)** *(Mil.)* sich aufstellen **(in[to]** in + *Dat.*); sich formieren **(in[to]** zu); **~ [up]** sich formieren

formal ['fɔːml] **1.** *adj.* **a)** formell; förmlich ⟨*Person, Art, Einladung, Begrüßung*⟩; steif ⟨*Person, Begrüßung*⟩; *(official)* offiziell; *(regular)* regelmäßig angelegt ⟨*Garten*⟩; **wear ~ dress** *or* **clothes** Gesellschaftskleidung tragen; **~ call** Höflichkeitsbesuch, *der*; **b)** *(explicit)* formell; *(in recognized form)* traditionell; herkömmlich; **a ~ 'yes'/'no'** eine bindende Zusage/endgültige Absage; **~ education/knowledge** ordentliche Schulbildung/reales Wissen; **make a ~ apology** sich in aller Form entschuldigen; **c)** *(of the outward form)* formal; äußerlich; *(Philos., Logic)* formal. **2.** *n. (Amer.)* **a)** *(event)* gesellschaftliches Ereignis; **b)** *(dress)* Gesellschaftskleidung, *die*

formaldehyde [fɔː'mældɪhaɪd] *n. (Chem.)* Formaldehyd, *der*

formalise *see* **formalize**

formalism ['fɔːməlɪzm] *n.* Formalismus, *der*

formality [fɔː'mælɪtɪ] *n.* **a)** *(requirement)* Formalität, *die*; **drop the** *or* **dispense with the formalities** sich nicht mit Formalitäten aufhalten; **b)** *no pl. (being formal, ceremony)* Förmlichkeit, *die*

formalize ['fɔːməlaɪz] *v.t.* **a)** *(specify and systematize)* formalisieren; **b)** *(make official)* formell bekräftigen

formally ['fɔːməlɪ] *adv.* **a)** *(ceremoniously)* formell; förmlich; feierlich ⟨*empfangen*⟩; *(officially)* offiziell; *(regularly)* regelmäßig; **b)** *(explicitly)* ausdrücklich ⟨*formulieren, wünschen*⟩; in aller Form ⟨*sich entschuldigen*⟩; **c)** *(in form)* formal; äußerlich

format ['fɔːmæt] **1.** *n.* **a)** *(of book) (general appearance, layout)* Aufmachung, *die*; *(shape and size)* Format, *das*; **b)** *(Telev., Radio: of programme)* Aufbau, *der*; **c)** *(Computing)* Format, *das.* **2.** *v.t.*, **-tt-** *(Computing)* formatieren

formation [fɔː'meɪʃn] *n.* **a)** *no pl. (forming) (of substance, object)* Bildung, *die; (of character)* Formung, *die; (of handwriting)* Ausbildung, *die*; Ausformung, *die; (of plan)* Entstehung, *die; (Ling.)* Bildung, *die; (establishing)* Gründung, *die*; **b)** *(thing formed; also Ling.)* Bildung, *die*; **c)** *(Mil., Aeronaut., Dancing)* Formation, *die; (Footb.)* Aufstellung, *die*; **battle ~:** Gefechtsordnung, *die*; **in close ~:** in geschlossener Formation; **~ flying** Formationsflug, *der*; **~ dancing** Formationstanz, *der*; **d)** *(Geol.)* Formation, *die*; **rock ~s** Gesteinsformationen *Pl.*; **e)** *(structure)* Aufbau, *der*; Struktur, *die*

formative ['fɔːmətɪv] *adj.* **a)** formend, prägend ⟨*Einfluß*⟩; **the ~ years of life** die entscheidenden Lebensjahre; **b)** *(Ling.)* wortbildend; **~ element** Wortbildungselement, *das*; Formativ, *das*

former ['fɔːmə(r)] *attrib. adj.* **a)** *(earlier)* früher; *(ex-)* ehemalig; Ex-; **in ~ times** früher; **b)** *(first-mentioned)* **the ~:** der/die/das erstere; *pl.* die ersteren; **in the ~ case** im ersteren Fall

-former [fɔːmə(r)] *n. in comb. (Brit. Sch.)* -kläßler, *der*/-kläßlerin, *die*; **third-~:** Drittkläßler, *der*/-kläßlerin, *die*; *see also* **sixth-former**

formerly ['fɔːməlɪ] *adv.* früher; **Mrs Bloggs, ~ Miss Smith** Frau Bloggs, früher Fräulein Smith

Formica, (P) [fɔː'maɪkə] *n.* ≈ Resopal, *das* Ⓦᶻ; **surfaced with ~:** kunststoffbeschichtet

formidable ['fɔːmɪdəbl] *adj.* gewaltig; ungeheuer; bedrohlich, gefährlich ⟨*Herausforderung, Gegner*⟩; *(arousing dread)* furchterregend; *(awe-inspiring)* formidabel; beeindruckend

formless ['fɔːmlɪs] *adj.* formlos; *(having no physical existence)* immateriell; körperlos

form: ~ letter *n.* vorgedruckter Brief; **~-master** *n. (Brit. Sch.)* Klassenlehrer, *der*; **~-mate** *n. (Brit. Sch.)* Klassenkamerad, *der*/-kameradin, *die*; Mitschüler, *der*/-schülerin, *die*; **~-mistress** *n. (Brit. Sch.)* Klassenlehrerin, *die*; **~-room** *n. (Brit. Sch.)* Klassenraum, *der*

formula ['fɔːmjʊlə] *n., pl.* **~s** *or (esp. as tech. term)* **~e** ['fɔːmjʊliː] **a)** *(Math., Chem., Phys.)* Formel, *die*; **b)** *(fixed form of words)* Formel, *die*; **trite ~s** nichtssagende Floskeln; **find a ~** *(to reconcile differences)* einen gemeinsamen Nenner finden; **c)** *(set form)* Schema, *das*; **d)** *(prescription, recipe)* Rezeptur, *die*; Formel, *die; (fig.)* Rezept, *das*; Formel, *die*; **no sure ~ exists** es gibt kein Patentrezept; **e)** *(Motor-racing)* Formel, *die*; **f)** *(Amer.: infant's food)* Säuglingsmilchpräparat, *das*

formulate ['fɔːmjʊleɪt] *v.t.* formulieren; *(devise)* entwickeln; **~ in words/writing** in Worte fassen/schriftlich formulieren

formulation [fɔːmjʊ'leɪʃn] *n.* Formulierung, *die*; **the ~ of a question** eine Fragestellung

'formwork *n.* Schalung, *die*

fornicate ['fɔ:nɪkeɪt] *v. i.* Unzucht treiben; huren *(abwertend)*
fornication [fɔ:nɪ'keɪʃn] *n.* Unzucht, *die;* Hurerei, *die (abwertend)*
forsake [fə'seɪk] *v. t.*, **forsook** [fə'sʊk], **~n** [fə'seɪkn] **a)** *(give up)* entsagen *(geh.)* (+ *Dat.*); verzichten auf (+ *Akk.*); **b)** *(desert)* verlassen
forsaken [fə'seɪkn] *adj.* verlassen
forsook *see* **forsake**
forsooth [fə'su:θ] *adv. (arch./iron./derog.)* fürwahr *(geh.)*
forswear [fɔ:'sweə(r)] *v. t., forms as* **swear** abschwören (+ *Dat.*); *(deny)* ableugnen; abschwören *(veralt.)*
forswore, forsworn *see* **forswear**
forsythia [fɔ:'saɪθɪə] *n. (Bot.)* Forsythie, *die*
fort [fɔ:t] *n. (Mil.)* Fort, *das;* **hold the ~** *(fig.)* die Stellung halten *(fig.)*
[1]**forte** ['fɔ:teɪ, fɔ:t] *n.* Stärke, *die;* starke Seite *(ugs.)*
[2]**forte** ['fɔ:tɪ] *(Mus.)* **1.** *adj.* laut; forte *nicht attr.;* forte gespielt/gesungen; forte. **2.** *adv.* forte. **3.** *n.* Forte, *das*
fortepiano [fɔ:tɪpɪ'ænəʊ] *n., pl.* **~s** *(Mus.)* Fortepiano, *das*
forth [fɔ:θ] *adv.* **a) and so ~:** und so weiter; **b) from this/that day** *etc.* **~:** von diesem/jenem Tag *usw.* an; von Stund an *(geh.)*; **c)** *(literary)* **stretch ~:** ausstrecken; **give ~:** von sich geben; **go ~:** hinausgehen; ⟨*Befehl:*⟩ ausgehen; *(emerge)* hervorgehen; **ride ~:** losreiten; **show ~:** zeigen
Forth Bridge [fɔ:θ 'brɪdʒ] *n.* **it's like [painting] the ~** *(fig.)* es ist eine Arbeit, mit der man nie zum Ende kommt
forthcoming ['fɔ:θkʌmɪŋ, fɔ:θ'kʌmɪŋ] *adj.* **a)** *(approaching)* bevorstehend; *(about to appear)* in Kürze zu erwartend; in Kürze anlaufend ⟨*Film*⟩; in Kürze erscheinend ⟨*Ausgabe, Buch usw.*⟩; **be ~:** bevorstehen; *(about to appear)* in Kürze zu erwarten sein/anlaufen/erscheinen; **~ events** *(Journ.)* „Veranstaltungskalender"; **b)** *pred. (made available)* **be ~** ⟨*Geld, Antwort:*⟩ kommen; ⟨*Ware:*⟩ geliefert werden; ⟨*Hilfe:*⟩ geleistet werden; **not be ~:** ausbleiben; **c)** *(responsive)* mitteilsam, gesprächig ⟨*Person*⟩; **she wasn't very ~ with hard facts** mit der Mitteilung von Tatsachen hielt sie sich ziemlich zurück
forthright ['fɔ:θraɪt] *adj.* direkt; offen ⟨*Blick*⟩
forthwith [fɔ:θ'wɪθ, fɔ:θ'wɪð] *adv.* unverzüglich
fortieth ['fɔ:tɪɪθ] **1.** *adj.* vierzigst...; *see also* **eighth 1. 2.** *n. (fraction)* Vierzigstel, *das; see also* **eighth 2**
fortification [fɔ:tɪfɪ'keɪʃn] *n.* **a)** *no pl. (Mil.: fortifying)* Befestigung, *die;* **b)** *usu. in pl. (Mil.: defensive works)* Befestigung, *die;* Festungsanlage, *die;* **c)** *(of wine)* Aufspriten, *das*
fortify ['fɔ:tɪfaɪ] *v. t.* **a)** *(Mil.)* befestigen; **b)** *(strengthen, lit. or fig.)* stärken; **c)** aufspriten ⟨*Wein*⟩; anreichern ⟨*Nahrungsmittel*⟩
fortissimo [fɔ:'tɪsɪməʊ] *(Mus.)* **1.** *adj.* fortissimo *nicht attr.;* fortissimo gespielt/gesungen; Fortissimo-. **2.** *adv.* fortissimo. **3.** *n., pl.* **~s** *or* **fortissimi** [fɔ:'tɪsɪmi:] Fortissimo, *das*
fortitude ['fɔ:tɪtju:d] *n., no pl.* innere Stärke
fortnight ['fɔ:tnaɪt] *n.* vierzehn Tage; zwei Wochen; **a ~ [from] today** heute in vierzehn Tagen; **a ~ on Monday** *etc.* Montag *usw.* in vierzehn Tagen; **a ~ ago today** heute vor vierzehn Tagen; **in a ~['s time]** in vierzehn Tagen; **stay/go away for a ~:** vierzehn Tage [lang] bleiben/[für] vierzehn Tage verreisen; **take a ~'s leave** [sich *(Dat.)*] vierzehn Tage Urlaub nehmen; **once a ~, every ~:** alle vierzehn Tage *od.* zwei Wochen
fortnightly ['fɔ:tnaɪtlɪ] **1.** *adj.* vierzehntäglich; zweiwöchentlich; **~ magazine** *see* **3; at ~ intervals** in Abständen von zwei Wochen; alle zwei Wochen. **2.** *adv.* alle vierzehn Tage; alle zwei Wochen. **3.** *n.* Halbmonatsschrift, *die*
fortress ['fɔ:trɪs] *n. (lit. or fig.)* Festung, *die*
fortuitous [fɔ:'tju:ɪtəs] *adj.*, **fortuitously** [fɔ:'tju:ɪtəslɪ] *adv.* zufällig
fortunate ['fɔ:tʃʊnət, 'fɔ:tʃənət] *adj.* glücklich; **it is ~ for sb. [that ...]** es ist jmds. Glück[, daß ...]; **sb. is ~ to be alive** jmd. kann von Glück sagen *od.* reden, daß er noch lebt; **it was very ~ that ...:** es war ein Glück, daß ...; **how ~!, this is ~!** welch ein Glück!
fortunately ['fɔ:tʃʊnətlɪ, 'fɔ:tʃənətlɪ] *adv.* **a)** *(luckily)* glücklicherweise; zum Glück; **~ for everybody/me** zum Glück [aller]/zu meinem Glück; **b)** *(favourably, advantageously)* gut ⟨*dastehen, gestellt sein*⟩
fortune ['fɔ:tʃən, 'fɔ:tʃu:n] *n.* **a)** *(private wealth)* Vermögen, *das;* **family/private ~:** Familien-/Privatvermögen, *das;* **make one's ~:** sein Glück machen; **come into a ~:** ein Vermögen erben; **his brains are his/her face is her ~** *(fig. joc.)* sein Verstand ist sein/ihr Gesicht ist ihr Kapital; **a [small] ~:** ein [kleines] Vermögen; **make a ~:** ein Vermögen machen; **b)** *(prosperous condition)* Glück, *das; (of country)* Wohl, *das;* **seek one's ~:** sein Glück suchen; **c)** *(luck, destiny)* Schicksal, *das;* **bad/good ~:** Pech/Glück, *das;* **that was a piece of good ~:** das war Glück; **by sheer good ~ there was ...:** es war reines Glück, daß ... war; **he's had a change of ~:** das Blatt hat sich [für ihn] gewendet *(ugs.)*; **thank one's good ~ that ...:** dem Glück dafür danken, daß ...; **F~** *(personified)* das Glück; Fortuna *(die)*; **~ favours the brave** *(prov.)* das Glück ist auf der Seite der Mutigen; **~ smiles on sb.** das Glück lächelt *od.* lacht jmdm.; **tell sb.'s ~:** jmdm. wahrsagen *od.* sein Schicksal vorhersagen; **tell ~s** wahrsagen; *see also* **soldier 1; d)** *in pl. (ups and downs, good or bad luck befalling sb., sth.)* Schicksal, *das;* **the ~s of war** das Kriegsglück *(geh.)*; **the changing ~s of the combatants** der wechselnde Erfolg der Kämpfer
fortune: ~ cookie *n. (Amer. Cookery) Plätzchen mit einer eingebackenen Weissagung;* **~-hunter** *n. (derog.)* Mitgiftjäger, *der (abwertend)*; **~-teller** *n.* Wahrsager, *der*/Wahrsagerin, *die;* **~-telling** *n., no pl.* Wahrsagerei, *die*
forty ['fɔ:tɪ] **1.** *adj.* vierzig; **have ~ 'winks** ein Nickerchen *(fam.)* machen *od.* halten; **one-and-~** *(arch.) see* **~-one 1**; *see also* **eight 1. 2.** *n.* Vierzig, *die;* **the roaring forties** *(Geog.) stürmisches Ozeangebiet zwischen dem 40. und 50. Breitengrad;* Roaring forties *Pl.;* **the Forties** *(Brit. Geog.) Seegebiet zwischen der Nordostküste Schottlands und der Südwestküste Norwegens;* **one-and-~** *(arch.) see* **~-one 2**; *see also* **eight 2 a; eighty 2**
forty: ~-'first *etc. adj.* einundvierzigst... *usw.; see also* **eighth 1; ~-'five** *n. (record)* Single[platte], *die;* **~fold** *adj., adv.* vierzigfach; *see also* **eightfold; ~-'one** *etc.* **1.** *adj.* einundvierzig *usw.; see also* **eight 1; 2.** *n.* Einundvierzig *usw., die; see also* **eight 2 a**
forum ['fɔ:rəm] *n. (also Roman Hist.)* Forum, *das;* **~ for discussion** [Diskussions]forum, *das;* **the ~ of public opinion** das Forum der Öffentlichkeit
forward ['fɔ:wəd] **1.** *adv.* **a)** *(in direction faced, onwards in progress)* vorwärts; **bend ~:** sich vorbeugen; **take three steps ~:** drei Schritte vortreten; **~ march!** *(Mil.)* vorwärts marsch!; **b)** *(towards end of room etc. faced)* nach vorn; vor⟨*laufen, -rücken, -schieben*⟩; **work one's way ~:** sich nach vorn durcharbeiten; **the seat is too far ~:** der Sitz ist zu weit vorn; **c)** *(closer)* heran; **rush ~ to help sb.** jmdm. zu Hilfe eilen; **he came ~ to greet me** er kam auf mich zu, um mich zu begrüßen; **d)** *(ahead, in advance)* voraus⟨*schicken, -gehen*⟩; **e)** *(into better state)* **the country began to move ~:** mit dem Land ging es allmählich aufwärts; **f)** *(into future)* voraus⟨*schauen, -denken*⟩; **from that day/time ~:** von dem *od.* jenem Tag an/von da an; **from this day/time ~:** von heute/jetzt an; **date ~** *(Commerc.)* vordatieren; **g)** *(into prominence)* in den Vordergrund; **come ~** *(present oneself)* ⟨*Zeuge, Helfer:*⟩ sich melden; **h)** *(indicating motion) (Naut.)* nach vorn [zum Bug]; *(Aeronaut.)* nach vorn [in den Bug]; **i)** *(Naut., Aeronaut.: indicating position) (inside)* vorn [im Bug]; *(outside)* vorn [am Bug]; **j)** *(Cricket)* **play ~:** nach vorn treten, um zu schlagen. *See also* **backward 1 b; bring forward; carry forward; go forward; go forward with; look forward to; push forward; put forward; set forward. 2.** *adj.* **a)** *(directed ahead)* vorwärts gerichtet; nach vorn *nachgestellt;* **~ movement** Vorwärtsbewegung, *die;* **~ pass** *(Rugby)* Vorpaß, *der;* **~ somersault** Salto vorwärts; **b)** *(at or to the front)* Vorder-; vorder...; **c)** *(lying in one's line of motion)* vor einem *nachgestellt;* **the ~ horizon** der vor einem liegende Horizont; **d)** *(advanced)* frühreif ⟨*Kind, Pflanze, Getreide*⟩; fortschrittlich ⟨*Vorstellung, Ansicht, Maßnahme*⟩; [früh]zeitig, verfrüht ⟨*Frühling, Blüte*⟩; **be well ~ with one's work/in one's plans** mit seiner Arbeit/seinen Plänen gut vorangekommen *od.* weit gediehen sein; **e)** *(bold)* dreist; **f)** *(Commerc.)* Termin⟨*geschäft, -verkauf*⟩; Zukunfts⟨*planung*⟩; **g)** *(Naut.)* zum Vor[der]schiff gehörend. **3.** *n. (Sport)* Stürmer, *der*/Stürmerin, *die.* **4.** *v. t.* **a)** *(send on)* nachschicken ⟨*Brief, Paket, Post*⟩ **(to** an + *Akk.*); *(dispatch)* abschicken ⟨*Waren*⟩ **(to** an + *Akk.*); **'please ~', 'to be ~ed'** „bitte nachsenden"; **b)** *(pass on)* weiterreichen, weiterleiten ⟨*Vorschlag, Plan*⟩ **(to** an + *Akk.*); **c)** *(promote)* voranbringen ⟨*Karriere, Vorbereitung*⟩; **~ one's own interests** seine eigenen Interessen verfolgen; **d)** *(accelerate)* beschleunigen ⟨*Wachstum*⟩
forwarding ['fɔ:wədɪŋ]: **~ address** *n.* Nachsendeanschrift, *die;* **~ agent** *n.* Spediteur, *der;* **~ instructions** *n. pl.* Anweisung über die Nachsendung/*(for dispatch)* den Versand
forward: ~ line *n. (Sport)* Sturm, *der;* **~-looking** *adj.* vorausschauend
forwardly ['fɔ:wədlɪ] *adv.* dreist
forwardness ['fɔ:wədnɪs] *n., no pl.* **a)** *(boldness)* Dreistigkeit, *die;* **b)** *(advanced state) (of child, crop)* Frühreife, *die; (of season)* verfrühter *od.* [früh]zeitiger Beginn
forwards ['fɔ:wədz] *see* **forward 1 a, b, c**
forwent *see* **forgo**
fossil ['fɒsɪl] **1.** *n.* **a)** Fossil, *das;* **b)** *(fig. derog.) (antiquated person)* Fossil, *das; (antiquated thing)* verstaubtes Relikt; **c)** *(Ling.)* **[linguistic] ~:** Sprachrelikt, *das.* **2.** *attrib. adj.* fossil *(Paläont.)*; **~ fuel** fossiler Brennstoff
fossilisation, fossilise *see* **fossiliz-**
fossilization [fɒsɪlaɪ'zeɪʃn] *n.* Fossilisation, die *(Paläont.)*
fossilize ['fɒsɪlaɪz] **1.** *v. t.* fossilisieren lassen *(Paläont.)*; versteinern lassen *(auch fig.)*; **become ~d** *see* **2; ~d** fossil *(Paläont.)*; *(fig.)* antiquiert; verstaubt *(abwertend)*; **~d remains** Fossilien *Pl.* **2.** *v. i.* fossilisieren *(Paläont.)*; versteinern *(auch fig.)*
foster ['fɒstə(r)] **1.** *v. t.* **a)** *(encourage)* fördern; pflegen ⟨*Freundschaft*⟩; *(harbour)* hegen *(geh.)*; **b)** *(rear as ~-child)* in Pflege haben ⟨*Kind*⟩; **the child was ~ed from the age of two** das Kind war seit seinem dritten Lebensjahr in Pflege *od.* bei Pflegeeltern. **2.** *adj.* **~-:** Pflege⟨*bruder, -eltern, -sohn usw.*⟩; **~ home** Pflegestelle, *die;* **put a child into ~ care** ein Kind in Pflege geben; **be in ~ care** in Pflege sein
'**foster-child** *n.* Pflegekind, *das*

'**foster-mother** *n.* **a)** Pflegemutter, *die;* **b)** *(Brit.: for chickens)* künstliche Glucke
fought *see* **fight 1, 2**
foul [faʊl] **1.** *adj.* **a)** *(offensive to the senses, loathsome)* abscheulich; übel ⟨*Geruch, Geschmack*⟩; **b)** *(polluted)* verschmutzt ⟨*Wasser, Luft*⟩; *(putrid)* faulig ⟨*Wasser*⟩; stickig ⟨*Luft*⟩; **c)** *(sl.: awful)* scheußlich *(ugs.);* mies *(ugs. abwertend);* **d)** *(morally vile)* anstößig, unanständig ⟨*Sprache, Gerede*⟩; lose ⟨*Maul, Mundwerk*⟩; schmutzig ⟨*Phantasie, Gedanke, Gewerbe*⟩; niederträchtig ⟨*Verleumdung, Tat*⟩; feige, abscheulich ⟨*Mord*⟩; gemein, schäbig ⟨*Behandlung*⟩; böse, *(geh.)* übel ⟨*Streich*⟩; ~ **deed** Schandtat, *die;* **e)** *(unfair)* unerlaubt, unredlich ⟨*Mittel*⟩; *(Sport)* regelwidrig, verboten ⟨*Schlag, Hieb*⟩; ~ **play** *(Sport)* Foulspiel, *das; (fig.: unfair dealing)* Betrug, *der;* **the police do not suspect ~ play** die Polizei vermutet kein Verbrechen; **there was a lot of ~ play** *(Sport)* es ging recht unfair zu; *see also* **[2]fair 1 a; f) fall** *or* **run ~ of** *(Naut.)* zusammenstoßen *od.* kollidieren mit; *(fig.)* kollidieren *od.* in Konflikt geraten mit ⟨*Vorschrift, Gesetz, Polizei*⟩; aneinandergeraten mit ⟨*Person*⟩; **g)** *(Naut.: entangled)* unklar; **h)** *(clogged up)* verstopft. **2.** *n. (Sport)* Foul, *das;* Regelverstoß, *der;* **commit a ~:** foulen; ein Foul *od.* einen Regelverstoß begehen. **3.** *v. t.* **a)** *(make foul)* beschmutzen *(auch fig.);* verunreinigen *(abwertend);* verpesten ⟨*Luft*⟩; *see also* **nest 1 a; b)** *(be entangled with)* sich verfangen in (+ *Dat.*); **c)** *see* **~ up b; d)** *(Sport)* foulen
~ **'up** *v. t.* **a)** *(coll.: spoil)* vermasseln *(salopp);* verderben ⟨*Atmosphäre, Beziehung*⟩; **b)** *(block)* blockieren. *See also* **foul-up**
foully ['faʊllɪ] *adv. (wickedly)* skrupellos ⟨*ermorden, verurteilen*⟩; schlecht ⟨*behandeln*⟩; böswillig ⟨*verleumden*⟩
foul-mouthed ['faʊlmaʊðd] *adj.* unanständig; unflätig
foulness ['faʊlnɪs] *n., no pl.* **a)** Abscheulichkeit, *die;* **b)** *(state of being polluted)* Verschmutzung, *die; (putridness)* Fauligkeit, *die*
foul: ~-smelling *adj.* übelriechend; **~-up** *n.* Durcheinander, *das;* Schlamassel, *der (ugs.)*
[1]found [faʊnd] *v. t.* **a)** *(establish)* gründen; begründen ⟨*Wissenschaft, Religion, Glauben, Kirche*⟩; **F~ing Fathers** *Mitglieder der verfassunggebenden Versammlung der USA von 1787;* Gründerväter; **b)** *(fig.: base)* begründen; ~ **sth. [up]on sth.** etw. auf etw. *(Akk.)* gründen; **be ~ed [up]on sth.** [sich] auf etw. *(Akk.)* gründen; auf etw. *(Dat.)* beruhen; *see also* **ill-founded; well-founded**
[2]found *see* **find 1, 2**
[3]found *v. t. (Metallurgy)* gießen; *(Glassmaking)* gießen; *(melt)* schmelzen
foundation [faʊn'deɪʃn] *n.* **a)** *(establishing)* Gründung, *die; (of hospital, monastery)* Stiftung, *die; (of school of painting, of religion)* Begründung, *die;* **b)** *(institution)* Stiftung, *die;* **be on the ~** *(Brit.)* ein Stipendium erhalten; **c)** *usu. in pl.* **~[s]** *(underlying part, lit. or fig.) (of building)* Fundament, *das; (of road)* Unterbau, *der;* **lay the ~s** das Fundament legen; *(for road)* den Unterbau legen; **be without** *or* **have no ~** *(fig.)* unbegründet sein; der Grundlage entbehren; **lay the ~ of/for sth.** *(fig.)* das Fundament *od.* die Grundlage zu etw. legen; **shake sth. to its ~s** *(fig.)* etw. in seinen Grundfesten erschüttern; **d)** *(cosmetic)* Grundierung, *die;* **e)** *see* **foundation garment**
foundation: ~ course *n. (Univ. etc.)* Grundkurs, *der;* **~ cream** *n.* Grundierungscreme, *die;* **~ garment** *n.* Mieder, *das;* **~-stone** *n. (lit. or fig.)* Grundstein, *der*
[1]founder ['faʊndə(r)] *n.* Gründer, *der/*Gründerin, *die; (of hospital, or with an endowment)* Stifter, *der/*Stifterin, *die; (of sect, science, school, religion)* Begründer, *der/*Begründerin, *die;* **~ member** Gründungsmitglied, *das*
[2]founder *v. i.* **a)** ⟨*Schiff:*⟩ sinken, untergehen; ⟨*Pferd:*⟩ straucheln, stürzen; ⟨*Erdboden, Gebäude:*⟩ einstürzen; **b)** *(fig.: fail)* sich zerschlagen
foundling ['faʊndlɪŋ] *n.* Findelkind, *das;* Findling, *der*
foundry ['faʊndrɪ] *n. (Metallurgy)* Gießerei, *die; (Glass-making)* Glashütte, *die*
[1]fount [faʊnt, fɒnt] *n. (Printing)* Schrift, *die*
[2]fount [faʊnt] *n. (poet./rhet.: fountain)* Born, *der (dichter., auch fig. geh.)*
fountain ['faʊntɪn] *n.* **a)** *see* **drinking fountain; b)** *(jet[s] of water)* Fontäne, *die; (structure)* Springbrunnen, *der;* **c)** *(fig.: source)* Quelle, *die;* **~ of youth** Jungbrunnen, *der. See also* **soda-fountain**
fountain: ~-head *n.* Quelle, *die;* **~-pen** *n.* Füllfederhalter, *der;* Füller, *der (ugs.)*
four [fɔ:(r)] **1.** *adj.* vier; *see also* **eight 1. 2.** *n.* **a)** *(number, symbol)* Vier, *die;* **b)** *(set of ~ people)* Vierergruppe, *die; (Rowing)* Vierer, *der;* **the ~:** die vier; **make up a ~ at tennis/bridge** im Doppel Tennis spielen/der vierte Mitspieler beim Bridge sein; **c) on all ~s** auf allen vieren *(ugs.);* **be/crawl/move on all ~s** auf allen vieren kriechen *(ugs.);* **get down on all ~s** sich auf alle viere begeben *(ugs.). See also* **eight 2 a, c, d**
four: ~-ball *n. (Golf)* Vierball, *der;* **~-door** *attrib. adj.* viertürig ⟨*Auto*⟩; **~fold** ['fɔ:fəʊld] *adj., adv.* vierfach; *see also* **eightfold; ~-footed** ['fɔ:fʊtɪd] *adj.* vierfüßig; **~-handed** ['fɔ:hændɪd] *adj.* **a)** ⟨*Spiel*⟩ mit vier Mitspielern; **b)** *(Mus.)* zu vier Händen *nachgestellt;* vierhändig; **~-in-hand** *adj.* vierspännig; **~-in-hand tie** *(Amer.)* Schlips, *der;* Krawatte, *die;* **~-leaf clover, ~-leaved clover** *n.* vierblättriges Kleeblatt; **~-legged** ['fɔ:legɪd, 'fɔ:legd] *adj.* vierbeinig; **~-letter 'word** *n.* vulgärer Ausdruck; *(expressing anger)* ≈ Kraftausdruck, *der;* **~pence** ['fɔ:pəns] *n. (Brit.)* vier Pence; **~penny** ['fɔ:pənɪ] *adj. (Brit.) (costing 4p or 4d)* Vier-Pence-; **~-poster** *n.* Himmelbett, *das;* **~score** *adj. (arch.)* achtzig; **~some** ['fɔ:səm] *n.* **a)** Quartett, *das;* **go in** *or* **as a ~some** zu viert gehen; **b)** *(Golf)* Vierer, *der;* **~-square** *adj.* **a)** *(square)* quadratisch; **b)** *(fig.: resolute)* unerschütterlich; tatkräftig ⟨*Unterstützung*⟩; *(forthright)* direkt ⟨*Inangriffnahme*⟩; unverblümt ⟨*Schilderung*⟩; **~-stroke** *adj. (Mech. Engin.)* Viertakt⟨*motor, -verfahren*⟩
fourteen [fɔ:'ti:n] **1.** *adj.* vierzehn; *see also* **eight 1. 2.** *n.* Vierzehn, *die; see also* **eight 2 a, d; eighteen 2**
fourteenth [fɔ:'ti:nθ] **1.** *adj.* vierzehnt...; *see also* **eighth 1. 2.** *n. (fraction)* Vierzehntel, *das; see also* **eighth 2**
fourth [fɔ:θ] **1.** *adj.* **a)** viert...; **the ~ finger** der kleine Finger; *see also* **eighth 1; b) ~ dimension** vierte Dimension; *see also* **estate f. 2.** *n.* **a)** *(in sequence)* vierte, *der/die/das; (in rank)* Vierte, *der/die/das; (fraction)* Viertel, *das;* **b)** *(~ form)* vierte [Schul]klasse; Vierte, *die (Schuljargon);* **c)** *(Motor Veh.)* vierter Gang; **in ~:** im vierten [Gang]; **change up [in]to ~:** in den vierten Gang schalten; **d)** *(Mus.)* Quarte, *die;* **e)** *(person)* vierter Teilnehmer/vierte Teilnehmerin; *(in a game)* vierter Mitspieler/vierte Mitspielerin; **make a ~:** als vierter/vierte mitmachen; **f)** *(day)* **the ~ of May** der vierte Mai; **the ~ [of the month]** der Vierte [des Monats]; **F~ of July** *(Amer.) Unabhängigkeitstag der USA;* **F~ of June** *(Brit.) jährliche Feier in Eton. See also* **eighth 2**
fourth: ~ form *see* **form 1 d; ~ 'gear** *n., no pl. (Motor Veh.)* vierter Gang; *see also* **gear 1 d**
fourthly ['fɔ:θlɪ] *adv.* viertens
four-wheel 'drive *n. (Motor Veh.)* Vier- *od.* Allradantrieb, *der*
fowl [faʊl] **1.** *n. pl.* **~s** *or same* **a)** Haushuhn, *das; (collectively)* Geflügel, *das;* **b)** *(Gastr.)* Huhn, *das;* **boiling ~:** Suppenhuhn, *das;* **c)** *(literary: bird)* Vogel, *der; see also* **waterfowl; wildfowl. 2.** *v. i.* **go ~ing** auf die Vogeljagd gehen
fowler ['faʊlə(r)] *n.* Vogeljäger, *der*
fox [fɒks] **1.** *n., pl.* **~es** *or (esp. Hunting) same;* **a)** Fuchs, *der (auch fig. ugs.);* **as cunning as a ~:** schlau wie ein Fuchs; **b)** *(fur)* Fuchs[pelz], *der.* **2.** *v. t.* verwirren; **that's got you ~ed** *or* **that's ~ed you, hasn't it?** jetzt bist du verblüfft, was?
fox: ~ cub *n.* Fuchswelpe, *der;* **~ fur** *n.* Fuchspelz, *der;* **~glove** *n. (Bot.)* Fingerhut, *der;* **~hole** *n.* **a)** Fuchsbau, *der;* **b)** *(Mil.)* Schützenloch, *das; (fig.)* Versteck, *das;* **~hound** *n.* Foxhound, *der;* **~-hunt 1.** *n.* Fuchsjagd, *die;* **2.** *v. i.* **go ~-hunting** auf die Fuchsjagd gehen; **~-hunter** *n.* Fuchsjäger, *der;* **~-hunting** *n.* Fuchsjagd, *die;* **~tail** *n.* **a)** Fuchsschwanz, *der;* **b)** *(Bot.) (Alopecurus)* Fuchsschwanz, *der; (Hordeum)* Gerste, *die; (Setaria)* Borstenhirse, *die;* **~-'terrier** *n.* Foxterrier, *der;* **~trot 1.** *n.* Foxtrott, *der;* **2.** *v. i.* Foxtrott tanzen
foxy ['fɒksɪ] *adj.* **a)** [fuchs]schlau ⟨*Augen, Manöver*⟩; **b)** *(Amer. sl.: attractive)* dufte *(salopp)*
'**foxy-looking** *adj.* fuchsgesichtig
foyer ['fɔɪeɪ, 'fwɑjeɪ] *n.* Foyer, *das*
Fr. *abbr.* **a)** *(Eccl.)* **Father** P.; **b) French** frz.; fr.; franz.
fr. *abbr.* **franc[s]** fr
fracas ['frækɑ:] *n., pl. same* ['frækɑ:z] [lautstarke] Auseinandersetzung; Krawall, *der*
fraction ['frækʃn] *n.* **a)** *(Math.)* Bruch, *der;* **do ~s** bruchrechnen; *see also* **decimal fraction; improper d; proper fraction; vulgar c; b)** *(small part)* Bruchteil, *der; (tiny bit)* Kleinigkeit, *die (ugs.);* Stückchen, *das;* Idee, *die;* **the car missed the pedestrian by a ~ of an inch** das Auto hätte den Fußgänger um Haaresbreite überfahren; **c)** *(Chem.)* Fraktion, *die*
fractional ['frækʃənl] *adj.* **a)** *(Math.)* Bruch⟨*zahl, -rechnen*⟩; *(fig.: very slight)* geringfügig; **~ part** Bruchteil, *der;* **b)** *(Chem.)* **~ crystallization/distillation** fraktionierte Kristallisation/Destillation
fractionally ['frækʃənəlɪ] *adv. (fig.: very slightly)* geringfügig
fractious ['frækʃəs] *adj. (unruly)* aufsässig; ungebärdig *(geh.);* störrisch ⟨*Pferd*⟩; *(peevish)* quengelig ⟨*Kind*⟩
fracture ['fræktʃə(r)] **1.** *n. (also Med., Min.)* Bruch, *der;* **nose ~:** Nasenbeinbruch, *der.* **2.** *v. t. (also Med.)* brechen; *(break up)* aufspalten; **~ one's jaw** *etc.* sich *(Dat.)* den Kiefer *usw.* brechen; **~ one's skull** sich *(Dat.)* einen Schädelbruch zuziehen; **have a ~d jaw** *etc.* sich *(Dat.)* den Kiefer *usw.* gebrochen haben. **3.** *v. i. (Med.)* brechen
fragile ['frædʒaɪl] *adj.* **a)** zerbrechlich; zart ⟨*Teint, Hand*⟩; **'~ – handle with care'** „Vorsicht, zerbrechlich!"; **feel ~** *(coll.: ill, esp. because of hangover)* sich ganz zerschlagen fühlen; **b)** *(fig.)* fadenscheinig ⟨*Entschuldigung, Grund*⟩; heikel ⟨*Situation*⟩; unsicher ⟨*Frieden*⟩; zart ⟨*Glück, Gesundheit, Konstitution*⟩; gebrechlich ⟨*alte Frau*⟩; schwach ⟨*Selbstvertrauen*⟩
fragility [frə'dʒɪlɪtɪ] *n., no pl.* Zerbrechlichkeit, *die; (of health, constitution, frame, beauty)* Zartheit, *die; (fig.: of peace, situation)* Unsicherheit, *die*
fragment 1. ['frægmənt] *n.* Bruchstück, *das; (of document, conversation)* Fetzen, *der; (of china)* Scherbe, *die; (of rock)* Brocken, *der; (Lit., Mus.)* Fragment, *das;* Bruchstück, *das;* **it was in ~s** es war zerbrochen. **2.** [fræg'ment] *v. t. & i.* zersplittern

fragmentary ['frægməntərɪ] *adj.* bruchstückhaft; fragmentarisch
fragmentation [frægmən'teɪʃn] *n.* Zersplitterung, *die*
fragmen'tation bomb *n. (Mil.)* Splitterbombe, *die*
fragmented [fræg'mentɪd] *adj.* bruchstückhaft
fragrance ['freɪgrəns] *n.* Duft, *der*
fragrant ['freɪgrənt] *adj.* duftend; *(fig.)* angenehm ‹*Erinnerung, Gefühl*›; ~ **odour** *or* **smell** *or* **aroma** Wohlgeruch, *der;* **be ~ with sth.** nach etw. duften
frail [freɪl] *adj.* zerbrechlich; zart ‹*Gesundheit*›; gebrechlich ‹*Greis, Greisin*›; *(lacking force)* schwach ‹*Stimme*›; *(morally weak)* schwach, labil ‹*Mensch, Natur, Charakter*›; *(transient)* vergänglich ‹*Leben, Glück*›; *(slender)* schwach ‹*Hoffnung*›; gering ‹*Verständnis*›
frailty ['freɪltɪ] *n.* **a)** *no pl.* Zerbrechlichkeit, *die; (of health)* Zartheit, *die; (moral weakness)* Schwachheit, *die; (transience)* Vergänglichkeit, *die;* **b)** *esp. in pl. (fault)* Schwäche, *die*
frame [freɪm] **1.** *n.* **a)** *(of vehicle, bicycle)* Rahmen, *der; (of easel, rucksack, bed, umbrella)* Gestell, *das; (of ship, aircraft)* Gerüst, *das; (of building)* Tragwerk, *das (Bauw.);* **timber ~:** Fachwerk, *das;* Gebälk, *das; see also* **climbing-frame; b)** *(border)* Rahmen, *der;* **[spectacle] ~s** [Brillen]gestell, *das;* **c)** *(fig.: established order)* Struktur, *die;* ~ **of government/society** Regierungs-/Gesellschaftsform, *die;* ~ **of reference** *(Phys., Sociol.)* Bezugssystem, *das;* **d)** *(of person, animal)* Körper, *der;* **a man of gigantic ~:** ein Mann von hünenhafter Gestalt; **e)** *(Photog., Cinemat.)* [Einzel]bild, *das; (Telev.)* [einzelnes Fernseh]bild; **f)** *(of comic strip)* [Einzel]bild, *das;* **g)** *(Hort.)* Frühbeet, *das;* **h)** *(Snooker) (triangle)* [dreieckiger] Rahmen; *(round of play)* Spiel, *das;* [Spiel]runde, *die. See also* **mind 1 e. 2.** *v. t.* **a)** rahmen ‹*Bild, Spiegel*›; umrahmen ‹*Text usw. mit Verzierungen*›; **a face ~d in curls** ein von Locken umrahmtes Gesicht; **b)** *(compose)* formulieren ‹*Frage, Antwort, Satz*›; aufbauen ‹*Rede, Aufsatz*›; *(devise)* entwerfen ‹*Gesetz, Politik, Plan*›; ausarbeiten ‹*Plan, Methode, Denksystem*›; aufstellen ‹*Regel, Theorie*›; *(shape)* konstruieren; schaffen ‹*Bau[werk]*›; gestalten ‹*[Um]welt, Leben*›; ~ **one's words** sich ausdrücken; **her lips ~d a curse** ihre Lippen formten einen Fluch; **c)** *(sl.: incriminate unjustly)* ~ **sb.** jmdm. etwas anhängen *(ugs.)*
~ **'up** *v.t. (Amer. sl.)* manipulieren; türken *(ugs.); see also* **frame-up**
'frame house *n.* Haus mit Holzgerüst
framer ['freɪmə(r)] *n.* Rahmenschreiner, *der;* **picture-~:** Bildereinrahmer, *der*
frame: ~-up *n. (coll.)* abgekartetes Spiel *(ugs.);* **~work** *n. (of ship etc.)* Gerüst, *das; (of building)* Fachwerk, *das;* Gebälk, *das; (fig.: of project)* Gerüst, *das; (of novel)* Rahmen, *der; (of essay, lecture, etc.)* Aufbau, *der;* Gliederung, *die; (of society, government, system)* [Grund]struktur, *die;* Grundlagen *Pl.;* **[with]in the ~work of** *(as part of)* im Rahmen (+ *Gen.*); *(in relation to)* im Zusammenhang mit; **outside the ~work of** *(not as part of)* außerhalb (+ *Gen.*)
framing ['freɪmɪŋ] *n. (Building)* Fachwerk, *das*
franc [fræŋk] *n. (Swiss)* Franken, *der; (French, Belgian, Luxemburg)* Franc, *der*
France [frɑ:ns] *pr. n.* Frankreich *(das)*
franchise ['fræntʃaɪz] **1.** *n.* **a)** Stimmrecht, *das; (esp. for Parliament)* Wahlrecht, *das;* **b)** *(Commerc.)* Lizenz, *die.* **2.** *v.t. (Commerc.)* [die] Lizenz erteilen (+ *Dat.*)
Francis ['frɑ:nsɪs] *pr. n. (Hist., as name of ruler etc.)* Franz *(der);* **St ~:** der hl. Franziskus
Franciscan [fræn'sɪskn] **1.** *n.* Franziskaner, *der*/Franziskanerin, *die.* **2.** *adj.* franziskanisch/Franziskaner‹*mönch, -kloster*›
Franco- ['fræŋkəʊ] *in comb.* französisch-; franko‹*kanadisch*›; Franko‹*kanadier*›; **~-German** deutsch-französisch; **the ~-Prussian War** der Deutsch-Französische Krieg
Franconia [fræŋ'kəʊnɪə] *pr. n.* Franken, *das*
Franconian [fræŋ'kəʊnɪən] **1.** *adj.* fränkisch. **2.** *n. (person)* Franke, *der*/Fränkin, *die; (dialect)* Fränkisch, *das*
francophone ['fræŋkəfəʊn] **1.** *adj.* frankophon. **2.** *n.* Frankophone, *der/die*
franglais ['frɑ̃gleɪ] *n.* von englischen Ausdrücken durchsetztes Französisch; Franglais, *das*
Frank [fræŋk] *n. (Hist.)* Franke, *der*/Fränkin, *die*
[1]frank *adj.* **a)** *(candid)* offen ‹*Bekenntnis, Aussprache, Blick, Gesicht, Mensch*›; freimütig ‹*Geständnis, Äußerung*›; *(undisguised)* offen ‹*Abneigung, Widerwille*›; unverhohlen ‹*Bewunderung, Neugier, Verlangen*›; *(uninhibited)* unbefangen; **give me your ~ opinion** sag mir offen deine Meinung; **be ~ with sb.** zu jmdm. offen sein; jmdm. offen seine Meinung sagen; **to be [quite] ~** *(as sentence-modifier)* offen gesagt; ~ **and open** offen und ehrlich ‹*Gesicht*›; frei und ungezwungen ‹*Benehmen*›; **b)** *(Med.)* eindeutig; manifest *(fachspr.)*
[2]frank 1. *v.t. (Post)* **a)** *(in lieu of postage stamp)* freistempeln; **b)** *(put postage stamp on)* frankieren. **2.** *n.* Vermerk über Gebührenfreiheit
[3]frank *n. (Amer. coll.: frankfurter)* Frankfurter [Würstchen]
Frankenstein ['fræŋknstaɪn] **~['s 'monster]** *n. seinen Schöpfer vernichtendes Ungeheuer;* ≈ Monster, *das*
frankfurter ['fræŋkf3:tə(r)] *(Amer.:* **frankfurt** ['fræŋkf3:t]) *n.* Frankfurter [Würstchen]
frankincense ['fræŋkɪnsens] *n.* Weihrauch, *der; (turpentine)* Terpentin, *das*
franking-machine ['fræŋkɪŋməʃi:n] *n. (Brit. Post)* Frankiermaschine, *die;* Freistempler, *der*
Frankish ['fræŋkɪʃ] *adj. (Hist.)* fränkisch
frankly ['fræŋklɪ] *adv. (candidly)* offen; frank und frei; *(honestly)* offen *od.* ehrlich gesagt; *(openly, undisguisedly)* unverhohlen ‹*kritisch, materialistisch usw.*›; *(uninhibitedly)* unbefangen
frankness ['fræŋknɪs] *n., no pl.* Offenheit, *die;* Freimütigkeit, *die; (uninhibitedness)* Unbefangenheit, *die*
frantic ['fræntɪk] *adj.* **a)** *(nearly mad)* **be ~ with fear/rage** *etc.* außer sich *(Dat.)* sein vor Angst/Wut *usw.;* **drive sb. ~:** jmdn. in den Wahnsinn treiben *od.* wahnsinnig machen; **she was getting ~:** sie war am Durchdrehen *(ugs.);* sie geriet außer sich; **b)** *(very anxious, noisy, uncontrolled)* hektisch ‹*Aktivität, Suche, Getriebe*›; heftig ‹*Protest*›; tosend, stürmisch, *(geh.)* frenetisch ‹*Beifall*›; **c)** *(showing that sb. is ~)* erregt ‹*Schrei, Wort, Gebärde*›
frantically ['fræntɪkəlɪ], **franticly** ['fræntɪklɪ] *adv.* verzweifelt ‹*schreien, suchen, protestieren*›; stürmisch, *(geh.)* frenetisch ‹*applaudieren*›; wie angestochen, wie wild *(ugs.)* ‹*herumrennen*›; **the shops are ~ busy** in den Läden herrscht hektische Betriebsamkeit
frappé ['fræpeɪ] *adj.* geeist
fraternal [frə't3:nl] *adj.* brüderlich; ~ **twins** zweieiige Zwillinge
fraternisation, fraternise *see* **fraterniz-**
fraternity [frə't3:nɪtɪ] *n.* **a)** *(set of men with common interest)* Vereinigung, *die; (guild)* Gilde, *die (hist.);* Zunft, *die (hist.);* **the teaching/medical/legal ~:** die Lehrer-/Ärzte-/Juristenzunft; die Zunft der Lehrer/Ärzte/Juristen; **b)** *(Relig.)* Bruderschaft, *die;* Fraternität, *die (kath. Kirche);* **c)** *(Amer. Univ.: society)* [studentische] Verbindung; **d)** *no pl. (brotherliness)* Brüderlichkeit, *die*
fraternization [frætənaɪ'zeɪʃn] *n.* Verbrüderung, *die;* ~ **[with sb.]** *(Mil.)* Fraternisierung [mit jmdm.]
fraternize ['frætənaɪz] *v. i.* ~ **[with sb.]** sich verbrüdern [mit jmdm.]; *(Mil.)* fraternisieren [mit jmdm.]
Frau [fraʊ] *n.* Deutsche, *die;* deutsche Frau
fraud [frɔ:d] *n.* **a)** *no pl. (cheating, deceit)* Betrug, *der;* Täuschung, *die; (Law)* [arglistige] Täuschung; **b)** *(trick, false thing)* Schwindel, *der; (Law)* Betrug, *der;* **~s** Betrügereien; **pious ~:** frommer Betrug; **c)** *(person) (impostor, sham)* Betrüger, *der*/Betrügerin, *die;* Schwindler, *der*/Schwindlerin, *die; (hypocrite)* Heuchler, *der*/Heuchlerin, *die;* **you [old] ~!** *(coll.)* du alter Schlawiner! *(ugs.)*
fraudulent ['frɔ:djʊlənt] *adj.* betrügerisch; **with ~ intent** in betrügerischer Absicht; ~ **name** falscher Name
fraudulently ['frɔ:djʊləntlɪ] *adv.* in betrügerischer Weise
fraught [frɔ:t] *adj.* **a) be ~ with danger** voller Gefahren *od.* sehr gefahrvoll sein; ~ **with tension** spannungsgeladen; ~ **with meaning/memories** bedeutungsschwer/mit Erinnerungen befrachtet; ~ **with obstacles/difficulties** voller Hindernisse/Schwierigkeiten; **silence ~ with menace** bedrohliche Stille; **b)** *(coll.: distressingly tense)* stressig *(ugs.)* ‹*Atmosphäre, Situation, Diskussion*›; gestreßt *(ugs.)* ‹*Person*›
Fräulein ['frɔɪlaɪn] *n.* [junge] Deutsche; deutsche [junge] Frau
[1]fray [freɪ] *n. (fight)* [Kampf]getümmel, *das; (noisy quarrel)* Streit, *der;* **in the thick of the ~:** mitten im dicksten Getümmel; **plunge into the ~:** sich ins [Kampf]getümmel stürzen; **in the heat of the ~** *(fig.)* in der Hitze des Gefechts *(fig.);* **be eager/ready for the ~** *(lit. or fig.)* kampflustig/kampfbereit sein; **enter** *or* **join the ~** *(lit. or fig.)* sich in den Kampf *od.* ins Getümmel stürzen
[2]fray 1. *v. i.* [sich] durchscheuern; ‹*Hosenbein, Teppich, Seilende:*› ausfransen; **our nerves/tempers began to ~** *(fig.)* wir verloren langsam die Nerven/unsere Gemüter erhitzten sich. **2.** *v. t.* durchscheuern; ausfransen ‹*Hosenbein, Teppich, Seilende*›; *(fig.)* belasten; strapazieren
frayed [freɪd] *adj.* durchgescheuert; ausgefranst ‹*Hosenbein, Teppich, Seilende*›; *(fig.)* strapaziert ‹*Nerven, Geduld*›; erregt, erhitzt ‹*Gemüt*›; **his politeness was by now somewhat ~:** seine Höflichkeit war inzwischen etwas verkrampft
frazzle ['fræzl] *n. (coll.)* **to a ~:** völlig; total *(ugs.);* **my nerves were worn to a ~:** ich war mit den Nerven völlig am Ende
freak [fri:k] **1.** *n.* **a)** *(monstrosity) (person, animal)* Mißgeburt, *die; (plant)* mißgebildete Pflanze; Mutation, *die;* ~ **of nature** Laune der Natur; **b)** *(freakish thing or occurrence)* Laune, *die; (attrib.)* ungewöhnlich ‹*Wetter, Ereignis*›; völlig überraschend ‹*Sieg, Ergebnis*›; **c)** *(sl.: fanatic)* Freak, *der;* **health ~:** Gesundheitsfanatiker, *der;* **health-food ~:** Reformköstler, *der (ugs.);* Körnerfresser, *der (salopp);* **d)** *(coll.: eccentric person)* Freak, *der;* Ausgeflippte, *der/die (salopp); (derog.)* komischer Vogel *(ugs.);* **e)** *(caprice)* Laune, *die.* **2.** *v. i.* ~ **[out]** *(sl.) (with fury)* die Nerven verlieren; durchdrehen *(ugs.); (with ecstasy)* vor Freude [ganz] außer sich *(Dat.)* sein
freakish ['fri:kɪʃ] *adj. (capricious)* launisch; verrückt *(ugs.); (abnormal)* absonderlich; ~ **trick of fortune** Laune des Schicksals
freaky ['fri:kɪ] *adj.* **a)** *see* **freakish; b)** *(sl.: bizarre)* irre *(salopp);* verrückt *(ugs.)*

freckle ['frekl] *n.* Sommersprosse, *die*

freckled ['frekld], **freckle-faced** ['freklfeɪst], **freckly** ['freklɪ] *adjs.* sommersprossig

Frederick ['fredrɪk] *pr. n. (Hist., as name of ruler etc.)* Friedrich

free [friː] **1.** *adj.*, **freer** ['friːə(r)], **freest** ['friːɪst] **a)** frei; **get ~:** freikommen; sich befreien; **her heart is ~** *(fig.)* ihr Herz ist noch frei; **go ~** *(escape unpunished)* straffrei ausgehen; **let sb. go ~** *(leave captivity)* jmdn. freilassen; *(unpunished)* jmdn. freisprechen; **set ~:** freilassen; *(fig.)* erlösen; **as ~ as air** *or* **a bird** *or* **the wind** frei wie ein Vogel; **b)** *(Polit.)* frei; **it's a ~ country** *(coll.)* wir leben in einem freien Land; **c)** *(unrestricted, unconstrained, unrepressed)* frei; *(untrammelled)* frei; ungebunden; *(frank, open)* offen; freimütig; *(improper)* freizügig; *(forward, familiar)* ungezwungen; **~ of sth.** *(outside)* außerhalb etw.; *(without)* frei von etw.; **~ of prejudice/imperfections** vorurteils-/fehlerfrei; **~ of debts/tax/charge/cost** schulden-/steuer-/gebührenfrei/kostenlos; **be glad to be ~ of sth./sb.** froh sein, etw./jmdn. los zu sein; **~ and easy** ungezwungen; locker *(ugs.)*; **give sb. a ~ rein to do sth.** jmdm. freie Hand lassen, etw. zu tun; **give ~ rein to sth.** einer Sache *(Dat.)* freien Lauf lassen; **make ~ with sth.** mit etw. sehr großzügig umgehen; *(help oneself)* etw. ungeniert benutzen; **make [rather too] ~ with sb.** sich *(Dat.)* jmdm. gegenüber etwas [zuviel] herausnehmen; **be ~ with one's hands** *(hitting)* eine lockere Hand haben; *(stroking)* sich *(Dat.)* Freiheiten herausnehmen; **d)** *(Commerc., Econ.)* frei ⟨*Wirtschaft, Wettbewerb*⟩; **e)** *(not fixed, untied)* frei; lose; **work ~:** ⟨*Teil:*⟩ sich lösen; **she wrenched herself ~ from his arms** sie entwand sich seinen Armen; **get one hand ~:** eine Hand freibekommen; **f)** *(having liberty)* **sb. is ~ to do sth.** es steht jmdm. frei, etw. zu tun; **you're ~ to choose** du kannst frei [aus]wählen; **leave sb. ~ to do sth.** es jmdm. ermöglichen, etw. zu tun; **he's not ~ to marry** er kann/darf nicht heiraten; **our thoughts are ~ to roam** die Gedanken sind frei; **feel ~!** nur zu! *(ugs.)*; **Do you mind if I smoke? – Feel ~!** Stört es Sie, wenn ich rauche? – Nein, ganz und gar nicht!; **feel ~ to correct me** du darfst mich gerne korrigieren; **make sb. ~ of sth.** jmdm. etw. zur Verfügung stellen; **~ from sth.** frei von etw.; **~ from pain/troubles** schmerz-/sorgenfrei; **g)** *(provided without payment)* kostenlos; frei ⟨*Überfahrt, Unterkunft, Versand, Verpflegung*⟩; Frei⟨*karte, -exemplar, -fahrt*⟩; Gratis⟨*probe, -vorstellung*⟩; **they get ~ lunches** sie haben freies Mittagessen; **'admission ~':** „Eintritt frei"; **have a ~ ride on the train** umsonst mit der Bahn fahren; **have a ~ ride at sb.'s expense** *(fig. coll.)* auf jmds. Kosten faulenzen; **be out for a ~ ride** *(fig. coll.)* Trittbrettfahrer sein *(abwertend)*; **for ~** *(coll.)* umsonst; **publicity for ~** *(coll.)* kostenlose Werbung; **h)** *(not occupied, not reserved, not being used)* frei; **~ time** Freizeit, *die;* **when would you be ~ to start work?** wann könnten Sie mit der Arbeit anfangen?; **have a ~ period** *(Sch.)* eine Freistunde haben; **he's ~ in the mornings** er hat morgens Zeit; **when can you arrange to be ~?** wann könnten Sie sich freimachen?; **i)** *(generous)* **be ~ with sth.** mit etw. großzügig umgehen; **be a ~ spender** sein Geld mit vollen Händen ausgeben; **j)** *(not strict)* frei ⟨*Übersetzung, Interpretation, Bearbeitung usw.*⟩; **draw a ~ likeness of sb.** jmdn. mit künstlerischer Freiheit zeichnen; **k)** *(Chem., Phys.)* frei ⟨*Elektron, Energie*⟩. **2.** *adv.* **a)** *(without cost or payment)* gratis; umsonst; **he gets his accommodation ~:** er hat freies Logis; **b)** *(freely)* frei; **c)** *(Naut.)* auf raumem Kurs. **3.** *v. t.* *(set at liberty)* freilassen; *(disentangle)* befreien (**of, from** von); **~ sb./oneself from** jmdn./sich befreien von ⟨*Tyrannei, Unterdrückung, Tradition*⟩; jmdn./sich befreien aus ⟨*Gefängnis, Sklaverei, Umklammerung*⟩; *(make secure)* jmdn./sich schützen vor (+ *Dat.*) ⟨*Gefahr, Infektion*⟩; **~ oneself from debt/obligations** sich seiner Schulden/Verpflichtungen entledigen; **~ sb./oneself of** jmdn./sich befreien *od.* freimachen von

-free [friː] *in comb.* -frei

freebie ['friːbɪ] *(Amer. coll.)* **1.** *n.* Gratisgeschenk, *das.* **2.** *adj.* Gratis⟨*essen, -getränk*⟩; **~ ticket** Freikarte, *die*

'freeboard *n. (Naut.)* Freibord, *der*

freebooter ['friːbuːtə(r)] *n.* Freibeuter, *der (hist.)*

free: ~-born *adj.* frei *(hist.)*; **F~ 'Church** *n.* Freikirche, *die*

freedom ['friːdəm] *n.* **a)** Freiheit, *die;* **give sb. his ~:** jmdn. freigeben; *(from prison, slavery)* jmdn. freilassen; **~ of the press** Pressefreiheit, *die;* **~ of action/speech/movement** Handlungs-/Rede-/Bewegungsfreiheit, *die;* **~ from taxes/pain** Steuer-/Schmerzfreiheit, *die;* **b)** *(frankness)* Ungezwungenheit, *die; (over-familiarity)* Vertraulichkeit, *die;* **c)** *(ease)* **~ of operation of the mechanism** Leichtgängigkeit des Mechanismus; **d)** *(privilege)* **[give sb.** *or* **present sb. with] the ~ of the city** [jmdm.] die Ehrenbürgerrechte [verleihen]; **e)** *(use)* **give sb. the ~ of sth.** jmdm. etw. zur freien Verfügung überlassen. *See also* **conscience**

'freedom fighter *n.* Freiheitskämpfer, *der*/-kämpferin, *die*

free: ~ 'enterprise *n.* freies Unternehmertum; **~ 'fall** *n.* freier Fall; **~-fall parachuting** Fallschirmspringen mit freiem Fall; **~ 'fight** *n.* Kampf jeder gegen jeden; **~-for-all** **1.** *n.* [allgemeine] Schlägerei; *(less violent)* [allgemeines] Gerangel; **the discussion soon became a ~-for-all** bei der Diskussion redeten bald alle wild durcheinander; **2.** *adj.* **a)** allgemein ⟨*Schlägerei, Gerangel*⟩; **b)** *(observing no rules)* wild ⟨*Diskussion, Schlägerei*⟩; ⟨*Spiel*⟩ ohne [feste] Regeln; **~ 'gift** *n.* Gratisgabe, *die;* **~ 'hand** *n.* **a) I picked it up with my ~ hand** ich hob es mit der freien Hand auf; **b)** *(fig.)* freier [Handlungs]spielraum; **give sb. a ~ hand** jmdm. freie Hand lassen; **c) with a ~ hand** *(generously)* großzügig; **~-hand** *adj.* freihändig; **~ 'hit** *n. (Hockey, Polo)* Freischlag, *der;* **~hold** **1.** *n.* Besitzrecht, *das;* **2.** *adj.* Eigentums-; **~hold land** freier Grundbesitz; **~holder** *n.* Grundeigentümer, *der;* **~ house** *n. (Brit.)* *brauereiunabhängiges Wirtshaus;* **~ 'kick** *n. (Footb.)* Freistoß, *der;* **~-lance** **1.** *n.* **a)** freier Mitarbeiter/freie Mitarbeiterin; **b)** *(Hist.: mercenary)* Söldner, *der;* **2.** *adj.* freiberuflich; **~-lance translating** freiberufliche Arbeit als Übersetzer; **3.** *v. i.* freiberuflich arbeiten; **~-'loader** *n. (sl.)* Nassauer, *der (ugs., meist abwertend);* **~ 'love** *n.* freie Liebe

freely ['friːlɪ] *adv.* **a)** *(willingly)* großzügig; freimütig ⟨*eingestehen*⟩; **b)** *(without restriction, loosely)* frei; **c)** *(frankly)* offen; **d)** *(abundantly)* reichlich

free: ~man ['friːmən] *n., pl.* **~men** ['friːmən] **a)** Freie, *der (hist.)*; **b)** *(who has freedom of city etc.)* Ehrenbürger, *der;* **~ 'market** *n. (Econ.)* freier Markt; **F~mason** *n.* Freimaurer, *der;* **~masonry** *n.* **a) F~masonry** Freimaurerei, *die;* **b)** *(fig.: corporate feeling)* Zusammengehörigkeitsgefühl, *das;* **~ on 'board** **1.** *adv.* frei Schiff; **2.** *adj.* frei Schiff geliefert; **~ 'pass** *n.* Freikarte, *die; (Railw.)* Freifahrschein, *der;* **~ 'play** *n.* **a)** *(Mech.)* Spiel, *das;* **b)** *(fig.)* **give ~ play to sth.** etw. sich frei entfalten lassen; **allow one's imagination ~ play** der Phantasie freien Lauf lassen; **~ port** *n.* Freihafen, *der;* **~post** *n. (Brit.)* '**~post'** „Gebühr zahlt Empfänger"

freer *see* **free 1**

'free-range *adj.* freilaufend ⟨*Huhn*⟩; **~ eggs** Eier von freilaufenden Hühnern

freesia ['friːzɪə] *n. (Bot.)* Freesie, *die*

free: ~ 'speech *n.* Redefreiheit, *die;* **~-spoken** *adj.* freimütig

freest *see* **free 1**

free: ~-standing *adj.* frei stehend; **~-style** *n. (Sport)* Freistil, *der;* **~thinker** *n.* Freidenker, *der;* **~-thinking** **1.** *n.* Freidenkertum, *das;* **2.** *adj.* freidenkerisch; **~ 'trade** *n.* Freihandel, *der;* **~ 'verse** *n. (Lit.)* freie Verse; **~ 'vote** *n. (Brit. Parl.)* [dem Fraktionszwang nicht unterworfene] freie Stimmabgabe; **~way** *n. (Amer.)* Autobahn, *die;* **~ 'wheel** *n.* Freilauf, *der;* **~-wheel** *v. i.* im Freilauf fahren; *(fig.: drift)* sich treiben lassen; **~ 'will** *n.* **a)** *no art. (power)* Willensfreiheit, *die;* **b)** *(choice)* **do sth. of one's own ~ will** etw. aus freiem Willen tun; **be left to sb.'s own ~ will** jmds. freier Entscheidung *(Dat.)* überlassen sein; **~ 'world** *n.* freie Welt

freeze [friːz] **1.** *v. i.*, **froze** [frəʊz], **frozen** ['frəʊzn] **a)** frieren; **it will ~** *(Meteorol.)* es wird Frost geben; **it froze hard last night** heute nacht war starker Frost; **b)** *(become covered with ice)* ⟨*See, Fluß, Teich:*⟩ zufrieren; ⟨*Straße:*⟩ vereisen; **c)** *(solidify)* ⟨*Flüssigkeit:*⟩ gefrieren; ⟨*Rohr, Schloß:*⟩ einfrieren; **the pond has frozen solid** der Teich ist ganz zugefroren; **d)** *(become rigid)* steif frieren; *(fig.)* ⟨*Lächeln:*⟩ gefrieren *(geh.)*; **e)** *(become fastened)* festfrieren (**to** an + *Dat.*); **~ together** aneinander festfrieren; **f)** *(be or feel cold)* sehr frieren; *(fig.)* erstarren (**with** vor + *Dat.*); ⟨*Blut:*⟩ gefrieren *(geh.)*; **he is freezing** er *od.* ihn friert sehr; **my hands are freezing** meine Hände sind eiskalt; **~ to death** erfrieren; *(fig.)* bitterlich frieren; **g)** *(make oneself motionless)* erstarren; **~!** keine Bewegung!. **2.** *v. t.*, **froze, frozen** **a)** zufrieren lassen ⟨*Teich, Fluß*⟩; gefrieren lassen ⟨*Rohr*⟩; *(fig.)* erstarren lassen; **~ sb.'s blood** *(fig.)* jmdm. das Blut in den Adern gefrieren lassen *(geh.)*; **you look absolutely frozen** *(fig.)* du siehst ganz durchgefroren aus; **we were frozen stiff** *(fig.)* wir waren steif gefroren; **b)** *(preserve)* tiefkühlen, tiefgefrieren ⟨*Lebensmittel*⟩; **c)** *(make unrealizable or unchangeable)* einfrieren ⟨*Kredit, Guthaben, Gelder, Löhne, Preise usw.*⟩; **d)** *(Cinemat.)* in einem Stehkader festhalten; **e)** *(stiffen)* gefrieren lassen ⟨*Erdboden*⟩; festfrieren lassen ⟨*Wäsche*⟩ (**to** an + *Dat.*); **f)** *(deaden)* ⟨*Spritze:*⟩ taub machen; ⟨*Spray:*⟩ vereisen; **g)** *(kill)* erfrieren lassen ⟨*Pflanzen*⟩; **h)** *(fig.)* erstarren lassen; gefrieren lassen *(geh.)* ⟨*Lächeln*⟩. **3.** *n.* **a)** *see* **freeze-up a**; **b)** *(fixing)* Einfrieren, *das* (**on** *Gen.*); **price/wage/nuclear ~:** Preis-/Lohn-/Atomwaffenstopp, *der;* **c)** *(Cinemat.)* **~[-frame]** Stehkader, *der*

~ 'out *v. t. (socially)* hinausekeln

~ 'over *v. i.* ⟨*Teich, Fluß:*⟩ zufrieren; ⟨*Fenster-, Windschutzscheibe, Straße*⟩ vereisen

~ 'up **1.** *v. i.* ⟨*Fluß, Teich:*⟩ zufrieren; ⟨*Schloß, Rohr:*⟩ einfrieren; ⟨*Fenster:*⟩ vereisen. **2.** *v. t. see* **1:** zufrieren/einfrieren/vereisen lassen. *See also* **freeze-up**

'freeze-dry *v. t.* gefriertrocknen

freezer ['friːzə(r)] *n. (deep-freeze)* Tiefkühltruhe, *die;* Gefriertruhe, *die;* **[upright] ~:** Tiefkühlschrank, *der;* Gefrierschrank, *der;* **~ compartment** Tiefkühlfach, *das;* Gefrierfach, *das;* **~ [room]** Kühlraum, *der;* **[ice-cream] ~:** Eismaschine, *die*

'freeze-up *n.* **a)** *(period)* Dauerfrost, *der;* Frostperiode, *die;* **b)** *(fig.)* Stillstand, *der*

freezing ['friːzɪŋ] **1.** *adj. (lit. or fig.)* frostig; **~ temperatures** Temperaturen unter null Grad; **it is ~ in here** es ist eiskalt hier drinnen. **2.** *n.* **a)** *no pl.* (**~-point**) **above/below ~:** über/unter dem/den Gefrierpunkt; **b)** *(of food)* Einfrieren, *das*

'freezing-point *n.* Gefrierpunkt, *der*

freight [freɪt] **1.** *n.* **a)** Fracht, *die;* ~ **charges** Frachtgeld, *das;* Frachtkosten *Pl.;* **b)** *(transport)* Frachtsendung, *die;* **send goods** ~: Waren als Frachtgut senden; **c)** *(hire)* Charter, *die.* **2.** *v.t.* **a)** befrachten; **b)** *(hire)* chartern; *(hire out)* vermieten

freightage ['freɪtɪdʒ] *n., no pl.* Frachtkosten *Pl.*

'**freight car** *n. (Amer. Railw.)* Güterwagen, *der*

freighter ['freɪtə(r)] *n.* **a)** *(ship)* Frachter, *der;* Frachtschiff, *das; (aircraft)* Frachtflugzeug, *das;* **b)** *(Amer. Railw.)* Güterwagen, *der*

freight: ~-liner *n. (Railw.)* [Container]güterzug, *der;* ~ **train** *n. (Railw.)* Güterzug, *der*

French [frentʃ] **1.** *adj.* französisch; **he/she is** ~: er ist Franzose/sie ist Französin; **the ~ people** die Franzosen; ~ **lessons** *(lit. or euphem.)* Französischstunden; *see also* **English 1. 2.** *n.* **a)** Französisch, *das;* **b)** *(euphem.: bad language)* **pardon** *or* **excuse my** ~: entschuldigen Sie die Ausdrucksweise!; **c)** *constr. as pl.* **the** ~: die Franzosen. *See also* **English 2 a**

French: ~ '**bean** *n. (Brit.)* Gartenbohne, *die;* [grüne] Bohne; ~ '**bread** *n.* französisches [Stangen]weißbrot; ~ **Ca'nadian** *n.* Frankokanadier, *der/*-kanadierin, *die;* **~-Ca'nadian** *adj.* frankokanadisch; ~ '**chalk** *n.* Schneiderkreide, *die;* ~ '**dressing** *n.* Vinaigrette, *die;* ~ **fried po'tatoes,** ~ '**fries** *ns. pl.* Pommes frites *Pl.;* ~ '**horn** *n. (Mus.)* [Wald-]horn, *das*

Frenchified ['frentʃɪfaɪd] *adj.* französiert

French: ~ '**kiss** *n.* französischer Kuß *(ugs.);* Zungenkuß, *der;* ~ '**leave** *n.* **take ~ leave** *(without giving notice)* sich [auf] französisch empfehlen *od.* verabschieden *(ugs.); (without permission)* sich heimlich davonstehlen; ~ '**letter** *n. (Brit. coll.)* Pariser, *der (salopp);* **~man** ['frentʃmən] *n., pl.* **~men** ['frentʃmən] Franzose, *der;* ~ '**mustard** *n. (Brit.)* französischer Senf; ~ '**polish** *n.* Schellackpolitur, *die;* **~-'polish** *v.t.* [mit Schellackpolitur] polieren; ~ **Revo'lution** *n. (Hist.)* Französische Revolution; ~ '**toast** *n.* **a)** *(toasted)* einseitig geröstete Toastscheibe; **b)** *(fried)* arme Ritter; ~ **ver'mouth** *n.* trockener Wermut; ~ '**window** *n., in sing. or pl.* französisches Fenster; **~woman** *n.* Französin, *die*

Frenchy ['frentʃɪ] *(coll.)* **1.** *adj.* [betont] französisch. **2.** *n.* Franzose, *der;* Franzmann, *der (ugs. veraltend)*

frenetic [frɪ'netɪk] *adj.* **a)** *(frantic)* verzweifelt ⟨*Hilferuf, Versuch*⟩; **b)** *(fanatic)* frenetisch, rasend ⟨*Beifall*⟩; fanatisch ⟨*Sekte*⟩

frenzied ['frenzɪd] *adj.* rasend; wahnsinnig ⟨*Tat*⟩

frenzy ['frenzɪ] *n.* **a)** *(derangement)* Wahnsinn, *der;* **b)** *(fury, agitation)* Raserei, *die;* **in a ~ of despair/passion** in einem Anfall von Verzweiflung/von wilder Leidenschaft übermannt

frequency ['fri:kwənsɪ] *n.* **a)** Häufigkeit, *die;* **b)** *(of pulse)* Puls, *der;* [Puls]frequenz, *die (Med.);* **c)** *(Phys., Statistics)* Frequenz, *die*

'**frequency modulation** *n. (Radio, Telev.)* Frequenzmodulation, *die*

frequent 1. ['fri:kwənt] *adj.* **a)** häufig; **it's a ~ practice/occurrence** es ist üblich/kommt häufig vor; **become less** ~: seltener werden; **b)** *(habitual, constant)* eifrig ⟨*[Kino-, Theater]besucher, Briefschreiber*⟩; **he is a ~ visitor to our restaurant** er ist Stammgast in unserem Restaurant; **c)** *(abundant)* zahlreich. **2.** [frɪ'kwent] *v.t.* frequentieren *(geh.);* häufig besuchen ⟨*Café, Klub usw.*⟩; häufig aufsuchen ⟨*Futterplatz*⟩; **much ~ed** stark frequentiert *(geh.);* vielbefahren ⟨*Straße*⟩

frequently ['fri:kwəntlɪ] *adv.* häufig

fresco ['freskəʊ] *n., pl.* ~**es** *or* ~**s a)** *no pl., no art. (method)* Freskomalerei, *die;* **b)** *(a painting)* Fresko, *das*

fresh [freʃ] **1.** *adj.* **a)** neu; frisch, ausgeruht ⟨*Truppen*⟩; frisch, neu ⟨*Energie, Mut*⟩; *(lately made or arrived)* frisch; *(raw, inexperienced)* [jung und] unerfahren; **a ~ series of attacks** eine neuerliche Serie von Angriffen; **make a ~ start** noch einmal von vorn anfangen; *(fig.)* neu beginnen; ~ **from school/India** frisch von der Schule/gerade aus Indien gekommen; ~ **from** *or* **off the press** druckfrisch; frisch aus der Presse; ~ **from the oven** ofenfrisch; frisch aus dem Ofen; **b)** *(not preserved or stale or faded)* frisch ⟨*Obst, Fisch, Gemüse, Fleisch, Eier, Tee, Blumen usw.*⟩; **c)** *(clean, bright)* frisch ⟨*Aussehen, Gesichtsfarbe, Hemd, Wäsche*⟩; **d)** *(pure, cool)* frisch ⟨*Luft, Wasser, Wind*⟩; **go out for some ~ air** nach draußen gehen, um Luft zu schöpfen *(geh.);* **the wind became** ~: der Wind frischte auf; **e)** *(vigorous, fit)* frisch; *(refreshed)* erfrischt; **as ~ as a daisy/as paint** ganz frisch; *(in appearance)* frisch wie der junge Morgen *(meist scherzh.);* **f)** *(cheeky)* keck; **get ~ with sb.** jmdm. frech kommen *(ugs.). See also* **¹ground 1 b. 2.** *adv.* frisch; **we're ~ out of eggs** *(coll.)* uns sind gerade die Eier ausgegangen; **~-ground/-painted** frisch gemahlen/gestrichen

freshen ['freʃn] **1.** *v.i.* **a)** frisch[er] werden; *(increase)* ⟨*Wind:*⟩ auffrischen; **b)** *(brighten)* ein frisch[er]es Aussehen bekommen. **2.** *v.t.* *(ventilate)* durchlüften ⟨*Zimmer*⟩

~ '**up 1.** *v.i.* sich frisch machen. **2.** *v.t.* erfrischen; ~ **oneself/sb. up** sich/jmdn. frisch machen

fresher ['freʃə(r)] *(Brit. Univ. sl.) see* **freshman a**

freshly ['freʃlɪ] *adv.* frisch

freshman ['freʃmən] *n., pl.* **freshmen** ['freʃmən] **a)** Erstsemester, *das;* Frischling, *der (scherzh.);* **b)** *(Amer.) (in school)* Anfänger, *der/*Anfängerin, *die; (person beginning)* Neuling, *der*

freshness ['freʃnɪs] *n., no pl.* Frische, *die; (of idea, metaphor, etc.)* Neuartigkeit, *die; (originality)* Originalität, *die*

fresh 'water *n.* Süßwasser, *das*

'**freshwater** *adj.* Süßwasser-; ~ **sailor** Binnenschiffer, *der*

¹fret [fret] **1.** *v.i.,* **-tt-** *(worry)* beunruhigt sein; besorgt sein; **don't** ~: sei unbesorgt!; ~ **at** *or* **about** *or* **over sth.** sich über etw. *(Akk.) od.* wegen etw. aufregen; ~ **and fume** *(anxiously/impatiently)* voller Unruhe/Ungeduld sein. **2.** *v.t.,* **-tt-: a)** *(distress)* beunruhigen; quälen; ~ **oneself** sich beunruhigen; sich *(Dat.)* Sorgen machen **(about** wegen); **b)** *(chafe)* [wund] scheuern. **3.** *n.* Ärger, *der;* **be in a** ~: voll Verdruß sein

²fret *n. (Mus.)* Bund, *der*

fretful ['fretfl] *adj. (peevish)* verdrießlich; mürrisch; quengelig *(ugs.)* ⟨*Kleinkind*⟩; *(restless)* unruhig; *(impatient)* ungeduldig; *(ill-humoured)* übellaunig

fret: ~saw *n.* Laubsäge, *die;* **~work** *n.* **a)** *(Archit.)* durchbrochene Arbeit; **b)** *(wood)* Laubsägearbeit, *die*

Freudian ['frɔɪdɪən] *adj.* freudianisch; ~ **interpretation** Freudsche Interpretation; ~ **slip** Freudsche Fehlleistung; Freudscher Versprecher *(ugs.)*

Fri. *abbr.* **Friday** Fr.

friable ['fraɪəbl] *adj.* bröck[e]lig

friar ['fraɪə(r)] *n.* Ordensbruder, *der;* **Black/Grey/White F~:** Dominikaner/Franziskaner/Karmeliter, *der;* **F~ Peter** Bruder Peter

fricassee ['frɪkəsi:, frɪkə'si:] *(Cookery)* **1.** *n.* Frikassee, *das.* **2.** *v.t.* frikassieren

fricative ['frɪkətɪv] *(Phonet.)* **1.** *adj.* frikativ. **2.** *n.* Frikativ, *der (fachspr.);* Reibelaut, *der*

friction ['frɪkʃn] *n.* **a)** Reibung, *die; attrib.* Reibungs-; **b)** *(fig.: between persons)* Reibereien; **c)** *(of body or scalp)* Einreibung, *die;* Friktion, *die (Med.)*

Friday ['fraɪdeɪ, 'fraɪdɪ] **1.** *n.* Freitag, *der;* **on** ~: [am] Freitag; **on a** ~, **on ~s** freitags; **we got married on a** ~: wir haben an einem Freitag geheiratet; ~ **13 August** Freitag, der 13. August; *(at top of letter etc.)* Freitag, den 13. August; **on ~ 13 August** am Freitag, den *od.* dem 13. August; **next/last** ~: [am] nächsten/letzten *od.* vergangenen Freitag; **[on] ~ next/last** kommenden/vergangenen Freitag; **we were married a year [ago] last/next** ~: vergangenen/kommenden Freitag vor einem Jahr haben wir geheiratet; **[last] ~'s mail/newspaper** die Post/Zeitung vom [letzten] Freitag; **our ~ session** unsere Freitagssitzung; *(this ~)* unsere Sitzung am Freitag; **Good** ~: Karfreitag, *der;* **man/girl** ~: Mädchen für alles *(ugs.).* **2.** *adv. (coll.)* **a)** ~ **[week]** Freitag [in einer Woche]; **b)** ~**s** freitags; Freitag *(ugs.);* **she comes ~s** sie kommt freitags

fridge [frɪdʒ] *n. (Brit. coll.)* Kühlschrank, *der;* **~-freezer** Kühl- und Gefrier-Kombination, *die*

fried *see* **¹fry 2, 3**

friend [frend] *n.* **a)** Freund, *der/*Freundin, *die;* **~s and relations** Verwandte und Freunde; **be ~s with sb.** mit jmdm. befreundet sein; **I'm not ~s with you any more!** *(joc. or child language)* du bist nicht mehr mein Freund!; **let's be ~s again** wir wollen uns wieder vertragen; **make ~s [with sb.]** [mit jmdm.] Freundschaft schließen; **he makes ~s easily** er findet leicht Anschluß; **make a ~ of sb.** sich mit jmdm. anfreunden; **a ~ in need is a ~ indeed** *(prov.)* Freunde in der Not gehn hundert *od.* tausend auf ein Lot *(Spr.);* **between ~s** unter Freunden; **b)** *(helper, patron)* Freund, *der* **(of,** to *Gen.*); **~s in high places** *or* **at court** einflußreiche Freunde; Freunde höheren Orts; **the F~s of Covent Garden** der Freundes- *od.* Förderkreis des Covent Garden; **c)** *(Quaker)* **the Society of F~s** die Quäker; die Gesellschaft der Freunde; **d) my honourable/noble** ~ *(Brit. Parl.)* mein verehrter Freund; **my learned** ~ *(Law)* mein verehrter *od.* werter Kollege

friendless ['frendlɪs] *adj.* ohne Freund[e] *nachgestellt*

friendliness ['frendlɪnɪs] *n., no pl.* Freundlichkeit, *die*

friendly ['frendlɪ] **1.** *adj.* **a)** freundlich **(to** zu); freundschaftlich ⟨*Rat, Beziehungen, Wettkampf, Gespräch*⟩; **be on ~ terms** *or* **be ~ with sb.** mit jmdm. auf freundschaftlichem Fuße stehen; **we're very ~ with our neighbours** wir sind mit unseren Nachbarn sehr gut befreundet; *see also* **neighbourhood d; b)** *(not hostile)* freundlich [gesinnt] ⟨*Bewohner*⟩; befreundet ⟨*Staat*⟩; zutraulich ⟨*Tier*⟩; ~ **game** *(Sport)* Freundschaftsspiel, *das;* **c)** *(well-wishing)* wohlwollend ⟨*Erwähnung*⟩; günstig gestimmt ⟨*Götter*⟩. **2.** *n.* *(Sport)* Freundschaftsspiel, *das*

'**Friendly Society** *n. (Brit.)* Versicherungsverein auf Gegenseitigkeit

friendship ['frendʃɪp] *n.* Freundschaft, *die;* **[feelings of]** ~: freundschaftliche Gefühle; **strike up a ~ with sb.** sich mit jmdm. anfreunden

frier *see* **fryer**

Friesian ['fri:zɪən, 'fri:ʒən] *(Agric.)* **1.** *adj.* schwarzbunt. **2.** *n.* Schwarzbunte, *die*

¹frieze [fri:z] *n. (Textiles)* Fries, *der;* Friese, *die (fachspr.)*

²frieze *n. (Archit.)* Fries, *der*

frigate ['frɪgət] *n. (Naut.)* Fregatte, *die*

fright [fraɪt] *n.* **a)** Schreck, *der;* Schrecken, *der;* **in his** ~: vor Schreck; **take** ~: erschrecken; **the ~ of one's life** der Schock seines Lebens; **give sb. a** ~: jmdm. einen Schreck[en] einjagen; **get** *or* **have a** ~: einen Schreck[en] bekommen; **b)** *(grotesque per-*

son or thing) **be** *or* **look a ~:** zum Fürchten aussehen *(ugs.)*

frighten ['fraɪtn] *v. t.* ‹*Explosion, Schuß:*› erschrecken; ‹*Gedanke, Drohung:*› angst machen (+ *Dat.*); **be ~ed at** *or* **by sth.** vor etw. *(Dat.)* erschrecken; **she is not easily ~ed** sie fürchtet sich nicht so schnell; **~ sb. out of his wits/life** jmdn. furchtbar/zu Tode erschrecken; **~ sb. to death** *(fig.)* jmdn. zu Tode erschrecken; **be ~ed to death** *(fig.)* zu Tode erschrocken sein; **~ sb. into doing sth.** jmdm. solche Angst machen, daß er etw. tut

~ a'way, ~ 'off *v. t.* vertreiben; *(put off)* abschrecken

frightened ['fraɪtnd] *adj.* verängstigt; angsterfüllt ‹*Stimme*›; **be ~ [of sth.]** [vor etw. *(Dat.)*] Angst haben

frightening ['fraɪtnɪŋ] *adj.* furchterregend

frightful ['fraɪtfl] *adj.* furchtbar; schrecklich; *(coll.: terrible)* furchtbar *(ugs.)*

frightfully ['fraɪtfəlɪ] *adv.* furchtbar; schrecklich; *(coll.: extremely)* furchtbar *(ugs.)*

frigid ['frɪdʒɪd] *adj.* **a)** *(very cold)* eisig kalt; **b)** *(formal, unfriendly)* frostig; *(sexually unresponsive)* frigid[e] ‹*Frau*›

frigidity [frɪ'dʒɪdɪtɪ] *n., no pl.* **a)** *(coldness)* eisige Kälte; **b)** *(formality, unfriendliness)* Frostigkeit, *die; (of woman)* Frigidität, *die*

frill [frɪl] *n.* **a)** *(ruffled edge)* Rüsche, *die;* **b)** *(on animal, plant)* Kragen, *der; (on bird)* Halskrause, *die;* **c)** *in pl. (embellishments)* Beiwerk, *das;* Ausschmückungen *(fig.);* **with no ~s** ‹*Ferienhaus, Auto*› ohne besondere Ausstattung

frilly ['frɪlɪ] **1.** *adj.* mit Rüschen besetzt; Rüschen‹*kleid, -bluse*›. **2.** *n. in pl. (coll.)* Rüschenunterwäsche, *die*

fringe [frɪndʒ] **1.** *n.* **a)** *(bordering)* Fransen; Fransenkante, *die* **(on** an + *Dat.*); **b)** *(hair)* [Pony]fransen *(ugs.);* Pony, *der;* **c)** *(edge)* Rand, *der; attrib.* Rand‹*geschehen, -gruppe, -gebiet*›; **~ benefits** zusätzliche Leistungen; **live on the ~[s] of the city** am Stadtrand *od.* in den Randgebieten der Stadt wohnen; **lunatic ~:** Extremisten. **2.** *v. t.* säumen *(auch fig. geh.)*

frippery ['frɪpərɪ] *n.* Putz, *der;* Zierat, *der (geh.); (knick-knacks, trifles)* Tand, *der (geh.);* Kinkerlitzchen *Pl. (ugs.)*

Frisco ['frɪskəʊ] *pr. n. (Amer. sl.)* San Francisco *(das)*

Frisian ['frɪzɪən] **1.** *adj.* friesisch; *see also* **English 1. 2.** *n.* **a)** *(language)* Friesisch, *das;* **b)** *(person)* Friese, *der*/Friesin, *die. See also* **English 2 a**

frisk [frɪsk] **1.** *v. i.* **~ [about]** [herum]springen; **~ away** davonspringen. **2.** *v. t. (coll.)* filzen *(ugs.).* **3.** *n.* **a)** *(frolic)* Hüpfer, *der;* **b)** *(coll.: body search)* Filzung, *die (ugs.)*

frisky ['frɪskɪ] *adj.* munter; **as ~ as a kitten** so ausgelassen wie ein Füllen *(geh.)*

frisson ['fri:sõ] *n.* Schauer, *der*

fritillary [frɪ'tɪlərɪ] *n.* **a)** *(Bot.)* Fritillaria, *die (fachspr.);* Kaiserkrone, *die;* **b)** *(Zool.)* Fleckenfalter, *der*

¹fritter ['frɪtə(r)] *n. (Cookery)* **apple/sausage ~s** Apfelstücke/Würstchen in Pfannkuchenteig

²fritter *v. t.* **~ away** vergeuden; verplempern *(ugs.)*

frivolity [frɪ'vɒlɪtɪ] *n.* **a)** *no pl.* Oberflächlichkeit, *die;* Leichtfertigkeit, *die;* **b)** *(thing)* Tand, *der (geh.); (act)* **he watched these frivolities with contempt** er beobachtete dieses leichtfertige Treiben mit Verachtung

frivolous ['frɪvələs] *adj.* **a)** *(not serious)* frivol; extravagant ‹*Kleidung*›; **b)** *(trifling, futile)* belanglos

frivolously ['frɪvələslɪ] *adv.* frivol; extravagant ‹*gekleidet*›

frizzle ['frɪzl] **1.** *v. i.* brutzeln; braten. **2.** *v. t.* brutzeln *(ugs.);* braten

frizzy ['frɪzɪ] *adj.* kraus

fro [frəʊ] *adv. see* **to 2 b**

frock [frɒk] *n.* **a)** Kleid, *das;* **b)** *(Mil.)* Uniformrock, *der*

'frock-coat *n.* Gehrock, *der*

¹frog [frɒg] *n.* **a)** Frosch, *der;* **have a ~ in the** *or* **one's throat** *(coll.)* einen Frosch im Hals haben *(ugs.);* **b)** *(sl. derog.: Frenchman)* Franzmann, *der (ugs., veralt.)*

²frog *n.* **a)** *(coat-fastening)* Posamentenverschluß, *der;* **b)** *(on belt)* Schlaufe, *die*

froggy ['frɒgɪ] **1.** *adj.* Frosch‹*gesicht, -stimme*›. **2.** *n. (sl. derog.) see* **¹frog b**

frog: ~man ['frɒgmən] *n., pl.* **~men** ['frɒgmən] Froschmann, *der;* **~-march** *v. t.* *(carry)* zu viert an Händen und Füßen [mit dem Gesicht nach unten] tragen; *(hustle)* ≈ im Polizeigriff abführen; **~-spawn** *n.* Froschlaich, *der*

frolic ['frɒlɪk] **1.** *v. i.,* **-ck-:** **~ [about** *or* **around]** [herum]springen. **2.** *n. (prank, lark)* Spaß, *der; (fun, merriment)* Ausgelassenheit, *die*

frolicsome ['frɒlɪksəm] *adj. (dated)* ausgelassen

from [frəm, *stressed* frɒm] *prep.* **a)** *expr. starting-point* von; *(~ within)* aus; **[come] ~ Paris/Munich** aus Paris/München [kommen]; **~ Paris to Munich** von Paris nach München; **where have you come ~?** woher kommen Sie?; wo kommen Sie her?; **b)** *expr. beginning* von; **~ the year 1972 we never saw him again** seit 1972 haben wir ihn nie mehr [wieder]gesehen; **~ tomorrow [until ...]** von morgen an [bis ...]; **start work ~ 2 August** am 2. August anfangen zu arbeiten; vom 2. August an arbeiten; **~ now on** von jetzt an; ab jetzt; **~ then on** seitdem; *(relating to a place)* von da an; *see also* **as 4; c)** *expr. lower limit* von; **blouses [ranging] ~ £2 to £5** Blusen [im Preis] zwischen 2 und 5 Pfund; **dresses ~ £20 [upwards]** Kleider von 20 Pfund aufwärts *od.* ab 20 Pfund; **~ 4 to 6 eggs** 4 bis 6 Eier; **~ the age of 18 [upwards]** ab 18 Jahre *od.* Jahren; **~ a child** *(since childhood)* schon als Kind; **d)** *expr. distance* von; **be a mile ~ sth.** eine Meile von etw. entfernt sein; **away ~ home** von zu Hause weg; **e)** *expr. removal, avoidance* von; *expr. escape* vor (+ *Dat.*); **release the bomb ~ the aircraft** die Bombe aus dem Flugzeug ausklinken; **f)** *expr. change* von; **~ ... to ...:** von ... zu ...; *(relating to price)* von ... auf ...; **~ crisis to crisis, ~ one crisis to another** von einer Krise zur anderen; **g)** *expr. source, origin* aus; **pick apples ~ a tree** Äpfel vom Baum pflücken; **buy everything ~ Harrods/the same shop** alles bei Harrods/im selben Laden kaufen; **where do you come ~?, where are you ~?** woher kommen Sie?; **~ the country/another planet** vom Land/von einem anderen Planeten; **h)** *expr. viewpoint* von [... aus]; **i)** *expr. giver, sender* von; **take it ~ me that ...:** laß dir gesagt sein, daß ...; **j)** *(after the model of)* **painted ~ life/nature** nach dem Leben/nach der Natur gemalt; **k)** *expr. reason, cause* **she was weak ~ hunger/tired ~ so much work** sie war schwach vor Hunger/müde von der vielen Arbeit; **~ his looks you might think ...:** so wie er aussieht, könnte man denken ...; **~ what I can see/have heard ...:** wie ich das sehe/wie ich gehört habe, ...; **~ the look of things ...:** wie es aussieht, ...; **l)** *with adv.* von ‹*unten, oben, innen, außen*›; **m)** *with prep.* **~ behind/under[neath] sth.** hinter/unter etw. *(Dat.)* hervor; **~ amidst the trees** zwischen den Bäumen hervor; **~ before the marriage** aus der Zeit vor der Heirat; **the cries came ~ inside/outside the house** die Schreie kamen aus dem Inneren des Hauses/von draußen

frond [frɒnd] *n. (Bot.)* Wedel, *der;* Blatt, *das*

front [frʌnt] **1.** *n.* **a)** Vorderseite, *die; (of door)* Außenseite, *die; (of house)* Vorderfront, *die;* Frontseite, *die; (of dress)* Vorderteil, *das; (of queue)* vorderes Ende; *(of procession)* Spitze, *die; (of book)* vorderer Deckel; *(of cloth)* rechte Seite; **in** *or* **at the ~ [of sth.]** vorn [in etw. *position: Dat., movement: Akk.*]; **sit in the ~ of the car** vorne sitzen; **the index is at the ~:** das Register ist vorn; **to the ~:** nach vorn; **the living-room is at** *or* **in the ~ of the house** das Wohnzimmer liegt zur Straße hin *od. (ugs.)* nach vorn[e] raus; **lie on one's ~:** auf dem Bauch liegen; **a spot on the ~ of her dress** ein Fleck vorne am Kleid; **in ~:** vorn[e]; **be in ~ of sth./sb.** vor etw./jmdm. sein; **walk in ~ of sb.** *(preceding)* vor jmdm. gehen; *(to position)* vor jmdn. gehen; **look in ~ of one** nach vorn sehen; **he was murdered in ~ of his wife** er wurde vor den Augen seiner Frau ermordet; **b)** *(Mil.; also fig.)* Front, *die;* **on the Western ~:** an der Westfront; **send sb. to the ~:** jmdn. an die Front schicken; **be attacked on all ~s** an allen Fronten/*(fig.)* von allen Seiten angegriffen werden; **change of ~** *(fig.)* Gesinnungswandel; Frontwechsel *(Politik);* **on the international/home ~:** im Ausland/Inland; **on the sports ~:** im sportlichen Bereich; **on the entertainment ~:** auf dem Unterhaltungssektor; **the workers'/people's ~:** die Arbeiter-/Volksfront; **c)** *(promenade) (at seaside)* Strandpromenade, *die; (inland)* Uferpromenade, *die;* **d)** *(Theatre)* **~ of [the] house** Foyer und Zuschauerraum; **e)** *(Archit.)* ‹*West-, Garten-usw.*›seite, *die;* **f)** *(Meteorol.)* Front, *die;* **cold/warm ~:** Kalt-/Warmluftfront, *die;* **g)** *see* **shirt-front; h)** *(outward appearance)* Aussehen, *das; (bluff)* Fassade, *die (oft abwertend); (pretext, façade)* Tarnung, *die;* **put on** *or* **show** *or* **present a bold/brave ~:** sich nach außen unerschrocken zeigen/nach außen hin gefaßt bleiben; **preserve a calm ~:** nach außen hin ruhig bleiben; **it's all a ~:** das ist alles nur Fassade *(abwertend);* **i)** *(used as cover) (person)* Strohmann, *der; (organization)* Tarnorganisation, *die.* **2.** *adj.* **a)** vorder...; Vorder‹*rad, -zimmer, -zahn, -eingang, -ansicht*›; **~ garden** Vorgarten, *der;* **the ~ four coaches of a train** die ersten vier *od.* vier vorderen Wagen eines Zuges; **~ row** erste Reihe; **b)** *(Phonet.)* **~ vowel** Vorderzungenvokal, *der.* **3.** *v. i.* **a)** **~ on to the street/upon the lake** zur Straße/zum See hin liegen; **b)** *(sl.: act as cover)* **~ for sb.** für jmdn. den Strohmann spielen. **4.** *v. t. (furnish with façade)* **~ a building with stone** ein Gebäude mit einer Fassade aus Stein versehen

frontage ['frʌntɪdʒ] *n.* **a)** *(land)* Grundstück[steil] zwischen Gebäude und Straße; **river/street ~:** an den Fluß/die Straße grenzender Teil des Grundstücks; **b)** *(extent)* Frontbreite, *die;* **c)** *(façade)* Fassade, *die*

frontal ['frʌntl] *adj.* **a)** Frontal-; **b)** *(Art)* frontal ‹*Darstellung*›; **[full] ~:** frontal dargestellt ‹*Akt*›; **c)** *(Anat.)* Stirn‹*bein, -hirn, -höhle, -lappen*›

frontally ['frʌntəlɪ] *adv.* frontal

front: ~ 'bench *n. (Brit. Parl.)* vorderste Bank; **~-bencher** [frʌnt'bentʃə(r)] *n.* *(Brit. Parl.)* führender Politiker; **~ 'door** *n. (of flat)* Wohnungstür, *die; (of house; also fig.)* Haustür, *die*

frontier ['frʌntɪə(r)] *n.* **a)** *(lit. or fig.)* Grenze, *die; attrib.* Grenz‹*stadt, -posten, -streitigkeiten*›; **at** *or* **on the ~:** an der Grenze; **push the ~s of science forward** *(fig.)* wissenschaftliches Neuland erobern; **b)** *(Amer.: borders of civilization)* Grenzland, *das*

frontispiece ['frʌntɪspi:s] *n.* Frontispiz, *das;* Titelbild, *das*

front: ~ 'line *n.* Front[linie], *die;* **~ man** *n.* Strohmann, *der;* **~ 'page** *n.* Titelseite, *die;* **make the ~ page** auf die Titelseite kommen; **~-page** *adj.* ‹*Artikel*› auf der ersten Seite; **~ passage** *n. (Anat. coll.)* Scheide, *die;* **~-rank** *adj. (fig.)* herausragend; **~ runner** *n.* **a)** *(in race)* Läufer, der gern an der Spitze *läuft;* **b)** *(in any competition)* Spitzenkandidat, *der;* ~ **'seat** *n. (in theatre)* Platz in den ersten Reihen; *(in car)* Vordersitz, *der; (in bus, coach)* vorderer Sitzplatz

frost [frɒst] **1.** *n.* **a)** Frost, *der; (frozen dew or vapour)* Reif, *der;* **windows covered with ~:** vereiste Fensterscheiben; **white/black ~:** Frost mit/ohne Reif; **early/late ~s** Herbst-/Frühlingsfröste; **ten degrees of ~** *(Brit.)* zehn Grad minus; **there is still ~ in the ground** der Boden ist noch gefroren; **b)** *(fig.: hostility)* Frostigkeit, *die;* **c)** *(sl.: failure)* Reinfall, *der (ugs.);* Pleite, *die (salopp).* **2.** *v. t.* **a)** *(esp. Amer. Cookery)* mit Zucker bestreuen; *(ice)* glasieren; **b)** *(give ~like surface to)* mattieren ‹*Glas, Metall*›; **~ed glass** Mattglas, *das*

~ **'over 1.** *v. t.* **be ~ed over** vereist sein. **2.** *v. i.* vereisen

frost: ~bite *n.* Erfrierung, *die;* **~bitten** *adj.* durch Frost geschädigt; **sb. is ~bitten** jmd. hat Erfrierungen; **his toes are ~bitten** er hat Frost *od.* Erfrierungen in den Zehen

frostily ['frɒstɪlɪ] *adv.* frostig

frosting ['frɒstɪŋ] *n. (esp. Amer. Cookery)* Zucker, *der; (icing)* Glasur, *die*

frosty ['frɒstɪ] *adj. (lit. or fig.)* frostig; *(covered with hoar-frost)* bereift; *(fig.: white)* schneeweiß

froth [frɒθ] **1.** *n.* **a)** *(foam)* Schaum, *der;* **b)** *(worthless matter)* Tand, *der (geh.).* **2.** *v. i.* schäumen; **~ at the mouth** Schaum vor dem Mund haben; **~ at the mouth with rage** *(fig.)* vor Wut schäumen *(geh.).* **3.** *v. t. (Cookery)* **[beat and] ~ the eggs** die Eier schaumig schlagen

frothy ['frɒθɪ] *adj.* schaumig; schäumend ‹*Bier, Brandung, Maul*›; *(fig.: empty, shallow)* oberflächlich ‹*Mensch*›; seicht *(abwertend)* ‹*Unterhaltung, Roman*›

frown [fraʊn] **1.** *v. i.* **a)** die Stirn runzeln; **~ at sth./sb.** etw./jmdn. stirnrunzelnd ansehen; **b)** *(express disapproval)* die Stirn runzeln **(at, [up]on** über + *Akk.*); **~ [up]on a suggestion** über einen Vorschlag die Nase rümpfen; **gambling is very much ~ed upon here** das Glücksspiel ist hier streng verpönt; **c)** *(present gloomy aspect)* **~ [down]** düster herabblicken **(upon** auf + *Akk.*). **2.** *n.* Stirnrunzeln, *das;* **with a [deep/worried/puzzled] ~:** mit [stark/sorgenvoll/verwirrt] gerunzelter Stirn; **a ~ of disapproval** ein mißbilligender Blick

froze *see* **freeze 1, 2**

frozen ['frəʊzn] **1.** *see* **freeze 1, 2. 2.** *adj.* **a)** gefroren, zugefroren ‹*Fluß, See*›; erfroren ‹*Tier, Mensch, Pflanze*›; eingefroren ‹*Wasserleitung*›; **I am ~ stiff/through** *(fig.)* ich bin ganz steif gefroren/völlig durchgefroren; **my hands are ~** *(fig.)* meine Hände sind eiskalt; **b)** *(to preserve)* tiefgekühlt; **~ food** Tiefkühlkost, *die*

FRS *abbr.* **Fellow of the Royal Society**

fructose ['frʌktəʊs] *n. (Chem.)* Fructose, *die (fachspr.);* Fruchtzucker, *der*

frugal ['fru:gl] *adj.* **a)** *(careful, economical)* sparsam ‹*Hausfrau*›; genügsam ‹*Lebensweise, Mensch, Wesen*›; **b)** *(costing little)* frugal, karg ‹*Mahl*›; einfach, karg ‹*Zimmer, Einrichtung*›

frugally ['fru:gəlɪ] *adv.* frugal, genügsam ‹*leben, essen*›; einfach ‹*eingerichtet*›

fruit [fru:t] **1.** *n.* **a)** Frucht, *die; (collectively)* Obst, *das;* Früchte; **~s of the earth** Früchte des Feldes; **bear ~** *(lit. or fig.)* Früchte tragen; **b)** *(Bot.: seed with envelope)* Frucht, *die;* **c)** *(fig.) (product of action)* Frucht, *die (geh.);* Früchte *(geh.);* **~s** *(revenues produced)* Früchte *(geh.);* **this book is the ~ of long study** dieses Buch ist die Frucht langjähriger Arbeit *(geh.);* **d)** *(Bibl.: offspring)* Frucht, *die (geh.);* **the ~ of her womb/his loins** die Frucht ihres Leibes/seiner Lenden *(geh.).* **2.** *v. i.* [Früchte] tragen; *(fig.)* Früchte tragen

fruit: ~-cake *n.* englischer Teekuchen; **he is as nutty as a ~-cake** *(sl.) (eccentric)* er ist ein verrücktes Huhn *(ugs.); (insane)* er ist völlig übergeschnappt *(ugs.);* ~ **'cocktail** *n.* Früchtecocktail, *der*

fruiterer ['fru:tərə(r)] *n.* Obsthändler, *der/-händlerin, die*

fruitful ['fru:tfl] *adj.* **a)** fruchtbar; *(fig.)* fruchtbar ‹*Diskussion, Lebensabschnitt, Anregung*›; erfolgreich ‹*Karriere, Leben, Bemühungen*›; **be ~ and multiply** *(Bibl.)* seid fruchtbar und mehret euch; **b)** *(beneficial)* ertragreich ‹*Beschäftigung*›; nützlich ‹*Entdeckung*›

fruitfully ['fru:tfəlɪ] *adv.* nutzbringend

fruition [fru:'ɪʃn] *n. (of plan, aim)* Verwirklichung, *die; (of hope)* Erfüllung, *die;* **bring to ~:** verwirklichen ‹*Plan, Ziel*›; **come to ~** ‹*Plan:*› Wirklichkeit werden; ‹*Hoffnung:*› sich erfüllen

fruit: ~ juice *n.* Fruchtsaft, *der;* **~-knife** *n.* Obstmesser, *das*

fruitless ['fru:tlɪs] *adj. (unprofitable)* nutzlos ‹*Versuch, Gespräch*›; fruchtlos ‹*Verhandlung, Bemühung, Suche*›; **the investigation was ~:** die Untersuchung verlief ergebnislos; **it is ~ to ...:** es ist nutzlos zu ...

fruitlessly ['fru:tlɪslɪ] *adv.* umsonst ‹*versuchen, sich bemühen, suchen*›; fruchtlos, ergebnislos ‹*verhandeln, diskutieren*›

fruit: ~ machine *n. (Brit.)* Spielautomat, *der;* ~ **'salad** *n.* Obstsalat, *der;* **~ salts** *n. pl.* Magenpulver, *das;* **~-tree** *n.* Obstbaum, *der*

fruity ['fru:tɪ] *adj.* **a)** fruchtig ‹*Duft, Geschmack, Wein*›; **b)** *(coll.) (rich in tone)* volltönend ‹*Stimme*›; herzhaft ‹*Lachen*›; *(full of scandalous interest)* saftig *(ugs.)* ‹*Geschichte, Buch, Witz*›

frump [frʌmp] *n. (derog.)* Vogelscheuche, *die (ugs.)*

frumpy ['frʌmpɪ] *adj. (derog.)* ohne jeden Schick *nachgestellt*

frustrate [frʌ'streɪt, 'frʌstreɪt] *v. t.* vereiteln, durchkreuzen ‹*Plan, Vorhaben, Versuch*›; zunichte machen ‹*Hoffnung, Bemühungen*›; enttäuschen ‹*Erwartung, Hoffnung*›; **he was ~d in his attempts/efforts** seine Versuche/Bemühungen waren vergebens

frustrated [frʌ'streɪtɪd, 'frʌstreɪtɪd] *adj.* frustriert

frustrating [frʌ'streɪtɪŋ, 'frʌstreɪtɪŋ] *adj.* frustrierend; ärgerlich ‹*Angewohnheit*›; **he is a ~ person to deal with** es ist frustrierend, mit ihm zu tun zu haben

frustration [frʌ'streɪʃn] *n.* Frustration, *die; (defeat)* Enttäuschung, *die; (of plans, efforts)* Scheitern, *das*

[1]**fry** [fraɪ] **1.** *n.* **a)** Pfannengericht, *das;* **b)** *(internal parts of animals)* [gebratene] Innereien; *see also* **lamb's fry; c)** *(Amer.: social gathering)* Grillparty, *die.* **2.** *v. t.* braten; **fried eggs/potatoes** Spiegeleier/Bratkartoffeln; *see also* **fish 1 a. 3.** *v. i.* braten; *(coll.: burn)* **~ in the sun** in der Sonne schmoren *(ugs.)*

~ **'up** *v. t.* aufbraten ‹*Reste*›; **let's ~ up something** laß uns schnell was brutzeln *(ugs.); see also* **fry-up**

[2]**fry** *n. (young fishes etc.)* Brut, *die;* **'small ~** *(fig.)* unbedeutende Leute; *(children)* junges Gemüse *(ugs.);* **compared with him all the others are 'small ~** *(fig.)* im Vergleich mit ihm sind alle anderen unbedeutend

fryer ['fraɪə(r)] *n.* **a)** *(vessel)* Friteuse, *die;* **b)** *(Amer.: chicken)* Brathühnchen, *das;* Brathähnchen, *das*

frying-pan ['fraɪɪŋpæn] *n.* Bratpfanne, *die;* **[fall/jump] out of the ~ into the fire** vom Regen in die Traufe [kommen] *(ugs.)*

fry: ~pan *(Amer.) see* **frying-pan; ~-up** *n.* Pfannengericht, *das*

ft. *abbr.* **feet, foot** ft.

fuchsia ['fju:ʃə] *n. (Bot.)* Fuchsie, *die*

fuck [fʌk] *(coarse)* **1.** *v. t.* **a)** ficken *(vulg.);* **b)** *(damn)* **~ ...:** zum Teufel mit ... *(derb);* **~ you!** leck mich am Arsch! *(derb).* **2.** *v. i.* ficken *(vulg.).* **3.** *n.* **a)** *(act)* Fick, *der (vulg.);* **b)** *(person)* **be a good ~:** gut ficken *(vulg.);* **c)** *(damn)* **I don't give/care a ~:** es ist mir scheißegal *(derb)*

~ about, ~ around *(coarse)* **1.** *v. i.* rumgammeln *(ugs.);* **~ about** *or* **around with sth.** an etw. *(Dat.)* rumfummeln *(ugs.).* **2.** *v. t.* verarschen *(derb)*

~ **'off** *v. i. (coarse)* **~ off!** verpiß dich! *(salopp)*

~ **'up** *(coarse) v. t.* versauen *(derb)*

fucking ['fʌkɪŋ] *(coarse)* **1.** *adj.* Scheiß- *(salopp);* **what the ~ hell's that for?** wofür ist das denn, verdammte Scheiße? *(derb).* **2.** *adv.* verdammt *(ugs.)*

fuddle ['fʌdl] *v. t.* **a)** *(intoxicate)* benebeln ‹*Sinne*›; **they were slightly ~d** sie waren [leicht] beschwipst *od.* angesäuselt *(ugs.);* **b)** *(confuse)* verwirren

fuddy-duddy ['fʌdɪdʌdɪ] *(sl.)* **1.** *adj.* verkalkt *(ugs.).* **2.** *n.* Fossil, *das (fig.)*

[1]**fudge** [fʌdʒ] *n. (sweet)* Karamelbonbon, *der od. das;* [weiche] Karamelle, *die*

[2]**fudge 1.** *v. t.* frisieren *(ugs.)* ‹*Geschäftsbücher*›; ausweichen (+ *Dat.*) ‹*Problem*›; sich *(Dat.)* aus den Fingern saugen ‹*Ausrede, Geschichte, Entschuldigung*›. **2.** *v. i.* ausweichen. **3.** *n.* Schwindel, *der*

fuel ['fju:əl] **1.** *n.* Brennstoff, *der; (for vehicle)* Kraftstoff, *der; (for ship, aircraft, spacecraft)* Treibstoff, *der; (for cigarette-lighter)* Gas, *das; (petrol)* Benzin, *das; (Nucl. Engin.)* Kernbrennstoff, *der;* Spaltstoff, *der;* **add ~ to the flames** *or* **fire** *(fig.)* Öl ins Feuer gießen. **2.** *v. t., (Brit.)* **-ll-** heizen ‹*Ofen*›; beschicken ‹*Hochofen*›; auftanken ‹*Schiff, Flugzeug*›; betreiben ‹*Kraftwerk, Motor*›; *(fig.: stimulate)* Nahrung geben (+ *Dat.*) ‹*Verdacht, Hoffnung, Spekulationen*›; anheizen ‹*Inflation*›; fördern ‹*Entwicklung*›. **3.** *v. i., (Brit.)* **-ll-** auftanken

fuel: ~ cell *n.* Brennstoffzelle, *die;* **~ consumption** *n.* Brennstoffverbrauch, *der; (of vehicle)* Kraftstoffverbrauch, *der; (of aircraft, rocket)* Treibstoffverbrauch, *der;* **~ element** *n. (Nucl. Engin.)* Brenn[stoff]element, *das;* **~ injection** *n.* Treibstoffeinspritzung, *die; (in vehicle)* Benzineinspritzung, *die;* **~ oil** *n.* Heizöl, *das;* **~ pump** *n.* Kraftstoffpumpe, *die;* **~ tank** *n. (of motor cycle, vehicle)* Kraftstofftank, *der; (of aircraft, spacecraft)* Treibstofftank, *der; (of ship)* Treiböltank, *der; (for storage)* Kraftstoffbehälter, *der*

fug [fʌg] *n. (coll.)* Mief, *der (salopp)*

fugitive ['fju:dʒɪtɪv] **1.** *adj.* **a)** *(lit. or fig.)* flüchtig; **b)** *(flitting, shifting)* unstet ‹*Wesen, Charakter*›. **2.** *n.* **a)** Flüchtige, *der/die;* **be a ~ from justice/from the law** auf der Flucht vor der Justiz/dem Gesetz sein; **b)** *(exile)* Flüchtling, *der*

fugue [fju:g] *n. (Mus.)* Fuge, *die*

fulcrum ['fʊlkrəm] *n., pl.* **fulcra** ['fʊlkrə] **a)** *(Mech.)* Drehpunkt, *der;* **b)** *(fig.: factor)* [Dreh- und] Angelpunkt, *der*

fulfil *(Amer.:* **fulfill)** [fʊl'fɪl] *v. t.,* **-ll-** erfüllen; stillen ‹*Verlangen, Bedürfnisse*›; entsprechen (+ *Dat.*) ‹*Erwartungen*›; erhören ‹*Gebet*›; ausführen ‹*Befehl*›; beenden ‹*Arbeit, Werk*›; halten ‹*Versprechen*›; **be fulfilled** ‹*Traum:*› in Erfüllung gehen; ‹*Wunsch, Hoffnung, Prophezeiung:*› sich erfüllen; **~ oneself** sich selbst verwirklichen; **be** *or* **feel fulfilled [in one's job]** [in seinem Beruf] Erfüllung finden

fulfilling [fʊl'fɪlɪŋ] *adj. (giving satisfaction)* befriedigend

fulfilment *(Amer.:* **fulfillment)** [fʊl'fɪlmənt] *n. see* **fulfil:** Erfüllung, *die;* Erhörung, *die;* Ausführung, *die;* Beendigung, *die;* **bring sth. to ~:** etw. erfüllen; **sth. reaches ~:** etw. erfüllt sich; **find ~ in one's work** Erfüllung in seiner Arbeit finden

¹full [fʊl] **1.** *adj.* **a)** voll; **the jug is ~ of water** der Krug ist voll Wasser; **his pockets are ~ of money** er hat die Taschen voller Geld; **the bus was completely ~:** der Bus war voll besetzt; **~ of hatred/holes** voller Haß/Löcher; **my heart is too ~ for words** mir ist das Herz so voll, daß ich keine Worte finde; **be ~ up** *(coll.)* voll [besetzt] sein; ⟨*Behälter:*⟩ randvoll sein; ⟨*Liste:*⟩ voll sein; ⟨*Flug:*⟩ völlig ausgebucht sein; **b) ~ of** *(engrossed with):* **be ~ of oneself/one's own importance** sehr von sich eingenommen sein/sich sehr wichtig nehmen; **ever since this event she's been ~ of it** seit diesem Ereignis spricht sie von nichts anderem [mehr]; **the newspapers are ~ of the crisis** die Zeitungen sind voll von Berichten über die Krise; **he is ~ of his subject** er geht völlig in seinem Fachgebiet auf; **c)** *(replete with food)* voll ⟨*Magen*⟩; satt ⟨*Person*⟩; **I'm ~ [up]** *(coll.)* ich bin voll [bis obenhin] *(ugs.)*; **d)** *(comprehensive)* ausführlich, umfassend ⟨*Bericht, Beschreibung*⟩; *(abundant, satisfying)* vollwertig ⟨*Mahlzeit*⟩; erfüllt ⟨*Leben*⟩; *(complete)* geschlagen *(ugs.)*, ganz ⟨*Stunde*⟩; ganz ⟨*Jahr, Monat, Semester, Seite*⟩; voll ⟨*Gehalt, Bezahlung, Unterstützung, Mitgefühl, Verständnis*⟩; **weigh a ~ ten tons** volle zehn Tonnen wiegen; **the event received ~ TV coverage** das Fernsehen berichtete in aller Ausführlichkeit über das Ereignis; **with illustrations in ~ colour** durchgehend farbig illustriert; **the ~ details of the case** alle Einzelheiten des Falls; **in ~ daylight** am hellichten Tag; **the moon is ~:** es ist Vollmond; **in ~ bloom** in voller Blüte; **they were in ~ flight** *(fleeing)* sie flohen, so schnell sie konnten; *(impressive)* sie waren in Hochform; **this will require a ~ day's work** dazu braucht man einen ganzen Tag; **~ member** Vollmitglied, *das;* **~ membership** Vollmitgliedschaft, *die;* **in ~ possession of one's faculties** im Vollbesitz seiner Kräfte; **in ~ view of sb.** [direkt] vor jmds. Augen; **we were in ~ view of the house** wir konnten vom Haus aus ohne weiteres gesehen werden; **the ship came into ~ view** man konnte das Schiff allmählich richtig sehen; **at ~ speed** mit Höchstgeschwindigkeit; **~ speed** *or* **steam ahead!** *(lit. or fig.)* volle Kraft *od.* Volldampf voraus!; **the machine was operating at ~ capacity** die Maschine lief auf Hochtouren; **the team/cabinet was at ~ strength** die Mannschaft spielte in ihrer besten Besetzung/das Kabinett war vollzählig; **bound in ~ leather** in Ganzleder gebunden; **pay the ~ fare** voll bezahlen; den vollen Fahrpreis bezahlen; **~ name** voller Name; **~ sister/brother** leibliche Schwester/leiblicher Bruder; **e)** *(intense in quality)* hell, voll ⟨*Licht*⟩; satt ⟨*Farbe*⟩; voll ⟨*Klang, Stimme, Aroma*⟩; **f)** *(rounded, plump)* voll ⟨*Gesicht, Busen, Lippen, Mund*⟩; füllig ⟨*Figur*⟩; weit geschnitten ⟨*Rock*⟩; voll ⟨*Segel*⟩; **be ~ in the face** ein volles Gesicht haben. **2.** *n.* **a) in ~:** vollständig; **write your name [out] in ~:** schreiben Sie Ihren Namen aus; **b) satisfy sb./enjoy sth. to the ~:** jmdn. vollauf zufriedenstellen/etw. in vollen Zügen genießen; **c) the moon is at/past the ~:** es ist Vollmond/abnehmender Mond. **3.** *adv.* **a)** *(very)* **know ~ well that ...:** ganz genau *od.* sehr wohl wissen, daß ...; **b)** *(exactly, directly)* genau; voll *(ugs.)*; **~ in the face** direkt ins Gesicht ⟨*schlagen, scheinen*⟩; **look sb. ~ in the face** jmdn. voll ansehen

²full *v. t. (Textiles)* walken ⟨*Tuche*⟩

full: ~ 'age *n.* Volljährigkeit, *die;* **~ back** *n. (Sport)* Verteidiger, *der*/Verteidigerin, *die;* **~-blooded** ['fʊlblʌdɪd] *adj.* **a)** *(pure-bred)* reinrassig ⟨*Tier*⟩; reinblütig ⟨*Mensch*⟩; **b)** *(vigorous, hearty, sensual)* vollblütig; **~-blown** *adj.* **a)** *(at height of bloom)* voll aufgeblüht; **b)** *(fig.)* ausgewachsen ⟨*Skandal*⟩; ausgereift ⟨*Theorie, Plan, Gedanke*⟩; umfassend ⟨*Bericht*⟩; **~ 'board** *n.* Vollpension, *die;* **~-bodied** *adj.* vollmundig, *(fachspr.)* körperreich ⟨*Wein*⟩; voll ⟨*Ton, Klang*⟩; **~-cream** *adj.* **~-cream milk/cheese** Vollmilch, *die*/Vollfettkäse, *der;* **~ 'dress** *n.* Gesellschaftsanzug, *der;* **~-dress** *adj.* Gala⟨*uniform, -diner*⟩; *(fig.)* großangelegt; **~-dress occasion** feierliche Veranstaltung; **~ em'ployment** *n.* Vollbeschäftigung, *die*

fuller's earth [fʊləz 'ɜːθ] *n. (Min.)* Fullererde, *die;* Walkerde, *die*

full: ~ 'face *n. (Art, Photog.)* **in ~ face** en face; **~-face 1.** *adv. (Art, Photog.)* en face; **2.** *adj.* **a)** *(Art, Photog.)* En-face-; **b) ~-face helmet** Integralhelm, *der;* **~-faced** *adj.* mit vollem Gesicht *nachgestellt;* **~-grown** *adj.* ausgewachsen ⟨*Mensch, Tier*⟩; **~ 'house** *n.* **a)** *(Theatre)* ausverkauftes *od.* volles Haus; **play to ~ houses every night** jeden Abend vor ausverkauftem Haus spielen; **b)** *(Poker)* Full house, *das; (Bingo)* Voll, *das;* **~ 'length 1.** *n.* **at ~ length** *(in ~ detail)* in aller Ausführlichkeit; *(unabridged)* ungekürzt; **[stretched out] at ~ length** der Länge nach *od. (ugs.)* längelang ausgestreckt; **2.** *adv.* längelang *(ugs.)*, der Länge nach ⟨*hinfallen, liegen*⟩; **~-length** *adj.* abendfüllend ⟨*Film, Theaterstück*⟩; **~-length novel** größerer Roman; **~-length mirror** großer Spiegel *(in dem man sich ganz sehen kann);* **~-length portrait** Ganzporträt, *das;* **~-length dress** langes Kleid; **~ 'marks** *n. pl., no art.* die höchste Bewertung; *(Sch., Univ.)* die besten Noten; **~ marks!** *(fig. coll.)* ausgezeichnet!; **you get ~ marks for observation** das hast du ausgezeichnet beobachtet; **give sb. ~ marks** *(fig.)* jmdm. höchstes Lob zollen; **~ 'moon** *n.* Vollmond, *der*

fullness ['fʊlnɪs] *n., no pl. (of skirt)* weiter Schnitt; *(of figure)* Fülligkeit, *die; (of face)* Rundheit, *die;* **a feeling of ~:** ein Völlegefühl; **in the ~ of time** *(literary)* wenn die Zeit dafür gekommen ist/als die Zeit dafür gekommen war

full: ~-page *adj.* ganzseitig; **~ pitch** *see* **~ toss;** **~ 'play** *n.* **give sth. ~ play** einer Sache *(Dat.)* freien Lauf lassen; **give sb. ~ play** jmdm. völlig freie Hand lassen; **~ 'point** *n.* Punkt, *der;* **~ pro'fessor** *n.* ordentlicher Professor; **~-scale** *adj.* **a)** in Originalgröße *nachgestellt;* **b)** großangelegt ⟨*Werbekampagne, Untersuchung, Suchaktion*⟩; umfassend ⟨*Umarbeitung, Revision*⟩; **a ~-scale war/novel** ein richtiger Krieg/größerer Roman; **~ 'score** *n. (Mus.)* Partitur, *die;* **~-size** *see* **-size;** **~ 'stop** *n.* **a)** Punkt, *der;* **b)** *(fig. coll.)* **come to a ~ stop** zum Stillstand kommen; **I'm not going, ~ stop** ich gehe nicht, [und damit] basta! *(ugs.)*; **~ 'time 1.** *adv.* ganztags ⟨*arbeiten*⟩; **2.** *n. (Sport)* Spielende, *das;* **~-time** *adj.* ganztägig; Ganztags⟨*arbeit, -beschäftigung*⟩; **sb. is ~-time** jmd. arbeitet ganztags; **~-time teacher** Lehrer mit vollem Deputat; **this is a ~-time job** *(fig.)* das hält einen den ganzen Tag auf Trab *(ugs.)*; **~-'timer** *n.* Ganztagsbeschäftigte, *der/die;* **become a ~-timer** anfangen, ganztags zu arbeiten; **~ 'toss** *(Cricket) n. Ball, der den Schlagmann erreicht, ohne den Boden zu berühren*

fully ['fʊlɪ] *adv.* **a)** voll [und ganz]; fest ⟨*entschlossen*⟩; reich ⟨*belohnt*⟩; ausführlich ⟨*erklären usw.*⟩; **~ convinced** restlos überzeugt; **b)** *(at least)* **~ two hours** volle zwei Stunden; **~ three weeks ago** vor gut drei Wochen

fully: ~-fledged *attrib. adj.* flügge ⟨*Vogel*⟩; *(fig.)* [ganz] selbständig; **~-qualified** *attrib. adj.* vollqualifiziert

fulmar ['fʊlmə(r)] *n. (Ornith.)* Eissturmvogel, *der*

fulminate ['fʌlmɪneɪt] *v. i. (protest)* **~ against sb./sth.** gegen jmdn./etw. Sturm laufen

fulsome ['fʊlsəm] *adj.* übertrieben, *(ugs. abwertend)* dick aufgetragen ⟨*Lob, Kompliment, Schmeichelei*⟩

fulsomely ['fʊlsəmlɪ] *adv.* übertrieben ⟨*loben, schmeicheln*⟩

fumble ['fʌmbl] **1.** *v. i.* **~ at** *or* **with** [herum]fingern an (+ *Dat.*); **~ with one's papers** in seinen Papieren kramen *(ugs.)*; **~ in one's pockets for sth.** in seinen Taschen nach etw. fingern *od. (ugs.)* kramen; **~ for the light-switch** nach dem Lichtschalter tasten; **~ [about** *or* **around] in the dark** im Dunkeln herumtasten; **~ [about] for the right words** *(fig.)* nach den richtigen Worten suchen. **2.** *v. t.* **a)** nesteln an (+ *Dat.*); **b)** *(Games)* nicht sicher fangen ⟨*Ball*⟩

fume [fjuːm] **1.** *n.* **a)** *in pl.* **petrol/ammonia ~s** Benzin-/Ammoniakdämpfe; **~s of wine/whisky** Alkohol-/Whiskydunst, *der;* **[cigarette/cigar] ~s** [Zigaretten-/Zigarren]rauch, *der;* **b)** *(fit of anger);* **be in a ~:** vor Wut schäumen. **2.** *v. i.* **a)** ⟨*Feuer, Ofen:*⟩ rauchen; **b)** *(be angry)* vor Wut schäumen; **~ at** *or* **over sb.** auf *od.* über jmdn. wütend sein; **~ at** *or* **over** *or* **about sth.** wegen etw. wütend sein. **3.** *v. t.* **~d oak** geräuchertes Eichenholz *(Holzverarb.)*

fumigate ['fjuːmɪgeɪt] *v. t.* **a)** ausräuchern; **b)** *(apply fumes to)* begasen ⟨*Pflanzen*⟩

fumigation [fjuːmɪ'geɪʃn] *n. see* **fumigate:** Ausräucherung, *die;* Begasung, *die*

fun [fʌn] **1.** *n.* Spaß, *der;* **be half the ~:** [mit] das Schönste sein; **have ~ doing sth.** Spaß daran haben, etw. zu tun; **I/we had great ~ playing with the dog** es hat [mir/uns] viel Spaß gemacht, mit dem Hund zu spielen; **have ~!** viel Spaß!; **[are you] having ~?** *(iron.)* macht Spaß, was? *(ugs. iron.)*; **we'll have great ~:** es wird bestimmt sehr lustig; **I was just having a bit of ~:** ich habe nur Spaß gemacht; **be full of ~:** ein fröhliches Wesen haben; ⟨*Tier:*⟩ sehr verspielt sein; **make ~ of** *or* **poke ~ at sb./sth.** sich über jmdn./etw. lustig machen; **in ~:** im Spaß; **the things he said were only in ~:** was er gesagt hat, war nur Spaß; **for ~, for the ~ of it** zum Spaß; **what ~!** toll!; wie schön!; **spoil the** *or* **sb.'s ~:** jmdm. den Spaß verderben; **sounds like ~!** das wird sicher toll werden!; **like ~** *(very much)* wie verrückt *(salopp); (iron.: not at all)* von wegen!; **sth. is [good** *or* **great/no] ~:** etw. macht [großen/keinen] Spaß; **he is [good** *or* **great] ~ to have at a party** eine Party mit ihm ist immer sehr lustig; **sb. is [great] ~/no ~ to be with** es macht [großen] Spaß/keinen Spaß, mit jmdm. zusammenzusein; **it's no ~ being unemployed** es ist kein Vergnügen, arbeitslos zu sein; **~ and games** *(coll.)* Vergnügungen; **we had the usual ~ and games with him** *(iron.: trouble)* wir hatten wieder das übliche Theater mit ihm *(ugs.)*; **enjoy** *or* **have the ~ of the fair** *(fig.)* sich vergnügen; *see also* **figure 1d. 2.** *adj. (coll.)* lustig; amüsant; **have a ~ time at a party** sich auf einer Party gut amüsieren

function ['fʌŋkʃn] **1.** *n.* **a)** *(role)* Aufgabe, *die;* **in his ~ as surgeon** in seiner Funktion *od.* Eigenschaft als Chirurg; **b)** *(mode of action)* Funktion, *die;* **c)** *(formal event)* Veranstaltung, *die; (reception)* Empfang, *der; (official ceremony)* Feierlichkeit, *die;* **d)** *(Math.)* Funktion, *die.* **2.** *v.i.* ⟨*Maschine, System, Organisation:*⟩ funktionieren; ⟨*Organ:*⟩ arbeiten; **~ as** *(have the ~ of)* fungieren als; *(serve as)* dienen als; **I just don't ~ early in the morning** *(coll.)* am frühen Morgen bin ich zu nichts zu gebrauchen

functional ['fʌŋkʃənl] *adj.* **a)** *(useful, practical)* funktionell; funktional ⟨*Erziehung*⟩; **~ building** Zweckbau, *der;* **b)** *(working)* funktionsfähig; **be ~ again** wieder funktionieren; **c)** *(Physiol.)* **~ disease** Funktionsstörung eines Organs

functionalism ['fʌŋkʃənəlɪzm] *n.* Funktionalismus, *der*

functionally ['fʌŋkʃənəlɪ] *adv.* funktionell
functionary ['fʌŋkʃənərɪ] *n.* Funktionär, *der*/Funktionärin, *die*
fund [fʌnd] **1.** *n.* **a)** *(collection of money)* Fonds, *der;* **b)** *(fig.: stock, store)* Fundus, *der* (**of** von, an + *Dat.*); **c)** *in pl. (resources)* Mittel *Pl.;* Gelder *Pl.;* **public ~s** öffentliche Mittel; **be in ~s** bei Kasse sein *(ugs.);* **be pressed for** *or* **short of ~s** knapp *od.* schlecht bei Kasse sein *(ugs.).* **2.** *v. t.* **a)** finanzieren; **b)** *(invest)* anlegen; investieren
fundamental [fʌndə'mentl] **1.** *adj.* **a)** grundlegend (**to** für); fundamental, grundlegend ‹*Unterschied, Bedeutung, Bestandteil*›; elementar ‹*Bedürfnisse*›; *(primary, original)* Grund‹*struktur, -form, -typus*›; **b)** *(Mus.)* **~ note** Grundton, *der; (Acoustics)* **~ tone** Grundton, *der.* **2.** *n.* **a)** *in pl.* Grundlage, *die;* Fundament, *das;* **b)** *(Mus.) (note)* Grundton, *der; (tone)* Fundamentalbaß, *der*
fundamentalism [fʌndə'mentəlɪzm] *n.* Fundamentalismus, *der*
fundamentalist [fʌndə'mentəlɪst] *n.* Fundamentalist, *der*/Fundamentalistin, *die*
fundamentally [fʌndə'mentəlɪ] *adv.* grundlegend; von Grund auf ‹*verschieden, ehrlich*›; völlig ‹*abhängig*›; **I am ~ opposed to this** ich bin grundsätzlich dagegen; **man is ~ good/evil** der Mensch ist von Natur aus gut/böse
fundamental 'particle *see* **elementary particle**
funeral ['fju:nərl] *n.* **a)** Beerdigung, *die;* Beisetzung, *die (geh.);* **b)** *(procession)* Leichenzug, *der (geh.);* Trauerzug, *der;* **c)** *attrib.* **~ director** Bestattungsunternehmer, *der;* **~ home** *(Amer.) or* **parlour** Bestattungsunternehmen, *das;* **~ march** Trauermarsch, *der;* **~ procession** Leichenzug, *der (geh.)* Trauerzug, *der;* **~ service** Trauerfeier, *die;* **~ pile** *or* **pyre** Scheiterhaufen, *der;* **~ expenses** Bestattungskosten *Pl.;* **d)** *(sl.: one's concern)* **that's his/not my ~:** das ist sein/ nicht mein Problem; **e)** *(Amer.: service)* Trauerfeier, *die;* **preach sb.'s ~:** die Trauerfeier für jmdn. abhalten
funereal [fju:'nɪərɪəl] *adj.* **a)** *(of funeral)* Trauer-; **b)** *(gloomy)* düster; **~ voice** Grabesstimme, *die (ugs.);* **~ expression** Trauermiene, *die (ugs.);* trauervolle Miene; **~ pace** Geschwindigkeit eines Trauerzuges
'fun-fair *n. (Brit.)* Jahrmarkt, *der*
fungal ['fʌŋgl] *see* **fungous**
fungicide ['fʌndʒɪsaɪd] *n. (Hort.)* Fungizid, *das; (Pharm.)* Antimykotikum, *das*
fungous ['fʌŋgəs] *adj.* pilzartig; *(Med.)* Hautpilz-; **~ infection** Pilzinfektion, *die*
fungus ['fʌŋgəs] *n., pl.* **fungi** ['fʌŋgaɪ, 'fʌndʒaɪ] *or* **~es a)** Pilz, *der;* **b)** *(Med.)* Hautpilz, *der;* **c)** *(disease of fish)* Fischschimmel, *der;* **d)** *(sl.: beard)* **[face-] ~:** Sauerkohl, *der (salopp scherzh.)*
funicular [railway] [fju:'nɪkjʊlə(r) (reɪlweɪ)] *n.* [Stand]seilbahn, *die*
funk [fʌŋk] *(sl.)* **1.** *n.* Bammel, *der (salopp);* Schiß, *der (salopp);* **be in/go into a [blue] ~:** [mächtig] Bammel *od.* Schiß haben/kriegen *(salopp);* **put sb. in a [blue] ~:** jmdm. Angst einjagen. **2.** *v. t.* kneifen vor (+ *Dat.*) *(ugs.);* **he ~ed it** er hat gekniffen *(ugs.)*
funky ['fʌŋkɪ] *adj. (sl.)* irre *(salopp)* ‹*Musik*›
'fun-loving *adj.* lebenslustig
funnel ['fʌnl] **1.** *n.* **a)** *(cone)* Trichter, *der;* **b)** *(of ship etc.)* Schornstein, *der.* **2.** *v. t., (Brit.)* **-ll-** konzentrieren ‹*Aufmerksamkeit, Anstrengung, Bemühungen*›; schleusen ‹*Daten, Verkehr*›; lenken ‹*Verkehr*›. **3.** *v. i., (Brit.)* **-ll-** strömen
funnily ['fʌnɪlɪ] *adv.* komisch; **~ enough** komischerweise *(ugs.)*
funny ['fʌnɪ] **1.** *adj.* **a)** *(comical)* komisch; lustig; witzig ‹*Mensch, Einfall, Bemerkung*›; **are you being** *or* **trying to be ~?** das soll wohl ein Witz sein?; **b)** *(strange)* komisch; seltsam; **don't get any ~ ideas** *(coll.)* komm bloß nicht auf komische Gedanken! *(ugs.);* **be ~ about money** in Gelddingen komisch *od.* eigen sein; **that's ~, he's gone** komisch, er ist weg; **the ~ thing 'is that ...:** das Komische [daran] ist, daß ...; **have a ~ feeling that ...:** das komische Gefühl haben, daß ...; **there's something ~ going on here** hier ist doch was faul *(ugs.);* **c)** *(coll.: unwell)* **I feel ~:** mir ist komisch *od. (ugs.)* blümerant; **he's a bit ~ in the head** er ist nicht ganz richtig im Kopf *(ugs.).* **2.** *n. (coll.)* **a)** *in pl. (comic section)* Comicseite, *die;* **b)** *(joke)* Witz, *der*
funny: ~-bone *n. (Anat.)* Musikantenknochen, *der;* **~ business** *n.* **a)** *(comic behaviour)* Alberei, *die;* **b)** *(sl.: misbehaviour, deception)* krumme Touren *(ugs.);* **~-face** *n. (joc./coll.)* Krümel, *der (fam.);* **~-ha-'ha** *adj. (coll.)* [zum Lachen] komisch; **~ man** *n.* Komiker, *der;* **~-pe'culiar** *adj. (coll.)* seltsam
fur [fɜ:(r)] **1.** *n.* **a)** *(coat of animal)* Fell, *das; (for or as garment)* Pelz, *der;* **trimmed/lined with ~:** mit Pelz besetzt *od.* verbrämt/gefüttert; **make the ~ fly** *(fig.)* hohe Wellen schlagen; *attrib.* **~ coat/hat** Pelzmantel, *der*/-mütze, *die;* **~ rug** Fell, *das (als Vorleger);* **b)** *(coating)* Belag, *der; (formed by hard water)* Wasserstein, *der; (in kettle)* Kesselstein, *der.* **2.** *v. t.,* **-rr-: hard water will ~ [up] the kettle/pipes** bei hartem Wasser bildet sich Kesselstein im Kessel/Wasserstein in den Rohren. **3.** *v. i.,* **-rr-: the kettle has/pipes have ~red [up]** im Kessel hat sich Kesselstein/in den Rohren hat sich Wasserstein gebildet
furbelow ['fɜ:bɪləʊ] *n.* **frills and ~s** *(lit. or fig.)* Kinkerlitzchen *Pl. (ugs. abwertend)*
furbish ['fɜ:bɪʃ] *v. t.* blank reiben; polieren
'fur-clad *adj.* in Pelz gekleidet
furious ['fjʊərɪəs] *adj.* wütend; heftig ‹*Streit, Kampf, Sturm, Lärm*›; wild ‹*Tanz, Sturm, Tempo, Kampf*›; **be ~ with sb./at sth.** wütend auf jmdn./über etw. *(Akk.)* sein; **the fun was fast and ~:** der Spaß war in vollem Gange
furiously ['fjʊərɪəslɪ] *adv.* wütend; wild ‹*kämpfen, tanzen*›; wie wild *(ugs.)* ‹*arbeiten, in die Pedale treten*›; heftig ‹*erröten, kämpfen*›
furl [fɜ:l] *v. t.* einrollen ‹*Segel, Flagge*›; zusammenrollen ‹*Schirm*›
furlong ['fɜ:lɒŋ] *n.* Achtelmeile, *die*
furlough ['fɜ:ləʊ] *n. (Mil.)* Urlaub, *der;* **be/go on ~:** Urlaub haben/in Urlaub gehen
furnace ['fɜ:nɪs] *n.* Ofen, *der; (blast-~)* Hochofen, *der; (smelting-~)* Schmelzofen, *der; (pottery-kiln)* Brennofen, *der;* **this room is like a ~:** hier ist eine Hitze wie im Treibhaus *od.* Backofen
furnish ['fɜ:nɪʃ] *v. t.* **a)** möblieren; **live in ~ed accommodation** möbliert wohnen; **~ing fabrics** Möbel- und Vorhangstoffe; **b)** *(provide, supply)* liefern ‹*Vorräte*›; **~ sb. with sth.** jmdm. etw. liefern; **the army was ~ed with supplies** die Armee wurde mit Vorräten versorgt *od.* beliefert
furnishings ['fɜ:nɪʃɪŋz] *n. pl.* Einrichtungsgegenstände; **including ~ and fittings** mit kompletter Einrichtung
furniture ['fɜ:nɪtʃə(r)] *n., no pl.* Möbel *Pl.;* **piece of ~:** Möbel[stück], *das;* **the house has hardly any ~:** das Haus ist kaum eingerichtet; **a bed and a chair were all the ~:** ein Bett und ein Stuhl waren das ganze Mobiliar; **be [a] part of the ~** *(fig. coll.)* zum lebenden Inventar gehören *(scherzh.)*
furniture: ~ beetle *n.* Totenuhr, *die;* **~ polish** *n.* Möbelpolitur, *die;* **~ van** *n.* Möbelwagen, *der*
furore [fjʊə'rɔ:rɪ] *(Amer.:* **furor** ['fjʊərɔ:(r)]) *n.* **create** *or* **cause a ~:** Furore machen; *(cause a scandal)* einen Skandal verursachen; **when the ~ died down** als allmählich Gras über die Sache gewachsen war
furred [fɜ:d] *adj. (Med.)* belegt ‹*Zunge*›
furrier ['fʌrɪə(r)] *n. (dresser)* Kürschner, *der*/Kürschnerin, *die; (dealer)* Pelzhändler, *der*/-händlerin, *die*
furrow ['fʌrəʊ] **1.** *n. (lit. or fig.)* Furche, *die;* **cut a ~ through the waves** ‹*Schiff:*› die Wellen durchpflügen; *see also* **plough 2 c. 2.** *v. t.* **a)** *(plough)* pflügen; **b)** *(make ~s in)* durchpflügen; **c)** *(mark with wrinkles)* **~ed face** zerfurchtes Gesicht
furry ['fɜ:rɪ] *adj.* haarig; flauschig ‹*Mantel, Stofftier*›; belegt ‹*Zunge*›; **it has a ~ feel** es fühlt sich weich und flauschig an
further ['fɜ:ðə(r)] **1.** *adj. compar. of* **far: a)** *(of two)* ander...; *(in space)* weiter entfernt; **on the ~ bank of the river/side of town** am anderen Ufer/Ende der Stadt; **b)** *(additional)* weiter...; **till ~ notice/orders** bis auf weiteres; **I could eat this until ~ orders** *(fig. joc.)* ich könnte das bis in alle Ewigkeit essen *(ugs.);* **will there be anything ~?** darf es noch etwas sein?; haben Sie sonst noch einen Wunsch?; **~ details** *or* **particulars** weitere *od.* nähere Einzelheiten. **2.** *adv. compar. of* **far: a)** weiter; **before it goes any ~:** bevor es sich weiter ausbreitet; **not let it go any ~:** es nicht weitersagen; **one could go ~ and fare worse** es gibt Schlimmeres; **he never got ~ than secondary school** er ist über die Hauptschule nicht hinausgekommen; **until you hear ~ from us** bis Sie wieder von uns hören; **nothing was ~ from his thoughts** nichts lag ihm ferner; **b)** *(moreover)* außerdem; **c)** *(euphem.: in hell)* **I'll see you/him** *etc.* **~ first!** ich denke nicht im Traum daran! **3.** *v. t.* fördern; **in order to ~ one's career** um beruflich voranzukommen
furtherance ['fɜ:ðərəns] *n., no pl.* Förderung, *die;* Unterstützung, *die;* **in ~ of sth.** zur Förderung *od.* Unterstützung einer Sache *(Gen.)*
further edu'cation *n.* Weiterbildung, *die; (for adults also)* Erwachsenenbildung, *die*
furthermore [fɜ:ðə'mɔ:(r)] *adv.* außerdem; überdies
furthermost ['fɜ:ðəməʊst] *adj.* äußerst...; entlegenst...; **to the ~ ends of the earth** bis ans Ende der Welt
furthest ['fɜ:ðɪst] **1.** *adj. superl. of* **far** am weitesten entfernt; **take sb. to ~ Siberia** jmdn. ins hinterste Sibirien bringen; **to the ~ limits of the kingdom** bis in die entlegensten *od.* entferntesten Winkel des Königreichs; **ten miles at the ~:** höchstens zehn Meilen. **2.** *adv. superl. of* **far** am weitesten ‹*springen, laufen*›; am weitesten entfernt ‹*sein, wohnen*›
furtive ['fɜ:tɪv] *adj.* verstohlen; **the fox is ~ in its movements** der Fuchs bewegt sich unauffällig; **he is a ~ person** er wirkt schuldbewußt und bemüht, nicht aufzufallen
furtively ['fɜ:tɪvlɪ] *adv.* verstohlen
fury ['fjʊərɪ] *n.* **a)** Wut, *die; (of storm, sea, battle, war)* Wüten, *das;* **in a ~:** wütend; **in a terrible ~:** in heller Wut; **in a blind ~:** blindwütig; **fly into a/be in a ~:** einen Wutanfall bekommen/haben; **exposed to the ~ of the elements** dem Wüten der Elemente ausgeliefert; **b) like ~** *(coll.)* wie wild *(ugs.);* **c) Furies** *(Mythol.)* Furien; **[avenging] furies** Rachegeister
furze [fɜ:z] *n. (Brit. Bot.)* Stechginster, *der*
¹fuse [fju:z] **1.** *v. t.* **a)** *(blend)* verschmelzen (**into** zu); **b)** *(melt)* schmelzen. **2.** *v. i.* **a)** *(blend)* **~ together** miteinander verschmelzen; **~ with sth.** *(fig.)* sich mit etw. verbinden; **b)** *(melt)* schmelzen
²fuse 1. *n.* **[time-]~:** [Zeit]zünder, *der; (cord)* Zündschnur, *die;* **be on a short ~** *(fig.)* leicht explodieren *(fig.).* **2.** *v. t.* **~ a bomb** *etc.* einen Zünder an einer Bombe *usw.* anbringen
³fuse *(Electr.)* **1.** *n.* Sicherung, *die.* **2.** *v. t.* **a) ~ the lights** die Sicherung [für die Lampen] durchbrennen lassen; **b)** *(provide with ~)*

mit einer Sicherung versehen; absichern. **3.** *v.i.* **the lights have ~d** die Sicherung [für die Lampen] ist durchgebrannt

'fuse-box *n. (Electr.)* Sicherungskasten, *der*

fuselage ['fju:zəlɑ:ʒ] *n. (Aeronaut.)* [Flugzeug]rumpf, *der*

fusible ['fju:zɪbl] *adj.* schmelzbar

fusillade [fju:zɪ'leɪd] *n.* Gewehrfeuer, *das*

fusion ['fju:ʒn] *n.* **a)** *(blending)* Verschmelzung, *die; (fig.) (of political groups, enterprises)* Verbindung, *die;* Fusion, *die; (of ideas, ideologies, races)* Verschmelzung, *die;* **b)** *(melting)* Schmelzen, *das;* **c)** *(Phys.)* Fusion, *die*

fuss [fʌs] **1.** *n.* Theater, *das (ugs.);* **stop this silly ~:** hör mit dem Theater auf! *(ugs.);* **~ and bother** Rummel, *der (ugs.);* **without any ~:** ohne großes Theater *(ugs.);* **kick up a ~:** ein großes Theater machen; **make a ~ [about sth.]** Aufhebens [von etw.] *od.* einen Wirbel [um etw.] machen; **make a ~ of** *or* **over** [einen] Wirbel machen um ⟨*Person, Tier*⟩; **he is made a ~ of** um ihn wird Wirbel gemacht. **2.** *v.i.* Wirbel machen; *(get agitated)* sich [unnötig] aufregen; **she is always ~ing over sb./sth.** sie macht immer ein Theater mit jmdm./etw. *(ugs.).* **3.** *v.t.* **don't ~ me!** mach mich nicht verrückt! *(ugs.)*

fussily ['fʌsɪlɪ] *adv.* **a)** *(bustlingly)* übereifrig; rührig; **b)** *(fastidiously)* mäklig *(ugs.);* **c)** *(with undue detail)* überladen

'fuss-pot *n. (coll.)* **be a ~:** Theater machen *(ugs.);* **don't be a ~:** mach kein Theater! *(ugs.)*

fussy ['fʌsɪ] *adj.* **a)** *(bustling)* übereifrig; rührig; *(easily flustered)* reizbar; überempfindlich; **don't be so ~!** mach nicht so ein Theater! *(ugs.);* **b)** *(fastidious)* eigen; penibel; **be ~ about one's food** *or* **what one eats** mäklig im Essen sein *(ugs.);* **I'm not ~** *(in answer: I don't mind)* ich bin nicht wählerisch; **c)** *(full of undue detail)* überladen; *(full of unnecessary decoration)* verspielt

fusty ['fʌstɪ] *adj.* **a)** *(mouldy)* schimmelig; **b)** *(stuffy)* muffig; **c)** *(old-fashioned)* verstaubt

futile ['fju:taɪl] *adj.* vergeblich ⟨*Versuch, Bemühungen, Vorschlag usw.*⟩; zum Scheitern verurteilt ⟨*Plan, Vorgehen usw.*⟩

futilely ['fju:taɪllɪ] *adv.* vergeblich

futility [fju:'tɪlɪtɪ] *n., no pl. (of effort, attempt, etc.)* Vergeblichkeit, *die; (of plan)* Zwecklosigkeit, *die; (of war)* Sinnlosigkeit, *die*

futon ['fu:tɒn] *n.* Futon, *der*

future ['fju:tʃə(r)] **1.** *adj.* **a)** [zu]künftig; **at some ~ date** zu einem späteren Zeitpunkt; **b)** *(Ling.)* futurisch; **~ tense** Futur, *das;* Zukunft, *die; see also* **perfect 1 h; c) the ~ life** das Leben im Jenseits; das Leben nach dem Tod. **2.** *n.* **a)** Zukunft, *die;* **sth. is a thing of the ~:** etw. ist Zukunftsmusik; **what will her ~ be?** wie wird ihre Zukunft aussehen?; **a man with a ~:** ein Mann mit Zukunft; **in ~:** in Zukunft; künftig; **in the distant ~:** in ferner Zukunft; **sth. is still very much in the ~:** etw. liegt noch in weiter Ferne; **see sb. in the near ~:** jmdn. demnächst sehen; **there's no/little ~ in it** das hat keine/wenig Zukunft; **b)** *(Ling.)* Futur, *das;* Zukunft, *die;* **c)** *in pl. (Commerc.)* Terminware, *die; (contracts)* Lieferungsverträge

future 'shock *n.* Zukunftsschock, *der*

futurism ['fju:tʃərɪzm] *n.* Futurismus, *der*

futuristic [fju:tʃə'rɪstɪk] *adj.* futuristisch

futurology [fju:tʃə'rɒlədʒɪ] *n.* Futurologie, *die*

fuze *(Amer.) see* [2]**fuse**

fuzz [fʌz] *n.* **a)** *(fluff)* Flaum, *der;* **b)** *(frizzy hair)* Kraushaar, *das;* **a ~ of black curls** schwarzes Kraushaar; **c)** *no pl. (sl.) (police)* Polente, *die (salopp); (policeman)* Polyp, *der (salopp)*

fuzzy ['fʌzɪ] *adj.* **a)** *(like fuzz)* flaumig; **b)** *(frizzy)* kraus; wuschelig *(ugs.);* **c)** *(blurred)* verschwommen; unscharf

fuzzy-wuzzy ['fʌzɪwʌzɪ] *n. (sl. derog.)* Krauskopf, *der*

G

G, g [dʒi:] *n., pl.* **Gs** *or* **G's a)** *(letter)* G, g, *das;* **b) G** *(Mus.)* G, g, *das;* **G sharp** gis, Gis, *das;* **G flat** ges, Ges, *das*

g. *abbr.* **a) gram[s]** g; **b) gravity** *g*

gab [gæb] *(coll.)* **1.** *n.* Gequatsche, *das (ugs. abwertend);* **have the gift of the ~:** reden können. **2.** *v.i.,* **-bb-** quatschen *(salopp)*

gabardine ['gæbədi:n] *n.* Gabardine, *der;* **~ [coat/suit]** Gabardinemantel/-anzug, *der*

gabble ['gæbl] **1.** *v.i. (inarticulately)* brabbeln *(ugs.); (volubly)* schnattern *(fig.).* **2.** *v.t.* herunterschnurren *(salopp)* ⟨*Gebet, Gedicht*⟩; herunterhaspeln *(ugs.)* ⟨*Entschuldigung*⟩. **3.** *n.* Gebrabbel, *das (ugs.)*

gable ['geɪbl] *n.* **a)** Giebel, *der;* **b)** *see* **gable-end**

gabled ['geɪbld] *adj.* gegiebelt; Giebel⟨*dach, -haus*⟩

'gable-end *n.* Giebelseite, *die*

Gabon [gə'bɒn] *pr. n.* Gabun *(das)*

[1]**gad** [gæd] *int.* **[by] ~!** bei Gott!

[2]**gad** *v.i.,* **-dd-** *(coll.)* **~ about** *or* **around** herumziehen; sich herumtreiben *(ugs. abwertend);* **~ about** *or* **around the country** im Land herumreisen

'gadabout *(coll.) n.* Herumtreiber, *der/*-treiberin, *die (ugs. abwertend)*

'gadfly *n.* Bremse, *die*

gadget ['gædʒɪt] *n.* Gerät, *das; (larger)* Apparat, *der;* **~s** *(derog.: knick-knack)* [technischer] Krimskrams *(ugs.)*

gadgetry ['gædʒɪtrɪ] *n., no pl.* [hochtechnisierte] Ausstattung

Gael [geɪl] *n.* Gäle, *der*/Gälin, *die*

Gaelic ['geɪlɪk, 'gælɪk] **1.** *adj.* gälisch; *see also* **English 1. 2.** *n.* Gälisch, *das; see also* **English 2 a**

Gaelic 'coffee *n.* Irish coffee, *der*

[1]**gaff** [gæf] **1.** *n.* **a)** *(Fishing)* Speer, *der; (stick with iron hook)* Gaff, *das;* **b)** *(Naut.)* Gaffel, *die.* **2.** *v.t.* mit dem Speer/Gaff erlegen

[2]**gaff** *n. (sl.)* **blow the ~:** plaudern (on über + *Akk.*); **I'm not going to blow the ~:** ich werde dichthalten *(ugs.);* **stand the ~** *(Amer.)* durchhalten; **stand the ~ for sth.** etw. büßen

gaffe [gæf] *n.* Fauxpas, *der;* Fehler, *der;* **make** *or* **commit a ~:** einen Fauxpas begehen; ins Fettnäpfchen treten *(ugs. scherzh.)*

gaffer ['gæfə(r)] *n. (coll.)* **a)** *(old fellow)* Alte, *der;* **some old ~:** so'n alter Typ *(ugs.);* **b)** *(Brit.: foreman)* Vorarbeiter, *der*

gag [gæg] **1.** *n.* **a)** Knebel, *der; (Med.)* Mundsperrer, *der;* **b)** *(joke)* Gag, *der.* **2.** *v.t.,* **-gg-: a) ~ sb.** jmdn. knebeln; *(Med.)* jmdm. einen Mundsperrer anlegen; *(fig.: silence sb.)* jmdn. zum Schweigen bringen; **b)** *(cause to choke or retch)* **~ sb.** jmdn. würgen. **3.** *v.i.,* **-gg-: a)** Späße machen; witzeln; **b)** *(choke, retch)* würgen

gaga ['gɑ:gɑ:] *adj. (sl.)* übergeschnappt *(ugs.); (senile)* senil, *(ugs.)* verkalkt; **be [a bit] ~:** nicht mehr ganz dicht sein *(ugs.);* **go ~:** überschnappen *(ugs.); (become senile)* senil werden, *(ugs.)* verkalken; **she is really ~ about him** sie ist total vernarrt in ihn *(ugs.)*

gage *(Amer./Naut.) see* **gauge**

gaggle ['gægl] *n.* **a) ~ [of geese]** Schar [Gänse], *die;* **b)** *(fig.: disorderly group)* Schwarm, *der;* Pulk, *der*

gaiety ['geɪətɪ] *n., no pl.* **a)** Fröhlichkeit, *die;* **b)** *(merry-making)* Festivität, *die;* Vergnügung, *die*

gaily ['geɪlɪ] *adv.* **a)** *(merrily)* fröhlich; **b)** *(brightly, showily)* in leuchtenden Farben ⟨*gekleidet, bemalt, geschmückt*⟩; **~ coloured** farbenfroh; **c)** *(airily, without thinking)* fröhlich; unbekümmert

gain [geɪn] **1.** *n.* **a)** Gewinn, *der;* **be to sb.'s ~:** für jmdn. von Vorteil sein; **ill-gotten ~s** unrechtmäßig erworbener Besitz; *see also* **capital gain; b)** *(increase)* Zunahme, *die* **(in** an + *Dat.*); **a ~ of ten kilograms in weight** eine Gewichtszunahme von zehn Kilogramm; **a ~ in efficiency/value** eine Effektivitäts-/Wertsteigerung; **c)** *(Electronics)* Verstärkung, *die.* **2.** *v.t.* **a)** *(obtain)* gewinnen; finden ⟨*Zugang, Zutritt*⟩; sich *(Dat.)* schaffen ⟨*Feind*⟩; erwerben ⟨*Wissen, Ruf*⟩; erlangen ⟨*Freiheit, Ruhm*⟩; erzielen ⟨*Vorteil, Punkte*⟩; verdienen ⟨*Lebensunterhalt, Geldsumme*⟩; erreichen ⟨*Ziel*⟩; **~ possession of sth.** in den Besitz einer Sache *(Gen.)* kommen; **~ nothing** nichts erreichen; **~ time** Zeit gewinnen; **b)** *(win)* gewinnen ⟨*Preis, Schlacht*⟩; erringen ⟨*Sieg*⟩; **c)** *(obtain as increase)* **~ weight/five pounds [in weight]** zunehmen/fünf Pfund zunehmen; **~ speed** schneller werden; **~ momentum** in Schwung kommen; ⟨*Idee:*⟩ an Boden gewinnen; **d)** *(reach)* gewinnen *(geh.),* erreichen ⟨*Gipfel, Ufer*⟩; **e)** *(become fast by)* ⟨*Uhr:*⟩ vorgehen um ⟨*zwei Minuten täglich*⟩. *See also* [1]**ground 1 b; upper 1 a. 3.** *v.i.* **a)** *(make a profit)* **~ by sth.** von etw. profitieren; bei etw. gewinnen; **~ in influence/prestige** an Einfluß/Prestige gewinnen; **~ in health/speed/wealth/wisdom** gesünder/schneller/reicher/weiser werden; **~ in knowledge** sein Wissen vergrößern; **~ in weight** zunehmen; **b)** *(be improved)* gewinnen; **~ by comparison** durch einen Vergleich gewinnen; **c)** *(become fast)* ⟨*Uhr:*⟩ vorgehen; **d) ~ [up]on sb.** *(come closer)* jmdm. [immer] näher kommen; *(increase lead)* den Vorsprung zu jmdm. vergrößern

gainful ['geɪnfl] *adj.* bezahlt; *(profitable)* gewinnbringend; **~ employment** Erwerbstätigkeit, *die*

gainfully ['geɪnfəlɪ] *adv.* **~ employed** erwerbstätig

gainsay [geɪn'seɪ] *v.t.,* **gainsaid** [geɪn'seɪd, geɪn'sed] *(arch./literary)* leugnen

gait [geɪt] *n.* **a)** Gang, *der;* **with a slow ~:** mit langsamen Schritten; **b)** *(of horse)* Gangart, *die*

gaiter ['geɪtə(r)] *n.* **a)** Gamasche, *die;* **b)** *(Amer.) see* **galosh**

gal [gæl] *n. (sl.)* Mädchen, *das;* **you're a nice ~:** du bist ein netter Käfer *(ugs.)*

gal. *abbr.* **gallon[s]** gal.; gall.

gala ['gɑ:lə, 'geɪlə] *n.* **a)** *(fête)* Festveranstaltung, *die; attrib.* Gala⟨*abend, -diner, -vorstellung*⟩; **b)** *(Brit.: sports festival)* Sportfest, *das;* **swimming ~:** Schwimmfest, *das*

galactic [gə'læktɪk] *adj. (of a galaxy)* galaktisch; *(of the Galaxy)* Milchstraßen-

Galahad ['gæləhæd] *n.* edler Ritter

galantine ['gælənti:n] *n. (Cookery)* Galantine, *die*

galaxy ['gæləksɪ] *n.* **a)** *(Milky Way)* **the G~:** die Galaxis *(Astron.);* die Milchstraße; **b)** *(independent system of stars)* Galaxie, *die;* **c)** *(fig.: outstanding group)* illustre Schar *(geh.)*

gale [geɪl] *n.* **a)** Sturm, *der;* **it's blowing a ~ outside** draußen stürmt es *od.* tobt ein Sturm; ~ **force** Sturmstärke, *die;* **b)** *(fig.: outburst)* Sturm, *der;* **~s of laughter** Lachsalven

[1]**Galicia** [gə'lɪʃə] *pr. n. (in Spain)* Galicien *(das)*

[2]**Galicia** *pr. n. (in SW Poland and W. Russia)* Galizien *(das)*

Galilee ['gælɪli:] *pr. n.* Galiläa *(das);* **Sea of ~:** See Genezareth, *der*

[1]**gall** [gɔ:l] *n.* **a)** *(Physiol.)* Galle, *die;* **b)** *(fig.: bitterness)* Bitternis, *die (geh.);* **be ~ and wormwood** [bitter wie] Galle und Wermut sein; **c)** *(sl.: impudence)* Unverschämtheit, *die;* Frechheit, *die*

[2]**gall** **1.** *n. (sore)* Schürfwunde, *die.* **2.** *v. t.* wund scheuern; *(fig.) (annoy)* ärgern; *(vex)* schmerzen; **be ~ed by sth.** unter etw. *(Dat.)* leiden

[3]**gall** *see* **gall-nut**

gallant ['gælənt] **1.** *adj.* **a)** *(brave)* tapfer; *(chivalrous)* ritterlich; **b)** *(grand, stately)* stattlich ⟨*Schiff*⟩; **c)** ['gælənt, gə'lænt] *(attentive to women, amatory)* galant; **say ~ things** Galanterien *od.* Artigkeiten sagen *(geh.).* **2.** ['gælənt, gə'lænt] *n. (dated: ladies' man)* Kavalier, *der (veralt.)*

gallantly ['gæləntlɪ] *adv.* **a)** *(bravely)* tapfer; **b)** *(grandly)* stattlich; **c)** ['gæləntlɪ, gə'læntlɪ] *(with courtesy)* galant

gallantry ['gæləntrɪ] *n.* **a)** *(bravery)* Tapferkeit, *die;* **b)** *(courtliness, polite act or speech)* Galanterie, *die (geh.)*

'**gall-bladder** *n. (Anat.)* Gallenblase, *die*

galleon ['gælɪən] *n. (Hist.)* Galeone, *die*

gallery ['gælərɪ] *n.* **a)** Galerie, *die; see also* **shooting-gallery; b)** *(Theatre)* dritter Rang; Olymp, *der (ugs. scherzh.); (esp. Golf: group of spectators)* Zuschauer; **play to the ~** *(fig. coll.)* für die Galerie spielen; **c)** *(displaying works of art) (building)* Galerie, *die; (room)* Ausstellungsraum, *der;* **d)** *(Mining)* Stollen, *der*

'**gallery tray** *n.* Galerietablett, *das*

galley ['gælɪ] *n.* **a)** *(Hist.)* Galeere, *die;* **b)** *(kitchen) (of ship)* Kombüse, *die; (of aircraft)* Bordküche, *die;* **c)** *(Printing)* Satzschiff, *das;* ~ **[proof]** [Druck]fahne, *die*

'**galley-slave** *n.* Galeerensklave, *der*

Gallic ['gælɪk] *adj.* **a)** *(of the Gauls)* gallisch; **b)** *(often joc.: French)* französisch; gallisch ⟨*Witz*⟩

Gallicism ['gælɪsɪzm] *n.* **a)** *(word or idiom)* Gallizismus, *der;* **b)** *(characteristic)* französische Eigenart

galling ['gɔ:lɪŋ] *adj.* äußerst unangenehm

gallivant [gælɪ'vænt] *v. i. (coll.)* herumziehen *(ugs.);* ~ **about** *or* **around the country/Europe** im Lande/in Europa herumziehen

'**gall-nut** *n. (Bot.)* Gallapfel, *der*

gallon ['gælən] *n.* Gallone, *die;* **[imperial] ~** *(Brit.)* britische Gallone (4,546 l); **wine ~** *(Brit.),* ~ *(Amer.)* amerikanische Gallone (3,785 l); **drink ~s of water** *etc. (fig. coll.)* literweise *od.* eimerweise Wasser *usw.* trinken

galloon [gə'lu:n] *n.* Galone, *die;* Galon, *der*

gallop ['gæləp] **1.** *n.* **a)** Galopp, *der;* **at a ~/at full ~:** im Galopp/in vollem Galopp; **b)** *(ride)* Galoppritt, *der;* **c)** *(track)* Galopp[renn]bahn, *die.* **2.** *v. i.* **a)** ⟨*Pferd, Reiter:*⟩ galoppieren; **b)** *(fig.)* ~ **through** im Galopp *(ugs.)* durchlesen ⟨*Buch*⟩; rasch herunterspielen ⟨*Musikstück*⟩; im Galopp *(ugs.)* erledigen ⟨*Arbeit*⟩; **~ing consumption/inflation** *(fig.)* galoppierende Schwindsucht/Inflation

gallows ['gæləʊz] *n. sing.* Galgen, *der;* **be sent to the ~:** zum [Tod am] Galgen verurteilt werden

gallows: ~-bird *n.* Galgenvogel, *der (ugs. abwertend);* ~ **humour** *n.* Galgenhumor, *der*

'**gallstone** *n. (Med.)* Gallenstein, *der*

Gallup poll ['gæləp pəʊl] *n.* Meinungsumfrage, *die*

galop ['gæləp] *n. (Mus.)* Galopp, *der*

galore [gə'lɔ:(r)] *adv.* im Überfluß; in Hülle und Fülle

galosh [gə'lɒʃ] *n.* [Gummi]überschuh, *der;* [Gummi]galosche, *die*

galumph [gə'lʌmf] *v. i. (coll.)* **a)** *(in triumph)* stolzieren; **b)** *(noisily, clumsily)* stapfen

galvanic [gæl'vænɪk] *adj. (fig.) (sudden remarkable)* elektrisierend; Blitz⟨*wirkung, -reaktion*⟩; *(stimulating, full of energy)* mitreißend ⟨*Aufführung, Rede, Persönlichkeit*⟩

galvanize (galvanise) ['gælvənaɪz] *v. t.* **a)** *(fig.: rouse)* wachrütteln ⟨*Volk, Partei usw.*⟩; ~ **sb. into action/activity** jmdn. veranlassen, sofort aktiv zu werden; ~ **sb. into life** jmdn. aufrütteln; **b)** *(coat with zinc)* verzinken

Gambia ['gæmbɪə] *pr. n.* Gambia *(das)*

gambit ['gæmbɪt] *n. (Chess)* Gambit, *das; (fig.: trick, device)* Schachzug, *der;* **[opening] ~** *(fig.)* einleitender Schachzug; *(in a conversation)* einleitende Bemerkung; **conversational ~** *(fig.)* Gesprächseinstieg *od.* -aufhänger, *der*

gamble ['gæmbl] **1.** *v. i.* **a)** [um Geld] spielen; ~ **at cards/on horses** mit Karten um Geld spielen/auf Pferde wetten; **b)** *(fig.)* spekulieren; ~ **on the Stock Exchange/in oil shares** an der Börse/in Öl[aktien] spekulieren; ~ **on sth.** sich auf etw. *(Akk.)* verlassen; auf etw. *(Akk.)* spekulieren *(ugs.).* **2.** *v. t.* **a)** verspielen; ~ **money on horses** Geld für Pferdewetten einsetzen; **b)** *(fig.)* riskieren, aufs Spiel setzen ⟨*Vermögen*⟩. **3.** *n. (lit. or fig.)* Glücksspiel, *das;* **he likes the occasional ~:** er spielt gelegentlich ganz gern; **take a ~:** ein Wagnis eingehen *od.* auf sich *(Akk.)* nehmen

~ **a'way** *v. t.* verspielen ⟨*Vermögen, Geld, Geschäft, Haus*⟩; *(on the Stock Exchange)* verspekulieren ⟨*Vermögen*⟩

gambler ['gæmblə(r)] *n.* Glücksspieler, *der; (risk-taker)* Glücksritter, *der;* **born ~:** Spieler- *od.* Abenteurernatur, *die*

gambling ['gæmblɪŋ] *n.* Spiel[en], *das;* Glücksspiel, *das; (on horses, dogs)* Wetten, *das*

gambling: ~ debts *n. pl.* Spielschulden; **~-den** *n.* Spielhölle, *die (abwertend);* **~-machine** *n.* Spielautomat, *der*

gambol ['gæmbl] **1.** *n.* **~[s]** Herumspringen, *das.* **2.** *v. i., (Brit.)* **-ll-** ⟨*Kind, Lamm:*⟩ herumspringen

[1]**game** [geɪm] **1.** *n.* **a)** *(form of contest)* Spiel, *das; (contest) (with ball)* Spiel, *das; (at [table-]tennis, chess, cards, billiards, cricket)* Partie, *die;* **have** *or* **play a ~ of tennis/chess** *etc.* **[with sb.]** eine Partie Tennis/Schach *usw.* [mit jmdm.] spielen; **give sb. a ~ of tennis/chess** *etc.* eine Partie Tennis/Schach *usw.* mit jmdm. spielen; **have** *or* **play a ~ of football [with sb.]** Fußball [mit jmdm.] spielen; **play a good/poor ~ [of cards** *etc.*] gut/schlecht [Karten *usw.*] spielen; ein guter [Karten- *usw.*]spieler sein; **be back in/get back into the ~ again** *(have a chance of winning)* wieder Gewinnchancen haben/bekommen; **it's all in the ~:** das ist alles dabei möglich; das kann alles dazugehören; **be on/off one's ~:** gut in Form/nicht in Form sein; **beat sb. at his own ~** *(fig.)* jmdn. mit seinen eigenen Waffen schlagen *(geh.);* **play the ~** *(fig.)* sich an die Spielregeln halten *(fig.);* **I'll show her that two can play [at] that ~** *or* **that it's a ~ that two can play** *(fig.)* was sie kann, kann ich auch; *see also* **name 1 a; b)** *(fig.: scheme, undertaking)* Vorhaben, *das;* **sb.'s ~ is to do sth.** jmd. führt etw. im Schilde; *(policy)* jmds. Taktik ist es, etw. zu tun; **play a [double] ~:** ein [falsches] Spiel treiben; **play sb.'s ~:** jmdm. in die Hände arbeiten; *(for one's own benefit)* jmds. Spiel mitspielen; **the ~ is up** *(coll.)* das Spiel ist aus; **give the ~ away** alles verraten; **so that's your little ~!** ach, das führst du im Schilde!; **what's his ~?** *(coll.)* was hat er vor?; **what's the ~?** *(coll.)* was soll das?; **c)** *(policy, line of action)* Gewerbe, *das;* Branche, *die;* **the ~ of politics** die Politik; **the publishing/newspaper ~:** das Verlags-/Zeitungs- *od.* Pressewesen; **be new to the ~** *(fig.)* neu im Geschäft sein *(auch fig. ugs.);* **go [out]/be on the ~** *(Brit. sl.)* ⟨*Dieb, Prostituierte:*⟩ anschaffen *od.* auf die Anschaffe gehen *(salopp); see also* **candle 1 a; d)** *(diversion)* Spiel, *das; (piece of fun)* Scherz, *der;* Spaß, *der;* **don't play ~s with me** versuch nicht, mich auf den Arm zu nehmen *(ugs.);* **make ~ of sb./sth.** *(dated)* sich über jmdn./etw. lustig machen; jmdn./etw. zum Gelächter machen *(geh. veralt.);* **e)** *in pl. (athletic contests)* Spiele; *(in school) (sports)* Schulsport, *der; (athletics)* Leichtathletik, *die;* **good at ~s** gut im Sport; **f)** *(portion of play)* Spiel, *das; (winning score)* **21 points is ~:** zum Gewinn eines Spiels sind 21 Punkte erforderlich; ~ **all** eins beide; eins zu eins; **two ~s all** zwei beide; zwei zu zwei; ~ **to Graf** *(Tennis)* Spiel Graf; **~, set, and match** *(Tennis)* Spiel, Satz und Sieg; *(fig.: complete and decisive victory)* voller Erfolg **(to** für); Sieg auf der ganzen Linie **(to** für); **g)** *no pl. (Hunting, Cookery)* Wild, *das;* **fair ~:** jagdbares Wild; *(fig.)* Freiwild, *das;* **easy ~** *(fig. coll.)* leichte Beute; **big ~:** Großwild, *das.* **2.** *v. i.* [um Geld] spielen

[2]**game** *adj.* mutig; ~ **spirit/manner** Unverzagtheit, *die;* **remain ~:** sich nicht entmutigen lassen; **be ~ to do sth.** *(be willing)* bereit sein, etw. zu tun; **are you ~?** machst du mit?; **be ~ for sth./anything** zu etw./allem bereit sein

[3]**game** *adj. (crippled)* lahm ⟨*Arm, Bein*⟩

game: ~-bag *n.* Tragetasche, *die;* ~ **bird** *n.* **the pheasant is a ~ bird** Fasane sind Federwild; ~ **birds** Federwild, *das;* **~cock** *n.* Kampfhahn, *der;* **~keeper** *n.* Wildheger, *der*

gamely ['geɪmlɪ] *adv.* mutig ⟨*kämpfen*⟩

game: ~ **park** *n.* Wildreservat, *das;* ~ **point** *n. (Sport)* Spielpunkt, *der;* ~ **reserve** *n.* Wildreservat, *das*

gamesmanship ['geɪmzmənʃɪp] *n., no pl.* Gerissen- *od.* Gewieftheit *(ugs.)* beim Spiel

gamete ['gæmi:t] *n. (Biol.)* Gamet, *der;* Geschlechtszelle, *die*

'**game-warden** *n.* Wildhüter, *der*

gamin ['gæmɪn, 'gæmæ̃] *n.* Gamin, *der (veralt.);* Gassenjunge, *der (abwertend)*

gamine [gə'mi:n] *n. (small mischievous young woman)* schelmisches Mädchen; kesse Motte *(salopp)*

gaming ['gəɪmɪŋ]: **~-house** *n.* Spielbank, *die;* **~-machine** *n.* Münzspielgerät, *das;* **~-table** *n.* Spieltisch, *der*

gamma ['gæmə] *n.* **a)** *(letter)* Gamma, *das;* **b)** *(Sch., Univ.: mark)* Drei, *die*

gamma: ~ **radiation** *n. (Phys.)* Gammastrahlung, *die;* ~ **rays** *n. pl. (Phys.)* Gammastrahlen *Pl.*

gammon ['gæmən] *n. (ham cured like bacon)* Räucherschinken, *der*

gammy ['gæmɪ] *adj. (sl.)* lahm ⟨*Arm, Bein, Fuß*⟩

gamut ['gæmət] *n.* **a)** *(Mus.) (series of notes, compass)* Tonumfang, *der; (recognized scale)* Skala, *die;* Tonleiter, *die;* **b)** *(fig.: range)* Skala, *die;* **run the whole ~ of ...:** die ganze Skala von ... durchgehen

gamy ['geɪmɪ] *adj.* **a)** *(having flavour or scent of game)* nach Wild ⟨*schmecken*⟩; ~ **taste** Wildgeschmack, *der;* **b)** *(spirited)* mutig; **c)** *(Amer.: scandalous)* pikant

gander ['gændə(r)] *n.* **a)** *(Ornith.)* Gänserich, *der;* **what's sauce for the goose is sauce for the ~** *(prov.)* was dem einen recht ist, ist dem andern billig *(Spr.);* **b)** *(sl.: look, glance)* Blick, *der;* **take** *or* **have a ~ at/round sth.** sich *(Dat.)* etw. ansehen

[1]gang [gæŋ] **1.** *n.* **a)** *(of workmen, slaves, prisoners)* Trupp, *der;* **b)** *(of criminals)* Bande, *die;* Gang, *die;* ~ **of thieves/criminals/terrorists** Diebes-/Verbrecher-/Terroristenbande, *die;* **c)** *(coll.: band causing any kind of disapproval)* Gang, *die;* Bande, *die (abwertend, oft scherzh.);* **d)** *(coll.: group of friends etc.)* Haufen, *der;* Bande, *die (scherzh.).* **2.** *v.i.* **a)** ~ **up [with sb.]** *(join)* sich [mit jmdm.] zusammentun *(ugs.);* **b)** ~ **up against** *or* **on** *(coll.: combine against)* sich verbünden *od.* zusammenschließen gegen

[2]gang *v.i. (Scot.: go)* gehen; ~ **agley** [ə'gleɪ] ‹*Plan:*› scheitern

'gang-bang *n. (sl.)* Bandenfick, *der (derb)*

ganger ['gæŋə(r)] *n. (Brit.)* Vorarbeiter, *der*

gangling ['gæŋglɪŋ] *adj.* schlaksig *(ugs.)* ‹*Person, Gang, Gestalt*›

ganglion ['gæŋglɪən] *n., pl.* **ganglia** ['gæŋglɪə] *or* ~**s** *(Anat.)* Ganglion, *das (fachspr.);* Nervenknoten, *der*

gangly ['gæŋglɪ] *see* **gangling**

gang: ~**plank** *n. (Naut.)* Laufplanke, *die;* ~ **rape** *n.* Vergewaltigung durch eine Gruppe

gangrene ['gæŋgri:n] *n.* **a)** *(Med.)* Gangrän, *die od. fachspr. das;* [Faul]brand, *der;* **b)** *(fig.: corruption)* Krebsgeschwür, *das (fig.)*

gangrenous ['gæŋgrɪnəs] *adj. (Med.)* gangränös *(fachspr.);* brandig

gangster ['gæŋstə(r)] *n.* Gangster, *der (abwertend); attrib.* Gangster‹*film*›

'gang warfare *n.* Bandenkrieg, *der*

'gangway 1. *n.* Gangway, *die; (Brit.: between rows of seats)* Gang, *der;* **leave a** ~ *(fig.)* einen Durchgang freilassen. **2.** *int.* Platz

ganja ['gændʒə] *n. (Bot.)* Indischer Hanf

gannet ['gænɪt] *n.* **a)** *(Ornith.)* Tölpel, *der;* **b)** *(sl.: greedy person)* Raffke, *der (salopp abwertend)*

gantlet ['gæntlɪt] *(Amer.) see* **[2]gauntlet**

gantry ['gæntrɪ] *n. (crane)* Portal, *das; (on road)* Schilderbrücke, *die; (Railw.)* Signalbrücke, *die; (Astronaut.)* Startrampe, *die*

gaol [dʒeɪl] *n., v.t. (Brit. in official use) see* **jail**

gaoler ['dʒeɪlə(r)] *(Brit. in official use) see* **jailer**

gap [gæp] *n.* **a)** Lücke, *die; (in sparking plug)* Elektrodenabstand, *der;* **a** ~ **in the curtains** ein Spalt im Vorhang; **b)** *(Geog.: gorge, pass)* Joch, *das;* **c)** *(fig.: contrast, divergence in views etc.)* Kluft, *die;* **that is a** ~ **in his education/knowledge** er hat hier eine Bildungs-/Wissenslücke; **fill a** ~: eine Lücke füllen *od.* schließen; **stop** *or* **close** *or* **bridge a** ~: eine Kluft überbrücken *od.* überwinden; **close the** ~ **[on sb.]** den Abstand [zu jmdm.] aufholen

gape [geɪp] **1.** *v.i.* **a)** *(open mouth)* den Mund aufsperren; *([be] open wide)* ‹*Schnabel, Mund:*› aufgesperrt sein; ‹*Loch, Abgrund, Wunde:*› klaffen; **gaping** klaffend ‹*Wunde*›; gähnend ‹*Loch*›; ~ **at the seams** ‹*Kleid:*› in den Nähten aufgeplatzt sein; **b)** *(stare)* Mund und Nase aufsperren *(ugs.);* ~ **at sb./sth.** jmdn./etw. mit offenem Mund anstarren *od.* anstieren; **what are you gaping at?** worauf stierst du so?; **gaping** erstaunt starrend ‹*Person*›. **2.** *n.* stierer Blick

gap-toothed ['gæptu:θt] *adj.* ‹*Person*› mit Zahnlücken

gar [gɑ:(r)] *see* **garfish**

garage ['gærɑ:ʒ, 'gærɪdʒ] **1.** *n.* **a)** *(for parking)* Garage, *die;* **bus** ~: Busdepot, *das;* **b)** *(for selling petrol)* Tankstelle, *die; (for repairing cars)* [Kfz-]Werkstatt, *die; (for selling cars)* Autohandlung, *die.* **2.** *v.t.* in die Garage stellen ‹*Fahrzeug*›; **be kept** ~**d** in der Garage stehen; **where do you** ~ **your car?** wo parken Sie Ihr Auto?

garb [gɑ:b] **1.** *n.* Tracht, *die;* **strange** ~: seltsame Kleidung; **official** ~: Amtstracht, *die.* **2.** *v.t.* kleiden; *(fig.: invest)* verleihen *(Dat.);* ~**ed in white robes** in Weiß gekleidet

garbage ['gɑ:bɪdʒ] *n.* **a)** Abfall, *der;* Müll, *der;* **b)** *(fig.: foul or rubbishy literature)* Schund, *der;* **c)** *(coll.: nonsense)* Quatsch, *der (salopp);* ~ **in,** ~ **out** *(Computing fig. coll.)* wenn der Input nichts taugt, ist auch der Output entsprechend

garbage: ~ **can** *(Amer.) see* **dustbin;** ~ **collection** *n. (Amer.)* Müllabfuhr, *die;* ~ **collector** *(Amer.) see* **dustman;** ~ **dis'posal unit,** ~ **disposer** *ns.* Abfallvernichter, *der;* Müllwolf, *der*

garble ['gɑ:bl] *v.t.* **a)** verstümmeln, entstellen ‹*Bericht, Korrespondenz, Tatsache*›; **b)** *(confuse)* durcheinanderbringen; durcheinanderwerfen; **get** ~**d** durcheinandergeraten

garden [gɑ:dn] **1.** *n.* **a)** Garten, *der;* **everything in the** ~ **is lovely** *(fig. coll.)* es ist alles in Butter *(ugs.);* **lead sb. up the** ~ **[path]** *(fig. coll.)* jmdn. an der Nase herumführen *(ugs.);* **tea** ~: Gartencafé, *das;* **a small amount of** ~: ein kleines Stück Garten; **b)** *usu. in pl., with name prefixed (Brit.) (park)* -park, *der; (street, square)* -garten, *der;* **c)** *(land for raising crops)* Plantage, *die;* **d)** *(Amer.: large hall)* Halle, *die;* **e)** *attrib. (Bot.: cultivated)* Garten‹*pflanze, -kresse, -gemüse*›. *See also* **kitchen garden; market garden; zoological garden[s]. 2.** *v.i.* gärtnern

garden: ~ **centre** *n.* Gartencenter, *das;* ~ **chair** *n.* Gartenstuhl, *der;* ~ **'city** *n.* Gartenstadt, *die*

gardener ['gɑ:dnə(r)] *n.* Gärtner, *der*/Gärtnerin, *die*

garden 'gnome *n.* Gartenzwerg, *der*

gardenia [gɑ:'di:nɪə] *n. (Bot.)* **a)** *(tree, shrub)* Gardenie, *die;* **b)** *(flower)* Gardenienblüte, *die*

gardening ['gɑ:dnɪŋ] *n.* Gartenarbeit, *die; attrib.* Garten‹*gerät, -buch, -handschuh*›; **he likes** ~: er gärtnert gern

garden: ~ **party** *n.* Gartenfest, *das;* ~ **'shed** *n.* Geräteschuppen, *der;* ~ **'suburb** *n. (Brit.)* Gartenstadt, *die*

garfish ['gɑ:fɪʃ] *n., pl. same (Zool.) (needlefish)* Hornhecht, *der; (gar)* Knochenhecht, *der; (halfbeak)* Halbschnabelhecht, *der*

gargantuan [gɑ:'gæntjʊən] *adj.* gigantisch; riesig ‹*Mensch, Hunger, Gelächter*›; Riesen‹*größe, -hunger, -gebrüll*›

gargle ['gɑ:gl] **1.** *v.i.* gurgeln. **2.** *n.* **a)** *(liquid)* Gurgelmittel, *das;* Gargarisma, *das (fachspr.);* **b)** *(act)* Gurgeln, *das*

gargoyle ['gɑ:gɔɪl] *n. (Archit.)* Wasserspeier, *der*

garish ['geərɪʃ] *adj.* **a)** *(bright, showy)* grell ‹*Farbe, Licht, Beleuchtung*›; knallbunt ‹*Kleidung, Verzierung*›; protzig *(abwertend)* ‹*Lebensstil*›; **b)** *(over-decorated)* protzig *(abwertend)* ‹*Gebäude, Baustil, Aussehen*›; grellbunt, knallbunt ‹*Muster*›

garishly ['geərɪʃlɪ] *adv.* grell ‹*beleuchten*›; protzig *(abwertend)* ‹*einrichten*›; grellbunt, knallbunt ‹*kleiden, tapezieren*›; grell-, knall‹*bunt*›

garland ['gɑ:lənd] **1.** *n. (wreath of flowers etc.; Art: festoon)* Girlande, *die; (of laurel)* Kranz, *der;* ~ **of flowers/laurel/oak-leaves** Blumen-/Lorbeer-/Eichenkranz, *der.* **2.** *v.t.* bekränzen

garlic ['gɑ:lɪk] *n.* Knoblauch, *der*

garlicky ['gɑ:lɪkɪ] *adj.* nach Knoblauch riechend ‹*Atem*›; nach Knoblauch ‹*riechen, schmecken*›

garment ['gɑ:mənt] *n.* **a)** Kleidungsstück, *das; in pl. (clothes)* Kleidung, *die;* Kleider; **b)** *(fig.: covering)* Gewand, *das (geh.)*

garner ['gɑ:nə(r)] *v.t.* speichern ‹*Getreide*›; *(fig.: collect)* sammeln ‹*Kenntnisse usw.*›

garnet ['gɑ:nɪt] *n. (Min.)* Granat, *der*

garnish ['gɑ:nɪʃ] **1.** *v.t. (lit. or fig.)* garnieren. **2.** *n. (Cookery)* Garnierung, *die*

garotte *see* **garrotte**

garret ['gærɪt] *n. (room on top floor)* Dachkammer, *die;* Mansarde, *die; (attic)* [Dach]boden, *der*

garrison ['gærɪsn] **1.** *n.* Garnison, *die.* **2.** *v.t. (furnish with* ~*)* in Garnison legen; garnisonieren *(fachspr.); (occupy as* ~*)* mit einer Garnison belegen; garnisonieren *(fachspr.)*

garrison: ~ **duty** *n.* Garnison[s]dienst, *der;* ~ **town** *n.* Garnison[s]stadt, *die*

garrotte [gə'rɒt] *v.t.* **a)** garrottieren; **b)** *(throttle to rob)* [er]würgen [und ausrauben]

garrulous ['gærʊləs] *adj.* **a)** *(talkative)* gesprächig; geschwätzig; **b)** *(wordy)* wortreich; weitschweifig, langatmig ‹*Rede, Kommentar*›

garrulously ['gærʊləslɪ] *adv.* geschwätzig

garter ['gɑ:tə(r)] *n.* **a)** Strumpfband, *das;* **b)** **the [Order of the] G**~ *(Brit.)* der Hosenbandorden; **c)** *(Amer.: suspender)* Sockenhalter, *der*

'garter stitch *n.* Kraus[gestrick], *das;* **knit in** ~: kraus rechts stricken

gas [gæs] **1.** *n., pl.* ~**es** ['gæsɪz] **a)** Gas, *das;* **natural** ~: Erdgas, *das;* **cook by** *or* **with** ~: mit Gas kochen; **on a low/high** ~: auf kleiner/großer Flamme; **b)** *(Amer. coll.: petrol)* Benzin, *das;* **step on the** ~: Gas geben; *(fig.: hurry)* einen Zahn zulegen *(salopp);* **c)** *(anaesthetic)* Narkotikum, *das;* Lachgas, *das;* **d)** *(for lighting)* Leuchtgas, *das;* **e)** *(to fill balloon)* [Trag]gas, *das;* **f)** *(Mining)* Grubengas, *das;* **g)** *(coll.: idle talk)* leeres Geschwätz *(abwertend);* Blabla, *das (salopp);* **h)** *(sl.: sb./sth. attractive and impressive)* Wucht, *die (salopp).* **2.** *v.t.,* **-ss-** *esp. in p.p.* mit Gas vergiften; *(in Third Reich)* vergasen; ~ **oneself** den Gashahn aufdrehen *(ugs. verhüll.).* **3.** *v.i.,* **-ss-** *(coll.)* schwatzen *(abwertend),* schwafeln *(ugs. abwertend)* **(about** von)

gas: ~**bag** *n.* **a)** Gaszelle, *die;* **b)** *(derog.: talker)* Schwätzer, *der*/Schwätzerin, *die (abwertend);* Schwafler, *der*/Schwaflerin, *die (ugs. abwertend);* ~ **chamber** *n.* Gaskammer, *die;* ~**-cooled** *adj.* gasgekühlt; ~ **cylinder** *n.* Gasflasche, *die*

gaseous ['gæsɪəs, 'geɪsɪəs] *adj.* gasförmig

gas: ~ **'fire** *n.* Gasofen, *der;* ~**-fired** ['gæsfaɪəd] *adj.* mit Gas betrieben; Gas‹*boiler, -ofen usw.*›; ~**-fitter** *n.* Gasinstallateur, *der*

gash [gæʃ] **1.** *n. (slash, cut)* Schnittwunde, *die; (cleft)* [klaffende] Spalte; *(in sack etc.)* Schlitz, *der.* **2.** *v.t.* eine Schnittwunde beibringen *(+ Dat.);* aufritzen ‹*Haut*›; aufschlitzen ‹*Sack*›; ~ **one's finger/knee** sich *(Dat. od. Akk.)* in den Finger schneiden/sich *(Dat.)* das Knie aufschlagen

gas: ~ **heater** *n.* Gasofen, *der;* ~ **holder** *n.* Gasometer, *der;* Gasbehälter, *der;* ~ **jet** *n.* Gasflamme, *die; (burner)* Gasbrenner, *der*

gasket ['gæskɪt] *n.* **a)** *(sheet, ring)* Dichtung, *die;* **b)** *(packing)* Packung, *die*

gas: ~ **lamp** *n.* Gaslampe, *die; (in street etc.)* Gaslaterne, *die;* ~**light** *n.* **a)** *see* ~ **lamp; b)** *no pl. (illumination)* Gaslicht, *das;* Gasbeleuchtung, *die;* ~ **lighter** *n.* **a)** [Gas]anzünder, *der;* **b)** *(cigarette-lighter)* Gasfeuerzeug, *das;* ~ **main** *n.* Hauptgasleitung, *die;* ~**man** *n. (fitter)* Gasinstallateur, *der; (meter-reader, collector)* Gasableser, *der;* Gasmann, *der (ugs.);* ~**-mantle** *n.* Glühstrumpf, *der;* ~ **mask** *n.* Gasmaske, *die;* ~ **meter** *n.* Gaszähler, *der*

gasoline (gasolene) ['gæsəli:n] *n. (Amer.)* Benzin, *das*

gasometer [gæ'sɒmɪtə(r)] *n.* Gasometer, *der*

'gas oven *n.* **a)** *see* **gas stove a; b)** *see* **gas chamber**

gasp [gɑ:sp] **1.** *v.i.* nach Luft schnappen **(with** vor); **make sb.** ~ *(fig.)* jmdm. den Atem nehmen; **leave sb.** ~**ing [with sth.]** jmdm. [vor etw.] den Atem verschlagen *od.*

rauben; **he was ~ing for air** *or* **breath/under the heavy load** er rang nach Luft/keuchte unter der schweren Last. **2.** *v. t.* ~ **out** hervorstoßen ‹*Bitte, Worte*›; ~ **[one's] life away,** ~ **[one's] breath away** sein Leben aushauchen *(geh.)*. **3.** *n.* Keuchen, *das;* **give a ~ of fear/surprise** vor Furcht/Überraschung die Luft einziehen; **she gave a ~ of joy** es verschlug ihr vor Freude den Atem; **be at one's last ~**: in den letzten Zügen liegen *(ugs.)*; **sth. is at its last ~**: etw. tut's nicht mehr lange *(ugs.)*; **fight** *etc.* **to the last ~** *(fig.)* bis zum letzten Atemzug kämpfen *usw.*

gas: ~-pipe *n.* Gasleitung, *die;* **~ pistol** *n.* Gasanzünder, *der;* **~ poker** *n.* Gasanzünder, *der (für Kohle);* **~-proof** *adj.* gasdicht; **~ ring** *n.* Gasbrenner, *der;* **~ station** *n.* *(Amer.)* Tankstelle, *die;* **~ stove** *n.* **a)** Gasherd, *der;* **b)** *(portable)* Gaskocher, *der*

gassy ['gæsɪ] *adj.* **a)** gasig; *(containing gas)* gashaltig; **b)** *(fizzy)* sprudelnd; schäumend ‹*Bier*›; **be ~**: sprudeln

gas: ~ tank *n.* **a)** Gastank, *der;* **b)** *(Amer.: petrol tank)* Benzintank, *der;* **~ tap** *n.* Gashahn, *der;* **~-tight** *adj.* gasdicht

gastric ['gæstrɪk] *adj.* gastrisch *(fachspr.)*; Magen‹*beschwerden, -wand, -säfte usw.*›

gastric: ~ 'flu *(coll.)*, **~ influ'enza** *ns.* Darmgrippe, *die;* **~ 'ulcer** *n.* Magengeschwür, *das*

gastritis [gæ'straɪtɪs] *n. (Med.)* Magenschleimhautentzündung, *die;* Gastritis, *die (fachspr.)*

gastro-enteritis [gæstrəʊentə'raɪtɪs] *n. (Med.)* Gastroenteritis, *die (fachspr.)*; Magen-Darm-Katarrh, *der*

gastronomic [gæstrə'nɒmɪk] *adj.* gastronomisch; kulinarisch ‹*Genüsse*›

gastronomy [gæ'strɒnəmɪ] *n.* Gastronomie, *die;* **French ~**: französische Küche

gastropod ['gæstrəpɒd] *n. (Zool.)* Gastropode, *der*

gas: ~ turbine *n.* Gasturbine, *die;* **~works** *n. sing., pl. same* Gaswerk, *das*

gate [geɪt] *n.* **a)** *(lit. or fig.)* Tor, *das; (barrier)* Sperre, *die; (of animal pen)* Gatter, *das; (in garden fence)* [Garten]pforte, *die; (of lift)* [Scheren]gitter, *das; (Railw.: of level crossing)* [Bahn]schranke, *die; (in airport)* Flugsteig, *der;* **the ~s of heaven/hell** die Himmelspforte *(dichter.)*/die Pforten der Hölle *(geh.)*; **pay at the ~**: am Eingang bezahlen; **b)** *(Sport) (number to see match)* Besucher[zahl], *die; (money) see* **gate-money; c)** *(Amer. sl.: dismissal)* **give sb. the ~**: jmdn. vor die Tür setzen *(ugs.)*; jmdn. rausschmeißen *(salopp)*; **get the ~**: vor die Tür gesetzt werden *(ugs.)*; rausgeschmissen werden *(salopp)*; **d)** *(of gear in vehicle)* Kulisse, *die;* **e)** *(Cinemat.)* Bildfenster, *das*

gateau [gæ'təʊ] *n., pl.* **~s** *or* **~x** [gæ'təʊz] Torte, *die*

gate: ~crash 1. *v. t.* ohne Einladung einfach hingehen zu; **2.** *v. i.* ohne Einladung einfach hingehen; **~crasher** *n.* Eindringling, *der; (at party)* ungeladener Gast; **~house** *n.* Torhaus, *das;* **~keeper** *n. (attendant)* Torwächter, *der;* Pförtner, *der;* **~leg[ged]** ['geɪtleg(d)] *adj.* **~leg[ged] table** Klapptisch, *der;* **~man** *see* **~keeper; ~-money** *n.* Eintrittsgelder *Pl.;* Einnahmen *Pl.;* **~post** *n.* Torpfosten, *der;* **between you and me and the ~post** *(coll.)* unter uns *(Dat.)* gesagt; **~way** *n.* **a)** *(gate)* Tor, *das;* **b)** *(Archit.) (structure)* Torbau, *der; (frame)* Torbogen, *der;* **c)** *(fig.)* Tor, *das* **(to** zu)

gather ['gæðə(r)] **1.** *v. t.* **a)** *(bring together)* sammeln; zusammentragen ‹*Informationen*›; pflücken ‹*Obst, Blumen*›; **~ sth. [together]** etw. zusammensuchen *od.* -sammeln; **~ [in] potatoes/the harvest** Kartoffeln ernten/die Ernte einbringen; **be ~ed to one's fathers** zu seinen Vätern versammelt werden *(veralt., scherzh.)*; **b)** *(infer, deduce)* schließen **(from** aus); **~ from sb. that ...**: von jmdm. erfahren, daß ...; **I ~ he's doing a good job** ich höre, daß er gute Arbeit leistet; **not much can be ~ed from the facts/his statement** aus den Fakten/seiner Erklärung läßt sich nicht viel entnehmen; **as far as I can ~**: soweit ich weiß; **as you will have ~ed** wie Sie sicherlich vermutet haben; **c) it is just ~ing dust** das ist bloß ein Staubfänger; **~ speed/momentum** *or* **force/strength** schneller/stärker werden/zu Kräften kommen; **d)** *(summon up)* **~ [together]** zusammennehmen ‹*Kräfte, Mut*›; **~ oneself [together]** sich zusammennehmen; **~ one's thoughts** seine Gedanken ordnen; **~ one's breath/strength** [wieder] zu Atem kommen/Kräfte sammeln; **e)** *(draw)* **~ sb. into one's arms** jmdn. in die Arme nehmen *od. (geh.)* schließen; **she ~ed her shawl round her neck** sie schlang den Schal um den Hals; **~ oneself for a jump** sich zum Sprung sammeln; **f)** *(Sewing)* ankrausen. **2.** *v. i.* **a)** sich versammeln; ‹*Wolken:*› sich zusammenziehen; ‹*Staub:*› sich ansammeln; ‹*Schweißperlen:*› sich sammeln; **be ~ed [together]** versammelt sein; **~ round** zusammenkommen; **~ round sb./sth.** sich um jmdn./etw. versammeln; **tears/beads of perspiration ~ed in her eyes/on her forehead** Tränen/Schweißperlen traten ihr in die Augen/auf die Stirn; **b)** *(increase)* zunehmen; **~ing dangers** wachsende Gefahren; **darkness was ~ing round him** es wurde dunkler um ihn [herum]; **c)** *(Sewing)* angekraust sein; **d)** *(Med.)* ‹*Furunkel:*› reif werden. **3.** *n. in pl. (Sewing)* Kräusel[falten]

~ 'up *v. t.* **a)** *(bring together and pick up)* aufsammeln; auflesen; zusammenpacken ‹*Habseligkeiten, Werkzeug*›; **be left to ~ up the pieces of one's life** *(fig.)* vor dem Scherbenhaufen seines Lebens stehen; **b)** *(draw)* hochraffen ‹*Rock*›; **~ oneself up to one's full height** sich zu seiner vollen Größe aufrichten; **c)** *(sum up)* zusammentragen ‹*Fakten*›; **d)** *(summon)* sammeln ‹*Kräfte, Gedanken usw.*›

gathering ['gæðərɪŋ] *n.* **a)** *(group)* Gruppe, *die;* **b)** *(assembly, meeting)* Versammlung, *die; (in Scottish Highlands)* Volksfest, *das;* **social ~**: gesellschaftliches Ereignis; **c)** *(Sewing)* Kräusel[falten]

GATT [gæt] *abbr.* **General Agreement on Tariffs and Trade** GATT, *das*

gauche [gəʊʃ] *adj.* linkisch; *(clumsy)* schwerfällig; *(tactless)* plump

gaucheness ['gəʊʃnɪs] *n., no pl. see* **gauche:** Linkische, *das;* Schwerfälligkeit, *die;* Plumpheit, *die;* **~ of manner** linkische Art

gaucherie ['gəʊʃəri:] *n.* **a)** *no pl. (manner)* linkische Art; **b)** *(action)* Plumpheit, *die*

gaucho ['gaʊtʃəʊ] *n., pl.* **~s** Gaucho, *der*

gaudily ['gɔ:dɪlɪ] *adv.* prunkvoll ‹*dekoriert*›; übertrieben aufwendig; protzig *(abwertend)*; **~ coloured** knallbunt

¹gaudy ['gɔ:dɪ] *adj.* protzig *(abwertend)*; grell, *(ugs.)* knallig ‹*Farben*›

²gaudy *n. (Brit. Univ.) (jährliches)* [College]fest

gauge [geɪdʒ] **1.** *n.* **a)** *(standard measure)* [Normal]maß, *das; (of textile)* Gauge, das *(fachspr.)*; *(of bullet)* Kaliber, *das; (of rail)* Spurweite, *die;* **standard/broad/narrow ~**: Normal- *od.* Regel-/Breit-/Schmalspur, *die;* **b)** *(instrument)* Meßgerät, *das; (to measure water-level)* Pegel, *der;* Wasserstandsanzeiger, *der; (for dimensions of tools or wire)* Lehre, *die; see also* **oil-gauge; petrol-gauge; c)** *(Naut.) Schiffsposition in bezug auf den Wind;* **have the weather ~ [of sb.]** in Luv [von jmdm.] liegen; *(fig.)* die Oberhand [über jmdn.] haben; **d)** *(fig.: criterion, test)* Kriterium, *das;* Maßstab, *der.* **2.** *v. t.* **a)** *(measure)* messen; **b)** *(fig.)* beurteilen **(by** nach)

Gaul [gɔ:l] *n. (Hist.)* **a)** *(country)* Gallien, *das;* **b)** *(person)* Gallier, *der*/Gallierin, *die*

gauleiter ['gaʊlaɪtə(r)] *n.* **a)** *(Hist.)* Gauleiter, *der;* **b)** *(fig.: local or petty tyrant)* Ortstyrann, *der*

gaunt [gɔ:nt] *adj.* **a)** *(haggard)* hager; *(from suffering)* verhärmt; **b)** *(grim, desolate)* öde; kahl ‹*Baum*›; karg ‹*Landschaft*›

¹gauntlet ['gɔ:ntlɪt] *n.* **a)** Stulpenhandschuh, *der;* **b)** *(wrist-part of glove)* Stulpe, *die;* **c)** *(Hist.: armoured glove)* Panzerhandschuh, *der;* **d) fling** *or* **throw down the ~** *(fig.)* jmdm. den Fehdehandschuh hinwerfen *od.* vor die Füße werfen; **pick** *or* **take up the ~** *(fig.)* den Fehdehandschuh aufnehmen *od.* aufheben

²gauntlet *n.* **run the ~**: Spießruten laufen

gauss [gaʊs] *n., pl. same or* **~es** *(Phys.)* Gauß, *das*

gauze [gɔ:z] *n.* **a)** Gaze, *die;* **b)** *(of wire etc.)* Drahtgeflecht, *das;* Gaze, *die*

gave *see* **give 1, 2**

gavel ['gævl] *n.* Hammer, *der*

gavotte [gə'vɒt] *n. (Mus.)* Gavotte, *die*

gawk [gɔ:k] *v. i. (coll.)* gaffen *(abwertend)*; **~ at sth./sb.** etw./jmdn. begaffen

gawky ['gɔ:kɪ] *adj.* linkisch; unbeholfen; *(with disproportionately long limbs)* schlaksig *(ugs.)*

gawp [gɔ:p] *see* **gawk**

gay [geɪ] **1.** *adj.* **a)** fröhlich; *(sportive)* fidel *(ugs.)* ‹*Person, Gesellschaft*›; **b)** *(showy, bright-coloured)* farbenfroh ‹*Stoff, Ausstattung*›; fröhlich, lebhaft ‹*Farbe*›; **~ with flowers/flags** mit Blumen/Fahnen fröhlich geschmückt; **c)** *(coll.: homosexual)* schwul *(ugs.)*; Schwulen‹*lokal, -blatt*›; **d)** *(euphem.: immoral)* locker; **a ~ dog** ein lockerer Vogel *(salopp, oft scherzh.)*. **2.** *n. (coll.)* Schwule, *der (ugs.)*

gayety *(Amer.) see* **gaiety**

gayness ['geɪnɪs] *see* **gaiety**

Gaza [strip] ['gɑ:zə (strɪp)] *pr. n.* Gazastreifen, *der*

gaze [geɪz] **1.** *v. i.* blicken; *(more fixedly)* starren; **~ at sb./sth.** jmdn./etw. anstarren *od.* ansehen; **~ after sb./sth.** jmdm./einer Sache hinterhersehen; **~ around** *or* **about** um sich blicken. **2.** *n.* Blick, *der*

gazelle [gə'zel] *n.* Gazelle, *die*

gazette [gə'zet] **1.** *n.* **a)** *(Brit.: official journal)* **London G~**: Londoner Amtsblatt; **b)** *(newspaper)* Anzeiger, *der.* **2.** *v. t. (Brit.: announce)* [amtlich] bekanntgeben

gazetteer [gæzɪ'tɪə(r)] *n.* alphabetisches [Orts]verzeichnis

gazump [gə'zʌmp] *v. t. (sl.) durch nachträgliches Überbieten um die Chance bringen, ein Haus zu kaufen*

GB *abbr.* **Great Britain** GB

GC *abbr. (Brit.)* **George Cross**

GCE *abbr. (Brit. Hist.)* **General Certificate of Education**

GCSE *abbr. (Brit.)* **General Certificate of Secondary Education**

GDP *abbr.* **gross domestic product** BIP

GDR *abbr. (Hist.)* **German Democratic Republic** DDR, *die*

gear [gɪə(r)] **1.** *n.* **a)** *(Motor Veh.)* Gang, *der; (transmission)* Übersetzung, *die;* **first/second** *etc.* **~** *(Brit.)* der erste/zweite *usw.* Gang; **top/bottom ~** *(Brit.)* der höchste/erste Gang; **high/low ~**: hoher/niedriger Gang; **change** *or* **shift ~**: schalten; **change** *or* **shift [up] a ~** *(fig.)* einen Gang zulegen *(ugs.)*; **change into second/a higher/lower ~**: in den zweiten Gang/in einen höheren/niedrigeren Gang schalten; **a bicycle with ten-speed ~s** ein Fahrrad mit Zehngangschaltung; **put** *or* **get** *or* **shift the car into ~**: den Wagen in Gang setzen; einen Gang einlegen; **in ~** *(fig.)* in Ordnung; im Gleis; **out of ~**: im Leerlauf; *(fig.)* in Unordnung; aus dem Gleis [geraten]; **the car is in/out of ~**: es ist ein/kein Gang eingelegt; **leave the**

car in ~: den Gang drin lassen; **b)** *(combination of wheels, levers, etc.)* Getriebe, *das;* **c)** *(clothes)* Aufmachung, *die;* **travelling ~:** Reisekleidung, *die; see also* **headgear; d)** *(equipment, tools)* Gerät, *das;* Ausrüstung, *die;* **e)** *(apparatus)* Vorrichtung, *die;* **f)** *(harness)* [Sielen]geschirr, *das.* **2.** *v. t. (adjust, adapt)* anpassen (**to** *Dat.*); abstimmen, ausrichten (**to** auf + *Akk.*)

gear: ~box, ~case *ns.* Getriebekasten, *der;* **five-speed ~box** Fünfganggetriebe, *das;* **~-change** *n. (Brit.)* **an upward/a downward ~-change** ein Hoch-/Herunterschalten; **have a smooth/awkward ~-change** ⟨*Fahrrad, Auto:*⟩ sich leicht/schlecht schalten

gearing ['gɪərɪŋ] *n.* **a)** Getriebe, *das;* **b)** *(Brit. Finance) Verhältnis von Ausschüttung auf Vorzugsaktien zu Ausschüttung auf Stammaktien*

gear: ~-lever, *(Amer.)* **~-shift, ~-stick** *ns.* Schalthebel, *der;* Schaltknüppel, *der;* **~wheel** *n.* Zahnrad, *das*

gecko ['gekəʊ] *n., pl.* **~s** *(Zool.)* Gecko, *der*

geddit ['gedɪt] *v. i. (sl.)* **~?** verstanden? *(ugs.);* kapiert? *(salopp)*

¹gee [dʒi:] *int. (to horse)* hü

²gee *int. (coll.)* Mann *(salopp);* Mensch [Meier] *(salopp)*

'gee-gee *n. (Brit. coll.: horse)* Hottehü, *das (Kinderspr.)*

geese *pl. of* goose

'gee-up *int. see* **¹gee**

gee 'whiz *int. (coll.) see* **²gee**

geezer ['gi:zə(r)] *n.* **a)** *(sl.: old man)* Opa, *der (ugs. scherzh. od. abwertend);* **b)** *(coll.: fellow)* Typ, *der (ugs.)*

Geiger counter ['gaɪgə kaʊntə(r)] *n. (Phys.)* Geigerzähler, *der*

geisha ['geɪʃə] *n., pl.* **~s** *or same* Geisha, *die*

gel [dʒel] **1.** *n.* Gel, *das.* **2.** *v. i.,* **-ll-: a)** gelatinieren; gelieren; **b)** *(fig.)* Gestalt annehmen

gelatin ['dʒelətɪn], *(esp. Brit.)* **gelatine** ['dʒeləti:n] *n.* Gelatine, *die;* **blasting ~:** Sprenggelatine, *die*

gelatinous [dʒɪ'lætɪnəs] *adj.* **a)** *(resembling gelatin)* gelatineartig; **b)** *(consisting of gelatin)* gelatinös

geld [geld] *v. t.* kastrieren; *(spay)* sterilisieren

gelding ['geldɪŋ] *n.* kastriertes Tier; *(male horse)* Wallach, *der*

gelignite ['dʒelɪgnaɪt] *n.* Gelatinedynamit, *das*

gem [dʒem] *n.* **a)** Edelstein, *der; (cut also)* Juwel, *das od. der; ([semi-]precious stone with engraved design)* Gemme, *die;* **b)** *(fig.)* Juwel, *das;* Perle, *die; (choicest part)* Glanzstück, *das*

Geminean [dʒemɪ'ni:ən] *n. (Astrol.)* Zwilling, *der*

Gemini ['dʒemɪnaɪ, 'dʒemɪnɪ] *n. (Astrol., Astron.)* Zwillinge *Pl.;* Gemini *Pl.; see also* **Aries**

'gemstone *n.* Edelstein, *der*

gen [dʒen] *(Brit. sl.)* **1.** *n.* notwendige Angaben; **give sb. the ~ on** *or* **about sth.** jmdn. über etw. *(Akk.)* informieren. **2.** *v. t.,* **-nn-: ~ oneself/sb. up on** *or* **about sth.** sich/jmdn. über etw. *(Akk.)* informieren. **3.** *v. i.,* **-nn-: ~ up on** *or* **about sth.** sich über etw. *(Akk.)* informieren

Gen. *abbr.* **General** Gen.

gendarme ['ʒɒndɑ:m] *n.* Gendarm, *der*

gender ['dʒendə(r)] *n.* **a)** *(Ling.)* [grammatisches] Geschlecht; Genus, *das;* **b)** *(joc.: one's sex)* Geschlecht, *das*

gene [dʒi:n] *n. (Biol.)* Gen, *das*

genealogical [dʒi:nɪə'lɒdʒɪkl, dʒenɪə'lɒdʒɪkl] *adj.* genealogisch; **~ tree** Stammbaum, *der*

genealogist [dʒi:nɪ'ælədʒɪst, dʒenɪ'ælədʒɪst] *n.* Genealoge, *der*/Genealogin, *die;* Ahnenforscher, *der*/-forscherin, *die*

genealogy [dʒi:nɪ'ælədʒɪ, dʒenɪ'ælədʒɪ] *n.* **a)** Genealogie, *die (fachspr.); (pedigree)* Ahnentafel, *die (geh.); (investigation)* Ahnenforschung, *die;* **b)** *(Zool., Bot.)* Stammbaum, *der*

genera *pl. of* **genus**

general ['dʒenrl] **1.** *adj.* **a)** allgemein; **the ~ public** weite Kreise der Öffentlichkeit *od.* Bevölkerung; **in ~ use** allgemein verbreitet; **be in ~ use as sth.** allgemein als etw. benutzt werden; **not for ~ use** *(not to be used by everybody)* nicht für den allgemeinen Gebrauch bestimmt; **his ~ health/manner** sein Allgemeinbefinden/sein Benehmen im allgemeinen; **he has had a good ~ education** er hat eine gute Allgemeinbildung; **a ~ view of the building** eine Gesamtansicht des Gebäudes; **come to a ~ agreement** sich grundsätzlich einigen; **reach a ~ decision** eine grundsätzliche Entscheidung treffen; **in a ~ state of decay** in einem Zustand allgemeinen Verfalls; **~ matters** allgemeine Angelegenheiten; **the cold weather has been ~ in England** es ist in ganz England kalt gewesen; **b)** *(prevalent, widespread, usual)* allgemein; weitverbreitet ⟨*Übel, Vorurteil, Aberglaube, Ansicht*⟩; häufig ⟨*Leiden*⟩; **it is the ~ custom** *or* **rule** es ist allgemein üblich *od.* ist Sitte *od.* Brauch; **c)** *(not limited in application)* allgemein; *(true of [nearly] all cases)* allgemeingültig; generell; **as a ~ rule** im allgemeinen; **in the ~ way [of things]** normalerweise; **in ~:** im allgemeinen; **'G~ Enquiries'** „Auskunft"; **d)** *(not detailed, vague)* allgemein; ungefähr, vage ⟨*Vorstellung, Beschreibung, Ähnlichkeit usw.*⟩; allgemein gehalten ⟨*Übersetzung, Bestimmung, Vertrag*⟩; oberflächlich ⟨*Ähnlichkeit*⟩; **in its ~ form** im großen und ganzen; **in the most ~ terms, in a very ~ way** nur ganz allgemein; **the ~ idea** *or* **plan is that we ...:** wir haben uns das so vorgestellt, daß wir ...; **yes, that was the ~ idea** ja, so war es gedacht; **e)** *(Mil.)* Generals⟨*rang, -streifen usw.*⟩; **~ officer** General, *der;* **f)** *(chief, head)* General⟨*direktor, -vertretung*⟩. **2.** *n. (Mil.)* General, *der; (tactician, strategist)* Stratege, *der;* **~ of the army/air force** *(Amer.)* Fünfsternegeneral, *der*

general: G~ A'merican *n.* General American, *das;* amerikanische Standardsprache; **~ anaes'thetic** *n. see* **anaesthetic 2; G~ As'sembly** *n.* Generalversammlung, *die;* Vollversammlung, *die;* **G~ Certificate of Edu'cation** *n. (Brit. Hist.) (ordinary level)* ≈ mittlere Reife; *(advanced level)* ≈ Abitur, *das;* **G~ Certificate of Secondary Edu'cation** *n. (Brit.) Abschluß der Sekundarstufe;* **~ 'dealer** *n.* Gemischtwarenhändler, *der;* **~ de'livery** *n. (Amer.)* Schalter für postlagernde Sendungen; *written in address* postlagernd; **~ e'lection** *n. see* **election; ~ head'quarters** *n. sing. or pl.* Generalkommando, *das;* **~ hospital** *n.* Allgemeinkrankenhaus, *das; (Mil.)* Lazarett, *das*

generalist ['dʒenrəlɪst] *n.* Generalist, *der*

generality [dʒenə'rælɪtɪ] *n.* **a)** *(applicability)* allgemeine Anwendbarkeit; *(of conclusion)* Allgemeingültigkeit, *die;* **a method of great ~:** eine vielseitig anwendbare Methode; **b)** *(vagueness)* Allgemeinheit, *die;* **c) talk in/of generalities** verallgemeinern/über Allgemeines sprechen; **d)** *(main, body, bulk, majority) (of mankind, electorate, etc.)* Großteil, *der; (of voters, individuals, etc.)* Mehrheit, *die*

generalisation, generalise *see* **generaliz-**

generalization [dʒenrəlaɪ'zeɪʃn] *n.* Generalisierung, *die;* Verallgemeinerung, *die;* **hasty ~:** voreilige Verallgemeinerung

generalize ['dʒenrəlaɪz] **1.** *v. t.* **a)** generalisieren; verallgemeinern; **b)** *(infer)* ableiten; **c)** *(base general statement on)* eine allgemeingültige Feststellung treffen anhand von; **d)** *(Math., Philos.)* generalisieren; **e)** *(bring into use)* verbreiten. **2.** *v. i.* **~ [about sth.]** [etw.] verallgemeinern; **~ about the French people** die Franzosen alle in einen Topf werfen *(ugs.) od.* über einen Kamm scheren; **you can't ~; each one is different** man soll nicht verallgemeinern – jeder einzelne ist wieder anders

general 'knowledge *n.* Allgemeinwissen, *das;* **it is ~ that ...:** es ist allgemein bekannt, daß ...; **~ exam/questions** das Allgemeinwissen betreffende Prüfung/Fragen

generally ['dʒenrəlɪ] *adv.* **a)** *(extensively)* allgemein; **~ available** überall erhältlich; **b) ~ speaking** im allgemeinen; **c)** *(usually)* im allgemeinen; normalerweise; **d)** *(summarizing the situation)* ganz allgemein

general: ~ 'manager *n.* [leitender] Direktor/[leitende] Direktorin; **~ 'meeting** *n.* Generalversammlung, *die;* Hauptversammlung, *die;* **G~ 'Post Office** *n. (Brit.)* Hauptpost[amt, *das*], *die;* **~ 'practice** *n. (Med.)* Allgemeinmedizin, *die;* **~ prac'titioner** *n. (Med.)* Arzt/Ärztin für Allgemeinmedizin; **~ 'public** *n.* Öffentlichkeit, *die;* Allgemeinheit, *die;* **the lecture is open to the ~ public** die Vorlesung *od.* der Vortrag ist öffentlich; **~ reader** *n.* Durchschnittsleser, *der*/-leserin, *die*

generalship ['dʒenrlʃɪp] *n., no pl. (strategy)* Führung, *die;* Kommando, *das; (fig.)* Leitung, *die*

general: ~ shop *see* **~ store; ~ 'staff** *n.* Generalstab, *der;* **~ store** *n.* Gemischtwarenhandlung, *die (veralt.);* **~ 'strike** *n.* Generalstreik, *der*

generate ['dʒenəreɪt] *v. t. (produce)* erzeugen (**from** aus); *(result in)* führen zu

generating station ['dʒenəreɪtɪŋ steɪʃn] *n.* Elektrizitätswerk, *das*

generation [dʒenə'reɪʃn] *n.* **a)** Generation, *die;* **the present/rising ~:** die heutige/heranwachsende *od.* junge Generation; **~ gap** Generationsunterschied, *der;* **first-/second-~ computers** *etc.* Computer *usw.* der ersten/zweiten Generation; **b)** *(production)* Erzeugung, *die;* **~ of electricity** Stromerzeugung, *die;* **c)** *(procreation)* **organs of ~:** Geschlechtsorgane; Fortpflanzungsorgane

generative ['dʒenərətɪv] *adj.* generativ; Zeugungs⟨*fähigkeit, -kraft usw.*⟩

generator ['dʒenəreɪtə(r)] *n.* **a)** Generator, *der; (in motor car also)* Lichtmaschine, *die;* **b)** *(originator)* Schöpfer, *der;* **be a ~ of new ideas** neue Ideen entwickeln

generic [dʒɪ'nerɪk] *adj.* **a)** gattungsmäßig; generisch *(fachspr.);* **~ term** *or* **name** *or* **heading** Ober- *od.* Gattungsbegriff, *der;* **b)** *(Biol.)* Gattungs⟨*name, -bezeichnung*⟩

generosity [dʒenə'rɒsɪtɪ] *n.* Großzügigkeit, *die;* Generosität, *die (geh.); (magnanimity)* Großmut, *die;* Generosität, *die (geh.)*

generous ['dʒenərəs] *adj.* **a)** großzügig; generös *(geh.); (noble-minded)* edel *(geh.);* großmütig; **he is ~ with compliments** er spart nicht mit Komplimenten; **b)** *(ample, abundant)* großzügig; reichhaltig ⟨*Mahl*⟩; reichlich ⟨*Nachschub, Vorrat, Portion*⟩; üppig ⟨*Figur, Formen, Mahl*⟩; weit ⟨*Ärmel, Kleidungsstück*⟩; breit ⟨*Saum*⟩; **~ size 12** groß ausgefallene Größe 12

generously ['dʒenərəslɪ] *adv.* großzügig; generös *(geh.); (magnanimously)* großmütig; **'please give ~'** „wir bitten um großzügige Spenden"

genesis ['dʒenɪsɪs] *n., pl.* **geneses** ['dʒenɪsi:z] **a) G~** *no pl.* das erste Buch Mose; Schöpfungsgeschichte, *die;* **b)** *(origin)* Ursprung, *der;* Herkunft, *die; (development into being)* Entstehung, *die*

genetic [dʒɪ'netɪk] *adj.* **a)** genetisch; **~ code** genetischer Code; **~ engineering** Gentechnologie, *die;* **b)** *(concerning origin)* entwicklungsgeschichtlich; **~ development** Entwicklungsgeschichte, *die*

genetically [dʒɪ'netɪkəlɪ] *adv.* **a)** *(according to genetics)* genetisch; **b)** *(according to origin)* entwicklungsgeschichtlich

geneticist [dʒɪ'netɪsɪst] *n.* Genetiker, *der*/Genetikerin, *die*

genetics [dʒɪ'netɪks] *n., no pl.* Genetik, *die;* Erbbiologie, *die*

Geneva [dʒɪ'ni:və] **1.** *pr. n.* Genf *(das);* **Lake ~:** der Genfer See. **2.** *attrib. adj.* Genfer

genial ['dʒi:nɪəl] *adj. (mild)* angenehm; mild ⟨*Klima, Luft*⟩; *(jovial, kindly)* freundlich; *(sociable)* jovial, leutselig ⟨*Person, Art*⟩; *(amiable)* liebenswürdig; *(cheering, enlivening)* anregend; belebend

geniality [dʒi:nɪ'ælɪtɪ] *n., no pl.* Freundlichkeit, *die;* **hearty ~:** Herzlichkeit, *die*

genially ['dʒi:nɪəlɪ] *adv.* freundlich; **be ~ disposed towards sb.** jmdm. freundlich gesinnt sein

genie ['dʒi:nɪ] *n., pl.* **genii** ['dʒi:nɪaɪ] Flaschenteufel, *der*

genital ['dʒenɪtl] **1.** *n. in pl.* Geschlechtsorgane; Genitalien. **2.** *adj.* Geschlechts⟨*teile, -organe, -drüse*⟩

genitalia [dʒenɪ'teɪlɪə] *n. pl. see* **genital 1**

genitival [dʒenɪ'taɪvl] *adj. (Ling.)* genitivisch; Genitiv-

genitive ['dʒenɪtɪv] *(Ling.)* **1.** *adj.* Genitiv-; genitivisch; **~ case** Genitiv, *der.* **2.** *n.* Genitiv, *der; see also* **absolute c**

genius ['dʒi:nɪəs] *n., pl.* **~es** *or* **genii** ['dʒi:nɪaɪ] **a)** *pl.* **~es** *(person)* Genie, *das;* **b)** *(natural ability; also iron.)* Talent, *das;* Begabung, *die; (extremely great)* Genius, *der (geh.);* Genie, *das;* **a man of ~:** ein genialer Mensch; ein Genie; **~ for languages** Sprachbegabung, *die;* **c)** *(special character; prevalent feeling, opinions, or taste)* Geist, *der; (of people)* Charakter, *der;* Wesen, *das;* **d)** *(spirit)* [Schutz]geist, *der;* Genius, *der; (of place, country)* Geist, *der;* Genius, *der;* **good/evil ~:** guter/böser Geist

Genoa ['dʒenəʊə] *pr. n.* Genua *(das)*

genocide ['dʒenəsaɪd] *n.* Völkermord, *der;* Genozid, *der (geh.)*

genre [ʒɑ̃r] *n.* **a)** Genre, *das;* Gattung, *die;* **b)** *see* **~-painting a**

'**genre-painting** *n.* **a)** Genremalerei, *die;* **b)** *(picture)* Genrebild, *das*

gent [dʒent] *n.* **a)** *(coll./joc.)* Gent, der *(iron.);* **b)** *(in shops etc.)* **~s'** Herren⟨*friseur, -ausstatter*⟩; **c)** **the G~s** *(Brit. coll.)* die Herrentoilette

genteel [dʒen'ti:l] *adj.* vornehm; fein; **they lived in ~ poverty** sie lebten in vornehmer Armut

genteelly [dʒen'ti:llɪ] *adv.* vornehm

gentian ['dʒenʃn, 'dʒenʃɪən] *n. (Bot.)* Enzian, *der*

Gentile ['dʒentaɪl] **1.** *n.* Nichtjude, *der*/-jüdin, *die; (Bibl.)* Heide, *der*/Heidin, *die.* **2.** *adj.* nichtjüdisch; *(Bibl.)* heidnisch

gentility [dʒen'tɪlɪtɪ] *n., no pl.* **a)** *(condition)* Zugehörigkeit zum niederen Adel; **b)** *(members)* niederer Adel; **c)** *(superiority)* Vornehmheit, *die;* **appearance of ~:** vornehme Erscheinung

gentle ['dʒentl] *adj.,* **~r** ['dʒentlə(r)], **~st** ['dʒentlɪst] **a)** sanft; sanftmütig ⟨*Wesen*⟩; liebenswürdig, freundlich ⟨*Person, Verhalten, Ausdrucksweise*⟩; *(not stormy, rough, or violent)* leicht, schwach ⟨*Brise*⟩; ruhig ⟨*Fluß, Wesen*⟩; *(not loud)* leise ⟨*Geräusch*⟩; *(moderate)* gemäßigt ⟨*Tempo*⟩; mäßig ⟨*Hitze*⟩; gemächlich ⟨*Tempo, Schritte, Spaziergang*⟩; *(gradual)* sanft ⟨*Abhang usw.*⟩; *(mild, not drastic)* mild ⟨*Reinigungsmittel, Shampoo usw.*⟩; wohlig ⟨*Wärme*⟩; *(easily managed)* zahm, lammfromm ⟨*Tier*⟩; **be ~ with sb./sth.** sanft mit jmdm./etw. umgehen; **with ~ care** äußerst vorsichtig *od.* behutsam; **a ~ reminder/hint** ein zarter Wink/eine zarte Andeutung; **the ~ sex** das zarte Geschlecht *(ugs. scherzh.);* **the ~ art** *or* **craft** die edle Kunst; **b)** *(dated: honourable, well-born)* edel *(veralt.);* **of ~ birth** von hoher *od.* edler Geburt; **c)** **~ reader** *(arch.)* lieber *od.* geneigter Leser

'**gentlefolk[s]** *n. pl.* feine Leute; vornehme Leute

gentleman ['dʒentlmən] *n., pl.* **gentlemen** ['dʒentlmən] **a)** *(man of good manners and breeding)* Herr, *der;* Gentleman, *der;* **~ scholar** Privatgelehrter; **a country ~:** ein Landedelmann; **b)** *(man)* Herr, *der;* **Gentlemen!** meine Herren!; **Ladies and Gentlemen!** meine Damen und Herren!; **Gentlemen, ...** *(in formal, business letter)* Sehr geehrte Herren!; **the gentlemen of the jury/press** die Herren Geschworenen/von der Presse; **gentlemen's** Herren⟨*schneider, -friseur*⟩; **c)** *(man attached to household of sovereign etc.)* Höfling, *der;* **d)** *in pl., constr. as sing.* **the Gentlemen['s]** *(Brit.)* die Herrentoilette; **'Gentlemen'** „Herren"

gentleman 'farmer *n.* Gutsherr, *der*

gentlemanly ['dʒentlmənlɪ] *adj.* gentlemanlike *nicht attrib.;* eines Gentlemans *nachgestellt;* **~ person** Gentleman, *der*

'**gentleman's** *or* '**gentlemen's agreement** *n.* Gentleman's *od.* Gentlemen's Agreement, *das;* Vereinbarung auf Treu und Glauben

gentleness ['dʒentlnɪs] *n., no pl.* Sanftheit, *die; (of nature)* Sanftmütigkeit, *die; (of nurse, words, action)* Behutsamkeit, *die; (of shampoo, cleanser, etc.)* Milde, *die; (of animal)* Zahmheit, *die*

'**gentlepeople** *see* **gentlefolk[s]**

'**gentlewoman** *n. (arch.)* **a)** *(woman of good birth or breeding)* Dame von Stand; **b)** *(lady)* Dame, *die*

gently ['dʒentlɪ] *adv. (tenderly)* zart; zärtlich; *(mildly)* sanft; *(carefully)* vorsichtig; behutsam; *(quietly, softly)* leise; *(moderately)* sanft; *(slowly)* langsam; **she ~ broke the news to him** sie brachte ihm die Nachricht schonend bei; **a ~ teasing/sarcastic manner** eine leicht neckende/sarkastische Art; **she took things very ~:** sie ließ es langsam angehen *(ugs.);* **~ does it!** immer sachte! *(ugs.);* **~!** [sachte] sachte!

gentrification [dʒentrɪfɪ'keɪʃn] *n. Einzug von sozial Höherstehenden in heruntergekommene Wohnviertel*

gentry ['dʒentrɪ] *n. pl.* **a)** niederer Adel; Gentry, *die;* **b)** *(derog.: people)* Leute *Pl.;* **light-fingered ~:** Taschendiebe *Pl.*

genuflect ['dʒenju:flekt] *v. i.* niederknien; das Knie *od.* die Knie beugen

genuflection, genuflexion [dʒenju:'flekʃn] *n.* Kniefall, *der;* [Nieder]knien, *das*

genuine ['dʒenjʊɪn] *adj.* **a)** *(actually from reputed source or author)* echt; authentisch ⟨*Text*⟩; **the ~ article** die echte Ausgabe *(fig.);* **b)** *(true)* aufrichtig; wahr ⟨*Zuneigung, Grund, Not*⟩; echt ⟨*Tränen*⟩; ernsthaft, ernstgemeint ⟨*Angebot*⟩; echt, überzeugt ⟨*Skeptiker, Kommunist usw.*⟩

genuinely ['dʒenjʊɪnlɪ] *adv.* wirklich; **it is ~ antique** es ist echt antik

genus ['dʒi:nəs, 'dʒenəs] *n., pl.* **genera** ['dʒenərə] **a)** *(Biol., Logic)* Gattung, die; **b)** *(in popular use)* Gattung, *die;* Art, *die*

geodesic [dʒi:ə'desɪk, dʒi:ə'di:sɪk] *adj.* geodätisch

geodesy [dʒi:'ɒdɪsɪ] *n.* Geodäsie, *die*

geodetic [dʒi:ə'detɪk, dʒi:ə'di:tɪk] *see* **geodesic**

geographer [dʒɪ'ɒgrəfə(r)] *n.* Geograph, *der*/Geographin, *die*

geographic [dʒi:ə'græfɪk], **geographical** [dʒi:ə'græfɪkl] *adj.* geographisch; **~ latitude** [geographische] Breite

geographically [dʒi:ə'græfɪkəlɪ] *adv.* geographisch

geography [dʒɪ'ɒgrəfɪ] *n.* Geographie, *die;* Erdkunde, *die (Schulw.);* **physical/political/regional ~:** physische Geographie *od.* Naturgeographie, *die*/politische Geographie *od.* Staatengeographie, *die*/Landeskunde, *die;* **show sb. the ~ of the house** *(coll.)* jmdm. zeigen, wo sich die einzelnen Räume befinden; *(location of WC)* jmdm. zeigen, wo das [gewisse] Örtchen ist *(fam. verhüll.)*

geological [dʒi:ə'lɒdʒɪkl] *adj.,* **geologically** [dʒi:ə'lɒdʒɪkəlɪ] *adv.* geologisch

geologist [dʒɪ'ɒlədʒɪst] *n.* Geologe, *der*/Geologin, *die*

geology [dʒɪ'ɒlədʒɪ] *n.* Geologie, *die; (features)* geologische Beschaffenheit

geometric [dʒi:ə'metrɪk], **geometrical** [dʒi:ə'metrɪkl] *adj.* geometrisch; **geometric mean** geometrisches Mittel; **geometrical progression** *or* **series** geometrische Reihe

geometrically [dʒi:ə'metrɪkəlɪ] *adv.* geometrisch

geometry [dʒɪ'ɒmɪtrɪ] *n.* Geometrie, *die*

ge'ometry set *n.* Reißzeug, *das*

geophysical [dʒi:ə'fɪzɪkl] *adj.* geophysikalisch

geophysics [dʒi:ə'fɪzɪks] *n., no pl.* Geophysik, *die*

Geordie ['dʒɔ:dɪ] *n. (Brit.)* Geordie, *der; Einwohner von Tyneside*

George [dʒɔ:dʒ] *n.* **a)** *(Hist., as name of ruler etc.)* Georg; **b)** **by ~!** *(Brit. dated coll.)* potz Blitz!; bei Gott!

George: **~ 'Cross** *n. (Brit.)* Georgskreuz, *das;* **~ 'Medal** *n. (Brit.)* Georgsmedaille, *die*

georgette [dʒɔ:'dʒet] *n. (Textiles)* [Crêpe] Georgette, *der*

Georgia ['dʒɔ:dʒɪə] *pr. n. (in USSR)* Georgien *(das); (in US)* Georgia *(das)*

[1]**Georgian** ['dʒɔ:dʒɪən] *adj. (Brit. Hist.)* georgianisch

[2]**Georgian** *adj. (USSR)* georgisch; *(US)* aus/in/von Georgia *nachgestellt*

geostationary [dʒi:ə'steɪʃənərɪ] *adj.* geostationär

Ger. *abbr.* **German** dt.

geranium [dʒə'reɪnɪəm] *n.* **a)** *(in popular use)* Geranie, *die;* Pelargonie, *die;* **b)** *(herb or shrub Geranium)* Storchschnabel, *der;* Geranie, *die;* Geranium, *das*

gerbil ['dʒɜ:bɪl] *n. (Zool.)* Wüstenmaus, *die;* Rennmaus, *die*

gerfalcon *see* **gyrfalcon**

geriatric [dʒerɪ'ætrɪk] **1.** *adj.* geriatrisch. **2.** *n. (also joc.)* Greis, *der*/Greisin, *die*

geriatrician [dʒerɪə'trɪʃn] *n.* Geriater, *der*/Geriaterin, *die*

geriatrics [dʒerɪ'ætrɪks] *n., no pl.* Geriatrie, *die;* Altersheilkunde, *die*

germ [dʒɜ:m] *n. (lit. or fig.)* Keim, *der;* **I don't want to catch your ~s** ich möchte mich nicht bei dir anstecken; **I don't want you to spread your ~s around** behalte deine Bazillen für dich!; **wheat ~:** Weizenkeim, *der;* **a ~ of truth is contained in this legend** *(fig.)* diese Legende enthält einen wahren Kern

German ['dʒɜ:mən] **1.** *adj.* deutsch; **a ~ person** ein Deutscher/eine Deutsche; **the ~ people** die Deutschen; **he/she is ~:** er ist Deutscher/sie ist Deutsche; **have a ~ degree** *(in subject)* einen Universitätsabschluß in Germanistik haben; *(from country)* einen akademischen Grad von einer deutschen Universität haben; **he is a native ~ speaker** seine Muttersprache ist Deutsch; **he is a '~ translator** *(translator from German)* er ist Übersetzer für Deutsch; **'~ teacher/student** Deutschlehrer/-student, *der;* **~ 'teacher/student** deutscher Lehrer/Student; **~ studies** Germanistik, *die;* **~ department** Germanistisches Institut. *See also* **East German 1; English 1; West German 1.** **2.** *n.* **a)** *(person)* Deutsche, *der/die;* **he/she is a ~:** er ist Deutscher/sie ist Deutsche; **b)** *(language)* Deutsch, *das;* **High ~:** Hochdeutsch, *das;* **Low ~:** Niederdeutsch, *das.* *See also* **East German 2; English 2 a; West German 2**

german *adj. postpos.* leiblich

German Democratic Re'public *pr. n. (Hist.)* Deutsche Demokratische Republik

germane [dʒɜ:'meɪn] *adj.* ~ **to** von Bedeutung für

Germanic [dʒɜ:'mænɪk] **1.** *adj.* germanisch; *(having German characteristics)* deutsch; ~ **Confederation/Empire** *(Hist.)* Deutscher Bund/Deutsches Reich; ~ **people** Germanen. **2.** *n. (Ling.)* **East/North/West ~:** Ost-/Nord-/Westgermanisch, *das*

Germanise *see* **Germanize**

Germanism ['dʒɜ:mənɪzm] *n.* **a)** *(word or idiom)* Germanismus, *der;* **b)** *(German ideas or actions)* deutsche Eigenart *od.* Sitte

Germanist ['dʒɜ:mənɪst] *n.* Germanist, *der*/Germanistin, *die*

germanium [dʒɜ:'meɪnɪəm] *n. (Chem.)* Germanium, *das*

Germanize ['dʒɜ:mənaɪz] **1.** *v.t.* eindeutschen; germanisieren *(abwertend).* **2.** *v.i.* deutsch werden

German: ~'measles *n. sing.* Röteln *Pl.;* ~ **'sausage** *n.* ≈ Fleischwurst, *die;* ~ **'shepherd [dog]** *n.* [deutscher] Schäferhund; ~ **'silver** *n.* Neusilber, *das*

Germany ['dʒɜ:mənɪ] *pr. n.* Deutschland *(das);* **Federal Republic of ~:** Bundesrepublik Deutschland, *die; see also* **East Germany; West Germany**

'germ-cell *n.* Keimzelle, *die*

germicide ['dʒɜ:mɪsaɪd] *n.* keimtötendes Mittel; Bakterizid, *das (fachspr.)*

germinal ['dʒɜ:mɪnl] *adj.* **a)** *(in earliest stage of development)* noch unentwickelt; ~ **form** Anfangsstadium, *das;* **b)** *(of germ)* germinal *(Bot.);* Keim-

germinate ['dʒɜ:mɪneɪt] **1.** *v.i.* keimen; *(fig.)* entstehen. **2.** *v.t.* zum Keimen bringen; *(fig.)* hervorbringen

germination [dʒɜ:mɪ'neɪʃn] *n.* Keimung, *die;* Keimen, *das; (fig.)* Entstehung, *die*

germ 'warfare *n.* Bakterienkrieg, *der;* biologische Kriegführung

gerrymander [dʒerɪ'mændə(r)] **1.** *v.t. willkürlich in Wahlbezirke aufteilen, um einer politischen Partei Vorteile zu verschaffen.* **2.** *n.* Wahlkreisschiebungen *Pl. (ugs.)*

gerund ['dʒerənd] *n. (Ling.)* Gerundium, *das*

Gestapo [ge'stɑ:pəʊ] *n.* Gestapo, *die*

gestation [dʒe'steɪʃn] *n.* **a)** *(of animal)* Trächtigkeit, *die; (of woman)* Schwangerschaft, *die;* ~ **period** Tragezeit, *die*/Zeit der Schwangerschaft; **b)** *(fig.)* Reifung, *die;* Heranreifen, *das*

gesticulate [dʒe'stɪkjʊleɪt] *v.i.* gestikulieren; **he ~d to the lorry-driver to stop reversing** er signalisierte dem Lkw-Fahrer, nicht weiter rückwärts zu fahren

gesticulation [dʒestɪkjʊ'leɪʃn] *n.* Gesten; **wild ~:** wildes Gestikulieren

gesture ['dʒestʃə(r)] **1.** *n.* Geste, *die (auch fig.);* Gebärde, *die (geh.);* **a ~ of resignation** eine resignierte Geste. **2.** *v.i.* gestikulieren; ~ **to sb. to do sth.** jmdm. zu verstehen geben *od. (geh.)* jmdm. bedeuten, etw. zu tun. **3.** *v.t.* zu verstehen geben; ~ **sb. to do sth.** jmdm. zu verstehen geben *od. (geh.)* jmdm. bedeuten, etw. zu tun

get [get] **1.** *v.t.,* **-tt-,** *p.t.* **got** [gɒt], *p.p.* **got** *or (in comb./arch./ Amer. except in sense* **m)** **gotten** ['gɒtn] **(got** *also coll. abbr. of* **has got** *or* **have got) a)** *(obtain)* bekommen; kriegen *(ugs.); (by buying)* kaufen; sich *(Dat.)* anschaffen ⟨*Auto usw.*⟩; *(by one's own effort for special purpose)* sich *(Dat.)* besorgen ⟨*Visum, Genehmigung, Arbeitskräfte*⟩; sich *(Dat.)* beschaffen ⟨*Geld*⟩; einholen ⟨*Gutachten*⟩; *(by contrivance)* kommen zu; *(find)* finden ⟨*Zeit*⟩; *(extract)* fördern ⟨*Kohle, Öl*⟩; ~ **an income from sth.** ein Einkommen aus etw. beziehen; **where did you ~ that?** wo hast du das her?; **the bogy man will come and ~ you** der schwarze Mann kommt und holt dich; **he got him by the leg/arm** er kriegte ihn am Bein/Arm zu fassen; ~ **sb. a job/taxi,** ~ **a job/taxi for sb.** jmdm. einen Job verschaffen/ein Taxi besorgen *od.* rufen; ~ **oneself sth./a rich man/a job** sich *(Dat.)* etw. zulegen/einen reichen Mann finden/einen Job finden; **I need to ~ some bread** ich muß Brot besorgen *od.* holen; **you can't ~ this kind of fruit in the winter months** dieses Obst gibt es im Winter nicht zu kaufen; ~ **water from a well** das Wasser vom Brunnen holen; *see also* **best 3c; better 3a; kick 1c; upper 1a; ¹wind 1f; worst 3a; b)** *(fetch)* holen; **what can I ~ you?** was kann ich Ihnen anbieten?; **is there anything I can ~ you in town?** soll ich dir etwas aus der Stadt mitbringen?; ~ **sb. from the station** jmdn. vom Bahnhof abholen; **c)** ~ **the bus** *etc. (be in time for, catch)* den Bus *usw.* erreichen *od. (ugs.)* kriegen; *(travel by)* den Bus nehmen; **d)** *(prepare)* machen *(ugs.),* zubereiten ⟨*Essen*⟩; **e)** *(coll.: eat)* essen; zu sich nehmen ⟨*Imbiß*⟩; ~ **something to eat** etwas zu essen holen; *(be given)* etwas zu essen bekommen; **f)** *(gain)* erreichen; **what do I ~ out of it?** was habe ich davon?; **g)** *(by calculation)* erhalten; **h)** *(receive)* bekommen; erhalten, *(ugs.)* kriegen ⟨*Geldsumme, Belohnung*⟩; ernten ⟨*Lob*⟩; **the country ~s very little sun/rain** die Sonne scheint/es regnet nur sehr wenig in dem Land; **he got the full force of the blow** er bekam die volle Wucht des Schlages ab; **she got some bruises from the fall** sie hat sich *(Dat.)* mehrere Prellungen bei dem Sturz zugezogen; **he got his jaw broken in a fight** bei einer Schlägerei wurde ihm der Kiefer gebrochen; ~ **nothing but ingratitude** nichts als Undank ernten; **i)** *(receive as penalty)* bekommen, *(ugs.)* kriegen ⟨*6 Monate Gefängnis, lebenslänglich, Geldstrafe, Tracht Prügel*⟩; **that's what I ~ for trying to be helpful** *(iron.)* das hat man nun davon, daß man helfen will; **you'll ~ it** *(coll.)* du kriegst Prügel *(ugs.);* es setzt was *(ugs.); (be scolded)* du kriegst was zu hören *(ugs.);* **you'll really ~ it this time** diesmal wirst du nicht ungeschoren davonkommen; *see also* **best 3d; boot 1a; neck 1a; ¹sack 1b; j)** *(kill)* töten; erlegen ⟨*Wild*⟩; *(hit, injure)* treffen; erwischen; **I'll ~ you for that** das wirst du mir büßen; **they've got me** jetzt haben sie mich; ich bin getroffen *(Milit.);* ~ **him, boy!** *(to dog)* faß!; **k)** *(win)* bekommen; finden ⟨*Anerkennung*⟩; sich *(Dat.)* verschaffen ⟨*Ansehen*⟩; erzielen ⟨*Tor, Punkt, Treffer*⟩; gewinnen ⟨*Spiel, Preis, Belohnung*⟩; belegen ⟨*ersten usw. Platz*⟩; ~ **fame** berühmt werden; ~ **permission** die Erlaubnis erhalten; **he got his fare paid by the firm** seine Firma hat [ihm] die Fahrt bezahlt; **l)** *(come to have)* finden ⟨*Schlaf, Ruhe*⟩; bekommen ⟨*Einfall, Vorstellung, Gefühl*⟩; gewinnen ⟨*Eindruck*⟩; *(contract)* bekommen ⟨*Kopfschmerzen, Grippe, Malaria*⟩; ~ **some rest** sich ausruhen; ~ **one's freedom** seine Freiheit wiederhaben; ~ **an idea/a habit from sb.** von jmdm. eine Idee/Angewohnheit übernehmen; **I hope I don't ~ the flu from you** hoffentlich steckst du mich nicht mit deiner Grippe an; *see also* **brain 1a; religion b; m)** **have got** *(coll.: have)* haben; **give it all you've got** gib dein Bestes; **have got a toothache/a cold** Zahnschmerzen/eine Erkältung haben *od.* erkältet sein; **have got to do sth.** etw. tun müssen; **something has got to be done [about it]** dagegen muß etwas unternommen werden; **n)** *(succeed in bringing, placing, etc.)* bringen; kriegen *(ugs.);* ~ **sth. through the door** *etc.* etw. durch die Tür *usw.* bekommen; **she could hardly ~ herself out of bed** sie kam kaum aus dem Bett hoch; **that bike won't ~ you very far** mit dem Fahrrad wirst du nicht weit kommen; **I must ~ a message to her** ich muß ihr eine Nachricht zukommen lassen; **he's got you where he wants you** er hat dich genau da[hin] gekriegt, wo er dich hin haben wollte *(ugs.);* **o)** *(bring into some state)* **this music will ~ the party going** diese Musik wird Schwung in die Party bringen; ~ **a project going** ein Projekt in Gang bringen; ~ **a machine going** eine Maschine in Gang setzen *od.* bringen; ~ **things going** *or* **started** die Dinge in Gang bringen; ~ **everything packed/prepared** alles [ein]packen/vorbereiten; ~ **sth. ready/done** etw. fertig machen; ~ **oneself talked about** sich ins Gerede bringen; ~ **one's feet wet** nasse Füße kriegen; ~ **one's hands dirty** sich *(Dat.)* die Hände schmutzig machen; **I want to ~ the work done** ich möchte die Arbeit fertig haben; **I didn't ~ much done today** ich habe heute nicht viel geschafft; ~ **with child** *(dated)* schwängern; **he's got his sums right** er hat richtig gerechnet; **I need to ~ my house painted** ich muß mein Haus streichen lassen; **you'll ~ yourself thrown out/arrested** du schaffst es noch, daß du rausgeworfen/verhaftet wirst; **I got myself lost** ich habe mich verlaufen; ~ **sb. talking/drunk/interested** jmdn. zum Reden bringen/betrunken machen/jmds. Interesse wecken; ~ **one's hair cut/clothes dry-cleaned** sich *(Dat.)* die Haare schneiden lassen/seine Sachen reinigen lassen; **p)** *(induce)* ~ **sb. to do sth.** jmdn. dazu bringen, etw. zu tun; ~ **sth. to do sth.** es schaffen, daß etw. etw. tut; **I can never ~ you to listen to me** nie hörst du mir zu!; **I can't ~ the car to start/the door to shut** ich kriege das Auto nicht in Gang/die Tür nicht zu; **q)** *(bring in)* einbringen ⟨*Ernte*⟩; **r)** *(Radio, Telev.: pick up)* empfangen ⟨*Sender*⟩; **he's trying to ~ BBC 2** er versucht, BBC 2 reinzukriegen *(ugs.);* **s)** *(get in touch with by telephone)* ~ **sb. [on the phone]** jmdn. [telefonisch] erreichen; **please ~ me this number** bitte verbinden Sie mich mit dieser Nummer; **t)** *(answer)* **I'll ~ it!** ich geh' schon!; *(answer doorbell)* ich mach' auf; *(answer the phone)* ich gehe ran *(ugs.) od.* nehme ab; **u)** *(coll.: perplex)* in Verwirrung bringen; **this question will ~ him** mit dieser Frage kriegen wir ihn *(ugs.);* **you've got me there; I don't know** da bin ich überfragt – ich weiß es nicht; **v)** *(coll.) (understand)* kapieren *(ugs.);* verstehen ⟨*Personen*⟩; *(hear)* mitkriegen *(ugs.);* ~ **it?** alles klar? *(ugs.);* **w)** *(coll.: annoy)* aufregen *(ugs.);* **x)** *(coll.: attract, involve emotionally)* packen. **2.** *v.i.,* **-tt-, got, gotten a)** *(succeed in coming or going)* kommen; ~ **to London/the top before dark** London/den Gipfel vor Einbruch der Dunkelheit erreichen; **we got as far as Oxford** wir kamen bis Oxford; **we have got as far as quadratic equations** wir sind bis zu quadratischen Gleichungen gekommen; **how did that ~ here?** wie ist das hierher gekommen?; **b)** *(come to be)* ~ **working** sich an die Arbeit machen; ~ **talking [to sb.]** [mit jmdm.] ins Gespräch kommen; ~ **to talking about sth./sb.** auf etw./jmdn. zu sprechen kommen; **I got [to] thinking how nice ...:** ich habe mir überlegt, wie nett ...; ~ **going** *or* **started** *(leave)* losgehen; aufbrechen; *(start talking)* loslegen *(ugs.); (become lively or operative)* in Schwung kommen; **once he ~s going** wenn er einmal anfängt; ~ **going on** *or* **with sth.** mit etw. anfangen; sich hinter etw. *(Akk.)* klemmen *(ugs.);* ~ **going on sb.** jmdn. bearbeiten; **I can't ~ started in the mornings** ich komme morgens nicht in Gang; *see also* **way 1f; c)** ~ **to know sb.** jmdn. kennenlernen; **he got to like/hate her** mit der Zeit mochte er sie/begann er, sie zu hassen; ~ **to hear of sth.** von etw. erfahren; **I never ~ to see you any more** dich sieht man ja gar nicht mehr *od.* bekommt man ja gar nicht mehr zu Gesicht; ~ **to do sth.** *(succeed in doing)* etw. tun können; dazu kommen, etw. zu tun; **d)** *(become)* werden; ~ **ready/washed** sich fertigmachen/waschen; ~ **frightened/hungry** Angst/Hunger kriegen; **the time is ~ting near** die Zeit naht; ~ **excited about sth.** sich auf etw. *(Akk.)* freuen; ~ **interested in sth.** sich für etw. interessieren; ~ **caught in the rain** vom Regen überrascht werden; ~ **well soon!** gute Besserung!; *see also* **better 1; e)** *(sl.: be off, clear out)* verschwinden *(ugs.)*

~ **a'bout** *v. i.* **a)** *(move)* sich bewegen; *(travel)* herumkommen; **b)** *(spread)* sich herumsprechen; ‹*Gerücht:*› sich verbreiten

~ **across 1.** [--'-] *v. i.* **a)** *(to/from other side)* rüberkommen *(ugs.)*; **b)** *(coll.: be communicated)* rüberkommen *(ugs.)*; ~ **across [to sb.]** ‹*Person:*› sich [jmdm.] verständlich machen; ‹*Witz, Idee:*› [bei jmdm.] ankommen. **2.** *[stress varies] v. t.* **a)** *(cross)* überqueren; ~ **sb./sth. across [sth.]** *(transport to/from other side)* jmdn./etw. [über etw. *(Akk.)*] hin-/herüberbringen; **b)** *(coll.: communicate)* vermitteln, klarmachen (**to** *Dat.*); ~ **a joke across to sb.** mit einem Witz bei jmdm. ankommen

~ **a'long** *v. i.* **a)** *(advance, progress)* ~ **along well** [gute] Fortschritte machen; **how is he ~ting along with his work/is his work ~ting along?** wie kommt er mit seiner Arbeit voran/kommt seine *od.* geht es mit seiner Arbeit voran?; **the patient is ~ting along very well** mit dem Patienten geht es aufwärts; **b)** *(manage)* zurechtkommen; **c)** *(agree or live sociably)* auskommen; ~ **along with each other** *or* **together** miteinander auskommen; **d)** *(leave)* sich auf den Weg machen; ~ **along with you!** *(fig. coll.)* ach, geh *od.* komm! *(ugs.)*; ach, erzähl mir doch nichts! *(ugs.)*

~ **a'round 1.** *v. i.* **a)** *see* ~ **round 1 b; b)** *see* ~ **about a. 2.** *v. t. see* ~ **round 2 a, b, d**

~ **at** *v. t.* **a)** herankommen an (+ *Akk.*); **let sb. ~ at sth.** jmdn. an etw. *(Akk.)* [heran]lassen; **woodworm has got at the wardrobe** in dem Schrank ist der Holzwurm; **b)** *(coll.: start work on)* sich machen an (+ *Akk.*); **c)** *(~ hold of; ascertain)* [he]rausfinden ‹*Wahrheit, Ursache usw.*›; **d)** *(coll.)* **what are you/is he getting at?** worauf wollen Sie/will er hinaus?; *(referring to)* worauf spielen Sie/spielt er jetzt an?; **e)** *(sl.: tamper with)* sich zu schaffen machen an (+ *Dat.*); *(bribe)* bestechen; *(influence)* unter Druck setzen; **f)** *(sl.: attack, taunt)* anmachen *(salopp)*; **I have the feeling that I'm being got at** ich habe das Gefühl, daß man mich anpflaumen will *(ugs.)*

~ **a'way 1.** *v. i.* **a)** wegkommen; *(stand back)* zurücktreten; **you need to ~ away [from here]** du müßtest einmal [von hier] fort; **I can't ~ away from work** ich kann nicht von der Arbeit weg; ~ **away from the field** *(Racing)* sich vom Feld absetzen; **there is no ~ting away from the fact that ...:** man kommt nicht um die Tatsache *od.* darum herum, daß ...; ~ **away from it all** *see* **all 1 a; b)** *(escape)* entkommen; entwischen *(ugs.)*; **that's the one that got away** *(fig.)* das/der/die ist mir/dir *usw.* durch die Lappen gegangen *(ugs.)*; **c)** *(start)* aufbrechen; ‹*Läufer:*› losrennen; ‹*Schwimmer:*› losschwimmen; **d)** *in imper. (coll.)* ~ **away [with you]!** ach, geh *od.* komm! *(ugs.)*; ach, erzähl mir doch nichts! *(ugs.)*. **2.** *v. t.* **a)** *(remove, move)* wegnehmen; entfernen, *(ugs.)* wegkriegen ‹*Fleck*›; wegräumen ‹*Besteck, Geschirr*›; ~ **sth. away from sb.** jmdm. etw. wegnehmen; **we've got to ~ her away from here/his influence/her boy-friend** wir müssen sie von hier fortbringen/seinem Einfluß entziehen/von ihrem Freund fernhalten; **b)** *(post)* zur Post bringen; abschicken; wegkriegen *(ugs.)*. *See also* **get-away**

~ **a'way with** *v. t.* **a)** *(steal and escape with)* entkommen mit; **b)** *(as punishment)* davonkommen mit; **c)** *(coll.: go unpunished for)* ungestraft davonkommen mit; **the things he ~s away with!** was der sich *(Dat.)* alles erlauben kann!; ~ **away with it** es sich *(Dat.)* erlauben können; *(succeed)* damit durchkommen; **he can ~ away with anything** *or (fig.)* **murder** er kann sich *(Dat.)* alles erlauben

~ **'back 1.** *v. i.* **a)** *(return)* zurückkommen; ~ **back home** nach Hause kommen; **b)** *(stand away)* zurücktreten. **2.** *v. t.* **a)** *(recover)* wieder- *od.* zurückbekommen; wieder- *od.* zurückkriegen *(ugs.)*; zurückgewinnen ‹*Kraft, Ehefrau, Freund usw.*›; ~ **one's strength back** wieder zu Kräften kommen; **b)** *(return)* zurücktun; **I can't ~ the lid back on it** ich kriege den Deckel nicht wieder drauf *(ugs.)*; ~ **the children back home** die Kinder nach Hause zurückbringen; **c)** ~ **one's 'own back [on sb.]** *(sl.)* sich [an jmdm.] rächen

~ **'back at** *v. t. (coll.)* ~ **back at sb. for sth.** jmdm. etw. heimzahlen

~ **'back to** *v. t.* ~ **back to sb./sb.'s question** auf jmdn./jmds. Frage zurückkommen; **I'll ~ back to you on that** ich komme darauf noch zurück; ~ **back to one's work/to work/to the office** wieder an seine Arbeit/an die Arbeit/ins Büro gehen; **[~ting back to what I was saying ...:** um [noch einmal] auf das, was ich gesagt habe, zurückzukommen

~ **behind 1.** [--'-] *v. i.* zurückbleiben; ins Hintertreffen geraten *(ugs.)*; *(with payments)* in Rückstand geraten. **2.** *[stress varies] v. t.* **a)** ~ **behind sb./sth.** sich hinter jmdn./etw. stellen; **b)** *(not progress as fast as)* ~ **behind sb./sth.** hinter jmdm./etw. zurückbleiben

~ **'by 1.** *v. i.* **a)** *(move past)* passieren; vorbeikommen; **let sb. ~ by** jmdn. vorbeilassen; **b)** *(coll.: be acceptable, adequate)* **she should [just about] ~ by in the exam** sie müßte die Prüfung [gerade so] schaffen; **his essay isn't very good but it will ~ by** sein Aufsatz ist nicht sehr gut, aber es reicht noch; **c)** *(coll.: survive, manage)* über die Runden kommen *(ugs.)* (**on** mit). **2.** *v. t.* **a)** *(move past)* ~ **by sb./sth.** an jmdm./etw. vorbeikommen; **he got by the car in front** er überholte den vorderen Wagen; **b)** *(pass unnoticed)* entgehen (+ *Dat.*); unbemerkt vorbeikommen an (+ *Dat.*)

~ **down 1.** [-'-] *v. i.* **a)** *(come down)* heruntersteigen; *(go down)* hinuntersteigen; *(from bus etc.)* aussteigen (**from** aus); *(from horse)* absteigen (**from** von); **help sb. ~ down from the horse/bus** jmdm. vom Pferd/aus dem Bus helfen; **b)** *(leave table)* aufstehen; **c)** *(bend down)* sich bücken; ~ **down on one's knees** niederknien; sich hinknien. **2.** *[stress varies] v. t.* **a)** *(come down)* heruntersteigen; herunterkommen; *(go down)* hinuntersteigen; hinuntergehen; **b)** ~ **sb./sth. down** *(manage to bring down)* jmdn./etw. hin-/herunterbringen; *(with some difficulty)* jmdn./etw. hin-/herunterbekommen; *(take down from above)* jmdn./etw. hin-/herunterholen; **c)** ~ **one's trousers ~:** die Hose herunterziehen; **d)** *(swallow)* hinunterschlucken; **e)** *(write, record)* ~ **sth. down [on paper]** etw. schriftlich festhalten *od.* zu Papier bringen; **f)** *(coll.: depress)* fertigmachen *(ugs.)*; **g)** *(reduce)* kürzen ‹*Aufsatz*› (**to** auf + *Akk.*); senken ‹*Fieber, Preis*›; *(by bargaining)* herunterdrücken ‹*Preis*›; **I got him down [to £40]** ich habe ihn [auf 40 Pfund] heruntergehandelt

~ **'down to** *v. t.* ~ **down to sth.** sich an etw. *(Akk.)* machen; ~ **down to writing a letter** sich hinsetzen und einen Brief schreiben; **let's ~ down to the facts now** wenden wir uns nun den Fakten zu!; *see also* **brass tacks; business f**

~ **'in 1.** *v. i.* **a)** *(enter) (into bus etc.)* einsteigen; *(into bath)* hineinsteigen; *(into bed)* sich hinlegen; *(into room, house, etc.)* eintreten; *(intrude)* eindringen; **b)** *(arrive)* ankommen; *(get home)* heimkommen; **c)** *(be elected)* gewählt werden; ~ **in for Islington** als Abgeordneter für Islington ins Unterhaus einziehen; **d)** *(obtain place) (at institution etc.)* angenommen werden; *(at university)* einen Studienplatz bekommen; *(as employee)* genommen werden; **e)** *(coll.: gain an advantage)* ~ **in first/before sb.** die Nase vorn haben *(ugs.)*/schneller als jmd. sein. **2.** *v. t.* **a)** *(bring in)* einbringen ‹*Ernte*›; hineinbringen, ins Haus bringen ‹*Einkäufe, Kind*›; einlagern ‹*Kohlen, Kartoffeln*›; hineinfahren, in die Garage fahren ‹*Auto*›; reinholen ‹*Wäsche*›; einholen ‹*Netze, Hummerkörbe*›; *(Brit.: fetch and pay for)* holen ‹*Getränke*›; **b)** *(coll.: enter)* einsteigen in (+ *Akk.*) ‹*Auto, Zug*›; **c)** *(submit)* abgeben ‹*Artikel, Hausarbeit*›; einreichen ‹*Bewerbung, Bericht*›; **d)** *(receive)* erhalten; reinkriegen *(ugs.)*; **e)** *(send for)* holen; rufen ‹*Arzt, Polizei*›; hinzuziehen ‹*Spezialist*›; **f)** *(plant, sow)* in die Erde kriegen *(ugs.)*; auspflanzen ‹*Blumenzwiebeln*›; aussäen ‹*Samen*›; **g)** *(fit in)* reinkriegen *(ugs.)*; einschieben ‹*Unterrichtsstunde*›; **try to ~ in a word about sth.** sich zu etw. äußern wollen; *see also* **edgeways c; h)** *(cause to be admitted)* ~ **sb. in** *(as member, pupil, etc.)* jmdm. die Aufnahme ermöglichen; jmdn. reinbringen *(ugs.)*; **his good results should ~ him in** mit seinen guten Noten müßte er reinkommen; **you can ~ him in as a guest** du kannst ihn als Gast mitbringen; **i)** *(Boxing)* ~ **a blow/punch in** einen Schlag *od.* Treffer landen; *(fig.: coll.)* einen Schlag versetzen. *See also* **eye 1 a; hand 1 k**

~ **'in on** *v. t. (coll.)* sich beteiligen an (+ *Dat.*); *see also* **act 1 e**

~ **into** *v. t.* **a)** *(bring into)* fahren ‹*Auto usw.*› in (+ *Akk.*) ‹*Garage*›; bringen in (+ *Akk.*) ‹*Haus, Bett, Hafen*›; **b)** *(enter)* gehen/*(as intruder)* eindringen in (+ *Akk.*) ‹*Haus*›; [ein]steigen in (+ *Akk.*) ‹*Auto usw.*›; [ein]treten in (+ *Akk.*) ‹*Zimmer*›; steigen in (+ *Akk.*) ‹*Wasser*›; **the coach ~s into the station at 9 p.m.** der Bus kommt um 21.00 Uhr am Busbahnhof an; **it's getting into the hundreds** das geht schon in die Hunderte; **c)** *(gain admission to)* eingelassen werden in (+ *Akk.*); angenommen werden in (+ *Dat.*) ‹*Schule*›; einen Studienplatz erhalten an (+ *Dat.*) ‹*Universität*›; genommen werden von ‹*Firma*›; ~ **sb. into a school/firm/club** dafür sorgen, daß jmd. von einer Schule angenommen/einer Firma genommen/einem Verein aufgenommen wird; ~ **into Parliament** ins Parlament einziehen; **d)** *(coll.: make put on)* hineinkriegen in (+ *Akk.*); ~ **into one's clothes** sich anziehen; **I can't ~ into these trousers** ich komme in diese Hose nicht mehr rein *(ugs.)*; **e)** *(penetrate)* [ein]dringen in (+ *Akk.*); **sand got into my eyes** ich habe Sand in die Augen bekommen; **how did the fly ~ into the jam?** wie ist die Fliege in die Marmelade gekommen?; **f)** *(begin to undergo)* geraten in (+ *Akk.*); kommen in (+ *Akk.*) ‹*Schwierigkeiten*›; *(cause to undergo)* stürzen in (+ *Akk.*) ‹*Schulden, Unglück*›; bringen in (+ *Akk.*) ‹*Schwierigkeiten*›; **g)** *(accustom to, become accustomed to)* annehmen ‹*Gewohnheit*›; ~ **into the job/work** sich einarbeiten; **once you've got into the book, ...:** wenn man sich einmal eingelesen hat, ...; *see also* **habit 1 a; way 1 l, o; h)** *(change in mood to)* geraten in (+ *Akk.*) ‹*Wut, Panik*›; *(cause to change in mood to)* bringen in (+ *Akk.*) ‹*Wut*›; stürzen in (+ *Akk.*) ‹*Verzweiflung, Panik*›; **i) what's got into him?** was ist nur in ihn gefahren?; **something must have got into him** irgend etwas muß in ihn gefahren sein. *See also* **act 1 e**

~ **'in with** *v. t. (coll.)* ~ **in [well] with sb.** sich mit jmdm. gut stellen; **he got in with a bad crowd** er geriet in schlechte Gesellschaft; **he got in with a pretty girl** er bändelte mit einem hübschen Mädchen an

~ off 1. [-'-] *v. i.* **a)** *(alight)* aussteigen; *(dismount)* absteigen; **tell sb. where he ~s off** *or* **where to ~ off** *(fig. coll.)* jmdn. in seine Grenzen verweisen; **she told him where to ~ off in no uncertain terms** sie machte ihm unmißverständlich klar, daß er zu weit gegangen war; **b)** *(not remain on sb./sth.)* runtergehen; *(from chair)* aufstehen; *(from ladder, tree, table, lawn, carpet)* herunterkommen; *(let go)* loslassen; **~ off, you filthy dog!** verschwinde, du dreckiger Köter!; **c)** *(start)* aufbrechen; **~ off to school/to work** zur Schule/Arbeit losgehen/-fahren; **we hope to ~ off before seven** wir hoffen, noch vor sieben wegzukommen; **~ off to an early start** früh aufbrechen *od.* wegkommen; **~ off to a good** *etc.* **start** einen guten *usw.* Start haben; *see also* **foot 1 a**; **d)** *(be sent)* ‹*Brief:*› abgeschickt werden; ‹*Paket, Telegramm:*› aufgegeben werden; **e)** *(escape punishment or injury)* davonkommen; **~ off lightly** glimpflich davonkommen; **f)** *(fall asleep)* einschlafen; **g)** *(leave)* [weg]gehen; **~ off early** [schon] früh [weg]gehen. **2.** *[stress varies] v. t.* **a)** *(dismount from)* [ab]steigen von ‹*Fahrrad*›; steigen von ‹*Pferd*›; *(alight from)* aussteigen aus ‹*Bus, Zug usw.*›; steigen aus ‹*Boot*›; **b)** *(not remain on)* herunterkommen von ‹*Rasen, Teppich, Mauer, Leiter, Tisch*›; aufstehen von ‹*Stuhl*›; verschwinden von, verlassen ‹*Gelände*›; **~ off my toes!** geh von meinem Fuß runter! *(ugs.)*; **~ off the subject** vom Thema abkommen; **c)** *(cause to start)* [los]schicken; **it takes ages to ~ the children off to school** es dauert eine Ewigkeit, die Kinder für die Schule fertigzumachen; **~ sth. off to a good** *etc.* **start** einer Sache *(Dat.)* zu einem guten *usw.* Start verhelfen; **d)** *(remove)* ausziehen ‹*Kleidung usw.*›; entfernen ‹*Fleck, Farbe usw.*›; abbekommen ‹*Deckel, Ring*›; **~ sth. off sth.** etw. von etw. entfernen/abbekommen; **~ sb./an animal off [sth.]** jmdn./ein Tier [von etw.] wegjagen; **I can't ~ my shoes off** ich kriege die Schuhe nicht aus *(ugs.)*; **~ that cat off my desk/me!** schaff mir die Katze vom Tisch/Leib!; **~ sb. off a subject** jmdn. von einem Thema abbringen; **e)** *(send, dispatch)* abschicken; aufgeben ‹*Telegramm, Paket*›; **f)** *(cause to escape punishment)* davonkommen lassen; **the lawyer got his client off with a small fine** der Rechtsanwalt konnte für seinen Klienten ein niedriges Bußgeld durchsetzen; **g)** *(not have to do, go to, etc.)* frei haben; **~ off school/doing one's homework** nicht zur Schule zu gehen/keine Hausaufgaben zu machen brauchen; **~ time/a day off [work]** frei/einen Tag frei bekommen; **~ off work [early]** [früher] Feierabend machen; **I have got the afternoon off** ich habe den Nachmittag frei; **h)** *(cause to fall asleep)* zum Einschlafen bringen; **i)** *(coll.: obtain from)* bekommen von; kriegen von *(ugs.)*; **I got that recipe off my mother** das Rezept habe ich von meiner Mutter

~ 'off with *v. t. (Brit. coll.)* aufreißen *(salopp)*; anbändeln mit *(ugs.)*; **~ sb. off with sb.** jmdn. mit jmdm. zusammenbringen *od.* verkuppeln

~ on 1. [-'-] *v. i.* **a)** *(climb on) (on bicycle)* aufsteigen; *(on horse etc.)* aufsitzen; *(enter vehicle)* einsteigen; **you can't ~ on, the bus is full** Sie können nicht mehr rein *(ugs.)*, der Bus ist voll; **b)** *(make progress)* vorankommen; **~ on in life/the world** es zu etwas [im Leben] bringen; **you're ~ting on very nicely** Sie machen gute Fortschritte; **c)** *(fare)* **how did you ~ on there?** wie ist es dir dort ergangen?; **he's ~ting on well** es geht ihm gut; **I didn't ~ on too well in my exams** meine Prüfungen sind nicht besonders gut gelaufen *(ugs.)*; **d)** *(become late)* vorrücken; **it's ~ting on for five** es geht auf fünf zu; **it's ~ting on for six months since ...:** es sind bald sechs Monate, seit ...; **time is ~ting on** es wird langsam spät; **e)** *(advance in age)* älter werden; **be ~ting on in years/for seventy** langsam älter werden/auf die Siebzig zugehen; **f) there were ~ting on for fifty people** es waren an die fünfzig Leute da; **g)** *(manage)* zurechtkommen; **h)** *see* **~ along c. 2.** *[stress varies] v. t. (coll.)* **a)** *(climb on)* steigen auf (+ *Akk.*) ‹*Fahrrad, Pferd*›; *(cause to climb on)* setzen auf (+ *Akk.*); *(enter, board)* einsteigen in (+ *Akk.*) ‹*Zug, Bus, Flugzeug*›; gehen auf (+ *Akk.*) ‹*Schiff*›; *(cause to enter or board)* setzen in (+ *Akk.*) ‹*Bus, Zug, Flugzeug*›; bringen auf (+ Akk.) ‹*Schiff*›; **b)** *(put on)* anziehen ‹*Kleider, Schuhe*›; aufsetzen ‹*Hut, Kessel*›; *(load)* [auf]laden auf (+ *Akk.*); **~ the cover [back] on** den Deckel [wieder] drauftun; *(with some difficulty)* den Deckel [wieder] draufbekommen; **c)** *(coll.)* **~ something on sb.** *(discover sth. incriminating)* etwas gegen jmdn. in der Hand haben. *See also* **foot 1 a; move 1 f; nerve 1 b**

~ 'on to *v. t.* **a)** *see* **~ on 2 a**; **b)** *(contact)* sich in Verbindung setzen mit; *(by telephone)* anrufen; *(more insistently)* **~ on to sb.** jmdm. auf die Pelle rücken *(ugs.)*; **c)** *(trace, find)* ausfindig machen; **~ on to sb.'s trail/scent** jmdm. auf die Spur kommen/jmds. Fährte aufnehmen; **d)** *(realize)* **~ on to sth.** hinter etw. *(Akk.)* kommen; **~ on to the fact that ...:** dahinterkommen, daß ...; **e)** *(move or pass to)* übergehen zu; *(unintentionally in conversation)* kommen auf (+ *Akk.*); **we don't ~ on to anatomy until next year** zur Anatomie kommen wir erst im nächsten Jahr

~ 'on with *v. t.* **a)** weitermachen mit; **let sb. ~ on with it** *(coll.)* jmdn. [allein weiter]machen lassen; **enough to be ~ting on with** genug für den Anfang *od.* fürs erste; **b) = ~ along with** *see* **~ along a, c**

~ 'out 1. *v. i.* **a)** *(go away) (walk out)* rausgehen (**of** aus); *(drive out)* rausfahren (**of** aus); *(alight)* aussteigen (**of** aus); *(climb out)* rausklettern (**of** aus); **~ out from under** *(fig. coll.)* noch einmal davonkommen; **~ out [of my room]!** raus [aus meinem Zimmer]!; **we'd better ~ out, and quick!** wir verschwinden hier besser, und zwar schnell!; **you need to ~ out a bit more** du müßtest hier öfter mal raus; **she likes to ~ out for a breath of fresh air** sie geht gern mal vor die Tür, um frische Luft zu schnappen; **b)** *(leak)* austreten (**of** aus); *(escape from cage, jail)* ausbrechen, entkommen (**of** aus); *(fig.)* ‹*Geheimnis:*› herauskommen; ‹*Nachrichten:*› durchsickern; **c) ~ out [of it]!** *(sl.)* ach, geh *od.* komm!; ach, erzähl mir doch nichts! *(ugs.)*; **d)** *(Cricket)* ausgeschlagen werden. **2.** *v. t.* **a)** *(cause to leave)* rausbringen (**of** aus); *(send out)* rausschicken (**of** aus); *(throw out)* rauswerfen (**of** aus); **~ all the passengers out** alle Passagiere aussteigen lassen; **~ a nail out/out of the wall** einen Nagel herauskriegen/aus der Wand kriegen *(ugs.)*; **~ a stain out/out of sth.** einen Fleck wegbekommen/aus etw. herausbekommen; **b)** *(bring or take out)* herausholen (**of** aus); herausziehen ‹*Korken*›; *(drive out)* herausfahren (**of** aus); **you only ~ out what you put in** *(fig.)* man kriegt nur raus, was man reingesteckt hat *(ugs.)*; **c)** *(withdraw)* abheben ‹*Geld*› (**of** von); **d)** *(publish)* herausbringen; **e)** *(speak, utter)* hervorbringen ‹*Entschuldigung, Gruß usw.*›; herausbringen ‹*Wort*›; **f)** *(Cricket)* ausschlagen; **g)** *(work out)* herausbekommen, *(ugs.)* herauskriegen ‹*Rechenaufgabe, Summe, Rätsel*›. *See also* **get-out**

~ 'out of *v. t.* **a)** *(leave)* verlassen ‹*Zimmer, Haus, Stadt, Land*›; *(cause to leave)* entfernen aus; *(extract from)* herausziehen aus; *(bring or take out of)* herausholen; *(leak from)* austreten aus; *(withdraw from)* abheben von; **~ a book out of the library** ein Buch aus der Bibliothek ausleihen; **~ a lazy person out of bed** einen Faulpelz aus dem Bett kriegen *(ugs.)*; **~ him out of my sight!** schaff ihn mir aus den Augen!; **~ me out of this mess** hol mich aus diesem Schlamassel heraus! *(ugs.)*; **~ sth. out of one's head** *or* **mind** sich *(Dat.)* etw. aus dem Kopf schlagen; **he can't ~ the idea out of his head** er wird den Gedanken nicht los; *see also* **~ out 1 a, b, c, 2 a, b, c**; **b)** *(draw out of)* herausbringen *(ugs.) od.* herausbekommen ‹*Wahrheit, Worte*› aus; **c)** *(escape)* herauskommen aus; *(avoid)* herumkommen um *(ugs.)*; sich drücken vor (+ *Dat.*) *(ugs.)*‹*Arbeit*›; **I can't ~ out of it now** jetzt muß ich mich auch daran halten; **d)** *(gain from)* herausholen ‹*Geld*› aus; machen *(ugs.) od.* erzielen ‹*Gewinn*› bei; **I couldn't ~ much out of this book** das Buch hat mir nicht viel gegeben; **~ a word/the truth/a confession out of sb.** aus jmdm. ein Wort/die Wahrheit/ein Geständnis herausbringen; **~ the best/most/utmost out of sb./sth.** das Beste/Meiste/Äußerste aus jmdm./etw. herausholen. *See also* **bed 1 a; depth d; habit 1 a; hand 1 b; way 1 l**

~ outside [of] *v. t. (sl.: eat)* sich reinziehen *(ugs.)*

~ 'over 1. *v. i.* **a)** *(cross)* **~ over to the other side** auf die andere Seite gehen; **manage to ~ over to the other side** es schaffen, auf die andere Seite zu kommen; **I need to talk to you. When can you ~ over here?** ich muß dich sprechen – wann kannst du mal vorbeikommen?; **b)** *(coll.) see* **~ across 1 b. 2.** *v. t.* **a)** *(cross)* gehen über (+ *Akk.*); setzen über (+ *Akk.*) ‹*Fluß*›; *(climb)* klettern über (+ *Akk.*); *(cause to cross)* [hinüber]bringen über (+ *Akk.*); **we got ourselves safely over the river** wir kamen sicher über den Fluß; **manage to ~ over the road** es schaffen, über die Straße zu kommen; **b)** *see* **~ across 2 b**; **c)** *(surmount)* überwinden; **d)** *(overcome)* überwinden; hinwegkommen über (+ *Akk.*); **e)** *(recover from)* überwinden; hinwegkommen über (+ *Akk.*); verwinden *(geh.)* ‹*Verlust*›; sich erholen von ‹*Krankheit*›; **f)** *(fully believe)* **I can't ~ over his cheek/the fact that ...:** solche Frechheit kann ich nicht begreifen/ich kann gar nicht fassen, daß ...; **g)** *(travel over)* zurücklegen ‹*Strecke*›; **h)** *(coll.: do, so as not to have still to come)* hinter sich bringen; **you might as well ~ it over and done with** je eher du es tust, desto schneller hast du es hinter dir

~ 'over with *v. t. (coll.)* **~ sth. over with** etw. hinter sich bringen

~ 'past 1. *v. i. see* **~ by 1 a. 2.** *v. t. see* **~ by 2 a, b**

~ 'round 1. *v. i.* **a)** *see* **~ about**; **b) ~ round to doing sth.** dazu kommen, etw. zu tun. **2.** *v. t.* **a) she got round the shops very quickly** sie erledigte ihre Besorgungen sehr schnell; **b)** *(avoid)* umgehen ‹*Gesetz, Bestimmungen*›; **c) ~ sb. round, ~ round sb.** *(get one's way with)* jmdn. herumkriegen *(ugs.)*; *(persuade)* jmdn. überzeugen (**to** von); **d)** *(overcome)* lösen ‹*Problem usw.*›; überwinden ‹*Hindernis usw.*›; umgehen ‹*Schwierigkeit usw.*›. *See also* **table 1 a; tongue c**

~ there *v. i.* **a)** *(reach a place)* dorthin kommen; **b)** *(sl.: succeed)* es schaffen; **c)** *(understand)* verstehen, was gemeint ist; dahinterkommen *(ugs.)*

~ through 1. [-'-] *v. i.* **a)** *(pass obstacle)* durchkommen; *(make contact by radio or telephone)* durchkommen *(ugs.)*; Verbindung bekommen (**to** mit); **b)** *(be transmitted)* durchkommen *(ugs.)*; durchdringen (**to** bis zu *od.* nach); **c)** *(win heat or round)* gewinnen; **~ through to the finals** in die Endrunde kommen; **d) ~ through [to**

sb.] *(make sb. understand)* sich [jmdm.] verständlich machen; **e)** *(pass)* bestehen; durchkommen *(ugs.)*; **f)** ~ **through on** auskommen mit ‹*Gehalt*›; **g)** *(be approved)* angenommen werden; durchkommen *(ugs.)*. **2.** *[stress varies] v. t.* **a)** *(pass through)* [durch]kommen durch; ~ **sth. through sth.** etw. durch etw. [durch]bekommen *od. (ugs.)* [durch]kriegen; **b)** *(help to make contact)* ~ **sb. through to** jmdn. verbinden mit; **c)** *(bring)* [durch]bringen; übermitteln ‹*Nachricht*› **(to** *Dat.*); ~ **food/a message through to sb.** jmdm. Nahrungsmittel/eine Nachricht zukommen lassen; **d)** *(bring as far as)* ~ **a team through to the finals** eine Mannschaft in die Endrunde bringen; **e)** *(communicate)* ~ **sth. through to sb.** jmdm. etw. klarmachen; **f)** *(pass)* durchkommen bei *(ugs.)*, bestehen ‹*Prüfung*›; *(help to pass)* durchbringen ‹*Prüfling*›; **g)** *(Parl.: cause to be approved)* durchbringen; **h)** *(consume, use up)* verbrauchen; verqualmen *(ugs. abwertend)* ‹*Zigaretten*›; aufessen ‹*Essen*›; ablatschen *(salopp)* ‹*Schuhe*›; abtragen ‹*Kleidung*›; *(spend)* durchbringen ‹*Geld, Vermögen*›; **i)** *(survive)* durchstehen; überstehen; kommen durch; **j)** *(manage to deal with)* fertig werden mit, erledigen ‹*Arbeit*›; durchkriegen ‹*Buch*›; **let me ~ through this work first** laß mich erst diese Arbeit fertigmachen!; ~ **through reading a book/writing a letter** ein Buch auslesen/einen Brief fertigschreiben

~ **'through with** *v. t.* **a)** *(finish)* fertig werden mit ‹*Arbeit*›; erledigen ‹*Formalitäten*›; auslesen ‹*Buch*›; **b)** *(coll.: finish dealing with sb.)* **wait till I ~ through with him!** warte, bis ich mit ihm fertig bin!

~ **to** *v. t.* **a)** *(reach)* kommen zu ‹*Gebäude*›; erreichen ‹*Person, Ort*›; **I've got to here** ich bin bis hierher gekommen; **he is ~ting to the age when ...:** er wird bald das Alter erreicht haben, wo ...; **where have you got to in German/in this book?** wie weit bist du gekommen in Deutsch/mit *od.* in dem Buch?; **I haven't got to the end [of the novel] yet** ich habe [den Roman] noch nicht zu Ende gelesen; **where has the child/the book got to?** wo ist das Kind hin/das Buch hingekommen?; **b)** *(begin)* ~ **to doing sth.** anfangen, etw. zu tun; **c)** *(annoy)* ~ **to sb.** *(coll.)* jmdm. auf die Nerven gehen *(ugs.)*; **don't let him ~ to you!** laß dir von ihm nicht auf den Nerven rumtrampeln! *(salopp)*

~ **to'gether 1.** *v. i.* zusammenkommen; **we must ~ together again sometime** wir müssen uns bald mal wiedersehen; **why not ~ together after work?** wollen wir uns nach Feierabend treffen? **2.** *v. t.* **a)** *(collect)* zusammenbringen; ~ **one's things together** seine Sachen zusammenpacken; ~ **one's thoughts together** seine Gedanken sammeln; **b)** *(sl.: organize)* ~ **it** *or* **things together** die Dinge auf die Reihe kriegen *(ugs.)*; ~ **oneself together** sich am Riemen reißen *(ugs.)*. *See also* **get-together**

~ **'under** *v. t.* *(shelter)* gehen unter (+ *Akk.*); kriechen unter (+ *Akk.*) ‹*Decke, Bett*›; ~ **sth. under sth.** etw. unter etw. *(Akk.)* tun; **how did my passport manage to ~ under your books?** wie ist mein Paß nur unter deine Bücher gekommen?

~ **up 1.** [-'-] *v. i.* **a)** *(rise from bed, chair, floor; leave table)* aufstehen; **please don't ~ up!** bitte bleiben Sie sitzen!; **b)** *(climb)* [auf]steigen, aufsitzen **(on** auf + *Dat. od. Akk.*); **c)** *(rise, increase in force)* zunehmen; **the sea is ~ting up** die See wird immer wilder; **d)** *(Cricket)* ‹*Ball:*› steil hochfliegen; **e)** ~ **up and go** *(coll.)* in Gang kommen. **2.** *[stress varies] v. t.* **a)** *(call, awaken)* wecken; *(cause to leave bed)* aus dem Bett holen; ~ **oneself up** aufwachen; *(leave bed)* aus dem Bett kommen; **b)** *(cause to stand up)* aufhelfen (+ *Dat.*); hochkriegen *(ugs.)*; **c)** *(cause to mount)* ~ **sb. up on the horse** jmdm. aufs Pferd helfen; **d)** *(climb)* hinaufsteigen; **your car will not ~ up that hill** dein Auto kommt den Berg nicht hinauf *od.* schafft den Berg nicht; **water got up my nose** ich habe Wasser in die Nase gekriegt *(ugs.)*; **e)** *(carry up)* ~ **sb./sth. up [sth.]** jmdn./etw. [etw.] her-/hinaufbringen; *(with some difficulty)* jmdn. etw. [etw.] her-/hinaufbekommen; **f)** *(organize)* organisieren; auf die Beine stellen; auf die Beine bringen ‹*Personen*›; **g)** *(arrange appearance of, dress up)* zurechtmachen; herrichten ‹*Zimmer*›; hübsch aufmachen ‹*Buch, Geschenk*›. *See also* **back 1 a; get-up; get-up-and-go; steam 1; ¹wind 1 e**

~ **'up to** *v. t.* **a)** *(reach)* erreichen ‹*Leistungsniveau*›; *(cause to reach)* bringen auf (+ *Akk.*); **b)** *(indulge in)* aussein auf (+ *Akk.*); ~ **up to mischief** etwas anstellen; **what have you been ~ting up to?** was hast du getrieben *od.* angestellt?

get: ~-'at-able *adj.* zugänglich; **~-away** *n.* Flucht, *die; attrib.* Flucht‹*plan, -wagen*›; **make one's ~-away** entkommen; **~-out** *n.* **a)** *(coll.: evasion)* Ausweg, *der;* **b) as** *or* **like [all] ~-out** *(sl.)* wie nur irgend etwas; **~-rich-'quick** *adj.* **~-rich-quick manual/methods** Handbuch/Methoden, wie man schnell reich wird

gettable ['getəbl] *adj.* erhältlich

get: ~-together *n. (coll.)* Zusammenkunft, *die; (informal social gathering)* gemütliches Beisammensein; **have a ~-together** sich treffen; zusammenkommen; **~-up** *n. (coll.)* Aufmachung, *die;* **buy a new ~-up** sich neu einkleiden; **~-up-and-'go** *n. (coll.)* Elan, *der;* Schwung, *der*

geyser *n.* **a)** ['gi:zə(r), 'geɪzə(r)] *(hot spring)* Geysir, *der;* **b)** ['gi:zə(r)] *(Brit.: water-heater)* Durchlauferhitzer, *der*

Ghana ['gɑ:nə] *pr. n.* Ghana *(das)*

Ghanaian [gɑ:'neɪən] **1.** *adj.* ghanaisch; **sb. is ~:** jmd. ist Ghanaer/Ghanaerin. **2.** *n.* Ghanaer, *der*/Ghanaerin, *die*

ghastly ['gɑ:stlɪ] *adj.* **a)** grauenvoll; gräßlich; entsetzlich ‹*Verletzungen*›; schrecklich ‹*Geschichte, Fehler, Irrtum*›; **b)** *(coll.: objectionable, unpleasant)* scheußlich *(ugs.);* gräßlich *(ugs.)*; **I feel ~:** ich fühle mich scheußlich; **c)** *(pale)* leichenblaß; leichenhaft ‹*Blässe*›; gespenstisch ‹*Weiß*›; **d)** *(forced)* verzerrt ‹*Grinsen, Grimasse*›

Ghent [gent] *pr. n.* Gent *(das)*

gherkin ['gɜ:kɪn] *n.* Essiggurke, *die*

ghetto ['getəʊ] *n., pl.* **~s** Getto, *das*

ghetto-blaster ['getəʊblɑ:stə(r)] *n. (sl.)* [lauter] Radiorecorder

ghost [gəʊst] **1.** *n.* **a)** Geist, *der;* Gespenst, *das;* **b) give up the ~:** den *od.* seinen Geist aufgeben *(veralt., scherzh.)*; *(fig.: give up hope)* die Hoffnung aufgeben; **c)** *(shadowy outline)* Schatten, *der; (trace)* Spur, *die;* **the ~ of a smile** der Anflug eines Lächelns; **not have the** *or* **a ~ of a chance/an idea** nicht die geringste Chance/Ahnung haben; **d)** *(Telev.)* Geisterbild, *das.* **2.** *v. t.* ~ **sb.'s speech** *etc.* für jmdn. eine Rede *usw.* [als Ghostwriter] schreiben. **3.** *v. i.* ~ **[for sb.]** [für jmdn.] als Ghostwriter arbeiten

ghosting ['gəʊstɪŋ] *n., no pl. (Telev.)* ein Geisterbild

'ghostlike *adj.* gespenstisch

ghostly ['gəʊstlɪ] *adj.* gespenstisch; geisterhaft; **a ~ presence** die Anwesenheit eines Geistes

ghost: ~ story *n.* Gespenstergeschichte, *die;* **~ town** *n.* Geisterstadt, *die;* **~ train** *n.* Geisterbahn, *die;* **~ writer** *n.* Ghostwriter, *der*

ghoul [gu:l] *n. Mensch mit einem Hang zum Makabren*

ghoulish ['gu:lɪʃ] *adj.* teuflisch ‹*Freude*›; schaurig ‹*Gelächter*›; makaber ‹*Geschichte*›

GHQ *abbr.* **General Headquarters** HQ; H.-Qu.

GI ['dʒi:aɪ, dʒi:'aɪ] **1.** *adj.* GI-‹*Uniform, Haarschnitt*›; ~ **bride** Amibraut, *die (ugs.)*; ~ **Joe** Amisoldat, *der (ugs.)*. **2.** *n.* GI, *der*

giant ['dʒaɪənt] **1.** *n.* **a)** *(legendary being)* Riese, *der; (Greek Mythol.)* Gigant, *der;* **b)** *(person)* Riese, *der; (animal, plant)* besonders großes Exemplar; **a ~ of a man/plant** ein Riese von einem Mann/eine riesengroße Pflanze; **c)** *(person of extraordinary ability)* Größe, *die;* **he was one of the ~s of his time** er war einer der Großen seiner Zeit; **d)** *(sth. with power)* Koloß, *der;* **a ~ among rivers** ein gigantischer Strom; **e)** *(Astron.)* Riese[nstern], *der.* **2.** *attrib. adj.* riesig; Riesen- *(ugs.)*; Riesen‹*tier, -pflanze*›

giantess ['dʒaɪəntɪs] *n.* Riesin, *die*

giant: ~-killer *n.* Riesenbezwinger, *der;* ~ **'panda** *n.* Bambusbär, *der;* Riesenpanda, *der;* ~ **'slalom** *n.* Riesenslalom, *der*

Gib. [dʒɪb] *pr. n. (coll.)* Gibraltar *(das)*

gibber ['dʒɪbə(r)] *v. i.* plappern; ‹*Affe:*› schnattern; **I just stood there like a ~ing idiot** ich stand da wie ein Idiot

gibberish ['dʒɪbərɪʃ] *n.* **a)** *(unintelligible chatter)* Kauderwelsch, *das;* **b)** *(nonsense)* Geschwafel, *das (ugs.)*; **talk ~:** schwafeln *(ugs.)*

gibbet ['dʒɪbɪt] *n. (Hist.)* Galgen, *der*

gibbon ['gɪbən] *n. (Zool.)* Gibbon, *der*

gibe [dʒaɪb] **1.** *n.* Spöttelei, *die (ugs.)*; Stichelei, *die (ugs.)*; **make ~s at sb.** jmdn. verspotten; gegen jmdn. sticheln *(ugs.)*. **2.** *v. i.* ~ **at sb./sth.** über jmdn./etw. spötteln; sich über jmdn./etw. lustig machen

giblets ['dʒɪblɪts] *n. pl.* [Geflügel]klein, *das*

Gibraltar [dʒɪ'brɔ:ltə(r)] *pr. n.* Gibraltar *(das);* **the Rock/Straits of ~:** der Felsen/die Straße von Gibraltar

giddiness ['gɪdɪnɪs] *n., no pl.* Schwindel, *der;* **a feeling of ~:** ein Schwindelgefühl; **fits of ~:** Schwindelanfälle

giddy ['gɪdɪ] *adj.* **a)** *(dizzy)* schwind[e]lig; **I feel ~, I have a ~ feeling** mir ist schwindlig; mir schwindelt; **b)** *(causing vertigo)* schwindelerregend ‹*Höhe, Abgrund*›; atemberaubend ‹*Geschwindigkeit*›; **c)** *(fig.: frivolous)* ausgelassen; verrückt *(ugs.)*; **d) my ~ aunt!** *(fig. sl.)* ach, du dicker Vater! *(ugs.)*; ach, du dickes Ei! *(ugs.)*; *see also* **goat a**

gift [gɪft] *n.* **a)** *(present)* Geschenk, *das;* Gabe, *die (geh.)*; *(to an organization)* Schenkung, *die;* **make sb. a ~ of sth., make a ~ of sth. to sb.** jmdm. etw. schenken *od.* zum Geschenk machen; **it was given to me as a ~:** ich habe es geschenkt bekommen; **a ~ box/pack** eine Geschenkpackung; **I wouldn't [even] have it as a ~:** das würde ich nicht mal geschenkt nehmen; **b)** *(money given to charity)* Spende, *die;* **c)** *(talent etc.)* Begabung, *die;* **a person of many ~s** ein vielseitig begabter Mensch; **have a ~ for languages/mathematics** sprachbegabt/mathematisch begabt sein; *see also* **gab 1; tongue c; d)** *(easy task etc.)* **be a ~:** geschenkt sein *(ugs.)*; **e)** *(right to give)* **sth. is in the ~ of sb.** jmd. hat das Recht, etw. zu vergeben; etw. kann von jmdm. vergeben werden; **f)** *(Law)* Schenkung, *die*

gifted ['gɪftɪd] *adj.* begabt **(in, at** für); **highly ~:** hochbegabt; begnadet ‹*Künstler*›; **be ~ in** *or* **at languages** sprachbegabt sein

gift: ~-horse *n.* **never** *or* **don't look a ~-horse in the mouth** *(prov.)* einem geschenkten Gaul schaut man nicht ins Maul *(Spr.)*; **~ shop** *n.* Geschenkboutique, *die;* Geschenkladen, *der;* ~ **tax** *n. (Amer.)* Schenkungssteuer, *die;* ~ **token,** ~ **voucher** *ns.* Geschenkgutschein, *der;* **~-wrap** *v. t.* als Geschenk einpacken; in Geschenkpapier einpacken

¹gig [gɪg] *n. (boat, vehicle)* Gig, *das*

²gig *n. (coll.: performance)* Gig, *der*

giga- ['gɪgə] *pref.* giga-/Giga-

gigantic [dʒaɪ'gæntɪk] *adj.* gigantisch; riesig; enorm, gewaltig ‹*Verbesserung, Appetit,*

Portion〉; **a ~ success/effort** ein Riesenerfolg/eine Riesenanstrengung; **grow to a ~ size** riesengroß werden

giggle ['gɪgl] **1.** *n.* **a)** Kichern, *das;* Gekicher, *das;* **have a ~ about sth.** über etw. *(Akk.)* kichern; **with a ~:** kichernd; **[a fit of] the ~s** ein Kicheranfall; **get/have the ~s** kichern müssen; **b)** *(coll.) (amusing person)* Witzbold, *der; (amusing thing, joke)* Spaß, *der;* **it was a bit of a ~:** es war ganz amüsant; **for a ~:** aus Spaß; **we did it for a ~:** wir wollten unseren Spaß haben. **2.** *v. i.* kichern

¹gild [gɪld] *v. t.* vergolden; *(with gold-coloured paint)* mit Goldbronze überziehen; **~ed cage** *(fig.)* goldener Käfig *(fig.);* **~ed youth** Jeunesse dorée, *die (veralt.);* **~ the lily** etwas Vollkommenes [unnötigerweise] noch vervollkommnen [wollen]; des Guten zuviel tun

²gild *see* **guild**

gilding ['gɪldɪŋ] *n.* Goldauflage, *die; (process)* Vergoldung, *die; (paint)* Goldfarbe, *die*

¹gill [gɪl] *n., usu. in pl.* **a)** *(of fish etc.)* Kieme, *die;* **green about the ~s** *(fig.)* grün *od.* blaß um die Nase[nspitze] *(ugs.);* **b)** *(of mushroom etc.)* Lamelle, *die*

²gill *n.* *(Brit.)* **a)** *(ravine)* [bewaldete] Schlucht; **b)** *(torrent)* Wildbach, *der*

³gill [dʒɪl] *n.* Viertelpint, *das (0,142 l)*

gillie ['gɪlɪ] *n. (Hunting)* Jagdgehilfe, *der*

gilt [gɪlt] **1.** *n.* **a)** *(gilding)* Goldauflage, *die; (paint)* Goldfarbe, *die;* **take the ~ off the gingerbread** *(fig.)* der Sache den Reiz nehmen; **b)** *in pl.* = **gilt-edged securities** *see* **gilt-edged. 2.** *adj.* vergoldet

gilt-edged *adj. (Commerc.)* **~ securities/stocks** mündelsichere Wertpapiere

gimcrack ['dʒɪmkræk] *adj.* schäbig

gimlet ['gɪmlɪt] *n.* [Hand]bohrer, *der;* **~ eye** Luchsauge, *das; (fig.)* Scharfblick, *der*

gimme ['gɪmɪ] *(coll.)* = **give me**

gimmick ['gɪmɪk] *n. (coll.)* Gag, *der;* **a publicity/public relations/promotional ~:** ein Werbegag

gimmickry ['gɪmɪkrɪ] *n. (coll.)* Firlefanz, *der (ugs.);* Pipifax, *der (ugs.);* **advertising ~:** Werbetricks *od.* -gags

gimmicky ['gɪmɪkɪ] *adj. (coll.)* vergagt; **~ publicity stunts** verrückte Werbegags

¹gin [dʒɪn] *n. (drink)* Gin, *der;* **~ and tonic** Gin [und] Tonic, *der;* **~ and it** *(Brit. coll.)* Gin und [italienischer] Wermut; **pink ~:** Gin und Angostura

²gin *n. (trap)* Falle, *die; (snare)* Schlinge, *die*

ginger ['dʒɪndʒə(r)] **1.** *n.* **a)** Ingwer, *der;* **b)** *(colour)* Rötlichgelb, *das;* **his hair was a bright shade of ~:** er hatte helles rötliches Haar; **c)** *(vigour)* Feuer, *das;* Schwung, *der.* **2.** *adj.* **a)** *(flavour)* Ingwer〈*gebäck, -geschmack*〉; **b)** *(colour)* rötlichgelb; rotblond 〈*Bart, Haare*〉. **3.** *v. t.* **~ up** *(fig.)* in Schwung bringen

ginger: ~-'ale *n.* Ginger-ale, *das;* **~-'beer** *n.* Ingwerbier, *das;* Ginger-beer, *das;* **~-beer plant** *Mischung aus Hefe und Bakterie zur Gärung von Ginger-beer;* **~bread 1.** *n.* **a)** Pfefferkuchen, *der; see also* **gilt 1 a; b)** *(Archit. etc.)* überflüssiger [geschmackloser] Schmuck; **2.** *adj. (fig.)* überladen; zuckerbäckerhaft 〈*[Bau]stil*〉; **~ group** *n. (Brit.)* Initiative, *die;* Aktionsgruppe, *die*

gingerly ['dʒɪndʒəlɪ] *adv.* behutsam; [übertrieben] vorsichtig

ginger: ~-nut *n.* Pfeffernuß, *die;* **~-snap** *n.* Ingwerkeks, *der;* **~ 'wine** *n.* Ingwerwein, *der*

gingery ['dʒɪndʒərɪ] *adj.* ingwerartig

gingham ['gɪŋəm] *n. (Textiles)* Gingan, *der*

gingivitis [dʒɪndʒɪ'vaɪtɪs] *n. (Med.)* Gingivitis, *die (fachspr.);* Zahnfleischentzündung, *die*

ginormous [dʒaɪ'nɔːməs] *adj. (Brit. sl.)* elefantös *(ugs. scherzh.)*

gin: ~-palace *n.* auffällig aufgemachte Kneipe; **~ 'rummy** *n.* Rommé mit Zehn

ginseng ['dʒɪnseŋ] *n. (Bot., Med.)* Ginseng, *der*

gin 'sling *n.* Gin-Sling, *der*

gippy tummy [dʒɪpɪ 'tʌmɪ] *n. (sl.)* Durchfall, *der;* Durchmarsch, *der (salopp)*

gipsy *see* **gypsy**

giraffe [dʒɪ'rɑːf, dʒɪ'ræf] *n.* Giraffe, *die*

gird [gɜːd] *v. t.,* **~ed** *or* **girt** [gɜːt] **a)** *(encircle)* **~ sb./sb.'s waist with sth.** jmdn./jmds. Taille mit etw. gürten; etw. um jmdn./jmds. Taille als Gürtel legen; **b)** *(surround)* umgeben; **c)** *(secure)* **~ on one's armour/sword** seine Rüstung anlegen/sich *(Dat.)* sein Schwert umgürten; **d)** *(prepare)* **~ oneself for sth.** sich zu etw. rüsten; **be ~ed for sth.** für etw. gewappnet sein

~ up *v. t.* gürten; **~ up one's loins** *(literary)* seine Lenden gürten *(veralt.);* sich gürten

girder ['gɜːdə(r)] *n.* [Eisen-/Stahl]träger, *der*

¹girdle ['gɜːdl] **1.** *n.* **a)** *(corset)* Hüfthalter, *der;* Hüftgürtel, *der;* **b)** *(belt, cord, etc.)* Gürtel, *der; (sash)* Schärpe, *die;* **a ~ of trees/forests** eine Baumkette *od.* ein Gürtel von Bäumen/ein Waldgürtel; **c)** *(Anat.)* 〈*Schulter-, Becken*〉gürtel, *der.* **2.** *v. t.* umgeben; 〈*Bäume:*〉 umstehen; 〈*Fluß, Wasser:*〉 umfließen, umströmen

²girdle *(Scot.) see* **griddle**

girl [gɜːl] *n.* **a)** Mädchen, *das; (teenager)* junges Mädchen; *([young] woman)* Frau, *die; (daughter)* Mädchen, *das (ugs.);* Tochter, *die;* **baby ~:** kleines Mädchen; **~s' school** Mädchenschule, *die;* **a ~'s name** ein Mädchenname; **a little Italian ~:** eine kleine Italienerin; ein kleines italienisches Mädchen; **[my] ~** *(as address)* [mein] Mädchen; **the ~s** *(female friends)* meine/ihre *usw.* Freundinnen; **the Smith ~s** die Mädchen von Smiths; *see also* **old girl; b)** *(worker)* Mädchen, *das; (secretary)* Sekretärin, *die; (maid)* [Haus-/Dienst]mädchen, *das;* **the ~ at the cash-desk/switchboard** die Kassiererin/Telefonistin; **c)** *(sweetheart)* Mädchen, *das;* Freundin, *die*

girl: ~ 'Friday *n. see* **Friday 1; ~-friend** *n.* Freundin, *die;* **~ 'guide** *see* **guide 1 e**

girlhood ['gɜːlhʊd] *n.* Kindheit, *die*

girlie ['gɜːlɪ] **1.** *adj.* mit nackten Mädchen *nachgestellt.* **2.** *n.* [kleines] Mädchen

girlish ['gɜːlɪʃ] *adj. (coll.)* mädchenhaft; **a ~ voice** eine Mädchenstimme; **~ laughter** Mädchenlachen, *das*

girl 'scout *n. (Amer.)* Pfadfinderin, *die*

giro ['dʒaɪərəʊ] *n., pl.* **~s** Giro, *das; attrib.* Giro〈*bank, -geschäft, -konto, -scheck*〉; **post office/bank ~:** Postgiro- *od. (veralt.)* Postscheck-/Giroverkehr, *der*

girt *see* **gird**

girth [gɜːθ] *n.* **a)** *(circumference)* Umfang, *der; (at waist)* Taillenumfang, *der; (at belly)* Bauchumfang, *der; (of ship)* Spantumfang, *der;* **in ~:** im Umfang *usw.;* **b)** *(band round horse)* Bauchgurt, *der*

gismo ['gɪsməʊ] *n. (sl.)* Ding, *das (ugs.)*

gist [dʒɪst] *n.* Wesentliche, *das; (of tale, argument, question, etc.)* Kern, *der;* **this is the ~ of what he said** das hat er im wesentlichen gesagt; **get the ~ of sth.** das Wesentliche einer Sache mitbekommen; **could you give me the ~ of it/what's been going on?** könntest du mir sagen, worum es hier geht?/was losgewesen ist?

git [gɪt] *n. (Brit. sl. derog.)* Idiot, *der (salopp);* **stupid ~:** Blödmann, *der (derb); (woman)* blöde Kuh *(derb)*

give [gɪv] **1.** *v. t.,* **gave** [geɪv], **given** ['gɪvn] **a)** *(hand over, pass)* geben; *(transfer from one's authority, custody, or responsibility)* überbringen; übergeben (**to** an + *Akk.*); **she gave him her bag to carry** sie gab ihm ihre Tasche zum Tragen; **G~ it to me! I'll do it** Gib her! Ich mache das; **~ me ...** *(on telephone)* geben Sie mir ...; verbinden Sie mich mit ...; **b)** *(as gift)* schenken; *(donate)* spenden; geben; *(bequeath)* vermachen; **~ sb. sth., ~ sth. to sb.** jmdm. etw. schenken; **~ sb. sth.** *or* **~ sth. [to] sb. as a present** jmdm. etw. schenken; *(sth. of great value)* jmdm. etw. zum Geschenk machen; **each of the boys was ~n a book** die Jungen bekamen jeder ein Buch [geschenkt]; **the book was ~n me by my son** das Buch hat mir mein Sohn geschenkt; **I was ~n it by my son** mein Sohn hat es mir geschenkt; ich habe es von meinem Sohn [geschenkt] bekommen; *abs.* **I wouldn't have it if it was ~n [to] me** ich würde es nicht mal geschenkt nehmen; **it is more blessed to ~ than to receive** *(Bibl.)* Geben ist seliger denn Nehmen *(Spr.);* **~ alms/to the poor** Almosen/den Armen geben; **~ towards sth.** zu etw. beisteuern; **~ blood** Blut spenden; **~ [a donation] to charity** für wohltätige Zwecke spenden; **'please ~ generously'** „wir bitten um großzügige Spenden"; **~ and take** *(fig.)* Kompromisse eingehen; *(in marriage etc.)* geben und nehmen; **c)** *(sell)* verkaufen; geben; *(pay)* zahlen; geben *(ugs.); (sacrifice)* geben; opfern; **I'll ~ you the machine for £2** für 2 Pfund gebe ich dir *od.* hast du die Maschine; **what will you ~ me for this watch?** was *od.* wieviel geben Sie mir für diese Uhr?; **I'll ~ you anything you ask for it** ich zahle Ihnen jeden Preis dafür; **~ sb. sth. [in exchange] for sth.** jmdm. etw. für etw. [im Tausch] geben; **I would ~ anything** *or* **my right arm/a lot to be there** ich würde alles/viel darum geben, wenn ich dort sein könnte; **d)** *(assign)* aufgeben 〈*Hausaufgaben, Strafarbeit usw.*〉; *(sentence to)* geben 〈*10 Jahre Gefängnis usw.*〉; **~ sb. a translation to do/an essay to write for homework** jmdm. eine Übersetzung/einen Aufsatz aufgeben; **he was ~n ten years** er bekam zehn Jahre; **e)** *(grant, award)* geben 〈*Erlaubnis, Arbeitsplatz, Interview, Rabatt, Fähigkeit, Kraft*〉; verleihen 〈*Preis, Titel, Orden usw.*〉; **be ~n sth.** etw. bekommen; **he was ~n the privilege/honour of doing it** ihm wurde das Vorrecht/die Ehre zuteil, es zu tun; **~ me strength to do it** gib mir Kraft, es zu tun; **it is ~n to few/her** es ist wenigen/ihr gegeben *od. (geh.)* beschieden; **~ sb. to understand** *or* **believe that ...:** jmdn. glauben lassen, daß ...; **he gave me to understand** *or* **believe that ...** *(unintentionally)* was er sagte, ließ mich glauben, daß ...; **f)** *(entrust sb. with)* übertragen (**to** *Dat.*); **~ sb. the power to do sth.** jmdn. ermächtigen, etw. zu tun; **g)** *(allow sb. to have)* geben 〈*Recht, Zeit, Arbeit*〉; überlassen 〈*seinen Sitzplatz*〉; lassen 〈*Wahl, Zeit*〉; **be ~n little freedom** wenig Freiheit haben; **~ sb./a horse a rest** jmdm./einem Pferd eine Pause gönnen; **they gave me [the use of] their car for the weekend** sie überließen mir übers Wochenende ihr Auto; **~ it time and it will work out well** gut Ding will Weile haben *(Spr.);* **I will ~ you a day to think it over** ich lasse dir einen Tag Bedenkzeit; **I can ~ you an hour. Then I must go** Ich habe [für Sie] eine Stunde Zeit. Dann muß ich gehen; **~ yourself time to think about it** laß dir Zeit, und denk darüber nach; **~ me the good old times** *(fig. coll.)* es geht doch nichts über die guten alten Zeiten; **~ me London any day** *or* **time** *or* **every time** *(fig. coll.)* London ist mir zehnmal lieber; **I['ll] ~ you/him** *etc.* **that** *(fig. coll.: grant)* das gebe ich zu; zugegeben; **you've got to ~ it to him** *(fig. coll.)* das muß man ihm lassen; **~ or take** *(coll.)* mehr oder weniger; **it cost £5, ~ or take a few pence** es hat fünf Pfund gekostet, vielleicht ein paar Pence mehr oder weniger; **~ or take a few errors, this book is ...:** abgesehen von ein paar Fehlern ist dieses Buch ...; **~ oneself to sb.** *(yield sexually)* sich jmdm. hingeben; **~n that** *(because)* da; *(if)* wenn; **~n the right**

tools mit dem richtigen Werkzeug; **~n time/the cash, I'll do/buy it** wenn ich Zeit/das nötige Geld habe, mache/kaufe ich es; **h)** *(offer to sb.)* geben, reichen ⟨*Arm, Hand usw.*⟩; **~ sb. one's attention/confidence** jmdm. seine Aufmerksamkeit/sein Vertrauen schenken; **please ~ me your attention** ich bitte um Ihre Aufmerksamkeit; **~ sb. in marriage** jmdn. verheiraten; **my heart is ~n to another** mein Herz gehört einer/einem anderen; **she gave him an infection/a cold** sie hat ihn angesteckt/mit ihrer Erkältung angesteckt; **she gave him four sons** sie hat ihm vier Söhne geschenkt *(geh.)*; *see also* **way; i)** *(cause sb./sth. to have)* geben; verleihen ⟨*Charme, Reiz, Gewicht, Nachdruck*⟩; bereiten, machen ⟨*Freude, Mühe, Kummer*⟩; bereiten, verursachen ⟨*Schmerz*⟩; bieten ⟨*Abwechslung, Schutz*⟩; leisten ⟨*Hilfe*⟩; gewähren ⟨*Unterstützung*⟩; erteilen ⟨*Absolution*⟩; **~ sb. sth./be ~n sth. to eat** jmdm. etw. zu essen geben/etw. zu essen bekommen; **~ sb. some refreshment** jmdm. eine Erfrischung reichen; **~ sb. pork for dinner** jmdm. Schweinefleisch zum Abendessen geben *od.* reichen; **I was ~n the guestroom** man gab mir das Gästezimmer; **~ a clear picture/~ good reception** *(Telev.)* ein gutes Bild/einen guten Empfang haben; **the answer was ~n me in a dream** die Antwort kam mir im Traum; **her words gave me much pain/quite a shock** ihre Worte schmerzten/schockierten mich sehr; **~ hope to sb.** jmdm. Hoffnung machen; **~ sb. the name of Jim** jmdn. Jim nennen; jmdm. den Namen Jim geben; **the village gave its name to the battle** die Schlacht wurde nach dem Dorf benannt; **Latin, which has ~n the English language so many words** das Lateinische, aus dem so viele englische Wörter stammen; **~ sb. something to cry for/to complain about** jmdm. einen Grund zum Weinen/Klagen geben; **~ one's labour [free of charge]** unbezahlt arbeiten; seine Arbeit unentgeltlich machen; **~ sb. what for** *(sl.)* es jmdm. geben *(ugs.)*; **j)** *(convey in words, tell, communicate)* angeben ⟨*Namen, Anschrift, Alter, Grund, Zahl*⟩; nennen ⟨*Grund, Einzelheiten, Losungswort*⟩; geben ⟨*Rat, Beispiel, Befehl, Anweisung, Antwort*⟩; fällen ⟨*Urteil, Entscheidung*⟩; sagen ⟨*Meinung*⟩; erlassen ⟨*Gesetze*⟩; bekanntgeben ⟨*Nachricht, Ergebnis*⟩; machen ⟨*Andeutung*⟩; erteilen ⟨*Verweis, Rüge*⟩; *(present, set forth)* ⟨*Wörterbuch, Brief:*⟩ enthalten; ⟨*Zeitung:*⟩ bringen ⟨*Bericht*⟩; **~ details of sth.** Einzelheiten einer Sache *(Gen.)* darlegen; **~ sth. a mention** etw. erwähnen; **~ a brief history of sth.** einen kurzen Abriß der Geschichte einer Sache *(Gen.)* geben; **~ sb. the facts** jmdn. mit den Fakten vertraut *od.* bekannt machen; **she gave us the news/the news of her engagement** sie teilte es uns mit/teilte uns ihre Verlobung mit; **~ it as one's opinion that ...:** die Meinung äußern, daß ...; **~ sb. a decision** jmdm. eine Entscheidung mitteilen; **~ sb. the right time** jmdm. die genaue Zeit sagen; **~ him my best wishes** richte ihm meine besten Wünsche aus; **the average wage is ~n as £6,000** der Durchschnittslohn wird mit 6 000 Pfund angegeben; **don't ~ me 'that** *(coll.)* erzähl mir [doch] nichts! *(ugs.)*; **don't ~ me that legal jargon** laß mich mit deinem Juristenkauderwelsch in Ruhe!; **~!** *(coll.: disclose what you know)* [nun] red schon!; **~n** *(in formal dating)* ausgefertigt; **k) ~n** *(specified)* gegeben; **l)** *(perform, read, sing, etc.)* geben ⟨*Vorstellung, Konzert*⟩; halten ⟨*Vortrag, Seminar*⟩; vorlesen ⟨*Gedicht, Erzählung*⟩; singen ⟨*Lied*⟩; spielen ⟨*Schauspiel, Oper, Musikstück*⟩; **~ us a song** sing mal was; **m)** *(in speeches)* ausbringen ⟨*Toast, Trinkspruch*⟩; *(as toast)* **ladies and gentlemen, I ~ you the Queen** meine Damen, meine Herren, auf die Königin *od.* das Wohl der Königin; *(as speaker)* **I ~ you the Lord Mayor** das Wort hat der Oberbürgermeister; **n)** *(produce)* geben ⟨*Licht, Milch*⟩; tragen ⟨*Früchte*⟩; ergeben ⟨*Zahlen, Resultat*⟩; erbringen ⟨*Ernte*⟩; **~ your answer to the third decimal place** berechnen Sie das Ergebnis auf die dritte Stelle hinter dem Komma; **~ a high yield** sehr ertragreich sein; reichen Ertrag bringen; **o)** *(cause to develop)* machen; **sth. ~s me a headache** von etw. bekomme ich Kopfschmerzen; **running ~s me an appetite** Laufen macht mich hungrig; **he did this to ~ himself courage** er tat das, um sich *(Dat.)* Mut zu machen; **p)** *(make sb. undergo)* geben; versetzen ⟨*Schlag, Stoß*⟩; verabreichen *(geh.)*, geben ⟨*Arznei*⟩; **~ sb. a hammering** *(Sport)* jmdm. eine schwere Schlappe beibringen; **~ sb. a [friendly] look** jmdm. einen [freundlichen] Blick zuwerfen; **he gave her hand a squeeze** er drückte ihr die Hand; **~ it to sb.** *(thrash or scold him)* es jmdm. geben *(ugs.)*; **~ as good as one gets** *(coll.)* es jmdm. mit gleicher Münze heimzahlen; **q)** *(execute, make, show)* geben ⟨*Zeichen, Stoß, Tritt*⟩; machen ⟨*Satz, Ruck*⟩; ausstoßen ⟨*Schrei, Seufzer, Pfiff*⟩; **~ a [little] smile** [schwach] lächeln; **the flame gave a final flicker** die Flamme flackerte noch einmal auf; **~ sth./sb. a look** sich *(Dat.)* etw./jmdn. ansehen; **r)** *(devote, dedicate)* widmen; **be ~n to sth./doing sth.** zu etw. neigen/etw. gern tun; **~ [it] all one's got** *(coll.)* sein möglichstes tun; **s)** *(be host at)* geben ⟨*Party, Ball, Empfang, Essen usw.*⟩; **t)** *(predict time remaining as)* **~ sb./sth. two months/a year** jmdm./einer Sache zwei Monate/ein Jahr geben; **u) ~ birth, ~ chase,** *etc. see the nouns.* **2.** *v.i.,* **gave, given a)** *(yield, bend)* nachgeben *(auch fig.)*; ⟨*Knie:*⟩ weich werden; ⟨*Bett:*⟩ federn; *(break down)* zusammenbrechen; ⟨*Eisdecke, Boden:*⟩ einbrechen; ⟨*Brücke:*⟩ einstürzen; *(fig.)* nachlassen; **something's got to ~:** irgendwo muß man zurückstecken; **b)** *(lead)* **~ on to the street/garden/into a room** ⟨*Tür usw.:*⟩ auf die Straße hinaus-/in den Garten/ein Zimmer führen; **c) what ~s [with you]?** *(coll.)* was ist los [bei dir]?; **d) ~ of sth.** etw. opfern; **~ of oneself** sich [auf]opfern. **3.** *n.* **a)** Nachgiebigkeit, *die; (elasticity)* Elastizität, *die;* **have [no] ~:** [nicht] nachgeben; **b) ~ and take** *(exchange of ideas)* Gedankenaustausch, *der; (compromise)* Kompromiß, *der;* Entgegenkommen, *das; (exchange of benefits or mutual concessions)* Geben und Nehmen, *das;* **with a bit of ~ and take** mit etwas Kompromißbereitschaft

~ a'way *v.t.* **a)** *(without charge, as gift)* verschenken; *(fig.: lose by negligence)* verschenken ⟨*Punkt, Tor usw.*⟩; vergeben ⟨*Chance, Tor, Elfmeter*⟩; **b)** *(in marriage)* dem Bräutigam zuführen; **c)** *(distribute)* verteilen, vergeben ⟨*Preise*⟩; überreichen ⟨*Zeugnisse usw.*⟩; **d)** *(fig.: betray)* verraten. *See also* **'game 1 b; give-away**

~ 'back *v.t. (lit. or fig.)* zurückgeben, wiedergeben

~ 'forth *see* **forth c**

~ in 1. ['--] *v.t.* abgeben; **~ sb.'s name in for sth.** jmdn. zu etw. anmelden. **2.** [-'-] *v.i.* nachgeben **(to** *Dat.*); *(in guessing-game)* aufgeben; **~ in to temptation/blackmail/a superior force** der Versuchung *(Dat.)* erliegen/auf Erpressung *(Akk.)* eingehen/sich einer Übermacht *(Dat.)* ergeben; **~ in to persuasion** sich überzeugen lassen

~ 'off *v.t.* ausströmen ⟨*Rauch, Geruch*⟩; aussenden ⟨*Strahlen*⟩

~ out 1. ['--] *v.t.* **a)** *(distribute)* verteilen ⟨*Prospekte, Flugblätter, Karten, Preise*⟩; austeilen ⟨*Stifte, Hefte, Papier usw.*⟩; vergeben ⟨*Arbeit*⟩; **b)** *(declare)* bekanntgeben ⟨*Nachricht*⟩; *(pretend)* vorgeben; **~ oneself out to be ...:** sich als ... ausgeben. **2.** [-'-] *v.i.* ⟨*Vorräte:*⟩ ausgehen; ⟨*Maschine:*⟩ versagen; ⟨*Kraft:*⟩ nachlassen; **my patience/voice gave out** ich war mit meiner Geduld am Ende/mir versagte die Stimme

~ 'over *v.t.* **a) be ~n over to sth.** für etw. beansprucht werden; **the rest of the day was ~n over to pleasure** der Rest des Tages war dem Vergnügen gewidmet; **b)** *(abandon)* **~ sth./sb. over to sb.** etw. jmdm. überlassen/jmdn. jmdm. ausliefern; **~ oneself over to sb./sth.** sich jmdm./einer Sache ergeben *od.* hingeben; jmdm./einer Sache verfallen; **c)** *(coll.: stop)* **~ over [doing sth.]** aufhören[, etw. zu tun]

~ 'up 1. *v.i.* aufgeben. **2.** *v.t.* **a)** *(abandon, renounce)* aufgeben; ablegen ⟨*Gewohnheit*⟩; abschaffen ⟨*Auto, Fernsehgerät, Putzfrau*⟩; widmen ⟨*Zeit*⟩; *(relinquish, stop using)* verzichten auf (+ *Akk.*) ⟨*Territorium, Kinder, Süßigkeiten*⟩; **~ sth. up/~ up doing sth.** *(abandon habit)* sich *(Dat.)* etw. abgewöhnen/sich abgewöhnen, etw. zu tun; **~ sb./sth. up as a bad job** *(coll.)* jmdn./etw. abschreiben *(ugs.)*; **~ oneself up to sth.** sich einer Sache *(Dat.)* hingeben; **b) ~ sb. up** *(as not coming)* jmdn. nicht mehr erwarten; mit jmdm. nicht mehr rechnen; *(as beyond help)* jmdn. aufgeben; **~ up for lost/dead** verloren geben/für tot halten; **c)** *(hand over to police etc.)* übergeben **(to** *Dat.*); ausliefern ⟨*Spion usw.*⟩; **~ oneself up [to sb.]** sich [jmdm.] stellen

~ 'way *v.i.* **a)** *(yield, lit. or fig.)* nachgeben; *(collapse)* ⟨*Brücke, Balkon:*⟩ einstürzen; **his legs gave way under him** er knickte [in den Knien] ein; **~ way to sth.** einer Sache *(Dat.)* nachgeben; **~ way to tears** seinen Tränen freien Lauf lassen; **~ way to anger** seinem Ärger Luft machen; **~ way to persuasion** sich überzeugen lassen; **~ way to fear** der Angst erliegen; **his health gave way under this stress** seine Gesundheit hielt dieser Belastung nicht stand; **b)** *(in traffic)* **~ way [to traffic from the right]** [dem Rechtsverkehr] die Vorfahrt lassen; **'G~ Way'** „Vorfahrt beachten"; **c)** *(be succeeded by)* **~ way to sth.** einer Sache *(Dat.)* weichen; von etw. abgelöst werden; **winter gives way to spring** auf den Winter folgt der Frühling

'give-away *n. (coll.)* **a)** *(what betrays)* **the tremble in her voice was the ~:** mit ihrer zitternden Stimme hat sie sich verraten; **it was a dead ~:** es verriet alles; **b)** *attrib. (Commerc.)* **~ prices** Schleuderpreise

given *see* **give 1, 2**

'given name *n. (Amer.)* Vorname, *der*

giver ['gɪvə(r)] *n.* Geber, *der*/Geberin, *die; (donor)* Spender, *der*/Spenderin, *die*

give-'way sign *n. (Brit.)* Vorfahrtsschild, *das*

gizmo *see* **gismo**

gizzard ['gɪzəd] *n. (of bird)* Muskelmagen, *der; (of insect, fish, etc.)* Kaumagen, *der;* **stick in sb.'s ~** *(fig.)* jmdm. gegen den Strich gehen *(ugs.)*

Gk. *abbr.* **Greek** griech./Griech.

glacé ['glæseɪ] *adj.* **a)** glasiert ⟨*Früchte*⟩; *(candied)* kandiert; **b) ~ leather** Glacéleder, *das;* **~ kid gloves** Glacéhandschuhe

glacial ['gleɪsɪəl, 'gleɪʃl] *adj.* **a)** *(icy)* eisig; *(fig.)* eiskalt; **b)** *(Geol.)* Gletscher-; **~ epoch** *or* **period** Eiszeit, *die;* Glazialzeit, *die (fachspr.)*

glaciation [gleɪsɪ'eɪʃn, glæsɪ'eɪʃn] *n. (Geol.)* Vergletscherung, *die*

glacier ['glæsɪə(r)] *n.* Gletscher, *der*

glad [glæd] *adj.* **a)** *pred.* froh; **be ~ about sth.** sich über etw. *(Akk.)* freuen; **be ~ that ...:** sich freuen, daß ...; *(be relieved)* froh sein [darüber], daß ...; **[I'm] ~ to meet you** es freut mich *od.* ich freue mich, Sie kennenzulernen; **be ~ to hear sth.** sich freuen, etw. zu hören; *(relieved)* froh sein, etw. zu hören; **I am always ~ to see her** ich freue mich jedesmal, wenn ich sie sehe; **Don't mention it. I was ~ to be of assistance** Keine

Ursache. Das habe ich doch gern [für Sie] getan; **I'm ~ to know that ...:** zu meiner Freude erfahre ich, daß ...; **he's ~ to be alive** er ist froh, daß er lebt; **..., you'll be ~ to know/hear:** ..., das freut Sie sicherlich; **I'd be ~ to [help you]** aber gern [helfe ich Ihnen]; **we shall be ~ to come/give further information** wir werden gern kommen/wir geben Ihnen gerne weitere Informationen; **be ~ of sth.** über etw. *(Akk.)* froh sein; für etw. dankbar sein; **Take your gloves. You'll be ~ of them** Nimm deine Handschuhe mit. Du wirst sie gebrauchen können; **a sight which makes one ~ to be alive** ein Anblick, der einem Freude am Leben gibt; **I'd be ~ if you'd do some work** *(iron.)* ich hätte nichts dagegen, wenn du dich jetzt etwas nützlich machst *(iron.)*; **b)** *(giving joy)* froh ⟨*Botschaft*⟩; freudig ⟨*Nachricht, Ereignis, Tag usw.*⟩; *(marked by joy)* fröhlich; *(bright, beautiful)* herrlich ⟨*Morgen*⟩

gladden ['glædn] *v.t.* erfreuen

glade [gleɪd] *n.* Lichtung, *die*

glad 'eye *n.* **give sb. the ~** *(coll.)* jmdm. schöne Augen machen *(ugs.)*

glad 'hand *n.* **give sb. the ~** *(coll.)* jmdm. die Hand schütteln

gladiator ['glædɪeɪtə(r)] *n. (Roman Ant.)* Gladiator, *der*

gladiolus [glædɪ'əʊləs] *n., pl.* **gladioli** [glædɪ'əʊlaɪ] *or* **~es** *(Bot.)* Gladiole, *die*

gladly ['glædlɪ] *adv.* **a)** *(willingly)* gern; **b)** *(with joy)* freudig

gladness ['glædnɪs] *n., no pl.* Freude, *die; (of voice etc.)* Fröhlichkeit, *die*

'glad rags *n. pl. (coll.)* Festkleidung, *die*

Gladstone bag [glædstən 'bæg] *n.* zweiteiliger Reisehandkoffer

glamor *(Amer.) see* **glamour**

glamorize (glamorise) ['glæməraɪz] *v.t. (add glamour to)* [mehr] Glanz verleihen (+ *Dat.*); *(idealize)* verherrlichen (**into** zu); glorifizieren

glamorous ['glæmərəs] *adj.* glanzvoll; glamourös ⟨*Filmstar, Lebenswandel usw.*⟩; schillernd ⟨*Name, Persönlichkeit*⟩; mondän ⟨*Kleidung*⟩; **a ~ job** ein Traumberuf

glamorously ['glæmərəslɪ] *adv.* mondän ⟨*gekleidet sein*⟩; glanzvoll ⟨*darstellen*⟩

glamour ['glæmə(r)] *n.* Glanz, *der; (of person)* Ausstrahlung, *die*

glamour: ~ boy *n.* Schönling, *der;* **~ girl** *n.* Glamourgirl, *das*

glamourize *(Brit.) see* **glamorize**

'glamour puss *n. (sl.)* Glitzermieze, *die*

glance [glɑ:ns] **1.** *n.* **a)** *(quick look)* Blick, *der;* **cast** *or* **take** *or* **have a [quick] ~ at sth./sb.** einen [kurzen] Blick auf etw./jmdn. werfen; **cast** *etc.* **a quick ~ at the newspaper/letter** die Zeitung durchblättern/den Brief überfliegen; **cast** *etc.* **a hasty ~ round the room** sich hastig im Zimmer umsehen; **give sb. a [knowing/quick** *etc.*] **~:** jmdm. einen [wissenden/kurzen *usw.*] Blick zuwerfen; **not give sb./sth. so much as a ~:** jmdn./eine Sache keines Blickes würdigen; **at a ~:** auf einen Blick; **at first/a casual ~:** auf den ersten Blick/wenn man flüchtig hinsieht; **b)** *(Cricket)* Streifschlag, *der.* **2.** *v.i.* **a)** blicken; schauen; **~ at sb./sth.** jmdn./etw. anblicken; **~ at one's watch** auf seine Uhr blicken; **she ~d at herself in the mirror** sie warf einen Blick in den Spiegel; **~ over/across at sb. [nervously** *etc.*] jmdm. einen [nervösen *usw.*] Blick zuwerfen; **~ down/up [at sth.]** [auf etw. *(Akk.)*] hinunter-/[zu etw.] aufblicken; **~ over** *or* **through the newspaper** *etc.* die Zeitung *usw.* durchblättern; **~ at the newspaper** *etc.* einen Blick in die Zeitung *usw.* werfen; **~ round [the room]** sich [im Zimmer] umsehen; **~ around/from one thing to another** ⟨*Augen, Blick:*⟩ umherwandern/von einem Gegenstand zum anderen wandern; **b)** *(allude briefly)* **~ at sth.** etw. nur kurz streifen *od.* ansprechen; **c) ~ [off sth.]** abprallen [an etw. *(Dat.)*]; ⟨*Messer, Schwert:*⟩ abgleiten [an etw. *(Dat.)*]; **strike sb. a glancing blow** jmdn. nur streifen

¹gland [glænd] *n.* Drüse, *die*

²gland *n. (Mech.)* Dichtung, *die*

glandular ['glændjʊlə(r)] *adj.* Drüsen-; **~ swelling** geschwollene Drüse/Drüsen

glandular 'fever *n.* Drüsenfieber, *das*

glans [glænz] *n.* **~ [penis]** *(Anat.)* Eichel, *die*

glare [gleə(r)] **1.** *n.* **a)** *(dazzle)* grelles Licht; **shine with a ~:** grell scheinen; **the ~ of the sun** die grelle Sonne; das grelle Sonnenlicht; **amidst the ~/in the full ~ of publicity** *(fig.)* im Rampenlicht der Öffentlichkeit; **b)** *(hostile look)* feindseliger Blick; **with a ~:** feindselig; **c)** *(gaudiness)* Grellheit, *die.* **2.** *v.i.* **a)** *(glower)* [finster] starren; **~ at sb./sth.** jmdn./etw. anstarren; **b)** ⟨*Licht:*⟩ grell scheinen; *(shine by reflection)* ⟨*Strand, Straße:*⟩ flimmern; **~ down** ⟨*Sonne:*⟩ herunterbrennen. **3.** *v.t.* **~ contempt/defiance/hate** *etc.* **at sb.** jmdn. verächtlich/herausfordernd/haßerfüllt *usw.* anstarren

glaring ['gleərɪŋ] *adj. (dazzling)* grell [strahlend/scheinend *usw.*]; gleißend hell ⟨*Licht*⟩; *(fig.: conspicuous)* schreiend; eklatant; grob ⟨*Fehler*⟩; kraß ⟨*Gegensatz*⟩

glaringly ['gleərɪŋlɪ] *adv.* **a)** grell; **~ bright** gleißend hell; **b)** *(fig.)* **be ~ obvious** überdeutlich sein

glasnost ['glæsnɒst] *n.* Glasnost, *die*

glass [glɑ:s] **1.** *n.* **a)** *no pl. (substance)* Glas, *das;* **pieces of/broken ~:** Glasscherben *Pl.; (smaller)* Glassplitter *Pl.;* **a pane/sheet of ~:** eine Glasscheibe/Glasplatte; **b)** *(drinking ~)* Glas, *das;* **a ~ of milk** ein Glas Milch; **a friendly ~:** ein Gläschen unter Freunden; **he's fond of his ~:** er trinkt gern ein Gläschen; **wine by the ~:** offener Wein; **raise one's ~ [to sb.]** *(fig.)* [auf jmdn.] das Glas erheben; **c)** *(of spectacles, watch)* Glas, *das; (pane, covering picture)* [Glas]scheibe, *die;* **d)** *in pl. (spectacles)* **[a pair of] ~es** eine Brille; **she wears thick ~es** sie trägt eine Brille mit dicken Gläsern; **driving-/reading-~es** Fahr-/Lesebrille, *die;* **e)** *(binoculars)* Fernglas, *das;* **~es** *Pl.* ein Fernglas; **f)** *(barometer)* Barometer, *das;* **g)** *see* **looking-glass.** *See also* **dark glasses; eyeglass; field-glasses; ground glass; hourglass; magnifying glass; opera-glasses; plate glass; water-glass. 2.** *attrib. adj.* Glas-; **people who live in ~ houses should not throw stones** *(prov.)* wer im Glashaus sitzt, soll nicht mit Steinen werfen *(Spr.).* **3.** *v.t., usu. in p.p.* verglasen; **~ed in** verglast

glass: ~-blower *n.* Glasbläser, *der*/Glasbläserin, *die;* **~-blowing** *n.* Glasblasen, *das;* **~ 'case** *n.* Vitrine, *die;* Glaskasten, *der;* **~cloth** *n.* Gläsertuch, *das;* **~ 'fibre** *n.* Glasfaser, *die*

glassful ['glɑ:sfʊl] *n.* Glas, *das* (**of** von); **a ~ of milk** ein Glas Milch

glass: ~house *n.* **a)** *(~works)* Glashütte, *die;* **b)** *(Brit.: greenhouse)* Gewächshaus, *das;* Glashaus, *das;* **c)** *(Brit. sl.: military prison)* Bunker, *der (Soldatenspr. salopp);* **~-making** *n.* Glasherstellung, *die;* **~-paper** *n.* Glaspapier, *das;* **~ware** *n.* Glas, *das;* **~ wool** *n.* Glaswolle, *die;* **~works** *n. sing.* Glashütte, *die*

glassy ['glɑ:sɪ] *adj.* gläsern; *(fig.)* glasig ⟨*Blick*⟩; spiegelglatt ⟨*Wasseroberfläche*⟩

'glassy-eyed *adj.* glasig; ⟨*Person*⟩ mit glasigem Blick; **begin to look ~:** einen glasigen Blick bekommen

Glaswegian [glæz'wi:dʒn] **1.** *adj.* Glasgower. **2.** *n.* Glasgower, *der*/Glasgowerin, *die*

glaucoma [glɔ:'kəʊmə] *n. (Med.)* Glaukom, *das (fachspr.);* grüner Star

glaze [gleɪz] **1.** *n. (on food or pottery)* Glasur, *die; (of paint)* Lasur, *die; (on paper, fabric)* Appretur, *die.* **2.** *v.t.* **a)** *(cover with ~)* glasieren ⟨*Eßwaren, Töpferwaren*⟩; satinieren ⟨*Papier, Leder, Kunststoff, Tuch*⟩; lasieren ⟨*Farbe, bemalte Fläche*⟩; **~d tile** Kachel, *die;* **b)** *(fit with glass)* **~ [in]** verglasen ⟨*Fenster, Haus usw.*⟩; hinter Glas setzen ⟨*Bild*⟩. **3.** *v.i.* **~ [over]** ⟨*Augen:*⟩ glasig werden

glazed [gleɪzd] *adj.* glasig ⟨*Blick*⟩

glazier ['gleɪzɪə(r), 'gleɪʒə(r)] *n.* Glaser, *der*

glazing ['gleɪzɪŋ] *n. (pane)* [Glas]scheibe, *die; (layer)* Glasur, *die; see also* **double glazing**

gleam [gli:m] **1.** *n.* **a)** Schein, *der; (fainter, transient, or more subdued)* Schimmer, *der;* **~ of light** Lichtschein, *der;* **b)** *(fig.: faint trace)* Anflug, *der* (**of** von); **~ of hope/truth** Hoffnungsschimmer, *der*/Funke Wahrheit; **there was a ~ of anticipation in his eyes** seine Augen leuchteten erwartungsvoll. **2.** *v.i.* ⟨*Sonne, Licht:*⟩ scheinen; ⟨*Fußboden, Fahrzeug, Stiefel:*⟩ glänzen; ⟨*Zähne:*⟩ blitzen; ⟨*Augen:*⟩ leuchten

gleaming ['gli:mɪŋ] **1.** *adj.* glänzend ⟨*Wasser, Metall, Fahrzeug*⟩; schimmernd ⟨*Licht*⟩; leuchtend ⟨*Augen*⟩. **2.** *adv.* **~ white** leuchtend *od.* strahlend weiß; blendend *od.* blitzend weiß ⟨*Zähne*⟩

glean [gli:n] **1.** *v.t.* **a)** zusammentragen ⟨*Angaben, Informationen, Nachrichten usw.*⟩; herausfinden ⟨*Inhalt eines Briefes, Gesprächs usw.*⟩; **~ sth. from sth.** einer Sache *(Dat.)* etw. entnehmen; **b)** *(Agric.)* nachlesen ⟨*Getreide, Feld*⟩. **2.** *v.i.* Ähren lesen

gleaner ['gli:nə(r)] *n.* Ährenleser, *der*/Ährenleserin, *die*

gleanings ['gli:nɪŋz] *n. pl.* **a)** *(of news)* zusammengeklaubte Informationen; *(of research, study)* Ausbeute, *die;* **b)** *(of corn etc.)* Nachlese, *die*

glee [gli:] *n.* **a)** Freude, *die; (gloating joy)* Schadenfreude, *die;* Häme, *die;* **do sth. with** *or* **in ~:** etw. voll [Schaden]freude tun; **b)** *(Mus.)* Glee, *der*

'glee club *n.* Gesangverein, *der*

gleeful ['gli:fl] *adj.* freudig; vergnügt; *(gloatingly joyful)* schadenfroh; hämisch; **be ~:** sich [hämisch] freuen

gleefully ['gli:fəlɪ] *adv.* freudig; vor Freude ⟨*lachen usw.*⟩; *(gloatingly)* schadenfroh; hämisch

glen [glen] *n.* [schmales] Tal

glib [glɪb] *adj. (derog.)* aalglatt ⟨*Person*⟩; *(impromptu, offhand)* leicht dahingesagt, unbedacht ⟨*Antwort*⟩; *(unreflecting)* vorschnell ⟨*Schluß, Verallgemeinerung*⟩; *(voluble)* gewandt, geschickt ⟨*Redner, Politiker, Verkäufer*⟩; *(facile in the use of words)* zungenfertig ⟨*Person*⟩; flink ⟨*Zunge*⟩; flinkzüngig ⟨*Antwort*⟩; **be ~ in finding excuses** schnell Entschuldigungen bei der Hand haben

glide [glaɪd] **1.** *v.i.* **a)** gleiten; *(through the air)* schweben; *(slip, steal, creep)* schleichen; ⟨*Gespenst:*⟩ huschen; **b)** *(Aeronaut.)* ⟨*Segelflugzeug:*⟩ gleiten, schweben; ⟨*Flugzeug:*⟩ im Gleitflug fliegen; ⟨*Person:*⟩ segelfliegen; **~ down** im Gleitflug niedergehen. **2.** *n.* **a)** *(Dancing)* Schleifschritt, *der;* **b)** *(Mus.)* Portamento, *das (fachspr.);* **c)** *(Phonet.)* Gleitlaut, *der*

'glide path *n. (Aeronaut.)* Gleitflugbahn, *die*

glider ['glaɪdə(r)] *n.* Segelflugzeug, *das;* **~ [pilot]** Segelflieger, *der*/-fliegerin, *die*

gliding ['glaɪdɪŋ] *n. (Sport)* Segelfliegen, *das; attrib.* Segelflug-

glimmer ['glɪmə(r)] **1.** *n. (of light etc.)* [schwacher] Schein; Glimmer, *der (selten);* Schimmer, *der* (**of** von) *(auch fig.); (of fire, candle)* Glimmen, *das;* **~ of light** Lichtschimmer, *der;* **~ of hope** Hoffnungsschimmer, *der.* **2.** *v.i.* glimmen; ⟨*Satin usw.:*⟩ schimmern

glimmering ['glɪmərɪŋ] *n. (lit. or fig.)* Schimmer, *der* (**of** von)

glimpse [glɪmps] **1.** *n.* [kurzer] Blick; **catch** *or* **have** *or* **get a ~ of sb./sth.** jmdn./etw. [kurz] zu sehen *od.* zu Gesicht bekommen;

(fig.) einen Eindruck von jmdm./Einblick in etw. *(Akk.)* bekommen; **it gives us a ~ of what life must have been like then** es gibt uns einen Einblick in das damalige Leben. **2.** *v. t.* flüchtig sehen; *(fig.)* einen Einblick bekommen in (+ *Akk.*); einen Eindruck gewinnen von

glint [glɪnt] **1.** *n.* Schimmer, *der; (reflected flash)* Glitzern, *das; (of eyes)* Funkeln, *das; (of knife, dagger)* Blitzen, *das.* **2.** *v. i.* blinken; glitzern

glissando [glɪˈsændəʊ] *n., pl.* **glissandi** [glɪˈsændi:] *or* **~s** *(Mus.)* Glissando, *das*

glisten [ˈglɪsn] *v. i.* glitzern; *see also* **glitter 1 a**

glitch [glɪtʃ] *n. (sl.)* Panne, *die*

glitter [ˈglɪtə(r)] **1.** *v. i.* **a)** glitzern; ‹*Augen, Juwelen, Sterne:*› funkeln; **the sky ~s with stars, stars ~ in the sky** am Himmel funkeln Sterne; **all that ~s** *or* **glistens is not gold** *(prov.)* es ist nicht alles Gold, was glänzt *(Spr.)*; **b)** *esp. in pres. p. (fig.)* glänzen; **~ing prizes** verlockende *od.* attraktive Preise. **2.** *n.* **a)** Glitzern, *das; (of diamonds)* Funkeln, *das;* **b)** *(fig.: ~ing attractiveness)* verlockende Aussicht (**of** auf + *Akk.*); **c)** *(tinsel etc.)* Flitterwerk, *das;* Glitzerwerk, *das*

glitz [glɪts] *n.* Glanz, *der*

glitzy [ˈglɪtsɪ] *adj.* glanzvoll

gloaming [ˈgləʊmɪŋ] *n., no pl.* **the ~:** die Abenddämmerung

gloat [gləʊt] *v. i.* **~ over sth.** *(look at with selfish delight)* sich an etw. *(Dat.)* weiden *od.* ergötzen; *(derive sadistic pleasure from)* sich hämisch über etw. *(Akk.)* freuen

gloatingly [ˈgləʊtɪŋlɪ] *adv. (with delight)* selbstgefällig; genüßlich; *(with sadistic pleasure)* hämisch

global [ˈgləʊbl] *adj.* **a)** *(world-wide)* global; weltweit; weltumspannend ‹*Kommunikationssystem*›; **~ warming** globaler Temperaturanstieg; **~ peace/warfare** Weltfrieden/-krieg, *der;* **~ strategy** Globalstrategie, *die;* **the ~ village** das Weltdorf; **b)** *(comprehensive)* Gesamt-; umfassend ‹*Berichterstattung*›; **take a ~ view** die Dinge global betrachten

globally [ˈgləʊbəlɪ] *adv.* **a)** *(on a world-wide basis)* global; weltweit; **b)** *(comprehensively)* umfassend

globe [gləʊb] *n.* **a)** *(sphere)* Kugel, *die;* **b)** *(sphere with map)* Globus, *der;* **c)** *(world)* **the ~:** der Globus; der Erdball; **d)** *(spherical object)* Kugel, *die*

globe: ~ ˈartichoke *see* **artichoke; ~-fish** *n.* Kugelfisch, *der;* **~-flower** *n.* Trollblume, *die;* **~-trotter** *n.* Globetrotter, *der;* Weltenbummler, *der;* **~-trotting** *n.* Globetrotten, *das;* Weltreisen, *das*

globular [ˈglɒbjʊlə(r)] *adj.* kugelförmig

globule [ˈglɒbju:l] *n.* Kügelchen, *das; (of liquid)* Tröpfchen, *das*

globulin [ˈglɒbjʊlɪn] *n. (Biochem.)* Globulin, *das*

glockenspiel [ˈglɒkənspi:l, ˈglɒkənʃpi:l] *n. (Mus.)* Glockenspiel, *das*

gloom [glu:m] *n.* **a)** *(darkness)* Dunkel, *das (geh.);* **b)** *(despondency)* düstere Stimmung; **cast a ~ over sth.** einen Schatten auf etw. *(Akk.)* werfen *(fig.)*

gloomily [ˈglu:mɪlɪ] *adv.* finster; düster

gloomy [ˈglu:mɪ] *adj.* **a)** *(dark)* düster; finster; dämmrig ‹*Tag, Nachmittag usw.*›; **b)** *(depressing)* düster, finster [stimmend]; bedrückend; *(depressed)* trübsinnig ‹*Person*›; bedrückt ‹*Gesicht*›; **he always tends to see the ~ side of things** er sieht immer gleich schwarz; **have a ~ outlook on life** dem Leben erwartungslos *od.* pessimistisch gegenüberstehen; **feel ~ about the future** der Zukunft pessimistisch entgegensehen; **be in a ~ mood** düsterer Stimmung *od.* niedergeschlagen sein; **look ~:** niedergeschlagen *od.* bedrückt aussehen; ein bedrücktes Gesicht machen

glorification [glɔ:rɪfɪˈkeɪʃn] *n.* **a)** *(praise)* Verherrlichung, *die;* Glorifizierung, *die;* **b)** *(worship)* Verehrung, *die;* Anbetung, *die;* **c)** *(exaltation)* Verehrung, *die*

glorify [ˈglɔ:rɪfaɪ] *v. t.* **a)** *(extol)* verherrlichen; glorifizieren; *(misrepresent thus)* **glorified** besser *(ugs.)*; **he's no more than a glorified messenger-boy** er ist nichts weiter als *od.* doch nur ein besserer Botenjunge; **b)** *(worship)* verehren; anbeten; **c)** *(exalt)* verehren; ehren ‹*Helden, Andenken*›

glorious [ˈglɔ:rɪəs] *adj.* **a)** *(illustrious)* ruhmreich ‹*Held, Sieg, Geschichte*›; rühmlich ‹*Tat, Rolle*›; verehrungswürdig ‹*Heilige*›; **b)** *(honourable)* ehrenhaft ‹*Sache, Angelegenheit*›; ehrenvoll, rühmlich ‹*Tod, Kampf, Sieg, Tat*›; glorreich, glanzvoll ‹*Ende einer Karriere, Errungenschaft*›; **c)** *(delightful)* wunderschön; herrlich; *(iron.)* schön; **it was ~ fun** es war ein prächtiger *od.* köstlicher Spaß

gloriously [ˈglɔ:rɪəslɪ] *adv.* **a)** *(honourably)* rühmlich; *(illustriously)* glanzvoll; **die ~:** in Ehren sterben; **b)** *(splendidly)* wunderschön; herrlich

glory [ˈglɔ:rɪ] **1.** *n.* **a)** *(splendour)* Schönheit, *die; (majesty)* Herrlichkeit, *die;* **the Empire at the height of its ~:** das Imperium auf dem Höhepunkt seiner Macht; **a lily in all its ~:** eine Lilie in ihrer vollen Pracht; **in all one's ~** *(iron.)* in all seiner Pracht und Herrlichkeit *(iron.)*; **b)** *(honour)* Ehre, *die; (credit)* Verdienst, *das; (fame)* Ruhm, *der;* **they did all the work and he got all the ~:** sie haben die ganze Arbeit getan, und ihm wird es als Verdienst angerechnet; **cover oneself with ~:** sich mit Ruhm bedecken *(geh.)*; sich mit Ruhm bekleckern *(ugs., iron.)*; **c)** *(worshipful praise)* Ehre, *die;* Ruhm, *der;* **~ [be] to God in the highest** Ehre sei Gott in der Höhe; **[built] to the ~ of God** [erbaut] zur Ehre/zum Ruhme Gottes; **~ be!** *(dated sl.) expr. surprise* ach du lieber Himmel! *(ugs.)*; *expr. annoyance* Himmel noch mal! *(ugs.)*; *expr. delight* himmlisch!; **d)** *(source of distinction)* Größe, *die; (deed)* Ruhmestat, *die; (achievement)* Glanzleistung, *die;* **be the ~ of a nation** der Stolz *od.* die Zierde eines Volkes sein; *see also* **Old Glory; e)** *(heavenly bliss)* ewige Seligkeit; **Christ in ~:** Christus in seiner Herrlichkeit; **go/send to ~** *(arch. sl.)* abfahren *(veralt.)*/ins Jenseits befördern *(salopp)*. **2.** *v. i.* **~ in sth./doing sth.** *(be pleased by)* etw. genießen/es genießen, etw. zu tun; *(be proud of)* sich einer Sache *(Gen.)* rühmen/sich rühmen, etw. zu tun; **~ in the name/title of ...:** den stolzen Namen/Titel ... besitzen *od.* führen

ˈglory-hole *n. (sl.)* Rumpelkammer, *die*

¹gloss [glɒs] **1.** *n.* **a)** *(sheen)* Glanz, *der;* **~ paint** Lackfarbe, *die;* **~ finish** Glanz, *der;* **paper/photo with a ~ finish** Glanzpapier, *das*/Glanzabzug, *der;* **give sth. a high ~:** einer Sache *(Dat.)* Hochglanz verleihen; **b)** *(fig.)* Anstrich, *der.* **2.** *v. t.* polieren; auf Hochglanz bringen

~ over *v. t.* bemänteln; beschönigen ‹*Fehler*›; *(conceal)* unter den Teppich kehren *(ugs.)*

²gloss 1. *n.* **a)** *(comment)* [Wort]erklärung, *die; (Ling.)* Glosse, *die (fachspr.)*; **b)** *(misrepresentation of another's words)* [bewußt] falsche Auslegung; **c)** *(glossary)* Glossar, *das; (translation)* Interlinearübersetzung, *die; (continuous explanation)* Kommentar, *der.* **2.** *v. t.* glossieren

glossary [ˈglɒsərɪ] *n.* Glossar, *das*

glossy [ˈglɒsɪ] **1.** *adj.* **a)** glänzend; *(printed on ~ paper)* Hochglanz-; auf Glanzpapier gedruckt; **~ paper, paper with a ~ finish** Glanzpapier, *das;* **~ [photographic] print** Glanzabzug, *der;* **b)** *(fig.)* glanzvoll. **2.** *n. (coll.)* **a)** *(magazine)* auf [Hoch]glanzpapier gedruckte Zeitschrift; Hochglanzzeitschrift, *die;* **b)** *(photograph)* Glanzabzug, *der*

glottal [ˈglɒtl] *adj. (Phonet.)* glottal; Stimmritzen‹*laut, -verschluß usw.*›

glottal ˈstop *n. (Phonet.)* Glottisschlag, *der;* Knacklaut, *der*

glottis [ˈglɒtɪs] *n. (Anat.)* Glottis, *die*

glove [glʌv] *n.* **a)** Handschuh, *der;* **sth. fits sb. like a ~:** etw. paßt jmdm. wie angegossen *(ugs.)*; *(fig.)* etw. trifft auf jmdn. haargenau zu; **throw down/take up the ~** *(fig.)* den Fehdehandschuh werfen/aufnehmen *(geh.)*; **b)** *see* **boxing-glove; argue sth. with the ~s off** sich in allem Ernst *od.* offen und ehrlich über etw. *(Akk.)* auseinandersetzen. *See also* **hand 1 a**

glove: ~ box *n.* **a)** *see* **~ compartment; b)** *(for toxic material etc.)* Handschuhkasten, *der;* **~ compartment** *n.* Handschuhfach, *das*

gloved [glʌvd] *adj.* behandschuht

ˈglove puppet *n.* Handpuppe, *die*

glow [gləʊ] **1.** *v. i.* **a)** glühen; ‹*Lampe, Leuchtfarbe:*› schimmern, leuchten; **b)** *(fig.) (with warmth or pride)* ‹*Gesicht, Wangen:*› glühen (**with** vor + *Dat.*); *(with health or vigour)* strotzen (**with** vor + *Dat.*); *(with pleasure or excitement)* strahlen (**with** vor + *Dat.*); *(with rage or fervour)* glühen (**with** vor + *Dat.*); **c)** *(be suffused with warm colour)* [warm] leuchten; **~ with the tints of autumn** in allen Herbstfarben leuchten. **2.** *n.* **a)** Glühen, *das; (of candle, lamp)* Schein, *der; (of embers, lava, sunset)* Glut, *die;* **b)** *(fig.)* Glühen, *das;* **feel a ~ of pride** vor Stolz glühen; **his cheeks had a healthy ~:** seine Wangen hatten eine blühende Farbe; **~ of youth/health** blühende Jugend/Gesundheit; **feel a ~ of happiness/passion** ein warmes Glücksgefühl/glühende Leidenschaft verspüren

glower [ˈglaʊə(r)] *v. i.* finster dreinblicken; **~ at sb.** jmdn. finster anstarren

glowing [ˈgləʊɪŋ] *adj.* glühend *(auch fig.)*; [warm] leuchtend ‹*Herbstfarben*›; *(fig.: enthusiastic)* begeistert ‹*Bericht, Beschreibung*›; überschwenglich ‹*Lob*›; **be in ~ health** sich blühender Gesundheit *(Gen.)* erfreuen; **describe sth. in ~ colours/terms** *(fig.)* etw. in glühenden *od.* leuchtenden Farben/glühenden Worten beschreiben; **~ promises** glänzende Versprechungen

glow: ~-lamp *n. (Electr.)* Glühlampe, *die;* **~-worm** *n.* Glühwürmchen, *das*

gloxinia [glɒkˈsɪnɪə] *n. (Bot.)* Gloxinie, *die*

glucose [ˈglu:kəʊs, ˈglu:kəʊz] *n.* Glucose, *die;* **~ [powder]** *(Med.)* Traubenzucker, *der*

glue [glu:] **1.** *n.* Klebstoff, *der;* Leim, *der;* Kleber, *der (ugs.)*; **like ~** *(fig.)* wie festgeklebt; **cling like ~ to sth./sb.** *(fig.)* an etw./jmdm. kleben *(ugs.)*. **2.** *v. t.* **a)** kleben; leimen; **~ sth. together/on** etw. zusammen-/ankleben; **~ sth. to sth.** etw. an etw. *(Dat.)* an- *od.* festkleben; **as though ~d to the spot** wie angewurzelt; **b)** *(fig.)* **be ~d to sth./sb.** an etw./jmdm. kleben *(ugs.)*; **their eyes** *or* **they were ~d to the TV screen** sie starrten auf den Bildschirm

glue: ~-pot *n.* Leimtopf, *der;* **~-sniffing** *n.* Schnüffeln, *das (ugs.)*; Sniefen, *das (ugs.)*

glug [glʌg] *v. i.,* **-gg-** gluckern; glucksen

glum [glʌm] *adj.,* **glumly** [ˈglʌmlɪ] *adv.* verdrießlich; mißgelaunt

glut [glʌt] **1.** *n. (Commerc.)* Überangebot, *das* (**of** an, von + *Dat.*); **a ~ of apples/talent** eine Apfelschwemme/eine Menge Talente. **2.** *v. t.,* **-tt-** **a)** *(Commerc.)* überschwemmen; **b)** *(gorge)* **~ oneself** sich vollstopfen *(ugs.)* (**with, on** mit); **be ~ted with sth.** *(fig.)* einer Sache *(Gen.)* überdrüssig sein

glutamate [ˈglu:təmeɪt] *n. (Chem.)* Glutamat, *das;* **monosodium ~:** [Mono]natriumglutamat, *das*

gluten ['glu:tən] *n.* Gluten, *das;* Kleber, *der (fachspr.);* ~ **bread** Glutenbrot, *das*
glutinous ['glu:tɪnəs] *adj.* klebrig
glutton ['glʌtən] *n.* **a)** Vielfraß, *der (ugs.);* a ~ **for books/punishment** *(iron.)*/**work** *(fig.)* eine Leseratte *(ugs.)*/ein Masochist *(fig.)*/ ein Arbeitstier *(fig.);* **b)** *(Zool.)* Vielfraß, *der*
gluttonous ['glʌtənəs] *adj.* gefräßig
gluttony ['glʌtənɪ] *n.* Gefräßigkeit, *die*
glycerine ['glɪsəri:n] *(Amer.:* **glycerin** ['glɪsərɪn]) *n.* Glyzerin, *das*
glycogen ['glaɪkədʒən] *n. (Med., Biol.)* Glykogen, *das*
glycol ['glaɪkɒl] *n. (Chem.)* Glykol, *das*
gm. *abbr.* **gram[s]** g
G-man ['dʒi:mæn] *n., pl.* **G-men** ['dʒi:men] *(Amer. sl.)* G-man, *der*
GMT *abbr.* **Greenwich mean time** GMT; WEZ
gnarled [nɑ:ld], **gnarly** ['nɑ:lɪ] *adjs.* knorrig; knotig ‹*Finger, Hand*›
gnash [næʃ] *v. t.* ~ **one's teeth [in anger]** [vor Zorn] mit den Zähnen knirschen; ~**ing of teeth** Zähneknirschen, *das*
gnat [næt] *n.* [Stech]mücke, *die; see also* [1]**strain 3 b**
gnaw [nɔ:] **1.** *v. i.* **a)** ~ **[away] at sth.** an etw. *(Dat.)* nagen; ~ **through sth.** durch etw. ein Loch nagen; sich durch etw. fressen; **b)** *(fig.)* ~ **[away] at sth./sb.'s savings** an etw. *(Dat.)* nagen/an jmds. Ersparnissen zehren. **2.** *v. t.* **a)** nagen an (+ *Dat.*); abnagen ‹*Knochen*›; kauen an *od.* auf *(Dat.)* ‹*Fingernägeln*›; ~ **a hole in sth.** ein Loch in etw. *(Akk.)* nagen; **b)** *(fig.)* nagen an (+ *Dat.*) ‹*Gewissen*›; zehren an ‹*Herzen*›
gnawing ['nɔ:ɪŋ] *adj.* nagend ‹*Hunger, Schmerz, Zweifel, Kummer usw.*›; quälend ‹*Zahnschmerzen, Angst*›
gneiss [gnaɪs, naɪs] *n. (Geol.)* Gneis, *der*
gnome [nəʊm] *n.* **a)** Gnom, *der; (in garden)* Gartenzwerg, *der;* **b)** *(fig. coll.)* **the** ~**s of Zurich** die Zürcher Gnome; die Schweizer Bankiers
gnomic ['nəʊmɪk] *adj.* gnomisch
gnostic ['nɒstɪk] **1.** *adj.* **a)** *(relating to or having knowledge)* kognitiv; *(Relig.)* erleuchtet; **b)** **G**~ *(Relig. Hist.)* gnostisch. **2.** *n.* **G**~ *(Relig. Hist.)* Gnostiker, *der*
Gnosticism ['nɒstɪsɪzm] *n. (Relig. Hist.)* Gnostizismus, *der*
GNP *abbr.* **gross national product** BSP
gnu [nu:, nju:] *n. (Zool.)* Gnu, *das*
[1]**go** [gəʊ] **1.** *v. i., pres.* **he goes** [gəʊz], *p. t.* **went** [went], *pres. p.* **going** ['gəʊɪŋ], *p. p.* **gone** [gɒn, gɔ:n] **a)** gehen; ‹*Fahrzeug:*› fahren; ‹*Flugzeug:*› fliegen; ‹*Vierfüßer:*› laufen; ‹*Reptil:*› kriechen; *(on horseback etc.)* reiten; *(on skis, roller-skates)* laufen; *(in wheelchair, pram, lift)* fahren; **go by bicycle/car/bus/train** *or* **rail/boat** *or* **sea** *or* **ship** mit dem [Fahr]rad/Auto/Bus/Zug/Schiff fahren; **go by plane** *or* **air** fliegen; **go by Lufthansa/Concorde** mit der Lufthansa/der Concorde fliegen; **go on foot** zu Fuß gehen; laufen *(ugs.);* **as one goes [along]** *(fig.)* nach und nach; **do sth. as one goes [along]** *(lit.)* etw. beim Gehen *od.* unterwegs tun; **go on a journey** eine Reise machen; verreisen; **go first-class/at 50 m.p.h.** erster Klasse reisen *od.* fahren/80 Stundenkilometer fahren; **go with sb.** mit jmdm. gehen; jmdn. begleiten; ‹*Hund:*› jmdm. folgen; **have far to go** weit zu gehen *od.* zu fahren haben; es weit haben; **the doll/dog goes everywhere with her** sie hat immer ihre Puppe/ihren Hund dabei; **who goes there?** *(sentry's challenge)* wer da?; **there you go** *(coll., giving sth.)* bitte!; da! *(ugs.);* **b)** *(proceed as regards purpose, activity, destination, or route)* ‹*Bus, Zug, Lift, Schiff:*› fahren; *(use means of transportation)* fahren; *(fly)* fliegen; *(proceed on outward journey)* weg-, abfahren; *(travel regularly)* ‹*Verkehrsmittel:*› verkehren (**from** ... **to** zwischen + *Dat.* ... und); **know where one is going** *(fig.)* wissen, was man will; **his hand went to his pocket** er griff nach seiner Tasche; **go to the toilet/cinema/moon/a museum/a funeral** auf die Toilette/ins Kino gehen/zum Mond fliegen/ins Museum/zu einer Beerdigung gehen; **go to a dance** tanzen gehen; **go [along] to the doctor['s]** *etc.* zum Arzt *usw.* gehen; **go [out] to China** nach China gehen; **go [over] to America** nach Amerika [hinüber]fliegen/-fahren; **go [off] to London** nach London [ab]fahren/[ab]fliegen; **go [over** *or* **across] to the mainland** zum Festland [hinüber]fahren/-fliegen; **last year we went to Italy** letztes Jahr waren wir in Italien; **go this/that way** hier/da entlanggehen/-fahren; **go out of one's way** einen Umweg machen; *(fig.)* keine Mühe scheuen; **go towards sth./sb.** auf etw./jmdn. zugehen; **don't go on the grass** geh nicht auf den Rasen; **go by sth./sb.** ‹*Festzug usw.:*› an etw./jmdm. vorbeiziehen; ‹*Bus usw.:*› an etw./jmdm. vorbeifahren; **go in/out** hinein-/hinausgehen; **go in and out [of sth.]** [in etw. *(Dat.)*] ein- und ausgehen; **go into sth.** in etw. *(Akk.)* [hinein]gehen; **I'd never go on motorways** ich würde niemals [auf der] Autobahn fahren; **go out for some fresh air** frische Luft schöpfen gehen; **go out to the post-box** zum Briefkasten gehen; **go [out] for a walk** einen Spaziergang machen; spazierengehen; **go bathing** baden gehen; **go cycling** radfahren; **go looking for sb.** jmdn. suchen gehen; **go chasing after sth./sb.** hinter etw./jmdm. herrennen *(ugs.);* **go to do sth.** gehen, um etw. zu tun; *(while standing still)* etw. tun wollen; **go to live in Berlin** nach Berlin ziehen; **go to sea** in See stechen; *(become sailor)* zur See gehen *(ugs.);* **go to see sb.** jmdn. aufsuchen; **I went to water the garden** ich ging den Garten sprengen; **go and do sth.** [gehen und] etw. tun; **you ought to go and find a flat** du solltest dir eine Wohnung suchen; **I'll go and get my coat** ich hole jetzt meinen Mantel; **I'll just go and put my shoes on** ich ziehe mir nur eben Schuhe an; **go and see whether ...:** nachsehen [gehen], ob ...; **go on a pilgrimage** *etc.* eine Pilgerfahrt *usw.* machen; **go on TV/the radio** im Fernsehen/Radio auftreten; **I'll go!** ich geh schon!; *(answer phone)* ich geh ran *od.* nehme ab; *(answer door)* ich mache auf; **'you go** *(to the phone)* geh du mal ran!; **c)** *(start)* losgehen; *(in vehicle)* losfahren; **let's go!** *(coll.)* fangen wir an!; **here goes!** *(coll.)* dann mal los!; **whose turn is it to go?** *(in game)* wer ist an der Reihe?; **go first** *(in game)* anfangen; **from the word go** *(fig. coll.)* [schon] von Anfang an; **d)** *(pass, circulate, be transmitted)* gehen; **a shiver went up** *or* **down my spine** ein Schauer lief mir über den Rücken *od.* den Rücken hinunter; **go to** *(be given to)* ‹*Preis, Sieg, Gelder, Job:*› gehen an (+ *Akk.*); ‹*Titel, Krone, Besitz:*› übergehen auf (+ *Akk.*); ‹*Ehre, Verdienst:*› zuteil werden *(Dat.);* **go towards** *(be of benefit to)* zugute kommen (+ *Dat.*); **go according to** *(be determined by)* sich richten nach; *see also* **head 1 a; e)** *(make specific motion, do something specific)* **go round** ‹*Rad:*› sich drehen; **there he** *etc.* **goes again** *(coll.)* da, schon wieder!; **here we go again** *(coll.)* jetzt geht das wieder los!; **f)** *(act, work, function effectively)* gehen; ‹*Mechanismus, Maschine:*› laufen; **get the car to go** das Auto ankriegen *(ugs.) od.* starten; **at midnight we were still going** um Mitternacht waren wir immer noch dabei *od.* im Gange; **go by electricity** mit Strom betrieben werden; **the clock doesn't go** die Uhr geht nicht; **go to it!** *(coll.)* an die Arbeit!; **keep going** *(in movement)* weitergehen/-fahren; *(in activity)* weitermachen; *(not fail)* sich aufrecht halten; **the car still keeps going** das Auto läuft noch immer; **keep oneself going** durchhalten; **keep sb. going** *(enable to continue)* jmdn. aufrecht halten; **that'll keep me going** das reicht mir; damit komme ich aus; **keep sth. going** etw. in Gang halten; **make sth. go, get/set sth. going** etw. in Gang bringen; **set sb. going** *(iron.)* jmdn. aufs Thema bringen *(ugs.);* jmdn. in Fahrt bringen *(ugs.);* **g) go to** *(attend):* **go to work** zur Arbeit gehen; **go to church/kindergarten/school** in die Kirche/den Kindergarten/die Schule gehen; **go to Eton/Oxford** Eton besuchen/in Oxford studieren; **go to a comprehensive school** eine Gesamtschule besuchen; auf eine Gesamtschule gehen; **go as a witch** *etc.* als Hexe *usw.* gehen; **what should I go in?** was soll ich anziehen?; **h)** *(have recourse)* **go to the police** zur Polizei gehen; **go to the originals** auf die Quellen zurückgreifen; **go to the relevant authority/UN** sich an die zuständige Behörde/UN wenden; **go on hunger strike** in den Hungerstreik treten; **go into the army** zur Armee gehen; **where do we go from here?** *(fig.)* und was nun? *(ugs.);* **i)** *(depart)* gehen; ‹*Bus, Zug:*› [ab]fahren; ‹*Post:*› rausgehen *(ugs.); (resign)* zurücktreten; *(abdicate)* abdanken; **go away** weggehen; *(move away)* wegziehen; **he/the bus has gone** er/der Bus ist schon weg *(ugs.);* **I must go** ich muß gehen; **I must be going now** ich muß allmählich gehen; **time to go!** wir müssen/ihr müßt *usw.* gehen!; **'gone away'** *(on envelope)* „verzogen"; **Oh no! There goes my quiet weekend** Oh nein, jetzt ist mein geruhsames Wochenende dahin!; **to go** *(Amer.)* ‹*Speisen, Getränke*› zum Mitnehmen; **my headache has gone** mein Kopfweh ist weg; **j)** *(euphem.: die)* sterben; **be dead and gone** tot sein; **after I go** wenn ich einmal nicht mehr bin; **k)** *(fail)* [dahin]schwinden; nachlassen; *(cease to function)* kaputtgehen; ‹*Maschine, Computer usw.:*› ausfallen; ‹*Sicherung:*› durchbrennen; *(break)* brechen; ‹*Seil usw.:*› reißen; *(collapse)* einstürzen; ‹*Mast:*› umstürzen; *(fray badly)* ausfransen; **the jacket has gone at the elbows** die Jacke ist an den Ellbogen durchgescheuert *od.* abgewetzt; **his memory is going** sein Gedächtnis läßt nach; **l)** *(disappear)* weggehen; ‹*Mantel, Hut, Fleck:*› verschwinden; ‹*Zahn:*› ausfallen; ‹*Kultur:*› vergehen; ‹*Geruch, Rauch:*› sich verziehen; ‹*Geld, Zeit:*› draufgehen *(ugs.)* **(in, on** für); *(be relinquished)* aufgegeben werden; ‹*Absatz usw.:*› gestrichen werden; ‹*Unterrichtsfach:*› entfallen; ‹*Tradition:*› abgeschafft werden; *(be dismissed)* ‹*Arbeitskräfte:*› entlassen werden; *(Cricket) (be out)* aussein; **be gone from sight** außer Sicht geraten sein; **my coat/the stain has gone** mein Mantel/der Fleck ist weg; **where has my hat gone?** wo ist mein Hut [geblieben]?; **I don't know where my money goes** ich weiß nicht, wo das Geld bleibt; **that aid to developing countries goes on the growing of food** diese Entwicklungshilfe wird für den Anbau von Nahrungsmitteln verwendet; **this paragraph will have to go** dieser Absatz muß gestrichen werden; **all his money goes on women** er gibt sein ganzes Geld für Frauen aus; **all hope has gone** alle Hoffnung ist dahin; **m)** *(elapse)* ‹*Zeit:*› vergehen; ‹*Interview usw.:*› vorüber-, vorbeigehen; **that has all gone by** das ist jetzt alles vorbei; **in days gone by** in längst vergangenen Zeiten; **n) to go** *(still remaining)* **have sth. [still] to go** [noch] etw. übrig haben; **he has two years to go before he can retire** an der Rente fehlen ihm noch zwei Jahre; **there's hours to go** es dauert noch Stunden; **one week** *etc.* **to go to ...:** noch eine Woche *usw.* bis ...; **there's only another mile to go** [es ist] nur noch eine Meile; **have still a mile to go** noch eine Meile vor sich *(Dat.)* haben; **one down, two to go** einer ist bereits erledigt, bleiben noch zwei

übrig *(salopp)*; **o)** *(be sold)* weggehen *(ugs.)*; verkauft werden; **it went for £1** es ging für 1 Pfund weg; **I shan't let it go for less** für weniger gebe ich es nicht her; **go to sb.** an jmdn. gehen; **going! going! gone!** zum ersten! zum zweiten! zum dritten!; **p)** *(run)* ‹*Grenze, Straße usw.*:› verlaufen, gehen; *(afford access, lead)* gehen; führen; *(extend)* reichen; *(fig.)* gehen; **go high[er]** ‹*Preis*:› [noch weiter] steigen, [noch weiter] in die Höhe gehen; **the line goes across the page/to the corner/upwards** der Strich geht quer über die Seite/bis in die Ecke/verläuft nach oben; **my holiday goes from ... to ...**: ich habe Urlaub von ... bis ...; **as** *or* **so far as he/it goes** soweit; **sth. is correct as** *or* **so far as it goes** etw. ist soweit in Ordnung; **go a long way** ‹*Geld, Vorräte*:› lange reichen; **he will go a long way** *(fig.)* er wird es weit bringen; **go some/a long way to[wards] achieving sth.** ein kleines/ganzes Stück weiterhelfen *od.* einiges/eine Menge dazu beitragen, etw. zu erreichen; **ten pounds in those days went a long way** damals waren zehn Pfund noch etwas wert; **a little of his company goes a long way** *(coll. derog.)* wenn man nur kurze Zeit mit ihm verbracht hat, reicht das erst mal für eine Weile *od.* *(salopp)* ist man erst mal für eine Weile bedient; **q)** *(fig.: advance)* **we'll go half-way to meet the cost** wir kommen ihnen *usw.* bei den Kosten halbwegs entgegen; **I'll go as high as £100** *(at auction)* ich gehe *od.* biete bis zu 100 Pfund [mit]; *see also* **bother 3b; expense 1a; trouble a; way 1e; r)** *(turn out, progress)* ‹*Ereignis, Projekt, Interview, Abend*:› verlaufen; **go for/against sb./sth.** ‹*Wahl, Kampf*:› zu jmds./einer Sache Gunsten/Ungunsten ausgehen; ‹*Entscheidung, Urteil*:› zu jmds./einer Sache Gunsten/Ungunsten ausfallen; ‹*Rechtsfall*:› zu jmds./einer Sache Gunsten/Ungunsten entschieden werden; **how did your holiday/party go?** wie war Ihr Urlaub/Ihre Party?; **how is the book going?** was macht [denn] das Buch?; **how are the rehearsals going?** was machen die Proben?; wie läuft es mit den Proben?; **go according to plan** nach Plan gehen; planmäßig verlaufen; **things have been going well/badly/smoothly** *etc.* **of late** in der letzten Zeit läuft alles gut/schief/glatt *usw.*; **the way things are going, ...**: so wie es aussieht *od.* so wie die Dinge liegen, ...; **how are things going?, how is it going?,** *(coll. joc.)* **how goes it?** wie stehen die Aktien? *(ugs. scherzh.)*; wie steht's?; **s)** *(be, have form or nature, be in temporary state)* sein; ‹*Sprichwort, Gedicht, Titel*:› lauten; **this is how things go, that's the way it goes** so ist es nun mal; **go against sth.** mit etw. nicht übereinstimmen; **go against one's principles** gegen seine Prinzipien gehen; **go against logic** der Logik widersprechen; gegen alle Logik sein; **go armed/naked** bewaffnet sein/nackt herumlaufen; **go in rags** in Lumpen *od.* zerlumpt gehen; **go hungry** hungern; hungrig bleiben; **go without food/water** es ohne Essen/Wasser aushalten; **go in fear of one's life** in beständiger Angst um sein Leben leben; **may the blessings of God go with you** möge der Segen des Herrn dich begleiten; der Segen des Herrn sei mit dir; **how does the tune/song/wording go [now]?** wie geht die Melodie/das Lied/lauten die Worte [denn nun]?; **the argument goes like this** das Argument ist folgendes; **now the tale/rumour/theory goes that ...**: es wird erzählt/es geht das Gerücht/es wird die Theorie vertreten, daß ...; **go to the tune of ...**: der Melodie von ... folgen; **this noun/verb goes like ...**: dieses Substantiv/Verb geht genauso wie ...; **as things/canteens/actors** *etc.* **go** verglichen mit anderen Dingen/Kantinen/Schauspielern *usw.*; **as things go, it's not expensive** das ist verhältnismäßig billig; **go by** *or* **under the name of ...**: unter dem Namen ... bekannt sein; **t)** *(become)* werden; **the tyre has gone flat** der Reifen ist platt; **the phone has gone dead** die Leitung ist tot; **go on the blink** kaputtgehen *(ugs.)*; **go all freaky/Indian** *etc.* völlig ausflippen *(ugs.)*/ganz auf indisch *usw.* machen; **go serious/arty on sb.** jmdm. auf die ernste/Künstlertour kommen *(ugs.)*; **go nuclear/metric** *(coll.)* zur Atommacht werden/das metrische System einführen; **the constituency/York went Tory** der Wahlkreis/York ging an die Tories; **u)** *(have usual place)* kommen; *(belong)* gehören; **where does the box go?** wo kommt *od.* gehört die Kiste hin?; **where do you want this chair to go?** wo soll *od.* kommt der Stuhl hin?; **that chair will go nicely in the corner** dieser Stuhl macht sich gut *od.* paßt gut in die Ecke; **this goes under a different heading** das gehört unter eine andere Überschrift; **each drink goes** *or* **all drinks go on the bill** alle Getränke kommen *od.* gehen auf die Rechnung; **the cheque is to go in[to] my account** der Scheck geht auf mein Konto; **v)** *(fit)* passen; **go in[to] sth.** in etw. *(Akk.)* gehen *od.* [hinein]passen; **it won't go [in]** es geht nicht rein *(ugs.)*; **go through sth.** durch etw. [hindurch]gehen *od.* [hindurch]passen; **six into twelve goes twice** sechs geht zweimal in zwölf; **five goes into forty exactly** vierzig durch fünf geht auf; **w)** *(harmonize, match)* passen **(with** zu); **the two colours don't go** die beiden Farben passen nicht zusammen *od.* beißen sich; **x)** *(serve, contribute)* dienen; **the qualities that go to make a leader** die Eigenschaften, die einen Führer ausmachen; **the sounds that go to make up a language** die Laute, aus denen eine Sprache besteht; **this fact goes to prove that ...** folgende Tatsache belegt, daß ...; **it just goes to show that ...**: daran zeigt sich, daß ...; **y)** *(make sound of specified kind)* machen; *(emit sound)* ‹*Turmuhr, Gong*:› schlagen; ‹*Glocke*:› läuten; **There goes the bell. School is over** Es klingelt. Die Schule ist aus; **the fire alarm went at 3 a.m.** der Feueralarm ging um 3 Uhr morgens los; **a police car with its siren going** ein Polizeiwagen mit eingeschalteter Sirene; **z)** *as intensifier (coll.)* **don't go making** *or* **go and make him angry** verärgere ihn bloß nicht; **he might go and hang himself** nachher hängt er sich womöglich auf; **don't go and make a fool of yourself** mach dich doch nicht lächerlich; **don't go looking for trouble** such keinen Streit; **don't go thinking ...**: glaube doch ja nicht, daß ....; **I gave him a £10 note and, of course, he had to go and lose it** ich gab ihm einen 10-Pfund-Schein, und er mußte ihn natürlich prompt verlieren; **now you've been and gone and done it** *(sl.)* du hast ja was Schönes angerichtet! *(ugs. iron.)*; **go tell him I'm ready** *(coll./Amer.)* geh und sag ihm, daß ich fertig bin; **she said to her dog 'Go fetch it'** sie sagte zu ihrem Hund: „Los, hol's!"; **let's go get ourselves a drink** *(coll./Amer.)* holen wir uns was zu trinken; **aa)** *(coll.: be acceptable or permitted)* erlaubt sein; gehen *(ugs.)*; **everything/anything goes** es ist alles erlaubt; **it/that goes without saying** es/das ist doch selbstverständlich; es/das versteht sich von selbst; **what he** *etc.* **says, goes** was er *usw.* sagt, gilt; wenn er *usw.* etwas sagt, dann gilt es auch; *see also* [1]**let 1a; bb)** *(coll. euphem.: defecate or urinate)* auf die Toilette gehen; **really have to go** wirklich müssen *(ugs.)*; **I want to go somewhere** ich muß mal wohin *od.* verschwinden *(ugs.)*; **cc) go astray, go into action, go blackberrying, go to the country,** *etc. see the noun, adverb, etc. See also* **going; gone. 2.** *v. t., forms as* **1: a)** *(Cards)* spielen; **b)** *(sl.)* **go it** es toll treiben; *(work hard)* rangehen; **he has been going it a bit too hard** er hat es etwas zu weit getrieben; **go it!** los!; weiter!; **100 m.p.h.? That's really going it!** 160 km/h? Das ist wirklich ein tolles Tempo; *see also* **alone 1. 3.** *n., pl.* **goes** [gəʊz] *(coll.)* **a)** *(attempt, try)* Versuch, *der;* *(chance)* Gelegenheit, *die;* **have a go** es versuchen *od.* probieren; **have a go at doing sth.** versuchen, etw. zu tun; **have a go at sth.** sich an etw. *(Dat.)* versuchen; **someone has had a go at this lock** jmd. hat sich an dem Schloß zu schaffen gemacht; **he's had several goes at the driving test** er hat schon mehrere Anläufe genommen, den Führerschein zu bekommen; **have a good go with the vacuum cleaner** gründlich saugen; **let me have/can I have a go?** laß mich [auch ein]mal/kann ich [auch ein]mal? *(ugs.)*; **it's my go** ich bin an der Reihe *od.* dran; **I've had my go already** ich hab[e] schon *(ugs.)*; ich war schon dran *(ugs.)*; **it's your turn to have a go** du bist jetzt dran *(ugs.)*; **now 'you have a go** jetzt mach du mal; **you missed one go** du hast einmal ausgesetzt; du bist einmal übersprungen worden; **in two/three goes** bei zwei/drei Versuchen; **at one go** auf einmal; **at the first go** auf Anhieb; **give sth. a go** etw. mal versuchen *(ugs.)*; **b) have a go at sb.** *(scold)* sich *(Dat.)* jmdn. vornehmen *od.* vorknöpfen *(ugs.)*; *(attack)* über jmdn. herfallen; **have a go at a policeman** sich mit einem Polizisten anlegen *(ugs.)*; **c)** *(period of activity)* **in one go** auf einmal; **he downed his beer in one go** er trank sein Bier in einem Zug aus; **the dentist said he'd fill the teeth in two goes** der Zahnarzt meinte, daß er die Füllungen in zwei Sitzungen machen würde; **d)** *(energy)* Schwung, *der;* **be full of go** voller Schwung *od.* Elan sein; **have plenty of** *or* **a lot of go** einen enormen Schwung *od.* Elan haben; **e)** *(vigorous activity)* **it's all go** es ist alles eine einzige Hetzerei *(ugs.)*; **it's all go at work** es ist ganz schön was los bei der Arbeit; wir müssen ganz schön ran bei der Arbeit; **be on the go** auf Trab sein *(ugs.)*; **keep sb. on the go** jmdn. auf Trab halten *(ugs.)*; **have two jobs** *etc.* **on the go** zwei Jobs *usw.* gleichzeitig haben; **f)** *(success)* Erfolg, *der;* **make a go of sth.** *(turn sth. into a success)* mit etw. Erfolg haben; eine Sache zum Erfolg führen; *(not let sth. be a failure)* das Beste aus etw. machen; **it's no go** da ist nichts zu machen; **it's a go** *(dated coll.)* [es ist] abgemacht; *see also* **no-go; g) be all the go** der letzte Schrei sein *(ugs.)*; groß in Mode sein; **h) that was a near go** das war knapp; das wäre beinahe schiefgegangen; **i)** *(dated coll.: incident)* Geschichte, *die;* **a rum go** eine komische Geschichte. **4.** *adj. (coll.)* **all systems go** alles in Ordnung; alles klar

go about 1. ['--'-] *v. i.* **a)** *(move from place to place)* herumgehen; *(by vehicle)* herumfahren; **go about in groups** in Gruppen herumziehen; **go about in leather gear/dressed like a tramp** in Lederkleidung/wie ein Landstreicher herumlaufen; **go about doing sth.** *(be in the habit of)* etw. immer tun; **b)** *(circulate)* ‹*Gerücht, Geschichte, Grippe*:› umgehen; **c)** *(Naut.)* wenden. **2.** ['---] *v. t.* **a)** *(set about)* erledigen ‹*Arbeit*›; angehen ‹*Problem*›; **how does one go about it?** wie geht man da vor?; wie stellt man das am besten an?; **go about it [in] the right way** es richtig angehen; **go about it tactfully** *etc.* taktvoll *usw.* vorgehen; **b)** *(busy oneself with)* nachgehen (+ *Dat.*) ‹*Arbeit usw.*›

'go after *v. t. (hunt)* jagen; zu stellen versuchen; *(fig.)* anstreben; sich bemühen um ‹*Job*›; **decide what you want and go after it** werd dir darüber klar, was du willst, und dann versuche, es auch zu bekommen

'go against *v. t.* zuwiderhandeln (+ *Dat.*); handeln gegen ‹*Prinzip, Gesetz*›; **go against sb.** sich jmdm. in den Weg stellen *od.* widersetzen; *see also* [1]**go 1r, s**

go a'head *v. i.* **a)** *(in advance)* vorausgehen (of *Dat.*); *(Sport)* an die Spitze gehen; die Führung übernehmen; **the runner went ahead of the others** der Läufer zog an den anderen vorbei; **You go ahead. I'll meet you there** Geh mal schon vor. Wir treffen uns dann dort; **b)** *(proceed)* weitermachen; *(make progress)* ⟨*Arbeit:*⟩ fortschreiten, vorangehen; **go ahead with a plan** einen Plan durchführen; **go ahead and do it** es einfach machen; **go ahead!** nur zu!; **May I explain it to you? – OK. Go ahead** Darf ich es Ihnen erklären? – Ja, schießen Sie nur los *(ugs.)*. *See also* **go-ahead**

go a'long 1. *v. i.* dahingehen/-fahren; *(attend)* hingehen. **2.** *v. t.* entlanggehen/-fahren

go a'long with *v. t.* **a) go along with sth.** *(share sb.'s opinion)* einer Sache *(Dat.)* zustimmen; *(agree to)* sich einer Sache *(Dat.)* anschließen; **b) go along with you!** *(coll.)* ach, geh *od.* komm *(ugs.)*; ach, erzähl mir doch nichts! *(ugs.)*

go a'round *see* **go about 1 a, b; go round**

'go at *v. t.* **go at sb.** *(attack)* über jmdn. herfallen; auf jmdn. losgehen; **go at sth./it** *(work at)* sich hinter etw. *(Akk.)* klemmen/sich dahinterklemmen *(ugs.)*; sich an etw. *(Akk.)* machen/sich dranmachen

go a'way *v. i.* weggehen; *(on holiday or business)* wegfahren; verreisen; **what did the bride wear to go away in?** was trug die Braut, als sie auf Hochzeitsreise ging?; **the problem won't go away** das Problem kann man nicht einfach ignorieren; *see also* **[1]go 1 i; going-away**

go 'back *v. i.* **a)** *(return)* zurückgehen/-fahren; *(restart)* ⟨*Schule, Fabrik:*⟩ wieder anfangen; *(fig.)* zurückgehen; **I wouldn't want to go back to that place** dorthin wollte ich auf keinen Fall wieder zurück; **go back to a subject** auf ein Thema zurückkommen; **go back to the beginning** noch mal von vorne anfangen; **there'll be/there's no going back** da gibt es kein Zurück mehr; **b)** *(be returned)* zurückgegeben werden; ⟨*Waren:*⟩ zurückgehen (**to** an + *Akk.*); **c)** *(be put back)* ⟨*Uhren:*⟩ zurückgestellt werden

go 'back on *v. t.* nicht [ein]halten ⟨*Versprechen, Wort*⟩

go before 1. [--'-] *v. i.* *(live before)* früher leben; *(happen before)* vorher *od.* früher geschehen. **2.** ['---] *v. t.* **a)** *(live before)* **go before sb.** vor jmds. Zeit *(Dat.)* leben; **b)** *(appear before)* **go before sth./sb.** ⟨*Person:*⟩ vor etw./jmdm. erscheinen; ⟨*Sache:*⟩ vor etw./jmdn. kommen

'go by *v. t.* **go by sth.** sich nach etw. richten; *(adhere to)* sich an etw. *(Akk.)* halten; **if the report is anything to go by** wenn man nach dem Bericht gehen kann; **go by appearances** nach dem Äußeren gehen *od.* urteilen; *see also* **[1]go 1 b, m; go-by**

go 'down *v. i.* **a)** hinuntergehen/-fahren; ⟨*Taucher:*⟩ [hinunter]tauchen; *(set)* ⟨*Sonne:*⟩ untergehen; *(sink)* ⟨*Schiff:*⟩ sinken, untergehen; *(drown)* ⟨*Person:*⟩ untergehen, ertrinken; *(fall to ground)* ⟨*Flugzeug usw.:*⟩ abstürzen; **go down to the bottom of the garden/to the doctor/to the beach** zum hinteren Ende des Gartens gehen/zum Arzt gehen/an den Strand gehen; **b)** *(be digested)* verdaut werden; *(be swallowed)* hinuntergeschluckt werden; **go down the wrong way** in die falsche Kehle geraten; **sugar helps the medicine go down** mit Zucker kriegt man die Arznei besser hinunter *(ugs.)*; **c)** *(become less)* sinken; ⟨*Umsatz, Schwellung:*⟩ zurückgehen; ⟨*Vorräte usw.:*⟩ abnehmen; ⟨*Währung:*⟩ fallen; *(become lower)* fallen; *(subside)* ⟨*Wind usw.:*⟩ nachlassen; **go down in sb.'s estimation/in the world** in jmds. Achtung *(Dat.)* sinken/sich verschlechtern; **d) go down well/all right** *etc.* **[with sb.]** [mit jmdm.] gut *usw.* klarkommen *(ugs.)*; ⟨*Film, Schauspieler, Vorschlag:*⟩ [bei jmdm.] gut *usw.* ankommen *(ugs.)*; **that didn't go down [at all] well with his wife** das hat ihm seine Frau nicht abgenommen; **e)** *(be defeated)* unterliegen; **go down to sb.** gegen jmdn. verlieren; **f)** *(be recorded in writing)* niedergeschrieben werden; schriftlich vermerkt werden; **g)** *(Bridge)* den Kontrakt nicht erfüllen; *(Cards)* [seine Karten] aufdecken; **h)** *(Brit. Univ.)* abgehen; *(at end of term)* in die Semesterferien gehen; **i)** ⟨*Maschine, Computer usw.:*⟩ ausfallen

go 'down with *v. t.* bekommen ⟨*Krankheit*⟩; *see also* **go down d**

'go for *v. t.* **a)** *(go to fetch)* **go for sb./sth.** jmdn./etw. holen; **b)** *(apply to)* **go for sb./sth.** für jmdn./etw. gelten; **that goes for me too** das gilt auch für mich; ich auch; **what goes for me goes for you too** was für mich gilt, gilt auch für dich; **c)** *(attack)* **go for sb. [with a knife** *etc.***]** [mit einem Messer *usw.*] auf jmdn. losgehen; **d)** *(pass for)* **go for sth.** als etw. durchgehen; **e)** *(like)* **go for sb./sth.** jmdn./etw. gut finden; **I could ~ for 'him** der könnte mir gefallen; **f)** *(count for)* **go for nothing/little** nichts/wenig gelten *od.* zählen; **g)** *(aim at)* es abgesehen haben auf (+ *Akk.*). *See also* **[1]go 1 o, r**

go 'forth *see* **forth c**

go 'forward *v. i.* weitergehen/-fahren; *(fig.)* voranschreiten; ⟨*Uhren:*⟩ vorgestellt werden

go 'forward with *v. t.* weiter durchführen; weiter verfolgen ⟨*Plan usw.*⟩

go 'in *v. i.* **a)** *(go indoors)* hineingehen; reingehen *(ugs.)*; **b)** *(be covered by cloud)* verschwinden; weggehen *(ugs.)*; **c)** *(be learnt)* [in den Kopf] reingehen *(ugs.)*; **it just won't go in** es will einfach nicht in den Kopf; **d)** *(Cricket)* zum Schlagen drankommen; **e) go in and win!** Bangemachen gilt nicht! *(fam.)*; nur Mut! *See also* **[1]go 1 b, v**

go 'in for *v. t.* **go in for sth.** *(choose as career)* etw. [er]lernen wollen; *(enter)* an etw. *(Dat.)* teilnehmen; *(indulge in, like)* für etw. zu haben sein; *(have as one's hobby, pastime, etc.)* sich auf etw. *(Akk.)* verlegen; **so you'd like to go in for teaching** du willst also Lehrer/Lehrerin werden; **I don't really go in for jogging** ich habe nicht viel übrig fürs Joggen; **go in for wearing loud colours** gern knallige Farben tragen

'go into *v. t.* **a)** *(join)* eintreten in (+ *Akk.*) ⟨*Streitkräfte, Orden, Geschäft usw.*⟩; gehen in (+ *Akk.*) ⟨*Industrie, Politik*⟩; gehen zu ⟨*Film, Fernsehen*⟩; beitreten (+ *Dat.*) ⟨*Bündnis*⟩; **go into law/the church** Jurist/Geistlicher werden; **go into nursing** Krankenschwester/-pfleger werden; **go into publishing** ins Verlagswesen gehen; **go into general practice** *(Med.)* sich als allgemeiner Mediziner niederlassen; **b)** *(go and live in)* gehen in (+ *Akk.*) ⟨*Krankenhaus, Heim usw.*⟩; ziehen in (+ *Akk.*) ⟨*Wohnung, Heim*⟩; **go into digs/lodgings** sich *(Dat.)* eine Bude *(ugs.)*/ein Zimmer nehmen; **c)** *(consider)* eingehen auf *(Akk.)*; *(investigate, examine)* sich befassen mit; *(explain)* darlegen; **d)** *(crash into)* [hinein]fahren in (+ *Akk.*); fahren gegen ⟨*Baum usw.*⟩; **e)** *(pass into specified state)* verfallen in (+ *Akk.*); **go into hysterics/a fit** hysterisch werden/einen Anfall bekommen; **go [off] into laughter** *etc.* in Lachen *usw.* ausbrechen; **the book is going into paperback/its fifth edition** das Buch erscheint als Paperback/in der fünften Auflage; **f)** *([begin to] wear)* tragen. *See also* **[1]go 1 b, v**

go 'in with *v. t.* **go in with sb.** [mit jmdm.] mitmachen

go off 1. [-'-] *v. i.* **a)** *(Theatre)* abgehen; **b) go off with sb./sth.** sich mit jmdm./etw. auf- und davonmachen *(ugs.)*; **his wife has gone off with the milkman** seine Frau ist mit dem Milchmann durchgebrannt *(ugs.)*; **c)** ⟨*Alarm, Schußwaffe, Klingel:*⟩ losgehen; ⟨*Wecker:*⟩ klingeln; ⟨*Bombe:*⟩ hochgehen; **d)** *(turn bad)* schlecht werden; *(turn sour)* sauer werden; *(fig.)* sich verschlechtern; **e)** ⟨*Licht, Gas, Wasser:*⟩ ausfallen; **f) go off [to sleep]** einschlafen; **g)** *(be sent)* abgehen (**to** an + *Akk.*); **h) go off well** *etc.* gut *usw.* verlaufen. *See also* **[1]go 1 b. 2.** ['--, -'-] *v. t.* **a)** *(begin to dislike)* **go off sth.** von etw. abkommen; **go off sb.** jmdn. nicht mehr mögen; **go off beer/the cinema** sich *(Dat.)* nichts mehr aus Bier/Kino machen; **b) go off the gold standard** vom Goldstandard abgehen; **c) go off into** *see* **go into f**

go on 1. [-'-] *v. i.* **a)** weitergehen/-fahren; *(by vehicle)* die Reise/Fahrt *usw.* fortsetzen; *(go ahead)* vorausgehen; *(drive ahead)* vorausfahren; **b)** *(continue)* weitergehen; ⟨*Kämpfe:*⟩ anhalten; ⟨*Verhandlungen, Arbeiten:*⟩ [an]dauern; *(continue to act)* weitermachen; *(continue to live)* weiterleben; **I can't go on** ich kann nicht mehr; ich weiß nicht mehr weiter; **go on for weeks** *etc.* Wochen *usw.* dauern; **this has been going on for months** das geht schon seit Monaten so; **the case went on for years** der Prozeß hat sich jahrelang hingezogen; **go on to say** *etc.* fortfahren und sagen *usw.*; **'moreover', he went on, ...:** „außerdem", fuhr er fort, ...; **go on and on** dauern und dauern; kein Ende nehmen wollen; sich endlos hinziehen; **go on [and on]** *(coll.)* *(chatter)* reden und reden; **she does go on so** sie redet unaufhörlich; **go on about sb./sth.** stundenlang von jmdm./etw. erzählen; *(complain)* sich ständig über jmdn./etw. beklagen; **go on at sb.** *(coll.)* auf jmdm. herumhacken *(ugs.)*; **c)** *(elapse)* ⟨*Zeit:*⟩ vergehen; **as time/the years went on** im Laufe der Zeit/Jahre; **d)** *(happen)* passieren; vor sich gehen; **there's more going on in the big cities** in den großen Städten ist mehr los; **the things that go on there** die Dinge, die da vor sich gehen; **what's going on?, what goes on?** was geht vor?; was ist los?; **e) be going on [for] ...** *(be nearly)* fast ... sein; **he is going on [for] ninety** er geht auf die Neunzig zu; **he is seven going on [for] eight** er ist fast acht; **it is going on [for] ten o'clock** es geht auf 10 Uhr zu; **f)** *(behave)* sich benehmen; sich aufführen; **g)** ⟨*Kleidung:*⟩ passen; **my dress wouldn't go on** ich kriegte mein Kleid nicht an *(ugs.)*; ich kam nicht in mein Kleid rein *(ugs.)*; **this hat won't go on** diesen Hut kriege ich nicht auf *(ugs.)*; **h)** *(Theatre)* auftreten; *(Cricket)* mit dem Werfen beginnen; **i)** *see* **go forward; j)** *(be lit)* ⟨*Licht:*⟩ angehen; *(be supplied)* ⟨*Strom, Wasser:*⟩ kommen; **go on again** ⟨*Strom, Gas, Wasser:*⟩ wiederkommen; **k) go on!** *(proceed)* los, mach schon! *(ugs.)*; *(resume)* fahren Sie fort!; *(coll.: stop talking nonsense)* ach, geh *od.* komm *(ugs.)*; ach, erzähl mir doch nichts! *(ugs.)*; *see also* **goings-on. 2.** ['--] *v. t.* **a)** *(ride on)* fahren mit; **go on the roundabout/swings/Big Dipper** Karussell/Schiffschaukel/Achterbahn fahren; **b)** *(continue)* **go on working/talking** *etc.* weiterarbeiten/weiterreden *usw.*; **go on trying** es weiter[hin] versuchen; **c)** *(coll.: be guided by)* sich stützen auf (+ *Akk.*); **there's little evidence to go on** es gibt wenig Beweismaterial, auf das man sich stützen kann; **d)** *(begin to receive)* bekommen, erhalten ⟨*Arbeitslosengeld, Sozialfürsorge*⟩; *see also* **dole 1; e)** *see* **go on to b; f)** *(start to take)* nehmen ⟨*Medikament, Drogen*⟩; **go on a diet** eine Abmagerungs- *od.* Schlankheitskur machen; **g)** *(coll.: like)* *see* **much 2.** *See also* **[1]go 1 l; stage 1 b**

go 'on for *see* **go on 1 e**

go 'on to *v. t.* **a)** *(proceed to)* übergehen zu; **he went on to become ...:** er wurde schließlich ...; **b)** *(change working arrangements to)* übergehen zu ⟨*Kurzarbeit, Überstunden*⟩

go 'on with *v. t.* **a) go on with sth.** mit

etw. weitermachen; **something/enough to go on with** *or* **be going on with** etwas/genug für den Anfang *od.* fürs erste; **here's something to be going on with** hiermit kann man schon [ein]mal anfangen; **here's £10 to be going on with** hier sind erst [ein]mal 10 Pfund [für den Anfang] *(ugs.)*; **here's a cup of tea to be going on with** hier hast du erst einmal eine Tasse Tee; **b)** *see* **go along with b**

go 'out *v. i.* **a)** *(from home)* ausgehen; **go out to work/go out charring/for a meal** arbeiten/putzen/essen gehen; **go out and about** unterwegs sein; auf den Beinen sein; **out you go!** hinaus *od. (ugs.)* raus mit dir!; **go out with sb.** *(regularly)* mit jmdm. gehen *(ugs.)*; **b) go out [on strike]** in den Ausstand treten; **c)** *(be extinguished)* ‹*Feuer, Licht, Zigarre usw.*:› ausgehen; **go out like a light** *(fig. coll.: fall asleep)* sofort weg sein *(ugs.) od.* einschlafen; **d)** *(ebb)* ‹*Ebbe, Wasser*:› ablaufen, zurückgehen; **the tide has gone out** es ist Ebbe; **e)** *(Polit.)* [aus der Regierung] ausscheiden; ‹*Regierung*:› abgelöst werden; **f)** *(be issued)* verteilt werden; *(Radio, Telev.: be transmitted)* übertragen werden; ausgestrahlt werden; **g)** *(euphem.: die)* [hinüber]gehen *(verhüll.)*; **he went out peacefully in his sleep** er ist sanft entschlafen *(geh.)*; **h)** *(end)* ‹*Monat, Jahr*:› zu Ende gehen; **i)** *(of fashion)* unmodern werden; ‹*Brauch*:› aussterben; **j)** *(Sport: be defeated)* unterliegen (**to** *Dat.*). *See also* **¹go 1 b; business b; walk 3 a**

go 'out to *v. t.* ‹*Sympathie*:› sein mit; **my heart/sympathy goes out to them** ich fühle mit ihnen mit. *See also* **go out j**

go over 1. ['--] *v. i.* **a) he went over to the fireplace/man in the corner** er ging zum Kamin/zu dem Mann in der Ecke hinüber; **we're going over to our friends** wir fahren zu unseren Freunden; **I'm just going over to the shop** ich gehe kurz ins Geschäft hinüber; **b)** *(be received)* ‹*Rede, Ankündigung, Plan*:› ankommen (**with** bei); **c)** *(Radio, Telev.)* **go over to sb./sth./Belfast** zu jmdm./in etw. *(Akk.)*/nach Belfast umschalten. *See also* **¹go 1 b. 2.** ['---] *v. t.* **a)** *(re-examine, think over, rehearse)* durchgehen; **go over sth./the facts in one's head** *or* **mind** etw. im Geiste durchgehen/die Fakten überdenken; **b)** *(clean)* saubermachen; *(inspect and repair)* durchsehen ‹*Maschine, Auto usw.*›; **go over the house with the Hoover/duster** durchsaugen/mit dem Staubtuch durchs Haus gehen; **c)** *(survey)* begutachten; sich *(Dat.)* ansehen; **d) go over sth. with a pen** etw. mit dem Stift nachziehen. *See also* **going-over**

go 'over to *v. t.* **a)** hinübergehen zu; übertreten zu ‹*Glauben, Partei*›; überwechseln zu ‹*Revolutionären*›; ‹*Verräter*:› überlaufen zu ‹*Feind*›; überlaufen in (+ *Akk.*) ‹*Lager des Feindes*›; **b)** *(change to)* übergehen zu. *See also* **¹go 1 b**

go round 1. [-'-] *v. i.* **a)** *(call)* **go round and** *or* **to see sb.** jmdn. besuchen; bei jmdm. vorbeigehen *(ugs.)*; **go round to sb.'s house** *(call at)* jmdn. aufsuchen; **b)** *(look round)* sich umschauen; **c)** *(suffice)* reichen; langen *(ugs.)*; **enough coffee to go round** genug Kaffee für alle; **d)** *(spin)* sich drehen; **my head is going round** mir dreht sich alles; **e)** *(circulate)* **the word went round that ...**: es ging die Parole um, daß ...; **f)** *(Golf)* **go round in 70** eine 70er Runde spielen. **2.** ['--] *v. t.* **a)** *(inspect)* besichtigen; **b)** *(encompass)* ‹*Gürtel*:› herumreichen um ‹*Taille*›; **the trousers won't go round my waist** die Hose paßt mir nicht in der Taille *od.* um die Taille herum; **c) have enough food to go round [so many people]** [für so viele Leute] genügend zu essen haben

go through 1. [-'-] *v. i.* ‹*Ernennung, Gesetzesvorlage*:› durchkommen; ‹*Geschäft*:› [erfolgreich] abgeschlossen werden; ‹*Antrag, Bewerbung*:› durchgehen; **go through to the final** in die Endrunde kommen; **as soon as his divorce has gone through** sobald seine Scheidung durch ist. **2.** ['--] *v. t.* **a)** *(execute, undergo)* erledigen ‹*Formalität, Anforderung*›; abwickeln ‹*Geschäft*›; absolvieren ‹*Kurs, Lehre*›; durchziehen *(ugs.)* ‹*Programm*›; **go through a marriage ceremony/divorce proceedings** sich trauen lassen/die Scheidung durchmachen; **b)** *(rehearse)* durchgehen; **c)** *(examine)* durchsehen ‹*Post, Unterlagen*›; *(search)* durchsuchen ‹*Taschen*›; **d)** *(endure)* durchmachen ‹*schwere Zeiten*›; durchstehen ‹*Belastung*›; *(suffer)* erleiden ‹*Schmerzen*›; **e)** *(use up)* verbrauchen; durchbringen ‹*Erbschaft*›; aufbrauchen ‹*Vorräte*›; **f)** *(be published in)* erleben ‹*Auflagen*›. *See also* **¹go 1 v**

go 'through with *v. t.* zu Ende führen; ausführen ‹*Hinrichtung*›; **she realized that she would have to go through with it** sie sah ein, daß sie jetzt nicht mehr zurückkonnte; **she told him that she couldn't go through with the wedding** sie sagte ihm, daß aus der Hochzeit nichts würde

go to'gether *v. i.* **a)** *(coincide)* zusammengehen; **b)** *(match)* zusammenpassen; **c)** *(date regularly)* miteinander gehen *(ugs.)*

go 'under *v. i.* *(sink below surface)* untergehen; *(fig.: fail)* ‹*Geschäftsmann*:› scheitern; ‹*Unternehmen*:› eingehen; **~ under to sth.** einer Sache *(Dat.)* zum Opfer fallen

go 'up *v. i.* **a)** hinaufgehen/-fahren; ‹*Ballon*:› aufsteigen; ‹*Flugzeug, Flieger*› fliegen; *(Theatre)* ‹*Vorhang*:› aufgehen, hochgehen; ‹*Lichter*:› angehen; **b)** *(increase)* ‹*Bevölkerung, Zahl*:› wachsen; ‹*Preis, Wert, Zahl, Niveau*:› steigen; **everything is going up these days** heutzutage wird alles teurer; **c)** *(be constructed)* ‹*Gebäude, Barrikade*:› errichtet werden; **d)** *(be destroyed)* in die Luft fliegen *(ugs.)*; hochgehen *(ugs.)*; *see also* **flame 1 a; smoke 1 a; e)** *(Brit. Univ.)* sein Studium aufnehmen; **go up to Oxford** sein Studium in Oxford aufnehmen; *(at beginning of term)* nach den Semesterferien nach Oxford zurückkehren; **f) go up to sb.** *(approach for talk)* auf jmdn. zugehen; **g) go up in the world** [gesellschaftlich] aufsteigen

'go with *v. t.* **a)** *(be concomitant with)* einhergehen mit; **b)** *(be included with)* gehören zu; **c)** *(date regularly)* gehen mit *(ugs.)*. *See also* **¹go 1 a, w**

go without 1. ['---] *v. t.* verzichten auf (+ *Akk.*); **have to go without sth.** ohne etw. auskommen müssen. **2.** [--'-] *v. i.* *(receive nothing)* **if you won't eat that dinner, you'll have to go without** wenn du das Essen nicht ißt, mußt du eben ohne auskommen

²go *n. (game)* Go, *das*

goad [gəʊd] **1.** *v. t.* **a) ~ sb. into sth./doing sth.** jmdn. zu etw. anstacheln/dazu anstacheln, etw. zu tun; **~ sb. into a fury** jmdn. in Wut bringen; **b)** antreiben ‹*Vieh usw.*›. **2.** *n.* Stachelstock, *der; (fig.)* Stachel, *der; (stimulus)* Ansporn, *der*

~ 'on *v. t.* **~ sb. on** jmdn. anstiften

'go-ahead 1. *adj. (enterprising)* unternehmungslustig; *(progressive)* fortschrittlich; **~ spirit** Unternehmungsgeist, *der.* **2.** *n.* grünes Licht *(fig.)*; **give sb./sth. the ~**: jmdm./einer Sache grünes Licht geben

goal [gəʊl] *n.* **a)** *(aim)* Ziel, *das;* **what do you have as your ~?** welches Ziel hast du dir gesetzt?; **attain** *or* **reach** *or* **accomplish one's ~**: sein Ziel erreichen; **b)** *(Assoc. Footb., Hockey)* Tor, *das; (Rugby)* Mal, *das;* **keep ~**: das Tor hüten; **[play] in ~**: im Tor [stehen]; **score/kick a ~**: einen Treffer erzielen; **win by two ~s to one** zwei zu eins gewinnen; **c)** *(of race)* Ziellinie, *die;* Ziel, *das*

goal: ~ area *n.* Torraum, *der;* **~ average** *n.* **on ~ average** nach Toren; **~ difference** *n.* Tordifferenz, *die*

goalie ['gəʊlɪ] *n. (coll.)* Tormann, *der;* Schlußmann, *der (ugs.)*

goal: ~keeper *n.* Torwart, *der;* **~-'kick** *n.* *(Assoc. Footb.)* Abstoß, *der; (Rugby)* Tritt nach dem Mal

goalless ['gəʊllɪs] *adj.* torlos; **end in a ~ draw** torlos [unentschieden] enden

goal: ~-line *n. (Assoc. Footb., Hockey)* Torlinie, *die; (Rugby)* Mallinie, *die;* **~-minder** *n. (Amer.)* Torwart, *der;* **~-mouth** *n.* Raum unmittelbar vor dem Tor; **~-post** *n.* Torpfosten, *der;* **move the ~-posts** *(fig. coll.)* sich nicht an die vereinbarten Bedingungen halten; **~-tender** *n. (Amer.)* Torwart, *der*

go-as-you-'please *adj.* ungezwungen

goat [gəʊt] *n.* **a)** Ziege, *die;* **act** *or* **play the [giddy] ~**: den Clown spielen; herumalbern; **get sb.'s ~** *(sl.)* jmdn. aufregen *(ugs.)*; **b)** *(Astrol.)* **the G~** der Steinbock; *see also* **archer b; c)** *(coll.: fool)* Idiot, *der (ugs. abwertend);* Esel, *der (ugs.)*; **d)** *(coll.: licentious man)* **old ~**: alter [geiler] Bock *(salopp)*; **e)** *(Amer.: scapegoat)* Sündenbock, *der (ugs.)*

goatee [gəʊ'ti:] *n.* **~ [beard]** Kinnbart, *der;* Spitzbart, *der*

'goatherd *n.* Ziegenhirt[e], *der*

goatish ['gəʊtɪʃ] *adj. (fig.)* geil

goat: ~skin *n.* Ziegenleder, *das; (bottle)* Ziegenlederflasche, *die;* **~'s milk** *n.* Ziegenmilch, *die;* **~sucker** *see* **nightjar**

¹gob [gɒb] *n. (sl.)* Gosche, *die (landsch. derb);* Schnauze, *die (derb abwertend);* Maul, *das (derb abwertend);* **shut your ~!** halt's Maul! *(derb);* halt die Schnauze! *(derb)*

²gob *v. i. (coarse: spit)* rotzen *(derb)*

¹gobble ['gɒbl] **1.** *v. t.* **~ [down** *or* **up]** hinunterschlingen. **2.** *v. i.* schlingen

~ up *v. t. (fig. coll.)* verschlingen; ‹*Land, Imperium*:› sich *(Dat.)* einverleiben ‹*kleineres Land usw.*›

²gobble *v. i. (make sound)* kollern

gobbledegook, gobbledygook ['gɒbldɪgʊk, 'gɒbldɪgu:k] *n.* Kauderwelsch, *das*

'go-between *n.* Vermittler, *der*/Vermittlerin, *die; (in love affair)* Postillon d'amour, *der*

Gobi ['gəʊbɪ] *pr. n.* **the ~ [Desert]** die [Wüste] Gobi

goblet ['gɒblɪt] *n.* Kelchglas, *das*

goblin ['gɒblɪn] *n.* Kobold, *der*

'gob-stopper *n. (Brit.)* Riesenlutscher, *der;* Maulstopfer, *der (ugs.)*

goby ['gəʊbɪ] *n. (Zool.)* Grundel, *die*

'go-by *n.* **give the ~ to sb., give sb. the ~**: jmdn. schneiden

'go-cart *n.* **a)** *(handcart)* Handwagen, *der;* **b)** *(for child)* Sport[kinder]wagen, *der*

god [gɒd] *n.* **a)** Gott, *der;* **the drink of the ~s** der Göttertrank; **be** *or* **lie in the lap** *or* **on the knees of the ~s** im Schoß der Götter liegen; **a feast [fit] for the ~s** ein göttliches Mahl; **a gift from the ~s** ein Geschenk des Himmels; **a sight [fit] for the ~s** eine Augenweide; *(with grandeur)* ein majestätischer Anblick; *(iron.)* ein Bild für die Götter *(ugs. scherzh.)*; **ye ~s [and little fishes]!** mein Gott!; **b) God** *no pl. (Theol.)* Gott; **Almighty God** der allmächtige Gott; **God the Father, Son, and Holy Ghost** Gott Vater, Sohn und Heiliger Geist; **God moves in a mysterious way** *(prov.)* die Wege des Herrn sind unerforschlich; **God helps those who help themselves** *(prov.)* hilf dir selbst, so hilft dir Gott *(Spr.)*; **God knows** *(as God is witness)* weiß Gott *(ugs.)*; **God knows, I tried** ich habe es, weiß Gott, versucht; **God [only] knows** *(nobody knows)* weiß der Himmel *(ugs.)*; **God willing, if it is God's will** so Gott will; **an act of God** höhere Gewalt; **before God** bei Gott; **play God** sich zum Gott aufwerfen; **under God** auf Erden *(geh.)*; **God's gift** ein Geschenk Gottes; ein Gottesgeschenk; **she thinks she's God's gift to men** sie denkt, sie ist der Traum aller Männer; **God's truth** [nichts als] die reine Wahrheit *(geh.)*; **be with God** bei Gott sein *(bibl.)*; **God's [own]**

country Paradies auf Erden; **God's earth** Gottes [weite] Erde; **God!/good God!/my God!/oh God!/God in Heaven!** [ach] Gott!/großer *od.* allmächtiger *od.* guter Gott!/mein Gott!/o Gott!/[guter] Gott im Himmel!; **dear God!** lieber Gott!; **for God's sake!** um Himmels *od.* Gottes willen!; **I hope to God that ...:** ich hoffe bei Gott, daß ...; **God be with you** Gott mit euch; **God, he's so stupid!** [mein] Gott, ist er dumm!; **by God** bei Gott; **thank God!** Gott sei Dank!; **God damn it!** zum Teufel noch mal! *(ugs.)*; **God damn you/him** *etc.* Gott verfluche dich/ihn *usw.*; **God help you/him** *etc.* möge Gott dir/ihm *usw.* helfen; Gott steh dir/ihm *usw.* bei; **God grant ...:** Gott gebe ...; **please God!** so es Gott gefällt; **as God is my witness/judge** Gott ist mein Zeuge; *see also* **bless a; forbid b; help 1 e; man 1 a, b; name 1 d; c)** *(fig.)* Gott, *der;* Götze, *der (geh., abwertend); see also* **tin god; d)** *(Theatre)* **the ~s** der Olymp *(ugs. scherzh.)*

'God-awful *adj. (sl.)* fürchterlich

god: ~child *n.* Patenkind, *das;* **~-dam, ~-damn, ~-damned 1.** *adj.* gottverdammt *(derb);* **[it is] none of your ~-dam business** das geht dich einen Dreck an *(salopp);* **2.** *adv.* gottverdammt *(derb);* **you're ~-dam right!** du hast, verdammt noch mal, recht! *(derb);* **~-daughter** *n.* Patentochter, *die*

goddess ['gɒdɪs] *n.* Göttin, *die*

'godfather *n.* **a)** Pate, *der;* Patenonkel, *der;* **my ~s!** [ach] du meine *od.* liebe Güte!; **b)** *(fig.)* Boß, *der (ugs.); (of Mafia etc.)* Pate, *der*

'God-fearing *adj.* gottesfürchtig

'God-forsaken *adj.* gottverlassen

'God-given *adj.* gottgegeben

godhead ['gɒdhed] *n.* Göttlichkeit, *die;* **the G~:** die Gottheit; Gott, *der*

godless ['gɒdlɪs] *adj.* gottlos

godlike ['gɒdlaɪk] *adj.* göttlich; göttergleich *(geh.)*

godliness ['gɒdlɪnɪs] *n., no pl.* Gottgefälligkeit, *die*

godly ['gɒdlɪ] *adj.* gottgefällig; gottergeben

god: ~mother *n.* Patin, *die;* Patentante, *die;* **~parent** *n. (male)* Pate, *der; (female)* Patin, *die;* **~send** *n.* Gottesgabe, *die;* **be a ~send to sb.** für jmdn. ein Geschenk des Himmels sein; **~son** *n.* Patensohn, *der*

God'speed *n. (dated)* **wish** *or* **bid sb. ~:** jmdm. eine glückliche Reise wünschen

godwit ['gɒdwɪt] *n. (Ornith.)* Pfuhlschnepfe, *die*

goer ['gəʊə(r)] *n.* **a)** *(horse)* Geher, *der;* **be a good ~:** gut gehen; **b)** *(active person)* Energiebündel, *das (ugs.);* **c)** *in comb.* -gänger, *der;* -besucher, *der; see also* **church-goer, film-goer,** *etc.*

goes *see* [1]**go 1, 2**

Goethian (Goethean) ['gɜːtɪən] *adj. (of Goethe)* Goethisch; Goethesch; *(having characteristics of Goethe)* goethisch; goethesch

'go-getter *n. (coll.)* Ellbogenmensch, *der (abwertend);* Draufgänger, *der*

'go-getting *adj.* draufgängerisch; Ellbogen gebrauchend

goggle ['gɒgl] **1.** *n. in pl.* **[a pair of] ~s** eine Schutzbrille. **2.** *adj.* **~ eyes** Glupschaugen *(nordd.);* Froschaugen *(ugs.).* **3.** *v. i.* glotzen *(ugs.);* **~ at sb./sth.** jmdn./etw. anglotzen *(ugs.)*

goggle: ~-box *n. (sl.)* Glotze, *die (salopp);* Glotzkiste, *die (salopp);* **~-eyed** *adj.* glotzäugig *(ugs.)*

'go-go *adj. (coll.)* Go-go-; **~ dancer** *or* **girl** Go-Go-Girl, *das*

going ['gəʊɪŋ] **1.** *n.* **a)** *vbl. n. of* [1]**go 1; b)** *(progress)* Vorankommen, *das; (Horse-racing, Hunting, etc.)* Geläuf, *das;* **150 miles in two hours, that is good ~:** 150 Meilen in zwei Stunden, das ist wirklich gut; **the ~ was slow/heavy** man kam nur langsam/schwer voran; **the journey was slow ~:** die Reise zog sich [in die Länge]; **interviewing her is heavy ~:** ein Gespräch mit ihr ist ganz schön mühsam *od.* ein schwieriges Geschäft; **this book is heavy ~:** dieses Buch liest sich schwer; **while the ~ is good** solange noch Zeit dazu ist *od.* es noch geht. **2.** *adj.* **a)** *pres. p. of* [1]**go 1, 2; b)** *(available)* erhältlich; **there is sth. ~:** es gibt etw.; **take any job ~:** jede Arbeit annehmen, die es nur gibt; **this cabbage was the best one ~:** das war der beste Kohl, den man bekommen konnte; **c) be ~ to do sth.** etw. tun [werden/wollen]; **he's ~ to be a ballet-dancer when he grows up** wenn er groß ist, wird er Ballettänzer; **I was ~ to say** ich wollte sagen; **I was not ~** *(did not intend)* **to do sth.** ich hatte nicht die Absicht, etw. zu tun; **it's ~ to snow** es wird schneien; **d)** *(current)* üblich; **the ~ rate of exchange** der augenblickliche Wechselkurs; **e) a ~ concern** eine gesunde Firma; **f) have a lot/nothing** *etc.* **~ for one** *(coll.)* viel/nichts *usw.* haben, was für einen spricht; **g) to be ~ on with** *see* **go on with; set/keep sth. ~, keep sb. ~** *see* [1]**go 1 f; get ~** *see* **get 1 o, 2 b; be ~ on fifteen** *etc. see* **go on 1 e; ~ strong** *see* **strong 2; ~ great guns** *see* **gun 1 a**

going: ~-a'way *attrib. adj.* ⟨Ausstattung, Kleid⟩ für die Hochzeitsreise; **~-over** *n.* **a)** *(coll.: overhaul) (of list etc.)* Durchsicht, *die; (of engine etc.)* Überholung, *die;* Überprüfung, *die;* **give sth. a [good etc.] ~-over** eine Sache [gründlich *usw.*] durchgehen *od.* durchsehen; **give the room a ~-over with the Hoover/duster** das Zimmer durchsaugen/im Zimmer Staub wischen; **b)** *(sl.: thrashing)* **give sb. a [good] ~-over** jmdn. [ordentlich] verprügeln *(ugs.);* **c)** *(Amer. coll.: scolding)* **give sb. a [good] ~-over** sich *(Dat.)* jmdn. [einmal ordentlich] vorknöpfen *(ugs.)*

goings-on [gəʊɪŋz'ɒn] *n. pl.* Ereignisse; Vorgänge; **there have been some strange ~:** seltsame Dinge sind da passiert; **be disgusted by sb.'s ~:** empört über jmds. Treiben *od.* Geschichten *(Akk.)* sein

goitre *(Brit.; Amer.:* **goiter)** ['gɔɪtə(r)] *n. (Med.)* Kropf, *der*

'go-kart *n.* Go-Kart, *der*

gold [gəʊld] **1.** *n.* **a)** *no pl., no indef. art.* Gold, *das;* **the price of ~:** der Goldpreis; **be worth one's weight in ~:** nicht mit Gold aufzuwiegen sein; **a heart of ~:** ein goldenes Herz; **she is pure ~:** sie ist Gold wert; **b)** *no pl., no indef. art. (wealth)* Geld, *das; (coins)* Goldmünzen *Pl.;* **a crock** *or* **pot of ~ at the end of the rainbow** ein Krug/Topf voll Gold am Ende des Regenbogens *(ein unerfüllbarer Wunsch);* **c)** *(colour)* Gold, *das;* **the ~ of her hair** ihr goldenes Haar; **d)** *(medal)* Gold, *das;* **win six Olympic ~s** sechsmal olympisches Gold gewinnen; **e)** *(Archery)* Gold, *das. See also* **glitter 1 a; good 1 f. 2.** *attrib. adj.* golden; Gold⟨münze, -stück, -kette, -krone *usw.*⟩

gold: ~ 'brick *n.* **a)** *(sl.: fraud)* Schwindel, *der;* **sell sb. a ~ brick** jmdn. übers Ohr hauen *(ugs.);* jmdm. etwas andrehen *(ugs.);* **b)** *(Amer. sl.: shirker)* Drückeberger, *der (ugs. abwertend);* **~-coloured** *adj.* goldfarben; **~crest** *n. (Ornith.)* Wintergoldhähnchen, *das;* **~-digger** *n.* Goldgräber, *der;* **she's a ~-digger** *(fig. sl.)* sie ist nur auf das Geld der Männer aus; **~ 'disc** *n.* Goldene Schallplatte; **~-dust** *n.* **a)** Goldstaub, *der;* **be like ~-dust** eine Rarität sein; **b)** *(Bot.)* Felsensteinkraut, *das*

golden ['gəʊldn] *adj.* **a)** golden; **~ brown/yellow** goldbraun/goldgelb; **b)** *(fig.)* golden; einmalig ⟨Gelegenheit⟩

golden: ~ 'age *n.* goldenes Zeitalter; **~ boy** *n.* Goldjunge, *der;* **~ 'calf** *n.* Goldenes Kalb; **~ 'disc** *see* **gold disc; ~ 'eagle** *n.* Steinadler, *der;* **G~ 'Fleece** *n. (Greek Mythol.)* Goldenes Vlies; **G~ 'Gate** *pr. n. (Geog.)* Goldenes Tor; **the ~ Gate Bridge** die Golden-Gate-Brücke; **~ girl** *n.* Goldmädchen, *das;* **~-haired** *adj.* mit goldenem Haar *nachgestellt (dichter.);* **~ 'hamster** *n.* Goldhamster, *der;* **~ 'handshake** *n.* Abfindung[ssumme], *die;* **~ 'jubilee** *n.* goldenes Jubiläum; **~ 'mean** *n.* goldene Mitte; **~ re'triever** *n.* Golden Retriever, *der;* **~ rod** *n. (Bot.)* Goldrute, *die;* **~ 'rule** *n.* goldene Regel; **~ 'syrup** *n. (Brit.)* Sirup, *der;* **~ 'wedding** *n.* goldene Hochzeit

gold: ~-fever *n.* Goldrausch, *der;* **~-field** *n.* Goldfeld, *das;* **~finch** *n.* Stieglitz, *der;* Distelfink, *der;* **~fish** *n.* Goldfisch, *der;* **~fish bowl** *n.* Goldfischglas, *das;* **like being in a ~fish bowl** *(fig.)* wie auf dem Präsentierteller; **~ 'foil** *n.* Goldfolie, *die*

goldilocks ['gəʊldɪlɒks] *n.* Blondkopf, *der*

gold: ~ leaf *n.* Blattgold, *das;* **~ medal** *n.* Goldmedaille, *die;* **~ 'medallist** *n.* Goldmedaillengewinner, *der/*-gewinnerin, *die;* **~-mine** *n.* Goldmine, *die; (fig.)* Goldgrube, *die;* **~ 'plate** *n., no pl., no indef. art.* **a)** vergoldete Ware; *(coating)* Goldauflage, *die;* **be ~ plate** vergoldet sein; **b)** *(vessels, tableware)* Goldgeschirr, *das;* **~-plate** *v. t.* vergolden; **~ reserve** *n.* Goldreserve, *die;* **~-rush** *n.* **the ~-rush to Alaska** der Strom von Goldgräbern nach Alaska; **~smith** *n.* Goldschmied, *der/*-schmiedin, *die;* **~ standard** *n.* Goldstandard, *der; see also* **go off 2 b; ~ 'thread** *n.* Goldfaden, *der*

golf [gɒlf] **1.** *n., no pl.* Golf, das; *attrib.* Golf⟨*platz, -schlag usw.*⟩. **2.** *v. i.* Golf spielen; **his ~ing friends** seine Golffreunde

golf: ~-bag *n.* Golftasche, *die;* **~ ball** *n.* **a)** Golfball, *der;* **b)** *(coll.: in typewriter)* Kugelkopf, *der;* **~-club** *n.* **a)** *(implement)* Golfschläger, *der;* **b)** *(association)* Golfclub, *der;* **~-course** *n.* Golfplatz, *der*

golfer ['gɒlfə(r)] *n.* Golfer, *der/*Golferin, *die;* Golfspieler, *der/*Golfspielerin, *die*

golf-links *n. pl.* Golfplatz, *der*

Goliath [gə'laɪəθ] *n. (lit. or fig.)* Goliath, *der*

golliwog ['gɒlɪwɒg] *n.* Negerpuppe, *die;* **have hair like a ~:** wie ein Struwwelpeter aussehen

[1]**golly** ['gɒlɪ] *see* **golliwog**

[2]**golly** *int.* meine Güte!; **by ~:** Menschenskind!

golosh *(Brit.) see* **galosh**

gonad ['gəʊnæd] *n. (Anat., Zool.)* Gonade, *die*

gondola ['gɒndələ] *n.* **a)** *(boat)* Gondel, *die;* **b)** *(Amer. Railw.)* **~ [car]** offener Güterwagen; offener Flachwagen; **c)** *(of ski-lift, airship)* Gondel, *die;* **d)** *(in shop)* Gondel, *die;* Verkaufsregal, *das*

gondolier [gɒndə'lɪə(r)] *n.* Gondoliere, *der*

gone [gɒn, gɔːn] **1.** *p. p. of* [1]**go 1. 2.** *pred. adj.* **a)** *(away)* weg; **it's time you were ~:** es ist *od.* wird Zeit, daß du gehst; **he has been ~ ten minutes** *(coll.)* er ist seit zehn Minuten fort *od.* weg; **he will be ~ a year** er wird ein Jahr lang weg sein; **no, it's ~ again** *(fig.: forgotten)* es ist mir schon wieder entfallen; **b)** *(of time: after)* nach; **not be back until ~ ten o'clock** erst nach zehn Uhr zurückkommen; **it's ~ ten o'clock** es ist zehn Uhr vorbei; **at ~ midnight** nach Mitternacht; **c)** *(used up)* **be all ~:** alle sein *(ugs.);* **d)** *(coll.: pregnant)* **be six** *etc.* **months ~:** im sechsten *usw.* Monat sein; **e) be ~ on sb./sth.** *(sl.)* ganz weg von jmdm./etw. sein *(ugs.). See also* **far 1 d; forget 1 a;** [1]**go 1 k**

goner ['gɒnə(r)] *n. (sl.)* **he is a ~:** er hat die längste Zeit gelebt *(ugs.);* **the ship is a ~:** das Schiff macht es nicht mehr lange *od.* wird bald seinen Geist aufgeben *(ugs.)*

gong [gɒŋ] *n.* **a)** Gong, *der;* **b)** *(sl.: medal)* Orden, *der; in pl.* Blech, *das (ugs.);* Lametta, *das (ugs.)*

gonna ['gɒnə] *(sl./Amer. coll.)* = **going to;** *see* **going 2 c**

gonorrhoea (*Amer.:* **gonorrhea**) [gɒnəˈrɪə] *n. (Med.)* Gonorrhöe, *die (fachspr.);* Tripper, *der*

goo [gu:] *n. (coll.)* Schmiere, *die (ugs.); (fig.)* Gefühlsduselei, *die (ugs. abwertend); (in film etc.)* Schmalz, *der (ugs. abwertend)*

good [gʊd] **1.** *adj.,* **better** [ˈbetə(r)], **best** [best] **a)** *(satisfactory)* gut; *(reliable)* gut; zuverlässig; *(sufficient)* gut; ausreichend ⟨*Vorrat*⟩; ausgiebig ⟨*Mahl*⟩; *(competent)* gut; geeignet; **his ~ eye/leg** sein gesundes Auge/Bein; **in ~ health** bei guter Gesundheit; **come in a ~ third** einen guten dritten Platz belegen; **come ~** *(sl.)* groß rauskommen *(ugs.);* **Late again! It's just not ~ enough** *(coll.)* Schon wieder zu spät. So geht es einfach nicht!; **your excuse is not ~ enough** diese Entschuldigung reicht nicht; **in ~ time** frühzeitig; **all in ~ time** alles zu seiner Zeit; **take ~ care of sb.** gut für jmdn. sorgen; **be ~ at sth.** in etw. *(Dat.)* gut sein; **be ~ at doing sth.** etw. gut können; **speak ~ English** gut[es] Englisch sprechen; **be ~ with people** *etc.* mit Menschen *usw.* gut *od.* leicht zurechtkommen; **the ~ ship 'Victory'** die gute, alte „Victory"; **b)** *(favourable, advantageous)* gut; günstig ⟨*Gelegenheit, Augenblick, Angebot*⟩; **a ~ chance of succeeding** gute Erfolgschancen; **too ~ to be true** zu schön, um wahr zu sein; **in the ~ sense** im positiven Sinn; **I've heard so many ~ things about you** ich habe schon soviel Gutes von Ihnen gehört; **the ~ thing about it is that ...:** das Gute daran ist, daß ...; **be on to a ~ thing** was Gutes aufgetan haben *(ugs.);* **be too much of a ~ thing** zuviel des Guten sein; **you can have too much of a ~ thing** man kann es auch übertreiben; **be ~ for sb./sth.** gut für jmdn./etw. sein; **apples are ~ for you** Äpfel sind gesund; **eat more than is ~ for one** mehr essen, als einem guttut; **know what is ~ for one** wissen, was sich gehört; **it's a ~ thing you told him** nur gut, daß du es ihm gesagt hast; **make a ~ death** *or* **end** einen schönen Tod haben; **the water isn't ~ to drink** das Wasser kann man nicht trinken; **c)** *(prosperous)* gut; **~ times** eine schöne Zeit; **have it ~:** es gut haben; **d)** *(enjoyable)* schön ⟨*Leben, Urlaub, Wochenende*⟩; **the ~ things** alles, was gut und schön ist; **the ~ things in life** Annehmlichkeiten; **the ~ old days** die gute alte Zeit; **the ~ life** das angenehme[, sorglose] Leben; **have a ~ time!** viel Spaß *od.* Vergnügen!; **did you have a ~ time in Spain?** war es schön in Spanien?; **be after a ~ time** auf sein Vergnügen aussein; **have a ~ journey!** gute Reise!; **it's ~ to be alive** es ist eine Lust zu leben; **it's ~ to be home again** es ist schön, wieder zu Hause zu sein; **ox liver is not very ~ to eat** Rinderleber ist nicht gut zum Verzehr geeignet; **Did you have a ~ day at the office?** Wie war es heute im Büro?; **e)** *(cheerful)* gut; angenehm ⟨*Patient*⟩; **~ humour** *or* **spirits** *or* **mood** gute Laune; **feel ~:** sich wohl fühlen; **I'm not feeling too ~** *(coll.)* mir geht es nicht sehr gut; **f)** *(well-behaved)* gut; brav; **be ~!, be a ~ girl/boy!** sei brav *od.* lieb!; **[as] ~ as gold** ganz artig *od.* brav; **g)** *(virtuous)* rechtschaffen; *(kind)* nett; gut ⟨*Absicht, Wünsche, Benehmen, Tat*⟩; **the ~ guy** der Gute; **be ~ to sb.** gut zu jmdm. sein; **would you be so ~ as to** *or* **~ enough to do that?** wären Sie so freundlich *od.* nett, das zu tun?; **how ~ of you!** wie nett von Ihnen!; **that/it is ~ of you** das/es ist nett *od.* lieb von dir; **a ~ nature** Gutmütigkeit, *die;* **he has a very ~ nature** er ist sehr gutmütig; **~ works** gute Taten *od.* Werke; *see also* **turn 1 l; h)** *(commendable)* gut; **~ for 'you** *etc. (coll.),* **~ 'on you** *etc. (esp. Austral. and NZ coll.)* bravo!; **~ old Jim** *etc. (coll.)* der gute alte Jim *usw. (ugs.);* **~ man!** *(coll.)* mein lieber Mann!; alle Achtung!; **my ~ man/friend** *(coll.)* mein lieber Herr/Freund *(ugs.; auch iron.);* **the ~ man/woman** *(dated)* der werte Herr/die werte Dame *(geh.);* **your ~ man/lady** Ihr lieber Mann/Ihre liebe Frau; Ihr werter Gatte/Ihre werte Gattin; **~ men and true** rechtschaffene Leute; **that's a ~ one** *(sl.)* der ist gut! *(ugs.); (iron.);* das ist'n Ding! *(ugs.); see also* **fellow 1 a; i)** *(attractive)* schön; gut ⟨*Figur, Haltung*⟩; gepflegt ⟨*Erscheinung, Äußeres*⟩; wohlgeformt ⟨*Nase, Beine*⟩; **look ~:** gut aussehen; **~ looks** gutes Aussehen; **j)** *(thorough)* gut; **take a ~ look round** sich gründlich umsehen; **give sb. a ~ beating/scolding** jmdn. tüchtig verprügeln/ausschimpfen; **give sth. a ~ polish** etw. ordentlich polieren; **have a ~ weep/rest/sleep** sich richtig ausweinen/ausruhen/[sich] richtig ausschlafen *(ugs.);* **k)** *(considerable)* [recht] ansehnlich ⟨*Menschenmenge*⟩; ganz schön, ziemlich *(ugs.)* ⟨*Stück Wegs, Entfernung, Zeitraum, Strecke*⟩; gut, anständig ⟨*Preis, Erlös*⟩; hoch ⟨*Alter*⟩; **a ~ bit better** *(coll.)* ein ganzes Stück besser; **a ~ dose of ...:** eine gute Dosis ...; *(fig.)* eine gehörige Portion ...; **take a ~ long time** ziemlich *od.* recht lange dauern; seine Zeit brauchen; **have a ~ long sleep** [sich] richtig ausschlafen; **live to a ~ old age** ein recht hohes Alter erreichen; **a ~ four hours** *etc.* volle *od.* ganze vier Stunden *usw.;* gut vier Stunden *usw.;* **a ~ half pound** ein gutes halbes Pfund; **he is a ~ seventy** *(coll.)* er ist gute siebzig *(ugs.);* **l)** *(sound, valid)* gut ⟨*Grund, Rat, Gedanke*⟩; berechtigt ⟨*Anspruch*⟩; *(Commerc.)* solide ⟨*Kunde*⟩; sicher ⟨*Anleihe, Kredit*⟩; gedeckt ⟨*Scheck*⟩; **~ sense** Vernunft, *die;* **have the ~ sense to do sth.** so vernünftig sein, etw. zu tun; **be ~ for a year** es ein Jahr machen; ⟨*Gerät usw.:*⟩ ein Jahr halten; ⟨*Ticket:*⟩ ein Jahr gelten; **~ for five journeys** gültig für fünf Fahrten; **I'm ~ for another hour's walk** ich kann noch eine Stunde weiterlaufen; **he's ~ for £5,000** er wird bestimmt 5 000 Pfund geben *(ugs.);* **how much is he ~ for?** wieviel wird er wohl geben? *(ugs.);* **the draft is ~ for ...:** der Wechsel ist auf ... *(Akk.)* ausgestellt; **m)** *in greeting* gut; **~ afternoon/day** guten Tag!; **~ evening/morning** *or (Brit. arch.)* **morrow** guten Abend/Morgen!; **~ night** gute Nacht!; **a ~-night kiss** ein Gutenachtkuß; **n)** *in exclamation* gut; **very ~, sir** sehr wohl!; **~ God/Lord** *etc. see the nouns;* **o)** *(best)* gut ⟨*Geschirr, Anzug*⟩; **p)** *(serious)* ernst ⟨*Musik*⟩; schön ⟨*Künste*⟩; **q)** *(orthodox)* gut ⟨*Christ, Moslem*⟩; **r)** *(correct, fitting)* gut; *(appropriate)* angebracht; ratsam; **s)** *(socially prestigious)* gut; **be of a ~/very ~ family** aus guter Familie/bestem Hause stammen; **t) as ~ as** so gut wie; *see also* **give 1 p; u) make ~** *(succeed)* erfolgreich sein; *(effect)* in die Tat umsetzen; ausführen ⟨*Plan*⟩; erfüllen ⟨*Versprechen*⟩; *(compensate for)* wiedergutmachen ⟨*Fehler*⟩; *(indemnify)* ersetzen ⟨*Schaden, Ausgaben*⟩; *(prove)* belegen ⟨*Behauptung, Anschuldigung*⟩; **the film made ~ at the box office** der Film war ein Kassenerfolg; **they soon made ~ in Australia** sie brachten es bald zu was in Australien *(ugs.). See also* **best 1; better 1; ¹egg; form 1 f, h; luck a; temper 1 a. 2.** *adv.* **a)** *(coll.) as intensifier* **~ and ...:** richtig ...; **~ and angry** *(Amer.)* richtig böse; **hit sb. ~ and proper** jmdn. ordentlich verprügeln; **it was raining ~ and hard** es hat [so] richtig gegossen; **they quizzed him ~ and proper** sie haben ihn ordentlich in die Mangel genommen *(ugs.);* **b)** *(Amer. coll.: well)* gut; **get along ~:** gut zurechtkommen; **he's doing pretty ~ these days** es geht ihm in letzter Zeit sehr gut. *See also* **best 2; better 2. 3.** *n.* **a)** *(use)* Nutzen, *der;* **be some ~ to sb./sth.** jmdm./einer Sache nützen; **he'll never be any ~:** aus dem wird nichts Gutes werden; **is this book any ~?** taugt dieses Buch etwas?; **you're a lot of ~, I must say!** *(iron.)* du bist mir vielleicht einer! *(ugs.);* **be no ~ to sb./sth.** für jmdn./etw. nicht zu gebrauchen sein; **not be any ~ for work** nicht zur Arbeit taugen *od.* geeignet sein; **it is no/not much ~ doing sth.** es hat keinen/kaum einen Sinn, etw. zu tun; **what's the ~ of ...?, what ~ is ...?** was nützt ...?; **what's the ~ of knowing Latin?** was nützt einem Latein?; wozu ist Latein gut?; *see also* **no-good; b)** *(benefit)* **for your/his** *etc.* **own ~:** zu deinem/seinem *usw.* Besten *od.* eigenen Vorteil; **for the ~ of mankind/the country** zum Wohl[e] der Menschheit/des Landes; **for ~ or ill** *see* **ill 2 a; do no/little ~:** nichts/wenig helfen *od.* nützen; **do sb./sth. ~:** jmdm./einer Sache nützen; ⟨*Ruhe, Erholung:*⟩ jmdm./einer Sache guttun; ⟨*Arznei:*⟩ jmdm./einer Sache helfen; **I'll tell him, but what ~ will that do?** ich sag es ihm, aber was nützt *od.* hilft das schon?; **do sb. a lot/a world of ~:** jmdm. sehr guttun; **just sitting there won't do you any ~:** einfach dasitzen hilft dir auch nicht weiter; **you aren't doing yourself any ~:** du tust dir keinen Gefallen; **much ~ may it do you** *(iron.)* [na, dann] viel Vergnügen; **look what ~** *or* **a lot of ~** *or* **much ~ it did him** *(iron.)* [und] was hat es ihm genützt?; und das hat er nun davon gehabt *(iron.);* **to the ~** *(for the best)* zum Guten; *(in profit)* plus; **this development was all to the ~:** diese Entwicklung war nur von Vorteil; **the delay was partly to the ~:** die Verspätung hatte auch ihr Gutes; **end up [a game** *etc.***] £10 to the ~:** [bei einem Spiel *usw.*] 10 Pfund gutmachen; **come home £10 to the ~:** mit 10 Pfund plus nach Hause kommen; **be 4 points/wins to the ~:** 4 Punkte/Siege voraus *od.* im Vorteil sein; **finish the work with two days to the ~:** zwei Tage früher mit der Arbeit fertig sein; **come to no ~:** kein gutes Ende nehmen; **c)** *(goodness)* Gute, *das;* **the highest ~** *(Philos.)* das Höchste Gut; **there's ~ and bad in everyone** in jedem steckt Gutes und Böses; **the difference between ~ and bad** *or* **evil** der Unterschied zwischen Gut und Böse; **d)** *(kind acts)* Gute, *das;* **be up to** *or* **after no ~:** nichts Gutes im Sinn haben *od.* im Schilde führen; **do ~:** Gutes tun; **e) for ~ [and all]** *(finally)* ein für allemal; *(permanently)* für immer [und ewig]; endgültig; **f)** *constr. as pl. (virtuous people)* **the ~:** die Guten; **g)** *in pl. (wares etc.)* Waren; *(belongings)* Habe, *die; (Brit. Railw.)* Fracht, *die; attrib.* Fracht⟨*büro, -tarif, -schiff, -flugzeug, -zettel usw.*⟩; Güter⟨*abfertigung, -produktion, -verkehr, -wagen usw.*⟩; **~s and chattels** Sachen; **canned/manufactured ~s** Konserven/Fertigwaren; **stolen ~s** gestohlene Waren; Diebesgut, *das;* **by ~s** per Bahnfracht; als Frachtgut; **h)** *in pl.* **the ~s** *(coll.: what is wanted)* das Gewünschte; das Verlangte; **deliver the ~s** *(fig.)* halten, was man verspricht; **sb. is the ~s** jmd. ist der Richtige; **he's got the ~s** er ist der richtige Mann

good: ~'bye (*Amer.:* **~'by**) [gʊdˈbaɪ] **1.** *int.* auf Wiedersehen!; *(on telephone)* auf Wiederhören!; **2.** *n., pl.* **~byes** (*Amer.:* **~bys**) *(farewell remark or gesture)* Lebewohl, *das (geh.); (taking of leave)* Abschied, *der;* **say ~bye to sb.** jmdm. auf Wiedersehen sagen; **say ~bye, say one's ~byes** sich verabschieden; **nod/wave ~bye** zum Abschied nicken/winken; **kiss sb. ~bye** jmdm. einen Abschiedskuß geben; **say ~bye to sth.** Abschied nehmen von etw.; **say ~bye to sth., kiss sth. ~bye** *(fig.: have lost it)* etw. abschreiben *(ugs.);* **~-'fellowship** *n.* Kameradschaftlichkeit, *die;* **~-for-nothing** *(derog.)* **1.** *adj.* nichtsnutzig; **2.** *n.* Taugenichts, *der;* **G~ 'Friday** *see* **Friday 1; ~-hearted** [ˈgʊdhɑ:tɪd] *adj.* gutherzig; gutgemeint ⟨*Bemühungen*⟩; **~-humoured** [gʊdˈhju:məd] *adj.,* **~-humouredly** [gʊdˈhju:mədlɪ] *adv.* gutmütig

goodies ['gʊdɪz] *n. pl. (coll.) (food)* Naschereien; *(sweets)* Süßigkeiten; *(attractive things)* Attraktionen; tolle Sachen
goodish ['gʊdɪʃ] *adj.* **a)** *(quite good)* ganz gut; recht gut; **b)** *(considerable)* ganz schön
good: ~-looker *n.* flotte Erscheinung *(ugs.);* **be a ~-looker** gut aussehen; **~-'looking** *adj.* gutaussehend
goodly ['gʊdlɪ] *adj.* stattlich; ansehnlich
good: ~-'natured *adj.* gutwillig; gutmütig; **~-naturedly** [gʊd'neɪtʃədlɪ] *adv.* gutmütig; **~-'neighbour** *attrib. adj.* gutnachbarlich; **a ~-neighbour policy** eine Politik der guten Nachbarschaft
goodness ['gʊdnɪs] **1.** *n., no pl.* **a)** *(virtue)* Güte, *die;* **have the ~ to do sth.** die Güte haben, etw. zu tun *(geh., auch iron.);* **b)** *(of food)* Nährgehalt, *der;* Güte, *die; (of soil)* Fruchtbarkeit, *die;* Güte, *die.* **2.** *int.* **[my] ~** *expr. surprise* meine Güte! *(ugs.);* **[oh] my ~** *expr. shock* lieber Himmel!; **~ gracious** *or* **me!** [ach] du lieber Himmel *od.* liebe Güte! *(ugs.);* **for ~' sake** um Himmels willen; **~ [only] knows** weiß der Himmel *(ugs.);* **I hope to ~ that ...:** gebe Gott, daß ...; **I wish to ~ I'd never met him** wenn ich ihn doch bloß nie kennengelernt hätte!; **surely to ~ you don't mean that** das ist doch wohl nicht dein Ernst?; **thank ~:** Gott sei Dank
good: ~-o, ~-oh *int. (coll.)* toll! prima!
goods *see* **good 3 g, h**
good: ~-sized *see* **-sized; ~s station** *n. (Brit. Railw.)* Güterbahnhof, *der;* **~s train** *n. (Brit. Railw.)* Güterzug, *der;* **~s vehicle** *n.* Nutzfahrzeug, *das;* **~s yard** *n. (Brit. Railw.)* Güterbahnhof, *der;* **~-'tempered** *adj.* ausgeglichen; gutmütig; verträglich ⟨*Person*⟩; **~-time** *adj.* **a ~-time girl** ein leichtes Mädchen *(abwertend);* **~ 'will** *n.* gute Absicht; **~'will** *n.* **a)** *(friendly feeling)* guter Wille; *attrib.* Goodwill⟨*botschaft, -reise usw.*⟩; **men of ~will** Menschen, die guten Willens sind; **b)** *(willingness)* Bereitwilligkeit, *die;* **with ~will** bereitwillig; **c)** *(Commerc.)* Goodwill, *der*
¹goody ['gʊdɪ] *n. (coll.: hero)* Gute, *der/die; see also* **goodies**
²goody *int. (coll.)* toll; prima; **~, ~ gumdrops!** juhu!; juchhe!
goody: ~-goody 1. *n.* Tugendbold, *der (iron.);* **2.** *adj.* [scheinheilig] tugendhaft; musterhaft *(iron.);* **~-'two-shoes** *n.* Tugendlamm, *das (iron.)*
gooey ['gu:ɪ] *adj.,* **gooier** ['gu:ɪə(r)], **gooiest** ['gu:ɪɪst] *(coll.)* klebrig; *(fig.)* rührselig; schnulzig *(ugs. abwertend)*
goof [gu:f] *(sl.)* **1.** *n.* **a)** *(fool)* Döskopp, *der (salopp);* Doofi, *der (ugs.);* **b)** *(gaffe)* Schnitzer, *der (ugs.);* Patzer, *der (ugs.).* **2.** *v. i.* Mist machen *od.* bauen *(salopp).* **3.** *v. t.* vermasseln *(salopp);* Murks machen bei *(salopp)*
~ about, ~ around *v. i. (sl.)* herumpfuschen *(ugs. abwertend); (spend time idly)* herumhängen *(salopp);* herumtrödeln
goofy ['gu:fɪ] *adj. (sl.)* **a)** dämlich *(ugs.);* bescheuert *(salopp);* **b)** vorstehend ⟨*Zähne*⟩
googly ['gu:glɪ] *n. (Cricket) (zur Täuschung des Schlagmanns)* gedrehter Ball
gook [gu:k, gʊk] *n. (Amer. sl. derog.)* Schlitzauge, *das (salopp abwertend)*
goon [gu:n] *n. (sl.)* **a)** *(hatchet man)* Schläger, *der (abwertend);* **b)** *(fool)* Blödmann, *der (salopp)*
goosander [gu:'sændə(r)] *n. (Ornith.)* Gänsesäger, *der*
goose [gu:s] *n., pl.* **geese** [gi:s] **a)** Gans, *die;* **all mothers think their geese are swans** jede Mutter glaubt, ihre Kinder seien etwas Besonderes; **kill the ~ that lays the golden eggs** *(fig.)* das Huhn, das goldene Eier legt, schlachten; **roast ~:** Gänsebraten, *der; see also* **boo 1; cook 2 a; b)** *(simpleton)* Gans, *die (ugs.)*
gooseberry ['gʊzbərɪ] *n.* **a)** *(berry, shrub)* Stachelbeere, *die;* **b) play ~:** das fünfte Rad am Wagen sein *(ugs.)*
'gooseberry bush *n.* Stachelbeerstrauch, *der;* **we found you under a ~** *(fig.)* dich hat uns der Klapperstorch gebracht *(Kinderspr.)*
goose: ~ bumps *n. pl. (Amer.)* Gänsehaut, *die;* **~-egg** *n.* Gänseei, *das;* **~-flesh** *n., no pl.* Gänsehaut, *die;* **~-foot** *n., pl.* **~-foots** *(Bot.)* Gänsefuß, *der;* **~-grass** *n.* Klebkraut, *das;* **~-neck** *n.* Schwanenhals, *der (fig.);* **~-pimples** *n. pl.* **have ~-pimples** eine Gänsehaut haben; **~ step 1.** *n.* Stechschritt, *der;* **2.** *v. i.* im Stechschritt marschieren
gopher ['gəʊfə(r)] *n. (Zool.)* **a)** Taschenratte, *die;* **b)** *(squirrel)* Ziesel, *der*
gorblimey [gɔ:'blaɪmɪ] *int. (Brit. sl.)* Mensch! *(salopp)*
Gordian knot [gɔ:dɪən 'nɒt] *n.* gordischer Knoten; **cut the ~:** den gordischen Knoten durchhauen
¹gore [gɔ:(r)] *v. t.* [mit den Hörnern] aufspießen *od.* durchbohren; **be ~d to death by a bull** von den Hörnern eines Stieres durchbohrt [und tödlich verletzt] werden
²gore *n. (blood)* Blut, *das*
³gore *n.* Keil, *der; (of skirt)* [Rock]bahn, *die*
gorge [gɔ:dʒ] **1.** *n.* **a)** Schlucht, *die;* Klamm, *die;* **b) sb.'s ~ rises at sth.** *(fig.)* jmdm. wird schlecht *od.* übel von *od.* bei etw.; **c)** *(rhet.: throat) (of person)* Kehle, *die; (of animal)* Schlund, *der.* **2.** *v. i.* sich vollstopfen **(on** mit) *(ugs.);* ⟨*Tier:*⟩ sich vollfressen **(on** mit). **3.** *v. t.* **a)** *(satiate)* vollstopfen *(ugs.);* **~ oneself with** *or* **on sth.** sich mit etw. vollstopfen *(ugs.);* **b)** *(fill full)* anfüllen **(with** mit)
gorgeous ['gɔ:dʒəs] *adj.* **a)** *(magnificent)* prächtig; hinreißend ⟨*Frau, Mann, Lächeln*⟩; *(richly coloured)* farbenprächtig; **the ~ colours of sth.** die Farbenpracht einer Sache; **b)** *(coll.: splendid)* sagenhaft *(ugs.)*
gorgeously ['gɔ:dʒəslɪ] *adv.* **a)** prächtig; hinreißend ⟨*lächeln*⟩; **b)** *(coll.: splendidly)* sagenhaft
gorgon ['gɔ:gən] *n.* **a)** *(Greek Mythol.)* Gorgo, *die;* **b)** *(person)* Drachen, *der (ugs. abwertend)*
gorilla [gə'rɪlə] *n.* Gorilla, *der*
gormandize (gormandise) ['gɔ:məndaɪz] *v. i.* prassen; schlemmen
gormless ['gɔ:mlɪs] *adj. (Brit. coll.)* dämlich *(ugs.)*
gorse [gɔ:s] *n.* Stechginster, *der*
gory ['gɔ:rɪ] *adj.* **a)** blutbefleckt ⟨*Hände*⟩; blutbeschmiert ⟨*Waffe*⟩; blutig ⟨*Schlacht*⟩; **b)** *(fig.: sensational)* blutrünstig
gosh [gɒʃ] *int. (coll.)* Gott
goshawk ['gɒshɔ:k] *n. (Ornith.)* [Hühner]habicht, *der*
gosling ['gɒzlɪŋ] *n.* Gänseküken, *das;* Gössel, *das (nordd.)*
'go-slow *n. (Brit.)* Bummelstreik, *der*
gospel ['gɒspl] *n.* **a)** *(Relig.)* Evangelium, *das; (reading)* Lesung, *die;* **b)** *(fig.)* Evangelium, *das;* **take sth. for** *or* **as ~:** etw. für bare Münze nehmen; **preach the ~ of non-violence** Gewaltlosigkeit predigen
gospel: ~ 'oath *n.* Eid auf die Bibel; **~ singer** *n.* Gospelsänger, *der/*-sängerin, *die;* **~ 'truth** *n.* absolute *od.* reine Wahrheit
gossamer ['gɒsəmə(r)] *n.* **a)** Altweibersommer, *der;* **like ~:** wie Spinnfäden; **b)** *(fig.)* Spinnfäden *(fig.); attrib.* hauchdünn ⟨*Flügel*⟩
gossip ['gɒsɪp] **1.** *n.* **a)** *(person)* Klatschweib, *das (ugs. abwertend);* **b)** *(talk)* Schwatz, *der; (malicious)* Klatsch, *der (ugs. abwertend);* **the latest ~ is that ...:** seit neustem wird geklatscht, daß ... **2.** *v. i.* schwatzen; *(maliciously)* klatschen *(ugs. abwertend)*
gossip: ~ column *n.* Klatschspalte, *die (ugs. abwertend);* **~ columnist** *n.* Klatschspaltenkolumnist, *der/*-kolumnistin, *die (abwertend)*
gossiper ['gɒsɪpə(r)] *see* **gossip 1 a**
'gossip-monger *n. (derog.)* Klatschmaul, *das (ugs. abwertend)*
gossipy ['gɒsɪpɪ] *adj.* geschwätzig *(abwertend); (conversational)* plaudernd ⟨*Ton, Stil*⟩; im Plauderton geschrieben ⟨*Buch, Brief*⟩
got *see* **get**
Goth [gɒθ] *n.* Gote, *der*
Gothic ['gɒθɪk] **1.** *adj.* **a)** gotisch; **b)** *(Lit.) für den Schauerroman charakteristisch;* **~ novel** Schauerroman, *der;* **c)** *(Printing)* gotisch. **2.** *n.* **a)** *(Ling.)* Gotisch[e], *das;* **b)** *(Archit.)* Gotik, *die;* **c)** *(type, script)* Gotisch, *das*
Gothic Re'vival *n. (Archit.)* Neugotik, *die*
gotta ['gɒtə] *(coll.)* = **got to, got a; I['ve] ~** go ich muß gehen; **I['ve] ~ present for you** ich habe da ein Geschenk für dich
gotten *see* **get**
gouache [gu:'ɑ:ʃ] *n. (Art)* Gouache, *die*
gouge [gaʊdʒ, gu:dʒ] **1.** *v. t.* **a)** aushöhlen; ausmeißeln; **~ a channel** ⟨*Fluß:*⟩ eine Rinne auswaschen; **b)** *(Amer.: overcharge)* betrügen. **2.** *n.* **a)** Hohleisen, *das;* Hohlmeißel, *der;* **b)** *(Amer.: overcharging)* Betrug, *der*
~ out *v. t.* ausschneiden; ausstechen; **~ sb.'s eye out** jmdm. ein Auge ausstechen
goulash ['gu:læʃ] *n. (Gastr.)* Gulasch, *das od. der*
gourd [gʊəd] *n.* **a)** *(fruit, plant)* [Flaschen]kürbis, *der;* **b)** *(bottle, bowl)* Kürbisflasche, *die;* Kalebasse, *die*
gourmand ['gʊəmənd] *n. (glutton)* Gourmand, *der*
gourmet ['gʊəmeɪ] *n.* Gourmet, *der; attrib.* **~ meal/restaurant** Feinschmeckergericht, *das/*-lokal, *das*
gout [gaʊt] *n. (Med.)* Gicht, *die*
gouty ['gaʊtɪ] *adj. (Med.)* gichtkrank; gichtig
Gov. *abbr.* **a) Government** Reg.; Rg.; **b) Governor** Gouv.
govern ['gʌvn] **1.** *v. t.* **a)** *(rule)* regieren ⟨*Land, Volk*⟩; *(administer)* verwalten ⟨*Provinz, Kolonie*⟩; **b)** *(dictate)* bestimmen; **be ~ed by sth.** sich von etw. leiten lassen; **self-interest ~s all his actions** Eigennutz beherrscht all sein Tun; **c)** *(regulate proceedings of)* leiten ⟨*Geschäft, Unternehmen*⟩; ⟨*Vorschriften:*⟩ regeln; **d)** *(be in command of)* den Befehl haben über (+ *Akk.*) ⟨*Festung, Stadt*⟩; **e)** *(restrain)* zügeln ⟨*Temperament, Leidenschaften*⟩; **f)** *(constitute a law or principle for)* ⟨*Prinzipien:*⟩ die Grundlage bilden für; **the laws which ~ the animal kingdom** die Gesetze, denen das Tierreich unterworfen ist; **g)** *(Ling.)* verlangen; regieren ⟨*Kasus*⟩. **2.** *v. i.* regieren
governable ['gʌvənəbl] *adj.* regierbar
governance ['gʌvənəns] *n.* Regieren, *das; (office, function)* Regierungsgewalt, *die; (control)* Herrschaft, *die*
governess ['gʌvənɪs] *n.* Gouvernante, *die (veraltet);* Hauslehrerin, *die*
governing ['gʌvənɪŋ] *adj.* **a)** *(ruling)* regierend; **b)** *(guiding)* dominierend ⟨*Einfluß*⟩; geltend ⟨*Vorschriften*⟩; **sb.'s ~ principle** das Prinzip, von dem jmd. sich leiten läßt; **~ body** leitendes Gremium
government ['gʌvnmənt] *n.* **a)** Regierung, *die;* **form a G~:** die Regierung bilden; **b)** *(system, form)* Regierungsform, *die;* **c)** *(an administration or ministry)* **[central] ~:** Zentralregierung, *die; attrib.* Regierungs-; **~ money** Staatsgelder *Pl.;* **~ securities** *or* **stocks** Staatspapiere *od.* -anleihen; **~-controlled establishment** staatlich kontrollierte Einrichtung; *see also* **body 1 d**
governmental [gʌvn'mentl] *adj.* Regierungs-
government: ~ de'partment *n.* Regierungsstelle, *die;* **~ 'surplus** *n.* Waren aus

Regierungsbeständen; *attrib.* ~ **surplus radio** Radio aus Regierungsbeständen

governor ['gʌvənə(r)] *n.* **a)** *(ruler)* Herrscher, *der;* **b)** *(of province, town, etc.)* Gouverneur, *der;* Statthalter, *der (hist.);* **c)** *(of State of US)* Gouverneur, *der;* **d)** *(of institution)* Direktor, *der*/Direktorin, *die;* **[board of] ~s** Vorstand, *der; (of school)* Schulleitung, *die; (of bank, company)* Direktorium, *das;* Direktion, *die;* **e)** *(of prison)* Gefängnisdirektor, *der*/-direktorin, *die;* **f)** *(commandant)* Kommandant, *der;* Gouverneur, *der;* **g)** *(sl.) (employer)* Boß, *der (ugs.); (father)* Alte, *der (salopp);* **hey, ~!** *(as voc.: mister)* hallo, Chef! *(salopp);* **h)** *(Mech.)* Regler, *der*

Governor-'General *n.* Generalgouverneur, *der*

governorship ['gʌvənəʃɪp] *n.* Gouverneursamt, *das*

Govt. *abbr.* **Government** Reg.; Rg.

gown [gaʊn] *n.* **a)** [elegantes] Kleid; **bridal/baptismal ~:** Braut-/Taufkleid, *das;* **b)** *(official or uniform robe)* Talar, *der;* Robe, *die;* **town and ~:** Bürger und Studenten; **c)** *(surgeon's overall)* [Operations]kittel, *der*

GP *abbr.* **a) general practitioner; b) Grand Prix**

GPO *abbr.* **a)** *(Hist.)* **General Post Office** Post, *die;* **b)** *(Amer.)* **Government Printing Office** Staatsdruckerei, *die*

gr. *abbr.* **a) grain[s]** Gran, *der (veralt.);* **b) gram[s]** g; **c) gross** bto.

grab [græb] **1.** *v. t.*, **-bb-: a)** greifen nach; *(seize)* packen; *(capture, arrest)* schnappen *(ugs.);* **~ sth. away from sb.** jmdm. etw. entreißen; **~ sb. by the arm** *etc.* jmdn. am Arm *usw.* packen; **should we ~ some food** *or* **a bite to eat?** *(coll.)* sollen wir schnell etwas essen?; **could you ~ a table while I ...** *(coll.)* versuch du, einen Tisch zu ergattern, während ich ... *(ugs.);* **I managed to ~ her before she got on the bus** *(stop her)* ich konnte sie gerade noch aufhalten, bevor sie in den Bus stieg; **~ the chance** die Gelegenheit ergreifen; **I would ~ an offer like that** ein solches Angebot würde ich mir nicht entgehen lassen; **~ hold of sb./sth.** sich *(Dat.)* jmdn./etw. schnappen *(ugs.);* **b)** *(sl.: impress)* **how does that ~ you?** wie findest du das?; **this doesn't [really] ~ me** das läßt mich [im Grunde] kalt. **2.** *v. i.*, **-bb- a) ~ at sth.** nach etw. greifen; **don't ~ like that!** grapsch nicht so! *(ugs.);* **b)** *(act jerkily)* ‹*Bremse:*› ruckartig greifen. **3.** *n.* **a) make a ~ at** *or* **for sb./sth.** nach jmdm./etw. greifen *od. (ugs.)* grapschen; **be up for ~s** *(sl.)* zu erwerben sein; ‹*Posten:*› frei sein; **b)** *(sl.: robbery)* Raubüberfall, *der; (burglary)* Bruch, *der (ugs.);* **c)** *(Mech.)* Greifer, *der.* *See also* **smash-and-grab [raid]**

grab: ~-bag *n. (Amer.)* Grabbelsack, *der (ugs.);* **~ handle** *n.* Haltegriff, *der;* **~ rail** *n.* Haltestange, *die*

grace [greɪs] **1.** *n.* **a)** *(charm)* Anmut, *die (geh.);* Grazie, *die;* **b)** *(attractive feature)* Charme, *der;* **airs and ~s** vornehmes Getue *(ugs. abwertend);* affektiertes Benehmen; **c)** *(accomplishment)* **social ~s** Umgangsformen *Pl.;* **d)** *(decency)* Anstand, *der;* **have the ~ to do sth.** so anständig sein und etw. tun; **he didn't even have the ~ to apologize** er brachte es nicht einmal fertig, sich zu entschuldigen; *(civility)* **with [a] good/bad ~:** bereitwillig/widerwillig; **he accepted my criticism with good/bad ~:** er trug meine Kritik mit Fassung/nahm meine Kritik mit Verärgerung hin; **e)** *(favour)* Wohlwollen, *das;* Gunst, *die; (Theol.)* Gnade, *die;* **be in sb.'s good ~s** in jmds. Gunst stehen; bei jmdm. gut angeschrieben sein *(ugs.);* **~ and favour house/residence** *etc. von der Regierung od. Krone zur Verfügung gestelltes Haus/gestellte Residenz usw.;* **act of ~:** Gnadenakt, *der;* **there, but for the ~ of God, go I** es hätte leicht auch mich erwischen können; **by the ~ of God Queen of ...:** von Gottes Gnaden Königin von ...; **state of ~** *(Theol.)* Stand der Gnade; **he fell from ~:** er fiel in Ungnade; **in the year of ~ 1892** *(literary)* im Jahr des Herrn 1892; **f)** *(favour shown by granting delay)* Frist, *die; (Commerc.)* Zahlungsfrist, *die;* **give sb. a day's ~:** jmdm. einen Tag Aufschub gewähren; **we will grant you two weeks' ~:** wir lassen Ihnen zwei Wochen Zeit; **g)** *(prayers)* Tischgebet, *das;* **say ~:** das Tischgebet sprechen; **h)** *in address* **Your G~:** Euer Gnaden; **i)** *(Mus.) see* **grace-note; j)** *(Greek Mythol.)* **the G~s** die Grazien. *See also* **saving grace. 2.** *v. t.* **a)** *(adorn)* zieren *(geh.);* schmücken; **b)** *(honour)* auszeichnen; ehren; **~ a première by** *or* **with one's presence** eine Premiere mit seiner Anwesenheit beehren *(geh.)*

graceful ['greɪsfl] *adj.* elegant; graziös ‹*Bewegung, Eleganz*›; geschmeidig ‹*Katze, Pferd*›

gracefully ['greɪsfəlɪ] *adv.* elegant; graziös ‹*tanzen, sich bewegen*›; **grow old ~:** mit Würde alt werden

gracefulness ['greɪsflnɪs] *n., no pl.* Eleganz, *die; (of movement, form, style)* Grazie, *die*

graceless ['greɪslɪs] *adj.* *(lacking sense of decency)* taktlos; *(lacking charm and elegance)* ungehobelt, schroff ‹*Benehmen, Person*›

'grace-note *n. (Mus.)* Verzierung, *die;* Manier, *die (fachspr.)*

gracious ['greɪʃəs] **1.** *adj.* **a)** liebenswürdig; freundlich; *(iron./joc.)* gütig; **~ living** kultivierter Lebensstil; **our ~ Queen** unsere gnädige Königin; **b)** *(merciful)* gnädig. **2.** *int.* **~!, good[ness] ~!, [goodness] ~ me!** [ach] du meine *od.* liebe Güte!

graciously ['greɪʃəslɪ] *adv.* liebenswürdig; freundlich; *(with condescension)* gnädig

gradation [grə'deɪʃn] *n.* **a)** *usu. in pl. (stage)* **~s of madness/an illness** Stufen *od.* Grade des Wahnsinns/einer Krankheit; **b)** *(degree in rank, merit, intensity, etc.)* Stufung, *die;* **~s of colour** Farbskala, *die;* **~ on a thermometer** Gradeinteilung, *die*

grade [greɪd] **1.** *n.* **a)** Rang, *der; (Mil.)* Dienstgrad, *der; (salary ~)* Gehaltsstufe, *die; (in things: degree of quality, size, or value)* [Handels-, Güte]klasse, *die; (of textiles)* Qualität, *die; (position, level)* Stufe, *die; (intensity of illness)* Grad, *der;* **what ~ is your job?** in welcher Gehaltsklasse sind Sie?; **a high ~ of intelligence** ein hohes Maß an Intelligenz; **b)** *(Amer. Sch.: class)* Klasse, *die;* **c)** *(Sch., Univ.: mark)* Note, *die;* Zensur, *die;* **attain ~ B or a higher ~:** eine Zwei oder eine bessere Note erreichen; **d)** *(Amer.: gradient) (ascent)* Steigung, *die; (descent)* Neigung, *die;* **at ~:** auf gleicher Höhe; ebenerdig ‹*Wohnung usw.*›; **e) on the up/down ~** *(lit.)* ansteigend/abfallend; *(fig.)* auf dem auf-/absteigenden Ast; **make the ~:** es schaffen. **2.** *v. t.* **a)** einstufen ‹*Arbeit nach Gehalt, Schüler nach Fähigkeiten, Leistungen*›; [nach Größe/Qualität] sortieren ‹*Eier, Kartoffeln*›; **b)** *(mark)* benoten; zensieren. **3.** *v. i. (pass gradually)* übergehen **(into** in + *Akk.*)

'grade crossing *n. (Amer.)* Kreuzung, *die; (of railroad tracks and road)* schienengleicher Bahnübergang

grader ['greɪdə(r)] *n. (Amer. Sch.)* **a ninth/tenth-~:** ein Schüler der 9./10. Klasse; ein Neunt-/Zehntkläßler *(südd., schweiz.)*

'grade school *n. (Amer.)* Grundschule, *die*

gradient ['greɪdɪənt] *n.* **a)** *(amount of slope) (ascent)* Steigung, *die; (descent)* Gefälle, *das; (inclined part of road)* Neigung, *die;* **a ~ of 1 in 10** eine Steigung/ein Gefälle von 10%; **b)** *([rate of] rise or fall of temperature etc.)* Gradient, *der (bes. Math.); (ascent)* Anstieg, *der; (descent)* Abfall, *der*

gradual ['grædʒʊəl] *adj.* allmählich; sanft ‹*Steigung, Gefälle usw.*›

gradually ['grædʒʊəlɪ] *adv.* allmählich; sanft ‹*ansteigen, abfallen*›

graduate 1. ['grædʒʊət] *n.* **a)** Graduierte, *der/die; (who has left university)* Akademiker, *der*/Akademikerin, *die;* **university ~:** Hochschulabsolvent, *der*/-absolventin, *die;* **he is an Oxford ~:** er hat seinen Universitätsabschluß in Oxford gemacht; **b)** *(Amer. Sch.)* Schulabgänger, *der*/-abgängerin, *die.* **2.** ['grædʒʊeɪt] *v. i.* **a)** einen akademischen Grad/Titel erwerben; **he ~d from Oxford University** er schloß sein Studium an der Universität von Oxford ab; **b)** *(Amer. Sch.)* die [Schul]abschlußprüfung bestehen **(from** an + *Dat.*); **c)** *(move up)* **he's ~d from comics to detective stories** er hat sich vom Comicleser zum Krimileser entwickelt; **d)** *(pass by degrees)* **~ into** allmählich übergehen in (+ *Akk.*). **3.** ['grædʒʊeɪt] *v. t.* **a)** *(mark out)* mit Gradeinteilung versehen; graduieren *(bes. Technik)* ‹*Thermometer*›; *(arrange in gradations)* gradweise abstufen; **b)** *(Amer. Univ.)* graduieren; *(Amer. Sch.)* aus der Schule entlassen

graduated ['grædʒʊeɪtɪd] *adj.* *(marked with lines)* mit einer Skala versehen; *(arranged in grades)* abgestuft; **~ markings** unterteilte Markierung

graduate school ['grædʒʊət sku:l] *n.* *(Amer.) Hochschulabteilung für Fortgeschrittenenstudium*

graduation [grædʒʊ'eɪʃn] *n.* **a)** *(Univ.)* Graduierung, *die;* **b)** *(Amer. Sch.)* Entlassung, *die;* **c)** *attrib.* Abschluß-; **d)** *(mark on a scale)* Graduation, *die (bes. Technik)*

graffiti [grə'fi:ti:] *n. sing. or pl.* Graffiti *Pl.*

¹graft [grɑ:ft] **1.** *n.* **a)** *(Bot.) (shoot, scion)* Edelreis, *das;* Pfropfreis, *das; (process)* Pfropfung, *die; (place)* Pfropfstelle, *die;* **b)** *(Med.)* Transplantat, *das;* **c)** *(Brit. sl.: work)* Plackerei, *die (ugs.).* **2.** *v. t.* **a)** *(Bot.)* pfropfen; **b)** *(fig.)* **~ sth. on to sth.** etw. einer Sache *(Dat.)* aufpfropfen; **c)** *(Med.)* transplantieren *(fachspr.);* verpflanzen. **3.** *v. i.* **a)** *(Bot.)* pfropfen; **b)** *(Brit. sl.: work)* schuften *(ugs.)*

²graft *(coll.)* **1.** *n. (dishonesty)* Gaunerei, *die; (profit)* Fischzug, *der.* **2.** *v. i.* mit kleinen Gaunereien Geld machen

grafter ['grɑ:ftə(r)] *n. (Brit. coll.)* **a)** *(dishonest person)* Gauner, *der;* **b)** *(worker)* Wühler, *der (ugs.);* Arbeitstier, *das (ugs.)*

Grail [greɪl] *n.* **[Holy] ~:** [Heiliger] Gral

grain [greɪn] **1.** *n.* **a)** Korn, *das; (collect.: [species of] corn)* Getreide, *das;* Korn, *das;* **b)** *(particle)* Korn, *das;* **c)** *(unit of weight)* Gran, *das (veralt.); (fig.: small amount)* **a ~ of truth** ein Gran *od.* Körnchen Wahrheit; **not a ~ of love/sense** kein Fünkchen Liebe/Funke [von] Verstand; **d)** *(texture)* Korn, *das (fachspr.);* Griff, *der; (of fibre in wood)* Maserung, *die; (in paper)* Faser, *die;* Faserverlauf, *der; (in leather)* Narbung, *die;* **go against the ~ [for sb.]** *(fig.)* jmdm. gegen den Strich gehen *(ugs.).* **2.** *v. t.* körnen ‹*Papier*›; masern ‹*Holz*›; narben ‹*Leder*›

grained [greɪnd] *adj.* gekörnt ‹*Papier*›; genarbt ‹*Leder*›; maserig, gemasert ‹*Holz*›

'grain elevator *n.* Getreideheber, *der*

grainy ['greɪnɪ] *adj.* körnig; gemasert ‹*Holz*›; genarbt ‹*Leder*›

gram [græm] *n.* Gramm, *das*

grammar ['græmə(r)] *n.* **a)** *(also book)* Grammatik, *die;* **sth. is [bad] ~:** etw. ist grammat[ikal]isch [nicht] richtig *od.* korrekt; **b)** *(Brit. coll.) see* **grammar school a**

'grammar book *n.* Grammatik, *die;* Sprachlehre, *die*

grammarian [grə'meərɪən] *n.* Grammatiker, *der*/Grammatikerin, *die*

'grammar school *n.* **a)** *(Brit.)* ≈ Gymnasium, *das;* **b)** *(Amer.)* ≈ Realschule, *die*

grammatical [grə'mætɪkl] *adj.* **a)** gram-

mat[ikal]isch richtig *od.* korrekt; **b)** *(of grammar)* grammatisch
grammatically [grə'mætɪkəlɪ] *adv.* grammat[ikal]isch ‹*richtig, falsch*›; **speak English ~:** grammatisch richtiges *od.* korrektes Englisch sprechen
gramme *see* **gram**
gramophone ['græməfəʊn] *n.* Plattenspieler, *der*
'**gramophone record** *n.* Schallplatte, *die*
gran [græn] *n. (coll./child lang.)* Oma, *die (Kinderspr./ugs.)*
granary ['grænərɪ] *n.* **a)** Getreidesilo, *der od. das;* Kornspeicher, *der;* **b)** ~ **[loaf]** Vollkornbrot, *das (mit in die Kruste eingebackenen Getreidekörnern)*
grand [grænd] **1.** *adj.* **a)** *(in official titles: chief)* Groß‹*meister, -herzog usw.*›; *see also* **cross 1 g; lodge 1 c; b)** *(most or very important)* groß; ~ **finale** großes Finale; *see also* **²slam; c)** *(final)* ~ **total** Gesamtsumme, *die;* **d)** *(main)* Haupt‹*eingang, -raum, -halle usw.*›; **e)** *(great)* groß ‹*Armee, Leidenschaft usw.*›; **f)** *(splendid)* grandios; *(impressive)* eindrucksvoll ‹*Erscheinung, Figur, Person*›; *(conducted with solemnity, splendour, etc.)* glanzvoll; **live in ~ style** auf großem Fuß leben; **g)** *(distinguished)* vornehm; **put on a ~ air** die Nase hoch tragen *(ugs. abwertend);* **h)** *(dignified, lofty)* erhaben; groß ‹*Versprechungen, Pläne, Worte*›; *(noble, admirable)* ehrwürdig; **i)** *(coll.: excellent)* großartig. **2.** *n.* **a)** *(piano)* Flügel, *der;* **b)** *pl. same (sl.: thousand pounds or (Amer.) dollars)* Riese, *der (salopp)*
grand: ~aunt *n.* Großtante, *die;* **~child** *n.* Enkel, *der*/Enkelin, *die;* Enkelkind, *das;* **~-dad[dy]** ['grændæd(ɪ)] *n. (coll./child lang.)* Großpapa, *der (fam.);* Opa, *der (Kinderspr./ugs.);* **~daughter** *n.* Enkelin, *die;* Enkeltochter, *die;* ~ '**duchess** *n.* Großherzogin, *die;* ~ '**duchy** *n.* Großherzogtum, *das;* ~ '**duke** *n.* Großherzog, *der*
grandee [græn'di:] *n.* Grande, *der*
grandeur ['grændʒə(r), 'grændjə(r)] *n.* **a)** Erhabenheit, *die;* **b)** *(splendour of living, surroundings, etc.)* Großartigkeit, *die;* Glanz, *der;* **live a life of ~:** in Glanz und Herrlichkeit leben; **c)** *(nobility of character)* Größe, *die;* Erhabenheit, *die;* **d)** *(power, rank)* Größe, *die;* Macht, *die*
'**grandfather** *n.* Großvater, *der;* ~ **clock** Standuhr, *die*
grandiloquence [græn'dɪləkwəns] *n., no pl.* Großsprecherei, *die (abwertend); (of style)* Pathos, *das*
grandiloquent [græn'dɪləkwənt] *adj.* großtönend *(geh. abwertend);* hochtrabend *(abwertend)* ‹*Stil, Worte, Rede*›
grandiose ['grændɪəʊs] *adj.* **a)** *(impressive)* grandios; **b)** *(pompous)* bombastisch *(abwertend);* großtönend *(geh. abwertend)* ‹*Worte, Art*›
grand 'jury *n. (Hist./Amer.)* Großes Geschworenengericht
grandly ['grændlɪ] *adv.* großartig; aufwendig ‹*sich kleiden*›; in großem Stil ‹*leben*›
grand: ~ma[ma] *n. (coll./child lang.)* Großmama, *die (fam.);* Oma, *die (Kinderspr./ugs.);* ~ '**master** *n.* Großmeister, *der;* **~mother** *n.* Großmutter, *die; see also* '**egg; G~ 'National** *n. (Brit. Horse-racing)* Grand National, *das;* **~nephew** *n.* Großneffe, *der*
grandness ['grændnɪs] *n., no pl.* Großartigkeit, *die; (pomp)* Pracht[fülle], *die*
grand: ~niece *n.* Großnichte, *die;* ~ **old man** *n.* Grand Old Man, *der; älteste bedeutende männliche Persönlichkeit in einem bestimmten Bereich;* **G~ Old Party** *n. (Amer.)* Republikanische Partei; ~ '**opera** *n.* große Oper; **~pa[pa]** *n. (coll./child lang.)* Großpapa, *der (fam.);* Opa, *der (Kinderspr./ugs.);* **~parent** *n. (male)* Großvater, *der; (female)* Großmutter, *die;* **~parents** Großeltern *Pl.;* ~ **pi'ano** *n.* [Konzert]flügel, *der;* **G~ Prix** [grɑ̃ 'pri:] *n.* Grand Prix, *der;* **~sire** *n. (arch.) (grandfather)* Großvater, *der; (ancestor)* Ahne, *der (geh.);* **~son** *n.* Enkel, *der;* Enkelsohn, *der;* **~stand** *n.* [Haupt]tribüne, *die;* **~stand finish** packendes Finish; **~stand view** guter Überblick **(of** über + *Akk.*); **~stand play** *(Amer.)* Effekthascherei, *die;* ~ '**tour** *n.* **a)** *(Hist.)* Bildungsreise, *die;* Kavalierstour, *die;* **b)** *(fig.)* große Fahrt *od.* Reise *(scherzh.);* **make the ~ tour of** auf große Fahrt *od.* Reise gehen zu *(scherzh.);* **~uncle** *n.* Großonkel, *der*
grange [greɪndʒ] *n.* Gutshof, *der;* Landsitz, *der*
granite ['grænɪt] *n.* **a)** Granit, *der;* **b)** *(fig.: unyieldingness)* Unnachgiebigkeit, *die*
granny (grannie) ['grænɪ] *n.* **a)** *(coll./child lang.)* Großmama, *die (fam.);* Oma, *die (Kinderspr./ugs.);* **b)** *see* **granny knot**
granny: ~ flat *n.* Einliegerwohnung, *die;* ~ **knot** *n.* Altweiberknoten, *der (Seemannsspr.)*
grant [grɑ:nt] **1.** *v. t.* **a)** *(consent to fulfil)* erfüllen ‹*Wunsch*›; erhören ‹*Gebet, Flehen*›; stattgeben (+ *Dat.*) ‹*Gesuch*›; gewähren ‹*Gunst*›; ~ **sb. his wish** jmdm. seinen Wunsch erfüllen; **b)** *(concede, give)* gewähren; gestatten ‹*Blick*›; geben ‹*Zeit*›; bewilligen ‹*Geldmittel*›; verleihen ‹*akademischen Grad, Auszeichnung*›; zugestehen ‹*Recht*›; erteilen ‹*Erlaubnis*›; *(transfer legally)* übertragen **(to** auf + *Akk.*); **c)** *(in argument)* zugeben; einräumen *(geh.);* **~ed that ...:** zugegeben, daß ...; **~ing this to be true** *or* **that this is true** nehmen wir einmal an, daß das stimmt; **take sb./sth. [too much] for ~ed** sich *(Dat.)* jmds. [allzu] sicher sein/etw. für [allzu] selbstverständlich halten; **he's a good fellow, [that] I ~ you** er ist ein guter Kumpel *od.* Kerl, das gebe ich zu; **I beg your pardon – G~ed** Entschuldigen Sie! – Bitte; **nobody likes to be taken for ~ed** keiner mag es, wenn man sich nicht um ihn bemüht. **2.** *n.* **a)** *(sum of money)* Zuschuß, *der; (financial aid [to student])* [Studien]beihilfe, *die; (scholarship)* Stipendium, *das;* **b)** *(conceding, allowing) (of request, respite)* Gewährung, *die; (of pension, holiday)* Bewilligung, *die; (of award, degree)* Verleihung, *die; (of permission)* Erteilung, *die*
'**grant-aided school** *n. (Brit.)* subventionierte Schule
grant-in-'aid *n., pl.* **grants-in-aid** *(Educ.)* [staatlicher Schul]zuschuß
granular ['grænjʊlə(r)] *adj.* körnig; granulös *(Med.)*
granulate ['grænjʊleɪt] *v. t.* granulieren *(bes. Technik);* **~d sugar** [Zucker]raffinade, *die;* Kristallzucker, *der*
granule ['grænju:l] *n.* Körnchen, *das*
grape [greɪp] *n.* Weintraube, *die;* Weinbeere, *die;* **a bunch of ~s** eine Traube; **the juice of the ~** *(literary)* der Saft der Rebe[n] *(dichter.);* **[it's] sour ~s** *(fig.)* die Trauben hängen zu hoch
grape: ~fruit *n., pl. same* Grapefruit, *die;* ~ **harvest** *n.* Weinlese, *die;* ~ '**hyacinth** *n.* Traubenhyazinthe, *die;* **~-juice** *n.* Traubensaft, *der;* **~-shot** *n., pl. same (Mil. Hist.)* Kartätsche, *die;* **~vine** *n.* **a)** Wein, *der;* **b)** *(fig.)* **the ~vine** die Flüsterpropaganda; **I heard [it] on the ~-vine that they were getting married** es wird geflüstert, daß sie heiraten wollen
graph [græf, grɑ:f] **1.** *n.* graphische Darstellung; Graph, *der (Math.).* **2.** *v. t.* graphisch darstellen
graphic ['græfɪk] **1.** *adj.* **a)** graphisch; ~ **art** Graphik, *die;* ~ **artist** Graphiker, *der*/Graphikerin, *die;* **b)** *(clear, vivid)* plastisch; anschaulich; **in ~ detail** in allen Einzelheiten. **2.** *n.* **a)** *(product)* Graphik, *die;* **b)** *in pl. see* **graphics**
graphical ['græfɪkl] *see* **graphic 1**
graphically ['græfɪkəlɪ] *adv.* **a)** *(clearly, vividly)* plastisch; anschaulich; **b)** *(by use of graphic methods)* graphisch
graphic 'arts *n. pl.* Graphik, *die*
graphics ['græfɪks] *n. (design and decoration)* graphische Gestaltung; *(use of diagrams)* graphische Darstellung; **computer ~:** Computergraphik, *die*
graphite ['græfaɪt] *n.* Graphit, *der*
graphologist [grə'fɒlədʒɪst] *n.* Graphologe, *der*/Graphologin, *die*
graphology [grə'fɒlədʒɪ] *n.* Graphologie, *die*
'**graph paper** *n.* Diagrammpapier, *das*
grapnel ['græpnəl] *n.* Draggen, *der (bes. Seew.);* Dreghaken, *der; (to seize ship)* Enterhaken, *der*
grapple ['græpl] **1.** *v. i. (in fighting)* handgemein werden; **they ~d together** *(Wrestling)* sie rangen miteinander; ~ **with** *(fig.)* sich auseinandersetzen *od. (ugs.)* herumschlagen mit; ~ **with death** mit dem Tode ringen. **2.** *v. t.* **a)** *(seize, fasten)* [mit Enterhaken] festhaken ‹*Schiff*›; *(drag)* [mit Dreghaken] absuchen ‹*Fluß*›; **b)** *(grip with hands)* packen
grappling ['græplɪŋ]: **~-hook, ~-iron** *ns. see* **grapnel**
grasp [grɑ:sp] **1.** *v. i.* ~ **at** *(lit. or fig.)* ergreifen; sich stürzen auf (+ *Akk.*) ‹*Angebot*›; *see also* **straw b. 2.** *v. t.* **a)** *(clutch at, seize)* ergreifen *(auch fig.);* **manage to ~:** zu fassen bekommen; **b)** *(hold firmly)* festhalten; ~ **sb. in one's arms** jmdn. [fest] in den Armen halten; ~ **the nettle** *(fig.)* das Problem beherzt anpacken; **c)** *(understand)* verstehen; erfassen ‹*Bedeutung*›. **3.** *n.* **a)** *(firm hold)* Griff, *der;* **twist from sb.'s ~:** sich jmds. Griff *(Dat.)* entwinden; **he had my hand in a firm ~:** er hielt meine Hand mit festem Griff; **tighten/loosen one's ~:** fester zupacken/den Griff lockern; **sth. is within/beyond sb.'s ~:** etwas ist in/außer jmds. Reichweite; **success was almost within/was completely beyond his ~** *(fig.)* der Erfolg war zum Greifen nah/in unerreichbarer Ferne; **b)** *(mental hold)* **have a good ~ of sth.** etw. gut beherrschen; **his ~ of this subject is remarkable** er beherrscht das Thema außergewöhnlich gut; **sth. is beyond/within sb.'s ~:** etw. überfordert jmds. [intellektuelle] Fähigkeiten/kann von jmdm. verstanden werden
graspable ['grɑ:spəbl] *adj. (fig.)* verständlich
grasping ['grɑ:spɪŋ] *adj. (greedy)* habgierig
grass [grɑ:s] **1.** *n.* **a)** Gras, *das;* **be as green as ~** *(fig.)* noch feucht hinter den Ohren sein *(ugs.);* **not let the ~ grow under one's feet** *(fig. coll.)* die Sache nicht auf die lange Bank schieben *(ugs.);* **the ~ is always greener on the other side [of the hill** *or* **fence]** *(prov.)* die Kirschen aus Nachbars Garten schmecken immer viel besser; **b)** *no pl. (lawn)* Rasen, *der;* **c)** *no pl. (grazing, pasture)* Weide, *die; (pasture land)* Weideland, *das;* **be out at ~:** auf der Weide sein; **put** *or* **turn out to ~:** auf die Weide treiben *od.* führen; *(fig.)* in den Ruhestand versetzen; nicht mehr zur Arbeit einsetzen ‹*Pferd*›; **d)** *(sl.: marijuana)* Grass, *das (ugs.);* **e)** *(Brit. sl.: police informer)* Spitzel, *der.* **2.** *v. t.* **a)** *(cover with turf)* mit Rasen bedecken; **b)** *(Brit. sl.: betray)* verpfeifen *(ugs.).* **3.** *v. i. (Brit. sl.: inform police)* singen *(salopp);* ~ **on sb.** jmdn. verpfeifen *(ugs.)*
grass: ~-box *n.* Grasfangkorb, *der;* ~ '**court** *n.* Rasenplatz, *der;* Grasplatz, *der;* **~-green** *adj.* grasgrün; **~hopper** *n.* Grashüpfer, *der; see also* **knee-high; ~land** *n.* Grasland, *das; (for grazing)* Weideland, *das;* **~-root[s]** *attrib. adj. (Polit.)* Basis-; ~ **roots** *n. pl. (fig.) (source)* Wurzeln; *(Polit.)* Basis, *die;* **~-seed** *n.* Grassamen, *der;* ~ '**skirt** *n.* Baströckchen, *das;*

~ **snake** *n.* **a)** *(Brit.: ringed snake)* Ringelnatter, *die;* **b)** *(Amer.: green snake)* Grasnatter, *die;* ~ **widow** *n.* Strohwitwe, *die (ugs. scherzh.);* ~ **widower** *n.* Strohwitwer, *der (ugs. scherzh.)*

grassy ['grɑːsɪ] *adj.* mit Gras bewachsen

[1]**grate** [greɪt] *n.* Rost, *der; (fireplace)* Kamin, *der*

[2]**grate 1.** *v. t.* **a)** *(reduce to particles)* reiben; *(less finely)* raspeln; **b)** *(grind)* ~ **one's teeth in anger/in one's sleep** vor Wut/im Schlaf mit den Zähnen knirschen; **c)** *(utter in harsh tone)* [durch die Zähne] knirschen. **2.** *v. i.* **a)** *(rub)* knirschen; **the door ~s [up]on its hinges** die Tür knirscht in den Angeln; **b)** *(have irritating effect)* ~ **[up]on sb./sb.'s nerves** jmdm. auf die Nerven gehen; **c)** *(sound harshly)* knirschen; **her shrill voice ~d [up]on our ears** ihre schrille Stimme gellte uns in den Ohren

grateful ['greɪtfl] *adj.* **a)** dankbar (**to** *Dat.*); **a ~ word of thanks** ein herzliches Wort des Dankes; **b)** *(pleasant, agreeable)* wohltuend

gratefully ['greɪtfəlɪ] *adv.* dankbar; **thank sb. ~:** jmdm. aufrichtig danken

grater ['greɪtə(r)] *n.* Reibe, *die; (less fine)* Raspel, *die*

gratification [grætɪfɪ'keɪʃn] *n.* **a)** *(pleasure)* Genugtuung, *die;* **the ~ of doing sth.** die Genugtuung, etw. zu tun; **b)** *(satisfaction) see* **gratify b:** Befriedigung, *die;* Erfüllung, *die;* Stillung, *die*

gratify ['grætɪfaɪ] *v. t.* **a)** *(please)* freuen; **be gratified by** *or* **with** *or* **at sth.** über etw. *(Akk.)* erfreut sein; **I was gratified** *or* **it gratified me to hear that ...:** mit Genugtuung erfuhr ich, daß ...; **b)** *(satisfy)* befriedigen ‹*Neugier, Bedürfnis, Eitelkeit*›; erfüllen ‹*Wunsch*›; stillen ‹*Sehnsucht, Verlangen*›

gratifying ['grætɪfaɪɪŋ] *adj.* erfreulich

gratin ['grætæ̃] *n. (Cookery)* Gratin, *das;* **cauliflower au ~** [əʊ 'grætæ̃] gratinierter Blumenkohl

grating ['greɪtɪŋ] *n. (framework)* Gitter, *das*

gratis ['greɪtɪs, 'grætɪs, 'grɑːtɪs] **1.** *adv.* gratis, kostenlos ‹*bekommen, abgeben*›; umsonst, unentgeltlich ‹*tun*›. **2.** *adj.* gratis *nicht attr.;* Gratis‹*mahlzeit, -vorstellung usw.*›

gratitude ['grætɪtjuːd] *n., no pl.* Dankbarkeit, *die* (**to** gegenüber); **show one's ~ to sb.** sich jmdm. gegenüber dankbar zeigen

gratuitous [grə'tjuːɪtəs] *adj.* **a)** *(uncalled-for, motiveless)* grundlos; unnötig; *(without logical reason)* unbegründet; **b)** *(got or given free)* unentgeltlich ‹*Dienstleistung*›

gratuitously [grə'tjuːɪtəslɪ] *adv.* **a)** *(without motive or reason)* ohne Grund; **b)** *(free of cost)* unentgeltlich

gratuity [grə'tjuːɪtɪ] *n.* **a)** *(formal: tip)* Trinkgeld, *das;* **b)** *(Brit.: bounty)* Sonderzuwendung, *die*

graunch [grɔːnʃ] **1.** *v. t.* ~ **the gears** knirschend schalten. **2.** *v. i. (make grinding sound)* knirschen

[1]**grave** [greɪv] *n.* Grab, *das;* **the house was as quiet** *or* **silent** *or* **still as the ~:** im Haus herrschte Grabesstille; **dig one's own ~** *(fig.)* sich *(Dat.)* selbst sein Grab graben *(fig.);* **he would turn in his ~** *(fig.)* er würde sich im Grabe herumdrehen; **sb. is walking on** *or* **over my/his** *etc.* ~ *(fig.)* es überläuft mich/ihn *usw.* eiskalt; **carry a scar** *etc.* **to one's ~:** eine Narbe *usw.* bis an sein Lebensende tragen; **a message from beyond the ~:** eine Botschaft aus dem Jenseits; **take a secret to the ~:** ein Geheimnis mit ins Grab nehmen; *see also* **cradle 1 a; foot 1 a**

[2]**grave** *adj.* **a)** *(important, dignified, solemn)* ernst; **b)** *(formidable, serious)* schwer, gravierend ‹*Fehler, Irrtum, Verfehlung*›; ernst ‹*Situation, Lage, Schwierigkeit*›; groß ‹*Gefahr, Risiko, Verantwortung*›; schlimm ‹*Nachricht, Zeichen*›

[3]**grave** [grɑːv, greɪv] *adj. (Ling.)* ~ **accent** Accent grave, *der;* Gravis, *der*

grave-digger ['greɪvdɪgə(r)] *n.* Totengräber, *der*

gravel ['grævl] **1.** *n.* **a)** *(small stones)* Kies, *der; attrib.* ~ **path/pit** Kiesweg, *der*/-grube, *die;* **b)** *(Geol., Mining)* Geröll, *das;* **c)** *(Med.)* **[bladder/kidney]** ~**:** Harn-/Nierengrieß, *der.* **2.** *v. t., (Brit.)* **-ll-** kiesen

gravelly ['grævəlɪ] *adj.* **a)** kieshaltig ‹*Boden*›; **b)** rauh, heiser ‹*Stimme*›

gravely ['greɪvlɪ] *adv.* **a)** *(in grave manner)* ernst; **b)** *(seriously)* ernstlich; **be ~ mistaken** sich schwer irren *(ugs.)*

graven image [greɪvn 'ɪmɪdʒ] *n.* Götzenbild, *das*

grave [greɪv]: **~side** *n.* **at the ~side** am Grab; **~stone** *n.* Grabstein, *der;* **~yard** *n.* Friedhof, *der;* **be a ~yard of reputations** manch einen guten Ruf zerstört haben

graving dock ['greɪvɪŋ dɒk] *see* **dry dock**

gravitas ['grævɪtɑːs] *n. (literary)* Gravität, *die (veralt.)*

gravitate ['grævɪteɪt] *v. i.* gravitieren *(Phys., Astron., geh.);* **young people ~ to[wards] the cities** junge Leute zieht es in die Städte

gravitation [grævɪ'teɪʃn] *n.* Gravitation, *die;* Schwerkraft, *die; (fig.)* Streben, *das*

gravitational [grævɪ'teɪʃənl] *adj.* Gravitations‹*feld, -energie usw.*›; ~ **pull** Anziehungskraft, *die;* ~ **force** Schwerkraft, *die*

gravity ['grævɪtɪ] *n.* **a)** *(solemnity)* Feierlichkeit, *die;* **b)** *(importance) (of mistake, offence)* Schwere, *die; (of situation)* Ernst, *der;* **c)** *(seriousness, staidness)* Ernst, *der;* **the ~ of his manner** seine Ernsthaftigkeit; **keep** *or* **preserve one's ~:** ernst bleiben; **d)** *(Phys., Astron.)* Gravitation, *die;* Schwerkraft, *die;* **the law/force of ~:** das Gravitationsgesetz/die Schwerkraft; **centre of ~** *(lit. or fig.)* Schwerpunkt, *der;* **specific ~** *(Phys.)* spezifisches Gewicht; Wichte, *die (fachspr.)*

'**gravity feed** *n.* Schwerkraftzufuhr, *die (Technik)*

gravy ['greɪvɪ] *n.* **a)** *(juices)* Bratensaft, *der;* **b)** *(dressing)* [Braten]soße, *die;* **c)** *(sl.: money)* Nebenverdienst, *der; (tip)* Trinkgeld, *das*

gravy: ~-boat *n.* Sauciere, *die;* Soßenschüssel, *die;* **~ train** *n.* **ride/board the ~ train** *(sl.)* leichtes Geld machen *(ugs.)*

gray *etc. (Amer.) see* **grey** *etc.*

grayling ['greɪlɪŋ] *n., pl. same (Zool.)* Äsche, *die*

[1]**graze** [greɪz] **1.** *v. i.* grasen; weiden. **2.** *v. t.* **a)** *(feed)* weiden ‹*Schafe, Rinder*›; **b)** *(feed on)* abweiden ‹*Feld, Wiese*›

[2]**graze 1.** *n.* Schürfwunde, *die.* **2.** *v. t.* **a)** *(touch lightly)* streifen; **b)** *(scrape)* abschürfen ‹*Haut*›; zerkratzen ‹*Oberfläche*›; ~ **one's knee/elbow** sich *(Dat.)* das Knie/den Ellbogen aufschürfen. **3.** *v. i.* ~ **against/by** *or* **past the wall** an der Mauer entlang-/vorbeischrammen

grazier ['greɪzɪə(r), 'greɪʒə(r)] *n.* **a)** Viehzüchter, *der;* **b)** *(Austral.: sheep-farmer)* Schafzüchter, *der*

grazing ['greɪzɪŋ] **1.** *n. (feeding)* Weiden, *das; (land)* Weide, *die;* Weideland, *das.* **2.** *adj.* weidend; ~ **land** Weideland, *das;* ~ **rights** Weiderecht, *das*

grease 1. [griːs] *n.* Fett, *das; (lubricant)* Schmierfett, *das.* **2.** [griːz, griːs] *v. t.* einfetten; einreiben ‹*Haut, Rücken usw.*›; *(lubricate)* schmieren; **like ~d lightning** *(coll.)* wie ein geölter Blitz *(ugs.);* ~ **sb.'s palm** *(fig.)* jmdn. schmieren *(salopp abwertend);* ~ **the wheels** *(fig.)* der Sache *(Dat.)* nachhelfen

grease: ~-gun *n.* Fettpresse, *die (Technik);* ~ **monkey** *n. (sl.)* Schmiermaxe, *der (ugs.);* **~-paint** *n.* [Fett]schminke, *die;* **~-proof** *adj.* fettdicht; **~-proof paper** Pergament- *od.* Butterbrotpapier, *das*

greasy ['griːzɪ, 'griːsɪ] *adj.* **a)** fettig; fett ‹*Essen*›; speckig ‹*Kleidung*›; *(lubricated)* geschmiert; *(slippery, dirty with lubricant)* schmierig; **b)** *(fig.: unctuous)* schmierig *(abwertend)*

great [greɪt] **1.** *adj.* **a)** *(large)* groß; ~ **big** *(coll.)* riesengroß *(ugs.);* ~ **thick** *(coll.)* mordsdick *(ugs.);* **give sb. a ~ big hug** *(coll.)* jmdn. mit großer Herzlichkeit umarmen; **a ~ many** sehr viele; **a ~ amount of patience** eine Menge Geduld *(ugs.); see also* [2]**deal; b)** *(beyond the ordinary)* groß; sehr gut ‹*Freund*›; sehr schwer ‹*Krise*›; **a ~ [old] age** ein hohes Alter; **take ~ care of/a ~ interest in** sich sehr kümmern um/interessieren für; **c)** *(important)* groß ‹*Tag, Ereignis, Attraktion, Hilfe*›; *(powerful, influential, of remarkable ability)* groß ‹*Person, Komponist, Schriftsteller*›; *(impressive)* großartig; **the ~ thing is** die Hauptsache ist; *in titles or names* **Peter the G~:** Peter der Große; *in excl.* **G~ Scott!** großer Gott!; *(having much skill)* **be ~ at sth.** in etw. *(Dat.)* ganz groß sein *(ugs.); (having much knowledge)* **be ~ on modern music** in zeitgenössischer Musik sehr beschlagen sein *(ugs.);* **be a ~ one for sth.** etw. sehr gern tun; *see also* **spirit 1 h; d)** *(coll.: splendid)* großartig; **e)** *(in relationship)* Groß‹*onkel, -tante, -neffe, -nichte*›; Ur‹*großmutter, -großvater, -enkel, -enkelin*›; **~-~-:** Urgroß‹*onkel, -tante, -neffe, -nichte*›; Urur‹*großmutter, -großvater, -enkel, -enkelin*›. **2.** *n.* **a)** *(person)* Größe, *die;* **literary/football ~s** literarische Größen/Fußballgrößen; *as pl.* **the ~:** die Großen [der Geschichte/Literatur *usw.*]; **the ~est** *(sl.)* der/die Größte/die Größten *(ugs.);* **b) G~s** *(Brit. Univ.)* klassische Philologie

Great: ~ '**Bear** *n. (Astron.)* Großer Bär; ~ '**Britain** *pr. n.* Großbritannien *(das);* **g~coat** *n.* [Winter]mantel, *der;* ~ '**Dane** *n.* deutsche Dogge

Greater: ~ '**London** *pr. n.* Groß-London; ~ **London** '**Council** *n. (Hist.)* Stadtrat von Groß-London

great: ~-hearted *adj.* hochherzig; großmütig; ~ '**house** *n.* Gutshaus, *das;* Herrenhaus, *das;* **the ~ houses of England** englische Schlösser und Adelssitze; **G~** '**Lakes** *pr. n. pl.* Große Seen *Pl.*

greatly ['greɪtlɪ] *adv.* sehr; höchst ‹*verärgert*›; stark ‹*beeinflußt, beunruhigt*›; weit ‹*überlegen*›; bedeutend ‹*verbessert*›; **sth. is ~ to be feared** etw. muß ernstlich befürchtet werden; **it doesn't ~ matter** es ist nicht so wichtig

greatness ['greɪtnɪs] *n., no pl.* Größe, *die; (extent, degree)* Ausmaß, *das;* ~ **of heart/mind/soul** Hochherzigkeit, *die*/Großmut, *die*/Seelengröße, *die*

Great: ~ '**Power** *n.* Großmacht, *die;* ~ **Salt** '**Lake** *pr. n.* Großer Salzsee; **g~ tit** *n. (Ornith.)* Kohlmeise, *die;* **g~** '**toe** *n.* großer Zeh; ~ '**War** *n.* erster Weltkrieg

grebe [griːb] *n. (Ornith.)* Lappentaucher, *der*

Grecian ['griːʃn] **1.** *adj.* griechisch. **2.** *n.* Grieche, *der*/Griechin, *die*

Greece [griːs] *pr. n.* Griechenland *(das)*

greed [griːd] *n.* Gier, *die* (**for** nach); *(gluttony)* Gefräßigkeit, *die (abwertend); (of animal)* Freßgier, *die;* ~ **for money/power** Geld-/Machtgier, *die*

greedily ['griːdɪlɪ] *adv.* gierig

greediness ['griːdɪnɪs] *n., no pl.* Gier, *die*

greedy ['griːdɪ] *adj.* gierig; *(gluttonous)* gefräßig *(abwertend); (eager)* begierig; **be ~ for sth.** nach etw. gieren; ~ **for money/power/success** geldgierig/machthungrig/erfolgshungrig; **be ~ to do/get sth.** etw. unbedingt tun/bekommen wollen

'**greedy-guts** *n. sing. (coll.)* Vielfraß, *der (ugs.)*

Greek [griːk] **1.** *adj.* griechisch; **sb. is ~:** jmd. ist Grieche/Griechin; *see also* **calends; English 1. 2.** *n.* **a)** *(person)* Grieche, *der*/Griechin, *die;* **b)** *(language)* Griechisch, *das;* **modern ~:** Neugriechisch, *das;* **it's all ~ to me** *(fig.)* das sind mir *od.* für mich böhmische Dörfer; *see also* **English 2 a**

Greek: ~ 'Church *see* **~ Orthodox Church; ~ 'god** *n. (fig.)* Adonis, *der;* **~ Orthodox 'Church** *n.* griechisch-orthodoxe Kirche

green [gri:n] **1.** *adj.* **a)** grün; **have ~ fingers** *or* **a ~ thumb** *(fig.)* eine grüne Hand haben *(ugs.);* **~ vegetables** Grüngemüse, *das;* **b)** *(Polit.)* **G~:** grün; **he/she is ~:** er ist ein Grüner/sie ist eine Grüne; **the G~s** die Grünen; **c)** *(environmentally safe)* ökologisch; **d)** *(unripe, young, tender)* grün ‹*Obst, Apfel, Banane, Zweig*›; **e)** *(not dried, seasoned, smoked, or tanned)* grün ‹*Holz, Speck, Heringe*›; nicht gegerbt ‹*Fell*›; **f)** *(pale)* **his face turned ~ at the sight of the blood** beim Anblick des Blutes wurde er ganz grün im Gesicht; **be/turn ~ with envy/jealousy** vor Neid/Eifersucht grün sein/werden; **g)** *(immature, naïve)* unreif; *(gullible)* naiv; einfältig; *(inexperienced)* grün. **2.** *n.* **a)** *(colour)* Grün, *das;* **b)** *(piece of land)* Grünfläche, *die;* **village ~:** Dorfanger, *der;* **c)** *in pl. (green vegetables)* Grüngemüse, *das;* **d)** *(verdure, vegetation)* Grün, *das;* **e)** *(Snooker)* grüne Kugel; **f)** *(~ clothes)* **dressed in ~:** grün gekleidet; **g)** *(traffic-light)* Grün, *das;* **the traffic-light is at ~:** die Ampel steht auf Grün. **3.** *v. i.* grünen

green: ~back *n. (Amer.)* [Geld]schein, *der;* **~ 'belt** *n.* Grüngürtel, *der;* **~ 'card** *n. (Insurance)* grüne Karte *(Verkehrsw.)*

greenery ['gri:nərı] *n., no pl.* Grün, *das*

green: ~-eyed *adj.* grünäugig; *(fig.)* neidisch; **be ~-eyed** grüne Augen haben; **~-'field site** *n.* Bauplatz im Grünen; **~finch** *n.* Grünfink, *der;* **~fly** *n. (Brit.)* grüne Blattlaus; **~gage** *n.* Reineclaude, *die;* **~grocer** *n. (Brit.)* Obst- und Gemüsehändler, *der*/-händlerin, *die; see also* **baker; ~grocery** *n. (Brit.)* **a)** Obst- und Gemüsehandlung, *die;* **b)** *in sing. or pl. (goods)* Obst und Gemüse; **~horn** *n.* Greenhorn, *das;* **~house** *n.* Gewächshaus, *das;* **~house effect** *(Ecol.)* Treibhauseffekt, *der*

greenish ['gri:nıʃ] *adj.* grünlich

'greenkeeper *n. (Golf)* Golfwart, *der*

Greenland ['gri:nlənd] *pr. n.* Grönland *(das)*

Greenlander ['gri:nləndə(r)] *n.* Grönländer, *der*/Grönländerin, *die*

green 'light *n.* **a)** grünes Licht; *(as signal)* Grün, *das;* **it's a ~ light** die Ampel ist grün; **b)** *(fig. coll.)* **give sb./get the ~ light** jmdm. grünes Licht geben/grünes Licht erhalten

greenness ['gri:nnıs] *n., no pl.* **a)** *(of colour)* Grün, *das;* grüne Farbe; **b)** *(of sth. covered with herbage)* Grün, *das;* **c)** *(unripeness)* grüner Zustand; **d)** *(fig.: youth, immaturity)* Unreife, *die; (inexperience)* Unerfahrenheit, *die; (gullibility)* Naivität, *die;* Einfalt, *die*

green: G~ 'Paper *n. (Brit.) öffentliches Diskussionspapier über die Regierungspolitik;* **G~ Party** *n. (Polit.)* die Grünen; **~ 'pepper** *see* **pepper 1 b; ~ revo'lution** *n.* grüne Revolution; **~-room** *n. (Theatre)* Konversationszimmer, *das;* **~sward** *n. (literary)* Grünfläche, *die*

Greenwich ['grınıdʒ, 'grenıdʒ, 'grınıtʃ, 'grenıtʃ] *n.* **~ [mean] time** Greenwicher Zeit; [mittlere] Greenwich-Zeit

'greenwood *n.* [grüner] Wald

greet [gri:t] *v. t.* **a)** begrüßen; *(in passing)* grüßen; *(receive)* empfangen; **~ sb. with sth.** jmdn. mit etw. begrüßen/grüßen/empfangen; **b)** *(meet)* empfangen; **~ sb.'s eyes/ears** sich jmds. Augen *(Dat.)* darbieten/an jmds. Ohr *(Akk.)* dringen

greeting ['gri:tıŋ] *n.* Begrüßung, *die; (in passing)* Gruß, *der; (words)* Grußformel, *die; (reception)* Empfang, *der;* **please give my ~s to your parents** grüßen Sie bitte Ihre Eltern von mir; **my husband also sends his ~s** mein Mann läßt auch grüßen

greeting: ~[s] card *n.* Grußkarte, *die; (for anniversary, birthday)* Glückwunschkarte, *die;* **~[s] telegram** *n.* Glückwunschtelegramm, *das*

gregarious [grı'geərıəs] *adj.* **a)** *(Zool.)* gesellig; Herden‹*tier, -trieb*›; **b)** *(fond of company)* gesellig

gregariousness [grı'geərıəsnıs] *n., no pl.* **a)** *(Zool.)* Herdenleben, *das;* **b)** *(of person)* Geselligkeit, *die*

Gregorian [grı'gɔ:rıən] *adj.* gregorianisch; **~ calendar/chant** Gregorianischer Kalender/Gesang

Gregory ['gregərı] *pr. n. (Hist., as name of pope)* Gregor

gremlin ['gremlın] *n. (coll. joc.)* ≈ Kobold, *der*

grenade [grı'neıd] *n.* Granate, *die; see also* **hand-grenade**

Grenadier Guards [grenədıə(r) 'gɑ:dz] *n. pl. (Brit.)* Grenadiergarde, *die*

grew *see* **grow**

grey [greı] **1.** *adj.* **a)** *(lit. or fig.)* grau; **he** *or* **his hair went** *or* **turned ~:** er wurde grau *od.* ergraute; **grow ~ in sb.'s service** *(fig.)* in jmds. Diensten ergrauen; **~ area** *(fig.)* Grauzone, *die;* **b)** *(anonymous)* gesichtslos ‹*Person*›. **2.** *n.* **a)** Grau, *das;* **b)** *(~ clothes)* **dressed in ~:** grau gekleidet; **c)** *(horse)* Grauschimmel, *der*

grey: ~beard *n.* Graubart, *der (ugs.);* **~ cells** *n. pl.* graue Substanz *(Anat.);* **~ 'éminence** *see* **éminence grise; G~ Friar** *n.* Franziskaner, *der;* **~ goose** *n.* Graugans, *die;* **~-haired, ~-headed** *adjs.* grauhaarig; **~-hen** *n.* Birkhenne, *die*

'greyhound *n.* Windhund, *der*

'greyhound-racing *n.* Windhundrennen, *das*

greyish ['greııʃ] *adj.* gräulich

greylag ['greılæg] *n.* **~ [goose]** Graugans, *die*

grey: ~ matter *n.* graue Substanz *(Anat.); (fig.: intelligence)* graue Zellen; **~ 'squirrel** *n.* Grauhörnchen, *das*

grid [grıd] *n.* **a)** *(grating)* Rost, *der;* **b)** *(of lines)* Gitter[netz], *das;* **c)** *(for supply)* [Versorgungs]netz, *das;* **d)** *see* **gridiron a; e)** *(Motor-racing)* Startmarkierung, *die;* **f)** *(of town streets)* rechtwinkliges Straßennetz; **~ pattern** rechtwinkliges Straßensystem; **g)** *(Electronics)* Gitter, *das*

griddle ['grıdl] *n. [beheizbare] runde Eisenplatte zum Backen;* **~ cake** Crêpe, *die*

'gridiron *n.* **a)** *(Cookery)* Bratrost, *der;* **b)** *(Amer.: football field)* Footballfeld, *das*

grief [gri:f] *n.* **a)** Kummer, *der* **(over, at** über + *Akk.,* um); *(at loss of sb.)* Trauer, *die* **(for** um); **she felt [real] ~:** es bekümmerte sie sehr; **be a [great] ~ to sb.** jmdm. [großen *od.* viel] Kummer machen; **come to ~** *(fail)* scheitern; **the car came to ~:** das Auto wurde beschädigt *(ugs. scherzh.);* **b) good** *or* **great ~!** guter *od.* großer Gott!

'grief-stricken *adj.* untröstlich **(at** über + *Akk.*); **say sth. in a ~ voice** etw. mit vor Kummer erstickter Stimme sagen; **the ~ look on his face** sein gramvolles Gesicht

grievance ['gri:vəns] *n. (complaint)* Beschwerde, *die;* Klage, *die; (resentment, grudge)* Groll, *der;* **air one's ~s** seine Beschwerden vorbringen/seinem Groll Luft machen; **I have no ~s against him personally** ich habe nichts gegen ihn persönlich

'grievance procedure *n.* Schlichtungsverfahren, *das*

grieve [gri:v] **1.** *v. t.* betrüben; bekümmern. **2.** *v. i.* trauern **(for um)** ; **my heart ~s** *or* **I ~ for you** *(sympathize)* ich trauere mit dir; **~ over sb./sth.** jmdm./einer Sache nachtrauern

grievous ['gri:vəs] *adj.* **a)** *(causing grief)* schmerzlich; **b)** *(flagrant, heinous)* schwer; **~ wrong[s]** schreiendes Unrecht; **c)** *(severe)* schwer ‹*Verwundung, Krankheit*›; groß ‹*Schmerz*›; **d)** *(bringing serious trouble)* folgenschwer ‹*Irrtum, Dummheit*›; schwer ‹*Autounfall*›; **~ bodily harm** *(Law)* schwere Körperverletzung

grievously ['gri:vəslı] *adv.* **a)** *(seriously)* schwer ‹*verletzt, benachteiligt*›; **b)** *(strongly, exceedingly)* stark, ernstlich ‹*beunruhigt*›

griffin ['grıfın] *n.* Greif, *der*

[1]**grill** [grıl] **1.** *v. t.* **a)** *(cook)* grillen; **b)** *(fig.: question)* in die Mangel nehmen *(ugs.).* **2.** *v. i.* grillen; **be ~ing in the hot sun** *(fig.)* sich von *od.* in der heißen Sonne braten lassen *(ugs.).* **3.** *n.* **a)** *(Gastr.)* Grillgericht, *das;* **mixed ~:** Mixed grill, *der;* gemischte Grillplatte; **b)** *(restaurant)* Grillrestaurant, *das;* **c)** *(on cooker)* Grill, *der;* **d)** *see* **gridiron a**

grille ([2]grill) *n.* **a)** *(grating)* Gitter, *das;* **b)** *(Motor Veh.)* [Kühler]grill, *der*

'grill-room *see* [1]**grill 3 b**

grim [grım] *adj. (stern)* streng; grimmig ‹*Lächeln, Gesicht, Blick, Schweigen, Humor*›; furchterregend ‹*Krieger*›; *(unrelenting, merciless, severe)* erbittert ‹*Widerstand, Kampf, Schlacht*›; grimmig ‹*Entschlossenheit, Winter*›; eisern ‹*Vorsatz*›; *(sinister, ghastly)* grauenvoll ‹*Aufgabe, Anblick, Nachricht*›; grausig ‹*Wetter, Zeiten*›; trostlos ‹*Wetter, Winter, Tag, Landschaft, Aussichten*›; *(mirthless)* grimmig ‹*Humor, Spaß*›; **hold** *or* **hang** *or* **cling on [to sth.] like ~ death** sich mit aller Kraft [an etw. *(Dat.)*] festklammern; *see also* **reaper b**

grimace [grı'meıs] **1.** *n.* Grimasse, *die;* **make a ~:** eine Grimasse machen *od.* schneiden. **2.** *v. i.* Grimassen machen *od.* schneiden; **~ with pain/disgust** vor Schmerz/Ekel das Gesicht verziehen

grime [graım] *n.* Schmutz, *der; (soot)* Ruß, *der*

grimly ['grımlı] *adv.* grimmig; eisern ‹*entschlossen sein, sich festhalten*›; verbissen, erbittert ‹*kämpfen*›

Grimm's Law ['grımz lɔ:] *n. (Ling.)* germanische *od.* erste Lautverschiebung

grimy ['graımı] *adj.* schmutzig; schwarz *(ugs.);* **buildings ~ with soot** rußgeschwärzte Gebäude

grin [grın] **1.** *n.* Grinsen, *das.* **2.** *v. i.,* **-nn-** grinsen; **~ at sb.** jmdn. angrinsen; **~ and bear it** gute Miene zum bösen Spiel machen; *see also* **Cheshire cat. 3.** *v. t.,* **-nn-: ~ approval/satisfaction** *etc.* beifällig/zufrieden *usw.* grinsen

grind [graınd] **1.** *v. t.,* **ground** [graʊnd] **a)** *(reduce to small particles)* **~ [up]** zermahlen; pulverisieren ‹*Metall*›; mahlen ‹*Kaffee, Pfeffer, Getreide*›; **~ sth. to dust/[a] powder/into flour** *etc.* etw. zu Staub/[einem] Pulver/zu Mehl *usw.* zermahlen; **b)** *(sharpen)* schleifen ‹*Schere, Messer*›; schärfen ‹*Klinge*›; *(smooth, shape)* schleifen ‹*Linse, Edelstein*›; **~ sth. to a sharp edge** etw. scharf schleifen; *see also* **axe 1 a; c)** *(rub harshly)* zerquetschen; **~ a cigarette-end into the ground** einen Zigarettenstummel austreten; **~ facts into pupils** Schülern Fakten einhämmern; **~ dirt into sth.** Schmutz in etw. *(Akk.)* treten; **~ one's teeth** mit den Zähnen knirschen; **d)** *(produce by grinding)* mahlen ‹*Mehl*›; **e)** *(turn, cause to work)* drehen ‹*Leier*›; **~ the coffee-mill** den Kaffee mahlen; **~ a barrel-organ** eine Drehorgel spielen; **f)** *(fig.: oppress, harass)* auspressen *(fig.);* **~ the faces of the poor** *(literary)* die Armen [grausam] ausbeuten; **~ing poverty/tyranny** erdrückende Armut/Tyrannei. **2.** *v. i.,* **ground a)** *(toil)* hart arbeiten; *(study)* büffeln *(ugs.);* **b)** *(rub gratingly)* knirschen **(on** auf + *Dat.*); **bring sth. ~ing to a halt** etw. lahmlegen; **~ to a halt, come to a ~ing halt** ‹*Fahrzeug:*› quietschend zum Stehen kommen; *(fig.)* ‹*Verkehr:*› zum Erliegen kommen; ‹*Maschine:*› stehenbleiben; ‹*Projekt:*› sich festfahren. **3.** *n.* Plackerei, *die*

(ugs.); **the daily ~** (coll.) der alltägliche Trott
~ **a'way** 1. v.t. abschleifen. 2. v.i. (fig.) hart arbeiten (**at** an + Dat.); (study) büffeln (ugs.) (**at** Akk.)
~ **'down** v.t. a) zermahlen; pulverisieren ‹Metall›; mahlen ‹Kaffee›; b) (fig.: oppress) ‹Tyrann, Regierung:› unterdrücken; ‹Armut, Verantwortung:› erdrücken; c) (sharpen) abschleifen
~ **'in** v.t. a) (Mech.) einschleifen ‹Ventil›; b) **~ the dirt in** den Schmutz ein- od. festtreten; **~ in facts** (fig. coll.) Fakten einhämmern
~ **'on** v.i. sich mühsam voranarbeiten
~ **'out** v.t. (fig.) sich (Dat.) abquälen ‹Verse, Melodie, Aufsatz›
grinder ['graındə(r) n. a) Schleifmaschine, die; (pulverizing machine) Mühle, die; b) in comb. (person) ‹Messer-, Scheren›schleifer, der; c) (tooth) Mahlzahn, der; d) (millstone) Läufer, der. See also **organ-grinder**
'grindstone n. Schleifstein, der; **hold** or **keep one's/sb.'s nose to the ~** (fig.) sich dahinterklemmen (ugs.)/dafür sorgen, daß jmd. sich dahinterklemmt (ugs.); **get back to the ~**: sich wieder an die Arbeit machen
gringo ['grıŋgəʊ] n., pl. **~s** (often derog.) Gringo, der (abwertend)
grip [grıp] 1. n. a) (firm hold) Halt, der; (fig.: power) Umklammerung, die; **hold sth. with a firm ~**: etw. mit festem Griff halten; **have a ~ on sth.** etw. festhalten; **loosen one's ~**: loslassen; **take a ~**: festhalten (**on** Akk.); **get** or **take a ~ on oneself** (fig.) sich zusammenreißen (ugs.); **gain a ~**: einen Halt finden; ‹Reifen:› greifen; **have/get a ~ on sth.** (fig.) etw. im Griff haben/in den Griff bekommen; **winter tightened its ~**: der Winter wurde noch strenger; **come** or **get to ~s with sth./sb.** (fig.) mit etw. fertigwerden/sich (Dat.) jmdn. vorknöpfen od. vornehmen (ugs.); **be in the ~ of** (fig.) beherrscht werden von ‹Angst, Leidenschaft, Furcht›; heimgesucht werden von ‹Naturkatastrophe, Armut, Krieg›; **lose one's ~** (fig.) nachlassen; **lose one's ~ on reality** (fig.) den Bezug zur Realität verlieren; **the Prime Minister is losing his ~** (fig.) der Premierminister hat die Situation nicht mehr richtig im Griff; b) (strength or way of ~ping) Griff, der; **shorten/lengthen one's ~**: den Schläger o.ä. kürzer/länger fassen; c) (holding-device) Klammer, die; (part which is held) Griff, der; (of oar) Holm, der; d) see **hair-grip**; e) (bag) Reisetasche, die. 2. v.t., **-pp-** greifen nach; ‹Reifen:› greifen; (fig.) ergreifen; fesseln ‹Publikum, Aufmerksamkeit›; **~ sb.'s collar/hand** or **sb. by the collar/hand** jmdn. am Kragen packen/sich an jmds. Hand klammern; **~ sb.'s imagination** (fig.) jmdn. fesseln. 3. v.i., **-pp-** ‹Räder, Bremsen usw.:› greifen; **~ at** greifen nach
gripe [graıp] 1. n. a) (sl.: complaint) Meckern, das (ugs. abwertend); **one more ~ about my driving ...**: noch ein Wort über meinen Fahrstil ...; **his favourite ~ is ...**: am liebsten schimpft er über (+ Akk.) ...; **have a good ~ about sth./at sb.** sich über etw. (Akk.) ausschimpfen/jmdn. tüchtig ausschimpfen; b) in pl. (colic) **get/have the ~s** Bauchschmerzen od. (ugs.) Bauchweh bekommen/haben. 2. v.i. (sl.) meckern (ugs. abwertend) (**about** über + Akk.)
gripping ['grıpıŋ] adj. (fig.) packend
grisly ['grızlı] adj. grausig
Grisons ['gri:zɔ̃] pr. n. Graubünden (das)
grist [grıst] n. a) Mahlgut, das; (Brewing) Malzschrot, der od. das; b) (fig.) **it's all ~ to the/sb.'s mill** man kann aus allem etwas machen/jmd. versteht es, aus allem etwas zu machen
gristle ['grısl] n. Knorpel, der
gristly ['grıslı] adj. knorp[e]lig
grit [grıt] 1. n. a) Sand, der; b) see **gritstone**; c) (coll.: courage, endurance) Schneid, der (ugs.). 2. v.t., **-tt-**: a) streuen ‹vereiste Straßen›; b) **~ one's teeth** die Zähne zusammenbeißen (ugs.)
grits [grıts] n. pl. a) (oats) geschälte Haferkörner; b) (oatmeal) Haferschrot, der od. das
'gritstone n. (Geol.) Grit, der (fachspr.); Sandstein, der
gritty ['grıtı] adj. a) (containing grit) sandig ‹Weg, Boden, Butterbrot›; (full of hard particles) grobkörnig ‹Struktur, Sand›; b) (fig.: courageous) **be ~**: Schneid haben
grizzle ['grızl] v.i. (Brit. coll.) quengeln (ugs.)
grizzled ['grızld] adj. grau ‹Haar, Bart›; grauhaarig ‹Person›; (partly grey) graumeliert ‹Haar›
grizzly ['grızlı] n. **~ [bear]** Grislybär, der
groan [grəʊn] 1. n. (of person) Stöhnen, das; (of thing) Ächzen, das (fig.); **give a ~ of pain** vor Schmerz stöhnen; **a ~ rose from the crowd** die Menge stöhnte auf. 2. v.i. a) ‹Person:› [auf]stöhnen (**at** bei); ‹Tisch, Planken:› ächzen (fig.); **~ inwardly** innerlich aufstöhnen; **a ~ing board** (literary) ein reichgedeckter Tisch; b) (fig.: be oppressed) stöhnen. 3. v.t. stöhnen
groats [grəʊts] n. pl. (hulled) geschälte [Hafer]körner; (hulled and crushed) [Hafer]grütze, die
grocer ['grəʊsə(r)] n. Lebensmittelhändler, der/-händlerin, die; see also **baker**
grocery ['grəʊsərı] n. a) in pl. (goods) Lebensmittel Pl.; b) **~ [store]** Lebensmittelgeschäft, das; c) (trade) Lebensmittelhandel, der
grog [grɒg] n. Grog, der; (Austral. and NZ coll.: alcoholic liquor) Schnaps, der (ugs.)
groggily ['grɒgılı] adv. benommen ‹sprechen, gehen›; auf unsicheren od. (ugs.) auf wackeligen Beinen ‹gehen›
groggy ['grɒgı] adj. wackelig auf den Beinen (ugs.) präd.; groggy (ugs.) präd.
groin [grɔın] n. a) (Anat.) Leistengegend, die; (euphem.: genitals) Weichteile, die (verhüll.); b) (Archit.) Grat, der (fachspr.)
grommet see **grummet**
groom [gru:m, grʊm] 1. n. a) (stable-boy) Stallbursche, der; Stallknecht, der (veralt.); (stable-girl) Stallgehilfin, die; b) (bride~) Bräutigam, der; c) (Brit.: officer of Royal Household) Bediensteter des britischen Hofes. 2. v.t. a) striegeln ‹Pferd›; (smarten) pflegen ‹Kleidung›; **~ oneself** sich zurechtmachen; **well/badly ~ed** gepflegt/ungepflegt; b) (fig.: prepare) **~ sb. for/as sth.** jmdn. für/als etw. aufbauen; **~ sb. for a career** jmdn. auf od. für eine Laufbahn vorbereiten
groove [gru:v] 1. n. a) (channel) Nut, die (bes. Technik); (of gramophone record) Rille, die; b) (fig.: routine) **get into a ~** ‹Arbeit:› routinemäßig ablaufen; ‹Person:› zum Gewohnheitsmenschen werden; **be stuck in a ~**: aus dem Trott nicht mehr herauskommen; c) **be in the ~** (dated sl.) gut drauf sein (salopp); (perform excellently) groß in Form sein (ugs.); (be appreciative) ‹Publikum:› begeistert mitgehen. 2. v.t. nuten
groovy ['gru:vı] adj. (dated sl.) (excellent, very good) klasse (ugs.); **be ~** (Jazz) in Form sein (ugs.); gut drauf sein (salopp)
grope [grəʊp] 1. v.i. tasten (**for** nach); **~ for the right word/truth** nach dem richtigen Wort/der Wahrheit suchen; **~ after sth.** (fig.) etw. herauszufinden versuchen. 2. v.t. a) **~ one's way [along]** sich [entlang]tasten; (fig.) [sich durch]lavieren (ugs. abwertend); b) (sl.: caress) **~ sb.** jmdn. betatschen (ugs. abwertend)
grosgrain ['grəʊgreın] n. (Textiles) grob gerippter Stoff; Grosgrain, der (fachspr.)
gros point ['grəʊ pwæ̃] n. a) (embroidery) Kreuzstichstickerei, die; b) (stitch) Kreuzstich, der
[1]**gross** [grəʊs] 1. adj. a) (flagrant) grob ‹Fahrlässigkeit, Fehler, Irrtum›; übel ‹Laster, Beleidigung›; schwer ‹Verbrechen, Beleidigung›; schreiend ‹Ungerechtigkeit›; b) (obese) fett (abwertend); (luxuriant) üppig, dicht ‹Vegetation›; c) (coarse, rude) ordinär (abwertend); (coll.: disgusting) **that's really ~!** das ist wirklich ekelhaft!; d) (total) Brutto-; Gesamt‹umsatz, -absatz›; **~ national product** Bruttosozialprodukt, das; e) (dull, not delicate) grob ‹Person, Geschmack›; f) (coarse) deftig ‹Mahlzeit, Essen›. 2. v.t. a) (yield) [insgesamt] einbringen ‹Geld›; b) **~ up** einbeziehen; **~ed up** Brutto‹dividende, -rendite›
[2]**gross** n., pl. same Gros, das; **by the ~**: en gros
grossly ['grəʊslı] adv. a) (flagrantly) äußerst; grob ‹übertreiben›; schwer ‹beleidigen›; b) (coarsely, rudely) ordinär ‹sich benehmen, sprechen›; ohne Manieren ‹essen›
grotesque [grəʊ'tesk] 1. adj. grotesk. 2. n. a) (decoration) Groteske, die; b) (Printing) Grotesk, die
grotesquely [grəʊ'tesklı] adv. grotesk
grotto ['grɒtəʊ] n., pl. **~es** or **~s** Grotte, die
grotty ['grɒtı] adj. (Brit. sl.) mies (ugs.); (dirty) dreckig (ugs.); **the bathroom looks ~**: das Bad ist total versifft (salopp)
grouch [graʊtʃ] (coll.) 1. v.i. schimpfen; mosern (ugs.). 2. n. a) (person) Miesepeter, der (ugs. abwertend); b) (cause) Ärger, der; **have a ~ against sb.** auf jmdn. sauer sein (salopp)
grouchy ['graʊtʃı] adj. (coll.) griesgrämig
[1]**ground** [graʊnd] 1. n. a) Boden, der; **work above/below ~**: über/unter der Erde arbeiten; **1,000 feet above the ~**: 1 000 Fuß über dem Erdboden; **deep under the ~**: tief unter der Erde; **uneven, hilly ~**: unebenes, hügeliges Gelände; **on high ~**: in höheren Lagen; **cover much ~** (distance) eine weite Strecke zurücklegen; b) (fig.) **be above/below ~**: am Leben od. unter den Lebenden sein/unter der Erde sein od. liegen; **cut the ~ from under sb.'s feet** jmdm. den Wind aus den Segeln nehmen (ugs.); **be** or **suit sb. down to the ~** (coll.) genau das richtige für jmdn. sein; **Friday suits me down to the ~**: Freitag paßt mir prima (ugs.); **that's Billy down to the ~** (coll.) das ist typisch Billy (ugs.); **fall to the ~**: zunichte werden; **be dashed to the ~**: [mit einem Schlag] zunichte werden; **from the ~ up** (coll.) (thoroughly) von der Pike auf (ugs.) ‹lernen›; (entirely anew) ganz von vorne ‹anfangen›; **get off the ~** (coll.) konkrete Gestalt annehmen; **get sth. off the ~** (coll.) etw. in die Tat umsetzen; **go to ~**: ‹Fuchs usw.:› im Bau verschwinden; ‹Person:› untertauchen; **run to ~**: aufstöbern; **run sb./oneself into the ~** (coll.) jmdn./sich kaputtmachen (ugs.); **run sth. into the ~** (coll.: overdo sth.) es mit etw. übertreiben; **on the ~** (in practice) an Ort und Stelle; **be/not be on firm** or **solid ~**: sich auf sicherem/schwankendem Boden bewegen; **thin/thick on the ~**: dünn/dicht gesät; **break fresh** or **new ~**: Neuland betreten; **cover much** or **a lot of ~**: weit vorankommen; **cover the ~** ‹Student:› den Stoff erarbeiten; ‹Buch:› eine umfassende Darstellung geben; **cover the same ~** ‹Vorträge, Buch:› denselben Stoff behandeln; **gain** or **make ~**: Boden gewinnen (**on** gegenüber); (become established) Fuß fassen; **give** or **lose ~**: an Boden verlieren; **hold** or **keep** or **stand one's ~**: nicht nachgeben; **shift one's ~**: umschwenken; see also **foot 1 a**; c) (special area) Gelände, das; **[sports] ~**: Sportplatz, der; **[cricket] ~**: Cricketfeld, das; see also **common ground**; **forbidden 2**; d) in pl. (attached to house) Anlage, die; e) (Brit.: floor)

Boden, *der;* **f)** *(motive, reason)* Grund, *der;* **on the ~[s] of, on ~s of** auf Grund (+ *Gen.*); *(giving as one's reason)* unter Berufung auf (+ *Akk.*); **on the ~s that ...:** unter Berufung auf die Tatsache, daß ...; **on health/religious** *etc.* **~s** aus gesundheitlichen/religiösen *usw.* Gründen; **on what ~s do you suspect him?** mit welcher Begründung verdächtigen Sie ihn?; **the ~s for divorce are ...:** als Scheidungsgrund gilt ...; **there are no ~s for this assumption** es besteht kein Grund zu dieser Annahme; **have/give [no] ~s for sth.** [k]einen Grund für etw. haben/[keine] Gründe für etw. angeben; **have no ~s for sth./to do sth.** keinen Grund für etw. haben/keinen Grund haben, etw. zu tun; **have no ~s for complaint** keinen Grund zur Klage haben; **have good ~s for doing sth.** allen Grund haben, etw. zu tun; **g)** *(in embroidery, painting, etc.)* Grund, *der;* **on a white ~:** auf weißem Grund; **h)** *in pl. (sediment)* **~s** Satz, *der; (of coffee)* Kaffeesatz, *der;* **i)** *(Electr.)* Erde, *die;* **~ed plug** *(Amer.)* Schukostecker, *der;* **j)** *(bottom of sea)* Grund, *der;* **touch ~** *(fig.)* wieder Grund unter den Füßen haben. **2.** *v. t.* **a)** *(cause to run ashore)* auf Grund setzen; **be ~ed** auf Grund gelaufen sein; **b)** *(base, establish)* gründen (**on** auf + *Akk.*); **be ~ed on** gründen auf (+ *Dat.*); **well ~ed** wohlbegründet; **c)** *(instruct)* **~ sb. [in the essentials]** jmdn. in die Anfangsgründe einführen; **be well/not well ~ed in a subject** über gute/keine guten Grundkenntnisse auf einem Gebiet verfügen; **d)** *(Mil.)* niederlegen; **e)** *(Aeronaut.)* am Boden festhalten; *(prevent from flying)* nicht fliegen lassen ‹*Piloten*›; **be ~ed by bad weather/owing to a defect** *etc.* wegen schlechten Wetters/eines Defekts *usw.* nicht starten können; **f)** *(Electr.)* erden. **3.** *v. i. (run ashore)* ‹*Schiff:*› auf Grund laufen

[2]**ground 1.** *see* **grind 1, 2. 2.** *adj.* gemahlen ‹*Kaffee, Getreide*›; pulverisiert ‹*Holz, Gummi*›; **~ meat** *(Amer.)* Hackfleisch, *das;* **~ coffee** Kaffeepulver, *das;* **fine-/coarse-/medium-~ coffee** fein-/grobgemahlener/mittelfein gemahlener Kaffee

ground: ~-bait *n.* Grundköder, *der;* **~ bass** ['graʊnd beɪs] *n. (Mus.)* Basso ostinato, *der;* Ground, *der;* **~ control** *n. (Aeronaut.)* **a)** *(personnel, equipment, etc.)* Flugsicherungskontrolldienst, *der;* **b)** *(directing)* **~ control approach** GCA-Verfahren, *das;* **~ crew** *n. (Aeronaut.)* Bodenpersonal, *das;* **~ effect** *n.* Bodeneffekt, *der (Technik);* **~ 'floor** *see* **floor 1 b; ~ forces** *n. pl.* Bodentruppen *Pl.;* **~ frost** *n.* Bodenfrost, *der;* **~ 'glass** *n.* Mattglas, *das*

grounding ['graʊndɪŋ] *n.* **a)** Grundkenntnisse *Pl.;* Grundwissen, *das;* **b)** *(Aeronaut.)* **the ~ of the plane was ordered** dem Flugzeug wurde Startverbot erteilt

ground: ~ ivy *n.* Gundelrebe, *die;* **~keeper** *(Amer.) see* **groundsman**

groundless ['graʊndlɪs] *adj.* unbegründet; **these reports/rumours/statements are ~:** diese Berichte/Gerüchte/Aussagen entbehren jeder Grundlage

ground: ~ 'level *n.* **above/below ~ level** oberhalb/unterhalb der ebenen Erde; **on** *or* **at ~ level** ebenerdig; ‹*Wohnung, Fenster*› zu ebener Erde; **~-nut** *n. (Brit.)* Erdnuß, *die;* **~-plan** *n.* Grundriß, *der; (fig.)* Grundstruktur, *die;* **~-rent** *n.* Grundrente, *die;* **~ 'rice** *n.* Reismehl, *das;* **~ rule** *n.* **a)** *(Sport)* Platzregel, *die;* **b)** *(basic principle)* Grundregel, *die*

groundsel ['graʊnsl] *n. (Bot.)* Greiskraut, *das*

ground: ~sheet *n.* Bodenplane, *die;* **~sman** ['graʊndzmən] *n., pl.* **~smen** ['graʊndzmən] *(Sport)* Platzwart, *der;* **~ speed** *n. (Aeronaut.)* Grundgeschwindigkeit, *die;* **~-squirrel** *n.* Erdhörnchen, *das;* **~ staff** *n. (Aeronaut.)* Bodenpersonal, *das;* **~ station** *n. (Astronaut., Communications)* Bodenstation, *die;* **~ swell** *n.* schwere Dünung; **the ~ swell of public opinion** *(fig.)* der wachsende Druck der öffentlichen Meinung; **~ traffic** *n.* Bodenverkehr, *der;* **~ water** *n.* Grundwasser, *das;* **~work** *n.* Vorarbeiten; *(fig.)* Grundlage, *die;* **do the ~work for sth.** die Vorarbeiten für etw. machen; **~ 'zero** *n.* [Boden]nullpunkt, *der*

group [gru:p] **1.** *n.* **a)** Gruppe, *die; attrib.* Gruppen‹*verhalten, -dynamik, -bewußtsein*›; **~ of houses/trees/islands** Häuser-/Baum-/Inselgruppe, *die;* **the Germanic ~ of languages** die germanische Sprachfamilie; **b)** *(Commerc.)* [Unternehmens]gruppe, *die;* **c)** *(Polit.)* Gruppe, *die; (Parl.)* Fraktion, *die;* **d)** *see* **pop group; e)** *(Math., Chem.)* Gruppe, *die.* **2.** *v. t.* gruppieren; **~ books according to their subjects** Bücher nach ihrer Thematik ordnen; **~ flowers together** Blumen zusammenstellen; **you can't ~ all criminals together** man kann nicht alle Verbrecher in einen Topf werfen *(ugs.);* **be ~ed into classes** Klassen zugeordnet werden

group: ~ captain *n. (Air Force)* Oberst der Luftwaffe; **~ discussion** *n.* Gruppendiskussion, *die*

groupie ['gru:pɪ] *n. (sl.)* Groupie, *das*

grouping ['gru:pɪŋ] *n. (placing in groups)* Gruppierung, *die; (classification)* Klassifizierung, *die;* **blood ~:** Bestimmung der Blutgruppe; *([belonging to a] blood group)* Blutgruppe[nzugehörigkeit], *die*

group: ~ practice *n.* Gemeinschaftspraxis, *die;* **~ sex** *n.* Gruppensex, *der;* **~ therapy** *n.* Gruppentherapie, *die*

[1]**grouse** [graʊs] *n.* **a)** *pl. same* Rauhfußhuhn, *das;* **[red] ~** *(Brit.)* Schottisches Moorschneehuhn; **b)** *no pl. (as food)* Waldhuhn, *das;* schottisches Moorhuhn

[2]**grouse** *(coll.)* **1.** *v. i.* meckern *(ugs.),* mosern *(ugs.)* **(about** über + *Akk.*). **2.** *n.* Meckerei, *die (ugs.);* Moserei, *die (ugs.);* **my only ~ is that ...:** mir stinkt nur, daß ... *(salopp)*

grouser ['graʊsə(r)] *n. (coll.)* Meckerer, *der;* Meckerfritze, *der*/-liese, *die (ugs.)*

'grouse-shooting *n.* Jagd auf Moorhühner

grout [graʊt] **1.** *n.* Mörtelschlamm, *der.* **2.** *v. t.* verstreichen ‹*Fugen, Löcher*›; [aus]fugen ‹*Mauer, Fliesen*›

grove [grəʊv] *n.* Wäldchen, *das;* Hain, *der (dichter. veralt.)*

grovel ['grɒvl] *v. i., (Brit.)* **-ll-: a)** *(lie prone)* auf dem Bauch liegen; *(go down on one's knees)* sich auf die Knie werfen; **be ~ling on the floor** auf dem Fußboden kriechen; **b)** *(fig.: be subservient)* katzbuckeln *(abwertend); (in apology)* zu Kreuze kriechen *(abwertend)* **(before** vor + *Dat.*)

grovelling *(Amer.:* **groveling)** ['grɒvəlɪŋ] *adj.* kriechend; *(fig.)* kriecherisch *(abwertend)*

grow [grəʊ] **1.** *v. i.,* **grew** [gru:], **grown** [grəʊn] **a)** *(sprout)* ‹*Pflanze:*› wachsen; **leaves are beginning to ~ on the trees** an den Bäumen bilden sich allmählich Blätter; **b)** *(in size etc.)* wachsen; **haven't you ~n!** du bist aber gewachsen *od.* groß geworden!; **~ing lad** Junge, der noch im Wachsen ist *od.* noch wächst; **it just ~ed** *(coll.)* es hat sich einfach so entwickelt; **c)** *(develop, expand)* wachsen; *(increase numerically)* ‹*Bevölkerung:*› zunehmen, wachsen; **~ out of** *or* **from sth.** sich aus etw. entwickeln; *(from sth. abstract)* aus etw. erwachsen; von etw. herrühren; ‹*Situation, Krieg usw.:*› die Folge von etw. sein; ‹*Plan:*› aus etw. erwachsen; **~ in** zunehmen *od.* gewinnen an (+ *Dat.*) ‹*Größe, Bedeutung, Autorität, Ansehen, Weisheit*›; gewinnen an (+ *Dat.*) ‹*Popularität, Format*›; **d)** *(become)* werden; **~ used to sth./sb.** sich an etw./jmdn. gewöhnen; **~ like sb.** jmdm. ähnlich werden; **~ apart** *(fig.)* sich auseinanderleben; **~ away from sb.** *(fig.)* sich jmdm. entfremden; **~ to be sth.** allmählich etw. werden; **he grew to be a man** er wuchs zum Manne heran *(geh.);* **~ to love/hate** *etc.* **sb./sth.** jmdn./etw. liebenlernen/hassenlernen *usw.;* **~ to like sb./sth.** nach und nach Gefallen an jmdm./etw. finden; **~ old [gracefully]** [mit Würde] alt werden. *See also* **growing; grown 2. 2.** *v. t.,* **grew, grown a)** *(cultivate) (on a small scale)* ziehen; *(on a large scale)* anpflanzen; züchten ‹*Blumen*›; *(produce)* züchten ‹*Kristalle*›; **b) ~ one's hair [to a great length]** sich *(Dat.)* die Haare [sehr lang] wachsen lassen; **~ a beard** sich *(Dat.)* einen Bart wachsen lassen; **the lizard will ~ a new tail** der Eidechse wächst ein neuer Schwanz

~ into *v. t.* **a)** *(become)* werden zu; **b)** *(become big enough for)* hineinwachsen in (+ *Akk.*) ‹*Kleidungsstück*›

~ on *v. t.* **it ~s on you** man findet mit der Zeit Geschmack *od.* Gefallen daran; **he grew on us** wir haben ihn schätzengelernt

~ 'out of *v. t.* **a)** *(become too big for)* herauswachsen aus ‹*Kleidungsstück*›; **b)** *(lose in the course of time)* ablegen ‹*Angewohnheit*›; entwachsen (+ *Dat.*) ‹*Kindereien*›; überwinden ‹*Zustand*›; *see also* **~ 1 c**

~ 'up *v. i.* **a)** *(spend early years)* aufwachsen; *(become adult)* erwachsen werden; **she grew up to be a gifted pianist** sie wuchs zu einer begabten Pianistin heran; **what do you want to be** *or* **do when you ~ up?** was willst du denn mal werden, wenn du groß bist?; **b)** *(fig.: become mature)* erwachsen werden; **~ up!** werde endlich erwachsen!; **c)** *(develop)* ‹*Freundschaft, Feindschaft, Streit:*› sich entwickeln; ‹*Legende:*› entstehen, sich bilden; ‹*Tradition, Brauch:*› sich herausbilden

~ 'up into *v. t.* werden *od.* sich entwickeln zu

grower ['grəʊə(r)] *n.* **a)** *usu. in comb. (person)* Produzent, *der*/Produzentin, *die;* **fruit-/apple-/vegetable-~:** Obst-/Apfel-/Gemüsebauer, *der;* **coffee-/tobacco-~:** Kaffee-/Tabakpflanzer, *der;* **b)** *(plant)* **be a slow/free ~:** langsam/schnell wachsen; eine langsam/schnell wachsende Pflanze sein

growing ['grəʊɪŋ] **1.** *adj.* wachsend; sich verdichtend ‹*Anzeichen*›; immer umfangreicher werdend ‹*Sachgebiet*›; sich immer mehr verbreitend ‹*Praktik*›. **2.** *n.* Anbau, *der; attrib.* **~ season** Vegetationsperiode, *die;* **good/bad ~ weather** dem Pflanzenwachstum förderliches/abträgliches Wetter

'growing pains *n. pl.* Wachstumsschmerzen *Pl.; (fig.)* Anfangsschwierigkeiten *Pl.*

growl [graʊl] **1.** *n. (of dog, lion)* Knurren, *das; (of bear)* Brummen, *das;* **a ~ of disapproval** ein mißbilligendes Knurren. **2.** *v. i.* **a)** ‹*Hund, Löwe:*› knurren; ‹*Bär:*› [böse] brummen; **~ at sb.** jmdn. anknurren/anbrummen; **b)** *(murmur angrily)* knurren. **3.** *v. t.* **~ [out]** knurren

grown [grəʊn] **1.** *see* **grow. 2.** *adj.* erwachsen; **fully ~:** ausgewachsen

'grown-up 1. *n* Erwachsene, *der/die.* **2.** *adj.* erwachsen; **~ books/clothes** Bücher/Kleider für Erwachsene; **act in a ~ way** sich wie ein Erwachsener verhalten

growth [grəʊθ] *n.* **a)** *(of industry, economy, population)* Wachstum, *das* **(of, in** *Gen.*); *(of interest, illiteracy)* Zunahme, *die* **(of, in** *Gen.*); *attrib.* Wachstums‹*hormon, -rate*›; **b)** *(growing of organisms, crystals)* Wachstum, *das; (cultivation)* Anbau, *der;* **c)** *(amount grown)* Wachstum, *das;* **d)** *(thing grown)* Vegetation, *die;* Pflanzenwuchs, *der; (in classification of vineyards)* Lage, *die;* **a thick ~ of weeds** dicht wucherndes Unkraut; **cut away the old ~:** die alten Triebe ab- *od.* wegschneiden; **a four days' ~ [of beard]** ein vier Tage alter Bart; **e)** *(Med.)* Geschwulst, *die;* Gewächs, *das*

growth: ~ industry *n.* Wachstumsindustrie, *die;* **~ stock** *n.* Wachstumsaktien *Pl.*

groyne [grɔɪn] *n.* Buhne, *die*

grub [grʌb] **1.** *n.* **a)** Larve, *die; (maggot)* Made, *die; (ugs.)* Wurm, *der; (caterpillar)* Raupe, *die; (larva of cockchafer etc.)* Engerling, *der;* **b)** *(sl.: food)* Futterage, *die (ugs.); Fressen, das (salopp); (victuals)* Fressalien *Pl. (ugs.);* **~['s] up!** ran an die Futterkrippe! *(ugs.);* **lovely ~!** ein Spitzenfraß! *(salopp);* **pub ~** *(Brit.)* Kneipenessen, *das (ugs.).* **2.** *v.i.,* **-bb-: a)** *(dig)* wühlen, buddeln *(ugs.)* **(for** nach); **b)** *(search) (in bag, cupboard, etc.)* wühlen, kramen **(for** nach); **~ about** [herum]wühlen; [herum]kramen; **~ about for sth.** nach etw. wühlen *od.* kramen. **3.** *v.t.,* **-bb- a)** *(dig)* umgraben ⟨*Land, Boden*⟩; ⟨*Tier:*⟩ aufwühlen; *(remove roots or stumps from)* roden ⟨*Land*⟩; *(extract by digging)* ausgraben; *(uproot)* [aus]roden ⟨*Buschwerk, Baum*⟩; **b)** *(fig.)* **barely ~bing a subsistence** gerade eben in der Lage zu existieren

~ 'out *v.t.* roden ⟨*Land*⟩; [aus]roden ⟨*Wurzelstock*⟩; *(fig.)* zutage fördern

~ 'up *v.t.* ausgraben; [aus]jäten ⟨*Unkraut*⟩; [aus]roden ⟨*Wurzelstock*⟩

grubby ['grʌbɪ] *adj. (dirty)* schmudd[e]lig *(ugs. abwertend); (slovenly)* schlampig *(ugs. abwertend)*

'grub-screw *n. (Mech. Engin.)* Gewindestift, *der*

grudge [grʌdʒ] **1.** *v.t.* **~ sb. sth.** jmdm. etw. mißgönnen *od.* nicht gönnen; **I don't ~ him his success** ich gönne ihm seinen Erfolg; **~ every penny that is taken in tax** der Steuer jeden Pfennig mißgönnen; **~ doing sth.** *(be unwilling to do sth.)* nicht bereit sein, etw. zu tun; *(do sth. reluctantly)* etw. ungern tun; **I ~ paying £20 for this** es geht mir gegen den Strich, dafür 20 Pfund zu zahlen *(ugs.).* **2.** *n.* Groll, *der;* **have** *or* **hold a ~ against sb.** einen Groll *od. (ugs.)* Haß auf jmdn. haben; jmdm. grollen; **I owe him a ~:** den habe ich gefressen *(ugs.); see also* **[2]bear 1 h**

grudging ['grʌdʒɪŋ] *adj.* widerwillig ⟨*Lob, Bewunderung, Unterstützung*⟩; widerwillig gewährt ⟨*Zuschuß*⟩; **be ~ in one's approval** nur widerwillig zustimmen

grudgingly ['grʌdʒɪŋlɪ] *adv.* widerwillig

gruel ['gru:əl] *n.* [Hafer]schleim, *der;* Schleimsuppe, *die*

gruelling *(Amer.:* **grueling)** ['gru:əlɪŋ] **1.** *adj.* aufreibend; zermürbend; [äußerst] strapaziös ⟨*Reise, Marsch*⟩; mörderisch *(ugs.)* ⟨*Tempo, Rennen*⟩. **2.** *n. (Brit.)* **the boxer got a ~:** der Boxer bezog tüchtig Prügel *(ugs.);* **take a ~ from sth.** durch etw. sehr leiden

gruesome ['gru:səm] *adj.,* **gruesomely** ['gru:səmlɪ] *adv.* grausig; schaurig

gruff [grʌf] *adj.* barsch; schroff; ruppig, bärbeißig ⟨*Benehmen, Wesen*⟩; *(low-pitched, hoarse)* rauh ⟨*Stimme, Lachen*⟩

grumble ['grʌmbl] **1.** *v.i.* **a)** murren; **~ at sb. about** *or* **over sth.** sich bei jmdm. über etw. *(Akk.) od.* wegen etw. beklagen; **put up with sth. without grumbling** etw. ohne Murren ertragen; **b)** *(rumble)* ⟨*[Geschütz]donner:*⟩ grollen. **2.** *n.* **a)** *(act)* Murren, *das; (complaint)* Klage, *die;* **without a ~:** ohne Murren; **she's always full of ~s** sie hat immer etwas zu murren; **my chief ~ is that ...:** vor allem mißfällt mir, daß ...; am meisten stört mich, daß ...; **b)** *(rumble of thunder or cannon)* Grollen, *das*

grumbler ['grʌmblə(r)] *n.* Querulant, *der*/Querulantin, *die*

grumbling a'ppendix *n. (Med.)* Blinddarmreizung, *die*

grummet ['grʌmɪt] *n.* **a)** *(Naut.)* Grummet, *das;* Grummetstropp, *der;* **b)** *(washer)* Durchführung, *die;* **c)** *(in cap)* Versteifungsring, *der*

grumpily ['grʌmpɪlɪ] *adv.* unleidlich; grantig *(ugs.)*

grumpiness ['grʌmpɪnɪs] *n., no pl.* Unleidlichkeit, *die;* Grantigkeit, *die (ugs.)*

grumpy ['grʌmpɪ] *adj.* unleidlich; grantig *(ugs.)*

grunt [grʌnt] **1.** *n.* Grunzen, *das;* **give a ~:** grunzen. **2.** *v.i.* grunzen; **he only ~ed in answer** er gab nur ein Grunzen zur Antwort. **3.** *v.t.* **~ [out]** grunzen

gruyère ['gru:jeə(r)] *n.* Gruyère[käse], *der;* Greyerzer [Käse], *der*

gryphon ['grɪfn] *see* **griffin**

'G-string *n.* **a)** *(Mus.)* G-Saite, *die;* **b)** *(garment) (of showgirl)* ≈ Cache-sex, *das;* G-String, *die od. der; (of tribesman)* Lendenschurz, *der*

'G-suit *n. (Aeronaut.)* Anti-g-Anzug, *der*

Gt. *abbr.* **Great** Gr.

guano ['gwɑ:nəʊ] *n., pl.* **~s** Guano, *der*

guarantee [gærən'ti:] **1.** *v.t.* **a)** garantieren; garantieren für, bürgen für ⟨*Echtheit usw.*⟩; **~ sth. to sb.** jmdm. etw. zusichern; **b)** *(by formal agreement)* garantieren für; [eine] Garantie geben auf (+ *Akk.*); **~ sth. for a year** auf etw. *(Akk.)* ein Jahr Garantie geben; **is the clock ~d?** hat die Uhr Garantie?; gibt es auf die Uhr Garantie?; **the clock is ~d for a year** die Uhr hat ein Jahr Garantie; **~ sb. regular employment** jmdm. eine Beschäftigungsgarantie geben; **~d wage** Garantielohn, *der;* **~d genuine** *etc.* garantiert echt *usw.;* **c)** *(Law: take responsibility for)* bürgen für ⟨*Darlehen, Schuld usw.*⟩; **d)** *(in popular use) (promise)* garantieren *(ugs.); (ensure)* bürgen für ⟨*Qualität*⟩; garantieren ⟨*Erfolg*⟩; **be ~d to do sth.** etw. garantiert tun; **there's no ~ing he'll get a work permit** es ist gar nicht gesagt, daß er eine Arbeitserlaubnis kriegt. **2.** *n.* **a)** *(Commerc. etc.)* Garantie, *die; (document)* Garantieschein, *der; (Law)* Bürgschaft, *die;* **there's a year's ~ on this radio, this radio has** *or* **carries a year's ~:** auf dieses Radio gibt es *od.* dieses Radio hat ein Jahr Garantie; **is it still under ~?** ist noch Garantie darauf?; **come under** *or* **be covered by the ~:** unter die Garantie fallen; **b)** *(guarantor)* Garant, *der; (Law)* Bürge, *der*/Bürgin, *die;* **c)** *(in popular use: promise)* Garantie, *die (ugs.);* **give sb. a ~ that ...:** jmdm. garantieren, daß ...; **you have my ~:** das garantiere ich dir; **be a ~ of sth.** eine Garantie für etw. sein

guarantor ['gærəntə(r), gærən'tɔ:(r)] *n.* Bürge, *der*/Bürgin, *die;* **be** *or* **stand ~ for sb., be sb.'s ~** eine Bürgschaft für jmdn. übernehmen; für jmdn. bürgen

guaranty ['gærəntɪ] *n.* **a)** *(undertaking)* Garantie, *die; (to pay another's debt)* Bürgschaft, *die;* **b)** *(basis of security)* Garantie, *die;* Gewähr, *die*

guard [gɑ:d] **1.** *n.* **a)** *(Mil.: guardsman)* Wachtposten, *der;* **b)** *no pl. (Mil.: group of soldiers)* Wache, *die;* Wachmannschaft, *die;* **~ of honour** Ehrenwache, *die;* Ehrengarde, *die;* **change ~:** Wachablösung machen; **relieve ~:** die Wache ablösen; **mount ~:** Wache beziehen; *see also* **old guard; c) G~s** *(Brit. Mil.: household troops)* Garderegiment, *das;* Garde, *die; see also* **Foot Guards; Horse Guards; Life Guards; d)** *(watch; also Mil.)* Wache, *die;* **be on ~:** Wache haben; **keep** *or* **stand ~:** Wache halten *od.* stehen; **keep** *or* **mount** *or* **stand ~ over sth./sb.** etw./jmdn. bewachen; **be on [one's] ~ [against sb./sth.]** *(lit. or fig.)* [vor jmdm./etw.] auf der Hut sein; sich [vor jmdm./etw.] hüten; **be off [one's] ~** *(fig.)* nicht auf der Hut sein; **be caught** *or* **taken off [one's] ~ [by sth.]** *(fig.)* [von etw.] überrascht werden; **put sb. on [his/her] ~:** jmdn. mißtrauisch machen; **put** *or* **throw sb. off [his/her] ~:** jmdn. überrumpeln *(ugs.);* **under ~:** unter Bewachung; **be [kept/held] under ~:** bewacht werden; unter Bewachung stehen; **keep** *or* **hold/put under ~:** bewachen/unter Bewachung stellen; **put a ~ on sb./sth.** jmdn./etw. bewachen lassen; **e)** *(Brit. Railw.)* [Zug]schaffner, *der*/-schaffnerin, *die;* **f)** *(Amer.: prison warder)* [Gefängnis]wärter, *der*/-wärterin, *die;* **g)** *(safety device)* Schutz, *der;* Schutzvorrichtung, *die; (worn on body)* Schutz, *der;* Schützer, *der; (crossbar on sword)* Parierstange, *die; (of rapier)* Stichblatt, *das; (Fencing: of weapon)* Glocke, *die;* **h)** *(posture) (Boxing, Fencing)* Deckung, *die; (Cricket)* Abwehrhaltung, *die;* **on ~!** *(Fencing)* en garde!; **take ~:** in Verteidigungsstellung gehen; **drop** *or* **lower one's ~:** die Deckung fallen lassen; *(fig.)* seine Reserve aufgeben; **have one's ~ down** *(fig.)* sich ungezwungen verhalten *od.* bewegen. *See also* **security guard. 2.** *v.t.* **a)** *(watch over)* bewachen; *(keep safe)* hüten ⟨*Geheimnis, Schatz, Juwelen*⟩; schützen ⟨*Leben*⟩; beschützen ⟨*Blinden, Schwächeren, Prominenten*⟩; **~ sb./oneself against sth.** jmdn. vor etw. *(Dat.)* beschützen/sich vor etw. *(Dat.)* schützen; **b)** *(keep in check)* hüten, im Zaum halten ⟨*Zunge*⟩; mäßigen ⟨*Worte*⟩

~ against *v.t.* sich hüten vor (+ *Dat.*); verhüten ⟨*Unfall*⟩; vorbeugen (+ *Dat.*) ⟨*Krankheit, Gefahr, Irrtum*⟩; **~ against doing sth.** sich [davor] hüten, etw. zu tun

guard: ~ dog *n.* Wachhund, *der;* **~ duty** *n.* Wachdienst, *der;* **be on** *or* **do ~ duty** Wachdienst haben

guarded ['gɑ:dɪd] *adj.,* **guardedly** ['gɑ:dɪdlɪ] *adv.* zurückhaltend; vorsichtig

'guardhouse *n. (Mil.)* Wache, *die;* Wach[t]haus, *das*

guardian ['gɑ:dɪən] *n.* **a)** Hüter, *der;* Wächter, *der;* **b)** *(Law)* Vormund, *der;* **place sb. under the care of a ~:** jmdm. einen Vormund geben

guardian 'angel *n.* Schutzengel, *der*

guardianship ['gɑ:dɪənʃɪp] *n.* **a)** *no pl.* Schutz, *der;* **b)** *(Law)* Vormundschaft, *die;* **have [legal] ~ of sb.** jmds. Vormund sein

guard: ~-rail *n.* Geländer, *das; (Railw.)* Radlenker, *der;* **~room** *n. (Mil.)* Wachstube, *die;* Wachlokal, *das*

guardsman ['gɑ:dzmən] *n., pl.* **guardsmen** ['gɑ:dzmən] *(belonging to guard)* Wachtposten, *der; (belonging to Guards)* Gardist, *der;* Gardesoldat, *der*

'guard's van *n. (Brit. Railw.)* Gepäckwagen *(mit Dienstabteil)*

Guatemala [gwætɪ'mɑ:lə] *pr. n.* Guatemala *(das)*

Guatemalan [gwætɪ'mɑ:lən] **1.** *adj.* guatemaltekisch; **sb. is ~:** jmd. ist Guatemalteke/Guatemaltekin. **2.** *n.* Guatemalteke, *der*/Guatemaltekin, *die*

guava ['gwɑ:və] *n.* **a)** *(fruit)* Guave, *die;* Guajave, *die;* **b)** *(tree)* Guajavabaum, *der*

gubbins ['gʌbɪnz] *n. (Brit.)* **a)** *no pl. (trash)* Schund, *der (ugs. abwertend);* Ramsch, *der (ugs. abwertend); (personal effects)* Kram, *der (ugs.);* Krempel, *der (ugs.); (gadgetry)* Zeug, *das;* **b)** *(coll.: fool)* Simpel, *der (ugs.)*

gubernatorial [gju:bənə'tɔ:rɪəl] *adj. (Amer.)* Gouverneurs-

gudgeon ['gʌdʒn] *n. (Zool.)* Gründling, *der*

'gudgeon-pin *n. (Mech. Engin.)* Kolbenbolzen, *der*

guelder rose ['geldə rəʊz] *n. (Bot.)* Schneeball, *der*

guerilla *see* **guerrilla**

Guernsey ['gɜ:nzɪ] *n.* **a)** *pr. n.* Guernsey *(das);* **b)** *(animal)* Guernseyrind, *das*

guerrilla [gə'rɪlə] *n.* Guerillakämpfer, *der*/-kämpferin, *die; (in Latin America)* Guerillero, *der*/Guerillera, *die; attrib.* Guerilla-

guess [ges] **1.** *v.t.* **a)** *(estimate)* schätzen; *(surmise)* raten; *(surmise correctly)* erraten; raten ⟨*Rätsel*⟩; **I ~ her [age] to be ten** ich schätze sie auf zehn; **can you ~ his weight?** schätz mal, wieviel er wiegt; **~ who's here!** rate mal, wer da ist!; **~ what!** *(coll.)* stell dir vor!; **he ~ed from their manner that ...:** er entnahm aus ihrem Verhalten, daß ...; **you'd never ~ that ...:** man würde nie vermuten, daß ...; **I ~ed as much** das habe ich mir schon gedacht; **b)** *(esp. Amer.: suppose)* **I ~:** ich glaube; ich schätze *(ugs.)*; **I ~ I ought to apologize** ich sollte mich wohl entschuldigen; **I ~ we'll have to** wir müssen wohl; **I ~ so/not** ich glaube schon *od.* ja/nicht *od.* kaum. **2.** *v. i. (estimate)* schätzen; *(make assumption)* vermuten; *(surmise correctly)* es erraten; **~ at sth.** etw. schätzen; *(surmise)* über etw. *(Akk.)* Vermutungen anstellen; **I'm just ~ing** das ist nur eine Schätzung/eine Vermutung; **you've ~ed right/wrong** deine Vermutung ist richtig/falsch; **Do you know what he said? – No, but I can ~:** Weißt du, was er gesagt hat? – Nein, aber ich kann es mir denken; **well, ~!** na, rate mal!; **keep sb. ~ing** *(coll.)* jmdn. im unklaren *od.* ungewissen lassen; **how did you ~?** wie hast du das nur erraten?; **you'll never ~!** darauf kommst du nie!. **3.** *n.* Schätzung, *die;* **at a ~:** schätzungsweise; **what's your ~?** was schätzen Sie?; **make** *or* **have a ~:** schätzen; **have a ~!** rate *od.* schätz mal!; **my ~ is [that] ...:** ich schätze, daß ...; **miss one's ~** *(Amer.)* sich verschätzen; **I'll give you three ~es** *(coll.)* dreimal darfst du raten *(ugs.)*; **have another ~ coming** *(coll.)* sich verrechnet haben *(ugs.)*; *see also* **anybody b**

guessing-game ['gesɪŋgeɪm] *n.* Ratespiel, *das*

guesstimate ['gestɪmət] *n. (coll.)* grobe Schätzung

'guesswork *n., no pl., no indef. art.* **be ~:** eine Vermutung sein; **rely largely on ~:** [weitgehend] auf Vermutungen angewiesen sein; **How did you know? – Oh, it was only [by] ~:** Woher wußtest du das? – Ach, ich habe nur geraten

guest [gest] *n.* Gast, *der; attrib.* Gast⟨*auftritt, -spiel, -vortrag, -redner*⟩; Gäste⟨*handtuch*⟩; **be my ~** *(fig. coll.)* tun Sie sich/tu dir keinen Zwang an; **as [the] ~ of** als Gast (+ *Gen.*); **~ of honour** Ehrengast, *der*

guest: ~-house *n.* Pension, *die;* **~ list** *n.* Gästeliste, *die* **(at** *Gen.***)**; **~-night** *n.* Gästeabend, *der;* **~-room** *n.* Gästezimmer, *das;* **~ worker** *n.* Gastarbeiter, *der*/-arbeiterin, *die*

guff [gʌf] *n. (sl.)* Mumpitz, *der (ugs.)*

guffaw [gʌ'fɔ:, 'gʌfɔ:] **1.** *n.* brüllendes Gelächter; **give a [great] ~:** in brüllendes Gelächter ausbrechen. **2.** *v. i.* brüllend lachen

guidance ['gaɪdəns] *n., no pl., no indef. art.* **a)** *(leadership, direction)* Führung, *die; (by teacher, tutor, etc.)* [An]leitung, *die;* **pray for God's ~:** Gott bitten, einem den rechten Weg zu weisen; **b)** *(advice)* Rat, *der;* **turn to sb. for ~:** jmdn. um Rat fragen *od.* bitten; **give sb. ~ on sth.** jmdn. in etw. *(Dat.)* beraten; **financial/vocational ~:** Finanz-/Berufsberatung, *die*

guide [gaɪd] **1.** *n.* **a)** Führer, *der*/Führerin, *die; (Tourism)* [Fremden]führer, *der*/-führerin, *die; (professional mountain-climber)* [Berg]führer, *der*/-führerin, *die;* **b)** *(fig.: mentor)* Lehrer, *der*/Lehrerin, *die;* **God is my ~:** Gott leitet mich; **c)** *(directing principle)* Richtschnur, *die;* **always let your conscience be your ~:** laß dich stets von deinem Gewissen leiten; **d)** *(indicator)* **be a [good/bad] ~ to sth.** ein [guter/schlechter] Anhaltspunkt für etw. sein; **be no/little ~ to sth.** keine/nur begrenzte Rückschlüsse auf etw. *(Akk.)* zulassen; **e)** *(Brit.: member of girls' organization)* **[Girl] G~:** Pfadfinderin, *die;* **the G~s** *(organization)* die Pfadfinderinnen; **King's/Queen's G~:** *(im Britischen Commonwealth) Pfadfinderin der höchsten Rangstufe;* **f)** *(handbook)* Handbuch, *das;* **a ~ to healthier living** ein Ratgeber für ein gesünderes Leben; **g)** *(book for tourists)* [Reise]führer, *der; (on entertainment, with dates)* Veranstaltungskalender, *der;* **a ~ to York/the cathedral/the museum** ein Führer für *od.* durch York/für die Kathedrale/ein Museumsführer; **h)** *(Mech. Engin.)* Führung, *die.* **2.** *v. t.* **a)** führen ⟨*Personen, Pflug, Maschinenteil usw.*⟩; **b)** *(fig.)* bestimmen ⟨*Handeln, Urteil*⟩; anleiten ⟨*Schüler, Lehrling*⟩; **be ~d by sth./sb.** sich von etw./jmdm. leiten lassen; **guiding star** *(fig.)* Leitstern, *der (geh.);* **guiding hand** *(fig.)* leitende Hand; **c)** *(conduct affairs of)* führen, lenken ⟨*Land, Staat*⟩; lenken ⟨*Angelegenheit*⟩; führen ⟨*Finanzen*⟩

'guidebook *see* **guide 1 g**

guided missile [gaɪdɪd 'mɪsaɪl] *n.* Lenkflugkörper, *der*

'guide-dog *n.* **~ [for the blind]** Blinden[führ]hund, *der*

guided tour [gaɪdɪd 'tʊə(r)] *n.* Führung, *die* **(of** durch**)**

guide: ~line *n. (fig.)* Richtlinie, *die; (model)* Vorlage, *die;* **~-post** *n.* Wegweiser, *der*

Guider ['gaɪdə(r)] *n. (Brit.)* Pfadfinderführerin, *die*

guild [gɪld] *n.* **a)** Verein, *der;* Vereinigung, *die;* **b)** *(Hist.) (of merchants)* Gilde, *die; (of artisans)* Zunft, *die*

'guild-hall *n.* **a)** *(town hall)* Rathaus, *das;* **[the] Guildhall** *(Brit.)* die Guildhall *(in London);* **b)** *(Hist.) (for merchants)* Gildehaus, *das; (for artisans)* Zunfthaus, *das*

guile [gaɪl] *n., no pl.* Arglist, *die (geh.);* Hinterlist, *die; (wiliness)* List, *die;* **be without ~:** ohne Arg *od.* Falsch sein *(geh.)*

guileful ['gaɪlfl] *adj.* arglistig *(geh.);* hinterlistig; *(wily)* listig

guileless [gaɪllɪs] *adj.* arglos

guillemot ['gɪlɪmɒt] *n. (Ornith.) (Uria)* Lumme, *die; (Cepphus)* Teiste, *die*

guillotine ['gɪləti:n] **1.** *n.* **a)** Guillotine, *die;* Fallbeil, *das;* **b)** *(for paper)* Papierschneidemaschine, *die; (for metal)* Schlagschere, *die;* **c)** *(Brit. Parl.)* Begrenzung der Beratungszeit *(im Gesetzgebungsverfahren).* **2.** *v.t.* **a)** *(behead)* guillotinieren; mit der Guillotine *od.* dem Fallbeil hinrichten; **b)** *(cut)* schneiden

guilt [gɪlt] *n., no pl.* **a)** Schuld, *die* **(of, for** an + *Dat.***)**; **bear the ~ of** *or* **for sth.** die Schuld für etw. auf sich *(Akk.)* tragen; **b)** *(awareness of being in the wrong)* Schuldbewußtsein, *das; (guilty feeling)* Schuldgefühle *Pl.;* **feel [full of] ~:** [starke] Schuldgefühle haben; **~ was written all over his face** sein schlechtes Gewissen stand ihm im Gesicht geschrieben; **~ complex** *(Psych.)* Schuldkomplex, *der;* **~-feelings** Schuldgefühle

guiltily ['gɪltɪlɪ] *adv.* schuldbewußt

guiltless ['gɪltlɪs] *adj.* unschuldig **(of an** + *Dat.***)**

guilty ['gɪltɪ] *adj.* **a)** schuldig; **the ~ person** der/die Schuldige; **be ~ of murder** des Mordes schuldig sein; **find sb. ~/not ~ [of sth.]** jmdn. [an etw. *(Dat.)*] schuldig sprechen/[von etw.] freisprechen; **~ thoughts** böse Gedanken; **[return** *or* **find a verdict of] ~/not ~:** [auf] „schuldig"/„nicht schuldig" [erkennen]; **feel ~ about sth./having done sth.** *(coll.)* ein schlechtes Gewissen haben wegen etw./, weil man etw. getan hat; **everyone is/we're all ~ of that** *(coll.)* das tut jeder/das tun wir alle; **I've often been ~ of that myself** *(coll.)* das habe ich auch schon oft gemacht; **be ~ of bad taste** eine Geschmacklosigkeit begangen haben; **b)** *(prompted by guilt)* schuldbewußt ⟨*Miene, Blick, Verhalten*⟩; schlecht ⟨*Gewissen*⟩

Guinea ['gɪnɪ] *pr. n.* Guinea *(das)*

guinea *n. (Hist.)* Guinee, *die*

guinea: ~-fowl, ~-hen *ns.* Perlhuhn, *das*

Guinean ['gɪnɪən] **1.** *adj.* guineisch. **2.** *n.* Guineer, *der*/Guineerin, *die*

'guinea-pig *n.* **a)** *(animal)* Meerschweinchen, *das;* **b)** *(fig.: subject of experiment) (person)* Versuchsperson, *die;* Versuchskaninchen, *das (ugs. abwertend); (thing)* Versuchsobjekt, *das;* **act as ~:** Versuchskaninchen spielen

guise [gaɪz] *n.* **a)** *(semblance)* Gestalt, *die;* **in** *or* **under the ~ of** in Gestalt (+ *Gen.*); **b)** *(pretence)* Vorwand, *der;* **c)** *(external appearance)* Äußere, *das*

guitar [gɪ'tɑ:(r)] *n.* Gitarre, *die; attrib.* Gitarren⟨*musik, -spieler, -konzert*⟩; **electric ~:** elektrische Gitarre; Elektrogitarre, *die*

guitarist [gɪ'tɑ:rɪst] *n.* Gitarrist, *der*/Gitarristin, *die*

Gujarati [gu:dʒə'rɑ:tɪ] **1.** *adj.* gudscharatisch. **2.** *n.* **a)** *(person)* Gudscharate, *der*/Gudscharatin, *die;* **b)** *(language)* Gudscharati, *das*

gulch [gʌltʃ] *n. (Amer.)* Schlucht, *die;* Klamm, *die*

gules [gju:lz] *(esp. Her.)* **1.** *n.* Rot, *das.* **2.** *adj.* rot

gulf [gʌlf] *n.* **a)** *(portion of sea)* Golf, *der;* Meerbusen, *der;* **the [Arabian** *or* **Persian] G~:** der Persische Golf; **the G~ of Bothnia/Mexico** der Bottnische Meerbusen/der Golf von Mexiko; **b)** *(wide difference, impassable gap)* Kluft, *die;* **there is a great ~ between them** es besteht eine tiefe Kluft zwischen ihnen; **c)** *(chasm)* Abgrund, *der*

Gulf: ~ States *pr. n. pl.* Golfstaaten *Pl.;* **~ Stream** *pr. n.* Golfstrom, *der*

gull [gʌl] *n.* Möwe, *die*

gullet ['gʌlɪt] *n.* **a)** *(food-passage)* Speiseröhre, *die;* **b)** *(throat)* Kehle, *die;* Gurgel, *die*

gullible ['gʌlɪbl] *adj.* leichtgläubig; *(trusting)* gutgläubig

'gull-wing *adj.* **~ door** Flügeltür, *die*

gully ['gʌlɪ] *n.* **a)** *(artificial channel)* Abzugskanal, *der;* Abzugsrinne, *die;* **b)** *(drain)* Gully, *der;* **c)** *(water-worn ravine)* [Erosions]rinne, *die;* Runse, *die (Geol.);* **d)** *(Cricket) Position/Feldspieler seitlich hinter dem Schlagmann*

'gully-hole *see* **gully b**

gulp [gʌlp] **1.** *v. t.* hinunterschlingen; hinuntergießen ⟨*Getränk*⟩. **2.** *v. i. (swallow with difficulty)* würgen; *(choke, swallow on account of shock)* schlucken; **~ for air** nach Luft ringen *od.* schnappen. **3.** *n.* **a)** *(act of ~ing, effort to swallow)* Schlucken, *das;* **swallow in** *or* **at one ~:** mit einem Schluck herunterstürzen ⟨*Getränk*⟩; in einem Bissen herunterschlingen ⟨*Speise*⟩; **b)** *(large mouthful) (of drink)* kräftiger Schluck; *(of food)* großer Bissen; **c)** *(act of swallowing due to shock)* **give a ~:** schlucken

~ 'back *v. t.* hinunterschlucken ⟨*Tränen*⟩; unterdrücken ⟨*Schluchzer*⟩

~ 'down *v. t.* hinunterschlingen; hinuntergießen ⟨*Getränk*⟩

¹gum [gʌm] *n., usu. in pl. (Anat.)* **~[s]** Zahnfleisch, *das*

²gum 1. *n.* **a)** *(viscous secretion)* Gummi, *das; (glue)* Klebstoff, *der;* **b)** *(sweet)* Gummibonbon, *der od. das;* **c)** *(Amer.) see* **chewing-gum; d)** *(tree) see* **gum-tree. 2.** *v. t.*, **-mm-: a)** *(smear with ~)* mit Klebstoff bestreichen; gummieren ⟨*Briefmarken, Etiketten usw.*⟩; **b)** *(fasten with ~)* kleben

~ 'up *v. t.* aufkleben; **~ up the works** *(fig. sl.)* alles vermasseln *(salopp)*

gum: ~ 'arabic *see* **Arabic 1; ~boil** *n.* Zahnfleischabszeß, *der;* **~boot** *n.* Gummistiefel, *der*

gummy ['gʌmɪ] *adj.* **a)** *(sticky)* klebrig; **b)** *(covered with gum)* mit Klebstoff verschmiert

gumption ['gʌmpʃn] *n., no pl., no indef. art. (coll.)* **a)** *(resourcefulness)* Grips, *der (ugs.); (enterprising spirit)* Unternehmungsgeist, *der;* **she had the ~ to open the door** sie war clever genug, die Tür zu öffnen; **b)** *(practical sense)* praktische Veranlagung; **have a lot of ~:** sehr praktisch veranlagt sein

gum: ~-shield *n.* Mundschutz, *der;* **~-tree** *n.* Gummiharz liefernder Baum; *(eucalyptus)* [Australischer] Gummibaum; **be up a ~-tree** *(fig.)* in der Klemme sitzen *(ugs.)*

gun [gʌn] **1.** *n.* **a)** Schußwaffe, *die; (piece of artillery)* Geschütz, *das; (rifle)* Gewehr, *das; (pistol)* Pistole, *die; (revolver)* Revolver, *der;* **big ~** *(sl.: important person)* hohes *od.* großes Tier *(ugs.);* **be going great ~s** laufen wie geschmiert *(ugs.);* ⟨*Person:*⟩ toll in Schwung sein *(ugs.);* **son of a ~** *(coll.)* Hund, *der (salopp); (joc.)* alter Hund *(salopp);* **stick to one's ~s** auf seinem Posten bleiben; *(fig.)* auf seinem Standpunkt beharren; **give it the ~!** *(coll.)* drück auf die Tube! *(ugs.);* **~s or butter** *(fig.)* Macht oder Wohlleben; **b)** *(starting-pistol)* Startpistole, *die;* **wait for the ~:** auf den Startschuß warten; **beat** *or* **jump the ~:** einen Fehlstart verursachen; *(fig.)* vorpreschen; *(by saying sth.)* vorzeitig etwas bekanntwerden lassen; **c)** *(member of shooting-party)* Schütze, *der.* **2.** *v. t.,* **-nn- a)** *(Amer. coll.)* erschießen; umlegen *(salopp);* **b)** *(coll.)* **~ the engine** den Motor hochdrehen

~ 'down *v. t.* niederschießen

~ for *v. t.* **a)** *(seek with gun)* Jagd machen auf (+ *Akk.*); **b)** *(fig.)* auf dem Kieker haben *(ugs.)*

gun: ~-battle *n.* Schießerei, *die;* **~boat** *n.* Kanonenboot, *das;* **~boat diplomacy** Kanonenbootpolitik, *die;* **~-carriage** *n.* [fahrbare] Geschützlafette; **~-cotton** *n.* Schießbaumwolle, *die;* **~ crew** *n.* Geschützbedienung, *die;* **~ dog** *n.* Jagdhund, *der;* **~-fight** *n. (Amer. coll.)* Schießerei, *die;* **~fighter** *n.* Revolverheld, *der;* **~-fire** *n.* Geschützfeuer, *das; (of small arms)* Schießerei, *die*

gunge [gʌndʒ] *(Brit. coll.)* **1.** *n.* Schmiere, *die.* **2.** *v.t.* **~ up** verschmieren; **be/get ~d up** schmierig werden

gung-ho [gʌŋ'həʊ] *adj.* wild entschlossen; **be very ~ for sth.** ein leidenschaftlicher Verfechter einer Sache *(Gen.)* sein

gungy ['gʌndʒɪ] *adj. (Brit. coll.)* schmierig

gunk [gʌŋk] *n. (sl.)* Schmiere, *die*

gun: ~man ['gʌnmən] *n., pl.* **~men** ['gʌnmən] [mit einer Schußwaffe] bewaffneter Mann; **~-metal** *n.* Geschützbronze, *die; (colour)* Metallgrau, *das;* **~ moll** *n. (Amer. sl.)* **a)** *(armed woman criminal)* Revolverbraut, *die (salopp);* **b)** *see* **moll**

gunnel ['gʌnl] *see* **gunwale**

gunner ['gʌnə(r)] *n.* Artillerist, *der; (private soldier)* Kanonier, *der*

gunnery ['gʌnərɪ] *n., no pl.* Geschützwesen, *das*

gunny ['gʌnɪ] *n.* Rupfen, *der;* **~ cloth** Rupfenleinwand, *die;* **~-sack** Rupfensack, *der*

gun: ~-play *n., no pl., no indef. art.* Schießereien; *(single fight)* Schießerei, *die;* **~point** *n. see* **point 1 b;** **~powder** *n.* Schießpulver, *das;* **Gunpowder Plot** *(Hist.)* Pulververschwörung, *die;* **~room** *n.* **a)** *(in house)* Waffenkammer, *die;* **b)** *(in warship)* Kadettenmesse, *die;* **~-runner** *n.* Waffenschmuggler, *der*/-schmugglerin, *die;* **~-running** *n.* Waffenschmuggel, *der;* **~ship** *n.* Kampfhubschrauber, *der;* **~shot** *n.* **a)** *(shot)* Schuß, *der;* **~shot wound** Schußwunde, *die;* **b) within/out of ~shot** in/außer Schußweite; **~slinger** *see* **gunman;** **~smith** *n.* Büchsenmacher, *der*

gunwale ['gʌnl] *n. (Naut.)* Schandeck, *das;* Schandeckel, *der; (of rowing-boat)* Dollbord, *der*

guppy ['gʌpɪ] *n. (Zool.)* Guppy, *der*

gurgle ['gɜ:gl] **1.** *n.* Gluckern, *das; (of brook)* Plätschern, *das; (of baby)* Lallen, *das; (with delight)* Glucksen, *das.* **2.** *v. i.* gluckern; ⟨*Bach:*⟩ plätschern; ⟨*Baby:*⟩ lallen/glucksen. **3.** *v. t.* glucksen

Gurkha ['gɜ:kə, 'gʊəkə] *n.* Gurkha, *der*

gurnard ['gɜ:nəd], **gurnet** ['gɜ:nɪt] *n. (Zool.)* Knurrhahn, *der*

guru ['gʊru:] *n.* **a)** Guru, *der;* **b)** *(mentor)* Mentor, *der*

gush [gʌʃ] **1.** *n.* **a)** *(sudden stream)* Schwall, *der;* **b)** *(effusiveness)* Überschwenglichkeit, *die;* **c)** *(sentimental affectation)* Schmalz, *der (abwertend).* **2.** *v. i.* **a)** strömen; schießen; *(fig.: speak or act effusively)* überschwenglich sein; **~ out** herausströmen; herausschießen; **water ~ed down through the ceiling** das Wasser floß in Strömen durch die Decke; **b)** *(fig.: speak or act with sentimental affectation)* schwärmen. **3.** *v. t.* **a) sth. ~es water/oil/blood** Wasser/Öl/Blut schießt aus etw. hervor; **b) '...' she ~ed** „...", sagte sie begeistert

gusher ['gʌʃə(r)] *n.* **a)** *(oil-well)* [natürlich sprudelnde] Ölquelle; **b)** *(person)* exaltierter Mensch

gushing ['gʌʃɪŋ] *adj.* **a)** reißend ⟨*Strom*⟩; strömend ⟨*Regen*⟩; **b)** *(effusive)* exaltiert

gusset ['gʌsɪt] *n. (strengthening)* Verstärkung, *die; (enlarging)* Einsatz, *der; (triangular)* Zwickel, *der;* Keil, *der*

gust [gʌst] **1.** *n.* **a)** *(rush of wind)* **~ [of wind]** Windstoß, *der;* Bö[e], *die;* **b) ~ of rain** Regenbö[e], *die.* **2.** *v. i.* böig wehen

gusto ['gʌstəʊ] *n., no pl. (enjoyment)* Genuß, *der; (vitality)* Schwung, *der*

gusty ['gʌstɪ] *adj.* böig; **~ rain** Regenböen

gut [gʌt] **1.** *n.* **a)** *(material)* Darm, *der; (for fishing-line)* Seidenwurmdarm, *der; (Med.: for stitches)* Katgut, *das;* **b)** *in pl. (bowels)* Eingeweide *Pl.;* Gedärme *Pl.;* **hate sb.'s ~s** *(coll.)* jmdn. auf den Tod nicht ausstehen können; **sweat** *or* **work one's ~s out** *(coll.)* sich dumm und dämlich schuften *(ugs.);* **c)** *in pl. (fig.: substantial contents)* Innereien *Pl. (scherzh.); (of problem, matter)* Kern, *der;* **sth. has no ~s in it** etw. ist ohne Saft und Kraft; etw. ist fad[e]; **d)** *in pl. (coll.: pluck)* Schneid, *der (ugs.);* Mumm, *der (ugs.);* **e)** *(intestine)* Darm, *der;* **large/small ~:** Dick-/Dünndarm, *der;* **bust a ~** *(sl.)* sich totarbeiten *(ugs.);* **f)** *(narrow water-passage) (of sea)* Meerenge, *die;* Sund, *der; (of river)* Fluß-, Stromenge, *die.* **2.** *v. t.,* **-tt- a)** *(take out ~s of)* ausnehmen; **b)** *(remove or destroy fittings in)* ausräumen; **the fire ~ted the house** bei dem Feuer ist das Haus ausgebrannt; **it was ~ted [by the fire]** es brannte aus; **c)** *(extract essence of)* ≈ exzerpieren ⟨*Buch*⟩. **3.** *attrib. adj.* **a)** *(fundamental)* grundlegend ⟨*Problem*⟩; **b)** *(instinctive)* gefühlsmäßig ⟨*Reaktion*⟩

gutsy ['gʌtsɪ] *adj. (coll.: courageous)* mutig

gutta-percha [gʌtə'pɜ:tʃə, gʌtə'pɜ:kə] *n.* Guttapercha, *die od. das*

gutter ['gʌtə(r)] **1.** *n.* **a)** *(below edge of roof)* Dach- *od.* Regenrinne, *die; (at side of street)* Rinnstein, *der;* Gosse, *die; (open conduit)* Rinne, *die;* **the ~** *(fig.)* die Gosse; **b)** *(track worn by water)* Rinne, *die.* **2.** *v. i.* ⟨*Kerze:*⟩ tropfen; ⟨*Flamme:*⟩ [immer schwächer] flackern

guttering ['gʌtərɪŋ] *n. (on roof)* Dachrinnen; *(in floor)* Rinnen

gutter: ~ press *n.* Sensationspresse, *die (abwertend);* **~snipe** *n.* Gassenjunge, *der (abwertend)*

guttural ['gʌtərl] **1.** *adj.* **a)** *(from the throat)* guttural; kehlig; **b)** *(of the throat)* Kehl-; *(of the larynx)* Kehlkopf-; **c)** *(Phonet.)* Kehl-; guttural *(Sprachw. veralt.).* **2.** *n. (Phonet.)* Gaumensegellaut, *der;* Guttural[laut], *der (Sprachw. veralt.)*

guv [gʌv], **guv'nor** ['gʌvnə(r)] *(Brit. sl.) see* **governor g**

¹guy [gaɪ] *n. (rope, wire)* Halteseil, *das; (for hoisted things)* Lenkseil, *das*

²guy 1. *n.* **a)** *(sl.: man)* Typ, *der (ugs.);* **b)** *in pl. (Amer.: everyone)* **[listen,] you ~s!** [hört mal,] Kinder! *(ugs.);* **c)** *(Brit.: effigy)* Guy-Fawkes-Puppe, *die;* **Guy Fawkes Day** *Festtag (5. November) zum Gedenken an die Pulververschwörung.* **2.** *v. t. (ridicule)* sich lustig machen über (+ *Akk.*)

Guyana [gaɪ'ænə] *pr. n.* Gu[a]yana *(das)*

Guyanese [gaɪə'ni:z] **1.** *adj.* gu[a]yanisch. **2.** *n.* Gu[a]yaner, *der*/Gu[a]yanerin, *die*

guy: ~-rope *n.* Zelt[spann]leine, *die;* **~-wire** *n.* Spanndraht, *der;* Drahtseilabspannung, *die*

guzzle ['gʌzl] **1.** *v. t. (eat)* hinunterschlingen; *(drink)* hinuntergießen; *(eat or drink up)* wegputzen *(ugs.).* **2.** *v. i.* schlingen

gybe [dʒaɪb] *(Naut.)* **1.** *v. i.* **a)** *(swing across)* übergehen; **b)** *(change course)* halsen; *(accidentally)* eine Patenthalse machen. **2.** *n. (change of course)* Halse, *die; (accidental)* Patenthalse, *die; (swing of boom)* Schwenken, *das;* **~-oh!** rund achtern!

gym [dʒɪm] *n. (coll.)* **a)** *(gymnasium)* Turnhalle, *die;* **b)** *no pl., no indef. art. (gymnastics)* Turnen, *das;* **~ teacher** Turnlehrer, *der*/Turnlehrerin, *die*

gymkhana [dʒɪm'kɑ:nə] *n.* **a)** *(meeting)* Gymkhana, *das;* **b)** *(display)* Sportfest, *das*

gymnasium *n.* **a)** [dʒɪm'neɪzɪəm] *pl.* **~s** *or* **gymnasia** [dʒɪm'neɪzɪə] Turnhalle, *die;* **b)** [dʒɪm'neɪzɪəm, gɪm'nɑ:zɪʊm] *pl.* **~s** *(German school)* Gymnasium, *das*

gymnast ['dʒɪmnæst] *n.* Turner, *der*/Turnerin, *die*

gymnastic [dʒɪm'næstɪk] *adj.* turnerisch ⟨*Können*⟩; **~ exercise** gymnastische Übung; *(esp. with apparatus)* Turnübung, *die;* **~ equipment** Turngeräte; *(portable)* gymnastische Geräte

gymnastics [dʒɪm'næstɪks] *n., no pl.* **a)** *(exercise)* Gymnastik, *die; (esp. with apparatus)* Turnen, *das; attrib.* Gymnastik-/Turn⟨*stunde, -lehrer*⟩; **b)** *(fig.)* **mental ~:** Gehirnakrobatik, *die (ugs. scherzh.);* **verbal ~:** Wortakrobatik, *die (ugs. scherzh.)*

gym: ~-shoe *n.* Turnschuh, *der;* **~-slip, ~-tunic** *ns.* Trägerrock, *der (für die Schule)*

gynaecological [gaɪnɪkə'lɒdʒɪkl] *adj. (Med.)* gynäkologisch

gynaecologist [gaɪnɪ'kɒlədʒɪst] *n. (Med.)* Gynäkologe, *der*/Gynäkologin, *die;* Frauenarzt, *der*/Frauenärztin, *die*

gynaecology [gaɪnɪ'kɒlədʒɪ] *n. (Med.)* Gynäkologie, *die;* Frauenheilkunde, *die*

gynecological *etc. (Amer.) see* **gynaec-**

gyp [dʒɪp] *n.* **give sb. ~** *(coll.) (scold sb.)* jmdn. zusammenstauchen *(ugs.); (pain sb.)* jmdm. sehr zu schaffen machen *(ugs.)*

gypsophila [dʒɪp'sɒfɪlə] *n. (Bot.)* Gipskraut, *das*

gypsum ['dʒɪpsəm] *n.* Gips, *der*

gypsy, Gypsy ['dʒɪpsɪ] *n.* Zigeuner, *der*/Zigeunerin, *die;* **family of gypsies** Zigeunerfamilie, *die*

gypsy: ~ moth *n. (Zool.)* Schwammspinner, *der;* **~ rose** *n. (Bot.)* Krätz[en]kraut, *das*

gyrate [dʒaɪə'reɪt] *v. i.* sich drehen; kreiseln

gyration [dʒaɪə'reɪʃn] *n.* Drehung, *die;* kreiselnde Bewegung

gyratory ['dʒaɪərətərɪ] *adj.* kreiselnd

gyrfalcon ['dʒɜ:fɔ:lkn, 'dʒɜ:fɒlkn] *n. (Ornith.)* Gerfalke, *der*

gyro ['dʒaɪərəʊ] *n., pl.* **~s** *(coll.) see* **gyroscope**

'gyro-compass *n.* Kreiselkompaß, *der*

gyroscope ['dʒaɪərəskəʊp] *n. (Phys., Naut., Aeronaut.)* Kreisel, *der; (for scientific purposes)* Gyroskop, *das*

gyroscopic [dʒaɪərə'skɒpɪk] *adj.* Kreisel-

gyro-'stabilizer *n.* Schiffskreisel, *der*

H

[1]H, h [eɪtʃ] *n., pl.* **Hs** *or* **H's** ['eɪtʃɪz] *(letter)* H, h, *das; see also* **drop 3g**
[2]H *abbr. (on pencil)* **hard** H
h. *abbr.* **a) hecto-** h; **b) hour[s]** Std[n].; **at 17^{00}h** um 17.00 h
ha [hɑ:] **1.** *int. expr. surprise, triumph* ha; *expr. hesitation* hm. **2.** *v. i. see* **hum 1a. 3.** *n., pl.* **ha's** *see* **hum 3b**
ha. *abbr.* **hectare[s]** ha
habeas corpus [heɪbɪəs 'kɔ:pəs] *n., no pl. (Law)* Anordnung eines Haftprüfungstermins; **Habeas Corpus Act** Habeaskorpusakte, *die*
haberdasher ['hæbədæʃə(r)] *n.* **a)** *(Brit.)* Kurzwarenhändler, *der*/-händlerin, *die;* **b)** *(Amer.) (dealer in men's accessories)* Inhaber eines Geschäfts für Herrenartikel; *(dealer in menswear)* Herrenausstatter, *der;* **c) ~'s** *see* **haberdashery b**
haberdashery ['hæbədæʃərɪ] *n.* **a)** *(goods) (Brit.)* Kurzwaren *Pl.; (Amer.: men's accessories)* Herrenartikel; *(Amer.: menswear)* Herrenmoden; **b)** *(shop) (Brit.)* Kurzwarengeschäft, *das;* Kurzwarenhandlung, *die; (Amer.)* Geschäft für Herrenartikel/Herrenmodengeschäft, *das;* **c)** *(department) (Brit.)* Kurzwarenabteilung, *die; (Amer.)* Abteilung für Herrenartikel/Herrenmodenabteilung, *die*
habit ['hæbɪt] **1.** *n.* **a)** *(set practice)* Gewohnheit, *die;* **good/bad ~:** gute/schlechte [An]gewohnheit; **the ~ of smoking** das [gewohnheitsmäßige] Rauchen; **have a** *or* **the ~ of doing sth.** die Angewohnheit haben, etw. zu tun; **the sun has a ~ of disappearing at the weekend** *(iron.)* zum Wochenende verzieht sich die Sonne regelmäßig; **make a [regular] ~ of doing sth.** sich *(Dat.)* angewöhnen, etw. [regelmäßig] zu tun; **you shouldn't make a ~ of it** du solltest es nicht zur Gewohnheit werden lassen; **let sth. become** *or (coll.)* **get to be a ~:** etw. zur Gewohnheit werden *od. (ugs.)* einreißen lassen; **out of** *or* **from [force of] ~:** aus Gewohnheit; **old ~s die hard** der Mensch ist ein Gewohnheitstier *(ugs.);* **be in the ~ of doing sth.** die Gewohnheit haben, etw. zu tun; **not be in the ~ of doing sth.** es nicht gewohnt sein, etw. zu tun; **I'm not in the ~ of accepting lifts from strangers** ich pflege mich nicht von Fremden im Auto mitnehmen zu lassen; **get** *or* **fall into a** *or* **the ~ of doing sth.** [es] sich *(Dat.)* angewöhnen, etw. zu tun; **get into** *or* **form** *or* **acquire good ~s** gute Angewohnheiten annehmen; **get** *or* **fall into** *or (coll.)* **pick up bad ~s** schlechte [An]gewohnheiten annehmen; **get out of** *or* **give up** *or* **stop a/the ~:** sich *(Dat.)* etwas/das abgewöhnen; eine/die Angewohnheit ablegen; **get out of the ~ of doing sth.** [es] sich *(Dat.)* abgewöhnen, etw. zu tun; **b)** *(coll.) (addiction)* Süchtigkeit, *die;* [Drogen]abhängigkeit, *die; (craving)* Sucht, *die;* **have got the ~:** süchtig sein; User sein *(Drogenjargon);* **c)** *(dress)* Habit, *der od. das; (woman's riding-dress)* Reitkostüm, *das; (arch.: clothing)* Gewand, *das;* **d)** *(Psych.)* Habit, *das od. der;* **e)** *(Biol., Chem.)* Habitus, *der.* **2.** *v. t. (formal: clothe)* kleiden
habitable ['hæbɪtəbl] *adj.* bewohnbar
habitat ['hæbɪtæt] *n.* **a)** *(of animals, plants)* Habitat, *das (Zool., Bot.);* Lebensraum, *der;* Standort, *der (Bot.); (of humans)* Lebensraum, *der;* **b)** *see* **habitation b**
habitation [hæbɪ'teɪʃn] *n.* **a)** *(inhabiting)* [Be]wohnen, *das;* **fit/unfit** *or* **not fit for human ~:** bewohnbar/unbewohnbar; **b)** *(place)* Wohnstätte, *die (geh.)*
habit-forming ['hæbɪtfɔ:mɪŋ] *adj.* Abhängigkeit erzeugend; **be ~:** Abhängigkeit erzeugen; abhängig machen; *(fig.)* leicht zur Gewohnheit werden [können]
habitual [hə'bɪtjʊəl] *adj.* **a)** *(customary)* gewohnt; üblich; **b)** *(continual, recurring)* ständig; **that's a ~ problem of hers** das ist immer wieder ihr Problem; **c)** *(given to habit)* gewohnheitsmäßig; Gewohnheits‹*trinker*›; notorisch *(abwertend),* gewohnheitsmäßig ‹*Lügner*›
habitually [hə'bɪtjʊəlɪ] *adv.* **a)** *(regularly, recurrently)* regelmäßig; **b)** *(incessantly)* ständig
habituate [hə'bɪtjʊeɪt] *v. t.* **~ sb./oneself to sth./sb.** jmdn./sich an etw./jmdn. gewöhnen; **~ sb./oneself to doing sth.** jmdn./sich daran gewöhnen, etw. zu tun; **become [too] ~d to sth.** sich [zu sehr] an etw. *(Akk.)* gewöhnen
habitué [hə'bɪtjʊeɪ] *n.* Habitué, *der (veralt.);* regelmäßiger Besucher; *(of hotel, casino, etc.)* Stammgast, *der*
Habsburg ['hæpsbɜ:g] *pr. n.* **a)** *(place)* Habsburg *(das);* **b)** *(family name)* Habsburger, *der;* **the ~ family** die Habsburger *Pl.;* **the ~ emperors** die habsburgischen Kaiser; die Habsburgerkaiser
[1]hack [hæk] **1.** *v. t.* **a)** *(cut)* hacken ‹*Holz*›; **~ sb./sth. to bits** *or* **pieces** jmdn. zerstückeln/etw. in Stücke hacken; **~ to bits** *or* **pieces** *(fig.)* zerpflücken; kaputtmachen ‹*Ruf*›; verreißen ‹*Artikel*›; **~ sth. out of sth.** etw. aus etw. heraushacken; **~ one's way [through/along/out of sth.]** sich *(Dat.)* einen Weg [durch etw./etw. entlang/aus etw. heraus] [frei]schlagen; **b)** *(Footb.)* **~ sb.'s shin** jmdm. *od.* jmdn. vors *od.* gegen das Schienbein treten. **2.** *v. i.* **a)** *(deal blows)* **~ at** herumhacken auf (+ *Dat.*); **~ through the undergrowth** sich *(Dat.)* einen Weg durchs Unterholz schlagen; **b) ~ing cough** trockener Husten; Reizhusten, *der*
~ a'bout *v. t.* verpfuschen *(ugs.); (fig.)* zurechtstutzen
~ a'way 1. *v. i.* **~ away at sth.** auf etw. *(Akk.)* einhacken; *(fig.)* etw. aushöhlen. **2.** *v. t.* weghacken
~ 'off *v. t.* abhacken; abschlagen
~ 'out *v. t.* heraushauen **(from** aus); *(fig.: work out)* zustande bringen
[2]hack 1. *n.* **a)** *(drudge)* ≈ Gelegenheitsarbeiter, *der;* Mietling, *der (veralt. abwertend); (uninspired worker)* Arbeitstier, *das; (writer)* Schreiberling, *der (abwertend);* **newspaper ~:** Zeitungsschreiber, *der;* **publisher's ~:** Lohnschreiber, *der;* Auftragsschreiber, *der;* **b)** *(hired horse)* Mietpferd, *das;* **c)** *(horse for ordinary riding)* Reitpferd, *das;* **d)** *see* **[1]jade 1a; e)** *(Amer.) (taxi)* Taxi, *das; (taxi-driver)* Taxifahrer, *der.* **2.** *adj.* **a) ~ writer** Lohnschreiber, *der;* **b)** *(mediocre)* Nullachtfünfzehn- *(ugs. abwertend)*
hacker ['hækə(r)] *n. (Computing)* Hacker, *der*
hacking ['hækɪŋ]: **~ coat, ~ jacket** *ns.* Reitjackett, *das; (sports jacket)* Sportjacke, *die*
hackle ['hækl] *n.* **a)** *(long feather/feathers)* Schmuckfeder, *die*/Schmuckfedern; *(neck plumage)* Kragen, *der;* Kragenfedern; **b)** *in pl. (animal's hair)* Nacken[- und Rücken]haare *Pl.;* **a cock's/a dog's ~s are up** ein Hahn sträubt die Federn *od.* stellt die Federn auf/einem Hund sträubt sich das Fell; **sb.'s ~s rise/are up** *(fig.)* jmd. gerät/ist in Harnisch; **get sb.'s ~s up, make sb.'s ~s rise** *(fig.)* jmdn. wütend machen; **that kind of thing always gets his ~s up** bei so was sieht er immer rot *(ugs.);* so etwas bringt ihn immer in Harnisch; **c)** *(comb)* Hechel, *die (Landw.)*
hackney ['hæknɪ] *n.* [gewöhnliches] Pferd; Gaul, *der (ugs.)*
hackney: ~ 'cab, ~ 'carriage *ns.* Droschke, *die (veralt.);* Taxe, *die;* **~ 'coach** *n. (Hist.)* [Pferde]droschke, *die*
hackneyed ['hæknɪd] *adj.* abgegriffen; abgedroschen *(ugs.)*
'hack-saw *n.* [Metall]bügelsäge, *die*
had *see* **have 1, 2**
haddie ['hædɪ] *(Scot.) see* **haddock**
haddock ['hædək] *n., pl. same* Schellfisch, *der;* **smoked ~:** Haddock, *der*
Hades ['heɪdi:z] *n., no pl.* **a)** *(Greek Mythol.)* Hades, *der;* **to/in ~:** in den/im Hades; **b)** *(coll. euphem.) see* **hell a**
hadji ['hædʒɪ] *n.* Hadschi, *der*
hadn't ['hædnt] *(coll.)* = **had not;** *see* **have 1, 2**
Hadrian's Wall [heɪdrɪənz 'wɔ:l] *n. (Hist.)* Hadrianswall, *der*
haematology [hi:mə'tɒlədʒɪ] *n. (Med.)* Hämatologie, *die*
haemoglobin [hi:mə'gləʊbɪn] *n. (Anat., Zool.)* Hämoglobin, *das*
haemophilia [hi:mə'fɪlɪə] *n. (Med.)* Hämophilie, *die (fachspr.);* Bluterkrankheit, *die*
haemophiliac [hi:mə'fɪlɪæk] *n. (Med.)* Bluter, *der*/Bluterin, *die*
haemorrhage ['hemərɪdʒ] *(Med.)* **1.** *n.* Hämorrhagie, *die (fachspr.);* Blutung, *die.* **2.** *v. i.* starke Blutungen haben
haemorrhoid ['hemərɔɪd] *n., usu. in pl. (Med.)* Hämorrhoide, *die*
haft [hɑ:ft] *n.* Griff, *der;* Heft, *das (geh.)*
hag [hæg] *n.* **a)** *(old woman)* [alte] Hexe; **b)** *(witch)* Hexe, *die;* **c)** *see* **hagfish**
'hagfish *n.* Inger, *der;* Schleimaal, *der*
haggard ['hægəd] *adj. (worn)* ausgezehrt; *(with worry)* abgehärmt; *(tired)* abgespannt
haggis ['hægɪs] *n. (Gastr.)* Haggis, *der; gefüllter Schafsmagen*
haggle ['hægl] **1.** *v. i.* sich zanken **(over, about** wegen); *(over price)* feilschen *(abwertend)* **(over, about** um). **2.** *n.* Gezänk, *das (abwertend); (over price)* Gefeilsche, *das (abwertend)*
hagiography [hægɪ'ɒgrəfɪ] *n.* Hagiographie, *die*
'hag-ridden *adj.* **be ~ by sth.** von etw. geplagt *od.* gequält werden; **look ~:** niedergedrückt aussehen
Hague [heɪg] *pr. n.* **The ~:** Den Haag *(das);* der Haag *(geh.);* **The ~ Conventions** die Haager Konventionen
ha ha [hɑ: 'hɑ:] *int.* haha!
ha-ha ['hɑ:hɑ:] *n.* Umfassungsgraben, *der;* Aha, *das (Bauw.)*
haiku ['haɪku:] *n., pl. same (Lit.)* Haiku, *das*
[1]hail [heɪl] **1.** *n.* **a)** *no pl., no indef. art. (Meteorol.)* Hagel, *der;* **b)** *(fig.: shower)* Hagel, *der; (of curses, insults, questions, praise)* Schwall, *der;* Flut, *die;* **a ~ of bullets/missiles/stones/arrows** ein Kugel-/Geschoß-/Stein-/Pfeilhagel *od.* -regen. **2.** *v. i.* **a)** *(impers.) (Meteorol.)* **it ~s** *or* **is ~ing** es hagelt; **b)** *(fig.: descend)* **~ down** niederprasseln **(on** auf + *Akk.*); **~ down on sb.** ‹*Beschimpfungen, Vorwürfe usw.:*› auf jmdn. einprasseln. **3.** *v. t.* niederhageln *od.* niederprasseln lassen
[2]hail 1. *v. t.* **a)** *(call out to)* anrufen, *(fachspr.)* anpreien ‹*Schiff*›; *(signal to)* heranwinken, anhalten ‹*Taxi*›; **within/not within ~ing distance** in/außer Rufweite; **b)** *(salute)* grüßen; *(receive, welcome)* begrüßen; empfangen; **c)** *(acclaim)* zujubeln (+ *Dat.*); bejubeln **(as** als); **~ sb. king** jmdm. als König zujubeln. **2.** *v. i.* **a)** rufen; **b) where does the ship ~ from?** woher kommt das Schiff?; **where do you ~ from?** woher kommst du?; wo bist du her? *(ugs.).* **3.** *n.* **a)** *(salutation)*

Gruß, *der; (shout of acclamation)* Jubelruf, *der;* **b)** *(call)* [Zu]ruf, *der;* **within/out of ~:** in/außer Rufweite. **4.** *int. (arch.)* sei gegrüßt *(geh.);* **~ Macbeth/to thee, O Caesar** Heil Macbeth/dir, o Cäsar; **H~ Mary** = Ave Maria *see* **ave a; ~-fellow-well-met** kumpelhaft; **be ~-fellow-well-met with sb.** jmdn. kumpelhaft behandeln; **say ~ and farewell to sb.** jmdn. begrüßen und von ihm [zugleich] Abschied nehmen; *see also* **all 1 a**

hail: ~stone *n. (Meteorol.)* Hagelkorn, *das;* **~storm** *n. (Meteorol.)* heftiger Hagelfall; Hagelschauer, *der*

hair [heə(r)] *n.* **a)** *(one strand)* Haar, *das;* **a dog's ~:** ein Hundehaar; **without turning a ~** *(fig.)* ohne eine Miene zu verziehen; **not harm a ~ of sb.'s head** *(fig.)* jmdm. kein Haar krümmen; *see also* **dog 1 a; hang 2 a; short 1 a; split 3 b; b)** *collect., no pl. (many strands, mass)* Haar, *das;* Haare *Pl.; attrib.* Haar-; *(horse~)* Roßhaar-; **the cat has a lovely coat of black ~:** die Katze hat ein wunderschönes schwarzes Fell; **do one's/sb.'s ~:** sich/jmdm. das Haar machen *(ugs.);* **do one's own ~:** sich *(Dat.)* das Haar selbst machen *(ugs.);* **have** *or* **get one's ~ done** sich *(Dat.)* das Haar *od.* die Haare machen *(ugs.)* lassen; **where did you get your ~ done?** bei welchem Friseur warst du?; **pull sb.'s ~:** jmdn. an den Haaren ziehen; **he's losing his ~:** ihm gehen die Haare aus; **he has still not lost his ~:** er hat seine Haare noch [alle]; **keep your ~ on!** *(sl.),* **don't lose your ~!** *(coll.)* geh [mal] nicht gleich an die Decke! *(ugs.);* **let one's ~ down** sein Haar aufmachen *od.* lösen; *(fig. coll.)* [ganz] locker sein *(ugs.);* sich [ganz] locker geben *(ugs.); (give free expression to one's feelings etc.)* aus sich herausgehen; *(have a good time)* auf den Putz hauen *(ugs.);* die Sau rauslassen *(salopp);* **sb.'s ~ stands on end** *(fig.)* jmdm. stehen die Haare zu Berge *(ugs.);* **get in sb.'s ~** *(fig. coll.)* jmdm. auf die Nerven *od.* den Wecker gehen *od.* fallen *(ugs.);* **get out of my ~!** *(coll.)* laß mich in Ruhe! *(ugs.);* **keep out of sb.'s ~** *(coll.)* jmdn. in Ruhe lassen; *see also* **curl 1 a, 2 a; ¹tear 2 b; c)** *(Bot.)* Haar, *das;* **d)** *(thin filament)* Faden, *der;* **e)** *(minute amount)* **a ~:** eine Idee; **by a ~:** knapp ‹*gewinnen*›; **to a ~:** haargenau; *(in every detail)* haarklein

hair: ~breadth 1. *n.* winzige Kleinigkeit; **by [no more than] a ~breadth** [nur] um Haaresbreite ‹*verfehlen*›; nur knapp ‹*gewinnen*›; **the firm was within a ~breadth of bankruptcy** die Firma wäre um ein Haar *(ugs.)* bankrott gegangen; **2.** *adj.* minimal; hauchdünn *(ugs.)* ‹*Chance*›; **that was a ~breadth escape** das war äußerst *od. (ugs.)* verdammt knapp; **~brush** *n.* Haarbürste, *die;* **~-conditioner** *n.* Frisiermittel, *das;* **~-cream** *n.* Haarcreme, *die;* Pomade, *die;* **~-curler** *n.* Lockenwickler, *der;* **~cut** *n.* **a)** *(act)* Haareschneiden, *das;* **go for/need a ~cut** zum Friseur gehen/müssen; **give sb. a ~cut** jmdm. die Haare schneiden; **get/have a ~cut** sich *(Dat.)* die Haare schneiden lassen; **b)** *(style)* Haarschnitt, *der;* **~-do** *n. (coll.)* **a) get a ~-do** sich *(Dat.)* das Haar machen lassen *(ugs.);* **give sb. a ~-do** jmdm. das Haar machen *(ugs.);* **b)** *(style)* Frisur, *die;* **~dresser** *n.* **a)** *(Brit.)* Friseur, *der/* Friseuse, *die;* **men's ~dresser** Herrenfriseur, *der/*-friseuse, *die;* **ladies' ~dresser** Damenfriseur, *der/*-friseuse, *die;* **go to the ~dresser['s]** zum Friseur gehen; **b)** *(Amer.: for women)* Damenfriseur, *der/*-friseuse, *die;* **~dresser's** Damen[frisier]salon, *der;* **go to the ~dresser['s]** zum Friseur gehen; **~dressing** *n.* der Friseurberuf; *attrib.* **~dressing salon** Friseursalon, *der;* **~-drier** *n.* Haartrockner, *der;* Fön ®, *der; (with a hood)* Trockenhaube, *die;* **~-dye** *n.* Haarfärbemittel, *das;* **use ~-dye** sich *(Dat.)* das Haar färben

-haired [heəd] *adj. in comb.* **black-/dark-/frizzy-~:** schwarz-/dunkel-/kraushaarig; **greasy-~:** mit fettigem Haar *nachgestellt*

hair: ~ follicle *n.* Haarbalg, *der;* **~-grip** *n. (Brit.)* Haarklammer, *die;* **~ lacquer** *see* **~spray**

hairless ['heəlɪs] *adj.* unbehaart ‹*Körper[teil], Pflanze, Blatt*›; kahlköpfig ‹*Person*›; kahl ‹*Kopf*›

hair: ~-line *n.* **a)** *(edge of hair)* Haaransatz, *der;* **his ~-line is receding, he has a receding ~-line** er bekommt eine Stirnglatze; **b)** *(narrow line)* haarfeine Linie; haarfeiner Strich; **c)** *(crack)* haarfeiner Riß; **~-line crack** *(esp. Metallurgy, Mech. Engin.)* Haarriß, *der;* **~-line fracture** *(Med.)* Fissur, *die;* **d)** *(in writing or printing)* Haarstrich, *der;* **~-net** *n.* Haarnetz, *das;* **~-piece** *n.* Haarteil, *das;* **~pin** *n.* Haarnadel, *die;* **~pin 'bend** *n.* Haarnadelkurve, *die;* **~-raising** ['heəreɪzɪŋ] *adj.* furchterregend; *(very bad)* haarsträubend; mörderisch ‹*Rennstrecke; Abstieg vom Berg usw.*›; **~-restorer** *n.* Haarwuchsmittel, *das;* **~'s breadth** *see* **~breadth; ~ 'shirt** *n.* härenes Hemd *(geh.);* Härenhemd, *das (veralt.); (worn as a penance)* Büßerhemd, *das;* **~-slide** *n. (Brit.)* Haarspange, *die;* **~-space** *n. (Printing)* Haarspatium, *das;* **~-splitting** *(derog.)* **1.** *adj.* haarspalterisch *(abwertend);* **2.** *n.* Haarspalterei, *die (abwertend);* **~spray** *n.* Haarspray, *das;* **~spring** *n. (Horol.)* Unruhfeder, *die;* **~-style** *n.* Frisur, *die;* **~-stylist** *n.* Friseur, *der/*Friseuse, *die;* Hair-Stylist, *der/*-Stylistin, *die;* **~-trigger** *n. (Arms)* Stecher, *der*

hairy ['heərɪ] *adj.* **a)** *(having hair)* behaart; flauschig ‹*Schal, Pullover, Teppich*›; **you're beginning to get a ~ chest** du bekommst Haare auf der Brust; **a very ~ dog** ein Hund mit einem dichten Fell; *(having very long hair)* ein sehr langhaariger Hund; **be all ~:** voller Haare sein; **b)** *(made of hair)* aus Haar *(nachgestellt);* hären *(geh.)*‹*Gewand*›; **c)** *(sl.: difficult, dangerous)* haarig; **d)** *(sl.: unpleasant, frightening)* eklig *(ugs.);* **e)** *(sl.: crude, clumsy)* unmöglich *(ugs.)*

Haiti [hɑː'iːtɪ, 'heɪtɪ] *pr. n.* Haiti *(das)*

Haitian [hɑː'iːʃn, 'heɪʃn] **1.** *adj.* haitianisch; **sb. is ~:** jmd. ist Haitianer/Haitianerin. **2.** *n.* Haitianer, *der/*Haitianerin, *die*

hajji *see* **hadji**

hake [heɪk] *n., pl. same (Zool.)* Seehecht, *der*

halal [hɑː'lɑːl] *(Islam)* **1.** *v. t.* nach muslimischem Ritus schlachten. **2.** *n.* Fleisch von einem nach muslimischem Ritus geschlachteten Tier. **3.** *adj.* ‹*Fleisch*› von einem nach muslimischem Ritus geschlachteten Tier

halberd ['hælbəd] *n. (Arms Hist.)* Hellebarde, *die*

halbert ['hælbət] *see* **halberd**

'halcyon days ['hælsɪən deɪz] *n. pl. (happy days)* glückliche Tage *Pl.;* glückliche Zeiten *Pl.*

¹hale [heɪl] *adj.* kräftig ‹*Körper, Konstitution*›; rege ‹*Geist*›; **~ and hearty** gesund und munter

²hale *v. t. (literary)* **~ sb. to prison** jmdn. ins Gefängnis werfen *(geh.);* **~ sb. before the magistrate** jmdn. vor den Friedensrichter *od.* das Schiedsgericht zerren

half [hɑːf] **1.** *n., pl.* **halves** [hɑːvz] **a)** *(part)* Hälfte, *die;* **~ [of sth.]** die Hälfte [von etw.]; **~ of Europe** halb Europa; **I've only ~ left** ich habe nur noch die Hälfte; **~ [of] that** die Hälfte [davon]; **I don't believe ~ of it!** ich glaube nicht die Hälfte davon; **cut sth. in ~** *or* **into [two] halves** etw. in zwei Hälften schneiden; **divide sth. in ~** *or* **into halves** etw. halbieren; **one/two and a ~ hours, one hour/two hours and a ~:** anderthalb *od.* eineinhalb/zweieinhalb Stunden; **she is three and a ~:** sie ist dreieinhalb; **that was a performance/game/job and a ~** *(fig. coll.)* das war vielleicht eine Vorstellung/ein Spiel/eine Arbeit *(ugs.);* **an idiot/a joker/a fool/a woman and a ~** *(fig. coll.)* ein Oberidiot/-witzbold/-trottel *(ugs.)*/eine Superfrau *(ugs.);* **not/never do anything/things by halves** keine halben Sachen machen; **you don't do things by halves, do you?** *(iron.)* du meinst wohl, wenn schon, denn schon?; **be too cheeky/big by ~:** entschieden zu frech/groß sein; **be too clever by ~** *(iron.)* oberschlau *(ugs. iron.) od.* superklug *(ugs. iron.)* sein; **go halves** *or* **go ~ and ~ [with sb.] in** *or* *(coll.)* **on sth.** sich *(Dat.)* etw. [mit jmdm.] teilen; bei etw. halbe-halbe [mit jmdm.] machen *(ugs.);* **how the other ~ lives** wie andere Leute leben; **that's only** *or* **just** *or* **not the ~ of it** das ist noch nicht alles; **you don't know the ~ of it** [ja,] wenn es nur das wäre!; **my other ~** *(coll.)* meine bessere Hälfte *(ugs.); see also* **better 1; b)** *(coll.: ~ pint)* kleines Glas; *(of beer)* kleines Bier; Kleine, *das (ugs.);* **a ~ of bitter/lager/cider** ein kleines Bitter/ein kleines Lager/ein kleiner Apfelwein; **c)** *(Brit. Hist. coll.: ~ a new penny)* Halbe, *der (ugs.);* **d)** *(child's ticket)* Fahrkarte zum halben Preis; halbe Fahrkarte; **one and a ~ to Oxford** eineinhalbmal nach Oxford; **two halves to Oxford** zwei halbe [Fahrkarten] nach Oxford; **e)** *(Brit. Sch.: term)* Halbjahr, *das;* **f)** *(Footb. etc.) (period)* Halbzeit, *die; (of pitch)* [Spielfeld]hälfte, *die; (coll.: ~-back)* Läufer, *der/*Läuferin, *die;* **g)** *(Golf)* halbiertes Loch; **the outward/inward ~:** die Löcher 1–9/10–18. **2.** *adj.* **a)** *(equal to a ~)* halb; **~ the house/books/staff/time** die Hälfte des Hauses/der Bücher/des Personals/der Zeit; **~ the world** die halbe Welt; **he is drunk ~ the time** *(very often)* er ist fast immer betrunken; **she knits ~ the time/the day** *(a lot of, a good deal of)* sie strickt die ganze Zeit/den halben Tag; **~ an hour** eine halbe Stunde; **be only ~ the man/woman one used to be** *(fig.)* längst nicht mehr der/die alte sein; **b)** *(forming a ~)* **they each have a ~ share in the boat** das Boot gehört jedem [von ihnen] zur Hälfte; **be given a ~ day's holiday** einen halben Tag freibekommen; **c)** *(Bookbinding)* Halb‹*leder, -leinen*›; *see also* **battle 1 c; ¹ear a; eye 1 a; mind 1 b. 3.** *adv.* **a)** *(to the extent of ~)* zur Hälfte; halb ‹*öffnen, schließen, aufessen, fertig, voll, geöffnet*›; *(almost)* fast ‹*fallen, ersticken, tot sein*›; **our journey was now ~ done** die Hälfte der Reise lag hinter uns; **~ as much/many/big/heavy** halb so viel/viele/groß/schwer; **~ run [and] ~ walk** teils laufen, teils gehen; **~ cough and ~ sneeze** halb husten, halb niesen; **we had only ~ entered the room when ...:** wir waren noch nicht ganz eingetreten, als ...; **I ~ wished/hoped that ...:** ich wünschte mir/hoffte fast, daß ...; **only ~ hear what ...:** nur zum Teil hören, was ...; **~ listen for/to** mit halbem Ohr horchen auf (+ *Akk.*)/zuhören (+ *Dat.*); **I ~ laughed** *(almost)* ich hätte fast [los]gelacht; **I felt ~ dead** *(fig.)* ich war halbtot; **be only ~ ready** *or* **done** *(Cookery)* erst halb gar sein; **~ cook sth.** etw. halb gar werden lassen; **be ~ happy, ~ worried about sth.** teils glücklich, teils besorgt über etw. *(Akk.)* sein; **leave the food ~ eaten** die Hälfte von dem Essen übriglassen; **go ~ crazy/wild** halb verrückt *(ugs.)* werden; **not ~ cooked yet** noch lange nicht gar; **not ~ finished yet** noch lange nicht fertig; **not ~ long/strong enough** bei weitem nicht lang/stark genug; **not ~** *(sl.) (most certainly)* und ob!; *(extremely)* irrsinnig *(ugs.);* **not ~ bad** *(coll.)* toll *(ugs.);* **not ~ a bad fellow/meal** *(coll.)* ein toller Typ/ein tolles Essen *(ugs.);* **not ~ he wouldn't!** *(coll.)* und ob er das wäre/tun würde!; **it wasn't ~ a problem** *(coll.)* es war ein großes *od. (ugs.)* wahnsinniges Problem; **she can't ~ be stubborn**

(coll.) sie ist wahnsinnig *(ugs.)* dickköpfig; **there won't ~ be trouble** *(coll.)* es wird einen Riesenkrach geben; *see also* **again a; b)** *(by the amount of a ~-hour)* halb; **at ~ past the hour** um halb; **from eight o'clock till ~ past** von acht bis halb neun; **~ past** *or (coll.)* **~ one/two/three** *etc.* halb zwei/drei/vier *usw.*; **~ past twelve** halbeins; **~ past midday/midnight** halb eins mittags/nachts

half- *in comb.* halb ⟨*gar, verbrannt, betrunken, voll, leer*⟩; **~-cold** fast kalt; **~-starved** halb verhungert; **a ~-dozen** ein halbes Dutzend; **~-pound bag/~-litre glass** Halbpfundtüte, *die*/-literglas, *das;* **a ~-mile** eine halbe Meile; **~-year** Halbjahr, *das;* halbes Jahr

half: ~-and-'~ 1. *n.* **Does it contain a or b? – H~-and-~:** Enthält es a oder b? – Halb und halb; **it is all silver, not ~-and-~:** es ist reines Silber, nicht halb Silber und halb etwas anderes; **settle for ~-and-~:** sich für eine Kombination aus beidem entscheiden; **2.** *adj.* **a)** *(equal)* **take a ~-and-~ share in the duties** sich mit jmdm. in die Pflichten teilen; **~-and-~ mixture of a and b** Mischung, die je zur Hälfte aus a und b besteht; **b)** *(indecisive)* halb ⟨*Maßnahme*⟩; **3.** *adv.* zu gleichen Teilen; **they divide their earnings/share the duties ~-and-~:** sie teilen ihre Einkünfte/die Pflichten gleichmäßig untereinander auf; **~-arse[d]** ['hɑːfɑːs(t)] *adj. (sl.)* bescheuert *(salopp);* beknackt *(salopp);* **do a ~-arse[d] job** Murks machen *(ugs.);* pfuschen *(ugs.);* **~-back** *n.* *(Footb., Hockey)* Läufer, *der*/Läuferin, *die;* **~-baked** [hɑːf'beɪkt] *adj.* **a)** *(Cookery)* nicht richtig durchgebacken; **b)** *(fig.) (not thorough[ly planned])* unausgegoren *(abwertend),* unausgereift ⟨*Plan, Aufsatz*⟩; *(not earnest, lacking in strength of purpose)* lasch ⟨*Haltung, Person*⟩; **c)** *(~-witted)* nicht ganz gar *od.* dicht *(ugs.);* **~-binding** *n.* *(Bookbinding)* Halbledereinband, *der;* Halbfranzeinband, *der;* **~-blood** *see* **~-breed a; ~-'blue** *n. (Brit. Univ.)* **get a** *or* **one's ~-blue** die Universität bei weniger wichtigen Sportwettkämpfen oder als Reservespieler vertreten; **~-'board** *n.* Halbpension, *die;* **~-board accommodation** [Unterkunft mit] Halbpension; **~-boot** *n.* Halbstiefel, *der;* **~-breed** *n.* **a)** Mischling, *der;* Halbblut, *das;* **b)** *see* **cross-breed 1; ~-brother** *n.* Halbbruder, *der;* **be ~-brother to sb.** jmds. Halbbruder sein; **~-caste 1.** *n.* Mischling, *der;* Halbblut, *das;* **2.** *adj.* Mischlings-; **~'cock** *see* **¹cock 1e; ~-cocked** [hɑːf'kɒkt] *adj., adv.* *(Amer.)* = **at ~ cock** *see* **¹cock 1e; ~-'crown** *n. (Brit. Hist.)* Half-crown, *die;* **~-'hardy** *adj. (Hort.)* [bedingt] winterhart; **~-hearted** [hɑːf'hɑːtɪd] *adj.,* **~-heartedly** [hɑːf'hɑːtɪdlɪ] *adv.* halbherzig; **~ hitch** *see* **hitch 3b; ~'holiday** *n.* halber freier Tag; **I'll take a ~ holiday on Wednesday** ich werde [am] Mittwoch einen halben Tag Urlaub nehmen; **there will be a ~ holiday in May** im Mai gibt es einen halben Tag frei; **~-hose** *see* **hose 1b; ~-'hour** *n.* halbe Stunde; **at the ~-hour** um halb; **the clock chimes at the ~-hour** die Uhr schlägt jeweils um halb; **~-'hourly 1.** *adj.* halbstündlich; halbstündlich verkehrend ⟨*Bus usw.*⟩; **the bus service is ~-hourly** der Bus verkehrt halbstündlich; **2.** *adv.* jede halbe Stunde; halbstündlich; **~-hunter** *see* **hunter e; ~-'inch 1.** *n.* halber Inch; halber Zoll; *attrib.* ['--] halbzollig; Halbzoll⟨*bohrer, -schraube*⟩; **2.** *v. t. (Brit. sl.)* klauen *(ugs.);* klemmen *(salopp);* **~-landing** *n.* Treppenabsatz, *der;* Zwischenpodest, *das (Bauw.);* **~-life** *n. (Phys.)* Halbwertszeit, *die;* **~-light** *n.* Halblicht, *das;* **~-'mast** *n.* **be [flown] at ~-mast** ⟨*Flagge:*⟩ auf halbmast gehißt sein *od.* stehen; **raise/lower to ~-mast** auf halbmast hissen/setzen ⟨*Flagge*⟩; **~-measure** *n.* **a) a ~ measure of whisky** ein halber Whisky; **b)** *in pl.* halbe Maßnahme; Halbheit, *die (abwertend);* **there are no ~ measures with him** er macht keine halben Sachen *(ugs.);* bei ihm gibt es keine Halbheiten; **~ 'moon** *n.* **a)** Halbmond, *der;* **b)** *(Anat.)* Möndchen, *das;* **the ~ moons of his nails** seine Nagelmöndchen; **~ 'nelson** *n.* *(Wrestling)* Halbnelson, *der;* **get/have got a ~ nelson on sb./sth.** *(fig.)* jmdn./etw. unter Kontrolle bringen/haben; ⟨*Erpresser usw.:*⟩ jmdn./etw. in die Hand kriegen/in der Hand haben; **~-note** *(Amer. Mus.) see* **minim a; ~ 'pay** *n.* Ruhegehalt, *das;* Pension, *die;* **be on ~ pay** Ruhegehalt *od.* Pension beziehen; **~penny** ['heɪpnɪ], *pl. usu.* **~pennies** ['heɪpnɪz] *for separate coins,* **~pence** ['heɪpəns] *for sum of money (Brit. Hist.) (coin)* Halfpenny, *der; (sum)* halber Penny; **~pennyworth** ['heɪpəθ] *n. (Brit.)* **a)** *(Hist.: amount)* **a ~pennyworth of ...:** für einen halben Penny ...; **b)** *(fig.: small amount)* **not a** *or* **one ~pennyworth of** nicht für fünf Pfennig *(ugs.)* ⟨*Verstand*⟩; nicht das kleinste bißchen ⟨*Ruhe, Gastfreundschaft, Entgegenkommen usw.*⟩; **~-'pint** *n.* **a)** *(quantity)* halbes Pint; **b)** *(coll.: small or insignificant person)* halbe Portion *(ugs. spött.);* **~-'price 1.** *n.* halber Preis; **all articles are at ~-price** alle Artikel gibt es zum halben Preis; **bring sth. down** *or* **reduce sth. to ~-price** etw. um die Hälfte heruntersetzen *od.* reduzieren; **2.** *adj.* zum halben Preis *nachgestellt;* **~-price air fares** um die Hälfte herabgesetzte Flugpreise; **3.** *adv.* zum halben Preis; **~-seas-over** [hɑːfsiːz'əʊvə(r)] *adj. (sl.)* angesäuselt *(ugs.);* **~-shell** *n.* Austernschale, *die:* **lobster on the ~-shell** *(Gastr.)* auf einer Austernschale servierter Hummer; **~-sister** *n.* Halbschwester, *die;* **be ~-sister to sb.** jmds. Halbschwester sein; **~-size 1.** *n.* Zwischengröße, *die;* halbe Größe; **a ~-size larger** eine halbe Nummer größer; **2.** *adj.* halb ⟨*Portion*⟩; klein ⟨*Blumentopf, Spaten*⟩; **~-'staff** *(Amer.) see* **~-mast; ~-step** *(Amer. Mus.) see* **semitone; ~-'term** *n.* *(Brit.)* **a) it is nearly ~-term** das Trimester ist fast zur Hälfte vorüber; **by/at/towards ~-term** bis zur/in der/gegen die Mitte des Trimesters; **b)** *(holiday)* **~-term [holiday/break]** Ferien in der Mitte des Trimesters; **before ~-term** in der ersten Trimesterhälfte; **~-timbered** [hɑːf'tɪmbəd] *adj.* Fachwerk⟨*haus, -bauweise*⟩; **be ~-timbered** ein Fachwerkbau sein; **~-'time 1.** *n.* **a)** *(Sport)* Halbzeit, *die; attrib.* ['--] Halbzeit⟨*pfiff, -stand*⟩; **blow the whistle for ~-time** die erste Halbzeit abpfeifen; **by/to ~-time** bis zur Halbzeit; **at ~-time** bei *od.* bis zur Halbzeit; *(during interval)* in der Halbzeitpause; **b)** *(Industry)* Kurzarbeit, *die (mit um 50 Prozent gekürzter Arbeitszeit);* **~-time working** Kurzarbeit, *die;* **several cotton-mills were put on ~-time** in mehreren Baumwollspinnereien wurde Kurzarbeit eingeführt; **1,150 workers were put on ~-time** *or* **had to go on ~-time schedules** 1 150 Arbeiter mußten kurzarbeiten; **2.** *adv. (Industry)* kurz⟨*arbeiten*⟩; **~-title** *n. (Printing)* **a)** Schmutztitel, *der;* Vortitel, *der;* **b)** *(section title)* Zwischentitel, *der;* **~-tone** *n.* **a)** *(Printing etc.)* Rasterbild, *das;* **b)** *(Amer. Mus.) see* **semitone; ~-track** *n.* **a)** *(system)* Halbkettenantrieb, *der;* **b)** *(vehicle)* Halbkettenfahrzeug, *das;* **~-truth** *n.* Halbwahrheit, *die;* **you've only told us a ~-truth** du hast uns nur die halbe Wahrheit gesagt; **~-'volley** *see* **volley 1c; ~-'way 1.** *adj.* halb ⟨*Maßnahme*⟩; **~-way point** Mitte, *die;* **we're well over the ~-way mark** wir haben gut die Hälfte geschafft; **~-way house** Gasthaus auf halbem Weg; *(fig.: compromise)* Kompromiß, *der;* Mittelweg, *der;* **~-way line** *(Footb.)* Mittellinie, *die;* **2.** *adv.* die Hälfte des Weges ⟨*begleiten, fahren*⟩; **not ~-way satisfactory** nicht einmal halbwegs zufriedenstellend; **by midday they had climbed ~-way up the mountain** bis zum Mittag hatten sie den halben Aufstieg hinter sich; *see also* **¹go 1q; ¹meet 1b; ~-wit** *n.* Schwachkopf, *der;* *(scatter-brain)* Schussel, *der;* **~-witted** ['hɑːfwɪtɪd] *adj.* dumm; *(mentally deficient)* debil; schwachsinnig; **~-witted person** Schwachkopf, *der;* **~-'yearly 1.** *adj.* halbjährlich; **at ~-yearly intervals** in halbjährigen Abständen; halbjährlich; **2.** *adv.* halbjährlich; jedes halbe Jahr

halibut ['hælɪbət] *n., pl. same (Zool.)* Heilbutt, *der*

halide ['heɪlaɪd, 'hælaɪd] *n. (Chem.)* Halogenid, *das;* Halid, *das*

halitosis [hælɪ'təʊsɪs] *n., pl.* **halitoses** [hælɪ'təʊsiːz] *(Med.)* Halitose, *die (fachspr.);* schlechter Atem

hall [hɔːl] *n.* **a)** *(large [public] room)* Saal, *der; (public building)* Halle, *die; (for receptions, banquets)* Festsaal, *der; (in medieval house: principal living-room)* Wohnsaal, *der;* **school/church ~:** Aula, *die*/Gemeindehaus, *das; see also* **servants' hall; b)** *(mansion)* Herrenhaus, *das;* Herrensitz, *der;* **c)** *(Univ.) (residential building)* **~ [of residence]** Studentenwohnheim, *das; (Hist.: college)* Kolleg, *das;* **live in ~:** im [Studenten]wohnheim wohnen; **d)** *(Univ.: dining-room)* Speisesaal, *der;* Mensa, *die;* **in ~:** im Speisesaal; in der Mensa; **e)** *no art. (dinner taken in ~)* Abendessen in der Mensa; **f)** *see* **guild-hall b; g)** *in pl. (music-~s)* Varieté, *das;* **be on the ~s** im Varieté auftreten; **do a turn on the ~s** mit einer Nummer im Varieté auftreten; **h)** *(entrance-passage)* Diele, *die;* Flur, *der;* **i)** *(Amer.: corridor)* Korridor, *der;* Flur, *der*

hallal *see* **halal**

halliard *see* **halyard**

'hallmark 1. *n.* [Feingehalts]stempel, *der;* Repunze, *die; (fig.: distinctive mark)* Kennzeichen, *das;* **be the ~ of quality/perfection** *(fig.)* für Qualität/Vollkommenheit bürgen *od.* stehen. **2.** *v. t.* stempeln; repunzieren

hallo [hə'ləʊ] **1.** *int.* **a)** *(to call attention)* hallo!; **b)** *(Brit.) see* **hello. 2.** *n., pl.* **~s** Hallo, *das;* Halloruf, *der;* **give a ~:** hallo rufen. **3.** *v. i.* hallo rufen; **~ to sb.** jmdn. anrufen

hall of 'fame *n.* Ruhmeshalle, *die*

halloo [hə'luː] **1.** *int.* **a)** *(Hunting)* horrido!; **b)** *see* **hallo 1a. 2.** *n.* **a)** *(Hunting)* Horrido, *das;* **b)** *see* **hallo 2. 3.** *v. i. (Hunting)* horrido rufen. **4.** *v. t. (Hunting)* anfeuern ⟨*Jagdhund*⟩

hallow ['hæləʊ] **1.** *n.* **All H~s, H~mas = All Saints' Day** *see* **all 1b. 2.** *v. t.* **a)** *(sanctify)* heiligen; **~ed** geheiligt *(auch fig.);* heilig ⟨*Boden*⟩; **b)** *(honour)* als heilig verehren; **~ed be Thy Name** *(in Lord's Prayer)* geheiligt werde Dein Name

Hallowe'en [hæləʊ'iːn] *n.* Halloween, *das;* *Abend vor Allerheiligen;* **on** *or* **at ~:** [an] Halloween

hall: ~'porter *n. (Brit.)* [Hotel]portier, *der;* **~-stand** *n.* [Flur]garderobe, *die*

hallucinant [hə'luːsɪnənt] **1.** *adj. see* **hallucinogenic. 2.** *n. see* **hallucinogen**

hallucinate [hə'luːsɪneɪt] *v. i.* halluzinieren *(Med., Psych.);* Halluzinationen haben

hallucination [həluːsɪ'neɪʃn] *n. (act)* Halluzinieren, *das; (instance, imagined object)* Halluzination, *die;* Sinnestäuschung, *die*

hallucinatory [hə'luːsɪneɪtərɪ] *adj.* **a)** *(producing hallucinations) see* **hallucinogenic; b)** *(associated with hallucinations)* halluzinatorisch *(Med., Psych.);* **c)** *(unreal)* imaginär *(geh.);* **be purely ~:** reine Einbildung sein

hallucinogen [hə'luːsɪnədʒen] *n. (Med.)* Halluzinogen, *das*

hallucinogenic [həluːsɪnə'dʒenɪk] *adj.* *(Med.)* halluzinogen

'hallway *n.* **a)** *see* **hall h; b)** *(corridor)* Flur, *der;* Korridor, *der;* Gang, *der (bes. südd., österr., schweiz.)*

halm *see* **haulm**

halo ['heɪləʊ] *n., pl.* **~es a)** *(Meteorol.)* Halo, *der (fachspr.);* Hof, *der;* **there was a ~ round** *or* **a ~ surrounded the moon** der Mond hatte einen Hof *od. (fachspr.)* Halo; **b)** *(circle)* Ring, *der; (of light)* Lichthof, *der;* **c)** *(around head)* Heiligen-, Glorienschein, *der;* **d)** *(fig.: aura)* Nimbus, *der;* **put a romantic ~ about sth.** etw. mit einer romantischen Gloriole umgeben

halogen ['hælədʒən] *n. (Chem.)* Halogen, *das (fachspr.);* Salzbildner, *der*

[1]**halt** [hɒlt, hɔ:lt] **1.** *n.* **a)** *(temporary stoppage)* Pause, *die; (on march or journey)* Rast, *die;* Pause, *die; (esp. Mil. also)* Halt, *der;* **make a ~:** Rast/eine Pause machen/haltmachen; **call a ~:** eine Pause machen lassen/haltmachen lassen; **let's call a ~:** machen wir eine Pause!; **b)** *(interruption)* Unterbrechung, *die;* **come to a ~ = come to a standstill** *see* **standstill;** *see also* **call 2f; come 1h; grind 2b; c)** *(Brit. Railw.)* Haltepunkt, *der.* **2.** *v.i.* **a)** *(stop)* ‹*Fußgänger, Tier:*› stehenbleiben; ‹*Fahrer:*› anhalten; *(for a rest)* eine Pause machen; *(esp. Mil.)* haltmachen; *(to collect one's thoughts etc.)* innehalten; **~, who goes there?** *(Mil.)* halt, wer da?; **b)** *(end)* eingestellt werden. **3.** *v.t.* **a)** *(cause to stop)* anhalten; haltmachen lassen ‹*Marschkolonne usw.*›; **he could not be ~ed** *(fig.)* er war nicht aufzuhalten *od. (ugs.)* zu bremsen; **b)** *(cause to end)* stoppen ‹*Inflation, Diskussion*›; beenden ‹*Herrschaft*›; einstellen ‹*Projekt*›

[2]**halt** *v.i. (not progress smoothly)* ‹*Argument:*› schwach sein; ‹*Verse, Übersetzung:*› holprig sein; **~ing** schleppend ‹*Stimme, Redeweise, Fortschritt*›; holprig ‹*Verse*›; zögernd ‹*Antwort*›; schwach ‹*Argument*›; **in a ~ing way** *or* **manner** schleppend ‹*sprechen*›

halter ['hɒltə(r), 'hɔ:ltə(r)] *n.* **a)** *(for horse)* Halfter, *das; (for cattle)* **[rope] ~:** Strick, *der;* **b)** *(for hanging)* Strick, *der;* Strang, *der;* **you'll find a ~ round your neck if ...:** du findest dich am Galgen wieder, wenn ...; **the ~** *(arch./literary: hanging)* Strang, *der (geh.);* **c)** *(Dressmaking) (strap)* Nackenträger, *der;* Nackenband, *das; (top with a ~)* Oberteil *od.* Top mit Nackenträger; **~ dress/bodice/top/bra** Kleid/Mieder/Oberteil *od.* Top/Büstenhalter mit Nackenträger; **~ neck** Nackenband, *das*

halting *see* [2]**halt**

haltingly ['hɒltɪŋlɪ, 'hɔ:ltɪŋlɪ] *adv.* schleppend ‹*vorankommen*›; *(with uncertain steps)* mit unsicheren Schritten ‹*gehen*›; *(hesitantly)* zögernd; **come ~ to the point** nur auf Umwegen zur Sache kommen

halve [hɑ:v] *v.t.* **a)** *(divide)* halbieren; **b)** *(share)* [ehrlich] teilen; **they ~d the cake [between them]** sie haben sich *(Dat.)* den Kuchen ehrlich geteilt; **c)** *(reduce)* halbieren; auf *od.* um die Hälfte verringern; **'sale – all prices ~d!'** „Ausverkauf – alles zum halben Preis!"; **~ the amount of beer one drinks/number of nights one goes out** nur noch halb soviel Bier trinken/halb sooft abends ausgehen; **d)** *(Golf)* mit der gleichen Anzahl von Schlägen erreichen ‹*Loch*› **(with** wie); durchspielen ‹*Runde*›; beenden ‹*Spiel*›; **the hole was ~d in 5** beide Spieler erreichten das Loch mit fünf Schlägen; **be ~d** ‹*Spiel:*› unentschieden enden

halves *pl. of* **half**

halyard ['hæljəd] *n. (Naut.)* Fall, *das; (for flag)* Flagg[en]leine, *die*

ham [hæm] **1.** *n.* **a)** *([meat from] thigh of pig)* Schinken, *der;* **b)** *usu. in pl. (back of thigh)* Hinterseite des Oberschenkels; **squat** *or* **sit on one's ~s** in der Hocke sitzen; **c)** *(sl.) (amateur)* Amateur, *der; (poor actor)* Schmierenkomödiant, *der (abwertend);* **radio ~:** Funkamateur, *der;* **d)** *no pl., no art. (sl.: inexpert acting)* Schmierentheater, *das (abwertend).* **2.** *adj. (sl.)* überzogen; **a very ~ performance** ein ziemliches Schmierentheater *(abwertend).* **3.** *v.i.,* **-mm-** *(sl.)* überziehen. **4.** *v.t.,* **-mm-** *(sl.)* überzogen spielen

~ 'up *v.t. (sl.)* überzogen spielen ‹*Stück*›; **~ it up** überziehen

hamadryad [hæmə'draɪæd] *n.* **a)** *(Greek and Roman Mythol.)* Hamadryade, *die;* **b)** *(Zool.: cobra)* Königskobra, *die;* **c)** *(Zool.: baboon)* Mantelpavian, *der*

Hamburg ['hæmbɜ:g] **1.** *pr.n.* Hamburg *(das).* **2.** *attrib. adj.* Hamburger

hamburger ['hæmbɜ:gə(r)] *n.* **a)** *(beef cake)* Hacksteak, *das; (filled roll)* Hamburger, *der;* **b) H~** *(person)* Hamburger, *der*/Hamburgerin, *die*

Hamelin ['hæməlɪn] *pr.n.* Hameln *(das)*

ham: ~-fisted [hæm'fɪstɪd], **~-handed** [hæm'hændɪd] *adjs. (sl.)* tolpatschig *(ugs.)* ‹*Mensch, Art*›; dilettantisch ‹*Bearbeitung, Vorgehensweise*›; plump *(abwertend)* ‹*Vorstellung, Humor*›; **~-fisted** *or* **~-handed actions** Tolpatschigkeiten

Hamitic [hə'mɪtɪk] *adj. (Ling.)* hamitisch

hamlet ['hæmlɪt] *n.* Weiler, *der*

hammer ['hæmə(r)] **1.** *n.* **a)** *(tool; also Anat.)* Hammer, *der;* **the H~ and Sickle** Hammer und Sichel; **go** *or* **be at sth. ~ and tongs** sich bei etw. schwer ins Zeug legen *(ugs.);* **go** *or* **be at it ~ and tongs** *(quarrel)* sich streiten, daß die Fetzen fliegen; **b)** *(of gun)* Hahn, *der;* **c)** *(auctioneer's mallet)* Hammer, *der;* **come under the ~:** unter den Hammer kommen; **d)** *(Athletics)* [Wurf]hammer, *der;* **[throwing] the ~** *(event)* das Hammerwerfen. **2.** *v.t.* **a)** *(strike with ~)* hämmern; *(fig.)* hämmern auf *(Akk.)* ‹*Tasten, Tisch*›; einhämmern auf *(Akk.)* ‹*Gegner, Opfer*›; **~ a nail into sth.** einen Nagel in etw. *(Akk.)* hämmern *od.* schlagen; **~ sth. into sb.['s head]** *(fig.)* jmdm. etw. einhämmern; **~ home** einschlagen ‹*Nagel, Bolzen usw.*›; **He must not do that. We'll ~ it home** Er darf das nicht tun. Wir werden es ihm einbleuen; **b)** *(coll.: inflict heavy defeat on)* abservieren *(ugs.)* ‹*Gegner*›; vernichtend schlagen ‹*Feind*›; ausstechen ‹*Konkurrenten*›; **c)** *(St. Exch.)* für zahlungsunfähig erklären. **3.** *v.i.* **a)** *(give blows)* hämmern; klopfen; **~ at sth.** an etw. *(Dat.)* [herum]hämmern; **~ at** *or* **on the door** an *od.* gegen die Tür hämmern; **b)** *(fig. coll.: travel fast)* düsen *(ugs.);* kacheln *(salopp)*

~ a'way *v.i.* hämmern; **~ away at** herumhämmern *od. (ugs.)* -kloppen auf (+ *Dat.*); *(fig.: work hard at)* sich hineinknien in (+ *Akk.*) *(ugs.)* ‹*Tätigkeit*›; [herum]bosseln an (+ *Dat.*) *(ugs.)* ‹*Aufsatz*›

~ 'down *v.t.* festhämmern, -klopfen

~ 'out *v.t.* **a)** *(make smooth)* ausklopfen ‹*Delle, Beule*›; ausbeulen ‹*Kotflügel usw.*›; glatt klopfen ‹*Blech usw.*›; **b)** *(fig.: devise)* ausarbeiten ‹*Plan, Methode, Vereinbarung*›; kommen zu ‹*Entscheidung, Entschluß*›

hammock ['hæmək] *n.* Hängematte, *die*

hammy ['hæmɪ] *adj.* **a)** *(resembling ham)* schinkenartig; Schinken‹*geschmack, -geruch*›; **have a ~ taste** nach Schinken schmecken; **b)** *(sl.: of ham actors)* theatralisch *(abwertend)* ‹*Nummer, Rolle, Aufführung, Darstellung*›

[1]**hamper** ['hæmpə(r)] *n.* **a)** *(basket)* [Deckel]korb, *der;* **b)** *(consignment of food)* Präsentkorb, *der;* **Christmas ~:** Weihnachtsgeschenkkorb, *der*

[2]**hamper** *v.t.* behindern; hemmen ‹*Entwicklung, Wachstum usw.*›; **~ sb. in his progress, ~ sb.'s progress** ‹*Hindernis:*› jmdn. aufhalten; **~ sb. in his movements** jmdn. behindern *od.* in seiner Bewegungsfreiheit beeinträchtigen

hamster ['hæmstə(r)] *n.* Hamster, *der; see also* **golden hamster**

'hamstring 1. *n. (Anat.)* **a)** *(in man, ape)* Kniesehne, *die;* **b)** *(in quadruped)* Achillessehne, *die.* **2.** *v.t.,* **hamstrung** *or* **~ed a)** *(cripple)* die Kniesehnen/Achillessehnen durchtrennen (+ *Dat.*); **b)** *(fig.: destroy efficiency of)* lähmen

hand [hænd] **1.** *n.* **a)** *(Anat., Zool.)* Hand, *die;* **eat from** *or* **out of sb.'s ~** *(lit. or fig.)* jmdm. aus der Hand fressen; **I need an extra/a strong pair of ~s** ich brauche noch jmdn., der/eine kräftige Person, die mir hilft; **get one's ~s dirty, dirty** *or* **soil one's ~s** *(lit. or fig.)* sich *(Dat.)* die Hände schmutzig machen; **give sb. one's ~** *(reach, shake)* jmdm. die Hand geben *od.* reichen; **give** *or* **lend [sb.] a ~ [with** *or* **in sth.]** [jmdm.] [bei etw.] helfen; **not/never do a ~'s turn** keine/niemals eine Hand rühren *(ugs.);* keinen/niemals einen Finger krumm machen *(ugs.);* **pass** *or* **go through sb.'s ~s** *(fig.)* durch jmds. Hand *od.* Hände gehen; **pass through many/several ~s** durch viele/etliche Hände gehen; **many ~s make light work** *(prov.)* viele Hände machen der Arbeit bald ein Ende *(Spr.);* **~ in ~:** Hand in Hand; **go ~ in ~ [with sth.]** *(fig.)* [mit etw.] Hand in Hand gehen; **the problem/project/matter in ~:** das vorliegende Problem/Projekt/die vorliegende Angelegenheit; *see also* **d; hold ~s** Händchen halten *(ugs. scherzh.);* sich bei den Händen halten; **hold sb.'s ~:** jmds. Hand halten; jmdm. die Hand halten; *(fig.: give sb. close guidance)* jmdn. bei der Hand nehmen; *(fig.: give sb. moral support or backing)* jmdn. moralisch unterstützen; jmdm. das Händchen halten *(iron.);* **take one's child's/big brother's ~:** ‹*Erwachsener:*› sein Kind an die Hand nehmen/‹*Kind:*› sich von seinem großen Bruder an die Hand nehmen lassen; **~s off!** Hände *od.* Finger weg!; **~s off my wife/Chile!** Hände weg von meiner Frau/Chile!; **take/keep one's ~s off sb./sth.** jmdn./etw. loslassen/nicht anfassen; **take your ~s off me this instant!** nimm sofort die Finger weg!; **keep one's ~s off sth.** *(fig.)* die Finger von etw. lassen *(ugs.);* **show of ~s** Handzeichen, *das;* **~s up [all those in favour]** *(as sign of assent)* wer dafür ist, hebt die Hand!; **~s up!** *(as sign of surrender)* Hände hoch!; **~s down** *(fig.) (easily)* mit links *(ugs.); (without a doubt, by a large margin)* ganz klar *(ugs.);* eindeutig *(ugs.);* **be good with one's ~s** [handwerklich] geschickt sein; **change** *or (coll.)* **swap ~s** die Hand wechseln; die andere Hand nehmen; *see also* **c; turn one's ~ to sth.** sich einer Sache *(Dat.)* zuwenden; **put** *or* **set one's ~ to** sich machen an (+ *Akk.*) ‹*Arbeit, Aufgabe*›; *see also* **l; put** *or* **set one's ~ to doing sth.** sich daran machen, etw. zu tun; **have sth. at ~:** etw. zur Hand haben; **have sb. at ~:** jmdn. bei sich haben; **be at ~** *(be nearby)* in der Nähe sein; *(be about to happen)* unmittelbar bevorstehen; **out of ~** *(without delay)* unverzüglich; *(summarily)* kurzerhand; *see also* **b; be to ~** *(be readily available, within reach)* zur Hand sein; *(be received)* ‹*Brief, Notiz, Anweisung:*› vorliegen; **come to ~** *(turn up)* sich finden; *(be received)* ‹*Brief, Mitteilung:*› eingehen; **she uses whatever comes to ~:** sie nimmt, was gerade da ist; **fight ~ to ~:** Mann gegen Mann kämpfen; **go/pass from ~ to ~:** von Hand zu Hand gehen; **~ over ~** *or* **fist** Zug um Zug ‹*hinaufklettern, einziehen*›; **~ over fist** *(fig.) (with steady progress)* laufend; *(with rapid progress)* rapide; **live from ~ to mouth** von der Hand in den Mund leben; **be ~ in glove [with]** unter einer Decke stecken [mit]; **bind sb. ~ and foot** jmdn. an Händen und Füßen fesseln; **wait on** *or* **serve sb. ~ and foot** *(fig.)* jmdn. vorn und hinten bedienen *(ugs.);* **on [one's] ~s and knees** auf Händen und Knien; **crawl on [one's] ~s and knees** auf allen vieren kriechen *(ugs.);* **get down on one's ~s and knees**

auf die Knie gehen; **his ~s are tied** *(fig.)* ihm sind die Hände gebunden; **have one's ~s full** die Hände voll haben; *(fig.: be fully occupied)* alle Hände voll zu tun haben *(ugs.)*; **~ on** *or* **over heart** *(fig.)* Hand aufs Herz; **get one's ~s on sb./sth.** jmdn. erwischen *od. (ugs.)* in die Finger kriegen/etw. auftreiben; **lay** *or* **put one's ~ on sth.** etw. finden; **lay [one's] ~s on sth.** sich einer Sache bemächtigen; **everything** *or* **anything** *or* **all they could lay [their] ~s on** alles, wessen sie habhaft werden konnten; **lay ~s on sb.** jmdm. etw. tun; Hand an jmdn. legen *(geh.)*; *(violate)* sich an jmdm. vergreifen; **by ~** *(manually)* mit der *od.* von Hand; *(in handwriting)* handschriftlich; *(by messenger)* durch Boten; **be made by ~**: Handarbeit sein; **bring up by ~**: mit der Flasche aufziehen; *see also* **banana a; clean 1b; finger 1a; hand-to-hand; hand-to-mouth; join 1a; shake 2a; sit 1b; wash 1a; b)** *(fig.: authority)* **with a strict/firm/iron ~**: mit fester/starker Hand/eiserner Faust ‹*regieren*›; **with a heavy ~**: mit eiserner Strenge; **he needs a father's ~**: er braucht die väterliche Hand; **hold one's ~**: abwarten; **hold one's ~ and not do sth.** davon Abstand nehmen, etw. zu tun; **keep in ~**: unter Kontrolle behalten ‹*Schüler, Demonstranten*› *(see also* **d)**; **get out of ~**: außer Kontrolle geraten; *see also* **a**; *see also* **free hand; take 1a; upper 1a; c)** *in pl. (custody)* **in sb.'s ~s, in the ~s of sb.** *(in sb.'s possession)* in jmds. Besitz; *(in sb.'s care)* in jmds. Obhut; **I am in your ~s** die Entscheidungen überlasse ich Ihnen; **put oneself in sb.'s ~s** sich jmdm. anvertrauen; **be in the ~s of the police** ‹*Verdächtiger:*› sich in Polizeigewahrsam befinden; **may I leave the matter in your ~s?** darf ich die Angelegenheit Ihnen überlassen?; **the matter/the decision is now out of my ~s** ich bin für die Angelegenheit/die Entscheidung nicht mehr zuständig; **take sth. out of sb.'s ~s** *(withdraw sth. from sb.)* jmdm. etw. entziehen *od.* aus der Hand nehmen; *(relieve sb. of sth.)* jmdm. etw. abnehmen; **fall into sb.'s ~s** ‹*Person, Geld:*› jmdm. in die Hände fallen; ‹*Verantwortung:*› jmdm. zufallen; **be in good/bad ~s** in guten/schlechten Händen sein; **have [got] sth./sb. on one's ~s** sich um etw./jmdn. kümmern müssen; **he's got such a lot/enough on his ~s at the moment** er hat augenblicklich so viel/genug um die Ohren *(ugs.)*; **suddenly we had a riot on our ~s** plötzlich sahen wir uns mit Ausschreitungen konfrontiert; **have time on one's ~s** [viel] Zeit haben; *(too much)* mit seiner Zeit nichts anzufangen wissen; **they are off our ~s at last** endlich sind wir sie los *(ugs.)*; **have [got] sth./sb. off one's ~s** etw./jmdn. lossein *(ugs.)*; **take sb./sth. off sb.'s ~s** jmdm. jmdn./etw. abnehmen; **change ~s** den Besitzer wechseln; *see also* **a; d)** *(disposal)* **have sth. in ~**: etw. zur Verfügung haben; *(not used up)* etw. [übrig] haben; **keep in ~**: in Reserve halten ‹*Geld*› *(see also* **b)**; **have on ~**: dahaben; **be on ~**: dasein; **e)** *(share)* **have a ~ in sth.** bei etw. seine Hände im Spiel haben; **take a ~ [in sth.]** sich [an etw. *(Dat.)*] beteiligen; **take a ~ [at bridge]** [Bridge] mitspielen; *see also* **²bear 1k; f)** *(agency)* Wirken, *das (geh.)*; **the ~ of a thief/artist/craftsman has been at work here** hier war ein Dieb/Künstler/Handwerker am Werk; **the ~ of God** die Hand Gottes; **these two paintings are by the same ~**: diese beiden Gemälde stammen von derselben Hand; **suffer/suffer injustice at the ~s of sb.** unter jmdm./jmds. Ungerechtigkeit zu leiden haben; **die by one's own ~[s]** *(literary)* Hand an sich *(Akk.)* legen *(geh.)*; **g)** *(pledge of marriage)* **ask for** *or* **seek sb.'s ~ [in marriage]** um jmds. Hand bitten *od. (geh.)* anhalten; um jmdn. anhalten *(geh.)*; **ask sb. for his daughter's ~**: jmdn. um die Hand seiner Tochter bitten; bei jmdm. um die Hand seiner Tochter anhalten *(geh.)*; **win sb.'s ~**: jmdn. zur Frau *od.* jmds. Hand gewinnen; **h)** *(worker)* Arbeitskraft, *die;* Arbeiter, *der; (Naut.: seaman)* Hand, *die (fachspr.)*; Matrose, *der;* **the ship sank with all ~s** das Schiff sank mit der gesamten Mannschaft; **i)** *(person having ability)* **be a good/poor/rotten ~ at [playing] tennis** ein guter/schwacher/miserabler Tennisspieler sein; **I'm no ~ at painting** ich kann nicht malen; *see also* **old 1b; j)** *(source)* Quelle, *die;* **at first/second/third ~**: aus erster/zweiter/dritter Hand; *see also* **firsthand; second-hand; k)** *(skill)* Geschick, *das; (characteristic style)* Handschrift, *die;* **get one's ~ in** wieder in Übung kommen *od. (ugs.)* reinkommen; **get one's ~ in at sth.** etw. lernen; **keep one's ~ in [at singing/dancing]** [im Singen/Tanzen] in der Übung bleiben *od.* nicht aus der Übung kommen; *see also* **try 2b; l)** *(style of handwriting)* Handschrift, *die;* Hand, *die (veralt.)*; *(signature)* Unterschrift, *die;* **witness the ~ of J.C.** laut eigener Unterschrift – J.C.; **set one's ~ to sth.** seine Unterschrift unter etw. *(Akk.)* setzen; *see also* **a; m)** *(of clock or watch)* Zeiger, *der;* **n)** *(side)* Seite, *die;* **on the right/left ~**: rechts/links; rechter/linker Hand; **on sb.'s right/left ~**: rechts/links von jmdm.; zu jmds. Rechten/Linken; **on either ~**: zu *od.* auf beiden Seiten; **on every ~, on all ~s** von allen Seiten ‹*umringt sein*›; ringsum ‹*etw. sehen*›; von überallher ‹*eintreffen*›; **on the one ~ ..., [but] on the other [~] ...**: einerseits ..., andererseits ...; auf der einen Seite ..., auf der anderen Seite ...; **[but] on the other ~**: aber andererseits *od.* auf der anderen Seite; *see also* **left-hand; right-hand; o)** *(measurement)* Handbreit, *die;* **p)** *(Cards)* Karte, *die; (player)* Mitspieler, *der/*-spielerin, *die; (period of play)* Runde, *die;* **have a good/bad ~**: ein gutes/schlechtes Blatt haben; eine gute/schlechte Karte haben; **play a good ~**: gut spielen; *see also* **¹force 2b; play 2a; show 2a; q)** *(coll.: applause)* Beifall, *der;* Applaus, *der;* **give him a big ~, let's have a big ~ for him** viel Applaus *od.* Beifall für ihn! **2.** *v.t.* **a)** *(deliver)* geben; ‹*Überbringer:*› übergeben ‹*Sendung, Lieferung*›; **~ sth. from one to another** etw. von einem zum anderen weitergeben *od.* -reichen; **~ sth. [a]round [to sb.]** *(offer for distribution)* [jmdm.] etw. anbieten; **~ sth. [a]round** *(pass round, circulate)* etw. herumgeben *od.* -reichen; *(among group)* etw. herumgehen lassen; **you've got to ~ it to them/her** *etc. (fig. coll.)* das muß man ihnen/ihr *usw.* lassen; **b)** *(help)* helfen; **~ sb. out of/into/over sth.** jmdm. aus etw./in etw. *(Akk.)*/über etw. *(Akk.)* helfen

~ 'back *v.t. (return)* zurückgeben

~ 'down *v.t.* **a)** *(pass on)* überliefern ‹*Geschichte, Information, Tradition*›; weitergeben ‹*Gegenstand*› **(to** an + *Akk.*); [weiter]vererben ‹*Erbstück*› **(to** an + *Akk.*); **that ring has been ~ed down from your great-great-grandmother** der Ring ist ein Erbstück von deiner Ururgroßmutter; **b)** *(Law)* verhängen ‹*Strafe*› **(to** über + *Akk.*); fällen ‹*Entscheidung*›; verkünden ‹*Urteil*›; **~ down a fine to sb.** jmdn. mit einer Geldstrafe belegen; **c)** *(give to person below)* hinunter-/herunterreichen

~ 'in *v.t.* abgeben ‹*Klausur, Arbeit, Aufsatz*› **(to, at** bei); einreichen ‹*Petition, Bewerbung*› **(to, at** bei)

~ 'on *v.t.* weitergeben ‹*Rundschreiben, Nachricht, Erfahrungen, Information*› **(to** an + *Akk.*); **at 65 he ~ed the business on to his son** mit 65 hat er das Geschäft seinem Sohn übergeben

~ 'out *v.t.* aus-, verteilen **(to** an + *Akk.*, **among** unter + *Dat.*); geben ‹*Ratschläge, Tips, Winke*› **(to** an + *Akk.*); verteilen ‹*Komplimente, Lob*› **(to** an + *Akk.*); *see also* **hand-out**

~ 'over 1. *v.t.* **a)** *(deliver)* übergeben **(to** *Dat.*); freilassen ‹*Geisel*›; **~ over your guns/money!** Waffen/Geld her!; gebt eure Waffen/euer Geld her!; **he ~ed the housekeeping money over to his wife** er händigte seiner Frau das Haushaltsgeld aus; **b)** *(transfer)* übergeben *od.* -reichen **(to** *Dat.*); *(pass)* herüber- *od.* rübergeben *od.* -reichen **(to** *Dat.*); *(allow to have)* abgeben. **2.** *v.i. (to next speaker/one's successor)* das Wort/die Arbeit übergeben **(to** an + *Akk.*)

~ 'up *v.t.* heraufreichen **(to** *Dat.*)

hand- *in comb.* **a)** *(operated by hand, held in the hand)* Hand‹*hammer, -hebel, -gepäck, -werkzeug, -mixer*›; **b)** *(done by hand)* hand‹*gestickt*›; mit der Hand *od.* von Hand ‹*glasiert, verziert, gebacken*›

hand: ~bag *n.* Handtasche, *die;* **~-baggage** *n.* Handgepäck, *das;* **~bell** *n.* Handglocke, *die; (musical instrument)* Glocke, *die;* **~bill** *n.* Handzettel, *der;* **~book** *n.* Handbuch, *das; (guidebook)* Führer, *der;* **~-brake** *n.* Handbremse, *die*

h & c *abbr.* **hot and cold running water** fl. h. u. k. W.

hand: ~cart *n.* Handwagen, *der;* **~clap** *n.* **a)** *(single clap)* In-die-Hände-Klatschen, *das;* **give three ~claps** dreimal in die Hände klatschen; **b)** *(applause)* [Hände]klatschen, *das; see also* **slow handclap; ~clasp** *n.* Händedruck, *der;* **~craft 1.** *n. see* **handicraft a; 2.** *v.t.* in Handarbeit herstellen; **~cream** *n.* Handcreme, *die;* **~cuff 1.** *n., usu. in pl.* Handschelle, *die;* **2.** *v.t.* in Handschellen *(Akk.)* legen ‹*Hände*›; **~cuff sb.** jmdm. Handschellen anlegen

handed-'down *adj.* abgelegt ‹*Kleidungsstück*›; *(to posterity)* überliefert

hand-'finished *adj. see* **finish 1f**: mit der Hand *od.* von Hand geglättet/appretiert/glasiert/poliert/lackiert *usw.*

handful ['hændfʊl] *n.* **a)** *(quantity, or fig.: small number)* Handvoll, *die;* **a few ~s of nuts** ein paar Handvoll *od.* ein paar Hände voll Nüsse; **they picked them up by the ~**: sie sammelten ganze Hände voll davon auf; **come out in ~s** *or* **by the ~** ‹*Haar:*› büschelweise ausgehen; **b)** *(fig. coll.: troublesome person[s] or thing[s])*; **these children are/this dog is a real ~**: die Kinder halten/der Hund hält einen ständig auf Trab *(ugs.)*; **it's quite a ~ looking after the children** mit der Versorgung der Kinder hat man alle Hände voll zu tun; **that car is quite a ~ to steer** das Auto zu lenken ist Schwerarbeit *(ugs.)*

hand: ~-grenade *n. (Mil.)* Handgranate, *die;* **~-gun** *n. (Arms)* Faustfeuerwaffe, *die;* **~-held** *adj.* **~-held camera** Handkamera, *die;* **~hold** *n.* Halt, *der;* **provide ~holds/a ~hold for sb.** jmdm. Halt bieten; **use sth. as a ~hold** sich an etw. *(Dat.)* festhalten

handicap ['hændɪkæp] **1.** *n.* **a)** *(Sport) (advantage)* Handikap, *das (fachspr.)*; Vorgabe, *die; (disadvantage)* **carry a ~** ‹*Jockey:*› ein Ergänzungsgewicht mitführen; ‹*Pferd:*› ein Ergänzungsgewicht tragen; **b)** *(race, competition)* Handikaprennen, *das;* Ausgleichsrennen, *das;* **c)** *(fig.: hindrance)* Handikap, *das;* **have a mental/physical ~**: geistig behindert/körperbehindert sein; **be a ~/more of a ~ than a help** hinderlich/eher hinderlich als eine Hilfe sein; **don't let the child become a ~ to you** laß dich durch das Kind nicht zu sehr einschränken. **2.** *v.t.,* **-pp- a)** *(Sport: impose a ~ on)* ein Handikap festlegen für; **b)** *(fig.: put at a disadvantage)* benachteiligen; handikapen *(ugs.)*; *(fig.: obstruct)* ein Hemmnis darstellen für

handicapped ['hændɪkæpt] **1.** *adj.* behindert; **mentally/physically ~**: geistig behindert/körperbehindert. **2.** *n. pl.* **the [mentally/physically] ~**: die [geistig/körperlich]

Behinderten; **a home for the ~:** ein Heim für Behinderte; ein Behindertenheim

handicapper ['hændɪkæpə(r)] *n. (Sport) (person)* Handikapper, *der*/Handikapperin, *die;* Ausgleicher, *der*/Ausgleicherin, *die*

handicraft ['hændɪkrɑ:ft] *n.* **a)** *(craft)* [Kunst]handwerk, *das; (knitting, weaving, needlework)* Handarbeit, *die;* **b)** *no pl. (manual skill)* Handfertigkeit, *die*

handily ['hændɪlɪ] *adv.* praktisch; günstig ‹*gelegen*›; deutlich ‹*gewinnen, schlagen*›

handiness ['hændɪnɪs] *n., no pl.* **a)** *(convenience)* Vorteil, *der; (nearness)* günstige Lage; **b)** *(adroitness)* Geschicklichkeit, *die*

handiwork ['hændɪwɜ:k] *n., no pl., no indef. art.* **a)** *(working)* handwerkliche Arbeit; **he enjoys ~:** er arbeitet gern handwerklich; **a nice piece of ~!** *(fig.)* gute Arbeit!; **b)** *(piece of work)* [Hand]arbeit, *die;* **this painting is the ~ of a master** dieses Bild ist das Werk eines Meisters *od.* ein Meisterwerk; **this ring/newly decorated kitchen is all my own ~:** diesen Ring habe ich selbst gemacht *od. (geh.)* gearbeitet/diese Küche habe ich selbst renoviert; **c)** *(derog.: bad piece of work)* Werk, *das (ugs.);* **whose ~ is this?** wer hat das [denn] verbrochen? *(ugs.)*

handkerchief ['hæŋkətʃɪf, 'hæŋkətʃi:f] *n., pl.* **~s** *or* **handkerchieves** ['hæŋkətʃi:vz] Taschentuch, *das*

handle ['hændl] **1.** *n.* **a)** *(part held)* [Hand]griff, *der; (of bag etc.)* [Trag]griff, *der; (of knife, chisel)* Heft, *das;* Griff, *der; (of axe, brush, comb, broom, saucepan)* Stiel, *der; (of handbag)* Bügel, *der; (of door)* Klinke, *die; (of bucket, watering-can, cup, jug)* Henkel, *der; (of pump)* Schwengel, *der;* **fly off the ~** *(fig. coll.)* an die Decke gehen *(ugs.);* ausflippen *(salopp);* **b)** *(coll.: title)* Titel, *der;* **have a ~ to one's name** einen Titel haben; **c)** *(fact used against one)* Handhabe, *die;* **d)** *(feel)* Griff, *der;* **have a natural/give a warm ~:** sich natürlich/warm anfühlen. **2.** *v. t.* **a)** *(touch, feel)* anfassen; **'Fragile! H~ with care!'** „Vorsicht! Zerbrechlich!"; **mind how you ~ those glasses** geh bitte vorsichtig mit den Gläsern um; **b)** *(deal with)* umgehen mit ‹*Person, Tier, Situation*›; führen ‹*Verhandlung*›; erledigen ‹*Korrespondenz, Telefonat usw.*›; *(cope with)* fertigwerden *od.* zurechtkommen mit ‹*Person, Tier, Situation*›; **train sb. to ~ dogs** jmdn. zum Hundeführer ausbilden; **c)** *(control)* handhaben ‹*Fahrzeug, Flugzeug*›; **d)** *(treat)* behandeln ‹*Person*›; **e)** *(process, transport)* umschlagen ‹*Fracht*›; **Heathrow ~s x passengers per year** in Heathrow werden pro Jahr x Passagiere abgefertigt; **the railway ~s x tons of coal a week** die Bahn befördert wöchentlich x Tonnen Kohle; **f)** *(discuss)* behandeln ‹*Thema, Ansicht, Frage*›; **g)** *(deal in)* handeln mit. **3.** *v. i.* ‹*Gerät:*› sich handhaben lassen; ‹*Fahrzeug, Boot:*› sich fahren; ‹*Flugzeug:*› sich fliegen

handlebar ['hændlbɑ:(r)] *n.* Lenkstange, *die;* Lenker, *der;* **~ moustache** Schnauzbart, *der*

handler ['hændlə(r)] *n.* **a)** *(of police-dog)* Hundeführer, *der*/-führerin, *die;* **b)** *(dealer)* **be a ~ of sth.** mit etw. handeln; **a ~ of stolen goods** ein Hehler

handling ['hændlɪŋ] *n., no pl.* **a)** *(management)* Handhabung, *die; (of troops, workforce, bargaining, discussion)* Führung, *die; (of situation, class, crowd)* Umgang, *der* **(of** mit); **b)** *(use)* Handhabung, *die; (Motor Veh.)* Fahrverhalten, *das;* Handling, *das;* **what's your car's ~ like?** wie fährt sich dein Auto?; **c)** *(treatment)* Behandlung, *die;* **the child needs firm/considerate ~:** das Kind braucht eine feste Hand/muß rücksichtsvoll behandelt werden; **come in for some rough ~** ‹*Sache:*› schlecht behandelt werden; ‹*Person:*› ganz schön etwas abbekommen *(ugs.);* **d)** *(processing)* Beförderung, *die; (of passengers)* Abfertigung, *die*

hand: ~list *n.* Aufstellung, *die;* Liste, *die;* **~ luggage** *n.* Handgepäck, *das;* **~made** *adj.* handgearbeitet; in Handarbeit hergestellt; handgeschöpft ‹*Papier*›; **~maid, ~maiden** *ns.* **a)** *(arch.: female attendant)* Kammerfrau, *die;* [Kammer]zofe, *die;* **b)** *(fig.: subordinate)* Dienerin, *die;* **~-me-down 1.** *n.* **a)** *(garment ~ed down)* abgelegtes *od.* getragenes *od.* gebrauchtes Kleidungsstück **(from** *Gen.***)**; **I got the hat/ring as a ~-me-down from my aunt** den Hut/Ring habe ich von meiner Tante übernommen *od. (scherzh.)* geerbt; **b)** *(ready-made garment)* [billiges] Kleidungsstück von der Stange; **2.** *adj.* gebraucht; alt; **~-out** *n.* **a)** *(alms)* Almosen, *das;* Gabe, *die;* **b)** *(information)* Handout, *das; (press release)* Presseerklärung, *die;* **~-painted** *adj.* handbemalt ‹*Gegenstand*›; handgemalt ‹*Muster, Bild*›; **~-'picked** *adj.* sorgfältig ausgewählt; handverlesen *(ugs. scherzh.);* **~rail** *n.* Geländer, *das;* Handlauf, *der (Bauw.); (on ship)* Handläufer, *der;* **~set** *n. (Teleph.)* Handapparat, *der;* **~shake** *n.* Händedruck, *der;* Handschlag, *der; see also* **golden handshake**

handsome ['hænsəm] *adj.*, **~r** ['hænsəmə(r)], **~st** ['hænsəmɪst] **a)** *(good-looking)* gutaussehend ‹*Mann, Frau*›; schön, edel ‹*Tier, Möbel, Vase usw.*›; **~ is as ~ does** *(prov.)* man soll nicht nach dem Äußeren urteilen; **b)** *(generous)* großzügig ‹*Geschenk, Belohnung, Mitgift*›; nobel ‹*Behandlung, Verhalten, Empfang*›; *(considerable)* stattlich, ansehnlich ‹*Vermögen, Summe, Preis*›; stolz ‹*Preis, Summe*›

handsomely ['hænsəmlɪ] *adv.* großzügig; mit großem Vorsprung ‹*gewinnen*›

hand: ~s-'on *adj.* praktisch; **~spring** *n.* Handstandüberschlag, *der;* **~stand** *n.* Handstand, *der;* **~-to-~** *adj.* **~-to-~ combat** ein Kampf Mann gegen Mann; **~-to-mouth** *adj.* **a)** *(meagre)* kärglich, kümmerlich ‹*Leben, Dasein*›; **eke out/lead a ~-to-mouth life/existence** von der Hand in den Mund leben; **b)** *(precarious)* Gelegenheits‹*arbeit*›; **operate on a ~-to-mouth basis** von der Hand in den Mund leben *(fig.);* **~-towel** *n.* [Hände]handtuch, *das;* **~work** *n., no pl.* Handarbeit, *die;* **~writing** *n.* [Hand]schrift, *die;* **his style of ~writing** seine [Hand]schrift; **~-'written** *adj.* handgeschrieben; handschriftlich

handy ['hændɪ] *adj.* **a)** *(ready to hand)* griffbereit; greifbar; **keep/have sth. ~:** etw. griffbereit *od.* greifbar haben; **there is a ~ socket just by my bed** ich habe direkt am Bett eine Steckdose; **the house is very ~ for the market/town centre** *etc.* von dem Haus aus ist man sehr schnell auf dem Markt/in der Stadt *usw.;* **b)** *(useful)* praktisch; nützlich; **come in ~:** sich als nützlich erweisen; **that'll come in ~!** das kann ich gebrauchen!; **c)** *(adroit)* geschickt; **be ~ about the house** handwerklich geschickt sein; **be [quite/very] ~ with sth.** [ganz gut/sehr gut] mit etw. umgehen können; **he is too ~ with his gun/fists** er greift zu schnell zum Gewehr/ihm sitzen die Fäuste allzu locker

'handyman *n.* Handwerker, *der;* **[home]~:** Heimwerker, *der;* **be a ~:** handwerklich geschickt sein

hang [hæŋ] **1.** *v. t.*, **hung** [hʌŋ] *(see also* **f)**: **a)** *(support from above)* hängen; aufhängen ‹*Gardinen*›; **~ sth. from sth.** etw. an etw. *(Dat.)* aufhängen; **~ sth. on sb.** *(fig. sl.)* jmdm. etw. anhängen *(ugs. abwertend);* **b)** *(place on wall)* aufhängen ‹*Bild, Gemälde, Zeichnung*›; **~ a picture from a nail** ein Bild an *od.* mit einem Nagel aufhängen; **c)** *(paste up)* ankleben ‹*Tapete*›; **~ [the] wallpaper** tapezieren; **d)** *(install)* aufhängen ‹*Glocke*›; einhängen ‹*Tür, Tor*›; **e)** *(Cookery)* abhängen lassen ‹*Fleisch, Wild*›; **be well hung** gut abgehangen sein; **f)** *p. t., p.p.* **hanged** *(execute)* hängen, *(ugs.)* aufhängen **(for** wegen); **~ oneself** sich erhängen *od. (ugs.)* aufhängen; **be ~ed, drawn, and quartered** *(Hist.)* gehängt werden*(, die Eingeweide herausgenommen bekommen)* und gevierteilt werden; **I'll be** *or* **I am ~ed if ...** *(fig.)* der Henker soll mich holen, wenn ...; **[well,] I'm ~ed!** beim *od.* zum Henker! *(derb);* **I'm ~ed if I will** *(said as a retort)* den Teufel werd' ich *(salopp);* **~ it!** zum Henker! *(derb);* **~ the expense!** die Kosten interessieren mich nicht; **g)** *(let droop)* **~ one's head in** *or* **for shame** beschämt den Kopf senken; **h)** *(decorate)* schmücken; **i) ~ fire** ‹*Schußwaffe:*› mit Verzögerung losgehen; **he won't ~ fire in doing it** *(fig.)* er wird keinen Augenblick zögern, es zu tun. **2.** *v. i.*, **hung a)** *(be supported from above)* hängen; ‹*Kleid usw.*› fallen; **~ from the ceiling** an der Decke hängen; von der Decke [herab]hängen; **~ by a rope** an einem Strick hängen; **~ in folds** ‹*Haut, Segel, Markise, Zelt:*› Falten werfen; **~ loose** lose sein; **~ tough** *(coll.)* hart bleiben; **~ in there!** *(sl.)* halte durch!; **~ by a hair** *(fig.)* an einem seidenen Faden hängen; **he had the threat of prison ~ing over his head** ihm drohte eine Gefängnisstrafe; **time ~s heavily** *or* **heavy** die Zeit wird einem lang; **time ~s heavily** *or* **heavy on sb.** die Zeit wird jmdm. lang; *see also* **balance 1 c; lip a; thereby; thread 1 b; b)** *(be executed)* hängen; **let sth. go ~** *(coll.)* etw. schleifen lassen *(ugs.);* **let things go ~:** alles schleifen lassen *(ugs.);* **let sb. go ~:** jmdn. abschreiben *(ugs.);* **c)** *(droop)* **the dog's ears and tail hung [down]** der Hund ließ die Ohren und den Schwanz hängen; **his head hung** er hielt den Kopf gesenkt; **with his head ~ing** mit gesenktem Kopf. **3.** *n., no pl.* **a)** *(how sth. ~s)* Sitz, *der;* **the ~ of those clothes is perfect** die Kleider sitzen perfekt; **get the ~ of** *(fig. coll.) (get the knack of, understand)* klarkommen mit *(ugs.)* ‹*Gerät, Arbeit*›; *(see the meaning of)* kapieren *(ugs.)* ‹*Sprache, Argument*›; **you'll soon get the ~ of it/doing it** du wirst den Bogen bald raushaben *(ugs.)*/wirst bald raushaben, wie man es macht; **b) I don't give** *or* **care a ~ about that/him** *(coll.)* das/er kümmert mich nicht die Bohne *(ugs.)*

~ about *(Brit.)*, **~ around 1.** [--'-] *v. i.* **a)** *(loiter about)* herumlungern *(salopp);* **we ~ about** *or* **around there all evening** wir hängen da den ganzen Abend rum *(ugs.);* **b)** *(coll.: wait)* warten; **keep sb. ~ing about** *or* **around** jmdn. warten lassen; **don't ~ about, get a move on!** trödel nicht, beeile dich!; **~ about!** *(sl.)* wart mal!; Sekunde mal! *(ugs.).* **2.** ['---] *v. t.* herumlungern an/in/*usw.* (+ *Dat.*) *(salopp);* **~ about the exit** am Ausgang herumlungern

~ 'back *v. i.* **a)** *(be reluctant)* sich zieren; **don't ~ back!** na komm schon!; **b)** *(keep rearward position)* zurückbleiben

~ on 1. [-'-] *v. i.* **a)** *(hold fast)* sich festhalten; **~ on to** *(lit.: grasp)* sich festhalten an (+ *Dat.*) ‹*Gegenstand*›; *(fig. coll.: retain)* behalten ‹*Eigentum, Stellung*›; **b)** *(stand firm, survive)* durchhalten; **c)** *(sl.: wait)* warten; **~ on [a minute]!** Moment *od. (ugs.)* Sekunde mal!; **d)** *(coll.: not ring off)* dranbleiben *(ugs.).* **2.** ['--] *v. t.* **~ on sth.** *(fig.)* von etw. abhängen; **~ on sb.'s words** jmdm. gespannt zuhören

~ 'out 1. *v. t.* **a)** *(suspend)* aufhängen ‹*Wäsche*›; **b)** *(cause to protrude)* heraushängen lassen ‹*Zunge, Tentakel*›. **2.** *v. i.* **a)** *(protrude)* heraushängen; **the dog's tongue hung out** dem Hund hing die Zunge heraus; **let it all ~ out** *(fig. sl.)* die Sau rauslassen *(ugs.);* **just let it all ~ out!** mach einfach das, wozu du lustig bist! *(ugs.);* **b)** *(sl.) (reside)* wohnen; seine Bude haben *(ugs.); (be often pres-*

ent) sich herumtreiben *(ugs.)*; rumhängen *(ugs.)*

~ **to'gether** *v.i.* **a)** *(be coherent)* ‹*Handlung:*› stimmig sein; ‹*Teile eines Ganzen:*› sich zusammenfügen; ‹*Aussagen:*› zusammenstimmen; **b)** *(be or remain associated)* zusammenhalten

~ **'up 1.** *v.t.* **a)** *(suspend)* aufhängen; ~ **up sth. on a hook** etw. an einen Haken hängen *od.* an einem Haken aufhängen; **b)** *(fig.: put aside)* an den Nagel hängen *(ugs.)*; **c)** *(postpone)* aufschieben, vertagen ‹*Entscheidung*›; *(indefinitely)* auf die lange Bank schieben; **d)** *(cause delay to)* aufhalten ‹*Person*›; **the negotiations were hung up for a week** die Verhandlungen kamen für eine Woche zum Stillstand; **e)** *(sl.: cause inhibition to)* **be hung up about sth.** ein gestörtes Verhältnis zu etw. haben. *See also* **hang-up. 2.** *v.i. (Teleph.)* einhängen; auflegen; ~ **up on sb.** einfach einhängen *od.* auflegen

hangar ['hæŋə(r), 'hæŋgə(r)] *n.* Hangar, *der;* Flugzeughalle, *die*

'hangdog *adj.* zerknirscht

hanger ['hæŋə(r)] *n.* **a)** *(for clothes)* Bügel, *der;* **b)** *(loop on clothes etc.)* Aufhänger, *der*

hanger-'on *n.* **there are many hangers-on in every political party** in jeder politischen Partei gibt es viele, denen es nur um den persönlichen Vorteil geht; **the rock group with its usual [crowd of] hangers-on** die Rockgruppe mit ihrem üblichen Anhang

hang: ~-glider *n.* Hängegleiter, *der;* Drachen, *der;* **~-glider pilot** Drachenflieger, *der*/-fliegerin, *die;* **~-gliding** *n.* Drachenfliegen, *das*

hanging ['hæŋıŋ] **1.** *n.* **a)** *see* **hang 1:** [Auf]hängen, *das;* Ankleben, *das;* Einhängen, *das;* Abhängen, *das;* **b)** *(execution)* Hinrichtung [durch den Strang]; ~ **is too good for sb.** der Strang wäre noch eine zu milde Strafe [für jmdn.]; **this is a ~ matter** *or* **crime** darauf steht der Tod durch Erhängen; **it's/that's not a** *or* **no ~ matter** *(fig.)* das ist doch kein Beinbruch! *(ugs.)*; **c)** *in pl. (drapery)* Behang, *der.* **2.** *adj.* ~ **basket/staircase/balcony** Hängekorb, *der*/freitragende Treppe/vorstehender Balkon

hanging: ~ 'gardens *n. pl.* hängende Gärten; ~ **judge** *n. Richter, der schnell mit der Todesstrafe bei der Hand ist;* ~ **'paragraph** *n. (Printing) Absatz mit ausgerückter erster Zeile;* ~ **'valley** *n. (Geog.)* Hängetal, *das;* ~ **'wardrobe** *n.* Kleiderschrank, *der*

hang: ~man ['hæŋmən] *n., pl.* **~men** ['hæŋmən] Henker, *der;* **~over** *n.* **a)** *(aftereffects)* Kater, *der (ugs.)*; **b)** *(remainder)* Relikt, *das;* **~-up** *n. (sl.)* **a)** *(difficulty)* Problem, *das;* **we have no ~-ups about morals** die Moral ist bei uns kein Thema; **b)** *(inhibition)* Macke, *die (ugs.)*; **have a ~-up about sth.** ein gestörtes Verhältnis zu etw. haben; **c)** *(fixation)* Komplex, *der* **(about** wegen); **he has a ~-up about his mother** er hat einen Mutterkomplex

hank [hæŋk] *n.* Strang, *der*

hanker ['hæŋkə(r)] *v.i.* ~ **after** *or* **for** ein [heftiges] Verlangen haben nach ‹*Person, etwas Neuem, Zigarette*›; sich *(Dat.)* sehnlichst wünschen ‹*Gelegenheit*›

hankering ['hæŋkərıŋ] *n. (craving)* Verlangen, *das* **(after, for** nach); *(longing)* Sehnsucht, *die* **(after, for** nach)

hanky ['hæŋkı] *n. (coll.)* Taschentuch, *das*

hanky-panky [hæŋkı'pæŋkı] *n., no pl., no indef. art. (sl.)* **a)** *(underhand dealing)* Mauschelei, *die (abwertend)*; **there's been some ~/there was some ~ going on** es ist gemauschelt worden *(ugs. abwertend)*; **b)** *(love affair)* Techtelmechtel, *das;* **be involved in some ~ with sb.** ein Techtelmechtel mit jmdm. haben; **c)** *(illicit sexual activity)* Knutscherei, *die (ugs.)*; Gefummel, *das (ugs. abwertend)*; **there was some ~ going on** es wurde geknutscht *od.* gefummelt *(ugs.)*

Hanover ['hænəʊvə(r)] *pr. n.* Hannover *(das)*; **the House of ~** *(Hist.)* das Haus Hannover

Hanoverian [hænə'vıərıən] **1.** *n. (Hist.)* Hannoveraner, *der*/Hannoveranerin, *die;* **be a ~:** aus dem Haus Hannover sein. **2.** *adj.* hannoversch

Hansard ['hænsɑ:d] *n.* Hansard, *der; die britischen Parlamentsberichte*

Hanse ['hæns] *n. (Hist.)* Hanse, *die*

Hanseatic [hænsı'ætık] *adj. (Hist.)* hansisch; ~ **town** Hansestadt, *die;* **the ~ League** der Hansebund

hansom [cab] ['hænsəm (kæb)] *n. (Hist.)* Hansom, *der*

Hants *abbr.* **Hampshire**

haphazard [hæp'hæzəd] **1.** *adj.* willkürlich ‹*Auswahl*›; unbedacht ‹*Bemerkung*›; **arranged in a ~ fashion** willkürlich *od.* wahllos angeordnet; **the whole thing was rather ~:** das Ganze geschah ziemlich planlos. **2.** *adv. (at random)* willkürlich; wahllos

haphazardly [hæp'hæzədlı] *adv.* willkürlich; wahllos; ~ **planned** planlos

hapless ['hæplıs] *adj.* unglückselig

ha'p'orth ['heıpəθ] *see* **halfpennyworth**

happen ['hæpn] *v.i.* **a)** *(occur)* geschehen; ‹*Vorhergesagtes:*› eintreffen; **these things [do] ~:** das kommt vor; **it was the only thing that 'could ~:** es konnte [gar] nicht anders kommen; **what's ~ing?** was ist los?; **what's ~ing this evening?** was ist für heute abend geplant?; **I can't** *or* **don't see 'that ~ing** das kann ich mir nicht vorstellen; **it all ~ed like this ...:** das war so ...; **nothing ever ~s here** hier ist nichts los; **don't let it ~ again!** daß mir das nicht wieder vorkommt!; **that's what ~s!** das kommt davon!; **~ to sb.** jmdm. passieren; **what has ~ed to him/her arm?** was ist mit ihm/ihrem Arm?; **what can have ~ed to him?** was mag mit ihm los sein?; **it all ~ed so quickly that ...:** es ging alles so schnell, daß ...; **it's all ~ing** *(sl.)* es ist was los *(ugs.)*; **it's all ~ing for him** *(sl.)* es läuft gut bei ihm *(ugs.)*; **b)** *(chance)* ~ **to do sth./be sb.** zufällig etw. tun/jmd. sein; **it so ~s** *or* **as it ~s I have ...:** zufällig habe ich *od.* ich habe zufällig ...; **how does it ~ that ...?** wie kommt es, daß ...?; **do you ~ to know him?** kennen Sie ihn zufällig?

~ **'by** *v.i.* zufällig vorbeikommen

~ **[up]on** *v.t.* zufällig treffen ‹*Person*›; zufällig finden ‹*Arbeit, Gegenstand*›

happening ['hæpnıŋ] *n.* **a)** *usu. in pl. (event)* Ereignis, *das;* **a regrettable ~:** ein bedauerlicher Vorfall; **such ~s cannot be tolerated** solche Vorfälle können nicht toleriert werden; **b)** *(improvised performance)* Happening, *das*

happenstance ['hæpnstæns, 'hæpnstɑ:ns] *n. (Amer.)* Zufall, *der*

happily ['hæpılı] *adv.* **a)** glücklich ‹*lächeln*›; fröhlich, vergnügt ‹*spielen, lachen*›; gut ‹*zurechtkommen*›; **they lived ~ ever after[wards]** *(at end of fairy-tale)* sie lebten fortan glücklich und zufrieden[, und wenn sie nicht gestorben sind, dann leben sie noch heute]; **b)** *(gladly)* mit Vergnügen; **c)** *(aptly)* gut; treffend, passend ‹*ausdrücken, formulieren*›; **d)** *(fortunately)* glücklicherweise; zum Glück; **it ended ~:** es ging gut aus

happiness ['hæpınıs] *n., no pl. see* **happy a:** Glück, *das;* Heiterkeit, *die;* Zufriedenheit, *die;* **I wish you every ~:** [ich wünsche Ihnen] alles Gute

happy ['hæpı] *adj.* **a)** *(joyful)* glücklich; heiter ‹*Bild, Veranlagung, Ton*›; *(contented)* zufrieden; *(causing joy)* erfreulich ‹*Gedanke, Erinnerung, Szene*›; froh ‹*Ereignis*›; glücklich ‹*Zeiten*›; **I'm not ~ with her work** ich bin mit ihrer Arbeit nicht zufrieden; **not be ~ about sth./doing sth.** nicht froh über etw. *(Akk.)* sein/etw. nicht gern tun; **are you ~?** *(not needing help)* kommen Sie allein zurecht?; ~ **birthday!** herzlichen Glückwunsch zum Geburtstag!; ~ **anniversary!** herzlichen Glückwunsch! *(zum Jahrestag)*; ~ **Christmas!** frohe Weihnachten!; ~ **New Year!** ein glückliches neues Jahr!; ~ **days/landings!** *(dated coll.)* viel Glück!; ~ **event** *(euphem.: birth)* freudiges Ereignis *(verhüll.)*; **[strike] a ~ medium** den goldenen Mittelweg [wählen]; ~ **release** *(death)* Erlösung, *die; see also* **day a; 'lark; return 3 a; sandboy; b)** *(glad)* **be ~ to do sth.** etw. gern *od.* mit Vergnügen tun; **[I'm] ~ to meet you** [es] freut mich, Sie kennenzulernen; **I'm ~ for you** das freut mich für dich; **make sb. ~:** jmdn. zufriedenstellen; **yes, I'd be ~ to** *(as reply to request)* ja, gern *od.* mit Vergnügen; **I'd be only too ~ to do that** ich würde das nur zu gern tun; **c)** *(lucky)* glücklich; **by a ~ chance/accident/coincidence** durch einen glücklichen Zufall; **d)** *(apt)* glücklich ‹*Einfall*›; gut ‹*Wahl, Methode*›; **e)** *in comb. (quick to use sth.)* **bomb-~:** mit Bomben schnell bei der Hand *nur präd.*; **gun-~** schießwütig *(ugs.)*; *see also* **slap-happy; trigger-happy**

happy: ~ 'ending *n.* Happy-End, *das;* ~ **'families** *n. sing. (Cards)* Quartett, *das;* **~-go-'lucky** *adj.* sorglos; unbekümmert; ~ **hour** *n. Zeitspanne am frühen Abend, in der die Getränke in einer Bar o. ä. billiger verkauft werden;* ~ **'hunting-ground[s]** *n. [pl.]* **a)** *(N. Amer. Ind. Mythol.)* **the ~ hunting-grounds** die ewigen Jagdgründe; **b)** *(fig.)* Eldorado, *das*

hara-kiri [hærə'kırı] *n.* Harakiri, *das*

harangue [hə'ræŋ] **1.** *n.* Tirade, *die (abwertend).* **2.** *v.t.* eine Ansprache halten an (+ *Akk.*); **stop haranguing me about how ...:** hör auf, mir ständig zu predigen *(ugs.)*, wie ...

harass ['hærəs] *v.t.* schikanieren; **constantly ~ the enemy** den Feind nicht zur Ruhe kommen lassen; ~ **sb. with complaints** jmdn. mit [ständigen] Beschwerden belästigen; ~ **sb. into doing sth.** jmdm. so sehr zusetzen, daß er etw. tut

harassed ['hærəst] *adj.* geplagt **(with** von); gequält ‹*Blick, Ausdruck*›

harassment ['hærəsmənt] *n.* Schikanierung, *die;* **constant ~ of/by the enemy** ständiger Kleinkrieg mit dem Feind; **sexual ~:** [sexuelle] Belästigung

harbinger ['hɑ:bındʒə(r)] *n.* Vorbote, *der*/Vorbotin, *die*

harbour *(Brit.; Amer.:* **harbor)** ['hɑ:bə(r)] **1.** *n.* **a)** *(for ships)* Hafen, *der;* **in ~:** im Hafen; **b)** *(shelter)* Unterschlupf, *der.* **2.** *v.t.* beherbergen; Unterschlupf gewähren (+ *Dat.*) ‹*Verbrecher, Flüchtling*›; *(fig.)* hegen *(geh.)* ‹*Hoffnung, Groll, Verdacht*›

'harbour-master *n.* Hafenmeister, *der*

hard [hɑ:d] **1.** *adj.* **a)** hart; fest ‹*Gelee, Eiskrem, Preis*›; stark, heftig ‹*Regen*›; hart, streng ‹*Frost*›; gesichert ‹*Beweis, Zahlen, Daten, Information*›; ~ **water area** Gebiet mit hartem Wasser; **drive a ~ bargain** hart verhandeln; **a drop of the ~ stuff** *(coll.)* etw. Hochprozentiges; **the ~ fact is that ...;** es ist einfach eine Tatsache, daß ...; ~ **facts** nackte *od.* unumstößliche Tatsachen; *see also* **cheese c; iron 1 a; liquor a; nail 1 b; nut a; b)** *(difficult)* schwer; schwierig; **this is ~ to believe** das ist kaum zu glauben; es fällt schwer, das zu glauben; **it is ~ to do sth.** es ist schwer, etw. zu tun; **he's ~ to get on with** mit ihm ist schwer auszukommen; **this is a [very] ~ thing [for me] to say** es fällt mir [sehr] schwer, das zu sagen; **make it ~ for sb. [to do sth.]** es jmdm. schwermachen[, etw. zu tun]; **make sth. ~ for sb.** jmdm. etw. schwermachen; **[choose to] go about/do sth. the ~ way** es sich *(Dat.)* bei etw. unnötig schwermachen; **learn sth. the ~ way** etw. durch schlechte Erfahrungen lernen; **be [a] ~ [person] to please/prove wrong/catch out** schwer zufriedenzustellen/zu widerlegen/zu überführen sein; **be ~ to convince [of sth.]** schwer [von etw.] zu überzeugen sein; **be ~ to understand** schwer zu verstehen sein; **have a ~ row to hoe** *(fig. dated)* es nicht leicht haben; **be ~ of hearing** schwerhörig sein; **be ~ going** ‹*Buch:*› sich schwer lesen; ‹*Arbeit:*› anstrengend sein; **play ~ to get** *(coll.)* so tun, als sei man nicht interessiert; **have a ~ time doing sth.** Schwierigkeiten haben, etw. zu tun; **give sb. a ~ time** jmdm. das Leben schwermachen; **it's a ~ life** *(joc.)* das Leben ist schwer; **c)** *(involving suffering)* hart, anstrengend, beschwerlich ‹*Marsch*›; **it is [a bit] ~ on him** es ist [schon] schlimm für ihn; **~ luck** *(coll.)* Pech; *see also* **[1]line 1 a; d)** *(strenuous)* hart; beschwerlich ‹*Reise*›; konzentriert ‹*Gespräch, Diskussion*›; leidenschaftlich ‹*Spieler*›; **be a ~ drinker** viel trinken; **this is really ~ work!** *(coll.)* das ist wirklich nicht leicht; **go in [too much] for ~ drinking/gambling** zu viel trinken/spielen; **be a ~ worker/campaigner** sehr viel arbeiten/sich im Wahlkampf voll einsetzen; **try one's ~est to do sth.** sich nach Kräften bemühen, etw. zu tun; **I worked my very ~est** ich arbeitete, so hart ich konnte; **e)** *(vigorous)* heftig ‹*Angriff, Schlag*›; kräftig ‹*Schlag, Stoß, Tritt, Klaps*›; *(severe)* streng ‹*Winter*›; *(strong)* hart, hochprozentig ‹*alkoholisches Getränk*›; **f)** *(unfeeling)* hart; streng ‹*Kritiker*›; **be ~ [up]on sb.** streng mit jmdm. sein; **take a ~ line [with sb. on sth.]** [in bezug auf etw. *(Akk.)*] eine harte Linie [gegenüber jmdm.] vertreten; *see also* **nail 1 b; g)** *(harsh)* hart; **be ~ on sb./sth.** jmdn./etw. strapazieren; **h)** *(Phonet.)* hart. **2.** *adv.* **a)** *(strenuously)* hart ‹*arbeiten, trainieren*›; schnell ‹*laufen*›; fleißig ‹*lernen, studieren, üben*›; genau ‹*überlegen, beobachten, ansehen*›; scharf ‹*nachdenken*›; gut ‹*aufpassen, zuhören, sich festhalten*›; fest ‹*kleben*›; **he drinks ~:** er ist ein starker Trinker; **concentrate ~/~er** sich sehr/mehr konzentrieren; **try ~:** sich sehr bemühen; **work ~ and play ~:** intensiv arbeiten und leben; **be ~ at work on sth.** an etw. *(Dat.)* intensiv *od.* konzentriert arbeiten; **go ~ at it** sich richtig hineinknien *(ugs.)*; **be ~ 'at it** schwer arbeiten; **we found him already ~ 'at it** wir fanden ihn schon mitten in der Arbeit; **it's freezing ~ outside** es friert Stein und Bein draußen *(ugs.)*; **b)** *(vigorously)* heftig; herzhaft ‹*küssen*›; laut ‹*rufen*›; fest ‹*schlagen, drücken, klopfen*›; **c)** *(severely, drastically)* hart; streng ‹*zensieren*›; **come down ~ on sb.** jmdn. zusammenstauchen *(ugs.)*; **cut back** *or* **down ~ on sth.** etw. drastisch einschränken; **he took the news very ~:** die Nachricht traf ihn hart *od.* sehr; **be ~ up** knapp bei Kasse sein *(ugs.)*; **be ~ up for sth.** um etw. verlegen sein; **d)** *(with difficulty)* **it goes ~ with sb.** jmd. bekommt Schwierigkeiten; **be ~ put to it [to do sth.]** große Schwierigkeiten haben[, etw. zu tun]; **e)** hart ‹*kochen*›; fest ‹*gefrieren [lassen]*›; **bake ~:** abbacken; **set ~:** fest werden; **f)** *(close)* **darkness/trouble is ~ at hand** es wird gleich dunkel/gibt gleich Ärger; **follow ~ upon sth.** unmittelbar auf etw. *(Akk.)* folgen; **~ by** in nächster Nähe; **~ by sth.** nahe an etw. *(Dat.)*; *see also* **[1]heel 1 a; trail 1 b; g)** *(Naut.)* hart; **~ a-port!** hart backbord!

hard: ~ and 'fast *see* **[2]fast 1 a; ~back** *(Printing)* **1.** *n.* gebundene Ausgabe; Hardcover-Ausgabe, *die; attrib.* Hard-cover ‹*-Verlag, -Verkäufe*›; **in ~back** gebunden; mit festem Einband; **2.** *adj.* gebunden; Hard-cover-; **~backed** ['hɑ:dbækt] *adj. see* **~back 2; ~bitten** *adj.* hartgesotten; abgebrüht *(ugs.)* ‹*Veteran, Journalist, Karrieremacher*›; **~board** *n.* Hartfaserplatte, *die; attrib.* Hartfaser‹*trennwand, -unterlage*›; **~-boiled** *adj.* **a)** *(boiled solid)* hartgekocht; **b)** *(fig.)* *(shrewd)* ausgekocht *(ugs.)*; *(realistic, unsentimental)* realistisch; *(tough)* hartgesotten; **~ 'case** *n.* *(intractable person)* ausgebuffter Typ *(ugs.)*; *(criminal)* Gangster, *der;* **~ 'cash** *n.* **a)** *(coins)* Hartgeld, *das;* **b)** *(actual money)* Bargeld, *das;* **in ~ cash** in bar ‹*bezahlen*›; **~ 'coal** *n.* Anthrazit, *der;* ≈ Steinkohle, *die;* **~ 'copy** *n.* *(Computing)* Hardcopy, *die;* Papierausdruck, *der;* **~ 'core** *n.* **a)** *(nucleus)* harter Kern; *(of a problem)* Kern, *der;* **b)** *(Brit.: material)* Packlage, *die (Bauw.)*; **~-core** *attrib. adj.* hart ‹*Pornographie*›; zum harten Kern gehörend ‹*Terrorist*›; **~ 'court** *n.* *(Tennis)* Hartplatz, *der;* **~ 'cover** *n.* Hardcover-Einband, *der; attrib.* Hard-cover ‹*-Ausgabe*›; **in ~ covers** als Hard cover ‹*herauskommen*›; **~ 'currency** *n.* *(Econ.)* harte Währung; *attrib.* ‹*Markt, Land*› mit harter Währung; **~-currency shop** Geschäft, in dem nur harte Währungen angenommen werden; **~ 'disc** *see* **disc c; ~-drinking** *attrib. adj.* ‹*Mann/Frau,*› der/die viel [Alkohol] trinkt; **~ drug** *n.* harte Droge; **~-earned** *adj.* schwer verdient

harden ['hɑ:dn] **1.** *v. t.* **a)** *(make hard)* härten; **b)** *(fig.: reinforce)* bestärken (**in** in + *Dat.*); **~ sb.'s attitude/conviction** jmdn. in seiner Haltung/Überzeugung bestärken; **c)** *(make robust)* abhärten (**to** gegen); **d)** *(make tough)* unempfindlich machen (**to** gegen); **~ sb./oneself to sth.** jmdn./sich gegenüber etw. hart machen; **~ sb. to killing** jmdn. an das Töten gewöhnen; **he ~ed his heart against her** er verhärtete sich gegen sie. **2.** *v. i.* **a)** *(become hard)* hart werden; härten; **b)** *(become confirmed)* sich verhärten; **c)** ‹*Preis:*› sich festigen; **d)** *(become severe)* ‹*Gesicht:*› einen harten Ausdruck annehmen; ‹*Gesichtsausdruck:*› hart werden; **his face ~ed into anger** sein Gesicht verhärtete sich zornig

~ 'off *v. t.* widerstandsfähig machen ‹*Pflanze*›

hardened ['hɑ:dnd] *adj.* **a)** verhärtet ‹*Arterie*›; **b)** *(grown tough)* abgehärtet, unempfindlich (**to, against** gegen); hartgesotten ‹*Verbrecher, Sünder, Krieger*›; **be ~ to sth.** gegen etw. unempfindlich sein; **become** *or* **get ~ to sth.** gegen etw. unempfindlich werden; **a ~ drinker** jemand, der viel verträgt; **c)** *(seasoned)* eingefleischt

hardener ['hɑ:dnə(r)] *n.* Härter, *der*

hardening ['hɑ:dnɪŋ] *n.* **a)** *(of steel)* Härten, *das;* *(of arteries)* Verhärtung, *die;* **b)** *(making callous)* Verhärtung, *die*

hard: ~-featured *adj.* ‹*Person*› mit harten Gesichtszügen; hart ‹*Gesicht*›; **~ 'feeling[s]** *n.* *[pl.]* *(coll.)* **no ~ feelings** schon gut; **make sure there are no ~ feelings** dafür sorgen, daß er/sie/*usw.* nicht mehr böse ist; **with no ~ feelings on either side** ohne daß es einer dem anderen nachtrug; **~-fought** *adj.* heftig ‹*Kampf*›; hart ‹*Spiel, Wettbewerb*›; **~ 'hat** *n.* **a)** *(Brit.: bowler hat)* Bowler, *der;* **b)** *(protective headgear)* Schutzhelm, *der;* **~-headed** *adj.* sachlich; nüchtern; **be ~-headed about what one wants** genau wissen, was man will; **~-hearted** [hɑ:d'hɑ:tɪd] *adj.* hartherzig (**towards** gegenüber); **~-'hitting** *adj.* schlagkräftig; *(fig.)* aggressiv ‹*Rede, Politik, Kritik*›

hardiness ['hɑ:dɪnɪs] *n., no pl.* Widerstandsfähigkeit, *die*

hard: ~ 'labour *n.* Zwangsarbeit, *die;* **~ 'landing** *n.* *(Astronaut.)* harte Landung; **~-line** *adj.* kompromißlos; **~-'liner** *n.* Befürworter einer harten Linie (**on** gegenüber); **~-'luck story** *n.* Leidensgeschichte, *die*

hardly ['hɑ:dlɪ] *adv.* kaum; **he can ~ have arrived yet** er kann kaum jetzt schon angekommen sein; **~ anyone** *or* **anybody/anything** kaum jemand/etwas; fast niemand/nichts; **~ any wine/beds** kaum Wein/Betten; fast kein Wein/keine Betten; **~ ever** so gut wie nie; **~ at all** fast überhaupt nicht

hard 'money *n.* *(Amer.)* Hartgeld, *das*

hardness ['hɑ:dnɪs] *n., no pl.* Härte, *die;* *(of blow)* Heftigkeit, *die;* *(of person)* Strenge, *die;* **~ of hearing** Schwerhörigkeit, *die*

hard: ~ 'news *n. sing.* gesicherte Fakten; **~-nose[d]** ['hɑ:dnəʊz(d)] *adj.* *(coll.)* abgebrüht; **~-on** *n.* *(sl.)* Ständer, *der (ugs.)*; **~ 'palate** *n.* *(Anat.)* harter Gaumen; **~ 'pressed** *adj.* hart bedrängt; **be ~ pressed** große Schwierigkeiten haben; **~ 'rock** *n.* *(Mus.)* Hard Rock, *der;* **~-scrabble** *(Amer.)* **1.** *n.* karger Boden; **2.** *adj.* ertragsarm ‹*Bauernhof*›; karg ‹*Boden, Feld, Acker*›; **~ sell** *n.* aggressive Verkaufsmethoden; *attrib.* aggressiv ‹*Werbung, [Verkaufs]methode*›

hardship ['hɑ:dʃɪp] *n.* **a)** *no pl., no indef. art.* Not, *die;* Elend, *das;* **life of ~:** entbehrungsreiches *od.* hartes Leben; **b)** *(instance)* Notlage, *die;* **~s** Not, *die;* Entbehrungen; **if it's not too much of a ~ for you** wenn es nicht zuviel verlangt ist; **c)** *(sth. causing suffering)* Unannehmlichkeit, *die*

hard: ~ 'shoulder *n.* Standspur, *die;* **~ 'standing** *n.* befestigter Abstellplatz; **~ 'tack** *n.* Schiffszwieback, *der;* **it'll be ~ tack from now on** *(fig.)* von jetzt an gibt es nur noch trocken Brot *(fig.)*; **~-top** *n.* Hardtop, *das;* **~ware** *n., no pl., no indef. art.* **a)** *(goods)* Eisenwaren *Pl.*; *(for domestic use also)* Haushaltswaren *Pl.*; *attrib.* Eisen-/Haushaltswaren‹*geschäft*›; **b)** *(sl.: weapons)* Schießeisen *(ugs.)*; **military ~ware** Waffen *Pl.*; **c)** *(Computing)* Hardware, *die;* **~-wearing** *adj.* strapazierfähig; **~ 'wheat** *n.* Hartweizen, *der;* **~-wired** *adj.* *(Computing)* festverdrahtet; **~-won** *adj.* schwer errungen *od.* erkämpft ‹*Sieg*›; mühsam gewonnen ‹*Schlacht*›; schwer erarbeitet ‹*Reichtum*›; **~wood** *n.* Hartholz, *das; attrib.* Hartholz‹*möbel, -fußboden, -baum*›; **~ 'words** *n. pl.* **a)** *(difficult to understand)* schwierige Wörter; **b)** *(angry)* harte Worte; **~-working** *adj.* fleißig ‹*Person*›

hardy ['hɑ:dɪ] *adj.* **a)** *(robust)* abgehärtet; zäh, robust ‹*Rasse*›; **b)** *(Hort.)* winterhart; **c)** *(bold)* unerschrocken

hardy: ~ 'annual *n.* **a)** *(Hort.)* winterharte einjährige Pflanze; **b)** *(fig. joc.)* nicht totzukriegendes Thema *(scherzh.)*; **~ per'ennial** *n.* **a)** *(Hort.)* winterharte mehrjährige Pflanze; **b)** *(fig. joc.)* Dauerbrenner, *der (ugs.)*

hare [heə(r)] **1.** *n.* Hase, *der;* **run like a ~:** wie ein geölter Blitz laufen *(ugs.)*; **[as] mad as a March ~** *(fig.)* völlig verrückt *(ugs.)*; **run with the ~ and hunt with the hounds** *(fig.)* auf beiden Schultern *od.* Achseln Wasser tragen *(veralt.)*. **2.** *v. i.* sausen *(ugs.)*; **go haring about** herumsausen *(ugs.)*

hare: ~ and 'hounds *n. sing.* Schnitzeljagd, *die;* **~bell** *n.* *(Bot.)* **a)** *(Scottish bluebell)* Rundblättrige Glockenblume; **b)** *(English bluebell)* Hasenglöckchen, *das;* **~-brained** *adj.* unüberlegt; **~'lip** *n.* Hasenscharte, *die*

harem ['hɑ:ri:m, hɑ:'ri:m] *n.* Harem, *der*

haricot ['hærɪkəʊ] *n.* **a)** *(Cookery)* Ragout, *das;* **~ of veal** Kalbsragout, *das;* **b)** *see* **haricot bean**

haricot bean *n.* Gartenbohne, *die;* *(pod also)* grüne Bohne; *(seed also)* weiße Bohne

hark [hɑ:k] *v. i.* **a)** *(arch.: listen)* **~ [to sb.]** hören [auf jmdn.]; **~!** horch!/horcht!; **b)** *(coll.)* **just ~ at him!** hör ihn dir/hört ihn euch nur an!

~ 'back *v. i.* **~ back to** *(come back to)* zurückkommen auf (+ *Akk.*); zurückgreifen auf (+ *Akk.*) ‹*Tradition*›; wieder anfangen von ‹*alten Zeiten*›; *(go back to)* ‹*Idee, Brauch:*› zurückgehen auf (+ *Akk.*)

Harlequin ['hɑ:lɪkwɪn] *n.* Harlekin, *der*

harlot ['hɑ:lət] *(arch./derog.)* *n.* Metze, *die (veralt.)*

harlotry ['hɑːlətrɪ] *n. (arch./derog.)* Prostitution, *die*

harm [hɑːm] **1.** *n.* Schaden, *der;* **do ~:** Schaden anrichten; **do ~ to sb., do sb. ~:** jmdm. schaden; *(injure)* jmdn. verletzen; **the blow didn't do him any ~:** der Schlag war harmlos; **the dog won't do you any ~:** der Hund tut dir nichts; **it will do you no** *or* **won't do you any ~** *(iron.)* es würde dir nichts schaden; **do ~ to sth.** einer Sache *(Dat.)* schaden; **sb./sth. comes to no ~:** jmdm./einer Sache passiert nichts; **there is no ~ done** nichts ist passiert; **there's no ~ in doing sth., it will do no ~ to do sth.** *(could be of benefit)* es kann nicht schaden, etw. zu tun; **there's no ~ in asking** Fragen kostet nichts; **it will do more ~ than good** es wird mehr schaden als nützen; **where's** *or* **what's the ~ in it?** was ist denn schon dabei?; **see no ~ in it/sth./doing sth.** nichts dabei/bei etw. finden/dabei finden, etw. zu tun; **let's hope no ~ will come of it** wir wollen hoffen, daß es sich nicht negativ auswirkt; **stay here, out of ~'s way** bleib hier, wo dir nichts passieren kann; **keep out of ~'s way** der Gefahr fernbleiben; an einem sicheren Ort aufbewahren ⟨*Medikamente*⟩; von der Gefahr fernhalten ⟨*Person*⟩; **get sb. out of ~'s way** jmdn. in Sicherheit bringen; *see also* **intend a; [3]mean a. 2.** *v.t.* etwas [zuleide] tun (+ *Dat.*); schaden (+ *Dat.*) ⟨*Beziehungen, Land, Karriere, Ruf*⟩

harmful ['hɑːmfl] *adj.* schädlich **(to** für); schlecht ⟨*Angewohnheit*⟩

harmfulness ['hɑːmflnɪs] *n., no pl.* Schädlichkeit, *die*

harmless ['hɑːmlɪs] *adj.* harmlos; **make** *or* **render ~:** unschädlich machen; entschärfen ⟨*Bombe*⟩

harmlessly ['hɑːmlɪslɪ] *adv.* ohne Schaden anzurichten

harmlessness ['hɑːmlɪsnɪs] *n., no pl.* Harmlosigkeit, *die*

harmonic [hɑː'mɒnɪk] **1.** *adj. (also Mus., Math.)* harmonisch. **2.** *n.* **a)** *(Mus.)* Oberton, *der;* **b)** *(component frequency)* Harmonische, *die (Physik);* **upper ~s** harmonische Oberschwingungen *(Physik)*

harmonica [hɑː'mɒnɪkə] *n. (Mus.)* Mundharmonika, *die*

harmonious [hɑː'məʊnɪəs] *adj.,* **harmoniously** [hɑː'məʊnɪəslɪ] *adv.* harmonisch

harmonise *see* **harmonize**

harmonium [hɑː'məʊnɪəm] *n. (Mus.)* Harmonium, *das*

harmonize ['hɑːmənaɪz] **1.** *v. t.* **a)** *(bring into harmony)* aufeinander abstimmen; **~ sth. with sth.** etw. mit etw. in Einklang bringen *od.* auf etw. *(Akk.)* abstimmen; **b)** *(Mus.)* harmonisieren. **2.** *v.i. (be in harmony)* harmonieren **(with** mit); ⟨*Interessen, Ansichten, Wort und Tat:*⟩ miteinander im *od.* in Einklang stehen; **~ well together** ⟨*Farben, Klänge:*⟩ gut harmonieren

harmony ['hɑːmənɪ] *n.* **a)** Harmonie, *die;* **live in perfect ~:** völlig harmonisch *od.* in vollkommener Harmonie zusammenleben; **peace and ~:** Friede und Eintracht; **be in ~** *see* **harmonize 2; be in ~ with sth.** mit etw. im *od.* in Einklang stehen; **be out of ~ with sth.** mit etw. nicht im *od.* in Einklang stehen; **b)** *(Mus.)* Harmonie, *die; (theory of ~)* Harmonielehre, *die;* **sing in ~:** mehrstimmig singen; *see also* **sphere c**

harness ['hɑːnɪs] **1.** *n.* **a)** Geschirr, *das;* **b)** *(on parachute)* Gurtzeug, *das; (for toddler, dog)* Laufgeschirr, *das; (for window-cleaner, steeplejack, etc.)* Sicherheitsgürtel, *der;* **in ~** *(fig.) (in the daily routine)* in der Tretmühle *(ugs. abwertend); (together)* gemeinsam; **die in ~:** in den Sielen sterben; **out of ~** *(fig.)* außer Dienst; *see also* **double harness. 2.** *v. t.* **a)** *(put ~ on)* anschirren; **~ a horse to a cart** ein Pferd vor einen Wagen spannen; **b)** *(fig.)* nutzen

'harness-racing Trabrennen, *das*

harp [hɑːp] **1.** *n.* Harfe, *die.* **2.** *v.i.* **~ on [about] sth.** [immer wieder] von etw. reden; *(critically)* auf etw. *(Dat.)* herumreiten *(salopp); (complainingly)* über etw. *(Akk.)* lamentieren *(ugs.);* **don't ~ on about it!** hör auf damit!

harpist ['hɑːpɪst] *ns.* Harfenist, *der*/Harfenistin, *die;* Harfenspieler, *der*/-spielerin, *die*

harpoon [hɑː'puːn] **1.** *n.* Harpune, *die.* **2.** *v.t.* harpunieren

harpoon-'gun *n.* Harpunengeschütz, *das*

'harp-seal *n. (Zool.)* Sattelrobbe, *die*

harpsichord ['hɑːpsɪkɔːd] *n. (Mus.)* Cembalo, *das*

harpy ['hɑːpɪ] *n.* **a)** *(grasping person)* Hyäne, *die (ugs. abwertend);* **b)** *(Greek and Roman Mythol.)* Harpyie, *die*

harridan ['hærɪdən] *n.* Schreckschraube, *die (ugs. abwertend)*

harrier ['hærɪə(r)] *n.* **a)** *(Ornith.)* Weihe, *die;* **b)** *(Hunting)* Harrier, *der (Hund für die Hasenjagd);* **c)** *(Sport)* Querfeldeinläufer, *der*/-läuferin, *die*

Harris tweed [hærɪs 'twiːd] *n.* Harris-Tweed, *der; attrib.* Harris-Tweed⟨*-Jackett*⟩

harrow ['hærəʊ] **1.** *n.* Egge, *die.* **2.** *v.t.* **a)** eggen; **b)** *(distress)* quälen

harrowing ['hærəʊɪŋ] *adj.* entsetzlich; *(horrific)* grauenhaft ⟨*Anblick, Geschichte*⟩

harry ['hærɪ] *v. t.* **a)** ~ **[continuously]** wiederholt angreifen; **b)** *(harass)* bedrängen; **be harried by telephone calls** von Anrufern belästigt *od.* behelligt werden

harsh [hɑːʃ] *adj.* **a)** rauh ⟨*Gewebe, Oberfläche, Gegend, Land, Klima*⟩; schrill ⟨*Ton, Stimme*⟩; grell ⟨*Licht, Farbe, Ton*⟩; schroff, stark ⟨*Kontrast*⟩; scharf ⟨*Geschmack*⟩; stechend, streng ⟨*Geruch*⟩; hart ⟨*Bedingungen, Leben*⟩; **b)** *(excessively severe)* [sehr] hart; [äußerst] streng ⟨*Richter, Disziplin*⟩; rücksichtslos ⟨*Tyrann, Herrscher, Verhalten, Politik*⟩; **back to ~ reality** zurück zur grauen Wirklichkeit; **don't be ~ on him** sei nicht zu streng mit ihm

harshly ['hɑːʃlɪ] *adv.* **a)** *(disagreeably)* grell ⟨*klingen*⟩; in schroffem Ton ⟨*reden*⟩; **b)** *(extremely severely)* [sehr] hart

harshness ['hɑːʃnɪs] *n., no pl.* **a)** *see* **harsh a:** Rauheit, *die;* schriller Klang; Grelle, *die;* Schroffheit, *die;* Schärfe, *die; (of life conditions)* Härte, *die;* **b)** *see* **harsh b:** Härte, *die;* Strenge, *die;* Rücksichtslosigkeit, *die*

hart [hɑːt] *n.* Hirsch, *der*

harum-scarum [heərəm'skeərəm] *(coll.)* **1.** *adj.* unbesonnen. **2.** *n.* Wildfang, *der*

harvest ['hɑːvɪst] **1.** *n.* **a)** Ernte, *die;* **timber ~:** Holzschlag, *der;* **find/reap a [rich] harvest** *(fig.)* einen [tollen] Fang machen; **b)** *(time)* Ernte[zeit], *die.* **2.** *v. t.* ernten; schlagen ⟨*Holz*⟩; lesen ⟨*Weintrauben*⟩; fangen ⟨*Fisch*⟩; *(fig.)* gewinnen ⟨*Energie*⟩; ansammeln ⟨*Vermögen*⟩; **~ the crops** die Ernte einbringen; **~ the fruits of one's labours** *(fig.)* die Früchte seiner Arbeit ernten

harvester ['hɑːvɪstə(r)] *n.* **a)** *(machine)* Erntemaschine, *die; see also* **combine 3 b; b)** *(person)* Erntearbeiter, *der*/-arbeiterin, *die*

harvest: ~ 'festival *n.* Erntedankfest, *das;* **~ 'home** *n.* Erntefest, *das;* **~man** ['hɑːvɪstmən] *n., pl.* **-men** ['hɑːvɪstmən] *(Zool.)* Weberknecht, *der;* **~ 'moon** *n. Vollmond zur Zeit der Herbst-Tagundnachtgleiche;* **~ mouse** *n.* Zwergmaus, *die*

has *see* **have 1, 2**

has-been ['hæzbiːn] *n. (coll.)* **be [a bit of] a ~:** seine besten Jahre hinter sich haben; **a seedy ~ of an actor** ein abgetakelter Schauspieler

[1]hash [hæʃ] **1.** *n. (Cookery)* Haschee, *das; (fig.)* Aufguß, *der (abwertend);* **make a ~ of sth.** *(coll.)* etw. verpfuschen *od.* verpatzen *(ugs.);* **settle sb.'s ~** *(coll.)* jmdn. zur Vernunft bringen; *(by forceful methods)* jmdn. unschädlich machen; **I'll settle his ~:** dem werd' ich's zeigen *(ugs.).* **2.** *v. t.* haschieren; *(fig. coll.)* verpfuschen *(ugs.);* verpatzen *(ugs.);* **~ and rehash sth.** etw. x-mal durchkauen *(ugs.)*

~ 'up *v.t.* zerkleinern; *(fig. coll.)* verpfuschen *(ugs.);* verpatzen *(ugs.)*

[2]hash *n. (coll.: drug)* Hasch, *das (ugs.)*

hashish ['hæʃɪʃ] *n.* Haschisch, *das*

Hasidic [hə'sɪdɪc] *adj.* chassidisch

hasn't ['hæznt] = **has not;** *see* **have 1, 2**

hasp [hɑːsp] *n.* Haspe, *die; (fastener snapping into a lock)* [Schnapp]schloß, *das; (fastener for book or cape)* Schließe, *die*

hassle ['hæsl] *(coll.)* **1.** *n.* **~[s]** Krach, *der (ugs.); (trouble, problem)* Ärger, *der;* **get involved in ~s with sb.** mit jmdm. Ärger kriegen *(ugs.);* **no end of ~[s]** nichts als Ärger; **it's a real ~:** das ist ein echtes Problem; **it's too much [of a]/such a ~:** das macht zuviel/soviel Umstände. **2.** *v.t.* schikanieren; **don't ~ me** nerv mich nicht *(ugs.)*

hassock ['hæsək] *n.* **a)** *(cushion)* Kniekissen, *das;* **b)** *(tuft of grass)* Grasbüschel, *das*

haste [heɪst] *n., no pl.* Eile, *die; (rush)* Hast, *die;* **in his ~:** in seiner Hast; **no need for ~:** kein Grund zur Eile; **more ~, less speed** *(prov.)* eile mit Weile *(Spr.);* **do sth. in ~:** etw. eilig tun; **yours in ~** *(at end of letter)* in Eile, Dein/Deine; **make ~:** sich beeilen

hasten ['heɪsn] **1.** *v. t. (cause to hurry)* drängen; *(accelerate)* beschleunigen. **2.** *v.i.* eilen; *(precipitately)* hasten *(geh.);* **~ away** davoneilen; **~ to do sth.** sich beeilen, etw. zu tun; **I ~ to add/say** ich muß *od.* möchte gleich hinzufügen/sagen

hastily ['heɪstɪlɪ] *adv. (hurriedly)* eilig; *(precipitately)* hastig; *(rashly)* übereilt; *(quick-temperedly)* heftig; hitzig; **judge sb. too ~:** jmdn. vorschnell beurteilen

hasty ['heɪstɪ] *adj. (hurried)* eilig; flüchtig ⟨*Skizze, Blick*⟩; *(precipitate)* hastig; *(rash)* übereilt; *(quick-tempered)* heftig; hitzig; **beat a ~ retreat** sich schnellstens zurückziehen *od. (ugs.)* aus dem Staub machen; *(fig.)* schnell einen Rückzieher machen; **he's a man of ~ temper/disposition** er hat eine recht hitzige Art

hasty 'pudding *n. (Brit.)* Mehlbrei, *der; (Amer.)* Maismehlbrei, *der*

hat [hæt] *n.* **a)** Hut, *der;* **[sailor's/woollen/knitted] ~:** [Matrosen-/Woll-/Strick]mütze, *die;* **without a ~:** ohne Hut/Mütze; **doff** *or* **raise one's ~ to sb.** vor jmdm. den Hut ziehen; **take off one's ~, take one's ~ off** seinen *od.* den Hut abnehmen; **take one's ~ off** *or* **take off one's ~ to sb./sth.** *(lit. or fig.)* vor jmdm./etw. den Hut ziehen; **~s off to him!** Hut ab vor ihm!; **b)** *(fig.)* **bad ~** *(Brit. sl.)* übler Kunde *(ugs.);* **at the drop of a ~:** auf der Stelle; **sb. will/would eat his ~ if ...:** jmd. frißt einen Besen/will einen Besen fressen, wenn ... *(salopp);* **somewhere** *or* **a place to hang [up] one's ~:** ein Ort, an dem man zu Hause ist; **throw one's ~ in the ring** seine Kandidatur anmelden; **my ~!** *expr. surprise* ist es/[denn] das die Möglichkeit! *(ugs.); expr. disbelief* daß ich nicht lache!; **be old ~** *(coll.)* ein alter Hut sein *(ugs.);* **become old ~** *(coll.)* aus der Mode kommen; **they pulled his name out of a ~:** er wurde ganz zufällig ausgewählt; **produce sth. out of a ~:** etw. aus dem Ärmel schütteln; **pass** *or* **send round the ~** *or* **the ~ round** *(coll.)* den Hut herumgehen lassen; **with ~ in hand** demütig; **talk through one's ~** *(sl.)* dummes Zeug reden *(ugs.);* **keep sth. under one's ~:** etw. für sich behalten; **[when he is] wearing his ... ~:** in seiner Rolle als ...; **switch ~s** die Rollen vertauschen; **wear two ~s** zwei Interessen gleichzeitig vertreten

hat: ~band *n.* Hutband, *das;* **~box** *n.* Hutschachtel, *die*

[1]hatch [hætʃ] *n.* **a)** *(opening)* Luke, *die;*

under ~es unter Deck; **down the ~!** *(fig. sl.)* runter damit! *(ugs.)*; **b)** *(serving-~)* Durchreiche, *die. See also* **escape-hatch**

²hatch 1. *v. t. (lit. or fig.)* ausbrüten. **2.** *v. i.* [aus]schlüpfen; *see also* **chicken 1 a. 3.** *n.* **a)** *(act of ~ing)* Schlüpfen, *das;* **b)** *(brood ~ed)* Brut, *die*

~ 'out 1. *v. i.* ausschlüpfen; **the eggs have ~ed out** die Eier sind ausgebrütet. **2.** *v. t.* ausbrüten

~ 'up *v. t.* ausbrüten *(fig.)*; aushecken *(ugs.)*

³hatch *v. t. (Art)* schraffieren

'hatchback *n.* **a)** *(door)* Heckklappe, *die;* **a ~ model** ein Modell mit Heckklappe; **b)** *(vehicle)* Schräghecklimousine, *die*

hatchery ['hætʃərɪ] *n. (for birds)* Brutplatz, *der; (for fish)* Laichplatz, *der*

hatchet ['hætʃɪt] *n.* Beil, *das;* **bury the ~** *(fig.)* das Kriegsbeil begraben

hatchet: ~ face *n.* scharfgeschnittenes Gesicht; **~-faced** *adj.* mit scharfen Gesichtszügen *nachgestellt;* **~ job** *n.* **do a ~ job on sb./sth.** jmdn./etw. in der Luft zerreißen *(salopp)*; **~ man a)** *(professional killer)* Killer, *der;* **be a real ~ man** *(fig.)* kein Pardon kennen; **b)** *(henchman)* Erfüllungsgehilfe, *der (fig. abwertend)*

hatchling ['hætʃlɪŋ] *n.* Junge, *das*

hatchment ['hætʃmənt] *n. (Her.)* Totenschild, *der od. das*

hate [heɪt] **1.** *n.* **a)** Haß, *der;* **~ for sb.** Haß auf *od.* gegen jmdn.; **b)** *(coll.: object of dislike)* **be sb.'s ~:** jmdm. verhaßt sein; **my pet ~ at the moment is ...:** ... hasse ich zur Zeit am meisten. **2.** *v. t.* hassen; **I ~ having to get up at seven** ich hasse es, um sieben Uhr aufstehen zu müssen; **I ~ to say this** *(coll.)* ich sage das nicht gern; **I ~ [having] to trouble you** *(coll.)* tut mir leid, daß ich Sie damit behelligen muß; **I ~ to think what would have happened if .../I ~ the thought of having to leave this job** *(coll.)* ich darf gar nicht daran denken, was geschehen wäre, wenn .../wie es wäre, wenn ich die Stelle aufgeben müßte

hateful ['heɪtfl] *adj.* abscheulich; verabscheuenswürdig *(geh.)*; **that would be a ~ thing to do** das [zu tun] wäre abscheulich

hatful ['hætfʊl] *n.* **a) a ~ of eggs** ein Hut voll[er] Eier; **b)** *(fig.: considerable number/amount)* **a ~ of** eine ganze Menge *(ugs.)*

hatless ['hætlɪs] *adj.* ohne Hut *nachgestellt*

hat: ~-peg *n.* Huthaken, *der;* **~-pin** *n.* Hutnadel, *die*

hatred ['heɪtrɪd] *n.* Haß, *der;* **feel ~ for** *or* **of sb./sth.** Haß auf *od.* gegen jmdn./etw. empfinden

'hat-stand *n.* Hutständer, *der*

hatter ['hætə(r)] *n.* Hutmacher, *der;* **[as] mad as a ~** *(fig.)* völlig verrückt *(ugs.)*

'hat trick *n.* Hattrick, *der;* **make** *or* **score a ~:** einen Hattrick erzielen; **be on a ~:** vor einem Hattrick stehen

haughtily ['hɔːtɪlɪ] *adv.* hochmütig

haughtiness ['hɔːtɪnɪs] *n., no pl.* Hochmut, *der*

haughty ['hɔːtɪ] *adj.* hochmütig

haul [hɔːl] **1.** *v. t.* **a)** *(pull)* ziehen; schleppen; *(Fishing)* einholen ⟨*Netze*⟩; **~ sth. up the wall** etw. die Mauer hochziehen; **~ the boat up on the beach** das Boot auf den Strand ziehen; **be ~ed before the court** *(fig. coll.)* vor Gericht gestellt werden; **~ down** einholen ⟨*Flagge, Segel*⟩; *see also* **coal b; b)** *(transport)* transportieren; befördern; **c)** *(Naut.) (mit geändertem Kurs)* steuern; **~ the ship into the wind** anluven. **2.** *v. i.* ziehen; **~ [up]on** *or* **at sth.** an etw. *(Dat.)* [kräftig] ziehen. **3.** *n.* **a)** Ziehen, *das;* Schleppen, *das; (Fishing)* Einholen, *das;* **b)** *(catch)* Fang, *der; (fig.)* Beute, *die;* **c)** *(distance)* Strecke, *die; see also* **long haul; short haul**

haulage ['hɔːlɪdʒ] *n., no pl.* **a)** *(hauling)* Transport, *der;* **b)** *(charges)* Transportkosten *Pl.*

hauler ['hɔːlə(r)] *(Amer.),* **haulier** ['hɔːlɪə(r)] *(Brit.) n. (person)* Spediteur, *der; (firm)* Spedition[sfirma], *die*

haulm [hɔːm, hɑːm] *n.* **a)** *no pl., no indef. art. (Agric.)* Kraut, *das;* **b)** *(stem) (of grass, straw)* Halm, *der; (of leaf, fruit)* Stiel, *der*

haunch [hɔːnʃ] *n.* **a) sit on one's/its ~es** auf seinem Hinterteil sitzen; **b)** *(Gastr.)* Keule, *die;* **c)** *(Archit.)* [Bogen]schenkel, *der*

haunt [hɔːnt] **1.** *v. t.* **a) ~ a house/castle** in einem Haus/Schloß spuken *od.* umgehen; **the old farmhouse is ~ed by ghosts** in dem alten Bauernhaus spuken Geister; **b)** *(fig.: trouble)* ⟨*Erinnerung, Gedanke:*⟩ plagen, verfolgen; **c)** *(frequent)* häufig besuchen ⟨*Ort, Lokal*⟩. **2.** *n.* **a favourite ~ of artists** ein beliebter Treffpunkt für Künstler; **these are my old ~s** hier habe ich mich früher immer herumgetrieben *(ugs.)*

haunted ['hɔːntɪd] *adj.* **a) a ~ house** ein Haus, in dem es spukt; **a ~ castle** ein Spukschloß; **b)** *(fig.: troubled)* gehetzt ⟨*Blick, Eindruck*⟩

haunting ['hɔːntɪŋ] *adj.* sehnsüchtig ⟨*Klänge, Musik*⟩; lastend ⟨*Erinnerung*⟩; drückend ⟨*Schuld*⟩

Hausa ['haʊsə] *n., pl. same* **a)** *(person)* Haus[s]a, *der*/Haus[s]afrau, *die;* **b)** *(language)* Hausa, *das*

hausfrau ['haʊsfraʊ] *n.* [biedere] Hausfrau

haute couture [əʊt kuː'tjʊə(r)] *n., no pl.* Haute Couture, *die*

haute école [əʊt eɪ'kɒl] *n., no pl.* [die] Hohe Schule

hauteur [əʊ'tɜː(r)] *n., no pl.* Stolz, *der*

Havana [hə'vænə] *n.* **a)** *(cigar)* Havanna, *die;* **b)** *pr. n.* Havanna *(das)*

have 1. [hæv] *v. t., pres.* **he has** [hæz], *p. t. & p. p.* **had** [hæd] **a)** *(possess)* haben; **I ~ it!** ich hab's[!]; **and what ~ you** *(coll.)* und so weiter; **I ~ something to say [to you]** ich habe Ihnen etwas zu sagen; **~ nothing to do/wear/say** nichts zu tun/anzuziehen/zu sagen haben; **they ~ some French** sie können etwas Französisch; **I still ~ some work to do** ich muß noch etwas arbeiten; **you ~ some explaining to do** du schuldest mir eine Erklärung; **you ~ five minutes [in which] to do it** Sie haben fünf Minuten [Zeit], um es zu tun; **b)** *(obtain)* bekommen; **there was no money/help to be had** es war kein Geld/keine Hilfe zu bekommen *od. (ugs.)* aufzutreiben; **we shall ~ snow** es wird schneien; **let's not ~ any ...:** laß uns ... vermeiden; **come on, let's ~ it!** *(coll.)* rück schon raus damit! *(ugs.)*; **c)** *(take)* nehmen; **~ a cigarette** nehmen Sie eine Zigarette; *see also* **e; d)** *(keep)* behalten; haben; **you can ~ that pencil** Sie können den Bleistift behalten *od.* haben; **e)** *(eat, drink, etc.)* **~ breakfast/dinner/lunch** frühstücken/zu Abend/zu Mittag essen; **~ a cup of tea** eine Tasse Tee trinken; **~ a cigarette** eine Zigarette rauchen; *see also* **c; f)** *(experience)* haben ⟨*Spaß, Vergnügen*⟩; **g)** *(suffer)* haben ⟨*Krankheit, Schmerz, Enttäuschung, Abenteuer*⟩; erleiden ⟨*Schock*⟩; *(feel)* haben ⟨*Gefühl, Idee*⟩; *(show)* haben ⟨*Güte, Freundlichkeit, Frechheit*⟩; **let him/them ~ it** *(coll.)* gib's ihm/ihnen *(ugs.)*; **h)** *(engage in)* **~ a game of football** Fußball spielen; **~ a try** es [einmal] versuchen; **~ it [with sb.]** *(sl.: copulate)* es [mit jmdm.] machen *(salopp)*; **i)** *(accept)* **I won't ~ it** das lasse ich mir nicht bieten; **I won't ~ him in the house** er kommt mir nicht ins Haus; **I won't ~ you behaving like that** so kannst du dich nicht benehmen; **j)** *(give birth to)* **~ a baby/children** ein Baby/Kinder bekommen; **~ pups** *etc.* Junge bekommen; **k)** *(sl.: copulate with)* **he had her on the sofa** er machte es mit ihr auf dem Sofa *(salopp)*; **l)** *(coll.: beat)* **you ~ me there** da bringen Sie mich aber in Verlegenheit; **m)** *(coll.: swindle)* **I was had** ich bin [he]reingelegt worden *(ugs.)*; **ever been had!** da bist du ganz schön reingefallen *(ugs.)*; **n)** *(know)* **I ~ it on good authority that ...:** ich weiß es aus zuverlässiger Quelle, daß ...; **she 'will ~ it that ...:** sie besteht darauf, daß ...; **she won't ~ it that ...:** sie will nichts davon hören, daß ...; **rumour/legend/tradition has it that they escaped** einem Gerücht/der Legende/der Überlieferung zufolge sind sie entkommen; **as Goethe has it** wie Goethe sagt; **o)** *(as guest)* **~ sb. to stay** jmdn. zu Besuch haben; **thanks for having me** danke für die Einladung; **p)** *(summon)* **he had me into his office** er hat mich in sein Büro beordert; **q)** *(in coll. phrases)* **you've had it now** *(coll.)* jetzt ist es aus *(ugs.)*; **if you want another drink, you've had it** *(coll.)* falls du noch was trinken willst, da geht nichts mehr *(ugs.)*; **this car/dress has had it** *(coll.)* dieser Wagen/dieses Kleid hat ausgedient. **2.** [həv, əv, *stressed* hæv] *v. aux.,* **he has** [həz, əz, *stressed* hæz], **had** [həd, əd, *stressed* hæd] **a)** *forming past tenses* **I've** *or* **I ~/I had read** ich habe/hatte gelesen; **I've** *or* **I ~/I had gone** ich bin/war gegangen; **having seen him** *(because)* weil ich ihn gesehen habe/hatte; *(after)* wenn ich ihn gesehen habe/nachdem ich ihn gesehen hatte; **if I had known ...:** wenn ich gewußt hätte ...; **b)** *(cause to be)* **~ sth. made/repaired** etw. machen/reparieren lassen; **~ the painters in** die Maler haben; **~ sb. do sth.** jmdn. etw. tun lassen; **~ a tooth extracted** sich *(Dat.)* einen Zahn ziehen lassen; **~ oneself tattooed** sich tätowieren lassen; **c) she had her purse stolen** man hat ihr das Portemonnaie gestohlen; **d)** *expr. obligation* **~ to** müssen; **you don't ~ to** du brauchst *od.* mußt nicht; **I only ~ to do the washing-up** ich muß nur noch den Abwasch machen; **I ~ only to see him to feel annoyed** ich brauche ihn nur zu sehen, und ich ärgere mich; **he 'has to be guilty** er ist fraglos schuldig. **3.** [hæv] *n. in pl.* **the ~s and the have-nots** die Besitzenden und die Besitzlosen

~ a'way *see* **~ off b**

~ 'off *v. t.* **a)** abmachen; **b) ~ it off [with sb.]** *(sl.)* es [mit jmdm.] treiben *(salopp)*

~ 'on *v. t.* **a) ~ the light on** das Licht anhaben; **b)** *(wear)* **~ a dress/hat on** ein Kleid/einen Hut tragen; ein Kleid anhaben/einen Hut aufhaben *(ugs.)*; **c)** *(Brit. coll.: deceive)* **~ sb. on** jmdn. auf den Arm nehmen *(ugs.)*

~ 'out *v. t.* **a)** entfernen; **~ a tooth/one's tonsils out** sich *(Dat.)* einen Zahn ziehen lassen/sich *(Dat.)* die Mandeln herausnehmen lassen; **b)** *(discuss and settle)* **~ sth. out** sich über etw. *(Akk.)* offen [mit jmdm.] aussprechen; **~ it out with sb.** mit jmdm. offen sprechen

~ 'up *v. t.* **a)** aufgehängt haben ⟨*Vorhang, Bild*⟩; **b)** *(coll.: bring to court)* **~ sb. up** jmdn. rankriegen *(ugs.)*

haven ['heɪvn] *n.* **a)** *(mooring)* geschützte Anlegestelle, *die; (fig.)* Zufluchtsort, *der;* **a ~ of peace** eine Insel des Friedens; **b)** *(arch.: harbour)* Port, *der (veralt.)*

have-not ['hævnɒt] *see* **have 3**

haven't ['hævnt] = **have not;** *see* **have 1, 2**

haver ['heɪvə(r)] *v. i.* **a)** *(talk foolishly)* **~ [on] about sth.** über etw. *(Akk.)* schwafeln *(ugs.)*; **b)** *(vacillate)* zögern

haversack ['hævəsæk] *n.* Brotbeutel, *der*

havoc ['hævək] *n., no pl.* **a)** *(devastation)* Verwüstungen; **cause** *or* **create** *or* **wreak ~:** Verwüstungen anrichten; **play ~ with** ruinieren ⟨*Gesundheit, Frisur usw.*⟩; **b)** *(confusion)* Chaos; **play ~ with sth.** etw. völlig durcheinanderbringen

¹haw [hɔː] *n. (Bot.)* **a)** *(tree) (white)* Weißdorn, *der; (red)* Rotdorn, *der;* **b)** *(fruit)* Weißdorn-/Rotdornfrucht, *die*

²haw *v. i., n. see* **hum 1 a, 3 b**

Hawaii [hə'waɪɪ] *pr. n.* Hawaii *(das)*

Hawaiian [hə'waɪən] **1.** *adj.* hawaiisch. **2.** *n.* **a)** *(person)* Hawaiianer, *der*/Hawaiianerin, *die;* **b)** *(language)* Hawaiisch, *das*

haw-haw ['hɔ:hɔ:] **1.** *int. (laughter)* haha. **2.** *n.* **let out a loud ~:** laut auflachen
[1]**hawk** [hɔ:k] **1.** *n. (Ornith., Polit.)* Falke, *der;* **watch sb. like a ~:** jmdn. mit Argusaugen beobachten. **2.** *v. i.* mit dem Falken jagen; beizen *(Jägerspr.)*
[2]**hawk** *v. t. (peddle)* **~ sth.** *(at door)* mit etw. hausieren [gehen]; *(in street)* etw. [auf der Straße] verkaufen; **~ sth. around** *(fig.)* mit etw. hausieren [gehen]
[3]**hawk 1.** *v. t.* **~ [up] phlegm** Schleim auswerfen. **2.** *v. i.* Schleim hochziehen [im Hals]
hawker ['hɔ:kə(r)] *n.* Hausierer, *der*/Hausiererin, *die; (in street)* fliegender Händler
'**hawk-eyed** *adj.* adleräugig; **be ~:** Falkenaugen *od.* Adleraugen haben
hawkish ['hɔ:kɪʃ] *adj.* raubvogelartig ⟨*Aussehen*⟩; *(Polit.)* militant
'**hawklike** *adj.* falkenartig
hawk: ~-moth *n. (Zool.)* Schwärmer, *der;* **~-nosed** *adj.* hakennasig; **be ~-nosed** eine Hakennase *od.* Habichtsnase haben
hawser ['hɔ:zə(r)] *n. (Naut.)* Trosse, *die*
hawthorn ['hɔ:θɔ:n] *n. (Bot.) (white)* Weißdorn, *der; (red)* Rotdorn, *der*
hay [heɪ] *n., no pl.* Heu, *das;* **make ~:** Heu machen; **make ~ while the sun shines** *(prov.)* die Zeit nutzen; *see also* **hit 1 i**
hay: ~cock *n.* Heuhaufen, *der;* **~ fever** *n., no pl.* Heuschnupfen, *der;* **~field** *n.* Heuwiese, *die;* **~maker** *n.* **a)** Heumacher, *der;* **b)** *(coll.: blow)* weit ausholender Schlag; Heumacher, *der (Boxen Jargon);* **~making** *n., no pl.* Heuernte, *die;* **~rick** *see* **~stack; ~seed** *n.* **a)** Heublumen *Pl.;* **b)** *(Amer. derog.: yokel)* Bauerntölpel, *der;* **~stack** *n.* Heuschober, *der (südd.);* Heudieme, *die (nordd.); see also* **needle 1**
haywire ['heɪwaɪə(r)] *adj. (coll.)* **go ~** ⟨*Instrument:*⟩ verrückt spielen *(ugs.);* ⟨*Plan:*⟩ über den Haufen geworfen werden *(ugs.);* ⟨*Person:*⟩ durchdrehen *(ugs.)*
hazard ['hæzəd] **1.** *n.* **a)** *(danger)* Gefahr, *die; (on road)* Gefahrenstelle, *die;* **occupational ~:** Berufsrisiko, *das; see also* **fire hazard; b)** *(chance)* Schicksal, *das;* **c)** *(Golf)* Hindernis, *das.* **2.** *v. t.* **a)** *(endanger)* in Gefahr bringen; **b)** *(venture)* riskieren; **~ a guess** mit Raten probieren
hazardous ['hæzədəs] *adj. (dangerous)* gefährlich; *(risky)* riskant
hazardously ['hæzədəslɪ] *adv. (dangerously)* gefährlich; *(riskily)* riskant
hazard 'warning lights *n.pl. (Motor Veh.)* Warnblinkanlage, *die*
haze [heɪz] **1.** *n.* Dunst[schleier], *der; (fig.)* Nebel, *der.* **2.** *v. t.* vernebeln
hazel ['heɪzl] **1.** *n.* **a)** *(Bot.)* Haselnußstrauch, *der; (wood)* Haselholz, *das (veralt.);* **b)** *(colour)* Haselnußbraun, *das.* **2.** *adj.* haselnußbraun
'**hazel-nut** *n.* Haselnuß, *die*
hazily ['heɪzɪlɪ] *adv. (lit. or fig.)* verschwommen; unscharf; vage ⟨*verstehen*⟩; unklar ⟨*sich vorstellen*⟩
haziness ['heɪzɪnɪs] *n., no pl.* Dunst, *der; (fig.)* Vagheit, *die*
hazy ['heɪzɪ] *adj.* dunstig, diesig ⟨*Wetter, Tag[eszeit]*⟩; verschwommen, unscharf ⟨*Konturen*⟩; *(fig.)* vage; **I have a ~ recollection that ...:** ich erinnere mich dunkel, daß ...
H-bomb ['eɪtʃbɒm] *n.* H-Bombe, *die*
HE *abbr.* **a) high explosive; b) His Eminence; c) His/Her Excellency**
[1]**he** [hɪ, *stressed* hi:] **1.** *pron.* er; *referring to personified things or animals which correspond to German feminines/neuters* sie/es; **it was he** *(formal)* er war es; **he who** wer; *(Games)* **be 'he'** dran sein; *see also* **him; himself; his. 2.** *n., pl.* **hes** [hi:z] Er, der *(ugs.)*
[2]**he** [hi:] *int.* haha!
he- [hi:] *pref.* männlich; **he-goat** [Ziegen]bock, *der*
head [hed] **1.** *n.* **a)** Kopf, *der;* Haupt, *das (geh.);* **count ~s** die Anzahl feststellen; **mind your ~!** Vorsicht, dein Kopf!; *(on sign)* Vorsicht – geringe Durchgangshöhe!; **turn sb.'s ~** *(fig.)* jmdm. den Kopf verdrehen; **laugh/scream one's ~ off** wie verrückt lachen/schreien; **from ~ to foot** von Kopf bis Fuß; **get one's ~ down** *(coll.)* sich aufs Ohr hauen *(ugs.);* **keep one's ~ down** *(lit. or fig.)* in Deckung bleiben; **stand on one's ~:** [einen] Kopfstand machen; **I could do that [standing] on my ~** *(fig. coll.)* das kann *od.* mache ich mit links *(ugs.);* **he has a price on his ~:** auf seinen Kopf ist eine Belohnung *od.* ein Preis ausgesetzt; **have a [bad] ~** *(fig. coll.: headache)* einen Brummschädel haben *(ugs.);* **the crowned ~s of Europe** die gekrönten Häupter Europas; **taller by a ~, a ~ taller** einen Kopf größer; **win by a ~/short ~:** mit einer Kopflänge/Nasenlänge gewinnen; **be** *or* **stand ~ and shoulders above sb.** *(fig.)* jmdm. haushoch überlegen sein; **give a horse its ~:** einem Pferd die Zügel schießen lassen; **give sb.** *or* **let sb. have his/her ~** *(fig.)* jmdm. freie Hand lassen; **go to sb.'s ~:** jmdm. in den *od.* zu Kopf steigen; **have a [good] ~ for heights** schwindelfrei sein; **~ first** mit dem Kopf zuerst/voran; *(fig.)* kopfüber; **not know whether one is [standing] on one's ~ or one's heels** nicht wissen, wo einem der Kopf steht; **~ over heels** kopfüber; **~ over heels in love** bis über beide Ohren verliebt *(ugs.);* **I can hold up my ~ [again]** ich brauche mich nicht [mehr] zu schämen; **keep one's ~:** einen klaren Kopf behalten; **keep one's ~ above water** *(fig.)* sich über Wasser halten; **put our/your/their ~s together [on sth.]** sich [wegen etw.] zusammensetzen; **lose one's ~:** enthauptet werden; *(fig.)* den Kopf verlieren; **~ to tail** in einer Reihe dicht hintereinander; *(~ beside tail)* nebeneinander in umgekehrter Richtung; **be unable to make ~ or tail of sth./sb.** aus etw./jmdm. nicht klug werden; **be off one's ~** *(coll.)* übergeschnappt sein *(ugs.);* **off the top of one's ~** *(coll.)* aus dem Stegreif; *(as estimate)* über den Daumen gepeilt; **on your** *etc.* **[own] ~ be it** das hast du *usw.* selbst zu verantworten; **promote sb. over sb.'s ~:** jmdn. jmdm. bei der Beförderung vorziehen; **go over sb.'s ~:** jmdn. übergehen; *see also* **[1]ear a; hole 1 a; raise 1 a; b)** *(mind)* Kopf, *der;* **in one's ~:** im Kopf; **enter sb.'s ~:** jmdm. in den Sinn kommen; **two ~s are better than one** *(prov.)* zwei Köpfe sind besser als einer; **it went right out of my ~:** ich habe das völlig vergessen; **take it into one's ~ [to do sth.]** auf die Idee kommen[, etw. zu tun]; **put sth. into sb.'s ~:** jmdn. auf etw. *(Akk.)* bringen; **it went above** *or* **over my ~** *(fig.)* das war zu hoch für mich *(ugs.);* **talk over sb.'s ~:** sich zu kompliziert für jmdn. ausdrücken; **I've got a good/bad ~ for figures** ich kann gut rechnen/rechnen kann ich überhaupt nicht; **use your ~:** gebrauch deinen Verstand; **not quite right in the ~** *(coll.)* nicht ganz richtig [im Kopf] *(ugs.);* **get sth. into one's ~:** etw. begreifen; **get this into your ~!** schreib dir das hinter die Ohren! *(ugs.);* **have got it into one's ~ that ...:** fest [davon] überzeugt sein, daß ...; **the first thing that comes into sb.'s ~:** das erste, was jmdm. einfällt; **you ought to have your ~ examined** *(joc.)* ich glaube, du mußt mal deinen Kopf untersuchen lassen *(ugs. scherzh.);* **the ~ rules the heart** der Verstand kontrolliert die Gefühle; **c)** *(person)* **a** *or* **per ~:** pro Kopf; **d)** *pl. same (in counting)* Stück [Vieh], *das;* **e)** *in pl. (on coin)* **~s or tails?** Kopf oder Zahl?; **~s [it is]** Kopf; **~s I go, tails I stay** bei Kopf gehe ich, bei Zahl bleibe ich; **~s I win, tails you lose** es läuft auf dasselbe hinaus; **f)** *(working end etc.; also Mus.)* Kopf, *der; (of axe)* Blatt, *das; (of spear)* Spitze, *die; (of cylinder)* Zylinderkopf, *der;* **drilling/cutting ~:** Bohr-/Schneidkopf, *der;* **playback/erasing ~:** Wiedergabe-/Löschkopf, *der;* **g)** *(of plant)* Kopf, *der; (of grain)* Ähre, *die;* **~ of lettuce** Salatkopf, *der;* **h)** *(on beer)* Blume, *die;* **i)** *(highest part)* Kopf, *der; (of stairs)* oberes Ende; *(of list, column)* oberste Reihe; *(of mast)* Topp, *der;* **j)** *(upper or more important end)* Kopf, *der; (of table)* Kopf, *der;* Kopfende, *das; (of lake, valley)* oberes Ende; *(of river)* Quelle, *die; (of bed)* Kopfende, *das;* **k)** *(of boil etc.)* Spitze, *die; (fig.: crisis)* **come to a ~:** sich zuspitzen; **bring matters to a ~:** die Sache auf die Spitze treiben; *(force a decision)* die Entscheidung herbeiführen; **l)** *(leader)* Leiter, *der*/Leiterin, *die; (of church, family)* Oberhaupt, *das;* **~ of government** Regierungschef, *der*/-chefin, *die;* **~ of state** Staatsoberhaupt, *das;* **m)** *see* **headmaster; headmistress; n)** *(leadership)* Spitze, *die;* **he is at the ~ of his profession** er hat eine Spitzenstellung in seinem Beruf; **o)** *(of ship)* Bug, *der;* **p)** *see* **headland; q)** *(body of water)* gestautes Wasser; Oberwasser, *das; (height of liquid)* Höhe, *die; (pressure)* Druck, *der;* **under a full ~ of steam** mit Volldampf; **r)** *(title)* Überschrift, *die; (fig.: category)* Rubrik, *die.* **2.** *attrib. adj. (senior)* **~ boy/girl** ≈ Schulsprecher, *der*/-sprecherin, *die (vom Lehrkörper eingesetzt);* **~ waiter** Oberkellner, *der;* **~ clerk** Bürovorsteher, *der; (main)* **~ office** Hauptverwaltung, *die; (Commerc.)* Hauptbüro, *das; (Banking, Insurance)* Hauptgeschäftsstelle, *die.* **3.** *v. t.* **a)** *(provide with heading)* überschreiben; betiteln; **~ed notepaper** Briefpapier mit Kopf; **b)** *(stand at top of)* anführen ⟨*Liste*⟩; *(lead)* leiten; führen ⟨*Bewegung*⟩; **c)** *(precede)* anführen; **d)** *(direct)* **~ sth. towards sth.** etw. auf etw. zusteuern; **we were ~ed towards Plymouth** wir fuhren mit Kurs auf Plymouth; **e)** *(Football)* köpfen; **f)** *(overtake and stop)* **~ sb./sth. [off]** jmdn./etw. abdrängen; **g)** *(surpass)* überholen. **4.** *v. i.* steuern; **~ for London** ⟨*Flugzeug, Schiff:*⟩ Kurs auf London nehmen; ⟨*Auto:*⟩ in Richtung London fahren; **~ towards** *or* **for sb./the buffet** auf jmdn./das Buffet zusteuern; **where are you ~ing?** wo gehst du hin?; **you're ~ing in the wrong direction** *(fig.)* du bist auf dem Holzweg; **you're ~ing for trouble** du wirst Ärger bekommen
~ 'up *v. t. (Amer.)* leiten
head: ~ache *n.* Kopfschmerzen *Pl.; (fig. coll.)* Problem, *das;* **~achy** *adj. (coll.)* drückend ⟨*Wetter*⟩; **feel ~achy** einen Druck im Kopf haben; **~band** *n.* Stirnband, *das;* **~board** *n. (of bed)* Kopfende, *das;* **~butt 1.** *n.* Kopfstoß, *der;* **2.** *v. t.* einen Kopfstoß geben (+ *Dat.*); **~ count** *n.* **a) take a ~ count** abzählen; die Anzahl feststellen; **b)** *(number of people)* Kopfzahl, *die;* **~-covering** *n.* Kopfbedeckung, *die;* **~-dress** *n.* Kopfschmuck, *der*
-headed ['hedɪd] *adj. in comb.* -köpfig
header ['hedə(r)] *n.* **a)** *(Football)* Kopfball, *der;* **b)** *(dive)* Kopfsprung, *der;* **c)** *(Building)* Binder, *der*
head: ~gear *n., no pl.* **a)** Kopfbedeckung, *die; (hats)* Kopfbedeckungen *Pl.;* **protective ~gear** Kopfschutz, *der;* **b)** *(Mining)* Fördergerüst, *das;* **~-hunter** *n. (lit. or fig.)* Kopfjäger, *der*
heading ['hedɪŋ] *n.* **a)** *(title)* Überschrift, *die; (in encyclopaedia)* Stichwort, *das; (fig.: category)* Rubrik, *die;* **come under the ~ [of] X** unter die Rubrik X fallen; **let's discuss these problems under separate ~s** diese Probleme sollten gesondert behandelt werden; **b)** *(direction)* Kurs, *der*
head: ~lamp *n.* Scheinwerfer, *der;* **~land** ['hedlənd, 'hedlænd] *n.* **a)** *(Geog.)* Landspitze, *die;* **b)** *(Agric.)* Vorgewende, *das*
headless ['hedlɪs] *adj.* ohne Kopf
head: ~light *n.* Scheinwerfer, *der;* **~line** *n.* Schlagzeile, *die;* **be ~line news, make**

[the] ~lines, *(coll.)* **hit the ~lines** Schlagzeilen machen; **the [news] ~lines** *(Radio, Telev.)* die Kurznachrichten; *(within news programme)* der [Nachrichten]überblick; *see also* **running head[line]; ~liner** *n. (Amer.)* Star *(der ständig in den Schlagzeilen ist)*; **~lock** *n. (Wrestling)* Schwitzkasten, *der*

ˈheadlong 1. *adv.* **a)** *(head first)* **fall/plunge ~ into sth.** kopfüber in etw. fallen/springen; **b)** *(uncontrollably)* blindlings; **rush ~ into sth.** *(fig.)* etw. überstürzen. **2.** *adj.* **a)** *(head first)* **~ dive** Kopfsprung, *der;* **b)** *(impetuous)* überstürzt ‹*Flucht, Entscheidung*›

head: ~man *n.* Häuptling, *der;* **~ˈmaster** *n.* Schulleiter, *der; (in secondary school)* Direktor, *der; (in primary school)* Rektor, *der;* **~ˈmistress** *n. see* **~master:** Schulleiterin, *die;* Direktorin, *die;* Rektorin, *die;* **~-on 1.** [ˈ--] *adj.* frontal; offen ‹*Konfrontation, Konflikt*›; **a ~-on collision** *or* **crash** ein Frontalzusammenstoß; **2.** [-ˈ-] *adv.* frontal; **meet sth./sb. ~-on** *(fig.: resolutely)* einer Sache/jmdm. entschieden entgegentreten; **~phones** *n. pl.* Kopfhörer, *der;* **~ˈquarters** *n. sing. or pl.* Hauptquartier, *das; (of firm)* Zentrale, *die;* **police ~quarters** Polizeidirektion, *die;* **~-rest** *n.* Kopfstütze, *die;* **~room** *n., no pl.* [lichte] Höhe, *die; (in car)* Kopffreiheit, *die;* **low ~room** geringe Durchfahrtshöhe; **~scarf** *n.* Kopftuch, *das;* **~-set** *n.* Kopfhörer, *der*

headship [ˈhedʃɪp] *n.* Posten des Schulleiters/der Schulleiterin

head: ~shrinker *n.* **a)** Kopfjäger, *der;* **b)** *(sl.: psychiatrist)* Seelenklempner, *der (salopp);* **~square** *n.* [viereckiges] Kopftuch; **~ˈstart** *n.* **a ~ start [over sb.]** eine Vorgabe [gegenüber jmdm.]; **~stock** *n.* Spindelstock, *der;* **~stone** *n.* **a)** *(gravestone)* Grabstein, *der;* **b)** *(of building)* Grundstein, *der; (fig.)* Grundpfeiler, *der;* **~strong** *adj.* eigensinnig; störrisch ‹*Pferd, Esel*›; **~ tax** *n. (Amer.)* Kopfsteuer, *die;* **~ ˈteacher** *n. see* **headmaster; headmistress; ~-voice** *n.* Kopfstimme, *die;* **~water** *n., usu. in pl.* Quellfluß, *der;* **~way** *n., no pl. (progress)* **make ~way** Fortschritte machen; **~ wind** *n.* Gegenwind, *der;* **~word** *n.* **a)** Stichwort, *das;* **b)** *(Ling.)* Nukleus, *der;* **~-work** *n., no pl.* Kopfarbeit, *die*

heady [ˈhedɪ] *adj.* **a)** vorschnell; unbesonnen; **b)** *(intoxicating)* berauschend

¹heal [hi:l] **1.** *v. t.* **a)** *(lit. or fig.)* heilen; **time ~s all** *(fig.)* die Zeit heilt [alle] Wunden; **b)** *(arch.) see* **cure 2 a. 2.** *v. i.* **~ [up]** [ver]heilen

²heal *see* **hele**

healer [ˈhi:lə(r)] *n. (person)* Heilkundige, *der/die;* **time is a great ~:** die Zeit heilt alle Wunden

healing [ˈhi:lɪŋ] **1.** *n.* Heilung, *die;* **powers of ~:** Heilkräfte. **2.** *attrib. adj.* **~ effect** Heilwirkung, *die;* **~ influence** heilsamer Einfluß; **~ ointment** Heilsalbe, *die*

health [helθ] *n.* **a)** *no pl. (state)* Gesundheitszustand, *der; (healthiness)* Gesundheit, *die;* **in good/very good ~:** bei guter/bester Gesundheit; **sb. suffers from poor** *or* **bad ~:** jmdm. geht es gesundheitlich schlecht; **be restored to ~:** wiederhergestellt sein; **be in poor ~:** in schlechtem gesundheitlichen Zustand sein; **[not] be in the best of ~:** [nicht] bei bester Gesundheit sein; **in my state of ~:** in meinem Gesundheitszustand; **I'm not doing it for [the good of] my ~:** ich mache das nicht meiner Gesundheit zuliebe *od. (fig.)* nicht zum Vergnügen; **at least you have your ~:** du bist wenigstens gesund; **b)** *(toast)* **drink sb.'s ~** *or* **a ~ to sb.** auf jmds. Gesundheit trinken; **good** *or* **your ~!** auf deine Gesundheit!; zum Wohl!; pros[i]t!

health: ~ authority *n.* Gesundheitsbehörde, *die;* **~ centre** *n.* medizinisches Versorgungszentrum; Poliklinik, *die (DDR);* **~ certificate** *n.* Gesundheitszeugnis, *das;* **~ education** *n.* Gesundheitslehre, *die;* **~ farm** *n.* Gesundheitsfarm, *die (ugs.);* **~ food** *n.* Reformhauskost, *die;* **~-food shop** Reformhaus, *das;* **~-giving** *adj.* gesund

healthily [ˈhelθɪlɪ] *adv.* gesund

healthiness [ˈhelθɪnɪs] *n., no pl. (lit. or fig.)* Gesundheit, *die*

health: ~ insurance *n.* Krankenversicherung, *die;* **~ ˈphysics** *n.* Strahlenhygiene, *die;* **~ resort** *n.* Kurort, *der;* **~ salts** *n. pl.* leichtes Magenmittel; **~ service** *n.* Gesundheitsdienst, *der;* **~ visitor** *n.* Krankenschwester/-pfleger im Sozialdienst

healthy [ˈhelθɪ] *adj.* **a)** gesund; *(fig.)* **the engine sounds ~:** der Motor hat einen gesunden Klang; **a ~ attitude towards sex** ein gesundes *od.* natürliches Verhältnis zum Sex; **b)** *(salutary)* gut ‹*Zeichen*›; **~ living** ein gesundes Leben; *(safe)* **stay at a ~ distance** in sicherer Entfernung bleiben

heap [hi:p] **1.** *n.* **a)** *(pile)* Haufen, *der;* **a ~ of clothes** ein Kleiderhaufen; **at the bottom/top of the ~** *(fig.)* bei den Verlierern/Gewinnern; **lying in a ~/in ~s** auf einem/in Haufen liegen; **he was lying in a ~ on the ground** er lag zusammengesackt am Boden; **b)** *(fig. coll.: quantity)* **a [whole] ~ of** eine [ganze] Menge; **~s of** jede Menge *(ugs.);* **c)** *(fig. coll. derog.: vehicle)* Klapperkiste, *die (ugs.).* **2.** *v. t. (pile)* aufhäufen; **a ~ed spoonful of sugar** ein gehäufter Löffel Zucker; **~ sth. up** etw. aufhäufen; **~ sth. with sth.** etw. mit etw. [hoch] beladen; **~ sth. on sb.** *(fig.)* jmdn. mit etw. überhäufen

hear [hɪə(r)] **1.** *v. t.,* **heard** [hɜ:d] **a)** hören; **they ~d the car drive away** sie hörten den Wagen abfahren; **did you ~ him leaving** *or* **leave?** hast du ihn weggehen gehört *od.* hören?; **I have ~d it said that ...:** ich habe sagen hören, daß ...; **I can hardly ~ myself think/speak** ich kann keinen klaren Gedanken fassen/kann mein eigenes Wort nicht verstehen; **let's ~ it!** nun sag's schon!; **from what one ~s** wie man hört; **what's this I ~?** was muß ich da hören?; **you haven't ~d the last of this matter** das letzte Wort in dieser Sache ist noch nicht gesprochen; *see also* **end 1 g; ¹last 3 a; b)** *(understand)* verstehen; **c)** *(Law)* [an]hören; verhandeln ‹*Fall*›; **d)** *(answer)* **our prayers have been ~d** unsere Gebete sind erhört worden. **2.** *v. i.,* **heard: ~ about sb./sth.** von jmdm./etw. [etwas] hören; **I've ~d all aˈbout you** ich habe schon viel von Ihnen gehört; **~ from sb.** von jmdm. hören; **have you ~d from Tokyo/Smith yet?** haben Sie schon Nachricht aus Tokio/von Smith?; **I never ~d of such a thing!** hat man so was schon gehört!; **he was never ~d of again** von ihm hat man nie wieder [etwas] gehört; **he wouldn't ~ of it** er wollte davon nichts hören. **3.** *int.* **H~! H~!** bravo!; richtig!

~ ˈout *v. t.* ausreden lassen

heard *see* **hear 1, 2**

hearer [ˈhɪərə(r)] *n.* Hörer, *der*/Hörerin, *die*

hearing [ˈhɪərɪŋ] *n.* **a)** *no pl., no art. (faculty)* Gehör, *das;* **have good ~:** gut hören können; **be hard of ~:** schwerhörig sein; **b)** *no pl. (distance)* **within/out of ~:** in/außer Hörweite; **c)** *no pl.* **a fair ~:** eine faire Chance zu sprechen; **get a ~:** sich *(Dat.)* Gehör verschaffen können; **d)** *(Law etc.)* Hearing, *das*

ˈhearing-aid *n.* Hörgerät, *das*

hearken [ˈhɑ:kn] *v. i. (arch./literary)* **~ to sb./sth.** jmdm./einer Sache lauschen

hearsay [ˈhɪəseɪ] *n., no pl.* Gerücht, *das;* Klatsch, *der (abwertend);* **~ evidence** *(Law)* Beweis vom Hörensagen

hearse [hɜ:s] *n.* Leichenwagen, *der*

heart [hɑ:t] *n.* **a)** *(Anat.; also ~-shaped object)* Herz, *das;* **he has a weak ~** *(Med.)* er hat ein schwaches Herz; **know/learn sth. by ~:** etw. auswendig wissen/lernen; **b)** *(seat of feeling)* **at ~:** im Grunde seines/ihres Herzens; **sb. has sth. at ~, sth. is near** *or* **close to sb.'s ~:** jmdm. liegt etw. am Herzen; **a matter near** *or* **close to sb.'s ~:** ein Herzensanliegen; **go to sb.'s ~:** jmdm. ans Herz gehen; **in one's ~ [of ~s]** im tiefsten Herzen; **from the** *or* **one's ~:** von Herzen; **from the bottom of one's ~:** aus tiefstem Herzen; **with all one's ~ [and soul]** von ganzem Herzen; **put one's ~ and soul into sth.** etw. mit Leib und Seele tun; **put one's ~ into sth.** mit ganzem Herzen bei einer Sache sein; **cry one's ~ out** sich *(Dat.)* die Augen ausweinen *od.* aus dem Kopf weinen; **eat one's ~ out** sich vor Gram/Sehnsucht/Trauer *usw.* verzehren; **eat your ~ out!** da kannst du grün vor Neid werden!; **set one's ~ on sth./on doing sth.** sein Herz an etw. *(Akk.)* hängen/daran hängen, etw. zu tun; **to one's ~'s content** nach Herzenslust; **take sth. to ~:** sich *(Dat.)* etw. zu Herzen nehmen; *(accept)* beherzigen ‹*Rat*›; **take sb. to one's ~:** jmdn. in sein *od.* ins Herz schließen; **my ~ goes out to them** ich verspüre großes Mitleid mit ihnen; **my ~ bleeds for him** ich habe tiefstes Mitgefühl mit ihm; *(iron.)* mir blutet das Herz; **it does my ~ good** es erfreut mein Herz; **somebody after my own ~:** jemand ganz nach meinem Herzen; **have a ~ to ~ talk** offen und ehrlich miteinander sprechen; **her ~ is in the right place** sie hat das Herz auf dem rechten Fleck; **lose one's ~ to sb./sth.** sein Herz an jmdn./etw. verlieren; **give one's ~:** sein Herz schenken; **be sick at ~:** verzweifelt sein; **with a light/heavy ~:** leichten/schweren Herzens; **his ~ is not in it** er ist nicht mit dem Herzen dabei; **all the ~ could desire** alles, was das Herz begehrt; **bless his/her ~:** das liebe Kind!; **wear one's ~ [up]on one's sleeve** das Herz auf der Zunge tragen; **find it in one's ~ to do sth.** es übers Herz bringen, etw. zu tun; **have a ~!** hab' Erbarmen!; **not have the ~ to do sth.** nicht das Herz haben, etw. zu tun; **c)** *(seat of courage)* **take ~:** Mut schöpfen **(from** bei); **put new ~ into sb.** jmdm. neuen Mut geben; **in good ~:** voll Zuversicht; **lose ~:** den Mut verlieren; **his ~ stood still** ihm stand das Herz still; **my ~ was in my boots** ich war am Boden zerstört *(ugs.);* **my ~ sank** mein Mut sank; **d)** *(Cards)* Herz, *das; see also* **club 1 d; e)** *(centre) (of cabbage)* Strunk, *der; (of lettuce)* Herz, *das; (of tree)* Kernholz, *das;* **the ~ of the matter** der wahre Kern der Sache; **go to the ~ of a problem** zum Kern eines Problems kommen; **in the ~ of the forest/England** mitten im Wald/im Herzen Englands. *See also* **¹break 1 h, 2 a; change 1 a; dear 1 a; desire 1 c; gold 1 a; stone 1 a**

heart: ~ache *n.* [seelische] Qual; **~ attack** *n.* Herzanfall, *der; (fatal)* Herzschlag, *der;* **~beat** *n.* Herzschlag, *der;* **~['s]-blood** *n. (fig.)* Herzblut, *das (geh.);* **~-break** *n.* Herzeleid, *das (geh.);* tiefer Kummer; **~-breaking** *adj.* herzzerreißend; **~-broken** *adj.* **she was ~-broken** ihr Herz war gebrochen; **~burn** *n., no pl.* **a)** Groll, *der;* **b)** *(Med.)* Sodbrennen, *das;* **~ disease** *n.* Herzkrankheit, *die*

hearten [ˈhɑ:tn] *v. t.* ermutigen

heartening [ˈhɑ:tənɪŋ] *adj.* ermutigend; **~ news** erfreuliche Nachrichten

heart: ~ failure *n.* Herzversagen, *das;* **~felt** *adj.* tiefempfunden ‹*Beileid*›; aufrichtig ‹*Dankbarkeit*›; **a ~felt wish** ein Herzenswunsch

hearth [hɑ:θ] *n.* **a)** *[gekachelter o. ä.] Platz vor dem Kamin;* **~ and home** *(fig.)* der heimische Herd; **b)** *(in furnace)* Ofenraum, *der; (smith's ~)* Esse, *die*

hearth-rug *n.* Kaminvorleger, *der*

heartily [ˈhɑ:tɪlɪ] *adv.* von Herzen; **eat ~:** tüchtig essen; **be ~ sick of sth.** etw. herzlich leid sein

'**heartland** *n.* Landesinnere, *das*
heartless ['hɑ:tlɪs] *adj.*, **heartlessly** ['hɑ:tlɪslɪ] *adv.* herzlos; unbarmherzig
heartlessness ['hɑ:tlɪsnɪs] *n.*, *no pl.* Unbarmherzigkeit, *die*
heart: ~-'lung machine *n. (Med.)* Herz-Lungen-Maschine, *die;* **~-rending** *adj.* herzzerreißend; **~-searching** *n.* Gewissenserforschung, *die;* **~'s-ease** *n. (Bot.)* Veilchen, *das; (Viola tricolor)* Stiefmütterchen, *das;* **~-shaped** *adj.* herzförmig; **~sick** *adj.* verzweifelt; **~-strings** *n. pl.* **touch sb.'s ~-strings** jmdm. zu Herzen gehen; **~-throb** *n. (person)* Idol, *das;* **~-to-~** *n.* **have a ~-to-~:** offen und ehrlich miteinander sprechen; **~ trouble** *n.* Probleme mit dem Herzen; **~-warming** *adj.* herzerfreuend; **~wood** *n. (Bot.)* Kernholz, *das*
hearty ['hɑ:tɪ] **1.** *adj.* **a)** *(whole-hearted)* ungeteilt ‹*Unterstützung, Zustimmung*›; *(enthusiastic, unrestrained)* herzlich; begeistert ‹*Gesang*›; **a ~ eater** ein guter Esser; **b)** *(large)* herzhaft ‹*Mahlzeit*›; gesund ‹*Appetit*›; **c)** *(vigorous)* herzhaft ‹*Ruck, Tritt*›; *see also* **'hale. 2.** *n. (Naut.)* **come on, my hearties!** auf geht's, Jungs!
heat [hi:t] **1.** *n.* **a)** *(hotness)* Hitze, *die; (temperature)* Temperatur, *die; (temperature setting)* Temperaturstufe, *die; (fig.: sensation)* Brennen, *das;* **remove sth. from/return sth. to the ~:** etw. vom Feuer nehmen/wieder erhitzen; **b)** *(Phys.)* Wärme, *die;* **latent ~:** Umwandlungswärme, *die;* **specific ~:** spezifische Wärme; **c)** *(fig.) (anger)* Erregung, *die;* **generate a lot of ~/more ~ than light** die Gemüter erregen/mehr Erregung als Erleuchtung erzeugen; **take the ~ out of a situation** eine Situation entschärfen; **in the ~ of the moment** in der Hitze des Gefechts; *(coll.: pressure)* **the ~ is on** die Sache ist heiß *(ugs.);* **put the ~ on** Druck machen; **put the ~ on sb.** jmdn. unter Druck setzen; **the ~ is off** die Lage hat sich entspannt; **d)** *(Zool.)* Brunst, *die;* **come into** *or* **on/be in** *or* **on ~:** brünstig werden/sein; ‹*Stute:*› rossig werden/sein; ‹*Hündin:*› läufig werden/sein; ‹*Katze:*› rollig werden/sein; **e)** *(Sport)* Vorlauf, *der; see also* **dead heat. 2.** *v.t.* heizen ‹*Raum*›; erhitzen ‹*Substanz, Lösung*›; vorheizen ‹*Backofen*›. **3.** *v.i.* warm werden
~ 'up *v.t.* heiß machen ‹*Essen, Wasser*›
heated ['hi:tɪd] *adj.* erhitzt; *(fig.: angry)* hitzig; **a ~ exchange** ein heftiger Schlagabtausch *(fig.)*
heatedly ['hi:tɪdlɪ] *adv.* hitzig
heater ['hi:tə(r)] *n.* **a)** Ofen, *der; (for water)* Boiler, *der;* **b)** *(sl.: firearm)* Kanone, *die (salopp)*
'**heat-exchanger** *n.* Wärmetauscher, *der*
heath [hi:θ] *n.* **a)** Heide, *die;* **b)** *(Bot.) (Calluna)* Heidekraut, *das; (Erica)* Erika, *die;* Glockenheide, *die*
heathen ['hi:ðn] **1.** *adj.* heidnisch. **2.** *n.* Heide, *der*/Heidin, *die; (fig. derog.)* gottloser Mensch
heather ['heðə(r)] *n.* **a)** *(plant)* Heidekraut, *das;* **b)** *(colour)* Erikarot, *das*
heating ['hi:tɪŋ] *n.*, *no pl.* Heizung, *die*
heat: ~-proof *adj.* feuerfest; **~-pump** *n.* Wärmepumpe, *die;* **~-rash** *n. (Med.)* Hitzebläschen *Pl.;* **~-resistant** *adj.* hitzebeständig; **~ shield** *n. (Astronaut.)* Hitzeschild, *der;* **~-stroke** *n.* Hitzschlag, *der;* **~ treatment** *n. (Metall., Med.)* Wärmebehandlung, *die;* **~wave** *n.* Hitzewelle, *die*
heave [hi:v] **1.** *v.t.* **a)** *(lift)* heben; wuchten *(ugs.);* **b)** *p.t. & p.p.* **hove** [həʊv] *(coll.: throw)* werfen; schmeißen *(ugs.); (Naut.: cast, haul up)* hieven; **c)** *(utter)* **~ a sigh [of relief]** [erleichtert] aufseufzen. **2.** *v.i.* **a)** *(pitch)* [auf und nieder] schwanken; ‹*Schiff:*› stampfen *(Seemannsspr.); (rise)* sich heben; **b)** *(pull)* ziehen; **~ ho!** hau ruck!; holt auf *(Seemannsspr.);* **c)** *(pant)* keuchen; **d)** *(retch)* sich übergeben; **e)** *p.t. & p.p.* **hove** *(move)* **~ in sight** in Sicht kommen; **~ to** *(Naut.)* beidrehen. **3.** *n.* **a)** *(pull)* Zug, *der;* **b)** *(throw)* Schwung, *der*
heaven ['hevn] *n.* **a)** Himmel, *der;* **in ~:** im Himmel; **go** *or* **ascend to ~:** in den Himmel kommen; **~ on earth** *(fig.)* der Himmel auf Erden; **be sent from ~** *(fig.)* ein Geschenk des Himmels sein; **it was ~ [to her]** *(fig.)* es war der Himmel auf Erden [für sie]; **seventh ~** *(fig.)* der siebte Himmel; **move ~ and earth** *(fig.)* Himmel und Erde in Bewegung setzen; **b)** *in pl., (poet.) in sing. (sky)* Firmament, *das;* Himmelszelt, *das (dichter.);* **in the ~s** am Himmel; **the ~s opened** es prasselte los; **c)** *(God, Providence)* **by H~!** bei Gott; **[good] H~s!** gütiger Himmel!; **H~s above!** du lieber Himmel!; **H~ [only] knows** weiß der Himmel; **H~ help us** der Himmel steh uns bei; **for H~'s sake** um Gottes *od.* Himmels willen; **thank H~[s]** Gott sei Dank; **I hope to H~ that ...:** ich hoffe zu Gott, daß ...; *see also* **forbid b; name 1 d**
heavenly ['hevnlɪ] *adj.* **a)** *(also coll.: delightful)* himmlisch; **b) ~ body** Himmelskörper, *der;* **c)** *(of heaven)* himmlisch; **the H~ City** das Himmelreich
'**heaven-sent** *adj.* **a ~ opportunity** eine Gelegenheit, die wie gerufen kommt/kam
heavenward[s] ['hevnwəd(z)] *adv.* himmelwärts
heavily ['hevɪlɪ] *adj.* **a)** *(with great weight, severely, with difficulty)* schwer ‹*beladen, bestraft, atmen*›; **~ guarded** streng bewacht; **b)** *(to a great extent)* stark; schwer ‹*bewaffnet*›; tief ‹*schlafen*›; dicht ‹*bevölkert*›; **smoke/drink ~:** ein starker Raucher/Trinker sein; **eat too ~:** zu schwer essen; **gamble ~:** ein [leidenschaftlicher] Spieler sein; **rely ~ on sb./sth.** von jmdn./etw. [vollkommen] abhängig sein; **c)** *(with great force)* **it rained/snowed ~:** es regnete/schneite stark; **fall ~:** hart fallen; **~ underlined** dick unterstrichen; **weigh ~ [up]on sb.** *(fig.)* schwer auf jmdm. lasten; **~ built** kräftig gebaut
heaviness ['hevɪnɪs] *n.*, *no pl.* **a)** *(weight)* Gewicht, *das;* **b)** *(great extent)* Ausmaß, *das; (severity)* Härte, *die;* **c)** *(clinging quality)* Schwere, *die;* **d)** *(tiredness)* Schwerfälligkeit, *die*
heavy ['hevɪ] **1.** *adj.* **a)** *(in weight)* schwer; dick ‹*Mantel*›; fest ‹*Schuh*›; **~ traffic** Schwerlastverkehr, *der; (dense)* hohes Verkehrsaufkommen; **~ work** Schwerarbeit, *die;* **a ~ crop** *(fig.)* eine [sehr] reiche Ernte; **a ~ silence** eine atemlose Stille; **b)** *(severe)* schwer ‹*Schaden, Verlust, Strafe, Kampf*›; hoch ‹*Steuern, Schulden, Anforderungen*›; massiv ‹*Druck, Unterstützung*›; **~ responsibilities** schwere Verantwortungen; **c)** *(excessive)* unmäßig ‹*Trinken, Essen, Rauchen*›; ausgiebig ‹*Necking, Petting*›; **be ~ on the sugar/petrol** *(coll.)* viel Zucker nehmen/viel Benzin verbrauchen; **a ~ smoker/drinker** ein starker Raucher/Trinker; **a ~ gambler** ein [leidenschaftlicher] Spieler; **be a ~ sleeper** sehr fest schlafen; **d)** *(violent)* schwer ‹*Schlag, Sturm, Regen, Sturz, Seegang*›; hart ‹*Aufprall*›; **~ weather** ungünstiges Wetter; **make ~ weather of sth.** *(fig.)* die Dinge unnötig komplizieren; **e)** *(clinging)* schwer ‹*Boden*›; *see also* **going 1 b; f)** *(hard to digest)* schwer ‹*Mahlzeit*›; **g)** *(overcast)* bedeckt ‹*Himmel*›; **h)** *(in sound)* **~ footsteps** schwere Schritte; **i)** *(clumsy)* plump; *(intellectually slow)* schwerfällig; **~ with sleep** schlaftrunken; **our eyes were ~ with sleep** wir konnten [vor Müdigkeit] kaum noch die Augen offenhalten; **j)** *(tedious)* schwerfällig; *(serious)* seriös ‹*Zeitung*›; ernst ‹*Musik, Theaterrolle*›; *(stern)* streng; gestreng *(veralt.)* ‹*Vater, Ehemann*›; **lie ~ on sb.'s stomach/conscience** jmdm. schwer im Magen liegen/auf der Seele liegen; **time lies ~ on my hands** mir wird die Zeit lang; *see also* **hand 1 b; k)** *(Phys.)* **~ hydrogen/water** schwerer Wasserstoff/schweres Wasser. **2.** *n. (coll.)* **a)** *(newspaper)* seriöse Zeitung; **b)** *(coll.: thug)* Schlägertyp, *der (ugs.)*
heavy: ~-duty *adj.* strapazierfähig ‹*Kleidung, Material*›; schwer ‹*Werkzeug, Maschine*›; **~-'footed** *adj.* schwerfällig; **~ 'goods vehicle** *n.* Schwerlastwagen, *der;* **~-'handed** *adj. (clumsy)* ungeschickt ‹*Person*›; umständlich ‹*Stil*›; *(oppressive)* unbarmherzig ‹*Tyrannei, Diktatur*›; **~-'hearted** *adj.* traurig; **~ 'industry** *n.* Schwerindustrie, *die;* **~ 'metal** *n.* **a)** Schwermetall, *das;* **b)** *(Mus.)* Heavy metal, *das;* **a ~-metal band** eine Heavy-metal-Band; **~ 'type** *n. (Printing)* fette Schrift; **~weight** *n. (Boxing etc.)* Schwergewicht, *das; (person also)* Schwergewichtler, *der; (fig.)* Größe, *die*
Hebraic [hi:'breɪɪk] *adj.* hebräisch
Hebrew ['hi:bru:] **1.** *adj.* hebräisch; *see also* **English 1. 2.** *n.* **a)** *(Israelite)* Hebräer, *der*/Hebräerin, *die;* **b)** *no pl. (language)* Hebräisch, *das;* **a ~ scholar** ein Hebraist; *see also* **English 2 a**
Hebrides ['hebrɪdi:z] *pr. n. pl.* Hebriden *Pl.;* **Inner/Outer ~:** Innere/Äußere Hebriden
heck [hek] *(coll. euphem.) see* **hell b**
heckle ['hekl] *v.t.* **~ sb./a speech** jmdn./eine Rede durch Zwischenrufe unterbrechen
heckler ['heklə(r)] *n.* Zwischenrufer, *der*
hectare ['hektɑ:(r), 'hekteə(r)] *n.* Hektar, *das od. der*
hectic ['hektɪk] *adj.* hektisch
hecto- ['hektə] *pref.* hekto-/Hekto-
hector ['hektə(r)] **1.** *v.t.* einschüchtern. **2.** *v.i.* bramarbasieren *(geh.)*
hectoring ['hektərɪŋ] *adj.* überheblich
he'd [hɪd, *stressed* hi:d] **a) = he had; b) = he would**
hedge [hedʒ] **1.** *n. (of bushes, trees, etc.)* Hecke, *die; (fig.: barrier)* Mauer, *die; (fig.: means of protection)* Schutzwall, *der; (against financial loss)* Absicherung, *die.* **2.** *v.t.* **a)** *(surround with ~)* mit einer Hecke umgeben; **~ sb. [in** *or* **round]** *(fig.)* jmdn. in seiner Handlungsfreiheit einschränken; **b)** *(protect)* **~ one's bets** mit verteiltem Risiko wetten; *(fig.)* nicht alles auf eine Karte setzen. **3.** *v.i. (avoid commitment)* sich nicht festlegen; **stop hedging and give me a straight answer** weich nicht dauernd aus, und gib mir eine klare Antwort
'**hedge-clippers** *n. pl.* Heckenschere, *die*
hedgehog ['hedʒhɒg] *n.* Igel, *der*
'**hedge-hop** *v.i.* im Tiefflug fliegen
hedge: ~row *n.* Hecke, *die* [als Feldbegrenzung]; **~-sparrow** *n.* Heckenbraunelle, *die*
hedonism ['hi:dənɪzm] *n.*, *no pl.* Hedonismus, *der*
hedonist ['hi:dənɪst] *n.* Hedonist, *der*/Hedonistin, *die*
hedonistic [hi:də'nɪstɪk] *adj.* hedonistisch
heebie-jeebies ['hi:bɪdʒi:bɪz] *n. pl. (sl.)* **give sb. the ~:** jmdn. kribblig machen *(ugs.)*
heed [hi:d] **1.** *v.t.* beachten; beherzigen ‹*Rat, Lektion*›; **~ the danger/risk** sich *(Dat.)* der Gefahr/des Risikos bewußt sein. **2.** *n.*, *no art.*, *no pl.* **give** *or* **pay ~ to, take ~ of** Beachtung schenken (+ *Dat.*); **give** *or* **pay no ~ to, take no ~ of** nicht beachten
heedful ['hi:dfl] *adj.* achtsam; **be ~ of sth.** etw. beachten; **be ~ of the danger/necessity** sich *(Dat.)* der Gefahr/Notwendigkeit *(Gen.)* bewußt sein; **be ~ of sb.'s warning** jmds. Warnung beherzigen
heedless ['hi:dlɪs] *adj.* unachtsam; **be ~ of sth.** auf etw. *(Akk.)* nicht achten; **be ~ of the danger/risks** die Gefahr/Risiken nicht beachten
hee-haw ['hi:hɔ:] **1.** *int.* iah. **2.** *n.* Iah, *das.* **3.** *v.i.* iahen; *(fig.)* wiehern
'**heel** [hi:l] **1.** *n.* **a)** Ferse, *die;* **~ of the hand**

Handballen, *der;* **Achilles' ~** *(fig.)* Achillesferse, *die;* **bring a dog to ~:** einen Hund bei Fuß rufen; **bring sb. to ~** *(fig.)* jmdn. auf Vordermann bringen *(ugs.);* **come to ~:** bei Fuß gehen; *(fig.)* parieren *(ugs.);* **[to] ~!** bei Fuß!; **at ~:** bei Fuß; **be on sb.'s ~s** *(fig.)* jmdm. auf den Fersen sein *(ugs.);* **[hard** *or* **close] on** *or* **at the ~s of sb./sth.** [dicht] hinter jmdm./etw.; *(in time or quality)* gleich nach jmdm./etw.; **show a clean pair of ~s** *(fig.)* sich aus dem Staub machen *(ugs.);* **show sb. a clean pair of ~s** *(fig.)* jmdn. abhängen *(ugs.);* **take to one's ~s** *(fig.)* Fersengeld geben *(ugs.);* **cool one's ~s** *(fig. coll.)* lange warten [müssen]; **kick one's ~s** *(fig. coll.)* rumhängen *(ugs.);* **be under the ~ of sb.** *(fig.)* unter jmds. Herrschaft sein; *see also* **dig in 2 b; b)** *(of shoe)* Absatz, *der; (of stocking)* Ferse, *die;* **down at ~:** abgetreten; *(fig.)* heruntergekommen *(ugs.);* **turn on one's ~:** auf dem Absatz kehrtmachen; *see also* **high heel; c)** *(of violin bow)* Frosch, *der; (of golf-club)* Ferse, *die; (of ski)* hinteres Ende; *(of loaf)* Endstück, *das;* **d)** *(sl.: person)* Schuft, *der (abwertend).* **2.** *v. t.* **a) ~ a shoe** einen Schuh mit einem [neuen] Absatz versehen; **b)** *(Golf)* mit der Ferse schlagen; **c)** *(Rugby)* mit dem Absatz spielen

[2]heel *(Naut.)* **1.** *v. i.* krängen. **2.** *v. t.* zum Krängen bringen. **3.** *n.* Krängung, *die*

[3]heel *see* **hele**

heel: ~ bar *n.* Absatzschnelldienst, *der;* **~ bone** *n. (Anat.)* Fersenbein, *das*

heelless ['hi:llɪs] *adj.* ‹*Schuhe*› ohne Absatz

heft [heft] **1.** *v. t.* anheben *(und dabei das Gewicht feststellen).* **2.** *n. (Amer.)* Gewicht, *das*

heftily ['heftɪlɪ] *adv.* kräftig; *(fig.)* stark

hefty ['heftɪ] *adj.* kräftig; *(heavy)* schwer; *(fig.: large)* hoch ‹*Rechnung, Summe, Strafe, Anteil*›; deutlich ‹*Mehrheit*›; stark ‹*Erhöhung*›

Hegelian [he'gi:lɪən, heɪ'gi:lɪən] *(Philos.)* **1.** *adj.* hegelianisch. **2.** *n.* Hegelianer, *der*/Hegelianerin, *die*

hegemony [hɪ'gemənɪ, hɪ'dʒemənɪ] *n.* Hegemonie, *die*

hegira ['hedʒɪrə] *n.* Hedschra, *die; (fig. literary)* Exodus, *der*

heh [heɪ] *int.* he

he-he [hi:'hi:] *int.* haha

heifer ['hefə(r)] *n.* Färse, *die*

heigh-ho [heɪ'həʊ] *int.* ach ja

height [haɪt] *n.* **a)** Höhe, *die; (of person, animal, building)* Größe, *die;* **lose ~** *(Aeron.)* an Höhe verlieren; **be three metres in ~:** drei Meter hoch sein; **at a ~ of three metres** in einer Höhe von drei Metern; **be six feet in ~** ‹*Person:*› 1,80 m groß sein; **what is your ~?** wie groß sind Sie?; **b)** *usu. in pl. (high place)* **the ~s** die Anhöhe; **be afraid of ~s** nicht schwindelfrei sein; **~ of land** *(Amer. Geog.)* Wasserscheide, *die;* **c)** *(fig.: highest point)* Höhepunkt, *der;* **at the ~ of one's fame** auf dem Gipfel seines Ruhms; **the ~ of luxury** das Nonplusultra an Luxus; **the ~ of folly** der Gipfel der Dummheit; **at the ~ of summer** im Hochsommer; *see also* **fashion 1 b**

heighten ['haɪtn] **1.** *v. t.* aufstocken; *(fig.: intensify)* verstärken. **2.** *v. i. (fig.)* sich verstärken

heinous ['heɪnəs] *adj.* schändlich; ruchlos *(geh., veralt.)*

heir [eə(r)] *n. (lit. or fig.)* Erbe, *der*/Erbin, *die;* **the ~ to the throne** der Thronerbe/die Thronerbin; *see also* **apparent a; presumptive**

heiress ['eərɪs] *n.* Erbin, *die (bes. eines Vermögens); see also* **heir**

heirloom ['eəlu:m] *n.* **a)** Erbstück, *das; (fig.)* Erbe, *das;* **b)** *(Law)* von einem Erbe nicht abtrennbarer Teil

heist [haɪst] *(Amer. sl.)* **1.** *n.* Raubüberfall, *der.* **2.** *v. t. (steal)* rauben; *(rob)* ausrauben

hejira *see* **hegira**

held *see* **[2]hold 1, 2**

hele [hi:l] *v. t. (Hort.)* **~ sth. [in]** etw. einpflanzen

Helen ['helən] *pr. n.* **~ of Troy** [die schöne] Helena

heli- ['helɪ] *in comb.* Heli-

helical ['helɪkl] *adj.* spiralförmig; spiralig; **~ gear** Schrägstirnrad, *das;* **~ spring** Schraubenfeder, *die*

helices *pl. of* **helix**

helicopter ['helɪkɒptə(r)] *n.* Hubschrauber, *der*

Heligoland ['helɪgəlænd] *pr. n.* Helgoland *(das)*

helio- ['hi:lɪə] *in comb.* helio-/Helio-

'heliograph 1. *n.* Heliograph, *der.* **2.** *v. t.* mit dem Heliographen übermitteln

heliotrope ['hi:lɪətrəʊp, 'helɪətrəʊp] **1.** *n.* **a)** *(Bot., Min.)* Heliotrop, *das;* **b)** *(colour)* Bläulichviolett, *das;* Heliotrop, *das.* **2.** *adj.* bläulichviolett; heliotrop

heliport ['helɪpɔ:t] *n.* Heliport, *der*

helium ['hi:lɪəm] *n.* Helium, *das*

helix ['hi:lɪks] *n., pl.* **helices** ['hi:lɪsi:z] **a)** Spirale, *die;* **b)** *(Archit.)* Volute, *die;* **c)** *(Anat.)* Helix, *die*

hell [hel] *n.* **a)** Hölle, *die;* **suffer the torments of ~:** Höllenqualen erleiden; **make sb.'s life [a] ~, make life ~ for sb.** jmdm. das Leben zur Hölle machen; **all ~ was let loose** *(fig.)* es war die Hölle los; **~ on earth** *(fig.)* die Hölle auf Erden; **b)** *(coll.: in imprecations and phrases)* **[oh] ~!** verdammter Mist! *(ugs.);* **what the ~!** ach, zum Teufel! *(ugs.);* **to** *or* **the ~ with it!** ich hab's satt *(ugs.);* **who the ~ are you?** wer, zum Teufel, sind Sie? *(ugs.);* **~'s bells!** *(sl.)* Mensch, Scheiße! *(salopp);* **get the ~ 'out of here!, go to ~!** scher dich zum Teufel! *(ugs.);* **play [merry] ~ with sth.** etw. [ganz schön] ins Schleudern bringen *(ugs.);* **there'll be ~ to pay if you get caught** wenn sie dich erwischen, ist der Teufel los *(ugs.);* **as tired/angry as ~:** unheimlich müde/wütend; **a** *or* **one ~ of a** *or* **a helluva [good] party** eine unheimlich gute Party *(ugs.);* **a ~ of a** *or* **a helluva noise** ein Höllenlärm *(salopp);* **like sb./sth. a ~ of a lot** jmdn./etw. wahnsinnig gern mögen *(ugs.);* **a ~ of a lot of money** wahnsinnig viel Geld *(ugs.);* **he thinks he's a ~ of a fellow** er denkt, er ist ein Teufelskerl *(ugs.);* **that was a ~ of a thing to do** das war ungeheuerlich *(abwertend)/(praising)* grandios; **work/run like ~:** wie der Teufel arbeiten/rennen *(ugs.);* **like ~!** nie im Leben! *(ugs.);* **it hurt like ~:** es tat höllisch weh *(ugs.);* **beat** *or* **knock [the] ~ out of sb.** jmdn. grün und blau schlagen *(ugs.);* **give sb. ~:** jmdm. die Hölle heiß machen *(ugs.);* ‹*Schmerzen usw.:*› jmdn. verrückt machen *(ugs.);* **get ~:** großen Ärger kriegen *(ugs.);* **come ~ or high water** [völlig] egal, was passieren sollte *(ugs.);* **do sth. [just] for the ~ of it** etw. [nur so] aus Jux und Tollerei tun *(ugs.);* **~ for leather** wie der Teufel *(ugs.);* **I'll see you in ~ first** ich denke nicht im Traum daran!; *see also* **hope 1; raise 1 g**

he'll [hɪl, *stressed* hi:l] = **he will**

hell: ~bender *n. (Amer. Zool.)* Schlammteufel, *der;* **~-'bent** *adj.* **be ~-bent on doing sth.** *(coll.)* wild entschlossen sein, etw. zu tun *(ugs.);* **~-cat** *n. (derog.)* Wildkatze, *die*

hellebore ['helɪbɔ:(r)] *n. (Bot.)* Nieswurz, *die*

Hellenic [he'li:nɪk] *adj.* hellenisch

Hellenist ['helɪnɪst] *n.* Hellenist, *der*/Hellenistin, *die*

Hellenistic [helɪ'nɪstɪk] *adj.* hellenistisch

'hellfire *n.* Höllenfeuer, *das*

'hell-hound *n.* Höllenhund, *der; (fig.)* Teufel, *der*

hellish ['helɪʃ] **1.** *adj.* höllisch ‹*Qual, Schmerz*›; scheußlich ‹*Arbeit, Zeit*›. **2.** *adv. (coll.)* verdammt *(ugs.)*

hellishly ['helɪʃlɪ] *adv.* höllisch; scheußlich; *(coll. as intensive)* verdammt *(ugs.)*

hello [hə'ləʊ, he'ləʊ] **1.** *int. (greeting)* hallo!; *(surprise)* holla! **2.** *n.* Hallo, *das*

hell's 'angel *n.* Rocker, *der*

helluva ['heləvə] = **hell of a;** *see* **hell b**

[1]helm [helm] *n. (Naut.)* Ruder, *das;* **be at the ~** *(lit. or fig.)* am Ruder sein; **take the ~** *(lit. or fig.)* das Ruder übernehmen

[2]helm *n. (arch.: helmet)* Helm, *der*

helmet ['helmɪt] *n.* Helm, *der*

helmeted ['helmɪtɪd] *adj.* behelmt

helmsman ['helmzmən] *n., pl.* **helmsmen** ['helmzmən] *(Naut.)* Rudergänger, *der*

helot ['helət] *n.* Helot, *der*

help [help] **1.** *v. t.* **a) ~ sb. [to do sth.]** jmdm. helfen[, etw. zu tun]; **~ [sb.] with sth.** [jmdm.] bei etw. helfen; **~ oneself** sich *(Dat.)* selbst helfen; **can I ~ you?** was kann ich für Sie tun?; *(in shop also)* was möchten Sie bitte?; **~sb. over a difficulty** jmdm. über eine Schwierigkeit hinweghelfen; **~ sb. on/off with his coat** jmdm. in den/aus dem Mantel helfen; **every little ~s** auch der kleinste Beitrag hilft weiter; **it would ~ [matters], if ...:** es wäre von Nutzen, wenn ...; **how does that ~?** was sollte *od.* könnte das nützen?; **b)** *(serve)* **~ oneself** sich *(Dat.)* nehmen; sich bedienen; **~ oneself to sth.** sich *(Dat.)* etw. nehmen; *(coll.: steal)* etw. mitgehen lassen *(ugs.);* **~ sb. to some soup** jmdm. etwas Suppe geben; **c)** *(avoid)* **if I/you can ~ it** wenn es irgend zu vermeiden ist; **not if I can ~ it** nicht wenn ich es verhindern kann; **it can't be ~ed** es läßt sich nicht ändern; *(remedy)* **I can't ~ it** ich kann nichts dafür *(ugs.);* **d)** *(refrain from)* **I can't ~ it** *or* **myself** ich kann mir nicht helfen; **I can't ~ thinking** *or* **can't ~ but think that ...:** ich kann mir nicht helfen, ich glaube, ...; **I couldn't ~ hearing what you said** ich konnte nicht umhin, zu hören, was Sie sagten; **I can't ~ laughing** ich muß einfach lachen; **e)** *(in oath)* **so ~ me [God]** so wahr mir Gott helfe. **2.** *n.* **a)** Hilfe, *die;* **can I be of ~?** kann ich Ihnen behilflich sein?; **a cry for ~:** ein Hilferuf; **give sb. some ~:** jmdm. helfen **(with** bei**); be of [some]/no/much ~ to sb.** jmdm. eine gewisse/keine/eine große Hilfe sein; **with the ~ of sth./sb.** mit Hilfe einer Sache/mit jmds. Hilfe; mit Hilfe von etw./jmdm.; **walk without the ~ of a stick** ohne Stock gehen; **that's no ~:** das hilft nicht; **there's no ~ for it** daran läßt sich nichts ändern; **be a great ~ to sb.** jmdm. eine große Hilfe sein; **b)** *(employee)* Aushilfskraft, *die;* **home ~** *(Brit.)* Haushaltshilfe, *die*

~ 'out 1. *v. i.* aushelfen. **2.** *v. t.* **~ sb. out** jmdm. helfen

helper ['helpə(r)] *n.* Helfer, *der*/Helferin, *die; (paid assistant)* Aushilfskraft, *die*

helpful ['helpfl] *adj. (willing)* hilfsbereit; *(useful)* hilfreich; nützlich

helpfully ['helpfəlɪ] *adv.* hilfsbereit

helpfulness ['helpflnɪs] *n., no pl. (willingness)* Hilfsbereitschaft, *die; (usefulness)* Nützlichkeit, *die*

helping ['helpɪŋ] **1.** *adj.* **lend [sb.] a ~ hand [with sth.]** *(fig.)* [jmdm.] [bei etw.] helfen; **need a ~ hand** jmdn. brauchen, der einem hilft; **be ready with a ~ hand** bereit sein zu helfen. **2.** *n.* Portion, *die*

helpless ['helplɪs] *adj.* hilflos; *(powerless)* machtlos

helplessly ['helplɪslɪ] *adv.* hilflos

helplessness ['helplɪsnɪs] *n., no pl.* Hilflosigkeit, *die; (powerlessness)* Machtlosigkeit, *die*

helpmate ['helpmeɪt], **helpmeet** ['helpmi:t] *n.* Gefährte, *der*/Gefährtin, *die (geh.)*

helter-skelter [heltə'skeltə(r)] **1.** *adv.* in wildem Durcheinander. **2.** *adj.* unkontrolliert. **3.** *n.* **a)** wildes Durcheinander; **b)** *(in fun-fair)* [spiralförmige] Rutschbahn

helve [helv] *n.* Stiel, *der*

¹hem [hem] **1.** *n.* Saum, *der.* **2.** *v.t.*, **-mm- a)** säumen; **b)** *(surround)* ~ **sb./sth. in** *or* **about** jmdn./etw. einschließen; **feel ~med in** *(fig.)* sich eingeengt fühlen

²hem [hem, həm, hm] **1.** *int.* hm! **2.** *n. (sound)* Räuspern, *das;* **give a loud ~:** sich laut räuspern. **3.** *v.i.*, **-mm-** sich räuspern; **~ and haw** *(coll.)* herumdrucksen *(ugs.)*

he-man ['hi:mæn] *n.* **a real ~:** ein richtiger Mann

hematology *(Amer.) see* **haematology**

hemi- ['hemı] *pref.* hemi-/Hemi-

hemiplegia [hemı'pli:dʒıə] *n. (Med.)* Halbseitenlähmung, *die;* Hemiplegie, *die (fachspr.)*

hemiplegic [hemı'pli:dʒık] *adj. (Med.)* halbseitig gelähmt

'hemisphere *n.* **a)** Halbkugel, *die;* Hemisphäre, *die;* **the Southern ~** *(Geog., Astron.)* die südliche Halbkugel; **b)** *(Anat.)* Hemisphäre, *die*

hemi'spherical *adj.* halbkugelig; halbkugelförmig

'hem-line *n.* Saum, *der;* **~s are up/down** die Röcke sind kurz/lang; **Yves St. Laurent's new ~:** die neue Rocklänge bei Yves St. Laurent

hemlock ['hemlɒk] *n.* Schierling, *der*

hemlock ['fir, 'spruce] *ns. (Amer. Bot.)* Hemlocktanne, *die*

hemo- *(Amer.) see* **haemo-**

hemp [hemp] *n.* **a)** *(Bot., Textiles)* Hanf, *der;* **b)** *(drug)* Haschisch, *das od. der*

'hem-stitch 1. *n.* Hohlsaum, *der.* **2.** *v.t.* mit Hohlsaum versehen

hen [hen] *n.* **a)** *(Ornith.)* Huhn, *das;* Henne, *die (bes. im Gegensatz zu „Hahn");* **b)** *(Zool.) (lobster, crab)* weiblicher Hummer/Krebs; *(salmon)* Lachsweibchen, *das*

'henbane *n., no pl. (Bot., Med.)* Bilsenkraut, *das*

hence [hens] *adv.* **a)** *(therefore)* daher; **b)** *(from this time)* **a week/ten years ~:** in einer Woche/zehn Jahren; **c)** *(arch./poet.: from here)* **[from] ~:** von hinnen *(veralt.)*

hence'forth, hence'forward *advs.* von nun an; fürderhin *(veralt.)*

henchman ['hentʃmən] *n., pl.* **henchmen** ['hentʃmən] *(derog.)* Handlanger, *der*

'hen-coop *n.* Hühnerstall, *der*

hendeca- [hen'dekə] *in comb.* elf-/Elf-

'hen-house *n.* Hühnerhaus, *das;* Hühnerstall, *der*

henna ['henə] *n. (dye)* Henna, *das*

hen: ~-party *n. (coll.)* [Damen]kränzchen, *das;* **~pecked** ['henpekt] *adj.* **a ~pecked husband** ein Pantoffelheld *(ugs.);* **be ~pecked** unter dem Pantoffel stehen *(ugs.);* **~-run** *n.* [Hühner]auslauf, *der*

Henry ['henrı] *pr. n. (Hist., as name of ruler etc.)* Heinrich *(der)*

hep *adj. (dated sl.)* [über alles Moderne] informiert; **be ~ to sth.** über etw. *(Akk.)* auf dem laufenden sein

hepatic [hı'pætık] *adj. (Anat., Med.)* Leber-

hepatitis [hepə'taıtıs] *n. (Med.)* Leberentzündung, *die;* Hepatitis, *die (fachspr.)*

heptagon ['heptəgən] *n. (Geom.)* Siebeneck, *das;* Heptagon, *das (fachspr.)*

heptagonal [hep'tægənl] *adj. (Geom.)* siebeneckig; heptagonal *(fachspr.)*

¹her [hə(r), *stressed* hɜ:(r)] *pron.* sie; *as indirect object* ihr; *reflexively* sich; *referring to personified things or animals which correspond to German masculines/neuters* ihn/es; *as indirect object* ihm; **it was ~:** sie war's; **~ and me** *(coll.)* sie und ich; **if I were ~** *(coll.)* wenn ich sie wäre

²her *poss. pron. attr.* ihr; *referring to personified things or animals which correspond to German masculines/neuters* sein; **she opened ~ eyes/mouth** sie öffnete die Augen/den Mund; **~ father and mother** ihr Vater und ihre Mutter; **she has problems of her own** sie hat ihre eigenen Probleme; **she has a room of ~ own** sie hat ein eigenes Zimmer; **he complained about ~ being late** er beklagte sich darüber, daß sie zu spät kam; er beklagte sich über ihr Zuspätkommen

herald ['herəld] **1.** *n.* **a)** Herold, *der;* **b)** *(messenger)* Bote, *der; (fig.: forerunner)* Vorbote, *der;* **c)** *(Brit.: official of Heralds' College) Beamter des Heroldamtes.* **2.** *v.t. (lit. or fig.)* ankündigen

heraldic [he'rældık] *adj.* heraldisch; **~ animal** Wappentier, *das*

heraldry ['herəldrı] *n., no pl.* **a)** Wappenkunde, *die;* Heraldik, *die;* **b)** *(armorial bearings)* Wappenschmuck, *der*

herb [hɜ:b] *n.* **a)** Kraut, *das; (Cookery)* Gewürzkraut, *das;* **b)** *(Med.)* [Heil]kraut, *das*

herbaceous [hɜ:'beıʃəs] *adj. (Bot.)* krautartig ⟨*Pflanze*⟩; krautig ⟨*Stiel*⟩; **~ border** Staudenrabatte, *die*

herbage ['hɜ:bıdʒ] *n., no pl. (Agric.) (herbs)* Weide, *die; (succulent parts)* Kraut, *das*

herbal ['hɜ:bl] **1.** *attrib. adj.* Kräuter⟨*tee, -arznei*⟩; ⟨*Behandlung*⟩ mit Heilkräutern. **2.** *n.* Pflanzenbuch, *das*

herbalist ['hɜ:bəlıst] *n.* **a)** Kräuterhändler, *der*/Kräuterhändlerin, *die* [für Heilkräuter]; **b)** *(Hist.)* Herbalist, *der*

herbarium [hɜ:'beərıəm] *n., pl.* **herbaria** [hɜ:'beərıə] Herbarium, *das*

'herb garden *n.* Kräutergarten, *der*

herbicide ['hɜ:bısaıd] *n.* Unkrautvertilgungsmittel, *das;* Herbizid, *das*

herbivore ['hɜ:bıvɔ:(r)] *n. (Zool.)* Pflanzenfresser, *der;* Herbivore, *der (fachspr.)*

herbivorous [hɜ:'bıvərəs] *adj.* pflanzenfressend; herbivor *(fachspr.)*

'herb-tea *n.* Kräuteraufguß, *der*

herby ['hɜ:bı] *adj.* **a ~ taste/smell** ein Geschmack/Geruch nach Kräutern

Herculean [hɜ:kjʊ'li:ən, hɜ:'kju:lıən] *adj.* übermenschlich ⟨*Anstrengung*⟩; bärenstark ⟨*Person*⟩; herkulisch *(geh.)*, ungeheuer ⟨*Kraft*⟩; **~ labour** Herkulesarbeit, *die*

Hercules ['hɜ:kjʊli:z] *pr. n.* Herakles, *der;* Herkules, *der (auch fig.);* **the labours of ~:** die zwölf Arbeiten des Herakles

herd [hɜ:d] **1.** *n.* **a)** Herde, *die; (of wild animals)* Rudel, *das;* **a ~ of sheep/elephants** eine Herde Schafe/Elefanten; eine Schaf-/Elefantenherde; **ride ~ on sb.** *(Amer.)* jmdn. im Auge behalten; **b)** *(fig.)* Masse, *die;* **the common ~** *(derog.)* die breite Masse; **the ~ instinct** der Herdentrieb. **2.** *v.t.* **a)** *(lit. or fig.)* treiben; **~ [people] together** *(fig.)* [Menschen] zusammenpferchen; **b)** *(tend)* hüten. **3.** *v.i.* sich zu einer Herde zusammenschließen; *(fig.)* sich drängen

'herdsman ['hɜ:dzmən] *n., pl.* **~smen** ['hɜ:dzmən] Hirt[e], *der*

here [hıə(r)] **1.** *adv.* **a)** *(in or at this place)* hier; **Schmidt ~** *(on telephone)* Schmidt; **spring is ~:** der Frühling ist da; **stay ~:** hierbleiben; **down/in/up ~:** hier unten/drin/oben; **~ below** *(fig. literary)* hienieden *(geh.);* auf dieser Erde; **~ goes!** *(coll.)* dann mal los! *(ugs.);* **~'s to you!** auf dein Wohl!; **~, there, and everywhere** überall; **that's neither ~ nor there** *(coll.)* das ist völlig nebensächlich; **~ today and gone tomorrow** *(of traveller)* heute hier, morgen dort; *(of money)* wie gewonnen, so zerronnen; **~ you are** *(coll.: giving sth.)* hier; **~ we are** *(on arrival)* da sind *od.* wären wir; **~ we go again** *(coll.)* jetzt geht das wieder los! *(ugs.);* **b)** *(to this place)* hierher; **in[to] ~:** hierherein; **come/bring ~:** [hier]herkommen/-bringen; **put sth. ~:** etw. hierhin- *od.* hierhertun; **~ comes the bus** hier *od.* da kommt der Bus. **2.** *n.* **leave ~:** von hier abreisen; **near ~:** hier in der Nähe; **up to ~, as far as ~:** bis hierhin; **he is up to ~ in problems** die Probleme sind ihm über den Kopf gewachsen; **from ~ on** von nun an; **where do we go from ~?** *(fig.)* was machen wir jetzt? **3.** *int. (attracting attention)* he; *(at roll-call)* hier

here: ~a'bout[s] *adv.* hier [in dieser Gegend]; **~'after** *adv. (formal)* im folgenden; *(in the future)* fürderhin *(veralt.); (literary: in the next world)* dereinst *(geh.);* **the life ~after** das Leben im Jenseits; **~'at** *adv. (arch.)* daraufhin; **~'by** *adv. (formal)* hiermit

hereditary [hı'redıtərı] *adj.* **a)** erblich ⟨*Titel, Amt*⟩; ererbt ⟨*Reichtum*⟩; **~ monarchy/right** Erbmonarchie, *die*/Erbrecht, *das;* **b)** *(Biol.)* angeboren ⟨*Instinkt, Verhaltensweise*⟩; **~ disease** Erbkrankheit, *die;* **c)** *(of a family)* **~ feud/enemy** Erbfehde, *die*/-feind, *der*

heredity [hı'redıtı] *n. (Biol.)* **a)** *(transmission of qualities)* Vererbung, *die;* **b)** *(genetic constitution)* Erbgut, *das*

here: ~'in *adv. (formal)* hierin; **~in'after** *adv. (formal)* im folgenden; **~'of** *adv. (formal)* davon

heresy ['herısı] *n.* Ketzerei, *die;* Häresie, *die (geh.)*

heretic ['herıtık] *n.* Ketzer, *der*/Ketzerin, *die;* Häretiker, *der*/Häretikerin, *die (geh.)*

heretical [hı'retıkl] *adj.* ketzerisch; häretisch *(geh.)*

here: ~'to [hıə'tʊ, hıə'tu:] *adv. (formal)* darauf/hierauf; **~to'fore** *adv. (formal) (up to now)* bisher; *(up until that time)* bis dahin; **~'under** *adv. (formal)* im folgenden; **~u'pon** *adv.* hierauf; **~'with** *adv.* **a)** *(with this)* in der Anlage; **we enclose ~with your cheque** wir legen Ihren Scheck diesem Schreiben bei; **b)** *see* **~by**

heritage ['herıtıdʒ] *n. (lit. or fig.)* Erbe, *das*

hermaphrodite [hɜ:'mæfrədaıt] **1.** *n.* Zwitter, *der (auch fig.);* Hermaphrodit, *der.* **2.** *adj.* zwittrig; hermaphroditisch

hermeneutics [hɜ:mı'nju:tıks] *n., no pl.* Hermeneutik, *die*

hermetic [hɜ:'metık] *adj. (airtight)* luftdicht; *(fig.)* hermetisch *(geh.)*

hermetically [hɜ:'metıkəlı] *adv.* hermetisch

hermit ['hɜ:mıt] *n.* **a)** Einsiedler, *der*/Einsiedlerin, *die;* **b)** *(Relig.)* Eremit, *der*

hermitage ['hɜ:mıtıdʒ] *n.* Einsiedelei, *die*

'hermit-crab *n.* Einsiedlerkrebs, *der*

hernia ['hɜ:nıə] *n., pl.* **~s** *or* **~e** ['hɜ:nıi:] *(Med.)* Bruch, *der;* Hernie, *die (Med.)*

hero ['hıərəʊ] *n., pl.* **~es** Held, *der; (demigod)* Heros, *der;* **~ of the hour** Held des Tages

heroic [hı'rəʊık] *adj.* **a)** heldenhaft; heroisch *(geh.);* **b)** *(Lit.)* **~ epic/legend** Heldenepos, *das*/-legende, *die;* **~ couplet** Heroic couplet, *das;* **~ verse** heroischer Vers; **c)** *(high-flown)* erhaben; *(very large)* gewaltig

heroically [hı'rəʊıkəlı] *adv.* heldenhaft

heroics [hı'rəʊıks] *n. pl.* **a)** *(language)* Theatralische, *das; (foolhardiness)* Draufgängertum, *das;* **b)** *(Lit.)* heroischer Vers

heroin ['herəʊın] *n., no pl.* Heroin, *das*

heroine ['herəʊın] *n. fem.* Heldin, *die;* Heroin, *die (geh.);* Heroine, *die (Theater)*

heroism ['herəʊızm] *n., no pl.* Heldentum, *das*

heron ['hern] *n.* Reiher, *der*

hero: ~-worship 1. *n.* Heldenverehrung, *die;* **2.** *v.t.* vergöttern; **~-worshipper** *n.* Heldenverehrer, *der*/-verehrerin, *die*

herpes ['hɜ:pi:z] *n. (Med.)* Herpes, *der*

herring ['herıŋ] *n.* Hering, *der*

herring: ~-bone 1. *n.* **a)** *(Textiles) (stitch)* Fischgrätenstich, *der; (cloth)* Fischgrat, *der;* **b)** *(Archit.)* Fischgrätenverband, *der;* **2.** *adj.* **~-bone pattern** *(Textiles)* Fischgrätenmuster, *das;* **~-gull** *n.* Silbermöwe, *die;* **~-pond** *n. (joc.)* Atlantik, *der*

hers [hɜ:z] *poss. pron. pred.* ihrer/ihre/ihres; der/die/das ihre *od.* ihrige *(geh.);* **the book is ~:** das Buch gehört ihr; **that car is ~:** das ist ihr Wagen; der Wagen gehört ihr; **some friends of ~:** ein paar Freunde von ihr; **a book of ~:** ein Buch von ihr; eins ihrer Bücher; **those children of ~:** ihre Gören *(ugs.);*

~ **is a difficult job** sie hat einen schwierigen Job *(ugs.)*

herself [hɜː'self] *pron.* **a)** *emphat.* selbst; **she ~ said so** sie selbst hat das gesagt; **she saw it ~:** sie hat es selbst gesehen; **she wanted to be ~:** sie wollte sie selbst sein; **she was just being ~:** sie gab sich einfach so wie sie ist; **she is [quite] ~ again** sie ist wieder ganz die alte; *(after an illness)* sie ist wieder auf der Höhe *(ugs.)*; **all right in ~:** im wesentlichen gesund; **she's not quite ~:** sie ist nicht ganz in Ordnung; **[all] by ~** *(on her own, by her own efforts)* [ganz] allein[e]; **b)** *refl.* sich; allein[e] ⟨*tun, wählen*⟩; **she wants it for ~:** sie will es für sich [selbst]; **she won't believe anything that she hasn't seen for ~:** sie glaubt nichts, was sie nicht selbst gesehen hat; **younger than/as heavy as ~:** jünger als/ so schwer wie sie selbst; **... she thought to ~:** ... dachte sie sich [im stillen]; ... dachte sie bei sich

hertz [hɜːts] *n., pl. same (Phys.)* Hertz, *das*

he's [hɪz, *stressed* hiːz] **a)** = **he is; b)** = **he has**

hesitance ['hezɪtəns], **hesitancy** ['hezɪtənsɪ] *n., no pl.* Unschlüssigkeit, *die*

hesitant ['hezɪtənt] *adj.* zögernd ⟨*Politik, Reaktion*⟩; stockend ⟨*Rede*⟩; unsicher ⟨*Person, Stimme*⟩; **be ~ to do sth.** *or* **about doing sth.** Bedenken haben, etw. zu tun

hesitantly ['hezɪtəntlɪ] *adv.* zögernd ⟨*handeln, reagieren*⟩; stockend ⟨*sprechen*⟩

hesitate ['hezɪteɪt] *v. i.* **a)** *(show uncertainty)* zögern; **he who ~s is lost** *(prov.)* man muß die Gelegenheit beim Schopfe fassen; **b)** *(falter)* ins Stocken geraten; **c)** *(show reluctance)* **~ to do sth.** Bedenken haben, etw. zu tun

hesitation [hezɪ'teɪʃn] *n.* **a)** *no pl. (indecision)* Unentschlossenheit, *die;* **without the slightest ~:** ohne im geringsten zu zögern; **have no ~ in doing sth.** nicht zögern, etw. zu tun; **b)** *(instance of faltering)* Unsicherheit, *die;* **c)** *no pl. (reluctance)* Bedenken *Pl.*

Hesse ['hesə] *pr. n.* Hessen *(das)*

Hessian ['hesɪən] **1.** *adj.* hessisch. **2.** *n.* Hesse, *der*/Hessin, *die*

hessian *n.* Sackleinen, *das;* Hessian, *das (fachspr.)*

het [het] *adj. (coll.)* **~ up** aufgeregt; **get ~ up over sth.** sich über etw. *(Akk.)* aufregen

hetero- ['hetərə] *in comb.* hetero-/Hetero-

heterodox ['hetərədɒks] *adj.* heterodox

heterodoxy ['hetərədɒksɪ] *n.* Heterodoxie, *die*

heterogeneity [hetərədʒɪ'niːɪtɪ] *n.* Ungleichartigkeit, *die;* Heterogenität, *die*

heterogeneous [hetərə'dʒiːnɪəs, hetərə'dʒenɪəs] *adj.* ungleichartig; heterogen

heterosexual 1. *adj.* heterosexuell. **2.** *n.* Heterosexuelle, *der/die*

heuristic [hjʊə'rɪstɪk] **1.** *adj.* heuristisch. **2.** *n. (procedure)* heuristische Methode

hew [hjuː] **1.** *v.t., p.p.* **~n** [hjuːn] *or* **~ed** [hjuːd] **a)** *(cut)* hacken ⟨*Holz*⟩; fällen ⟨*Baum*⟩; losschlagen ⟨*Kohle, Gestein*⟩; **~ away** *or* **off** abschlagen; **b)** *(shape)* hauen ⟨*Stufen*⟩; behauen ⟨*Holz, Stein*⟩. **2.** *v.i., p.p.* **~n** *or* **~ed a)** zuschlagen; **~ at sth.** auf etw. *(Akk.)* einschlagen; **b)** *(Amer.: conform)* **~ to sth.** sich an etw. *(Akk.)* halten

hex [heks] *(Amer.)* **1.** *v.t. (lit. or fig.)* verhexen. **2.** *n.* **a) put a ~ on sb./sth.** jmdn./etw. verhexen; **b)** *(witch, lit. or fig.)* Hexe, *die*

hexagon ['heksəgən] *n. (Geom.)* Sechseck, *das;* Hexagon, *das (fachspr.)*

hexagonal [hek'sægənl] *adj. (Geom.)* sechseckig; hexagonal *(fachspr.)*

hexameter [hek'sæmɪtə(r)] *n. (Pros.)* Hexameter, *der*

hey [heɪ] *int.* he!; **~ presto!** simsalabim!

heyday ['heɪdeɪ] *n., no pl.* Blütezeit, *die*

HF *abbr.* **high frequency** HF

hf. *abbr.* **half**

HGV *abbr. (Brit.)* **heavy goods vehicle**

HH *abbr.* **a) Her/His Highness** I. H./S. H.; **b) His Holiness**

hi [haɪ] *int.* hallo *(ugs.)*

hiatus [haɪ'eɪtəs] *n.* **a)** *(gap)* Bruch, *der; (interruption)* Unterbrechung, *die;* **b)** *(Ling.)* Hiatus, *der*

hibernate ['haɪbəneɪt] *v.i.* Winterschlaf halten

hibernation [haɪbə'neɪʃn] *n.* Winterschlaf, *der;* **go into/come out of ~:** sich zum Winterschlaf zurückziehen/aus dem Winterschlaf erwachen

Hibernian [haɪ'bɜːnɪən] **1.** *adj.* irisch. **2.** *n.* Ire, *der*/Irin, *die*

hibiscus [hɪ'bɪskəs] *n. (Bot.)* Hibiskus, *der*

hic [hɪk] *int.* hick *(ugs.)*

hiccup ['hɪkəp] **1.** *n.* **a)** Schluckauf, *der;* **have/get [the] ~s** [den] Schluckauf haben/ bekommen; **give a ~:** schlucksen *(ugs.)*; hick machen *(ugs.)*; hicksen *(landsch.)*; **an attack of [the] ~s** ein Schluckaufanfall; **b)** *(fig.: stoppage)* Störung, *die;* **without any ~s** reibungslos. **2.** *v.i.* schlucksen *(ugs.)*; hicksen *(landsch.)*; hick machen *(ugs.)*; *(many times)* den Schluckauf haben

hick [hɪk] *n. (Amer. coll.)* **[country] ~:** Provinzler, *der (ugs. abwertend)*; Hinterwäldler, *der (spött.)*; **~ town** Provinzstadt, *die;* Provinznest, *das (ugs. abwertend)*

hickey ['hɪkɪ] *n. (Amer.)* Dings, *das (ugs.)*

hickory ['hɪkərɪ] *n.* **a)** *(tree)* Hickory[baum], *der;* **b)** *(wood)* Hickory[holz], *das*

hid *see* **¹hide 1, 2**

hidden *see* **¹hide 1, 2**

hidden re'serve *n. (Econ.)* stille Reserve *od.* Rücklage

¹hide [haɪd] **1.** *v. t.,* **hid** [hɪd], **hidden** ['hɪdn] **a)** *(put or keep out of sight)* verstecken ⟨*Gegenstand, Person usw.*⟩ **(from** vor + *Dat.*); **~ one's head [in embarrassment/shame]** *(fig.)* sich [vor Verlegenheit/Scham *(Dat.)*] verstecken; **~ one's face in one's hands** sein Gesicht in den Händen bergen; *see also* **bushel; b)** *(keep secret)* verbergen ⟨*Gefühle, Sinn, Freude usw.*⟩ **(from** vor + *Dat.*); verheimlichen ⟨*Tatsache, Absicht, Grund usw.*⟩ **(from** *Dat.*); **have nothing to ~:** nichts zu verbergen haben; **the future is hidden from us** die Zukunft ist uns verborgen; **c)** *(obscure)* verdecken; **~ sth. [from view]** etw. verstecken; *(by covering)* etw. verdecken; ⟨*Nebel, Rauch usw.:*⟩ etw. einhüllen. **2.** *v. i.,* **hid, hidden** sich verstecken *od.* verbergen **(from** vor + *Dat.*); **where is he hiding?** wo hält er sich versteckt *od.* verborgen? **3.** *n. (Brit.)* Versteck, *das; (hunter's ~)* Ansitz, *der (Jägerspr.)*

~ a'way *v. i.* sich verstecken *od.* verbergen; *see also* **hideaway**

~ 'out, ~ 'up *v. i.* sich versteckt *od.* verborgen halten; *see also* **hide-out**

²hide *n. (animal's skin)* Haut, *die; (of furry animal)* Fell, *das; (dressed)* Leder, *das; (joc.: human skin)* Haut, *die;* Fell, *das;* **tan sb.'s ~:** jmdm. das Fell gerben *od.* versohlen *(salopp)*; **save one's own ~:** die eigene Haut retten *(ugs.)*; **when I returned I could find neither ~ nor hair of them** als ich zurückkam, waren sie spurlos verschwunden

hide: ~-and-'seek *(Amer.:* **~-and-go-'seek)** *n.* Versteckspiel, *das;* **play ~-and-seek** Verstecken spielen; **~away** *see* **~-out; ~bound** *adj.* engstirnig, borniert *(abwertend)* ⟨*Person, Ansicht*⟩

hideous ['hɪdɪəs] *adj.* **a)** *(extremely ugly, offensive to the ear)* scheußlich; *(repulsive, horrific)* entsetzlich; grauenhaft; **b)** *(coll.: unpleasant)* furchtbar *(ugs.)*, schrecklich *(ugs.)*

hideously ['hɪdɪəslɪ] *adv.* **a)** entsetzlich, grauenhaft ⟨*verstümmelt, entstellt, schreien*⟩; **b)** *(coll.: unpleasantly)* furchtbar *(ugs.)*, schrecklich *(ugs.)* ⟨*langweilig, teuer, kalt, laut usw.*⟩

'hide-out *n.* Versteck, *das; (of bandits, partisans, etc.)* Versteck, *das;* Unterschlupf, *der; (retreat)* Refugium, *das*

hidey-hole *see* **hidy-hole**

¹hiding ['haɪdɪŋ] *n.* **go into ~:** sich verstecken; *(to avoid police, public attention)* untertauchen; **be/stay in ~:** sich versteckt halten/sich weiterhin versteckt halten; *(to avoid police, public attention)* untergetaucht sein/bleiben; **come out of ~:** aus seinem Versteck kommen; *(no longer avoid police, public attention)* wieder auftauchen

²hiding *n. (coll.: beating)* Tracht Prügel; *(fig.)* Schlappe, *die;* **give sb. a [good] ~:** jmdm. eine [ordentliche] Tracht Prügel verpassen; *(fig.)* jmdm. eine [klare] Abfuhr erteilen; **get/be given/take a real ~ [from sb.]** [von jmdm.] gehörige Prügel beziehen *od.* einstecken müssen; *(fig.)* sich *(Dat.)* [von jmdm.] eine klare Abfuhr holen; **be on a ~ to nothing** eine undankbare Rolle haben

'hiding-place *n.* Versteck, *das*

hidy-hole ['haɪdɪhəʊl] *n. (coll.)* Versteck, *das*

hierarchic [haɪə'rɑːkɪk], **hierarchical** [haɪə'rɑːkɪkl] *adj.* hierarchisch

hierarchy ['haɪərɑːkɪ] *n.* Hierarchie, *die*

hieroglyph ['haɪərəglɪf] *n.* **a)** Hieroglyphe, *die;* **b)** *in pl. (joc.: scrawl)* Hieroglyphen *(scherzh.)*

hieroglyphic [haɪərə'glɪfɪk] **1.** *adj.* **a)** *(composed of hieroglyphs)* hieroglyphisch; **b)** *(symbolical)* geheimnisvoll ⟨*Zeichen*⟩. **2.** *n. in pl. (also joc.)* Hieroglyphen

hi-fi ['haɪfaɪ] *(coll.)* **1.** *adj.* Hi-Fi-. **2.** *n.* **a)** *(equipment)* Hi-Fi-Anlage, *die;* **b)** *(use of ~)* Hi-Fi, *das; attrib.* Hi-Fi-⟨*fan usw.*⟩

higgledy-piggledy [hɪgldɪ'pɪgldɪ] **1.** *adv.* wie Kraut und Rüben *(ugs.)*. **2.** *adj.* wirr, kunterbunt ⟨*Ansammlung usw.*⟩

high [haɪ] **1.** *adj.* **a)** *(reaching far up)* hoch ⟨*Berg, Gebäude, Mauer*⟩; **a wall eight feet** *or* **foot ~:** eine acht Fuß hohe Mauer; **I've known him since he was only so ~** *(coll.)* ich kannte ihn schon, als er [noch] so [klein] war; **b)** *(above normal level)* hoch ⟨*Stiefel*⟩; **a dress with a ~ neckline** ein hochgeschlossenes Kleid; **the river/water is ~:** der Fluß/ das Wasser steht hoch; **~ and dry** ⟨*Boot:*⟩ auf dem Trockenen; hoch und trocken *(Seemannsspr.)*; **be left ~ and dry** *(fig.)* auf dem trock[e]nen sitzen *(ugs.)*; *(be stuck without transport)* festsitzen *(ugs.)*; **c)** *(far above ground or sea level)* hoch ⟨*Gipfel, Punkt*⟩; groß ⟨*Höhe*⟩; Hoch⟨*ebene, -moor*⟩; **be ~** ⟨*Ort:*⟩ hoch liegen; ⟨*Sonne, Mond:*⟩ hoch stehen; **d)** *(to or from far above the ground)* hoch ⟨*Aufstieg, Sprung*⟩; **~ diving** Turmspringen, *das;* **a ~ dive** ein Sprung vom Turm; *see also* **¹bar 1 b; e)** *(of exalted rank)* hoch ⟨*Beamter, Amt, Gericht*⟩; **the Most H~** *(Bibl.)* der Allerhöchste; **~ and low** arm und reich *(veralt.)*; **a ~er court** eine höhere Instanz; **~er mammals/plants** höhere Säugetiere/Pflanzen; **~ and mighty** *(coll.: ~-handed)* selbstherrlich; *(coll.: self-important)* wichtigtuerisch; *(coll.: superior)* hochnäsig *(ugs.)*; *(arch.: exalted)* hoch ⟨*Adlige*⟩; groß ⟨*Häuptling*⟩; **aim for ~er things** *(fig.)* nach Höherem streben; **be born** *or* **destined for ~er things** zu Höherem geboren *od.* bestimmt sein; **in ~ places** an höherer Stelle; höheren Orts; **people in ~ places** Leute in hohen Positionen; **those in ~ places** die Oberen; **f)** *(great in degree)* hoch; groß ⟨*Gefallen, Bedeutung*⟩; stark ⟨*Wind*⟩; **be ~ in iodine** einen hohen Jodgehalt aufweisen; **be held in ~ regard/esteem** hohes Ansehen/ hohe Wertschätzung genießen; hoch angesehen/geschätzt sein; **~ blood pressure** Bluthochdruck, *der;* **~ vacuum** Hochvakuum, *das;* **her ~est aspiration** ihr größter Wunsch; **get a nice ~ polish on the car** das Auto auf Hochglanz polieren; **a/his** *etc.* **~ colour** ein/sein *usw.* rotes Gesicht; **have a ~ opinion of sb./sth.** eine hohe Meinung von jmdm./etw. haben *(geh.)*; viel von jmdm./etw. halten; **g)** *(extreme in opinion)* extrem; **h)** *(noble, virtuous)* hoch ‹*Ideal, Ziel, Prinzip, Berufung*›; edel ‹*Charakter*›; **of ~ birth** von hoher Geburt *(geh.)*; **~ art/comedy** hohe Kunst/Komödie; **i)** *(Geog.)* **~ latitudes** hohe Breiten; **j)** *(of time, season)* **it is ~ time you left** es ist *od.* wird höchste Zeit, daß du gehst; **~ noon** Mittag; **it was ~ noon** es war genau Mittag; **~ summer** Hochsommer, *der;* **k)** *(fully developed)* hoch; Hoch‹*mittelalter, -renaissance usw.*›; **l)** *(long since passed)* fern ‹*Vergangenheit*›; **m)** *(luxurious, extravagant)* üppig ‹*Leben*›; **n)** *(enjoyable)* **have a ~ [old] time** sich bestens amüsieren; **have a ~ [old] time doing sth.** Spaß damit haben, etw. zu tun; **o)** *(coll.) (under the influence) (of a drug)* high *nicht attr. (ugs.)* **(on** von); angeturnt *(ugs.)* **(on** von); *(on cannabis)* bekifft *(ugs.)*; *(on alcohol)* blau *(ugs.)* **(on** von); **get ~ on** sich anturnen mit *(ugs.)* ‹*Haschisch, LSD usw.*›; sich besaufen mit *(salopp)* ‹*Whisky, Bier usw.*›; **p)** *(in pitch)* hoch ‹*Ton, Stimme, Lage, Klang usw.*›; **q)** *(slightly decomposed)* angegangen *(landsch.)* ‹*Fleisch*›; ‹*Wild*› mit Hautgout; **r)** *(Cards)* hoch; **ace is ~**: As ist hoch; **I'm queen** *etc.* **~**: Dame *usw.* ist das Höchste, was ich habe; **s)** *(Ling.) see* **close 1 n.** *See also* **horse 1 a. 2.** *adv.* **a)** *(in or to a ~ position)* hoch; **~ on our list of priorities** weit oben auf unserer Prioritätenliste; **~er up the valley** weiter oben im Tal; **we climbed ~er up the cliff** wir kletterten das Kliff ein Stück höher hinauf; **search** *or* **hunt** *or* **look ~ and low** überall suchen; **search** *or* **hunt** *or* **look ~ and low for sb./sth.** jmdn./etw. suchen wie eine Stecknadel; *see also* **aim 2 a; b)** *(to a ~ level)* hoch; **prices have gone too ~**: die Preise sind zu stark gestiegen; **I'll go as ~ as two thousand pounds** ich gehe bis zweitausend Pfund; **c)** *(at or to a ~ pitch)* hoch ‹*singen*›; **d) play ~** *(Cards)* etwas Hohes spielen; *(Gambling)* mit hohen Einsätzen spielen. **3.** *n.* **a)** *(~est level/figure)* Höchststand, *der; see also* **all-time; b)** *(Meteorol.)* Hoch, *das;* **c)** *(Amer. coll.: ~ school)* Oberschule, *die;* **in junior ~**: in der Unterstufe [der Oberschule]; **d)** *(sl.: drug-induced euphoria)* Rausch[zustand], *der;* **give sb. a ~** ‹*Droge:*› jmdn. high machen *(ugs.)*; **e)** *(~ position)* **on ~**: hoch oben *od. (geh., südd., österr.)* droben; *(in heaven)* im Himmel; **from on ~**: von hoch oben; *(from heaven)* vom Himmel; *(fig.: from a ~ authority)* von oben; **a judgement from on ~**: eine Strafe des Himmels

high: ~ 'altar *n. (Eccl.)* Hochaltar, *der;* **~-altitude** *adj.* Höhen-; **~ball** *n. (Amer.)* **a)** *(drink)* Highball, *der;* **b)** *(Railw.: signal)* Freie-Fahrt-Signal, *das;* **~ 'beam** *n.* Fernlicht, *das;* **I was on ~ beam most of the time** ich fuhr die meiste Zeit mit Fernlicht; **~binder** *n. (Amer.)* **a)** *(thug)* Schläger, *der;* **b)** *(assassin)* [chinesischer] Killer; **c)** *(swindler)* Schwindler, *der;* Ganove, *der (ugs.)*; **~-born** *adj.* hochgeboren *(veralt.)*; **~boy** *n. (Amer.) (hochbeinige)* hohe Kommode; Highboy, *der (fachspr.)*; **~brow** *(coll.)* **1.** *n.* Intellektuelle, *der/die;* **2.** *adj.* intellektuell ‹*Person, Gerede usw.*›; hochgestochen *(abwertend)* ‹*Person, Gerede, Musik, Literatur usw.*›; hochgeistig ‹*Interessen, Beschäftigung, Gerede*›; **~ chair** *n. (for baby)* Hochstuhl, *der;* **H~ 'Church** *n.* High Church, *die;* Hochkirche, *die; attrib.* hochkirchlich; **~-class** *adj.* hochwertig ‹*Erzeugnis*›; erstklassig ‹*Unterkunft, Konditor usw.*›; **~ com'mand** *n. (Mil.)* Oberkommando, *das;* **H~ Com'mission** *n.* Hohe Kommission; **H~ Com'missioner** *n.* Hoher Kommissar; **H~ 'Court [of Justice]** *n. (Brit. Law) oberster Gerichtshof für Zivil- und Strafsachen;* **~ day** *n.* **on ~ days and holidays** zu besonderen Anlässen

higher ['haɪə(r)]: **~ edu'cation** *n., no pl., no art.* Hochschul[aus]bildung, *die;* **he works in ~ education** er ist im Hochschulbereich tätig; **more funds are needed for ~ education** das Hochschulwesen braucht mehr Mittel; **~ mathe'matics** *n.* höhere Mathematik

high: ~ ex'plosive *see* **explosive 2; ~-falutin** [haɪfə'lu:tɪn], **~-faluting** [haɪfə'lu:tɪŋ] *adj. (coll. derog.)* hochtrabend ‹*Gerede, Stil, Sprache usw.*›; aufgeblasen *(ugs. abwertend)* ‹*Person*›; **~ 'fashion** *see* **haute couture; ~ fi'delity** *n.* High-Fidelity, *die;* **reproduce sth. in ~ fidelity** etw. in Hi-Fi-Qualität wiedergeben; **~ fi'nance** *n.* Hochfinanz, *die;* **~-'flier** *see* **~-flyer; ~-flown** *adj.* geschwollen *(abwertend)* ‹*Stil, Ausdrucksweise*›; hochfliegend ‹*Ideen, Pläne*›; **~-'flyer** *n.* **a)** *(ambitious person)* Ehrgeizling, *der (ugs., abwertend)*; **be a ~-flyer** große Rosinen im Kopf haben *(ugs.)*; hoch hinaus wollen; **b)** *(able person)* Hochbegabte, *der/die;* **~-'flying** *adj.* hoch fliegend; *(fig.: ambitious)* hochfliegend ‹*Pläne, Ideen*›; ehrgeizig ‹*Person*›; **~ 'frequency** *n.* hohe Frequenz; *(radiofrequency)* Hochfrequenz, *die;* **~-frequency** *adj.* hochfrequent ‹*Welle, Schwingung, Strahlung, Strom, Ton, Signal*›; Hochfrequenz‹*welle, -schwingung, -signal, -gerät, -sender usw.*›; ‹*Sendung*› ≈ auf Kurzwelle; ‹*Verluste*› im Hochfrequenzbereich; **~ 'German** *see* **German 2 b; ~-grade** *adj.* hochwertig; **~-grade ore** hochhaltiges Erz; Reicherz, *das;* **~-grade steel** Edelstahl, *der;* **~-handed** [haɪ'hændɪd] *adj.* selbstherrlich; **~ 'hat** *n.* **a)** *(tall hat)* Zylinder, *der;* **b)** *(fig.: snobbish person)* dünkelhafter Mensch; **~ 'heel** *n.* **a)** hoher Absatz; **b)** *in pl. (shoes)* hochhackige Schuhe; **~-heeled** [haɪ'hi:ld] *adj.* ‹*Schuhe*› mit hohen Absätzen; **~ 'holiday** *n. (Relig.) einer der beiden höchsten jüdischen Feiertage;* höchster Feiertag; **~ 'jinks** ['haɪ dʒɪŋks] *n. pl.* [übermütige] Ausgelassenheit; **~ jump** *n., no pl.* **a)** *(Sport)* Hochsprung, *der;* **b)** *(fig.: reprimand, punishment)* **he is for the ~ jump, it's the ~ jump for him** er kann sich auf was gefaßt machen *(ugs.)*; **~-jumper** *n. (Sport)* Hochspringer, *der*/-springerin, *die;* **~-'key** *adj. (Photog.)* High-key-‹*Bild, Aufnahme usw.*› *(fachspr.)*; **~ 'kick** *n.* hoher Beinwurf; **~land** ['haɪlənd] **1.** *n., usu. in pl.* Hochland, *das;* **the H~lands** *(in Scotland)* die Highlands; **2.** *adj.* hochländisch; **H~land 'cattle** *n. pl.* schottische Hochlandrinder; **H~land 'dress** *n., no pl.* [schottische] Hochlandtracht; **~lander** ['haɪləndə(r)] *n.* Hochländer, *der*/-länderin, *die;* **H~lander** schottischer Hochländer/schottische Hochländerin; **~-level** *adj.* ‹*Verhandlungen usw.*› auf hoher Ebene; **~-level talks** Spitzengespräche; **~-level computer language** problemorientierte Programmiersprache; **~ life** *n., no pl.* **a)** *(life of upper class)* das Leben der Oberschicht; **b)** *(luxurious living)* **the ~ life** das Leben auf großem Fuße; **~light 1.** *n.* **a)** *(outstanding moment)* Höhepunkt, *der;* **the ~light of the week's events** das herausragende Ereignis der Woche; **b)** *(bright area)* Licht, *das;* **c)** *(in hair) usu. pl.* Strähnchen, *das;* **2.** *v. t.*, **~lighted** ein Schlaglicht werfen auf (+ *Akk.*) ‹*Probleme usw.*›; **~lighter** *n.* Textmarker, *der*

highly ['haɪlɪ] *adv.* **a)** *(to a high degree)* sehr; äußerst; hoch‹*begabt, -interessant, -angesehen, -bezahlt, -gebildet, -modern, -aktuell*›; leicht ‹*entzündlich*›; stark ‹*gewürzt*›; **feel ~ honoured** sich hoch geehrt fühlen; **I can ~ recommend the restaurant** ich kann dieses Restaurant sehr empfehlen; *see also* **polish 1 b; b)** *(favourably)* **think ~ of sb./sth., regard sb./sth. ~**: eine hohe Meinung von jmdm./etw. haben; **speak/write ~ of sb./sth.** jmdn./etw. sehr loben

'highly-strung *adj.* übererregbar

high: ~ 'mass *see* **[1]mass; ~-minded** [haɪ'maɪndɪd] *adj.* hochgesinnt ‹*Person*›; hoch, *(geh.)* hehr ‹*Prinzipien, Dienstauffassung usw.*›; **~-necked** *adj.* hochgeschlossen ‹*Kleidungsstück*›

Highness ['haɪnɪs] *n.* Hoheit, *die;* **His/Her/Your [Royal] ~**: Seine/Ihre/Eure [Königliche] Hoheit

high: ~-octane *adj.* hochoktanig; **~-performance** *adj.* Hochleistungs-; **~-pitched** *adj.* **a)** hoch ‹*Ton, Stimme*›; **b)** *(Archit.)* steil ‹*Dach*›; **c)** *(lofty)* anspruchsvoll; hochgeistig ‹*Unterhaltung*›; **be too ~-pitched intellectually for sb.** jmdm. *od.* für jmdn. zu hoch sein *(ugs.)*; **~ point** *n.* Höhepunkt, *der;* Gipfelpunkt, *der;* **~-powered** ['haɪpaʊəd] *adj.* **a)** *(powerful)* stark ‹*Fahrzeug, Motor, Glühbirne usw.*›; **b)** *(forceful)* dynamisch ‹*Geschäftsmann, Manager usw.*›; **c)** *(authoritative)* mit umfangreichen Vollmachten ausgestattet; *(intellectually excellent)* [äußerst] fähig; hochkarätig *(ugs.)* ‹*Examen*›; **~ 'pressure** *n.* **a)** *(Meteorol.)* Hochdruck, *der;* **an area of ~ pressure** ein Hochdruckgebiet; **b)** *(Mech. Engin.)* Überdruck, *der;* **c)** *(fig.: high degree of activity)* Hochdruck, *der;* **work at ~ pressure** mit Hochdruck arbeiten *(ugs.)*; **~-pressure** *adj.* Hochdruck-; *(fig.: persuasive)* aggressiv ‹*Verkaufsmethoden*›; aufdringlich ‹*Vertreter*›; **~-priced** [haɪ'praɪst] *adj.* teuer; **~ 'priest** *n.* Hohepriester, *der;* **~ 'profile** *see* **profile 1 g; ~-ranking** *adj.* hochrangig; von hohem Rang *nachgestellt;* hoch ‹*Beamter, Offizier*›; **~ re'lief** *see* **[2]relief a; ~-rise** *adj.* Hochhaus-; **~-rise building** Hochhaus, *das;* **~-rise [block of] flats/office block** Wohn-/Bürohochhaus, *das;* **~ road** *n.* Hauptstraße, *die;* **the ~ road to ruin** der sichere Weg zum Ruin; **a ~ road to happiness** ein sicherer Weg zum Glück; **~ school** *n.* ≈ Oberschule, *die;* **~ 'seas** *n. pl.* **the ~ seas** die hohe See; **~ season** *n.* Hochsaison, *die;* **~ sign** *n. (Amer. coll.)* **give sb. the ~ sign** jmdm. signalisieren, daß die Luft rein ist; **~-sounding** *adj.* hochtönend; hochtrabend *(abwertend)*; **~-speed** *adj.* **a)** schnell[fahrend]; **~-speed train** Hochgeschwindigkeitszug, *der;* **~-speed steel** Schnell[arbeits]stahl, *der;* **b)** *(Photog.) see* **[2]fast 1 h; ~-spirited** *see* **spirited b; ~ 'spirits** *see* **spirit 1 h; ~ spot** *n. (coll.)* Höhepunkt, *der;* **~ street** *n.* Hauptstraße, *die;* **~-street shop/office** Geschäft/Büro in der Hauptstraße; **~-street banks** Großbanken; **~-'strung** *see* **highly-strung; ~ 'table** *n.* **a)** *(at public dinner)* erhöhte Speisetafel; **b)** *(table for college fellows)* Dozententisch, *der;* **~tail** *v. i. & t. (Amer. sl.)* **~tail [it]** abhauen *(salopp)*; verduften *(ugs.)*; sich aus dem Staub machen *(ugs.)*; **~ 'tea** *see* **tea b; ~-tech** *adj. (coll.)* High-Tech-; **~ 'tech** *(coll.)*, **~ tech'nology** *ns.* Spitzentechnologie, *die;* Hochtechnologie, *die;* **~-technology** *adj.* hochtechnisiert, High-Tech-; **~ 'tension** ≈ **~ voltage** *see* **voltage; ~-'tension** *see* **~-voltage; ~ 'tide** *see* **tide 1 a; ~ 'treason** *see* **treason a; ~-up** *n. (coll.)* hohes Tier *(ugs.)*; **~ 'voltage** *see* **voltage; ~-'voltage** *adj. (Electr.)* Hochspannungs-; **~ 'water** *n.* Hochwasser, *das;* **~-'water mark** *n.* **a)** *(level reached by tide)* Hochwassermarke, *die;* **b)** *(maximum value)* höchster Stand; Höchststand, *der;* *(highest point of excellence)* Höhepunkt, *der;* **~way** *n.* **a)** *(public road)* öffentliche Straße; *(public path)* öffentlicher Weg; **H~ways Department** Straßenbauamt, *das;* **the King's/Queen's ~way** *(Brit.) eine öffentliche Straße;* **b)** *(main route)* Verkehrsweg, *der;* **the spinal cord is the ~way for all nervous impulses** das Rückenmark ist die Bahn, die alle Nervenimpulse nehmen; **c)** *(fig.:*

course of action) **the ~way to ruin** der sichere Weg zum Ruin; **H~way 'Code** *n. (Brit.)* Straßenverkehrsordnung, *die;* **~wayman** ['haɪweɪmən] *n., pl.* **~waymen** ['haɪweɪmən] *(Hist.)* Straßenräuber, *der;* Wegelagerer, *der;* **~ 'wire** *n.* [Hoch]seil, *das*

hijack ['haɪdʒæk] **1.** *v.t.* **a)** *(seize)* in seine Gewalt bringen; **they ~ed an aircraft to Cuba** sie haben ein Flugzeug nach Kuba entführt; **he ~ed the lorry to London** er zwang den Fahrer des LKW, nach London zu fahren; **b)** *(coll.: steal)* sich *(Dat.)* unter den Nagel reißen *(ugs.).* **2.** *n. (of aircraft)* Entführung, *die* **(of** *Gen.***)**; *(of vehicle)* Überfall, *der* **(of** auf + *Akk.***)**

hijacker ['haɪdʒækə(r)] *n.* Entführer, *der; (of aircraft)* Hijacker, *der;* Flugzeugentführer, *der;* **be seized by ~s** entführt werden

hike [haɪk] **1.** *n.* **a)** *(long walk)* Wanderung, *die;* **go on a ~:** eine Wanderung machen; wandern gehen; **be on a ~:** auf einer Wanderung sein; eine Wanderung machen; **b)** *(esp. Amer.: increase)* Anstieg, *der;* Erhöhung, *die* **(in** *Gen.***)**. **2.** *v.i.* **a)** wandern; eine Wanderung machen; **b)** *(walk vigorously)* wandern; marschieren. **3.** *v.t.* **a)** *(hoist)* hieven *(ugs.);* **b)** *(esp. Amer.: raise)* erhöhen, anheben ‹*Preise usw.*› **(to** auf + *Akk.***)**

~ 'up *v.i.* ‹*Kleidungsstück:*› hochrutschen *(ugs.),* sich hochschieben

hiker ['haɪkə(r)] *n.* Wanderer, *der*/Wanderin, *die*

hilarious [hɪ'leərɪəs] *adj.* **a)** *(extremely funny)* urkomisch; rasend komisch *(ugs.);* **b)** *(boisterously merry)* ausgelassen ‹*Party, Stimmung*›

hilariously [hɪ'leərɪəslɪ] *adv.* **be ~ funny** rasend komisch sein *(ugs.);* zum Schreien sein *(ugs.)*

hilarity [hɪ'lærɪtɪ] *n., no pl.* **a)** *(gaiety)* Fröhlichkeit, *die;* **b)** *(merriment)* übermütige Ausgelassenheit; *(loud laughter)* Heiterkeit, *die*

Hilary term [hɪlərɪ 'tɜ:m] *n. (Brit. Univ.)* Frühjahrstrimester, *das*

hill [hɪl] *n.* **a)** Hügel, *der; (higher)* Berg, *der;* **walk in the ~s** in den Bergen gehen; **built on a ~:** am Hang gebaut; **be over the ~** *(fig. coll.)* auf dem absteigenden Ast sein *(ugs.); (past the crisis)* über den Berg sein *(ugs.);* **[as] old as the ~s** *(fig.)* uralt; ‹*Person*› [so] alt wie Methusalem; *see also* **up 2 a; uphill; b)** *(heap)* Hügel, *der; (ant~, dung~, mole~)* Haufen, *der;* **c)** *(sloping road)* Steigung, *die;* **park on a ~:** am Berg parken

hill: ~-billy *n. (Amer.)* **a)** Hinterwäldler, *der*/Hinterwäldlerin, *die (spött.);* Landpomeranze, *die (ugs. abwertend, auch scherzh.); (of the SE US)* Hillbilly, *der;* **b)** *(Mus.)* Hillbilly, *der;* **~ climb** *n. (Motor Racing)* Bergrennen, *das;* **~-fort** *n.* Bergfestung, *die; (Archaeol.)* Hillfort, *das;* **~-man** *n.* Bergbewohner, *der*

hillock ['hɪlək] *n.* [kleiner] Hügel

hill: ~side *n.* Hang, *der;* **~ start** *n. (Motor Veh.)* Anfahren am Berg, *das;* **do a ~ start** am Berg anfahren; **~top** *n.* [Berg]gipfel, *der*

hilly ['hɪlɪ] *adj.* hüg[e]lig; *(higher)* bergig

hilt [hɪlt] *n.* Griff, *der;* Heft, *das (geh., fachspr.);* **[up] to the ~** *(fig.)* voll und ganz ‹*unterstützen usw.*›; schlagend, stichhaltig ‹*beweisen*›

him [ɪm, *stressed* hɪm] *pron.* ihn; *as indirect object* ihm; *reflexively* sich; *referring to personified things or animals which correspond to German feminines/neuters* sie/es; *as indirect object* ihr/ihm; **it was ~:** er war's; *see also* ^{1}**her**

Himalayan [hɪmə'leɪən] *adj.* Himalaya-

Himalayas [hɪmə'leɪəz] *pr. n. pl.* Himalaya, *der*

himself [hɪm'self] *pron.* **a)** *emphat.* selbst; **b)** *refl.* sich. *See also* **herself**

^{1}**hind** [haɪnd] *n.* Hirschkuh, *die*

^{2}**hind** *adj.* hinter...; **~ legs** Hinterbeine; **get up on one's ~ legs** *(fig. joc.)* sich hinstellen; *see also* **donkey**

hinder ['hɪndə(r)] **1.** *v.t. (impede)* behindern; *(delay)* verzögern ‹*Vollendung einer Arbeit, Vorgang*›; aufhalten ‹*Person*›; **~ sb. in his work** jmdn. bei der Arbeit behindern; **~ sb. from doing sth.** jmdn. daran hindern, etw. zu tun. **2.** *v.i.* **will it help or ~?** bedeutet es eine Erleichterung oder eine Erschwernis?

Hindi ['hɪndi:] **1.** *adj.* Hindi-; *see also* **English 1. 2.** *n.* Hindi, *das; see also* **English 2 a**

hind: ~most *adj. (furthest behind)* hinterst...; *see also* **devil 1 c; ~quarters** *n. pl.* Hinterteil, *das; (of large quadruped)* Hinterteil, *das;* Hinterhand, *die (fachspr.)*

hindrance ['hɪndrəns] *n.* **a)** *(action)* Behinderung, *die; see also* ^{2}**let a; b)** *(obstacle)* Hindernis, *das* **(to** für**)**; **he is more of a ~ than a help** er stört mehr, als daß er hilft; **be a ~ to navigation** ein Hindernis für die Schiffahrt sein *od.* darstellen

'hindsight *n.* **in ~, with [the benefit of] ~:** im nachhinein

Hindu ['hɪndu:, hɪn'du:] **1.** *n.* Hindu, *der.* **2.** *adj.* hinduistisch; Hindu‹*gott, -tempel*›

Hinduism ['hɪndu:ɪzm] *n., no pl.* Hinduismus, *der*

Hindustani [hɪndə'stɑ:ni:] **1.** *adj.* **a)** hindustanisch; **b)** *(Ling.)* Hindustani-; hindustanisch; *see also* **English 1. 2.** *n.* Hindustani, *das; see also* **English 2 a**

hinge [hɪndʒ] **1.** *n.* **a)** Scharnier, *das; (continuous)* Klavierband, *das;* **off its ~s** ‹*Tür*› aus den Angeln gehoben; **b)** *(Zool.: of bivalve)* Schloß, *das;* **c)** *(Philat.)* **[stamp-]~:** Klebefalz, *der.* **2.** *v.t.* mit Scharnieren/einem Scharnier versehen; **~ sth. to sth.** etw. mit Scharnieren/einem Scharnier an etw. *(Dat.)* befestigen. **3.** *v.i.* **a)** *(hang and turn)* **~ [up]on sth.** mit Scharnieren/einem Scharnier an etw. *(Dat.)* befestigt sein; **b)** *(fig.: depend)* abhängen **([up]on** von**)**; hängen *(ugs.)* **([up]on** an + *Dat.***)**

hinged [hɪndʒd] *adj.* mit Scharnieren/einem Scharnier versehen; **~ lid** Klappdeckel, *der*

hinny ['hɪnɪ] *n. (Zool.)* Maulesel, *der*

hint [hɪnt] **1.** *n.* **a)** *(suggestion)* Wink, *der;* Hinweis, *der;* **give a ~ that ...:** andeuten, daß ...; **give no ~ that ...:** nicht einmal andeutungsweise zu erkennen geben, daß ...; **is that a ~?** ist das ein Wink mit dem Zaunpfahl? *(scherzh.);* **~, ~!** *(joc.)* wenn ich mal mit dem Zaunpfahl winken darf *(scherzh.); see also* **broad 1 b; drop 3 d; take 1 v; b)** *(slight trace)* Spur, *die* **(of** von**)**; **the ~/no ~ of a smile** der Anflug/nicht die Spur eines Lächelns; **there was a ~ of sadness in his smile** in seinem Lächeln zeigte sich ein Anflug von Traurigkeit; **a ~ of aniseed** ein Hauch von Anis; **c)** *(practical information)* Tip, *der* **(on** für**)**; **car repair ~s** Tips für die Autoreparatur. **2.** *v.t.* andeuten; **nothing has yet been ~ed about it** darüber hat man noch nichts herausgelassen *(ugs.).* **3.** *v.i.* **~ at** andeuten

hinterland ['hɪntəlænd] *n.* Hinterland, *das; (area surrounding city)* Umland, *das*

^{1}**hip** [hɪp] *n.* **a)** Hüfte, *die;* **with one's hands on one's ~s** die Arme in die Hüften gestemmt; **shoot from the ~** *(lit. or fig.)* aus der Hüfte schießen; **b)** *in sing. or pl. (~-measurement)* Hüftumfang, *der;* Hüftweite, *die; (of man, boy)* Gesäßumfang, *der;* Gesäßweite, *die;* **have thirty-seven-inch ~s** *or* **a thirty-seven-inch ~:** eine Hüftweite/Gesäßweite von vierundneunzig Zentimetern haben; **how large are your ~s?** welche Hüftweite/Gesäßweite hast du?; **c)** *(Archit.)* Grat, *der*

^{2}**hip** *n. (Bot.)* Hagebutte, *die*

^{3}**hip** *int. see* **hurrah 1**

^{4}**hip** *see* **hep**

hip: ~-bath *n.* Sitzbad, *das;* **~-bone** *n. (Anat.)* Hüftbein, *das;* Hüftknochen, *der;* **~-flask** *n.* Taschenflasche, *die;* Flachmann, *der (ugs. scherzh.);* **~-joint** *n. (Anat.)* Hüftgelenk, *das;* **~-length** *adj.* hüftlang ‹*Kleidungsstück*›; **~-measurement** *n.* Hüftumfang, *der;* Hüftweite, *die; (of man, boy)* Gesäßumfang, *der;* Gesäßweite, *die*

hippie ['hɪpɪ] *n. (coll.)* Hippie, *der*

hippo ['hɪpəʊ] *n., pl.* **~s** *(coll.) see* **hippopotamus**

hip-'pocket *n.* Gesäßtasche, *die*

Hippocratic oath [hɪpəkrætɪk 'əʊθ] *n. (Med.)* Eid des Hippokrates

hippopotamus [hɪpə'pɒtəməs] *n., pl.* **~es** *or* **hippopotami** [hɪpə'pɒtəmaɪ] *(Zool.)* Nilpferd, *das;* Flußpferd, *das*

hippy ['hɪpɪ] *n. see* **hippie**

hip: ~-roof *n. (Archit.)* Walmdach, *das;* **~ size** *n. see* **~-measurement**

hipster ['hɪpstə(r)] **1.** *adj.* auf der Hüfte sitzend ‹*Hose*›. **2.** *in pl.* Hüfthose, *die*

hire [haɪə(r)] **1.** *n.* **a)** *(action)* Mieten, *das; (of servant)* Einstellen, *das;* **conditions of ~:** Mietbedingungen; **b)** *(condition)* **be on ~ [to sb.]** [an jmdn.] vermietet sein; **for** *or* **on ~:** zu vermieten; **'for ~'** „frei"; **there are boats for** *or* **on ~:** man kann Boote mieten; **c)** *(amount)* Leihgebühr, *die;* **d)** *(arch.: wages)* Lohn, *der;* **the labourer is worthy of his ~** *(prov.)* jede Arbeit ist ihres Lohnes wert *(Spr.).* **2.** *v.t.* **a)** *(employ)* anwerben; engagieren ‹*Anwalt, Berater usw.*›; **~d assassin** gedungener Mörder; **b)** *(obtain use of)* mieten; **~ sth. from sb.** etw. bei jmdm. mieten; **c)** *(grant use of)* vermieten; **~ sth. to sb.** etw. jmdm. *od.* an jmdn. vermieten

~ 'out *v.t.* vermieten

'hire-car *n.* Mietwagen, *der;* Leihwagen, *der*

hired [haɪəd]: **~ car** *see* **hire-car; ~ girl** *n. (Amer.)* Hausmädchen, *das; (on farm)* Magd, *die (veralt.);* **~ man** *n. (Amer.)* Gehilfe, *der; (on farm)* Knecht, *der (veralt.)*

hireling ['haɪəlɪŋ] *n.* Söldling, *der (abwertend);* Mietling, *der (abwertend)*

hire-'purchase *n., no pl., no art. (Brit.)* Ratenkauf, *der;* Teilzahlungskauf, *der; attrib.* Raten-; Teilzahlungs-; **pay for/buy sth. on ~:** etw. in Raten bezahlen/auf Raten *od.* Teilzahlung kaufen

hirer ['haɪərə(r)] *n.* Mieter, *der*/Mieterin, *die; (who grants use)* Vermieter, *der*/Vermieterin, *die*

hirsute ['hɜ:sju:t] *adj.* behaart; *(unkempt)* zottelig; struppig

hirsuteness ['hɜ:sju:tnɪs] *n., no pl.* starke Behaarung; *(unkempt appearance)* Struppigkeit, *die*

his [ɪz, *stressed* hɪz] *poss. pron.* **a)** *attrib.* sein; *referring to personified things or animals which correspond to German feminines/neuters* ihr/sein; *see also* ^{2}**her; b)** *pred. (the one[s] belonging to him)* seiner/seine/sein[e]s; der/die/das seine *od.* seinige *(geh.);* **towels labelled '~' and 'hers'** mit „Er" und „Sie" gekennzeichnete Handtücher; *see also* **hers**

Hispanic [hɪ'spænɪk] **1.** *adj.* lateinamerikanisch; **~ studies** Hispanistik, *die;* **~ Americans** Hispanoamerikaner. **2.** *n.* Lateinamerikaner, *der*/-amerikanerin, *die;* Hispanoamerikaner, *der*/-amerikanerin, *die*

Hispanicist [hɪ'spænɪsɪst], **Hispanist** ['hɪspənɪst] *n.* Hispanist, *der*/Hispanistin, *die*

hiss [hɪs] **1.** *n. (of goose, snake, escaping steam, crowd, audience)* Zischen, *das; (of cat, locomotive)* Fauchen, *das.* **2.** *v.i.* ‹*Gans, Schlange, Dampf, Publikum, Menge:*› zischen; ‹*Katze, Lokomotive:*› fauchen. **3.** *v.t.* **a)** *(express disapproval of)* auszischen ‹*Redner, Schauspieler*›; **b)** *(utter with a hiss)* zischen

histamine ['hɪstəmɪn, 'hɪstəmi:n] *n. (Physiol.)* Histamin, *das*
histogram ['hɪstəgræm] *n. (Statistics)* Histogramm, *das*
histology [hɪ'stɒlədʒɪ] *n. (Biol.)* Histologie, *die*
historian [hɪ'stɔ:rɪən] *n.* **a)** *(writer of history)* Geschichtsschreiber, *der*/-schreiberin, *die;* **b)** *(scholar of history)* Historiker, *der*/Historikerin, *die*
historic [hɪ'stɒrɪk] *adj.* **a)** *(famous)* historisch; **b)** *(Ling.)* historisch ‹*Tempus usw.*›
historical [hɪ'stɒrɪkl] *adj.* **a)** historisch; geschichtlich ‹*Belege, Hintergrund*›; ~ **research** Geschichtsforschung, *die;* **of ~ interest** von historischem *od.* geschichtlichem Interesse; **b)** *(belonging to the past)* in früheren Zeiten üblich ‹*Methode*›; **be ~:** der Geschichte angehören
historically [hɪ'stɒrɪkəlɪ] *adv.* **a)** *(with respect to history)* historisch; **b)** *(as a matter of history)* in der Geschichte
history ['hɪstərɪ] *n.* **a)** *(continuous record)* Geschichte, *die;* **histories** historische Darstellungen; **b)** *no pl., no art.* Geschichte, *die; (study of past events)* Geschichte, *die;* Geschichtswissenschaft, *die;* **~ relates ...:** die Geschichte erzählt ...; **that's [all] [past] ~** das ist [alles] [längst] vergangen [und vergessen]; das gehört [alles] [längst] der Vergangenheit an; **~ repeats itself** die Geschichte wiederholt sich; **make [boxing] ~:** Geschichte [im Boxen] machen; **go down in ~:** in die Geschichte eingehen; **c)** *(train of events)* Geschichte, *die; (of person)* Werdegang, *der;* **have a ~ of asthma/shop-lifting** schon lange an Asthma leiden/eine Vorgeschichte als Ladendieb haben; **d)** *(eventful past career)* Geschichte, *die;* **he has quite a ~:** er hat eine bewegte Vergangenheit; **e)** *(Theatre)* historisches Drama; **Shakespeare's histories** Shakespeares Historien. *See also* **ancient 1a; case history; life history; medieval history; natural history**
'**history book** *n.* Geschichtsbuch, *das*
histrionic [hɪstrɪ'ɒnɪk] **1.** *adj.* **a)** schauspielerisch ‹*Talent, Fähigkeiten*›; **~ art** Schauspielkunst, *die;* **b)** *(stagy)* theatralisch *(abwertend).* **2.** *n. in pl.* **a)** *(theatrical art)* Schauspielkunst, *die;* Schauspielerei, *die;* **b)** *(melodramatic behaviour)* theatralisches Getue *(abwertend);* **forget the ~s!** laß die Schauspielerei! *(ugs. abwertend)*
hit [hɪt] **1.** *v. t.*, **-tt-, hit a)** *(strike with blow)* schlagen; *(strike with missile)* treffen; ‹*Geschoß, Ball usw.:*› treffen; **I've been ~!** *(struck by bullet)* ich bin getroffen!; **I could ~ him** *(fig. coll.)* ich könnte ihm eine runterhauen *(ugs.);* **the ball ~ me in the face** der Ball traf mich ins Gesicht; **~ sb. over the head** jmdm. eins überziehen *(ugs.);* **~ one's thumb** sich *(Dat.)* auf den Daumen schlagen; **~ by lightning** vom Blitz getroffen; **~ a man when he's down** *(fig.)* jmdn. treten, der schon am Boden liegt; *see also* **belt 1a; nail 1b; note 1a; b)** *(come forcibly into contact with)* ‹*Fahrzeug:*› prallen gegen ‹*Mauer usw.*›; ‹*Schiff:*› laufen gegen ‹*Felsen usw.*›; **the aircraft ~ the ground** das Flugzeug schlug auf den Boden auf; **the noise of the hammer ~ting the anvil** das Geräusch des Hammers beim Auftreffen auf den Amboß; **~ the roof** *or* **ceiling** *(fig. coll.: become angry)* an die Decke *od.* in die Luft gehen *(ugs.);* **c)** *(cause to come into contact)* [an]stoßen; [an]schlagen; **~ one's head on sth.** mit dem Kopf gegen etw. stoßen; sich *(Dat.)* den Kopf an etw. *(Dat.)* stoßen; **d)** *(deliver)* **~ a blow at sb., ~ sb. a blow** jmdm. einen Schlag verpassen *(ugs.);* **e)** *(fig.: cause to suffer)* **~ badly** *or* **hard** schwer treffen; **I will ~ them very hard** *(take severe measures against)* ich werde mit aller Schärfe gegen sie vorgehen; **f)** *(fig.: affect)* treffen; **have been ~ by frost/rain** *etc.* durch Frost/Regen *usw.* gelitten haben; **g)** *(fig.: light upon)* finden; stoßen *od.* treffen auf (+ *Akk.*); finden ‹*Bodenschätze*›; **you've ~ it!** du sagst es!; **h)** *(fig.: characterize) see* **~ off; i)** *(fig. coll.) (encounter)* Bekanntschaft machen mit (+ *Dat.*) *(ugs.); (arrive at)* erreichen ‹*Höchstform, bestimmten Ort, bestimmte Höhe, bestimmtes Alter usw.*›; **I think we've ~ a snag** ich glaube, jetzt gibt's Probleme; **~ a pool of water** ‹*Auto:*› in eine [Wasser]pfütze fahren; **~ an all-time high** ‹*Preis:*› eine Rekordhöhe erreichen; **the car can ~ 100 miles an hour** das Auto schafft 100 Meilen in der Stunde *(ugs.);* **they ~ all the night-spots** sie statteten allen Nachtlokalen einen Besuch ab *(ugs.);* **~ town** ankommen; **~ the trail** *(Amer. sl.) or* **the road** sich auf den Weg *od. (ugs.)* die Socken machen; **~ the hay** *(sl.)* in die Falle gehen *(ugs.);* sich in die Falle hauen *(ugs.);* **j)** *(fig. coll.: indulge in)* zuschlagen bei (+ *Dat.*) *(salopp);* **[begin to] ~ the bottle** das Trinken anfangen; **k)** *(Cricket)* erzielen ‹*Lauf*›; **~ the ball for six** *(Brit.)* sechs Läufe auf einmal erzielen; **~ sb. for six** *(Brit.)* gegen jmdn. sechs Läufe erzielen; *(fig.: defeat)* jmdn. übertrumpfen; **~ the enemy for six** *(Brit.)* den Feind zerschmettern. **2.** *v. i.*, **-tt-, hit a)** *(direct a blow)* schlagen; **~ hard** fest *od.* hart zuschlagen; **~ at sb./sth.** auf jmdn./etw. einschlagen; *(fig.: criticize)* jmdn./etw. kritisieren; **~ at sth. as being extravagant** etw. als extravagant geißeln; **~ and run** ‹*Autofahrer:*› Fahrer- *od.* Unfallflucht begehen; ‹*Angreifer:*› einen Blitzüberfall machen; *see also* **hit-and-run; b)** *(come into forcible contact)* **~ against** *or* **upon sth.** gegen *od.* auf etw. *(Akk.)* stoßen. **3.** *n.* **a)** *(blow)* Schlag, *der;* **b)** *(sarcastic remark)* Seitenhieb, *der* **(at** gegen); Spitze, *die* **(at** gegen); *(censure, rebuke)* Angriff, *der;* **that's a ~ at me** das geht gegen mich; **c)** *(shot or bomb striking target)* Treffer, *der;* **d)** *(success)* Erfolg, *der;* Knüller, *der (ugs.); (success in entertainment)* Schlager, *der;* Hit, *der (ugs.);* **make a ~:** gut ankommen; **make** *or* **be a ~ with sb.** bei jmdm. einschlagen *od.* gut ankommen; **I'm sure she'll be** *or* **make a [big] ~:** ich bin sicher, sie wird [ganz] groß herauskommen *(ugs.);* **e)** *(stroke of luck)* Glückstreffer, *der*
~ 'back 1. *v. t.* zurückschlagen. **2.** *v. i.* zurückschlagen; *(verbally)* kontern; sich wehren; **~ back at sb.** *(fig.)* jmdm. Kontra geben
~ 'off *v. t.* **a)** *(characterize)* genau treffen; treffend charakterisieren; **b) ~ it off [with each other]** miteinander auskommen; sich verstehen; **~ it off with sb.** mit jmdm. auskommen; sich mit jmdm. verstehen
~ on *see* **~ upon**
~ 'out *v. i.* **a)** *(aim blows)* drauflosschlagen; **b) ~ out at** *or* **against sb./sth.** *(fig.)* jmdn./etw. scharf angreifen *od.* attackieren
~ upon *v. t.* stoßen auf (+ *Akk.*); finden ‹*richtige Antwort, Methode*›; kommen auf (+ *Akk.*) ‹*Idee*›
hit: ~-and-'miss *see* **~-or-miss; ~-and-'run** *adj.* **a)** unfallflüchtig ‹*Fahrer*›; **~-and-run accident** Unfall mit Fahrerflucht; **b)** Blitz‹*angriff, -überfall*›; **~-and-run tactics** Taktik des Blitzüberfalls
hitch [hɪtʃ] **1.** *v. t.* **a)** *(move by a jerk)* rücken; **b)** *(fasten)* [fest]binden ‹*Tier*› **(to** an + *Akk.*); binden ‹*Seil*› **(round** um + *Akk.*); [an]koppeln ‹*Anhänger usw.*› **(to** an + *Akk.*); spannen ‹*Zugtier, -maschine usw.*› **(to** vor + *Akk.*); **get ~ed** *(sl.)* heiraten; *see also* **wagon a; c) ~ a lift** *or* **ride** *(coll.)* per Anhalter fahren; trampen; **he was trying to ~ a lift** *or* **ride** er wollte mitgenommen werden. **2.** *v. i. see* **hitch-hike 1. 3.** *n.* **a)** *(jerk)* Ruck, *der;* **give sth. a ~:** an etw. *(Dat.)* rucken; **b)** *(Naut.: knot)* Stek, *der (Seemannsspr.);* **half ~:** halber Schlag; *see also* **clove hitch; c)** *(stoppage)* Unterbrechung, *die;* **go off without a ~:** glatt *od.* reibungslos über die Bühne gehen; **d)** *(impediment)* Problem, *das;* Schwierigkeit, *die;* **have one ~:** einen Haken haben *(ugs.);* **e)** *see* **hitch-hike 2**
~ 'up *v. t.* **a)** hochheben ‹*Rock*›; **~ up one's trousers** seinen Hosenbund hochziehen; **b)** *(Amer.: attach)* anspannen
hitch: ~-hike 1. *v. i.* per Anhalter fahren; trampen; **2.** *n.* Tramptour, *die;* **~-hiker** *n.* Anhalter, *der*/Anhalterin, *die;* Tramper, *der*/Tramperin, *die;* **~-hiking** *n.* Trampen, *das*
hitching-post ['hɪtʃɪŋpəʊst] *n.* Pfosten, *der (zum Anbinden von Zug- und Reittieren)*
hi-tech *adj. see* **high-tech**
hither ['hɪðə(r)] *adv. (literary)* hierher; **~ and thither** *or* **yon** hierhin und dorthin; *see also* **come-hither**
hitherto ['hɪðətʊ, hɪðə'tu:] *adv. (literary)* bisher; bislang; *(up to that time)* bis dahin
hit: ~ list *n.* **a)** *(charts) see* **~ parade; b)** *(victims)* Abschußliste, *die (fig.);* **~ man** *n. (Amer.)* Killer, *der (salopp);* **~-or-'miss** *adj. (coll.) (random)* unsicher, unzuverlässig ‹*Methode*›; *(careless)* schlampig, schluderig *(ugs. abwertend)* ‹*Arbeit*›; **it was a very ~-or-miss affair** das ging alles aufs Geratewohl *(ugs.);* **~ parade** *n.* Hitparade, *die;* Schlagerparade, *die;* **~ 'record** *n.* Hit, *der (ugs.)*
Hittite ['hɪtaɪt] **1.** *n.* **a)** Hethiter, *der*/Hethiterin, *die;* **b)** *(Ling.)* Hethitisch, *das.* **2.** *adj.* hethitisch
HIV *abbr. (Med.)* **human immunodeficiency virus** HIV; **HIV-positive/-negative** HIV-positiv/-negativ
hive [haɪv] **1.** *n.* **a)** [Bienen]stock, *der; (of straw)* Bienenkorb, *der;* **frame ~:** Bienenkasten, *der;* **b)** *(fig.: busy place)* **what a ~ of industry!** der reinste Bienenstock! *(ugs.);* **the office is a [regular] ~ of industry** in dem Büro geht es zu wie in einem Bienenstock. **2.** *v. t.* in einen Stock bringen, einfangen ‹*Bienen*›
~ 'off *(Brit.)* **1.** *v. i.* ‹*Firma, Abteilung:*› sich abspalten **(from** von). **2.** *v. t. (separate and make independent)* verselbständigen; *(assign)* zuweisen, übertragen ‹*Aufgabe usw.*› **(to** *Dat.*); **the firm was ~d off from the parent company** die Firma wurde aus der Muttergesellschaft ausgegliedert
hiya ['haɪjə] *int. (coll.)* hallo!
HM *abbr.* **a) Her/His Majesty** I. M./S. M.; **b) Her/His Majesty's; c) headmaster/headmistress** ≈ Dir.
HMG *abbr. (Brit.)* **Her/His Majesty's Government**
HMI *abbr. (Brit.)* **Her/His Majesty's Inspector [of Schools]**
HMS *abbr. (Brit.)* **Her/His Majesty's Ship** H.M.S.
HMSO *abbr. (Brit.)* **Her/His Majesty's Stationery Office**
HNC *abbr. (Brit.)* **Higher National Certificate**
HND *abbr. (Brit.)* **Higher National Diploma**
ho [həʊ] *int.* **a)** *expr. surprise* oh; nanu; *expr. admiration* oh; *expr. triumph* ha; *drawing attention* he; heda; *expr. derision* haha; **land ~!** Land in Sicht!; **b)** *(Naut.: rallying cry)* **westward ~!** auf nach Westen!
hoard [hɔ:d] **1.** *n.* **a)** *(store laid by)* Vorrat, *der;* **make/collect a ~ of sth.** etw. horten; **b)** *(fig.: amassed stock)* Sammlung, *die;* **he had accumulated a ~ of grievances** bei ihm hatten sich eine Menge Klagen angehäuft *od.* angestaut; **c)** *(Archaeol.)* Hort, *der (fachspr.).* **2.** *v. t.* **~ [up]** horten ‹*Geld, Brennmaterial, Lebensmittel usw.*›; hamstern ‹*Lebensmittel*›. **3.** *v. i.* horten
hoarder ['hɔ:də(r)] *n.* Hamsterer, *der*/Hamsterin, *die*
¹hoarding ['hɔ:dɪŋ] *n.* Horten, *das;* Hamstern, *das*

[2]**hoarding** *n.* **a)** *(fence)* Bretterzaun, *der;* Bretterwand, *die; (round building-site)* Bauzaun, *der;* **b)** *(Brit.: for advertisements)* Reklamewand, *die;* Plakatwand, *die*

hoar-frost ['hɔ:frɒst] *n.* [Rauh]reif, *der*

hoarse [hɔ:s] *adj.* **a)** *(rough, husky)* heiser ⟨*Laut*⟩; heiser, rauh ⟨*Stimme*⟩; *(croaking)* krächzend ⟨*Laut*⟩; *(with emotion)* belegt ⟨*Stimme*⟩; **b)** *(having a dry, husky voice)* heiser; **shout oneself ~**: sich heiser schreien

hoarsely ['hɔ:slɪ] *adv. (in a hoarse voice)* heiser ⟨*sprechen*⟩; mit heiserer Stimme ⟨*reden, schreien, singen*⟩; *(in an emotional voice)* mit belegter Stimme

hoarseness ['hɔ:snɪs] *n.* Heiserkeit, *die*

hoary ['hɔ:rɪ] *adj.* **a)** *(grey)* grau; ergraut *(geh.); (white)* [schloh]weiß; **become ~**: grau werden, *(geh.)* ergrauen/weiß werden; **b)** *(having grey hair)* grauhaarig; ergraut *(geh.); (having white hair)* weißhaarig; **c)** *(very old)* altehrwürdig ⟨*Gebäude*⟩; **~ old joke** uralter Witz

hoax [həʊks] **1.** *v.t.* anführen *(ugs.);* foppen; zum besten haben *od.* halten; **I'd been ~ed** ich hatte mich anführen *(ugs.) od.* foppen lassen; **~ sb. into believing sth.** jmdm. etw. weismachen. **2.** *n. (deception)* Schwindel, *der; (false report)* Falschmeldung, *die;* Ente, *die (ugs.); (practical joke)* Streich, *der; (false alarm)* blinder Alarm

hoaxer ['həʊksə(r)] *n.* Schwindler, *der*/Schwindlerin, *die*

hob [hɒb] *n.* **a)** *(of cooker)* Kochmulde, *die (Fachspr.);* [Koch]platte, *die;* Kochstelle, *die;* **b)** *(at side of fireplace)* Kamineinsatz, *der;* **c)** *(peg)* Zielpflock, *der*

hobble ['hɒbl] **1.** *v.i.* **~ [about]** [herum]humpeln *od.* -hinken. **2.** *v.t.* **a)** *(cause to ~)* [beim Gehen] behindern; **b)** *(tie together legs of)* an den Füßen fesseln ⟨*Pferd usw.*⟩; **c)** *(tie together)* fesseln ⟨*Vorderbeine*⟩. **3.** *n.* **a)** *no pl. (uneven gait)* Humpeln, *das;* Hinken, *das;* **b)** *(device for hobbling)* [Fuß]fessel, *die*

[1]**hobby** ['hɒbɪ] *n.* Hobby, *das;* Steckenpferd, *das;* **do sth. as a ~**: etw. als Hobby tun

[2]**hobby** *n. (Ornith.)* Baumfalke, *der*

'**hobby-horse** *n.* **a)** *(wicker horse)* Pferdemaske, *die;* **b)** *(child's toy)* Steckenpferd, *das;* **c)** *see* **rocking-horse; d)** *(favourite topic)* Lieblingsthema, *das;* **get on to/start on one's ~**: anfangen, sein Steckenpferd zu reiten *(scherzh.)*

hob: ~goblin *n.* **a)** *(mischievous imp)* Kobold, *der;* Puck, *der;* **b)** *(bogy)* Schreckgespenst, *das;* **~nail** *n.* [starker] Schuh- *od.* Stiefelnagel; **~nailed** ['hɒbneɪld] *adj.* Nagel⟨*schuh, -stiefel*⟩; **~-nob** *v.i.*, **-bb-: I've seen them ~-nobbing [together] a lot recently** ich habe sie in letzter Zeit viel zusammen gesehen; **he's always ~-nobbing with the aristocracy** er verkehrt viel in adeligen Kreisen

hobo ['həʊbəʊ] *n., pl.* **~es** *(Amer.)* Landstreicher, *der*/-streicherin, *die*

Hobson's choice [hɒbsnz 'tʃɔɪs] *n.* **it was [a case of] ~**: es gab eigentlich gar keine Wahl

[1]**hock** [hɒk] *(joint of quadruped's leg)* Sprunggelenk, *das*

[2]**hock** *n. (Brit.: wine)* Rheinwein, *der*

[3]**hock** *(Amer. coll.)* **1.** *v.t.* versetzen. **2.** *n.* **be in ~** *(in pawn)* versetzt sein; *(in prison)* [im Kittchen *od.* Knast] sitzen *(ugs.);* Knast schieben *(salopp); (in debt)* in Schulden stecken; **put sth. in ~**: etw. versetzen; **put sb. in ~** *(in debt)* jmdn. in Schulden stürzen; *(in prison)* jmdn. einlochen *(salopp);* **be in ~ to sb.** bei jmdm. in der Kreide stehen *(ugs.)*

hockey ['hɒkɪ] *n.* **a)** Hockey, *das;* **b)** *(Can.) see* **ice hockey**

hockey: ~-player *n.* Hockeyspieler, *der*/-spielerin, *die;* **~-stick** *n.* Hockeystock, *der;* Hockeyschläger, *der*

hocus-pocus [həʊkəs'pəʊkəs] *n. (deception)* Zauberei, *die*

hod [hɒd] *n.* **a)** *(Building)* Tragmulde, *die;* **b)** *(for coal)* Kohlenschütte, *die*

hodgepodge ['hɒdʒpɒdʒ] *see* **hotchpotch**

hoe [həʊ] **1.** *n.* Hacke, *die; see also* **Dutch hoe. 2.** *v.t.* hacken ⟨*Beet, Acker*⟩; **~ up** weg- *od.* heraushacken ⟨*Unkraut*⟩; **~ down** weg- *od.* umhacken ⟨*Büsche*⟩; **~ in** einhacken; *see also* **hard 1b. 3.** *v.i.* hacken

'**hoe-down** *n. (Amer.)* **a)** *(dance)* Hoedown, *der;* **b)** *(party)* Schwof, *der (ugs.)*

hog [hɒg] **1.** *n.* **a)** *(domesticated pig)* [Mast]schwein, *das;* **go the whole ~** *(coll.)* Nägel mit Köpfen machen *(ugs.);* **go the whole ~ with sb.** so weit wie jmd. gehen; **live high off** *or* **on the ~** *(Amer.)* aus dem vollen leben; **b)** *(Zool.: animal of family Suidae)* Schwein, *das;* **c)** *(fig.: person)* Schwein, *das (derb);* Sau, *die (derb);* Ferkel, *das (derb).* **2.** *v.t.*, **-gg-** *(coll.)* sich *(Dat.)* unter den Nagel reißen; **~ the middle of the road** ⟨*Fahrer:*⟩ die ganze Straße für sich beanspruchen; **~ the bathroom** das Badezimmer mit Beschlag belegen

'**hog-back** *n. (Geog.)* [scharfer, steiler und langer] Grat

hoggish ['hɒgɪʃ] *adj.* verfressen *(salopp abwertend)*

Hogmanay ['hɒgmənei] *n. (Scot., N. Engl.)* Silvester, *der od. das*

hog's back ['hɒgz bæk] *see* **hog-back**

hogshead ['hɒgzhed] *n.* **a)** *(cask)* [großes] Faß; Oxhoftfaß, *das;* **b)** *(measure)* Oxhoft, *das*

hog: ~-tie *v.t. (Amer.)* **a)** *(secure)* an Händen und Füßen fesseln ⟨*Person*⟩; an allen vieren fesseln ⟨*Tier*⟩; **b)** *(fig.: impede)* in ein zu enges Korsett zwängen; **sb. is ~-tied** jmdm. sind Hände und Füße gebunden; **~-wash** *n.* **a)** *(coll.: nonsense)* Quatsch, *der (salopp);* **b)** *(pigswill)* Schweinefutter, *das;* **~weed** *n. (Bot.)* Wiesenbärenklau, *der*

ho-'ho *int. expr. surprise* ach ne!; *expr. triumph, derision* haha!

hoick [hɔɪk] *v.t. (sl.)* wuchten ⟨*[schweren] Gegenstand*⟩ **(over** über + *Akk.*, **into** in + *Akk.*)

hoi polloi [hɔɪ pə'lɔɪ] *n. pl. (literary)* **[the] ~**: das [gemeine] Volk; die Masse; der Pöbel *(abwertend)*

hoist [hɔɪst] **1.** *v.t.* **a)** *(raise aloft)* hoch-, aufziehen, hissen ⟨*Flagge usw.*⟩; heißen *(Seemannsspr.)* ⟨*Flagge usw.*⟩; setzen *(Seemannsspr.)* ⟨*Signal usw.*⟩; **~ sth. up a mast** etw. an einem Mast hoch-/aufziehen/hissen/heißen/setzen; **b)** *(raise by tackle etc.)* hieven ⟨*Last*⟩; setzen ⟨*Segel*⟩. **2.** *n.* **a)** *(act of hoisting)* [Hoch]hieven, *das;* **b)** *(part of flag)* Liek, *das;* **c)** *(goods lift)* [Lasten]aufzug, *der.* **3.** *adj.* **be ~ with one's own petard** sich in seiner eigenen Schlinge fangen

hoity-toity [hɔɪtɪ'tɔɪtɪ] *adj. (coll.)* hochnäsig *(abwertend);* eingebildet; *(petulant)* pikiert

hokum ['həʊkəm] *n. (sl.)* Humbug, *der*

[1]**hold** [həʊld] *n. (of ship)* Laderaum, *der; (of aircraft)* Frachtraum, *der*

[2]**hold 1.** *v.t.*, **held** [held] **a)** *(grasp)* halten; *(carry)* tragen; *(keep fast)* festhalten; **~ sb. by the arm** jmdn. am Arm festhalten; **they held each other tight** sie hielten sich fest umschlungen; **~ one's belly/head** *etc.* sich *(Dat.)* den Bauch/Kopf *usw.* halten; **~ tight!** *(in bus etc.)* festhalten!; *see also* **baby 1a; clock 1a; hand 1a; nose 1a; b)** *(support)* ⟨*tragendes Teil:*⟩ halten, stützen, tragen ⟨*Decke, Dach usw.*⟩; aufnehmen ⟨*Gewicht, Kraft*⟩; **c)** *(keep in position)* halten; **~ the door open for sb.** jmdm. die Tür aufhalten; **~ sth. in place** etw. halten; **~ sth. over sb.** *(fig.)* jmdm. ständig mit etw. drohen; *see also* **candle 1a; d)** *(grasp to control)* halten ⟨*Kind, Hund, Zügel*⟩; **e)** *(keep in particular attitude)* **~ oneself well/badly/straight** sich gut/schlecht/gerade halten; **~ oneself still** stillhalten; **~ oneself ready** *or* **in readiness** sich bereit *od.* in Bereitschaft halten; **~ oneself ready** *or* **in readiness to do sth.** jederzeit bereit sein, etw. zu tun; **~ one's head high** *(fig.) (be confident)* selbstbewußt sein *od.* auftreten; *(be proud)* den Kopf hoch tragen; **f)** *(contain)* enthalten; bergen ⟨*Gefahr, Geheimnis*⟩; *(be able to contain)* fassen ⟨*Liter, Personen usw.*⟩; **the bag ~s flour** in dem Sack wird Mehl aufbewahrt; **the room ~s ten people** in dem Raum haben 10 Leute Platz; der Raum bietet 10 Leuten Platz; **the box won't ~ these books** diese Bücher gehen nicht in die Kiste; **the disaster may ~ lessons for the future** aus dem Unglück kann man vielleicht Lehren für die Zukunft ziehen; **no one knows what the future will ~**: niemand weiß, was die Zukunft bringt *od.* bringen wird; **~ water** ⟨*Behälter:*⟩ wasserdicht sein; Wasser halten; *(fig.)* ⟨*Argument, Theorie:*⟩ stichhaltig sein, hieb- und stichfest sein; ⟨*Annahme, Theorie, Alibi:*⟩ haltbar sein; **g)** *(not be intoxicated by)* **he can/can't ~ his drink** *or* **liquor** er kann etwas/nichts vertragen; **h)** *(possess)* besitzen; haben; halten *(Wirtsch.)* ⟨*Aktien, Anteile*⟩; **i)** *(Cards: have in one's hand)* [auf der Hand] haben; **j)** *(have gained)* halten ⟨*Rekord*⟩; haben ⟨*Diplom, Doktorgrad*⟩; **k)** *(keep possession of)* halten ⟨*Stützpunkt, Stadt, Stellung*⟩; *(Mus.: sustain)* [aus]halten ⟨*Ton*⟩; **~ one's own** *(fig.)* sich behaupten; **~ one's position** *(fig.)* auf seinem Standpunkt beharren; **~ the line on the price/over one's demands** den Preis [stabil] halten/in seinen Forderungen hart *od.* fest bleiben; *see also* **l; fort; [1]ground 1b; l)** *(occupy)* innehaben, *(geh.)* bekleiden ⟨*Posten, Amt, Stellung*⟩; **~ office** im Amt sein; **~ the line** *(Teleph.)* am Apparat bleiben; *see also* **k; ~ the road** nicht von der Straße abkommen; **~ the road well** ⟨*Auto:*⟩ eine gute Straßenlage haben; **m)** *(engross)* fesseln, *(geh.)* gefangenhalten ⟨*Aufmerksamkeit, Publikum*⟩; **n)** *(dominate)* **~ the stage** *or* **house** das Publikum *od.* ganze Haus in Bann halten *(geh.);* **~ the floor** das Wort führen; das Gespräch/die Diskussion/Debatte *usw.* beherrschen *od.* bestimmen; *see also* **field 1e; o)** *(keep in specified condition)* halten; **~ the ladder steady** die Leiter festhalten; **~ the audience in suspense** das Publikum fesseln; *see also* **[4]bay 1; ransom 1; p)** *(detain) (in custody)* in Haft halten, festhalten; *(imprison)* festsetzen; inhaftieren; *(arrest)* festnehmen; **be held in a prison** in einem Gefängnis einsitzen; **~ a [connecting] train** einen [Anschluß]zug warten lassen; **there was nothing to ~ me there** da hielt mich nichts mehr; **q)** *(oblige to adhere)* **~ sb. to the terms of the contract/to a promise** darauf bestehen, daß jmd. sich an die Vertragsbestimmungen hält/daß jmd. ein Versprechen hält *od.* einlöst; **You can have the car when I go abroad – I'll ~ you to that** Du kannst das Auto haben, wenn ich ins Ausland gehe – Ich werde dich beim Wort nehmen; **r)** *(Sport: restrict)* **~ one's opponent [to a draw]** ein Unentschieden [gegen den Gegner] halten *od.* verteidigen; **~ one's opponents to three goals** die Zahl der gegnerischen Tore bei drei halten; **s)** *(cause to take place)* stattfinden lassen; abhalten ⟨*Veranstaltung, Konferenz, Gottesdienst, Sitzung, Prüfung*⟩; veranstalten ⟨*Festival, Auktion*⟩; austragen ⟨*Meisterschaften*⟩; führen ⟨*Unterhaltung, Gespräch, Korrespondenz*⟩; durchführen ⟨*Untersuchung*⟩; geben ⟨*Empfang*⟩; halten ⟨*Vortrag, Rede*⟩; **be held** stattfinden; **~ a conversation with sb.** eine Unterhaltung mit jmdm. führen *od.* haben; sich mit jmdm. unterhalten; *see also* **court 1c; t)** *(restrain)* [fest]halten; **~ sb. from doing sth.** jmdn. davon abhalten, etw. zu tun; **~ one's noise** leise sein; **~ one's fire** [noch] nicht schießen; *(fig.: refrain from*

criticism) mit seiner Kritik zurückhalten; ~ **your fire!** nicht schießen!; *(fig.)* nun mal sachte! *(ugs.)*; **there is/was no ~ing sb.** jmdn. ist/war nicht mehr zu halten *od.* *(ugs.)* bremsen; für jmdn. gibt/gab es kein Halten mehr; *see also* **breath a; hand 1 b; peace b; u)** *(coll.: withhold)* zurückhalten; ~ **one's payments** mit der Abzahlung säumig sein; ~ **it!** [einen] Moment mal!; ~ **everything!** stopp! *(ugs.)*; *see also* **horse 1 a; v)** *(think, believe)* ~ **a view** *or* **an opinion** eine Ansicht haben **(on** über + *Akk.*); ~ **that ...:** dafürhalten, daß ...; der Ansicht sein, daß ...; ~ **sb. to be ...:** jmdn. für ... halten; glauben, daß jmd. ... ist; ~ **sb./oneself guilty/blameless** jmdn./sich für schuldig/unschuldig halten **(for** an + *Dat.*); ~ **oneself responsible for sth.** sich für etw. verantwortlich fühlen; ~ **sb. in high/low regard** *or* **esteem** viel/wenig von jmdm. halten; jmdn. hochschätzen *(geh.)*/geringschätzen; ~ **sth. against sb.** jmdm. etw. vorwerfen; ~ **it against sb. that ...:** jmdm. vorwerfen, daß ...; *see also* **cheap 1 c; dear 1 a; responsible a; w)** *(Law: pronounce)* ~ **that ...:** entscheiden, daß ... **2.** *v. i.*, **held a)** *(not give way)* ⟨*Seil, Nagel, Anker, Schloß, Angeklebtes:*⟩ halten; ⟨*Damm:*⟩ [stand]halten; **b)** *(remain unchanged)* anhalten; [an]dauern; ⟨*Wetter:*⟩ sich halten, so bleiben; ⟨*Angebot, Versprechen:*⟩ gelten; **his luck held** er hatte auch weiterhin Glück; **c)** *(remain steadfast)* ~ **to sth.** bei etw. bleiben; an etw. *(Dat.)* festhalten; ~ **to** *or* **by one's family** zur Familie stehen *od.* halten; ~ **by one's beliefs/convictions** tun, was man für richtig hält; **he still ~s to the view that ...:** er ist nach wie vor der Ansicht, daß ...; *see also* **aloof 1; d)** *(be valid)* ~ **[good** *or* **true]** gelten; Gültigkeit haben; **e)** *(arch.: wait)* einhalten; ~ **[hard]!** halt[et] ein! *See also* **¹still 1 a. 3.** *n.* **a)** *(grasp)* Griff, *der;* **grab** *or* **seize ~ of sth.** etw. ergreifen; **get** *or* **lay** *or* **take ~ of sth.** etw. fassen *od.* packen; *(manage to gain a grip on sth.)* etw. zu fassen kriegen *(ugs.)* *od.* bekommen; *(in order to carry it)* etw. nehmen; **keep ~ of sth.** etw. festhalten; **keep/lose one's ~:** den Halt nicht verlieren/den Halt verlieren; **lose one's ~ on reality** den Sinn für die Realität verlieren; **take ~** *(fig.)* sich durchsetzen; ⟨*Krankheit:*⟩ fortschreiten; **get ~ of sth.** *(fig.)* etw. bekommen *od.* auftreiben; **if the newspapers get ~ of the story** wenn die Zeitungen Wind von der Sache bekommen *(ugs.)*; **get ~ of sb.** *(fig.)* jmdn. erreichen; **get a ~ on oneself** sich fassen; **have a ~ over sb.** jmdn. in der Hand halten; *see also* **catch 1 a; b)** *(influence)* Einfluß, *der* **(on, over** auf + *Akk.*); **lose one's ~:** seinen Einfluß verlieren; **gain a ~:** zu Einfluß gelangen; **c)** *(Sport)* Griff, *der;* **there are no ~s barred** *(fig.)* alles ist erlaubt; **d)** *(thing to hold by)* Griff, *der;* **e) put on ~:** auf Eis legen ⟨*Plan, Programm*⟩

~ **'back 1.** *v. t.* **a)** *(restrain)* zurückhalten; ~ **sb. back from doing sth.** jmdn. [daran] hindern, etw. zu tun; **b)** *(impede progress of)* hindern; **nothing can ~ him back** er ist nicht mehr aufzuhalten; **c)** *(withhold)* zurückhalten; zurückhalten mit ⟨*Bekanntgabe von Ergebnissen, Veröffentlichung eines Berichts*⟩; ~ **sth. back from sb.** jmdm. etw. vorenthalten. **2.** *v. i.* zögern; ~ **back from doing sth.** zögern, etw. zu tun

~ **'down** *v. t.* **a)** festhalten; *(repress)* unterdrücken; niederhalten ⟨*Volk*⟩; *(fig.: keep at low level)* niedrig halten ⟨*Preise, Löhne usw.*⟩; **b)** *(keep)* sich halten in (+ *Dat.*) ⟨*Stellung, Position*⟩

~ **'forth 1.** *v. t. (offer)* anpreisen. **2.** *v. i.* sich in langen Reden ergehen *(oft abwertend)*; ~ **forth about** *or* **on sth.** sich über etw. *(Akk.)* auslassen *(abwertend)*

~ **'in** *v. t.* zügeln ⟨*Pferd, Temperament*⟩; einziehen ⟨*Bauch*⟩; ~ **oneself in** *(temper, emotions)* sich beherrschen; an sich *(Akk.)* halten; *(stomach)* den Bauch einziehen

~ **'off 1.** *v. t. (keep at bay)* von sich fernhalten, *(ugs.)* sich *(Dat.)* vom Leib halten ⟨*Fans, Presse*⟩; in Schach halten ⟨*gegnerische Stürmer*⟩; abwehren ⟨*Angriff*⟩; Einhalt gebieten (+ *Dat.*) ⟨*Inflation, Arbeitslosigkeit*⟩; **he's been ~ing her off for years** er hat sie jahrelang immer wieder abgewiesen; ~ **your dog off!** halten Sie Ihren Hund zurück! **2.** *v. i. (restrain oneself)* ⟨*Käufer usw.:*⟩ sich zurückhalten; ⟨*Feind:*⟩ sich ruhig verhalten; *(be delayed)* ⟨*Regen, Monsun, Winter:*⟩ ausbleiben; auf sich *(Akk.)* warten lassen

~ **'on 1.** *v. t. (keep in position)* [fest]halten. **2.** *v. i.* **a)** *(continue)* andauern; weitergehen; **b)** *(stand firm)* durchhalten; aushalten; ⟨*Regierung:*⟩ sich halten; **c)** ~ **on to sb./sth.** sich an jmdm./etw. festhalten; *(fig.: retain)* jmdn./etw. behalten; **the firm should make every effort to ~ on to him** die Firma sollte alles versuchen, ihn zu halten; **d)** *(Teleph.)* am Apparat bleiben; dranbleiben *(ugs.)*; **e)** *(coll.: wait)* warten; ~ **on!** einen Moment!; **just [you] ~ on now!** *(calm yourself)* nun mal ganz ruhig!; Moment mal!

~ **'out 1.** *v. t.* **a)** *(stretch forth)* ausstrecken ⟨*Hand, Arm usw.*⟩; ausbreiten ⟨*Arme*⟩; hinhalten ⟨*Tasse, Teller*⟩; **b)** *(fig.: offer)* in Aussicht stellen **(to** *Dat.*); **he did not ~ out much hope of the patient's recovery** er hat mir/uns/ihm *usw.* keine großen Hoffnungen gemacht, daß der Patient wieder gesund wird. **2.** *v. i.* **a)** *(maintain resistance)* sich halten; **b)** *(last)* ⟨*Vorräte:*⟩ vorhalten; ⟨*Motor:*⟩ halten; durchhalten *(ugs.)*; **c)** ~ **out for sth.** etw. herauszuschinden versuchen *(ugs.)*; **d)** ~ **out [on sb.]** *(coll.: withhold knowledge)* [jmdm.] etwas verschweigen

~ **'over** *v. t.* vertagen **(till** auf + *Akk.*)

~ **to'gether 1.** *v. t.* zusammenhalten. **2.** *v. i. (lit. or fig.)* zusammenhalten

~ **'under** *v. t.* unter Wasser drücken; *(fig.)* unterdrücken ⟨*Land, Volk, usw.*⟩

~ **'up 1.** *v. t.* **a)** *(raise)* hochhalten; hochheben ⟨*Person*⟩; [hoch]heben ⟨*Hand, Kopf*⟩; ~ **sth. up to the light** etw. ins Licht/*(to see through it)* gegen das Licht halten; ~ **up one's head** *(fig.)* seine Selbstachtung nicht verlieren; **he'd never be able to ~ his head up again** er könnte seine Selbstachtung niemals mehr wiedergewinnen; **b)** *(fig.: offer as an example)* ~ **sb. up as ...:** jmdn. als ... hinstellen; ~ **sb. up as an example** jmdn. als [leuchtendes] Vorbild hinstellen; ~ **sb./sth. up to ridicule/scorn** jmdn./etw. dem Spott/Hohn preisgeben; **c)** *(support)* stützen; tragen ⟨*Dach usw.*⟩; *(fig.: give support to)* stützen ⟨*Regime*⟩; ~ **sth. up with sth.** etw. mit etw. abstützen; **d)** *(delay)* aufhalten; behindern ⟨*Verkehr, Versorgung*⟩; verzögern ⟨*Friedensvertrag*⟩; *(halt)* ins Stocken bringen ⟨*Produktion*⟩; **e)** *(rob)* überfallen [und ausrauben]. *See also* **hold-up. 2.** *v. i.* **a)** *(under scrutiny)* sich als stichhaltig erweisen; **b)** ⟨*Wetter:*⟩ schön bleiben, sich halten

~ **with** *v. t.* ~**/not ~ with sth.** mit etw. einverstanden sein/etw. ablehnen

holdall ['həʊldɔ:l] *n.* Reisetasche, *die*

holder ['həʊldə(r)] *n.* **a)** *(of post)* Inhaber, *der*/Inhaberin, *die;* **b)** *(of title)* Träger, *der*/Trägerin, *die;* Inhaber, *der*/Inhaberin, *die; (Sport)* Titelhalter, -inhaber, *der; (shareholder)* Aktionär, *der;* Aktieninhaber, *der;* **in the Cup Final, the ~s were beaten** im Pokalendspiel wurden die Pokalverteidiger geschlagen; **c)** ⟨*Zigaretten*⟩spitze, *die;* ⟨*Schirm*⟩ständer, *der;* ⟨*Papier-, Feder-, Zahnputzglas*⟩halter, *der;* **flowerpot-~:** Übertopf, *der*

holding ['həʊldɪŋ] *n.* **a)** *(tenure)* Land-, Grundbesitz, *der;* **b)** *(land held)* Gut, *das; see also* **smallholding; c)** *(property held)* Besitz, *der; (stocks or shares)* Anteil, *der*

holding: ~ **company** *n. (Commerc.)* Holding[gesellschaft], *die;* ~ **operation** *n.* Aktion zur Schadensbegrenzung

'hold-up *n.* **a)** *(robbery)* [Raub]überfall, *der;* **b)** *(stoppage)* Unterbrechung, *die; (delay)* Verzögerung, *die;* **run into a traffic ~** in einen [Verkehrs]stau geraten; **there are ~s on the motorway** auf der Autobahn kommt es zu erheblichen Behinderungen

hole [həʊl] **1.** *n.* **a)** Loch, *das;* **make a ~ in sth.** *(fig.)* eine ganze Menge von etw. verschlingen; **be a round/square peg in a square/round ~** *(fig.)* es nicht gut getroffen haben; **be in ~s** voller Löcher sein; **pick ~s in** Löcher machen in (+ *Akk.*) ⟨*Pullover usw.*⟩; *(fig.: find fault with)* zerpflücken *(ugs.)*; auseinandernehmen *(ugs.)*; madig machen *(ugs.)* ⟨*Person*⟩; **be full of ~s** *(fig.)* viele Schwächen haben; ~ **in the heart** Loch in der Herzscheidewand; Septumdefekt, *der (fachspr.)*; **they need it like a ~ in the head** *(coll.)* das ist das Letzte, was sie gebrauchen können *(ugs.)*; **b)** *(burrow) (of fox, badger, rabbit)* Bau, *der; (of mouse)* Loch, *das;* **c)** *(coll.) (dingy abode)* Loch, *das (salopp abwertend); (wretched place)* Kaff, *das (ugs. abwertend);* Nest, *das (ugs. abwertend);* **d)** *(sl.: awkward situation)* Klemme, *die (ugs.)*; Patsche, *die (ugs.)*; **be in a ~:** in der Klemme sein *od.* Patsche sitzen; **e)** *(Golf)* Loch, *das; (space between tee and ~)* [Spiel]bahn, *die; (point scored)* Loch, *das;* ~ **in one** Hole-in-One, *das;* As, *das. See also* **¹burn 2 a. 2.** *v. t.* **a)** Löcher/ein Loch machen in (+ *Akk.*); **be ~d** Löcher/ein Loch haben; **b)** *(Naut.: pierce side of)* **be ~d** leckschlagen *(Seemannsspr.)*; **c)** *(Golf) see* ~ **out**

~ **'out** *v. t. (Golf)* einlochen; *abs.* ~ **out in one** ein Hole-in-One *od.* As spielen

~ **'up** *v. i. (Amer. coll.)* sich verkriechen *(ugs.)*

hole-and-'corner *adj.* zwielichtig; anrüchig

holiday ['hɒlɪdeɪ, 'hɒlɪdɪ] **1.** *n.* **a)** *(day of recreation)* [arbeits]freier Tag; *(day of festivity)* Feiertag, *der;* **the whole country was given a ~:** das ganze Land bekam einen Tag [arbeits]frei; **tomorrow is a ~:** morgen ist frei/Feiertag; *see also* **bank holiday; national holiday; public holiday; b)** *in sing. or pl. (Brit.: vacation)* Urlaub, *der; (Sch.)* [Schul]ferien *Pl.*; **need a ~:** urlaubsreif sein; **have a good ~!** schönen Urlaub!; *(at Christmas etc.)* schöne Feiertage!; **go to Cornwall for one's ~[s]** im Urlaub/in den Ferien nach Cornwall fahren; in Cornwall urlauben *(ugs.)*; **take** *or* **have a/one's ~:** Urlaub nehmen *od.* machen/seinen Urlaub nehmen; **on ~, on one's ~s** im *od.* in seinem Urlaub; **be [away] on ~** *or* **on one's ~s** in *od.* im *od.* auf Urlaub sein; **go on [a] ~** *or* **on one's ~s** *(leave work)* in Urlaub gehen; *(go away)* in Urlaub fahren; *see also* **busman. 2.** *attrib. adj.* Urlaubs-/Ferien⟨*stimmung, -pläne*⟩; Freizeit⟨*kleidung*⟩. **3.** *v. i.* Urlaub/Ferien machen; urlauben *(ugs.)*

holiday: ~ **camp** *n.* Feriendorf, *das;* Ferienpark, *der;* ~**-maker** *n.* Urlauber, *der*/Urlauberin, *die;* ~ **resort** *n.* Ferienort, *der;* ~ **season** *n.* Urlaubszeit, *die*

holier-than-thou [həʊlɪəðən'ðaʊ] *adj. (coll.)* selbstgerecht

holiness ['həʊlɪnɪs] *n., no pl.* Heiligkeit, *die;* **His H~:** Seine Heiligkeit

holism ['hɒlɪzm, 'həʊlɪzm] *n., no pl. (Philos.)* Holismus, *der*

holistic [hɒ'lɪstɪk, həʊ'lɪstɪk] *adj. (Philos.)* holistisch

Holland ['hɒlənd] *pr. n.* Holland *(das)*

hollandaise ['hɒləndeɪz] *n. (Gastr.)* ~ **[sauce]** holländische Soße; Sauce hollandaise, *die*

holler ['hɒlə(r)] *(Amer.)* **1.** *v. i.* schreien; brüllen. **2.** *v. t.* schreien

hollow ['hɒləʊ] **1.** *adj.* **a)** *(not solid)* hohl; Hohl⟨*ziegel, -mauer, -zylinder, -kugel*⟩; **have**

~ **legs** *(joc.)* nicht satt zu kriegen sein *(ugs.)*; **b)** *(sunken)* eingefallen ‹*Wangen, Schläfen*›; hohl, tiefliegend ‹*Augen*›; nach innen gewölbt ‹*Stück Blech usw.*›; **a ~ place in the ground/road** *etc.* eine Vertiefung im Boden/in der Straße *usw.*; **c)** *(hungry)* **feel ~**: ein Loch im Bauch haben *(ugs.)*; **d)** *(echoing)* hohl ‹*Ton, Klang*›; **speak with a ~ voice** mit Grabesstimme sprechen; **e)** *(fig.: empty)* wertlos; eitel *(geh.)* ‹*Reichtum*›; oberflächlich ‹*Person*›; **f)** *(fig.: cynical)* verlogen; leer ‹*Versprechen*›; gequält ‹*Lachen*›. **2.** *n.* [Boden]senke, *die;* [Boden]vertiefung, *die; (area below general level)* Niederung, *die;* **hold sth. in the ~ of one's hand** etw. in der hohlen Hand halten. **3.** *adv.* **beat sb. ~** *(coll.)* jmdn. um Längen schlagen *(ugs.)*. **4.** *v.t.* **~ out** aushöhlen; graben ‹*Höhle*›; bohren, graben ‹*Tunnel*›

'hollow-eyed *adj.* hohläugig

hollowly ['hɒləʊlɪ] *adv.* hohl ‹*widerhallen*›

hollowness ['hɒləʊnɪs] *n. no pl.* **a)** Hohlheit, *die;* **b)** *(of voice)* Hohlheit, *die;* **c)** *(fig.) (emptiness)* Hohlheit, *die; (falseness)* Verlogenheit, *die*

'hollow-ware *n., no pl.* Geschirr, *das;* Gefäße *Pl.*

holly ['hɒlɪ] *n.* **a)** *(tree)* Stechpalme, *die;* Ilex, *der (fachspr.)*; **b)** *(foliage)* Stechpalmenzweige *Pl.*

'hollyhock *n. (Bot.)* Stockrose, *die*

¹holm [həʊm] *n. (Brit.) (islet)* kleine Insel; Holm, *der (nordd.)*; *(in a river)* Werder, *der*

²holm *n.* **~ [oak]** *(Bot.)* Steineiche, *die*

holocaust ['hɒləkɔ:st] *n. (destruction)* Massenvernichtung, *die;* **the H~**: der Holocaust; die Judenvernichtung; **nuclear ~**: atomarer Holocaust

Holocene ['hɒləsi:n] *n. (Geol.)* Holozän, *das*

hologram ['hɒləgræm] *n.* Hologramm, *das*

holography [hɒ'lɒgrəfɪ] *n., no pl., no art.* Holographie, *die*

hols [hɒlz] *n. pl. (Brit. coll.)* Ferien *Pl.*

holster ['həʊlstə(r)] *n.* [Pistolen]halfter, *die od. das*

holy ['həʊlɪ] *adj.* heilig; fromm ‹*Zweck*›; **~ saints** Heilige; **~ smoke** *or* **cow!** *(coll.)* heiliger Bimbam *(ugs.) od. (salopp)* Strohsack!

holy: H~ 'Bible *n.* Heilige Schrift; **H~ 'City** *n.* Heilige Stadt; **H~ Com'munion** *see* **communion a**; **~ 'cross** *n.* Kreuz Christi, *das;* **the sign of the ~ cross** das Kreuzzeichen; **~ day** *n.* religiöser Feiertag; **H~ 'Family** *n.* Heilige Familie; **H~ 'Father** *see* **father 1f**; **H~ 'Ghost** *see* **H~ Spirit**; **H~ Grail** *see* **Grail**; **~ 'Joe** *n. (sl. derog.)* Pfaffe, *der (abwertend)*; **H~ Land** *n.* **a)** **the H~ Land** das Heilige Land; **b)** *(revered land)* geheiligtes *od.* heiliges Land; **~ of 'holies** *n. (inner chamber, fig.: sacred place)* Allerheiligste, *das;* **~ 'orders** *see* **order 1h**; **~ place** *n.* **a)** Heilige, *das;* **b)** *in pl. (places of pilgrimage)* heilige Stätten *Pl.*; **H~ Roman 'Empire** *see* **Roman Empire**; **H~ 'Sacrament** *see* **sacrament a**; **H~ 'Saturday** *n.* Karsamstag, *der;* **H~ 'Scripture** *see* **scripture**; **H~ 'See** *see* **²see**; **H~ 'Spirit** *n. (Relig.)* Heiliger Geist; **~ 'terror** *see* **terror c**; **H~ 'Trinity** *see* **Trinity a**; **~ 'war** *n.* heiliger Krieg; **~ 'water** *n. (Eccl.)* Weihwasser, *das;* **H~ Week** *n.* Karwoche, *die*

homage ['hɒmɪdʒ] *n. (tribute)* Huldigung, *die* (to an + *Akk.*); **pay** *or* **do ~ to sb./sth.** jmdm./einer Sache huldigen

Homburg ['hɒmbɜ:g] *n.* **~ [hat]** Homburg, *der*

home [həʊm] **1.** *n.* **a)** *(place of residence)* Heim, *das; (flat)* Wohnung, *die; (house)* Haus, *das; (household)* [Eltern]haus, *das;* **my ~ is in Leeds** ich bin in Leeds zu Hause *od.* wohne in Leeds; **a ~ of one's own** ein eigenes Zuhause; **give sb./an animal a ~**: jmdm./einem Tier ein Zuhause geben; **work/be away from ~**: auswärts arbeiten/nicht zu Hause sein; **leave/have left ~**: aus dem Haus gehen/sein; **have a good ~**: ein gutes Zuhause haben; **live at ~**: im Elternhaus wohnen; **they had no ~/~s [of their own]** sie hatten kein Zuhause; **safety in the ~**: Sicherheit im Haus[halt]; **make one's ~ in the country/abroad** aufs Land ziehen/ins Ausland gehen; **at ~**: zu Hause; *(not abroad)* im Inland; **be at ~ [to sb.]** *(be available to caller)* [für jmdn.] zu sprechen sein *od.* dasein; *(Sport: play on one's own ground)* auf eigenem Platz *od.* zu Hause [gegen jmdn.] spielen; **who/what is X when he's/it's at ~?** *(joc.)* wer/was ist das denn?; **is our next match at ~ or away?** ist unser nächstes Spiel ein Heimspiel oder ein Auswärtsspiel?; **be/feel at ~** *(fig.)* sich wohl fühlen; **make sb. feel at ~**: es jmdm. behaglich machen; **make yourself at ~**: fühl dich wie zu Hause; **he is quite at ~ in French** er ist im Französischen ganz gut zu Hause; *see also* **d**; **get at-home**; **there's no place like ~** *(prov.)* es geht [doch] nichts über das eigene Zuhause; **~ from ~**: zweites Zuhause; **b)** *(fig.)* **this was something very near ~**: das war etwas, das einen sehr direkt betraf; **to take an example nearer ~, ...**: um ein Beispiel zu nehmen, das uns näher liegt, ...; *see also* **from d**; **second home**; **c)** *(Amer., Austral., NZ: dwelling-house)* Haus, *das;* **d)** *(native country)* die Heimat; **at ~**: zu Hause; in der Heimat; *see also* **a**; **e)** *(place where thing is native)* Heimat, *die;* **f)** *(institution)* Heim, *das; (coll.: mental ~)* Anstalt, *die (salopp)*; **you ought to be in a ~**: du gehörst in die Klapsmühle; *see also* **mental home**; **nursing home**; **g)** *no art. (Games: safe place)* das Mal; *(in Ludo etc.)* das Haus; *(finishing-point)* das Ziel; **h)** *(Sport: ~ win)* Heimsieg, *der.* **2.** *adj.* **a)** *(connected with home)* Haus-; Haushalts‹*gerät usw.*›; **she enjoyed her ~ life** sie genoß das Zuhausesein; **b)** *(done at home)* häuslich; Selbst‹*backen, ~brauen usw.*›; **c)** *(in the neighbourhood of home)* nahegelegen; **d)** *(Sport)* Heim‹*spiel, -sieg, -mannschaft*›; ‹*Anhänger, Spieler*› der Heimmannschaft; **~ ground** eigener Platz; **e)** *(not foreign)* [ein]heimisch; inländisch; *see also* **trade**. **3.** *adv.* **a)** *(to home)* nach Hause; **find one's way ~**: nach Hause finden; **on one's way ~**: auf dem Weg nach Hause *od.* Nachhauseweg; **get ~**: nach Hause kommen; *(to the finishing-point)* das Ziel erreichen; **get ~ by inches** um eine Nasenlänge gewinnen; **Pierre is going ~ to France tomorrow** Pierre fährt morgen nach Frankreich zurück; **be going ~** *(fig.: be becoming unserviceable)* den Geist aufgeben *(ugs.)*; **he takes ~ £200 a week after tax** er verdient 200 Pfund netto in der Woche; **nothing to write ~ about** *(coll.)* nichts Besonderes *od.* Aufregendes; **b)** *(arrived at home)* zu Hause; **the first competitor ~ was Paul** als erster [Teilnehmer] traf Paul am Ziel ein *od.* ging Paul durchs Ziel; **be ~ and dry** *(fig.)* aus dem Schneider sein *(ugs.)*; **c)** *(Amer.: at home)* zu Hause; **d)** *(to the point aimed at)* **go ~** ‹*Schlag usw.*:› sitzen *(ugs.)*; ‹*Schuß*:› treffen; *(fig.)* ‹*Bemerkungen usw.*:› ins Schwarze treffen, *(ugs.)* sitzen; **e)** *(as far as possible)* **push ~**: [ganz] hineinschieben ‹*Schublade*›; forcieren ‹*Angriff*›; ausnutzen ‹*Vorteil*›; **press ~**: [ganz] hinunterdrücken ‹*Hebel*›; forcieren ‹*Angriff*›; [voll] ausnutzen ‹*Vorteil*›; **drive ~**: [ganz] einschlagen ‹*Nagel*›; **f)** **come** *or* **get ~ to sb.** *(become fully realized)* jmdm. in vollem Ausmaß bewußt werden; **bring sth. ~ to sb.** jmdm. etw. klarmachen *od.* vor Augen führen; *see also* **roost 1. 4.** *v.i.* **a)** ‹*Vogel usw.*:› zurückkehren; **b)** *(be guided)* **these missiles ~ [in] on their targets** diese Flugkörper suchen sich *(Dat.)* ihr Ziel; **c)** **~ in/on sth.** *(fig.)* etw. herausgreifen

home: ~ address *n.* Privatanschrift, *die;* **~-based** ['həʊmbeɪst] *adj.* zu Hause arbeitend; **be ~-based** zu Hause arbeiten; seinen Arbeitsplatz zu Hause haben; **~ bird** *n.* häuslicher Mensch; **~ 'brew** *n.* selbstgebrautes Bier; **~-brewed** ['həʊmbru:d] *adj.* selbstgebraut; **~ 'comforts** *n. pl.* häuslicher Komfort; **~-coming** *n.* Heimkehr, *die;* **~ com'puter** *n.* Heimcomputer, *der;* **H~ Counties** *n. pl. (Brit.)* **the H~ Counties** die Home Counties; *die Grafschaften um London;* **~ eco'nomics** *n. sing. see* **domestic science**; **~ farm** *n. (Brit.)* Herrenhof, *der;* **~ 'ground** *n.* **on [one's] ~ ground** auf heimischem Boden; *(fig.)* zu Hause *(ugs.)*; **~-grown** *adj.* selbstgezogen ‹*Gemüse, Obst*›; **H~ 'Guard** *n. (Brit. Hist.)* **a)** *(army)* Bürgerwehr, *die;* **b)** *(person)* Mitglied der Bürgerwehr; **~ 'help** *(Brit.) see* **help 2b**; **~land** *n.* **a)** *(native land)* Heimat, *die;* Heimatland, *das;* **b)** *(in South Africa)* Homeland, *das;* **~ leave** *n.* Heimaturlaub, *der*

homeless ['həʊmlɪs] **1.** *adj.* obdachlos. **2.** *n.* **the ~**: die Obdachlosen

homelessness ['həʊmlɪsnɪs] *n.* Obdachlosigkeit, *die*

'homelike *adj.* wohnlich

'home-loving *adj.* häuslich

homely ['həʊmlɪ] *adj.* **a)** *(unpretentious, simple)* einfach, schlicht ‹*Worte, Stil, Sprache usw.*›; warmherzig ‹*Person*›; bescheiden ‹*kleines Haus*›; **b)** *(Amer.: not attractive)* nicht sehr attraktiv; wenig attraktiv

home: ~-made *adj.* selbstgemacht; selbstgebacken ‹*Brot*›; hausgemacht ‹*Lebensmittel*›; **~-maker** *n.* Hausfrau, *die; (man)* Hausmann, *der;* **~ 'movie** *n.* Amateurfilm, *der;* **H~ Office** *n. (Brit.)* Innenministerium, *das*

homeopathic *etc. (Amer.) see* **homoeo-**

home: ~ 'perm *n.* selbstgemachte Dauerwelle; **~ 'plate** *see* **plate 11**; **~ 'port** *n.* Heimathafen, *der*

Homer *pr. n.* Homer *(der)*

Homeric [hə'merɪk, həʊ'merɪk] *adj.* Homerisch; *(in the style of Homer)* homerisch

home: ~ 'rule *n.* Autonomie, *die;* Selbstbestimmung, *die;* **~ 'run** *n. (Baseball)* Homerun, *der;* **H~ 'Secretary** *n. (Brit.)* Innenminister, *der;* **~sick** *adj.* heimwehkrank; **become/be ~sick** Heimweh bekommen/haben; **~sickness** *n., no pl.* Heimweh, *das;* **~spun** *adj.* **a)** *(spun [and woven] at ~)* selbstgesponnen [und -gewoben]; *(of ~ manufacture)* in Heimarbeit gesponnen; **b)** *(unsophisticated)* schlicht; einfach; **~spun philosophy** Lebensweisheiten; **~stead** *n.* **a)** *(house with land)* Anwesen, *das; (farm)* Gehöft, *das;* **b)** *(Austral., NZ: residence)* Herrenhaus, *das;* **c)** *(Amer.: area of land)* Parzelle, *die;* ≈ Heimstätte, *die;* **~ 'straight** *(Amer.:* **~ 'stretch)** *n. (lit. or fig.)* Zielgerade, *die;* **~ 'town** *n.* Heimatstadt, *die;* Vaterstadt, *die (geh.)*; *(town of residence)* Wohnort, *der;* **~ 'truth** *n.* unangenehme Wahrheit; **tell** *or* **give sb. a few ~ truths** jmdm. [gehörig] die Meinung sagen; **now you're going to listen to a few ~ truths** jetzt hörst du mir mal zu!

homeward ['həʊmwəd] **1.** *adj.* nach Hause *nachgestellt;* Nachhause‹*weg*›; *(return)* Rück‹*fahrt, -reise, -weg*›; *see also* **³bound**. **2.** *adv.* nach Hause; heimwärts

homewards ['həʊmwədz] *see* **homeward 2**

'homework *n. (Sch.)* Hausaufgabe, *die;* **Latin ~**: Hausaufgaben in Latein; **be given ~**: Hausaufgaben aufbekommen *od.* aufhaben; **give/set sb. too much ~**: jmdm. zuviel [Hausaufgaben] aufgeben; **for ~**: als Hausaufgabe; **do one's ~** *(fig.)* sich mit der Materie vertraut machen; seine Hausaufgaben machen *(scherzh.)*

homicidal [hɒmɪ'saɪdl] *adj.* gemeingefährlich; **~ tendency** Drang zum Töten

homicide ['hɒmɪsaɪd] *n.* **a)** *(act)* Tötung,

die; (manslaughter) Totschlag, der; b) (person) jemand, der einen Menschen getötet hat
homily ['hɒmɪlɪ] n. a) (sermon) Homilie, die (Theol.); b) (tedious discourse) Moralpredigt, die; Predigt, die (ugs.); **give sb. a ~**: jmdm. eine [Moral]predigt halten
homing ['həʊmɪŋ] attrib. adj. zielsuchend ⟨Flugkörper, Torpedo⟩; Zielsuch⟨einrichtung, -kopf⟩; **~ instinct/sense** Heimfindevermögen, das
'**homing pigeon** n. Brieftaube, die
hominid ['hɒmɪnɪd] (Zool.) 1. adj. zu den Hominiden gehörend. 2. n. Hominide, der
homo ['həʊməʊ] (coll.) 1. adj. homosexuell; homo nicht attr. (ugs.). 2. n., pl. **~s** Homo, der (ugs.)
homo- [həʊməʊ, hɒməʊ] in comb. homo-/Homo-
homoeopathic [həʊmɪə'pæθɪk, hɒmɪə'pæθɪk] adj. homöopathisch
homoeopathy [həʊmɪ'ɒpəθɪ, hɒmɪ'ɒpəθɪ] n. Homöopathie, die
homogeneity [hɒmədʒɪ'ni:ɪtɪ, həʊmədʒɪ'ni:ɪtɪ] n., no pl. Homogenität, die
homogeneous [hɒmə'dʒi:nɪəs, həʊmə'dʒi:nɪəs] adj. homogen
homogenisation, homogenise, homogeniser see **homogeniz-**
homogenization [həmɒdʒɪnaɪ'zeɪʃn] n. Homogenisierung, die
homogenize [hə'mɒdʒɪnaɪz] v. t. (lit. or fig.) homogenisieren
homogenizer [hə'mɒdʒɪnaɪzə(r)] n. Homogenisator, der
'**homograph** n. (Ling.) Homograph, das
homologous [hə'mɒləgəs] adj. homolog
homonym ['hɒmənɪm] n. (Ling.) Homonym, das
homonymous [hə'mɒnɪməs] adj. homonym
'**homophone** n. (Ling.) Homophon, das
Homo sapiens [hɒməʊ 'sæpɪenz] n., no pl. Homo sapiens, der
homo'sexual 1. adj. homosexuell. 2. n. Homosexuelle, der/die; **he is a ~**: er ist homosexuell
homosexu'ality n. Homosexualität, die
homy ['həʊmɪ] adj. wohnlich; heimelig (veralt.) ⟨Zimmer, Haus⟩; vertraut ⟨Anblick⟩
Hon. [ɒn] abbr. a) **Honorary**; b) **Honourable**
honcho ['hɒntʃəʊ] n. (Amer. sl.) Boß, der (ugs.)
Honduran [hɒn'djʊərən] 1. adj. honduranisch; **sb. is ~**: jmd. ist Honduraner/Honduranerin. 2. n. Honduraner, der/Honduranerin, die
Honduras [hɒn'djʊərəs] pr. n. Honduras (das)
hone [həʊn] 1. n. Wetzstein, der. 2. v. t. wetzen ⟨Messer, Klinge usw.⟩; **~ a razor to a sharp edge** ein Rasiermesser wetzen, bis die Schneide scharf ist
honest ['ɒnɪst] adj. a) (acting fairly) ehrlich; **~ broker** ehrlicher Makler; b) (sincere) ehrlich; **the ~ truth** die reine Wahrheit; **to be ~ [with you]** offen od. ehrlich gesagt; c) (showing righteousness) redlich; ehrenhaft ⟨Absicht, Tat, Plan⟩; ehrlich ⟨Arbeit⟩; d) (blameless) rechtschaffen; **he made an ~ woman of her** (joc.) er heiratete sie; e) (got by fair means) ehrlich erworben ⟨Besitz⟩; ehrlich verdient ⟨Geld⟩; ehrlich erwirtschaftet ⟨Gewinn⟩; **make an ~ living** sein Leben auf ehrliche Weise verdienen; **earn** or **turn an ~ penny** sich (Dat.) sein Brot ehrlich verdienen; f) (unsophisticated) [gut und] einfach; (unadulterated) rein; **~ bread** gutes, einfaches Brot; g) **~ [to God], ~ to goodness!** (coll.) ehrlich! (ugs.); see also **honest-to-God**
honestly ['ɒnɪstlɪ] adv. a) (fairly) ehrlich; redlich ⟨handeln⟩; b) (frankly) ehrlich; offen; c) (genuinely, really) ehrlich (ugs.); wirklich; **~!** ehrlich!; (annoyed) also wirklich!
honest: ~-to-God, ~-to-goodness adjs. echt
honesty ['ɒnɪstɪ] n. a) (truthfulness) Ehrlichkeit, die; Aufrichtigkeit, die; **in all ~**: ganz ehrlich; **in all ~, I have to admit ...**: ich muß ehrlicherweise zugeben ...; b) (upright conduct) Redlichkeit, die; Anständigkeit, die; **~ is the best policy** (prov.) ehrlich währt am längsten (Spr.); c) (Bot.) Silberblatt, das
honey ['hʌnɪ] n. a) Honig, der; b) (colour) Honiggelb, das; c) (fig.: sweetness) Lieblichkeit, die; d) **sb. is a [real] ~**: jmd. ist ein Schatz (ugs.); e) (Amer., Ir.: darling) Schatz, der (ugs.)
honey: ~-bee n. Honigbiene, die; **~ blonde** adj. honigblond; **~-coloured** adj. honigfarben; **~comb** n. Bienenwabe, die; (filled with honey) Honigwabe, die; **~combed** ['hʌnɪkəʊmd] adj. (with cavities) wabenartig durchsetzt od. durchzogen; **~dew** n. (lit. or fig.) Honigtau, der; **~dew [melon]** Honigmelone, die
honeyed ['hʌnɪd] adj. honigsüß ⟨Worte⟩
honey: ~moon 1. n. a) Flitterwochen Pl.; Honigmond, der (scherzh.); (journey) Hochzeitsreise, die; **where did you go for your ~moon?** wohin habt ihr eure Hochzeitsreise gemacht?; **be a ~moon couple** sich auf der Hochzeitsreise befinden; b) (fig.: initial period) anfängliche Begeisterung; **the ~moon period** die Phase der Begeisterung; 2. v. i. seine Flitterwochen verbringen; flittern (ugs. scherzh.); **~-pot** n. Honigtopf, der; **~suckle** n. (Bot.) Geißblatt, das; **~-sweet** adj. honigsüß
honk [hɒŋk] 1. n. a) (of horn) Hupen, das; **I gave him a ~ [on my horn]** ich hupte ihn an; **~s** Hupsignale; b) (of goose or seal) Schrei, der. 2. v. i. a) ⟨Fahrzeug, Fahrer:⟩ hupen; b) ⟨Gans, Seehund:⟩ schreien. 3. v. t. **~ one's horn** see **horn 1 d**
honky-tonk ['hɒŋkɪtɒŋk] n. (coll.) a) (nightclub) Schuppen, der (ugs.); b) (music) Ragtime, der
honor, honorable, honorably (Amer.) see **honour** etc.
honorarium [ɒnə'reərɪəm] n., pl. **~s** or **honoraria** [ɒnə'reərɪə] Honorar, das
honorary ['ɒnərərɪ] adj. a) ehrenamtlich; Ehren⟨mitglied, -präsident, -doktor, -bürger⟩; b) (conferred as an honour) Ehren-; **~ degree** ehrenhalber verliehener akademischer Grad; **the position is an ~ one** der Posten ist ehrenamtlich
honour ['ɒnə(r)] (Brit.) 1. n. a) no indef. art. (reputation) Ehre, die; **win/achieve ~**: zu Ehren kommen; **to his ~, he refused** es ehrt ihn, daß er abgelehnt hat; **do ~ to sb./sth.** jmdm./einer Sache zur Ehre gereichen (geh.); jmdm./einer Sache Ehre machen; b) (respect) Hochachtung, die; **he was treated with** or **shown ~**: ihm wurde große Achtung entgegengebracht; **hold sb./sth. in ~**: jmdn./etw. achten; **do sb. ~, do ~ to sb.** jmdm. Ehre erweisen; (show appreciation of) jmdn. würdigen; **do ~ to sth.** etw. würdigen; **in ~ of sb.** jmdm. zu Ehren; **in ~ of sth.** um etw. gebührend zu feiern; c) (privilege) Ehre, die; **have the ~ to do** or **of doing sth.** die Ehre haben, etw. zu tun; **may I have the ~ [of the next dance]?** darf ich [um den nächsten Tanz] bitten?; **do sb. an ~**: jmdm. eine Ehre erweisen; **you do me too great an ~**: Sie tun mir zuviel Ehre an; **do sb. the ~ of doing sth.** jmdm. die Ehre erweisen, etw. zu tun; d) no art. (ethical quality) Ehre, die; **he is a man of ~** or **with a sense of ~**: er ist ein Ehrenmann od. Mann von Ehre; **feel [in] ~ bound to do sth.** sich moralisch verpflichtet fühlen, etw. zu tun; **promise [up]on one's ~**: sein Ehrenwort geben; **be on one's ~**: sein Ehrenwort gegeben haben; **[up]on my ~!** Ehrenwort!; bei meiner Ehre! (geh.); **the prisoner was put [up]on his ~ not to escape** der Gefangene mußte sich auf Ehrenwort verpflichten, nicht zu fliehen; **~ bright** (coll.) großes Ehrenwort! (ugs.); **[there is] ~ among thieves** [es gibt so etwas wie] Ganovenehre; e) (chastity) Ehre, die (veralt.); f) (distinction) Auszeichnung, die; (title) Ehrentitel, der; see also **birthday**; **new year**; g) in pl. (recognition) Auszeichnungen; h) in pl. (Univ.) **she gained ~s in her exam, she passed [the exam] with ~s** sie hat das Examen mit Auszeichnung bestanden; i) in pl. **do the ~s** (coll.) (introduce guests) die Honneurs machen; (serve guests) den Gastgeber spielen; j) (ceremony) **funeral** or **last ~s** Trauerfeierlichkeiten Pl.; **pay the last ~s to sb.** jmdm. die letzte Ehre erweisen (geh.); **military ~s** militärische Ehren; k) in title **your H~** (Brit. Law) hohes Gericht; Euer Ehren; l) (person or thing that brings credit) **be an ~ to sb./sth.** jmdm./einer Sache Ehre machen; m) (Cards) Honneur, das; **~s are even** es gibt keinen Verlierer. See also **affair f**; **code 1 a**; **[1]companion c**; **debt**; **guard 1 b**; **guest**; **legion c**; **maid of honour**; **matron b**; **point 1 c**; **word 1 c**. 2. v. t. a) ehren; würdigen ⟨Verdienste, besondere Eigenschaften⟩; **be ~ed as an artist** als Künstler Anerkennung finden; **~ your father and your mother** du sollst Vater und Mutter ehren; **be ~ed with a knighthood** in den Ritterstand erhoben werden; **~ sb. with one's presence** (iron.) jmdn. mit seiner Gegenwart beehren; b) (acknowledge) beachten ⟨Vorschriften⟩; respektieren ⟨Gebräuche, Rechte⟩; c) (fulfil) sich halten an (+ Akk.); (Commerc.) honorieren; begleichen ⟨Rechnung, Schuld⟩
honourable ['ɒnərəbl] adj. (Brit.) a) (worthy of respect) ehrenwert (geh.); ehrbar (geh.); b) (bringing credit) achtbar; (consistent with honour) ehrenvoll ⟨Frieden, Rückzug, Entlassung⟩; c) (ethical) rechtschaffen; redlich ⟨Geschäftsgebaren⟩; **sb.'s intentions are ~**: jmd. hat ehrliche Absichten; d) in title **the H~ ...**: ≈ der/die ehrenwerte ...; **the ~ gentleman/lady, the ~ member [for X]** (Brit. Parl.) der Herr/die Frau Abgeordnete [für den Wahlkreis X]; ≈ der [verehrte] Herr Kollege/die [verehrte] Frau Kollegin; **the Most H~ ...** (Brit.) ≈ der/die höchst ehrenwerte ...; **the Right H~ ...** (Brit.) ≈ der sehr ehrenwerte ... See also **mention 1 b**
honourably ['ɒnərəblɪ] adv. (Brit.) a) (with credit) ehrenvoll; b) (ethically) ehrenhaft ⟨handeln⟩
honours: ~ degree n. Examen mit Auszeichnung; **~ list** n. a) (Univ.) Liste der Kandidaten, die das Examen mit Auszeichnung bestanden haben; b) (of sovereign) Liste der Titel- und Rangverleihungen
Hon. Sec. [ɒn 'sek] abbr. **Honorary Secretary**
hooch [hu:tʃ] n. (Amer. coll.) [schwarz gebrannter] Schnaps; Fusel, der (ugs. abwertend)
[1]hood [hʊd] n. a) Kapuze, die; b) (of vehicle) (Brit.: waterproof top) Verdeck, das; (Amer.: bonnet) [Motor]haube, die; (of pram) Verdeck, das; **drive with the ~ down** mit offenem Verdeck fahren; c) (over hearth) [Rauch]abzug, der; (over stove) Abzugshaube, die
[2]hood [hʊd, hu:d] n. (sl.: gangster) Gangster, der
hooded ['hʊdɪd] adj. (wearing hood) mit einer Kapuze bekleidet; (with hood attached) ⟨Mantel usw.⟩ mit Kapuze; **a ~ figure** eine Gestalt mit [einer] Kapuze
hooded 'crow n. (Ornith.) Nebelkrähe, die
hoodlum ['hu:dləm] n. a) (young thug) Rowdy, der (abwertend); b) (Amer.: gangster) see **[2]hood**
hoodoo ['hu:du:] n. a) (bad spell) Fluch, der; **there is a ~ on that house** es liegt ein Fluch über diesem Haus; **put a ~ on sb.** ⟨Hexe:⟩ jmdn. verwünschen; b) (bringer of bad luck) **be a ~**: Unglück bringen

hoodwink ['hʊdwɪŋk] *v. t.* hinters Licht führen; täuschen

hooey ['hu:ɪ] *(sl.)* **1.** *n.* Quatsch, *der (ugs.);* Blödsinn, *der (ugs.).* **2.** *int.* Quatsch [mit Soße]! *(ugs.)*

hoof [hu:f] **1.** *n., pl.* **~s** *or* **hooves** [hu:vz] **a)** Huf, *der; (sl. derog.: human foot)* Pedal, *das (ugs. scherzh.);* **b) buy cattle on the ~** *(for meat)* Lebendvieh kaufen. *See also* **cloven 2. 2.** *v. t. (sl.)* **a)** *(kick)* **he ~ed him out of** *or* **through the door** er gab ihm einen Tritt, daß er durch die Tür flog; **get ~ed out of the army** *(fig.)* aus der Armee fliegen *(ugs.);* **b)** *(walk)* **~ it** tippeln *(ugs.)*

'hoofbeat *n.* Hufschlag, *der*

hoo-ha ['hu:hɑ:] *n. (coll.)* Wirbel, *der;* **make a [lot of** *or* **big] ~ [about sth.]** [viel] Wind [um etw.] machen *(ugs.)*

hook [hʊk] **1.** *n.* **a)** Haken, *der; (Fishing)* [Angel]haken, *der;* **~ and eye** Haken und Öse; **swallow sth. ~, line, and sinker** *(fig.)* etw. blind glauben; **they fell for it ~, line, and sinker** *(fig.)* sie sind voll und ganz darauf hereingefallen; **get sb. off the ~** *(fig. sl.)* jmdn. herauspauken *(ugs.);* **get oneself off the ~** *(fig. sl.)* den Kopf aus der Schlinge ziehen; **that lets me/him off the ~** *(fig. sl.)* da bin ich/ist er noch einmal davongekommen; verduften *(ugs.);* **by ~ or by crook** mit allen Mitteln; **b)** *(telephone cradle)* Gabel, *die;* **the telephone was off the ~:** das Telefon war ausgehängt; **c)** *(Agric.) (for cutting grass or grain)* Sense, *die; (for cutting and lopping)* Hippe, *die;* **d)** *(Boxing)* Haken, *der;* **e)** *(Baseball, Bowling, Cricket, Golf)* Hook, *der;* **f)** *(Geog., Geol.) (in river)* [scharfe] Krümmung; *(sand-spit)* spitz zulaufende Sandbank; *(projecting land)* gekrümmte Landzunge; **the H~** *(coll.) see* **Hook of Holland; g)** *(Mus.)* [Noten]fähnchen, *das.* **2.** *v. t.* **a)** *(grasp)* mit Haken/mit einem Haken greifen; **b)** *(fasten)* mit Haken/mit einem Haken befestigen **(to** an + *Dat.*); festhaken ⟨*Tor*⟩ **(to** an + *Akk.*); haken ⟨*Bein, Finger*⟩ **(over** über + *Akk.*, **in** in + *Akk.*); **~ a caravan to a car** einen Wohnwagen an ein Auto hängen; **c) be ~ed [on sth./sb.]** *(sl.) (addicted harmfully)* [von etw./jmdm.] abhängig sein; *(addicted harmlessly)* [auf etw./jmdn.] stehen *(ugs., bes. Jugendspr.); (captivated)* [von etw./jmdm.] fasziniert sein; **be ~ed on heroin/drugs** heroin-/drogenabhängig sein; **d)** *(catch)* an die Angel bekommen ⟨*Fisch*⟩; *(fig.)* sich *(Dat.)* angeln; **e) ~ it** *(sl.: leave)* abhauen *(salopp);* **f)** *(Boxing)* einen Haken versetzen *od.* geben (+ *Dat.*); **g)** *(Rugby)* hakeln; *(Golf)* einen Linksdrall geben (+ *Dat.*), nach links verziehen ⟨*Ball*⟩; *(Cricket) mit waagerechtem Schläger in Schulterhöhe hinter sich schlagen* ⟨*Ball*⟩

~ 'on 1. *v. t.* anhaken **(to** an + *Akk.*); anhängen ⟨*Wagen, Anhänger, Schiff*⟩ **(to** an + *Akk.*). **2.** *v. i.* angehakt werden **(to** an + *Akk.*)

~ 'up 1. *v. t.* **a)** festhaken **(to** an + *Akk.*); zuhaken ⟨*Kleid*⟩; **b)** *(Radio and Telev. coll.)* zusammenschalten ⟨*Sender*⟩; *see also* **hook-up. 2.** *v. i.* ⟨*Kleid:*⟩ mit Haken geschlossen werden

hookah ['hʊkə] *n.* Huka, *die;* [indische] Wasserpfeife

hooked [hʊkt] *adj.* **a)** *(hook-shaped)* hakenförmig; **~ nose** Hakennase, *die;* **b)** *(having hook[s])* mit Haken/mit einem Haken versehen. *See also* **hook 2 c**

hooker ['hʊkə(r)] *n.* **a)** *(Rugby)* Hakler, *der;* **b)** *(Amer. sl.: prostitute)* Nutte, *die (salopp)*

hookey ['hʊkɪ] *n. (Amer. sl.)* **play ~:** [die] Schule schwänzen *(ugs.)*

hook: ~-'nose *n.* Hakennase, *die;* **~-nosed** ['hʊknəʊzd] *adj.* mit einer Hakennase *nachgestellt;* hakennasig; **be ~-nosed** eine Hakennase haben; **H~ of 'Holland** *pr. n.* Hoek van Holland *(das);* **~-up** *n. (Radio and Telev. coll.)* Zusammenschaltung, *die (zu einer Gemeinschaftssendung);* **~worm** *n.* **a)** *(worm)* Hakenwurm, *der;* **b)** *no art. (disease)* die Hakenwurmkrankheit

hooky *see* **hookey**

hooligan ['hu:lɪgən] *n.* Rowdy, *der*

hooliganism ['hu:lɪgənɪzm] *n., no pl.* Rowdytum, *das*

hoop [hu:p] *n.* **a)** *(circular band)* Reifen, *der; (of barrel)* Faßreifen, *der;* Faßband, *das;* **b)** *(toy)* Reifen, *der;* **c)** *(Croquet)* [Krocket]tor, *das;* **d)** *(in circus, show, etc.)* Springreifen, *der;* **go** *or* **be put/put sb. through the hoop[s]** *(fig.)* durch die Mangel gedreht werden/jmdn. durch die Mangel drehen *(salopp)*

hoop-la ['hu:plɑ:] *n.* Ringwerfen, *das*

hoopoe ['hu:pu:] *n. (Ornith.)* Wiedehopf, *der*

hooray *see* **hurray**

Hooray 'Henry *n. (Brit.)* [reicher, extrovertierter] Schickimicki *(ugs.)*

hoosegow ['hu:sgaʊ] *n. (Amer. sl.)* Knast, *der (ugs.)*

hoot [hu:t] **1.** *v. i.* **a)** *(call out)* johlen; **~ with laughter** in johlendes Gelächter ausbrechen; **b)** ⟨*Eule:*⟩ schreien; **c)** ⟨*Fahrzeug, Fahrer:*⟩ hupen, tuten; ⟨*Sirene, Nebelhorn usw.:*⟩ heulen, tuten; **~ at sb./sth.** jmdn./etw. anhupen. **2.** *v. t.* **a)** *(assail with derision)* ausbuhen *(ugs.);* **b)** heulen *od.* tuten lassen ⟨*Sirene, Nebelhorn*⟩; **~ one's horn** *see* **horn 1 d. 3.** *n.* **a)** *(shout)* **~s of derision/scorn** verächtliches Gejohle; **~s of laughter** johlendes Gelächter; **b)** *(owl's cry)* Schrei, *der;* **c)** *(signal) (of vehicle)* Hupen, *das; (of siren, fog-horn)* Heulen, *das;* Tuten, *das;* **give a ~ of** *or* **on one's horn** ⟨*Fahrer:*⟩ hupen; **d)** *(coll.)* **I don't care** *or* **give a ~** *or* **two ~s what you do** es ist mir völlig piepegal *od.* schnuppe *(ugs.),* was du tust; **not matter a ~** *or* **two ~s [to sb.]** [jmdm.] völlig schnuppe sein *(ugs.);* **e)** *(coll.: cause of laughter)* **what a ~!** zum Kaputtlachen! *(ugs.);* **be a ~:** zum Schießen sein *(ugs.)*

hooter ['hu:tə(r)] *n. (Brit.)* **a)** *(siren)* Sirene, *die;* **b)** *(motor horn)* Hupe, *die;* **sound one's ~:** hupen; **c)** *(sl.: nose)* Zinken, *der (ugs. scherzh.)*

hoots [hu:ts] *int. (Scot., N. Engl.)* ach was!

hoover ['hu:və(r)] *(Brit.)* **1.** *n.* **a) H~ (P)** [Hoover]staubsauger, *der;* **b)** *(made by any company)* Staubsauger, *der.* **2.** *v. t. (coll.)* staubsaugen; saugen ⟨*Boden, Teppich*⟩; absaugen ⟨*Möbel*⟩. **3.** *v. i. (coll.)* [staub]saugen

[1]hop [hɒp] *n.* **a)** *(Bot.) (plant)* Hopfen, *der; in pl. (cones)* Hopfendolden; **b)** *in pl. (Brewing)* Hopfen, *der*

[2]hop 1. *v. i.,* **-pp- a)** hüpfen; ⟨*Hase:*⟩ hoppeln; **be ~ping mad [about** *or* **over sth.]** *(coll.)* [wegen etw.] fuchsteufelswild sein *(ugs.);* **b)** *(fig. coll.)* **~ out of bed** aus dem Bett springen; **~ into the car/on [to] the bus/train/bicycle** sich ins Auto/in den Bus/Zug/aufs Fahrrad schwingen *(ugs.);* **~ into bed with sb.** mit jmdm. ins Bett steigen *(ugs.);* **~ off/out** aussteigen; **c)** *(coll.: change location)* **be always ~ping [about] from place to place/country to country** ständig unterwegs sein. **2.** *v. t.,* **-pp- a)** *(jump over)* springen über (+ *Akk.*); **b)** *(coll.: jump aboard)* aufspringen auf (+ *Akk.*); **c) ~ it** *(Brit. sl.: go away)* sich verziehen *(ugs.). See also* **hedgehop. 3.** *n.* **a)** *(action)* Hüpfer, *der;* Hopser, *der (ugs.);* **~, step, and jump** *see* **triple jump; b) be on the ~** *(Brit. coll.: be bustling about)* auf Trab sein *(ugs.);* **keep sb. on the ~** *(Brit. coll.)* jmdn. in Trab halten *(ugs.);* **c) catch sb. on the ~** *(Brit. coll.) (unprepared)* jmdn. überraschen *od.* überrumpeln; *(in the act)* jmdn. auf frischer Tat ertappen; **d)** *(coll.: dance)* Schwof, *der (ugs.);* **e)** *(distance flown)* Flugstrecke, *die; (stage of journey)* Teilstrecke, *die;* Etappe, *die; (flight)* kurzer Flug; *(trip)* kurze Reise

hope [həʊp] **1.** *n.* Hoffnung, *die;* **~ springs eternal [in the human breast]** *(prov.)* der Mensch hofft, solange er lebt; **give up ~:** die Hoffnung aufgeben; **that is my [dearest] ~:** darauf setze ich meine [ganze] Hoffnung; **hold out ~ [for sb.]** [jmdm.] Hoffnung machen; **I don't hold out much ~ for his recovery** ich habe nicht viel Hoffnung, daß er sich wieder erholt; **beyond** *or* **past ~:** hoffnungslos; **in the ~/in ~[s] of sth./doing sth.** in der Hoffnung auf etw. *(Akk.)*/, etw. zu tun; **live in ~[s] of sth.** in der Hoffnung auf etw. *(Akk.)* leben; **sb.'s ~[s] of sth.** jmds. Hoffnung auf etw. *(Akk.);* **I have some ~[s] of success** *or* **of succeeding** *or* **that I shall succeed** es besteht die Hoffnung, daß ich Erfolg habe; **set** *or* **put** *or* **place one's ~s on** *or* **in sth./sb.** seine Hoffnung auf etw./jmdn. setzen; **raise sb.'s ~s** jmdm. Hoffnung machen; **raise sb.'s ~s too much** *or* **high** jmdm. zu große Hoffnungen machen; **high ~s** große Hoffnungen; **have high ~s of sth./doing sth.** sich *(Dat.)* große Hoffnungen auf etw. *(Akk.)* machen/sich *(Dat.)* große Hoffnungen machen, etw. zu tun; **there is no/some/little ~ that ...:** es besteht keine/einige/wenig Hoffnung, daß ...; **not have a ~ [in hell] [of sth.]** *(coll.)* sich *(Dat.)* keine[rlei] Hoffnung [auf etw. *(Akk.)*] machen können; **there's not a ~ in hell that ...** *(coll.)* es besteht nicht die leiseste Chance, daß ...; **not a ~ [in hell]!** *(coll. iron.)* völlig ausgeschlossen!; **what a ~!** *(coll.),* **some ~[s]!** *(coll. iron.)* schön wär's!; **be hoping against ~ that ...:** trotz allem die Hoffnung nicht aufgeben, daß ...; **be the great new tennis ~:** die große neue Hoffnung im Tennis sein; **hard work is our only ~ for** *or* **of a better way of life** nur wenn wir hart arbeiten, können wir auf ein besseres Leben hoffen; **my ~ is that ...:** ich hoffe, daß ...; *see also* **alive a; forlorn a. 2.** *v. i.* hoffen **(for** auf + *Akk.*); **I ~ so/not** hoffentlich/hoffentlich nicht; ich hoffe es/ich hoffe nicht; **~ for the best** das Beste hoffen. **3.** *v. t.* **~ to do sth./that sth. may be so** hoffen, etw. zu tun/daß etw. so eintrifft; **I ~ to go to Paris** *(am planning)* ich habe vor, nach Paris zu fahren; **I ~ [that] that is true** hoffentlich stimmt das; **hoping to see you soon** in der Hoffnung, Sie bald zu sehen

'hope chest *n. (Amer.)* Aussteuertruhe, *die*

hoped-for ['həʊptfɔ:(r)] *attrib. adj.* erhofft

hopeful ['həʊpfl] **1.** *adj.* **a)** zuversichtlich; **I'm ~/not ~ that ...:** ich hoffe zuversichtlich/bezweifle, daß ...; **feel ~:** zuversichtlich sein; **be** *or* **feel ~ about the future** hoffnungsvoll *od.* zuversichtlich in die Zukunft blicken; **if you think he will help you, you are very ~ indeed** wenn du denkst, daß er dir helfen wird, dann bist du wirklich ein Optimist; **be ~ of sth./of doing sth./that sth. may be so** auf etw. *(Akk.)* hoffen/voller Hoffnung sein, etw. zu tun/daß etw. so eintrifft; **b)** *(promising)* vielversprechend; aussichtsreich ⟨*Kapitalanlage, Kandidat*⟩. **2.** *n.* **[young] ~:** hoffnungsvoller junger Mensch

hopefully ['həʊpfəlɪ] *adv.* **a)** *(expectantly)* voller Hoffnung; **b)** *(promisingly)* vielversprechend; **c)** *(coll.: it is hoped that)* hoffentlich; **~, all our problems should now be over** wir wollen hoffen, daß unsere ganzen *(ugs.)* Probleme jetzt beseitigt sind; **~, it will be available in the autumn** wir hoffen, daß es im Herbst zur Verfügung steht

hopeless ['həʊplɪs] *adj.* **a)** hoffnungslos; **b)** *(inadequate, incompetent)* miserabel; **be ~, be a ~ case** ein hoffnungsloser Fall sein *(ugs.)* **(at** in + *Dat.*); **be ~ at doing sth.** etw. überhaupt nicht können

hopelessly ['həʊplɪslɪ] *adv.* **a)** hoffnungslos; **be ~ in love** *(fig.)* rettungslos verliebt sein *(ugs.);* **I'm ~ bad at maths** in Mathematik bin ich ein hoffnungsloser Fall *(ugs. scherzh.);* **b)** *(inadequately)* miserabel

hopelessness ['həʊplɪsnɪs] *n., no pl.* Hoffnungslosigkeit, *die*

'hop-garden *n. (Brit. Agric.)* Hopfengarten, *der*

hopper ['hɒpə(r)] *n. (Mech.)* Trichter, *der*

hop: ~sack *n.* **a)** *(bag)* Hopfensack, *der;* **b)** *(Textiles)* Sackleinen, *das;* Sackleinwand, *die;* **~scotch** *n.* Himmel-und-Hölle-Spiel, *das;* **play ~scotch** „Himmel und Hölle" spielen

horde [hɔ:d] *n. (huge number)* große Menge; *(derog./of wild animals)* Horde, *die;* **in [their] ~s** in Scharen; **~s of tourists** Scharen von Touristen

horizon [hə'raɪzn] *n.* **a)** Horizont, *der;* **on/over the ~:** am Horizont; **the sun dropped below the ~:** die Sonne verschwand hinter dem Horizont; **there is trouble on the ~** *(fig.)* am Horizont tauchen Probleme auf; **there's nothing on the ~** *(fig.)* da ist nichts in Sicht *(ugs.); see also* **artificial horizon; b)** *(fig.: perceptual limit)* Horizont, *der;* Gesichtskreis, *der;* **broaden one's/sb.'s ~s** seinen/jmds. Horizont erweitern; **c)** *(Geol.)* Horizont, *der;* **d)** *(Archaeol.)* Kulturschicht, *die;* **e)** *(Soil Science)* Bodenhorizont, *der*

horizontal [hɒrɪ'zɒntl] **1.** *adj.* horizontal; waagerecht; *see also* **¹bar 1 b; integration d. 2.** *n.* Horizontale, *die;* Waagerechte, *die*

horizontally [hɒrɪ'zɒntəlɪ] *adv.* horizontal; *(flat)* waagerecht; flach ‹*liegen*›

hormonal [hɔ:'məʊnl, 'hɔ:mənl] *adj. (Biol., Pharm.)* hormonal; hormonell; **~ deficiency** Hormonmangel, *der*

hormone ['hɔ:məʊn] *n. (Biol., Pharm.)* Hormon, *das*

horn [hɔ:n] **1.** *n.* **a)** *(of animal or devil)* Horn, *das; (of deer)* Geweihstange, *die (Jägerspr.);* **~s** Geweih, *das;* **lock ~s [with sb.]** *(fig.)* [mit jmdm.] die Klinge[n] kreuzen *(geh.);* **b)** *(substance)* Horn, *das; attrib.* Horn-; **c)** *(Mus.)* Horn, *das;* **[French] ~:** [Wald]horn, *das; see also* **English horn; d)** *(of vehicle)* Hupe, *die; (of ship)* [Signal]horn, *das; (of factory)* [Fabrik]sirene, *die;* **sound** *or* **blow** *or* **hoot** *or* **honk the** *or* **one's ~ [at sb.]** ‹*Fahrer:*› [jmdn. an]hupen; **e)** *(of snail)* Horn, *das; (of insect)* Fühler, *der;* **draw in one's ~s** *(fig.)* sich zurückhalten; *(restrain one's ambition)* zurückstecken; **f)** *(vessel)* Horn, *das; (to drink from)* Trinkhorn, *das (hist.); (for gunpowder)* Pulverhorn, *das (hist.);* **~ of plenty** Füllhorn, *das;* **g)** *(loudspeaker)* [Schall]trichter, *der;* **h)** *(of crescent)* Horn, *das;* **the ~s of the moon** die Hörnerspitzen des Mondes; **i)** *(Geog.) (of land)* Horn, *das (veralt.);* **the H~:** das Kap Hoorn; **j)** *(coarse: erect penis)* Latte, *die (salopp). See also* **¹bull 1 a; dilemma; fog-horn; shoehorn. 2.** *v. i. (sl.)* **~ in [on sth.]** sich [in etw. *(Akk.)*] reinhängen *(salopp)*

horn: ~beam *n. (Bot.)* Hainbuche, *die;* Hornbaum, *der;* **~bill** *n. (Ornith.)* Nashornvogel, *der*

horned [hɔ:nd] *adj.* **a)** gehörnt; *(with antlers)* geweihtragend; **b)** *(poet.: crescent-shaped)* sichelförmig

horned: ~ 'owl *n.* Ohreule, *die;* **~ 'toad** *n.* Texaskrötenechse, *die*

hornet ['hɔ:nɪt] *n.* Hornisse, *die;* **stir up** *or* **walk into a ~s' nest** *(fig.)* in ein Wespennest stechen *od.* greifen *(ugs.);* **bring a ~s' nest about one's ears** *(fig.)* sich in ein Wespennest setzen *(ugs.)*

hornless ['hɔ:nlɪs] *adj.* hornlos; *(without antlers)* geweihlos

'hornpipe *n. (Mus.)* Hornpipe, *die*

'horn-rimmed *adj.* **~ spectacles** *or* **glasses** Hornbrille, *die*

horny ['hɔ:nɪ] *adj.* **a)** *(hard)* hornig ‹*Fußsohlen, Haut, Hände*›; **b)** *(made of horn)* aus Horn *nachgestellt; (like horn)* hornartig; **c)** *(sl.: sexually aroused)* spitz *(ugs.);* geil *(oft abwertend)*

horology [hə'rɒlədʒɪ] *n., no pl.* **a)** *(science)* Lehre von der Zeitmessung; **b)** *(clock-making)* Uhrmacherkunst, *die*

horoscope ['hɒrəskəʊp] *n. (Astrol.)* Horoskop, *das;* **draw up** *or* **cast sb.'s ~:** jmdm. das Horoskop stellen

horrendous [hə'rendəs] *adj. (coll.)* schrecklich *(ugs.);* entsetzlich *(ugs.)* ‹*Dummheit*›; horrend ‹*Preis*›

horrendously [hə'rendəslɪ] *adv. (coll.)* entsetzlich *(ugs.);* horrend ‹*teuer*›

horrible ['hɒrɪbl] *adj.* **a)** grauenhaft; grausig ‹*Monster, Geschichte*›; grauenvoll ‹*Verbrechen, Alptraum*›; schauerlich ‹*Maske*›; **I find all insects ~:** mir graust vor jeder Art von Insekten; **b)** *(coll.: unpleasant, excessive)* grauenhaft *(ugs.);* horrend ‹*Ausgaben, Kosten*›; **have a ~ surprise** eine ganz böse Überraschung erleben *(ugs.);* **don't be so ~ to me** sei nicht so garstig zu mir; **I have a ~ feeling that ...:** ich habe das ungute Gefühl, daß ...

horribly ['hɒrɪblɪ] *adv.* **a)** entsetzlich ‹*entstellt*›; scheußlich ‹*grinsen*›; **it was a ~ frightening story** es war eine überaus grausige Geschichte; **b)** *(coll.: unpleasantly, excessively)* entsetzlich *(ugs.);* fürchterlich *(ugs.)* ‹*aufregen*›; horrend ‹*teuer*›

horrid ['hɒrɪd] *adj.* scheußlich; **don't be so ~ to me** *(coll.)* sei nicht so garstig zu mir

horrific [hə'rɪfɪk] *adj.* schrecklich; grausig ‹*Geistergeschichte*›; *(coll.)* horrend ‹*Preis*›

horrify ['hɒrɪfaɪ] *v. t.* **a)** *(excite horror in)* mit Schrecken erfüllen; **it horrifies me to think what ...:** ich denke mit Schrecken daran, was ...; **I was horrified to see my car rolling into the river** voller Entsetzen sah ich, wie mein Auto in den Fluß rollte; **b)** *(shock, scandalize)* **be horrified** entsetzt sein **(at, by** über + *Akk.*)

horrifying ['hɒrɪfaɪɪŋ] *adj.* grauenhaft; grausig ‹*Film*›; **it is ~ to think that ...:** der Gedanke, daß ..., ist schrecklich

horrifyingly ['hɒrɪfaɪɪŋlɪ] *adv.* erschreckend

horror ['hɒrə(r)] **1.** *n.* **a)** Entsetzen, *das* **(at** über + *Akk.*); *(repugnance)* Grausen, *das;* **she screamed in ~:** sie schrie voller Entsetzen; **there was [an expression of] ~ on her face** Entsetzen/Grauen stand ihr im Gesicht geschrieben; **have a ~ of sb./sth./doing sth.** einen Horror vor jmdm./etw. haben/einen Horror davor haben, etw. zu tun *(ugs.);* **have a fit of the ~s** weiße Mäuse sehen *(ugs.);* **spiders gave her the ~s** vor Spinnen hatte sie eine panische Angst; **he gives me the ~s** er ist mir unheimlich; **b)** *(coll.: dismay)* Entsetzen, *das* **(at** über + *Akk.*); **c)** *(horrifying quality)* Grauenhaftigkeit, *die; (horrifying thing)* Greuel, *der; (horrifying person)* Scheusal, *das;* **'Six Die in Blaze H~'** „Sechs Tote in flammendem Inferno"; **Chamber of H~s** *(lit. or fig.)* Schreckenskabinett, *das.* **2.** *adj.* Horror‹*comic, -film, -geschichte*›. **3.** *int.* **~[s]!** wie schrecklich!; o Graus! *(ugs. scherzh.);* **~ of ~s!** o Schreck, o Graus! *(ugs. scherzh.)*

horror: ~-stricken, ~-struck *adjs.* von Entsetzen gepackt; **be ~-stricken** *or* **-struck at sth.** über etw. *(Akk.)* furchtbar entsetzt sein

hors de combat [ɔ: də 'kɔ̃bɑ:] *pred. adj.* kampfunfähig; **put** *or* **render sb./sth. ~:** jmdn./etw. außer Gefecht setzen

hors-d'œuvre [ɔ:'dɜ:vr, ɔ:'dɜ:v] *n. (Gastr.)* Horsd'œuvre, *das;* ≈ Vorspeise, *die*

horse [hɔ:s] **1.** *n.* **a)** Pferd, *das; (adult male)* Hengst, *der;* **be/get on one's high ~** *(fig.)* auf dem hohen Roß sitzen/sich aufs hohe Roß setzen *(ugs.);* **get [down] off one's high ~** *(fig.)* von seinem hohen Roß herunterkommen *od.* -steigen *(ugs.);* **hold your ~s!** *(fig.)* immer sachte mit den jungen Pferden! *(ugs.);* **he ought to hold his ~s** er sollte erst einmal abwarten; **that's/he is a ~ of a different** *or* **of another colour** *(fig.)* das ist etwas anderes/mit ihm sieht die Sache anders aus; **as strong as a ~:** bärenstark *(ugs.);* **eat/work like a ~:** wie ein Scheunendrescher essen *(salopp)*/wie ein Pferd arbeiten; **I could eat a ~** *(coll.)* ich habe einen Bärenhunger *(ugs.);* **[right** *or* **straight] from the ~'s mouth** *(fig.)* aus erster Hand *od.* Quelle; **change** *or* **swap ~s in midstream** *(fig.)* auf halbem Wege die Richtung ändern; **to ~!** aufgesessen!; **it's [a question** *or* **matter of] ~s for courses** *(fig.)* jeder sollte die Aufgaben übernehmen, für die er am besten geeignet ist; **you can lead** *or* **take a ~ to water, but you can't make it drink** *(prov.)* man kann ein Pferd zur Tränke bringen, aber es nicht zwingen zu trinken; **b)** *constr. as pl. (Mil.)* Kavallerie, *die;* Reiterei, *die;* **800 ~:** 800 Reiter *od.* Berittene; **c)** *(Gymnastics)* **[vaulting-]~:** [Sprung]pferd, *das;* **d)** *(framework)* Gestell, *das; (for planks or beams)* [Auflager]bock, *der;* **[clothes-]~:** Wäscheständer, *der;* **e)** *(coll.: horsepower)* PS, *das. See also* **cart 1; cart-horse; dark horse; flog a; gift-horse; hobby-horse; light horse; ²lock 2 a; marine 2 a; pommel-horse; rocking-horse; sea-horse; Trojan horse; white horse; wild horse; wooden horse. 2.** *v. i.* **~ about** *or* **around** *(coll.)* herumalbern *(ugs.)*

horse: ~-and-'buggy *adj. (Amer. fig.)* aus der Zeit der Postkutschen *(fig.) nachgestellt;* **~back 1.** *n.* **a) on ~back** zu Pferd; **ride on ~back** reiten; **b)** *attrib. (Amer.)* **~back riding** Reiten, *das;* **go in for** *or* **enjoy ~back rides** gerne reiten; **2.** *adv.* **go ~back** reiten; **~-box** *n. (trailer)* Pferdeanhänger, *der; (Motor Veh.)* Pferdetransporter, *der;* **~-brass** *see* **brass 1 c; ~-breaker** *n.* Zureiter, *der;* **~-breeder** *see* **breeder; ~-'chestnut** *n. (Bot.)* Roßkastanie, *die;* **~-drawn** *attrib. adj.* pferdebespannt; von Pferden gezogen; **~-drawn vehicle** Pferdewagen, *der;* Pferdefuhrwerk, *das;* **~flesh** *n.* **a)** *(meat)* Pferdefleisch, *das;* **b)** *(horses)* Pferde; **~-fly** *n. (Zool.)* Pferdebremse, *die;* **H~ Guards** *n. pl. (Brit. Mil.) (brigade)* Gardekavallerie, *die;* **~hair** *n.* **a)** *(single hair)* Pferdehaar, *das;* **b)** *no pl., no indef. art. (mass of hairs)* Roßhaar, *das;* **c)** *(fabric)* Roßhaar, *das;* **~ latitudes** *n. pl. (Geog.)* Roßbreiten *Pl.;* **~-laugh** *n.* laute Lache *(ugs.);* **~man** ['hɔ:smən] *n., pl.* **~men** ['hɔ:smən] **a)** *([skilled] rider)* [guter] Reiter; **b)** *(Amer.: breeder)* Pferdezüchter, *der*

horsemanship ['hɔ:smənʃɪp] *n., no pl.* **[skills of] ~:** reiterliches Können

horse: ~ opera *n. (Amer. sl.)* Pferdeoper, *die (ugs.);* **~play** *n.* Balgerei, *die;* Alberei, *die;* **~power** *n., pl. same (Mech.)* Pferdestärke, *die;* **a 40 ~power car** ein Auto mit 40 PS; **what ~power is your car?** wieviel PS hat dein Auto?; **~-race** *n.* Pferderennen, *das;* **~-racing** *n.* Pferderennsport, *der;* **~-radish** *n.* Meerrettich, *der;* **~ sense** *n. (coll.)* [gesunder Menschen]verstand; **~shoe** *n.* Hufeisen, *das; (Archit.)* Hufeisenbogen, *der; attrib.* hufeisenförmig; **~shoe magnet** Hufeisenmagnet, *der;* **~shoe crab** *(Amer. Zool.)* Königskrabbe, *die;* **~ show** *n.* Pferdeschau, *die;* **~tail** *n.* **a)** *(Bot.)* Schachtelhalm, *der;* **b)** *see* **pony-tail; ~-trader** *n.* Pferdehändler, *der;* **~-trading** *n.* **a)** *(Amer.: dealing in horses)* Pferdehandel, *der;* **b)** *(fig.: bargaining)* Kuhhandel, *der (ugs. abwertend);* **~whip 1.** *n.* Reitpeitsche, *die;* **2.** *v. t.* auspeitschen; **~woman** *n.* Reiterin, *die*

horsy (horsey) ['hɔ:sɪ] *adj.* **a)** *(horselike)* pferdeähnlich; **~ face/laugh** Pferdegesicht, *das*/wieherndes Lachen *(ugs.);* **b)** *(much concerned with horses)* pferdenärrisch; **~ people** Pferdenarren

horticultural [hɔ:tɪ'kʌltʃərl] *adj.* gartenbaulich; Gartenbau‹*zeitschrift, -ausstellung*›; **~ society** Gesellschaft für Gartenbau; **~ show** Gartenschau, *die*

horticulture ['hɔːtɪkʌltʃə(r)] *n.* Gartenbau, *der*

horticulturist [hɔːtɪ'kʌltʃərɪst] *n.* Gärtner, *der*/Gärtnerin, *die*

hosanna [həʊ'zænə] *(Bibl.)* **1.** *int.* hosianna. **2.** *n.* Hosianna, *das*

hose [həʊz] **1.** *n.* **a)** *(flexible tube)* Schlauch, *der;* **garden ~:** Gartenschlauch, *der;* **b)** *constr. as pl. (stockings)* Strümpfe; **half-~:** Socken; **c)** *constr. as pl. (Hist.) (tights)* Strumpfhose, *die; (breeches)* Kniehose, *die; see also* **doublet a. 2.** *v. t.* sprengen

~ **'down** *v. t.* abspritzen

'hose-pipe *n. see* **hose 1 a**

hosiery ['həʊʒərɪ] *n., no pl.* Strumpfwaren *Pl.*

hospice ['hɒspɪs] *n.* **a)** *(Brit.) (for the destitute)* Heim für Mittellose; *(for the terminally ill)* Sterbeklinik, *die;* **b)** *(for travellers or students)* Hospiz, *das*

hospitable ['hɒspɪtəbl] *adj.* **a)** *(welcoming)* gastfreundlich ⟨*Person, Wesensart*⟩; gastlich ⟨*Haus, Hotel, Klima*⟩; freundlich ⟨*Einladung*⟩; **be ~ to sb.** jmdn. gastfreundlich *od.* gastlich aufnehmen; **b)** *(fig.: favourably disposed)* **be ~ [to sth.]** aufgeschlossen [gegenüber etw.] sein

hospitably ['hɒspɪtəblɪ] *adv. (welcomingly)* gastlich; gastfreundlich

hospital ['hɒspɪtl] *n.* Krankenhaus, *das;* **in ~** *(Brit.),* **in the ~** *(Amer.)* im Krankenhaus; **into** *or* **to ~** *(Brit.),* **to the ~** *(Amer.)* ins Krankenhaus ⟨*gehen, bringen*⟩; **veterinary/dolls' ~:** Tier-/Puppenklinik, *die*

hospital: ~ **bed** *n.* Krankenhausbett, *das;* ~ **case** *n.* Fall fürs Krankenhaus

hospitalisation, hospitalise *see* **hospitaliz-**

hospitality [hɒspɪ'tælɪtɪ] *n., no pl. (of person)* Gastfreundschaft, *die; (of thing, action, environment)* Freundlichkeit, *die*

hospitalization [hɒspɪtəlaɪ'zeɪʃn] *n.* Einweisung ins Krankenhaus; **long periods of ~:** lange Krankenhausaufenthalte

hospitalize ['hɒspɪtəlaɪz] *v. t.* ins Krankenhaus einweisen

hospital: ~ **nurse** *n.* Krankenschwester, *die*/Krankenpfleger, *der;* ~ **porter** *n.* ≈ Krankenpflegehelfer, *der*/-helferin, *die;* ~ **ship** *n.* Lazarettschiff, *das*

¹host [həʊst] *n.* **a)** *(large number)* Menge, *die;* **in [their] ~s** in Scharen; **a ~ of people/children** eine Menge Leute/eine Schar von Kindern; **he has ~s** *or* **a ~ of things to do/friends** er hat eine Menge zu erledigen/eine Menge Freunde; **b)** *(arch.: army)* Heer, *das;* **c)** *(Bibl.)* **the Lord [God] of ~s** der Herr der Heerscharen; **the heavenly ~** *(angels)* die himmlischen Heerscharen *(bibl.)*

²host 1. *n.* **a)** Gastgeber, *der*/Gastgeberin, *die;* **be** *or* **play ~ to sb.** jmdn. zu Gast haben; ~ **country** Gastland, *das;* **b)** *(landlord)* [Gast]wirt, *der;* **mine ~** *(arch./joc.)* der Herr Wirt; **c)** *(compère)* Moderator, *der;* **your ~ for the show is ...:** durch die Show führt Sie ...; *(for chat show)* Gastgeber ist heute abend ...; **d)** *(Biol.: with parasite)* Wirt, *der;* **e)** *(Biol./Med.: recipient)* Empfänger [eines Transplantats]; *(of organ)* [Organ]empfänger, *der.* **2.** *v. t.* **a)** *(act as host at)* Gastgeber sein bei; **China is to ~ the Olympic Games** China soll die Olympischen Spiele ausrichten; **b)** *(compère)* moderieren; ~ **a programme** durch ein Programm führen

³host *n. (Eccl.: bread)* Hostie, *die*

hostage ['hɒstɪdʒ] *n.* Geisel, *die;* **hold/take sb. ~:** jmdn. als Geisel festhalten/nehmen; **a ~ to fortune** etwas, was einem das Schicksal nehmen kann; **give ~s to fortune** *or* **history** *or* **time** sich dem Schicksal in die Hand geben *(geh.)*

hostel ['hɒstl] *n. (Brit.)* **a)** Wohnheim, *das;* **b)** *see* **youth hostel**

hostelry ['hɒstlrɪ] *n. (arch./literary)* Herberge, *die (veralt.)*

hostess ['həʊstɪs] *n.* **a)** Gastgeberin, *die;* **take flowers for the ~:** der Dame des Hauses Blumen mitbringen; **b)** *(in night-club)* Animierdame, *die;* **c)** *(euphem.: prostitute)* Hostess, *die (verhüll.);* **d)** *(in passenger transport)* Hostess, *die; see also* **air hostess; e)** *(compère)* Moderatorin, *die*

'hostess gown *n.* Hausmantel, *der*

hostile ['hɒstaɪl] *adj.* **a)** feindlich; **b)** *(unfriendly)* feindselig **(to[wards]** gegenüber); **give sb. a ~ look** jmdn. feindselig ansehen; **be ~ to** *or* **towards sb.** jmdm. mit Feindseligkeit begegnen; **be ~ to sth.** etw. ablehnen; **a government ~ to change** eine Veränderungen ablehnende Regierung; **c)** *(inhospitable)* unwirtlich; feindselig ⟨*Atmosphäre*⟩; rauh ⟨*Wirklichkeit*⟩

hostility [hɒ'stɪlɪtɪ] *n.* **a)** *no pl. (enmity)* Feindschaft, *die;* **b)** *no pl. (antagonism)* Feindseligkeit, *die* **(to[wards]** gegenüber); **feel no ~ towards anybody** niemandem feindlich gesinnt sein; **show ~ to sth.** einer Sache *(Dat.)* feindlich gegenüberstehen; **c)** *(state of war, act of warfare)* Feindseligkeit, *die;* **an act of ~:** eine feindselige Handlung

hot [hɒt] **1.** *adj.* **a)** heiß; *(cooked)* warm ⟨*Mahlzeit, Essen*⟩; *(fig.: potentially dangerous, difficult)* heiß *(ugs.)* ⟨*Thema, Geschichte*⟩; ungemütlich, gefährlich ⟨*Lage*⟩; **bake in a ~ oven** bei hoher Temperatur backen; **the room is much too ~:** in dem Zimmer ist es viel zu heiß; **~ and cold running water** fließend warm und kalt Wasser; **I've climbed more mountains than you've had ~ dinners** *(coll.)* ich habe schon mehr Berge bestiegen, als du dir vorstellen kannst; **be too ~ to handle** *(fig.)* eine zu heiße Angelegenheit sein *(ugs.);* **things were getting too ~ for him [to handle]** *(fig.)* die Sache wurde ihm zu brenzlig *(ugs.);* **make it** *or* **things [too] ~ for sb.** *(fig.)* jmdm. die Hölle heiß machen *(ugs.);* **b)** *(feeling heat)* **I am/feel ~:** mir ist heiß; **I got ~:** mir wurde heiß; **I went ~ and cold all over** es überlief mich heiß und kalt; **c)** *(pungent)* scharf ⟨*Gewürz, Senf usw.*⟩; scharf gewürzt ⟨*Essen*⟩; **d)** *(suggesting heat)* grell, flammend ⟨*Farbe*⟩; **e)** *(passionate, lustful)* glühend ⟨*Begeisterung*⟩; heiß ⟨*Küsse, Tränen, Umarmung*⟩; **be ~ for sth.** heiß auf etw. *(Akk.)* sein *(ugs.);* **be ~ on sth./sb.** *(keen)* auf etw./jmdn. wild sein *(ugs.);* auf etw./jmdn. versessen sein; **he's really ~ on her** *(sexually)* er ist richtig scharf auf sie *(ugs.);* **have a ~ temper** ein hitziges Temperament haben; **f)** *(agitated, angry)* hitzig; **get ~ over sth.** sich an etw. *(Dat.)* erhitzen; **be [all] ~ and bothered** ganz aufgelöst sein; **get [all] ~ and bothered** sich [fürchterlich *(ugs.)*] aufregen; **g)** *(intense)* heiß ⟨*[Wett]kampf, Auseinandersetzung*⟩; **h)** *(coll.: good, skilful)* toll *(ugs.);* **be ~ at sth.** in etw. *(Dat.)* [ganz] groß sein *(ugs.);* **I'm not too ~ at that** darin bin ich nicht besonders umwerfend *(ugs.);* **be ~ on sth.** *(interested)* sich in *od.* mit etw. *(Dat.)* gut auskennen; **not so** *or* **too ~** *(coll.)* nicht gerade berauschend *(ugs.);* **i)** *(recent) (Hunting)* warm, frisch ⟨*Fährte*⟩; *(fig.)* noch warm ⟨*Nachrichten*⟩; **this is really ~ [news]** das ist wirklich das Neueste vom Neuen; **~ off the press[es]** *(Journ., Printing)* frisch aus der Presse; **j)** *(close)* **you are getting ~/are ~** *(in children's games)* es wird schon wärmer/[jetzt ist es] heiß; **follow ~ on sb.'s heels** jmdm. dicht auf den Fersen folgen *(ugs.);* **be ~ on sb.'s track** *or* **trail** jmdm. dicht auf den Fersen sein *(ugs.);* **in ~ pursuit** dicht auf den Fersen *(ugs.);* **k)** *(Mus.: rhythmical)* heiß; schräg *(ugs.)* ⟨*Musik*⟩; **he is a really ~ saxophonist** er spielt ein heißes Saxophon; **l)** *(coll.: in demand)* zugkräftig; **they are the ~test items just now** sie sind die augenblicklichen Renner *(ugs.);* **a ~ property** *(singer, actress, etc.)* eine ertragreiche Zugnummer; *(company, invention, etc.)* eine ertragreiche Geldanlage; **m)** *(sl.: radioactive)* heiß *(Kernphysik);* **n)** *(Sport; also fig.)* heiß *(ugs.)* ⟨*Tip, Favorit*⟩; **o)** *(sl.: illegally obtained)* heiß ⟨*Ware, Geld*⟩. *See also* **¹blow 1 b; cake 1 b; collar 1 a; potato a; red-hot; white-hot. 2.** *adv.* heiß. **3.** *n. in pl.* **have the ~s for sb.** *(sl.)* richtig scharf auf jmdn. sein *(ugs.)*

~ **'up** *(Brit. coll.)* **1.** *v. t.* **a)** *(heat)* warm machen; **b)** *(excite)* auf Touren bringen *(ugs.);* **c)** *(make more exciting)* in Schwung bringen; *(make more dangerous)* verschärfen; **d)** *(intensify)* anheizen *(ugs.);* **e)** *(Motor Veh.)* frisieren *(ugs.).* **2.** *v. i.* **a)** *(rise in temperature)* heiß werden; **the weather ~s up** es wird wärmer; **b)** *(become exciting)* in Schwung kommen; *(become dangerous)* sich verschärfen; **c)** *(become more intense)* sich verstärken; ⟨*Wortgefecht:*⟩ zunehmend heißer *od.* hitziger werden

hot: ~ **'air** *n. (sl.: idle talk)* leeres Gerede *(ugs.);* **talk ~ air** dummes Gewäsch von sich geben *(ugs. abwertend); see also* **balloon 1 a;** ~**bed** *n. (Hort.)* Mistbeet, *das;* Frühbeet, *das; (fig.: place favouring growth)* Nährboden, *der* **(of** für); *(of vice, corruption, etc.)* Brutstätte, *die* **(of** für); ~**-blooded** ['hɒtblʌdɪd] *adj.* heißblütig

hotchpotch ['hɒtʃpɒtʃ] *n. (mixture)* Mischmasch, *der (ugs.)* **(of** aus); **a ~ of people** eine bunte Mischung von Leuten *(scherzh.)*

hot: ~ **cross 'bun** *n. mit einem Kreuz aus Teig verziertes Rosinenbrötchen, das am Karfreitag gegessen wird;* ~ **'dog** *n. (coll.)* Hot dog, *das od. der; attrib.* **a ~-dog stand** ≈ eine Würstchenbude

hotel [hə'tel, həʊ'tel] *n.* **a)** Hotel, *das; see also* **private hotel; b)** *(Austral., NZ: public house)* Wirtshaus, *das*

hotelier [hə'telɪə(r)] *n.* Hotelier, *der*

hot: ~ **'flush** *n. (Med.)* **suffer from ~ flushes** unter fliegender Hitze leiden; ~**foot 1.** *adv.* stehenden Fußes; **2.** *adj.* **in ~foot pursuit** dicht auf den Fersen *(ugs.);* **3.** *v. i. (Amer. coll.)* **~foot home** machen, daß man nach Hause kommt *(ugs.);* **4.** *v. t.* **~foot it** sich hastig davonmachen; ~**head** *n.* Hitzkopf, *der;* ~**-headed** *adj.* hitzköpfig; ~**house** *n.* Treibhaus, *das; attrib. (lit. or fig.)* Treibhaus-; ~ **line** *n. (Polit.)* heißer Draht

hotly ['hɒtlɪ] *adv.* heftig; **they were hotly pursued by the police** die Polizei war ihnen dicht auf den Fersen *(ugs.);* **his cheeks flushed ~:** er wurde über und über rot

hot: ~**-'metal** *adj. (Printing)* Bleisatz-; ~ **'money** *n. (Finance)* heißes Geld

hotness ['hɒtnɪs] *n., no pl.* **a)** *(temperature)* Hitze, *die;* **test the ~:** die Wärme prüfen; **b)** *(hot sensation)* Hitze, *die;* **c)** *(pungency)* Schärfe, *die;* **d)** *(ardour)* Feuer, *das;* Glut, *die (geh.)*

hot: ~**plate** *n.* Kochplatte, *die; (for keeping food hot)* Warmhalteplatte, *die;* ~**pot** *n. (Gastr.)* **[Lancashire] ~pot** *Fleischeintopf mit Kartoffeleinlage;* ~ **rod** *n. (Motor Veh.)* hochfrisiertes Auto *(ugs.);* ~ **seat** *n. (sl.)* **a)** *(electric chair)* elektrischer Stuhl; **b)** *(uneasy situation)* Folterbank, *die (fig.); (involving heavy responsibility)* **be in the ~ seat** den Kopf hinhalten müssen *(ugs.);* ~ **shoe** *n. (Photog.)* [Blitzlicht]mittenkontakt, *der;* ~**-shot** *n. (coll.)* As, *das (ugs.);* ~ **spot** *n.* **a)** heiße Gegend; **b) a ~ spot of political instability** *(fig.)* ein politischer Krisenherd; **c)** *(night-club)* Nachtlokal, *das;* **d)** *(difficult situation)* **find oneself** *or* **be in/get into a ~ spot** in der Bredouille sein/in die Bredouille kommen *od.* geraten *(ugs.);* ~ **'spring** *n.* heiße Quelle; Thermalquelle, *die;* ~ **'stuff** *n., no pl., no art. (sl.)* **sb./sth. is ~ stuff** jmd./etw. ist große Klasse *(ugs.);* ~**-tempered** *adj.* heißblütig

Hottentot ['hɒtntɒt] *n. (person)* Hottentotte, *der*/Hottentottin, *die; attrib.* ⟨*Gebräuche, Lebensweise*⟩ der Hottentotten

hot: ~ **'water** *n. (fig. coll.)* **be in/get into ~ water** in der Bredouille sein/in die Bredouille geraten *(ugs.)*; **he got into ~ water with the authorities** er bekam Ärger mit den Behörden; **~-'water bag** *(Amer.)*, **~-'water bottle** *ns.* Wärmflasche, *die*

hound [haʊnd] **1.** *n.* **a)** Jagdhund, *der;* **the [pack of] ~s** *(Brit. Hunting)* die Meute *(Jägerspr.)*; **ride to ~s** mit der Meute jagen; **b)** *(despicable man)* Lump, *der.* **2.** *v. t.* jagen; *(fig.)* verfolgen; **they were ~ed from country to country** sie wurden von einem Land ins andere gejagt

~ **'down** *v. t. (lit. or fig.)* zur Strecke bringen

~ **'on** *v. t.* antreiben; **~ sb. on to do sth.** jmdn. [dazu] antreiben, etw. zu tun

~ **'out** *v. t.* **a)** *(hunt out)* aufspüren; **b)** *(force to leave)* vertreiben **(of** aus); verjagen **(of** aus)

hound's-tooth *n. (Textiles) (pattern)* Hahnentritt, *der; (fabric)* Stoff mit Hahnentrittmuster

hour ['aʊə(r)] *n.* **a)** Stunde, *die;* **half an ~:** eine halbe Stunde; **an ~ and a half** anderthalb Stunden; **be paid by the ~:** stundenweise bezahlt werden; **it takes her ~s to get ready** sie braucht Stunden, bis sie fertig ist; **I did two ~s' work** ich habe zwei Stunden [lang] gearbeitet; **there aren't enough ~s in the day** der Tag hat nicht genug Stunden [für all die Dinge, die man erledigen möchte], **an eight-~ day** ein Achtstundentag; **a two-~ session** eine zweistündige Sitzung; **the 24-~ clock** die Vierundzwanzigstundenuhr; *see also* **lunch-hour; b)** *(time o'clock)* Zeit, *die;* **the ~ grows late** *(literary)* es wird spät; **strike the ~:** die volle Stunde schlagen; **on the ~:** zur vollen Stunde; **every ~ on the ~:** jede volle Stunde; **at this late ~:** zu so später Stunde *(geh.)*; **at an early/a late ~:** zu früher/später *od.* vorgerückter Stunde *(geh.)*; **at all ~s** zu jeder [Tages- oder Nacht]zeit; *(late at night)* spät in der Nacht; **till all ~s [of the morning/night]** bis zum Morgengrauen/bis in die späte Nacht; **the small ~s [of the morning]** die frühen Morgenstunden; **0100/0200/1700/1800 ~s** *(on 24-~ clock)* 1.00/2.00/17.00/18.00 Uhr; **c)** *in pl.* **doctor's ~s** Sprechstunde, *die;* **post-office ~s** Schalterstunden der Post; **what ~s do you work?, what are your working ~s?** wie ist deine Arbeitszeit?; **strike for shorter ~s** für eine kürzere Arbeitszeit streiken; **work long ~s** einen langen Arbeitstag haben; **during school ~s** während der Schulstunden *od.* des Unterrichts; **out of/after ~s** *(in office, bank, etc.)* außerhalb der Dienstzeit; *(of doctor)* außerhalb der Sprechstunde; *(in shop)* außerhalb der Geschäftszeit; *(in pub)* außerhalb der Ausschankzeit; *(in school)* außerhalb der Unterrichtszeit; **keep regular/irregular ~s** geregelte/keine geregelten Zeiten einhalten; **what sort of ~s do you keep?** was hast du für einen Tagesrhythmus?; **be accustomed to late ~s** gewöhnlich lange aufbleiben; **d)** *(particular time)* Stunde, *die;* **don't desert me in my ~ of need** verlaß mich nicht in der Stunde der Not; **~ of glory** Stunde des Ruhmes; **sb.'s finest ~:** jmds. größte Stunde; **one's dying** *or* **final ~** *or* **~ of death** jmds. letzte Stunde *od.* Todesstunde; **at an unhappy/a happy ~:** in einer unglücklichen/glücklichen Stunde; **e)** *(present)* **the question** *etc.* **of the ~:** das Problem *usw.* der Stunde; **f)** *(distance)* Stunde, *die;* **they are two ~s from us by train** sie wohnen zwei Bahnstunden von uns entfernt; **he lives an ~ from the sea** er wohnt eine Stunde vom Meer entfernt; **g)** *in pl. (RC Ch.) (times)* Gebetsstunden; *(prayers)* Stundengebete; **book of ~s** Stundenbuch, *das. See also* **eleventh 1**

hour: ~glass *n.* Sanduhr, *die;* Stundenglas, *das (veralt.)*; **a woman with an ~glass figure** eine kurvenreiche Frau *(ugs. scherzh.)*; **~-hand** *n.* Stundenzeiger, *der;* kleiner Zeiger

houri ['hʊərɪ] *n. (Muslim Mythol.)* Huri, *die*

'hour-long 1. *attrib. adj.* einstündig. **2.** *adv.* eine Stunde [lang]

hourly ['aʊəlɪ] **1.** *adj.* **a)** *(happening every hour)* stündlich; **at ~ intervals** jede Stunde; stündlich; **there are ~ trains to London** jede *od.* alle Stunde fährt ein Zug nach London; **the bus service is ~:** der Bus verkehrt stündlich; **b)** *(reckoned by the hour)* **he is paid an ~ rate of £6** er hat einen Stundenlohn von 6 Pfund; **on an ~ basis** stundenweise ⟨*mieten*⟩; **c)** *(continual)* ständig; **d) two-~** zweistündlich. **2.** *adv.* stündlich; **be paid ~:** stundenweise bezahlt werden

house 1. [haʊs] *n., pl.* **~s** ['haʊzɪz] **a)** *(dwelling, occupants)* Haus, *das;* **a collection from ~ to ~:** eine Haussammlung; **to/at my ~:** zu mir [nach Hause]/bei mir [zu Hause]; **~ of cards** *(lit. or fig.)* Kartenhaus, *das;* **H~ of God** Gotteshaus, *das;* **~ and home** Haus und Hof; **keep ~ [for sb.]** [jmdm.] den Haushalt führen; **keep open ~:** ein offenes Haus haben *od.* führen; **set up ~:** einen eigenen Hausstand gründen; **put** *or* **set one's ~ in order** *(fig.)* seine Angelegenheiten in Ordnung bringen; **[as] safe as ~s** absolut sicher; **[get on] like a ~ on fire** *(fig.)* prächtig [miteinander auskommen]; **go all [a]round the ~s** *(fig.)* überall herumlaufen; *(in discussion)* sich lange im Kreise drehen; **man/lady** *or* **woman of the ~:** Hausherr, *der*/Dame des Hauses; **b)** *in comb. (for animals)* **lion-/reptile-/monkey-~:** Löwen-/Reptilien-/Affenhaus, *das;* **c)** *(Parl.) (building)* Parlamentsgebäude, *das; (assembly)* Haus, *das;* **the H~** *(Brit.)* das Parlament; **H~ of Keys** *Unterhaus der Insel Man; see also* **commons a; lord 1c; Lower House; parliament; representative 1b; Upper House; d)** *(institution)* Haus, *das;* **fashion ~:** Modehaus, *das;* **Broadcasting H~:** das Funkhaus; **Congress H~:** das Gewerkschaftshaus; **e)** *(inn etc.)* Wirtshaus, *das;* **keep a good ~:** ein gepflegtes Haus führen; **on the ~:** auf Kosten des Hauses; **~ of ill fame** *or* **repute** *(arch./joc.)*, **~** *(Amer.) (brothel)* öffentliches Haus *(verhüll.)*; *see also* **free house; tied; f)** *(Relig.) (residence)* Ordenshaus, *das; (members)* Ordensgemeinschaft, *die;* Orden, *der;* **a ~ of friars** ein Mönchskloster; **she entered a ~ of nuns** sie ging in ein Kloster; **g)** *(Univ.)* College, *das;* **h)** *(Sch.) eine von mehreren Schülergruppen innerhalb einer Privatschule;* **i)** *(Theatre) (building)* Haus, *das; (audience)* Publikum, *das; (performance)* Vorstellung, *die;* **an empty ~:** ein leeres Haus; **a good/bad ~:** eine gut/schlecht besuchte Vorstellung; **bring the ~ down, bring down the ~:** stürmischen Beifall auslösen; *(cause laughter)* Lachstürme entfesseln; *see also* **full house a; j)** *(family)* Haus, *das;* Geschlecht, *das;* **the H~ of Windsor** das Haus Windsor; **k)** *(Astrol.)* Haus, *das.* **2.** [haʊz] *v. t.* **a)** *(provide with home)* ein Heim geben (+ *Dat.*); **be ~d in sth.** in etw. *(Dat.)* untergebracht sein; **b)** *(receive in ~)* beherbergen; **be ~d by sb.** bei jmdm. unterkommen *od.* Unterkunft finden; **c)** *(keep, store)* unterbringen; einlagern ⟨*Waren*⟩; **d)** *(fig.: encase)* in sich *(Dat.)* bergen *(geh.)*

house [haʊs]: **~-agent** *n. (Brit.)* Häusermakler, *der;* **~ arrest** *n.* Hausarrest, *der;* **~boat** *n.* Hausboot, *das;* **~-bound** *adj.* ans Haus gefesselt; **~boy** *n.* Boy, *der;* **~breaker** *n. (burglar)* Einbrecher, *der;* **~breaking** *n., no pl. (burglary)* Einbruch, *der;* **~coat** *n.* Hausmantel, *der;* Morgenmantel, *der;* **~craft** *n., no pl., no art. (Brit.)* Hauswirtschaft, *die;* **~-father** *n.* Hausvater, *der;* **~-flag** *n. (Naut.)* Hausflagge, *die;* **~-fly** *n.* Stubenfliege, *die*

houseful ['haʊsfʊl] *n.* **a ~ of guests** ein Haus voll[er] Gäste; **we've already got a ~:** wir haben das Haus schon voll *(ugs.)*

house guest ['haʊs gest] *n.* Logiergast, *der*

household ['haʊshəʊld] *n.* **a)** Haushalt, *der; attrib.* Haushalts-; **~ chores** Hausarbeit, *die;* **b) the H~** *(Brit.: royal family)* die königliche Hofhaltung

household 'cavalry *n. (Brit. Mil.)* berittene königliche Leibgarde

householder ['haʊshəʊldə(r)] *n.* **a)** *(home-owner)* Wohnungsinhaber, *der*/-inhaberin, *die;* **b)** *(head of household)* Haushaltsvorstand, *der*

household: ~ **'gods** *n. pl. (Roman Ant.; also fig.)* Hausgötter; ~ **'management** *n.* Hauswirtschaft, *die;* ~ **'name** *n.* geläufiger Name; **be a ~ name** ein Begriff sein; ~ **'troops** *n. pl. (Brit. Mil.)* königliche Leibgarde; ~ **'word** *n.* geläufiger Ausdruck

house [haʊs]: **~-hunter** *n.* Haussuchende, *der/die;* **~-hunting** *n., no indef. art.* Suche nach einem Haus; **go ~-hunting** sich nach einem Haus umsehen; **~-husband** *n.* Hausmann, *der;* **~keep** *v. i. (coll.)* den Haushalt führen **(for** *Dat.*); **~keeper** *n.* *(woman managing household affairs)* Haushälterin, *die;* Wirtschafterin, *die; (person running own home)* Hausfrau, *die*/Hausmann, *der; (person in charge)* Hausmeister, *der*/-meisterin, *die;* **~keeping** *n.* **a)** *(management)* Hauswirtschaft, *die,* Haushaltsführung, *die;* **he does most of/helps with the ~keeping** er besorgt fast den ganzen Haushalt/hilft im Haushalt; **~keeping money,** *(coll.)* **~keeping** Haushalts- *od.* Wirtschaftsgeld, *das;* **b)** *(fig.: maintenance, record-keeping, etc.)* Wirtschaften, *das;* **~leek** *n. (Bot.)* Hauswurz, *die;* ~ **lights** *n. pl. (Theatre)* Lichter im Zuschauerraum; ~ **magazine** *n.* Hauszeitschrift, *die;* **~maid** *n.* Hausgehilfin, *die;* **~maid's 'knee** *n.* *(Med.)* Dienstmädchenknie, *das;* **~man** ['haʊsmən] *n., pl.* **~men** ['haʊsmən] **a)** Hausdiener, *der;* **b)** *(Brit. Med.)* Medizinalassistent, *der;* **~-martin** *see* **martin; ~master** *n. (Sch.) für ein „house" zuständiger Lehrer;* **~mistress** *n. (Sch.) für ein „house" zuständige Lehrerin;* **~-mother** *n.* Hausmutter, *die;* **~-painter** *n.* Maler, *die*/Malerin, *die;* Anstreicher, *der*/Anstreicherin, *die;* ~ **party** *n.* ≈ Gesellschaft, *die; mehrtägiges Fest in einem Landhaus;* ~ **physician** *n. (in hospital) im Krankenhaus wohnender Arzt; (elsewhere)* Hausarzt, *der;* Anstaltsarzt, *der;* **~-plant** *n.* Zimmerpflanze, *die;* ~ **prices** *n. pl.* Immobilienpreise; **~-proud** *adj.* **he/she is ~-proud** Ordnung und Sauberkeit [im Haushalt] gehen ihm/ihr über alles; **~-room** *n., no pl., no indef. art.* **find ~-room for sth.** einen Platz für etw. [in der Wohnung] finden; **I wouldn't give it ~-room** so etwas wollte ich nicht im Haus haben; ~ **'style** *n. (Printing, Publishing)* hauseigener Stil; ~ **surgeon** *n. (in hospital) im Krankenhaus wohnender Chirurg; (elsewhere)* Hauschirurg, *der;* Anstaltschirurg, *der;* **~-to-~: 1.** *adj.* **make ~-to-~ enquiries** von Haus zu Haus gehen und fragen; **a ~-to-~ delivery** eine Lieferung von Haus zu Haus; **2.** *adv.* von Haus zu Haus ⟨*gehen usw.*⟩; **~-top** *n.* [Haus]dach, *das;* **cry** *or* **proclaim** *or* **shout sth. from the ~-tops** *(fig.)* etw. öffentlich verkünden; **~-train** *v. t. (Brit.)* **~-train a cat/child** eine Katze/ein Kleinkind dazu bringen, daß sie/es stubenrein/sauber wird; **~-trained** *adj.* *(Brit.)* stubenrein ⟨*Hund, Katze*⟩; sauber ⟨*Kleinkind*⟩; **~-training** *n. (of pet)* Stubenreinmachen, *das; (of child)* Sauberkeitserziehung, *die;* Sauberkeitsgewöhnung, *die;* **~-warming** ['haʊswɔ:mɪŋ] *n.* **~-warming [party]** Einzugsfeier, *die;* **~wife** *n.* Hausfrau, *die;* **~wifely** *adj.* hausfraulich; **~work** *n., no pl.* Hausarbeit, *die*

housey[-housey], housie[-housie] ['haʊsɪ (haʊsɪ)] *n.* Lotto, *das*
housing ['haʊzɪŋ] *n.* **a)** *no pl. (dwellings collectively)* Wohnungen; *(provision of dwellings)* Wohnungsbeschaffung, *die; attrib.* Wohnungs-; **there was insufficient ~:** es gab zuwenig Wohnungen; **this piece of land has been set aside for ~:** auf diesem Stück Land sollen neue Wohnungen gebaut werden; **~ programme** Wohnungsbauprogramm, *das;* **b)** *no pl. (shelter)* Unterkunft, *die;* **c)** *(Mech. Engin.)* Gehäuse, *das*
housing: ~ association *n. (Brit.)* Gesellschaft für sozialen Wohnungsbau; **~ benefit** *n. (Brit.)* Wohngeld, *das;* **~ estate** *n. (Brit.)* Wohnsiedlung, *die*
hove *see* **heave 1 b, 2 e**
hovel ['hɒvl] *n.* [armselige] Hütte; *(joc.)* Bruchbude, *die (ugs. abwertend)*
hover ['hɒvə(r)] *v.i.* **a)** *(hang in air)* schweben; **b)** *(linger)* sich herumdrücken *(ugs.);* **~ about** *or* **round sb./sth.** um jmdn./etw. herumschleichen *(ugs.);* **c)** *(move to and fro)* herumstrolchen *(ugs. abwertend);* **d)** *(waver)* schwanken; **~ between doing this and doing that** schwanken, ob man dieses oder jenes tun soll; **~ between life and death** *(fig.)* zwischen Leben und Tod schweben
hover: ~craft *n., pl. same* Hovercraft, *das;* Luftkissenfahrzeug, *das;* **~port** *n.* Anlegestelle [für Hovercrafts]; **~train** *n.* Luftkissenzug, *der; (magnetic)* Magnetschwebebahn, *die*
how [haʊ] **1.** *adv.* wie; **learn ~ to ride a bike/swim** *etc.* radfahren/schwimmen *usw.* lernen; **this is ~ to do it** so macht man das; **~ do you know that?** woher weißt du das?; **~ to find the answer?** wie soll man die Lösung finden?; **~ should I know?** woher soll ich das wissen?; **~ 'could you?** wie konntest du nur?; **here's ~!** *(as toast)* zum Wohl!; **~ is it/does it happen that ...:** wie kommt es, daß ...; **~'s that?** *(~ did that happen?)* wie kommt das [denn]?; *(is that as it should be?)* ist es so gut?; *(will you agree to that?)* was hältst du davon?; *(Cricket)* ist der Schlagmann aus?; **~'s that for impudence?** ist das nicht eine Unverschämtheit?; **~ so?** wieso [das]?; **~ can that be?** wie kommt das?; **~ would it be if ...?** wie wäre es, wenn ...?; **~ would this dress be?** wie wäre es mit diesem Kleid?; **~ now?** *(arch.)* wie?; **[I know/see] ~ it is** [ich weiß,] wie das ist; **~ is she/the car?** *(after accident)* wie geht es ihr?/was ist mit dem Auto?; **~ 'are you?** wie geht es dir?; *(greeting)* guten Morgen/Tag/Abend!; **~ do you 'do?** *(formal)* guten Morgen/Tag/Abend!; **~ 'do?** *(coll.)* Morgen/Tag/'n Abend! *(ugs.);* **~ much?** wieviel?; *(joc.: I did not hear)* wie bitte?; **~ many?** wieviel?; wie viele?; **~ many times?** wie oft?; **~ crazy** *etc.* **can you get?** verrückter *usw.* geht's wohl nicht! *(ugs.);* **~ far** *(to what extent)* inwieweit; **~ marvellous/perfect!** wie herrlich *od.* wunderbar!**~ right/wrong you are!** da hast du völlig recht/da irrst du dich gewaltig!; **~ naughty of him** das war aber frech von ihm; **and ~!** *(coll.)* und wie! *(ugs.);* **we must earn a living ~ [best] we can** wir müssen uns unseren Lebensunterhalt, so gut es geht, verdienen; **~ about ...?** wie ist es mit ...?; *(in invitation, proposal, suggestion)* wie wäre es mit ...?; **~ about all the overtime I've done?** wie ist das eigentlich mit meinen ganzen Überstunden?; **~ about having a drink?** wie wäre es mit etwas zu trinken?; **~ about getting up?** wie wäre es, wenn du aufstehst/wir aufstehen?; **~ about [giving me] a lift?** wie sieht's aus, kannst du mich mitnehmen? *(ugs.);* **~ about tomorrow?** wie sieht's morgen aus? *(ugs.);* **~ about it/that?** na, wie ist das?/was sagst du nun?; *(is that acceptable?)* was hältst du davon?; *see also* **come m; ¹do 2 f; ever e; ¹go 1 r, s. 2.** *n.* Wie, *das*
howbeit [haʊ'bi:ɪt] *adv. (arch./literary)* nichtsdestominder
howdah ['haʊdə] *n. [baldachinartig überdachter] Sitz auf einem Elefanten*
how-de-do [haʊdɪ'du:], **how-do-you-do** [haʊdjʊ'du:] *ns.* **[this is] a fine** *or* **pretty ~ [we have landed in]** das ist ja eine schöne Bescherung *(ugs. iron.)*
howdy ['haʊdɪ] *int. (Amer.)* = **how do;** *see* **how 1**
how-d'ye-do [haʊdjə'du:] *see* **how-de-do**
however [haʊ'evə(r)] *adv.* **a)** wie ... auch; egal, wie *(ugs.);* **it's a long journey ~ you choose to travel, whether by train or by car** es ist eine lange Fahrt, ganz gleich, ob du mit dem Zug oder mit dem Auto fährst; **~ beautiful she is** wie schön sie auch ist; ganz gleich, wie schön sie ist; **I shall never win this race, ~ hard I try** ich werde dieses Rennen nie gewinnen, und wenn ich mich noch so anstrenge *od.* wie sehr ich mich auch anstrenge; **b)** *(nevertheless)* jedoch; aber; **I don't like him very much. H~, he has never done me any harm** Ich mag ihn nicht sehr. Er hat mir allerdings noch nie etwas getan; **~, the rain soon stopped, and ...:** es hörte jedoch *od.* aber bald auf zu regnen, und ...; **this, ~, seems not to be true** das scheint jedoch *od.* aber nicht wahr zu sein; **c)** *(coll.)* = **how ever** *see* **ever e**
howitzer ['haʊɪtsə(r)] *n. (Mil.)* Haubitze, *die*
howl [haʊl] **1.** *n.* **a)** *(of animal)* Heulen, *das; (of distress)* Schrei, *der;* **the repeated ~s of the dog** das wiederholte Heulen des Hundes; **a ~ of pain** *or* **agony** ein Schmerzensschrei; **~s of protest/rage** Protestgeschrei, *das*/wütendes Geschrei; **~s of laughter** brüllendes Gelächter; **~s of delight/merriment** Freudengeheul, *das;* **~s of derision/scorn** verächtliches Gejohle; **b)** *(Electr.)* Pfeifgeräusch, *das.* **2.** *v.i.* ⟨*Tier, Wind:*⟩ heulen; *(with distress)* schreien; **~ in** *or* **with pain/hunger** *etc.* vor Schmerz/Hunger *usw.* schreien; **~ with laughter** vor Lachen brüllen. **3.** *v.t.* [hinaus]schreien
~ 'down *v.t.* niederbrüllen
howler ['haʊlə(r)] *n.* **a)** *(coll.: blunder)* Schnitzer, *der (ugs.);* **make a ~:** sich *(Dat.)* einen Schnitzer leisten; **b)** *(Zool.) see* **~ monkey**
'howler monkey *n. (Zool.)* Brüllaffe, *der*
howling ['haʊlɪŋ] **1.** *n.* Heulen, *das; (of distress)* Schreien, *das.* **2.** *adj.* **a)** heulend ⟨*Tier, Wind*⟩; *(crying with distress)* schreiend; *(with laughter)* johlend; **the ~ mob** der johlende Pöbel; **five ~ brats/children** fünf Schreihälse *(ugs.);* **there is a ~ draught in this room** *(coll.)* hier im Zimmer zieht es höllisch *(ugs.);* **b)** *(sl.: extreme)* enorm; fürchterlich ⟨*Katastrophe*⟩; **a ~ mistake** ein Riesenfehler *(ugs.)*
howso'e'er *(poet.),* **howso'ever** *adv.* **a)** *(arch.)* wie auch immer; **b)** *(to whatsoever extent)* wie ... auch immer
hoy [hɔɪ] *int.* he! *(ugs.)*
HP *abbr.* **a)** [eɪtʃ'pi:] *(Brit.)* **hire-purchase; on ~:** auf Teilzahlungsbasis; **b)** horsepower PS; **c)** high pressure
HQ *abbr.* **headquarters** HQ
hr[s]. *abbr.* **hour[s]** Std[n].; **at 0800 hrs.** um 8.00 Uhr
HRH *abbr.* **Her/His Royal Highness** I./S. Kgl. H.
HT *abbr.* **high tension**
hub [hʌb] *n.* **a)** *(of wheel)* [Rad]nabe, *die;* **b)** *(fig.: central point)* Mittelpunkt, *der;* Zentrum, *das;* **the ~ of the universe** *(fig.)* der Nabel der Welt *(geh.)*
hubbub ['hʌbʌb] *n.* **a)** *(din)* Lärm, *der;* **a ~ of conversation/voices** ein Stimmengewirr; **b)** *(disturbance)* Tumult, *der;* **be in a ~:** sich in Aufruhr befinden
hubby ['hʌbɪ] *n. (coll.)* Mann, *der; (iron./joc.)* der Herr des Hauses
'hub-cap *n.* Radkappe, *die*
hubris ['hju:brɪs] *n., no pl.* Überheblichkeit, *die;* Hybris, *die (geh.)*
huckleberry ['hʌklbərɪ] *n. (Bot.)* **a)** *(Gaylussacia)* Gaylussacie, *die (fachspr.);* ≈ Heidelbeere, *die; attrib.* ≈ Heidelbeer-; **b)** *(Vaccinium)* Heidel- *od.* Blaubeere, *die*
huckster ['hʌkstə(r)] *n.* **a)** *(pedlar)* Straßenhändler, *der; (from door to door)* Hausierer, *der;* **b)** *(mercenary person)* Profitjäger, *der (abwertend);* **c)** *(Amer.) (salesman using showmanship)* Werbefachmann, *der; (Radio, Telev.: presenter)* Propagandist, *der*
huddle ['hʌdl] **1.** *v.i.* sich drängen; *(curl up, nestle)* sich kuscheln; **~ against each other/together** sich aneinanderdrängen/sich zusammendrängen; **a few cottages ~d on the hillside** ein paar kleine Häuser kauerten sich an den Hang. **2.** *v.t.* **a)** *(put on)* **~ one's coat around one** sich in den Mantel hüllen; **b)** *(crowd together)* [eng] zusammendrängen; **the sheep were ~d against the fence/together** die Schafe drängten sich gegen den Zaun/aneinander. **3.** *v. refl.* **~ oneself against sb./sth.** sich an jmdn./etw. kuscheln; **~ oneself up** sich zusammenkauern. **4.** *n.* **a)** *(tight group)* dichtgedrängte Menge *od.* Gruppe; **[stand] in a ~:** dicht zusammengedrängt [stehen]; **b)** *(coll.: conference)* Besprechung, *die;* **be in a ~/go [off] in[to] a ~:** die Köpfe zusammenstecken *(ugs.)*
~ 'up *v.i. (nestle up)* sich zusammenkauern; *(crowd together)* sich [zusammen]drängen; **~ up to sb./sth.** sich an jmdn./etw. kuscheln
¹hue [hju:] *n.* **a)** Farbton, *der;* **his face was of** *or* **had** *or* **looked a very sickly ~:** er hatte eine sehr ungesunde Gesichtsfarbe; **the sky took on a reddish ~:** der Himmel färbte sich rötlich; **b)** *(fig.: aspect)* Schattierung, *die;* Couleur, *die*
²hue *n.* **~ and cry** *(outcry)* lautes Geschrei; *(protest)* Gezeter, *das (abwertend);* **raise a ~ and cry against sb./sth.** ein lautes Geschrei/Gezeter über jmdn./etw. anstimmen
huff [hʌf] **1.** *v.i.* **~ and puff** schnaufen und keuchen; *(fig.: speak threateningly and bombastically)* sich aufblasen *(ugs.).* **2.** *n.* **be in a ~:** beleidigt *od. (ugs.)* eingeschnappt sein; **get into a ~:** einschnappen *(ugs.);* den Beleidigten/die Beleidigte spielen *(ugs.);* **go off in a ~:** beleidigt *od.* eingeschnappt abziehen *(ugs.)*
huffy ['hʌfɪ] *adj.* **a)** *(indignant)* ungehalten *(geh.);* **get ~ [about** *or* **over sth.]** [wegen etw.] beleidigt *od. (ugs.)* eingeschnappt sein; *(become irritated)* [über etw. *(Akk.)*] aufgebracht sein; **b)** *(easily offended)* empfindlich; gereizt ⟨*Stimmung, Laune*⟩
hug [hʌg] **1.** *n. (squeeze)* Umarmung, *die; (of animal)* Umklammerung, *die;* **give sb. a ~:** jmdn. umarmen. **2.** *v.t.,* **-gg-** **a)** *(squeeze)* umarmen; ⟨*Tier:*⟩ umklammern; **~ sb./sth. to oneself** jmdn./etw. an sich *(Akk.)* drücken *od.* pressen; **~ one's knees** seine Knie umfassen; **the bear ~ged him to death** der Bär drückte ihn zu Tode; **b)** *(keep close to)* sich dicht halten an *(+ Dat.);* ⟨*Schiff, Auto usw.:*⟩ dicht entlangfahren an *(+ Dat.);* **c)** *(fit tightly around)* eng anliegen an *(+ Dat.);* **a pullover that ~s the figure** ein Pullover, der die Figur betont. **3.** *v. refl.,* **-gg-** die Arme um sich schlagen; **we ~ged ourselves for** *or* **on managing to win** *(fig.)* wir beglückwünschten uns dazu, den Sieg errungen zu haben
huge [hju:dʒ] *adj.* riesig; gewaltig ⟨*Unterschied, Verbesserung, Interesse*⟩; **the problem is ~:** das Problem ist außerordentlich schwierig; **she is not just fat: she is ~:** sie ist nicht einfach dick: sie ist ein Monstrum; **tell ~ lies** wie gedruckt lügen *(ugs.)*
hugely ['hju:dʒlɪ] *adv.* gewaltig; riesig ⟨*sich freuen, sich amüsieren*⟩; außerordentlich ⟨*intelligent*⟩; ungeheuer ⟨*erfolgreich*⟩
Huguenot ['hju:gənɒt, 'hju:gənəʊ] *pr. n.*

Hugenotte, *der*/Hugenottin, *die; attrib.* Hugenotten-

huh [hʌ] *int. (Amer.)* pah!

hula hoop ['hu:lə hu:p] *n.* Hula-Hoop-Reifen, *der*

hulk [hʌlk] *n.* **a)** *(body of ship)* [Schiffs]rumpf, *der; (as store etc.)* Hulk, *die od. der (Seew.);* **b)** *(wreck) (of car, machine, etc.)* Wrack, *das; (of house)* Ruine, *die;* **c)** *(unwieldy ship)* dicker Pott *(ugs.);* **d)** *(fig.) (big thing)* Klotz, *der; (big person)* Koloß, *der (ugs. scherzh.);* **a ~ of a man** ein Klotz von [einem] Mann *(fig. ugs.)*

hulking ['hʌlkɪŋ] *adj. (coll.) (bulky)* wuchtig; *(clumsy)* klotzig *(abwertend);* **a ~ great person/thing** ein klobiger Mensch/ein klobiges Etwas; **a ~ great brute of a man/dog** ein grobschlächtiger, brutaler Kerl/ein scheußliches Ungetüm von einem Hund

¹hull [hʌl] *n. (Naut.)* Schiffskörper, *der; (Aeronaut.)* Rumpf, *der;* **be ~ down on the horizon** ‹*Schiff:*› am Horizont entschwinden/auftauchen

²hull 1. *n. (Bot.) (pod, husk)* Hülse, *die; (of peas)* Schote, *die; (of barley, oats, etc.)* Spelze, *die.* **2.** *v.t.* enthülsen ‹*Erbsen, Bohnen, Korn*›; entstielen ‹*Erdbeeren*›

hullabaloo [hʌləbə'lu:] *n.* **a)** *(noise)* Radau, *der (ugs.);* Lärm, *der; (of show-business life, city)* Trubel, *der;* **b)** *(controversy)* Aufruhr, *der;* **make a ~ about sth.** viel Lärm um etw. machen; **I don't see what all the ~ is about** ich verstehe nicht, was das ganze Theater *(ugs.)* eigentlich soll

hullo [hə'ləʊ] *see* **hallo; hello**

hum [hʌm] **1.** *v. i.*, **-mm- a)** summen; ‹*Motor, Maschine, Kreisel:*› brummen; **~ and ha** *or* **haw** *(coll.)* herumdrucksen *(ugs.);* **the workshop was ~ming with the noise of machinery** die Werkstatt war vom Brummen der Maschinen erfüllt; **b)** *(coll.: be in state of activity)* voller Leben *od.* Aktivität sein; **things are ~ming** die Sache ist in Schwung gekommen *od.* läuft *(ugs.);* **make things ~, set things ~ming** die Sache in Schwung bringen *(ugs.);* **c)** *(Brit. sl.: smell)* riechen. **2.** *v.t.*, **-mm-** summen ‹*Melodie, Lied*›. **3.** *n.* **a)** Summen, *das; (of spinning-top, machinery, engine)* Brummen, *das;* **b)** *(inarticulate sound)* Hm, *das;* **~s and ha's** *or* **haws** verlegenes Geräusper; **c)** *(of voices, conversation)* Gemurmel, *das; (of insects and small creatures)* Gesumme, *das; (of traffic)* Brausen, *das;* **d)** *(Electronics)* Brummen, *das;* **e)** *(Brit. sl.: smell)* Geruch, *der.* **4.** *int.* hm

human ['hju:mən] **1.** *adj.* menschlich; **~ biology** Humanbiologie, *die;* **result in a terrible loss of ~ life** ‹*Katastrophe:*› erschreckend viele Menschenleben fordern *(geh.);* **untouched by ~ hand** hygienisch verpackt ‹*Lebensmittel*›; **the ~ condition** das Menschsein; **the ~ race** die menschliche Rasse; das Menschengeschlecht *(geh.);* **~ sacrifice** Menschenopfer, *das;* **~ dustbin** *(joc.)* Resteesser, *der;* **they formed a ~ chain** sie bildeten eine Kette; *(as demonstration)* sie bildeten eine Menschenkette; **do everything within ~ power** alles menschenmögliche tun; **that is not ~:** das ist unmenschlich; **I sometimes wonder if he's ~** *(iron.)* manchmal frage ich mich, ob er überhaupt ein Mensch ist; **I'm only ~:** ich bin auch nur ein Mensch; **it's only ~:** es ist menschlich; **~ error** menschliches Versagen; **the ~ element** *or* **factor** das menschliche Element; der menschliche Faktor; **lack the ~ touch** menschliche Wärme vermissen lassen; **be ~!** sei kein Unmensch!; *see also* **nature d. 2.** *n.* Mensch, *der*

human: ~ 'being *n.* Mensch, *der;* **~ 'comedy** *n.* menschliche Komödie *(fig.)*

humane [hju:'meɪn] *adj.* **a)** human; **b)** *(tending to civilize)* humanistisch

humane 'killer *n. Instrument zur schmerzlosen Tötung von Tieren (bes. im Schlachthof)*

humanely [hju:'meɪnlɪ] *adv.* human

human: ~ engi'neering *n. (Industry)* Human engineering, *das;* Ergonomie, *die;* **~ 'interest** *n., no pl.* **a story full of/an occupation with a lot of ~ interest** eine Geschichte, in der/ein Beruf, in dem das Menschliche eine große Rolle spielt; **~-interest story** Geschichte aus dem Leben

humanise *see* **humanize**

humanism ['hju:mənɪzm] *n., no pl.* **a)** Humanität, *die;* Menschlichkeit, *die;* **b)** *(literary culture; also Philos.)* Humanismus, *der*

humanist ['hju:mənɪst] *n.* Humanist, *der*/Humanistin, *die*

humanistic [hju:mə'nɪstɪk] *adj.* **a)** *(Philos.)* humanistisch; **b)** *(humanitarian)* humanitär ‹*Einstellung, Zwecke*›; von Menschlichkeit zeugend ‹*Äußerung*›; **c)** *(of classical study)* humanistisch; *(as opposed to scientific study)* geisteswissenschaftlich

humanitarian [hju:mænɪ'teərɪən] **1.** *adj.* humanitär. **2.** *n. (philanthropist)* Menschenfreund, *der; (promoter of human welfare)* Humanitarist, *der*/Humanitaristin, *die*

humanitarianism [hju:mænɪ'teərɪənɪzm] *n., no pl.* Humanitarismus, *der*

humanity [hju:'mænɪtɪ] *n.* **a)** *no pl.* Menschsein, *das;* **he was a pathetic specimen of ~:** er war ein jämmerliches Exemplar der Gattung Mensch; **b)** *no pl., no art. (mankind)* Menschheit, *die; (people collectively)* Menschen; **c)** *no pl. (being humane)* Humanität, *die;* Menschlichkeit, *die;* **d)** *in pl. (cultural learning)* **[the] humanities** [die] Geisteswissenschaften; *(study of Latin and Greek classics)* [die] Altphilologie; [die] klassische Philologie

humanize ['hju:mənaɪz] *v.t.* **a)** *(make human)* vermenschlichen; **b)** *(adapt to human use)* den menschlichen Bedürfnissen anpassen; humanisieren ‹*Industrie*›; **c)** *(make humane)* humanisieren ‹*Strafvollzug*›; zivilisieren ‹*Wilde*›; geistig bilden ‹*Gesellschaft*›

'humankind *n., no pl., no art.* die Menschheit; **all ~:** die ganze Menschheit

humanly ['hju:mənlɪ] *adv.* menschlich; *(by human means)* mit menschlichen Mitteln; **do everything ~ possible** alles menschenmögliche tun; **would it be ~ possible to obtain a copy?** wäre es zuviel verlangt, ein Exemplar zu bekommen?

human: ~ re'lations *n. pl. (Social Psych., Industry)* Human Relations *Pl.;* **~ 'right** *n.* **~ rights** Menschenrechte *Pl.;* **fundamental ~ right** Grundrecht, *das;* **Court of H~ Rights** Europäischer Gerichtshof für Menschenrechte

humble ['hʌmbl] **1.** *adj.* **a)** *(modest)* bescheiden; ergeben ‹*Untertan, Diener, Gefolgsmann*›; bescheiden ‹*Vorschlag, Meinung*›; demütig ‹*Gebet*›; ehrfurchtsvoll ‹*Bewunderung*›; unterwürfig *(oft abwertend)* ‹*Haltung, Knechtschaft*›; **when I look up at the vast universe, it makes me feel very ~:** wenn ich das unermeßliche Universum betrachte, komme ich mir sehr klein und unbedeutend vor; **may I offer** *or* **please accept my ~ apologies** ich bitte ergebenst um Verzeihung; **eat ~ pie** klein beigeben; *see also* **servant c; b)** *(low-ranking)* einfach; niedrig ‹*Status, Rang usw.*›; **he stems from very ~ stock/origins** er ist von sehr niedriger Geburt *od.* Herkunft; **c)** *(unpretentious)* einfach; bescheiden ‹*Zuhause, Wohnung, Anfang*›; **the meal/gift was a very ~ offering** es war ein sehr einfaches Essen/nur eine bescheidene Gabe. **2.** *v.t.* **a)** *(abase)* demütigen; **feel ~d** sich *(Dat.)* klein vorkommen; **~ oneself** sich demütigen *od.* erniedrigen; **b)** *(remove power of)* entmachten; *(defeat decisively)* [vernichtend] schlagen; **~ oneself** sich [selbst] erniedrigen

'humble-bee *n.* Hummel, *die*

humbly ['hʌmblɪ] *adv.* **a)** *(with humility)* demütig; ergebenst ‹*um Verzeihung bitten*›; ergeben ‹*dienen*›; *(meekly)* unterwürfig; *(in formal address)* höflichst ‹*bitten, ersuchen*›; **b)** *(in low rank)* **~ born** von niedriger Herkunft; **c)** *(unpretentiously)* einfach; bescheiden; spärlich ‹*ausgestattet*›

humbug ['hʌmbʌg] *n.* **a)** *no pl., no art. (deception, nonsense)* Humbug, *der (ugs. abwertend);* **b)** *(fraud)* Schwindel, *der;* Betrug, *der;* **c)** *(impostor)* Schwindler, *der*/Schwindlerin, *die (abwertend);* **d)** *(Brit.: sweet)* [Pfefferminz]bonbon, *der od. das*

humdinger ['hʌmdɪŋə(r), hʌm'dɪŋə(r)] *n. (sl.)* **be a ~:** Spitze *od.* große Klasse sein *(ugs.);* **she's a real ~:** sie ist absolute Spitze; **when we have a quarrel, it's a real ~:** wenn wir uns streiten, fliegen die Fetzen *(ugs.)*

humdrum ['hʌmdrʌm] *adj.* **a)** alltäglich; eintönig ‹*Leben*›; langweilig ‹*Person*›; **b)** *(monotonous)* stumpfsinnig; **the ~ routine of life/things** das tägliche Einerlei

humerus ['hju:mərəs] *n., pl.* **humeri** ['hju:məraɪ] *(Anat., Zool.)* Humerus, *der*

humid ['hju:mɪd] *adj.* feucht; humid *(Geogr.)*

humidifier [hju:'mɪdɪfaɪə(r)] *n.* Luftbefeuchter, *der*

humidify [hju:'mɪdɪfaɪ] *v.t.* befeuchten

humidity [hju:'mɪdɪtɪ] *n.* **a)** *no pl.* Feuchtigkeit, *die;* **I don't mind the heat but I cannot stand ~:** die Hitze macht mir nichts aus, aber die [hohe] Luftfeuchtigkeit kann ich nicht vertragen; **the ~ of the atmosphere** die [hohe] Luftfeuchtigkeit; **b)** *(degree of moisture)* **~ [of the atmosphere]** Luftfeuchtigkeit, *die (Met.);* Luftfeuchte, *die (bes. fachspr.)*

humiliate [hju:'mɪlɪeɪt] *v.t.* demütigen; **I was** *or* **felt totally ~d** ich war zutiefst beschämt

humiliation [hju:mɪlɪ'eɪʃn] *n.* Demütigung, *die*

humility [hju:'mɪlɪtɪ] *n.* Demut, *die; (of servant)* Ergebenheit, *die; (absence of pride or arrogance)* Bescheidenheit, *die*

humming ['hʌmɪŋ]: **~-bird** *n.* Kolibri, *der;* **~-top** *n.* Brummkreisel, *der*

hummock ['hʌmək] *n.* **a)** *(hillock)* [kleiner] Hügel; **b)** *(Amer.: rise)* Waldinsel, *die;* **c)** *(in ice-field)* Eishügel, *der*

humor *(Amer.) see* **humour**

humoresque [hju:mə'resk] *n. (Mus.)* Humoreske, *die*

humorist ['hju:mərɪst] *n.* **a)** *(facetious person)* Spaßvogel, *der;* Komiker, *der (fig.);* **b)** *(talker, writer)* Humorist, *der*/Humoristin, *die*

humorless *(Amer.) see* **humourless**

humorous ['hju:mərəs] *adj.* **a)** *(comic)* lustig, komisch ‹*Geschichte, Name, Situation*›; witzig ‹*Bemerkung*›; **I fail to see anything ~ in the situation** ich finde die Situation überhaupt nicht komisch *od.* lustig; **the ~ side of the situation** das Komische der Situation; **stop trying to be ~:** hör auf damit, komisch wirken zu wollen!; **b)** *(showing sense of humour)* humorvoll ‹*Person*›; **be/not be in a ~ mood** in heiterer Stimmung sein/nicht zum Lachen aufgelegt sein

humorously ['hju:mərəslɪ] *adv.* **a)** *(comically)* komisch; lustig; **his remarks were meant ~, not offensively** seine Bemerkungen sollten belustigen und nicht verletzen; **~ enough, ...:** lustigerweise ...; **b)** *(with sense of humour)* humorvoll; **look ~ at the problems of life** den Problemen des Alltags mit Humor begegnen

humour ['hju:mə(r)] *(Brit.)* **1.** *n.* **a)** *no pl., no indef. art. (faculty, comic quality)* Humor, *der; (of situation)* Komische, *das;* **see the ~ of sth.** einer Sache *(Dat.)* die komische Seite abgewinnen; **sense of ~:** Sinn für Humor; **he has no sense of ~:** er hat keinen Humor; **b)** *no pl., no indef. art. (facetiousness)* Witzigkeit, *die;* **a funeral is no place for ~:** bei einer Beerdigung macht man keine Witze; **c)** *(mood)* Laune, *die;* **his ~ is sometimes melancholy** er ist manchmal [in] melancholisch[er Stimmung]; **be in a good/bad ~:** in guter Stimmung sein/schlechte Laune haben; **what sort of ~ are you in?** wie ist deine Stimmung?; **in good ~:** gutgelaunt; **be out of ~:** schlechte Laune haben; **a fit of ill ~:** ein Anfall von schlechter Laune; **have recovered one's good ~:** wieder bei Laune sein; **d)** *(disposition)* Temperament, *das;* **be of a pleasant/jovial ~:** eine angenehme/joviale Art haben; **e)** *(Hist.: body fluid)* Körpersaft, *der;* Humor, *der (Med. veralt.);* **the cardinal ~s** die Hauptsäfte des Körpers; *see also* **aqueous humour; vitreous b. 2.** *v. t.* *(indulge)* willfahren *(geh.)* (+ *Dat.*); **~ sb.** jmdm. seinen Willen lassen; **~ sb.'s taste** jmds. Geschmack *od.* Vorliebe *(Dat.)* entsprechen; **don't [try to] ~ me!** sei nicht so übertrieben rücksichtsvoll!; **do it just to ~ her/him** tu's doch, damit sie ihren/er seinen Willen hat

humourless ['hju:məlɪs] *adj. (Brit.)* humorlos; todernst ⟨*Gesicht*⟩; trocken ⟨*Buch*⟩

humous ['hju:məs] *adj.* humos *(Bodenk.)*

hump [hʌmp] **1.** *n.* **a)** *(human)* Buckel, *der;* Höcker, *der (ugs.); (of animal)* Höcker, *der;* **he has a ~ on his back** er hat einen Buckel; **live on one's ~** *(fig.)* von seinen Reserven leben; **b)** *(mound)* Hügel, *der; (Railw.)* Ablaufberg, *der;* **c)** *(fig.: critical point)* Wendepunkt, *der;* **be over the ~:** über den Berg sein *(ugs.);* **d)** *(Brit. sl.)* **have the ~:** sauer sein *(ugs.);* **get the ~:** [stink]sauer werden *(ugs.).* **2.** *v. t.* *(Brit. sl.)* *(carry)* schleppen; *(hoist)* **~ a sack on to one's shoulders** einen Sack buckeln *od.* auf den Buckel nehmen *(ugs.)*

hump: ~back *n.* **a)** *see* **hunchback; b)** *see* **~back whale; ~back 'bridge** *n.* gewölbte Brücke; **~backed** ['hʌmpbækt] *adj. see* **hunchbacked; ~back 'whale** *n.* Buckelwal, *der;* **~ 'bridge** *see* **~back bridge**

humph [hmf] **1.** *int.* hm. **2.** *n.* Hm, *das;* Grunzen, *das (ugs.)*

humus ['hju:məs] *n.* Humus, *der*

Hun [hʌn] *n.* **a)** *(Hist.)* Hunne, *der*/Hunnin, *die; attrib.* Hunnen-; **b)** *(derog.: German)* Sauerkrautfresser, *der (ugs. abwertend);* **the ~** *(collect.)* der Teutone *(abwertend)*

¹hunch [hʌntʃ] **1.** *v. t.* hochziehen ⟨*Schultern*⟩; **sit ~ed in a corner** zusammengekauert in einer Ecke sitzen; **he/the cat ~ed his/its back** er/die Katze machte einen Buckel. **2.** *v. i.* *(Amer.)* **a)** *(adopt bent posture)* sich krümmen; *(curl up)* sich zusammenrollen; **~ in a chair** gebeugt *od.* mit krummem Rücken auf einem Stuhl sitzen; **b)** *(rise in hump)* sich buckelartig erheben; sich nach oben wölben; **his shoulders ~ed** er zog die Schultern hoch

~ 'up 1. *v. t.* hochziehen; **don't sit ~ed up like that** sitz nicht so krumm da!; **~ oneself up** einen Buckel machen. **2.** *v. i.* *(Amer.) see* **~ 2**

²hunch *n.* *(intuitive feeling)* Gefühl, *das;* **I have a ~ that ..., my ~ is that ...:** ich habe das [leise] Gefühl, daß ...; **the detective followed a ~:** der Detektiv folgte einem inneren Gefühl

hunch: ~back *n.* **a)** *(back)* Buckel, *der;* **b)** *(person)* Bucklige, *der/die;* **be a ~back** einen Buckel haben; **the H~back of Notre Dame** der Glöckner von Notre-Dame; **~backed** ['hʌntʃbækt] *adj.* buck[e]lig; höckerig ⟨*Kamel*⟩

hundred ['hʌndrəd] **1.** *adj.* **a)** hundert; **a** *or* **one ~:** [ein]hundert; **two/several ~:** zweihundert/mehrere hundert; **a** *or* **one ~ and one** [ein]hundert[und]eins; **a** *or* **one ~ and one people** hundert[und]ein Menschen *od.* Mensch; **the ~ metres race** der Hundertmeterlauf; **the H~ Years War** *(Hist.)* der Hundertjährige Krieg; **eighteen ~ hours** 18.00 Uhr; **b) a ~ [and one]** *(fig.: innumerable)* hundert *(ugs.);* **I've told you a ~ times** ich habe es dir schon hundertmal gesagt; **never** *or* **not in a ~ years** nie im Leben; **I've got a ~ [and one] things to do** ich habe hunderterlei zu tun *(ugs.);* **c) a** *or* **one ~ per cent** hundertprozentig; **I'm not a ~ per cent at the moment** *(fig.)* momentan geht es mir nicht sehr gut. *See also* **eight 1; mile a. 2.** *n.* **a)** *(number)* hundert; **a** *or* **one/two ~:** [ein]hundert/zweihundert; **count up to a** *or* **one ~:** bis hundert zählen; **not if I live to be a ~:** nie im Leben; **in** *or* **by ~s** hundertweise; **the seventeen-~s** *etc.* das achtzehnte *usw.* Jahrhundert; **a ~ and one** *etc.* [ein]hundert[und]eins *usw.;* **a** *or* **one/two ~ of the men died** einhundert/zweihundert der Männer starben; **there are five ~ of us** wir sind zu fünfhundert; **it's a ~ to one that ...:** die Chancen stehen hundert zu eins, daß ...; **b)** *(symbol, written figure)* Hundert, *die; in adding numbers by columns* Hunderter, *der (Math.); (set or group of 100)* Hundert, *das; (~-pound etc. note)* Hunderter, *der;* **c)** *(indefinite amount)* **~s** Hunderte *Pl.;* **tourists flock to Rome by the ~[s]** *or* **in their ~s:** die Touristen reisen zu Hunderten nach Rom; **~s of times** hundertmal; **d)** *(Brit. Hist.: county division)* Zent, *die; see also* **Chiltern Hundreds.** *See also* **eight 2 a**

hundredfold ['hʌndrədfəʊld] **1.** *adv.* hundertfach. **2.** *adj.* hundertfach. **3.** *n.* Hundertfache, *das;* **improve a ~** *(fig.)* sich um ein Vielfaches verbessern; **she had repaid his kindness a ~:** sie hatte seine Güte tausendfach vergolten; **by a ~:** um das Hundertfache. See also **eightfold**

hundreds and 'thousands *n. pl. (sweets)* Liebesperlen *Pl.*

hundredth ['hʌndrədθ] **1.** *adj.* hundertst...; **the one-/two-~ person** der [ein]hundertste/zweihundertste Mensch; **a ~ part** ein Hundertstel; *see also* **eighth 1. 2.** *n.* **a)** *(fraction)* Hundertstel, *das;* **a ~ of a second** eine Hundertstelsekunde; **b)** *(in sequence)* hundertste, *der/die/das; (in rank)* Hundertste, *der/die/das;* **Old H~** *(Eccl.)* der hundertste Psalm. *See also* **eighth 2**

hundredweight ['hʌndrədweɪt] *n., pl. same or* **~s a)** *(Brit.)* **[long] ~:** 50,8 kg; ≈ Zentner, *der;* **b)** *(in metric weight)* **[metric] ~:** Zentner, *der;* **c)** *(Amer.)* **[short] ~:** 45,36 kg; ≈ Zentner, *der (45,36 kg)*

hung *see* **hang 1, 2**

Hungarian [hʌŋ'geərɪən] **1.** *adj.* ungarisch; **sb. is ~:** jmd. ist Ungar/Ungarin; *see also* **English 1. 2.** *n.* **a)** *(person)* Ungar, *der*/Ungarin, *die;* **b)** *(language)* Ungarisch, *das; see also* **English 2 a**

Hungary ['hʌŋgərɪ] *pr. n.* Ungarn *(das)*

hunger ['hʌŋgə(r)] **1.** *n. (lit. or fig.)* Hunger, *der;* **pang[s] of ~:** quälender Hunger; **the pangs of ~ were getting stronger** der Hunger plagte mich *usw.* immer mehr; **~ is the best sauce** *(prov.)* Hunger ist der beste Koch *(Spr.);* **die of ~:** verhungern; *(fig.: be very hungry)* vor Hunger sterben *(ugs.);* **~ for sth.** *(lit. or fig.)* Hunger nach etw. *(geh.);* **~ for revenge/knowledge** Rache-/Wissensdurst, *der.* **2.** *v. i.* *(have craving);* **~ after** *or* **for sb./sth.** [heftiges] Verlangen nach jmdm./etw. haben

hunger: ~-march *n.* Hungermarsch, *der;* **~-marcher** *n.* Hungermarschierer, *der;* **~-strike 1.** *n.* Hungerstreik, *der;* **stage a/go on ~-strike** in den Hungerstreik treten; **2.** *v. i.* in den Hungerstreik treten; **be ~-striking** sich im Hungerstreik befinden; **~-striker** *n.* Hungerstreikende, *der/die*

hung: ~ 'jury *n. Geschworenengericht, das zu keinem einstimmigen Urteil/keinem Mehrheitsurteil gelangen kann;* **~-'over** *adj. (coll.)* verkatert *(ugs.);* **~ 'parliament** *n. Parlament, in dem keine Partei die absolute Mehrheit hat*

hungrily ['hʌŋgrɪlɪ] *adv.* **a)** hungrig; **my stomach was rumbling/growling ~:** mir knurrte vor Hunger der Magen; **b)** *(fig.: longingly)* sehnsüchtig ⟨*an etw. denken*⟩; [be]gierig ⟨*etw. verfolgen*⟩

hungry ['hʌŋgrɪ] *adj.* **a)** *(feeling hunger)* hungrig; *(regularly feeling hunger or lacking food)* hungernd; *(showing hunger)* hungrig, gierig ⟨*Augen, Blick*⟩; **be ~:** Hunger haben; hungrig sein; **we were poor and ~:** wir waren arm und litten Hunger; **[as] ~ as a hunter** *or* **lion** *or* **wolf** hungrig wie ein Löwe *od.* Wolf; **go ~:** hungern; hungrig bleiben; **I don't like fish. – Go ~, then!** Ich mag keinen Fisch. – Dann mußt du eben hungern; **~ years** Hungerjahre *Pl.;* **b)** *(inducing hunger)* hungrig machend; **c)** *(fig.: eager, avaricious)* [hab]gierig ⟨*Spekulant*⟩; stürmisch ⟨*Liebhaber*⟩; brennend, glühend ⟨*Verlangen*⟩; hungrig ⟨*Ozean, Kriegsmaschine usw.*⟩; **be ~ for sb./sth.** sich nach jmdm. sehnen/nach etw. hungern *(geh.);* **be ~ to do sth.** darauf brennen, etw. zu tun; **~ for success/power/knowledge/love** erfolgs-/macht-/bildungs-/liebeshungrig; **~ to learn** lernbegierig; **be ~ after sth.** nach etw. hungern *(geh.);* **success-/war-/freedom-~:** erfolgshungrig/kriegslustig/freiheitsdurstig; **d)** *(barren)* karg

hunk [hʌŋk] *n.* **a)** *(large piece)* [großes] Stück; *(clumsy piece)* Brocken, *der; (of bread)* Brocken, *der;* Ranken, *der (landsch.);* **~s of wood** große Holzscheite; **b)** *(coll.: large person)* stattliche Erscheinung; **he is a gorgeous great ~:** er ist ein blendend aussehender, stattlicher Mann; **a great ~ of a weight-lifter** ein Koloß *(ugs. scherzh.)* von einem Gewichtheber

hunky ['hʌŋkɪ] *adj. (coll.)* stattlich

hunky-dory [hʌŋkɪ'dɔ:rɪ] *adj. (Amer. sl.)* prima *(ugs.);* **everything's ~, it's all ~:** es ist alles in [bester] Ordnung

hunt [hʌnt] **1.** *n.* **a)** *(pursuit of game)* Jagd, *die;* **the ~ is up** *(Sport)* die Jagd ist eröffnet; Jagd frei! *(Jägerspr.);* **badger-/deer-~:** Dachs-/Hirschjagd, *die;* **b)** *(search)* Suche, *die; (strenuous search)* Jagd, *die;* **be on the ~ for sb./sth.** auf der Suche/Jagd nach jmdm./etw. sein; **the ~ is on/up [for sb./sth.]** die Suche/Jagd [nach jmdm./etw.] hat begonnen/die Jagd [nach jmdm./etw.] ist eröffnet; **c)** *(body of fox-hunters)* Jagd[gesellschaft], *die; (association)* Jagdverband, *der;* **the local ~:** der örtliche Jägerverein; **d)** *(district)* Jagd, *die;* Jagdrevier, *das.* **2.** *v. t.* **a)** jagen; Jagd machen auf (+ *Akk.*); **he spends his weekends ~ing foxes** am Wochenende geht er auf die Fuchsjagd; **b)** *(search for)* Jagd machen auf (+ *Akk.*) ⟨*Mörder usw.*⟩; fahnden nach ⟨*vermißter Person*⟩; **~ the thimble/slipper** *(Games)* Fingerhutverstecken, *das*/Pantoffelverstecken, *das;* **c)** *(drive, lit. or fig.)* jagen; **he was ~ed from office/out of society** er wurde aus dem Amt gejagt/aus der Gesellschaft ausgestoßen; **d)** *(Amer.: shoot)* schießen ⟨*Wildenten*⟩. **3.** *v. i.* **a)** jagen; **go ~ing** jagen; auf die Jagd gehen; **~ after** *or* **for** Jagd machen auf (+ *Akk.*), jagen ⟨*Tier*⟩; **b)** *(seek)* **~ after** *or* **for sb./sth.** nach jmdm./etw. suchen; **he ~ed through his pockets for a coin** er durchsuchte seine Taschen nach einer Münze; **the police are ~ing for him** die Polizei ist auf der Suche nach ihm; **c)** *(operate irregularly)* abwechselnd zu schnell und zu langsam laufen; pendeln *(Technik)*

~ a'bout, ~ a'round *v. i.* **~ about** *or* **around for sb./sth.** [überall] nach jmdm./etw. suchen

~ 'down *v. t.* **a)** *(bring to bay)* hetzen und stellen; **the animal was finally ~ed down** das Tier wurde schließlich zur Strecke gebracht *(Jägerspr.);* **b)** *(pursue and overcome)* zur Strecke bringen ⟨*Person*⟩; abschießen ⟨*feindliches Flugzeug*⟩; **c)** *(fig.: track down)* aufstöbern

~ **'out** *v. t.* **a)** *(drive from cover)* aufstöbern; **b)** *(seek out)* suchen; **c)** *(fig.: track down)* ausfindig machen ⟨*Tatsachen, Antworten*⟩

~ **'up** *v. t.* aufspüren

hunt 'ball *n. Ball eines Jagdverbandes*

hunted ['hʌntɪd] *adj.* **a)** *(pursued)* gejagt; **the deer is a much ~ beast** der Hirsch ist ein vielbejagtes *od.* intensiv bejagtes Tier; **b)** *(fig.: sought)* gesucht; **c)** *(expressing fear)* gejagt, gehetzt ⟨*Blick, Gesichtsausdruck*⟩

hunter ['hʌntə(r)] *n.* **a)** Jäger, *der;* **big-game ~:** Großwildjäger, *der;* **whale-~:** Walfänger, *der;* **b)** *(fig.: seeker)* **be a ~ after glory/truth** dem Ruhm nachjagen/der Wahrheit nachspüren; **autograph-~:** Autogrammjäger, *der;* **bargain-~s** *Leute, die ständig auf der Suche nach Sonderangeboten, nach einem Gelegenheitskauf sind;* **treasure-~:** Schatzsucher, *der; see also* **fortune-hunter; c)** *(horse)* Jagdpferd, *das;* **d)** *(dog)* Jagdhund, *der;* **e)** *(watch)* Sprungdeckeluhr, *die;* **half-~:** *Sprungdeckeluhr mit teilweise durchsichtigem Deckel*

hunter-'killer *n. zur Jagd auf Schiffe eingesetztes U-Boot*

hunter's 'moon *n. Vollmond nach dem „harvest moon"*

hunting ['hʌntɪŋ] **1.** *n., no pl.* **a)** die Jagd **(of** auf + *Akk.*); das Jagen **(of** *Gen.*); **there's good ~** *or* **the ~ is good in this forest** dieser Wald ist ein gutes Jagdgebiet; **~, shooting, [and] fishing,** *(iron.)* **huntin', shootin', and fishin'** Fischen und Jagen; **otter-~:** Otterjagd, *die; see also* **fox-hunting; b)** *(fig.: searching)* Suche, *die* **(for** nach); **the ~ of a criminal** die Verbrecherjagd; **after months of/much ~:** nach monatelanger/langer Suche; **[I wish you] good ~** *(fig.)* [ich wünsche dir] viel Glück bei der Suche; *see also* **house-hunting; job-hunting; c)** *(searching through) (of house)* Durchsuchen, *das; (of area)* Absuchen, *das; (in pursuit of game)* Jagen, *das* **(of** in + *Dat.*); **d)** *(Amer.: shooting)* Schießen, *das.* **2.** *adj.* jagend

hunting: ~-box *n. (Brit.)* Jagdhütte, *die;* **~-crop** *see* **crop 1 c; ~-ground** *n. (lit. or fig.)* Jagdrevier, *das; see also* **happy hunting-ground[s]; ~-horn** *n.* Jagdhorn, *das;* **~-lodge** *n.* Jagdhaus, *das;* **~-'pink** *n.* Rot des Jagdrocks

huntsman ['hʌntsmən] *n., pl.* **huntsmen** ['hʌntsmən] **a)** *(hunter)* Jäger, *der; (riding to hounds)* Jagdreiter, *der;* **b)** *(manager of hunt)* Rüdemeister, *der (Jagdw. hist.); (in fox-hunting)* Pikör, *der (Jagdw. hist.)*

huntswoman ['hʌntswʊmən] *n.* Jägerin, *die; (riding to hounds)* Jagdreiterin, *die*

hurdle ['hɜ:dl] **1.** *n.* **a)** *(Athletics)* Hürde, *die;* **~ race, ~s** Hürdenlauf, *der; (for horses)* Hürdenrennen, *das;* **the 200 metres ~s** der 200-m-Hürdenlauf; die 200 m Hürden *(Sportjargon);* **b)** *(fig.: obstacle)* Hürde, *die;* **fall at the last ~:** an der letzten Hürde scheitern; **get over** *or* **negotiate a ~:** eine Hürde nehmen; **c)** *(for fence)* Hürde, *die.* **2.** *v. t.* überspringen ⟨*Zaun, Hecke usw.*⟩

hurdler ['hɜ:dlə(r)] *n. (Athletics)* Hürdenläufer, *der/* läufcrin, *die*

hurdy-gurdy ['hɜ:dɪgɜ:dɪ] *n.* **a)** *(Mus. Hist.)* Drehleier, *die (hist.);* **b)** *(coll.: barrel-organ)* Drehorgel, *die;* Leierkasten, *der (ugs.)*

hurl [hɜ:l] **1.** *v. t.* **a)** *(throw)* werfen; *(violently)* schleudern; *(throw down)* stürzen; **~ sb. [down] into the street** jmdn. auf die Straße hinunterstürzen; **she ~ed herself to her death from a 15th-floor window** sie stürzte sich aus einem Fenster im 15. Stock zu Tode; **b)** *(fig.)* **~ insults at sb.** jmdm. Beleidigungen ins Gesicht schleudern; **~ defiant looks/glances at sb.** trotzige Blicke auf jmdn. schleudern; **c)** *(drive)* werfen; **be ~ed around the ship/against each other** durch das Schiff geschleudert/gegeneinandergeschleudert werden; **~ oneself at** *or* **upon sb.** sich auf jmdn. stürzen; **~ oneself into a new job** *(fig.)* sich in eine neue Arbeit stürzen. **2.** *n. (throwing)* Stürzen, *das; (violent)* Schleudern, *das*

hurling ['hɜ:lɪŋ] *n. (Sport)* Hurling, *das;* irisches Hockey; *attrib.* Hurling-

hurly-burly ['hɜ:lɪbɜ:lɪ] *n.* Tumult, *der;* **the ~ of city life** der Großstadtrummel *(ugs.)*

hurrah [hə'rɑ:, hʊ'rɑ:], **hurray** [hə'reɪ, hʊ'reɪ] **1.** *int.* hurra; **~ for sb./sth.!** jmd./etw. lebe hoch!; **~ for the Queen!** ein Hoch der Königin!; **hip, hip, ~!** hipp, hipp, hurra!. **2.** Hurra, *das;* **their joyous ~s** ihre freudigen Hurrarufe. **3.** *v. i.* Hurra rufen

hurricane ['hʌrɪkən] *n.* **a)** *(tropical cyclone)* Hurrikan, *der; (storm, lit. or fig.)* Orkan, *der;* **it's/the wind is blowing a ~ outside** draußen tobt ein Orkan; **b)** *(Meteorol.)* Orkan, *der; attrib.* **~ force** Orkanstärke, *die;* **~ force winds** Winde, die Orkanstärke erreichen

hurricane: ~-lamp *n.* Sturmlaterne, *die;* **~ season** *n. Jahreszeit, in der Hurrikane am häufigsten auftreten*

hurried ['hʌrɪd] *adj.* eilig; überstürzt ⟨*Abreise*⟩; eilig *od.* hastig geschrieben ⟨*Brief, Aufsatz*⟩; eilig vollzogen ⟨*Zeremonie*⟩; in Eile ausgeführt ⟨*Arbeit*⟩; **our farewells were ~:** wir verabschiedeten uns eilig

hurriedly ['hʌrɪdlɪ] *adv.* eilig; überstürzt ⟨*abreisen*⟩; in Eile ⟨*ausführen*⟩

hurry ['hʌrɪ] **1.** *n.* **a)** *(great haste)* Eile, *die;* **what is** *or* **why the [big] ~?** warum die Eile?; **amongst all the ~ at the airport** in der allgemeinen Hetze am Flughafen; **in a ~:** eilig; **be in a [great** *or* **terrible] ~:** es [furchtbar] eilig haben; in [großer] Eile sein; **do sth. in a ~:** etw. in Eile tun; **leave in a ~:** davoneilen; **I have to get there in a ~:** ich muß so schnell wie möglich dort sein; **I need it in a ~:** ich brauche es dringend; **the handle won't come off again in a ~** *(coll.)* der Griff wird so schnell nicht wieder abgehen; **I shall not ask again in a ~** *(coll.)* ich frage so schnell nicht wieder; **be in a/not be in a** *or* **be in no ~ to do sth.** es eilig/nicht eilig haben, etw. zu tun; **b)** *(urgent requirement)* **there is a ~ for sth.** etw. ist sehr gefragt; **there is a ~ for us to get out** wir müssen uns beeilen, hinauszukommen; **what's the [big] ~?** wozu die Eile?; **there's no ~:** es eilt nicht; es hat keine Eile; **is there any ~ for this letter [to be sent off]?** ist dieser Brief eilig?. **2.** *v. t. (transport fast)* schnell bringen; *(urge to go or act faster)* antreiben; *(quicken process of)* beschleunigen; *(consume fast)* hinunterschlingen ⟨*Essen*⟩; hinunterstürzen ⟨*Getränk*⟩; **~ sb. out of the house** dafür sorgen, daß jmd. bald aus dem Haus herauskommt; **~ dinner** sich mit dem Abendessen beeilen; **~ a soufflé** ein Soufflé zu schnell zubereiten; **~ one's work** seine Arbeit in zu großer Eile erledigen. **3.** *v. i.* sich beeilen; *(to or from place)* eilen; **~ downstairs/out/in** nach unten/nach draußen/nach drinnen eilen; **she hurried from shop to shop** sie hastete von einem Laden zum andern

~ **a'long 1.** *v. i. (coll.)* sich beeilen. **2.** *v. t.* zur Eile antreiben; beschleunigen ⟨*Vorgang*⟩

~ **'on 1.** *v. i.* weitereilen; **the teacher is ~ing on too fast** *(fig.)* der Lehrer geht zu schnell weiter; **I must ~ on** ich muß [rasch] weiter. **2.** *v. t.* antreiben; beschleunigen ⟨*Vorgang*⟩

~ **through** *v. t.* **a)** [--'-] beschleunigen; **b)** ['---] schnell durcheilen; *(fig.)* möglichst schnell durchziehen *(ugs.); (Parl.)* durchpeitschen ⟨*Gesetz*⟩

~ **'up 1.** *v. i. (coll.)* sich beeilen. **2.** *v. t.* antreiben; beschleunigen, vorantreiben ⟨*Vorgang*⟩

'hurry-scurry 1. *adv.* in wilder Hast. **2.** *n.* Hektik, *die.* **3.** *v. i.* in wilder Hast laufen

hurt [hɜ:t] **1.** *v. t.,* **hurt a)** *(cause pain to)* weh tun (+ *Dat.*); *(injure physically)* verletzen; **~ one's arm/leg/head/back** sich *(Dat.)* am Arm/Bein/Kopf/Rücken weh tun; *(injure)* sich *(Dat.)* den Arm/das Bein/am Kopf/am Rücken verletzen; **you are ~ing me/my arm** du tust mir weh/am Arm weh; **my arm is ~ing me** mein Arm tut [mir] weh; mir tut der Arm weh; **it ~s me to move my arm** es tut [mir] weh, wenn ich den Arm bewege; **it ~s my ears to listen to that noise** dieser Lärm tut meinen Ohren weh; **he wouldn't ~ a fly** *(fig.)* er tut keiner Fliege etwas zuleide; **sth. won't** *or* **wouldn't ~ sb.** etw. tut nicht weh; *(fig.)* etw. würde jmdm. nichts schaden *(ugs.);* **~ oneself** sich *(Dat.)* weh tun; *(injure oneself)* sich verletzen; **b)** *(damage, be detrimental to)* schaden (+ *Dat.*); **sth. won't** *or* **wouldn't ~ sth.** etw. würde einer Sache *(Dat.)* nichts schaden; **c)** *(distress emotionally)* verletzen, kränken ⟨*Person*⟩; verletzen ⟨*Ehrgefühl, Stolz*⟩; **~ sb.'s feelings** jmdn. verletzen; **it ~s me to have to tell you this** es ist mir schmerzlich, Ihnen dies sagen zu müssen; **~ sb.'s sense of honour** jmdn. in seiner Ehre kränken. **2.** *v. i.,* **hurt a)** *(cause pain)* weh tun; schmerzen; **b)** *(cause damage, be detrimental)* schaden; **does it ~ to drive the car with the hand-brake on?** schadet es dem Auto, wenn man mit angezogener Handbremse fährt?; **I don't think it really ~s** ich glaube nicht, daß es wirklich etwas schadet; **publicity never ~s** Publicity kann nie schaden *(ugs.);* **sth. won't** *or* **wouldn't ~** *(also iron.)* etw. würde nichts schaden *(ugs.);* **it won't ~ to have another biscuit** noch ein Keks kann doch nichts schaden; **c)** *(cause emotional distress)* weh tun; ⟨*Worte, Beleidigungen:*⟩ verletzen; ⟨*Person:*⟩ verletzend sein; **d)** *(coll.: suffer)* **I ~ all over** es tut mir überall weh; **my leg ~s** mein Bein tut [mir] weh; **does your hand ~?** tut dir die Hand weh?; **I ~ inside** *(emotionally)* es tut mir innerlich weh. **3.** *n.* **a)** *(bodily injury)* Verletzung, *die;* **b)** *(detriment)* Schaden, *der;* **c)** *(emotional pain)* Schmerz, *der; (emotional injury)* Kränkung, *die*

hurtful ['hɜ:tfl] *adj.* **a)** *(physically harmful, detrimental)* schädlich **(to** für); **be ~ to sb./sth.** jmdm./einer Sache schaden; **b)** *(fig.: painful)* schmerzlich; **c)** *(emotionally wounding)* verletzend; **be ~ [in what one says] about sth.** sich in verletzender Form über etw. äußern; **what a ~ thing to say/do!** wie kann man nur so etwas Verletzendes sagen/tun!

hurtle ['hɜ:tl] **1.** *v. i.* **a)** *(move rapidly)* rasen *(ugs.);* **he went hurtling down the street/round the corner** er raste die Straße hinunter/um die Ecke; **the car was hurtling along** das Auto brauste *od.* sauste dahin; **b)** *(move with clattering sound)* **the saucepans came hurtling to the floor** die Kochtöpfe fielen mit lautem Klappern auf den Boden. **2.** *v. t.* schleudern

husband ['hʌzbənd] **1.** *n.* Ehemann, *der;* **my/your/her ~:** mein/dein/ihr Mann; **give my regards to your ~:** grüßen Sie Ihren Mann *od. (geh.)* Gatten von mir; **~ and wife** Mann und Frau; **they are a ~-[and-]wife team of interior decorators** die Eheleute arbeiten gemeinsam als Innenarchitekten. **2.** *v. t.* regeln ⟨*Angelegenheiten*⟩; haushalten mit ⟨*Mitteln*⟩; bewirtschaften ⟨*Land*⟩

husbandry ['hʌzbəndrɪ] *n., no pl.* **a)** *(farming)* Landwirtschaft, *die; (application of farming technique)* Bewirtschaftung, *die;* **animal/dairy ~:** Viehzucht, *die*/Milchviehhaltung, *die;* **b)** *(management)* **bad/good ~:** schlechtes/sparsames Wirtschaften; **bad/good ~ of sth.** verschwenderischer/haushälterischer Umgang mit etw.; **c)** *(careful management)* sparsames Wirtschaften

hush [hʌʃ] **1.** *n.* **a)** *(silence)* Schweigen, *das;* **a sudden ~ fell over them** sie verstummten plötzlich; **can we have a bit of ~ now, please?** *(coll.)* ein bißchen mehr Ruhe jetzt, wenn ich bitten dürfte!; **b)** *(stillness)* Stille, *die;* **dead ~:** Totenstille, *die;* **c)** *(secrecy)* Geheimhaltung, *die;* **why all the ~?** wozu die ganze Geheimnistuerei? *(ugs.).* **2.** *v.t. (silence)* zum Schweigen bringen; zum Verstummen bringen ‹*Vogelgesang, Gerüchte*›; *(still)* beruhigen; besänftigen; *(quieten)* dämpfen ‹*Stimme*›; **she tried to ~ her baby to sleep/her baby's crying** sie versuchte, ihr Baby zum Schlafen zu bringen/ihr schreiendes Baby zu beruhigen. **3.** *v.i.* still sein; *(become silent)* verstummen; **~!** still!

~ 'up *v.t.* **a)** *(make silent)* zum Schweigen bringen; **b)** *(keep secret)* **~ sth. up** etw. vertuschen

hushaby[e] ['hʌʃəbaɪ] *int.* eiapopeia

hushed [hʌʃt] *adj.* schweigend ‹*Publikum*›; gedämpft ‹*Flüstern, Stimme*›; **~ atmosphere** Stille, *die;* **there was a ~ silence** alles schwieg; **with ~ respect/attention** mit respektvollem/gespanntem Schweigen

hush: ~-hush *adj. (coll.)* geheim; **strictly/terribly/very ~-hush** streng geheim; **keep sth. ~-hush** etw. geheimhalten; **~ money** *n.* Schweigegeld, *das*

husk [hʌsk] **1.** *n.* Schale, *die; (of wheat, grain, rice)* Spelze, *die; (Amer.: of maize)* Hüllblatt, *das;* Liesche, *die (Bot.); (fig.: useless remainder)* Hülse, *die.* **2.** *v.t.* schälen

huskily ['hʌskɪlɪ] *adv.* heiser

¹husky ['hʌskɪ] **1.** *adj.* **a)** *(hoarse)* heiser; **her voice has a natural/an attractive ~ quality** ihre Stimme ist von Natur aus rauh/sie hat eine anziehende rauchige Stimme; **b)** *(coll.: tough)* bärenstark *(ugs.).* **2.** *n. (Amer. coll.: strong person)* bärenstarker Typ *(ugs.)*

²husky *n. (dog)* Eskimohund, *der; (Siberian ~)* Husky, *der; (sledge-dog)* Schlittenhund, *der*

hussar [hʊ'zɑ:(r)] *n. (Mil.)* Husar, *der*

hussy ['hʌsɪ, 'hʌzɪ] *n. fem.* **a)** *(improper woman)* Flittchen, *das (ugs. abwertend);* **b)** *(pert girl)* Göre, *die (nordd.);* Fratz, *der (fam.)*

hustings ['hʌstɪŋz] *n. pl.* **a)** *constr. as sing. or pl. (proceedings)* Wahlveranstaltungen; **b)** *(Hist.: platform) Rednerbühne für die Kandidaten einer Wahl;* **c)** *(fig.)* **he gave a good speech from the ~:** er hielt eine gute Wahlrede

hustle ['hʌsl] **1.** *v.t.* **a)** drängen **(into** zu); **b)** *(jostle)* anrempeln *(salopp);* schubsen *(ugs.); (thrust)* [hastig] drängen; **the guide ~d the tourists along/from one church to another** der Führer scheuchte die Touristen voran/von einer Kirche zur anderen *(ugs.);* **~ a Budget through the Senate** ein Budget im Senat durchpeitschen *(ugs.);* **c)** *(sl.: exert pressure on)* bedrängen; **~ sb. to do sth.** jmdn. dazu bringen wollen, etw. zu tun. **2.** *v.i.* **a)** *(push roughly)* **~ against sb./sth.** jmdn. anrempeln/gegen etw. stoßen; **~ through the crowds** sich durch die Menge drängeln; **b)** *(hurry)* hasten; **~ about the house** durchs Haus wirbeln; **we'll have to ~:** wir müssen uns beeilen; **~ and bustle about** geschäftig hin und her eilen *od.* sausen; **c)** *(sl.: strive for business)* **~ for sth.** etw. zu kriegen versuchen *(ugs.);* **d)** *(sl.: solicit)* **~ [on the street]** auf den Strich gehen *(salopp);* **he ~s for her** er besorgt ihr die Freier *(ugs.).* **3.** *n.* **a)** *(jostling)* Gedränge, *das;* **b)** *(hurry)* Hetze, *die;* **~ and bustle** Geschäftigkeit, *die; (in street)* geschäftiges Treiben

hustler ['hʌslə(r)] *n. (sl.: prostitute)* Strichmädchen, *das*/Strichjunge, *der (salopp)*

hut [hʌt] *n.* Hütte, *die; (Mil.)* Baracke, *die*

hutch [hʌtʃ] *n.* **a)** *(for rabbit)* Stall, *der; (for guinea-pig)* Käfig, *der;* **b)** *(derog.: hut, small house)* Hütte, *die*

hyacinth ['haɪəsɪnθ] *n.* **a)** *(Bot.)* Hyazinthe, *die;* **wild** *or* **wood ~:** Hasenglöckchen, *das; see also* **grape hyacinth; b)** *(colour)* **~ [blue]** Hyazinthblau, *das*

hybrid ['haɪbrɪd] **1.** *n.* **a)** *(Biol.)* Hybride, *die od. der* (**between** aus); Kreuzung, *die;* **b)** *(Ethnol.)* Mischling, *der;* **c)** *(fig.: mixture)* Mischung, *die;* **d)** *(Ling.)* hybride Bildung. **2.** *adj.* **a)** *(Biol.)* hybrid ‹*Züchtung*›; **this is a ~ rose** diese Rose ist eine Hybride; **a ~ species/animal/plant** eine Hybridzüchtung; ein[e] Hybride; **b)** *(Ethnol.)* mischerbig; **c)** *(fig.: mixed)* gemischt; Misch‹*kultur, -sprache*›; **d)** *(Ling.)* hybrid

hybridize (hybridise) ['haɪbrɪdaɪz] *v.t.* **a)** *(Biol.)* hybridisieren *(fachspr.);* kreuzen; **b)** *(Ling.)* **~ words** hybride Wörter bilden

hydra ['haɪdrə] *n.* **a)** *(Greek Mythol.)* Hydra, *die;* **b)** *(Zool.: polyp)* Süßwasserpolyp, *der;* Hydra, *die*

hydrangea [haɪ'dreɪndʒə] *n. (Bot.)* Hortensie, *die;* Hydrangea, *die (fachspr.)*

hydrant ['haɪdrənt] *n.* Hydrant, *der*

hydrate ['haɪdreɪt] *n. (Chem.)* Hydrat, *das*

hydration [haɪ'dreɪʃn] *n.* **a)** *(addition of fluid)* Flüssigkeitszufuhr, *die;* **b)** *(Chem.)* Hydra[ta]tion, *die*

hydraulic [haɪ'drɔ:lɪk] *adj. (Mech. Engin.)* hydraulisch; **~ engineer** Wasserbauingenieur, *der;* **~ engineering** Wasserbau, *der*

hydraulic: ~ 'brake *n. (Mech. Engin.)* hydraulische Bremse; **~ 'fluid** *n. (Mech. Engin.)* hydraulische Flüssigkeit; *(in brake system)* Bremsflüssigkeit, *die;* **~ 'ram** *n. (Mech. Engin.)* **a)** *(pump)* hydraulischer Widder; **b)** *(piston)* Hydraulikkolben, *der*

hydride ['haɪdraɪd] *n. (Chem.)* Hydrid, *das*

hydrocarbon [haɪdrə'kɑ:bən] *n. (Chem.)* Kohlenwasserstoff, *der*

hydrochloric acid [haɪdrəklɔ:rɪk 'æsɪd] *n. (Chem.)* Salzsäure, *die*

hydrodynamics [haɪdrədaɪ'næmɪks] *n., no pl. (Phys.)* Hydrodynamik, *die*

hydroelectric [haɪdrəʊɪ'lektrɪk] *adj. (Electr.)* hydroelektrisch; **~ power plant** *or* **station** Wasserkraftwerk, *das*

hydrofoil ['haɪdrəfɔɪl] *n. (Naut.)* **a)** *(structure)* Tragfläche, *die;* Tragflügel, *der;* **b)** *(vessel)* Tragflächenboot, *das;* Tragflügelboot, *das*

hydrogen ['haɪdrədʒən] *n.* Wasserstoff, *der;* Hydrogen[ium], *das (fachspr.);* **a ~-filled balloon** ein mit Wasserstoff gefüllter Ballon; *see also* **peroxide 1 b**

'hydrogen bomb *n.* Wasserstoffbombe, *die*

hydrolyse ['haɪdrəlaɪz] *v.t. (Chem.)* hydrolysieren

hydrolysis [haɪ'drɒlɪsɪs] *n., pl.* **hydrolyses** [haɪ'drɒlɪsi:z] *(Chem.)* Hydrolyse, *die*

hydrolyze *(Amer.) see* **hydrolyse**

hydrometer [haɪ'drɒmɪtə(r)] *n.* Hydrometer, *das*

hydrophobia [haɪdrə'fəʊbɪə] *n.* **a)** *(Med.) (rabies)* Tollwut, *die; (symptom)* Hydrophobie, *die (Med.);* **b)** *(Psych.)* Hydrophobie, *die (fachspr.);* krankhafte Wasserscheu

hydrophobic [haɪdrə'fəʊbɪk] *adj.* **a)** *(Med.)* tollwutkrank, tollwutinfiziert ‹*Tier, Person*›; tollwütig ‹*Tier*›; **be ~:** Tollwut haben; **b)** *(water-resistant)* hydrophob *(Chemie, Technik)*

hydroplane ['haɪdrəpleɪn] *n.* **a)** *(Naut.: finlike device)* Gleitfläche, *die; (of submarine)* Tiefenruder, *das;* **b)** *(motor boat)* Gleitboot, *das*

hydroponics [haɪdrə'pɒnɪks] *n., no pl. (Hort.)* Hydroponik, *die (fachspr.);* Hydrokultur, *die*

hydrosphere ['haɪdrəsfɪə(r)] *n. (Geog.)* Hydrosphäre, *die*

hydrostatic [haɪdrə'stætɪk] *adj. (Phys.)* hydrostatisch

hydrostatics [haɪdrə'stætɪks] *n., no pl. (Phys.)* Hydrostatik, *die*

hydrous ['haɪdrəs] *adj. (Chem., Min.)* wasserhaltig ‹*Salz, Substanz*›

hydroxide [haɪ'drɒksaɪd] *n. (Chem.)* Hydroxid, *das*

hydrozoan [haɪdrə'zəʊən] *(Zool.)* **1.** *adj.* zu den Hydrozoen gehörend; **~ polyp** Hydroidpolyp, *der.* **2.** *n.* Hydrozoon, *das*

hyena [haɪ'i:nə] *n.* **a)** *(Zool.)* Hyäne, *die;* **laughing** *or* **spotted ~:** Tüpfel- *od.* Fleckenhyäne, *die;* **laugh like a ~:** wie eine Hyäne kreischen; ≈ wiehernd lachen; **b)** *(fig.: person)* Hyäne, *die (ugs. abwertend);* **c)** *(Austral. Zool.)* Beutelwolf, *der*

hygiene ['haɪdʒi:n] *n., no pl.* **a)** Hygiene, *die;* **conditions of bad ~:** schlechte hygienische Verhältnisse; **domestic ~:** häusliche Hygiene; **feminine ~:** Monatshygiene, *die;* **b)** *no art. (science)* Hygiene, *die (Med.);* **dental ~:** Zahnhygiene, *die*

hygienic [haɪ'dʒi:nɪk] *adj.* hygienisch; **not ~:** unhygienisch

hygienically [haɪ'dʒi:nɪkəlɪ] *adv.* hygienisch

hygienist [haɪ'dʒi:nɪst] *n.* Hygieniker, *der*/Hygienikerin, *die;* **dental ~:** Zahnhygieniker, *der*/-hygienikerin, *die*

hygrometer [haɪ'grɒmɪtə(r)] *n. (Meteorol.)* Hygrometer, *das*

hymen ['haɪmen] *n. (Anat.)* Hymen, *das od. der (fachspr.);* Jungfernhäutchen, *das*

hymn [hɪm] **1.** *n.* **a)** *(Relig.)* Hymne, *die;* Loblied, *das; (sung in service)* Kirchenlied, *das;* **Easter ~, ~ for Easter** Osterlied, *das;* **b)** *(song of praise, lit. or fig.)* Hymne, *die;* **a ~ to nature** eine Hymne an die Natur; **a ~ to Venus/England/the new age** eine Hymne auf Venus/England/das neue Zeitalter. **2.** *v.t. (praise with songs)* besingen *(geh.);* lobpreisen *(dichter.)*‹*Gott, Werke Gottes*›; *(fig.: praise)* preisen *(geh.)*

hymnal ['hɪmnl], **hymnary** ['hɪmnərɪ] *ns.* Gesangbuch, *das;* Hymnar[ium], *das*

'hymn-book *n.* Gesangbuch, *das*

hyoid ['haɪɔɪd] *(Anat.) adj. & n.* **~ [bone]** Zungenbein, *das*

hype [haɪp] *(sl.)* **1.** *n.* **a)** *(deception)* Schwindel, *der (ugs.);* **b)** *(misleading publicity)* Reklameschwindel, *der (ugs.);* **media ~:** Medienrummel, *der.* **2.** *v.t.* **a)** *(cheat)* reinlegen *(ugs.);* **~ sb. into sth./doing sth.** jmdn. [durch Tricks] zu etw. bringen/jmdn. [durch Tricks] dazu bringen, etw. zu tun; **b) ~ [up]** *(publicize excessively)* groß herausbringen

~ up *v.t. (sl.)* hochputschen *(ugs.);* **feel ~d up** überdreht sein *(ugs.)*

hyperactive [haɪpə'ræktɪv] *adj.* überaktiv

hyperbola [haɪ'pɜ:bələ] *n., pl.* **~s** *or* **~e** [haɪ'pɜ:bəli:] *(Geom.)* Hyperbel, *die*

hyperbole [haɪ'pɜ:bəlɪ] *n. (Rhet.)* Hyperbel, *die*

hyperbolic [haɪpə'bɒlɪk] *adj.* **a)** *(Geom.)* hyperbolisch; **b)** *see* **hyperbolical a**

hyperbolical [haɪpə'bɒlɪkl] *adj.* **a)** *(Rhet.)* hyperbolisch ‹*Stil, Wendung usw.*›; **b)** *see* **hyperbolic a**

hypermarket ['haɪpəmɑ:kɪt] *n.* Verbrauchermarkt, *der*

hypermarket ['haɪpəmɑ:kɪt] *n.* Großmarkt, *der; großer Supermarkt*

hypersensitive [haɪpə'sensɪtɪv] *adj.* hypersensibel; überempfindlich; **be ~ to sth.** überempfindlich auf etw. *(Akk.)* reagieren

hypersensitivity [haɪpəsensɪ'tɪvɪtɪ] *n., no pl.* Überempfindlichkeit, *die*

hypertension [haɪpə'tenʃn] *n. (Med.)* Hypertonie, *die (fachspr.);* Bluthochdruck, *der*

hypertensive [haɪpə'tensɪv] *adj. (Med.)* hypertonisch

hypertrophied [haɪ'pɜ:trəfɪd] *adj.* hypertroph ‹*Organ*›; *(fig.: excessive)* hypertroph[isch] *(geh.);* hypertrophiert *(geh.)*

hypha ['haɪfə] *n., pl* **~e** ['haɪfi:] *(Bot.)* Hyphe, *die (fachspr.);* Pilzfaden, *der*

hyphen ['haɪfn] **1.** *n.* **a)** Bindestrich, *der;* **b)** *(connecting separate syllables)* Trennungsstrich, *der;* Divis, *das (fachspr.).* **2.** *v.t.* mit Bindestrich schreiben

hyphenate ['haɪfəneɪt] *see* **hyphen 2**

hyphenation [haɪfə'neɪʃn] *n., no pl.* Kopplung, *die*

hypnosis [hɪp'nəʊsɪs] *n., pl.* **hypnoses** [hɪp'nəʊsi:z] Hypnose, *die; (act, process)* Hypnotisierung, *die;* **under ~:** in Hypnose *(Dat.)*

hypnotic [hɪp'nɒtɪk] **1.** *adj.* hypnotisch; *(producing hypnotism)* hypnotisch; hypnotisierend ⟨*Wirkung, Blick*⟩; **have a ~ effect on sb.** hypnotisierend *od.* einschläfernd auf jmdn. wirken. **2.** *n.* Schlafmittel, *das; (Med. also)* Hypnotikum, *das (fachspr.)*

hypnotism ['hɪpnətɪzm] *n.* Hypnotik, *die; (act)* Hypnotisieren, *das*

hypnotist ['hɪpnətɪst] *n.* Hypnotiseur, *der*/Hypnotiseuse, *die*

hypnotize ['hɪpnətaɪz] *v. t. (lit. or fig.)* hypnotisieren; *(fig.: fascinate)* faszinieren

hypo ['haɪpəʊ] *n. (Photog.)* Fixiernatron, *das;* Fixiersalz, *das*

hypocaust ['haɪpəkɔ:st] *n. (Roman Ant.)* Hypokaustum, *das*

hypochondria [haɪpə'kɒndrɪə] *n.* Hypochondrie, *die*

hypochondriac [haɪpə'kɒndrɪæk] **1.** *adj.* hypochondrisch. **2.** *n.* Hypochonder, *der*

hypocrisy [hɪ'pɒkrɪsɪ] *n.* **a)** *(simulation of virtue)* Scheinheiligkeit, *die;* **b)** *(dissimulation)* Heuchelei, *die;* Hypokrisie, *die (geh.)*

hypocrite ['hɪpəkrɪt] *n.* **a)** *(person feigning virtue)* Scheinheilige, *der/die;* **b)** *(dissembler)* Heuchler, *der*/Heuchlerin, *die;* Hypokrit, *der (geh. veralt.)*

hypocritical [hɪpə'krɪtɪkl] *adj.* heuchlerisch; scheinheilig; hypokritisch *(geh. veralt.)*

hypodermic [haɪpə'dɜ:mɪk] *(Med.)* **1.** *adj.* subkutan ⟨*Injektion*⟩; subkutan verabreicht ⟨*Medikament*⟩; **~ syringe** Injektionsspritze, *die.* **2.** *n.* **a)** *(injection)* subkutane Injektion; **b)** *(syringe)* Injektionsspritze, *die*

hypotension [haɪpəʊ'tenʃn] *n. (Med.)* Hypotonie, *die (fachspr.);* zu niedriger Blutdruck

hypotensive [haɪpəʊ'tensɪv] *adj. (Med.)* hypotonisch; *(tending to lower the blood pressure)* blutdrucksenkend ⟨*Medikament*⟩

hypotenuse [haɪ'pɒtənju:z] *n. (Geom.)* Hypotenuse, *die;* **square on the ~:** Hypotenusenquadrat, *das*

hypothermia [haɪpə'θɜ:mɪə] *n. (Med.)* Hypothermie, *die (fachspr.);* Unterkühlung, *die*

hypothesis [haɪ'pɒθɪsɪs] *n., pl.* **hypotheses** [haɪ'pɒθɪsi:z] Hypothese, *die; (unproved assumption also)* Annahme, *die*

hypothesize (hypothesise) [haɪ'pɒθɪsaɪz] **1.** *v. i.* eine Hypothese aufstellen; mutmaßen; spekulieren. **2.** *v. t.* annehmen

hypothetical [haɪpə'θetɪkl] *adj.* hypothetisch; angenommen; **it will remain ~:** darüber wird man nur mutmaßen *od.* spekulieren können

hypothetically [haɪpə'θetɪkəlɪ] *adv.* hypothetisch

hyrax ['haɪəræks] *n. (Zool.)* Klippschliefer, *der*

hyssop ['hɪsəp] *n. (Bot.)* Ysop, *der*

hysterectomy [hɪstə'rektəmɪ] *n. (Med.)* Hysterektomie, *die (fachspr.);* operative Entfernung der Gebärmutter

hysteria [hɪ'stɪərɪə] *n.* Hysterie, *die*

hysterical [hɪ'sterɪkl] *adj.* hysterisch

hysterically [hɪ'sterɪkəlɪ] *adv.* hysterisch; **~ funny** urkomisch

hysterics [hɪ'sterɪks] *n. pl. (laughter)* hysterischer Lachanfall; *(crying)* hysterischer Weinkrampf; **have ~:** hysterisch lachen/weinen

Hz *abbr.* **hertz** Hz

I

[1]I, i [aɪ] *n., pl.* **Is** *or* **I's a)** *(letter)* I, i, *das; see also* **dot 2 b; b)** *(Roman numeral)* I

[2]I 1. *pron.* ich; **it was I** *(formal)* ich bin es; **it was I who locked the door** *(formal)* ich war es, der die Tür abgeschlossen hat; ich habe die Tür abgeschlossen; *see also* **[1]me; [2]mine; my; myself. 2.** *n., no pl.* **the I** *(Philos.)* das Ich

I. *abbr.* **a) Island[s]** I.; **b) Isle[s] I.**

iamb ['aɪæm] *see* **iambus**

iambic [aɪ'æmbɪk] *(Pros.)* **1.** *adj.* jambisch; **~ pentameter** fünffüßiger Jambus. **2.** *n. in pl.* Jamben

iambus [aɪ'æmbəs] *n., pl.* **~es** *or* **iambi** [aɪ'æmbaɪ] *(Pros.)* Jambus, *der*

IATA [ɪ'ɑ:tə, aɪ'ɑ:tə] *abbr.* **International Air Transport Association** IATA, *die*

IBA *abbr. (Brit.)* **Independent Broadcasting Authority** *Kontrollgremium für den privaten Rundfunk und das Privatfernsehen*

Iberia [aɪ'bɪərɪə] *pr. n. (Hist., Geog.)* Iberische Halbinsel

Iberian [aɪ'bɪərɪən] **1.** *adj.* iberisch. **2.** *n. (inhabitant of [ancient] Iberia)* Iberer, *der*/Ibererin, *die*

Iberian Pe'ninsula *pr. n. (Geog.)* Iberische Halbinsel

ibex ['aɪbeks] *n. (Zool.)* Steinbock, *der*

ibid. *abbr.* **ibidem** ib.; ibd.; ibid.

ibidem ['ɪbɪdem, ɪ'baɪdəm] *adv.* ibidem; ebenda; ebendort

ibis ['aɪbɪs] *n. (Ornith.)* Ibis, *der*

i/c *abbr.* **a) in charge; b) in command**

ICBM *abbr.* **intercontinental ballistic missile**

ice [aɪs] **1.** *n.* **a)** *no pl.* Eis, *das;* **become ~:** [zu Eis] gefrieren; **feel/be like ~** *(be very cold)* eiskalt sein; **there was ~ over the pond** eine Eisschicht bedeckte den Teich; **fall through the ~:** auf dem Eis einbrechen; **be on ~** *(coll.) (be held in reserve)* ⟨*Plan:*⟩ auf Eis *(Dat.)* liegen *(ugs.);* **put on ~** *(coll.)* auf Eis *(Akk.)* legen *(ugs.);* **be on thin ~** *(fig.)* sich auf dünnes Eis begeben haben; **break the ~** *(fig.: make a beginning)* den Anfang machen; *(break through reserve)* das Eis brechen; *see also* **cut 1 b; [2]skate 2; b)** *(confection)* [Speise]eis, *das;* Eiscreme, *die;* **an ~/two ~s** ein/zwei Eis; **c)** *no pl., no indef. art. (Amer. sl.: diamonds)* Diamanten. **2.** *v. t.* **a)** *(freeze)* einfrieren, tiefkühlen ⟨*Lebensmittel*⟩; *see also* **lolly a; b)** *(cool with ~)* [mit Eis] kühlen; **~d coffee/tea** Eiskaffee, *der*/Tee mit Eis; **be ~d** eisgekühlt sein; **c)** glasieren ⟨*Kuchen*⟩

~ 'over *v. i.* ⟨*Gewässer:*⟩ zufrieren; ⟨*Straße, Flugzeug:*⟩ vereisen

~ 'up *v. i.* **a)** *(freeze)* ⟨*Wasserleitung:*⟩ einfrieren; **b)** *see* **~ over**

ice: **~ age** *n.* Eiszeit, *die;* **~-axe** *n.* Pickel, *der*

iceberg ['aɪsbɜ:g] *n.* Eisberg, *der;* **the tip of the ~** *(fig.)* die Spitze des Eisbergs

ice: **~-blue 1.** [-'-] *n.* Eisblau, *das;* **2.** ['--] *adj.* eisblau; **~-bound** *adj.* eingefroren ⟨*Schiff*⟩; durch Vereisung abgeschnitten ⟨*Hafen, Küste*⟩; **~box** *n. (Amer.)* Kühlschrank, *der;* **~-breaker** *n. (Naut.)* Eisbrecher, *der;* **~-cap** *n.* Eisdecke, -schicht, *die; (polar)* Eiskappe, *die;* **~-cold** *adj.* eiskalt; **~-'cream** *n.* Eis, *das;* Eiscreme, *die;* **one ~-cream/two/too many ~-creams** ein/zwei/zuviel Eis; **~-cube** *n.* Eiswürfel, *der;* **~-floe** *see* **floe; ~ hockey** *n.* Eishockey, *das*

Iceland ['aɪslənd] *pr. n.* Island *(das)*

Icelander ['aɪsləndə(r)] *n.* Isländer, *der*/Isländerin, *die*

Icelandic [aɪs'lændɪk] **1.** *adj.* isländisch; *see also* **English 1. 2.** *n.* Isländisch, *das; see also* **English 2 a**

ice: **~ 'lolly** *see* **lolly a; ~-machine** *n.* Gefrierapparat, *der;* **~-pack** *n.* **a)** *(to relieve pain)* Eispackung, *die;* **b)** *(to keep food cool)* Kälteakku *od.* Kühlakku, *der (ugs.);* **c)** *(sea ice)* [Pack]eisdecke, *die;* **~-rink** *n.* Schlittschuh-, Eisbahn, *die;* **~-skate 1.** *n.* Schlittschuh, *der;* **2.** *v. i.* Schlittschuh laufen; eislaufen; **~-skater** *n.* Schlittschuhläufer, *der;* **~-skating** *n.* Schlittschuhlaufen, *das;* **~-water** *n.* Eiswasser, *das*

ichthyologist [ɪkθɪ'ɒlədʒɪst] *n.* Ichthyologe, *der*/Ichthyologin, *die;* Fischkundler, *der*/-kundlerin, *die*

ichthyology [ɪkθɪ'ɒlədʒɪ] *n.* Ichthyologie, *die;* Fischkunde, *die*

icicle ['aɪsɪkl] *n.* Eiszapfen, *der*

icily ['aɪsɪlɪ] *adv.* eisig; *(fig.)* kalt ⟨*ablehnend, lächelnd*⟩; eisig, frostig ⟨*empfangen, begrüßen, anblicken*⟩; **~ cold** eiskalt

iciness ['aɪsɪnɪs] *n., no pl.* Eis[es]kälte, *die; (of road)* Eisglätte, *die*

icing ['aɪsɪŋ] *n.* **a)** *no pl.* Vereisen, *das; (cooling)* Kühlen, *das; (of cake)* Überziehen mit Zuckerguß; **b)** *(Cookery: sugar coating)* Zuckerguß, *der;* Zuckerglasur, *die;* **[the] ~ on the cake** *(fig.)* das Tüpfelchen auf dem i

'icing sugar *n. (Brit.)* Puderzucker, *der*

icon ['aɪkən, 'aɪkɒn] *n.* **a)** *(statue)* Standbild, *das;* **b)** *(Orthodox Ch.)* Ikone, *die*

iconoclast [aɪ'kɒnəklæst] *n. (lit. or fig.)* Bilderstürmer, *der*

iconoclastic [aɪkɒnə'klæstɪk] *adj. (lit. or fig.)* bilderstürmerisch

icterus ['ɪktərəs] *n. (Med.)* Ikterus, *der (fachspr.);* Gelbsucht, *die*

icy ['aɪsɪ] *adj.* **a)** vereist ⟨*Berge, Landschaft, Straße, See*⟩; eisreich ⟨*Region, Land*⟩; **in ~ conditions** bei Eis; **b)** *(very cold)* eiskalt; eisig; *(fig.)* frostig ⟨*Benehmen, Ton*⟩

ID [aɪ'di:] *n.* **~ card/disc/plate** *etc. see* **identification c; have you [got] some** *or* **any ID?** können Sie sich ausweisen?

id [ɪd] *n. (Psych.)* Es, *das*

I'd [aɪd] **a) = I had; b) = I would**

idea [aɪ'dɪə] *n.* **a)** *(conception)* Idee, *die;* Gedanke, *der;* **arrive at an ~:** auf eine Idee *od.* einen Gedanken kommen; **get one's** *or* **the ~ from sth.** sich durch etw. anregen *od.* inspirieren lassen; **the ~ of going abroad** der Gedanke *od.* die Vorstellung, ins Ausland zu fahren; **have a good ~ of sth.** über etw. *(Akk.)* Bescheid wissen; **give/get some ~ of sth.** einen Überblick über etw. *(Akk.)* geben/einen Eindruck von etw. bekommen; **get the ~ [of sth.]** verstehen, worum es [bei etw.] geht; **be getting the ~ quickly** schnell [damit] zurechtkommen; **sb.'s ~ of sth.** *(coll.)* jmds. Vorstellung von etw.; **not my ~ of ...** *(coll.)* nicht, was ich mir unter ... *(Dat.)* vorstelle; **he has no ~** *(coll.)* er hat keine Ahnung *(ugs.);* **b)** *(mental picture)* Vorstellung, *die;* **what gave you 'that ~?** wie bist du darauf gekommen?; **get the ~ that ...:** den Eindruck bekommen, daß ...; **I don't want her to get the ~ that ...:** ich will nicht, daß sie glaubt *od.* den Eindruck bekommt, daß ...; **he's got the ~ that ...:** er bildet sich *(Dat.)* ein, daß ...; **get** *or* **have ~s** *(coll.) (be rebellious)* auf dumme Gedanken kommen *(ugs.); (be ambitious)* sich *(Dat.)* Hoffnungen machen; **put ~s into sb.'s head** jmdn. auf dumme Gedanken bringen; **c)** *(vague notion)* Ahnung, *die;* Vorstellung, *die;* **have you any ~ [of] how ...?** weißt du ungefähr, wie ...?; **have no ~ [of] where ...:** keine Ahnung haben, wo ...; **you can have no ~ [of]**

how ...: du kannst dir gar nicht vorstellen, wie ...; **not have the remotest** *or* **slightest** *or* **faintest** *or (coll.)* **foggiest ~:** nicht die entfernteste *od.* mindeste *od.* leiseste Ahnung haben; keinen blassen Schimmer haben *(ugs.)*; **I suddenly had the ~ that ...:** mir kam plötzlich der Gedanke, daß ...; **I've an ~ that ...:** ich habe so eine Ahnung, daß ...; **the ~ of his having committed a murder** die Vorstellung, daß er einen Mord begangen hat *od.* er könne einen Mord begangen haben; **the [very] ~!, what an ~!** *(coll.)* unvorstellbar!; allein die Vorstellung!; **d)** *(way of thinking)* Vorstellung, *die;* **e)** *(plan)* Idee, *die;* **man of ~s** kluger Kopf; einfallsreicher Mensch; **have you any ~s for the future?** hast du [irgendwelche] Zukunftspläne?; **be full of good/new ~s** viele gute/neue Ideen haben; voller guter/neuer Ideen sein; **good ~!** [das ist eine] gute Idee!; **'that's an ~** *(coll.)* das ist eine gute Idee; **that gives me an ~:** das hat mich auf eine Idee gebracht; **the ~ was that ...:** der Plan war, daß ...; **have big ~s** große Rosinen im Kopf haben; **what's the big ~?** *(iron.)* was soll das?; was soll der Blödsinn? *(ugs.)*; **f)** *(archetype)* Leitgedanke, *der; (Platonic Philos.)* Idee, *die*

ideal [aɪ'dɪəl] **1.** *adj.* **a)** ideal; vollendet ⟨*Genuß, Ehemann, Gastgeber, Rittertum*⟩; vollkommen ⟨*Glück, Welt*⟩; **b)** *(embodying an idea, existing only in idea)* ideell; gedacht; **c)** *(visionary)* idealistisch. **2.** *n.* **a)** *(perfect type)* Ideal, *das;* Idealvorstellung, *die;* **b)** *(standard for imitation)* Vorbild, *das*

ideal 'gas *n. (Phys.)* ideales Gas

idealise *see* **idealize**

idealism [aɪ'dɪəlɪzm] *n., no pl.* **a)** Idealismus, *der;* **b)** *(representation of things in idealized form)* Idealisierung, *die*

idealist [aɪ'dɪəlɪst] *n.* Idealist, *der*/Idealistin, *die*

idealistic [aɪdɪə'lɪstɪk] *adj.* idealistisch; **~ young people** junge Idealisten *Pl.*

idealize [aɪ'dɪəlaɪz] *v. t.* **a)** *(exalt)* idealisieren; verklären; **b)** *(represent in ideal form)* idealisieren; idealisierend darstellen

ideally [aɪ'dɪəlɪ] *adv.* ideal; **~, the work should be finished in two weeks** im Idealfalle *od.* idealerweise sollte die Arbeit in zwei Wochen abgeschlossen sein

idée fixe [i:deɪ 'fi:ks] *n., pl.* **idées fixes** [i:deɪ 'fi:ks] fixe Idee; Idée fixe, *die (geh.)*

identical [aɪ'dentɪkl] *adj.* **a)** identisch; **the ~ species** dieselbe Art; **he is the ~ convict who ...:** er ist genau der Sträfling, der ...; **b)** *(agreeing in every detail)* identisch; sich *(Dat.)* gleichend; **be ~:** sich *(Dat.)* völlig gleichen; **~ twins** eineiige Zwillinge

identically [aɪ'dentɪkəlɪ] *adv.* völlig, genau ⟨*gleich, übereinstimmend*⟩; völlig gleich, völlig einheitlich ⟨*bauen usw.*⟩

identifiable [aɪ'dentɪfaɪəbl] *adj.* erkennbar (**by** an + *Dat.*); nachweisbar ⟨*Stoff, Substanz*⟩; bestimmbar ⟨*Pflanzen-, Tierart*⟩; diagnostizierbar ⟨*Krankheit*⟩

identification [aɪdentɪfɪ'keɪʃn] *n.* **a)** *(treating as identical)* Gleichsetzung, *die;* **b)** *(association)* Identifikation, *die;* Identifizierung, *die;* **c)** *(determination of identity) (of person)* Identifizierung, *die;* Wiedererkennen, *das; (of plants or animals)* Bestimmung, *die;* **means of ~:** Ausweispapiere *Pl.;* **have you any means of ~?** können Sie sich ausweisen?; **~ card** [Personal]ausweis, *der;* **~ disc** Erkennungsmarke, *die;* **~ plate** Kennzeichenschild, *das;* **~ badge** Ausweisplakette, *die;* Legitimationsabzeichen, *das*

identifi'cation parade *n. (Brit.)* Gegenüberstellung [zur Identifizierung], *die*

identify [aɪ'dentɪfaɪ] **1.** *v. t.* **a)** *(treat as identical)* gleichsetzen; **b)** *(associate)* identifizieren; **Guy Fawkes will always be identified with the Gunpowder Plot** bei Guy Fawkes wird jeder sofort an die Pulververschwörung denken; **c)** *(recognize)* identifizieren; bestimmen ⟨*Pflanze, Tier*⟩; **d)** *(establish)* ermitteln. **2.** *v. i.* **~ with sb.** sich mit jmdm. identifizieren

Identikit, (P) [aɪ'dentɪkɪt] *n.* Phantombild, *das*

identity [aɪ'dentɪtɪ] *n.* **a)** *(sameness)* Übereinstimmung, *die;* **b)** *(individuality, being specified person)* Identität, *die;* **proof of ~:** Identitätsnachweis, *der;* **[case of] mistaken ~:** [Personen]verwechslung, *die;* **c)** *(Math.)* Identität, *die;* identische Gleichung; **d)** **~ card/disc/plate** *etc. see* **identification c**

identity: ~ crisis *n.* Identitätskrise, *die;* **~ parade** *see* **identification parade**

ideogram ['ɪdɪəgræm], **ideograph** ['ɪdɪəgrɑ:f] *ns.* Ideogramm, *das;* Begriffszeichen, *das*

ideological [aɪdɪə'lɒdʒɪkl, ɪdɪə'lɒdʒɪkl] *adj.*, **ideologically** [aɪdɪə'lɒdʒɪkəlɪ, ɪdɪə'lɒdʒɪkəlɪ] *adv.* ideologisch; weltanschaulich

ideologue ['aɪdɪəlɒg, 'ɪdɪəlɒg] *n.* Ideologe, *der*/Ideologin, *die*

ideology [aɪdɪ'ɒlədʒɪ, ɪdɪ'ɒlədʒɪ] *n.* Ideologie, *die;* Weltanschauung, *die*

ides [aɪdz] *n. pl.* Iden *Pl.;* **the ~ of March** die Iden des März

idiocy ['ɪdɪəsɪ] *n.* **a)** *(foolishness)* Dummheit, *die;* Idiotie, *die (abwertend);* **b)** *no pl. (Med.)* Idiotie, *die;* hochgradiger Schwachsinn

idiolect ['ɪdɪəlekt] *n. (Ling.)* Idiolekt, *der*

idiom ['ɪdɪəm] *n.* **a)** *(set phrase)* [Rede]wendung, *die;* idiomatischer Ausdruck; **b)** *(expression peculiar to a group)* Ausdrucksweise, *die; (expression peculiar to a person)* Stil, *der;* Diktion, *die (geh.);* **the legal ~:** die Juristensprache; **c)** *(national language)* Idiom, *das;* [National]sprache, *die;* **d)** *(style of artistic expression)* Ausdrucksform, *die;* **the New Orleans ~:** der New-Orleans-Stil

idiomatic [ɪdɪə'mætɪk] *adj.*, **idiomatically** [ɪdɪə'mætɪkəlɪ] *adv.* idiomatisch

idiosyncrasy [ɪdɪə'sɪŋkrəsɪ] *n.* **a)** *(mental constitution)* [geistige] Einstellung; **b)** *(view, behaviour)* Eigentümlichkeit, *die;* Eigenheit, *die*

idiosyncratic [ɪdɪəsɪŋ'krætɪk] *adj.*, **idiosyncratically** [ɪdɪəsɪŋ'krætɪkəlɪ] *adv.* eigenwillig

idiot ['ɪdɪət] *n.* **a)** *(coll.: fool)* Idiot, *der (ugs.);* Trottel, *der (ugs.);* **b)** *(Med.)* Schwachsinnige, *der/die;* Idiot, *der*/Idiotin, *die (veralt.)*

idiotic [ɪdɪ'ɒtɪk] *adj.* idiotisch *(ugs. abwertend);* schwachsinnig *(abwertend);* **what an ~ thing to do/say** was für ein Schwachsinn

idiotically [ɪdɪ'ɒtɪkəlɪ] *adv.* idiotisch *(ugs.);* schwachsinnig

idle ['aɪdl] **1.** *adj.* **a)** *(lazy)* faul; träge; **b)** *(not in use)* außer Betrieb *nachgestellt; (unemployed)* unbeschäftigt, arbeitslos ⟨*Person*⟩; **be ~** ⟨*Maschinen, Fabrik:*⟩ stillstehen; **be ~ for an hour** eine Stunde lang untätig sein *od.* nichts tun; *see also* **²lie 2 b**; **c)** *(having no special purpose)* bloß ⟨*Neugier*⟩; nutzlos, leer ⟨*Geschwätz*⟩; **d)** *(groundless)* unbegründet ⟨*Annahme, Mutmaßung*⟩; bloß, rein ⟨*Spekulation, Angeberei, Gerücht, Behauptung*⟩; **no ~ jest** kein Scherz; **no ~ boast** *or* **jest** *(iron.)* kein leeres Versprechen; **e)** *(ineffective)* sinnlos, *(geh.)* müßig ⟨*Diskussion, Streit*⟩; fruchtlos, vergeblich ⟨*Versuch*⟩; leer ⟨*Versprechen*⟩; **f)** *(unoccupied)* frei ⟨*Zeit, Stunden, Tag*⟩; **Satan** *or* **the devil finds** *or* **makes work for ~ hands [to do]** *(prov.)* Müßiggang ist aller Laster Anfang *(Spr.)*. **2.** *v. i.* **a)** faulenzen; **b)** ⟨*Motor:*⟩ leer laufen, im Leerlauf laufen

~ a'way *v. t.* vertun ⟨*Zeit, Leben, Chancen*⟩

idleness ['aɪdlnɪs] *n., no pl. (being unoccupied)* Untätigkeit, *die; (avoidance of work)* Müßiggang, *der (geh.)*

idler ['aɪdlə(r)] *n.* Faulenzer, *der*/Faulenzerin, *die;* Faulpelz, *der (fam.)*

idly ['aɪdlɪ] *adv.* **a)** *(carelessly)* leichtsinnig; gedankenlos; **b)** *(inactively)* untätig; **stand ~ by while ...** *(fig.)* untätig zusehen, wie ...; **c)** *(indolently)* faul; **spend one's time ~:** seine Zeit mit Faulenzen verbringen

idol ['aɪdl] *n.* **a)** *(false god)* Götze, *der; (image of deity)* Götzenbild, *das;* **b)** *(person venerated)* Idol, *das; (thing venerated)* Götze, *der*

idolater [aɪ'dɒlətə(r)] *n.* **a)** *(worshipper of idols)* Götzendiener, *der;* **b)** *(devoted admirer)* Verehrer, *der*/Verehrerin, *die*

idolatrous [aɪ'dɒlətrəs] *adj.* götzendienerisch ⟨*Religion, Person*⟩; abgöttisch, götzenhaft ⟨*Verehrung*⟩

idolatry [aɪ'dɒlətrɪ] *n.* **a)** *(worship of false gods)* Götzenverehrung, *die;* **b)** *(veneration of person or thing)* Vergötterung, *die*

idolize (idolise) ['aɪdəlaɪz] *v. t.* **a)** *(make an idol of)* anbeten; verehren; **b)** *(fig.: venerate)* vergöttern; zum Idol erheben

idyll (idyl) ['ɪdɪl] **a)** *(description of scene)* Idylle, *die;* **prose ~:** Idylle in Prosa; **b)** *(episode)* Idyll, *das*

idyllic [aɪ'dɪlɪk, ɪ'dɪlɪk] *adj.* idyllisch

i.e. [aɪ'i:] *abbr.* **that is** d. h.; i. e.

if [ɪf] **1.** *conj.* **a)** wenn; **if anyone should ask ...:** falls jemand fragt, ...; wenn jemand fragen sollte, ...; **if you were a bird ...:** wenn du ein Vogel wärest; **if you would lend me some money ...:** wenn du mir Geld leihen würdest, ...; **if I knew what to do ...:** wenn ich wüßte, was ich tun soll ...; **if I were you** an deiner Stelle; **if and when ...:** im Falle, daß ...; unter der Voraussetzung, daß ...; **write down the items you wish to buy, if any** schreib auf, welche Artikel du kaufen willst, wenn *od.* falls du etwas möchtest; **better, if anything** vielleicht etwas besser; **tell me what I can do to help, if anything** falls ich irgendwie helfen kann, sag es mir; **if so/not** wenn ja/nein *od.* nicht; **if then/that/at all** wenn überhaupt; **if only for today** wenn auch nur für heute; **if only because/to ...:** schon allein, weil/um ... zu ...; **as if** als ob; **he nodded, as if to say ...:** er nickte, als ob er sagen wollte *od.* wie um zu sagen ...; **as if you didn't know!** als ob du es nicht gewußt hättest!; **it isn't** *or* **it's not as if we were** *or (coll.)* **we're rich** es ist nicht etwa so, daß wir reich wären; **b)** *(whenever)* [immer] wenn; **c)** *(whether)* ob; **d)** *in excl. of wish* **if I only knew, if only I knew!** wenn ich das nur wüßte!; das wüßte ich gern!; **if only he arrives in time!** wenn er nur rechtzeitig ankommt!; **if only you could** *or* **if you could only have seen it!** wenn du es nur hättest sehen können!; **e)** *expr. surprise etc.* **if it isn't Ronnie!** das ist doch Ronnie!; **and if he didn't try to knock me down!** und er hat doch tatsächlich versucht, mich niederzuschlagen!; **f)** *in polite request* **if you will wait a moment** wenn Sie einen Augenblick warten wollen; **if you wouldn't mind holding the door open** wenn Sie so freundlich wären und die Tür aufhielten; wenn Sie freundlicherweise die Tür aufhielten; **g)** *(though)* und wenn; auch *od.* selbst wenn; **if I'm mistaken, you're mistaken too** wenn ich mich auch irre, du irrst dich genauso; **even if he did say that, ...:** selbst wenn er das gesagt hat, ...; **h)** *(despite being)* wenn auch; **likeable, if somewhat rough** liebenswürdig, wenn auch etwas derb. **2.** *n.* Wenn, *das;* Einschränkung, *die;* **ifs and buts** Wenn und Aber, *das*

iffish ['ɪfɪʃ], **iffy** ['ɪfɪ] *adjs. (coll.)* ungewiß; zweifelhaft

igloo ['ɪglu:] *n.* Iglu, *der od. das*

igneous ['ɪgnɪəs] *adj.* **~ rock** *(Geol.)* Extrusivgestein, *das;* Eruptivgestein, *das*

ignite [ɪg'naɪt] **1.** *v. t.* **a)** anzünden; entzünden *(geh.)*; **b)** *(Chem.: heat)* [bis zur Verbrennung] erhitzen. **2.** *v. i.* sich entzünden

ignition [ɪg'nɪʃn] *n.* **a)** *(igniting)* Zünden, *das;* Entzünden, *das (geh.); (being ignited)*

Entzündung, *die;* **we have ~:** wir haben gezündet; **b)** *(Motor Veh.)* Zündung, *die*
ignition: ~ key *n. (Motor Veh.)* Zündschlüssel, *der;* **~ system** *n. (Motor Veh.)* Zündanlage, *die*
ignoble [ɪg'nəʊbl] *adj.* niedrig ‹*Geburt, Herkunft*›; niederträchtig ‹*Person*›; schändlich ‹*Tat*›
ignominious [ɪgnə'mɪnɪəs] *adj.* **a)** verwerflich *(geh.)* ‹*Tat, Idee, Praktik*›; schändlich, verworfen ‹*Person*›; **b)** *(humiliating)* schändlich; schmachvoll *(geh.)*
ignominiously [ɪgnə'mɪnɪəslɪ] *adv. (in a humiliating manner)* auf entehrende *od.* erniedrigende Weise; schmachvoll *(geh.)*
ignominy ['ɪgnəmɪnɪ] *n.* Schande, *die*
ignoramus [ɪgnə'reɪməs] *n.* Ignorant, *der;* Nichtswisser, *der*
ignorance ['ɪgnərəns] *n., no pl.* Ignoranz, *die (abwertend);* Unwissenheit, *die;* **keep sb. in ~ of sth.** jmdn. in Unkenntnis über etw. *(Akk.)* lassen; **~ is bliss** das ist das Glück der Unwissenden; was ich nicht weiß, macht mich nicht heiß *(Spr.);* **his ~ of physics** seine mangelnden Kenntnisse in Physik
ignorant ['ɪgnərənt] *adj.* **a)** *(lacking knowledge)* unwissend; ungebildet; **b)** *(behaving in uncouth manner)* unkultiviert *(abwertend);* **c)** *(uninformed)* **be ~ of sth.** über etw. *(Akk.)* nicht informiert sein; von etw. keine Ahnung haben; **remain ~ of sth.** über etw. *(Akk.)* nie etwas erfahren; **be ~ in** *or* **of mathematics** mangelnde Kenntnisse in Mathematik haben *od. (geh.)* aufweisen
ignorantly ['ɪgnərəntlɪ] *adv.* unwissend; in Unwissenheit; **behave ~:** sich ungehobelt benehmen
ignore [ɪg'nɔ:(r)] *v.t.* ignorieren; nicht beachten; nicht befolgen ‹*Befehl, Rat*›; übergehen, überhören ‹*Frage, Bemerkung*›; **he ~d me in the street** er ist [auf der Straße] einfach an mir vorbeigegangen; **I shall ~ that remark!** ich habe das nicht gehört!
iguana [ɪ'gwɑ:nə] *n. (Zool.)* Leguan, *der*
ikon *see* **icon**
Iliad ['ɪlɪæd] *n.* Ilias, *die*
ilk [ɪlk] *n.* **a)** *(coll.)* **Bill and [others of] his ~:** Bill und seinesgleichen; **... and that ~:** ... und dergleichen; **he's another of the same ~:** er gehört auch zu *od.* ist auch von derselben Sorte; **people of that ~:** solche Leute; **b) of that ~** *(Scot.)* aus dem Clan/Ort gleichen Namens
ill [ɪl] **1.** *adj.*, **worse** [wɜ:s], **worst** [wɜ:st] **a)** *(sick)* krank; **be ~ with flu** an Grippe *(Dat.)* erkrankt sein; [die] Grippe haben; **be ~ with worry** vor Sorgen [ganz] krank sein; sich vor Sorgen verzehren *(geh.);* **b)** *(morally bad)* schlecht, zweifelhaft ‹*Ruf, Ansehen*›; *see also* **fame; c)** *(hostile)* schlimm, böse ‹*Gerücht*›; schlecht, übel ‹*Laune, Stimmung*›; **d)** *(harmful)* **~ effects** schädliche Wirkungen; **do an ~ turn to sb.** jmdm. Schaden zufügen; **e)** *(unfavourable)* ungünstig ‹*Zeitpunkt*›; widrig ‹*Schicksal, Umstand*›; **~ fate** *or* **fortune** *or* **luck** Pech, *das;* **it's an ~ wind that blows nobody [any] good** *(prov.)* des einen Leid, des andern Freud' *(Spr.);* **as ~ luck would have it** wie es das Unglück wollte; **f)** *(improper)* schlecht ‹*Benehmen, Manieren*›. **2.** *n.* **a)** *(evil)* Übel, *das;* **for good or ~:** komme, was will; **through good and ~:** im Glück wie im Unglück; **b)** *(harm)* Schlechte, *das;* Unglück, *das;* **wish sb. ~:** jmdm. nichts Gutes *od.* nur das Schlechteste wünschen; **speak ~ of sb./sth.** Schlechtes über jmdn. *od.* von jmdm./von etw. sagen; **let's not speak ~ of the dead** die Toten soll man ruhen lassen; **c)** *in pl. (misfortunes)* Mißstände *Pl.;* **the ~s that flesh is heir to** die Leiden, mit denen die Menschheit geschlagen ist. **3.** *adv.*, **worse, worst a)** *(badly)* schlecht, unschicklich ‹*sich benehmen*›; *see also* **take 1 i; b)** *(unfavourably)* ungünstig ‹*gelegen*›; **it goes ~ with sb.** es geht jmdm. schlecht; **c)** *(imperfectly)* schlecht, unzureichend ‹*versorgt, ausgestattet*›; **he can ~ afford it** er kann es sich *(Dat.)* kaum leisten; **it ~ becomes sb. to do sth.** es ist nicht jmds. Sache *od.* steht jmdm. nicht zu, etw. zu tun; **~ at ease** verlegen
I'll [aɪl] **a) = I shall; b) = I will**
ill: ~-advised *adj.* unklug; schlechtberaten ‹*Kunde*›; **be ~-advised** ‹*Person:*› schlecht beraten sein; **~-ad'visedly** *adv.* in unüberlegter Weise; unüberlegt, unklug ‹*handeln*›; **~-assorted** *adj.* schlecht zusammenpassend; nicht harmonierend, unverträglich ‹*Ehepaar usw.*›; bunt zusammengewürfelt ‹*Sammlung*›; **~-behaved** ['ɪlbɪheɪvd] *adj. see* **behave 1 a; ~-bred** *adj.* schlecht erzogen ‹*Kind, Jugendlicher*›; unkultiviert *(abwertend)* ‹*Leute, Kerl usw.*›; **~-conceived** ['ɪlkənsi:vd] *adj.* schlecht durchdacht; **~-defined** ['ɪldɪfaɪnd] *adj.* ungenau definiert, unklar ‹*Verfahren, Vorgehen*›; verschwommen [formuliert] ‹*Gesetz, Verordnung, Vertrag*›; nicht klar *od.* fest umrissen ‹*Aufgabenbereich*›; **~ disposed** ['ɪldɪspəʊzd] *adj. see* **disposed**
illegal [ɪ'li:gl] *adj.* ungesetzlich; illegal; *(Games, Sport: contrary to rules)* regelwidrig; unerlaubt; **it is ~ to drive a car without a licence** es ist verboten, ohne Führerschein Auto zu fahren
illegality [ɪlɪ'gælɪtɪ] *n.* **a)** *no pl.* Ungesetzlichkeit, *die;* **be unaware of the ~ of sth.** nicht wissen, daß etw. verboten ist; **b)** *(illegal act)* Gesetzesübertretung, *die*
illegally [ɪ'li:gəlɪ] *adv.* illegal; **bring sth. into the country ~:** etw. illegal *od.* auf illegalem Wege einführen
illegibility [ɪledʒɪ'bɪlɪtɪ] *n., no pl.* Unleserlichkeit, *die*
illegible [ɪ'ledʒɪbl] *adj.*, **illegibly** [ɪ'ledʒɪblɪ] *adv.* unleserlich
illegitimacy [ɪlɪ'dʒɪtɪməsɪ] *n., no pl. see* **illegitimate: a)** Unehelichkeit, *die;* Illegitimität, *die;* **b)** Unrechtmäßigkeit, *die;* **c)** Unzulässigkeit, *die*
illegitimate [ɪlɪ'dʒɪtɪmət] *adj.* **a)** *(not from wedlock)* unehelich; illegitim; **b)** *(not authorized by law)* unrechtmäßig ‹*Machtergreifung, Geschäft*›; mit dem Gesetz unvereinbar ‹*Maßnahme, Vorgehen, Beweggrund*›; **c)** *(wrongly inferred)* unzulässig
illegitimately [ɪlɪ'dʒɪtɪmətlɪ] *adv. see* **illegitimate: a)** unehelich; **b)** zu Unrecht; **c)** auf unzulässige Weise
ill: ~ 'fated *adj.* unglückselig; verhängnisvoll ‹*Entscheidung, Stunde, Tag*›; **~-'favoured** *adj. (unattractive)* unansehnlich ‹*Person*›; **~ 'feeling** *n.* Verstimmung, *die;* **cause ~ feeling** böses Blut machen *od.* schaffen; **no ~ feeling[s]?** sind Sie jetzt verstimmt *od. (fam.)* böse?; **no ~ feeling[s]** das macht [doch] nichts; ich nehme es nicht übel; **~-founded** ['ɪlfaʊndɪd] *adj.* haltlos ‹*Theorie, Gerücht*›; **be ~-founded** völlig haltlos sein; jeder Grundlage entbehren; **~-gotten** *adj.* unrechtmäßig erworben; **~ 'health** *n.* schwache Gesundheit; **~ humour** *n.* schlechte Laune; Gereiztheit, *die;* **~-humoured** [ɪl'hju:məd] *adj.* schlecht gelaunt
illicit [ɪ'lɪsɪt] *adj.* verboten ‹*Glücksspiel*›; unerlaubt ‹*[Geschlechts]verkehr, Beziehung*›; Schwarz‹*handel, -verkauf, -arbeit, -brennerei*›; **~ traffic in drugs** illegaler Drogenhandel
illicitly [ɪ'lɪsɪtlɪ] *adv.* illegal ‹*Handel treiben, Schnaps brennen*›
'ill-informed *adj.* schlecht informiert; auf Unkenntnis beruhend ‹*Bemerkung, Schätzung, Urteil*›
illiteracy [ɪ'lɪtərəsɪ] *n., no pl.* Analphabetentum, *das;* Analphabetismus, *der*
illiterate [ɪ'lɪtərət] **1.** *adj.* **a)** des Lesens und Schreibens unkundig; analphabetisch ‹*Bevölkerung*›; **he is ~:** er ist Analphabet; **b)** *(showing lack of learning)* primitiv *(abwertend);* **musically ~:** auf musikalischem Gebiet *od.* musikalisch völlig unbedarft; **he is politically ~:** er ist ein politischer Analphabet. **2.** *n.* Analphabet, *der*/Analphabetin, *die*
ill: ~-judged [ɪl'dʒʌdʒd] *adj.* unklug; *(rash)* unüberlegt; leichtfertig; **~-mannered** [ɪl'mænəd] *adj.* rüpelhaft *(abwertend);* ungezogen ‹*Kind*›; **an ~-mannered fellow** ein Rüpel; **~-matched** *adj.* schlecht zusammenpassend; **~-natured** [ɪl'neɪtʃəd] *adj.*, **~ naturedly** [ɪl'neɪtʃədlɪ] *adv.* übellaunig
illness ['ɪlnɪs] *n.* **a)** *(a disease)* Krankheit, *die;* Erkrankung, *die;* **children's ~:** Kinderkrankheit, *die;* **b)** *no pl.* Krankheit, *die;* **because of ~:** wegen [einer] Krankheit
illogical [ɪ'lɒdʒɪkl] *adj.* unlogisch; unbegründet ‹*Ärger, Verstimmung*›
illogicality [ɪlɒdʒɪ'kælɪtɪ] *n.* **a)** *no pl.* Unlogik, *die;* **b)** *(illogical thing)* Ungereimtheit, *die;* logischer Fehler
illogically [ɪ'lɒdʒɪkəlɪ] *adv.* auf unlogische Weise; ohne jede Logik
ill: ~-omened [ɪl'əʊmənd] *adj.* unheilvoll; **~-starred** ['ɪlstɑ:d] *adj.* unglücklich ‹*Liebesverhältnis*›; unheilvoll, verhängnisvoll ‹*Tag, Jahr, Zufall*›; **the trip was ~-starred** die Reise stand unter einem Unstern *od.* ungünstigen Stern; **~ 'temper** *see* **ill humour; ~-tempered** [ɪl'tempəd] *see* **ill-humoured; ~-timed** [ɪl'taɪmd] *adj.* [zeitlich] ungelegen; ungünstig; unpassend, unbesonnen ‹*Bemerkung*›; **~-'treat** *v.t.* mißhandeln ‹*Lebewesen*›; nicht schonend behandeln, schlecht umgehen mit ‹*Gegenstand*›; **~-'treatment** *n., no pl. (of living thing)* Mißhandlung, *die; (of object)* wenig pflegliche Behandlung; **suffer/receive ~-treatment** mißhandelt/wenig schonend *od.* pfleglich behandelt werden
illuminate [ɪ'lju:mɪneɪt, ɪ'lu:mɪneɪt] *v.t.* **a)** *(light up)* ‹*Lampe usw.:*› beleuchten; ‹*Mond, Sonne:*› erleuchten; **b)** *(give enlightenment to)* erleuchten; **c)** *(help to explain)* erhellen; [näher] beleuchten; **~ a period of history** Licht in eine Geschichtsepoche bringen; **d)** *(decorate with lights)* festlich beleuchten; illuminieren; **~d advertisements** Leuchtreklamen; **e)** *(decorate with colours)* ausmalen, *(fachspr.)* illuminieren ‹*Handschriften usw.*›; **~d initial letters** verzierte *od.* ausgemalte Initialen
illuminating [ɪ'lju:mɪneɪtɪŋ, ɪ'lu:mɪneɪtɪŋ] *adj.* aufschlußreich
illumination [ɪlju:mɪ'neɪʃn, ɪlu:mɪ'neɪʃn] *n.* **a)** *(lighting)* Beleuchtung, *die;* **b)** *(enlightenment)* Erleuchtung, *die;* **c)** *(decorative lights) often in pl.* **~[s]** Festbeleuchtung, *die;* Illumination, *die;* **d)** *(of manuscript)* Buchmalerei, *die;* Illumination, *die (fachspr.)*
illumine [ɪ'lju:mɪn, ɪ'lu:mɪn] *v.t. (literary)* **a)** *(light up)* erhellen; illuminieren *(geh.);* **b)** *(enlighten)* erleuchten; Erleuchtung bringen (+ *Dat.*); illuminieren *(geh.)*
ill-use 1. [ɪl'ju:z] *v.t. see* **ill-treat. 2.** [ɪl'ju:s] *n. see* **ill-treatment**
illusion [ɪ'lju:ʒn, ɪ'lu:ʒn] *n.* **a)** *(false sense-perception)* [Sinnes]täuschung, *die;* Illusion, *die;* **have the ~ of seeing sth.** sich *(Dat.)* einbilden, etw. zu sehen; etw. zu sehen glauben; **the ointment produces an ~ of warmth** die Salbe ruft die Empfindung *od.* Illusion von Wärme hervor; **b)** *(deception)* Wunschbild, *das;* Illusion, *die;* *(misapprehension)* falsche Vorstellung; Illusion, *die;* **be under an ~:** sich Illusionen *(Dat.)* hingeben; sich *(Dat.)* Illusionen machen; **be under the ~ that ...:** sich *(Dat.)* einbilden, daß ...; **have no ~s about sb./sth.** sich *(Dat.)* über jmdn./etw. keine Illusionen machen *od.* nichts vormachen
illusionist [ɪ'lju:ʒənɪst, ɪ'lu:ʒənɪst] *see* **conjurer**

illusory [ɪ'lju:sərɪ, ɪ'lu:sərɪ] *adj.* **a)** *(deceptive)* illusorisch; trügerisch; **b)** *(of the nature of an illusion)* imaginär *(geh.)* ‹*Gestalt*›; Wahn‹*bild, -idee, -vorstellung*›; irrig ‹*Lehre, Ansicht, Annahme*›

illustrate ['ɪləstreɪt] *v. t.* **a)** *(serve as example of)* veranschaulichen; illustrieren; **b)** *(elucidate by pictures)* [bildlich] darstellen ‹*Vorgang, Ablauf*›; illustrieren ‹*Buch, Erklärung*›; **c)** *(explain)* verdeutlichen; erläutern; *(make clear by examples)* anschaulicher machen; illustrieren; **d)** *(ornament)* illustrieren; bebildern

illustration [ɪlə'streɪʃn] *n.* **a)** *(example)* Beispiel, *das* **(of** für); *(drawing)* Abbildung, *die;* bildliche Darstellung; **b)** *(picture)* Abbildung, *die;* Illustration, *die;* **c)** *no pl. (with example)* Illustration, *die;* Erläuterung, *die; (with picture)* Illustration, *die;* Illustrierung, *die;* **by way of ~:** zur Illustration *od.* Verdeutlichung

illustrative ['ɪləstrətɪv] *adj.* erläuternd; illustrativ; **be ~ of sth.** beispielhaft *od.* typisch für etw. sein; **~ material** Beispielmaterial, *das*

illustrator ['ɪləstreɪtə(r)] *n.* Illustrator, *der*/Illustratorin, *die*

illustrious [ɪ'lʌstrɪəs] *adj.* berühmt ‹*Person*› **(for** wegen); ruhmreich ‹*Tat, Herrschaft*›

ill 'will *n.* Böswilligkeit, *die*

I'm [aɪm] = **I am**

image ['ɪmɪdʒ] *n.* **a)** Bildnis, *das (geh.); (statue)* Standbild, *das;* Statue, *die;* **b)** *(Optics, Math.)* Bild, *das;* **c)** *(semblance)* Bild, *das; (counterpart)* Ebenbild, *das (geh.); (archetype)* Verkörperung, *die;* **God created man in his own ~** *(Bibl.)* Gott schuf den Menschen nach seinem Bilde; **she is the [very] ~ of her mother** sie ist das [getreue] Ebenbild ihrer Mutter; **d)** *(Lit.: simile, metaphor)* Bild, *das;* Metapher, *die (fachspr.);* **e)** *(mental representation)* Bild, *das; (conception)* Vorstellung, *die;* **f)** *(perceived character)* Image, *das;* **improve one's ~:** sein Image aufbessern; **public ~:** Image [in der Öffentlichkeit], *das*

imagery ['ɪmɪdʒərɪ, 'ɪmɪdʒrɪ] *n., no pl.* **a)** *(images)* Bilder *Pl.;* bildliche Darstellungen *Pl.; (statues)* Statuen *Pl.;* Standbilder *Pl.;* **b)** *(mental images)* Vorstellungen *Pl.;* **c)** *(Lit.: figurative illustration)* Metaphorik, *die*

imaginable [ɪ'mædʒɪnəbl] *adj.* erdenklich; **the biggest lie ~:** die unverschämteste Lüge, die man sich *(Dat.)* vorstellen kann

imaginary [ɪ'mædʒɪnərɪ] *adj.* **a)** imaginär *(geh.);* konstruiert ‹*Bildnis*›; eingebildet ‹*Krankheit*›; **b)** *(Math.)* imaginär

imagination [ɪmædʒɪ'neɪʃn] *n.* **a)** *no pl., no art.* Phantasie, *die;* **do/see sth. in one's ~:** sich *(Dat.)* vorstellen, etw. zu tun/etw. vor seinem geistigen Auge sehen; **use your ~!** hab doch ein bißchen Phantasie! *(ugs.);* entwickel doch mal etwas Phantasie!; **b)** *no pl., no art. (fancy)* Einbildung, *die;* **catch sb.'s ~:** jmdn. begeistern; **it's just your ~:** das bildest du dir nur ein; **it's all in your ~:** das bildest du dir alles [nur] ein

imaginative [ɪ'mædʒɪnətɪv] *adj.* **a)** imaginativ *(geh.);* **~ faculties** Vorstellungsvermögen, *das;* **b)** *(given to using imagination)* phantasievoll; **be too ~:** zuviel Phantasie haben; **c)** *(showing imagination)* einfallsreich

imaginatively [ɪ'mædʒɪnətɪvlɪ] *adv.* **a)** einfallsreich; **b)** *(using imagination)* phantasievoll

imagine [ɪ'mædʒɪn] *v. t.* **a)** *(picture to oneself)* sich *(Dat.)* vorstellen; **can you ~?** stell dir vor!; **it cannot be ~d** es ist unvorstellbar; **~ things** sich *(Dat.)* Dinge einbilden[, die gar nicht stimmen]; **..., or am I imagining things?** ..., oder bilde ich mir das bloß ein?; **b)** *(think)* sich *(Dat.)* vorstellen; **~ sb./sth. to be/do ...:** denken *od.* sich *(Dat.)* vorstellen, daß jmd./etw. ... ist/tut; **~ sth. to be easy/difficult** *etc.* sich *(Dat.)* etw. leicht/schwer *usw.* vorstellen; **~ oneself to be sth.** sich *(Dat.)* einbilden, etw. zu sein; **do not ~ that ...:** bilden Sie sich *(Dat.)* bloß nicht ein, daß ...; **c)** *(guess)* sich *(Dat.)* vorstellen; **as you can ~, as may be ~d** wie du dir denken *od.* vorstellen kannst/wie man sich denken *od.* vorstellen kann; **d)** *(coll.: suppose)* glauben; **e)** *(get the impression)* **~ [that] ...:** sich *(Dat.)* einbilden[, daß] ...

imago [ɪ'meɪgəʊ] *n., pl.* **imagines** [ɪ'meɪdʒɪni:z] *or* **~s** *or (Amer.)* **~es** *(Biol., Psych.)* Imago, *die*

imam [ɪ'mɑ:m] *n. (Muslim Rel.)* Imam, *der*

imbalance [ɪm'bæləns] *n.* Unausgeglichenheit, *die*

imbecile ['ɪmbɪsi:l, 'ɪmbɪsaɪl] **1.** *adj.* **a)** *(stupid)* schwachsinnig *(ugs. abwertend);* **b)** *(Med.)* imbezil[l]. **2.** *n.* **a)** *(stupid person)* Idiot, *der (ugs.);* Schwachkopf, *der;* **b)** *(Med.)* Imbezil[l]e, *der/die*

imbibe [ɪm'baɪb] *v. t.* **a)** *(drink)* trinken; **b)** *(fig.: assimilate)* in sich *(Akk.)* aufsaugen

imbroglio [ɪm'brəʊljəʊ] *n., pl.* **~s a) a financial ~:** ein finanzielles Chaos; ein Finanzchaos; **b)** *(dramatic situation)* Verwicklungen *Pl.; (political situation)* Wirrwarr, *das*

imbue [ɪm'bju:] *v. t.* **a)** *(tinge)* färben; **b)** *(permeate)* durchdringen; **~d with sth.** von etw. durchdrungen

IMF *abbr.* **International Monetary Fund** IWF, *der*

imitate ['ɪmɪteɪt] *v. t.* **a)** *(mimic)* nachahmen; nachmachen *(ugs.);* **~ sb.** *(follow example of)* es jmdm. gleichtun; **b)** *(produce sth. like)* kopieren; **c)** *(be like)* imitieren

imitation [ɪmɪ'teɪʃn] **1.** *n.* **a)** *(imitating)* Nachahmung, *die;* **Tim's ~ of his brother** die Art und Weise, wie Tim seinen Bruder nachahmt/nachahmte; **a style developed in ~ of classical models** ein nach klassischen Vorbildern entwickelter Stil; **do ~s of sb.** jmdn. imitieren *od.* nachahmen; **he sings, tells jokes, and does ~s** er singt, erzählt Witze und ahmt andere Leute nach; **~ is the sincerest [form of] flattery** nachgeahmt zu werden ist das größte Kompliment; **b)** *(copy)* Kopie, *die;* Nachbildung, *die; (counterfeit)* Imitation, *die.* **2.** *adj.* imitiert; Kunst‹*leder, -horn*›; **~ marble/ivory/teak/fur** *etc.* Marmor-/Elfenbein-/Teak-/Pelzimitation *usw., die*

imitative ['ɪmɪtətɪv, 'ɪmɪteɪtɪv] *adj.* **a)** uneigenständig; epigonal *(geh.);* **be ~ of sb./sth.** jmdn./etw. nachahmen; **~ arts** bildende Künste; **b)** *(prone to copy)* imitativ *(geh.)*

imitator ['ɪmɪteɪtə(r)] *n.* Nachahmer, *der*/Nachahmerin, *die; (one who mimics another)* Imitator, *der*/Imitatorin, *die;* **be an ~ of sb.** jmdn. nachahmen

immaculate [ɪ'mækjʊlət] *adj.* **a)** *(spotless)* makellos ‹*Kleidung, Weiß*›; **b)** *(faultless)* tadellos

Immaculate Con'ception *n. (RC Ch.)* Unbefleckte Empfängnis

immaculately [ɪ'mækjʊlətlɪ] *adv.* **a)** *(spotlessly)* makellos; **~ white** blütenweiß; **b)** *(faultlessly)* tadellos

immanence ['ɪmənəns] *n., no pl.* Immanenz, *die*

immanent ['ɪmənənt] *adj.* **a)** immanent; **be ~ in sth.** einer Sache *(Dat.)* innewohnen *(geh.);* **b)** *(Theol.)* allgegenwärtig

immaterial [ɪmə'tɪərɪəl] *adj.* **a)** *(unimportant)* unerheblich; **it's quite ~ to me** das ist für mich vollkommen uninteressant; **b)** *(not consisting of matter)* immateriell *(geh.);* körperlos ‹*Wesen*›

immature [ɪmə'tjʊə(r)] *adj.* **a)** noch nicht voll entwickelt ‹*Lebewesen*›; noch nicht voll ausgereift ‹*Begabung, Talent*›; noch etwas unausgegoren ‹*Kunststil*›; unreif ‹*Persönlichkeit, Einstellung*›; **b)** *(Biol.: unripe)* unreif; noch nicht voll entwickelt ‹*Organ*›

immaturity [ɪmə'tjʊərɪtɪ] *n.* **a)** *no pl.* Unreife, *die;* **b)** *no pl. (Biol.: unripeness)* Unreife, *die;* **in ~:** vor der Reife

immeasurable [ɪ'meʒərəbl] *adj.* unermeßlich; unmeßbar ‹*Entfernung*›

immeasurably [ɪ'meʒərəblɪ] *adv.* **a)** unmeßbar; unendlich ‹*lang*›; **b)** *(immensely)* ungeheuer

immediate [ɪ'mi:djət] *adj.* **a)** unmittelbar; *(nearest)* nächst... ‹*Nachbar[schaft], Umgebung, Zukunft*›; engst... ‹*Familie*›; unmittelbar ‹*Kontakt*›; **your ~ action must be to ...:** als erstes müssen Sie ...; **~ inference** direkter Schluß; **his ~ plan is to ...:** zunächst einmal will er ...; **b)** *(occurring at once)* prompt; unverzüglich ‹*Handeln, Maßnahmen*›; umgehend ‹*Antwort*›

immediately [ɪ'mi:djətlɪ] **1.** *adv.* **a)** unmittelbar; direkt; **b)** *(without delay)* sofort. **2.** *conj. (coll.)* sobald

immemorial [ɪmɪ'mɔ:rɪəl] *adj.* undenklich; **from time ~:** seit undenklichen Zeiten

immense [ɪ'mens] *adj.* **a)** ungeheuer; immens; **b)** *(coll.: great)* enorm

immensely [ɪ'menslɪ] *adv.* **a)** ungeheuer; **b)** *(coll.: very much)* unheimlich *(ugs.)*

immensity [ɪ'mensɪtɪ] *n., no pl. (great size)* Ungeheuerlichkeit, *die*

immerse [ɪ'mɜ:s] *v. t.* **a)** *(dip)* [ein]tauchen; **he ~d his head in cold water** er tauchte den Kopf in kaltes Wasser; **b)** *(cause to be under water)* versenken; *(Eccl.)* untertauchen; **~d in water** unter Wasser; **c) be ~d in thought/one's work** *(fig.: involved deeply)* in Gedanken versunken/in seine Arbeit vertieft sein

immersion [ɪ'mɜ:ʃn] *n.* **a)** Eintauchen, *das;* **b)** *(Relig.)* Untertauchen, *das;* **c)** *(fig.) (in work)* Vertiefung, *die; (in thought)* Versunkenheit, *die (geh.)*

im'mersion heater *n.* Heißwasserbereiter, *der; (small, portable)* Tauchsieder, *der*

immigrant ['ɪmɪgrənt] **1.** *n.* Einwanderer, *der*/Einwanderin, *die;* Immigrant, *der*/Immigrantin, *die.* **2.** *adj.* Einwanderer-; **~ population** Einwanderer *Pl.;* **~ workers** ausländische Arbeitnehmer

immigrate ['ɪmɪgreɪt] *v. i.* einwandern, immigrieren **(into** nach, **from** aus)

immigration [ɪmɪ'greɪʃn] *n.* Einwanderung *die,* Immigration, *die* **(into** nach, **from** aus); *attrib.* Einwanderungs‹*kontrolle, -beschränkung, -gesetz*›; **~ officer** Beamte/Beamtin der Einwanderungsbehörde

imminence ['ɪmɪnəns] *n., no pl.* Bevorstehen, *das*

imminent ['ɪmɪnənt] *adj.* unmittelbar bevorstehend; drohend ‹*Gefahr*›; **be ~:** unmittelbar bevorstehen/drohen

imminently ['ɪmɪnəntlɪ] *adv.* unmittelbar; **the President's arrival is expected ~:** die Ankunft des Präsidenten wird jeden Moment erwartet

immiscible [ɪ'mɪsɪbl] *adj.* nicht mischbar

immobile [ɪ'məʊbaɪl] *adj.* **a)** *(immovable)* unbeweglich; *(Mil.)* immobil; **b)** *(motionless)* bewegungslos

immobilisation, immobilise *see* **immobiliz-**

immobility [ɪmə'bɪlɪtɪ] *n., no pl.* **a)** *(immovableness)* Unbeweglichkeit, *die; (of army)* Immobilität, *die;* **b)** *(motionlessness)* Bewegungslosigkeit, *die*

immobilization [ɪməʊbɪlaɪ'zeɪʃn] *n.* **a)** *(fixing immovably)* Verankerung, *die;* **b)** *(Med.: restricting in movement)* Ruhigstellung, *die*

immobilize [ɪ'məʊbɪlaɪz] *v. t.* **a)** *(fix immovably)* verankern; *(fig.)* lähmen; **b)** *(restrict movement of)* feststellen ‹*Tür usw.*›; ruhigstellen ‹*Tier, Körperteil, Patienten*›; **c)** gegen Wegfahren sichern ‹*Fahrzeug*›

immoderate [ɪ'mɒdərət] *adj.* **a)** *(excessive)* unmäßig ‹*Rauchen, Trinken*›; überhöht ‹*Geschwindigkeit, Preis*›; übermäßig ‹*Lärm*›; **b)** *(extreme)* extrem ‹*Ansichten, Politiker*›; maßlos ‹*Lebensstil*›

immoderately [ɪ'mɒdərətlɪ] *adv.* **a)** *(excessively)* übermäßig ‹*hoch*›; unmäßig ‹*essen, trinken usw.*›; übertrieben ‹*schnell, laut*›; **b)** *(to an extreme degree)* extrem

immodest [ɪ'mɒdɪst] *adj.* **a)** *(impudent)* unbescheiden; **b)** *(improper)* unanständig

immodestly [ɪ'mɒdɪstlɪ] *adv.* **a)** *(impudently)* unbescheidenerweise; **b)** *(improperly)* unanständig

immodesty [ɪ'mɒdɪstɪ] *n., no pl.* **a)** *(impudence)* Unbescheidenheit, *die;* **b)** *(impropriety)* Unanständigkeit, *die;* **the ~ of her short skirt** ihr unanständig kurzer Rock

immolate ['ɪməleɪt] *v.t. (literary)* **a)** *(kill)* opfern (**to** *Dat.*); **b)** *(fig.: sacrifice)* zum Opfer bringen, aufopfern *(geh.)* (**to** *Dat.*)

immolation [ɪmə'leɪʃn] *n. (literary)* **a)** Opferung, *die;* **b)** *(fig.)* Aufopferung, *die*

immoral [ɪ'mɒrəl] *adj.* **a)** *(not conforming to morality)* unmoralisch; unsittlich; sittenwidrig *(Rechtsspr.)*; **b)** *(morally evil)* pervers; *(unchaste)* sittenlos; **c)** *(dissolute)* zügellos

immoral 'earnings *n. pl. (Law)* Einkünfte aus gewerbsmäßiger Unzucht

immorality [ɪmə'rælɪtɪ] *n.* **a)** *no pl.* Unsittlichkeit, *die;* Unmoral, *die;* Sittenwidrigkeit, *die (Rechtsspr.)*; **b)** *no pl. (wickedness)* Verdorbenheit, *die; (unchastity)* Sittenlosigkeit, *die;* **c)** *no pl. (dissoluteness)* Zügellosigkeit, *die;* **d)** *(morally evil or unchaste act)* Unsittlichkeit, *die;* **e)** *(dissolute act)* Ausschweifung, *die*

immorally [ɪ'mɒrəlɪ] *adv.* **a)** *(without regard for morality)* unmoralisch; unsittlich; **b)** *(wickedly)* unmoralisch; *(unchastely)* sittenlos; **c)** *(dissolutely)* ausschweifend; zügellos

immortal [ɪ'mɔ:tl] **1.** *adj.* **a)** *(living for ever)* unsterblich; **b)** *(divine)* ewig; **~ life, the life ~:** das ewige Leben; **c)** *(incorruptible)* unvergänglich; **d)** *(famous for all time)* unsterblich, unvergänglich ‹*Kunstwerk*›. **2.** *n.* **a)** Unsterbliche, *der/die;* **b)** *in pl. (Greek and Roman Mythol.)* Unsterbliche; Götter

immortality [ɪmɔ:'tælɪtɪ] *n., no pl. see* **immortal 1 a, c, d:** Unsterblichkeit, *die;* Unvergänglichkeit, *die*

immortalize [ɪ'mɔ:təlaɪz] *v.t.* unsterblich machen

immortally [ɪ'mɔ:təlɪ] *adv.* **a)** *(eternally)* ewig[lich]; **b)** *(perpetually)* [immer und] ewig

immovable [ɪ'mu:vəbl] *adj.* **a)** unbeweglich; **be ~:** sich nicht bewegen lassen; **b)** *(motionless)* bewegungslos; **c)** *(not subject to change)* unveränderbar; *see also* **feast 1 a; d)** *(steadfast)* unerschütterlich; unverrückbar ‹*Entschluß*›; **e)** *(emotionless)* unbewegt; **f)** *(Law)* unbeweglich

immovably [ɪ'mu:vəblɪ] *adv.* **a)** fest; **be ~ stuck** feststecken; **b)** *(in a motionless manner)* bewegungslos; **c)** *(unchangeably)* unveränderbar; **d)** *(steadfastly)* unerschütterlich; **be ~ resolved** fest entschlossen sein; **e)** *(in an emotionless manner)* unbewegt

immune [ɪ'mju:n] *adj.* **a)** *(exempt)* sicher (**from** vor + *Dat.*); geschützt (**from, against** vor + *Dat.*); gefeit *(geh.)* (**from, against** gegen); **~ from criminal liability** nicht strafmündig; **make oneself ~ from criticism** sich gegen Kritik abschirmen; **b)** *(insusceptible)* unempfindlich (**to** gegen); *(to hints, suggestions, etc.)* unempfänglich (**to** für); immun (**to** gegen); **c)** *(Med.) (resistant to disease)* immun (**to** gegen); *(relating to immunity)* Immun‹*defekt, -körper, -schwäche, -serum, -system*›

immunisation, immunise *see* **immuniz-**

immunity [ɪ'mju:nɪtɪ] *n.* **a)** *(freedom)* **~ from criminal liability** Strafunmündigkeit, *die;* **~ from prosecution** Schutz vor Strafverfolgung; **give sb. ~ from punishment** ‹*Person:*› jmdn. von der Bestrafung ausnehmen; ‹*Umstand:*› jmdn. vor Strafe schützen; **b)** *see* **immune b:** Unempfindlichkeit, *die* (**to** gegen); Unempfänglichkeit, *die* (**to** für); Immunität, *die* (**to** gegen); **c)** *(Law)* Immunität, *die* (**from** vor + *Dat.*); **d)** *(Med.: capacity to resist disease)* Immunität, *die;* **have ~ to infection** gegen Infektion immun sein

immunization [ɪmjʊnaɪ'zeɪʃn] *n. (Med.)* Immunisierung, *die*

immunize ['ɪmjʊnaɪz] *v.t. (Med.)* immunisieren

immunology [ɪmjʊ'nɒlədʒɪ] *n. (Med.)* Immunologie, *die*

immure [ɪ'mjʊə(r)] *(literary)* **1.** *v.t.* einkerkern *(geh.)*. **2.** *v. refl.* **~ oneself** sich abkapseln

immutability [ɪmju:tə'bɪlɪtɪ] *n., no pl.* Unveränderlichkeit, *die*

immutable [ɪ'mju:təbl] *adj.* unveränderlich

imp [ɪmp] *n.* **a)** Kobold, *der;* **b)** *(fig.: mischievous child)* Racker, *der (fam.)*

impact 1. ['ɪmpækt] *n.* **a)** Aufprall, *der* (**on, against** auf + *Akk.*); *(of shell or bomb)* Einschlag, *der; (collision)* Zusammenprall, *der;* **b)** *(fig.: effect)* Wirkung, *die;* **the ~ of plastics on modern life** die Auswirkung von Kunststoffen auf das moderne Leben; **have an ~ on sb./sth.** Auswirkungen auf jmdn./etw. haben; **make an ~ on sb./sth.** Eindruck auf jmdn./etw. machen. **2.** [ɪm'pækt] *v.t.* pressen

impacted [ɪm'pæktɪd] *adj.* **a)** *(Dent.)* impaktiert ‹*Zahn*›; **b)** *(Med.)* **~ fracture** Knocheneinkeilung, *die*

'impact strength *n. (Metallurgy)* Stoßfestigkeit, *die*

impair [ɪm'peə(r)] *v.t.* **a)** *(damage)* beeinträchtigen; schaden (+ *Dat.*) ‹*Gesundheit*›; **b)** *(weaken)* beeinträchtigen; **~ed vision** Sehschwäche, *die;* **~ed hearing** Schwerhörigkeit, *die*

impairment [ɪm'peəmənt] *n.* Beeinträchtigung, *die;* **~ of memory** Gedächtnisschwäche, *die*

impale [ɪm'peɪl] *v.t.* **a)** aufspießen; *(Hist.)* pfählen; **b)** *(Her.)* spalten ‹*Wappen*›

impalpable [ɪm'pælpəbl] *adj.* **a)** *(imperceptible to touch)* nicht fühlbar; **b)** *(not easily grasped by the mind)* unfaßbar

impart [ɪm'pɑ:t] *v.t.* **a)** *(give)* [ab]geben (**to** an + *Akk.*); vermachen (**to** *Dat.*); **b)** *(communicate)* kundtun *(geh.)* (**to** *Dat.*); vermitteln ‹*Kenntnisse*› (**to** *Dat.*)

impartial [ɪm'pɑ:ʃl] *adj.* unparteiisch; gerecht ‹*Entscheidung, Behandlung, Urteil*›

impartiality [ɪmpɑ:ʃɪ'ælɪtɪ] *n., no pl.* Unparteilichkeit, *die*

impartially [ɪm'pɑ:ʃəlɪ] *adv.* unparteiisch

impassable [ɪm'pɑ:səbl] *adj.* unpassierbar (**to** für); *(to vehicles)* unbefahrbar (**to** für)

impasse ['æmpɑ:s] *n. (lit. or fig.)* Sackgasse, *die;* **the negotiations have reached an ~:** die Verhandlungen sind in eine Sackgasse geraten

impassioned [ɪm'pæʃnd] *adj.* leidenschaftlich

impassive [ɪm'pæsɪv] *adj.* **a)** ausdruckslos; **b)** *(incapable of feeling emotion)* leidenschaftslos

impassively [ɪm'pæsɪvlɪ] *adv. see* **impassive: a)** ausdruckslos; **b)** leidenschaftslos

impatience [ɪm'peɪʃəns] *n., no pl.* **a)** Ungeduld, *die* (**at** über + *Akk.*); **b)** *(intolerance)* Unduldsamkeit, *die* (**of** gegen); **c)** *(eager desire)* [ungeduldige] Erwartung (**for** *Gen.*)

impatient [ɪm'peɪʃənt] *adj.* **a)** ungeduldig; **~ at sth./with sb.** ungeduldig über etw. *(Akk.)*/mit jmdm.; **b)** *(intolerant)* unduldsam (**of** gegen); **be ~ of sth.** etw. nicht ertragen können; **c)** *(eagerly desirous)* **be ~ for sth.** etw. kaum erwarten können; **be ~ to do sth.** unbedingt etw. tun wollen

impatiently [ɪm'peɪʃəntlɪ] *adv.* **a)** ungeduldig; **b)** *(intolerantly)* unduldsam; **c)** *(with eager desire)* begierig

impeach [ɪm'pi:tʃ] *v.t.* **a)** *(call in question)* in Frage stellen; **b) ~ sb. with sth.** jmdn. einer Sache *(Gen.)* beschuldigen; **c)** *(find fault with)* anzweifeln; in Zweifel ziehen; **d)** *(Law)* anklagen (**of** *Gen.*, wegen)

impeachment [ɪm'pi:tʃmənt] *n.* **a)** *(calling in question)* Infragestellung, *die;* **b)** *(finding of fault)* Anzweif[e]lung, *die;* **c)** *(Law)* Impeachment, *das*

impeccable [ɪm'pekəbl] *adj.* makellos; tadellos ‹*Manieren*›

impeccably [ɪm'pekəblɪ] *adv.* tadellos; makellos ‹*rein*›

impecunious [ɪmpɪ'kju:nɪəs] *adj.* mittellos

impedance [ɪm'pi:dəns] *n. (Electr.)* Impedanz, *die*

impede [ɪm'pi:d] *v.t.* behindern

impediment [ɪm'pedɪmənt] *n.* **a)** Hindernis, *das* (**to** für); **b)** *(speech defect)* Sprachfehler, *der*

impedimenta [ɪmpedɪ'mentə] *n. pl. (also Mil.)* Gepäck, *das*

impel [ɪm'pel] *v.t.,* **-ll- a)** *(drive by moral action)* treiben; **feel ~led to do sth.** sich genötigt *od.* gezwungen fühlen, etw. zu tun; **~ sb. to greater efforts** jmdn. zu größeren Bemühungen anspornen; **b)** *(drive forward)* treiben; antreiben ‹*Turbine usw.*›

impend [ɪm'pend] *v.i.* **a)** *(be about to happen)* bevorstehen; ‹*Gefahr:*› drohen

impenetrable [ɪm'penɪtrəbl] *adj.* **a)** undurchdringlich (**by, to** für); unbezwingbar, uneinnehmbar ‹*Festung*›; **b)** *(inscrutable)* unergründlich

impenetrably [ɪm'penɪtrəblɪ] *adv.* **a)** undurchdringlich; **b)** *(inscrutably)* unergründlich; **c)** hoffnungslos ‹*dumm*›

impenitent [ɪm'penɪtənt] *adj.* reu[e]los; **be quite ~:** keine Spur von Reue zeigen

impenitently [ɪm'penɪtəntlɪ] *adv.* reu[e]los

imperative [ɪm'perətɪv] **1.** *adj.* **a)** *(commanding)* gebieterisch *(geh.)* ‹*Stimme, Geste*›; **b)** *(urgent)* dringend erforderlich; **c)** *(obligatory)* zwingend ‹*Verpflichtung*›; **d)** *(Ling.)* imperativisch; **~ mood** Imperativ, *der.* **2.** *n.* **a)** *(command)* Befehl, *der;* **b)** *(Ling.)* Imperativ, *der;* Befehlsform, *die*

imperceptible [ɪmpə'septɪbl] *adj.* **a)** nicht wahrnehmbar (**to** für); unsichtbar ‹*Schranke (fig.)*›; **be ~ to sb./the senses** von jmdm./den Sinnen nicht wahrgenommen werden können; **b)** *(very slight or gradual)* unmerklich; *(subtle)* kaum zu erkennen *nicht attr.*; kaum zu erkennend *nicht präd.*; minimal ‹*Unterschied*›

imperceptibly [ɪmpə'septɪblɪ] *adv.* **a)** unmerklich; kaum wahrnehmbar ‹*sich bewegen*›; **b)** *(very gradually)* unmerklich; *(very slightly)* geringfügig

imperfect [ɪm'pɜ:fɪkt] **1.** *adj.* **a)** *(not fully formed)* unfertig; *(incomplete)* unvollständig; **drainage in this region is ~:** die Entwässerung in dieser Gegend ist mangelhaft; **slightly ~ stockings/pottery** *etc.* Strümpfe/Keramik *usw.* mit kleinen Fehlern; **b)** *(faulty)* mangelhaft; **human beings are ~:** der Mensch ist unvollkommen; **c)** *(Ling.)* Imperfekt-; **the ~ tense** das Imperfekt. **2.** *n. (Ling.)* Imperfekt, *das*

imperfection [ɪmpə'fekʃn] *n.* **a)** *no pl. (incompleteness)* Unvollständigkeit, *die;* **b)** *no pl. (faultiness)* Mangelhaftigkeit, *die; (of human beings)* Unvollkommenheit, *die;* **c)** *(fault)* Mangel, *der*

imperfectly [ɪm'pɜ:fɪktlɪ] *adv.* **a)** *(incompletely)* unvollständig; **b)** *(faultily)* fehlerhaft; mangelhaft

imperial [ɪm'pɪərɪəl] *adj.* **a)** kaiserlich; imperial *(geh.)*; Reichs‹*adler, -insignien*›; **I~ Rome** das Rom der Kaiserzeit; das kaiserliche Rom; **b)** *(Brit. Hist.)* des Britischen Weltreiches *nachgestellt;* **c)** *(of an emperor)* Kaiser-; **the I~ Court** der Kaiserhof; der kaiserliche Hof; **Her I~ Majesty** Ihre Kaiserliche Hoheit; **d)** *(majestic)* majestätisch; *(haughty)* hochmütig; erhaben *(iron.)*; **e)**

(magnificent) fürstlich; glanzvoll ‹*Stadt*›; **f)** *(fixed by statute)* britisch ‹*Maße, Gewichte*›; *see also* **gallon**

imperialism [ɪm'pɪərɪəlɪzm] *n., no pl.* *(derog.)* Imperialismus, *der;* **US/Soviet ~:** der US-/Sowjetimperialismus

imperialist [ɪm'pɪərɪəlɪst] *n. (derog.)* Imperialist, *der*/Imperialistin, *die;* **~ countries** imperialistische Länder

imperialistic [ɪmpɪərɪə'lɪstɪk] *adj. (derog.)* imperialistisch

imperil [ɪm'perl] *v. t., (Brit.)* **-ll-** gefährden

imperious [ɪm'pɪərɪəs] *adj.* **a)** *(overbearing)* herrisch; **b)** *(urgent)* zwingend; mächtig ‹*Triebe usw.*›

imperiously [ɪm'pɪərɪəslɪ] *adv.* **a)** *(overbearingly)* herrisch; **b)** *(urgently)* zwingend

imperishable [ɪm'perɪʃəbl] *adj.* **a)** *(immortal)* unvergänglich; **b)** *(not decaying)* alterungsbeständig ‹*Material*›; unverderblich ‹*Lebensmittel*›

imperishably [ɪm'perɪʃəblɪ] *adv.* unvergänglich

impermanence [ɪm'pɜ:mənəns] *n., no pl.* Vergänglichkeit, *die*

impermanent [ɪm'pɜ:mənənt] *adj.* vorübergehend; vergänglich ‹*Leben*›

impermeable [ɪm'pɜ:mɪəbl] *adj.* undurchlässig; impermeabel *(fachspr.)*

impermissible [ɪmpə'mɪsɪbl] *adj.* unzulässig

impersonal [ɪm'pɜ:sənl] *adj.* **a)** *(having no personality)* **an ~ thing** etwas [rein] Dingliches; **b)** *(not connected with any particular person)* unpersönlich ‹*Art, Zimmer usw.*›

impersonality [ɪmpɜ:sə'nælɪtɪ] *n., no pl.* Unpersönlichkeit, *die*

impersonal: ~ 'pronoun *see* **pronoun; ~ 'verb** *n. (Ling.)* unpersönliches Verb; Impersonale, *das (fachspr.)*

impersonate [ɪm'pɜ:səneɪt] *v. t. (pretend to be) (for entertainment)* imitieren; nachahmen; *(for purpose of fraud)* sich ausgeben als

impersonation [ɪmpɜ:sə'neɪʃn] *n.* **a)** *(personification)* Verkörperung, *die;* **b)** *(imitation)* Imitation, *die;* Nachahmung, *die;* **he does ~s** er ist Imitator; **her ~ of Margaret Thatcher** ihre Margaret-Thatcher-Imitation; **do an ~ of sb.** jmdn. imitieren *od.* nachahmen; **~ of sb.** *(for purpose of fraud)* Auftreten als jmd.

impersonator [ɪm'pɜ:səneɪtə(r)] *n.* *(entertainer)* Imitator, *der*/Imitatorin, *die;* *(sb. with fraudulent intent)* Betrüger, *der*/Betrügerin, *die;* **an ~ posing as a policeman** jemand, der sich als Polizist ausgibt; *see also* **female 1 a**

impertinence [ɪm'pɜ:tɪnəns] *n.* Unverschämtheit, *die;* Impertinenz, *die (geh.)*

impertinent [ɪm'pɜ:tɪnənt] *adj.* unverschämt; impertinent *(geh.)*

impertinently [ɪm'pɜ:tɪnəntlɪ] *adv.* unverschämterweise; **behave ~:** sich unverschämt benehmen

imperturbability [ɪmpətɜ:bə'bɪlɪtɪ] *n., no pl.* Gelassenheit, *die*

imperturbable [ɪmpə'tɜ:bəbl] *adj.* gelassen; **be completely ~:** durch nichts zu erschüttern sein; die Ruhe weghaben *(ugs.)*

imperturbably [ɪmpə'tɜ:bəblɪ] *adv.* gelassen; **..., he said ~:** ..., sagte er in aller Ruhe

impervious [ɪm'pɜ:vɪəs] *adj.* **a)** undurchlässig; **~ to water/bullets/rain** wasserdicht/kugelsicher/regendicht; **b)** *(fig.: impenetrable)* unergründlich; **c) be ~ to sth.** *(fig.)* unempfänglich für etw. sein; **be ~ to argument** Argumenten unzugänglich sein

impetigo [ɪmpɪ'taɪgəʊ] *n. (Med.)* Impetigo, *die (fachspr.);* Eiterflechte, *die*

impetuosity [ɪmpetjʊ'ɒsɪtɪ] *n.* **a)** *no pl.* *(quality)* Impulsivität, *die;* **b)** *(act, impulse)* Ausbruch, *der*

impetuous [ɪm'petjʊəs] *adj.* impulsiv ‹*Person*›; unüberlegt ‹*Handlung, Entscheidung*›; *(vehement)* stürmisch; ungestüm ‹*Person, Angriff*›

impetuousness [ɪm'petjʊəsnɪs] *see* **impetuosity a**

impetus ['ɪmpɪtəs] *n.* **a)** Kraft, *die;* *(of impact)* Wucht, *die;* **b)** *(fig.: impulse)* Motivation, *die;* **give an ~ to sth.** einer Sache *(Dat.)* Impulse geben; **give sth. new** *or* **fresh ~:** einer Sache *(Dat.)* neuen Auftrieb geben; **the ~ behind the development of nuclear power** die treibende Kraft bei der Entwicklung der Kernkraft

impiety [ɪm'paɪətɪ] *n.* **a)** *no pl. (ungodliness)* Gottlosigkeit, *die;* **b)** *no pl. (lack of dutifulness)* Respektlosigkeit, *die;* **c)** *(act)* Pietätlosigkeit, *die*

impinge [ɪm'pɪndʒ] *v. i.* **a)** *(make impact)* **~ [up]on sth.** auf etw. *(Akk.)* auftreffen; **b)** *(encroach)* **~ [up]on sth.** auf etw. *(Akk.)* Einfluß nehmen

impious ['ɪmpɪəs] *adj.* **a)** *(wicked)* gottlos; **b)** *(lacking in respect)* respektlos

impish ['ɪmpɪʃ] *adj.* lausbübisch; diebisch ‹*Freude*›; verschmitzt ‹*Grinsen, Blick*›

impishly ['ɪmpɪʃlɪ] *adv.* lausbübisch; diebisch ‹*sich freuen*›; verschmitzt ‹*grinsen*›

implacable [ɪm'plækəbl] *adj.* unversöhnlich; erbittert ‹*Gegner*›; erbarmungslos ‹*Verfolgung*›; unerbittlich ‹*Schicksal*›

implacably [ɪm'plækəblɪ] *adv.* unerbittlich; unaufhaltsam ‹*voranschreiten*›

implant 1. [ɪm'plɑ:nt] *v. t.* **a)** *(Med.)* implantieren *(fachspr.),* einpflanzen **(in** *Dat.*); **~ sb./sth. with sth.** jmdm./einer Sache etw. einpflanzen; **b)** *(Physiol.)* **be ~ed** sich einnisten; **c)** *(fig.: instil)* einpflanzen **(in** *Dat.*); **d)** *(plant)* [ein]pflanzen. **2.** ['ɪmplɑ:nt] *n.* *(Med.)* Implantat, *das*

implantation [ɪmplɑ:n'teɪʃn] *n.* **a)** *(Med.)* Implantation, *die (fachspr.);* Einpflanzung, *die;* **b)** *(fig.: instilling)* Einpflanzung, *die*

implausibility [ɪmplɔ:zɪ'bɪlɪtɪ] *n., no pl.* Unglaubwürdigkeit, *die*

implausible [ɪm'plɔ:zɪbl] *adj.,* **implausibly** [ɪm'plɔ:zɪblɪ] *adv.* unglaubwürdig

implement 1. ['ɪmplɪmənt] *n.* Gerät, *das.* **2.** ['ɪmplɪment] *v. t.* **a)** *(fulfil, complete)* erfüllen ‹*Versprechen, Vertrag*›; einhalten ‹*Termin usw.*›; vollziehen ‹*Erlaß usw.*›; **b)** *(put into effect)* [in die Tat] umsetzen ‹*Politik, Plan usw.*›

implementation [ɪmplɪmen'teɪʃn] *n.* *see* **implement 2:** Erfüllung, *die;* Einhaltung, *die;* Vollzug, *der;* Umsetzung [in die Tat], *die*

implicate ['ɪmplɪkeɪt] *v. t.* **a)** *(show to be involved)* belasten ‹*Verdächtigen usw.*›; **be ~d in a scandal** in einen Skandal verwickelt sein; **b)** *(affect)* **be ~d in sth.** von etw. betroffen sein

implication [ɪmplɪ'keɪʃn] *n.* **a)** *no pl. (implying)* Implikation, *die (geh.);* **by ~:** implizit; implizite *(geh.);* **b)** *no pl. (being involved)* Verwicklung, *die* **(in** in + *Akk.*); **c)** *no pl. (being affected)* Betroffenheit, *die* **(in** von); **d)** *(thing implied)* Implikation, *die*

implicit [ɪm'plɪsɪt] *adj.* **a)** *(implied)* implizit *(geh.);* unausgesprochen ‹*Drohung, Zweifel*›; **b)** *(virtually contained)* **be ~ in sth.** in etw. *(Dat.)* enthalten sein; **c)** *(resting on authority)* unbedingt; blind ‹*Vertrauen*›

implicitly [ɪm'plɪsɪtlɪ] *adv.* **a)** *(by implication)* implizit *(geh.);* **b)** *(unquestioningly)* blind ‹*vertrauen, gehorchen usw.*›

implode [ɪm'pləʊd] **1.** *v. i.* implodieren. **2.** *v. t.* implodieren lassen; **be ~d** implodieren

implore [ɪm'plɔ:(r)] *v. t.* **a)** *(beg for)* erflehen *(geh.);* flehen um; **'please', she ~d** „bitte", flehte sie; **b)** *(entreat)* anflehen **(for** um); **~ sb. to do/not to do sth.** jmdn. anflehen *od.* inständig bitten, etw. zu tun/nicht zu tun

imploring [ɪm'plɔ:rɪŋ] *adj.* flehend

imploringly [ɪm'plɔ:rɪŋlɪ] *adv.* flehentlich *(geh.)*

imply [ɪm'plaɪ] *v. t.* **a)** *(involve the existence of)* implizieren *(geh.);* *(by inference)* schließen lassen auf (+ *Akk.*); **be implied in sth.** in etw. *(Dat.)* enthalten sein; **silence sometimes implies consent** Schweigen bedeutet manchmal Zustimmung; **b)** *(express indirectly)* hindeuten auf (+ *Akk.*); *(insinuate)* unterstellen; **are you ~ing that ...?** willst du damit etwa sagen, daß ...?

impolite [ɪmpə'laɪt] *adj.,* **~r** [ɪmpə'laɪtə(r)], **~st** [ɪmpə'laɪtɪst] unhöflich; ungezogen ‹*Kind*›

impolitely [ɪmpə'laɪtlɪ] *adv.* unhöflich

impoliteness [ɪmpə'laɪtnɪs] *n., no pl.* Unhöflichkeit, *die;* *(of child)* Ungezogenheit, *die*

impolitic [ɪm'pɒlɪtɪk] *adj. (inexpedient)* unklug; unratsam

imponderable [ɪm'pɒndərəbl] **1.** *adj.* unwägbar; imponderabel *(geh. veralt.).* **2.** *n.* Unwägbarkeit, *die;* **~s** Unwägbarkeiten; Imponderabilien *(geh.)*

import 1. [ɪm'pɔ:t] *v. t.* **a)** importieren, einführen ‹*Waren*› **(from** aus, **into** nach); importieren ‹*Kulturgüter*›; **~ing country** Einfuhrland, *das;* **oil-~ing countries** [erd]ölimportierende Länder; **b)** *(signify)* bedeuten. **2.** ['ɪmpɔ:t] *n.* **a)** *(process, amount imported)* Import, *der;* Einfuhr, *die;* **~s of beef/sugar** Zucker-/Rindfleischimporte *od.* -einfuhren; **ban on the ~ of sth.** Einfuhrverbot für etw.; **b)** *(article imported)* Importgut, *das;* **c)** *(meaning)* Bedeutung, *die;* Sinn, *der;* **the ~ of his speech was that ...:** was aus seiner Rede hervorging, war, daß ...; **d)** *(importance)* Bedeutung, *die;* **an event of great ~:** ein sehr bedeutungsvolles Ereignis

importance [ɪm'pɔ:təns] *n., no pl.* **a)** Bedeutung, *die;* Wichtigkeit, *die;* **be of great ~ to sb./sth.** für jmdn./etw. äußerst wichtig sein; **b)** *(significance)* Bedeutung, *die;* *(of decision)* Tragweite, *die;* **increase in ~:** an Bedeutung zunehmen; **be of/without ~:** wichtig/unwichtig sein; **c)** *(personal consequence)* Bedeutung, *die;* Gewicht, *das;* **a man of considerable ~:** ein sehr wichtiger Mann; **speak with an air of ~:** mit gewichtiger Miene sprechen; **full of one's own ~:** von seiner eigenen Wichtigkeit überzeugt

important [ɪm'pɔ:tənt] *adj.* **a)** bedeutend; *(in a particular matter)* wichtig **(to** für); **the most ~ thing is ...:** die Hauptsache ist ...; **b)** *(momentous)* wichtig ‹*Entscheidung*›; bedeutsam ‹*Tag*›; **c)** *(having high rank)* wichtig ‹*Persönlichkeit*›; **very ~ person** wichtige Persönlichkeit; VIP; **d)** *(considerable)* beträchtlich; erheblich; **e)** *(pompous)* wichtigtuerisch; gewichtig *(iron.)*

importantly [ɪm'pɔ:təntlɪ] *adv.* **a) bear ~ [up]on sth.** auf etw. bedeutsame Auswirkungen haben; **more/most ~** *as sentence-modifier* was noch wichtiger/am wichtigsten ist; **b)** *(pompously)* wichtigtuerisch

importation [ɪmpɔ:'teɪʃn] *see* **import 2 a**

'import duty *n.* Einfuhrzoll, *der*

importer [ɪm'pɔ:tə(r)] *n.* Importeur, *der;* **be an ~ of cotton** Baumwollimporteur sein; ‹*Land:*› Baumwolle importieren

'import permit *n.* Einfuhrerlaubnis, *die*

importunate [ɪm'pɔ:tjʊnət] *adj.* zudringlich

importunately [ɪm'pɔ:tʃʊnətlɪ] *adv.* zudringlich; nachdrücklich ‹*beharren auf, instruieren*›

importune [ɪmpɔ:'tju:n] **1.** *v. t.* **a)** behelligen; **she ~d her neighbours and relatives for money** sie belästigte ihre Nachbarn und Verwandten mit Bitten um Geld; **b)** *(solicit for immoral purpose)* belästigen. **2.** *v. i.* sich aufdrängen; lästig fallen

importunity [ɪmpɔ:'tju:nɪtɪ] *n.* Aufdringlichkeit, *die*

impose [ɪm'pəʊz] **1.** *v. t.* **a)** auferlegen *(geh.)* ‹*Bürde, Verpflichtung*› **([up]on** *Dat.*); erheben ‹*Steuer, Zoll*› **(on** auf + *Akk.*); verhängen ‹*Kriegsrecht*›; anordnen ‹*Rationie-*

rung⟩; ~ **a ban on sth.** etw. mit einem Verbot belegen; ~ **a tax on sth.** etw. mit einer Steuer belegen; ~ **a nervous strain on sb.** jmdn. nervlich belasten; **b)** *(compel compliance with)* ~ **sth. [up]on sb.** jmdm. etw. aufdrängen; ~ **one's company [up]on sb.** sich jmdm. aufdrängen; ~ **restraints [up]on sb.** jmdm. Grenzen setzen; **c)** *(Printing)* ausschießen ⟨*Seiten*⟩. **2.** *v. i.* **a)** *(exert influence)* imponieren; Eindruck machen; **b)** *(take advantage)* **I would** *or* **do not want** *or* **wish to** ~: ich will nicht aufdringlich sein. **3.** *v. refl.* ~ **oneself on sb.** sich jmdm. aufdrängen

~ **on** *v. t.* **a)** *(take advantage of)* ausnutzen ⟨*Gutmütigkeit, Toleranz usw.*⟩; ~ **on sb. for help** jmdn. mit der Bitte um Hilfe belästigen; **b)** *(force oneself on)* ~ **on sb.** sich jmdm. aufdrängen

~ **upon** *see* ~ **on**

imposing [ɪm'pəʊzɪŋ] *adj.* imposant

imposition [ɪmpə'zɪʃn] *n.* **a)** *no pl. (action)* Auferlegung, *die; (of tax)* Erhebung, *die;* **b)** *no pl. (enforcement)* Durchsetzung, *die;* **c)** *no pl. (Printing)* Ausschießen, *das;* **d)** *(tax)* Abgabe, *die;* Steuer, *die;* **e)** *(piece of advantage-taking)* Ausnützung, *die;* **I am weary of the ~s of my relatives** ich bin es leid, mich von meinen Verwandten ausnützen zu lassen; **I hope it's not too much of an** ~: ich hoffe, es macht nicht zu viele Umstände; **f)** *(Brit. Sch.: work set as punishment)* Strafarbeit, *die*

impossibility [ɪmpɒsɪ'bɪlɪtɪ] *n.* **a)** *no pl.* Unmöglichkeit, *die;* **the ~ of a man's flying** die Tatsache, daß der Mensch nicht fliegen kann *od.* daß es dem Menschen nicht möglich ist zu fliegen; **b) go after impossibilities** das Unerreichbare wollen; **that's an absolute** ~: das ist völlig unmöglich *od.* ausgeschlossen *od.* ein Ding der Unmöglichkeit *(ugs.)*

impossible [ɪm'pɒsɪbl] **1.** *adj.* **a)** unmöglich; **it is ~ for me to do it** es ist mir nicht möglich, es zu tun; **b)** *(not easy)* schwer; *(not easily believable)* unmöglich *(ugs.);* **his car is becoming ~ to start** sein Auto läßt sich kaum noch starten; **c)** *(coll.: intolerable)* unmöglich *(ugs.).* **2.** *n.* **the** ~: das Unmögliche; Unmögliches; **achieve the** ~: das Unmögliche erreichen

impossibly [ɪm'pɒsɪblɪ] *adv.* **a)** unmöglich; **the stone was ~ heavy to lift** der Stein war so schwer, daß man ihn unmöglich anheben konnte; **b)** *(to an inconvenient degree)* unheimlich *(ugs.)* ⟨*schwierig, teuer usw.*⟩; **c)** *(coll.: intolerably)* unmöglich *(ugs.);* **he is ~ idealistic** er ist unmöglich mit seinem Idealismus *(ugs.)*

impost ['ɪmpəʊst] *n.* **a)** *(tax)* Abgabe, *die;* **b)** *(Archit.)* Kämpfer[stein], *der*

impostor [ɪm'pɒstə(r)] *n.* Hochstapler, *der*/-staplerin, *die; (swindler)* Betrüger, *der*/Betrügerin, *die*

imposture [ɪm'pɒstʃə(r)] *n.* **a)** *no pl. (practice of deception)* Hochstapelei, *die; (swindling)* Betrügerei, *die;* **b)** *(act of deception)* Betrug, *der;* Schwindel, *der;* **c)** *(fake)* Fälschung, *die*

impotence ['ɪmpətəns], **impotency** ['ɪmpətənsɪ] *n., no pl.* **a)** *(powerlessness)* Machtlosigkeit, *die;* **b)** *(helplessness)* Hilflosigkeit, *die;* **c)** *(lack of sexual power; in popular use: sterility)* Impotenz, *die*

impotent ['ɪmpətənt] *adj.* **a)** *(powerless)* machtlos; kraftlos ⟨*Argument*⟩; **be ~ to do sth.** nicht in der Lage sein, etw. zu tun; **b)** *(helpless)* hilflos; **c)** *(lacking in sexual power; in popular use: sterile)* impotent

impotently ['ɪmpətəntlɪ] *adv.* **a)** *(powerlessly)* machtlos; **b)** *(helplessly)* hilflos

impound [ɪm'paʊnd] *v. t.* **a)** *(shut up)* einpferchen ⟨*Vieh*⟩; einsperren ⟨*streunende Hunde usw.*⟩; *(fig.: confine)* einsperren ⟨*Person*⟩; **b)** *(take possession of)* beschlagnahmen; requirieren *(Milit.)*

impoverish [ɪm'pɒvərɪʃ] *v. t.* **a)** verarmen lassen; **be/become ~ed** verarmt sein/verarmen; **b)** *(exhaust)* auslaugen ⟨*Boden*⟩

impoverishment [ɪm'pɒvərɪʃmənt] *n., no pl.* **a)** *(making poor)* Verarmung, *die; (being poor)* Armut, *die;* **b)** *(exhaustion) (process)* Auslaugung, *die; (state)* Ausgelaugtheit, *die*

impracticability [ɪmpræktɪkə'bɪlɪtɪ] *n.* **a)** *no pl. (of plan)* Undurchführbarkeit, *die; (of prediction)* Unmöglichkeit, *die;* **b)** *(thing)* **be an** ~: undurchführbar sein; **it's an** ~: es läßt sich nicht durchführen

impracticable [ɪm'præktɪkəbl] *adj.* undurchführbar ⟨*Plan*⟩; impraktikabel *(geh.)*

impractical [ɪm'præktɪkl] **a)** *see* **unpractical; b)** *see* **impracticable**

impracticality [ɪmpræktɪ'kælɪtɪ] *see* **impracticability**

imprecation [ɪmprɪ'keɪʃn] *n.* Verwünschung, *die*

imprecise [ɪmprɪ'saɪs] *adj.*, **imprecisely** [ɪmprɪ'saɪslɪ] *adv.* ungenau; unpräzise *(geh.)*

imprecision [ɪmprɪ'sɪʒn] *n.* Ungenauigkeit, *die*

impregnability [ɪmpregnə'bɪlɪtɪ] *n., no pl.* Uneinnehmbarkeit, *die; (of strong-room etc.)* Einbruch[s]sicherheit, *die; (fig.)* Unanfechtbarkeit, *die*

impregnable [ɪm'pregnəbl] *adj.* uneinnehmbar ⟨*Festung, Bollwerk*⟩; einbruch[s]sicher ⟨*Tresorraum usw.*⟩; *(fig.)* unanfechtbar ⟨*Ruf, Tugend, Stellung*⟩

impregnate ['ɪmpregneɪt, ɪm'pregneɪt] *v. t.* **a)** imprägnieren; **b)** *(make pregnant)* schwängern; *(Biol.: fertilize)* befruchten; **Mary was ~d by the Holy Ghost** Maria empfing vom Heiligen Geist

impregnation [ɪmpreg'neɪʃn] *n., no pl.* **a)** Imprägnierung, *die;* **b)** *(making pregnant)* Schwängerung, *die; (Biol.: fertilization)* Befruchtung, *die*

impresario [ɪmprɪ'sɑːrɪəʊ] *n., pl.* ~s Intendant, *der*/Intendantin, *die;* Impresario, *der (veralt.)*

impress 1. [ɪm'pres] *v. t.* **a)** *(apply)* drücken; ~ **a pattern** *etc.* **on/in sth.** ein Muster *usw.* auf etw. *(Akk.)* aufdrücken *od.* aufprägen/in etw. *(Akk.)* eindrücken *od.* einprägen; **b)** *(arouse strong feeling in)* beeindrucken; Eindruck machen auf (+ *Akk.*); *abs.* Eindruck machen **(with** mit**)**; **be ~ed by** *or* **with sth.** von etw. beeindruckt sein; **c)** *(affect favourably)* beeindrucken; *abs.* Eindruck machen; **d)** *(mark)* stempeln ⟨*Dokument*⟩; ~ **a child with the right attitude** *(fig.)* einem Kind die richtige Einstellung vermitteln; **e)** *(affect)* ~ **sb. favourably/unfavourably** auf jmdn. einen günstigen/ungünstigen Eindruck machen. **2.** ['ɪmpres] *n.* **a)** Druck, *der;* **b)** *(mark)* Abdruck, *der;* **bear the ~ of sth.** *(fig.)* den Stempel *od. (geh.)* das Gepräge von etw. tragen

~ **[up]on** *v. t.* einprägen, einschärfen (+ *Dat.*); **they have had ~ed [up]on them the danger of doing that** ihnen ist eingeschärft worden, wie gefährlich es sei, das zu tun; ~ **sth. [up]on sb.'s memory** jmdm. etw. einprägen *od.* einschärfen

impression [ɪm'preʃn] *n.* **a)** *(impressing)* Druck, *der;* **b)** *(mark)* Abdruck, *der;* **c)** *(print)* Druck, *der;* **take an ~ of sth.** einen Abzug von etw. machen; *(of painting, engraving, etc.)* Druck, *der;* **d)** *(Printing) (quantity of copies)* Auflage, *die; (unaltered reprint)* Nachdruck, *der;* **e)** *(effect on persons)* Eindruck, *der* **(of** von**)**; *(effect on inanimate things)* Wirkung, *die;* **make an ~ on sb.** Eindruck auf jmdn. machen; **make a good/bad/strong** *etc.* ~ **on sb.** einen guten/schlechten/starken *usw.* Eindruck auf jmdn. machen; bei jmdm. einen guten/schlechten/starken *usw.* Eindruck hinterlassen; **he had made quite an ~ on the weed-choked flower-bed** nachdem er sich des im Unkraut erstickenden Blumenbeets angenommen hatte, war es kaum noch wiederzuerkennen; **first ~/~s** erster Eindruck/erste Eindrücke; **f)** *(impersonation)* **do ~s** andere Leute imitieren; **g)** *(notion)* Eindruck, *der;* **it's my ~ that ...:** ich habe den Eindruck, daß ...; **what's your ~ of him?** welchen Eindruck hast du von ihm *od.* macht er auf dich?; **form an ~ of sb.** sich *(Dat.)* ein Bild von jmdm. machen; **it's only an** ~: es ist nur eine Vermutung; **give [sb.] the ~ that .../of being bored** [bei jmdm.] den Eindruck erwecken, als ob .../als ob man sich langweile; **be under the ~ that ...:** der Auffassung *od.* Überzeugung sein, daß ...; *(less certain)* den Eindruck haben, daß ...

impressionable [ɪm'preʃənəbl] *adj.* beeinflußbar; **have an ~ mind, be** ~: sich leicht beeinflussen lassen; **children who are at the ~ age** Kinder in dem Alter, in dem sie noch formbar sind

impressionism [ɪm'preʃənɪzm] *n., no pl.* Impressionismus, *der*

impressionist [ɪm'preʃənɪst] *n.* Impressionist, *der*/Impressionistin, *die; attrib.* impressionistisch ⟨*Kunst usw.*⟩

impressionistic [ɪmpreʃə'nɪstɪk] *adj.* impressionistisch

impressive [ɪm'presɪv] *adj.* beeindruckend; imponierend; **be ~ on account of** *or* ~ **for sth.** durch etw. beeindrucken

impressively [ɪm'presɪvlɪ] *adv.* beeindruckend; imponierend

imprimatur [ɪmprɪ'mɑːtə(r), ɪmpraɪ'meɪtə(r)] *n.* **a)** *(RC Ch.)* Imprimatur, *das;* **b)** *(fig.: sanction)* **put the ~ of approval on sth.** etw. gutheißen *od.* billigen; **bear the ~ of sth./an institution** jmds. Plazet/das Plazet einer Institution haben *(geh.)*

imprint 1. ['ɪmprɪnt] *n.* **a)** Abdruck, *der;* **publisher's/printer's** ~: Impressum, *das;* **b)** *(fig.)* Stempel, *der;* **leave one's ~ on sb./sth.** jmdm./einer Sache seinen Stempel aufdrücken; **the ~ of suffering upon sb.'s face** die Spuren des Leidens in jmds. Gesicht. **2.** [ɪm'prɪnt] *v. t.* **a)** *(stamp)* aufdrucken; aufdrücken ⟨*Poststempel*⟩; *(on metal)* aufprägen; **b)** *(fix indelibly)* **sth. is ~ed in** *or* **on sb.'s memory** etw. hat sich jmdm. [unauslöschlich] eingeprägt; **c)** *(Ethol.)* ~ **on** *or* **to** prägen auf (+ *Akk.*)

imprison [ɪm'prɪzn] *v. t.* **a)** in Haft nehmen; **be ~ed** sich in Haft befinden; eine Freiheitsstrafe verbüßen; **be ~ed for three months** eine dreimonatige Freiheitsstrafe erhalten; **b)** *(fig.: confine)* einsperren; *(hold)* festhalten

imprisonment [ɪm'prɪznmənt] *n.* **a)** Haft, *die;* **a long term** *or* **period of** ~: eine langjährige Haft- *od.* Freiheitsstrafe; **serve a sentence of** ~: eine Gefängnisstrafe verbüßen; **b)** *(fig.: being confined)* Gefangenschaft, *die;* ~ **by sb./sth.** Gefangensein durch jmdn./etw.

improbability [ɪmprɒbə'bɪlɪtɪ] *n.* Unwahrscheinlichkeit, *die*

improbable [ɪm'prɒbəbl] *adj.* **a)** *(not likely)* unwahrscheinlich; **b)** *(incongruous)* unmöglich *(ugs.);* **he is an ~ person to be in charge of a large company** es ist eigentlich erstaunlich, daß er der Chef einer großen Firma ist

impromptu [ɪm'prɒmptjuː] **1.** *adj.* improvisiert; **an ~ speech** eine Stegreifrede; **an ~ visit** ein Überraschungsbesuch; ein unangekündigter Besuch. **2.** *adv.* aus dem Stegreif. **3.** *n.* **a)** Improvisation, *die;* **b)** *(Mus.)* Impromptu, *das*

improper [ɪm'prɒpə(r)] *adj.* **a)** *(wrong)* unrichtig; ungeeignet ⟨*Werkzeug*⟩; **b)** *(unseemly)* ungehörig; unpassend; *(indecent)* unanständig; **c)** *(not in accordance with rules of conduct)* unangebracht; unzulässig ⟨*Gebühren*⟩; **d)** ~ **fraction** *(Math.)* unechter Bruch

improperly [ɪm'prɒpəlɪ] *adv.* **a)** *(wrongly)*

unrichtig; **use sth. ~:** etw. unsachgemäß gebrauchen; **b)** *(in unseemly fashion)* unpassend; *(indecently)* unanständig; **c)** *(in contravention of rules of conduct)* unzulässigerweise; **use sth. ~:** etw. mißbrauchen

impropriety [ɪmprəˈpraɪətɪ] *n.* **a)** *no pl.* Unrichtigkeit, *die; (unfitness)* Ungeeignetheit, *die;* **say/state** *etc.* **without ~ that ...:** mit Recht sagen/behaupten *usw.*, daß ...; **b)** *no pl. (unseemliness)* Unpassende, *das; (indecency)* Unanständigkeit, *die;* **the ~ of sb.'s clothing** jmds. unpassende/unschickliche Kleidung; **c)** *no pl. (lack of accordance with rules of conduct)* Unrechtmäßigkeit, *die;* Unredlichkeit, *die;* **see no ~ in doing sth.** nichts Unrechtmäßiges *od.* Unredliches darin sehen, etw. zu tun; **d)** *(instance of improper conduct)* Unanständigkeit, *die;* **moral ~:** moralisches Fehlverhalten

improvable [ɪmˈpruːvəbl] *adj.* verbesserungsfähig

improve [ɪmˈpruːv] **1.** *v.i.* sich verbessern; besser werden; ⟨*Person, Wetter:*⟩ sich bessern; *(become more attractive)* sich zu seinem Vorteil verändern; **he was ill, but he's improving now** er war krank, aber es geht ihm jetzt schon besser; **things are improving** es sieht schon besser aus. **2.** *v.t.* verbessern; erhöhen, steigern ⟨*Produktion*⟩; ausbessern ⟨*Haus usw.*⟩; verschönern ⟨*öffentliche Anlage usw.*⟩; **~d health** ein besserer Gesundheitszustand; **~ one's mind** sich [weiter]bilden; **~ one's situation** sich verbessern. **3.** *v. refl.* **~ oneself** sich weiterbilden

~ [up]on *v.t.* überbieten ⟨*Rekord, Angebot*⟩; verbessern ⟨*Leistung*⟩

improvement [ɪmˈpruːvmənt] *n.* **a)** *no pl.* Verbesserung, *die;* Besserung, *die; (in trading)* Steigerung, *die;* **there is need for ~ in your handwriting** deine Handschrift müßte besser werden; **an ~ on** *or* **over sth.** eine Verbesserung gegenüber etw.; **b)** *(addition)* Verbesserung, *die;* **make ~s to sth.** Verbesserungen an etw. *(Dat.)* vornehmen

improvidence [ɪmˈprɒvɪdəns] *n., no pl.* **a)** Sorglosigkeit, *die;* **b)** *(heedlessness)* Leichtsinn, *der;* **c)** *(thriftlessness)* Verschwendungssucht, *die*

improvident [ɪmˈprɒvɪdənt] *adj.* **a)** sorglos; leichtsinnig; **he is ~:** er ist ein unbekümmerter Mensch; **~ action** unbedachtes Handeln; **b)** *(heedless)* leichtsinnig; **c)** *(thriftless)* verschwenderisch

improvidently [ɪmˈprɒvɪdəntlɪ] *adv.* **a)** leichtsinnigerweise; **b)** *(thriftlessly)* verschwenderisch

improvisation [ɪmprəvaɪˈzeɪʃn, ɪmprɒvɪˈzeɪʃn] *n.* **a)** *no pl.* Improvisieren, *das; (composing while performing)* Improvisation, *die;* **his talent for ~:** sein Improvisationstalent; *(in speaking)* sein Talent für Stegreifreden; **b)** *(thing)* Improvisation, *die;* **the speech was an ~:** die Rede war improvisiert *od.* aus dem Stegreif vorgetragen; **the bench was only an ~:** die Bank war nur ein Provisorium

improvise [ˈɪmprəvaɪz] *v.t.* improvisieren; aus dem Stegreif vortragen ⟨*Rede*⟩

imprudence [ɪmˈpruːdəns] *n.* **a)** *no pl.* Unüberlegtheit, *die;* **with great ~:** sehr unüberlegt; **b)** *(rash act)* Unbesonnenheit, *die*

imprudent [ɪmˈpruːdənt] *adj.* unklug; *(showing rashness)* unbesonnen

imprudently [ɪmˈpruːdəntlɪ] *adv.* unbesonnenerweise; bedenklich ⟨*nah, schnell*⟩

impudence [ˈɪmpjʊdəns] *n.* **a)** Unverschämtheit, *die;* **b)** *(brazenness)* Dreistigkeit, *die*

impudent [ˈɪmpjʊdənt] *adj.*, **impudently** [ˈɪmpjʊdəntlɪ] *adv.* unverschämt; *(brazen)* dreist

impugn [ɪmˈpjuːn] *v.t.* in Zweifel ziehen; anfechten ⟨*Anspruch*⟩

impulse [ˈɪmpʌls] *n.* **a)** *(act of impelling)* Stoß, *der;* Impuls, *der; (fig.: motivation)* Impuls, *der;* **give an ~ to sth.** einer Sache *(Dat.)* neue Impulse geben; **b)** *(mental incitement)* Impuls, *der;* **be seized with an irresistible ~ to do sth.** von einem unwiderstehlichen Drang ergriffen werden, etw. zu tun; **c)** *(tendency to act without reflection)* Impulsivität, *die;* **from pure ~:** rein impulsiv; **be ruled/guided by ~:** impulsiv sein; **be a creature of ~:** ein impulsives Wesen haben; **act/do sth. on [an] ~:** impulsiv handeln/etw. tun; **d)** *(impetus)* Stoßkraft, *die;* **e)** *(Biol., Electr., Phys.)* Impuls, *der*

'impulse buying *n.* Spontankäufe *Pl.*

impulsion [ɪmˈpʌlʃn] *n.* **a)** *(impelling push)* Stoß, *der;* **b)** *(mental impulse)* Antrieb, *der;* **c)** *(impetus)* Impuls, *der;* **give an ~ to sth.** einer Sache *(Dat.)* neue Impulse geben

impulsive [ɪmˈpʌlsɪv] *adj.* **a)** impulsiv; **b)** *(driving)* vorwärts treibend; **~ force** Antriebskraft, *die;* **c)** *(Phys.)* stoßartig

impulsively [ɪmˈpʌlsɪvlɪ] *adv.* impulsiv

impulsiveness [ɪmˈpʌlsɪvnɪs] *n., no pl.* Impulsivität, *die*

impunity [ɪmˈpjuːnɪtɪ] *n., no pl.* Straffreiheit, *die;* **be able to do sth. with ~:** etw. gefahrlos tun können; *(without being punished)* etw. ungestraft tun können

impure [ɪmˈpjʊə(r)] *adj.* **a)** *(dirty)* unsauber; schmutzig ⟨*Wasser*⟩; **b)** *(unchaste)* unrein; unanständig ⟨*Person, Sprache*⟩; schmutzig ⟨*Gedanke*⟩; **c)** *(mixed with extraneous substance)* unrein; *(fig.: of mixed nature)* unrein; uneinheitlich ⟨*Stilform*⟩

impurity [ɪmˈpjʊərɪtɪ] *n.* **a)** *no pl. (being dirty)* Unsauberkeit, *die; (of water)* Verschmutzung, *die;* **b)** *no pl. (not being chaste)* Unreinheit, *die;* **moral ~:** moralische Verfehlung; **c)** *no pl. (being mixed with extraneous substance)* Unreinheit, *die;* **d)** *in pl. (dirt)* Schmutz, *der;* **e)** *(foreign matter)* Fremdkörper, *der;* Fremdstoff, *der*

imputation [ɪmpjʊˈteɪʃn] *n.* **a)** *no pl.* Zuschreibung, *die; (accusing)* Bezichtigung, *die;* [ungerechtfertigte] Beschuldigung; Imputation, *die (veralt.)*; **b)** *(charge)* Anschuldigung, *die;* Beschuldigung, *die*

impute [ɪmˈpjuːt] *v.t.* **~ sth. to sb./sth.** jmdm./einer Sache etw. zuschreiben; **~ bad intentions to sb.** jmdm. schlechte Absichten unterstellen

in [ɪn] **1.** *prep.* **a)** *(position; also fig.)* in (+ *Dat.*); **I looked into all the boxes, but there was nothing in them** ich sah in alle Kisten hinein, aber es war nichts darin; **in the 'Mauretania'** auf der „Mauretania"; **in the fields** auf den Feldern; **a ride in a motor car** eine Autofahrt; **shot/wounded in the leg** ins Bein geschossen/am Bein verwundet; **in this heat** bei dieser Hitze; **the highest mountain in the world** der höchste Berg der Welt; *see also* **bed 1 a; clover; country b; dark 2 a; prison b; rage 1 a; sky 1; sleep 1 b; street a; ²tear; b)** *(wearing as dress)* in (+ *Dat.*); *(wearing as headgear)* mit; **in brown shoes** mit braunen Schuhen; **a lady in black** eine Dame in Schwarz; **a group of youths in leather jackets** eine Gruppe Jugendlicher in *od.* mit Lederjacken; *see also* **shirt-sleeve 1; c)** *(with respect to)* **two feet in diameter** mit einem Durchmesser von zwei Fuß; **young in years** jung an Jahren; *see also* **herself a; itself a; d)** *(as a proportionate part of)* **eight dogs in ten** acht von zehn Hunden; **pay 33 pence in the pound as interest** 33 Prozent Zinsen zahlen; *see also* **gradient a; e)** *(as a member of)* in (+ *Dat.*); **be in the Scouts** bei den Pfadfindern sein; **be employed in the Civil Service** als Beamter/Beamtin beschäftigt sein; **f)** *(as content of)* **there are three feet in a yard** ein Yard hat drei Fuß; **is there anything in the notion of ...?** ist an der Vorstellung ... etwas dran?; **what is there in this deal for me?** was springt für mich bei dem Geschäft heraus? *(ugs.)*; **there is nothing of the hero in him** er hat nichts von einem Helden an sich *(Dat.)*; **there is nothing/not much** *or* **little in it** *(difference)* da ist kein/kein großer Unterschied [zwischen ihnen]; **there is something in what you say** an dem, was Sie sagen, ist etwas dran *(ugs.)*; **g)** *(coll.: as a kind of)* in (+ *Dat.*); **the latest thing in fashion/in luxury** der letzte Modeschrei/der neueste Luxus; **h)** *expr. identity* in (+ *Dat.*); **have a faithful friend in sb.** an jmdm. einen treuen Freund haben; **we have lost a first-rate teacher in Jim** wir haben mit Jim einen erstklassigen Lehrer verloren; **i)** *(concerned with)* in (+ *Dat.*); **what line of business are you in?** in welcher Branche sind Sie?; **he's in politics** er ist Politiker; **she's in insurance** sie ist in der Versicherungsbranche tätig; **j) be [not] in it** *(as competitor)* [nicht] dabei *od.* im Rennen sein; **k)** *(Mus.)* in; **in [the key of] D flat** in Des; **l)** *(Ling.) (ending with)* [endend] auf (+ *Akk.*); *(beginning with)* beginnend mit; **m)** *(with arrangement of)* in (+ *Dat.*); **sell eggs in half-dozens** Eier im halben Dutzend verkaufen; *see also* **order 1 a; n)** *(with the means of; having as material, colour)* **a message in code** eine verschlüsselte Nachricht; **in writing** schriftlich; **in this way** auf diese Weise; so; **in a few words** mit wenigen Worten; **bind in leather** in Leder binden; **a dress in velvet** ein Kleid aus Samt; **this sofa is also available in leather/blue** dieses Sofa gibt es auch in Leder/Blau; **write sth. in red** etw. in Rot schreiben; **write in red** mit Rot schreiben; **pay in pounds/dollars** in Pfund/Dollars bezahlen; **draw in crayon/ink** *etc.* mit Kreide/Tinte *usw.* zeichnen; **be cast in brass** *etc.* aus Messing *usw.* gegossen sein; *see also* **English 2 a; o)** *(while, during)* **in crossing the river** beim Überqueren des Flusses; **in fog/rain** *etc.* bei Nebel/Regen *usw.*; **in the 20th century** im 20. Jahrhundert; **in the eighties/nineties** in den Achtzigern/Neunzigern; **4 o'clock in the morning/afternoon** 4 Uhr morgens/abends; **in 1990** [im Jahre] 1990; **p)** *(after a period of)* in (+ *Dat.*); **in three minutes/years** in drei Minuten/Jahren; **q)** *(within the ability of)* **have it in one [to do sth.]** fähig sein[, etw. zu tun]; **I didn't know you had it in you** das hätte ich dir nicht zugetraut; **he has in him the makings of a good soldier** er hat das Zeug zu einem guten Soldaten; **be in human nature** in der menschlichen Natur liegen; **there is no malice in him** er hat nichts Bösartiges an sich *(Dat.)*; **r)** *(into)* in (+ *Akk.*); **get the whole of sth. in a photo** etwas ganz auf ein Foto kriegen *(ugs.) od.* bekommen; **s) in that** insofern als; *see also* **far 1 d; t) in doing this** *(by so doing)* indem jmd. das tut/tat; dadurch; hierdurch. **2.** *adv.* **a)** *(inside)* hinein⟨*gehen usw.*⟩; *(towards speaker)* herein⟨*kommen usw.*⟩; **when the animal is in, shut the cage door** wenn das Tier drin ist, mach die Käfigtür zu; **is everyone in?** sind alle drin? *(ugs.)*; **in with you!** rein mit dir! *(ugs.)*; **'In'** „Einfahrt"/„Eingang"; **the children have been in and out all day** die Kinder sind den ganzen Tag raus- und reingerannt *(ugs.)*; **b)** *(at home, work, etc.)* **be in** dasein; **find sb. in** jmdn. antreffen; **ask sb. in** jmdn. hereinbitten; **he's been in and out all day** er war den ganzen Tag über mal da und mal nicht da; **c)** *(included)* darin; drin *(ugs.)*; **cost £50 all in** 50 Pfund kosten, alles inbegriffen; **the word is not in** das Wort ist nicht aufgeführt; **your article is not in** dein Artikel steht nicht drin *(ugs.)*; **d)** *(inward)* innen; **e)** *(in fashion)* in *(ugs.)*; in Mode; **f)** *(elected)* **be in** gewählt sein; **the Tories are in** die Tories sind am Ruder; **the Tories are in by three votes** die Tories haben die Wahl mit einer Mehrheit von drei Stimmen gewonnen; **g)** *(Cricket)* **our team is in** unsere Mannschaft ist am Schlag; **h)** *(Brit.: burning)* **be in** ⟨*Feuer:*⟩ ansein, brennen; **keep the fire in** das Feuer brennen lassen; **i)** *(having arrived)* **be in** ⟨*Zug, Schiff, Ware, Bewerbung:*⟩ dasein; ⟨*Ernte:*⟩ eingebracht sein; **the coach is not due in for another hour** der Bus wird nicht vor einer Stunde dasein; **j)** *(present)* **be in at the start/climax** beim Start/Höhepunkt dabeisein; **k) sb. is in for sth.** *(about to undergo sth.)* jmdm. steht etw. bevor; *(in competition for sth.)* jmd. nimmt im Wettbewerb um etw. teil; *(taking part in sth.)* jmd. nimmt an etw. *(Dat.)* teil; **we're in for it now!** *(coll.)* jetzt blüht uns was! *(ugs.)*; **have it in for sb.** es auf jmdn. abgesehen haben *(ugs.)*; **l)** *(coll.: as participant, accomplice, observer, etc.)* **be in on the secret/discussion** in das Geheimnis eingeweiht sein/bei der Diskussion dabei sein; **be in on the action** dabeisein; **be [well] in with sb.** mit jmdm. [gut] auskommen; **be in with the right/wrong people** mit den richtigen/falschen Leuten verkehren; **m)** *(Sport)* **be in** ⟨*Ball:*⟩ drin sein. *See also* **all 3; eye 1 a; far 1 d; luck b; penny c; tide 1 a. 3.** *attrib. adj. (fashionable)* Mode-; **the in crowd** die Clique, die gerade in ist *(ugs.)*; **in joke** Insiderwitz, *der.* **4.** *n.* **know the ins and outs of a matter** sich in einer Sache genau auskennen; **I don't know the ins and outs of the argument** ich weiß nicht [genau], worum es bei diesem Streit geht

in. *abbr.* **inch[es]**

inability [ɪnəˈbɪlɪtɪ] *n., no pl.* **a)** *(being unable)* Unfähigkeit, *die;* **b)** *(lack of power)* Unvermögen, *das*

in absentia [ɪn æbˈsentɪə, ɪn æbˈsenʃɪə] *adv.* in absentia *(bes. Rechtsw.)*

inaccessibility [ɪnəksesɪˈbɪlɪtɪ] *n., no pl.* **a)** *(unreachableness)* Unzugänglichkeit, *die;* **b)** *(unapproachableness)* Unnahbarkeit, *die*

inaccessible [ɪnəkˈsesɪbl] *adj.* **a)** *(that cannot be reached)* unzugänglich; **b)** *(unapproachable)* unnahbar; unzugänglich

inaccuracy [ɪnˈækjʊrəsɪ] *n.* **a)** *(incorrectness)* Unrichtigkeit, *die;* **an example of ~ in the use of ...:** ein Beispiel für den unrichtigen Gebrauch von ...; **b)** *(imprecision)* Ungenauigkeit, *die*

inaccurate [ɪnˈækjʊrət] *adj.* **a)** *(incorrect)* unrichtig; **b)** *(imprecise)* ungenau

inaccurately [ɪnˈækjʊrətlɪ] *adv.* **a)** *(incorrectly)* falsch; **b)** *(imprecisely)* ungenau

inaction [ɪnˈækʃn] *n., no pl., no indef. art.* **a)** Untätigkeit, *die;* **b)** *(sluggishness)* Trägheit, *die*

inactive [ɪnˈæktɪv] *adj.* **a)** untätig; **b)** *(sluggish)* träge

inactivity [ɪnækˈtɪvɪtɪ] *n., no pl.* **a)** Untätigkeit, *die;* **b)** *(sluggishness)* Trägheit, *die*

inadequacy [ɪnˈædɪkwəsɪ] *n.* **a)** Unzulänglichkeit, *die;* **b)** *(incompetence)* mangelnde Eignung

inadequate [ɪnˈædɪkwət] *adj.* **a)** unzulänglich; **his response was ~ [to the situation]** seine Antwort war [der Situation] nicht angemessen; **the resources are ~ to his needs** die Mittel reichen für seine Bedürfnisse nicht aus; **b)** *(incompetent)* ungeeignet; **feel ~:** sich überfordert fühlen

inadequately [ɪnˈædɪkwətlɪ] *adv.* **a)** unzulänglich; **b)** *(incompetently)* mangelhaft

inadmissibility [ɪnədmɪsɪˈbɪlɪtɪ] *n., no pl.* Unzulässigkeit, *die*

inadmissible [ɪnədˈmɪsɪbl] *adj.* unzulässig

inadvertent [ɪnədˈvɜːtənt] *adj.* ungewollt; versehentlich

inadvertently [ɪnədˈvɜːtəntlɪ] *adv.* versehentlich

inadvisability [ɪnədvaɪzəˈbɪlɪtɪ] *n., no pl.* *(inappropriateness)* Unangebrachtheit, *die;* *(foolishness)* Unvernünftigkeit, *die;* **see the ~ of sth.** sehen, daß etw. nicht ratsam ist

inadvisable [ɪnədˈvaɪzəbl] *adj.* nicht ratsam; unratsam

inalienable [ɪnˈeɪlɪənəbl] *adj.* unveräußerlich ⟨*Recht*⟩

inane [ɪˈneɪn] *adj.*, **inanely** [ɪˈneɪnlɪ] *adv.* dümmlich

inanimate [ɪnˈænɪmət] *adj.* unbelebt

inanity [ɪˈnænɪtɪ] *n.* Dümmlichkeit, *die*

inapplicability [ɪnæplɪkəˈbɪlɪtɪ] *n., no pl.* Nichtanwendbarkeit, *die*

inapplicable [ɪnˈæplɪkəbl, ɪnəˈplɪkəbl] *adj.* nicht anwendbar (**to** auf + *Akk.*)

inappropriate [ɪnəˈprəʊprɪət] *adj.* unpassend; **be ~ for sth.** für etw. nicht geeignet sein; **be ~ to the occasion** dem Anlaß nicht angemessen sein; **this translation is ~:** diese Übersetzung ist nicht angemessen

inappropriately [ɪnəˈprəʊprɪətlɪ] *adv.* unpassend

inapt [ɪnˈæpt] *adj.*, **inaptly** [ɪnˈæptlɪ] *adv.* unpassend

inarticulate [ɪnɑːˈtɪkjʊlət] *adj.* **a)** unverständlich; inartikuliert *(geh.)*; **b)** *(dumb)* unfähig zu sprechen

inarticulately [ɪnɑːˈtɪkjʊlətlɪ] *adv.* inartikuliert *(geh.)*; unverständlich ⟨*murmeln*⟩

inartistic [ɪnɑːˈtɪstɪk] *adj.* unkünstlerisch ⟨*Person*⟩

inasmuch [ɪnəzˈmʌtʃ] *adv.* **~ as a)** insofern als; **b)** *(because)* da

inattention [ɪnəˈtenʃn] *n., no pl.* Unaufmerksamkeit, *die* (**to** gegenüber); **~ to detail** Ungenauigkeit im Detail

inattentive [ɪnəˈtentɪv] *adj.* unaufmerksam (**to** gegenüber)

inattentiveness [ɪnəˈtentɪvnɪs] *n., no pl.* Unaufmerksamkeit, *die*

inaudible [ɪnˈɔːdɪbl] *adj.*, **inaudibly** [ɪnˈɔːdɪblɪ] *adv.* unhörbar

inaugural [ɪˈnɔːgjʊrl] *adj.* **a)** *(first in series)* Eröffnungs-; **b)** *(given at inauguration)* **~ lecture** *or* **address** Antrittsrede, *die; (of professor)* Antrittsvorlesung, *die*

inaugurate [ɪˈnɔːgjʊreɪt] *v. t.* **a)** *(admit to office)* in sein Amt einführen; inaugurieren *(geh.)*; **b)** *(begin)* einführen; aufnehmen ⟨*Frachtverkehr usw.*⟩; in Angriff nehmen ⟨*Projekt*⟩; **c)** *(officially open)* seiner Bestimmung übergeben; *(with ceremony)* einweihen

inauguration [ɪnɔːgjʊˈreɪʃn] *n.* **a)** *(admission to office)* Amtseinführung, *die;* Inauguration, *die (geh.)*; **b)** *(beginning)* Einführung, *die; (of service)* Aufnahme, *die; (of project)* Inangriffnahme, *die;* **c)** *(official opening)* Übergabe, *die; (with ceremony)* Einweihung, *die*

inauspicious [ɪnɔːˈspɪʃəs] *adj.* **a)** *(ominous)* unheilverkündend; unheilvoll; **we made an ~ start to the project** schon der Beginn des Projekts verhieß nichts Gutes; **b)** *(unlucky)* unglücklich

ˈinboard *(Naut., Aeronaut., Motor Veh.)* **1.** *adv.* binnenbords. **2.** *adj.* Innen[bord]-

ˈinborn *adj.* angeboren (**in** *Dat.*)

inˈbred *adj.* **a)** angeboren; **b)** *(impaired by inbreeding)* **they are/have become ~:** bei ihnen herrscht Inzucht

inˈbreeding *n.* Inzucht, *die*

ˈin-built *adj.* jmdm./einer Sache eigen

Inc. *abbr. (Amer.)* **Incorporated** e. G.

Inca [ˈɪŋkə] **1.** *n.* Inka, *der/die.* **2.** *adj.* der Inkas *nachgestellt*

incalculable [ɪnˈkælkjʊləbl] *adj.* **a)** *(very great)* unermeßlich; **b)** *(unpredictable)* unabsehbar; unberechenbar ⟨*Person, Temperament*⟩

in camera *see* **camera b**

incandescent [ɪnkænˈdesənt] *adj.* glühend; **~ lamp** Glühlampe, *die*

incantation [ɪnkænˈteɪʃn] *n.* **a)** *(words)* Zauberspruch, *der;* **b)** *(spell)* Beschwörung, *die*

incapability [ɪnkeɪpəˈbɪlɪtɪ] *n., no pl.* Unvermögen, *das;* Unfähigkeit, *die*

incapable [ɪnˈkeɪpəbl] *adj.* **a)** *(lacking ability)* **be ~ of doing sth.** außerstande sein, etw. zu tun; **be ~ of sth.** zu etw. unfähig sein; **she is ~ of such an act** sie ist zu einer solchen Tat nicht fähig; **b) be ~ of** *(not allow)* nicht zulassen ⟨*Beweis, Messung usw.*⟩; **sb. is ~ of any improvement** jmd. ist zu keiner Besserung fähig; **a statement that is ~ of proof** eine Feststellung, die nicht beweisbar ist; **c)** *(incompetent)* unfähig; **he was drunk to the point of being completely ~:** er war so betrunken, daß er zu nichts mehr fähig war

incapacitate [ɪnkəˈpæsɪteɪt] *v. t.* **a)** *(render unfit)* unfähig machen; **~ sb. for** *or* **from doing sth.** es jmdm. unmöglich machen, etw. zu tun; **physically ~d/~d by illness** körperlich/durch Krankheit behindert; **b)** *(disqualify)* ausschließen (**for** von)

incapacity [ɪnkəˈpæsɪtɪ] *n., no pl.* Unfähigkeit, *die* (**for** zu); **civil ~** *(Law)* Geschäftsunfähigkeit, *die*

incarcerate [ɪnˈkɑːsəreɪt] *v. t.* einkerkern *(geh.)*

incarceration [ɪnkɑːsəˈreɪʃn] *n.* Einkerkerung, *die (geh.)*

incarnate [ɪnˈkɑːnət] *adj.* **a) be the devil ~:** der leibhaftige Satan *od.* der Teufel in Person sein; **the Word I~** *(Theol.)* das fleischgewordene Wort; **b)** *(in perfect form)* **be beauty/wisdom** *etc.* **~:** die personifizierte Schönheit/Weisheit *usw.* sein

incarnation [ɪnkɑːˈneɪʃn] *n.* Inkarnation, *die*

incautious [ɪnˈkɔːʃəs] *adj.*, **incautiously** [ɪnˈkɔːʃəslɪ] *adv.* unbedacht

incendiary [ɪnˈsendɪərɪ] **1.** *adj.* **a) ~ attack** Brandstiftung, *die;* **~ device** Brandsatz, *der;* **~ bomb** *see* **2 b**; **b)** *(fig.)* aufwieglerisch; Hetz-. **2.** *n.* **a)** *(person)* Brandstifter, *der*/-stifterin, *die; (fig.)* Aufwiegler, *der*/Aufwieglerin, *die;* **b)** *(bomb)* Brandbombe, *die*

¹incense [ˈɪnsens] *n.* Weihrauch, *der*

²incense [ɪnˈsens] *v. t.* erzürnen; erbosen; **be ~d at** *or* **by sth./with sb.** über etw./jmdn. erbost *od.* erzürnt sein

incentive [ɪnˈsentɪv] *n.* **a)** *(motivation)* Anreiz, *der;* **~ to achievement** Leistungsanreiz, *der; attrib.* **~ payment system** System des finanziellen Anreizes; **b)** *(payment)* finanzieller Anreiz

inception [ɪnˈsepʃn] *n.* Einführung, *die;* **from** *or* **since/at its ~:** von Beginn an/zu Beginn

incessant [ɪnˈsesənt] *adj.*, **incessantly** [ɪnˈsesəntlɪ] *adv.* unablässig; unaufhörlich

incest [ˈɪnsest] *n.* Inzest, *der;* Blutschande, *die*

incestuous [ɪnˈsestjʊəs] *adj. (lit. or fig.)* inzestuös

inch [ɪntʃ] **1.** *n.* **a)** Inch, *der;* Zoll, *der (veralt.)*; **a 2½-~ map** eine Landkarte im Maßstab 1 Meile: 2½ Inches; **he could hardly see an ~ in front of him** er konnte kaum die Hand vor Augen sehen; **miss sth./sb. by ~es** etw./jmdn. um Haaresbreite verfehlen; **b)** *(small amount)* **~ by ~:** ≈ Zentimeter um Zentimeter; **by ~es** ≈ zentimeterweise; **escape death by an ~:** dem Tod mit knapper Not entrinnen; **she came within an ~ of winning** sie hätte um ein Haar gewonnen; **give him an ~ and he will take a mile** wenn man ihm den kleinen Finger reicht, nimmt er gleich die ganze Hand; **not give** *or* **yield an ~:** keinen Fingerbreit nachgeben; keinen Zoll weichen *(geh.)*; **he is every ~ a soldier** er ist Zoll für Zoll ein Soldat *(geh.)*; **he was flogged within an ~ of his life** er wurde fast zu Tode geprügelt; **c)** *in pl. (stature)* Körpergröße, *die.* **2.** *v. t.* ≈ zentimeterweise bewegen; **~ one's way forward** sich Zoll für Zoll vorwärtsbewegen. **3.** *v. i.* ≈ sich zentimeterweise bewegen; **~ along/forward** sich ganz langsam entlang-/vorwärtsbewegen

inchoate [ˈɪnkəʊət] *adj.* **a)** *(just begun)* beginnend; **b)** *(undeveloped)* unausgereift

incidence [ˈɪnsɪdəns] *n.* **a)** *(occurrence)* Auftreten, *das;* Vorkommen, *das;* **b)** *(man-*

ner or range of occurrence) Häufigkeit, *die;* ~ **of crime/accidents** Verbrechens-/Unfallrate, *die;* **c)** *(Phys.)* Einfall, *der;* **angle of** ~: Einfall[s]winkel, *der;* Inzidenzwinkel, *der (fachspr.)*

incident ['ɪnsɪdənt] **1.** *n.* **a)** *(notable event)* Vorfall, *der; (minor occurrence)* Begebenheit, *die;* Vorkommnis, *das;* **the evening passed without** ~: der Abend verging ohne besondere Vorkommnisse; **b)** *(clash)* Zwischenfall, *der;* **frontier** ~: Grenzzwischenfall, *der;* **c)** *(in play, novel, etc.)* Episode, *die.* **2.** *adj.* **a)** *(attaching)* ~ **to** verbunden mit; **b)** *(falling)* einfallend ⟨*Licht, Strahl*⟩

incidental [ɪnsɪ'dentl] **1.** *adj.* **a)** *(casual)* beiläufig ⟨*Art, Bemerkung*⟩; Neben⟨*ausgaben, -einnahmen, -gewinn*⟩; **b)** *(attaching)* ~ **to** verbunden mit. **2.** *n., in pl.* Nebensächlichkeiten; *(expenses)* Nebenausgaben

incidentally [ɪnsɪ'dentəlɪ] *adv.* **a)** *(by the way)* nebenbei [bemerkt]; **b)** *(by chance)* zufällig; **c)** *(as not essential)* am Rande

inci'dental music *n.* Begleitmusik, *die*

'incident room *n. [temporäres] lokales Einsatzzentrum der Polizei*

incinerate [ɪn'sɪnəreɪt] *v. t.* verbrennen

incinerator [ɪn'sɪnəreɪtə(r)] *n.* Verbrennungsofen, *der; (in garden)* Abfallverbrenner, *der*

incipient [ɪn'sɪpɪənt] *adj.* anfänglich; einsetzend ⟨*Schmerzen*⟩; aufkommend ⟨*Zweifel, Angst*⟩

incise [ɪn'saɪz] *v. t.* einschneiden

incision [ɪn'sɪʒn] *n.* **a)** *(cutting)* Einschneiden, *das;* **b)** *(cut)* Einschnitt, *der;* **abdominal** ~: Bauchschnitt, *der*

incisive [ɪn'saɪsɪv] *adj.* schneidend ⟨*Ton*⟩; scharf ⟨*Verstand*⟩; scharfsinnig ⟨*Genie, Kritik, Methode, Frage, Bemerkung, Argument*⟩; präzise ⟨*Sprache, Stil*⟩

incisively [ɪn'saɪsɪvlɪ] *adv.* scharfsinnig; präzise ⟨*sich ausdrücken*⟩

incisor [ɪn'saɪzə(r)] *n. (Anat., Zool.)* Schneidezahn, *der*

incitation [ɪnsɪ'teɪʃn] *n. see* **incitement a**

incite [ɪn'saɪt] *v. t.* anstiften; aufstacheln, aufwiegeln ⟨*Massen, Volk*⟩

incitement [ɪn'saɪtmənt] *n.* **a)** *(act)* Anstiftung, *die; (of masses, crowd)* Aufstachelung, *die;* Aufwiegelung, *die;* **b)** *(encouragement)* Antrieb, *der*

incivility [ɪnsɪ'vɪlɪtɪ] *n.* Unhöflichkeit, *die;* **it is gross** ~ **to refuse** es ist eine grobe Unhöflichkeit abzulehnen

incl. *abbr.* **including** inkl.; einschl.

inclement [ɪn'klemənt] *adj.* unfreundlich ⟨*Wetter*⟩

inclination [ɪnklɪ'neɪʃn] *n.* **a)** *(slope)* [Ab]hang, *der; (of roof)* Neigung, *die;* **b)** *(preference, desire)* Neigung, *die;* **have a strong** ~ **to[wards]** *or* **for sth.** eine ausgeprägte Neigung für etw. haben; **my** ~ **is to let the matter rest** ich neige dazu, die Sache auf sich beruhen zu lassen; **by** ~ **he tended to be a recluse** er hatte eine Neigung zum Einsiedlertum; **have neither the time nor the** ~ **to pursue the matter** weder die Zeit noch die Lust haben, die Sache zu verfolgen; **my immediate** ~ **was to throw him out** mein erster Gedanke war, ihn hinauszuwerfen; **show no** ~ **to go to bed** keine Anstalten machen, ins Bett zu gehen; **c)** *(liking)* ~ **for sb.** Zuneigung für jmdn.; **d)** *(bow, nod)* Neigung, *die*

incline 1. [ɪn'klaɪn] *v. t.* **a)** *(bend)* neigen; **b)** *(dispose)* veranlassen; **all her instincts** ~**d her to stay** alles in ihr drängte sie zu bleiben. **2.** *v. i.* **a)** *(be disposed)* neigen **(to[wards]** zu); ~ **to believe that ...:** geneigt sein zu glauben, daß ...; ~ **to suppose that ...:** zu der Annahme neigen, daß ...; **b)** *(lean)* sich neigen. **3.** ['ɪnklaɪn] *n.* Steigung, *die*

inclined [ɪn'klaɪnd] *adj.* **a)** *(disposed)* geneigt; **be mathematically** ~: sich für Mathematik interessieren; **he is not very much** ~ **to believe me** er zeigt wenig Neigung, mir zu glauben; **they are** ~ **to be slow** sie neigen zur Langsamkeit; **if you feel [so]** ~: wenn Sie Lust dazu haben; **if you are that way** ~: wenn das Ihren Neigungen entspricht; **he is that way** ~: er neigt dazu; **be** ~ **to believe that ...:** geneigt sein zu glauben, daß ...; **the door is** ~ **to bang** die Tür schlägt leicht zu; **b)** *(sloping)* abfallend

inclined 'plane *n. (Phys.)* schiefe Ebene

inclose *see* **enclose**

include [ɪn'klu:d] *v. t.* einschließen; *(contain)* enthalten; **his team** ~**s a number of people who ...:** zu seiner Mannschaft gehören einige, die ...; **..., [the] children** ~**d** ..., [die] Kinder eingeschlossen; **does that** ~ **'me?** gilt das auch für mich?; **the list** ~**d several prominent politicians** die Liste enthielt mehrere prominente Politiker; **your name is not** ~**d in the list** dein Name steht nicht auf der Liste; **have you** ~**d the full amount?** haben Sie den vollen Betrag einbezogen?; ~ **sth. in an essay** *etc.* etw. in einen Aufsatz *usw.* aufnehmen; ~**d in the price** im Preis inbegriffen; **postage** ~**d** einschließlich Porto

~ **'out** *v. t. (coll. joc.)* auslassen; **[you can]** ~ **me out** ohne mich!

including [ɪn'klu:dɪŋ] *prep.* einschließlich; **I make that ten** ~ **the captain** mit dem Kapitän sind das nach meiner Rechnung zehn; **up to and** ~ **the last financial year** bis einschließlich des letzten Geschäftsjahres; ~ **VAT** inklusive Mehrwertsteuer; **the lights cost me £10,** ~ **the batteries** die Lampen kosteten mich, einschließlich Batterien, 10 Pfund

inclusion [ɪn'klu:ʒn] *n.* Aufnahme, *die*

inclusive [ɪn'klu:sɪv] *adj.* **a)** inklusive *(bes. Kaufmannsspr.);* einschließlich; **be** ~ **of sth.** etw. einschließen; **the rent is not** ~ **of gas and electricity charges** in der Miete sind Gas und Strom nicht enthalten; **from 2 to 6 January** ~: vom 2. bis einschließlich 6. Januar; **pages 7 to 26** ~: Seite 7 bis 26 einschließlich; **b)** *(including everything)* Pauschal-; Inklusiv-; ~ **terms** Pauschalpreis, *der;* **cost £50** ~: 50 Pfund kosten, alles inbegriffen

incognito [ɪnkɒg'ni:təʊ] **1.** *adj., adv.* inkognito. **2.** *n.* Inkognito, *das*

incoherent [ɪnkəʊ'hɪərənt] *adj.* zusammenhanglos; ~ **person/talk** sich ohne Zusammenhang ausdrückende Person/zusammenhangloses Gerede

incoherently [ɪnkəʊ'hɪərəntlɪ] *adv.* zusammenhanglos

incombustible [ɪnkəm'bʌstɪbl] *adj.* unbrennbar

income ['ɪnkəm] *n.* Einkommen, *das;* ~**s** *(receipts)* Einkünfte *Pl.;* **live within/beyond one's** ~: entsprechend seinen Verhältnissen/über seine Verhältnisse leben

income: ~ **group** *n.* Einkommensklasse, *die;* ~**s policy** *n.* Einkommenspolitik, *die;* ~ **support** *n. (Brit.)* zusätzliche Hilfe zum Lebensunterhalt; ~ **tax** *n.* Einkommensteuer, *die; (on wages, salary)* Lohnsteuer, *die;* ~ **tax return** Einkommensteuererklärung, *die*/Lohnsteuererklärung, *die*

'incoming *adj.* **a)** *(arriving)* ankommend; einlaufend ⟨*Zug, Schiff*⟩; landend ⟨*Flugzeug*⟩; einfahrend ⟨*Zug*⟩; eingehend ⟨*Telefongespräch, Auftrag*⟩; **the** ~ **post** *or* **mail** der Posteingang *(Bürow.)*; **the** ~ **tide** die Flut; **b)** *(succeeding)* neu ⟨*Vorsitzender, Präsident, Mieter, Regierung*⟩

incomings ['ɪnkʌmɪŋz] *n. pl. (revenue, income)* Einnahmen *Pl.;* Einkünfte *Pl.*

incommensurable [ɪnkə'menʃərəbl] *adj.* inkommensurabel

incommensurate [ɪnkə'menʃərət] *adj. (not comparable)* **be** ~ **with** *or* **to sth.** einer Sache *(Gen.)* unangemessen sein

incommode [ɪnkə'məʊd] *v. t. (formal)* **a)** *(annoy)* belästigen; inkommodieren *(geh. veralt.);* **b)** *(inconvenience)* behindern

incommunicado [ɪnkəmju:nɪ'kɑ:dəʊ] *pred. adj.* von der Außenwelt abgeschnitten; **hold sb.** ~: jmdn. ohne Verbindung zur Außenwelt halten

incomparable [ɪn'kɒmpərəbl] *adj.*, **incomparably** [ɪn'kɒmpərəblɪ] *adv.* unvergleichlich

incompatibility [ɪnkəmpætɪ'bɪlɪtɪ] *n., no pl.* **a)** *(inability to harmonize)* Unverträglichkeit, *die;* **divorce on grounds of** ~: Scheidung wegen unüberwindlicher Abneigung; **b)** *(unsuitability for use together)* Nichtübereinstimmung, *die; (of medicines)* Unverträglichkeit, *die;* **c)** *(inconsistency)* Unvereinbarkeit, *die*

incompatible [ɪnkəm'pætɪbl] *adj.* **a)** *(unable to harmonize)* unverträglich; **they were** ~ **and they separated** sie paßten nicht zueinander und trennten sich; **b)** *(unsuitable for use together)* unvereinbar; inkompatibel *(Technik);* unverträglich ⟨*Medikamente*⟩; **c)** *(inconsistent)* unvereinbar

incompetence [ɪn'kɒmpɪtəns], **incompetency** [ɪn'kɒmpɪtənsɪ] *n.* Unfähigkeit, *die;* Unvermögen, *das*

incompetent [ɪn'kɒmpɪtənt] **1.** *adj.* unfähig; unzulänglich ⟨*Arbeit*⟩; **he was** ~ **at his job** in seinem Beruf war er völlig unfähig. **2.** *n.* Unfähige, *der/die*

incompetently [ɪn'kɒmpɪtəntlɪ] *adv.* stümperhaft

incomplete [ɪnkəm'pli:t] *adj.*, **incompletely** [ɪnkəm'pli:tlɪ] *adv.* unvollständig

incompleteness [ɪnkəm'pli:tnɪs] *n., no pl.* Unvollständigkeit, *die*

incomprehensible [ɪnkɒmprɪ'hensɪbl] *adj.* unbegreiflich; unverständlich ⟨*Sprache, Rede, Theorie, Argument*⟩

incomprehension [ɪnkɒmprɪ'henʃn] *n., no pl.* Verständnislosigkeit, *die* **(of** gegenüber)

inconceivable [ɪnkən'si:vəbl] *adj.*, **inconceivably** [ɪnkən'si:vəblɪ] *adv.* **a)** *(coll.: remarkable/remarkably)* unfaßbar; **b)** *(unimaginable/unimaginably)* unvorstellbar

inconclusive [ɪnkən'klu:sɪv] *adj.* ergebnislos; nicht schlüssig ⟨*Beweis, Argument*⟩; **the result was** ~: das Ergebnis gab keinen Aufschluß

inconclusively [ɪnkən'klu:sɪvlɪ] *adv.* ergebnislos; nicht schlüssig ⟨*argumentieren*⟩

incongruity [ɪnkɒŋ'gru:ɪtɪ] *n.* **a)** *no pl. (quality)* Deplaziertheit, *die;* **without** ~: ohne deplaziert zu wirken; **b)** *(instance)* Absurdität, *die*

incongruous [ɪn'kɒŋgrʊəs] *adj.* **a)** *(inappropriate)* unpassend; **b)** *(inharmonious)* unvereinbar; nicht zusammenpassend ⟨*Farben, Kleidungsstücke*⟩

incongruously [ɪn'kɒŋgrʊəslɪ] *adv.* *(inappropriately)* unpassend; *as sentence-modifier* unpassenderweise

incongruousness [ɪn'kɒŋgrʊəsnɪs] *see* **incongruity a**

inconsequent [ɪn'kɒnsɪkwənt] *adj.* **a)** *(irrelevant)* sprunghaft ⟨*Abweichung, Eingebung*⟩; zusammenhanglos ⟨*Bemerkung*⟩; **b)** *(illogical)* unlogisch; **c)** *(disconnected)* unzusammenhängend

inconsequential [ɪnkɒnsɪ'kwenʃl] *adj.* **a)** *(unimportant)* belanglos; **b)** *see* **inconsequent a**

inconsiderable [ɪnkən'sɪdərəbl] *adj.* unbeträchtlich; unerheblich; **the costs were not** ~: die Kosten waren nicht unerheblich

inconsiderate [ɪnkən'sɪdərət] *adj.* **a)** *(unkind)* rücksichtslos; **b)** *(rash)* unbedacht; unüberlegt

inconsiderately [ɪnkən'sɪdərətlɪ] *adv.* *(unkindly)* rücksichtslos; *as sentence-modifier* rücksichtsloserweise

inconsistency [ɪnkən'sɪstənsɪ] *n.* **a)** *(incompatibility, self-contradiction)* Widersprüchlichkeit, *die* **(with** zu); **b)** *(illogicality)*

Inkonsequenz, *die;* **c)** *(irregularity)* Unbeständigkeit, *die;* Inkonsistenz, *die (geh.)*
inconsistent [ɪnkən'sɪstənt] *adj.* **a)** *(incompatible, self-contradictory)* widersprüchlich; **be ~ with sth.** zu etw. im Widerspruch stehen; **results ~ with the others** Ergebnisse, die nicht zu den anderen passen; **b)** *(illogical)* inkonsequent; **c)** *(irregular)* unbeständig; inkonsistent *(geh.)*
inconsistently [ɪnkən'sɪstəntlɪ] *adv.* **a)** *(in a self-contradictory manner)* widersprüchlich; **b)** *(illogically)* inkonsequent; **c)** *(irregularly)* unbeständig; inkonsistent *(geh.)*
inconsolable [ɪnkən'səʊləbl] *adj.* untröstlich
inconspicuous [ɪnkən'spɪkjʊəs] *adj.* unauffällig; **make oneself ~:** sich so verhalten, daß man nicht auffällt
inconspicuously [ɪnkən'spɪkjʊəslɪ] *adv.* unauffällig
inconstancy [ɪn'kɒnstənsɪ] *n., no pl. see* **inconstant:** Unstetigkeit, *die;* Wankelmut, *der (geh.);* Ungleichmäßigkeit, *die*
inconstant [ɪn'kɒnstənt] *adj.* **a)** *(fickle)* unstet; wankelmütig *(geh.);* **b)** *(irregular)* ungleichmäßig
incontestable [ɪnkən'testəbl] *adj.* unbestreitbar; unwiderlegbar ‹*Beweis*›
incontinence [ɪn'kɒntɪnəns] *n. (Med.)* Inkontinenz, *die*
incontinent [ɪn'kɒntɪnənt] *adj. (Med.)* inkontinent; **be ~:** an Inkontinenz leiden
incontrovertible [ɪnkɒntrə'vɜ:tɪbl] *adj.* unbestreitbar; unwiderlegbar ‹*Beweis*›
incontrovertibly [ɪnkɒntrə'vɜ:tɪblɪ] *adv.* unbestreitbar; unwiderlegbar ‹*beweisen*›
inconvenience [ɪnkən'vi:nɪəns] **1.** *n.* **a)** *no pl. (discomfort, disadvantage)* Unannehmlichkeiten **(to** für); **put sb. to a lot of ~:** jmdm. große Unannehmlichkeiten bereiten; **go to a great deal of ~:** große Unannehmlichkeiten auf sich *(Akk.)* nehmen; **b)** *(instance)* **if it's no ~:** wenn es keine Umstände macht; **it is rather an ~ to have to wait** es ist ziemlich unangenehm, warten zu müssen. **2.** *v. t.* Unannehmlichkeiten bereiten (+ *Dat.*); *(disturb)* stören; **don't ~ yourself just for me** *or* **on my account** mach [dir] meinetwegen nur keine Umstände!
inconvenient [ɪnkən'vi:nɪənt] *adj.* unbequem; ungünstig ‹*Lage, Standort*›; unpraktisch ‹*Design, Konstruktion, Schnitt*›; **a very ~ time** eine sehr ungünstige Zeit; **come at an ~ time** zu ungelegener Zeit kommen; **if it is not ~ [to you]** wenn es Ihnen recht ist
inconveniently [ɪnkən'vi:nɪəntlɪ] *adv.* ungünstig ‹*gelegen*›; unbequem ‹*klein*›
incorporate [ɪn'kɔ:pəreɪt] *v. t.* **a)** *(make a legal corporation)* vereinigen; **~ a company** eine Gesellschaft gründen; **be ~d as a company** zu einer Gesellschaft zusammengeschlossen sein; **b)** *(include)* aufnehmen **(in[to], with** in + *Akk.*); **your suggestion will be ~d in the plan** dein Vorschlag wird in den Plan eingehen; **the new plan ~s many of your suggestions** in dem neuen Plan sind viele deiner Vorschläge enthalten; **c)** *(unite)* verbinden **(into** zu); **~ one's ideas in an essay** seine Gedanken in einem Essay zusammenfassen
incorporated [ɪn'kɔ:pəreɪtɪd] *adj.* eingetragen ‹*[Handels]gesellschaft*›
incorporation [ɪnkɔ:pə'reɪʃn] *n.* **a)** *(formation)* Gründung, *die;* **b)** *(inclusion)* Eingliederung, *die; (of material, chemical)* Aufnahme, *die;* **c)** *(union)* Verbindung, *die* **(into** zu)
incorporeal [ɪnkɔ:'pɔ:rɪəl] *adj. (not composed of matter; also Law)* unkörperlich; geisterhaft ‹*Erscheinung, Wesen*›
incorrect [ɪnkə'rekt] *adj.* **a)** unrichtig; inkorrekt; **be ~:** nicht stimmen; **it is ~ to say that ...:** es stimmt nicht, daß ...; **you are ~ in believing that ...:** du irrst, wenn du glaubst, daß ...; **b)** *(improper)* inkorrekt; unschicklich
incorrectly [ɪnkə'rektlɪ] *adv.* **a)** unrichtigerweise; falsch ‹*beantworten, aussprechen*›; **b)** *(improperly)* inkorrekt; unschicklich
incorrectness [ɪnkə'rektnɪs] *n., no pl.* **a)** Unrichtigkeit, *die;* Inkorrektheit, *die;* **b)** *(impropriety)* Inkorrektheit, *die;* Unschicklichkeit, *die*
incorrigible [ɪn'kɒrɪdʒɪbl] *adj.,* **incorrigibly** [ɪn'kɒrɪdʒɪblɪ] *adv.* unverbesserlich
incorruptible [ɪnkə'rʌptɪbl] *adj.* **a)** *(upright)* unbestechlich; **b)** *(not subject to decay)* unzerstörbar
increase 1. [ɪn'kri:s] *v. i.* zunehmen; ‹*Schmerzen:*› stärker werden; ‹*Lärm:*› größer werden; ‹*Verkäufe, Preise, Nachfrage:*› steigen; **~ in skill** größere Fertigkeit gewinnen; **~ in weight/size/price** schwerer/größer/teurer werden; **~ in maturity/value/popularity** an Reife/Wert/Popularität *(Dat.)* gewinnen. **2.** *v. t.* **a)** *(make greater)* erhöhen; vermehren ‹*Besitz*›; **wages are ~d** die Löhne steigen; **b)** *(intensify)* verstärken; **~ one's efforts/commitment** sich mehr anstrengen/engagieren. **3.** ['ɪnkri:s] *n.* **a)** *(becoming greater)* Zunahme, *die* **(in** *Gen.*); *(in measurable amount)* Anstieg, *der* **(in** *Gen.*); *(deliberately caused)* Steigerung, *die* **(in** *Gen.*); **~ in weight/size** Gewichtszunahme, *die*/Vergrößerung, *die;* **~ in popularity** Popularitätsgewinn, *der;* **be on the ~:** [ständig] zunehmen; **b)** *(by reproduction)* Zunahme, *die;* Zuwachs, *der;* **c)** *(amount)* Erhöhung, *die; (of growth)* Zuwachs, *der*
increasing [ɪn'kri:sɪŋ] *adj.* steigend; wachsend; **an ~ number of people** mehr und mehr Menschen
increasingly [ɪn'kri:sɪŋlɪ] *adv.* in zunehmendem Maße; **become ~ apparent** immer deutlicher werden; **I am ~ of the opinion that ...:** ich bin immer mehr der Meinung, daß ...; **~, the husband looks after the children** immer häufiger kümmert sich der Mann um die Kinder
incredibility [ɪnkredɪ'bɪlɪtɪ] *n., no pl.* Unglaublichkeit, *die*
incredible [ɪn'kredɪbl] *adj.* **a)** *(beyond belief)* unglaublich; **b)** *(coll.) (remarkable)* unglaublich *(ugs.); (wonderful)* toll *(ugs.)*
incredibly [ɪn'kredɪblɪ] *adv.* **a)** unglaublich; **b)** *(coll.: remarkably)* unglaublich *(ugs.);* unwahrscheinlich *(ugs.);* **c)** *as sentence-modifier* es ist/war kaum zu glauben, aber ...
incredulity [ɪnkrɪ'dju:lɪtɪ] *n., no pl.* Ungläubigkeit, *die*
incredulous [ɪn'kredjʊləs] *adj.* ungläubig; **be ~ of sth.** einer Sache *(Dat.)* keinen Glauben schenken
incredulously [ɪn'kredjʊləslɪ] *adv.* ungläubig
increment ['ɪnkrɪmənt] *n.* Erhöhung, *die; (amount of growth)* Zuwachs, *der*
incriminate [ɪn'krɪmɪneɪt] *v. t.* belasten; **incriminating evidence** belastendes Material
incriminatory [ɪn'krɪmɪnətərɪ] *adj.* belastend
incrustation [ɪnkrʌs'teɪʃn] *n.* **a)** *(encrusting)* Überkrustung, *die;* **b)** *(deposit)* Inkrustation, *die (Geol.);* Verkrustung, *die*
incubate ['ɪnkjʊbeɪt] **1.** *v. t.* bebrüten; *(to hatching; also fig.)* ausbrüten. **2.** *v. i.* **a)** ‹*Henne:*› brüten; **b)** *(be developed)* ‹*Kulturen:*› bebrütet werden
incubation [ɪnkjʊ'beɪʃn] *n.* **a)** Inkubation, *die (Biol.);* Bebrütung, *die; (fig.)* Ausbrüten, *das;* **b)** *(Med.)* Inkubation, *die;* **~ period** Inkubationszeit, *die*
incubator ['ɪnkjʊbeɪtə(r)] *n.* Inkubator, *der (Biol., Med.); (for babies also)* Brutkasten, *der; (for eggs)* Brutapparat, *der*
incubus ['ɪŋkjʊbəs] *n., pl.* **~es** *or* **incubi** ['ɪnkjʊbaɪ] **a)** Alpdruck, *der;* **b)** *(spirit)* Inkubus, *der*
inculcate ['ɪnkʌlkeɪt] *v. t.* **~ sth. in[to] sb., ~ sb. with sth.** jmdm. etw. einpflanzen
inculpate ['ɪnkʌlpeɪt] *v. t.* **a)** *(accuse)* **~ sb. [for a crime]** jmdn. [eines Verbrechens] beschuldigen; **b)** *(involve)* **~ sb. [in sth.]** jmdn. der Mittäterschaft *(Gen.)* [bei etw.] beschuldigen
inculpation [ɪnkʌl'peɪʃn] *n.* Beschuldigung, *die*
incumbency [ɪn'kʌmbənsɪ] *n.* Amt, *das*
incumbent [ɪn'kʌmbənt] **1.** *n.* **a)** *(Eccl.)* **the ~ of the parish** der Inhaber der Pfarrstelle; **b)** *(office-holder)* Amtsinhaber, *der.* **2.** *adj. (imposed)* **the duty ~ on me** die mir obliegende Pflicht; **it is ~ on sb. to do it** es ist jmds. Pflicht *od.* obliegt jmdm., es zu tun; **I feel it ~ on me** ich sehe es als meine Pflicht an
incur [ɪn'kɜ:(r)] *v. t.,* **-rr-** sich *(Dat.)* zuziehen ‹*Unwillen, Ärger*›; **~ a loss** einen Verlust erleiden; **~ debts/expenses/risks** Schulden machen/Ausgaben haben/Risiken eingehen; **they had ~red fines** sie waren mit Geldstrafen belegt worden
incurable [ɪn'kjʊərəbl] **1.** *adj.* **a)** *(Med.)* unheilbar; **b)** *(fig.)* unheilbar *(ugs.);* unstillbar ‹*Sehnsucht, Verlangen*›; unüberwindbar ‹*Scheu, Zurückhaltung*›. **2.** *n.* unheilbar Kranker/Kranke
incurably [ɪn'kjʊərəblɪ] *adv.* unheilbar ‹*krank*›
incurious [ɪn'kjʊərɪəs] *adj.* uninteressiert
incursion [ɪn'kɜ:ʃn] *n. (invasion)* Eindringen, *das; (by sudden attack)* Einfall, *der*
indebted [ɪn'detɪd] *pred. adj.* **a) be/feel deeply ~ to sb.** tief in jmds. Schuld *(Dat.)* stehen *(geh.);* **he was ~ to the book/a friend for this information** er verdankte dem Buch/einem Freund diese Information; **be [much] ~ to sb. for sth.** jmdm. für etw. [sehr] verbunden sein *(geh.) od.* zu Dank verpflichtet sein; **b)** *(owing money)* **be ~ to the bank for a large sum** bei der Bank mit einer hohen Summe verschuldet sein; **be [heavily] ~ to a friend** bei einem Freund [große] Schulden haben
indebtedness [ɪn'detɪdnɪs] *n.* **a)** *(something owed)* Dankesschuld, *die (geh.)* **(to** bei); **b)** *(condition of owing money)* Verschuldung, *die*
indecency [ɪn'di:sənsɪ] *n.* Unanständigkeit, *die*
indecent [ɪn'di:sənt] *adj.* **a)** *(immodest, obscene)* unanständig; *see also* **exposure a; b)** *(unseemly)* ungehörig; **with ~ haste** mit unziemlicher Hast *(geh.)*
indecent as'sault *n. (Law)* Notzucht, *die (Rechtsw.)*
indecently [ɪn'di:səntlɪ] *adv.* unanständig
indecipherable [ɪndɪ'saɪfərəbl] *adj.* unentzifferbar
indecision [ɪndɪ'sɪʒn] *n., no pl.* Unentschlossenheit, *die*
indecisive [ɪndɪ'saɪsɪv] *adj.* **a)** *(not conclusive)* ergebnislos ‹*Streit, Diskussion*›; nichts entscheidend ‹*Krieg, Schlacht*›; nichtssagend ‹*Ergebnis, Beobachtung*›; **b)** *(hesitating)* unentschlossen; **be ~ about one's plans** keine festen Pläne haben; **~ about which line of action to choose** unschlüssig, wie man vorgehen soll
indecisively [ɪndɪ'saɪsɪvlɪ] *adv.* **a)** *(inconclusively)* ohne Entscheidung; **b)** *(hesitatingly)* unentschlossen
indecisiveness [ɪndɪ'saɪsɪvnɪs] *n., no pl.* **a)** Ergebnislosigkeit, *die;* Unentschlossenheit, *die;* **b)** *(hesitation)* **~ over a crucial issue** Unentschlossenheit in einer äußerst wichtigen Sache
indeclinable [ɪndɪ'klaɪnəbl] *adj. (Ling.)* indeklinabel
indecorous [ɪn'dekərəs] *adj. (improper)* ungehörig; *(in bad taste)* unschicklich
indeed [ɪn'di:d] *adv.* **a)** *(in truth)* in der Tat; tatsächlich; **~ that is correct** das stimmt tatsächlich *od.* in der Tat; **b)** *emphat.* **thank you very much ~:** haben Sie vielen herzli-

chen Dank; **it was very kind of you ~**: es war wirklich sehr freundlich von Ihnen; **I shall be very glad ~ when ...**: ich bin wirklich sehr froh, wenn ...; **~ it is** in der Tat; allerdings; **yes ~, it certainly is/I certainly did** *etc.* ja, das kann man wohl sagen; **no, ~**: nein, ganz bestimmt nicht; **c)** *(in fact)* ja sogar; **~, he can ...**: ja, er kann sogar ...; **if ~ such a thing is possible** wenn so etwas überhaupt möglich ist; **I feel, ~ I know, she will come** ich habe das Gefühl, [ja] ich weiß sogar, daß sie kommen wird; **d)** *(admittedly)* zugegebenermaßen; zwar; **e)** *interrog.* **~?** wirklich?; ist das wahr?; **f)** *expr. irony, surprise, interest, etc.* **He expects to win – Does he ~!** Er glaubt, daß er gewinnt – Tatsächlich?; **I want a fortnight off work – [Do you] ~!** Ich möchte 14 Tage freihaben – Ach wirklich?; **smoked salmon, ~!** soso *od.* sieh mal einer an, geräucherter Lachs [also]!; **g)** *echoing question* **Who is this Mr Smith? – Who is he, ~!** *(you may well ask)* Wer ist denn dieser Mr. Smith? – Ja, wer ist er eigentlich?

indefatigable [ɪndɪˈfætɪgəbl] *adj.* unermüdlich

indefensible [ɪndɪˈfensɪbl] *adj.* **a)** *(insecure)* unhaltbar; **b)** *(untenable)* unvertretbar; unhaltbar; **c)** *(intolerable)* unverzeihlich

indefinable [ɪndɪˈfaɪnəbl] *adj.* undefinierbar; **have a certain ~ something** etwas Gewisses haben

indefinite [ɪnˈdefɪnɪt] *adj.* **a)** *(vague)* unbestimmt; **she was rather ~ about it** sie äußerte sich ziemlich vage darüber; **b)** *(unlimited)* unbegrenzt; **~ leave** Urlaub auf unbestimmte Zeit; **c)** *(Ling.)* unbestimmt; indefinit *(fachspr.)*; infinit *(fachspr.)* ⟨*Verbform*⟩; *see also* **article 1 c; pronoun**

indefinitely [ɪnˈdefɪnɪtlɪ] *adv.* **a)** *(vaguely)* unbestimmt; **b)** *(unlimitedly)* unbegrenzt; **it can't go on ~**: es kann nicht endlos so weitergehen; **postponed ~**: auf unbestimmte Zeit verschoben; **it would be easy to prolong the list ~**: die Liste ließe sich beliebig verlängern

indelible [ɪnˈdelɪbl] *adj.* unauslöschlich *(auch fig.)*; nicht zu entfernend ⟨*Fleck*⟩; **~ ink** Wäschetinte, *die;* **~ pencil** Kopierstift, *der;* Tintenstift, *der*

indelibly [ɪnˈdelɪblɪ] *adv.* unauslöschlich

indelicacy [ɪnˈdelɪkəsɪ] *n. see* **indelicate**: Ungehörigkeit, *die;* Geschmacklosigkeit, *die;* Mangel an Feingefühl

indelicate [ɪnˈdelɪkət] *adj. (coarse)* ungehörig; *(almost indecent)* geschmacklos; *(slightly tactless)* nicht sehr feinfühlig

indelicately [ɪnˈdelɪkətlɪ] *adv. see* **indelicate**: ungehörig; geschmacklos; wenig feinfühlend

indemnification [ɪndemnɪfɪˈkeɪʃn] *n.* Entschädigung, *die*

indemnify [ɪnˈdemnɪfaɪ] *v. t.* **a)** *(protect)* **~ sb. against sth.** jmdn. gegen etw. absichern; **b)** *(compensate)* entschädigen

indemnity [ɪnˈdemnɪtɪ] *n.* **a)** *(security)* Absicherung, *die;* **b)** *(compensation)* Entschädigung, *die*

inˈdemnity policy *n.* Haftpflichtversicherung, *die*

¹indent 1. [ˈɪndent] *n.* **a)** *(incision)* Einschnitt, *der;* **b)** *(Brit.: requisition)* Requisition, *die;* **c)** *see* **indentures. 2.** [ɪnˈdent] *v. t.* **a)** *(make notches in)* einkerben; **b)** *(form recesses in)* einschneiden in (+ *Akk.*); **an ~ed coastline** eine Küste mit tiefen Einschnitten; **c)** *(from margin)* einrücken; **d)** *(Brit.: order)* requirieren. **3.** *v. i.* *(Brit.: make requisition)* **~ [on sb.] for sth.** etw. [bei jmdm.] requirieren

²indent [ɪnˈdent] *v. t. (imprint)* eindrücken

indentation [ɪndenˈteɪʃn] *n.* **a)** *(indenting, notch)* Einkerbung, *die;* **b)** *(recess)* Einschnitt, *der*

indentures [ɪnˈdentʃəz] *n. pl.* Ausbildungsvertrag, *der*

independence [ɪndɪˈpendəns] *n.* Unabhängigkeit, *die;* **declaration of ~**: Unabhängigkeitserklärung, *die;* **~ of mind/spirit** geistige Selbständigkeit

Indeˈpendence Day *n. (Amer.)* Unabhängigkeitstag, *der*

independent [ɪndɪˈpendənt] **1.** *adj.* **a)** unabhängig; **~ income/means** eigenes Einkommen; **b)** *(not wanting obligations)* selbständig. **2.** *n. (Polit.)* Unabhängige, *der/die*

independently [ɪndɪˈpendəntlɪ] *adv.* unabhängig **(of** von); **they work ~**: sie arbeiten unabhängig voneinander

indeˈpendent school *n. (Brit.)* Schule in nichtstaatlicher Trägerschaft

ˈin-depth *adj. see* **depth c**

indescribable [ɪndɪˈskraɪbəbl] *adj.*, **indescribably** [ɪndɪˈskraɪbəblɪ] *adv.* unbeschreiblich

indestructible [ɪndɪˈstrʌktɪbl] *adj.* unzerstörbar; unerschütterlich ⟨*Glaube*⟩

indeterminable [ɪndɪˈtɜːmɪnəbl] *adj.* unbestimmbar

indeterminacy [ɪndɪˈtɜːmɪnəsɪ] *n., no pl.* Unbestimmtheit, *die*

indeterminate [ɪndɪˈtɜːmɪnət] *adj.* **a)** *(not fixed, vague)* unbestimmt ⟨*Form, Menge*⟩; unklar ⟨*Konzept, Bedeutung*⟩; **b)** *(left undecided)* ergebnislos; offen ⟨*Rechtsfrage*⟩; **c)** *(Math.)* unbestimmt

index [ˈɪndeks] **1.** *n.* **a)** *(list)* Index, *der;* Register, *das;* **~ of sources** Quellenverzeichnis, *das; see also* **card index; b)** *pl.* **indices** [ˈɪndɪsiːz] *(Phys.)* **refractive ~**: Brechzahl, *die;* Brechungsindex, *der;* **c)** *pl.* **indices** *(Math.)* Index, *der;* *(exponent)* Exponent, *der;* **d)** *(pointer on scale)* Zeiger, *der;* **e)** *(Econ.)* Index, *der;* **f)** *pl.* **indices** *(indication)* [An]zeichen, *das;* **g) the I~** *(Hist.)* der Index; **put on the I~**: auf den Index setzen. **2.** *v. t.* **a)** *(furnish with ~)* mit einem Register *od.* Index versehen; **b)** *(enter in ~)* ins Register aufnehmen; **c)** *(Econ.)* indexieren; **~ pensions** Renten dynamisieren

indexation [ɪndekˈseɪʃn] *n. (Econ.)* Indexierung, *die*

indexer [ˈɪndeksə(r)] *n.* Verfasser eines Registers/von Registern

index: ~ finger *n.* Zeigefinger, *der;* Index, *der (Anat.);* **~-linked** *adj. (Econ.)* indexiert; dynamisch ⟨*Rente*⟩; **~-linking** *n. (Econ.)* Indexierung, *die;* **~-linking of pensions** ≈ Rentenanpassung, *die;* **~ number** *n.* Indexzahl, *die (bes. Statistik)*

India [ˈɪndɪə] *pr. n.* Indien *(das);* **~ ink** *(Amer.) see* **Indian ink**

Indian [ˈɪndɪən] **1.** *adj.* **a)** indisch; **b) [American] ~**: indianisch. *See also* **³file 1 a; Red Indian; West Indian 1. 2.** *n.* **a)** Inder, *der/*Inderin, *die;* **b) [American] ~**: Indianer, *der/*Indianerin, *die*

Indian: ~ ˈclub *n.* Keule, *die;* **~ ˈcorn** *n.* Mais, *der;* **~ ˈink** *n. (Brit.)* Tusche, *die;* **~ ˈOcean** *pr. n.* Indischer Ozean; **~ ˈrope-trick** *n.* indischer Seiltrick; **~ ˈsummer** *n.* Altweibersommer, *der;* Nachsommer, *der (auch fig.)*

ˈIndia rubber *see* **¹rubber a, b**

indicate [ˈɪndɪkeɪt] **1.** *v. t.* **a)** *(be a sign of)* erkennen lassen; **this ~s something about his attitude** dies gibt Aufschlüsse über seine Haltung; **b)** *(state briefly)* andeuten; **~ the rough outlines of a project** ein Projekt kurz umreißen *od.* in groben Umrissen darstellen; **they ~d that they might take action** sie gaben zu verstehen, daß sie Schritte unternehmen könnten; **c)** *(mark, point out)* anzeigen; **d)** *(suggest, make evident)* zum Ausdruck bringen **(to** gegenüber); **e)** *(Med.)* **be ~d** indiziert sein. **2.** *v. i.* blinken *(bes. Verkehrsw.)*

indication [ɪndɪˈkeɪʃn] *n.* **a)** *(sign, guide)* [An]zeichen, *das* **(of** *Gen.*, für); **he gave no ~ that he understood** nichts wies darauf hin, daß er verstand; **there is every/no ~ that ...**: alles/nichts weist darauf hin, daß ...; **give a clear ~ of one's intentions** seine Absichten klar zum Ausdruck bringen; **first ~s are that ...**: die ersten Anzeichen deuten darauf hin, daß ...; **that is some ~ of his feelings/the seriousness of the situation** das läßt seine Gefühle erkennen/das deutet darauf hin, wie ernst die Lage ist; **give me a rough ~ of when you will arrive** sagen Sie mir ungefähr, wann Sie kommen; **b)** *(Med.)* Indikation, *die*

indicative [ɪnˈdɪkətɪv] **1.** *adj.* **a)** *(suggestive)* **be ~ of sth./that ...**: auf etw. *(Akk.)* schließen lassen/darauf schließen lassen, daß ...; **b)** *(Ling.)* indikativisch; **~ mood** Indikativ, *der.* **2.** *n. (Ling.)* Indikativ, *der*

indicator [ˈɪndɪkeɪtə(r)] *n.* **a)** *(instrument)* Anzeiger, *der;* **b)** *(board)* Anzeigetafel, *die;* **c)** *(on vehicle)* Blinker, *der;* **d)** *(fig.: pointer)* Indikator, *der (bes. Wirtsch.);* **e)** *(Chem.)* Indikator, *der*

indices *pl. of* **index 1 b, c, f**

indict [ɪnˈdaɪt] *v. t.* anklagen **(for, on a charge of** *Gen.*)

indictable [ɪnˈdaɪtəbl] *adj.* strafrechtlich verfolgbar ⟨*Person*⟩; strafbar ⟨*Handlung*⟩

indictment [ɪnˈdaɪtmənt] *n.* **a)** *(Law)* Anklageerhebung, *die;* **~ for** *or* **on a charge of murder** Mordanklage, *die;* **bring an ~ against sb.** Anklage gegen jmdn. erheben; **[bill of] ~**: Anklageschrift, *die;* **b)** *(fig.: accusation)* **~ of sth.** Anklage gegen etw. *(geh.)*

Indies [ˈɪndɪz] *pr. n. pl.* **a) the ~** *(arch.)* Indien; der indische Subkontinent; **b) East ~**: Malaiischer Archipel; Ostindischer Archipel *(veralt.);* **West ~**: Westindische Inseln

indifference [ɪnˈdɪfərəns] *n., no pl.* **a)** *(unconcern)* Gleichgültigkeit, *die* **(to[wards]** gegenüber); **b)** *(neutrality)* Indifferenz, *die;* **c)** *(unimportance)* **a matter of ~**: eine Belanglosigkeit; **this is a matter of complete ~ to** *or* **for him** das ist für ihn völlig belanglos

indifferent [ɪnˈdɪfərənt] *adj.* **a)** *(without concern or interest)* gleichgültig; unbeteiligt ⟨*Beobachter*⟩; **be ~ to[wards] sb./sth.** sich für jmdn./etw. nicht interessieren; **b)** *(not good)* mittelmäßig; *(fairly bad)* mäßig; *(neither good nor bad)* durchschnittlich; **very ~**: schlecht

indifferently [ɪnˈdɪfərəntlɪ] *adv.* **a)** *(unconcernedly)* gleichgültig; **b)** *(badly)* mäßig

indigence [ˈɪndɪdʒəns] *n., no pl.* Armut, *die*

indigenous [ɪnˈdɪdʒɪnəs] *adj.* einheimisch; eingeboren ⟨*Bevölkerung*⟩; **a species ~ to India** eine in Indien heimische *od.* beheimatete Art; **~ inhabitant** Ureinwohner, *der*

indigent [ˈɪndɪdʒənt] *adj.* arm

indigestible [ɪndɪˈdʒestɪbl] *adj. (lit. or fig.)* unverdaulich

indigestion [ɪndɪˈdʒestʃn] *n., no pl., no indef. art.* Magenverstimmung, *die;* *(chronic)* Verdauungsstörungen

indignant [ɪnˈdɪgnənt] *adj.* entrüstet **(at, over, about** über + *Akk.*); indigniert ⟨*Blick, Geste*⟩; **grow ~**: sich entrüsten; **it makes me ~**: es regt mich auf; **he was ~ with his wife** er ärgerte sich über seine Frau; **it's no use getting ~**: es hat keinen Zweck, sich aufzuregen

indignantly [ɪnˈdɪgnəntlɪ] *adv.* entrüstet; indigniert

indignation [ɪndɪgˈneɪʃn] *n., no pl.* Entrüstung, *die* **(about, at, against, over** über + *Akk.*); **feel great ~ at sb.** sehr entrüstet über jmdn. sein

indignity [ɪnˈdɪgnɪtɪ] *n.* **a)** *no pl., no art.* *(humiliation)* Demütigung, *die;* **be treated with great ~**: äußerst demütigend behandelt werden; **b)** *no pl. (lack of dignity)* **the ~ of my position** das Demütigende [an] meiner Situation; **oh, the ~ of it!** o Schmach und Schande!; **the ~ of having to do sth.** die Demütigung, etw. tun zu müssen

indigo ['ɪndɪgəʊ] **1.** *n., pl.* ~**s a)** *(dye)* Indigo, *der od. das;* **b)** *(plant)* Indigopflanze, *die;* **c)** *(colour)* ~ **[blue]** Indigoblau, *das.* **2.** *adj.* ~ **[blue]** indigoblau

indirect [ɪndɪ'rekt, ɪndaɪ'rekt] *adj.* indirekt; *(long-winded)* umständlich; **follow an ~ route** nicht den direkten Weg nehmen; **that's the more ~ way** das ist der weniger direkte *od.* gradlinige Weg; **that road is rather ~:** diese Straße ist ein ziemlicher Umweg; **by ~ means** auf Umwegen *(fig.)*

indirectly [ɪndɪ'rektlɪ, ɪndaɪ'rektlɪ] *adv.* indirekt; auf Umwegen ⟨*hören, herausfinden*⟩

indirect: ~ 'object *n. (Ling.)* indirektes Objekt; *(in German)* Dativobjekt, *das;* ~ **'question** *n. (Ling.)* indirekte Frage; ~ **'speech** *n. (Ling.)* indirekte Rede

indiscernible [ɪndɪ'sɜːnɪbl] *adj.* unmerklich; **the sound was virtually ~:** das Geräusch war kaum wahrnehmbar

indiscipline [ɪn'dɪsɪplɪn] *n., no pl., no indef. art.* Disziplinlosigkeit, *die*

indiscreet [ɪndɪ'skriːt] *adj.* indiskret; taktlos ⟨*Benehmen*⟩; **she was ~ to do that** es war indiskret von ihr, das zu tun

indiscreetly [ɪndɪ'skriːtlɪ] *adv.* indiskret; taktlos ⟨*sich benehmen*⟩

indiscretion [ɪndɪ'skreʃn] *n.* **a)** *(conduct)* Indiskretion, *die; (tactlessness)* Taktlosigkeit, *die;* **b)** *(imprudence)* Unbedachtheit, *die;* **c)** *(action)* Unbedachtsamkeit, *die; (love affair)* Affäre, *die;* **d)** *(revelation of official secret etc.)* Indiskretion, *die*

indiscriminate [ɪndɪ'skrɪmɪnət] *adj.* **a)** *(undiscriminating)* unkritisch; **hand out ~ condemnations** unterschiedslos alles verurteilen; **b)** *(unrestrained, promiscuous)* wahllos; willkürlich ⟨*Anwendung*⟩; unüberlegt ⟨*Ausgaben*⟩

indiscriminately [ɪndɪ'skrɪmɪnətlɪ] *adv. see* **indiscriminate:** unkritisch; wahllos; willkürlich; unüberlegt

indispensability [ɪndɪspensə'bɪlɪtɪ] *n., no pl.* Unentbehrlichkeit, *die* **(to** für)

indispensable [ɪndɪ'spensəbl] *adj.* unentbehrlich **(to** für); unabdingbar ⟨*Voraussetzung*⟩; **make oneself ~:** sich unentbehrlich machen

indispose [ɪndɪ'spəʊz] *v. t. (make averse)* einnehmen **(towards** gegen)

indisposed [ɪndɪ'spəʊzd] *adj.* **a)** *(unwell)* unpäßlich; indisponiert ⟨*Sänger, Schauspieler*⟩; **b)** *(disinclined)* **be ~ to do sth.** abgeneigt sein, etw. zu tun; **she was ~d to be polite** sie war nicht geneigt, höflich zu sein

indisposition [ɪndɪspə'zɪʃn] *n.* **a)** *(ill health)* Unpäßlichkeit, *die; (of singer, actor)* Indisposition, *die;* **b)** *(disinclination)* **an ~ to do sth.** eine Abneigung dagegen, etw. zu tun

indisputable [ɪndɪ'spjuːtəbl] *adj.,* **indisputably** [ɪndɪ'spjuːtəblɪ] *adv.* unbestreitbar

indissoluble [ɪndɪ'sɒljʊbl] *adj.,* **indissolubly** [ɪndɪ'sɒljʊblɪ] *adv.* unauflöslich

indistinct [ɪndɪ'stɪŋkt] *adj.* undeutlich; *(blurred)* verschwommen; **grow ~ in the twilight** in der Dämmerung verschwimmen

indistinctly [ɪndɪ'stɪŋktlɪ] *adv.* undeutlich ⟨*sprechen*⟩; verschwommen ⟨*sich erinnern*⟩

indistinguishable [ɪndɪ'stɪŋgwɪʃəbl] *adj.* **a)** *(not distinguishable)* nicht unterscheidbar; **the twins are ~:** die Zwillinge sind nicht voneinander zu unterscheiden; **b)** *(imperceptible)* nicht erkennbar; nicht wahrnehmbar ⟨*Geräusch*⟩

individual [ɪndɪ'vɪdjʊəl] **1.** *adj.* **a)** *(single)* einzeln; **b)** *(special, personal)* besonder... ⟨*Vorteil, Merkmal*⟩; **give ~ attention to one's pupils** seine Schüler individuell betreuen; ~ **case** Einzelfall, *der;* **c)** *(intended for one)* für eine [einzelne] Person bestimmt; ~ **portions** Einzelportionen; ~ **pie** Pastete für eine [einzelne] Person; **d)** *(distinctive)* eigentümlich; individuell; **be ~ in one's view** individuelle *od.* eigene Ansichten vertreten; **e)** *(characteristic)* eigen; individuell. **2.** *n.* **a)** *(one member)* einzelne, *der/die; (animal)* Einzeltier, *das;* einzelnes Tier; ~**s** einzelne; **b)** *(one being)* Individuum, *das;* einzelne, *der/die;* **the rights of ~s** die Rechte des Individuums *od.* des einzelnen; **c)** *(coll.: person)* Individuum, *das (abwertend);* **who is that ~?** wer ist dieses Individuum?

individualise *see* **individualize**

individualist [ɪndɪ'vɪdjʊəlɪst] *n.* Individualist, *der*/Individualistin, *die*

individualistic [ɪndɪvɪdjʊə'lɪstɪk] *adj.* individualistisch

individuality [ɪndɪvɪdjʊ'ælɪtɪ] *n., no pl.* **a)** *(character)* eigene Persönlichkeit; Individualität, *die;* **b)** *(separate existence)* individuelle Existenz

individualize [ɪndɪ'vɪdjʊəlaɪz] *v. t.* ~ **sth.** einer Sache *(Dat.)* einen eigenen Charakter geben

individually [ɪndɪ'vɪdjʊəlɪ] *adv.* **a)** *(singly)* einzeln; **b)** *(distinctively)* individuell; **c)** *(personally)* persönlich

indivisibility [ɪndɪvɪzɪ'bɪlɪtɪ] *n., no pl.* Unteilbarkeit, *die*

indivisible [ɪndɪ'vɪzɪbl] *adj.* **a)** *(not divisible)* unteilbar; **b)** *(not distributable)* nicht aufteilbar

indivisibly [ɪndɪ'vɪzɪblɪ] *adv.* unteilbar

Indo- [ɪndəʊ] *in comb.* Indo-

Indo-'China *pr. n.* Indochina *(das)*

indoctrinate [ɪn'dɒktrɪneɪt] *v. t.* indoktrinieren *(abwertend)*

indoctrination [ɪndɒktrɪ'neɪʃn] *n.* Indoktrination, *die (abwertend)*

Indo: ~-Euro'pean, ~-Ger'manic 1. *adjs.* indoeuropäisch; indogermanisch. **2.** *ns. (Ling.)* Indogermanisch, *das*

indolence ['ɪndələns] *n., no pl.* Trägheit, *die;* Indolenz, *die (geh.)*

indolent ['ɪndələnt] *adj.,* **indolently** ['ɪndələntlɪ] *adv.* träge; indolent *(geh.)*

indomitable [ɪn'dɒmɪtəbl] *adj.* unbeugsam; unbezähmbar ⟨*Begeisterung*⟩

Indonesia [ɪndə'niːʃə] *pr. n.* Indonesien *(das)*

Indonesian [ɪndə'niːʃn] **1.** *adj.* indonesisch; **sb. is ~:** jmd. ist Indonesier/Indonesierin; *see also* **English 1. 2.** *n.* **a)** *(person)* Indonesier, *der*/Indonesierin, *die;* **b)** *(language)* Indonesisch, *das; see also* **English 2 a**

'indoor *adj.* ~ **shoes** Schuhe für zu Hause; ~ **swimming-pool/sports/tennis** Hallenbad, *das*/-sport, *der*/-tennis, *das;* ~ **plants** Zimmerpflanzen; ~ **games** Spiele im Haus; *(Sport)* Hallenspiele; ~ **aerial** Innenantenne, *die; (in room)* Zimmerantenne, *die;* **I don't enjoy ~ work** ich arbeite nicht gern drinnen *od.* im Haus/Büro *usw.*; **he's not one for [the] ~ life** er ist lieber draußen als drinnen

indoors [ɪn'dɔːz] *adv.* drinnen; im Haus; **come/go ~:** nach drinnen *od.* ins Haus kommen/gehen

indorse *see* **endorse**

indubitable [ɪn'djuːbɪtəbl] *adj.* unzweifelhaft

indubitably [ɪn'djuːbɪtəblɪ] *adv.* zweifellos; zweifelsohne

induce [ɪn'djuːs] *v. t.* **a)** *(persuade)* ~ **sb. to do sth.** jmdn. dazu bringen, etw. zu tun; **b)** *(bring about)* hervorrufen; verursachen, führen zu ⟨*Krankheit*⟩; **c)** *(Med.)* einleiten ⟨*Wehen, Geburt*⟩; herbeiführen ⟨*Schlaf*⟩; **d)** *(Electr., Phys., Philos.)* induzieren

inducement [ɪn'djuːsmənt] *n.* *(incentive)* Anreiz, *der;* **as an added ~:** als besonderer Anreiz *od.* Ansporn; **no ~ would persuade her to give up her home** kein noch so verlockendes Angebot könnte sie dazu bewegen, ihr Zuhause aufzugeben

induct [ɪn'dʌkt] *v. t.* **a)** einführen **(to** in + *Akk.*); **b)** *(Amer. Mil.)* einziehen; einberufen

inductance [ɪn'dʌktəns] *n. (Electr.)* Induktanz, *die*

inductee [ɪndʌk'tiː] *n. (Amer. Mil.)* Einberufene, *der/die*

induction [ɪn'dʌkʃn] *n.* **a)** *(formal introduction)* Amtseinführung, *die;* **b)** *(initiation)* Einführung, *die* **(into** in + *Akk.*); ~ **course** Einführungskurs[us], *der;* **c)** *(Med.)* Einleitung, *die; (of sleep)* Herbeiführen, *das;* **d)** *(Electr., Phys., Math., Philos.)* Induktion, *die;* **e)** *(Amer. Mil.)* Einberufung, *die*

induction: ~-coil *n. (Electr.)* Induktionsspule, *die;* ~ **heating** *n.* Induktionsheizung, *die*

inductive [ɪn'dʌktɪv] *adj.,* **inductively** [ɪn'dʌktɪvlɪ] *adv. (Electr., Phys., Math., Logic)* induktiv

indue *see* **endue**

indulge [ɪn'dʌldʒ] **1.** *v. t.* **a)** *(yield to)* nachgeben (+ *Dat.*) ⟨*Wunsch, Verlangen, Verlockung*⟩; frönen *(geh.)* (+ *Dat.*) ⟨*Leidenschaft, Neigung*⟩; **b)** *(please)* verwöhnen; ~ **sb. in sth.** jmdm. in etw. *(Dat.)* nachgeben; ~ **oneself in** schwelgen in *(geh.)* (+ *Dat.*); sich gütlich tun an (+ *Dat.*) ⟨*Speisen, Leckereien*⟩. **2.** *v. i.* **a)** *(allow oneself pleasure)* ~ **in** frönen *(geh.)* (+ *Dat.*) ⟨*Leidenschaft, Neigung*⟩; sich gütlich tun an (+ *Dat.*) ⟨*Speisen, Leckereien*⟩; **b)** *(coll.: take alcoholic drink)* sich *(Dat.)* einen genehmigen *(ugs.)*; **I'd better not ~:** ich halte mich besser zurück

indulgence [ɪn'dʌldʒəns] *n.* **a)** Nachsicht, *die; (humouring)* Nachgiebigkeit, *die* **(with** gegenüber); **b) sb.'s ~ in sth.** jmds. Hang zu etw.; **constant ~ in bad habits** ständiges Nachgeben gegenüber schlechten Gewohnheiten; **c)** *(thing indulged in)* Luxus, *der;* **d)** *(privilege)* Vorrecht, *das;* **e)** *(Relig.: remission)* Ablaß, *der*

indulgent [ɪn'dʌldʒənt] *adj.* nachsichtig **(with, to[wards]** gegenüber); **she's so ~ with that dog of hers** sie verhätschelt ihren Hund so sehr

indulgently [ɪn'dʌldʒəntlɪ] *adv.* nachsichtig

industrial [ɪn'dʌstrɪəl] *adj.* **a)** industriell; betrieblich ⟨*Ausbildung, Forschung*⟩; Arbeits⟨*unfall, -medizin, -psychologie*⟩; **b)** *(intended for industry)* Industrie⟨*alkohol, -diamant usw.*⟩; **c)** *(characterized by industry)* industrialisiert; **the ~ nations** die Industrienationen. *See also* **archaeology; estate b**

industrial: ~ 'action *n.* Arbeitskampfmaßnahmen *Pl.*; **take ~ action** in den Ausstand treten; ~ **di'spute** *n.* Arbeitskonflikt, *der;* ~ **'espionage** *n.* Industriespionage, *die;* ~ **exhibition** *n.* Industrieausstellung, *die;* ~ **'injury** *n.* Arbeitsverletzung, *die*

industrialisation, industrialise *see* **industrializ-**

industrialist [ɪn'dʌstrɪəlɪst] *n.* Industrielle, *der/die*

industrialization [ɪndʌstrɪəlaɪ'zeɪʃn] *n.* Industrialisierung, *die*

industrialize [ɪn'dʌstrɪəlaɪz] *v.i. & t.* industrialisieren

industrially [ɪn'dʌstrɪəlɪ] *adv.* industriell

industrial: ~ park *n.* Industriegebiet, *das;* ~ **plant** *n.* Industrieanlage, *die;* ~ **re'lations** *n. pl.* Industrial relations *Pl. (Wirtsch.)*; *Beziehungen zwischen Arbeitgebern und Gewerkschaften;* **I~ Revo'lution** *n. (Hist.)* industrielle Revolution; ~ **'town** *n.* Industriestadt, *die;* ~ **un'rest** *n.* Unruhe in der Arbeitnehmerschaft; ~ **'waste** *n.* Industriemüll, *der*

industrious [ɪn'dʌstrɪəs] *adj.* fleißig; *(busy)* emsig

industriously [ɪn'dʌstrɪəslɪ] *adv.* fleißig; *(busily)* emsig

industry ['ɪndəstrɪ] *n.* **a)** Industrie, *die;* **several industries** mehrere Industriezweige; **steel/coal ~:** Stahl-/Kohleindustrie, *die;* **the nation's ~:** die Industrie des Landes; **in-**

centives to ~: Maßnahmen zur Förderung des industriellen Wachstums; **the leaders of ~:** die Industriebosse *(ugs.)*; die Industriemanager; **~ is thriving** die Industrie blüht; **his experience of ~:** seine Erfahrungen auf dem industriellen Sektor; **the Shakespeare/abortion ~** *(coll.)* die Vermarktung Shakespeares/das Geschäft mit der Abtreibung; **b)** *see* **industrious:** Fleiß, *der;* Emsigkeit, *die*

inebriated [ɪ'ni:brɪeɪtɪd] *adj.* **a)** *(drunk)* betrunken; **b)** *(fig.)* berauscht **(with** von); trunken *(geh.)* **(with** von, vor + *Dat.*)

inedible [ɪn'edɪbl] *adj.* ungenießbar

ineducable [ɪn'edjʊkəbl] *adj.* lernunfähig

ineffable [ɪn'efəbl] *adj.* unbeschreiblich

ineffective [ɪnɪ'fektɪv] *adj.* **a)** unwirksam; ineffektiv; fruchtlos ⟨*Anstrengung, Versuch*⟩; ineffizient ⟨*Produktionsmethoden*⟩; wirkungslos ⟨*Argument*⟩; **b)** *(inefficient)* untauglich; **c)** *(lacking artistic effect)* reizlos

ineffectively [ɪnɪ'fektɪvlɪ] *adv.* unwirksam; ineffektiv

ineffectiveness [ɪnɪ'fektɪvnɪs] *n., no pl. see* **ineffective:** Unwirksamkeit, *die;* Ineffizienz, *die;* Fruchtlosigkeit, *die;* Wirkungslosigkeit, *die;* Untauglichkeit, *die;* Reizlosigkeit, *die*

ineffectual [ɪnɪ'fektjʊəl] *adj.* unwirksam; ineffektiv; fruchtlos ⟨*Versuch, Bemühung*⟩; ineffizient ⟨*Methode, Person*⟩

ineffectually [ɪnɪ'fektjʊəlɪ] *adv.* vergebens; ohne Aussagekraft ⟨*schreiben*⟩

inefficacious [ɪnefɪ'keɪʃəs] *adj.* unwirksam; wirkungslos

inefficacy [ɪn'efɪkəsɪ] *n., no pl.* *(of measures)* Unwirksamkeit, *die;* Wirkungslosigkeit, *die*

inefficiency [ɪnɪ'fɪʃənsɪ] *n.* Ineffizienz, *die; (incapability)* Unfähigkeit, *die*

inefficient [ɪnɪ'fɪʃənt] *adj.* ineffizient; *(incapable)* unfähig; **the worker/machine is ~:** der Arbeiter/die Maschine leistet nicht genug

inefficiently [ɪnɪ'fɪʃəntlɪ] *adv.* ineffizient; **do one's job too ~:** zu wenig leisten

inelastic [ɪnɪ'læstɪk, ɪnɪ'lɑ:stɪk] *adj.* **a)** *(not elastic)* unelastisch; **b)** *(unadaptable)* nicht flexibel

inelegance [ɪn'elɪgəns] *n., no pl.* **a)** *(of dress)* Mangel an Eleganz; *(of gestures, movements, gait)* Schwerfälligkeit, *die;* **b)** *(lack of refinement, polish)* Ungeschliffenheit, *die (abwertend)*

inelegant [ɪn'elɪgənt] *adj.* **a)** unelegant; schwerfällig ⟨*Bewegung, Gang*⟩; **b)** *(unrefined, unpolished)* ungeschliffen *(abwertend)*

inelegantly [ɪn'elɪgəntlɪ] *adv.* **a)** unelegant; schwerfällig ⟨*sich bewegen*⟩; **b)** *(without refinement or polish)* ungeschliffen *(abwertend)*

ineligible [ɪn'elɪdʒɪbl] *adj.* ungeeignet; **be ~ for** nicht in Frage kommen für ⟨*Beförderung, Position, Mannschaft*⟩; nicht berechtigt sein zu ⟨*Leistungen des Staats usw.*⟩; **be ~ for a pension** nicht pensionsberechtigt sein

ineluctable [ɪnɪ'lʌktəbl] *adj. (literary) (remorseless)* unbarmherzig; *(not to be opposed)* unausweichlich; unentrinnbar *(geh.)* ⟨*Schicksal*⟩

inept [ɪ'nept] *adj.* **a)** *(unskilful, clumsy)* unbeholfen; **b)** *(inappropriate)* unangemessen, unpassend ⟨*Vergleich*⟩; unpassend, unangebracht ⟨*Bemerkung, Eingreifen*⟩; **c)** *(foolish)* albern

ineptitude [ɪ'neptɪtju:d] *n., no pl.* **a)** *(unskilfulness, clumsiness)* Unbeholfenheit, *die;* **b)** *(inappropriateness) (of comparison)* Unangemessenheit, *die; (of remark, intervention)* Unangebrachtheit, *die;* **c)** *(foolishness)* Albernheit, *die*

ineptly [ɪ'neptlɪ] *adv.* **a)** *(unskilfully, clumsily)* unbeholfen; **b)** *(inappropriately)* **intervene ~:** in unangebrachter Weise eingreifen; **c)** *(foolishly)* albern

ineptness *see* **ineptitude**

inequable [ɪn'ekwəbl] *adj.* **a)** *(not uniform)* ungleichmäßig; **b)** *(not fair)* ungleich

inequality [ɪnɪ'kwɒlɪtɪ] *n.* **a)** *(lack of equality)* Ungleichheit, *die;* **great inequalities between rich and poor** große Ungleichheit zwischen arm und reich; **educational ~:** Ungleichheit der Bildungschancen; **the inequalities in income** die ungleiche Einkommensverteilung; **b)** *(variableness)* Veränderlichkeit, *die; (in time)* Unbeständigkeit, *die;* **c)** *(irregularity)* Unebenheit, *die;* **d)** *(Math.)* Ungleichheit, *die; (expression)* Ungleichung, *die*

inequitable [ɪn'ekwɪtəbl] *adj.*, **inequitably** [ɪn'ekwɪtəblɪ] *adv.* ungerecht

inequity [ɪn'ekwɪtɪ] *n.* Ungerechtigkeit, *die*

ineradicable [ɪnɪ'rædɪkəbl] *adj.* unausrottbar ⟨*Vorurteil, Aberglaube*⟩

inert [ɪ'nɜ:t] *adj.* **a)** reglos; *(sluggish)* träge; *(passive)* untätig; **b)** *(Chem.: neutral)* inert

inert 'gas *n. (Chem.)* Edelgas, *das*

inertia [ɪ'nɜ:ʃə, ɪ'nɜ:ʃjə] *n. (also Phys.)* Trägheit, *die; see also* **moment c**

inertial [ɪ'nɜ:ʃl] *adj.* **a)** Trägheits-; **b)** *(performed automatically)* Automatik-

inertia: ~ reel *n.* Aufrollautomatik, *die;* **~ reel seat-belt** Automatikgurt, *der;* **~ selling** *n.* unverlangte Warenzusendung

inertly [ɪ'nɜ:tlɪ] *adv.* reglos; *(sluggishly)* träge; *(passively)* untätig

inescapable [ɪnɪ'skeɪpəbl] *adj.* unausweichlich ⟨*Schlußfolgerung, Logik*⟩; **the facts were ~:** man konnte sich den Tatsachen nicht entziehen

inessential [ɪnɪ'senʃl] **1.** *adj. (not necessary)* unwesentlich; *(dispensable)* entbehrlich. **2.** *n.* Nebensächlichkeit, *die*

inestimable [ɪn'estɪməbl] *adj.* unschätzbar

inevitability [ɪnevɪtə'bɪlɪtɪ] *n., no pl.* Unvermeidlichkeit, *die; (of fate, event)* Unabwendbarkeit, *die*

inevitable [ɪn'evɪtəbl] *adj.* unvermeidlich; unabwendbar ⟨*Ereignis, Krieg, Schicksal*⟩; zwangsläufig ⟨*Ergebnis, Folge*⟩; **bow to the ~:** sich in das Unvermeidliche fügen

inevitably [ɪn'evɪtəblɪ] *adv.* zwangsläufig

inexact [ɪnɪg'zækt] *adj.* ungenau

inexactitude [ɪnɪg'zæktɪtju:d] *see* **inexactness**

inexactly [ɪnɪg'zæktlɪ] *adv.* ungenau

inexactness [ɪnɪg'zæktnɪs] *n.* Ungenauigkeit, *die*

inexcusable [ɪnɪk'skju:zəbl] *adj.*, **inexcusably** [ɪnɪk'skju:zəblɪ] *adv.* unverzeihlich; unentschuldbar

inexhaustible [ɪnɪg'zɔ:stɪbl] *adj.* unerschöpflich ⟨*Reserven, Quelle, Energie*⟩; unverwüstlich ⟨*Person*⟩

inexorable [ɪn'eksərəbl] *adj.*, **inexorably** [ɪn'eksərəblɪ] *adv.* unerbittlich

inexpediency [ɪnɪk'spi:dɪənsɪ] *n., no pl.* Unklugheit, *die; (of plan, measure)* Ungeeignetheit, *die*

inexpedient [ɪnɪk'spi:dɪənt] *adj.* unklug ⟨*Entscheidung, Politik*⟩; ungeeignet ⟨*Plan, Maßnahme*⟩; **she thought it somewhat ~ to reveal the names** es erschien ihr wenig ratsam, die Namen preiszugeben

inexpensive [ɪnɪk'spensɪv] *adj.* preisgünstig; **the car is ~ to run** der Wagen ist sparsam im Verbrauch

inexpensively [ɪnɪk'spensɪvlɪ] *adv.* günstig ⟨*kaufen*⟩; unaufwendig ⟨*leben*⟩; ohne viel Geld ⟨*einrichten*⟩

inexperience [ɪnɪk'spɪərɪəns] *n.* Unerfahrenheit, *die;* Mangel an Erfahrung; **his ~ with this machine** seine mangelnde Vertrautheit mit dieser Maschine

inexperienced [ɪnɪk'spɪərɪənst] *adj.* unerfahren; **~ at doing sth.** wenig damit vertraut, etw. zu tun; **~ in sth.** wenig vertraut mit etw.

inexpert [ɪn'ekspɜ:t] *adj.* unerfahren; *(unskilled)* ungeschickt; unsachgemäß ⟨*Behandlung*⟩

inexpertly [ɪn'ekspɜ:tlɪ] *adv.* ungeschickt; unsachgemäß ⟨*behandeln*⟩

inexplicable [ɪnek'splɪkəbl] *adj.* unerklärlich

inexplicably [ɪnek'splɪkəblɪ] *adv.* unerklärlich ⟨*hoch, langsam*⟩; *as sentence-modifier* unerklärlicherweise

inexpressible [ɪnɪk'spresɪbl] *adj.*, **inexpressibly** [ɪnɪk'spresɪblɪ] *adv.* unbeschreiblich

inextinguishable [ɪnɪk'stɪŋgwɪʃəbl] *adj.* nicht löschbar ⟨*Feuer, Flamme*⟩; unauslöschlich ⟨*Liebe, Hoffnung, Sehnsucht, Verlangen*⟩

in extremis [ɪn ek'stri:mɪs] *adv.* **a)** *(in great difficulties)* in äußerster Not; **b)** *(at point of death)* in extremis *(Med.)*; **be ~:** im Sterben liegen

inextricable [ɪn'ekstrɪkəbl] *adj.* **a)** *(that cannot be unravelled)* unentwirrbar; **b)** unüberschaubar ⟨*Durcheinander*⟩

inextricably [ɪn'ekstrɪkəblɪ] *adv.* **become ~ entangled** sich vollkommen verheddern *(ugs.)*; **[be] ~ linked** untrennbar verbunden [sein]

INF *abbr.* **intermediate-range nuclear force** Mittelstrecken-Nuklearkräfte *Pl.*

infallibility [ɪnfælɪ'bɪlɪtɪ] *n., no pl.* Unfehlbarkeit, *die;* **Papal I~:** päpstliche Unfehlbarkeit; Infallibilität, *die (kath. Kirche)*

infallible [ɪn'fælɪbl] *adj.*, **infallibly** [ɪn'fælɪblɪ] *adv.* unfehlbar

infamous ['ɪnfəməs] *adj.* **a)** berüchtigt; **of ~ repute** verrufen; **b)** *(wicked)* infam; niederträchtig

infamy ['ɪnfəmɪ] *n.* **a)** Verrufenheit, *die;* **b)** *(wickedness)* Infamie, *die;* Niederträchtigkeit, *die*

infancy ['ɪnfənsɪ] *n.* **a)** frühe Kindheit; **b)** *(fig.: early state)* Frühzeit, *die;* **be in its ~:** noch in den Anfängen *od.* Kinderschuhen stecken; **c)** *(Law)* Minderjährigkeit, *die*

infant ['ɪnfənt] **1.** *n.* **a)** kleines Kind; **teach ~s** ≈ Vorschulklassen unterrichten; **b)** *(Law)* Minderjährige, *der/die.* **2.** *adj.* **a)** kindlich; **b)** *(fig.: not developed)* in den Anfängen steckend

infanta [ɪn'fæntə] *n. (Hist.)* Infantin, *die*

infanticide [ɪn'fæntɪsaɪd] *n.* Kindesmord, *der; (custom)* Kindestötung, *die*

infantile ['ɪnfəntaɪl] *adj.* **a)** *(relating to infancy)* kindlich; **b)** *(childish)* kindisch *(abwertend)*; infantil *(abwertend)*

infant: ~ mor'tality *n.* Säuglingssterblichkeit, *die;* **~ 'prodigy** *n.* Wunderkind, *das*

infantry ['ɪnfəntrɪ] *n. constr. as sing. or pl.* Infanterie, *die*

infantryman ['ɪnfəntrɪmən] *n., pl.* **infantrymen** ['ɪnfəntrɪmən] Infanterist, *der*

'infant school *n. (Brit.)* ≈ Vorschule, *die; Grundschule für die ersten beiden Jahrgänge*

infarction ['ɪnfɑ:kʃn] *n. (Med.)* Infarkt, *der*

infatuated [ɪn'fætjʊeɪtɪd] *adj.* betört *(geh.)*; verzaubert; **be ~ with sb./oneself** in jmdn./sich selbst vernarrt sein

infatuation [ɪnfætjʊ'eɪʃn] *n.* Vernarrtheit, *die* **(with** in + *Akk.*)

infect [ɪn'fekt] *v. t.* **a)** *(contaminate)* verseuchen; **b)** *(affect with disease)* infizieren *(Med.)*; **~ sb. with sth.** jmdn. mit etw. infizieren *od.* anstecken; **the wound became ~ed** die Wunde entzündete sich; **be ~ed with sth.** *(fig.)* von etw. infiziert sein; **c)** *(imbue)* anstecken

infection [ɪn'fekʃn] *n.* Infektion, *die;* **throat/ear/eye ~:** Hals-/Ohren-/Augenentzündung, *die*

infectious [ɪn'fekʃəs] *adj.* **a)** infektiös *(Med.)*, ansteckend ⟨*Krankheit*⟩; **be ~** ⟨*Person:*⟩ eine ansteckende Krankheit haben; ansteckend sein *(ugs.)*; **b)** *(fig.)* ansteckend ⟨*Heiterkeit, Begeisterung, Lachen*⟩

infectiously [ɪn'fekʃəslɪ] *adv.* ansteckend ⟨*lachen usw.*⟩
infectiousness [ɪn'fekʃəsnɪs] *n., no pl.* **a)** Infektiosität, *die (Med.);* Ansteckungsfähigkeit, *die;* **b)** *(fig.)* **the ~ of her enthusiasm** ihre ansteckend wirkende *od.* mitreißende Begeisterung
infelicitous [ɪnfɪ'lɪsɪtəs] *adj.*, **infelicitously** [ɪnfɪ'lɪsɪtəslɪ] *adv.* unangebracht
infelicity [ɪnfɪ'lɪsɪtɪ] *n.* Unangebrachtheit, *die;* **infelicities of style** stilistische Ungeschicklichkeiten
infer [ɪn'fɜ:(r)] *v. t.*, **-rr-** schließen **(from** aus); erschließen ⟨*Voraussetzung*⟩; gewinnen ⟨*Kenntnisse*⟩; ziehen ⟨*Schlußfolgerung*⟩
inference ['ɪnfərəns] *n.* [Schluß]folgerung, *die;* **make ~s** [Schluß]folgerungen ableiten *od.* ziehen; **by ~:** schlußfolgernd
inferential [ɪnfə'renʃl] *adj.* **a)** auf [Schluß]folgerungen beruhend; schlußfolgernd; **b)** *(deduced by inference)* gefolgert
inferior [ɪn'fɪərɪə(r)] **1.** *adj.* **a)** *(of lower quality)* minderwertig ⟨*Ware*⟩; minder... ⟨*Qualität*⟩; gering ⟨*Kenntnis*⟩; unter..., nieder... ⟨*Klasse, Kaste*⟩; unterlegen ⟨*Gegner*⟩; **~ to sth.** schlechter als etw.; **feel ~:** Minderwertigkeitsgefühle haben; **feel ~ to sb.** sich jmdm. gegenüber unterlegen fühlen; **b)** *(having lower rank)* untergeordnet **(to** *Dat.***)**; **c)** *(Printing)* tiefgestellt ⟨*Buchstabe, Zahl*⟩. **2.** *n.* Untergebene, *der/die;* **his social ~s** die gesellschaftlich unter ihm Stehenden
inferiority [ɪnfɪərɪ'ɒrɪtɪ] *n., no pl.* Unterlegenheit, *die* **(to** gegenüber); *(of goods)* schlechtere Qualität
inferi'ority complex *n. (Psych.)* Minderwertigkeitskomplex, *der*
infernal [ɪn'fɜ:nl] *adj.* **a)** *(of hell)* höllisch; ⟨*Regionen, Geister, Götter*⟩ der Unterwelt; **b)** *(hellish)* teuflisch; **c)** *(coll.: detestable)* verdammt *(salopp)*
infernally [ɪn'fɜ:nəlɪ] *adv. (coll.)* verdammt; **he is too ~ clever for me** er ist, verdammt noch mal, zu clever für mich *(ugs.)*
inferno [ɪn'fɜ:nəʊ] *n., pl.* **~s** Inferno, *das;* **a blazing ~:** ein flammendes Inferno; **the ~ of the blazing house** das Flammenmeer des brennenden Hauses
infertile [ɪn'fɜ:taɪl] *adj.* unfruchtbar
infertility [ɪnfɜ:'tɪlɪtɪ] *n., no pl.* Unfruchtbarkeit, *die*
infest [ɪn'fest] *v. t.* ⟨*Ungeziefer, Schädlinge:*⟩ befallen; ⟨*Unkraut:*⟩ überwuchern; *(fig.)* heimsuchen; **~ed with** befallen/überwuchert/heimgesucht von
infestation [ɪnfes'teɪʃn] *n.* **~ of rats/insects** Ratten-/Insektenplage, *die*
infidel ['ɪnfɪdəl] *n. (Relig. Hist.)* Ungläubige, *der/die*
infidelity [ɪnfɪ'delɪtɪ] *n.* Untreue, *die* **(to** gegenüber); **infidelities** *(to lover, wife, husband)* Seitensprünge
'infighting *n.* **a)** *(in organization)* interne Machtkämpfe; **b)** *(Boxing)* Nahkampf, *der*
infiltrate ['ɪnfɪltreɪt] **1.** *v. t.* **a)** *(penetrate into)* infiltrieren ⟨*feindliche Reihen*⟩; unterwandern ⟨*Partei, Organisation*⟩; **b)** *(cause to enter)* einschleusen ⟨*Agenten*⟩; **c)** *(esp. Biol., Med.: pass into, permeate)* infiltrieren. **2.** *v. i.* **a)** *(penetrate)* einsickern *(fig.);* **~ into** unterwandern ⟨*Partei, Organisation*⟩; infiltrieren ⟨*feindliche Reihen*⟩; **b)** ⟨*Flüssigkeit:*⟩ eindringen
infiltration [ɪnfɪl'treɪʃn] *n.* **a)** *(penetration) (of enemy lines)* Infiltration, *die; (of party, organization)* Unterwanderung, *die* **(into** *Gen.***)**; **b)** *(of spies, agents)* Einschleusung, *die;* **c)** *(of liquid)* Einsickern, *das*
infiltrator ['ɪnfɪltreɪtə(r)] *n.* Eindringling, *der; (of party, organization)* Unterwanderer, *der*
infinite ['ɪnfɪnɪt] *adj.* **a)** *(endless)* unendlich; **I don't have an ~ amount of time/money** ich habe nicht unbegrenzt Zeit/keine unbegrenzten Mittel; **b)** *(very great)* ungeheuer; unendlich groß; **c)** *(very many)* endlos; **his problems seemed to be ~:** seine Probleme schienen kein Ende zu nehmen; **d)** *(Math.)* unendlich
infinitely ['ɪnfɪnɪtlɪ] *adv.* **a)** *(endlessly)* unendlich ⟨*mitfühlend, dumm usw.*⟩; endlos ⟨*sich erstrecken, teilbar*⟩; **b)** *(vastly)* unendlich; unendlich viel ⟨*weiser, stärker, besser*⟩
infinitesimal [ɪnfɪnɪ'tesɪml] *adj.* **a)** *(Math.)* infinitesimal; *see also* **calculus a; b)** *(very small)* äußerst gering; winzig ⟨*Menge*⟩; **be of ~ value** so gut wie wertlos sein
infinitive [ɪn'fɪnɪtɪv] *(Ling.)* **1.** *n.* Infinitiv, *der.* **2.** *adj.* Infinitiv-
infinity [ɪn'fɪnɪtɪ] *n.* **a)** *(boundlessness, boundless extent)* Unendlichkeit, *die;* **b)** *(indefinite amount)* **an ~ of [stars** *etc.***]** unendlich viele [Sterne *usw.*]; **c)** *(Geom.: infinite distance)* **at ~:** im Unendlichen ⟨*sich schneiden*⟩; **focus on ~** *(Photog.)* auf unendlich stellen; **d)** *(Math.: infinite quantity)* unendliche Menge
infirm [ɪn'fɜ:m] *adj.* **a)** *(weak)* gebrechlich; **b)** *(irresolute)* schwach; **~ of purpose** *(literary)* willensschwach
infirmary [ɪn'fɜ:mərɪ] *n.* **a)** *(hospital)* Krankenhaus, *das;* **b)** *(sick-quarters)* Krankenstation, *die; (room)* Krankenzimmer, *das*
infirmity [ɪn'fɜ:mɪtɪ] *n.* **a)** *no pl. (feebleness)* Gebrechlichkeit, *die;* **b)** *(malady)* Gebrechen, *das (geh.);* **c)** *(weakness of character)* Schwäche, *die*
in flagrante [delicto] [ɪn flæ'græntɪ (de'lɪktəʊ)] *adv.* in flagranti
inflame [ɪn'fleɪm] *v. t.* **a)** *(excite)* entflammen *(geh.);* **~d with patriotic fever** in patriotischem Fieber entbrannt; **b)** *(aggravate)* schüren ⟨*Feindschaft, Haß*⟩; **c)** *(Med.)* **become/be ~d** ⟨*Auge, Wunde:*⟩ sich entzünden/entzündet sein; **d)** *(make hot)* erhitzen; **his face was ~d with anger/passion** sein Gesicht glühte vor Zorn/Leidenschaft
inflammability [ɪnflæmə'bɪlɪtɪ] *n., no pl.* Feuergefährlichkeit, *die;* Entflammbarkeit, *die (Chemie)*
inflammable [ɪn'flæməbl] *adj.* **a)** *(easily set on fire)* feuergefährlich; leicht entzündlich *od.* entflammbar; **'highly ~'** „feuergefährlich"; **b)** explosiv ⟨*Situation*⟩
inflammation [ɪnflə'meɪʃn] *n.* **a)** *(Med.)* Entzündung, *die;* Inflammation, *die (fachspr.);* **b)** *(fig.: of feeling etc.)* Entfachung, *die (geh.)*
inflammatory [ɪn'flæmətərɪ] *adj.* **a)** aufrührerisch; **an ~ speech** eine Hetzrede *(abwertend);* **b)** *(Med.)* entzündlich
inflatable [ɪn'fleɪtəbl] **1.** *adj.* aufblasbar; **~ dinghy** Schlauchboot, *das.* **2.** *n.* **a)** *(boat)* Schlauchboot, *das;* **b)** *(to jump around on)* Luftkissen, *das*
inflate [ɪn'fleɪt] *v. t.* **a)** *(distend)* aufblasen; *(with pump)* aufpumpen; **b)** *(Econ.)* in die Höhe treiben ⟨*Preise, Kosten*⟩; inflationieren ⟨*Währung*⟩; **~ the economy** Inflationspolitik betreiben; **c)** *(fig.: puff up)* **be ~d with pride** von Stolz geschwellt sein
inflated [ɪn'fleɪtɪd] *adj. (lit or fig.)* aufgeblasen; geschwollen ⟨*Stil*⟩; **have an ~ opinion of oneself** aufgeblasen sein *(ugs. abwertend);* **have an ~ ego** ein übertriebenes Selbstbewußtsein haben
inflation [ɪn'fleɪʃn] *n.* **a)** Aufblasen, *das; (with pump)* Aufpumpen, *das;* **b)** *(Econ.)* Inflation, *die*
inflationary [ɪn'fleɪʃənərɪ] *adj. (Econ.)* inflationär; **~ policies** Inflationspolitik, *die*
in'flation-proofed *adj.* mit Inflationsausgleich *nachgestellt*
inflect [ɪn'flekt] *v. t.* **a)** *(Ling.)* flektieren; beugen; **b)** *(change pitch)* modulieren ⟨*Stimme*⟩
inflection *see* **inflexion**
inflectional *see* **inflexional**
inflective [ɪn'flektɪv] *see* **inflexional**
inflexibility [ɪnfleksɪ'bɪlɪtɪ] *n., no pl.* **a)** *(stiffness)* Unbiegsamkeit, *die;* **b)** *(obstinacy)* [geistige] Unbeweglichkeit; *(lack of versatility)* mangelnde Flexibilität
inflexible [ɪn'fleksɪbl] *adj.* **a)** *(stiff)* unbiegsam; **b)** *(obstinate)* [geistig] unbeweglich ⟨*Person*⟩; wenig flexibel ⟨*Einstellung, Meinung*⟩
inflexion [ɪn'flekʃn] *n. (Brit.)* **a)** *(in voice)* Tonfall, *der;* **a rising ~:** ein Heben der Stimme; **b)** *(bending)* Biegung, *die;* **c)** *(Ling.) (form)* Flexionsform, *die; (suffix)* Flexionsendung, *die*
inflexional [ɪn'flekʃənl] *adj. (Brit. Ling.)* flektierend ⟨*Sprache*⟩; **~ ending** Flexionsendung, *die*
inflict [ɪn'flɪkt] *v. t.* zufügen ⟨*Leid, Schmerzen*⟩, beibringen ⟨*Wunde*⟩, versetzen ⟨*Schlag*⟩ **(on** *Dat.***)**; **~ punishment [on sb.]** eine Strafe [über jmdn.] verhängen; [jmdm.] eine Strafe auferlegen *(geh.);* **~ oneself** *or* **one's company on sb.** sich jmdm. aufdrängen
infliction [ɪn'flɪkʃn] *n.: see* **inflict:** Zufügen, *das;* Beibringen, *das;* Versetzen, *das;* Verhängung, *die*
'in-flight *adj.* Bord⟨*verpflegung, -programm*⟩
inflorescence [ɪnflə'resəns] *n. (Bot.)* Blütenstand, *der*
'inflow *n.* Zustrom, *der*
influence ['ɪnflʊəns] **1.** *n. (also thing, person)* Einfluß, *der;* **exercise ~:** Einfluß ausüben (**over** *just* **+** *Akk.*); **owe sth. to ~:** etw. seinen guten Beziehungen verdanken; **have ~ with/over sb.** Einfluß bei jmdm./auf jmdn. haben; **use one's ~ to do sth.** seinen Einfluß nutzen, um etw. zu tun; **you have to have ~ to get a job** man muß Beziehungen haben, um eine Stelle zu bekommen; **a person of ~:** eine einflußreiche Persönlichkeit; **be a good/bad/major ~ [on sb.]** einen guten/schlechten/bedeutenden Einfluß [auf jmdn.] ausüben; **under the ~ of alcohol** unter Alkoholeinfluß; **be under the ~** *(coll.)* betrunken sein; **steal a car while under the ~** *(coll.)* in betrunkenem Zustand ein Auto stehlen. **2.** *v. t.* beeinflussen; **be too easily ~d** sich zu leicht beeinflussen lassen
influential [ɪnflʊ'enʃl] *adj.* einflußreich ⟨*Person*⟩; **be ~ in sb.'s decision/on sb.'s career** jmdn. in seiner Entscheidung beeinflussen/jmds. Karriere beeinflussen; **have been ~ in the successful outcome of sth.** den erfolgreichen Ausgang einer Sache *(Gen.)* beeinflußt haben
influenza [ɪnflʊ'enzə] *n.* Grippe, *die; see also* **gastric influenza**
influx ['ɪnflʌks] *n.* Zustrom, *der*
info ['ɪnfəʊ] *n., no pl. (coll.)* Informationen
inform [ɪn'fɔ:m] **1.** *n.* **a)** informieren **(of, about** über + *Akk.***)**; **I am pleased to ~ you that ...:** ich freue mich, Ihnen mitteilen zu können, daß ...; **keep sb./oneself ~ed** jmdn./sich auf dem laufenden halten; **he is not very well ~ed** er ist nicht besonders gut informiert; **why wasn't I ~ed?** warum wurde ich nicht [darüber] informiert?; **b)** *(animate, inspire)* durchdringen; **c)** *(give character or essence to)* prägen. **2.** *v. i.* **~ against** *or* **on sb.** jmdn. anzeigen *od. (abwertend)* denunzieren **(to** bei)
informal [ɪn'fɔ:ml] *adj.* **a)** *(without formality)* zwanglos; ungezwungen ⟨*Ton, Sprache*⟩; leger ⟨*Kleidungsstück*⟩; **'dress: ~'** „keine festliche Garderobe"; **b)** *(unofficial)* informell ⟨*Gespräch, Treffen*⟩
informality [ɪnfɔ:'mælɪtɪ] *n. no pl.* Zwanglosigkeit, *die;* Ungezwungenheit, *die*
informally [ɪn'fɔ:məlɪ] *adv.* **a)** *(casually)* zwanglos; leger ⟨*gekleidet*⟩; **b)** *(unofficially)* informell; **talks are proceeding ~:** die Gespräche laufen auf informeller Ebene
informant [ɪn'fɔ:mənt] *n.* Informant, *der/* Informantin, *die;* Gewährsmann, *der*

informatics [ɪnfə'mætɪks] *n. sing.* *(Brit.)* Informatik, *die*
information [ɪnfə'meɪʃn] *n., no pl.* **a)** *no indef. art.* Informationen; **give ~ on sth.** Auskunft über etw. *(Akk.)* erteilen; **piece** *or* **bit of ~:** Information, *die;* **some/any ~:** einige/irgendwelche Informationen; **source of ~:** Informationsquelle, *die;* **where can we get hold of some ~?** wo können wir uns informieren?; wo können wir Auskunft bekommen?; **have ~ about sth.** über etw. *(Akk.)* informiert sein; **have no ~ on sb.** nichts über jmdn. wissen; **we have ~ that ...:** uns *(Dat.)* liegen Informationen [darüber] vor, daß ...; **for your ~:** zu Ihrer Information; *(iron.)* damit du Bescheid weißt!; **b)** *(Law)* Anklage, *die*
information: ~ bureau, ~ centre *ns.* Auskunftsbüro, *das;* **~ desk** *n.* Informationsschalter, *der;* **~ explosion** *n.* Informationsflut, *die;* **~ office** *see* **~ bureau; ~ retrieval** *n.* Information Retrieval, *das (DV);* Wiederauffinden von Informationen; **~ science** *n.* Informatik, *die;* **~ scientist** *n.* Informatiker, *der*/Informatikerin, *die;* **~ technology** *n.* Informationstechnologie, *die;* Informationstechnik, *die;* **~ theory** *n.* Informationstheorie, *die*
informative [ɪn'fɔ:mətɪv] *adj.* informativ; **not very ~:** nicht sehr aufschlußreich ‹*Dokument, Schriftstück*›; **he was not very ~ about his qualifications** er war nicht sehr mitteilsam, was seine Qualifikationen anbelangte
informed [ɪn'fɔ:md] *adj.* **a)** informiert; fundiert ‹*Schätzung*›; **very ~:** sehr gut informiert; *see also* **ill-informed; well-informed; b)** *(educated)* kultiviert; **~ opinion suggests that ...:** Kundige meinen, daß ...
informer [ɪn'fɔ:mə(r)] *n.* Denunziant, *der*/Denunziantin, *die (abwertend);* Informant, *der*/Informantin, *die;* **police ~:** Polizeispitzel, *der (abwertend)*
infraction [ɪn'frækʃn] *n.* Übertretung, *die;* Regelverstoß, *der (Sport)*
infra dig. [ɪnfrə'dɪg] *pred. adj.* *(coll.)* unter meiner/seiner *usw.* Würde
infra-red [ɪnfrə'red] *adj.* **a)** infrarot; **b)** *(using ~ radiation)* Infrarot-
infrastructure ['ɪnfrəstrʌktʃə(r)] *n.* Infrastruktur, *die*
infrequency [ɪn'fri:kwənsɪ] *n., no pl.* Seltenheit, *die*
infrequent [ɪn'fri:kwənt] *adj.* **a)** *(uncommon)* selten; **b)** *(sparse)* vereinzelt
infrequently [ɪn'fri:kwəntlɪ] *adv.* selten
infringe [ɪn'frɪndʒ] **1.** *v. t.* verstoßen gegen. **2.** *v. i.* **~ [up]on** verstoßen gegen ‹*Recht, Gesetz usw.*›; unbefugt betreten ‹*Privatgelände usw.*›; **~ upon sb.'s privacy** jmds. Privatsphäre verletzen
infringement [ɪn'frɪndʒmənt] *n.* **a)** *(violation)* Verstoß, *der* **(of** gegen); **~ of the contract** Vertragsverletzung, *die;* Vertragsbruch, *der;* **b)** *(encroachment)* Übergriff, *der* **(on** auf + *Akk.*); *(on privacy)* Eingriff, *der* **(on** in + *Akk.*)
infuriate [ɪn'fjʊərɪeɪt] *v. t.* wütend machen; **be ~d** wütend sein **(by** über + *Akk.*)
infuriating [ɪn'fjʊərɪeɪtɪŋ] *adj.* **she is an ~ person** sie kann einen zur Raserei bringen; **it is ~ when/that ...:** es ist wahnsinnig ärgerlich, wenn/daß ... *(ugs.);* **he has some ~ habits** er hat einige Angewohnheiten, die einen rasend machen können; **~ calmness/slowness** aufreizende Gelassenheit/Langsamkeit
infuriatingly [ɪn'fjʊərɪeɪtɪŋlɪ] *adv.* aufreizend ‹*gleichgültig, langsam*›
infuse [ɪn'fju:z] **1.** *v. t.* **a)** *(instil)* **~ sth. into sb., ~ sb. with sth.** jmdm. etw. einflößen *od.* *(geh.)* eingeben; **~ new life into an ancient institution** eine altehrwürdige Institution mit neuem Leben erfüllen; **~ vitality into** mit Vitalität erfüllen; **be ~d with new hope** neue Hoffnung schöpfen; **b)** *(steep)* aufgießen ‹*Tee usw.*›. **2.** *v. i.* ‹*Tee usw.*:› ziehen; **let the tea [stand to] ~:** den Tee ziehen lassen
infusion [ɪn'fju:ʒn] *n.* **a)** *(Med.)* Infusion, *die;* **an ~ of new blood into the organization is essential** *(fig.)* die Organisation braucht dringend frisches Blut; **b)** *(imparting)* Einflößen, *das;* **c)** *(steeping)* Aufgießen, *das;* **d)** *(liquid)* Aufguß, *der*
ingenious [ɪn'dʒi:nɪəs] *adj.* **a)** *(resourceful)* einfallsreich; *(skilful)* geschickt; **b)** *(cleverly constructed)* genial ‹*Methode, Idee*›; raffiniert ‹*Spielzeug, Werkzeug, Maschine*›
ingeniously [ɪn'dʒi:nɪəslɪ] *adv.* genial; raffiniert ‹*konstruiert*›
ingénue ['æʒeɪnju:] *n.* unschuldiges junges Mädchen; *(Theatre)* Naive, *die*
ingenuity [ɪndʒɪ'nju:ɪtɪ] *n., no pl.* **a)** *(resourcefulness)* Einfallsreichtum, *der;* *(skill)* Geschicklichkeit, *die;* **b)** *(cleverness of construction)* Genialität, *die;* **a plan of some ~:** ein recht raffinierter Plan
ingenuous [ɪn'dʒenjʊəs] *adj.* **a)** *(frank)* freimütig; **b)** *(innocent)* naiv; unschuldig ‹*Augen, Lächeln*›
ingenuously [ɪn'dʒenjʊəslɪ] *adv.* freimütig
ingest [ɪn'dʒest] *v. t.* aufnehmen
ingestion [ɪn'dʒestʃn] *n.* Aufnahme, *die;* **~ of food** Nahrungsaufnahme, *die*
inglenook ['ɪŋglnʊk] *n.* Kaminecke, *die*
inglorious [ɪn'glɔ:rɪəs] *adj.* unrühmlich; schmählich *(geh.)* ‹*Niederlage*›
ingot ['ɪŋgət] *n.* Ingot, *der (Metall.)*
ingrained ['ɪngreɪnd, ɪn'greɪnd] *adj.* **a)** *(embedded)* **the stain was deeply ~ in the fibres** der Fleck war tief in die Fasern eingedrungen; **hands ~ with dirt** stark verschmutzte Hände; **b)** *(fig.)* tief eingewurzelt ‹*Vorurteil usw.*›; **c)** *(thorough)* eingefleischt ‹*Skeptiker usw.*›
ingrate ['ɪngreɪt, ɪn'greɪt] *n.* *(arch.)* Undankbare, *der/die;* **be an ~:** undankbar sein
ingratiate [ɪn'greɪʃɪeɪt] *v. refl.* **~ oneself with sb.** sich bei jmdm. einschmeicheln
ingratiating [ɪn'greɪʃɪeɪtɪŋ] *adj.* schmeichlerisch
ingratitude [ɪn'grætɪtju:d] *n., no pl.* Undankbarkeit, *die* **(to[wards]** gegenüber)
ingredient [ɪn'gri:dɪənt] *n.* Zutat, *die;* Ingredienz, *die;* **the ~s of a successful marriage** *(fig.)* die Voraussetzungen für eine gute Ehe; **all the ~s of success** *(fig.)* alles, was man zum Erfolg braucht
'in-group *n.* Ingroup, *die (Soziol.);* Eigengruppe, *die (Soziol.)*
ingrowing ['ɪngrəʊɪŋ] *adj.* eingewachsen ‹*Zehennagel usw.*›
inhabit [ɪn'hæbɪt] *v. t.* bewohnen; **the region was ~ed by penguins/the Celts** in der Gegend lebten Pinguine/die Kelten; **a region ~ed by a rich flora** eine Gegend mit einer reichen Flora
inhabitable [ɪn'hæbɪtəbl] *adj.* bewohnbar
inhabitant [ɪn'hæbɪtənt] *n.* Bewohner, *der*/Bewohnerin, *die;* *(of village etc. also)* Einwohner, *der*/Einwohnerin, *die;* **that district has few ~s** in diesem Bezirk leben nur wenige Menschen
inhalant [ɪn'heɪlənt] *n.* *(Med.)* Inhalationsmittel, *das*
inhalation [ɪnhə'leɪʃn] *n.* *(Med.)* Inhalation, *die*
inhale [ɪn'heɪl] **1.** *v. t.* *(breathe in)* einatmen; *(take into the lungs)* inhalieren *(ugs.)* ‹*Zigarettenrauch usw.*›; *(Med.)* inhalieren. **2.** *v. i.* einatmen; *(Med.)* inhalieren; ‹*Raucher:*› inhalieren *(ugs.),* über die Lunge rauchen
inhaler [ɪn'heɪlə(r)] *n.* *(Med.)* Inhalationsapparat, *der*
inharmonious [ɪnhɑ:'məʊnɪəs] *adj.* **a)** disharmonisch; mißtönend; **b)** *(fig.)* unharmonisch
inharmoniously [ɪnhɑ:'məʊnɪəslɪ] *adv.* **a)** disharmonisch; **b)** *(fig.)* unharmonisch
inhere [ɪn'hɪə(r)] *v. i.* **~ in sth.** einer Sache *(Dat.)* innewohnen *(geh.);* einer Sache *(Dat.)* inhärieren *(Philos.)*
inherent [ɪn'hɪərənt, ɪn'herənt] *adj.* *(belonging by nature)* innewohnend *(geh.);* natürlich ‹*Anmut, Eleganz*›; inhärent *(Philos.);* **our ~ indolence** die uns *(Dat.)* innewohnende Trägheit
inherently [ɪn'hɪərəntlɪ, ɪn'herəntlɪ] *adv.* von Natur aus
inherit [ɪn'herɪt] *v. t.* erben
inheritable [ɪn'herɪtəbl] *adj.* erblich; **~ disease** Erbkrankheit, *die*
inheritance [ɪn'herɪtəns] *n.* **a)** *(what is inherited)* Erbe, *das;* **come into one's ~:** sein Erbe antreten; **b)** *no pl.* *(inheriting)* Erbschaft, *die*
in'heritance tax *n.* Erbschaftssteuer, *die*
inhibit [ɪn'hɪbɪt] *v. t.* hemmen; **~ sb. from doing sth.** jmdn. daran hindern, etw. zu tun
inhibited [ɪn'hɪbɪtɪd] *adj.* gehemmt
inhibition [ɪnhɪ'bɪʃn] *n.* **a)** Unterdrückung, *die;* **b)** *(Psych.)* Hemmung, *die;* **c)** *(coll.: emotional resistance)* Hemmung, *die;* **without ~:** hemmungslos; **have no ~s about doing sth.** keine Hemmungen haben, etw. zu tun
inhomogeneity [ɪnhɒmədʒɪ'ni:ɪtɪ, ɪnhəʊmədʒɪ'ni:ɪtɪ] *n.* **a)** *no pl.* *(lack of homogeneity)* Inhomogenität, *die;* **b)** *(irregularity)* Unregelmäßigkeit, *die*
inhomogeneous [ɪnhɒmə'dʒi:nɪəs, ɪnhəʊmə'dʒi:nɪəs] *adj.* inhomogen
inhospitable [ɪnhɒs'pɪtəbl] *adj.* **a)** ungastlich ‹*Person, Verhalten*›; **b)** unwirtlich ‹*Gegend, Klima*›
'in-house *adj.* hausintern
inhuman [ɪn'hju:mən] *adj.* **a)** *(brutal)* unmenschlich ‹*Tyrann, Grausamkeit, Strenge*›; inhuman ‹*Arbeitgeber, Verhalten*›; **b)** *(not human)* nicht menschlich
inhumane [ɪnhju:'meɪn] *adj.* unmenschlich; inhuman *(geh.);* menschenunwürdig ‹*Zustände, Behandlung*›
inhumanity [ɪnhju:'mænɪtɪ] *n.* *see* **inhumane:** Unmenschlichkeit, *die;* Inhumanität, *die (geh.);* Menschenunwürdigkeit, *die;* **man's ~ to man** die Unmenschlichkeit unter den Menschen
inimical [ɪ'nɪmɪkl] *adj.* **a)** *(hostile)* feindselig ‹*Blick, Beziehungen*›; feindlich [gesinnt] ‹*Macht*›; **be ~ to sb.** jmdm. feindlich gesinnt sein; jmdm. feind sein *(geh.);* **b)** *(harmful)* abträglich **(to** *Dat.*) *(geh.);* nachteilig **(to** für); schädlich **(to** für)
inimitable [ɪ'nɪmɪtəbl] *adj.* unnachahmlich ‹*Gabe, Fähigkeit*›; einzigartig ‹*Persönlichkeit*›
iniquitous [ɪ'nɪkwɪtəs] *adj.* **a)** *(wicked)* schändlich; **b)** *(unjust)* ungerecht ‹*Urteil*›; ungeheuer hoch ‹*Preis*›
iniquity [ɪ'nɪkwɪtɪ] *n.* **a)** *(wickedness)* Schändlichkeit, *die;* *(sin)* Missetat, *die;* **b)** *(injustice)* Ungerechtigkeit, *die*
initial [ɪ'nɪʃl] **1.** *adj.* anfänglich; zu Anfang auftretend ‹*Symptome*›; Anfangs‹*stadium, -schwierigkeiten*›; **~ costs** *or* **expenses** Startkosten. **2.** *n. esp. in pl.* Initiale, *die;* **what do the ~s s.a.e. stand for?** wofür steht *od.* was bedeutet die Abkürzung s.a.e.?. **3.** *v. t.,* *(Brit.)* **-ll-** abzeichnen ‹*Scheck, Quittung, Beleg*›; paraphieren ‹*Vertrag, Abkommen usw.*›
initial 'letter *n.* Anfangsbuchstabe, *der*
initially [ɪ'nɪʃəlɪ] *adv.* anfangs; am *od.* zu Anfang
initiate 1. [ɪ'nɪʃɪeɪt] *v. t.* **a)** *(admit)* [feierlich] aufnehmen; initiieren *(Soziol., Völkerk.);* *(introduce)* einführen **(into** in + *Akk.*); **~ sb. into sth.** *(into club, group, etc.)* jmdn. in etw. *(Akk.)* aufnehmen; *(into knowledge, mystery, etc.)* jmdn. in etw. *(Akk.)* einweihen; **b)** *(begin)* initiieren *(geh.);* in die Wege leiten ‹*Vorhaben*›; einleiten ‹*Verhandlungen, Reformen*›; eröffnen ‹*Diskussion, Ver-*

handlung, Feierlichkeiten, Feindseligkeiten⟩; anstrengen ⟨*Prozeß, Klage*⟩. **2.** [ɪ'nɪʃɪət] *n.* Eingeweihte, *der/die*

initiation [ɪnɪʃɪ'eɪʃn] *n.* **a)** *(beginning)* Initiierung, *die (geh.); (of hostilities, discussion, negotiation, festivities)* Eröffnung, *die; (of reforms, negotiations)* Einleitung, *die;* **b)** *(admission)* Aufnahme, *die* (**into** in + *Akk.*); *(into knowledge, mystery, etc.)* Einweihung, *die;* Initiation, *die (Soziol., Völkerk.); (introduction)* Einführung, *die* (**into** in + *Akk.*); ~ **ceremony** Aufnahmezeremonie, *die;* Initiationsritus, *der (Soziol., Völkerk.)*

initiative [ɪ'nɪʃətɪv, ɪ'nɪʃɪətɪv] *n.* **a)** *(power)* **the ~ is ours/lies with them** die Initiative liegt bei uns/ihnen; **have the ~** *(Mil.)* den Kampf bestimmen; **b)** *no pl., no indef. art. (ability)* Initiative, *die;* **lack ~:** keine Initiative haben *od.* besitzen; **c)** *(first step)* Initiative, *die;* **take the ~:** die Initiative ergreifen; den ersten Schritt tun; **on one's own ~:** aus eigener Initiative; **d)** *(citizen's right to initiate legislation)* Gesetzesinitiative, *die*

initiator [ɪ'nɪʃɪeɪtə(r)] *n.* Initiator, *der*/Initiatorin, *die*

inject [ɪn'dʒekt] *v. t.* **a)** [ein]spritzen; injizieren *(Med.);* **b)** *(put fluid into)* **~ a vein with sth.** etw. in eine Vene spritzen *od. (Med.)* injizieren; **~ a mould with plastic** Plastik in eine Form spritzen; **c)** *(administer sth. to)* **~ sb. with sth.** jmdm. etw. spritzen *od. (Med.)* injizieren; **~ sb. against smallpox** jmdn. gegen Pocken impfen; **d)** *(fig.)* pumpen ⟨*Geld*⟩; **~ new life/vigour into sth.** einer Sache *(Dat.)* neues Leben geben/neue Kraft verleihen

injection [ɪn'dʒekʃn] *n.* **a)** *(injecting)* Einspritzung, *die;* Injektion, *die (Med.);* **give sb. an ~:** jmdm. eine Spritze *od.* Injektion geben; **b)** *(liquid injected)* Injektion, *die;* Injektionslösung, *die;* **c)** *(fig.)* **~ of money/capital, financial ~:** Geldzuschuß, *der;* Finanzspritze, *die (ugs.); see also* **fuel injection**

in'jection moulding *n.* Spritzguß, *der*

injudicious [ɪndʒu:'dɪʃəs] *adj.* unklug; ungünstig ⟨*Moment*⟩

Injun ['ɪndʒən] *n. (coll.)* Indianer, *der*/Indianerin, *die*

injunction [ɪn'dʒʌŋkʃn] *n.* **a)** *(order)* Verfügung, *die;* **b)** *(Law)* [richterliche] Verfügung; **a court ~:** eine richterliche Verfügung

injure ['ɪndʒə(r)] *v. t.* **a)** *(hurt)* verletzen; *(fig.)* verletzen ⟨*Stolz, Gefühle*⟩; kränken ⟨*Person*⟩; **his leg was ~d** er wurde/*(state)* war am Bein verletzt; **six people were badly ~d** es gab sechs Schwerverletzte; **b)** *(impair)* schaden (+ *Dat.*); schädigen ⟨*Gesundheit*⟩; beeinträchtigen ⟨*Beziehungen*⟩; **c)** *(do harm to)* schädigen ⟨*Ruf, Ansehen*⟩

injured ['ɪndʒəd] *adj.* **a)** *(hurt, lit. or fig.)* verletzt; verwundet ⟨*Soldat*⟩; **because of his ~ hand** wegen seiner Handverletzung; **the ~:** die Verletzten/Verwundeten; **b)** *(wronged)* geschädigt; hintergangen, betrogen ⟨*Ehemann*⟩; **the ~ party** *(Law)* der/die Geschädigte; **c)** *(showing offence)* gekränkt ⟨*Stimme, Blick*⟩; verletzt, beleidigt ⟨*Person*⟩; **with an ~ air** mit gekränkter Miene; **speak in an ~ voice** mit gekränkter Stimme sprechen

injurious [ɪn'dʒʊərɪəs] *adj.* **a)** *(wrongful)* ungerecht ⟨*Behandlung*⟩; **b)** *(hurtful)* schädlich; **be ~ to sb./sth.** jmdm./einer Sache schaden; **smoking is ~ to health** Rauchen schadet der Gesundheit

injury ['ɪndʒərɪ] *n.* **a)** *(harm)* Verletzung, *die* (**to** *Gen.*); **risk ~ to life and limb** Leben und Gesundheit aufs Spiel setzen; **b)** *(instance of harm)* Verletzung, *die* (**to** *Gen.*); *(fig.)* Kränkung, *die* (**to** *Gen.*); **add insult to ~:** das Ganze noch schlimmer machen; **do sb./oneself an ~:** jmdm./sich weh tun; **I'll do him an ~ if he doesn't shut up!** *(coll.)* ich tu ihm jetzt [gleich] was, wenn er nicht ruhig ist!; **c)** *(wrongful action)* Verletzung, *die* (**to** *Gen.*)

'injury time *n. (Brit. Footb.)* Nachspielzeit, *die;* **be into/play ~:** nachspielen

injustice [ɪn'dʒʌstɪs] *n.* **a)** *(unfairness)* Ungerechtigkeit, *die;* **fight against ~:** gegen die Ungerechtigkeit *od.* das Unrecht kämpfen; **protest at the ~ of a statement** gegen eine ungerechte Behauptung protestieren; **b)** *(wrong act)* Ungerechtigkeit, *die;* **do sb. an ~:** jmdm. unrecht tun

ink [ɪŋk] **1.** *n.* **a)** Tinte, *die; (for stamp-pad)* Farbe, *die; (for drawing)* Tusche, *die;* **my ball-point has run out of ~:** meine [Kugelschreiber]mine ist leer; **b)** *(in printing)* Druckfarbe, *die; (in duplicating, newsprint)* Druckerschwärze, *die;* **c)** *(Zool.)* Tinte, *die.* **2.** *v. t.* **a)** **~ in** mit Tinte/Tusche nachziehen ⟨*Bleistiftstrich usw.*⟩; mit Tusche ausmalen ⟨*Teil eines Bildes*⟩; **~ over** mit Tusche übermalen ⟨*Papier, Blatt*⟩; **b)** *(apply ink to)* einfärben ⟨*Druckform*⟩; mit Farbe schwärzen ⟨*Stempel*⟩

'ink-bottle *n.* Tintenfaß, *das*

inkling ['ɪŋklɪŋ] *n.* Ahnung, *die;* **I haven't an ~:** ich habe nicht die leiseste Ahnung *od. (ugs.)* keinen blassen Schimmer; **have an ~ of sth.** etw. ahnen; **get an ~ of sth.** etw. merken; Wind von etw. bekommen *(ugs.)*

ink: ~-pad *n.* Stempelkissen, *das;* **~well** *n.* [eingelassenes] Tintenfaß

inky ['ɪŋkɪ] *adj.* **a)** *(covered with ink)* tintenbeschmiert; tintig; **I have ~ fingers** meine Finger sind voller Tinte; **b)** *(black)* tintenschwarz; tintig

inlaid *see* **inlay 1**

inland 1. ['ɪnlənd, 'ɪnlænd] *adj.* **a)** *(placed ~)* Binnen-; binnenländisch; **~ town** Stadt im Landesinneren; **an ~ state** ein Binnenstaat; **b)** *(carried on ~)* inländisch; Binnen⟨*handel, -verkehr*⟩; Inlands⟨*brief, -paket, -gebühren*⟩. **2.** [ɪn'lænd] *adv.* landeinwärts; im Landesinneren ⟨*leben*⟩

inland: ~ navi'gation *n.* Binnenschiffahrt, *die;* **~ 'revenue** *n.* Steuereinnahmen *Pl.;* **I~ 'Revenue** *n. (Brit.)* ≈ Finanzamt, *das;* **~ 'sea** *n.* Binnenmeer, *das*

'in-law *n., usu. in pl. (coll.)* angeheirateter Verwandter/angeheiratete Verwandte; **~s** *(parents-in-law)* Schwiegereltern

inlay 1. [-'-] *v. t.,* **inlaid a)** *(embed)* einlassen; **b)** *(ornament)* einlegen. **2.** ['--] *n.* **a)** *(work)* Einlegearbeit, *die;* Intarsie, *die;* **b)** *(material)* **~s** Intarsien *Pl.* (**of** aus); **c)** *(Dent.)* Inlay, *das*

inlet ['ɪnlet, 'ɪnlɪt] *n.* **a)** [schmale] Bucht; **b)** *(piece inserted)* eingelegtes Stück; Einsatz, *der;* **c)** *(way of entry)* Einlaßöffnung, *die;* **~ pipe** Zuleitungsrohr, *das;* Zuleitung, *die;* **~ valve** Einlaßventil, *das*

'inmate *n. (of hospital, prison, etc.)* Insasse, *der*/Insassin, *die; (of house)* Bewohner, *der*/Bewohnerin, *die*

in memoriam [ɪn mɪ'mɔ:rɪæm] *n.* Gedenkinschrift, *die*

inmost ['ɪnməʊst, 'ɪnməst] *adj.* **a)** *(deepest)* tiefst...; **b)** *(fig.: most inward)* innerst... ⟨*Gefühle, Wesen*⟩

inn [ɪn] *n.* **a)** *(hotel)* Herberge, *die (veralt.);* Gasthof, *der;* **no room at the ~** *(fig.)* alles ausgebucht *(scherzh.);* **b)** *(pub)* Wirtshaus, *das;* Gastwirtschaft, *die;* **'The Swan Inn'** „Wirtshaus zum Schwan"

innards ['ɪnədz] *n. pl. (coll.)* Eingeweide *Pl.; (in animals for slaughter)* Innereien *Pl.*

innate [ɪ'neɪt, 'ɪneɪt] *adj.* **a)** *(inborn)* angeboren; natürlich ⟨*Schönheit, Fähigkeit*⟩; **be ~ in sb.** jmdm. angeboren sein; **we all have an ~ desire for happiness** das Streben nach Glück ist uns allen angeboren; **b)** *(Philos.)* angeboren ⟨*Ideen*⟩

inner ['ɪnə(r)] *adj.* **a)** inner...; Innen⟨*hof, -tür, -fläche, -seite usw.*⟩; **~ ear** *(Anat.)* Innenohr, *das;* **b)** *(fig.)* inner... ⟨*Gefühl, Wesen, Zweifel, Ängste*⟩; verborgen ⟨*Bedeutung*⟩; **~ life** Seelenleben, *das;* **~ circle of friends** engster Freundeskreis; *see also* **¹bar 1 i**

inner: ~ 'city *n.* Innenstadt, *die;* City, *die;* **~ city areas** Innenbezirke; Innenstadtgebiete; **~ man** *n.* **a)** *(soul, mind)* Innere, *das;* **the needs of the ~ man** die inneren Bedürfnisse; **b)** *(joc.: stomach)* Magen, *der;* **satisfy the ~ man** für sein leibliches Wohl sorgen

innermost ['ɪnəməʊst] *adj.* innerst...; **one's ~ thoughts** seine geheimsten Gedanken; **in the ~ depths of the forest** im tiefsten Wald

inner: ~-spring *(Amer.) see* **interior-sprung; ~ tube** *n.* Schlauch, *der*

'inner woman *see* **inner man**

inning ['ɪnɪŋ] *n. (Amer. Baseball)* Inning, *das*

innings ['ɪnɪŋz] *n., pl. same or (coll.)* **~es a)** *(Cricket)* Durchgang, *der;* Innings, *das (fachspr.);* **b)** *(period of office)* Amtszeit, *die; (dominance of political party)* Legislaturperiode, *die;* **c)** *(period of life etc.)* **a good ~:** eine gute Gelegenheit; **he had a good/long ~:** er hatte ein langes, ausgefülltes Leben

'innkeeper *n.* [Gast]wirt, *der*/-wirtin, *die*

innocence ['ɪnəsəns] *n., no pl.* **a)** Unschuld, *die;* **a presumption of ~:** eine Unschuldsvermutung; **lose one's ~:** die Unschuld verlieren; **b)** *(freedom from cunning)* Naivität, *die;* **c)** *(lack of knowledge)* Unkenntnis, *die;* **in all ~:** in aller Unschuld; **in all ~ of the fact that ...:** ohne die leiseste Ahnung davon zu haben, daß ...

innocent ['ɪnəsənt] **1.** *adj.* **a)** unschuldig (**of** an + *Dat.*); **be ~ of the charge/accusation** unschuldig sein; **the ~ party** der/die Unschuldige; **he is not as ~ as he appears** er ist nicht der Unschuldsengel, der er scheint *(ugs.);* **b)** *(simple)* einfältig; naiv ⟨*Wortwahl*⟩; **c)** *(harmless)* harmlos; **d)** *(naïve)* unschuldig; **he is ~ about the ways of the world** er ist völlig unerfahren; **e)** *(pretending to be guileless)* arglos, unschuldig ⟨*Blick, Erscheinung*⟩; **adopt an ~ air** eine Unschuldsmiene aufsetzen. **2.** *n. (innocent person)* Unschuldige, *der/die;* **he was such an ~ when he went to London** er war noch so unschuldig *od.* unverdorben, als er nach London ging

innocently ['ɪnəsəntlɪ] *adv.* unschuldig ⟨*blicken*⟩; in aller Unschuld ⟨*etw. sagen, tun*⟩

innocuous [ɪ'nɒkjʊəs] *adj.* *(not injurious)* unschädlich ⟨*Tier, Mittel*⟩; *(inoffensive)* harmlos

innocuously [ɪ'nɒkjʊəslɪ] *adv.* harmlos

Inn of 'Court *n., pl.* **Inns of Court** *(Brit.) (society)* englischer Anwaltsverband; *(building)* Gebäude dieses Verbandes

innovate ['ɪnəveɪt] *v. i.* **a)** *(bring in novelties)* Innovationen vornehmen; innovieren *(fachspr.);* **b)** *(make changes)* Änderungen vornehmen

innovation [ɪnə'veɪʃn] *n.* **a)** *(introduction of something new)* Innovation, *die (geh., fachspr.); (thing introduced)* Neuerung, *die;* **b)** *(change)* [Ver]änderung, *die;* Neuerung, *die;* Innovation, *die (geh., fachspr.)*

innovator ['ɪnəveɪtə(r)] *n.* Neuerer, *der*/Neuerin, *die*

'inn-sign *n.* Gasthausschild, *das*

innuendo [ɪnju:'endəʊ] *n., pl.* **~es** *or* **~s** versteckte Andeutung; Anspielung, *die;* Innuendo, *das (geh.);* **make ~es about sb.** über jmdn. Andeutungen fallenlassen *od.* machen

innumerable [ɪ'nju:mərəbl] *adj.* unzählig; zahllos; *(uncountable)* unzählbar

innumeracy [ɪ'nju:mərəsɪ] *n., no pl. (Brit.)* Nicht-Rechnen-Können, *das*

innumerate [ɪ'nju:mərət] *adj. (Brit.)* **be ~:** nicht rechnen können; des Rechnens unkundig sein *(geh.)*

inoculate [ɪ'nɒkjʊleɪt] *v. t.* **a)** *(treat by injection)* impfen (**against, for** gegen); **b)** *(im-*

plant) einimpfen (**into** in + *Akk.*); ~ **sb. with a virus** jmdm. einen Virus einimpfen

inoculation [ɪnɒkjʊ'leɪʃn] *n.* Impfung, *die,* Inokulation, *die (Med.)* (**against, for** gegen); **give sb. an ~:** jmdn. impfen

inoffensive [ɪnə'fensɪv] *adj.* **a)** *(unoffending)* harmlos; gutartig ‹*Tier*›; **b)** *(not objectionable)* harmlos ‹*Bemerkung*›; unaufdringlich ‹*Geruch, Art, Person*›; **be ~ to the eye** dem Auge nicht weh tun

inoffensively [ɪnə'fensɪvlɪ] *adv.* harmlos

inoperable [ɪn'ɒpərəbl] *adj.* **a)** *(Surg.)* inoperabel *(fachspr.);* nicht operierbar; **b)** *(fig.)* undurchführbar ‹*Politik*›

inoperative [ɪn'ɒpərətɪv] *adj.* ungültig; außer Kraft *nicht attr.*; **render sth. ~:** etw. außer Betrieb setzen

inopportune [ɪn'ɒpətju:n] *adj.* inopportun *(geh.);* unpassend, unangebracht ‹*Bemerkung*›; ungelegen, unpassend ‹*Augenblick, Besuch*›; **it was very ~ that ...:** es kam sehr ungelegen, daß ...

inopportunely [ɪn'ɒpətju:nlɪ] *adv.* zur Unzeit ‹*kommen*›; unpassenderweise, im unpassenden Moment ‹*vorbringen, äußern*›

inordinate [ɪ'nɔ:dɪnət] *adj.* *(immoderate)* unmäßig; ungeheuer ‹*[Menschen]menge*›; überzogen, übertrieben ‹*Forderung*›; **an ~ amount of work/money** ungeheuer viel Arbeit/eine Unmenge Geld

inordinately [ɪ'nɔ:dɪnətlɪ] *adv.* unmäßig; ungeheuer ‹*groß, hoch, weit usw.*›; **he is ~ fond of ...:** seine Zuneigung zu ... ist übertrieben

inorganic [ɪnɔ:'gænɪk] *adj.* **a)** *(Chem.)* anorganisch; **b)** *(fig.)* unorganisch *(geh.)*

inorganic 'chemist *n.* Anorganiker, *der*/Anorganikerin, *die*

'in-patient *n.* stationär behandelter Patient/behandelte Patientin; **be an ~:** stationär behandelt werden

'input 1. *n.* **a)** *(esp. Computing: what is put in)* Input, *der od. das; (of capital)* Investition, *die; (of manpower)* [Arbeits]aufwand, *der; (of electricity)* Energiezufuhr, *die;* **b)** *(esp. Computing: place where information etc. enters system)* Eingang, *der.* **2.** *v. t.*, **-tt-, ~** *or* **~ted** *(esp. Computing)* eingeben ‹*Daten, Programm*›; zuführen ‹*Strom, Energie*›; **~ data to the computer** Daten in den Computer eingeben

input: ~ circuit *n.* Eingangsstromkreis, *der;* Primärstromkreis, *der;* **~ data** *n. pl.* Eingabedaten *Pl.*; Rechnerdaten *Pl.*

inquest ['ɪnkwest, 'ɪŋkwest] *n.* **a)** *(legal inquiry)* gerichtliche Untersuchung; **b)** *(inquiry by coroner's court)* **~ [into the causes of death]** gerichtliche Untersuchung der Todesursache; **c)** *(coll.: discussion) see* **postmortem 3 b; d)** *(inquisition)* Untersuchung, *die* (**into** *Gen.*)

inquietude [ɪn'kwaɪɪtju:d, ɪŋ'kwaɪɪtju:d] *n., no pl.* Unruhe, *die*

inquire [ɪn'kwaɪə(r), ɪŋ'kwaɪə(r)] **1.** *v. i.* **a)** *(make search)* Untersuchungen anstellen (**into** über + *Akk.*); **~ into a matter** eine Angelegenheit untersuchen *od.* prüfen; **b)** *(seek information)* sich erkundigen (**about, after** nach, **of** bei); **c)** *(ask)* fragen (**for** nach). **2.** *v. t.* sich erkundigen nach, fragen nach ‹*Weg, Namen*›; **~ how/whether** *etc.* **...:** fragen *od.* sich erkundigen, wie/ob *usw.* ...

inquirer [ɪn'kwaɪərə(r), ɪŋ'kwaɪərə(r)] *n. (for the way, a name, etc.)* Fragende, *der/die; (into a matter)* Untersuchende, *der/die;* Nachforschende, *der/die*

inquiring [ɪn'kwaɪərɪŋ, ɪŋ'kwaɪərɪŋ] *adj.* fragend; forschend ‹*Geist*›

inquiry [ɪn'kwaɪərɪ, ɪŋ'kwaɪərɪ] *n.* **a)** *(asking)* Anfrage, *die;* **on ~:** auf Anfrage; **give sb. a look of ~:** jmdn. fragend ansehen; **b)** *(question)* Erkundigung, *die* (**into** über + *Akk.*); **make inquiries** Erkundigungen einziehen; Nachforschungen anstellen; **c)** *(investigation)* Untersuchung, *die; (research)* Forschung, *die;* **hold an ~:** eine Untersuchung durchführen (**into** *Gen.*); **court of ~** *(Mil.)* Untersuchungskommission, *die*

inquiry: ~ agent *n. (Brit.)* Privatdetektiv, *der;* **~ desk, ~ office** *ns.* Auskunft, *die*

inquisition [ɪnkwɪ'zɪʃn, ɪŋkwɪ'zɪʃn] *n.* **a)** *(search)* Nachforschung, *die* (**into** über + *Akk.*); **b)** *(judicial inquiry)* gerichtliche Untersuchung; *(fig. coll.)* Verhör, *das;* **c) I~** *(Hist.)* Inquisition, *die*

inquisitive [ɪn'kwɪzɪtɪv, ɪŋ'kwɪzɪtɪv] *adj.* **a)** *(unduly inquiring)* neugierig; **b)** *(inquiring)* wißbegierig; **be ~ about sth.** alles über etw. *(Akk.)* wissen wollen; **give sb. an ~ look** jmdn. forschend ansehen

inquisitively [ɪn'kwɪzɪtɪvlɪ, ɪŋ'kwɪzɪtɪvlɪ] *adv. see* **inquisitive a, b:** neugierig; wißbegierig

inquisitiveness [ɪn'kwɪzɪtɪvnɪs, ɪŋ'kwɪzɪtɪvnɪs] *n., no pl. see* **inquisitive a, b:** Neugier[de], *die;* Wißbegier[de], *die*

inquorate [ɪn'kwɔ:reɪt, ɪŋ'kwɔ:reɪt] *adj.* nicht beschlußfähig

'inroad *n.* **a)** *(intrusion)* Eingriff, *der* (**on, into** in + *Akk.*); **make ~s into the market** in den Markt eindringen; **make ~s into sb.'s savings** jmds. Ersparnisse angreifen; **b)** *(hostile incursion)* Einfall, *der* (**into** in + *Akk.*); Überfall, *der* (**[up]on** auf + *Akk.*); **make ~s on a country** in ein Land einfallen

'inrush *n.* Zustrom, *der; (of water)* Einbruch, *der;* **an ~ of air/water** ein Luftzug/Wassereinbruch

insane [ɪn'seɪn] *adj.* **a)** *(not of sound mind)* geisteskrank; **b)** *(extremely foolish)* wahnsinnig *(ugs.);* irrsinnig *(ugs.)*

insanely [ɪn'seɪnlɪ] *adv.* **a)** *(in a mad manner)* wahnsinnig *(ugs.)* ‹*eifersüchtig*›; irr[e] ‹*reden*›; **b)** *(very foolishly)* verrückt ‹*sich benehmen*›

insanitary [ɪn'sænɪtərɪ] *adj.* unhygienisch

insanity [ɪn'sænɪtɪ] *n.* **a)** Geisteskrankheit, *die;* Wahnsinn, *der;* **b)** *(extreme folly)* Irrsinn, *der;* Wahnsinn, *der (ugs.); (instance)* Verrücktheit, *die*

insatiable [ɪn'seɪʃəbl] *adj.* unersättlich; unstillbar ‹*Verlangen, Neugierde*›; **he has an ~ thirst for knowledge** er ist unersättlich in seinem Wissensdurst

inscribe [ɪn'skraɪb] *v. t.* **a)** *(write)* schreiben; *(on ring etc.)* eingravieren; *(on stone, rock)* einmeißeln; **~ sth. on sth.** etw. auf etw. *(Akk.)* schreiben/in etw. *(Akk.)* eingravieren/einmeißeln; **b)** *(enter)* eintragen ‹*Namen*› (**on** in + *Akk.*); **~ one's name in the Visitors' Book** sich in das Gästebuch eintragen; **c)** *(mark)* mit einer Inschrift versehen ‹*Denkmal, Grabstein*›; **~ a tombstone/locket with a name** einen Namen in einen Grabstein einmeißeln/ein Medaillon eingravieren; **d)** *(with informal dedication)* **~ sth. to sb.** jmdm. etw. widmen

inscription [ɪn'skrɪpʃn] *n.* **a)** *(words inscribed)* Inschrift, *die; (on coin)* Aufschrift, *die;* **b)** *(informal dedication)* Widmung, *die*

inscrutability [ɪnskru:tə'bɪlɪtɪ] *n., no pl.* Unergründlichkeit, *die; (of facial expression)* Undurchdringlichkeit, *die*

inscrutable [ɪn'skru:təbl] *adj.* **a)** *(mysterious)* unergründlich; geheimnisvoll ‹*Lächeln*›; undurchdringlich ‹*Miene*›; **he remained ~:** seine Miene *od.* sein Gesichtsausdruck blieb undurchdringlich; **b)** *(incomprehensible)* unerforschlich *(geh.)*

inscrutably [ɪn'skru:təblɪ] *adv.* unergründlich; geheimnisvoll ‹*lächeln*›

insect ['ɪnsekt] *n.* Insekt, *das;* Kerbtier, *das*

insect: ~ bite *n.* Insektenstich, *der;* **~-borne** *adj.* durch Insekten übertragen ‹*Krankheit*›; **~-control** *n.* Insektenbekämpfung, *die*

insecticide [ɪn'sektɪsaɪd] *n.* Insektizid, *das*

insectivore [ɪn'sektɪvɔ:(r)] *n. (Zool.)* Insektenfresser, *der*

insect: ~-powder *n.* Insektenpulver, *das;* **~-proof** *adj.* insektensicher; **~-repellent** *n.* Insektenschutzmittel, *das*

insecure [ɪnsɪ'kjʊə(r)] *adj.* **a)** *(unsafe)* unsicher; **b)** *(not firm, liable to give way)* nicht sicher; nicht fest ‹*Knoten*›; unstabil, instabil ‹*Regal*›; **c)** *(Psych.)* unsicher; **feel ~:** sich nicht sicher fühlen

insecurely [ɪnsɪ'kjʊəlɪ] *adv.* nicht sicher ‹*befestigt*›; nicht fest ‹*verschlossen*›

insecurity [ɪnsɪ'kjʊərɪtɪ] *n., no pl. (also Psych.)* Unsicherheit, *die;* **the ~ of his job** sein unsicherer Arbeitsplatz

inseminate [ɪn'semɪneɪt] *v. t.* inseminieren *(Med., Zool., Landw.);* befruchten ‹*Frau*›; besamen ‹*Vieh*›

insemination [ɪnsemɪ'neɪʃn] *n.* Insemination, *die (Med., Zool., Landw.); (of woman)* Befruchtung, *die; (of animal)* Besamung, *die; see also* **artificial insemination**

insensibility [ɪnsensɪ'bɪlɪtɪ] *n., no pl.* **a)** *(lack of emotional feeling, indifference)* Gefühllosigkeit, *die* (**to** gegenüber); **b)** *(unconsciousness)* Bewußtlosigkeit, *die;* **c)** *(lack of physical feeling)* Unempfindlichkeit, *die* (**to** gegen); **~ to pain** Schmerzunempfindlichkeit, *die*

insensible [ɪn'sensɪbl] *adj.* **a)** *(imperceptible)* unmerklich; nicht wahrnehmbar; **b)** *(unconscious)* bewußtlos; **they drank themselves ~:** sie betranken sich bis zur Bewußtlosigkeit; **c)** *(unaware)* **be ~ of** *or* **to sth.** sich *(Dat.)* einer Sache *(Gen.)* nicht bewußt sein; **d)** *(deprived of sensation)* unempfindlich (**to** gegen); **be ~ to the cold/to pain** keine Kälte/keinen Schmerz empfinden; **e)** *(emotionless)* gefühllos ‹*Person, Art*›; unempfindlich (**to** für)

insensitive [ɪn'sensɪtɪv] *adj.* **a)** *(lacking feeling)* gefühllos ‹*Person, Art*›; **be ~ to the needs of others** kein Gefühl für die Bedürfnisse anderer haben; **b)** *(unappreciative)* unempfänglich (**to** für); **c)** *(not physically sensitive)* unempfindlich (**to** gegen); **~ to light/heat** licht-/hitzeunempfindlich

insensitively [ɪn'sensɪtɪvlɪ] *adv.* gefühllos, ohne Gefühl ‹*reagieren, sprechen*›

insensitiveness [ɪn'sensɪtɪvnɪs], **insensitivity** [ɪnsensɪ'tɪvɪtɪ] *ns., no pl.* **a)** *(lack of feeling)* Gefühllosigkeit, *die* (**to** gegenüber); **b)** *(unappreciativeness)* Unempfindlichkeit, *die* (**to** für); **c)** *(lack of physical sensitiveness)* Unempfindlichkeit, *die* (**to** gegen); **~ to heat** Hitzeunempfindlichkeit, *die*

inseparable [ɪn'sepərəbl] *adj.* **a)** untrennbar; *(fig.)* unzertrennlich ‹*Freunde, Zwillinge usw.*›; **sth. is ~ from sth.** etw. ist mit etw. untrennbar verbunden; **he is ~ from his teddy bear** der Junge und sein Teddybär sind unzertrennlich; **b)** *(Ling.)* untrennbar

inseparably [ɪn'sepərəblɪ] *adv.* untrennbar

insert 1. [ɪn'sɜ:t] *v. t.* **a)** einlegen ‹*Film*›; einwerfen ‹*Münze*›; einsetzen ‹*Herzschrittmacher*›; einstechen ‹*Nadel*›; **~ a piece of paper into the typewriter** ein Blatt Papier in die Schreibmaschine einspannen; **~ sth. in/between sth.** etw. in/zwischen etw. *(Akk.)* stecken/legen *usw.*; **~ the key [into the lock]** den Schlüssel ins Schloß stecken; **~ a page into a book** ein Blatt in ein Buch einlegen; **b)** *(introduce into)* einfügen ‹*Wort, Satz usw.*› (**in** in + *Akk.*); **~ an advertisement in 'The Times'** eine Anzeige in die „Times" setzen; in der „Times" inserieren. **2.** ['ɪnsɜ:t] *n. (in magazine)* Beilage, *die; (in garment)* Einsatz, *der; (in book)* Einlage, *die; (printed in newspaper)* Inserat, *das*

insertion [ɪn'sɜ:ʃn] *n.* **a)** *(inserting) see* **insert 1 a:** Einlegen, *das;* Einwerfen, *das;* Einsetzen, *das;* Einstechen, *das;* **b)** *(thing inserted) (words, sentences in a text)* Einfügung, *die;* Beifügung, *die; (in newspaper)* Inserat, *das;* **c)** *(each appearance of an advertisement)* Insertion, *die*

inset 1. ['--] *n. (small map)* Nebenkarte, *die;*

(small photograph, diagram) Nebenbild, *das.* **2.** ['-'] *v. t.*, **-tt-**, ~ *or* ~**ted** einfügen ⟨*Karte, Seite*⟩ (**in** in + *Akk.*)

inshore 1. ['--] *adj.* Küsten⟨*fischerei, -gewässer, -schiffahrt*⟩; ~ **currents** sich auf die Küste zubewegende Strömungen. **2.** [-'-] *adv.* auf die Küste zu ⟨*treiben*⟩; in Küstennähe ⟨*sein, fischen*⟩; **close** ~: dicht an der Küste ⟨*sein, liegen*⟩; dicht an die Küste ⟨*heranfahren*⟩

inside 1. [-'-, '--] *n.* **a)** *(internal side)* Innenseite, *die;* **on the** ~: innen; **to/from the** ~: nach/von innen; **overtake sb. on the** ~ *(in driving)* jmdn. auf der falschen Seite überholen; **on the** ~ **of the door** innen an der Tür; **lock the door from the** ~: die Tür von innen abschließen; **b)** *(inner part)* Innere, *das;* **the** ~ **of the cupboard needs a good clean-out** der Schrank muß innen richtig saubergemacht werden; **c)** *in sing. or pl. (coll.: stomach and bowels)* Eingeweide *Pl.*; Innere, *das;* **have a pain in one's** ~**[s]** Bauch- *od.* Leibschmerzen haben; **d)** *(position affording* ~ *information)* **he knows Parliament from the** ~: er kennt das Parlament von innen; **be on the** ~: eingeweiht *od.* ein Insider sein; **e) the wind blew her umbrella** ~ **out** der Wind hat ihren Regenschirm umgestülpt; **wear one's sweater** ~ **out** seinen Pullover verkehrt *od.* falsch herum anhaben; **know sth.** ~ **out** etw. in- und auswendig kennen; **turn a jacket** ~ **out** eine Jacke nach links wenden; **turn sth.** ~ **out** *(fig.)* etw. auf den Kopf stellen *(ugs.).* **2.** ['--] *adj. (of, on, nearer the* ~*)* inner...; Innen⟨*wand, -einrichtung, -ansicht, -reparatur, -durchmesser*⟩; *(fig.)* intern; **be on an** ~ **page** im Inneren [der Zeitung] stehen; **give the** ~ **story of sth.** etw. von innen beleuchten *(fig.)*; ~ **information** interne Informationen; **the burglary was an** ~ **job** *(coll.)* der Einbruch war das Werk von Leuten, die sich auskannten; ~ **pocket** Innentasche, *die;* ~ **lane** Innenspur, *die;* ~ **track** *(Racing)* Innenbahn, *die.* **3.** [-'-] *adv.* **a)** *(on or in the* ~*)* innen; *(to the* ~*)* nach innen hinein/herein; *(indoors)* drinnen; **come** ~: hereinkommen; **take a look** ~: hineinsehen; *(in search of sth.)* innen nachsehen; **go** ~: [ins Haus] hineingehen; **see** ~ **for further details** weitere Informationen finden Sie in diesem Brief/in dieser Broschüre; **b)** *(sl.: in prison)* **be** ~: sitzen *(ugs.)*; **put sb.** ~: jmdn. einlochen *(salopp)*; **c)** ~ **of** *see* **4. 4.** [-'-] *prep.* **a)** *(on inner side of)* [innen] in (+ *Dat.*); *(with direction)* in (+ *Akk.*) hinein; **sit/get** ~ **the house** im Haus sitzen/ins Haus hineinkommen; **what's** ~ **that package?** was ist in diesem Paket?; **leave your shoes just** ~ **the door** laß deine Schuhe gerade [innen] an der Tür stehen; **b)** *(in less than)* ~ **an hour** innerhalb [von] einer Stunde; in weniger als einer Stunde

inside: ~ **edge** *n. (Skating, Cricket)* Innenkante, *die;* ~ **'forward** *n. (Footb., Hockey)* Halbstürmer, *der;* Innenstürmer, *der;* Inside, *der (schweiz. Fußball)*; ~ **'left** *n. (Footb., Hockey)* Halblinke, *der/die;* ~**-leg** *adj.* ~**-leg measurement** Schrittlänge, *die*

insider [ɪn'saɪdə(r)] *n.* **a)** *(within a society)* Mitglied, *das;* Zugehörige, *der/die;* **b)** *(person privy to secret)* Eingeweihte, *der/die;* Insider, *der;* ~ **dealing** *or* **trading** *(Stock Exch.)* Insiderhandel, *der*

inside 'right *n. (Footb., Hockey)* Halbrechte, *der/die*

insidious [ɪn'sɪdɪəs] *adj.* heimtückisch; **an** ~ **disease** eine heimtückische *od. (fachspr.)* insidiöse Krankheit

insidiously [ɪn'sɪdɪəslɪ] *adv.* auf heimtückische Weise

insidiousness [ɪn'sɪdɪəsnɪs] *n., no pl.* Heimtücke, *die*

'insight *n.* **a)** *(penetration, discernment)* Verständnis, *das;* **be lacking in** ~: einen Mangel an Verständnis zeigen; ~ **into human nature** Menschenkenntnis, *die;* **b)** *(instance)* Einblick, *der* (**into** in + *Akk.*); **be** *or* **give an** ~ **into sth.** einen Einblick in etw. *(Akk.)* geben; **gain an** ~ **into sth.** [einen] Einblick in etw. *(Akk.)* gewinnen *od.* bekommen

insignia [ɪn'sɪgnɪə] *n., pl. same* Insigne, *das*

insignificance [ɪnsɪg'nɪfɪkəns] *n., no pl.* **a)** *(unimportance)* Bedeutungslosigkeit, *die;* Unwichtigkeit, *die;* **b)** *(contemptibility)* Unscheinbarkeit, *die;* **c)** *(meaninglessness)* Belanglosigkeit, *die*

insignificant [ɪnsɪg'nɪfɪkənt] *adj.* **a)** *(unimportant)* unbedeutend; geringfügig ⟨*Summe*⟩; unbedeutend, geringfügig ⟨*Unterschied*⟩; unscheinbar ⟨*Äußeres*⟩; **b)** *(contemptible)* unscheinbar ⟨*Person*⟩; **c)** *(meaningless)* belanglos ⟨*Bemerkung*⟩

insincere [ɪnsɪn'sɪə(r)] *adj.* unaufrichtig; falsch ⟨*Lächeln*⟩

insincerely [ɪnsɪn'sɪəlɪ] *adv.* unaufrichtig; falsch ⟨*lächeln*⟩

insincerity [ɪnsɪn'serɪtɪ] *n.* Unaufrichtigkeit, *die; (of smile, person)* Falschheit, *die*

insinuate [ɪn'sɪnjʊeɪt] *v. t.* **a)** *(introduce)* [auf geschickte Art] einflößen ⟨*Propaganda*⟩; insinuieren *(veralt.)*; ~ **doubts into sb.'s mind** jmdm. geschickt Zweifel einpflanzen; **b)** *(convey)* andeuten (**to sb.** jmdm. gegenüber); unterstellen; insinuieren *(geh.)*; **how dare you** ~ **that ...?** wie können Sie es wagen, zu behaupten, daß ...?; **insinuating remarks** Andeutungen; Unterstellungen; **c)** ~ **oneself into sb.'s favour** sich bei jmdm. einschmeicheln

insinuation [ɪnsɪnjʊ'eɪʃn] *n.* Anspielung, *die* (**about** auf + *Akk.*); versteckte Andeutung; **by** ~: andeutungsweise

insipid [ɪn'sɪpɪd] *adj.* **a)** *(tasteless)* fad[e] ⟨*Essen*⟩; schal ⟨*Getränk*⟩; **b)** *(lacking liveliness)* fad[e] *(ugs.)*, geistlos ⟨*Person*⟩; schal, fad[e] *(ugs.)* ⟨*Witz, Spaß*⟩; geistlos ⟨*Gespräch*⟩; langweilig ⟨*Farbe, Musik*⟩

insist [ɪn'sɪst] **1.** *v. i.* bestehen (**[up]on** auf + *Dat.*); ~ **on doing sth./on sb.'s doing sth.** darauf bestehen, etw. zu tun/daß jmd. etw. tut; **if you** ~: wenn du darauf bestehst; **he will** ~ **on ringing us late at night** er ruft uns beharrlich spätabends an; **she** ~**s on her innocence** sie behauptet beharrlich, unschuldig zu sein. **2.** *v. t.* **a)** ~ **that ...**: darauf bestehen, daß ...; **b)** *(maintain positively)* **they keep** ~**ing that ...**: sie beharren *od.* bestehen beharrlich darauf, daß ...; **he** ~**ed that he was right** er bestand darauf, daß er recht habe

insistence [ɪn'sɪstəns], **insistency** [ɪn'sɪstənsɪ] *n., no pl.* Bestehen, *das* (**on** auf + *Dat.*); **I only came here at your** ~: ich kam nur auf dein Drängen hierher

insistent [ɪn'sɪstənt] *adj.* **a)** beharrlich, hartnäckig ⟨*Person*⟩; aufdringlich ⟨*Musik*⟩; nachdrücklich ⟨*Forderung*⟩; **be most** ~ **that .../about sth.** hartnäckig darauf bestehen, daß .../auf etw. *(Dat.)* bestehen; **b)** *([annoyingly] persistent)* penetrant *(abwertend)*

insistently [ɪn'sɪstəntlɪ] *adv.* **a)** mit Nachdruck ⟨*betonen, fordern*⟩; **b)** *(persistently)* penetrant *(abwertend)*

in situ [ɪn 'sɪtju:] *adv.* in situ; in natürlicher Lage *(Med.)*; in originaler Lage *(Archäol.)*

insobriety [ɪnsə'braɪətɪ] *n., no pl.* Trunkenheit, *die*

insofar [ɪnsəʊ'fɑ:(r)] *adv.* = **in so far;** *see* **far 1 d**

insole ['ɪnsəʊl] *n.* **a)** Einlegesohle, *die;* **b)** *(part of shoe or boot)* Brandsohle, *die*

insolence ['ɪnsələns] *n., no pl.* Unverschämtheit, *die;* Frechheit, *die;* Insolenz, *die (geh.)*

insolent ['ɪnsələnt] *adj.*, **insolently** ['ɪnsələntlɪ] *adv.* **a)** *(contemptuous[ly])* anmaßend; überheblich; **b)** *(insulting[ly])* unverschämt; frech; insolent *(geh.)*

insolubility [ɪnsɒljʊ'bɪlɪtɪ] *n., no pl. see* **insoluble:** Unlösbarkeit, *die;* Unlöslichkeit, *die*

insoluble [ɪn'sɒljʊbl] *adj.* **a)** unlösbar ⟨*Problem, Rätsel usw.*⟩; **b)** unlöslich ⟨*Substanz*⟩; insolubel *(Chem.)* ⟨*Verbindung*⟩

insolvency [ɪn'sɒlvənsɪ] *n.* Insolvenz, *die (bes. Wirtsch.)*; Zahlungsunfähigkeit, *die*

insolvent [ɪn'sɒlvənt] **1.** *adj. (unable to pay debts)* insolvent *(bes. Wirtsch.)*; zahlungsunfähig. **2.** *n.* zahlungsunfähiger Schuldner

insomnia [ɪn'sɒmnɪə] *n.* Schlaflosigkeit, *die;* Insomnie, *die (Med.)*

insomniac [ɪn'sɒmnɪæk] *n.* an Schlaflosigkeit Leidender/Leidende; **be an** ~: an Schlaflosigkeit leiden

insomuch [ɪnsəʊ'mʌtʃ] *adv.* **a)** *(to such an extent)* ~ **that** so sehr *od.* dermaßen, daß; **b)** *(inasmuch)* insofern (**as** als)

insouciance [ɪn'su:sɪəns, ɛ̃'su:sjɑ̃s] *n., no pl.* Unbekümmertheit, *die;* Sorglosigkeit, *die*

insouciant [ɪn'su:sɪənt, ɛ̃'su:sjɑ̃] *adj.* unbekümmert; sorglos

inspect [ɪn'spekt] *v. t.* **a)** *(view closely)* prüfend betrachten; **let me** ~ **your hands** laß mich mal deine Hände sehen; zeig mal deine Hände vor; ~ **a cat for fleas** eine Katze auf Flöhe untersuchen; **b)** *(examine officially)* überprüfen; inspizieren, kontrollieren ⟨*Räumlichkeiten*⟩; abschreiten ⟨*Ehrenformation*⟩

inspection [ɪn'spekʃn] *n.* Überprüfung, *die; (of premises)* Kontrolle, *die;* Inspektion, *die;* **tour of** ~: Inspektionsrunde, *die; (on foot also)* Inspektionsgang, *der* (**of** durch); **present/show/submit sth. for** ~: etw. zur Prüfung vorlegen; **hold out your hands for** ~: zeigt eure Hände vor; **on [closer]** ~: bei näherer Betrachtung *od.* Prüfung

in'spection copy *n.* Ansichtsexemplar, *das; (for teachers)* Lehrerprüfstück, *das*

inspector [ɪn'spektə(r)] *n.* **a)** *(official) (on bus, train, etc.)* Kontrolleur, *der*/Kontrolleurin, *die;* ~ **[of schools]** Schulrat, *der*/-rätin, *die;* **health** ~: *Beamter/Beamtin in der Gesundheitsfürsorge;* **b)** *(Brit.: police officer)* ≈ Polizeiinspektor, *der*

inspector: ~ **'general** *n.* Oberinspektor, *der;* ~ **of 'taxes** *n. (Brit.)* Finanzbeamte, *der*/Finanzbeamtin, *die*

inspiration [ɪnspə'reɪʃn] *n.* **a)** Inspiration, *die (geh.)*; **get one's** ~ **from sth.** sich von etw. inspirieren lassen; **I have just had an** ~: ich hatte gerade eine [plötzliche] Eingebung; mir ist gerade eine Erleuchtung gekommen *(oft iron.)*; **sth. is an** ~ **to sb.** etw. inspiriert jmdn.; **b)** *(drawing in of breath)* Inspiration, *die (Med.)*; Einatmung, *die*

inspire [ɪn'spaɪə(r)] *v. t.* **a)** *(instil thought or feeling into)* inspirieren *(geh.)*; **in an** ~**d moment** *(coll.)* in einem Augenblick der Erleuchtung; **b)** *(breathe in)* einatmen ⟨*Luft*⟩; **c)** *(animate)* inspirieren; anregen; *(encourage)* anspornen; ~ **sb. with hope/confidence/respect** jmdn. mit Hoffnung/Vertrauen/Respekt erfüllen; ~**d playing** beseeltes Spiel; ~**d idea** genialer Gedanke; ~**d guess** intuitiv richtige Vermutung; **d)** *(instil)* einflößen ⟨*Mut, Angst, Respekt*⟩ (**in** *Dat.*); [er]wecken ⟨*Vertrauen, Gedanke, Hoffnung*⟩ (**in** in + *Dat.*); hervorrufen ⟨*Haß, Abneigung*⟩ (**in** bei); *(incite)* anstiften; anzetteln *(abwertend)* ⟨*Unruhen usw.*⟩; **what** ~**d this piece of music?** woher kamen die Anregungen zu diesem Musikstück?

inspiring [ɪn'spaɪərɪŋ] *adj.* inspirierend *(geh.)*; **his speech was not particularly** ~: seine Rede riß einen nicht gerade vom Stuhl *(ugs.)*

inst. *abbr. (Commerc.)* **instant** d. M.

instability [ɪnstə'bɪlɪtɪ] *n. (mental, physical)* Labilität, *die; (inconstancy)* Instabilität, *die*

install [ɪn'stɔ:l] *v. t.* **a)** *(establish)* ~ **oneself**

sich installieren; *(in a chair etc.)* sich niederlassen; sich pflanzen *(ugs.)*; *(in a house etc.)* sich einrichten; **when we're ~ed in our new house** wenn wir in unserem neuen Haus eingerichtet sind; **b)** *(set up for use)* installieren ‹*Heizung, Leitung*›; anschließen ‹*Telefon*›; einbauen ‹*Badezimmer*›; aufstellen, anschließen ‹*Herd*›; **c)** *(place ceremonially)* installieren *(geh.)*; **~ sb. in an office/a post** jmdn. in ein Amt einführen *od.* einsetzen

installation [ɪnstəˈleɪʃn] *n.* **a)** *(installing) (in an office or post)* Amtseinsetzung, *die;* Amtseinführung, *die;* Installation, *die (schweiz., sonst veralt.)*; *(setting up for use)* Installation, *die; (of bathroom etc.)* Einbau, *der; (of telephone, cooker)* Anschluß, *der;* **~ charges** Installationskosten; **b)** *(apparatus etc. installed)* Anlage, *die;* **kitchen ~:** Kücheneinrichtung, *die*

instalment (*Amer.:* **installment**) [ɪnˈstɔːlmənt] *n.* **a)** *(part-payment)* Rate, *die;* **pay by** *or* **in ~s** in Raten *od.* ratenweise zahlen; **monthly ~:** Monatsrate, *die;* **b)** *(of serial, novel)* Fortsetzung, *die; (of film, radio programme)* Folge, *die;* **c) ~ plan** *(Amer.)* Ratenzahlung, *die;* Teilzahlung, *die;* **buy on an ~ plan** auf Raten kaufen

instance [ˈɪnstəns] **1.** *n.* **a)** *(example)* Beispiel, *das* (**of** für); **as an ~ of ...:** als [ein] Beispiel für ...; **for ~:** zum Beispiel; **b)** *(particular case)* **in your/this ~:** in deinem/diesem Fall[e]; **in many ~s** in vielen Fällen; **isolated ~s** Einzelfälle; **c) at the ~ of ...:** auf Ersuchen *od.* Betreiben (+ *Gen.*); **at his ~:** auf seine Veranlassung [hin]; auf sein Betreiben; **court of first ~** *(Law)* erste Instanz; **d) in the first ~:** zuerst *od.* zunächst einmal; *(at the very beginning)* gleich zu Anfang; **it will be for six months in the first ~:** es ist zunächst auf sechs Monate befristet. **2.** *v. t.* **a)** *(cite as an ~)* anführen; **b)** *usu. in pass. (exemplify)* exemplifizieren

instant [ˈɪnstənt] **1.** *adj.* **a)** *(occurring immediately)* unmittelbar; sofortig ‹*Wirkung, Linderung, Ergebnis*›; **these new showers give you ~ hot water** mit diesen neuen Duschen hat man sofort heißes Wasser; **b) ~ coffee/tea** Instant- *od.* Pulverkaffee/Instanttee, *der;* **~ potatoes** fertiger Kartoffelbrei; **~ cake-mix** fertige Backmischung; **~ meal** Fertiggericht, *das;* **c)** *(fig.: hurriedly produced)* eilig angefertigt/geschrieben *usw.*; **d)** *(Commerc.)* dieses Monats. **2.** *n.* Augenblick, *der;* **at that very ~:** genau in dem Augenblick; **come here this ~:** komm sofort *od.* auf der Stelle her; **we were just this ~ talking about you** wir haben gerade eben von dir gesprochen; **the ~ he walked in at the door ...:** in dem Augenblick, als er hereintrat, ...; **in an ~:** augenblicklich; sofort; **not [for] an ~:** keinen Augenblick

instantaneous [ɪnstənˈteɪnɪəs] *adj.* unmittelbar; **his reaction was ~:** er reagierte sofort; **death was ~:** der Tod trat sofort *od.* unmittelbar ein

instantaneously [ɪnstənˈteɪnɪəslɪ] *adv.* sofort; unverzüglich

instantly [ˈɪnstəntlɪ] *adv.* sofort; **he is ~ likeable** er ist einem sofort sympathisch

instant ˈreplay *n. (Sport)* [sofortige] Wiederholung

instead [ɪnˈsted] *adv.* statt dessen; **~ of doing sth.** [an]statt etw. zu tun; **~ of sth.** anstelle einer Sache *(Gen.)*; **I will go ~ of you** ich gehe an deiner Stelle; **Friday ~ of Saturday** Freitag anstelle von *od.* [an]statt Sonnabend

ˈinstep *n.* **a)** *(of foot)* Spann, *der;* Fußrücken, *der;* **b)** *(of shoe)* Blatt, *das*

instigate [ˈɪnstɪgeɪt] *v. t.* **a)** *(urge on)* anstiften (**to** zu); **~ sb. to do sth.** jmdn. dazu anstiften, etw. zu tun; **b)** *(bring about)* initiieren *(geh.)* ‹*Reformen, Projekt usw.*›; anzetteln *(abwertend)* ‹*Streik usw.*›

instigation [ɪnstɪˈgeɪʃn] *n.* **a)** *(urging)* Anstiftung, *die;* **at sb.'s ~:** auf jmds. Betreiben *(Akk.)*; **b)** *(bringing about)* Anzettelung, *die (abwertend); (of reforms etc.)* Initiierung, *die (geh.)*

instigator [ˈɪnstɪgeɪtə(r)] *n.* **a)** *(of bank raid etc.)* Anstifter, *der*/Anstifterin, *die;* **b)** *(of riot, strike)* Anzettler, *der*/Anzettlerin, *die (abwertend); (of reforms)* Initiator, *der*/Initiatorin, *die (geh.)*

instil (*Amer.:* **instill**) [ɪnˈstɪl] *v. t.*, **-ll- a)** *(introduce gradually)* einflößen (**in** *Dat.*); einimpfen (**in** *Dat.*); beibringen ‹*gutes Benehmen, Wissen*› (**in** *Dat.*); **b)** *(put in by drops)* einträufeln (**into** in + *Akk.*)

instinct [ˈɪnstɪnkt] *n.* **a)** Instinkt, *der;* **~ for survival, survival ~:** Überlebenstrieb, *der; see also* **herd 1 b**; **b)** *(intuition)* Instinkt, *der;* instinktives Gefühl (**for** für); *(unconscious skill)* natürliche Begabung (**for** für); Sinn, *der* (**for** für); **~ warns them when danger is near** der Instinkt warnt sie bei drohender Gefahr; **have an ~ for business** Geschäftssinn *od.* -instinkt haben; **c)** *(innate impulse)* angeborener *od.* natürlicher *od.* instinktiver Drang

instinctive [ɪnˈstɪnktɪv] *adj.*, **instinctively** [ɪnˈstɪnktɪvlɪ] *adv.* instinktiv

institute [ˈɪnstɪtjuːt] **1.** *n.* Institut, *das; see also* **Women's Institute.** **2.** *v. t.* einführen ‹*Reform, Brauch, Beschränkung*›; einleiten ‹*Suche, Verfahren, Untersuchung*›; gründen ‹*Gesellschaft*›; anstrengen ‹*Prozeß, Klage*›; schaffen ‹*Posten*›; einrichten ‹*Ausstellung*›; **his wife ~d divorce proceedings against him** seine Ehefrau reichte die Scheidung [gegen ihn] ein

institution [ɪnstɪˈtjuːʃn] *n.* **a)** *(instituting)* Einführung, *die;* **b)** *(law, custom)* Institution, *die;* **c)** *(coll.: familiar object)* Institution, *die;* **become an ~:** zur Institution werden; **he's one of the ~s of the place** er gehört dort/hier schon zum Inventar *(scherzh.)*; **d)** *(institute)* Heim, *das;* Anstalt, *die;* **charitable/educational ~:** Wohltätigkeitseinrichtung/Erziehungsanstalt, *die*

institutional [ɪnstɪˈtjuːʃənl] *adj.* **a)** *(of, like, organized through institutions)* institutionell *(geh.)*; **b)** *(suggestive of typical charitable institutions)* Heim-; Anstalts-; **~ care/catering** Heim-/Anstaltsfürsorge, *die*/Heim-/Anstaltsverpflegung, *die;* **c)** *(Amer.)* **~ advertising** Prestigewerbung, *die;* institutionelle Werbung *(fachspr.)*

instruct [ɪnˈstrʌkt] *v. t.* **a)** *(teach)* unterrichten ‹*Klasse, Fach*›; **b)** *(direct, command)* anweisen; die Anweisung erteilen (+ *Dat.*); instruieren; **we were ~ed to do it in this way** wir hatten Weisung *(Amtsspr.) od.* Anweisung, es so zu machen; **c)** *(inform)* unterrichten; in Kenntnis setzen; instruieren *(geh.)*; **d)** *(Law: appoint)* beauftragen ‹*Anwalt*›

instruction [ɪnˈstrʌkʃn] *n.* **a)** *(teaching)* Unterricht, *der;* **a course of ~:** ein Lehrgang; **give ~ in judo** Judounterricht erteilen; **'Driver under ~'** ≈ „Fahrschule"; **b)** *esp. in pl. (direction, order)* Anweisung, *die;* Instruktion, *die;* **~ manual/~s for use** Gebrauchsanleitung, *die; (for machine etc.)* Betriebsanleitung, *die;* **they had precise ~s as to where to go** sie hatten genaue Anweisung, wo sie hinzugehen hatten; **under ~s from** *or* **on the ~s of the committee** auf Anweisung *od.* Anordnung des Komitees; **be under strict ~s to do sth.** strenge Anweisung haben, etw. zu tun; **c)** *(Computing)* Befehl, *der*

instructional [ɪnˈstrʌkʃənl] *adj.* Schulungs-; lehrreich ‹*Erfahrung*›; **an ~ film** ein Lehrfilm

instructive [ɪnˈstrʌktɪv] *adj.* aufschlußreich; instruktiv; lehrreich ‹*Erfahrung, Buch*›

instructively [ɪnˈstrʌktɪvlɪ] *adv.* aufschlußreich; instruktiv; **an ~ written book** ein lehrreiches Buch

instructor [ɪnˈstrʌktə(r)] *n.* **a)** Lehrer, *der*/Lehrerin, *die; (Mil.)* Ausbilder, *der;* **riding ~:** Reitlehrer, *der*/-lehrerin, *die;* **b)** *(Amer. Univ.)* Dozent, *der*/Dozentin, *die*

instrument [ˈɪnstrʊmənt] *n.* **a)** *(tool, implement)* Instrument, *das;* **~s of torture** Folterwerkzeuge *od.* -instrumente; **b)** *(measuring-device)* Instrument, *das;* **~ failure** Versagen der Instrumente; **c)** *(Mus.)* Instrument, *das;* **d)** *(person)* Werkzeug, *das;* Instrument, *das (geh.)*; **e)** *(means, cause)* Mittel, *das;* **f)** *(Law)* Urkunde, *die;* **~ of abdication** Abdankungsurkunde, *die*

instrumental [ɪnstrʊˈmentl] *adj.* **a)** *(serving as instrument or means)* dienlich (**to** *Dat.*); förderlich (**to** *Dat.*); **he was ~ in finding me a post** er hat mir zu einer Stelle verholfen; **b)** *(Mus.)* instrumental; Instrumental- ‹*musik, -version, -nummer*›; **c)** *(Ling.)* instrumental

instrumentalist [ɪnstrʊˈmentəlɪst] *n.* Instrumentalist, *der*/Instrumentalistin, *die*

instrumentation [ɪnstrʊmenˈteɪʃn] *n.* **a)** *(Mus.)* Instrumentation, *die;* **b)** *(provision)* Instrumentierung, *die; (use)* Anwendung von Instrumenten

instrument: ~ board, ~ panel *ns.* Instrumentenbrett, *das;* Paneel, *das*

insubordinate [ɪnsəˈbɔːdɪnət] *adj.* aufsässig; widersetzlich; *(Mil.)* ungehorsam; **~ behaviour** Widersetzlichkeit, *die; (Mil.)* Ungehorsam, *der*

insubordination [ɪnsəbɔːdɪˈneɪʃn] *n.*, *no pl.* Aufsässigkeit, *die;* Widersetzlichkeit, *die; (Mil.)* Gehorsamsverweigerung, *die*

insubstantial [ɪnsəbˈstænʃl] *adj.* **a)** *(lacking solidity)* wenig substantiell *(geh.)*; gegenstandslos ‹*Anschuldigung*›; dürftig ‹*Essen, Kleidung*›; gering[fügig] ‹*Menge, Betrag*›; **b)** *(not real)* unwirklich; gegenstandslos ‹*Hoffnung, Angst*›

insufferable [ɪnˈsʌfərəbl] *adj.* **a)** *(unbearably arrogant)* unausstehlich; **b)** *(intolerable)* unerträglich

insufferably [ɪnˈsʌfərəblɪ] *adv.* unerträglich

insufficiency [ɪnsəˈfɪʃənsɪ] *n.* **a)** Unzulänglichkeit, *die; (of money, provisions, information)* Mangel, *der* (**of** an + *Dat.*); *(inability, incompetence)* Unfähigkeit, *die;* mangelnde Eignung; **an ~ of money** Geldknappheit, *die;* **b)** *(Med.)* Insuffizienz, *die;* **cardiac/renal ~:** Herz-/Niereninsuffizienz, *die*

insufficient [ɪnsəˈfɪʃənt] *adj.* nicht genügend ‹*Arbeit, Gründe, Geld*›; unzulänglich ‹*Beweise*›; unzureichend ‹*Versorgung, Beleuchtung*›; **we have ~ membership** wir haben nicht genügend *od.* zuwenig Mitglieder; **give sb. ~ notice** jmdm. nicht rechtzeitig Bescheid geben

insufficiently [ɪnsəˈfɪʃəntlɪ] *adv.* ungenügend; unzulänglich; unzureichend ‹*versorgen*›

insular [ˈɪnsjʊlə(r)] *adj.* **a)** *(of an island)* Insel-; insular *(fachspr.)*; **an ~ people** *or* **race** ein Inselvolk; **b)** *(fig.: narrow-minded)* provinziell *(abwertend)*

insularity [ɪnsjʊˈlærɪtɪ] *n.* Provinzialität, *die (abwertend)*

insulate [ˈɪnsjʊleɪt] *v. t.* **a)** *(isolate)* isolieren (**against, from** gegen); **~ floors against noise** Fußböden schallisolieren *od.* gegen Schall isolieren; **b)** *(detach from surrounding)* isolieren (**from** von)

insulating [ˈɪnsjʊleɪtɪŋ]: **~ material** *n.* Isoliermaterial, *das;* **~ tape** *n.* Isolierband, *das*

insulation [ɪnsjʊˈleɪʃn] *n.* Isolierung, *die;* **put ~ in the loft** den Dachboden isolieren

insulator [ˈɪnsjʊleɪtə(r)] *n.* Isolator, *der*

insulin [ˈɪnsjʊlɪn] *n. (Med.)* Insulin, *das*

ˈinsulin shock *n. (Med.)* Insulinschock, *der*

insult 1. [ˈɪnsʌlt] *n.* Beleidigung, *die* (**to**

Gen.); **fling an ~ in sb.'s face** jmdm. eine Beleidigung an den Kopf werfen *(ugs.); see also* **injury b. 2.** [ɪn'sʌlt] *v. t.* beleidigen

insulting [ɪn'sʌltɪŋ] *adj.* beleidigend

insuperable [ɪn'su:pərəbl, ɪn'sju:pərəbl] *adj.*, **insuperably** [ɪn'su:pərəblɪ, ɪn'sju:pərəblɪ] *adv.* unüberwindlich

insupportable [ɪnsə'pɔ:təbl] *adj.* **a)** *(unendurable)* unerträglich; **b)** *(unjustifiable)* nicht zu rechtfertigen *präd.*; nicht zu rechtfertigend *nicht präd.*

insurance [ɪn'ʃʊərəns] *n.* **a)** *(insuring)* Versicherung, *die; (fig.)* Sicherheit, *die;* Gewähr, *die;* **take out ~ against/on sth.** eine Versicherung gegen etw. abschließen/etw. versichern lassen; **travel ~:** Reisegepäck- und -unfallversicherung, *die;* **~ against fire/theft/accident** Feuer-/Diebstahl-/Unfallversicherung, *die;* **b)** *(sum received)* Versicherungssumme, *die; (sum paid)* Versicherungsbetrag, *der;* **I got £15 ~ when my bike was stolen** ich bekam 15 Pfund von der Versicherung, als mein Fahrrad gestohlen wurde; **I've been paying ~ for the last 15 years** ich zahle jetzt schon 15 Jahre in die Versicherung ein; **claim the ~:** den Versicherungsanspruch geltend machen

insurance: ~ agent Versicherungsvertreter, *der*/-vertreterin, *die;* Versicherungsagent, *der*/-agentin, *die;* **~ broker** *n.* Versicherungsmakler, *der;* **~ company** *n.* Versicherungsgesellschaft, *die;* **~ policy** *n.* Versicherungspolice, *die; (fig.)* Sicherheit, *die;* Gewähr, *die;* **take out an ~ policy** eine Versicherung abschließen; **~ stamp** *n. (Brit.)* Versicherungsmarke, *die*

insure [ɪn'ʃʊə(r)] *v. t.* **a)** *(secure payment to)* versichern ‹*Person*› **(against** gegen); **~ [oneself] against sth.** sich gegen etw. versichern; **the ~d** der/die Versicherte; der Versicherungsnehmer/die Versicherungsnehmerin *(fachspr.);* **b)** *(secure payment for)* ‹*Versicherungsgesellschaft:*› versichern; ‹*Versicherungsnehmer:*› versichern lassen ‹*Gepäck, Gemälde usw.*›; **~ one's life** eine Lebensversicherung abschließen; **c)** *(Amer.) see* **ensure**

insurer [ɪn'ʃʊərə(r)] *n.* Versicherer, *der;* Versicherungsgeber, *der (fachspr.)*

insurgent [ɪn'sɜ:dʒənt] **1.** *attrib. adj.* aufständisch. **2.** *n.* Aufständische, *der/die*

insurmountable [ɪnsə'maʊntəbl] *adj.* unüberwindlich

insurrection [ɪnsə'rekʃn] *n. (uprising)* Aufstand, *der*

intact [ɪn'tækt] *adj.* **a)** *(entire)* unbeschädigt; unversehrt; intakt ‹*Uhr, Maschine usw.*›; **keep one's capital ~:** sein Kapital unangetastet lassen; **b)** *(unimpaired)* unversehrt; **keep one's reputation ~:** sich *(Dat.)* einen guten Ruf bewahren; **c)** *(untouched)* unberührt; unangetastet; **the package was returned to me ~:** das Paket wurde ungeöffnet an mich zurückgesandt

intaglio [ɪn'tælɪəʊ, ɪn'tɑ:lɪəʊ] *n., pl.* **~s a)** *(engraved design)* eingeschnittene Figur; **b)** *(carving in hard material)* Steinschneidekunst, *die;* Glyptik, *die;* **in ~:** in negativer Gravierung; **c)** *(printing process)* Tiefdruck, *der;* **d)** *(gem with incised design)* Intaglio, *das*

'**intake** *n.* **a)** *(action)* Aufnahme, *die;* **~ of breath** Atemholen, *das;* **b)** *(where water enters channel or pipe)* Einströmungsöffnung, *die; (where air or fuel enters engine)* Ansaugöffnung, *die; (airway into mine)* Einziehschacht, *der;* **c)** *(persons or things taken in)* Neuzugänge; *(amount taken in)* aufgenommene Menge; *(number of persons taken in)* Zahl der aufgenommenen Personen; **~ of alcohol** Alkoholkonsum, *der;* **~ of calories** Kalorienzufuhr, *die;* aufgenommene Kalorienmenge; **~ of students** Zahl der Studienanfänger

intangible [ɪn'tændʒɪbl] *adj.* **a)** *(that cannot be touched)* nicht greifbar; **feel an ~ presence in the room** spüren, daß etwas Unwirkliches anwesend ist; **b)** *(that cannot be grasped mentally)* unbestimmbar; unbestimmt ‹*Gefühl*›; vage ‹*Vorstellung*›; **~ assets** *(Econ.)* immaterielle Anlagewerte

integer ['ɪntɪdʒə(r)] *n. (Math.)* ganze Zahl

integral ['ɪntɪgrl] **1.** *adj.* **a)** *(of a whole)* wesentlich, integral ‹*Bestandteil*›; **b)** *(whole, complete)* vollständig; vollkommen; **c)** *(forming a whole)* ein Ganzes bildend; integrierend; **an ~ group** eine aus verschiedenen integrierenden Teilen zusammengesetzte Gruppe; **d)** *(Math.) (of or denoted by an integer)* ganzzahlig; *(involving only integers)* Integral-; *see also* **calculus a. 2.** *n. (Math.)* Integral, *das*

integrate ['ɪntɪgreɪt] **1.** *v. t.* **a)** *(combine into a whole)* integrieren; **an ~d Europe** ein vereintes Europa; **an ~d personality** eine in sich *(Dat.)* ausgewogene Persönlichkeit; **b)** *(into society)* integrieren; **~ sb. into a society** jmdn. in eine Gesellschaft integrieren *od.* eingliedern; **c)** *(open to all racial groups)* **~ a school/college** eine Schule/ein College für alle Rassen zugänglich machen; **an ~d school** eine Schule ohne Rassentrennung; **d)** *(Math.)* integrieren. **2.** *v. i.* integrieren; ‹*Schulen:*› auch für Farbige zugänglich werden

integrated 'circuit *n. (Electronics)* integrierter Schaltkreis

integration [ɪntɪ'greɪʃn] *n.* **a)** *(integrating; also Math.)* Integration, *die;* **b)** *(ending of segregation)* Integration, *die* **(into** in + *Akk.*); **the ~ of the schools** die Aufhebung der Rassentrennung an den Schulen; **racial ~:** Rassenintegration, *die;* **c)** *(Psych.)* Integration, *die;* **d)** *(Commerc.)* **horizontal ~:** horizontale Integration; **vertical ~:** Vertikalkonzentration, *die*

integrationist [ɪntɪ'greɪʃənɪst] *n.* Integrationist, *der*/Integrationistin, *die*

integrity [ɪn'tegrɪtɪ] *n.* **a)** *(uprightness, honesty)* Redlichkeit, *die; (of business, venture)* Seriosität, *die; (of style)* Echtheit, *die;* Unverfälschtheit, *die;* **intellectual ~:** intellektuelle Redlichkeit *od.* Integrität; **business ~:** honoriges Geschäftsgebaren; **a writer of ~:** ein redlicher Autor; **b)** *(wholeness) (of country, empire)* Einheit, *die; (of person)* Ganzheit, *die; (of fossil etc.)* Unversehrtheit, *die;* **territorial ~:** territoriale Integrität; **c)** *(soundness)* Intaktheit, *die*

integument [ɪn'tegjʊmənt] *n. (Biol.)* Integument, *das*

intellect ['ɪntəlekt] *n.* **a)** *(faculty)* Verstand, *der;* Intellekt, *der;* **~ distinguishes man from the animals** das Denkvermögen unterscheidet den Menschen vom Tier; **b)** *(understanding)* Intelligenz, *die;* **powers of ~:** Verstandeskräfte; intellektuelle Fähigkeiten; **c)** *(person)* großer Geist

intellectual [ɪntə'lektjʊəl] **1.** *adj.* **a)** *(of intellect)* intellektuell; geistig ‹*Klima, Interessen, Waffe, Arbeit*›; abstrakt ‹*Mitgefühl, Sympathie*›; **~ powers** intellektuelle Fähigkeiten; **b)** *(possessing good understanding or intelligence)* geistig anspruchsvoll ‹*Person, Publikum*›. **2.** *n.* Intellektuelle, *der/die*

intellectually [ɪntə'lektjʊəlɪ] *adv.* intellektuell; geistig; **it's ~ stimulating** es regt den Geist an

intelligence [ɪn'telɪdʒəns] *n.* **a)** *(quickness of understanding)* Intelligenz, *die;* **have the ~ to do sth.** so intelligent sein, etw. zu tun; **have ~:** intelligent sein; **b)** *(intellect, understanding)* Intelligenz, *die;* **a man of no mean ~:** ein sehr intelligenter Mann; **c)** *(being)* Geist, *der; (spirit)* Geistwesen, *das;* **d)** *(information)* Informationen *Pl.; (news)* Nachrichten *Pl.;* Meldungen *Pl.;* **a source of ~:** eine Informationsquelle; **e)** *([persons employed in] collecting information)* Nachrichtendienst, *der;* **military ~:** militärischer Geheimdienst; **be in ~:** dem Nachrichtendienst angehören

intelligence: ~ department *n.* Nachrichtendienst, *der;* **~ officer** *n.* Nachrichtenoffizier, *der;* **~ quotient** *n.* Intelligenzquotient, *der;* **~ service** *n.* Nachrichtendienst, *der;* **~ test** *n.* Intelligenztest, *der*

intelligent [ɪn'telɪdʒənt] *adj.* intelligent; intelligent geschrieben, geistreich ‹*Buch*›; *(clever also)* klug; gescheit; **is there ~ life on other planets?** gibt es intelligente *od.* vernunftbegabte Lebewesen auf anderen Planeten?

intelligently [ɪn'telɪdʒəntlɪ] *adv.* intelligent

intelligentsia [ɪntelɪ'dʒentsɪə] *n.* Intelligentsia, *die (geh.);* Intelligenz, *die*

intelligibility [ɪntelɪdʒɪ'bɪlɪtɪ] *n., no pl.* Verständlichkeit, *die*

intelligible [ɪn'telɪdʒɪbl] *adj.* verständlich **(to** für); intelligibel *(Philos.);* **is their language ~ to you?** verstehst du ihre Sprache?

intelligibly [ɪn'telɪdʒɪblɪ] *adv.* deutlich

intemperance [ɪn'tempərəns] *n.* Maßlosigkeit, *die;* Unmäßigkeit, *die; (addiction to drinking)* Trunksucht, *die*

intemperate [ɪn'tempərət] *adj.* **a)** *(immoderate)* maßlos; überzogen, übertrieben ‹*Verhalten, Bemerkung*›; unmäßig, maßlos ‹*Verlangen, Appetit, Konsum*›; übermäßig ‹*Eifer*›; ausschweifend ‹*Leben*›; **his ~ conduct** seine Maßlosigkeit; **b)** *(addicted to drinking)* trunksüchtig

intemperately [ɪn'tempərətlɪ] *adv.* unmäßig

intend [ɪn'tend] *v. t.* **a)** *(have as one's purpose)* beabsichtigen; **~ doing sth.** *or* **to do sth.** beabsichtigen, etw. zu tun; **did you ~ that [to happen]?** hattest du das beabsichtigt?; **we ~ed no harm** wir haben nichts Böses damit bezweckt; *(we didn't mean to cause offence)* wir haben es nicht böse gemeint; **it isn't really what we ~ed** es ist eigentlich nicht das, was wir wollten; **longer than was ~ed** länger als geplant *od.* beabsichtigt; **b)** *(design, mean)* **we ~ed it as a stopgap** das sollte eine Notlösung sein; **we ~ him to go** wir wollen, daß er geht; er soll gehen; **this dish is ~ed to be cooked slowly** dieses Gericht sollte langsam gekocht werden; **it was ~ed as a joke** das sollte ein Witz sein; **what do you ~ by that remark?** was willst du mit dieser Bemerkung sagen?; **what does the author ~ here?** was will der Autor hier sagen? *See also* **intended**

intended [ɪn'tendɪd] **1.** *adj.* beabsichtigt ‹*Wirkung*›; erklärt ‹*Ziel*›; absichtlich ‹*Beleidigung*›; **be ~ for sb./sth.** für jmdn./etw. bestimmt *od.* gedacht sein; **~ for adults/beginners** für Erwachsene/Anfänger; **~ for drinking** zum Trinken [gedacht]. **2.** *n. (coll.)* Zukünftige, *der/die (ugs.)*

intense [ɪn'tens] *adj.*, **~r** [ɪn'tensə(r)], **~st** [ɪn'tensɪst] **a)** intensiv; stark ‹*Hitze, Belastung*›; stark, heftig ‹*Schmerzen*›; kräftig, intensiv ‹*Farbe*›; äußerst groß ‹*Aufregung*›; ungeheuer ‹*Kälte, Helligkeit*›; **the day before the play opens is a period of ~ activity** am Tag vor der Premiere herrscht große Geschäftigkeit; **b)** *(eager, ardent)* eifrig, lebhaft ‹*Diskussion*›; stark, ausgeprägt ‹*Interesse*›; brennend, glühend ‹*Verlangen*›; äußerst groß ‹*Empörung, Aufregung, Betrübnis*›; tief ‹*Gefühl*›; rasend ‹*Haß, Eifersucht*›; **c)** *(with strong emotion)* stark gefühlsbetont ‹*Person, Brief*›; *(earnest)* ernst

intensely [ɪn'tenslɪ] *adv.* äußerst ‹*schwierig, verärgert, enttäuscht, kalt*›; ernsthaft, intensiv ‹*studieren*›; intensiv ‹*fühlen*›

intensification [ɪntensɪfɪ'keɪʃn] *n.* Intensivierung, *die*

intensifier [ɪn'tensɪfaɪə(r)] *n. (Ling.)* intensivierendes Wort

intensify [ɪn'tensɪfaɪ] **1.** *v. t.* intensivieren. **2.** *v. i.* zunehmen; ‹*Hitze, Schmerzen:*› stärker werden; ‹*Kampf:*› sich verschärfen

intensity [ɪn'tensɪtɪ] *n.* **a)** Intensität, *die; (of feeling also)* Heftigkeit, *die;* **the heat had lost some of its ~:** die Hitze hatte etwas abgenommen *od.* nachgelassen; **b)** *(measurable amount)* Intensität, *die*
intensive [ɪn'tensɪv] **1.** *adj.* **a)** *(vigorous, thorough)* intensiv; Intensiv‹*kurs*›; **b)** *(Ling.)* verstärkend; intensivierend; **c)** *(concentrated, directed to a single point or area)* intensiv; heftig ‹*Beschuß*›; gezielt ‹*Entwicklung*›; **d)** *(Econ.)* intensiv ‹*Landwirtschaft*›; **e)** *in comb.* **capital-~/labour-~:** kapital-/arbeitsintensiv. **2.** *n. see* **intensifier**
intensive 'care *n.* Intensivpflege, *die (Med.);* **be in ~:** auf der Intensivstation sein; **~ unit** Intensivstation, *die*
intensively [ɪn'tensɪvlɪ] *adv.* intensiv
intent [ɪn'tent] **1.** *n.* Absicht, *die;* **by ~:** beabsichtigt; **with good/malicious ~:** in guter/schlechter Absicht; **with ~ to do sth.** *(Law)* in der Absicht *od.* mit dem Vorsatz, etw. zu tun; **do sth. with ~:** etw. vorsätzlich tun; **to all ~s and purposes** im Grunde; praktisch. **2.** *adj.* **a)** *(resolved)* erpicht, versessen (**[up]on** auf + *Akk.*); **be ~ on achieving sth.** etw. unbedingt erreichen wollen; **be ~ upon revenge** auf Rache sinnen; **b)** *(attentively occupied)* eifrig beschäftigt (**on** mit); **be ~ on one's work** auf seine Arbeit konzentriert sein; in seine Arbeit vertieft sein; **c)** *(earnest, eager)* aufmerksam; konzentriert; forschend ‹*Blick*›
intention [ɪn'tenʃn] *n.* **a)** Absicht, *die;* Intention, *die;* **have no ~/every ~ of doing sth.** nicht die Absicht haben/die feste Absicht haben, etw. zu tun; **it was my ~ to visit him** ich hatte die Absicht *od.* beabsichtigte, ihn zu besuchen; **with the best of ~s** in der besten Absicht; **the road to hell is paved with good ~s** *(prov.)* der Weg zur Hölle ist mit guten Vorsätzen gepflastert *(Spr.);* **what is the author's ~ here?** was will der Autor hier sagen?; **b)** *in pl. (coll.: in respect of marriage)* [Heirats]absichten
intentional [ɪn'tenʃənl] *adj.* absichtlich; vorsätzlich *(bes. Rechtsspr.);* **it wasn't ~:** es war keine Absicht
intentionally [ɪn'tenʃənəlɪ] *adv.* absichtlich; mit Absicht
intently [ɪn'tentlɪ] *adv.* aufmerksam ‹*zuhören, lesen, beobachten*›
inter [ɪn'tɜː(r)] *v. t.,* **-rr-** *(literary)* bestatten *(geh.)* ‹*Leichnam*›
interact [ɪntər'ækt] *v. i.* **a)** ‹*Ideen:*› sich gegenseitig beeinflussen; ‹*Chemikalien usw.:*› aufeinander einwirken, miteinander reagieren; **b)** *(Sociol., Psych.)* interagieren
interaction [ɪntər'ækʃn] *n.* **a)** gegenseitige Beeinflussung; *(Chem., Phys.)* Wechselwirkung, *die;* Reaktion, *die;* **b)** *(Sociol., Psych.)* Interaktion, *die*
interactive [ɪntər'æktɪv] *adj.* **a)** *(Chem.)* miteinander reagierend; **b)** *(Sociol., Psych., Computing)* interaktiv
inter alia [ɪntər'eɪlɪə] *adv.* unter anderem
interbreed [ɪntə'briːd] **1.** *v. t.,* **interbred** [ɪntə'bred] bastardieren *(fachspr.);* kreuzen ‹*Pflanzen, Tiere*›. **2.** *v. i.,* **interbred** bastardisieren *(fachspr.);* sich kreuzen
intercede [ɪntə'siːd] *v. i.* sich einsetzen (**with** bei; **for, on behalf of** für)
intercept [ɪntə'sept] *v. t.* **a)** *(seize)* abfangen; **~ the enemy** dem Feind den Weg abschneiden; **b)** *(check, stop)* abwehren ‹*Schlag, Angriff*›; **c)** *(listen in to)* abhören ‹*Gespräch, Funkspruch*›
interception [ɪntə'sepʃn] *n. see* **intercept:** Abfangen, *das;* Abwehr, *die;* Abhören, *das*
interceptor [ɪntə'septə(r)] *n. (Air Force)* Abfangjäger, *der*
intercession [ɪntə'seʃn] *n. (mediation)* Vermittlung, *die, (entreaty)* Fürsprache, *die* (**for, on behalf of** für)
interchange 1. ['ɪntətʃeɪndʒ] *n.* **a)** *(reciprocal exchange)* Austausch, *der;* **b)** *(road junction)* [Autobahn]kreuz, *das.* **2.** [ɪntə'tʃeɪndʒ] *v. t.* **a)** *(exchange with each other)* austauschen; wechseln ‹*Briefe, Blicke, Worte, Grüße*›; **b)** *(put each in the other's place)* [miteinander] vertauschen; **they can be ~d** sie sind austauschbar; **c)** *(alternate)* wechseln; [aus]wechseln ‹*Kulissen usw.*›
interchangeable [ɪntə'tʃeɪndʒəbl] *adj.* austauschbar; synonym ‹*Wörter, Ausdrücke*›
inter-city [ɪntə'sɪtɪ] *adj.* Intercity-; **~ train** Intercity[-Zug], *der*
intercom ['ɪntəkɒm] *n. (coll.)* Gegensprechanlage, *die; (Aeronaut.)* Eigenverständigungsanlage, *die*
intercommunicate [ɪntəkə'mjuːnɪkeɪt] *v. i.* **a)** ‹*Räume:*› miteinander verbunden sein; **b)** ‹*Personen, Organisationen:*› Kontakt haben zueinander
interconnect [ɪntəkə'nekt] **1.** *v. t.* miteinander verbinden; zusammenschalten ‹*Stromkreise, Verstärker, Lautsprecher*›; **~ed facts/results** zusammenhängende Tatsachen/Ergebnisse; **the events are ~ed** es besteht ein Zusammenhang zwischen den Ereignissen. **2.** *v. i.* miteinander in Zusammenhang stehen; **~ing rooms** miteinander verbundene Zimmer
interconnection [ɪntəkə'nekʃn] *n. (of parts, components)* Zusammenwirken, *das; (of circuits)* Zusammenschalten, *das; (of facts, events, ideas)* Zusammenhang, *der*
intercontinental [ɪntəkɒntɪ'nentl] *adj.* interkontinental; Interkontinental‹*rakete, -flug, -reise*›
intercourse ['ɪntəkɔːs] *n., no pl.* **a)** *(social communication)* Umgang, *der;* **social ~:** gesellschaftlicher Verkehr; **human ~:** menschliche Kontakte; die Beziehungen der Menschen; **b)** *(sexual ~)* [Geschlechts]verkehr, *der*
interdenominational [ɪntədɪnɒmɪ'neɪʃənl] *adj.* interkonfessionell
interdepartmental [ɪntədiːpɑːt'mentl] *adj.* ‹*Konferenz, Zusammenarbeit, Streit*› zwischen den Abteilungen/Fachbereichen
interdependence [ɪntədɪ'pendəns] *n.* gegenseitige Abhängigkeit; Interdependenz, *die*
interdependent [ɪntədɪ'pendənt] *adj.* voneinander abhängig; interdependent
interdict ['ɪntədɪkt] *n.* **a)** *(authoritative prohibition)* Verbot, *das;* **b)** *(RC Ch.)* Interdikt, *das*
interdisciplinary [ɪntədɪsɪ'plɪnərɪ] *adj.* fachübergreifend; interdisziplinär
interest ['ɪntrəst, 'ɪntrɪst] **1.** *n.* **a)** *(concern, curiosity)* Interesse, *das;* Anliegen, *das;* **take** *or* **have an ~ in sb./sth.** sich für jmdn./etw. interessieren; **show/develop a [lively] ~ in sb./sth.** [lebhaftes] Interesse an jmdm./etw. zeigen/entwickeln; **take** *or* **have/show no further ~ in sb./sth.** das Interesse an jmdm./etw. verloren haben/kein Interesse mehr an jmdm./etw. zeigen; **[just] for** *or* **out of ~:** [nur] interessehalber; **with ~:** interessiert *(see also* **e**); **lose ~ in sb./sth.** das Interesse an jmdm./etw. verlieren; **~ in life/food** Lust am Leben/Essen; **b)** *(quality of sth.)* Interesse, *das;* Bedeutung, *die;* **this has no great ~ for me** das ist nicht sehr wichtig für mich; **be of ~:** interessant *od.* von Interesse sein (**to** für); **this is of no ~ to me** das ist belanglos für mich; **c)** *(advantage, profit)* Interesse, *das;* **act in one's own/sb.'s ~[s]** im eigenen/in jmds. Interesse handeln; **it is in your ~ to go** es liegt in deinem Interesse zu gehen; **in the ~[s] of humanity** zum Wohle der Menschheit; **d)** *(thing in which one is concerned)* Angelegenheit, *die;* Belange *Pl.;* **have a wide range of ~s** viele Interessen haben; **e)** *(Finance)* Zinsen *Pl.;* **rate of ~, ~ rate** Zinssatz, *der;* **~ on one's capital** Zinsen auf sein Kapital; **~ on a mortgage** Hypothekenzinsen *Pl.;* **at ~:** gegen *od.* auf Zinsen; **at 6 % ~:** zu 6 % Zinsen; **with ~** *(fig.: with increased force etc.)* überreichlich; doppelt und dreifach *(ugs.) (see also* **a**); **give back** *or* **return blows with ~** *(fig.)* Schläge mit doppelter Härte zurückgeben; **f)** *(financial stake)* Beteiligung, *die;* Anteil, *der;* **have [financial] ~s all over the world** an Firmen *od.* Unternehmungen in der ganzen Welt finanziell beteiligt sein; **American ~s in the Caribbean** amerikanische Interessen in der Karibik; **declare an ~:** seine Interessen darlegen; **g)** *(legal concern)* [Rechts]anspruch, *der;* **h)** *(party having common interest)* Interessengruppe, *die;* **banking ~s** Bankkreise *Pl.;* die Banken; **business ~s** die Großindustrie. *See also* **compound interest; simple interest; vested. 2.** *v. t.* interessieren (**in** für); **be ~ed in sb./sth.** sich für jmdn./etw. interessieren; **~ oneself in ...:** sich für ... interessieren; **sb. is ~ed by sb./sth.** jmd./etw. erregt jmds. Interesse; *see also* **interested**
interested ['ɪntrəstɪd, 'ɪntrɪstɪd] *adj.* **a)** *(taking or showing interest)* interessiert; **be ~ in music/football/sb.** sich für Musik/Fußball/jmdn. interessieren; **I shall be ~ to hear about your trip** ich bin gespannt darauf, von deiner Reise zu hören; **I should be ~ to know why ...:** es würde mich interessieren, warum ...; **be ~ in doing sth.** sich dafür interessieren, etw. zu tun; **he is ~ in buying a car** er würde gern ein Auto kaufen; **not ~ in his work** nicht an seiner Arbeit interessiert; **the ~ parties** die beteiligten Parteien; **he looked ~:** er zeigte sich interessiert; **b)** *(not impartial)* voreingenommen; eigennützig ‹*Beweggründe*›; befangen ‹*Zeuge*›
interest: ~-free *adj., adv.* unverzinslich; **~ group** *n.* Interessengruppe, *die*
interesting ['ɪntrəstɪŋ, 'ɪntrɪstɪŋ] *adj.* interessant
interestingly ['ɪntrəstɪŋlɪ, 'ɪntrɪstɪŋlɪ] *adv.* interessant; **~ [enough], ...:** interessanterweise ...
'interest rate *n.* Zinssatz, *der;* Zinsfuß, *der*
interface ['ɪntəfeɪs] *n.* **a)** *(surface)* Grenzfläche, *die;* **b)** *(place where interaction occurs)* Nahtstelle, *die;* Schnittstelle, *die; (fig.)* Verbindung, *die;* Kontakt, *der;* **c)** *(Computing)* Schnittstelle, *die*
interfacing ['ɪntəfeɪsɪŋ] *n. (Dressm.)* Einlage, *die*
interfere [ɪntə'fɪə(r)] *v. i.* **a)** *(meddle)* sich einmischen (**in** in + *Akk.*); **~ with sth.** sich an etw. *(Dat.)* zu schaffen machen; **b)** *(come into opposition)* in Konflikt geraten (**with** mit); **~ with sth.** etw. beeinträchtigen; **~ with sb.'s plans** jmds. Pläne durchkreuzen; **c)** *(Radio, Telev.)* stören (**with** *Akk.*); **d)** **~ with sb.** *(sexually)* jmdn. sexuell mißbrauchen; **e)** *(Phys.)* interferieren
interference [ɪntə'fɪərəns] *n.* **a)** *(interfering)* Einmischung, *die;* **b)** *(Radio, Telev.)* Störung, *die;* **~ suppressor** Siebkreis, *der;* Entstörgerät, *das;* **c)** *(sexual)* Notzucht, *die (veralt.);* Mißbrauch, *der;* **d)** *(Phys.)* Interferenz, *die*
interfering [ɪntə'fɪərɪŋ] *attrib. adj.* sich einmischend; **she is an ~ old busybody** sie mischt sich in alles und jedes ein
intergovernmental [ɪntəgʌvn'mentl] *adj.* zwischenstaatlich; **~ agreement/conference** Regierungsabkommen, *das*/-konferenz, *die;* **~ discussions** Gespräche auf Regierungsebene; **~ co-operation** internationale Zusammenarbeit
interim ['ɪntərɪm] **1.** *n.* **in the ~:** in der Zwischenzeit. **2.** *adj.* **a)** *(intervening)* dazwischenliegend; **the ~ period** die Zwischenzeit; **b)** *(temporary, provisional)* vorläufig ‹*Vereinbarung, Bericht, Anordnung, Zustand, Maßnahme*›; Zwischen‹*lösung, -abkommen, -kredit, -finanzierung, -zinsen*›; Übergangs‹*regierung, -regelung, -hilfe*›
interim 'dividend *n. (Finance)* Abschlagsdividende, *die*

interior [ɪn'tɪərə(r)] **1.** *adj.* **a)** inner...; Innen⟨*fläche, -einrichtung, -wand*⟩; **b)** *(inland)* im Landesinneren befindlich; **c)** *(internal, domestic)* Inlands-; Binnen⟨*markt, -handel*⟩; **d)** *(Cinemat.)* ~ **shots/photography** Innenaufnahmen *Pl.* **2.** *n.* **a)** *(inland region)* [Landes]innere, *das;* **b)** *(~ part)* Innere, *das;* **redecorate the ~ of the shop** den Laden innen renovieren; **c)** *([picture of] inside of building, room, etc.)* Innere, *das; (picture)* Interieur, *das;* **d)** *(Cinemat.)* Innenaufnahme, *die; (Theatre)* Szene eines Innenraumes; **e)** *(home affairs)* **Department of the I~** *(US, Canada),* **Ministry of the I~** *(France, Germany, etc.)* Innenministerium, *das;* Ministerium des Innern

interior: ~ **deco'ration** *n.* Raumgestaltung, *die;* ~ **'decorator** *n.* Raumgestalter, *der*/-gestalterin, *die;* ~ **de'sign** *n.* Innenarchitektur, *die;* ~ **de'signer** *n.* Innenarchitekt, *der*/-architektin, *die;* **~-sprung** *adj.* *(Brit.)* **~-sprung mattress** Federkernmatratze, *die*

interject [ɪntə'dʒekt] *v. t.* **a)** *(interpose)* einwerfen ⟨*Behauptung, Bemerkung, Frage*⟩; ~ **remarks** Einwürfe *od.* Zwischenbemerkungen machen; **..., he ~ed ...,** rief er dazwischen; **b)** *(remark parenthetically)* einflechten; nebenbei bemerken

interjection [ɪntə'dʒekʃn] *n.* **a)** *(exclamation)* Ausruf, *der; (Ling.)* Interjektion, *die;* **b)** *(interposed remark)* Einwurf, *der;* Zwischenbemerkung, *die*

interlace [ɪntə'leɪs] *v. t.* **a)** *(bind together)* zusammenfügen; **b)** *(interweave)* [miteinander] verflechten; *(fig.)* [miteinander] verbinden; **cloth ~d with gold threads** mit Goldfäden durchwirktes Tuch; **c)** *(mingle)* [miteinander] kombinieren ⟨*zwei Muster*⟩; spicken ⟨*Rede, Schreiben*⟩ **(with** mit)

interlard [ɪntə'lɑ:d] *v. t.* spicken **(with** mit); **be heavily ~ed with quotations** von Zitaten strotzen

interleave [ɪntə'li:v] *v. t.* *(Printing)* durchschießen **(with** mit); *(fig.)* abwechseln **(with** mit)

inter-library loan [ɪntəlaɪbrərɪ 'ləʊn] *n.* Fernleihe, *die;* **get a book on ~:** ein Buch über die Fernleihe bekommen

interlink [ɪntə'lɪŋk] *v. t.* miteinander verbinden

interlock [ɪntə'lɒk] **1.** *v. i.* sich ineinanderhaken; ⟨*Teile eines Puzzles:*⟩ sich zusammenfügen. **2.** *v. t.* **a)** *(lock together)* zusammenfügen; verflechten ⟨*Fasern*⟩; **b)** *(connect) (Railw.)* verriegeln; *(Cinemat.)* synchronisieren

interloper ['ɪntələʊpə(r)] *n.* Eindringling, *der*

interlude ['ɪntəlu:d, 'ɪntəlju:d] *n.* **a)** *(Theatre: break)* Pause, *die;* **b)** *(occurring in break)* Zwischenspiel, *das;* Intermezzo, *das;* **musical ~:** musikalisches Zwischenspiel; **c)** *(intervening time)* kurze Phase *od.* Periode; **a few brief ~s of sleep** wenige kurze Schlafpausen; **d)** *(event interposed)* Intermezzo, *das*

intermarriage [ɪntə'mærɪdʒ] *n.* **a)** *(between groups)* Mischehen *Pl.;* **b)** *(within groups)* Heirat untereinander; *(between related persons)* Verwandtenehe, *die*

intermarry [ɪntə'mærɪ] *v. i.* **a)** *(between groups)* Mischehen schließen; **b)** *(within groups)* untereinander heiraten; *(between related persons)* Verwandtenehen schließen

intermediary [ɪntə'mi:dɪərɪ] *n.* Vermittler, *der*/Vermittlerin, *die*

intermediate [ɪntə'mi:djət] **1.** *adj.* **a)** Zwischen-; ~ **level/point between ...:** Niveau/Punkt zwischen ...; **b)** *(Educ.)* Mittel⟨*stufe, -schule*⟩; ~ **education** ≈ Realschulausbildung, *die;* mittlere Reife; ~ **French** Französisch für fortgeschrittene Anfänger. **2.** *n.* **a)** fortgeschrittener Anfänger; **b)** *(Chem.)* Zwischenprodukt, *das*

intermediate-range [ballistic] 'missile *n.* Mittelstreckenrakete, *die*

interment [ɪn'tɜ:mənt] *n.* Bestattung, *die (geh.);* Beisetzung, *die (geh.)*

intermesh [ɪntə'meʃ] *v. i.* ⟨*Zahnräder:*⟩ ineinandergreifen; ⟨*Fäden, Garne:*⟩ sich ineinanderfügen

intermezzo [ɪntə'metsəʊ] *n., pl.* **intermezzi** [ɪntə'metsi:] *or* ~**s** Intermezzo, *das*

interminable [ɪn'tɜ:mɪnəbl] *adj.,* **interminably** [ɪn'tɜ:mɪnəblɪ] *adv.* *(lit. or fig.)* endlos

intermingle [ɪntə'mɪŋgl] **1.** *v. i.* sich vermischen; ⟨*Personen:*⟩ miteinander in Kontakt treten. **2.** *v. t.* vermischen

intermission [ɪntə'mɪʃn] *n.* **a)** *(pause)* Unterbrechung, *die;* **b)** *(period of inactivity)* Pause, *die;* **c)** *(Amer.: interval in performance)* Pause, *die*

intermittent [ɪntə'mɪtənt] *adj.* in Abständen auftretend ⟨*Signal, Fehler, Geräusch*⟩; **be ~:** in Abständen auftreten; **there was ~ rain all day** es hat den ganzen Tag mit kurzen Unterbrechungen geregnet; ~ **fever** Wechselfieber, *das;* intermittierendes Fieber *(fachspr.)*

intermittently [ɪntə'mɪtəntlɪ] *adv.* in Abständen

intern 1. [ɪn'tɜ:n] *v. t.* gefangenhalten; internieren ⟨*Kriegsgefangenen usw.*⟩. **2.** ['ɪntɜ:n] *n.* *(Amer.)* **a)** *(Med.)* Medizinalassistent, *der*/-assistentin, *die;* **b)** *(teacher)* Lehramtskandidat, *der*/-kandidatin, *die*

internal [ɪn'tɜ:nl] *adj.* **a)** inner...; Innen⟨*winkel, -durchmesser, -fläche, -druck, -gewinde, -abmessungen*⟩; **b)** *(Physiol.)* inner... ⟨*Blutung, Sekretion, Verletzung*⟩; ~ **temperature** Innentemperatur, *die;* **c)** *(intrinsic)* inner... ⟨*Logik, Stimmigkeit*⟩; **d)** *(within country)* inner... ⟨*Angelegenheiten, Frieden, Probleme*⟩; Binnen⟨*handel, -markt*⟩; innenpolitisch ⟨*Angelegenheiten, Streitigkeiten, Probleme*⟩; *(within organization)* [betriebs-/partei]intern ⟨*Auseinandersetzung, Post, Praxis, Verfahren[sweise]*⟩; inner[betrieblich/-kirchlich/-gewerkschaftlich *usw.*] ⟨*Streitigkeiten*⟩; ~ **telephone** Haustelefon, *das;* **e)** *(Med.)* innerlich ⟨*Anwendung*⟩; **f)** *(of the mind)* inner... ⟨*Monolog, Bewegung, Regung, Widerstände, Groll*⟩; **g)** *(Univ.)* ordentlich ⟨*Student*⟩; ~ **examination** *an der Universität, an der man immatrikuliert ist, abgelegte Prüfung*

internal: ~ **'clock** *n.* innere Uhr; ~**com'bustion engine** *n.* Verbrennungsmotor, *der;* ~ **'evidence** *n.* impliziter Beweis

internalize (internalise) [ɪn'tɜ:nəlaɪz] *v. t.* *(Psych.)* verinnerlichen; internalisieren *(fachspr.)*

internally [ɪn'tɜ:nəlɪ] *adv.* innerlich; *(within organization)* [partei-/betriebs]intern; **not to be taken ~:** nicht zum Einnehmen; nur zur äußerlichen Anwendung; **bleed ~:** innere Blutungen haben; ~ **inconsistent** in sich *(Dat.)* unstimmig

internal: ~ **'medicine** *n.* innere Medizin; ~ **'revenue** *n.* *(Amer.)* Steuereinnahmen *Pl.;* **I~ 'Revenue Service** *n.* *(Amer.)* ≈ Finanzamt, *das;* ~ **'rhyme** *n.* *(Pros.)* Binnenreim, *der*

international [ɪntə'næʃənl] **1.** *adj.* international; **it was a very ~ gathering** das Treffen hatte ausgesprochen internationalen Charakter; ~ **travel** Auslandsreisen *Pl.;* ~ **team** *(Sport)* Nationalmannschaft, *die.* **2.** *n.* **a)** *(Sport: contest)* Länderkampf, *der; (in team sports)* Länderspiel, *das;* **b)** *(Sport: participant)* Internationale, *der/die; (in team sports)* Nationalspieler, *der*/-spielerin, *die;* **c)** **I~** *(Polit.)* Internationale, *die*

international: ~ **call** *n.* *(Teleph.)* Auslandsgespräch, *das;* ~ **'code** *n.* *(Naut.)* internationales Signalbuch; **I~ Court of 'Justice** *n.* Internationaler Gerichtshof; ~ **date-line** *see* **date-line;** ~ **'driving licence** *or* **permit** *n.* internationaler Führerschein

internationalism [ɪntə'næʃənəlɪzm] *n.* Internationalismus, *der*

internationalize (internationalise) [ɪntə'næʃənəlaɪz] *v. t.* internationalisieren

international 'law *n.* Völkerrecht, *das*

internationally [ɪntə'næʃənəlɪ] *adv.* international

international: I~ 'Monetary Fund *n.* Internationaler Währungsfonds; ~ **re'ply coupon** *see* **reply coupon;** ~ **system of 'units** *n.* *(Phys.)* Internationales Einheitensystem

internecine [ɪntə'ni:saɪn] *adj.* *(mutually destructive)* [für beide Seiten] vernichtend; *(bloody)* Vernichtungs⟨*krieg, -feldzug*⟩; *(internal)* intern ⟨*Streitigkeiten, Zwist*⟩

internee [ɪntɜ:'ni:] *n.* Internierte, *der/die*

internist [ɪn'tɜ:nɪst] *n.* **a)** *(specialist)* Facharzt/-ärztin für innere Krankheiten; Internist, *der*/Internistin, *die;* **b)** *(Amer.: general practitioner)* praktischer Arzt/praktische Ärztin

internment [ɪn'tɜ:nmənt] *n.* Internierung, *die;* ~ **camp** Internierungslager, *das*

interpersonal [ɪntə'pɜ:sənl] *adj.* interpersonal; interpersonell

interplanetary [ɪntə'plænɪtərɪ] *adj.* *(Astron., Astronaut.)* interplanetar[isch] ⟨*Rakete, Raum, Raumfahrt*⟩

interplay ['ɪntəpleɪ] *n.* **a)** *(interaction)* Wechselwirkung, *die;* **b)** *(reciprocal action)* Zusammenspiel, *das*

Interpol ['ɪntəpɒl] *n.* Interpol, *die*

interpolate [ɪn'tɜ:pəleɪt] *v. t.* **a)** *(interpose orally)* einwerfen ⟨*Satz, Bemerkung*⟩; *(in programme)* einschieben ⟨*Warnung usw.*⟩; **b)** *(introduce by insertion)* einfügen ⟨*Worte*⟩; **c)** *(Math.)* interpolieren

interpolation [ɪntɜ:pə'leɪʃn] *n.* **a)** Einfügung, *die;* **his ~ of that remark** sein Einwurf; **b)** *(Math.)* Interpolation, *die*

interpose [ɪntə'pəʊz] **1.** *v. t.* **a)** *(insert)* dazwischenlegen; ~ **sth. between sb./sth. and sb./sth.** etw. zwischen jmdn./etw. und jmdn./etw. bringen; **b)** *(say as interruption)* einwerfen ⟨*Frage, Bemerkung*⟩; **c)** *(exercise, advance)* ~ **one's veto** sein Veto einlegen; von seinem Veto[recht] Gebrauch machen; ~ **one's authority** seinen Einfluß geltend machen; ~ **an objection** einen Einwand vorbringen; Einspruch einlegen *(Rechtsw.).* **2.** *v. i.* **a)** *(intervene)* ~ **on sb.'s side** *or* **behalf** sich für jmdn. einsetzen; ~ **in sth.** in etw. *(Akk.)* [vermittelnd] eingreifen; **b)** *(make an interruption)* [kurz] unterbrechen

interpret [ɪn'tɜ:prɪt] **1.** *v. t.* **a)** interpretieren; deuten ⟨*Traum, Zeichen*⟩; auslegen ⟨*Heilige Schrift*⟩; **b)** *(between languages)* dolmetschen; **c)** *(decipher)* entziffern ⟨*Schrift, Inschrift*⟩. **2.** *v. i.* dolmetschen

interpretation [ɪntɜ:prɪ'teɪʃn] *n.* **a)** Interpretation, *die; (of dream, symptoms)* Deutung, *die; (of biblical passage)* Auslegung, *die;* **b)** *(deciphering)* Entzifferung, *die*

interpretative [ɪn'tɜ:prɪtətɪv] *adj.* erläuternd ⟨*Artikel, Aufsatz*⟩; interpretativ ⟨*Kraft, Talent*⟩; interpretierend ⟨*Künstler*⟩

interpreter [ɪn'tɜ:prɪtə(r)] *n.* **a)** *(between languages)* Dolmetscher, *der*/Dolmetscherin, *die;* **b)** *(of dreams, hieroglyphics)* Deuter, *der;* **c)** *(performer on stage etc.)* Interpret, *der*/Interpretin, *die*

interpretive [ɪn'tɜ:prɪtɪv] *see* **interpretative**

interregnum [ɪntə'regnəm] *n., pl.* ~**s** *or* **interregna** [ɪntə'regnə] **a)** *(period)* Zwischenregierung, *die;* Interregnum, *das (Politik);* **b)** *(interval)* Unterbrechung, *die*

interrelated [ɪntərɪ'leɪtɪd] *adj.* zusammenhängend ⟨*Tatsachen, Ereignisse, Themen*⟩; verwandt ⟨*Sprachen, Fachgebiete*⟩; **be ~:** zusammenhängen/verwandt sein

interrelation [ɪntərɪ'leɪʃn] *n.* Wechselbeziehung, *die; (between events)* Zusammenhang, *der*

interrogate [ɪn'terəgeɪt] *v. t.* vernehmen ‹*Zeugen, Angeklagten*›; verhören ‹*Angeklagten, Verdächtigen, Spion, Gefangenen*›; ausfragen ‹*Freund, Kind, Schüler usw.*›

interrogation [ɪnterə'geɪʃn] *n. (interrogating)* Verhör, *das; attrib.* Verhör-; **under ~:** beim Verhör; **be under ~:** verhört werden

interrogative [ɪntə'rɒgətɪv] *adj.* **a)** *(having question form)* Frage-; fragend ‹*Tonfall*›; **b)** *(inquiring)* fragend ‹*Ton, Blick*›; **c)** *(Ling.)* Interrogativ‹*pronomen, -adverb, -form*›

interrogator [ɪn'terəgeɪtə(r)] *n.* Vernehmer, *der*

interrupt [ɪntə'rʌpt] **1.** *v. t.* unterbrechen; **~ sb.'s sleep** jmds. Schlaf stören; **don't ~ me when I'm busy** stör mich nicht, wenn ich zu tun habe; **~ sb.'s view** jmdm. die Sicht versperren. **2.** *v. i.* stören; unterbrechen; **stop ~ing!** stör *od.* unterbrich nicht dauernd!

interruption [ɪntə'rʌpʃn] *n. (of work etc.)* Unterbrechung, *die;* Störung, *die; (of peace, sleep)* Störung, *die; (of services)* [zeitweiliger] Ausfall; **without ~:** ohne Unterbrechung; ununterbrochen

intersect [ɪntə'sekt] **1.** *v. t.* **a)** ‹*Kanäle, Schluchten, [Quarz]adern:*› durchziehen ‹*Land, Boden*›; **streets ~ing each other** einander kreuzende Straßen; **b)** *(Geom.)* schneiden; **~ each other** sich schneiden. **2.** *v. i.* **a)** ‹*Straßen:*› sich kreuzen; **b)** *(Geom.)* sich schneiden

intersection [ɪntə'sekʃn] *n.* **a)** *(intersecting; road etc. junction)* Kreuzung, *die;* **b)** *(Geom.)* **[point of] ~:** Schnittpunkt, *der;* **c)** *(Logic, Math.)* Schnittmenge, *die*

intersperse [ɪntə'spɜ:s] *v. t.* **a)** *(scatter)* [hier und da] einfügen; **b) be ~d with** durchsetzt sein mit; ‹*Erzählung, Arbeit, Routine:*› unterbrochen werden durch ‹*Pausen, Ruhe, Aufregungen*›

interstate ['ɪntəsteɪt] *adj. (Amer.)* zwischen den [Bundes]staaten *nachgestellt;* zwischenstaatlich; **~ highway** Fernstraße *(die durch mehrere Bundesstaaten führt)*

interstellar [ɪntə'stelə(r)] *adj.* interstellar ‹*Materie, Staub, Raum*›; **~ travel** [Welt-]raumfahrt, *die*

interstice [ɪn'tɜ:stɪs] *n. (intervening space)* Zwischenraum, *der; (of net)* Masche, *die; (between panels etc.)* Fuge, *die*

intertribal [ɪntə'traɪbl] *adj.* ‹*Krieg, Streitigkeiten usw.*› zwischen verschiedenen Stämmen

intertwine [ɪntə'twaɪn] **1.** *v. t.* flechten **(in** in + *Akk.*); **he ~d his fingers with hers** er schlang *od.* flocht seine Finger zwischen ihre *od.* die ihren *(geh.).* **2.** *v. i.* sich [ineinander] verschlingen

interval ['ɪntəvl] *n.* **a)** *(intervening space)* Zwischenraum, *der; (intervening time)* [Zeit]abstand, *der;* **at ~s** in Abständen; **at 20-minute ~s** in Abständen von 20 Minuten; **at frequent** *or* **short/wide ~s** in kurzen/weiten Abständen; **at ~s along the road/river** hier und da an der Straße/am Flußufer; **after an ~ of three years** nach [Ablauf von] drei Jahren; **b)** *(break; also Brit. Theatre etc.)* Pause, *die;* **an ~ of silence** eine Schweige- *od.* Gedenkminute; **an ~ in the shooting** eine Unterbrechung der Schießereien; **sunny** *or* **bright ~s** *(Meteorol.)* Aufheiterungen *Pl.;* **~ music** Pausenmusik, *die;* **c)** *(period)* Pause, *die;* **~s of sanity** lichte Momente; **d)** *(Mus.)* Intervall, *das;* **perfect ~:** reines Intervall

'interval signal *n. (Broadcasting)* Pausenzeichen, *das*

intervene [ɪntə'vi:n] *v. i.* **a)** [vermittelnd] eingreifen **(in** in + *Akk.*); *(come between persons)* vermitteln **(between** zwischen + *Dat.*); **if nothing ~s** wenn nichts dazwischenkommt; **if fate had not ~d** wenn das Schicksal nicht eingegriffen hätte; **b)** *(occur)* **the years that ~d, the intervening years** die dazwischenliegenden Jahre; **c)** *(Law)* **~ in** eintreten in (+ *Akk.*) ‹*Vertrag usw.*›; beitreten (+ *Dat.*) ‹*Verfahren*›

intervention [ɪntə'venʃn] *n.* Eingreifen, *das;* Intervention, *die (bes. Politik);* **surgical ~:** chirurgischer Eingriff; **at my ~:** auf mein Eingreifen/meine Intervention [hin]; **I~ Board** ≈ Interventionsstelle, *die*

interventionist [ɪntə'venʃənɪst] **1.** *n.* Interventionist, *der.* **2.** *adj.* interventionistisch

interview ['ɪntəvju:] **1.** *n.* **a)** *(for job etc.)* Vorstellungsgespräch, *das;* **b)** *(Journ., Radio, Telev.)* Interview, *das;* **c)** *(discussion)* Gespräch, *das;* Unterredung, *die.* **2.** *v. t.* Vorstellungsgespräch[e] führen mit ‹*Stellen-, Studienbewerber*›; interviewen ‹*Politiker, Filmstar, Konsumenten usw.*›; vernehmen ‹*Zeugen*›

interviewee [ɪntəvju:'i:] *n. (for opinion poll)* Befragte, *der/die; (candidate, applicant)* [Stellen-, Studien]bewerber, *der/*-bewerberin, *die; (politician, celebrity, etc.)* Interviewpartner, *der/*-partnerin, *die;* Interviewte, *der/die*

interviewer ['ɪntəvju:ə(r)] *n. (reporter, pollster, etc.)* Interviewer, *der/*Interviewerin, *die; (for job etc.)* Leiter/Leiterin des Vorstellungsgesprächs

inter-war ['ɪntəwɔ:(r)] *attrib. adj.* ‹*Zeit, Jahre*› zwischen den [Welt]kriegen

interweave [ɪntə'wi:v] *v. t.*, **interwove** [ɪntə'wəʊv], **interwoven** [ɪntə'wəʊvn] [miteinander] verweben ‹*Fäden, Wolle, Seide usw.*›; [miteinander] verflechten ‹*Zweige, Bänder*›; **our lives are interwoven** unsere Lebenswege sind miteinander verschlungen

intestacy [ɪn'testəsɪ] *n.* Sterben ohne Hinterlassung eines Testaments

intestate [ɪn'testət] *adj.* Intestat‹*erbe, -erbfolge, -nachlaß*›; **die ~:** ohne Hinterlassung eines Testaments sterben

intestinal [ɪn'testɪnl] *adj. (Med.)* Darm-; intestinal *(fachspr.)*

intestine [ɪn'testɪn] *n. in sing. or pl. (Anat.)* Darm, *der;* Gedärme *Pl.;* **large/small ~:** Dick-/Dünndarm, *der*

intimacy ['ɪntɪməsɪ] *n.* **a)** *(state)* Vertrautheit, *die; (close personal relationship)* enges [Freundschafts]verhältnis; **b)** *(euphem.: sexual intercourse)* Intimität, *die;* **~ took place** es kam zu Intimitäten; **c)** *in pl. (caresses)* Intimitäten; Vertraulichkeiten

intimate 1. ['ɪntɪmət] *adj.* **a)** *(close, closely acquainted)* eng ‹*Freund, Freundschaft, Beziehung, Verhältnis*›; vertraulich ‹*Ton*›; **be on ~ terms with sb.** zu jmdm. ein enges *od.* vertrautes Verhältnis haben; **b)** *(euphem.: having sexual intercourse)* intim ‹*Beziehungen*›; **be/become ~ with sb.** mit jmdm. intim sein/werden; **c)** *(from close familiarity)* **~ knowledge of sth.** genaue *od.* intime Kenntnis einer Sache; **~ acquaintance with sth.** enge Vertrautheit mit etw.; **d)** *(closely personal)* persönlich ‹*Problem*›; privat ‹*Angelegenheit, Gefühl, Dinge*›; geheim ‹*Gedanken*›; *(euphem.)* Intim‹*bereich, -spray*›; **e)** innig ‹*Verbindung, Verschmelzung, Zusammenhang*›; **f)** intim ‹*Tagebuch, Brief, Darstellung, Raum, Theater, Restaurant, Musik, Feier, Treffen*›; **the party was a small, ~ affair** die Feier fand im intimsten Kreis statt. **2.** *n. (close friend)* Vertraute, *der/die.* **3.** ['ɪntɪmeɪt] *v. t.* **a) ~ sth. [to sb.]/[to sb.] that ...** *(make known)* [jmdm.] etw. mitteilen/[jmdm.] mitteilen, daß ...; *(show clearly)* [jmdm.] etw. deutlich machen *od.* zu verstehen geben/[jmdm.] zu verstehen geben, daß ...; **b)** *(imply)* andeuten

intimately ['ɪntɪmətlɪ] *adv.* genau[estens] ‹*kennen*›; bestens ‹*vertraut*›; gründlich ‹*vermischen*›; eng ‹*verbinden*›; **he is ~ involved in the planning of the project** er ist an der Planung des Projekts maßgeblich beteiligt; **we know each other, but not ~:** wir kennen uns, aber nicht näher

intimation [ɪntɪ'meɪʃn] *n.* **a)** Mitteilung, *die; (of sb.'s death etc.)* Anzeige, *die;* **give an ~:** eine Mitteilung machen; **b)** *(hint)* Andeutung, *die; (of trouble, anger, pain)* Anzeichen, *das;* **give ~s** Andeutungen machen

intimidate [ɪn'tɪmɪdeɪt] *v. t.* einschüchtern; **~ sb. into doing sth.** jmdn. einschüchtern *od.* unter Druck setzen, damit er etw. tut; **use intimidating behaviour** zum Mittel der Einschüchterung greifen

intimidation [ɪntɪmɪ'deɪʃn] *n.* Einschüchterung, *die*

into [*before vowel* 'ɪntʊ, *before consonant* 'ɪntə] *prep.* **a)** *expr. motion or direction* in (+ *Akk.*); *(against)* gegen; **I went out ~ the street** ich ging auf die Straße hinaus; **they disappeared ~ the night** sie verschwanden in die Nacht hinein; **you don't have to go ~ London** *(coll.)* du brauchst nicht nach London rein *(ugs.);* **he was [straight] ~ the biscuit-tin** er machte sich über die Keksdose her; **baptized ~ the Catholic Church** katholisch getauft; **they were soon ~ their clothes and on deck** sie waren in kurzer Zeit angekleidet auf Deck; **4 [divided] ~ 20 = 5** 20 [geteilt] durch 4 = 5; **until well ~ this century** bis weit in unser Jahrhundert hinein; **it was 15 minutes ~ the second half before ...:** erst in der 15. Minute der zweiten Halbzeit ...; **b)** *expr. change, result* **translate sth. ~ English** etw. ins Englische übersetzen; **the book is ~ its third edition** das Buch liegt schon in dritter Auflage vor; **poke the fire ~ a blaze** das Feuer [durch Schüren] zum Auflodern bringen; **c)** *(coll.)* **be ~ sth./sb.** *(interested in)* auf etw./jmdn. stehen *(ugs.);* auf etw./jmdn. abfahren *(salopp);* **be ~ sth.** *(knowledgeable about)* mit etw. vertraut sein; **he's heavily ~ meditation** er ist völlig auf Meditation abgefahren *(salopp)*

intolerable [ɪn'tɒlərəbl] *adj.* unerträglich; **it's ~:** es ist nicht auszuhalten; **an ~ place to live in** ein Ort, an dem das Leben unerträglich ist

intolerably [ɪn'tɒlərəblɪ] *adv.* unerträglich

intolerance [ɪn'tɒlərəns] *n., no pl.* Intoleranz, *die;* Unduldsamkeit, *die* **(of** gegenüber); *(Med.)* [Über]empfindlichkeit, *die* **(to, of** gegen)

intolerant [ɪn'tɒlərənt] *adj.* intolerant, unduldsam **(of** gegenüber)

intonation [ɪntə'neɪʃn] *n. (modulation)* Intonation, *die (Sprachw.);* Sprachmelodie, *die;* **speak with a Russian ~:** in russischem Tonfall sprechen

intone [ɪn'təʊn] *v. t.* intonieren; psalmodieren *(Rel.)*

intoxicant [ɪn'tɒksɪkənt] **1.** *n.* Rauschmittel, *das.* **2.** *adj.* berauschend

intoxicate [ɪn'tɒksɪkeɪt] *v. t.* **a)** *(make drunk)* betrunken machen; **be/become ~d** betrunken sein/werden; **b)** *(excite)* berauschen; **be ~d by/with sth.** durch/von etw. berauscht sein

intoxicating [ɪn'tɒksɪkeɪtɪŋ] *adj.* berauschend ‹*Wirkung, Schönheit*›; mitreißend ‹*Worte, Rhythmus*›; **~ liquors** alkoholische Getränke

intoxication [ɪntɒksɪ'keɪʃn] *n.* **a)** Rausch, *der;* **in a state of ~:** in betrunkenem Zustand; im Rausch; **b)** *(excitement)* Hochgefühl, *das;* Euphorie, *die (geh.)*

intra- [ɪntrə] *pref.* inner-; *(mit Fremdwörtern meist)* intra-

intractable [ɪn'træktəbl] *adj.* widerspenstig ‹*Verhalten, Kind, Tier*›; aufrührerisch ‹*[Menschen]menge, -masse*›; unbeugsam ‹*Wille*›; hartnäckig ‹*Krankheit, Schmerzen, Problem*›

intra'mural *adj. (Univ.)* innerhalb der Universität; inneruniversitär

intra'muscular *adj. (Med.)* intramuskulär

intransigence [ɪn'trænsɪdʒəns, ɪn'trænzɪ-

dʒəns] *n., no pl. see* **intransigent:** Kompromißlosigkeit, *die;* Unnachgiebigkeit, *die;* Intransigenz, *die (geh.);* Unerschütterlichkeit, *die*
intransigent [ɪn'trænsɪdʒənt, ɪn'trænzɪdʒənt] **1.** *adj.* kompromißlos, unnachgiebig, *(geh.)* intransigent ⟨*Haltung, Einstellung*⟩; unerschütterlich ⟨*Wille, Grundsätze, Glaube*⟩. **2.** *n. (in politics)* Radikale, *der/die*
intransitive [ɪn'trænsɪtɪv, ɪn'trɑːnsɪtɪv] *adj.*, **intransitively** [ɪn'trænsɪtɪvlɪ, ɪn'trɑːnsɪtɪvlɪ] *adv. (Ling.)* intransitiv
intra-uterine [ɪntrə'juːtəraɪn] *adj. (Med.)* intrauterin; ~ **[contraceptive] device** Intrauterinpessar, *das*
intra'venous *adj. (Med.)* intravenös
'in-tray *n.* Ablage für Eingänge
intrepid [ɪn'trepɪd] *adj.*, **intrepidly** [ɪn'trepɪdlɪ] *adv.* unerschrocken
intricacy ['ɪntrɪkəsɪ] *n.* **a)** *no pl. (quality)* Kompliziertheit, *die;* **increase the ~ of sth.** etw. [noch] komplizierter machen; **b)** *in pl. (things)* Feinheiten *Pl.*
intricate ['ɪntrɪkət] *adj.* verschlungen ⟨*Pfad, Windung*⟩; kompliziert ⟨*System, Muster, Fabel, Werkstück, Maschinenteil, Aufgabe*⟩; *(obscure)* schwer verständlich
intricately ['ɪntrɪkətlɪ] *adv.* kompliziert; **an ~ designed pattern** ein kompliziertes Muster
intrigue [ɪn'triːg] **1.** *v. t.* faszinieren; **I'm ~d to find out what ...:** ich bin gespannt darauf, zu erfahren, was ... **2.** *v. i.* **~ against sb.** gegen jmdn. intrigieren; **~ with sb.** mit jmdm. Ränke schmieden *od.* Intrigen spinnen. **3.** [ɪn'triːg, 'ɪntriːg] *n.* Intrige, *die;* **~s** Machenschaften *Pl. (abwertend)*
intriguer [ɪn'triːgə(r)] *n.* Intrigant, *der*/Intrigantin, *die*
intriguing [ɪn'triːgɪŋ] *adj.*, **intriguingly** [ɪn'triːgɪŋlɪ] *adv.* faszinierend
intrinsic [ɪn'trɪnsɪk, ɪn'trɪnzɪk] *adj. (inherent)* innewohnend; inner... ⟨*Verdorbenheit, Aufbau, Logik*⟩; immanent *(geh.); (essential)* wesentlich, *(Philos.)* essentiell ⟨*Eigenschaft, Bestandteil, Mangel*⟩; **be ~ in** *or* **to a thing** wesentliches Merkmal einer Sache sein; **~ value** innerer Wert; *(of sth. concrete)* Eigenwert, *der*
intrinsically [ɪn'trɪnsɪkəlɪ, ɪn'trɪnzɪkəlɪ] *adv.* im wesentlichen; *(Philos.)* essentiell
intro ['ɪntrəʊ] *n., pl.* **~s** *(coll.) (presentation)* Vorstellung, *die; (Mus.)* Einleitung, *die;* Intro, *das (fachspr.)*
introduce [ɪntrə'djuːs] *v. t.* **a)** *(bring in)* [erstmals] einführen ⟨*Ware, Tier, Pflanze*⟩ **(into** in + *Akk.*, **from ... into** von ... nach); einleiten ⟨*Maßnahmen*⟩; einflechten ⟨*Episoden in Roman*⟩; einschleppen ⟨*Krankheit*⟩; **~ irrelevancies into the discussion** Unwesentliches in die Diskussion bringen; **b)** einführen ⟨*Katheter, Schlauch*⟩ **(into** in + *Akk.*); stecken ⟨*Schlüssel, Draht, Rohr, Schlauch*⟩ **(into** in + *Akk.*); **~ sth. into the flame** etw. der Flamme aussetzen; **c)** *(bring into use)* einführen ⟨*Neuerung, Verfahren, Brauch, Mode, Kalender, Nomenklatur*⟩; aufbringen ⟨*Gerücht, Schlagwort, Mode*⟩; **d)** *(make known)* vorstellen; einführen ⟨*Vortragenden*⟩; **~ oneself/sb. [to sb.]** sich/jmdn. [jmdm.] vorstellen; **I ~d them to each other** ich machte sie miteinander bekannt *od.* stellte sie einander vor; **I don't think we've been ~d** ich glaube, wir kennen uns noch nicht; **~ sb. to a hobby/to drugs** jmdn. in ein Hobby einführen/mit Drogen bekannt machen; **e)** *(usher in, begin, precede)* einleiten ⟨*Buch, Thema, Musikstück, Epoche*⟩; **f)** *(present)* ankündigen ⟨*Programm, Darsteller*⟩; **g)** *(Parl.)* einbringen ⟨*Antrag, Entwurf, Gesetz*⟩; einleiten ⟨*Reform*⟩
introduction [ɪntrə'dʌkʃn] *n.* **a)** *(of methods, measures, process, machinery)* Einführen, *das;* Einführung, *die; (of rules)* Aufstellung, *die; (of fashion)* Aufbringen, *das;* **b)** *(of tube, catheter)* Einführen, *das;* **c)** **an ~ to London night-life** eine Einführung ins Londoner Nachtleben; **~ to heroin** erste Bekanntschaft mit Heroin; **d)** *(formal presentation)* Vorstellung, *die; (into society)* Einführung, *die; (of reform)* Einleiten, *das; (of parliamentary bill)* Einbringen, *das;* **X needs no ~ from me** ich brauche X nicht vorzustellen; **do the ~s** die Anwesenden miteinander bekannt machen; **letter of ~:** Empfehlungsschreiben, *das;* **e)** *(preliminary matter)* Einleitung, *die;* Introduktion, die *(Musik);* **f)** *(introductory treatise)* Einführung, *die* **(to** in + *Akk.*); Leitfaden, *der* **(to** *Gen.*); **g)** *(thing introduced)* Eingeführte, *das; (exotic plant or animal)* Eingebürgerte, *der/die/das;* **mechanized sowing was a later ~:** [die] maschinelle Aussaat wurde [erst] später eingeführt
introductory [ɪntrə'dʌktərɪ] *adj.* einleitend; Einführungs⟨*kurs, -vortrag*⟩; Einleitungs⟨*kapitel, -rede*⟩
introspection [ɪntrə'spekʃn] *n.* Selbstbeobachtung, *die;* Introspektion, *die (geh., Psych.)*
introspective [ɪntrə'spektɪv] *adj.* in sich *(Akk.)* gerichtet; verinnerlicht; introspektiv *(geh., Psych.)*
introvert 1. ['ɪntrəvɜːt] *n.* Introvertierte, *der/die;* introvertierter Mensch; **be an ~:** introvertiert sein. **2.** *adj.* introvertiert; **have ~ tendencies** zur Introvertiertheit neigen
introverted [ɪntrə'vɜːtɪd] *adj.* introvertiert
intrude [ɪn'truːd] **1.** *v. i.* stören; **~ [up]on sb.'s grief/leisure time/privacy** jmdn. in seiner Trauer stören/ jmds. Freizeit beanspruchen/in jmds. Privatsphäre *(Akk.)* eindringen; **~ [up]on sb.'s time** jmds. Zeit in Anspruch nehmen; **~ in[to] sb.'s affairs/conversation** sich in jmds. Angelegenheiten/Unterhaltung *(Akk.)* einmischen. **2.** *v. t.* aufdrängen **(into, [up]on** *Dat.*); **the idea** *or* **thought ~d itself into my mind** der Gedanke drängte sich mir auf; **~ oneself** *or* **one's presence upon sb.** sich jmdm. aufdrängen
intruder [ɪn'truːdə(r)] *n.* Eindringling, *der; (Mil.)* Intruder, *der*
intrusion [ɪn'truːʒn] *n.* **a)** *(intruding)* Störung, *die;* **an ~/numerous ~s upon** *or* **into sb.'s privacy** ein/wiederholtes Eindringen in jmds. Privatsphäre *(Akk.);* **~ on sb.'s leisure time** Inanspruchnahme von jmds. Freizeit; **b)** *(into building, country, etc.)* [gewaltsames] Eindringen; *(Mil.)* Einmarsch, *der* **(into** in + *Akk.*); **c)** *(forcing oneself in)* Einmischung, *die* **(upon** in + *Akk.*); **d)** *(Geol.)* Intrusion, *die*
intrusive [ɪn'truːsɪv] *adj.* **a)** aufdringlich ⟨*Person*⟩; aggressiv ⟨*Bemerkung, Kultur, Journalismus*⟩; **b)** *(Phonet.)* intrusiv; **c)** *(Geol.)* **~ rock** Intrusivgestein, *das*
intuition [ɪntjuː'ɪʃn] *n.* Intuition, *die;* **know sth. by ~:** etw. intuitiv wissen; **have an ~ that ...:** eine Eingebung haben *od.* intuitiv spüren, daß ...
intuitive [ɪn'tjuːɪtɪv] *adj.* intuitiv; gefühlsmäßig ⟨*Ablehnung, Beurteilung*⟩; instinktiv ⟨*Annahme, Gefühl*⟩
intuitively [ɪn'tjuːɪtɪvlɪ] *adv.* intuitiv; gefühlsmäßig
inundate ['ɪnəndeɪt] *v. t.* überschwemmen; ⟨*Meer:*⟩ überfluten; *(fig.) (with inquiries, letters, complaints, goods, information)* überschwemmen; *(with work, praise, advice)* überhäufen; **~d with tourists** von Touristen überlaufen; **we've been ~d with letters** eine Flut von Zuschriften ist bei uns eingegangen
inundation [ɪnən'deɪʃn] *n.* Überschwemmung, *die; (by the sea)* Überflutung, *die; (fig.)* Flut, *die*
inure [ɪ'njʊə(r)] *v. t.* gewöhnen **(to** an + *Akk.*); *(toughen)* abhärten **(to** gegen); **become ~d to/~ oneself to sth.** sich an etw. *(Akk.)* gewöhnen
in vacuo [ɪn 'vækjʊəʊ] *adv. (fig.)* im luftleeren Raum; *(lit.)* in einem Vakuum
invade [ɪn'veɪd] *v. t.* **a)** einfallen in ⟨*Gebiet, Staat*⟩; **Poland was ~d by the Germans** die Deutschen marschierten in Polen *(Akk.)* ein; **b)** *(swarm into)* ⟨*Touristen, Kinder:*⟩ überschwemmen ⟨*Land, Strand, Schwimmbad*⟩; **c)** *(fig.)* ⟨*unangenehmes Gefühl, Krankheit, Schwäche:*⟩ befallen ⟨*Personen, Gewebe, Körper*⟩; ⟨*Krankheit, Seuche, Unwetter:*⟩ heimsuchen ⟨*Person, Stadt, Gebiet*⟩; ⟨*Glücksgefühl, Geruch:*⟩ durchströmen ⟨*Person, Raum*⟩; ⟨*Thema, Vorstellung:*⟩ Eingang finden in (+ *Akk.*) ⟨*Literatur, Sprache*⟩; **d)** *(encroach upon)* verletzen ⟨*Rechte*⟩; stören ⟨*Ruhe, Frieden*⟩; eindringen in (+ *Akk.*) ⟨*Haus, Bereich, Privatsphäre*⟩
invader [ɪn'veɪdə(r)] *n. (hostile)* Angreifer, *der;* Invasor, *der (bes. Milit.); (intruder)* Eindringling, *der* **(of** in + *Akk.*)
[1]invalid 1. ['ɪnvəlɪd] *n. (Brit.)* Kranke, *der/die; (disabled person)* Körperbehinderte, *der/die; (from war injuries)* Kriegsinvalide *der*/-invalidin, *die.* **2.** *adj. (Brit.)* körperbehindert; *(from war injuries)* kriegsbeschädigt; kriegsinvalide. **3.** ['ɪnvəliːd, ɪnvə'liːd] *v. t.* **~ home** *or* **out** als dienstuntauglich entlassen; **~ out of the army** wegen Dienstuntauglichkeit aus der Armee entlassen
[2]invalid [ɪn'vælɪd] *adj.* nicht schlüssig ⟨*Argument, Behauptung, Folgerung, Theorie*⟩; nicht zulässig ⟨*Annahme*⟩; ungerechtfertigt ⟨*Forderung, Vorwurf*⟩; nichtig ⟨*Entschuldigung*⟩; ungültig ⟨*Fahrkarte, Garantie, Vertrag, Testament, Ehe*⟩
invalidate [ɪn'vælɪdeɪt] *v. t.* aufheben; widerlegen ⟨*Theorie, These, Behauptung*⟩
invalid ['ɪnvəlɪd]: **~ carriage** *n.* Kranken[fahr]stuhl, *der;* **~ chair** *n.* Rollstuhl, *der;* **~ diet** *n.* Krankenkost, *die*
invalidity [ɪnvə'lɪdɪtɪ] *n., no pl. see* **[2]invalid:** mangelnde Schlüssigkeit; Unzulässigkeit, *die;* Ungerechtigkeit, *die;* Nichtigkeit, *die;* Ungültigkeit, *die*
invalidly [ɪn'vælɪdlɪ] *adv.* nicht ordnungsgemäß
invaluable [ɪn'væljʊəbl] *adj.* unbezahlbar; unersetzlich ⟨*Mitarbeiter, Person*⟩; unschätzbar ⟨*Dienst, Verdienst, Hilfe, Bedeutung*⟩; außerordentlich wichtig ⟨*Rolle, Funktion*⟩; außerordentlich wertvoll ⟨*Rat[schlag]*⟩; **be ~ to sb.** für jmdn. von unschätzbarem Wert sein
invariable [ɪn'veərɪəbl] *adj.* **a)** *(fixed)* unveränderlich ⟨*Wert, Einheit*⟩; **b)** *(always the same)* [stets] gleichbleibend ⟨*Druck, Temperatur, Höflichkeit, gute Laune*⟩; ständig ⟨*Pech*⟩
invariably [ɪn'veərɪəblɪ] *adv.* immer; ausnahmslos ⟨*falsch, richtig*⟩; **it's ~ wet when I am on holiday** wenn ich Urlaub habe, regnet es garantiert
invasion [ɪn'veɪʒn] *n.* **a)** *(of troops, virus, locusts)* Invasion, *die; (of weeds etc.)* massenweise Ausbreitung; *(intrusion)* [überfallartiges] Eindringen **(of** in + *Akk.*); **the ~ of Belgium by German troops** der Einmarsch deutscher Truppen in Belgien; **the Viking ~ of Britain** der Einfall der Wikinger in Britannien; **b)** *(encroachment) see* **invade d:** Verletzung, *die;* Störung, *die;* Eindringen, *das*
invective [ɪn'vektɪv] *n.* **a)** *(abusive language)* Beschimpfungen *Pl.* **b)** *(violent attack in words)* Schmähung, *die;* Invektive, *die (geh.)*
inveigh [ɪn'veɪ] *v. i.* **~ against sb./sth.** über jmdn./etw. schimpfen *od.* sich empören; **~ against fate/the elements** gegen das Schicksal/die Elemente aufbegehren
inveigle [ɪn'viːgl, ɪn'veɪgl] *v. t.* **a)** *(entice)* **~ sb. into sth./doing sth.** jmdn. zu etw. verleiten/dazu verleiten, etw. zu tun; **~ sb. into the house** jmdn. ins Haus locken; **b)** *(cajole)*

~ **sb. into doing sth.** jmdn. überreden *od. (ugs.)* beschwatzen, etw. zu tun
invent [ɪn'vent] *v. t.* **a)** *(create)* erfinden ‹*Maschine, Verfahren, Spiel*›; ersinnen ‹*Melodie*›; entwickeln ‹*Schrift*›; **b)** *(concoct)* erfinden; sich *(Dat.)* ausdenken
invention [ɪn'venʃn] *n.* **a)** *(thing invented, inventing)* Erfindung, *die; (concept)* Idee, *die;* **it's a device of my own ~:** das habe ich mir selbst ausgedacht; **a story of his own ~:** eine von ihm [selbst] erfundene Geschichte; **b)** *(inventiveness)* Erfindungsgabe, *die;* [schöpferische] Phantasie; **c)** *(fictitious story)* Erfindung, *die;* Lüge, *die*
inventive [ɪn'ventɪv] *adj.* **a)** schöpferisch ‹*Person, Kraft, Geist, Begabung*›; phantasievoll ‹*Künstler, Kind*›; **b)** *(produced with originality)* originell; einfallsreich
inventiveness [ɪn'ventɪvnɪs] *n., no pl.* Erfindungsgabe, *die;* Kreativität, *die*
inventor [ɪn'ventə(r)] *n.* Erfinder, *der*/Erfinderin, *die*
inventory ['ɪnvəntərɪ] **1.** *n.* **a)** *(list)* Bestandsliste, *die;* **make** *or* **take an ~ of sth.** von etw. ein Inventar aufstellen; Inventur machen; **b)** *(stock)* Lagerbestand, *der;* **c)** *(Amer.: trader's stock)* Warenbestand, *der.* **2.** *v. t.* **a)** *(make ~ of)* eine Bestandsliste *od.* ein Inventar aufstellen von; **b)** *(enter in ~)* inventarisieren
inverse [ɪn'vɜ:s, 'ɪnvɜ:s] **1.** *adj.* umgekehrt ‹*Reihenfolge*›. **2.** *n. (opposite)* Gegenteil, *das; (inversion)* Umkehrung, *die*
inversely [ɪn'vɜ:slɪ, 'ɪnvɜ:slɪ] *adv.* umgekehrt
inverse: ~ **pro'portion** *n.* umgekehrtes Verhältnis; **be in ~ proportion to sth.** im umgekehrten Verhältnis zu etw. stehen; ~ **'ratio** *n.* umgekehrtes Verhältnis; ~ **'square law** *n. (Phys.)* [quadratisches] Abstandsgesetz
inversion [ɪn'vɜ:ʃn] *n.* **a)** *(turning upside down)* Umdrehen, *das;* **b)** *(reversal of role, relation)* Umkehrung, *die;* **c)** *(Ling., Meteorol., Mus.)* Inversion, *die*
invert [ɪn'vɜ:t] *v. t.* **a)** *(turn upside down)* umstülpen; ~ **sth. over sth.** etw. über etw. *(Akk.)* stülpen; **b)** umkehren ‹*Wortstellung*›; vertauschen ‹*Wörter, Filmrollen usw.*›; **c)** *(Mus.)* umkehren
invertebrate [ɪn'vɜ:tɪbrət, ɪn'vɜ:tɪbreɪt] *(Zool.)* **1.** *adj.* wirbellos. **2.** *n.* wirbelloses Tier; Evertebrat, *der (fachspr.)*
inverted: ~ **'commas** *n. pl. (Brit.)* Anführungszeichen *Pl.;* Gänsefüßchen *Pl. (ugs.);* **in ~ commas** *(also iron.)* in Anführungszeichen; ~ **'pleat** *n.* Kellerfalte, *die;* ~ **'snob** *n.* Edelproletarier, *der (salopp);* ~ **'snobbery** *n.* Edelproletariertum, *das (salopp)*
invest [ɪn'vest] **1.** *v. t.* **a)** *(Finance)* anlegen **(in** in + *Dat.***)**; investieren **(in** in + *Dat. od. Akk.***)**; ~ **time and effort in sth.** Zeit und Mühe in etw. *(Akk.)* investieren; **b)** ~ **sb. with** *(cause to have)* jmdm. übertragen ‹*Aufgabe, Amt, Leitung*›; jmdm. verleihen ‹*Orden, Titel, Amt, Rechte, Kraft*›; jmdn. ausstatten mit ‹*Geldmitteln, Vollmacht, Insignien*›; **c)** ~ **sth. with sth.** einer Sache *(Dat.)* etw. verleihen; **be ~ed with [an air of] mystery** den Anschein des Geheimnisvollen haben; **d)** *(Mil.)* belagern. **2.** *v. i.* investieren **(in** in + *Akk.*, **with** bei**)**; ~ **in sth.** *(coll.: buy)* sich *(Dat.)* etw. zulegen *(ugs.)*
investigate [ɪn'vestɪgeɪt] **1.** *v. t.* untersuchen; überprüfen; prüfen ‹*Rechtsfrage, Material, Methode*›; ermitteln ‹*Produktionskosten*›; ~ **a case** einen Fall untersuchen; in einem Fall ermitteln; ~ **a crime** ein Verbrechen untersuchen; wegen eines Verbrechens ermitteln. **2.** *v. i.* nachforschen; ‹*Kripo, Staatsanwaltschaft:*› ermitteln; ~ **into sth.** etw. untersuchen
investigation [ɪnvestɪ'geɪʃn] *n. see* **investigate:** Untersuchung, *die;* Überprüfung, *die;* Prüfung, *die;* Ermittlung, *die;* **sth. is under ~:** etw. wird überprüft; **sb. is under ~:** gegen jmdn. wird ermittelt; **a scientific ~:** eine wissenschaftliche Untersuchung
investigative [ɪn'vestɪgətɪv] *adj.* detektivisch; ~ **journalism** Enthüllungsjournalismus, *der*
investigator [ɪn'vestɪgeɪtə(r)] *n.* Ermittler, *der*/Ermittlerin, *die; (government official)* Untersuchungsbeamte, *der*/-beamtin, *die;* **[private] ~:** [Privat]detektiv, *der*/-detektivin, *die*
investigatory [ɪn'vestɪgeɪtərɪ] *adj.* ~ **proceedings/tests/studies** Untersuchungen *Pl.*
investiture [ɪn'vestɪtʃə(r)] *n.* Investitur, *die;* ~ **with the Order of the Garter** Verleihung des Hosenbandordens
investment [ɪn'vestmənt] *n.* **a)** *(of money)* Investition, *die (auch fig.);* Anlage, *die; (fig.)* Einsatz, *der;* Aufwand, *der; attrib.* Investitions-; Anlage-; ~ **of capital** Kapitalanlage, *die;* **make an ~ [of £1,000 in sth.]** [1 000 Pfund in etw. *(Akk.)*] investieren; ~ **advice** Anlageberatung, *die;* ~ **income** Kapitaleinkommen, *das;* ~ **capital** Anlagekapital, *das;* ~ **trust** Investmenttrust, *der;* Investmentgesellschaft, *die;* **b)** *(money invested)* angelegtes Geld; **his large ~ in the company** seine hohe Beteiligung an dem Unternehmen; **c)** *(property)* Kapitalanlage, *die;* **be a good ~** *(fig.)* sich bezahlt machen; eine gute Investition sein; **d)** *see* **investiture; e)** *(Mil.) (siege)* Belagerung, *die; (blockade)* Blockade, *die*
investor [ɪn'vestə(r)] *n.* Investor, *der*/Investorin, *die;* [Kapital]anleger, *der*/-anlegerin, *die;* **~s in that company** Anteilseigner dieser Firma; **small ~s** Kleinanleger
inveterate [ɪn'vetərət] *adj.* **a)** *(deep-rooted)* unüberwindbar ‹*Vorurteil, Mißtrauen*›; unversöhnlich ‹*Haß*›; unverbesserlich ‹*Faulheit usw.*›; **b)** *(habitual)* eingefleischt ‹*Trinker, Raucher, Individualist, Spieler*›; unverbesserlich ‹*Lügner*›
invidious [ɪn'vɪdɪəs] *adj.* undankbar ‹*Aufgabe*›; unpassend, unfair ‹*Vergleich, Bemerkung*›
invidiously [ɪn'vɪdɪəslɪ] *adv. see* **invidious:** auf eine undankbare/unpassende *od.* unfaire Art; *as sentence-modifier* unfairerweise
invigilate [ɪn'vɪdʒɪleɪt] *v. i. (Brit.: in examination)* Aufsicht führen
invigilation [ɪnvɪdʒɪ'leɪʃn] *n. (Brit.)* Aufsichtführung, *die*
invigilator [ɪn'vɪdʒɪleɪtə(r)] *n. (Brit.)* Aufsichtsperson, *die;* Aufsichtführende, *der/die;* **there were no ~s** es gab keine Aufsicht
invigorate [ɪn'vɪgəreɪt] *v. t.* **a)** *(make vigorous)* stärken; *(physically)* kräftigen; **b)** *(animate)* beleben; anregen ‹*Phantasie*›
invigorating [ɪn'vɪgəreɪtɪŋ] *adj.* kräftigend ‹*Getränk, Mahlzeit, Klima*›; stärkend ‹*Schlaf, Mittel*›; belebend ‹*Brise, Dusche, Rasierwasser*›; *(fig.)* anregend ‹*Idee, Erfahrung*›
invincibility [ɪnvɪnsɪ'bɪlɪtɪ] *n., no pl.* Unbesiegbarkeit, *die*
invincible [ɪn'vɪnsɪbl] *adj.* unbesiegbar; unerschütterlich ‹*Entschlossenheit, Mut, Überzeugung, Stolz*›; unüberwindlich ‹*Schwierigkeiten, Unwissenheit, Skepsis*›
inviolable [ɪn'vaɪələbl] *adj.* **a)** *(not to be violated)* unantastbar; **maintain ~ secrecy** unverbrüchliches Stillschweigen bewahren; **b)** *(to be kept sacred)* unantastbar; sakrosankt *(geh.)*
inviolate [ɪn'vaɪələt] *adj.* **a)** *(not violated)* unversehrt; ungestört ‹*Friede, Ruhe*›; nicht verletzt ‹*Abkommen*›; **b)** *(unbroken)* ungetrübt ‹*Freundschaft*›; unerschüttert ‹*Glaube*›; **c)** *(unprofaned)* unangetastet
invisibility [ɪnvɪzɪ'bɪlɪtɪ] *n.* Unsichtbarkeit, *die*
invisible [ɪn'vɪzɪbl] *adj. (also Econ.)* unsichtbar; *(hidden because of fog etc.; too small)* nicht sichtbar; **almost ~:** kaum zu sehen; ~ **mending** Kunststopfen, *das*
invisibly [ɪn'vɪzɪblɪ] *adv.* [für das Auge] nicht sichtbar; ~ **repaired** *or* **mended** so repariert, daß man nichts [davon] sieht; kunstgestopft ‹*Gewebe*›
invitation [ɪnvɪ'teɪʃn] *n. (lit. or fig.)* Einladung, *die;* **at sb.'s ~:** auf jmds. Einladung; **admission by ~ only** Einlaß nur mit Einladung; **an [open] ~ to thieves** eine Aufforderung zum Diebstahl
invite 1. [ɪn'vaɪt] *v. t.* **a)** *(request to come)* einladen; ~ **oneself** *(iron.)* sich selbst einladen; **before an ~d audience** vor geladenen Gästen; ~ **sb. in/over/round** jmdn. hereinbitten/herüberbitten/[zu sich] einladen **(for, to** zu**)**; **b)** *(request to do sth.)* auffordern; **she ~d him to accompany her** sie forderte ihn auf *od.* lud ihn ein, sie zu begleiten; **they ~d him to ascend the throne** sie boten ihm an, den Thron zu besteigen; sie trugen ihm den Thron an *(geh.);* **c)** *(ask for)* erbitten; bitten um; **d)** *(bring on)* herausfordern ‹*Kritik, Verhängnis, Spott, Verachtung, Protest*›; **you're inviting ridicule** du machst dich lächerlich *od.* zum Gespött; **e)** *(attract)* einladen; ~ **interest in sth.** Interesse an etw. *(Dat.)* wecken. **2.** ['ɪnvaɪt] *n. (coll.)* Einladung, *die*
invitee [ɪnvaɪ'ti:] *n.* geladener Gast
inviting [ɪn'vaɪtɪŋ] *adj.* einladend; verlockend ‹*Gedanke, Vorstellung, Aussicht*›; freundlich ‹*Klima*›; ansprechend ‹*Anblick, Schriftbild*›; **make sth. ~ to sb.** etw. für jmdn. attraktiv machen
invitingly [ɪn'vaɪtɪŋlɪ] *adv.* einladend
invocation [ɪnvə'keɪʃn] *n.* Anrufung, *die;* Invokation, *die (geh.)*
invoice ['ɪnvɔɪs] **1.** *n. (bill)* Rechnung, *die; (list)* Lieferschein, *der.* **2.** *v. t.* **a)** *(make ~ for)* eine Rechnung ausstellen für; *(enter in ~)* in Rechnung stellen ‹*Waren*›; **b)** *(send ~ to)* ~ **sb.** jmdm. eine Rechnung schicken; ~ **sb. for sth.** jmdm. etw. in Rechnung stellen; **be ~d for sth.** für etw. eine Rechnung erhalten
invoke [ɪn'vəʊk] *v. t.* **a)** *(call on)* anrufen; **b)** *(appeal to)* sich berufen auf (+ *Akk.*); ~ **an example/sth. as an example** ein Beispiel/etw. als Beispiel anführen; ~ **sth. to justify/explain sth.** etw. bemühen, um etw. zu rechtfertigen/erklären; **c)** *(summon)* beschwören; **d)** *(ask earnestly for)* erbitten; bitten um
involucre ['ɪnvəlu:kə(r)] *n. (Bot.)* Hülle, *die*
involuntarily [ɪn'vɒləntərɪlɪ] *adv.*, **involuntary** [ɪn'vɒləntərɪ] *adj.* unwillkürlich
involve [ɪn'vɒlv] *v. t.* **a)** *(implicate)* verwickeln; ~ **sb. in a charge** jmdn. zum Mitangeklagten machen; **b)** *(draw in as a participant)* ~ **sb. in a game/fight** jmdn. an einem Spiel beteiligen/in eine Schlägerei [mit] hineinziehen; **become** *or* **get ~d in a fight** in eine Schlägerei verwickelt *od.* hineingezogen werden; **be ~d in a project** *(employed)* an einem Projekt mitarbeiten; **get ~d with sb.** sich mit jmdm. einlassen; *(sexually, emotionally)* eine Beziehung mit jmdm. anfangen; **sth. is ~d** *(concerned)* etw. kommt mit ins Spiel; **no other vehicle was ~ in the accident** kein anderes Fahrzeug war an dem Unfall beteiligt; **c)** *(include)* enthalten; *(contain implicitly)* beinhalten; **this event ~s us all** dieses Ereignis betrifft uns alle *od.* geht uns alle an; **d)** *(be necessarily accompanied by)* mit sich bringen; *(require as accompaniment)* erfordern; *(cause, mean)* bedeuten
involved [ɪn'vɒlvd] *adj.* verwickelt; *(complicated)* kompliziert; *(complex)* komplex
involvement [ɪn'vɒlvmənt] *n.* **a)** **my ~ in this affair began only recently** ich habe mit dieser Angelegenheit erst seit kurzem zu tun; **his ~ in the company** seine Beteiligung an der Firma; **I don't know the extent of his**

~ **in this affair** ich weiß nicht, inwieweit er mit dieser Sache zu tun hat; **b)** *(implication)* ~ **in a conflict** Einmischung in einen Konflikt; **his increasing** ~ **in public life** die Rolle, die er in zunehmendem Maße im öffentlichen Leben spielt; **have an** ~ **with sb.** *(sexually)* eine Affäre mit jmdm. haben; **you may not take on any other** ~: Sie dürfen sich nicht anderweitig engagieren

invulnerable [ɪn'vʌlnərəbl] *adj.* unverwundbar ‹*Lebewesen, Waffensystem*›; *(impregnable)* uneinnehmbar ‹*Festung, Stadt usw.*›; *(fig.)* unantastbar ‹*Würde, Stellung*›; **be** ~ **to sth.** gegen etw. gefeit sein *(geh.)*

inward ['ɪnwəd] **1.** *adj.* **a)** *(situated within)* inner...; **b)** *(mental, spiritual)* inner... ‹*Impuls, Regung, Friede, Kampf*›; innerlich *(geh.)* ‹*Leben*›; **his** ~ **thoughts** seine innersten *od.* geheimsten Gedanken; **c)** *(directed inside)* nach innen gehend; nach innen gerichtet; **'goods** ~' „Eingänge"; ~ **slope** Innenneigung, *die;* Neigung nach innen. **2.** *adv.* einwärts ‹*gerichtet, gebogen*›; **open** ~: nach innen öffnen; **an** ~**-looking person** *(fig.)* ein in sich *(Akk.)* gekehrter Mensch

inwardly ['ɪnwədlɪ] *adv.* im Inneren; innerlich

inwards ['ɪnwədz] *see* **inward 2**

iodide ['aɪədaɪd] *n. (Chem.)* Jodid, *das*

iodine ['aɪədi:n, 'aɪədɪn] *n.* Jod, *das*

IOM *abbr.* **Isle of Man**

ion ['aɪən] *n. (Phys., Chem.)* Ion, *das*

ion ex'change *n.* Ionenaustausch, *der*

ionic [aɪ'ɒnɪk] *adj. (Phys., Chem.)* Ionen-; in Ionenform vorliegend ‹*Grundstoff*›; ionisch ‹*Bindung, Verbindung usw.*›

ionisation, ionise *see* **ioniz-**

ionization [aɪənaɪ'zeɪʃn] *n.* Ionisation, *die*

ionize ['aɪənaɪz] *v.t.* ionisieren

ionosphere [aɪ'ɒnəsfɪə(r)] *n.* Ionosphäre, *die*

iota [aɪ'əʊtə] *n.* **a)** *(smallest amount)* Jota, *das (geh.);* **not an** *or* **one** ~: nicht ein Jota *(geh.);* kein Jota *(geh.);* **there's not an** ~ **of truth in that** daran ist nicht ein Fünkchen Wahrheit; **b)** *(Greek letter)* Jota, *das*

IOU [aɪəʊ'ju:] *n.* Schuldschein, *der*

IOW *abbr.* **Isle of Wight**

IPA *abbr.* **International Phonetic Alphabet/Association** IPA

i.p.s. *abbr.* **inches per second** inch/s

ipso facto [ɪpsəʊ 'fæktəʊ] *adv.* **a)** *(by that very fact)* eo ipso *(geh.);* eben dadurch; **b)** *(thereby)* auf Grund dessen; **c)** *(by the very nature of the case)* eo ipso; naturgemäß

IQ *abbr.* **intelligence quotient** IQ, *der;* **IQ-test** IQ-Test, *der*

IRA *abbr.* **Irish Republican Army** IRA, *die*

Iran [ɪ'rɑ:n] *pr. n.* Iran, *der*

Iranian [ɪ'reɪnɪən] **1.** *adj.* iranisch; **sb. is** ~: jmd. ist Iraner/Iranerin. **2.** *n.* **a)** *(person)* Iraner, *der*/Iranerin, *die;* **b)** *(Ling.)* Iranisch, *das;* **speak** ~: eine iranische Sprache sprechen

Iraq [ɪ'rɑ:k] *pr. n.* Irak, *der*

Iraqi [ɪ'rɑ:kɪ] **1.** *adj.* irakisch; **sb. is** ~: jmd. ist Iraker/Irakerin. **2.** *n.* **a)** *(person)* Iraker, *der*/Irakerin, *die;* **b)** *(dialect)* Irakisch, *das*

irascible [ɪ'ræsɪbl] *adj. (hot-tempered)* aufbrausend; *(irritable)* reizbar

irate [aɪ'reɪt] *adj.* wütend ‹*Person, Tier, Menge*›; erbost *(geh.)* ‹*Person*›

irately [aɪ'reɪtlɪ] *adv.* wütend

ire [aɪə(r)] *n. (rhet./poet.)* Zorn, *der*

Ireland ['aɪələnd] *pr. n.* **[Republic of]** ~: Irland *(das)*

iridescence [ɪrɪ'desəns] *n.* Schillern, *das;* Irisieren, *das*

iridescent [ɪrɪ'desənt] *adj.* regenbogenfarben; *(changing colour with position)* schillernd; irisierend

iridium [ɪ'rɪdɪəm] *n. (Chem.)* Iridium, *das*

iris ['aɪərɪs] *n.* **a)** *(Anat.)* Iris, *die;* Regenbogenhaut, *die;* **b)** *(Bot.)* Iris, *die;* Schwertlilie, *die;* **c)** *(Optics)* Irisblende, *die*

Irish ['aɪərɪʃ] **1.** *adj.* **a)** irisch; **sb. is** ~: jmd. ist Ire/Irin; ~ **joke** Irenwitz, *der; see also* **English 1; b)** *(coll.: contradictory)* komisch. **2.** *n.* **a)** *(language)* Irisch, *das; see also* **English 2 a; b)** *constr. as pl.* **the** ~: die Iren

Irish: ~ **'bull** *n.* Widerspruch in sich; Paradox, *das (geh.);* ~ **'coffee** *n.* Irish coffee, *der;* ~ **'Gaelic** *n.* Irisch-Gälisch, *das;* ~**man** ['aɪərɪʃmən] *n., pl.* ~**men** ['aɪərɪʃmən] Ire, *der;* ~ **Re'public** *pr. n.* Irische Republik; ~ **'Sea** *pr. n.* Irische See; ~ **'stew** *n.* Irish-Stew, *das;* ~ **'whisk[e]y** *n.* irischer Whisk[e]y; ~**woman** *n.* Irin, *die*

irk [ɜ:k] *v.t.* ärgern

irksome ['ɜ:ksəm] *adj.* lästig

iron ['aɪən] **1.** *n.* **a)** *(metal)* Eisen, *das;* ~ **tablets** Eisentabletten; **man of** ~ *(fig.)* stahlharter Mann; **with a grip of** ~: mit eisernem Griff; **as hard as** ~: eisenhart; **will of** ~: eiserner Wille; **strike while the** ~ **is hot** *(prov.)* das Eisen schmieden, solange es heiß ist *(Spr.); see also* **pyrites, rod c; b)** *(tool)* Eisen, *das;* **have several** ~**s in the fire** mehrere Eisen im Feuer haben *(ugs.);* **have too many** ~**s in the fire** sich verzetteln; sich *(Dat.)* zuviel auf einmal vornehmen; **c)** *(Golf)* Eisen, *das;* Eisenschläger, *der;* **d)** *(for smoothing)* Bügeleisen, *das;* **e)** *usu. in pl. (fetter)* Eisen, *das;* **put sb. in** ~**s** jmdn. in Eisen legen *(dichter., veralt.).* **2.** *attrib. adj.* **a)** *(of iron)* eisern; Eisen‹*platte usw.*›; **b)** *(very robust)* eisern ‹*Konstitution*›; stählern ‹*Muskeln*›; **c)** *(unyielding)* eisern; ehern *(geh.)* ‹*Stoizismus*›; ~ **rule/his** ~ **rule** ein/sein eisernes Regiment. **3.** *v.t.* bügeln. **4.** *v.i.* **a)** ‹*Kleidungsstück:*› sich bügeln lassen; **b)** ‹*Person:*› bügeln

~ **'on** *v.t.* aufbügeln; *see also* **iron-on**

~ **'out** *v.t.* herausbügeln ‹*Falten*›; *(flatten)* glätten ‹*Papier*›; *(fig.)* beseitigen ‹*Kurve, Unregelmäßigkeit*›; aus dem Weg räumen ‹*Schwierigkeit, Problem*›; ausgleichen ‹*Interessengegensatz*›

iron: **I~ Age** *n.* Eisenzeit, *die;* ~**clad 1.** *adj.* **a)** *(clad in iron)* eisenbewehrt; gepanzert ‹*Schiff*›; **b)** *(fig.) (rigorous)* eisern; unverbrüchlich ‹*Eid*›; unnachsichtig ‹*Kontrolle*›; **there are no** ~**clad rules in this matter** dafür gibt es keine starren Regeln; **2.** *n. (Navy Hist.)* Panzerschiff, *das;* **I~ 'Cross** *n.* Eisernes Kreuz; **I~ 'Curtain** *n. (fig.)* Eiserner Vorhang; ~**-grey 1.** *adj.* eisengrau; grau ‹*Herbsttag*›; **2.** *n.* Eisengrau, *das*

ironic [aɪ'rɒnɪk], **ironical** [aɪ'rɒnɪkl] *adj.* ironisch; **it is** ~ **that ...**: es ist paradox, daß ...

ironically [aɪ'rɒnɪkəlɪ] *adv.* ironisch; *as sentence-modifier* ironischerweise

ironing ['aɪənɪŋ] *n.* Bügeln, *das; (things [to be] ironed)* Bügelwäsche, *die;* **do the** ~: bügeln

'ironing-board *n.* Bügelbrett, *das*

iron 'lung *n.* eiserne Lunge

ironmonger ['aɪənmʌŋgə(r)] *n. (Brit.)* Eisenwarenhändler, *der*/-händlerin, *die; see also* **baker**

ironmongery ['aɪənmʌŋgərɪ] *n. (Brit.)* **a)** *(hardware)* Eisenwaren *Pl.;* **b)** *(sl.: firearms)* Schießeisen *(ugs.)*

iron: ~**-on** *adj.* aufbügelbar; zum Aufbügeln *nachgestellt;* ~ **ore** *n.* Eisenerz, *das;* ~ **'ration** *n.* eiserne Ration; ~**ware** *n., no pl.* Eisenwaren *Pl.; (household utensils)* Haushaltswaren *Pl.;* ~**work** *n., no pl.* Eisenarbeit, *die; (part)* Eisenwerk, *das; (articles)* Eisenwaren *Pl.;* ~**works** *n. sing., pl. same* Eisenhüttenwerk, *das;* Eisenhütte, *die*

irony ['aɪrənɪ] *n.* Ironie, *die;* **one of life's [little] ironies** eine Ironie des Schicksals; **the** ~ **was that ...**: die Ironie lag darin, daß ...; das Ironische war, daß ...; *see also* **tragic b**

irradiate [ɪ'reɪdɪeɪt] *v.t.* **a)** *(shine upon)* bescheinen; **b)** *(light up)* erstrahlen lassen; zum Leuchten bringen; **c)** *(Phys., Med., Gastr.)* bestrahlen

irradiation [ɪreɪdɪ'eɪʃn] *n.* **a)** *(illumination)* Leuchten, *das;* **b)** *(fig.)* Erleuchtung, *die;* **c)** *(Phys., Med.)* Bestrahlung, *die;* **d) [food]** ~: [Lebensmittel]bestrahlung, *die*

irrational [ɪ'ræʃənl] **1.** *adj.* **a)** *(unreasonable)* irrational *(geh.);* vernunftwidrig; **b)** *(incapable of reasoning)* nicht vernunftbegabt; **c)** *(Math.)* irrational ‹*Zahl*›

irrationality [ɪræʃə'nælɪtɪ] *n.* Irrationalität, *die (geh.); (of situation)* Absurdität, *die*

irrationally [ɪ'ræʃənəlɪ] *adv.* irrationalerweise *(geh.);* ohne vernünftigen Grund

irreconcilable [ɪ'rekənsaɪləbl] *adj.* **a)** *(implacably hostile)* unversöhnlich; unüberwindlich ‹*Abneigung*›; **b)** *(incompatible)* unvereinbar; unversöhnlich ‹*Gegensätze*›; **theory and practice are completely** ~: Theorie und Praxis widersprechen sich total

irrecoverable [ɪrɪ'kʌvərəbl] *adj.* unwiederbringlich verloren; endgültig ‹*Verlust*›; nicht eintreibbar ‹*Schuld*›; **the situation was** ~: die Situation war nicht mehr zu retten

irredeemable [ɪrɪ'di:məbl] *adj.* nicht wiedergutzumachend ‹*Fehler*›; **be** ~: nicht wiedergutzumachen sein; **the mistake is not yet** ~: noch kann der Fehler wiedergutgemacht werden

irreducible [ɪrɪ'dju:sɪbl] *adj.* nicht [mehr *od.* weiter] reduzierbar; Mindest‹*menge*›

irrefutable [ɪ'refjʊtəbl, ɪrɪ'fju:təbl] *adj.* unwiderlegbar

irregular [ɪ'regjʊlə(r)] **1.** *adj.* **a)** *(not conforming)* unkorrekt ‹*Verhalten, Handlung usw.*›; **this is most** ~! das ist eigentlich nicht erlaubt!; **b)** *(uneven in duration, order, etc.)* unregelmäßig; *see also* **hour c; c)** *(abnormal)* sonderbar; eigenartig; **d)** *(not symmetrical)* unregelmäßig; uneben ‹*Oberfläche, Gelände*›; **e)** *(disorderly)* ungeregelt ‹*Leben[sweise]*›; *(lawless)* zwielichtig; **f)** *(Mil.)* irregulär ‹*Truppen*›; **g)** *(Ling., Bot.)* unregelmäßig. **2.** *n. in pl. (Mil.)* Irreguläre *Pl.*

irregularity [ɪregjʊ'lærɪtɪ] *n.* **a)** *(lack of conformity)* Unkorrektheit, *die; (instance also)* Unregelmäßigkeit, *die;* **b)** *(uneveness in duration, order, etc.)* Unregelmäßigkeit, *die;* **c)** *(abnormality)* Sonderbarkeit, *die;* Eigenartigkeit, *die;* **d)** *(disorderliness)* Ungeregeltheit, *die; (lawlessness)* Zwielichtigkeit, *die;* **e)** *(lack of symmetry)* Unregelmäßigkeit, *die; (of surface)* Unebenheit, *die*

irregularly [ɪ'regjʊləlɪ] *adv.* **a)** *(not in conformity)* unkorrekt; *(lawlessly)* unzulässigerweise; **b)** *(unevenly)* unregelmäßig

irrelevance [ɪ'relɪvəns], **irrelevancy** [ɪ'relɪvənsɪ] *n. (being irrelevant)* Belanglosigkeit, *die;* Irrelevanz, *die (geh.); (irrelevant detail, information, etc.)* Belanglosigkeit, *die*

irrelevant [ɪ'relɪvənt] *adj.* belanglos; irrelevant *(geh.);* **be** ~ **to a subject** für ein Thema ohne Belang *od. (geh.)* irrelevant sein

irreligious [ɪrɪ'lɪdʒəs] *adj.* irreligiös *(geh.),* ungläubig ‹*Person*›; gottlos ‹*Verhaltensweise, Idee, Person*›

irremediable [ɪrɪ'mi:dɪəbl] *adj.* nicht wiedergutzumachend *nicht präd.* ‹*Tat, Verlust, Schaden, Fehler, Irrtum*›; nicht wettzumachend *nicht präd.* ‹*Verschlechterung*›; nicht zu behebend *nicht präd.* ‹*Mangel*›; nicht zu verbessernd *nicht präd.* ‹*Situation*›; **be** ~: nicht wiedergutzumachen/wettzumachen/zu beheben/zu verbessern sein

irreparable [ɪ'repərəbl] *adj.* nicht wiedergutzumachend *nicht präd.;* irreparabel *(geh., Med.)*

irreparably [ɪ'repərəblɪ] *adv.* irreparabel *(geh.);* **be** ~ **damaged** einen nicht behebbaren *od. (geh.)* irreparablen Schaden haben

irreplaceable [ɪrɪ'pleɪsəbl] *adj.* **a)** *(not replaceable)* nicht ersetzbar; nicht nachlieferbar ‹*Waren*›; **b)** *(of which the loss cannot be made good)* unersetzlich

irrepressible [ɪrɪ'presɪbl] *adj.* nicht zu unterdrückend *nicht präd.;* unbezähmbar ‹*Neugier, Verlangen*›; unerschütterlich ‹*Op-*

timismus⟩; unbändig ⟨*Freude, Entzücken*⟩; unbezwingbar ⟨*Neigung*⟩; sonnig ⟨*Gemüt*⟩; **he/she is ~:** er/sie ist nicht unterzukriegen *(ugs.)*; **an ~ chatterbox** eine unentwegte Quasselstrippe *(ugs.)*

irreproachable [ɪrɪ'prəʊtʃəbl] *adj.* untadelig ⟨*Charakter, Lebenswandel, Benehmen*⟩; unanfechtbar ⟨*Ehrlichkeit*⟩; tadellos ⟨*Kleidung, Manieren*⟩; makellos ⟨*Vergangenheit [eines Menschen]*⟩

irresistible [ɪrɪ'zɪstɪbl] *adj.* unwiderstehlich; bestechend ⟨*Argument*⟩

irresistibly [ɪrɪ'zɪstɪblɪ] *adv.* unwiderstehlich; unaufhaltsam ⟨*näherkommen*⟩

irresolute [ɪ'rezəlu:t, ɪ'rezəlju:t] *adj.* **a)** *(undecided)* unentschlossen; unschlüssig; **b)** *(lacking in resoluteness)* unentschlossen

irresolutely [ɪ'rezəlu:tlɪ, ɪ'rezəlju:tlɪ] *adv.* unentschlossen; unschlüssig

irresoluteness [ɪ'rezəlu:tnɪs, ɪ'rezəlju:tnɪs], **irresolution** [ɪrezə'lu:ʃn, ɪrezə'lju:ʃn] *ns., no pl.* **a)** *(being undecided)* Unentschlossenheit, *die;* Unschlüssigkeit, *die;* **b)** *(lack of resoluteness)* Unentschlossenheit, *die;* Entschlußlosigkeit, *die*

irrespective [ɪrɪ'spektɪv] *adj.* **~ of** ungeachtet (+ *Gen.*); *(independent of)* unabhängig von; **~ of what ...:** unabhängig davon, was ...; **~ of the consequences** ungeachtet der *od.* ohne Rücksicht auf die Folgen

irresponsibility [ɪrɪspɒnsɪ'bɪlɪtɪ] *n., no pl. see* **irresponsible:** Verantwortungslosigkeit, *die;* Unverantwortlichkeit, *die;* **it is sheer ~ to ...:** es ist einfach unverantwortlich, zu ...

irresponsible [ɪrɪ'spɒnsɪbl] *adj.* verantwortungslos ⟨*Person*⟩; unverantwortlich ⟨*Benehmen*⟩; *(mentally inadequate to bear responsibility)* der Verantwortung nicht gewachsen; **[financially] ~:** zahlungsunwillig

irresponsibly [ɪrɪ'spɒnsɪblɪ] *adv.* verantwortungslos; unverantwortlich; in verantwortungsloser Weise

irretrievable [ɪrɪ'tri:vəbl] *adj.* nicht mehr wiederzubekommen *nicht attr.*; nicht mehr korrigierbar ⟨*Fehler*⟩; *(irreversible)* endgültig ⟨*Ruin, Verfall, Verlust*⟩; unheilbar ⟨*Zerrüttung einer Ehe*⟩; ausweglos ⟨*Situation*⟩

irretrievably [ɪrɪ'tri:vəblɪ] *adv.* unwiederbringlich ⟨*verloren*⟩; *(for ever)* endgültig; für alle Zeiten; **the marriage has ~ broken down** die Ehe ist unheilbar zerrüttet

irreverence [ɪ'revərəns] *n. see* **irreverent:** Respektlosigkeit, *die;* Pietätlosigkeit, *die (geh.)*; **an [act of] ~:** eine Respektlosigkeit/Pietätlosigkeit *(geh.)*

irreverent [ɪ'revərənt] *adj.*, **irreverently** [ɪ'revərəntlɪ] *adv.* respektlos; *(towards religious values or the dead)* pietätlos *(geh.)*

irreversible [ɪrɪ'vɜ:sɪbl] *adj.* **a)** *(unalterable)* unabänderlich, unumstößlich ⟨*Entscheidung, Entschluß, Tatsache*⟩; unwiderruflich ⟨*Entschluß, Entscheidung, Anordnung, Befehl usw.*⟩; **b)** *(not reversible)* irreversibel *(geh.)* ⟨*Vorgang*⟩; *(inexorable)* unaufhaltsam ⟨*Entwicklung, Verfall*⟩; **~ damage** nicht wiedergutzumachender *od. (geh.)* irreparabler Schaden

irrevocable [ɪ'revəkəbl] *adj.* **a)** *(unalterable, final)* unwiderruflich ⟨*Gelübde, Entscheidung, Entschluß, Befehl*⟩; unabänderlich ⟨*Entschluß*⟩; **b)** *(gone beyond recall)* unwiederbringlich ⟨*Vergangenheit, Augenblick*⟩

irrevocably [ɪ'revəkəblɪ] *adv.* unwiederbringlich, unwiderruflich ⟨*verloren, vorüber*⟩

irrigate ['ɪrɪgeɪt] *v.t.* **a)** bewässern; **b)** *(Med.)* [aus]spülen

irrigation [ɪrɪ'geɪʃn] *n.* **a)** Bewässerung, *die;* **overhead ~:** Beregnung, *die;* **b)** *(Med.)* Spülung, *die;* Irrigation, *die (fachspr.)*

irritability [ɪrɪtə'bɪlɪtɪ] *n. see* **irritable a:** Reizbarkeit, *die;* Gereiztheit, *die*

irritable ['ɪrɪtəbl] *adj.* **a)** *(quick to anger)* reizbar; *(temporarily)* gereizt; **b)** *(of organ)* empfindlich; **~ to the touch** empfindlich gegen Berührung; **c)** *(Biol.)* reizbar

irritably ['ɪrɪtəblɪ] *adv.* gereizt

irritant ['ɪrɪtənt] **1.** *adj.* Reiz-; **be ~:** reizen. **2.** *n.* Reizstoff, *der;* **the spicy food proved to be an ~ to his stomach** sein Magen vertrug das scharf gewürzte Essen nicht; **be an ~ to sb./sb.'s nerves** *(fig.)* jmdm. auf die Nerven gehen *(ugs.)*

irritate ['ɪrɪteɪt] *v.t.* **a)** ärgern; **get ~d** ärgerlich werden; **be ~d** sich ärgern; ungehalten sein *(geh.)*; **be ~d by** *or* **feel ~d at sth.** sich über etw. *(Akk.)* ärgern; **be ~d with sb.** sich über jmdn. aufregen *od.* ärgern; **be ~d that ...:** verärgert *od. (geh.)* ungehalten [darüber] sein, daß ...; **she was ~d to hear this** sie war ärgerlich *od. (geh.)* ungehalten, als sie dies hörte; **b)** *(Med., Biol.)* reizen

irritating ['ɪrɪteɪtɪŋ] *adj.* lästig; **I find him ~:** er geht mir auf die Nerven *(ugs.)*

irritatingly ['ɪrɪteɪtɪŋlɪ] *adv.* ärgerlich; *as sentence-modifier* ärgerlicherweise; **the tap was dripping ~:** der Wasserhahn tropfte nervtötend

irritation [ɪrɪ'teɪʃn] *n.* **a)** Ärger, *der;* **[source** *or* **cause of] ~:** Ärgernis, *das;* **b)** *(Med., Biol.)* Reizung, *die*

is *see* **be**

Is. *abbr.* **Island[s]; Isle[s]** I[n].

Isaac ['aɪzək] *pr. n. (Bibl.)* Isaak *(der)*

Isaiah [aɪ'zaɪə] *pr. n. (Bibl.)* Jesaja *(der)*

ISBN *abbr.* **international standard book number** ISBN

isinglass ['aɪzɪŋglɑ:s] *n.* Hausenblase, *die;* Fischleim, *der*

Islam ['ɪzlɑ:m, 'ɪzlæm, ɪz'lɑ:m] *n.* Islam, *der*

Islamic [ɪz'læmɪk] *adj.* islamisch

island ['aɪlənd] *n. (lit. or fig.)* Insel, *die; see also* **traffic island**

islander ['aɪləndə(r)] *n.* Inselbewohner, *der*/-bewohnerin, *die;* Insulaner, *der*/Insulanerin, *die*

isle [aɪl] *n.* Insel, *die;* Eiland, *das (dichter.)*

Isle of Man [aɪl əv 'mæn] *pr. n.* Insel Man, *die*

Isle of Wight [aɪl əv 'waɪt] *pr. n.* Insel Wight, *die*

islet ['aɪlɪt] *n.* **a)** *(little island)* kleine Insel; kleines Eiland *(dichter.)*; **b)** *(isolated spot)* Insel, *die;* **c)** *(Anat.)* Insel, *die*

ism [ɪzm] *n. (derog.)* Ismus, *der (abwertend)*

isn't [ɪznt] *(coll.)* = **is not;** *see* **be**

ISO *abbr.* **International Organization for Standardization** ISO, *die*

isobar ['aɪsəbɑ:(r)] *n. (Meteorol., Phys.)* Isobare, *die*

isolate ['aɪsəleɪt] *v.t.* isolieren; *(Electr.)* vom Stromkreis trennen; **~ sb. from sb.** jmdn. von jmdm. trennen; **he felt completely ~d** er kam sich *(Dat.)* völlig verloren vor

isolated ['aɪsəleɪtɪd] *adj.* **a)** *(single)* einzeln; *(occasional)* vereinzelt; *(unique)* einmalig; **~ instances/cases** Einzelfälle; **b)** *(solitary)* einsam; *(remote)* abgelegen **(from** von); *(cut off)* abgeschnitten **(from** von)

isolation [aɪsə'leɪʃn] *n.* **a)** *(act)* Isolierung, *die;* Absonderung, *die;* **b)** *(state)* Isoliertheit, *die;* Isolation, *die;* Abgeschnittenheit, *die;* *(remoteness)* Abgeschiedenheit, *die;* **examine/look at/treat sth. in ~:** etw. isoliert *od.* gesondert betrachten; **~ hospital** Infektionskrankenhaus, *das;* **~ ward** Isolierstation, *die;* Infektionsabteilung, *die*

isolationism [aɪsə'leɪʃənɪzm] *n. (Polit.)* Isolationismus, *der*

isolationist [aɪsə'leɪʃənɪst] *n. (Polit.)* Isolationist, *der*/Isolationistin, *die*

isomer ['aɪsəmə(r)] *n. (Chem.)* Isomer[e], *das*

isometric [aɪsə'metrɪk] *adj. (Geom., Physiol.)* isometrisch

isometrics [aɪsə'metrɪks] *n., no pl.* isometrisches Muskeltraining; Isometrik, *die*

isomorph ['aɪsəmɔ:f] *n.* Isomorphe, *die*

isomorphic [aɪsə'mɔ:fɪk] *adj.* isomorph

isomorphism [aɪsə'mɔ:fɪzm] *n.* Isomorphie, *die;* *(of crystals)* Isomorphismus, *der*

isomorphous [aɪsə'mɔ:fəs] *adj.* isomorph

isosceles [aɪ'sɒsəli:z] *adj. (Geom.)* gleichschenklig

isotherm ['aɪsəθɜ:m] *n. (Meteorol., Phys.)* Isotherme, *die*

isothermal [aɪsə'θɜ:ml] *adj. (Meteorol., Phys.)* isotherm

isotope ['aɪsətəʊp] *n. (Chem., Phys.)* Isotop, *das*

isotropic [aɪsə'trɒpɪk] *adj. (Phys.)* isotrop

Israel ['ɪzreɪl] *pr. n.* Israel *(das)*

Israeli [ɪz'reɪlɪ] **1.** *adj.* israelisch. **2.** *n.* Israeli, *der/die*

Israelite ['ɪzrɪəlaɪt] *n.* Israelit, *der*/Israelitin, *die*

issue ['ɪʃu:, 'ɪsju:] **1.** *n.* **a)** *(point in question)* Frage, *die;* **the ~ of the day** das Thema des Tages; **contemporary ~s** aktuelle Fragen *od.* Themen; **make an ~ of sth.** etw. aufbauschen; **the real ~s in today's world** die Kernprobleme der heutigen Zeit; **become an ~:** zum Problem werden; **evade** *or* **dodge** *or* **duck the ~:** ausweichen; **~ of fact** *(Law)* Tatsachenfrage, *die;* **the point at ~:** der strittige Punkt; worum es geht; **what is at ~ is whether we should stay** es geht darum, ob wir hierbleiben; die Frage ist: sollen wir hierbleiben?; **that's not at ~:** das steht nicht zur Debatte; darum geht es nicht; **be at ~ over sth.** wegen etw. miteinander im Streit liegen; wegen etw. Meinungsverschiedenheiten haben; **join** *or* **take ~ with sb. over sth.** sich mit jmdm. auf eine Diskussion über etw. *(Akk.)* einlassen; **b)** *(giving out)* Ausgabe, *die;* *(of document)* Ausstellung, *die;* *(of shares)* Emission, *die;* **date of ~:** Ausgabedatum, *das;* Ausgabetag, *der;* *(of document)* Ausstellungsdatum, *das;* *(of stamps)* Ausgabetag, *der;* **c)** *(of magazine, journal, etc.)* Ausgabe, *die;* **d)** *(total number of copies)* Auflage, *die;* **e)** *(quantity of coins)* Emissionszahl, *die;* *(quantity of stamps)* Auflage, *die;* **f)** *(result, outcome)* Ergebnis, *das;* Ausgang, *der;* **decide the ~:** den Ausschlag geben; **force the ~:** eine Entscheidung erzwingen; **g)** *(termination)* Ende, *das;* **h)** *(Law: progeny)* Nachkommen *Pl.*; **i)** *(outgoing, outflow)* Austritt, *der.* **2.** *v.t.* **a)** *(give out)* ausgeben; ausstellen ⟨*Paß, Visum, Lizenz, Zeugnis*⟩; erteilen ⟨*Lizenz, Befehl*⟩; **~ sb. with sth.** etw. an jmdn. austeilen; **b)** *(publish)* herausgeben ⟨*Publikation*⟩; herausbringen ⟨*Publikation, Münze, Briefmarke*⟩; emittieren ⟨*Wertpapiere*⟩; geben ⟨*Warnung*⟩; **c)** *(supply)* ausgeben **(to** an + *Akk.*); **~ sb. with sth.** jmdn. mit etw. ausstatten; **be ~d with sth.** etw. erhalten. **3.** *v.i.* **a)** *(go or come out)* ⟨*Personen:*⟩ herausströmen **(from** aus); ⟨*Gas, Flüssigkeit:*⟩ austreten **(from** aus); ⟨*Rauch:*⟩ heraus-, hervorquellen **(from** aus); ⟨*Ton, Geräusch:*⟩ hervor-, herausdringen **(from** aus); **b)** *(be derived)* entspringen **(from** *Dat.*); **c)** *(result)* sich ergeben **(from** aus)

isthmus ['ɪsməs, 'ɪsθməs] *n. (Geog.)* Landenge, *die;* Isthmus, *der*

IT *abbr.* **information technology**

[1]**it** [ɪt] *pron.* **a)** *(the thing, animal, young child previously mentioned)* er/sie/es; *as direct obj.* ihn/sie/es; *as indirect obj.* ihm/ihr/ihm; **the book was not in the cupboard but behind it** das Buch war nicht im Schrank, sondern dahinter; **the animal turned and snarled at the huntsman behind it** das Tier drehte sich um und knurrte den Jäger hinter sich *(Dat.)* an; **the cathedral and the buildings around it** der Dom und die umliegenden Gebäude; **b)** *(the person in question)* **who is it?** wer ist da?; **it was the children** es waren die Kinder; **is it you, father?** bist du es, Vater?; **Are you the one responsible for all this mess? – No, it's him**

Sind Sie für dieses Durcheinander verantwortlich? – Nein, er; **c)** *subj. of impers. v.* es; **it is snowing/warm** es schneit/ist warm; **it is winter/midnight/ten o'clock** es ist Winter/Mitternacht/zehn Uhr; **it is ten miles to Oxford** es sind zehn Meilen bis Oxford; **it says in the Bible that ...:** in der Bibel heißt es, daß ...; in der Bibel steht, daß ...; **had it not been a Sunday ...:** wenn nicht Sonntag gewesen wäre ...; **if it hadn't been for you ...:** wenn du nicht gewesen wärst, ...; **d)** *anticipating subj. or obj.* es; **it is typical of her to do that** es ist typisch für sie, so etwas zu tun; **it is absurd talking** *or* **to talk like that** es ist absurd, so zu reden; **it is a difficult time, winter** es ist eine schwierige Zeit, der Winter; **it is not often that we see them** wir sehen sie nicht oft; **it was for our sake that he did it** um unseretwillen hat er es getan; **it is to him that you must apply** an ihn mußt du dich wenden; **e)** *as antecedent to relative* es; **it was us who saw him** wir waren es, die ihn gesehen haben; wir haben ihn gesehen; **it was a large sum of money that he found** was er fand, war ein großer Geldbetrag; **f)** *as indef. obj.* es; **I can't cope with it any more** ich halte das nicht mehr länger aus; **have a hard time of it** eine schwere Zeit haben; **what is it?** was ist los?; was ist denn?; **g)** *(exactly what is needed)* **That's it! That's exactly what I've been looking for** Das ist es! Genau das habe ich gesucht; **a gift that is really 'it** das ideale Geschenk *(ugs.)*; **he thinks he's really 'it** er denkt, er ist der Größte *(ugs.)*; **h)** *(the extreme limit of achievement)* **this is really 'it** das ist wirklich [einsame *od.* absolute] Spitze *(ugs.)*; **i)** *(coll.: sexual appeal)* das gewisse Etwas *(ugs.)*; **j) that's 'it** *(coll.) (that's the problem)* das ist es [eben]; *(that's the end)* jetzt ist Schluß; *(that's true)* genau *(ugs.)*; **when you've done your stint, that's 'it!** wenn du deinen Anteil geleistet hast, dann fertig *od.* dann war's das; **this is 'it** *(coll.) (the time for action)* es ist soweit; *(the real problem)* das ist es [eben]; **k)** *(in children's games)* **you're 'it!** du bist! *(ugs.)*. *See also* **its; itself**

²it *n. (Brit. coll.)* [italienischer] Wermut

Italian [ɪ'tæljən] **1.** *adj.* italienisch; **sb. is ~:** jmd. ist Italiener/Italienerin; *see also* **English 1. 2.** *n.* **a)** *(person)* Italiener, *der*/Italienerin, *die;* **b)** *(language)* Italienisch, *das; see also* **English 2 a**

Italianate [ɪ'tæljənət, ɪ'tæljəneɪt] *adj.* italienisch beeinflußt

italic [ɪ'tælɪk] **1.** *adj.* kursiv. **2.** *n. in pl.* Kursivschrift, *die;* **in ~s** kursiv; **my ~s** Hervorhebung von mir

italicize (italicise) [ɪ'tælɪsaɪz] *v. t.* kursiv setzen

italic: ~ 'script *n.* Kursive, *die;* **~ 'type** *n. (Printing)* Kursivschrift, *die*

Italy ['ɪtəlɪ] *pr. n.* Italien *(das)*

itch [ɪtʃ] **1.** *n.* **a)** Juckreiz, *der;* Jucken, *das;* **I have an ~:** es juckt mich; ich habe einen Juckreiz; **when you get an ~:** wenn es [dich] juckt; **b)** *(disease)* Krätze, *die;* **c)** *(restless desire)* Drang, *der;* **I have an ~ to do it** es juckt *(ugs.) od.* reizt mich, es zu tun; **an ~ for money/success** ein Verlangen nach Geld/Erfolg. **2.** *v. i.* **a)** einen Juckreiz haben; **I'm ~ing** es juckt mich; **woollen jumpers make me ~:** Wollpullover jucken mich; **this heat makes me ~ all over** bei der Hitze juckt es mich überall; **it ~es** es juckt; **my back ~es** mein Rücken juckt; es juckt mich am Rücken; *see also* **finger 1 a; b)** *(feel a desire)* **~** *or* **be ~ing to do sth.** darauf brennen, etw. zu tun; **~ for sth.** sich nach etw. sehnen

itching-powder ['ɪtʃɪŋpaʊdə(r)] *n.* Juckpulver, *das*

itchy ['ɪtʃɪ] *adj.* kratzig ‹*Socken, Laken*›; **be ~** ‹*Körperteil:*› jucken; **I feel ~:** es juckt mich; **I've got ~ feet** *(fig. coll.)* mich hält es hier nicht länger; *(by temperament)* mich hält es nirgends lange

it'd ['ɪtəd] *(coll.)* **a)** = **it had; b)** = **it would**

item ['aɪtəm] *n.* **a)** Ding, *das;* Sache, *die; (in shop, catalogue)* Artikel, *der; (in variety show, radio, TV)* Nummer, *die;* **~ of clothing/furniture** Kleidungs-/Möbelstück, *das;* **~ of equipment** Ausrüstungsgegenstand, *der;* **b) ~ [of news]** Nachricht, *die;* **c)** *(in account or bill)* Posten, *der; (in list, programme, agenda)* Punkt, *der*

itemize (itemise) ['aɪtəmaɪz] *v. t.* einzeln aufführen; spezifizieren ‹*Rechnung*›; **~ the stock** den Bestand auflisten

iterative ['ɪtərətɪv] *adj.*, **iteratively** ['ɪtərətɪvlɪ] *adv. (Ling.)* iterativ

itinerant [ɪ'tɪnərənt, aɪ'tɪnərənt] **1.** *adj.* reisend; umherziehend; Wander‹*prediger, -arbeiter*›; fahrend ‹*Sänger*›. **2.** *n.* Landfahrer, *der*/Landfahrerin, *die*

itinerary [aɪ'tɪnərərɪ, ɪ'tɪnərərɪ] *n.* **a)** *(route)* [Reise]route, *die;* [Reise]weg, *der;* **b)** *(record of travel)* Reisebericht, *der;* Reisebeschreibung, *die;* **c)** *(guidebook)* Reiseführer, *der*

it'll [ɪtl] *(coll.)* = **it will**

its [ɪts] *poss. pron. attrib.* sein/ihr/sein; *see also* **²her**

it's [ɪts] **a)** = **it is; b)** = **it has**

itself [ɪt'self] *pron.* **a)** *emphat.* selbst; **by ~** *(automatically)* von selbst; *(alone)* allein; *(taken in isolation)* für sich; **in ~:** für sich genommen; **which ~ is reason enough** was allein schon Grund genug ist; **he is generosity ~:** er ist die Großzügigkeit in Person; **b)** *refl.* sich; **the rocket destroys ~:** die Rakete zerstört sich selbst; **the machine switches ~ off** die Maschine schaltet sich [von] selbst aus. *See also* **herself**

itsy-bitsy [ɪtsɪ'bɪtsɪ], **itty-bitty** [ɪtɪ'bɪtɪ] *adjs. (coll.)* klitzeklein *(ugs.)*; **~ little** klitzeklitzeklein *(ugs.)*

ITV *abbr. (Brit.)* **Independent Television** *kommerzielles britisches Fernsehprogramm*

Ivan ['aɪvn] *pr. n. (Hist., as name of ruler etc.)* Iwan *(der);* **~ the Terrible** Iwan der Schreckliche

I've [aɪv] = **I have**

ivory ['aɪvərɪ] *n.* **a)** *(substance)* Elfenbein, *das; attrib.* elfenbeinern; Elfenbein-; **b)** *(object)* Elfenbeinschnitzerei, *die;* **c)** *(colour)* Elfenbein, *das; attrib.* elfenbeinfarbig; **d) tickle the ivories** *(coll.)* ein bißchen auf dem Klavier spielen

ivory: I~ 'Coast *pr. n.* Elfenbeinküste, *die;* **~ 'tower** *n.* Elfenbeinturm, *der*

ivy ['aɪvɪ] *n.* Efeu, *der; see also* **ground ivy**

'ivy-clad *adj.* efeubewachsen

'Ivy League *n. (Amer.) Eliteuniversitäten im Osten der USA*

J

J, j [dʒeɪ] *n., pl.* **Js** *or* **J's** J, j, *das*

J. *abbr.* **a)** *(Cards)* **jack** B; **b)** *(Phys.)* **joule[s]** J

jab [dʒæb] **1.** *v. t.*, **-bb- a)** *(poke roughly)* stoßen; **he ~bed my arm with his finger** er pikste mir mit dem Finger in den Arm; **he ~bed his elbow into my side** er stieß mir den Ellbogen in die Seite; **b)** *(stab)* stechen; **he ~bed the needle into my leg** er stach mir mit der Nadel ins Bein; **c)** *(thrust abruptly)* stoßen. **2.** *v. i.*, **-bb-: ~ at sb. [with sth.]** auf jmdn. [mit etw.] einhauen; *(stab at)* auf jmdn. [mit etw.] einstechen. **3.** *n.* **a)** *(abrupt blow)* Schlag, *der; (with stick, elbow)* Stoß, *der; (with needle)* Stich, *der; (Boxing)* Jab, *der;* **give sb. a ~:** jmdm. einen Schlag/Stoß/Stich versetzen; **b)** *(Brit. coll.: hypodermic injection)* Spritze, *die;* **give sb./oneself a ~:** jmdm./sich eine Spritze verpassen *(ugs.)*; **have you had your cholera ~s yet?** bist du schon gegen Cholera geimpft worden?

jabber ['dʒæbə(r)] **1.** *v. i.* plappern *(ugs.)*; **~ at sb.** auf jmdn. einreden. **2.** *v. t.* brabbeln *(ugs.)*. **3.** *n.* **a)** *(fast)* Geplapper, *das (ugs.)*; **b)** *(unclear)* Gebrabbel, *das (ugs. abwertend)*; Kauderwelsch, *das*

jabot ['ʒæbəʊ] *n.* Jabot, *das*

jack [dʒæk] **1.** *n.* **a)** *(Cards)* Bube, *der;* **~ of hearts** Herzbube, *der;* **b)** *(for lifting vehicle wheel)* Wagenheber, *der;* **c) J~** *(man)* Hans; **every man ~ [of them]** *(coll.)* alle miteinander; allesamt; **on one's J~ [Jones]** *(sl.)* ganz allein; **all work and no play makes J~ a dull boy** *(prov.)* zuviel Arbeit ist ungesund; **I'm all right, J~** *(fig. coll.)* was kümmern *od.* interessieren mich die anderen?; **d)** *see* **Jack tar; e)** *(for turning spit)* Bratenwender, *der;* **f)** *(on clock)* Glockenschläger, *der;* **g)** *(Teleph. etc.)* Buchse, *die;* Klinke, *die (Postw.)*; *(wall socket)* Steckdose, *die;* **h)** *(Bowls)* Malkugel, *die;* **i)** *(Zool.)* Männchen, *das;* **j)** *(ship's flag)* Gösch, *die (Seemannsspr.)*. *See also* **Union Jack. 2.** *v. t.* **a) ~ in** *or* **up** *(Brit. sl.: abandon)* [auf]stecken *(ugs.)*; **b) ~ up** *(lift)* aufbocken ‹*Fahrzeug*›; *(fig. sl.: increase)* was draufsatteln auf (+ *Akk.*) *(ugs.)*

jackal ['dʒækl] *n. (Zool.)* Schakal, *der*

jackanapes ['dʒækəneɪps] *n. (arch.: impertinent fellow)* Laffe, *der (veralt. abwertend)*

jackass ['dʒækæs] *n.* **a)** *(male ass)* Eselhengst, *der;* **b)** *(stupid person)* Esel, *der (ugs.)*; **c) laughing ~** *(Austral. Ornith.)* Lachender Hans

jack: ~boot *n.* **a)** [Stulpen]stiefel, *der;* **b)** *(fig.)* **be under the ~boot** brutalen *od.* rücksichtslosen Methoden ausgeliefert sein; **~daw** ['dʒækdɔː] *n. (Ornith.)* Dohle, *die*

jacket ['dʒækɪt] *n.* **a)** Jacke, *die; (of suit)* Jackett, *das;* **sports ~:** Sakko, *der;* **a new ~ and trousers** ein neues Jackett und Hosen; eine neue Kombination; **~ pocket** Jackentasche, *die*/Jackettasche, *die;* **b)** *(round a boiler etc.)* Mantel, *der;* **c)** *(of book)* Schutzumschlag, *der;* **d)** *(of a potato)* Schale, *die;* **~ potatoes** in der Schale gebackene Kartoffeln; **e)** *(Amer.) see* **sleeve b**

jack: J~ 'Frost *n.* Väterchen Frost *(scherzh.)*; **~-in-the-box** *n.* Schachtelteufel, *der;* Kastenteufel, *der;* **~-knife 1.** *n.* **a)** *(large clasp-knife)* Klappmesser, *das;* **b)** *(dive)* Hechtsprung, *der;* **c)** *(Motor Veh.)* Querstellen des Anhängers; **2.** *v. i.* **the lorry ~-knifed** der Anhänger des Lastwagens stellte sich quer; **~ of 'all trades** *n.* Hansdampf [in allen Gassen]; **he is a ~ of all trades and master of none** er versteht von allem ein bißchen was, aber von nichts sehr viel; **~pot** *n.* Jackpot, *der;* **hit the ~pot** *(fig.)* das große Los ziehen; **J~ Robinson** [dʒæk 'rɒbɪnsn] *n.* **before you can/could say J~ Robinson** im Nu *(ugs.)*; in Null Komma nichts *(ugs.)*; **J~ Russell** [dʒæk 'rʌsl] *n. eine Terrierart;* **J~ 'tar** *n.* Teerjacke, *die (scherzh.)*

Jacob ['dʒeɪkəb] *pr. n. (Bibl.)* Jakob *(der);* **~'s ladder** *(Bot.)* Jakobsleiter, *die;* Sperrkraut, *das*

Jacobean [dʒækə'biːən] *adj. (Hist.)* [aus] der Zeit Jakobs I. *nachgestellt*

Jacobite ['dʒækəbaɪt] *n. (Hist.)* Jakobit, *der*
Jacquard [loom] ['dʒækɑ:d (lu:m)] *n.* Jacquardwebstuhl, *der*
jacuzzi, *(Amer.:* P) [dʒə'ku:zɪ] *n.* ≈ Whirlpool, *der*
[1]**jade** [dʒeɪd] **1.** *n. (derog.)* **a)** *(horse)* alter Klepper *(abwertend);* Schindmähre, *die (abwertend);* **b)** *(woman)* Weib, *das;* Weibsbild, *das (abwertend).* **2.** *v.t., esp. in p.p. (tire)* ermüden; abstumpfen ⟨*Geschmacksnerven*⟩; **look ~d** abgespannt *od.* erschöpft aussehen
[2]**jade** *n.* **a)** *(stone)* Jade, *der od. die; (carvings)* Jade[arbeiten], *die;* **b)** *(colour)* Jadegrün, *das*
Jaffa ['dʒæfə], **Jaffa orange** [dʒæfə 'ɒrɪndʒ] *n.* Jaffaapfelsine, *die*
Jag [dʒæg] *n. (Brit. coll.: car)* Jaguar, *der*
[1]**jag** *n.* Zacke, *die;* Spitze, *die*
[2]**jag** *n. (sl.: drinking-bout)* Besäufnis, *das (salopp);* Sauferei, *die (derb abwertend);* **go on a ~:** saufen *(derb);* **be on a ~:** am Saufen sein *(derb)*
jagged ['dʒægɪd] *adj.* **a)** *(irregularly cut)* gezackt; ausgefranst ⟨*Loch/Riß in Kleidungsstücken*⟩; ⟨*Wunde*⟩ mit [unregelmäßig] gezackten *od.* zerfetzten Rändern; **b)** *(deeply indented)* zerklüftet ⟨*Küste*⟩
jaguar ['dʒægjʊə(r)] *n. (Zool.)* Jaguar, *der*
jail [dʒeɪl] **1.** *n. (place)* Gefängnis, *das; (confinement)* Haft, *die;* **in ~:** im Gefängnis; **be sent to ~:** ins Gefängnis kommen; eingesperrt werden; **go to ~:** ins Gefängnis gehen. **2.** *v.t.* ins Gefängnis bringen; einsperren
jail: ~bird *n.* Knastbruder, *der (ugs.);* **~break** *n.* Gefängnisausbruch, *der*
jailer, jailor ['dʒeɪlə(r)] *n.* Gefängniswärter, *der*/Gefängniswärterin, *die*
jalopy [dʒə'lɒpɪ] *n. (coll.)* Klapperkiste, *die (ugs.)*
[1]**jam** [dʒæm] **1.** *v.t.,* **-mm- a)** *(squeeze and fix between two surfaces)* einklemmen; **~ sth. into sth.** etw. in etw. *(Akk.)* zwängen; **the key had become ~med in the lock** der Schlüssel hatte sich im Schloß verklemmt; **b)** *(make immovable)* blockieren; *(fig.)* lähmen; lahmlegen; **I seem to ~ the car door every time I lock it** die Autotür verklemmt sich anscheinend jedes Mal, wenn ich sie abschließe; **c)** *(squeeze together in compact mass)* stopfen **(into** in + *Akk.*); **~ together** zusammenpferchen ⟨*Personen*⟩; **d)** *(thrust into confined space)* stopfen **(into** in + *Akk.*); stecken ⟨*Schlüssel, Münze*⟩ **(into** in + *Akk.*); **e)** *(block by crowding)* blockieren; versperren, blockieren ⟨*Eingang*⟩; verstopfen, blockieren ⟨*Rohr*⟩; **the switchboard was ~med with calls** sämtliche Leitungen waren durch Anrufe blockiert; **f)** *(Radio)* stören. **2.** *v.i.,* **-mm- a)** *(become tightly wedged)* sich verklemmen; **b)** *(become unworkable)* ⟨*Maschine:*⟩ klemmen. **3.** *n.* **a)** *(crush, stoppage)* Blockierung, *die;* Klemmen, *das;* **b)** *(crowded mass)* Stau, *der;* **c)** *(coll.: dilemma)* Klemme, *die (ugs.);* Patsche, *die (ugs.);* **be in a ~:** in der Klemme stecken; in der Patsche sitzen; **get into a ~:** in die Klemme geraten; **d)** *see* **jam session.** *See also* **log jam; traffic jam**
~ **'in** *v.t.* hineinzwängen; **we were ~med in** wir waren eingepfercht
~ **'on** *v.t.* **~ the brakes [full] on** [voll] auf die Bremse steigen *(ugs.);* eine Vollbremsung machen
~ **'up** *v.t.* verstopfen ⟨*Straße usw.*⟩; lahmlegen ⟨*System*⟩; verklemmen ⟨*Mechanismus*⟩
[2]**jam** *n.* **a)** Marmelade, *die;* Konfitüre, *die (bes. Kaufmannsspr.);* **make ~:** Marmelade einmachen; **[promises of] ~ tomorrow** *(fig.)* schöne Zukunftsverheißungen; **sb. wants ~ on it** *(fig. coll.)* jmdm. genügt etw. noch nicht; **b)** *(Brit. coll.: sth. easy)* kinderleichte Sache *(fam.);* Kinderspiel, *das; see also* **money a**

Jamaica [dʒə'meɪkə] *pr. n.* Jamaika *(das)*
Jamaican [dʒə'meɪkən] **1.** *adj.* jamaik[an]isch; **sb. is ~:** jmd. ist Jamaikaner/Jamaikanerin. **2.** *n.* Jamaikaner, *der*/Jamaikanerin, *die*
jamb [dʒæm] *n. (of doorway, window)* Pfosten, *der*
jamboree [dʒæmbə'ri:] *n.* **a)** fröhliches Beisammensein; Fete, *die (ugs. scherzh.); (carousal)* Zechgelage, *das (veralt.);* **b)** *(large rally of Scouts)* Jamboree, *das*
James [dʒeɪmz] *pr. n. (Hist., as name of ruler etc.)* Jakob *(der)*
'jam-jar *n.* Marmeladenglas, *das*
jammy ['dʒæmɪ] *adj.* **a)** *(sticky with jam)* von Marmelade klebrig; marmeladeverklebt; **b)** *(Brit. coll.) (easy)* kinderleicht *(fam.); (lucky)* **that was ~:** das war Schwein *(ugs.);* **~ beggar** Glückspilz, *der (ugs.)*
jam: ~-packed *adj. (coll.)* knallvoll *(ugs.),* proppenvoll *(ugs.)* **(with** von); **~ session** *n. (Jazz coll.)* Jam session, *die;* **~ 'tart** *n.* Marmeladentörtchen, *das*
Jan. *abbr.* **January** Jan.
jane [dʒeɪn] *n. (sl.)* Mieze, *die (salopp); see also* **plain 1 d**
jangle ['dʒæŋgl] **1.** *v.i.* klimpern; ⟨*Klingel:*⟩ bimmeln. **2.** *v.t.* **a)** *(sound)* rasseln mit; bimmeln mit ⟨*Glocke*⟩; **b)** *(irritate)* **~ sb.'s nerves** jmdn. nerven *(salopp);* jmdm. auf die Nerven gehen. **3.** *n.* Geklapper, *das; (of bell)* Schrillen, *das*
janitor ['dʒænɪtə(r)] *n.* **a)** *(door-keeper)* Portier, *der;* **b)** *(caretaker)* Hausmeister, *der*
January ['dʒænjʊərɪ] *n.* Januar, *der; see also* **August**
Jap [dʒæp] *n. (coll., often derog.)* Japs, *der (ugs., oft abwertend)*
Japan [dʒə'pæn] *n.* Japan *(das)*
japan 1. *n.* Japanlack, *der.* **2.** *v.t.,* **-nn-** mit Japanlack überziehen; **a ~ned table** ein Lacktisch
Japanese [dʒæpə'ni:z] **1.** *adj.* japanisch; **sb. is ~:** jmd. ist Japaner/Japanerin; *see also* **English 1. 2.** *n., pl. same* **a)** *(person)* Japaner, *der*/Japanerin, *die;* **b)** *(language)* Japanisch, *das; see also* **English 2 a**
Japanese: ~ [flowering] 'cherry *n.* Japanische Kirsche; **~ 'quince** *n.* Japanische Quitte; **~ 'silk** *n.* Japanseide, *die*
jape [dʒeɪp] **1.** *v.i.* spotten **(with** über + *Akk.*); **~ at** verspotten. **2.** *n.* Scherz, *der;* Spaß, *der; (practical joke)* Streich, *der*
japonica [dʒə'pɒnɪkə] *n. (Bot.)* Japanische Quitte
[1]**jar** [dʒɑ:(r)] **1.** *n.* **a)** *(harsh or grating sound)* Quietschen, *das;* **b)** *(thrill of nerves, shock)* Schlag, *der;* **stop with a ~:** mit einem Ruck halten; **c)** *(lack of harmony)* Mißton, *der.* **2.** *v.i.,* **-rr- a)** *(sound discordantly)* quietschen; *(rattle)* ⟨*Fenster:*⟩ scheppern *(ugs.);* **~ on** *or* **against sth.** über etw. *(Akk.)* knirschen; **b)** *(have discordant or painful effect)* **~ [up]on sb./sb.'s nerves** jmdm. auf die Nerven gehen; **~ on the ears** durch Mark und Bein gehen *(ugs. scherzh.);* **these two colours ~:** diese beiden Farben beißen sich *(ugs.);* **c)** *(fig.: be out of harmony)* **~ with sth.** sich mit etw. nicht vertragen. **3.** *v.t.,* **-rr- a)** *(cause to vibrate)* erschüttern; **b)** *(send shock through)* **~ sb.'s nerves** jmdm. auf die Nerven gehen; **~ one's elbow** sich *(Dat.)* den Ellbogen anschlagen
[2]**jar** *n.* **a)** *(vessel)* Topf, *der; (of glass)* Glas, *das;* **~ of jam** *etc.* Topf/Glas Marmelade *usw.;* **b)** *(Brit. coll.: glass of beer)* Bierchen, *das (fam.)*
[3]**jar** *n. (arch./coll.)* **on the ~** *(ajar)* angelehnt
jardinière [ʒɑ:dɪ'njeə(r)] *n.* Jardinière, *die;* **à la ~:** nach Gärtnerinart
jarful ['dʒɑ:fʊl] *n.* Topf, *der; (contents of glass jar)* Glas, *das;* **a ~ of jam** ein Topf/Glas Marmelade; **a ~ of pebbles** ein Topf/Glas voll Kieselsteine
jargon ['dʒɑ:gən] *n.* **a)** *(speech familiar only to a particular group)* Jargon, *der;* **b)** *(unintelligible words)* Gebrabbel, *das (ugs. abwertend)*
Jas. *abbr.* **James**
jasmin[e] ['dʒæsmɪn, 'dʒæzmɪn] *n.* Jasmin, *der;* **common** *or* **white ~:** echter Jasmin; Kletterjasmin, *der;* **red ~:** rotblühende Plumeria; **winter ~:** Winterjasmin, *der*
jasper ['dʒæspə(r)] *n. (Min.)* Jaspis, *der*
jaundice ['dʒɔ:ndɪs] **1.** *n. (Med.)* Gelbsucht, *die.* **2.** *v.t.* **a)** *(Med.)* **be [badly] ~d** eine [schwere] Gelbsucht bekommen; **b)** *usu. in p.p. (fig.: affect with bitterness)* verbittern; **~ sb. against sth./towards sb.** jmdn. gegen etw./jmdn. einnehmen; **with [a] ~d eye** *(enviously)* neidvoll; mit Neid; **a very ~d view of life** eine durch große Verbitterung gekennzeichnete Lebenseinstellung
jaunt [dʒɔ:nt] **1.** *n.* Ausflug, *der;* **be off on/go for a ~:** einen Ausflug machen. **2.** *v.i.* **~ [about]** herumziehen; **are you ~ing off again on some new trip?** geht es mal wieder auf Tour?
jauntily ['dʒɔ:ntɪlɪ] *adv.* unbeschwert
jaunty ['dʒɔ:ntɪ] *adj.* unbeschwert; keck ⟨*Hut*⟩; **with a ~ gait** beschwingten Schrittes; **he wore his hat at a ~ angle** er hatte sich *(Dat.)* den Hut keck aufs Ohr gesetzt
Java ['dʒɑ:və] *pr. n.* Java *(das)*
javelin ['dʒævəlɪn, 'dʒævlɪn] *n.* **a)** Speer, *der;* **throwing the ~** *(Sport)* Speerwerfen, *das;* **b)** *(Sport: event)* Speerwerfen, *das*
jaw [dʒɔ:] **1.** *n.* **a)** *(Anat.)* Kiefer, *der;* **his ~ dropped** er ließ die Kinnlade herunterfallen; **upper/lower ~:** Ober-/Unterkiefer, *der;* **set one's ~:** ein entschlossenes Gesicht machen; **b)** *in pl. (of valley, channel)* Schlund, *der;* **c)** *(of machine)* [Klemm]backe, *die;* **d)** *in pl. (large dangerous mouth)* Rachen, *der; (fig.: of fate, death, etc.)* Klauen; **snatch sb. from the ~s of death** jmdn. vor dem sicheren Tod retten; **snatch victory from the ~s of defeat** kurz vor der drohenden Niederlage doch noch den Sieg erringen. **2.** *v.i. (sl.)* quatschen *(ugs.);* **~ at sb.** jmdn. vollquatschen *(ugs.)*
jaw: ~bone *n.* Kieferknochen, *der;* **~-breaker** *n. (coll.)* Zungenbrecher, *der*
jay [dʒeɪ] *n. (Ornith.)* **a)** *(Garrulus glandarius)* Eichelhäher, *der;* **b)** *(Garrulinae)* Häher, *der*
jay: ~-walk *v.i.* verkehrswidrig die Straße überqueren; **~-walker** *n.* verkehrswidrig die Fahrbahn überquerender Fußgänger
jazz [dʒæz] **1.** *n.* **a)** Jazz, *der; attrib.* Jazz⟨*musik, -musiker*⟩; **b)** *(sl.: nonsense)* Quatsch, *der (ugs. abwertend);* Gewäsch, *das (ugs. abwertend);* **and all that ~** *(coll.)* und der ganze Kram *(ugs.).* **2.** *v.t.* **~ up** aufpeppen *(ugs.);* aufmotzen *(ugs.)*
'jazz band *n.* Jazzband, *die*
jazzy ['dʒæzɪ] *adj.* poppig; **a ~ sports car** ein aufgemotzter Sportwagen *(ugs.)*
JCR *abbr. (Brit. Univ.)* **Junior Common Room; Junior Combination Room**
jealous ['dʒeləs] *adj.* **a)** *(feeling resentment)* eifersüchtig **(of** auf + *Akk.*); **b)** *(possessive)* eifersüchtig ⟨*Liebe*⟩; **be ~ of sth.** eifersüchtig über etw. *(Akk.)* wachen; **be ~ for sth.** peinlich auf etw. *(Akk.)* bedacht sein; **he kept a ~ eye on her** er wachte eifersüchtig über sie
jealously ['dʒeləslɪ] *adv.* eifersüchtig
jealousy ['dʒeləsɪ] *n.* Eifersucht, *die;* **little jealousies** [kleine] Eifersüchteleien
jean [dʒi:n] *n.* **a)** *(cloth)* Baumwolldrell, *der;* **b)** *in pl. (trousers)* Jeans *Pl.;* Jeans, *die;* **a pair of ~s** ein Paar Jeans; eine Jeans; *see also* **blue jeans**
Jeep, (P) [dʒi:p] *n.* Jeep ⓦ, *der*
jeer [dʒɪə(r)] **1.** *v.i.* höhnen *(geh.);* **~ at sb.** jmdn. verhöhnen. **2.** *v.t.* verhöhnen; **the crowd ~ed every tackle he made** die Menge johlte höhnisch bei jedem Tackling, das er machte. **3.** *n.* höhnisches Johlen; *(remark)*

höhnische Bemerkung; ~s höhnisches Gejohle/höhnische Bemerkungen
jehad *see* **jihad**
Jehovah [dʒɪ'həʊvə] *n. (Relig.)* Jehovah *(der)*
Jehovah's 'Witness *n. (Relig.)* Zeuge Jehovas
jejune [dʒɪ'dʒu:n] *adj.* **a)** *(intellectually unsatisfying)* unergiebig; unzulänglich ⟨*Erklärung, Begründung, Leistung*⟩; **b)** *(puerile)* läppisch *(abwertend)*; infantil *(abwertend)*
jejunum [dʒɪ'dʒu:nəm] *n. (Anat.)* Leerdarm, *der*
jell [dʒel] *v. i.* **a)** *(set as jelly)* fest werden; gelieren; **b)** *(fig.: take definite form)* Gestalt annehmen; **not ~ as a group** als Gruppe nicht zusammenpassen
jelly ['dʒelɪ] **1.** *n.* **a)** Gelee, *das; (dessert)* Götterspeise, *die;* **b)** *(substance of similar consistency)* gallertartige Masse; **her legs felt like ~:** ihr schlotterten die Knie; sie hatte Pudding in den Knien *(ugs.)*; **c)** *(sl.: gelignite)* Plastiksprengstoff, *der.* **2.** *v. t.* **a)** zu einer gallertartigen Masse erstarren lassen; Gelee machen aus ⟨*Obst*⟩; **b) jellied eels** Aal in Aspik. **3.** *v. i. (become ~)* gelieren
jelly: ~ **baby** *n.* ≈ Gummibärchen, *das;* ~ **bean** *n.* [bohnenförmiges] Geleebonbon; ~**fish** *n.* Qualle, *die;* ~**-like** *adj.* gallertartig; gallertig ⟨*Konsistenz*⟩
jemmy ['dʒemɪ] *n. (Brit.)* Brecheisen, *das*
jeopardize (jeopardise) ['dʒepədaɪz] *v. t.* gefährden
jeopardy ['dʒepədɪ] *n., no pl.* Gefahr, *die;* **put** *or* **place sth./sb. in ~:** etw. aufs Spiel setzen/jmdn. in Gefahr bringen; etw./jmdn. gefährden; **in ~:** in Gefahr; gefährdet; **her life is in ~:** sie schwebt in Lebensgefahr
jerbil *see* **gerbil**
jerboa [dʒɜ:'bəʊə] *n. (Zool.)* Springmaus, *die*
Jeremiah [dʒerɪ'maɪə] *n.* **a)** *(Bibl.)* Jeremia[s] *(der);* **b)** *(fig.)* Schwarzseher, *der*
Jericho ['dʒerɪkəʊ] *pr. n. (Geog.)* Jericho *(das)*
jerk [dʒɜ:k] **1.** *n.* **a)** *(sharp sudden pull)* Ruck, *der;* ruckartige Bewegung; **with a series of ~s** ruckartig; ruckend; **with a ~ of his thumb, he indicated the direction in which ...:** mit einer kurzen Daumenbewegung zeigte er die Richtung, in die ...; **give sth. a ~:** einer Sache *(Dat.)* einen Ruck geben; an etw. *(Dat.)* rucken; **b)** *(involuntary movement)* Zuckung, *die;* Zucken, *das;* **c)** *(sl.: person)* Null, *die (ugs.)*; Blödmann, *der (ugs.)*. **2.** *v. t.* **a)** reißen an (+ *Dat.*) ⟨*Seil usw.*⟩; ~ **sth. away/back** *etc.* etw. weg-/zurückreißen *usw.*; ~ **sth. off/out of sth.** *etc.* etw. von etw. [herunter]reißen/aus etw. [heraus]reißen *usw.*; **he ~ed his thumb in the direction of the town** er zeigte mit einer kurzen Bewegung seines Daumens in Richtung Stadt; **a noise ~ed him out of his reverie** ein Geräusch riß ihn aus seinen Träumereien; **b)** *(Weight-lifting)* stoßen. **3.** *v. i.* ruckeln; *(move in a spasmodic manner)* zucken; **the lever ~ed out of his hand** der Hebel sprang ihm aus der Hand; **his head ~ed back** sein Kopf zuckte zurück
~ **'off** *(coarse)* **1.** *v. t.* ~ **sb. off** jmdm. einen abwichsen *(vulg.)*. **2.** *v. i.* wichsen *(derb)*
jerkily ['dʒɜ:kɪlɪ] *adv.* ruckartig; eckig ⟨*gehen, sich verbeugen*⟩
jerkin ['dʒɜ:kɪn] *n.* ≈ Wams, *das; (modern)* Weste, *die*
jerky ['dʒɜ:kɪ] *adj.* **a)** abgehackt, holprig ⟨*Art zu schreiben/sprechen*⟩; holprig ⟨*Busfahrt*⟩; holpernd ⟨*Fahrzeug*⟩; ruckartig ⟨*Bewegung*⟩; **b)** *(spasmodic)* zuckend; **the ~ movements of a puppet** die eckigen Bewegungen einer Marionette
Jerome [dʒə'rəʊm] *pr. n.* St ~: der heilige Hieronymus
jerrican *see* **jerry-can**
Jerry ['dʒerɪ] *n. (Brit. dated sl.)* **a)** *(soldier)* Deutsche, *der;* **b)** *no pl. (Germans collectively)* der Deutsche
jerry: ~**-builder** *n.* Baupfuscher, *der (ugs. abwertend);* ~**-building** *n.* Pfusch am Bau *(ugs. abwertend);* ~**-built** *adj.* unsolide gebaut; ~**-can** *n.* Kanister, *der*
jersey ['dʒɜ:zɪ] *n.* **a)** Pullover, *der; (Sport)* Trikot, *das;* Jersey, *das;* **b)** *(vest)* Unterhemd, *das;* **c)** *(fabric)* Jersey, *der;* **d) J~** *(cow)* Jerseyrind, *das;* **e) J~** *pr. n. (island)* Jersey *(das)*
Jerusalem [dʒə'ru:sələm] *pr. n.* Jerusalem *(das)*
Jerusalem 'artichoke *n.* Topinambur, *der*
jest [dʒest] **1.** *n.* **a)** *(joke)* Scherz, *der;* Witz, *der;* **make ~s** scherzen; Witze machen; **b)** *no pl. (fun)* Spaß, *der;* **in ~:** im Scherz. **2.** *v. i.* scherzen; Witze machen
jester ['dʒestə(r)] *n.* Spaßmacher, *der; (at court)* Hofnarr, *der; (fool)* Hanswurst, *der*
Jesuit ['dʒezjʊɪt] *n.* Jesuit, *der*
Jesuitical [dʒezjʊ'ɪtɪkl] *adj.* jesuitisch
Jesus ['dʒi:zəs] **1.** *pr. n.* Jesus *(der).* **2.** *interj. (sl.)* ~ **[Christ]!** Herrgott noch mal! *(ugs.)*
[1]**jet** [dʒet] **1.** *n.* **a)** *(stream)* Strahl, *der;* ~ **of flame/steam/water** Feuer-/Dampf-/Wasserstrahl, *der;* **b)** *(spout, nozzle)* Düse, *die;* **c)** *(aircraft)* Düsenflugzeug, *das;* Jet, *der; (engine)* Düsentriebwerk, *das.* **2.** *v. i.,* **-tt- a)** *(spurt out)* ⟨*Wasser:*⟩ herausschießen **(from** aus); ⟨*Gas, Dampf:*⟩ ausströmen **(from** aus); **b)** *(coll.: travel by ~ plane)* jetten *(ugs.)*; ~ **in/out** *or* **off** [per Jet] einfliegen/abfliegen
[2]**jet** *n. (Min.)* Jett, *der od. das;* Gagat, *der*
jet: ~**-black** *adj.* pechschwarz; kohlrabenschwarz; ~ **engine** *n.* Düsen- *od.* Strahltriebwerk, *das;* ~ **fighter** *n.* Düsenjäger, *der;* ~ **lag** *n.* ≈ Zeitverschiebung, *die;* Jettravel-Syndrom, *das (Med.)*; ~ **plane** *n.* Düsenflugzeug, *das;* ~**-propelled** *adj.* düsen- *od.* strahlgetrieben; mit Düsen- *od.* Strahlantrieb *nachgestellt;* ~ **pro'pulsion** *n.* Düsen- *od.* Strahlantrieb, *der*
jetsam ['dʒetsəm] *n.* sinkendes Seewurfgut *(Seew.); (on seashore)* Strandgut, *das*
jet: ~ **set** *n.* Jet-set, *der;* ~ **stream** *n.* **a)** *(Meteorol.)* Jetstream, *der;* Strahlstrom, *der;* **b)** *(of ~ engine)* Düsenstrahl, *der*
jettison ['dʒetɪsən] *v. t.* **a)** *(from ship)* über Bord werfen; *(from aircraft)* abwerfen ⟨*Ballast, Bombe*⟩; *(discard)* wegwerfen; *(Astronaut.) (separate)* abtrennen; *(blast off)* absprengen; **b)** *(fig.: abandon)* aufgeben; über Bord werfen ⟨*Plan*⟩
jetty ['dʒetɪ] *n.* **a)** *(protecting harbour or coast)* [Hafen]mole, *die;* **b)** *(landing-pier)* Landungsbrücke, *die;* Anleger, *der (Seemannsspr.); (smaller)* [Landungs]steg, *der*
Jew [dʒu:] *n.* **a)** Jude, *der*/Jüdin, *die;* **b)** *(coll. derog.: person who drives hard bargains)* Geldschneider, *der (abwertend). See also* **wandering Jew**
'Jew-baiting *n.* Judenhetze, *die;* Judenverfolgung, *die*
jewel ['dʒu:əl] **1.** *n.* **a)** *(ornament)* [kostbares] Schmuckstück; **~s** *collect.* Schmuck, *der;* Juwelen *Pl.*; **b)** *(precious stone)* Juwel, *das od. der;* [wertvoller] Edelstein; *(of watch)* Stein, *der;* **c)** *(fig.) (person)* Goldstück, *das;* Juwel, *das; (thing)* Kleinod, *das.* **2.** *v. t., (Brit.)* **-ll-**; *esp. in p.p.* **a)** *(adorn with jewels)* mit Juwelen besetzen; **~led hand** juwelengeschmückte Hand; **b)** *(fit with ~s)* mit Steinen versehen
jewel: ~**-box,** ~**-case** *ns.* Schmuckkasten, *der*
jeweller *(Amer.:* **jeweler)** ['dʒu:ələ(r)] *n.* Juwelier, *der;* **~'s rouge** Polierrot, *das; see also* **baker**
jewellery *(Brit.),* **jewelry** ['dʒu:əlrɪ] *n.* Schmuck, *der*
jewellery (box) *(Brit.),* **jewelry box** *n.* Schmuckkasten, *der*
Jewess ['dʒu:ɪs] *n.* Jüdin, *die*
Jewish ['dʒu:ɪʃ] *adj.* jüdisch; **he/she is ~:** er ist Jude/sie ist Jüdin
Jewry ['dʒʊərɪ] *n.* Judentum, *das;* Judenheit, *die*
Jew's 'harp *n. (Mus.)* Maultrommel, *die*
[1]**jib** [dʒɪb] *n.* **a)** *(Naut.) (on sailing ship)* Stagsegel, *das (Seew.); (on sailing yacht or dinghy)* Fock, *die (Seew.);* **I don't like the cut of his ~** *(fig.)* mir gefällt sein Gesicht *od.* *(ugs.)* seine Nase nicht; **b)** *(of crane)* Ausleger, *der*
[2]**jib** *v. i.,* **-bb- a)** *(refuse to go on)* ⟨*Pferd usw.:*⟩ bocken; *(because of fright)* scheuen; **b)** *(fig.)* sich sträuben; streiken *(ugs.)*; ~ **at sth./at doing sth.** sich gegen etw. sträuben/sich dagegen sträuben, etw. zu tun; **he ~bed at the idea** er wollte nichts davon wissen
[1]**jibe** [dʒaɪb] *v. i. (Amer.) (fit)* sich decken; *(match)* zusammenpassen
[2]**jibe** *see* **gibe; gybe**
jiff [dʒɪf], **jiffy** ['dʒɪfɪ] *n. (coll.)* Augenblick, *der;* Moment, *der;* **in a ~:** sofort; gleich; **half a ~:** ein Momentchen!
'Jiffy bag, (P) *n.* gefütterte Versandtasche
jig [dʒɪg] **1.** *n.* **a)** *(dance, music)* Jig, *die; (movement of suite)* Gigue, *die;* **dance** *or* **do a ~:** einen Freudentanz vollführen; **b)** *(appliance)* Einspannvorrichtung, *die.* **2.** *v. i.,* **-gg-** *(dance a ~/gigue)* eine Jig/eine Gigue tanzen; *(fig.)* herumhüpfen; ~ **up and down** herumhüpfen
jigger ['dʒɪgə(r)] *n.* *Meßbecher für alkoholische Getränke*
jiggered ['dʒɪgəd] *adj. (coll.)* **I'll be ~:** gibt's denn sowas! *(ugs.);* **I'll be ~ if ...:** der Teufel soll mich holen, wenn ... *(salopp)*
jiggery-pokery [dʒɪgərɪ'pəʊkərɪ] *n. (Brit. coll.)* **a)** *(underhand scheming)* Schmu, *der (ugs.)*; **there is some [sort of] ~ going on** hier ist was faul; **he's up to some [sort of] ~:** er hat 'n krummes Ding vor *(ugs.)*; **b)** *(nonsense)* Stuß, *der (ugs. abwertend)*
jiggle ['dʒɪgl] **1.** *v. t.* rütteln an, wackeln an (+ *Dat.*). **2.** *v. i.* rütteln; wackeln
'jigsaw *n.* **a)** Dekupiersäge, *die; (electric)* Stichsäge, *die;* **b)** ~ **[puzzle]** Puzzle, *das*
jihad [dʒɪ'hæd, dʒɪ'hɑ:d] *n. (war)* Dschihad, *der*
jilt [dʒɪlt] *v. t.* sitzenlassen *(ugs.)*
Jim Crow [dʒɪm 'krəʊ] *n. (Amer. derog.)* **a)** *(a Black)* Nigger, *der (abwertend);* **b)** *no pl. (racial segregation)* Rassentrennung, *die; (racial discrimination)* Rassendiskriminierung, *die*
jim-jams ['dʒɪmdʒæmz] *n. pl. (sl.: fit of depression)* Muffe, *die (ugs.)*; **she got [an attack of] the ~:** ihr ging die Muffe
jimmy ['dʒɪmɪ] *(Amer.) see* **jemmy**
jimson [weed] ['dʒɪmsən (wi:d)] *n. (Amer. Bot.)* Stechapfel, *der*
jingle ['dʒɪŋgl] **1.** *n.* **a)** Klingeln, *das;* Bimmeln, *das (ugs.)*; *(of cutlery, chains, spurs)* Klirren, *das; (of coins, keys)* Geklimper, *das;* **b)** *(repetition)* Aneinanderreihen lautähnlicher Wörter; *(trivial verse)* Wortgeklingel, *das (abwertend)*; *(Commerc.)* Werbespruch, *der;* Jingle, *der (Werbespr.)*; **c)** *(thing designed to ~)* Schelle, *die.* **2.** *v. i.* **a)** ⟨*Metallgegenstände:*⟩ klimpern; ⟨*Kasse, Schelle:*⟩ klingeln; ⟨*Glöckchen:*⟩ bimmeln; **b)** *(be full of alliterations, rhymes, etc.)* ⟨*Text:*⟩ sich reimen und stabreimen. **3.** *v. t.* klingeln mit, *(ugs.)* bimmeln mit ⟨*Glöckchen*⟩; klimpern mit ⟨*Münzen, Schlüsseln, Armreifen*⟩
'jingle-jangle *n.* Geklimper, *das (abwertend)*
jingo ['dʒɪŋgəʊ] *n., pl.* **~es a)** Chauvinist, *der (abwertend);* Hurrapatriot, *der (ugs. abwertend);* **b) by ~!** beim Zeus!; bei Gott!
jingoism ['dʒɪŋgəʊɪzm] *n., no pl.* Chauvinismus, *der (abwertend);* Hurrapatriotismus, *der (ugs. abwertend)*
jingoist ['dʒɪŋgəʊɪst] *see* **jingo a**

jink *see* **high jinks**

jinx [dʒɪŋks] **1.** *n. (coll.)* Fluch, *der;* **there seemed to be a ~ on him** er schien vom Pech verfolgt zu sein; **break the ~:** den Bann brechen. **2.** *v. t.* verhexen

jitterbug ['dʒɪtəbʌg] **1.** *n.* **a)** Nervenbündel, *das (ugs.);* **b)** *(dance)* Jitterbug, *der.* **2.** *v. i.* Jitterbug tanzen

jitters ['dʒɪtəz] *n. pl. (coll.)* großes Zittern; Bammel, *der (salopp);* **an attack** *or* **a case of the ~:** ein Bammel *(salopp);* **give sb. the ~:** jmdm. Schiß machen *(salopp)*

jittery ['dʒɪtərɪ] *adj. (nervous)* nervös; *(frightened)* verängstigt

jive [dʒaɪv] **1.** *n.* Jive, *der.* **2.** *v. i.* Jive tanzen

Jnr. *abbr.* **Junior** jr.; jun.

Joan of Arc [dʒəʊn əv 'ɑːk] *pr. n.* die Jungfrau von Orleans

Job [dʒəʊb] *pr. n.* Hiob *(der);* **he would try the patience of ~:** bei ihm braucht man eine Engelsgeduld; **~'s 'comforter** schlechter Trostspender

job [dʒɒb] **1.** *n.* **a)** *(piece of work)* **~ [of work]** Arbeit, *die;* **we have five ~s to do today** wir haben heute fünf Dinge zu erledigen; *(orders to be fulfilled)* wir haben heute fünf Aufträge zu erledigen; **I have a little ~ for you** ich habe eine kleine Aufgabe *od.* einen kleinen Auftrag für dich; **do a ~ for sb.** für jmdn. etw. erledigen; **try to do sb.'s ~ for him** *(fig. coll.)* jmdm. ins Handwerk pfuschen *(ugs.);* **it is sb.'s ~ to do sth.** es ist jmds. Arbeit, etw. zu tun; **you've got a really tough ~ on your hands!** da hast du aber eine Heidenarbeit *od.* ein schönes Stück Arbeit!; **you're doing an excellent ~:** Sie machen das ausgezeichnet; **nose ~** *(coll.)* Nasenoperation, *die;* **b)** *(position of employment)* Stelle, *die;* Anstellung, *die;* Job, *der (ugs.);* **he is, after all, only doing his ~!** er tut schließlich nur seine Pflicht; **he knows his ~:** er versteht sein Handwerk *od.* versteht etwas von der Sache; **~ vacancies** offene Stellen; *(in newspaper)* „Stellenangebote"; **have ~ security** einen sicheren Arbeitsplatz haben; **~ situation** Arbeitsmarktsituation, *die;* **it's as much as my ~'s worth** es würde mich meinen Job kosten; **it's not my ~** *(fig.)* es ist nicht meine Sache *od.* Aufgabe; **the man for the ~:** der richtige Mann; **~s for the boys** *(coll.)* ≈ wer gute Beziehungen hat, kriegt einen Job *(ugs.);* **it is a case** *or* **matter of ~s for the boys** alle Posten *od. (ugs.)* Jobs werden unterderhand vergeben; **just the ~** *(fig. sl.)* genau das richtige; die Sache *(ugs.);* **on the ~:** bei der Arbeit; **out of a ~:** arbeitslos; ohne Stellung; **c)** *(sl.: crime)* [krummes] Ding *(ugs.);* **do a [bank] ~:** ein Ding [in einer Bank] drehen *(ugs.);* **this was a professional ~:** hier war ein Profi/hier waren Profis am Werk; **d)** *(result of work)* Ergebnis, *das;* **make a [good] ~ of sth.** bei etw. gute Arbeit leisten; **make a thorough ~ of it** ganze Arbeit machen; **be a good** *etc.* **~:** gut *usw.* sein; **this respray/rebuilt car is a superb ~!** diese Neulackierung/dieses restaurierte Auto ist großartig geworden!; **e)** *(coll.: difficult task)* [schönes] Stück Arbeit; **I had a [hard** *or* **tough] ~ convincing** *or* **to convince him** es war gar nicht so einfach für mich *od.* ich hatte [einige] Mühe, ihn zu überzeugen; **f)** *(state of affairs)* **a bad ~:** eine schlimme *od.* üble Sache; **it's a bad ~: the company is virtually bankrupt** es sieht schlecht aus: die Firma ist praktisch pleite; **give sb./sth. up as a bad ~** *see* **give up 2 a; a good ~:** ein Glück; **we've finished, and a good ~ too!** wir sind fertig, zum Glück; **what** *or* **it's a good ~ he doesn't know about it!** nur gut, daß er nichts davon weiß! **2.** *v. i.*, **-bb- a)** *(do ~s)* Gelegenheitsarbeiten verrichten; jobben *(ugs.);* **b)** *(deal in stocks)* als Börsenhändler arbeiten; **c)** *(turn position of trust to private advantage)* sein Amt [zum eigenen Vorteil] mißbrauchen; **d)** *(buy and sell as middleman)* als Vermittler Geschäfte machen; *(Amer.: trade in wholesale lots)* als Zwischenhändler tätig sein. **3.** *v. t.*, **-bb-** im Zwischenhandel verkaufen; makeln ⟨*Häuser, Grundstücke*⟩

jobber ['dʒɒbə(r)] *n.* **a)** *(Amer.: wholesaler)* Zwischenhändler, *der;* **b)** *(stock~)* Börsen- *od.* Effektenhändler, *der;* Jobber, *der*

jobbery ['dʒɒbərɪ] *n.* Schiebung, *die*

jobbing ['dʒɒbɪŋ] *adj.* Gelegenheits-; **~ gardener** Gelegenheits- *od.* Aushilfsgärtner, *der;* **~ printer** Akzidenzdrucker, *der*

job: ~centre *n. (Brit.)* Arbeitsvermittlungsstelle, *die;* **~ creation** *n.* Schaffung von Arbeitsplätzen; **~ description** *n.* Arbeitsplatzbeschreibung, *die;* Tätigkeitsbeschreibung, *die;* **~ evaluation** *n.* Arbeitsbewertung, *die;* **~-hunt** *v. i.* **go/be ~-hunting** auf Arbeits- *od.* Stellensuche gehen/sein; **~-hunter** *n.* Stellen- *od.* Arbeitssuchende, *der/die;* **~-hunting** *n.* Arbeitssuche, *die;* Stellensuche, *die*

jobless ['dʒɒblɪs] *adj.* beschäftigungslos; arbeitslos

job: ~ 'lot *n.* Partieware, *die (Kaufmannsspr.); (fig.)* Sammelsurium, *das (abwertend);* **~ satisfaction** *see* **satisfaction b; ~-sharing** *n.* Job-sharing, *das;* **~-sheet** *n.* Arbeitsbericht, *der*

Jock [dʒɒk] *n. (Brit. sl.)* Schotte, *der*

jock *(coll.) see* **jockey**

jockey ['dʒɒkɪ] **1.** *n.* Jockei, *der;* Jockey, *der.* **2.** *v. i.* rangeln **(for** um); **~ for position** *(lit. or fig.)* alles daransetzen, eine möglichst gute Position zu erringen; **all the ~ing behind the scenes** das ganze Gerangel hinter den Kulissen. **3.** *v. t.* **~ sb. into/out of doing sth.** jmdn. dazu bringen, etw. zu tun/nicht mehr zu tun

jockey: ~ cap *n.* Jockeymütze, *die;* **J~ Club** *n. (Brit.) oberste Behörde des Galoppsports in England*

jock-strap ['dʒɒkstræp] *n.* [Sport]suspensorium, *das*

jocose [dʒə'kəʊs] *adj.* **a)** *(playful, fond of joking)* launig ⟨*Stimmung, Bemerkung, Wesensart*⟩; **~ person** Spaßvogel, *der;* **b)** *(waggish)* schalkhaft

jocular ['dʒɒkjʊlə(r)] *adj.* lustig, witzig ⟨*Bemerkung, Antwort*⟩; spaßig, scherzhaft ⟨*Person*⟩; **his ~ conversation bored her** seine Witze langweilten sie

jocularly ['dʒɒkjʊləlɪ] *adv.* scherzhaft

jocund ['dʒɒkənd] *adj. (literary)* fröhlich

jodhpurs ['dʒɒdpəz] *n. pl.* Reithose, *die;* Jodhpur[hose], *die*

Joe [dʒəʊ] *n.* **~ [Q.] Public** *(coll.)* Otto Normalverbraucher *(der) (ugs.)*

joey ['dʒəʊɪ] *n. (Austral.)* junges Känguruh

jog [dʒɒg] **1.** *v. t.*, **-gg- a)** *(shake with push or jerk)* rütteln; schütteln; **the horse ~ged its rider up and down** das Pferd schüttelte seinen Reiter durch; **b)** *(nudge)* [an]stoßen; **~ sb.'s elbow** jmdn. [am Ellbogen] anstoßen; **c)** *(stimulate)* **~ sb.'s memory** jmds. Gedächtnis *(Dat.)* auf die Sprünge helfen. **2.** *v. i.*, **-gg- a)** *(move up and down)* auf und ab hüpfen; **~ around/about** herumhüpfen; **his holster was ~ging against his hip** sein Halfter schlug ihm im Rhythmus gegen die Hüfte; **b)** *(move at ~trot)* ⟨*Pferd:*⟩ [dahin]trotten; **c)** *(run at slow pace)* [in mäßigem Tempo] laufen; traben *(Sport); (for physical exercise)* joggen; [einen] Dauerlauf machen; laufen; **~ along** *or* **on** *(fig.)* ⟨*Geschäft, Projekt:*⟩ laufen, seinen Gang gehen; ⟨*Person:*⟩ vor sich hin wursteln *(ugs.).* **3.** *n.* **a)** *(shake, nudge)* Stoß, *der;* Schubs, *der (ugs.);* **b)** *(slow walk or trot) (of horse)* Trott, *der; (of person for physical exercise)* Dauerlauf, *der;* **go for a ~:** joggen gehen; **he went off at a ~:** er trabte davon

jogger ['dʒɒgə(r)] *n.* Jogger, *der*/Joggerin, *die*

jogging ['dʒɒgɪŋ] *n.* Jogging, *das;* Joggen, *das*

joggle ['dʒɒgl] **1.** *v. t.* schütteln; wackeln an (+ *Dat.*) ⟨*Tisch*⟩. **2.** *v. i.* wackeln **(to and fro** hin und her); wippen **(up and down** auf und ab); *(in the air)* taumeln. **3.** *n. (slight shake)* Holpern, *das*

'jogtrot *n. (lit. or fig.)* Trott, *der*

John [dʒɒn] *pr. n. (Hist., as name of ruler etc.)* Johann *(der); see also* **Baptist b**

john *n. (Amer. sl.: lavatory)* Lokus, *der (salopp)*

John: ~ 'Bull *n.* John Bull *(der);* **a real ~ Bull** ein typischer Engländer; **~ 'Citizen** *n.* Otto Normalverbraucher *(der);* **~ 'Doe** *n.* **a)** *(Law)* ≈ Meier *(der);* ≈ die Partei A; *fiktiver Name einer Prozeßpartei;* **b)** *(Amer.: average man)* Otto Normalverbraucher *(der)*

johnny ['dʒɒnɪ] *n. (Brit. coll.: chap)* Heini, *der (ugs.)*

Johnny-come-'lately *n. (coll.)* Neuankömmling, *der*

joie de vivre [ʒwɑː də 'viːvr] *n.* Lebensfreude, *die;* Lebenslust, *die*

join [dʒɔɪn] **1.** *v. t.* **a)** *(put together, connect)* verbinden **(to** mit); **~ two things [together]** zwei Dinge miteinander verbinden; zwei Dinge zusammenfügen; **~ hands** sich *(Dat.)* die Hände reichen; **~ hands [with sb.]** *(fig.)* ⟨*Nation, Partei usw.:*⟩ sich [mit jmdm.] vereinen; **~ sb. [with** *or* **to sb.] in marriage/in holy matrimony** jmdn. [mit jmdm.] ehelich verbinden/durch das heilige Band der Ehe vereinen *(geh.); see also* **'force 1 d; b)** *(come into company of)* sich gesellen zu; sich zugesellen (+ *Dat.*); *(meet)* treffen; *(come with)* mitkommen mit; sich anschließen (+ *Dat.*); **you go on ahead – I'll ~ you in a minute** geh nur schon voraus – ich komme gleich nach; **may I ~ you [at the table]?** kann ich mich zu euch [an den Tisch] setzen?; **do ~ us for lunch** iß doch mit uns zu Mittag; **would you like to ~ me in a drink?** hast du Lust, ein Glas mit mir zu trinken?; **if you can't beat them, ~ them** wenn man mit dem Gegner nicht fertig wird, läuft man eben zu ihm über; **c)** *(become member of)* eintreten in (+ *Akk.*) ⟨*Armee, Firma, Orden, Verein, Partei*⟩; beitreten (+ *Dat.*) ⟨*Verein, Partei, Orden*⟩; **I thought of ~ing the Army/the Scouts** ich dachte daran, zur Armee/zu den Pfadfindern zu gehen; **d)** *(take one's place in)* sich einreihen in (+ *Akk.*) ⟨*Umzug, Demonstrationszug*⟩; **~ one's ship** an Bord seines Schiffs gehen; **~ one's regiment** sich bei seinem Regiment einfinden; **e)** ⟨*Fluß, Straße:*⟩ münden in (+ *Akk.*). *See also* **battle 1 a. 2.** *v. i.* **a)** *(come together)* ⟨*Flüsse:*⟩ sich vereinigen, zusammenfließen; ⟨*Straßen:*⟩ sich vereinigen, zusammenlaufen; ⟨*Grundstücke:*⟩ aneinandergrenzen, aneinanderstoßen; ⟨*gebrochener Knochen:*⟩ zusammenwachsen; ⟨*Einzelteile:*⟩ zusammenpassen; **b)** *(take part)* **~ with sb.** sich jmdn. anschließen; **my wife ~s with me in wishing you ...:** auch meine Frau wünscht Ihnen ...; **c)** *(become member)* Mitglied werden; *(become employee)* in die Firma eintreten. **3.** *n.* Verbindung, *die; (line)* Nahtstelle, *die*

~ in 1. [-'-] *v. i.* mitmachen **(with** bei); *(in conversation)* sich beteiligen **(with** an + *Dat.*); *(in singing)* einstimmen; mitsingen; **they all ~ed in together** sie machten/sangen alle mit. **2.** ['--] *v. t.* mitmachen bei ⟨*Spiel, Spaß*⟩; sich beteiligen an (+ *Dat.*) ⟨*Spiel, Festlichkeiten, Gespräch*⟩; mitsingen ⟨*Refrain*⟩; sich einreihen in (+ *Akk.*), sich anschließen (+ *Dat.*) ⟨*Demonstrations-, Umzug*⟩

~ 'on *v. i.* befestigt werden **(to** an + *Dat.*); ⟨*Grundstück:*⟩ [an]grenzen **(to** an + *Akk.*)

~ 'up 1. *v. i.* **a)** *(Mil.)* einrücken; Soldat werden; **b)** ⟨*Straßen:*⟩ zusammenlaufen;

⟨*Nebenstraße:*⟩ [ein]münden in (+ *Akk.*); ⟨*Straße:*⟩ zusammenlaufen mit. **2.** *v. t.* miteinander verbinden

joiner ['dʒɔɪnə(r)] *n.* Tischler, *der*/Tischlerin, *die*

joinery ['dʒɔɪnərɪ] *n., no pl.* **a)** *no art.* *(craft)* Tischlerei, *die;* Tischlerhandwerk, *das;* **b)** *no indef. art.* *(products)* Tischlerarbeiten

joint [dʒɔɪnt] **1.** *n.* **a)** *(place of joining)* Verbindung, *die; (line)* Nahtstelle, *die; (Building)* Fuge, *die;* **b)** *(Anat.)* Gelenk, *das;* **be out of ~** ⟨*Körperteil:*⟩ ausgerenkt sein; *(fig.: be out of order)* ⟨*Zeit, Welt:*⟩ aus den Fugen sein; *see also* **nose 1a;** **c)** *(Bot.)* Knoten, *der;* **d)** *(Mech. Engin. etc.)* Gelenk, *das;* **e)** *(part of carcass)* **a ~ [of meat]** ein Stück Fleisch; *(for roasting, roast)* ein Braten; **a roast ~:** ein Braten; **a ~ of roast beef** ein Rinderbraten; **chicken ~s** Hähnchenteile *Pl.;* **carve/cut sth. into ~s** etw. tranchieren/zerlegen; **f)** *(sl.: place)* Kaschemme, *die (abwertend);* Spelunke, *die (abwertend); (public place)* Laden, *der (ugs.); (dwelling)* Bude, *die (ugs.);* **jazz ~:** Jazzschuppen, *der (ugs.);* **g)** *(sl.: marijuana cigarette)* Joint, *der;* **h)** *(Amer. sl.: prison)* Knast, *der (ugs.).* **2.** *adj.* **a)** *(of two or more)* gemeinsam ⟨*Anstrengung, Bericht, Besitz, Projekt, Ansicht, Konto*⟩; **~ venture** Gemeinschaftsunternehmen, *das;* Joint-venture, *das (Wirtsch.); see also* **several 1b;** **b)** Mit⟨*autor, -erbe, -besitzer*⟩. **3.** *v. t.* **a)** *(connect)* verbinden; **b)** *(Building)* [aus-, ver-]fugen ⟨*Wand, Decke, Belag*⟩; **c)** *(divide)* zerlegen ⟨*Tier*⟩

jointed ['dʒɔɪntɪd] *adj.* Glieder⟨*puppe, -tier*⟩; knotig ⟨*Stamm*⟩

jointly ['dʒɔɪntlɪ] *adv.* gemeinsam; **he is ~ responsible** er ist mitverantwortlich

joint 'stock *n. (Econ.)* Gesellschafts- *od.* Aktienkapital, *das;* **~ bank/company** Aktienbank, *die*/Aktiengesellschaft, *die*

joist [dʒɔɪst] *n. (Building)* Deckenbalken, *der; (steel)* [Decken]träger, *der*

joke [dʒəʊk] **1.** *n.* **a)** Witz, *der;* Scherz, *der;* **sb.'s little ~** *(iron.)* jmds. Scherzchen; **make a ~:** einen Scherz machen; **do sth. for a ~:** etw. spaßeshalber *od.* zum Spaß tun; **tell a ~:** einen Witz erzählen; **have a ~ with sb.** mit jmdm. scherzen *od.* spaßen; **play a ~ on sb.** jmdm. einen Streich spielen; **he can/can't take a ~:** er versteht Spaß/keinen Spaß; **the ~ was on him** er war der Narr; **a ~ is a ~:** das ist gar nicht so komisch; **this is getting beyond/is** *or* **goes beyond a ~:** da hört der Spaß auf/das ist kein Spaß mehr; **this is no ~:** das ist nicht zum Lachen; **b)** *(ridiculous thing or circumstance)* Witz, *der (ugs.); (ridiculous person)* Witzfigur, *die;* **he/it is a standing ~:** alle Welt lacht nur noch über ihn/darüber; **treat sth. as a ~:** etw. nicht weiter ernst nehmen. **2.** *v. i.* scherzen, Witze machen (**about** über + *Akk.*); **I was only joking** ich habe nur Spaß gemacht *(ugs.);* **joking apart** Scherz *od.* Spaß beiseite!; **you are/must be** *or (coll.)* **have [got] to be joking!** das soll wohl ein Witz sein!; mach keine Witze!

joker ['dʒəʊkə(r)] *n.* **a)** *(person fond of making jokes)* Spaßvogel, *der;* Witzbold, *der (ugs.);* **b)** *(sl.: person)* Vogel, *der (salopp);* **c)** *(Cards)* Joker, *der;* **~ in the pack** *(fig.)* Unsicherheitsfaktor, *der;* **d)** *(Amer.: clause)* versteckte Klausel; **e)** *(unexpected factor)* Pferdefuß, *der;* Haken, *der (ugs.)*

jokey ['dʒəʊkɪ] *adj.* witzig; spaßig

jokingly ['dʒəʊkɪŋlɪ] *adv.* im Scherz; **..., he said ~:** ..., scherzte er

joky *see* **jokey**

jollification [dʒɒlɪfɪ'keɪʃn] *n. (coll.)* Vergnügen, *das*

jollity ['dʒɒlɪtɪ] *n.* Fröhlichkeit, *die;* Lustigkeit, *die; (merry-making, festivity)* Festlichkeit, *die*

jolly ['dʒɒlɪ] **1.** *adj.* **a)** *(cheerful)* fröhlich; knallig ⟨*Farbe*⟩; *(multicoloured)* bunt; **b)** *(euphem.: drunk)* angeheitert; **c)** *(festive)* lustig; **d)** *(coll.: delightful)* klasse *(ugs.);* prima *(ugs.).* **2.** *adv. (Brit. coll.)* ganz schön *(ugs.);* sehr ⟨*nett*⟩; **~ good** wirklich gut; **~ good!** ausgezeichnet! **I should ~ well think so!** das möchte ich auch meinen!; **we ~ well 'are coming!** und ob wir kommen! **3.** *v. t. (coll.)* aufmuntern; **~ sb. into doing sth.** jmdn. dazu überreden, etw. zu tun

~ a'long *v. t.* bei Laune halten

~ 'up *v. t.* aufmuntern

'jolly-boat *n.* Jolle, *die*

Jolly 'Roger *n.* Piratenflagge, *die;* Totenkopfflagge, *die*

jolt [dʒəʊlt] **1.** *v. t.* **a)** *(shake)* ⟨*Fahrzeug:*⟩ durchrütteln, durchschütteln; **~ sb./sth. out of/on to sth.** jmdn./etw. aus etw./auf etw. *(Akk.)* schleudern *od.* werfen; **b)** *(shock)* aufschrecken; **~ sb. into action** jmdn. auf Trab bringen *(ugs.);* **~ sb. into doing sth.** jmdn. so aufschrecken, daß er etw. tut. **2.** *v. i.* ⟨*Fahrzeug:*⟩ holpern, rütteln, rumpeln *(ugs.).* **3.** *n.* **a)** *(jerk)* Stoß, *der;* Ruck, *der;* **b)** *(fig.) (shock)* Schock, *der;* Schreck, *der; (surprise)* Überraschung, *die;* **give sb. a ~:** jmdm. einen Schock versetzen *od.* einen Schreck[en] einjagen/jmdn. überraschen

Jonah ['dʒəʊnə] *n.* **a)** Unglücksvogel, *der;* **b)** *(Bibl.)* Jonas *(der)*

Joneses ['dʒəʊnzɪz] *see* **keep up 1a**

jonquil ['dʒɒŋkwɪl] *n. (Bot.)* Jonquille, *die*

Jordan ['dʒɔ:dn] *pr. n.* **a)** *(river)* Jordan, *der;* **b)** *(country)* Jordanien *(das)*

Jordanian [dʒɔ:'deɪnɪən] **1.** *adj.* jordanisch; **sb. is ~:** jmd. ist Jordanier/Jordanierin. **2.** *n.* Jordanier, *der*/Jordanierin, *die*

josh [dʒɒʃ] *(coll.)* **1.** *v. t.* aufziehen. **2.** *v. i.* scherzen

jostle ['dʒɒsl] **1.** *v. i.* **a)** *(knock)* **~ [against each other]** aneinanderstoßen; **b)** *(struggle)* [sich] streiten (**for** um, **with** mit); **~ with each other** [miteinander *od.* sich] streiten. **2.** *v. t.* **a)** stoßen; **~ sb.'s arm** jmdn. [am Arm] anstoßen; **~ sb. aside/off the pavement** jmdn. zur Seite/vom Bürgersteig stoßen; **the defender ~d the forward off the ball** der Verteidiger trennte den Stürmer mit einem Rempler vom Ball; **b)** *(Racing)* behindern

jot [dʒɒt] **1.** *n.* **[not] a ~:** [k]ein bißchen; *(of truth, sympathy also)* [k]ein Fünkchen; **not one ~ or tittle** *(coll.)* nicht das kleinste bißchen. **2.** *v. t.,* **-tt-** [rasch] aufschreiben *od.* notieren; **~ sth. on a piece of paper** etw. rasch auf einen Zettel schreiben

~ 'down *v. t.* [rasch] aufschreiben *od.* notieren; **~ down notes** [sich *(Dat.)*] rasch Notizen machen

jotter ['dʒɒtə(r)] *n. (pad)* Notizblock, *der; (notebook)* Notizbuch, *das*

jotting ['dʒɒtɪŋ] *n.* Notiz, *die*

joule [dʒu:l] *n. (Phys.)* Joule, *das*

journal ['dʒɜ:nl] *n.* **a)** *(newspaper)* Zeitung, *die; (periodical)* Zeitschrift, *die;* **weekly ~:** Wochenzeitung, *die;* **b)** *(Bookk.)* Journal, *das;* Tagebuch, *das;* **c)** *(daily record of events)* Tagebuch, *das;* **d)** *(Naut.)* **[captain's/ship's] ~:** Schiffstagebuch, *das;* Journal, *das (veralt.);* **e)** *(part of shaft or axle)* Zapfen, *der*

'journal-bearing *n. (Mech. Engin.)* Zapfenlager, *das*

journalese [dʒɜ:nə'li:z] *n. (derog.)* [schlechter] Zeitungsstil

journalism ['dʒɜ:nəlɪzm] *n.* Journalismus, *der*

journalist ['dʒɜ:nəlɪst] *n.* Journalist, *der*/Journalistin, *die*

journalistic [dʒɜ:nə'lɪstɪk] *adj.* journalistisch ⟨*Stil*⟩; **~ circles** Journalistenkreise

journey ['dʒɜ:nɪ] **1.** *n.* **a)** *(distance)* Weg, *der;* **London is three hours' ~ from here** man fährt drei Stunden von hier nach London; **a three-hour ~:** eine Fahrt von drei Stunden; eine dreistündige Fahrt; *(on foot)* ein dreistündiger Weg; **b)** *(expedition)* Reise, *die;* **a fruitless ~:** ein vergeblicher Gang; **a ~ by car/train/ship** eine Auto-/Bahn-/Schiffsreise; eine Reise mit dem Auto/der Bahn/dem Schiff; **go on a ~:** verreisen; eine Reise machen; **~'s end** die Endstation *(fig.);* **go on a train/car ~:** eine Reise mit dem Zug *od.* Zugreise/eine Reise mit dem Auto *od.* Autoreise machen; **c)** *(fig.)* Weg, *der;* **~ through life** Lebensreise, *die (geh.);* **a ~ into history** ein Ausflug in die Geschichte; **d)** *(of vehicle)* Fahrt, *die;* **~ time** Fahrtzeit, *die.* **2.** *v. i. (formal/literary)* fahren; ziehen

journeyman ['dʒɜ:nɪmən] *n., pl.* **journeymen** ['dʒɜ:nɪmən] Geselle, *der;* **a ~ butcher** ein Fleischergeselle

joust [dʒaʊst] **1.** *n.* Tjost, *die.* **2.** *v. i.* tjostieren

Jove [dʒəʊv] *n.* **a)** *(Mythol.)* Jupiter *(der);* **b)** **by ~!** *(dated coll.) expr. surprise* potztausend! *(veralt.); expr. approval* Hut ab! *(ugs.);* alle Achtung!

jovial ['dʒəʊvɪəl] *adj.* *(hearty)* herzlich, freundlich ⟨*Gruß*⟩; *(merry)* fröhlich ⟨*Ausdruck, Person*⟩; launig ⟨*Bemerkung*⟩; *(convivial)* lustig ⟨*Versammlung, Gesellschaft*⟩

jovially ['dʒəʊvɪəlɪ] *adv.* fröhlich ⟨*zustimmen, rufen*⟩; herzlich, freundlich ⟨*begrüßen*⟩

jowl [dʒaʊl] *n. (jaw)* Unterkiefer, *der; (lower part of face)* Kinnbacken *Pl.; (double chin)* Doppelkinn, *das; (flabby cheek)* Hängebacke, *die; (of cattle)* Wamme, *die; (of bird)* Kehllappen, *der; see also* **cheek 1a**

joy [dʒɔɪ] *n.* **a)** Freude, *die;* **wish sb. ~:** jmdm. viel Spaß *od.* Vergnügen wünschen; **I wish you ~ of it** *(also iron.)* ich wünsche dir viel Vergnügen damit; **sing for/weep with ~:** vor Freude *(Dat.)* singen/weinen; **we heard with ~ that ...:** wir haben zu unserer Freude erfahren, daß ...; **the ~s of hunting** das Vergnügen des Jagens; **be full of the ~s of spring** *(fig. coll.)* vor Freude ganz aus dem Häuschen sein *(ugs.);* **that is the ~ of the Highlands** das ist der Reiz *od.* das Reizvolle an den Highlands; **it was a ~ to look at** es war eine Augenweide; *see also* **jump 2c;** **b)** *no pl., no art. (coll.: success, satisfaction)* Erfolg, *der;* **he didn't get much ~ out of it** es hat ihm nicht viel gebracht; **any ~?** Erfolg gehabt?; was erreicht? *(ugs.)*

joyful ['dʒɔɪfl] *adj.* froh[gestimmt] ⟨*Person*⟩; froh ⟨*Gesicht*⟩; freudig ⟨*Blick, Ereignis, Umarmung, Gesang, Beifall*⟩; freudig, froh ⟨*Nachricht, Kunde*⟩; erfreulich ⟨*Nachricht, Ergebnis, Anblick*⟩; Freuden⟨*tag, -schrei*⟩; **she was ~ [at his return]** sie freute sich [über seine Rückkehr]

joyfully ['dʒɔɪfəlɪ] *adv.* freudig

joyless ['dʒɔɪlɪs] *adj.* traurig ⟨*Ausdruck, Nachricht, Ergebnis, Anlaß*⟩; freudlos ⟨*Zeit, Leben*⟩; verdrossen ⟨*Person*⟩

joyous ['dʒɔɪəs] *adj.* freudig ⟨*Anlaß, Ereignis*⟩; froh ⟨*Lachen, Herz*⟩; Freuden⟨*tag, -schrei*⟩

joy: **~-ride** *n. (coll.)* Spritztour [im gestohlenen Auto]; **~-rider** *n.* Autodieb *(der den Wagen nur für eine Spritztour gestohlen hat);* **~stick** *n.* **a)** *(Aeronaut. coll.)* Knüppel, *der;* **b)** *(on computer etc.)* Hebel, *der;* Joystick, *der (DV)*

JP *abbr.* **Justice of the Peace**

Jr. *abbr.* **Junior** jun.; jr.

jt. *abbr.* **joint;** *see* **joint 2**

jubilant ['dʒu:bɪlənt] *adj.* jubelnd; *(exultingly glad)* freudestrahlend ⟨*Miene*⟩; *(triumphant)* triumphierend ⟨*Miene*⟩; **be ~** ⟨*Person:*⟩ frohlocken

jubilation [dʒu:bɪ'leɪʃn] *n.* Jubel, *der*

jubilee ['dʒu:bɪli:] *n.* *(anniversary)* Jubiläum, *das; see also* **diamond jubilee; golden jubilee; silver jubilee**

Judaism ['dʒu:deɪɪzm] *n., no pl., no art.* Judentum, *das;* Judaismus, *der*

Judas ['dʒu:dəs] *n.* *(traitor)* Judas, *der*

'Judas-tree *n. (Bot.)* Judasbaum, *der*

judder ['dʒʌdə(r)] **1.** *v. i.* rattern. **2.** *n.* Rattern, *das;* **give a ~:** rattern; **with a ~:** ratternd

judge [dʒʌdʒ] **1.** *n.* **a)** Richter, *der*/Richterin, *die;* **[the Book of] J~s** *(Bibl.)* das Buch der Richter; **~ and jury** das Gericht; **be ~ and jury** *(fig.)* sich zum alleinigen Richter aufwerfen; *see also* **sober a; b)** *(in contest)* Juror, *der*/Jurorin, *die;* Preisrichter, *der*/-richterin, *die; (Sport)* Kampfrichter, *der*/-richterin, *die;* Schiedsrichter, *der*/-richterin, *die; (in cycle-racing)* Zielrichter, *der*/-richterin, *die; (in dispute)* Schiedsrichter, *der*/-richterin, *die;* **c)** *(fig.: connoisseur, critic)* Kenner, *der*/Kennerin, *die;* **~ of character/poetry** Menschen-/Lyrikkenner, *der;* **be a good ~ of sth.** etw. gut beurteilen können; **if I'm any ~/any ~ of sth.** soweit ich das/etw. beurteilen kann; **d)** *(person who decides question)* Schiedsrichter, *der;* **be the ~ of sth.** über etw. *(Akk.)* entscheiden *od.* befinden. **2.** *v. t.* **a)** *(pronounce sentence on)* richten *(geh.);* **~ sb.** *(Law)* jmds. Fall entscheiden; in jmds. Fall das Urteil fällen; **b)** *(try)* verhandeln ‹*Fall*›; **c)** *(act as adjudicator of)* Juror/Jurorin *od.* Preisrichter/-richterin sein bei; *(Sport)* Kampfrichter/-richterin *od.* Schiedsrichter/-richterin sein bei; **d)** *(form opinion about)* urteilen *od.* ein Urteil fällen über (+ *Akk.*); beurteilen; **~ a book to be worth reading** ein Buch für lesenswert erachten *od.* befinden; **~ sth. [to be] necessary** etw. für *od.* als notwendig erachten; **~d by modern standards** nach heutigen Maßstäben; **e)** *(decide)* entscheiden ‹*Angelegenheit, Frage*›; **f)** *(conclude)* **I ~d that the meat was done** ich war der Meinung, daß das Fleisch gar war; **I can't ~ whether it's any good** ich kann nicht beurteilen, ob er/sie/es etwas taugt. **3.** *v. i.* **a)** *(form a judgement)* urteilen; **to ~ by its size, ...:** der Größe nach zu urteilen, ...; **judging** *or* **to ~ by the look on his face ...:** nach dem Gesicht zu schließen, das er macht/machte, ...; **judging from what you say, ...:** nach dem, was du sagst, ...; **as far as I can ~, ...:** soweit ich es beurteilen kann, ...; **as near as I could ~, ...:** nach meiner Schätzung ...; **b)** *(act as ~) see* **1 a, b:** Richter/Richterin sein; Kampfrichter/-richterin sein; Schiedsrichter/-richterin sein

judgement, judgment ['dʒʌdʒmənt] *n.* **a)** Urteil, *das;* **the J~ of Paris** *(Greek Mythol.)* das Urteil des Paris; **~ was given in favour of/against sb.** das Urteil fiel zu jmds. Gunsten/Ungunsten aus; **pass [a] ~:** ein Urteil abgeben (**on** über + *Akk.*); **give one's ~:** ein Urteil fällen; **in** *or* **according to my ~:** meines Erachtens; **in the ~ of most people** nach Meinung der meisten Leute; **form a ~:** sich *(Dat.)* ein Urteil *od.* eine Meinung bilden; **against one's better ~:** entgegen seiner besseren Einsicht; *see also* **sit 1 b; Solomon; b)** *(critical faculty)* Urteilsfähigkeit, *die;* Urteilsvermögen, *das;* **error of ~:** Fehlurteil, *das;* Fehleinschätzung, *die;* **a man of ~:** ein urteilsfähiger Mann; **critical ~:** Kritikfähigkeit, *die;* **I leave it to your ~:** ich stelle das in Ihr Ermessen; **use your own ~:** verfahren Sie nach Ihrem Gutdünken; **c)** *(trial by God)* Gericht, *das;* **day of ~, J~ Day** Tag des Jüngsten Gerichts; *(fig.)* Stunde der Wahrheit; **the last ~:** das Jüngste *od.* Letzte Gericht; **d)** *(misfortune)* **it's a ~ on you for ...** *(joc.)* das ist die Strafe dafür, daß du ...

judicature ['dʒu:dɪkətʃə(r)] *n. (Law)* Judikatur, *die (fachspr.);* Rechtsprechung, *die;* **Supreme Court of J~** *(Brit.) Oberster Gerichtshof*

judicial [dʒu:'dɪʃl] *adj.* **a)** gerichtlich; richterlich ‹*Gewalt*›; Recht sprechend ‹*Versammlung*›; **~ error** Justizirrtum, *der;* **~ murder** Justizmord, *der;* **take** *or* **bring ~ proceedings against sb.** gegen jmdn. gerichtlich vorgehen; **b)** *(of a judge)* richterlich; **in his ~ capacity** in seiner Eigenschaft als Richter; **c)** *(expressing judgement)* kritisch; **d)** *(impartial)* unvoreingenommen

judiciary [dʒu:'dɪʃərɪ] *n. (Law)* Richterschaft, *die*

judicious [dʒu:'dɪʃəs] *adj.* **a)** *(discerning)* klarblickend; **b)** *(sensible)* besonnen

judiciously [dʒu:'dɪʃəslɪ] *adv.* mit Bedacht

judo ['dʒu:dəʊ] *n., pl.* **~s** Judo, *das*

jug [dʒʌg] **1.** *n.* **a)** Krug, *der; (with lid, water-~)* Kanne, *die; (small milk-~)* Kännchen, *das;* **a ~ of water** ein Krug/eine Kanne Wasser; **b)** *(sl.: prison)* Loch, *das (salopp);* **put/be in ~:** ins Loch stecken/im Loch sitzen. **2.** *v. t.,* **-gg-** *(Cookery)* schmoren; **~ged hare** Hasenpfeffer, *der*

jugful ['dʒʌgfʊl] *n. see* **jug 1 a:** Krug, *der;* Kanne, *die;* Kännchen, *das;* **a ~ of ...:** ein Krug/eine Kanne/ein Kännchen [voll] ...

juggernaut ['dʒʌgənɔ:t] *n.* **a)** *(institution, notion)* Moloch, *der (geh.);* **b)** *(large object)* Ungetüm, *das;* **~ [lorry]** *(Brit.)* schwerer Brummer *(ugs.)*

juggins ['dʒʌgɪnz] *n. (sl.)* Dämel, *der (salopp);* Dämlack, *der (salopp)*

juggle ['dʒʌgl] **1.** *v. i.* **a)** jonglieren; *(perform conjuring tricks)* zaubern; **b) ~ with** *(misrepresent)* jonglieren mit ‹*Fakten, Zahlen*›. **2.** *v. t. (lit., or fig.: manipulate)* jonglieren [mit]

juggler ['dʒʌglə(r)] *n.* **a)** Jongleur, *der*/Jongleuse, *die;* **b)** *(conjurer)* Zauber[künstl]er, *der*/Zauber[künstler]in, *die;* **c)** *(trickster)* Betrüger, *der*/Betrügerin, *die*

Jugoslav, Jugoslavia *see* **Yugoslav** *etc.*

jugular ['dʒʌgjʊlə(r)] *(Anat.)* **1.** *adj.* jugular *(fachspr.);* **~ vein** Jugularvene, *die (fachspr.);* Drosselvene, *die.* **2.** *n.* Jugularvene, *die (fachspr.);* Drosselvene, *die;* **go for the ~** *(fig.)* versuchen, den Lebensnerv zu treffen

juice [dʒu:s] *n.* **a)** Saft, *der; see also* **stew 3 a; b)** *(sl.) (electricity)* Saft, *der (salopp); (petrol)* Sprit, *der (ugs.)*

juicy ['dʒu:sɪ] *adj.* **a)** saftig; **b)** *(coll.) (racy)* saftig *(ugs.)* ‹*Anekdote, Witz, Geschichte, Skandal*›; *(suggestive)* schlüpfrig; *(profitable)* fett *(ugs.)* ‹*Vertrag, Geschäft usw.*›

ju-jitsu [dʒu:'dʒɪtsu:] *n.* Jiu-Jitsu, *das*

juke-box ['dʒu:kbɒks] *n.* Jukebox, *die;* Musikbox, *die*

Jul. *abbr.* **July** Jul.

julep ['dʒu:lep] *n.* Julep, *das od. der*

Julian ['dʒu:lɪən] *adj.* **~ calendar** Julianischer Kalender

July [dʒʊ'laɪ] *n.* Juli, *der; see also* **August**

jumble ['dʒʌmbl] **1.** *v. t.* **~ up** *or* **together** *or* **about** durcheinanderbringen; durcheinanderwerfen; **~ sth. up with sth.** etw. mit etw. durcheinanderbringen *od.* -werfen; **they've got my clothes ~d up with yours** sie haben meine und deine Sachen durcheinandergebracht. **2.** *n.* **a)** Wirrwarr, *der;* Gewirr, *das; (muddle)* Durcheinander, *das;* **the cupboard was in a complete ~:** im Schrank herrschte ein heilloses Durcheinander; **a ~ of clothes, books, and toys** ein kunterbuntes Durcheinander von Kleidungsstücken, Büchern und Spielsachen; **b)** *no pl., no indef. art. (Brit.: articles for ~ sale)* alte *od.* gebrauchte Sachen

'jumble sale *n. (Brit.)* Trödelmarkt, *der; (for charity)* Wohltätigkeitsbasar, *der*

jumbo ['dʒʌmbəʊ] **1.** *n., pl.* **~s a)** *(very large specimen)* riesiges Exemplar; **b)** *(jet)* Jumbo, *der.* **2.** *adj.* **~[-sized]** riesig; Riesen- *(ugs.)*

jumbo 'jet *n.* Jumbo-Jet, *der*

jump [dʒʌmp] **1.** *n.* **a)** Sprung, *der;* **be on the ~** *(fig. coll.)* in Bewegung *od.* in Aktion sein; **keep sb. on the ~** *(fig. coll.)* jmdn. auf Trab halten *(ugs.);* **take a running ~ [at oneself]** *(fig. coll.)* verschwinden; **get the ~ on sb.** *(sl.)* sich *(Dat.)* einen Vorsprung vor jmdm. verschaffen; **always be one ~ ahead of sb.** jmdm. immer um eine Nasenlänge voraus sein *(ugs.);* **b)** *(sudden movement)* **give a ~:** zusammenzucken *od.* -fahren; **have got the ~s** *(sl.)* ganz zapp[e]lig *od. (landsch.)* fick[e]rig sein; **give sb. the ~s** *(sl.)* jmdn. ganz zapp[e]lig *od. (landsch.)* fick[e]rig machen; **c)** *(sudden transition)* Sprung, *der;* sprunghafter Wechsel; *(gap)* Lücke, *die;* **d)** *(abrupt rise)* sprunghafter Anstieg; **~ in value/temperature** plötzliche Wertsteigerung/plötzlicher Temperaturanstieg; **there has been a considerable ~ in prices** die Preise sind beträchtlich in die Höhe geschnellt; **e)** *(Sport: obstacle) (in steeplechase)* Sprung, *der; (in athletics)* Hindernis, *das;* **set of ~s** Sprungkombination, *die;* **f)** *(Parachuting)* Absprung, *der. See also* **broad jump; high jump; long jump. 2.** *v. i.* **a)** springen; ‹*Fallschirmspringer:*› abspringen; **~ to one's feet/from one's seat** aufspringen/vom Sitz aufspringen; **~ down sb.'s throat** *(fig. coll.)* jmdn. anblaffen *(salopp);* **~ in the lake** *or* **off a cliff** *(fig. coll.)* sich zum Teufel scheren *(ugs.);* **~ on sb.** *or (Amer.)* **all over sb.** *(fig. coll.)* jmdn. zur Minna machen *(salopp); see also* **skin 1 a; b)** *(fig.: come over-hastily)* voreilig gelangen **(to conclusion)** ‹*Annahme, Lösung*›; **~ to the conclusion that ...:** den voreiligen Schluß ziehen, daß ...; **~ to conclusions** voreilige Schlüsse ziehen; **c)** *(make sudden movement)* springen; *(start)* zusammenzucken; **~ for joy** einen Freudensprung/Freudensprünge machen; *(fig.)* vor Freude ganz aus dem Häuschen sein; wahre Freudentänze vollführen; **~ up and down with excitement** aufgeregt herumspringen *od.* -hüpfen; **her heart ~ed** ihr Herz machte einen Sprung; **d)** *(rise suddenly)* ‹*Kosten, Preise usw.*› sprunghaft steigen, in die Höhe schnellen; **e)** *(rise in status, prominence)* plötzlich aufsteigen; **f) ~ to it** *(coll.)* zupacken; **~ to it!** *(coll.)* mach/macht schon! **3.** *v. t.* **a)** springen über (+ *Akk.*); überspringen ‹*Mauer, Zaun usw.*›; **b)** springen lassen ‹*Pferd*›; **~ one's horse over a fence** mit dem Pferd über einen Zaun setzen; **c)** *(move to point beyond)* überspringen; **d)** *(not stop at)* überfahren ‹*rote Ampel*›; **e) ~ the rails** *or* **track** ‹*Zug:*› entgleisen; **f) ~ ship** ‹*Seemann:*› [unter Bruch des Heuervertrages vorzeitig] den Dienst quittieren; **g) ~ the starting signal by half a second** eine halbe Sekunde vor dem Startsignal starten; **~ the [bus-]queue** *(Brit.)* sich [an der Bushaltestelle] vordrängeln; **h)** *(skip over)* überspringen ‹*Seite, Kapitel usw.*›; **i)** *(attack)* herfallen über (+ *Akk.*). *See also* **'bail 1 a; gun 1 b**

~ at *v. t.* **a)** anspringen; *(fig.: rebuke)* anfahren; **b)** *(fig.: seize, accept eagerly)* sofort [beim Schopf] ergreifen ‹*Gelegenheit*›; sofort zugreifen *od. (ugs.)* zuschlagen bei ‹*Angebot*›; sofort aufgreifen *od. (ugs.)* anspringen auf ‹*Vorschlag*›

~ 'in *v. i.* reinspringen *(ugs.)*

~ 'off 1. *v. i.* **a)** abspringen; **he ~ed off from his horse/bicycle** er sprang vom Pferd/Rad; **b)** *(Show-jumping)* am Stechen teilnehmen; *see also* **jump-off. 2.** *v. t.* **~ off sth.** von etw. springen

~ on 1. [-'-] *v. i.* aufspringen; **~ on to a bus/train** in einen Bus/Zug springen; **~ on to one's bicycle/horse** sich aufs Fahrrad/Pferd schwingen. **2.** ['--] *v. t.* **~ on a bus/train** in einen Bus/Zug springen; **~ on one's bicycle** sich aufs Fahrrad schwingen

~ 'out *v. i.* hinaus-/herausspringen; **~ out of** springen aus

~ 'up *v. i.* aufspringen **(from** von); **the dog ~ed up at him** der Hund sprang an ihm hoch; **~ up on to sth.** auf etw. *(Akk.)* springen; *see also* **~ 2 c**

jumped-up ['dʒʌmptʌp] *adj. (coll.)* emporgekommen

jumper ['dʒʌmpə(r)] *n.* **a)** *(Brit.: pullover)* Pullover, *der;* Pulli, *der (ugs.);* **b)** *(loose jacket)* Jumper, *der;* Buseruntje, *die (Seemannsspr.);* **c)** *(Amer.: pinafore dress)* Trägerkleid, *das*
jumping ['dʒʌmpɪŋ]: ~ **bean** *n.* Springbohne, *die;* ~ **jack** *n.* **a)** Hampelmann, *der;* **b)** *(firework)* Knallfrosch, *der;* ~-'**off place** *n.* Ausgangsbasis, *die*
jump: ~-**jet** *n. (Aeronaut.)* Senkrechtstarter, *der;* ~ **leads** *n. pl. (Brit. Motor Veh.)* Starthilfekabel; ~-**off** *n. (Show-jumping)* Stechen, *das;* ~ **seat** *n. (Amer. Motor Veh.)* Klappsitz, *der;* ~ **suit** *n.* Overall, *der*
jumpy ['dʒʌmpɪ] *adj.* nervös; aufgeregt
Jun. *abbr.* **a) June** Jun.; **b) Junior** jun.
junction ['dʒʌŋkʃn] *n.* **a)** Verbindungspunkt, *der;* Verbindungsstelle, *die; (of rivers)* Zusammenfluß, *der; (of railway lines, roads)* ≈ Einmündung, *die; (Electr.)* [Leitungs]verbindung, *die; (of motorway)* Anschlußstelle, *die;* **the ~ of two roads** ≈ eine Straßeneinmündung; **b)** *(Electronics)* Übergang, *der*
'**junction box** *n. (Electr.)* Verteilerkasten, *der*
juncture ['dʒʌŋktʃə(r)] *n.* **at this ~:** unter diesen Umständen; *(at this point of time)* zu diesem Zeitpunkt
June [dʒu:n] *n.* Juni, *der; see also* **August**
jungle ['dʒʌŋgl] *n.* Dschungel, *der (auch fig.);* Urwald, *der;* **tropical ~:** tropischer Urwald; **~ life** das Leben im Dschungel; **the law of the ~:** das Gesetz des Dschungels; **concrete ~:** Betondschungel, *der (ugs.)*
junior ['dʒu:nɪə(r)] **1.** *adj.* **a)** *(below a certain age)* jünger; **~ team** Juniorenmannschaft, *die;* **~ member** ≈ Mitglied der Jugendabteilung; **be ~ to sb.** jünger sein als jmd.; **b)** *(of lower rank)* rangniedriger ⟨*Person*⟩; niedriger ⟨*Rang*⟩; einfach ⟨*Angestellter*⟩; **be ~ to sb.** eine niedrigere Stellung haben als jmd.; **be ~ to sb. by two years** zwei Jahre kürzer im Dienst sein als jmd.; **c)** *appended to name (the younger)* **Mr Smith J~:** Mr. Smith junior; **d)** *(Brit. Sch.)* Grundschul⟨*klasse*⟩; Grund⟨*schule*⟩; **e)** *(Brit. Univ.)* **~ combination** *or* **common room** Gemeinschaftsraum für Studenten; **f)** *(Amer. Sch., Univ.)* **~ year** vorletztes Jahr vor der Abschlußprüfung. **2.** *n.* **a)** *(younger person)* Jüngere, *der/die; (person of lower rank)* Untergebene, *der/die; (in an office) jmd., der in einem Büro die niedrigste Stellung hat;* **be sb.'s ~ [by six years]** *or* **[six years] sb.'s ~:** [sechs Jahre] jünger sein als jmd.; **b)** *(Brit. Sch.) (at primary school)* Grundschüler, *der/*-schülerin, *die; (at secondary school)* Unterstufenschüler, *der/*-schülerin, *die;* **c)** *(Amer.) (Univ.)* Student/Studentin im vorletzten Studienjahr; *(Sch.)* Schüler/Schülerin im vorletzten Schuljahr; **d)** *no art. (Amer. coll.: son in the family)* der Junge; der Junior *(scherzh.);* **come on, ~:** komm, Junior *(scherzh.) od.* Junge!
junior: ~ '**minister** *n. (Brit.)* ≈ Ministerialdirektor, *der/*-direktorin, *die;* ~ '**partner** *n.* Juniorpartner, *der/*-partnerin, *die*
juniper ['dʒu:nɪpə(r)] *n. (Bot.)* Wacholder, *der;* **oil of ~:** Wacholderöl, *das*
¹**junk** [dʒʌŋk] **1.** *n.* **a)** *(discarded material)* Trödel, *der (ugs.);* Gerümpel, *das; (trash)* Plunder, *der (ugs.);* Ramsch, *der (ugs.);* **b)** *(Naut.) (cables or ropes)* [altes] Tauwerk; Junk, *der (fachspr.); (cable or rope)* [alter] Tampen *(fachspr.);* **c)** *(sl.: drug, esp. heroin)* Junk, *der (Drogenjargon).* **2.** *v.t.* wegwerfen; ausmisten *(ugs.); (fig.)* aufgeben
²**junk** *n. (ship)* Dschunke, *die*
'**junk bonds** *n. pl.* Junk bonds *Pl. (Wirtsch.)*
junket ['dʒʌŋkɪt] **1.** *n.* **a)** *(dessert of set milk)* Dickmilchdessert, *das;* **b)** *(dated: feast)* [Fest]schmaus, *der (veralt.);* Festmahl, *das (geh.);* **c)** *(Amer.) (pleasure outing)* Vergnügungsfahrt, *die; (official's tour)* Vergnügungsreise auf Kosten des Steuerzahlers. **2.** *v.i.* **a)** *(dated: feast, banquet)* schlemmen; **b)** *(esp. Amer.: tour)* eine Vergnügungsreise/Vergnügungsreisen machen
junketing ['dʒʌŋkɪtɪŋ] *n.* **a)** *(dated)* Schlemmerei, *die;* **b)** *(esp. Amer.: by official[s])* Vergnügungsreisen auf Kosten des Steuerzahlers
junk: ~ **food** *n.* minderwertige Kost; ~-**heap** *n.* **a)** *see* **scrap-heap; b)** *(sl.: old car etc.)* Schrotthaufen, *der (ugs.)*
junkie ['dʒʌŋkɪ] *n. (sl.)* Junkie, *der (Drogenjargon)*
junk: ~ **mail** *n.* Reklame, *die;* ~-**shop** *n.* Trödelladen, *der (ugs.);* ~-**yard** *see* **scrap-yard**
junta ['dʒʌntə] *n.* Junta, *die;* **military ~:** Militärjunta, *die*
Jupiter ['dʒu:pɪtə(r)] *pr. n.* **a)** *(Astron.)* Jupiter, *der;* **b)** *(Roman Mythol.)* Jupiter *(der)*
Jura ['dʒʊərə] *pr. n.* Jura, *der*
Jurassic [dʒʊə'ræsɪk] *(Geol.)* **1.** *adj.* jurassisch; Jura-. **2.** *n.* Jura, *der*
juridical [dʒʊə'rɪdɪkl] *adj.* **a)** *(of judicial proceedings)* gerichtlich; **b)** *(of law)* juristisch
jurisdiction [dʒʊərɪs'dɪkʃn] *n. (authority)* Jurisdiktion, *die;* Gerichtsbarkeit, *die; (authority of a sovereign power)* Hoheit, *die; (extent)* Zuständigkeit, *die; (territory)* Zuständigkeitsbereich, *der;* **fall** *or* **come under** *or* **within the ~ of sth./sb.** in die Zuständigkeit *od.* den Zuständigkeitsbereich von etw./jmdm. fallen; **have ~ over sb./in a matter** für jmdn./in einer Angelegenheit zuständig sein
jurisprudence [dʒʊərɪs'pru:dəns] *n., no pl.* Rechtswissenschaft, *die;* Jurisprudenz, *die*
jurist ['dʒʊərɪst] *n.* **a)** Rechtswissenschaftler, *der/*-wissenschaftlerin, *die;* Jurist, *der/*Juristin, *die;* **b)** *(Amer.: lawyer)* [Rechts]anwalt, *der/*-anwältin, *die*
juror ['dʒʊərə(r)] *n.* Geschworene, *der/die; (in Germany, in some Austrian courts)* Schöffe, *der/*Schöffin, *die*
jury ['dʒʊərɪ] *n.* **a)** *(in court)* **the ~:** die Geschworenen; *(in Germany, in some Austrian courts)* die Schöffen; **sit on the ~:** auf der Geschworenen-/Schöffenbank sitzen; **do ~ service** das Amt eines Geschworenen/Schöffen ausüben; **a ~ consists of ...:** eine Geschworenen-/Schöffenbank besteht aus ...; **trial by ~:** Schwurgerichtsverfahren, *das;* **the ~ of public opinion** *(fig.)* die Instanz der öffentlichen Meinung; *see also* **grand jury; judge 1 a; b)** *(in competition)* Jury, *die;* Preisgericht, *das; (Sport)* Schiedsgericht, *das;* Kampfgericht, *das*
jury: ~-**box** *n.* Geschworenenbank, *die; (in Germany, in some Austrian courts)* Schöffenbank, *die;* ~**man** ['dʒʊərɪmən] *n., pl.* ~**men** ['dʒʊərɪmən] Geschworene, *der; (in Germany, in some Austrian courts)* Schöffe, *der;* ~**woman** *n.* Geschworene, *die; (in Germany, in some Austrian courts)* Schöffin, *die*
just [dʒʌst] **1.** *adj.* **a)** *(morally right, deserved)* gerecht; anständig, korrekt ⟨*Verhalten, Benehmen*⟩; *see also* ¹**desert a; b)** *(legally right)* rechtmäßig; **c)** *(well-grounded)* berechtigt ⟨*Angst, Zorn, Groll*⟩; gerechtfertigt ⟨*Verhalten*⟩; begründet ⟨*Verdacht, Ansicht*⟩; **d)** *(right in amount)* recht, richtig ⟨*Proportion, Maß, Verhältnis*⟩. **2.** *adv.* **a)** *(exactly)* genau; **~ then/enough** gerade da/genug; **~ as** *(exactly as, in the same way as)* genauso wie; *(when)* gerade, als; **~ as you like** *or* **please** ganz wie Sie wünschen/du magst; **~ as good/tidy** *etc.* genauso gut/ordentlich *usw.;* **come ~ as you are** komm so, wie du bist; **~ as fast as I can** so schnell wie ich nur kann; **~ about** *(coll.)* so ziemlich *(ugs.);* **it'll ~ about be enough** *(coll.)* es wird in etwa reichen; **I've had ~ about enough of you** *(coll.)* ich hab' langsam genug von dir; **that is ~ 'it** das ist es ja gerade; genau das ist es ja; **that's ~ like him** das ist typisch er *od.* für ihn; **~ 'so** *(in an orderly manner)* ordentlich; *expr. agreement* ganz recht; **be ~ 'so** *(be exactly arranged)* tadellos in Ordnung sein; **~ what ...?** was genau ...?; **I wonder ~ how good he is** ich frage mich, wie gut er eigentlich wirklich ist; **b)** *(barely)* gerade [eben]; *(with very little time to spare)* gerade [eben] noch; *(no more than)* nur; **~ under £10** nicht ganz zehn Pfund; **we had only ~ enough time for a cup of tea** wir hatten gerade [genug] Zeit, eine Tasse Tee zu trinken; **it's ~ possible** das ist gerade noch möglich; **there will be enough, but only ~:** es wird reichen, aber [nur] gerade eben *od.* [nur] gerade so; **it's ~ on/before/after 8 a.m.** es ist fast 8 Uhr/es ist kurz vor/nach 8 Uhr; **it's ~ after/before the traffic-lights** es ist direkt hinter/vor der Verkehrsampel; **c)** *(exactly or nearly now or then, in immediate past)* gerade [eben]; [so]eben; *(at this moment)* gerade; **I have ~ seen him** *(Brit.),* **I ~ saw him** *(Amer.)* ich habe ihn gerade [eben] *od.* eben gesehen; **~ now** *(at this moment)* [im Moment] gerade; *(a little time ago)* gerade eben; **not ~ now** im Moment nicht; **d)** *(coll.) (simply)* einfach; *(only)* nur; *esp. with imperatives* mal [eben]; **it ~ so happens that ...:** es ist ganz zufällig, daß ...; **it is ~ that I don't like them** ich mag sie einfach nicht; **I've come here ~ to see you** ich bin nur gekommen, um dich zu besuchen; **~ [you] wait till I catch you!** warte nur *od.* na warte, wenn ich dich erwische!; **~ anybody** irgend jemand; **~ another car** ein ganz gewöhnliches Auto; **~ look at that!** guck dir das mal an!; **could you ~ turn round?** kannst du dich mal [eben] umdrehen?; **~ come here a moment** komm [doch] mal einen Moment her; **~ a moment, please** einen Moment mal; **~ like that** einfach so; ohne weiteres; **~ in case** für alle Fälle; **~ in case it rains** falls es regnet; **e)** *(coll.: positively)* einfach; echt *(ugs.);* **that's ~ ridiculous/fantastic** das ist einfach lächerlich/phantastisch; **f)** *(quite)* **not ~ yet** noch nicht ganz; **it is ~ as well that ...:** [es ist] nur gut *od.* es ist doch gut, daß ...; **you might ~ as well ...:** du könntest genausogut ...; **g)** *(coll.: really, indeed)* wirklich; echt *(ugs.);* **You wouldn't dare do that! – Oh, wouldn't I ~?** Das würdest du nicht wagen! – Und ob!; **That's lovely. – Isn't it ~?** Das ist schön. – Ja, und wie; **~ the same** *(nevertheless)* trotzdem; **that's ~ too bad** das ist Pech. **3.** *n. pl.* **the ~:** die Gerechten; *see also* **sleep 3 a**
justice ['dʒʌstɪs] *n.* **a)** Gerechtigkeit, *die;* **administer ~:** Recht sprechen; **poetic[al] ~:** ausgleichende Gerechtigkeit; **treat sb. with ~:** jmdn. gerecht behandeln; **do ~ to sth.** einer Sache *(Dat.)* gerecht werden; *(to food or drink)* einer Sache *(Dat.)* gebührend zusprechen; **~ was done in the end** der Gerechtigkeit wurde schließlich Genüge getan; **do oneself ~:** sich richtig zur Geltung bringen; **in ~ to sb.** um jmdm. gerecht zu werden; **with ~:** mit Recht; **in all ~:** um gerecht zu sein; *see also* **rough justice; b)** *(judicial proceedings)* **bring sb. to [a court of] ~:** jmdn. vor Gericht bringen *od.* stellen; **let ~ take its course, not interfere with the course of ~:** der Gerechtigkeit ihren Lauf lassen; **Department of J~** *(Amer.)* Justizministerium, *das;* **c)** *(magistrate)* Schiedsrichter, *der/*-richterin, *die;* Schiedsmann, *der/*-männin, *die; (Brit.: judge of Supreme Court) Richter/Richterin des Obersten Gerichtshofs;* **Mr/Mrs J~ Smith** *(Brit.)* Richter/Richterin Smith; **J~ of the Peace** Friedensrichter, *der/*-richterin, *die; see also* **chief 2 a**
justifiable [dʒʌstɪ'faɪəbl] *adj.* berechtigt; gerechtfertigt ⟨*Maßnahme, Handlung*⟩; **it is ~ to state that ...:** man kann mit Recht behaupten, daß ...

justifiably [dʒʌstɪ'faɪəblɪ] *adv.* zu Recht; berechtigterweise *(Papierdt.)*; **and ~ so** und das zu Recht
justification [dʒʌstɪfɪ'keɪʃn] *n.* **a)** Rechtfertigung, *die; (condition of being justified)* Berechtigung, *die;* **with some ~:** mit einigem Recht; **in sb.'s ~:** zu jmds. Rechtfertigung; **b)** *(Printing)* Randausgleich, *der*
justify ['dʒʌstɪfaɪ] *v.t.* **a)** *(show justice of, vindicate)* rechtfertigen; *(demonstrate correctness of)* belegen, beweisen ⟨*Behauptung, Argument, Darstellung*⟩; *(offer adequate grounds for)* begründen ⟨*Verhalten, Vorstellung, Behauptung*⟩; **~ oneself/sth. to sb.** sich/etw. jmdm. gegenüber *od.* vor jmdm. rechtfertigen; **the end justifies the means** der Zweck heiligt die Mittel; **be justified in doing sth.** etw. zu Recht tun; **this cannot be justified** das ist nicht zu rechtfertigen; **b)** *(Printing)* ausschließen
justly ['dʒʌstlɪ] *adv. (with justice, fairly)* gerecht; *(rightly)* mit *od.* zu Recht
jut [dʒʌt] *v.i.*, **-tt-: ~ [out]** [her]vorragen; herausragen; **his chin ~s out rather a lot** er hat ein ziemlich stark vorspringendes Kinn
Jute [dʒu:t] *n. (Ethnol., Hist.)* Jüte, *der*/Jütin, *die*
jute *n.* Jute, *die*
Jutland ['dʒʌtlənd] *pr. n.* Jütland *(das)*
juvenile ['dʒu:vənaɪl] **1.** *adj.* **a)** *(young, characteristic of youth)* jugendlich, *(geh.)* juvenil ⟨*Geschmack, Einstellung*⟩; Jugend⟨*literatur, -mode*⟩; **~ crime** Jugendkriminalität, *die;* **b)** *(immature)* kindisch *(abwertend);* infantil *(abwertend).* **2.** *n.* Jugendliche, *der/die; attrib.* **~ lead** *(Theatre)* jugendlicher Held
juvenile: ~ court *n. (Law)* Jugendgericht, *das;* **~ de'linquency** *n.* Jugendkriminalität, *die;* **~ de'linquent** *n.* jugendlicher Straftäter/jugendliche Straftäterin
juxtapose [dʒʌkstə'pəʊz] *v.t.* nebeneinanderstellen **(with, to** und)
juxtaposition [dʒʌkstəpə'zɪʃn] *n. (action)* Nebeneinanderstellung, *die; (condition)* Nebeneinander, *das;* **be in ~:** nebeneinandergestellt sein

K

¹K, ¹k [keɪ] *n., pl.* **Ks** *or* **K's** K, k, *das*
²K *abbr.* **a)** King[**'s**] kgl.; **b)** *(Phys.)* **kelvin[s]** K; **c)** *(Computing)* **kilobyte** K; **d)** *(Chess)* **king** K; **e)** *(£1,000)* Tsd. £; **earn 35K a year** 35 000 im Jahr verdienen
²k *abbr.* **kilo-** k-
Kaffir ['kæfə(r)] **1.** *n.* **a)** *(Ethnol.)* Kaffer, *der*/Kaffernfrau, *die;* **b)** *(derog.: South African Black)* Kaffer, *der*/Kaffernweib, *das (abwertend).* **2.** *adj.* Kaffern-
Kafkaesque [kæfkə'esk] *adj.* kafkaesk *(geh.)*
kale [keɪl] *n. (Bot.)* **[curly/Scotch] ~:** Grünkohl, *der;* Krauskohl, *der; see also* **sea-kale**
kaleidoscope [kə'laɪdəskəʊp] *n. (lit. or fig.)* Kaleidoskop, *das*
kaleidoscopic [kəlaɪdə'skɒpɪk] *adj. (lit. or fig.)* kaleidoskopisch
kamikaze [kæmɪ'kɑ:zɪ] *n. (Hist.)* **a)** *(pilot)* Kamikaze[flieger], *der;* **b)** *(aircraft)* Kamikazeflugzeug, *das*
Kampuchea [kæmpʊ'tʃi:ə] *pr. n.* Kamputschea *(das)*
kangaroo [kæŋgə'ru:] *n.* Känguruh, *das*
kanga'roo court *n.* Femegericht, *das;* Feme, *die*
Kantian ['kæntɪən] *(of Kant)* Kantisch; *(of Kantianism)* kant[ian]isch
kaolin ['keɪəlɪn] *n.* Kaolin, *das od. (fachspr.) der*
kaput [kæ'pʊt] *pred. adj. (sl.)* kaputt *(ugs.)*
karate [kə'rɑ:tɪ] *n., no pl., no indef. art.* Karate, *das*
ka'rate chop *n.* Karateschlag, *der;* Handkantenschlag, *der*
karma ['kɑ:mə] *n. (Buddhism, Hinduism)* Karma[n], *das*
karst [kɑ:st] *n. (Geog.)* Karst, *der*
kart [kɑ:t] *see* **go-kart**
Kashmir [kæʃ'mɪə(r)] *pr. n.* Kaschmir *(das)*
Katherine ['kæθrɪn] *pr. n. (Hist., as name of ruler etc.)* Katharina *(die)*
kayak ['kaɪæk] *n.* Kajak, *der*
KC *abbr. (Brit.)* **King's Counsel**
kc *abbr.* **kilocycle[s]** kHz
kc/s *abbr.* **kilocycles per second** kHz
kebab [kɪ'bæb] *n. (Cookery)* Kebab, *der*
kedgeree ['kedʒəri:, kedʒə'ri:] *n. (Gastr.)* Kedgeree, *das; indisches Reisgericht mit Hülsenfrüchten, Zwiebeln, Eiern; (European dish) Reisgericht mit Fisch und Eiern*
keel [ki:l] **1.** *n. (Naut.)* Kiel, *der;* **lay down a ~:** ein Schiff auf Kiel legen; *see also* **¹even 1 b. 2.** *v.i.* **~ over a)** *(overturn)* umstürzen; ⟨*Schiff:*⟩ kentern; **b)** *(fall)* ⟨*Person:*⟩ umkippen; **he ~ed over on to the bed** er fiel aufs Bett. **3.** *v.t.* **~ over** *(Naut.)* zum Kentern bringen; kieloben legen *(Seemannsspr.); (on one side)* kielholen *(Seemannsspr.)*
'keel-haul *v.t.* kielholen *(Seemannsspr.); (fig.)* zusammenstauchen *(ugs.)*
¹keen [ki:n] *adj.* **a)** *(sharp)* scharf ⟨*Messer, Klinge, Schneide*⟩; *(fig.)* scharf ⟨*Hohn, Spott*⟩; beißend ⟨*Sarkasmus*⟩; **b)** *(piercingly cold)* scharf, schneidend ⟨*Wind, Kälte*⟩; *(penetrating, strong)* grell ⟨*Licht*⟩; durchdringend, stechend ⟨*Geruch*⟩; **c)** *(eager)* begeistert, leidenschaftlich ⟨*Fußballfan, Amateurfotograf, Sportler*⟩; ausgeprägt, lebhaft ⟨*Interesse*⟩; heftig ⟨*Konkurrenz, Verlangen*⟩; **be ~ to do sth.** darauf erpicht sein, etw. zu tun; **he's really ~ to win** er will unbedingt gewinnen; **although he's inexperienced, he's really ~:** obwohl er unerfahren ist, ist er doch wirklich sehr interessiert; **she was not particularly ~ to see the play** sie war nicht besonders scharf darauf, das Stück zu sehen *(ugs.);* **be [as] ~ as mustard** mit Feuereifer dabei sein; **not be ~ on sth.** nicht gerade begeistert von etw. sein; **I'm not too** *or* **not very** *or* **not madly ~ on it** ich bin nicht so wild darauf *(ugs.);* **my father's very ~ on my going to college** mein Vater will unbedingt, daß ich aufs College gehe; **be ~ on sb.** scharf auf jmdn. sein *(ugs.);* **d)** *(highly sensitive)* scharf ⟨*Augen*⟩; fein ⟨*Sinne*⟩; ausgeprägt ⟨*Sinn für etw.*⟩; **e)** *(intellectually sharp)* scharf ⟨*Verstand, Intellekt*⟩; clever ⟨*Geschäftsmann*⟩; scharfsinnig, geistreich ⟨*Bemerkung, Frage usw.*⟩; rasch ⟨*Auffassungsgabe*⟩; **~ wit** Scharfsinn, *der;* **f)** *(acute)* heftig, stark ⟨*Schmerzen, Qualen*⟩; **g)** *(Brit.: exceptionally low)* niedrig, günstig ⟨*Preis*⟩; günstig ⟨*Angebot*⟩; **h)** *(coll.: excellent)* [einfach] klasse *(ugs.)*
²keen 1. *n.* Totenklage, *die.* **2.** *v.i.* die Totenklage halten *od.* singen **(over** für)
keenly ['ki:nlɪ] *adv.* **a)** *(sharply)* scharf ⟨*geschliffen*⟩; **b)** *(coldly)* scharf; **c)** *(eagerly)* eifrig ⟨*arbeiten*⟩; brennend ⟨*interessiert sein*⟩; **look forward ~ to sth.** auf etw. *(Akk.)* sehr gespannt sein; **d)** *(piercingly)* scharf ⟨*ansehen*⟩; **e)** *(acutely)* **be ~ aware of sth.** sich *(Dat.)* einer Sache *(Gen.)* voll bewußt sein; **feel sth. ~:** etw. deutlich fühlen
keenness ['ki:nnɪs] *n., no pl.* **a)** *(sharpness, coldness, acuteness of sense)* Schärfe, *die;* **b)** *(eagerness)* Eifer, *der;* **c)** *(of intellect)* Schärfe, *die;* **the ~ of his wit** seine Scharfsinnigkeit; **d)** *(of pain etc.)* Heftigkeit, *die*
keep [ki:p] **1.** *v.t.*, **kept** [kept] **a)** *(observe)* halten ⟨*Versprechen, Schwur usw.*⟩; einhalten ⟨*Verabredung, Vereinbarung, Vertrag, Sonntagsruhe, Zeitplan*⟩; begehen, feiern ⟨*Fest*⟩; halten, einhalten ⟨*Sabbat, Fasten*⟩; *see also* **hour c; b)** *(guard)* behüten, beschützen ⟨*Person*⟩; hüten ⟨*Herde, Schafe*⟩; schützen ⟨*Stadt, Festung*⟩; verwahren ⟨*Wertgegenstände*⟩; **may God ~ you!** Gott beschütze dich!; **~ sb. [safe] from sth.** jmdn. vor etw. *(Dat.)* bewahren; **~ sb. safe** jmdn. beschützen; **~ sth. locked away** etw. unter Verschluß halten *od.* aufbewahren; **c)** *(have charge of)* aufbewahren; verwahren; **d)** *(retain possession of)* behalten; *(not lose or destroy)* aufheben ⟨*Quittung, Rechnung*⟩; **I'll give you that book to ~:** ich schenke dir das Buch; **~ one's position** seine Stellung behaupten *od.* halten; **you can ~ it** *(coll.: I do not want it)* das kannst du behalten *od.* dir an den Hut stecken *(ugs.);* **Another talk on architecture? You can ~ it** Noch ein Vortrag über Architektur? Nein danke, kein Bedarf *(ugs.);* **e)** *(maintain)* unterhalten, instandhalten ⟨*Gebäude, Straße usw.*⟩; pflegen ⟨*Garten*⟩; **neatly kept** gut gepflegt; **f)** *(carry on, manage)* unterhalten, führen, betreiben ⟨*Geschäft, Lokal, Bauernhof*⟩; **g)** halten ⟨*Schweine, Bienen, Hund, Katze usw*⟩; sich *(Dat.)* halten ⟨*Diener, Auto*⟩; **h)** führen ⟨*Tagebuch, Liste usw.*⟩; **~ an account of expenditure** über seine Ausgaben Buch führen; **~ the books** die Bücher führen; **i)** *(provide for sustenance of)* versorgen, unterhalten ⟨*Familie*⟩; **~ sb./oneself in cigarettes** *etc.* jmdn./sich mit Zigaretten *usw.* versorgen; **~ sb. in luxury** jmdm. ein Leben in Luxus bieten; **~ sb. in the style to which he is accustomed** jmdm. den gewohnten Lebensstil bieten; **she has to ~ herself on £20 a week** sie muß mit 20 Pfund pro Woche auskommen; **j)** sich *(Dat.)* halten ⟨*Geliebte, Mätresse usw.*⟩; sich *(Dat.)* als Geliebte halten ⟨*Frau*⟩; sich *(Dat.)* als Liebhaber halten ⟨*Mann*⟩; **she is a kept woman** sie läßt sich von einem Mann aushalten; **k)** *(have on sale)* führen ⟨*Ware*⟩; **~ a stock of sth.** etw. [am Lager] haben; **we always ~ a bit of cheese** wir haben immer ein bißchen Käse da; **l)** *(maintain in quality, state, or position)* halten ⟨*Rhythmus*⟩; **~ one's hands in one's pockets** die Hände in den Taschen behalten; **~ sth. in one's head** etw. [im Kopf] behalten; sich *(Dat.)* etw. merken; **~ sth. in a cool place** etw. an einem kühlen Ort aufbewahren; **a cold kept her in bed** eine Erkältung zwang sie, im Bett zu bleiben; **~ sb. to his word/promise** jmdn. beim Wort nehmen; **~ sb. waiting** jmdn. warten lassen; **~ the water boiling** das Wasser am Kochen halten; **~ the office running smoothly** dafür sorgen, daß im Büro weiterhin alles reibungslos [ab]läuft; **~ sb. alive** jmdn. am Leben halten; **~ the traffic moving** den Verkehr in Fluß halten; **~ a plant watered** eine Pflanze feucht halten; **~ sth. shut/tidy** etw. geschlossen/in Ordnung halten; **~ the engine running** den Motor laufen lassen; **~ sth. under [the] water** etw. unter Wasser halten; **m)** *(maintain as quality)* **~ silence** schweigen; **~ its shape** seine Form nicht verlieren; **~ one's beauty** sich *(Dat.)* seine Schönheit bewahren; **n)** *(detain)* festhalten; **there was no longer anything to ~ him there** es hielt ihn dort nichts mehr; **what kept you [so long]?** wo bleibst du denn [so lange]?;

don't let me ~ you, I mustn't ~ you laß dich [von mir] nicht aufhalten; **~ sb. in prison** jmdn. in Haft halten; **~ sb. in hospital a few days longer** jmdn. noch ein paar Tage länger im Krankenhaus behalten; **~ sb. indoors** jmdn. nicht aus dem Haus lassen; **the teacher kept Peter behind after the lesson** der Lehrer rief Peter nach der Stunde zu sich; **~ sb. from doing sth.** jmdn. davon abhalten *od.* daran hindern, etw. zu tun; **~ sth. from doing sth.** verhindern, daß etw. etw. tut; **to ~ myself from falling** um nicht zu fallen; **I couldn't ~ myself from laughing** [ich konnte mir nicht helfen,] ich mußte einfach lachen; **we must ~ them from seeing each other** wir müssen verhindern, daß sie sich sehen; **o)** *(reserve)* aufheben; aufsparen; **I asked him to ~ a seat for me** ich bat ihn, mir einen Platz freizuhalten; **~ it for oneself** es für sich behalten; **~ sth. for later** *etc.* sich *(Dat.)* etw. für später *usw.* aufheben *od.* aufsparen; **let's ~ the business talk for later** verschieben wir das Geschäftliche erst mal auf später; **p)** *(conceal)* **~ sth. to oneself** etw. für sich behalten; **~ sth. a mystery** ein Geheimnis aus etw. machen; **~ sth. from sb.** jmdm. etw. verheimlichen; **he kept the news from them** er verschwieg ihnen die Neuigkeit; **q)** *(continue to follow)* folgen (+ *Dat.*) ⟨*Straße, Weg*⟩; **~ a straight path** immer geradeaus gehen. **2.** *v.i.*, **kept a)** *(remain in specified place, condition)* bleiben; **~ warm/clean** sich warm/sauber halten; **how are you ~ing?** *(coll.)* wie geht's [dir] denn so? *(ugs.)*; **are you ~ing well?** geht's dir gut?; *see also* **calm 2a; cool 1b;** ^{2}**fit 1e; silent a; b)** *(continue in course, direction, or action)* **~ [to the] left/[to the] right/straight ahead** *or* **straight on** sich links/rechts halten/immer geradeaus fahren/gehen *usw.*; **~ on until you get to the traffic lights** geh/fahr *usw.* weiter bis zur Ampel; **'~ left'** *(traffic sign)* „links vorbeifahren"; *(sign to pedestrians)* „links gehen"; **traffic in Britain ~s [to the] left** in Großbritannien herrscht Linksverkehr *od.* fährt man links; **the lorry kept to the middle of the road** der Lastwagen fuhr die ganze Zeit auf der Straßenmitte; **~ behind me** halte dich *od.* bleib hinter mir; **~ doing sth.** *(not stop)* etw. weiter tun; *(repeatedly)* etw. immer wieder tun; *(constantly)* etw. dauernd *od.* immer tun; **~ talking/working** *etc.* **until ...:** weiterreden/-arbeiten *usw.*, bis ...; *see also* **smile 2; c)** *(remain good)* ⟨*Lebensmittel:*⟩ sich halten; *(fig.)* ⟨*Geheimnis:*⟩ gewahrt bleiben; **that story can ~:** diese Geschichte kann warten *od.* eilt nicht; **your report will have to ~ until the next meeting** mit Ihrem Bericht müssen wir bis zum nächsten Treffen warten; **what I have to say won't ~:** was ich zu sagen habe, ist eilig *od.* eilt; **will your news ~ till tomorrow?** haben ihre Neuigkeiten Zeit bis morgen?. *See also* ^{1}**go 1f; touch 3h. 3.** *n.* **a)** *(maintenance)* Unterhalt, *der;* **you don't earn your ~:** du bist nichts als ein unnützer Esser; **sth. doesn't earn its ~:** etw. zahlt sich nicht aus *(ugs.)*; **b) for ~s** *(coll.)* auf Dauer; *(to be retained)* zum Behalten; **you can have it** *or* **it's yours for ~s** du kannst es behalten; **c)** *(Hist.: tower)* Bergfried, *der*

~ 'after *v.t.* verfolgen; jagen; *(fig.: chivvy)* antreiben

~ at *v.t.* **a)** *(work persistently)* weitermachen mit; **~ 'at it!** nicht nachlassen!; **b)** *(cause to work at)* **~ sb. at sth.** jmdn. dazu anhalten, daß er etw. weitermacht; **c)** [-'-] *(nag)* nicht in Ruhe lassen; [ständig] zusetzen (+ *Dat.*); **don't ~ at me all the time!** laß mich endlich einmal in Ruhe!; **they kept at him for the money he owed** sie lagen ihm ständig wegen des Geldes, das er ihnen schuldete, in den Ohren *(ugs.)*

~ a'way 1. *v.i.* wegbleiben *(ugs.)* **(from** von); sich fernhalten **(from** von); **I just can't ~ away** es zieht mich immer wieder hin. **2.** *v.t.* fernhalten **(from** von); **~ them away from each other!** halte sie auseinander!; **~ him away from me!** halte ihn mir vom Hals! *(ugs.)*; **what kept you away?** warum bist du nicht gekommen?

~ 'back 1. *v.i.* zurückbleiben; **~ back from sth.** sich von etw. fernhalten; von etw. wegbleiben *(ugs.)*; **~ back!** bleib, wo du bist!; **~ back and wait your turn** halte dich zurück und warte, bis du an der Reihe bist. **2.** *v.t.* **a)** *(restrain)* zurückhalten ⟨*Menschenmenge, Tränen*⟩; **~ sb. back from sb./sth.** jmdn. von jmdm./etw. fernhalten; **b)** *(withhold)* verschweigen ⟨*Informationen, Tatsachen*⟩ **(from** *Dat.*); einbehalten ⟨*Geld, Zinsen, Zahlung*⟩; **don't try to ~ any secrets back** versuch nicht, etwas zu verheimlichen

~ 'down 1. *v.i.* unten bleiben; *(Mil.: lie low in skirmishing)* in Deckung bleiben; ⟨*Wind:*⟩ nicht stärker werden; **~ down!** bleib unten!; duck dich! **2.** *v.t.* **a)** *(oppress, suppress)* unterdrücken ⟨*Volk, Person, Tränen*⟩; bändigen ⟨*Hund*⟩; niederhalten ⟨*rebellische Person*⟩; **you can't ~ a good man down** *(prov.)* er/sie *usw.* läßt/lassen sich nicht unterkriegen *(ugs.)*; **b)** *(prevent increase of)* niedrig halten ⟨*Steuern, Preise, Zinssatz, Ausgaben, usw.*⟩; eindämmen ⟨*Epidemie*⟩; **~ one's weight down** nicht zunehmen; **~ the weeds down** dafür sorgen, daß das Unkraut nicht überhandnimmt; **~ down insects** Insekten bekämpfen; **c)** *(not raise)* unten lassen ⟨*Kopf*⟩; **~ that noise/your voice down** sei/rede nicht so laut; **could you ~ the volume down on your radio?** könntest du dein Radio leiser stellen?; **d)** *(not vomit)* bei sich behalten ⟨*Essen*⟩

~ from *v.t.* **~ from doing sth.** etw. nicht tun; *(avoid doing)* es vermeiden, etw. zu tun; **I couldn't ~ from smiling** ich mußte einfach lächeln *od.* konnte ein Lächeln nicht unterdrücken; **it is impossible to ~ from getting wet** es ist nicht zu vermeiden, daß man naß wird

~ 'in 1. *v.i.* **a)** *(remain indoors)* drinnen bleiben; im Haus bleiben; **b)** *(remain in favour)* **~ in with sb.** sich mit jmdm. gut stellen; sich *(Dat.)* jmdn. warmhalten *(ugs.)*. **2.** *v.t.* **a)** *(confine)* unterdrücken ⟨*Gefühle*⟩; verbergen ⟨*Überraschung*⟩; einziehen ⟨*Bauch*⟩; **b)** *(keep burning)* am Brennen halten ⟨*Feuer*⟩; *(not extinguish)* anlassen ⟨*Feuer*⟩; **c)** *(Sch.)* nachsitzen lassen ⟨*Schüler*⟩; **be kept in [after school]** nachsitzen müssen. *See also* **hand 1k**

~ 'off 1. *v.i.* ⟨*Person:*⟩ wegbleiben; ⟨*Regen, Sturm usw.:*⟩ ausbleiben; **let's hope the snow ~s off** hoffen wir, daß es nicht anfängt zu schneien *od.* keinen Schnee gibt; **'~ off'** *(on building-site etc.)* „Betreten verboten". **2.** *v.t.* **a)** fernhalten ⟨*Person, Tier*⟩; abhalten ⟨*Sonne*⟩; **~ sb./sth. off sth.** jmdn./etw. von etw. fernhalten/abhalten; **~ your dog off our lawn** lassen Sie Ihren Hund nicht auf unseren Rasen; **b)** *(not go on)* nicht betreten; nicht begehen/befahren ⟨*Weg, Straße usw.*⟩; **~ off the flower-beds** nicht in die Blumenbeete treten; **'~ off the grass'** „Betreten des Rasens verboten"; **c)** *(not touch)* **~ off my whisky!** Hände *od.* Finger weg von meinem Whisky!; **d)** *(not eat or drink)* **~ off chocolates/brandy** keine Schokolade essen/keinen Brandy trinken; **~ off cigarettes/drinking** keine Zigaretten rauchen/nicht trinken; **if you don't ~ off drugs ...:** wenn du die Finger nicht von den Drogen läßt, ... *(ugs.)*; wenn du Drogen nimmst, ...; **e)** *(not mention)* **~ off a subject** ein Thema vermeiden; **do ~ off religion when the vicar comes to tea** sprich nicht über Religion, wenn der Pfarrer zum Tee kommt

~ 'on 1. *v.i.* **a)** *(continue, persist)* weitermachen **(with** *Akk.*); **~ on doing sth.** etw. [immer] weiter tun; *(repeatedly)* etw. immer wieder tun; *(constantly)* etw. dauernd *od.* immer tun; **I ~ on telling you this** das sage ich dir ja immer; **~ on driving down this road until ...:** fahr diese Straße immer weiter [entlang], bis ...; **I hope you'll ~ on coming to visit us** ich hoffe, du wirst uns auch weiterhin besuchen kommen; **b)** *(Brit.: talk tiresomely)* **he does ~ on** er redet von nichts anderem; **~ on about sth.** immer wieder von etw. anfangen; **~ on at sb. about sth.** jmdm. mit etw. ständig in den Ohren liegen *(ugs.)*. **2.** *v.t.* **a)** weiterbeschäftigen, behalten ⟨*Angestellten*⟩; behalten ⟨*Wohnung, Auto*⟩; verlängern ⟨*Ausstellung, Film*⟩; anlassen, laufen lassen ⟨*Radio, Fernseher*⟩; **the film was kept on for another three months/till Easter** der Film blieb drei weitere Monate/bis Ostern im Programm; **b)** anbehalten, anlassen ⟨*Kleid, Mantel*⟩; aufbehalten ⟨*Hut*⟩; *see also* **hair b**

~ 'out 1. *v.i.* draußen bleiben; **'~ out'** „Zutritt verboten". **2.** *v.t.* **a)** *(not let enter)* nicht hereinlassen ⟨*Person, Tier*⟩; **b)** abhalten ⟨*Kälte*⟩; abweisen ⟨*Nässe*⟩; **central heating helps ~ out the cold** eine Zentralheizung sorgt dafür, daß es nie zu kalt wird

~ 'out of *v.t.* **a)** *(stay outside)* **~ out of a room/an area/a country** ein Zimmer/eine Gegend nicht betreten/nicht in ein Land reisen; **b)** *(avoid)* **~ out of danger** Gefahren meiden; sich nicht in Gefahr begeben; **~ out of the rain/sun** *etc.* nicht in den Regen/die Sonne *usw.* gehen; **~ out of a quarrel** sich aus einem Streit heraushalten; **~ out of sb.'s way** jmdm. aus dem Weg gehen; **~ out of the way of those boys!** halt dich von diesen Jungen fern!; **~ out of trouble** zurechtkommen; **c)** *(not let enter)* nicht hereinlassen in (+ *Akk.*); **d)** *(cause to avoid)* **~ him/the dog out of my way** halte mir ihn/den Hund vom Leibe *(salopp)*; **~ sb. out of danger** jmdn. vor Gefahr bewahren; **~ the plants out of the sun** die Pflanzen vor Sonne schützen; **I want to ~ him out of it** ich möchte ihn da heraushalten; **he wanted his name to be kept out of the papers** er wollte, daß sein Name in den Zeitungen nicht erwähnt wird

~ to *v.t.* **a)** *(not leave)* bleiben auf (+ *Dat.*) ⟨*Straße, Weg*⟩; **~ to the left!** halte dich links!; bleib links!; **b)** *(follow, observe)* sich halten an (+ *Akk.*) ⟨*Regeln, Muster, Gesetz, Diät, usw.*⟩; einhalten ⟨*Zeitplan*⟩; halten ⟨*Versprechen*⟩; **~ to one's word** Wort halten; **c)** *(remain in)* **~ to one's bed** im Bett bleiben; **d) ~ [oneself] to oneself** für sich bleiben; **they ~ themselves to themselves** sie bleiben unter sich; **he ~s to himself [most of the time]** er bleibt [meist] für sich allein. *See also* **~ 1l, 2b**

~ 'under *v.t.* **a)** *(hold in subjection)* unterdrücken; **b)** *(maintain in state of unconsciousness etc.)* unter Narkose halten

~ 'up 1. *v.i.* **a)** *(proceed equally)* **~ up with sb./sth.** mit jmdm./etw. Schritt halten; **he can't ~ up with the rest** er kommt mit den anderen nicht mit; **~ up with the Joneses** mit den andern gleichziehen; **b)** *(maintain contact)* **~ up with sb.** mit jmdm. Kontakt halten; **~ up with sth.** sich über etw. *(Akk.)* auf dem laufenden halten; **~ up with fashions/the times** *(follow)* mit der Mode/Zeit gehen; **c)** ⟨*Regen, Wetter:*⟩ anhalten. **2.** *v.t.* **a)** *(prevent from falling)* festhalten ⟨*Leiter, Zelt usw.*⟩; **wear a belt to ~ one's trousers up** einen Gürtel tragen, damit die Hosen nicht rutschen; **b)** *(prevent from sinking)* aufrechterhalten ⟨*Produktion, Standard usw.*⟩; auf gleichem Niveau halten ⟨*Preise, Löhne usw.*⟩; **c)** *(maintain)* aufrechterhalten ⟨*Bräuche, Traditionen, Freundschaft, Lebensstil, Tempo, jmds. Moral*⟩; *(provide means for the maintenance of)* unterhalten ⟨*Anwesen*⟩; *(keep in repair)* instand *od. (ugs.)* in Schuß halten ⟨*Haus*⟩; *(keep in* *proper condition)* in Ordnung *od. (ugs.)* in Schuß halten ⟨*Garten*⟩; **d)** *continue)* fortsetzen ⟨*Angriff, Belagerung*⟩; weiterhin zahlen ⟨*Raten*⟩; **such old customs are no longer kept up** solche alten Bräuche werden nicht mehr gepflegt; **~ one's courage/spirits up** den Mut nicht sinken lassen; **~ one's strength up** sich bei Kräften halten; **~ it up** weitermachen; **~ it up!** weiter so!; **he'll never be able to ~ it up** er wird es nicht durchhalten [können]; **I'm trying to ~ up my French** ich versuche, mit meinem Französisch nicht aus der Übung zu kommen; **~ up one's chess/painting** weiterhin Schach spielen/malen; **they kept up a correspondence for many years** sie haben jahrelang [miteinander] im Briefwechsel gestanden; *see also* **appearance b; chin; end 1 a; e)** *(prevent from going to bed)* am Schlafengehen hindern; **are we ~ing you up?** halten wir dich vom Schlafengehen ab?; **they kept me up all night** sie haben mich die ganze Nacht nicht schlafen lassen; **they were kept up by their baby crying** wegen ihres schreienden Babys kamen sie nicht zum Schlafen

keeper ['ki:pə(r)] *n.* **a)** *see* **gamekeeper; b)** *see* **goalkeeper; wicket-keeper; c)** *(custodian)* Wärter, *der*/Wärterin, *die; (zoo~)* Tierwärter, *der*/-wärterin, *die;* **~ of the keys** Schlüsselverwahrer, *der (veralt.);* **am I my brother's ~?** *(Bibl.)* soll ich meines Bruders Hüter sein? *(bibl.);* **d)** *(fruit that keeps)* **these apples are good ~s** diese Äpfel halten sich gut

keep-'fit class *n.* Fitneßgruppe, *die;* **go to ~es** zu Fitneßübungen gehen

keeping ['ki:pɪŋ] *n., no pl.* **a)** *no art.* **be in ~ with sth.** einer Sache *(Dat.)* entsprechen; *(be suited to sth.)* zu etw. passen; **be out of ~ with sth.** einer Sache *(Dat.)* nicht entsprechen; **the dress she wore was rather out of ~:** das Kleid, das sie anhatte, war ziemlich unpassend; **b)** *(custody)* **give sth. into sb.'s ~:** jmdm. etw. zur Aufbewahrung [über]geben; **the keys are in his ~:** er bewahrt die Schlüssel auf; **take sth. into one's ~:** etw. in Gewahrsam nehmen; **leave sb. in sb.'s ~:** jmdn. jmds. Obhut anvertrauen; **c) the apples will improve with ~:** die Äpfel werden besser, wenn man sie eine Zeitlang liegen läßt

'keepsake *n.* Andenken, *das;* **take it as** *or* **for a ~ [to remind you] of me** nimm es als *od.* zum Andenken an mich

keg [keg] *n.* **a)** *(barrel)* [kleines] Faß; Fäßchen, *das;* **b)** *attrib.* **~ beer** *aus luftdichten Metallbehältern gezapftes, mit Kohlensäure versetztes Bier;* ≈ Faßbier, *das*

kelp [kelp] *n.* [See]tang, *der*

kelvin ['kelvɪn] *n. (Phys.)* Kelvin, *das*

'Kelvin scale *n. (Phys.)* Kelvinskala, *die*

[1]**ken** [ken] *n.* **this is beyond** *or* **outside my ~:** das geht über meinen Horizont; das ist zu hoch für mich *(ugs.); (beyond range of knowledge)* das übersteigt mein Wissen

[2]**ken** *v.t.,* **~ned** *or* **kent** [kent], **~ned** *(Scot.) see* **know 1**

kennel ['kenl] *n.* **a)** Hundehütte, *die;* **b)** *in pl.* **[boarding] ~s** Hundepension, *die;* **[breeding] ~s** Zwinger, *der*

Kentish ['kentɪʃ] *adj.* kentisch

Kenya ['kenjə, 'ki:njə] *pr. n.* Kenia *(das)*

Kenyan ['kenjən, 'ki:njən] **1.** *adj.* kenianisch; **sb. is ~:** jmd. ist Kenianer/Kenianerin. **2.** *n.* Kenianer, *der*/Kenianerin, *die*

kepi ['kepɪ, 'keɪpɪ] *n.* Käppi, *das*

kept *see* **keep 1, 2**

kerb [kɜ:b] *n. (Brit.)* Bordstein, *der*

kerb: ~-crawling *n. (Brit.) langsames Fahren mit dem Auto am Straßenrand, um jemanden „aufzureißen";* **~ drill** *n. (Brit.)* richtiges [Verhalten beim] Überqueren der Fahrbahn; **~stone** *n. (Brit.)* Bordstein, *der;* **~ weight** *n. (Brit.)* [Fahrzeug]leergewicht, *das*

kerchief ['kɜ:tʃɪf, 'kɜ:tʃi:f] *n. (worn on the head)* Kopftuch, *das; (worn around the neck)* [Hals]tuch, *das*

kerfuffle [kə'fʌfl] *n. (Brit. coll.)* Wirbel, *der;* Affenzeck, *der (ugs. abwertend)*

kernel ['kɜ:nl] *n. (lit. or fig.)* Kern, *der;* **a ~ of truth** ein Körnchen Wahrheit

kerosene, kerosine ['kerəsi:n] *n. (Amer., Austral., NZ/as tech. term)* Paraffin[öl], *das; (for jet engines)* Kerosin, *das; (for lamps etc.)* Petroleum, *das;* **~ lamp** Petroleumlampe, *die*

kestrel ['kestrəl] *n. (Ornith.)* Turmfalke, *der*

ketch [ketʃ] *n. (Naut.)* Ketsch, *die*

ketchup ['ketʃʌp] *n.* Ketchup, *der od. das*

ketone ['ki:təʊn] *n. (Chem.)* Keton, *das*

kettle ['ketl] *n.* [Wasser]kessel, *der;* **a pretty** *or* **fine ~ of fish** *(iron.)* eine schöne Bescherung *(ugs. iron.);* **a different** *or* **another ~ of fish** eine ganz andere Sache

kettle: ~-drum *n. (Mus.)* [Kessel]pauke, *die;* **~-drummer** *n. (Mus.)* Paukist, *der*/Paukistin, *die*

kettleful ['ketlfʊl] *n.* Kessel, *der;* **a ~ of water** ein Kessel [voll] Wasser

[1]**key** [ki:] **1.** *n.* **a)** *(lit. or fig.)* Schlüssel, *der;* **the ~ to success** der Schlüssel zum Erfolg; **the ~ to the mystery** des Rätsels Lösung; der Schlüssel zum Geheimnis; **b)** *(place)* Schlüsselstellung, *die (Milit.);* **c)** *(set of answers)* [Lösungs]schlüssel, *der; (to map etc.)* Zeichenerklärung, *die; (to cipher)* Schlüssel, *der;* **d)** *(translation)* [wörtliche] Übersetzung; **e)** *(on piano, typewriter, etc.)* Taste, *die; (on wind instrument)* Klappe, *die;* **f)** *(Electr.)* Taste, *die;* **g)** *(Mus.)* Tonart, *die; (fig.: of speech or writing)* Ton, *der;* Tonart, *die;* **sing/play in/off ~:** richtig/falsch singen/spielen; **h)** *(Bot.)* Flügelfrucht, *die;* **i)** *(for grasping screws etc.)* [Schrauben]schlüssel, *der; (for winding a clock etc.)* Schlüssel, *der. See also* **house 1 c. 2.** *attrib. adj.* entscheidend; Schlüssel⟨*frage, -position, -rolle, -figur, -industrie*⟩. **3.** *v. t. (Computing)* eintasten

~ up a) *(stimulate)* **~ sb. up to sth./to a state of excitement** jmdn. zu etw. hinreißen/in einen Zustand der Erregung versetzen; **the crowd was ~ed up for the match** die Menge war auf das Spiel eingestimmt; **b)** *(make extremely tense)* **be all ~ed up** ganz aufgeregt sein; **he was all ~ed up for the great event** er fieberte dem großen Ereignis entgegen

[2]**key** *n. (Geog.)* [Korallen]insel, *die*

key: ~bar *n.* Typenhebel, *der;* **~board 1.** *n. (of piano etc.)* Klaviatur, *die; (of typewriter etc.)* Tastatur, *die;* **~board instrument** Tasteninstrument, *das;* **2.** *v. t.* tasten; **~boarder, ~board operator** *ns.* Taster, *der*/Tasterin, *die;* **~hole** *n.* Schlüsselloch, *das;* **~note** *n.* **a)** *(Mus.)* Grundton, *der;* **b)** *(fig.)* Grundgedanke, *der;* [Grund]tenor, *der; attrib.* **~note speech** programmatische Rede; **~-pad** *n.* Tastenfeld, *das;* **~punch operator** *n.* Locher, *der*/Locherin, *die;* **~ring** *n.* Schlüsselring, *der;* **~ signature** *n. (Mus.)* Tonartvorzeichnung, *die;* **~stone** *n. (Archit.)* Schlußstein, *der; (fig.)* Grundpfeiler, *der;* **~stroke** *n. (Computing)* Anschlag, *der;* **~word** *n.* **a)** *(key to cipher)* Schlüsselwort, *das;* **b)** *(significant word in indexing)* Stichwort, *das;* Schlüsselwort, *das (bes. DV)*

KG *abbr. (Brit.)* **Knight [of the Order] of the Garter**

kg. *abbr.* **kilogram[s]** kg

khaki ['kɑ:kɪ] **1.** *adj.* khakifarben; **~ colour/cloth** Khaki, *das*/Khaki, *der.* **2.** *n. (cloth)* Khaki, *der;* **~-coloured** khakifarben

kHz *abbr.* **kilohertz** kHz

kibbutz [kɪ'bʊts] *n., pl.* **kibbutzim** [kɪbʊt'si:m] Kibbuz, *der*

kibitzer ['kɪbɪtsə(r), kɪ'bɪtsə(r)] *n. (coll.)* Kiebitz, *der (ugs.); (meddlesome person)* wichtigtuerischer Besserwisser

kibosh ['kaɪbɒʃ] *n. (sl.)* **put the ~ on sth.** etw. vermasseln *(salopp);* **that's put the ~ on his hopes, hasn't it?** damit sind seine Hoffnungen wohl im Eimer, was? *(salopp)*

kick [kɪk] **1.** *n.* **a)** [Fuß]tritt, *der; (Footb.)* Schuß, *der;* **give sb. a ~:** jmdm. einen Tritt geben *od.* versetzen; **give a ~ at sth., give sth. a ~:** gegen etw. treten; **give sb. a ~ in the pants** *(fig. coll.)* jmdm. Feuer unterm Hintern machen *(salopp);* **a ~ in the teeth** *(fig.)* ein Schlag ins Gesicht; **give sb. a ~ in the teeth** *(fig. coll.)* jmdn. vor den Kopf stoßen; **b)** *(Sport: burst of speed)* Spurt, *der;* **c)** *(coll.: sharp effect, thrill)* Kitzel, *der; (of wine)* Feuer, *das;* **give sb. a ~:** jmdm. Spaß machen; **this beer has plenty of ~ in it** dieses Bier hat es in sich *(Dat.);* **he gets a ~ out of it** er hat Spaß daran; es macht ihm Spaß; **do sth. for ~s** etw. zum Spaß tun; **d)** *(coll.: temporary interest)* Fimmel, *der (ugs. abwertend);* Tick, *der (ugs.);* **be on a** *or* **the fitness ~:** auf einem *od.* dem Fitneßtrip sein *(ugs.);* **e)** *(recoil of gun)* Rückstoß, *der.* **2.** *v. i.* **a)** treten; ⟨*Pferd:*⟩ ausschlagen; ⟨*Baby:*⟩ strampeln; ⟨*Tänzer:*⟩ das Bein hochwerfen; **~ at sth.** gegen etw. treten; **you have to ~ with your legs when doing the crawl** beim Kraulen mußt du mit den Beinen schlagen; **~ing and screaming** *(fig.)* in heftigem *od.* wildem Protest; **b)** *(show opposition)* sich zur Wehr setzen **(at, against** gegen). *See also* **alive d; prick 3 e;** [2]**trace. 3.** *v. t.* **a)** einen Tritt geben (+ *Dat.*) ⟨*Person, Hund*⟩; treten gegen ⟨*Gegenstand*⟩; kicken *(ugs.),* schlagen, schießen ⟨*Ball*⟩; **~ the door open/shut** die Tür auf-/zutreten; **he ~ed the ball straight at me** er kickte den Ball genau in meine Richtung; **~ sb. in the teeth** *(fig. coll.)* jmdn. vor den Kopf stoßen; **~ sb. upstairs** *(fig. coll.) jmdm. eine nach außen bessere Position geben, aber seinen Einflußbereich einschränken;* ≈ jmdn. fortloben; **~ a goal** ein Tor schießen; **I could ~ myself!** *(coll.)* ich könnte mir *od.* mich in den Hintern beißen *(salopp);* **b)** *(sl.: abandon)* ablegen ⟨*schlechte Angewohnheit*⟩; aufgeben ⟨*Rauchen*⟩; **~ the habit** es aufstecken *(ugs.). See also* **bucket 1 a;** [1]**heel 1 a**

~ a'bout, ~ a'round 1. *v. t.* **a)** [in der Gegend] herumkicken *(ugs.);* **b)** *(treat badly)* herumstoßen; schikanieren; **c)** *(coll.: discuss unsystematically)* bekakeln *(ugs.);* bequatschen *(salopp).* **2.** *v. i.* **a)** *(coll.: wander about)* rumziehen *(ugs.);* **b) be ~ing about** *or* **around** *(coll.: be present, alive)* rumhängen *(ugs.);* **old Thompson is still ~ing around** *(is still alive)* der alte Thompson macht's immer noch *(ugs.);* **c) be ~ing about** *or* **around** *(coll.: lie scattered)* rumliegen *(ugs.),* rumfliegen *(salopp);* **is there a sandwich ~ing around?** gibt's hier irgendwo 'n Sandwich? *(ugs.)*

~ 'back 1. *v. i.* **a)** *(~ in retaliation)* zurücktreten; *(fig.)* zurückschlagen; **b)** *(recoil)* ⟨*Gewehr:*⟩ zurückschlagen. **2.** *v. t.* **a)** zurückschlagen ⟨*Ball*⟩; mit dem Fuß zurückschlagen ⟨*Bettdecke*⟩; **b)** *(~ in retaliation)* wiedertreten. *See also* **kickback**

~ 'in *v. t. (break, damage)* eintreten

~ 'off 1. *v. t.* von sich schleudern ⟨*Kleidungsstück, Schuhe*⟩. **2.** *v. i. (Footb.)* anstoßen; ⟨*Spiel:*⟩ beginnen; *(fig. coll.: start)* anfangen; *see also* **kick-off**

~ 'out *v. t. (force to leave)* hinauswerfen; rausschmeißen *(ugs.);* **get ~ed out** rausfliegen *(ugs.);* **get ~ed out of one's job** [aus der Stellung] fliegen *(ugs.)*

~ 'up *v. t.* **a)** *(raise by ~ing)* [mit den Füßen] aufwirbeln ⟨*Sand, Staub*⟩; ⟨*Autoreifen:*⟩ hochschleudern ⟨*Steine*⟩; mit dem Fuß umschlagen ⟨*Teppich*⟩; **b)** *(coll.: create)* vom Zaun brechen ⟨*Streit*⟩; **~ up a shindy/stink** Radau machen *(ugs.)*/Stunk machen od. anfangen *(ugs.)*

kick: ~back *n. (coll.: bribe)* Prozente *(fig.*

*ugs.); ~-***down** *n. (Motor Veh.)* Kickdown, *der;* ~-**off** *n.* **a)** *(Footb.)* Anstoß, *der; (fig.: start)* Beginn, *der;* **for a ~-off** *(coll.)* zunächst einmal; **b)** *(inaugural event)* Eröffnung, *die;* ~-**start[er]** *n. (Motor Veh.)* Kickstarter, *der;* ~-**turn** *n. (Skiing)* Spitzkehre, *die*

kid [kɪd] **1.** *n.* **a)** *(young goat)* Kitz, *das;* Zickel, *das;* **b)** *(leather)* Ziegenleder, *das; attrib.* Ziegenleder-; **c)** *(coll.: child)* Kind, *das; (Amer. coll.: young person)* Jugendliche, *der/die;* Kid, *das (ugs.);* **these ~s are driving me mad today** diese Bälger machen mich heute verrückt *(ugs.);* **you're still only a ~:** du bist noch zu jung [dazu]; **OK, ~s, let's go** *(Amer.)* also gut, Leute, gehen wir *(ugs.);* **college ~** *(Amer.)* Student, *der*/Studentin, *die;* **what a great ~ she is!** *(Amer.)* sie ist wirklich schwer in Ordnung *(ugs.);* **it's ~[s'] stuff** *(sl.: easy)* das ist ein Kinderspiel; **I'm too old for that ~s' stuff** ich bin zu alt für diese Kindereien; **~ brother/sister** *(sl.)* kleiner Bruder/kleine Schwester; Brüderchen, *das*/Schwesterchen, *das.* **2.** *v. t.,* **-dd-** *(coll.) (hoax)* anführen *(ugs.);* auf den Arm nehmen *(ugs.); (deceive)* was vormachen (+ *Dat.*) *(ugs.); (tease)* aufziehen *(ugs.);* **I ~ you 'not** ehrlich!; **~ oneself** sich *(Dat.)* was vormachen *(ugs.).* **3.** *v. i.,* **-dd-** *(coll.)* **be ~ding** Spaß machen *(ugs.);* **you've got to be ~ding!** das ist doch nicht dein Ernst!; **no ~ding** [ganz] im Ernst *od.* ohne Scherz

kiddie ['kɪdɪ] *(coll.)* Kindchen, *das;* **all right ~s, off to bed with you** okay, Kinder, ab ins Bett *(ugs.);* **I wish had some ~s of my own** ich wünschte, ich hätte selbst kleine Kinder

kid 'glove *n.* Glacéhandschuh, *der;* **handle** *or* **treat sb. with ~s** *(fig.)* jmdn. mit Samt- *od.* Glacéhandschuhen anfassen *(ugs.)*

kid-'glove *adj.* sanft; behutsam; **give sb. the ~ treatment** jmdn. mit Samt- *od.* Glacéhandschuhen anfassen *(ugs.)*

kidnap ['kɪdnæp] *v. t., (Brit.)* **-pp-** entführen ‹*Person*›; stehlen ‹*Tier*›; *(to obtain ransom)* kidnappen; entführen

kidnapper ['kɪdnæpə(r)] *n.* Entführer, *der*/Entführerin, *die;* Kidnapper, *der*/Kidnapperin, *die*

kidney ['kɪdnɪ] *n.* **a)** *(Anat., Gastr.)* Niere, *die;* **steak and ~ pie/pudding** *see* **steak; b)** *(fig.: temperament)* [Menschen]schlag, *der;* **of the same/right** *etc.* **~:** vom gleichen/richtigen *usw.* Schlag

kidney: ~ bean *n.* Gartenbohne, *die; (scarlet runner bean)* Feuerbohne, *die;* **red ~ bean** Kidneybohne, *die;* **~ dish** *n.* Nierenschale, *die;* **~ machine** *n.* künstliche Niere; Dialysegerät, *das;* **~-shaped** *adj.* nierenförmig; **~ table** *n.* Nierentisch, *der;* **~-vetch** *n.* Gemeiner Wundklee; gelber Klee

Kiel Canal [ki:l kə'næl] *pr. n.* Nord-Ostsee-Kanal, *der*

Kilkenny cat [kɪlkenɪ 'kæt] *n.* **fight like ~s** wie zwei Wildkatzen kämpfen; *(fig.)* sich bis zum letzten Blutstropfen bekämpfen

kill [kɪl] **1.** *v. t.* **a)** töten; *(deliberately)* umbringen; ‹*Rauchen usw.:*› tödliche Folgen haben für; sterben lassen ‹*Romanfigur usw.*›; **be ~ed in action/war** im Kampf/Krieg fallen; **shoot to ~:** gezielt schießen; **too much drink can ~ you** zuviel Alkohol kann tödlich sein; **~ or cure sb./sth.** jmdn./etw. entweder umbringen oder wieder auf die Beine bringen; **be ~ed in a car crash** bei einem Autounfall umkommen *od.* ums Leben kommen; **grief/the shock almost ~ed her** sie wäre vor Gram/Schreck fast gestorben; **it won't ~ you** *(iron.)* es wird dich [schon] nicht *od.* nicht gleich umbringen; **that last stretch [nearly] ~ed me!** das letzte Stück hat mich fast umgebracht; **~ oneself** sich umbringen; **I'm ~ing myself with this work** ich arbeite mich [dabei] zu Tode; **~ oneself laughing** *(fig.)* sich totlachen; **b)** *(coll.: cause severe pain to)* **it is ~ing me** das bringt mich noch um; **c)** abtöten ‹*Krankheitserreger, Schmerz, Ungeziefer, Hefe*›; erfolgreich bekämpfen ‹*Krankheit*›; absterben lassen ‹*Bäume, Pflanzen*›; totschlagen ‹*Geschmack, Farbe*›; verderben ‹*Witz*›; *(put an end to)* [ab]töten ‹*Gefühl*›; zerstören ‹*Glauben*›; **~ sb.'s ambition** jmdn. resignieren lassen; jmds. Ehrgeiz erkalten lassen *(geh.);* **d) ~ time** sich *(Dat.)* die Zeit vertreiben; die Zeit totschlagen *(abwertend);* **I've got such a lot of time to ~ at the moment** ich habe zur Zeit soviel Leerlauf; **~ an hour** sich *(Dat.)* eine Stunde lang die Zeit vertreiben; **e)** *(obtain meat from)* schlachten ‹*Tier*›; **~ meat** schlachten; **f)** *(overwhelm)* überwältigen; **dress to ~:** sich herausputzen; **g)** *(switch off)* ausschalten; *(extinguish)* ausdrücken, *(ugs.)* töten ‹*Zigarette*›; **h)** *(coll.) (eat)* verdrücken *(ugs.); (drink)* leer machen ‹*Flasche*›; **i)** *(Footb.)* stoppen ‹*Ball*›; *(Tennis)* unretournierbar schlagen ‹*Ball*›; **j)** *(defeat, veto)* zu Fall bringen; abschmettern *(ugs.). See also* **bird a. 2.** *n.* **a)** *(~ing of game)* Abschuß, *der; (prey)* Beute, *die;* **the tiger has made a ~/is on the ~:** der Tiger hat eine Beute geschlagen/ist auf der Jagd; **move in for the ~** ‹*Raubtier:*› die Beute anschleichen, zum Sprung auf die Beute ansetzen; *(fig.)* zum entscheidenden Schlag ausholen; **be in at the ~ = be in at the death** *see* **death a; b)** *(Hunting: amount)* Strecke, *die (Jägerspr.);* **c)** *(destruction) (of aircraft)* Abschuß, *der; (of ship)* Versenkung, *die*

~ 'off *v. t.* vernichten ‹*Feinde, Konkurrenz*›; ausrotten ‹*Tierart*›; abschlachten ‹*Vieh*›; sterben lassen ‹*Romanfigur usw.*›; vertilgen ‹*Ungeziefer, Unkraut*›; scheitern lassen ‹*Projekt*›; ‹*Frost:*› eingehen lassen ‹*Pflanze*›

killer ['kɪlə(r)] *n.* Mörder, *der*/Mörderin, *die; (murderous ruffian)* Killer, *der (salopp);* **be a ~** ‹*Krankheit:*› tödlich sein; *attrib.* **the ~ instinct** der Instinkt zum Töten; der Killerinstinkt *(Sportjargon); see also* **humane killer**

'killer whale *n.* Mörderwal, *der*

killing ['kɪlɪŋ] **1.** *n.* **a)** Töten, *das;* Tötung, *die;* **the ~ of the three children** der Mord an den drei Kindern; **b)** *(fig. coll.: great success)* Coup, *der (ugs.);* **make a ~** *(make a great profit)* einen [Mords]reibach machen *(ugs.).* **2.** *adj.* **a)** tödlich; **b)** *(coll.: exhausting)* mörderisch *(ugs.);* **c)** *(coll.: attractive, amusing, etc.)* umwerfend

killingly ['kɪlɪŋlɪ] *adv.* **~ funny** zum Totlachen [komisch] *(ugs.)*

'killjoy *n.* Spielverderber, *der*/-verderberin, *die*

kiln [kɪln] *n. (for burning/drying)* [Brenn-/Trocken]ofen, *der; (hop-~)* Darre, *die*

'kiln-dry *v. t.* [im Ofen] brennen ‹*Keramik*›; darren ‹*Hopfen, Getreide usw.*›

kilo ['ki:ləʊ] *n., pl.* **~s** Kilo, *das*

kilo- ['kɪlə] *pref.* kilo-/Kilo-

'kilobyte *n. (Computing)* Kilobyte, *das*

'kilocycle *n. (frequency unit)* Kilohertz, *das*

'kilogram, 'kilogramme *n.* Kilogramm, *das*

'kilohertz *n. (Phys.)* Kilohertz, *das*

kilometre *(Brit.; Amer.:* **kilometer**) ['kɪləmi:tə(r) *(Brit.),* kɪ'lɒmɪtə(r)] *n.* Kilometer, *der*

'kilowatt *n. (Electr., Phys.)* Kilowatt, *das*

'kilowatt-hour *n. (Electr., Phys.)* Kilowattstunde, *die*

kilt [kɪlt] *n.* **a)** *(Scot.)* Kilt, *der;* **b)** *(women's garment)* Schottenrock, *der;* Kiltrock, *der*

kilted ['kɪltɪd] *adj.* kiltbekleidet; kilttragend; **be ~:** einen Kilt tragen

kilter ['kɪltə(r)] *n. (Amer.)* **be out of ~** *(out of order)* nicht in Ordnung sein; *(out of alignment)* schief sein

kimono [kɪ'məʊnəʊ] *n., pl.* **~s** Kimono, *der*

kin [kɪn] **1.** *n. (ancestral stock)* Geschlecht, *das; (relatives)* Verwandte; *(relation)* Verwandte, *der/die; see also* **kith; next 3c. 2.** *pred. adj.* verwandt (to mit)

[1]**kind** [kaɪnd] *n.* **a)** *(class, sort)* Art, *die;* **several ~s of apples** mehrere Sorten Äpfel; **all ~s of things/excuses** alles mögliche/alle möglichen Ausreden; **all ~s of people enjoy that programme** das Programm gefällt den verschiedensten Leuten; **no ... of any ~** keinerlei ...; **good of its ~:** auf seine Art ganz gut; **books of every ~:** Bücher aller Art; **be [of] the same ~:** von derselben Sorte *od.* Art sein; **I know [you and] your ~:** deine Sorte kenne ich; **people/things of this ~:** diese Art Leute/solche Dinge; **she's not the ~ [of person] to talk scandal** es ist nicht ihre Art, zu tratschen; **something/nothing of the ~:** so etwas Ähnliches/nichts dergleichen; **you'll do nothing of the ~!** das kommt gar nicht in Frage!; **two of a ~:** zwei gleiche; **they differ** *or* **are different in ~:** sie unterscheiden sich wesentlich; **I suppose it was art of a ~** *(derog.)* das sollte wohl Kunst sein; **Was there any entertainment? – Well, of a ~** *(derog.)* Gab es irgendwelche Unterhaltung? – Na ja, es sollte wohl so was sein; **what ~ is it?** was für einer/eine/eins ist es?; **what ~ of [a] tree is this?** was für ein Baum ist das?; **what ~ of people are they?** was für Leute sind sie?; **what ~ of thing are you going to wear?** was ziehst du an?; **what ~ of [a] fool do you take me for?** für wie dumm hältst du mich?; **what ~ of [a] person do you think I am?** für wen hältst du mich?; **the ~ of person we need** der Typ, den wir brauchen; **this is exactly the ~ of house we're looking for** genau so ein Haus suchen wir; **they are the ~ of people who ...:** sie gehören zu der Sorte von Leuten, die ...; das sind solche Leute, die ...; **this ~ of food/atmosphere** diese Art *od.* solches Essen/solch *od.* so eine Stimmung; **these ~ of people/things** *(coll.)* solche Leute/Sachen; **b)** *(implying vagueness)* **a ~ of ...:** [so] eine Art ...; **~ of interesting/cute** *etc. (coll.)* irgendwie interessant/niedlich *usw. (ugs.);* **c)** *(race)* **the human ~:** die Menschheit; das Menschengeschlecht; **one's own ~:** seinesgleichen; **d) in ~** *(not in money)* in Sachwerten; **pay in ~:** in Naturalien zahlen/bezahlen; **benefits in ~:** Sachbezüge *Pl.;* **pay back** *or* **repay sth. in ~** *(fig.)* etw. mit *od.* in gleicher Münze zurückzahlen

[2]**kind** *adj. (of gentle nature)* liebenswürdig; *(showing friendliness)* freundlich; *(affectionate)* lieb; **if the weather is ~:** bei schönem Wetter; **have a ~ heart** gutherzig sein; **would you be so ~ as to** *or* **~ enough to do that?** wären Sie so freundlich *od.* nett, das zu tun?; **be ~ to animals/children** gut zu Tieren/Kindern sein; **oh, you 'are ~!, that 'is ~ of you** sehr nett *od.* liebenswürdig von Ihnen; **how ~ !** wie nett [von ihm/ihr/Ihnen *usw.*]!

kinda ['kaɪndə] *(coll.)* = **kind of; I ~ like that** ich mag das irgendwie *od. (ugs.)* irgendwo; **that ~ thing** so was *(ugs.)*

kindergarten ['kɪndəgɑ:tn] *n.* Kindergarten, *der; (forming part of a school)* ≈ Vorklasse, *die*

kind-hearted [kaɪnd'hɑ:tɪd] *adj.* gutherzig; liebenswürdig ‹*Geste, Handlung*›

kindle ['kɪndl] **1.** *v. t.* **a)** *(light)* anzünden, *(geh.)* entzünden ‹*Holz, Feuer*›; entfachen *(geh.)* ‹*Flamme*›; *(fig.: inflame)* entzünden, entfachen *(geh.)* ‹*Zorn, Leidenschaft*›; wecken ‹*Interesse, Gefühl*›; **b)** *(make bright)* erglühen lassen *(geh.).* **2.** *v. i.* **a)** *(catch fire)* sich entzünden; *(fig.: become animated)* aufleben; *(fig.: flare up)* aufflammen; entbrennen *(geh.);* **b)** *(become bright)* ‹*Augen:*› aufflammen *(geh.)* (**with** vor + *Dat.*); ‹*Licht:*› aufscheinen *(geh.); (start to glow)* erglühen *(geh.)*

kindliness ['kaɪndlɪnɪs] *n., no pl.* Freund-

lichkeit, *die; (gentleness of nature)* Liebenswürdigkeit, *die*
kindling ['kɪndlɪŋ] *n., no pl., no indef. art. (for lighting fire)* Anmachholz, *das*
kindly ['kaɪndlɪ] **1.** *adv.* **a)** freundlich; nett; **..., she said ~:** ..., sagte sie freundlich; **b)** *in polite request etc.* freundlicherweise; **c) take sth. ~:** etw. gern annehmen; **take ~ to sth./sb.** sich mit etw./jmdm. schnell anfreunden; **he didn't take at all ~ to the suggestion** er konnte sich mit dem Vorschlag gar nicht recht anfreunden; **I wouldn't take ~ to anything like that** für dergleichen könnte ich mich kaum erwärmen; **d) thank sb. ~:** jmdm. herzlich danken; **thank you ~:** herzlichen Dank. **2.** *adj.* **a)** freundlich; nett; liebenswürdig; *(good-natured, kind-hearted)* gütig; wohlwollend; gut ‹*Herz, Tat*›; **b)** *(pleasant)* angenehm ‹*Wetter, Klima*›; *(favourable)* günstig; gut
kindness ['kaɪndnɪs] *n.* **a)** *no pl. (kind nature)* Freundlichkeit, *die;* Liebenswürdigkeit, *die;* **do sth. out of ~:** etw. aus Gefälligkeit tun; **out of the ~ of one's heart** aus reiner Freundlichkeit; **b)** *(kind act)* Gefälligkeit, *die;* **do sb. a ~:** jmdm. eine Gefälligkeit erweisen *od.* einen Gefallen tun
kindred ['kɪndrɪd] **1.** *n., no pl.* **a)** *(blood relationship)* Blutsverwandtschaft, *die;* **b)** *(one's relatives)* Verwandtschaft, *die;* Verwandte. **2.** *adj.* **a)** *(related by blood)* blutsverwandt; **b)** *(fig.) (connected)* verwandt; *(similar)* ähnlich
kindred 'spirit *n.* Gleichgesinnte, *der/die;* verwandte Seele *(geh.)*
kinetic [kɪ'netɪk, kaɪ'netɪk] *adj.* kinetisch
king [kɪŋ] *n.* **a)** König, *der;* **live like a ~:** leben wie ein Fürst; **a feast fit for a ~:** ein königliches Mahl; **[the First/Second Book of] K~s** *(Bibl.)* [das erste/zweite Buch der] Könige; **K~ of ~s** *(God)* König aller Könige; **K~ of the Castle** *ein Kinderspiel, bei dem man versucht, den Gegner von einem Hügel zu verdrängen;* **be the ~ of the castle** *(fig.)* das Sagen haben; **~ of beasts/birds** König der Tiere/Vögel; **b)** *(great merchant, player, etc.)* König, *der;* **oil ~:** Ölkönig, *der;* Ölmagnat, *der;* **c)** *(Chess, Cards)* König, *der; (Draughts)* Dame, *die;* **~'s bishop/knight/pawn/rook** Königsläufer/-springer/-bauer/-turm, *der;* **~ of hearts** Herzkönig, *der. See also* **bench h; colour 1 j; counsel 1 c; English 2 a; evidence 1 b; guide 1 e; highway a; messenger b; ransom 1; save 1 c; [1]scout 1 a; shilling**
king: ~ 'cobra *n.* Königskobra, *die;* **~-crab** *n.* **a)** Königskrabbe, *die;* **b)** *(Amer.: edible spider-crab)* Steinkrabbe, *die;* **~cup** *n. (Bot.)* **a)** *(buttercup)* Hahnenfuß, der; **b)** *(Brit.: marsh marigold)* Sumpfdotterblume, *die*
kingdom ['kɪŋdəm] *n.* **a)** Königreich, *das;* **the ~ of Naples** das Königreich Neapel; *see also* **United Kingdom; b)** *(reign of God, sphere of reign)* Reich, *das;* **the ~ of God** das Reich Gottes; **thy ~ come** dein Reich komme; **the ~ of heaven** das Himmelreich; **wait till ~ come** *(sl.)* bis in alle Ewigkeit warten *(ugs.);* **blast sb. to ~ come** *(sl.)* jmdn. umnieten *(salopp);* **c)** *(domain)* Welt, *die;* **the ~ of thought** das Reich der Gedanken; **d)** *(province of nature)* Reich, *das;* **animal/vegetable/mineral ~:** Tier-/Pflanzen-/Mineralreich, *das;* **~ of nature** Naturreich, *das*
king: ~fisher *n. (Ornith.)* Eisvogel, *der;* **K~ 'James['s] Bible** *or* **Version** *(Amer.)* = **Authorized Version;** *see* **authorize b**
kingly ['kɪŋlɪ] *adj.* königlich
king: ~maker *n.* Königsmacher, *der;* **~ 'penguin** *n.* Königspinguin, *der;* **~pin** *n. (lit., or fig.: essential person or thing)* Hauptstütze, *die; (most prominent person or organization)* Nummer eins; **he's the ~pin in the team** mit ihm steht und fällt die Mannschaft
kingship ['kɪŋʃɪp] *n.* **a)** *no pl., no art. (office of king)* Königsamt, *das;* **b)** *(rule of king)* Königtum, *das*
'king-size[d] *adj.* extragroß; King-size- ‹*Zigaretten*›
kink [kɪŋk] **1.** *n.* **a)** *(in pipe, wire, etc.)* Knick, *der; (in rope)* Kink, *der (Seemannsspr.); (in hair, wool)* Welle, *die;* **b)** *(fig.: mental peculiarity)* Tick, *der (ugs.);* Spleen, *der.* **2.** *v. i.* Knicke kriegen; ‹*Haar:*› sich wellen. **3.** *v. t.* knicken; Knicke machen in (+ *Akk.*); einen Kink machen in (+ *Akk.*) *(Seemannsspr.)*
kinkajou ['kɪŋkədʒu:] *n. (Zool.)* Kinkaju, *der;* Wickelbär, *der*
kinky ['kɪŋkɪ] *adj.* **a)** geknickt; wellig ‹*Haar*›; **b)** *(coll.: bizarre, perverted)* spleenig; *(sexually)* abartig
kinsfolk ['kɪnzfəʊk] *n. pl.* Verwandtschaft, *die;* Verwandte
kinship ['kɪnʃɪp] *n.* **a)** *(blood relationship)* Blutsverwandtschaft, *die;* **b)** *(similarity)* Ähnlichkeit, *die; (spiritual)* Verwandtschaft, *die*
kinsman ['kɪnzmən] *n., pl.* **kinsmen** ['kɪnzmən] Verwandte, *der*
kinswoman ['kɪnzwʊmn] *n.* Verwandte, *die*
kiosk ['ki:ɒsk] *n.* **a)** *(outdoor structure)* Kiosk, *der; (Brit.: indoor structure)* [Verkaufs]stand, *der;* **b)** *(public telephone booth)* [Telefon]zelle, *die*
kip [kɪp] *(Brit. sl.)* **1.** *n.* **a)** *(sleep)* Schlaf, *der;* **have a** *or* **get some ~:** eine Runde pennen *(salopp);* **b)** *(bed)* Falle, *die (salopp).* **2.** *v. i.*, **-pp-** pennen *(salopp);* **~ down** sich hinhauen *(salopp)*
kipper ['kɪpə(r)] **1.** *n.* Kipper, *der;* ≈ Bückling, *der.* **2.** *v. t.* räuchern ‹*Fisch*›; **~ed** Räucher‹*fisch, -lachs, -hering*›
kirk [kɜ:k] *n. (Brit.)* **a)** *(Scot., N. Engl.: church)* Kirche, *die;* **b) the K~ [of Scotland]** die Kirche von Schottland
kirsch[wasser] ['kɪəʃ(vʌsə(r))] *n.* Kirsch, *der;* Kirschwasser, *das*
kiss [kɪs] **1.** *n.* Kuß, *der;* **the ~ of death** *(apparently friendly act causing ruin)* ein Danaergeschenk; *(act putting an end to sth.)* der Todesstoß; **give sb./***(fig.)* **sth. the ~ of life** *(Brit.)* jmdn. von Mund zu Mund beatmen/versuchen, etw. wiederzubeleben; **by administering the ~ of life** durch Mund-zu-Mund-Beatmung; **the ~ of peace** der Friedenskuß; *see also* **[1]blow 2 b. 2.** *v. t.* küssen; **~ sb. good night/goodbye** jmdm. einen Gutenacht-/Abschiedskuß geben; **it hurts, mummy – ~ it better** *(child lang.)* es tut weh, Mami – puste mal; **~ sb.'s hand** jmdm. einen Handkuß geben. **3.** *v. i.* sich küssen; **~ and make up** sich mit einem Kuß versöhnen **~ a'way** *v. t.* wegküssen; **~ away sb.'s tears** jmdm. die Tränen wegküssen
kissable ['kɪsəbl] *adj.* **~ lips/mouth** Kußmund, *der*
kisser ['kɪsə(r)] *n. (sl.: mouth, face)* Fresse, *die (derb);* Schnauze, *die (derb)*
kissing ['kɪsɪŋ] **1.** *adj.* Kuß-. **2.** *n.* Küsserei, *die (ugs.);* Geküsse, *das (oft abwertend)*
kissogram ['kɪsəgræm] *n. Glückwunsch o. ä., der mit Küssen überbracht wird*
'kiss-proof *adj.* kußecht
kit [kɪt] **1.** *n.* **a)** *(personal equipment)* Sachen; **have you got all your ~ together?** hast du deine Siebensachen beisammen? *(ugs.);* **b)** *(Brit.: set of items)* Set, *das;* **construction/self-assembly ~:** Bausatz, *der;* **repair ~:** Reparatursatz, *der;* Reparaturset, *das; see also* **tool-kit; c)** *(Brit.: clothing etc.)* **sports ~:** Sportzeug, *das;* Sportsachen *Pl.;* **riding-/skiing-/shooting-~:** Reit-/Ski-/Jagdausrüstung, *die;* **d)** *(Brit. Mil.)* Ausrüstung, *die; (pack)* [Feld]gepäck, *das; (uniform)* Montur, *die.* **2.** *v. t.*, **-tt-** *(Brit.)* **~ out** *or* **up** *(equip)* ausrüsten; *(give clothes or uniforms to)* einkleiden
'kitbag *n. (knapsack)* Knappsack, *der (veralt.);* Tornister, *der; (travelling-bag)* Reisetasche, *die*
kitchen ['kɪtʃɪn] *n.* Küche, *die; attrib.* Küchen-; *see also* **soup-kitchen**
kitchenette [kɪtʃɪ'net] *n.* kleine Küche; Kitchenette, *die; (alcove)* Kochnische, *die*
kitchen: ~ 'garden *n.* Küchengarten, *der;* Nutzgarten, *der;* **~-maid** *n.* Küchenmädchen, *das;* Küchenhilfe, *die;* **~ police** *n. pl. (Amer. Mil.)* Küchendienst, *der;* **~ 'sink** *n.* [Küchen]ausguß, *der;* Spüle, *die;* **everything but the ~ sink** *(fig.)* der halbe Hausrat; *attrib. (Brit.)* ≈ neonaturalistisch ‹*Drama, Kunst usw.*›; **~ unit** *n.* Küchenelement, *das;* **~ units** Küchenmöbel; **~ utensil** *n.* Küchengerät, *das;* **~-ware** *n.* Küchengeräte
kite [kaɪt] *n.* **a)** *(toy)* Drachen, *der;* **b)** *(Ornith.)* habichtartiger Greifvogel; *(species)* Roter Milan; Gabelweihe, *die;* **c)** *(Brit. sl.: aeroplane)* Vogel, *der;* Kiste, *die (salopp). See also* **[2]fly 2 b**
kith [kɪθ] *n.* **~ and kin** Freunde und Verwandte
kitsch [kɪtʃ] *n.* Kitsch, *der;* **it's a piece of ~:** es ist Kitsch
kitschy ['kɪtʃɪ] *adj.* kitschig
kitten [kɪtn] *n.* **a)** [Katzen]junge, *das;* Kätzchen, *das;* **the cat has had ~s** die Katze hat Junge bekommen; **as weak as a ~:** schwach und matt; **be as nervous as a ~:** furchtbar ängstlich sein; *(be easily startled)* vor dem eigenen Schatten erschrecken; **b)** *(coll.)* **have ~s** *(be upset)* Zustände kriegen *(ugs.);* **be having ~s** *(be nervous)* am Rotieren sein *(ugs.)*
kittenish ['kɪtənɪʃ] *adj.* verspielt; kokett ‹*junges Mädchen*›
kittiwake ['kɪtɪweɪk] *n. (Ornith.)* Dreizehenmöwe, *die*
[1]kitty ['kɪtɪ] *n. (kitten)* Kätzchen, *das; (child lang.)* Miez[e], *die (fam.);* Miezekätzchen, *das (fam.);* **~, ~, ~!** Miez, Miez, Miez!
[2]kitty *n.* **a)** *(Cards)* [Spiel]kasse, *die;* **b)** *(joint fund)* Kasse, *die;* **raid the ~:** die Kasse plündern *(scherzh.)*
kiwi ['ki:wi:] *n.* **a)** *(Ornith.)* Kiwi, *der;* **b) K~** *(coll.: New Zealander)* Neuseeländer, *der/*Neuseeländerin, *die*
kiwi: ~ berry, ~ fruit *ns.* Kiwi[frucht], *die*
klaxon, (P) ['klæksn] *n.* Horn, *das*
Kleenex, (P) ['kli:neks] *n.* Papier[taschen]tuch, *das*
kleptomania [kleptə'meɪnɪə] *n., no pl. (Psych.)* Kleptomanie, *die*
km. *abbr.* **kilometre[s]** km
knack [næk] *n.* **a)** *(faculty)* Talent, *das;* **have a ~ for** *or* **of doing sth.** das Talent haben, etw. zu tun; **get the ~ [of doing sth.]** den Bogen rauskriegen[, wie man etw. macht] *(ugs.);* **there's a [real] ~ in doing sth.** es gehört schon [einiges] Geschick dazu, etw. zu tun; **have lost the ~:** es nicht mehr zustande bringen *od. (ugs.)* hinkriegen; **b)** *(habit)* **have a ~ of doing sth.** es [mit seltenem Talent] verstehen, etw. zu tun *(iron.)*
knacker ['nækə(r)] *n. (Brit.) (horse-slaughterer)* Abdecker, *der;* **~'s yard** Abdeckerei, *die*
knackered ['nækəd] *adj. (Brit. sl.)* geschlaucht *(ugs.)*
knapsack ['næpsæk] *n.* Rucksack, *der; (Mil.)* Tornister, *der*
knave [neɪv] *n.* **a)** *(rogue)* Schurke, *der;* **b)** *(Cards) see* **jack 1 a**
knavery ['neɪvərɪ] *n.* Schurkerei, *die*
knavish ['neɪvɪʃ] *adj.* schurkisch
knead [ni:d] *v. t.* **a)** kneten; **~ sth. with sth.** etw. mit etw. verkneten; **~ together** miteinander verkneten; **b)** *(manipulate)* kneten ‹*Muskeln*›
knee [ni:] *n.* **a)** Knie, *das;* **the ~s of his trousers were torn** seine Hose war an den Knien zerrissen; **bend** *or* **bow the ~:** das

Knie beugen (to vor + *Dat.*); *(fig.: behave humbly)* sich beugen (**to** *Dat.*); **on one's ~s/on bended ~[s]** auf Knien; **be on one's ~s** knien; *(fig.: be defeated)* in die Knie gezwungen sein *(geh.)*; **bring** *or* **force sb. to his ~s** *(fig.)* jmdn. in die Knie zwingen *(geh.)*; **go down on one's ~s [to** *or* **before sb.]** [vor jmdm.] auf die Knie sinken *(geh.)*; **b)** *(of animal)* Kniegelenk, *das;* **c)** *(thigh)* **hold a child** *etc.* **on one's ~:** ein Kind *usw.* auf den Knien *od.* auf dem Schoß haben; **put a child** *etc.* **over one's ~:** ein Kind *usw.* übers Knie legen *(ugs.)*

knee: ~-breeches *n. pl.* Kniebundhose, *die;* **~cap** *n.* **a)** *(Anat.)* Kniescheibe, *die;* **b)** *(protective covering)* Knieschoner, *der;* **~capping** *n.* Knieschuß, *der;* **~-deep** *adj.* **a)** knietief; **b)** *(fig.: deeply involved)* **be ~-deep in sth.** bis über den Hals in etw. *(Dat.)* stecken *(ugs.)*; **~-high** *adj.* kniehoch; **be ~-high to a grasshopper** *(coll.)* ein Dreikäsehoch sein *(ugs. scherzh.)*; **~-jerk** *n.* Kniesehnenreflex, *der; attrib.* **~-jerk reaction** *(fig.)* automatische Reaktion; **~-joint** *n.* Kniegelenk, *das*

kneel [ni:l] *v. i.,* **knelt** [nelt] *or (esp. Amer.)* **~ed** knien; **~ down** niederknien; **~ [down] to do sth.** niederknien *od.* sich [hin]knien, um etw. zu tun; **~ to sb.** vor jmdm. [nieder]knien

'knee-length *adj.* knielang

kneeler ['ni:lə(r)] *see* **hassock a**

knees-up ['ni:zʌp] *n. (coll.)* Schwof, *der (ugs.)*

knell [nel] *n.* Glockengeläut, *das; (at funeral)* Totengeläut, *das;* **ring** *or* **sound the ~ of sth.** *(fig.)* das Ende einer Sache *(Gen.)* einläuten

knelt *see* **kneel**

knew *see* **know 1**

knickerbockers ['nɪkəbɒkəz] *n. pl.* Knickerbocker *Pl.*

knickers ['nikəz] **1.** *n. pl.* **a)** *(Brit.: undergarment)* [Damen]schlüpfer, *der;* **get one's ~ in a twist** *(Brit. fig. sl.)* sich aufregen; **b)** *(Amer.) see* **knickerbockers. 2.** *int. (Brit. sl.)* was soll's *(ugs.)*

knick-knack ['nɪknæk] *n.* **a)** *(dainty thing)* **~s** Schnickschnack, *der (ugs.)*; **b)** *(ornament)* Nippfigur, *die*

knife [naɪf] **1.** *n., pl.* **knives** [naɪvz] Messer, *das;* **put a ~ into sb.** jmdm. ein Messer zwischen die Rippen jagen; **like a ~ through butter** mühelos; **have got one's ~ into sb.** *(fig.)* einen Haß auf jmdn. haben *(ugs.)*; **you could [have] cut the atmosphere** *(fig.)*/**air with a ~** *(coll.)* die Atmosphäre war zum Zerreißen gespannt/die Luft war zum Schneiden; **before you can say ~** *(coll.)* ehe man sich's versieht; **turn** *or* **twist the ~ [in the wound]** *(fig.)* Salz in die Wunde streuen; **the knives are out [for sb.]** *(fig.)* das Messer wird [für jmdn.] gewetzt; *see also* **fork 1 a. 2.** *v. t. (stab)* einstechen auf (+ *Akk.*); *(kill)* erstechen; **~ sb. in the chest** jmdm. ein/das Messer in die Brust stoßen

knife: ~-edge *n.* Schneide, *die;* **be [balanced] on a ~-edge** *(fig.)* auf des Messers Schneide stehen; **~-grinder** *n.* Messerschleifer, *der;* **~-pleat** *n. (Dressm.)* Plisseefalte, *die;* **~-point** *see* **point 1 b**; **~ sharpener** *n.* Messerschärfer, *der; (steel)* Wetzstahl, *der;* **~-throwing** *n., no pl., no indef. art.* Messerwerfen, *das*

knifing ['naɪfɪŋ] *n.* **there were three ~s on one day** an einem Tag wurden drei Menschen niedergestochen

knight [naɪt] **1.** *n.* **a)** *Träger des Titels „Sir";* **b)** *(Hist.)* Ritter, *der;* **~ in shining armour** *(fig.)* Märchenprinz, *der;* **c)** *(Chess)* Springer, *der;* **d) ~ of the road** *(lorry-driver)* Kapitän der Landstraße *(ugs.)*. *See also* **bachelor c; Templar. 2.** *v. t.* adeln; zum Ritter schlagen *(hist.)*; in den Ritterstand erheben *(hist.)*

knight: ~ 'errant *n. (lit. or fig.)* fahrender Ritter; *(fig.)* Don Quichotte, *der;* **~-'errantry** [naɪt'erəntrɪ] *n., no pl.* ≈ höfisches Rittertum; *(fig.: quixotic behaviour)* Donquichotterie, *die*

knighthood ['naɪthʊd] *n.* **a)** *(rank)* Ritterwürde, *die;* **receive one's ~:** geadelt werden; in den Ritterstand erhoben werden *(hist.)*; **b)** *(Hist.: vocation)* Rittertum, *das;* **c)** *(Hist.: body of knights)* Ritterschaft, *die*

knightly ['naɪtlɪ] *adj.* ritterlich

knit [nɪt] **1.** *v. t.,* **-tt-, -ted** *or (esp. fig.)* **knit a)** stricken ⟨*Kleidungsstück usw.*⟩; **b) ~ a stitch** eine [rechte] Masche stricken; **~ 2, purl 2** zwei rechts, zwei links [stricken]; **c) ~ one's brow** die Stirn runzeln; **d)** *(make compact)* zusammenfügen (**into** zu); **closely** *or* **tightly ~** *(fig.)* festgefügt; hieb- und stichfest ⟨*Argument*⟩; *see also* **well-knit. 2.** *v. i.* sich verbinden; ⟨*Teile:*⟩ zusammenhalten; ⟨*Knochenbruch:*⟩ verheilen; ⟨*Knochen:*⟩ zusammenwachsen. **3.** *n. (garment)* Strickware, *die;* **this pattern is for a heavy ~:** dieses Muster eignet sich für Grobgestricktes

~ to'gether 1. *v. t.* zusammenhalten ⟨*Familie, Gemeinschaft*⟩. **2.** *v. i.* ⟨*Knochen:*⟩ zusammenwachsen; ⟨*Knochenbruch:*⟩ zusammenheilen

knitter ['nɪtə(r)] *n.* Stricker, *der*/Strickerin, *die*

knitting ['nɪtɪŋ] *n., no pl., no indef. art.* Stricken, *das; (work in process of being knitted)* Strickarbeit, *die;* **carry on with one's ~:** weiterstricken

knitting: ~-machine *n.* Strickmaschine, *die;* **~-needle** *n.* Stricknadel, *die;* **~-pattern** *n.* Strickmuster, *das*

'knitwear *n., no pl., no indef. art.* Strickwaren *Pl.*

knives *pl. of* **knife 1**

knob [nɒb] *n.* **a)** *(protuberance)* Verdickung, *die; (on club, tree-trunk, etc.)* Knoten, *der;* **b)** *(on door, walking-stick, etc.)* Knauf, *der; (control on radio etc.)* Knopf, *der;* **the same to you with [brass] ~s on!** *(coll.)* danke gleichfalls! *(iron.)*; **c)** *(of butter, sugar)* Klümpchen, *das; (of coal)* Brocken, *der*

knobbly ['nɒblɪ] *adj.* knotig ⟨*Finger, Stock*⟩; knorrig ⟨*Baum*⟩; **~ knees competition** Knubbelkniewettbewerb, *der*

knock [nɒk] **1.** *v. t.* **a)** *(strike) (lightly)* klopfen gegen *od.* an (+ *Akk.*); *(forcefully)* schlagen gegen *od.* an (+ *Akk.*); *see also* **wood b; b)** *(make by striking)* schlagen; **~ two rooms/houses into one** zwei Zimmer/Häuser zu einem umbauen; **~ a hole in sth.** ein Loch in etw. *(Akk.)* schlagen; **c)** *(drive by striking)* schlagen; **~ sb.'s brains out** jmdm. den Schädel einschlagen; **I'll ~ those ideas out of your head** *(fig.)* diese Flausen werde ich dir austreiben *(ugs.)*; **~ the handle off a cup** von einer Tasse den Henkel abschlagen; **I'd like to ~ their heads together** *(lit.)* ich könnte ihre Köpfe gegeneinanderschlagen; *(fig.: reprove them)* ich möchte ihnen mal gehörig die Leviten lesen; **~ sb. into the middle of next week** *(coll.)* jmdm. ein Ding verpassen, daß ihm Hören und Sehen vergeht *(ugs.)*; **~ for six** = **hit for six** *see* **hit 1 k**; *see also* **bottom 1 a; 'cock 2 c; spot 1 d; d) ~ sb. cold** jmdn. bewußtlos schlagen; *(fig.)* jmdn. am Boden zerstören; **~ sb. on the head** jmdm. eins über *od.* auf den Schädel geben; **~ sth. on the head** *(fig.: put an end to)* einer Sache *(Dat.)* ein Ende setzen; **e)** *(sl.: criticize)* herziehen über (+ *Akk.*) *(ugs.)*; **don't ~ it** halt dich zurück; **f)** *(Brit. sl.: astonish)* umhauen *(salopp)*. **2.** *v. i.* **a)** *(strike) (lightly)* klopfen; *(forcefully)* schlagen; *see also* **wood b; b)** *(seek admittance)* klopfen (**at** an + *Akk.*); **c)** *(Mech. Engin.)* klappern; **d)** *(Motor Veh.)* klopfen. **3.** *n.* **a)** *(rap)* Klopfen, *das;* **there was a ~ on** *or* **at the door** es klopfte an der Tür; **give sb. a ~:** bei jmdm. klopfen; **b)** *(blow)* Schlag, *der; (gentler)* Stoß, *der;* **have had a ~:** einen Schlag/Stoß abbekommen haben; **he got a bad ~ when he fell** er schlug beim Fallen hart auf; **~ for ~ agreement** *(Insurance)* gegenseitige Regreßverzichtserklärung; **c)** *(fig.: blow of misfortune)* [Schicksals]schlag, *der;* **take a [bad** *or* **hard] ~:** einen [schweren *od.* harten] Schlag erleiden; **d)** *(Mech. Engin.)* Klappern, *das;* **make a ~:** klappern; **e)** *(Motor Veh.: high-pitched explosive sound)* Klopfen, *das*

~ a'bout 1. *v. t.* **a)** schlagen; verprügeln; **be ~ed about** Schläge *od.* Prügel einstecken müssen; **the building has been ~ed about** das Haus ist ziemlich ramponiert worden; **b) ~ about the world** in der Welt herumkommen. **2.** *v. i.* herumhängen *(ugs.)*; ⟨*Gegenstand:*⟩ herumfliegen *(ugs.)*; **he's ~ed about a bit** er hat sich in der Welt umgetan; **~ about with sb.** sich mit jmdm. herumtreiben *(ugs.)*. *See also* **knockabout**

~ against *v. t.* stoßen gegen; **~ against each other** gegeneinanderstoßen; gegeneinanderprallen

~ a'round *see* **~ about**

~ 'back *v. t. (coll.)* **a)** *(eat quickly)* verputzen *(ugs.)*; *(drink quickly)* hinunterkippen *(ugs.)*; **b)** *(cost)* **~ sb. back a thousand** jmdn. um einen Tausender ärmer machen; **c)** *(disconcert)* einen Schlag versetzen (+ *Dat.*)

~ 'down *v. t.* **a)** *(strike to the ground)* niederreißen, umstürzen ⟨*Zaun, Hindernis*⟩; *(with fist or weapon)* niederschlagen; *(with car etc.)* umfahren; **b)** *(demolish)* abreißen; abbrechen; **c)** *(fig.: defeat)* bezwingen; **d)** *(sell by auction)* zuschlagen; **~ sth. down to sb.** jmdm. etw. zuschlagen; **e)** *(coll.: lower)* heruntersetzen *(ugs.)* ⟨*Preis*⟩; herunterdrücken *(ugs.)* ⟨*Kosten*⟩; **f)** *(Amer. sl.: steal)* mitgehen lassen *(ugs.)*; klauen *(salopp)*. *See also* **feather 1 a; knock-down**

~ 'off 1. *v. t.* **a)** *(leave off)* aufhören mit; **~ off painting** zu malen *od.* mit dem Malen aufhören; **~ off work** Feierabend machen; **~ it off!** *(coll.)* hör auf [damit]!; **b)** *(coll.) (produce rapidly)* aus dem Ärmel schütteln *(ugs.)*; *(dispatch rapidly)* schnell erledigen; **c)** *(deduct)* **~ five pounds off the price** es fünf Pfund billiger machen; **how much will you ~ off for me?** wieviel billiger kriege ich es denn?; **d)** *(sl.) (steal)* mitgehen lassen *(ugs.)*; klauen *(salopp)*; *(rob)* ausräumen ⟨*Bank, Laden, Kasse*⟩; **e)** *(sl.: copulate with)* bumsen *(salopp)*; **f)** *(sl.: kill)* umlegen *(salopp)*. **2.** *v. i.* Feierabend machen; **~ off for an hour/for lunch** eine Stunde aussetzen/Mittag machen

~ 'on *v. t. (Rugby)* **~ on a pass** bei der Annahme eines Passes ein Vorfallen verursachen; *see also* **knock-on 1**

~ 'out *v. t.* **a)** *(make unconscious)* bewußtlos umfallen lassen; **he collided with a lamppost and ~ed himself out** er stieß mit einem Laternenpfahl zusammen und fiel bewußtlos um; **b)** *(Boxing)* k.o. schlagen; kampfunfähig schlagen; **c)** *(fig.: defeat)* **be ~ed out [of the Cup]** [aus dem Pokal] ausscheiden *od. (ugs.)* rausfliegen; **they ~ed us out of the Cup** sie warfen uns aus dem Pokal; **d)** *(make useless)* außer Funktion setzen; **e)** *(sl.: astonish)* umhauen *(salopp)*; **be [completely** *or* **totally] ~ed out** [völlig] fertig sein *(ugs.)*; **f)** *(sl.: exhaust)* kaputtmachen *(ugs.)*; **g)** *(coll.: produce rapidly)* aus dem Ärmel schütteln; **h)** *(empty)* ausklopfen ⟨*Pfeife*⟩; **~ the ashes out** die Asche herausklopfen. *See also* **knock-out**

~ 'over *v. t.* umstoßen; ⟨*Fahrer, Fahrzeug:*⟩ umfahren ⟨*Person*⟩

~ to'gether 1. *v. t.* zusammenzimmern *(ugs.)* ⟨*Hütte, Tisch, Bühne*⟩; *see also* **knock 1 c. 2.** *v. i.* **my knees were ~ing together** mir schlotterten die Knie

~ 'up 1. *v. t.* **a)** *(make hastily)* zusammenzimmern *(ugs.)* ⟨*Hütte, Schrank*⟩; [her]zaubern

⟨Mahlzeit, Imbiß⟩; grob skizzieren ⟨Plan⟩; **b)** *(score)* erzielen; **c)** *(Brit.: awaken)* durch Klopfen wecken; *(unexpectedly)* herausklopfen; **d)** *(exhaust)* fertigmachen *(ugs.)*; **be ~ed up** fertig *od.* groggy sein *(ugs.)*; **e)** *(sl.: make pregnant)* dick machen *(derb)*. **2.** *v.i.* *(Sport)* sich warmspielen; *see also* **knock-up**

knock: ~about *adj.* **a)** *(boisterous)* Klamauk⟨*film, -stück, -szene*⟩; burlesk ⟨*Komödie, Komik*⟩; wild ⟨*Spiel*⟩; **b)** *(for rough use)* strapazierfähig; **~-down** *adj.* **a)** *(low)* **~-down cost/prices** minimale Kosten/ Schleuderpreise; **b)** *(minimum)* Mindest⟨*preis, -gebot*⟩; **c)** *(easily disassembled)* zerlegbar ⟨*Möbelstück, Boot*⟩; **d)** niederschmetternd ⟨*Schlag, Hieb*⟩; *(fig.: conclusive)* hieb- und stichfest, schlagend ⟨*Argument*⟩

knocker ['nɒkə(r)] *n.* **a)** *(on door)* [Tür]klopfer, *der;* **b)** *in pl. (coarse: breasts)* **[pair of] ~s** Vorbau, *der (salopp scherzh.)*; Titten *(derb)*; **c)** *(sl.: critic)* Beckmesser, *der*

'knocking-shop *n. (Brit. sl.)* Puff, *der od. das (salopp)*

knock: ~-kneed ['nɒkni:d] *adj.* X-beinig ⟨*Person usw.*⟩; kuhhessig ⟨*Pferd*⟩; **~ 'knees** *n. pl.* X-Beine *Pl.*; **~-on 1.** *n. (Rugby)* Vorfallen, *das;* **2.** *attrib. adj.* **~-on effect** mittelbare Auswirkung; **~-out 1.** *n.* **a)** *(blow)* Knockout[schlag], *der;* K.-o.[-Schlag], *der; (to armed forces)* vernichtender Schlag; **b)** *(competition)* Ausscheidungs[wett]kampf, *der;* **c)** *(sl.: outstanding person or thing)* **sb./sth. is a [real] ~-out** jmd./etw. ist eine Wucht *(salopp)*; **2.** *adj.* **a)** *(that stuns)* betäubend; *(that incapacitates)* vernichtend; **~-out blow** K.-o.-Schlag, *der;* **~-out drops** K.-o.-Tropfen *(ugs.)*; **b)** Ausscheidungs⟨*spiel, -[wett]kampf, -runde*⟩; **~-up** *n. (Sport)* Warmspielen, *das;* **have a ~-up** sich warmspielen

knoll [nəʊl] *n.* Anhöhe, *die*

knot [nɒt] **1.** *n.* **a)** Knoten, *der;* **the wool has got into a [complete] ~:** die Wolle hat sich völlig verheddert; **tie sb. [up] in ~s** *(fig. coll.)* jmdn. in Widersprüche verwickeln; **b)** *(ornament)* Schleife, *die; (cockade)* Kokarde, *die; (epaulette)* Schulterstück, *das;* **c)** *(problem)* Verwicklung, *die;* Haken, *der (ugs.)*; **d)** *(cluster)* Pulk, *der;* **e)** *(in wood)* Ast, *der;* **f)** *(speed unit)* Knoten, *der;* **make** *or* **log ten ~s** zehn Knoten machen *od.* fahren; **at a rate of ~s** *(coll.)* mit einem Affenzahn *(salopp)*; **g)** *(Naut.: unit of length)* Knotenlänge, *die;* **h)** *(in popular use: nautical mile)* Seemeile, *die;* **i)** *(bond)* Bund, *der;* **tie the ~** *(marry)* den Bund der Ehe eingehen *(geh.)*; den Bund fürs Leben schließen *(geh.)*; **j)** *(lump)* Knoten, *der;* Verdickung, *die.* **2.** *v.t.*, **-tt- a)** *(tie)* knoten ⟨*Seil, Faden usw.*⟩; knoten ⟨*Schnürsenkel*⟩; knoten, binden ⟨*Krawatte*⟩; **~ threads together** Fäden verknoten; **~ clothes into a bundle** Kleider zu einem Bündel zusammenknoten; **~ a rope** Knoten in ein Seil machen; **b)** *(entangle)* verfilzen; **c) get ~ted!** *(sl.)* rutsch mir den Buckel runter! *(ugs.)*; **d)** *see* **knit 1 c**; **e)** *(unite closely)* verknüpfen **(into** zu)

knot: ~-garden *n.* Boskettgarten, *der;* **~-hole** *n.* Astloch, *das*

knotty ['nɒtı] *adj.* **a)** *(full of knots)* ⟨*Seil, Peitsche*⟩ mit Knoten; knotig ⟨*Stock, Gewebe, Finger*⟩; ineinandergewachsen ⟨*Gestrüpp, Kriechpflanzen, Ausläufer*⟩; knorrig, astig ⟨*Holz, Baumstamm*⟩; **b)** *(fig.: puzzling)* verwickelt

know [nəʊ] **1.** *v.t.*, **knew** [nju:], **~n** [nəʊn] **a)** *(recognize)* erkennen **(by** an + *Dat.*, **for** als + *Akk.*); **b)** *(be able to distinguish)* **~ sth. from sth.** etw. von etw. unterscheiden können; **~ right from wrong, ~ the difference between right and wrong** den Unterschied zwischen Gut und Böse kennen; **he wouldn't ~ the difference** er wüßte den Unterschied nicht; *see also* **Adam; c)** *(be aware of)* wissen; kennen ⟨*Person*⟩; **I ~ who she is** ich weiß, wer sie ist; **I ~ for a fact that ...:** ich weiß ganz bestimmt, daß ...; **it is ~n that ...:** man weiß, daß ...; es ist bekannt, daß ...; **they knew they could never become rich** sie wußten [nur zu gut], daß sie niemals reich werden konnten; **~ sb./sth. to be ...:** wissen, daß jmd./etw. ... ist; **I ~ him to be an honest man** ich weiß, daß er ein ehrlicher Mensch ist; **that's/that might be worth ~ing** das ist gut/wäre wichtig zu wissen; **it's worth ~ing whether ...:** es ist wichtig zu wissen, ob ...; **he doesn't want to ~:** er will nichts davon wissen *od.* hören; **not if I ~ it** nicht mit mir; **I 'knew it** ich hab's ja geahnt; **'I ~ what** ich weiß was *(ugs.)*; **you ~** *(coll.) (as reminder)* weißt du [noch]; *(as conversational filler)* **they think we might be, you ~, glamorous or something** sie meinen, wir wären vielleicht, na ja, superschick oder so *(ugs.)*; **I went to see the doctor, you ~:** ich war beim Arzt, weißt du; **you ~ something** *or* **what?** weißt du was?; **you never ~:** man kann nie wissen *(ugs.)*; **sb. has [never] been ~n to do sth.** jmd. hat bekanntlich [noch nie] etw. getan; **for all** *or (arch.)* **aught I ~ they may be looking for us** ich könnte mir gut denken, daß sie uns suchen; **and I don't ~ what [all]** *(coll.)* und ich weiß nicht, was noch alles *(ugs.)*; **and he ~s it** und er weiß das auch; **don't I ~ it!** *(coll.)* das weiß ich nur zu gut; **I don't ~ that ...** *(coll.: don't believe)* ich glaube nicht, daß ...; **before sb. ~s where he is** ehe jmd. sich's versieht; **what do you ~ [about that]?** *(coll.: that is surprising)* was sagst du dazu?; **sb. is not to ~** *(is not to be told)* jmd. soll nichts wissen **(about, of** von); *(has no way of learning)* jmd. kann nicht wissen; **I was not to ~ until years later** ich sollte erst Jahre später davon erfahren; **not ~ what hit one** *(fig.)* gar nicht begreifen, was geschehen ist; **that's all 'you ~ [about it]** das glaubst du vielleicht; **I'll have you ~ that ...:** ich möchte Sie darauf hinweisen, daß ...; **if you 'must ~:** wenn du es unbedingt wissen willst; **~ different** *or* **otherwise** es besser wissen; **~ what's what** wissen, wie es in der Welt zugeht; **how should I ~?** woher soll ich das wissen?; **I might have ~n** das hätte ich mir denken können; **do you ~, ...:** stell dir [mal] vor, ...; *see also* **best 2; better 2 d; god b; heaven c; [1]let 1 b; lord 1 b; thing c; who a; you a; d)** *(have understanding of)* können ⟨*ABC, Einmaleins, Deutsch usw.*⟩; beherrschen ⟨*Grundlagen, Regeln, Grammatik*⟩; sich auskennen mit ⟨*Gerät, Verfahren, Gesetz*⟩; **they ~ their Latin well** sie haben gute Kenntnisse in Latein; **do you ~ any German?** können Sie etwas Deutsch?; **~ 'how** wissen, wie das geht; **~ how to mend fuses** wissen, wie man Sicherungen repariert; **~ how to drive a car** Auto fahren können; **~ how to write vividly** [es] verstehen, lebendig zu schreiben; **do all one ~s [how]** sein Bestes geben; *see also* **onion; rope 1 c; stuff 1 e; e)** *(be acquainted with)* kennen; **we have ~n each other for years** wir kennen uns [schon] seit Jahren; **surely you ~ me better than that** du müßtest mich eigentlich besser kennen; **you don't really ~ him** du kennst ihn nicht gut genug; **you ~ what he/it is** *(is like)* du kennst ihn ja/du weißt ja, wie es ist; **you ~ what it is to be an adolescent** du weißt ja, wie man als Jugendlicher ist; *see also* **get 2 c; sight 1 a; f)** *(have experience of)* erleben; erfahren; **he ~s no fear, he doesn't ~ what it is to be afraid** er kennt keine Furcht; **~ what it is to be hungry** wissen, was es heißt, Hunger zu haben. **2.** *n. (coll.)* **be in the ~:** Bescheid wissen; **those in the ~:** die Eingeweihten

~ about *v.t.* wissen über (+ *Akk.*); **oh, I didn't ~ about it/that** oh, das habe ich nicht gewußt; **did you ~ about your son's behaviour?** haben Sie gehört, wie sich Ihr Sohn benommen hat?; **not much is ~n about some of the tribes** über einige Stämme weiß man fast nichts; **I didn't ~ anything about any committee meeting** ich habe nichts von irgendeiner Ausschußsitzung gewußt; **I don't ~ about 'that** na, ich weiß nicht [so recht]; **I don't ~ about beautiful, but it certainly is old** schön – na, ich weiß nicht, auf jeden Fall ist es alt

~ of *v.t.* wissen von ⟨*Plänen, Vorhaben*⟩; kennen, wissen ⟨*Lokal, Geschäft*⟩; **~ of sb.** von jmdm. gehört haben; **~ of sb. who ...:** jmdn. wissen, der ...; **not that I ~ of** nicht, daß ich wüßte

knowable ['nəʊəbl] *adj.* [mit dem Verstand] erkennbar

know: ~-all *n. (derog.)* Neunmalkluge, *der/die (spöttisch)*; **~-how** *n., no pl., no indef. art.* praktisches Wissen; *(technical expertise)* Know-how, *das*

knowing ['nəʊıŋ] **1.** *adj.* **a)** *(shrewd)* verschmitzt ⟨*Blick, Lachen, Lächeln*⟩; ⟨*Person*⟩ mit wachem Verstand; *(indicating possession of inside information)* vielsagend, wissend ⟨*Blick, Lächeln*⟩; beredt *(iron.)* ⟨*Schweigen*⟩; **b)** *(derog.: cunning)* verschlagen *(abwertend)*. **2.** *n.* **there is no ~:** niemand weiß; es läßt sich nicht vorhersagen

knowingly ['nəʊıŋlı] *adv.* **a)** *(intentionally)* wissentlich ⟨*lügen, verletzen*⟩; bewußt ⟨*planen*⟩; **b)** *(in a shrewd manner)* verschmitzt ⟨*lachen, blicken*⟩; *(indicating possession of inside information)* vielsagend ⟨*lächeln, anblicken, zwinkern, nicken*⟩; **c)** *(derog.: cunningly)* verschlagen *(abwertend)*

'know-it-all *see* **know-all**

knowledge ['nɒlıdʒ] *n., no pl.* **a)** *(familiarity)* Kenntnisse **(of** in + *Dat.*); **a ~ of this field** Kenntnisse auf diesem Gebiet; **a little ~ is a dangerous thing** *(prov.)* Halbwissen ist gefährlich; **gain ~ of sb./sth.** Kenntnisse über jmdn./etw. gewinnen; **~ of human nature** Menschenkenntnis, *die; see also* **carnal knowledge; b)** *(awareness)* Wissen, *das;* **have no ~ of sth.** nichts von etw. wissen; keine Kenntnis von etw. haben *(geh.)*; **she had no ~ of it** sie wußte nichts davon; sie war völlig ahnungslos; **the ~ that it was really important** die Gewißheit, daß es wirklich wichtig war; **sth. came to my ~:** etw. ist mir zu Ohren gekommen; **[not] to my** *etc.* **~:** meines *usw.* Wissens [nicht]; **to my certain ~:** wie ich mit Bestimmtheit weiß; **without sb.'s ~:** ohne jmds. Wissen; **c)** *(understanding)* **[a] ~ of languages/French** Sprach-/Französischkenntnisse *Pl.*; **sb. with [a] ~ of computers** jmd., der sich mit Computern auskennt; **d)** *no art. (what is known)* Wissen, *das;* **in the present state of ~:** beim derzeitigen Wissensstand; **branch of ~:** Wissenszweig, *der*

knowledgeable ['nɒlıdʒəbl] *adj.* sachkundig; **be ~ about** *or* **on sth.** viel über etw. *(Akk.)* wissen

known [nəʊn] **1.** *see* **know. 2.** *adj.* bekannt; *(generally recognized)* anerkannt

knuckle ['nʌkl] *n.* **a)** *(Anat.)* [Finger]knöchel, *der;* **b)** *(joint of meat) (pork)* Eisbein, *das; (veal or pork)* Hachse, *die;* Haxe, *die (südd.)*; **c) near the ~** *(coll.)* hart an der Grenze [des guten Geschmacks]. *See also* **[1]rap 1 a, 2 a**

~ 'down *v.i. (apply oneself)* **~ down to sth.** sich hinter etw. *(Akk.)* klemmen *(ugs.)*

~ 'under *v.i.* klein beigeben **(to** gegenüber)

knuckle: ~-bone *n.* **a)** *(Anat.)* Fingerknochen, *der;* **b)** *(Zool.)* Knochen [mit Gelenkkopf]; **~duster** *n.* Schlagring, *der*

knurled [nɜ:ld] *adj.* geriffelt; kordiert *(Technik)*

KO *abbr.* **a) kick-off; b) knock-out** K. o.; **c) knocked out** k. o.

koala [kəʊ'ɑ:lə] *n.* **~ [bear]** *(Zool.)* Koala, *der;* Beutelbär, *der*

KO'd [keɪ'əʊd] *see* **KO c**
kohlrabi [kəʊl'rɑːbɪ] *n.* Kohlrabi, *der*
kook [kuːk] *(Amer. sl.)* **1.** *n.* Spinner, *der*/Spinnerin, *die (ugs. abwertend).* **2.** *adj. see* **kooky**
kookaburra ['kʊkəbʌrə] *n. (Austral. Ornith.)* Lachender Hans
kooky ['kuːkɪ] *adj. (Amer. sl.)* überkandidelt *(ugs.);* idiotisch *(ugs. abwertend)* ‹*Leben*›
Koran [kɔː'rɑːn, kə'rɑːn] *n. (Muslim Relig.)* Koran, *der*
Korea [kə'rɪə] *pr. n.* Korea *(das)*
Korean [kə'riːən] **1.** *adj.* koreanisch; **sb. is ~:** jmd. ist Koreaner/Koreanerin; *see also* **English 1. 2.** *n.* **a)** *(person)* Koreaner, *der*/Koreanerin, *die;* **b)** *(language)* Koreanisch, *das; see also* **English 2 a**
kosher ['kəʊʃə(r), 'kɒʃə(r)] **1.** *adj. (lit. or fig.)* koscher. **2.** *n., no pl., no art. (food)* Koschere, *das;* **eat ~:** koscher essen
kowtow [kaʊ'taʊ] (**kotow** [kəʊ'taʊ]) *v. i.* ~ **[to sb./sth.]** [vor jmdm./etw.] [s]einen Kotau machen
k.p.h. *abbr.* **kilometres per hour** km/h
kraal [krɑːl] *n.* Kral, *der*
Kraut [kraʊt] *n. & adj. (sl. derog.) angelsächsische abwertende Bez. für „Deutscher" und „deutsch"*
Kremlin ['kremlɪn] *n.* **the K~:** der Kreml
Kremlinology [kremlɪ'nɒlədʒɪ] *n., no pl., no indef. art.* Sowjetforschung, *die;* Kremlastrologie, *die (ugs.)*
krill [krɪl] *n., no pl., no indef. art. (Zool.)* Krill, *der*
kris [kriːs] *n.* Kris, *der*
krugerrand ['kruːgərɑːnt] *n.* Krügerrand, *der*
krypton ['krɪptɒn] *n. (Chem.)* Krypton, *das*
Kt. *abbr.* **knight**
kudos ['kjuːdɒs] *n., no pl., no indef. art. (coll.)* Prestige, *das*
kümmel ['kʊml] *n.* Kümmellikör, *der*
kung fu [kʊŋ'fuː, kʌŋ'fuː] *n.* Kung-Fu, *das*
Kurd [kɜːd] *n.* Kurde, *der*/Kurdin, *die*
Kurdish ['kɜːdɪʃ] **1.** *adj.* kurdisch. **2.** *n.* Kurdisch, *das*
kW *abbr.* **kilowatt[s]** kW
kWh *abbr.* **kilowatt-hour[s]** kWh

L

L, l [el] *n., pl.* **Ls** *or* **L's a)** *(letter)* L, l, *das;* **b)** *(Roman numeral)* L
L. *abbr.* **a) Lake; b) Liberal** Lib.; **c)** *lire* L.
£ *abbr.* **pound[s]** £; **cost £5** 5 £ *od.* Pfund kosten
l. *abbr.* **a) litre[s]** l; **b) left** l.; **c) line** Z.
LA *abbr.* **Los Angeles** L. A.
la *see* **lah**
lab [læb] *n. (coll.)* Labor, *das*
Lab. *abbr.* **Labour**
label ['leɪbl] **1.** *n.* **a)** *(slip)* Schildchen, *das; (on goods, bottles, jars, in clothes)* Etikett, *das; (tied/stuck to an object)* Anhänger/Aufkleber, *der;* **b)** *(on record)* Label, *das; (record company)* Plattenfirma, *die;* **record on a new ~:** die Plattenfirma *od. (Fachjargon)* das Label gewechselt haben; **c)** *(fig.: classifying phrase)* Etikett, *das;* **hang the ~ ... on sb.** jmdn. als ... etikettieren; **acquire/be given the ~ of ...:** als ... etikettiert werden. **2.** *v. t., (Brit.)* **-ll- a)** *(attach ~ to)* etikettieren; *(attach price-tag to)* auszeichnen ‹*Waren*›; *(write on)* beschriften; *(attach stamp or sticker to)* mit einem Aufkleber versehen; *(tie ~ to)* mit einem Anhänger versehen; **b)** *(fig.: classify)* **~ sb./sth. [as] sth.** jmdn./etw. als etw. etikettieren; **he doesn't like being ~led** er läßt sich nicht gern etikettieren
labial ['leɪbɪəl] **1.** *adj.* Lippen-; *(Anat., Zool., Phonet.)* labial; **~ consonant** *see* **2. 2.** *n. (Phonet.)* Labial, *der;* Lippenlaut, *der*
labia majora/minora [leɪbɪə mə'dʒɔːrə/ mɪ'nɔːrə] *n. pl. (Anat.)* äußere *od.* große/innere *od.* kleine Schamlippen
labor *(Amer.) see* **labour**
laboratory [lə'bɒrətərɪ] *n. (lit. or fig.)* Labor[atorium], *das;* **~ animal** Versuchstier, *das; see also* **language laboratory**
labored, laborer *(Amer.) see* **labour-**
laborious [lə'bɔːrɪəs] *adj.* **a)** mühsam; mühevoll ‹*Forschung, Aufgabe usw.*›; **b)** *(not fluent)* schwerfällig, umständlich ‹*Stil*›; schleppend ‹*Rede*›
laboriously [lə'bɔːrɪəslɪ] *adv.* **a)** *(with difficulty)* mühevoll; **~ slow** mühsam und schleppend; **b)** *(not fluently)* schwerfällig; schleppend ‹*vorangehen*›
laborite *(Amer.) see* **labourite**
'labor union *(Amer.) see* **trade union**
labour ['leɪbə(r)] *(Brit.)* **1.** *n.* **a)** *(task)* Arbeit, *die;* **sth. is/they did it as a ~ of love** etw. geschieht/sie taten es aus Liebe zur Sache; **~ of Hercules** Herkulesarbeit, *die;* **b)** *(exertion)* Mühe, *die;* **~ in vain, lost ~:** vergebliche *od.* verlorene Mühe; *see also* **hard labour; c)** *(work)* Arbeit, *die;* **cost of ~:** Arbeitskosten *Pl.;* **withdraw one's ~:** die Arbeit niederlegen; **d)** *(body of workers)* Arbeiterschaft, *die;* **immigrant ~:** eingewanderte Arbeitskräfte; **e) L~** *(Polit.)* die Labour Party; **f)** *(childbirth)* Wehen *Pl.;* **be in ~:** in den Wehen liegen; **go into ~:** die Wehen bekommen. *See also* **intensive 1 e. 2.** *v. i.* **a)** *(work hard)* hart arbeiten **(at, on** an + *Dat.*); *(slave away)* sich abmühen **(at, over** mit); **b)** *(strive)* sich einsetzen **(for** für); **~ to do sth.** sich bemühen, etw. zu tun; **c)** *(be troubled)* leiden; sich quälen; **~ under sth.** sich mit etw. quälen; **~ under a delusion** sich einer Täuschung *(Dat.)* hingeben; **d)** *(Naut.: pitch)* ‹*Schiff:*› stampfen *(Seemannsspr.);* **e)** *(advance with difficulty)* sich quälen *od.* kämpfen; *(run too slowly)* ‹*Motor:*› untertourig laufen; **~ up the stairs** sich die Treppe hinaufquälen. **3.** *v. t. (elaborate needlessly)* auswalzen *(ugs.);* **I don't want to ~ the point** ich möchte mich über diesen Punkt nicht weiter verbreiten; **I do hate the way he ~s every point** ich hasse es, wie er jeden Punkt auswalzt *(ugs.)*
labour: ~ camp *n.* Arbeitslager, *das;* **L~ Day** *n.* Tag der Arbeit *(in Amerika: erster Montag im September)*
laboured ['leɪbəd] *adj. (Brit.)* mühsam; schwerfällig ‹*Stil*›; mühsam zusammengetragen ‹*Argumente*›; **his breathing was ~:** er atmete schwer
labourer ['leɪbərə(r)] *n. (Brit.)* Arbeiter, *der*/Arbeiterin, *die; (assisting skilled worker)* Hilfsarbeiter, *der*/-arbeiterin, *die;* **bricklayer's ~:** Maurergehilfe, *der;* **builder's ~:** Bau[hilfs]arbeiter, *der*
labour: L~ Exchange *(Hist./coll.) see* **employment exchange; ~ force** *n.* Arbeitskräfte; **a considerable ~ force** eine beträchtliche Anzahl von Arbeitskräften
labourite ['leɪbəraɪt] *n. (Brit. Polit.)* Anhänger/Anhängerin der Labour Party; *(member)* Mitglied der Labour Party
labour: ~-market *n.* Arbeitsmarkt, *der;* **~ pains** *n. pl.* Wehenschmerzen; **L~ Party** *n. (Polit.)* Labour Party, *die;* **~ relations** *n. pl.* Beziehungen zwischen Arbeitgebern und Arbeitnehmern; *(within one company)* Betriebsklima, *das;* **~-saving** *adj.* arbeit[s]sparend ‹*Methode, Vorrichtung*›
Labrador ['læbrədɔː(r)] *n.* **~ [dog** *or* **retriever]** Labrador[hund], *der*
laburnum [lə'bɜːnəm] *n. (Bot.)* Goldregen, *der*
labyrinth ['læbərɪnθ] *n.* Labyrinth, *das*
labyrinthine [læbə'rɪnθaɪn] *adj.* **a)** labyrinthisch; labyrinthartig; **b)** *(complex)* verschachtelt
¹lac [læk] *n.* Stocklack, *der;* **~ insect** Lackschildlaus, *die*
²lac *see* **lakh**
lace [leɪs] **1.** *n.* **a)** *(for shoe)* Schuhband, *das (bes. südd.);* Schnürsenkel, *der (bes. nordd.);* **b)** *(fabric)* Spitze, *die; attrib.* Spitzen-; **c)** *(braid)* **gold/silver ~:** Gold-/Silberlitze, *die.* **2.** *v. t.* **a)** *(fasten)* **~ [up]** [zu]schnüren; **b)** *(interlace)* durchwirken *(geh.);* **c)** *(pass through)* [durch]ziehen; **d) ~ sth. with alcohol** einen Schuß Alkohol in etw. *(Akk.)* geben; **~d with brandy** mit einem Schuß Weinbrand; **~ sb.'s drink** einen Schuß Alkohol/eine Droge in jmds. Getränk *(Akk.)* geben
lacerate ['læsəreɪt] *v. t.* **a)** *(tear)* aufreißen; **her arm was badly ~d** sie hatte tiefe Wunden am Arm; **b)** *(fig.: afflict)* verletzen
laceration [læsə'reɪʃn] *n.* **a)** *no pl.* Verletzung, *die (durch Aufreißen);* **b)** *(wound)* Rißwunde, *die; (from glass)* Schnittwunde, *die*
lace: ~-up 1. *attrib. adj.* zum Schnüren *nachgestellt;* **~-up boot** Schnürstiefel, *der;* **2.** *n.* Schnürschuh/-stiefel, *der;* **~wing** *n. (Zool.)* Netzflügler, *der*
lachrymal ['lækrɪml] *adj. (Anat.)* Tränen-
lachrymose ['lækrɪməʊs] *adj.* weinerlich; tränenselig, rührselig ‹*Geschichte, Theaterstück, Abschied*›
lacing ['leɪsɪŋ] *n.* **a)** Schnur, *die; (on shoes)* Schuhband, *das (bes. südd.);* Schnürsenkel, *der (bes. nordd.); (of corset)* Schnüre *Pl.;* **b)** *(quantity of spirits)* Schuß, *der;* **coffee with a ~ of whisky** Kaffee mit einem Schuß Whisky
lack [læk] **1.** *n.* Mangel, *der* **(of** an + *Dat.*); **his ~ of enemies makes his task easier** daß er keine Feinde hat, macht seine Aufgabe leichter; **her ~ of aggression makes her easy to live with** da ihr jegliche Aggressivität abgeht, kann man gut mit ihr zusammenleben; **~ of self-consciousness** Unbefangenheit, *die;* **~ of obedience** mangelnder Gehorsam; **~ of work** Arbeitsmangel, *der;* **there is no ~ of it [for them]** es fehlt [ihnen] nicht daran; **he has no ~ of confidence** an Vertrauen mangelt *od.* fehlt es ihm nicht; **for ~ of sth.** aus Mangel an etw. *(Dat.);* **for ~ of time** aus Zeitmangel. **2.** *v. t.* **sb./sth. ~s sth.** jmdm./einer Sache fehlt es an etw. *(Dat.);* **sb. ~s the creativity/ability to do sth.** jmdm. fehlt die Kreativität/Fähigkeit, etw. zu tun; **what he ~s is ...:** woran es ihm fehlt, ist ...; **his life ~ed something** seinem Leben fehlte etwas; **~ content** inhaltsarm sein. **3.** *v. i.* **sb. ~s for sth.** *(formal)* jmdm. fehlt es an etw. *(Dat.); see also* **lacking**
lackadaisical [lækə'deɪzɪkl] *adj. (unenthusiastic)* gleichgültig; desinteressiert; *(listless)* lustlos
lackadaisically [lækə'deɪzɪkəlɪ] *adv. see* **lackadaisical:** gleichgültig; desinteressiert; lustlos
lackey ['lækɪ] *n.* **a)** *(footman)* Lakai, *der;* **b)** *(servant)* Diener, *der;* **c)** *(toady)* Speichellecker, *der (abwertend);* **d)** *(derog.: political follower)* Lakai, *der (fig.: abwertend)*
lacking ['lækɪŋ] *adj.* **a) be ~** ‹*Geld, Ressourcen usw.:*› fehlen; **he was found to be ~** *(incapable)* es erwies sich, daß er den Ansprü-

chen nicht genügte; **he is ~ in stamina/confidence** ihm fehlt es an Stehvermögen *(Dat.)*/er hat nicht genug Selbstvertrauen; **b)** *(coll.: deficient in intellect)* **be ~:** [geistig] unterbelichtet sein *(salopp)*

'lacklustre *adj.* trüb; glanzlos ‹*Augen*›; matt ‹*Lächeln*›; langweilig ‹*Aufführung, Party*›

laconic [lə'kɒnɪk] *adj.* **a)** *(concise)* lakonisch; **b)** wortkarg ‹*Person, Naturell*›

laconically [lə'kɒnɪkəlɪ] *adv.* lakonisch

lacquer ['lækə(r)] **1.** *n.* Lack, *der.* **2.** *v.t.* lackieren; **~ed wood** Lackholz, *das*

lacrosse [lə'krɒs] *n. (Sport)* Lacrosse, *das*

lactation [læk'teɪʃn] *n. (Physiol.)* Laktation, *die*

lactic acid [læktɪk 'æsɪd] *n. (Chem.)* Milchsäure, *die*

lactose ['læktəʊs] *n. (Chem.)* Laktose, *die;* Milchzucker, *der*

lacuna [lə'kju:nə] *n., pl.* **~e** [lə'kju:ni:] *or* **~s** Lücke, *die; (in text)* Lakune, *die (Sprachw.);* Textlücke, *die*

lacy ['leɪsɪ] *adj.* Spitzen-; *(of metalwork)* spitzenartig; Filigran-

lad [læd] *n.* **a)** *(boy)* Junge, *der;* **young ~:** kleiner Junge; **when I was a ~:** als ich noch ein Junge war; **these are my ~s** das sind meine Jungen *od. (ugs.)* Jungs; **b)** *(man)* Typ, *der;* **the ~s** die Jungs *(ugs.);* **he always goes out for a drink with the ~s** er geht immer mit seinen Kumpels einen trinken *(ugs.);* **my ~:** mein Junge *(ugs.);* **c)** *(spirited person)* **be a bit of** *or* **quite a ~:** kein Kind von Traurigkeit sein *(ugs.);* **he's a bit of a ~ with the girls** *or* **ladies** *(coll.)* er ist ein Charmeur; **d)** *see* **stable-lad**

ladder ['lædə(r)] **1.** *n.* **a)** *(lit. or fig.)* Leiter, *die; (fig.: means of advancement)* Aufstiegsmöglichkeit, *die;* **the ~ to political power** der Weg zu politischer Macht; **have a foot on the ~:** die erste Sprosse auf der Leiter des Erfolgs erklommen haben *(geh.); see also* **¹rung a; snake 1a; step-ladder; ¹top 1a; b)** *(Brit.: in tights etc.)* Laufmasche, *die.* **2.** *v.i. (Brit.)* Laufmaschen/eine Laufmasche bekommen. **3.** *v.t. (Brit.)* Laufmaschen/eine Laufmasche machen in (+ *Akk.*)

'ladder-proof *adj. (Brit. Textiles)* maschenfest; laufmaschensicher

laddie ['lædɪ] *n.* Jungchen, *das (fam.);* Bubi, *der (bes. südd.)*

lade [leɪd] *v.t., p.p.* **~n** ['leɪdn] *(Naut.)* **a)** *(load with cargo)* laden; **b)** *(load on to ship)* verladen

laden ['leɪdn] **a)** *(loaded)* beladen (**with** mit); **the air was ~ with moisture** die Luft war schwer von Feuchtigkeit; **trees ~ with blossom** Bäume, schwer von Blüten; **b)** *(burdened)* bedrückt; lastend ‹*Stille*›; bedrückend ‹*Schweigen*›; **~ with grief/guilt** gramerfüllt/schuldbeladen *(geh.)*

la-di-da [lɑ:dɪ'dɑ:] *adj.* affektiert; **~ manners** Vornehmtuerei, *die (abwertend)*

ladies' ['leɪdɪz]: **~ man** *n.* Frauenheld, *der;* **~ night** *n.* Damenabend, *der;* **~ room** *n.* Damentoilette, *die*

ladified *see* **ladyfied**

lading ['leɪdɪŋ] *n.* **a)** *(loading)* Laden, *das; see also* **³bill 1h; b)** *(freight)* Ladung, *die*

ladle ['leɪdl] **1.** *n.* **a)** *(utensil)* Schöpfkelle, *die;* Schöpflöffel, *der;* **b)** *(Metallurgy)* Pfanne, *die.* **2.** *v.t.* schöpfen

~ 'out *v.t. (lit. or fig.)* austeilen

lady ['leɪdɪ] *n.* **a)** Dame, *die; (English, American, etc. also)* Lady, *die;* **~-in-waiting** *(Brit.)* Hofdame, *die;* **ladies' hairdresser** Damenfriseur, *der;* **b)** *in pl., constr. as sing.* **the Ladies[']** *(Brit.)* die Damentoilette; **'Ladies'** „Damen"; **c)** *as form of address in sing. (poet.)* Herrin *(veralt.); in pl.* meine Damen; **Ladies and Gentlemen!** meine Damen und Herren!; **my dear** *or* **good ~:** meine Gnädigste; **d)** *(Brit.) as title* **L~:** Lady; **my ~:** Mylady; **e)** *(ruling woman)* Herrin, *die;* **~ of the house** Dame des Hauses; **our sovereign ~[, Queen Elizabeth]** *(Brit.)* unsere gnädige Herrin[, Königin Elisabeth]; **Our L~** *(Relig.)* Unsere Liebe Frau; **find the ~** = **three-card trick; f)** *(object of a man's devotion)* Angebetete, *die; (~-love)* Herzenskönigin, *die (dichter.);* Liebste, *die (veralt.);* **your/his** *etc.* **~:** die Dame deines/seines *usw.* Herzens; **g)** *(titled married woman)* Gemahlin, *die (geh.);* **h) my/your ~ wife** meine Frau/Ihre Gattin *od. (geh.)* Frau Gemahlin; **your good ~:** die Frau Gemahlin *(geh.);* **i)** *attrib. (female)* **~ clerk** Angestellte, *die;* **~ doctor** Ärztin, *die;* **~ friend** Freundin, *die;* **~ dog** Hundedame, *die (scherzh.). See also* **easy 1c; first 2a; mayoress; old lady; painted lady; young lady**

lady: ~bird, *(Amer.)* **~bug** *ns. (Zool.)* Marienkäfer, *der;* **L~ chapel** *n. (Eccl.)* Marienkapelle, *die;* **L~ Day** *n., no art.* Mariä Verkündigung; **~-fern** *n. (Bot.)* Waldfrauenfarn, *der*

ladyfied ['leɪdɪfaɪd] *adj.* [aufgesetzt] damenhaft; **be ~:** sich [allzu] damenhaft geben

lady: ~-killer *n. (coll.)* Herzensbrecher, *der;* Ladykiller, *der (scherzh.);* **~like** *adj.* **a)** damenhaft; **be ~like** sich wie eine Dame benehmen; **b)** *(effeminate)* feminin *(abwertend);* **~-love** *n.* Liebste, *die (veralt.);* **L~'s 'bedstraw** *see* **bedstraw**

ladyship ['leɪdɪʃɪp] *n.* **her/your ~/their ~s** Ihre/Eure Ladyschaft/Ihre Ladyschaften

lady: ~'s-maid *n.* [Kammer]zofe, *die;* **~'s man** *see* **ladies' man; ~-smock** *see* **cuckoo flower; ~'s 'slipper** *n. (Bot.)* Frauenschuh, *der*

¹lag [læg] **1.** *v.i.,* **-gg-** *(lit. or fig.)* zurückbleiben; *see also* **behind 1b, 2c. 2.** *n.* **a)** *(delay)* Verzögerung, *die; (falling behind)* Zurückbleiben, *das;* **there was a ~ before ...:** es verging einige Zeit, bevor ...; **b)** *(Phys.: retardation)* Verzögerung, *die* (**behind** gegenüber); *(amount of retardation)* Verzögerungszeit, *die. See also* **jet lag; time-lag**

²lag *n. (sl.: convict)* Knastbruder, *der (ugs.);* Knacki, *der (ugs.);* **old ~:** alter Knastbruder *(ugs.)*

³lag *v.t.,* **-gg-** *(insulate)* isolieren

lager ['lɑ:gə(r)] *n.* Lagerbier, *das;* **a small ~** ≈ ein kleines Helles

laggard ['lægəd] **1.** *n.* Nachzügler, *der; (with work)* Bummelant, *der (ugs. abwertend).* **2.** *adj.* langsam

¹lagging *n.* **no ~!** nicht zurückbleiben!

²lagging *n. (insulation)* Isolierung, *die*

lagoon [lə'gu:n] *n.* **a)** Lagune, *die;* **b)** *(Amer., Austral., NZ: small lake)* kleiner [abflußloser] See; **c)** *(in sewage-works)* Klärteich, *der*

lah [lɑ:] *n. (Mus.)* la

laid *see* **²lay 1, 2**

'laid-back *adj. (coll.)* gelassen

lain *see* **²lie 2**

lair [leər] *n.* *(of wild animal)* Unterschlupf, *der;* Lager, *das (Jägerspr.); (fig.: hiding-place) (of pirates, bandits)* Schlupfwinkel, *der; (of children etc.)* Versteck, *das*

laird [leəd] *n. (Scot.)* Gutsbesitzer, *der*

laisser-faire, laissez-faire [leɪseɪ'feə(r)] *n., no pl., no indef. art.* Laisser-faire, *das; attrib.* Laisser-faire‹*-Kapitalismus, -Einstellung*›

laity ['leɪɪtɪ] *n. pl.* Laien; **many of the ~:** viele aus dem Laienstand

¹lake [leɪk] *n.* See, *der;* **the Great L~s** die Großen Seen

²lake *n. (pigment from cochineal)* Koschenillerot, *das;* Karmin, *das*

lake: L~ Constance [leɪk 'kɒnstəns] *pr. n.* der Bodensee; **L~-country, L~ District** *pr. ns. (Brit.)* Lake District, *der (Seenlandschaft im Nordwesten Englands);* **~-dwelling** *n.* Pfahlbau, *der;* **L~land** ['leɪklənd] *see* **L~ District; L~ Lucerne** *see* **Lucerne; L~ Lugano** [leɪk lu:'gɑ:nəʊ] *pr. n.* der Luganer See; **~side** *n.* Seeufer, *das;* **by the ~side** am See[ufer]; **a ~side hotel/promenade** ein Hotel am See/eine Seeuferpromenade; **L~ Su'perior** *pr. n.* der Obere See

lakh [læk] *n. (Ind.)* Lakh, *der;* **a ~ of rupees** [ein]hunderttausend Rupien

lam [læm] *(sl.)* **1.** *v.i.,* **-mm-:** **~ into sb.** auf jmdn. eindreschen *(ugs.); (verbally)* jmdn. zur Schnecke machen *(ugs.).* **2.** *v.t.,* **-mm-** dreschen *(salopp)* ‹*Ball*›; verdreschen *(salopp)* ‹*Person*›

lama ['lɑ:mə] *n.* Lama, *der*

lamasery ['lɑ:məserɪ] *n.* Lamakloster, *das*

lamb [læm] **1.** *n.* **a)** Lamm, *das;* **as gentle/meek as a ~:** sanft wie ein Lamm; **one may** *or* **might as well be hanged** *or* **hung for a sheep as [for] a ~** *(fig.)* darauf kommt es jetzt auch nicht mehr an; **like a ~ [to the slaughter]** wie ein Lamm [zur Schlachtbank *(geh.)*]; **b)** *no pl. (flesh)* Lamm[fleisch], *das;* **c)** *(mild person)* Lamm, *das; (dear person)* Schatz, *der (ugs.); (pitiable person)* armes Geschöpf; **the L~ [of God]** *(Bibl.)* das Lamm Gottes. **2.** *v.i.* lammen; **~ing season** Lammzeit, *die*

lambaste [læm'beɪst] (**lambast** [læm'bæst]) *v.t. (coll.: thrash, lit. or fig.)* fertigmachen *(ugs.)*

lamb: ~ 'chop *n.* Lammkotelett, *das;* **~ 'cutlet** *n.* Kammkotelett vom Lamm

Lambda probe ['læmdə prəʊb] *n. (Motor Veh.)* Lambdasonde, *die*

lambkin ['læmkɪn] *n.* **a)** *(animal)* Lämmchen, *das;* **b)** *(person)* Schäfchen, *das (fam.)*

lamb: ~like *adj.* sanftmütig ‹*Wesen, Aussehen*›; **~'s fry** *n., no pl., no indef. art.* Gekröse vom Lamm; **~skin** *n. (with wool on)* Lammfell, *das; (as leather)* Schafleder, *das;* **~'s 'lettuce** *n., no pl., no indef. art. (Bot.)* Feldsalat, *der;* **~'s-tails** *n. pl. (Brit. Bot.)* Haselkätzchen; **~'s-wool** *n.* Lambswool, *die (Textilw.)*

lame [leɪm] **1.** *adj.* **a)** *(disabled)* lahm; **go ~:** lahm werden; **be ~ in one's right leg** ein lahmes rechtes Bein haben; **the horse was ~ in one leg** das Pferd lahmte auf einem Bein; **b)** *(fig.: unconvincing)* lahm *(ugs. abwertend);* **c)** *(fig.: halting)* holprig ‹*Vers, Versmaß*›. **2.** *v.t.* lahm reiten ‹*Pferd usw.*›; *(fig.: hinder)* lähmen ‹*Person, Fähigkeiten, Kraft*›

lamé ['lɑ:meɪ] *(Textiles)* **1.** *n.* Lamé, *der.* **2.** *adj.* lamé; Lamé-

lame: ~-brain *n. (Amer.)* Schwachkopf, *der (abwertend);* **~ dog** *see* **dog 1a; ~ 'duck** *n.* **a)** *(incapable person)* Versager, *der*/Versagerin, *die;* **b)** *(firm)* zahlungsunfähige Firma; **the ~ ducks of industry** die bankrotten Industrieunternehmen; **c)** *(Amer.: official about to retire)* *Politiker, der nicht wiedergewählt worden ist*

lamella [lə'melə] *n., pl.* **~e** [lə'meli:] Lamelle, *die*

lamely ['leɪmlɪ] *adv.* **a)** hinkend; **the horse walks ~:** das Pferd geht lahm; **b)** *(fig.: unconvincingly)* lahm *(ugs. abwertend);* **she ~ mumbled an excuse** sie murmelte eine lahme Entschuldigung

lameness ['leɪmnɪs] *n., no pl. (lit.; also fig.: unconvincingness)* Lahmheit, *die*

lament [lə'ment] **1.** *n.* **a)** *(expression of grief)* Klage, *die* (**for** um); **his great ~ is ...:** sein großer Kummer ist ...; **b)** *(dirge)* Klagegesang, *der.* **2.** *v.t.* klagen über (+ *Akk.*) *(geh.);* klagen um *(geh.)* ‹*Freund, Heimat, Glück*›; **~ that ...:** beklagen, daß ... **3.** *v.i.* klagen *(geh.);* **~ over** *or* **for sth.** etw. beklagen *(geh.);* etw. beweinen; **~ over** *or* **for sb.** jmdn. beweinen; um jmdn. weinen

lamentable ['læməntəbl] *adj.* beklagenswert; kläglich ‹*Versuch, Leistung*›

lamentably ['læməntəblɪ] *adv.* beklagenswert; kläglich ‹*scheitern*›; **be ~ ignorant of**

sth. beklagenswert wenig über etw. *(Akk.)* wissen

lamentation [læmən'teɪʃn] *n.* **a)** *no pl., no art. (lamenting)* Wehklagen, *das (geh.)*; **b)** *(lament)* [Weh]klage, *die (geh.)*; **c) L~s [of Jeremiah]** *(Bibl.)* Klagelieder [Jeremiä]

lamented [lə'mentɪd] *adj.* betrauert; **the late ~ President** der verschiedene Präsident

laminate 1. ['læmɪneɪt] *v. t.* **a)** *(construct)* lamellieren *(Technik)*; **b)** *(make into thin plates)* laminieren *(Metall.)*; **c)** *(split)* in [flache] Platten spalten; **d)** *(overlay)* beschichten; laminieren *(Technik)*. **2.** *v. i.* sich [in flache Platten] spalten. **3.** ['læmɪnət] *n.* Schicht[preß]stoff, *der (Technik)*; Laminat, *das (Technik)*; **fibreglass ~:** Glasfaserschichtstoff, *der (Technik)*

laminated ['læmɪneɪtɪd] *adj.* lamelliert *(Technik)*; **~ glass** Verbundglas, *das*; **~ fibreglass** Glasfasergewebe, *das*

lamination [læmɪ'neɪʃn] *n.* **a)** *(process)* Laminierung, *die (Technik)*; **b)** *(layer of material)* Schicht, *die*

lammergeyer ['læməgaɪə(r)] *n. (Ornith.)* Lämmergeier, *der*; Bartgeier, *der*

lamp [læmp] *n.* Lampe, *die*; *(in street)* [Straßen]laterne, *die*; [Straßen]lampe, *die*; *(of vehicle)* Licht, *das*; *(car headlamp)* Scheinwerfer, *der*; *(fig.: source of hope etc.)* Licht, *das*; *see also* **fluorescent lamp; neon lamp; spirit lamp; sun-lamp**

lamp: ~black *n.* Lampenruß, *der*; **~-holder** *n.* [Glühlampen]fassung, *die*; **~light** *n.* Lampenlicht, *das*; **~lighter** *n.* Laternenanzünder, *der*

lampoon [læm'pu:n] **1.** *n.* Spottschrift, *die*; Pasquill, *das (geh.)*. **2.** *v. t.* verhöhnen; verspotten

'lamp-post *n.* Laternenpfahl, *der*; *(taller)* Lichtmast, *der*

lamprey ['læmprɪ] *n. (Zool.)* Neunauge, *das*

lamp: ~shade *n.* Lampenschirm, *der*; **~-standard** *n.* Lichtmast, *der*

Lancastrian [læŋ'kæstrɪən] **1.** *adj.* **a)** *(of Lancashire)* Lancashire-; ⟨*Abstammung*⟩ aus Lancashire; **b)** *(Hist.)* zum Hause Lancaster gehörig; des Hauses Lancaster *nachgestellt*. **2.** *n.* **a)** *(native of Lancashire)* **be a ~:** aus Lancashire stammen; **b)** *(Hist.)* Mitglied/Anhänger des Hauses Lancaster; **the ~s** die Partei der Lancaster

lance [lɑ:ns] **1.** *n.* **a)** *(weapon)* Lanze, *die*; **b)** *(Fishing)* Stoßharpune, *die*; **c)** *(pipe)* Sprührohr, *das*; *(for burning a hole)* **[oxygen] ~:** [Sauerstoff]lanze, *die*; **d)** *(Mil.) see* **lancer a. 2.** *v. t.* **a)** *(Med.)* mit der Lanzette öffnen; **b)** *(pierce with ~)* mit der Lanze durchbohren

lance: ~-bombar'dier *n. (Mil.)* Obergefreiter der Artillerie; **~-'corporal** *n. (Mil.)* Obergefreite, *der*

lancer ['lɑ:nsə(r)] *n.* **a)** *(Mil. Hist.)* Lanzenreiter, *der*; **b)** *in pl. (dance)* Lancier, *der*

lancet ['lɑ:nsɪt] *n.* **a)** *(Med.)* Lanzette, *die*; **b)** *(Archit.)* **~ [arch/light** *or* **window]** Lanzettbogen, *der*/Lanzettfenster, *das*

land [lænd] **1.** *n.* **a)** *no pl., no indef. art. (solid part of the earth)* Land, *das*; **by ~:** auf dem Landweg; **by ~ or by sea** zu Lande oder zu Wasser ⟨*reisen*⟩; auf dem Landweg oder auf dem Seeweg ⟨*schicken, transportieren*⟩; **on ~:** zu Lande; *(not in air)* auf dem Boden; *(not in or on water)* an Land; **~ travel** das Reisen zu Lande; **b)** *no indef. art. (expanse of country)* Land, *das*; **see/find out how the ~ lies** *(fig.)* herausfinden, wie die Dinge liegen; **how does the ~ lie?** *(fig.)* wie ist die Lage?; *see also* **²lay 3 b; ²lie 1 a; c)** *no pl., no indef. art. (ground for farming or building)* Land, *das*; **work the ~:** das Land bebauen; **back to the ~:** zurück aufs Land; **live off the ~:** sich von dem ernähren, was das Land hergibt; **d)** *(country)* Land, *das*; **the greatest in the ~:** der/die Größte im ganzen Land; **out of the ~ of Egypt** *(Bibl.)* aus Ägyptenland *(bibl.)*; **~ of hope and glory** Land der Hoffnung und des Ruhms; *see also* **living 1 e; promised land; e)** *no indef. art. (landed property)* Land, *das*; **have or own ~:** Grundbesitz haben; **~s** *(estates)* Ländereien *Pl.* **2.** *v. t.* **a)** *(set ashore)* [an]landen ⟨*Truppen, Passagiere, Waren, Fang*⟩; **b)** *(Aeronaut.)* landen ⟨*[Wasser]flugzeug*⟩; **they were ~ed at an airstrip** ihr Flugzeug landete auf einer Piste; **c)** *(bring into a situation)* **~ oneself in trouble** sich in Schwierigkeiten bringen; sich *(Dat.)* Ärger einhandeln *(ugs.)*; **this will ~ him in bankruptcy** das wird ihn [noch] bankrott machen; **his recklessness ~ed him in danger** durch seinen Leichtsinn hat er sich in Gefahr gebracht; **~ sb. in [the thick of] it** jmdn. [ganz schön] reinreiten *(salopp)*; **d)** *(deal)* landen ⟨*Schlag*⟩; **~ a blow on sb., ~ sb. one** jmdm. einen Schlag versetzen *od. (ugs.)* verpassen; **~ sb. one right in the eye** jmdm. eins aufs Auge geben *(ugs.)*; **e)** *(burden)* **~ sb. with sth., ~ sth. on sb.** jmdm. etw. aufhalsen *(ugs.)*; **be ~ed with sb./sth.** jmdn. auf dem Hals haben *(ugs.)*/etw. aufgehalst bekommen *(ugs.)*; **this ~ed me with a huge problem** dies stellte mich vor ein ungeheures Problem; **f) ~ a fish** einen Fisch an Land ziehen; **g)** *(fig.: obtain in face of competition)* an Land ziehen *(ugs.)*. **3.** *v. i.* **a)** ⟨*Boot usw.:*⟩ anlegen, landen; ⟨*Passagier:*⟩ aussteigen **(from** aus); **we ~ed at Dieppe** wir gingen in Dieppe an Land; **b)** *(Aeronaut.)* landen; *(on water)* [auf dem Wasser] aufsetzen; wassern; **be about to ~:** zur Landung angesetzt haben; gerade landen; **c)** *(alight)* landen; ⟨*Ball:*⟩ aufkommen; **~ on one's feet** auf den Füßen landen; *(fig.)* [wieder] auf die Füße fallen; **d)** *(find oneself in a situation)* landen *(ugs.)* **(at, in** in + *Dat.*); **~ in the middle of a dispute** [mitten] in eine Auseinandersetzung hineingeraten

~ 'back *v. i.* wieder landen *(ugs.)*

~ on *v. t.* **~ on sb.** *(impose oneself)* jmdn. heimsuchen *(fig.)*

~ 'up *v. i.* landen *(ugs.)*

'land-agent *n.* **a)** *(Brit.: steward)* Liegenschaftsverwalter, *der*/-verwalterin, *die*; **b)** *(selling land)* Grundstücksmakler, *der*/-maklerin, *die*

landau ['lændɔ:] *n.* Landauer, *der*

land: ~-breeze *n.* Landwind, *der*; **~-crab** *n. (Zool.)* Landkrabbe, *die*

landed ['lændɪd] *adj.* **a)** *(having land)* **~ gentry/aristocracy** Landadel, *der*; **the ~ interest** die Großgrundbesitzer; **b)** *(consisting of land)* Land⟨*besitz, -gut*⟩

lander ['lændə(r)] *n. (Astronaut.)* Landefahrzeug, *das*; Landefähre, *die*

land: ~fall *n. (Naut.)* Landfall, *der*; **~fill** *n.* **a)** *(material)* Müll, *der*; Schutt, *der (zur Geländeauffüllung)*; **b)** *(process)* Geländeauffüllung, *die*; **~ fill site** *(mit Erde wieder aufgefüllte)* Müllgrube; **~ force** *n.* **~ force[s** *pl.*]Landstreitkräfte *Pl.*; **~-girl** *n. (Brit.)* Landarbeiterin, *die*; Landwirtschaftsgehilfin, *die*

landing ['lændɪŋ] *n.* **a)** *(of ship)* Landung, *die*; **on ~** *(disembarkation)* beim Verlassen des Schiffs; **b)** *(of aircraft)* Landung, *die*; **emergency ~:** Notlandung, *die*; *see also* **hard landing; soft landing; c)** *(place for disembarkation)* Anlegestelle, *die*; **d)** *(between flights of stairs)* Treppenabsatz, *der*; *(passage)* Treppenflur, *der*

landing: ~-card *n.* Landekarte, *die*; **~-craft** *n. (Navy)* Landungsboot, *das*; **~-flap** *n.* Landeklappe, *die*; **~-gear** *n.* Fahrwerk, *das*; **~-net** *n.* Kescher, *der*; **~-place** *see* **landing c; ~-stage** *n.* Landungssteg, *der*; Landungsbrücke, *die*; *(floating)* Anlegeponton, *der*; **~-strip** *see* **airstrip**

land: ~lady *n.* **a)** *(of rented property)* Vermieterin, *die*; *(of flat also)* Hauswirtin, *die*; *(of room also)* Zimmerwirtin, *die*; **b)** *(of public house)* [Gast]wirtin, *die*; **c)** *(of lodgings etc.)* [Pensions]wirtin, *die*; **~-line** *n.* Landkabel, *das*; **~-locked** *adj.* vom Land eingeschlossen ⟨*Bucht, Hafen*⟩; ⟨*Staat*⟩ ohne Zugang zum Meer; **~lord** *n.* **a)** *(of rented property)* Vermieter, *der*; [Haus]wirt, *der*; **b)** *(of public house)* [Gast]wirt, *der*; **c)** *(of lodgings etc.)* [Pensions]wirt, *der*; **~lubber** ['lændlʌbə(r)] *n. (Naut.)* Landratte, *die (ugs.)*; **~mark** *n.* **a)** *(boundary mark)* Grenzzeichen, *das*; *(stone)* Grenzstein, *der*; **b)** *(conspicuous object)* weithin sichtbares Erkennungszeichen; *(Naut.)* Landmarke, *die*; **c)** *(fig.: significant event)* Markstein, *der*; **stand as a ~mark** einen Meilenstein bedeuten; **~ mass** *n. (Geog.)* Landmasse, *die*; **~-mine** *n. (Mil.)* **a)** *(on ground)* Landmine, *die*; **b)** *(parachute mine)* Fallschirmmine, *die*; **~owner** *n.* **[large** *or* **big] ~owner** [Groß]grundbesitzer, *der*/-besitzerin, *die*

landscape ['lændskeɪp, 'lænskeɪp] **1.** *n.* **a)** Landschaft, *die*; **b)** *(picture)* Landschaftsbild, *das*; Landschaft, *die*. **2.** *v. t.* landschaftsgärtnerisch gestalten ⟨*Garten, Park*⟩

landscape: ~ architect *n.* Landschaftsarchitekt, *der*/-architektin, *die*; **~ architecture** *n.* Landschaftsgestaltung, *die*; **~ gardener** *n.* Landschaftsgärtner, *der*/-gärtnerin, *die*; **~ gardening** *n.* Landschaftsgärtnerei, *die*; **~ painter** *n.* Landschaftsmaler, *der*/-malerin, *die*

land: ~slide *n.* **a)** Erdrutsch, *der*; **b)** *(fig.: majority)* Erdrutsch[wahl]sieg, *der*; *attrib.* **a ~slide victory** ein Erdrutsch[wahl]sieg; **~slip** *see* **~slide a; ~-tax** *n. (Admin.)* Grundsteuer, *die*

landward ['lændwəd] **1.** *adj.* **~ side** Landseite, *die*; **~ view** Blick zur Landseite hin. **2.** *adv.* land[ein]wärts. **3.** *n.* **to [the] ~:** zur Landseite hin

landwards ['lændwədz] *see* **landward 2**

'land-wind *n.* Landwind, *der*

lane [leɪn] *n.* **a)** *(in the country)* Landsträßchen, *das*; *(unmetalled)* [Hecken]weg, *der*; **it's a long ~ that has no turning** *(prov.)* alles muß einmal ein Ende haben; **b)** *(in town)* Gasse, *die*; **lovers' ~:** Seufzerallee, *die (scherzh.)*; **c)** *(part of road)* [Fahr]spur, *die*; **slow ~** *(in Britain)* linke Spur; *(on the continent)* rechte Spur; **'get in ~'** „bitte einordnen"; *see also* **fast lane; d) aircraft ~:** Flugroute, *die*; **shipping ~:** Schiffahrtsweg, *der*; **ocean ~:** Schiffahrtsstraße, *die*; **e)** *(for race)* Bahn, *die*

-lane[d] [leɪn(d)] *adj. in comb.* -spurig

language ['læŋgwɪdʒ] *n.* **a)** Sprache, *die*; **speak the same ~** *(fig.)* die gleiche Sprache sprechen; *see also* **artificial language; dead language; foreign language; sign language; b)** *no pl., no art. (words, wording)* Sprache, *die*; **[style of] ~:** [Sprach]stil, *der*; **use of ~:** Sprachgebrauch, *der*; **c)** *(style)* Ausdrucksweise, *die*; Sprache, *die*; **use uncompromising ~:** eine unmißverständliche Sprache sprechen; **mind your ~:** drück dich gefälligst anständig aus; **~ of the gutter** Gossensprache, *die*; *see also* **bad 1 d; strong language; d)** *(professional vocabulary)* [Fach]sprache, *die*; **the ~ of diplomacy** die Sprache der Diplomatie; **medical ~:** medizinische Fachsprache; **e)** *(Computing)* Sprache, *die*; **computer ~s** Computersprachen; **f)** *no pl., no art. (faculty of speech)* Sprachfähigkeit, *die*

language: ~ course *n.* Sprachkurs[us], *der*; **~ laboratory** *n.* Sprachlabor, *das*; **~-teacher** *n.* Sprachlehrer, *der*/-lehrerin, *die*

languid ['læŋgwɪd] *adj.* **a)** *(indisposed to exertion, sluggish)* träge; **b)** *(inert)* matt; **c)** *(apathetic)* lahm

languidly ['læŋgwɪdlɪ] *adv.* **a)** *(without vigour, sluggishly)* träge; **b)** *(inertly)* matt; **c)** *(apathetically)* lustlos

languish ['læŋgwɪʃ] *v. i.* **a)** *(lose vitality)* ermatten *(geh.)*; ‹*Pflanzen:*› kümmern; **b)** *(live wretchedly)* ~ **under sth.** unter etw. *(Dat.)* schmachten *(geh.)*; ~ **in prison** im Gefängnis schmachten *(geh.)*; **c)** *(pine)* dahinvegetieren; ~ **for sth.** nach etw. schmachten *(geh.)*; ~ **for sb.** sich nach jmdm. verzehren *(geh.)*
languor [læŋgə(r)] *n. see* **languorous:** Mattigkeit, *die;* Trägheit, *die;* Verträumtheit, *die*
languorous ['læŋgərəs] *adj.* **a)** *(faint)* matt; **b)** *(inert)* träge; **c)** *(dreamy)* verträumt
lank [læŋk] *adj.* **a)** *(tall)* hager; **b)** *(thin)* abgemagert; **c)** *(limp)* glatt herabhängend ‹*Haar*›
lanky ['læŋkɪ] *adj.* schlaksig *(ugs.)*; [dürr und] lang ‹*Arm, Bein*›
lanolin ['lænəlɪn] *n.* Lanolin, *das*
lantern ['læntən] *n.* Laterne, *die; see also* **Chinese lantern; magic lantern**
lantern: ~-jawed ['læntəndʒɔ:d] *adj.* mit langgeschnittenem Gesicht; **~-slide** *n. bemalte Glasplatte oder Dia für die Laterna magica*
lanyard ['lænjəd] *n.* **a)** *(Naut.)* Bändsel, *das; (in tackle)* Taljenreep, *das;* **b)** *(loop of cord)* Kordel, *die;* **c)** *(to fire gun)* Abzugsleine, *die*
Laos ['laʊs, 'lɑ:ɒs] *pr. n.* Laos *(das)*
Laotian [laʊʃn] **1.** *adj.* laotisch; **sb. is ~:** jmd. ist Laote/Laotin. **2.** *n.* **a)** *(person)* Laote, *der*/Laotin, *die;* **b)** *(language)* laotische Sprache
[1]lap [læp] *n.* **a)** *(part of body)* Schoß, *der;* **live in the ~ of luxury** *(fig.)* im Überfluß leben; **fall** *or* **drop** *or* **be dropped into sb.'s ~** *(fig.)* jmdm. in den Schoß fallen; **end up on** *or* **in sb.'s ~** *(fig.)* bei jmdm. landen *(ugs.)*; bei jmdm. abgeladen werden *(fig.)*; *see also* **god a;** **b)** *(flap)* [Rock]schoß, *der*
[2]lap 1. *n.* **a)** *(Sport)* Runde, *die;* **on the last ~** *(fig. coll.)* auf der Zielgeraden *(fig.)*; **~ of honour** Ehrenrunde, *die;* **b)** *(amount of overlap)* Überlappung, *die* **(of** um); *(overlapping part)* überlappender Teil. **2.** *v. t.*, **-pp- a)** *(Sport)* überrunden; **b)** *(cause to overlap)* überlappen; **c)** *(wrap)* wickeln (**[a]round** um); **d)** *(swathe)* umwickeln **(in** mit); wickeln ‹*Baby*› **(in** in + *Akk.*). **3.** *v. i.*, **-pp-:** ~ **over sth.** etw. überlappen
[3]lap 1. *v. i.*, **-pp- a)** *(drink)* schlappen; schlecken; **b)** ‹*See, Wasser, Wellen:*› plätschern. **2.** *v. t.*, **-pp- a)** *(drink)* ~ **[up]** [auf]schlappen; [auf]schlecken; **b)** *see* ~ **up b;** **c)** *see* ~ **up c;** **d)** ‹*See, Wasser, Wellen:*› plätschern an (+ *Akk.*)
~ **'up** *v. t.* **a)** *(drink) see* ~ **2 a;** **b)** *(consume greedily)* hinunterschütten; **c)** *(fig.: receive eagerly)* schlucken *(ugs.)*; begierig aufnehmen ‹*Lob*›; sich stürzen auf (+ *Akk.*) ‹*Sensation*›
lap: ~ belt *n.* Beckengurt, *der;* **~-dog** *n.* Schoßhund, *der;* Schoßhündchen, *das*
lapel [lə'pel] *n.* Revers, *das od. (österr.) der*
lapidary ['læpɪdərɪ] *adj.* **a)** *(of gems)* ~ **art** *(cutting gems)* Steinschneidekunst, *die; (polishing gems)* Kunst des Steinschleifens; **b)** *(engraved)* in Stein gehauen; **c)** *(dignified and concise)* lapidar
lapis [lazuli] ['læpɪs ('læzjʊlɪ), 'leɪpɪs ('læzjʊlaɪ)] *n., no pl., no indef. art.* **a)** *(gem)* Lapislazuli, *der;* Lasurstein, *der;* **b)** *(pigment, colour)* Ultramarin, *das;* Lasurblau, *das*
'lap-joint *n.* Überlappung, *die;* Überlappungsverbindung, *die*
Lapland ['læplænd] *pr. n.* Lappland *(das)*
Laplander ['læplændə(r)] *n.* Lappländer, *der*/Lappländerin, *die*
Lapp [læp] **1.** *n.* **a)** *(person)* Lappe, *der*/Lappin, *die;* **b)** *(language)* lappische Sprache. **2.** *adj.* **a)** lappisch; lappländisch; **b)** *(of language)* lappisch
Lappish ['læpɪʃ] *see* **Lapp 2**
lapse [læps] **1.** *n.* **a)** *(interval)* **a/the ~ of ...:** eine/die Zeitspanne von ...; **a ~ in the conversation** eine Gesprächspause; **b)** *(mistake)* Fehler, *der;* Lapsus, *der (geh.)*; ~ **of memory** Gedächtnislücke, *die;* **c)** *(deviation)* Verstoß, *der* **(from** gegen); **momentary ~ of concentration** momentane Konzentrationsschwäche; **a ~ from his high standard** eine Abweichung von seinem hohen Standard; ~ **from good taste** Geschmacksverirrung, *die;* **d)** *(Law: termination of right) (of patent)* Erlöschen, *das; (of legacy)* Heimfall, *der.* **2.** *v. i.* **a)** *(fail)* versagen; ~ **from sth.** etw. vermissen lassen; **b)** *(sink)* ~ **into** verfallen in (+ *Akk.*); fallen in (+ *Akk.*) ‹*Schlaf, Koma*›; verfallen (+ *Dat.*) ‹*Sucht, Ketzerei*›; **c)** *(become void)* ‹*Vertrag, Versicherungspolice usw.:*› ungültig werden; ‹*Plan, Projekt:*› hinfällig werden; ‹*Anspruch:*› verfallen; **d)** ~ **to sb.** *(Law)* auf jmdn. übergehen; an jmdn. fallen
lapsed [læpst] *adj.* **a)** *(disused)* in Vergessenheit geraten; **b)** *(having defected)* abgefallen ‹*Christ, Katholik usw.*›; **c)** abgelaufen, ungültig ‹*Paß, Führerschein, Versicherungspolice*›; frei geworden ‹*Lehen*›
lap: ~-top 1. *adj.* tragbar, Laptop‹*gerät, -PC*›; **2.** *n.* Laptop, *der;* tragbarer PC; **~-weld** *(Metalw.)* **1.** *n.* Überlapp-[schweiß]naht, *die;* **2.** *v. t.* überlappt schweißen; **~wing** *n. (Ornith.)* Kiebitz, *der*
larboard ['lɑ:bəd] *see* **[1]port 1 c, 2**
larcenous ['lɑ:sənəs] *adj.* diebisch
larceny ['lɑ:sənɪ] *n. (Law)* Diebstahl, *der*
larch [lɑ:tʃ] *n.* Lärche, *die*
lard [lɑ:d] **1.** *n.* Schweineschmalz, *das;* Schweinefett, *das.* **2.** *v. t.* **a)** *(Cookery)* spicken; **b)** *(fig.: garnish)* spicken *(ugs.)*
larder ['lɑ:də(r)] *n. (room)* Speisekammer, *die; (cupboard)* Speiseschrank, *der*
lardy ['lɑ:dɪ] *adj.* fett
'lardy-cake *n.* ≈ Rosinenbrot, *das*
large [lɑ:dʒ] **1.** *adj.* **a)** groß; **a ~ lady** eine stattliche Dame; ~ **importer/user** Großimporteur, *der*/Großverbraucher, *der; see also* **intestine; life d;** **b)** *(comprehensive, broad)* umfassend; **taking the ~ view** im großen ganzen gesehen. **2.** *n.* **a) at ~** *(at liberty)* frei; *(not in prison etc.)* auf freiem Fuß; in Freiheit; *(at full length)* ausführlich; *(as a body)* insgesamt; *(Amer. Polit.: representing whole State)* für den ganzen Staat ‹*gewählt*›; **society at ~:** die Gesellschaft in ihrer Gesamtheit; **students/teachers/doctors at ~:** die [gesamte] Studenten-/Lehrer-/Ärzteschaft; **ambassador at ~** *(Amer.)* Sonderbotschafter, *der*/-botschafterin, *die;* **b) in [the] ~:** im großen. **3.** *adv. see* **bulk 2; [1]by 2 d; [2]loom; write 2 d**
'large-hearted *adj.* großherzig *(geh.)*
largely ['lɑ:dʒlɪ] *adv.* weitgehend
largeness ['lɑ:dʒnɪs] *n., no pl.* Größe, *die; (of person)* Stattlichkeit, *die*
larger-than-'life *attrib. adj.* überlebensgroß
large: ~-scale *attrib. adj.* großangelegt; groß ‹*Erfolg, Mißerfolg*›; ‹*Katastrophe*› großen Ausmaßes; ‹*Modell*› in großem Maßstab; **~-scale manufacture** Massenproduktion, *die;* **~-size** *see* **-size**
largess[e] [lɑ:'ʒes] *n., no pl.* **a)** *(gifts)* Geschenke; **government ~:** staatliche Geschenke; **b)** *(bestowal)* [großzügige] Unterstützung *od.* Förderung
largish ['lɑ:dʒɪʃ] *adj.* ziemlich groß; recht stattlich ‹*Person*›
largo ['lɑ:gəʊ] *(Mus.)* **1.** *adv. & adj.* largo. **2.** *n., pl.* **~s** Largo, *das*
lariat ['lærɪət] *n.* **a)** *(lasso) (lateinamerikanisches)* Lasso; **b)** *(tethering-rope)* Seil zum Anpflocken
[1]lark [lɑ:k] *n. (Ornith.)* Lerche, *die;* **be up with the ~:** beim *od.* mit dem ersten Hahnenschrei aufstehen; **gay** *or* **happy as a ~:** lustig und vergnügt
[2]lark *(coll.)* **1.** *n.* **a)** *(frolic)* Jux, *der (ugs.)*; **they were only having a ~:** sie haben sich *(Dat.)* nur einen Jux gemacht *(ugs.)*; **be a real ~:** eine Mordsgaudi sein *(ugs.)*; **it'll be a bit of a ~:** es wird bestimmt lustig; **do sth. for a ~:** etw. aus Jux machen *(ugs.)*; **what a ~!** das ist/war spitze *(ugs.)*; **b)** *(Brit.) (form of activity)* Blödsinn, *der (ugs.)*; *(affair)* Geschichte, *die (ugs.)*; **blow** *or (sl.)* **sod** *or (coarse)* **bugger this for a ~:** zum Teufel!; verdammte Scheiße *(derb).* **2.** *v. i.* ~ **[about** *or* **around]** herumalbern *(ugs.)*
'larkspur *n. (Bot.)* Rittersporn, *der*
larva ['lɑ:və] *n., pl.* **~e** ['lɑ:vi:] Larve, *die*
larval ['lɑ:vl] *adj.* Larven-; larval *(fachspr.)*; **a ~ fly/frog** eine Fliegen-/Froschlarve
laryngeal [lə'rɪndʒɪəl] **1.** *adj.* **a)** *(Anat.)* Kehlkopf-; laryngeal *(fachspr.)*; **b)** *(Ling.)* Kehl[kopf]-; laryngal *(fachspr.)*. **2.** *n. (Ling.)* Kehl[kopf]laut, *der;* Laryngal, *der (fachspr.)*
laryngitis [lærɪn'dʒaɪtɪs] *n. (Med.)* Kehlkopfentzündung, *die;* Laryngitis, *die (fachspr.)*
larynx ['lærɪŋks] *n., pl.* **larynges** [lə'rɪndʒi:z] *(Anat.)* Kehlkopf, *der;* Larynx, *der (fachspr.)*
lasagne [lə'sænjə, lə'sɑ:njə] *n. (Gastr.)* Lasagne *Pl.*
lascivious [lə'sɪvɪəs] *adj.* **a)** *(lustful)* lüstern *(geh.)*; **b)** *(inciting to lust)* lasziv
lasciviously [lə'sɪvɪəslɪ] *adv. see* **lascivious:** lüstern *(geh.)*; lasziv
lasciviousness [lə'sɪvɪəsnɪs] *n., no pl. see* **lascivious:** Lüsternheit, *die (geh.)*; Laszivität, *die*
laser ['leɪzə(r)] *n.* Laser, *der*
laser: ~ beam *n.* Laserstrahl, *der;* **~ printer** *n.* Laserdrucker, *der*
lash [læʃ] **1.** *n.* **a)** *(stroke)* [Peitschen]hieb, *der;* **b)** *(part of whip) biegsamer Teil der Peitsche; (whipcord)* Peitschenschnur, *die; (as punishment)* **the ~:** die Peitsche; **c)** *(on eyelid)* Wimper, *die.* **2.** *v. i.* **a)** *(make violent movement)* schlagen; ‹*Peitsche, Schlange:*› zuschlagen; **b)** *(strike)* ‹*Welle, Regen:*› peitschen **(against** gegen, **on** auf + *Akk.*); ‹*Person:*› [mit der Peitsche] schlagen **(at** nach). **3.** *v. t.* **a)** *(fasten)* festbinden **(to** an + *Dat.*); *(Naut.)* festzurren *(bes. Seemannsspr.)*; laschen *(Seemannsspr.)*; ~ **together** zusammenbinden; **b)** *(flog)* mit der Peitsche schlagen; *(as punishment)* auspeitschen; ~ **oneself** sich geißeln; **c)** *(rebuke)* abkanzeln; geißeln ‹*Mißstand, Laster, Fehler*›; *(satirize)* verhöhnen; **d)** *(move violently)* schlagen mit; **e)** *(beat upon)* peitschen; **the rain ~ed the windows/roof** der Regen peitschte gegen die Fenster/auf das Dach; **f)** *(drive)* ~ **sb. into sth.** jmdn. zu etw. anstacheln
~ **a'bout** *v. i.* wild um sich schlagen
~ **'down 1.** *v. t.* festbinden; *(Naut.)* festzurren *(bes. Seemannsspr.)*. **2.** *v. i.* ‹*Regen:*› niederprasseln
~ **'into** *v. t.* ~ **into sb.** über jmdn. herfallen
~ **'out** *v. i.* **a)** *(hit out)* um sich schlagen; ‹*Pferd:*› ausschlagen; ~ **out at sb.** nach jmdm. schlagen; *(fig.)* über jmdn. herziehen *(ugs.)*; **b)** ~ **out on sth.** *(coll.) (spend freely)* sich *(Dat.)* etw. leisten *od.* gönnen; *(pay a lot)* viel Geld für etw. ausgeben
lashing ['læʃɪŋ] *n.* **a)** *see* **lash 2:** Schlagen, *das usw.;* **b)** *(cord)* Zurring, *der (Seemannsspr.)*; **c)** *in pl. (large amounts)* **~s of sth.** Unmengen von etw.
'lash-up 1. *adj.* behelfsmäßig; **~ procedures** provisorische Maßnahmen. **2.** *n. (improvised structure)* Notbehelf, *der*
lass [læs] *n.* **a)** *(Scot./N. Engl./poet.: girl)* Mädchen, *das;* Maid, *die (dichter.)*; **b)** *(sweetheart)* Liebste, *die (veralt.)*; Mädchen, *das (ugs.)*
lassie ['læsɪ] *n. (Scot., N. Engl.)* Mädchen, *das; (sweetheart)* Schätzchen, *das (ugs.)*
lassitude ['læsɪtju:d] *n.* Mattigkeit, *die*
lasso [lə'su:, 'læsəʊ] **1.** *n., pl.* **~s** *or* **~es** Lasso, *das.* **2.** *v. t.* mit dem Lasso fangen

[1]**last** [lɑːst] **1.** *adj.* letzt...; **be [the] ~ to arrive** als letzter/letzte ankommen; **for the [very] ~ time** zum [aller]letzten Mal; **who was ~?** wer war letzter?; **the ~ two/three** *etc.* die letzten beiden/drei *usw.*; **he came ~ in the race** er war letzter bei dem Rennen; **second ~, ~ but one** vorletzt...; **~ but not least** last, not least; nicht zuletzt; **~ evening/night was windy** gestern abend/gestern *od.* heute nacht war es windig; **~ week/month/year was cold** letzte Woche/letzten Monat/letztes Jahr war es kalt; **~ month was a memorable one** der letzte Monat war bedeutungsvoll; **~ evening/week we were out** gestern abend/letzte Woche waren wir aus; **I thought my ~ hour had come** ich dachte, mein letztes Stündlein hätte geschlagen; **sb.'s ~ crust** *(fig.)* jmds. letztes Stück Brot *(fig.)*; **I was down to my ~ crust** *(fig.)* ich war völlig abgebrannt *(ugs.)*; **I should be the '~ person to do such a thing** ich wäre der letzte, der so etwas täte; **the '~ thing** das Letzte; **that would be the '~ thing to do in this situation** das wäre das Letzte, was man in dieser Situation tun würde; *see also* **ditch 1; honour 1 j; judgment c; leg 1 a; ; quarter 1 j; resort 1 a; respect 1 e; straw b. 2.** *adv.* **a)** [ganz] zuletzt; als letzter/letzte ‹*sprechen, ankommen*›; **come ~ with sb.** *(fig.)* für jmdn. an letzter Stelle rangieren; **b)** *(on ~ previous occasion)* das letzte Mal; zuletzt; **when did you ~ see him** *or* **see him ~?** wann hast du ihn zuletzt *od.* das letzte Mal gesehen? **3.** *n.* **a)** *(mention, sight)* **I shall never hear the ~ of it** das werde ich ständig zu hören bekommen; **you haven't heard the ~ of this matter** das letzte Wort in dieser Sache ist noch nicht gesprochen; **I hope we shall soon see the ~ of him** wir werden ihn hoffentlich bald zum letzten Mal gesehen haben; **that's the ~ we'll see of that old car** jetzt sehen wir dieses alte Auto wohl zum letzten Mal; **that was the ~ we ever saw of him** das war das letzte Mal, daß wir ihn gesehen haben; **b)** *(person or thing)* letzter...; **these ~**: letztere; **which ~**: welch letzt...; **I'm always the ~ to be told** ich bin immer der letzte, der etwas erfährt; **she was the ~ to know about it** sie erfuhr es als letzte; **the ~ shall be first** *(Bibl.)* die Letzten werden die Ersten sein; **c)** *(day, moment[s])* **towards** *or* **at the ~ he was serene** *(just before his death)* am Ende war er gelassen; **to** *or* **till the ~**: bis zuletzt; **d) look one's ~ on** einen letzten Blick werfen auf (+ *Akk.*); *see also* **breathe 2 a; e) at [long] ~**: endlich; schließlich [doch noch]

[2]**last** *v.i.* **a)** *(continue)* andauern; ‹*Wetter, Ärger:*› anhalten; **~ all night** die ganze Nacht dauern; **~ till** dauern bis; **~ from ... to ...**: von ... bis ... dauern; **built to ~**: dauerhaft gebaut; **a book that will ~**: ein Buch, das bleibt; **he will not ~ very much longer** *(live)* er hat nicht mehr lange zu leben; *(in job)* ihm wird bald gekündigt werden; **make one's money ~**: mit seinem Geld haushalten; **it can't/won't ~**: das geht nicht mehr lange so; **it's too good to ~**: es ist zu schön, um von Dauer zu sein; **~ sb.'s time** halten, solange jmd. es braucht; **b)** *(manage to continue)* es aushalten; **c)** *(suffice)* reichen; **while stocks ~**: solange Vorrat reicht; **this knife will ~ [me] a lifetime** dies Messer hält mein ganzes Leben; **memories to ~ a lifetime** Erinnerungen für das ganze Leben

~ 'out 1. *v.t. (complete task)* durchhalten; *(survive)* überstehen; **~ out the winter/journey** ‹*Vorräte usw.:*› den Winter über/für die Reise ausreichen; **he would probably not ~ out the afternoon** er würde wahrscheinlich den Nachmittag nicht überleben. **2.** *v.i.* durchhalten; ‹*Vorräte usw:*› ausreichen

[3]**last** *n. (for shoemaker)* Leisten, *der;* **the cobbler should stick to his ~** *(prov.)* Schuster, bleib bei deinem Leisten

Last: **~ 'Day** *n. (Relig.)* **the ~ Day** der Jüngste Tag; **l~-ditch** *adj.* **l~-ditch attempt** letzter verzweifelter Versuch

lasting ['lɑːstɪŋ] *adj.* **a)** *(permanent)* bleibend; dauerhaft ‹*Beziehung*›; nachhaltig ‹*Eindruck, Wirkung, Bedeutung*›; nicht nachlassend ‹*Interesse*›; **be of no ~ benefit to sb.** sich für jmdn. auf die Dauer nicht auszahlen; **b)** *(durable)* haltbar; **[made] in a ~ material** aus haltbarem Material

lastly ['lɑːstlɪ] *adv.* schließlich

last: **~-mentioned** *attrib. adj.* letztgenannt; **~ 'minute** *n.* **at the ~ minute** in letzter Minute; **up to the ~ minute** bis zum letzten Augenblick; **~-minute** *attrib. adj.* in letzter Minute vorgebracht ‹*Plan, Aufruf, Ergänzung, Gesuch, Bewerbung*›; ‹*Sinneswandel*› in letzter Minute; **make a ~-minute dash to the airport** in letzter Minute zum Flughafen rasen; **in the ~-minute rush** kurz vor Toresschluß; **~ name** *n.* Zuname, *der;* Nachname, *der;* **~-named** *attrib. adj.* zuletzt genannt; **~ 'rites** *n. pl.*, **~ 'sacrament** *n. (Relig.)* Letzte Ölung; **~ 'sleep** *n., no pl. (literary)* ewiger Schlaf *(geh.)*; **L~ 'Supper** *n., no pl. (Relig.)* **the L~ Supper** das Abendmahl; **~ 'thing** *adv. (coll.)* als letztes; **~ 'trump** *n. (Relig.)* letzte Posaune; **~ 'will** *n.* **~ will [and testament]** letzter Wille; **~ 'word** *n., no pl., no indef. art.* **a)** letztes Wort; **be the ~ word** *(fig.)* nicht zu überbieten sein (**in** an + *Dat.*); das letzte sein (**in** an + *Dat.*); **sth. is the ~ word on sth.** mit etw. ist das letzte Wort über etw. *(Akk.)* gesprochen; **b)** *(latest fashion)* **the ~ word** das Allerneueste; der letzte Schrei *(ugs.)*; **~ 'words** *n. pl.* **her/his ~ words** ihre/seine letzten Worte; **[there's] famous ~ words [for you]** *(joc. iron.)* das wollen wir erst mal sehen

lat. *abbr.* **latitude** Br.

latch [lætʃ] **1.** *n.* **a)** *(bar)* Riegel, *der;* **b)** *(spring-lock)* Schnappschloß, *das;* **c) on the ~** *(held by bar)* nur mit einem Riegel verschlossen; *(with lock not in use)* nur eingeklinkt. **2.** *v.t.* zuschnappen lassen. **3.** *v.i.* zuschnappen

~ 'on *v.i. (coll.)* **a)** *(attach oneself)* sich [ungefragt] anschließen; **b)** *(understand)* es mitkriegen *(ugs.)*

~ 'on to *v.t. (coll.)* **a)** *(attach oneself to)* **~ on to sb.** sich an jmdn. hängen *(ugs.)*; **b)** *(understand)* kapieren *(ugs.)*; **c)** *(be enthusiastic about)* abfahren auf (+ *Akk.*) *(salopp)*

'latchkey *n.* Hausschlüssel, *der;* **~ child** *(fig.)* Schlüsselkind, *das*

late [leɪt] **1.** *adj.* **a)** spät; *(after proper time)* verspätet; **am I ~?** komme ich zu spät?; **I am rather ~**: ich bin ziemlich spät dran *(ugs.) od.* habe mich etwas verspätet; **be ~ for the train** den Zug verpassen; **the train is [ten minutes] ~**: der Zug hat [zehn Minuten] Verspätung; **spring is ~ this year** dieses Jahr haben wir einen späten Frühling; **be [very] ~ for dinner** mit [großer] Verspätung zum Essen kommen; **what makes you so ~ today?** warum kommst du heute so spät?; **~ riser** Spätaufsteher, *der/*-aufsteherin, *die;* **~ entry** verspätete Anmeldung; **~ shift** Spätschicht, *die;* **in the ~ evening** spät am Abend; spätabends; **it is ~**: es ist [schon] spät; **have a ~ dinner** [erst] spät zu Abend essen; **~ summer** Spätsommer, *der;* **~ spring holidays** Ferien im späten Frühjahr; **in ~ July** Ende Juli; **~ Gothic/Victorian** spätgotisch/-viktorianisch; **~ seventeenth-century paintings** Gemälde aus dem späten siebzehnten Jahrhundert; *see also* **hour b; b)** *(deceased)* verstorben; *see also* **lamented; c)** *(former)* ehemalig; vormalig; **d)** *(recent)* letzt...; **in ~ times** in letzter Zeit; **of ~ years** in den letzten Jahren; **e)** *(backward in flowering, ripening, etc.)* spät ‹*Sorte, Nelken*›; **be ~** ‹*Blumen:*› spät blühen. *See also* **later; latest. 2.** *adv.* **a)** *(after proper time)* verspätet; **[too] ~**: zu spät; **they got home very ~**: sie kamen [erst] sehr spät nach Hause; **better ~ than never** lieber spät als gar nicht; **b)** *(far on in time)* spät; **not until quite ~ this year** dieses Jahr erst recht spät; **~ in August** Ende August; **~ last century** [gegen] Ende des letzten Jahrhunderts; **~ in life** erst spät im Leben; erst im fortgeschrittenen Alter; **c)** *(at or till a ~ hour)* spät; **be up/sit up ~**: bis spät in die Nacht *od.* lange aufbleiben; **work ~ at the office** [abends] lange im Büro arbeiten; **wait up ~ for sb./sth.** jmds./einer Sache wegen lange aufbleiben; **d)** *(formerly)* **~ of ...**: ehemals wohnhaft in ...; ehemaliger Mitarbeiter ‹*einer Firma*›; **e)** *(at ~ stage)* **traces remained as ~ as the seventeenth century** Überreste blieben noch bis ins siebzehnte Jahrhundert erhalten; **she was seen as ~ as yesterday** sie wurde gestern noch gesehen; **[a bit** *or* **somewhat** *or* **rather] ~ in the day** *(fig. coll.)* reichlich spät; **too ~ in the day** *(lit. or fig.)* zu spät. **3.** *n.* **of ~**: in letzter Zeit

late: **~ bird** *n. (fig. coll.)* Nachtmensch, *der;* Nachteule, *die (ugs. scherzh.)*; **~comer** *n.* Zuspätkommende, *der/die*

lateen [lə'tiːn] *adj. (Naut.)* **a) ~ sail** Lateinersegel, *das;* **b)** *(rigged with a ~ sail)* Lateinersegel-; mit Lateinersegel *nachgestellt*

lately ['leɪtlɪ] *adv.* in letzter Zeit; **only ~**: erst vor kurzem; **till ~**: bis vor kurzem

lateness ['leɪtnɪs] *n., no pl.* **a)** *(being after due time)* Verspätung, *die;* **b)** *(being far on in time)* **the ~ of the performance** der späte Beginn der Vorstellung; **the ~ of the hour** die späte *od.* vorgerückte Stunde

'late-night *attrib. adj.* Spät‹*programm, -vorstellung*›

latent ['leɪtənt] *adj.* **a)** latent [vorhanden]; **b)** *(Med.)* latent. *See also* **heat 1 b**

latent 'image *n. (Photog.)* latentes Bild

later ['leɪtə(r)] **1.** *adv.* später; **~ on** später; **it must be ready no ~ than next week** es muß bis spätestens nächste Woche fertig sein; **~ [on] the same day** im weiteren Verlauf des Tages; später am Tag; **see you ~**: bis nachher; bis später; *see also* **soon b. 2.** *adj.* später; *(more recent)* neuer; jünger; **at a ~ date/time** zu einem späteren Zeitpunkt; später; **be ~, be of ~ date** neueren *od.* jüngeren Datums sein

lateral ['lætərəl] *adj.* **a)** seitlich (**to** von); Seiten‹*flügel, -ansicht*›; **~ thinking** Querdenken, *das;* **b)** *(Anat.)* lateral; **c)** *(Bot.)* seitenständig; **~ shoot** Seitentrieb, *der*

laterally ['lætərəlɪ] *adv.* seitlich

latest ['leɪtɪst] *adj.* **a)** *(modern)* neu[e]st...; **the very ~ thing** das Allerneu[e]ste; **the ~ in fashion** der letzte Schrei *(ugs.)*; die neu[e]ste Mode; **b)** *(most recent)* letzt...; **have you heard the ~?** wissen Sie schon das Neu[e]ste?; **what's the ~?** was gibt's Neues?; **c) at [the] ~/the very ~**: spätestens/allerspätestens

latex ['leɪteks] *n., pl.* **~es** *or* **latices** ['leɪtɪsiːz] Latex, *der*

lath [lɑːθ] *n., pl.* **~s** [lɑːθs, lɑːðz] Latte, *die;* **~s** *(arrangement)* Lattung, *die;* **~ and plaster** Putzträger und Putz

lathe [leɪð] *n.* Drehbank, *die;* Drehmaschine, *die (Technik)*

lather ['lɑːðə(r), 'læðə(r)] **1.** *n.* **a)** *(froth)* [Seifen]schaum, *der;* **b)** *(sweat)* Schweiß, *der;* Schaum, *der (veralt.)*; **get [oneself] into a ~ [about sth.]** *(fig.)* sich [über etw. *(Akk.)*] aufregen. **2.** *v.t.* **a)** *(cover with froth)* einschäumen; einseifen; **b)** *(coll.: thrash)* verprügeln

Latin ['lætɪn] **1.** *adj.* **a)** lateinisch; *see also* **English 1; b)** *(of ancient Romans)* römisch; **c)** *(of RC Ch.)* lateinisch; **d)** *(of Southern Europeans)* romanisch; südländisch ‹*Temperament, Charme*›. **2.** *n.* Latein, *das;* **medieval ~**: Mittellatein, *das;* **modern ~**: Neulatein, *das;* **thieves' ~**: Gaunersprache, *die;* *see also* **English 2 a**

Latin: ~ **A'merica** *pr. n.* Lateinamerika *(das);* ~-**A'merican 1.** *adj.* lateinamerikanisch; **2.** *n.* Lateinamerikaner, *der*/Lateinamerikanerin, *die*
Latinate ['lætɪneɪt] *adj. (derived from Latin)* aus dem Lateinischen stammend
'**Latin Church** *n.* lateinische Kirche
Latinism ['lætɪnɪzm] *n.* Latinismus, *der*
Latinist ['lætɪnɪst] *n.* Latinist, *der*/Latinistin, *die*
Latinize ['lætɪnaɪz] *v. t.* latinisieren
Latino [lə'ti:nəʊ] *n., pl.* ~s *(Amer.)* Lateinamerikaner/-amerikanerin [in den USA]
Latin: ~ **Quarter** *n.* Quartier Latin, *das;* ~ **rite** *n. (Eccl.)* lateinischer Ritus
latish ['leɪtɪʃ] *adj. & adv.* ziemlich spät
latitude ['lætɪtju:d] *n.* **a)** *(freedom)* Freiheit, *die; (for differences)* Spielraum, *der;* **b)** *(Geog.)* [geographische] Breite; *(of a place)* Breite, *die;* ~s *(regions)* Breiten *Pl.;* ~ **40° N.** 40° nördlicher Breite; **c)** *(Astron.)* Breite, *die*
latrine [lə'tri:n] *n.* Latrine, *die*
latter ['lætə(r)] *attrib. adj.* **a)** letzter...; **the** ~: der/die/das letztere; *pl.* die letzteren; **b)** *(later)* letzt...; **the** ~ **half of the century** die zweite Hälfte des Jahrhunderts; **the** ~ **part of the year** die zweite Jahreshälfte; **the** ~ **end** das Ende
latter: ~ '**day** *n.* Jüngster Tag; ~-**day** *adj.* modern; **L**~-**day 'Saints** *n. pl.* Heilige der Letzten Tage
latterly ['lætəlɪ] *adv.* **a)** *(later)* später; gegen Ende; **b)** *(lately)* in letzter Zeit
lattice ['lætɪs] *n. (also fig., Phys.)* Gitter, *das*
lattice: ~ **frame,** ~ **girder** *ns.* Gitterträger, *der;* ~-**work** *n., no pl.* Gitterwerk, *das*
Latvia ['lætvɪə] *pr. n.* Lettland *(das)*
Latvian ['lætvɪən] **1.** *adj.* lettisch; *see also* **English 1. 2.** *n.* **a)** *(person)* Lette, *der*/Lettin, *die;* **b)** *(language)* Lettisch, *das; see also* **English 2 a**
laud [lɔ:d] *v. t. (literary)* preisen *(geh.);* rühmen; **much-**~**ed** vielgepriesen
laudable ['lɔ:dəbl] *adj.* lobenswert
laudably ['lɔ:dəblɪ] *adv.* lobenswert; löblich
laudanum ['lɔ:dnəm, 'lɒdnəm] *n. (Pharm.)* Laudanum, *das*
laugh [lɑ:f] **1.** *n.* **a)** Lachen, *das; (loud and continuous)* Gelächter, *das;* **have a [good]** ~ **about sth.** [herzlich] über etw. *(Akk.)* lachen; **give a loud** ~: laut auflachen; **this line in the play always gets/raises a** ~: diese Zeile im Stück bringt immer einen Lacher; **join in the** ~: mitlachen; **have the last** ~: derjenige sein, der zuletzt lacht *(fig.);* **have** *or* **get the** ~ **of** *or* **on sb.** jmdn. auslachen können; **the** ~ **is on me** ich stehe dumm da *(ugs.);* **he is always good for a** ~: bei ihm gibt es immer etwas zu lachen; **it should be good for a** ~: dabei gibt es sicher etwas zu lachen; **sb./sth. is a** ~ **a minute** bei jmdm./etw. muß man alle Augenblicke lachen; **that sounds like a** ~ **a minute** *(iron.)* da wird man sicher viel zu lachen haben; **for** ~**s** zum *od.* aus Spaß; **play Mephisto for** ~**s** *(Theatre coll.)* aus Mephisto eine komische Figur machen; **for a** ~: [so] zum Spaß; **anything for a** ~: ich bin für alles *od.* für jeden Spaß zu haben *(ugs.);* **b)** *(type of* ~*)* Lachen, *das;* Art zu lachen; **c)** *(coll.: comical thing)* **it would be a** ~ **if ...**: es wäre ja zum [Tot]lachen, wenn ... *(ugs.);* **that's a** *or* **what a** ~! das ist ja zum [Tot]lachen! *(ugs.); (iron.)* das ist zum Lachen *(ugs.);* daß ich nicht lache!; **he's a [good]** ~: er ist urkomisch. **2.** *v. i.* lachen; ~ **out loud** laut auflachen; **I thought I'd die** ~**ing** ich hätte mich beinahe totgelacht *(ugs.);* **I** ~**ed till I cried** ich habe Tränen gelacht; **be** ~**ing all over one's face** über das ganze Gesicht lachen; ~ **at sb./sth.** *(in amusement)* über jmdn./etw. lachen; *(jeer)* jmdn. auslachen/etw. verlachen; über jmdn./etw. lachen; ~ **in sb.'s face** jmdm. ins Gesicht lachen; ~ **in** *or* **up one's sleeve** sich *(Dat.)* ins Fäustchen lachen; **he'll** ~ **on the other side of his face when ...**: ihm wird das Lachen [noch] vergehen, wenn ...; **he who** ~**s last** ~**s longest** *(prov.)* wer zuletzt lacht, lacht am besten *(Spr.);* **don't make me** ~ *(coll. iron.)* daß ich nicht lache!; ~ **and the world** ~**s with you, weep and you weep alone** *(prov.)* Freunde in der Not gehn hundert *od.* tausend auf ein Lot *(Spr.); see also* **laughing. 3.** *v. t.* lachen; **he was** ~**ed out of town/off the stage** mit Hohnlachen wurde er aus der Stadt/von der Bühne gejagt; ~ **oneself sick** *or* **silly** sich krank- *od.* schieflachen *(ugs.)*
~ **'off** *v. t.* mit einem Lachen abtun
laughable ['lɑ:fəbl] *adj.* lachhaft *(abwertend);* lächerlich
laughing ['lɑ:fɪŋ] **1.** *n.* **be no** ~ **matter** nicht zum Lachen sein. **2.** *adj. (sl.: fortunate)* **be** ~ **[all over one's face]** fein raussein *(ugs.); see also* **hyena a; jackass c**
'**laughing-gas** *n.* Lachgas, *das*
laughingly ['lɑ:fɪŋlɪ] *adv.* lachend; **what is** ~ **called ...** *(iron.)* was sich ... nennt *(spött.)*
'**laughing-stock** *n.* **make sb. a** ~, **make a** ~ **of sb.** jmdn. zum Gespött machen; **he became the** ~ **of the whole neighbourhood** er wurde zum Gespött der ganzen Nachbarschaft
laughter ['lɑ:ftə(r)] *n.* Lachen, *das; (loud and continuous)* Gelächter, *das;* ~ **is the best medicine** *(prov.)* Lachen ist die beste Medizin
'**laughter lines** *n. pl.* Lachfältchen
[1]**launch** [lɔ:nʃ] **1.** *v. t.* **a)** zu Wasser lassen, aussetzen ⟨*Rettungsboot, Segelboot*⟩; vom Stapel lassen ⟨*neues Schiff*⟩; *(propel)* werfen, abschießen ⟨*Harpune*⟩; schleudern ⟨*Speer*⟩; abschießen ⟨*Torpedo*⟩; ~ **a rocket into space** eine Rakete ins All schießen; **b)** *(fig.)* lancieren *(bes. Wirtsch.);* auf den Markt bringen ⟨*Produkt*⟩; vorstellen ⟨*Buch, Schallplatte, Sänger*⟩; auf die Bühne bringen ⟨*Theaterstück*⟩; gründen ⟨*Firma*⟩; ~ **an attack** einen Angriff durchführen. **2.** *v. i.* ~ **into a song** ein Lied anstimmen; ~ **into a long speech/a stream of insults** eine lange Rede/eine Flut von Beschimpfungen vom Stapel lassen *od.* loslassen *(ugs.).* **3.** *n.* **a)** *(of spacecraft)* Start, *der; (of rocket)* Abschuß, *der; (of new ship)* Stapellauf, *der; (of boat)* Aussetzen, *das;* **b)** *(of product)* Lancieren, *das; (of book, record, singer)* Vorstellung, *die; (of play)* Premiere, *die; (of firm)* Gründung, *die*
~ **'out** *v. i. (fig.)* **we can really** ~ **out now** jetzt können wir aus dem vollen schöpfen *od.* brauchen wir nicht zu sparen; ~ **out at sb.** jmdn. anfahren
[2]**launch** *n. (boat)* Barkasse, *die*
launcher ['lɔ:nʃə(r)] *n.* **a)** *(rocket)* Trägerrakete, *die;* **b)** *(structure)* Startrampe, *die*
launching: ~ **pad** *n.* [Raketen]abschußrampe, *die;* ~ **site** *n.* [Raketen]abschußbasis, *die*
'**launch pad** *see* **launching pad**
launder ['lɔ:ndə(r)] *v. t.* **a)** waschen und bügeln; **I have sent the sheets away to be** ~**ed** ich habe die Bettlaken zum Waschen weggegeben; **b)** *(fig.)* waschen ⟨*Geld*⟩
launderette [lɔ:ndə'ret], **laundrette** [lɔ:n'dret], *(Amer.)* **laundromat** ['lɔ:ndrəmæt] *ns.* Waschsalon, *der*
laundry ['lɔ:ndrɪ] *n.* **a)** *(place)* Wäscherei, *die;* **b)** *(clothes etc.)* Wäsche, *die;* **do the** ~: Wäsche waschen
laundry: ~-**bag** *n.* Wäschebeutel, *der;* ~-**basket** *n.* Wäschekorb, *der;* ~**man** *n.* Wäschemann, *der*
laureate ['lɔ:rɪət, 'lɒrɪət] *n.* Laureat, *der;* **[Poet] L**~: Hofdichter, *der;* Poeta laureatus, *der;* **Nobel** ~: Nobelpreisträger, *der*
laurel ['lɒrl] *n.* **a)** *(emblem of victory)* Lorbeer[kranz], *der;* **win one's** ~**[s]** *(fig.)* Lorbeeren ernten; **have to look to one's** ~**s** *(fig.)* sich nicht auf seinen Lorbeeren ausruhen dürfen; **rest on one's** ~**s** *(fig.)* sich auf seinen Lorbeeren ausruhen *(ugs.);* **b)** *(Bot.)* **[cherry-]**~: Kirschlorbeer, *der;* Lorbeerkirsche, *die;* **mountain** ~: Lorbeerrose, *die;* see also **spurge laurel**
lav [læv] *n. (coll.)* Klo, *das (ugs.)*
lava ['lɑ:və] *n.* Lava, *die*
lavage ['lævɪdʒ] *n. (Med.)* Spülung, *die*
lavatory ['lævətərɪ] *n.* Toilette, *die; see also* **toilet a**
lavatory: ~-**attendant** *n.* Toilettenmann, *der*/Toilettenfrau, *die;* ~ **humour** *n.* Fäkalhumor, *der;* ~-**paper** *see* **toilet-paper;** ~-**seat** *see* **toilet-seat**
lavender ['lævɪndə(r)] **1.** *n.* **a)** *(Bot.)* Lavendel, *der;* **b)** *(colour)* Lavendel[blau], *das.* **2.** *adj.* lavendel[blau]
'**lavender-water** *n.* Lavendel[wasser], *das*
lavish ['lævɪʃ] **1.** *adj. (generous)* großzügig; überschwenglich ⟨*Lob, Liebe*⟩; verschwenderisch ⟨*Ausgaben*⟩; *(abundant)* üppig; **be** ~ **of** *or* **with sth.** nicht mit etw. geizen; **be too** ~ **with sth.** mit etw. übertreiben. **2.** *v. t.* ~ **sth. on sb.** jmdn. mit etw. überhäufen *od.* überschütten; ~ **too much time and money on a project** zuviel Zeit und Geld an ein Projekt verschwenden; ~ **care on sth.** seine ganze Mühe auf etw. *(Akk.)* verwenden
lavishly ['lævɪʃlɪ] *adv.* großzügig; überschwenglich ⟨*loben, lieben*⟩; verschwenderisch ⟨*Geld ausgeben*⟩; herrschaftlich ⟨*eingerichtet*⟩
law [lɔ:] *n.* **a)** *no pl. (body of established rules)* Gesetz, *das;* Recht, *das;* **the** ~ **forbids/allows sth. to be done** nach dem Gesetz ist es verboten/erlaubt, etw. zu tun; **the** ~ **is an ass** das Gesetz ist absurd; **according to/under British** *etc.* ~: nach britischem *usw.* Recht; **break the** ~: gegen das Gesetz verstoßen; **be against the** ~: gegen das Gesetz sein; **the** ~ **is the** ~: Gesetz ist Gesetz; **be well versed in the** ~: gesetzeskundig *od.* rechtskundig sein; sich gut mit den Gesetzen auskennen; **history of** ~: Rechtsgeschichte, *die;* **laid down by [the]** ~: gesetzlich festgelegt; **under the** *or* **by** *or* **in** ~: nach dem Gesetz; **be/become** ~: vorgeschrieben sein/werden; **one** ~ **for the rich and another for the poor** zweierlei Recht für Reiche und Arme; **his word is** ~ *(fig.)* sein Wort ist Gesetz; **lay down the** ~ **[about politics]** *(fig. coll.)* [in Sachen Politik] den Ton angeben; **lay down the** ~ **to sb.** *(fig. coll.)* jmdm. Vorschriften machen; **point** *or* **issue of** ~: Rechtsfrage, *die (Rechtsw.);* ~ **enforcement** Durchführung der Gesetze/des Gesetzes; **b)** *no pl., no indef. art. (control through* ~*)* Gesetz, *das;* ~ **and order** Ruhe und Ordnung; **be above the** ~: über dem Gesetz stehen; **outside the** ~: außerhalb der Legalität; **c)** *(statute)* Gesetz, *das;* **what are the** ~**s on drinking and driving?** wie sind die gesetzlichen Bestimmungen bei Trunkenheit am Steuer?; **there ought to be a** ~ **against it/people like you** so etwas sollte/Leute wie du sollten verboten werden; **be a** ~ **unto itself** seinen eigenen Gesetzen folgen; **be a** ~ **unto oneself** machen, was man will; **necessity knows** *or* **has no** ~**[s]** *(prov.)* Not kennt kein Gebot *(Spr.);* **d)** *no pl., no indef. art. (litigation)* Rechtswesen, *das;* Gerichtswesen, *das;* **go to** ~ **[over sth.]** [wegen etw.] vor Gericht gehen; [wegen etw.] den Rechtsweg beschreiten; **have the** ~ **on sb. [over sth.]** jmdn. [wegen etw.] verklagen; gegen jmdn. [wegen etw.] gerichtlich vorgehen; **take the** ~ **into one's own hands** sich *(Dat.)* selbst Recht verschaffen; **e)** *no pl., no indef. art. (profession)* **practise** ~: Jurist/Juristin sein; **go into [the]** ~: die juristische Laufbahn einschlagen; Jurist/Juristin werden; **f)** *no pl., no art. (Univ.: jurisprudence)* Jura *o. Art.;* Rechtswissenschaft, *die; attrib.* Rechts-; **Faculty of Law** juristische Fa-

kultät; ~ **school** *(Amer.)* juristische Fakultät; ~ **student** Jurastudent, *der*/-studentin, *die;* **g)** *no indef. art. (branch of ~)* **commercial ~:** Handelsrecht, *das;* ~ **of contract** Vertragsrecht, *das;* ~ **of nations** Völkerrecht, *das;* **bachelor/doctor of ~s** Bakkalaureus/Doktor der Rechte; **h)** *(Sci., Philos., etc.)* Gesetz, *das; (regularity in nature)* Gesetzmäßigkeit, *die;* ~ **of nature, natural ~** *(lit., or fig. iron.)* Naturgesetz, *das;* ~ **of supply and demand** Gesetz von Angebot und Nachfrage; ~ **of gravity** *or* **gravitation** Gravitationsgesetz, *das;* **i)** *(rule of game, etiquette, or art)* Regel, *die;* **~s of tennis/chess** Tennis-/Schachregeln; **j)** *(Relig.)* Gebot, *das;* Gesetz, *das;* **Divine/God's ~:** göttliche Gebote/Gebote Gottes; **k)** *(enforcing agent)* **the ~:** die Rechtsordnung; *(coll.: police, policeman)* Polente, *die (salopp);* **be in trouble with the ~:** mit dem Gesetz in Konflikt geraten; **I'll set the ~ on you!** ich hole die Polizei!; **the long arm of the ~** *(rhet./iron.)* der Arm des Gesetzes; **officer of the ~:** Vertreter des Gesetzes

law: ~-abiding *adj.* gesetzestreu; ~ **agent** *n. (Scot.) see* **solicitor a; ~-breaker** *n.* Gesetzesbrecher, *der*/-brecherin, *die;* Rechtsbrecher, *der*/-brecherin, *die;* **~court** *n.* Gerichtsgebäude, *das; (room)* Gerichtssaal, *der;* **L~ Courts** *n. pl. (Brit.) Gebäudekomplex von Gerichtshöfen;* ~ **firm** *n. (Amer.)* Anwaltskanzlei, *die*

lawful ['lɔ:fl] *adj.* rechtmäßig, legitim ⟨*Besitzer, Erbe*⟩; legitim, ehelich ⟨*Tochter, Sohn, Nachkomme*⟩; legal, gesetzmäßig ⟨*Vorgehen, Maßnahme*⟩; **by ~ means** mit legitimen Mitteln; *see also* **wife**

lawfully ['lɔ:fəlı] *adv.* legal; auf legalem Weg[e] ⟨*erwerben*⟩

'lawgiver *n.* Gesetzgeber, *der*

lawless ['lɔ:lıs] *adj.* **a)** gesetzlos; **b)** *(unbridled)* zügellos

law: L~ Lord *n. (Brit.) Mitglied des obersten brit. Berufungsgerichts;* Law Lord, *der;* **~maker** *n.* Gesetzgeber, *der;* **~man** *n. (Amer.)* Vertreter des Gesetzes

lawn [lɔ:n] *n. (grass)* Rasen, *der;* **~s** Rasenflächen; **area of ~:** Rasenfläche, *die*

lawn: ~-mower *n.* Rasenmäher, *der;* **~-seed** *n.* Grassamen, *der;* **~-sprinkler** *n.* Rasensprenger, *der;* ~ **'tennis** *n.* Rasentennis, *das*

law: ~ officer *n.* **a)** Justizbeamte, *der*/Justizbeamtin, *die;* **b)** *(Brit.: member of Government)* Kronanwalt, *der*/Kronanwältin, *die;* **~suit** *n.* Prozeß, *der*

lawyer ['lɔ:jə(r),'lɔıə(r)] *n.* **a)** *(solicitor etc.)* Rechtsanwalt, *der*/Rechtsanwältin, *die;* **b)** *(expert in law)* Jurist, *der*/Juristin, *die*

lax [læks] *adj.* lax; **the guards are ~ about whom they allow to enter** die Wachen nehmen es nicht sehr genau damit, wen sie hineinlassen

laxative ['læksətıv] *(Med.)* **1.** *adj.* abführend; stuhlgangfördernd. **2.** *n.* Abführmittel, *das;* Laxativ[um] *das (fachspr.)*

laxity ['læksıtı], **laxness** ['læksnıs] *ns.* Laxheit, *die;* **moral ~:** laxe Moral

[1]**lay** [leı] *adj.* **a)** *(Relig.)* laikal; Laien⟨*bruder, -schwester, -predigt*⟩; *see also* **vicar; b)** *(inexpert)* laienhaft; **in ~ opinion** nach Ansicht des Laien; **to the ~ mind** für den Nichtfachmann *od.* Laien

[2]**lay 1.** *v. t.,* **laid** [leıd] **a)** *(deposit, put)* legen, [ver]legen ⟨*Teppichboden, Rohr, Gleis, Steine, Kabel, Leitung*⟩; legen ⟨*Parkett, Fliesen, Fundament*⟩; anlegen ⟨*Straße, Gehsteig*⟩; ~ **to rest** *(euphem.: bury)* zur letzten Ruhe betten *(geh. verhüll.);* ~ **eyes on sb.** jmdn. sehen *od.* erblicken; *see also* **hand 1a; b)** *(fig.)* **feel oneself laid under an obligation** sich verpflichtet fühlen; ~ **one's case before sb.** jmdm. seinen Fall vortragen; ~ **one's plans/ideas before sb.** jmdm. seine Pläne/Vorstellungen unterbreiten; **the facts are laid before us** die Fakten liegen vor uns; ~ **sth. before the Commons** *or* **on the table** *(Brit. Parl.)* etw. dem Unterhaus vorlegen; ~ **damages at £900** *(Law)* 900 Pfund Schadensersatz fordern; **c)** *(impose)* auferlegen ⟨*Verantwortung, Verpflichtung, Geldbuße, Steuern*⟩ **(on** *Dat.*); verhängen ⟨*Strafe*⟩ **(on** über + *Akk.*); ~ **a penalty/a tax on sth.** etw. mit einer Strafe/einer Steuer belegen; ~ **a burden of responsibility on sb.'s shoulders** jmdm. Verantwortung aufbürden; **that ~s an obligation on me to do it** das verpflichtet mich, es zu tun; ~ **weight on sth.** Gewicht auf etw. *(Akk.)* legen; **d)** *(wager)* **I'll ~ you five to one that ...:** ich wette mit dir fünf zu eins, daß ...; **I'll ~ you £10 that he'll come** ich wette mit dir um 10 Pfund, daß er kommt; ~ **a wager on sth.** eine Wette auf etw. *(Akk.)* abschließen; auf etw. *(Akk.)* wetten; **e)** *(prepare)* ~ **the table/cloth** den Tisch decken/die Tischdecke auflegen; ~ **three places for lunch** drei Gedecke zum Mittagessen auflegen; ~ **[for] breakfast,** ~ **the breakfast things** den Frühstückstisch decken; *see also* **fire 1d; f)** *(Biol.)* legen ⟨*Ei*⟩; **g)** *(apply)* auftragen ⟨*Farbe usw.*⟩ **(on to, over** auf + *Akk.*); *(cover)* ~ **a floor with lino** *etc.* einen Boden mit Linoleum *usw.* auslegen; **h)** *(devise)* schmieden, ersinnen ⟨*Plan*⟩; **i)** *(bring into a state)* ~ **idle** stillegen ⟨*Fabrik*⟩; ~ **land under water** Land überfluten; **j)** *(cause to subside)* glätten ⟨*See*⟩; binden ⟨*Staub*⟩; beruhigen ⟨*Sturm*⟩; *(fig.)* zerstreuen ⟨*Bedenken, Befürchtungen*⟩; bannen ⟨*Geist, Gespenst*⟩; **k)** *(bring down)* ~ **one on sb.** *(sl.: hit sb.)* jmdm. eine reinschlagen *(salopp);* **the crops were laid [flat] by the rain** der Regen hat das Getreide zu Boden gedrückt; **l)** *(sl.: copulate with)* ~ **a woman** eine Frau vernaschen *od.* aufs Kreuz legen *(salopp);* **m)** *(make by twisting)* drehen ⟨*Seil*⟩. **2.** *v. i.,* **laid a)** *(Naut.)* liegen; ~ **at anchor** vor Anker liegen; **b)** *(used erroneously for 'lie')* liegen; ~ **down** sich hinlegen. **3.** *n.* **a)** *(sl.: sexual partner)* **she's a good/an easy ~:** sie ist gut im Bett/steigt mit jedem ins Bett *(ugs.);* **b)** *(way sth. lies)* Lage, *die;* **the ~ of the land** *(Amer.)* ≈ **the lie of the land** *see* [2]**lie 1a**

~ **a'bout** *v. t. (coll.)* ~ **about sb.** auf jmdn. einschlagen; *(scold)* jmdn. ausschimpfen; ~ **about one** um sich schlagen; *see also* **layabout**

~ **a'side** *v. t.* beiseite *od.* zur Seite legen, weglegen ⟨*angefangene Arbeit*⟩; *(fig.)* beilegen ⟨*Streit, Differenzen*⟩; beiseite *od.* auf die Seite legen ⟨*Geld*⟩; ablegen ⟨*Gewohnheiten, Untugenden*⟩

~ **'back** *v. t.* zurückstellen ⟨*Autositz, Behandlungsstuhl*⟩; *see also* **laid-back**

~ **'by** *v. t.* beiseite *od.* auf die Seite legen; **have some money laid by** etwas [Geld] auf der hohen Kante haben *(ugs.)*

~ **'down** *v. t.* **a)** hinlegen; ~ **sth. down on the table** etw. auf den Tisch legen; **b)** *(give up)* niederlegen ⟨*Amt, Waffen*⟩; ablegen ⟨*Amtskette*⟩; *(deposit)* hinterlegen ⟨*Geld*⟩; *(wager)* wetten ⟨*Betrag*⟩; ~ **down one's arms** sich ergeben; die Waffen strecken *(geh.);* ~ **down one's life for sth./sb.** sein Leben für etw./jmdn. [hin]geben; **c)** *(build)* bauen; auf Kiel legen ⟨*Schiff*⟩; **d)** *(formulate)* festlegen ⟨*Regeln, Richtlinien, Bedingungen*⟩; aufstellen ⟨*Grundsätze, Regeln, Norm*⟩; festsetzen ⟨*Preis*⟩; *(in a contract, constitution)* verankern; niederlegen; **e)** ~ **the land/field down to pasture** das Land/Feld in Weideland umwandeln; **f)** *(store)* einlagern ⟨*Wein*⟩

~ **'in** *v. t.* einlagern; sich eindecken mit

~ **'into** *v. t. (coll.)* ~ **into sb.** auf jmdn. losgehen; über jmdn. herfallen; *(fig.)* jmdn. zusammenstauchen *(ugs.)*

~ **'off 1.** *v. t.* **a)** *(from work)* vorübergehend entlassen; **be laid off [from one's job]** Feierschichten einlegen müssen; **b)** *(coll.) (stop)* ~ **off shouting!** hör auf zu schreien!; ~ **off it!** laß das!; hör auf damit!; *(stop attacking, lit. or fig.)* ~ **off him!** laß ihn in Ruhe! **2.** *v. i. (coll.: stop)* aufhören. *See also* **lay-off**

~ **'on** *v. t.* **a)** *(provide)* sorgen für ⟨*Getränke, Erfrischungen, Unterhaltung*⟩; bereitstellen ⟨*Auto, Transportmittel*⟩; organisieren ⟨*Theaterbesuch, Stadtrundfahrt*⟩; anschließen ⟨*Gas, Wasser, Strom*⟩; **b)** *(apply)* auftragen ⟨*Farbe usw.*⟩; ~ **it on** *(fig.: exaggerate)* dick auftragen *(ugs.); see also* **thick 1a; trowel a; c)** *(impose)* erheben ⟨*Steuer, Gebühr*⟩; verhängen ⟨*Strafe*⟩; **d) ~ing on of hands** *(Eccl.)* Handauflegung, *die*

~ **'out 1.** *v. t.* **a)** *(spread out)* ausbreiten; *(ready for use)* zurechtlegen; **the books were laid out on the table** die Bücher waren *od.* lagen auf dem Tisch ausgebreitet; ~ **out sth. for sb. to see** etw. vor jmdm. ausbreiten; **b)** *(for burial)* aufbahren; **c)** *(arrange)* anlegen ⟨*Garten, Park, Wege*⟩; das Layout machen für ⟨*Buch*⟩; *see also* **layout; d)** *(coll.: knock unconscious)* ~ **sb. out** jmdn. außer Gefecht setzen; **e)** *(spend)* ausgeben; investieren *(ugs.).* **2.** *v. refl.* ~ **oneself out to do sth.** sich anstrengen *od. (ugs.)* sich mächtig ins Zeug legen, etw. zu tun

~ **'up** *v. t.* **a)** *(store)* lagern; **you're ~ing up trouble/problems for yourself [later on]** *(fig.)* du handelst dir [für später] nur Ärger/Schwierigkeiten ein; **b)** *(put out of service)* [vorübergehend] aus dem Verkehr ziehen ⟨*Fahrzeug*⟩; *(through illness)* außer Gefecht setzen; **I was laid up in bed for a week** ich mußte eine Woche das Bett hüten

[3]**lay** *n.* **a)** *(of medieval minstrel)* Leich, *der (Literaturw.);* **b)** *(narrative poem, song)* Ballade, *die*

[4]**lay** *see* [2]**lie 2**

lay: ~about *n. (Brit.)* Gammler, *der (ugs. abwertend);* Nichtstuer, *der (abwertend);* **~-by** *n., pl.* **~-bys** *(Brit.)* Parkbucht, *die;* Haltebucht, *die;* ~ **clerk** *n.* Kantoreisänger, *der*

layer ['leıə(r)] *n.* **a)** Schicht, *die;* **wear several ~s of clothing** mehrere Kleidungsstücke übereinander tragen; **several ~s of paper** mehrere Lagen Papier; ~ **of dust** Staubschicht, *die;* **b)** *(Hort.)* Ableger, *der;* **c)** *(poultry)* Leg[e]henne, *die;* **this hen is a poor ~:** dieses Huhn legt schlecht

'layer cake *n.* Schichttorte, *die*

layered ['leıəd] *adj.* stufig ⟨*Haarschnitt*⟩; **three-~ cake** dreischichtige Torte; ~ **skirt** Stufenrock, *der;* ~ **clouds** Schichtwolken

layette [leı'et] *n.* **[baby's] ~:** Babyausstattung, *die*

lay: ~ figure *n.* **a)** *(Art)* Gliederpuppe, *die;* **b)** *(in dramatic work)* Phantom, *das;* **~man** ['leımən] *n., pl.* **~men** ['leımən] Laie, *der;* **~-off** *n.* **a)** *(temporary dismissal)* vorübergehende Entlassung; **the ~-offs lasted longer than expected** es mußten länger als erwartet Feierschichten gefahren werden; **b)** *(Sport; coll.: break from work)* Pause, *die;* **take a ~-off** [eine] Pause machen; **~out** *n. (of house, office)* Raumaufteilung, *die; (of garden, park)* Gestaltung, *die;* Anlage, *die; (of book, magazine, poster, advertisement)* Gestaltung, *die;* Layout, *das; (of letter)* äußere Form; ~ **reader** *n. Laie, der Teile des Gottesdienstes halten darf;* ≈ Lektor, *der (ev. Kirche);* ≈ Diakon, *der (kath. Kirche);* **~shaft** *n. (Mech. Engin.)* Vorgelegewelle, *die (Technik)*

laze [leız] **1.** *v. i.* faulenzen; ~ **around** *or* **about** herumfaulenzen *(ugs.);* **spend the whole day lazing in bed** den ganzen Tag faul im Bett liegen. **2.** *v. t.* ~ **the day/one's life away** den ganzen Tag/sein ganzes Leben vertrödeln *od.* verbummeln *(ugs. abwertend)*

lazily ['leızılı] *adv.* faul; *(sluggishly)* träge

laziness ['leızınıs] *n., no pl.* Faulheit, *die; (sluggishness)* Trägheit, *die*

lazy ['leɪzɪ] *adj.* faul; träge ‹*Rhythmus, Musik, Geste, Sprechweise*›; träge fließend ‹*Fluß*›; **physically ~:** träge; **mentally ~:** geistig träge; denkfaul; **have a ~ day on the beach** einen Tag am Strand faulenzen; **be in a ~ mood** sich träge fühlen; **be ~ about writing [letters]** schreibfaul sein

lazy: ~-bones *n. sing.* Faulpelz, *der;* ~ **'eye** *n. Auge mit Sehschwäche, das [beim Schielen] weniger belastet wird und deshalb in der Sehkraft weiter nachläßt*

lb. *abbr.* **pound[s]** ≈ Pfd.

l.b.w. [elbi:'dʌblju] *abbr. (Cricket)* **leg before wicket**

LCD *abbr.* **liquid crystal display** LCD

L/Cpl. *abbr.* **Lance-Corporal** OG

L-driver ['eldraɪvə(r)] *(Brit.) see* **learner-driver**

LEA *abbr.* **Local Education Authority** ≈ Schulamt, *das*

lea [li:] *n. (poet.)* Wiese, *die*

leach [li:tʃ] **1.** *v. t. (make percolate)* durchsickern lassen; *(subject to percolation)* auslaugen; *(remove by percolation)* extrahieren; auslaugen. **2.** *v. i. (percolate through)* durchsickern; *(be removed by percolation)* ausgelaugt werden

¹lead [led] **1.** *n.* **a)** *(metal)* Blei, *das;* **white ~:** Bleiweiß, *das;* **[as] heavy as ~:** schwer wie Blei; bleischwer; *see also* **blacklead; red lead; b)** *(in pencil)* [Bleistift]mine, *die;* **c)** *(bullets)* Blei, *das (veralt.);* **I'll fill** *or* **pump you full of ~:** ich pumpe dich mit Blei voll; **d)** *(Naut.)* Lot, *das;* Senkblei, *das;* **cast** *or* **heave the ~:** das Lot [aus]werfen; **swing the ~** *(fig. Brit. sl.)* sich drücken; **e)** *in pl. (of window)* Bleifassung, *die;* **f)** *(Printing)* Reglette, *die.* **2.** *attrib. adj.* Blei-. **3.** *v. t.* **a)** in Blei fassen ‹*Fenster*›; **~ed** bleigefaßt; **b) ~ed petrol** bleihaltiges Benzin

²lead [li:d] **1.** *v. t.,* **led** [led] **a)** führen; **~ sb. a miserable life** *or* **existence** jmdm. das Leben zur Qual machen; **~ sb. through the procedures** *(fig.)* jmdn. mit dem Verfahren vertraut machen; **~ sb. to do sth.** *(fig.)* jmdn. dazu bringen, etw. zu tun; **~ sb. by the hand** jmdn. an der Hand führen; **~ sb. by the nose** *(fig.)* jmdn. nach seiner Pfeife tanzen lassen; **let oneself be led by the nose** *(fig.)* sich an der Nase herumführen lassen; **~ sb. into trouble/difficulties** *(fig.)* jmdm. Ärger einbringen/jmdn. in Schwierigkeiten bringen; **this is ~ing us nowhere** *(fig.)* das führt zu nichts; *see also* **astray 1; dance 3 a; garden 1 a; way 1 b; b)** *(fig.: influence, induce)* **~ sb. to do sth.** jmdn. veranlassen, etw. zu tun; **be easily led** sich leicht beeinflussen lassen; **~ sb. into bad habits** jmdn. zu schlechten Gewohnheiten verleiten; **children are easier led than driven** bei Kindern erreicht man im Guten mehr als im Bösen; **that ~s me to believe that ...:** das läßt mich glauben, daß ...; **I was led to the conclusion that ...:** ich gelangte zu dem Schluß, daß ...; **this leads me to the conclusion that ...:** daraus schließe ich, daß ...; **Is it true that she was married before? – So I am led to believe** Stimmt es, daß sie schon einmal verheiratet war? – Soweit ich weiß, ja; **he led me to suppose/believe that ...:** er gab mir Grund zu der Annahme/er machte mich glauben, daß ...; **c)** führen ‹*Leben*›; **~ a life of misery/a wretched existence** ein erbärmliches Dasein führen/eine kümmerliche Existenz fristen; **d)** *(be first in)* anführen; **~ the world in electrical engineering** auf dem Gebiet der Elektrotechnik in der ganzen Welt führend sein; **Smith led Jones by several yards/seconds** *(Sport)* Smith hatte mehrere Yards/Sekunden Vorsprung vor Jones; *see also* **field 1 l; e)** *(direct, be head of)* anführen ‹*Bewegung, Abordnung*›; leiten ‹*Diskussion, Veranstaltung, Ensemble*›; ‹*Dirigent:*› leiten ‹*Orchester, Chor*›; ‹*Konzertmeister:*› führen ‹*Orchester*›; **~ a party** Vorsitzender/Vorsitzende einer Partei sein; **~ the government** an der Spitze der Regierung stehen; Regierungschef/-chefin sein; **Napoleon led his army into Italy/to a great victory** Napoleon führte seine Armee nach Italien/zu einem großen Sieg; **f)** *(cause to pass)* **~ water through sth.** Wasser durch etw. [hindurch]leiten; **~ a rope through a pulley** ein Seil über die Rolle[n] eines Flaschenzugs führen; **g)** *(Cards)* ausspielen; **~ a spade** Pik ausspielen. **2.** *v. i.,* **led a)** ‹*Straße usw., Tür:*› führen; **~ to the town/to the sea/out of the town** zur Stadt/ans Meer/aus der Stadt führen; **~ to confusion** Verwirrung stiften; **one thing led to another** es kam eins zum anderen; **what will it all ~ to?** wo soll das alles [noch] hinführen?; **b)** *(be first)* führen; *(go in front)* vorangehen; *(fig.: be leader)* an der Spitze stehen; **~ by 3 metres** mit 3 Metern in Führung liegen; 3 Meter Vorsprung haben; **~ in the race** das Rennen anführen; **it's Smith ~ing from Jones and Brown** Smith führt vor Jones und Brown; **c)** *(Journ.)* **a good story to ~ with** eine gute Titelgeschichte; **~ with the latest spy scandal** die jüngste Spionageaffäre groß herausbringen; **d)** *(Cards)* ausspielen; **~ with a spade** Pik ausspielen. **3.** *n.* **a)** *(precedent)* Beispiel, *das;* *(clue)* Anhaltspunkt, *der;* **follow sb.'s ~, take one's ~ from sb.** jmds. Beispiel *(Dat.)* folgen; **give sb. a ~** *(precedent)* jmdm. mit gutem Beispiel vorangehen; *(clue)* jmdm. einen Anhaltspunkt geben; **b)** *(first place)* Führung, *die;* **be in the ~:** in Führung liegen; an der Spitze liegen; **move** *or* **go into the ~:** sich an die Spitze setzen; in Führung gehen; **keep one's ~:** sich an der Spitze *od.* seine Führungsposition behaupten; **we mustn't lose our ~:** wir dürfen unsere Führungsposition nicht verlieren; **hold the ~ in export sales** mit seinen Exportgeschäften die Spitze halten; **take the ~ from sb.** jmdm. den Rang ablaufen; *(in race)* sich vor jmdm. an die Spitze setzen; vor jmdm. in Führung gehen; **c)** *(amount)* Vorsprung, *der;* **have a ~ of two metres/minutes over sb.** einen Vorsprung von zwei Metern/Minuten vor jmdm. haben; **d)** *(leash)* Leine, *die;* **on a ~:** an der Leine; **let a dog off the** *or* **its ~:** einen Hund von der Leine losmachen; **put a dog on the ~:** einen Hund anleinen; **e)** *(Electr.)* Kabel, *das;* Leitung, *die;* **f)** *(Theatre)* Hauptrolle, *die;* *(player)* Hauptdarsteller, *der*/-darstellerin, *die;* **g)** *(Cards)* **whose ~ is it?** wer spielt aus?; **the ~ was the jack of clubs** Kreuzbube war gespielt. **4.** *adj.* Lead‹*gitarre, -gitarrist usw.*›

~ a'way *v. t.* abführen ‹*Gefangenen, Verbrecher*›

~ 'off 1. *v. t.* **a)** *(take away)* abführen; **b)** *(begin)* beginnen. **2.** *v. i.* beginnen

~ 'on 1. *v. t.* **a)** *(entice)* **~ sb. on** jmdn. reizen; **he's ~ing you on** er versucht, dich zu reizen; **b)** *(take further)* **that ~s me on to my next point** das bringt mich zu meinem nächsten Punkt; **~ sb. on to do sth.** jmdn. darauf bringen, etw. zu tun. **2.** *v. i.* **a)** *imper. (go first)* **~ on!** geh vor!; **b) ~ing on from what you have just said, ...:** um fortzuführen, was Sie eben sagten, ...; **~ on to the next topic** *etc.* zum nächsten Thema *usw.* führen; **~ on to better things** jmdn. weiterbringen

~ 'up to *v. t.* hinführen zu; *(aim at)* hinauswollen auf (+ *Akk.*); **~ up to a very funny punch-line** in einer köstlichen Pointe gipfeln; **just as I was ~ing up to the main point of my speech** gerade als ich zum Hauptpunkt meiner Rede kommen wollte

leaden ['ledn] *adj.* **a)** bleiern; **b)** *(fig.) (heavy)* bleiern ‹*Schlaf, Augenlider, Glieder*›; schleppend ‹*Tempo*›; bang ‹*Herz*›; *(oppressive)* drückend ‹*Atmosphäre*›; lähmend ‹*Einfluß*›; starr ‹*Regeln, Haltung*›

leader ['li:də(r)] *n.* **a)** Führer, *der*/Führerin, *die;* *(of political party)* Vorsitzende, *der/die;* *(of gang, hooligans, rebels)* Anführer, *der*/Anführerin, *die;* *(of expedition, project, troupe)* Leiter, *der*/Leiterin, *die;* *(of deputation)* Sprecher, *der*/Sprecherin, *die;* *(of tribe)* [Stammes]häuptling, *der;* Stammesführer, *der;* **the Egyptian/Labour ~:** der ägyptische Präsident/der Vorsitzende der Labour Party; **union/the Labour ~s** Gewerkschaftsvorsitzende/die Führenden der Labour Party; **L~ of the House of Commons/Lords** *(Brit. Polit.)* Führer des Unterhauses/Oberhauses; **have the qualities of a ~:** Führungsqualitäten haben; *see also* **follow-my-leader; b)** *(one who is first)* **this scientist is a ~ in his field** dieser Wissenschaftler ist eine führende Kapazität auf seinem Gebiet; **be the ~ in a race** in einem Rennen in Führung liegen; **catch up with the ~s** *(in race)* sich an die Spitze des Feldes vorarbeiten; **be no longer amongst the ~s of world tennis** nicht mehr zur internationalen Spitze[nklasse] im Tennis gehören; **c)** *(Brit. Journ.)* Leitartikel, *der;* **d)** *(tab on film or tape)* Startband, *das;* **e)** *(Mus.) (leading performer)* Leader, *der*/Leaderin, *die;* *(Brit.: principal first violinist)* Konzertmeister, *der*/-meisterin, *die;* *(Amer.: conductor)* Dirigent, *der*/Dirigentin, *die;* **f)** *(Hort.)* Haupttrieb, *der*

leaderless ['li:dəlɪs] *adj.* führerlos

leadership ['li:dəʃɪp] *n.* **a)** Führung, *die;* *(capacity to lead)* Führungseigenschaften *Pl.;* **under the ~ of** unter [der] Führung von; **b)** *(leaders)* Führung[sspitze], *die;* **~ of the party** Parteivorsitz, *der*

'leader writer *n.* Leitartikelschreiber, *der*/-schreiberin, *die;* Leitartikler, *der*/-artiklerin, *die (Pressejargon)*

lead-free ['ledfri:] *adj.* bleifrei

lead-in ['li:dɪn] *n.* Einleitung, *die* **(to** *Gen.*); **as a ~-in to the film/programme** zur Einleitung des Films/Programms

leading ['li:dɪŋ] *adj.* führend; *(in first position)* ‹*Läufer, Pferd, Auto*› an der Spitze; **~ role** Hauptrolle, *die;* *(fig.)* führende Rolle

leading: ~ 'article *n. (Brit. Journ.)* Leitartikel, *der;* **~ 'counsel** *n. (Brit. Law)* Kronanwalt, *der*/-anwältin, *die;* *(of the defence)* Hauptverteidiger, *der*/-verteidigerin, *die;* **~ 'edge** *n. (foremost edge)* Vorderkante, *die;* *(of sail)* Vorliek, *das;* **~ 'lady** *n.* Hauptdarstellerin, *die;* **his ~ lady** seine Partnerin *(als Hauptdarstellerin);* **~ 'light** *n.* herausragende Persönlichkeit; *(expert)* führende Kapazität; **~ 'man** *n.* Hauptdarsteller, *der;* **her ~ man** ihr Partner *(als Hauptdarsteller);* **~ 'question** *n.* Suggestivfrage, *die;* **~-rein** *n.* Leitzügel, *der*

lead: ~ pencil [led 'pensl] *n.* Bleistift, *der;* **~-poisoning** ['ledpɔɪzənɪŋ] *n.* Bleivergiftung, *die;* **~ screw** ['li:d skru:] *n.* Leitspindel, *die (Technik);* **~ shot** [led 'ʃɒt] *n.* **a)** *no pl. (Angling)* Bleikugeln *Pl.;* **b)** *no pl. (for shotgun)* Schrot, *der od. das;* **c)** *(single projectile)* Blei- *od.* Schrotkugel, *die;* **~ singer** [li:d 'sɪŋə(r)] *n.* Leadsänger *der*/-sängerin, *die;* **~ story** ['li:d stɔ:rɪ] *n. (Journ.)* Titelgeschichte, *die;* **~ time** ['li:d taɪm] *n. (Econ.)* Entwicklungszeit, *die;* **~-up** ['li:dʌp] *n.* Vorfeld, *das (fig.);* **in/during the ~-up to the election/revolution** im Vorfeld der Wahlen/der Revolution

leaf [li:f] **1.** *n., pl.* **leaves** [li:vz] **a)** Blatt, *das;* **the falling leaves** die fallenden Blätter; das fallende Laub; **shake like a ~:** zittern wie Espenlaub; **be in ~:** grün sein; **come into ~:** grün werden; ausschlagen; **b)** *(of paper)* Blatt, *das;* **a ~ of paper** ein Blatt Papier; **turn over a new ~** *(fig.)* einen neuen Anfang machen; sich ändern; *see also* **book 1 a; c)** *(of door)* Flügel, *der;* *(of table) (hinged/sliding flap)* Platte, *die;* *(for inserting)* Einlegebrett, *das.* **2.** *v. i.* **~ through sth.** etw. durchblättern; in etw. *(Dat.)* blättern

leaf: ~-green 1. ['--] *adj.* laubgrün; **2.** [-'-]

n. Laubgrün, *das;* **~-insect** *n.* Wandelndes Blatt

leafless ['li:flɪs] *adj.* blattlos, kahl ‹*Baum*›

leaflet ['li:flɪt] **1.** *n.* **a)** [Hand]zettel, *der; (with manufacturer's instructions)* Gebrauchsanweisung, *die;* Bedienungsanleitung, *die; (advertising)* Reklamezettel, *der; (political)* Flugblatt, *das;* **b)** *(Bot.)* Blättchen, *das.* **2.** *v. t.* [Hand]zettel verteilen an (+ *Akk.*)

leaf: ~-mould *n.* Laubkompost, *der;* **~ spring** *n. (Mech. Engin.)* Blattfeder, *die (Technik);* **~-stalk** *n.* Blattstiel, *der*

leafy ['li:fɪ] *adj.* belaubt; **~ vegetable** Blattgemüse, *das;* **a ~ country lane** eine baumbestandene Landstraße

¹league [li:g] *n.* **a)** *(agreement)* Bündnis, *das;* Bund, *der; (in history)* Liga, *die;* **enter into** *or* **form a ~:** ein Bündnis eingehen *od.* schließen; einen Bund schließen; **be in ~ with sb.** mit jmdm. im Bunde sein *od.* stehen; **those two are in ~ [together]** die beiden stecken unter einer Decke *(ugs.);* **b)** *(Sport)* Liga, *die;* **the ~ championship** die Ligameisterschaft; **I am not in his ~, he is out of my ~** *(fig.)* ich komme nicht an ihn heran; mit ihm kann ich mich nicht messen; **be in the big ~** *(fig.)* es geschafft haben; *see also* **Rugby League**

²league *n. (arch.: distance)* ≈ drei Meilen; **travel many a ~:** viele Meilen reisen

league: ~ 'football *n.* Ligafußball, *der;* **~ game** *n.* Ligaspiel, *das;* **~ 'leaders** *n. pl. (Sport)* Tabellenführer, *der;* **~ match** *n.* Ligaspiel, *das;* **L~ of 'Nations** *n. (Hist.)* Völkerbund, *der;* **~ table** *n.* Tabelle, *die (Sport);* **be at the top/bottom of the ~ table** an der Tabellenspitze/am Tabellenende sein *(fig.);* an der Spitze rangieren/das Schlußlicht bilden *(ugs.)* (**of** unter + *Dat.*)

leak [li:k] **1.** *n.* **a)** *(hole)* Leck, *das; (in roof, ceiling, tent)* undichte Stelle; **there's a ~ in the tank** der Tank hat ein Leck; **spring a ~** ‹*Schiff:*› leckschlagen *(Seemannsspr.);* ‹*Gas-, Flüssigkeitsbehälter:*› ein Leck bekommen; **stop the ~:** das Leck abdichten *od.* stopfen; **b)** *(escaping fluid/gas)* durch ein Leck austretende Flüssigkeit/austretendes Gas; **I can smell a gas ~:** hier riecht es nach Gas; **c)** *(fig.: of information)* undichte Stelle; **government ~s** undichte Stellen in der Regierung; **there has been a ~ to the press/from reliable sources** der Presse sind Informationen zugespielt worden/aus verläßlichen Quellen sind Informationen durchgesickert; **who was responsible for the ~?** wer war dafür verantwortlich, daß Informationen durchgesickert sind?; **d)** *(Electr.)* Elektrizitätsverlust, *der; (path or point)* Fehlerstelle, *die;* **e) have a/go for a ~** *(sl.)* pinkeln/pinkeln gehen *(salopp).* **2.** *v. t.* **a)** austreten lassen; **the pipe is ~ing water/gas** aus dem lecken Rohr tritt Wasser/Gas aus; **b)** *(fig.: disclose)* durchsickern lassen; **~ sth. to sb.** jmdm. etw. zuspielen; **details of the plan have been ~ed** man hat Einzelheiten des Plans durchsickern lassen. **3.** *v. i.* **a)** *(escape)* austreten (**from** aus); *(enter)* eindringen (**in** in + *Akk.*); **b)** ‹*Faß, Tank, Schiff:*› lecken; ‹*Rohr, Leitung, Dach:*› undicht sein; ‹*Gefäß, Füller:*› auslaufen; **the roof ~s** es regnet durch das Dach; **c)** *(fig.)* **~ [out]** durchsickern

leakage ['li:kɪdʒ] *n.* **a)** Auslaufen, *das; (of fluid, gas)* Ausströmen, *das; (fig.: of information)* Durchsickern, *das;* **b)** *(substance, amount)* **the ~ is increasing** das Leck wird größer; **mop up the ~:** das ausgelaufene Wasser *usw.* aufwischen; **~ to the Press** *(fig.)* Indiskretionen der Presse gegenüber

leaky ['li:kɪ] *adj.* undicht; leck ‹*Schiff, Boot, Tank*›

¹lean [li:n] **1.** *adj.* mager; hager ‹*Person, Gesicht*›; **we had a ~ time [of it] during the War** es ging uns sehr schlecht während des Krieges. **2.** *n. (meat)* Magere, *das*

²lean 1. *v. i.*, **~ed** [li:nd, lent] *or (Brit.)* **~t** [lent] **a)** sich beugen; **~ against the door** sich gegen die Tür lehnen; **~ out of the window** sich aus dem Fenster lehnen *od.* beugen; **~ down/forward** sich herab-/vorbeugen; **~ backwards** sich zurückbeugen; sich nach hinten beugen; **~ back in one's chair** sich im Sessel zurücklehnen; **b)** *(support oneself)* **~ against/on sth.** sich gegen/an etw. *(Akk.)* lehnen; **~ on sth.** *(from above)* sich auf etw. *(Akk.)* lehnen; **~ on sb.'s arm** sich auf jmds. Arm *(Akk.)* stützen; **c)** *(be supported)* lehnen (**against** an + *Dat.*); **d)** *(fig.: rely)* **~ [up]on sb.** auf jmdn. bauen; **I ~ on my friends for moral support** ich baue auf den Beistand meiner Freunde; **e)** *(stand obliquely)* sich neigen; **the L~ing Tower of Pisa** der Schiefe Turm von Pisa; **f)** *(fig.: tend)* **~ to[wards] sth.** zu etw. neigen; **he ~s to the left politically** er tendiert politisch nach links. **2.** *v. t.*, **~ed** *or (Brit.)* **~t** lehnen (**against** gegen *od.* an + *Akk.*). **3.** *n.* Neigung, *die;* **have a definite ~ to the right** deutlich nach rechts geneigt sein; eine deutliche Neigung nach rechts aufweisen; **be on the ~:** schief sein; **have a ~ of 15°** einen Neigungswinkel von 15° haben

~ on *v. t. (fig. sl.)* unter Druck setzen; **he just needs ~ing on a little** man muß ihm nur ein bißchen gut zureden *(iron.), see also* **²lean 1 b, d**

~ over 1. ['---] *v. t.* sich neigen über (+ *Akk.*). **2.** [-'--] *v. i.* ‹*Person:*› sich hinüberbeugen; *(forwards)* sich verbeugen; ‹*Gegenstand:*› sich neigen; **he ~ed over backwards/ sideways** er beugte sich nach hinten/zur Seite; *see also* **backwards a**

lean-burn 'engine *n. (Motor Veh.)* Mager[mix]motor, *der*

leaning ['li:nɪŋ] *n.* Hang, *der;* Neigung, *die;* **have Marxist/homosexual ~s** zum Marxismus tendieren/homosexuelle Neigungen haben

leanness ['li:nnɪs] *n., no pl.* Hagerkeit, *die; (of times)* Dürftigkeit, *die*

leant *see* **²lean**

lean-to ['li:ntu:] *n., pl.* **~s** Anbau, *der*

leap [li:p] **1.** *v. i.*, **~ed** [li:pt, lept] *or* **~t** [lept] **a)** springen; ‹*Herz:*› hüpfen; **~ to one's feet** aufspringen; **~ out of/up from one's chair** aus seinem Sessel/von seinem Stuhl aufspringen; **~ down off the table** vom Tisch herunterspringen; **~ back in shock** vor Entsetzen zurückspringen; **~ up and down in excitement** aufgeregt herumspringen; **~ around** *or* **about** herumspringen; **b)** *(fig.)* **~ to conclusions** voreilige Schlüsse ziehen; **~ to sb.'s defence** jmdm. beispringen *(geh.);* **~ at the chance** *or* **opportunity** die Gelegenheit beim Schopf packen; **~ to stardom/into prominence** mit einem Schlag zum Star/berühmt werden; **~ at an offer** sofort zugreifen; **~ to the eye** ins Auge *od.* in die Augen springen. *See also* **look 1 a. 2.** *v. t.*, **~ed** *or* **~t a)** *(jump over)* überspringen; springen *od.* setzen über (+ *Akk.*); **b)** *(cause to ~)* springen lassen. **3.** *n.* Sprung, *der;* **take a [great] ~ at the fence** [mit einem großen Satz] am Zaun hochspringen; *(successfully)* einen [großen] Satz über den Zaun machen; **with** *or* **in one ~:** mit einem Satz; **by ~s and bounds** *(fig.)* mit Riesenschritten ‹*vorangehen*›; sprunghaft ‹*zunehmen*›; *see also* **dark 2 c**

'leap-frog 1. *n.* Bockspringen, *das.* **2.** *v. i.*, **-gg-** Bockspringen machen; **~ over sb.** einen Bocksprung über jmdn. machen. **3.** *v. t.*, **-gg-** *(fig.)* überspringen

leapt *see* **leap**

'leap year *n.* Schaltjahr, *das*

learn [lɜ:n] **1.** *v. t.*, **~ed** [lɜ:nd, lɜ:nt] *or* **~t** [lɜ:nt] **a)** lernen; *(with emphasis on completeness of result)* erlernen; **~ sth. by** *or* **from experience** etw. durch [die] *od.* aus der Erfahrung lernen; **~ sth. from** *or* **of sb./from a book/an example** etw. von jmdm./aus einem Buch/am Beispiel lernen; **~ one's craft from** *or* **through hard study** seine beruflichen Fähigkeiten durch fleißiges Lernen erwerben; **have you never ~ed any manners/ sense?** hat man dir keine Manieren beigebracht/wo hast du nur deinen Verstand?; **I am ~ing [how] to play tennis** ich lerne Tennis spielen; **Can you swim? – No, I never ~ed how [to]** Kannst du schwimmen? – Nein, ich habe es nie gelernt; *see also* **lesson c; rope 1 e; b)** *(find out)* erfahren; lernen; *(by oral information)* hören; *(by observation)* erkennen; merken; *(by thought)* erkennen; *(be informed of)* erfahren; **I ~ed from the newspaper that ...:** ich habe in der Zeitung gelesen *od.* aus der Zeitung erfahren, daß ...; **I ~ed from his manner what sort of person he was** seine Art verriet mir, was für ein Mensch er war; **c)** *(arch./joc./uneducated: teach)* lernen (+ *Dat.*) *(mundartl., ugs. [standardsprachlich nicht korrekt]);* **that'll ~ you!** das wird dir 'ne Lehre sein!; **I'll ~ you!** *(threat)* ich werd' dir helfen! *(ugs.).* **2.** *v. i.*, **~ed** *or* **~t a)** lernen; **be slow to ~:** langsam lernen; **you'll soon ~:** du wirst es bald lernen; **will you never ~?** du lernst es wohl nie!; **~ from the experience/mistakes of others** aus den Erfahrungen/Fehlern anderer lernen; **some people never ~:** mancher lernt's nie; **~ by one's mistakes** aus seinen Fehlern lernen; **I had to ~ by my mistakes** ich konnte nur aus meinen eigenen Fehlern lernen; **~ about sth.** etwas über etw. *(Akk.)* lernen; **you're never too old** *or* **it's never too late to ~:** man kann immer noch [etwas] dazulernen; zum Lernen ist es nie zu spät; **b)** *(get to know)* erfahren (**of** von); **I have ~t about what you get up to** ich habe erfahren, was du so treibst

~ 'up *v. t.* **a) ~ up some law** sich *(Dat.)* einige juristische Kenntnisse aneignen; einiges über das Rechtswesen lernen; **b)** *(refresh knowledge of)* **~ up one's history** seine Geschichtskenntnisse auffrischen

learned ['lɜ:nɪd] *adj.* **a)** gelehrt; **very ~ in ancient history** in Alter Geschichte sehr bewandert; **b)** *(associated with ~ persons)* wissenschaftlich ‹*Gesellschaft, Zeitschrift*›; akademisch ‹*Stil*›; *see also* **profession a; c)** *(Brit. Law: in address or reference)* verehrt; geschätzt; **my ~ colleague** *etc.* mein verehrter Herr Kollege/meine verehrte Frau Kollegin *usw.; see also* **friend d**

learnedly ['lɜ:nɪdlɪ] *adv.* gelehrt

learner ['lɜ:nə(r)] *n.* Lernende, *der/die; (beginner)* Anfänger, *der*/Anfängerin, *die;* **be a slow/quick ~:** langsam/schnell lernen; **the car is driven by a ~:** ein Fahrschüler steuert den Wagen; **I'm only a ~ still** ich lerne noch

learner-'driver *n. (Brit.)* Fahrschüler/ -schülerin *(der/die unter Aufsicht fährt)*

learning ['lɜ:nɪŋ] *n. (scholarship)* Wissen, *das; (of person)* Gelehrsamkeit, *die;* **the new ~:** der Humanismus

learnt *see* **learn**

lease [li:s] **1.** *n. (of land, business premises)* Pachtvertrag, *der; (of house, flat, office)* Mietvertrag, *der;* **be on [a] ~:** gepachtet/gemietet sein; **have sth. on a 99-year** *etc.* **~:** etw. auf 99 Jahre *usw.* gepachtet/gemietet haben; **take a ~ on** pachten ‹*Grundstück, Geschäft*›; mieten ‹*Haus, Wohnung, Büro*›; **enjoy a new ~ of** *or (Amer.)* **on life** neuen Auftrieb bekommen; **give sb./sth. a new ~ of life** jmdm. Auftrieb geben/etw. wieder in Schuß bringen *(ugs.).* **2.** *v. t.* **a)** *(grant ~ on)* verpachten ‹*Grundstück, Geschäft, Rechte*›; vermieten ‹*Haus, Wohnung, Büro*›; **b)** *(take ~ on)* pachten ‹*Grundstück, Geschäft, Rechte*›; mieten ‹*Haus, Wohnung, Büro*›; leasen ‹*Auto*›

lease: ~back *n.* Verpachtung an den Verkäufer; ~**hold** *see* **lease 2: 1.** *n.* **have the ~hold of** *or* **on sth.** etw. gepachtet *od.* in Pacht/gemietet haben; **2.** *adj.* gepachtet/gemietet; **3.** *adv.* **own a property ~hold** einen Besitz in Pacht/gemietet haben; ~**holder** *n. see* **lease 2:** Pächter, *der*/Pächterin, *die;* Mieter, *der*/Mieterin, *die*

leash [li:ʃ] *n.* **a)** *see* **²lead 3d; b) be straining at the ~ to do sth.** *(fig.)* darauf brennen, etw. zu tun; **he was straining at the ~:** er war voller Ungeduld

least [li:st] **1.** *adj.* **a)** *(smallest)* kleinst...; *(in quantity)* wenigst...; *(in status)* geringst...; **be ~ in size** am kleinsten sein; **every ~ indication** jedes noch so geringe Anzeichen; **I haven't the ~ idea** ich habe nicht die geringste Ahnung; **not the ~ bit hungry** kein bißchen hungrig; **that's the ~ of our problems** das ist unser geringstes Problem; *see also* **common denominator; common multiple; ¹last 1; resistance a; b)** *(Bot., Ornith., Zool.)* Zwerg-. **2.** *n.* Geringste, *das;* **the ~ I can do** das mindeste, was ich tun kann; **the ~ he could do would be to apologize** er könnte sich wenigstens entschuldigen; **pay the ~:** den niedrigsten Preis zahlen; **to say the ~ [of it]** gelinde gesagt; **~ said, soonest mended** *(prov.)* vieles Reden macht die Sache nur schlimmer; **at ~:** mindestens; *(if nothing more; anyway)* wenigstens; **at the [very] ~:** [aller]mindestens; **not [in] the ~:** nicht im geringsten. **3.** *adv.* am wenigsten; **not ~ because ...:** nicht zuletzt deshalb, weil ...; **~ of all** am allerwenigsten; **the ~ likely answer** die unwahrscheinlichste Lösung

leastways ['li:stweɪz], **leastwise** ['li:stwaɪz] *adv. (dial.)* wenigstens

leather ['leðə(r)] **1.** *n.* **a)** Leder, *das; (things made of ~)* Lederwaren *Pl.;* **these shoes are genuine ~:** diese Schuhe sind echt Leder *od.* aus echtem Leder; *see also* **chamois b; hell b; patent leather; b)** *(used for polishing)* Leder, *das;* Lederlappen, *der;* **c)** *(strap)* Lederriemen, *der; (for stirrup)* Steigriemen, *der.* **2.** *adj.* ledern; Leder⟨*jacke, -mantel, -handschuh*⟩. **3.** *v. t.* **a)** *(polish)* [ab]ledern; **b)** *(thrash, whip)* **~ sb.** jmdm. das Leder gerben

'leather-jacket *n. (Brit. Zool.)* Schnakenlarve, *die*

leathery ['leðərɪ] *adj.* ledern

¹leave [li:v] *n., no pl.* **a)** *(permission)* Erlaubnis, *die; (official approval)* Genehmigung, *die;* **grant** *or* **give sb. ~ to do sth.** jmdm. gestatten, etw. zu tun; **beg ~ to do sth.** um Erlaubnis bitten, etw. tun zu dürfen; **be absent without ~:** sich unerlaubt entfernt haben; **get ~ from sb. to do sth.** von jmdm. die Erlaubnis bekommen, etw. zu tun; **by ~ of sb.** mit jmds. Genehmigung; **by your ~** *(formal)* mit Ihrer Erlaubnis; *(iron.)* mit Ihrer gütigen Erlaubnis *(iron.);* **without so much as a by your ~** *(coll.)* ohne auch nur zu fragen; **take ~ to do sth.** sich *(Dat.)* erlauben, etw. zu tun; **b)** *(from duty or work)* Urlaub, *der;* **~ [of absence]** Beurlaubung, *die;* Urlaub, *der (auch Mil.);* **a fortnight's ~:** vierzehn Tage Urlaub; **book one's ~:** seinen Urlaub anmelden; **when do you intend to go on ~?** wann nehmen Sie Ihren *od.* gehen Sie in Urlaub?; **I've got ~ [of absence] for a couple of days** ich bin für einige Tage beurlaubt; **be on ~:** Urlaub haben; in Urlaub sein; **c) take one's ~** *(say farewell)* sich verabschieden; Abschied nehmen *(geh.);* **take [one's] ~ of sb.** sich von jmdm. verabschieden; von jmdm. Abschied nehmen *(geh.);* **have you taken ~ of your senses?** bist du noch bei Sinnen?; **he must have taken ~ of his senses** er muß von Sinnen sein. *See also* **French leave; sick-leave**

²leave *v. t.,* **left** [left] **a)** *(make or let remain, lit. or fig.)* hinterlassen; **may I ~ my dog/son with you?** kann ich meinen Hund/Sohn bei dir lassen?; **he left a message with me for Mary** er hat bei mir eine Nachricht für Mary hinterlassen; **~ sb. to do sth.** es jmdm. überlassen, etw. zu tun; **I am always left to make the decisions** ich muß immer alles entscheiden; **if he likes the work, ~ him to get on with it** wenn ihm die Arbeit Spaß macht, überläßt du ihn am besten sich *(Dat.)* selbst; **~ be** *(coll.)* sich raushalten *(ugs.);* **6 from 10 ~s 4** 10 weniger 6 ist 4; *(in will)* **~ sb. sth., ~ sth. to sb.** jmdm. etw. hinterlassen; *see also* **desire 2c; b)** *(by mistake)* vergessen; **I left my gloves in your car/my umbrella at the butcher's** ich habe meine Handschuhe in deinem Auto liegenlassen *od.* vergessen/meinen Schirm beim Fleischer stehenlassen *od.* vergessen; **c) be left with** nicht loswerden ⟨*Gefühl, Verdacht*⟩; übrigbehalten ⟨*Geld*⟩; zurückbleiben mit ⟨*Schulden, Kind*⟩; **I was left with the job/task of clearing up** es blieb mir überlassen, aufzuräumen; **d)** *(refrain from doing, using, etc., let remain undisturbed)* stehenlassen ⟨*Abwasch, Essen*⟩; sich *(Dat.)* entgehen lassen ⟨*Gelegenheit*⟩; *(spare)* verschonen; **e)** *(let remain in given state)* lassen; **~ the door open/the light on** die Tür offenlassen/das Licht anlassen; **~ the curtains drawn/the water running** die Vorhänge zugezogen lassen/das Wasser laufen lassen; **~ the book lying on the table** das Buch auf dem Tisch liegenlassen; **~ sb. in the dark** *(fig.)* jmdn. im dunkeln lassen; **~ sb. unharmed** jmdm. nichts zuleide tun; **~ one's clothes around** *or* **about/all over the room** seine Kleider überall/im ganzen Zimmer herumliegen lassen; **this ~s me free to do sth.** das erlaubt mir, etw. zu tun; **~ sb. alone** *(allow to be alone)* jmdn. allein lassen; *(stop bothering)* jmdn. in Ruhe lassen; **~ sth. alone** etw. in Ruhe lassen; **~ sb. be** jmdn. in Ruhe *od.* Frieden lassen; **~ him** *etc.* **'be** laß ihn *usw.* [in Ruhe]; **~ go [of] sth.** *(coll.),* **~ hold of sth.** etw. loslassen; **~ it at that** *(coll.)* es dabei bewenden lassen; **how shall we ~ it?** wie verbleiben wir?; **we left it that he'd phone me tomorrow** wir sind so verblieben, daß er mich morgen anruft; *see also* **²well 2b; f)** *(station for a purpose)* postieren; **g)** *(refer, entrust)* **~ sth. to sb./sth.** etw. jmdm./einer Sache überlassen; **I ~ the matter entirely in your hands** ich lege diese Angelegenheit ganz in Ihre Hand/Hände; **I ~ the decision to** *or* **with you** ich überlasse dir die Entscheidung; **sit back and ~ the worrying to me** laß mich nur machen; **~ it to me** laß mich nur machen; **~ sb. to himself** *or* **to his own devices** *or* **resources** *or* **to it** jmdn. sich *(Dat.)* selbst überlassen; **h)** *(go away from)* verlassen; **~ home at 6 a.m.** um 6 Uhr früh von zu Hause weggehen/-fahren; **the plane ~s Bonn at 6 p.m.** das Flugzeug fliegt um 18 Uhr von Bonn ab; **~ Bonn at 6 p.m.** *(by car, in train)* um 18 Uhr von Bonn abfahren; *(by plane)* um 18 Uhr in Bonn abfliegen; **please may I ~ the room?** *(to go to toilet)* darf ich bitte mal austreten? *(ugs.);* **~ the rails** *or* **tracks** entgleisen; **the train ~s the station** der Zug rollt aus dem Bahnhof; **let's ~ here** laß uns hier weggehen; **I left her at the bus stop** *(parted from)* an der Bushaltestelle haben wir uns getrennt; *(set down)* ich habe sie an der Bushaltestelle abgesetzt; **I left her much happier/I left her in tears** als ich ging, war sie schon wieder viel zuversichtlicher/weinte sie; **~ the table** vom Tisch aufstehen; *abs.* **the train ~s at 8.30 a.m.** der Zug fährt *od.* geht um 8.30 Uhr; **~ for Paris** nach Paris fahren/fliegen; **it is time to ~:** wir müssen gehen *od.* aufbrechen; **we're just leaving** wir wollen gerade weggehen; **~ on the 8 a.m. train/flight** mit dem Acht-Uhr-Zug fahren/der Acht-Uhr-Maschine fliegen; **i)** *(quit permanently)* verlassen; **~ school** die Schule verlassen; *(prematurely)* von der Schule abgehen; **~ work** aufhören zu arbeiten; **~ this world for the next** diese Welt verlassen *(geh. verhüll.);* **all my children have left home now** meine Kinder sind jetzt alle aus dem Haus; *abs.* **I am leaving at Easter** ich gehe zu Ostern; **j)** *(desert)* verlassen; **~ sb. for another man/woman** jmdn. wegen eines anderen Mannes/einer anderen Frau verlassen; **~ a house to rot** ein Haus dem Verfall überlassen; **she was left at the altar** der Bräutigam erschien nicht zur Trauung; **~ one's studies half-way through the course** das Studium mittendrin abbrechen; **he was left for dead** man ließ ihn zurück, weil man ihn für tot hielt; *see also* **mercy 1b; ¹post 1c; k)** *(pass)* **branch off, leaving the farm on one's right** den Bauernhof rechts liegen lassen und abbiegen

~ **a'side** *v. t.* beiseite lassen

~ **be'hind** *v. t.* **a)** zurücklassen; **b)** *(by mistake) see* **leave b**

~ **'off** *v. t.* **a)** *(cease to wear)* auslassen *(ugs.);* nicht anziehen; **in summer we can ~ off our coats** im Sommer brauchen wir keine Mäntel [anzuziehen]; **b)** *(discontinue)* aufhören mit; *abs.* aufhören; **~ off smoking** mit dem Rauchen aufhören; aufhören zu rauchen; **~ off the habit of smoking** sich *(Dat.)* das Rauchen abgewöhnen; **has it left off raining?** hat es aufgehört zu regnen?

~ **'out** *v. t.* auslassen

~ **'over** *v. t.* **a)** *(Brit.: not deal with till later)* zurückstellen; **b) be left over** übrig[geblieben] sein; *see also* **left-over; left-overs**

-leaved [li:vd] *adj. in comb.* -blätt[e]rig

leaven ['levn] **1.** *n.* **a)** Treibmittel, *das; (fermenting dough)* Sauerteig, *der;* **b)** *(fig.) (transforming influence)* Sauerteig, *der (geh. veralt.).* **2.** *v. t.* **a)** mit Treibmittel/Sauerteig ansetzen ⟨*Teig*⟩; **b)** *(fig.: transform)* durchsetzen

'leave-taking *n.* Abschied, *der; attrib.* Abschieds-

leaving ['li:vɪŋ] **1.** *n. in pl.* Überbleibsel, *das (ugs.);* Rest, *der.* **2.** *attrib. adj.* Abschieds⟨*party, -geschenk*⟩; **~ certificate** Abschlußzertifikat, *das; (from school)* Abgangszeugnis, *das*

Lebanese [lebə'ni:z] **1.** *adj.* libanesisch; **sb. is ~:** jmd. ist Libanese/Libanesin. **2.** *n., pl. same* Libanese, *der*/Libanesin, *die*

Lebanon ['lebənən] *pr. n.* **[the] ~:** [der] Libanon; *see also* **cedar a**

lecher ['letʃə(r)] *n.* Wüstling, *der (abwertend)*

lecherous ['letʃərəs] *adj.,* **lecherously** ['letʃərəslɪ] *adv.* lüstern *(geh.);* geil *(abwertend)*

lechery ['letʃərɪ] *n.* Wollust, *die (geh.)*

lecithin ['lesɪθɪn] *n. (Chem.)* Lezithin, *das*

lectern ['lektɜ:n] *n.* **a)** *(in church) (for Bible etc.)* Lektionar[ium], *das; (for singers)* Notenpult, *das;* **b)** *(Amer.: for lecturer etc.)* Katheder, *das od. der;* Pult, *das*

lector ['lektə(r)] *n.* Lektor, *der*/Lektorin, *die*

lecture ['lektʃə(r)] **1.** *n.* **a)** Vortrag, *der; (Univ.)* Vorlesung, *die;* **give [sb.] a ~ on sth.** [vor jmdm.] einen Vortrag/eine Vorlesung über etw. *(Akk.)* halten; **b)** *(reprimand)* Strafpredigt, *die (ugs.);* **give** *or* **read sb. a ~:** jmdm. eine Strafpredigt halten *(ugs.);* jmdm. die Leviten lesen *(ugs.).* **2.** *v. i.* **~ [to sb.] [on sth.]** [vor jmdm.] einen Vortrag/ *(Univ.)* eine Vorlesung [über etw. *(Akk.)*] halten; *(give ~s)* [vor jmdm.] Vorträge/ *(Univ.)* Vorlesungen [über etw. *(Akk.)*] halten. **3.** *v. t. (scold)* **~ sb.** jmdm. eine Strafpredigt halten *(ugs.);* **he ~d me about** *or* **for** *or* **over being lazy** er hielt mir eine Strafpredigt wegen meiner Faulheit; **stop lecturing me all the time!** mach mir nicht dauernd Vorhaltungen!

lecture: ~-**hall** *n.* Hörsaal, *der;* ~ **notes** *n. pl.* Manuskript, *das*

lecturer ['lektʃərə(r)] *n.* **a)** Vortragende, *der/die;* **b)** *(Univ.)* Lehrbeauftragte, *der/*

die; **senior ~:** Dozent, *der*/Dozentin, *die;* **be a ~ in French** Dozent/Dozentin für Französisch sein

ˈlecture-room *n.* Vortragsraum, *der; (Univ.)* Vorlesungsraum, *der*

lectureship [ˈlektʃəʃɪp] *n.* Dozentur, *die*

lecture: ~ theatre *n.* Hörsaal, *der;* **~ tour** *n.* Vortragsreise, *die;* **a ~ tour of America** eine Vortragsreise durch Amerika

led *see* [2]**lead 1, 2**

ledge [ledʒ] *n.* **a)** Vorsprung, *der;* Sims, *der od. das;* **b)** *(of rock)* [schmaler] Vorsprung; Band, *das (Bergsteigen)*

ledger [ˈledʒə(r)] **1.** *n. (Commerc.)* Hauptbuch, *das.* **2.** *adj. (Mus.)* **~ line** Hilfslinie, *die*

lee [li:] *n.* **a)** *(shelter)* Schutz, *der;* **in/under the ~ of** im Schutz (+ *Gen.*); **b)** **~ [side]** *(Naut.)* Leeseite, *die*

ˈlee-board *n.* Seitenschwert, *das (Seew.)*

leech [li:tʃ] *n.* **a)** [Blut]egel, *der;* **stick like a ~** *(fig.)* jmdm. nicht von der Pelle gehen *(ugs.);* **b)** *(fig.: sponger)* Blutsauger, *der (abwertend)*

leek [li:k] *n.* Porree, *der;* Lauch, *der; (as Welsh emblem)* Lauch, *der;* **I like ~s** ich mag Porree *od.* Lauch; **three ~s** drei Stangen Porree/Lauch

leek ˈsoup *n.* Lauch[creme]suppe, *die*

leer [lɪə(r)] **1.** *n.* **[suggestive/sneering] ~:** anzüglicher/spöttischer Blick; **give sb. a ~ of desire** jmdn. begehrlich ansehen. **2.** *v.i.* [anzüglich/spöttisch/begehrlich] blicken; **he just ~ed in reply** ein anzüglicher/spöttischer/begehrlicher [Seiten]blick war seine ganze Antwort; **~ at sb.** jmdm. einen anzüglichen/spöttischen/begehrlichen [Seiten]blick zuwerfen

leery [ˈlɪərɪ] *adj. (sl.)* mißtrauisch **(of** gegenüber)

lees [li:z] *n. pl.* Bodensatz, *der*

leeward [ˈli:wəd, *(Naut.)* ˈlu:əd] *(esp. Naut.)* **1.** *adj.* **to/on the ~ side of the ship** nach/in Lee; **to/on the ~ side of the mountain** in den/im Windschatten des Berges; in das Lee/im Lee *(Geogr.);* **L~ Islands** *pr. n. pl.* die Inseln unter dem Winde. **2.** *adv.* leewärts; nach Lee. **3.** *n.* Leeseite, *die;* **to ~:** leewärts; nach Lee

ˈleeway *n.* **a)** *(Naut.)* Leeweg, *der;* Abdrift, *die;* **b)** *(fig.)* Spielraum, *der;* **allow** *or* **give sb. ~:** jmdm. Spielraum lassen; **make up ~:** den Zeitverlust aufholen; **have a great deal of ~ to make up** einiges aufzuholen haben

[1]**left** *see* [2]**leave**

[2]**left** [left] **1.** *adj.* **a)** *(opposite of right)* link...; **on the ~ side** auf der linken Seite; links; **~ field** *(Baseball)* linkes Außenfeld; **have two ~ feet** *(fig.)* zwei linke Füße haben *(ugs.); see also* **turn 1 c; b) L~** *(Polit.)* link...; **her views are very L~:** sie hat sehr linke Ansichten. **2.** *adv.* nach links; **~ of the road** links von der Straße; *see also* **right 4 b. 3.** *n.* **a)** *(~-hand side)* linke Seite; **move to the ~:** nach links rücken; **crowds lined the street to ~ and right** eine Menschenmenge säumte links und rechts die Straße; **on** *or* **to the ~ [of sb./sth.]** links [von jmdm./etw.]; **on** *or* **to my ~, to the ~ of me** links von mir; zu meiner Linken; **b)** *(Polit.)* **the L~:** die Linke; *(radicals)* die Linken; **be on the L~ of the Party** dem linken Flügel der Partei angehören; **c)** *(Theatre)* **[stage] ~:** rechte Bühnenseite; **d)** *(Boxing)* Linke, *die;* **e)** *(in marching)* **~, right, ~, right, ~, ...** *(Mil.)* links, zwo, drei, vier, links, ...

left: ~ ˈback *n. (Footb.)* linker Verteidiger/linke Verteidigerin; **~ ˈbank** *n.* linkes Ufer; *(in Paris)* Rive Gauche; **~-ˈfooted** *adj.* mit dem linken Fuß geschickter; linksfüßig ⟨*Fußballspieler*⟩; **~ ˈhand** *n.* **a)** linke Hand; Linke, *die;* **b)** *(left side)* **on** *or* **at sb.'s ~ hand** zu jmds. Linken; links von jmdm.; **on sb.'s ~ hand** *(not close)* linker Hand; links; **~-hand** *adj.* link...; linksgängig, linksdrehend ⟨*Schraube*⟩; **~-hand bend** Linkskurve, *die;* **on your ~-hand side you see ...:** links *od.* zur Linken sehen Sie ...; **drive on the ~-hand side** links *od.* auf der linken Seite fahren; *see also* **drive 1 i; ~-handed** [leftˈhændɪd] **1.** *adj.* **a)** linkshändig; ⟨*Werkzeug*⟩ für Linkshänder; ⟨*Schlag*⟩ mit der Linken; **be ~-handed** Linkshänder/Linkshänderin sein; **b)** *(turning to left)* links angeschlagen ⟨*Tür*⟩; Links⟨*gewinde, -drehung*⟩; linksgängig, linksdrehend ⟨*Schraube*⟩; **c)** *(fig.: ambiguous)* zweifelhaft ⟨*Kompliment, Gefallen*⟩; **d)** *(fig.: clumsy)* ungeschickt; unbeholfen; **2.** *adv.* linkshändig; mit der linken Hand; **~-handedness** [leftˈhændɪdnɪs] *n.* Linkshändigkeit, *die;* **~-hander** [leftˈhændə(r)] *n.* **a)** *(person)* Linkshänder, *der*/-händerin, *die;* **b)** *(blow)* Schlag mit der Linken; *(Boxing)* Linke, *die*

leftie *see* **lefty**

leftish [ˈleftɪʃ] *adj. (Polit.)* nach links tendierend; **be ~, have ~ opinions/views** links angehaucht sein; nach links tendieren

leftism [ˈleftɪzm] *n., no pl. (Polit.)* linksorientierte Haltung; *(movement)* linke [politische] Strömungen

leftist [ˈleftɪst] *(Polit.)* **1.** *adj.* linksorientiert. **2.** *n.* Linke, *der/die*

left: ~ ˈluggage [office] *n. (Brit. Railw.)* Gepäckaufbewahrung, *die;* **~-over** *attrib. adj.* übriggeblieben; **~-overs** *n pl.* Reste; *(fig.)* Relikte; Überbleibsel *(ugs.)*

leftward [ˈleftwəd] **1.** *adv.* [nach] links ⟨*abbiegen*⟩; nach links ⟨*blicken, sich wenden*⟩; **lie ~ of sth.** links von etw. liegen. **2.** *adj.* linker Hand *nachgestellt*

leftwards [ˈleftwədz] *see* **leftward 1**

left: ~ ˈwing *n.* linker Flügel; **~-wing** *adj.* **a)** *(Sport)* Linksaußen⟨*spieler, -position*⟩; **b)** *(Polit.)* link...; linksgerichtet; Links⟨*intellektueller, -extremist, -radikalismus*⟩; **~-ˈwinger** *n.* **a)** *(Sport)* Linksaußen, *der;* **b)** *(Polit.)* Angehöriger/Angehörige des linken Flügels; **extreme ~-winger** Linksaußen, *der/die (Jargon);* Linksradikale, *der/die*

lefty [ˈleftɪ] *n. (coll.)* **a)** *(Polit.)* Linke, *der/die;* Rote, *der/die (ugs., oft abwertend);* **b)** *see* **left-hander a**

leg [leg] **1.** *n.* **a)** Bein, *das;* **upper/lower ~:** Ober-/Unterschenkel, *der;* **artificial ~:** Beinprothese, *die;* **wooden ~:** Holzbein, *das;* **as fast as my ~s would carry me** so schnell mich die Füße trugen; **give sb. a ~ up on to a horse/into the saddle/over the gate** jmdm. auf ein Pferd/in den Sattel/über das Gatter helfen; **give sb. a ~ up in his career** *(fig.)* jmds. Karriere fördern; **be on one's last ~s** sich kaum noch auf den Beinen halten können; *(be about to die)* mit einem Fuß *od.* Bein im Grabe stehen; **the car is on its last ~s** das Auto macht es nicht mehr lange *(ugs.);* **the firm is on its last ~s** die Firma liegt in den letzten Zügen; **on one's ~s** auf den Beinen; **pull sb.'s ~** *(fig.)* jmdn. auf den Arm nehmen *(ugs.);* **pull the other ~, it's got bells on** *(coll.)* das kannst du einem andern erzählen; **be all ~s** staksig sein; **shake a ~** *(fig. sl.)* das Tanzbein schwingen *(ugs. scherzh.);* **show a ~!** *(sl.)* aus den Federn! *(ugs.);* **not have a ~ to stand on** *(fig.)* nichts in der Hand haben *(fig.);* **stretch one's ~s** sich *(Dat.)* die Beine vertreten; **b)** *(of table, chair, etc.)* Bein, *das; (of machine)* Stütze, *die;* **c)** *(of garment)* Bein, *das; (of boot)* Schaft, *der;* **trouser-~s** Hosenbeine; **d)** *(Gastr.)* Keule, *die;* Schlegel, *der (südd., österr.);* **~ of lamb/veal** Lamm-/Kalbskeule, *die;* **e)** *(of journey)* Etappe, *die;* Teilstrecke, *die;* **f)** *(of forked object)* Schenkel, *der;* **g)** *(Sport coll.)* Durchgang, *der; (of relay race)* Teilstrecke, *die;* **h)** *(Cricket) Spielfeldhälfte rechts bzw., bei linkshändigem Schlagmann, links vom Werfer;* **i)** *(Geom.)* Schenkel, *der;* **j)** *(straight run) (Naut.)* Schlag, *der; (Aeronaut.)* Etappe, *die.* **2.** *adj. (Cricket)* ⟨*Seite, Torstab*⟩ rechts vom Werfer, *(if batsman is left-handed)* links vom Werfer. **3.** *v. t.,* **-gg-: ~ it** die Beine in die Hand *od.* unter die Arme nehmen *(ugs.)*

legacy [ˈlegəsɪ] *n.* Vermächtnis, *das (Rechtsspr.);* Erbschaft, *die; (fig.)* Erbe, *das;* **leave sb. sth. as a ~** *(lit. or fig.)* jmdm. etw. hinterlassen; **leave sb. a ~ of £30,000** jmdm. 30 000 Pfund vermachen *od.* hinterlassen

legal [ˈli:gl] *adj.* **a)** *(concerning the law)* juristisch; Rechts⟨*beratung, -berater, -streit, -experte, -angelegenheit, -schutz*⟩; gesetzlich ⟨*Vertreter*⟩; rechtlich ⟨*Gründe, Stellung*⟩; *(of the law)* Gerichts⟨*kosten*⟩; **in ~ matters/affairs** in Rechtsfragen/-angelegenheiten; **seek ~ advice** sich juristisch beraten lassen; **he is a member of the ~ profession** er ist Jurist; **a ~ friend of mine** ein Freund von mir, der Jurist ist; **b)** *(required by law)* gesetzlich vorgeschrieben ⟨*Mindestalter, Zeitraum*⟩; gesetzlich ⟨*Verpflichtung*⟩; gesetzlich verankert ⟨*Recht*⟩; **I know my ~ rights** ich kenne meine Rechte; **c)** *(lawful)* legal; rechtsgültig ⟨*Vertrag, Testament*⟩; gesetzlich zulässig ⟨*Grenze, Höchstwert*⟩; **it is ~/not ~ to do sth.** es ist rechtlich zulässig/gesetzlich verboten, etw. zu tun; **it is not ~ for children to marry** nach dem Gesetz dürfen Kinder nicht heiraten; **make sth. ~:** etw. legalisieren. *See also* **proceeding c; separation a;** [3]**tender 3 b**

legal: ~ ˈaction *n.* Gerichtsverfahren, *das;* Prozeß, *der;* **take ~ action against sb.** gerichtlich gegen jmdn. vorgehen; eine Klage gegen jmdn. anstrengen; **take/have recourse to ~ action** den Rechtsweg beschreiten *od.* einschlagen; **~ ˈaid** *n.* ≈ Prozeßkostenhilfe, *die;* **~ ˈfiction** *n.* juristische Fiktion *(Rechtsw.);* **~ ˈholiday** *(Amer.) see* **bank holiday b**

legalistic [li:gəˈlɪstɪk] *adj.* legalistisch *(geh.);* stur legalistisch *(abwertend)*

legality [lɪˈgælɪtɪ] *n.* Legalität, *die;* Rechtmäßigkeit, *die*

legalization [li:gəlaɪˈzeɪʃn] *n. (lit. or fig.)* Legalisierung, *die*

legalize [ˈli:gəlaɪz] *v. t. (lit. or fig.)* legalisieren

legally [ˈli:gəlɪ] *adv.* rechtlich ⟨*zulässig, verpflichtet, begründet, unhaltbar, möglich*⟩; gesetzlich ⟨*verankert, verpflichtet*⟩; vor dem Gesetz ⟨*verantwortlich*⟩; legal ⟨*durchführen, abwickeln, erwerben*⟩; **~ and morally** aus rechtlicher und moralischer Sicht; **~ speaking** rechtlich gesehen; vom rechtlichen Standpunkt aus; **~ valid/binding** rechtsgültig/-verbindlich; **be ~ entitled to sth.** einen Rechtsanspruch auf etw. *(Akk.)* haben

legate [ˈlegət] *n. (RC Ch.)* Legat, *der*

legatee [legəˈti:] *n.* Legatar, *der*/Legatarin, *die (Rechtsw.);* Vermächtnisnehmer, *der*/-nehmerin, *die (Rechtsw.)*

legation [lɪˈgeɪʃn] *n. (Diplom.)* Gesandtschaft, *die; (residence also)* Gesandtschaftsgebäude, *das*

legato [lɪˈgɑ:təʊ] *(Mus.)* **1.** *adj.* Legato-. **2.** *adv.* legato. **3.** *n., pl.* **~s** Legato, *das*

legend [ˈledʒənd] *n.* **a)** *(myth)* Sage, *die; (of life of saint etc.; unfounded belief)* Legende, *die;* **read sb. tales from** *or* **out of Greek ~:** jmdm. aus den griechischen Sagen vorlesen; **~ has it that ...:** es geht die Sage, daß ...; **become a ~ in one's own lifetime** *(fig.)* schon zu Lebzeiten zur Legende werden; **turn sb. into a ~** *(fig.)* jmdn. legendär machen; **b)** *(inscription)* Inschrift, *die; (Num.)* Randinschrift, *die;* **c)** *(Printing) (caption)* Bildunterschrift, *die; (on map)* Legende, *die*

legendary [ˈledʒəndərɪ] *adj.* **a)** legendenhaft; *(described in legend)* legendär; sagenhaft; **b)** *(coll.: famous)* sagenhaft *(ugs.);* legendär; **become ~:** zur Legende werden

legerdemain ['ledʒədəmeɪn] *n.* Taschenspielerei, *die;* **diplomatic ~** *(fig.)* diplomatische Kunstgriffe

leger line ['ledʒə laɪn] *n. (Mus.)* Hilfslinie, *die*

-legged [legd, legɪd] *adj. in comb.* -beinig; **two-~:** zweibeinig

leggings ['legɪŋz] *n. pl.* Ledergamaschen *(veralt.); (of child)* Gamaschenhose, *die; (of baby)* Strampelhose, *die*

leggy ['legɪ] *adj.* langbeinig; hochbeinig; ⟨*Junge, Fohlen, Welpe*⟩ mit [staksigen] langen Beinen

legibility [ledʒɪ'bɪlɪtɪ] *n., no pl.* Leserlichkeit, *die*

legible ['ledʒɪbl] *adj.* leserlich; **easily/scarcely ~:** leicht/kaum lesbar

legibly ['ledʒɪblɪ] *adv.* leserlich

legion ['li:dʒn] *n.* **a)** *(Roman Ant.)* Legion, *die;* **b) [Royal] British L~:** *Veteranenvereinigung der britischen Streitkräfte;* **American L~:** *Veteranenvereinigung der amerikanischen Streitkräfte;* **c) L~ of Honour** Ehrenlegion, *die;* **d)** *(vast number)* Legion, *die;* **they are ~** *(rhet.)* sie sind Legion *(geh.). See also* **foreign legion**

legionary ['li:dʒənərɪ] *n.* **a)** *(Mil.)* Legionär, *der;* **b)** *(of Legion of Honour)* Ritter der Ehrenlegion

legionnaire [li:dʒə'neə(r)] *n.* Legionär, *der; (of British or American Legion)* ≈ Veteran, *der*

legion'naires' disease *n., no pl., no art. (Med.)* Legionärskrankheit, *die*

legislate ['ledʒɪsleɪt] *v.i.* Gesetze verabschieden; **it is the job of Parliament to ~:** dem Parlament obliegt die Gesetzgebung *od. (fachspr.)* Legislatur; **~ for/against sth.** Gesetze zum Schutz von/gegen etw. einbringen; **you cannot ~ for everything** *(fig.)* man kann nicht für alles Vorschriften erlassen

legislation [ledʒɪs'leɪʃn] *n.* **a)** *(laws)* Gesetze; **in German ~:** in den deutschen Gesetzen; **rent-control ~ was extended for another year** die Gesetze zur Mietkontrolle blieben ein weiteres Jahr in Kraft; **b)** *(legislating)* Gesetzgebung, *die;* Legislatur, *die (fachspr.)*

legislative ['ledʒɪslətɪv] *adj.* gesetzgebend; legislativ *(fachspr.); (created by legislature)* gesetzgeberisch

legislative: ~ as'sembly *n.* gesetzgebende Versammlung; **~ 'council** *n.* [gesetzgebender] Rat

legislator ['ledʒɪsleɪtə(r)] *n.* Mitglied der Legislative; *(lawgiver)* Gesetzgeber, *der*

legislature ['ledʒɪsleɪtʃə(r)] *n.* Legislative, *die*

legit [lɪ'dʒɪt] *adj. (coll.) see* **legitimate 1 a**

legitimacy [lɪ'dʒɪtɪməsɪ] *n., no pl.* **a)** Rechtmäßigkeit, *die;* Legitimität, *die;* **b)** *(of child)* Ehelichkeit, *die*

legitimate 1. [lɪ'dʒɪtɪmət] *adj.* **a)** *(lawful)* legitim; rechtmäßig ⟨*Besitzer, Regierung*⟩; legal ⟨*Vorgehen, Weg, Geschäft, Gewinn*⟩; **I've turned ~:** ich bin jetzt ein gesetzestreuer Bürger; **b)** *(valid)* berechtigt; stichhaltig; legitim *(geh.)* ⟨*Argument*⟩; ausreichend ⟨*Entschuldigung*⟩; triftig ⟨*Grund*⟩; **c)** *(from wedlock)* ehelich, legitim ⟨*Kind*⟩; leiblich ⟨*Vater*⟩. **2.** [lɪ'dʒɪtɪmeɪt] *v.t.* **a)** legitimieren; **b)** *(justify)* rechtfertigen

legitimately [lɪ'dʒɪtɪmətlɪ] *adv.* **a)** *(lawfully)* legal; **be ~ entitled to sth.** einen legitimen Anspruch auf etw. *(Akk.)* haben; **b)** *(justifiably)* zu Recht; **c)** *(in wedlock)* ehelich, legitim ⟨*geboren*⟩

legitimatize (legitimatise) [lɪ'dʒɪtɪmətaɪz], **legitimize (legitimise)** [lɪ'dʒɪtɪmaɪz] *v.t.* legitimieren; [durch Heirat] ehelich machen ⟨*Kind*⟩

legless ['leglɪs] *adj.* **a)** *(without legs)* ohne Beine *nachgestellt;* **b)** *(sl.: drunk)* sternhagelvoll *(salopp)*

leg: ~man *n. (Journ.)* Reporter, *der;* **~-of-mutton** *adj.* **~-of-mutton sleeve** Keulenärmel, *der;* Gigot, *das (Mode);* **~-pull** *n. (coll.)* Jux, *der (ugs.);* **~-pulling** *n., no pl., no indef. art.* Aufziehen, *das;* **~-room** *n., no pl., no indef. art.* Beinfreiheit, *die;* **~-show** *n.* Revue, *die*

leguminous [lɪ'gju:mɪnəs] *adj. (Bot.)* **~ plant** Hülsenfrucht, *die;* Leguminose, *die (fachspr.)*

leg: ~-warmer *n.* Überstrumpf, *der;* Legwarmer, *der;* **~work** *n., no pl., no indef. art.* Lauferei, *die (ugs.); (running errands)* Botengänge; **do a lot of ~work** viel herumlaufen

leisure ['leʒə(r)] *n.* Freizeit, *die; (for relaxation)* Muße, *die; attrib.* Freizeit⟨*kleidung, -beschäftigung, -zentrum, -industrie*⟩; **a life/day of ~:** ein Leben/Tag der Muße *(geh.);* **I haven't a moment's ~:** ich habe keine freie Minute; **have [the] ~ to do sth./for sth.** [die] Zeit haben, etw. zu tun/Zeit für etw. haben; **lady/gentleman of ~:** Müßiggängerin, *die*/Müßiggänger, *der;* **she has become a lady of ~:** sie verbringt jetzt ihr Leben im Müßiggang; **do sth. at ~:** etw. in Ruhe tun; **do sth. at one's ~:** sich *(Dat.)* Zeit mit etw. lassen; **~ time** *or* **hours** Freizeit, *die*

leisured ['leʒəd] *adj.* müßig *(geh.);* **the ~ classes** das Müßiggängertum

leisurely ['leʒəlɪ] **1.** *adj.* gemächlich; **walk in a ~ manner** gemächlich gehen; **work at a more ~ rate** langsamer *od.* geruhsamer arbeiten; **they made a ~ start** sie ließen es gemächlich angehen. **2.** *adv.* langsam; ohne Hast

'leisurewear *n., no pl., no indef. art.* Freizeitkleidung, *die*

leitmotiv (leitmotif) ['laɪtməʊti:f] *n. (Mus. etc.; also fig.)* Leitmotiv, *das*

lemma ['lemə] *n., pl.* **~ta** ['lemətə] *or* **~s** *(Math., Logic, etc.)* Lemma, *das*

lemming ['lemɪŋ] *n. (Zool.; also fig.)* Lemming, *der;* **rush like ~s** rennen wie die Lemminge

lemon ['lemən] **1.** *n.* **a)** *(fruit)* Zitrone, *die;* **b)** *(tree)* Zitronenbaum, *der;* **c)** *(colour)* Zitronengelb, *das;* **d)** *(sl.: fool)* Trottel, *der (ugs. abwertend);* **e)** *(dud)* Reinfall, *der.* **2.** *adj.* **a)** *(in colour)* zitronengelb; zitronenfarben; **b)** *(in taste)* Zitronen⟨*geschmack, -tee*⟩. *See also* **verbena**

lemonade [lemə'neɪd] *n.* [Zitronen]limonade, *die*

lemon: ~ balm *n. (Bot.)* Zitronenmelisse, *die;* **~ 'cheese, ~ 'curd** *ns.* Zitronencreme, *die;* **~-juice** *n.* Zitronensaft, *der;* **~ meringue 'pie** *n.* Zitronenbaisertorte, *die;* **~ 'sole** *n.* Seezunge, *die;* **~ 'squash** *n. (Brit.)* Zitronensaftgetränk, *das; (concentrated)* Zitronensaftkonzentrat, *das;* **~-squeezer** *n.* Zitronenpresse, *die;* **~-tree** *n. see* **lemon 1 b;** **~-yellow** *adj.* zitronengelb

lemur ['li:mə] *n. (Zool.)* Lemure, *der*

lend [lend] **1.** *v.t.,* **lent** [lent] **a)** leihen; **~ sth. to sb.** jmdm. etw. leihen; **b)** *(give, impart)* geben; zur Verfügung stellen ⟨*Dienste*⟩; verleihen ⟨*Würde, Glaubwürdigkeit, Zauber*⟩; **~ one's support to sth.** etw. unterstützen; **~ one's name/authority to sth.** seinen Namen/guten Namen für etw. hergeben; *see also* **credence a; ¹ear a; hand 1 a. 2.** *v. refl.,* **lent: ~ oneself to sth.** sich für etw. zur Verfügung stellen; *(degradingly)* sich für etw. hergeben; **the book ~s itself/does not ~ itself to use as a learning aid** das Buch eignet sich/eignet sich nicht als Lehrmittel; **the system ~s itself to manipulation** das System bietet sich zur Manipulation an. **3.** *n. (sl.)* **give me a ~ of your bicycle** leih mir mal dein Fahrrad

lender ['lendə(r)] *n.* Verleiher, *der*/Verleiherin, *die*

lending ['lendɪŋ] **1.** *n.* **~ charge** Leihgebühr, *die.* **2.** *adj.* **~ library** *(esp. Brit.)* Leihbücherei, *die. See also* **public lending right**

length [leŋθ, leŋkθ] *n.* **a)** *(also Horse-racing, Rowing, Swimming, Phonet., Pros., Tennis, Fashion)* Länge, *die;* **the river was navigable for most of its ~:** der Fluß war fast in seiner ganzen Länge schiffbar; **a road four miles in ~:** eine vier Meilen lange Straße; **be six feet** *etc.* **in ~:** sechs Fuß *usw.* lang sein; **the room is twice the ~ of yours** das Zimmer ist doppelt so lang wie deins; **travel the ~ and breadth of the British Isles** überall auf den Britischen Inseln herumreisen; **walk the ~ of the street** die ganze Straße entlang laufen; **a list the ~ of my arm** *(fig.)* eine ellenlange Liste; **win by a ~:** mit einer Länge siegen; **b)** *(of time)* Länge, *die;* **a short ~ of time** kurze Zeit; **in that ~ of time** in dieser Zeit; **for some ~ of time** für einige Zeit; **I shouldn't care to live here for any ~ of time** auf die Dauer möchte ich hier nicht wohnen; **spend a ridiculous ~ of time in the bath** unmöglich viel Zeit im Badezimmer verbringen; **the play was three hours in ~:** das Stück dauerte drei Stunden; **depend on ~ of service with the company** von der Dauer der Betriebszugehörigkeit abhängen; **c) at ~** *(for a long time)* lange; *(eventually)* schließlich; **at [great] ~** *(in great detail)* lang und breit; sehr ausführlich; **at some ~:** ziemlich ausführlich; **write at undue ~:** übertrieben ausführlich schreiben; **d) go to any/great** *etc.* **~s** alles nur/alles Erdenkliche tun; **she went to absurd ~s to save money** sie kam auf die seltsamsten Ideen, nur um Geld zu sparen; **carry sth. to dangerous ~s** mit etw. gefährlich weit gehen; **he even went to the ~ of phoning the police** er ging sogar so weit, die Polizei anzurufen; **e)** *(piece of material)* Länge, *die;* Stück, *das;* **six-foot ~s of wood** sechs Fuß lange Holzstücke; **f)** *(full extent of body)* [Körper]länge, *die. See also* **¹arm a; full length; measure 1 a, 2 e**

-length *adj. in comb.* -lang

lengthen ['leŋθən, 'leŋkθən] **1.** *v.i.* länger werden. **2.** *v.t.* **a)** verlängern; länger machen ⟨*Kleid*⟩; **b)** *(Phonet., Pros.)* längen

lengthily ['leŋθɪlɪ, leŋkθɪlɪ] *adv.* ausführlich; lange und gründlich ⟨*planen*⟩

lengthiness ['leŋθɪnɪs, 'leŋkθɪnɪs] *n., no pl.* Überlänge, *die*

lengthways ['leŋθweɪz, 'leŋkθweɪz] *adv.* der Länge nach

lengthwise ['leŋθwaɪz, 'leŋkθwaɪz] **1.** *adv. see* **lengthways. 2.** *adj.* längs angeordnet/verlaufend *usw.*

lengthy ['leŋθɪ, 'leŋkθɪ] *adj.* überlang

leniency ['li:nɪənsɪ] *n., no pl.* Nachsicht, *die;* Milde, *die;* **show ~:** Milde walten lassen; Nachsicht zeigen

lenient ['li:nɪənt] *adj.* **a)** *(tolerant)* nachsichtig; milde, nachsichtig ⟨*Richter*⟩; **take a ~ view of sth.** Verständnis für etw. haben; **b)** *(mild)* mild ⟨*Urteil, Strafe*⟩

leniently ['li:nɪəntlɪ] *adv.* nachsichtig; mit Nachsicht

lens [lenz] *n.* **a)** *(Optics, Phys., Anat.)* Linse, *die; (in spectacles)* Glas, *das;* **b)** *(Photog.)* Objektiv, *das;* **c)** *(Zool.)* Einzelauge, *das*

lens: ~ cap *n. (Photog.)* Objektivdeckel, *der;* **~hood** *n. (Photog.)* Gegenlichtblende, *die*

Lent [lent] *n.* Fastenzeit, *die;* **~ term** *(Brit. Univ.)* Frühjahrstrimester, *das*

lent *see* **lend 1, 2**

Lenten ['lentən] *attrib. adj.* Fasten-; **~ fare** Fastenspeise, *die*

lentil ['lentɪl] *n.* Linse, *die*

lentil 'soup *n.* Linsensuppe, *die*

Leo ['li:əʊ] *n., pl.* **~s** *(Astrol., Astron.)* der Löwe; der Leo; *see also* **Aries**

leopard ['lepəd] *n. (Zool.)* Leopard, *der;* **hunting ~:** Gepard, *der;* **a ~ can't change** *or* **never changes its spots** niemand kann aus seiner Haut heraus *(ugs.)*

'leopard skin *n.* Leopardenfell, *das*

leotard ['li:ətɑ:d] *n.* Turnanzug, *der*

leper ['lepə(r)] *n.* Leprakranke, *der/die;* Aussätzige, *der/die (auch fig.)*

'leper colony *n.* Leprakolonie, *die*

lepidopterist [lepɪ'dɒptərɪst] *n.* Lepidopterologe, *der*/Lepidopterologin, *die*

leprechaun ['leprəkɔ:n] *n. (Ir. Mythol.)* Kobold, *der*

leprosy ['leprəsɪ] *n.* **a)** *(Med.)* Lepra, *die;* **b)** *(fig.)* Seuche, *die*

leprous ['leprəs] *adj. (Med.)* leprös; lepros

lesbian ['lezbɪən] **1.** *n.* Lesbierin, *die.* **2.** *adj.* lesbisch

lesbianism ['lezbɪənɪzm] *n., no pl.* lesbische Liebe; Lesbianismus, *der (geh.)*

lèse-majesté [leɪz'mæʒesteɪ], **lese-majesty** [li:z'mædʒɪstɪ] *n. (Law)* Majestätsbeleidigung, *die (auch scherzh.); (treason)* Majestätsverbrechen, *das (Rechtsw.)*

lesion ['li:ʒn] *n. (Med.)* Läsion, *die (fachspr.);* Verletzung, *die; (abnormal change)* krankhafte Veränderung

less [les] **1.** *adj.* weniger; **of ~ value/importance/account** *or* **note** weniger wertvoll/wichtig/bedeutend; von geringerem Wert/geringerer Wichtigkeit/Bedeutung; **his chances are ~ than mine** seine Chancen sind geringer als meine; **for ~ time** kürzere Zeit; **the pain is getting ~:** der Schmerz läßt nach; **~ talking, please** etwas mehr Ruhe, bitte. **2.** *adv.* weniger; **I like him ~ than I used to** ich mag ihn [heute] weniger als früher; **I think ~/no ~ of him after what he did** ich halte nicht mehr so viel/nicht weniger von ihm, seit er das getan hat; **~ and ~:** immer weniger; **~ and ~ [often]** immer seltener; **~ so** weniger; **the ~ so because ...:** um so weniger, als *od.* weil ...; **even** *or* **still/far** *or* **much ~:** noch/viel weniger; **not ..., even** *or* **still** *or* **far** *or* **much ~ ...:** ..., geschweige denn ...; *see also* **more 3g; no 2a; none 2. 3.** *n., no pl., no indef. art.* weniger; **~ and ~:** immer weniger; **the ~ said [about it] the better** je weniger man darüber sagt, um so besser; **this is ~ of a house than a cottage** das ist weniger ein Haus als ein Cottage *od.* Häuschen; **parking is ~ of a problem with a small car** mit einem kleinen Auto ist das Parken weniger problematisch; **in ~ than no time** *(joc.)* in Null Komma nichts *(ugs.);* **~ of that!** *(coll.)* Schluß damit!; **[I'll have] ~ of your clever remarks** *(coll.)* deine schlauen Bemerkungen kannst du dir sparen *(ugs.);* **~ of your cheek!** *(coll.)* sei nicht so frech!; *see also* **little 3; more 2c. 4.** *prep. (deducting)* **ten ~ three is seven** zehn weniger drei ist sieben; **work every weekend ~ two Saturdays** bis auf zwei Sonnabende an jedem Wochenende arbeiten; **~ £2/tax** abzüglich 2 Pfund/Steuer

-less [lɪs] *adj. suf. (without)* -los; **error~:** fehlerlos; **parent~:** elternlos; **window~:** fensterlos; **hat~/trouser~:** ohne Hut/Hose

lessee [le'si:] *n. see* **lease 2:** Pächter, *der*/Pächterin, *die;* Mieter, *der*/Mieterin, *die*

lessen ['lesn] **1.** *v.t. (reduce)* verringern; lindern ⟨*Schmerz*⟩; dämpfen ⟨*Lärm*⟩; abschwächen ⟨*Aufprall*⟩. **2.** *v.i. (become less)* sich verringern; ⟨*Fieber:*⟩ sinken, fallen; ⟨*Schwierigkeiten:*⟩ abnehmen; ⟨*Zorn:*⟩ sich legen; ⟨*Schmerz:*⟩ nachlassen

lesser ['lesə(r)] *attrib. adj.* geringer...; weniger bedeutend... ⟨*Schauspieler, Werk*⟩; **~ in rank, of ~ rank** rangniedriger; **be a ~ man than ...:** kein so großer Mensch sein wie ...; *see also* **evil 2b**

lesson ['lesn] *n.* **a)** *(class)* [Unterrichts]stunde, *die; (teaching unit in textbook)* Lektion, *die;* **I like her ~s** mir gefällt ihr Unterricht; **give ~s** Privatstunden *od.* -unterricht geben; **give Italian ~s** Italienischunterricht *od.* -stunden geben; **give [sb.] a [riding] ~:** [jmdm.] eine [Reit]stunde geben; **[give] ~s in/on** Unterricht [erteilen] in (+ *Dat.*); **take piano ~s with sb.** bei jmdm. Klavierstunden nehmen; **b)** *(thing to be learnt)* Lektion, *die;* **the first ~ to be learnt** das erste, was man lernen muß; **c)** *(fig.: example, warning)* Lektion, *die;* Lehre, *die;* **teach sb. a ~:** jmdm. eine Lektion erteilen; ⟨*Vorfall usw.:*⟩ jmdm. eine Lehre sein; **he needs to be taught a ~:** er braucht einen Denkzettel; **do that again and I'll teach you a ~ you won't forget!** wenn du das noch mal machst, verpasse ich dir einen Denkzettel, den du nicht vergißt!; **be a ~ to sb.** jmdm. eine Lehre sein; **learn one's** *or* **a ~ from sth.** aus etw. eine Lehre ziehen; **I have learnt my ~:** das soll mir eine Lehre sein; **let that be a ~ to you** laß dir das eine Lehre sein!; **d)** *(Eccl.)* Lesung, *die;* **read the ~:** die Lesung halten

lessor [le'sɔ:(r)] *n. see* **lease 2:** Verpächter, *der*/Verpächterin, *die;* Vermieter, *der*/Vermieterin, *die*

lest [lest] *conj. (literary)* damit ... nicht; [auf] daß ... nicht *(geh.);* **he ran away ~ he [should] be seen** er rannte weg, um nicht gesehen zu werden; **I was afraid ~ he [should] come back before I was ready** ich fürchtete, daß er zurückkommen würde, bevor ich fertig war

¹let [let] **1.** *v.t.,* **-tt-, let a)** *(allow to)* lassen; **~ sb. do sth.** jmdn. etw. tun lassen; **don't ~ things get you down/worry you** laß dich nicht entmutigen/mach dir keine Sorgen; **don't ~ him upset you** reg dich seinetwegen nicht auf; **I'll come if you will ~ me** ich komme, wenn ich darf; **~ sb./sth. alone** jmdn./etw. in Ruhe lassen; **~ alone** *(far less)* geschweige denn; **~ sb. be** jmdn. in Ruhe *od.* Frieden lassen; **Let it be. We can't alter things** Laß doch! Wir können die Dinge nicht ändern; **~ go [of] sth./sb.** *(release hold)* etw./jmdn. loslassen; **~ sb. go** *(from captivity)* jmdn. freilassen; **~ go** *(release hold)* loslassen; *(abandon self-restraint)* sich gehenlassen; *(neglect)* herunterkommen lassen ⟨*Haus*⟩; *(~ pass)* durchgehen lassen ⟨*Bemerkung*⟩; **~ it go [at that]** es dabei belassen *od.* bewenden lassen; **~ oneself go** *(neglect oneself)* sich vernachlässigen; nicht auf sich achten; *(abandon self-restraint)* sich gehenlassen; **~ loose** loslassen; **b)** *(cause to)* **~ sb. know** jmdn. wissen lassen; **~ sb. think that ...:** jmdn. in dem Glauben lassen, daß ...; **I will ~ you know as soon as ...:** ich gebe Ihnen Bescheid, sobald ...; **I have ~ it be known that ...:** ich habe alle wissen lassen, daß ...; **c)** *(release)* ablassen ⟨*Wasser*⟩ **(out of, from** aus); lassen ⟨*Luft*⟩ **(out of** aus); **the practice of ~ting blood** der Brauch des Aderlasses; **d)** *(Brit.: rent out)* vermieten ⟨*Haus, Wohnung, Büro*⟩; verpachten ⟨*Gelände, Grundstück*⟩; **~ a flat to sb. for a year** jmdm. *od.* an jmdn. eine Wohnung für ein Jahr vermieten; **there were plenty of houses to ~:** es gab viele Häuser, die zu vermieten waren; **'to ~'** „zu vermieten"; **e)** *(award)* vergeben ⟨*Arbeit, Rechte usw.*⟩. *See also* **²fly 1g; ¹rip 3b; ¹see 1f, 2c; slip 1b; ²well 2b. 2.** *v. aux.,* **-tt-, let a)** *in exhortations* lassen; **~ us [just] suppose that ...:** lassen Sie uns einmal annehmen, daß ...; nehmen wir [nur] einmal an, daß ...; **Let's go to the cinema. – Yes, ~'s/No, ~'s not** *or* **don't ~'s** Komm/Kommt, wir gehen ins Kino. – Ja, gut/Nein, lieber nicht; **~'s pretend** *(coll.)* tun wir so, als ob; **~'s have a go on your bike** *(coll.)* laß mich mal mit deinem Rad fahren; **b)** *in command, challenge, prayer* lassen; **~ them come in** sie sollen hereinkommen; lassen Sie sie herein; **~ there be light** *(Bibl.)* es werde Licht!; **~ the bells be rung** laßt die Glocken erklingen; **~ him go to the devil!** er soll zum Teufel gehen!; **~ it be said that ...:** es muß gesagt werden, daß ...; **never ~ it be thought/said that ...:** keiner soll glauben/sagen, daß ...; **[just] ~ him try!** das soll er [nur] mal wagen!; **~ him get well** *(in prayer)* laß ihn gesund werden; **~ x be equal to 3a + b²** *(Math.)* x sei 3a + b²; *see also* **pray 1. 3.** *n. (Brit.)* **holiday ~s** ≈ Ferienwohnungen; **rent a flat on a short ~:** eine Wohnung für kurze Zeit mieten

~ 'down *v.t.* **a)** *(lower)* herunter-/hinunterlassen; herunterkurbeln ⟨*Autofenster*⟩; **~ sb. down gently** *(fig.)* es jmdm. schonend beibringen *(ugs.); see also* **hair b; b)** *(deflate)* die Luft [heraus]lassen aus; **c)** *(Dressm.)* auslassen ⟨*Saum, Ärmel, Kleid, Hose*⟩; **d)** *(disappoint, fail)* im Stich lassen; **~ oneself down** sich unter sein Niveau begeben; **I ~ myself down in the exam** ich habe in der Prüfung enttäuschend abgeschnitten; *see also* **let-down**

~ 'in *v.t.* **a)** *(admit)* herein-/hineinlassen; *(fig.)* die Tür öffnen (+ *Dat.*); **~ oneself/sb. in** sich *(Dat.)* [die Tür] aufschließen/jmdm. aufmachen; **my shoes are ~ting in water** meine Schuhe sind undicht; **b)** *(Dressm.)* enger machen; einnähen; **c) ~ oneself in for sth.** sich auf etw. *(Akk.)* einlassen; **~ oneself in for a lot of work/trouble** sich *(Dat.)* viel Arbeit aufhalsen *(ugs.)*/Ärger einhandeln; **~ sb. in for sth.** jmdm. etw. einbrocken *(ugs.);* **d) ~ sb. in on a secret/plan** *etc.* jmdn. in ein Geheimnis/einen Plan *usw.* einweihen

~ into *v.t.* **a)** *(admit into)* lassen in (+ *Akk.*); **b)** *(fig.: acquaint with)* **~ sb. into a secret** jmdn. in ein Geheimnis einweihen; **c)** *(set into)* **a safe ~ into the wall** ein in die Wand eingelassener Safe

~ 'off *v.t.* **a)** *(excuse)* laufenlassen *(ugs.); (allow to go)* gehen lassen; **~ sb. off lightly/with a fine** jmdn. glimpflich/mit einer Geldstrafe davonkommen lassen; **~ sb. off sth.** jmdm. etw. erlassen; *see also* **let-off; b)** *(fire, explode)* abbrennen ⟨*Feuerwerk*⟩; abfeuern ⟨*Kanone, Gewehrsalve*⟩; **c)** *(allow to escape)* ablassen ⟨*Dampf, Flüssigkeit*⟩; **d)** *(Brit.: rent out)* einzeln vermieten; **e)** *(allow to alight)* aussteigen lassen

~ 'on *(sl.)* **1.** *v.i.* **~ on about sth. [to sb.]** [jmdm.] etwas verraten; **don't ~ on!** nichts verraten! **2.** *v.t.* **a) sb. ~ on to me that ...:** man hat mir gesteckt, daß ... *(ugs.);* **b)** *(pretend)* **~ on that ...:** so tun, als ob ... *(ugs.);* **she's not as sick as she ~s on** sie ist nicht so krank, wie sie tut *(ugs.)*

~ 'out *v.t.* **a)** *(open door for)* **~ sb./an animal out** jmdn./ein Tier heraus-/hinauslassen; **Don't get up. I'll ~ myself out** Bleiben Sie sitzen. Ich finde schon allein hinaus; **b)** *(allow out)* rauslassen *(ugs.);* gehen lassen; **c)** *(emit)* ausstoßen ⟨*Schrei*⟩; hören lassen ⟨*Lachen, Seufzer*⟩; **~ out a groan** aufstöhnen; **d)** *(reveal)* verraten, ausplaudern ⟨*Geheimnis*⟩; **~ out that ...:** durchsickern lassen, daß ...; **e)** *(Dressm.)* auslassen; **f)** *(Brit.: rent out) see* **¹let 1d; g)** *(from duty)* **On Saturday? That ~s me out** Samstag? Da falle ich schon mal aus; **that ~s me out of having to go** dann muß ich nicht hin *(ugs.); see also* **let-out**

~ 'through *v.t.* durchlassen

~ 'up *v.i. (coll.)* nachlassen; **don't you ever ~ up?** wirst du überhaupt nicht müde?; *see also* **let-up**

²let *n.* **a) without ~ [or hindrance]** *(formal/Law)* ohne jede Behinderung; **b)** *(Tennis)* Let, *der*

'let-down *n.* Enttäuschung, *die*

lethal [li:θl] *adj.* tödlich; letal *(Med.); (fig.)* vernichtend; **that knife looks ~:** das Messer sieht sehr gefährlich aus

lethargic [lɪ'θɑ:dʒɪk] *adj.* **a)** träge; *(apathetic)* lethargisch; *(causing lethargy)* träge machend; einschläfernd ⟨*Atmosphäre, Musik*⟩; **b)** *(Med.)* lethargisch

lethargically [lɪ'θɑ:dʒɪkəlɪ] *adv.* träge; *(apathetically)* lethargisch

lethargy ['leθədʒɪ] *n.* **a)** Trägheit, *die; (apathy)* Lethargie, *die;* **b)** *(Med.)* Lethargie, *die*

let: **~-off** *n.* **have a ~-off** noch einmal davonkommen; **that was a [lucky] ~-off** da habe ich/hast du *usw.* noch einmal Glück gehabt; **~-out** *n.* Ausrede, *die*

Lett [let] *n.* **a)** *(person)* Lette, *der*/Lettin, *die;* **b)** *(language)* Lettisch, *das*

letter [letə(r)] **1.** *n.* **a)** *(written communication)* Brief, *der* (**to** an + *Akk.*); *(official communication)* Schreiben, *das;* **a ~ of appointment** eine [briefliche] Anstellungszusage; **by ~:** brieflich; schriftlich; **'~s to the editor'** „Leserbriefe"; *see also* **credit 1 e;** **b)** *(of alphabet)* Buchstabe, *der;* **how many ~s are there in the word?** wie viele Buchstaben hat das Wort?; **learn one's ~s** die Buchstaben lernen; **write in capital/small ~s** mit Groß-/Kleinbuchstaben schreiben; **have ~s after one's name** Ehrentitel/einen Ehrentitel haben; **c)** *(fig.)* **to the ~:** buchstabengetreu; aufs Wort; **the ~ of the law** der Buchstabe des Gesetzes; **in ~ and in spirit** in Geist und Buchstabe; **d)** *in pl. (literature)* Literatur, *die;* **world of ~s** literarische Welt; **man of ~s** Homme de lettres, *der;* Literat, *der;* **Doctor of L~s** Lit[t]erarum Humaniorum Doctor; **e)** *(Printing: type-fount)* Letter, *die;* Type, *die;* **f)** *(Amer. Sport: mark of proficiency)* Leistungsabzeichen, *das.* **2.** *v.t.* **a)** *(classify alphabetically)* mit Buchstaben kennzeichnen; **b)** *(inscribe on)* beschriften

letter: **~-bomb** *n.* Briefbombe, *die;* **~-box** *n.* Briefkasten, *der; (slit)* Briefschlitz, *der;* **come** *or* **be put through the ~-box** in den Briefkasten gesteckt werden; **~-card** *n.* Kartenbrief, *der*

lettered ['letəd] *adj.* **a)** *(well read, educated)* gebildet; **b)** *(inscribed)* beschriftet

letter: **~-head, ~-heading** *ns.* Briefpapier mit Briefkopf; *(heading)* Briefkopf, *der*

lettering ['letərɪŋ] *n. (letters)* Typographie, *die; (on book-cover)* Aufschrift, *die; (carved)* Inschrift, *die*

letter: **~-pad** *n.* Briefblock, *der;* **~-paper** *n.* Briefpapier, *das;* **~ post** *n. (Brit. Post)* Briefpost, *die (veralt.);* **~press** *n.* **a)** *(Brit.: text)* Text, *der;* **b)** *(Printing)* Hochdruck, *der;* **~s page** *n.* Leserbriefseite, *die;* **~s 'patent** *n. pl.* Patent, *das;* **~-writer** *n.* Briefschreiber, *der*/Briefschreiberin, *die*

Lettish ['letɪʃ] **1.** *adj.* lettisch. **2.** *n. see* **Lett b**

lettuce ['letɪs] *n.* [Kopf]salat, *der;* [grüner] Salat; **a [head of] ~:** ein Kopf Salat

'let-up *n. (coll.) (in fighting)* Nachlassen, *das; (in work)* Pause, *die;* **there was no ~-up in the fighting/bombardment** die Kämpfe ließen/der Beschuß ließ nicht nach

leucocyte [lu:kəsaɪt] *n. (Anat.)* Leukozyt, *der (fachspr.);* weißes Blutkörperchen

leucotomy [lu:'kɒtəmɪ] *n. (Med.)* Leukotomie, *die*

leukaemia (*Amer.:* **leukemia**) [lu:'ki:mɪə] *n. (Med.)* Leukämie, *die*

Levant [lɪ'vænt] *pr. n.* **the ~** die Levante

Levantine [lɪ'væntaɪn, 'levəntaɪn] **1.** *adj.* levantinisch. **2.** *n.* Levantiner, *der*/Levantinerin, *die*

levee ['levɪ] *n. (Amer. Geog.)* Fluß-, Uferdamm, *der*

level ['levl] **1.** *n.* **a)** Höhe, *die; (storey)* Etage, *die; (fig.: steady state)* Niveau, *das; (fig.: basis)* Ebene, *die;* **the water rose to the ~ of the doorsteps** das Wasser stieg bis zur Türschwelle; **live on the same ~:** in *od.* auf derselben Etage wohnen; **prices are at a high/low ~:** die Preise sind hoch/niedrig; **be on a ~ [with sb./sth.]** sich auf gleicher *od.* einer Höhe [mit jmdm./etw.] befinden; *(fig.)* auf dem gleichen Niveau sein *od.* der gleichen Stufe stehen [wie jmd./etw.]; **on the ~** *(fig. coll.)* ehrlich; **he's on the ~:** man kann ihm durchaus trauen; **water finds/seeks its ~:** Wasser verteilt sich gleichmäßig; **find one's ~** *(fig.)* seinen Platz finden; **b)** *(height)* at **waist/roof-top** *etc.* **~:** in Taillen-/Dachhöhe *usw.;* **c)** *(relative amount)* **sugar/alcohol ~:** [Blut]zucker-/Alkoholspiegel, *der;* **noise ~:** Geräuschpegel, *der;* **high ~s of CO_2 in the atmosphere** ein hoher CO_2-Gehalt in der Atmosphäre; **d)** *(social, moral, or intellectual plane)* Niveau, *das; (degree of achievement etc.)* Grad, *der* (**of** an + *Dat.*); *(plane of significance)* Ebene, *die;* **the lower ~s** die unteren Schichten; **on a personal/moral ~:** auf persönlicher/moralischer Ebene; **expenditure is running at high ~s** die Aufwendungen bewegen sich auf einem hohen Niveau; **high ~ of intellect** hoher Intelligenzgrad; **pupils of varying ~s of ability** Schüler unterschiedlicher Begabung; **he has reached an advanced ~ in his course** er hat in seinem Kurs ein fortgeschrittenes Niveau erreicht; **talks at the highest ~ [of government]** Gespräche auf höchster [Regierungs]ebene; **e)** *(instrument to test horizontal)* Wasserwaage, *die;* **f)** *(Surv.: telescope)* Nivellierinstrument, *das;* **g)** *(Mining)* Sohle, *die.* **2.** *adj.* **a)** waagerecht; flach ‹*Land*›; eben ‹*Boden, Land*›; **a ~ spoonful of flour** ein gestrichener Löffel Mehl; **the picture is not ~:** das Bild hängt nicht gerade; **b)** *(on a ~)* **be ~ [with sth./sb.]** auf gleicher Höhe [mit etw./jmdm.] sein; *(fig.)* [mit etw./jmdm.] gleichauf liegen; **the two pictures are not ~:** die beiden Bilder hängen nicht gleich hoch; **draw/keep ~ with a rival** mit einem Gegner gleichziehen/auf gleicher Höhe bleiben; **~ race** Kopf-an-Kopf-Rennen, *das; see also* **peg 2 c;** **c)** *(fig.: steady, even)* ausgeglichen ‹*Leben, Temperament*›; ausgewogen ‹*Stil*›; **keep a ~ head** einen kühlen Kopf bewahren; **d) do one's ~ best** *(coll.)* sein möglichstes tun. **3.** *v.t., (Brit.)* **-ll-** **a)** *(make ~ 2 a)* ebnen; **b)** *(aim)* richten ‹*Blick, Gewehr, Rakete*› (**at, against** auf + *Akk.*); *(fig.)* richten ‹*Kritik usw.*› (**at, against** gegen); erheben ‹*Anklage, Vorwurf*› (**at, against** gegen); **c)** *(raze)* dem Erdboden gleichmachen ‹*Stadt, Gebäude*›; **d)** *(knock down)* zu Boden schlagen ‹*Person*›; **e)** *(abolish)* aufheben, nivellieren ‹*Unterschiede*›; **f)** *(Surv.)* nivellieren. **4.** *v.i., (Brit.)* **-ll-** *(sl.)* **I'll ~ with you** ganz im Ernst; ehrlich *(ugs.);* **~ with sb.** mit jmdm. ehrlich sein

~ 'down *v.t.* herabsetzen; abbauen ‹*Privilegien, Gehälter, Einkommen*›

~ 'off 1. *v.t.* glatt machen. **2.** *v.i. (Aeronaut.)* die Flughöhe beibehalten

~ 'out 1. *v.t.* einebnen. **2.** *v.i.* **a)** *see* **~ off 2;** **b)** *(fig.)* sich ausgleichen; ‹*Preise, Markt:*› sich beruhigen

~ 'up *v.t.* anheben ‹*Niveau, Leistungsstand, Gehalt, Einkommen*›

level 'crossing *n. (Brit. Railw.)* [schienengleicher] Bahnübergang

leveler *(Amer.) see* **leveller**

level-'headed *adj.* besonnen; **remain ~:** einen kühlen Kopf bewahren

leveller ['levələ(r)] *n.* Gleichmacher, *der*

levelling-screw (*Amer.:* **leveling-screw**) ['levəlɪŋskru:] *n.* Stellschraube, *die*

lever ['li:və(r)] **1.** *n.* **a)** Hebel, *der; (crowbar)* Brechstange, *die; (Mech.)* Hebel[arm], *der;* **b)** *(fig.: means of persuasion)* Druckmittel, *das.* **2.** *v.t.* **~ sth. open** etw. aufhebeln; **~ sth. up** etw. hochhebeln

leverage ['li:vərɪdʒ] *n.* **a)** Hebelwirkung, *die; (action of lever)* Hebelkraft, *die; (system of levers)* Hebelwerk, *das;* **I need more ~ to move this cupboard** ich brauche einen günstigeren Ansatzpunkt, um den Schrank bewegen zu können; **b)** *(fig.: influence)* **give sb. [a lot of] ~:** jmds. Position [sehr] stärken

leveret ['levərɪt] *n. (Zool.)* Junghase, *der*

leviathan [lɪ'vaɪəθən] *n.* **a)** *(sea monster)* Seeungeheuer, *das;* **b)** *(fig.: huge thing)* Riese, *der; (ship)* Ozeanriese, *der*

Levis, (P) ['li:vaɪz] *n. pl.* Levis, *die* Ⓦ

levitate ['levɪteɪt] *v.i. & t.* levitieren

levitation [levɪ'teɪʃn] *n.* Levitation, *die*

levity ['levɪtɪ] *n.* **a)** *(frivolity)* Unernst, *der;* **b)** *(inconstancy)* Unbeständigkeit, *die;* Wankelmut, *der (geh.);* **c)** *(undignified behaviour)* Leichtfertigkeit, *die*

levy ['levɪ] **1.** *n.* **a)** [Steuer]erhebung, *die;* **b)** *(tax)* Steuer, *die;* **make** *or* **impose a ~ on sth.** eine Steuer auf etw. *(Akk.)* erheben; **c)** *(Mil.: conscription)* Einberufung, *die; (number of conscripts)* Anzahl von Einberufenen; *in pl. (conscripts)* Einberufene. **2.** *v.t.* **a)** *(exact)* erheben ‹*Steuern, Beträge*›; *(seize)* beschlagnahmen; einziehen; *(extort)* erpressen ‹*Geld*›; **~ a fine on sb./a tax on sth.** jmdn. mit einer Geldstrafe/etw. mit einer Steuer belegen; **b)** *(Mil.: conscript)* aufstellen ‹*Armee, Truppe*›; einberufen ‹*Soldat*›

lewd [lju:d] *adj.* geil *(oft abwertend),* lüstern *(geh.)* ‹*Person*›; anzüglich ‹*Blick, Geste*›; schlüpfrig, unanständig ‹*Lied, Ausdruck, Witz*›

lewdly ['lju:dlɪ] *adv.* lüstern *(geh.);* anzüglich

lewdness ['lju:dnɪs] *n., no pl. (of person)* Geilheit, *die (oft abwertend);* Lüsternheit, *die (geh.); (of look, remark)* Anzüglichkeit, *die; (of language, joke)* Schlüpfrigkeit, *die*

lexical ['leksɪkl] *adj.* lexikalisch

lexicographer [leksɪ'kɒgrəfə(r)] *n.* Lexikograph, *der*/Lexikographin, *die*

lexicography [leksɪ'kɒgrəfɪ] *n., no pl.* Lexikographie, *die*

lexicon ['leksɪkən] *n.* **a)** *(dictionary)* Wörterbuch, *das;* Lexikon, *das (veralt.);* **b)** *(vocabulary)* Wortschatz, *der*

lexis ['leksɪs] *n.* Wortschatz, *der*

l. h. *abbr.* **left hand** l.

liability [laɪə'bɪlɪtɪ] *n.* **a)** *no pl. (legal obligation)* Haftung, *die;* **limited ~** *(Brit.)* beschränkte Haftung; **~ to pay tax[es]** *or* **for taxation** Steuerpflicht, *die;* **~ for military service** Dienstpflicht, *die;* **b)** *no pl. (proneness) (to disease etc.)* Anfälligkeit, *die* (**to** für); **c)** *(sth. one is liable for)* Verpflichtung, *die;* **liabilities** *(debts)* Verbindlichkeiten *(Kaufmannsspr.);* **d)** *(cause of disadvantage)* Belastung, *die* (**to** für)

liable ['laɪəbl] *pred. adj.* **a)** *(legally bound)* **be ~ for sth.** für etw. haftbar sein *od.* haften; **~ for military service** militärdienstpflichtig; **be ~ to pay tax[es]** steuerpflichtig sein; **b)** *(prone)* **be ~ to sth.** ‹*Sache:*› leicht etw. haben; ‹*Person:*› zu etw. neigen; **be ~ to do sth.** ‹*Sache:*› leicht etw. tun; ‹*Person:*› dazu neigen, etw. zu tun; **c)** *(likely)* **difficulties are ~ to occur** mit Schwierigkeiten muß man rechnen; **she is ~ to change her mind** es kann durchaus sein, daß sie ihre Meinung ändert; **it is ~ to be cold there** im allgemeinen ist es dort kalt

liaise [lɪ'eɪz] *v.i. (coll.)* eine Verbindung herstellen; **~ on a project** bei einem Projekt zusammenarbeiten; **they ~ on a regular basis** sie haben regelmäßig Kontakt

liaison [lɪ'eɪzɒn] *n.* **a)** *(co-operation)* Zusammenarbeit, *die; (connection)* Verbindung, *die;* **be in ~ with** in Verbindung stehen mit; **b)** *(illicit relation)* Verhältnis, *das;* Liaison, *die (geh.);* **form** *or* **enter into a ~:** ein Verhältnis anfangen; **c)** *(Phonet.)* Liaison, *die*

li'aison officer *n.* Verbindungsmann, *der; (Mil.)* Verbindungsoffizier, *der*

liana [lɪ'ɑ:nə] *n. (Bot.)* Liane, *die*

liar ['laɪə(r)] *n.* Lügner, *der*/Lügnerin, *die*

Lib [lɪb] *abbr.* **a) Liberal** Lib.; **b)** *(coll.)* **liberation**

libation [laɪ'beɪʃn, lɪ'beɪʃn] *n.* Libation, *die;* Trankopfer, *das*

libel ['laɪbl] **1.** *n.* **a)** [schriftliche] Verleumdung; **[public] ~:** [blasphemische, obszöne, aufrührerische od. landesverräterische] Verleumdung; **b)** *(misrepresentation that*

discredits) diffamierende Entstellung **(on** *Gen.*). **2.** *v. t., (Brit.)* **-ll-** [öffentlich] verleumden
libellous (*Amer.:* **libelous**) ['laɪbələs] *adj.* verleumderisch
liberal ['lɪbərl] **1.** *adj.* **a)** *(generous, abundant)* großzügig; freigebig, großzügig ‹*Person, Wesen*›; **a ~ amount of** reichlich; **b)** *(generally educative)* allgemeinbildend; **~ education** *or* **culture** Allgemeinbildung, *die;* **~ studies** *geisteswissenschaftliches Nebenfach bei naturwissenschaftlicher, technischer oder berufsspezifischer Ausbildung;* **c)** *(not strict)* liberal; frei ‹*Auslegung*›; **d)** *(open-minded)* liberal; aufgeschlossen; **e)** *(Polit.)* liberal. **2.** *n.* **a)** liberal denkender Mensch; **b) L~** *(Polit.)* Liberale, *der/die*
liberal 'arts *n. pl.* **a)** *(Hist.)* Artes liberales *Pl.;* die Sieben Freien Künste; **b)** *(Amer.: arts)* Geisteswissenschaften *Pl.*
liberalism ['lɪbərəlɪzm] *n.* **a)** Liberalität, *die;* **b) L~** *(Polit.)* Liberalismus, *der*
liberality [lɪbə'rælɪtɪ] *n., no pl.* **a)** *(generosity)* Großzügigkeit, *die* **(to** gegenüber); Freigebigkeit, *die;* **b)** *(open-mindedness)* Liberalität, *die;* **~ of mind** liberale Gesinnung
liberalize ['lɪbərəlaɪz] *v. t.* liberalisieren
liberally ['lɪbərəlɪ] *adv. (generously)* großzügig; *(abundantly)* reichlich
liberate ['lɪbəreɪt] *v. t.* **a)** befreien **(from** aus); **b)** *(Chem.)* freisetzen; **c)** *(joc. sl.: steal)* mitgehen lassen *(ugs.)*
liberation [lɪbə'reɪʃn] *n.* **a)** Befreiung, *die;* **~ theology** Theologie der Befreiung; *see also* **Women's Liberation; b)** *(Chem.)* Freisetzung, *die*
liberator ['lɪbəreɪtə(r)] *n.* Befreier, *der/*Befreierin, *die*
Liberia [laɪ'bɪərɪə] *pr. n.* Liberia *(das)*
Liberian [laɪ'bɪərɪən] **1.** *adj.* liber[ian]isch. **2.** *n.* Liberi[an]er, *der/*Liberi[an]erin, *die*
libertine ['lɪbəti:n] *n.* Libertin, *der*
liberty ['lɪbətɪ] *n.* Freiheit, *die;* **the Statue of L~:** die Freiheitsstatue; **you are at ~ to come and go as you please** es steht Ihnen frei, zu kommen und zu gehen, wie Sie wollen; **be at ~:** auf freiem Fuß sein; **set sb. at ~:** jmdn. auf freien Fuß setzen; **~ of the subject** Recht als Staatsbürger; **~ of action/movement** Handlungs-/Bewegungsfreiheit, *die;* **take the ~ to do** *or* **of doing sth.** sich *(Dat.)* die Freiheit nehmen, etw. zu tun; **take liberties with sb.** sich *(Dat.)* Freiheiten gegen jmdn. herausnehmen *(ugs.);* **take liberties with sth.** mit etw. allzu frei umgehen; **if you'll pardon the ~:** wenn ich mir die Bemerkung erlauben darf; *see also* **conscience**
liberty: L~ Bell *n. (Amer.)* Freiheitsglocke, *die;* **~ boat** *n. (Brit. Naut.) Boot, mit dem Seeleute zu einem kurzen Landurlaub an Land gebracht werden;* **~ horse** *n.* Freiheitsdressurpferd, *das*
libidinal [lɪ'bɪdɪnl] *adj. (Psych.)* libidinös
libidinous [lɪ'bɪdɪnəs] *adj.* triebhaft
libido [lɪ'bi:dəʊ] *n. (Psych.)* Libido, *die*
Libra ['li:brə, 'lɪbrə] *n. (Astrol., Astron.)* die Waage; die Libra; *see also* **Aries**
Libran ['li:brən, 'lɪbrən] *n. (Astrol.)* Waage, *die*
librarian [laɪ'breərɪən] *n.* Bibliothekar, *der/*Bibliothekarin, *die*
librarianship [laɪ'breərɪənʃɪp] *n.* **a)** *(subject)* Bibliothekswesen, *das;* Bibliothekskunde, *die;* **b)** *(work)* bibliothekarische Tätigkeit
library ['laɪbrərɪ] *n.* **a)** Bibliothek, *die;* Bücherei, *die;* **reference ~:** Präsenzbibliothek, *die;* **public ~:** öffentliche Bücherei; **b)** *(collection of films, records, etc.)* Sammlung, *die. See also* **lending 2; rental library**
library: ~ book *n.* Buch aus der Bibliothek *od.* Bücherei; **~ edition** *n.* Ausgabe mit Bibliothekseinband; **~ school** *n.* Bibliotheksschule, *die;* **~ science** *n.* Bibliothekswissenschaft, *die;* **~ ticket** *n.* Lesekarte, *die*
librettist [lɪ'bretɪst] *n.* Librettist, *der/*Librettistin, *die*
libretto [lɪ'bretəʊ] *n., pl.* **libretti** [lɪ'breti:] *or* **~s** Libretto, *das*
Libya ['lɪbɪə] *pr. n.* Libyen *(das)*
Libyan ['lɪbɪən] **1.** *adj.* libysch; **sb. is ~:** jmd. ist Libyer/Libyerin. **2.** *n.* Libyer, *der/*Libyerin, *die*
lice *pl. of* **louse 1 a**
licence ['laɪsəns] **1.** *n.* **a)** *(official permit)* [behördliche] Genehmigung; Lizenz, *die;* Konzession, *die (Amtsspr.);* **hunting ~:** Jagdschein, *der;* **gun ~:** Waffenschein, *der;* **~ to marry** *see* **marriage licence; b)** *([excessive] liberty of action)* [uneingeschränkte] Handlungsfreiheit; **c)** *(licentiousness)* Unzüchtigkeit, *die;* Zügellosigkeit, *die;* **d)** *(artist's irregularity)* Freiheit, *die;* **poetic ~:** dichterische Freiheit. **2.** *v. t. see* **license 1**
'licence-dodger *n. (car owner)* Schwarzfahrer, *der; (TV)* Schwarzseher, *der*
license ['laɪsəns] **1.** *v. t.* ermächtigen; **~ a building for use as a theatre** ein Gebäude zur Nutzung als Theater freigeben; **~d to sell alcoholic beverages** *(formal)* [für den Ausschank von alkoholischen Getränken] konzessioniert; **~d to sell tobacco** berechtigt, Tabakwaren zu verkaufen; **the restaurant is ~d to sell drinks** das Restaurant hat eine Schankerlaubnis *od.* -konzession; **~d house** Gastwirtschaft, *die;* **licensing hours** *(in public house)* Ausschankzeiten; **licensing laws** Schankgesetze; ≈ Gaststättengesetz, *das;* **~d premises** Gaststätte mit Schankerlaubnis; **~ a book/play** *etc.* **[for publication]** ein Buch/Stück *usw.* [zur Veröffentlichung] freigeben; *see also* **victualler. 2.** *n. (Amer.) see* **licence 1**
licensee [laɪsən'si:] *n.* Lizenzinhaber, *der;* Konzessionsinhaber, *der; (of bar)* Wirt, *der/*Wirtin, *die*
'license plate *n. (Amer.)* Nummernschild, *das*
licentiate [laɪ'senʃɪət] *n.* **a)** *(person)* Inhaber eines Diploms; **b)** *(certificate)* Diplom, *das*
licentious [laɪ'senʃəs] *adj.* zügellos, ausschweifend ‹*Leben, Person*›; unzüchtig ‹*Benehmen, Reden*›; freizügig ‹*Buch, Theaterstück*›
lichen ['laɪkn, 'lɪtʃn] *n.* Flechte, *die*
lich-gate ['lɪtʃgeɪt] *n.* überdachtes Friedhofstor
licit ['lɪsɪt] *adj.* legal
lick [lɪk] **1.** *v. t.* **a)** lecken; **~ a stamp** eine Briefmarke anlecken *od.* belecken; **~ one's chops** *(coll.) or* **lips** *(lit. or fig.)* sich *(Dat.)* die Lippen lecken; **~ sth./sb. into shape** *(fig.)* etw./jmdn. auf Vordermann bringen *(ugs.);* **~ sb.'s boots** *(fig.)* jmdm. die Stiefel lecken; **~ sb.'s arse** *(fig. coarse)* jmdm. hinten reinkriechen *(derb);* **~ one's wounds** *(lit. or fig.)* seine Wunden lecken; **b)** *(play gently over)* ‹*Flammen, Feuer:*› [empor]züngeln an (+ *Dat.*); ‹*Wasser, Wellen:*› plätschern über (+ *Akk.*); **c)** *(sl.: beat)* verdreschen *(ugs.); (fig.)* bewältigen, meistern ‹*Problem*›; *(in contest)* eine Abfuhr erteilen (+ *Dat.*); **this crossword/problem has [got] me ~ed** bei diesem Kreuzworträtsel/Problem steck' ich fest *(ugs.).* **2.** *n.* **a)** *(act)* Lecken, *das;* **have a ~ at sth.** an etw. *(Dat.)* lecken; **give a door a ~ of paint** eine Tür [oberflächlich] überstreichen; **give the shoes a ~ of polish** die Schuhe flüchtig putzen; **give sth./oneself a ~ and a promise** *(fig. coll.)* kurz über etw. *(Akk.)* hinhuschen/Katzenwäsche machen *(ugs.);* **b)** *(sl.: fast pace)* **at a great** *or* **at full ~:** mit einem Affenzahn *(ugs.);* **at quite a ~:** mit einem ganz schönen Zahn *(ugs.);* **c)** *see* **salt-lick**
~ 'off *v. t.* ablecken; **~ the cream off the cake** die Sahne vom Kuchen lecken
~ 'up *v. t.* auflecken
lickety-split [lɪkətɪ'splɪt] *adv. (coll.)* wie der Blitz *(ugs.)*
licking ['lɪkɪŋ] *n. (sl.: beating)* Abreibung, *die (ugs.);* **give sb. a good ~:** jmdn. kräftig durchbleuen *(ugs.);* **take a ~:** eine Abreibung kriegen *(ugs.)*
'lickspittle *n.* Speichellecker, *der (abwertend)*
licorice *see* **liquorice**
lid [lɪd] *n.* **a)** Deckel, *der;* **with the ~ off** *(fig.)* unter Aufdeckung aller Mängel/Schwächen/Mißstände; **take the ~ off sth.** *(fig.)* etw. aufdecken; **put the [tin] ~ on sth.** *(Brit. sl.) (be the final blow)* einer Sache *(Dat.)* die Krone aufsetzen; *(put an end to)* etw. stoppen; **that [really] puts the tin ~ on it** das schlägt dem Faß den Boden aus; *see also* **¹flip 3; b)** *(eyelid)* Lid, *das*
lido ['li:dəʊ] *n., pl.* **~s** Freibad, *das*
¹lie [laɪ] **1.** *n.* **a)** *(false statement)* Lüge, *die;* **tell ~s/a ~:** lügen; **no, I tell a ~, ...** *(coll.)* nein, nicht daß ich jetzt lüge, ... *(ugs.);* **white ~:** Notlüge, *die;* **tell a white ~:** eine Notlüge gebrauchen; **give sb. the ~ [in his throat]** jmdn. der Lüge bezichtigen; **give the ~ to sth.** etw. Lügen strafen; **b)** *(thing that deceives)* [einzige] Lüge *(fig.);* Schwindel, *der (abwertend);* **he lived a ~:** sein Leben war eine einzige Lüge. **2.** *v. i.,* **lying** ['laɪɪŋ] lügen; **~ to sb.** jmdn. be- *od.* anlügen; **~ through one's teeth** *(joc.)* das Blaue vom Himmel herunterlügen *(ugs.).* **3.** *v. t.,* **lying: ~ one's way out of sth.** sich aus etw. herauslügen
²lie 1. *n.* **a)** *(direction, position)* Lage, *die;* **the ~ of the land** *(Brit. fig.: state of affairs)* die Lage der Dinge; die Sachlage; **b)** *(Golf)* Lage [des Balles]. **2.** *v. i.,* **lying** ['laɪɪŋ], **lay** [leɪ], **lain** [leɪn] **a)** liegen; *(assume horizontal position)* sich legen; **many obstacles ~ in the way of my success** *(fig.)* viele Hindernisse verstellen mir den Weg zum Erfolg; **~ resting** ruhen; **she lay asleep/resting on the sofa** sie lag auf dem Sofa und schlief/ruhte sich aus; **~ still/dying** still liegen/im Sterben liegen; **~ sick** [krank] daniederliegen; **~ dead/helpless** tot/hilflos [da]liegen; **b)** *(be or remain in specified state)* **~ in prison** im Gefängnis sitzen; **~ idle** ‹*Feld, Garten:*› brachliegen; ‹*Maschine, Fabrik:*› stillstehen; ‹*Gegenstand:*› [unbenutzt] herumstehen *(ugs.);* **the money is lying idle in the bank** das Geld liegt ungenutzt auf der Bank; **let sth./things ~:** etw./die Dinge ruhen lassen; **how do things ~?** wie liegen die Dinge?; *see also* **close 1 k; doggo; ¹fallow 2; heavy 1 j; ¹low 2 e; wait 3 b; waste 4 b; c)** *(be buried)* [begraben] liegen; *see also* **state 1 g; d)** *(be situated)* liegen; **Austria ~s to the south of Germany** Österreich liegt südlich von Deutschland; **our road ~s northwards/along the river** unsere Straße führt nach Norden/verläuft entlang dem Fluß; *see also* **land 1 b; e)** *(be spread out to view)* **the valley/plain/desert lay before us** vor uns lag das Tal/die Ebene/die Wüste; **a brilliant career lay before him** *(fig.)* eine glänzende Karriere lag vor ihm; **these suggestions now ~ open to discussion** *(fig.)* diese Vorschläge können jetzt diskutiert werden; **f)** *(Naut.)* **~ at anchor/in harbour** vor Anker/im Hafen liegen; **g)** *(fig.)* ‹*Gegenstand:*› liegen; **her interest ~s in languages** ihr Interesse liegt auf sprachlichem Gebiet; **I will do everything that ~s in my power to help** ich werde alles tun, was in meiner Macht steht, um zu helfen; **I will ... as far as in me ~s** *(literary)* was an mir liegt, so will ich ...; **it ~s with you** es liegt bei dir; **h)** *(Law: be admissible or sustainable)* zulässig sein; **no objection will ~:** Einspruch kann nicht erhoben werden; **i) ~ with sb.** *(arch.: have sexual intercourse)* jmdm. beiliegen *(geh. veraltet)*
~ a'bout, ~ a'round *v. i.* herumliegen *(ugs.)*

~ '**back** *v.i. (recline against sth.)* sich zurücklegen; *(in sitting position)* sich zurücklehnen

~ '**down** *v.i.* sich hinlegen; **take sth. lying down** *(fig.)* etw. ruhig *od.* tatenlos hinnehmen; *see also* **lie-down**

~ '**in** *v.i.* **a)** *(arch.: labour in childbirth)* in den Wehen liegen *(veralt.)*; **b)** *(Brit. coll.: stay in bed)* liegenbleiben; *see also* **lie-in**

~ '**over** *v.i.* ‹*Arbeit:*› liegenbleiben; ‹*Tagesordnungspunkt, Entscheidung:*› vertagt werden

~ '**to** *v.i. (Naut.)* beidrehen

~ '**up** *v.i.* **a)** *(hide)* sich versteckt halten; **b)** *(stay in bed)* das Bett hüten

'**lie-abed** *n.* Langschläfer, *der*/-schläferin, *die*

lied [li:t] *n., pl.* **~er** ['li:də(r)] Lied, *das; (genre)* Kunstlied, *das*

lie: **~-detector** *n.* Lügendetektor, *der;* **~-down** *n. (coll.)* **have a ~-down** sich hinlegen

Liège [lɪ'eɪʒ] *pr. n.* Lüttich *(das)*

liege [li:dʒ] *n. (Hist.)* **a)** *(lord)* Lehnsherr, *der;* **my ~:** *as form of address* mein gnädiger Herr; **b)** *usu. in pl. (vassal)* Lehnsmann, *der*

'**lie-in** *n. (coll.)* **a)** *(Brit.: extra time in bed)* **have a ~** [sich] ausschlafen; **b)** *(protest) Demonstration, bei der sich die Protestierenden auf den Boden legen;* Lie-in, *das*

lien ['li:ən] *n. (Law)* Zurückbehaltungsrecht, *das;* Retentionsrecht, *das*

lieu [lju:, lu:] *n.* **in ~ of sth.** anstelle einer Sache *(Gen.)*; **get money/holidays in ~:** statt dessen Geld/Urlaub bekommen

Lieut. *abbr.* **Lieutenant**

lieutenant [lef'tenənt, ləf'tenənt] *n.* **a)** *(Army)* Oberleutnant, *der; (Navy)* Kapitänleutnant, *der;* **first ~** *(Amer. Air Force)* Oberleutnant, *der;* **b)** *(Amer.: policeman)* ≈ Polizeioberkommissar, *der*

lieutenant: **~-'colonel** *n.* Oberstleutnant, *der;* **~-com'mander** *n.* Korvettenkapitän, *der;* **~-'general** *n.* Generalleutnant, *der;* **~-'governor** *n.* Vizegouverneur, *der*

life [laɪf] *n., pl.* **lives** [laɪvz] **a)** Leben, *das;* **sign of ~:** Lebenszeichen, *das;* **essential for ~:** lebensnotwendig; **it is a matter of ~ and death** es geht [dabei] um Leben und Tod; *(fig.: it is of vital importance)* es ist äußerst wichtig **(to** für); **come to ~** ‹*Bild, Statue:*› lebendig werden; ‹*die Natur:*› zu neuem Leben erwachen; *(after unconsciousness)* wieder zu sich kommen; **then the match came to ~:** dann kam Leben in das Spiel; **run** *etc.* **for one's ~:** um sein Leben rennen *usw.;* **I cannot for the ~ of me** ich kann beim besten Willen nicht; **lay down one's ~:** sein Leben [hin]geben; **lose one's ~:** sein Leben verlieren; **they lost their lives** sie verloren ihr Leben; **many lives were lost** viele Menschen kamen ums Leben; **risk [losing] one's ~:** sein Leben riskieren; **without loss of ~:** ohne Todesopfer; **~ begins at forty** das Leben beginnt mit 40; **~ is not worth living** das Leben ist nicht lebenswert; **not on your ~** *(coll.)* nie im Leben! *(ugs.);* **save one's/sb.'s ~:** sein Leben/jmdm. das Leben retten; **sth. is as much as sb.'s ~ is worth** mit etw. setzt jmd. sein Leben aufs Spiel; **take [sb.'s] ~:** jmdn. töten; **take one's [own] ~:** sich *(Dat.)* das Leben nehmen; **take one's ~ in one's hands** sein Leben riskieren; **upon my ~:** meiner Treu *(veralt.);* bei Gott; *see also* **book 1a, lease 1; limb a; price 1a; sell 1a; staff 1g; b)** *(energy, animation)* Leben, *das;* **be the ~ and soul of the party** der Mittelpunkt der Party sein; **full of ~:** energiegeladen ‹*Person*›; lebendig ‹*Stadt, Straße*›; **there is still ~ in sth.** in etw. *(Dat.)* steckt noch Leben; **put some ~ into it!** *(coll.)* ein bißchen flotter!; **c)** *(living things and their activity)* Leben, *das;* **is there ~ on Mars?** gibt es Leben auf dem Mars?; **support ~:** organisches Leben tragen; **bird/insect ~:** die Vogelwelt/die Insekten; **d)** *(living form or model)* **draw sb. from ~:** jmdn. nach dem Leben zeichnen; **as large as ~** *(life-size)* lebensgroß; *(in person)* in voller Schönheit *(ugs. scherzh.);* **larger than ~:** überzeichnet; **larger-than-~ faces** überlebensgroße Gesichter; **true to ~:** wahrheitsgetreu; **to the ~:** lebensgetreu; **e)** *(period from birth to death, from specified time to death)* Leben, *das;* **marry early in ~:** früh heiraten; **late in ~:** erst im fortgeschrittenen Alter; **sb.'s ~ and times** jmds. Leben und die Zeit, in der er *usw.* lebte; **for ~:** auf Lebenszeit; lebenslänglich ‹*inhaftiert*›; **he's doing ~** *(coll.)* er sitzt lebenslänglich *(ugs.);* **get ~** *(sl.)* lebenslänglich kriegen *(ugs.);* **expectation of ~:** Lebenserwartung, *die;* **get the fright/shock of one's ~** *(coll.)* zu Tode erschrekken/den Schock seines Lebens bekommen *(ugs.);* **have the time of one's ~:** sich hervorragend amüsieren; **f)** *(chance, fresh start)* **a cat has nine lives** eine Katze hat neun Leben; **a player has three lives** *(Sport)* ein Spieler hat drei Versuche; **g)** *(form of existence)* Leben, *das;* **he will do anything for a quiet ~:** für ihn ist die Hauptsache, daß er seine Ruhe hat; **nothing in ~:** nichts auf der Welt; **make ~ easy for oneself/sb.** es sich *(Dat.)*/jmdm. leichtmachen; **make ~ difficult for oneself/sb.** sich *(Dat.)*/jmdm. das Leben schwermachen; **this is the ~!** *expr. content* so läßt sich's leben!; **what a ~!** *expr. discontent* so ein Hundeleben! *(ugs.);* **that's ~, ~'s like that** so ist das Leben [nun mal]; **h)** *(specific aspect)* ‹*Privat-, Wirtschafts-, Dorf*›leben, *das;* **military/national ~:** das militärische/öffentliche Leben; **the bustle of street ~:** das pulsierende Leben in den Straßen; **in this ~** *(on earth)* in diesem Leben; **the other** *or* **the future** *or* **the next ~** *(in heaven)* das zukünftige Leben [nach dem Tode]; **eternal** *or* **everlasting ~:** ewiges Leben; *see also* **depart 1d, 2; simple a; i)** *(biography)* Lebensbeschreibung, *die;* **j)** *(active part of existence)* das Leben; **daily ~:** das Alltagsleben; **see ~:** etwas von der Welt sehen; *see also* **high life; k)** *(of battery, lightbulb, etc.)* Lebensdauer, *die*

life: **~-and-death** *adj.* ‹*Kampf*› auf Leben und Tod; *(fig.)* überaus wichtig ‹*Frage, Brief*›; **~ an'nuity** *n.* Leibrente, *die;* **~ assurance** *n. (Brit.)* Lebensversicherung, *die;* **~belt** *n.* Rettungsring, *der;* **~-blood** *n.* Blut, *das;* Lebenssaft, *der (dichter.); (fig.)* Lebensnerv, *der;* **~boat** *n.* Rettungsboot, *das;* **~buoy** *n. (ring-shaped)* Rettungsring, *der;* **~ cycle** *n.* Lebenszyklus, *der;* **~ expectancy** *n.* Lebenserwartung, *die;* **~ force** *n.* Elan vital, *der;* **~-giving** *adj.* lebenspendend *(geh.);* **~-guard** *n.* **a)** *(soldiers)* Leibwache, *die;* **b)** *(expert swimmer)* Rettungsschwimmer, *der*/-schwimmerin, *die;* **L~ Guards** *n. pl. (Brit.: regiment)* [Leib]garde, *die;* **~ 'history** *n.* **a)** *(of person)* Lebensgeschichte, *die;* **b)** *(of organism)* Entwicklungsgeschichte, *die;* **~ insurance** *n.* Lebensversicherung, *die;* **~-jacket** *n.* Schwimmweste, *die*

lifeless ['laɪflɪs] *adj.* **a)** leblos; unbelebt ‹*Gegend, Planet*›; **b)** *(lacking animation)* farblos ‹*Stimme, Rede, Aufführung*›; ‹*Stadt*› ohne Leben

life: **~like** *adj.* lebensecht; **~line** *n.* **a)** *(rope)* Rettungsleine, *die;* Manntau, *das; (of diver)* Signalleine, *die;* **b)** *(fig.)* [lebenswichtige] Verbindung; *(support)* Rettungsanker, *der;* **c)** *(Palmistry)* Lebenslinie, *die;* **~long** *adj.* lebenslang; **sb.'s ~long friend** *(future)* jmds. Freund fürs Leben; *(past)* jmds. Freund seit der Kindheit; **~ 'member** *n.* Mitglied auf Lebenszeit; **~ 'membership** *n.* lebenslange Mitgliedschaft; Mitgliedschaft auf Lebenszeit; **~ 'peer** *n.* Peer auf Lebenszeit; **~ 'peerage** *n.* nicht erbliche Peerswürde; **~-preserver** *n.* **a)** *(~-jacket)* Schwimmweste, *die; (~buoy)* Rettungsring, *der;* **b)** *(stick)* Totschläger, *der*

lifer ['laɪfə(r)] *n. (sl.)* Lebenslängliche, *der/die (ugs.)*

life: **~-raft** *n.* Rettungsfloß, *das;* **~-saver** *n.* **a)** *(Austral., NZ: ~-guard)* Rettungsschwimmer, *der;* **b)** *(thing that saves)* Lebensretter, *der (fig.);* **it's been a ~-saver** es war die letzte Rettung; **~-saving** *n.* Rettungsschwimmen, *das; attrib.* Rettungs‹*gerät, -technik*›; lebensrettend ‹*Medikament*›; **~ sciences** *n. pl.* Biowissenschaften *Pl.;* **~ sentence** *n.* lebenslängliche Freiheitsstrafe; **get a ~ sentence** lebenslänglich bekommen; **~-size, ~-sized** *adj.* lebensgroß; in Lebensgröße *nachgestellt;* **~-span** *n.* Lebenserwartung, *die; (Biol.)* Lebensdauer, *die;* **~ story** *n.* Lebensgeschichte, *die;* **~-style** *n.* Lebensstil, *der;* **~-support** *n.* **~-support system** lebenserhaltende Apparate; **~time** *n.* Lebenszeit, *die; (Phys.)* Lebensdauer, *die; attrib.* lebenslang; **once in a ~time** einmal im Leben; **during my ~time** während meines Lebens; **the chance of a ~time** eine einmalige Gelegenheit; die Chance meines/deines *usw.* Lebens; **~-vest** *n.* Schwimmweste, *die;* **~-work** *n.* Lebenswerk, *das*

lift [lɪft] **1.** *v.t.* **a)** heben; *(slightly)* anheben; *(fig.)* erheben ‹*Seele, Gemüt, Geist*›; **have one's face ~ed** sich *(Dat.)* das Gesicht liften lassen; **~ sb.'s spirits** jmds. Stimmung heben; **not ~ a hand to do sth.** keine Hand rühren *(ugs.);* **~ a hand against sb.** die Hand gegen jmdn. heben; *see also* **finger 1a; b)** *(sl.: steal)* klauen *(salopp);* **c)** *(sl.: plagiarize)* abkupfern *(salopp)* **(from** aus); **d)** *(dig up)* ernten ‹*Kartoffeln*›; aus der Erde nehmen ‹*Blumenzwiebeln, -knollen*›; **e)** *(end)* aufheben ‹*Verbot, Beschränkung, Blockade*›. **2.** *v.i.* **a)** *(disperse)* sich auflösen; *(fig.)* ‹*schlechte Stimmung, Unmut:*› verfliegen; **b)** *(rise)* ‹*Stimmung:*› sich aufhellen; ‹*Herz:*› höher schlagen. **3.** *n.* **a)** *(free ride in vehicle)* Mitfahrgelegenheit, *die;* **get a ~ [with** *or* **from sb.]** [von jmdm.] mitgenommen werden; **give sb. a ~:** jmdn. mitnehmen; **would you like a ~?** möchtest du mitfahren?; **b)** *(Brit.: machine for vertical movement)* Aufzug, *der;* Fahrstuhl, *der;* **c)** *(~ing)* Heben, *das; (of eyebrow)* Hochziehen, *das; (of prices)* Anstieg, *der;* **d)** *(Mil.)* Lufttransport, *der;* **e)** *(emotional boost)* Auftrieb, *der;* **give sb. a ~:** jmdm. Auftrieb geben; ‹*Droge:*› jmdn. anturnen *(ugs.);* **get a ~ from sth.** durch etw. Aufschwung bekommen; **f)** *(Mech. Engin.)* Hub, *der;* **g)** *(upward pressure of air)* Auftrieb, *der*

~ '**down** *v.t.* herunterheben

~ '**off** *v.t. & i.* abheben; *see also* **lift-off**

~ '**up 1.** *v.i.* ‹*Sitz:*› hochklappbar sein. **2.** *v.t. (raise)* hochheben; *(turn upwards)* heben ‹*Kopf*›; **~ up one's hands** die Hände erheben *(geh.);* **~ up your hearts** erhebet die Herzen! *(geh.);* **~ up one's voice** die Stimme erheben

lift: **~-attendant, ~-boy, ~-man** *ns. (Brit.)* Aufzugführer, *der;* **~-off 1.** *adj.* abhebbar; *(from backing)* abnehmbar; **2.** *n. (Aeronaut., Astronaut.)* Abheben, *das;* **soon after ~-off** bald nach dem Abheben; **we have ~-off** wir haben abgehoben

ligament ['lɪgəmənt] *n. (Anat.)* Band, *das;* Ligament[um], *das (fachspr.)*

ligature ['lɪgətʃə(r)] **1.** *n.* **a)** Bandage, *die; (in surgery)* Ligaturfaden, *der;* **b)** *(Med.: tying; Mus., Printing)* Ligatur, *die.* **2.** *v.t. (bind)* abbinden

¹**light** [laɪt] **1.** *n.* **a)** Licht, *das;* **in a good ~:** bei gutem Licht; *see also* **j; be in sb.'s ~:** jmdm. im Licht sein; **get out of my ~:** geh mir aus dem Weg!; **stand in sb.'s ~** *(fig.)* jmdm. im Weg stehen *(fig.);* **at first ~:** bei Tagesanbruch; **while the ~ lasts** solange es

[noch] hell ist; noch bei Tageslicht; ~ **of day** *(lit. or fig.)* Tageslicht, *das;* **she was the ~ of his life** *(fig.)* sie war die Sonne seines Lebens; **b)** *(electric lamp)* Licht, *das; (fitting)* Lampe, *die;* **~s out** *(in school etc.)* Bettruhe *die; (Mil.)* Zapfenstreich, *der;* **go out like a ~** *(fig.)* sofort weg sein *(ugs.);* **c)** *(signal to ships)* Leuchtfeuer, *das;* **d)** *in sing. or pl. (signal to traffic)* Ampel, *die;* **at the third set of ~s** an der dritten Ampel; *see also* **green light; red light; traffic lights; e)** *(to ignite)* Feuer, *das;* **have you got a ~?** haben Sie Feuer?; **put a/set ~ to sth.** etw. anzünden; **strike a ~** *(produce spark or flame)* Feuer schlagen; *(with match)* ein Streichholz anzünden; *(Brit. dated sl. int.) expr. surprise* potz Blitz! *(veralt.);* **f)** *(eminent person)* Größe, *die;* **be a literary ~:** eine literarische Berühmtheit sein; **lesser ~s** weniger berühmte *od.* bekannte Personen; *see also* **leading light; g)** *(look in eyes)* Leuchten, *das;* **h)** *(fig.: mental illumination)* **throw** *or* **shed ~ [up]on sth.** Licht in etw. *(Akk.)* bringen ; **the ~ of nature** *or* **reason** natürliche Verstandeskräfte; **bring sth. to ~:** etw. ans [Tages]licht bringen; **come to ~:** ans [Tages]licht kommen; *see also* **[1]see 1 a; i)** *in pl. (beliefs, abilities, convictions)* **according to one's ~s** nach bestem Wissen [und Gewissen]; **j)** *(aspect)* **in that ~:** aus dieser Sicht; **seen in this ~:** so gesehen; wenn man es so sieht; **in the ~ of** *(taking into consideration)* angesichts (+ *Gen.*); **show sb. in a bad ~:** ein schlechtes Licht auf jmdn. werfen; **put sb. in a good/bad ~:** jmdn. in einem guten/schlechten Licht erscheinen lassen; **k)** *(Crosswords)* Lösung, *die;* **l)** *(Theol.)* Erleuchtung, *die;* Licht, *das;* **m)** *(window)* Fenster, *das; (skylight)* Oberlicht, *das; (division in mullion)* Teilfenster, *das.* **2.** *adj.* hell; licht *(geh.);* **~-blue/-brown** *etc.* hellblau/-braun *usw.; see also* **[1]blue 2 e. 3.** *v. t.,* **lit** [lɪt] *or* **~ed a)** *(ignite)* anzünden; **b)** *(illuminate)* erhellen; **~ sb.'s/one's way** jmdm./sich leuchten. **4.** *v. i.,* **lit** *or* **~ed** ⟨*Feuer, Zigarette:*⟩ brennen, sich anzünden lassen

~ 'up 1. *v. i.* **a)** *(become lit)* erleuchtet werden; **b)** *(become bright)* aufleuchten **(with** vor); *(become flushed)* aufglühen **(with** vor); **his face lit up in a smile** sein Gesicht hellte sich zu einem Lächeln auf; **c)** *(begin to smoke)* sich *(Dat.)* eine anstecken *(ugs.).* **2.** *v. t.* **a)** *(illuminate)* erleuchten; **~ up with floodlights** mit Flutlicht anstrahlen; **b)** *(make bright)* erhellen; **c)** *(ignite)* anzünden ⟨*Zigarette usw.*⟩; **d) lit up** *(sl.: drunk)* blau *(ugs.);* sternhagelvoll *(salopp)*

[2]light 1. *adj.* **a)** leicht; Leicht⟨*metall, -öl, -benzin*⟩; **[for] ~ relief** [als] kleine Abwechslung; **be a ~ sleeper** einen leichten Schlaf haben; **b)** *(small in amount)* gering; **traffic is ~ on these roads** auf diesen Straßen herrscht nur wenig Verkehr; **c)** *(Printing)* mager ⟨*Schrift*⟩; **d)** *(not important)* leicht; **sth. is no ~ matter** etw. ist keine leichte Sache; **make ~ of sth.** etw. bagatellisieren; **e)** *(jesting, frivolous)* leichtfertig; **f)** *(nimble)* leicht ⟨*Schritt, Bewegungen*⟩; gewandt ⟨*Hände*⟩; **be ~ of foot** leichtfüßig sein; **have ~ fingers** *(steal)* gern lange Finger machen *(ugs.);* **g)** *(easily borne)* leicht ⟨*Krankheit, Strafe*⟩; gering ⟨*Steuern*⟩; unbedeutend ⟨*Mißgeschick*⟩; *(Law)* mild ⟨*Strafe, Urteil*⟩; **h) with a ~ heart** *(carefree)* leichten *od.* frohen Herzens; **i) feel ~ in the head** *(giddy)* leicht benommen sein. **2.** *adv.* **travel ~:** mit wenig *od.* leichtem Gepäck reisen

[3]light *v. i.,* **lit** [lɪt] *or* **~ed a)** *(come by chance)* **~ [up]on sth.** auf etw. *(Akk.)* kommen *od.* stoßen; **b)** *(sl.: attack)* **~ into sb./sth.** über jmdn./etw. herfallen; **c)** *(sl.: depart)* sich auf den Weg machen **(for** nach/zu)

light: ~-bulb *n.* Glühbirne, *die;* Glühlampe, *die (fachspr.);* **~-coloured** *adj.* hell

lighted ['laɪtɪd] *adj.* brennend ⟨*Kerze, Zigarette*⟩; angezündet ⟨*Streichholz*⟩; beleuchtet ⟨*Zimmer, Pfad, Schild, Vitrine*⟩

[1]lighten ['laɪtn] **1.** *v. t.* **a)** *(make less heavy)* leichter machen; leichtern ⟨*Schiff*⟩; **b)** *(make less oppressive)* lindern ⟨*Not*⟩; mildern ⟨*Zorn, Erregung*⟩; leichter machen ⟨*Arbeit, Aufgabe*⟩; verringern ⟨*Arbeitslast*⟩; kurzweilig gestalten ⟨*Weg, Reise*⟩; erleichtern ⟨*Gewissen*⟩; **~ sb.'s burden** jmdn. entlasten; **~ sb.'s duties** jmdm. leichtere Aufgaben zuteilen. **2.** *v. i. (become less heavy)* leichter werden; *(fig.)* ⟨*Stimmung:*⟩ sich aufheitern

[2]lighten 1. *v. t.* **a)** *(make brighter)* aufhellen; heller machen ⟨*Raum*⟩; **b)** *(arch.: illuminate)* erhellen. **2.** *v. i.* **a)** *(become brighter)* sich aufhellen; ⟨*Auge:*⟩ aufleuchten; **b)** *(emit lightning)* blitzen

[1]lighter ['laɪtə(r)] *n. (device)* Feuerzeug, *das; (in car)* Zigarettenanzünder, *der*

[2]lighter *n. (boat)* Leichter, *der*

lighterman ['laɪtəmən] *n., pl.* **lightermen** ['laɪtəmən] Leichterschiffer, *der*

light: ~er-than-'air *adj.* **~er-than-air aircraft/dirigible** Luftschiff, *das*/lenkbares Luftschiff; **~-face** *adj. see* **[2]light 1 d; ~-fingered** ['laɪtfɪŋgəd] *adj.* langfing[e]rig; **~ fitting** *n.* Lampe, *die;* **~-footed** ['laɪtfʊtɪd] *adj.* leichtfüßig; **~-'headed** *adj.* **a)** *(slightly giddy)* leicht benommen; **b)** *(frivolous)* leichtfertig; **~-hearted** *adj.* **a)** *(gay, humorous)* unbeschwert; heiter; **b)** *(optimistic, casual)* unbekümmert; **~-heartedly** [laɪt'hɑ:tɪdlɪ] *adv.* unbeschwert ⟨*lachen*⟩; unbekümmert ⟨*sich verhalten*⟩; **~ 'heavyweight** *n. (Boxing)* Halbschwergewicht, *das; (person also)* Halbschwergewichtler, *der;* **~ 'horse** *n., constr. as pl. (Mil.)* leichte Kavallerie; **~ 'horseman** *n. (Mil.)* leichter Kavallerist; **~house** *n.* Leuchtturm, *der;* **~house-keeper** *n.* Leuchtturmwärter, *der;* **~ 'industry** *n.* Leichtindustrie, *die;* **~ 'infantry** *n. (Mil.)* leichte Infanterie

lighting ['laɪtɪŋ] *n.* **a)** *(supply of light)* Beleuchtung, *die;* **b)** *(setting alight)* Anzünden, *das*

lighting-'up time *n.* Zeit zum Einschalten der Beleuchtung; **at ~:** ≈ wenn es dunkel wird

lightish ['laɪtɪʃ] *adj.* **a)** *(in colour)* ziemlich hell; hell ⟨*Farbe, Haare usw.*⟩; **~-blue/-skinned** [eher] hellblau/-häutig; **b)** *(in weight)* ziemlich leicht

lightly ['laɪtlɪ] *adv.* **a)** *(not heavily)* leicht; **sleep ~:** einen leichten Schlaf haben; **fall ~:** sacht fallen; **touch ~ on a topic** ein Thema kurz streifen; **b)** *(in a small degree)* leicht; **c)** *(without serious consideration)* leichtfertig; **d)** *(cheerfully, deprecatingly)* leichthin; **not treat sth. ~:** etw. nicht auf die leichte Schulter nehmen; **take sth. ~:** etw. nicht [so] ernst nehmen; **e)** *(nimbly)* behend; **f) get off ~** *(not receive heavy penalty)* glimpflich davonkommen; **let sb. off ~** *(not inflict heavy penalty)* jmdn. mit Nachsicht behandeln

light: ~ meter *n.* Lichtmesser, *der; (exposure meter)* Belichtungsmesser, *der;* **~-minded** *adj.* gedankenlos; oberflächlich

[1]lightness ['laɪtnɪs] *n., no pl.* **a)** *(having little weight, lit. or fig.)* Leichtigkeit, *die;* **the pianist's ~ of touch** der weiche Anschlag des Pianisten; **b)** *(of penalty, weather)* Milde, *die; (of infection)* Geringfügigkeit, *die;* **c)** *(absence of anxiety)* **~ of heart/spirit** Heiterkeit/Unbekümmertheit, *die;* **d)** *(lack of concern)* Leichtfertigkeit, *die;* **e)** *(agility of movement)* Leichtigkeit, *die*

[2]lightness *n. (brightness, paleness of colour)* Helligkeit, *die*

lightning ['laɪtnɪŋ] **1.** *n., no pl., no indef. art.* Blitz, *der;* **flash of ~:** Blitz, *der;* **like ~** *(coll.)* wie der Blitz *(ugs.);* **[as] quick as ~** *(coll.)* schnell wie der Blitz *(ugs.);* **like greased ~** *(coll.)* wie ein geölter Blitz *(ugs.); see also* **ball lightning; sheet lightning; summer lightning. 2.** *adj.* Blitz-; **with ~ speed** blitzschnell; **events moved with ~ speed** die Ereignisse überschlugen sich

lightning: ~-bug *n. (Amer.)* Leuchtkäfer, *der;* Glühwürmchen, *das (ugs.);* **~-conductor** *n. (lit. or fig.)* Blitzableiter, *der;* **~-rod** *n. (Amer.)* Blitzableiter, *der;* **[1]~ strike** *n. (~ hitting object)* Blitzschlag, *der;* **[2]~ 'strike** *n. (Industry)* überraschender [Kurz]streik

light: ~ 'opera *see* **[1]opera c; ~ pen** *n.* Lichtstift, *der;* **~-proof** *adj.* lichtundurchlässig; **~ 'railway** *n.* Kleinbahn, *die*

lights [laɪts] *n. pl. (lungs)* Lunge, *die*

light: ~ship *n.* Feuerschiff, *das;* **~ show** *n.* Light-Show, *die*

light: ~-tight *adj.* lichtdicht; **~weight 1.** *adj.* **a)** leicht; **b)** *(fig.: of little consequence)* unmaßgeblich; **c)** *(Boxing etc.)* Leichtgewichts⟨*boxer, -kampf*⟩; **2.** *n.* **a)** *(Boxing etc.)* Leichtgewicht, *das; (person also)* Leichtgewichtler, *der;* **b)** *(fig.: person of little ability or importance)* Leichtgewicht, *das (fig.);* **~-year** *n.* Lichtjahr, *das;* **~-years [removed] from sth.** *(fig.)* meilenweit von etw. entfernt

ligneous ['lɪgnɪəs] *adj. (Bot.)* holzig; **~ plants** Holzgewächse

lignite ['lɪgnaɪt] *n.* Braunkohle, *die*

[1]like [laɪk] **1.** *adj.* **a)** *(resembling)* wie; **your dress is ~ mine** dein Kleid ist so ähnlich wie meins; dein Kleid gleicht meinem *(geh.);* **your dress is very ~ mine** dein Kleid ist meinem sehr ähnlich; **in a case ~ that** in so einem Fall; **there was nothing ~ it** es gab nichts Vergleichbares; **who do you think he's ~?** wem sieht er deiner Ansicht nach ähnlich?; **what is sb./sth. ~?** wie ist jmd./etw.?; **what's he ~ to talk to?** wie redet es sich mit ihm?; **what's it ~ to go up in a balloon?** wie ist es, wenn man im Ballon aufsteigt?; **more ~ twelve** eher zwölf; **that's [a bit] more ~ it** *(coll.: better)* das ist schon [etwas] besser; *(coll.: nearer the truth)* das stimmt schon eher; **a man ~ you** ein Mann [so] wie du; **they are nothing ~ each other** sie sind sich *(Dat.)* nicht im geringsten ähnlich; **nothing ~ as** *or* **so good/bad/many** *etc.* **as ...:** bei weitem nicht so gut/schlecht/viele *usw.* wie ...; **no, nothing ~:** nein, längst *od.* bei weitem nicht; **Have you finished it yet? – Nothing ~:** Bist du schon damit fertig? – Noch längst nicht; *see also* **feel 2 c; look 1 d; something f; b)** *(characteristic of)* typisch für ⟨*dich, ihn usw.*⟩; **it's just ~ you to be late!** du mußt natürlich wieder zu spät kommen!; **it would be [just] ~ her to do that** das sähe ihr [wieder einmal] ähnlich; **just ~ a woman** typisch Frau *(ugs.);* **c)** *(similar)* ähnlich; **in ~ manner** auf die gleiche Weise; **be as ~ as two peas in a pod** sich *(Dat.)* gleichen wie ein Ei dem andern; **~ father, ~ son** *(prov.)* der Apfel fällt nicht weit vom Stamm *(Spr.);* **d)** *(Math., Phys.)* **~ signs** gleiche Vorzeichen; **~ charges** gleiche Ladungen; **~ quantities** gleiche Größen. **2.** *prep. (in the manner of)* wie; **[just] ~ that** [einfach] so; **you do it ~ so** *(coll.)* so mußt du das machen; *see also* **hell b; mad a, f; shot 1 d. 3.** *adv.* **a)** *(arch./coll.)* **[as] ~ as not, ~ enough** wahrscheinlich; **b)** *(sl.: so to speak)* also; irgendwie; **he kind of hit me, ~:** also, der hat mich irgendwie geschlagen *(ugs.);* **all friendly ~:** ganz freundlich und so *(ugs.).* **4.** *conj. (coll.)* **a)** *(in same or similar manner as)* wie; **he is not shy ~ he used to be** er ist nicht mehr so schüchtern wie früher; **b)** *(coll.: for example)* etwa; beispielsweise; **c)** *(Amer.: as if)* als ob; **d) tell it ~ it is** sagen Sie die ganze Wahrheit! **5.** *n.* **a)** *(equal)* **his/her ~:** seines-/ihresgleichen; **the ~ of it** so etwas; dergleichen; **I've never known the ~ [of it]** so etwas habe ich noch nie gehört; ~ **attracts ~:** gleich und gleich gesellt sich gern; **compare ~ with ~:** Vergleichbares miteinander vergleichen; **the ~s of me/you** *(coll.)* meines-/deinesgleichen; Leute wie ich/du; **if it weren't for the ~s of them ...** *(coll.)* wenn solche wie die nicht wären, ... *(ugs.)*; **that's not for the ~s of us** *(coll.)* das ist nichts für unsereinen *(ugs.)*; **I know you and your ~** *or* **the ~s of you** *(coll.)* deine Sorte/Leute von deiner Sorte kenne ich *(ugs.)*; **b)** *(similar things)* **the ~:** so etwas; **and the ~:** und dergleichen; **or the ~:** oder so etwas; oder so *(salopp)*

²like 1. *v. t. (be fond of, wish for)* mögen; **~ it or not** ob es dir/ihm *usw.* gefällt oder nicht; **~ vegetables** Gemüse mögen; gern Gemüse essen; **~ doing sth.** etw. gern tun; **would you ~ a drink/to borrow the book?** möchtest du etwas trinken/dir das Buch leihen?; **would you ~ me to do it?** möchtest du, daß ich es tue?; **I'd ~ it back soon** ich hätte es gern bald zurück; **I don't ~ this affair** die Sache gefällt mir nicht; **I didn't ~ to disturb you** ich wollte dich nicht stören; **perhaps you would ~ time to consider it** vielleicht brauchst du etwas Bedenkzeit; **I ~ 'that!** *(iron.)* so was hab' ich gern! *(ugs. iron.)*; **I ~ his cheek!** *(iron.)* er hat vielleicht Nerven! *(ugs. iron.)*; **how do you ~ it?** wie gefällt es dir?; **how does he ~ living in America?** wie gefällt es ihm in Amerika?; **how would you ~ an ice-cream?** was hältst du von einem Eis?; **how would 'you ~ it if ...?** wie würdest du es [denn] finden, wenn ...?; **how do you ~ 'that?** was sagst du dazu?; **but what happens 'then, I should ~ to know** *(iron.)* aber was dann passiert, wüßte ich gern; **I'd ~ to see you try!** *(iron.)* das möchte ich sehen!; **I should ~ to see them do it** ich möchte mal sehen, wie sie das machen wollen; **if you ~** *expr. assent* wenn du willst *od.* möchtest; *expr. limited assent* wenn man so will; **if one ~s that sort of thing** wenn einem so was gefällt *(ugs.)*. **2.** *n., in pl.* **~s and dislikes** Vorlieben und Abneigungen; **tell me your ~s and dislikes** sag mir, was du magst und was nicht

-like *adj. suf.* -artig; **bird~:** wie ein Vogel *nachgestellt*

likeable ['laɪkəbl] *adj.* nett; sympathisch

likelihood ['laɪklɪhʊd] *n.* Wahrscheinlichkeit, *die;* **what is the ~ of this happening?** wie wahrscheinlich ist es, daß dies geschieht?; **there is little ~ of his seeing this** *or* **that he will see this** es ist kaum anzunehmen, daß er das sieht; **he saw no ~ of the plan being approved** er hielt es für ausgeschlossen, daß der Plan Zustimmung finden könnte; **in all ~:** aller Wahrscheinlichkeit nach

likely ['laɪklɪ] **1.** *adj.* **a)** *(probable)* wahrscheinlich; glaubhaft ⟨*Geschichte*⟩; voraussichtlich ⟨*Bedarf, Zukunft*⟩; **be the ~ reason/source** wahrscheinlich der Grund/die Ursache sein; **do you think it ~?** hältst du es für wahrscheinlich?; **is it ~ that he'd do that?** ist ihm so etwas zuzutrauen?; **[that's] a ~ story** *(iron.)* du kannst mir viel erzählen! *(ugs.)*; **b)** *(to be expected)* wahrscheinlich; **there are ~ to be [traffic] hold-ups** man muß mit [Verkehrs]staus rechnen; **he is ~ to meet the same fate** er könnte leicht das gleiche Schicksal erleiden; **they are [not] ~ to come** sie werden wohl *od.* wahrscheinlich [nicht] kommen; **am I ~ to do something like that?** sehe ich aus, als ob ich so etwas tun würde?; **is it ~ to rain tomorrow?** wird es morgen wohl regnen?; **this is not ~ to happen** es ist unwahrscheinlich, daß das geschieht; das wird wohl kaum geschehen; **he is ~ to be our next president** er wird voraussichtlich unser nächster Präsident sein; **it seems ~ to have been an accident** es dürfte wohl ein Unfall gewesen sein; **the candidate most ~ to succeed** der Kandidat mit den größten Erfolgsaussichten; **c)** *(promising, apparently suitable)* geeignet ⟨*Person, Ort, Methode, Weg*⟩; **we've looked in all the ~ places** wir haben an allen in Frage kommenden Stellen gesucht; **this looks a ~ place to find mushrooms** es sieht so aus, als ob man hier Pilze finden könnte; **this restaurant seems a ~-looking place** dieses Restaurant sieht ganz annehmbar aus; **d)** *(strong, capable-looking)* fähig; *(showing promise)* vielversprechend ⟨*Kandidat, Anwärter*⟩; begabt ⟨*Student usw.*⟩; **we need a couple of ~ lads** wir brauchen ein paar tüchtige Burschen. **2.** *adv. (probably)* wahrscheinlich; **very** *or* **more than** *or* **quite** *or* **most ~:** höchstwahrscheinlich; sehr wahrscheinlich; **as ~ as not** höchstwahrscheinlich; **not ~!** *(coll.)* auf keinen Fall!

'like-minded *adj.* gleichgesinnt; **~ people** Gleichgesinnte

liken ['laɪkn] *v. t.* **~ sth./sb. to sth./sb.** etw./jmdn. mit etw./jmdm. vergleichen

likeness ['laɪknɪs] *n.* **a)** *(resemblance)* Ähnlichkeit, *die* **(to** mit); **b)** *(guise)* Aussehen, *das;* Gestalt, *die;* **take on the ~ of a swan** die Gestalt eines Schwanes annehmen; **c)** *(portrait)* Bild, *das;* Bildnis, *das (geh.)*; **take sb.'s ~** *(arch.)* jmdn. porträtieren

likewise ['laɪkwaɪz] *adv.* ebenso; **do ~:** das gleiche tun; **if we all did ~:** wenn [wir] das alle machen würden; **I'm not going – L~:** Ich gehe nicht hin – Ich auch nicht

liking ['laɪkɪŋ] *n.* Vorliebe, *die;* **they expressed a ~ for her cakes** sie lobten ihre Kuchen; **take a ~ to sb./sth.** an jmdm./etw. Gefallen finden; **sth. is [not] to sb.'s ~:** etw. ist [nicht] nach jmds. Geschmack

lilac ['laɪlək] **1.** *n.* **a)** *(Bot.)* Flieder, *der;* **b)** *(colour)* Zartlila, *das.* **2.** *adj.* zartlila; fliederfarben

lilliputian [lɪlɪ'pju:ʃn] **1.** *adj.* Liliput-; winzig ⟨*Format, Figur*⟩. **2.** *n.* Liliputaner, *der*/Liliputanerin, *die*

Lilo, (P) ['laɪləʊ] *n.* Luftmatratze, *die*

lilt [lɪlt] *(Scot./literary)* **1.** *n.* **a)** *(cadence, swing)* schwingender Rhythmus; *(of voice)* singender Tonfall; **speak with a ~:** mit singendem Tonfall sprechen; **b)** *(song, tune)* [fröhliche] Weise; Lied[chen], *das.* **2.** *v. t.* trällern ⟨*Lied, Melodie*⟩

lilting ['lɪltɪŋ] *adj.* heiter, beschwingt ⟨*Melodie, Walzer, Lied*⟩; singend ⟨*Tonfall*⟩

lily ['lɪlɪ] *n.* Lilie, *die;* **~ of the valley** Maiglöckchen, *das; see also* **¹gild**

lily: ~-livered ['lɪlɪlɪvəd] *adj. (literary)* feige; **~-pad** *n.* Seerosenblatt, *das;* **~-white** *adj.* lilienweiß; *(Amer.: excluding Blacks)* rein weiß

limb [lɪm] *n.* **a)** *(Anat.)* Glied, *das;* **~s** Glieder; Gliedmaßen; **a danger to life and ~:** eine Gefahr für Leib und Leben; **tear sb. ~ from ~** *(lit. or fig.)* jmdm. alle Glieder einzeln ausreißen; **b)** *(of tree)* Ast, *der;* **be out on a ~** *(fig.)* exponiert sein; **go out** *or* **put oneself out on a ~:** sich exponieren; **c)** *(of cross, sea)* Arm, *der*

¹limber ['lɪmbə(r)] *(Mil.) n.* Protze, *die*

²limber 1. *adj.* **a)** *(flexible)* biegsam ⟨*Zweig*⟩; elastisch ⟨*Seil, Leder*⟩; **b)** *(nimble)* geschmeidig; elastisch. **2.** *v. t. & i. see* **~ up**

~ up 1. *v. t.* warm machen; aufwärmen *(Sport)*; **~ oneself up** *(fig.)* sich fit machen *(fig.)* **(for** für); sich vorbereiten **(for** auf + *Akk.*). **2.** *v. i.* = **~ oneself up** *see* **~ up 1**

limbless ['lɪmlɪs] *adj.* ⟨*Person, Tier*⟩ ohne Gliedmaßen; ⟨*Baum*⟩ ohne Äste

¹limbo ['lɪmbəʊ] *n., pl.* **~s a)** *(region)* Vorhölle, *die;* Limbus, *der (Rel.)*; **b)** *(fig.)* Vergessenheit, *die;* **vanish into ~:** spurlos verschwinden; **be in ~** *(be pending)* in der Schwebe sein; *(be abandoned)* abgeschrieben sein; **live in ~:** in einer Art Niemandsland leben

²limbo *n., pl.* **~s** *(dance)* Limbo, *der*

¹lime [laɪm] *n.* **a) [quick]~:** [ungelöschter] Kalk; **slaked ~:** gelöschter Kalk; Löschkalk, *der;* **b)** *see* **birdlime**

²lime *n.* **a)** *(fruit)* Limone, *die;* **b)** *(juice)* Limonensaft, *der;* **c)** *see* **lime-green**

³lime *see* **lime-tree**

lime: ~-green 1. *adj.* [leuchtend] hellgrün; **2.** *n.* Hellgrün, *das;* **~-juice** *n.* Limonensaft, *der;* **~-kiln** *n.* Kalkofen, *der;* **~light** *n.* **a)** *(light)* Kalklicht, *das;* **b)** *(fig.: attention)* **be in the ~light** im Rampenlicht [der Öffentlichkeit] stehen

limerick ['lɪmərɪk] *n.* Limerick, *der*

lime: ~stone *n.* Kalkstein, *der;* **~-tree** *n.* Linde, *die;* Lindenbaum, *der (geh.)*; **~wood** *n.* Lindenholz, *das*

Limey ['laɪmɪ] *n. (Amer. sl. derog.)* Engländer, *der; (esp. soldier)* Tommy, *der; attrib.* englisch

limit ['lɪmɪt] **1.** *n.* **a)** *usu. in pl. (boundary)* Grenze, *die;* **within [the] city ~s** innerhalb der Stadtgrenzen; **b)** *(point or line that may not be passed)* Limit, *das; (of ability, love, etc.)* Grenze, *die;* **set** *or* **put a ~ on sth.** etw. begrenzen *od.* beschränken; **be over the ~** ⟨*Autofahrer:*⟩ zu viele Promille haben; ⟨*Reisender:*⟩ Übergepäck haben; **£400 is my upper ~:** 400 Pfund sind für mich das Äußerste; **there is a ~ to what I can spend/do** ich kann nicht unbegrenzt Geld ausgeben/meine Möglichkeiten sind auch nur begrenzt; **there is a ~ to everything** alles hat seine Grenzen; **there is a ~ to my patience** meine Geduld ist begrenzt; **there is no ~ to his impudence, his impudence knows no ~s** seine Unverschämtheit kennt keine Grenzen; **lower/upper ~:** Untergrenze/Höchstgrenze, *die;* **without ~:** unbegrenzt; **within ~s** innerhalb gewisser Grenzen; **'off ~s'** *(esp. Amer.)* „Zutritt [für Soldaten] verboten"; **this bar is off ~s** zu dieser Bar haben Soldaten keinen Zutritt; **c)** *(coll.)* **this is the ~!** das ist [doch] die Höhe!; **he/she is the [very] ~:** er/sie ist [einfach] unmöglich *(ugs.)*; **d)** *(Math.)* Grenzwert, *der.* **2.** *v. t.* begrenzen **(to** auf + *Akk.*); einschränken ⟨*Freiheit*⟩

limitation [lɪmɪ'teɪʃn] *n.* **a)** *(act)* Beschränkung, *die; (of freedom)* Einschränkung, *die;* **b)** *(condition) (of extent)* Begrenzung, *die; (of amount)* Beschränkung, *die;* **know one's ~s** seine Grenzen kennen; **c)** *(restrictive circumstance)* Beschränkung, *die;* **due to ~s of space** aus Platzmangel *od.* Platzgründen; **d)** *(Law)* Verjährung, *die*

limited ['lɪmɪtɪd] *adj.* **a)** *(restricted)* begrenzt; **~ company** *(Brit.)* Gesellschaft mit beschränkter Haftung; **~ edition** limitierte Auflage; **~ train** *(Amer.)* ≈ Schnellzug, *der;* **b)** *(intellectually narrow)* beschränkt *(abwertend)*; **~ outlook/mind** beschränkter Horizont/Verstand

limitless ['lɪmɪtlɪs] *adj.* grenzenlos

limo ['lɪməʊ] *n., pl.* **~s** *(Amer. coll.)* Limousine, *die*

limousine ['lɪmʊzi:n] *n.* Limousine, *die (mit Trennscheibe)*

¹limp [lɪmp] **1.** *v. i. (lit. or fig.)* hinken; **the ship managed to ~ into port** das Schiff schaffte es mit Müh und Not *od.* gerade so in den Hafen. **2.** *n.* Hinken, *das;* **walk with a ~:** hinken; **have a slight/pronounced ~:** leicht/stark hinken

²limp *adj.* **a)** *(not stiff, lit. or fig.)* schlaff; welk ⟨*Blumen*⟩; **I feel ~ at the thought of it** beim bloßen Gedanken daran wird mir schwach *(ugs.)*; **b)** *(flexible)* flexibel ⟨*Einband*⟩

limpet ['lɪmpɪt] *n. (Zool.)* Napfschnecke, *die*

'limpet mine *n.* Haftmine, *die*

limpid ['lɪmpɪd] *adj.* klar

limply ['lɪmplɪ] *adv.* schlaff; *(weakly)* schwach

limpness ['lɪmpnɪs] *n., no pl.* Schlaffheit, *die; (weakness)* Schwäche, *die*

linchpin ['lɪntʃpɪn] *n.* **a)** *(pin)* Lünse, *die;* Achsnagel, *der;* **b)** *(fig.: essential element)* Kernstück, *das;* **he is the ~ of the company** er ist das Herz der Firma; mit ihm steht und fällt die Firma

linctus ['lɪŋktəs] *n. (Med.)* Hustensaft, *der*

linden ['lɪndən] *n.* Linde, *die;* Lindenbaum, *der (geh.)*

^{1}**line** [laɪn] **1.** *n.* **a)** *(string, cord, rope, etc.)* Leine, *die;* **[fishing-]~:** [Angel]schnur, *die;* **the ~s** *(Amer.: reins)* die Zügel; **hard ~s** *(sl.)* ein schwerer Schlag; **[that's] hard ~s, old chap!** Schicksal, alter Junge!; **b)** *(telephone or telegraph cable)* Leitung, *die;* **our company has 20 ~s** unsere Firma hat 20 Anschlüsse; **get me a ~ to Washington** verbinden Sie mich mit Washington; **bad ~:** schlechte Verbindung; **be on the ~:** am Apparat sein; *see also* **cross 2a; ^{2}hold 1l; party line a; c)** *(long mark; also Math., Phys.)* Linie, *die; (less precise or shorter)* Strich, *der; (Telev.)* Zeile, *die;* **capture sth. in a few ~s** etw. mit wenigen Strichen einfangen; **the L~:** die Linie *(Seemannsspr.);* der Äquator; **~ of force** *(Phys.)* Kraftlinie, *die;* **~ of life/fortune** *(Palmistry)* Lebenslinie, *die*/Schicksalslinie, *die;* **straight ~:** gerade Linie; *(Geom.)* Gerade, *die;* **walk in a straight ~:** in einer geraden Linie gehen; **~ of sight** *or* **vision** Blickrichtung, *die;* **the ~s of her face** ihre Gesichtszüge/*(wrinkles)* ihre Falten; *see also* **yellow line; d)** *in pl. (outline of car, ship, etc.)* Linien *Pl.;* **e)** *(boundary)* Linie, *die; (fig.)* **somewhere on the ~:** irgendwo dazwischen; **lay sth. on the ~ [for sb.]** [jmdm.] etw. rundheraus sagen; **put sth. on the ~:** etw. aufs Spiel setzen; **put oneself on the ~:** ein Risiko eingehen; **your job is on the ~:** deine Stelle steht auf dem Spiel; *see also* **draw 1g; f)** *(row)* Reihe, *die; (Amer.: queue)* Schlange, *die;* **~ of trees** Baumreihe, *die;* **arrange the chairs in a straight ~:** die Stühle in einer Reihe aufstellen; **bring sb. into ~:** dafür sorgen, daß jmd. nicht aus der Reihe tanzt *(ugs.);* **come** *or* **fall into ~:** sich in die Reihe stellen; ‹*Gruppe:*› sich in einer Reihe aufstellen; *(fig.)* nicht mehr aus der Reihe tanzen *(ugs.);* **be in ~ [with sth.]** [mit etw.] in einer Linie liegen; **be in ~ for promotion** Aussicht auf Beförderung haben; **be in/out of ~ with sth.** *(fig.)* mit etw. in/nicht in Einklang stehen; **all along the ~:** auf der ganzen Linie; **somewhere along the ~:** irgendwann einmal; **stand in ~** *(Amer.: queue)* Schlange stehen; *see also* **toe 2; g)** *(Naut.)* **~ abreast** Dwarslinie, *die;* **~ ahead** Kiellinie, *die;* **~ [of battle]** [Kampf]linie, *die;* **h)** *(row of words on a page)* Zeile, *die;* **~s** *(actor's part)* Text, *der;* **drop me a ~:** schreib mir ein paar Zeilen; **she has only a few ~s** *(Theatre)* sie hat nur ein paar Worte zu sprechen; **he gave the boy 100 ~s** *(Sch.)* er ließ den Jungen 100 Zeilen abschreiben; *see also* **read 1c; i)** *(system of transport)* Linie, *die;* **[shipping] ~:** Schiffahrtslinie, *die;* **j)** *(series of persons or things)* Reihe, *die; (generations of family)* Linie, *die;* **be third in ~ to the throne** dritter in der Thronfolge sein; **k)** *(direction, course)* Richtung, *die;* **on these ~s** in dieser Richtung; **on the ~s of** nach Art (+ *Gen.*); **on similar ~s** auf ähnliche Art; **be on the right/wrong ~s** in die richtige/falsche Richtung gehen; **along** *or* **on the same ~s** in der gleichen Richtung; **be on the same ~s** die gleiche Richtung verfolgen; **~ of thought/march** Gedankengang, *der*/Marschrichtung, *die;* **what ~ shall we take with her?** wie sollen wir uns ihr gegenüber verhalten?; **take a strong ~ with sb.** jmdm. gegenüber bestimmt *od.* energisch auftreten; **~ of action** Vorgehensweise, *die;* **get a ~ on sb./sth.** *(coll.)* etwas über jmdn./etw. herausfinden; *see also* **assembly line; hard 1f; hard-line; party line b; resistance a; l)** *(Railw.)* Bahnlinie, *die; (track)* Gleis, *das;* **cross the ~:** die Gleise überqueren; **the ~ was blocked** die Strecke war blockiert; **the Waterloo ~, the ~ to Waterloo** die Linie nach Waterloo; **this is the end of the ~ [for you]** *(fig.)* dies ist das Aus [für dich]; **m)** *(field of activity)* Branche, *die; (academic)* Fachrichtung, *die;* **what's your ~?** in welcher Branche sind Sie?/was ist Ihre Fachrichtung?; **he's in the building ~:** er ist in der Baubranche; **that's not my ~:** das ist nicht mein Gebiet; **be in the ~ of duty/business** zu den Pflichten/zum Geschäft gehören; *see also* **shoot 2d; n)** *(Commerc.: product)* Artikel, *der;* Linie, *die (fachspr.);* **o)** *(Fashion)* Linie, *die;* **p)** *(Mil.: series of defences)* Linie, *die;* **draw the ~s** Stellungen beziehen; **enemy ~s** feindliche Stellungen *od.* Linien; *see also* **^{2}hold 1k. 2.** *v.t.* **a)** *(mark with lines)* linieren ‹*Papier*›; **a ~d face** ein faltiges Gesicht; **a face ~d with worry** ein von Sorgen gezeichnetes Gesicht; **b)** *(stand at intervals along)* säumen *(geh.)* ‹*Straße, Strecke*›

~ 'up 1. *v.t.* antreten lassen ‹*Gefangene, Soldaten usw.*›; [in einer Reihe] aufstellen ‹*Gegenstände*›; *(fig.)* **I've got a nice little job/a surprise ~d up for you** ich hab da eine nette kleine Beschäftigung/eine Überraschung für dich *(ugs.);* **have you got anything ~d up for this evening?** haben Sie heute abend schon etwas vor?; *see also* **line-up. 2.** *v.i.* ‹*Gefangene, Soldaten:*› antreten; ‹*Läufer:*› Aufstellung nehmen; *(queue up)* sich anstellen

^{2}**line** *v.t.* füttern ‹*Kleidungsstück*›; auskleiden ‹*Magen, Nest*›; ausschlagen ‹*Schublade usw.*›; **~ one's pockets** *(fig.)* sich *(Dat.)* die Taschen füllen

lineage ['lɪnɪɪdʒ] *n.* Abstammung, *die*

lineal ['lɪnɪəl] *adj.* **a)** *(in direct line of descent)* geradlinig ‹*Abstammung*›; direkt ‹*Nachkomme, Vorfahr*›; **b)** *(linear)* linear

lineament ['lɪnɪəmənt] *n., usu. in pl.* [Gesichts]zug, *der; (distinctive feature)* Grundzug, *der*

linear ['lɪnɪə(r)] *adj.* linear; **~ perspective** Linearperspektive, *die;* **~ extent** Längenausdehnung, *die;* **~ measure** Längenmaß, *das*

linear ac'celerator *n. (Phys.)* Linearbeschleuniger, *der*

line: ~-backer *n. (Amer. Footb.)* Gedrängehalbspieler, *der;* **~-drawing** *n.* Strichzeichnung, *die;* **~-engraving** *n.* Strichätzung, *die;* **~ fishing** *n.* Angeln, *das;* **~man** ['laɪnmən] *n., pl.* **linemen** ['laɪnmən] *(Amer. Footb.)* Stürmer, *der*

linen ['lɪnɪn] **1.** *n.* **a)** Leinen, *das;* **b)** *(shirts, sheets, clothes, etc.)* Wäsche, *die;* **wash one's dirty ~ in public** *(fig.)* seine schmutzige Wäsche vor anderen Leuten waschen. **2.** *adj.* Leinen‹*faden, -bluse, -laken*›; Lein‹*tuch*›

linen: ~-basket *n. (Brit.)* Wäschekorb, *der;* **~ cupboard** *n.* Wäscheschrank, *der*

line: ~-out *n. (Sport)* Gasse, *die;* **~ printer** *n. (Computing)* Zeilendrucker, *der*

^{1}**liner** ['laɪnə(r)] *n. (removable metal lining)* Auskleidung, *die; (in engine)* Laufbuchse, *die;* **carpet ~:** rutschfeste Teppichunterlage; **[bin-]~:** Müllbeutel, *der*

^{2}**liner** *n. (ship)* Linienschiff, *das; (aircraft)* Linienflugzeug, *das;* **ocean ~:** [Ozean-]Liner, *der*

'liner train *n.* Containerzug, *der*

linesman ['laɪnzmən] *n., pl.* **linesmen** ['laɪnzmən] **a)** *(Sport)* Linienrichter, *der;* **b)** *(Brit. Railw.)* Streckenarbeiter, *der;* **c)** *see* **lineman**

'line-up *n.* **a)** Aufstellung, *die;* **~ of cabaret acts** Zusammenstellung von Kabarettauftritten; **b)** *(Amer.) see* **identification parade**

^{1}**ling** [lɪŋ] *n. (Zool.)* Leng[fisch], *der*

^{2}**ling** *n. (Bot.)* Heidekraut, *das*

linger ['lɪŋgə(r)] *v.i.* **a)** *(remain, wait)* verweilen *(geh.);* bleiben; *(persist)* fortbestehen; ‹*Erkältung, Diskussion, Schmerzen:*› andauern; ‹*Lied:*› nachklingen; **her scent still ~ed in the room** ihr Duft hing noch im Raum; **b)** *(dwell)* **~ over** *or* **up[on] a subject** *etc.* bei einem Thema *usw.* verweilen; **~ over a meal** lange beim Essen sitzen

lingerie ['læ̃ʒəri:] *n.* **[women's] ~:** Damenunterwäsche, *die*

lingering ['lɪŋgərɪŋ] *adj.* anhaltend; verbleibend ‹*Zweifel*›; langwierig ‹*Krankheit*›; langsam ‹*Tod*›; nachklingend ‹*Melodie*›; **one last ~ look** ein letzter sehnsuchtsvoller Blick; **any ~ hope was abandoned** alle noch vorhandene Hoffnung schwand dahin *(geh.)*

lingo ['lɪŋgəʊ] *n., pl.* **~es a)** *(derog./joc.: language)* Sprache, *die;* Kauderwelsch, *das (abwertend);* **b)** *(jargon)* Fachjargon, *der*

lingua franca [lɪŋgwə 'fræŋkə] *n.* Lingua franca, *die (geh.);* Verkehrssprache, *die*

linguist ['lɪŋgwɪst] *n.* **a)** Sprachkundige, *der/die;* **she's a good ~:** sie kann mehrere Sprachen; **I'm no ~:** Sprachen liegen mir nicht; **b)** *(philologist)* Linguist, *der*/Linguistin, *die;* Sprachwissenschaftler, *der*/-wissenschaftlerin, *die*

linguistic [lɪŋ'gwɪstɪk] *adj.* *(of ~s)* linguistisch; sprachwissenschaftlich; *(of language)* sprachlich; Sprach-; **~ science** *see* **linguistics; ~ skills** Sprachbegabung, *die;* **~ fluency** Sprachgewandtheit, *die*

linguistically [lɪŋ'gwɪstɪkəlɪ] *adv.* sprachwissenschaftlich; linguistisch

linguistics [lɪŋ'gwɪstɪks] *n., no pl.* Linguistik, *die;* Sprachwissenschaft, *die*

liniment ['lɪnɪmənt] *n.* Liniment, *das (Med.);* Einreib[e]mittel, *das*

lining ['laɪnɪŋ] *n. (of clothes)* Futter, *das; (of stomach)* Magenschleimhaut, *die; (of objects, containers, machines, etc.)* Auskleidung, *die*

'lining paper *n.* Schrankpapier, *das*

link [lɪŋk] **1.** *n.* **a)** *(of chain)* Glied, *das;* **b)** *see* **cuff-link; c)** *(connecting part)* Bindeglied, *das;* Verbindung, *die;* **radio ~:** Funkverbindung, *die;* **road/rail ~:** Straßen-/Zugverbindung, *die;* **what is the ~ between these two?** was verbindet diese beiden?; **~ between two countries** Verbindung zwischen zwei Ländern; **sever all ~s with sb.** alle Bindungen zu jmdm. lösen; **have ~s with the Mafia** Verbindungen zur Mafia haben; *see also* **cut 1b; d)** *see* **linkman. 2.** *v.t.* **a)** *(connect)* verbinden; **how are these events ~ed?** was haben diese Ereignisse miteinander zu tun?; **~ sb. with sth.** jmdn. mit etw. in Verbindung bringen; **his name has been ~ed with hers** sein Name wurde mit ihrem in Verbindung gebracht; **be ~ed by telephone to Oslo** telefonisch mit Oslo verbunden sein; **b)** *(clasp or hook together)* **~ hands** sich bei den Händen halten; **~ arms** sich unterhaken. **3.** *v.i.* **~ together** sich zusammenfügen; **~ with sth.** sich verbinden mit etw.; ‹*Firma:*› sich zusammenschließen mit etw.

~ 'up 1. *v.t.* miteinander verbinden; ankoppeln ‹*Wagen, Raumschiff usw.*› **(to** an + *Akk.*); miteinander in Verbindung bringen ‹*Fakten usw.*›; **~ up A with B** A mit B verbinden. **2.** *v.i.* **~ up with sb.** sich mit jmdm. zusammentun *od.* zusammenschließen; **~ up with American TV** sich dem amerikanischen Fernsehen anschließen; **the spacecraft ~ed up** die Raumschiffe wurden angekoppelt; **this road ~s up with the M3** diese Straße mündet in die M3 *od.* geht in die M3 über. *See also* **link-up**

linkage ['lɪŋkɪdʒ] *n.* **a)** Verbindung, *die;* **b)** *(system of links or bars)* Gestänge, *das;* **steering ~:** Lenkgestänge, *das;* **c)** *(Chem.)* Verknüpfung, *die;* Verbindung, *die;* **d)** *(Genetics)* Kopplung, *die*

linkman ['lɪŋkmən] *n., pl.* **linkmen** ['lɪŋkmən] **a)** Verbindungsmann, *der;* **b)** *(Radio, Telev.)* Moderator, *der*/Moderatorin, *die;* **c)** *(Hockey, Footb.)* Mittelfeldspieler, *der*

links [lɪŋks] *sing. or pl.* [golf] ~: Golfplatz, *der*
ˈ**link-up** *n.* Verbindung, *die; (of spacecraft etc.)* Ankopplung, *die*
linnet [ˈlɪnɪt] *n. (Ornith.)* Hänfling, *der*
lino [ˈlaɪnəʊ] *n., pl.* ~s Linoleum, *das*
linocut *n.* Linolschnitt, *der*
linoleum [lɪˈnəʊlɪəm] *n.* Linoleum, *das*
linseed [ˈlɪnsi:d] *n.* Leinsamen, *der*
linseed: ~ **cake** *n. (Agric.)* Leinkuchen, *der;* ~ ˈ**oil** *n.* Leinöl, *das*
lint [lɪnt] *n.* **a)** Mull, *der;* **b)** *(fluff)* Fussel, *die*
lintel [ˈlɪntl] *n. (Archit.)* Sturz, *der*
lion [ˈlaɪən] *n.* **a)** Löwe, *der;* **put one's head into the ~'s mouth** *(fig.)* sich in höchste Gefahr begeben; **the ~'s share** der Löwenanteil; **b)** *(celebrity)* **literary ~ [of the day]** literarischer Löwe des Tages *(veralt.);* **c)** *(Astrol.)* **the L~:** der Löwe; *see also* **archer b**
lioness [ˈlaɪənɪs] *n.* Löwin, *die*
lion: ~**-heart** *n.* Löwenherz, *das (dichter. veralt.);* **Richard [the] L~-heart** Richard Löwenherz; ~**-hearted** *adj.* wagemutig; löwenherzig *(dichter. veralt.)*
lionize (lionise) [ˈlaɪənaɪz] *v.t.* [als Berühmtheit] feiern
ˈ**lion-tamer** *n.* Löwenbändiger, *der*
lip [lɪp] *n.* **a)** Lippe, *die;* **lower/upper ~:** Unter-/Oberlippe, *die;* **bite one's ~** *(lit. or fig.)* sich *(Dat.)* auf die Lippen beißen; **escape sb.'s ~s** jmds. Lippen *(Dat.)* entschlüpfen; **hang on sb.'s ~s** an jmds. Lippen *(Dat.)* hängen; **lick one's ~s** *(lit. or fig.)* sich *(Dat.)* die Lippen lecken; **not let a word pass one's ~s** kein Wort über seine Lippen kommen lassen; **not a morsel passed his ~s** er rührte nichts an; **keep a stiff upper ~** *(fig.)* Haltung bewahren; *see also* **button 2;** ²**seal 2 b;** ²**smack 2 b; b)** *(of saucer, cup, crater)* [Gieß]rand, *der; (of jug)* Schnabel, *der;* Tülle, *die;* **c)** *(sl.: impudence)* **give sb. some ~:** jmdm. gegenüber eine dicke Lippe riskieren *(ugs.);* **none of your ~!** keine frechen Bemerkungen!
lipped [lɪpt] *adj.* **thick-/thin-~:** dick-/dünnlippig; ~ **vessel** Gefäß mit Schnabel *od.* Gießrand
lippy [ˈlɪpɪ] *adj. (sl.)* **be ~:** ein freches Mundwerk haben
lip: ~**-read 1.** *v.i.* von den Lippen lesen; **2.** *v.t.* **be able to ~-read what sb. says** jmdm. von den Lippen ablesen können, was er/sie sagt; ~**-reading** *n.* Lippenlesen, *das;* ~**-service** *n.* **pay** *or* **give ~-service to sth.** ein Lippenbekenntnis zu etw. ablegen; ~**stick** *n.* Lippenstift, *der*
liquefaction [lɪkwɪˈfækʃn] *n.* Verflüssigung, *die*
liquefier [ˈlɪkwɪfaɪə(r)] *n.* Verflüssiger, *der*
liquefy [ˈlɪkwɪfaɪ] **1.** *v.t.* verflüssigen. **2.** *v.i.* sich verflüssigen
liqueur [lɪˈkjʊə(r)] *n.* Likör, *der*
liqueur: ~ ˈ**brandy** *n. gut gealterter, hochwertiger Brandy;* ~ ˈ**chocolate** *n.* Likörpraline, *die;* ~**-glass** *n.* Likörglas, *das*
liquid [ˈlɪkwɪd] **1.** *adj.* **a)** flüssig; glänzend ‹*Augen*›; hellklingend ‹*Töne, Laute*›; ~ **air** Flüssigluft, *die;* ~ **blue** wasserblau; **b)** *(Commerc.)* liquid; ~ **assets** flüssige Mittel; **c)** *(Phonet.)* ~ **consonant** Fließlaut, *der;* Liquida, *die (fachspr.).* **2.** *n.* **a)** Flüssigkeit, *die;* **he can only take ~s** er kann nur Flüssiges zu sich nehmen; **b)** *(Phonet.)* Fließlaut, *der;* Liquida, *die (fachspr.)*
liquidate [ˈlɪkwɪdeɪt] **1.** *v.t.* **a)** *(Commerc.)* liquidieren; tilgen ‹*Schuld*›; ~**d damages** *(Law)* Konventionalstrafe, *die;* **b)** *(eliminate, kill)* liquidieren; beseitigen. **2.** *v.i.* *(Commerc.)* liquidieren
liquidation [lɪkwɪˈdeɪʃn] *n.* **a)** *(Commerc.)* Liquidation, *die; (of debt)* Tilgung, *die;* **go into ~:** in Liquidation gehen; **b)** *(eliminating, killing)* Liquidierung, *die;* Beseitigung, *die*
liquidator [ˈlɪkwɪdeɪtə(r)] *n. (Commerc.)* Liquidator, *der*
liquid: ~ ˈ**crystal** *n.* Flüssigkristall, *der;* ~ **crystal disˈplay** *n.* Flüssigkristallanzeige, *die*
liquidity [lɪˈkwɪdɪtɪ] *n., no pl.* **a)** flüssiger Zustand; **b)** *(Commerc.)* Liquidität, *die*
liquidize [ˈlɪkwɪdaɪz] *v.t.* auflösen; *(Cookery)* [im Mixer] pürieren
liquidizer [ˈlɪkwɪdaɪzə(r)] *n.* Mixer, *der*
liquid ˈ**measure** *n.* Flüssigkeitsmaß, *das*
liquor [ˈlɪkə(r)] *n.* **a)** *(drink)* Alkohol, *der;* Spirituosen; **be able to carry** *or* **hold one's ~:** etwas vertragen können; **hard** *or* **strong ~:** hochprozentiger Alkohol; scharfe Sachen *(ugs.);* **be the worse for ~:** betrunken sein; **b)** *(Industry)* Beize, *die*
~ ˈ**up** *(sl.) v.t.* besoffen machen *(derb);* **get/be ~ed up** sich *(Dat.)* einen ansaufen/besoffen sein *(derb)*
liquorice [ˈlɪkərɪs] *n.* **a)** *(root)* Süßholz, *das; (preparation)* Lakritze, *die;* **b)** *(plant)* Süßholzstrauch, *der*
ˈ**liquor store** *n. (Amer.)* Spirituosenladen, *der*
lira [ˈlɪərə] *n., pl.* **lire** [ˈlɪərə, ˈlɪərɪ] *or* ~s Lira, *die*
Lisbon [ˈlɪzbən] *pr. n.* Lissabon *(das)*
lisle [laɪl] *n.* ~ **[thread]** Florgarn, *das (Textilw.)*
lisp [lɪsp] **1.** *v.i. & t.* lispeln. **2.** *n.* Lispeln, *das;* **speak with a ~:** lispeln; **have a bad ~:** stark lispeln
lissom[e] [ˈlɪsəm] *adj.* geschmeidig
¹**list** [lɪst] **1.** *n.* **a)** Liste, *die;* **active ~** *(Mil.)* Liste der Reserve; **publisher's ~:** Verlagsprogramm, *das;* **shopping ~:** Einkaufszettel, *der;* **b)** *in pl.* **enter the ~s [against sb./sth.]** *(fig.)* den Kampf [gegen jmdn./etw.] antreten. **2.** *v.t.* aufführen; auflisten; *(verbally)* aufzählen; ~**ed securities/stock** an der Börse zugelassene Wertpapiere/Aktien
²**list 1.** *n.* **a)** *(Naut.: tilt)* Schlagseite, *die;* **have/develop a pronounced ~:** deutlich Schlagseite haben/bekommen; **b)** *(of building, fence, etc.)* Neigung, *die;* **develop a ~:** sich neigen. **2.** *v.i.* **a)** *(Naut.)* ~ **[to port/starboard]** Schlagseite [nach Backbord/Steuerbord] haben; **b)** ‹*Gebäude, Zaun usw.:*› sich neigen
listed ˈ**building** *n. (Brit.)* Gebäude unter Denkmalsschutz
listen [ˈlɪsn] *v.i.* zuhören; ~ **to music/the radio** Musik/Radio hören; **just ~ to the noise they are making!** hör dir bloß mal an, was sie für einen Lärm machen!; ~, **nitwit** hör zu, du Trottel; **they ~ed to his words** sie hörten ihm zu; **you never ~ to what I say** du hörst mir nie zu; **we stopped and ~ed** wir hielten inne und horchten; ~ **[out] for sth./sb.** auf etw. *(Akk.)* horchen/horchen, ob jmd. kommt; ~ **to sth./sb.** *(pay heed)* auf etw./jmdn. hören; **he wouldn't ~** *(heed)* er wollte nicht hören; ~ **to sb.'s grievances** sich *(Dat.)* jmds. Beschwerden anhören
~ ˈ**in** *v.i.* **a)** *(Radio)* hören **(on, to** *Akk.***); b)** *(tap line)* mithören; **c)** *(eavesdrop)* mithören **(on, to** *Akk.***)**
listener [ˈlɪsnə(r)] *n.* **a)** Zuhörer, *der*/Zuhörerin, *die;* **be a good ~:** ein guter Zuhörer sein; **b)** *(Radio)* Hörer, *der*/Hörerin, *die*
listening-post [ˈlɪsnɪŋpəʊst] *n. (Mil.; also fig.)* Horchposten, *der*
listing [ˈlɪstɪŋ] *n.* Aufführung, *die;* Auflistung, *die; (verbal)* Aufzählung, *die*
listless [ˈlɪstlɪs] *adj.,* **listlessly** [ˈlɪstlɪslɪ] *adv.* lustlos
listlessness [ˈlɪstlɪsnɪs] *n., no pl.* Lustlosigkeit, *die*
ˈ**list price** *n.* Katalogpreis, *der*
lit [lɪt] *see* ¹**light 4;** ³**light**
litany [ˈlɪtənɪ] *n. (lit. or fig.)* Litanei, *die;* **the L~:** *die Litanei im Book of Common Prayer*
litchi [ˈlaɪtʃɪ, ˈlɪtʃɪ] *n.* Litschi, *die*
liter *(Amer.) see* **litre**
literacy [ˈlɪtərəsɪ] *n., no pl.* Lese- und Schreibfertigkeit, *die;* **adult ~ classes** Kurse für Analphabeten; ~ **is low** das Analphabetentum ist groß
literal [ˈlɪtərl] **1.** *adj.* **a)** wörtlich; **take sth. in a ~ sense** etw. wörtlich nehmen; **b)** *(not exaggerated)* buchstäblich; **the ~ truth** die reine Wahrheit; **c)** *(coll.: with some exaggeration)* wahr; **d)** *(prosaic)* nüchtern; prosaisch; **e)** *(in text)* ~ **error** Tippfehler, *der; (misprint)* Druckfehler, *der.* **2.** *n.* **a)** *(error)* Tippfehler, *der; (misprint)* Druckfehler, *der;* **b)** *(Computing)* Literal, *das*
literally [ˈlɪtərəlɪ] *adv.* **a)** wörtlich; **take sth./sb. ~:** etw./was jmd. sagt, wörtlich nehmen; **b)** *(actually)* buchstäblich; **c)** *(coll.: with some exaggeration)* geradezu
literal: ~-ˈ**minded** *adj.* nüchtern [denkend *nicht präd.*]; ~**-mindedness** [lɪtərlˈmaɪndɪdnɪs] *n., no pl.* Nüchternheit [des Denkens]
literary [ˈlɪtərərɪ] *adj.* literarisch; *(not colloquial)* gewählt; **be of a ~ turn of mind** sich für Literatur interessieren
literary: ~ ˈ**agent** *n.* Literaturagent, *der*/-agentin, *die;* ~ ˈ**critic** *n.* Literaturkritiker, *der*/-kritikerin, *die;* ~ **exˈecutor** *see* **executor;** ~ **gent** *n. (coll.)* Literat, *der (oft abwertend);* ~ **hiˈstorian** *n.* Literaturhistoriker, *der*/-historikerin, *die;* ~ ˈ**history** *n.* Literaturgeschichte, *die;* ~ ˈ**luncheon** *n.* literarischer Lunch *(mit Schriftstellern und Verlegern);* ~ **man** *n.* Schriftsteller, *der; (versed in literature)* Literaturkenner, *der*
literate [ˈlɪtərət] **1.** *adj. (able to read and write)* des Lesens und Schreibens kundig; *(educated)* gebildet; **not be ~:** nicht lesen und schreiben können. **2.** *n.* Alphabet, *der*
literature [ˈlɪtərətʃə(r), ˈlɪtrətʃə(r)] *n.* **a)** Literatur, *die;* **b)** *(writings on a subject)* [Fach]literatur, *die* **(on** zu**); c)** *(coll.: printed matter)* Literatur, *die;* Informationsmaterial, *das;* **advertising ~:** Werbeschriften *od.* -material
lithe [laɪð] *adj.* geschmeidig
lithium [ˈlɪθɪəm] *n. (Chem.)* Lithium, *das*
litho [ˈlaɪθəʊ] *(coll.)* **1.** *n., pl.* ~s Litho, *das.* **2.** *adj.* Litho-; ~ **print/printing** Litho, *das.* **3.** *v.t.* lithographieren
lithograph [ˈlɪθəgrɑ:f] **1.** *n.* Lithographie, *die.* **2.** *v.t.* lithographieren
lithographer [lɪˈθɒgrəfə(r)] *n.* Lithograph, *der*/Lithographin, *die*
lithographic [lɪθəˈgræfɪk] *adj.* lithographisch
lithography [lɪˈθɒgrəfɪ] *n.* Lithographie, *die*
Lithuania [lɪθjʊˈeɪnɪə] *pr. n.* Litauen *(das)*
Lithuanian [lɪθjʊˈeɪnɪən] **1.** *adj.* litauisch; **sb. is ~:** jmd. ist Litauer/Litauerin; *see also* **English 1. 2.** *n.* **a)** *(person)* Litauer, *der*/Litauerin, *die;* **b)** *(language)* Litauisch, *das; see also* **English 2 a**
litigant [ˈlɪtɪgənt] **1.** *n.* Prozeßpartei, *die.* **2.** *adj.* ~ **party** Prozeßpartei, *die*
litigate [ˈlɪtɪgeɪt] **1.** *v.i.* prozessieren. **2.** *v.t.* vor Gericht verhandeln
litigation [lɪtɪˈgeɪʃn] *n.* Rechtsstreit, *der;* **in ~:** rechtshängig
litigious [lɪˈtɪdʒəs] *adj.* prozeßsüchtig; **a ~ person** ein Prozeßhansel *(ugs.)*
litmus [ˈlɪtməs] *n.* Lackmus, *das od. der*
ˈ**litmus-paper** *n.* Lackmuspapier, *das*
litotes [ˈlaɪtəti:z] *n. (Rhet.)* Litotes, *die*
litre [ˈli:tə(r)] *n. (Brit.)* Liter, *der od. das*
Litt. D. [lɪt ˈdi:] *see* **D. Litt.**
litter [ˈlɪtə(r)] **1.** *n.* **a)** *(rubbish)* Abfall, *der;* Abfälle; **'do not leave ~'** „bitte keine Abfälle zurücklassen"; **her desk was strewn with a ~ of books** ihr Schreibtisch war mit Büchern übersät; **b)** *(vehicle)* Sänfte, *die;* **c)** *(stretcher)* Trage, *die;* Tragbahre, *die;* **d)** *(bedding for animals)* Streu, *die;* Einstreu, *die (Landw.);* **e)** *(young)* Wurf, *der.* **2.** *v.t.* verstreuen; **papers were ~ed about the room** im Zimmer lagen überall Zeitungen herum;

~ **the room with one's books** seine Bücher im Zimmer verstreuen. 3. *v. i.* **'do not ~'** „bitte keine Abfälle zurücklassen"

litter: ~-basket *n.* Abfallkorb, *der;* **~-bin** *n.* Abfalleimer, *der;* **~bug, ~-lout** *ns.* Schmutzfink, *der (ugs.)*

little ['lɪtl] 1. *adj.*, **~r** ['lɪtlə(r)], **~st** ['lɪtlɪst] (*Note: it is more common to use the compar. and superl. forms* **smaller, smallest**) **a)** *(small)* klein; ~ **town/book/dog** kleine Stadt/kleines Buch/kleiner Hund; *(showing affection or amusement)* Städtchen, *das*/Büchlein, *das*/Hündchen, *das;* ~ **toe** kleine Zehe; **the ~ woman** *(coll.: my wife)* mein kleines Frauchen *(ugs.);* **you poor ~ thing!** du armes kleines Ding!; **don't worry your ~ head** zerbrich dir nicht dein Köpfchen!; **I know your ~ ways** ich kenne deine Tricks; **do one's ~ best** sein Bestes tun; **L~ Venice** Klein-Venedig, *das;* **the ~ people** *(fairies)* die Elfen; *see also* [1]**bear c;** [2]**slam a; b)** *(young)* klein; **the ~ Joneses** die Jones-Kinder; **~ man/woman** *(child)* Kleiner/Kleine; **the ~ ones** die Kleinen; **my ~ sister** meine kleine Schwester; **c)** *(short)* klein ⟨*Zwerg*⟩; **a ~ way** ein kleines *od.* kurzes Stück; **after a ~ while** nach kurzer Zeit; nach einer kleinen Weile *(veralt.);* **d)** *(not much)* wenig; **you have ~ time left** dir bleibt nicht mehr viel Zeit; **there is very ~ tea left** es ist kaum noch Tee *od.* nur noch ganz wenig Tee da; **make a nice ~ profit** *(coll. iron.)* einen hübschen Gewinn machen *(ugs.);* **a ~ ...** *(a small quantity of)* etwas ...; ein wenig *od.* bißchen ...; **speak a ~ German** etwas Deutsch sprechen; **speak only a ~ German** nur wenig Deutsch sprechen; **a ~ goes a long way** ein bißchen reicht lange; *(fig.)* ein bißchen hat eine große Wirkung; **no ~ ...:** nicht wenig ...; **e)** *(trivial)* klein; **get annoyed about ~ things** sich über Kleinigkeiten aufregen; **of course, this 'would occur to your mean ~ mind** einem miesen Kleingeist wie dir muß natürlich so etwas einfallen; **~ things please ~ minds** kleine Geister erfreuen sich an kleinen Dingen. *See also* **Englander; old 1 e; Russian 2 b.** 2. *n.* wenig; **but ~:** nur wenig; **~ or nothing** kaum etwas; so gut wie nichts; **[do] not a ~:** einiges [tun]; **not a ~ angry** *etc.* ziemlich verärgert *usw.;* **there was ~ we could do** wir konnten nur wenig tun; **a ~** *(a small quantity)* etwas; ein wenig *od.* bißchen; *(somewhat)* ein wenig; **too ~ too late** zu wenig [und] zu spät; **think ~ of sb.** gering von jmdm. denken; **after a ~:** nach einer Weile; **a ~ after eight** kurz nach acht; **for a ~:** ein Weilchen; *(a short way)* ein Stückchen; **we see very ~ of one another** wir sehen sehr wenig voneinander; **~ by ~:** nach und nach; **the ~ I know** das wenige, was ich weiß; *see also* **help 1 a; make 1 m; what 6 a.** 3. *adv.*, **less** [les], **least** [li:st] **a)** *(not at all)* **she ~ thought that ...:** sie dachte nicht im geringsten daran, daß ...; **he ~ suspected/knew what ...:** er hatte nicht die geringste Ahnung/wußte überhaupt nicht, was ...; **b)** *(to only a small extent)* **~ as he liked it** sowenig es ihm auch gefiel; **he writes ~ now** er schreibt nur noch wenig; **~ more/less than ...:** kaum mehr/weniger als ...; **that is ~ less than ...:** das grenzt schon an (+ *Akk.*) ...; **the holiday was ~ less than a disaster** der Urlaub war ein ziemlicher Reinfall *(ugs.);* **his behaviour is ~ less than disgraceful** sein Benehmen ist schon fast skandalös zu nennen

little: ~ end *n. (Brit. Motor Veh.)* Pleuelauge, *das (Technik);* **~ 'finger** *n.* kleiner Finger; **twist sb. round one's ~ finger** jmdn. um den [kleinen] Finger wickeln *(ugs.);* **~-known** *adj.* wenig bekannt

littleness ['lɪtlnɪs] *n., no pl.* Kleinheit, *die*

'little theatre *n.* Kleinbühne, *die*

littoral ['lɪtərl] 1. *adj.* litoral *(Geogr.).* 2. *n.* Litoral, *das (Geogr.);* Küstengebiet, *das*

liturgical [lɪ'tɜ:dʒɪkl] *adj.* liturgisch

liturgy ['lɪtədʒɪ] *n.* **a)** Liturgie, *die;* **b)** *(Book of Common Prayer)* **the ~:** das Book of Common Prayer

[1]**live** [laɪv] 1. *adj.* **a)** *attrib. (alive)* lebend; **b)** *(Radio, Telev.)* **~ performance** Live-Aufführung, *die;* **~ broadcast** Live-Sendung, *die;* Direkt- *od.* Originalübertragung, *die;* **we go ~ tomorrow** *(fig.)* morgen machen wir Ernst; **c)** *(topical)* aktuell ⟨*Thema, Frage*⟩; **d)** *(Electr.)* stromführend; **e)** *(unexploded)* scharf ⟨*Munition usw.*⟩; **f)** *(glowing)* glühend ⟨*Kohle*⟩; **g)** *(joc.: actual)* **real ~:** richtig; **h)** *(Mech. Engin.)* Trieb⟨*rad, -feder*⟩; Antriebs⟨*achse, -rad, -welle*⟩. 2. *adv. (Radio, Telev.)* live ⟨*übertragen usw.*⟩

[2]**live** [lɪv] 1. *v. i.* **a)** leben; **~ and let ~:** leben und leben lassen; **~ by sth.** von etw. leben; **will he ~?** wird er am Leben bleiben?; **you'll ~** *(iron.)* du wirst's [schon] überleben *(iron.);* **as long as I ~ I shall never understand why ...:** mein Leben lang werde ich nicht begreifen, warum ...; **~ to see** [mit]erleben; **she will ~ to regret her stupidity** sie wird ihre Dummheit noch bereuen; **you ~ and learn** man lernt nie aus; **~ for sth./sb.** für etw./jmdn. leben; **~ through sth.** etw. durchmachen *(ugs.); (survive)* etw. überleben; **~ to a ripe old age/to be a hundred** ein hohes Alter erreichen/hundert Jahre alt werden; **long ~ the queen!** lang lebe die Königin!; **they ~d violently** ihr Leben stand im Zeichen der Gewalt; **~ beyond one's means** über seine Verhältnisse leben; **~ well** *(eat well)* es sich *(Dat.)* gutgehen lassen; *see also* **hand 1 a; b)** *(make permanent home)* wohnen; leben; **the room seems ~d in** das Zimmer scheint bewohnt zu sein; **~ together** zusammenleben; **~ with sb.** mit jmdm. zusammenleben; **~ with sth.** *(lit. or fig.)* mit etw. leben. 2. *v. t.* **a)** leben; **~ one's own life** sein eigenes Leben leben; **~ an honest life** ein ehrbares Leben führen; **~ it up** das Leben in vollen Zügen genießen; *(have a good time)* einen draufmachen *(ugs.);* **b)** *(express)* **~ one's convictions** nach seiner Überzeugung leben; **what others were preaching, he ~d** was andere nur predigten, lebte er vor

~ 'down *v. t.* Gras wachsen lassen über (+ *Akk.*); **he will never be able to ~ it down** das wird ihm ewig anhängen

~ 'in *v. i. (Brit.)* ⟨*Personal, Koch usw.:*⟩ im Haus wohnen; ⟨*Student, Krankenschwester:*⟩ im Wohnheim wohnen

~ on 1. ['--] *v. t.* leben von; *(fig.)* zehren von ⟨*Ruf*⟩; leben von ⟨*Hoffnung*⟩; **~ on air** *(joc.)* von der Luft *od. (ugs. scherzh.)* von Luft und Liebe leben; *see also* **fat 2.** 2. [-'-] *v. i.* weiterleben

~ out 1. [-'-] *v. i. (Brit.)* außerhalb wohnen. 2. ['--] *v. t.* **a)** *(survive)* überleben; überstehen ⟨*Winter, Woche*⟩; **b)** *(complete, spend)* verbringen; **they had ~d out their lives as fishermen** sie waren ihr Leben lang Fischer gewesen

~ 'up to *v. t.* gerecht werden (+ *Dat.*); **~ up to one's principles/faith** nach seinen Prinzipien/seinem Glauben leben; **he's a bright lad – I hope he ~s up to his promise** er ist ein aufgeweckter Bursche – ich hoffe, er hält, was er verspricht; **~ up to one's reputation** seinem Ruf Ehre machen; **~ up to one's income** seinen Verhältnissen entsprechend leben

liveable ['lɪvəbl] *adj.* lebenswert, erträglich ⟨*Leben*⟩

live birth [laɪv 'bɜ:θ] *n.* Lebendgeburt, *die*

live-in ['lɪvɪn] *attrib. adj.* **~ cook** Koch *(der im Haus wohnt);* **~ lover** Geliebter, der/Geliebte, die bei ihr/ihm *usw.* wohnt

livelihood ['laɪvlɪhʊd] *n.* Lebensunterhalt, *der;* **gain a ~ from sth.** sich *(Dat.)* seinen Lebensunterhalt mit etw. verdienen; **her ~ is her painting** sie lebt von der Malerei

liveliness ['laɪvlɪnɪs] *n., no pl.* Lebhaftigkeit, *die*

livelong ['lɪvlɒŋ] *adj. (poet./rhet.)* **all the ~ day/night** den lieben langen Tag/die ganze Nacht [hindurch]

lively ['laɪvlɪ] *adj.* **a)** lebhaft; lebendig ⟨*Gegenwart*⟩; rege ⟨*Handel*⟩; **things start to get ~ at 9 a.m.** um 9 Uhr wird es lebhaft; **have a ~ sense of humour** immer zu Späßen aufgelegt sein; **look ~** *(coll.)* sich ranhalten *(ugs.);* **b)** *(vivid)* lebendig, anschaulich ⟨*Bericht, Schilderung*⟩; **c)** *(joc.: exciting, dangerous, difficult)* **things were getting ~:** die Sache wurde gefährlich; **give sb. a ~ time, make things ~ for sb.** jmdm. zu schaffen machen; **d)** *(fresh)* lebhaft ⟨*Farbe*⟩

liven *see* **~ up 1**

liven up [laɪvn 'ʌp] 1. *v. t.* Leben bringen in (+ *Akk.*). 2. *v. i.* ⟨*Person:*⟩ aufleben; **things will ~ when ...:** es wird Leben in die Bude kommen *(ugs.),* wenn ...

[1]**liver** ['lɪvə(r)] *n. (Anat., Gastr.)* Leber, *die*

[2]**liver** *n.* **be a fast/clean ~:** ein flottes/solides Leben führen

'liver-coloured *adj.* leberbraun

liveried ['lɪvərɪd] *adj.* livriert

liverish ['lɪvərɪʃ] *adj.* **a)** *(unwell)* elend; unwohl; **b)** *(grumpy)* mürrisch

Liverpudlian [lɪvə'pʌdlɪən] 1. *adj.* Liverpooler. 2. *n.* Liverpooler, *der*/Liverpoolerin, *die*

liver: ~ salts *n. pl. (Brit.)* ≈ Magenmittel, *das;* **~ sausage** *n.* Leberwurst, *die;* **~-wort** *n.* Lebermoos, *das;* **~wurst** ['lɪvəwɜ:st] *(Amer.) see* **~ sausage**

livery ['lɪvərɪ] *n.* Livree, *die;* **in/out of ~:** livriert/nicht livriert

livery: ~ company *n. (Brit.) Londoner Zunft;* **~ stable** *n.* Mietstall, *der*

live [laɪv]: **~stock** *n. pl.* Vieh, *das;* **large number of ~stock** großer Viehbestand; **~ weight** *n.* Lebendgewicht, *das;* **~ 'wire** *n. (Electr.)* stromführender Draht; *(fig.)* Energiebündel, *das (ugs.)*

livid ['lɪvɪd] *adj.* **a)** *(bluish)* bleigrau; **b)** *(Brit. coll.: furious)* fuchtig *(ugs.)*

living ['lɪvɪŋ] 1. *n.* **a)** Leben, *das; see also* **cost of living; standard 1 b; b)** *(livelihood)* Lebensunterhalt, *der;* **make a ~:** seinen Lebensunterhalt verdienen; **earn one's [own] ~:** sich *(Dat.)* seinen Lebensunterhalt [selbst] verdienen; **make one's ~ out of farming** von der Landwirtschaft leben; **make a good ~:** viel verdienen; **it's a ~** *(joc.)* man kann davon leben; **c)** *(Brit. Eccl.)* Pfründe, *die;* **d)** *(way of life)* Lebensstil, *der;* **the art of ~:** die Kunst zu leben; **good ~:** üppiges Leben; *(pious)* guter Lebenswandel; **high ~:** hoher Lebensstandard; **e)** *in pl.* **the ~:** die Lebenden; **be still/back in the land of the ~:** noch/wieder unter den Lebenden weilen. 2. *adj.* **a)** lebend; **~ things** Lebewesen; **not a ~ soul** keine Menschenseele; **no man ~:** niemand auf der Welt; **it was a ~ death for him** er fühlte sich dort wie lebendig begraben; **within ~ memory** seit Menschengedenken; **be the ~ image of sb.** jmds. Ebenbild sein; **a ~ monument** ein lebendiges Zeugnis **(to** *Gen.***)**; *see also* **daylight c; b)** *(uncut, unquarried)* gewachsen ⟨*Stein, Fels*⟩; **c)** *(still in vernacular use)* lebend ⟨*Sprache*⟩

living: ~-room *n.* Wohnzimmer, *das;* **~-space** *n.* **a)** Lebensraum, *der;* **b)** *(in dwelling)* Wohnraum, *der;* **~ 'wage** *n.* Lohn, von dem man leben kann

Livy ['lɪvɪ] *pr. n.* Livius *(der)*

lizard ['lɪzəd] *n.* Eidechse, *die*

'll [l] *(coll.)* = **shall; will**

ll. *abbr.* **lines** Zz.

llama ['lɑ:mə] *n. (Zool., Textiles)* Lama, *das*

LL.B/LL.D/LL.M *abbrs.* **Bachelor/Doctor/Master of Laws;** *see also* **B. Sc.**

lo [ləʊ] *int.* **a)** **~ and behold** *(joc.)* sieh[e] da; **b)** *(arch.)* siehe/seh[e]t

loach [ləʊtʃ] *n. (Zool.)* Schmerle, *die*
load [ləʊd] **1.** *n.* **a)** *(burden, weight)* Last, *die; (amount carried)* Ladung, *die;* **a ~ of hay** eine Ladung Heu; **barrow-~ of apples** Karre voll Äpfel; **a ~ of [old] rubbish** *or* **tripe** *(fig. coll.)* ein einziger Mist *(ugs.);* **talk a ~ of rubbish** eine Menge Blödsinn reden *(ugs.);* **what a ~ of rubbish!** was für ein Quatsch *(ugs.) od. (ugs. abwertend)* Schmarren!; **get a ~ of this!** *(sl.) (listen)* hör einmal gut *od.* genau zu! *(ugs.); (look)* guck mal genau hin! *(ugs.);* **b)** *(weight)* Last, *die; (Electr.)* Belastung, *die;* **c)** *(fig.)* Last, *die;* Bürde, *die (geh.);* **a heavy ~ of work** eine große Arbeitsbelastung; **take a ~ off sb.'s mind** jmdm. eine Last von der Seele nehmen; **that's a ~ off my mind** damit fällt mir ein Stein vom Herzen; **teaching ~** *(Sch.)* Deputat, *das;* **d)** *usu. in pl. (coll.: plenty)* **~s of** jede Menge *od.* massenhaft *(ugs.)* ⟨*Nahrungsmittel usw.*⟩; **have ~s of sense** sehr vernünftig sein. **2.** *v. t.* **a)** *(put ~ on)* beladen; **~ sb. with work** *(fig.)* jmdm. Arbeit auftragen *od. (ugs. abwertend)* aufhalsen *od. (geh.)* aufbürden; **b)** *(put as ~)* laden; **c)** *(weight with lead)* mit Blei beschweren; **~ed dice** präparierte Würfel; **the dice were ~ed against him** *(fig.)* er hatte schlechte Karten; **d)** *(charge)* laden ⟨*Gewehr*⟩; **~ a camera** einen Film [in einen Fotoapparat] einlegen; **e)** *(insert)* einlegen ⟨*Film, Tonband usw.*⟩ **(into** in + *Akk.*); **f)** *(strain)* schwer belasten; **a table ~ed with food** ein mit Speisen beladener Tisch; **g)** *(overwhelm) (with praise, presents, etc.)* überhäufen; *(with abuse)* überschütten. **3.** *v. i.* laden **(with** *Akk.*); Ladung übernehmen
~ 'up *v. i.* laden **(with** *Akk.*)
'load-bearing *adj.* tragend ⟨*Wand, Balken, Konstruktion*⟩
loaded ['ləʊdɪd] *adj.* **a)** *(sl.: rich)* **be ~:** [schwer] Kohle haben *(salopp);* **b)** *(sl.: drunk)* voll *(ugs.);* **c)** *(Amer. sl.: drugged)* high *(Jargon verhüll.);* **be ~ [up] on heroin** sich mit Heroin vollgepumpt haben *(ugs.);* **d) ~ for bear** *(Amer. coll.)* für alles gerüstet; **e) emotionally ~ words** emotional befrachtete Wörter; **a ~ question** eine suggestive Frage. *See also* **load 2**
loader ['ləʊdə(r)] *n.* **a)** *(person who loads gun)* [Gewehr]lader, *der;* **b)** *(machine)* Lader, *der;* **c)** *in comb. (gun etc.)* ⟨*Vorder-, Hinter*⟩lader, *der*
'loading bay *n.* Ladeplatz, *der*
load: ~ line *n.* Ladelinie, *die (Seew.);* **~-shedding** *n. (Electr.)* Stromabschaltung, *die;* **~star** *see* **lodestar; ~stone** *n.* **a)** *(oxide)* Magnetit, *der;* **b)** *(piece)* Magnet[eisen]stein, *der;* **c)** *(fig.)* Magnet, *der*
¹loaf [ləʊf] *n., pl.* **loaves** [ləʊvz] **a)** Brot, *das;* [Brot]laib, *der;* **a ~ of bread** ein Laib Brot; **a brown/white ~:** ein dunkles Brot/Weißbrot; **half a ~ is better than no bread** *or* **none** *(prov.)* wenig ist besser als gar nichts; **b)** *(sl.: head)* **use one's ~:** seinen Grips anstrengen *(ugs.);* **c) ~ sugar** Hutzucker, *der*
²loaf 1. *v. i.* **a) ~ round town/the house** in der Stadt/zu Hause herumlungern *(ugs.);* **b)** *(saunter)* trödeln *(ugs.).* **2.** *v. t.* **~ away** vertrödeln ⟨*Zeit*⟩
loafer ['ləʊfə(r)] *n.* **a)** *(idler)* Faulenzer, *der;* **b) L~, (P)** *bequemer [mokassinartiger] Halbschuh*
loam [ləʊm] *n.* **a)** *(paste)* Lehm, *der;* **b)** *(soil)* Lehmboden, *der*
loamy ['ləʊmɪ] *adj.* lehmig
loan [ləʊn] **1.** *n.* **a)** *(thing lent)* Leihgabe, *die;* **b)** *(lending)* **let sb. have/give sb. the ~ of sth.** jmdm. etw. leihen; **may I have the ~ of your mower?** könnte ich mir mal Ihren Rasenmäher ausleihen?; **be [out] on ~** ⟨*Buch, Schallplatte:*⟩ ausgeliehen sein; **have sth. on ~ [from sb.]** etw. [von jmdm.] geliehen haben; **c)** *(money lent)* Darlehen, *das;* Kredit, *der; (public ~)* Anleihe, *die.* **2.** *v. t.* **~ sth. to sb.** jmdm. etw. leihen; etw. an jmdn. verleihen
loan: ~ collection *n.* Leihgaben; **~ shark** *n. (coll.)* Kredithai, *der (ugs. abwertend);* **~-translation** *n.* Lehnübersetzung, *die;* **~-word** *n.* Lehnwort, *das*
loath [ləʊθ] *pred. adj.* **be ~ to do sth.** etw. ungern tun; **be nothing ~:** nicht abgeneigt sein
loathe [ləʊð] *v. t.* verabscheuen; nicht ausstehen können; **he ~s eggs** er mag Eier überhaupt nicht; **I ~ ironing** ich kann Bügeln nicht ausstehen; **I ~d having to tell her** ich fand es gräßlich, ihr das sagen zu müssen
loathing ['ləʊðɪŋ] *n.* Abscheu, *der* **(of, for** vor + *Dat.*); **have a ~ of sth.** Abscheu vor etw. *(Dat.)* haben; etw. verabscheuen
loathsome ['ləʊðsəm] *adj.* abscheulich; widerlich; verhaßt ⟨*Tätigkeit, Pflicht*⟩
loaves *pl. of* **¹loaf**
lob [lɒb] **1.** *v. t.,* **-bb-** in hohem Bogen werfen; *(Tennis)* lobben. **2.** *n. (Tennis)* Lob, *der*
lobby ['lɒbɪ] **1.** *n.* **a)** *(pressure group)* Lobby, *die;* Interessenvertretung, *die;* **b)** *(of hotel)* Eingangshalle, *die; (of theatre)* Foyer, *das; (anteroom) (narrow)* Flur, *der; (larger)* Vorraum, *der;* **c)** *(esp. Brit. Parl.: hall)* Lobby, *die;* Wandelhalle, *die.* **2.** *v. t. (als Lobby)* zu beeinflussen suchen ⟨*Abgeordnete*⟩. **3.** *v. i. (als Lobby)* seinen Einfluß geltend machen; **~ for/against sth.** *(als Lobby)* sich für etw. einsetzen/gegen etw. wenden
lobbyist ['lɒbɪɪst] *n.* Lobbyist, *der*/Lobbyistin, *die*
lobe [ləʊb] *n.* *(ear~)* Ohrläppchen, *das; (of liver, lung, brain)* Lappen, *der;* Lobus, *der (fachspr.); (of leaf)* Ausbuchtung, *die*
lobed [ləʊbd] *adj.* gelappt
lobelia [lə'bi:lɪə] *n. (Bot.)* Lobelie, *die*
lobotomy [ləʊ'bɒtəmɪ] *see* **leucotomy**
lobster ['lɒbstə(r)] *n.* Hummer, *der*
'lobster-pot *n.* Hummerkorb, *der*
local ['ləʊkl] **1.** *adj.* **a)** lokal *(bes. Zeitungsw.);* Lokal⟨*teil, -nachrichten, -sender*⟩; Kommunal⟨*politiker, -wahl, -abgaben*⟩; *(of this area)* hiesig; *(of that area)* dortig; ortsansässig ⟨*Firma, Familie*⟩; ⟨*Wein, Produkt, Spezialität*⟩ [aus] der Gegend; *(Bot.)* örtlich begrenzt [vorkommend]; lokal [verbreitet]; **~ knowledge** Ortskenntnis, *die;* **go into your ~ branch** gehen Sie zu Ihrer Filiale; **our ~ hairdresser** der Friseur bei uns in der Nähe/ *(in village)* bei uns im Dorf; **she's a ~ girl** sie ist von hier/dort; **~ resident** Anwohner, *der*/Anwohnerin, *die;* **~ bus** hiesiger/dortiger Bus; *(serving immediate area)* Nahverkehrsbus, *der;* **your ~ candidate** der Kandidat Ihres Wahlkreises; **~ opinion** die Meinung der unmittelbar betroffenen Bevölkerung; **b)** *(Med.)* lokal ⟨*Schmerzen, Entzündung*⟩; örtlich ⟨*Betäubung*⟩; **c)** *(Post)* innerstädtisch ⟨*Briefzustellung, Post*⟩. **2.** *n.* **a)** *(inhabitant)* Einheimische, *der/die;* **b)** *(Brit. coll.: pub)* [Stamm]kneipe, *die*
local: ~ anaes'thetic *n.* Lokalanästhetikum, *das (Med.);* **[be treated] under a ~ anaesthetic** unter örtlicher Betäubung *od. (Med.)* Lokalanästhesie [behandelt werden]; **~ au'thority** *n. (Brit.)* Kommunalverwaltung, *die; attrib.* kommunal; **~ call** *n. (Teleph.)* Ortsgespräch, *das;* Nahbereichsgespräch, *das (Postw.);* **~ 'colour** *see* **colour 1 g; ~ 'Derby** *see* **Derby a**
locale [ləʊ'kɑ:l] *n.* Ort, *der; (of crime etc.)* Schauplatz, *der*
local 'government *n.* Kommunalverwaltung, *die;* **~ elections/officials** Kommunalwahlen/-beamte
localise *see* **localize**
locality [lə'kælɪtɪ] *n.* **a)** *(position) (of thing)* Position [im Raum]; *(of person)* Aufenthaltsort, *der; (of mineral)* Vorkommen, *das;* **b)** *(district)* Ort, *der;* Gegend, *die*
localize ['ləʊkəlaɪz] *v. t.* **a)** *(restrict)* eingrenzen **(to** auf + *Akk.*); lokalisieren *(bes. Politik, Med.);* **b)** *(decentralize)* lokalisieren
locally ['ləʊkəlɪ] *adv.* im/am Ort; in der Gegend
'local time *n.* Ortszeit, *die;* **[it's] 3 p.m. ~:** [es ist] 15 Uhr Ortszeit
locate [lə'keɪt] *v. t.* **a)** *(position)* plazieren; **be ~d** liegen; gelegen sein; **the factory is to be ~d on the edge of the town** die Fabrik soll am Stadtrand errichtet werden; **b)** *(determine position of)* ausfindig machen; lokalisieren *(fachspr.);* orten *(Flugw., Seew.)*
location [lə'keɪʃn] *n.* **a)** *(position)* Lage, *die; (place)* Ort, *der; (of ship, aircraft, police car)* Position, *die; (of person, building, etc.)* Standort, *der;* **discover the ~ of sth.** etw. ausfindig machen; **b)** *(positioning)* Positionierung, *die;* **c)** *(determination of position of)* Lokalisierung, *die;* **succeed in the ~ of the buried treasure** den vergrabenen Schatz ausfindig machen; **d)** *(Cinemat.)* Drehort, *der;* **be on ~:** bei Außenaufnahmen sein; **shoot on ~:** Außenaufnahmen drehen; **e)** *(S. Afr.)* [Bantu]siedlung, *die*
loc. cit. [lɒk 'sɪt] *abbr.* **in the passage already quoted** loc. cit.; a. a. O.
loch [lɒx, lɒk] *n. (Scot.)* See, *der; (in Scotland)* Loch, *der; (arm of sea)* Meeresarm, *der; (in Scotland)* Loch, *der*
Loch Ness [lɒx 'nes, lɒk 'nes] *pr. n.* Loch Ness *(der);* **~ monster** Ungeheuer von Loch Ness
¹lock [lɒk] *n.* **a)** *(tress of hair)* [Haar]büschel, *das;* [Haar]strähne, *die; (ringlet)* Locke, *die;* **b)** *in pl. (hair)* Haar, *das;* **c)** *(of wool, cotton, etc.)* Flocke, *die*
²lock 1. *n.* **a)** *(of door etc.)* Schloß, *das;* **under ~ and key** unter [strengem] Verschluß; **b)** *(on canal etc.)* Schleuse, *die;* **c)** *(on wheel)* Sperrvorrichtung, *die;* Sperre, *die;* **d)** *(Wrestling)* Fesselgriff, *der;* Klammergriff, *der;* **e)** *(of gun)* Schloß, *das;* **~, stock, and barrel** *(fig.)* mit allem Drum und Dran *(ugs.);* **condemn sth. ~, stock, and barrel** *(fig.)* etw. in Bausch und Bogen verurteilen; **f)** *(Motor Veh.)* Lenkeinschlag, *der;* **full [left/right] ~:** voller Lenk[rad]einschlag [nach links/rechts]; **g)** *(Rugby)* **~ [forward]** Gedrängespieler in der zweiten Reihe; **h)** *see* **airlock b. 2.** *v. t.* **a)** *(fasten)* zuschließen, abschließen; **~** *or* **shut the stable-door after the horse has bolted** *(fig.)* den Brunnen erst zudecken, wenn das Kind hineingefallen ist; **b)** *(shut)* **~ sb./sth. in sth.** jmdn./etw. in etw. *(Akk.)* [ein]schließen; **~ sb./sth. out of sth.** jmdn./etw. aus etw. aussperren; **c)** *(Mech. Engin.: engage)* befestigen **(in** in + *Dat.*); **d)** *in p.p. (joined)* **the wrestlers were ~ed in combat** die Ringer hielten sich im Fesselgriff; **the lovers were ~ed in an embrace** die Liebenden hielten sich fest umschlungen. *See also* **horn 1 a. 3.** *v. i.* ⟨*Tür, Kasten usw.:*⟩ sich ab-/zuschließen lassen
~ a'way *v. t.* einschließen; wegschließen; einsperren ⟨*Person, Tier*⟩; **he ought to be ~ed away** er gehört hinter Schloß und Riegel
~ 'in *v. t.* einschließen; *(deliberately)* einsperren ⟨*Person, Tier*⟩
~ 'on to *v. t.* **a)** ⟨*Rakete:*⟩ erfassen ⟨*Ziel*⟩; **b)** ⟨*Teleskop:*⟩ sich einstellen auf (+ *Akk.*) ⟨*Objekt*⟩
~ 'out *v. t.* **a)** aussperren; **~ oneself out** sich aussperren; **b)** *(Industry)* aussperren ⟨*Arbeiter*⟩; *see also* **lock-out**
~ 'up 1. *v. i.* abschließen. **2.** *v. t.* **a)** abschließen ⟨*Haus, Tür*⟩; **b)** *(imprison)* einsperren; **he ought to be ~ed up** er gehört hinter Schloß und Riegel; **c)** *(store inaccessibly)* binden ⟨*Kapital*⟩; *(fig.)* unterdrücken ⟨*Gefühle*⟩; **~ sth. up in one's heart** *(fig.)* etw. ganz für sich behalten. *See also* **lock-up**
locker ['lɒkə(r)] *n.* **a)** Schließfach, *das;* **b)** *(Naut.)* Schapp, *das od. der (Seemannsspr.)*

'locker-room *n.* Umkleideraum, *der*

locket ['lɒkɪt] *n.* Medaillon, *das*

lock: ~-gate *n.* Schleusentor, *das;* **~jaw** *n. (Med.)* Kieferklemme, *die; (disease)* Wundstarrkrampf, *der;* **~-keeper** *n.* Schleusenwärter, *der;* **~-nut** *n. (Mech.)* Kontermutter, *die;* **~-out** *n.* Aussperrung, *die;* **~smith** *n.* Schlosser, *der;* **~-stitch 1.** *n.* Doppelsteppstich, *der;* **2.** *v. t. & i.* steppen; **~-up 1.** *n.* **a)** *(closing-time)* Toresschluß, *der;* **b)** *(jail)* Gewahrsam, *das (veralt.);* **2.** *adj.* **a)** *(Brit.)* **~-up shop/garage** *Laden in einem Gebäude, in dem der Inhaber nicht wohnt/nicht unmittelbar bei der Wohnung gelegene Garage;* **b) ~-up time** Toresschluß, *der*

locomotion [ləʊkə'məʊʃn] *n.* Fortbewegung, *die;* Lokomotion, *die (fachspr.)*

locomotive ['ləʊkəməʊtɪv, ləʊkə'məʊtɪv] **1.** *n.* Lokomotive, *die.* **2.** *adj.* **a)** *(of locomotion)* lokomotorisch *(fachspr.);* **b)** *(not stationary)* fahrbar ⟨*Kran*⟩; **~ engine** Lokomotive, *die*

locum ['ləʊkəm] *n., (coll.),* **locum tenens** [ləʊkəm 'tenenz] *n., pl.* **locum tenentes** [ləʊkəm te'nenti:z] [Stell]vertreter, *der/-*vertreterin, *die*

locus ['ləʊkəs] *n., pl.* **loci** ['ləʊsaɪ] **a)** *(Math.)* geometrischer Ort; **b)** *(Biol.)* Genort, *der*

locust ['ləʊkəst] *n.* **a)** [Wander]heuschrecke, *die;* **b)** *(Amer.: cicada)* Zikade, *die;* **c)** *(Bot.)* **~ [bean]** Johannisbrot, *das;* **~ [tree]** *(carob tree)* Johannisbrotbaum, *der; (false acacia)* Robinie, *die;* Scheinakazie, *die*

locution [lə'kju:ʃn] *n.* Lokution, *die (geh.); (style)* Ausdrucksweise, *die; (idiom)* Ausdruck, *der;* Redewendung, *die*

lode [ləʊd] *n. (Min.)* Erzgang, *der*

loden ['ləʊdn] *n. (cloth)* Loden, *der*

lode: ~star *n.* Leitstern, *der; (esp.)* Polarstern, *der; (fig.)* Leitbild, *das;* **~stone** *see* **loadstone**

lodge [lɒdʒ] **1.** *n.* **a)** *(servant's cottage)* Pförtner-/Gärtnerhaus, *das; (Sport)* [Jagd-/Ski]hütte, *die; (hotel)* Hotel, *das;* **b)** *(porter's room)* [Pförtner]loge, *die; (at gate of school etc.)* Pedelloge, *die;* **c)** *(Freemasonry)* Loge, *die;* **grand ~:** Großloge, *die;* **d)** *(lair)* Bau, *der;* **e)** *(of trade union)* Ortsgruppe, *die.* **2.** *v. t.* **a)** *(deposit formally)* einlegen ⟨*Beschwerde, Protest, Berufung usw.*⟩; *(bring forward)* erheben ⟨*Einspruch, Protest*⟩; einreichen ⟨*Klage*⟩; **~ information against sb.** jmdn. anzeigen; **b)** *(house)* unterbringen; *(receive as guest)* beherbergen; bei sich unterbringen; *(establish as resident)* einquartieren; **c)** *(leave)* **~ sth. with sb./in a bank** *etc.* etw. bei jmdm./in einer Bank *usw.* hinterlegen *od.* deponieren; **d) ~ power** *etc.* **in the hands of** *or* **with sb.** jmdm. Macht *od.* Befugnis[se] *usw.* übertragen; **e)** *(put, fix)* stecken; [hinein]stoßen ⟨*Schwert, Messer usw.*⟩; **be ~d in sth.** in etw. *(Dat.)* stecken; **become ~d in sth.** ⟨*Kugel, Messer:*⟩ steckenbleiben in etw. *(Dat.);* **the idea became ~d in his mind** der Gedanke setzte sich in ihm fest. **3.** *v. i.* **a)** *(be paying guest)* [zur Miete] wohnen; **b)** *(enter and remain)* steckenbleiben **(in** in + *Dat.*); hängenbleiben **(on** an + *Dat.*); **~ in sb.'s memory** jmdm. im Gedächtnis bleiben; **c)** *(reside)* wohnen; *(pass the night)* übernachten; nächtigen *(geh.)*

lodger ['lɒdʒə(r)] *n.* Untermieter, *der/*Untermieterin, *die; see also* **take in d**

lodging ['lɒdʒɪŋ] *n.* **a)** *usu. in pl. (rented room)* [möbliertes] Zimmer; **b)** *(accommodation)* Unterkunft, *die;* **board** *or* **food and ~:** Unterkunft und Verpflegung; Kost und Logis

'lodging-house *n.* Pension, *die*

loess ['ləʊes] *n. (Geol.)* Löß, *der*

loft [lɒft] **1.** *n.* **a)** *(attic)* [Dach]boden, *der; (Amer.: room)* Dachzimmer, *das;* **~ conversion** Dachausbau, *der;* **b)** *(over stable)* Heuboden, *der;* **c)** *(pigeon-house)* Taubenschlag, *der;* **d)** *(gallery in church)* Empore, *die.* **2.** *v. t. (Sport)* hochspielen ⟨*Ball*⟩; **~ a ball over sth.** einen Ball über etw. *(Akk.)* heben

loftily ['lɒftɪlɪ] *adv.* **a)** *(grandiosely)* feierlich ⟨*schreiben, sprechen*⟩; **b)** *(haughtily)* hochmütig; überheblich

lofty ['lɒftɪ] *adj.* **a)** *(exalted, grandiose)* hoch; hehr *(geh.);* hochfliegend ⟨*Ideen*⟩; hochgesteckt ⟨*Ziele*⟩; *(fig.: elevated)* feierlich ⟨*Stil*⟩; **b)** *(high)* hoch [aufragend]; hoch ⟨*Flug, Raum*⟩; **c)** *(haughty)* hochmütig; überheblich

¹log [lɒg] **1.** *n.* **a)** *(rough piece of timber)* [geschlagener] Baumstamm; *(part of treetrunk)* Klotz, *der; (as cut for firewood)* [Holz]scheit, *das;* **be as easy as falling off a ~:** kinderleicht sein; **sleep like a ~:** schlafen wie ein Klotz; **b) ~[-book]** Tagebuch, *das; (Naut.)* Logbuch, *das; (Aeronaut.)* Bordbuch, *das;* **c)** *(Naut.: float etc.)* Log, *das.* **2.** *v. t.,* **-gg- a)** *(record)* Buch führen über *(Akk.); (Naut.)* ins Logbuch eintragen; **b)** *(achieve)* verbuchen

~ 'off *v. i.* sich abmelden

~ 'on *v. i.* sich anmelden

²log *n. (Math.)* Logarithmus, *der*

loganberry ['ləʊgnbərɪ] *n.* Loganbeere, *die*

logarithm ['lɒgərɪðm] *n. (Math.)* Logarithmus, *der*

logarithmic [lɒgə'rɪðmɪk] *adj. (Math.)* logarithmisch

log: ~-book *n.* **a)** *(Brit.: of car)* Zulassung, *die;* **b)** *see* **¹log 1 b; ~ 'cabin** *n.* Blockhütte, *die;* **~-'fire** *n.* Holzfeuer, *das*

loggerheads ['lɒgəhedz] *n. pl.* **be at ~ with sb.** mit jmdm. im Clinch liegen; **they were constantly at ~:** sie lagen ständig miteinander im Clinch

loggia ['ləʊdʒə, 'lɒdʒjə] *n.* Loggia, *die*

logic ['lɒdʒɪk] *n.* Logik, *die*

logical ['lɒdʒɪkl] *adj.* **a)** logisch; **she has a ~ mind** sie denkt logisch; **b)** *(clear-thinking)* logisch denkend; klar denkend

logicality [lɒdʒɪ'kælɪtɪ] *n.* Logik, *die*

logically ['lɒdʒɪkəlɪ] *adv.* logisch

logical 'positivism *n. (Philos.)* logischer Empirismus

logician [lə'dʒɪʃn] *n. (Philos.)* Logiker, *der/* Logikerin, *die*

logistic [lə'dʒɪstɪk] *adj.* logistisch

logistics [lə'dʒɪstɪks] *n. pl.* Logistik, *die*

'log jam *n. Stau von treibendem Holz/Flößholz;* **the talks failed to move** *or* **break the ~** *(fig.)* die Gespräche haben keinen Durchbruch gebracht

logo ['lɒgəʊ, 'ləʊgəʊ] *n., pl.* **~s** Signet, *das;* Logo, *das*

'log tables *n. pl.* Logarithmentafeln

loin [lɔɪn] *n.* **a)** *in pl. (Anat.)* Lende, *die; see also* **gird up; b)** *(meat)* Lende, *die*

'loincloth *n.* Lendenschurz, *der*

loiter ['lɔɪtə(r)] *v. i.* trödeln; bummeln; *(linger suspiciously)* herumlungern; **~ with intent** sich mit krimineller Absicht irgendwo aufhalten

~ a'way *v. t.* vertrödeln ⟨*Zeit*⟩

loiterer ['lɔɪtərə(r)] *n.* Herumtreiber, *der;* Herumlungerer, *der (salopp)*

loll [lɒl] *v. i.* **a)** *(lounge)* sich lümmeln *(ugs. abwertend);* **don't ~!** lümmel dich nicht so!; **b)** *(droop)* ⟨*Zunge:*⟩ heraushängen; ⟨*Kopf:*⟩ hängen

~ a'bout, ~ a'round *v. i.* sich herumlümmeln *(ugs. abwertend)*

lollipop ['lɒlɪpɒp] *n.* Lutscher, *der*

lollipop: ~ man/woman *ns. (Brit. coll.) Mann/Frau in der Funktion eines Schülerlotsen*

lollop ['lɒləp] *v. i. (coll.) (bob up and down)* ⟨*Kaninchen usw.:*⟩ hoppeln; *(proceed by clumsy bounds)* zotteln *(ugs.);* trotten

lolly ['lɒlɪ] *n.* **a)** *(Brit. coll.: lollipop)* Lutscher, *der;* **ice[d] ~:** Eis am Stiel; **b)** *no pl., no indef. art. (sl.: money)* Kohle, *die (salopp)*

Lombardy ['lɒmbədɪ] *pr. n.* Lombardei, *die;* **~ poplar** *(Bot.)* Pyramidenpappel, *die*

London ['lʌndən] **1.** *pr. n.* London *(das).* **2.** *attrib. adj.* Londoner

Londoner ['lʌndənə(r)] *pr. n.* Londoner, *der/*Londonerin, *die*

lone [ləʊn] *attrib. adj.* **a)** *(poet./rhet.: solitary)* einsam; **b)** *(lonesome)* einsam; **c) ~ hand** *(Cards: player)* Einzelspieler, *der/ -*spielerin, *die;* **play** *or* **hold a ~ hand** allein spielen; **play a ~ hand** *(fig.)* einen Alleingang machen

loneliness ['ləʊnlɪnɪs] *n., no pl.* Einsamkeit, *die; (remoteness)* Abgeschiedenheit, *die*

lonely ['ləʊnlɪ] *adj.* einsam; *(remote)* abgeschieden; **~ heart** einsames Herz

loner ['ləʊnə(r)] *n.* Einzelgänger, *der/-*gängerin, *die*

lonesome ['ləʊnsəm] *adj.* einsam; **by** *or* **on one's ~:** ganz allein

lone 'wolf *n. (fig.)* Einzelgänger, *der/-*gängerin, *die*

¹long [lɒŋ] **1.** *adj.,* **~er** ['lɒŋgə(r)], **~est** ['lɒŋgɪst] **a)** lang; weit ⟨*Reise, Weg*⟩; **be ~ in the tooth** nicht mehr der/die Jüngste sein; **she's getting a bit ~ in the tooth for that** dafür ist sie allmählich vielleicht doch etwas zu alt; **in two days at the ~est** in spätestens zwei Tagen; **it will take two hours at the ~est** es wird höchstens zwei Stunden dauern; **take a ~ view of sth.** etw. auf lange *od.* weite Sicht sehen; **two inches/weeks ~:** zwei Zoll/ Wochen lang; *see also* **law k; way 1 e; b)** *(elongated)* länglich; schmal; **pull** *or* **make a ~ face** *(fig.)* ein langes Gesicht ziehen *od.* machen *(ugs.);* **c)** *(of extended duration)* lang; **~ service** *(esp. Mil.)* langjähriger Dienst; **in the '~ run** auf die Dauer; auf lange Sicht; **in the '~ term** auf lange Sicht; langfristig; **for a '~ time** lange; *(still continuing)* seit langem; **what a ~ time you've been away!** du warst aber lange [Zeit] fort!; **~ time no see!** *(coll.)* lange nicht gesehen! *(ugs.);* **d)** *(tediously lengthy)* lang[atmig]; weitschweifig; **e)** *(lasting)* lang; langjährig ⟨*Gewohnheit, Freundschaft*⟩; alt ⟨*Brauch, Gewohnheit*⟩; **f)** klein, gering ⟨*Chance*⟩; **it would be a ~ chance that ...:** es ist ziemlich unwahrscheinlich, daß ...; **g)** *(seemingly more than stated)* lang ⟨*Minute, Tag, Jahre usw.*⟩; **h)** *(coll.: tall)* lang *(ugs.)* ⟨*Person*⟩; hoch ⟨*Fenster*⟩; **i)** lang ⟨*Gedächtnis*⟩; **have a ~ memory for sth.** etw. nicht so schnell vergessen; **j)** *qualifying number or measure:* **~ dozen** dreizehn [Stück]; **~ hundred** hundertzwanzig [Stück]; Großhundert, *das (veralt.);* **~ hundredweight** englischer Zentner; **~ ton** Longton, *die;* **k)** *(consisting of many items)* lang ⟨*Liste usw.*⟩; hoch ⟨*Zahl*⟩; **l)** *(Phonet., Pros.)* lang; **m)** *(Cards)* **~ suit** lange Farbe; **be sb.'s ~ suit** *(fig.)* jmds. Stärke sein; **n) be ~ on sth.** *(coll.)* ein Ausbund an etw. *(Dat.)* sein *(ugs.).* **2.** *n.* **a)** *(long interval)* **take ~:** lange dauern; **for ~:** lange; *(since ~ ago)* seit langem; **before ~:** bald; **it is ~ since ...:** es ist lange her, daß ...; **b) the ~ and the short of it is ...:** der langen Rede kurzer Sinn ist ... **3.** *adv.,* **~er, ~est a)** lang[e]; **as** *or* **so ~ as** solange; **the shop hasn't ~ been open** den Laden gibt es noch nicht lange; **you should have finished ~ before now** du hättest schon längst *od.* viel früher fertig sein sollen; **I knew her ~ before I met you** ich kenne sie schon viel länger als dich; **not ~ before that** kurz davor *od.* zuvor; **not ~ before I ...:** kurz bevor ich ...; **~ since** [schon] seit langem; **all day/night/ summer ~:** den ganzen Tag/die ganze Nacht/den ganzen Sommer [über *od.* lang]; **a quiet resort, ~ the gathering place of ...:** ein ruhiger Ferienort, lange/*(still continuing)* schon lange Versammlungsort von ...; **not be ~ for this world** nicht mehr lange zu leben haben; **I shan't be ~:** ich bin gleich fertig; *(departing)* bis gleich!; **don't be ~!**

beeil dich!; **don't be ~ about [doing] it!** laß dir nicht zuviel Zeit damit!; **sb. is ~ [in** *or* **about doing sth.]** jmd. braucht lange *od.* viel Zeit[, um etw. zu tun]; **the opportunity was not ~ in coming** es dauerte nicht lange, bis sich die Gelegenheit bot; **much ~er** viel länger; **not wait any/much ~er** nicht mehr länger/viel länger warten; **no ~er** nicht mehr; nicht länger ⟨*warten usw.*⟩; **we no ~er had any hope** wir hatten keine Hoffnung mehr; **play can't go on much ~er** das Spiel muß bald abgebrochen werden; **how much ~er is he going to sleep?** wie lange schläft er denn noch?; *see also* **ago**; **¹so 1 a**; **b) as** *or* **so ~ as** *(provided that)* solange; wenn

²long *v. i.* **~ for sb./sth.** sich nach jmdm./etw. sehnen; **~ for the end of sth./for the summer to come** das Ende einer Sache/den Sommer herbeisehnen; **~ for sb. to do sth.** sich *(Dat.)* [sehr] wünschen, daß jmd. etw. tut; **I ~ for you to come home** ich warte sehnsüchtig darauf, daß du nach Hause kommst; **~ to do sth.** sich danach sehnen, etw. zu tun; **he ~ed to ask his mother the meaning of it** es drängte ihn, seine Mutter zu fragen, was das bedeutete; **[much] ~ed-for** [lang]ersehnt

long. *abbr.* **longitude** Lg.

long: ~-ago 1. *n.* längst vergangene Zeit[en]; **2.** *adj.* längst vergangen; **~boat** *n.* Barkasse, *die;* Langboot, *das;* **~bow** *n. (Mil.)* Langbogen, *der;* **~-case 'clock** *n.* Standuhr, *die;* **~-dated** *adj. (Finance)* langfristig; **~-distance 1.** ['---] *adj.* Fern⟨*gespräch, -verkehr usw.*⟩; Langstrecken⟨*lauf, -läufer, -flug usw.*⟩; **~-distance coach** Reise- *od.* Überlandbus, *der;* **~-distance lorry-driver** Fern[last]fahrer, *der;* **2.** [-'--] *adv.* **phone ~-distance** ein Ferngespräch führen; **~ division** *see* **division g**; **~-drawn[-out]** *adj.* langgezogen ⟨*Schrei, Ton*⟩; langatmig ⟨*Erklärung, Diskussion*⟩; ausgedehnt ⟨*Wanderung*⟩; **~ drink** *n.* Longdrink, *der*

longevity [lɒn'dʒevɪtɪ] *n., no pl.* Langlebigkeit, *die*

long: ~-forgotten *adj.* längst vergessen; **~-haired** *adj.* langhaarig; Langhaar⟨*dackel, -katze*⟩; **~hand** *n.* Langschrift, *die;* **~ haul** *n.* Langstreckentransport, *der;* [Güter]ferntransport, *der;* **it's a ~ haul** das ist ein weiter Weg; **~-haul** *adj.* Fern⟨*verkehr, -lastwagen*⟩; Langstrecken⟨*[flug]verkehr*⟩; Fernverkehrs⟨*bus, -verbindung*⟩; **~ hop** *n. (Cricket) kurz aufgesetzter und dann weit fliegender Ball;* **~horn** *n.* **a)** *(cattle)* Longhorn, *das;* **b)** *(beetle)* Bockkäfer, *der*

longing ['lɒŋɪŋ] **1.** *n.* Verlangen, *das;* Sehnsucht, *die; (craving)* Gelüst, *das (geh.);* **I had a sudden ~ for a cigarette** ich hatte plötzlich Lust auf eine Zigarette. **2.** *adj.* sehnsüchtig

longingly ['lɒŋɪŋlɪ] *adv.* voll Sehnsucht; sehnsüchtig

longish ['lɒŋɪʃ] *adj.* ziemlich lang

longitude ['lɒndʒɪtju:d, 'lɒŋgɪtju:d] *n.* **a)** *(Geog.)* [geographische] Länge; *(of a place)* Länge, *die;* **~ 40° E** 40° östlicher Länge; **b)** *(Astron.)* Länge, *die*

longitudinal [lɒndʒɪ'tju:dɪnl, lɒŋgɪ'tju:dɪnl] *adj.* **a)** Längen⟨*ausdehnung, -messung*⟩; **b)** *(running lengthwise)* längsgerichtet; **~ stripe** Längsstreifen, *der;* **c) ~ wave** *(Phys.)* Longitudinalwelle, *die*

long: ~ johns *n. pl. (coll.)* lange Unterhosen; **~ jump** *n. (Brit. Sport)* Weitsprung, *der;* **~-lasting** *adj.* langandauernd; anhaltend ⟨*Niederschläge, Schneefälle usw.*⟩; dauerhaft ⟨*Beziehung, Freundschaft*⟩; **~-legged** *adj.* langbeinig; **~ 'lens** *n. (Photog.)* Fernobjektiv, *das;* **~-life** *adj.* haltbar [gemacht]; **~-life battery** Batterie mit langer Lebensdauer; **~-life milk** H-Milch, *die;* **~-lived** ['lɒŋlɪvd] *adj. (durable)* andauernd; *(having long life)* langlebig; **be ~-lived** sehr alt werden; **a ~-lived family** eine Familie, in der alle sehr alt werden; **~ 'odds** *n. pl. (Racing, also fig.)* geringe Gewinnchancen; **~ 'player, ~-playing 'record** *ns.* Langspielplatte, *die;* **~-range** *adj.* **a)** *(having a long range)* Langstrecken⟨*flugzeug, -rakete usw.*⟩; ⟨*Geschütz*⟩ mit großer Reichweite; **b)** *(relating to the future)* langfristig; **~-running** *adj.* anhaltend; Langzeit⟨*versuch*⟩; wochen-/monate-/jahrelang ⟨*Debatte, Streit usw.*⟩; lange laufend ⟨*Theaterstück*⟩; **~ ship** *n. (Hist.)* Wikingerschiff, *das;* **~-shoreman** ['lɒŋʃɔ:mən] *n., pl.* **~-shoremen** ['lɒŋʃɔ:mən] *n.* Schauermann, *der;* **~ shot** *n.* **a)** *(wild guess)* reine Spekulation; **b)** *(bet at long odds)* gewagter Versuch; **c)** *(Cinemat.)* Fernaufnahme, *die;* **d) not by a ~ shot** bei weitem nicht; **~ 'sight** *n.* Weitsichtigkeit, *die;* **have ~ sight** weitsichtig sein; **~-sighted** *adj.* weitsichtig; *(fig.)* weitblickend; vorausschauend; **~-sleeved** ['lɒŋsli:vd] *adj.* langärmelig; **~-standing** *attrib. adj.* seit langem bestehend; langjährig ⟨*Freundschaft usw.*⟩; alt ⟨*Schulden, Rechnung, Streit*⟩; **~stop** *n. (fig.)* Notnagel, *der;* **~-suffering** *adj.* schwer geprüft; *(meek)* geduldig; **~-term** *adj.* langfristig; **~-time** *adj.* seit langem bestehend; alt ⟨*Zwist, Freund*⟩; **~ va'cation** *n. (Brit.)* Sommer[semester]ferien *Pl.; (Law)* Sommerpause, *die;* **~ wave** *n. (Radio)* Langwelle, *die;* **~-wave** *adj. (Radio)* Langwellen-; **~ways** *adv.* längs; in Längsrichtung; **~-winded** [lɒŋ'wɪndɪd] *adj.* langatmig; weitschweifig

loo [lu:] *n. (Brit. coll.)* Klo, *das (ugs. fam.)*

loofah ['lu:fə] *n.* **a)** *(sponge)* Luffaschwamm, *der;* **b)** *(Bot.)* Luffa, *die*

look [lʊk] **1.** *v. i.* **a)** sehen; gucken *(ugs.);* schauen *(bes. südd., sonst geh.);* **~ down at one's feet** zu Boden blicken; **don't ~ now, but ...:** sieh jetzt nicht hin, aber ...; **~ before you leap** *(prov.)* erst wägen, dann wagen *(Spr.);* **~ the other way** *(fig.)* die Augen verschließen; **not know which way to ~:** nicht wissen, wohin man sehen soll; **as quick** *or* **soon as ~ [at you]** *(coll.: very readily)* ohne zu zögern; *see also* **eye 1 a**; **b)** *(search)* nachsehen; **c)** *(face)* zugewandt sein **(to[wards]** *Dat.*); **the windows ~ north** die Fenster liegen *od.* gehen nach Norden; **the room ~s on to the road/into the garden** das Zimmer liegt zur Straße/zum Garten hin *od.* geht zur Straße/zum Garten; **d)** *(appear)* aussehen; **~ as if** [so] aussehen, als ob; **~ well/ill** gut *od.* gesund/schlecht *od.* krank aussehen; **~ like** aussehen wie; **it ~s like rain** es sieht nach Regen aus; **he ~s like winning** es sieht so aus, als ob er gewinnt; **make sb. ~ small** jmdn. herabsetzen; jmdn. heruntermachen *(salopp); see also* **alive d**; **black 1 d**; **¹fool 1 a**; **e)** *(seem to be)* **she ~s her age/her 40 years** man sieht ihr ihr Alter/die 40 Jahre an; **you ~ yourself again** es scheint dir wieder gut zu gehen; **you don't ~ yourself** du siehst schlecht aus; **~ the part** *(lit. or fig.)* so aussehen; **she ~ed the part to perfection** sie war für die Rolle wie geschaffen; **f)** *(inquire)* **you haven't ~ed deep enough into it** du hast dich nicht eingehend genug damit befaßt; **~ [here]!** *(demanding attention)* hören Sie/hör zu; *(protesting)* passen Sie/paß ja *od.* bloß auf!; **~ sharp [about sth.]** *(hurry up)* sich [mit etw.] beeilen; **~ inwards** in sich *(Akk.)* hineinblicken; nach innen blicken; **g)** *(take care, make sure)* **~ that ...:** dafür sorgen *od.* zusehen *od.* darauf achten, daß ...; **~ to do sth.** *(expect)* erwarten *od.* hoffen, etw. zu tun. **2.** *v. t.* **a)** *(ascertain by sight)* nachsehen; *in exclamation of surprise etc.* sich *(Dat.)* ansehen; **~ what you've done!** sieh [dir mal an], was du getan *od.* angerichtet hast!; **~ who's here!** sieh mal, wer da *od.* gekommen ist!; **b)** *(express by one's ~s)* **~ a question at sb.** jmdn. fragend ansehen; **she ~ed her surprise** die Überraschung stand ihr im Gesicht geschrieben; *see also* **dagger a. 3.** *n.* **a)** Blick, *der;* **get a good ~ at sb.** jmdn. gut *od.* genau sehen [können]; **have** *or* **take a ~ at sb./sth.** sich *(Dat.)* jmdn./etw. ansehen; einen Blick auf jmdn./etw. werfen; **have a ~ at a town** sich *(Dat.)* eine Stadt ansehen; **let sb. have a ~ at sth.** jmdn. etw. sehen lassen; **if ~s could kill** wenn Blicke töten könnten; **b)** *in sing. or pl. (person's appearance)* Aussehen, *das; (facial expression)* [Gesichts]ausdruck, *der;* **from** *or* **by the ~[s] of sb.** von jmds. Aussehen zu schließen; **good ~s** gutes Aussehen; **she's lost her ~s** sie hat ihre Schönheit verloren; **have a hungry ~:** hungrig aussehen; **have the ~ of an artist** wie ein Künstler aussehen; **put on a ~ of innocence** eine Unschuldsmiene aufsetzen; **there were angry ~s from them** sie guckten *od. (geh.)* blickten böse; *see also* **black 1 f**; **c)** *(thing's appearance)* Aussehen, *das; (Fashion)* Look, *der;* **have a neglected ~:** verwahrlost aussehen; **from** *or* **by the ~ of the furniture** *etc.* [so] wie die Möbel *usw.* aussehen; **by the ~[s] of it** *or* **things** [so] wie es aussieht; **the house is empty, by the ~ of it** das Haus steht allem Anschein nach leer; **I don't like the ~ of this** das gefällt mir gar nicht; **the place has a European ~:** der Ort wirkt europäisch; **for the ~ of the thing** *(coll.)* um den Schein zu wahren

~ a'bout 1. *v. t.* **~ about a room** sich in einem Zimmer umsehen; **~ about one** sich umsehen *od.* umschauen. **2.** *v. i.* **a)** sich umsehen; **~ about everywhere** *(search)* überall gucken; **b)** *(be watchful)* sich vorsehen; **~ about for sth.** sich nach etw. umsehen

~ 'after *v. t.* **a)** *(follow with one's eyes)* nachsehen (+ *Dat.*); **b)** *(attend to)* sich kümmern um; **c)** *(care for)* sorgen für; **~ after oneself** allein zurechtkommen; für sich selbst sorgen; **~ 'after yourself!** paß auf dich auf!

~ a'head *v. i.* **a)** nach vorne sehen; **b)** *(fig.: plan for future)* an die Zukunft denken; vorausschauen; **~ ahead five years/to next year** an die Zeit in fünf Jahren/an nächstes Jahr denken

~ a'round *see* **~ about**

~ at *v. t.* **a)** *(regard)* ansehen; **~ at one's watch** auf seine Uhr sehen; **~ directly at the light** direkt ins Licht sehen; **don't ~ at me like that!** sieh mich nicht so an!; **be pleasing to ~ at** [recht] nett aussehen; **be good/not much to ~ at** nach etwas/nach nichts *od.* nicht nach viel aussehen *(ugs.);* **to ~ at him, you'd think ...:** wenn man ihn so sieht, würde man meinen, ...; **b)** *(examine)* sich *(Dat.)* ansehen; **c)** *(consider)* betrachten; in Betracht ziehen ⟨*Angebot*⟩; **that's the proper way to ~ at it** so muß man es sehen; **I wouldn't even ~ at such an offer** so ein Angebot wäre für mich völlig undiskutabel; **I can't ~ at any more caviare** ich kann Kaviar nicht mehr sehen

~ a'way *v. i.* weggucken *(ugs.);* wegsehen

~ 'back *v. i.* **a)** *(glance behind)* sich umsehen; sich umblicken *(geh.); (fig.: hesitate)* zurückschauen; **he's never ~ed back since then** seitdem läuft bei ihm alles bestens; **b)** *(cast one's mind back)* **~ back [up]on** *or* **to sth.** an etw. *(Akk.)* zurückdenken; auf etw. *(Akk.)* zurückblicken

~ 'down [up]on *v. t.* **a)** herunter-/hinuntersehen, *(ugs.)* runtergucken auf (+ *Akk.*); **b)** *(fig.: despise)* herabsehen auf (+ *Akk.*)

~ for *v. t.* **a)** *(expect)* erwarten; **b)** *(seek)* suchen nach; auf der Suche sein nach ⟨*neuen Ideen*⟩; **~ for trouble** Streit suchen; *(unintentionally)* sich *(Dat.)* Ärger einhandeln

~ 'forward to *v. t.* sich freuen auf (+ *Akk.*); **~ forward to doing sth.** sich darauf freuen, etw. zu tun

~ 'in *v. i.* **a)** hin-/hereinsehen; *(visit)* vorbeikommen **(on** bei); vorbei- *od.* hereinschauen (**on** bei) *(bes. südd. ugs.)*; ~ **in at the butcher's** beim Schlachter vorbeigehen; **the doctor ~ed in frequently** der Arzt kam häufig vorbei; **the nurse ~ed in on the patient every hour** die Schwester sah jede Stunde nach dem Patienten; **b)** *(coll.: watch television)* fernsehen. *See also* **look-in**

~ **into** *v. t.* **a)** sehen in (+ *Akk.*); **b)** *(fig.: investigate)* [eingehend] untersuchen; unter die Lupe nehmen *(ugs.)*; prüfen ⟨*Beschwerde*⟩

~ **on 1.** [-'-] *v. i.* zusehen; zugucken *(ugs.)*; *see also* **looker-on. 2.** ['--] *v. t.* ~ **on sb. as a hero** *etc.* jmdn. als Held[en] *usw.* betrachten; ~ **on sb. with distrust/suspicion** jmdn. mit Mißtrauen/Argwohn betrachten

~ **'out 1.** *v. i.* **a)** hinaus-/heraussehen (**of** aus); rausgucken *(ugs.)*; **b)** *(take care)* aufpassen; **c)** *(have view)* ~ **out on sth.** ⟨*Zimmer, Wohnung usw.:*⟩ zu etw. gehen *(ugs.)*; zu etw. hin liegen; **the house ~s out over the river** von dem Haus hat man einen Blick auf den Fluß; **a room ~ing out on the green** ein Zimmer mit Blick auf die Wiese. **2.** *v. t.* *(Brit.: select)* [her]aussuchen. *See also* **look-out**

~ **'out for** *v. t.* *(be prepared for)* aufpassen *od.* achten auf (+ *Akk.*); sich in acht nehmen vor (+ *Dat.*) ⟨*gefährliche Person, Sturm*⟩; *(keep watching for)* Ausschau halten nach ⟨*Arbeit, Gelegenheit, Partner, Sammelobjekt usw.*⟩

~ **'out of** *v. t.* sehen *od.* *(ugs.)* gucken aus

~ **'over** *v. t.* **a)** sehen über (+ *Akk.*) ⟨*Mauer usw.*⟩; überblicken ⟨*Tal usw.*⟩; **b)** *(survey)* inspizieren, sich *(Dat.)* ansehen ⟨*Haus, Anwesen*⟩; **c)** *(scrutinize)* mustern ⟨*Person*⟩; durchsehen ⟨*Text*⟩

~ **'round** *v. i.* sich umsehen; sich umgucken *(ugs.)*; ~ **round in search of sth.** nach etw. Ausschau halten

~ **through** *v. t.* **a)** ~ **through sth.** durch etw. [hindurch] sehen; **b)** *(inspect)* durchsehen ⟨*Papiere*⟩; prüfen ⟨*Antrag, Vorschlag, Aussage*⟩; **c)** *(glance through)* sich *(Dat.)* ansehen ⟨*Buch, Notizen*⟩; **d)** *(fig.: ignore deliberately)* ~ **straight 'through sb.** durch jmdn. hindurchsehen; jmdn. einfach übersehen; **e)** *(penetrate)* durchschauen ⟨*Person, Verhaltensweise*⟩

~ **to** *v. t.* **a)** *(rely on, count upon)* ~ **to sb./sth. for sth.** etw. von jmdm./etw. erwarten; ~ **to sb./sth. to do sth.** von jmdm./etw. erwarten, daß er/es etw. tut; **we ~ to him for help/to help us** wir zählen auf seine *od.* rechnen mit seiner Hilfe/zählen darauf *od.* rechnen damit, daß er uns hilft; **b)** *(be careful about)* sorgen für; *(keep watch upon)* aufpassen auf (+ *Akk.*); ~ **to it that ...:** zusehen *od.* dafür sorgen, daß ...; ~ **to your manners!** benimm dich! *(ugs.)*; *see also* **laurel a; c)** *(consider)* ~ **to sth.** etw. beachten; einer Sache *(Dat.)* Beachtung schenken; ~ **more to quality than to quantity** mehr auf Qualität als auf Quantität achten; **d)** *(take care of)* sich kümmern um ⟨*Wunde, Kind usw.*⟩

~ **towards** *v. t.* **a)** sehen *od.* *(ugs.)* gucken nach/zu; **b)** *(face)* **the balcony/room ~s towards the sea** der Balkon/das Zimmer liegt zum Meer hin; **c)** *(consider)* ~ **towards the future** an die Zukunft denken; **d)** *(hope for and expect)* sich *(Dat.)* erhoffen; **e)** *(aim at)* abzielen auf (+ *Akk.*)

~ **'up 1.** *v. i.* **a)** aufblicken; ~ **up into the sky** in den Himmel [hinauf]blicken; **b)** *(improve)* besser werden; ⟨*Aktien, Chancen:*⟩ steigen; **things are ~ing up** es geht bergauf; **business is ~ing up again** das Geschäft läuft wieder besser. **2.** *v. t.* **a)** *(search for)* nachschlagen ⟨*Wort*⟩; heraussuchen ⟨*Telefonnummer, Zugverbindung usw.*⟩; **b)** *(coll.: visit)* ~ **sb. up** bei jmdm. reingucken *(ugs.)*; bei jmdm. vorbeischauen *(bes. südd. ugs.)*; **c)** ~ **sb. up and down** jmdn. von Kopf bis Fuß mustern

~ **upon** *see* ~ **on 2**

~ **'up to** *v. t.* ~ **up to sb.** *(lit. or fig.)* zu jmdm. aufschauen *od.* aufsehen

'look-alike *n.* Doppelgänger, *der*/-gängerin, *die*; **be ~s** wie Zwillinge aussehen

looker ['lʊkə(r)] *n.* *(coll.: attractive woman)* gutaussehende Frau; **she's a ~:** sie sieht gut aus; *see also* **good-looker**

looker-'on *n.* Zuschauer, *der*/Zuschauerin, *die*

'look-in *n.* **a)** *(visit)* kurzer Besuch; **b)** *(opportunity)* Chance, *die*; **we didn't get a ~:** wir hatten überhaupt keine Chance

-looking [lʊkɪŋ] *adj. in comb.* aussehend; **dirty-~:** schmutzig wirkend; **European-/oriental-~:** europäisch/orientalisch aussehend; *see also* **good-looking**

'looking-glass *n.* Spiegel, *der*

'look-out *n.*, *pl.* **~s a)** *(keeping watch)* *(Naut.)* Ausschauhalten, *das*; *(guard)* Wache, *die*; **keep a ~** *or* **be on the ~ [for sth./sb.]** *(wanted)* [nach etw./jmdm.] Ausschau halten; *(not wanted)* [auf etw./jmdn.] aufpassen; **b)** *(observation post)* Ausguck, *der*; Beobachtungsstand, *der*; *(crow's nest)* Krähennest, *das (Seemannsspr.)*; Mastkorb, *der (Seemannsspr.)*; *(belvedere)* Aussichtsturm, *der*; **c)** *(person)* Wache, *die*; *(Mil.)* Wach[t]posten, *der*; Beobachtungsposten, *der*; *(scout, scouts)* Wachtposten, *der*; **d)** *(view)* Ausblick, *der*; *(esp. Brit. fig.: prospect)* Aussichten; **that's a bad ~:** das sind schlechte Aussichten; **it's a poor/bleak** *etc.* ~ **for sb./sth.** es sieht schlecht/düster *usw.* aus für jmdn./etw.; **e)** *(concern)* Sache, *die*; Problem, *das*; **that's his [own] ~:** das ist [allein] sein Problem *od.* seine Sache

¹loom [lu:m] *n.* *(Weaving)* Webstuhl, *der*

²loom *v. i.* auftauchen; *(as impending occurrence)* sich [bedrohlich] abzeichnen; ~ **large** [bedrohlich] auftauchen; *(fig.)* eine große Rolle spielen

~ **a'head** *v. i.* **a)** auftauchen (**of** vor + *Dat.*); **b)** ⟨*Prüfung:*⟩ unausweichlich bevorstehen (**of** *Dat.*); ⟨*Hindernis, Schwierigkeit, Problem:*⟩ sich [bedrohlich] abzeichnen (**of** für)

~ **'up** *v. i.* ~ **up [in front of sb.]** [unmittelbar] [vor jmdm.] auftauchen

loon [lu:n] *n.* **a** *(crazy person)* Idiot, *der (ugs. abwertend)*; **b)** *(Ornith.)* [See]taucher, *der*

loony ['lu:nɪ] *(sl.)* **1.** *n.* Verrückte, *der/die (ugs.)*. **2.** *adj.* verrückt *(ugs.)*; irr; **the ~ Left/Right** die hundertfünfzigprozentigen Linken/Rechten

'loony-bin *n.* *(sl.)* Klapsmühle, *die (salopp)*

loop [lu:p] **1.** *n.* **a)** Schleife, *die*; **b)** *(cord)* Schlaufe, *die*; **c)** *(for lifting or fastening)* Schlaufe, *die*; *(eye)* Öse, *die*; ~ **aerial** *or* *(Amer.)* **antenna** Rahmenantenne, *die*; **d)** *(contraceptive coil)* Spirale, *die*. **2.** *v. t.* **a)** *(form into a loop)* zu einer Schlaufe/Öse formen; **b)** *(enclose)* umschlingen; **c)** *(fasten)* ~ **up/together** *etc.* mit einer Schlaufe hoch-/zusammenbinden *usw.*; **d)** *(Aeronaut.)* ~ **the loop** einen Looping fliegen; loopen *(fachspr.)*

'loophole *n.* **a)** *(in wall)* Maueröffnung, *die*; *(for shooting through)* Schießscharte, *die*; **b)** *(fig.)* Lücke, *die*; ~ **in the law** Gesetzeslücke, *die*; Lücke im Gesetz; **tax ~:** Lücke im Steuergesetz

loopy ['lu:pɪ] *adj.* *(sl.)* verrückt *(ugs.)*

loose [lu:s] **1.** *adj.* **a)** *(unrestrained)* freilaufend ⟨*Tier*⟩; *(escaped)* ausgebrochen; *(bolted)* durchgegangen ⟨*Pferd*⟩; **he finally got one hand ~:** er bekam schließlich eine Hand frei; **run** *or* **be ~:** los sein; **set** *or* **turn ~:** freilassen; **cut the boat/dog ~:** das Boot/den Hund losschneiden; **cut ~ from sb.** *(fig.)* sich von jmdm. lösen; **cut ~** *(coll.: behave wildly)* verrückt spielen *(ugs.)*; *see also* **cast 1 a; ²fast 1 a; ¹let 1 a; b)** *(not firm)* locker ⟨*Zahn, Schraube, Mutter, Knopf, Messerklinge*⟩; **come/get/work ~** ⟨*Schraube, Mutter, Knoten, Knopf usw.:*⟩ sich lockern; *see also* **screw 1 a; c)** *(not fixed)* lose ⟨*Knopf, Buchseite, Brett, Stein*⟩; **the pages have come ~:** die Seiten haben sich gelöst; **d)** *(not bound together)* lose; offen ⟨*Haar*⟩; **e)** *(slack)* locker; schlaff ⟨*Haut, Gewebe usw.*⟩; beweglich ⟨*Glieder*⟩; ~ **tongue** loses Mundwerk *(salopp)*; ~ **bowels** [Neigung zu] Durchfall; ~ **build** *or* **frame** schlaksige Gestalt; **f)** *(not dense)* locker ⟨*Boden, Gewebe usw.*⟩; **g)** *(hanging free)* lose; **be at a ~ end** *or (Amer.)* **at ~ ends** *(fig.)* beschäftigungslos sein; *(not knowing what to do with oneself)* nichts zu tun haben; nichts anzufangen wissen; **tie up the ~ ends** *or* **threads** *(fig.)* die letzten Kleinigkeiten erledigen; **h)** *(inexact)* ungenau; schief ⟨*Vergleich*⟩; frei ⟨*Stil*⟩; unsauber ⟨*Denken*⟩; unklar, verwaschen ⟨*Aussage*⟩; **i)** *(lewd)* lose ⟨*Mundwerk, Person*⟩; liederlich ⟨*Leben[swandel], Person*⟩; locker ⟨*Moral, Lebenswandel, Mundwerk*⟩; **a ~ woman** ein leichtes Mädchen; **j)** *in comb.* lose; locker; **~-flowing hair** locker fallendes Haar. **2.** *v. t.* **a)** loslassen ⟨*Hund usw.*⟩; **b)** *(untie)* lösen; aufmachen *(ugs.)*; **c)** ~ **[off]** abschießen ⟨*Pfeil*⟩; abfeuern ⟨*Feuerwaffe, Salve*⟩; abgeben ⟨*Schuß, Salve*⟩; **d)** *(relax)* lockern; ~ **[one's] hold** loslassen; **e)** *(detach from moorings)* losmachen ⟨*Schiff*⟩; loswerfen *(Seemannsspr.)* ⟨*Tau*⟩. **3.** *n.* **a) be on the ~:** frei herumlaufen; **b)** *(Rugby)* **in the ~:** beim offenen Kombinationsspiel

loose: ~ **box** *see* **²box 1 g**; ~ **'change** *see* **change 1 d**; ~ **'cover** *n.* *(Brit.)* Überzug, *der*; Schoner, *der*; **~-fitting** *adj.* bequem geschnitten; **~-knit** *adj.* lose zusammenhängend ⟨*Organisation, Gemeinschaft usw.*⟩; **~-leaf** *attrib. adj.* Loseblatt-; **~-leaf file** Ringbuch, *das*; **~-limbed** ['lu:slɪmd] *adj.* gelenkig; geschmeidig; *(gawky)* schlaksig; **~-lipped** ['lu:slɪpt] *adj.* geschwätzig; **~-living** *adj.* mit lockerem *od.* liederlichem Lebenswandel *nachgestellt*

loosely ['lu:slɪ] *adv.* **a)** *(not tightly)* locker; lose; **b)** *(not strictly)* locker ⟨*gruppieren*⟩; lose ⟨*zusammenhängen*⟩; frei ⟨*übersetzen*⟩; ~ **speaking** grob gesagt; **use a word ~:** ein Wort in einem weiteren Sinne gebrauchen

loosen ['lu:sn] **1.** *v. t.* **a)** *(make less tight etc.)* lockern ; **b)** *(Med.)* lösen ⟨*Husten*⟩; ~ **the/sb.'s bowels** abführend wirken; **c)** *(fig.: relax)* lockern ⟨*Bestimmungen, Reglement usw.*⟩; ~ **sb.'s tongue** *(fig.)* jmds. Zunge lösen. **2.** *v. i.* *(become looser)* sich lockern

~ **up 1.** ['---] *v. t.* lockern ⟨*Glieder, Muskeln*⟩. **2.** [--'-] *v. i.* sich auflockern; *(relax)* auftauen

looseness ['lu:snɪs] *n.*, *no pl.* **a)** Lockerheit, *die*; **b)** *(Med.)* ~ **of the bowels** [Neigung zu] Durchfall

loot [lu:t] **1.** *v. t.* **a)** *(plunder)* plündern; **b)** *(carry off)* rauben. **2.** *n.* **a)** *(in war)* [Kriegs]beute, *die*; **b)** *(gain, esp. illicit)* Beute, *die*; **c)** *(sl.: money)* Zaster, *der (salopp)*; Knete, *die (salopp)*

looter ['lu:tə(r)] *n.* Plünderer, *der*

lop [lɒp] *v. t.*, **-pp- a)** stutzen, beschneiden ⟨*Baum, Hecke*⟩; **b)** ~ **sth. [off** *or* **away]** etw. abhauen *od.* abhacken

lope [ləʊp] *v. i.* ⟨*Hase, Kaninchen:*⟩ springen; ⟨*Wolf, Fuchs:*⟩ laufen; ⟨*Person:*⟩ beschwingten Schrittes gehen

lop-eared ['lɒpɪəd] *adj.* schlappohrig *(ugs.)*; hängeohrig

lopsided [lɒp'saɪdɪd] *adj.* schief; *(fig.)* einseitig

loquacious [lə'kweɪʃəs] *adj.* redselig; schwatzhaft *(abwertend)*

loquacity [lə'kwæsɪtɪ] *n.*, *no pl.* Redseligkeit, *die*; Geschwätzigkeit, *die (abwertend)*

lord [lɔ:d] **1.** *n.* **a)** *(master)* Herr, *der*; **the ~s of creation** *(fig.: mankind)* die Krone der Schöpfung; ~ **and master** *(joc.)* Herr und Gebieter *od.* Meister *(scherzh.)*; **b)** L~

(Relig.) Herr, *der;* **L~ God [Almighty]** unser Herr[, der allmächtige Gott]; **the L~ [God]** [Gott] der Herr; **Our/the L~** *(Christ)* unser Herr Jesus/der Herr; **in the year of Our L~ ...:** im Jahre des Herrn ...; **the L~'s Prayer** das Vaterunser; **the 'L~'s Day** der Tag des Herrn; **the L~'s Supper** das [Heilige] Abendmahl; **L~ only knows** *(coll.)* weiß der Himmel *(ugs.)*; **c)** *(Brit.: nobleman, or as title)* Lord, *der;* **live like a ~** *(fig.)* fürstlich leben; **treat sb. like a ~:** jmdn. fürstlich bewirten; **the L~s** *(Brit.)* die Lords; das Oberhaus; **the House of L~s** *(Brit.)* das Oberhaus; *see also* **drunk 1**; **d) My L~** *(Brit.) form of address (to earl, viscount)* Graf; *(to baron)* Baron; *(to bishop)* Exzellenz; *(to ~ mayor, ~ provost)* Herr Oberbürgermeister; *(to judge)* [mlʌd] Herr Richter; **e)** *(Brit.: feudal superior)* Lord, *der;* Lehnsherr, *der.* **2.** *int. (coll.)* Gott!; **oh/good L~!** du lieber Himmel *od.* Gott!; großer Gott!; **L~ bless my soul/me/us** *etc.* allmächtiger Gott! **3.** *v. t.* **~ it** *(rule)* das Zepter *od.* Regiment führen; *(put on airs)* sich groß aufspielen; **~ it over sb.** bei jmdm. den großen Herrn/die große Dame spielen

Lord: ~ 'Advocate *n. (Scot. Law)* Kronanwalt, *der;* **~ 'Bishop** *n. (Brit.)* Lordbischof, *der;* **~ 'Chamberlain** *n. (Brit.)* Haushofmeister, *der;* **~ 'Chancellor** *n. (Brit.)* Lord[groß]kanzler, *der;* **~ Chief 'Justice** *see* **chief 2a**; **~ Lieu'tenant** *n. (Brit.)* Lord Lieutenant, *der; Vertreter der Krone in einer Grafschaft*

lordly ['lɔ:dlɪ] *adj.* **a)** *(grand)* herrschaftlich; edel ⟨*Gegenstand*⟩; herrschaftlich ⟨*Gebäude*⟩; stattlich ⟨*Vermögen*⟩; **b)** *(haughty)* anmaßend; hochmütig

Lord: ~ 'Mayor *see* **mayor**; **~ President of the 'Council** *n. (Brit.)* Lordpräsident, *der;* **~ Privy 'Seal** *n. (Brit.)* Lordsiegelverwalter, *der;* **~ 'Provost** *n. (Scot.)* ≈ Oberbürgermeister, *der*

lordship ['lɔ:dʃɪp] *n.* **a)** *(title, estate)* Lordschaft, *die;* **his/your ~/their/your ~s** seine/Eure Lordschaft/ihre/Eure Lordschaften; **b)** *(dominion)* Herrschaft, *die* **(of, over** über + *Akk.)*

lore [lɔ:(r)] *n.* Wissen, *das;* Kunde, *die; (body of traditions)* Überlieferung, *die; (of a people, an area)* Folklore, *die;* **animal/bird/plant ~:** Tier-/Vogel-/Pflanzenkunde, *die*

lorgnette [lɔ:'njet] *n. in sing. or pl.* Lorgnette, *die*

Lorraine [lɒ'reɪn] *pr. n.* Lothringen *(das)*

lorry ['lɒrɪ] *n. (Brit.)* Lastwagen, *der;* Lkw, *der;* Laster, *der (ugs.);* **it fell off the back of a ~** *(joc.)* das ist mir/ihm *usw.* zugelaufen *(ugs. scherzh.)*

'lorry-driver *n. (Brit.)* Lastwagenfahrer, *der;* Lkw-Fahrer, *der*

lose [lu:z] **1.** *v. t.,* **lost** [lɒst] **a)** verlieren; kommen um, verlieren ⟨*Leben, Habe*⟩; **sb. has something/nothing to ~ [by doing sth.]** es kann jmdm. schaden/nicht schaden[, wenn er etw. tut]; *see also* **face 1a**; **grip 1a**; **'ground 1b**; **hold 3a, b**; **sight 1b**; **temper 1a**; **b)** *(fail to maintain)* verlieren; *(become slow by)* ⟨*Uhr:*⟩ nachgehen ⟨*zwei Minuten täglich usw.*⟩; **c)** *(become unable to find)* verlieren; **~ one's way** sich verlaufen/verfahren; **be lost/~ oneself in sth.** *(fig.)* ganz in etw. *(Dat.)* aufgehen; **d)** *(waste)* vertun ⟨*Zeit*⟩; *(miss)* versäumen, verpassen ⟨*Zeitpunkt, Gelegenheit, Ereignis*⟩; *see also* **time 1b**; **e)** *(fail to obtain)* nicht bekommen ⟨*Preis, Vertrag usw.*⟩; *(fail to hear)* nicht mitbekommen ⟨*Teil einer Rede usw.*⟩; *(fail to catch)* verpassen, versäumen ⟨*Zug, Bus*⟩; **the motion was lost** der Antrag kam nicht durch *od.* scheiterte; **f)** *(forfeit)* verlieren; verlieren, *(geh.)* verwirken ⟨*Recht*⟩; **g)** *(be defeated in)* verlieren ⟨*Kampf, Wette, Prozeß usw.*⟩; *see also* **fight 2c**; **toss 3a**; **h)** *(cause loss of)* **~ sb. sth.** jmdn. um etw. bringen; **you['ve] lost me** *(fig.)* ich komme nicht mehr mit; **i)** *(get rid of)* abschütteln ⟨*Verfolger*⟩; loswerden ⟨*Erkältung*⟩; **~ weight** abnehmen. *See also* **lost. 2.** *v. i.,* **lost a)** *suffer loss)* einen Verlust erleiden; *(in business)* Verlust machen **(on** bei); *(in match, contest)* verlieren; **heads you win, tails you ~:** bei Kopf hast du gewonnen, bei Zahl verloren; **~ in freshness** an Frische verlieren; **the story didn't ~ in the telling** die Geschichte wurde beim Weitererzählen eher noch aufgebauscht; **his poetry ~s in translation** seine Gedichte verlieren durch die Übersetzung; **you can't ~** *(coll.)* du kannst nur profitieren *od.* gewinnen; **b)** *(become slow)* ⟨*Uhr:*⟩ nachgehen

~ 'out *v. i.* verdrängt werden **(to** von)

loser ['lu:zə(r)] *n.* Verlierer, *der*/Verliererin, *die; (failure)* Versager, *der*/Versagerin, *die;* **we'd be the ~s by it** wir wären dabei die Dummen *(ugs.)*

loss [lɒs] *n.* **a)** *(process)* Verlust, *der* **(of** *Gen.*); **b)** *in sing. or pl. (what is lost)* Verlust, *der;* **sell at a ~:** mit Verlust verkaufen; *see also* **cut 1k**; **c)** *(state)* Verlust, *der;* **be a great/no ~ to sb.** für jmdn. ein großer *od.* schwerer/kein Verlust sein; **d) be at a ~:** nicht [mehr] weiterwissen; **be at a ~ what to do** nicht wissen, was zu tun ist; **be at a ~ [how] to do sth.** nicht wissen, wie man etwas machen soll; **be at a ~ to understand sth.** etw. nicht verstehen können; **be at a ~ for words/an answer** um Worte/eine Antwort verlegen sein. *See also* **dead loss**; **life a**; **profit 1a**

'loss-leader *n. (Commerc.)* [unter dem Selbstkostenpreis angebotener] Lockartikel

lost [lɒst] *adj.* **a)** *(perished)* verloren; ausgestorben ⟨*Kunst[fertigkeit]*⟩; **b)** *(astray)* verloren; vermißt ⟨*Person*⟩; **get ~:** sich verlaufen *od.* verirren/verfahren; **get ~!** *(sl.)* verdufte! *(salopp);* **he can get ~!** *(sl.)* er soll verduften! *(salopp);* **I'm ~** *(fig.)* ich verstehe gar nichts mehr; **feel ~ without sb./sth.** *(fig.)* sich *(Dat.)* ohne jmdn./etw. hilflos vorkommen; **~ generation** verlorene Generation; Lost generation, *die (Literaturw.);* **c)** *(wasted)* vertan ⟨*Zeit, Gelegenheit*⟩; verschwendet ⟨*Zeit, Mühe*⟩; verpaßt, versäumt ⟨*Gelegenheit*⟩; **d)** *(not won)* verloren; aussichtslos ⟨*Sache*⟩; *see also* **all 2d**; **cause 1d**; **e) ~ in admiration** überwältigt; **be ~ to sb.** für jmdn. verloren sein; **be ~ [up]on sb.** *(unrecognized by)* bei jmdm. keine Anerkennung finden; von jmdm. nicht gewürdigt werden; **sarcasm was ~ on him** mit Sarkasmus konnte er nichts anfangen; **be ~ to all sense of duty** jedes Pflichtgefühl vermissen lassen. *See also* **lose**; **property a**

lot [lɒt] *n.* **a)** *(method of choosing)* Los, *das;* **by ~:** durch das Los; **b)** *(destiny)* Los, *das;* **fall to the ~ of sb.** jmdm. bestimmt sein; **c)** *(item to be auctioned)* Posten, *der;* **bad ~** *(fig.: disreputable person)* üble Person; **d)** *(set of persons)* Haufen, *der;* **the ~:** [sie] alle; **'our/'your/'their ~** *(coll.)* wir/ihr/die; **not an honest man among the '~ [of them]** kein einziger anständiger Kerl in dem ganzen Haufen; **I'm bored with the '~ of you** *or* **with 'you ~:** ihr langweilt mich alle; **e)** *(set of things)* Menge, *die;* **we received a new ~ of hats** wir haben eine neue Sendung Hüte erhalten; **divide sth. into five ~s** etw. in fünf Stapel/Haufen *usw.* teilen; **the ~** *(whole set)* alle/alles; **that's the ~** *(coll.)* das ist alles; das wär's *(ugs.);* **'that little ~** *(coll. iron.)* diese Kleinigkeit; **f)** *(coll.: large number or quantity)* **~s** *or* **a ~ of money** *etc.* viel *od.* eine Menge Geld *usw.*; **~s of books/coins** eine Menge Bücher/Münzen; **he has a ~ to learn** er muß noch viel lernen; **I have a ~ to be thankful for** ich muß für vieles dankbar sein; **have ~s to do** viel zu tun haben; **we have ~s of time** wir haben viel *od.* *(ugs.)* massenweise Zeit; **sing** *etc.* **a ~:** viel singen *usw.*; **~s** *or* **a ~ better** viel besser; **not a ~ better** nicht viel besser; **like sth. a ~:** etw. sehr mögen; **Did you like it? – Not a ~:** Hat es dir gefallen? – Nicht sehr; **g)** *(for choosing)* Los, *das;* **draw/cast/throw ~s [for sth.]** das Los [über etw. *(Akk.)*] entscheiden lassen; [um etw.] losen; **cast/throw in one's ~ with sb.** sich mit jmdm. zusammentun; **draw ~s to determine sth.** etw. durch das Los entscheiden ; **h)** *(plot of land)* Gelände, *das;* Platz, *der; (measured piece of land)* Parzelle, *die;* **building ~** *(Amer.)* Bauplatz, *der;* **across ~s** *(Amer.)* querfeldein

lotion ['ləʊʃn] *n.* Lotion, *die*

lottery ['lɒtərɪ] *n.* Lotterie, *die; (fig.)* Glücksspiel, *das*

lotto ['lɒtəʊ] *n., no pl.* Lotto, *das*

lotus ['ləʊtəs] *n. (Nymphaea)* Seerose, *die; (Nelumbo)* Lotusblume, *die*

'lotus position *n.* Lotussitz, *der*

loud [laʊd] **1.** *adj.* **a)** laut; schreiend ⟨*Reklame*⟩; lautstark ⟨*Protest, Kritik*⟩; **he was ~ in his praise/criticism of the government** er lobte die Regierung in höchsten Tönen/er äußerte scharfe Kritik an der Regierung; *see also* **pedal 1a**; **b)** *(conspicuous)* aufdringlich; laut, aufdringlich ⟨*Farbe, Muster usw.*⟩; grell, schreiend ⟨*Farbe*⟩. **2.** *adv.* laut; **laugh out ~:** laut auflachen; **laugh ~ and long** in lautes, anhaltendes Gelächter ausbrechen; **say sth. out ~:** etw. aussprechen; *(fig.)* etw. laut verkünden

loud hailer ['laʊd heɪlə(r)] *n.* Megaphon, *das;* Flüstertüte, *die (ugs. scherzh.)*

loudly ['laʊdlɪ] *adv.* **a)** *(in a loud voice, clamorously)* laut; **he insisted ~ on his rights** er bestand entschieden auf seinen Rechten; **b)** *(flashily)* aufdringlich

loud: ~-mouth *n.* Großmaul, *das;* **~-mouthed** ['laʊdmaʊðd] *adj.* großmäulig *(ugs. abwertend);* großsprecherisch *(abwertend)*

loudness ['laʊdnɪs] *n., no pl.* Lautstärke, *die; (flashiness)* Aufdringlichkeit, *die*

loud'speaker *n.* Lautsprecher, *der*

lough [lɒx, lɒk] *n. (Ir.)* See, der

lounge [laʊndʒ] **1.** *v. i.* **~ [about** *or* **around]** [faul] herumliegen/-sitzen/-stehen; [faul] herumhängen *(ugs.); (in chair etc.)* sich lümmeln *(ugs.).* **2.** *n.* **a)** *(public room)* Lounge, *die; (in hotel)* Lounge, *die;* [Hotel]halle, *die; (at station)* Wartesaal, *der; (in theatre)* Foyer, *das; (at airport)* Lounge, *die;* Wartehalle, *die;* **b)** *(sitting-room)* Wohnzimmer, *das;* **c)** *(Brit.: bar)* **~ [bar]** *see* **saloon bar**

lounger ['laʊndʒə(r)] *n.* **a)** Nichtstuer, *der;* **b)** *(sun-bed)* Liege, *die*

'lounge suit *n. (Brit.)* Straßenanzug, *der*

lour ['laʊə(r)] *v. i.* mißmutig [drein]blicken; ein finsteres Gesicht machen; *(fig.)* ⟨*Wolken, Gewitter:*⟩ sich [bedrohlich] zusammenziehen; ⟨*Himmel:*⟩ sich [bedrohlich] verfinstern

louse [laʊs] **1.** *n.* **a)** *pl.* **lice** [laɪs] Laus, *die;* **b)** *pl.* **~s** *(sl.: person)* Ratte, *die (derb).* **2.** *v. t.* **~ up** *(sl.)* vermasseln *(salopp)*

lousy ['laʊzɪ] *adj.* **a)** *(infested)* verlaust; **be ~ with money** *(coll.)* im Geld schwimmen *(ugs.);* lausig viel Geld haben *(ugs.);* **places ~ with foreigners** von Ausländern wimmelnde Orte; **b)** *(sl.) (disgusting)* ekelhaft; widerlich; *(very poor)* lausig *(ugs.);* mies *(ugs.);* **feel ~:** sich mies *(ugs.)* od. miserabel fühlen; **men are ~ at housework** Männer stellen sich bei der Hausarbeit miserabel an

lout [laʊt] *n.* Rüpel, *der;* Flegel, *der; (bumpkin)* Tolpatsch, *der (ugs.);* Tölpel, *der*

loutish ['laʊtɪʃ] *adj.* rüpelhaft; flegelhaft

louver, louvre ['lu:və(r)] *n.* **a)** *(roof-turret)* Laterne, *die (Bauw.);* **b)** *(slat)* Jalousiebrettchen, *das;* **~ door** Jalousietür, *die;* **~ window** Jalousiefenster, *das;* **c)** *in pl. (blind)* Jalousie, *die; (for cooling engine etc.)* Lüftungslamellen

lovable ['lʌvəbl] *adj.* liebenswert

love [lʌv] **1.** *n.* **a)** *(affection, sexual ~)* Liebe, *die* (for zu); ~ **is blind** *(prov.)* die Liebe ist blind; ~**'s young dream** junges Liebesglück; **in ~ [with]** verliebt [in (+ *Akk.*)]; **fall in ~ [with]** sich verlieben [in (+ *Akk.*)]; **be/fall out of ~ with sb.** jmdn. nicht mehr lieben; **be/fall out of ~ with sth.** einer Sache *(Gen.)* überdrüssig sein/etw. nicht mehr mögen; **make ~ to sb.** *(court)* um jmdn. werben; jmdm. den Hof machen *(veralt., noch scherzh.)*; *(have sex)* mit jmdm. schlafen; jmdn. lieben; **they made ~**: sie schliefen miteinander; sie liebten sich; **for ~**: aus Liebe; *(free)* unentgeltlich; umsonst; *(for pleasure)* aus Spaß an der Freude *(ugs.)*; nur zum Vergnügen *od.* Spaß; **not for ~ or money** um nichts in der Welt; **[Happy Christmas,] ~ from Beth** [fröhliche Weihnachten und] herzliche Grüße von Beth; **give my ~ to her** grüß sie von mir; **send one's ~ to sb.** jmdn. grüßen lassen; **Peter sends [you] his ~**: Peter läßt [dich] grüßen; **there is no ~ lost between them** sie sind sich *(Dat.)* nicht grün *(ugs.)*; **sb.'s life and ~s** jmds. Lebens- und Liebesgeschichte; see also ²**fair 1 a**; **b)** *(devotion)* Liebe, *die* (of, for, to[wards] zu); ~ **of life/eating/learning** Freude am Leben/Essen/Lernen; **for [the] ~ of sb.** jmdm. zu Liebe; um jmds. willen; **for the ~ of God** um Gottes willen; *see also* **Mike**; **c)** *(sweetheart)* Geliebte, *der/die;* Liebste, *der/die (veraltet)*; **[my] ~** *(coll.: form of address)* [mein] Liebling *od.* Schatz; *(to sb. less close)* mein Lieber/meine Liebe; **sth. is sb.'s first ~**: etw. ist jmds. größte Leidenschaft; **can I help you, ~?** *(in shop)* was darf's denn sein?; **d)** *(Tennis)* **fifteen/thirty ~**: fünfzehn/dreißig null; **win the set six games to ~**: den Satz mit sechs zu null Spielen gewinnen; ~ **all** null beide; ~ **game/victory** *etc.* Zu-null-Spiel, *das*/-Sieg, *der usw.* **2.** *v. t.* **a)** lieben; **our/their ~d ones** unsere/ihre Lieben; **b)** *(like)* **I'd ~ a cigarette** ich hätte sehr gerne eine Zigarette; ~ **to do** *or* **doing sth.** etw. [leidenschaftlich] gern tun. **3.** *v. i.* lieben

love: ~ **affair** *n.* [Liebes]verhältnis, *das;* Liebschaft, *die;* ~**-bird** *n. (Ornith.)* Unzertrennliche, *der; (fig.)* Turteltaube, *die (ugs. scherzh.)*; ~**-child** *n. (euphem.)* Kind der Liebe *(geh. verhüll.)*; uneheliches Kind; ~**-'hate** *adj.* von Haßliebe geprägt; ~**-hate relationship** Haßliebe, *die;* ~**-in-a-'mist** *n. (Bot.)* Jungfer im Grünen; Gretel im Busch; ~**-knot** *see* **true-love knot**

loveless ['lʌvlɪs] *adj.* **a)** *(unloving)* lieblos; hart; **b)** *(unloved)* ohne Liebe *nachgestellt*

love: ~**-letter** *n.* Liebesbrief, *der;* ~**-lies-'bleeding** *n. (Bot.)* Fuchsschwanz, *der;* ~**-life** *n.* Liebesleben, *das*

loveliness ['lʌvlɪnɪs] *n., no pl.* Schönheit, *die*

lovelorn ['lʌvlɔːn] *adj.* liebeskrank *(geh.)*

lovely ['lʌvlɪ] **1.** *adj.* **a)** [wunder]schön; herrlich ⟨*Tag, Essen*⟩; **b)** *(lovable)* liebenswert; **c)** *(coll.: delightful)* toll *(ugs.)*; wunderbar; ~ **and warm/cool** *etc. (coll.)* schön warm/kühl *usw.* **2.** *n.* Schönheit, *die;* Schöne, *die*

love: ~**-making** *n.* **a)** *(courtship)* Liebeswerben, *das (geh.)*; **b)** *(sexual intercourse)* körperliche Liebe; ~**-match** *n.* Liebesheirat, *die;* ~**-nest** *n.* Liebesnest, *das;* ~ **potion** *n.* Liebestrank, *der*

lover ['lʌvə(r)] *n.* **a)** Liebhaber, *der;* Geliebte, *der; (woman)* Geliebte, *die;* **be ~s** ein Liebespaar sein; ~**'s knot** *see* **true-love knot**; **b)** *(person devoted to sth.)* Liebhaber, *der*/Liebhaberin, *die;* Freund, *der*/Freundin, *die;* ~ **of the arts** Kunstliebhaber, *der*/-liebhaberin, *die;* Kunstfreund, *der*/-freundin, *die;* **dog-~** Hundefreund, *der*/-freundin, *die*

love: ~**sick** *adj.* an Liebeskummer leidend; liebeskrank *(geh.)*; **be ~sick** Liebeskummer haben; liebeskrank sein *(geh.)*; ~**-song** *n.* Liebeslied, *das;* ~**-story** *n.* Liebesgeschichte, *die;* ~**-token** *n.* Liebespfand, *das*

lovey ['lʌvɪ] *n. (coll.) usu. as form of address* Liebling, *der;* Schatz, *der*

lovey-dovey [lʌvɪ'dʌvɪ] *adj.* **be ~**: den Verliebten/die Verliebte spielen *(ugs.)*; **be ~ with sb.** jmdn. umschmeicheln

loving *adj.* **a)** *(affectionate)* liebend; **b)** *(expressing love)* liebevoll; **your ~ father** *(in letter)* Dein Dich liebender Vater; in Liebe Dein Vater

loving: ~**-cup** *n.* Pokal, *der;* ~**-'kindness** *n.* Güte, *die*

lovingly ['lʌvɪŋlɪ] *adv.* liebevoll; *(painstakingly)* mit viel Liebe

¹**low** [ləʊ] **1.** *adj.* **a)** *(not reaching far up)* niedrig; niedrig, flach ⟨*Absätze, Stirn*⟩; flach ⟨*Relief*⟩; gering ⟨*Körpergröße*⟩; **b)** *(below normal level)* niedrig; tief ⟨*Flug*⟩; flach ⟨*Welle*⟩; tief ausgeschnitten ⟨*Kleid*⟩; tief ⟨*Ausschnitt*⟩; **c)** *(not elevated)* tiefliegend ⟨*Wiese, Grund, Land*⟩; tiefhängend ⟨*Wolke*⟩; tiefstehend ⟨*Gestirne*⟩; tief ⟨*Verbeugung*⟩; **the river/water is ~**: der Fluß/das Wasser ist niedrig; **the sun/moon is ~**: die Sonne/der Mond steht tief; **d)** *(of humble rank)* nieder...; niedrig; *see also* **high 1 e**; **e)** *(inferior)* niedrig; gering ⟨*Intelligenz, Bildung*⟩; gewöhnlich ⟨*Geschmack*⟩; *(vulgar)* gewöhnlich; **f)** *(not fair)* gemein; **g)** *(Cards)* niedrig; **h)** *(small in degree)* niedrig; gering ⟨*Sichtweite, Wert*⟩; leicht ⟨*Fieber*⟩; **be ~ in iodine** einen geringen Jodgehalt aufweisen; **have a ~ opinion of sb./sth.** von jmdm./etw. keine hohe Meinung haben; **temperatures will be in the ~ forties** die Temperaturen werden knapp über 40° [Fahrenheit] liegen; *see also* **common denominator**; **i)** *(in pitch)* tief ⟨*Ton, Stimme, Lage, Klang*⟩; *(in loudness)* leise ⟨*Ton, Stimme*⟩; **j)** *(Ling.) see* **open 1 m**; **k)** *(weak)* schwach; ~ **vitality** Kraftlosigkeit, *die;* **he is very ~** *(physically)* er ist sehr geschwächt; *(emotionally)* er ist sehr niedergeschlagen; **in a ~ state of mind** niedergeschlagen; in gedrückter Stimmung; **l)** *(nearly gone)* fast verbraucht *od.* aufgebraucht; **run ~**: allmählich ausgehen *od.* zu Ende gehen; **we are ~/getting ~ on petrol** wir haben nur noch wenig/bald kein Benzin mehr; **the bottle is getting ~**: die Flasche geht allmählich zu Ende *od.* ist bald leer; **m)** *(Geog.)* ~ **latitudes** niedere Breiten. *See also* ¹**lower 1.** **2.** *adv.* **a)** *(in or to a ~ position)* tief; niedrig, tief ⟨*hängen*⟩; **that comes ~ on my list of priorities** das hat für mich keine hohe Priorität; *see also* **high 2 a**; **b)** *(to a ~ level)* **prices have gone too ~**: die Preise sind zu weit gefallen; **if the temperature drops any ~er** wenn die Temperatur weiter sinkt; **c)** *(not loudly)* leise; **d)** *(at ~ pitch)* tief; **e) lay sb. ~** *(prostrate)* jmdn. niederstrecken *(geh.)*; *(confine to sick-bed)* jmdn. aufs Krankenlager werfen *(geh.)*; **lie ~**: am Boden liegen; *(hide)* untertauchen. *See also* **bring a**; ²**lower 2.** **3.** *n.* **a)** *(Meteorol.)* Tief, *das;* **b) hit** *or* **reach a new/an all-time ~**: einen neuen/absoluten Tiefststand erreichen

²**low** *v. i.* ⟨*Kuh:*⟩ muhen

low: ~**brow** *(coll.)* **1.** *n.* Nichtintellektuelle, *der/die;* **2.** *adj.* schlicht ⟨*Person*⟩; [geistig] anspruchslos ⟨*Buch, Programm*⟩; **Low 'Church** *n.* Low Church, *die;* ~**-class** *adj. (Brit.) (of ~ quality)* drittklassig; *(of ~ social class)* Unterschicht[s]-; ~ **'comedy** *n.* Schwank, *der;* Posse, *die;* ~**-cost** *adj.* preisgünstig; **Low Countries** *pr. n. pl. (Hist.)* Niederlande *Pl.;* ~**-cut** *adj.* [tief] ausgeschnitten ⟨*Kleid*⟩; ~**-cut neck** tiefer Ausschnitt; ~**-cut shoes** Halbschuhe; ~**-down 1.** *adj. (coll.: mean)* mies *(ugs.)*; **2.** *n. (coll.)* **give [sb.]/get the ~-down on sb./sth.** [jmdm.] sagen/rauskriegen, was es mit jmdm./etw. [wirklich] auf sich hat

¹**lower** ['ləʊə(r)] **1.** *v. t.* **a)** *(let down)* herab-/hinablassen; zu Wasser lassen ⟨*Boot*⟩; einholen ⟨*Flagge, Segel*⟩; ~ **oneself into** hinuntersteigen in (+ *Akk.*) ⟨*Kanalschacht, Keller*⟩; ~ **oneself into a chair** sich in einen Sessel sinken lassen; *abs.* ~ **[away]** *(Naut.)* (~ *boat)* das Boot aussetzen *od.* zu Wasser lassen; (~ *sail)* das Segel einholen; **b)** *(reduce in height)* senken ⟨*Blick*⟩; niederschlagen ⟨*Augen*⟩; niedriger machen ⟨*Wand*⟩; absenken ⟨*Zimmerdecke*⟩; tiefer hängen ⟨*Bild*⟩; auslassen ⟨*Saum*⟩; *see also* **sight 1 h**; **c)** *(lessen)* senken ⟨*Preis, Miete, Zins usw.*⟩; **d)** *(degrade)* herabsetzen; verderben ⟨*Geschmack*⟩; ~ **oneself** sich erniedrigen; ~ **oneself to do sth.** sich so weit erniedrigen, etw. zu tun; **e)** *(weaken)* schwächen; dämpfen ⟨*Licht, Stimme, Lärm*⟩; ~ **one's voice** leiser sprechen; die Stimme senken *(geh.)*. **2.** *v. i.* **a)** *(weaken)* ⟨*Stimme:*⟩ leiser werden; ⟨*Licht:*⟩ dunkler werden; **b)** *(sink)* sinken; ⟨*Wasservorrat:*⟩ weniger werden, abnehmen

²**lower 1.** *compar. adj.* **a)** unter... ⟨*Nil, Themse usw., Atmosphäre*⟩; Unter⟨*jura, -devon usw., -arm, -lippe usw.*⟩; Nieder⟨*rhein, -kalifornien*⟩; *see also* **jaw 1 a**; **b)** *(in rank)* unter...; ~ **mammals/plants** niedere Säugetiere/Pflanzen; **the ~ orders/classes** die Unterschichten/die unteren Klassen; ~ **middle class** untere Mittelschicht. **2.** *compar. adv.* tiefer ⟨*sinken, hängen usw.*⟩

³**lower** ['laʊə(r)] *see* **lour**

lower: ~ **case 1.** *n.* Kleinbuchstaben *Pl.;* **in ~ case** in Kleinbuchstaben; **2.** *adj.* klein ⟨*Buchstabe*⟩; **L~ 'Chamber** *n. (Parl.)* Unterhaus, *das;* ~ **court** *n.* unteres *od.* untergeordnetes Gericht; ~ **'deck** *n.* **a)** *(of ship)* Unterdeck, *das; (of bus)* unteres Deck; **b)** *(Brit.: seamen)* Mannschaft, *die;* **L~ House** *n. (Parl.)* Unterhaus, *das;* ~**most** *adj.* unterst...; **be ~most** zuunterst liegen; ~ **'regions** *n. pl. (Mythol.)* Unterwelt, *die;* **L~ 'Saxon** *adj.* niedersächsisch; **L~ 'Saxony** *pr. n.* Niedersachsen *(das);* ~ **'world** *n.* **a)** *(the earth)* Erde, *die;* **b)** *(hell)* Unterwelt, *die*

low: ~**-fat** *adj.* fettarm; ~**-flying** *adj.* tief fliegend; ~**-flying aircraft** Tiefflieger, *der;* ~ **'frequency** *n.* Niederfrequenz, *die;* ~**-frequency** *adj.* niederfrequent; **Low 'German** *see* **German 2 b**; ~**-grade** *adj.* minderwertig; leicht ⟨*Infektion*⟩; ~**-grade steel** Stahl minderer Güte; ~**-heeled** *adj.* flach ⟨*Schuh*⟩; ⟨*Schuhe*⟩ mit flachen Absätzen; ~**-key** *adj.* zurückhaltend; unaufdringlich ⟨*Beleuchtung, Unterhaltung*⟩; unauffällig ⟨*Einsatz*⟩; ~**land** ['ləʊlənd] **1.** *n.* Tiefland, *das;* **the Lowlands of Scotland** die Lowlands; das schottische Tiefland; **2.** *adj.* tiefländisch; Tiefland⟨*rasse, -farm*⟩; ~**lander** ['ləʊləndə(r)] *n.* Tieflandbewohner, *der*/-bewohnerin, *die; (Scot.)* Bewohner/Bewohnerin der Lowlands

lowly ['ləʊlɪ] *adj.* **a)** *(modest)* bescheiden; **b)** *(not highly evolved)* nieder...

low: ~**-lying** *adj.* tiefliegend; ~**-necked** *adj.* [tief] ausgeschnitten; ~**-'pitched** *adj.* **a)** tief ⟨*Stimme*⟩; **b)** *(Archit.)* wenig geneigt ⟨*Dach*⟩; ~ **point** *n.* Tiefpunkt, *der;* ~**-powered** ['ləʊpaʊəd] *adj.* schwach ⟨*Motor, Glühbirne*⟩; ~ **'pressure** Tiefdruck, *der;* **an area of ~ pressure** ein Tiefdruckgebiet; ~**-priced** [ləʊ'praɪst] *adj.* preisgünstig; ~ **'profile** *see* **profile 1 g**; ~ **re'lief** *see* ²**relief a**; ~**-rise** *adj.* ⟨*Gebäude*⟩ mit wenigen Stockwerken; ~ **season** *n.* Nebensaison, *die;* ~**-'spirited** *adj.* niedergeschlagen; ~ **'tension** = ~ **voltage** *see* **voltage**; ~**-tension** *see* ~**-voltage**; ~ **'tide** *see* **tide 1 a**; ~ **'voltage** *see* **voltage**; ~**-voltage** *adj. (Electr.)* Niederspannungs-; ~**-wage** *attrib. adj.* schlechtbezahlt; ~ **'water** *n.* Niedrigwasser, *das; (fig.)* Tiefpunkt, *der;* ~**-'water mark** *n.* Niedrigwassermarke, *die*

loyal ['lɔɪəl] *adj. (to person)* treu; *(to government etc.)* treu [ergeben]; loyal; ~ **address** Ergebenheitsadresse, *die*
loyalist ['lɔɪəlɪst] **1.** *n.* Loyalist, *der*/Loyalistin, *die.* **2.** *adj.* loyalistisch
loyally ['lɔɪəlɪ] *adv.* treu; loyal
loyalty ['lɔɪəltɪ] *n.* Treue, *die;* Loyalität, *die;* **brand ~:** Markentreue, *die*
lozenge ['lɒzɪndʒ] *n.* **a)** *(tablet)* Pastille, *die;* **b)** *(diamond shape)* Raute, *die;* Rhombus, *der*
LP *abbr.* **long-playing record** LP, *die*
'L-plate *n. (Brit.)* 'L'-Schild, *das;* ≈ „Fahrschule"-Schild, *das*
LSD *abbr.* **lysergic acid diethylamide** LSD, *das*
LSE *abbr.* **London School of Economics**
Lt. *abbr.* **Lieutenant**
Ltd. *abbr.* **Limited** GmbH; ... **Company ~:** ...gesellschaft mbH
lubricant ['lu:brɪkənt] **1.** *n.* Schmiermittel, *das.* **2.** *adj.* Schmier-
lubricate ['lu:brɪkeɪt] *v.t.* schmieren; einfetten ⟨*Haut*⟩
lubrication [lu:brɪ'keɪʃn] *n.* Schmierung, *die; attrib.* Schmier⟨*system, -vorrichtung*⟩
Lucerne [lu:'sɜ:n] *pr. n.* Luzern *(das);* **Lake ~:** der Vierwaldstätter See
lucerne *n. (Brit. Bot.)* [Blaue] Luzerne
lucid ['lu:sɪd] *adj.* klar; [leicht] verständlich; einleuchtend ⟨*Argumentation*⟩; ~ **interval** *(period of sanity)* lichter Augenblick *od.* Moment
lucidity [lu:'sɪdɪtɪ] *n., no pl.* Klarheit, *die*
lucidly ['lu:sɪdlɪ] *adv.* klar [und verständlich] ⟨*formulieren usw.*⟩
luck [lʌk] *n.* **a)** *(good or ill fortune)* Schicksal, *das;* **as ~ would have it** wie das Schicksal es wollte; **good ~:** Glück, *das;* **bad ~:** Pech, *das;* **bring [sb.] good/bad ~:** [jmdm.] Glück/Pech bringen; **better ~ next time** mehr Glück beim nächsten Mal; **good ~ [to you]!** viel Glück!; alles Gute!; viel Erfolg!; **good ~ to him, I say** ich wünsche ihm viel Glück; *(iron.)* na, dann viel Glück!; **it's the ~ of the game** Glück/Pech gehabt!; **just my ~:** typisch für mich; **try one's ~:** sein Glück versuchen; **you never know your ~:** vielleicht hast du ja Glück; *see also* **³down 1 mm; draw 3 a; hard 1 c; push 1 c; worse 1; b)** *(good fortune)* Glück, *das;* **with [any] ~:** mit ein bißchen *od.* etwas Glück; ~ **was with us all the way** wir hatten die ganze Zeit Glück; **I was in ~'s way** das war wirklich Glück; **wear sth. for ~:** etw. als Glücksbringer tragen; **do sth. for ~:** etw. tun, damit es einem Glück bringen soll; **have the ~ to do sth.** das Glück haben, etw. zu tun; **be in/out of ~:** Glück/kein Glück haben; **sb.'s ~ is in/out** jmd. hat Glück/kein Glück; **no such ~:** schön wär's; *see also* **¹stroke 1 c**
luckily ['lʌkɪlɪ] *adv.* glücklicherweise; ~ **for her** zu ihrem Glück
luckless ['lʌklɪs] *adj.* glücklos; *(unlucky, unfortunate)* unglücklich
lucky ['lʌkɪ] *adj.* **a)** *(favoured by chance)* glücklich; **be ~ [in love/at games]** Glück [in der Liebe/im Spiel] haben; **be ~ to be alive** von Glück sagen können, daß man noch am Leben ist; **be ~ enough to be rescued** das [große] Glück haben, gerettet zu werden; **I should be so ~:** schön wär's; **get ~:** Glück haben; **Could you lend me £100? – 'You'll be ~:** Könntest du mir 100 Pfund leihen? – So siehst du aus!; **it was ~ [for you/him *etc.*] the car stopped in time** dein/sein *usw.* Glück, daß das Auto rechtzeitig gehalten hat; **be a ~ dog** ein Glückspilz sein *(ugs.);* **b)** *(favouring sb. by chance)* glücklich ⟨*Umstand, Zufall, Zusammentreffen usw.*⟩; *see also* **escape 1 a; c)** *(bringing good luck)* Glücks⟨*zahl, -tag usw.*⟩; ~ **charm** Glücksbringer, *der;* **be born under a ~ star** ein Glückskind sein; **you can thank your ~ stars** du kannst von Glück sagen
lucky: ~ bag, *(Brit.)* **~ 'dip** *ns.* Glückstopf, *der; (fig.)* Glücksspiel, *das*
lucrative ['lu:krətɪv] *adj.* einträglich; lukrativ
lucre ['lu:kə(r)] *n. (derog.)* Profit, *der; see also* **filthy 1 b**
Luddite ['lʌdaɪt] *n.* **a)** Maschinenstürmer, *der;* **b)** *(Hist.)* Luddit, *der*
ludicrous ['lu:dɪkrəs] *adj.* lächerlich ⟨*Anblick, Lohn, Argument, Vorschlag, Idee*⟩; lachhaft ⟨*Angebot, Ausrede*⟩; **a ~ speed/price** *(low)* eine lächerliche Geschwindigkeit/ein lächerlicher Preis; *(high)* eine haarsträubende Geschwindigkeit/ein haarsträubender Preis
ludicrously ['lu:dɪkrəslɪ] *adv.* lächerlich ⟨*wenig, billig, langsam, klein*⟩; haarsträubend ⟨*schnell, teuer*⟩
ludo ['lu:dəʊ] *n., no pl., no art.* Mensch-ärgere-dich-nicht[-Spiel], *das*
luff [lʌf] *(Naut.)* **1.** *v.t.* **a)** *(bring nearer wind)* luven ⟨*Schiff*⟩; **b)** *(turn)* ~ **the helm** anluven; **c)** *(Yacht-racing)* durch Luven den Wind nehmen (+ *Dat.*). **2.** *v.i.* anluven. **3.** *n.* Vorliek, *das*
¹lug [lʌg] **1.** *v.t.,* **-gg- a)** *(drag)* schleppen; **b)** *(force)* ~ **sb. along** jmdn. mit herumschleppen *(ugs.).* **2.** *v.i.,* **-gg-** ziehen, zerren **(at** an + *Dat.*)
²lug *see* **lugworm**
³lug *n.* **a)** *(projection)* Henkel, *der;* **b)** *(coll./joc.: ear)* Löffel, *der (ugs.)*
luge [lu:ʒ] *n.* [Rodel]schlitten, *der*
luggage ['lʌgɪdʒ] *n.* Gepäck, *das*
luggage: ~-carrier *n.* Gepäckträger, *der;* **~-locker** *n.* [Gepäck]schließfach, *das;* **~-rack** *n.* Gepäckablage, *die;* **~ trolley** *n.* Kofferkuli, *der;* **~-van** *n.* Gepäckwagen, *der*
lugger ['lʌgə(r)] *n. (Naut.)* Logger, *der*
'lughole *n. (sl.: ear)* Löffel, *der (ugs.)*
lugubrious [lu:'gu:brɪəs, lʊ'gu:brɪəs] *adj.* *(mournful)* kummervoll; traurig; *(dismal)* düster; trübselig
lugubriously [lu:'gu:brɪəslɪ, lʊ'gu:brɪəslɪ] *adv.* *(mournfully)* kummervoll; traurig; *(dismally)* düster
'lugworm *n.* Köderwurm, *der*
Luke [lu:k] *pr. n.* **St ~:** der hl. Lukas
lukewarm ['lu:kwɔ:m, lu:k'wɔ:m] *adj.* **a)** lauwarm; **b)** *(fig.)* lau[warm]; halbherzig
lull [lʌl] **1.** *v.t.* **a)** *(soothe)* lullen; ~ **a child to sleep** ein Kind in den Schlaf lullen; **b)** *(fig.)* einlullen; einschläfern ⟨*Mißtrauen*⟩; ~ **sb. into a false sense of security** jmdn. in einer trügerischen Sicherheit wiegen. **2.** *n.* Pause, *die;* **the ~ before the storm** *(fig.)* die Ruhe vor dem Sturm; **a ~ in the storm** ein vorübergehendes *od.* kurzes Nachlassen des Sturms
lullaby ['lʌləbaɪ] *n.* Schlaflied, *das;* Wiegenlied, *das*
lulu ['lu:lu:] *n. (sl.) (thing)* Hammer, *der (salopp); (person)* bombige Type *(ugs.)*
lumbago [lʌm'beɪgəʊ] *n., pl.* **~s** *(Med.)* Hexenschuß, *der;* Lumbago, *die (fachspr.)*
lumbar ['lʌmbə(r)] *adj. (Anat.)* Lenden-; lumbal *(fachspr.);* ~ **puncture** *(Med.)* Lumbalpunktion, *die*
¹lumber ['lʌmbə(r)] *v.i.* ⟨*Person:*⟩ schwerfällig gehen; ⟨*Fahrzeug:*⟩ rumpeln
²lumber 1. *n.* **a)** *(furniture)* Gerümpel, *das;* **b)** *(useless material)* Kram, *der (ugs. abwertend);* Krempel, *der (ugs. abwertend);* **c)** *(Amer.: timber)* [Bau]holz, *das.* **2.** *v.t.* *(fill up, encumber)* vollstopfen *(ugs.);* vollstellen ⟨*Zimmer*⟩; überladen ⟨*Stil, Buch*⟩; ~ **sb. with sth./sb.** jmdm. etw./jmdn. aufhalsen *(ugs.);* **get ~ed with sth./sb.** etw./jmdn. aufgehalst kriegen *(ugs.);* ~ **oneself with too many things** *(lit. or fig.)* sich *(Dat.)* zuviel Krempel *(ugs.)* anschaffen
lumbering ['lʌmbərɪŋ] *adj.* schwerfällig; *(graceless in appearance)* plump
lumber: ~-jack *n. (Amer.)* Holzfäller, *der;* **~-jacket** *n.* Lumberjack, *der;* **~-man** *see* **~-jack; ~-room** *n.* Abstellkammer, *die;* Rumpelkammer, *die (ugs.)*
luminary ['lu:mɪnərɪ] *n. (person)* Koryphäe, *die*
luminescence [lu:mɪ'nesəns] *n.* Leuchten, *das; (Phys.)* Lumineszenz, *die*
luminescent [lu:mɪ'nesənt] *adj.* leuchtend; *(Phys.)* lumineszierend
luminosity [lu:mɪ'nɒsɪtɪ] *n. (also Astron.)* Helligkeit, *die*
luminous ['lu:mɪnəs] *adj.* **a)** *(bright)* hell ⟨*Feuer, Licht usw.*⟩; [hell] leuchtend; Leucht⟨*anzeige, -zeiger usw.*⟩; ~ **paint** Leuchtfarbe, *die;* **b)** *(of light)* Leucht⟨*kraft, -stärke usw.*⟩; **c)** *(fig.)* brillant; *(enlightening)* erhellend
lummee ['lʌmɪ] *int. (Brit. sl.)* großer Gott
lummox ['lʌməks] *n. (Amer. coll.)* Tölpel, *der;* Tolpatsch, *der (ugs.)*
¹lump [lʌmp] **1.** *n.* **a)** *(shapeless mass)* Klumpen, *der; (of sugar, butter, etc.)* Stück, *das; (of wood)* Klotz, *der; (of dough)* Kloß, *der; (of bread)* Brocken, *der;* **a ~ of sugar/dough/bread** ein Stück Zucker/ein Teigkloß/ein Brocken Brot; **a ~ of wood/clay** ein Holzklotz/ein Klumpen Lehm *od.* Lehmklumpen; **have/get a ~ in one's throat** *(fig.)* einen Kloß im Hals haben *(ugs.);* **b)** *(swelling)* Beule, *die; (caused by cancer)* Knoten, *der;* **c)** *(sl.: heap)* Haufen, *der;* **d)** *(thickset person)* Klotz, *der (ugs.);* **a great ~ of a woman** ein Koloß von Frau; **e) the ~** *(Brit.: workers)* die Schwarzarbeiter im Baugewerbe; **f) [taken] in the ~:** im ganzen [gesehen]; **get payment in a ~:** die gesamte Summe auf einmal erhalten. **2.** *v.t.* *(mass together)* zusammentun; ~ **sth. with sth.** etw. und etw. zusammentun; ~ **sb./sth. with the rest** jmdn./etw. mit dem Rest in einen Topf werfen *(ugs.);* ~ **the archaeology books under History** die Archäologiebücher mit zur Geschichte stellen
~ **to'gether** *v.t.* zusammenfassen
²lump *v.t. (coll.)* sich abfinden mit; **he can [like it or] ~ it** er muß sich [wohl oder übel] damit abfinden; **if you don't like it you can ~ it** du mußt dich wohl oder übel damit abfinden
lumpenproletariat ['lʌmpənprəʊləteərɪət] *n. (derog.)* Lumpenproletariat, *das*
lumpish ['lʌmpɪʃ] *adj. (derog.)* **a)** *(clumsy)* plump; *(in movement, speech, action)* schwerfällig; **b)** *(dull)* dumpf; stumpf
lump: ~ payment *n.* einmalige Zahlung [einer größeren Summe]; **~-sucker** *n.* *(Zool.)* Scheibenbauch, *der;* Lumpfisch, *der; (Cyclopterus lumpus)* Seehase, *der;* ~ **'sugar** *n.* Würfelzucker, *der;* ~ **'sum** *n.* *(covering several items)* Pauschalsumme, *die; (paid at once)* einmalige Pauschale
lumpy ['lʌmpɪ] *adj.* klumpig ⟨*Brei, Lehm*⟩; ⟨*Kissen, Matratze*⟩ mit klumpiger Füllung
lunacy ['lu:nəsɪ] *n.* **a)** *(insanity)* Wahnsinn, *der; (Law)* geistige Unzurechnungsfähigkeit; **b)** *(mad folly)* Wahnsinn, *der (ugs.);* Irrsinn, *der*
lunar ['lu:nə(r)] *adj.* Mond-; lunar *(fachspr.)*
lunar: ~ e'clipse *n. (Astron.)* Mondfinsternis, *die;* ~ **'module** *n.* Mond[lande]fähre, *die*
lunatic ['lu:nətɪk] **1.** *adj.* **a)** *(mad)* wahnsinnig; irre *(veralt.); see also* **fringe 1 c; b)** *(foolish)* wahnwitzig; Wahnsinns- *(ugs.);* idiotisch *(ugs. abwertend).* **2.** *n.* Wahnsinnige, *der/die;* Irre, *der/die;* **be a ~:** wahnsinnig *od. (veralt.)* irre sein
'lunatic asylum *n. (Hist.)* Irrenanstalt, *die (veralt., ugs. abwertend)*
lunch [lʌnʃ] **1.** *n.* Mittagessen, *das;* **have** *or* **eat** *or (formal)* **take [one's] ~:** zu Mittag essen; das Mittagessen einnehmen *(geh.);* **get an hour for ~:** eine Stunde Mittag[spause] haben; **have sth. for ~:** etw. zu Mittag essen; **be at** *or* **eating** *or* **having [one's] ~:** gera-

de beim Mittagessen sein; zu Tisch sein; **there's no such thing as a free** ~ *(fig.)* es wird einem nichts geschenkt. **2.** *v. i.* zu Mittag essen

'lunch-break *see* **lunch-hour**

luncheon ['lʌnʃn] *n. (formal)* **a)** *(midday meal)* Mittagessen, *das;* **b)** *(Amer.: light meal)* Imbiß, *der*

luncheon: ~ **meat** *n.* Frühstücksfleisch, *das;* ~ **voucher** *n. (Brit.)* Essenmarke, *die;* Essensbon, *der*

lunch: ~**-hour** *n.* Mittagspause, *die;* ~**-room** *n.* Imbißraum, *der;* ~**-time** *n.* Mittagszeit, *die;* **at** ~**-time** mittags

lung [lʌŋ] *n.* Lunge, *die; (right or left)* Lungenflügel, *der;* **have good/weak** ~**s** eine gute *od.* kräftige/schwache Lunge haben; **the** ~**s of a city** *(fig.)* die grünen Lungen einer Stadt

'lung cancer *n. (Med.)* Lungenkrebs, *der*

lunge [lʌndʒ] **1.** *n.* **a)** *(Sport)* Ausfall, *der;* **b)** *(sudden forward movement)* Sprung nach vorn; **make a** ~ **at sb.** sich auf jmdn. stürzen. **2.** *v. i.* **a)** *(Sport)* einen Ausfall machen **(at** gegen); **b)** ~ **at sb. with a knife** jmdn. mit einem Messer angreifen

~ **'out** *v. i.* einen Ausfall machen **(at** gegen); ~ **out at sb.** *(make sudden forward movement)* sich auf jmdn. stürzen

lung: ~**-fish** *n.* Lungenfisch, *der;* ~**-power** *n.* Stimmkraft, *die*

lupin, [1]**lupine** ['lu:pɪn] *n.* [Edel]lupine, *die*

[2]**lupine** ['lu:paɪn, 'lju:paɪn] *adj.* Wolfs-; wölfisch; **have** ~ **features/a** ~ **appearance** ein Wolfsgesicht haben/wie ein Wolf aussehen

lupus ['lu:pəs] *n. (Med.)* Zehrflechte, *die;* Lupus, *der (fachspr.)*

[1]**lurch** [lɜ:tʃ] *n.* **leave sb. in the** ~: jmdn. im Stich lassen; jmdn. hängenlassen *(ugs.)*

[2]**lurch** **1.** *n.* Rucken, *das; (of ship)* Schlingern, *das;* **give a** ~: rucken; ⟨*Schiff:*⟩ schlingern. **2.** *v. i.* rucken; ⟨*Betrunkener:*⟩ torkeln; ⟨*Schiff:*⟩ schlingern

lurcher ['lɜ:tʃə(r)] *n. (Brit.) Kreuzung zwischen Collie und Windhund [besonders als Spürhund eines Wilderers];* ≈ Spürhund, *der*

lure [ljʊə(r), lʊə(r)] **1.** *v. t.* locken; ~ **away from/out of/into sth.** von etw. fortlocken/aus etw. [heraus]locken/in etw. *(Akk.)* [hinein]locken; ~ **sb. away from his duty** jmdn. [durch Lockungen] von seinen Pflichten abbringen. **2.** *n.* **a)** *(Falconry)* Federspiel, *das;* **b)** *(Hunting)* Lockvogel, *der; (fig.: thing)* Lockmittel, *das;* **c) the** ~ **of the sea** der Ruf *od.* die Lockung des Meeres *(geh.)*

lurid ['ljʊərɪd, 'lʊərɪd] *adj.* **a)** *(ghastly)* gespenstisch; *(highly coloured)* grell ⟨*Licht, Schein, Himmel*⟩; **b)** *(fig.) (horrifying)* gräßlich, schaurig ⟨*Einzelheiten, Beispiele*⟩; *(sensational)* reißerisch *(abwertend); (showy, gaudy)* reißerisch [aufgemacht] *(abwertend)* ⟨*Umschlag, Bild*⟩

luridly ['ljʊərɪdlɪ, 'lʊərɪdlɪ] *adv.* **a)** *(glaringly)* grell; **b)** *(fig.) (horrifyingly)* gräßlich; schaurig; *(showily, gaudily)* reißerisch

lurk [lɜ:k] *v. i.* **a)** lauern; ⟨*Raubtier:*⟩ auf Lauer liegen; ~ **about a place** an einem Ort herumschleichen; **b)** *(fig.)* ~ **in sb.'s** *or* **at the back of sb.'s mind** ⟨*Zweifel, Verdacht, Furcht:*⟩ an jmdm. nagen

lurking ['lɜ:kɪŋ] *attrib. adj.* heimlich ⟨*Zweifel, Verdacht, Angst, Mitgefühl*⟩

luscious ['lʌʃəs] *adj.* **a)** *(sweet in taste or smell)* köstlich [süß]; saftig [süß] ⟨*Obst*⟩; **b)** *(excessively sweet)* aufdringlich süß ⟨*Parfüm*⟩; **c)** *(appealing to senses)* üppig ⟨*Figur, Kurven*⟩; knackig *(ugs.)* ⟨*Mädchen*⟩; voll ⟨*Lippen*⟩; satt ⟨*Farbe*⟩

lush [lʌʃ] *adj.* saftig ⟨*Wiese*⟩; grün ⟨*Tal*⟩; üppig ⟨*Vegetation*⟩; *(fig.)* luxuriös, *(ugs.)* feudal ⟨*Atmosphäre, Räumlichkeiten*⟩

lust [lʌst] **1.** *n.* **a)** *(sexual drive)* Sinnenlust, *die;* sinnliche Begierde; **b)** *(passionate desire)* Gier, *die* **(for** nach); ~ **for power/glory/of battle** Machtgier, *die*/Ruhmsucht, *die*/Kampf[es]lust, *die;* **c)** *(Bibl., Theol.)* Fleischeslust, *die (geh.);* ~**s of the flesh** fleischliche Gelüste *(geh.).* **2.** *v. i.* ~ **after** [lustvoll] begehren *(geh.);* **he** ~**s after ...:** es gelüstet ihn nach ... *(geh.);* ~ **for glory** ruhmbegierig *(geh.) od.* ruhmsüchtig sein

luster *(Amer.) see* **lustre**

lustful ['lʌstfl] *adj.* lüstern *(geh.)*

lustily ['lʌstɪlɪ] *adv.* kräftig; forsch ⟨*sich bewegen, etw. angehen*⟩; herzhaft ⟨*lachen, gähnen*⟩; aus voller Kehle ⟨*rufen, singen*⟩; **he tucked** ~ **into his dinner** er langte kräftig *od.* tüchtig *od.* herzhaft zu

lustre ['lʌstə(r)] *n. (Brit.)* **a)** Schimmer, *der;* [schimmernder] Glanz; **shine with a** ~: einen schimmernden Glanz haben; **b)** *(fig.: splendour)* Glanz, *der;* **add** ~ **to** *or* **shed** ~ **on sth.** einer Sache *(Dat.)* Glanz verleihen; **lack** ~ ⟨*Augen:*⟩ glanzlos sein; ⟨*Lächeln:*⟩ matt sein; **c)** *(glaze)* Glasurglanz, *der;* Lüster, *der (fachspr.)*

lustreless ['lʌstəlɪs] *adj.* glanzlos; stumpf

'lustreware *n.* Lüsterkeramik, *die*

lustrous ['lʌstrəs] *adj.* schimmernd; *(fig.)* glanzvoll; erhaben *(geh.)* ⟨*Geist*⟩

lusty ['lʌstɪ] *adj.* **a)** *(healthy)* gesund; frisch ⟨*Gesichtsfarbe*⟩; *(strong, powerful)* kräftig; **b)** *(vigorous)* herzhaft ⟨*Applaus, Tritt*⟩; tüchtig, zupackend ⟨*Arbeiter*⟩; **a** ~ **girl from the country** ein strammes Landmädchen

lutanist ['lu:tənɪst, 'lju:tənɪst] *n. (Mus.)* Lautenist, *der*/Lautenistin, *die*

lute [lu:t, lju:t] *n. (Mus.)* Laute, *die*

lutenist *see* **lutanist**

Lutheran ['lu:θərən, 'lju:θərən] **1.** *adj.* lutherisch. **2.** *n.* Lutheraner, *der*/Lutheranerin, *die*

Luxembourg *etc. see* **Luxemburg** *etc.*

Luxemburg ['lʌksəmbɜ:g] *pr. n.* Luxemburg *(das)*

Luxemburger ['lʌksəmbɜ:gə(r)] *n.* Luxemburger, *der*/Luxemburgerin, *die*

Luxemburgian ['lʌksəmbɜ:gɪən] **1.** *adj.* luxemburgisch. **2.** *n.* Luxemburgisch, *das;* Letzeburgesch, *das (fachspr.)*

luxuriance [lʌg'zjʊərɪəns, lʌk'sjʊərɪəns] *n., no pl. (superabundance)* Üppigkeit, *die; (of hair)* Fülle, *die*

luxuriant [lʌg'zjʊərɪənt, lʌk'sjʊərɪənt] *adj.* **a)** *(growing profusely, exuberant)* üppig ⟨*Vegetation, Farbenpracht, Blattwerk*⟩; voll ⟨*Haar*⟩; ertragreich ⟨*Ernte*⟩; **b)** *(richly ornamented)* reich ausgeschmückt

luxuriantly [lʌg'zjʊərɪəntlɪ, lʌk'sjʊərɪəntlɪ] *adv.* üppig

luxuriate [lʌg'zjʊərɪeɪt, lʌk'sjʊərɪeɪt] *v. i.* ~ **in** sich aalen in (+ *Dat.*) ⟨*Sonne, Bett usw.*⟩; ~ **in the bath** sich genüßlich in der Badewanne rekeln *(ugs.)*

luxurious [lʌg'zjʊərɪəs, lʌk'sjʊərɪəs] *adj.* luxuriös; Luxus-; *(self-indulgent)* verwöhnt; luxuriös, verschwenderisch ⟨*Lebensstil*⟩

luxuriously [lʌg'zjʊərɪəslɪ, lʌk'sjʊərɪəslɪ] *adv.* luxuriös; mit allem Luxus; feudal *(ugs.)* ⟨*wohnen, essen*⟩

luxury ['lʌkʃərɪ] **1.** *n.* **a)** Luxus, *der;* **live** *or* **lead a life of** ~: ein Leben im Luxus führen; *see also* **'lap a; b)** *(article)* Luxusgegenstand, *der;* **luxuries** Luxus, *der;* **c)** *(sth. one enjoys)* Luxus, *der.* **2.** *attrib. adj.* Luxus-

LV *abbr. (Brit.)* **luncheon voucher**

LW *abbr. (Radio)* **long wave** LW

lychee ['laɪtʃɪ, 'lɪtʃɪ] *n.* Litschi, *die*

lych-gate *see* **lich-gate**

lye [laɪ] *n.* Lauge, *die*

lying ['laɪɪŋ] **1.** *adj.* **a)** *(given to falsehood)* verlogen; ~ **scoundrel** Lügenbold, *der;* **b)** *(false, untrue)* lügnerisch; lügenhaft; erlogen ⟨*Geschichte*⟩; falsch, verlogen ⟨*Sentimentalität*⟩. **2.** *n.* Lügen, *das;* **that would be** ~: das wäre gelogen. *See also* **'lie 2, 3**

lymph [lɪmf] *n.* **a)** *(Physiol.)* Lymphe, *die (fachspr.);* Gewebsflüssigkeit, *die;* **b)** *(Med.: exudation from sore)* Blutwasser, *das*

lymphatic [lɪm'fætɪk] **1.** *adj. (Physiol., Anat.)* Lymph-; lymphatisch. **2.** *n. (Anat.)* Lymphgefäß, *das*

lymph: ~ **gland,** ~ **node** *ns. (Anat.)* Lymphknoten, *der*

lymphocyte ['lɪmfəsaɪt] *n. (Anat.)* Lymphozyt, *der*

lynch [lɪnʃ] *v. t.* lynchen

'lynch law *n.* Lynchjustiz, *die*

lynx [lɪŋks] *n. (Zool.)* Luchs, *der*

'lynx-eyed *adj. (fig.)* luchsäugig; mit Luchsaugen *nachgestellt;* **be** ~: Luchsaugen haben

Lyons ['li:ɔ̃, 'laɪənz] *pr. n.* Lyon *(das)*

lyre ['laɪə(r)] *n. (Mus.)* Lyra, *die;* Leier, *die*

'lyre-bird *n. (Ornith.)* Leierschwanz, *der*

lyric ['lɪrɪk] **1.** *adj.* lyrisch; ~ **poet** Lyriker, *der*/Lyrikerin, *die;* ~ **poetry** Lyrik, *die.* **2.** *n.* **a)** *(poem)* lyrisches Gedicht; **b)** *in pl. (verses)* lyrische Passagen; *(of song)* Text, *der*

lyrical ['lɪrɪkl] *adj.* **a)** *see* **lyric 1; b)** *(like lyric poetry)* lyrisch; **c)** *(coll.: enthusiastic)* gefühlvoll; **become** *or* **grow** *or* **wax** ~ **about** *or* **over sth.** über etw. *(Akk.)* ins Schwärmen geraten

lyrically ['lɪrɪkəlɪ] *adv.* lyrisch

lyricism ['lɪrɪsɪzm] *n.* **a)** *(lyric character, a lyrical expression)* Lyrismus, *der;* **b)** *(high-flown sentiments)* Gefühlsbetontheit, *die;* Gefühlsseligkeit, *die;* Schwärmerei, *die*

lyricist ['lɪrɪsɪst] *n.* Texter, *der*/Texterin, *die*

M

M, m [em] *n., pl.* **Ms** *or* **M's a)** *(letter)* M, m, *das;* **b)** *(Roman numeral)* M

M. *abbr.* **a) Master/Member of/Monsieur** M.; **b) mega-** M; **c)** *(Brit.)* **motorway** A

m. *abbr.* **a) male** männl.; **b) masculine** m.; **c) married** verh.; **d) metre[s]** m; **e) milli-** m; **f) million[s]** Mill.; **g) minute[s]** Min.; **h) mile[s]** M

m' [mə] *poss. pron.* mein

MA *abbr.* **Master of Arts** M.A.; *see also* **B.Sc.**

ma [mɑ:] *n. (coll.)* Mama, *die;* Mutti, *die (fam.)*

ma'am [mɑ:m, mæm] *n.* gnädige Frau; *(in addressing Queen)* Majestät

Mac [mæk] *n. (coll.)* **a)** *(Scotsman)* Schotte, *der; (in address)* Mac; **b)** *(Amer.: fellow)* Kumpel, *der (ugs.);* **hi,** ~! Tag, Kumpel!

mac *see* **mack**

macabre [mə'kɑ:br] *adj.* makaber

macaque [mə'kæk] *n. (Zool.)* Makak, *der*

macaroni [mækə'rəʊnɪ] *n.* Makkaroni *Pl.;* ~ **and cheese** *(Amer.) see* **macaroni cheese**

macaroni 'cheese *n. (Brit.)* Käsemakkaroni *Pl.*

macaroon [mækə'ru:n] *n.* Makrone, *die*

macaw [mə'kɔ:] *n. (Ornith.)* Ara, *der;* Langschwanzpapagei, *der*

[1]**mace** [meɪs] *n.* **a)** *(Hist.: weapon)* Keule, *die;* **b)** *(staff of office)* Amtsstab, *der*

[2]**mace** *n. (Bot., Cookery)* Mazis, *der;* Mazisblüte, *die;* Muskatblüte, *die*

'mace-bearer *n.* Träger/Trägerin des Amtsstabes
macédoine ['mæsɪdwɑ:n] *n. (Cookery)* Macedoine, *das*
Macedonia [mæsɪ'dəʊnɪə] *pr. n.* Makedonien *(das)*
macerate ['mæsəreɪt] *v.t.* aufweichen ‹*Papier*›
Mach [mæk, mɑ:k] *n. (Phys., Aeronaut.)* ~ **[number]** Mach-Zahl, *die;* Machsche Zahl; ~ **one/two** *etc.* Geschwindigkeit von 1/2 *usw.* Mach
machete [mə'tʃetɪ, mə'tʃeɪtɪ] *n.* Machete, *die;* Buschmesser, *das*
machiavellian [mækɪə'velɪən] *adj.* machiavellistisch
machination [mækɪ'neɪʃn, mæʃɪ'neɪʃn] *n.* Machenschaft, *die (abwertend)*
machine [mə'ʃi:n] **1.** *n.* **a)** Maschine, *die;* **be made by ~:** maschinell hergestellt werden; **b)** *(bicycle)* [Fahr]rad, *das; (motor cycle)* Maschine, *die (ugs.);* **c)** *(computer)* Computer, *der;* **d)** *(fig.: person)* Roboter, *der;* Maschine, *die;* **e)** *(system of organization)* Apparat, *der;* **party/propaganda ~:** Partei-/Propagandaapparat, *der.* **2.** *v.t. (make with ~)* maschinell herstellen; *(operate on with ~)* maschinell bearbeiten ‹*Werkstück*›; *(sew)* mit *od.* auf der Maschine nähen
machine: ~ **age** *n.* Maschinenzeitalter, *das;* ~ **code** *n. (Computing)* Maschinensprache, *die;* **~-gun** *n.* Maschinengewehr, *das;* **~-made** *adj.* maschinell hergestellt; **~-minder** *n.* Maschinenwärter, *der;* **~-pistol** *n.* Maschinenpistole, *die;* **~-readable** *adj. (Computing)* maschinenlesbar; **~-room** *n.* Maschinenraum, *der*
machinery [mə'ʃi:nərɪ] *n.* **a)** *(machines)* Maschinen *Pl.;* **b)** *(mechanism)* Mechanismus, *der;* **c)** *(organized system)* Maschinerie, *die;* **d)** *(Lit.)* Kunstmittel *Pl.*
machine: ~ **tool** *n.* Werkzeugmaschine, *die;* **~-wash** *v.t.* in der Waschmaschine waschen; **~-washable** *adj.* waschmaschinenfest
machinist [mə'ʃi:nɪst] *n. (who makes machinery)* Maschinenbauer, *der; (who controls machinery)* Maschinist, *der*/Maschinistin, *die;* **[sewing-]~:** [Maschinen]näherin, *die*/-näher, *der*
machismo [mə'tʃɪzməʊ, mə'kɪzməʊ] *n., no pl.* Machismo, *der;* Männlichkeitswahn, *der*
macho ['mætʃəʊ] **1.** *n., pl.* **~s** Macho, *der.* **2.** *adj.* Macho-; **he is really ~:** er ist wirklich ein Macho
mack [mæk] *n. (Brit. coll.)* Regenmantel, *der;* Kleppermantel ®, *der (ugs. veralt.)*
mackerel ['mækərl] *n., pl. same or* **~s** *(Zool.)* Makrele, *die*
mackerel 'sky *n. (Meteorol.)* Zirrokumulusbewölkung, *die;* Schäfchenwolken *Pl.*
mackintosh ['mækɪntɒʃ] *n.* Regenmantel, *der*
macramé [mə'krɑ:mɪ] *n.* Makramee, *das*
macro- [mækrəʊ] *in comb.* makro-/Makro-
macrobiotic [mækrəʊbaɪ'ɒtɪk] *adj.* makrobiotisch
macron ['mækrɒn] *n.* übergesetzter waagerechter Strich *(zur Kennzeichnung langer Vokale)*
macroscopic [mækrəʊ'skɒpɪk] *adj.* makroskopisch
mad [mæd] *adj.* **a)** *(insane)* geisteskrank; irr ‹*Blick, Ausdruck*›; **you must be ~!** du bist wohl verrückt! *(ugs.);* **are you ~?** bist du völlig verrückt geworden? *(ugs.);* **like a ~ thing** *(coll.)* wie ein Verrückter/eine Verrückte *(ugs.);* **b)** *(frenzied)* wahnsinnig; verrückt *(ugs.);* **it's one ~ rush** *(coll.)* es ist eine einzige Hetze; **make a ~ dash for sth.** sich auf etw. *(Akk.)* stürzen; **drive sb. ~:** jmdn. um den Verstand bringen *od. (ugs.)* verrückt machen; **this noise is enough to drive anyone ~!** dieser Lärm ist ja zum Verrücktwerden! *(ugs.);* ~ **with joy/fear** außer sich vor Freude/Angst; **c)** *(foolish)* verrückt *(ugs.);* **that was a ~ thing to do** das war eine Dummheit *od. (ugs.)* verrückt; **a ~ hope** eine wahnwitzige Hoffnung; **d)** *(very enthusiastic)* **be/go ~ about** *or* **on sb./sth.** auf jmdn./etw. wild sein/werden *(ugs.);* **be ~ keen on sth.** *(sl.)* auf etw. *(Akk.)* ganz scharf *od.* wild sein *(ugs.);* **be ~ keen to do sth.** *(sl.)* ganz scharf *od.* wild darauf sein, etw. zu tun; **e)** *(coll.: annoyed)* ~ **[with** *or* **at sb.]** sauer [auf jmdn.] *(ugs.);* **be ~ about/at missing the train** wütend sein, weil man den Zug verpaßt hat; **f)** *(with rabies)* toll[wütig]; ~ **dog** *(fig.)* Verrückte, *der/die (ugs.);* **[run etc.] like ~:** wie wild *od.* wie ein Wilder/eine Wilde *(ugs.)* [laufen *usw.*]; **g)** *(frivolous)* ausgelassen, *(ugs.)* verrückt ‹*Stimmung*›
Madagascan [mædə'gæskən] **1.** *adj.* madagassisch. **2.** *n.* Madagasse, *der*/Madagassin, *die*
Madagascar [mædə'gæskə(r)] *pr. n.* Madagaskar *(das)*
madam ['mædəm] *n.* **a)** *(formal address)* gnädige Frau; **M~ Chairman** Frau Vorsitzende; **Dear M~** *(in letter)* Sehr verehrte gnädige Frau; **b)** *(euphem.: woman brothel-keeper)* Bordellwirtin, *die;* Puffmutter, *die (salopp);* **c)** *(derog.: conceited, pert young woman)* Kratzbürste, *die (ugs. scherzh.)*
Madame [mə'dɑ:m, 'mædəm] *n., pl.* **Mesdames** [meɪ'dæm, meɪ'dɑ:m] **a)** *(title)* Madame, *die;* **[the] Mesdames A and B** Madame A und Madame B; **b)** *(formal address)* gnädige Frau; meine Dame
'madcap 1. *adj.* unbesonnen. **2.** *n.* Heißsporn, *der*
madden ['mædn] *v.t.* **a)** *(make mad)* wahnsinnig machen *(ugs.);* um den Verstand bringen; **~ed with grief/loneliness** wahnsinnig vor Kummer/Einsamkeit; **b)** *(irritate)* [ver]ärgern; **be ~ed by sth.** sich über etw. *(Akk.)* [maßlos] aufregen; **it ~s me to think that ...:** es fuchst mich *(ugs.),* wenn ich daran denke, daß ...
maddening ['mædənɪŋ] *adj.* **a)** *(irritating, tending to infuriate)* [äußerst] ärgerlich; **b)** *(tending to craze)* unerträglich
maddeningly ['mædənɪŋlɪ] *adv. see* **maddening a, b:** [äußerst] ärgerlich; unerträglich
madder ['mædə(r)] *n.* **a)** *(Bot.)* Krapp, *der;* Färberröte, *die;* **b)** *(dye)* Krappfarbstoff, *der;* **c)** *(Chem.)* synthetisches Alizarin
made *see* **make 1, 2**
Madeira [mə'dɪərə] **1.** *n.* Madeira[wein], *der.* **2.** *pr. n.* Madeira *(das)*
Ma'deira cake *n.* Madeira-Kuchen, *der*
madeleine ['mædleɪn] *n. Butterkeks in Form einer Muschel*
made-to-'measure *attrib. adj.* Maß-; **a ~ suit** ein Maßanzug *od.* maßgeschneiderter Anzug; *see also* **measure 1 a**
'made-up *attrib. adj.* erfunden ‹*Geschichte*›
'madhouse *n.* Irrenanstalt, *die;* Irrenhaus, *das; (fig.)* Tollhaus, *das*
Madison Avenue [mædɪsən 'ævənju:] *n.* die amerikanische Werbeindustrie
madly ['mædlɪ] *adv.* **a)** wie ein Verrückter/eine Verrückte *(ugs.);* **b)** *(coll.: passionately, extremely)* wahnsinnig *(ugs.)*
madman ['mædmən] *n., pl.* **madmen** ['mædmən] Wahnsinnige, *der;* Irre, *der*
madness ['mædnɪs] *n., no pl.* Wahnsinn, *der; see also* **method b**
madonna [mə'dɒnə] *n. (Art, Relig.)* Madonna, *die*
madrigal ['mædrɪgl] *n. (Lit., Mus.)* Madrigal, *das*
'madwoman *n.* Wahnsinnige, *die;* Irre, *die*
maelstrom ['meɪlstrəm] *n. (lit. or fig.)* Ma[h]lstrom, *der;* Strudel, *der;* Sog, *der*
maestro ['maɪstrəʊ] *n., pl.* **maestri** ['maɪstri:] *or* **~s** *(Mus.)* Maestro, *der; (fig.: great performer)* Meister, *der*
Mae West [meɪ 'west] *n.* aufblasbare Schwimmweste
Mafia ['mæfɪə] *n.* **a)** *(secret criminal organization)* Mafia, *die;* **b) m~** *(organization exerting influence)* Mafia, *die*
mag [mæg] *n. (coll.: magazine)* Zeitschrift, *die;* **porno ~:** Pornoheft, *das*
magazine [mægə'zi:n] *n.* **a)** *(periodical)* Zeitschrift, *die; (news ~, fashion ~, etc.)* Magazin, *das;* **b)** *(Mil.: store) (for arms)* Waffenkammer, *die; (for ammunition)* Munitionsdepot, *das; (for provisions)* Proviantlager, *das; (for explosives)* Sprengstofflager, *das;* **c)** *(Arms, Photog.)* Magazin, *das*
magenta [mə'dʒentə] **1.** *n.* **a)** *(dye)* Fuchsin, *das;* Rosanilin, *das;* **b)** *(colour)* Magenta, *das;* Purpur, *das.* **2.** *adj.* purpurrot
maggot ['mægət] *n.* Made, *die*
maggoty ['mægətɪ] *adj.* madig
Magi ['meɪdʒaɪ] *n. pl.* **the [three] ~:** die drei Weisen aus dem Morgenland; die Heiligen Drei Könige
magic ['mædʒɪk] **1.** *n.* **a)** *(witchcraft, lit. or fig.)* Magie, *die;* **do ~:** zaubern; **as if by ~:** wie durch Zauberei; **black/white ~:** Schwarze/Weiße Magie; **work like ~:** wie ein Wunder wirken; **like ~** *(rapidly)* blitzartig; **b)** *(conjuring tricks)* Zauberei, *die;* **make sth. appear/disappear by ~:** etw. herbei-/wegzaubern; **c)** *(fig.: charm, enchantment)* Zauber, *der.* **2.** *adj.* **a)** *(of ~)* magisch ‹*Eigenschaft, Kraft*›; *(resembling ~)* zauberhaft; *(used in ~)* Zauber‹*spruch, -trank, -wort, -bann*›; **cast a ~ spell on sb.** jmdn. verzaubern; **b)** *(fig.: producing surprising results)* wunderbar. **3.** *v.t.,* **-ck-** zaubern; ~ **sth./sb. away** ‹*Zauberspruch:*› etw./jmdn. verschwinden lassen; ‹*Person:*› etw./jmdn. wegzaubern
magical ['mædʒɪkl] *adj. (of magic)* magisch; *(resembling magic)* zauberhaft; **the effect was ~:** das wirkte [wahre] Wunder
magically ['mædʒɪkəlɪ] *adv.* auf wunderbare Weise ‹*schützen, verwandeln, befördern*›; zauberhaft ‹*beleuchten*›
magic: ~ **'carpet** *n.* fliegender Teppich; ~ **'eye** *n.* **a)** *(Electr.: control device)* Photozelle, *die;* **b)** *(Radio)* magisches Auge
magician [mə'dʒɪʃn] *n. (lit. or fig.)* Magier, *der*/Magierin, *die; (conjurer)* Zauberer, *der*/Zauberin, *die;* **I'm not a ~:** ich kann doch nicht zaubern *od.* hexen *(ugs.)*
magic: ~ **'lantern** *n. (Optics)* Laterna Magica; ~ **'square** *n. (Math.)* magisches Quadrat; ~ **'wand** *n.* Zauberstab, *der*
magisterial [mædʒɪ'stɪərɪəl] *adj.* **a)** *(invested with authority)* gebieterisch *(geh.);* **b)** *(dictatorial)* diktatorisch *(abwertend);* herrisch; **c)** *(authoritative)* maßgebend
magistracy ['mædʒɪstrəsɪ] *n., no pl. (position)* Amt des Friedensrichters
magistrate ['mædʒɪstreɪt] *n.* Friedensrichter, *der*/Friedensrichterin, *die;* **~s' court** ≈ Schiedsgericht, *das*
magma ['mægmə] *n., pl.* **~ta** ['mægmətə] *or* **~s** *(Geol.)* Magma, *das*
Magna Carta, Magna Charta [mægnə 'kɑ:tə] *n. (Hist.; also fig.)* Magna Charta, *die*
magnanimity [mægnə'nɪmɪtɪ] *n., no pl.* Großmut, *die;* **with ~:** großmütig
magnanimous [mæg'nænɪməs] *adj.,* **magnanimously** [mæg'nænɪməslɪ] *adv.* großmütig **(towards** gegen)
magnate ['mægneɪt] *n.* Magnat, *der*/Magnatin, *die;* **cotton/steel ~:** Baumwoll-/Stahlmagnat, *der*
magnesia [mæg'ni:ʃə] *n.* Magnesiaweiß, *das; see also* **milk 1**
magnesium [mæg'ni:zɪəm] *n. (Chem.)* Magnesium, *das*
magnet ['mægnɪt] *n. (lit. or fig.)* Magnet, *der*
magnetic [mæg'netɪk] *adj. (lit. or fig.)* magnetisch; *(fig.: very attractive)* sehr anziehend, unwiderstehlich ‹*Person*›; ~ **power** *(fig.)* magnetische Anziehungskraft

magnetic: ~ **at'traction** *n. (Phys.)* magnetische Anziehungskraft; ~ **'compass** *n.* Magnetkompaß, *der;* ~ **'disc** *see* **disc c;** ~ **'field** *n. (Phys.)* Magnetfeld, *das;* ~ **'mine** *n.* Magnetmine, *die;* ~ **'needle** *n.* Magnetnadel, *die;* ~ **'north** *n.* magnetisch Nord, *das;* ~ **'pole** *n. (Phys.)* Magnetpol, *der; (Geog.)* magnetischer Pol; ~ **'storm** *n. (Phys.)* erdmagnetischer Sturm; ~ **'tape** *n.* Magnetband, *das*

magnetise *see* **magnetize**

magnetism ['mægnɪtɪzm] *n.* **a)** *(Phys.) (science)* Magnetik, *die; (force, lit. or fig.)* Magnetismus, *der;* **terrestrial ~:** Erdmagnetismus, *der;* **b)** *(fig.: personal charm and attraction)* Attraktivität, *die;* Anziehungskraft, *die;* Attraktion, *die*

magnetize ['mægnɪtaɪz] *v. t.* **a)** *(Phys.)* magnetisieren; **b)** *(fig.: attract)* in seinen Bann schlagen *od.* ziehen *(geh.);* **be ~d by sth.** von etw. ganz gebannt sein

magneto [mæg'ni:təʊ] *n., pl.* **~s** Magnetzünder, *der*

magnification [mægnɪfɪ'keɪʃn] *n.* Vergrößerung, *die;* **under high/low ~/at x ~s** in starker/geringer/x-facher Vergrößerung

magnificence [mæg'nɪfɪsəns] *n., no pl. (lavish display)* Pracht, *die;* Üppigkeit, *die; (splendour)* Prunk, *der;* Pracht, *die; (grandeur)* Stattlichkeit, *die;* Großartigkeit, *die; (beauty)* Herrlichkeit, *die*

magnificent [mæg'nɪfɪsənt] *adj.* **a)** *(stately, sumptuously constructed or adorned)* prächtig; prachtvoll; *(sumptuous)* prunkvoll; grandios, großartig ‹*Pracht, Herrlichkeit, Anblick*›; *(beautiful)* herrlich ‹*Garten, Umgebung, Kleidung, Vorhang, Kunstwerk, Wetter, Gestalt*›; *(lavish)* üppig ‹*Freigebigkeit, Mahl*›; **b)** *(coll.: fine, excellent)* fabelhaft *(ugs.)*

magnificently [mæg'nɪfɪsəntlɪ] *adv.* **a)** *(with great stateliness and grandeur)* prächtig; prachtvoll; *(sumptuously)* prunkvoll ‹*einrichten, schmücken*›; *(with lavishness)* üppig ‹*zubereitet*›; **b)** *(coll.: in fine manner)* fabelhaft *(ugs.)*

magnifier ['mægnɪfaɪə(r)] *n. (Optics)* Lupe, *die*

magnify ['mægnɪfaɪ] *v. t.* **a)** vergrößern; **b)** *(exaggerate)* aufbauschen; übertrieben darstellen ‹*Gefahren*›

'magnifying glass *n.* Lupe, *die;* Vergrößerungsglas, *das*

magnitude ['mægnɪtju:d] *n.* **a)** *(largeness, vastness)* Ausmaß, *das; (of explosion, earthquake)* Stärke, *die;* **b)** *(size)* Größe, *die;* **problems of this ~:** Probleme dieser Größenordnung; **order of ~:** Größenordnung, *die;* **c)** *(importance)* Wichtigkeit, *die; (of person)* Bedeutung, *die;* **sth. of the first ~:** etw. von höchster Wichtigkeit; **a writer of the first ~:** ein sehr bedeutender Schriftsteller; **d)** *(Astron.)* Helligkeit, *die*

magnolia [mæg'nəʊlɪə] *n. (Bot.)* Magnolie, *die*

magnum ['mægnəm] *n. (bottle)* Magnum, *die; (measure)* 1,5 l; **two ~s** 3 l

magnum 'opus *see* **opus b**

magpie ['mægpaɪ] *n. (Ornith.)* Elster, *die;* **chatter like a ~:** unaufhörlich schnattern *(ugs.);* **be like a ~** *(fig.)* alles mögliche sammeln [wie eine Elster]

Magyar ['mægjɑ:(r)] **1.** *adj.* madjarisch. **2.** *n.* **a)** *(person)* Madjar, *der*/Madjarin, *die;* **b)** *(language)* Madjarisch, *das*

maharaja[h] [mɑ:hə'rɑ:dʒə] *n. (Ind. Hist.)* Maharadscha, *der*

mah-jong[g] [mɑ:'dʒɒŋ] *n.* Mah-Jongg, *das*

mahogany [mə'hɒgənɪ] *n.* **a)** *(wood)* Mahagoni[holz], *das; attrib.* Mahagoni-; **b)** *(tree)* Mahagonibaum, *der;* **c)** *(colour)* Mahagonibraun, *das*

maid [meɪd] *n.* **a)** *(servant)* Dienstmädchen, *das;* Dienstmagd, *die (veralt.);* ~ **of 'all work** *(servant)* Hausangestellte, *die;* Hausmädchen, *das; (fig.: person doing many jobs)* Mädchen für alles *(ugs.);* **b)** *(arch.: unmarried woman)* unverheiratete Frau; Jungfer, *die (veralt., oft abwertend);* **c)** *(arch./poet.) (girl)* Maid, *die (dichter. veralt.); (young unmarried woman, virgin)* Jungfrau, *die;* **d)** *(rhet.: young woman)* Maid, *die (dichter. veralt.);* **the M~ [of Orleans]** die Jungfrau von Orleans. *See also* **old maid**

maiden ['meɪdn] **1.** *n.* **a)** *see* **maid c;** **the answer to a ~'s prayer** genau das Richtige; *(attractive man)* der Traum aller Frauen; **b)** *see* **maiden over. 2.** *adj.* **a)** *(unmarried)* unverheiratet; *(befitting a maid)* jungfräulich ‹*Unschuld, Schönheit, Anmut*›; mädchenhaft ‹*Bescheidenheit, Erröten*›; **b)** *(first)* ~ **voyage/speech** Jungfernfahrt/-rede, *die;* **c)** *(unmated)* nicht gedeckt, nicht begattet ‹*Tier*›; **d)** *(that has never won)* sieglos; ~ **horse** Maiden, *das;* ~ **race** Maidenrennen, *das*

maiden: **~hair** *n. (Bot.)* Frauenhaarfarn, *der;* **~hair tree** Gingko[baum], *der;* Fächerbaum, *der;* **~head** *n.* **a)** *(virginity)* Jungfräulichkeit, *die;* **b)** *(hymen)* Jungfernhäutchen, *das;* ~ **name** *n.* Mädchenname, *der;* ~ **'over** *n. (Cricket) Serie von sechs Würfen ohne erzielten Lauf*

maid: ~ **of 'honour** *n., pl.* **~s of honour a)** *(attendant of queen or princess)* Hof- *od.* Ehrendame, *die;* **b)** *(Amer.: chief bridesmaid)* Brautjungfer, *die;* **~servant** *n. (arch.)* Hausangestellte, *die;* Hausmädchen, *das*

¹mail [meɪl] **1.** *n.* **a)** *see* **²post 1;** **b)** *(vehicle carrying ~)* Postbeförderungsmittel, *das; (train)* Postzug, *der.* **2.** *v. t. see* **²post 2 a**

²mail *n.* **a)** *(armour)* Panzer, *der;* Rüstung, *die; (chain ~)* Kettenpanzer, *der;* **coat of ~:** Panzer- *od.* Kettenhemd, *das;* **b)** *(Zool.)* Panzer, *der*

mail: **~-bag** *n. (postman's bag)* Zustelltasche, *die; (sack for transporting ~)* Postsack, *der;* **my ~-bag is full of such requests** *(fig.)* ich habe jede Menge Anfragen dieser Art bekommen; **~-boat** *n.* Postschiff *od.* -boot, *das;* Postdampfer, *der;* **~box** *n. (Amer.)* Briefkasten, *der; (slot)* Briefschlitz, *der;* ~ **coach** *n.* **a)** *(Hist.)* Postkutsche, *die;* **b)** *(Railw.)* Post- *od.* Paketwagen, *der*

mailed [meɪld] *adj.* **a)** *(armed with mail)* gepanzert; **b)** ~ **fist** *([threat of] armed force)* gepanzerte Faust

mailing list ['meɪlɪŋ lɪst] *n.* Adressenliste, *die*

mail: **~man** *n. (Amer.)* Briefträger, *der;* Postbote, *der (ugs.);* ~ **order** *n.* postalische Bestellung; Mail-order, *die (Werbespr., Kaufmannsspr.);* **by ~ order** durch Bestellung *od.* Mail-order; **~-order catalogue** *n.* Versandhauskatalog, *der;* **~-order firm, ~-order house** *ns.* Versandhaus, *das;* ~ **shot** *n.* Versand von Werbeschriften; ~ **train** *n.* Postzug, *der;* ~ **van** *n. (Railw.)* Post- *od.* Paketwagen, *der*

maim [meɪm] *v. t. (mutilate)* verstümmeln; *(cripple)* zum Krüppel machen; ~ **sb. for life** jmdn. zeitlebens zum Krüppel machen

main [meɪn] **1.** *n.* **a)** *(channel, pipe)* Hauptleitung, *die;* **sewage ~:** Kanalisation, *die;* **~s [system]** öffentliches Versorgungsnetz; *(of electricity)* Stromnetz, *das;* **turn the gas/water off at the ~[s]** den Haupthahn [für das Gas/Wasser] abstellen; **turn the electricity off at the ~s** [den Strom] am Hauptschalter abschalten; **~s-operated** für Netzbetrieb *nachgestellt;* **the radio works on battery and on ~s** das Radio funktioniert mit Batterie- und Netzstrom; **b)** **in the ~:** im allgemeinen; im großen und ganzen. **2.** *attrib. adj.* Haupt-; **the ~ body of troops** das Gros der Truppen; **the ~ doubt/principle** der entscheidende Zweifel/oberste Grundsatz; ~ **office** Zentrale, *die;* ~ **theme** Hauptthema, *das;* **the ~ points of the news** die wichtigsten Meldungen; **the ~ thing is that ...:** die Hauptsache *od.* das Wichtigste ist, daß ...; **by ~ force** gewaltsam; **have an eye to the ~ chance** auf den eigenen Vorteil bedacht sein; **he married her with an eye to the ~ chance** er war auf seinen eigenen Vorteil bedacht, als er sie heiratete

main: ~ **beam** *n. (Motor Veh.)* **on ~ beam** aufgeblendet; ~ **brace** *n. (Naut.)* Großbrasse, *die;* **splice the ~ brace** *(Hist.)* eine Extraration Rum austeilen; ~ **'clause** *n. (Ling.)* Hauptsatz, *der;* **~frame** *n. (Computing)* Großrechner, *der;* **~land** ['meɪnlənd] *n.* Festland, *das;* ~ **'line** *n.* **a)** *(principal line of a railway)* Hauptstrecke, *die;* **~-line station/train** Fernbahnhof/-zug, *der;* **~-line train service** Fernverkehr, *der;* **b)** *(Amer.: chief road or street)* Hauptstraße, *die;* **~line** *(sl.)* **1.** *v. i.* an der Spritze hängen *(ugs.);* **2.** *v. t.* spritzen ‹*Heroin*›

mainly ['meɪnlɪ] *adv.* hauptsächlich; in erster Linie; *(for the most part)* vorwiegend

main: **~mast** *n. (Naut.)* Großmast, *der;* ~ **'road** Hauptstraße, *die;* **~sail** ['meɪnseɪl, 'meɪnsl] *n. (Naut.)* Großsegel, *das;* **~spring** *n.* Hauptfeder, *die; (of clock, watch, etc.; also fig.)* Triebfeder, *die;* **~stay** *n. (Naut.)* Großstag, *das; (fig.)* [wichtigste] Stütze; ~ **'stem** *n. (Amer. coll.) (street)* Hauptstraße, *die; (Railw.)* Hauptstrecke, *die;* **~stream** *n.* **a)** *(principal current)* Hauptstrom, *der; (fig.)* Hauptrichtung, *die;* **the ~stream of fashion** der vorherrschende Trend in der Mode; **be in the ~stream** der Hauptrichtung angehören; **b)** *(Jazz)* Mainstream, *der;* ~ **'street** *n.* [*(Amer.)* '--] Hauptstraße, *die;* **M~ Street** *n., no pl., no art. (Amer. fig.)* Kleinbürgertum, *das*

maintain [meɪn'teɪn] *v. t.* **a)** *(keep up)* aufrechterhalten; bewahren ‹*Anschein, Haltung, Einstellung, Frieden, Fassung*›; unterhalten ‹*Beziehungen, Briefwechsel*›; [bei-be]halten ‹*Preise, Geschwindigkeit, Standard, Temperatur*›; wahren ‹*Rechte, Ruf*›; **in order to ~ security** aus Sicherheitsgründen; **b)** *(provide for)* ~ **sb.** für jmds. Unterhalt aufkommen; **c)** *(preserve)* instand halten; warten ‹*Maschine, Gerät*›; unterhalten ‹*Straße*›; **the car is too expensive to ~:** der Wagen ist in der Unterhaltung *od.* im Unterhalt zu teuer; **d)** *(give aid to)* unterstützen ‹*Partei, Wohlfahrtsorganisation, Sache*›; **e)** *(assert as true)* vertreten ‹*Meinung, Lehre*›; beteuern ‹*Unschuld*›; ~ **that ...:** behaupten, daß ...

main'tained school *n. (Brit.)* staatliche Schule

maintenance ['meɪntənəns] *n.* **a)** *see* **maintain a:** Aufrechterhaltung, *die;* Bewahrung, *die;* Unterhaltung, *die;* [Beibe]halten, *das;* Wahrung, *die;* **b)** *(furnishing with means of subsistence)* Unterhaltung, *die;* **c)** *(assertion as true)* Vertretung, *die; (of innocence)* Beteuerung, *die;* **d)** *(Law: money paid to support sb.)* Unterhalt, *der; see also* **separate maintenance;** **e)** *(preservation)* Instandhaltung, *die; (of machinery)* Wartung, *die;* ~ **instructions** *(for car)* Wartungs- und Pflegeanleitung, *die;* **f)** *(aiding)* Unterstützung, *die*

maintenance: **~-'free** *adj.* wartungsfrei; ~ **manual** *n.* Wartungsbuch, *das;* ~ **order** *n.* Unterhaltsurteil, *das;* ~ **worker** *n.* Wartungsmonteur, *der*

main 'verb *n.* Hauptverb, *das*

maison[n]ette [meɪzə'net] *n.* [zweistöckige] Wohnung; Maison[n]ette, *die*

maître d'hôtel [meɪtr dəʊ'tel] *n.* **a)** *(head steward)* Haushofmeister, *der;* **b)** *(head waiter)* Oberkellner, *der*

maize [meɪz] *n.* Mais, *der;* ~ **cob** Maiskolben, *der;* **grain of ~:** Maiskorn, *das;* **field of ~:** Maisfeld, *das*

Maj. abbr. Major[-] Maj.

majestic [mə'dʒestɪk] adj. majestätisch; hoheitsvoll (geh.); erhaben ‹Erscheinung, Schlichtheit, Schönheit›; gemessen ‹Auftreten, Schritt›; getragen ‹Musik›; (stately) stattlich; (possessing grandeur) grandios

majestically [mə'dʒestɪkəlɪ] adv. majestätisch; gemessen[en Schritts] ‹gehen›

majesty ['mædʒɪstɪ] n. a) Majestät, die (geh.); (of verse, music) Erhabenheit, die; (of appearance) Stattlichkeit, die; (of person, bearing) Würde, die; b) (sovereign power) Hoheit, die; Majestät, die; c) Your/His/Her M~: Eure/Seine/Ihre Majestät

major ['meɪdʒə(r)] 1. adj. a) attrib. (greater of two) größer...; ~ part Großteil, der; b) attrib. (important) bedeutend...; (serious) schwer ‹Unfall, Krankheit, Unglück, Unruhen›; größer... ‹Krieg, Angriff, Durchbruch›; not a ~ poet kein bedeutender Dichter; kein Dichter von Bedeutung; of ~ interest/importance von größerem Interesse/von größerer Bedeutung; ~ road (important) Hauptverkehrsstraße, die; (having priority) Vorfahrtsstraße, die; c) attrib. (Med.) schwer, größer... ‹Operation›; d) (Brit. Sch.) Jones ~: der ältere Jones; Jones Nr. 1 (ugs.); e) (Mus.) Dur-; ~ key/scale/chord Durtonart, die/Durtonleiter, die/Durakkord, der; C ~: C-Dur; in a ~ key in Dur; ~ third etc. große Terz usw. 2. n. a) (Mil.) (officer above captain) Major, der; (officer in charge of section of band instruments) Leiter der Trommler/Trompeter usw. einer Regimentskapelle; see also sergeant-major; b) (Amer. Univ.) Hauptfach, das; with ~ in maths mit Mathematik als Hauptfach; be an economics ~: Wirtschaftswissenschaft als Hauptfach studieren. 3. v.i. (Amer. Univ.) ~ in sth. etw. als Hauptfach studieren

major 'axis n. (Geom.) große Achse; Hauptachse, die

Majorca [mə'jɔ:kə] pr. n. Mallorca (das)

major-domo [meɪdʒə'dəʊməʊ] n., pl. ~s (butler, house-steward) Haushofmeister, der

majorette [meɪdʒə'ret] see drum majorette

major-'general n. (Mil.) Generalmajor, der

majority [mə'dʒɒrɪtɪ] n. a) (greater number or part) Mehrheit, die; the great ~: die überwiegende Mehrheit; der größte Teil; the ~ of people think ...: die meisten Menschen denken ...; be in the ~: in der Mehr- od. Überzahl sein; überwiegen; b) (in vote) [Stimmen]mehrheit, die; Majorität, die; (party with greater/greatest number of votes) Mehrheitspartei, die; two-thirds ~: Zweidrittelmehrheit, die; be elected by a narrow or small ~/a ~ of 3,000 mit knapper Mehrheit/einer Mehrheit von 3 000 Stimmen gewählt werden; c) (full age) Volljährigkeit, die; attain or reach one's ~: volljährig werden; the age of ~: das Volljährigkeitsalter

majority: ~ de'cision n. Mehrheitsentscheid, der; **~ 'holding** n. (Finance) Mehrheitsanteile Pl.; **~ 'rule** n. Mehrheitsregierung, die; **~ 'verdict** n. Mehrheitsentscheid, der; return a ~ verdict mehrheitlich zu einem Urteil kommen

major: ~ 'league n. (Amer.) Oberliga, die; **~ 'planet** n. Riesenplanet, der; **~ 'prophet** n. (Bibl.) Großer Prophet; **~ 'suit** n. (Bridge) hohe Farbe

make [meɪk] 1. v.t., made [meɪd] a) (construct) machen, anfertigen (of aus); bauen ‹Damm, Straße, Flugzeug, Geige›; anlegen ‹See, Teich, Weg usw.›; zimmern ‹Tisch, Regal›; basteln ‹Spielzeug, Vogelhäuschen, Dekoration usw.›; nähen ‹Kleider›; durchbrechen ‹Türöffnung›; (manufacture) herstellen; (create) [er]schaffen ‹Welt›; (prepare) zubereiten ‹Mahlzeit›; machen ‹Frühstück, Grog›; machen, kochen ‹Kaffee, Tee, Marmelade›; backen ‹Brot, Kuchen›; (compose, write) schreiben, verfassen ‹Buch, Gedicht, Lied, Bericht›; machen ‹Eintrag, Zeichen, Kopie, Zusammenfassung, Testament›; anfertigen ‹Entwurf›; aufsetzen ‹Bewerbung, Schreiben, Urkunde›; ~ a film einen Film drehen; as tough/clever/stupid as they ~ them (coll.) zäh/schlau/dumm wie sonstwas (ugs.); ~ a dress out of the material, ~ the material into a dress aus dem Stoff ein Kleid machen; ~ wine from grapes/a frame with timber aus Trauben Wein/Holz einen Rahmen machen; ~ milk into butter aus Milch Butter machen; ~ a sofa into a bed aus einem Sofa ein Bett machen; a table made of wood/of the finest wood ein Holztisch/ein Tisch aus feinstem Holz; made in Germany in Deutschland hergestellt; be German-made deutsche Ware sein; show what one is made of zeigen, was in einem steckt (ugs.); see what sb. is made of sehen, was in jmdm. steckt (ugs.); be [simply] 'made of money (coll.) ein [wahrer] Krösus sein (ugs.); im Geld [nur so] schwimmen (ugs.); be 'made for sth./sb. (fig.: ideally suited) wie geschaffen für etw./jmdn. sein; 'made for one another wie für einander geschaffen; that's the way he's made so ist er nun einmal; be 'made for doing sth. (fig.) dazu geschaffen sein, etw. zu tun; be made [so as] to ...: so beschaffen sein, daß ...; a made dish ein aus mehreren Zutaten bereitetes Gericht; made road befestigte od. gepflasterte Straße; ~ a bed (for sleeping) ein Bett bauen (ugs.); ~ the bed (arrange after sleeping) das Bett machen; have it made (sl.) ausgesorgt haben (ugs.); she has it made (is sure of success) ihr ist der Erfolg sicher; see also best 3 e; [1]hash 1; hay; head 1 e; [2]light 1 f; [1]meal; measure 1 a; most 2 c; nothing 1 a; order 1 e; b) (combine into) sich verbinden zu; bilden; blue and yellow ~ green aus Blau und Gelb wird Grün; ~ it a foursome eine Vierergruppe bilden; c) (cause to exist) machen ‹Ärger, Schwierigkeiten, Lärm, Aufhebens›; ~ enemies sich (Dat.) Feinde machen od. schaffen; ~ time for sb./sth. sich (Dat.) für jmdn./etw. Zeit nehmen; ~ time for doing or to do sth. sich (Dat.) die Zeit dazu nehmen, etw. zu tun; see also bone 1 a, d; book 1 g; conversation; friend a; fun 1; [1]game 1 d; [1]mark 1 a, b; name 1 e; peace b; point 1 g; room 1 b; sport 1 d; [1]stir 3 a; d) (result in, amount to) machen ‹Unterschied, Summe›; ergeben ‹Resultat›; it ~s a difference es ist ein od. (ugs.) macht einen Unterschied; two and two ~ four zwei und zwei ist od. macht od. sind vier; twelve inches ~ a foot zwölf Inches sind ein Fuß; these two gloves don't ~ a pair diese beiden Handschuhe ergeben kein Paar od. gehören nicht zusammen; that would ~ a nice Christmas present das wäre ein schönes Weihnachtsgeschenk; ~ an unusual sight ein ungewöhnlicher Anblick sein; they ~ a handsome pair sie geben ein hübsches Paar ab; sie sind ein hübsches Paar; qualities that ~ a man Eigenschaften, die einen Mann ausmachen; see also change 1 a, c, d; [2]swallow; e) (establish, enact) bilden ‹Gegensatz›; treffen ‹Unterscheidung, Übereinkommen›; ziehen ‹Vergleich, Parallele›; erlassen ‹Gesetz, Haftbefehl›; aufstellen ‹Regeln, Behauptung›; stellen ‹Forderung›; geben ‹Bericht›; schließen ‹Vertrag›; vornehmen ‹Zahlung›; machen ‹Geschäft, Vorschlag, Geständnis›; erheben ‹Anschuldigung, Protest, Beschwerde›; f) (cause to be or become) ~ angry/happy/known etc. wütend/glücklich/bekannt usw. machen; ~ sb. captain/one's wife jmdn. zum Kapitän/(veralt.) zu seiner Frau machen; ~ a good husband of sb. aus jmdm. einen guten Ehemann machen; ~ a star of sb. aus jmdm. einen Star machen; ~ a friend of sb. sich mit jmdm. anfreunden; ~ something of oneself/sth. etwas aus sich/etw. machen; ~ oneself heard/respected sich (Dat.) Gehör/Respekt verschaffen; ~ oneself understood sich verständlich machen; ~ oneself/sb. feared bewirken, daß man/jmd. gefürchtet ist; ~ a weekend of it ein Wochenende daraus machen; es zu einem Wochenende verlängern; he was made director/the heir er wurde Direktor/zum Erben; shall we ~ it Tuesday then? sagen wir also Dienstag?; that ~s it one pound exactly das macht genau ein Pfund; ~ it a round dozen ein rundes Dutzend daraus machen; das Dutzend voll machen; ~ it a shorter journey by doing sth. die Reise abkürzen, indem man etw. tut; see also example b; exhibition c; [1]fool 1 a; habit 1 a; night a; [1]practice a, d; scarce 1 b; g) ~ sb. do sth. (cause) jmdn. dazu bringen, etw. zu tun; (compel) jmdn. zwingen, etw. zu tun; he made her cry seinetwegen mußte sie weinen; er brachte sie zum Heulen (ugs.); ~ sb. repeat the sentence jmdn. den Satz wiederholen lassen; be made to do sth. etw. tun müssen; you can't ~ me du kannst mich nicht zwingen; ~ oneself do sth. sich überwinden, etw. zu tun; what ~s you think that? wie kommst du darauf?; ~ sth. do sth. es fertigbringen, daß etw. etw. tut; h) (form, be counted as) this ~s the tenth time you've failed das ist nun [schon] das zehnte Mal, daß du versagt hast; du hast nun schon zum zehnten Mal versagt; will you ~ one of the party? wirst du dabei od. (ugs.) mit von der Partie sein?; i) (serve for) abgeben; this story ~s good reading diese Geschichte ist guter Lesestoff; j) (become by development or training) the site would ~ a good playground der Platz würde einen guten Spielplatz abgeben od. würde sich gut als Spielplatz eignen; he will ~ a good officer/husband aus ihm wird noch ein guter Offizier/Ehemann; ~ a reliable partner ein verläßlicher Partner sein; k) (gain, acquire, procure) machen ‹Vermögen, Profit, Verlust›; machen (ugs.) ‹Geld›; verdienen ‹Lebensunterhalt›; sich (Dat.) erwerben ‹Ruf›; (obtain as result) kommen zu od. auf, herausbekommen ‹Ergebnis, Endsumme›; (Cricket: score) erzielen; (Cards: win) machen ‹Stich›; erfüllen ‹Kontrakt›; how much did you ~? wieviel hast du verdient?; that ~s one pound exactly das macht genau ein Pfund; that ~s a hundred you've scored damit hast du insgesamt 100 Punkte; l) (execute by physical movement) machen ‹Geste, Bewegung, Verbeugung, Knicks, Satz›; schlagen ‹Purzelbaum›; (perform as action) machen ‹Reise, Besuch, Ausnahme, Fehler, Angebot, Entdeckung, Witz, Bemerkung›; begehen ‹Irrtum›; vornehmen ‹Änderung, Stornierung›; vorbringen ‹Beschwerde›; tätigen, machen ‹Einkäufe›; geben ‹Versprechen, Kommentar›; halten ‹Rede›; ziehen ‹Vergleich›; durchführen, machen ‹Experiment, Analyse, Inspektion›; (wage) führen ‹Krieg›; (accomplish) schaffen ‹Strecke pro Zeiteinheit›; ~ a good breakfast etc. (dated: eat) gut frühstücken usw.; see also back 1 a; [2]bow 3; face 1 a; love 1 a; shift 3 d; m) ~ much of sth. etw. betonen; ~ little of sth. (play down) etw. herunterspielen; they could ~ little of his letter (understand) sie konnten mit seinem Brief nicht viel anfangen; I couldn't ~ much of the book (understand) ich konnte mit dem Buch nicht viel anfangen; das Buch sagte mir nicht viel; I don't know what to ~ of him/it ich werde aus ihm/daraus nicht schlau od. klug; what do you ~ of him? was hältst du von ihm?; wie schätzt du ihn ein?; n) (arrive at) erreichen ‹Bestimmungsort›; (achieve place in) kommen in (+ Akk.) ‹Hitparade›; aufsteigen in (+ Akk.) ‹1. Liga usw.›; (coll.: catch) [noch] kriegen (ugs.) ‹Zug usw.›; (sl.: se-

duce) ins Bett kriegen *(ugs.)*; ~ **it** *(succeed in arriving)* es schaffen; ~ **it in business** es geschäftlich zu etwas bringen; ~ **it through the winter/night** über den Winter/durch die Nacht kommen; **I can't ~ it tomorrow** *(coll.)* morgen paßt es mir nicht; ~ **it with sb.** *(sl.: seduce)* es mit jmdm. machen *(ugs.)*; mit jmdm. ins Bett steigen *(ugs.)*; **o)** *(frame in mind)* ~ **a judgement/an estimate of sth.** sich *(Dat.)* ein Urteil über etw. *(Akk.)* bilden/etw. [ab- *od.* ein]schätzen; **p)** *(secure advancement of)* machen *(ugs.)* ‹*Popstar usw.*›; zum Erfolg verhelfen (+ *Dat.*); **a made man** ein gemachter Mann; **sth. ~s or breaks** *or* **mars sb.** etw. entscheidet über jmds. Glück oder Verderben *(Akk.)*; ~ **sb.'s day** jmdm. einen glücklichen Tag bescheren; **q)** *(consider to be)* **What do you ~ the time? – I ~ it five past eight** Wie spät hast du es *od.* ist es bei dir? – Auf meiner Uhr ist es fünf nach acht; **he made the answer/total £10** er bekam 10 Pfund als Antwort heraus/kam zu einer Gesamtsumme von 10 Pfund; **r)** *(Electr.)* herstellen ‹*Kontakt*›; schließen ‹*Stromkreis*›; **s)** *(Naut.)* *(discern)* sichten ‹*Land, Hafen usw.*›; ~ **sail** Segel setzen; *(start on voyage)* lossegeln; **t)** ~ **do** vorliebnehmen; ~ **do and mend** mit den vorhandenen Sachen vorliebnehmen und sie ausbessern; ~ **do with/without sth.** mit/ohne etw. auskommen. **2.** *v.i.*, **made a)** *(proceed)* ~ **toward sth./sb.** auf etw./jmdn. zusteuern; **b)** *(act as if with intention)* ~ **to do sth.** Anstalten machen, etw. zu tun; ~ **as if** *or* **as though to do sth.** so tun, als wolle man etw. tun; **c)** *(profit)* ~ **on a deal** bei einem Geschäft Gewinn machen. *See also* **bold b; certain b; free 1c; good 1u; merry a; sure 1e. 3.** *n.* **a)** *(kind of structure)* Ausführung, *die; (of clothes)* Machart, *die;* **b)** *(type of manufacture)* Fabrikat, *das; (brand)* Marke, *die;* ~ **of car** Automarke, *die;* **a camera of Japanese ~**: eine Kamera japanischer Herstellung *od.* Fabrikation; **c) on the ~** *(sl.: intent on gain)* hinter dem Geld her *(abwertend)*

~ **a'way with** *see* ~ **off with**

~ **for** *v.t.* **a)** *(move towards)* zusteuern auf (+ *Akk.*); zuhalten auf (+ *Akk.*); *(rush towards)* losgehen auf (+ *Akk.*); zustürzen auf (+ *Akk.*); ~ **for home** heimwärts steuern; **b)** *(be conducive to)* führen zu, herbeiführen ‹*gute Beziehungen, Erfolg, Zuversicht*›

~ **'off** *v.i.* sich davonmachen

~ **'off with** *v.t.* ~ **off with sb./sth.** sich mit jmdm./etw. [auf und] davonmachen

~ **'out 1.** *v.t.* **a)** *(write)* ausstellen ‹*Scheck, Dokument, Rechnung*›; aufstellen ‹*Liste*›; ausfertigen *(Amtsspr.)* ‹*Schreiben, Antrag*›; **b)** *(claim, assert)* behaupten; **the novel wasn't as good as the review had made it out to be** *or* **made out** der Roman war nicht so gut, wie in der Rezension behauptet wurde; ~ **out a case for/against sth.** für/gegen etw. argumentieren; **you've made out a convincing case** deine Argumente sind überzeugend; **you ~ me out to be a liar** du stellst mich als Lügner hin; **how do you ~ that out?** wie kommst du darauf?; **c)** *(understand)* verstehen; ~ **out what sb. wants/whether sb. wants help or not** herausbekommen, was jmd. will/ob jmd. Hilfe möchte oder nicht; **d)** *(manage to see or hear)* ausmachen; *(manage to read)* entziffern; **e)** *(pretend, assert falsely)* vorgeben. **2.** *v.i.* *(coll.)* *(make progress)* zurechtkommen **(at** bei); **how are you making out with your girl-friend?** wie läuft es denn so mit deiner Freundin? *(ugs.)*

~ **'over** *v.t.* **a)** *(transfer)* übereignen, überschreiben ‹*Geld, Geschäft, Eigentum*› **(to** *Dat.*); **b)** *(change, convert)* umändern, umarbeiten ‹*Kleidung*›; umbauen ‹*Haus*› **(into** zu); umgestalten ‹*Garten, Zimmer*›

~ **'up 1.** *v.t.* **a)** *(replace)* ausgleichen ‹*Fehlmenge, Verluste*›; ~ **up lost ground/time** Boden gut- *od.* wettmachen *(ugs.)*/den Zeitverlust aufholen; **b)** *(complete)* komplett machen; **c)** *(prepare, arrange)* zubereiten ‹*Arznei usw.*›; zusammenstellen ‹*Picknickkorb usw.*›; zurechtmachen ‹*Bett*›; *(prepare by mixing)* vermischen **(into** zu); *(process material)* verarbeiten **(into** zu); ~ **up into bundles** bündeln; **d)** *(apply cosmetics to)* schminken; ~ **up one's face/eyes** sich schminken/sich *(Dat.)* die Augen schminken; *see also* **make-up a**; **e)** *(assemble, compile)* zusammenstellen; aufstellen ‹*Liste usw.*›; bilden ‹*ein Ganzes*›; **f)** *(Printing)* umbrechen; *see also* **make-up d**; **g)** *(invent)* erfinden; sich *(Dat.)* ausdenken; **you're just making it up!** das hast du dir doch nur ausgedacht!; **h)** *(reconcile)* beilegen ‹*Streit, Meinungsverschiedenheit*›; ~ **up the quarrel** *or* ~ **it up with sb.** sich wieder mit jmdm. vertragen; sich mit jmdm. aus- *od.* versöhnen; **they've made it up [again]** sie vertragen sich wieder *od.* haben sich ausgesöhnt; *see also* **mind 1b**; **i)** *(form, constitute)* bilden; ~ **up a man's character** den Charakter eines Menschen ausmachen; **be made up of ...:** bestehen aus ...; *see also* **make-up b, c**; **j)** ~ **up the fire** [Holz *usw.* aufs Feuer] nachlegen. **2.** *v.i.* **a)** *(apply cosmetics etc.)* sich schminken; *see also* **make-up a**; **b)** *(be reconciled)* sich wieder vertragen

~ **'up for** *v.t.* **a)** *(outweigh, compensate)* wettmachen; **b)** *(~ amends for)* wiedergutmachen; **c)** ~ **up for lost time** Versäumtes nachholen *od.* *(ugs.)* wettmachen

~ **'up to** *v.t.* **a)** *(raise to, increase to)* bringen auf (+ *Akk.*); **b)** *(coll.: act flirtatiously towards)* sich heranmachen an (+ *Akk.*) *(ugs.)*; **c)** *(coll.: give compensation to)* ~ **it/this up to sb.** jmdn. dafür entschädigen

~ **with** *v.t.* *(Amer. coll.: supply, produce)* ~ **with the drinks!** [los,] her mit den Getränken!; **start making with the ideas!** laß dir mal was einfallen!

'make-believe 1. *n.* **it's only ~** das ist bloß Phantasie; **a world of ~** eine Scheinwelt. **2.** *adj.* nicht echt; **a ~ world/story** eine Scheinwelt/Phantasiegeschichte

make-or-'break *attrib. adj.* alles entscheidend

maker ['meɪkə(r)] *n.* **a)** *(manufacturer)* Hersteller, *der;* ~ **of laws/rules/regulations** *jmd., der Gesetze macht/Regeln aufstellt/Verordnungen erläßt;* **b) M~** *(God)* Schöpfer, *der;* **meet one's M~**: vor seinen Schöpfer treten *(verhüll.)*

-maker *n. in comb.* -macher, *der*/-macherin, *die; (by machine)* -hersteller, *der*/-herstellerin, *die*

make: ~shift 1. *adj.* behelfsmäßig; **a ~shift shelter/bridge** eine Behelfsunterkunft/-brücke; **2.** *n.* Notbehelf, *der;* **~-up** *n.* **a)** *(Cosmetics)* Make-up, *das; (Theatre)* Maske, *die;* **put on one's ~-up** Make-up auflegen; sich schminken; *(Theatre)* Maske machen; **wear heavy ~-up/one's stage ~-up** stark geschminkt/in Maske sein; **b)** *(composition)* Zusammensetzung, *die;* **c)** *(character, temperament)* Veranlagung, *die;* **physical ~-up** Konstitution, *die;* **national ~-up** Nationalcharakter, *der;* **honesty is/is not part of his ~-up** er ist seinem Wesen nach aufrichtig/Aufrichtigkeit liegt nicht in seinem Wesen; **d)** *(Printing: arrangement of type)* Umbruch, *der;* **~weight** *n.* Gewichtszugabe, *die; (fig.: insignificant thing or person)* Lückenbüßer, *der; (unimportant point) unbedeutender Punkt zur Unterstützung eines Arguments;* **use X as [a] ~weight to Y** Y durch X schwerer machen; *(fig.)* Y durch X mehr Gewicht verleihen

making ['meɪkɪŋ] *n.* **a)** *(production)* Herstellung, *die;* **the ~ of the English working class** die Entstehung der englischen Arbeiterklasse; **in the ~**: im Entstehen; im Werden; **a minister in the ~**: ein angehender Minister; **be the ~ of victory/sb.'s career/sb.'s future** zum Sieg/zu jmds. Karriere führen/jmds. Zukunft sichern; **b)** *in pl.* *(profit)* Gewinn, *der* **(from** aus); *(earnings)* Verdienst, *der* **(on** für); **c)** *in pl.* *(qualities)* Anlagen; Voraussetzungen; **have all the ~s of sth.** alle Voraussetzungen für etw. haben; **have the ~s of a leader** über Führerqualitäten verfügen; das Zeug zum Führer haben *(ugs.)*; **d)** *(Amer., Austral.)* **the ~s for cigarettes** Zigarettenpapier und Tabak

malachite ['mæləkaɪt] *n.* *(Min.)* Malachit, *der; attrib.* aus Malachit *nachgestellt*

maladjusted [mælə'dʒʌstɪd] *adj.* *(Psych., Sociol.)* **[psychologically/socially]** ~: verhaltensgestört

maladjustment [mælə'dʒʌstmənt] *n.* *(Psych., Sociol.)* **[psychological/social]** ~: Verhaltensgestörtheit, *die*

maladministration [mælədmɪnɪ'streɪʃn] *n.* Mißwirtschaft, *die*

maladroit [mælə'drɔɪt, 'mælədrɔɪt] *adj.* ungeschickt; taktlos ‹*Bemerkung*›

malady ['mælədɪ] *n.* Leiden, *das; (fig.: of society, epoch)* Übel, *das*

Malaga ['mæləgə] *n.* *(wine)* Malaga, *der*

Malagasy [mælə'gæsɪ] **1.** *adj.* madagassisch. **2.** *n.* *(person)* Madagasse, *der*/Madagassin, *die; (language)* Malagassi, *das;* Madagassisch, *das*

malaise [mə'leɪz] *n.* *(bodily discomfort)* Unwohlsein, *das; (feeling of uneasiness)* Unbehagen, *das;* Malaise, *die (geh.)*

malapropism ['mæləprɒpɪzm] *n.* Malapropismus, *der (Literaturw.); irrtümlicher Gebrauch eines [schwierigen] Wortes anstelle eines ähnlich klingenden*

malaria [mə'leərɪə] *n.* Malaria, *die*

malarkey [mə'lɑːkɪ] *n., no pl., no indef. art.* *(sl.)* Blabla, *das (salopp);* **a load of ~**: reinstes Geschwafel *(ugs.)*

Malawi [mə'lɑːwɪ] *pr. n.* Malawi *(das)*

Malawian [mə'lɑːwɪən] **1.** *adj.* malawisch. **2.** Malawier, *der*/Malawierin, *die*

Malay [mə'leɪ] **1.** *adj.* malaiisch; **sb. is ~**: jmd. ist Malaie/Malaiin; *see also* **English 1. 2.** *n.* **a)** *(person)* Malaie, *der*/Malaiin, *die;* **b)** *(language)* Malaiisch, *das; see also* **English 2a**

Malaya [mə'leɪə] *pr. n.* Malaya *(das)*

Malayan [mə'leɪən] *see* **Malay 1, 2a**

Malaysia [mə'leɪzɪə] *pr. n.* Malaysia *(das)*

Malaysian [mə'leɪzɪən] **1.** *adj.* malaysisch. **2.** *n.* Malaysier, *der*/Malaysierin, *die*

malcontent ['mælkəntent] **1.** *adj.* unzufrieden; malkontent *(landsch., sonst veralt.)*. **2.** *n.* Nörgler, *der*/Nörglerin, *die (abwertend)*

Maldives ['mɔːldiːvz] *pr. n. pl.* Malediven *Pl.*

male [meɪl] **1.** *adj.* **a)** männlich; Männer‹*stimme, -chor, -verein*›; ~ **child/dog/cat/doctor/nurse/student** Junge/Rüde/Kater/Arzt/Krankenpfleger/Student, *der;* ~ **prostitute** *Mann, der der Prostitution nachgeht;* Strichjunge, *der (salopp);* Stricher, *der (salopp);* ~ **animal/bird/fish/insect** Männchen, *das;* ~ **ward** Männerstation, *die;* **b)** ~ **screw** Schraube, *die;* ~ **thread** Außengewinde, *das. See also* **chauvinism; chauvinist; menopause a. 2.** *n.* *(person)* Mann, *der; (foetus, child)* Junge, *der; (animal)* Männchen, *das*

malediction [mælɪ'dɪkʃn] *n.* Fluch, *der;* Verwünschung, *die*

malefactor ['mælɪfæktə(r)] *n.* Übeltäter, *der*

maleficent [mə'lefɪsənt] *adj.* böse ‹*Geist, Macht*›

male voice 'choir *n.* Männerchor, *der*

malevolence [mə'levələns] *n., no pl. see* **malevolent**: Bosheit, *die;* Übelwollen, *das;* Böswilligkeit, *die;* Boshaftigkeit, *die;* **feel ~ towards sb.** Mißgunst gegenüber jmdm. empfinden

malevolent [mə'levələnt] *adj.* böse ‹*Macht, Tat*›; übelwollend ‹*Gott*›; boshaft, hämisch ‹*Gelächter*›; böswillig ‹*Lüge*›; boshaft ‹*Person*›

malevolently [mə'levələntlı] *adv.* boshaft ‹*anstarren*›; böswillig ‹*verhindern, durchkreuzen*›; in böser Absicht ‹*überreden*›; hämisch ‹*lachen*›

malformation [mælfɔ:'meıʃn] *n. (Med.)* Mißbildung, *die*

malformed [mæl'fɔ:md] *adj. (Med.)* mißgebildet

malfunction [mæl'fʌŋkʃn] **1.** *n.* Störung, *die; (Med.)* Dysfunktion, *die (fachspr.);* Funktionsstörung, *die.* **2.** *v.i.* ‹*Mechanismus, System, Gerät:*› nicht richtig funktionieren; ‹*Prozeß, Vorgang:*› nicht richtig ablaufen; **the nervous system/liver ~s** die Funktion des Nervensystems/der Leber ist gestört

Mali ['mɑ:lı] *pr. n.* Mali *(das)*

Malian ['mɑ:lıən] **1.** *adj.* malisch. **2.** *n.* Malier, *der*/Malierin, *die*

malice ['mælıs] *n.* **a)** *(active ill will)* Bosheit, *die;* Böswilligkeit, *die; (desire to tease)* Schalkhaftigkeit, *die (geh.);* **bear ~ to** *or* **towards** *or* **against sb.** jmdm. übelwollen; **b)** *(Law)* böse Absicht; Dolus, *der (fachspr.);* böser Vorsatz; *see also* **aforethought**

malicious [mə'lıʃəs] *adj.* **a)** böse ‹*Klatsch, Tat, Person, Wort*›; böswillig ‹*Gerücht, Lüge, Verleumdung*›; boshaft ‹*Person*›; hämisch ‹*Vergnügen, Freude*›; **b)** *(Law)* böswillig ‹*Sachbeschädigung, Verleumdung*›

maliciously [mə'lıʃəslı] *adv.* **a)** mit [böser] Absicht; böse ‹*lächeln*›; **b)** *(Law)* böswillig

malign [mə'laın] **1.** *v.t. (slander)* verleumden; *(speak ill of)* schlechtmachen; **~ sb.'s character** jmdm. Übles nachsagen; ‹*Klatsch, Verleumdung:*› jmdn. in Verruf bringen. **2.** *adj.* **a)** *(injurious)* böse ‹*Macht, Geist*›; schlecht, unheilvoll ‹*Eigenschaft, Einfluß*›; **b)** *(Med.: malignant)* maligne *(fachspr.),* bösartig ‹*Krankheit*›; schwer ‹*Verletzung*›; **c)** *(malevolent)* böse ‹*Absicht*›; niederträchtig ‹*Motiv*›

malignancy [mə'lıgnənsı] *n. (Med.)* Bösartigkeit, *die;* Malignität, *die (fachspr.)*

malignant [mə'lıgnənt] *adj.* **a)** *(Med.)* maligne *(fachspr.),* bösartig ‹*Krankheit, Geschwür*›; **~ cancer** Karzinom, *das (fachspr.);* Krebs, *der;* **b)** *(harmful)* böse ‹*Macht*›; ungünstig ‹*Einfluß*›; **c)** *(feeling or showing ill will)* böse ‹*Geist, Zunge, Klatsch*›; bösartig, boshaft ‹*Verleumdung*›

malinger [mə'lıŋgə(r)] *v.i.* simulieren

malingerer [mə'lıŋgərə(r)] *n.* Simulant, *der*/Simulantin, *die*

mall [mæl, mɔ:l] *n.* **a)** *(promenade)* Promenade, *die;* **b)** *(Amer.: shopping precinct)* Einkaufszentrum, *das;* Einkaufsstraße, *die*

mallard ['mælɑ:d] *n. (Ornith.)* Stockente, *die*

malleable ['mælıəbl] *adj.* formbar ‹*Material, Person*›

mallet ['mælıt] *n.* **a)** *(hammer)* Holzhammer, *der;* Schlegel, *der; (of stonemason)* Klöpfel, *der; (of carpenter)* Klopfholz, *das;* **b)** *(Croquet)* Hammer, *der; (Polo)* Schläger, *der*

mallow ['mæləʊ] *n. (Bot.)* Malve, *die*

malnutrition [mælnju:'trıʃn] *n.* Unterernährung, *die*

malodorous [mæl'əʊdərəs] *adj.* übelriechend

malpractice [mæl'præktıs] *n.* **a)** *(wrongdoing)* Übeltat, *die (geh.);* **b)** *(Law, Med.: improper treatment of patient)* Kunstfehler, *der;* **c)** *(Law: wrongdoing by official etc.)* Amtsvergehen, *das*

malt [mɔ:lt, mɒlt] **1.** *n.* **a)** Malz, *das;* **b)** *(coll.: malt whisky)* Malzwhisky, *der.* **2.** *v.t.* mälzen ‹*Gerste*›

Malta ['mɔ:ltə, 'mɒltə] *pr. n.* Malta *(das)*

malted ['mɔ:ltıd, 'mɒltıd] *attrib. adj.* Malz-

Maltese [mɔ:l'ti:z, mɒl'ti:z] **1.** *adj.* maltesisch; **sb. is ~:** jmd. ist Malteser/Malteserin. **2.** *n., pl. same* **a)** *(person)* Malteser, *der*/Malteserin, *die;* **b)** *(language)* Maltesisch *(das)*

Maltese: ~ 'cat *n. blaugraue, kurzhaarige Hauskatze;* **~ 'cross** *n.* Malteserkreuz, *das*

malt: ~ 'extract *n.* Malzextrakt, *der;* **~-house** *n.* Mälzerei, *die;* **~ 'liquor** *n.* Bier, *das*

maltreat [mæl'tri:t] *v.t.* mißhandeln

maltreatment [mæl'tri:tmənt] *n.* Mißhandlung, *die*

malt 'whisky *n.* Malzwhisky, *der*

mam [mæm] *n. (Brit. coll./child lang.)* Mama, *die (fam.);* Mami, *die (fam.)*

mama *see* **mamma**

mamba ['mæmbə] *n. (Zool.)* Mamba, *die*

mamma [mə'mɑ:] *n. (coll./child lang.)* Mama, *die (fam.);* Mami, *die (fam.);* **~'s boy** *(coll.)* Muttersöhnchen, *das (ugs.)*

mammal ['mæml] *n. (Zool.)* Säugetier, *das;* Säuger, *der*

mammalian [mə'meılıən] *(Zool.)* **1.** *adj.* Säugetier-; eines Säugetiers *nachgestellt.* **2.** *n.* Säugetier, *das;* Säuger, *der*

mammary ['mæmərı] *adj. (Anat., Zool.)* Brust-; **~ gland** Brustdrüse, *die*

Mammon ['mæmən] *n.* **a)** *(wealth regarded as idol)* Mammon, *der;* **ye cannot serve God and ~** *(Bibl.)* ihr könnt nicht Gott dienen und dem Mammon; **b)** *(the rich)* die Reichen

mammoth ['mæməθ] **1.** *n. (Zool., Palaeont.)* Mammut, *das.* **2.** *adj.* Mammut-; riesig ‹*Menge*›; gigantisch ‹*Vorhaben*›

mammy ['mæmı] *n.* **a)** *(child lang.: mother)* Mama, *die (fam.);* Mami, *die (fam.);* **b)** *(Amer.: black nurse)* schwarze Kinderfrau

man [mæn] **1.** *n., pl.* **men** [men] **a)** *no art., no pl. (human being, person)* Mensch, *der; (the human race)* der Mensch; **as a ~:** als Mensch; **God was made ~:** Gott ward Mensch *(bibl.);* **~ is a political animal** der Mensch ist ein politisches Wesen; **everything a ~ needs** alles, was der Mensch braucht; **what can a ~ do?** was kann man tun?; **every ~ for himself** rette sich, wer kann; **as one ~:** wie ein Mann; *(unanimously)* geschlossen; **any ~ who ...:** wer ...; jeder, der ...; **no ~:** niemand; **always get one's ~:** den Täter immer finden; **[all] to a ~:** allesamt; **to the last ~:** bis zum letzten Mann; **they were killed to a ~:** sie wurden bis auf den letzten Mann getötet; **the ~ in** *or (Amer.)* **on the street** der Mann auf der Straße; **the rights of ~:** die Menschenrechte; **Heidelberg Man** der Homo heidelbergensis; der Heidelbergmensch; **Java/Peking Man** der Java-/Pekingmensch; **b)** *(adult male, individual male)* Mann, *der;* **every ~, woman, and child** ausnahmslos jeder *od.* alle; **the right ~:** der richtige Mann; der Richtige; **the [very] ~ for sth.** der richtige Mann *od.* der Richtige; **he is your ~:** er ist der richtige Mann *od.* der Richtige für dich; **you have arrested the wrong ~:** Sie haben den Falschen verhaftet; **a ~'s life** ein Leben für Männer; **a ~'s ~:** ein Mann, der sich nur in männlicher Gesellschaft wohl fühlt; **make a ~ out of sb.** *(fig.)* einen Mann aus jmdm. machen; **be only half a ~:** nur ein halber Mann sein; **like a ~:** wie ein Mann; **that's just like a ~:** typisch Mann!; **a ~ of property/great strength** ein vermögender/sehr kräftiger Mann; **that ~ Oakfield** dieser Oakfield; **play the ~:** ein Mann sein; **men's clothing/outfitter** Herrenkleidung, *die*/Herrenausstatter, *der;* **be ~ enough to ...:** Manns genug sein, um zu ...; **a '~'s voice** eine männliche Stimme; **'the deodorant for men'** „das Herrendeodorant"; **I have lived here, ~ and boy** ich habe hier von frühester Jugend an gewohnt; **sth. sorts out** *or* **separates the men from the boys** *(coll.)* an etw. *(Dat.)* zeigt sich, wer ein ganzer Kerl ist und wer nicht; **~ of God** Gottesmann, *der (geh.);* **the ~ in the moon** der Mann im Mond; **he's a local ~:** er ist von hier; **a whisky ~:** ein Whiskytrinker; **he's [not] a drinking ~:** er trinkt [nicht]; **be one's own ~:** wissen, was man will; **you've come to the right ~:** bei mir sind Sie richtig; **men's toilet** Herrentoilette, *die;* **'Men'** „Herren"; **my [good] ~:** mein Guter; **fight ~ to ~:** Mann gegen Mann kämpfen; **~ friend** Freund, *der;* **c)** *(husband)* Mann, *der;* **be ~ and wife** verheiratet sein; **d)** *(work~)* Mann, *der;* **e)** *usu. in pl. (soldier, sailor, etc.)* Mann, *der;* **f)** *(Chess)* Figur, *die; (Draughts)* Stein, *der;* **g)** *(sl.: as int. of surprise or impatience, as mode of address)* Mensch! *(salopp);* **nonsense, ~!** Unsinn!; **hurry up, ~!** Mensch, beeil dich!; **h)** *(type of ~)* Mann, *der;* Typ, *der;* **a ~ of the people/world/of action** ein Mann des Volkes/von Welt/der Tat; **he is not a** *or* **the ~ to do something like that** er ist nicht der Mann *od.* Typ, der so etwas tut; **he is not a ~ I could trust** ihm könnte ich nicht trauen; **be an Oxford ~:** aus Oxford kommen; *(Univ.)* in Oxford studiert haben; **i)** *(~servant)* Diener, *der. See also* **action a; alive a; best man; Clapham; handyman; honour 1 d; house 1 a; inner man; jack 1 c; letter 1 d; little 1 b; moment a; old man; outer b; part 1 i; substance b; town a; word 1 b; world a. 2.** *v.t.,* **-nn-** bemannen ‹*Schiff, Spill*›; besetzen ‹*Büro, Stelle, Posten, Pumpe, Kontrollpunkt*›; bedienen ‹*Telefon, Geschütz*›; ‹*Soldaten:*› Stellung beziehen in (+ *Dat.*) ‹*Festung*›; mit Personal besetzen ‹*Fabrik, Werk*›; **be ~ned by a crew of 50** ‹*Schiff:*› eine Besatzung von 50 Mann haben

manacle ['mænəkl] **1.** *n., usu. in pl.* [Hand]fessel, *die;* Kette, *die.* **2.** *v.t.* Handfesseln anlegen (+ *Dat.*)

manage ['mænıdʒ] **1.** *v.t.* **a)** *(handle, wield)* handhaben ‹*Werkzeug, Segel, Boot*›; bedienen ‹*Schaltbrett*›; **the tool is too heavy for him to ~:** er kommt mit dem schweren Gerät nicht zurecht; **b)** *(conduct, organize)* durchführen ‹*Operation, Unternehmen*›; erledigen ‹*Angelegenheit*›; verwalten ‹*Geld, Grundstück*›; leiten ‹*Geschäft, Büro, Schule, Krankenhaus*›; führen ‹*Haushalt*›; **c)** *(Sport etc.: be manager of)* managen, betreuen ‹*Team, Mannschaft*›; **d)** *(cope with)* schaffen; **I could/couldn't ~ another apple** *(coll.)* ich könnte noch einen Apfel schaffen/noch einen Apfel schaffe ich nicht; **I can/can't ~ this suitcase** den Koffer kann ich [alleine] tragen/ich werde mit diesem Koffer nicht fertig; **we can ~ another person in the car** einer hat noch Platz im Wagen; **he can't ~ the stairs** er kommt die Treppe nicht rauf/runter; **e)** *(gain one's ends with)* für sich gewinnen ‹*Person*›; **f)** *(succeed in achieving)* zustandebringen ‹*Lächeln*›; **g)** *(contrive)* **~ to do sth.** *(also iron.)* es fertigbringen, etw. zu tun; **he ~d to do it** es gelang ihm, es zu tun; **I don't know how you ~d it** ich weiß nicht, wie du das bewerkstelligt hast; **I'll ~ it somehow** ich werde es schon irgendwie hinkriegen *(ugs.);* **I ~d to get a word in** ich kam endlich zu Wort; **can you ~ to be there at 10 a.m.?** *(coll.)* kannst du um 10 Uhr dort sein?; **how could you ~ to eat all that?** *(coll.)* wie hast du es [bloß] geschafft, das alles zu essen?; **can you ~ 7 [o'clock]?** paßt dir 7 Uhr?; **h)** *(be in charge of)* hüten ‹*Herde*›; **i)** *(control)* bändigen ‹*Person, Tier, Haar*›. **2.** *v.i.* zurechtkommen; **~ without sth.** ohne etw. auskommen; **~ on** zurecht- *od.* auskommen mit ‹*Geld, Einkommen*›; **~ by oneself** allein zurechtkommen; **I can ~:** es geht; **can you ~?** geht's?; geht es?

manageable ['mænıdʒəbl] *adj.* leicht frisierbar ‹*Haar*›; fügsam ‹*Person, Tier*›; regierbar ‹*Land, Staat*›; überschaubar

⟨*Größe, Menge*⟩; zu bewältigend ⟨*Portion*⟩; lenkbar ⟨*Firma*⟩

management ['mænɪdʒmənt] *n.* **a)** Durchführung, *die; (of a business)* Leitung, *die;* Management, *das; (of money)* Verwaltung, *die;* ~ **studies** Betriebsführung und -organisation *(als Teilgebiet der Betriebswirtschaftslehre);* **it was bad ~ to ...:** es war ein Fehler der Geschäftsleitung, zu ...; **b)** *(managers)* Leitung, *die;* Management, *das; (of theatre etc.)* Direktion, *die;* **the ~:** die Geschäftsleitung; **'under new ~'** „unter neuer Leitung"; **c)** *(Med.)* Behandlung, *die*

manager ['mænɪdʒə(r)] *n. (of branch of shop or bank)* Filialleiter, *der*/-leiterin, *die;* Geschäftsstellenleiter, *der*/-leiterin, *die; (of football team)* [Chef]trainer, *der*/-trainerin, *die; (of tennis-player, boxer, pop group)* Manager, *der*/Managerin, *die; (of restaurant, shop, hotel)* Geschäftsführer, *der*/-führerin, *die; (of estate, grounds)* Verwalter, *der*/Verwalterin, *die; (of department; sales or publicity ~)* Leiter, *der*/Leiterin, *die; (of theatre)* Direktor, *der*/Direktorin, *die*

manageress ['mænɪdʒəres, mænɪdʒə'res] *n. (of restaurant, shop, hotel)* Geschäftsführerin, *die; see also* **manager**

managerial [mænə'dʒɪərɪəl] *adj.* führend, leitend ⟨*Stellung*⟩; geschäftlich ⟨*Aspekt, Seite*⟩; ⟨*Pflicht, Fähigkeiten*⟩ als Führungskraft; ~ **skills** Führungsqualitäten; **the ~ class** die Führungsschicht

managing ['mænɪdʒɪŋ] *attrib. adj.* geschäftsführend; leitend; ~ **director** Geschäftsführer, *der*

Manchuria [mæn'tʃʊərɪə] *pr. n.* die Mandschurei

Mancunian [mæŋ'kju:nɪən] **1.** *adj.* Manchesterer. **2.** *n.* Manchesterer, *der*/Manchesterin, *die*

mandala ['mændələ] *n. (Hinduism, Buddhism, Psych.)* Mandala, *das*

¹mandarin ['mændərɪn] *n.* ~ **[orange]** Mandarine, *die*

²mandarin *n.* **a)** *(Hist.: Chinese official)* Mandarin, *der;* **b) M~** *(language)* Hochchinesisch, *das;* **c)** *(party leader)* Parteiboß, *der (ugs.);* [Partei]bonze, *der (abwertend);* **d)** *(bureaucrat)* Bürokrat, *der*/Bürokratin, *die (abwertend);* Apparatschik, *der (abwertend)*

mandarin: ~ 'collar *n.* Mandarinkragen, *der;* ~ **'duck** *n.* Mandarinente, *die*

mandarine ['mændəri:n] *see* **¹mandarin**

mandarin 'sleeve *n.* Bouffonärmel, *der*

mandate 1. ['mændeɪt] *n.* **a)** *(judicial or legal command)* Verfügung, *die;* **b)** *(commission to act for another)* Mandat, *das;* **c)** *(Polit.)* Mandat, *das;* **electoral ~:** Wählerauftrag, *der.* **2.** [mæn'deɪt] *v. t.* **~ a territory to a country** ein Gebiet der Verwaltung eines Landes unterstellen

mandatory ['mændətərɪ] *adj.* obligatorisch; **be ~:** Pflicht od. obligatorisch sein; **it is ~ for sb. to do sth.** jmd. muß etw. tun

'man-day *n. (Work Study)* Manntag, *der;* Arbeitstag pro Mann

mandible ['mændɪbl] *n. (Zool.)* **a)** *(of mammal, fish)* Unterkiefer, *der;* **b)** *(of bird)* Schnabel, *der;* **lower ~:** Unterschnabel, *der;* **c)** *(of insect)* Zange, *die;* Kiefer, *der*

mandolin, mandoline [mændə'lɪn] *n. (Mus.)* Mandoline, *die*

mandrake ['mændreɪk] *n. (Bot.)* Mandragore, *die;* Alraunwurzel, *die*

mandrel ['mændrəl] *n. (Mech. Engin.)* **a)** *(shaft in lathe)* Drehspindel, *die;* **b)** *(rod)* Horn, *das*

mandrill ['mændrɪl] *n. (Zool.)* Mandrill, *der*

mane [meɪn] *n. (lit. or fig.)* Mähne, *die*

man: ~-eater *n. (tiger)* menschenfressender Tiger; *(shark)* Menschenhai, *der; (cannibal)* Kannibale, *der*/Kannibalin, *die; (fig.: woman)* Frau, die Männer aussaugt; **~-eating** *adj.* menschenfressend ⟨*Löwe, Tiger*⟩; **a ~-eating shark** ein Menschenhai

maneuver, maneuverable *(Amer.) see* **manœuvr-**

man 'Friday *see* **Friday 1**

manful ['mænfl] *adj.* mannhaft

manfully ['mænfəlɪ] *adv.* mannhaft; wie ein Mann

manganese ['mæŋgəni:z, mæŋgə'ni:z] *n.* **a)** *(Min.)* Braunstein, *der;* Manganoxid, *das (fachspr.);* **b)** *(Chem.)* Mangan, *das*

mange [meɪndʒ] *n. (Vet. Med.)* Räude, *die*

mangel[-wurzel] ['mæŋgl(wɜ:zl)] *n. (Agric.)* Runkelrübe, *die*

manger ['meɪndʒə(r)] *n.* Futtertrog, *der; (Bibl.)* Krippe, *die; see also* **dog 1 a**

mange-tout [mɑ̃ʒ'tu:] *n.* Zuckererbse, *die*

¹mangle ['mæŋgl] **1.** *n.* Mangel, *die.* **2.** *v. t.* mangeln ⟨*Wäsche*⟩

²mangle *v. t.* verstümmeln, [übel] zurichten ⟨*Person*⟩; demolieren ⟨*Sache*⟩; verstümmeln, entstellen ⟨*Zitat, Musikstück*⟩

mango ['mæŋgəʊ] *n., pl.* **~es** *or* **~s a)** *(tree)* Mangobaum, *der;* **b)** *(fruit)* Mango[frucht], *die*

mangrove ['mæŋgrəʊv] *n. (Bot.)* Mangrovebaum, *der*

mangy ['meɪndʒɪ] *adj.* **a)** *(Vet. Med.)* räudig; **b)** *(squalid, shabby)* verwahrlost, schäbig ⟨*Äußeres, Kleidung*⟩; abgenutzt, schäbig ⟨*Teppich, Decke, Stuhl*⟩

man: ~handle *v. t.* **a)** *(move by human effort)* von Hand bewegen ⟨*Gegenstand*⟩; **b)** *(handle roughly)* grob behandeln ⟨*Person*⟩; **~-hater** *n. (misanthrope)* Menschenhasser, *der*/-hasserin, *die; (hater of male sex)* Männerfeind, *der*/-feindin, *die;* **~hole** *n.* Mannloch, *das; (in tank)* Einstiegsluke, *die; (to cables under pavement)* Kabelschacht, *der*

manhood ['mænhʊd] *n., no pl.* **a)** *(state)* Mannesalter, *das;* **b)** *(courage)* Männlichkeit, *die;* **c)** *(men of a country)* Männer *Pl.*

man: ~-hour *n. (Work Study)* Arbeitsstunde, *die;* **~-hunt** *n.* Menschenjagd, *die; (for criminal)* Verbrecherjagd, *die*

mania ['meɪnɪə] *n.* **a)** *(madness)* Wahnsinn, *der;* **b)** *(enthusiasm)* Manie, *die;* **~ for detective novels** Leidenschaft für Krimis; **have a ~ for doing sth.** etw. wie besessen *od.* leidenschaftlich gern tun; **there was a ~ at that time for wearing ear-rings** damals waren die Leute ganz verrückt nach Ohrringen

-mania *n. in comb. (Psych.)* -manie, *die*

maniac ['meɪnɪæk] **1.** *adj.* wahnsinnig; krankhaft, *(geh.)* manisch ⟨*Phantasie, Verlangen*⟩. **2.** *n.* **a)** *(Psych.)* Besessene, *der/die; (madman/-woman)* Wahnsinnige, *der/die;* **b)** *(person with passion for sth.)* Fanatiker, *der*/Fanatikerin, *die;* **a nation of tennis ~s** ein Volk von Tennisfanatikern

maniacal [mə'naɪəkl] *adj.* wahnsinnig

manic ['mænɪk] *adj. (Psych.)* manisch

manic-de'pressive *(Psych.)* **1.** *adj.* manisch-depressiv. **2.** *n.* manisch-depressiver Mensch; **be a ~:** manisch-depressiv sein

manicure ['mænɪkjʊə(r)] **1.** *n.* Maniküre, *die;* **give sb. a ~:** jmdn. maniküren. **2.** *v. t.* maniküren

manicurist ['mænɪkjʊərɪst] *n.* Maniküre, *die*

manifest ['mænɪfest] **1.** *adj.* offenkundig; offenbar ⟨*Mißverständnis*⟩; sichtbar ⟨*Erfolg, Fortschritt*⟩; sichtlich ⟨*Freude*⟩. **2.** *v. t.* **a)** *(show, display)* zeigen, bekunden *(geh.)* ⟨*Interesse, Mißfallen, Begeisterung, Zuneigung*⟩; **b)** *(reveal)* offenbaren *(meist geh.);* **~ itself** ⟨*Geist:*⟩ erscheinen; ⟨*Natur, Wahrheit:*⟩ sich offenbaren; ⟨*Symptom, Krankheit:*⟩ manifest werden. **3.** *n.* **a)** *(cargo-list)* Frachtgutliste, *die;* Ladeverzeichnis, *das;* **ship's ~:** [Schiffs]manifest, *das;* **b)** *(list) (of passengers in aircraft)* Passagierliste, *die; (of trucks etc. in goods train)* Fahrzeugliste, *die*

manifestation [mænɪfe'steɪʃn] *n. (of ill-will, favour, disapproval)* Ausdruck, *der;* Bekundung, *die (geh.);* Bezeugung, *die; (appearance)* Erscheinung, *die; in pl.* Erscheinungsformen; *(visible expression, sign)* [An]zeichen, *das* **(of** von)

manifestly ['mænɪfestlɪ] *adv.* offenkundig; **it is ~ unjust that ...:** es ist ganz offensichtlich ungerecht, daß ...

manifesto [mænɪ'festəʊ] *n., pl.* **~s** Manifest, *das*

manifold ['mænɪfəʊld] **1.** *adj. (literary)* mannigfaltig *(geh.);* vielfältig; vielseitig ⟨*Erzählperspektive, Gehalt, Verwendung*⟩. **2.** *(Mech. Engin.)* Verteilerrohr, *das;* **[inlet] ~:** [Ansaug]krümmer, *der;* **[exhaust] ~:** [Auspuff]krümmer, *der*

manikin ['mænɪkɪn] *n.* **a)** *(dwarf)* Zwerg, *der;* **b)** *(Art)* Gliederpuppe, *die;* **c)** *(Med.)* anatomisches Modell

Manila [mə'nɪlə] *n.* **a)** *(cigar)* Manilazigarre, *die;* **b)** *(fibre)* ~ **[hemp]** *see* **hemp a; c)** *(paper)* ~ **[paper]** Manilapapier, *das;* ~ **[envelope]** Briefumschlag aus Manilapapier; brauner Briefumschlag

manioc ['mænɪɒk] *n.* **a)** *(plant)* Maniok, *der;* **b)** *(flour)* Mandioka, *die*

manipulate [mə'nɪpjʊleɪt] *v. t.* **a)** *(also Med.)* manipulieren; **~ sb. into doing sth.** jmdn. dahin gehend manipulieren, daß er etw. tut; **b)** *(handle)* handhaben

manipulation [mənɪpjʊ'leɪʃn] *n.* **a)** *(also Med.)* Manipulation, *die;* **b)** *(handling)* Handhabung, *die*

manipulative [mə'nɪpjʊlətɪv] *adj.* manipulativ

mankind [mæn'kaɪnd] *n.* Menschheit, *die*

'manlike *adj.* **a)** *(like a male, mannish)* männlich; **b)** *(like a human)* menschenähnlich

manly ['mænlɪ] *adj.* männlich; *(brave)* mannhaft *(geh.)*

'man-made *adj.* künstlich ⟨*See, Blumen, Schlucht*⟩; vom Menschen geschaffen ⟨*Gesetze*⟩; *(synthetic)* Kunst⟨*faser, -stoff*⟩

manna ['mænə] *n. (Bibl.)* Manna, *das;* **be ~ [from heaven]** *(fig.)* ein wahrer Segen sein

manned [mænd] *adj.* bemannt ⟨*Raumschiff usw.*⟩

mannequin ['mænɪkɪn] *n.* **a)** *(person)* Mannequin, *das;* **b)** *(dummy)* Schaufensterpuppe, *die*

manner ['mænə(r)] *n.* **a)** *(way, fashion)* Art, *die;* Weise, *die; (more emphatic)* Art und Weise, *die;* **in this ~:** auf diese Art und Weise; **he did it in a very unorthodox ~:** er machte es auf [eine ganz] unorthodoxe Art; **he acted in such a ~ as to offend her** er benahm sich so, daß sie beleidigt war; **in the French ~:** auf französische Art; **celebrate in the grand ~:** im großen Stil feiern; **[as] to the ~ born** *(coll.)* wie dafür geschaffen; **in a ~ of speaking** mehr oder weniger; **adverb of ~** *(Ling.)* Umstandsbestimmung der Art und Weise; **b)** *no pl. (bearing)* Art, *die; (towards others)* Auftreten, *das;* **c)** *in pl. (social behaviour)* Manieren *Pl.;* Benehmen, *das;* **teach sb. some ~s** jmdm. Manieren beibringen; **forget one's ~s** seine guten Manieren zu Hause lassen; **where are your ~s?** wo hast du deine Manieren gelassen?; **that's good ~s** das gehört sich so; **that's bad ~s** das gehört sich nicht; das macht man nicht; **mind** *or* **watch your ~s!** benimm dich!; **~s maketh man** *(prov.)* es kommt vor allem auf gutes Benehmen an; *see also* **mend 1 b; d)** *in pl. (modes of life)* Sitten *Pl.;* **e)** *(artistic style)* Stil, *der;* **~s** Stilrichtungen; **f)** *(type)* **all ~ of** *see* **all 1 b; no ~ of** keinerlei; **what ~ of man is he?** *(arch.)* was für ein Mensch ist er?; *see also* **means c**

mannered ['mænəd] *adj.* **a)** *(showing mannerism)* manieriert; **b)** *in comb.* **...-~:** mit ... Manieren *nachgestellt;* **be well-~/bad-~:** gute/schlechte Manieren haben; **he's a mild-~ man** er hat ein sanftes Wesen

mannerism ['mænərɪzm] *n.* **a)** *(addiction to*

a manner) Manieriertheit, *die;* **b)** *(trick of style)* Manierismus, *der;* **c)** *(in behaviour)* Eigenart, *die;* **d)** *no pl., no art. (Art)* Manierismus, *der*

manning ['mænɪŋ] *n. (of ship, aircraft)* Bemannung, *die; (of factory, industry, etc.)* Personalausstattung, *die*

mannish ['mænɪʃ] *adj.* männlich; männlich, maskulin ‹*Kleidung*›; **a ~ woman** ein Mannweib *(abwertend)*

manœuvrable [mə'nu:vrəbl] *adj. (Brit.)* manövrierfähig ‹*Schiff, Flugzeug, Auto*›; **be easily ~:** leicht zu manövrieren *od.* zu lenken sein

manœuvre [mə'nu:və(r)] *(Brit.)* **1.** *n.* **a)** *(Mil., Navy)* Manöver, *das;* **be/go on ~s** im Manöver sein/ins Manöver ziehen *od.* rücken; **b)** *(deceptive movement, scheme; also of vehicle, aircraft)* Manöver, *das;* **room for ~** *(fig.)* Spielraum, *der.* **2.** *v. t.* **a)** *(Mil., Navy)* führen; dirigieren; **b)** *(bring by ~s)* manövrieren; bugsieren ‹*Sperriges*›; **~ sb./oneself/sth. into a good position** *(fig.)* jmdn./sich/etw. in eine gute Position manövrieren; **c)** *(manipulate)* beeinflussen; **~ sb. into doing sth.** jmdn. dazu bringen, etw. zu tun; **~ sb. away from sth.** jmdn. von etw. abbringen. **3.** *v. i.* **a)** *(Mil., Navy)* [ein] Manöver durchführen; **b)** *(move, scheme)* manövrieren; **room to ~:** Platz zum Manövrieren; *(fig.)* Spielraum, *der;* **~ for power** auf Machtgewinn hinarbeiten

man-of-'war *n., pl.* **men-of-war** Kriegsschiff, *das; see also* **Portuguese man-of-war**

manor ['mænə(r)] *n.* **a)** *(land)* [Land]gut, *das;* **lord/lady of the ~:** Gutsherr, *der*/Gutsherrin, *die;* **b)** *(house)* Herrenhaus, das; **c)** *(Brit. sl.: police area)* Revier, *das*

'manor-house *see* **manor b**

manorial [mə'nɔ:rɪəl] *adj.* Guts‹*hof, -besitz*›; gutsherrschaftlich ‹*System, Rechte*›

'manpower *n.* **a)** *(available power)* Arbeitspotential, *das; (workers)* Arbeitskräfte *Pl.; attrib.* Personal‹*mangel, -planung*›; **b)** *(Mil.)* Stärke, *die*

'man-powered *adj.* **~ flight** Flug mit [menschlicher] Muskelkraft

manqué ['mɑ̃keɪ] *adj. postpos.* verhindert ‹*Poet, Künstler, Intellektueller usw.*›

mansard ['mænsɑ:d] *n.* **~ [roof]** *(Archit.)* Mansard[en]dach, *das*

manse [mæns] *n.* Pfarrhaus, *das*

'manservant *n., pl.* **'menservants** Diener, *der*

mansion ['mænʃn] *n.* Villa, *die; (of lord of the manor)* Herrenhaus, *das*

man: ~-size, ~-sized *adj. (suitable for a man)* ‹*Mahlzeit, Steak*› für einen [ganzen] Mann; *(large)* groß; **~slaughter** *n. (Law)* Totschlag, *der*

manta ['mæntə] *n. (Zool.)* Teufelsrochen, *der;* Manta, *der*

mantel ['mæntl] *see* **mantelpiece**

mantel: ~piece *n.* **a)** *(above fireplace)* Kaminsims, *der od. das;* **b)** *(around fireplace)* Kamineinfassung, *die;* **~shelf** *see* **~piece a**

mantis ['mæntɪs] *n., pl. same (Zool.)* Fang[heu]schrecke, *die;* **praying ~:** Gottesanbeterin, *die*

mantle ['mæntl] **1.** *n.* **a)** *(cloak)* Umhang, *der; (fig.)* Mantel, *der;* **~ of snow** Schneedecke, *die;* **b)** *(Geol.)* Mantel, *der.* **2.** *v. t. (literary: cover)* bedecken

'man-to-man *adj.* von Mann zu Mann *nachgestellt*

mantra ['mæntrə] *n. (Relig.)* Mantra, *das*

'mantrap *n.* Fußangel, *die*

manual ['mænjʊəl] **1.** *adj.* **a)** manuell; **~ work/labour** manuelle Tätigkeit *od.* Handarbeit/körperliche Arbeit *od.* Schwerarbeit; **~ worker/labourer** Handarbeiter/Schwerarbeiter, *der;* **b)** *(not automatic)* handbetrieben; ‹*Bedienung, Kontrolle, Schaltung*› von Hand; **~ steering/signals** Handsteuerung, *die*/-zeichen. **2.** *n.* **a)** *(handbook)* Handbuch, *das;* **b)** *(Mus.)* Manual, *das*

manually ['mænjʊəlɪ] *adv.* manuell; von Hand; mit der Hand; **a ~ operated machine** eine handbetriebene Maschine

manufacture [mænjʊ'fæktʃə(r)] **1.** *n.* Herstellung, *die;* **cost/country of ~:** Herstellungskosten, *Pl.*/-land, *das;* **articles of home/foreign/British ~:** inländische/ausländische/britische Erzeugnisse. **2.** *v. t.* **a)** *(Commerc.)* herstellen; **~ iron into steel/cloth into garments** Eisen zu Stahl verarbeiten/aus Stoff Kleidungsstücke herstellen; **~d goods** Fertigprodukte *Pl.;* **manufacturing costs/firm/fault** Herstellungskosten *Pl.*/Herstellerfirma, *die*/Produktionsfehler, *der;* **manufacturing town** Industriestadt, *die;* **b)** *(invent)* erfinden ‹*Geschichte, Ausrede usw.*›

manufacturer [mænjʊ'fæktʃərə(r)] *n.* Hersteller, *der;* **'~'s recommended [retail] price'** „unverbindliche Preisempfehlung"

manure [mə'njʊə(r)] **1.** *n. (dung)* Dung, *der; (fertilizer)* Dünger, *der.* **2.** *v. t.* düngen

manuscript ['mænjʊskrɪpt] **1.** *n.* **a)** Handschrift, *die;* **b)** *(not yet printed)* Manuskript, *das;* **the novel is still in ~:** der Roman liegt [erst] im *od.* als Manuskript vor. **2.** *adj.* handschriftlich

'man-week *n. (Work Study)* Mannwoche, *die*

Manx [mæŋks] **1.** *adj.* der Insel Man *nachgestellt.* **2.** *n. (Ling.)* Manx, *das*

Manx: ~ 'cat *n.* Man[x]katze, *die;* **~man** ['mæŋksmən] *n., pl.* **~men** ['mæŋksmən] Bewohner der Insel Man; Manx, *der*

many ['menɪ] **1.** *adj.* **a)** viele; *pred.* zahlreich; **how ~ people/books?** wie viele *od.* wieviel Leute/Bücher?; **as ~ as** so viele wie; **there were as ~ as 50 of them** es waren mindestens *od.* bestimmt 50; **three accidents in as ~ days** drei Unfälle in ebenso vielen *od.* ebensoviel Tagen; **~'s the tale/the time** so manche Geschichte/so manches Mal; **too ~ people/books** zu viele *od.* zuviel Leute/Bücher; **there were too ~ of them** es waren zu viele *od.* zuviel; **two [copies] too ~:** zwei [Exemplare] zuviel; **one is too ~/there is one too ~:** einer/eine/eins ist zuviel; **he/she is one too ~ here** er/sie ist hier überflüssig; **he's had one too ~** *(is drunk)* er hat einen *od.* ein Glas zuviel getrunken; **b) ~ a man** so mancher; manch einer; **~ a time** so manches Mal. **2.** *n.* viele [Leute]; **there weren't ~ of them there** es waren nicht viele da; **~ of us** viele von uns; **a good/great ~ [of them/of the books]** eine Menge/eine ganze Reihe [von ihnen/der Bücher]; **there were a good ~ there** eine Menge war *od.* waren da

'many-coloured *adj.* vielfarbig

'man-year *n. (Work Study)* Mannjahr, *das*

'many-sided *adj. (Geom.; also fig.)* vielseitig

Mao [maʊ] *adj.* ‹*Jacke, Schirmmütze*› im Mao-Look; Mao-‹*Jacke, Mütze*›

Maoism ['maʊɪzm] *n., no pl.* Maoismus, *der*

Maoist ['maʊɪst] *n.* Maoist, *der; attrib.* maoistisch

Maori ['maʊrɪ] **1.** *n.* **a)** *(person)* Maori, *der;* **b)** *(language)* Maori, *das.* **2.** *adj.* maorisch

map [mæp] **1.** *n.* **a)** [Land]karte, *die; (street plan)* Stadtplan, *der;* **b)** *(fig. coll.)* **off the ~:** abgelegen; **we're a bit off the ~ up here** wir leben hier ein bißchen hinter dem Mond *(ugs.);* **wipe off the ~:** ausradieren; **[put sth./sb.] on the ~:** [etw./jmdn.] populär [machen]. **2.** *v. t.,* **-pp-** *(make map of)* kartographieren; *(make survey of)* vermessen

~ 'out *v. t.* im einzelnen festlegen

maple ['meɪpl] *n.* Ahorn, *der*

maple: ~-leaf *n.* Ahornblatt, *das;* **~ sugar** *n.* Ahornzucker, *der;* **~ syrup** *n.* Ahornsirup, *der*

map: ~-maker *n.* Kartograph, *der*/Kartographin, *die;* **~-reader** *n.* Kartenleser, *der*/-leserin, *die;* **~-reading** *n., no pl.* Kartenlesen, *das*

mar [mɑ:(r)] *v. t.,* **-rr- a)** *(spoil, disfigure)* verderben; entstellen ‹*Aussehen*›; stören ‹*Veranstaltung*›; **the book was ~red by a number of small mistakes** die Qualität des Buches wurde durch eine Reihe kleiner Fehler beeinträchtigt; **b)** *(ruin) see* **make 1 p**

Mar. *abbr.* **March** Mrz.

marabou ['mærəbu:] *n. (Ornith.)* **a)** *(African)* Marabu, *der;* **b)** *see* **adjutant b**

maraschino [mærə'ski:nəʊ] *n., pl.* **~s** Maraschino, *der;* **~ cherry** Maraschinokirsche, *die*

marathon ['mærəθən] *n.* **a)** *(race)* Marathon[lauf], *der; attrib.* Marathon‹*läufer*›; **b)** *(fig.)* Marathon, *das; attrib.* Marathon‹*rede, -spiel, -sitzung*›; **a chess ~:** ein Schachmarathon

maraud [mə'rɔ:d] **1.** *v. i.* plündern; marodieren *(Soldatenspr.).* **2.** *v. t.* plündern

marauder [mə'rɔ:də(r)] *n.* Plünderer, *der;* Marodeur, *der (Soldatenspr.); (animal)* Räuber, *der*

marble ['mɑ:bl] *n.* **a)** *(stone)* Marmor, *der (auch fig.); attrib.* Marmor-; aus Marmor *nachgestellt;* marmorn *(dichter.; fig.);* **b)** *in pl. (statues)* Marmorskulpturen; **the Elgin M~s** die Elgin Marbles *(Kunstwiss.);* **c)** *(toy)* Murmel, *die;* **[game of] ~s** Murmelspiel, *das;* **play ~s** murmeln; [mit] Murmeln spielen; **d)** *in pl.* **not have all** *or* **have lost one's ~s** *(sl.)* nicht alle Tassen im Schrank haben *(ugs.)*

marbled ['mɑ:bld] *adj.* **a)** marmoriert ‹*Papier, Seife usw.*›; **b)** *(streaked)* durchwachsen ‹*Fleisch*›

March [mɑ:tʃ] *n.* März, *der; see also* **August; hare 1 a**

[1]march 1. *n.* **a)** *(Mil., Mus.; hike)* Marsch, *der; (gait)* Marschschritt, *der;* Marschtritt, *der;* **on the ~:** auf dem Marsch; *(fig.)* unterwegs; **~ past** Vorbeimarsch, *der;* Defilee, *das;* **a day's/three days' ~:** ein Tagesmarsch/drei Tagesmärsche; **an hour's ~ away** eine Marschstunde *od.* eine Stunde Marsch entfernt; *see also* **forced march; [1]line 1 k; steal 1 c; b)** *(in protest)* **[protest] ~:** Protestmarsch, *der;* **c)** *(progress of time, events, etc.)* Gang, *der;* **the onward ~ of science** der Vormarsch der Wissenschaft. **2.** *v. i. (also Mil.)* marschieren; *(fig.)* fortschreiten; **~ away** abmarschieren; **forward/quick ~!** vorwärts/im Eilschritt marsch!; **~ing song** Marschlied, *das;* **~ing order** *(Brit.)* Marschordnung, *die;* **~ing orders** Marschbefehl, *der;* **give sb. his/her ~ing orders** *(fig. coll.)* jmdm. den Laufpaß geben *(ugs.).* **3.** *v. t. (Mil.)* marschieren lassen

~ 'off 1. *v. i.* losmarschieren. **2.** *v. t.* ‹*Polizei usw.:*› abführen

~ on *v. t. (Mil.)* marschieren gegen ‹*Feind*›; marschieren auf (+ *Akk.*) ‹*Stadt*›

[2]march *n. (Hist.: frontier)* Mark, *die;* **the Welsh ~es** das Grenzland zwischen Wales und England

marcher ['mɑ:tʃə(r)] *n.* **[protest] ~:** Demonstrant, *der*/Demonstrantin, *die;* **~s on a demonstration** Teilnehmer an einem Demonstrationszug

marchioness [mɑ:ʃə'nes] *n.* Marquise, *die*

Mardi Gras [mɑ:di: 'grɑ:] *n.* **a)** *(Shrove Tuesday)* Fastnachtsdienstag, *der;* **b)** *(carnival)* Karneval, *der*

mare [meə(r)] *n.* Stute, *die*

Margaret ['mɑ:grɪt] *pr. n. (Hist., as name of ruler etc.)* Margarete *(die)*

margarine [mɑ:dʒə'ri:n, mɑ:gə'ri:n], *(coll.)* **marge** [mɑ:dʒ] *ns.* Margarine, *die*

margin ['mɑ:dʒɪn] *n.* **a)** *(of page)* Rand, *der;* **notes [written] in the ~:** Randbemerkungen; Anmerkungen am Rand; **~ release** Randlöser, *der;* Randfreigabe, *die;* **b)** *(extra amount)* Spielraum, *der;* **profit ~:** Gewinnspanne, *die;* **win by a narrow/wide ~:** knapp/mit großem Vorsprung gewinnen; **~ of error** Spielraum für mögliche Fehler; **allow for a considerable ~ of error** eine beachtliche Fehlerzahl mit einkalkulieren; **c)** *(edge)* Rand, *der;* Saum, *der (geh.);* **[be] on the ~ of sth.** *(fig.)* am Rande einer Sache *(Gen.)* [sein]

marginal ['mɑːdʒɪnl] *adj.* **a)** *(barely adequate, slight)* geringfügig; unwesentlich; **of ~ importance/use** von geringer Bedeutung/geringem Nutzen; **b)** *(close to limit)* marginal; *(of profitability)* kaum rentabel; **c)** knapp ‹*Wahlergebnis*›; **~ seat/constituency** *(Brit. Polit.)* wackeliger *(ugs.) od.* nur mit knapper Mehrheit gehaltener Parlamentssitz/Wahlkreis; **d) ~ cost** Grenzkosten *Pl.;* **e)** *(of or written in margin)* an den Rand geschrieben; **~ notes/references** Randbemerkungen/-verweise; **f)** *(of or at the edge)* Rand‹*gebiet, -bereich, -besitzung, -bepflanzung usw.*›

marginalia [mɑːdʒɪ'neɪlɪə] *n. pl.* Marginalien *Pl.*

marginally ['mɑːdʒɪnəlɪ] *adv.* geringfügig; unwesentlich; **only ~ profitable** kaum rentabel

marguerite [mɑːgə'riːt] *n. (Bot.)* Margerite, *die*

marigold ['mærɪgəʊld] *n. (Calendula)* Studentenblume, *die;* Ringelblume, *die; (Tagetes)* Studentenblume, *die; see also* **corn marigold; marsh marigold**

marijuana (marihuana) [mærɪ'hwɑːnə] *n.* Marihuana, *das; attrib.* Marihuana‹*zigarette, -raucher, -süchtiger*›

marimba [mə'rɪmbə] *n. (Mus.)* **a)** *(native xylophone)* Marimba, *die;* **b)** *(modern instrument)* Marimbaphon, *das*

marina [mə'riːnə] *n.* Marina, *die;* Jachthafen, *der*

marinade [mærɪ'neɪd] **1.** *n.* **a)** *(spiced mixture)* Marinade, *die;* **b)** *(marinaded meat)* **a ~ of beef/pork** mariniertes Rind-/Schweinefleisch; **a ~ of fish** marinierter Fisch; eine Marinade. **2.** *v. t.* marinieren

marinate ['mærɪneɪt] *see* **marinade 2**

marine [mə'riːn] **1.** *adj.* **a)** *(of the sea)* Meeres-; **~ life** Meeresflora und -fauna; **b)** *(of shipping)* See‹*versicherung, -recht, -schiffahrt*›; **~ engineering** Schiffsmaschinenbau, *der;* **~ engineer** Schiffbauingenieur, *der;* **c)** *(for use at sea)* Schiffs‹*ausrüstung, -chronometer, -kessel, -turbine usw.*›. **2.** *n.* **a)** *(person)* Marineinfanterist, *der;* **the M~s** die Marineinfanterie; die Marinetruppen; **tell that/it to the [horse] ~s** *(coll.)* das kannst du deiner Großmutter erzählen *(ugs.); see also* **Royal Marine; b)** *(shipping)* **merchant** *or* **mercantile ~:** Handelsmarine, *die*

mariner ['mærɪnə(r)] *n.* Seemann, *der;* **master ~:** Kapitän eines Handelsschiffes; *see also* **compass 1 b**

marionette [mærɪə'net] *n.* Marionette, *die*

marital ['mærɪtl] *adj.* ehelich ‹*Rechte, Pflichten, Harmonie*›; Ehe‹*beratung, -glück, -krach, -krise, -probleme*›; **~ status** Familienstand, *der*

maritime ['mærɪtaɪm] *adj.* **a)** *(found near the sea)* Küsten‹*bewohner, -gebiet, -stadt, -provinz*›; **~ climate** Meeresklima, *das;* **b)** *(connected with the sea)* See‹*recht, -versicherung, -volk, -wesen*›

marjoram ['mɑːdʒərəm] *n. (Bot., Cookery)* Majoran, *der*

Mark [mɑːk] *pr. n.* **St ~:** der hl. Markus

¹mark **1.** *n.* **a)** *(trace)* Spur, *die; (of finger, foot also)* Abdruck, *der; (stain etc.)* Fleck, *der; (scratch)* Kratzer, *der;* **dirty ~:** Schmutzfleck, *der;* **make/leave a ~ on sth.** auf etw. *(Dat. od. Akk.)* einen Fleck/einen Kratzer machen/auf etw. *(Dat.)* einen Fleck/eine Spur/einen Kratzer hinterlassen; **leave one's/its ~ on sth.** *(fig.)* einer Sache *(Dat.)* seinen Stempel aufdrücken; **leave its ~ on sb.** Spuren bei jmdm. hinterlassen; **make one's/its ~** *(fig.)* sich *(Dat.)* einen Namen machen *(see also* **b)**; **of ~** *postpos.* von Bedeutung *nachgestellt; see also* **birthmark; b)** *(affixed sign, indication, symbol)* Zeichen, *das; (in trade names)* Typ, *der (Technik); (made by illiterate)* Kreuz, *das;* **distinguishing ~:** Kennzeichen, *das;* **M~ 2 version/model** Version/Modell 2; **make one's ~:** ein Kreuz *od.* drei Kreuze machen *(see also* **a)**; **bear the ~ of sth.** *(lit. or fig.)* den Stempel von etw. tragen; **have all the ~s of sth.** alle Anzeichen von etw. haben; **be a ~ of good taste/breeding** ein Zeichen guten Geschmacks/guter Erziehung sein; **sth. is the ~ of a good writer** an etw. *(Dat.)* erkennt man einen guten Schriftsteller; **c)** *(Sch.: grade)* Zensur, *die;* Note, *die; (Sch., Sport: unit of numerical award)* Punkt, *der;* **get good/bad/35 ~s in** *or* **for a subject** gute/schlechte Noten *od.* Zensuren/35 Punkte in einem Fach bekommen; **there are no ~s for guessing that ...** *(fig. coll.)* es ist ja wohl nicht schwer zu erraten, daß ...; *see also* **black mark; full marks; pass-mark; d)** *(line etc. to indicate position)* Markierung, *die; (Naut.)* Marke, *die (an der Lotleine);* **be up to/below** *or* **not up to the ~** *(fig.)* den Anforderungen entsprechen/nicht entsprechen; **his work hasn't really been up to the ~ lately** seine Arbeit war in letzter Zeit wirklich nicht sonderlich; **[not] feel up to the ~:** [nicht] auf der Höhe sein; **e)** *(level)* Marke, *die;* **reach the 15%/25 million/£300 ~:** die 15%-Marke/25-Millionen-Marke/300-Pfund-Marke erreichen; **around the 300 ~:** ungefähr 300; **f)** *(Sport: starting position)* Startlinie, *die;* **on your ~s! [get set! go!]** auf die Plätze! [Fertig! Los!]; **get off the ~ quickly** *(fig.)* einen guten Start haben; **be quick/slow off the ~:** einen guten/schlechten Start haben; *(fig.)* fix *(ugs.)*/langsam sein; **he is usually the quickest/first off the ~:** er ist gewöhnlich der Schnellste/Erste; **g)** *(Rugby) (spot)* Marke, *die; (fair catch)* Freifang, *der;* **'~!'** „Marke!"; **h)** *(target, desired object)* Ziel, *das; (sl.: intended victim)* Opfer, *das;* **hit/miss the ~** *(fig.)* ins Schwarze treffen/danebenschießen *(ugs.) od.* -treffen; **be wide of the ~** *(lit. or fig.)* danebentreffen; **his calculations were wide of the ~:** mit seinen Berechnungen hat er völlig danebengetroffen; **my guess was off the ~:** mit meiner Schätzung lag ich daneben *(ugs.);* **be close to the ~** *(fig.)* der Sache nahekommen; *see also* **overshoot; overstep. 2.** *v. t.* **a)** *(stain, dirty)* Flecke[n] machen auf (+ *Dat.*); schmutzig machen; *(scratch)* zerkratzen; **be ~ed for life** bleibende Narben zurückbehalten; *(fig.)* fürs Leben gezeichnet sein; **b)** *(put distinguishing mark on, signal)* kennzeichnen, markieren **(with** mit); **the bottle was ~ed 'poison'** die Flasche trug die Aufschrift „Gift"; **~ sb.'s name on sth.** etw. mit jmds. Namen kennzeichnen; **~ an item with its price** eine Ware auszeichnen *od.* mit einem Preisschild versehen; **~ a route on a map** eine Route auf *od.* in einer *od.* in eine Landkarte einzeichnen; **ceremonies to ~ the tenth anniversary** Feierlichkeiten aus Anlaß des 10. Jahrestages; **c)** *(Sch.) (correct)* korrigieren; *(grade)* benoten; zensieren; **~ an answer wrong** eine Antwort als falsch bewerten; **d) ~ time** *(Mil.; also fig.)* auf der Stelle treten; **e)** *(characterize)* kennzeichnen; charakterisieren; **be ~ed by sth.** durch etw. gekennzeichnet *od.* charakterisiert sein; **his style is ~ed by a great variety of metaphors** sein Stil zeichnet sich durch eine reiche Metaphorik aus; **f)** *(heed)* hören auf (+ *Akk.*) ‹*Person, Wort*›; **~ carefully how it is done** paß genau auf, wie es gemacht wird; **[you] ~ my words** höre auf mich; eins kann ich dir sagen; *(as a warning)* laß dir das gesagt sein; **~ you, it may not be true** vielleicht stimmt es ja doch gar nicht; **g)** *(manifest)* bekunden ‹*Mißfallen, Zustimmung usw.*›; **h)** *(record)* notieren, aufschreiben ‹*Spielstand*›; **~ a pupil absent** einen Schüler als fehlend eintragen; **i)** *(Brit. Sport: keep close to)* markieren *(fachspr.),* decken ‹*Gegenspieler*›; **j)** *(choose as victim) see* **~ down a; k)** *(arch./literary: notice)* bemerken ‹*Vorfall, Vorgang*›

~ 'down *v. t.* **a)** *(choose as victim, lit. or fig.)* [sich *(Dat.)*] auswählen; ausersehen *(geh.);* **b)** [im Preis] herabsetzen ‹*Ware*›; herabsetzen ‹*Preis*›; *see also* **mark-down**

~ 'off *v. t.* abgrenzen **(from** von, gegen)

~ 'out *v. t.* **a)** *(trace out boundaries of)* markieren ‹*Spielfeld*›; **~ out a tennis-court** auf einen Tennisplatz die Spielfeldlinien markieren; **b)** *(plan)* festlegen ‹*Strategie, Vorgehen*›; **c)** *(destine)* vorsehen; ‹*Schicksal:*› bestimmen, ausersehen

~ 'up *v. t.* [im Preis] heraufsetzen ‹*Ware*›; heraufsetzen ‹*Preis*›; *see also* **mark-up**

²mark *n. (monetary unit)* Mark, *die*

'mark-down *n. (Econ.)* Preissenkung, *die;* **there has been a ~:** der Preis ist/die Preise sind gesenkt worden

marked [mɑːkt] *adj.* **a)** *(noticeable)* deutlich ‹*Gegensatz, Unterschied, [Ver]besserung, Veränderung*›; ausgeprägt ‹*Akzent, Sprachfehler, Kennzeichen, Merkmal, Fähigkeit, Neigung*›; **b)** *(given distinctive mark)* gezinkt ‹*Spielkarte*›; **c) be a ~ man** auf der schwarzen Liste stehen *(ugs.)*

markedly ['mɑːkɪdlɪ] *adv.* eindeutig; deutlich

marker ['mɑːkə(r)] *n.* **a)** *(to mark place)* Markierung, *die;* **b)** *see* **bookmark; c)** *(of examination etc.)* Korrektor, *der*/Korrektorin, *die;* **be a fair/severe ~:** gerecht/streng [korrigieren und] benoten; **d)** *(Aeronaut.: flare)* Marker, *der (fachspr.);* Sichtzeichen, *das*

'marker pen *n.* Markierstift, *der*

market ['mɑːkɪt] **1.** *n.* **a)** Markt, *der; attrib.* Markt‹*händler, -stand*›; **at the ~:** auf dem Markt; **go to ~:** auf den Markt gehen; **take sth. to ~:** etw. auf den Markt bringen; **there is a ~ every Friday** freitags *od.* jeden Freitag ist Markt; **b)** *(demand)* Markt, *der;* **find a [ready] ~:** [guten] Absatz finden; **price oneself/one's goods out of the ~:** sich/seine Waren durch Überteuerung konkurrenzunfähig machen; **c)** *(area of demand)* Absatzmarkt, *der; (persons)* Abnehmer *Pl.;* **d)** *(conditions for buying and selling, trade)* Markt, *der;* **the corn/coffee** *etc.* **~:** der Getreide-/Kaffeemarkt *usw.;* **be in the ~ for sth.** an etw. *(Dat.)* interessiert sein; **be on/come into** *or* **on to the ~** ‹*Haus:*› zum Verkauf stehen/kommen; ‹*neue Produkte:*› auf dem Markt sein/auf den Markt kommen; **put on the ~:** zum Verkauf anbieten ‹*Haus*›; **bring on to the ~:** auf den Markt bringen ‹*neues Produkt*›; **make a ~** *(St. Exch.)* [künstlich] Nachfrage erzeugen; **the M~** *(Brit. Polit.)* der Gemeinsame Markt; *see also* **buyer c; Common Market; corner 2 b; play 3 i; seller a. 2.** *v. t.* vermarkten

marketable ['mɑːkɪtəbl] *adj.* **a)** *(suitable for the market)* marktfähig; **b)** *(wanted by purchasers)* marktgängig; **~ securities** börsengängige Effekten

market: ~-day *n.* Markttag, *der;* **~ e'conomy** *n.* Marktwirtschaft, *die;* **~ 'forces** *n. pl.* Kräfte des freien Marktes; **~ 'garden** *n. (Brit.)* Gartenbaubetrieb, *der;* **~ 'gardener** *n. (Brit.)* Gemüseanbauer, *der*/-anbauerin, *die;* **~ 'gardening** *n. (Brit.)* Gemüseanbau, *der*

marketing ['mɑːkɪtɪŋ] *n. (Econ.)* Marketing, *das; attrib.* Marketing-; **~ research** Marketing-Research, *das*

market: ~-maker *n. (St. Exch.) die Preise bestimmender Wertpapierhändler;* **~-place**

n. Marktplatz, *der; (fig.)* Markt, *der;* ~ **'price** *n.* Marktpreis, *der;* ~ **'research** *n.* Marktforschung, *die;* ~**'square** *n.* Marktplatz, *der;* ~ **town** *n.* Marktort, *der;* ~ **'value** *n.* Marktwert, *der*

marking ['mɑ:kɪŋ] *n.* **a)** *(identification symbol)* Markierung, *die;* Kennzeichen, *das;* **b)** *(on animal)* Zeichnung, *die;* **c)** *(Sch.) (correcting)* Korrektur, *die; (grading)* Benotung, *die;* Zensieren, *das;* **I've got some ~ to do** ich muß noch korrigieren

'marking-ink *n.* Wäschetinte, *die*

marksman ['mɑ:ksmən] *n., pl.* **marksmen** ['mɑ:ksmən] Scharfschütze, *der*

marksmanship ['mɑ:ksmənʃɪp] *n., no pl.* Treffsicherheit, *die*

'mark-up *n. (Econ.)* **a)** *(price increase)* Preiserhöhung, *die;* **b)** *(amount added)* Handelsspanne, *die (Kaufmannsspr.)*

marl [mɑ:l] *n.* Mergel, *der*

marmalade ['mɑ:məleɪd] *n.* **[orange]** ~: Orangenmarmelade, *die;* **tangerine/lime** ~: Mandarinen-/Limonenmarmelade, *die*

marmalade 'cat *n.* orangefarbene Katze

marmoset ['mɑ:məzet] *n. (Zool.)* Marmosette, *die*

marmot ['mɑ:mət] *n. (Zool.)* Murmeltier, *das*

¹maroon [mə'ru:n] **1.** *adj.* kastanienbraun. **2.** *n.* Kastanienbraun, *das*

²maroon *v. t.* **a)** *(Naut.: put ashore)* aussetzen; **b)** ‹*Flut, Hochwasser:*› von der Außenwelt abschneiden; **she was ~ed at home without transport** ohne Transportmittel saß sie zu Hause fest

marque [mɑ:k] *n.* Marke, *die; (of cars also)* Fabrikat, *das*

marquee [mɑ:'ki:] *n.* **a)** *(large tent)* großes Zelt; *(for public entertainment)* Festzelt, *das;* **b)** *(Amer.: canopy)* Vordach, *das*

marquess *see* **marquis**

marquetry ['mɑ:kɪtrɪ] *n.* Marketerie, *die (Kunstwiss.);* Einlegearbeit, *die;* Intarsie, *die; attrib.* Intarsien‹*arbeit, -schrank*›

marquis ['mɑ:kwɪs] *n.* Marquis, *der*

marriage ['mærɪdʒ] *n.* **a)** Ehe, *die* **(to** mit); **state of ~:** Ehestand, *der;* **proposal** *or* **offer of ~:** Heiratsantrag, *der;* **his son by a former ~:** sein Sohn aus einer früheren Ehe; **related by ~:** verschwägert; **uncle/cousin by ~:** angeheirateter Onkel/Cousin; **take sb. in ~:** jmdn. zum Mann/zur Frau nehmen; *see also* **convenience a; give 1 h; b)** *(wedding)* Hochzeit, *die; (act of marrying)* Heirat, *die; (ceremony)* Trauung, *die;* ~ **ceremony** Trauzeremonie, *die;* Eheschließung, *die;* **church ~:** kirchliche Trauung; *see also* **civil marriage; c)** *(fig.)* Verbindung, *die*

marriageable ['mærɪdʒəbl] *adj.* heiratsfähig; **of ~ age** im heiratsfähigen Alter

marriage: ~**-broker** *n.* Heiratsvermittler, *der/*-vermittlerin, *die;* ~ **bureau** *n.* Eheanbahnungs- *od.* Ehevermittlungsinstitut, *das;* ~ **certificate** *n.* Trauschein, *der; (record of civil marriage also)* Heiratsurkunde, *die;* ~ **'guidance** *n.* Eheberatung, *die;* ~ **licence** *n.* Heirats- *od.* Eheerlaubnis, *die;* ~ **lines** *n. pl. (Brit.) see* ~ **certificate;** ~ **market** *n.* Heiratsmarkt, *der;* ~ **settlement** *n. (Law)* Ehevertrag, *der;* ~ **stakes** *n. pl. (joc.)* Heiratsmarkt, *der;* ~ **vows** *n. pl.* Ehegelöbnis, *das (geh.)*

married ['mærɪd] **1.** *adj.* **a)** verheiratet; ~ **couple** Ehepaar, *das;* **b)** *(marital)* ehelich ‹*Leben, Liebe*›; Ehe‹*leben, -name, -stand*›; ~ **quarters** Verheiratetenquartiere. **2.** *n.* Verheiratete, *der/die;* **young/newly ~s** Jungverheiratete

marron glacé [mærɒn 'glɑ:seɪ] *n.* kandierte Kastanie

marrow ['mærəʊ] *n.* **a) [vegetable]** ~ Speisekürbis, *der;* **b)** *(Anat.)* [Knochen]mark, *das;* **spinal ~:** Rückenmark, *das;* **to the ~** *(fig.)* durch und durch; **be chilled to the ~** *(fig.)* völlig durchgefroren sein

marrow: ~**bone** *n.* Markknochen, *der;* ~**fat** *n.* Markerbse, *die;* ~ **squash** *(Amer.) see* **marrow a**

marry ['mærɪ] **1.** *v. t.* **a)** *(take in marriage)* heiraten; ~ **money** Geld *od. (ugs.)* reich heiraten; *(for financial gain only)* jmds. Geld heiraten; **b)** *(join in marriage)* trauen; **they were** *or* **got married last summer** sie haben letzten Sommer geheiratet; **c)** *(give in marriage)* verheiraten ‹*Kind*› **(to** mit); **d)** *(fig.: unite intimately)* verquicken; eng miteinander verbinden; ~ **sth. with** *or* **to sth.** etw. mit etw. verquicken *od.* eng verbinden. **2.** *v. i.* heiraten; ~ **for money** wegen des Geldes heiraten; ~ **in haste, repent at leisure** *(prov.)* Heirat in Eile bereut man in Weile *(Spr.);* ~ **into a [rich] family** in eine [reiche] Familie einheiraten

~ **'off** *v. t.* verheiraten ‹*Tochter*› **(to** mit)

marrying ['mærɪɪŋ] *adj.* **he's not the ~ sort** *or* **kind** *or* **type** er ist nicht der Typ [von Mann], der heiratet

Mars [mɑ:z] *pr. n.* **a)** *(Astron.)* Mars, *der;* **b)** *(Roman Mythol.)* Mars *(der)*

Marsala [mɑ:'sɑ:lə] *n.* Marsala[wein], *der*

Marseillaise [mɑ:sə'leɪz, mɑ:seɪ'jeɪz] *n.* Marseillaise, *die*

Marseilles [mɑ:'seɪlz, mɑ:'seɪ] *pr. n.* Marseille *(das)*

marsh [mɑ:ʃ] *n.* Sumpf, *der; attrib. (Bot., Zool.)* Sumpf‹*klee, -kresse, -[kratz]distel, -krokodil, -hirsch*›

marshal ['mɑ:ʃl] **1.** *n.* **a)** *(officer of state)* [Hof]marschall, *der;* **b)** *(officer in army)* Marschall, *der; see also* **Field Marshal; c)** *(Sport)* Ordner, *der;* **d)** *(Amer.) (head of police department)* Polizeipräsident, *der; (head of fire department)* Branddirektor, *der. See also* **provost marshal. 2.** *v. t., (Brit.)* **-ll- a)** *(arrange in order)* aufstellen ‹*Truppen*›; sich *(Dat.)* zurechtlegen ‹*Argumente*›; ordnen ‹*Fakten*›; **the teacher ~led the children on to the coach** der Lehrer führte die Kinder zu ihren Plätzen im Bus; **b)** *(Her.)* vereinigen, verbinden ‹*Wappen*›

'marshalling yard ['mɑ:ʃəlɪŋ jɑ:d] *n. (Railw.)* Rangierbahnhof, *der*

marsh: ~ **gas** *n. (Chem.)* Sumpfgas, *das;* ~**'harrier** *n. (Ornith.)* Rohrweihe, *die;* ~**land** *n.* Sumpfland, *das;* ~ **mallow** *n.* **a)** *(Bot.)* Eibisch, *der;* **b)** *(confection)* Marshmallow, *das;* süßer Speck; ~**'mallow** *n. (sweet)* ≈ Mohrenkopf, *der;* ~ **'marigold** *n.* Sumpfdotterblume, *die;* ~ **tit** *n. (Ornith.)* Nonnenmeise, *die*

marshy ['mɑ:ʃɪ] *adj.* sumpfig; Sumpf‹*boden, -gebiet, -land*›

marsupial [mɑ:'sju:pɪəl, mɑ:'su:pɪəl] *(Zool.)* **1.** *adj.* Beutel‹*tier, -frosch, -mulle*›. **2.** *n.* Beuteltier, *das*

mart [mɑ:t] *n.* **a)** *(market-place)* Markt, *der;* **b)** *(auction-room)* Auktionsraum, *der;* **sale ~:** Verkaufsraum, *der*

marten ['mɑ:tɪn] *n. (Zool.)* Marder, *der;* **stone ~:** Steinmarder, *der; see also* **pine marten**

martial ['mɑ:ʃl] *adj.* kriegerisch; *see also* **court martial**

martial: ~ **'arts** *n. pl. (Sport)* Kampfsportarten; ~ **'law** *n.* Kriegsrecht, *das;* **state of ~ law** Kriegszustand, *der*

martin ['mɑ:tɪn] *n. (Ornith.)* **[house-]~:** Mehlschwalbe, *die*

martinet [mɑ:tɪ'net] *n.* Zuchtmeister, *der (veralt., noch scherzh.)*

Martini, (P) [mɑ:'ti:nɪ] *n.* Martini, *der;* **dry ~:** Martini dry, *der*

martyr ['mɑ:tə(r)] **1.** *n. (Relig.; also fig.)* Märtyrer, *der/*Märtyrerin, *die;* **die a ~'s death** den Märtyrertod erleiden *od.* sterben; **a ~ to** *or* **in the cause of sth.** Märtyrer/Märtyrerin einer Sache *(Gen.);* **be a ~ to rheumatism** entsetzlich unter Rheumatismus leiden; **make a ~ of oneself** den Märtyrer/die Märtyrerin spielen; **make sb. a ~, make a ~ of sb.** jmdn. zum Märtyrer/zur Märtyrerin machen. **2.** *v. t.* **a)** den Märtyrertod sterben lassen; **be ~ed** den Märtyrertod sterben; **b)** *(fig.: torment)* martern *(geh.);* **a ~ed expression** eine Duldermiene

martyrdom ['mɑ:tədəm] *n.* Martyrium, *das;* **suffer ~:** ein Martyrium durchleiden

marvel ['mɑ:vl] **1.** *n.* Wunder, *das;* **work ~s** Wunder wirken; **it's a ~ to me how ...:** es ist mir schleierhaft, wie ...; **it will be a ~ if ...:** es wäre ein Wunder, wenn ...; **be a ~ of patience/neatness** eine sagenhafte Geduld haben/sagenhaft ordentlich sein *(ugs.).* **2.** *v. i., (Brit.)* **-ll-** *(literary)* **a)** *(be surprised)* ~ **at sth.** über etw. *(Akk.)* staunen; etw. bestaunen; ~ **that ...:** erstaunt sein, daß ...; **b)** *(wonder)* sich wundern; sich fragen; ~ **how/why** *etc.* sich fragen *od. (bes. schweiz.)* sich wundern, wie/warum *usw.*

marvellous ['mɑ:vələs] *adj.*, **marvellously** ['mɑ:vələslɪ] *adv.* wunderbar

marvelous, marvelously *(Amer.) see* **marvell-**

Marxian ['mɑ:ksɪən] *see* **Marxist**

Marxism ['mɑ:ksɪzm] *n.* Marxismus, *der*

Marxist ['mɑ:ksɪst] **1.** *n.* Marxist, *der/*Marxistin, *die.* **2.** *adj.* marxistisch

Mary ['meərɪ] *pr. n. (Hist., as name of ruler, saint, etc.)* Maria *(die); see also* **Bloody Mary**

marzipan ['mɑ:zɪpæn] *n.* Marzipan, *das*

mascara [mæ'skɑ:rə] *n.* Mascara, *das*

mascot ['mæskɒt] *n.* Maskottchen, *das*

masculine ['mæskjʊlɪn] **1.** *adj.* **a)** *(of men)* männlich; **b)** *(manly, manlike)* maskulin; **c)** *(Ling.)* männlich; maskulin *(fachspr.).* **2.** *n. (Ling.)* Maskulinum, *das*

masculine 'rhyme *n. (Pros.)* männlicher *od.* stumpfer Reim

masculinity [mæskjʊ'lɪnɪtɪ] *n., no pl.* Männlichkeit, *die*

maser ['meɪzə(r)] *n. (Phys.)* Maser, *der*

mash [mæʃ] **1.** *n.* **a)** *(Brewing)* Maische, *die;* **b)** *(as fodder)* Mischfutter, *das;* **c)** *(pulp)* Brei, *der;* **d)** *(Brit. coll.: mashed potatoes)* Kartoffelbrei, *der.* **2.** *v. t.* zerdrücken, zerquetschen, stampfen ‹*Kartoffeln*›; zerdrücken, zerquetschen ‹*Gemüse, Obst*›; **~ed potatoes** Kartoffelbrei, *der*

mask [mɑ:sk] **1.** *n. (also fig., Phot.)* Maske, *die ; (worn by surgeon)* Gesichtsmaske, *die;* Mundschutz, *der;* **throw off the ~** *(fig.: abandon pretence)* die Maske fallen lassen. **2.** *v. t.* **a)** *(cover with mask)* maskieren; **b)** *(Mil.)* tarnen; **c)** *(fig.: disguise, conceal)* maskieren; ‹*Wolken, Bäume:*› verdecken; überdecken ‹*Geschmack*›; **d)** *(cover for protection)* abdecken

masked 'ball *n.* Maskenball, *der*

'masking tape *n.* Abdeckband, *das*

masochism ['mæsəkɪzm] *n.* Masochismus, *der*

masochist ['mæsəkɪst] *n.* Masochist, *der/*Masochistin, *die*

masochistic [mæsə'kɪstɪk] *adj.* masochistisch

mason ['meɪsn] *n.* **a)** *(builder)* Baumeister, *der;* Steinmetz, *der;* **b) M~** *(Free~)* [Frei]maurer, *der*

Masonic [mə'sɒnɪk] *adj.* [frei]maurerisch; ~ **lodge** [Frei]maurerloge, *die*

masonry ['meɪsnrɪ] *n.* **a)** *(stonework)* Mauerwerk, *das; (work of a mason)* Steinmetzarbeit, *die;* **b) M~** *(Free~)* [Frei]maurertum, *das*

masque [mɑ:sk] *n.* Maskenspiel, *das*

masquerade [mæskə'reɪd, mɑ:skə'reɪd] **1.** *n. (lit. or fig.)* Maskerade, *die.* **2.** *v. i.* ~ **as sb./sth.** sich als jmd./etw. ausgeben; vorgeben, jmd./etw. zu sein

¹mass [mæs] *n. (Eccl., Mus.)* Messe, *die; attrib.* Meß‹*buch, -gewand*›; **say/hear ~:** die Messe lesen/hören; **go to** *or* **attend ~:** zur Messe gehen; **high ~:** Hochamt, *das;* **low ~:** stille Messe; *see also* **black mass**

²mass **1.** *n.* **a)** *(solid body of matter)* Brocken, *der; (of dough, rubber)* Klumpen, *der;* **a ~ of rock/stone** ein Felsbrocken/Steinblock; **b)** *(dense aggregation of objects)* Masse, *die;* **a tangled ~ of threads** ein wirres Knäuel von Fäden; **a ~ of curls** eine Fülle von Locken; **a confused ~ of ideas** ein Wust von Ideen; **c)** *(large number or amount of)* **a ~ of ...:** eine Unmenge von ...; **a ~ of people** eine große Menschenmenge; **~es of ...:** massenhaft ... *(ugs.);* eine Masse ... *(ugs.);* **d)** *(unbroken expanse)* **a ~ of blossom/colour/red** ein Blütenmeer/Farbenmeer/Meer von Rot; **be a ~ of bruises/mistakes/inhibitions** *(coll.)* voll blauer Flecken sein/von Fehlern nur so wimmeln/nur aus Hemmungen bestehen; **e)** *(main portion)* Masse, *die;* **the [great] ~ of people/voters** die Masse des Volkes/der Wähler; **the ~es** die breite Masse; die Massen; **in the ~:** als Ganzes; **f)** *(Phys.)* Masse, *die;* **centre of ~:** Massenmittelpunkt, *der;* **g)** *(bulk)* massige Form; **the huge ~ of the pyramid** die riesige Größe der Pyramide; **h)** *attrib. (for many people)* Massen-. **2.** *v. t.* **a)** anhäufen; **~ed bands** mehrere gleichzeitig spielende Kapellen; **b)** *(Mil.)* massieren, zusammenziehen ‹*Truppen*›. **3.** *v. i.* sich ansammeln; ‹*Truppen:*› sich massieren, sich zusammenziehen; ‹*Wolken:*› sich zusammenziehen

massacre ['mæsəkə(r)] **1.** *n.* **a)** *(slaughter)* Massaker, *das;* **make a ~ of ...:** ein Massaker anrichten unter (+ *Dat.*) ...; **b)** *(coll.: defeat)* völlige Zerstörung. **2.** *v. t.* **a)** *(slaughter)* massakrieren; **b)** *(coll.: defeat heavily)* massakrieren *(ugs., meist scherzh.)*

massage ['mæsɑːʒ] **1.** *n.* Massage, *die;* **give sb./sb.'s back a ~:** jmdn./jmds. Rücken massieren; **~ parlour** *(often euphem.)* Massagesalon, *der.* **2.** *v. t.* massieren

mass communi'cations *n. pl.* Massenkommunikation, *die*

masseur [mæ'sɜː(r)] *n.* Masseur, *der*

masseuse [mæ'sɜːz] *n. fem.* Masseurin, *die;* Masseuse, *die (oft verhüll.)*

mass: ~ 'grave *n.* Massengrab, *das;* **~ hy'steria** *n.* Massenhysterie, *die*

massif [mæ'siːf] *n. (Geog.)* Massiv, *das*

massive ['mæsɪv] *adj. (lit. or fig.)* massiv; wuchtig ‹*Statur, Stirn*›; kräftig ‹*Augenbrauen, Gesicht*›; gewaltig ‹*Ausmaße, Aufgabe*›; enorm ‹*Schulden, Vermögen*›; **be [conceived] on a ~ scale** groß angelegt sein; **receive aid on a ~ scale** massive Unterstützung erhalten

massively ['mæsɪvlɪ] *adv. (lit. or fig.)* massiv

mass: ~ 'media *n. pl.* Massenmedien *Pl.;* **~ 'meeting** *n.* Massenversammlung, *die; (Pol.)* Massenkundgebung, *die; (Industry)* Belegschaftsversammlung, *die;* **~ 'murder** *n.* Massenmord, *der;* **~ 'murderer** *n.* Massenmörder, *der;* **~-pro'duced** *adj.* serienmäßig produziert *od.* hergestellt; Massen‹*artikel*›; **~-pro'ducer** *n.* Massenproduzent, *der;* **~ pro'duction** *n.* Massenproduktion, *die*

¹mast [mɑːst] *n. (for sail, flag, aerial, etc.)* Mast, *der;* **work** *or* **serve** *or* **sail before the ~:** als Matrose dienen; **[mooring-]~:** Ankermast, *der; see also* **colour 1 j; half-mast**

²mast *n. (for fodder)* Mast, *die*

mastectomy [mæ'stektəmɪ] *n. (Med.)* Mastektomie, *die (fachspr.);* Brustamputation, *die*

-masted [mɑːstɪd] *adj. in comb. (Naut.)* -mastig; **two-~:** zweimastig

master ['mɑːstə(r)] **1.** *n.* **a)** Herr, *der;* **be ~ of sth./oneself** Herr über etw. *(Akk.)*/sich selbst sein; **be ~ of the situation/[the] ~ of one's fate** Herr der Lage/seines Schicksals sein; **be one's own ~:** sein eigener Herr sein; **make oneself ~ of sth.** sich zum Herrn über etw. *(Akk.)* machen; **b)** *(of animal, slave)* Halter, *der; (of dog)* Herrchen, *das; (Hunting)* Master, *der; (of ship)* Kapitän, *der; (of college)* Rektor, *der; (of livery company, masonic lodge)* Meister, *der;* **~ of the house** Hausherr, *der;* **be ~ in one's own house** Herr im eigenen Hause sein; **~'s certificate** *or* **ticket** *(Naut.)* Kapitänspatent, *das; see also* **mariner; c)** *(Sch.: teacher)* Lehrer, *der;* **French ~:** Französischlehrer, *der;* **d) find** *or* **meet [in sb.] one's ~:** [in jmdm.] seinen Meister finden; **e)** *(employer)* Herr, *der;* **f)** *in titles* ‹*Hofkapell-, Schatz-, Ritt-, Waffen- usw.*›meister, *der;* **M~ of Ceremonies** Zeremonienmeister, *der; (for variety programme etc.)* Conférencier, *der;* **M~ of the Rolls** *(Brit. Law)* Präsident des Berufungsgerichts; **g)** *(original of document, film, etc.)* Original, *das;* **h)** *(expert, great artist)* Meister, *der* **(at** in + *Dat.*); **be a ~ of sth.** etw. meisterhaft beherrschen; *see also* **grand master; old master; past master; i)** *(skilled workman)* **~ craftsman/carpenter** Handwerks-/Tischlermeister, *der;* **j)** *(Univ.)* Magister, *der;* **~ of Arts/Science** Magister Artium/rerum naturalium; **he got his ~'s degree in 1971** er hat 1971 den *od.* seinen Magister gemacht; **k)** *(boy's title)* ≈ junger Herr *(veralt.);* **M~ Theo/Richard** *etc.* Master Theo/Richard *usw.* **2.** *adj.* **a)** *(commanding)* **the ~ race** die Herrenrasse; **~ card** Leitkarte, *die (DV);* **b)** *(principal)* Haupt‹*strategie, -liste*›; **~ bedroom** großes Schlafzimmer; ≈ Elternschlafzimmer, *das;* **~ tape/copy** Originalband, *das*/Original, *das;* **~ plan** Gesamtplan, *der.* **3.** *v. t.* **a)** *(learn)* erlernen; **have ~ed a language/subject/instrument** eine Sprache/ein Fach/ein Instrument beherrschen; **b)** *(overcome)* meistern ‹*Probleme usw.*›; besiegen ‹*Feind*›; beherrschen ‹*Natur*›; zügeln ‹*Emotionen, Gefühle*›

-master *n. in comb. (Naut.)* -master, *der;* **two-~:** Zweimaster, *der*

'master class *n. (Mus. etc.)* Meisterklasse, *die*

masterful ['mɑːstəfl] *adj.* **a)** *(imperious)* herrisch ‹*Haltung, Ton, Person*›; **b)** *(masterly)* meisterhaft ‹*Beherrschung, Fähigkeit*›

masterfully ['mɑːstəfəlɪ] *adv. see* **masterful:** herrisch; meisterhaft

master: ~-hand *n. (person)* Meister, *der* **(at** im + *Dat.*); **~-key** *n.* General- *od.* Hauptschlüssel, *der; (fig.)* Schlüssel, *der*

masterly ['mɑːstəlɪ] *adj.* meisterhaft

master: ~mind 1. *n.* führender Kopf; **2.** *v. t.* **~mind the plot/conspiracy** *etc.* der Kopf des Komplotts/der Verschwörung *usw.* sein; **~piece** *n. (work of art)* Meisterwerk, *das; (production showing masterly skill)* Meisterstück, *das;* **a ~piece of tact/irony** ein Meisterstück an Takt/Ironie *od.* des Taktes/der Ironie; **~singer** *n. (Hist.)* Meistersinger, *der;* **~-stroke** *n.* Meister- *od.* Glanzstück, *das;* **~ switch** *n.* Hauptschalter, *der;* **~-work** *see* **~piece**

mastery ['mɑːstərɪ] *n.* **a)** *(skill)* Meisterschaft, *die;* **b)** *(knowledge)* Beherrschung, *die* **(of** *Gen.*); **c)** *(upper hand)* Oberhand, *die;* **gain ~ over sb.** die Oberhand über jmdn. gewinnen; **d)** *(control)* Herrschaft, *die* **(of** über + *Akk.*)

'masthead *n.* **a)** *(Naut.)* [Mast]topp, *der;* **b)** *(Journ.)* Impressum, *das; (title)* Titel, *der*

mastic ['mæstɪk] *n.* **a)** *(gum, resin, asphalt)* Mastix, *der;* **b)** *(cement)* Mastik, *der*

masticate ['mæstɪkeɪt] *v. t.* zerkauen

mastication [mæstɪ'keɪʃn] *n.* Zerkauen, *das*

mastiff ['mæstɪf] *n. (Zool.)* Mastiff, *der*

mastitis [mæs'taɪtɪs] *n. (Med.)* Mastitis, *die*

mastodon ['mæstədɒn] *n. (Zool., Palaeont.)* Mastodon, *das*

mastoid ['mæstɔɪd] *n. (Anat.)* Mastoid, *das*

masturbate ['mæstəbeɪt] *v. i. & t.* masturbieren

masturbation [mæstə'beɪʃn] *n.* Masturbation, *die*

¹mat [mæt] **1.** *n.* **a)** *(on floor, Sport)* Matte, *die;* **pull the ~ from under sb.'s feet** *(fig.)* jmdm. den Boden unter den Füßen wegziehen; **be on the ~** *(sl.: be in trouble)* zusammengestaucht werden *(ugs.);* **b)** *(to protect table etc.)* Untersetzer, *der; (as decorative support)* Deckchen, *das;* **c)** *(tangled mess) (of hair)* Wust, *der (ugs.); (of weeds, foliage)* Gewirr, *das.* **2.** *v. t.,* **-tt- a)** *(furnish with mats)* mit Matten belegen ‹*Boden*›; mit Matten auslegen ‹*Zimmer*›; **b)** *usu. in p.p. (entangle)* verflechten ‹*Äste, Unkraut*›; verfilzen ‹*Haar*›; **~ted** verflochten; verfilzt. **3.** *v. i.,* **-tt-** ‹*Äste, Unkraut usw.:*› sich [ineinander] verflechten; ‹*Haare, Wolle:*› verfilzen

²mat *see* **matt**

matador ['mætədɔː(r)] *n.* Matador, *der*

¹match [mætʃ] **1.** *n.* **a)** *(equal)* Ebenbürtige, *der/die;* **be a/no ~ for sb.** es mit jmdm. aufnehmen/nicht aufnehmen [können]; sich mit jmdm. messen/nicht messen können; **she is more than a ~ for him** sie ist ihm mehr als gewachsen; **find** *or* **meet one's ~:** einen ebenbürtigen Gegner finden; *(be defeated)* seinen Meister finden; **b)** *(sb./sth. similar or appropriate)* **be a [good** *etc.*] **~ for sth.** [gut *usw.*] zu etw. passen; **the colours are a poor ~:** die Farben passen schlecht zueinander *od.* zusammen; **find a ~ for this paint** genau die gleiche Farbe finden; **c)** *(Sport)* Spiel, *das; (Football, Tennis, etc. also)* Match, *das; (Boxing)* Kampf, *der; (Athletics)* Wettkampf, *der;* **d)** *(marriage)* Heirat, *die; (marriage partner)* Partie, *die;* **make a ~:** sich verheiraten; **make a good ~:** eine gute Partie machen. **2.** *v. t.* **a)** *(equal)* **~ sb. at chess/in shooting/in argument/in originality** es mit jmdm. im Schach/Schießen/Argumentieren/an Originalität *(Dat.)* aufnehmen [können]; **can you ~ that for impudence?** das ist eine Unverschämtheit ohnegleichen!; **~ that if you can!** das mach [mir] erst mal einer nach!; **b)** *(pit)* **~ sb. with** *or* **against sb.** jmdn. jmdm. gegenüberstellen; **be ~ed against sb.** gegen jmdn. antreten; **~ one's skill/strength against sb.** sein Können/seine Kräfte mit jmdm. messen; **c) be well ~ed** ‹*Mann u. Frau:*› gut zusammenpassen; ‹*Spieler, Mannschaften:*› sich *(Dat.)* ebenbürtig sein; **they are a well ~ed couple/pair** die beiden passen gut zusammen; **d)** *(harmonize with)* passen zu; **a handbag and ~ing shoes** eine Handtasche und [dazu] passende Schuhe; **~ each other exactly** genau zueinander passen; **form a ~ing pair** [als Paar] gut zueinander passen; **e)** *(find matching material etc. for)* **~ sth. with sth.** etw. auf etw. abstimmen; **~ people with jobs** geeignete Personen für die Stellen finden. **3.** *v. i. (correspond)* zusammenpassen; **with a scarf** *etc.* **to ~:** mit [dazu] passendem Schal *usw.* **~ 'up 1.** *v. i.* **a)** *(correspond)* zusammenpassen; **b)** *(be equal)* **~ up to sth.** einer Sache *(Dat.)* entsprechen; **~ up to the situation** der Situation gewachsen sein. **2.** *v. t.* aufeinander abstimmen ‹*Farben usw.*›; passend zusammenfügen ‹*Teile, Hälften*›; **~ up one colour with another** eine Farbe auf eine andere abstimmen

²match *n. (for lighting)* Streichholz, *das;* Zündholz, *das (südd., österr.)*

match: ~box *n.* Streichholzschachtel, *die;* **~-fit** *adj. (Sport)* spielfähig

matchless ['mætʃlɪs] *adj.* unvergleichlich; beispiellos

match: ~maker *n.* Ehestifter, *der*/Ehestifterin, *die;* **~making** *n.* Ehestiftung, *die;* **~ point** *n. (Tennis etc.)* Matchball, *der;* **~stick** *n.* **a)** Streichholz, *das;* Zündholz, *das (südd., österr.);* **b) ~stick man** *see* **stick figure; ~wood** *n.* **make ~wood of sth., smash sth. to ~wood** Kleinholz aus etw. machen; **the storm had made ~wood of the boat** der Sturm hatte das Boot zertrümmert

[1]mate [meɪt] **1.** *n.* **a)** Kumpel, *der (ugs.); (friend also)* Kamerad, *der*/Kameradin, *die; (workmate also)* [Arbeits]kollege, *der*/-kollegin, *die;* **b)** *(coll.: as form of address)* Kumpel, *der (ugs.);* **look** *or* **listen, ~, ...:** jetzt hör [mir] mal gut zu, Freundchen, ...; **c)** *(Naut.: officer on merchant ship)* ≈ Kapitänleutnant, *der;* **chief** *or* **first/second ~:** Erster/Zweiter Offizier; **d)** *(workman's assistant)* Gehilfe, *der;* **e)** *(spouse)* Lebensgefährte, *der*/-gefährtin, *die (geh.);* **f)** *(Zool.) (male)* Männchen, *das; (female)* Weibchen, *das.* **2.** *v. i.* **a)** *(for breeding)* sich paaren; **b)** *(Mech.: fit well)* **~ with sth.** [genau] auf/in etw. *(Akk.)* passen. **3.** *v. t.* paaren ‹*Tiere*›; **~ a mare and** *or* **with a stallion** eine Stute von einem Hengst decken lassen

[2]mate *(Chess) see* **checkmate 1, 3**

material [məˈtɪərɪəl] **1.** *adj.* **a)** *(physical, tangible, bodily)* materiell; **b)** *(not spiritual)* materiell *(oft abwertend)* ‹*Mensch, Einstellung, Lebensführung*›; **c)** *(relevant, important)* wesentlich; **be not ~ to sth.** für etw. nicht relevant sein. **2.** *n.* **a)** *(matter from which thing is made)* Material, *das;* **cost of ~s** Materialkosten *Pl.; see also* **raw material; b)** *in sing. or pl. (elements)* Material, *das; (for novel, sermon also)* Stoff, *der;* **c)** *(cloth)* Stoff, *der;* **d)** *in pl.* **building/writing ~s** Bau-/Schreibmaterial, *das;* **cleaning ~s** Reinigungsmaterial; **reading ~:** Lesestoff, *der;* **e) be leadership/university/officer** *etc.* **~:** das Zeug für einen Führungsposten/zum Hochschulstudium/zum Offizier *usw.* haben

materialise *see* **materialize**

materialism [məˈtɪərɪəlɪzm] *n., no pl.* Materialismus, *der*

materialist [məˈtɪərɪəlɪst] *n.* Materialist, *der*/Materialistin, *die; attrib.* materialistisch ‹*Philosophie*›

materialistic [mətɪərɪəˈlɪstɪk] *adj.* materialistisch

materialize [məˈtɪərɪəlaɪz] *v. i.* **a)** ‹*Hoffnung:*› sich erfüllen; ‹*Plan, Idee:*› sich verwirklichen; ‹*Treffen, Versammlung:*› zustande kommen; **he promised help/money, but it never ~d** aus seiner versprochenen Hilfe/seinem versprochenen Geld wurde nichts; **this idea will never ~:** aus dieser Idee wird nie etwas; **problems kept materializing** dauernd traten Probleme auf; **b)** *(come into view, appear)* [plötzlich] auftauchen; *(coll.)* ‹*Person:*› sich blicken lassen *(ugs.),* kommen

materially [məˈtɪərɪəlɪ] *adv.* **a)** *(considerably)* wesentlich; **b)** *(in respect of material interests)* materiell

matériel [mətɪərɪˈel] *n.* Ausrüstung, *die*

maternal [məˈtɜːnl] *adj.* **a)** *(motherly)* mütterlich ‹*Liebe, Sorge, Typ*›; Mutter‹*instinkt*›; **b)** *(related)* ‹*Großeltern, Onkel, Tante*› mütterlicherseits

maternity [məˈtɜːnɪtɪ] *n. (motherhood)* Mutterschaft, *die*

maternity: ~ allowance *n.* Mutterschaftshilfe, *die;* **~ benefit** *n.* Mutterschaftsgeld, *das;* **~ dress** *n.* Umstandskleid, *das;* **~ home, ~ hospital** *ns.* Entbindungsheim, *das;* **~ leave** *n.* Mutterschaftsurlaub, *der;* **~ nurse** *n.* Hebamme, *die;* **~ pay** *n.* Mutterschaftsgeld, *das;* **~ unit, ~ward** *ns.* Entbindungsstation, *die;* **~ wear** *n.* Umstandskleidung, *die*

matey [ˈmeɪtɪ] *(Brit. coll.)* **1.** *adj.,* **matier** [ˈmeɪtɪə(r)], **matiest** [ˈmeɪtɪɪst] kameradschaftlich ‹*Typ, Atmosphäre*›; **be/get ~ with sb.** mit jmdm. vertraulich sein/werden. **2.** *n.* Kumpel, *der (ugs.);* **watch it, ~!** paß bloß auf, Freundchen!

math [mæθ] *(Amer. coll.) see* **maths**

mathematical [mæθɪˈmætɪkl] *adj.* **a)** mathematisch; **b)** *(precise)* mathematisch ‹*Genauigkeit, Exaktheit, Bestimmtheit*›; mathematisch genau ‹*Beweis*›

mathematically [mæθɪˈmætɪkəlɪ] *adv.* mathematisch; **prove sth. ~:** etw. mathematisch genau beweisen

mathematician [mæθɪməˈtɪʃn] *n.* Mathematiker, *der*/Mathematikerin, *die*

mathematics [mæθɪˈmætɪks] *n., no pl.* **a)** *(subject)* Mathematik, *die;* **pure/applied ~:** reine/angewandte Mathematik; **b)** *constr. as pl. (application)* **the ~ of this problem are complicated** diese Aufgabe ist mathematisch kompliziert; **your ~ are good** du bist gut in Mathematik

maths [mæθs] *n. (Brit. coll.)* Mathe, *die (Schülerspr.)*

matinée *(Amer.:* **matinee)** [ˈmætɪneɪ] *n.* Matinee, *die;* Frühvorstellung, *die; (in the afternoon)* Nachmittagsvorstellung, *die*

mating [ˈmeɪtɪŋ]: **~ call, ~ cry** *ns.* Paarungsruf, *der;* **~ season** *n.* Paarungszeit, *die*

matins [ˈmætɪnz] *n., constr. as sing. or pl.* **a)** *(RC Ch.)* Matutin, *die;* **b)** *(Anglican Ch.)* Früh- *od.* Morgenandacht, *die*

matriarchal [meɪtrɪˈɑːkl] *adj.* matriarchalisch

matriarchy [ˈmeɪtrɪɑːkɪ] *n.* Matriarchat, *das*

matrices *pl. of* **matrix**

matricide [ˈmætrɪsaɪd] *n.* **a)** *(murder)* Muttermord, *der;* **b)** *(murderer)* Muttermörder, *der*/-mörderin, *die*

matriculate [məˈtrɪkjʊleɪt] *(Univ.)* **1.** *v. t.* immatrikulieren (**in** an + *Dat.*). **2.** *v. i.* sich immatrikulieren

matriculation [mətrɪkjʊˈleɪʃn] *n.* *(Univ.)* Immatrikulation, *die*

matrimonial [mætrɪˈməʊnɪəl] *adj.* Ehe-

matrimony [ˈmætrɪmənɪ] *n.* **a)** *(rite of marriage)* Eheschließung, *die;* **sacrament of ~:** Ehesakrament, *das;* **b)** *(married state)* Ehestand, *der;* **enter into [holy] ~:** in den [heiligen] Stand der Ehe treten *(geh.)*

matrix [ˈmeɪtrɪks, ˈmætrɪks] *n., pl.* **matrices** [ˈmeɪtrɪsiːz, ˈmætrɪsiːz] *or* **~es a)** *(Geol., Math.)* Matrix, *die;* **b)** *(mould)* Matrize, *die*

matron [ˈmeɪtrən] *n.* **a)** *(in school)* ≈ Hausmutter, *die; (in hospital)* Oberin, *die;* Oberschwester, *die;* **b)** *(arch./literary: married woman)* Matrone, *die;* **~ of honour** *(verheiratete)* Brautführerin

matronly [ˈmeɪtrənlɪ] *adj.* matronenhaft *(meist abwertend)*

matt [mæt] *adj.* matt; **have a ~ finish** ‹*Fotografie:*› auf mattem Papier abgezogen sein

matter [ˈmætə(r)] **1.** *n.* **a)** *(affair)* Angelegenheit, *die;* **~s** die Dinge; **business ~s** geschäftliche Angelegenheiten *od.* Dinge; **money ~s** Geldangelegenheiten *od.* -fragen; **~s of state** Staatsangelegenheiten; **raise an important ~:** einen wichtigen Punkt ansprechen; **police investigation into the ~:** polizeiliche Ermittlung in dieser Sache; **it's only a minor** *or* **it's no great ~:** es ist nicht wichtig; **that's another** *or* **a different ~ altogether** *or* **quite another ~:** das ist etwas ganz anderes; **it will only make ~s worse** das macht die Sache nur schlimmer; **and to make ~s worse ...:** und was die Sache noch schlimmer macht/machte, ...; **b)** *(cause, occasion)* **a/no ~ for** *or* **of ...:** ein/kein Grund *od.* Anlaß zu ...; **it's a ~ of complete indifference to me** es ist mir völlig gleichgültig; **c)** *(topic)* Thema, *das;* Gegenstand, *der;* **~ on the agenda** Punkt der Tagesordnung; **it's a ~ for the committee [to decide]** das muß der [zuständige] Ausschuß entscheiden; **d) a ~ of ...** *(something that amounts to)* eine Frage (+ *Gen.*) ...; eine Sache von ...; **it's a ~ of taste/habit** das ist Geschmack-/Gewohnheitssache; **it's a ~ of common knowledge** es ist allgemein bekannt; **it's a ~ of policy with us** das ist für uns eine Grundsatzfrage; **a ~ of how fast I can type** eine Frage, wie schnell ich tippen kann; **[only] a ~ of time** [nur noch] eine Frage der Zeit; **it's a ~ of repairing the switch** der Schalter muß repariert werden; **it's just a ~ of working harder** man muß sich ganz einfach [bei der Arbeit] mehr anstrengen; **it's a ~ of a couple of hours** es wird ein paar Stunden dauern; das ist eine Sache von ein paar Stunden; **in a ~ of minutes** in wenigen Minuten; **it's only a ~ of seconds** das ist eine Sache von Sekunden; **a [plain] ~ of fact** eine [schlichte] Tatsache; **That's odd! As a ~ of fact, I was just thinking the same** Das ist komisch! Ich habe nämlich gerade dasselbe gedacht; **Do you know him? – Yes, as a ~ of fact, I do/I know him quite well** Kennst du ihn? – Ja, und ob [ich ihn kenne]/und sogar recht gut; **no, as a ~ of fact, you're wrong** nein, da irrst du dich aber; **~ of fact** *(Law)* Tatfrage, *die;* **~ of law** Rechtsfrage, *die; see also* **course 1 b; form 1 h; e) what's the ~?** was ist [los]?; **is something the ~?** stimmt irgend etwas nicht?; ist [irgend]was *(ugs.)*?; **there's nothing the ~:** gar nichts ist los; **there must be something the ~:** irgend etwas stimmt da nicht; **What's the ~ with you? – There's nothing the ~ with me** Was hast du *od.* ist [los] mit dir? – Gar nichts [ist los mit mir]; **there's nothing the ~ with him really, he's just pretending** es fehlt ihm eigentlich gar nichts, er tut nur so; **f) for that ~:** eigentlich; **... and for that ~ so am/do I ...** und ich eigentlich auch; **g) no ~!** [das] macht nichts!; **no ~ how/who/what/why** *etc.* ganz gleich *od.* egal *(ugs.),* wie/wer/was/warum *usw.;* **no ~ how hard he tried** sosehr er sich auch bemühte; **h) in the ~ of sth.** was etw. *(Akk.)* anbelangt; **in the ~ of A versus B** *(Law)* in Sachen *od.* in der Sache A gegen B; **i)** *(material, as opposed to mind, spirit, etc.)* Materie, *die;* **[in]organic/solid/vegetable ~:** [an]organische/feste/pflanzliche Stoffe; **the triumph of mind over ~:** der Sieg des Geistes über die Materie; **j)** *(Physiol.)* Substanz, *die; (pus)* Eiter, *der;* **faecal ~:** Fäzes *Pl.; see also* **grey matter; k)** *no pl., no indef. art. (written or printed material)* **reading ~:** Lesestoff, *der;* **advertising ~:** Reklame, *die;* **l)** *(material for thought etc.)* Material, *das;* **m)** *(content)* Inhalt, *der.* **2.** *v. i.* etwas ausmachen; **what does it ~?** was macht das schon?; was macht's? *(ugs.);* **what ~s is that ...:** worum es geht, ist ...; **not ~ a damn** vollkommen egal sein; **[it] doesn't ~:** [das] macht nichts *(ugs.);* **it ~s a great deal** es macht eine ganze Menge aus; **it doesn't ~ how/when** *etc.* es ist einerlei, wie/wann *usw.;* **does it ~ to you if ...?** macht es dir etwas aus, wenn ...?; **it doesn't ~ at all to me** es ist mir völlig einerlei; **some things ~ rather more than others** manche Dinge sind eben wichtiger als andere; **that's all that ~s** das ist die Hauptsache; **the things which ~ in life** [das,] worauf es im Leben ankommt; **she knows the people who really ~:** sie kennt die Leute, die wirklich etwas gelten

ˈmatter-of-fact *adj.* sachlich; nüchtern

matter-of-ˈfactly [mætərəvˈfæktlɪ] *adv.* sachlich; nüchtern

Matthew [ˈmæθjuː] *pr. n.* **St ~:** der hl. Matthäus *od. (ökumen.)* Mattäus

matting [ˈmætɪŋ] *n. (fabric)* **coconut/straw/reed ~:** Kokos-/Stroh-/Schilf- *od.* Rohrgeflecht, *das; (as floor-covering)* Kokos-/Stroh-/Schilfmatten; **a piece of ~:** ein Stück Matte

mattock [ˈmætək] *n. (Agric.)* Breithacke, *die*

mattress [ˈmætrɪs] *n.* Matratze, *die; see also* **spring mattress**

maturation [mætjʊˈreɪʃn] *n.* **a)** *(maturing)* Reifung, *die;* **b)** *(of fruit)* [Heran]reifen, *das*

mature [məˈtjʊə(r)] **1.** *adj.,* **~r** [məˈtjʊərə(r)], **~st** [məˈtjʊərɪst] **a)** reif; ausgereift ‹*Plan, Methode, Stil, Käse, Portwein, Sherry*›; durchgegoren ‹*Wein*›; ausgewachsen ‹*Pflanze, Tier*›; vollentwickelt ‹*Zellen*›; ~

student Spätstudierende, *der/die;* **a man of ~ years** ein Mann im reiferen Alter *od.* in reiferen Jahren; **b)** *(Finance)* fällig ⟨*Rechnung, Schuldschein usw.*⟩. **2.** *v. t.* reifen lassen ⟨*Frucht, Wein, Käse*⟩; reifer machen ⟨*Personen*⟩; ausreifen lassen ⟨*Plan*⟩; **port is ~d in oak casks** Portwein reift in Eichenfässern. **3.** *v. i.* **a)** ⟨*Frucht, Wein, Käse usw.:*⟩ reifen; **b)** ⟨*Person:*⟩ reifen, reifer werden; **c)** ⟨*Rechnung, Police usw.:*⟩ fällig werden

maturity [mə'tjʊərɪtɪ] *n.* **a)** Reife, *die;* **reach ~, come to ~** ⟨*Person:*⟩ erwachsen werden; ⟨*Tier:*⟩ ausgewachsen sein; **b)** *(Finance)* Fälligkeit, *die;* **come to ~:** fällig werden

maty *see* **matey**

maudlin ['mɔ:dlɪn] *adj.* gefühlsselig

maul [mɔ:l] **1.** *v. t.* **a)** ⟨*Tiger, Löwe, Bär usw.:*⟩ Pranken-/Tatzenhiebe versetzen (+ *Dat.*); *(fig.)* malträtieren; verreißen ⟨*Theaterstück, Buch*⟩; ⟨*Boxer:*⟩ losgehen auf (+ *Akk.*) ⟨*Gegner*⟩; **he was ~ed by a lion** er wurde von einem Löwen angefallen; **b)** *(fondle roughly)* betatschen *(ugs.)*. **2.** *n.* **a)** *(brawl)* Schlägerei, *die;* **b)** *(Rugby)* **[loose] ~:** offenes Gedränge

Maundy ['mɔ:ndɪ] *n. (Brit.) Verteilung von Almosen am Gründonnerstag*

Maundy: ~ money *n. (Brit.) englische silberne Sondermünzen, die am Gründonnerstag als Almosen verteilt werden;* Maundy money, *das;* **~ 'Thursday** *n.* Gründonnerstag, *der*

Mauritania [mɒrɪ'teɪnɪə] *pr. n.* Mauretanien *(das)*

Mauritian [mə'rɪʃn] **1.** *adj.* mauritisch; **sb. is ~:** jmd. ist Mauritier/Mauritierin. **2.** *n.* Mauritier, *der*/Mauritierin, *die*

Mauritius [mə'rɪʃəs] *pr. n.* Mauritius *(das)*

mausoleum [mɔ:sə'li:əm] *n.* Mausoleum, *das*

mauve [məʊv] *adj.* mauve

maverick ['mævərɪk] **1.** *n.* Einzelgänger, *der*/Einzelgängerin, *die; (Amer.: politician)* Alleingänger, *der.* **2.** *adj.* einzelgängerisch

maw [mɔ:] *n.* **a)** *(stomach)* Magen, *der; (of ruminant)* Labmagen, *der;* **b)** *(jaws)* Rachen, *der*

mawkish ['mɔ:kɪʃ] *adj. (sentimental)* rührselig

max. *abbr.* **maximum** *(adj.)* max., *(n.)* Max.

maxi ['mæksɪ] *n. (coll.) (dress)* Maxi, *das (ugs.); (skirt)* Maxi, *der (ugs.)*

maxi- *in comb.* Maxi⟨*kleid, -mantel, -rock*⟩

maxim ['mæksɪm] *n.* Maxime, *die*

maximal ['mæksɪml] *adj.,* **maximally** ['mæksɪməlɪ] *adv.* maximal

maximisation, maximise *see* **maximiz-**

maximization [mæksɪmaɪ'zeɪʃn] *n.* Maximierung, *die;* **~ of profit** Profitmaximierung, *die*

maximize ['mæksɪmaɪz] *v. t.* maximieren

maximum ['mæksɪməm] **1.** *n., pl.* **maxima** ['mæksɪmə] Maximum, *das;* **a ~ of happiness** ein Maximum *od.* Höchstmaß an Glück; **production is at a ~:** die Produktion befindet sich auf einem Höchststand. **2.** *adj.* maximal; Maximal-; **~ security prison** Hochsicherheitsgefängnis, *das*

May [meɪ] *n.* **a)** *(month)* Mai, *der; see also* **August; queen a; b) may** *(hawthorn)* Weißdorn, *der*

may *v. aux., only in pres.* **may,** *neg. (coll.)* **mayn't** [meɪnt], *past* **might** [maɪt], *neg. (coll.)* **mightn't** ['maɪtnt] **a)** *expr. possibility* können; **it ~ be true** das kann stimmen; **it ~ or ~ not be true** vielleicht stimmt's, vielleicht auch nicht; **I ~ be wrong** vielleicht irre ich mich; **they ~ be related** es kann sein, daß sie verwandt sind; vielleicht sind sie verwandt; **it ~ not be possible** das wird vielleicht nicht möglich sein; **he ~ have missed his train** vielleicht hat er seinen Zug verpaßt; **he ~ have finished already** vielleicht ist er schon fertig; **it ~ or might be true, though I doubt it** das kann schon *od.* könnte stimmen, obwohl ich es bezweifle; **it ~ or might rain** es könnte regnen; **he might come round later** vielleicht kommt er später noch vorbei; **they might decide to stay** womöglich beschließen sie zu bleiben; **he might have been right** vielleicht hat er [ja] recht gehabt; er könnte recht gehabt haben; **he might have agreed if ...:** vielleicht hätte er zugestimmt, wenn ...; **it's not so bad as it might have been** es hätte schlimmer kommen können; **that ~ well be** das ist durchaus möglich; das kann durchaus sein; **it ~ or might well be true** das kann *od.* könnte durchaus stimmen; **it ~ or might well turn out to be quite easy** es ist durchaus möglich, daß es sich als recht einfach herausstellt; **you ~ well say so** das kann man wohl sagen; **as well he ~/might** wozu er [auch] allen Grund hat/hatte; **we ~ or might as well go** wir könnten eigentlich ebensogut [auch] gehen; *(we are not achieving anything here)* dann können wir ja gehen; **that is as '~ be** das kann *od.* mag schon sein; **be that as it ~:** wie dem auch sei; **b)** *expr. permission* dürfen; **you ~ go now** du kannst *od.* darfst jetzt gehen; **~ I ask why ...?** darf ich fragen, warum ...?; **if I ~ say so ...:** wenn ich das sagen darf, ...; **~ or might I be permitted to ...?** *(formal)* gestatten Sie, daß ...?; **we ~ safely assert that ...:** wir dürfen wohl behaupten, daß ...; **~ or might I ask** *(iron.)* ..., wenn ich [mal] fragen darf?; **c)** *expr. wish* mögen; **~ you be happy together!** ich hoffe, ihr werdet glücklich miteinander!; **~ the best man win!** auf daß der Beste gewinnt!; **~ God bless you** Gott segne dich; **d)** *expr. request* **you might help me with this** du könntest mir dabei helfen; **you might offer to help instead of ...:** du solltest lieber helfen, statt ...; **you might at least try [it]** du könntest es wenigstens versuchen; **you might have asked permission** du hättest um Erlaubnis fragen können; **e)** *used concessively* **he ~ be slow but he's accurate** mag *od.* kann sein, daß er langsam ist, aber dafür ist er auch genau; **f)** *in clauses* **so that I ~/might do sth.** damit ich etw. tun kann; **I hope he ~ succeed** ich hoffe, es gelingt ihm; **I wish it might happen** ich wünschte, es würde geschehen; **you never know what ~ happen** man weiß nie, was passieren kann; **come what ~, whatever ~ happen** geschehe was will; was auch geschieht; **whatever you ~ say ...:** ganz gleich, was du sagst ...; **g) who ~ you be?** wer bist du denn *od.* bist denn du?; **how old might she be?** wie alt mag sie *od.* wird sie wohl sein?

maybe ['meɪbi:, 'meɪbɪ] *adv.* vielleicht

'May Day *n.* der Erste Mai; **~ celebrations/demonstrations** Maifeiern/-demonstrationen; **the ~ holiday** der Maifeiertag

'Mayday *n. (distress signal)* Mayday; **~ signal/call** Maydaysignal, *das*

'mayfly *n. (Zool.)* Eintagsfliege, *die*

mayhem ['meɪhem] *n.* **a)** *(confusion, chaos)* Chaos, *das;* **there was ~:** es gab ein Chaos; **cause** *or* **create ~:** ein Chaos verursachen *od.* hervorrufen; **b)** *(Brit. Hist./Amer.)* schwere Körperverletzung

mayn't [meɪnt] *(coll.)* = **may not;** *see* **may**

mayonnaise [meɪə'neɪz] *n.* Mayonnaise, *die;* **egg/fish ~:** Ei/Fisch in Mayonnaise

mayor [meə(r)] *n.* Bürgermeister, *der;* **Lord M~** *(Brit.)* Lord-Mayor, *der;* ≈ Oberbürgermeister, *der;* **Lord M~'s Show** *(Brit.) Festzug des Lord-Mayor durch die City von London*

mayoral ['meərl] *adj.* des Bürgermeisters *nachgestellt*

mayoralty ['meərltɪ] *n. (office)* Amt des Bürgermeisters; *(period of office)* Amtszeit eines Bürgermeisters

mayoress ['meərɪs] *n. (woman mayor)* Bürgermeisterin, *die; (mayor's wife)* [Ehe]frau des Bürgermeisters; **Lady M~** *(Brit.)* Oberbürgermeisterin, *die*/[Ehe]frau des Oberbürgermeisters

'maypole *n.* Maibaum, *der*

'May queen *n.* Maikönigin, *die*

maze [meɪz] *n. (lit. or fig.)* Labyrinth, *das*

mazurka [mə'zɜ:kə] *n. (Mus.)* Mazurka, *die*

MB *abbr.* **Bachelor of Medicine** ≈ zweites medizinisches Staatsexamen; *see also* **B. Sc.**

MBA *abbr.* **Master of Business Administration** graduierter Betriebswirt; *see also* **B. Sc.**

MBE *abbr. (Brit.)* **Member [of the Order] of the British Empire** Träger des Ordens des British Empire 5. Klasse

MC *abbr.* **a) Master of Ceremonies; b)** *(Brit.)* **Military Cross** *militärisches Verdienstkreuz*

MCC [emsɪ:'sɪ:] *n. britischer Kricketverband*

McCoy [mə'kɔɪ] **the real ~** *(coll.)* der/die/das Echte; *(not a fake or replica)* das Original

MCP *abbr. (coll.)* **male chauvinist pig**

MD *abbr.* **a) Doctor of Medicine** Dr. med.; *see also* **B. Sc.; b) Managing Director** Ltd. Dir.

[1]me [mɪ, *stressed* mi:] *pron.* mich; *as indirect object* mir; **bigger than/as big as me** größer als/so groß wie ich; **silly ~:** ich Dussel! *(salopp);* **why me?** warum ich/mich/mir?; **who, me?** wer, ich?; **not me** ich/mich/mir nicht; **it's me** ich bin's; **it isn't me** das bin ich nicht; **yes, me** ja, ich/mich/mir; **the real me** mein wahres Ich

[2]me [mi:] *n. (Mus.)* mi

[1]mead [mi:d] *n. (drink)* Met, *der*

[2]mead *n. (poet./arch.: meadow)* Aue, *die*

meadow ['medəʊ] *n.* Wiese, *die;* **in the ~:** auf der Wiese

meadow: ~-grass *n.* [Wiesen]rispengras, *das;* **~ pipit** *n. (Ornith.)* Wiesenpieper, *der;* **~ 'saffron** *n. (Bot.)* Herbstzeitlose, *die;* **~sweet** *n. (Bot.) (Brit.)* Mädesüß, *das; (Amer.)* Weidenblättriger Spierstrauch

meager, meagerly, meagerness *(Amer.) see* **meagre** *etc.*

meagre ['mi:gə(r)] *adj.* **a)** spärlich; dürftig *(auch fig.);* mager ⟨*Boden*⟩; **a ~ attendance** eine geringe Teilnehmerzahl; **b)** mager ⟨*Gesicht, Mensch*⟩; hager ⟨*Gestalt*⟩

meagrely ['mi:gəlɪ] *adv.* spärlich; dürftig ⟨*leben, sich ernähren, behandeln*⟩

meagreness ['mi:gənɪs] *n., no pl.* Spärlichkeit, *die;* Dürftigkeit, *die*

[1]meal [mi:l] *n.* Mahlzeit, *die;* **stay for a ~:** zum Essen bleiben; **go out for a ~:** essen gehen; **have a [hot/cold/light] ~:** [warm/kalt/etwas Leichtes essen; **enjoy your ~:** guten Appetit!; **did you enjoy your ~?** hat es Ihnen geschmeckt?; **~s on wheels** *(Brit.)* Essen auf Rädern; **make a ~ of sth.** etw. verzehren *od.* essen; *(fig.)* eine große Sache aus etw. machen

[2]meal *n.* **a)** *(ground grain)* Schrot[mehl], *das;* **b)** *(Scot.: oatmeal)* Hafermehl, *das;* **c)** *(Amer.: maize flour)* Maismehl, *das*

mealies ['mi:lɪz] *n. pl. (S. Afr.)* **a)** *(maize)* Mais, *der;* **b)** *(corn-cob)* Maiskolben, *der*

meal: ~-ticket *n.* Essenmarke, *die; (fig. coll.)* melkende Kuh *(ugs.);* **~time** *n.* Essenszeit, *die;* **at ~times** während des Essens; bei Tisch; **my usual ~time is ...:** ich esse gewöhnlich um ...

mealy ['mi:lɪ] *adj.* mehlig ⟨*Kartoffeln, Äpfel*⟩

mealy-mouthed ['mi:lɪmaʊðd] *adj. (derog.)* unaufrichtig

[1]mean [mi:n] **1.** *n.* **a)** Mittelweg, *der;* Mitte, *die;* **a happy ~:** der goldene Mittelweg; *see also* **golden mean; b)** *(Math.)* Mittelwert, *der*

[2]mean *adj.* **a)** *(niggardly)* schäbig *(abwertend);* **you ~ old thing!** du alter Geizhals! *(abwertend);* **b)** *(ignoble)* schäbig *(abwertend),* gemein ⟨*Person, Verhalten, Gesinnung*⟩; *(malicious)* hinterhältig ⟨*Blick*⟩; **c)** *(unimpressive)* schäbig *(abwertend)* ⟨*Haus,*

Wohngegend⟩; armselig ⟨*Verhältnisse*⟩; **be no ~ athlete/feat** kein schlechter Sportler/keine schlechte Leistung sein; **d)** *(coll.: ashamed)* **feel ~ [about sth.]** sich [wegen etw.] schäbig vorkommen; **he made me feel ~:** ich kam mir ihm gegenüber richtig schäbig vor; **e)** *(inferior)* minder... ⟨*Qualität*⟩; **this is clear to the ~est intelligence** das ist selbst dem Dümmsten klar; **f)** *(Amer.: vicious)* bösartig, heimtückisch ⟨*Person, Tier*⟩; **g)** *(Amer. coll.: unwell)* **feel ~:** sich mies fühlen *(ugs.)*; **h)** *(coll.: skilful)* spitze *(ugs.)*; klasse *(ugs.)*; **blow a ~ trumpet** spitze *od.* klasse Trompete spielen

³mean *v. t.*, **~t** [ment] **a)** *(have as one's purpose)* beabsichtigen; **~ well** es gut meinen; **~ sb. well, ~ well by** *or* **to** *or* **towards sb.** es gut mit jmdm. meinen; **I ~t no harm** ich hab's nicht böse gemeint; **I ~t him no harm** ich wollte ihm nichts Böses; **what do you ~ by [saying] that?** was willst du damit sagen?; **what do you ~ by entering without first knocking?** was fällt dir ein, einfach, ohne anzuklopfen, hereinzukommen? **I ~t it** *or* **it was ~t as a joke** das sollte ein Scherz sein; **~ to do sth.** etw. tun wollen; **I ~ to do it** ich bin fest dazu entschlossen; **I ~ to be obeyed** ich verlange, daß man mir gehorcht; **if he ~s to come ...:** wenn er [schon] unbedingt kommen will, ...; **I ~t to write, but forgot** ich hatte [fest] vor zu schreiben, aber habe es [dann] vergessen; **I only ~t to be helpful** ich wollte [doch] nur helfen; **I didn't ~ to be rude** ich wollte nicht unhöflich sein; **I never ~t to imply that** das habe ich niemals sagen wollen; **do you ~ to say that ...?** willst du damit sagen, daß ...?; *see also* **business f; b)** *(design, destine)* **these plates are ~t to be used** diese Teller sind zum Gebrauch bestimmt *od.* sind da, um benutzt zu werden; **what's this gadget ~t to be?** welche Funktion hat dieses Gerät?; **I ~t it to be a surprise/as a surprise for him** es sollte eine Überraschung für ihn sein; ich wollte ihn damit überraschen; **you were never ~t for a diplomat** du bist eben nicht der geborene Diplomat; **they are ~t for each other** sie sind füreinander bestimmt; **I am ~t for greater things than this** ich bin zu Höherem bestimmt; **is this ~t for me?** soll das für mich sein?; **I ~t you to read the letter** ich wollte, daß du den Brief liest; **be ~t to do sth.** etw. tun sollen; **you are ~t to arrive on time** es wird erwartet, daß Sie pünktlich eintreffen *od.* sind; **you weren't ~t to say that** das hättest du nicht sagen sollen; **I am ~t to be giving a lecture** ich soll einen Vortrag halten; **are we ~t to go this way?** *(permitted)* dürfen wir hier langgehen?; **the Russians are ~t to be good at chess** die Russen sollen gut im Schach sein; **c)** *(intend to convey, refer to)* meinen; **I ~ [to say], ...:** ich meine ...; **if you know** *or* **see what I ~:** du verstehst, was ich meine?; **what do you ~ by that?** was hast du damit gemeint?; **what I ~ is, will you marry me?** ich meine, willst du mich heiraten?; **I really ~ it, I ~ what I say** ich meine das ernst; es ist mir Ernst damit; **I didn't ~ it literally** ich habe das nicht wörtlich gemeint; **d)** *(signify, entail, matter)* bedeuten; **the name ~s/the instructions ~ nothing to me** der Name sagt mir nichts/ich kann mit der Anleitung nichts anfangen; **this ~s serious problems for him** das wird ihn in ernste Schwierigkeiten bringen

meander [mɪ'ændə(r)] **1.** *v. i.* **a)** ⟨*Fluß:*⟩ sich schlängeln *od.* winden; mäandern *(Geogr.)*; **b)** ⟨*Person:*⟩ schlendern. **2.** *n. in pl.* Windungen; *(of river also)* Mäander *(Geogr.)*

meanderings [mɪ'ændərɪŋz] *n. pl.* Windungen; *(of stream also)* Mäander *(Geogr.)*

meanie ['mi:nɪ] *n. (coll.)* Geizhals, *der (abwertend)*; Geizkragen, *der (ugs. abwertend)*

meaning ['mi:nɪŋ] **1.** *n.* Bedeutung, *die; (of text etc., life)* Sinn, *der;* **this sentence has no ~:** dieser Satz ergibt keinen Sinn; **if you get my ~:** du verstehst, was ich meine?; **I don't get your ~:** ich verstehe dich nicht; ich weiß nicht, was du meinst; **I mistook his ~:** ich habe ihn mißverstanden; **what's the ~ of this?** was hat [denn] das zu bedeuten?; **you don't know the ~ of suffering/of the word** du weißt ja gar nicht, was Leiden bedeutet *od.* ist/was das bedeutet; **with ~:** bedeutungsvoll. **2.** *adj.* bedeutungsvoll

meaningful ['mi:nɪŋfl] *adj.* sinntragend ⟨*Wort, Einheit*⟩; *(fig.)* bedeutungsvoll ⟨*Blick, Ergebnis, Folgerung*⟩; sinnvoll ⟨*Leben, Aufgabe, Arbeit, Gespräch*⟩

meaningless ['mi:nɪŋlɪs] *adj.* ⟨*Wort, Satz, Gespräch*⟩ ohne Sinn; *(fig.)* sinnlos ⟨*Aktivität, Leben, Leiden, Opfer, Verhalten*⟩

meanly ['mi:nlɪ] *adv.* schäbig *(abwertend)* gemein ⟨*sich verhalten, jmdn. behandeln*⟩; armselig, dürftig ⟨*bekleidet, ausgestattet, ausgerüstet*⟩; **live ~:** in armseligen Verhältnissen leben

meanness ['mi:nnɪs] *n., no pl.* **a)** *(stinginess)* Schäbigkeit, *die (abwertend)*; **b)** *(baseness)* Schäbigkeit, *die (abwertend)*; Gemeinheit, *die;* **c)** *(shabbiness) see* **²mean c:** Schäbigkeit, *die;* Armseligkeit, *die*

means [mi:nz] *n. pl.* **a)** *usu. constr. as sing. (way, method)* Möglichkeit, *die;* [Art und] Weise; **by this ~:** hierdurch; auf diese Weise; **by what ~?** wie? auf welche Weise?; **by some ~ or other** auf die eine oder andere Weise; irgendwie; **a ~ to an end** ein Mittel zum Zweck; **do the ends justify the ~?** heiligt der Zweck die Mittel?; **we have no ~ of doing this** wir haben keine Möglichkeit, dies zu tun; **he used poetry as a ~ of expressing his ideas** er benutzte Dichtung als Mittel, um seine Gedanken auszudrücken; **an easy ~ of escape** eine bequeme Fluchtmöglichkeit; **~ of transport** Transportmittel, *das;* **a ~ of communicating with sb.** eine Möglichkeit *od.* ein Weg, sich mit jmdm. zu verständigen; **how this happened we have no ~ of telling/knowing** wie es passierte *od. (geh.)* geschah, können wir nicht sagen/wissen; *see also* **way 1 c; b)** *(resources)* Mittel *Pl.;* **live within/beyond one's ~:** seinen Verhältnissen entsprechend/über seine Verhältnisse leben; **he/she is a man/woman of ~:** er/sie ist vermögend; **c) Will you help me? – By all ~:** Hilfst du mir? Selbstverständlich!; **May I go now? – By all ~:** Darf ich jetzt gehen? – Ja, gern *od.* sicher; **do so by all ~, but ...:** tu das ruhig, aber ...; **by no [manner of] ~, not by any [manner of] ~:** ganz und gar nicht; keineswegs; **by ~ of** durch; mit [Hilfe von]

'means test 1. *n.* Überprüfung der Bedürftigkeit. **2.** *v. t.* jmds. Bedürftigkeit überprüfen; **~ tested benefits** nach Bedürftigkeit gestaffelte Unterstützungszahlungen

meant *see* **³mean**

mean: ~time 1. *n.* **in the ~time** in der Zwischenzeit; inzwischen; **2.** *adv.* inzwischen; **~while** *adv.* inzwischen

meany *see* **meanie**

measles ['mi:zlz] *n., constr. as pl. or sing.* Masern *Pl.; see also* **German measles**

measly ['mi:zlɪ] *adj. (coll. derog.)* pop[e]lig *(ugs. abwertend)*; **a ~ little portion** eine mickrige Portion *(ugs. abwertend)*

measurable ['meʒərəbl] *adj.* meßbar ⟨*Anzahl, Menge, Größe*⟩; *(fig.)* merklich ⟨*Besserung, Veränderung, Fortschritte*⟩; **bring sb. within ~ distance of bankruptcy** jmdn. an den Rand des Bankrotts bringen

measurably ['meʒərəblɪ] *adv.* merklich ⟨*besser, größer*⟩

measure ['meʒə(r)] **1.** *n.* **a)** Maß, *das;* **~ of length** Längenmaß, *das;* **weights and ~s** Maße und Gewichte; **for good ~:** sicherheitshalber; *(as an extra)* zusätzlich; **give short/full ~** *(in public house)* zu wenig/vorschriftsmäßig ausschenken; *(in shop)* zu wenig/vorschriftsmäßig abwiegen; **made to ~** *pred. (Brit., lit. or fig.)* maßgeschneidert; **b)** *(degree)* Menge, *die;* **in some ~:** in gewisser Hinsicht; **in large/full ~:** in hohem/vollem Maße; **a ~ of freedom/responsibility** ein gewisses Maß an Freiheit/Verantwortung *(Dat.)*; **c)** *(instrument or utensil for measuring)* Maß, *das; (for quantity also)* Meßglas, *das;* Meßbecher, *der; (for size also)* Meßstab, *der;* Maßstab, *der (selten)*; *(fig.)* Maßstab, *der;* **be a/the ~ of sth.** Maßstab für etw. sein; **it gave us some ~ of the problems** das gab uns eine Vorstellung *od.* einen Begriff von den Problemen; **beyond [all] ~:** grenzenlos; über die *od.* alle Maßen *adv.*; **d)** *(Pros.)* Versmaß, *das;* Metrum, *das;* **e)** *(Mus.: time, bar)* Takt, *der;* **f)** *(step, law)* Maßnahme, *die; (Law: bill)* Gesetzesvorlage, *die;* **take ~s to stop/ensure sth.** Maßnahmen ergreifen *od.* treffen, um etw. zu unterbinden/sicherzustellen; *see also* **half measure b; g)** *(Geol.) see* **coal measures. 2.** *v. t.* **a)** messen ⟨*Größe, Menge usw.*⟩; ausmessen ⟨*Raum*⟩; **~ sb. for a suit** [bei] jmdm. Maß *od.* die Maße für einen Anzug nehmen; **b)** *(fig.: estimate)* abschätzen; **~ sb. by one's own standards** jmdn. an seinen eigenen Maßstäben messen; **c)** *(mark off)* **~ sth. [off]** etw. abmessen; **d)** *(fig.: put in competition)* messen *(geh.)*; **~ oneself against sb.** sich mit jmdm. messen *(geh.)*; **e) ~ one's length** *(fig.)* der Länge nach hinfallen. **3.** *v. i.* **a)** *(have a given size)* messen; **b)** *(take measurement[s])* Maß nehmen

~ 'out *v. t.* abmessen

~ 'up to *v. t.* entsprechen (+ *Dat.*) ⟨*Maßstäben, Erwartungen*⟩; gewachsen sein (+ *Dat.*) ⟨*Anforderungen*⟩

measured ['meʒəd] *adj.* rhythmisch, gleichmäßig ⟨*Geräusch, Bewegung*⟩; gemessen ⟨*Schritt, Worte, Ausdrucksweise*⟩; **speak in ~ terms** sich gemessen ausdrücken

measureless ['meʒəlɪs] *adj.* unermeßlich

measurement ['meʒəmənt] *n.* **a)** *(act, result)* Messung, *die;* **b)** *in pl. (dimensions)* Maße *Pl.;* **take sb.'s ~s** [bei] jmdm. Maß *od.* die Maße nehmen

measuring ['meʒərɪŋ]: **~-jug** *n.* Meßbecher, *der;* **~-tape** *n.* Bandmaß, *das*

meat [mi:t] *n.* **a)** Fleisch, *das;* **b)** *(arch.: food)* Essen, *das; (for animals)* Futter, *das;* **~ and drink** Speis und Trank *(geh.)*; **one man's ~ is another man's poison** *(prov.)* was dem einen sin Uhl, ist dem andern sin Nachtigall *(Spr.)*; **be ~ and drink to sb.** *(fig.)* genau das sein, was jmd. braucht; **c)** *(fig.: chief part, essence)* Substanz, *die*

meat: ~-axe *n.* Fleischbeil, *das;* Spalter, *der (fachspr.)*; **~ball** *n.* Fleischkloß, *der;* Fleischklößchen, *das;* **~-fly** *n.* Fleischfliege, *die;* **~ grinder** *(Amer.) see* **mincer**

meatless ['mi:tlɪs] *adj.* fleischlos

meat: ~ loaf *n.* Hackbraten, *der;* **~ 'pie** *n.* Fleischpastete, *die;* **~-safe** *n. (Brit.)* Fliegenschrank, *der*

meaty ['mi:tɪ] *adj.* **a)** *(full of meat)* fleischig; ⟨*Gulasch usw.*⟩ mit reichlich Fleisch; **have a ~ taste** nach Fleisch schmecken; **b)** *(fig.: full of substance)* gehaltvoll

Mecca ['mekə] *n.* Mekka, *das;* **the ~ of golfers** das Mekka für Golfer

mechanic [mɪ'kænɪk] *n.* Mechaniker, *der*

mechanical [mɪ'kænɪkl] *adj. (lit. or fig.)* mechanisch; **produced by ~ means** maschinell produziert; maschinell erzeugt ⟨*Strom*⟩; **~ contrivance** Mechanismus, *der*

mechanical: ~ engi'neer *n.* Maschinenbauer, *der/*-bauerin, *die; (graduate)* Maschinenbauingenieur, *der/*-ingenieurin, *die;* **~ engi'neering** *n.* Maschinenbau, *der*

mechanically [mɪ'kænɪkəlɪ] *adv. (lit. or fig.)* mechanisch; **~ inclined/minded** technisch interessiert/veranlagt

mechanical 'pencil *n. (Amer.)* Drehbleistift, *der*
mechanics [mɪ'kænɪks] *n., no pl.* **a)** Mechanik, *die;* **b)** *constr. as pl. (means of construction or operation)* Mechanismus, *der; (of writing, painting, etc.)* Technik, *die;* **understand the ~ of sth.** wissen, wie etw. funktioniert
mechanisation, mechanise *see* **mechaniz-**
mechanism ['mekənɪzm] *n.* Mechanismus, *der*
mechanization [mekənaɪ'zeɪʃn] *n.* Mechanisierung, *die*
mechanize ['mekənaɪz] *v.t.* **a)** mechanisieren; **b)** *(Mil.)* motorisieren
Med [med] *pr. n. (coll.)* **the ~:** das Mittelmeer
medal ['medl] *n.* Medaille, *die; (decoration)* Orden, *der;* **~ for bravery/pole-vaulting** Tapferkeitsmedaille, *die*/Medaille im Stabhochsprung; **the reverse of the ~** *(fig.)* die Kehrseite der Medaille
medalist *(Amer.) see* **medallist**
medallion [mɪ'dæljən] *n.* **a)** *(large medal)* [große] Medaille; **b)** *(thing shaped like medal)* Medaillon, *das*
medallist ['medəlɪst] *n.* Medaillengewinner, *der*/-gewinnerin, *die (Sport);* **be a ~:** eine Medaille gewonnen haben
meddle ['medl] *v.i.* **~ with sth.** sich *(Dat.)* an etw. *(Dat.)* zu schaffen machen; **~ in sth.** sich in etw. *(Akk.)* einmischen; **don't ~:** Finger weg! *(ugs.); (stop interfering)* misch dich nicht ein!; **she's always meddling** sie muß sich immer in alles einmischen
meddler ['medlə(r)] *n.* **he's [such] a ~:** *(with things)* er muß immer alles in die Finger nehmen *od. (ugs.)* an allem herumspielen; *(in things)* er muß sich immer in alles einmischen
meddlesome ['medlsəm] *adj.* **she is so ~** *or* **such a ~ person** *(interferes with things)* sie muß sich *(Dat.)* immer an was zu schaffen machen; *(interferes in things)* sie muß sich in alles einmischen
media ['mi:dɪə] *see* **mass media; medium 1 a**
mediaeval *see* **medieval**
medial ['mi:dɪəl] *adj.* mittler...; ⟨*Buchstabe, Zeichen*⟩ mitten im Wort
median ['mi:dɪən] **1.** *adj.* mittler...; median *(Anat.).* **2.** *n. (Statistics)* Median[wert], *der;* Zentralwert, *der*
median 'strip *n. (Amer.)* Mittelstreifen, *der*
mediate ['mi:dɪeɪt] **1.** *v.i.* vermitteln. **2.** *v.t.* **a)** *(settle)* vermitteln in (+ *Dat.*); **b)** *(bring about)* vermitteln
mediation [mi:dɪ'eɪʃn] *n.* Vermittlung, *die*
mediator ['mi:dɪeɪtə(r)] *n.* Vermittler, *der*/Vermittlerin, *die*
medic ['medɪk] *see* **medico**
Medicaid ['medɪkeɪd] *n. (Amer.) [bundes]staatliches Programm, das Unterstützungsbedürftigen Beihilfe zur Deckung von Arzt- und Heilmittelkosten gewährt*
medical ['medɪkl] **1.** *adj.* medizinisch; ärztlich ⟨*Behandlung*⟩; **~ ward** ≈ medizinische *od.* innere Abteilung. **2.** *n. (coll.) see* **medical examination**
medical: ~ attendant *n.* Leibarzt, *der*/-ärztin, *die;* **~ certificate** *n.* Attest, *das;* **~ exami'nation** *n.* ärztliche Untersuchung; **~ 'history** *n.* **a)** Geschichte der Medizin; **make ~ history** auf dem Gebiet der Medizin Geschichte machen; **b)** *(of person)* Krankengeschichte, *die*
medically ['medɪkəlɪ] *adv.* medizinisch
medical: ~ officer *n. (Brit.)* **a)** Amtsarzt, *der*/-ärztin, *die;* **b)** *(Mil.)* Sanitätsoffizier, *der;* **~ prac'titioner** *n.* praktischer Arzt/praktische Ärztin; Arzt/Ärztin für Allgemeinmedizin; **~ report** *n.* medizinisches Gutachten; **~ school** *n.* medizinische Hochschule; *(faculty)* medizinische Fakultät; **~ student** *n.* Medizinstudent, *der*/-studentin, *die*
medicament [mɪ'dɪkəmənt, 'medɪkəmənt] *n.* Medikament, *das*
Medicare ['medɪkeə(r)] *n. (Amer.) [bundes]staatliches Krankenversicherungssystem für Personen über 65 Jahre*
medicated ['medɪkeɪtɪd] *adj.* **~ shampoo/soap** medizinisches Haarwaschmittel/medizinische Seife; **~ gauze** imprägnierter Mull
medication [medɪ'keɪʃn] *n.* **a)** *(treatment)* Behandlung, *die;* Medikation, *die (Med.);* **b)** *(medicament)* Medikament, *das*
medicinal [mɪ'dɪsɪnl] *adj.* medizinisch; Arznei⟨*mittel, -kohle*⟩; **~ qualities** Heilkräfte
medicinally [mɪ'dɪsɪnəlɪ] *adv.* medizinisch; **use sth. ~:** etw. zu medizinischen Zwecken *od.* Heilzwecken verwenden
medicine ['medsən, 'medɪsɪn] *n. (science)* Medizin, *die; (preparation)* Medikament, *das;* Medizin, *die (veralt.);* **give sb. some** *or* **a little** *or* **a dose** *or* **a taste of his/her own ~** *(fig.)* es jmdm. mit gleicher Münze heimzahlen; **they got a taste of their own ~** *(fig.)* man zahlte es ihnen mit gleicher Münze heim; **take one's ~** *(fig.)* die bittere Pille schlucken *(ugs.); (bear the consequences)* die Suppe auslöffeln *(ugs.)*
medicine: ~ ball *n.* Medizinball, *der;* **~ chest** *n.* Medikamentenschränkchen, *das; (in home)* Hausapotheke, *die;* **~-man** *n.* Medizinmann, *der*
medico ['medɪkəʊ] *n., pl.* **~s** *(coll.)* **a)** *(doctor)* Doktor, *der (ugs.);* **b)** *(student)* Mediziner, *der*/Medizinerin, *die (ugs.)*
medieval [medɪ'i:vl] *adj. (lit. or fig.)* mittelalterlich; **the ~ period** das Mittelalter; **~ studies** Mediävistik, *die;* **in ~ times** im Mittelalter; **~ Latin** *see* **Latin 2**
medieval 'history *n.* Geschichte des Mittelalters; *(as subject)* mittelalterliche Geschichte
medievalist [medɪ'i:vəlɪst] *n.* Mediävist, *der*/Mediävistin, *die*
mediocre [mi:dɪ'əʊkə(r)] *adj.* mittelmäßig
mediocrity [mi:dɪ'ɒkrɪtɪ] *n.* **a)** *no pl.* Mittelmäßigkeit, *die;* **b)** *(person)* mittelmäßiger Mensch; **he is a ~/they are mediocrities** er ist/sie sind [ausgesprochenes] Mittelmaß
meditate ['medɪteɪt] **1.** *v.t. (consider)* denken an (+ *Akk.*); erwägen; *(design)* planen; **~ revenge** auf Rache *(Akk.)* sinnen *(geh.).* **2.** *v.i.* nachdenken, *(esp. Relig.)* meditieren **([up]on** über + *Akk.*)
meditation [medɪ'teɪʃn] *n.* **a)** *(act of meditating)* Nachdenken, *das;* **b)** *(Relig.)* Meditation, *die*
meditative ['medɪtətɪv] *adj.,* **meditatively** ['medɪtətɪvlɪ] *adv.* nachdenklich; *(esp. Relig.)* meditativ
Mediterranean [medɪtə'reɪnɪən] **1.** *pr. n.* **the ~:** das Mittelmeer. **2.** *adj.* mediterran *(Geogr.);* südländisch; **~ coast/countries** Mittelmeerküste, *die*/Mittelmeerländer
Mediterranean: ~ 'climate *n. (Geog.)* mediterranes Klima; **~ 'Sea** *pr. n.* Mittelmeer, *das*
medium ['mi:dɪəm] **1.** *n., pl.* **media** ['mi:dɪə] *or* **~s a)** *(substance)* Medium, *das; (fig.: environment)* Umgebung, *die;* **b)** *(intermediate agency)* Mittel, *das;* **by** *or* **through the ~ of** durch; **c)** *pl.* **~s** *(Spiritualism)* Medium, *das;* **d)** *(means of communication or artistic expression)* Medium, *das;* **e)** *in pl. (means of mass communication)* Medien *Pl.;* **f)** *(middle degree)* Mittelweg, *der; see also* **happy a; g)** *(liquid)* Bindemittel, *das.* **2.** *adj.* mittler...; medium *nur präd.,* halb durchgebraten ⟨*Steak*⟩; *see also* **-size**
medium: ~-size[d] *adj.* mittelgroß; **~ term** *see* **term 1 d; ~ wave** *n. (Radio)* Mittelwelle, *die*
medlar ['medlə(r)] *n. (Bot.)* Mispel, *die*
medley ['medlɪ] *n.* **a)** *(forming a whole)* buntes Gemisch; *(collection of items)* Sammelsurium, *das (abwertend); (of colours)* Kunterbunt, *das;* **his mind was confused with a ~ of thoughts** die verschiedensten Gedanken schossen durch seinen verwirrten Kopf; **b)** *(Mus.)* Potpourri, *das;* Medley, *das;* **c)** *see* **medley relay**
medley 'relay *n. (Athletics)* Schwellstaffel, *die; (Swimming)* Lagenstaffel, *die*
medulla [mɪ'dʌlə] *n. (Anat.)* **a)** Medulla, *die (fachspr.);* ⟨*Knochen-, Rücken-, Haar*⟩mark, *das;* **b)** *(of brain) see* **medulla oblongata**
medulla oblongata [mɪdʌlə ɒblɒŋ'gɑ:tə] *n. (Anat.)* verlängertes Rückenmark; Medulla oblongata, *die (fachspr.)*
meek [mi:k] *adj.* **a)** *(humble)* sanftmütig; **b)** *(tamely submissive)* zu nachgiebig; **be [far] too ~:** sich *(Dat.)* [viel] zu viel gefallen lassen; **[as] ~ as a lamb** fromm wie ein Lamm
meekly [mi:klɪ] *adv.* **a)** *(humbly)* demütig; **b)** *(submissively)* widerstandslos
meekness ['mi:knɪs] *n., no pl.* **a)** *(humbleness)* Sanftmütigkeit, *die;* **b)** *(submissiveness)* [zu große] Nachgiebigkeit
meerschaum ['mɪəʃəm] *n.* **a)** *(Min.)* Meerschaum, *der;* **b)** *(pipe)* Meerschaumpfeife, *die*
[1]**meet** [mi:t] **1.** *v.t.,* **met** [met] **a)** *(come face to face with or into the company of)* treffen; **I have to ~ my boss at 11 a.m.** ich muß um 11 Uhr zum Chef *(ugs.) od* habe um 11 Uhr einen Termin beim Chef; **arrange to ~ sb.** sich mit jmdm. verabreden; **b)** *(go to place of arrival of)* treffen; *(collect)* abholen; **I'll ~ your train** ich hole dich vom Zug ab; **~ sb. half-way** *(fig.)* jmdm. [auf halbem Wege] entgegenkommen; **~ trouble half-way** sich *(Dat.)* unnötig Sorgen machen; **c)** *(make the acquaintance of)* kennenlernen; **I'd like you to ~ my wife** ich möchte Sie gern meiner Frau vorstellen *od.* mit meiner Frau bekannt machen; **I have never met her** ich kenne sie nicht persönlich; **pleased to ~ you** [sehr] angenehm; sehr erfreut; **Maimie, ~ Charlene. Charlene, ~ Maimie** *(Amer.)* Maimie, [dies ist] Charlene. Charlene, [dies ist] Maimie; **d)** *(reach point of contact with)* treffen auf (+ *Akk.*); **~ the eye/sb.'s eye[s]** sich den/jmds. Blicken darbieten; **~ the ear/sb.'s ears** das/jmds. Ohr treffen; **she met his eye[s], her eyes met his** *(fig.)* sie sah ihn an, er sah sie an; **he could not ~ his father's eyes** er konnte seinem Vater nicht in die Augen sehen; **there's more to** *or* **in it/him** *etc.* **than ~s the eye** da ist *od.* steckt mehr dahinter, als man zuerst denkt/in ihm *usw.* steckt mehr, als man auf den ersten Blick denkt; **e)** *(oppose)* treffen auf (+ *Akk.*) ⟨*Feind, Herausforderer usw.*⟩; *(grapple with)* begegnen (+ *Dat.*); **f)** *(experience)* stoßen auf (+ *Akk.*) ⟨*Widerstand, Problem*⟩; ernten ⟨*Gelächter, Drohungen*⟩; **~ [one's] death** *or* **one's end/disaster/one's fate** den Tod finden *(geh.)*/von einer Katastrophe/seinem Schicksal ereilt werden *(geh.);* **~ one's fate bravely** sich seinem Schicksal tapfer stellen; **g)** *(satisfy)* entsprechen (+ *Dat.*) ⟨*Forderung, Wunsch, Bedürfnis, Erfordernis*⟩; einhalten ⟨*Termin, Zeitplan*⟩; Rechnung tragen (+ *Dat.*) ⟨*Einwand, Kritik*⟩; **~ the case** angemessen sein; **h)** *(pay)* decken ⟨*Kosten, Auslagen*⟩; bezahlen ⟨*Rechnung*⟩; **~ one's obligations** seinen Verpflichtungen nachkommen. **2.** *v.i.,* **met a)** *(come face to face) (by chance)* sich *(Dat.)* begegnen; *(by arrangement)* sich treffen; **goodbye, until we ~ again** auf Wiedersehen bis zum nächsten Mal; **we've met before** wir kennen uns bereits; **b)** *(assemble)* ⟨*Komitee, Ausschuß usw.:*⟩ tagen; **~ together** sich versammeln; **c)** *(be in opposition)* aufeinandertreffen; **d)** *(come together)* ⟨*Bahnlinien, Straßen usw.:*⟩ aufeinandertreffen; ⟨*Flüsse*⟩ zusammenfließen; **their eyes/lips met** ihre

Blicke/Lippen begegneten sich; **the tables don't quite ~:** die Tische stehen nicht ganz dicht aneinander; *see also* **end 1 h, n; e)** *(be united)* ~ **in sb.** in jmdm. zusammentreffen; sich in jmdm. vereinen *(geh.)*. **3.** *n. (Hunting)* Treffen, *das*

~ **'up** *v. i.* sich treffen; ~ **up with sb.** *(coll.)* jmdn. [zufällig] treffen

~ **with** *v. t.* **a)** *(encounter)* begegnen (+ *Dat.*); **b)** *(experience)* haben ‹*Erfolg, Unfall*›; finden ‹*Zustimmung, Verständnis, Tod*›; stoßen auf (+ *Akk.*) ‹*Widerstand*›; **be met with sth.** etw. hervorrufen; **all her attempts met with failure** alle ihre Bemühungen endeten in einem Mißerfolg; **c)** *(Amer.) see* ~ **1 a**

[2]**meet** *adj. (arch.)* **it is ~ to do sth.** es ziemt sich *(geh. veralt.)*, etw. zu tun

meeting ['mi:tɪŋ] *n.* **a)** Begegnung, *die (auch fig.)*; *(by arrangement)* Treffen, *das*; *(of rivers)* Zusammenfluß, *der*; **~ of minds** Verständigung, *die*; Annäherung der Standpunkte; **b)** *(assembly) (of shareholders, club members etc.; also Relig.)* Versammlung, *die*; *(of committee, Cabinet, council, etc.)* Sitzung, *die*; *(social gathering)* Treffen, *das*; **call a ~ of the committee** den Ausschuß einberufen; **c)** *(persons assembled)* Versammlung, *die*; **d)** *(Sport)* Treffen, *das*; *(Racing)* Rennen, *das*

meeting: ~-place *n.* Treffpunkt, *der*; **~-point** *n. (of lines, roads)* Schnittpunkt, *der*; *(of rivers)* Zusammenfluß, *der*; **at the ~-point of the roads** wo die Straßen zusammentreffen

mega- ['megə] *pref.* mega-/Mega-

'megacycle *n.* Megahertz, *das*

'megadeath *n.* Megatote *Pl.*; **one ~:** 1 Million Tote

'megahertz *n. (Phys.)* Megahertz, *das*

megalithic [megə'lɪθɪk] *adj. (Archaeol.)* megalithisch

megalomania [megələ'meɪnɪə] *n.* Größenwahn, *der*; Megalomanie, *die (Psych.)*

megalomaniac [megələ'meɪnɪæk] **1.** *n.* Größenwahnsinnige, *der/die*; Megalomane, *der/die (Psych.)*; **he's a ~:** er ist größenwahnsinnig. **2.** *adj.* größenwahnsinnig; megaloman[isch] *(Psych.)*

'megaphone *n.* Megaphon, *das*

'megastar *n. (coll.)* Megastar, *der (ugs.)*

'megaton[ne] *n.* Megatonne, *die*

'megawatt *n. (Electr.)* Megawatt, *das*

meiosis [maɪ'əʊsɪs] *n., pl.* **meioses** [maɪ'əʊsi:z] *(Biol.)* Meiose, *die*

Meissen ['maɪsn] *pr. n.* **~ [porcelain]** *see* **porcelain a**

melancholia [melən'kəʊlɪə] *n. (Med.)* Melancholie, *die*

melancholic [melən'kɒlɪk] *adj.* melancholisch; schwermütig

melancholy ['melənkəlɪ] **1.** *n.* Melancholie, *die*; *(pensive sadness)* Schwermut, *die*. **2.** *adj.* **a)** *(gloomy, expressing sadness)* melancholisch; schwermütig; **b)** *(saddening)* deprimierend

Melanesia [melə'ni:ʃə] *pr. n.* Melanesien *(das)*

Melanesian [melə'ni:ʃən] **1.** *adj.* melanesisch. **2.** *n.* **a)** *(person)* Melanesier, *der*/Melanesierin, *die*; **b)** *(language)* Melanesisch, *das*

melanin ['melənɪn] *n.* Melanin, *das*

Melba ['melbə] *see* **peach Melba**

Melba 'toast *n. dünner, knuspriger Toast*

meld [meld] *(Amer.)* **1.** *v. t.* verschmelzen **(into** zu). **2.** *v. i.* [miteinander] verschmelzen

mêlée *(Amer.:* **melee)** ['meleɪ] *n.* **a)** *(scuffle)* Handgemenge, *das*; **b)** *(muddle)* Durcheinander, *das*; *(of things or people moving to and fro)* Gewühl, *das*

mellifluous [me'lɪflʊəs] *adj.* einschmeichelnd ‹*Stimme, Melodie*›

mellow ['meləʊ] **1.** *adj.* **a)** *(softened by age or experience)* abgeklärt; **b)** *(ripe, well-matured)* reif; ausgereift ‹*Wein*›; **c)** *(genial)* freundlich; *(slightly drunk)* angeheitert; ~ **in mood** heiter gestimmt; aufgeräumt; **d)** *(full and soft)* weich ‹*Stimme, Ton, Licht, Farben*›. **2.** *v. t.* reifer machen ‹*Person*›; [aus]reifen lassen ‹*Wein*›. **3.** *v. i.* ‹*Person, Obst, Wein:*› reifen; ‹*Licht, Farbe:*› weicher werden

melodic [mɪ'lɒdɪk] *adj.* melodisch; **~ minor** melodisches Moll

melodious [mɪ'ləʊdɪəs] *adj.*, **melodiously** [mɪ'ləʊdɪəslɪ] *adv.* melodisch

melodrama ['melədrɑ:mə] *n. (lit. or fig.)* Melodrama, *das*

melodramatic [melədrə'mætɪk] *adj.*, **melodramatically** [melədrə'mætɪkəlɪ] *adv. (lit. or fig.)* melodramatisch

melody ['melədɪ] *n.* **a)** *(pleasing sound)* Gesang, *der*; **b)** *(tune)* Melodie, *die*; **c)** *no pl. (musical quality)* Melodik, *die*; **d)** *(Mus.: part in harmonized music)* Melodiestimme, *die*

melon ['melən] *n.* Melone, *die*

melt [melt] **1.** *v. i.* **a)** schmelzen; *(dissolve)* sich auflösen; **~ in one's** *or* **the mouth** *(coll.)* auf der Zunge zergehen; *see also* **butter 1; b)** *(fig.: be softened)* dahinschmelzen *(geh.)* **(at** bei); sich erweichen lassen **(at** durch); **her heart ~ed with pity** ihr Herz schmolz vor Mitleid; **~ into tears** in Tränen zerfließen. **2.** *v. t.* **a)** schmelzen ‹*Schnee, Eis, Metall*›; *(Cookery)* zerlassen ‹*Butter*›; **b)** *(fig.: make tender)* erweichen ‹*Person, Herz*›; **he was ~ed by her entreaties** er ließ sich durch ihre Bitten erweichen

~ **a'way** *v. i.* ‹*Schnee, Eis:*› [weg]schmelzen; *(fig.: dwindle away)* ‹*Nebel, Dunst, Menschenmenge:*› sich auflösen; ‹*Verdacht, Mehrheit, Furcht:*› dahinschwinden *(geh.)*; ‹*Geld:*› dahinschmelzen

~ **'down 1.** *v. i.* schmelzen. **2.** *v. t.* einschmelzen ‹*Metall, Glas*›. *See also* **melt-down**

~ **into** *v. t.* übergehen in (+ *Akk.*)

'melt-down *n.* Schmelzen, *das*

melting ['meltɪŋ]: **~-point** *n.* Schmelzpunkt, *der*; **~-pot** *n. (fig.)* Schmelztiegel, *der*; **be in the ~-pot** in rascher Veränderung begriffen sein

member ['membə(r)] *n.* **a)** Mitglied, *das*; *attrib.* Mitglieds‹*staat, -land*›; **be a ~ of the club** Mitglied des Vereins sein; Vereinsmitglied sein; **~ of the expedition** Expeditionsteilnehmer, *der*/-teilnehmerin, *die*; **be a ~ of an expedition** an einer Expedition teilnehmen; **~ of a/the family** Familienangehörige, *der/die*; **b) M~ [of Parliament)** *(Brit. Polit.)* Abgeordnete [des Unterhauses], *der/die*; **M~ of Congress** *(Amer. Polit.)* Kongreßabgeordnete, *der/die*; **c)** *(limb)* Gliedmaße, *die*; Glied, *das*; *(organ of the body)* [Körper]organ, *das*

membership ['membəʃɪp] *n.* **a)** *(being a member)* Mitgliedschaft, *die* **(of** in + *Dat.*); *attrib.* Mitglieds‹*karte, -ausweis, -beitrag*›; Mitglieder‹*liste, -verzeichnis*›; **he was elected to ~ of the Society** er wurde zum Mitglied der Gesellschaft gewählt; **b)** *(number of members)* Mitgliederzahl, *die*; **the club has a ~ of a few hundred** der Verein hat einige hundert Mitglieder; **c)** *(body of members)* Mitglieder *Pl.*

membrane ['membreɪn] *n. (Biol.)* Membran, *die*

membranous ['membrənəs] *adj. (Biol.)* membranös; **~ bag** Hautsack, *der*

memento [mɪ'mentəʊ] *n., pl.* **~es** *or* **~s** Andenken, *das* **(of** an + *Akk.*)

memo ['meməʊ] *n., pl.* **~s** *(coll.) see* **memorandum a, b**

memoir ['memwɑ:(r)] *n.* **a)** *in pl. (autobiography)* Memoiren *Pl.*; **b)** *(biography)* Biographie, *die*

memorabilia [memərə'bɪlɪə] *n. pl.* Erinnerungsstücke *Pl.*; Memorabilien *Pl. (veralt.)*

memorable ['memərəbl] *adj.* denkwürdig ‹*Ereignis, Gelegenheit, Tag*›; unvergeßlich ‹*Film, Buch, Aufführung*›; **not a very ~ play** kein sehr beeindruckendes Stück

memorably ['memərəblɪ] *adv.* nachhaltig ‹*beeindrucken*›; auf unvergeßliche Weise ‹*spielen*›

memorandum [memə'rændəm] *n., pl.* **memoranda** [memə'rændə] *or* **~s a)** *(note)* Notiz, *die*; **make a ~ of sth.** sich *(Dat.)* etw. notieren; **b)** *(letter)* Mitteilung, *die*; **c)** *(Diplom.)* Memorandum, *das*; **d)** *(Law)* rechtskräftiges Dokument

memorial [mɪ'mɔ:rɪəl] **1.** *adj.* Gedenk‹*stein, -gottesdienst, -ausstellung*›. **2.** *n.* **a)** *(monument)* Denkmal, *das* (to für); *(ceremony)* Gedenkzeremonie, *die*; **b)** *(statement of facts)* Denkschrift, *die* **(to** an + *Akk.*); **c)** *(Diplom.)* Memorandum, *das*

Me'morial Day *n. (Amer.) Trauertag zum Gedenken an die Gefallenen*; ≈ Volkstrauertag, *der*

memorize (memorise) ['meməraɪz] *v. t.* sich *(Dat.)* merken *od.* einprägen; *(learn by heart)* auswendig lernen

memory ['memərɪ] *n.* **a)** *(faculty or capacity, recovery of knowledge)* Gedächtnis, *das*; **have a good/poor ~ for faces** ein gutes/schlechtes Personengedächtnis haben; **commit sth. to ~:** *see* **memorize; b)** *(recollection, person or thing remembered, act of remembering)* Erinnerung, *die* **(of** an + *Akk.*); **have a vague ~ of sth.** sich nur ungenau *od.* vage an etw. *(Akk.)* erinnern; **to the best of my ~:** soweit ich mich erinnere *od.* erinnern kann; **if my ~ is right** wenn ich mich recht erinnere; **search one's ~:** versuchen, sich zu erinnern; **it slipped** *or* **escaped my ~:** es ist mir entfallen; **a trip down ~ lane** eine Reise in die Vergangenheit; **from ~:** aus dem Gedächtnis *od.* Kopf; **speaking from ~, ...:** soweit *od.* soviel ich mich erinnere, ...; **in ~ of** zur Erinnerung an (+ *Akk.*); **c)** *(remembered time)* **a time within the ~ of men still living** eine Zeit, an die sich heute lebende Menschen noch erinnern können; **it is beyond the ~ of anyone alive today** es lebt niemand mehr, der sich daran erinnern könnte; *see also* **living 2 a; d)** *(posthumous repute)* Andenken, *das* **(of** an + *Akk.*); **of happy** *or* **blessed ~:** seligen Angedenkens *(veralt.)*; **e)** *(Computing)* Speicher, *der*

men *pl. of* **man**

menace ['menɪs] **1.** *v. t.* bedrohen ‹*Person*›; androhen ‹*Strafe*›; **~ sb. with sth.** jmdm. mit etw. drohen. **2.** *v. i.* drohen. **3.** *n.* **a)** Plage, *die*; **an absolute** *or* **a public ~** *(fig. coll.) (dangerous person)* eine öffentliche Gefahr; *(obnoxious person)* ein [richtiges] Ekel *(ugs.)*, *(child)* ein kleiner Teufel; **b)** *(literary: threat)* Drohung, *die*; **a sense of ~:** ein Gefühl der Bedrohung; *see also* **demand 2 a**

menacing ['menɪsɪŋ] *adj.* drohend

ménage [meɪ'nɑ:ʒ] *n.* Haushalt, *der*; **~ à trois** [meɪnɑ:ʒ ɑ: 'trwɑ:] Menage à trois, *die*; ≈ Dreiecksverhältnis, *das*

menagerie [mɪ'nædʒərɪ] *n.* Tierschau, *die*; Menagerie, *die (veralt.)*; *(fig. iron.: collection of persons)* Gesellschaft, *die*

mend [mend] **1.** *v. t.* **a)** *(repair)* reparieren; ausbessern, flicken ‹*Kleidung, Fischernetz*›; kleben, kitten ‹*Glas, Porzellan, Sprung*›; beheben ‹*Schaden*›; beseitigen ‹*Riß*›; **b)** *(improve)* **~ one's manners** sich *(Dat.)* bessere Umgangsformen angewöhnen; **~ one's ways** sich bessern; **~ matters** die Sache bereinigen; **it is never too late to ~** *(prov.)* zum Bessermachen/Verbessern ist es nie zu spät; *see also* **fence 1 a; least 2. 2.** *v. i.* gesund werden; genesen *(geh.)*; *(knit together)* heilen; **has his leg ~ed yet?** ist sein Bein schon verheilt?. **3.** *n. (in glass, china etc.)* Kleb[e]stelle, *die*; *(in cloth)* ausgebesserte Stelle; *(repair)* Ausbesserung, *die*; **be on the**

~ ⟨*Person:*⟩ auf dem Wege der Besserung sein; ⟨*Verhältnisse, Lage:*⟩ sich bessern
mendacious [men'deɪʃəs] *adj.* unwahr ⟨*Bericht, Behauptung, Darstellung*⟩; verlogen *(abwertend)* ⟨*Person, Rede, Buch*⟩
mendacity [men'dæsɪtɪ] *n.* **a)** *no pl. (untruthfulness) see* **mendacious:** Unwahrheit, *die;* Verlogenheit, *die (abwertend);* **b)** *(a lie)* Lüge, *die*
Mendelian [men'di:lɪən] *adj. (Biol.)* Mendelsch
mender ['mendə(r)] *n.* Ausbesserer, *der/* Ausbesserin, *die; (of clocks, watches, machines)* Reparateur, *der;* **take one's watch/shoes to the ~'s** seine Uhr zum Uhrmacher *od.* zur Reparatur/seine Schuhe zum Schuster *od.* zur Reparatur
mendicant ['mendɪkənt] **1.** *adj.* bettelnd; **~ friar** Bettelmönch, *der.* **2.** *n.* **a)** *(beggar)* Bettler, *der*/Bettlerin, *die;* **b)** *(friar)* Bettelmönch, *der*
menfolk ['menfəʊk] *n. pl.* Männer
menial ['mi:nɪəl] **1.** *adj.* niedrig; untergeordnet ⟨*Aufgabe*⟩. **2.** *n. (derog.)* Domestik, *der (veralt. abwertend)*
meningitis [menɪn'dʒaɪtɪs] *n. (Med.)* Meningitis, *die (fachspr.);* Hirnhautentzündung, *die*
menopausal ['menəpɔ:zl] *adj. (Physiol.)* klimakterisch; menopausal
menopause ['menəpɔ:z] *n.* **a)** *(period of life)* Wechseljahre *Pl.;* Klimakterium, *das (fachspr.);* **male ~:** Wechseljahre des Mannes; **b)** *(Physiol.)* Menopause, *die*
menstrual ['menstrʊəl] *adj. (Physiol.)* menstrual *(fachspr.);* Menstruations-
menstruate ['menstrʊeɪt] *v. i. (Physiol.)* menstruieren
menstruation [menstrʊ'eɪʃn] *n. (Physiol.)* Menstruation, *die*
menswear ['menzweə(r)] *n., no pl.* Herrenbekleidung, *die; attrib.* Herrenbekleidungs-; für Herrenbekleidung *od.* -moden *nachgestellt*
mental ['mentl] *adj.* **a)** *(of the mind)* geistig; seelisch ⟨*Belastung, Labilität*⟩; Geistes⟨*zustand, -verfassung, -störung*⟩; **the previous ~ history of the patient** die Vorgeschichte der seelischen Erkrankungen des Patienten; **b)** *(done by the mind)* geistig; gedanklich; **make a quick ~ calculation** es im Kopf schnell überschlagen; **~ process** Denkprozeß, -vorgang, *der;* **make a ~ note of sth.** sich *(Dat.)* etw. merken; **make a ~ note to do sth.** versuchen, daran zu denken, etw. zu tun; **c)** *(Brit. coll.: mad)* verrückt *(salopp);* bekloppt *(salopp)*
mental: ~ age *n.* geistiger Entwicklungsstand; Intelligenzalter, *das (Psych.);* **~ a'rithmetic** *n.* Kopfrechnen, *das;* **~ asylum** *see* **~ hospital; ~ 'block** *see* **block 11; ~ case** *(coll.)* Verrückte, *der/die (salopp); (mental patient)* Geisteskranke, *der/ die;* **~ 'cruelty** *n., no pl.* seelische Grausamkeit; **~ de'fective** *n.* Schwachsinnige, *der/die;* **~ de'ficiency** *n.* Geistesschwäche, *die;* **~ 'health** *n.* seelische Gesundheit; **~ health services** psychiatrische Versorgung; **~ home** *n.* Nervenklinik, *die;* **~ hospital** *n.* psychiatrische Klinik; Nervenklinik, *die;* **~ 'illness** *n.* Geisteskrankheit, *die*
mentality [men'tælɪtɪ] *n.* **a)** *(outlook)* Mentalität, *die;* **b)** *(mental capacity)* geistige Fähigkeit
mentally ['mentəlɪ] *adv.* **a)** geistig; geistes⟨*gestört, -krank*⟩; **~ deficient** *or* **defective** schwachsinnig; **b)** *(inwardly)* innerlich *od.* im Geiste ⟨*fluchen, sich Vorwürfe machen*⟩; im Kopf ⟨*rechnen*⟩
mental: ~ patient *n.* Geisteskranke, *der/ die;* **~ reser'vation** *n.* geheimer Vorbehalt
menthol ['menθɒl] *n.* Menthol, *das*
mention ['menʃn] **1.** *n.* **a)** Erwähnung, *die;* **there is a brief/no ~ of sth.** etw. wird kurz/ nicht erwähnt; **the earliest ~ of this is in ...:** das wird zum ersten Mal in ... *(Dat.)* erwähnt; **get a ~:** erwähnt werden; **make [no] ~ of sth.** etw. [nicht] erwähnen; **b)** *(commendation)* Belobigung, *die;* **honourable ~:** ehrenvolle Erwähnung. **2.** *v. t.* **a)** erwähnen (to gegenüber); **~ as the reason for sth.** als Grund für etw. nennen; **now that you [come to] ~ it** jetzt, wo Sie es sagen; **not to ~ ...:** ganz zu schweigen von ...; **not to ~ the fact that ...:** ganz abgesehen davon, daß ...; **Thank you very much. – Don't ~ it** Vielen Dank. – Keine Ursache; **b)** *(commend)* **be ~ed** lobend erwähnt werden. *See also* **dispatch 2 a**
mentor ['mentɔ:(r)] *n.* Mentor, *der*/Mentorin, *die*
menu ['menju:] *n.* **a)** [Speise]karte, *die;* **ensure a varied ~:** für einen abwechslungsreichen Speiseplan sorgen; **a ~ at 40 marks** ein Menü zu 40 Mark; **b)** *(fig.: diet)* Nahrung, *die;* **c)** *(fig.: programme)* Angebot, *das;* **d)** *(Computing, Telev.)* Menü, *das*
MEP *abbr.* **Member of the European Parliament** MdEP
Mephistopheles [mefɪ'stɒfɪli:z] *n.* **a)** *pr. n.* Mephisto[pheles] *(der);* **b)** *n. (fiendish person)* Mephisto, *der*
mercantile ['mɜ:kəntaɪl] *adj.* **a)** *(commercial)* Handels-; **the ~ system** der Merkantilismus; das Merkantilsystem; **b)** *(trading)* handeltreibend *(nicht präd.)* ⟨*Nation*⟩; **~ marine** *see* **merchant navy**
Mercator [mɜ:'keɪtə(r)] *n.* **~'s projection** *(Geog.)* Mercatorprojektion, *die;* Zylinderprojektion, *die*
mercenary ['mɜ:sɪnərɪ] **1.** *adj.* **a)** gewinnsüchtig; **b)** *(hired)* Söldner-. **2.** *n.* Söldner, *der*
merchandise ['mɜ:tʃəndaɪz] **1.** *n., no pl., no indef. art.* [Handels]ware, *die.* **2.** *v. t.* auf den Markt bringen
merchant ['mɜ:tʃənt] *n.* **a)** *(trader)* Kaufmann, *der;* **corn-/timber-~:** Getreide-/ Holzhändler, *der*/-händlerin, *die; see also* **coal-merchant; scrap merchant; wine-merchant; b)** *(Amer., Scot.: retailer)* Einzelhändler, *der*/-händlerin, *die;* **c)** *(sl.: person engaged in specified activity)* **rip-off ~:** Halsabschneider, *der (ugs. abwertend);* **gloom ~:** Schwarzseher, *der*/-seherin, *die; see also* **speed merchant**
merchant: ~ 'bank *n.* Handelsbank, *die;* **~ 'banker** *n.* Leiter einer Handelsbank; ≈ Bankier, *der;* **~ 'fleet** *see* **~ navy; ~man** ['mɜ:tʃəntmən] *n., pl.* **~men** ['mɜ:tʃəntmən] *see* **~ ship; ~ ma'rine** *(Amer.),* **~ 'navy** *(Brit.) ns.* Handelsmarine, *die;* **~ 'prince** *n.* Großkaufmann, *der;* Handelsherr, *der (veralt.);* **~ 'seaman** *n.* Matrose bei der Handelsmarine; **~ service** *see* **~ navy; ~ ship** *n.* Handelsschiff, *das*
merciful ['mɜ:sɪfl] *adj.* gnädig; **his death must have come as a ~ release from his sufferings** der Tod muß für ihn eine Erlösung gewesen sein; **~ Heavens!** gütiger *od.* barmherziger Himmel!; **God is ~ to sinners** Gott ist den Sündern gnädig
mercifully ['mɜ:sɪfəlɪ] *adv.* gnädig; *as sentence-modifier (fortunately)* glücklicherweise
merciless ['mɜ:sɪlɪs] *adj.,* **mercilessly** ['mɜ:sɪlɪslɪ] *adv.* gnadenlos; unbarmherzig
mercurial [mɜ:'kjʊərɪəl] *adj. (quick-witted)* quecksilbrig; *(changeable)* wechselhaft
mercury ['mɜ:kjʊrɪ] *n.* **a)** Quecksilber, *das;* **the ~ is rising/falling** das Barometer steigt/ fällt; **b)** *pr. n.* **M~** *(Roman Mythol.)* Merkur *(der);* **c)** *pr. n.* **M~** *(Astron.)* Merkur, *der;* **d)** *(Bot.)* Bingelkraut, *das*
mercy ['mɜ:sɪ] **1.** *n.* **a)** *no pl., no indef. art. (compassion; also Theol.)* Erbarmen, *das* (on mit); **show sb. [no] ~:** mit jmdm. [kein] Erbarmen haben; **beg for ~:** um Gnade bitten *od.* flehen; **act of ~:** Gnadenakt, *der;* **God's great ~:** Gottes große Barmherzigkeit; **be at the ~ of sb./sth.** jmdm./einer Sache [auf Gedeih und Verderb] ausgeliefert sein; **the ship was at the ~ of the waves** das Schiff war den Wellen preisgegeben; **have ~!** Gnade!; **Lord have ~ [up]on us** *(Relig.)* Herr, erbarme Dich [unser]; **~ [me]!, ~ [up]on us** gütiger Himmel!; **b)** *(instance)* glückliche Fügung; **one** *or* **we must be thankful** *or* **grateful for small mercies** *(coll.)* man darf [ja] nicht zuviel verlangen; **leave sb. to the [tender] mercies of sb.** *(iron.)* jmdn. jmds. [liebevoller] Fürsorge überlassen; **it is a ~:** es ist ein Glück *od.* Segen; **what a ~ it is that ...:** welch ein Glück *od.* Segen, daß ... **2.** *attrib. adj.* Hilfs-, Rettungs⟨*einsatz, -flug*⟩; **~ killing** aktive Sterbehilfe; **~ killings** Fälle aktiver Sterbehilfe
[1]**mere** [mɪə(r)] *adj.* bloß; rein ⟨*Tautologie, Versehen*⟩; **he is a ~ child** er ist nur ein Kind; **it's a ~ copy** es ist bloß eine Kopie; **~ courage is not enough** Mut allein genügt nicht; **the ~st hint/trace of sth.** die kleinste Andeutung/Spur von etw.; **~ words won't help** Worte allein tun es nicht
[2]**mere** *n. (arch./literary)* See, *der*
merely ['mɪəlɪ] *adv.* bloß; lediglich; **not ~ ...:** nicht bloß ...
meretricious [merɪ'trɪʃəs] *adj.* trügerisch ⟨*Argument, Methode*⟩
merge [mɜ:dʒ] **1.** *v. t.* **a)** *(combine)* zusammenschließen ⟨*Firmen, Unternehmen*⟩ **(into** zu); zusammenlegen ⟨*Anteile, Abteilungen*⟩; **~ one firm/department with another** eine Firma mit einer anderen zusammenschließen/eine Abteilung mit einer anderen zusammenlegen; **b)** *(blend gradually)* verschmelzen **(with** mit); **his library should not be ~d with another collection** seine Bibliothek sollte nicht einer anderen Sammlung einverleibt werden. **2.** *v. i.* **a)** *(combine)* ⟨*Firma, Unternehmen:*⟩ sich zusammenschließen, fusionieren **(with** mit); ⟨*Abteilung:*⟩ zusammengelegt werden **(with** mit); **b)** *(blend gradually)* ⟨*Straße:*⟩ zusammenlaufen **(with** mit); **~ with sth.** ⟨*Kontur, Muster:*⟩ verschmelzen mit etw.; ⟨*Unterhaltung:*⟩ untergehen in etw. *(Dat.);* **~ into sth.** ⟨*Farbe usw.:*⟩ in etw. *(Akk.)* übergehen
merger ['mɜ:dʒə(r)] *n. (of departments, parties)* Zusammenschluß, *der;* Vereinigung, *die; (of companies)* Fusion, *die*
meridian [mə'rɪdɪən] *n. (Astron., Geog.)* Meridian, *der; see also* **prime meridian**
meringue [mə'ræŋ] *n.* Meringe, *die;* Baiser, *das*
merino [mə'ri:nəʊ] *n., pl.* **~s a) ~ [sheep]** Merinoschaf, *das;* Merino, *der;* **b)** *(material)* Merino, *der;* **c)** *(yarn)* Merinogarn, *das*
merit ['merɪt] **1.** *n.* **a)** *no pl. (worth)* Verdienst, *das;* **a man of great ~:** ein Mann von hohen Verdiensten *(geh.);* ein sehr verdienter Mann; **promotion is by ~:** Beförderung richtet sich nach Leistung; **there is no ~ in doing that** es ist nicht [sehr] sinnvoll, das zu tun; **be without ~:** ⟨*Buch, Film:*⟩ kein Niveau haben; **b)** *(good feature)* Vorzug, *der;* **on his/its ~s** nach seinen Vorzügen; **c)** *in pl. (rights and wrongs)* Für und Wider, *das;* **d)** *(Theol.)* Verdienst, *der;* **e) Order of M~** *(Brit.)* Order of Merit, *der; britischer Verdienstorden.* **2.** *v. t.* verdienen; **sb. ~s reward/punishment** jmd. hat eine Belohnung/ Strafe verdient
meritocracy [merɪ'tɒkrəsɪ] *n.* Meritokratie, *die;* Verdienstadel, *der (veralt.)*
meritorious [merɪ'tɔ:rɪəs] *adj.* verdienstvoll ⟨*Tat, Verhalten, Person*⟩; verdient ⟨*Person*⟩
'merit system *n. (Amer.)* Leistungsprinzip im öffentlichen Dienst
mermaid ['mɜ:meɪd] *n.* Nixe, *die*
merrie England *see* **merry England**
merrily ['merɪlɪ] *adv.* munter

merriment ['merɪmənt] *n., no pl.* Fröhlichkeit, *die;* **fall into fits of helpless ~:** sich vor Lachen nicht mehr halten können

merry ['merɪ] *adj.* **a)** *(full of laughter or gaiety)* fröhlich; **the M~ Widow/Wives of Windsor** die lustige Witwe/die lustigen Weiber von Windsor; **a ~ time was had by all** alle haben sich prächtig amüsiert; **make ~:** sich amüsieren; **make ~ over sb./sth.** sich über jmdn./etw. lustig machen; **the more the merrier** je mehr, desto besser; **~ 'Christmas!** frohe *od.* fröhliche Weihnachten!; **b)** *(coll.: tipsy)* beschwipst *(ugs.)*

merry: ~ 'England *pr. n.* das gute alte England; **~-go-round** *n.* Karussell, *das;* **~ 'hell** *see* **hell b; ~-making** *n.* **a)** *no pl., no indef. art.* Feiern, *das;* **the sound of ~-making** fröhlicher Festlärm; **b)** *(occasion)* Fest, *das;* **~ 'men** *n. pl.* Getreue; Kumpane *(ugs.)*

mesa ['meɪsə] *n. (Amer. Geog.)* Tafelberg, *der*

Mesdames *pl. of* **Madame; Mrs**

mesh [meʃ] **1.** *n.* **a)** Masche, *die;* **b)** *(netting; also fig.: network)* Geflecht, *das;* **wire ~ [fence]** Maschendraht[zaun], *der;* **c)** *in pl. (fig.: snare)* Maschen; **d)** *(fabric)* Netzgewebe, *das; attrib.* Netz‹*strumpf, -hemd, -vorhang*›; **e) be in ~** ‹*Zahnräder:*› ineinandergreifen, im Eingriff stehen *(Technik).* **2.** *v. i.* **a)** *(Mech. Engin.)* ‹*Zahnräder:*› ineinandergreifen; **~ with** eingreifen in *(Akk.);* **b)** *(fig.: be harmonious)* harmonisieren **(with** mit)

mesmerism ['mezmərɪzm] *n., no pl.* **a)** Mesmerismus, *der;* **b)** *(dated: influence)* hypnotische Kraft; **powers of ~:** hypnotische Fähigkeiten

mesmerize ['mezməraɪz] *v. t.* faszinieren; erstarren lassen ‹*Tier*›

Mesopotamia [mesəpə'teɪmɪə] *pr. n.* Mesopotamien *(das);* Zweistromland, *das*

Mesozoic [mesəʊ'zəʊɪk] *(Geol.)* **1.** *adj.* mesozoisch. **2.** *n.* Mesozoikum, *das*

mess [mes] **1.** *n.* **a)** *(dirty/untidy state)* **[be] a ~** *or* **in a ~:** schmutzig/unaufgeräumt [sein]; **[be] a complete** *or* **in an awful ~:** in einem fürchterlichen Zustand [sein]; **what a ~!** was für ein Dreck *(ugs.)*/Durcheinander; **look a ~:** schlimm aussehen; **your hair is a ~:** dein Haar ist ganz durcheinander; **don't make too much ~:** mach nicht zuviel Schmutz/Durcheinander; **b)** *(sth. out of place)* **leave a lot of ~ behind one** *(dirt)* viel Schmutz hinterlassen; *(untidiness)* eine große Unordnung hinterlassen; **I'm not tidying up your ~:** ich mache deinen Schmutz/räume deinen Kram nicht weg *(ugs.);* **make a ~ with sth.** mit etw. Schmutz machen; **c)** *(excreta)* **dog's/cat's ~es** Hunde-/Katzenkot, *der;* **make/leave a ~ on the carpet** auf den Teppich machen/gemacht haben *(ugs.);* **d)** *(bad state)* **be [in] a ~:** sich in einem schlimmen Zustand befinden; ‹*Person:*› schlimm dran sein; **get into a ~:** in Schwierigkeiten geraten; **clear up the ~:** die Dinge wieder in Ordnung bringen; **what a ~!** *(troubled situation)* das ist ja eine schöne Bescherung!; *(unpleasant sight)* das sieht ja schlimm aus!; **make a ~ of** verpfuschen *(ugs.)* ‹*Arbeit, Leben, Bericht, Vertrag*›; ruinieren ‹*Wirtschaft*›; durcheinanderbringen ‹*Pläne*›; **make a ~ of things** alles verpfuschen *(ugs.);* **e)** *(food)* **give sth. away for a ~ of pottage** *(fig. arch.)* etw. für ein Linsengericht hergeben *(geh.);* **f)** *(derog.: disagreeable concoction)* Mischmasch, *der (ugs.);* **g)** *(eating-place)* Kantine, *die; (for officers)* Kasino, *das; (on ship)* Messe, *die;* **officers' ~:** Offizierskasino, *das*/Offiziersmesse, *die.* **2.** *v. i. (Mil., Navy)* essen. **3.** *v. t. see* **~ up**

~ a'bout, ~ a'round 1. *v. i.* **a)** *(potter)* herumwerken; *(fool about)* herumalbern; **~ about with cars** an Autos herumbasteln *(ugs.);* **b)** *(interfere)* **~ about** *or* **around with** sich einmischen in (+ *Akk.*) ‹*Angelegenheit*›; herumspielen an (+ *Dat.*) ‹*Mechanismus, Stromkabel usw.*›. **2.** *v. t.* **~ sb. about** *or* **around** mit jmdm. nach Belieben umspringen *(abwertend);* **he's been ~ed about** *or* **around by the doctors** die Ärzte haben ihn in der Mangel gehabt *(ugs.)*

~ 'up *v. t.* **a)** *(make dirty)* schmutzig machen; *(make untidy)* in Unordnung bringen; **b)** *(bungle)* verpfuschen; **c)** *(interfere with)* durcheinanderbringen ‹*Plan*›. *See also* **mess-up**

message ['mesɪdʒ] *n.* **a)** *(communication)* Mitteilung, *die;* Nachricht, *die;* **send/take/leave a ~:** eine Nachricht übermitteln/entgegennehmen/hinterlassen; **give sb. a ~:** jmdm. etw. ausrichten; **did you give him my ~?** haben Sie ihm meine Nachricht übermittelt?; **can I take a ~?** kann *od.* soll ich etw. ausrichten?; **send sb. a ~ by sb.** *(orally)* jmdm. etwas durch jmdn. ausrichten lassen; *(in writing)* jmdm. durch jmdn. eine Nachricht zukommen lassen; **b)** *(teaching)* Aussage, *die; (Relig.)* Botschaft, *die;* **get the ~** *(fig. coll.)* verstehen; es schnallen *(salopp)*

messenger ['mesɪndʒə(r)] *n.* **a)** Bote, *der*/Botin, *die;* **b) King's/Queen's M~:** königlicher Kurier

'messenger-boy *n.* Botenjunge, *der*

Messiah [mɪ'saɪə] *n. (lit. or fig.)* Messias, *der*

Messianic [mesɪ'ænɪk] *adj.* messianisch

messily ['mesɪlɪ] *adv.* nachlässig; unordentlich ‹*arbeiten*›; **eat/drink ~:** sich beim Essen/Trinken bekleckern

mess: ~-jacket *n. (Mil., Navy)* Messjackett, *das;* **~mate** *n. (Mil., Navy)* Kamerad, *der;* **he was a ~mate of mine** er und ich waren Kameraden [in der Armee/Marine]

Messrs ['mesəz] *n. pl.* **a)** *(in name of firm)* ≈ Fa.; **b)** *pl. of* **Mr;** *(in list of names)* **~ A, B, and C** die Herren A, B und C

'mess-up *n.* Durcheinander, *das;* **there has been a ~ with your order** bei deiner Bestellung ist etwas durcheinandergeraten

messy ['mesɪ] *adj.* **a)** *(dirty)* schmutzig; *(untidy)* unordentlich; **be a ~ workman** unordentlich arbeiten; **be a ~ eater** sich beim Essen bekleckern; **b)** *(awkward)* vertrackt *(ugs.)*

¹met *see* **¹meet 1, 2**

²met [met] *(coll.)* **1.** *adj. see* **meteorological. 2.** *n.* **the Met: a)** *(Brit.)* **The Metropolitan Police** *see* **metropolitan 1 a; b)** *(Amer.: Metropolitan Opera)* die Met

metabolic [metə'bɒlɪk] *adj. (Physiol.)* metabolisch *(fachspr.);* Stoffwechsel‹*krankheit, -typ*›

metabolism [mɪ'tæbəlɪzm] *n. (Physiol.)* Metabolismus, *der (fachspr.);* Stoffwechsel, *der;* **basal ~:** Grundumsatz, *der*

metabolize [mɪ'tæbəlaɪz] *v. t. (Physiol.)* umsetzen

metal ['metl] **1.** *n.* **a)** Metall, *das; see also* **gun-metal; white metal; b)** *in pl. (Brit.: rails)* Schienen; Gleise; **leave the ~s** entgleisen. **2.** *adj.* Metall-; **be ~:** aus Metall sein. **3.** *v. t., (Brit.)* **-ll-** *(Brit.: surface)* schottern ‹*Straße*›

'metal-detector *n.* Metallsuchgerät, *das*

metalize *(Amer.) see* **metallize**

metallic [mɪ'tælɪk] *adj.* **a)** *(of metal)* metallisch ‹*Element, Substanz*›; Metall‹*salz, -oxid*›; **~ currency** Hart- *od.* Metallgeld, *das;* **b)** *(like metal)* metallisch ‹*Härte, Glanz, Farbe, Geräusch, Stimme*›; metallisch glänzend ‹*Glasur, Anstrich*›; **have a ~ taste** nach Metall schmecken

metallize (metallise) ['metəlaɪz] *v. t.* metallisieren

metallurgic [metə'lɜ:dʒɪk], **metallurgical** [metə'lɜ:dʒɪkl] *adj.* metallurgisch

metallurgist [mɪ'tælədʒɪst, 'metəlɜ:dʒɪst] *n.* Metallurg, *der*/Metallurgin, *die*

metallurgy [mɪ'tælədʒɪ, 'metəlɜ:dʒɪ] *n., no pl.* Metallurgie, *die*

metal: ~ polish *n.* Metallputzmittel, *das;* **~work** *n., no pl.* **a)** *(activity)* Metallbearbeitung, *die;* **b)** *(products)* Metallarbeiten; **a piece of ~work** eine Metallarbeit; **~worker** *n.* Metallarbeiter, *der*/-arbeiterin, *die*

metamorphic [metə'mɔ:fɪk] *adj. (Geol.)* metamorph ‹*Gestein*›

metamorphose [metə'mɔ:fəʊz] **1.** *v. t.* verwandeln **(into** in + *Akk.*). **2.** *v. i.* sich verwandeln **(into** in + *Akk.*)

metamorphosis [metə'mɔ:fəsɪs, metəmɔ:'fəʊsɪs] *n., pl.* **metamorphoses** [metə'mɔ:fəsi:z, metəmɔ:'fəʊsi:z] **a)** *(change of form or character)* Metamorphose, *die* **(into** in + *Akk.*); **undergo a [gradual] ~:** sich [allmählich] verändern; **b)** *(Zool.)* Metamorphose, *die*

metaphor ['metəfə(r)] *n.* **a)** *no pl., no art. (stylistic device)* **[the use of] ~:** der Gebrauch von Metaphern; **b)** *(instance)* Metapher, *die;* **mixed ~:** Bildbruch, *der;* Katachrese, *die (Literaturw.)*

metaphoric [metə'fɒrɪk], **metaphorical** [metə'fɒrɪkl] *adj.* metaphorisch

metaphorically [metə'fɒrɪkəlɪ] *adv.* metaphorisch; **be ~ true** metaphorisch betrachtet zutreffen; **~ speaking** bildlich gesprochen

metaphysical [metə'fɪzɪkl] *adj.* **a)** *(Philos.)* metaphysisch; **~ language/terminology** Sprache/Terminologie der Metaphysik; **b)** *(in popular use: abstract)* theoretisch

metaphysics [metə'fɪzɪks] *n., no pl.* **a)** *(Philos.)* Metaphysik, *die;* **b)** *(in popular use: abstract talk or theory)* abstrakte Theorie

metastasis [me'tæstəsɪs] *n., pl.* **metastases** [me'tæstəsi:z] *(Med.)* Metastasierung, *die*

mete [mi:t] *v. t. (literary)* **~ out** zuteil werden lassen *(geh.)* ‹*Belohnung*› **(to** *Dat.*); auferlegen ‹*Strafe*› **(to** *Dat.*); **~ out justice** Recht sprechen

meteor ['mi:tɪə(r)] *n. (Astron.)* Meteor, *der;* **~ shower** Meteorschauer, *der*

meteoric [mi:tɪ'ɒrɪk] *adj.* **a)** *(Astron.)* Meteor‹*schweif, -tätigkeit*›; meteorisch; **b)** *(fig.)* kometenhaft; meteorhaft

meteorite ['mi:tɪəraɪt] *n. (Astron.)* Meteorit, *der*

meteorological [mi:tɪərə'lɒdʒɪkl] *adj.* meteorologisch ‹*Instrument*›; Wetter‹*ballon, -bericht*›; **M~ Office** *(Brit.)* Meteorologisches Amt; Wetteramt, *das*

meteorologist [mi:tɪə'rɒlədʒɪst] *n.* Meteorologe, *der*/Meteorologin, *die*

meteorology [mi:tɪə'rɒlədʒɪ] *n.* **a)** *no pl.* Meteorologie, *die;* **b)** *(weather of region)* meteorologische Bedingungen

¹meter ['mi:tə(r)] **1.** *n.* **a)** *(measuring device)* Zähler, *der; (for coins)* Münzzähler, *der;* **humidity ~:** Hygrometer, *das; see also* **electricity meter; gas meter; water meter; b)** *(parking-~)* Parkuhr, *die;* **feed the ~** *(coll.)* Geld [in die Parkuhr] nachwerfen; **c)** *see* **taximeter. 2.** *v. t.* [mit einem Zähler] messen ‹*[Wasser-, Gas-, Strom]verbrauch*›

²meter *(Amer.) see* **¹metre**

³meter *(Amer.) see* **²metre**

'meter maid *n. (coll.)* Politesse, *die*

methadone ['meθədəʊn] *n.* Methadon, *das*

methane ['mi:θeɪn, 'meθeɪn] *n. (Chem.)* Methan, *das*

methinks [mɪ'θɪŋks] *v. i. impers., p. t.* **methought** [mɪ'θɔ:t] *(arch.)* mich dünkt *od.* deucht *(geh. veralt.)*

method ['meθəd] *n.* **a)** *(procedure)* Methode, *die;* **~ of proceeding** *or* **procedure** Vorgehensweise, *die;* **brew by the traditional ~:** nach traditionellem Verfahren brauen; **police ~s** die Arbeitsweise der Polizei; **b)** *no pl., no art. (arrangement of ideas, orderliness)* System, *das;* Systematik, *die;* **there was a lack of** *or* **was no ~ in the book** das Buch war unmethodisch *od.* unsystematisch aufgebaut; **a man of ~:** ein systematisch denkender Mensch; **use ~:** methodisch *od.* systematisch vorgehen; **there's ~ in his madness** *(fig. joc.)* der Wahnsinn hat Methode; **c)** *(scheme of classification)* System, *das*

methodic [mɪ'θɒdɪk] *adj. (Amer.)* **a)** *see* **methodical; b)** *(relating to methodology)* methodologisch

methodical [mɪ'θɒdɪkl] *adj.* methodisch; systematisch; **in a ~ way** methodisch; systematisch; **be ~:** methodisch *od.* systematisch vorgehen

methodically [mɪ'θɒdɪkəlɪ] *adv.* mit Methode; systematisch

Methodism ['meθədɪzm] *n., no pl. (Relig.)* Methodismus, *der*

Methodist ['meθədɪst] *n. (Relig.)* Methodist, *der*/Methodistin, *die; attrib.* Methodisten⟨*kapelle, -gottesdienst, -pfarrer*⟩

methodology [meθə'dɒlədʒɪ] *n.* **a)** *no pl., no art. (science of method)* Methodik, *die;* Methodologie, *die;* **b)** *(methods used)* Methodik, *die*

methought *see* **methinks**

meths [meθs] *n., no pl., no indef. art. (Brit. coll.)* [Brenn]spiritus, *der*

'meths-drinker *n. (Brit. coll.)* ≈ Fuseltrinker, *der*/-trinkerin, *die*

Methuselah [mɪ'θju:zələ] *n.* **a)** *pr. n. (Bibl.)* Methusalem *(der);* **b) [old] ~:** Methusalem, *der (ugs.)*

methyl ['meθɪl, 'mi:θaɪl] *n. (Chem.)* Methyl, *das*

methyl 'alcohol *n. (Chem.)* Methylalkohol, *der;* Methanol, *das*

methylated spirit[s] [meθɪleɪtɪd 'spɪrɪt(s)] *n. [pl.]* Brennspiritus, *der;* vergällter *od.* denaturierter Alkohol *(fachspr.)*

meticulous [mɪ'tɪkjʊləs] *adj.* **a)** *(scrupulous)* sorgfältig; *(over-scrupulous)* übergenau; pedantisch *(abwertend);* **be ~ about sth.** es peinlich genau mit etw. nehmen; **b)** *(coll.: careful)* pingelig *(ugs.);* **be a ~ person** es sehr genau nehmen

meticulously [mɪ'tɪkjʊləslɪ] *adv.* **a)** *(scrupulously)* sorgfältig; *(over-scrupulously)* übergenau; pedantisch *(abwertend);* **~ clean** peinlich sauber; **b)** *(coll.: carefully)* sehr sorgfältig; haargenau *(ugs.)* ⟨*abbilden, wiedergeben*⟩

métier ['metjeɪ] *n.* **a)** *(calling)* Metier, *das;* **b)** *(forte)* Stärke, *die*

metonymy [mɪ'tɒnɪmɪ] *n. (Rhet.)* Metonymie, *die*

[1]metre ['mi:tə] *n. (Brit.)* **a)** *(poetic rhythm)* Metrum, *das (Verslehre);* Versmaß, *das;* **written in an iambic ~:** in Jamben geschrieben; **b)** *(Pros.: metrical group)* Metrum, *das*

[2]metre *n. (Brit.: unit)* Meter, *der od. das;* **sell cloth by the ~:** Stoff meterweise verkaufen; *see also* **cubic b; square 2 b**

metric ['metrɪk] *adj.* metrisch; **~ system** metrisches System; **go ~** *(coll.)* das metrische System einführen; *see also* **hundredweight; ton a**

metrical ['metrɪkl] *adj.*, **metrically** ['metrɪkəlɪ] *adv.* metrisch

metricate ['metrɪkeɪt] *v. t. & i.* auf das metrische System umstellen

metrication [metrɪ'keɪʃn] *n.* Umstellung auf das metrische System

Metro, Métro ['metrəʊ] *n., pl.* **~s** *(coll.)* U-Bahn, *die;* **the Paris ~:** die [Pariser] Metro

metronome ['metrənəʊm] *n. (Mus.)* Metronom, *das*

metropolis [mɪ'trɒpəlɪs] *n. (capital)* Hauptstadt, *die; (chief city)* Metropole, *die;* **the ~** *(Brit.)* London *(das)*

metropolitan [metrə'pɒlɪtən] **1.** *adj.* **a)** *(of a metropolis)* **[the] ~ hotels/cinemas** die Hotels/Kinos der Metropole; **~ New York/Tokyo** der Großraum New York/Tokio; **~ London** Großlondon *(das);* **the M~ Police** die Londoner Polizei; **~ borough/district** *(Brit. Admin.)* Gemeinde/Bezirk im Großraum einer Großstadt; **~ county** *(Brit. Admin.) eines von sechs Ballungsgebieten außerhalb Großlondons;* **b)** *(not colonial)* mutterländisch; **~ France** das Mutterland Frankreich. **2.** *n. see* **metropolitan bishop**

metropolitan 'bishop *n. (Gk. Orthodox Ch., RC Ch.)* Metropolit, *der; (Anglican Ch.)* Erzbischof, *der*

mettle ['metl] *n.* **a)** *(quality of temperament)* Wesensart, *die;* **show one's ~:** zeigen, aus welchem Holz man [geschnitzt] ist; **b)** *(spirit)* Mut, *der;* **a man of ~:** ein mutiger Mann; **be on one's ~:** zeigen müssen, was man kann; **put sb./sth. on his/its ~:** jmdn./etw. fordern; **c)** *(animal's vigour)* Feuer, *das*

Meuse [mɜ:z] *pr. n. (Geog.)* Maas *(die)*

mew [mju:] **1.** *v. i.* ⟨*Katze:*⟩ miauen; ⟨*Möwe:*⟩ kreischen. **2.** *n. (of cat)* Miauen, *das; (of seagull)* Kreischen, *das*

mews [mju:z] *n., pl. same (Brit.)* Stallungen *Pl.; (converted into dwellings/garages) zu [eleganten] Wohnhäusern/Garagen umgebaute ehemalige Stallungen [in ruhigen Seitenstraßen]*

Mexican ['meksɪkən] **1.** *adj.* mexikanisch; **sb. is ~:** jmd. ist Mexikaner/Mexikanerin; *see also* **English 1. 2.** *n.* Mexikaner, *der*/Mexikanerin, *die*

Mexico ['meksɪkəʊ] *pr. n.* Mexiko *(das);* **~ City** Mexiko [City] *(das)*

mezzanine ['metsəni:n, 'mezəni:n] *n.* **a)** *(Archit.)* Mezzanin, *das (fachspr.);* Halbgeschoß, *das;* **b)** *(Amer. Theatre)* erster Rang

mezzotint ['medzəʊtɪnt, 'metsəʊtɪnt] *n. (Art)* Mezzotinto, *das; (method)* Mezzotinto, *das;* Schabkunst, *die*

mg. *abbr.* **milligram[s]** mg

MHz *abbr.* **megahertz** MHz

MI *n. (Brit. Hist./coll.)* **MI5** *die britische Spionageabwehr;* **MI6** *der britische Nachrichtendienst*

mi [mi:] *see* **[2]me**

mi. *abbr. (Amer.)* **mile[s]** M

miaow [mɪ'aʊ] **1.** *v. i.* miauen. **2.** *n.* Miauen, *das*

miasma [mɪ'æzmə, maɪ'æzmə] *n., pl.* **~ta** [mɪ'æzmətə, maɪ'æzmətə] *or* **~s** Miasma, *das;* Gestank, *der*

mica ['maɪkə] *n. (Min.)* Glimmer, *der*

mice *pl. of* **mouse**

Michaelmas ['mɪklməs] *n.* Michaeli[s] *(das);* Michaelistag, *der*

Michaelmas: ~ 'daisy *n. (Bot.)* Herbstaster, *die;* **~ term** *n. (Brit. Univ.)* Herbsttrimester, *das*

mickey ['mɪkɪ] *n. (Brit. sl.)* **take the ~ [out of sb./sth.]** jmdn./etw. durch den Kakao ziehen *(ugs.)*

Mickey 'Mouse *attrib. adj. (derog.)* lächerlich; **croquet is a bit of a ~ sport** Krocket ist doch gar kein richtiger Sport; **this is a ~ job** diese Arbeit ist ein Witz

mickle ['mɪkl] *(arch./Scot.)* **1.** groß. **2.** *n.* **many a ~ makes a muckle** *(prov.)* Kleinvieh macht auch Mist *(ugs.)*

micky *see* **mickey**

micro ['maɪkrəʊ] *n., pl.* **~s** *see* **microcomputer**

micro- [maɪkrəʊ] *in comb.* mikro-/Mikro-

microbe ['maɪkrəʊb] *n. (Biol.)* Mikrobe, *die*

micro: ~bi'ology *n.* Mikrobiologie, *die;* **M~card, (P)** *n.* Mikrokarte, *die;* **~chip** *n. (Electronics)* [Mikro]chip, *der;* **~com'puter** *n. (Computing)* Mikrocomputer, *der;* **~con'troller** *n. (Electronics)* Mikrocontroller, *der;* **~dot** *n. (Information Sci.)* Mikrat, *das;* **~-elec'tronics** *n.* Mikroelektronik, *die;* **~fiche** *n., pl. same or* **~fiches** Mikrofiche, *das od. der;* **~film 1.** *n.* Mikrofilm, *der;* **2.** *v. t.* auf Mikrofilm *(Akk.)* aufnehmen; **~light ['aircraft]** *n. (Aeronaut.)* Ultraleichtflugzeug, *das*

micrometer [maɪ'krɒmɪtə(r)] *n. (Mech. Engin.)* [Fein]meßschraube, *die*

micron ['maɪkrɒn] *n.* Mikrometer, *der od. das*

Micronesia [maɪkrə'ni:ʃə] *pr. n.* Mikronesien *(das)*

micro-'organism *n.* Mikroorganismus, *der;* Kleinstlebewesen, *das*

microphone ['maɪkrəfəʊn] *n.* Mikrophon, *das*

micro: ~'photograph *n.* Mikrokopie, *die;* **~ 'processor** *n. (Computing)* Mikroprozessor, *der*

microscope ['maɪkrəskəʊp] *n.* Mikroskop, *das;* **examine sth. through** *or* **under a ~:** etw. unter dem Mikroskop untersuchen; **put** *or* **have sth. under the ~** *(fig.)* etw. unter die Lupe nehmen *(ugs.);* **be under the ~** *(fig.)* unter die Lupe genommen werden *(ugs.);* auf den Zahn gefühlt werden *(ugs.)*

microscopic [maɪkrə'skɒpɪk] *adj.* **a)** mikroskopisch; sehr stark vergrößernd ⟨*Linse*⟩; **b)** *(fig.: very small)* winzig ⟨*Portion, Auto*⟩; mikroskopisch klein ⟨*Tier, Portion*⟩

microscopy [maɪ'krɒskəpɪ] *n., no pl., no art.* Mikroskopie, *die,* **by ~:** mikroskopisch; unter dem Mikroskop

micro: ~surgery *n., no pl., no art. (Med.)* Mikrochirurgie, *die;* **~wave** *n.* Mikrowelle, *die;* **~wave ['oven]** *n.* Mikrowellenherd, *der*

mid- [mɪd] *in comb.* **a)** in **~-air/-stream** in der Luft/Strommitte; **~-air collision** Zusammenstoß in der Luft; **in ~-flight/-sentence** mitten im Flug/Satz; **in ~-course** mittendrin; **[in] ~-afternoon** [mitten] am Nachmittag; **b)** *forming compound adj. used attrib.* **~-afternoon siesta** Nachmittagsschläfchen, *das;* **~-morning break** ≈ Frühstückspause, *die;* große Pause *(Schulw.);* **a ~-season game** ein Spiel in der Mitte der Saison; **~-term exams** Prüfungen in der Mitte des Trimesters; **~-term elections** *(Amer.)* Kongreß- und Kommunalwahlen in der Mitte der Amtszeit des Präsidenten; **c)** *with months, decades, persons' ages* **~-July** Mitte Juli; **the ~-60s** die Mitte der sechziger Jahre; **a man in the** *or* **his ~-fifties** ein Mittfünfziger; **be in one's ~-thirties** Mitte Dreißig sein

Midas touch ['maɪdəs tʌtʃ] *n.* **he has the ~:** was er anfaßt, wird zu Gold *(fig.)*

midday ['mɪddeɪ, mɪd'deɪ] *n.* **a)** *(noon)* zwölf Uhr; **round about ~:** um die Mittagszeit; **b)** *(middle of day)* Mittag, *der; attrib.* Mittags-

midden ['mɪdn] *n.* **a)** *(dunghill)* Misthaufen, *der;* **b)** *(refuse heap)* Abfallhaufen, *der*

middle ['mɪdl] **1.** *attrib. adj.* **a)** mittler...; **the ~ one** der/die/das mittlere; **~ space** Zwischenraum, *der;* **the ~ years of the 19th century** die Jahre in der Mitte des 19. Jahrhunderts; **man/house of ~ height/size** mittelgroßer Mann/-großes Haus; **b)** *(equidistant from extremities)* **~ point** Mittelpunkt, *der;* **c)** *(Ling.)* Mittel⟨*latein, -hochdeutsch*⟩; *see also* **English 2 a. 2.** *n.* **a)** Mitte, *die; (central part)* Mittelteil, *der;* **in the ~ of the room/the table** in der Mitte des Zimmers/des Tisches; *(emphatic)* mitten im Zimmer/auf dem Tisch; **right in the ~ of Manchester** genau im Zentrum von Manchester; **in the ~ of the forest** mitten im Wald; **the boat sank in the ~ of the Atlantic** das Schiff sank mitten im Atlantik; **grasp the ~ of sth.** etw. in der Mitte festhalten; **fold sth. down the ~:** etw. in der Mitte falten; **in the ~ of the day** mittags; **in the ~ of the morning/afternoon** mitten am Vor-/Nachmittag; **in the ~ of the night/week** mitten in der Nacht/Woche; **happen in the ~ of next week/month** Mitte nächster Woche/nächsten Monats geschehen; **the ~ of the day** die Mitte des Tages; **be in the ~ of doing sth.** *(fig.)* gerade mitten dabei sein, etw. zu tun; **in the ~ of the operation/washing her hair** *(fig.)* mitten in der Operation/im Haarewaschen; *see also* **knock 1 c; nowhere 2; b)** *(waist)* Taille, *die*

middle: ~ **'age** *n.* mittleres [Lebens]alter; **a man in ~ age** ein Mann mittleren Alters; **complaints of ~ age** Beschwerden von Menschen mittleren Alters; **~-aged** ['mɪdleɪdʒd] *adj.* mittleren Alters *nachgestellt;* **acquire a ~-aged spread** [in den mittleren Jahren] Speck ansetzen; **M~ 'Ages** *n. pl.* **the M~ Ages** das Mittelalter; **~-brow** *(coll.)* **1.** *adj.* für den [geistigen] Normalverbraucher *nachgestellt (ugs.);* **2.** *n.* [geistiger] Normalverbraucher *(ugs.);* ~ **'C** *n. (Mus.)* das eingestrichene C; ~ **'class** *n.* Mittelstand, *der;* Mittelschicht, *die;* **~-class** *adj.* bürgerlich ‹*Vorort, Einstellung, Moral, Werte*›; ‹*Moral, Werte*› des Mittelstandes; **~-class people** Mittelständler; ~ **'common room** *n. (Brit. Univ.)* Gemeinschaftsraum für graduierte Studenten; ~ **'course** *n.* Mittelweg, *der;* ~ **'distance** *see* **distance 1d; ~-distance runner** Mittelstreckenläufer, *der/*-läuferin, *die;* ~ **'ear** *n. (Anat.)* Mittelohr, *das;* **M~ 'East** *pr. n.* **the M~ East** der Nahe [und Mittlere] Osten; **M~ 'Eastern** *adj.* nahöstlich; des Nahen Ostens *nachgestellt;* ‹*Person*› aus dem Nahen Osten; ~ **finger** *n.* Mittelfinger, *der;* ~ **'life** *n., no pl.* mittleres Lebensalter; **~man** *n. (Commerc.)* Zwischenhändler, *der/*-händlerin, *die; (fig.)* Vermittler, *der/*Vermittlerin, *die;* ~ **'management** *n.* mittleres Management; ~ **'manager** *n.* **be a ~ manager** im mittleren Management arbeiten; ~ **name** *n.* **a)** zweiter Vorname; **b)** *(fig.: characteristic quality)* **carefulness is my ~ name** ich bin die Vorsicht in Person; **modesty is not his ~ name** Bescheidenheit ist nicht seine Stärke; **~-of-the-'road** *adj.* gemäßigt; moderat; **~-of-the-road politician/politics** Politiker/Politik der Mitte; ~ **school** *n. (Brit.)* **a)** *(State school) Schule für 9- bis 13jährige;* **b)** *(third and fourth forms) dritte und vierte Klasse einer höheren Schule;* **~-size[d]** *adj.* mittelgroß; ~ **'way** *n.* **a)** *see* ~ **course; b)** *(Buddhism)* **the ~ way** der mittlere Weg; **~weight** *n. (Boxing etc.)* Mittelgewicht, *das; (person also)* Mittelgewichtler, *der;* **M~ 'West** *pr. n. (Amer.)* **the M~ West** der Mittlere Westen; **M~ 'Western** *adj. (Amer.)* des Mittleren Westens *nachgestellt*

middling ['mɪdlɪŋ] **1.** *adj.* **a)** *(second-rate)* mittelmäßig; **b)** *(moderately good)* **[fair to] ~:** ganz ordentlich *(ugs.);* [ganz] passabel; **c)** *(coll.: in fairly good health)* mittelprächtig *(ugs. scherzh.);* **How are you? – Oh, ~:** Wie geht es dir? – Ach, so einigermaßen; **d)** *(Commerc.)* mittler... ‹*Qualität, Ware*›. **2.** *adv.* recht; *(only moderately)* ganz

middlingly ['mɪdlɪŋlɪ] *adv.* **a)** ganz ordentlich *od.* passabel; **b)** *(only moderately well)* mäßig

'Mideast *(Amer.) see* **Middle East**

Mid'eastern *(Amer.) see* **Middle Eastern**

'midfield *n. (Footb.)* Mittelfeld, *das;* **play in ~:** im Mittelfeld spielen; *attrib.* ~ **player** Mittelfeldspieler, *der*

midge [mɪdʒ] *n.* **a)** *(in popular use)* Stechmücke, *die;* **b)** *(Zool.)* Zuckmücke, *die*

midget ['mɪdʒɪt] **1.** *n.* **a)** *(person)* Liliputaner, *der/*Liliputanerin, *die;* Zwerg, *der/*Zwergin, *die;* **b)** *(thing)* Zwerg, *der (fig.); (animal)* Zwergform, *die.* **2.** *adj.* winzig; *(in design)* Mini‹*flugzeug, -U-Boot*›

midi ['mɪdɪ] *n.* Midi[rock], *der; (dress)* Midikleid, *das;* **~-length coat** Midimantel, *der*

midland ['mɪdlənd] **1.** *n.* Binnenland, *das;* **the M~s** *(Brit.)* Mittelengland. **2.** *adj.* im Landesinnern *nachgestellt;* **M~[s]** *(Brit.)* in den Midlands *nachgestellt;* ‹*Dialekt*› der Midlands

midlander ['mɪdləndə(r)] *n.* Bewohner/Bewohnerin des Binnenlandes; **M~** *(Brit.)* Bewohner/Bewohnerin der Midlands

midlife crisis [mɪdlaɪf 'kraɪsɪs] *n.* Midlife-crisis, *die*

'mid-line *n.* Mittellinie, *die*

'midnight *n.* Mitternacht, *die; attrib.* Mitternachts‹*stunde, -messe, -zug*›; mitternächtlich ‹*Festgelage, Feiern*›

midnight: ~ **'oil** *see* **oil 1a;** ~ **'sun** *n.* Mitternachtssonne, *die*

mid-'off *n. (Cricket)* Feldspieler links vom Werfer *(bei rechtshändigem Schlagmann)*

mid-'on *n. (Cricket)* Feldspieler rechts vom Werfer *(bei rechtshändigem Schlagmann)*

'midpoint *n.* Mitte, *die*

'midrib *n. (Bot.)* [mittlere] Blattrippe

midriff ['mɪdrɪf] *n.* **a) the bulge below his ~:** die Wölbung seiner Taillengegend; **with bare ~:** nabelfrei; **he landed a blow on his opponent's ~:** er traf seinen Gegner unterhalb des Brustkorbs; **b)** *(diaphragm)* Zwerchfell, *das;* **c)** *(Amer.: garment exposing ~)* die Taille freilassender Zweiteiler

midshipman ['mɪdʃɪpmən] *n., pl.* **midshipmen** ['mɪdʃɪpmən] *(Navy)* **a)** *(Brit.)* Midshipman, *der; unterster Seeoffiziersrang;* **b)** *(Amer.)* Midshipman, *der;* Seeoffiziersanwärter, *der*

midst [mɪdst] *n.* **in the ~ of sth.** mitten in einer Sache; **be in the ~ of doing sth.** gerade mitten dabei sein, etw. zu tun; **in our/their/your ~:** in unserer/ihrer/eurer Mitte

midsummer ['mɪdsʌmə(r), mɪd'sʌmə(r)] *n.* die [Zeit der] Sommersonnenwende; der Mittsommer; **[on] M~['s] Day** [am] Johannistag; ~ **madness** [heller] Wahnsinn *(ugs.)*

'midtown *n. (Amer.) am Rande des Zentrums gelegener Stadtbezirk; attrib.* am Rande des Zentrums *nachgestellt*

midway ['mɪdweɪ, mɪd'weɪ] *adv.* auf halbem Weg[e] ‹*sich treffen, sich befinden*›; ~ **through sth.** *(fig.)* mitten in etw. *(Dat.)*

midweek ['mɪdwi:k, mɪd'wi:k] *n.* **in ~:** in der Wochenmitte; ~ **flights** Flüge in der Wochenmitte

'Midwest *(Amer.) see* **Middle West**

Mid'western *(Amer.) see* **Middle Western**

midwife ['mɪdwaɪf] *n., pl.* **midwives** ['mɪdwaɪvz] Hebamme, *die*

midwifery ['mɪdwɪfrɪ, mɪd'wɪfərɪ] *n., no pl., no art.* Geburtshilfe, *die*

mid'winter *n.* die [Zeit der] Wintersonnenwende; der Mittwinter

mien [mi:n] *n. (literary) (look)* Miene, *die; (bearing)* Gebaren, *das*

miff [mɪf] *(coll.)* **1.** *n.* **a)** *(huff)* **get into a ~:** sich auf den Schlips getreten fühlen **(about** wegen) *(ugs.);* **be in a ~:** beleidigt *od.* eingeschnappt sein *(ugs.);* **b)** *(quarrel)* Knies, *der (ugs.);* **have a ~ with sb.** mit jmdm. Ärger *od. (ugs.)* Knies haben. **2.** *v. t.* verärgern; **be ~ed** beleidigt *od. (ugs.)* eingeschnappt sein

¹might [maɪt] *see* **may**

²might *n.* **a)** *(force)* Gewalt, *die; (inner strength)* Macht, *die;* **with all one's ~:** mit aller Kraft; **with ~ and main** mit aller Macht; **b)** *(power)* Macht, *die;* ~ **is right** Macht geht vor Recht

might-have-been ['maɪtəvbi:n] *n.* **a)** nicht verwirklichte Möglichkeit; **the ~s** das, was hätte sein können; **b)** *(person) jemand, der es zu etwas hätte bringen können;* **he is a ~:** er hat seine Chancen verpaßt

mightily ['maɪtɪlɪ] *adv.* **a)** mit aller Kraft; **b)** *(coll.: very)* überaus; **be ~ amused** sich köstlich amüsieren

mightn't ['maɪtnt] *(coll.)* = **might not;** *see* **may**

mighty ['maɪtɪ] **1.** *adj.* **a)** *(powerful)* mächtig; gewaltig ‹*Krieger, Anstrengung*›; **b)** *(massive)* gewaltig; **c)** *(coll.: great)* riesig; stark ‹*Trinker*›. *See also* **high 1e. 2.** *adv. (coll.)* verdammt *(ugs.)*

mignonette [mɪnjə'net] *n.* **a)** *(plant)* Reseda, *die; (Reseda odorata)* Gartenresede, *die;* **b)** *(colour)* Resedagrün, *das*

migraine ['mi:greɪn, 'maɪgreɪn] *n. (Med.)* Migräne, *die*

migrant ['maɪgrənt] **1.** *adj.* **a)** ~ **tribe** Nomadenstamm, *der;* ~ **worker** Wanderarbeiter, *der/*-arbeiterin, *die; (in EEC)* Gastarbeiter, *der/*-arbeiterin, *die;* **b)** *(coming and going with the seasons)* ~ **bird/fish** Zugvogel, *der/*Wanderfisch, *der;* ~ **herds** wandernde Herden. **2.** *n.* **a)** Auswanderer, *der/*Auswanderin, *die; (worker)* Wanderarbeiter, *der/*-arbeiterin, *die;* **b)** *(bird)* Zugvogel, *der; (fish)* Wanderfisch, *der*

migrate [maɪ'greɪt] *v. i.* **a)** *(from rural area to town)* abwandern; *(to another country)* auswandern; *(to another town)* übersiedeln **(to** nach); *(to another place of work)* überwechseln; **b)** *(with the seasons)* ‹*Vogel:*› fortziehen; ‹*Fisch:*› wandern; ~ **to the south/sea** nach Süden ziehen/zum Meer wandern

migration [maɪ'greɪʃn] *n.* **a)** *see* **migrate a:** Abwandern, *das;* Auswandern, *das;* Übersiedeln, *das;* Überwechseln, *das;* **a great ~:** eine große Auswanderungswelle; **b)** *(with the seasons) (of birds)* Fortziehen, *das; (of fish)* Wandern, *das; (instance) (of birds)* Zug, *der; (of fish)* Wanderung, *die*

migratory ['maɪgrətərɪ, maɪ'greɪtərɪ] *adj.* **a)** ~ **tribe** Nomadenstamm, *der;* **these workers are ~:** dies sind Wanderarbeiter/*(in EEC)* Gastarbeiter; **b)** *(moving according to seasons)* ~ **bird/fish** Zugvogel, *der/*Wanderfisch, *der*

Mike [maɪk] *pr. n.* **for the love of ~** *(coll.)* um Himmels willen

mike *n. (coll.)* Mikro, *das*

milady [mɪ'leɪdɪ] *n.* **a)** Lady, *die;* **b)** *(form of address)* Mylady; gnädige Frau

Milan [mɪ'læn] *pr. n.* Mailand *(das)*

Milanese [mɪlə'ni:z] **1.** *n.* Mailänder, *der/*Mailänderin, *die.* **2.** *adj.* mailändisch; Mailänder

milch [mɪltʃ] *attrib. adj.* ~ **cow** Milchkuh, *die*

mild [maɪld] **1.** *adj.* **a)** *(gentle)* sanft ‹*Person*›; **b)** *(not severe)* mild ‹*Urteil, Bestrafung, Kritik*›; leicht ‹*Erkrankung, Gefühlsregung*›; gemäßigt ‹*Ausdrucksweise, Sprache, Satire*›; *(moderate)* leicht ‹*Ermutigung, Aufregung*›; **c)** *(moderately warm)* mild ‹*Wetter, Winter*›; **d)** *(having gentle effect)* mild, leicht ‹*Arzneimittel, Stimulans*›; **e)** *(not strong in taste)* mild; leicht ‹*Bier*›; **f)** *(feeble)* zahm *(ugs.)* ‹*Versuch, Spiel*›. *See also* **draw 1c. 2.** *n. schwach gehopfte englische Biersorte;* ~ **and bitter** *(Brit.) Mischgetränk aus schwach und stark gehopftem Bier*

mildew ['mɪldju:] **1.** *n.* **a)** *(on paper, cloth, wood)* Schimmel, *der;* **be spotted with ~:** Stockflecke haben; **b)** *(on plant)* Mehltau, *der.* **2.** *v. t.* **be/become ~ed** schimm[e]lig sein/verschimmeln; ‹*Pflanze:*› von Mehltau befallen sein/werden

mildewy ['mɪldju:ɪ] *adj.* schimm[e]lig ‹*Papier, Stoff, Holz*›; von Mehltau befallen ‹*Pflanze*›; muffig, mod[e]rig ‹*Atmosphäre, Luft*›; *(spotted with mildew)* stock[fleck]ig

mildly ['maɪldlɪ] *adv.* **a)** *(gently)* mild[e]; **b)** *(slightly)* ein bißchen *od.* wenig ‹*enttäuscht, bestürzt, ermutigend, begeistert*›; **c) to put it ~:** gelinde gesagt; **and that's putting it ~:** und das ist noch gelinde ausgedrückt

mild 'steel *n.* weicher *od.* kohlenstoffarmer Stahl

mile [maɪl] *n.* **a)** Meile, *die;* ~ **after** *or* **upon ~** *or* **~s and ~s of sand/beaches** meilenweit Sand/Strände; **~s per hour** Meilen pro Stunde; **not a hundred** *or* **thousand** *or* **million ~s from** *(joc.)* nicht allzu weit von; **someone not a hundred** *etc.* **~s from here** *(joc.)* einer ganz hier in der Nähe; *see also* **square 2b; b) geographical** *or* **nautical** *or* **sea ~** *see* **nautical mile; c)** *(fig. coll.: great amount)* **win/miss by a ~:** haushoch gewinnen/meilenweit verfehlen; **~s better/too big** tausendmal besser/viel zu groß; **beat sb. by ~s** jmdn. haushoch schlagen; **be ~s ahead of sb.** jmdm. weit voraus sein; **be ~s out [in one's answers]** [mit seinen Antworten] völlig danebenliegen *(ugs.)*; **run a ~** *(fig.)* das Weite suchen; **you can see it a ~ off** *(fig.)* das sieht doch ein Blinder [mit dem Krückstock] *(ugs.)*; **sb. is ~s away** *(in thought)* jmd. ist mit seinen Gedanken ganz woanders; *see also* **stand out b**; **stick out 2 b**; **d)** *(race)* Meilenlauf, *der*; **run the ~ in under four minutes** die Meile in weniger als vier Minuten laufen

mileage ['maɪlɪdʒ] *n.* **a)** *(number of miles)* [Anzahl der] Meilen; **state the exact ~ travelled** die gefahrenen Meilen genau angeben; **a low ~** *(on milometer)* ein niedriger Meilenstand; **b)** *(number of miles per gallon)* [Benzin]verbrauch, *der*; **what ~ do you get with your car?** wieviel verbraucht dein Auto?; **c)** *(fig.: benefit)* Nutzen, *der*; **get ~ out of sth.** Nutzen aus etw. ziehen; **there is no ~ in the idea** dieser Vorschlag rentiert sich nicht; **d)** *(expenses)* ≈ Kilometergeld, *das*

mile: ~-post *n.* **a)** Meilenpfosten, *der*; **b)** *(Sport)* Meilenmarkierung, *die*; **by/at the ~-post** eine Meile vor dem Ziel; **~stone** *n.* *(lit. or fig.)* Meilenstein, *der*

milieu [mɪ'ljɜ:, 'mi:ljɜ:] *n.*, *pl.* **~x** [mɪ'ljɜ:z, 'mi:ljɜ:z] *or* **~s** Milieu, *das*

militancy ['mɪlɪtənsɪ] *n.*, *no pl.* Kampfbereitschaft, *die*; Militanz, *die*

militant ['mɪlɪtənt] **1.** *adj.* **a)** *(aggressively active)* kämpferisch; militant; *(less aggressive)* aktiv; **b)** *(engaged in warfare)* kriegführend. **2.** *n.* Militante, *der/die*

militaria [mɪlɪ'teərɪə] *n. pl.* Militaria *Pl.*

militarism ['mɪlɪtərɪzəm] *n.* Militarismus, *der*

militarize (militarise) ['mɪlɪtəraɪz] *v. t.* militarisieren; *(equip)* militärisch ausrüsten

military ['mɪlɪtərɪ] **1.** *adj.* militärisch; Militär⟨*regierung, -akademie, -uniform, -parade*⟩; **~ man** Soldat, *der*; **~ service** Militärdienst, *der*; Wehrdienst, *der*. **2.** *n.*, *constr. as sing. or pl.* **the ~**: das Militär

military: ~ 'band *n.* Militärkapelle, *die*; **~ po'lice** *n.* Militärpolizei, *die*

militate ['mɪlɪteɪt] *v. i.* **~ against/in favour of sth.** [deutlich] gegen/für etw. sprechen; *(have effect)* sich zuungunsten/zugunsten einer Sache *(Gen.)* auswirken

militia [mɪ'lɪʃə] *n.* Miliz, *die*; Bürgerwehr, *die (hist.)*

militiaman [mɪ'lɪʃəmən] *n.*, *pl.* **militiamen** [mɪ'lɪʃəmən] Milizionär, *der*

milk [mɪlk] **1.** *n.* Milch, *die*; **it's no use crying over spilt ~** *(prov.)* [was] passiert ist[, ist] passiert; **be [like] ~ and water** bieder und harmlos sein; **~-and-water** *(fig.)* nichtssagend ⟨*Rede, Predigt, Meinung, Buch*⟩; halbherzig ⟨*Politik*⟩; **a land of** *or* **flowing with ~ and honey** *(fig.)* ein Land, darin Milch und Honig fließt *(bibl. fig.)*; **the ~ of human kindness** die Milch der frommen Denkart *(dichter.)*; **M~ of Magnesia, (P)** Magnesiamilch, *die*; *see also* **condense 1 a**; **dried**; **powder 2 b**. **2.** *v. t.* *(draw ~ from)* melken; *(fig.: get money out of)* melken *(salopp)*; **be ~ed dry by sb.** von jmdm. ausgenommen werden *(ugs.)*

milk: ~ bar *n.* Milchbar, *die*; **~-bottle** *n.* Milchflasche, *die*; **~ 'chocolate** *n.* Milchschokolade, *die*; **~-churn** *n.* Milchkanne, *die*; **~-float** *n. (Brit.)* Milchwagen, *der*

milking ['mɪlkɪŋ] *n.* Melken, *das*

milking: ~-machine *n.* Melkmaschine, *die*; **~-stool** *n.* Melkschemel, *der*

milk: ~-jug *n.* Milchkrug, *der*; *(with tea, coffee, etc.)* Milchkännchen, *das*; **~-loaf** *n.* Milchbrot, *das*; **~maid** *n.* Melkerin, *die*; **~man** ['mɪlkmən] *n.*, *pl.* **~men** ['mɪlkmən] Milchmann, *der*; **~-powder** *n.* Milchpulver, *das*; **~ 'pudding** *n.* Milchpudding, *der*; **~ run** *n.* *(fig.)* [übliche] Tour; **~ shake** *n.* Milk-Shake, *der*; Milchshake, *der*; **~sop** *n.* Weichling, *der*; **~-tooth** *n.* Milchzahn, *der*; **~-white** *adj.* milchweiß

milky ['mɪlkɪ] *adj.* milchig; **~ coffee** Milchkaffee, *der*

Milky 'Way *n.* Milchstraße, *die*

mill [mɪl] **1.** *n.* **a)** Mühle, *die*; **he really went** *or* **was put through the ~** *(fig.)* er wurde ganz schön in die Mangel genommen *(ugs.)*; **b)** *(factory)* Fabrik, *die*; *(machine)* Maschine, *die*; **~ town** ≈ Textilstadt, *die*. **2.** *v. t.* **a)** mahlen ⟨*Getreide*⟩; **b)** fräsen ⟨*Metallgegenstand*⟩; rändeln ⟨*Münze*⟩. **3.** *v. i.* ⟨*Vieh:*⟩ im Kreis laufen; **crowds of customers were ~ing in the corridors** die Kunden schoben sich in Scharen durch die Gänge

~ a'bout *(Brit.)*, **~ a'round** *v. i.* durcheinanderlaufen; **a mass of people ~ing about** *or* **around in the square** eine Menschenmenge, die sich hin und her über den Platz schiebt/schob

milled [mɪld] *adj.* gemahlen ⟨*Korn*⟩; gerändelt ⟨*Münze*⟩

millennium [mɪ'lenɪəm] *n.*, *pl.* **~s** *or* **millennia** [mɪ'lenɪə] **a)** Millennium, *das*; **b)** *(Relig.)* Tausendjähriges Reich; Millennium, *das (fachspr.)*

millepede ['mɪlɪpi:d] *n.* *(Zool.)* **a)** *(myriapod)* Tausendfüß[l]er, *der*; **b)** *(crustacean)* Assel, *die*

miller ['mɪlə(r)] *n.* Müller, *der*

millet ['mɪlɪt] *n.* *(Bot.)* Hirse, *die*

milli- ['mɪlɪ] *pref.* milli-/Milli-

milliard ['mɪljəd] *n.* *(Brit.)* Milliarde, *die*

'millibar *n.* *(Meteorol.)* Millibar, *das*

'milligram *n.* Milligramm, *das*

'millilitre (*Brit.*; *Amer.*: **milliliter**) *n.* Milliliter, *der od. das*

'millimetre (*Brit.*; *Amer.*: **millimeter**) *n.* Millimeter, *der*

milliner ['mɪlɪnə(r)] *n.* Putzmacher, *der*/-macherin, *die*; Modist, *der*/Modistin, *die*

millinery ['mɪlɪnərɪ] *n.* **a)** *no pl.* *(articles)* Hüte; **b)** *no pl.* *(business)* Hutmacherei, *die*; **c)** *(shop)* Hutgeschäft, *das*

million ['mɪljən] **1.** *adj.* **a) a** *or* **one ~**: eine Million; **two/several ~**: zwei/mehrere Millionen; **a** *or* **one ~ and one** eine Million ein; **half a ~** eine halbe Million; **b) a ~ [and one]** *(fig.: innumerable)* tausend; **a ~ books/customers** eine Unmenge Bücher/Kunden; **never in a ~ years** nie im Leben *(ugs.)*; **I've got a ~ [and one] things to do** ich habe tausend Sachen zu erledigen; *see also* **dollar**; **mile a**. **2.** *n.* **a)** Million, *die*; **a** *or* **one/two ~**: eine Million/zwei Millionen; **a ~-to-one chance** eine Chance von einer Million zu eins; **in** *or* **by ~s**: millionenweise; **a ~ and one** *etc.* eine Million einer/eine/eins; **the starving ~s** die Millionen [von] Hungerleidenden; **make a ~**: eine Million machen; **b)** *(indefinite amount)* **there were ~s of people** eine Unmenge Leute waren da; **thanks a ~**: tausend Dank; **~s of times** tausendmal; x-mal *(ugs.)*; **he is a man/she is one in a ~**: so jemanden wie ihn/sie findet man nicht noch einmal; **the ~[s]** die breite Masse

millionaire [mɪljə'neə(r)] *n.* *(lit. or fig.)* Millionär, *der*/Millionärin, *die*

millionth ['mɪljənθ] **1.** *adj.* millionst...; **a ~ part** ein Millionstel. **2.** *n.* *(fraction)* Millionstel, *das*; **a ~ of a second** eine Millionstelsekunde

millipede *see* **millepede**

mill: ~-owner *n.* Textilfabrikant, *der*; **~-pond** *n.* Mühlteich, *der*; **the sea was like a ~-pond** die See war ruhig wie ein Teich; **~-race** *n.* Mühlbach, *der*; **~stone** *n.* Mühlstein, *der*; **be a ~stone round sb.'s neck** *(fig.)* jmdm. ein Klotz am Bein sein *(ugs.)*; **~-wheel** *n.* Mühlrad, *das*

milometer [maɪ'lɒmɪtə(r)] *n.* Meilenzähler, *der*

mime [maɪm] **1.** *n.* **a)** *(performance)* Pantomime, *die*; **b)** *no pl., no art.* *(art)* Pantomimik, *die*; Pantomime, *die (ugs.)*; **c)** *(performer)* Pantomime, *der*/Pantomimin, *die*. **2.** *v. i.* pantomimisch agieren. **3.** *v. t.* pantomimisch darstellen

mimeograph ['mɪmɪəgrɑ:f] **1.** *n.* *(machine)* Mimeograph, *der*. **2.** *v. t.* [auf einen Mimeographen] herstellen ⟨*Kopien*⟩/vervielfältigen ⟨*Vorlage*⟩

mimic ['mɪmɪk] **1.** *n.* Imitator, *der*; **that child is such a ~!** das Kind macht/plappert alles nach!. **2.** *v. t.*, **-ck- a)** nachahmen; imitieren; *(ridicule by imitating)* parodieren; **b)** *(resemble closely)* aussehen wie

mimicry ['mɪmɪkrɪ] *n.* **a)** *no pl.* Nachahmen, *das*; Nachäffen, *das (abwertend)*; **b)** *(instance of imitation) (of person)* Parodie, *die*; **c)** *(Zool.)* Mimikry, *die*

mimosa [mɪ'məʊzə] *n.* Mimose, *die*

Min. *abbr.* **Minister/Ministry** Min.

min. *abbr.* **a) minute[s]** Min; **b) minimum** *(adj.)* mind., *(n.)* Min.

mina ['maɪnə] *n.* *(Ornith.)* Maina, *der*; *(talking species)* Beo, *der*

minaret ['mɪnəret] *n.* Minarett, *das*

mince [mɪns] **1.** *n.* Hackfleisch, *das*; Gehackte, *das*. **2.** *v. t.* in kleine Stücke schneiden; *(chop)* kleinhacken; **~ beef in a machine** Rindfleisch durch den [Fleisch]wolf drehen; **~d meat** Hackfleisch, *das*; **not ~ matters** die Dinge beim Namen nennen; **there is no point in mincing matters** es hat keinen Sinn, etwas zu beschönigen; **she doesn't ~ her words** sie spricht ganz offen und unverblümt. **3.** *v. i.* trippeln

mince: ~meat *n.* **a)** Hackfleisch, *das*; Gehackte, *das*; **make ~meat of sb.** *(fig.)* Hackfleisch aus jmdm. machen *(ugs.)*; **make ~meat of sb.'s arguments** *(fig.)* jmds. Argumente zerpflücken; **b)** *(sweet) süße Pastetenfüllung aus Obst, Rosinen, Gewürzen, Nierenfett usw.*; **~ 'pie** *n. mit süßem „mincemeat" gefüllte Pastete*

mincer ['mɪnsə(r)] *n.* Fleischwolf, *der*

mind [maɪnd] **1.** *n.* **a)** *(remembrance)* **bear** *or* **keep sth. in ~**: an etw. *(Akk.)* denken; etw. nicht vergessen; **have [it] in ~ to do sth.** vorhaben, etw. zu tun; etw. zu tun gedenken *(geh.)*; **we have in ~ a new project** uns *(Dat.)* schwebt ein neues Projekt vor; **bring sth. to ~**: etw. in Erinnerung rufen; **call sth. to ~**: sich *(Dat.)* an etw. erinnern; **many things came to ~**: vielerlei kam mir/ihm *usw.* in den Sinn; **sth. comes into sb.'s ~**: jmdm. fällt etw. ein; **it went out of my ~**: ich habe es vergessen; es ist mir entfallen; **put sb. in ~ of sb./sth.** jmdn. an jmdn./etw. erinnern; **put sth./sb. out of one's ~**: etw./jmdn. aus seinem Gedächtnis streichen; *see also* **sight 1 f**; **time 1 b**; **b)** *(opinion)* **in** *or* **to my ~**: meiner Meinung *od.* Ansicht nach; **be of a** *or* **of one** *or* **of the same ~**, **be in one ~**: einer Meinung sein; **be in two ~s about sth.** [sich *(Dat.)*] unschlüssig über etw. *(Akk.)* sein; **change one's ~**: seine Meinung ändern; **have a ~ of one's own** seinen eigenen Kopf haben; **I have a good ~/a** *or* **half a ~ to do that** ich hätte große Lust/nicht übel Lust, das zu tun; **he doesn't know his own ~**: er weiß nicht, was er will; **make up one's ~**, **make one's ~ up** sich entscheiden; **make up one's ~ to do sth.** sich entschließen, etw. zu tun; **I've finally made up my ~**: ich bin zu einem Entschluß gekommen; **if your ~ is made up** wenn Sie einen Entschluß gefaßt haben; **he made up my ~ for me** er nahm mir die Entscheidung ab; *(made my decision easy)* er machte mir die Entscheidung leicht; **tell sb. one's ~ frankly** freimütig jmdm. seine Meinung sagen; **give sb. a piece of one's ~**: jmdm. gründlich die Meinung sagen; **read sb.'s ~**: jmds. Gedanken lesen; *see also* **speak 2 b**; **c)** *(direction of thoughts)* **his ~ is on other things** er ist mit den Gedanken woanders; **give** *or* **put** *or* **set** *or* **turn one's ~ to** sich konzentrieren auf (+ *Akk.*) ⟨*Arbeit, Aufgabe, Angelegenheit*⟩; **I have had sb./sth. on my ~**: jmd./etw.

hat mich beschäftigt; *(remembered)* ich habe an jmdn./etw. gedacht; *(worried)* ich habe mir Sorgen wegen jmdm./etw. gemacht; **she has a lot of things on her ~**: sie hat viele Sorgen; **sth. preys** *or* **weighs on sb.'s ~**: etw. macht jmdm. zu schaffen *od.* läßt jmdn. nicht los; **take sb.'s ~ off sth.** jmdn. von etw. ablenken; **keep one's ~ on sth.** sich auf etw. *(Akk.)* konzentrieren; **close one's ~ to sth.** sich einer Sache *(Dat.)* verschließen *(geh.)*; **have a closed ~**: sich entschieden haben; **set one's ~ on sth./on doing sth.** sich *(Dat.)* etw. in den Kopf setzen/sich *(Dat.)* in den Kopf setzen, etw. zu tun; *see also* **absence c; open 1g; presence e; d)** *(way of thinking and feeling)* Denkweise, *die;* **frame of ~**: [seelische] Verfassung; **state of ~**: [Geistes]zustand, *der;* **be in a frame of ~ to do sth.** in der Verfassung sein, etw. zu tun; **be in a calm frame of ~**: ruhig sein; **her state of ~ was confused** sie konnte nicht mehr klar denken; **have a logical ~**: logisch denken; **he has the ~ of a child** er hat ein kindliches Gemüt; **the secrets of the human ~**: die Geheimnisse des menschlichen Geistes; **the Victorian/Classical** *etc.* **~**: die Denkweise des viktorianischen Zeitalters/der Klassik *usw.*; **e)** *(seat of consciousness, thought, volition)* Geist, *der;* **a triumph/the power of ~ over matter** ein Triumph/die Macht des Geistes über die Materie; **it was a case of ~ over matter** der Geist hat über die Materie triumphiert; **it's all in the ~**: es ist alles nur Einstellung; **in one's ~**: im stillen; **in my ~'s eye** vor meinem geistigen Auge; im Geiste; **nothing could be further from my ~ than ...**: nichts läge mir ferner, als ...; **no such thought ever entered his ~**: so etwas kam ihm nie in den Sinn; **his ~ was filled with gloomy forebodings** er war von düsteren Vorahnungen erfüllt; **f)** *(intellectual powers)* Verstand, *der;* Intellekt, *der;* **have a very fine** *or* **good ~**: einen klaren *od.* scharfen Verstand haben; **[not] have a good ~**: [nicht] intelligent sein; **g)** *(normal mental faculties)* Verstand, *der;* **lose** *or* **go out of one's ~**: den Verstand verlieren; **be out of one's ~**: verrückt sein; den Verstand verloren haben; **in one's right ~**: im Vollbesitz seiner geistigen Kräfte; bei klarem Verstand; **h)** *(person)* Geist, *der;* **a fine ~**: ein großer Geist *od.* *(ugs.)* kluger Kopf. **2.** *v.t.* **a)** *(heed)* **don't ~ what he says** gib nichts auf sein Gerede *od.* *(geh.)* seine Worte; **~ what I say** glaub mir; **let's do it, and never ~ the expense** machen wir es doch, egal, was es kostet; **b)** *(concern oneself about)* **he ~s a lot what people think of him** es ist für ihn sehr wichtig, was die Leute von ihm denken; **I can't afford a bicycle, never ~ a car** ich kann mir kein Fahrrad leisten, geschweige denn ein Auto; **never ~ him/that** *(don't be anxious)* er/das kann dir doch egal sein *(ugs.)*; **never ~ him – what about me/my predicament?** es interessiert mich nicht – was ist mit mir/mit meinem Dilemma?; **never ~ how/where ...**: es tut nichts zur Sache, wie/wo ...; **never ~ your mistake** laß dir über diesen Fehler *od.* wegen dieses Fehlers keine grauen Haare wachsen *(ugs.)*; **don't ~ me** nimm keine Rücksicht auf mich; *(don't let my presence disturb you)* laß dich [durch mich] nicht stören; *(iron.)* nimm bloß keine Rücksicht auf mich; **~ the doors!** passen Sie auf die Türen auf!; **~ your back[s]** *(coll.)* Bahn frei! *(ugs.)*; **~ one's P's and Q's** sich anständig benehmen; *(follow the correct procedure)* sich nichts zuschulden kommen lassen; **c)** *(apply oneself to)* sich kümmern um; *see also* **business c; d)** *usu. neg. or interrog. (object to)* **did he ~ being woken up?** hat es ihm was ausgemacht, aufgeweckt zu werden?; **would you ~ opening the door?** würdest du bitte die Tür öffnen?; **do you ~?** *(may I?)* hätten Sie etwas dagegen?; *(please do not)* darf ich bitten! *(iron.)*; **if you don't ~**: wenn es Ihnen recht ist; *(iron.)* wenn ich bitten darf!; **do you ~ my asking you a personal question?** darf ich Sie etwas Persönliches fragen?; **do you ~ my smoking?** stört es Sie *od.* haben Sie etwas dagegen, wenn ich rauche?; **I don't ~ what he says** es ist mir gleichgültig *od.* egal, was er sagt; **I don't ~ him** ich habe nichts gegen ihn; **I wouldn't ~ a new car/a walk** ich hätte nichts gegen ein neues Auto/einen Spaziergang; **Have a cup of tea. – I don't ~ if I do** Eine Tasse Tee? – Ach ja, warum nicht?; **do you ~ not helping yourself to all the sweets?** *(iron.)* wie wär's, wenn du ein paar von den Süßigkeiten übrig ließest?; **e)** *(remember and take care)* **~ you don't go too near the cliff-edge!** paß auf, daß du nicht zu nah an den Klippenrand gehst!; **~ [that] you wash your hands before lunch!** denk daran *od.* vergiß nicht, vor dem Essen die Hände zu waschen!; **~ you don't leave anything behind** denk daran, nichts liegenlassen!; **~ how you go!** paß auf! sei vorsichtig!; *(as general farewell)* mach's gut! *(ugs.)*; **~ you get this work done** sieh zu, daß du mit dieser Arbeit fertig wirst!; **f)** *(have charge of)* aufpassen auf (+ *Akk.*); hüten ⟨*Schafe*⟩; **~ the shop** *or* *(Amer.)* **the store** *(fig.)* sich um den Laden kümmern *(ugs.)*; **g)** *(Amer.: be obedient to)* gehorchen (+ *Dat.*) ⟨*Person*⟩; befolgen ⟨*Befehl*⟩; **~ what they tell you** tu, was sie sagen!. **3.** *v.i.* **a) ~!** Vorsicht!; Achtung!; **b)** *usu. in imper. (take note)* **follow the signposts, ~, or ...**: denk daran und halte dich an die Wegweiser, sonst...; **I didn't know that, ~, or ...**: das habe ich allerdings nicht gewußt, sonst ...; wohlgemerkt, das habe ich nicht gewußt, sonst ...; **~ you, I could see he was good** daß er gut war, war mir durchaus klar; **c)** *(care)* **do you '~?** *(iron.)* ich muß doch sehr bitten!; **turn it on; nobody will ~**: mach es an – es wird keinen stören *od.* keiner wird etwas dagegen haben; **he doesn't ~ about your using the car** er hat nichts dagegen, wenn Sie den Wagen benutzen; **if you don't ~**: wenn es dir recht ist *od.* du nichts dagegen hast; **d)** *(give heed)* **never [you] ~** *(it's not important)* macht nichts; ist nicht schlimm; **never ~: I can do it** schon gut – das kann ich machen; **never you ~** *(do not be inquisitive)* das braucht dich nicht zu interessieren; **Never ~ about that now! This work is more important** Laß das jetzt mal [sein/liegen]! Dies hier ist wichtiger; **never ~ about him – what happened to her?** er interessiert mich nicht – was ist ihr passiert?

~ 'out *v.i.* **I told them to ~ out** ich sagte ihnen, sie sollten aufpassen; **~ out for sth.** auf etw. *(Akk.)* aufpassen; **~ out!** Vorsicht!

mind: ~-bending, *(sl.)* **~-blowing** *adjs.* bewußtseinsverändernd; **the concert was ~-blowing** das Konzert war wahnsinnig *(ugs.)*; **~-boggling** ['maɪndbɒglɪŋ] *adj.* *(coll.)* wahnsinnig *(ugs.)*

minded ['maɪndɪd] *adj.* **a)** *(disposed)* **be ~ to do sth.** bereit *od.* *(geh.)* geneigt sein, etw. zu tun; **he could do it if he were so ~**: er könnte es tun, wenn ihm der Sinn danach stünde; **b) mechanically ~**: technisch veranlagt; **he is not in the least politically ~**: er ist vollkommen unpolitisch; **romantically ~**: romantisch veranlagt; **religious-~**: religiös; **be Establishment-~**: sich nach dem Establishment richten

minder ['maɪndə(r)] *n.* **a)** *(for child)* **we need a ~ for the child** wir brauchen jemanden, der auf das Kind aufpaßt *od.* das Kind betreut; **b)** *(for machine)* Maschinenwart, *der;* **c)** *(sl.: protector of criminal)* Gorilla, *der* *(salopp)*

mindful ['maɪndfl] *adj.* **be ~ of sth.** *(take into account)* etw. bedenken *od.* berücksichtigen; *(give attention to)* an etw. *(Akk.)* denken

mindless ['maɪndlɪs] *adj.* geistlos, *(ugs.)* hirnlos ⟨*Mensch*⟩; sinnlos ⟨*Handlung, Gewalt*⟩

'mind: ~-reader *see* **thought-reader; ~-set** *n.* Denkart, *die*

¹mine [maɪn] **1.** *n.* **a)** *(for coal)* Bergwerk, *das;* *(for metal, diamonds, etc.)* Bergwerk, *das;* Mine, *die;* **go** *or* **work down the ~**: unter Tage arbeiten; **b)** *(fig.: abundant source)* unerschöpfliche Quelle; **he is a ~ of useful facts/of information** von ihm kann man eine Menge Nützliches/eine Menge erfahren; **c)** *(explosive device)* Mine, *die.* **2.** *v.t.* **a)** graben ⟨*Loch, unterirdischen Gang*⟩; **b)** schürfen ⟨*Gold*⟩; abbauen, fördern ⟨*Erz, Kohle, Schiefer*⟩; **c)** *(dig into for ore etc.)* **~ an area** in einem Gebiet Bergbau betreiben; **~ an area for ore** *etc.* in einem Gebiet Erz *usw.* abbauen *od.* fördern; **d)** *(Mil.: lay mines in)* verminen. **3.** *v.i.* *(dig the earth)* Bergbau betreiben; **~ for** *see* **2b**

²mine *poss. pron.* **a)** *pred.* meiner/meine/mein[e]s; der/die/das meinige *(geh.)*; **you do your best and I'll do ~**: du tust dein Bestes und ich auch; **look at that dog of ~!** sieh dir bloß mal meinen Hund an! *(ugs.)*; **those big feet of ~**: meine großen Quanten *(ugs.)*; **when will you be ~?** wann wirst du die Meine/der Meine sein? *(veralt.)*; **vengeance is ~**: die Rache ist mein *(geh., veralt.)*; *see also* **hers; b)** *attrib.* *(arch./poet.)* mein

mine: ~-detector *n.* Minensuchgerät, *das;* **~field** *n.* *(lit. or fig.)* Minenfeld, *das;* **~layer** *n.* Minenleger, *der*

miner ['maɪnə(r)] *n.* Bergmann, *der;* Kumpel, *der (Bergmannsspr.)*

mineral ['mɪnərl] **1.** *adj.* mineralisch; Mineral⟨*salz, -quelle*⟩; **~ wealth** Mineralienreichtum, *der;* Reichtum an Bodenschätzen; *see also* **kingdom d. 2.** *n.* **a)** *(mineral substance)* Mineral, *das;* **a country rich in ~s** ein an Bodenschätzen reiches Land; **b)** *esp. in pl.* *(Brit.: soft drink)* Erfrischungsgetränk, *das*

mineralize ['mɪnərəlaɪz] *v.t. & i.* mineralisieren

mineralogist [mɪnə'rælədʒɪst] *n.* Mineraloge, *der*/Mineralogin, *die*

mineralogy [mɪnə'rælədʒɪ] *n.* Mineralogie, *die*

mineral: ~ oil *n.* Mineralöl, *das;* **~ water** *n.* Mineralwasser, *das*

'mine-shaft *n.* [Gruben]schacht, *der*

minestrone [mɪnɪ'strəʊnɪ] *n.* *(Gastr.)* Minestrone, *die*

mine: ~sweeper *n.* Minensuchboot, *das;* **~worker** *n.* Bergmann, *der;* Kumpel, *der (Bergmannsspr.)*

mingle ['mɪŋgl] **1.** *v.t.* [ver]mischen. **2.** *v.i.* sich [ver]mischen (**with** mit); **~ with** *or* **among the crowds** sich unters Volk mischen; **he ~s with millionaires** er hat Umgang mit Millionären

mingy ['mɪndʒɪ] *adj.* *(Brit. coll.)* mick[e]rig *(ugs.)* ⟨*Gegenstand*⟩; knick[e]rig *(ugs.)* ⟨*Mensch*⟩; lumpig *(ugs.)* ⟨*Betrag*⟩

mini ['mɪnɪ] *n.* *(coll.)* **a)** *(car)* **M~, (P)** Mini, *der;* **b)** *(skirt)* Mini, *der (ugs.)*

mini- ['mɪnɪ] *in comb.* Mini-; Klein⟨*bus, -wagen, -taxi*⟩

miniature ['mɪnɪtʃə(r)] **1.** *n.* **a)** *(picture)* Miniatur, *die;* **b)** *no pl., no art.* *(branch of painting)* Miniaturmalerei, *die;* **a portrait in ~**: ein Miniaturportrait; **c)** *(small version)* Miniaturausgabe, *die;* **in ~**: im Kleinformat. **2.** *adj.* **a)** *(small-scale)* Miniatur-; **b)** *(smaller than normal)* Mini- *(ugs.)*; Kleinst-; **~ poodle** Zwergpudel, *der;* **~ golf** Minigolf, *das;* **~ camera** Kleinstbildkamera, *die;* **~ railway** Miniaturbahn, *die*

miniaturise *see* **miniaturize**

miniaturist ['mɪnɪtʃərɪst] *n.* Miniaturmaler, *der*/-malerin, *die*

miniaturize ['mɪnɪtʃəraɪz] *v. t.* verkleinern
mini: **~bus** *n.* Kleinbus, *der;* **~cab** *n.* Kleintaxi, *das;* Minicar, *das;* **~computer** *n.* Minicomputer, *der*
minim ['mɪnɪm] *n.* **a)** *(Brit. Mus.)* halbe Note; **b)** *(fluid measure)* Minim, *das (ca. 0,06 cm³)*
minimal ['mɪnɪml] *adj.* minimal
minimally ['mɪnɪməlɪ] *adv.* minimal
minimisation, minimise *see* **minimiz-**
minimization [mɪnɪmaɪ'zeɪʃn] *n.* **a)** Minimierung, *die;* **b)** *(understating)* Verharmlosung, *die*
minimize ['mɪnɪmaɪz] *v. t.* **a)** *(reduce)* minimieren; auf ein Mindestmaß reduzieren; **b)** *(understate)* bagatellisieren; verharmlosen ‹*Gefahr*›; herunterspielen ‹*Bedeutung*›
minimum ['mɪnɪməm] **1.** *n., pl.* **minima** ['mɪnɪmə] Minimum, *das* (**of** an + *Dat.*); **reduce to a ~:** auf ein Minimum reduzieren; **keep sth. to a ~:** etw. so gering/niedrig wie möglich halten; **a ~ of £5** mindestens 5 Pfund; **at the ~:** mindestens. **2.** *attrib. adj.* Mindest-; **~ temperatures tonight around 5°** nächtliche Tiefsttemperaturen um 5°
minimum: **~ 'lending rate** *n. (Finance) Mindestausleihsatz [der Bank von England];* ≈ Mindestdiskontsatz, *der;* **~ 'wage** *n.* Mindestlohn, *der*
mining ['maɪnɪŋ] *n.* Bergbau, *der; attrib.* Bergbau-; **~ area** *or* **district** Bergbaugebiet, *das;* Revier, *das*
mining: **~ engineer** *n.* Berg[bau]ingenieur, *der;* **~ engineering** *n.* Bergbautechnik, *die;* **~ industry** *n.* Montanindustrie, *die;* Bergbau, *der;* **~ town** *n.* Bergbaustadt, *die;* **~ village** *n.* Bergbaudorf, *das*
minion ['mɪnjən] *n. (derog.)* **a)** *(servile agent)* Ergebene, *der/die;* Lakai, *der (abwertend);* **b)** *(favourite of king etc.)* Günstling, *der (abwertend);* Protegé, *der*
'mini-roundabout *n. (Brit.) sehr kleiner, oft nur aufs Pflaster aufgezeichneter Kreisverkehr*
'miniskirt *n.* Minirock, *der*
minister ['mɪnɪstə(r)] **1.** *n.* **a)** *(Polit.)* Minister, *der*/Ministerin, *die;* **M~ of the Crown** *(Brit.)* Kabinettsminister, *der*/-ministerin, *die;* **M~ of State** *(Brit.)* ≈ Staatssekretär, *der*/-sekretärin, *die; see also* **portfolio b; prime minister; b)** *(diplomat)* Gesandte, *der*/Gesandtin, *die;* **c)** *(Eccl.)* **~ [of religion]** Geistliche, *der/die;* Pfarrer, *der*/Pfarrerin, *die.* **2.** *v. i.* **~ to sb.** sich um jmdn. kümmern; **~ to sb.'s wants/needs** jmds. Wünsche/Bedürfnisse befriedigen; **~ing angel** barmherziger Engel
ministerial [mɪnɪ'stɪərɪəl] *adj.* **a)** *(Eccl.)* geistlich; **~ candidate** Kandidat [für das Pfarramt]; **b)** *(Polit.)* Minister-; ministeriell
ministration [mɪnɪ'streɪʃn] *n.* **a)** *(giving aid)* Hilfe[leistung], *die;* Fürsorge, *die;* **under the ~s of sb.** durch jmds. Fürsorge *od.* Pflege; **b)** *(Relig.)* Seelsorge, *die;* seelsorgerischer Dienst (**to** an + *Dat.*)
ministry ['mɪnɪstrɪ] *n.* **a)** *(Government department or building)* Ministerium, *das;* **~ official** Ministerialbeamte, *der*/-beamtin, *die;* **b)** *(Polit.: body of ministers)* Kabinett, *das;* Regierung, *die;* **c)** *(Eccl.: body of ministers)* Geistlichkeit, *die;* **d)** *(profession of clergyman)* geistliches Amt; **go into** *or* **enter the ~:** Geistlicher werden; **e)** *(Relig.:) (office as minister)* geistliches Amt; *(period of tenure)* Amtszeit als Geistlicher; **perform a ~ among the poor** die Armen seelsorgerisch betreuen; **f)** *(Polit.: period of office)* Amtszeit [als Minister]
mink [mɪŋk] *n.* Nerz, *der;* **~ coat** Nerzmantel, *der*
minnow ['mɪnəʊ] *n. (Zool.)* Elritze, *die; (fig.)* kleiner Fisch
minor ['maɪnə(r)] **1.** *adj.* **a)** *(lesser)* kleiner...; leicht ‹*Operation, Verletzung, Anfall*›; Neben‹*figur, -rolle*›; **~ piece** *(Chess)* Leichtfigur, *die;* **b)** *(comparatively unimportant)* weniger bedeutend; geringer ‹*Bedeutung*›; **~ matter** Nebensächlichkeit, *die;* **c)** *(Brit. Sch.)* **Jones ~:** der jüngere Jones; Jones No. 2 *(ugs.);* **d)** *(Mus.)* Moll-; **~ key/scale/chord** Molltonart, *die*/Molltonleiter, *die*/Mollakkord, *der;* **A ~:** a-Moll; **in a ~ key** in Moll; **~ third** *etc.* kleine Terz *usw.* **2.** *n.* **a)** *(person)* Minderjährige, *der/die;* **be a ~:** minderjährig sein; **b)** *(Amer. Univ.)* Nebenfach, *das.* **3.** *v. i. (Amer.)* **~ in sth.** etw. als Nebenfach haben
minor 'axis *n. (Geom.)* kleine Achse
minority [maɪ'nɒrɪtɪ, mɪ'nɒrɪtɪ] *n.* **a)** Minderheit, *die;* Minorität, *die;* **be in a ~ of one** allein dastehen; **in the ~:** in der Minderheit; **b)** *attrib.* Minderheits‹*regierung, -bericht*›; **~ group** Minderheit, *die;* Minorität, *die;* **~ rights** Minderheitenrechte
minor: **~ league** *(Amer.) n.* untere Liga; *attrib.* Unterliga-; **~ planet** *see* **planet; ~ suit** *n. (Bridge)* niedrige Farbe
minster ['mɪnstə(r)] *n.* Münster, *das;* **York M~:** die Kathedrale von York
minstrel ['mɪnstrl] *n.* **a)** *(medieval singer or musician)* Spielmann, *der;* fahrender Sänger; **~s' gallery** Musikantengalerie, *die;* **b)** *(Hist.: entertainer)* Minstrel, *der (hist.)*
¹mint [mɪnt] **1.** *n.* **a)** *(place)* Münzanstalt, *die;* Münze, *die;* **Royal M~** *(Brit.)* Königlich-Britische Münzanstalt; **b)** *(sum of money)* **a ~ [of money]** eine schöne Stange *od.* ein Haufen Geld *(ugs.);* **have a ~ [of money]** Geld wie Heu haben *(ugs.);* im Geld schwimmen *(ugs.);* **c)** *(fig.: source)* Prägestätte, *die.* **2.** *adj.* funkelnagelneu *(ugs.);* vorzüglich ‹*Münze*› *(fachspr.);* ungestempelt ‹*Briefmarke*›; **in ~ condition** *or* **state** ‹*Auto, Bild usw.*› in tadellosem Zustand. **3.** *v. t. (lit. or fig.)* prägen
²mint *n.* **a)** *(plant)* Minze, *die;* **b)** *(peppermint)* Pfefferminz, *das; attrib.* Pfefferminz-
mint 'sauce *n.* Minzsoße, *die*
minty ['mɪntɪ] *adj.* Pfefferminz‹*aroma, -geschmack*›; **be/taste ~:** nach Pfefferminz schmecken
minuet [mɪnjʊ'et] *n. (Mus.)* Menuett, *das*
minus ['maɪnəs] **1.** *prep.* **a)** *(with the subtraction of)* minus; weniger; *(without)* ohne; abzüglich (+ *Gen.*); **b)** *(below zero)* minus; **a temperature of ~ 20 degrees** [eine Temperatur von] 20 Grad Kälte *od.* minus 20 Grad; **c)** *(coll.: lacking)* ohne. **2.** *adj.* **a)** *(Math.)* negativ ‹*Wert, Menge, Größe*›; Minus‹*zeichen, -betrag*›; **b)** *(Electr.)* **~ pole/terminal** Minuspol, *der.* **3.** *n.* **a)** *(Math.) (symbol)* Minus[zeichen], *das; (negative quantity)* negative Größe; **b)** *(disadvantage)* Minus, *das;* Nachteil, *der*
minuscule ['mɪnəskju:l] **1.** *adj.* winzig. **2.** *n. (lower-case letter)* Minuskel, *die (Druckw.);* Kleinbuchstabe, *der*
¹minute ['mɪnɪt] **1.** *n.* **a)** Minute, *die; (moment)* Moment, *der;* Augenblick, *der;* **I expect him [at] any ~ [now]** ich erwarte ihn jeden Augenblick; **for a ~:** eine Minute/einen Moment [lang]; **I'm not for a ~ saying you're wrong** ich will keinesfalls sagen, daß du unrecht hast; **in a ~** *(very soon)* gleich; **half a ~!** einen Augenblick!; **have not a ~ to spare** keine [Minute] Zeit haben; **have you got a ~?** hast du mal eine Minute *od.* einen Augenblick Zeit?; **can you just give me a ~'s peace?** kannst du mich mal eine Minute *od.* einen Augenblick in Frieden lassen?; **come back this ~!** komm sofort *od.* auf der Stelle zurück!; **at that very ~:** genau in diesem Augenblick; **at the ~** *(coll.)* momentan; im Moment; **to the ~:** auf die Minute; **up to the ~:** hochaktuell; **the ~ [that] I left** in dem Augenblick, als ich wegging; **the ~ he gets home, he's out in the garden** kaum ist er zu Hause, geht er in den Garten; **just a ~!, wait a ~!** *(coll.)* einen Augenblick!; *(objecting)* Augenblick mal! *(ugs.);* **would you mind waiting a ~?** würden Sie sich einen Moment gedulden?; **live ten ~s from town** zehn Minuten von der Stadt entfernt wohnen; **be five ~s' walk [away]** fünf Minuten zu Fuß entfernt sein; *see also* **last minute; b)** *(of angle)* Minute, *die;* **c)** *(draft)* Entwurf, *der; (note)* Notiz, *die;* Vermerk, *der;* **d)** *in pl. (brief summary)* Protokoll, *das;* **keep** *or* **take** *or* **record the ~s** das Protokoll führen; **e)** *(official memorandum)* Memorandum, *das.* **2.** *v. t.* **a)** *(record)* protokollieren ‹*Vernehmung, Aussage*›; zu Protokoll nehmen ‹*Bemerkung*›; **b)** *(send note to)* **~ sb. [about sth.]** jmdn. schriftlich [von etw.] unterrichten
²minute [maɪ'nju:t] *adj.* **, ~r** [maɪ'nju:tə(r)], **~st** [maɪ'nju:tɪst] **a)** *(tiny)* winzig; **not the ~st interest** nicht das geringste Interesse; **b)** *(petty)* [völlig] unbedeutend; **c)** *(precise)* minuziös; exakt; **with ~ care** mit peinlicher Sorgfalt
minute-hand ['mɪnɪthænd] *n.* Minutenzeiger, *der;* großer Zeiger
minutely [maɪ'nju:tlɪ] *adv. (with precision)* genauestens; sorgfältigst; **~ planned** bis ins kleinste Detail geplant; **a ~ detailed analysis** eine Untersuchung bis ins kleinste Detail
minuteman ['mɪnɪtmæn] *n. (Amer. Hist.) auf Abruf bereitstehender Freiwilliger im amerikanischen Unabhängigkeitskrieg;* Minuteman, *der (fachspr.)*
minute steak ['mɪnɪt steɪk] *n.* Minutensteak, *das*
minutiae [maɪ'nju:ʃɪi:, mɪ'nju:ʃɪi:] *n. pl.* Details
minx [mɪŋks] *n.* kleines Biest *(ugs.)*
miracle ['mɪrəkl] *n.* Wunder, *das;* **perform** *or* **work ~s** Wunder tun *od.* vollbringen/wirken; **be nothing short of a ~:** an ein Wunder *od.* ans Wunderbare grenzen; **the age of ~s is not past** es geschehen noch Zeichen und Wunder; **economic ~:** Wirtschaftswunder, *das;* **we'll do our best but we can't promise ~s!** wir tun unser Bestes, aber wir können nicht hexen *od.* zaubern; **be a ~ of ingenuity** ein Wunder an Genialität sein
'miracle play *n. (Hist.)* Mirakel[spiel], *das*
miraculous [mɪ'rækjʊləs] *adj.* **a)** wunderbar; wundersam *(geh.); (supernatural)* übernatürlich ‹*Ereignisse*›; *(having ~ power)* wunderkräftig; **b)** *(surprising)* erstaunlich; unglaublich
miraculously [mɪ'rækjʊləslɪ] *adv.* **a)** auf wunderbare *od. (geh.)* wundersame Weise; **~, he escaped injury** wie durch ein Wunder blieb er unverletzt; **b)** *(surprisingly)* erstaunlicherweise
mirage ['mɪrɑ:ʒ, mɪ'rɑ:ʒ] *n.* **a)** *(optical illusion)* Fata Morgana, *die;* Luftspiegelung, *die;* **b)** *(illusory thing)* Illusion, *die;* Trugbild, *das*
mire [maɪə(r)] *n.* Morast, *der;* **be** *or* **stick** *or* **find oneself in the ~** *(fig.)* im Dreck *od.* in der Klemme stecken *od.* sitzen *(ugs.);* **drag sb.'s name through the ~** *(fig.)* jmds. Namen in den Schmutz *od. (ugs.)* Dreck ziehen
mirror ['mɪrə(r)] **1.** *n. (lit. or fig.)* Spiegel, *der;* **hold the ~ up to sb./sth.** *(fig.)* jmdm./einer Sache den Spiegel vorhalten; **it's all done with ~s** *(coll.)* das Ganze ist nur ein Trick. **2.** *v. t. (lit. or fig.)* [wider]spiegeln; **be ~ed in sth.** sich in etw. *(Dat.)* [wider]spiegeln
mirror: **~ 'image** *n.* Spiegelbild, *das;* **~ writing** *n.* Spiegelschrift, *die*
mirth [mɜ:θ] *n. (literary)* Frohsinn, *der;* Fröhlichkeit, *die; (laughter)* Heiterkeit, *die*
mirthful ['mɜ:θfl] *adj. (literary)* heiter, fröhlich ‹*Lachen*›
misadventure [mɪsəd'ventʃə(r)] *n.* **a)** *(piece of bad luck)* Mißgeschick, *das;* **I had a ~:** mir ist ein Mißgeschick passiert; **b)** *(Law)* **death by ~:** Tod durch Unfall

misalliance [mɪsəˈlaɪəns] *n.* Mesalliance, *die (geh.);* Mißheirat, *die*

misanthrope [ˈmɪzənθrəʊp], **misanthropist** [mɪˈzænθrəpɪst] *ns.* Misanthrop, *der (geh.);* Menschenfeind, *der*

misanthropic [mɪzənˈθrɒpɪk] *adj.* misanthropisch *(geh.);* menschenfeindlich

misanthropy [mɪˈzænθrəpɪ] *n.* Menschenfeindlichkeit, *die*

misapprehend [mɪsæprɪˈhend] *v. t.* mißverstehen

misapprehension [mɪsæprɪˈhenʃn] *n.* Mißverständnis, *das;* **be under a ~:** einem Irrtum unterliegen; **have a lot of ~s about sth.** völlig falsche Vorstellungen von etw. haben

misappropriate [mɪsəˈprəʊprɪeɪt] *v. t.* unterschlagen, *(Rechtsspr.)* veruntreuen ⟨*Geld usw.*⟩; stehlen ⟨*Idee*⟩

misappropriation [mɪsəprəʊprɪˈeɪʃn] *n. (of money)* Unterschlagung, *die;* Veruntreuung, *die (Rechtsspr.)*

misbegotten [mɪsbɪˈgɒtn] *adj.* **a)** *(badly conceived)* schlecht konzipiert ⟨*Plan, Vorhaben, Projekt*⟩; **b)** *(dated: illigitimate)* unehelich ⟨*Kind*⟩

misbehave [mɪsbɪˈheɪv] **1.** *v. i.* sich schlecht benehmen. **2.** *v. refl.* **~ oneself** sich schlecht benehmen; sich danebenbenehmen *(ugs.);* **he and his girl-friend have been misbehaving themselves** *(euphem.)* er und seine Freundin haben sich miteinander eingelassen

misbehaviour (*Amer.:* **misbehavior**) [mɪsbɪˈheɪvɪə(r)] *n.* schlechtes Benehmen *od.* Betragen

miscalculate [mɪsˈkælkjʊleɪt] *v. t.* falsch berechnen ⟨*Menge*⟩; *(misjudge)* falsch einschätzen ⟨*Folgen, Auswirkungen, Stärke*⟩; **~ the distance/the budget** sich bei der Entfernung/beim Budget verkalkulieren *od.* verschätzen

miscalculation [mɪskælkjʊˈleɪʃn] *n. (arithmetical error)* Rechenfehler, *der; (misjudgement)* Fehleinschätzung, *die;* **make a ~ about sth.** *(misjudge sth.)* etw. falsch einschätzen

miscarriage [mɪsˈkærɪdʒ] *n.* **a)** *(Med.)* Fehlgeburt, *die;* **b)** *(of plans, projects, etc.)* Fehlschlagen, *das;* Mißlingen, *das;* **~ of justice** Justizirrtum, *der*

miscarry [mɪsˈkærɪ] *v. i.* **a)** *(Med.)* eine Fehlgeburt haben; **b)** ⟨*Plan, Vorhaben usw.:*⟩ fehlschlagen; **c)** *(not reach destination)* ⟨*Brief usw.:*⟩ fehlgeleitet werden

miscast [mɪsˈkɑːst] *v. t.,* **miscast** falsch *od.* schlecht besetzen ⟨*Rolle, Film, Theaterstück*⟩; fehlbesetzen ⟨*Rolle*⟩

miscellaneous [mɪsəˈleɪnɪəs] *adj.* **a)** *(mixed)* [kunter]bunt ⟨*[Menschen]menge, Sammlung*⟩; **b)** *with pl. n. (of various kinds)* verschieden; verschiedenerlei

miscellany [mɪˈselənɪ] *n.* **a)** *(mixture)* [bunte] Sammlung; [buntes] Gemisch; **b)** *(book)* Sammelband, *der*

mischance [mɪsˈtʃɑːns] *n.* **a)** *(piece of bad luck)* unglücklicher Zufall; **by a** *or* **some ~:** durch einen unglücklichen Zufall; **b)** *no pl., no art. (bad luck)* Pech, *das*

mischief [ˈmɪstʃɪf] *n.* **a)** Unsinn, *der;* Unfug, *der; (pranks)* [dumme] Streiche *Pl.; (playful malice)* Schalk, *der;* **mean ~:** etwas im Schilde führen; **be up to ~ again** wieder etwas im Schilde führen; **be** *or* **get up to [some] ~:** etwas anstellen; **keep out of ~:** keine Dummheiten *od.* keinen Unfug machen; **keep sb. out of ~:** jmdn. vor Dummheiten bewahren; **what ~ have you been up to now?** was hast du denn jetzt schon wieder angestellt?; **sb.'s eyes are full of ~:** jmdm. sieht *od.* schaut der Schalk aus den Augen; **b)** *(harm)* Schaden, *der;* **do sb./oneself a ~** *(coll.)* jmdm./sich etwas antun; **make** *or* **stir up ~:** Ärger machen; **c)** *(person)* Schlawiner, *der (ugs.); (child also)* Racker, *der*

ˈmischief-maker *n.* Böswillige, *der/die*

mischievous [ˈmɪstʃɪvəs] *adj.* **a)** spitzbübisch, schelmisch ⟨*Blick, Gesichtsausdruck, Lächeln*⟩; schalkhaft *(geh.);* **~ trick** Schabernack, *der;* [dummer] Streich; **b)** *(malicious)* boshaft ⟨*Person*⟩; böse ⟨*Absicht*⟩; **c)** *(harmful)* schädlich ⟨*Effekt*⟩; bösartig ⟨*Gerücht*⟩; böse ⟨*Zeitungsartikel*⟩

mischievously [ˈmɪstʃɪvəslɪ] *adv.* **a)** spitzbübisch; schalkhaft *(geh.);* **behave ~:** Schabernack treiben; Unfug anstellen; **b)** *(maliciously)* aus [reiner] Bosheit

miscible [ˈmɪsɪbl] *adj.* mischbar

misconceive [mɪskənˈsiːv] **1.** *v. i.* **~ of sth.** eine falsche Vorstellung von etw. haben; etw. verkennen. **2.** *v. t.* **be ~d** ⟨*Projekt, Vorschlag, Aktion:*⟩ schlecht konzipiert sein

misconception [mɪskənˈsepʃn] *n.* falsche Vorstellung (**about** von); **be [labouring] under a ~ about sth.** sich *(Dat.)* eine falsche Vorstellung von etw. machen; etw. verkennen; **it is a ~ to think that ...:** es ist ein Irrtum, anzunehmen, daß ...

misconduct **1.** [mɪsˈkɒndʌkt] *n., no pl.* **a)** *(improper conduct)* unkorrektes Verhalten; *(Sport)* unsportliches *od.* unfaires Verhalten; **he was accused of gross ~:** er wurde grober Verfehlungen bezichtigt; **professional ~:** standeswidriges Verhalten; **b)** *(bad management)* schlechte Verwaltung; **~ of the war** schlechte Kriegsführung. **2.** [mɪskənˈdʌkt] *v. refl.* sich unkorrekt verhalten

misconstrue [mɪskənˈstruː] *v. t.* mißdeuten; mißverstehen; **~ sb.'s meaning** jmdn. mißverstehen; **~ sth. as sth.** etw. irrtümlicherweise für etw. halten

miscount [mɪsˈkaʊnt] **1.** *n.* falsche Zählung; *(of votes)* falsche Auszählung; **there had been a ~:** bei der Zählung hatte es einen Fehler gegeben. **2.** *v. i.* sich verzählen; *(when counting votes)* falsch [aus]zählen; *(when calculating)* sich verrechnen. **3.** *v. t.* falsch zählen; falsch ausrechnen ⟨*Zahl*⟩

misdeal [mɪsˈdiːl] *(Cards)* **1.** *v. i., forms as* **¹deal 1** sich vergeben; falsch geben. **2.** *v. t., forms as* **¹deal 2** vergeben, falsch geben ⟨*Karten*⟩

misdeed [mɪsˈdiːd] *n.* **a)** *(evil deed)* Missetat, *die (geh. veralt.);* **b)** *(crime)* Verbrechen, *das;* Untat, *die*

misdemeanour (*Amer.:* **misdemeanor**) [mɪsdɪˈmiːnə(r)] *n.* **a)** *(misdeed)* Missetat, *die (geh. veralt.);* **b)** *(Law)* Vergehen, *das;* Übertretung, *die*

misdirect [mɪsdɪˈrekt, mɪsdaɪˈrekt] *v. t.* **a)** *(direct wrongly)* falsch adressieren ⟨*Brief*⟩; vergeuden, falsch einsetzen ⟨*Energien*⟩; in die falsche Richtung schicken ⟨*nach dem Weg Fragenden*⟩; **b)** *(Law)* falsch informieren; falsch belehren ⟨*Geschworene*⟩

miser [ˈmaɪzə(r)] *n.* Geizhals, *der;* Geizkragen, *der (ugs.)*

miserable [ˈmɪzərəbl] *adj.* **a)** *(unhappy)* unglücklich; erbärmlich, elend ⟨*Leben[sbedingungen]*⟩; **make sb.'s life ~:** jmdm. das Leben schwermachen; **feel ~:** sich elend fühlen; **b)** *(causing wretchedness)* trostlos; trist ⟨*Wetter, Urlaub*⟩; elend, armselig ⟨*Wohnviertel, Slums*⟩; öde ⟨*Beschäftigung*⟩; [sehr] unglücklich ⟨*Ehe*⟩; **c)** *(contemptible, mean)* armselig; **a ~ five pounds** klägliche *od. (ugs. abwertend)* miese fünf Pfund

miserably [ˈmɪzərəblɪ] *adv.* **a)** *(uncomfortably, unhappily)* unglücklich; elend, jämmerlich ⟨*leben, zugrunde gehen*⟩; elend ⟨*kalt, naß*⟩; **~ poor** bettelarm; **b)** *(meanly)* spärlich ⟨*beleuchtet, möbliert*⟩; miserabel, *(ugs.)* mies ⟨*bezahlt*⟩; **c)** *(to a deplorable extent)* kläglich, jämmerlich ⟨*versagen*⟩; völlig, total ⟨*verpfuscht, unzureichend*⟩

miserliness [ˈmaɪzəlɪnɪs] *n., no pl.* Geiz, *der*

miserly [ˈmaɪzəlɪ] *adj.* geizig; armselig ⟨*Portion, Essen*⟩; **~ creature** Geizhals, *der;* Geizkragen, *der (ugs.)*

misery [ˈmɪzərɪ] *n.* **a)** *(wretched state)* Elend, *das;* **make sb.'s life a ~:** jmdm. das Leben zur Qual *od.* zur Hölle machen; **live in ~, live a life of ~:** ein erbärmliches *od.* jämmerliches Leben führen; **put an animal out of its ~:** ein Tier von seinen Qualen erlösen; **put sb. out of his ~** *(fig.)* jmdn. nicht länger auf die Folter spannen; **b)** *(thing)* **the ~ of it was that ...:** das Unglück dabei war, daß ...; **miseries** Elend, *das;* Nöte; **c)** *(coll.: discontented person)* **~[-guts]** Miesepeter, *der (ugs. abwertend)*

misfire [mɪsˈfaɪə(r)] **1.** *v. i.* **a)** ⟨*Motor:*⟩ eine Fehlzündung/Fehlzündungen haben; ⟨*Kanone, Gewehr:*⟩ versagen, nicht losgehen; **b)** ⟨*Plan, Versuch:*⟩ fehlschlagen; ⟨*Streich, Witz:*⟩ danebengehen. **2.** *n.* **a)** *(of engine)* Fehlzündung, *die; (of gun)* Versager, *der;* **b)** *(of plan, attempt)* Fehlschlag, *der;* **c)** *(sth. that fails)* Schlag ins Wasser; *(book, play)* Flop, *der*

misfit [ˈmɪsfɪt] *n. (person)* Außenseiter, *der*/Außenseiterin, *die*

misfortune [mɪsˈfɔːtʃən, mɪsˈfɔːtʃuːn] *n.* **a)** *no pl., no art. (bad luck)* Mißgeschick, *das;* **suffer ~:** [viel] Unglück haben; **companions in ~:** Leidensgenossen; **b)** *(stroke of fate)* Schicksalsschlag, *der; (unlucky incident)* Mißgeschick, *das;* **bear one's ~s bravely** sein Schicksal tapfer tragen; **it was his ~** *or* **he had the ~ to ...:** er hatte das Pech, zu ...; **~s rarely come singly** ein Unglück kommt selten allein

misgiving [mɪsˈgɪvɪŋ] *n.* Bedenken *Pl.;* Zweifel, *der;* **have some ~s about sth.** wegen einer Sache Bedenken haben

misgovern [mɪsˈgʌvn] *v. t.* schlecht regieren

misgovernment [mɪsˈgʌvnmənt] *n., no pl.* politische Mißwirtschaft

misguided [mɪsˈgaɪdɪd] *adj.* töricht ⟨*Mensch*⟩; unangebracht ⟨*Eifer, Freundlichkeit*⟩; unsinnig ⟨*Bemühung, Maßnahme*⟩

misguidedly [mɪsˈgaɪdɪdlɪ] *adv. (in error)* irrigerweise; *(ill-advisedly)* törichterweise

mishandle [mɪsˈhændl] *v. t.* **a)** *(deal with incorrectly)* falsch behandeln ⟨*Angelegenheit*⟩; schlecht verwalten ⟨*Finanzen*⟩; **b)** *(handle roughly)* mißhandeln

mishap [ˈmɪshæp, mɪsˈhæp] *n.* Mißgeschick, *das;* **sb. suffers** *or* **meets with a ~:** jmdm. passiert ein Mißgeschick; **without further ~:** ohne weitere Zwischenfälle

mishear [mɪsˈhɪə(r)], **misheard** [mɪsˈhɜːd] **1.** *v. i.* sich verhören. **2.** *v. t.* falsch verstehen

mishit **1.** [ˈmɪshɪt] *n.* Fehlschlag, *der;* **have** *or* **make a ~:** [den Ball] verschlagen. **2.** [mɪsˈhɪt] *v. t., forms as* **hit 1** verschlagen ⟨*Ball*⟩

mishmash [ˈmɪʃmæʃ] *n.* Mischmasch, *der (ugs.)* (**of** aus)

misinform [mɪsɪnˈfɔːm] *v. t.* falsch informieren *od.* unterrichten

misinformation [mɪsɪnfəˈmeɪʃn] *n., no pl., no indef. art.* Fehlinformationen; *(on radio, in newspaper)* Falschmeldungen

misinterpret [mɪsɪnˈtɜːprɪt] *v. t.* **a)** *(interpret wrongly)* fehlinterpretieren, falsch auslegen ⟨*Text, Inschrift, Buch*⟩; ⟨*Übersetzung:*⟩ falsch wiedergeben ⟨*Sinn*⟩; **b)** *(make wrong inference from)* falsch deuten; mißdeuten; **he ~ed her letter as meaning that ...:** er las fälschlicherweise aus ihrem Brief heraus, daß ...

misinterpretation [mɪsɪntɜːprɪˈteɪʃn] *n.* Fehlinterpretation, *die;* **be open to ~:** leicht falsch ausgelegt werden können

misjudge [mɪsˈdʒʌdʒ] **1.** *v. t.* falsch einschätzen; falsch beurteilen ⟨*Person*⟩; **~ the height/distance/length of time** sich in der Höhe/Entfernung/Zeit verschätzen. **2.** *v. i.* sich verschätzen

misjudgement, misjudgment [mɪsˈdʒʌdʒmənt] *n.* Fehleinschätzung, *die; (of person)* falsche Beurteilung; *(of distance, length, etc.)* falsche Einschätzung

mislay [mɪs'leɪ] *v. t.*, **mislaid** [mɪs'leɪd] verlegen

mislead [mɪs'li:d] *v. t.*, **misled** [mɪs'led] irreführen; täuschen; **~ sb. about sth.** jmdm. ein falsches Bild von etw. vermitteln

misleading [mɪs'li:dɪŋ] *adj.* irreführend

mismanage [mɪs'mænɪdʒ] *v. t.* herunterwirtschaften ‹*Firma, Land*›; schlecht führen ‹*Haushalt*›; schlecht handhaben *od.* abwickeln ‹*Angelegenheit, Projekt, Sache*›; schlecht abwickeln ‹*Geschäft*›

mismanagement [mɪs'mænɪdʒmənt] *n.* Mißwirtschaft, *die; (of finances)* schlechte Verwaltung; *(of matters or affairs)* schlechte Handhabung *od.* Abwicklung

mismatch 1. [mɪs'mætʃ] *v. t.* **~ parts of sth.** Teile von etw. nicht richtig zusammenfügen; **~ colours/fabrics/patterns** Farben/Gewebe/Muster miteinander kombinieren, die nicht zusammenpassen; **a badly ~ed couple** ein Paar, das absolut nicht zusammenpaßt. **2.** ['mɪsmætʃ] *n.* Nichtübereinstimmung, *die; (Boxing)* ungleicher Kampf; **their marriage was a ~:** sie paßten als Eheleute nicht zusammen

misnomer [mɪs'nəʊmə(r)] *n.* **a)** *(use of wrong name)* falsche Bezeichnung *od.* Benennung; **this seems like a slight ~** *(iron.)* das ist wohl etwas danebengegriffen; **b)** *(wrong name)* unzutreffende Bezeichnung

misogynist [mɪ'sɒdʒɪnɪst] *n.* Frauenhasser, *der;* Misogyn, *der (geh.)*

misogyny [mɪ'sɒdʒɪnɪ] *n.* Frauenhaß, *der;* Misogynie, *die (geh.)*

misplace [mɪs'pleɪs] *v. t.* **a)** *(put in wrong place)* an die falsche Stelle *od.* den falschen Platz stellen/legen/setzen *usw.*; **b)** *(bestow on wrong object)* **~ one's affection/confidence** seine Zuneigung/sein Vertrauen dem Falschen/der Falschen schenken; **have a ~d reliance on sb./sth.** so töricht sein, fest auf jmdn./etw. zu vertrauen; **c) be ~d** *(inappropriate)* unangebracht *od.* fehl am Platz sein

misplay [mɪs'pleɪ] *v. t.* verschießen ‹*Elfmeter, Eckball usw.*›; schlecht spielen, verschlagen ‹*Ball, Return*›; **~ one's stroke** den Ball verschlagen

misprint 1. ['mɪsprɪnt] *n.* Druckfehler, *der.* **2.** [mɪs'prɪnt] *v. t.* verdrucken

mispronounce [mɪsprə'naʊns] *v. t.* falsch aussprechen

mispronunciation [mɪsprənʌnsɪ'eɪʃn] *n.* falsche Aussprache; *(mistake)* Aussprachefehler, *der*

misquotation [mɪskwəʊ'teɪʃn] *n.* falsches Zitat; **he is given to ~:** er zitiert oft falsch

misquote [mɪs'kwəʊt] *v. t.* falsch zitieren; **he was ~d as saying that ...:** man unterstellte ihm, gesagt zu haben, daß ...

misread [mɪs'ri:d] *v. t.*, **misread** [mɪs'red] *(read wrongly)* falsch *od.* nicht richtig lesen ‹*Text, Wort, Schrift*›; *(interpret wrongly)* falsch verstehen ‹*Anweisungen*›; mißdeuten ‹*Text, Absichten*›; **~ an 'a' as a 'b'** ein „a“ als „b“ lesen

misremember [mɪsrɪ'membə(r)] *v. t.* **~ sth.** etw. nicht richtig in Erinnerung haben

misrepresent [mɪsreprɪ'zent] *v. t.* falsch darstellen; verdrehen ‹*Tatsachen*›; **~ sb.'s character** ein falsches Bild von jmds. Charakter geben

misrepresentation [mɪsreprɪzen'teɪʃn] *n.* falsche Darstellung; *(of facts)* Verdrehung, *die*

Miss [mɪs] *n.* **a)** *(title of unmarried woman)* **~ Brown** Frau Brown; Fräulein Brown *(veralt.)*; *(girl)* Fräulein Brown; **the ~es Smith[s]** die Damen/Fräulein Smith; **b)** *(title of beauty queen)* **~ France** Miß Frankreich; **~ World Contest** Miß-Universum-Wahl, *die;* **c)** *(as form of address to teacher etc.)* Frau Schmidt *usw.*; *(from servant)* gnädiges Fräulein; **d) m~** *(derog. or playful: girl)* **the young ~es** die jungen Dinger *(ugs.)*; **she is a saucy [little] ~:** sie ist ein freches [junges] Ding *(ugs.)*

miss 1. *n.* **a)** *(failure to hit or attain)* Fehlschlag, *der; (shot)* Fehlschuß, *der; (throw)* Fehlwurf, *der;* **be a ~:** danebengehen *(ugs.)*; **a ~ is as good as a mile** *(prov.)* fast getroffen ist auch daneben; **b) give sb./sth. a ~:** sich *(Dat.)* jmdn./etw. schenken; **we'll give the pub a ~ tonight** wir werden heute abend mal nicht in die Kneipe gehen; *see also* **near 3c. 2.** *v. t.* **a)** *(fail to hit, lit. or fig.)* verfehlen; **~ed!** nicht getroffen!; **the car just ~ed the tree** das Auto wäre um ein Haar gegen den Baum geprallt; **we just ~ed having an accident** wir hätten um ein Haar einen Unfall gehabt; **b)** *(fail to get)* nicht bekommen; *(fail to find or meet)* verpassen; **they ~ed each other** sie verpaßten *od.* verfehlten sich; **~ a catch** einen Ball nicht fangen; **~ the goal** am Tor vorbeischießen; danebenschießen; **he just ~ed being first** er wäre um ein Haar Erster geworden; **c)** *(let slip)* verpassen; versäumen; **~ an opportunity** sich *(Dat.)* eine Gelegenheit entgehen lassen; **you don't know what you're ~ing** du weißt ja gar nicht, was dir entgeht; **it is too good to ~** *or* **is not to be ~ed** das darf man sich *(Dat.)* [einfach] nicht entgehen lassen; **an experience he would not have ~ed** eine Erfahrung, die er nicht hätte missen wollen; **d)** *(fail to catch)* versäumen, verpassen ‹*Bus, Zug, Flugzeug*›; **~ the boat** *or* **bus** *(fig.)* den Anschluß verpassen *(fig.)*; **e)** *(fail to take part in)* versäumen; **~ school** in der Schule fehlen; **f)** *(fail to see)* übersehen; *(fail to hear or understand)* nicht mitbekommen; **you can't ~ it** es ist nicht zu übersehen; **he doesn't ~ much** ihm entgeht so schnell nichts; **g)** *(feel the absence of)* vermissen; **she ~es him** er fehlt ihr; **h)** *(fail to keep or perform)* versäumen ‹*Verabredung, Vorstellung*›; **she ~ed her pill** sie hat vergessen, ihre Pille zu nehmen. **3.** *v. i.* **a)** *(not hit sth.)* nicht treffen; *(not catch sth.)* danebengreifen; **b)** ‹*Ball, Schuß usw.:*› danebengehen; **c)** ‹*Motor:*› aussetzen

~ 'out 1. *v. t.* weglassen; **his name was ~ed out from the list** sein Name fehlte auf der Liste. **2.** *v. i.* **~ out on sth.** *(coll.)* sich *(Dat.)* etw. entgehen lassen; **he can't afford to ~ out** er kann es sich nicht leisten, sich das entgehen zu lassen

missal ['mɪsl] *n.* **a)** *(RC Ch.)* Missal[e], *das;* **b)** *(book of prayers)* [illuminiertes] Gebetbuch

missel[-thrush] ['mɪsl(θrʌʃ)] *n. (Ornith.)* Misteldrossel, *die*

misshapen [mɪs'ʃeɪpn] *adj.* mißgebildet, mißgestaltet ‹*Körper[teil]*›; verwachsen ‹*Baum, Pflanze*›; verbogen ‹*Münze*›

missile ['mɪsaɪl] *n.* **a)** *(thrown)* [Wurf]geschoß, *das;* **b)** *(self-propelled)* Missile, *das;* Flugkörper, *der;* **intercontinental ballistic ~:** [ballistische] Interkontinentalrakete

missile: ~ base *n.* [Raketen]abschußbasis, *die;* **~launcher** *n.* [Raketen]abschußrampe, *die*

missilery ['mɪslrɪ] *n., no pl.* **a)** *(missiles)* Geschosse; *(modern)* Raketen; **b)** *(science)* Raketentechnik, *die*

'missile site *see* **missile base**

missing ['mɪsɪŋ] *adj.* vermißt; fehlend ‹*Seite, Kapitel, Teil, Hinweis, Indiz*›; **be ~** ‹*Kapitel, Wort, Seite:*› fehlen; ‹*Brille, Bleistift usw.:*› verschwunden sein; ‹*Mensch:*› vermißt werden; *(not be present)* nicht dasein; fehlen; **she went ~ two hours ago** sie wird seit zwei Stunden vermißt; **the jacket has two buttons ~:** an der Jacke fehlen zwei Knöpfe; **I am ~ £10** mir fehlen 10 Pfund; **the dead, wounded, and ~:** die Toten, Verwundeten und Vermißten; **~ person** Vermißte *der/die;* **~ link** *(Biol.)* Missing link, *das*

mission ['mɪʃn] *n.* **a)** *(task)* Mission, *die;* Auftrag, *der;* **b)** *(journey)* Mission, *die;* **go/come on a ~ to do sth.** mit dem Auftrag reisen/kommen, etw. zu tun; **c)** *(planned operation)* Einsatz, *der; (order)* Befehl, *der;* **space ~:** Weltraumflug, *der;* **d)** *(vocation)* Mission, *die;* **~ in life** Lebensaufgabe, *die;* **have a ~ to do sth.** dazu berufen sein, etw. zu tun; **e)** *(persons)* Mission, *die;* **f)** *(Relig.)* Mission, *die; (missionary post)* Mission[sstation], *die; (religious body)* Mission[sgesellschaft], *die;* **foreign/home ~** *(campaign)* äußere/innere Mission

missionary ['mɪʃənərɪ] **1.** *adj.* missionarisch; Missions‹*station, -arbeit, -schrift*›; **~ box** Opferbüchse [für die Mission]. **2.** *n.* Missionar, *der*/Missionarin, *die*

missis ['mɪsɪz, 'mɪsɪs] *n.* **a)** *(sl./joc.: wife)* **the** *or* **my/his/your ~:** die *od.* meine/seine/deine Alte *(salopp)*; meine/seine/deine bessere Hälfte *(ugs. scherzh.)*; **b)** *(sl.: as form of address)* **well, ~, ...:** na, die Dame, ... *(ugs.)*

missive ['mɪsɪv] *n. (formal/joc.)* Missiv, *das (veralt.)*; Schreiben, *das*

misspell [mɪs'spel] *v. t., forms as* **'spell** falsch schreiben

misspelling [mɪs'spelɪŋ] *n.* falsch geschriebenes Wort

misspend [mɪs'spend] *v. t., forms as* **spend** verschwenden; vergeuden; **his was a misspent youth** er hat seine Jugend vertan

misstate [mɪs'steɪt] *v. t.* falsch darstellen

misstatement [mɪs'steɪtmənt] *n.* falsche Darstellung

missus ['mɪsɪz] *see* **missis**

mist [mɪst] **1.** *n.* **a)** *(fog)* Nebel, *der; (haze)* Dunst, *der; (on windscreen etc.)* Beschlag, *der; see also* **Scotch mist**; **b) in the ~s of time** *or* **antiquity** *(fig.)* im Dunkel *od.* *(geh.)* Nebel der Vergangenheit; **c)** *(of spray, vapour, etc.)* Wolke, *die;* **d)** *(blurring of sight)* Schleier, *der.* **2.** *v. t.* beschlagen lassen ‹*Glas*›; ‹*Tränen:*› verschleiern ‹*Blick*›

~ 'over 1. *v. i.* ‹*Glas usw.:*› [sich] beschlagen; **his eyes ~ed over** Tränen verschleierten seinen Blick. **2.** *v. t.* beschlagen lassen

~ 'up *v. i.* ‹*Glas, Brille:*› [sich] beschlagen

mistakable [mɪ'steɪkəbl] *adj.* verwechselbar **(for** mit**)**

mistake [mɪ'steɪk] **1.** *n.* Fehler, *der; (misunderstanding)* Mißverständnis, *das;* **make a ~:** einen Fehler machen; *(in thinking)* sich irren; **there was a ~ about sth.** man hat sich in etw. *(Dat.)* geirrt; **there's some ~!** da liegt ein Irrtum *od.* Fehler vor!; **we all make ~s** jeder macht mal einen Fehler; *(in thinking)* jeder kann sich mal irren; **the ~ is mine** der Fehler liegt bei mir; **it is a ~ to assume that ...:** es ist ein Irrtum anzunehmen, daß ...; **by ~:** versehentlich; aus Versehen; **... and no ~:** ..., aber wirklich; **I was properly scared and no ~:** ich habe einen ganz schönen Schrecken gekriegt, kann ich dir sagen; **make no ~ about it, ...:** täusch dich nicht, ... **2.** *v. t., forms as* **take 1: a)** *(misunderstand meaning of)* falsch verstehen; mißverstehen; **~ sth./sb. as meaning that ...:** etw./jmdn. [fälschlicherweise] so verstehen, daß ...; **b)** *(wrongly take one for another)* **~ x for y** x mit y verwechseln; x [fälschlich] für y halten; **there is no mistaking what ought to be done** es steht außer Frage *od.* ist ganz klar, was getan werden muß; **there is no mistaking him** man kann ihn gar nicht verwechseln; **~ sb.'s identity** jmdn. [mit jmd. anderem] verwechseln; **c)** *(choose wrongly)* verfehlen ‹*Beruf, Weg*›

mistaken [mɪ'steɪkn] *adj.* **be ~:** sich täuschen; **you're ~ in believing that** wenn du das glaubst, täuschst du dich; **~ kindness/zeal** unangebrachte Freundlichkeit/unangebrachter Eifer; **or** *or* **unless I'm very much ~:** wenn mich nicht alles täuscht; **a case of ~ identity** eine Verwechslung

mistakenly [mɪ'steɪknlɪ] *adv.* irrtümlicherweise

mister ['mɪstə(r)] *n.* **a)** *(sl./joc.)* **hey, ~:** he, Meister *od.* Chef *(ugs.)*; **b)** *(person without title)* **a mere ~:** ein gewöhnlicher Bürger

mistime [mɪs'taɪm] *v. t.* einen ungünstigen Zeitpunkt wählen für; schlecht timen *(bes. Sport)*

mistletoe ['mɪsltəʊ] *n.* Mistel, *die; (sprig)* Mistelzweig, *der*

mistook *see* **mistake 2**

mistral [mɪs'trɑ:l] *n. (Meteorol.)* Mistral, *der*

mistranslate [mɪstræns'leɪt] *v. t.* falsch übersetzen

mistranslation [mɪstræns'leɪʃn] *n.* falsche Übersetzung; *(error)* Übersetzungsfehler, *der*

mistreat [mɪs'tri:t] *v. t.* schlecht behandeln; *(violently)* mißhandeln; **~ one's tools** nachlässig mit seinem Werkzeug umgehen

mistreatment [mɪs'tri:tmənt] *n.* schlechte Behandlung; *(violent)* Mißhandlung, *die*

mistress ['mɪstrɪs] *n.* **a)** *(of a household)* Hausherrin, *die;* **the ~ of the house** *or* **family** die Frau des Hauses; **b)** *(person in control, employer)* Herrin, *die;* **she is ~ of the situation** sie ist Herr der Lage; **she is her own ~:** sie ist ihr eigener Herr; **the dog's ~:** das Frauchen [des Hundes]; **c)** *(Brit. Sch.: teacher)* Lehrerin, *die;* **'French ~:** Französischlehrerin, *die;* **d)** *(man's illicit lover)* Geliebte, *die;* Mätresse, *die (veralt. abwertend);* **e)** *(expert)* Expertin, *die;* Meisterin, *die;* **f)** *(of college)* Rektorin, *die*

mistrial [mɪs'traɪəl] *n. (Law)* **a)** *(invalid trial)* fehlerhaft geführter Prozeß; **on the grounds that there had been a ~:** wegen Verfahrensfehlern in der Prozeßführung; **b)** *(Amer.: inconclusive trial)* ergebnisloser Prozeß

mistrust [mɪs'trʌst] **1.** *v. t.* mißtrauen (+ *Dat.*); **~ oneself** sich *(Dat.)* selbst mißtrauen. **2.** *n., no pl.* Mißtrauen, *das* (**of** gegenüber + *Dat.*); **[show] ~ towards sb.** Mißtrauen gegen jmdn. [hegen]

mistrustful [mɪs'trʌstfl] *adj.* mißtrauisch; **be ~ of sb./sth.** jmdm./einer Sache gegenüber mißtrauisch sein

misty ['mɪstɪ] *adj.* **a)** verschleiert ‹*Augen, Blick*›; neb[e]lig, dunstig ‹*Tag, Morgen*›; in Nebel *od.* Dunst gehüllt ‹*Berg, Hügel*›; nebelverhangen *(geh.)*, dunstig ‹*Tal*›; **~ blue** rauchiges Blau; **b)** *(indistinct in form)* unklar; verschwommen

'misty-eyed *adj.* mit verschleiertem Blick *nachgestellt;* **be ~:** einen [tränen]verschleierten Blick haben

misunderstand [mɪsʌndə'stænd] *v. t., forms as* **understand** mißverstehen; falsch verstehen; **~ the word x as meaning y** das Wort x im Sinne von y verstehen; **don't ~ me** versteh mich nicht falsch

misunderstanding [mɪsʌndə'stændɪŋ] *n.* Mißverständnis, *das;* **there has been a ~:** da lag ein Mißverständnis vor; **I don't want there to be any ~ about it** ich möchte nicht, daß deswegen ein Mißverständnis aufkommt

misunderstood [mɪsʌndə'stʊd] *adj.* unverstanden; verkannt ‹*Künstler, Genie*›; **be ~:** kein Verständnis finden

misuse 1. [mɪs'ju:z] *v. t.* mißbrauchen; zweckentfremden ‹*Werkzeug, Gelder*›; falsch bedienen ‹*Maschine*›; nichts Rechtes machen aus ‹*Gelegenheit, Talent*›; vergeuden, verschwenden ‹*Reserven, Zeit*›. **2.** [mɪs'ju:s] *n.* Mißbrauch, *der; (of funds)* Zweckentfremdung, *die; (of resources, time)* Vergeudung, *die;* Verschwendung, *die;* **a ~ of language** eine unangemessene *od.* unangebrachte Ausdrucksweise

mite [maɪt] *n.* **a)** *(Zool.)* Milbe, *die;* **b)** *(contribution)* Scherflein, *das;* **give one's ~ to sth.** sein Scherflein zu etw. beitragen; **the widow's ~:** das Scherflein der armen Witwe; **c)** *(small object)* Dingelchen, *das;* kleines Ding; *(small child)* Würmchen, *das (fam.);* **poor little ~:** armes Kleines; **d)** *(coll.: somewhat)* **a ~ too strong/outspoken** ein bißchen *od.* etwas zu stark/geradeheraus

miter, mitered *(Amer.) see* **mitre, mitred**

mitigate ['mɪtɪgeɪt] *v. t.* **a)** *(alleviate)* lindern; **b)** *(make less severe)* mildern; **mitigating circumstances** mildernde Umstände; **c)** *(appease)* besänftigen ‹*Zorn, Wut*›

mitigation [mɪtɪ'geɪʃn] *n. see* **mitigate**: Linderung, *die;* Milderung, *die;* Besänftigung, *die;* **it must be said, in ~ of his faults, that ...:** es muß zu seiner Verteidigung *od.* Entlastung gesagt werden, daß ...; **~ of punishment** Strafmilderung, *die*

mitre ['maɪtə(r)] *n. (Brit.)* **a)** *(Eccl.)* Mitra, *die;* **b)** *(joint)* Gehrung, *die (bes. Technik)*

mitred ['maɪtəd] *adj.* **a)** *(Brit. Eccl.)* eine Mitra tragend; **b) ~ joint** *(Carpentry)* Gehrungsverbindung, *die*

mitten ['mɪtn] *n.* Fausthandschuh, *der;* Fäustling, *der; (not covering fingers)* fingerloser Handschuh

Mitty ['mɪtɪ] *n., pl.* **~s: [Walter] ~ [figure]** *Mensch, der sich gern Tagträumen von eigenen Großtaten hingibt*

mix [mɪks] **1.** *v. t.* **a)** *(combine)* [ver]mischen; vermengen; verrühren ‹*Zutaten*›; verbinden ‹*Harmonien, Komponenten, Stilrichtungen*›; **~ one's drinks** alles durcheinander trinken; **~ an egg into the batter** ein Ei in den Teig rühren; **b)** *(prepare by ~ing)* mischen, mixen ‹*Cocktail*›; anrühren, ansetzen ‹*Lösung, Teig*›; zubereiten ‹*Medikament*›; **c) ~ it [with sb.]** *(coll.)* sich [mit jmdm.] prügeln. **2.** *v. i.* **a)** *(become ~ed)* sich vermischen; sich mischen lassen; **b)** *(be sociable, participate)* Umgang mit anderen [Menschen] haben; **~ well** kontaktfreudig *od.* gesellig sein; **you should ~ with other people** du solltest unter Leute gehen; **I don't ~ with that sort of people/in those circles** ich verkehre nicht mit solchen Leuten/in diesen Kreisen; **c)** *(be compatible)* zusammenpassen; sich [miteinander] vertragen; ‹*Ideen:*› sich verbinden lassen. **3.** *n.* **a)** *(coll.: mixture)* Mischung, *die* (**of** aus); **b)** *(proportion)* [Mischungs]verhältnis, *das;* **c)** *(ready ingredients)* [gebrauchsfertige] Mischung; **[cake-]~:** Backmischung, *die;* **d)** *(Radio, Cinemat., TV)* **~[es]** Mischung, *die*

~ 'in 1. *v. i.* **a)** *(be compatible)* zu jmdm./etw. passen; **b)** *(start fighting)* aufeinander losgehen. **2.** *v. t.* einrühren

~ 'up *v. t.* **a)** vermischen; verrühren ‹*Zutaten*›; **b)** *(make a muddle of)* durcheinanderbringen; *(confuse one with another)* verwechseln; *see also* **mix-up**; **c)** *in pass. (involve)* **be/get ~ed up in sth.** in etw. *(Akk.)* verwickelt sein/werden; **get ~ed up with a gang** sich mit einer Gang einlassen

mixed [mɪkst] *adj.* **a)** *(diverse)* unterschiedlich ‹*Reaktionen, Kritiken*›; **a ~ assortment** eine [bunte] Mischung (**of** von); **~ feelings** gemischte Gefühle; **get ~ reviews** sehr unterschiedliche Kritiken bekommen; **b)** *(containing people from various backgrounds etc.)* gemischt ‹*Gesellschaft*›; **a ~ bunch** ein bunt gemischter Haufen; **c)** *(for both sexes)* gemischt

mixed: ~ 'bag *n.* bunte Mischung; **a very ~ bag of people** eine bunt gemischte Gruppe [von Leuten]; **~ 'blessing** *n.* **be a ~ blessing** nicht nur Vorteile haben; **children are a ~ blessing** Kinder sind kein reiner Segen; **~ 'company** *n.* **in ~ company** in Gesellschaft von Damen [und Kindern]; **~ 'doubles** *see* **double 3j**; **~ 'farming** *n.* Kombination von Ackerbau und Viehzucht; **~ 'grill** *n.* Mixed grill, *der (Gastr.)*; gemischte Grillplatte; **~ 'marriage** *n.* Mischehe, *die;* **~ 'metaphor** *see* **metaphor b**; **~ 'up** *adj. (fig. coll.)* verwirrt, konfus ‹*Person*›; **be/feel very ~ up** völlig durcheinander sein; **[crazy] ~ up kids** Jugendliche ohne [jeden] inneren Halt

mixer ['mɪksə(r)] *n.* **a)** *(for foods)* Mixer, *der; (for cement, concrete)* Mischmaschine, *die;* **b)** *(merging pictures) (apparatus)* Mischpult, *das; (person)* Bildmischer, *der;* **c)** *(combining sounds) (apparatus)* Mischpult, *das;* Tonmischer, *der; (person)* Tonmischer, *der;* **d)** *(drink)* Getränk zum Mischen; **e)** *(in society)* **be a good ~:** mit den unterschiedlichsten Leuten gut zurechtkommen

mixture ['mɪkstʃə(r)] *n.* **a)** *(mixing, being mixed)* Mischen, *das; (of harmonies)* Verbinden, *das;* **b)** *(result)* Mischung, *die* (**of** aus); **~ of gases** Gasgemisch, *das;* **he is such a ~** *(fig.)* er ist so unausgeglichen; **c)** *(medicinal preparation)* Mixtur, *die;* **the ~ as before** *(fig.)* die altbekannte Mischung; **d)** *(Motor Veh.: gas or vaporized petrol)* Gemisch, *das;* **e)** *(ready ingredients) see* **mix 3c**; **f) [mechanical] ~:** *(act)* Vermengen, *das; (product)* Gemenge, *das*

'mix-up *n.* Durcheinander, *das; (misunderstanding)* Mißverständnis, *das;* **there has been some sort of ~:** da ist irgend etwas schiefgelaufen *(ugs.)*; **there's been a ~ about who should be invited** es gab einige Verwirrung darüber, wer eingeladen werden sollte

mizen ['mɪzn] *n. (Naut.)* Besan, *der*

mizen: ~-mast *n. (Naut.)* Besanmast, *der;* **~-sail** *n. (Naut.)* Besansegel, *das*

mizzen *see* **mizen**

Mk. *abbr.* **'mark 1 b**

ml. *abbr.* **a) millilitre[s]** ml; **b) mile[s]** M

MLR *abbr.* **minimum lending rate**

mm. *abbr.* **millimetre[s]** mm

mnemonic [nɪ'mɒnɪk] *n.* Gedächtnishilfe, *die;* Eselsbrücke, *die (ugs.)*

mo [məʊ] *n., pl.* **mos** [məʊz] *(sl.)* Moment, *der;* **half a ~, wait a ~:** Momentchen!

mo. *abbr. (Amer.)* **month** Mo.

moa ['məʊə] *n. (Ornith.)* Moa, *der*

moan [məʊn] **1.** *n.* **a)** Stöhnen, *das; (fig.: of wind)* Heulen, *das;* **b)** *(complaint)* **have a ~** *(complain at length)* jammern; *(have a grievance)* eine Beschwerde haben. **2.** *v. i.* **a)** stöhnen (**with** vor + *Dat.*); *(fig.)* ‹*Wind:*› heulen; **b)** *(complain)* jammern (**about** über + *Akk.*); **what is he ~ing [and groaning] about now?** was hat er denn jetzt wieder zu jammern?; **~ at sb.** jmdm. etwas vorjammern. **3.** *v. t.* stöhnen

moat [məʊt] **1.** *n.* [Wasser]graben, *der;* **[castle] ~:** Burggraben, *der.* **2.** *v. t.* mit einem Wassergraben umgeben

mob [mɒb] **1.** *n.* **a)** *(rabble)* Mob, *der (abwertend);* Pöbel, *der (abwertend);* **a ~ gathered outside the police station** eine aufgebrachte Menge versammelte sich vor der Polizeiwache; **b)** *(sl.: associated group)* **~ [of criminals]** Bande, *die (abwertend);* **Peter and his ~:** Peter und seine ganze Blase *(salopp)*; **~ law/rule** Gesetz/Herrschaft der Straße; **c)** *(derog.: populace)* **the ~:** die [breite] Masse. **2.** *v. t.,* **-bb- a)** *(crowd round)* belagern *(ugs.)* ‹*Schauspieler, Star*›; stürmen ‹*Kino*›; **b)** *(attack)* herfallen über (+ *Akk.*); sich stürzen auf (+ *Akk.*); **he was ~bed** sie fielen über ihn her

mobile ['məʊbaɪl] **1.** *adj.* **a)** *(able to move easily)* beweglich; *(on wheels)* fahrbar; **b)** lebhaft ‹*Gesicht[szüge]*›; **c)** *(Mil.)* mobil; **d)** *(accommodated in vehicle)* mobil; fahrbar; **~ library** Fahrbücherei, *die;* **~ canteen** Kantine auf Rädern; **e)** *(in social status)* mobil *(bes. Soziol.)*; *see also* **upwardly**. **2.** *n.* Mobile, *das*

mobile: ~ 'home *n.* transportable Wohneinheit; *(caravan)* Wohnwagen, *der;* **~ 'phone** *n.* Mobiltelefon, *das*

mobilisation, mobilise *see* **mobiliz-**

mobility [mə'bɪlɪtɪ] *n.* **a)** *(ability to move) (of person)* Beweglichkeit, *die; (on wheels)* Fahrbarkeit, *die;* **b)** *(in social status)* Mobilität, *die (bes. Soziol.)*

mo'bility allowance *n. (Brit.) staatliche Geldleistung, die Gehbehinderten gewährt werden kann*

mobilization [məʊbɪlaɪ'zeɪʃn] *n.* **a)** *(act of mobilizing)* Mobilisierung, *die;* **b)** *(Mil.)* Mobilmachung, *die*
mobilize ['məʊbɪlaɪz] *v.t.* **a)** *(render movable or effective)* mobilisieren; **b)** *(Mil.)* mobil machen; *abs.* **make preparations to ~:** die Mobilmachung vorbereiten
mobster ['mɒbstə(r)] *n. (sl.)* Gangster, *der*
moccasin ['mɒkəsɪn] *n.* Mokassin, *der*
mocha ['mɒkə] *n.* Mokka, *der*
mock [mɒk] **1.** *v.t.* **a)** *(subject to ridicule)* sich lustig machen über (+ *Akk.*); verspotten; **he was ~ed** man machte sich über ihn lustig; **b)** *(ridicule by imitation)* **~ sb./sth.** jmdn./etw. nachmachen[, um sich über ihn/darüber lustig zu machen]. **2.** *v.i.* **~ at sb./sth.** sich über jmdn./etw. mokieren *od.* lustig machen. **3.** *attrib. adj.* gespielt ‹*Feierlichkeit, Bescheidenheit, Ernst*›; Schein‹*kampf, -angriff, -ehe*›; **~ Tudor style** Pseudotudorstil, *der;* **~ examination** simulierte Prüfung; **~-turtle soup** Mockturtlesuppe, *die (Kochk.); see also* **orange 1b. 4.** *n. (thing deserving scorn)* **make [a] ~ of sb./sth.** sich über jmdn./etw. lustig machen
mocker ['mɒkə(r)] *n.* **a)** Spötter, *der*/Spötterin, *die;* **b) put the ~s on sb./sth.** *(sl.)* jmdm. alles vermasseln/etw. vermasseln *(salopp)*
mockery ['mɒkərɪ] *n.* **a)** *(inadequate form)* **be a ~ of justice/the truth** der Gerechtigkeit/Wahrheit *(Dat.)* hohnsprechen *(geh.);* **he received only the ~ of a trial** sein Verfahren war eine einzige Farce; **b)** *(futile action)* **it would be a ~ to ...** *(be absurd)* es wäre grotesk *od.* absurd, zu ...; *(be impudent)* es wäre geschmacklos *od.* unverschämt, zu ...; **c)** *no pl., no indef. art. (derision)* Spott, *der;* **d)** *(person or thing derided)* Gespött, *das*
mock-he'roic *adj.* komisch-heroisch *(Literaturw.);* **~ poem** komisches Heldengedicht *od.* Epos
mocking ['mɒkɪŋ] **1.** *adj.* spöttisch. **2.** *n.* Spott, *der*
'mocking-bird *n.* Spottdrossel, *die*
'mock-up *n.* Modell [in Originalgröße]; *(of book etc.)* Layout, *das*
MOD *abbr. (Brit.)* **Ministry of Defence** Verteidigungsministerium, *das*
Mod [mɒd] *n. (Brit.) sich modisch kleidender [Motorroller fahrender] Jugendlicher in den sechziger Jahren;* Mod, *der*
modal ['məʊdl] *adj.* **a)** *(of mode, form)* formal; **b)** *(Ling.)* modal; **~ auxiliary** *or* **verb** Modalverb, *das;* **c)** *(Mus.)* modal
modality [mə'dælɪtɪ] *n.* **the modalities are** *or* **the ~ is as follows** die Modalitäten sind wie folgt
mod cons [mɒd 'kɒnz] *n. pl. (Brit. coll.)* [moderner] Komfort; **have all ~:** mit allem Komfort *od. (ugs.)* allen Schikanen ausgestattet sein
mode [məʊd] *n.* **a)** *(way in which thing is done)* Art [und Weise], *die; (method of procedure)* Methode, *die; (Computing)* Betriebsart, *die;* **~ of behaviour** *or* **conduct/life** Verhaltens-/Lebensweise, *die;* **~ of transport** Transportmittel, *das;* **b)** *(fashion)* Mode, *die;* **the ~ for short skirts** die Mode der kurzen Röcke; **~s and fashions** Moden und Modetrends; **c)** *(Mus.)* Tonart, *die;* **d)** *(Statistics)* Modus, *der (fachspr.);* statistischer Mittelwert
model ['mɒdl] **1.** *n.* **a)** Modell, *das;* **a sports ~:** ein Sportmodell; *see also* **working model; b)** *(perfect example)* Muster, *das* (of an + *Dat.*); *(to be imitated)* Vorbild, *das;* **be a ~ of industry** ein Muster an Fleiß *(Dat.)* sein; **on the ~ of sth.** nach dem Vorbild einer Sache *(Gen.);* **make sth. on the ~ of sth.** etw. einer Sache *(Dat.)* nachbilden; **take sb. as a ~:** [sich *(Dat.)*] jmdn. zum Vorbild nehmen; **c)** *(person employed to pose)* Modell, *das; (Fashion)* Model, *das;* Mannequin, *das; (male)* Dressman, *der;* **photographer's ~:** Fotomodell, *das;* **be a painter's ~:** einem Maler Modell stehen/sitzen. **2.** *adj.* **a)** *(exemplary)* vorbildlich; mustergültig; Muster- *(oft iron.);* **~ child** Musterkind, *das; (boy)* Musterknabe, *der (iron.);* **b)** *(miniature)* Modell‹*stadt, -eisenbahn, -flugzeug*›. **3.** *v.t.*, *(Brit.)* **-ll- a)** *(shape figure of)* modellieren; formen; **~ sth. in clay** etw. in Ton modellieren; **delicately ~led features** *(fig.)* fein geschnittene Gesichtszüge; **b)** *(form in imitation of sth.)* **~ sth. after** *or* **[up]on sth.** etw. einer Sache *(Dat.)* nachbilden; **we ~led our system on the European one** wir haben unser System nach europäischem Vorbild aufgebaut; **~ oneself on sb.** sich *(Dat.)* jmdn. zum Vorbild nehmen; **c)** *(Fashion)* vorführen ‹*Kleid, Entwurf usw.*›. **4.** *v.i.*, *(Brit.)* **-ll- a)** *(Fashion)* als Mannequin *od.* Model arbeiten; ‹*Mann:*› als Dressman arbeiten; *(Photog.)* als [Foto]modell arbeiten; *(Art)* Modell stehen/sitzen; **b) ~ in clay** *etc.* in Ton *usw.* modellieren
modelling (*Amer.:* **modeling**) ['mɒdəlɪŋ] *n.* **a)** *no art. (posing)* **do ~** *(Fashion)* als Mannequin *od.* Model arbeiten; ‹*Mann:*› als Dressman arbeiten; *(Photog., Art)* als Modell arbeiten; **do [some] ~ for sb.** *(Fashion)* jmds. Kreationen vorführen; *(Photog., Art)* jmdm. Modell stehen/sitzen; **b)** *no indef. art. (sculpturing)* Modellieren, *das;* **~ clay** Modellierton, *der*
modem ['məʊdem] *n. (Communications)* Modem, *der*
moderate 1. ['mɒdərət] *adj.* **a)** *(avoiding extremes)* gemäßigt ‹*Partei, Ansichten*›; mäßig, maßvoll ‹*Mensch, bes. Trinker, Esser; Forderungen*›; mäßig ‹*Begeisterung, Interesse*›; **be ~ in one's demands** maßvolle Forderungen erheben *od.* stellen; **b)** *(fairly large or good)* mittler... ‹*Größe, Menge, Wert*›; nicht allzu groß ‹*Entfernung, Wert*›; **[only] ~:** mäßig ‹*Qualität, Ernte*›; **a ~ amount of coal** eine gewisse Menge Kohle; **the water was of only ~ depth** das Wasser war nicht besonders *od.* nur mäßig tief; **c)** *(reasonable)* angemessen, vernünftig ‹*Preis, Summe*›; **d)** mäßig ‹*Wind*›. **2.** ['mɒdərət] Gemäßigte, *der/die;* **be a ~ in politics** gemäßigte politische Ansichten vertreten. **3.** ['mɒdəreɪt] *v.t.* mäßigen ‹*Begierde, Ungeduld, Gefühl*›; lindern ‹*Schmerzen, Sorgen*›; dämpfen ‹*Eifer*›; zügeln ‹*Begeisterung*›; senken ‹*Stimme*›; mildern ‹*negativen Effekt*›; **~ one's demands** seine Forderungen einschränken *od.* abschwächen. **4.** ['mɒdəreɪt] *v.i.* nachlassen; ‹*Forderungen:*› gemäßigter *od.* maßvoller werden
moderately ['mɒdərətlɪ] *adv.* einigermaßen; mäßig ‹*begeistert, groß, begabt; rauchen*›; **there was only a ~ large audience** es waren nicht übermäßig viele Zuschauer da; **be only ~ enthusiastic/concerned about sth.** sich nicht allzu sehr *od.* übermäßig für etw. begeistern/sich keine allzu großen Sorgen um etw. machen
moderation [mɒdə'reɪʃn] *n.* **a)** *(moderating)* Mäßigung, *die; (of wind, fever)* Nachlassen, *das;* **b)** *no pl. (moderateness)* Mäßigkeit, *die; (of demands etc.)* Angemessenheit, *die;* Vernünftigkeit, *die;* **~ in all things** alles mit Maßen; **in ~:** mit *od.* in Maßen
moderator ['mɒdəreɪtə(r)] *n.* **a)** *(arbitrator)* Schlichter, *der; (mediator)* Vermittler, *der*/Vermittlerin, *die;* **b)** *(presiding officer)* Vorsitzende, *der/die;* **c)** *(Eccl.)* Moderator, *der*
modern ['mɒdn] **1.** *adj.* **a)** *(of the present)* modern; heutig ‹*Zeit[alter], Welt, Mensch*›; **~ jazz** Modern Jazz, *der;* **in ~ times** in der heutigen Zeit; **~ English** modernes Englisch; **~ history** neuere Geschichte; **~ languages** neuere Sprachen; *(subject of study)* Neuphilologie, *die;* **~ maths** die neue Mathematik; *see also* **Latin 2; b)** *(in current fashion)* modern; neumodisch *(oft abwertend);* **the ~ fashion is to wear a hat** es ist [jetzt] Mode, einen Hut zu tragen. **2.** *n. usu. in pl.* moderner Mensch; *(Art)* Modernist, *der*/Modernistin, *die; (person alive at present)* Zeitgenosse, *der*/-genossin, *die*
'modern-day *attrib. adj.* von heute *nachgestellt;* heutig
modernisation, modernise *see* **modernize**
modernism ['mɒdənɪzm] *n.* Modernismus, *der*
modernist ['mɒdənɪst] *n.* Modernist, *der*/Modernistin, *die*
modernistic [mɒdə'nɪstɪk] *adj.* modernistisch
modernity [mə'dɜ:nɪtɪ] *n.* Modernität, *die*
modernization [mɒdənaɪ'zeɪʃn] *n.* **a)** *(modernizing)* Modernisierung, *die;* **b)** *(version)* modernisierte Fassung
modernize ['mɒdənaɪz] **1.** *v.t.* modernisieren. **2.** *v.i.* sich der modernen Zeit anpassen
modest ['mɒdɪst] *adj.* **a)** *(not conceited)* bescheiden; *(shy)* bescheiden; zurückhaltend; **be ~ about one's achievements** nicht mit seinen Leistungen prahlen; **b)** *(not excessive)* bescheiden *(auch iron.);* genügsam, anspruchslos ‹*Mensch*›; vorsichtig ‹*Schätzung*›; **c)** *(unpretentious in appearance, amount, etc.)* bescheiden; einfach, unauffällig ‹*Haus, Kleidung*›; **have a ~ life-style** bescheiden *od.* einfach leben; **~ in appearance** unauffällig; **d)** *(decorous, chaste)* anständig ‹*Charakter*›; anständig, *(veralt.)* sittsam ‹*Mensch, Benehmen*›; schicklich ‹*Benehmen, Ausdrucksweise*›; dezent, unauffällig ‹*Kleidung*›
modestly ['mɒdɪstlɪ] *adv.* **a)** *(not conceitedly)* bescheiden; **b)** *(decently)* dezent, unauffällig *(sich kleiden);* schicklich, sittsam *(veralt.)* ‹*sich benehmen*›
modesty ['mɒdɪstɪ] *n., no pl.* **a)** *(freedom from conceit)* Bescheidenheit, *die;* **in all ~:** bei aller Bescheidenheit; **the [sheer] ~ of the man!** *(iron.)* die Bescheidenheit in Person!; **b) the ~ of their demands** ihre maßvollen Forderungen; **c)** *(regard for propriety) see* **modest d:** Anständigkeit, *die;* Sittsamkeit, *die (veralt.);* Schicklichkeit, *die;* Unauffälligkeit, *die;* Dezentheit, *die*
modicum ['mɒdɪkəm] *n.* Minimum, *das;* **a ~ of luck/truth** ein Quentchen Glück/ein Körnchen Wahrheit
modification [mɒdɪfɪ'keɪʃn] *n.* [Ab]änderung, *die;* Modifizierung, *die;* **without any sort of ~:** ohne jede Änderung
modifier ['mɒdɪfaɪə(r)] *n. (esp. Ling., Biol.)* Modifikator, *der*
modify ['mɒdɪfaɪ] *v.t.* **a)** *(make changes in)* [ab-, ver]ändern; modifizieren; **b)** *(tone down)* mäßigen; mildern ‹*Klima*›; **~ one's position** in seiner Haltung gemäßigter werden; **you'd better ~ your tone** mäßigen Sie sich mal in Ihrem Ton!; **c)** *(Ling.) (qualify sense of)* näher bestimmen ‹*Verb, Adjektiv usw.*›; *(change by umlaut)* umlauten ‹*Vokal*›
modish ['məʊdɪʃ] *adj.* modisch
modular ['mɒdjʊlə(r)] *adj.* **a)** *(employing module[s])* aus Elementen [zusammengesetzt]; *(in construction)* aus Baueinheiten *od.* -elementen [zusammengesetzt]; **~ system** Baukastensystem, *das;* **~ construction/design** Konstruktion/Entwurf nach dem Baukastensystem; **~ unit** [Bau-, Konstruktions]element, *das;* **b)** *(Educ.)* **~ course** *aus vielen verschiedenen, beliebig kombinierten Unterrichtseinheiten bestehender Kurs*
modulate ['mɒdjʊleɪt] **1.** *v.t.* **a)** *(regulate)* abstimmen (**to** auf + *Akk.*); anpassen (**to** *Dat.*, an + *Akk.*); **b)** *(adjust pitch)* modulieren ‹*Stimme, Sprache, Ton*›; **c)** *(Radio)* modulieren ‹*Welle, Sender*›. **2.** *v.i.* modulieren; **~ from one key to another** von einer Tonart in die andere übergehen

modulation [mɒdjʊˈleɪʃn] *n.* Modulation, *die*
modulator [ˈmɒdjʊleɪtə(r)] *n.* *(Electronics)* Modulator, *der*
module [ˈmɒdju:l] *n.* **a)** *(in construction or system)* Bauelement, *das; (Electronics)* Modul, *das;* **b)** *(Educ.)* Unterrichtseinheit, *die;* **c)** *(Astronaut.)* **command ~:** Kommandoeinheit *od.* -kapsel, *die; see also* **lunar module**
modulus [ˈmɒdjʊləs] *n., pl.* **moduli** [ˈmɒdjʊlaɪ] *(Math., Phys.)* Modul, *der*
modus operandi [məʊdəs ɒpəˈrændi:] *n.* Modus operandi, *der (geh.)*
modus vivendi [məʊdəs vɪˈvendɪ:] *n.* Modus vivendi, *der (geh.)*
mog [mɒg], **moggie** [ˈmɒgɪ] *ns. (Brit. sl.)* Katze, *die;* Katzenvieh, *das (abwertend)*
Mogul [ˈməʊgl, məʊˈgʌl] **1.** *n.* **a)** *(Hist.: Mongolian)* Mongole, *der*/Mongolin, *die;* **the Great** *or* **Grand ~:** der Großmogul; **b)** **m~** *(coll.: important person)* Mogul, *der (fig.).* **2.** *adj. (Hist.)* mongolisch; **the ~ empire** das Reich der Moguln
mohair [ˈməʊheə(r)] *n.* Mohair, *der; (yarn)* Mohair- *od.* Angorawolle, *die*
Mohammedan [məˈhæmɪdən] *see* **Muhammadan**
moist [mɔɪst] *adj.* feucht (**with** von)
moisten [ˈmɔɪsn] *v.t.* anfeuchten; feucht machen; **~ one's lips** sich *(Dat.)* die Lippen [mit der Zunge] befeuchten
moisture [ˈmɔɪstʃə(r)] *n.* Feuchtigkeit, *die;* **~ in the air** Luftfeuchtigkeit, *die;* **film of ~:** Feuchtigkeitsfilm, *der*
moisturise, moisturiser, moisturising *see* **moisturiz-**
moisturize [ˈmɔɪstjʊraɪz, ˈmɔɪstʃəraɪz] *v.t.* befeuchten; **~ the skin** der Haut *(Dat.)* Feuchtigkeit zuführen; ⟨*Creme:*⟩ der Haut *(Dat.)* Feuchtigkeit verleihen
moisturizer [ˈmɔɪstjʊraɪzə(r), ˈmɔɪstʃəraɪzə(r)], **ˈmoisturizing cream** *ns.* Feuchtigkeitscreme, *die*
moke [məʊk] *n. (Brit. sl.)* Esel, *der*
molar [ˈməʊlə(r)] **1.** *n.* Backenzahn, *der;* Molar[zahn], *der (Anat.);* Mahlzahn, *der (bes. Zool.).* **2.** *adj.* **~ tooth** *see* **1**
molasses [məˈlæsɪz] *n.* **a)** *(syrup drained from raw sugar)* Melasse, *die;* **b)** *(Amer.: treacle)* Sirup, *der*
mold *(Amer.) see* [1, 2, 3]**mould**
Moldavia [mɒlˈdeɪvɪə] *pr. n.* Moldau, *die*
molder, molding, moldy *(Amer.) see* **mould-**
[1]**mole** [məʊl] *n. (on skin)* Leberfleck, *der;* Pigmentfleck, *der (Med.); (prominent)* Muttermal, *das*
[2]**mole** *n.* **a)** *(animal)* Maulwurf, *der;* **b)** *(coll.: spy)* Maulwurf, *der (ugs.)*
[3]**mole** *n.* **a)** *(breakwater)* Mole, *die;* **b)** *(artificial harbour)* [künstlicher] Hafen
[4]**mole** *n. (Chem.)* Mol, *das*
molecular [məˈlekjʊlə(r)] *adj. (Phys., Chem.)* molekular; **~ weight/biology** Molekulargewicht, *das*/-biologie, *die*
molecule [ˈmɒlɪkju:l, ˈməʊlɪkju:l] *n.* **a)** *(Phys., Chem.)* Molekül, *das;* **b)** *(small particle)* winziges Teilchen
ˈmolehill *n.* Maulwurfshügel, *der;* **make a mountain out of a ~** *(fig.)* aus einer Mücke einen Elefanten machen *(ugs.)*
molest [məˈlest] *v.t.* **a)** belästigen; *(to rob)* überfallen; **b)** *(sexually)* [unsittlich] belästigen
molestation [məʊlɪˈsteɪʃn, mɒlɪˈsteɪʃn] *n.* **a)** Belästigung, *die; (to rob)* Überfallen, *das;* **b)** *(sexual)* [unsittliche] Belästigung
moll [mɒl] *n. (coll.)* Gangsterbraut, *die*
mollify [ˈmɒlɪfaɪ] *v.t.* besänftigen; beschwichtigen; **be finally mollified** sich schließlich beruhigen
mollusc *(Amer.:* **mollusk)** [ˈmɒləsk] *n. (Zool.)* Molluske, *die (fachspr.);* Weichtier, *das*

mollycoddle [ˈmɒlɪkɒdl] **1.** *v.t.* [ver]hätscheln *(oft abwertend);* verzärteln *(abwertend).* **2.** *n.* Weichling, *der (abwertend)*
molt *(Amer.) see* **moult**
molten [ˈməʊltn] *adj.* geschmolzen; flüssig ⟨*Lava*⟩
molybdenum [məˈlɪbdɪnəm] *n. (Chem.)* Molybdän, *das*
mom [mɒm] *(Amer. coll.) see* [2]**mum**
moment [ˈməʊmənt] *n.* **a)** Moment, *der;* Augenblick, *der;* **barely a ~ had elapsed ...:** es war kaum eine Minute vergangen ...; **help came not a ~ too soon** die Hilfe hätte keinen Moment später kommen dürfen; **for a ~ or two** für einen kurzen Augenblick; **for a few ~s** für ein paar Augenblicke; ein paar Augenblicke lang; **there was never a dull ~:** man langweilte sich keinen Augenblick lang; **at this ~ in time** in diesem Moment *od.* Augenblick; **after a ~'s hesitation** nach kurzem Zögern; **at any ~,** *(coll.)* **any ~:** jeden Augenblick *od.* Moment; **on the spur of the ~:** ganz spontan; **it was over in just a few ~s** es dauerte nur wenige Augenblicke *od.* war im Nu geschehen; **it is the ~ [for sth.]** es ist der richtige Zeitpunkt [für etw.]; **this is the ~!** dies ist der geeignete Augenblick!; **a few ~s of peace** ein paar Minuten der Ruhe; ein paar ruhige Minuten; **the film had its ~s** der Film hatte einige starke Stellen; **he has his ~s** manchmal ist er gar nicht so übel *(ugs.);* **at odd ~s** gelegentlich[, wenn ein wenig Zeit ist]; **a ~ to remember** ein denkwürdiger Augenblick; **at the precise ~ she came in ...:** genau in dem Augenblick *od.* gerade, als sie hereintrat, ...; **the ~ I get home** gleich *od.* sofort, wenn ich nach Hause komme; **one** *or* **half a** *or* **just a** *or* **wait a ~!** einen Moment *od.* Augenblick!; Moment[chen] *od.* Augenblick mal!; **in a ~** *(instantly)* im Nu *(ugs.); (very soon)* sofort; gleich; **for a ~:** einen Moment [lang]; für einen Moment; **not for a ~:** keinen Moment [lang]; **[at] the [very] ~ it happened** in dem *od.* im selben Augenblick, als es passierte; **the ~ of truth** die Stunde der Wahrheit; **at the ~:** im Augenblick; momentan; **for the ~:** im *od.* für den Augenblick; vorläufig; **I shan't be a ~** *(I'll be back very soon)* ich bin sofort zurück; *(I have very nearly finished)* ich bin sofort soweit; **have you got a ~?** hast du mal einen Augenblick Zeit?; **be the man of the ~:** der Mann des Tages sein; **come here this ~!** komm sofort *od.* auf der Stelle her!; **just this ~:** soeben; gerade *od.* eben [erst]; **from ~ to ~:** alle Augenblicke; **b)** *(formal: importance)* **of ~:** von Bedeutung; **of little** *or* **small/no ~:** von geringer/ohne Bedeutung; **c)** *(Phys.)* Moment, *das;* **~ of inertia** Trägheitsmoment, *das*
momentarily [ˈməʊməntərɪlɪ] *adv.* **a)** *(for a moment)* einen Augenblick lang; *(for a while)* vorübergehend; **b)** *(Amer.) (at any moment)* jeden Augenblick *od.* Moment; *(in a few minutes)* in wenigen Minuten
momentary [ˈməʊməntərɪ] *adj.* **a)** *(lasting only a moment)* kurz; **a ~ forgetfulness/aberration** ein Augenblick geistiger Abwesenheit/der Verwirrung; **b)** *(transitory)* vorübergehend
momentous [məˈmentəs] *adj. (important)* bedeutsam; bedeutungsvoll; *(of consequence)* folgenschwer; von großer Tragweite *nachgestellt;* **of ~ importance** von entscheidender Bedeutung
momentum [məˈmentəm] *n., pl.* **momenta** [məˈmentə] **a)** *(impetus)* Schwung, *der;* **lose ~:** Schwung *od.* Fahrt verlieren; *(fig.)* [an] Schwung *od.* Fahrt verlieren; *see also* **gain 2 c; gather 1 c; b)** *(Mech.)* Impuls, *der; see also* **angular c; conservation b**
mommy [ˈmɒmɪ] *(Amer. coll.) see* [2]**mummy**
Mon. *abbr.* **Monday** Mo.
Monaco [ˈmɒnəkəʊ] *pr. n.* Monaco *(das)*

monarch [ˈmɒnək] *n. (king, emperor, etc.)* Monarch, *der*/Monarchin, *die; (supreme ruler)* [Allein]herrscher, *der*/-herrscherin, *die*
monarchic [məˈnɑ:kɪk], **monarchical** [məˈnɑ:kɪkl] *adj.* **a)** *(of government)* monarchisch; **b)** *(of monarchy)* monarchistisch
monarchism [ˈmɒnəkɪzm] *n. (monarchical government)* Monarchie, *die; (attachment to monarchy)* Monarchismus, *der*
monarchist [ˈmɒnəkɪst] *n.* Monarchist, *der*/Monarchistin, *die*
monarchy [ˈmɒnəkɪ] *n.* Monarchie, *die; see also* **constitutional 1 b**
monastery [ˈmɒnəstrɪ] *n.* [Mönchs]kloster, *das*
monastic [məˈnæstɪk] *adj.* **a)** *(of or like monks)* mönchisch; **b)** *(of monasteries)* klösterlich; Kloster⟨*gebäude, -architektur*⟩
monasticism [məˈnæstɪsɪzm] *n.* Mönch[s]tum, *das*
Monday [ˈmʌndeɪ, ˈmʌndɪ] **1.** *n.* Montag, *der.* **2.** *adv. (coll.)* **she comes ~s** sie kommt montags. *See also* **Friday**
monetarism [ˈmʌnɪtərɪzm] *n. (Econ.)* Monetarismus, *der*
monetarist [ˈmʌnɪtərɪst] *n. (Econ.)* Monetarist, *der*/Monetaristin, *die*
monetary [ˈmʌnɪtərɪ] *adj.* **a)** *(of the currency in use)* monetär; Währungs⟨*politik, -system*⟩; **b)** *(of money)* finanziell; **~ gift** Geldgeschenk, *das*
money [ˈmʌnɪ] *n.* **a)** *no pl.* Geld, *das;* **your ~ or your life!** Geld oder Leben!; **be in the ~** *(coll.) (be winning ~ prizes)* am Scheffeln sein *(ugs.); (have plenty of ~)* im Geld schwimmen *(ugs.);* **there is ~ in sth.** mit etw. kann man [viel] Geld verdienen; **~ for jam** *or* **old rope** *(Brit. fig. coll.)* leicht *od.* schnell verdientes Geld; **make ~** ⟨*Person:*⟩ [viel] Geld verdienen, *(ugs.)* [das große] Geld machen; ⟨*Geschäft:*⟩ etwas einbringen, sich rentieren; **earn good ~:** gut verdienen; **come into ~:** zu Geld kommen; **~ talks** das Geld macht's *(ugs.);* **~ makes the world go round** Geld regiert die Welt; **put ~ into sth.** Geld in etw. *(Akk.)* investieren *od. (ugs.)* hineinstecken; **have ~ to burn** *(fig. coll.)* Geld wie Heu haben *(ugs.);* **[not] be made of ~** *(fig. coll.)* [k]ein Goldesel *od.* Krösus sein; **spend ~ like water** mit dem Geld nur so um sich werfen *(ugs.);* **good ~** *(earned/spent)* gutes/teueres Geld; **this would only be to throw** *or* **pour good ~ after bad** das wäre nur rausgeschmissenes *od.* rausgeworfenes Geld *(ugs.);* **for ˈmy ~:** wenn man mich fragt; **he/she is the one for my ~:** ich tippe auf ihn/sie; **put one's ~ on sth.** auf etw. *(Akk.)* wetten *od.* setzen; *(fig.)* [seine Hoffnung] auf etw. *(Akk.)* setzen; **the best that ~ can buy** das Beste, was es für Geld gibt; **~ can't buy happiness!** Geld allein macht nicht glücklich!; **~ supply** Geldmenge, *die;* **b)** *pl.* **~s** *or* **monies** [ˈmʌnɪz] *(sum of money)* Geld, *das;* [Geld]betrag, *der;* **the rent ~:** [das Geld für] die Miete; **c)** *(rich person[s])* **that's not where the real ~ lives** da ist nicht das große Geld zu Hause. *See also* **account 3 a; big 1 a; conscience money; cost 2 a; love 1 a; run 1 a**
money: ~-back *attrib. adj.* **~-back guarantee** Geld-zurück-Garantie, *die;* **~-bag** *n.* Geldsack, *der;* **~-bags** *n. sing. (coll.: person)* Geldsack, *der (ugs. abwertend);* **~-box** *n.* Sparbüchse, *die; (for collection)* Sammelbüchse, *die;* **~-changer** *n.* Geldwechsler, *der*
moneyed [ˈmʌnɪd] *adj. (rich)* vermögend; begütert; **the ~ classes** die besitzenden Klassen
money: ~-grubber *n.* Raffzahn, *der (ugs.);* **~-grubbing 1.** *adj.* geldgierig *(abwertend);* **2.** *n.* Geldgier, *die (abwertend);* **~-lender** *n.* Geldverleiher, *der;* **~-maker** *n.* **be a ~-maker** ⟨*Projekt, Produkt, Film:*⟩

Geld bringen; ~-**making** 1. *adj.* gewinnbringend, einträglich ‹*Geschäft, Beschäftigung*›; 2. *n., no pl.* Geldverdienen, *das;* ~-**market** *n.* Geldmarkt, *der;* ~ **order** *n.* Zahlungsanweisung, *die; (issued by Post Office)* Postanweisung, *die;* ~-**spinner** *n. (Brit.)* Verkaufsschlager, *der; (business)* Goldgrube, *die (ugs.);* **he turned that idea into a ~-spinner** er hat diese Idee versilbert *(ugs.);* ~'**s-worth** *n.* **get** *or* **have one's ~'s-worth** etwas für sein Geld bekommen

Mongol ['mɒŋgl] 1. *n.* a) Mongole, *der*/Mongolin, *die; (Anthrop.)* Mongolide, *der/die;* b) **m~** *(Med.)* Mongoloide, *der/die;* **she is a m~:** sie ist mongoloid. 2. *adj.* a) mongolisch; *(Anthrop.)* mongolid; b) **m~** *(Med.)* mongoloid

Mongolia [mɒŋ'gəʊlɪə] *pr. n.* Mongolei, *die*

Mongolian [mɒŋ'gəʊlɪən] 1. *adj.* a) mongolisch; b) *(Anthrop.)* mongolid *(fachspr.);* mongolisch. 2. *n.* a) *(person)* Mongole, *der*/Mongolin, *die;* b) *(Anthrop.)* Mongolide, *der/die;* c) *(language)* Mongolisch, *das;* das Mongolische

mongolism ['mɒŋgəlɪzm] *n. (Med.)* Mongolismus, *der*

mongoose ['mɒŋgu:s] *n. (Zool.)* Indischer Mungo

mongrel ['mʌŋgrəl, 'mɒŋgrəl] 1. *n.* a) *(Bot., Zool.)* Bastard, *der (fachspr.);* Hybride, *der (fachspr.);* Kreuzung, *die; (often derog.: dog)* Promenadenmischung, *die (scherzh., auch abwertend);* b) *(derog.: person)* Mischling, *der;* Bastard, *der (derb abwertend).* 2. *adj. (of mixed origin)* hybrid *(fachspr.)* ‹*Pflanze, Tier*›; ~ **animal/plant** [tierischer/pflanzlicher] Hybride *od.* Bastard *(fachspr.);* [Tier-/Pflanzen]kreuzung, *die*

moni[c]ker ['mɒnɪkə(r)] *n. (sl.)* Name, *der; (nickname)* Spitzname, *der*

monitor ['mɒnɪtə(r)] 1. *n.* a) *(Sch.)* Aufsichtsschüler, *der*/-schülerin, *die;* **pencil/milk/lunch ~:** Bleistift-/Milch-/Essen[s]wart, *der;* **school ~:** Präfekt, *der;* b) *(Zool.)* ~ **[lizard]** Waran, *der;* c) *(listener)* Mithörer, *der*/Mithörerin, *die;* d) *(Mech. Engin., Phys., Med., Telev.)* Monitor, *der.* 2. *v. t.* a) *(maintain surveillance over)* kontrollieren ‹*Strahlungsintensität*›; beobachten ‹*Wetter, Flugzeug, Gewohnheit, Bewegung*›; abhören ‹*Sendung, Telefongespräch*›; b) *(regulate)* kontrollieren ‹*Radio-, Fernsehempfang*›; überwachen ‹*Verteilung, Ein-/Ausfuhr*›

monk [mʌŋk] *n.* Mönch, *der;* **order of ~s** Mönchsorden, *der; see also* **White Monk**

monkey ['mʌŋkɪ] 1. *n.* a) Affe, *der;* **the three wise ~s** *(Mythol.)* die „Drei Affen"; **make a ~ of sb.** *(sl.)* jmdn. zum Gespött machen; **get one's ~ up** *(Brit. sl.)* auf die Palme gehen *(ugs.);* **sb.'s ~ is up** *(Brit. sl.)* jmd. ist auf der Palme; **I'll be a ~'s uncle!** *(sl.)* ich denk', mich laust der Affe *(ugs.);* b) *(in playful abuse)* Schlingel, *der (scherzh.);* **cheeky ~:** Frechdachs, *der (fam.);* c) *(sl.: £500, $500)* halber Riese *(salopp).* 2. *v. i.* ~ **about** *or* **around [with]** *(coll.)* herumalbern [mit] *(ugs.)* ‹*Person*›; *(interfere)* herumspielen [mit *od.* an (+ *Dat.*)] ‹*Gegenstand*›

monkey: ~ **business** *n. (coll.) (mischief)* Schabernack, *der; (unlawful or unfair activities)* krumme Touren *Pl. (ugs.);* ~-**jacket** *n. (Naut., Fashion)* Monkijacke, *die;* Affenjäckchen, *das (Soldatenspr. scherzh.);* ~-**nut** *n. (Bot.)* Erdnuß, *die;* ~-**puzzle** *n. (Bot.)* Chilefichte, *die;* Araukarie, *die (fachspr.);* ~-**tricks** *n. pl. (Brit. sl.)* **be up to one's ~-tricks** etw. aushecken; **no ~-tricks!** mach keinen Quatsch *(ugs.);* ~-**wrench** *n.* Rollgabelschlüssel, *der (fachspr.);* Universalschraubenschlüssel, *der*

monkish ['mʌŋkɪʃ] *adj.* a) mönchisch; Mönchs‹*kleidung*›; Kloster‹*leben, -bibliothek*›; b) *(derog.: sanctimonious)* pfäffisch *(abwertend);* c) *(modest)* anspruchslos; d) *(derog.: unsociable)* ungesellig

monkshood ['mʌŋkshʊd] *n. (Bot.)* Blauer Eisenhut

mono ['mɒnəʊ] *adj.* Mono‹*platte[nspieler], -wiedergabe*›

monochrome ['mɒnəkrəʊm] 1. *n.* a) *(picture)* monochromes *(fachspr.) od.* einfarbiges Bild; b) *(representation)* monochrome *(fachspr.) od.* einfarbige Darstellung; **in ~:** monochrom *(fachspr.);* einfarbig; Schwarzweiß- *(Ferns.).* 2. *adj.* monochrom *(fachspr.);* einfarbig; Schwarzweiß- *(Ferns.)*

monocle ['mɒnəkl] *n.* Monokel, *das;* Einglas, *das (veralt.)*

monocotyledon [mɒnəkɒtɪ'li:dn] *n. (Bot.)* Monokotyle[done], *die (fachspr.);* einkeimblättrige Pflanze

monocycle ['mɒnəsaɪkl] *n.* Einrad, *das*

monogamous [mə'nɒgəməs] *adj.* monogam

monogamy [mə'nɒgəmɪ] *n.* Monogamie, *die;* Einehe, *die*

monogram ['mɒnəgræm] *n.* Monogramm, *das*

monogrammed ['mɒnəgræmd] *adj.* monogrammiert; ‹*Taschentuch usw.:*› mit Monogramm

monograph ['mɒnəgra:f] *n.* Monographie, *die;* Einzeldarstellung, *die*

monohull ['mɒnəhʌl] *n. (Naut.)* Einrumpfschiff, *das;* Einkörperschiff, *das*

monolingual [mɒnə'lɪŋgwəl] *adj.* einsprachig

monolith ['mɒnəlɪθ] *n. (Prehist., Building; lit. or fig.)* Monolith, *der*

monolithic [mɒnə'lɪθɪk] *adj. (Prehist., Building; lit. or fig.)* monolithisch; Monolith‹*denkmal, -säule, -charakter, -beton*›

monologue (*Amer.:* **monolog**) ['mɒnəlɒg] *n. (lit. or fig.)* Monolog, *der*

monomania [mɒnə'meɪnɪə] *n.* a) *(Med., Psych.)* Monomanie, *die;* b) *(fig.)* übertriebene Begeisterung (**for** für); Leidenschaft, *die* (**for** für)

monophonic [mɒnə'fɒnɪk] *adj.* monophon

monoplane ['mɒnəpleɪn] *n. (Aeronaut.)* Eindecker, *der*

monopolisation, monopolise *see* **monopoliz-**

monopolistic [mənɒpə'lɪstɪk] *adj. (Econ.)* monopolistisch ‹*Wettbewerb usw.*›

monopolization [mənɒpəlaɪ'zeɪʃn] *n. (Econ.)* Monopolisierung, *die*

monopolize [mə'nɒpəlaɪz] *v. t. (Econ.)* monopolisieren; *(fig.)* mit Beschlag belegen; ~ **the conversation** den/die anderen nicht zu Wort kommen lassen

monopoly [mə'nɒpəlɪ] *n.* a) *(Econ.)* Monopol, *das* (**of** auf + *Dat.*); b) *(exclusive possession)* alleiniger Besitz; c) *(thing monopolized)* Monopol, *das;* d) **M~, (P)** *(game)* Monopoly Ⓦ, *das*

monorail ['mɒnəreɪl] *n.* a) *(single rail)* Einschienengleis, *das;* b) *(vehicle)* Einschienenbahn, *die;* c) *(overhead)* Schwebebahn, *die*

monosyllabic [mɒnəsɪ'læbɪk] *adj.* a) einsilbig ‹*Antwort, Person*›; aus einsilbigen Wörtern bestehend ‹*Rede, Dichtung, Schrift, Sprache*›; b) *(Ling.)* monosyllabisch

monosyllable ['mɒnəsɪləbl] *n.* a) einsilbiges Wort; **speak** *or* **talk/answer in ~s** einsilbig reden/antworten; b) *(Ling.)* Einsilber, *der*

monotheism ['mɒnəθi:ɪzm] *n. (Relig.)* **[doctrine of/belief in] ~:** Monotheismus, *der*

monotheistic [mɒnəθi:'ɪstɪk] *adj. (Relig.)* monotheistisch

monotone ['mɒnətəʊn] 1. *n.* a) gleichbleibender Ton; b) *(uniformity) (general)* Einerlei, *das; (of colour)* Einfarbigkeit, *die; (of style)* eintöniger *od.* monotoner Stil; **grey ~:** graues Einerlei; **engravings in ~:** einfarbige Stiche. 2. *adj.* a) *(monotonous)* eintönig, monoton ‹*Geräusch, Sprache, Akzent, Rezitation*›; b) *(in one colour)* einfarbig

monotonous [mə'nɒtənəs] *adj.* eintönig, monoton ‹*Laut, Leben, Landschaft usw.*›

monotonously [mə'nɒtənəslɪ] *adv.* eintönig

monotonousness [mə'nɒtənəsnɪs], **monotony** [mə'nɒtənɪ] *ns.* Eintönigkeit, *die;* Monotonie, *die*

monoxide [mə'nɒksaɪd] *n. (Chem.)* Monoxyd, *das;* Monoxid, *das (fachspr.)*

Monseigneur [mɔ̃se'njɜ:(r)] *n., pl.* **Messeigneurs** [mese'njɜ:(r)] Monseigneur, *der*

Monsignor [mɒn'si:njɔ:(r)] *n., pl.* ~i [mɒnsi:'njɔ:ri:] *(Eccl.)* Monsignore, *der*

monsoon [mɒn'su:n] *n. (Geog.)* a) *(wind)* **summer** *or* **wet/dry ~:** Sommer-/Wintermonsun, *der;* b) *(season)* Regenzeit, *die*

monster ['mɒnstə(r)] 1. *n.* a) *(imaginary or huge creature)* Ungeheuer, *das;* Monster, *das; (huge thing)* Ungetüm, *das;* Monstrum, *das;* **a ~ of a fish/car** ein Ungeheuer/Ungetüm von einem Fisch/Auto; **that's a real ~!, what a ~!** *(in surprise or admiration)* das ist ja ungeheuer!; b) *(inhuman person)* Unmensch, *der; (iron.: naughty child)* Monster, *das (scherzh.).* 2. *adj.* riesig; monströs; Mammut‹*sitzung, -veranstaltung*›

monstrance ['mɒnstrəns] *n. (RC Ch.)* Monstranz, *die*

monstrosity [mɒn'strɒsɪtɪ] *n.* a) *(physical deformity)* Mißbildung, *die; (deviation from the norm, unnatural thing)* Abnormität, *die;* Widernatürlichkeit, *die;* b) *(outrageous thing)* Ungeheuerlichkeit, *die; (hideous building etc.)* Ungetüm, *das;* c) *(imaginary or huge creature)* Ungeheuer, *das;* Monster, *das*

monstrous ['mɒnstrəs] *adj.* a) *(huge)* monströs *(geh.);* ungeheuer ‹*Lärm, Jubel, Menge*›; riesig ‹*Lkw, Kuchen, Buch*›; unnatürlich groß ‹*Gemüse, Person, Baum, Pflanze*›; b) *(outrageous)* ungeheuerlich *(abwertend)* ‹*Vorschlag, Vorstellung, Glaube, Einstellung, Wahl, Entscheidung*›; c) *(atrocious)* scheußlich *(emotional);* monströs *(meist abwertend);* d) *(misshapen)* mißgestaltet

monstrously ['mɒnstrəslɪ] *adv.* a) *(hugely)* schrecklich *(ugs.),* furchtbar *(ugs.)* ‹*hoch, beschäftigt, kurz, dick*›; b) *(outrageously)* unmöglich *(ugs. meist abwertend)* ‹*sich benehmen*›

mons Veneris [mɒnz 'venərɪs] *n. (Anat.)* Venushügel, *der (fachspr.);* weiblicher Schamberg

montage [mɒn'tɑ:ʒ] *n. (Photog., Art, Radio, Film)* Montage, *die; (Mus.)* Collage, *die;* **work in ~:** Montagen herstellen

month [mʌnθ] *n.* a) Monat, *der;* **last day of the ~:** Monatsletzte, *der;* Ultimo, *der (Kaufmannsspr.);* **on the last day of the ~:** ultimo; am Monatsletzten; **the ~ of January** der [Monat] Januar; **come every ~:** jeden Monat kommen; **for a ~/several ~s** einen Monat [lang]/mehrere Monate [lang] *od.* monatelang; **for ~s [on end]** monatelang; **I haven't seen him for ~s** ich habe ihn seit Monaten nicht mehr gesehen; **~s ago** vor Monaten; **every six ~s** alle sechs Monate; halbjährlich; **once every** *or* **a ~:** einmal monatlich *od.* im Monat; **in a ~['s time]** in einem Monat; **in two ~s[' time]** in zwei Monaten; **in alternate ~s** alle zwei Monate; **take a ~'s holiday** [sich *(Dat.)*] einen Monat Urlaub nehmen; **£10 a** *or* **per ~:** zehn Pfund im Monat; **from ~ to ~:** Monat um *od.* für Monat; **she is in the third/last ~ of her pregnancy** sie ist im dritten/neunten Monat schwanger; **a ~ from today** heute in einem Monat; **a three-~ period** ein Zeitraum von drei Monaten; **a six-~[s]-old baby/strike** ein sechs Monate altes *od.* sechsmonatiges Baby/ein bereits sechsmonatiger Streik; *see also* **calendar a; next 1 b; Sunday 1 a; this 1 e;** b) *(period of 28 days)* vier Wochen; 28 Tage

'month-long *attrib. adj.* einmonatig
monthly ['mʌnθlı] **1.** *adj.* **a)** *(of or relating to a month)* monatlich; Monats⟨*umsatz, -einkommen, -gehalt*⟩; **three-~:** dreimonatlich; vierteljährlich; **b)** *(lasting a month)* einmonatig ⟨*Abstand*⟩; Monats⟨*zyklus, -karte*⟩; **three-~ season ticket** Dreimonats- *od.* Vierteljahreskarte, *die;* **c)** *(happening every month)* monatlich; *(happening once a month)* [ein]monatlich; **a woman's ~ period** die Periode *od.* Monatsblutung einer Frau. **2.** *adv.* [ein]monatlich; einmal im Monat. **3.** *n. (publication)* monatlich erscheinende Zeitschrift; Monatsschrift, *die*
monument ['mɒnjʊmənt] *n.* **a)** Denkmal, *das; see also* **ancient 1 b; b)** *(on grave)* Grabmal, *das (geh.);* **c) the M~:** *in der Londoner Innenstadt stehende Säule zur Erinnerung an den großen Brand von 1666*
monumental [mɒnjʊ'mentl] *adj.* **a)** *(of a monument)* Denkmals⟨*architekt, -inschrift*⟩; **b)** *(massive)* gewaltig ⟨*Auffahrt, Skulptur*⟩; monumental ⟨*Plastik, Gemälde, Gebäude*⟩; **c)** *(extremely great)* kolossal *(ugs. emotional)*
monumentally [mɒnjʊ'mentəlı] *adv.* enorm ⟨*stur, schlau, kreativ*⟩; **~ boring/stupid** sterbenslangweilig/strohdumm
monumental 'mason *n.* Steinmetz, *der*
moo [mu:] **1.** *n.* Muhen, *das;* **give** *or* **utter a loud ~:** laut muhen. **2.** *v.i.* muhen
mooch [mu:tʃ] *(sl.)* **1.** *v.i.* **~ about** *or* **around/along** herumschleichen *(ugs.)*/zockeln *(ugs.).* **2.** *v.t. (Amer.)* **a)** *(steal)* mopsen *(fam.);* **b)** *(beg)* schnorren *(ugs.)*
'moo-cow *n. (child lang.)* Muhkuh, *die (Kinderspr.)*
[1]**mood** [mu:d] *n.* **a)** *(state of mind)* Stimmung, *die;* **there was a [general] ~ of optimism** es herrschte allgemeiner Optimismus; **be in a very good/good/bad ~:** [bei] bester/guter/schlechter Laune sein; **be in a cheerful ~:** froh gelaunt *od.* fröhlich gestimmt sein; **be in a militant ~:** in Kampfstimmung sein; **be in a serious/pensive ~:** ernst/nachdenklich gestimmt sein; **be in no ~ for joking/dancing** nicht zum Scherzen/Tanzen aufgelegt sein; **b)** *(fit of melancholy or bad temper)* Verstimmung, *die;* schlechte Laune; **have one's ~s** [seine] Launen haben
[2]**mood** *n. (Ling.)* Modus, *der (fachspr.);* Aussageweise, *die;* **the subjunctive ~:** der Konjunktiv *(fachspr.);* die Möglichkeitsform
moodily ['mu:dılı] *adv.* übelgelaunt; mißgestimmt; *(in a sullen manner)* mißmutig; verdrossen
'mood music *n.* stimmungsvolle Musik
moody ['mu:dı] *adj.* **a)** *(sullen)* mißmutig; verdrossen; *(gloomy)* niedergeschlagen; **b)** *(subject to moods)* launenhaft
moon [mu:n] **1.** *n.* **a)** Mond, *der;* **light of the ~:** Mondlicht, *das;* Mondschein, *der;* **the ~ is full/waning/waxing** es ist Vollmond/abnehmender/zunehmender Mond; **there is no ~ tonight** heute nacht ist der Mond nicht zu sehen; **be over the ~** *(fig. coll.)* im siebten Himmel sein *(ugs.);* **offer sb. the ~** *(fig.)* jmdm. ein Vermögen bieten; **promise sb. the ~** *(fig.)* jmdm. das Blaue vom Himmel versprechen *(ugs.);* **ask for the ~:** Unmögliches verlangen; *see also* **blue moon; cry 3 a; full moon; half moon; man 1 b; new moon; shoot 2 d; b)** *(poet.: month)* Mond, *der (dichter. veralt.);* **c) that was many ~s ago** das liegt schon lange zurück. **2.** *v.i. (coll.)* **~ about** *or* **around [the house]** trübselig [im Haus] herumschleichen *(ugs.)*
~ over *v.t.* in Gedanken an ... *(Akk.)* verloren *od.* versunken *od.* vertieft sein
moon: ~beam *n.* Mondstrahl, *der;* **~beams** Mondschein, *der;* Mondlicht, *das;* **~-face** *n.* Mondgesicht, *das*
Moonie ['mu:nı] *n. (coll.)* Anhänger der Mun-Sekte
moon: ~ landing *n.* Mondlandung, *die;* **~less** *adj.* mondlos ⟨*Nacht, Himmel*⟩; **~light 1.** *n.* Mondlicht, *das;* Mondschein, *der;* **2.** *attrib. adj.* mondhell *(geh.)* ⟨*Nacht*⟩; **do a ~light [flit]** *(Brit. coll.)* bei Nacht und Nebel wegziehen, ohne die Schulden zu bezahlen; **3.** *v.i. (coll.)* nebenberuflich abends arbeiten; *(hold two jobs at once)* zwei Jobs gleichzeitig haben; **~lit** *adj.* mondbeschienen *(geh.);* **~shine** *n.* **a)** *(visionary ideas)* Unsinn, *der;* **b)** *(liquor)* schwarzgebrannter Alkohol; **~shine whisky** schwarzgebrannter Whiskey; **~shot** *n. (Astronaut.)* Mondflug, *der;* **~stone** *n. (Min.)* Mondstein, *der;* Adular, *der (fachspr.)*
Moor [mʊə(r), mɔ:(r)] *n.* Maure, *der*/Maurin, *die*
[1]**moor** *n.* **a)** *(Geog.)* [Hoch]moor, *das;* **b)** *(for shooting) im Moor gelegenes Wildhegegebiet*
[2]**moor 1.** *v.t.* festmachen; vertäuen. **2.** *v.i.* festmachen
'moorhen *n. (Ornith.)* [Grünfüßiges] Teichhuhn
mooring ['mʊərıŋ, 'mɔ:rıŋ] *n.* **a)** *usu. in pl. (means of attachment)* Vertäuung, *die;* **b)** *usu. in pl. (place)* Anlegestelle, *die;* **set sail from one's ~:** ablegen; **c)** *(action of making fast)* Vertäuung, *die*
mooring: ~-line *n.* Festmacher, *der;* **~-mast** *see* [1]**mast; ~-post** *n.* Pfahl, *der;* ≈ Duckdalben, *der;* **~-rope** *n.* Festmachetrosse, *die*
Moorish ['mʊərıʃ, 'mɔ:rıʃ] *adj.* maurisch
moorland ['mʊələnd, 'mɔ:lənd] *n. (Geog.)* Moorland, *das*
moose [mu:s] *n., pl. same (Zool.)* Amerikanischer Elch
moot [mu:t] **1.** *adj.* umstritten; offen ⟨*Frage*⟩; strittig ⟨*Punkt*⟩. **2.** *v.t. (broach, suggest)* zur Sprache bringen ⟨*Maßnahme, Plan*⟩; anschneiden ⟨*Thema*⟩; erörtern ⟨*Frage, Punkt*⟩
mop [mɒp] **1.** *n.* **a)** Mop, *der; (for washing up)* ≈ Spülbürste, *die; (Naut.)* Dweil, *der;* **Mrs Mop[p]** *(Brit.)* [die/unsere] Parkettkosmetikerin *(ugs. scherzh.);* **b) ~ [of hair]** Wuschelkopf, *der.* **2.** *v.t.,* **-pp- a)** *(clean with ~)* moppen ⟨*Fußboden*⟩; **b)** *(wipe)* abwischen ⟨*Träne, Schweiß, Stirn*⟩; **c) ~ the floor with sb.** *(fig. sl.)* jmdn. fertigmachen *(ugs.)*
~ 'up *v.t.* **a)** *(wipe up)* aufwischen ⟨*Flüssigkeit*⟩; **here's some bread to ~ up the gravy** hier ist etwas Brot, um die Soße vom Teller zu wischen; **b)** *(Brit. sl.) (drink greedily)* wegschlabbern *(ugs.)* ⟨*Getränk*⟩; *(eat greedily)* reinstopfen *(ugs.)* ⟨*Essen*⟩; **c)** *(Mil.)* ausheben ⟨*Widerstandsnest*⟩; aufreiben ⟨*versprengte Truppen*⟩; säubern ⟨*Gebiet*⟩
'mopboard *n. (Amer.)* Fußleiste, *die*
mope [məʊp] *v.i.* Trübsal blasen *(ugs.);* **~ about** *or* **around** trübselig herumschleichen *(ugs.)*
moped ['məʊped] *n.* Moped, *das*
'mophead *n.* **a)** *(at end of mop)* Mop, *der;* **b)** *(of hair; person)* Wuschelkopf, *der (ugs.)*
Mopp *see* **mop 1 a**
moppet ['mɒpıt] *n.* **a)** *(endearing: baby, little girl)* Fratz, *der (fam.);* **b)** *(coll.: child)* Matz, *der (fam.)*
moquette [mɒ'ket] *n. (Textiles)* Mokett, *der (fachspr.);* Möbelplüsch aus Wolle
moraine [mə'reın] *n. (Geol.)* Moräne, *die*
moral ['mɒrl] **1.** *adj.* **a)** *(of right and wrong)* moralisch ⟨*Gefühl, Bewußtsein*⟩; sittlich ⟨*Wert*⟩; Moral⟨*begriff, -prinzip, -vorstellung*⟩; **b)** *(dealing with regulation of conduct)* moralisch ⟨*Erzählung, Rede*⟩; Lehr⟨*gedicht, -stück*⟩; **c)** *(concerned with rules of morality)* Moral⟨*philosoph[ie], -psychologie*⟩; **d)** *(virtuous)* moralisch, sittlich, *(veralt.)* tugendhaft ⟨*Leben, Person*⟩; **e)** *(founded on ~ law)* moralisch, sittlich ⟨*Verpflichtung, Pflicht*⟩; **be under a ~ obligation** eine moralische *od.* sittliche Pflicht haben; **f)** *(not physical)* moralisch ⟨*Stärke, Zusammenbruch*⟩. **2.** *n.* **a)** *(lesson)* Moral, *die;* **draw the ~ from sth.** die Lehre aus etw. ziehen; **b)** *in pl. (habits)* Moral, *die;* Moralvorstellungen; **c)** *(maxim)* Moral, *die;* Lehre, *die;* **point a ~:** einen moralischen Grundsatz aufstellen
moral: ~ 'certainty *n.* **it is a ~ certainty [that ...]** es ist so gut wie sicher[, daß ...]; **~ 'courage** *n.* Rückgrat, *das;* Zivilcourage, *die;* **~ 'cowardice** *n.* Mangel an Rückgrat *od.* Zivilcourage
morale [mə'rɑ:l] Moral, *die;* **high/low ~:** gute/schlechte Moral
moralise *see* **moralize**
moralist ['mɒrəlıst] *n.* **a)** *(one who practises morality)* moralischer *od.* sittlicher Mensch; **b)** *(philosopher)* Moralist, *der*/Moralistin, *die;* Moralphilosoph, *der*/Moralphilosophin, *die*
moralistic [mɒrə'lıstık] *adj.* moralistisch
morality [mə'rælıtı] *n.* **a)** *(conduct)* Moral, *die;* Sittlichkeit, *die;* Moralität, *die (geh.);* **b)** *(moral science)* Moralphilosophie, *die;* Ethik, *die;* Sittenlehre, *die;* **c)** *in pl. (moral principles)* Moralgesetze *Pl.;* Moralprinzipien *Pl.;* **d)** *(particular system)* Ethik, *die;* **e)** *(conformity to moral principles)* Sittlichkeit, *die;* Moralität, *die (geh.);* **f)** *(Hist., Lit.)* **~ [play]** Moralität, *die*
moralize ['mɒrəlaız] *v.i.* moralisieren *(geh.);* moralische Betrachtungen anstellen ([**up**]**on** über + *Akk.*); **do stop moralizing!** hör auf mit deinen Moralpredigten!
moral 'law *n.* Moralgesetz, *das*
morally ['mɒrəlı] *adv.* **a)** *(as regards right and wrong)* moralisch ⟨*verantwortlich*⟩; **b)** *(virtuously)* moralisch einwandfrei, integer ⟨*sich benehmen*⟩; **c)** *(virtually)* praktisch, so gut wie ⟨*sicher*⟩; **d)** *(not physically)* moralisch; psychisch
moral: ~ 'majority *n. vermutete Mehrheit, die für strengere öffentliche Moral eintritt;* **~ phi'losophy** *n.* Moralphilosophie, *die;* **~ 'pressure** *n.* moralischer Druck; **~ 'sense** *n.* moralisches *od.* sittliches Bewußtsein; **~ sup'port** *n.* moralische Unterstützung; **~ the'ology** *n.* Moraltheologie, *die;* **~ 'victory** *n.* moralischer Sieg
morass [mə'ræs] *n.* **a)** *(bog)* Morast, *der;* **b)** *(fig.: entanglement)* Wirrnis, *die (geh.);* Labyrinth, *das;* **a ~ of confusion** heillose Verwirrung
moratorium [mɒrə'tɔ:rıəm] *n., pl.* **~s** *or* **moratoria** [mɒrə'tɔ:rıə] **a)** vorläufige Einstellung (**on** *Gen.*); [vorläufiger] Stopp (**on** für); **declare a ~ on sth.** etw. vorläufig einstellen *od.* stoppen; **b)** *(authorized delay)* Moratorium, *das*
Moravia [mə'reıvıə] *pr. n.* Mähren *(das)*
morbid ['mɔ:bıd] *adj.* **a)** *(unwholesome, having such feelings)* krankhaft; makaber, morbid *(geh.)* ⟨*Freude, Faszination, Phantasie, Neigung*⟩; **b)** *(coll.: melancholy)* trübselig; **make sb. feel ~:** jmdn. trübselig machen; **c)** *(Med.)* pathologisch *(fachspr.)* ⟨*Anatomie*⟩; krankhaft ⟨*Zustand, Veränderung*⟩; krank ⟨*Körper*⟩; pathogen *(fachspr.)* ⟨*Substanz*⟩
morbidity [mɔ:'bıdıtı] *n., no pl.* **a)** Krankhaftigkeit, *die;* **b)** *(Med.) (diseased state)* Krankheit, *die; (rate of sickness)* Morbidität, *die (fachspr.)*
morbidly ['mɔ:bıdlı] *adv.* **a)** *(Med.)* krankhaft; **b)** *(coll.: in melancholy way)* trübselig
mordant ['mɔ:dənt] *adj.* bissig ⟨*Bemerkung, Rede*⟩; beißend ⟨*Humor*⟩; sarkastisch ⟨*Person*⟩
more [mɔ:(r)] **1.** *adj.* **a)** *(additional)* mehr; **would you like any** *or* **some/a few ~?** *(apples, books, etc.)* möchten Sie noch welche/ein paar?; **would you like any** *or* **some ~ apples?** möchten Sie noch Äpfel?; **would you like any** *or* **some/a little ~?** *(tea, paper, etc.)* möchten Sie noch etwas/ein wenig?; **would you like any** *or* **some ~ tea/paper?** möchten Sie noch Tee/Papier?; **I haven't any ~**

[apples/tea] ich habe keine [Äpfel]/keinen [Tee] mehr; ~ **and** ~: immer mehr; **offer** ~ **coffee** noch Kaffee anbieten; **for a few dollars** ~: für ein paar Dollar mehr; **[just] one ~ thing before I go** [nur] noch eins, bevor ich gehe; **one ~ word and ...**: noch ein Wort und ...; **many ~ things** noch viel mehr [Dinge]; **two/twenty ~ things** noch zwei/zwanzig Dinge; **some ~ things** noch einige Dinge; noch einiges; **b)** *(greater in degree)* größer; **~'s the pity** *(coll.)* leider!; **the ~ fool 'you** du bist vielleicht ein Dummkopf. **2.** *n., no pl., no indef. art.* **a)** *(greater amount or number or thing)* mehr; **he is ~ of a poet than a musician** er ist mehr Dichter als Musiker; ~ **and** ~: mehr und mehr; immer mehr; **six or** ~: mindestens sechs; **I hope to see ~ of you** hoffentlich sehen wir uns öfter; **the ~ the merrier** *see* **merry a; b)** *(additional number or amount or thing)* mehr; **what is ~...**: außerdem ...; **do no ~ than do sth.** nur etw. tun; **~ means worse** ein Mehr an Zahl heißt ein Weniger an Qualität; **water is no ~ than thawed ice** Wasser ist nichts weiter *od.* anderes als aufgetautes Eis; **and** ~: mindestens *vorangestellt;* oder mehr; **there's plenty ~ where that came from** es ist noch viel mehr da; man braucht keineswegs zu geizen; **there's no need to do/say [any] ~**: da braucht nichts weiter getan/gesagt zu werden; *see also* **say 1 a; c) ~ than** *(coll.: exceedingly)* über⟨*satt, -glücklich, -froh*⟩; hoch⟨*erfreut, willkommen*⟩; sehr ⟨*aufgeregt*⟩; tief⟨*traurig*⟩; **at least you enjoyed yourself, which is ~ than I did** im Gegensatz zu mir *od.* anders als ich hast du dich wenigstens noch amüsiert; **which is ~ than you** *or* **one can say of X** und das kann man nicht von X behaupten; **neither ~ nor less [than ridiculous** *etc.*] [lächerlich *usw.*,] nicht mehr und nicht weniger. **3.** *adv.* **a)** mehr ⟨*mögen, interessieren, gefallen, sich wünschen*⟩; *forming compar.* **a ~ interesting book** ein interessanteres Buch; **this book is ~ interesting** dieses Buch ist interessanter; **~ often** häufiger; **~ than a little tiresome** ziemlich langweilig; **~ than anything [else]** vor allem; **~ than sb. can say** mehr als jmd. sagen kann; **b)** *(nearer, rather)* eher; **~ ... than ...**: eher ... als ...; **~ dead than alive** mehr tot als lebendig; **c) you couldn't be ~** *(are extremely)* **mistaken** *or* **wrong** du irrst dich gewaltig; **I couldn't be ~** *(am extremely)* **sorry** es tut mir schrecklich leid; **d)** *(again)* wieder; **never ~**: nie wieder *od.* mehr; **not any ~**: nicht mehr; **once ~**: noch einmal; **a couple of times ~**: noch ein paarmal; **e) ~ and ~ ...**: mehr und mehr *od.* immer mehr ...; *with adj. or adv.* immer ... (+ *Komp.*); **become ~ and ~ absurd** immer absurder werden; **f) ~ or less** *(fairly)* mehr oder weniger; *(approximately)* annähernd; **g) ~ so** noch mehr; **Is she equally attractive? – Rather ~ so, if anything** Ist sie genauso attraktiv? – Ja, wenn nicht noch attraktiver; **the ~ so because ...**: um so mehr, als *od.* weil ...; **h) not any ~ [than]** nicht mehr [als]. *See also* **'like 1 a; little 3 b; 'no 2 a; the 2; what 6 a**

moreish ['mɔːrɪʃ] *adj. (coll.)* lecker; **this cake is rather ~**: dieser Kuchen schmeckt nach mehr

morel [mə'rel] *n. (Bot.: edible fungus)* [Speise]morchel, *die*

morello [mə'reləʊ] *n., pl.* **~s** *(Bot.)* Schattenmorelle, *die*

moreover [mɔː'rəʊvə(r)] *adv.* und außerdem; zudem *(geh.)*

mores ['mɔːriːz, 'mɔːreɪz] *n. pl.* Sitten *Pl.;* **sexual ~**: Sexualethik *od.* -moral, *die*

morganatic [mɔːgə'nætɪk] *adj.* morganatisch; **~ marriage** morganatische Ehe; Ehe zur linken Hand *(hist.)*

morgue [mɔːg] *n.* **a)** *see* **mortuary; b)** *(Journ.)* Archiv, *das*

moribund ['mɒrɪbʌnd] *adj. (lit. or fig.)* moribund *(Med.);* dem Tode geweiht *(geh.);* im Sterben liegend ⟨*Person*⟩; im Aussterben begriffen ⟨*Spezies*⟩; dem Untergang geweiht ⟨*Nation, Volk, Brauch*⟩

Mormon ['mɔːmən] **1.** *n.* Mormone, *der*/Mormonin, *die;* **Book of ~**: Buch Mormon. **2.** *adj.* mormonisch

morn [mɔːn] *n.* **a)** *(poet.: morning)* Morgen, *der;* **from ~ to** *or* **till night** von früh bis spät; **b)** *(poet.: dawn)* Morgengrauen, *das*

mornay ['mɔːneɪ] *n. (Gastr.)* Sauce Mornay, *die (eine Käsesoße)*

morning ['mɔːnɪŋ] *n.* **a)** Morgen, *der; (as opposed to afternoon)* Vormittag, *der;* **this ~**: heute morgen *od.* früh; **tomorrow ~**: morgen früh; **during the ~**: am Morgen/Vormittag; **[early] in the ~**: am [frühen] Morgen; *(regularly)* [früh] morgens; **at one** *etc.* **in the ~ = at one a.m.** *etc. see* **a.m. 1; begin next ~**: am anderen Morgen beginnen; **on Wednesday ~s/~**: Mittwoch morgens/[am] Mittwoch morgen *od.* früh; **one ~**: eines Morgens; **the other ~**: neulich morgens *od.* früh; **~, noon, and night** Tag und Nacht; **~ came** es wurde Morgen; **~s, of a ~**: morgens; *see also* **good 1 m; b) in the ~** *(coll.: next morning)* morgen früh; **see you in the ~!** bis morgen früh!; **c)** *(spent in a particular way)* **a ~ of shopping** ein mit Einkaufen verbrachter Morgen; **d)** *(coll. greeting)* **~, all!** Morgen, zusammen!; **e)** *(fig.)* Anfang, *der;* Beginn, *der;* **f)** *attrib.* morgendlich; Morgen⟨*kaffee, -spaziergang*⟩

morning: ~ 'after *n. (coll.: hangover)* **~-'after [feeling]** Katzenjammer, *der;* Kater, *der;* **~-'after pill** *n.* Pille [für den Morgen] danach; **~ coat** *n.* Cut[away], *der;* **~ dress** *n.* Stresemann, *der;* **~ 'glory** *n. (Bot.)* Winde, *die;* **~ 'paper** *n.* Morgenzeitung, *die;* **~ 'prayer** *n.* Morgenandacht, *die;* **~ 'service** *n. (Eccl.)* Morgenandacht, *die; (RC Ch.)* Frühmesse, *die;* **~ sickness** *n.* morgendliche Übelkeit; **~ 'star** *n.* Morgenstern, *der*

Moroccan [mə'rɒkən] **1.** *adj.* marokkanisch; **sb. is ~**: jmd. ist Marokkaner/Marokkanerin. **2.** *n.* Marokkaner, *der*/Marokkanerin, *die*

Morocco [mə'rɒkəʊ] *pr. n.* Marokko *(das)*

morocco *n., pl.* **~s** Maroquin, *der*

moron ['mɔːrɒn] *n.* **a)** *(coll.)* Trottel, *der (ugs. abwertend);* Schwachkopf, *der (ugs.);* **b)** *(mental defective)* Geistesschwache, *der/die;* Schwachsinnige, *der/die*

moronic [mə'rɒnɪk] *adj.* geistesschwach; schwachsinnig; debil *(fachspr.)*

morose [mə'rəʊs] *adj.,* **morosely** [mə'rəʊslɪ] *adv.* verdrießlich

morpheme ['mɔːfiːm] *n. (Ling.)* Morphem, *das*

morphia ['mɔːfɪə], **morphine** ['mɔːfiːn] *ns.* Morphin, *das (fachspr.);* Morphium, *das;* **be a ~ addict** morphiumsüchtig sein

morphological [mɔːfə'lɒdʒɪkl] *adj. (Biol., Ling.)* morphologisch

morphology [mɔː'fɒlədʒɪ] *n.* **a)** *(Biol.)* Morphologie, *die;* Gestaltlehre, *die;* **b)** *(Ling.)* Morphologie, *die (fachspr.);* Formen- und Wortbildungslehre, *die*

morris ['mɒrɪs]: **~ dance** *n.* Moriskentanz, *der;* **~ dancer** *n.* Moriskentänzer, *der;* **~ dancing** *n.* Moriskentanzen, *das*

morrow ['mɒrəʊ] *n. (literary)* **the ~** *(the next day)* der folgende *od.* kommende Tag; **on the ~**: tags drauf; am nächsten Tag. *See also* **good 1 m**

Morse [mɔːs] *n.* Morseschrift, *die;* Morsezeichen *Pl.;* **can you use ~?** können Sie morsen?

Morse 'code *n.* Morseschrift, *die;* Morsealphabet, *das*

morsel ['mɔːsl] *n.* **a)** *(of food)* Bissen, *der;* Happen, *der;* **b)** *(fragment)* Stückchen, *das;* Bröckchen, *das; (fig.)* Quentchen, *das*

mortal ['mɔːtl] **1.** *adj.* **a)** *(that must die)* sterblich; **b)** *(fatal, fought to the death, intense)* tödlich **(to** für); **~ combat** ein Kampf auf Leben und Tod; **give ~ offence to sb.** jmdn. tödlich beleidigen; **~ sin** Todsünde, *die;* **c)** *(implacable)* tödlich; erbittert; **~ enemy** Todfeind, *der;* **d)** *(sl.: whatsoever)* **every ~ thing** alles menschenmögliche; **e)** *(accompanying death)* Todes⟨*strudel, -kampf, -angst*⟩; **f)** *(human, earthly)* vergänglich; irdisch ⟨*Dasein*⟩; menschlich ⟨*Verlangen, Geist*⟩. **2.** *n.* Sterbliche, *der/die;* **be a mere ~**: auch nur ein Mensch sein

mortality [mɔː'tælɪtɪ] *n.* **a)** Sterblichkeit, *die;* **b)** *(loss of life)* [Dahin]sterben, *das;* **c)** *(number of deaths)* Sterblichkeit, *die;* Todesfälle *Pl.;* Mortalität, *die (Med.);* **d) ~ [rate]** Sterblichkeitsrate, *die;* Sterbeziffer, *die;* Mortalität, *die (Med.)*

mortally ['mɔːtəlɪ] *adv.* **a) ~ wounded** tödlich verletzt; **b)** *(intensely)* **~ offended** zutiefst *od.* tödlich beleidigt

mortar ['mɔːtə(r)] *n.* **a)** *(substance)* Mörtel, *der;* **b)** *(vessel)* Mörser, *der;* **c)** *(cannon)* Minenwerfer, *der;* Mörser, *der*

'mortar-board *n. (Univ.) bei bestimmten Anlässen zum Talar getragene viereckige Kopfbedeckung der Studenten und Lehrer an britischen und amerikanischen Universitäten;* ≈ Barett, *das*

mortgage ['mɔːgɪdʒ] **1.** *n.* **a)** Hypothek, *die;* **b)** *(deed)* Pfandverschreibung, *die;* Hypothekenbrief, *der;* **c)** *attrib.* Hypotheken⟨*schuld, -zinssatz, -darlehen, -geld*⟩; **~ repayment** Hypothekenzahlung, *die.* **2.** *v. t.* **a)** mit einer Hypothek *od.* hypothekarisch belasten; **b)** *(pledge)* verpfänden

mortgagee [mɔːgɪ'dʒiː] *n.* Hypothekar, *der;* Hypothekengläubiger, *der*

mortgager ['mɔːgɪdʒə(r)], **mortgagor** [mɔːgɪ'dʒɔː(r)] *n.* Hypothekenschuldner, *der*

mortice *see* **mortise**

mortician [mɔː'tɪʃn] *n. (Amer.)* Leichenbestatter, *der*/-bestatterin, *die; (firm)* Bestattungsinstitut, *das*

mortification [mɔːtɪfɪ'keɪʃn] *n. (humiliation)* Beschämung, *die;* Kränkung, *die;* **feel great ~ at sth.** etw. als eine große Schmach empfinden; tief beschämt über etw. *(Akk.)* sein

mortify ['mɔːtɪfaɪ] *v. t.* **a)** *(humiliate)* beschämen; kränken; **he felt mortified** er empfand es als beschämend; **b)** *(subdue desires of)* **~ the flesh/oneself** sich kasteien

mortise ['mɔːtɪs] *n.* **a)** *(Woodw.)* Zapfenloch, *das;* **~ and tenon [joint]** Zapfenverbindung, *die;* Verzapfung, *die;* **b)** *attrib.* **~ lock** Steckschloß, *das*

mortuary ['mɔːtjʊərɪ] *n.* Leichenschauhaus, *das*

mosaic [məʊ'zeɪɪk] *n. (lit. or fig.)* Mosaik, *das; attrib.* Mosaik⟨*fußboden, -arbeit, -stein usw.*⟩

Moscow ['mɒskəʊ] **1.** *pr. n.* Moskau *(das).* **2.** *attrib. adj.* Moskauer

Moselle [məʊ'zel] *pr. n.* Mosel, *die*

moselle *n. (wine)* Mosel[wein], *der*

Moses ['məʊzɪz] *pr. n. (Bibl.)* Moses *(der);* Mose *(der) (ökum.)*

Moslem ['mɒzləm] *see* **Muslim**

mosque [mɒsk] *n.* Moschee, *die*

mosquito [mɒs'kiːtəʊ] *n., pl.* **~es** Stechmücke, *die; (in tropics)* Moskito, *der;* **~ bite** Mücken-/Moskitostich, *der*

mos'quito-net *n.* Moskitonetz, *das*

moss [mɒs] *n.* **a)** Moos, *das;* **b)** *(Scot., N. Engl.: bog)* Moor, *das;* Sumpf, *der*

moss: ~-covered *adj.* bemoost; moosbedeckt; **~-green** *adj.* moosgrün

mossy ['mɒsɪ] *adj.* moosig; bemoost; moosbewachsen

most [məʊst] **1.** *adj. (in greatest number, the majority of)* die meisten; *(in greatest amount)* meist...; größt... ⟨*Fähigkeit, Macht,*

Bedarf, Geduld, Lärm›; **make the ~ mistakes/noise** die meisten Fehler/den meisten *od.* größten Lärm machen; **~ people** die meisten Leute; die Mehrheit [der Leute]; **he has the ~ need of it** er braucht es am nötigsten; **for the ~ part** größtenteils; zum größten Teil. **2.** *n.* **a)** *(greatest amount)* das meiste; **offer [the] ~ for it** das meiste *od.* am meisten dafür bieten; **pay the ~:** am meisten bezahlen; **want sth. the ~:** sich *(Dat.)* etw. am meisten wünschen; **the ~ one can say** das Beste, was man sagen kann; **b)** *(the greater part)* **~ of the girls** die meisten Mädchen; **~ of his friends** die meisten seiner Freunde; **~ of the poem** der größte Teil des Gedichts; **~ of the time** die meiste Zeit; *(on ~ occasions)* meistens; **lead for ~ of the race** während des größten Teils des Rennens führen; **be more enterprising than ~:** unternehmungslustiger als die meisten anderen sein; **~ of what he said** das meiste von dem, was er sagte; **c) make the ~ of sth., get the ~ out of sth.** etw. voll ausschöpfen; *(employ to the best advantage)* etw. voll ausnützen; *(represent at its best)* das Beste aus etw. machen; **d) at [the] ~:** höchstens; **at the very ~:** allerhöchstens. **3.** *adv.* **a)** *(more than anything else)* am meisten ‹*mögen, interessieren, gefallen, sich wünschen, verlangt*›; **~ of all** am allermeisten; **b)** *forming superl.* **the ~ interesting book** das interessanteste Buch; **this book is the ~ interesting** dieses Buch ist das interessanteste; **~ probably** höchstwahrscheinlich; **~ often** am häufigsten; **c)** *(exceedingly)* überaus; äußerst; **~ decidedly** ganz entschieden; ausgesprochen; **~ certainly** ohne jeden Zweifel; **d)** *(Amer. coll.: almost)* fast

mostly ['məʊstlɪ] *adv.* *(most of the time)* meistens; *(mainly)* größtenteils; hauptsächlich

MOT [eməʊ'ti:] *see* **MOT test**

mote [məʊt] *n.* **the ~ in sb.'s eye** *(fig. dated)* die Schwächen anderer

motel [məʊ'tel] *n.* Motel, *das*

motet [məʊ'tet] *n.* *(Mus.)* Motette, *die*

moth [mɒθ] *n.* Nachtfalter, *der;* *(in clothes)* Motte, *die;* **[the] ~** *(collect.)* die [Kleider]motten

moth: ~-ball 1. *n.* Mottenkugel, *die;* **in ~-balls** *(fig.: stored)* eingemottet ‹*Kleidung*›; *(Mil.)* eingelagert, eingemottet ‹*Schiffe, Waffen*›; beiseite geschoben ‹*Plan, Projekt*›; **put sth. in ~-balls** etw. einmotten; **2.** *v. t.* einmotten ‹*Kleider, alte Sachen, Vorschlag*›; einlagern, einmotten ‹*militärisches Gerät*›; beiseite schieben ‹*Plan, Projekt*›; **~-eaten** *adj.* von Motten zerfressen; vermottet; *(fig.: antiquated)* verstaubt ‹*Idee, Politik*›; altmodisch ‹*Person, System*›

mother ['mʌðə(r)] **1.** *n.* **a)** Mutter, *die;* **she is a** *or* **the ~ of six [children]** sie ist Mutter von sechs Kindern; **like ~ used to make** ‹*Essen*› wie bei Muttern *(ugs.);* **every ~'s son [of you]** jeder einzelne [von euch]; **~ animal** Muttertier, *das;* **~ hen** Glucke, *die; see also* **expectant b; b)** *(Relig.)* **M~ Superior** Äbtissin, *die;* **c)** *(fig.: source)* Ursprung, *der;* Wurzel, *die;* **necessity is the ~ of invention** *(prov.)* Not macht erfinderisch *(Spr.).* **2.** *v. t.* **a)** großziehen ‹*Familie*›; hervorbringen ‹*Idee, Gerücht*›; **b)** *(over-protect)* bemuttern

mother: M~ Church *n.* **a)** ['---] Mutterkirche, *die;* **b)** [--'-] *(authority)* Mutter Kirche *o. Art.;* die Kirche; **~ country** *n.* Mutterland, *das;* **~craft** *n., no pl.* Kinderpflege, *die;* **~ 'earth** *n.* Mutter Erde; **~ fixation** *n.* *(Psych.)* Mutterbindung, *die;* **M~ 'Goose rhyme** *n.* *(Amer.)* Kinderreim, *der*

motherhood ['mʌðəhʊd] *n., no pl.* Mutterschaft, *die*

Mothering Sunday ['mʌðərɪŋ sʌndɪ] *(Brit. Eccl.) see* **Mother's Day**

mother: ~-in-law *n., pl.* **~s-in-law** Schwiegermutter, *die;* **~-in-law's 'tongue** *n.* *(Bot.)* Bajonettpflanze, *die;* Frauenzunge, *die;* **~land** *n.* Vaterland, *das;* Heimatland, *das*

motherless ['mʌðəlɪs] *adj.* mutterlos; **the child was left ~:** das Kind verlor seine Mutter

motherly ['mʌðəlɪ] *adj.* mütterlich; **~ love** Mutterliebe, *die*

mother: M~ of 'God *n.* Mutter Gottes, *die;* Muttergottes, *die;* **~-of-'pearl** *n.* Perlmutt, *das;* **~'s boy** *or* **darling** *n.* *(coll. derog.)* Muttersöhnchen, *das (ugs.);* **M~'s Day** *n.* Muttertag, *der;* **~s' 'meeting** *n.* *(Brit.)* Müttertreffen [der Pfarrgemeinde], *das;* *(fig.)* aufgeregte Debatte; **~ 'tongue** *n.* Muttersprache, *die;* **~ wit** *n.* Mutterwitz, *der*

moth: ~-hole *n.* Mottenloch, *das;* **~-proof 1.** *adj.* mottenfest; **2.** *v. t.* mottenfest machen

motif [məʊ'ti:f] *n.* **a)** Motiv, *das;* **b)** *(on goods)* Markenzeichen, *das;* **the BMW ~:** das BMW-Zeichen; **c)** *(Mus.)* [Leit]motiv, *das;* **d)** *(on clothing)* Applikation, *die (fachspr.);* Aufnäher, *der*

motion ['məʊʃn] **1.** *n.* **a)** *(movement)* Bewegung, *die;* Gang, *der;* **be in ~:** in Bewegung sein; sich bewegen; ‹*Maschine:*› laufen; ‹*Fahrzeug:*› fahren; **set** *or* **put sth. in ~** *(lit. or fig.)* etw. in Bewegung *od.* Gang setzen; *see also* **perpetual motion; slow motion; b)** *(gesture)* Bewegung, *die;* Wink, *der;* **make a ~ to sb. to do sth.** jmdm. ein Zeichen geben, etw. zu tun; **a ~ of the hand** ein Zeichen mit der Hand; eine Handbewegung; **c)** *(formal proposal; also Law)* Antrag, *der;* **put forward** *or* **propose a ~:** einen Antrag stellen; **d)** *(of bowels)* Stuhlgang, *der;* **have** *or* **make a ~:** Stuhlgang haben; **e)** *in sing. or pl.* *(faeces)* Stuhl, *der;* **f)** *(manner of moving)* [Körper]haltung, *die;* **g)** *(change of posture)* Bewegung, *die;* **make a ~ to leave** Anstalten machen wegzugehen; **h) go through the ~s of doing sth.** *(coll.)* *(simulate)* so tun, als ob man etw. täte; *(do superficially)* etw. pro forma tun; **go through the ~s** *(coll.)* *(simulate)* nur so tun; *(do superficially)* es nur pro forma tun. **2.** *v. t.* **~ sb. to do sth.** jmdm. bedeuten *(geh.) od.* winken, etw. zu tun; **~ sb. to[wards]/away from sth.** jmdm. bedeuten *(geh.),* zu etw. [hin]zugehen/von etw. wegzugehen; **~ sb. aside/to a seat** jmdn. zur Seite winken/jmdm. bedeuten *(geh.),* Platz zu nehmen. **3.** *v. i.* winken; **~ to sb. to come in** jmdn. hereinwinken; **~ to** *or* **for sb. to do sth.** jmdm. bedeuten *(geh.),* etw. zu tun

motionless ['məʊʃnlɪs] *adj.* reg[ungs]los; bewegungslos; unbewegt ‹*See, Teich*›; **be/stay** *or* **remain ~:** sich nicht bewegen

'motion picture *n.* *(esp. Amer.)* Film, *der;* *attrib.* Film-

motivate ['məʊtɪveɪt] *v. t.* **a)** *(be motive of, stimulate)* motivieren; **b)** *(cause to act)* **~ sb. to do sth.** jmdn. veranlassen, etw. zu tun

motivation [məʊtɪ'veɪʃn] *n.* **a)** *(process)* Motivierung, *die;* **give/receive ~:** motivieren/motiviert werden; **b)** *(incentive)* Motivation, *die* **(for** zu); Anreiz, *der;* **c)** *(condition)* Motiviertheit, *die;* Motivation, *die;* **have good/poor** *or* **little ~:** sehr/wenig motiviert sein

motive ['məʊtɪv] **1.** *n.* **a)** Motiv, *das;* Beweggrund, *der;* **the ~ for the crime** das Tatmotiv; **do sth. from ~s of kindness** etw. aus Freundlichkeit tun; **b)** *see* **motif a, c. 2.** *adj.* *(moving to action)* treibend ‹*Geist, Kraft*›; *(productive of motion)* Antriebs-

motiveless ['məʊtɪvlɪs] *adj.* unmotiviert

'motive power *n.* Antriebskraft, *die*

mot juste [məʊ 'ʒu:st] *n., pl.* **mots justes** [məʊ 'ʒu:st] treffender *od.* passender Ausdruck

motley ['mɒtlɪ] **1.** *adj.* **a)** [bunt]gescheckt; *(multicoloured)* [kunter]bunt; **b)** *(varied)* buntgemischt; bunt ‹*Auswahl*›; *see also* **crew 1 b. 2.** *n.* *(Hist.: jester's dress)* Narrenkostüm, *das;* Narrenkleid, *das*

moto-cross ['məʊtəʊkrɒs] *n., no pl., no art.* Moto-Cross, *das*

motor ['məʊtə(r)] **1.** *n.* **a)** *(machine)* Motor, *der;* **b)** *(Brit.: ~ car)* Auto, *das.* **2.** *adj.* **a)** *(driven by engine or ~)* Motor‹*schlitten, -mäher, -jacht usw.*›; **b)** *(of ~ vehicles)* Kraftfahrzeug‹*ersatzteile, -mechaniker, -verkehr, -motor*›. **3.** *v. t.* *(Brit.)* fahren. **4.** *v. i.* *(Brit.)* [mit dem Auto] fahren

Motorail ['məʊtəreɪl] *n.* *(Brit.)* Autoreisezug, *der*

motor: ~ bike *(coll.) see* **motor cycle; ~ boat** *n.* Motorboot, *das*

motorcade ['məʊtəkeɪd] *n.* Fahrzeug- *od.* Wagenkolonne, *die*

motor: ~ car *n.* *(Brit.)* Kraftfahrzeug, *das;* Automobil, *das (geh.);* **~ caravan** *n.* *(Brit.)* Caravan, *der;* Omnibus, *der;* **~ cycle** *n.* Motorrad, *das;* Kraftrad, *das (Amtsspr.);* **~-cycle combination** *(Brit.)* Motorrad mit Beiwagen; **~-cyclist** *n.* Motorradfahrer, *der*/-fahrerin, *die;* **~ home** *n.* Reisemobil, *das;* **~ industry** *n.* Kraftfahrzeugindustrie, *die*

motoring ['məʊtərɪŋ] *n.* *(Brit.)* Autofahren, *das;* **~ correspondent** Motorjournalist, *der;* **school of ~:** Fahrschule, *die;* **~ offence** Verstoß gegen die [Straßen]verkehrsordnung; **~ organisation** Automobilklub, *der*

motorise *see* **motorize**

motorist ['məʊtərɪst] *n.* Autofahrer, *der*/-fahrerin, *die*

motorize ['məʊtəraɪz] *v. t.* motorisieren

motor: ~man *n.* Wagenführer, *der;* **~ nerve** *n.* *(Anat.)* motorischer Nerv; **~-racing** *n.* Autorennsport, *der;* **~ scooter** *see* **scooter b; ~ show** *n.* Auto[mobil]ausstellung, *die;* **~ trade** *n.* Kraftfahrzeughandel, *der;* **~ vehicle** *n.* Kraftfahrzeug, *das;* **~way** *n.* *(Brit.)* Autobahn, *die*

motte [mɒt] *n.* Motte, *die (fachspr.);* Erdhügelburg, *die*

MO'T test *n.* *(Brit.)* ≈ TÜV, *der*

mottle ['mɒtl] *v. t.* sprenkeln

mottled ['mɒtld] *adj.* gesprenkelt

motto ['mɒtəʊ] *n., pl.* **~es a)** Motto, *das;* **my ~ is 'live and let live'** meine Devise ist „leben und leben lassen"; **b)** *(in cracker)* Spruch, *der;* **c)** *(Mus.)* Leitmotiv, *das*

moufflon ['mu:flən] *n.* *(Zool.)* Mufflon, *der*

¹mould [məʊld] *n.* **a)** *(earth)* Erde, *die;* **b)** *(upper soil)* [Mutter]boden, *der*

²mould 1. *n.* **a)** *(hollow)* Form, *die;* *(Metallurgy)* Kokille, *die;* *(Plastics)* Preßform, *die;* *(Papermaking)* Schöpfform, *die;* **break the mould of sth.** *(fig.)* neue Wege in etw. *(Dat.)* gehen; **b)** *(Cookery: hollow utensil)* [Kuchen-/Back-/Pudding]form, *die;* **c)** *(fig.)* Wesensart, *die;* **be cast in heroic/pedantic** *etc.* **~:** von heldischer/pedantischer *usw.* Wesensart sein. **2.** *v. t.* formen **(out of, from** aus); **~ sth. into a certain shape** etw. in bestimmter Weise formen; **~ sb. into a fine character/person** einen feinen Menschen aus jmdm. machen

³mould *n.* *(Bot.)* Schimmel, *der;* *(in Roquefort, Stilton, etc. cheese)* Edelschimmelpilz, *der;* **grow [a]/get ~:** schimmlig werden

moulder ['məʊldə(r)] *v. i.* **~ [away]** *(lit. or fig.)* [ver]modern

moulding ['məʊldɪŋ] *n.* **a)** *(process of forming, lit. or fig.)* Formen, *das;* **b)** *(object)* Formteil, *das* **(of, in** aus); Formling, *der (fachspr.);* *(Archit.)* Zierleiste, *die;* **c)** *(wooden strip)* Leiste, *die*

mouldy ['məʊldɪ] *adj.* *(overgrown with mould)* schimmlig ‹*Lebensmittel*›; verschimmelnd, [ver]modernd ‹*Buch, Vorhang, Teppich*›; **a ~ smell** ein Modergeruch; **become** *or* **grow** *or* **get** *or* **go ~:** verschimmeln; schimmlig werden

moult [məʊlt] **1.** *v. t.* **a)** *(Ornith.)* verlieren

⟨*Federn, Gefieder*⟩; **b)** *(Zool.)* verlieren ⟨*Haar*⟩; abstreifen ⟨*Haut*⟩; abwerfen ⟨*Horn, Geweih*⟩. **2.** *v.i.* ⟨*Vogel:*⟩ sich mausern; ⟨*Hund, Katze:*⟩ sich haaren; ⟨*Schlange, Krebs usw.:*⟩ sich häuten. **3.** *n. (of bird)* Mauser, *die; (of snake, crab, etc.)* Häutung, *die*

mound [maʊnd] *n.* **a)** *(of earth)* Hügel, *der; (of stones)* Steinhaufen, *der;* **defensive ~:** Verteidigungshügel, *der;* **burial** *or* **sepulchral** *or* **grave ~:** Grabhügel, *der;* **b)** *(hillock)* Anhöhe, *die;* **c)** *(heap)* Haufen, *der;* **d)** *(Baseball)* [erhöhtes] Wurfmal

mount [maʊnt] **1.** *n.* **a)** *(mountain, hill)* Berg, *der;* **M~ Vesuvius/Everest** der Vesuv/der Mount Everest; *see also* **sermon a; b)** *(animal)* Reittier, *das; (horse)* Pferd, *das;* **c)** *(of picture, photograph)* Passepartout, *das; (backing)* Unterlage, *die;* **d)** *(for gem)* Fassung, *die;* **e)** *(Philat.)* [Klebe]falz, *der.* **2.** *v.t.* **a)** *(ascend)* hinaufsteigen ⟨*Treppe, Leiter, Stufe*⟩; steigen auf (+ *Akk.*) ⟨*Plattform, Berg, Kanzel*⟩; besteigen ⟨*Thron*⟩; **b)** *(get on)* steigen auf *(Akk.)* ⟨*Reittier, Fahrzeug*⟩; *abs.* aufsitzen; **~ the pavement** auf den Bürgersteig fahren; **c)** *(place on support)* montieren (**on** auf + *Akk.*); **d)** *(prepare)* aufstellen ⟨*Maschine, Apparat*⟩; präparieren ⟨*Exemplar, Haut, Skelett*⟩; *(fasten)* in ein Album einkleben ⟨*Briefmarke*⟩; *(for microscope)* fixieren; *(raise into position)* in Stellung bringen ⟨*Kanone, Geschütz, Mörser*⟩; **e)** *(Art)* aufziehen ⟨*Bild usw.*⟩; einfassen ⟨*Edelstein usw.*⟩; **f)** *(put on stage)* inszenieren ⟨*Stück, Show, Oper*⟩; organisieren ⟨*Festspiele, Ausstellung*⟩; **g)** *(carry out)* durchführen ⟨*Angriff, Operation usw.*⟩; *see also* **guard 1 b, d; h)** *(for copulation)* bespringen ⟨*Tier*⟩; besteigen *(salopp)* ⟨*Frau*⟩. **3.** *v.i.* **a)** *(move up, rise in rank)* aufsteigen; **b) ~ [up]** *(fig.: increase)* steigen (**to** auf + *Akk.*); ⟨*Unruhe, Besorgnis, Unwillen:*⟩ wachsen; **it all ~s up** es summiert sich

mountain ['maʊntɪn] *n.* **a)** *(lit. or fig.)* Berg, *der;* **in the ~s** im Gebirge; **~s high** *(fig.)* berg[e]hoch; **~s of books** *(fig.)* Berge von Büchern; **butter/grain** *etc.* **~** *(fig.)* Butter-/Getreideberg *usw., der;* **move ~s** *(fig.)* Berge versetzen; Himmel und Hölle in Bewegung setzen; *see also* **molehill; b)** *attrib.* Gebirgs-; **~ top/lake** Berggipfel/Bergsee, *der*

mountain: ~ 'ash *n. (Bot.)* Eberesche, *die;* **~ bike** *n.* Mountain-Bike, *das;* **~ chain** *n. (Geog.)* Gebirgskette, *die*

mountaineer [maʊntɪ'nɪə(r)] *n.* Bergsteiger, *der*/Bergsteigerin, *die*

mountaineering [maʊntɪ'nɪərɪŋ] *n.* Bergsteigen, *das;* **~ expedition/party** Bergpartie/Seilschaft, *die;* **~ experience** bergsteigerische Erfahrung; **~ equipment/club** Bergsteigerausrüstung, *die*/-verein, *der*

mountain 'goat *n.* Schneeziege, *die*

mountainous ['maʊntɪnəs] *adj.* **a)** *(characterized by mountains)* gebirgig; **b)** *(huge)* riesig ⟨*Gegenstand, Welle*⟩; riesenhaft ⟨*Person*⟩; groß ⟨*Leistung*⟩

mountain: ~ 'railway *n.* [Schienen]bergbahn, *die;* **~ 'range** *n.* Gebirgszug, *der;* **~ 'road** *n.* Gebirgsstraße, *die;* **~ sickness** *n.* Höhenkrankheit, *die;* **~side** *n.* [Berg][ab]hang, *der;* **~ top** *n.* Berggipfel, *der*

mountebank ['maʊntɪbæŋk] *n.* **a)** *(derog.: quack)* Quacksalber, *der (abwertend);* **b)** *(derog.: charlatan)* Scharlatan, *der (abwertend)*

mounted ['maʊntɪd] *adj.* **a)** *(on animal)* beritten; **b)** *(on support)* montiert ⟨*Gerät*⟩; aufgezogen ⟨*Stich*⟩; *(for display)* präpariert ⟨*Tier*⟩

Mountie ['maʊntɪ] *n. (coll.)* Mountie, *der;* *berittener kanadischer Polizist*

mounting ['maʊntɪŋ] *n.* **a)** *(of performance)* Inszenierung, *die; (of programme)* Durchführung, *die;* **b)** *(support) (Art: of drawing)* Passepartout, *das; (backing)* Unterlage, *die; (of engine, axle, etc.)* Aufhängung, *die (Technik)*

Mount of 'Olives *pr. n.* Ölberg, *der*

mourn [mɔːn] **1.** *v.i.* **a)** *(feel sorrow or regret)* trauern; **~ for** *or* **over** trauern um ⟨*Toten*⟩; nachtrauern (+ *Dat.*) ⟨*Jugend, Augenlicht, Haustier*⟩; betrauern ⟨*Verlust, Mißgeschick*⟩; **b)** *(observe conventions of ~ing)* trauern; Trauer tragen. **2.** *v.t.* betrauern; nachtrauern ⟨*etw. Verlorenem*⟩

mourner ['mɔːnə(r)] *n.* **a)** *(one who mourns)* Trauernde, *der/die;* Trauergast, *der;* **b)** *(person hired to attend funeral) (man)* Klagemann, *der; (woman)* Klageweib, *das*

mournful ['mɔːnfl] *adj.* traurig, bitter ⟨*Träne*⟩; klagend ⟨*Stimme, Ton, Schrei, Geheul*⟩; trauervoll *(geh.)* ⟨*Person*⟩

mournfully ['mɔːnfəlɪ] *adv.* traurig; klagend ⟨*sprechen, tönen*⟩

mourning ['mɔːnɪŋ] *n.* **a)** *(clothes)* Trauer[kleidung], *die;* **be [dressed] in** *or* **wear/put on** *or* **go into ~:** Trauer tragen/anlegen; *see also* **deep mourning; b)** *(sorrowing, lamentation)* Trauer, *die; (period)* Trauer[zeit], *die;* **a national day of ~:** eintägige Staatstrauer

mouse [maʊs] **1.** *n., pl.* **mice** [maɪs] **a)** Maus, *die;* **as quiet as a ~:** ganz leise; mucksmäuschenstill *(fam.)* ⟨*dasitzen*⟩; *(by nature)* sehr still; *see also* **cat a; church mouse; b)** *(fig.: timid person)* Angsthase, *der (ugs.);* **a man or a ~:** ein Mann oder ein Schwächling; **c)** *(Computing)* Maus, *die.* **2.** *v.i.* mausen; **go mousing** auf Mäusejagd gehen

mouse: ~-coloured *adj.* mausfarben; mausgrau; **~-hole** *n.* Mauseloch, *das*

mouser ['maʊsə(r)] *n.* Mäusefänger, *der*

'mousetrap *n.* **a)** Mausefalle, *die;* **b)** *(joc.: cheese)* billiger *od.* einfacher Käse

moussaka [mʊ'sɑːkə] *n. (Gastr.)* Moussaka, *die*

mousse [muːs] *n.* Mousse, *die*

moustache [mə'stɑːʃ] *n.* Schnurrbart, *der*

mousy ['maʊsɪ] *adj.* **a)** *(nondescript)* mattbraun ⟨*Haar*⟩; **b)** *(timid)* scheu ⟨*Blick, Wesen, Bewegung*⟩

mouth 1. [maʊθ] *n., pl.* **~s** [maʊðz] **a)** *(of person)* Mund, *der; (of animal)* Maul, *das;* **his ~ quivered/twitched/moved** seine Lippen zitterten/zuckten/bewegten sich; **hit sb. in the ~:** jmdn. auf den Mund schlagen; **with one's ~ open** mit offenem Mund; **keep one's ~ shut** *(fig. sl.)* die *od.* seine Klappe halten *(salopp);* **put one's money where one's ~ is** *(fig. sl.)* seinen Worten Taten folgen lassen; **shut sb.'s ~** *(fig. sl.)* jmdm. den Mund stopfen *(ugs.);* **with one's ~ full** mit vollem Mund; **my ~ feels dry** ich habe einen trockenen Mund; **out of sb.'s own ~** *(fig.)* aus jmds. eigenem Mund; von jmdm. selbst; **hear sb. say sth. out of his own ~:** hören, wie jmd. etw. selbst sagt; **out of the ~s of babes [and sucklings]!** *(fig.)* Kindermund tut Wahrheit kund *(Spr.);* **put words into sb.'s ~:** jmdm. etwas in den Mund legen; *(misrepresent)* jmdm. das Wort im Munde [her-]umdrehen; **have got many ~s to feed** viele hungrige Mäuler zu stopfen haben *(ugs.);* **take the words out of sb.'s ~:** jmdm. das Wort aus dem Mund *od.* von der Zunge nehmen; **go** *or* **be passed** *or* **be spread from ~ to ~:** von Mund zu Mund gehen; **b)** *(fig.) (entrance to harbour)* [Hafen]einfahrt, *die; (of valley, gorge, mine, burrow, tunnel, cave)* Eingang, *der; (of well)* Loch, *das; (of volcano)* Krater, *der; (of bottle, cannon)* Mündung, *die; (of pocket, womb, pit)* Öffnung, *die;* **c)** *(of river)* Mündung, *die. See also* **³down 1 dd; open 1 a, 3 a; shoot off 1; water 3 b; word 1 d. 2.** [maʊð] *v.t.* **a)** *(declaim)* schwülstig vortragen ⟨*Gedicht, Rede, Zitat, Satz*⟩; **b)** *(express by silent lip-movement)* mit Lippenbewegungen sagen; **~ sth. to oneself** etw. unhörbar vor sich *(Akk.)* hin sagen. **3.** [maʊð] *v.i.* **a)** *(grimace)* den Mund verziehen; **b)** *(move lips silently)* lautlos die Lippen bewegen; **~ to oneself** unhörbar vor sich *(Akk.)* hin sprechen

mouthful ['maʊθfʊl] *n.* **a)** *(bite)* Mundvoll, *der; (of solid food)* Bissen, *der; (of drink)* Schluck, *der;* **a ~ of abuse** ein Schwall Schimpfwörter; **b)** *(small quantity)* **a ~:** ein bißchen; **c)** *(sth. difficult to say)* Zungenbrecher, *der (ugs.);* **d)** *(Amer. sl.: sth. important)* etwas Wichtiges

mouth: ~-organ *n.* Mundharmonika, *die;* **~piece** *n.* **a)** *(Mus., Med.: for cigar[ette], pipe)* Mundstück, *das; (of telephone)* Sprechmuschel, *die;* **b)** *(speaker for others)* Sprachrohr, *das;* **act as the ~piece** Sprachrohr sein; **~-to-~ resusci'tation** *n.* Wiederbelebung durch Mund-zu-Mund-Beatmung; **~wash** *n.* Mundwasser, *das;* **~-watering** *adj.* appetitlich ⟨*Essen, Geruch, Anblick*⟩; lecker ⟨*Essen, Geruch, Geschmack*⟩

movable ['muːvəbl] *adj.* **a)** *(capable of being moved)* beweglich ⟨*Möbel, Teppich, Regal*⟩; **b)** *(Law)* beweglich ⟨*Vermögen, Güter*⟩; *(Scot. Law)* nicht vererbbar. *See also* **doh; feast 1 a**

move [muːv] **1.** *n.* **a)** *(change of residence)* Umzug, *der; (change of job)* **after three years with the same firm it was time for a ~:** nach drei Jahren bei derselben Firma war es Zeit, sich *(Dat.)* eine neue Stelle zu suchen; **b)** *(action taken)* Schritt, *der; (Footb. etc.)* Spielzug, *der;* **c)** *(turn in game)* Zug, *der; (fig.)* [Schach]zug, *der;* **make a ~:** ziehen; **it's your ~:** du bist am Zug; **d) be on the ~** *(moving about)* ⟨*Person:*⟩ unterwegs *od. (ugs.)* auf Achse sein; ⟨*Tier, Tramp:*⟩ umherziehen; *(progressing)* ⟨*Land usw.:*⟩ sich weiterentwickeln; ⟨*Person:*⟩ vorankommen; **e) make a ~** *(initiate action)* etwas tun *od.* unternehmen; *(~ from motionless position)* sich rühren; *(rise from table)* aufstehen; *(coll.: leave, depart)* losziehen *(ugs.);* **make the first ~:** den Anfang machen; **make no ~:** sich nicht rühren; **make no ~ to help sb.** keine Anstalten machen, jmdm. zu helfen; **f) get a ~ on** *(coll.)* einen Zahn zulegen *(ugs.);* **get a ~ on!** *(coll.)* [mach] Tempo! *(ugs.).* **2.** *v.t.* **a)** *(change position of)* bewegen; wegräumen ⟨*Hindernis, Schutt*⟩; *(transport)* befördern; **~ the chair over here** rück den Stuhl hier herüber!; **~ sth. somewhere else** etw. anderswohin tun; **~ sth. from the spot/its place** etw. von der Stelle/seinem Platz wegnehmen; **~ sth. to a new position** etw. an einen neuen Platz bringen; **~ house** umziehen; **~ the furniture about** umräumen; **who has ~d my papers?** wer war an meinen Papieren?; **please ~ your car** bitte fahren Sie Ihr Auto weg; **~ the luggage/equipment into the building** das Gepäck/die Ausrüstung ins Gebäude hineinbringen; **not ~ a muscle** sich nicht rühren; **~ one's/sb.'s bowels** Stuhlgang haben/jmds. Verdauung in Gang bringen; **please ~ your head [to one side]** bitte tun Sie Ihren Kopf zur Seite; **please ~ your legs out of the way** bitte nehmen Sie Ihre Beine aus dem Weg; **~ it!** *(coll.)* Beeilung! *(ugs.);* **~ yourself!** *(coll.)* Beeilung! *(ugs.);* **~ sb. to another department/job** jmdn. in eine andere Abteilung/Position versetzen; **the residents were ~d out of the area** die Bewohner wurden aus dem Gebiet evakuiert; **~ one's child to a different school** sein Kind in eine andere Schule schicken; **the patient was ~d to a different ward** der Patient wurde in eine andere Abteilung verlegt; **~ police/troops into an area** Polizeikräfte/Truppen in ein Gebiet schicken; **~ sb. into new accommodation** jmdn. in eine neue Unterkunft bringen lassen; **b)** *(in game)* ziehen; **c)** *(put or keep in motion)* bewegen; in Marsch setzen ⟨*Truppe*⟩; auseinandertreiben ⟨*Demonstran-*

ten›; in Bewegung setzen ‹*Mechanismus*›; **d)** *(provoke)* erregen ‹*Ärger, Eifersucht, Begierde*›; wecken ‹*Ehrgeiz, Haß*›; hervorrufen ‹*Gelächter*›; **~ sb. to laughter** jmdn. zum Lachen bringen; **~ sb. to anger** jmds. Ärger erregen; **e)** *(affect)* bewegen; berühren; **~ sb. to tears** jmdn. zu Tränen rühren; **~ sb. to pity/compassion** jmds. Mitleid erregen; **be ~d to pity/compassion** vor Mitleid gerührt sein; **be ~d by sth.** über etw. *(Akk.)* gerührt sein; **f)** *(prompt)* **~ sb. to do sth.** jmdn. dazu bewegen, etw. zu tun; **he was ~d by this** *or* **this ~d him to do it** das bewog ihn dazu, es zu tun; **~ sb. to action** jmdn. aktivieren *od.* mobilisieren; **I shall not be ~d** ich bleibe dabei; **sb. is not to be ~d** jmd. läßt sich nicht erschüttern; **g)** *(propose)* beantragen ‹*Beendigung, Danksagung*›; stellen ‹*Antrag*›; **~ that sth. should be done** beantragen, daß etw. getan wird; **h)** *(make formal application to)* einen Antrag stellen bei ‹*Gericht usw.*›; **i)** *(Commerc.: sell)* absetzen. **3.** *v.i.* **a)** *(go from place to place)* sich bewegen; *(by car, bus, train)* fahren; *(on foot)* gehen; *(coll.: start, leave)* gehen; ‹*Wolken*:› ziehen (**across** über + *Akk.*); **~ with the times** *(fig.)* mit der Zeit gehen; **it's time we got moving** es ist Zeit aufzubrechen; **get moving!** beeil dich!; **start to ~** ‹*Fahrzeug*:› sich in Bewegung setzen; **nobody ~d** niemand rührte sich von der Stelle; **keep moving!** bewegt euch!; *(~ on)* gehen Sie bitte weiter; **Don't ~. You're not in the way** Bleiben Sie sitzen/stehen. Sie sind nicht im Weg; **he has ~d to another department** er ist jetzt in einer anderen Abteilung; **Don't ~. I'll be back soon** Bleib hier *od.* Geh nicht weg. Ich bin gleich zurück; **in which direction are your thoughts moving?** in welche Richtung gehen Ihre Gedanken?; **b)** *(in games)* ziehen; **it's your turn to ~**: du bist am Zug; **White to ~** *(Chess)* Weiß zieht; **c)** *(fig.: initiate action)* handeln; aktiv werden; **~ quickly** *etc.* **to do sth.** schnell *usw.* handeln und etw. tun; **d)** *(be socially active) (in certain circles, part of society, part of town)* verkehren; *(in certain part of country)* sich aufhalten; **e)** *(change residence or accommodation)* umziehen (**to** nach); *(into flat etc.)* einziehen (**into** in + *Akk.*); *(out of town)* wegziehen (**out of** aus); *(out of flat etc.)* ausziehen (**out of** aus); **I want to ~ to London** ich will nach London ziehen; **I hate moving** ich hasse Umzüge; **f)** *(change posture or state)* sich bewegen; *(in order to make oneself comfortable etc.)* eine andere Haltung einnehmen; **don't ~ or I'll shoot** keine Bewegung, oder ich schieße; **nobody/nothing ~d** niemand/nichts rührte sich; **~ aside to make room** zur Seite gehen/rücken, um Platz zu machen; **~ back/forward in one's seat** sich auf seinem Sitz zurücklehnen/vorbeugen; **have your bowels ~d?** hatten Sie Stuhlgang?; haben Sie abgeführt?; **lie without moving** regungslos daliegen; **g)** *(operate)* ‹*Maschine*:› laufen; ‹*Pendel*:› schwingen; **h)** *(make progress)* vorankommen; **get things moving** vorankommen; **things are moving now** jetzt geht es voran; **~ towards** näherkommen (+ *Dat.*) ‹*Einigung, Höhepunkt, Kompromiß*›; **~ away from** abrücken von ‹*Standpunkt*›; **~ in the direction of sth.** sich auf etw. *(Akk.)* zubewegen; **i)** *(Commerc.: be sold)* ‹*Waren*:› Absatz finden, sich absetzen lassen; **j)** *(coll.: go fast)* **that car can really ~**: der Wagen ist enorm schnell *(ugs.)*; **that's really moving!** das nenn' ich Tempo! *(ugs.)*

~ a'bout 1. *v.i.* zugange sein; *(travel)* unterwegs sein; **I need more room to ~ about** ich brauche mehr Bewegungsfreiheit *od.* Spielraum. **2.** *v.t.* herumräumen ‹*Möbel, Bücher*›; herumschieben ‹*Teile einer Collage*›

~ a'long 1. *v.i.* **a)** gehen/fahren; **b)** *(make room)* Platz machen; **~ along, please!** gehen/fahren Sie bitte weiter; *(on bus etc.)* bitte weiter [durch]gehen. **2.** *v.t.* zum Weitergehen/-fahren auffordern

~ a'round *see* **~ about**

~ 'in 1. *v.i.* **a)** einziehen; *(to start work)* ‹*Bauarbeiter*:› kommen; **b)** *(come closer)* ‹*Truppen, Polizeikräfte*:› anrücken; ‹*Kamera*:› näher herangehen; **~ in on** ‹*Truppen, Polizeikräfte*:› vorrücken gegen; **~ in on a new market** beginnen, sich auf einem neuen Markt zu etablieren. **2.** *v.t.* einrücken lassen ‹*Truppen, Polizeikräfte*›; hineinbringen ‹*Gepäck, Ausrüstung*›

~ 'off *v.i.* sich in Bewegung setzen

~ 'on 1. *v.i.* weitergehen/-fahren; *(leave job)* sich verändern; **~ on to another question** *(fig.)* zu einer anderen Frage übergehen. **2.** *v.t.* zum Weitergehen/-fahren auffordern

~ 'out *v.i.* ausziehen (**of** aus); *(in car)* nach rechts/*(im Rechtsverkehr)* links ausbiegen

~ 'over *v.i.* rücken; **~ over!** *(said rudely)* Platz da!; **would you mind moving over a little?** würden Sie bitte ein Stück [weiter]rücken?

~ 'up 1. *v.i.* **a)** *(in queue, hierarchy)* aufrücken; ‹*Fahrzeug*:› vorfahren; *(to new class)* versetzt werden; *(to new school)* wechseln (**to** auf); **she's moving up in the world** sie kommt voran [im Leben]; **b)** *see* **~ over. 2.** *v.t.* versetzen ‹*Schüler*›

movement ['mu:vmənt] *n.* **a)** *(change of position or posture, or to and fro)* Bewegung, *die; (of people: towards city, country, etc.)* [Ab]wanderung, *die; (of clouds)* Zug, *der; (of air)* Regung, *die; (trend, tendency)* Tendenz, *die, (fashion)* Trend, *der* (**towards** zu); **a ~ of the head/arm/leg** eine Kopf-/Arm-/Beinbewegung; **without ~**: bewegungslos; **b)** *in pl.* Aktivitäten *Pl.*; **keep track of sb.'s ~s** jmdn. überwachen; **c)** *(Mus.)* Satz, *der;* **d)** *(concerted action for purpose)* Bewegung, *die;* **e)** *in sing. or pl. (Mech. esp. in clock, watch)* Räderwerk, *das;* **f)** *(Mil.)* Manöver, *das; (shifting)* Verlegung, *die; (advance)* Vorstoß, *der;* **g)** *(mental impulse)* Regung, *die;* **h)** *(progressive development) (of plot)* Fortgang, *der; (of story, poem, etc.)* Handlung, *die;* **i)** *(Commerc.: activity)* Geschäft, *das* (**in** mit); Bewegung im Handel (**in** mit); **j)** *(rise or fall in price)* Preisbewegung, *die;* **a downward/an upward ~ in shares** *or* **share prices/[the price of] coffee** ein Rückgang/Anstieg der Aktienkurse/des Kaffeepreises; **k)** *(of bowels) see* **motion 1 d**

mover ['mu:və(r)] *n.* **a)** *(of proposition)* Antragsteller, *der*/-stellerin, *die;* **b)** *(Amer.: of furniture)* Möbelspediteur, *der; (employee)* Möbelpacker, *der;* **firm** *or* **company of ~s** Möbelspedition, *die;* **c) prime ~** *(God)* Schöpfer, *der; (source of motive power)* Energiequelle, *die; (fig.: of plan etc.)* Urheber, *der*/Urheberin, *die;* **d) this animal is a slow** *etc.* **~**: die Bewegungen dieses Tieres sind langsam *usw.*; **she is a beautiful ~**: ihre Bewegungen sind anmutig; **be a slow ~** *(think slowly)* langsam schalten *(ugs.)*; *(work slowly)* langsam arbeiten; **be a fast ~**: von der schnellen Truppe sein *(ugs.)*

movie ['mu:vɪ] *n. (Amer. coll.)* Film, *der; attrib.* Film‹*publikum, -projektor, -studio usw.*›; **the ~s** *(art form, cinema industry)* der Film; *(cinema)* das Kino; **go to the ~s** ins Kino gehen

movie: ~-goer *n.* Kinogänger, *der*/-gängerin, *die;* **~-house, ~-theater** *n. (Amer. coll.)* Kino, *das*

moving ['mu:vɪŋ] *adj.* **a)** beweglich; **from a ~ car** ‹*sehen, erkennen*› von einem fahrenden Auto aus; ‹*fallen, werfen, schießen*› aus einem fahrenden Auto; **b)** *(affecting)* ergreifend; bewegend; rührend

movingly ['mu:vɪŋlɪ] *adv.* in rührender Weise; ergreifend ‹*schreiben, sprechen*›

moving: ~ 'pavement *n. (Brit.)* Rollbürgersteig, *der;* **~ 'picture** *n.* Film, *der;* **~ 'sidewalk** *(Amer.) see* **~ pavement; ~ 'spirit** *n.* treibende Kraft; **~ 'staircase** *see* **escalator a**

mow [məʊ] *v.t., p.p.* **~ed** [məʊd] *or* **~n** [məʊn] mähen ‹*Gras, Getreide, Rasen, Feld usw.*›; **newly-~n** frisch gemäht

~ 'down *v.t.* niedermähen ‹*Soldaten*›; überfahren ‹*Fußgänger*›; *(fig.: rout, smash)* zerschlagen ‹*Opposition*›

mower ['məʊə(r)] *n.* **a)** *(lawn-~)* Rasenmäher, *der;* **b)** *(Agric.)* Mäher, *der*

'mowing machine *see* **mower b**

Mozambican [məʊzəm'bi:kn] **1.** *adj.* mosambikisch. **2.** *n.* Mosambikaner, *der*/Mosambikanerin, *die*

Mozambique [məʊzəm'bi:k] *pr. n.* Mosambik *(das)*

MP *abbr.* **a) Member of Parliament; committee of MPs** Unterhausausschuß, *der;* **b) military police** MP; **c) military policeman/policewoman** Militärpolizist, *der*/-polizistin, *die;* **d) melting point** Schmp.

m.p.g. [empi:'dʒi:] *abbr. (Motor Veh.)* **miles per gallon; do/get 34 ~** *(Brit.)* 8,31 auf 100 km [ver]brauchen

m.p.h. [empi:'eɪtʃ] *abbr.* **miles per hour; How many ~ are we doing? – We are travelling at/driving at/doing 30 ~**: Wie schnell fahren wir? – Wir fahren 50 [km/h]

Mr ['mɪstə(r)] *n., pl.* **Messrs** ['mesəz] *(title)* Herr; *(third person also)* Hr.; *(in an address)* Herrn; Messrs Hrn.; *(firm)* Fa.; **Mr Right** *(joc.: destined husband)* der Richtige *(ugs.)*; Mr Big *(coll.)* der Boß *(ugs.)*

Mrs ['mɪsɪz] *n., pl. same or* **Mesdames** [meɪ'dæm, meɪ'dɑ:m] **a)** *(title)* Frau; *(third person also)* Fr.; **b)** *(coll.: wife)* **the** *or* **my/your** *etc.* **~**: meine/deine *usw.* Madam *(ugs. scherzh.)*. *See also* **Grundy; mop 1 a**

Ms [mɪz] *n., no pl.* Frau

MS *abbr.* **a) manuscript** Ms.; **b)** *(Med.)* **multiple sclerosis** MS

M.Sc. [emes'si:] *abbr.* **Master of Science** ≈ Mag. rer. nat. *(österr.)*; *see also* **B.Sc.**

MSS *abbr.* [em'esɪz] **manuscripts** Mss.

Mt. *abbr.* **Mount; ~ Etna/Everest/Sinai** *(Geog.)* der Ätna/der Mount Everest/der Berg Sinai

mth *abbr.* **month**

much [mʌtʃ] **1.** *adj.,* **more** [mɔ:(r)], **most** [məʊst] **a)** viel; groß ‹*Erleichterung, Sorge, Dankbarkeit, Verachtung*›; **with ~ love** voller Liebe; **with ~ love from ...** *(familiar ending to letter)* herzlichst, ...; **he never eats ~ breakfast/lunch/supper** er ißt nicht viel zum Frühstück/zu Mittag/zum Abendbrot; **too ~**: zuviel *indekl.*; **b) be a bit ~** *(coll.)* ein bißchen zuviel sein; *(fig.)* ein bißchen zu weit gehen. *See also* **good 3 b; how 1; nothing 1 a; so 1 a; this 3; too a. 2.** *n.; see also* **more 2; most 2;** vieles; **we don't see ~ of her any more** wir sehen sie kaum noch; **we haven't ~ to go on yet** bis jetzt haben wir noch nicht viel; **that doesn't come** *or* **amount to ~**: es kommt nicht viel dabei heraus; **he/this beer isn't up to ~** *(coll.)* mit ihm/diesem Bier ist nicht viel los *(ugs.)*; **spend ~ of the day/week/month doing sth.** den Großteil des Tages/der Woche/des Monats damit verbringen, etw. zu tun; **they have done ~ to improve the situation** sie haben viel für die Verbesserung der Situation getan; **not be ~ of a cinema-goer** *etc.* *(coll.)* kein großer Kinogänger *usw.* sein *(ugs.)*; **not have ~ of a singing voice/head for heights** keine besonders schöne Stimme haben/leicht schwindelig werden; **it isn't ~ of a bicycle/car/house** es ist kein besonders tolles Fahrrad/Auto/Haus *(ugs.)*; **not be ~ to look at** nicht sehr ansehnlich sein; **he/the plan/plant didn't come to ~**: aus ihm/dem Plan/der Pflanze ist nichts Richtiges geworden; **it's as ~ as she can do to get up the stairs** sie kommt gerade noch die Treppe hinauf; **I expected/thought as ~:** das habe ich erwartet/mir gedacht; **he stared at me as ~ as to say ...:** er starrte mich an, als ob er sagen wollte: ...; **you are as ~ to blame as he is** du bist ebensosehr schuld wie er; **she knows as ~ as we do** sie weiß genausoviel wie wir; **we didn't have so ~ as the bus fare home** wir hatten nicht einmal das Geld für den Bus nach Hause; **without so ~ as saying goodbye/a backward glance** ohne auch nur auf Wiedersehen zu sagen/einen Blick zurückzuwerfen; *see also* **again a; as 1; in a; make 1 m; so 1 a; think of g; up 1 v. 3.** *adv.*, **more, most a)** *modifying comparatives* viel ‹*besser*›; **~ more lively/happy/attractive** viel lebhafter/glücklicher/attraktiver; **b)** *modifying superlatives* mit Abstand ‹*der/die/das beste, schlechteste, klügste usw.*›; **c)** *modifying passive participles and predicative adjectives* sehr; **he is ~ improved** *(in behaviour)* er hat sich sehr gebessert; *(in health)* es geht ihm viel besser; **d)** *modifying verbs (greatly)* sehr ‹*lieben, mögen, genießen*›; *(often)* oft ‹*sehen, treffen, besuchen*›; *(frequently)* viel; **she loved him too ~:** sie liebte ihn zu sehr; **I don't ~ like him** *or* **like him ~:** ich mag ihn nicht besonders; **it doesn't matter ~:** es ist nicht so wichtig; **I don't very ~ want to come** ich habe keine sehr große Lust zu kommen; **I would ~ prefer to stay at home** ich würde viel lieber zu Hause bleiben; **~ to my surprise/annoyance, I found that ...:** zu meiner großen Überraschung/Verärgerung stellte ich fest, daß ...; **it's not so ~ a problem of money as of time** es ist nicht so sehr ein finanzielles als ein zeitliches Problem; **e)** *(approximately)* fast; **[pretty** *or* **very] ~ the same** fast [genau] der-/die-/dasselbe; **the old house was ~ as it had always been** das alte Haus hatte sich kaum verändert; **f)** *(for a large part of time)* viel ‹*gärtnern, lesen, spielen*›; *(often)* oft; häufig; **g) ~ as** *or* **though** *(although)* sosehr ... auch; **~ as he disliked the idea** sosehr ihm die Idee auch mißfiel; **~ as I should like to go** so gern ich auch gehen würde; **h) not ~** *(sl.: certainly not)* nicht die Bohne *(ugs.)*; denkste! *(ugs.)*. *See also* **less 2; oblige 1 d; same 1**

muchly ['mʌtʃlɪ] *adv.* *(joc.)* sehr ‹*beeindruckt*›; **ta** *or* **thanks ~!** tausend Dank! *(ugs.)*

muchness ['mʌtʃnɪs] *n., no pl., no def. art.* **be much of a ~** *(coll.)* sich *(Dat.)* so ziemlich gleichen *(ugs.)*; **they are much of a ~ when it comes to ...:** wenn es um ... geht, kann der eine es nicht besser als der andere

muck [mʌk] **1.** *n.* **a)** *(farmyard manure)* Mist, *der*; *see also* **common 1 e; b)** *(coll.: anything disgusting)* Dreck, *der (ugs.)*; *(liquid)* Brühe, *die (ugs. abwertend)*; **covered in ~:** verdreckt *(ugs.)*; **c)** *(coll.: defamatory remarks, nonsense)* Mist, *der (ugs.)*; Dreck, *der (ugs.)*; **d)** *(coll.: untidy state)* Schweinerei, *die (derb abwertend)*; **make a ~ of sth.** *(coll.)* [bei einer Sache] Mist bauen *(ugs.)*. **2.** *v. t. see* **muck up b**

~ a'bout, ~ a'round *(Brit. sl.)* **1.** *v. i.* **a)** herumalbern *(ugs.)*; **b)** *(tinker)* herumfummeln **(with** an + *Dat.*). **2.** *v. t.* **a)** herumstreifen *od.* umherstreifen in (+ *Dat.*) *(ugs.)* ‹*Stadt, Straße*›; **b) ~ sb. about** *or* **around** jmdn. verarschen *(derb)*; **the bank really ~ed us about** es war ein ewiges Hin und Her mit der Bank *(ugs.)*

~ 'in *v. i.* *(coll.)* mit zugreifen *od.* mit anpacken **(with** bei)

~ 'out *v. t.* ausmisten ‹*Stall*›; *(fig.)* aufräumen ‹*Haus, Garage, Zimmer*›

~ 'up *v. t.* **a)** *(Brit. sl.: bungle)* vermurksen, verbocken *(ugs.)*; **~ it up** Mist bauen *(ugs.)*; **b)** *(make dirty)* vollschmieren, dreckig machen *(ugs.)*; einsauen *(derb)*; **c)** *(spoil)* vermasseln *(salopp)*. *See also* **muck-up**

muckle ['mʌkl] *see* **mickle**

muck: ~raker ['mʌkreɪkə(r)] *n.* **he's just a ~raker** er ist nur auf Sensationen aus; **~raking** ['mʌkreɪkɪŋ] **1.** *adj.* skandalträchtig ‹*Rede, Brief, Angriff, Politik*›; skandalsüchtig *(abwertend)* ‹*Person*›; Skandal‹*artikel, -blatt, -journalismus, -presse*› *(abwertend)*; **2.** *n.* Skandalhascherei, *die (abwertend)*; Sensationsmache, *die (ugs. abwertend)*; **~-up** *n.* *(Brit. sl.) (confusing or confused situation)* Kuddelmuddel, *der od. das (ugs.)*; *(blunder, mess)* Mist, *der (ugs.)*; **make a ~-up of sth.** etw. vermasseln *(salopp)*

mucky ['mʌkɪ] *adj.* dreckig *(ugs.)*; *(with manure)* mistig; *(fig.)* schmierig ‹*Zeitung, Witz, usw.*›

mucous ['mju:kəs] *adj.* *(Med., Bot., Zool.)* schleimig; Schleim-; mukös *(fachspr.)*

mucous 'membrane *n.* Schleimhaut, *die*

mucus ['mju:kəs] *n.* *(Med., Bot., Zool.)* Schleim, *der*

mud [mʌd] *n.* **a)** Schlamm, *der*; Morast, *der*; **patch/expanse** *or* **area of ~:** schlammige *od.* morastige Stelle/Fläche; **covered with ~:** schlammbedeckt; **be as clear as ~** *(joc. iron.)* absolut unklar sein; **[here's] ~ in your eye!** *(dated sl.)* Prösterchen! *(fam.)*; **b)** *(hard ground)* Lehm, *der*; *attrib.* Lehm-; lehmig; **~ hut** Lehmhütte, *die*; **c)** *(fig.)* **be dragged through the ~:** in den Schmutz gezogen werden; **his name is ~** *(coll.)* er ist unten durch *(ugs.)* **(with** bei); **fling** *or* **sling** *or* **throw ~ at sb.** *(fig.)* jmdn. mit Dreck *(ugs.)* *od.* Schmutz bewerfen; *see also* **stick 1 e; stick-in-the-mud**

'mud-bath *n.* *(Med.; also fig.)* Schlammbad, *das*

muddle ['mʌdl] **1.** *n.* Durcheinander, *das*; **the room is in a hopeless ~:** in dem Zimmer herrscht ein heilloses Durcheinander *od.* eine heillose Unordnung; **get sth. in a ~:** etw. in Unordnung bringen; etw. durcheinanderbringen; **my mind/brain is in a ~:** ich bin ganz durcheinander; ich kann nicht klar denken; **get/get sb. in[to] a ~:** durcheinanderkommen *(ugs.)*/jmdn. durcheinanderbringen; **make a ~ of sth.** *(bungle)* etw. verpfuschen. **2.** *v. t.* **a) ~ [up]** durcheinanderbringen; **~ up** *(mix up)* verwechseln **(with** mit); **be ~d up** *(out of order)* durcheinandergeraten sein; **b)** *(mismanage)* verderben. **3.** *v. i.* wursteln *(ugs.)* **(with** an + *Dat.*)

~ a'long, ~ 'on *v. i.* vor sich *(Akk.)* hin wursteln *(ugs.)* **(with** bei); **~ on towards sth.** planlos auf etw. *(Akk.)* hinarbeiten

~ 'through *v. i.* sich durchwursteln *(ugs.)*

muddled ['mʌdld] *adj.* **a)** *(confused)* benebelt ‹*Person*›; konfus ‹*Verhalten, Denken*›; **b)** *(mixed-up, jumbled)* verworren ‹*Situation, Information, Ideen*›

muddle-'headed *adj.* wirr; **a ~ thinker/person** ein Wirrkopf

muddy ['mʌdɪ] **1.** *adj.* **a)** schlammig; **get** *or* **grow** *or* **become ~:** verschlammen; **b)** *(turbid, dull)* trübe ‹*Flüssigkeit, Licht, Farbe*›; grau ‹*Haut*›; **c)** *(obscure)* wirr; **a ~ thinker** ein Wirrkopf. **2.** *v. t.* *(cover with mud)* schmutzig machen; *(make turbid)* trüben ‹*Flüssigkeit*›

mud: ~-flap *n.* *(Motor Veh.)* Schmutzfänger, *der*; **~-flat[s]** *n.* *[pl.]* *(Geog.)* Watt, *das*; **~guard** *n.* Schutzblech, *das*; *(of car)* Kotflügel, *der*; **~pack** *n.* Schlammpackung [für das Gesicht]; Gesichtsmaske aus Schlamm; **~ 'pie** *n.* Kuchen *aus Sand usw.*; **~ vol'cano** *n.* *(Geog.)* Schlammvulkan, *der*; Salse, *die (fachspr.)*

muesli ['mju:zlɪ] *n.* Müsli, *das*

muezzin [mʊ'ezɪn] *n.* Muezzin, *der*

¹muff [mʌf] *n.* *(for hands)* Muff, *der*; *see also* **ear-muffs; foot-muff**

²muff 1. *n.* *(person)* Tölpel, *der (abwertend)*. **2.** *v. t.* **a)** *(bungle)* verderben; verpatzen *(ugs.)*; verhauen *(ugs.)* ‹*Examen*›; **I ~ed everything today** mir ging heute alles daneben *(ugs.)*; **b)** *(Theatre)* verpatzen *(ugs.)*; **~ a line** einen Patzer machen *(ugs.)*

muffin ['mʌfɪn] *n.* Muffin, *das*

muffle ['mʌfl] *v. t.* **a)** *(envelop)* **~ [up]** einhüllen; einmumme[l]n *(ugs.)*; **b)** *(deaden [sound of])* dämpfen ‹*Geräusch*›; [zur Schalldämpfung] umwickeln ‹*Fuß, Schuh, Ruder, Trommel, Glocke*›; **~ sb.'s cries/screams** ‹*Kopfkissen, Wand:*› jmds. Schreie dämpfen; ‹*Person:*› jmdn. am Schreien hindern; **c)** *(suppress sound of)* unterdrücken ‹*Fluch, Bemerkung*›; hinunterschlucken ‹*Fluch*›

muffler ['mʌflə(r)] *n.* **a)** *(wrap, scarf)* Schal, *der*; **b)** *(deadener of sound)* Dämpfer, *der*; **c)** *(Amer. Motor Veh.: silencer)* Schalldämpfer, *der*; Auspufftopf, *der*

mufti ['mʌftɪ] *n.* **a)** *(plain clothes)* Zivil, *das*; **in ~:** in Zivil **b)** *(Muslim priest)* Mufti, *der*

¹mug [mʌg] **1.** *n.* **a)** *(vessel, contents)* Becher, *der (meist mit Henkel)*; *(for beer etc.)* Krug, *der*; **a ~ of milk** ein Becher Milch; **b)** *(sl.: face, mouth)* Visage, *die (salopp)*; Fresse, *die (derb)*; **c)** *(Brit. sl.: simpleton)* Schwachkopf, *der (ugs.)*; **d)** *(Brit. sl.: gullible person)* Trottel, *der (ugs. abwertend)*; Doofi, *der (ugs.)*; **make a ~ of sb.** jmdn. anschmieren *od.* beschupsen *(salopp)*; **that's a '~'s game** das ist doch Schwachsinn *(ugs.)*; **e)** *(Amer. sl.: hoodlum)* Ganove, *der (ugs.)*. **2.** *v. t.*, **-gg-** *(rob)* überfallen und berauben

²mug *(Brit. sl.: study)* *v. t.*, **-gg-: ~ up** büffeln *(ugs.)* ‹*Fach, Zitate, Formeln*›; durchackern *(ugs.)* ‹*Buch, Notizen*›

mugful ['mʌgfʊl] *(contents) see* **¹mug 1 a**

mugger ['mʌgə(r)] *n.* Straßenräuber, *der*/Straßenräuberin, *die*

mugginess ['mʌgɪnɪs] *n., no pl.* Schwüle, *die*

mugging ['mʌgɪŋ] *n.* Straßenraub, *der* **(of** an + *Dat.*)

muggins ['mʌgɪnz] *n., pl.* **~es** *or same (coll.)* **a)** *(simpleton)* Dummkopf, *der (ugs.)*; Esel, *der (ugs.)*; **b)** *(myself, stupidly)* ich Dummkopf *(ugs.)*

muggy ['mʌgɪ] *adj.* schwül; drückend ‹*Klima, Zeit, Tag, Luft*›; **a ~ place** ein Ort mit schwülem Klima

'mug shot *n.* *(sl.)* **a) [police] ~s of criminals** Verbrecherfotos; **b)** *(passport photo etc.)* [Paß]foto, *das*

mugwort ['mʌgwɜ:t] *n.* *(Bot.)* Beifuß, *der*

Muhammadan [mə'hæmədn] *(Relig.)* **1.** *n.* Moslem, *der*. **2.** *adj.* moslemisch

Muhammadanism [mə'hæmədənɪzm] *n., no pl.* *(Relig.)* Islam, *der*

mulatto [mju:'lætəʊ] *n., pl.* **~s** *(Amer.:* **~es***)* Mulatte, *der*/Mulattin, *die*

mulberry ['mʌlbərɪ] *n.* **a)** *(fruit)* Maulbeere, *die*; *attrib.* Maulbeer-; **b)** *(tree)* Maulbeerbaum, *der*; *attrib.* Maulbeer-

mulch [mʌltʃ] *(Agric., Hort.)* **1.** *n.* Mulch, *der*. **2.** *v. t.* mulchen

mulct [mʌlkt] *v. t.* **a)** *(Law: fine)* eine Geldstrafe auferlegen *(geh.)* (+ *Dat.*); **b)** *(literary: deprive)* berauben *(geh.)* **(of** *Gen.*)

¹mule [mju:l] *n.* **a)** *(Zool.)* Maultier, *das*; **have a kick like a ~** *(fig.)* einen umwerfen; *see also* **obstinate; stubborn a; b)** *(coll.) (stupid person)* Esel, *der (ugs.)*; *(obstinate person)* Dickkopf, *der (ugs.)*; **c)** *(Textiles)* Mule-Maschine, *die*

²mule *n.* *(slipper)* Pantoffel, *der*

muleteer [mju:lɪ'tɪə(r)] *n.* Maultiertreiber, *der*/Maultiertreiberin, *die*

mulish ['mju:lɪʃ] *adj.* *(stubborn)* stur; **~ stubbornness/obstinacy** Sturheit, *die*

¹mull [mʌl] *v. t.* **~ over** nachdenken über (+ *Akk.*); *(in conversation)* diskutieren

²mull *v. t.* *(prepare)* erhitzen und würzen ‹*Wein*›; **~ wine** Glühwein zubereiten; **~ed wine** Glühwein, *der*

³mull *n.* *(Scot.: promontory)* Kap, *das*

mullah ['mʌlə] *n.* *(Islam)* Mullah, *der*

mullet ['mʌlɪt] *n., pl.* **~s** *or same (Zool.)* **red ~:** Gewöhnliche Meerbarbe; **grey ~:** Meeräsche, *die*

mulligatawny [mʌlɪgəˈtɔ:nɪ] *n.* ~ **[soup]** Mulligatawny-Suppe, *die (mit Curry scharf gewürzte, indische Geflügelsuppe)*
mullion [ˈmʌljən] *n.* **a)** *(Archit.)* Längspfosten, *der;* **b)** *in pl. (Gothic Archit.)* Stabwerk, *das*
mullioned [ˈmʌljənd] *adj.* längs unterteilt; ~ **windows** Fenster mit Stabwerk
multi- [ˈmʌltɪ] *pref. (several)* mehr-/Mehr-; *(many)* viel-/Viel-; multi-/Multi-, poly-/Poly- *(bes. mit Fremdwörtern)*
ˈmulticoloured *(Brit.; Amer.:* **multicolored**) *adj. (with several colours)* mehrfarbig, *(with many colours)* vielfarbig ⟨*Gegenstand, Tier, Pflanze*⟩; bunt ⟨*Stoff, Kleid*⟩
multifarious [mʌltɪˈfeərɪəs] *adj.* **a)** *(having great variety)* vielgestaltig; **b)** *(many and various)* mannigfach; vielfältig
ˈmultigrade *adj., n.* ~ **[oil]** Mehrbereichsöl, *das*
multiˈlateral *adj.* mehrseitig; *(Polit.)* multilateral
multilingual [mʌltɪˈlɪŋgwəl] *adj.* mehrsprachig
multimillioˈnaire *n.* Multimillionär, *der*/-millionärin, *die*
multiˈnational **1.** *adj.* multinational. **2.** *n. (Econ.)* multinationaler Konzern; Multi, *der (ugs.)*
multiple [ˈmʌltɪpl] **1.** *adj.* **a)** *(manifold)* mehrfach; ~ **birth** Mehrlingsgeburt, *die;* ~ **crash/pile-up** Massenkarambolage, *die;* **b)** *(many and various)* vielerlei; vielfältig; mannigfach; **c)** *(Bot.)* multipel; ~ **fruit** Sammelfrucht, *die. See also* **sclerosis a. 2.** *n.* **a)** *(Math.)* Vielfache, *das; see also* **common multiple; b)** *see* **multiple store**
multiple: ~-ˈ**choice** *adj.* Multiple-choice-⟨*Verfahren, Test, Frage*⟩; ~ ˈ**store** *n. (Brit. Commerc.)* Kettenladen, *der*
multiplication [mʌltɪplɪˈkeɪʃn] *n. (increase)* Vervielfachung, *die; (Math.)* Multiplikation, *die (fachspr.);* Malnehmen, *das; attrib.* Multiplikations-; **do/use** ~: multiplizieren *(fachspr.);* malnehmen; ~ **sign** Malzeichen, *das;* ~ **table** Multiplikationstabelle, *die;* **do** *or* **learn/recite** *or* **say/practise one's** ~ **table[s]** das Einmaleins lernen/aufsagen/üben
multiplicity [mʌltɪˈplɪsɪtɪ] *n.* **a)** *(manifold variety)* Vielfalt, *die* (**of, in** an, von + *Dat. Pl.*); ~ **in size/age** Größen-/Altersvielfalt, *die;* ~ **of habits/beliefs/ideas** vielfältige Gewohnheiten/Überzeugungen/Ideen; **b)** *(great number)* Vielzahl, *die* (**of** von, an + *Dat.*)
[1]multiply [ˈmʌltɪplaɪ] **1.** *v. t.* **a)** *(Math., also abs.)* multiplizieren *(fachspr.),* malnehmen (**by** mit); **b)** *(increase)* vervielfachen; **be multiplied** sich vervielfachen; **c)** *(Biol.)* fortpflanzen; züchten. **2.** *v. i. (Biol.)* sich vermehren; sich fortpflanzen; **be fruitful and** ~ *(Bibl.)* seid fruchtbar und mehret euch *(bibl.)*
[2]multiply [ˈmʌltɪplɪ] *adv.* mehrfach
ˈmulti-purpose *adj.* Mehrzweck-
multiˈracial *adj.* mehrrassig; gemischtrassig
ˈmulti-stage *adj.* mehrstufig; Mehrstufen-
ˈmulti-storey *adj.* mehrstöckig; mehrgeschossig; ~ **car park/block of flats** Parkhaus/Wohnhochhaus, *das*
multitude [ˈmʌltɪtju:d] *n.* **a)** *(crowd)* Menge, *die; (great number)* Vielzahl, *die;* **cover a** ~ **of sins** *(joc.)* ein weites Feld umfassen; *(compensate)* vieles aufwiegen; **a** ~ **of animals/vehicles/men** eine Vielzahl von Tieren/Fahrzeugen/Männern; **b) the [common]** ~: die [breite] Masse *(oft abwertend)*
multitudinous [mʌltɪˈtju:dɪnəs] *adj.* **a)** *(comprising many individuals)* vielköpfig ⟨*Herde, Versammlung*⟩; **b)** *(very many)* zahlreich
ˈmulti-volume *adj.* vielbändig

[1]mum [mʌm] *(coll.)* **1.** *int.* pst; ~**'s the word** nicht weitersagen!; *(I won't tell anyone else)* ich sag's nicht weiter. **2.** *adj.* leise; ruhig; still; **keep** ~: den Mund halten *(ugs.);* **keep** ~ **about sth.** etw. nicht weitersagen
[2]mum *n. (Brit. coll.: mother)* Mama, *die (fam.)*
mumble [ˈmʌmbl] **1.** *v. i.* nuscheln *(ugs.);* ~ **[away] about sth.** über etw. *(Akk.)* nuscheln *(ugs.).* **2.** *v. t.* **a)** *(utter indistinctly)* nuscheln *(ugs.);* ~ **one's words/phrases** *etc.* nuscheln *(ugs.);* **b)** *(chew)* mit zahnlosem Mund kauen. **3.** *n.* Nuscheln, *das*
mumbo-jumbo [mʌmbəʊˈdʒʌmbəʊ] *n., pl.* ~**s a)** *(meaningless ritual)* Brimborium, *das (ugs.);* Theater, *das (ugs. abwertend);* **b)** *(gibberish)* Kauderwelsch, *das;* **c)** *(object of senseless veneration)* Idol, *das;* Götze, *der*
mummer [ˈmʌmə(r)] *n. (Theatre)* Pantomime, *der*/Pantomimin, *die*
mummery [ˈmʌmərɪ] *n. (derog.)* Mummenschanz, *der (abwertend)*
mummify [ˈmʌmɪfaɪ] *v. t.* **a)** mumifizieren; **b)** *(shrivel)* austrocknen
[1]mummy [ˈmʌmɪ] *n.* Mumie, *die*
[2]mummy *n. (Brit. coll.: mother)* Mutti, *die (fam.);* Mami, *die (fam.);* Mama, *die (fam.)*
mumps [mʌmps] *n. sing. (Med.)* Mumps, *der*
munch [mʌnʃ] **1.** *v. t.* ~ **one's food** mampfen *(salopp);* schmatzend kauen. **2.** *v. i.* mampfen *(salopp);* ~ **[away] at sth.** an etw. *(Dat.)* kauen
mundane [mʌnˈdeɪn] *adj.* **a)** *(dull)* banal; profan *(geh.);* stumpfsinnig ⟨*Entschluß, Routine*⟩; **b)** *(worldly)* weltlich; irdisch
Munich [ˈmju:nɪk] *pr. n.* München *(das); attrib.* Münchner
municipal [mjʊˈnɪsɪpl] *adj.* gemeindlich; kommunal; Kommunal⟨*politik, -verwaltung*⟩; Gemeinde⟨*rat, -verwaltung, -beschluß*⟩; ~ **district** *(Can., Austral.)* Landgemeinde, *die*
municipality [mju:nɪsɪˈpælɪtɪ] *n.* **a)** *(political unit)* Gemeinde, *die;* **b)** *(governing body)* Gemeindeverwaltung, *die*
munificence [mjʊˈnɪfɪsəns] *n. (formal)* Generosität, *die;* Hochherzigkeit, *die (geh.)*
munificent [mjʊˈnɪfɪsənt] *adj.,* **munificently** [mjʊˈnɪfɪsəntlɪ] *adv. (formal)* generös *(geh.)*
munition [mjʊˈnɪʃn] *n., usu. in pl.* Kriegsmaterial, *das;* ~**[s] factory** Rüstungsbetrieb, *der;* ~**[s] worker** Arbeiter in einem Rüstungsbetrieb
muntjak (muntjac) [ˈmʌntdʒæk] *n. (Zool.)* Muntjak, *der*
mural [ˈmjʊərl] **1.** *adj. (on a wall)* Wand-; an Wänden *nachgestellt.* **2.** *n.* Wandbild, *das;* Wandgemälde, *das; (on ceiling)* Deckengemälde, *das*
murder [ˈmɜ:də(r)] **1.** *n.* **a)** *(Law)* Mord, *der* (**of** an + *Dat.*); ~ **investigation** Ermittlungen *Pl.* in dem/einem Mordfall; ~ **hunt** Fahndung nach dem/einem Mörder; **be accused of** ~: des Mordes beschuldigt werden; **be arrested on a charge of** ~: unter Mordverdacht verhaftet werden; ~ **will out** *(prov.: sth. cannot be hidden)* die Wahrheit kommt doch an den Tag; **b)** *(fig.)* **the exam/journey was** ~: die Prüfung/Reise war der glatte *od.* reine Mord *(ugs.). See also* **blue murder; get away with c; judicial a. 2.** *v. t.* **a)** *(kill unlawfully)* ermorden; ~ **sb. with a gun/knife** jmdn. erschießen/erstechen; **I could** ~ **him/a hamburger/a beer** *(fig. coll.)* ich könnte ihn umbringen/einen Hamburger vertragen/ein Bier vertragen *(ugs.);* **b)** *(kill inhumanly)* umbringen; **c)** *(coll.: spoil)* verhunzen *(ugs.);* **d)** *(coll.: defeat)* fertigmachen *(ugs.)*
murderer [ˈmɜ:dərə(r)] *n.* Mörder, *der*/Mörderin, *die;* **be accused of being a** ~: des Mordes beschuldigt werden
murderess [ˈmɜ:dərɪs] *n.* Mörderin, *die*

murderous [ˈmɜ:dərəs] *adj.* tödlich; Mord⟨*absicht, -drohung*⟩; vernichtend ⟨*Blick*⟩; mörderisch *(ugs.)* ⟨*Fahrweise, Wetter, Kampf, Bedingung*⟩; ~ **nature/mentality/psychology** Wesen/Mentalität/Psyche eines Mörders
murk [mɜ:k] *n.* Dunkelheit, *die;* Nebelnacht, *die (geh.)*
murky [ˈmɜ:kɪ] *adj.* **a)** *(dark)* düster; trüb ⟨*Tag, Wetter*⟩; **b)** *(dirty)* schmutzig-trüb ⟨*Wasser*⟩; **c)** *(thick, opaque)* trüb ⟨*Luft, Atmosphäre*⟩; verhangen ⟨*Himmel*⟩; tief ⟨*Dunkelheit*⟩; *(fig.: obscure)* dunkel; undurchsichtig; unergründlich ⟨*Geheimnis, Tiefen*⟩; ~ **past** dunkle Vergangenheit
murmur [ˈmɜ:mə(r)] **1.** *n.* **a)** *(subdued sound)* Rauschen, *das; (of brook also)* Murmeln, *das (dichter.); (of bee)* Summen, *das;* **b)** *(Med.)* **heart** ~: Herzgeräusch, *das;* Klappengeräusch, *das;* **c)** *(expression of discontent)* Murren, *das;* **raise a few** ~**s** einige unzufriedene Stimmen laut werden lassen; ~ **of disagreement/impatience** ablehnendes/ungeduldiges Murren; **without a** ~: ohne Murren; ohne zu murren; **d)** *(soft speech)* Murmeln, *das;* ~ **of approval/delight** beifälliges/freudiges Murmeln; **a** ~ **of voices** ein Gemurmel; **say sth. in a** ~: etw. murmeln. **2.** *v. t.* murmeln; raunen *(geh.),* hauchen ⟨*Zärtlichkeiten*⟩. **3.** *v. i.* **a)** ⟨*Person:*⟩ murmeln; *(make soft sound)* ⟨*Brise:*⟩ rauschen; **b)** *(complain)* murren (**against, at** über + *Akk.*)
murphy [ˈmɜ:fɪ] *n. (sl.)* Kartoffel, *die;* Knolle, *die (ugs.)*
muscadel *see* **muscatel**
muscat [ˈmʌskət] *n. (grape)* Muskattraube, *die; (vine)* Muskatrebe, *die*
muscatel [mʌskəˈtel] *n.* **a)** *(raisin)* Muskadinerosine, *die;* **b)** *(wine)* Muskateller[wein], *der*
muscle [ˈmʌsl] **1.** *n.* **a)** Muskel, *der;* **not move a** ~ *(fig.)* sich nicht rühren; **b)** *(tissue)* Muskeln *Pl.;* **be all** ~: nur aus Muskeln bestehen; **c)** *(muscular power)* [Muskel-, Körper]kraft, *die;* Muskeln *Pl.; (fig.: force, power, influence)* Stärke, *die;* **have financial** ~: finanzkräftig *od.* -stark sein; [finanziell] potent sein; **have industrial** ~: eine leistungsfähige Industrie haben. **2.** *v. i.* ~ ˈ**in** *(coll.)* sich hineindrängen (**on** in + *Akk.*); **they're muscling in on our market** sie machen sich auf unserem Markt breit *(ugs.);* **you're muscling in [on my territory** *(fig.)*] du kommst mir ins Gehege
muscle: ~**-bound** *adj.* **a)** *(with powerful muscles)* muskelbepackt *(ugs.);* **b)** *(with stiff muscles)* **be** ~**-bound** Muskelkater haben; *(fig.)* verknöchert sein; **become** ~**-bound** *(fig.)* verknöchern; ~**man** *n.* **a)** *(intimidator)* Gorilla, *der (ugs.);* **b)** *(sb. with powerful physique)* Muskelmann, *der (ugs.)*
Muscovite [ˈmʌskəvaɪt] **1.** *n.* Moskauer, *der*/Moskauerin, *die;* Moskowiter, *der*/Moskowiterin, *die (veralt.).* **2.** *adj.* moskauisch, Moskauer ⟨*Winter, Arbeiter*⟩
muscular [ˈmʌskjʊlə(r)] *adj.* **a)** *(Med.)* Muskel-; muskulär *(fachspr.);* **b)** *(sinewy)* muskulös. *See also* **dystrophy**
muscularity [mʌskjʊˈlærɪtɪ] *n., no pl.* Muskulosität, *die*
[1]muse [mju:z] *n.* **a) M**~ *(Greek and Roman Mythol.)* Muse, *die;* **b)** *(Lit.)* Genius, *der (geh.)*
[2]muse *(literary)* **1.** *v. i. (ponder)* grübeln; [nach]sinnen *(geh.),* sinnieren (**on, about, over** über + *Akk.*). **2.** *v. t.* sinnieren
museum [mju:ˈzi:əm] *n.* Museum, *das;* **an art** ~, **a** ~ **of art** ein Kunstmuseum ; **a** ~ **of modern art** ein Museum für moderne Kunst
muˈseum piece *n.* **a)** *(specimen of art)* Museumsstück, *das;* **b)** *(joc. derog.) (old-fashioned thing)* Museumsstück, *das (ugs. iron.); (old-fashioned person)* Fossil, *das*
[1]mush [mʌʃ] *n.* **a)** *(soft pulp)* Mus, *das;* Brei,

der; **boil into a ~** ⟨*Kartoffeln:*⟩ zu Mus kochen *od.* verkochen; **~ of mud/snow** Matsch, *der;* **b)** *(coll.: weak sentimentality)* Schmalz, *der (ugs. abwertend)*

²mush [mʊʃ] *n. (sl.: face, mouth)* Schnauze, *die (derb)*

mushroom ['mʌʃrʊm, 'mʌʃru:m] **1.** *n.* **a)** Pilz, *der; (edible)* [Speise]pilz, *der; (cultivated, esp. Agaricus campestris)* Champignon, *der; attrib.* Pilz-; **grow like ~s** *(fig.)* wie Pilze aus dem Boden schießen; **b)** *(fig.)* **~ of smoke** Rauchpilz, *der; see also* **mushroom cloud. 2.** *v. i.* **a)** *(spring up)* wie Pilze aus dem Boden schießen; *(grow rapidly)* **demand ~ed overnight** die Nachfrage schoß über Nacht in die Höhe; **b)** *(expand and flatten)* ⟨*Aschenwolke, Rauch:*⟩ sich pilzförmig ausbreiten

mushroom: ~ cloud *n.* Rauchpilz, *der; (after nuclear explosion)* Atompilz, *der;* **~-colour** *n.* blasses Gelbbraun; **~-coloured** *adj.* blaß gelbbraun

mushy ['mʌʃɪ] *adj.* **a)** *(soft)* breiig; matschig ⟨*Boden*⟩; **b)** *(coll.: feebly sentimental)* schmalzig *(abwertend);* gefühlsduselig *(ugs. abwertend)* ⟨*Mensch*⟩; **be full of ~ sentiment** vor Schmalz triefen *(abwertend)*

music ['mju:zɪk] *n.* **a)** Musik, *die;* **make ~:** Musik machen; musizieren; **student of ~:** Musikstudent, *der/*-studentin, *die;* **piece of ~:** Musikstück, *das;* Musik, *die;* **set** *or* **put sth. to ~:** etw. vertonen *od.* in Musik setzen; **have a gift for ~:** musikalisch begabt *od.* musikbegabt sein; **be ~ to sb.'s ears** *(fig. coll.)* Musik in jmds. Ohren sein *(ugs.); see also* **face 2 c; set 1 s; sphere c; b)** *(of waves, wind, brook)* Rauschen, *das; (of birds)* Gesang, *der;* **c)** *(score)* Noten *Pl.; (as merchandise also)* Musikalien *Pl.;* **sheet of ~:** Notenblatt, *das;* **play from ~:** nach Noten spielen

musical ['mju:zɪkl] **1.** *adj.* **a)** *(of music)* musikalisch ⟨*Abend, Begabung*⟩; Musik⟨*instrument, -verein, -verständnis, -notation, -abend*⟩; **b)** *(melodious)* musikalisch ⟨*Stimme, Klänge*⟩; melodiös, melodisch ⟨*Stück*⟩; **c)** *(fond of or skilled in music)* musikalisch; **d)** *(set to music)* musikalisch; Musik⟨*film, -theater*⟩. **2.** *n. (Mus., Theatre)* Musical, *das*

musical: ~ box *n. (Brit.)* Spieldose, *die;* **~ 'chairs** *n. sing.* Reise nach Jerusalem; **~ director** *n. (Theatre)* Musikdirektor, *der/*-direktorin, *die; (conductor)* Kapellmeister, *der/*-meisterin, *die*

musically ['mju:zɪkəlɪ] *adv. (with regard to music)* musikalisch; *(melodiously)* melodisch; melodiös; **~ gifted** musikalisch [begabt]; musikbegabt

music: ~ box *(Amer.) see* **musical box; ~ centre** *n.* Kompaktanlage, *die;* **~ drama** *n.* Musikdrama, *das;* **~-hall** *n. (Brit.)* **1.** *n.* Varieté, *das;* **2.** *attrib. adj.* Varieté-

musician [mju:'zɪʃn] *n.* Musiker, *der/*Musikerin, *die; (minstrel, street ~ etc.)* Musikant, *der/*Musikantin, *die*

'music-lesson *n.* Musikstunde, *die*

musicologist [mju:zɪ'kɒlədʒɪst] *n.* Musikwissenschaftler, *der/*-wissenschaftlerin, *die;* Musikologe, *der/*Musikologin, *die (geh.)*

musicology [mju:zɪ'kɒlədʒɪ] *n.* Musikwissenschaft, *die;* Musikologie, *die (geh.)*

music: ~-paper *n.* Notenpapier, *das;* **~-rest** *n.* Notenpult, *das;* **~-room** *n.* Musiksaal, *der; (for concerts)* Konzertsaal, *der;* **~-stand** *n.* Notenständer, *der;* **~-stool** *n.* Klavierhocker, *der;* Klavierschemel, *der;* **~-teacher** *n.* Musiklehrer, *der/*-lehrerin, *die*

musk [mʌsk] *n.* **a)** *(substance)* Moschus, *der;* **~-scented** mit Moschus parfümiert; **b)** *(odour)* Moschusgeruch, *der;* **c)** *(Bot.)* Moschusgauklerblume, *die*

'musk-deer *n. (Zool.)* Moschushirsch, *der*

musket ['mʌskɪt] *n. (Arms Hist.)* Muskete, *die*

musketeer [mʌskɪ'tɪə(r)] *n. (Hist.)* Musketier, *der*

musketry ['mʌskɪtrɪ] *n. (Hist.) (muskets)* Musketen *Pl.; (musketeers)* Musketiere *Pl.*

musk: ~-melon *n.* Zuckermelone, *die;* Gartenmelone, *die;* **~-ox** *n. (Zool.)* Moschusochse, *der;* **~-rat** *n.* **a)** *(Zool.)* Bisamratte, *die;* **b)** *(fur)* Bisam, *der;* **~-rose** *n. (Bot.)* Moschusrose, *die*

musky ['mʌskɪ] *adj.* moschusartig duftend; moschusartig ⟨*Duft, Geruch, Geschmack*⟩; Moschus⟨*duft, -parfüm*⟩

Muslim ['mʊslɪm, 'mʌzlɪm] **1.** *adj.* muslimisch *(bes. fachspr.);* moslemisch; **be ~** ⟨*Person:*⟩ Muslim/Muslime sein, Moslem/Moslime sein. **2.** *n.* Muslim, *der/*Muslime, *die (bes. fachspr.);* Moslem, *der/*Moslime, *die*

muslin ['mʌzlɪn] **1.** *n.* **a)** Musselin, *der.* **2.** *adj.* musselinen; Musselin-

musquash ['mʌskwɒʃ] *n.* **a)** *(Zool.)* Bisamratte, *die;* **b)** *(fur)* Bisam, *der*

muss [mʌs] *v. t. (Amer. coll.)* verstrubbeln *(ugs.)* ⟨*Haar, Frisur*⟩; zerknittern ⟨*Stoff*⟩

~ 'up *v. t.* durcheinanderbringen; verstrubbeln *(ugs.)* ⟨*Haar*⟩; zerknittern ⟨*Kleidung*⟩

mussel ['mʌsl] *n.* Muschel, *die;* **bed of ~s, ~ bed** Muschelbank, *die*

¹must [məst, *stressed* mʌst] **1.** *v. aux., only in pres. and past* **must**, *neg. (coll.)* **mustn't** ['mʌsnt] **a)** *(have to)* müssen; *with negative* dürfen; **you ~ not/never do that** das darfst du nicht/nie tun; **you ~ remember ...:** du darfst nicht vergessen, ...; du mußt daran denken, ...; **you ~ stop that noise/listen to me!** hör mit dem Lärm auf/hör mir zu!; **you mustn't do that again!** tu das [ja] nie wieder!; **I ~ get back to the office** ich muß wieder ins Büro; **I ~ go to London** ich muß nach London; **I ~ leave at 6 o'clock** ich muß um 6 Uhr weg *od.* los; **do it if you ~:** wenn es sein muß, tu es eben; tu, was du nicht lassen kannst *(ugs.);* **I will go if I ~** wenn es sein muß, gehe ich; **~ I?** muß das sein?; **'~ you shout so loudly?** mußt du denn so laut schreien?; **I ~ away** *(arch.)* ich muß fort; **I ~ have a new dress** ich brauche ein neues Kleid; **why ~ it always rain on Saturdays?** warum muß es ausgerechnet sonnabends immer regnen?; **I '~ say ...:** ich muß sagen ...; **[that] I '~ say** [das] muß ich schon sagen; **if you '~ know** wenn du es unbedingt wissen willst; **b)** *(ought to)* müssen; *with negative* dürfen; **I ~ ask you to leave** ich muß Sie bitten zu gehen; **you ~ think about it** du solltest [unbedingt] darüber nachdenken; **I ~ not sit here drinking coffee** ich sollte *od.* dürfte eigentlich nicht hier sitzen und Kaffee trinken; **c)** *(be certain to)* müssen; **you ~ be tired** du mußt müde sein; du bist bestimmt müde; **you ~ be crazy** du bist wohl wahnsinnig!; **there ~ be a reason** es muß einen Grund geben; **it ~ be about 3 o'clock** es wird wohl *od.* dürfte *od.* müßte etwa 3 Uhr sein; **I ~ have lost it** ich muß es verloren haben; **it ~ have stopped raining by now** es dürfte *od.* müßte inzwischen aufgehört haben zu regnen; **I think they ~ have left** ich denke, sie sind sicher *od.* bestimmt weggegangen; **20 people ~ have visited me** es haben mich bestimmt 20 Leute besucht; **there ~ have been forty of them** *(forty)* es müssen vierzig gewesen sein; *(probably about forty)* es dürften etwa vierzig gewesen sein; **you ~ have seen it** *(necessarily would have)* du hättest es sehen müssen; *expr. indignation or annoyance* **he ~ come just when ...:** er muß/mußte natürlich *od.* ausgerechnet kommen, wenn/als ...; **what ~ I do but break my leg?** Was mußte natürlich kommen? Ich mußte mir das Bein brechen; *see also* **joke 2. 2.** *n. (coll.)* Muß, *das;* **be a ~ for sb./sth.** ein Muß für jmdn./unerläßlich für etw. sein

²must *n.* **a)** *(wine)* neuer Wein; **b)** *(grape-juice)* Most, *der*

³must *see* **mustiness**

mustache *see* **moustache**

mustachio [mə'stɑ:ʃəʊ] *n., pl.* **~s** Schnauzbart, *der*

mustachioed [mə'stɑ:ʃəʊd] *adj.* schnauzbärtig

mustang ['mʌstæŋ] *n.* Mustang, *der*

mustard ['mʌstəd] *n.* **a)** Senf, *der; attrib.* Senf⟨*geschmack usw.*⟩; **~ and cress** *(Brit.)* Senfkeimlinge und Kresse; **b)** *(colour)* Senffarbe, *die; attrib.* senffarben; **c)** *(Amer. sl.: thing that provides zest)* Pep, *der (ugs.);* **cut the ~:** es bringen *(ugs.);* **I can't cut the ~:** ich bringe es nicht *(ugs.)*

mustard: ~-coloured *adj.* senffarben; **~ gas** *n. (Chem., Mil.)* Senfgas, *das;* **~ plaster** *n.* Senfpflaster, *das;* **~-pot** *n.* Senftopf, *der;* **~-yellow** *adj.* senfgelb

muster ['mʌstə(r)] **1.** *n.* **a)** *(Mil.)* Appell, *der;* **pass ~** *(fig.)* akzeptabel sein; **b)** *(assembly)* Zusammenkunft, *die.* **2.** *v. t.* **a)** *(summon)* versammeln; *(Mil., Naut.)* [zum Appell] antreten lassen; **b)** *(collect)* zusammenbringen; zusammenziehen ⟨*Streitkräfte, Truppen*⟩; zusammentreiben ⟨*Vieh*⟩; *(raise)* aufstellen ⟨*Armee*⟩; ausheben ⟨*Truppen*⟩; **c)** *(fig.: summon up)* zusammennehmen ⟨*Kraft, Mut, Verstand*⟩; aufbringen ⟨*Unterstützung*⟩; **~ [the] strength to do sth.** all seine Kräfte zusammennehmen, um etw. zu tun; **he couldn't ~ [the] courage to do it** er brachte nicht den Mut auf, es zu tun. **3.** *v. i.* sich [ver]sammeln; ⟨*Truppen:*⟩ aufmarschieren; *(for parade)* antreten

~ 'up *v. t.* aufbringen ⟨*Unterstützung, Mut, Verständnis*⟩; **~ up all one's courage** seinen ganzen *od.* all seinen Mut zusammennehmen

mustiness ['mʌstɪnɪs] *n., no pl.* **a)** *(of smell, taste)* Muffigkeit, *die;* Muff, der *(nordd.);* **b)** *(mouldiness)* Stockigkeit, *die*

mustn't ['mʌsnt] *(coll.)* = **must not**

musty ['mʌstɪ] *adj.* **a)** *(smelling or tasting stale)* muffig; **b)** *(mouldy)* stockig; **c)** *(fig.: stale, antiquated)* verstaubt

mutable ['mju:təbl] *adj.* **a)** *(formal: liable to change)* wandelbar *(geh.);* **b)** *(Ling., Biol.)* mutabel *(fachspr.)*

mutant ['mju:tənt] *(Biol.)* **1.** *adj.* mutiert ⟨*Gen, Zelle, Stamm*⟩. **2.** *n.* Mutante, *die*

mutate [mju:'teɪt] *(Biol.)* **1.** *v. t.* zur Mutation anregen; **be ~d** mutieren. **2.** *v. i.* mutieren

mutation [mju:'teɪʃn] *n.* **a)** *(formal: change)* Wandel, *der;* Wandlung, *die;* **b)** *(Biol.)* Mutation, *die; attrib.* Mutations-

mute [mju:t] **1.** *adj. (dumb, silent; also Ling.)* stumm; *(silent also)* schweigend; *(temporarily bereft of speech also)* sprachlos; **be ~ with rage/amazement/grief/from shock** vor Zorn/Staunen/Kummer/Entsetzen kein Wort hervorbringen *od.* über die Lippen bringen. **2.** *n.* **a)** *(dumb person)* Stumme, *der/die;* **b)** *(Mus.)* Dämpfer, *der.* **3.** *v. t.* dämpfen

muted ['mju:tɪd] *adj.* gedämpft; verhalten ⟨*Kritik, Begeisterung*⟩

mutely ['mju:tlɪ] *adv.* stumm; *(silently also)* schweigend

mute 'swan *n.* Höckerschwan, *der*

mutilate ['mju:tɪleɪt] *v. t. (deprive of limb; fig.: render imperfect)* verstümmeln; mutilieren *(Med.); (cut off)* abtrennen ⟨*Gliedmaße*⟩

mutilation [mju:tɪ'leɪʃn] *n. (deprivation of limb; fig.: rendering imperfect)* Verstümmelung, *die;* Mutilation, *die (Med.)*

mutineer [mju:tɪ'nɪə(r)] *n.* Meuterer, *der*

mutinous ['mju:tɪnəs] *adj.* rebellisch ⟨*Geist, Person*⟩; aufrührerisch ⟨*Rede, Gedanke*⟩; meuternd ⟨*Mannschaft eines Schiffs, Truppen*⟩; **~ acts** Akte der Meuterei; **become ~:** meutern

mutinously ['mju:tɪnəslɪ] *adj.* rebellisch, aufrührerisch ‹*sich benehmen*›
mutiny ['mju:tɪnɪ] **1.** *n.* Meuterei, *die.* **2.** *v. i.* meutern
mutt [mʌt] *n. (sl.)* **a)** *(person)* Schafskopf, *der (ugs.);* **poor ~:** armer Irrer *(salopp);* **b)** *(derog.: dog)* Köter, *der (abwertend)*
mutter ['mʌtə(r)] **1.** *v. i.* **a)** *(speak low)* murmeln; brummeln; **~ [away] to oneself** vor sich *(Akk.)* hin murmeln *od.* brummeln; **b)** *(grumble)* murren **(at, about** über + *Akk.*). **2.** *v. t. (utter)* murmeln ‹*Beleidigung, Gebet, Drohung*›; **~ sth. under one's breath/to oneself** sich *(Dat.)* etw. in den Bart/etw. vor sich *(Akk.)* hin murmeln. **3.** *n.* Gemurmel, *das;* **~ of voices** Gemurmel [von Stimmen]
muttering ['mʌtərɪŋ] *n.* **a)** *no pl. (low speech)* Gemurmel, *das;* **b) ~[s]** *(complaints)* Gemurre, *das*
mutton ['mʌtn] *n.* Hammelfleisch, *das;* Hammel, *der;* **[a case of] ~ dressed [up] as lamb** *(coll. derog.)* [eine] aufgetakelte Fregatte *(ugs. abwertend); see also* **dead 1 a**
mutton: ~ 'chop *n.* **a)** Hammelkotelett, *das;* **b) ~-chop [whiskers]** [Bart]koteletten *Pl.;* **~-head** *n. (coll. derog.)* Schafskopf, *der (ugs.)*
mutual ['mju:tjʊəl] *adj.* **a)** *(given and received)* gegenseitig; beiderseitig ‹*Einvernehmen, Vorteil, Bemühung*›; wechselseitig ‹*Abhängigkeit*›; **look at each other with ~ suspicion** sich argwöhnisch ansehen; **I can't bear you! – The feeling's ~:** Ich kann dich nicht riechen! – Das beruht auf Gegenseitigkeit; **to our ~ satisfaction/benefit** zu unser beider Zufriedenheit/Nutzen; **~ aid programme** Programm zur gegenseitigen Hilfe; **be ~ well-wishers** es gut miteinander meinen; **b)** *(coll.: shared)* gemeinsam ‹*Interesse, Freund, Abneigung usw.*›
mutual: ~ admi'ration society *n. (joc.) Kreis von Leuten, die alle eine ungerechtfertigt hohe Meinung voneinander haben;* **~ 'fund** *n. (Amer. Econ.)* Investmentgesellschaft, *die;* **~ in'surance company** *n.* Versicherungsverein auf Gegenseitigkeit
mutuality [mju:tjʊ'ælɪtɪ] *n., no pl.* Gegenseitigkeit, *die; (of interests)* Gemeinsamkeit, *die*
mutually ['mju:tjʊəlɪ] *adv.* **a)** gegenseitig; **be ~ exclusive** einander *(geh.) od.* sich [gegenseitig] ausschließen; **~ beneficial/accepted** für beide Seiten vorteilhaft/von beiden Seiten akzeptiert; **b)** *(in common)* gemeinsam
muzak ['mju:zæk] *n. (often derog.)* Hintergrundmusik, *die;* Berieselungsmusik, *die (ugs. abwertend)*
muzzle ['mʌzl] **1.** *n.* **a)** *(of dog)* Schnauze, *die; (of horse, cattle)* Maul, *das;* **b)** *(of gun)* Mündung, *die;* **c)** *(put over animal's mouth)* Maulkorb, *der.* **2.** *v. t.* **a)** einen Maulkorb umbinden *od.* anlegen (+ *Dat.*) ‹*Hund*›; **b)** *(fig.)* mundtot machen, einen Maulkorb anlegen *(ugs.)* (+ *Dat.*) ‹*Presse, Kritiker*›; knebeln ‹*Presse, Redefreiheit*›; unterdrücken ‹*Protest*›
muzzle: ~-loader *n.* Vorderlader, *der;* **~ velocity** *n.* Mündungsgeschwindigkeit, *die*
muzzy ['mʌzɪ] *adj.* **a)** *(mentally hazy, blurred)* verschwommen; verworren ‹*Verstand*›; **feel ~:** ein dumpfes Gefühl haben; **b)** *(from intoxication)* benebelt **(with** von)
MW *abbr.* **a)** *(Radio)* **medium wave** MW; **b)** *(Electr., Phys.)* **megawatt[s]** MW
my [maɪ] *poss. pron. attrib.* **a)** *(belonging to me)* mein; **b)** *in affectionate, jocular, patronizing, etc. use* mein; **my poor fellow** du Ärmster; *see also* **man 1 b; c)** *in excl. of surprise* **my[, my]!, [my] oh my!** [ach du] meine Güte! *(ugs.);* ach du grüne Neune! *(ugs.). See also* **god b; ²her; word 1 c**
mycelium [maɪ'si:lɪəm] *n., pl.* **mycelia** [maɪ'si:lɪə] *(Bot.)* Myzel[ium], *das*
Mycenaean [maɪsɪ'ni:ən] *adj. (Archaeol.)* mykenisch
mycology [maɪ'kɒlədʒɪ] *n.* Mykologie, *die*
myna, mynah *see* **mina**
myopia [maɪ'əʊpɪə] *n.* Kurzsichtigkeit, *die (auch fig.);* Myopie, *die (fachspr.)*
myopic [maɪ'əʊpɪk] *adj.* kurzsichtig *(auch fig.);* myopisch *(fachspr.)*
myriad ['mɪrɪəd] *(literary)* **1.** *adj.* unzählig; Myriaden von *(geh.)* ‹*Insekten, Sternen*›. **2.** *n. (great number)* Unzahl, *die;* Myriade, *die (geh.);* **a ~ of possibilities** Myriaden von Möglichkeiten
myriapod, myriopod ['mɪrɪəpɒd] *n. (Zool.)* Myriapode, *der;* Myriopode, *der*
myrrh [mɜ:(r)] *n.* Myrrhe, *die*
myrtle ['mɜ:tl] *n. (Bot.)* **a) common ~:** Myrte, *die;* **b)** *(Amer.: periwinkle)* Immergrün, *das*
myself [maɪ'self] *pron.* **a)** *emphat.* selbst; **I thought so ~:** das habe ich auch gedacht; **I haven't been there, ~:** ich war nicht selbst da; **[even] though/if I say it ~:** wenn ich es auch selbst sage; **I am quite ~ again** mir geht es wieder gut; **I want to be ~:** ich will ich selbst sein; **b) you know more than ~:** du weißt mehr als ich [selbst]; **there were the three of them and ~:** da waren die drei und ich [selbst]; **c)** *refl.* mich/mir; **I washed ~:** ich wusch mich; **I'm going to get ~ a car** ich werde mir ein Auto zulegen; **I said to ~:** ich sagte mir; **I need to have time to ~:** ich brauche Zeit für mich. *See also* **herself**
mysterious [mɪ'stɪərɪəs] *adj.* **a)** *(curious, strange)* mysteriös; rätselhaft; geheimnisvoll ‹*Fremder, Orient*›; **~-looking** geheimnisvoll aussehend; **he did it for some ~ reason of his own** er hat es aus irgendeinem unerfindlichen Grunde getan; **b)** *(secretive)* geheimnisvoll; **be very ~ about sth.** ein großes Geheimnis aus etw. machen; **why are you being so ~?** warum tust du so geheimnisvoll?
mysteriously [mɪ'stɪərɪəslɪ] *adv.* auf mysteriöse *od.* rätselhafte Weise; sonderbar ‹*erfreut usw.*›; geheimnisvoll ‹*lächeln usw.*›
mystery ['mɪstərɪ] *n.* **a)** *(hidden, inexplicable matter)* Rätsel, *das;* **it's a ~ to me why ...:** es ist mir schleierhaft *(ugs.) od.* ein Rätsel, warum ...; **make a ~ [out] of sth.** ein Geheimnis aus etw. machen; **make no ~ of sth.** kein *od.* keinen Hehl aus etw. machen; **the mysteries of a trade** die Geheimnisse eines Handwerks; **he's a bit of a ~:** er hat etwas Rätselhaftes *od.* Geheimnisvolles; **b)** *(secrecy)* Geheimnis, *das;* **wrapped in** *or* **shrouded in** *or* **surrounded by ~:** geheimnisumwittert *od.* -umwoben *(geh.);* **there's no ~ about it** das ist überhaupt kein Geheimnis; **~ man, man of ~:** rätselhafter Mann; **c)** *(making a secret of things)* Heimlichtuerei, *die;* **d)** *(religious truth)* Mysterium, *das (geh.);* **e)** *see* **mystery play; mystery story**
mystery: ~ novel *n.* ≈ Detektiv- *od.* Kriminalroman, *der;* **~ play** *n.* Mysterienspiel, *das;* **~ story** *n. (detective story)* ≈ Detektiv- *od.* Kriminalgeschichte, *die; (mysterious story)* rätselhafte Erzählung; **~ tour, ~ trip** *ns.* Fahrt ins Blaue *(ugs.);* **~ writer** Kriminalschriftsteller, *der*/-schriftstellerin, *die;* Krimi-Autor, *der*/-Autorin, *die (ugs.)*
mystic ['mɪstɪk] **1.** *adj.* **a)** mystisch; **b)** *(mysterious)* geheimnisvoll. **2.** *n.* Mystiker, *der*/Mystikerin, *die*
mystical ['mɪstɪkl] *adj.* mystisch
mysticism ['mɪstɪsɪzm] *n.* Mystik, *die;* Mystizismus, *der (geh.)*
mystification [mɪstɪfɪ'keɪʃn] *n.* Verwirrung, *die;* **add to sb.'s ~:** jmdn. noch mehr verwirren
mystify ['mɪstɪfaɪ] *v. t.* verwirren; **this mystifies me** das ist mir ein Rätsel *od.* rätselhaft; **the police are completely mystified** die Polizei steht vor einem absoluten Rätsel
mystique [mɪ'sti:k] *n.* geheimnisvoller Nimbus
myth [mɪθ] *n.* **a)** Mythos, *der;* **b)** *(fictitious thing or idea)* Mythos, *der; (untrue tale)* Legende, *die; (rumour)* Gerücht, *das*
mythical ['mɪθɪkl] *adj.* **a)** *(based on myth)* mythisch; **~ creatures** Sagengestalten; **the ~ land of Atlantis** das sagenhafte Land Atlantis; **b)** *(invented)* fiktiv
mythological [mɪθə'lɒdʒɪkl] *adj.* mythologisch
mythology [mɪ'θɒlədʒɪ] *n.* Mythologie, *die*
myxomatosis [mɪksəmə'təʊsɪs] *n., pl.* **myxomatoses** [mɪksəmə'təʊsi:z] *(Vet. Med.)* Myxomatose, *die*

N

N, n [en] *n., pl.* **Ns** *or* **N's a)** *(letter)* N, n, *das;* **b)** *(Math.)* n; **nth** [enθ]: **to the nth [degree]** in der n-ten Potenz; *(fig.: to the utmost)* in höchster Potenz *(ugs.);* **for the nth time** zum x-ten Mal *(ugs.)*
'n, 'n' [ən] *conj. (coll.: and)* und
N. *abbr.* **a) north** N; **b) northern** n.; **c)** *(Chess)* **knight** S; **d) nuclear; N-weapons** A-Waffen; **e)** *(Phys.)* **newton** N
n. *abbr.* **a) note** Anm.; **b) nano-** n; **c) neuter** n.
n/a *abbr.* **a) not available** n. bek.; **b) not applicable** entf.
NAAFI ['næfɪ] *abbr. (Brit.)* **Navy, Army and Air Force Institutes** *Kaufhaus für Angehörige der britischen Truppen*
nab [næb] *v. t.,* **-bb-** *(sl.)* **a)** *(arrest)* schnappen *(ugs.);* **b)** *(seize)* sich *(Dat.)* schnappen; **~ him before he goes** sieh zu, daß du ihn noch erwischst, bevor er geht *(ugs.);* **all the best seats had been ~bed** die besten Plätze waren alle schon weggeschnappt; **c)** *(steal)* klauen *(salopp);* krallen *(salopp)*
nacelle [næ'sel] *n.* Gondel, *die*
nacre ['neɪkə(r)] *see* **mother-of-pearl**
nadir ['neɪdɪə(r)] *n.* **a)** *(lowest point)* Tief[st]punkt, *der;* **at the ~:** auf dem Tiefpunkt; **he was at the ~ of despair** er war zutiefst verzweifelt; **b)** *(Astron.)* Nadir, *der*
naff [næf] *(sl.)* **1.** *adj.* ätzend *(ugs.).* **2.** *v. i.* **~ off** abhauen *(ugs.)*
¹nag [næg] **1.** *v. i.,* **-gg- a)** *(scold)* nörgeln *(abwertend);* meckern *(ugs. abwertend);* **~ at sb.** an jmdm. herumnörgeln *od.* -meckern; **~ at sb. to do sth.** jmdm. zusetzen *(ugs.),* daß er etw. tut; **b)** *(cause distress)* **~ at sb.** jmdn. plagen; jmdm. zusetzen *(ugs.) od.* keine Ruhe lassen. **2.** *v. t.,* **-gg- a)** *(scold)* herumnörgeln an (+ *Dat.*) *(abwertend);* herummeckern an (+ *Dat.*) *(abwertend);* **don't ~ me!** laß mich [mit deinem Genörgel *od. (ugs.)* Gemecker] in Ruhe!; **~ sb. about sth./to do sth.** jmdm. wegen etw. zusetzen *(ugs.)*/jmdm. zusetzen *(ugs.),* daß er etw. tut; **b)** *(cause distress)* plagen; keine Ruhe lassen (+ *Dat.*)
²nag *n.* **a)** *(coll.: horse)* Gaul, *der;* **b)** *(old or inferior horse)* Klepper, *der (abwertend)*

nagging ['nægɪŋ] **1.** *adj.* **a)** *(annoying)* nörglerisch *(abwertend);* ständig nörgelnd *(abwertend);* **b)** *(persistent)* quälend ‹*Durst, Angst, Sorge, Zweifel*›; bohrend ‹*Schmerz*›; **a ~ conscience** [quälende] Gewissensbisse *Pl.* **2.** *n.* Genörgel, *das (abwertend);* Gemecker, *das (ugs. abwertend);* **stop your ~:** hör auf zu nörgeln *od.* meckern

naiad ['naɪæd] *n., pl.* **~s** *or* **~es** ['naɪədi:z] Najade, *die*

naïf [nɑ:'i:f] **1.** *adj. see* **naïve. 2.** *n.* Naive, *der/die;* Naivling, *der (ugs. abwertend)*

nail [neɪl] **1.** *n.* **a)** *(on finger, toe)* Nagel, *der;* **cut one's ~s** sich *(Dat.)* die Nägel schneiden; **bite one's ~s** an den Nägeln kauen; *(fig.)* wie auf Kohlen sitzen; **b)** *(metal spike)* Nagel, *der;* **be hard as ~s** *(fig.)* steinhart sein; *(fit)* topfit sein; *(unfeeling, insensitive)* knallhart sein *(ugs.);* **hit the [right] ~ on the head** *(fig.)* den Nagel auf den Kopf treffen *(ugs.);* **be a ~ in sb.'s/sth.'s coffin, drive a ~ into sb.'s/sth.'s coffin** *(fig.)* ein Nagel zu jmds. Sarg/ein Sargnagel für etw. sein *(ugs.);* **on the ~** *(fig. coll.)* pünktlich ‹*bezahlen, sein Geld kriegen*›; **c)** *(claw, talon)* Kralle, *die. See also* **tooth a. 2.** *v.t.* **a)** *(fasten)* nageln (to an + *Akk.*); **~ planks over sth.** etw. mit Brettern vernageln; **~ two planks together** zwei Bretter zusammennageln; **b)** *(fig.: expose)* **~ sth. [to the counter** *or* **barn-door]** etw. anprangern; **c)** *(fig.: fix)* **be ~ed to the spot/ground** wie angenagelt sein *(ugs.);* **~ one's eyes/attention on sth.** seine Augen auf etw. *(Akk.)* heften *(geh.)*/seine Aufmerksamkeit auf etw. *(Akk.)* konzentrieren; **d)** *(fig.: secure, catch, engage)* an Land ziehen *(ugs.)* ‹*Vertrag, Auftrag*›; **e)** *(sl.: arrest)* einkassieren *(salopp). See also* **colour 1 j**

~ 'down *v.t.* **a)** festnageln; zunageln ‹*Kiste, Fenster*›; **b)** *(fig.) (define)* untermauern ‹*Argument*›; festlegen ‹*Strategie*›; *(bind)* **~ sb. down to sth.** jmdn. auf etw. *(Akk.)* festnageln

~ 'up *v.t.* **a)** *(close)* vernageln; **b)** *(affix with ~)* annageln (**against** an + *Akk.*)

nail: ~-biting 1. *n., no pl.* Nägelkauen, *das;* **2.** *adj. (fig.)* bang ‹*Minuten, Schweigen, Sorge*›; angstvoll ‹*Spannung*›; spannungsgeladen ‹*Spiel, Film*›; **~-brush** *n.* Nagelbürste, *die;* **~-clippers** *n. pl.* **[pair of] ~-clippers** Nagelknipser, *der;* **~ enamel** *(Amer.) see* **~ polish; ~-file** *n.* Nagelfeile, *die;* **~ polish** *n.* Nagellack, *der;* **~-polish remover** Nagellackentferner, *der;* **~-scissors** *n. pl.* **[pair of] ~-scissors** Nagelschere, *die;* **~ varnish** *(Brit.) see* **~ polish**

naïve, naive [nɑ:'i:v, naɪ'i:v] *adj.* naiv; einfältig

naïvely, naively [nɑ:'i:vlɪ, naɪ'i:vlɪ] *adv.* naiv; *as sentence-modifier* naiverweise

naïvety, naivety [nɑ:'i:vtɪ, naɪ'i:vtɪ], **(naïveté** [nɑ:'i:vteɪ]) *n.* **a)** *(state, quality)* Naivität, *die;* Einfalt, *die;* **b)** *(action)* Naivität, *die*

naked ['neɪkɪd] *adj.* **a)** nackt; **as ~ as the day I was born** wie Gott mich geschaffen hat *(scherzh.);* **go ~:** nackt herumlaufen; **strip sb. ~:** jmdn. nackt ausziehen; **I feel ~ without my make-up on** ohne mein Make-up fühle ich mich nackt; **b)** *(unshaded)* nackt ‹*Glühbirne*›; *(unshielded)* offen ‹*Licht, Flamme*›; **c)** *(defenceless)* wehrlos; **d)** *(without covering)* blank ‹*Schwert*›; bloß ‹*Faust*›; **e)** *(plain)* nackt ‹*Tatsache, Wahrheit, Aggression, Gier, Ehrgeiz*›

naked: ~ 'eye *n.* **visible to** *or* **with the ~ eye** mit bloßem Auge zu erkennen; **~-eye** *adj.* mit bloßem Auge sichtbar

nakedness ['neɪkɪdnɪs] *n., no pl.* Nacktheit, *die;* Blöße, *die (geh.)*

namby-pamby [næmbɪ'pæmbɪ] *adj.* seicht *(abwertend)* ‹*Literatur usw.*›; verzärtelt *(abwertend)* ‹*Person*›; lax *(oft abwertend)* ‹*Handhabung, Normen*›

name [neɪm] **1.** *n.* **a)** Name, *der;* **what's your ~/the ~ of this place?** wie heißt du/dieser Ort?; **my ~ is Jack** ich heiße Jack; mein Name ist Jack; **call sb. by his ~:** jmdn. bei seinem Namen rufen; **no one of** *or* **by that ~:** niemand mit diesem Namen *od. (geh.)* dieses Namens; **last ~:** Zuname, *der,* Nachname, *der;* **know sb./sth. by** *or* **under another ~:** jmdn./etw. unter einem anderen Namen kennen; **the ~ of Edwards** der Name Edwards; **mention no ~s** keine Namen nennen; **fill in one's ~ and address** Name und Adresse eintragen; **she took her mother's ~:** sie nahm den Mädchennamen ihrer Mutter an; **what ~ shall I say?** wen darf ich melden?; **I can't put a ~ to the plant/his face** ich kann die Pflanze nicht benennen/sein Gesicht mit keinem Namen in Verbindung bringen; **a man of** *or* **by the ~ of Miller** ein Mann namens Miller *od.* mit Namen Miller; **go** *or* **be known by** *or* **under the ~ of ...:** unter dem Namen ... bekannt sein; **by ~:** namentlich ‹*erwähnen, aufrufen usw.*›; **refer to sb./sth. by ~:** jmdn./etw. namentlich nennen; **know sb. by ~/by ~ only** jmdn. mit Namen/nur dem Namen nach kennen; **she goes by the ~ of Madame Lola** sie ist unter dem Namen Madame Lola bekannt; **that's the ~ of the game** *(coll.)* darum geht es; **with us speed is the ~ of the game** *(coll.)* bei uns heißt die Devise Schnelligkeit; **put one's/sb.'s ~ down for sth.** sich/jmdn. für etw. vormerken lassen; **put one's/sb.'s ~ down on the waiting-list** sich auf die Warteliste setzen lassen/jmdn. auf die Warteliste setzen; **take sb.'s ~ off the books** jmdn. ausschließen *od.* von der Mitgliederliste streichen; **without a penny to his ~:** ohne einen Pfennig in der Tasche; **he hasn't a pair of shoes to his ~:** er kann nicht einmal ein Paar Schuhe sein eigen nennen *(ugs.);* **what's in a ~?** Name ist Schall und Rauch; **... or my ~ is not John Smith** ... so wahr ich John Smith heiße; **if this doesn't work, my ~ is not Peter Brown** *etc.* wenn das nicht funktioniert, will ich Emil heißen *(ugs.);* **that bullet had my ~ [and number] on it** die Kugel war für mich bestimmt; **have/see one's ~ [up] in lights** ganz groß herauskommen *(ugs.); see also* **mud c; b)** *(word denoting object of thought)* Bezeichnung, *die;* Name, *der;* **~s cannot hurt me** Beschimpfungen tun mir nicht weh; **c) in ~ [only]** [nur] auf dem Papier; **a Christian/town in ~ only** nur dem Namen nach ein Christ/eine Stadt; **in all but ~:** im Grunde genommen; **d) in the ~ of** im Namen (+ *Gen.*); **in God's ~, in the ~ of God** um Gottes willen; **in Heaven's ~:** um Himmels willen; **in one's own ~:** im eigenen Namen; *(independently)* von sich aus; **e)** *(reputation)* Ruf, *der;* **have a ~ for honesty** für seine Ehrlichkeit bekannt sein; **make a ~ for oneself, win oneself a ~:** sich *(Dat.)* einen Namen machen; **make one's/sb.'s ~:** berühmt werden/jmdn. berühmt machen; **this book made his ~:** mit diesem Buch machte er sich einen Namen; **clear one's/sb.'s ~:** seine/jmds. Unschuld beweisen; **f)** *(famous person)* Name, *der;* **many great** *or* **big ~s** viele namhafte Persönlichkeiten; viele Größen; **be a big ~:** einen großen Namen haben; **g)** *attrib.* **~ brand** Markenartikel, *der;* **~ band** Starband, *die. See also* **assume c; bad 1 a; call 2 i; dog 1 a; false 1 b; proper name; take 1 y; use 2 a; what 5 a. 2.** *v.t.* **a)** *(give ~ to)* einen Namen geben (+ *Dat.*); **~ sb. John** jmdn. John nennen; jmdm. den Namen John geben; **~ a ship 'Mary'** ein Schiff [auf den Namen] „Mary" taufen; **~ sb./sth. after** *or (Amer.)* **for sb.** jmdn./etw. nach jmdm. benennen; **be ~d John** John heißen; **a man ~d Smith** ein Mann namens *od.* mit Namen Smith; **~ sb. John after** *or (Amer.)* **for sb.** jmdn. nach jmdm. John nennen; **b)** *(call by right ~)* benennen; **~ the capital of Zambia** nenne die Hauptstadt von Sambia; **can you ~ the books of the Bible?** kannst du die Bücher der Bibel aufzählen?; **c)** *(nominate)* ernennen; **~ sb. [as] sth.** jmdn. zu etw. ernennen; **~ sb. to an office/a post** jmdn. in ein Amt berufen *od.* einsetzen/auf einen Posten berufen; **~ one's successor/heir** seinen Nachfolger/Erben bestimmen; **he has been ~d as the winner** ihm wurde der Sieg zuerkannt; **be ~d actress of the year** zur Schauspielerin des Jahres gewählt werden; **d)** *(mention)* nennen; *(specify)* benennen; **~ sb. as witness** jmdn. als Zeugen benennen; **~ names** Namen nennen; **he was ~d as the thief** er wurde als der Dieb genannt; **~ the time and I'll meet you there** sag die Zeit, und dann treffen wir uns dort; **~ the day** *(choose wedding-day)* den Tag der Hochzeit festlegen *od.* -setzen; **to ~ but a few** um nur einige zu nennen; **we were given champagne, oysters, you ~ it** wir kriegten Champagner, Austern, und, und, und; **you ~ it, he's got/done** *etc.* **it** *(coll.)* es gibt nichts, was er nicht hat/noch nicht gemacht hat *usw.*

name: ~-calling *n.* Beschimpfungen *Pl.;* **the debate degenerated into mere ~-calling** die Debatte artete in bloße gegenseitige Beschimpfungen aus; **~-day** *n.* Namenstag, *der;* **~-drop** *v.i.* [scheinbar beiläufig] bekannte Namen fallen lassen; **she is always ~-dropping** sie läßt dauernd einfließen, wen sie alles kennt; **~-dropping** ['neɪmdrɒpɪŋ] *n.* Name-dropping, *das; Nennung bedeutender Namen, um Eindruck zu machen*

nameless ['neɪmlɪs] *adj.* **a)** *(having no name, obscure)* namenlos; **a ~ grave** das Grab eines Unbekannten *od.* Namenlosen; **b)** *(not mentioned by name)* **a person who shall remain ~:** eine Person, die ungenannt bleiben soll; **c)** *(anonymous)* namenlos; anonym; **a ~ woman** eine namentlich nicht bekannte Frau; eine Unbekannte; **d)** *(abominable)* unaussprechlich; unsäglich *(geh.);* **e)** *(inexpressible)* unbeschreiblich

namely ['neɪmlɪ] *adv.* nämlich

name: ~-part *n.* Titelrolle, *die;* **~-plate** *n.* Namensschild, *das;* **~sake** *n.* Namensvetter, *der/*-schwester, *die;* **~-tag** *n.* Namensschild, *das;* **~-tape** *n.* Namensschildchen, *das;* ≈ Wäschezeichen, *das*

Namibia [nə'mɪbɪə] *pr. n.* Namibia *(das)*

nan [næn] *n. (child lang./coll.)* Omi, *die (Kinderspr.)*

nancy ['nænsɪ] *(sl.)* **1.** *n.* **~ [boy]** Tunte, *die (salopp).* **2.** *adj.* tuntig *(salopp)*

nanny ['nænɪ] *n.* **a)** *(Brit.: nursemaid)* Kindermädchen, *das;* **b)** *(coll.: granny)* Großmama, *die (fam.);* **c)** *see* **nanny-goat**

'nanny-goat *n.* Ziege, *die;* Geiß, *die (südd., österr., schweiz., westmd.)*

¹nap [næp] **1.** *n.* Schläfchen, *das (ugs.);* Nickerchen, *das (fam.);* **take** *or* **have a ~:** ein Schläfchen *od.* Nickerchen machen *od.* halten; **have an afternoon ~:** ein [Nach]mittagsschläfchen machen *od.* halten. **2.** *v.i.,* **-pp-** dösen *(ugs.);* **catch sb. ~ping** *(fig.)* jmdn. überrumpeln

²nap *n. (of cloth)* Flor, *der*

³nap *n.* **a) go ~** *(Cards)* die höchste Zahl von Stichen ansagen; *(fig.: risk everything)* alles auf eine Karte setzen; **b)** *(Horse-racing etc. coll.: tip)* Tip auf Sieg

napalm ['neɪpɑ:m] *n.* Napalm, *das*

nape [neɪp] *n.* **~ [of the neck]** Nacken, *der;* Genick, *das*

naphtha ['næfθə] *n.* Naphta, *das*

naphthalene ['næfθəli:n] *n.* Naphtalin, *das*

napkin ['næpkɪn] *n.* **a)** Serviette, *die;* **b)** *(Brit.: nappy)* Windel, *die;* **c)** *(waiter's)* Serviertuch, *das. See also* **sanitary napkin**

'napkin-ring *n.* Serviettenring, *der*

Naples ['neɪplz] *pr. n.* Neapel *(das)*

Napoleonic [nəpəʊlɪ'ɒnɪk] *adj.* napoleonisch; **the ~ Wars** die Napoleonischen Kriege
nappy ['næpɪ] *n. (Brit.)* Windel, *die;* **when you were still in nappies** als du noch in den Windeln gelegen hast
narcissism [nɑ:'sɪsɪzm] *n., no pl. (Psych.)* Narzißmus, *der*
narcissistic [nɑ:sɪ'sɪstɪk] *adj. (Psych.)* narzißtisch
narcissus [nɑ:'sɪsəs] *n., pl.* **narcissi** [nɑ:'sɪsaɪ] *or* **~es** *(Bot.)* Narzisse, *die*
narcosis [nɑ:'kəʊsɪs] *n., pl.* **narcoses** [nɑ:'kəʊsi:z] Betäubung, *die; (Med.: general anaesthesia)* Narkose, *die*
narcotic [nɑ:'kɒtɪk] **1.** *n.* **a)** *(drug)* Rauschgift, *das;* Betäubungsmittel, *das (Rechtsw.);* **~s squad** Rauschgiftdezernat, *das;* **b)** *(active ingredient)* Betäubungsmittel, *das;* Narkotikum, *das (Med.); (fig.)* Narkotikum, *das;* Droge, *die.* **2.** *adj.* **a)** narkotisch; **~ drug** Rauschgift, *das;* Betäubungsmittel, *das (Rechtsw.);* **b)** *(inducing drowsiness, fig.)* einschläfernd
nark [nɑ:k] *(sl.)* **1.** *n.* **a)** *(Brit.: informer)* Spitzel, *der (abwertend);* **b)** *(Brit.: policeman)* Bulle, *der (salopp).* **2.** *v.t. (annoy)* stinken (+ *Dat.*) *(salopp);* **be ~ed [about sb./at** *or* **about sth.]** [auf jmdn./über etw. *(Akk.)*] sauer sein *(ugs.);* **that really got me ~ed** das hat mir echt gestunken *(salopp)*
narrate [nə'reɪt] *v.t.* **a)** *(give account of)* erzählen; schildern ‹*Ereignisse*›; **b)** kommentieren ‹*Film*›; *abs.* erzählen
narration [nə'reɪʃn] *n.* **a)** Erzählen, *das;* Erzählung, *die; (of events)* Schilderung, *die;* Schildern, *das;* **b)** *see* **narrative 1 a**
narrative ['nærətɪv] **1.** *n.* **a)** *(tale, story)* Geschichte, *die;* Erzählung, *die;* **b)** *no pl. (kind of composition)* **be written in ~:** in der Erzählform geschrieben sein; **writer of ~:** erzählender Autor; Erzähler, *der.* **2.** *adj.* narrativ *(Sprachw.);* erzählend; erzählerisch ‹*Gabe, Talent*›; Erzähl‹*kunst, -technik*›; **~ writer** Erzähler, *der*/Erzählerin, *die*
narrator [nə'reɪtə(r)] *n.* Erzähler, *der*/Erzählerin, *die; (of film)* Kommentator, *der*/Kommentatorin, *die;* **first-/third-person ~:** Ich-/Er-Erzähler, *der*
narrow ['nærəʊ] **1.** *adj.* **a)** schmal; schmal geschnitten ‹*Rock, Hose, Ärmel usw.*›; eng ‹*Tal, Gasse*›; **the road became ~:** die Straße verschmälerte sich; **b)** *(limited)* eng; begrenzt, schmal ‹*Auswahl*›; **in the ~est sense** im engsten Sinne; **c)** *(with little margin)* knapp ‹*Sieg, Führung, Mehrheit*›; **have a ~ escape** mit knapper Not entkommen **(from** *Dat.*); **win by a ~ margin** knapp gewinnen; **d)** *(not tolerant)* spießig *(abwertend);* engstirnig *(abwertend);* **have a ~ mind** engstirnig *od.* spießig sein; **a ~ existence** ein Spießerdasein; **e)** *(restricted)* eng ‹*Grenzen, Toleranzen*›; klein, begrenzt ‹*Freundeskreis*›; beengt ‹*Verhältnisse*›; schmal ‹*Einkommen*›; **f)** *(precise)* genau; gründlich, eingehend ‹*Prüfung, Befragung*›. **2.** *n. usu. in pl. (of sea)* Meerenge, *die.* **3.** *v.i.* sich verschmälern; ‹*Augen, Tal:*› sich verengen; *(fig.)* [zusammen]schrumpfen; **the road ~s to one lane** die Straße wird einspurig. **4.** *v.t.* verschmälern; *(fig.)* einengen; enger fassen ‹*Definition*›; **~ one's eyes** die Augen zusammenkneifen; **~ the field** *(fig.)* eine Vorauswahl treffen
~ 'down 1. *v.t.* einengen, beschränken **(to** auf + *Akk.*). **2.** *v.i.* sich reduzieren **(to** auf + *Akk.*); **the choice ~s down to two possibilities** es bleiben zwei Möglichkeiten [übrig]
narrow: ~ boat *n. (Brit.) besonders schmales Binnenschiff;* **~-gauge** *adj.* schmalspurig; Schmalspur-
narrowly ['nærəʊlɪ] *adv.* **a)** *(with little width)* schmal; **b)** *(only just)* knapp; mit knapper Not ‹*entkommen*›; **he ~ escaped being run over by a car** er wäre um ein Haar *(ugs.)* überfahren worden; **~ miss winning [the election/race]** [bei der Wahl/in dem Rennen] knapp unterliegen; **c)** *(closely)* genau; eng ‹*auslegen*›
narrow: ~-'minded *adj.*, **~-mindedly** [nærəʊ'maɪndɪdlɪ] *adv.* engstirnig *(abwertend);* **~-mindedness** [nærəʊ'maɪndɪdnɪs] *n., no pl.* Engstirnigkeit, *die (abwertend);* **~-'shouldered** *adj.* schmalschultrig; **~ 'squeak** *see* **squeak 1 b**
narwhal ['nɑ:wəl] *n. (Zool.)* Narwal, *der*
nary ['neərɪ] *adj. (coll./dial.)* **~ a ...:** kein einziger/keine einzige/kein einziges ...
NASA ['næsə] *abbr. (Amer.)* **National Aeronautics and Space Administration** NASA, *die*
nasal ['neɪzl] **1.** *adj.* **a)** *(Anat.)* Nasen-; **b)** näselnd; **speak in a ~ voice** durch die Nase sprechen; näseln; **have a ~ intonation** näselnd sprechen; näseln; **c)** *(Ling.)* nasal; Nasal-. **2.** *n. (Ling.)* Nasal[laut], *der*
nasalize ['neɪzəlaɪz] *v.t. (Ling.)* nasalieren
nascent ['næsnt] *adj.* **a)** *(literary: coming into existence)* werdend; im Entstehen begriffen; aufkommend, *(geh.)* aufkeimend ‹*Hoffnung, Stolz*›; **b)** *(Chem.)* naszierend
nastily ['nɑ:stɪlɪ] *adv.* **a)** *(disagreeably, unpleasantly)* scheußlich; **b)** *(ill-naturedly)* gemein; gehässig; ärgerlich ‹*etwas sagen*›; **behave ~:** häßlich sein; **c)** *(disgustingly)* eklig; widerlich
nasturtium [nə'stɜ:ʃəm] *n.* **a)** *(in popular use: garden plant)* Kapuzinerkresse, *die;* **b)** *(Bot.: cruciferous plant)* Brunnenkresse, *die*
nasty ['nɑ:stɪ] **1.** *adj.* **a)** *(disagreeable, unpleasant)* scheußlich ‹*Geruch, Geschmack, Arznei, Essen, Wetter*›; gemein ‹*Trick, Verhalten, Äußerung, Mensch*›; häßlich ‹*Angewohnheit*›; **her ~ little ways** ihre kleinen Gemeinheiten; **that was a ~ thing to say/do** das war gemein *od.* eine Gemeinheit; **that's a ~ one** *(awkward question)* das ist vertrackt; *(injury)* das ist übel *od.* sieht böse aus; **a ~ bit** *or* **piece of work** *(coll.) (man)* ein fieser Kerl *(ugs. abwertend); (woman)* ein fieses Weibsstück *(ugs. abwertend); see also* **cheap 1 a; b)** *(ill-natured)* böse; **be ~ to sb.** häßlich zu jmdm. sein; **he has a ~ temper** er ist jähzornig; **cut up** *or* **turn ~** *(coll.)* eklig werden *(ugs.);* **c)** *(serious)* übel; böse ‹*Verletzung, Husten usw.*›; schlimm ‹*Krankheit, Husten, Verletzung, Wende*›; **that's a ~-looking wound** die Wunde sieht übel *od.* böse aus; **she had a ~ fall** sie ist übel *od.* böse gefallen; **He had to have his leg amputated – N~!** Sein Bein mußte amputiert werden – Das ist schlimm!; **d)** *(disgusting)* eklig; widerlich; **don't touch that, it's ~:** pfui, faß das nicht an! *(fam.);* nicht anfassen, das ist bä bä *(Kinderspr.);* **e)** *(obscene)* schweinisch *(ugs. abwertend);* **call sb. ~ names** jmdn. mit schweinischen Ausdrücken beschimpfen. **2.** *n.* **a)** *(person)* Ekel, *das (ugs. abwertend);* Fiesling, *der (salopp abwertend);* **b)** *(thing)* ekliges Ding; *see also* **video nasty**
Nat. *abbr. (Polit.)* **Nationalist**
natal ['neɪtl] *adj.* Geburts-
natch [nætʃ] *adv. (coll.)* versteht sich *(ugs.);* logisch *(ugs.)*
nation ['neɪʃn] *n.* Nation, *die; (people)* Volk, *das;* **law of ~s** Völkerrecht, *das;* **throughout the ~:** im ganzen Land. *See also* **League of Nations; United Nations**
national ['næʃənl] **1.** *adj.* national; National‹*flagge, -denkmal, -held, -theater, -tanz, -gericht, -charakter, -kirche, -ökonomie, -einkommen*›; Landes‹*durchschnitt, -sprache*›; Volks‹*wirtschaft, -charakter, -held*›; Staats‹*sicherheit, -religion, -symbol*›; überregional ‹*Rundfunkstation, Zeitung*›; landesweit ‹*Streik*›; **the rose is the ~ flower of England** die Rose ist das Symbol Englands. **2.** *n.* **a)** *(citizen)* Staatsbürger, *der*/-bürgerin, *die;* **foreign ~:** Ausländer, *der*/Ausländerin, *die;* **b)** *(fellow-countryman)* Landsmann, *der*/-männin, *die;* **c)** *usu. in pl. (newspaper)* überregionale Zeitung; [großes] überregionales Blatt; **d)** *(Brit.: horse-race)* **the N~:** das Grand National
national: ~ 'anthem *n.* Nationalhymne, *die;* **N~ As'sembly** *n.* Nationalversammlung, *die;* **N~ As'sistance** *n. (Brit. dated)* Sozialhilfe, *die;* **be on N~ Assistance** Sozialhilfe beziehen; **~ 'bank** *n. (Amer.)* Nationalbank, *die;* **~ call** *n. (Brit. Teleph.)* Inlandsgespräch, *das;* **~ con'vention** *n. (Amer.)* Nationalkonvent, *der;* ≈ Bundeskongreß, *der;* **~ 'costume** *n.* Nationaltracht, *die;* Landestracht, *die;* **N~ 'Debt** *see* **debt; ~ 'dress** *see* **~ costume; ~ 'football** *n. (Austral.)* australischer Fußball; **N~ 'Front** *n. (Brit.)* National Front, *die (britische Organisation mit extremen reaktionären Positionen z. B. in bezug auf die Einwanderungspolitik); attrib.* National-Front-‹*Mitglied, Slogan usw.*›; **~ 'grid** *n. (Brit.)* **a)** *(Electr.)* nationales Verbundnetz; **~ grid system** nationales Verbundsystem; **b)** *(Geog.)* nationales Gitternetz; **N~ 'Guard** *n. (Amer.)* Nationalgarde, *die;* **N~ 'Health [Service]** *n. (Brit.) staatlicher Gesundheitsdienst;* **he had his teeth done on the N~ Health** er hat sich seine Zähne auf Kosten des staatlichen Gesundheitsdienstes in Ordnung bringen *od. (ugs.)* machen lassen; **N~ Health doctor/patient/spectacles** ≈ Kassenarzt, *der*/-patient, *der*/-brille, *die;* **~ 'holiday** *n.* Nationalfeiertag, *der; (statutory holiday)* gesetzlicher Feiertag; **N~ In'surance** *n. (Brit.)* Sozialversicherung, *die*
nationalisation, nationalise *see* **nationaliz-**
nationalism ['næʃənəlɪzm] *n.* Nationalismus, *der; (patriotism)* nationale Gesinnung; **feelings of ~:** nationale Gefühle
nationalist ['næʃənəlɪst] **1.** *n.* Nationalist, *der*/Nationalistin, *die.* **2.** *adj.* nationalistisch
nationalistic [næʃənə'lɪstɪk] *adj.* **a)** *(patriotic)* nationalistisch; **b)** *(national)* national
nationality [næʃə'nælɪtɪ] *n.* **a)** Staatsangehörigkeit, *die;* Nationalität, *die (geh.);* **be of** *or* **have British ~:** britischer Nationalität sein *(geh.);* die britische Staatsangehörigkeit haben; **what's his ~?** welche Staatsangehörigkeit hat er?; welcher Nationalität ist er? *(geh.);* **b)** *(ethnic group)* Nationalität, *die;* Volksgruppe, *die;* **c)** *(of ship, aircraft, company)* Nationalität, *die*
nationalization [næʃənəlaɪ'zeɪʃn] *n.* **a)** *(bringing under state control)* Verstaatlichung, *die;* Nationalisierung, *die;* **b)** *(making national)* Nationalisierung, *die*
nationalize ['næʃənəlaɪz] *v.t.* **a)** *(bring under state control)* verstaatlichen, nationalisieren ‹*Betriebe, Industriezweige*›; **b)** *(make national)* nationalisieren
nationally ['næʃənəlɪ] *adv.* als Nation; *(throughout the nation)* landesweit
National: n~ 'park *n.* Nationalpark, *der;* **~ 'Savings** *n. pl. (Brit.)* Staatsschuldverschreibungen *Pl.;* **~ Savings certificate** Sparkassengutschein, *der;* öffentlicher Sparbrief; **n~ 'service** *n. (Brit.)* Wehrdienst, *der;* **do n~ service** seinen Wehrdienst ableisten; **~ 'Socialist** *n.* Nationalsozialist, *der*/-sozialistin, *die; attrib.* nationalsozialistisch; **~ Trust** *n. (Brit.) nationale Einrichtung für Naturschutz und Denkmalpflege*
nationhood ['neɪʃnhʊd] *n.* nationale Selbständigkeit
nation-wide 1. ['---] *adj.* landesweit; national ‹*Bedeutung*›. **2.** [--'-] *adv.* landesweit; im ganzen Land
native ['neɪtɪv] **1.** *n.* **a)** *(of specified place)* **a ~ of Britain** ein gebürtiger Brite/eine gebürtige Britin; **speak English like a ~:** Eng-

lisch wie seine Muttersprache sprechen; **b)** *(indigenous person)* Eingeborene, *der/die;* **c)** *(local inhabitant)* Einheimische, *der/die;* **the ~s** die Einheimischen; die einheimische Bevölkerung; **d)** *(Zool., Bot.)* **be a ~ of a place** in einem Ort beheimatet *od.* heimisch sein; **e)** *(S. Afr.: Black)* Schwarze, *der/die.* **2.** *adj.* **a)** *(indigenous)* eingeboren; *(local)* einheimisch ⟨*Pflanze, Tier*⟩; **be a ~ American** gebürtiger Amerikaner/gebürtige Amerikanerin sein; **the ~ habitat of the zebra** die Heimat des Zebras; **~ inhabitant** Eingeborene/Einheimische, *der/die;* **b)** *(of one's birth)* Geburts-, Heimat⟨*land, -stadt*⟩; Vater⟨*land, -stadt*⟩ *(geh.);* Mutter⟨*sprache, -sprachler*⟩; heimatlich ⟨*Wälder*⟩; **one's ~ soil** die Heimaterde; **in his ~ France** in seiner Heimat Frankreich; **~ speaker** Muttersprachler, *der (fachspr.);* **he's not a ~ speaker of English** Englisch ist nicht seine Muttersprache; **c)** *(innate)* angeboren ⟨*Qualitäten, Schläue, Humor, Wissen*⟩; **d)** *(of the natives)* Eingeborenen-; **go ~:** die Lebensweise der Eingeborenen annehmen; **e)** *(Mining)* gediegen

native: ~ 'bear *(Austral., NZ) see* **koala bear; ~ 'rock** *n.* anstehendes Gestein; gewachsener Fels

nativity [nə'tɪvɪtɪ] *n.* **a)** Geburt, *die;* **the N~ [of Christ]** die Geburt Christi; **b)** *(festival)* **the N~ of Christ** das Fest der Geburt Christi; **c)** *(picture)* Geburt Christi

na'tivity play *n.* Krippenspiel, *das*

NATO, Nato ['neɪtəʊ] *abbr.* **North Atlantic Treaty Organization** NATO, *die*

natter ['nætə(r)] *(Brit. coll.)* **1.** *v.i.* quatschen *(ugs.);* quasseln *(ugs.).* **2.** *n.* Schwatz, *der (fam.);* Schwätzchen, *das (fam.);* **have a bit of a ~:** ein bißchen quatschen *(ugs.);* ein Schwätzchen halten *(fam.)*

natterjack ['nætədʒæk] *n.* *(Zool.)* **~ [toad]** Kreuzkröte, *die*

nattily ['nætɪlɪ] *adv.* *(coll.)* schick; flott *(ugs.)*

natty ['nætɪ] *adj.* *(coll.)* **a)** *(spruce)* schick, *(ugs.)* flott ⟨*Kleidungs[stück]*⟩; **be a ~ dresser** immer schick *od.* flott angezogen sein; **b)** *(handy)* praktisch ⟨*Gerät, Werkzeug usw.*⟩

natural ['nætʃrəl] **1.** *adj.* **a)** *(existing in or by nature)* natürlich; Natur⟨*zustand, -begabung, -talent, -seide, -schwamm, -faser, -gewalt, -erscheinung*⟩; gediegen ⟨*Gold, Mineralien*⟩; naturgetreu ⟨*Wiedergabe, Darstellung*⟩; **the ~ world** die Natur[welt]; **in its ~ state** im ursprünglichen Zustand *od.* Naturzustand; **be a ~ blonde** naturblondes Haar haben; von Natur aus blond sein; **b)** *(normal)* natürlich; **it is ~ for dogs to fight** es ist natürlich, daß Hunde kämpfen; **it is ~ for you to think that** es ist klar, daß du das denkst; **die of** *or* **from ~ causes** eines natürlichen Todes sterben; **have a ~ tendency to ...:** naturgemäß dazu neigen, ... zu ...; **c)** *(unaffected)* natürlich ⟨*Art, Lächeln, Stil*⟩; **d)** *(destined)* natürlich ⟨*Feinde*⟩; **be a ~ artist** *etc.* der geborene Künstler *usw.* sein; **e)** *(related by nature)* leiblich ⟨*Eltern, Kind usw.*⟩; natürlich *(Rechtsspr. veralt.)* ⟨*Kind*⟩; **f)** *(instinctive)* Natur⟨*recht*⟩; auf das Naturrecht gegründet ⟨*Gerechtigkeit*⟩. **2.** *n.* **a)** *(person naturally expert or endowed)* Naturtalent, *das;* **she's a ~ for the part** die Rolle ist ihr auf den Leib geschrieben; **he was a ~ for the job** er war der Mann für die Stelle; **b)** *(arch.: mentally deficient person)* Schwachsinnige, *der/die;* **c)** *(Mus.)* *(symbol)* Auflösungszeichen, *das;* *(note)* Stammton, *der;* *(white key on piano)* weiße Taste; **he played C sharp instead of C ~:** er hat cis statt c gespielt

natural: ~ 'childbirth *n.* natürliche Geburt; **~ 'death** *n.* natürlicher Tod; **die a ~ death** eines natürlichen Todes sterben; **let the gossip die a ~ death** warten, bis sich das Gerede von selber legt; **~ 'food** *n.* naturreines Nahrungsmittel; **~ food[s]** Naturkost, *die;* **~ 'gas** *see* **gas 1 a; ~ hi'storian** *n.* Naturkundler, *der*/-kundlerin, *die;* **~ 'history** *n.* **a)** *(study)* Naturkunde, *die; attrib.* Naturkunde-; naturkundlich ⟨*Museum*⟩; **b)** *(facts)* Naturgeschichte, *die*

naturalisation, naturalise *see* **naturaliz-**

naturalism ['nætʃrəlɪzm] *n.* Naturalismus, *der*

naturalist ['nætʃrəlɪst] *n.* **a)** Naturforscher, *der*/-forscherin, *die;* **b)** *(believer in naturalism)* Naturalist, *der*/Naturalistin, *die*

naturalistic [nætʃrə'lɪstɪk] *adj.* naturalistisch

naturalization [nætʃrəlaɪ'zeɪʃn] *n.* *(admission to citizenship)* Einbürgerung, *die;* Naturalisierung, *die; attrib.* Einbürgerungs-

naturalize ['nætʃrəlaɪz] **1.** *v.t.* **a)** *(admit to citizenship)* einbürgern; naturalisieren; **b)** *(adopt)* übernehmen ⟨*Fremdwort, Sitte*⟩; **c)** *(introduce)* naturalisieren, einbürgern ⟨*Tiere, Pflanzen*⟩; **this plant has become ~d here** diese Pflanze wurde hier heimisch. **2.** *v.i.* eingebürgert werden

natural: ~ 'language *n.* natürliche Sprache; **~-language programming** Programmieren in natürlicher Sprache; **~ 'law** *n.* Naturrecht, *das;* *(regularity)* Naturgesetz, *das;* **~ 'life** *n.* Erdenleben, *das (meist dichter., geh. od. veralt.);* **~ 'logarithm** *n.* natürlicher Logarithmus

naturally ['nætʃrəlɪ] *adv.* **a)** *(by nature)* von Natur aus ⟨*musikalisch, blaß, fleißig usw.*⟩; *(in a true-to-life way)* naturgetreu; *(with ease)* natürlich; *(in a natural manner)* auf natürliche Weise; **a ~ posed photograph** ein natürlich wirkendes Foto; **it comes ~ to her** es fällt ihr leicht; es liegt in ihrer Natur; **leadership comes so ~ to him** die Führungsrolle liegt ihm sehr; **lead ~ to sth.** naturgemäß zu etw. führen; **b)** *(of course)* natürlich

naturalness ['nætʃrəlnɪs] Natürlichkeit, *die*

natural: ~ note *n.* *(Mus.)* Stammton, *der;* **~ 'number** *n.* *(Math.)* natürliche Zahl; **~ 'order** *n.* *(Biol.)* natürliche Kategorie; **~ phi'losopher** *n.* Naturphilosoph, *der*/-philosophin, *die;* **~ phi'losophy** *n.* **a)** *(physics)* Naturphilosophie, *die;* **b)** *(~ science)* die Naturwissenschaften; **~ re'ligion** *n.* natürliche Religion; **~ re'sources** *n. pl.* natürliche Ressourcen; Naturschätze *Pl.;* **~ 'scale** *n.* *(Mus.)* Grundskala, *die;* **~ 'science** *n.* **~ science, the ~ sciences** die Naturwissenschaften; **~ se'lection** *n.* *(Biol.)* natürliche Auslese

nature ['neɪtʃə(r)] *n.* **a)** Natur, *die;* **a gift from N~:** ein Geschenk der Natur; **balance of ~:** Gleichgewicht der Natur; **against** *or* **contrary to ~:** wider die Natur *od.* widernatürlich; **back to ~:** zurück zur Natur; **get back** *or* **return to ~:** zu einer natürlichen Lebensweise zurückkehren; **paint from ~:** nach der Natur malen; **in ~** *(actually existing)* in der Wirklichkeit; *(anywhere)* auf Erden; **one of ~'s gentlemen** ein geborener Gentleman; **one of ~'s innocents** die Unschuld selbst; **in a state of ~** *(undomesticated, uncultivated)* in der Wildform; *see also* **call 3 f; course 1 a; law h; b)** *(essential qualities)* Beschaffenheit, *die;* **in the ~ of things** naturgemäß; **it is in** *or* **by the [very] ~ of the case/of things** es liegt in der Natur der Sache/Dinge; **c)** *(kind, sort)* Art, *die;* **things of this ~:** derartiges; Dinge dieser Art; **or something of that ~:** oder etwas in der Art; **it's in** *or* **of the ~ of a command** es hat Befehlscharakter; **d)** *(character)* [Wesens]art, *die;* Wesen, *das;* **have a happy ~:** eine Frohnatur sein; ein glückliches Naturell haben; **be of** *or* **have a placid ~:** eine ruhige Art haben; **have a jealous ~:** eifersüchtig sein; **it is not in her ~ to lie** es ist nicht ihre Art zu lügen; **be proud/friendly** *etc.* **by ~:** ein stolzes/freundliches *usw.* Wesen haben; **[human] ~:** menschliche Natur; **it's only human ~ to ...:** es ist nur menschlich, ... zu ...; *see also* **better 1; second nature; e)** *(inherent impulses)* Natur, *die;* **commit a sin/crime against ~:** sich wider die Natur versündigen *(geh.);* **f)** *(person)* Natur, *die*

'nature cure *n.* Naturheilverfahren, *das*

-natured ['neɪtʃəd] *adj. in comb.* -artig; *see also* **good-natured; ill-natured**

nature: ~-lover *n.* Naturfreund, *der*/-freundin, *die;* **~ reserve** *n.* Naturschutzgebiet, *das;* **~ study** *n.* Naturkunde, *die;* **~ trail** *n.* Naturlehrpfad, *der;* **~-worshipper** *n.* Naturanbeter, *der*/-anbeterin, *die*

naturism ['neɪtʃərɪzm] *n.* *(nudism)* Naturismus, *der;* Freikörperkultur, *die*

naturist ['neɪtʃərɪst] *n.* *(nudist)* Naturist, *der*/Naturistin, *die;* FKK-Anhänger, *der*/FKK-Anhängerin, *die*

naught [nɔ:t] *n.* *(arch./dial.)* **~ but nur; I care ~ for what they say** ich scher mich keinen Deut darum, was sie sagen; **bring to ~:** zunichte machen; **come to ~:** zunichte werden; **it matters ~:** es ist ohne Belang

naughtily ['nɔ:tɪlɪ] *adv.* ungezogen, unartig ⟨*sich benehmen*⟩; frech ⟨*etw. tun, bemerken*⟩

naughtiness ['nɔ:tɪnɪs] *n.* Ungezogenheit, *die;* Unartigkeit, *die*

naughty ['nɔ:tɪ] *adj.* **a)** *(disobedient)* unartig; ungezogen; **the dog has been ~ on the carpet** *(coll. euphem.)* der Hund hat auf den Teppich gemacht *(ugs.);* **you ~ boy/dog** du böser Junge/Hund; **b)** *(wicked)* keß; frech; *(indecent)* unanständig; **how ~ of him** das war aber frech *od.* keß von ihm; **~, ~!** du bist ja ein ganz Schlimmer!/eine ganz Schlimme!

nausea ['nɔ:sɪə, 'nɔ:zɪə] *n.* **a)** Übelkeit, *die;* **even the idea fills me with ~:** schon beim bloßen Gedanken daran wird mir übel; **b)** *(fig.: disgust)* Ekel, *der,* Abscheu, *der* **(with,** at vor + *Dat.*)

nauseate ['nɔ:sɪeɪt, 'nɔ:zɪeɪt] *v.t.* **a) ~ sb.** in jmdm. Übelkeit erregen; **the smell ~d him** bei dem Geruch wurde ihm übel; **b)** *(fig.: disgust)* anekeln; anwidern

nauseating ['nɔ:sɪeɪtɪŋ, 'nɔ:zɪeɪtɪŋ] *adj.* **a)** Übelkeit verursachend *od.* erregend; **b)** *(fig.: disgusting)* widerlich; ekelerregend ⟨*Anblick, Geruch, Essen*⟩; ekelhaft ⟨*Mensch*⟩

nauseatingly ['nɔ:sɪeɪtɪŋlɪ, 'nɔ:zɪeɪtɪŋlɪ] *adv.* *(lit. or fig.)* widerlich

nauseous ['nɔ:sɪəs, 'nɔ:zɪəs] *adj.* **a) she's ~:** ihr ist übel; **b)** *(fig.: nasty, disgusting)* widerlich

nautical ['nɔ:tɪkl] *adj.* nautisch; seemännisch ⟨*Ausdruck, Können*⟩; **~ map** Seekarte, *die;* **be interested in ~ matters** sich für die Seefahrt interessieren

nautically ['nɔ:tɪkəlɪ] *adv.* nautisch

nautical 'mile *n.* Seemeile, *die;* nautische Meile

nautilus ['nɔ:tɪləs] *n., pl.* **~es** *or* **nautili** ['nɔ:tɪlaɪ] *(Zool.)* Nautilus, *der*

naval ['neɪvl] *adj.* Marine-; Flotten⟨*parade, -abkommen*⟩; See⟨*schlacht, -macht, -streitkräfte*⟩; ⟨*Überlegenheit*⟩ zur See; **~ ship** Kriegsschiff, *das*

naval: ~ a'cademy *n.* Marineakademie, *die;* **~ 'architect** *n.* Schiffsbauingenieur, *der;* **~ base** *n.* Flottenstützpunkt, *der;* **~ officer** *n.* Marineoffizier, *der;* **~ 'stores** *n. pl.* Schiffsvorräte *Pl.;* **~ 'warfare** *n.* Seekrieg, *der;* Krieg zur See

nave [neɪv] *n.* *(Archit.)* [Mittel-, Haupt]schiff, *das*

navel ['neɪvl] *n.* Nabel, *der;* **contemplate one's ~** *(fig.)* Nabelschau halten *(ugs. abwertend)*

'navel orange *n.* Navelorange, *die*

navigable ['nævɪgəbl] *adj.* **a)** *(suitable for ships)* schiffbar; befahrbar; **b)** *(seaworthy)* seetüchtig ⟨*Schiff, Zustand*⟩; **c)** *(steerable)* lenkbar, steuerbar ⟨*Ballon, Luftschiff*⟩

navigate ['nævɪgeɪt] **1.** *v.t.* **a)** *(sail on)* beschiffen *(veralt.)*, befahren ⟨*Kanal, Fluß, Gewässer*⟩; **b)** *(direct course of)* navigieren ⟨*Schiff, Flugzeug*⟩; **c)** *(fig.)* ~ **one's way to the bar** sich *(Dat.)* einen Weg zur Bar bahnen. **2.** *v.i.* **a)** *(in ship, aircraft)* navigieren; **b)** *(assist driver)* den Lotsen spielen *(ugs.)*; franzen *(Rallyesport)*; **you drive, I'll ~:** du fährst, und ich dirigiere *od.* lotse dich

navigation [nævɪ'geɪʃn] *n.* **a)** *(navigating)* Navigation, *die;* Navigieren, *das; (sailing on river etc.)* Befahren, *das; (assisting driver)* Dirigieren, *das;* Lotsen, *das;* Franzen, *das (Rallyesport);* **I'm relying on you to do the ~:** ich verlasse mich darauf, daß du mich richtig dirigierst; **b)** *(art, science)* Navigation, *die;* **c)** *(voyage)* Fahrt, *die;* Reise, *die*

navi'gation lights *n. pl. (Naut.)* Lichter; *(Aeronaut.)* Kennlichter

navigator ['nævɪgeɪtə(r)] *n.* **a)** *(one skilled in navigation)* Navigator, *der*/Navigatorin, *die;* **his co-driver was acting as ~:** sein Beifahrer dirigierte *od.* lotste ihn; **b)** *(sea explorer)* Seefahrer, *der*

navvy ['nævɪ] *(Brit.)* **1.** *n. (labourer)* Bau-/Straßenarbeiter, *der.* **2.** *v.i.* Bau-/Straßenarbeiter sein

navy ['neɪvɪ] *n.* **a)** [Kriegs]marine, *die; (ships also)* [Kriegs]flotte, *die;* **b)** *see* **navy blue**

navy: ~ **'blue** *n.* Marineblau, *das;* **~-blue** *adj.* marineblau; **N~ Department** *n. (Amer.)* Marineministerium, *das;* **N~ List** *n. (Brit.)* Rangliste der Marine; ~ **yard** *n. (Amer.)* Marinewerft, *die*

nay [neɪ] **1.** *adv.* **a)** *(literary: or rather)* ja [sogar]; **b)** *(arch./dial.: no)* nein. **2.** *n.* **a)** *(negative vote)* Neinstimme, *die;* **b)** *(arch./dial.: no)* Nein, *das. See also* **yea 2**

Nazi ['nɑːtsɪ] **1.** *n.* **a)** *(party member)* Nationalsozialist, *der*/-sozialistin, *die;* Nazi, *der;* **b)** *(fig. derog.)* Faschist, *der*/Faschistin, *die (abwertend);* Nazi, *der (abwertend).* **2.** *adj.* **a)** nazistisch; Nazi-; **b)** *(fig. derog.)* faschistisch *(abwertend);* Nazi- *(abwertend)*

Naziism ['nɑːtsɪɪzm], **Nazism** ['nɑːtsɪzm] *n.* Nazismus, *der*

NB *abbr.* **nota bene** NB

NCO *abbr.* **non-commissioned officer** Uffz.

NE *abbr.* **a)** [nɔːθ'iːst] **north-east** NO; **b)** [nɔːθ'iːstən] **north-eastern** nö.

Neanderthal [nɪ'ændətɑːl] *adj.* Neandertaler-; *(fig.)* neandertalerhaft; ~ **man** Neandertaler, *der*

neap [niːp] *see* **neap-tide**

Neapolitan [niːə'pɒlɪtn] **1.** *n.* Neapolitaner, *der*/Neapolitanerin, *die.* **2.** *adj.* Neapolitaner; neapolitanisch

'neap-tide *n.* Nipptide, *die*

near [nɪə(r)] **1.** *adv.* **a)** *(at a short distance)* nah[e]; **stand/live [quite] ~:** [ganz] in der Nähe stehen/wohnen; **come** *or* **draw ~/~er** ⟨*Tag, Zeitpunkt:*⟩ nahen/näherrücken; **take the one ~est to you** nimm das am nächsten liegende; **get ~er together** näher zusammenrücken; ~ **at hand** in Reichweite *(Dat.);* ⟨*Ort*⟩ ganz in der Nähe; **be ~ at hand** ⟨*Ereignis:*⟩ nahe bevorstehen; ~ **by** in der Nähe; **so ~ and yet so far** so nah und doch so fern; **b)** *(closely)* **it is 7.10 or as ~ as makes no difference** *or* **matter** es ist ziemlich genau *od.* fast 7.10 Uhr; **as ~ as I can judge** soweit ich es beurteilen kann; **no, but ~ enough** nein, aber beinah[e] *od.* fast; **c)** ~ **to = 2a, b, c; he came ~ to being the winner/to tears** er hätte fast *od.* beinah[e] gewonnen/war den Tränen nahe; **we were ~ to being drowned** wir wären fast *od.* beinah[e] ertrunken. **2.** *prep.* **a)** *(in space) (position)* nahe an/bei (+ *Dat.*); *(motion)* nahe an (+ *Akk.*); *(fig.)* nahe *(geh.) nachgestellt* (+ *Dat.*); in der Nähe (+ *Gen.*); **go ~ the water's edge** nahe ans Ufer gehen; **keep ~ me** halte dich *od.* bleib in meiner Nähe; ~ **where ...:** in der Nähe *od.* unweit der Stelle *(Gen.)*, wo ...; **move it ~er her** rücke es näher zu ihr; **I won't go ~ the police** *(fig.)* ich gehe der Polizei aus dem Weg; **don't stand so ~ the fire** geh nicht so nahe *od.* dicht an das Feuer; **when we got ~er Oxford** als wir in die Nähe von Oxford kamen; **wait till we're ~er home** warte, bis wir nicht mehr so weit von zu Hause weg sind; **don't come ~ me** komm mir nicht zu nahe; **it's ~ here** es ist hier in der Nähe; **the man ~/~est you** der Mann, der bei dir/der dir am nächsten steht; **b)** *(in quality)* **nobody comes anywhere ~ him at swimming** im Schwimmen kommt bei weitem keiner an ihn heran; **we're no ~er solving the problem** wir sind der Lösung des Problems nicht nähergekommen; **be very ~ the original** dem Original sehr nahe kommen; **be ~ completion** kurz vor der Vollendung stehen; **c)** *(in time)* **it's getting ~ the time when I must leave** der Zeitpunkt, wo ich gehen muß, rückt näher; **ask me again ~er the time** frag mich, wenn der Zeitpunkt etwas näher gerückt ist, noch einmal; **the Monday ~est Christmas** der Montag, der dem Weihnachtstag am nächsten liegt; **it's drawing ~ Christmas** es geht auf Weihnachten zu; **come back ~er 8 o'clock/the appointed time** komm kurz vor 8 Uhr/dem verabredeten Zeitpunkt noch einmal zurück; ~ **the end/the beginning of sth.** gegen Ende/zu Anfang einer Sache *(Gen.)*; **d)** *in comb. (close in nature)* Beinahe⟨*unfall, -zusammenstoß, -katastrophe*⟩; **~-hysterical/-human** fast hysterisch/menschlich; **a state of ~-panic** ein panikähnlicher Zustand; **be in a state of ~-collapse** kurz vor dem Zusammenbruch stehen; **a ~-miracle** fast *od.* beinahe ein Wunder; **~-famine conditions** Zustände schon fast wie bei einer Hungersnot. *See also* **heart 1 b; knuckle c; nowhere 1 c; 'wind 1 a. 3.** *adj.* **a)** *(in space or time)* nahe; **in the ~ future** in nächster Zukunft; **the ~est man** der am nächsten stehende Mann; **the chair is ~er** der Stuhl steht näher; **our ~est neighbours** unsere nächsten Nachbarn; **b)** *(closely related)* nahe ⟨*Verwandte, Freunde*⟩; eng ⟨*Freund*⟩; ~ **and dear** lieb und teuer; *abs.* **my/your** *etc.* **~est and dearest** meine/deine *usw.* Lieben; **c)** *(in nature)* fast richtig ⟨*Vermutung*⟩; groß ⟨*Ähnlichkeit*⟩; genau ⟨*Übersetzung*⟩; **£30 or ~/~est offer** 30 Pfund oder nächstbestes Angebot; **this is the ~est equivalent** dies entspricht dem am ehesten; **that's the ~est you'll get to an answer** eine weitergehende Antwort wirst du nicht bekommen; ~ **escape** Entkommen mit knapper Not; **round it up to the ~est penny** runde es auf den nächsthöheren Pfennigbetrag; **be a ~ miss** ⟨*Schuß, Wurf:*⟩ knapp danebengehen; **I had a ~ miss** *(accident)* ich hätte um Haaresbreite einen Unfall gehabt; **that was a ~ miss** *(escape)* das war aber knapp!; **d) the ~ side** *(Brit.) (travelling on the left/right)* die linke/rechte Seite; **e)** *(direct)* **4 miles by the ~est road** 4 Meilen auf dem kürzesten Wege. **4.** *v.t.* sich nähern (+ *Dat.*); **the building is ~ing completion** das Gebäude geht seiner Vollendung entgegen *od.* steht kurz vor seiner Vollendung; **he's ~ing his end** sein Ende naht. **5.** *v.i.* ⟨*Zeitpunkt:*⟩ näherrücken, *(geh.)* nahen

'nearby *adj.* nahe gelegen

Near: ~ **'East** *n.* **a)** *see* **Middle East; b)** *(arch.: Turkey and Balkans)* Balkan, *der;* ~ **'Eastern** *adj.* nahöstlich

nearly ['nɪəlɪ] *adv.* **a)** *(almost)* fast; **it ~ fell over** es wäre fast umgefallen; **be ~ crying** *or* **in tears** den Tränen nahe sein; **it is ~ six o'clock** es ist kurz vor sechs Uhr; **are you ~ ready?** bist du bald fertig?; **b)** *(closely)* nah[e] ⟨*verwandt*⟩; sehr ⟨*ähneln*⟩; weitgehend ⟨*sich entsprechen*⟩; **c)** *(at all)* **not ~:** nicht annähernd; bei weitem nicht

nearness ['nɪənɪs] *n., no pl.* **a)** *(proximity)* Nähe, *die;* **their ~ in age** der geringe Altersunterschied zwischen ihnen; **b)** *(similarity)* große Ähnlichkeit

near: **~-sighted** *adj. (Amer.)* kurzsichtig; ~ **'thing** *n.* **that was a ~ thing/what a ~ thing [that was]!** das war knapp!/war das aber knapp!

neat [niːt] *adj.* **a)** *(tidy, clean)* sauber, ordentlich ⟨*Handschrift, Arbeit*⟩; gepflegt ⟨*Haar, Person*⟩; **keep one's desk ~:** auf seinem Schreibtisch Ordnung halten; **b)** *(undiluted)* pur ⟨*Getränk*⟩; **she drinks vodka ~:** sie trinkt Wodka pur; **c)** *(smart)* gepflegt ⟨*Erscheinung, Kleidung*⟩; elegant, schick ⟨*Anzug, Auto, Haus*⟩; **d)** *(deft)* geschickt; raffiniert ⟨*Diebstahl, Trick, Plan, Lösung, Gerät*⟩; **make a ~ job of sth./repairing sth.** etw. sehr geschickt machen/reparieren; **e)** *(brief, clear)* prägnant ⟨*Beschreibung, Antwort, Formulierung*⟩; **f)** *(esp. Amer. sl.: excellent)* toll; geil *(Jugendspr. salopp)*

neath [niːθ] *prep. (arch./poet.)* unter (+ *Dat.*); nid (+ *Dat.*) *(schweiz. veralt.)*

neatly ['niːtlɪ] *adv.* **a)** *(tidily)* ordentlich; [fein] säuberlich; **b)** *(smartly)* gepflegt; ~ **groomed** äußerst gepflegt; **c)** *(deftly)* geschickt; auf raffinierte [Art und] Weise; **d)** *(briefly, clearly)* prägnant; **a ~ turned phrase** eine prägnante Formulierung

neatness ['niːtnɪs] *n., no pl. see* **neat a, c, d, e:** Sauberkeit, *die;* Ordentlichkeit, *die;* Gepflegtheit, *die;* Eleganz, *die;* Geschick, *das;* Geschicktheit, *die;* Raffiniertheit, *die;* Prägnanz, *die*

nebula ['nebjʊlə] *n., pl.* **~e** ['nebjʊliː] *or* **~s** *(Astron.)* Nebel, *der*

nebular ['nebjʊlə(r)] *adj. (Astron.)* Nebel-

nebulous ['nebjʊləs] *adj.* **a)** *(hazy)* nebelhaft, *(geh.)* nebulös ⟨*Vorstellung, Werte*⟩; verschwommen ⟨*Grenze*⟩; unbestimmt, vage ⟨*Angst, Hoffnung*⟩; **b)** *(cloudlike)* wolkenartig ⟨*Form*⟩

necessarily [nesɪ'serɪlɪ] *adv.* notwendigerweise; zwangsläufig; **it is not ~ true** es muß nicht [unbedingt] stimmen; **Do we have to do it? Not ~:** Müssen wir es tun? – Nicht unbedingt

necessary ['nesɪsərɪ] **1.** *adj.* **a)** *(indispensable)* nötig; notwendig; unbedingt ⟨*Erfordernis*⟩; **be ~ to life** lebensnotwendig sein; **patience is ~ for a teacher** ein Lehrer muß Geduld haben; **it is not ~ for you to go** es ist nicht nötig *od.* notwendig, daß du gehst; du brauchst nicht zu *od.* mußt nicht gehen; **it may be ~ for him to leave** vielleicht muß er gehen; **they made it ~ for him to attend** ihretwegen mußte er hingehen; **do no more than is ~:** nur das Nötigste tun; **do everything ~** *(that must be done)* das Nötige *od.* Notwendige tun; **b)** *(inevitable)* zwangsläufig ⟨*Ergebnis, Folge*⟩; zwingend ⟨*Schluß*⟩; **c) a ~ evil** ein notwendiges Übel. **2.** *n.* **the necessaries of life** das Lebensnotwendige; **will he come up with the ~?** *(sl.: money)* wird er die Kohle auftreiben? *(salopp);* **will you do the ~?** kümmerst du dich drum?

necessitate [nɪ'sesɪteɪt] *v.t.* **a)** *(make necessary)* erforderlich machen; **b)** *(Amer.: force)* zwingen; nötigen; **be ~d to do sth.** gezwungen *od.* genötigt sein, etw. zu tun

necessitous [nɪ'sesɪtəs] *adj. (formal)* bedürftig

necessity [nɪ'sesɪtɪ] *n.* **a)** *(power of circumstances)* Not, *die;* äußerer Zwang; **bow to ~:** der Not gehorchen *(geh.);* **do sth. out of** *or* **from ~:** etw. notgedrungen *od.* gezwungenermaßen tun; **make a virtue of ~:** aus der Not eine Tugend machen; **of ~:** notwendigerweise; **b)** *(necessary thing)* Notwendigkeit, *die;* **the necessities of life** das Lebensnotwendige; **be a ~ of life** lebensnotwendig sein; **be a ~ for sth.** eine notwendige Voraussetzung für etw. sein; **c)** *(indispensability, imperative need)* Notwendigkeit, *die;* **there is no ~ for rudeness** es besteht keine Notwendigkeit *od.* es ist nicht notwendig, unhöflich zu sein; **if the ~ arises** wenn es unbedingt nötig ist; **in case of ~:** nötigenfalls; **~ is the mother of invention** *(prov.)* Not macht erfinderisch *(Spr.)*; **d)** *(want)* Not, *die;* Bedürftigkeit, *die;* **be/live in ~:** Not leiden

neck [nek] **1.** *n.* **a)** Hals, *der;* **be breathing down sb.'s ~** *(fig.) (be close behind sb.)* jmdm. im Nacken sitzen *(ugs.)*; *(watch sb. closely)* jmdm. ständig auf die Finger sehen; **get it in the ~** *(coll.)* eins auf den Deckel *od.* das Dach kriegen *(ugs.)*; **be** *or* **come down on sb.'s ~** *(coll.)* jmdm. eins auf den Deckel *od.* aufs Dach geben *(ugs.)*; **give sb./be a pain in the ~** *(coll.)* jmdm. auf die Nerven *od.* den Wecker gehen *(ugs.)*; **have sb. round one's ~** *(coll.)* jmdn. auf dem *od.* am Hals haben *(ugs.)*; **you'll bring the police down on our ~s** wir werden deinetwegen die Polizei auf den Hals kriegen *(ugs.)*; **break one's/sb.'s ~** *(fig. coll.)* sich/jmdm. den Hals brechen; **risk one's ~:** Kopf und Kragen riskieren; **save one's ~:** seinen Kopf retten; **be up to one's ~ in work** *(coll.)* bis über den Hals in Arbeit stecken *(ugs.)*; **be [in it] up to one's ~** *(coll.)* bis über den Hals drinstecken *(ugs.)*; **~ and ~:** Kopf an Kopf; **~ or nothing** alles oder nichts; **it's [a matter of] ~ or nothing** es geht um die Wurst *(ugs.)*; *see also* **dead 1 a; millstone; stick out 1 a; b)** *(length)* Halslänge, *die;* *(fig.)* Nasenlänge, *die;* **short ~** *(Horse-racing)* kurze Halslänge; **c)** *(cut of meat)* Hals, *der;* **~ of lamb/mutton** *etc.* Lammfleisch/Hammelfleisch *usw.* vom Hals; **d)** *(part of garment)* Kragen, *der;* **that dress has a high ~:** das Kleid ist hochgeschlossen; **e)** *(narrow part)* Hals, *der;* **f)** *(Geog.: isthmus)* Landenge, *die;* **~ of land** Landzunge, *die;* **g) ~ of the woods** *(coll.)* Breiten *Pl.* **2.** *v. i.* *(sl.)* knutschen *(ugs.)*

neck: ~band *n.* Halsbündchen, *das;* **~cloth** *n.* *(Hist.)* Halstuch, *das*

-necked [nekt] *adj. in comb.* **red/long-~:** rot-/langhalsig; **polo-~:** Rollkragen-

neckerchief ['nekətʃɪf] *n.* Halstuch, *das*

necklace ['neklɪs] *n.* [Hals]kette, *die;* *(with jewels)* Kollier, *das*

neck: ~line *n.* [Hals]ausschnitt, *der;* **~tie** *n.* Krawatte, *die;* Binder, *der*

necromancy ['nekrəmænsɪ] *n.* Nekromantie, *die*

necrophilia [nekrə'fɪlɪə] *n.* Nekrophilie, *die*

necrosis [ne'krəʊsɪs] *n., pl.* **necroses** [ne'krəʊsi:z] *(Med.)* Nekrose, *die*

nectar ['nektə(r)] *n.* **a)** *(Bot., Greek and Roman Mythol.)* Nektar, *der;* **b)** *(delicious drink)* Göttertrank, *der (scherzh.)*; *(drink of blended fruit-juices)* Nektar, *der (fachspr.)*

nectarine ['nektərɪn, 'nektəri:n] *n.* Nektarine, *die*

nectary ['nektərɪ] *n.* *(Bot.)* Nektarium, *das (fachspr.)*; Honigdrüse, *die*

NEDC *abbr.* *(Brit. Hist.)* **National Economic Development Council** Rat für Wirtschaftsentwicklung

neddy ['nedɪ] *n.* *(child lang.: donkey)* Esel, *der;* Langohr, *das (scherzh.)*

née *(Amer.:* **nee)** [neɪ] *adj.* geborene

need [ni:d] **1.** *n.* **a)** *no pl.* Notwendigkeit, *die* **(for, of** *Gen.*); *(demand)* Bedarf, *der* **(for, of** an + *Dat.*); **as the ~ arises** nach Bedarf; **if ~ arise/be** nötigenfalls; falls nötig; **the ~ for discussion** die Notwendigkeit zu diskutieren; **there's no ~ for that** *(as answer)* [das ist] nicht nötig; **there's no ~ to do sth.** es ist nicht nötig *od.* notwendig, etw. zu tun; **there is no ~ to worry/get angry** es besteht kein Grund zur Sorge/sich zu ärgern; **is there any ~ [for us] to hurry?** müssen wir uns beeilen?; **there was a ~ for caution** Vorsicht war geboten; **be in ~ of sth.** etw. brauchen *od.* nötig haben; **there is no ~ for such behaviour** solch ein Verhalten ist unnötig; **is there any ~ for all this hurry?** ist diese Eile nötig *od.* notwendig?; **there's no ~ for you to apologize** du brauchst dich nicht zu entschuldigen; **feel the ~ to do sth.** sich gezwungen *od.* genötigt sehen, etw. zu tun; **feel the ~ to confide in sb.** das Bedürfnis haben, sich jmdm. anzuvertrauen; **have ~ to do sth.** *(dated)* es nötig haben, etw. zu tun; **be badly in ~ of sth.** etw. dringend nötig haben; etw. nötig brauchen; **be in ~ of a coat of paint** einen Anstrich nötig haben; **be in ~ of repair** reparaturbedürftig sein; **have ~ of sb./sth.** jmdn./etw. brauchen *od.* nötig haben; **your ~ is greater than mine** du hast es nötiger als ich; du brauchst es dringender als ich; **b)** *no pl.* *(emergency)* Not, *die;* **in case of ~:** im Notfall; **in times of ~:** in Notzeiten; *see also* **friend a; c)** *no pl.* *(destitution)* Not, *die;* Bedürftigkeit, *die;* **be in ~:** Not leiden; **those in ~:** die Notleidenden *od.* Bedürftigen; **d)** *(thing)* Bedürfnis, *das;* **my ~s are few** ich brauche nicht viel; **each will receive according to his ~s** jeder bekommt, was er braucht. **2.** *v. t.* **a)** *(require)* brauchen; **sth. that urgently ~s doing** etw., was dringend gemacht werden muß; **much ~ed** dringend notwendig; **that's all I ~ed!** *(iron.)* auch das noch!; das hat mir gerade noch gefehlt!; **it ~s a coat of paint** es muß gestrichen werden; **it ~s careful consideration** es muß gut überlegt werden; **~ correction** berichtigt werden müssen; **Education? Who ~s it?** *(coll.)* Bildung? Wozu?; **b)** *expr. necessity* müssen; **I ~ to do it** ich muß es tun; **it needs/doesn't need to be done** es muß getan werden/es braucht nicht getan zu werden; **you don't need to do that** das brauchst du nicht zu tun; **I don't ~ to be reminded** du brauchst/ihr braucht mich nicht daran zu erinnern; **it ~ed doing** es mußte getan werden; **he ~s cheering up** er muß [ein bißchen] aufgeheitert werden; **he doesn't ~ to be told** das braucht man ihm nicht erst zu sagen; **you shouldn't ~ to be told** das solltest *od.* müßtest du eigentlich wissen; **it doesn't ~ me to tell you** das muß ich dir nicht sagen *od.* brauche ich dir nicht zu sagen; **she ~s everything [to be] explained to her** man muß ihr alles erklären; **you ~ only ask** du brauchst nur zu fragen; **don't be away longer than you ~ [be]** bleib nicht länger als nötig weg; **c)** *pres.* **he ~,** *neg.* **~ not** *or* *(coll.)* **~n't** ['ni:dnt] *expr. desirability* müssen; *with neg.* brauchen zu; **~ anybody be there?** muß jemand dort sein?; **~ I say more?** muß ich noch mehr sagen?; **~ she have come at all?** hätte sie überhaupt kommen müssen?; **N~ you go? – No, I ~n't** Mußt du gehen? – Nein; **I ~ hardly** *or* **hardly ~ say that ...:** ich brauche wohl kaum zu sagen, daß ...; **I don't think that ~ be considered** ich glaube, das braucht nicht berücksichtigt zu werden; **no one ~ know this** das braucht niemand zu wissen; **he ~n't be told** *(let's keep it secret)* das braucht er nicht zu wissen; **we ~n't** *or* **~ not have done it, if ...** wir hätten es nicht zu tun brauchen, wenn ...; **it ~ not follow that ...:** daraus folgt nicht unbedingt, daß ...; daraus muß nicht [unbedingt] folgen, daß ...; **that ~ not be the case** das muß nicht so sein *od.* der Fall sein

needful ['ni:dfl] *adj.* *(arch.)* nötig; **it is ~ to do it** es ist vonnöten *od.* *(geh., veralt.)* tut not, daß es getan wird; **everything/the ~:** alles/das Nötige

needle ['ni:dl] **1.** *n.* Nadel, *die;* **it is like looking/searching for a ~ in a haystack** es ist, als wollte man eine Stecknadel in einem Heuhaufen finden; **~ and thread** *or* **cotton** Nadel und Faden; **~'s eye** Nadelöhr, *das;* **give sb. the ~** *(Brit. sl.)* jmdn. ärgern; **get the ~** *(Brit. sl.)* sich ärgern; *see also* **pin 1 a. 2.** *v. t.* *(coll.)* ärgern; nerven *(ugs.)*; **what's needling him?** was fuchst ihn [denn so]? *(ugs.)*

needle: ~cord *n.* *(Textiles)* Feinkord, *der;* **~craft** *n.* Nadelarbeit, *die;* **~ game, ~ match** *ns.* *(Brit.)* erbitterter Fight *(Sportjargon)*; **~-point** *ns.* **a)** Nadelspitze, *die;* *(fig.)* springender Punkt; **b)** *(embroidery)* Stickerei, *die*

needless ['ni:dlɪs] *adj.* unnötig; *(senseless)* sinnlos; **~ to say** *or* **add, he didn't do it** überflüssig zu sagen, daß er es nicht getan hat

needlessly ['ni:dlɪslɪ] *adv.* unnötigerweise; *(senselessly)* sinnlos

needle: ~ valve *n.* *(Mech. Engin.)* Nadelventil, *das;* **~woman** *n.* *(seamstress)* Näherin, *die;* **be a good/bad ~woman** gut nähen [können]/schlecht nähen *od.* nicht gut nähen können; **~work** *n.* Handarbeit, *die;* Nadelarbeit, *die (veralt.)*; *(school subject)* Handarbeiten, *das;* Nadelarbeit, *die (veralt.)*; **do ~work** handarbeiten; **a piece of ~work** eine Handarbeit

needn't ['ni:dnt] *(coll.)* = **need not;** *see* **need 2 c**

needs [ni:dz] *adv.* *(dated)* **~ must when the devil drives** *(prov.)* was sein muß, muß sein; **if ~ must** wenn es [unbedingt] sein muß *od.* nötig ist

needy ['ni:dɪ] *adj.* **a)** *(poor)* notleidend, bedürftig ⟨*Person, Familie*⟩; **the neediest cases** die schlimmsten Fälle von Bedürftigkeit; **the ~:** die Notleidenden *od.* Bedürftigen; **b)** ärmlich, dürftig ⟨*Verhältnisse*⟩

ne'er [neə(r)] *adv.* *(poet.: never)* nimmer *(geh. veralt.)*; nie; **~ a ...:** kein einziger/keine einzige/kein einziges ...

ne'er-do-well ['neədʊwel] **1.** *n.* Tunichtgut, *der.* **2.** *adj.* nichtsnutzig *(veralt. abwertend)*; **~ fellow** Tunichtgut, *der*

nefarious [nɪ'feərɪəs] *adj.* ruchlos *(geh.)*; frevelhaft *(geh.)*

negate [nɪ'geɪt] *v. t.* **a)** *(formal: be negation of)* widersprechen (+ *Dat.*); **b)** *(nullify)* zunichte machen; **c)** *(Ling.)* negieren *(fachspr.)*; verneinen

negation [nɪ'geɪʃn] *n.* **a)** *(refusal to accept)* Ablehnung, *die;* *(refusal to accept existence of sth.)* Verleugnung, *die;* **b)** *(negative statement)* negative Aussage; **be the ~ of sth.** im Widerspruch zu etw. stehen; **c)** *(opposite of sth. positive)* Negation, *die;* **d)** *(Ling.)* Negation, *die (fachspr.)*; Verneinung, *die*

negative ['negətɪv] **1.** *adj.* **a)** negativ; **~ vote** Neinstimme, *die;* **b)** *(Ling.)* verneint; Negations⟨*partikel*⟩; **c)** *(Electr.)* **~ pole/terminal** Minuspol, *der;* **d)** *(Photog.)* negativ; Negativ-. *See also* **feedback b. 2.** *n.* **a)** *(Photog.)* Negativ, *das;* **b)** *(negative statement)* negative Aussage; *(answer)* Nein, *das;* **two ~s make an affirmative** doppelte Verneinung ergibt Bejahung; **be in the ~** ⟨*Antwort:*⟩ negativ *od.* „nein" sein; ⟨*Votum:*⟩ ablehnend ausfallen; **c)** *(negative quality)* negative Eigenschaft; fehlende Eigenschaft; **d)** *(Ling.)* Negation, *die (fachspr.)*; Verneinung, *die.* **3.** *v. t.* **a)** *(veto)* ablehnen; **b)** *(disprove)* widerlegen

negatively ['negətɪvlɪ] *adv.* **a)** *(in the negative)* negativ; **answer ~:** eine negative Antwort geben; **b)** *(unsympathetically)* negativ; ablehnend; **c)** *(Electr.)* negativ

'negative sign *n.* *(Math.)* negatives Vorzeichen; *(symbol)* Minuszeichen, *das*

neglect [nɪ'glekt] **1.** *v. t.* **a)** *(disregard, leave uncared for)* vernachlässigen; nicht hören auf (+ *Akk.*) ⟨*Rat*⟩; versäumen ⟨*Gelegenheit*⟩; **b)** *(leave undone)* unerledigt lassen, liegenlassen ⟨*Korrespondenz, Arbeit*⟩; **c)** *(omit)* versäumen; **she ~ed to write** sie hat es versäumt zu schreiben; **not ~ doing** *or* **to do sth.** es nicht versäumen, etw. zu tun. **2.** *n.* **a)** *(neglecting, disregard)* Vernachlässigung, *die;* **be in a state of ~** ⟨*Gebäude:*⟩ verwahrlost sein; **years of ~:** jahrelange Vernachlässigung; **suffer from ~:** vernachlässigt werden; **~ of duty** Pflichtvergessenheit, *die;* **b)** *(negligence)* Nachlässigkeit, *die;* Fahrlässigkeit, *die*

neglectful [nɪ'glektfl] *adj. (careless)* gleichgültig (**of** gegenüber); **be ~ of** sich nicht kümmern um

néglígé, negligee ['neglɪʒeɪ] *n.* Negligé, *das*

negligence ['neglɪdʒəns] *n., no pl. (carelessness)* Nachlässigkeit, *die; (Law, Insurance, etc.)* Fahrlässigkeit, *die; see also* **contributory a**

negligent ['neglɪdʒənt] *adj.* **a)** nachlässig; **be ~ about sth.** sich um etw. nicht kümmern; **be ~ of one's duties/sb.** seine Pflichten/jmdn. vernachlässigen; **b)** *(offhand)* ungezwungen, zwanglos

negligently ['neglɪdʒəntlɪ] *adv.* **a)** nachlässig ⟨*arbeiten*⟩; unvorsichtig ⟨*fahren*⟩; *as sentence-modifier* nachlässigerweise/unvorsichtigerweise; **b)** *(in an offhand manner)* lässig

negligible ['neglɪdʒɪbl] *adj.* unerheblich; unbedeutend ⟨*Fehler*⟩; *see also* **quantity e**

negotiable [nɪ'gəʊʃəbl] *adj.* **a)** *(open to discussion)* verhandlungsfähig ⟨*Forderung, Bedingungen*⟩; **b)** *(that can be got past)* zu bewältigend *nicht präd.*; zu bewältigen *nicht attr.*; passierbar ⟨*Straße, Fluß*⟩; **c)** *(Commerc.)* übertragbar ⟨*Sicherheit, Scheck usw.*⟩

negotiate [nɪ'gəʊʃɪeɪt] **1.** *v. i.* verhandeln (**for, on, about** über + *Akk.*); **the negotiating table** der Verhandlungstisch. **2.** *v. t.* **a)** *(arrange)* aushandeln; **b)** *(get past)* bewältigen; überwinden ⟨*Hindernis*⟩; passieren ⟨*Straße, Fluß*⟩; nehmen ⟨*Kurve*⟩; **~ the stairs** die Treppe schaffen *(ugs.)*; **c)** *(Commerc.) (convert into cash)* einlösen ⟨*Scheck*⟩; *(transfer)* übertragen ⟨*Wechsel, Papiere, usw.*⟩

negotiation [nɪgəʊʃɪ'eɪʃn, nɪgəʊsɪ'eɪʃn] *n.* **a)** *(discussion)* Verhandlung, *die* (**for, about** über + *Akk.*); **by ~:** durch Verhandeln *od.* Verhandlungen; **enter into ~:** in Verhandlungen *(Akk.)* eintreten; **be in ~ with sb.** mit jmdm. verhandeln; **be a matter of ~:** Verhandlungssache sein; **b)** *in pl. (talks)* Verhandlungen *Pl.*; **c)** *see* **negotiate 2 b**: Bewältigung, *die;* Überwindung, *die;* Passieren, *das;* **d)** *see* **negotiate 2 c**: Einlösung, *die;* Übertragung, *die*

negotiator [nɪ'gəʊʃɪeɪtə(r)] *n.* Unterhändler, *der*/-händlerin, *die*

Negress ['ni:grɪs] *n.* Negerin, *die*

Negro ['ni:grəʊ] **1.** *n., pl.* **~es** Neger, *der.* **2.** *adj.* Neger-; **~ woman** Negerin, *die;* **~ art/music** Kunst/Musik der Neger; *see also* **spiritual 2**

Negroid ['ni:grɔɪd] **1.** *adj.* negrid; *(akin to or resembling Negroes)* negroid. **2.** *n.* Negride, *der/die; (akin to or resembling Negro)* Negroide, *der/die*

neigh [neɪ] **1.** *v. i.* wiehern. **2.** *n.* Wiehern, *das*

neighbor *etc. (Amer.) see* **neighbour** *etc.*

neighbour ['neɪbə(r)] **1.** *n.* Nachbar, *der*/Nachbarin, *die; (at table)* [Tisch]nachbar, *der*/[Tisch]nachbarin, *die; (thing)* der/die/das daneben; *(building/country)* Nachbargebäude/-land, *das;* **we're next-door ~s** wir wohnen Tür an Tür; **my next-door ~s** meine unmittelbaren Nachbarn; meine Nachbarn von nebenan; **we were ~s at dinner** wir haben beim Essen nebeneinander gesessen. **2.** *v. t. & i.* **~ [upon]** grenzen an (+ *Akk.*)

neighbourhood ['neɪbəhʊd] *n.* **a)** *(district)* Gegend, *die;* **sb.'s ~:** jmds. Nachbarschaft; **the children from the ~:** die Kinder aus der Nachbarschaft *od.* Umgebung; **b)** *(nearness)* Nähe, *die;* **it was [somewhere] in the ~ of £100** es waren [so] um [die] 100 Pfund; **c)** *(neighbours)* Nachbarschaft, *die;* **d)** *attrib.* an der *od.* um die Ecke *nachgestellt (ugs.)*; **small ~ shop/store** [kleiner] Laden um die Ecke; **your friendly ~ bobby/milkman** *etc. (coll. joc.)* der freundliche Polizist/Milchmann *(ugs.)* von nebenan

'neighbourhood watch *n.* Bürgerwehr, *die*

neighbouring ['neɪbərɪŋ] *adj.* benachbart; Nachbar-; angrenzend ⟨*Felder*⟩

neighbourliness ['neɪbəlɪnɪs] *n., no pl.* gut- *od.* freundnachbarliche Art

neighbourly ['neɪbəlɪ] *adj.* **a)** *(characteristic of neighbours)* [gut]nachbarlich; **b)** *(friendly)* freundlich

neither ['naɪðə(r), ni:ðə(r)] **1.** *adj.* keiner/keine/keins der beiden; **in ~ case** in keinem Falle. **2.** *pron.* keiner/keine/keins von *od.* der beiden; **~ of them** keiner von *od.* der beiden; *(none)* keiner von ihnen; **~ of the accusations** keine der [beiden] Beschuldigungen; **Which will you have? – N~** Welches nehmen Sie? – Keins [von beiden]; **we ~ of us moved** keiner von uns [beiden] hat sich bewegt. **3.** *adv. (also not)* auch nicht; **I'm not going – N~ am I** *or (sl.)* **Me ~:** Ich gehe nicht – Ich auch nicht; **if you don't go, ~ shall I** wenn du nicht gehst, gehe ich auch nicht; **he didn't go and ~ did I** er ging nicht und ich auch nicht. **4.** *conj.* **a)** *(not either, not on the one hand)* weder; **~ ... nor** weder ... noch; **he ~ knows nor cares** weder weiß er es, noch will er es wissen; **he ~ ate, drank, nor smoked** er aß weder, noch trank, noch rauchte er; *see also* **here 1 a**; **b)** *(arch.: and also not)* noch

nelly ['nelɪ] *n.* **not on your ~** *(Brit. sl.)* nie im Leben *(ugs.)*; im Leben nicht *(ugs.)*

nelson ['nelsn] *n. (Wrestling)* Nelson, *der*

nem. con. [nem 'kɒn] *abbr.* **nemine contradicente** nem. con.

nemesis ['nemɪsɪs] *n., pl.* **nemeses** ['nemɪsi:z] **a)** *(formal: justice)* Nemesis, *die;* ausgleichende Gerechtigkeit; **b)** *(downfall)* gerechte Strafe (**of** für)

neo- [ni:əʊ] *in comb.* neo-/Neo-

neo'classic, neo'classical *adj.* klassizistisch

neo'classicism *n.* Klassizismus, *der*

neolithic [ni:ə'lɪθɪk] *adj. (Archaeol.)* neolithisch *(fachspr.)*; jungsteinzeitlich; *(fig.)* vorsintflutlich; **~ period** Neolithikum, *das;* Jungsteinzeit, *die;* **~ man** Neolithiker, *der*

neologism [nɪ'ɒlədʒɪzm] *n.* Neubildung, *die;* Neologismus, *der (Sprachw.)*

neon ['ni:ɒn] *n. (Chem.)* Neon, *das*

neon: ~ 'lamp *n.* Neonlampe, *die;* **~ 'light** *n.* Neonlicht, *das; (fitting)* Neonlampe, *die;* **~ 'sign** *n.* Neonreklame, *die*

neophyte ['ni:əfaɪt] *n.* **a)** *(Relig.)* Neophyt, *der;* **b)** *(beginner)* Anfänger, *der*

Nepal [nɪ'pɔ:l] *pr. n.* Nepal *(das)*

Nepalese [nepə'li:z], **Nepali** [nɪ'pɔ:lɪ] **1.** *adj.* nepalesisch. **2.** *n.* **a)** *pl.* **Nepalese, Nepalis** *(person)* Nepalese, *der*/Nepalesin, *die;* **b)** *(language)* Nepali, *das*

nephew ['nevju:, 'nefju:] *n.* Neffe, *der*

nephritis [nɪ'fraɪtɪs] *n. (Med.)* Nephritis, *die (fachspr.)*; Nierenentzündung, *die*

nepotism ['nepətɪzm] *n.* Nepotismus, *der (geh.)*; Vetternwirtschaft, *die (abwertend)*

Neptune ['neptju:n] *pr. n.* **a)** *(Roman Mythol.)* Neptun *(der)*; **b)** *(Astron.)* Neptun, *der*

NERC *abbr. (Brit.)* **Natural Environment Research Council** ≈ Umweltbundesamt

nerd [nɜ:d] *n. (sl. derog.)* Depp, *der (abwertend)*

nerve [nɜ:v] **1.** *n.* **a)** Nerv, *der;* **~ tissue** Nervengewebe, *das;* **b)** *in pl. (fig., of mental state)* **be suffering from ~s** nervös sein; **bundle of ~s** Nervenbündel, *das (ugs.)*; **have a fit of ~s** durchdrehen *(ugs.)*; sehr nervös werden; **get on sb.'s ~s** jmdm. auf die Nerven gehen *od.* fallen *(ugs.)*; **~s of steel** Nerven wie Drahtseile *(ugs.)*; **c) strain every ~** *(fig.)* alle Anstrengungen machen; **d)** *(coolness, boldness)* Kaltblütigkeit, *die;* Mut, *der;* **not have the ~ for sth.** für *od.* zu etw. nicht die Nerven haben; **lose one's ~:** die Nerven verlieren; **a man with an iron ~:** ein Mann mit eisernen Nerven; **e)** *(coll.: audacity)* **of all the ~!** das ist doch die Höhe!; **what [a] ~!** [so eine] Frechheit!; **have the ~ to do sth.** den Nerv haben, etw. zu tun *(ugs.)*; **he's got a ~:** der hat Nerven *(ugs.)*. **2.** *v. t.* **a)** *(give strength or courage to)* ermutigen; **~ oneself** *or* **one's heart** seinen ganzen Mut zusammennehmen; **b)** *(brace)* **~ oneself** *or* **one's mind** sich wappnen *(geh.)*

nerve: ~-cell *n.* Nervenzelle, *die;* **~-centre** *n.* **a)** *(Anat.)* Nervenzentrum, *das;* **b)** *(fig.)* Schaltzentrale, *die;* **~ gas** *n.* Nervengas, *das*

nerveless ['nɜ:vlɪs] *adj.* **a)** *(inert)* schwach; kraftlos ⟨*Arm, Hand*⟩; **b)** *(flabby)* kraftlos ⟨*Stil*⟩; **c)** *(cool, confident)* nervenstark

nerve: ~-racking *adj.* nervenaufreibend; **~-shattering** *adj.* nervenzerrüttend

nervous ['nɜ:vəs] *adj.* **a)** *(Anat., Med.)* Nerven-; **[central] ~ system** [Zentral]nervensystem, *das;* **~ breakdown** Nervenzusammenbruch, *der;* **b)** *(having delicate nerves)* nervös; **be a ~ wreck** mit den Nerven völlig am Ende sein; **c)** *(Brit.: timid)* **be ~ of** *or* **about** Angst haben vor (+ *Dat.*); **I'm ~ of offending him** ich habe Angst, ihn zu kränken; **be a ~ person** ängstlich sein

nervously ['nɜ:vəslɪ] *adv.* nervös

nervousness ['nɜ:vəsnɪs] *n., no pl.* Ängstlichkeit, *die; (temporary)* Angst, *die*

nervure ['nɜ:vjə(r)] *n.* **a)** *(Zool.)* [Flügel]ader, *die;* **b)** *(Bot.)* [Blatt]ader, *die*

nervy ['nɜ:vɪ] *adj.* **a)** *(jerky, nervous)* nervös; unruhig; **b)** *(Amer. coll.) (cool, confident)* dreist; *(impudent)* unverschämt

nest [nest] **1.** *n.* **a)** *(of bird, animal, insect)* Nest, *das;* **foul one's own ~** *(fig.) (denigrate one's own family)* das eigene *od.* sein eigenes Nest beschmutzen; *(harm one's own interests)* sich *(Dat.)* selbst schaden; *see also* **feather 2 a**; **b)** *(fig.: retreat, shelter, receptacle)* Nest, *das (fig.)*; Zufluchtsort, *der;* **leave the ~:** flügge werden; **c)** *(haunt of robbers etc.)* Nest, *das;* Schlupfwinkel, *der;* **d)** *(place fostering vice etc.)* Brutstätte, *die;* **e)** *(brood or swarm in a ~)* Nest, *das; (of rabbits)* Satz, *der (Jägerspr.)*; *(of wasps, hornets, ants)* Schwarm, *der;* **f)** *(group of machine-guns) (Mil.)* [MG-]Nest, *das;* **g)** *(set)* Satz, *der;* **~ of tables** Satz Tische. **2.** *v. i.* **a)** *(make or have ~)* nisten; **b)** *(take ~s)* Nester entfernen; *(take eggs)* Nester ausnehmen *od.* ausheben; **c)** *(fit together)* **~ [into one another]** ineinanderpassen. **3.** *v. t.* **a)** *(place as in ~)* einbetten; **b)** *(pack one inside the other)* ineinandersetzen ⟨*Töpfe usw.*⟩; *(fig.)* einbetten

'nest-egg *n.* **a)** Nestei, *das;* **b)** *(fig.)* Notgroschen, *der*

'nesting-box *n.* Nistkasten, *der*

nestle ['nesl] **1.** *v. i.* **a)** *(settle oneself)* sich kuscheln; **~ down in a sleeping-bag** sich in einen Schlafsack kuscheln; **b)** *(press oneself affectionately)* sich schmiegen (**to, up against** an + *Akk.*); **they ~d [up] together** sie schmiegten sich aneinander; **c)** *(lie half hidden)* eingebettet sein. **2.** *v. t.* **a)** *(push affectionately or snugly)* kuscheln, schmiegen (**against** an + *Akk.*); **b)** *(hold as in nest)* **~ a baby in one's arms** ein Baby schützend in den Armen halten

nestling ['nestlɪŋ] *n.* Nestling, *der*

[1]net [net] **1.** *n. (lit. or fig.)* Netz, *das;* **cast one's ~ wide** *(fig.)* seine Netze weit spannen; **spread one's ~** *(fig.)* seine Netze stellen *od.* spannen. **2.** *v. t.*, **-tt- a)** *(cover)* **~ [over]** mit einem Netz überziehen ⟨*Baum, Busch*⟩; *(catch)* [mit einem Netz] fangen ⟨*Tier*⟩; einfangen ⟨*Person*⟩; **~ sb. sth.** *(fig. coll.)* jmdm. etw. einbringen; **b)** *(put in net)* ins Netz schlagen; *(put in goal)* ins Tor schießen; **~ a goal** ein Tor schießen

[2]net 1. *adj.* **a)** *(free from deduction)* netto; Netto⟨*einkommen, -[verkaufs]preis usw.*⟩; **b)** *(not subject to discount)*; **~ price** gebundener Preis; ~ **book** preisgebundenes Buch; **Net 'Book Agreement** Vereinbarung zur Preisbindung bei Büchern; **c)** *(excluding weight of container etc.)* netto; ~ **weight** Nettogewicht, *das;* **d)** *(effective, ultimate)* End⟨*ergebnis, -effekt*⟩. **2.** *v. t.*, **-tt-** *(gain)* netto einnehmen; *(yield)* netto einbringen

net: ~ball *n.* Korbball, *der;* **~-cord** *n. (Tennis)* **a)** Spannseil, *das;* **b)** *(stroke)* Netzball, *der;* ~ **'curtain** *n.* Store [aus Gittertüll]; Tüllgardine, *die*

nether ['neðə(r)] *adj. (arch./joc.)* unter...; Unter⟨*lippe, -kiefer*⟩

Netherlands ['neðələndz] **1.** *pr. n. sing. or pl.* Niederlande *Pl.* **2.** *attrib. adj.* niederländisch

nether 'regions, ~ 'world *ns.* Unterwelt, *die*

net 'profit *n.* Reingewinn, *der*

nett *see* ²**net**

netting ['netɪŋ] *n.* **a)** *(making net)* Knüpfen, *das;* **b)** *([piece of] net)* Netz, *das; (needlework)* Filet- *od.* Netzarbeit, *die;* **cover with ~:** mit Netzen/mit einem Netz bedecken; **wire ~:** Drahtgeflecht, *das;* Maschendraht, *der*

nettle ['netl] **1.** *n.* Nessel, *die; see also* **grasp 2 b; stinging-nettle. 2.** *v. t.* reizen; aufbringen

'nettle-rash *n. (Med.)* Nesselsucht, *die;* Nesselausschlag, *der*

'network 1. *n.* **a)** *(of intersecting lines, electrical conductors)* Netzwerk, *das;* **b)** *(of railways etc., persons, operations)* Netz, *das;* **c)** *(of broadcasting stations)* [Sender]netz, *das; (company)* Sender, *der.* **2.** *v. t. (broadcast)* [im ganzen Sendebereich] ausstrahlen

Neuchâtel [nɜːʃæ'tel] *pr. n.* Neuenburg *(das)*

neural ['njʊərl] *adj. (Anat.)* neural *(fachspr.);* Nerven-

neuralgia [njʊə'rældʒə] *n. (Med.)* Neuralgie, *die (fachspr.);* Nervenschmerz, *der*

neuritis [njʊə'raɪtɪs] *n. (Med.)* Neuritis, *die (fachspr.);* Nervenentzündung, *die*

neurological [njʊərə'lɒdʒɪkl] *adj.* neurologisch

neurologist [njʊə'rɒlədʒɪst] *n.* Neurologe, *der*/Neurologin, *die;* Nervenarzt, *der*/Nervenärztin, *die*

neurology [njʊə'rɒlədʒɪ] *n.* Neurologie, *die*

neuron ['njʊərɒn], **neurone** ['njʊərəʊn] *n. (Anat.)* Neuron, *das*

neurosis [njʊə'rəʊsɪs] *n., pl.* **neuroses** [njʊə'rəʊsiːz] Neurose, *die*

neurosurgeon [njʊərəʊ'sɜːdʒn] *n.* Neurochirurg, *der*/-chirurgin, *die*

neurosurgery [njʊərəʊ'sɜːdʒərɪ] *n.* Neurochirurgie, *die*

neurotic [njʊə'rɒtɪk] **1.** *adj.* **a)** *(suffering from neurosis)* nervenkrank; **b)** *(of neurosis)* neurotisch; ~ **affection** *or* **ailment** Nervenkrankheit, *die;* **c)** *(coll.: unduly anxious)* neurotisch; **don't get ~ about it** laß es nicht zu einer Neurose werden. **2.** *n.* Neurotiker, *der*/Neurotikerin, *die*

neurotically [njʊə'rɒtɪkəlɪ] *adv.* neurotisch

neuter ['njuːtə(r)] **1.** *adj.* **a)** *(Ling.)* sächlich; neutral *(fachspr.);* **b)** *(Bot.: asexual)* weder männlich noch weiblich; ungeschlechtlich ⟨*Blüte*⟩; **c)** *(Zool.: sterile)* unfruchtbar. **2.** *n.* **a)** *(Ling.)* Neutrum, *das;* **b)** *(Zool.) (insect)* unfruchtbares Insekt; *(ant, bee)* Arbeiterin, *die;* **c)** *(castrated animal)* kastriertes Tier. **3.** *v. t.* kastrieren

neutral ['njuːtrl] **1.** *adj.* neutral; ~ **gear** Leerlauf, *der; see also* **equilibrium. 2.** *n.* **a)** Neutrale, *der/die;* **be ~s/a ~:** neutral sein; **b)** *(~ gear)* Leerlauf, *der;* **in ~:** im Leerlauf

neutralise *see* **neutralize**

neutrality [njuː'trælɪtɪ] *n.* Neutralität, *die*

neutralize ['njuːtrəlaɪz] *v. t.* **a)** *(Chem.)* neutralisieren; **b)** *(counteract)* neutralisieren; entkräften ⟨*Argument*⟩

neutrally ['njuːtrəlɪ] *adv.* neutral

neutrino [njuː'triːnəʊ] *n., pl.* **~s** *(Phys.)* Neutrino, *das*

neutron ['njuːtrɒn] *n. (Phys.)* Neutron, *das*

neutron: ~ bomb *n.* Neutronenbombe, *die;* ~ **star** *n.* Neutronenstern, *der*

never ['nevə(r)] *adv.* **a)** *(at no time)* nie; **I ~ thought I would see her again** ich hätte nie gedacht, daß ich sie wiedersehen würde; **the rain seemed as if it would ~ stop** der Regen schien gar nicht mehr aufhören zu wollen; **will the rain ~ stop?** hört denn der Regen überhaupt nicht mehr auf?; **he has ~ been abroad** er war [noch] nie im Ausland; **he ~ so much as apologized** er hat sich nicht einmal entschuldigt; **I ~ slept a wink all night** ich habe die ganze Nacht kein Auge zugetan; ~ **is a long time** man soll niemals nie sagen; **~, ~:** nie, nie; niemals; *(more emphatic)* nie im Leben; ~ **so** [auch] noch so; **be it ~ so great** wenn es auch noch so groß ist; mag es auch noch so groß sein; **~-to-be-forgotten** unvergeßlich; **~-satisfied** unersättlich; **~-ending** endlos; **~-failing** unfehlbar; unerschöpflich ⟨*Quelle*⟩; **b)** *(not ... at any time, not ... at all)* nie; **he was ~ one to do sth.** es war nicht seine Art, etw. zu tun; **he is ~ likely to succeed** er wird es nie schaffen; **I ~ remember her winning** ich kann mich nicht erinnern, daß sie je gewonnen hätte; ~ **a** *(not one)* kein einziger/keine einzige/kein einziges; **c)** *(coll.) expr. surprise* **you ~ believed that, did you?** du hast das doch wohl nicht geglaubt?; **He ate the whole turkey. – N~!** Er hat den ganzen Truthahn aufgegessen. – Nein! *(ugs.);* **well, I ~ [did]!** [na *od.* nein *od.* also] so was!

never: ~'more *adv.* nie wieder; **~-'never** *n. (Brit. coll.)* Abzahlungskauf, *der;* **on the ~-never [system]** auf Stottern *(ugs.);* auf Raten; **~the'less** *adv.* trotzdem; nichtsdestoweniger

new [njuː] **1.** *adj.* **a)** *(not existing before)* neu; **'~ boy/girl** *(lit. or fig.)* Neuling, *der;* **a ~ baby** ein neugeborenes Kind; ein Neugeborenes; **b)** *(unfamiliar)* neu; **flying was an experience ~ to him** Fliegen war für ihn eine neue Erfahrung; **that's a ~ one on me** *(coll.)* das ist mir neu; *(of joke etc.)* den habe ich noch nicht gehört; *(of style etc.)* das habe ich noch nicht gesehen; **visit ~ places** unbekannte Orte besuchen; **so what else is ~?** *(iron.)* sonst was Neues? *(ugs.);* **that is not** *or* **nothing ~ to me** das ist mir nichts Neues; **c)** *(renewed, additional, changed)* neu; *(in place-names)* Neu-; **the ~ mathematics** die neue Mathematik; **the ~ poor** die erst vor kurzem Verarmten; **the ~ rich** die Neureichen *(abwertend);* **the ~ woman** die moderne Frau; die Frau von heute; **be like a ~ man/woman** wie neugeboren sein; *see also* **birth a; broom a; 'deal 3 a; leaf 1 b; d)** *(of recent origin, growth, or manufacture)* neu; frisch ⟨*Brot, Gemüse*⟩; neu ⟨*Kartoffeln*⟩; neu, jung ⟨*Wein*⟩; neu, lebend ⟨*Sprache*⟩; **as good as ~:** so gut wie neu; **as ~:** neuwertig. **2.** *adv.* **a)** *(recently)* vor kurzem; frisch ⟨*gebacken, gewaschen, geschnitten*⟩; gerade erst ⟨*erblüht*⟩; **b)** *(afresh)* neu

'new-born *adj.* **a)** *(recently born)* neugeboren; **b)** *(regenerated)* neu gewonnen ⟨*Mut, Kraft usw.*⟩; neu ⟨*Person*⟩

'newcomer *n.* Newcomer, *der; (new arrival also)* Neuankömmling, *der; (one having no experience also)* Neuling, *der* **(to** in + *Dat.*); *(thing also)* Neuheit, *die* **(to** für)

New Delhi [njuː 'delɪ] *pr. n.* Neu-Delhi *(das)*

newel ['njuːəl] *n.* **a)** *(pillar)* Spindel, *die;* **b)** ~ **[post]** *(supporting stair-handrail)* [Treppen]pfosten, *der*

New 'England 1. *n.* Neuengland *(das).* **2.** *attrib. adj.* aus Neuengland; ⟨*Stadt usw.*⟩ in Neuengland

New Englander [njuː 'ɪŋgləndə(r)] *n.* Neuengländer, *der*/Neuengländerin, die

new: ~fangled [njuː'fæŋgld] *adj. (derog.)* neumodisch *(abwertend);* **~-found** *adj.* neu; *(recently discovered)* neu[entdeckt]

Newfoundland [njuː'faʊndlənd] **1. a)** *pr. n.* Neufundland *(das);* **b)** *n. (dog)* Neufundländer, *der.* **2.** *adj.* neufundländisch; ~ **dog** Neufundländer, *der*

Newfoundlander [njuː'faʊndləndə(r)] *n.* Neufundländer, *der*/Neufundländerin, *die*

New 'Guinea *pr. n.* Neuguinea *(das)*

newish ['njuːɪʃ] *adj.* ziemlich neu

new: ~-laid *adj.* frisch [gelegt]; **New 'Left** *n.* neue Linke; ~ **'look** *n. (coll.)* neuer Stil; **~-look** *adj.* neu

newly ['njuːlɪ] *adv.* **a)** *(recently)* neu; ~ **married** seit kurzem verheiratet; **b)** *(in new way)* neu

'newly-wed *n.* Jungverheiratete, *der/die*

new: ~ 'moon *n.* Neumond, *der;* **~-mown** *adj.* frisch gemäht

news [njuːz] *n., no pl.* **a)** *(new information)* Nachricht, *die;* **items** *or* **pieces** *or* **bits of ~:** Neuigkeiten; **be in the** *or* **make ~:** Schlagzeilen machen; **that's ~ to me** *(coll.)* das ist mir neu; **what's the latest ~?** was gibt es Neues?; **have you heard the/this ~?** hast du schon gehört/das schon gehört?; weißt du schon das Neueste? *(ugs.);* **have you had any ~ of your brother?** hast du etwas von deinem Bruder gehört?; hast du Nachricht von deinem Bruder?; **I have ~ for you** *(also iron.)* ich habe eine Neuigkeit für dich; **had/good ~:** schlechte/gute Nachrichten; **sb./sth. is good ~** *(coll.)* jmd./etw. ist wirklich toll *(ugs.);* **he/she/that firm is bad ~** *(coll.)* er/sie/diese Firma ist mit Vorsicht zu genießen *(ugs.);* **no ~ is good ~** *(prov.)* keine Nachricht, gute Nachricht; **b)** *(Radio, Telev.)* Nachrichten *Pl.;* **the 10 o'clock ~:** die 10-Uhr-Nachrichten; **listen to/watch the ~:** [die] Nachrichten hören/sehen; **I heard it on the ~:** ich habe es in den Nachrichten gehört; **here is the ~** *(Radio)* Sie hören Nachrichten; *(Telev.)* ≈ ich begrüße Sie zu den Nachrichten; **summary of the ~:** Nachrichtenüberblick, *der*

news: ~ agency *n.* Nachrichtenagentur, *die;* **~agent** *n.* Zeitungshändler, *der*/-händlerin, *die;* ~ **boy** *n.* Zeitungsjunge, *der;* ~ **bulletin** *n.* Nachrichten *Pl.;* **~cast** *n.* Nachrichtensendung, *die;* **~caster** *n.* Nachrichtensprecher, *der*/-sprecherin, *die;* ~ **conference** *n.* Pressekonferenz, *die;* **~dealer** *n. (Amer.)* Zeitungshändler, *der*/-händlerin, *die;* ~ **desk** *n.* Nachrichtenredaktion, *die;* **this is Joe Smith at the ~ desk** *(Radio)* hier ist Joe Smith met den Nachrichten; **~flash** *n.* Kurzmeldung, *die;* **~girl** *n. (delivering)* Zeitungsausträgerin, *die; (selling)* Zeitungsverkäuferin, *die;* **~hawk** *see* **~hound;** ~ **'headline** *n.* Schlagzeile, *die;* **~hound** *n. (Amer.)* Zeitungsmann, *der (ugs.);* Journalist, *der;* **~letter** *n.* Rundschreiben, *das;* **~man** *n.* Reporter, *der;* **~paper** ['njuːspeɪpə(r)] *n.* **a)** Zeitung, *die; attrib.* **~paper boy/girl** Zeitungsausträger, *der*/-austrägerin, *die;* **b)** *(material)* Zeitungspapier, *das;* **~paperman** *n.* Zeitungsmann, *der (ugs.);* Journalist, *der;* **~print** *n.* Zeitungspapier, *das; (ink)* Druckerschwärze, *die;* **~reader** *n.* Nachrichtensprecher, *der*/-sprecherin, *die;* **~reel** *n.* Wochenschau, *die;* **~room** *n.* Nachrichtenredaktion, *die;* **~-sheet** *n.* Informationsblatt, *das;* **~-stand** *n.* Zeitungskiosk, *der;* Zeitungsstand, *der;* ~ **summary** *n.* Kurznachrichten *Pl.*

new 'star *n. (Astron.)* Nova, *die*

news: ~-vendor *n.* Zeitungsverkäufer, *der*/-verkäuferin, *die;* **~worthy** *adj.* [für die Medien] interessant ⟨*Person, Ereignis*⟩; berichtenswert ⟨*Ereignis*⟩

newsy ['njuːzɪ] *adj. (coll.)* **a)** *(full of news)* voller Neuigkeiten *nachgestellt;* **b)** *(newsworthy)* interessant

newt [nju:t] *n.* [Wasser]molch, *der; see also* **pissed a**
New 'Testament *see* **testament a**
newton ['nju:tn] *n. (Phys.)* Newton, *das*
new: ~ town *n.: mit Unterstützung der Regierung völlig neu entstandene Ansiedlung;* ~ **'world** *see* **world a**; ~ **'year** *n.* Neujahr, *das;* **over the New Year** über Neujahr; **the Jewish New Year** das jüdische Neujahrsfest; **a Happy New Year** ein glückliches *od.* gutes neues Jahr; **New Year honours** *(Brit.)* Titel- und Ordensverleihungen am Neujahrstag; **bring in the New Year** Silvester feiern; *see also* **resolution b**; **New 'Year's** *(Amer.)*, **New Year's 'Day** *ns.* Neujahrstag, *der;* **New Year's 'Eve** *n.* Silvester, *der od. das;* Neujahrsabend, *der*
New Yorker [nju: 'jɔ:kə(r)] *n.* New Yorker, *der*/New Yorkerin, *die*
New Zealand [nju: 'zi:lənd] **1.** *pr. n.* Neuseeland *(das).* **2.** *attrib. adj.* neuseeländisch
New Zealander [nju: 'zi:ləndə(r)] *n.* Neuseeländer, *der*/Neuseeländerin, *die*
next [nekst] **1.** *adj.* **a)** *(nearest)* nächst...; **[the] ~ thing to sth.** fast *od.* beinahe etw.; **the seat ~ to me** der Platz neben mir; **the ~ room** das Nebenzimmer; **~ friend** *(Law)* ≈ Beistand, *der;* **the ~ but one** der/die/das übernächste; **be the one ~ to the door** der/die neben der Tür sein; **~ to** *(fig.: almost)* fast; nahezu; **get ~ to sb.** *(Amer. sl.: friendly)* sich an jmdn. ranmachen *(ugs.)*; **b)** *(in order)* nächst...; **within the ~ few days** in den nächsten Tagen; **~ week/month/year** nächste Woche/nächsten Monat/nächstes Jahr; **on the first of ~ month** am nächsten Ersten; **~ year's results** die Ergebnisse des nächsten Jahres; **during the ~ year** während der nächsten zwölf Monate; **we'll come ~ May** wir kommen im Mai nächsten Jahres; **the ~ largest/larger** der/die/das nächstkleinere/nächstgrößere; **[the] ~ time** das nächste Mal; **the ~ best** der/die/das nächstbeste; **taking one year** *etc.* **with the ~**: im ganzen gesehen; **am I ~?** komme ich jetzt dran?; **he's as able as the '~ man** er kann es wie jeder andere auch; *see also* **door a; world a. 2.** *adv. (in the next place)* als nächstes; *(on the next occasion)* das nächste Mal; **when I ~ see him** wenn ich ihn das nächste Mal sehe; **whose name comes ~?** wessen Name kommt als nächstes *od.* nächster?; **it is my turn ~**: ich komme als nächster dran; **what 'will they think of ~?** was fällt denen als nächstes ein?; **sit/stand ~ to sb.** neben jmdm. sitzen/stehen; **place sth. ~ to sb./sth.** etw. neben jmdn./etw. stellen. **3.** *n.* **a)** *(letter, issue, etc.)* nächster Brief/nächste Ausgabe *usw.*; **b)** *(period of time)* **from one day to the ~**: von einem Tag zum andern; **the week after ~**: [die] übernächste Woche; **c)** *(person)* **~ of kin** nächster/nächste Angehörige; **~ please!** der nächste, bitte!
'next-door *adj.* gleich nebenan *nachgestellt; see also* **neighbour 1**
nexus ['neksəs] *n.* Nexus, *der (fachspr.)*
NHS *abbr. (Brit.)* **National Health Service**
NI *abbr. (Brit.)* **National Insurance**
Niagara Falls [naıægərə 'fɔ:lz] *pr. n. pl.* Niagarafälle
nib [nıb] *n.* Feder, *die; (tip)* Spitze, *die*
nibble ['nıbl] **1.** *v.t.* knabbern; **~ off** abknabbern. **2.** *v.i.* knabbern **(at,** on an + *Dat.*); **the cheese had been ~d at** der Käse war angeknabbert worden; **they are nibbling at the idea** *(fig.)* sie beginnen, sich langsam für die Idee zu interessieren. **3.** *n.* **a)** *(lit. or fig.)* Anbeißen, *das;* **he didn't get a single ~**: bei ihm biß nicht einer an; **b)** *in pl. (coll.: things to eat)* etwas zum Knabbern
nibs [nıbz] *n. (sl./joc.)* **his ~**: der hohe Herr *(scherzh.)*
Nicaragua [nıkə'rægjʊə] *pr. n.* Nicaragua *(das)*
Nicaraguan [nıkə'rægjʊən] **1.** *adj.* nicaraguanisch; **sb. is ~**: jmd. ist Nicaraguaner/Nicaraguanerin. **2.** *n.* Nicaraguaner, *der*/Nicaraguanerin, *die*
Nice [ni:s] *pr. n.* Nizza *(das)*
nice [naıs] *adj.* **a)** *(pleasing)* nett; angenehm ⟨*Stimme*⟩; schön ⟨*Wetter*⟩; *(iron.: disgraceful, difficult)* schön; sauber *(iron.)*; **the hotel is ~ enough** das Hotel ist nicht schlecht *od.* ganz ordentlich; **she has a ~ smile** sie lächelt so nett; **a ~ friend you are!** *(iron.)* du bist mir [ja] ein schöner Freund!; **you're a ~ one, I must say** *(iron.)* du bist mir vielleicht einer; **be in a ~ mess** *(iron.)* in einem schönen Schlamassel sitzen *(ugs.)*; **[do a piece of] ~ work** saubere *od.* gute Arbeit [leisten]; **~ to meet you** freut mich, Sie kennenzulernen; **~ [and] warm/fast/high** schön warm/schnell/hoch; **a ~ long holiday** schöne lange Ferien; **~-looking** hübsch; gut aussehend, hübsch ⟨*Person*⟩; **not very ~** *(unpleasant)* nicht sehr nett; nicht sehr schön ⟨*Wetter*⟩; **he is not very ~ to his sister** er ist nicht gerade nett zu seiner Schwester; **~ one!** *(coll.)* nicht schlecht!; **~ one, Cyril!** *(Brit. sl.)* so ein Schlaumeier!; **~ work if you can get it** *(iron.)* das ließe ich mir auch gefallen!; **b)** *(fastidious)* anspruchsvoll; *(punctilious)* genau; **c)** *(requiring precision)* fein, genau ⟨*Unterscheidung*⟩; **d)** *(subtle)* fein ⟨*Bedeutungsunterschied*⟩
nicely ['naıslı] *adv. (coll.)* **a)** *(well)* nett; gut ⟨*arbeiten, sich benehmen, plaziert sein*⟩; **a ~ behaved child** ein wohlerzogenes Kind; **b)** *(all right)* gut; **he's got a new job and is doing very ~**: er hat eine neue Arbeit und kommt prima *(ugs.) od.* sehr gut damit zurecht; **the patient is doing ~**: der Patient macht gute Fortschritte; **that will do ~**: das reicht völlig; *see also* **thank**
nicety ['naısıtı] *n.* **a)** *no pl. (punctiliousness)* [peinliche] Genauigkeit; **b)** *no pl. (precision, accuracy)* Feinheit, *die;* Genauigkeit, *die;* **to a ~**: perfekt ⟨*arrangieren*⟩; sehr genau ⟨*schätzen*⟩; **c)** *no pl. (intricate or subtle quality)* Feinheit, *die;* **make a point of great ~** höchst subtil argumentieren; **d)** *in pl. (minute distinctions)* Feinheiten
niche [nıtʃ, ni:ʃ] *n.* **a)** *(in wall)* Nische, *die;* **b)** *(fig.: suitable place)* Platz, *der;* **there he soon carved out a ~ for himself** dort fand er bald den richtigen Platz für sich
Nicholas ['nıkələs] *pr. n. (Hist., as name of ruler etc.)* Nikolaus *(der)*
Nick [nık] *n.* **Old ~**: der Teufel; der Leibhaftige *(verhüll.)*
nick 1. *n.* **a)** *(notch)* Kerbe, *die;* **b)** *(sl.: prison)* Kittchen, *das (ugs.)*; Knast, *der (salopp)*; **c)** *(Brit. sl.: police station)* Wache, *die;* Revier, *das;* **d) in good/poor ~** *(coll.)* gut/nicht gut in Schuß *(ugs.)*; **e) in the ~ of time** gerade noch rechtzeitig. **2.** *v.t.* **a)** *(make ~ in)* einkerben ⟨*Holz*⟩; **~ one's chin** sich am Kinn schneiden; **b)** *(Brit. sl.) (catch)* schnappen *(ugs.)*; *(arrest)* einlochen *(salopp)*; **c)** *(Brit. sl.: steal)* klauen *(salopp)*; mitgehen lassen *(ugs.)*
nickel ['nıkl] *n.* **a)** *(metal)* Nickel, *das;* **b)** *(US coin)* Fünfcentstück, *das*
nickel-'plate *v.t.* vernickeln
nicker ['nıkə(r)] *n., pl. same (Brit. sl.)* Pfund, *das;* **it's a hundred ~** ≈ es sind dreihundert Eier *(salopp)*
nickname ['nıkneım] **1.** *n.* **a)** *(name added or substituted)* Spitzname, *der;* **b)** *(abbreviation)* Spitzname, *der; (affectionate)* Koseform, *die.* **2.** *v.t.* einen Spitznamen geben (+ *Dat.*); **~ sb. ...**: jmdm. den Spitznamen ... geben; jmdn. ... taufen
nicotine ['nıkəti:n] *n.* Nikotin, *das*
niece [ni:s] *n.* Nichte, *die*
nifty ['nıftı] *adj. (sl.)* **a)** *(smart, excellent)* klasse *(ugs.)*; flott ⟨*Kleidung*⟩; **b)** *(clever)* geschickt; clever ⟨*Plan, Idee*⟩
¹Niger ['naıdʒə(r)] *pr. n. (river)* Niger, *der*
²Niger [ni:'ʒeə(r)] *pr. n. (country)* Niger *(das od. der)*
Nigeria [naı'dʒıərıə] *pr. n.* Nigeria *(das)*
Nigerian [naı'dʒıərıən] **1.** *adj.* nigerianisch; **sb. is ~**: jmd. ist Nigerianer/Nigerianerin. **2.** *n.* Nigerianer, *der*/Nigerianerin, *die*
niggardly ['nıgədlı] *adj.* **a)** *(miserly)* knaus[e]rig *(ugs. abwertend)*; **b)** *(given in small amounts)* armselig, kümmerlich *(abwertend)* ⟨*Portion*⟩
nigger ['nıgə(r)] *n. (derog.: Negro, dark-skinned person)* Nigger, *der (abwertend)*; **there's a ~ in the woodpile** *or (Amer.)* **in the fence** *(fig.)* es gibt einen Haken bei *od.* an der Sache; **who's the ~ in the woodpile?** *(fig.)* wer schießt hier quer?
niggle ['nıgl] **1.** *v.i.* **a)** *(spend time on petty details)* **~ over** [endlos] herumtüfteln an (+ *Dat.*) ⟨*Vertrag, Klausel*⟩; **~ over every small point** sich mit jeder winzigen Einzelheit aufhalten; **b)** *(find fault pettily)* [herum]nörgeln *(ugs. abwertend)* **(at** an + *Dat.*). **2.** *v.t.* herumnörgeln an (+ *Dat.*); **be ~d** verärgert sein
niggling ['nıglıŋ] *adj.* **a)** *(petty)* belanglos; **b)** *(trivial)* nichtssagend; oberflächlich ⟨*Kritik*⟩; krittelig ⟨*Rezension, Rezensent*⟩; **c)** *(nagging)* nagend ⟨*Zweifel*⟩; quälend ⟨*Gefühl*⟩
niggly ['nıglı] *adj.* **a)** *(irritable)* gereizt; **b)** *see* **niggling a**
nigh [naı] *(arch./literary/dial.)* **1.** *adv.* nahe; **come** *or* **draw ~**: näherkommen; ⟨*Tag, Zeitpunkt:*⟩ nahen; **it's ~ on impossible** es ist nahezu unmöglich; *see also* **wellnigh. 2.** *prep.* nahe *(geh.) nachgestellt* (+ *Dat.*)
night [naıt] *n.* **a)** Nacht, *die; (evening)* Abend, *der;* **~ after ~**: Nacht für Nacht/Abend für Abend; **the following ~**: die Nacht/der Abend darauf; **the previous ~**: die vorausgegangene Nacht/der vorausgegangene Abend; **one ~ he came** eines Nachts/Abends kam er; **two ~s ago** vorgestern nacht/abend; **the other ~**: neulich abends/nachts; **far into the ~**: bis spät *od.* tief in die Nacht; **on Sunday ~**: Sonntag nacht/[am] Sonntag abend; **on Sunday ~s** Sonntag abends; **on the ~ of Friday the 13th** am Freitag, dem 13., nachts/abends; **[on] the ~ after/before** die Nacht danach/davor; **[on] the ~ after/before sth.** die Nacht nach/vor etw. *(Dat.)*; **for the ~**: über Nacht; **late at ~**: spätabends; **a ~ raid** ein nächtlicher Überfall; ein Nachtangriff *(Milit.)*; **a ~'s rest will make you feel better** wenn du eine Nacht richtig geschlafen hast, wirst du dich wieder besser fühlen; **take all ~** *(fig.)* den ganzen Abend brauchen; **at ~** *(in the evening, at ~fall)* abends; *(during the ~)* nachts; bei Nacht; **make a ~ of it** die Nacht durchfeiern; durchmachen *(ugs.)*; **as ~ and day** Tag und Nacht; **as ~ follows day** so sicher wie das Amen in der Kirche; **a ~ off** eine Nacht/ein Abend frei; **~ out** *(of servant)* freier Abend; **it is her ~ out** sie hat ihren freien Abend; **have a ~ out** *(festive evening)* [abends] ausgehen; **she works one ~ a week** sie arbeitet einen Abend/eine Nacht in der Woche; **spend the ~ with sb.** bei jmdm. übernachten; *(implying sexual intimacy)* die Nacht mit jmdm. verbringen; **stay the ~** *or* **over ~**: über Nacht bleiben; **work ~s** nachts arbeiten; *(be on ~shift)* ⟨*Krankenschwester:*⟩ Nachtdienst haben; ⟨*Schichtarbeiter:*⟩ Nachtschicht haben; *see also* **good 1 m; 'last 1; b)** *(darkness, lit. or fig.)* Nacht, *die;* **black as ~**: schwarz wie die Nacht; **it went as dark as ~**: es wurde stockdunkel; **c)** *(~fall)* Einbruch der Dunkelheit; **wait for ~**: darauf warten, daß es Nacht wird; **when ~ comes** wenn es dunkel wird; **d)** *(~'s sleep)* **have a good/bad ~**: gut/schlecht schlafen; **have a sleepless ~**: eine schlaflose Nacht haben; **e)** *(evening of performance etc.)*

Abend, *der;* **opening ~:** Premiere, *die; see also* **first night; ladies' night; f)** *attrib.* Nacht-/Abend-

night: ~-bell *n. (Brit.)* Nachtglocke, *die;* **~bird** *n. (person)* Nachteule, *die (ugs. scherzh.);* **~-blindness** *n.* Nachtblindheit, *die;* **~cap** *n.* **a)** Nachtmütze, *die; (woman's)* Nachthaube, *die;* **b)** *(drink)* Schlaftrunk, *der;* **~clothes** *n. pl.* Nachtwäsche, *die;* **in one's ~clothes** im Nachthemd/Schlafanzug; **~-club** *n.* Nachtklub, *der;* Nachtlokal, *das;* **~dress** *n.* Nachthemd, *das;* **~ duty** *n.* Nachtdienst, *der;* **be on ~ duty** Nachtdienst haben; **~fall** *n., no art.* Einbruch der Dunkelheit; **at/after ~fall** bei/nach Einbruch der Dunkelheit; **~ fighter** *n. (Air Force)* Nachtjäger, *der;* **~ flying** *n.* Nachtfliegen, *das;* **~gown** *see* **~dress**

nightie ['naɪtɪ] *n. (coll.)* Nachthemd, *das*

nightingale ['naɪtɪŋgeɪl] *n.* Nachtigall, *die*

night: ~jar *n. (Ornith.)* Ziegenmelker, *der;* **~-life** *n.* Nachtleben, *das;* **~-light** *n.* Nachtlicht, *das;* **~-long 1.** *adj.* sich über die ganze Nacht hinziehend; **keep a ~-long vigil** die ganze Nacht wachen; **2.** *adv.* die ganze Nacht [lang *od.* über]

nightly ['naɪtlɪ] **1.** *adj. (happening, done, etc. in the night/evening)* nächtlich/abendlich; *(happening every night/evening)* allnächtlich/allabendlich. **2.** *adv. (every night)* jede Nacht; *(every evening)* jeden Abend; **twice ~** *(Theatre etc.)* zweimal pro Abend

night: ~mare *n. (lit. or fig.)* Alptraum, *der;* **~marish** ['naɪtmeərɪʃ] *adj.* alptraumhaft; **~-'night** *int. (coll.)* [gute] Nacht; **~ nurse** *n.* Nachtschwester, *die;* **~-owl** *n.* **a)** *(Ornith.)* Eule, *die;* Nachteule, *die (veralt.);* **b)** *(coll.: person)* Nachteule, *die (ugs. scherzh.);* Nachtschwärmer, *der (scherzh.);* **~-porter** *n.* Nachtportier, *der;* **~-robe** *(Amer.) see* **~-dress; ~ safe** *n.* Nachttresor, *der;* **~-scented 'stock** *n. (Bot.)* Abendlevkoje, *die;* **~ school** *n.* Abendschule, *die;* **~shade** *n. (Bot.)* Nachtschatten, *der;* **black ~shade** Schwarzer Nachtschatten; **woody ~shade** Bittersüß, *das;* Bittersüßer Nachtschatten; *see also* **deadly; ~ shift** *n.* Nachtschicht, *die;* **be on ~ shift** Nachtschicht haben *od.* machen; **~-shirt** *n.* [Herren]nachthemd, *das;* **~ 'sky** *n.* Nachthimmel, *der;* **~-spot** *(coll.) see* **~-club; ~stick** *n. (Amer.)* Schlagstock, *der;* **~ 'storage heater** *n.* Nachtspeicherofen, *der;* **~-time** *n., no indef. art.* Nacht, *die;* **at ~-time** nachts; **wait until ~-time** warten, bis es Nacht *od.* dunkel wird; **in the ~-time** während der Nacht; nachts; **~-'watch** *n.* Nachtwache, *die;* **in the ~-watches** während der Nacht; **~-'watchman** *n.* **a)** Nachtwächter, *der;* **b)** *(Cricket) Auswechselspieler, der am Ende eines Tages eingesetzt wird, damit ein besserer Spieler geschont wird;* **~wear** *n. sing. see* **~-clothes**

nig-nog ['nɪgnɒg] *n. (Brit. derog.)* Nigger, *der (abwertend)*

nihilism ['naɪlɪzm, 'nɪhɪlɪzm] *n.* Nihilismus, *der*

nihilist ['naɪlɪst, 'nɪhɪlɪst] *n.* Nihilist, *der*

nihilistic [naɪ'lɪstɪk, nɪhɪ'lɪstɪk] *adj.* nihilistisch

nil [nɪl] *n.* **a)** nichts; **his chances were ~:** seine Chancen waren gleich Null; **our investment has shown a ~ return** unsere Investition hat keinen Gewinn gebracht; **b)** *(Sport)* null; **win one ~** *or* **by one goal to ~:** eins zu null gewinnen

Nile [naɪl] *pr. n.* Nil, *der*

nimble ['nɪmbl] *adj.* **a)** *(quick in movement)* flink; behende; **b)** *(quick in mind)* beweglich ⟨*Geist*⟩; lebhaft ⟨*Phantasie*⟩; **his mind remained ~:** er blieb geistig beweglich; **c)** *(dextrous)* geschickt

nimbly ['nɪmblɪ] *adv.* flink ⟨*arbeiten, sich bewegen*⟩

nimbus ['nɪmbəs] *n., pl.* **nimbi** ['nɪmbaɪ] *or* **~es a)** *(halo)* Nimbus, *der (bild. Kunst);* Heiligenschein, *der;* **b)** *(Meteorol.)* Nimbostratus, *der*

nincompoop ['nɪŋkəmpu:p] *n.* Trottel, *der (ugs. abwertend)*

nine [naɪn] **1.** *adj.* neun; **~-tenths of the time/inhabitants** *(fig.)* fast die ganze Zeit/fast *od.* so gut wie alle Einwohner; **~ times out of ten** *(fig.: nearly always)* in den weitaus meisten Fällen; **a ~ days' wonder** nur eine Eintagsfliege *(ugs.); see also* **eight 1. 2.** *n.* **a)** *(number, symbol)* Neun, *die;* **work from ~ to five** die übliche Arbeitszeit [von 9 bis 17 Uhr] haben; **the ~-to-five world** die Welt des geregelten Achtstundentags; **~-to-five mentality** Angestelltenmentalität, *die (abwertend);* **b)** *(Amer.: baseball team)* Mannschaft, *die;* „Neun", *die;* **c) the N~** *(literary: the Muses)* die neun Musen; **d) dressed [up] to the ~s** sehr festlich gekleidet; **~-nine-nine, 999** *(Brit.: emergency number)* ≈ eins, eins, null. *See also* **eight 2 a, c, d**

ninefold ['naɪnfəʊld] *adj., adv.* neunfach; *see also* **eightfold**

'ninepins *n. (Brit.)* **a)** *(game)* Kegeln, *das;* **play ~:** kegeln; **b)** *constr. as pl. (pins)* Kegel; **go down like ~** *(fig.)* reihenweise umfallen *(ugs.)*

nineteen [naɪn'ti:n] **1.** *adj.* neunzehn; *see also* **eight 1. 2.** *n.* **a)** Neunzehn, *die; see also* **eight 2 a; eighteen 2; b) talk ~ to the dozen** *(Brit.)* wie ein Wasserfall reden *(ugs.)*

nineteenth [naɪn'ti:nθ] **1.** *adj.* neunzehnt...; **~ hole** *(joc.: golf-club's bar)* neunzehntes Loch *(fig. scherzh.); see also* **eighth 1. 2.** *n. (fraction)* Neunzehntel, *das; see also* **eighth 2**

ninetieth ['naɪntɪɪθ] **1.** *adj.* neunzigst...; *see also* **eighth 1. 2.** *n. (fraction)* Neunzigstel, *das; see also* **eighth 2**

ninety ['naɪntɪ] **1.** *adj.* neunzig; **one-and-~** *(arch.) see* **~-one 1;** *see also* **eight 1. 2.** *n.* Neunzig, *die;* **one-and-~** *(arch.) see* **~-one 2.** *See also* **eight 2 a; eighty 2**

ninety: ~-'first *etc. adj.* einundneunzigst... *usw.; see also* **eighth 1; ~-'one** *etc.* **1.** *adj.* einundneunzig *usw.;* **~-nine times out of a hundred** *(fig.: nearly always)* so gut wie immer; *see also* **eight 1; 2.** *n.* Einundneunzig *usw., die; see also* **eight 2 a**

ninny ['nɪnɪ] *n.* Dummkopf, *der (ugs.);* Dussel, *der (ugs.)*

ninth [naɪnθ] **1.** *adj.* neunt...; *see also* **eighth 1. 2.** *n.* **a)** *(in sequence)* neunte, *der/die/das; (in rank)* Neunte, *der/die/das; (fraction)* Neuntel, *das;* **b)** *(Mus.)* None, *die;* **c)** *(day)* **the ~ of May** der neunte Mai; **the ~ [of the month]** der neunte [des Monats]. *See also* **eighth 2**

niobium [naɪ'əʊbɪəm] *n. (Chem.)* Niobium, *das*

Nip [nɪp] *n. (sl. derog.)* Japs, *der (ugs., oft abwertend)*

¹nip 1. *v.t.,* **-pp- a)** *(pinch, squeeze, bite)* zwicken; **~ sb.'s toe/sb. on the leg** jmdn. *od.* jmdm. in den Zeh/jmdn. am Bein zwicken; **b) ~ off** abzwicken; *(with scissors)* abknipsen. *See also* **bud 1. 2.** *v.i.,* **-pp-** *(Brit. sl.: step etc. quickly)* **~ in** hinein-/hereinflitzen *(ugs.);* **~ out** hinaus-/herausflitzen *(ugs.);* **~ up** hochflitzen *(ugs.);* **~ out to get a paper** kurz rausgehen, um eine Zeitung zu holen *(ugs.);* **~ across to Mrs Jones and ...:** spring mal zu Frau Jones rüber und ... **3.** *n.* **a)** *(pinch, squeeze)* Kniff, *der; (bite)* Biß, *der;* **give sb.'s cheek a ~, give sb. a ~ on the cheek** jmdn. in die Wange zwicken; **b)** *(coldness of air)* Kälte, *die;* **there's a ~ in the air** es ist frisch

²nip *n. (of spirits etc.)* Schlückchen, *das;* **have a ~ of wine** ein Schlückchen Wein nehmen

nip and 'tuck *n. (Amer.)* **it was ~** es war ganz knapp

nipper ['nɪpə(r)] *n.* **a)** *(Brit. coll.: child)* Gör, *das (nordd.);* Balg, *das (ugs.);* **b)** *in pl. (pincers)* Beißzange, *die;* Kneifzange, *die;* **c)** *(claw)* Schere, *die;* Zange, *die*

nipple ['nɪpl] *n.* **a)** *(on breast)* Brustwarze, *die;* **b)** *(of feeding-bottle)* Sauger, *der;* **c) [grease-]~:** [Schmier]nippel, *der*

Nippon ['nɪpɒn] *pr. n.* Nippon *(das)*

nippy ['nɪpɪ] *adj. (coll.)* **a)** *(nimble)* flink; spritzig ⟨*Auto*⟩; **b)** *(cold)* frisch; kühl

nirvana [nɜ:'vɑ:nə, nɪə'vɑ:nə] *n.* Nirwana, *das*

nisi ['naɪsaɪ] *adj. (Law)* vorläufig; mit Vorbehalt; *see also* **decree 1 b**

Nissen hut ['nɪsn hʌt] *n.* Nissenhütte, *die*

nit [nɪt] *n.* **a)** *(egg)* Nisse, *die;* **b)** *(sl.: stupid person)* Dussel, *der (ugs.);* Blödmann, *der (salopp)*

niter *(Amer.) see* **nitre**

'nit: ~-pick *v.i.* kritteln *(abwertend);* **~-picking** *(coll.)* **1.** *n.* Kritteleien *(abwertend);* **2.** *adj.* kleinlich *(abwertend)*

nitrate ['naɪtreɪt] *n.* **a)** *(salt)* Nitrat, *das;* **b)** *(fertilizer)* Nitratdünger, *der*

nitre ['naɪtə(r)] *n. (Brit.)* Salpeter, *der*

nitric ['naɪtrɪk] *adj. (Chem.: of or containing nitrogen)* stickstoffhaltig; Stickstoff-

nitric: ~ 'acid *n. (Chem.)* Salpetersäure, *die;* **~ 'oxide** *n. (Chem.)* Stickoxid, *das*

nitride ['naɪtraɪd] *n. (Chem.)* Nitrid, *das*

nitrite ['naɪtraɪt] *n. (Chem.)* Nitrit, *das*

nitrogen ['naɪtrədʒən] *n.* Stickstoff, *der*

nitrogen: ~ cycle *n. (Bot.)* Stickstoffkreislauf, *der;* **~ fixation** *n. (Bot.)* Bindung des freien Stickstoffs

nitrogenous [naɪ'trɒdʒɪnəs] *adj.* stickstoffhaltig

nitroglycerine [naɪtrəʊ'glɪsəri:n] *n.* Nitroglyzerin, *das*

nitrous ['naɪtrəs]: **~ 'acid** *n. (Chem.)* salpet[e]rige Säure; **~ 'oxide** *n. (Chem.)* Distickstoff[mon]oxid, *das*

nitty-gritty [nɪtɪ'grɪtɪ] *n. (sl.)* **the ~ [of the matter]** der Kern [der Sache]; **the ~ of the situation** das, worum es eigentlich geht; **get down to the ~:** zur Sache kommen

nitwit ['nɪtwɪt] *n. (coll.)* Trottel, *der (ugs.)*

nitwitted ['nɪtwɪtɪd] *adj.* dämlich *(ugs.)*

nix [nɪks] *n. (sl.)* **a)** *(nothing)* nix *(ugs.);* **b)** *see* **no 2 b**

NNE [nɔ:θnɔ:θ'i:st] *abbr.* **north-north-east** NNO

NNW [nɔ:θnɔ:θ'west] *abbr.* **north-north-west** NNW

no [nəʊ] **1.** *adj.* **a)** *(not any)* kein; **b)** *(not a)* kein; *(quite other than)* alles andere als; **she is no beauty** sie ist keine Schönheit *od.* nicht gerade eine Schönheit; **you are no friend** du bist kein [wahrer] Freund; **friend or no friend** Freund oder nicht; Freund hin oder her; *see also* **¹go 3 f; c)** *(hardly any)* **it's no distance from our house to the shopping centre** von unserem Haus ist es nicht weit bis zum Einkaufszentrum; *see also* **time b. 2.** *adv.* **a)** *(by no amount)* nicht; **we went no further than the Post Office** wir gingen nicht weiter als bis zum Postamt; **no fewer than** nicht weniger als; **no less [than]** nicht weniger [als]; **it is no different from before** es hat sich nichts geändert; **it was no less a person than Gladstone** *or* **Gladstone, no less** es war kein Geringerer als Gladstone; **I ask no more of you other than ...:** ich verlange nicht mehr von dir als ...; **no more wine?** keinen Wein mehr?; **no more war!** nie wieder Krieg!; **he is no more upper-class than I am** er ist auch nicht mehr *od.* nichts Besseres *(ugs.)* als ich; **I'm not entirely innocent in this matter – No more am 'I** Ich bin nicht ganz unschuldig in dieser Sache – Und ich [bin's] ebensowenig; **I saw no more of him** ich habe ihn nicht mehr gesehen; **he is no more** *(is dead)* er ist nicht mehr *(geh.);* **b)** *(equivalent to negative sentence)* nein; **say/answer 'no'** nein sagen/mit Nein antworten;

I won't take 'no' for an answer ein Nein lasse ich nicht gelten; **I won't say 'no'** da kann ich nicht nein sagen; **c)** *(not)* nicht; **like it or no** ob es mir *usw.* [nun] paßt/paßte oder nicht; **whether or no anyone else helps** [egal] ob sonst jemand hilft oder nicht; **d) no can do** *(coll.)* geht nicht *(ugs.)*. **3.** *n., pl.* **noes** [nəʊz] Nein, *das; (vote)* Neinstimme, *die;* **the ayes and noes** die Stimmen für und wider; **the noes have it** die Mehrheit ist dagegen

No. *abbr.* **a) number** Nr. ; **b)** *(Amer.)* **North** N

'**no-account** *adj.* unbedeutend

Noah's ark [nəʊəz 'ɑ:k] **a)** *(Bibl.)* die Arche Noah; **b)** *(toy)* Arche Noah *(als Spielzeug)*

[1]**nob** [nɒb] *n. (sl.: head)* Rübe, *die (salopp)*

[2]**nob** *n. (Brit. sl.: wealthy or upper-class person)* **the ~s** die besseren Leute

no-'ball *(Cricket)* **1.** *n.* Fehlball, *der.* **2.** *v.t.* **~ sb.** jmds. Wurf für ungültig erklären

nobble ['nɒbl] *v.t. (Brit. sl.)* **a)** *(tamper with) (durch Spritzen o.ä.)* langsam machen ‹*Rennpferd*›; **b)** *(get the favour of) (durch Bestechung o.ä.)* auf seine Seite ziehen ‹*Person*›; **c)** *(take dishonestly)* klauen *(salopp)* ‹*Geld, Schmuck*›; **d)** *(catch)* schnappen *(ugs.)* ‹*Dieb*›

nobbut ['nɒbət] *adv. (dial.)* bloß *(ugs.)*; nur; **it's ~ Thursday** es ist erst Donnerstag

Nobel prize [nəʊbel 'praɪz] *n.* Nobelpreis, *der*

nobility [nə'bɪlɪtɪ] *n.* **a)** *no pl. (character)* hohe Gesinnung; Adel, *der;* **a true ~ of character** ein wahrhaft nobler Charakter; **~ of soul** Seelenadel, *der (geh.)*; **b)** *(class)* Adel, *der;* **many of the ~:** viele Adlige; **be born into the ~:** von adliger Geburt sein *(geh.)*

noble ['nəʊbl] **1.** *adj.* **a)** *(by rank, title, or birth)* ad[e]lig; **be of ~ birth** von adliger *od.* edler Geburt sein *(geh.)*; adlig sein; **the ~ Lord/Earl** der edle Lord/Graf *(geh.)*; **b)** *(of lofty character)* edel ‹*Gedanken, Gefühle*›; **~ ideals** hohe Ideale; **c)** *(showing greatness of character)* edel; hochherzig *(geh.)*; **make ~ efforts** sich in hochherziger Weise bemühen *(geh.)*; **d)** *(splendid)* edel *(geh.)*; vortrefflich. **2.** *n.* Adlige, *der/die;* Edelmann, *der*/Edelfrau, *die (hist.)*; **the ~s** die Adligen; die Edelleute *(hist.)*

noble: ~man ['nəʊblmən] *n., pl.* **~men** ['nəʊblmən] Adlige, *der;* Edelmann, *der (hist.)*; **~ 'metal** *n. (Chem.)* Edelmetall, *das;* **~-'minded** *adj.* edelgesinnt; edel ‹*Tat*›; **~ 'savage** *n.* edler Wilder *(Literaturw.)*

noblesse [nə'bles] *n., no pl.* Noblesse, *die (veralt.)*; Adel, *der;* **~ oblige** [nəʊbles əʊ'bli:ʒ] noblesse oblige *(geh., oft scherzh.)*; Adel verpflichtet

'**noblewoman** *n.* Adlige, *die;* Edelfrau, *die (hist.)*; *(unmarried)* Edelfräulein, *das (hist.)*

nobly ['nəʊblɪ] *adv.* **a)** *(with noble spirit)* edel[gesinnt]; **b)** *(generously)* edelmütig *(geh.)*; **c)** *(splendidly)* edel *(geh.)*

nobody ['nəʊbədɪ] *n. & pron.* niemand; keiner; *(person of no importance)* Niemand, *der; see also* **business c;** [1]**fool 1 a**

no-'claim[s] bonus *n. (Insurance)* Schadenfreiheitsrabatt, *der*

nocturnal [nɒk'tɜ:nl] *adj.* nächtlich; nachtaktiv ‹*Tier*›; **~ animal/bird** Nachttier, *das*/-vogel, *der*

nocturne ['nɒktɜ:n] *n.* **a)** *(Mus.)* Nocturne, *das od. die;* **b)** *(Art)* Nachtstück, *das*

nod [nɒd] **1.** *v.i.,* **-dd- a)** *(as signal)* nicken; **~ to sb.** jmdm. zunicken; **have a ~ding acquaintance with sth.** nur über geringe Kenntnisse in etw. *(Dat.)* verfügen; **he's only a ~ding acquaintance** ich kenne ihn nur flüchtig; **he ~ded to him to take charge** er gab ihm durch ein Nicken zu verstehen, daß er das Kommando übernehmen solle; *see also* **goodbye 2; b)** *(in drowsiness)* **she sat ~ding by the fire** sie war neben dem Kamin eingenickt *(ugs.)*; **her head started to ~:** sie begann einzunicken *(ugs.)*; **c)** *(make a mistake)* patzen *(ugs.)*; einen Fehler machen; **d)** *(move up and down)* nicken *(fig. dichter.)*. **2.** *v.t.,* **-dd- a)** *(incline)* **~ one's head [in greeting]** [zum Gruß] mit dem Kopf nicken; **b)** *(signify by nod)* **~ approval** *or* **agreement** zustimmend nicken; **~ sb. a welcome, ~ a welcome to sb.** jmdm. zum Gruß *od.* zur Begrüßung zunicken. **3.** *n.* **a)** *(nodding)* [Kopf]nicken, *das;* **a ~ is as good as a wink [to a blind man** *or* **horse]** *(fig.)* es bedarf/bedurfte keiner weiteren Worte; **land of Nod** Land der Träume *(geh.)*; **on the ~** *(coll.) (on credit)* auf Pump *(salopp)*; *(with merely formal assent)* ohne große Diskussion; **b)** *(Amer.: sign of approval)* **get the ~ from sb.** von jmdm. grünes Licht bekommen; **give sth. the ~:** grünes Licht für etw. geben

~ 'off *v.i.* einnicken *(ugs.)*

noddle ['nɒdl] *n. (coll.: head)* Birne, *die (salopp)*

noddy ['nɒdɪ] *n.* Dummkopf, *der*

node [nəʊd] *n.* **a)** *(Bot., Astron.)* Knoten, *der;* **b)** *(Phys.)* Schwingungsknoten, *der;* **c)** *(Math.)* Knoten[punkt], *der*

nodule ['nɒdju:l] *n.* **a)** Klümpchen, *das;* **b)** *(Bot.)* Knötchen, *das*

Noel [nəʊ'el] *n. (esp. in carols)* Weihnachten, *das od. Pl.*; Weihnacht, *die (geh.)*

'**no 'entry'** *(for people)* „Zutritt verboten"; *(for vehicles)* „Einfahrt verboten"; **a '~' sign** ein Schild mit der Aufschrift „Zutritt/Einfahrt verboten"

'**no-fault insurance** *n. (Amer.)* ≈ Vollkaskoversicherung

noggin ['nɒgɪn] *n.* **a)** *(mug)* Becher, *der;* *(drink)* Schlückchen, *das;* **b)** *(Amer. sl.: head)* Birne, *die (salopp)*

no-'go *adj.* Sperr‹*gebiet, -zone*›

'**no-good** *adj. (coll.)* nichtsnutzig *(abwertend)*

nohow ['nəʊhaʊ] *adv. (coll.)* in keiner Weise

noise [nɔɪz] **1.** *n.* **a)** *(loud outcry)* Lärm, *der;* Krach, *der;* **don't make so much ~/such a loud ~:** sei nicht so laut/mach nicht solchen Lärm *od.* Krach; **make a ~ about sth.** *(fig.: complain)* wegen etw. Krach machen *od.* schlagen *(ugs.)*; **make a ~** *(fig.: be much talked about)* von sich reden machen; Aufsehen erregen; *see also* [2]**hold 1 t; b)** *(any sound)* Geräusch, *das;* *(loud, harsh, unwanted)* Lärm, *der;* **~s off** Geräuschkulisse, *die;* **c)** *(Communications: irregular fluctuations of signal)* Geräusch, *das;* *(hissing)* Rauschen, *das;* **d)** *in pl. (conventional remarks or sounds)* **make friendly** *etc.* **~s [at sb.]** [jmdm. gegenüber] freundliche *usw.* Bemerkungen von sich geben; **make ~s about doing sth.** davon reden, etw. tun zu wollen. **2.** *v.t. (dated/formal)* **~ sth. abroad** *or* **about** etw. verbreiten

'**noise abatement** *n.* Lärmbekämpfung, *die*

noiseless ['nɔɪzlɪs] *adj.,* **noiselessly** ['nɔɪzlɪslɪ] *adv.* **a)** *(silent[ly])* lautlos; **b)** *(making no avoidable noise)* geräuschlos

'**noise pollution** *n.* Lärmbelästigung, *die*

noisily ['nɔɪzɪlɪ] *adv.* laut; lärmend ‹*spielen*›; geräuschvoll ‹*stolpern, schlürfen*›

noisome ['nɔɪsəm] *adj. (literary)* **a)** *(harmful, noxious)* gefährlich; übel *(geh.)* ‹*Umgebung*›; **b)** *(evil-smelling)* übelriechend; **c)** *(objectionable, offensive)* unangenehm

noisy ['nɔɪzɪ] *adj.* laut; lärmend, laut ‹*Menschenmasse, Kinder*›; lautstark ‹*Diskussion, Begrüßung*›; geräuschvoll ‹*Aufbruch, Ankunft*›

nomad ['nəʊmæd] **1.** *n.* **a)** Nomade, *der;* **b)** *(wanderer)* jmd., der ein Nomadendasein führt. **2.** *adj.* **a)** nomadisch; **b)** *(wandering)* **~ existence** Nomadendasein, *das*

nomadic [nə'mædɪk] *adj.* nomadisch; **~ tribe** Nomadenstamm, *der*

'**no man's land** *n.* Niemandsland, *das*

nom de plume [nɒm də 'plu:m] *n., pl.* **noms de plume** [nɒm də 'plu:m] Schriftstellername, *der;* Pseudonym, *das*

nomenclature [nə'menklətʃə(r), 'nəʊmənkleɪtʃə(r)] *n.* **a)** *(system of names)* Vokabular, *das;* **b)** *(terminology, systematic naming, catalogue)* Nomenklatur, *die*

nominal ['nɒmɪnl] *adj.* **a)** *(in name only)* nominell; **b)** *(virtually nothing)* äußerst gering; äußerst niedrig ‹*Preis, Miete*›; **c)** *(Ling.)* nominal; Nominal‹*phrase, -präfix*›

nominalism ['nɒmɪnəlɪzm] *n. (Philos.)* Nominalismus, *der*

nominally ['nɒmɪnəlɪ] *adv.* namentlich

nominal 'value *n. (Econ.)* Nennwert, *der*

nominate ['nɒmɪneɪt] *v.t.* **a)** *(call by name of)* nennen; **b)** *(propose for election)* nominieren; **c)** *(appoint to office)* ernennen

nomination [nɒmɪ'neɪʃn] *n.* **a)** *(appointment to office)* Ernennung, *die;* **b)** *(proposal for election)* Nominierung, *die*

nominative ['nɒmɪnətɪv] *(Ling.)* **1.** *adj.* Nominativ-; nominativisch; **~ case** Nominativ, *der.* **2.** *n.* Nominativ, *der; see also* **absolute c**

nominee [nɒmɪ'ni:] *n.* **a)** *(candidate)* Kandidat, *der*/Kandidatin, *die;* **b)** *(representative)* Stellvertreter, *der*/-vertreterin, *die*

non- [nɒn] *pref.* nicht-

non-ac'ceptance *n. (Commerc.)* Annahmeverweigerung, *die*

nonagenarian [nəʊnədʒɪ'neərɪən] **1.** *adj.* neunzigjährig; *(more than 90 years old)* in den Neunzigern *nachgestellt.* **2.** *n.* Neunziger, *der*/Neunzigerin, *die*

non-ag'gression *n.* Gewaltverzicht, *der;* **~ pact** *or* **treaty** Nichtangriffspakt, *der*

non-alco'holic *adj.* alkoholfrei

non-a'ligned *adj.* blockfrei

non-a'lignment *n., no pl.* Blockfreiheit, *die*

non-bel'ligerent 1. *adj.* nicht kriegführend. **2.** *n.* nicht kriegführendes Land

nonce [nɒns] *n.* **for the ~:** einstweilen

'**nonce-word** *n.* Ad-hoc-Bildung, *die*

nonchalance ['nɒnʃələns] *n.* Nonchalance, *die (geh.)*; Unbekümmertheit, *die;* *(lack of interest)* Desinteresse, *das;* Gleichgültigkeit, *die*

nonchalant ['nɒnʃələnt] *adj.,* **nonchalantly** ['nɒnʃələntlɪ] *adv.* nonchalant *(geh.)*; unbekümmert; *(without interest)* desinteressiert; gleichgültig

non-'combatant 1. *n.* Nichtkämpfende, *der/die.* **2.** *adj.* nicht am Kampf beteiligt

non-com'missioned *adj.* ohne Patent *nachgestellt;* **~ officer** Unteroffizier, *der*

non-com'mittal *adj.* unverbindlich

non compos [mentis] [nɒn 'kɒmpɒs ('mentɪs)] *pred. adj.* nicht im Vollbesitz seiner/ihrer *usw.* geistigen Kräfte

non-con'ducting *adj. (Phys.)* nichtleitend

non-con'ductor *n. (Phys.)* Nichtleiter, *der*

noncon'formism *n.* Nonkonformismus, *der*

noncon'formist *n.* Nonkonformist, *der*/Nonkonformistin, *die*

noncon'formity *n.* **a)** Nonkonformismus, *der;* **b)** *(lack of correspondence or agreement)* Nonkonformität, *die*

non-con'tributory *adj.* beitragsfrei

non-co-oper'ation *n.* Verweigerung der Kooperation

non-denomi'national *adj.* konfessionslos

nondescript ['nɒndɪskrɪpt] *adj.* unscheinbar; undefinierbar ‹*Farbe*›

'**non-drip** *adj.* nicht tropfend ‹*Farbe*›

non-'driver *n.* Nicht[auto]fahrer, *der*

none [nʌn] **1.** *pron.* kein...; **I want ~ of your cheek!** sei nicht so frech!; **~ of them** keiner/keine/keines von ihnen; **~ of this money is mine** von diesem Geld gehört mir nichts; **~ of these houses** kein[e]s dieser Häuser; **~ but they/he** keiner *od.* niemand außer ihnen/ihm; nur sie/er; **~ other than ...:** kein anderer/keine andere als ...; **Is there any bread left? – No, ~ at all** Ist noch Brot da? – Nein, gar keins mehr; **it is ~ of my concern** das geht mich nichts an; **his understanding is ~ of the clearest** seine Auffassungsgabe ist nicht nicht gerade die beste. **2.** *adv.* keineswegs; **I'm ~ the wiser now** jetzt bin ich um nichts klüger; **~ the less** nichtsdestoweniger; *see also* **too a**

non'entity *n. (non-existent thing, person or thing of no importance)* Nichts, *das*

nonesuch *see* **nonsuch**

'non-event *n.* Reinfall, *der (ugs.)*; Enttäuschung, *die*

non-ex'istence *n., no pl.* Nichtvorhandensein, *das*

non-existent [nɒnɪg'zɪstənt] *adj.* nicht vorhanden

non-'ferrous *adj.* Nichteisen-

non-'fiction *n.* ~ **[literature]** Sachliteratur, *die;* ~ **novel** Tatsachenroman, *der*

non-'flammable *adj.* nicht entzündbar

non-inter'ference, non-inter'vention *ns., no pl.* Nichteinmischung, *die*

non-'iron *adj.* bügelfrei

non-'member *n.* Nichtmitglied, *das*

non-'metal *n. (Chem.)* Nichtmetall, *das*

non-me'tallic *adj. (Chem.)* nichtmetallisch

non-'net *adj.* nicht preisgebunden

non-'nuclear *adj.* Nichtnuklear-; ~ **club** Gruppe der Nichtnuklearstaaten; ~ **weapons** konventionelle Waffen

'no-no *n., pl.* **~es** *(coll.)* **be a ~:** nicht in Frage kommen *(ugs.)*; **that's a ~:** das kannste vergessen *(ugs.)*

no-'nonsense *see* **nonsense 1 c**

nonpareil [nɒnpə'reɪl] *n. (person)* jemand, der nicht seinesgleichen hat; Ausnahmeerscheinung, *die; (thing)* Nonplusultra, *das*

non-'party *adj.* **a)** *(not attached to a party)* parteilos; **b)** *(not related to a party)* überparteilich; **c)** *(nonpartisan)* unparteiisch

non-'payment *n.* Nichtzahlung, *die*

non-'playing *adj.* nicht mitspielend; zuschauend; ~ **captain** Mannschaftsführer, *der*

nonplus [nɒn'plʌs] *v. t.,* **-ss-** verblüffen; **he was ~sed by sth.** etw. verblüffte ihn

non-'profit[-making] *adj.* nicht auf Gewinn ausgerichtet

non-prolife'ration *n., no pl.* Nichtverbreitung von Atomwaffen; Nonproliferation, *die (Politik)*; ~ **treaty** Atom[waffen]sperrvertrag, *der*

non-'resident 1. *adj. (residing elsewhere)* nicht im Haus wohnend; *(outside a country)* nicht ansässig; **a ~ landlord** ein Vermieter, der nicht im [selben] Haus wohnt. **2.** *n.* nicht im Haus Wohnende, *der/die; (outside a country)* Nichtansässige, *der/die;* **the bar is open to ~s** die Bar ist auch für Gäste geöffnet, die nicht im Hotel wohnen

non-re'turnable *adj.* Einweg⟨*behälter, -flasche, -[ver]packung*⟩; nicht rückzahlbar ⟨*Anzahlung*⟩

nonsense ['nɒnsəns] **1.** *n.* **a)** *no pl., no art. (meaningless words, ideas, or behaviour)* Unsinn, *der;* **make ~ of sth.** etw. ad absurdum führen; **piece of ~:** Firlefanz, *der (ugs. abwertend)*; **talk ~:** Unsinn reden; **it's all a lot of ~:** das ist alles Unsinn; **b)** *(instance)* Unsinn, *der;* **~s** Unsinn; **make a ~ of** verpfuschen *(ugs.)*; ⟨*Ereignis:*⟩ unsinnig *od.* widersinnig machen; ad absurdum führen ⟨*Idee, Ideal*⟩; **c)** *(sth. one disapproves of)* Unsinn, *der; (trifles)* Firlefanz, *der (ugs. abwertend)*; **what's all this ~ about ...?** was soll das [dumme] Gerede über (+ *Akk.*) ...?; **let's have no more ~, stop your ~:** Schluß mit dem Unsinn; **stand no ~:** keinen Unfug dulden; **no-~:** nüchtern; **come along now, and no ~:** kommt jetzt, und mach keinen Unsinn. **2.** *int.* Unsinn!

'nonsense verses *n. pl. (Lit.)* Nonsensdichtung, *die*

nonsensical [nɒn'sensɪkl] *adj.* unsinnig

nonsensically [nɒn'sensɪkəlɪ] *adv.* unsinnigerweise; ohne Sinn und Verstand ⟨*handeln*⟩

non sequitur [nɒn 'sekwɪtə(r)] *n.* unlogische Folgerung

non-'skid *adj.* rutschfest

non-'slip *adj.* rutschfest

non-'smoker *n.* **a)** *(person)* Nichtraucher, *der*/Nichtraucherin, *die;* **b)** *(train compartment)* Nichtraucherabteil, *das*

non-'starter *n.* **a)** *(Sport)* Nichtstartende, *der/die;* **b)** *(fig. coll.)* Reinfall, *der (ugs.)*; *(person)* Blindgänger, *der (fig. salopp)*

non-'stick *adj.* ~ **frying-pan** *etc.* Bratpfanne *usw.* mit Antihaftbeschichtung

non-stop 1. ['--] *adj.* durchgehend ⟨*Zug, Busverbindung*⟩; Nonstop⟨*flug, -revue*⟩. **2.** [-'-] *adv.* ohne Unterbrechung ⟨*tanzen, reden, reisen, senden*⟩; nonstop, im Nonstop ⟨*fliegen, tanzen, fahren*⟩

nonsuch ['nʌnsʌtʃ] *n.* **a)** Ausnahmeerscheinung, *die;* **b)** *(plant)* Hopfenklee, *der*

non-U [nɒn'ju:] *adj. (coll.)* nicht vornehm

non-'union *adj.* nichtorganisiert; *(made by ~ members)* von Nichtorganisierten hergestellt ⟨*Fabrikat*⟩

non-'violence *n., no pl.* Gewaltlosigkeit, *die*

non-'violent *adj.* gewaltlos

non-'white 1. *adj.* farbig. **2.** *n.* Farbige, *der/die*

¹noodle ['nu:dl] *n. (pasta)* Nudel, *die*

²noodle *n. (dated coll.: simpleton)* Dummkopf, *der (ugs.)*; **gape like a ~:** dumm gucken *(ugs.)*

nook [nʊk] *n.* Winkel, *der;* Ecke, *die;* **in every ~ and cranny** in allen Ecken und Winkeln

nooky ['nʊkɪ] *n. (sl.)* Aufhupfer, *der (ugs.)*

noon [nu:n] *n.* Mittag, *der;* zwölf Uhr [mittags]; **at/before ~:** um/vor zwölf [Uhr mittags]

'noonday *n.* Mittag, *der; attrib.* Mittags⟨*sonne, -hitze*⟩; **at ~:** mittags

'no one 1. *pron.* **a)** **~ of them** keiner/keine/keines von ihnen; **b)** *see* **nobody. 2.** *adj.* ~ **person could do that** einer allein könnte das nicht tun

'noon-tide *(dated/rhet.)*, **'noon-time** *(Amer.) ns.* Mittagszeit, *die;* **at ~tide** zur Mittagszeit

noose [nu:s] **1.** *n.* Schlinge, *die;* **put one's head in a ~** *(fig.)* den Kopf in die Schlinge stecken. **2.** *v. t.* [mit einer Schlinge] fangen

nope [nəʊp] *adv. (Amer. coll.)* nee *(ugs.)*

'no place *adv. (Amer.) see* **nowhere 1**

nor [nə(r), *stressed* nɔ:(r)] *conj.* noch; **neither ... ~ ..., not ... ~ ...:** weder ... noch ...; **he can't do it, ~ can I, ~ can you** er kann es nicht, ich auch nicht und du auch nicht; **~ will I deny that ...:** [und] ich will auch nicht bestreiten, daß ...

Nordic ['nɔ:dɪk] **1.** *adj.* nordisch. **2.** *n.* nordischer Typus; Nordide, *der/die (Ethnol.)*

norm [nɔ:m] *n.* Norm, *die;* **IQ above the ~:** überdurchschnittlicher IQ; **rise above the ~:** über den Normalwert steigen; **behavioural ~:** Verhaltensnorm *od.* -regel, *die*

normal ['nɔ:ml] **1.** *adj.* **a)** normal; **be back to ~ working hours** wieder normal arbeiten; **recover one's ~ self** sein seelisches Gleichgewicht wiederfinden; **b)** *(Geom.)* senkrecht **(to** auf + *Dat.,* zu). **2.** *n.* **a)** *(normal value)* Normalwert, *der;* **b)** *(usual state)* normaler Stand; **everything is back to** *or* **has returned to ~:** es hat sich wieder alles normalisiert; **his temperature is above ~:** er hat erhöhte Temperatur; **c)** *(Geom.)* Normale, *die*

normalcy ['nɔ:mlsɪ] *n., no pl. (normality)* Normalität, *die*

normalise *see* **normalize**

normality [nɔ:'mælɪtɪ] *n., no pl.* Normalität, *die;* **return to ~ after Christmas** nach Weihnachten wieder zum gewohnten Alltag zurückkehren

normalize ['nɔ:məlaɪz] **1.** *v. t.* normalisieren. **2.** *v. i.* sich normalisieren

normally ['nɔ:məlɪ] *adv.* **a)** *(in normal way)* normal; **b)** *(ordinarily)* normalerweise

Norman ['nɔ:mn] **1.** *n.* **a)** Normanne, *der*/Normannin, *die;* **b)** *(king)* normannischer König; **c)** *(Ling.)* Normannisch, *das;* **d)** *(Archit.)* normannischer Baustil. **2.** *adj.* normannisch; *see also* **conquest a**

Normandy ['nɔ:məndɪ] *pr. n.* Normandie, *die*

Norman: ~ 'French *n. (Ling.)* Normannisch, *das;* **~ style** *n. (Archit.)* normannischer Baustil

normative ['nɔ:mətɪv] *adj.* normativ *(geh.)*

Norse [nɔ:s] **1.** *n. (Ling.)* **a)** *(Scandinavian language group)* nordische Sprachen; **b)** **[Old] N~:** Altnordisch, *das.* **2.** *adj.* nordisch

Norseman ['nɔ:smən] *n., pl.* **Norsemen** ['nɔ:smən] *(Hist.)* Wikinger, *der*

north [nɔ:θ] **1.** *n.* **a)** Norden, *der;* **the ~:** Nord *(Met., Seew.)*; **in/to[wards]/from the ~:** im/nach *od. (geh.)* gen/von Norden; **to the ~ of** nördlich von; nördlich (+ *Gen.*); **magnetic ~:** magnetischer Nordpol; **b)** *usu.* **N~** *(part lying to the ~)* Norden, *der;* **from the N~:** aus dem Norden; **the N~** *(Brit.: of England)* Nordengland; der Norden; *(the Arctic)* die Arktis, der Nordpol; *(Amer.: the Northern states)* die Nordstaaten; der Norden; **c)** *(Cards)* Nord. **2.** *adj.* nördlich; Nord⟨*wind, -fenster, -küste, -grenze, -tor*⟩. **3.** *adv.* nordwärts; nach Norden; **~ of** nördlich von; nördlich (+ *Gen.*); **~ and south** nach Norden und Süden ⟨*verlaufen, sich erstrecken*⟩; *see also* **¹by 1 d**

north: N~ 'Africa *pr. n.* Nordafrika *(das)*; **N~ A'merica** *pr. n.* Nordamerika *(das)*; **N~ A'merican 1.** *adj.* nordamerikanisch; **2.** *n.* Nordamerikaner, *der*/-amerikanerin, *die;* **N~ At'lantic** *pr. n.* Nordatlantik, *der;* **N~ Atlantic Treaty Organization** Nordatlantikpakt, *der;* **~bound** *adj.* ⟨*Zug, Verkehr usw.*⟩ in Richtung Norden; **~ country** *n. (Brit.)* Nordengland *(das)*; Norden, *der;* **~-country** *adj. (Brit.)* nordenglisch; **~-'countryman** *n. (Brit.)* Nordengländer, *der;* **~-'east 1.** *n.* Nordosten, *der;* **in/to[wards]/from the ~-east** im/nach *od. (geh.)* gen/von Nordosten; **to the ~-east of** nordöstlich von; nordöstlich (+ *Gen.*); **2.** *adj.* nordöstlich; Nordost⟨*wind, -fenster, -küste*⟩; **~-east passage** Nordostpassage, *die;* **3.** *adv.* nordostwärts; nach Nordosten; **~-east of** nordöstlich von; nordöstlich (+ *Gen.*); *see also* **¹by 1 d; ~-'easter** Nordostwind, *der;* **~-'easterly 1.** *adj.* nordöstlich; **2.** *adv. (position)* im Nordosten; *(direction)* nach Nordosten; **~-'eastern** *adj.* nordöstlich

northerly ['nɔ:ðəlɪ] **1.** *adj.* **a)** *(in position or direction)* nördlich; **in a ~ direction** nach Norden; **b)** *(from the north)* ⟨*Wind*⟩ aus nördlichen Richtungen; **the wind was ~:** der Wind kam aus nördlichen Richtungen. **2.** *adv.* **a)** *(in position)* nördlich; *(in direction)* nordwärts; **b)** *(from the north)* aus *od.* von Nord[en]. **3.** *n.* Nord[wind], *der*

northern ['nɔ:ðən] *adj.* nördlich; Nord⟨*grenze, -hälfte, -seite, -fenster, -wind*⟩

northerner ['nɔ:ðənə(r)] *n. (male)* Nordengländer/-deutsche *usw., der; (female)* Nordengländerin/-deutsche *usw., die; (Amer.)* Nordstaatler, *der*/-staatlerin, *die;* **he's a ~:** er kommt aus dem Norden

northern: N~ 'Europe *pr. n.* Nordeuropa *(das)*; **N~ Euro'pean 1.** *adj.* nordeuropäisch; **2.** *n.* Nordeuropäer, *der*/Nordeuropäerin, *die;* **N~ 'Ireland** *pr. n.* Nordirland *(das)*; **~ 'lights** *n. pl.* Nordlicht, *das*

northernmost ['nɔ:ðənməʊst] *adj.* nördlichst...

north: N~ 'German 1. *adj.* norddeutsch; **2.** *n.* Norddeutsche, *der/die;* **N~ 'Germany** *pr. n.* Norddeutschland *(das);* **N~ Ko'rea** *pr. n.* Nordkorea *(das);* **N~ Ko'rean 1.** *adj.* nordkoreanisch; **2.** *n.* Nordkoreaner, *der*/-koreanerin, *die;* **'N~land** *n. (poet.)* Nordland, *das (selten);* **~ 'light** *n.* Licht von Norden; **N~man** ['nɔ:θmən] *n., pl.* **N~men** ['nɔ:θmən] *see* **Norseman; ~-~-'east 1.** *n.* Nordnordosten, *der;* **2.** *adj.* nordnordöstlich; **3.** *adv.* nordnordostwärts; **~-~-'west 1.** *n.* Nordnordwesten, *der;* **2.** *adj.* nordnordwestlich; **3.** *adv.* nordnordwestwärts; **N~ of 'England** *pr. n.* Nordengland *(das); attrib.* nordenglisch; **N~ 'Pole** *pr. n.* Nordpol, *der;* **N~ Rhine West'phalia** *pr. n.* Nordrhein-Westfalen *(das);* **~ 'Sea** *pr. n.* Nordsee, *die;* **N~ Sea gas/oil** Nordseegas/-öl, *das;* **N~ 'star** *n.* Nordstern, *der*

northward ['nɔ:θwəd] **1.** *adj.* nach Norden gerichtet; *(situated towards the north)* nördlich; **in a ~ direction** nach Norden; [in] Richtung Norden. **2.** *adv.* nordwärts; **they are ~ bound** sie fahren nach *od.* [in] Richtung Norden. **3.** *n.* Norden, *der*

northwards ['nɔ:θwədz] *see* **northward 2**

north: ~-'west 1. *n.* Nordwesten, *der;* **in/to[wards]/from the ~-west** im/nach *od. (geh.)* gen/von Nordwesten; **to the ~-west of** nordwestlich von; nordwestlich (+ *Gen.*); **2.** *adj.* nordwestlich; Nordwest- ⟨*wind, -fenster, -küste*⟩; **~-west passage** Nordwestpassage, *die;* **3.** *adv.* nordwestwärts; nach Nordwesten; **~-west of** nordwestlich von; nordwestlich (+ *Gen.*); *see also* **[1]by 1 d; ~-wester** [nɔ:θ'westə(r)] *n.* Nordwestwind, *der;* **~-'westerly 1.** *adj.* nordwestlich; **2.** *adv. (position)* im Nordwesten; *(direction)* nach Nordwesten; **~-'western** *adj.* nordwestlich

Norway ['nɔ:weɪ] *pr. n.* Norwegen *(das)*

Norwegian [nɔ:'wi:dʒn] **1.** *adj.* norwegisch *see also* **English 1. 2.** *n.* **a)** *(person)* Norweger, *der*/Norwegerin, *die;* **b)** *(language)* Norwegisch, *das; see also* **English 2 a**

Nos. *abbr.* **numbers** Nrn.

nose [nəʊz] **1.** *n.* **a)** Nase, *die;* **have one's ~ [stuck] in a book** *(coll.)* die Nase in ein Buch stecken *(ugs.);* **it's as plain as the ~ on your face** *(coll.)* das sieht doch ein Blinder [mit dem Krückstock] *(ugs.);* **[win] by a ~:** mit einer Nasenlänge [gewinnen]; **follow one's ~** *(fig.) (be guided by instinct)* seinem Instinkt folgen; *(go forward)* der Nase nachgehen; **then just follow your ~:** dann einfach immer der Nase nach *(ugs.);* **get up sb.'s ~** *(sl.: annoy sb.)* jmdm. auf den Wecker gehen *od.* fallen *(salopp);* **hold one's ~:** sich *(Dat.)* die Nase zuhalten; **keep one's ~ clean** *(fig. sl.)* eine saubere Weste behalten *(ugs.);* **keep your ~ clean!** bleib sauber! *(ugs.);* **on the ~** *(Amer. sl.: on time)* pünktlich auf die Minute; **hit it** *or* **be right on the ~** *(Amer. sl.)* den Nagel auf den Kopf treffen *(ugs.);* **parson's** *or* **pope's ~** *(Gastr.)* Bürzel, *der;* **pay through the ~:** tief in die Tasche greifen müssen *(ugs.);* **poke** *or* **thrust** *etc.* **one's ~ into sth.** *(fig.)* seine Nase in etw. *(Akk.)* stecken *(fig. ugs.);* **put sb.'s ~ out of joint** *(fig. coll.)* jmdn. vor den Kopf stoßen *(ugs.);* **rub sb.'s ~ in it** *(fig.)* es jmdm. ständig unter die Nase reiben *(ugs.);* **see no further than one's ~** *(fig.)* nicht weiter sehen, als seine Nase reicht *(ugs.);* **speak through one's ~:** näseln; durch die Nase sprechen; **turn up one's ~ at sth.** *(fig. coll.)* die Nase über etw. *(Akk.)* rümpfen; **under sb.'s ~** *(fig. coll.)* vor jmds. Augen *(Dat.);* **go** *or* **walk about with one's ~ in the air** die Nase hoch tragen; *see also* **[1]blow 2 g; grindstone; [2]lead 1 a; spite 2; thumb 2 c; b)** *(sense of smell)* Nase, *die;* **have a good ~ for sth.** eine gute Nase für etw. haben; **c)** *(of ship, aircraft)* Nase, *die; (of torpedo)* Schnauze, *die (ugs.);* **d)** *(of wine)* Blume, *die.* **2.** *v. t.* **a)** *(detect, smell out)* **~ [out]** aufspüren; **b) ~ one's way** sich *(Dat.)* vorsichtig seinen Weg bahnen. **3.** *v. i.* sich vorsichtig bewegen; **~ out of sth.** sich vorsichtig aus etw. hinausbewegen

~ about, ~ around *v. i. (coll.)* herumschnüffeln *(ugs.)*

nose: ~bag *n.* Futterbeutel, *der;* **~band** *n.* Nasenriemen, *der;* **~bleed** *n.* Nasenbluten, *das;* **~-cone** *n.* [Rumpf]spitze, *die;* **~dive 1.** *n.* **a)** Sturzflug, *der;* **b)** *(fig.)* Einbruch, *der;* **take a ~dive** einen Einbruch erleben; **2.** *v. i.* im Sturzflug hinuntergehen; ⟨*Schiff:*⟩ mit dem Bug wegtauchen; **~-flute** *n.* Nasenflöte, *die;* **~gay** *n.* [duftender] Blumenstrauß; **~ring** *n.* Nasenring, *der;* **~-wheel** *n. (Aeronaut.)* Bugrad, *das*

nosey *see* **nosy**

nosh [nɒʃ] *(esp. Brit. sl.)* **1.** *v. t. & i. (eat)* futtern *(ugs.); (between meals)* naschen. **2.** *n. (snack)* Imbiß, *der; (food)* Futter, *das (salopp)*

'no-show *n. seine Buchung nicht wahrnehmender Fahr-/Fluggast*

'nosh-up *n. (Brit. sl.)* Essen, *das; (good meal)* Festessen, *das;* **have a ~:** spachteln *(ugs.)*

no 'side *n. (Rugby)* Spielende, *das*

nostalgia [nɒ'stældʒə] *n.* Nostalgie, *die;* **~ for sth.** Sehnsucht nach etw.

nostalgic [nɒ'stældʒɪk] *adj.* nostalgisch

nostril ['nɒstrɪl] *n.* Nasenloch, *das; (of horse)* Nüster, *die*

nostrum ['nɒstrəm] *n.* **a)** *(medicine)* Mittelchen, *das;* **his pet ~ is** er schwört auf (+ *Akk.*); **b)** *(pet scheme)* Patentrezept, *das*

nosy ['nəʊzɪ] *adj. (sl. derog.)* neugierig

Nosy 'Parker *n.* Schnüffler, *der*/Schnüfflerin, *die (ugs. abwertend)*

not [nɒt] *adv.* **a)** nicht; **he is ~ a doctor** er ist kein Arzt; **isn't she pretty?** ist sie nicht hübsch?; **I do ~ feel like doing it** ich habe keine Lust, es zu tun; **b)** *in ellipt. phrs.* nicht; **I hope ~:** hoffentlich nicht; **~ so** keineswegs; **~ at all** überhaupt nicht; *(in polite reply to thanks)* keine Ursache; gern geschehen; **~ that [I know of]** nicht, daß [ich wüßte]; **c)** *in emphat. phrs.* **~ ... but ...:** nicht ..., sondern ...; **it was ~ a small town but a big one** es war keine kleine Stadt, sondern eine große; **lazy he is ~:** faul ist er keineswegs; **~ I/they** *etc.* ich/sie *usw.* [bestimmt] nicht; **~ a moment/grey hair** nicht ein *od.* kein einziger Augenblick/einziges graues Haar; **~ a thing** gar nichts; **come ~ a day too soon** keinen Tag zu früh kommen; **~ a few/everybody** nicht wenige/jeder; **~ a small sacrifice** kein kleines Opfer; **~ once or** *or* **nor twice, but ...:** nicht nur ein- oder zweimal, sondern ...; **feel ~ so** *or* **too well** sich nicht besonders gut fühlen

notability [nəʊtə'bɪlɪtɪ] *n.* **a)** *no pl. (being notable)* Ansehen, *das;* **a painter of [some] ~:** ein [ziemlich] angesehener Maler; **b)** *(person) see* **notable 2**

notable ['nəʊtəbl] **1.** *adj.* bemerkenswert; bedeutend, angesehen ⟨*Person*⟩; **be ~ for sth.** für etw. bekannt sein. **2.** *n.* bekannte Persönlichkeit; Notabilität, *die (geh.)*

notably ['nəʊtəblɪ] *adv.* besonders

notarial [nəʊ'teərɪəl] *adj. (Law)* **a)** *(of a notary)* Notariats-; **b)** *(prepared by a notary)* notariell ⟨*Urkunde*⟩

notary ['nəʊtərɪ] *n.* **~ ['public]** Notar, *der*/Notarin, *die*

notation [nəʊ'teɪʃn] *n.* **a)** *(Math., Mus., Chem.)* Notation, *die (fachspr.);* Notierung, *die;* **b)** *(Amer.: annotation)* Anmerkung, *die. See also* **[3]scale 1 f**

notch [nɒtʃ] **1.** *n.* Kerbe, *die; (in damaged blade)* Scharte, *die; (in belt)* Loch, *das;* **be a ~ above the others** *(fig.)* eine Klasse besser als die anderen sein; **tighten one's belt another ~** *(lit. or fig.)* seinen Gürtel ein Loch enger schnallen. **2.** *v. t.* **a)** *(make ~es in)* kerben; **b)** *(score by ~es)* mit Kerben notieren; *(fig.: score, achieve)* erreichen; erzielen ⟨*Tor, Eckstoß*⟩; erringen ⟨*Sieg*⟩

~ 'up *v. t.* erreichen; aufstellen ⟨*Rekord*⟩; erringen ⟨*Sieg*⟩

notched [nɒtʃt] *adj.* kerbig; gekerbt ⟨*Blattrand*⟩

note [nəʊt] **1.** *n.* **a)** *(Mus.) (sign)* Note, *die; (key of piano)* Taste, *die; (single sound)* Ton, *der; (bird's song)* Gesang, *der;* **strike a false ~:** unangebracht sein; **strike the right ~** ⟨*Sprecher, Redner, Brief:*⟩ den richtigen Ton treffen; **hit the wrong ~:** einen falschen Ton anschlagen; **b)** *(tone of expression)* [Unter]ton, *der;* **~ of discord** Mißklang, *der;* **~ of caution/anger** warnender/ärgerlicher [Unter]ton; **sound a ~ of caution** eine Warnung aussprechen; **on a ~ of optimism, on an optimistic ~:** in optimistischem Ton; **his voice had a peevish ~:** seine Stimme klang gereizt; **a festive ~, a ~ of festivity** eine festliche Note; **c)** *(jotting)* Notiz, *die;* **take** *or* **make ~s** sich *(Dat.)* Notizen machen; **take** *or* **make a ~ of sth.** sich *(Dat.)* etw. notieren; **speak without ~s** frei sprechen; **d)** *(annotation, footnote)* Anmerkung, *die;* **author's ~:** Anmerkung des Verfassers; **e)** *(short letter)* [kurzer] Brief; **write a ~:** ein paar Zeilen schreiben; **f)** *(Diplom.)* Note, *die;* **g)** *(Finance)* **~ [of hand]** Schuldschein, *der;* **£10 ~:** Zehn-Pfund-Schein, *der;* **h)** *no pl., no art. (importance)* Bedeutung, *die;* **person/sth. of ~:** bedeutende Persönlichkeit/etw. Bedeutendes; **nothing of ~:** nichts von Bedeutung; **be of ~:** bedeutend sein; **i)** *no pl., no art. (attention)* Beachtung, *die;* **worthy of ~:** beachtenswert; **take ~ of sth.** *(heed)* einer Sache *(Dat.)* Beachtung schenken; *(notice)* etw. zur Kenntnis nehmen. **2.** *v. t.* **a)** *(register)* beobachten; **b)** *(pay attention to)* beachten; **c)** *(notice)* bemerken; **d)** *(set down)* **~ [down]** [sich *(Dat.)*] notieren

note: ~book *n.* Notizbuch, *das; (for lecture notes)* Kollegheft, *das;* **~case** *n.* Brieftasche, *die*

noted ['nəʊtɪd] *adj.* **a)** *(famous)* bekannt, berühmt **(for** für, wegen); **b)** *(significant)* beachtlich

notelet ['nəʊtlɪt] *n.* Grußkarte, *die*

note: ~pad *n.* Notizblock, *der;* **~paper** *n.* Briefpapier, *das;* **~-row** *n. (Mus.)* Tonreihe, *die;* **~worthy** *adj.* bemerkenswert

nothing ['nʌθɪŋ] **1.** *n.* **a)** nichts; **~ interesting** nichts Interessantes; **~ much** nichts Besonderes; **~ more than** nur; **~ more, ~ less** nicht mehr, nicht weniger; **I should like ~ more than sth./to do sth.** ich würde etw. nur zu gern haben/tun; **next to ~:** so gut wie nichts; **~ less than the best treatment** die bestmögliche Behandlung; **~ less than a miracle is needed to save ...:** nur ein Wunder kann ... retten; **it's ~ less than suicidal to do this** es ist reiner *od.* glatter Selbstmord, dies zu tun; **there's ~ so good as ...:** es gibt nichts Besseres als ...; **be ~ [when] compared to sth.** nichts sein im Vergleich zu etw.; **~ else than, ~ [else] but** nur; **do ~ [else] but grumble** nur murren; **there was ~ [else] for it but to do sth.** es blieb nichts anderes übrig, als etw. zu tun; **he is ~ if not active** wenn er eins ist, dann [ist er] aktiv; **be ~ if not conscientious/brutal** überaus gewissenhaft/brutal sein; **there is ~ in it** *(in race etc.)* es ist noch nichts entschieden; *(it is untrue)* es ist nichts daran wahr; **there's ~ 'of him** *(he is very thin)* an ihm ist nichts dran; **there is ~ 'to it** es ist kinderleicht *(fam.);* **he/she is ~ to me** er/sie interessiert mich nicht; **your problems are ~ compared to his** deine Probleme sind nichts im Vergleich zu seinen; **~ ventured ~ gained, ~ venture ~ win** *(prov.)* wer nicht wagt, der nicht gewinnt *(Spr.);* **£300 is ~ to him** 300 Pfund sind ein Klacks für ihn *(ugs.);* **have [got]** *or* **be ~ to do with sb./sth.**

(not concern) nichts zu tun haben mit jmdm./etw.; **have ~ to do with sb./sth.** *(avoid)* jmdm./einer Sache aus dem Weg gehen; **[not] for ~**: [nicht] umsonst; **count** *or* **go for ~** *(be unappreciated)* ⟨*Person:*⟩ nicht zählen; *(be profitless)* ⟨*Arbeit, Bemühung:*⟩ umsonst *od.* vergebens sein; **have [got] ~ on sb./sth.** *(be not better than; iron.: be inferior to)* nicht mit jmdm./etw. zu vergleichen sein; nichts sein im Vergleich zu jmdm./etw.; **have [got] ~ on sb.** *(know nothing bad about)* nichts gegen jmdn. in der Hand haben; **have ~ on** *(be naked)* nichts anhaben; *(have no engagements)* nichts vorhaben; **make ~ of sth.** *(make light of)* keine große Sache aus etw. machen; *(not understand)* nichts anfangen mit etw. [können]; **it means ~ to me** *(is not understood)* ich werde nicht klug daraus; *(is not loved)* es bedeutet mir nichts; **no ~** *(coll.)* kein gar nichts *(ugs.)*; **to say ~ of** ganz zu schweigen von; **b)** *(zero)* **multiply by ~**: mit null multiplizieren; **register ~** ⟨*Thermometer:*⟩ null Grad anzeigen; **c)** *(trifling event)* Nichtigkeit, *die; (trifling person)* Nichts, *das;* Niemand, *der;* **soft** *or* **sweet ~s** Zärtlichkeiten *Pl. See also* [1]**do 1 b, 2 j;** [1]**like 1 a; short 1 d; stop 1 c, 2 b; think of g. 2.** *adv.* keineswegs; **~ near so bad as ...**: nicht annähernd so schlecht wie ... **3.** *adj. (coll.: unimportant)* langweilig

nothingness ['nʌθɪŋnɪs] *n., no pl.* Nichts, *das*

notice ['nəʊtɪs] **1.** *n.* **a)** Anschlag, *der;* Aushang, *der; (in newspaper)* Anzeige, *die;* **no-smoking ~**: Rauchverbotsschild, *das;* **b)** *(warning)* **~ of a forthcoming strike** Meldungen über einen bevorstehenden Streik; **give [sb.] [three days'] ~ of one's arrival** [jmdm.] seine Ankunft [drei Tage vorher] mitteilen; **have [no] ~ [of sth.]** [von etw.] [keine] Kenntnis haben; **at short/a moment's/ten minutes' ~**: kurzfristig/von einem Augenblick zum andern/innerhalb von zehn Minuten; **c)** *(formal notification)* Ankündigung, *die;* **give ~ of appeal** Berufung einlegen; **until further ~**: bis auf weiteres; **~ is given of sth.** etw. wird angekündigt; *see also* **quit 2 b; d)** *(ending an agreement)* Kündigung, *die;* **give sb. a week's/month's ~**: jmdm. mit einer Frist von einer Woche/einem Monat kündigen; **hand in one's ~** *or* **give ~** *(Brit.),* **give one's ~** *(Amer.)* kündigen; **e)** *(attention)* Beachtung, *die;* **attract ~**: Beachtung finden; **bring sb./sth. to sb.'s ~**: jmdn. auf jmdn./etw. aufmerksam machen; **worthy of ~**: beachtenswert; **it has come to my ~ that ...**: ich habe bemerkt *od.* mir ist aufgefallen, daß ...; **not take much ~ of sb./sth.** jmdm./einer Sache keine große Beachtung schenken; **take no ~ of sb./sth.** *(not observe)* jmdn./etw. nicht bemerken; *(disregard)* keine Notiz von jmdm./etw. nehmen; **take no ~**: sich nicht darum kümmern; **take ~ of** wahrnehmen; hören auf ⟨*Rat*⟩; zur Kenntnis nehmen ⟨*Leistung*⟩; **f)** *(review)* Besprechung, *die;* Rezension, *die.* **2.** *v. t.* **a)** *(perceive, take notice of)* bemerken; **~ the details [on this painting]** beachten Sie die Einzelheiten [auf diesem Gemälde]; **he likes to get himself ~d** er drängt sich gern in den Vordergrund; **but not so you'd ~** *(coll.)* aber es fällt/fiel nicht auf; **b)** *(remark upon)* erwähnen; **c)** *(acknowledge)* Notiz nehmen von

noticeable ['nəʊtɪsəbl] *adj.* **a)** *(perceptible)* wahrnehmbar ⟨*Fleck, Schaden, Geruch*⟩; merklich ⟨*Verbesserung*⟩; spürbar ⟨*Mangel*⟩; **b)** *(worthy of notice)* bemerkenswert

noticeably ['nəʊtɪsəblɪ] *adv.* sichtlich ⟨*größer, kleiner*⟩; merklich ⟨*verändern*⟩; spürbar ⟨*kälter*⟩

'notice-board *n. (Brit.)* Anschlagtafel, *die*

notifiable ['nəʊtɪfaɪəbl] *adj.* meldepflichtig ⟨*Krankheit*⟩

notification [nəʊtɪfɪ'keɪʃn] *n.* Mitteilung, *die* **(of sb.** an jmdn.; **of sth.** über etw. *[Akk.]*); *(of disease)* Meldung, *die* **(of** über + *Akk.*)

notify ['nəʊtɪfaɪ] *v. t.* **a)** *(make known)* ankündigen; **b)** *(inform)* benachrichtigen **(of** über + *Akk.*)

notion ['nəʊʃn] *n.* **a)** Vorstellung, *die;* **not have the faintest/least ~ of how/what** *etc.* nicht die blasseste/geringste Ahnung haben, wie/was *usw.;* **he has no ~ of time** er hat kein Verhältnis zur Zeit; **b)** *(intention)* **have no ~ of doing sth.** nicht beabsichtigen *od.* vorhaben, etw. zu tun; **c)** *(knack, inkling)* **have no ~ of sth.** keine Ahnung von etw. haben; **d)** *in pl. (Amer.: haberdashery)* Kurzwaren *Pl.*

notional ['nəʊʃənl] *adj.* **a)** *(imaginary)* imaginär; **b)** *(theoretical)* theoretisch ⟨*Ansatz, Wissen, Gewinn*⟩; *(token)* symbolisch; *(hypothetical)* angenommen; **c)** *(vague, abstract)* abstrakt

notionally ['nəʊʃənəlɪ] *adv.* theoretisch

notoriety [nəʊtə'raɪətɪ] *n., no pl.* traurige Berühmtheit

notorious [nə'tɔ:rɪəs] *adj.* bekannt; *(infamous)* berüchtigt; notorisch ⟨*Lügner*⟩; niederträchtig ⟨*List*⟩; **be** *or* **have become ~ for sth.** wegen *od.* für etw. bekannt/berüchtigt sein

notoriously [nə'tɔ:rɪəslɪ] *adv.* notorisch

no 'trump *n. (Bridge)* Sans atout, *das*

notwithstanding [nɒtwɪθ'stændɪŋ, nɒtwɪð'stændɪŋ] **1.** *prep.* ungeachtet. **2.** *adv.* dennoch; dessenungeachtet. **3.** *conj.* **~ that ...**: ungeachtet dessen, daß ...

nougat ['nu:gɑ:] *n.* Nougat, *das od. der*

nought [nɔ:t] *n.* **a)** *(zero)* Null, *die;* **~s and crosses** *(Brit.) Spiel, bei dem innerhalb eines Feldes von Kästchen Dreierreihen von Kreisen bzw. Kreuzen zu erzielen sind;* **b)** *(poet./arch.: nothing) see* **naught**

noun [naʊn] *n. (Ling.)* Substantiv, *das;* Hauptwort, *das;* Nomen, *das (fachspr.)*

nourish ['nʌrɪʃ] *v. t.* **a)** ernähren **(on** mit); *(fig.)* nähren *(geh.);* **b)** *(in one's heart)* hegen, nähren *(geh.)* ⟨*Gefühl, Hoffnung*⟩

nourishing ['nʌrɪʃɪŋ] *adj.* nahrhaft

nourishment ['nʌrɪʃmənt] *n.* *(food)* Nahrung, *die; (fig.)* Förderung, *die*

nous [naʊs] *n. (coll.)* Grips, *der (ugs.);* **use a bit of ~**: seinen Grips ein bißchen anstrengen

nouveau riche [nu:vəʊ 'ri:ʃ] **1.** *n., pl.* **nouveaux riches** [nu:vəʊ 'ri:ʃ] Neureiche, *der/die.* **2.** *adj.* neureich

Nov. *abbr.* **November** Nov.

nova ['nəʊvə] *n., pl.* **~e** ['nəʊvi:] *or* **~s** *(Astron.)* Nova, *die*

Nova Scotia [nəʊvə 'skəʊʃə] *pr. n.* Neuschottland *(das)*

novel ['nɒvl] **1.** *n.* Roman, *der.* **2.** *adj.* neuartig

novelette [nɒvə'let] *n.* Novelette, *die (Literaturw.); (Brit. derog.)* Groschenroman, *der*

novelist ['nɒvəlɪst] *n.* Romanautor, *der/*-autorin, *die*

novella [nə'velə] *n.* Novelle, *die*

novelty ['nɒvltɪ] *n.* **a) be a/no ~**: etwas/nichts Neues sein; **b)** *(newness)* Neuheit, *die;* Neuartigkeit, *die;* **the ~ will wear off** der Reiz des Neuen wird nachlassen; **have a certain ~ value** den Reiz des Neuen haben; **c)** *(gadget)* Überraschung, *die;* **jokes and novelties** Scherzartikel

November [nə'vembə(r)] *n.* November, *der; see also* **August**

novice ['nɒvɪs] *n.* **a)** *(Relig.)* Novize, *der/*Novizin, *die;* **b)** *(new convert)* Neubekehrte, *der/die;* **c)** *(beginner)* Anfänger, *der/*Anfängerin, *die*

noviciate, novitiate [nə'vɪʃɪət] *n.* **a)** *(Relig.: period, quarters)* Noviziat, *das; (fig.: period or state of initiation)* Lehrzeit, *die;* Lehre, *die;* **b)** *see* **novice a, c**

now [naʊ] **1.** *adv.* **a)** jetzt; *(nowadays)* heutzutage; *(immediately)* [jetzt] sofort; *(this time)* jetzt [schon wieder]; **it's ten years ago ~ that** *or* **since he died** es ist schon zehn Jahre her, seit er gestorben ist; **just ~** *(very recently)* gerade eben; *(at this particular time)* gerade jetzt; **I can't see you just ~**: ich habe im Augenblick leider keine Zeit für Sie; **~ for a cup of tea** jetzt eine Tasse Tee; **[every] ~ and then** *or* **again** hin und wieder; **~ sunshine, ~ showers** bald Sonne, bald Regen; **[it's] ~ or never!** jetzt oder nie!; **b)** *(not referring to time)* **well ~**: also; **come ~**: na, komm *(ugs.);* **~, ~**: na, na; **~, what happened is this ...**: also, passiert ist folgendes: ...; **~ just listen to me** jetzt hör mir mal gut zu; **~ then** na *(ugs.);* **quickly ~!** nun aber schnell; **goodbye ~**: also dann, auf Wiedersehen; **He thinks he can stay here for nothing. – Does he, ~!** Er glaubt, er könnte hier umsonst bleiben. – Da hat er sich aber geirrt! **2.** *conj.* **~ [that] ...**: jetzt, wo *od.* da ... **3.** *n.* **the here and ~**: das Hier und Jetzt; **~ is the time to do sth.** es ist jetzt an der Zeit, etw. zu tun; **before ~**: früher; **up to** *or* **until ~**: bis jetzt; **never before ~**: noch nie; **by ~**: inzwischen; **a week from ~**: [heute] in einer Woche; **you've got from ~ till Friday to do it** du hast bis Freitag Zeit, es zu tun; **between ~ and Friday** bis Freitag; **from ~ on** von jetzt an; **as of ~**: jetzt; **that's all for ~**: das ist im Augenblick alles; **put it aside for ~**: leg es einstweilen zur Seite; **bye** *etc.* **for ~!** *(coll.)* bis bald!

nowadays ['naʊədeɪz] *adv.* heutzutage

nowhere ['nəʊweə(r)] **1.** *adv.* **a)** *(in no place)* nirgends; nirgendwo; **b)** *(to no place)* nirgendwohin; **c) ~ near** *(not even nearly)* nicht annähernd; **be ~ near prepared** völlig unzureichend vorbereitet sein. **2.** *pron.* **as if from ~**: wie aus dem Nichts; **live in the middle of ~** *(coll.)* am Ende der Welt *od.* *(ugs.)* j.w.d. wohnen; **the train stopped in the middle of ~**: der Zug hielt mitten in der Wildnis *(ugs.);* **start from ~**: bei Null anfangen; **come from ~**: wie aus dem Nichts auftauchen; **come [in]/be ~** *(in race etc.)* unter „ferner liefen" rangieren *(ugs.);* **get ~** *(make no progress)* nicht vorankommen; *(have no success)* nichts erreichen; **get sb. ~**: [jmdm.] nichts nützen

no-'win *attrib. adj.* Verlierer-

nowt [naʊt] *n. (Brit. dial. or coll.)* nix *(ugs.)*

noxious ['nɒkʃəs] *adj.* giftig

nozzle ['nɒzl] *n.* Düse, *die; (of gun)* Mündung, *die; (of petrol-pump)* Zapfhahn, *der*

nr. *abbr.* **near**

NSPCC *abbr. (Brit.)* **National Society for the Prevention of Cruelty to Children** ≈ Kinderschutzbund, *der*

NT *abbr.* **New Testament** N.T.

nth [enθ] *see* **N, n b**

nuance ['nju:ɑ̃s] **1.** *n.* Nuance, *die; (Mus.)* Nuancierung, *die;* **~s of meaning** Bedeutungsnuancen; **~ of colour** Farbnuance, *die;* Farbschattierung, *die.* **2.** *v. t.* nuancieren *(geh.)*

nub [nʌb] *n.* **a)** *(small lump)* Stückchen, *das; (stub)* Stummel, *der;* **b)** *(fig.)* Kernpunkt, *der*

nubile ['nju:baɪl] *adj.* **a)** *(marriageable)* heiratsfähig; **b)** *(sexy)* sexy *(ugs.);* anziehend

nuclear ['nju:klɪə(r)] *adj.* **a)** Kern-; **b)** *(using ~ energy or weapons)* Atom-; Kern⟨*explosion, -technik*⟩; atomar ⟨*Antrieb, Gefechtskopf, Bedrohung, Gegenschlag, Wettrüsten*⟩; nuklear ⟨*Abschreckungspotential, Sprengkörper, Streitkräfte*⟩; atomgetrieben ⟨*Unterseeboot, Schiff*⟩

nuclear: ~ 'bomb *n.* Atombombe, *die;* **~ de'terrent** *n.* atomare *od.* nukleare Abschreckung; **~ dis'armament** *n.* atomare *od.* nukleare Abrüstung; **~ 'energy** *n., no pl.* Atom- *od.* Kernenergie, *die;* **~ 'family** *n. (Sociol.)* Kernfamilie, *die;* **~ 'fission** *n.*

Kernspaltung, *die;* ~**-free** *adj.* atomwaffenfrei ⟨*Zone*⟩; ~ '**fuel** *n.* Kernbrennstoff, *der;* ~ '**fusion** *n.* Kernfusion, *die;* ~ '**physics** *n.* Kernphysik, *die;* ~ '**power** *n.* **a)** Atom- *od.* Kernkraft, *die;* **b)** *(country)* Atom- *od.* Nuklearmacht, *die;* ~**-'powered** *adj.* atomgetrieben; ~ '**power station** *n.* Atom- *od.* Kernkraftwerk, *das;* ~ **re'actor** *see* **reactor a;** ~ '**warfare** *n., no pl.* Atomkrieg, *der;* ~ '**waste** *n.* Atommüll, *der;* ~ '**winter** *n.* nuklearer Winter

nuclei *pl. of* **nucleus**

nucleic acid [nju:kli:ɪk 'æsɪd] *n. (Biochem.)* Nukleinsäure, *die*

nucleus ['nju:klɪəs] *n., pl.* **nuclei** ['nju:klɪaɪ] Kern, *der; (of collection)* Grundstock, *der*

nude [nju:d] **1.** *adj.* nackt; ~ **figure/revue** Akt, *der*/Nacktrevue, *die.* **2.** *n.* **a)** *(Art) (figure)* Akt, *der; (painting)* Aktgemälde, *das;* **b) in the ~:** nackt; **c)** *(person)* Nackte, *der/die*

nudge [nʌdʒ] **1.** *v. t.* **a)** *(push gently)* anstoßen; ~ **aside** zur Seite schieben; ~ **sth.** *(fig.)* einer Sache *(Dat.)* einen Schubs geben *(ugs.);* **b)** *(touch)* stoßen an (+ *Akk.*) ⟨*Mauer*⟩. **2.** *n.* Stoß, *der;* Puff, *der;* **give sb. a ~:** jmdn. anstoßen

nudism ['nju:dɪzm] *n.* Nudismus, *der;* Freikörperkultur, *die*

nudist ['nju:dɪst] *n.* Nudist, *der*/Nudistin, *die;* FKK-Anhänger, *der*/-Anhängerin, *die; attrib.* Nudisten-

nudity ['nju:dɪtɪ] *n.* Nacktheit, *die*

nugatory ['nju:gətərɪ] *adj. (literary)* belanglos

nugget ['nʌgɪt] *n.* **a)** *(Mining)* Klumpen, *der; (of gold)* Goldklumpen, *der;* Nugget, *das;* **b)** *(fig.)* ~**s of wisdom** goldene Weisheiten; ~**s of information** wertvolle Informationen

nuisance ['nju:səns] *n.* **a)** Ärgernis, *das;* Plage, *die;* **what a ~!** so etwas Dummes!; **be a bit of a ~:** eine ziemliche Plage sein; **make a ~ of oneself** lästig werden; **b)** *(Law)* Belästigung, *die*

nuke [nju:k] *(Amer. sl.)* **1.** *n. (bomb)* Atombombe, *die.* **2.** *v. t.* Atombomben/eine Atombombe werfen auf (+ *Akk.*)

null [nʌl] *adj. (Law)* **declare sth. ~ [and void]** etw. für null und nichtig erklären

nullify ['nʌlɪfaɪ] *v. t.* **a)** *(cancel)* für null und nichtig *od.* rechtsungültig erklären ⟨*Vertrag, Testament*⟩; **b)** *(neutralize)* zunichte machen; entkräften ⟨*Beweis*⟩

nullity ['nʌlɪtɪ] *n. (Law)* Ungültigkeit, *die*

numb [nʌm] **1.** *adj. (without sensation)* gefühllos, taub (**with** vor + *Dat.*); *(fig.) (without emotion)* benommen; *(unable to move)* starr; gelähmt; **go ~ with horror** vor Entsetzen *(Dat.)* erstarren. **2.** *v. t.* **a)** ⟨*Kälte, Schock:*⟩ gefühllos machen; ⟨*Narkosemittel:*⟩ betäuben; **b)** *(fig.)* **her emotions were ~ed** sie war betäubt *od.* benommen; **be ~ed by horror/with fear** vor Entsetzen/Angst *(Dat.)* erstarren

number ['nʌmbə(r)] **1.** *n.* **a)** *(in series)* Nummer, *die;* ~ **3 West Street** West Street [Nr.] 3; **my ~ came up** *(fig.)* ich war dran *(ugs.) od.* an der Reihe; **the ~ of sb.'s car** jmds. Autonummer; **you've got the wrong ~** *(Teleph.)* Sie sind falsch verbunden; **dial a wrong ~:** sich verwählen *(ugs.);* **what page ~ is it?** welche Seite ist es?; ~ **one** *(oneself)* man selbst; *attrib.* Nummer eins *nachgestellt;* erstklassig ⟨*Darstellung*⟩; Spitzen⟨*position, -platz*⟩; **take care of** *or* **look after ~ one** an sich *(Akk.)* selbst denken; **be sb.'s ~ one priority** bei jmdm. an erster Stelle stehen; ~ **two** *(in organisation)* zweiter Mann; *(of sb. else)* rechte Hand; **N~ Ten [Downing Street]** *(Brit.) Amtssitz des britischen Premierministers/der britischen Premierministerin;* **paint by ~s** nach einer Vorlage [mit numerierten Farbfeldern] malen; **have [got] sb.'s ~** *(fig. sl.)* jmdn. durchschaut haben; **sb.'s ~ is up** *(coll.)* jmds. Stunde hat geschlagen; **b)** *(esp. Math.: numeral)* Zahl, *die;* **memory for ~s** Zahlengedächtnis, *das;* **c)** *(sum, total, quantity)* [An]zahl, *die;* **a ~ of people/things** einige Leute/Dinge; **a ~ of times/on a ~ of occasions** mehrfach *od.* -mals; **a small ~:** eine geringe [An]zahl; **large ~s** eine große [An]zahl; **in [large** *or* **great] ~s** in großer Zahl; **in a small ~ of cases** in einigen wenigen Fällen; **a and b in equal ~s** a und b in gleicher Anzahl; **a fair ~:** eine ganze Anzahl *od.* Reihe; **any ~:** beliebig viele; **on any ~ of occasions** oft[mals]; **without** *or* **beyond ~:** ohne Zahl *(geh.);* **times without ~:** unzählige Male; **in ~[s]** zahlenmäßig ⟨*überlegen sein, überwiegen*⟩; **ten in ~:** zehn an der Zahl; **be few in ~:** gering an Zahl sein; **d)** *(person, song, turn, edition)* Nummer, *die;* **final/May ~:** Schluß-/Mainummer, *die;* **e)** *(coll.) (outfit)* Kluft, *die; (girl)* Mieze, *die (salopp); (job)* Job, *der (ugs.);* **it's not a bad little ~** *(job)* da kann man eine ruhige Kugel schieben *(ugs.);* **f)** *(Bibl.)* **[the Book of] N~s** das vierte Buch Mose; **g)** *(company)* [Personen]kreis, *der;* Gruppe, *die;* **he was [one] of our ~:** er war einer von uns; **h)** *in pl. (arithmetic)* Rechnen, *das;* **i)** *(Ling.)* Numerus, *der (fachspr.). See also* **eight 2 a; opposite number; round number. 2.** *v. t.* **a)** *(assign ~ to)* beziffern; numerieren; **b)** *(amount to, comprise)* zählen; **the nominations ~ed ten in all** es wurden insgesamt zehn Kandidaten nominiert; **a town ~ing x inhabitants** eine Stadt mit x Einwohnern; **c)** *(include, regard as)* zählen, rechnen (**among, with** zu); **d) be ~ed** *(be limited)* begrenzt sein; **sb.'s days** *or* **years are ~ed** jmds. Tage sind gezählt; **e)** *(count)* zählen

~ '**off** *v. i.* abzählen

numbering ['nʌmbərɪŋ] *n.* Numerierung, *die*

numberless ['nʌmbəlɪs] *adj.* unzählig; zahllos

'**number-plate** *n.* Nummernschild, *das*

numbly ['nʌmlɪ] *adv.* wie betäubt

numbness ['nʌmnɪs] *n., no pl. (caused by cold)* Gefühllosigkeit, *die;* Taubheit, *die; (caused by anaesthetic, sleeping-pill)* Betäubung, *die; (fig.: stupor)* Benommenheit, *die*

numbskull *see* **numskull**

numeracy ['nju:mərəsɪ] *n.* rechnerische Fähigkeiten

numeral ['nju:mərl] *n.* Ziffer, *die; (word)* Zahlwort, *das;* **cardinal ~:** Kardinal- *od.* Grundzahl, *die*

numerate ['nju:mərət] *adj.* rechenkundig; **be ~:** rechnen können

numerator ['nju:məreɪtə(r)] *n. (Math.)* Zähler, *der*

numerical [nju:'merɪkl] *adj.* Zahlen⟨*wert, -folge*⟩; numerisch ⟨*Reihenfolge, Stärke, Überlegenheit*⟩; zahlenmäßig ⟨*Überlegenheit*⟩; rechnerisch ⟨*Fähigkeiten*⟩

numerically [nju:'merɪkəlɪ] *adv.* numerisch; ~ **speaking, ...:** numerisch *od.* zahlenmäßig ...

numerous ['nju:mərəs] *adj.* zahlreich

numismatics [nju:mɪz'mætɪks] *n., no pl.* Numismatik, *die;* Münzkunde, *die*

numismatist [nju:'mɪzmətɪst] *n.* Numismatiker, *der*/Numismatikerin, *die*

numskull ['nʌmskʌl] *n.* Hohlkopf, *der (abwertend)*

nun [nʌn] *n.* Nonne, *die*

nuncio ['nʌnʃɪəʊ] *n., pl.* ~**s** *(RC Ch.)* Nuntius, *der*

nunnery ['nʌnərɪ] *n.* [Nonnen]kloster, *das*

nuptial ['nʌpʃl] **1.** *adj.* ehelich; ~ **vow/feast/day** Eheversprechen, *das*/Hochzeitsfest, *das*/Hochzeitstag, *der.* **2.** *n. in pl. (literary/ joc.)* Hochzeit, *die*

nurd *see* **nerd**

nurse [nɜ:s] **1.** *n.* Krankenschwester, *die;* **thank you, ~:** danke, Schwester; **hospital ~:** Krankenhausschwester, *die;* **[male] ~:** Krankenpfleger, *der;* ~**s' home/uniform** Schwesternwohnheim, *das*/-tracht, *die.* **2.** *v. t.* **a)** *(act as ~ to)* pflegen ⟨*Kranke*⟩; **take up nursing the handicapped/sick** in der Behinderten-/Krankenpflege tätig werden; ~ **sb. through an illness** jmdn. während seiner Krankheit pflegen; ~ **sb. back to health** jmdn. gesundpflegen; **b)** *(act as ~maid to)* betreuen ⟨*Kind*⟩; *(fig.: foster, tend)* hegen *(geh.)* ⟨*Projekt*⟩; fördern ⟨*Begabung*⟩; **c)** *(try to cure)* versorgen; auskurieren ⟨*Erkältung*⟩; **d)** *(suckle)* die Brust geben (+ *Dat.*), stillen ⟨*Säugling*⟩; **e)** *(manage carefully)* hegen, pflegen ⟨*Pflanze*⟩; **f)** *(cradle)* vorsichtig halten; wiegen ⟨*Baby*⟩; **g)** *(keep burning)* hüten ⟨*Feuer*⟩; **h)** *(treat carefully)* ~ **gently/carefully** behutsam *od.* schonend umgehen mit; **i)** *(fig.: harbour)* hegen *(geh.)* ⟨*Gefühl, Plan, Groll*⟩. **3.** *v. i.* **a)** *(act as wet-~)* stillen; **b)** *(be a sick-~)* Krankenschwester/-pfleger sein. *See also* **wet-nurse**

'**nursemaid** *n. (lit. or fig.)* Kindermädchen, *das*

nursery ['nɜ:sərɪ] *n.* **a)** *(room for children)* Kinderzimmer, *das;* **b)** *(crèche)* Kindertagesstätte, *die;* **c)** *see* **nursery school; d)** *(Agric.) (for plants)* Gärtnerei, *die; (for trees)* Baumschule, *die; (fig.: training-ground)* Schule, *die*

nursery: ~man ['nɜ:sərɪmən] *n., pl.* **~men** ['nɜ:sərɪmən] Gärtner, *der;* ~ **nurse** *n.* Kindermädchen, *das;* Kinderpflegerin, *die;* ~ **rhyme** *n.* Kinderreim, *der;* ~ **school** *n.* Kindergarten, *der;* ~**-school teacher** *n. (female)* Kindergärtnerin, *die;* Erzieherin, *die; (male)* Erzieher, *der;* ~ **slopes** *n. pl. (Skiing)* Idiotenhügel, *der (ugs. scherzh.)*

nursing ['nɜ:sɪŋ] *n., no pl., no art. (profession)* Krankenpflege, *die; attrib.* Pflege⟨*personal, -beruf*⟩

nursing: ~ auxiliary *n. (female)* Schwesternhelferin, *die; (male)* Hilfspfleger, *der;* ~ **home** *n. (Brit.) (for the aged, infirm)* Pflegeheim, *das; (for convalescents)* Genesungsheim, *das; (maternity hospital)* Entbindungsheim, *das;* ~ '**mother** *n.* stillende Mutter

nurture ['nɜ:tʃə(r)] **1.** *n.* **a)** *no pl. (bringing up)* Erziehung, *die;* **b)** *(nourishment, lit. or fig.)* Nahrung, *die.* **2.** *v. t.* **a)** *(rear)* aufziehen; **b)** *(fig.: foster)* nähren *(geh.);* **c)** *(train)* erziehen; schulen, bilden ⟨*Geist*⟩

nut [nʌt] *n.* **a)** Nuß, *die;* **she can't sing/spell for ~s** *(Brit. sl.)* sie kann nicht für fünf Pfennig *(ugs.)* singen/schreiben; **be a hard** *or* **tough ~ [to crack]** *(fig.)* eine harte Nuß sein *(ugs.);* ⟨*Person:*⟩ schwierig sein; **~s to you** *(sl.)* du kannst/ihr könnt mir den Buckel runterrutschen *(ugs.);* **b)** *(Mech. Engin.)* [Schrauben]mutter, *die;* **~s and bolts** *(fig.)* praktische Grundlagen; **c)** *(sl.: head)* Kürbis, *der (salopp);* **go/be off one's ~:** verrückt *(ugs.)* werden/sein; **do one's ~:** durchdrehen *(ugs.);* **d)** *(crazy person)* Verrückte, *der/die (ugs.);* **be a bit of a ~:** ein bißchen spinnen *(ugs.);* **e)** *in pl. (coarse: testicles)* Eier *(derb). See also* **nuts**

nut: ~-brown *adj.* nußbraun; ~**-'butter** *n.* [Erd]nußbutter, *die;* ~**-case** *n. (sl.)* Verrückte, *der/die (ugs.);* **~crackers** *n. pl.* Nußknacker, *der;* ~ **cutlet** *n.* Nußschnitzel, *das;* **~hatch** *n. (Ornith.)* Kleiber, *der;* ~**-house** *n. (sl.)* Klapsmühle, *die (salopp);* ~**-meat** *n. (Amer.)* Nußkern, *der*

nutmeg ['nʌtmeg] *n.* Muskatnuß, *die;* Muskat, *der*

nutrient ['nju:trɪənt] **1.** *adj.* **a)** *(serving as nourishment)* nahrhaft; **b)** *(providing nourishment)* Ernährungs-; Nähr⟨*lösung, -salze*⟩. **2.** *n.* Nährstoff, *der*

nutriment ['nju:trɪmənt] *n. (lit. or fig.)* Nahrung, *die*

nutrition [nju:'trɪʃn] *n.* **a)** *(nourishment, diet)* Ernährung, *die;* **b)** *(food, lit. or fig.)* Nahrung, *die*

nutritional [nju:'trɪʃənl] *adj.* nahrhaft; ~ **value** Nährwert, *der;* ~ **deficiency/deficiencies** Nährstoffmangel, *der*

nutritionist [nju:'trɪʃənɪst] *n.* Ernährungswissenschaftler, *der*/-wissenschaftlerin, *die*

nutritious [nju:'trɪʃəs] *adj.* nahrhaft

nutritive ['nju:trɪtɪv] *adj.* nahrhaft; ~ **value/function** Nährwert, *der*/Ernährungsfunktion, *die*

'nut roast *n.* Nußbraten, *der*

nuts [nʌts] *pred. adj. (sl.)* verrückt *(ugs.);* **be ~ about** *or* **on sb./sth.** nach jmdm./etw. verrückt sein *(ugs.)*

'nutshell *n.* **a)** Nußschale, *die;* **b)** *(fig.)* **in a ~:** in aller Kürze; **to put it** *or* **the matter** *or* **the whole thing in a ~:** kurz gesagt

nutter ['nʌtə(r)] *n. (sl.)* Verrückte, *der/die (ugs.);* **be a ~:** verrückt sein *(ugs.)*

'nut-tree *n.* Haselnußstrauch, *der; (walnut)* Nußbaum, *der*

nutty ['nʌtɪ] *adj.* **a)** *(tasting like nuts)* nussig; **b)** *(abounding in nuts)* voller Nüsse *nachgestellt;* **c)** *(sl.: crazy)* verrückt *(ugs.);* **be ~ about** *or* **on sb./sth.** *(sl.)* nach jmdm./etw. verrückt sein *(ugs.); see also* **fruit-cake**

nuzzle ['nʌzl] **1.** *v.i.* **a)** *(with nose)* ~ **in** *or* **into sth.** die Schnauze in etw. *(Akk.)* drücken; ~ **against sth.** die Schnauze gegen etw. drücken; **b)** *(nestle)* sich kuscheln **([up] to, at, against** an + *Akk.*). **2.** *v.t.* schmiegen ‹*Gesicht, Kopf, Schulter*›

NW *abbr.* **a)** ['nɔ:θwest] **north-west** NW; **b)** ['nɔ:θwestən] **north-western** nw.

NY *abbr.* New York

nylon ['naɪlɒn] *n.* **a)** *no pl. (Textiles)* Nylon, *das; attrib.* Nylon-; **b)** *in pl. (stockings)* Nylonstrümpfe; Nylons *(ugs.)*

nymph [nɪmf] *n. (Mythol., Zool.)* Nymphe, *die*

nymphet ['nɪmfet, nɪm'fet] *n.* Nymphchen, *das*

nympho ['nɪmfəʊ] *n., pl.* ~**s** *(coll.)* Nymphomanin, *die*

nymphomania [nɪmfə'meɪnɪə] *n.* Nymphomanie, *die;* Mannstollheit, *die (veralt.)*

nymphomaniac [nɪmfə'meɪnɪæk] **1.** *n.* Nymphomanin, *die.* **2.** *adj.* nymphoman; mannstoll *(veralt.)*

NZ *abbr.* **New Zealand**

O

[1]O, o [əʊ] *n., pl.* **Os** *or* **O's a)** *(letter)* O, o, *das;* **b)** *(zero)* Null, *die*

[2]O *int. (arch./poet./rhet.)* o; **O God** *etc.* o Herr *usw.; see also* **that 6c**

o' [ə] *prep. (esp. arch./poet./dial.)* **a)** = **of** von; **man-o'-war** Kriegsschiff, *das;* **cup o' tea** *(coll.)* Tasse Tee; *see also* **o'clock; b)** = **on: o' nights/Sundays** nachts/sonntags

oaf [əʊf] *n., pl.* ~**s** *or* **oaves** [əʊvz] **a)** *(stupid person)* Dummkopf, *der (ugs.);* **great ~:** Riesenrindvieh, *das (ugs.);* **b)** *(awkward lout)* Stoffel, *der (ugs.);* **you clumsy ~!** du Trampeltier! *(ugs.)*

oafish ['əʊfɪʃ] *adj.* stoffelig *(ugs.)*

oak [əʊk] *n.* Eiche, *die; attrib.* Eichen‹*wald, -möbel, -kiste, -blatt*›

'oak-apple *n. (Bot.)* Gallapfel, *der*

oaken ['əʊkn] *attrib. adj.* eichen

'oak-tree *n.* Eiche, *die*

OAP *abbr. (Brit.)* **old-age pensioner** Rentner, *der*/Rentnerin, *die;* ~ **[social] club** Seniorenklub, *der*

oar [ɔ:(r)] *n.* **a)** Ruder, *das;* Riemen, *der (Sport, Seemannsspr.);* **put in one's ~, put one's ~ in** *(fig. coll.)* seinen Senf dazugeben *(ugs.);* sich einmischen; **rest on one's ~s, lie** *or (Amer.)* **lay on one's ~s** die Riemen hoch nehmen; *(fig.: relax one's efforts)* sich ausruhen; **b)** *(rower)* Ruderer, *der*/Ruderin, *die*

-oared [ɔ:d] *adj. in comb.* mit ... Riemen *nachgestellt;* -ruderig

oarsman ['ɔ:zmən] *n., pl.* **oarsmen** ['ɔ:zmən] Ruderer, *der*

oarsmanship ['ɔ:zmənʃɪp] *n., no pl.* ruderisches Können

oarswoman ['ɔ:zwʊmn] *n.* Ruderin, *die*

oasis [əʊ'eɪsɪs] *n., pl.* **oases** [əʊ'eɪsi:z] *(lit. or fig.)* Oase, *die*

oast [əʊst] *n. (Agric., Brewing)* Darre, *die*

'oast-house *n. (Agric., Brewing)* Hopfendarre, *die*

oat [əʊt] *n.* **a)** ~**s** Hafer, *der;* **be off one's ~s** *(fig.)* keinen Appetit haben; **rolled ~s** Haferflocken *Pl.;* **b)** *(plant)* Haferpflanze, *die;* **field of ~s** Haferfeld, *das;* **wild ~:** Flug- *od.* Windhafer, *der;* **sow one's wild ~s** *(fig.)* sich *(Dat.)* die Hörner abstoßen *(ugs.)*

'oatcake *n.* [flacher] Haferkuchen

oath [əʊθ] *n., pl.* ~**s** [əʊðz] **a)** Eid, *der;* Schwur, *der;* **be bound by ~:** durch einen Eid *od.* Schwur gebunden sein; **take** *or* **swear an ~ [on sth.] that ...:** einen Eid [auf etw. *(Akk.)*] schwören, daß ...; **b)** *(Law)* **swear** *or* **take the ~:** vereidigt werden; **on** *or* **under ~:** unter Eid; **be on** *or* **under ~ to do sth.** geschworen haben, etw. zu tun; **put sb. on** *or* **under ~:** jmdn. vereidigen *od.* unter Eid nehmen; **[I swear] on my ~ I am telling the truth** ich schwöre, daß ich die Wahrheit sage; ~ **of office** Amts- *od.* Diensteid, *der;* ~ **of allegiance/supremacy** Treu-/Suprematseid, *der;* **c)** *(expletive)* Fluch, *der*

'oatmeal *n.* **a)** Hafermehl, *das;* **b)** *(colour)* Graubeige, *das*

OAU *abbr. (Polit.)* **Organization of African Unity** OAE

oaves *pl. of* **oaf**

obbligato [ɒblɪ'gɑ:təʊ] *(Mus.)* **1.** *adj.* obligat. **2.** *n., pl.* ~**s** Obligato, *das*

obduracy ['ɒbdjʊrəsɪ] *n., no pl. (hardheartedness)* Unerbittlichkeit, *die; (stubbornness)* Verstocktheit, *die*

obdurate ['ɒbdjʊərət] *adj. (hardened)* unerbittlich ‹*Brutalität*›; verstockt ‹*Herz, Sünder*›; *(stubborn)* verstockt; hartnäckig ‹*Weigerung, Ablehnung*›

OBE *abbr. (Brit.)* **Officer [of the Order] of the British Empire**

obedience [ə'bi:dɪəns] *n.* Gehorsam, *der;* **show ~:** gehorsam sein; **in ~ to** gemäß

obedient [ə'bi:dɪənt] *adj.* gehorsam; *(submissive)* fügsam; **teach a dog to be ~:** einem Hund Gehorsam beibringen; **be ~ to sb./sth.** jmdm./einer Sache gehorchen; *see also* **servant c**

obediently [ə'bi:dɪəntlɪ] *adv.* gehorsam; *(submissively)* fügsam

obeisance [əʊ'beɪsəns] *n.* **a)** *(gesture)* Verbeugung, *die;* Verneigung, *die (geh.); (prostration)* Fußfall, *der;* **b)** *no pl. (homage)* Ehrerbietung, *die (geh.);* Reverenz, *die (geh.);* **do** *or* **make** *or* **pay ~ to sb.** jmdm. seine Reverenz bezeigen *od.* erweisen *(geh.)*

obelisk ['ɒbəlɪsk, 'ɒbɪlɪsk] *n.* **a)** *(pillar)* Obelisk, *der;* **b)** *(Printing)* Kreuzchen, *das;* **double ~:** Doppelkreuzchen, *das*

obese [əʊ'bi:s] *adj.* fett *(abwertend);* fettleibig *(bes. Med.)*

obesity [əʊ'bi:sɪtɪ] *n., no pl.* Fettheit, *die (abwertend);* Fettleibigkeit, *die (bes. Med.);* Obesität, *die (Med.)*

obey [əʊ'beɪ] **1.** *v.t.* gehorchen (+ *Dat.*); ‹*Kind, Hund:*› folgen (+ *Dat.*), gehorchen (+ *Dat.*); sich halten an (+ *Akk.*) ‹*Vorschrift, Regel*›; befolgen ‹*Befehl*›; folgen (+ *Dat.*) ‹*Aufforderung*›; nachkommen *(geh.)* (+ *Dat.*), Folge leisten (+ *Dat.*) ‹*Vorladung*›. **2.** *v.i.* gehorchen; ‹*Kind, Hund:*› folgen, gehorchen; **refuse to ~:** den Gehorsam verweigern

obfuscate ['ɒbfəskeɪt] *v.t. (literary) (obscure)* vernebeln; *(confuse)* verwirren

obituary [ə'bɪtjʊərɪ] **1.** *n.* Nachruf, *der* **(to, of** auf + *Akk.*); *(notice of death)* Todesanzeige, *die.* **2.** *adj.* ~ **notice/memoir** Todesanzeige, *die*/Nachruf, *der;* **the ~ page/column** die Todesanzeigen

object 1. ['ɒbdʒɪkt] *n.* **a)** *(thing)* Gegenstand, *der; (Philos.)* Objekt, *das;* **he was no longer the ~ of her affections** ihre Zuneigung gehörte ihm nicht mehr; **b)** *(purpose)* Ziel, *das;* ~ **in life** Lebensziel, *das od.* -zweck, *der;* **with this ~ in mind** *or* **view** mit diesem Ziel [vor Augen]; **with the ~ of doing sth.** in der Absicht, etw. zu tun; **make it one's ~ [in life]** es sich *(Dat.)* zum Ziel setzen; es zu seinem Lebensziel machen; *see also* **defeat 1 b; exercise 1 b; c)** *(obstacle, hindrance)* **money/time** *etc.* **is no ~:** Geld/Zeit *usw.* spielt keine Rolle; **d)** *(Ling.)* Objekt, *das; see also* **direct object; indirect object. 2.** [əb'dʒekt] *v.i.* **a)** *(state objection)* Einwände/einen Einwand erheben **(to** gegen); *(protest)* protestieren **(to** gegen); **I ~, your Honour** *(Law)* Einspruch, Herr Vorsitzender!; **b)** *(have objection or dislike)* etwas dagegen haben; ~ **to sb./sth.** etwas gegen jmdn./etw. haben; **if you don't ~:** wenn Sie nichts dagegen haben; **I ~ to your smoking** es stört mich, daß du rauchst; ~ **to sb.'s doing sth.** etw. dagegen haben, daß jmd. etw. tut; **I strongly ~ to this tone** ich verbitte mir diesen Ton; **I ~ to being blamed for this error** ich verwahre mich dagegen, für diesen Fehler verantwortlich gemacht zu werden. **3.** *v.t.* einwenden

objectify [əb'dʒektɪfaɪ] *v.t.* objektivieren

objection [əb'dʒekʃn] *n.* **a)** Einwand, *der;* Einspruch, *der (Amtsspr., Rechtsw.);* **raise** *or* **make an ~ [to sth.]** einen Einwand *od. (Rechtsw.)* Einspruch [gegen etw.] erheben; **make no ~ to sth.** nichts gegen etw. einzuwenden haben; **b)** *(feeling of opposition or dislike)* Abneigung, *die;* **have an/no ~ to sb./sth.** etw./nichts gegen jmdn./etw. haben; **have an/no ~:** etwas/nichts dagegen haben; **have no ~ to sb.'s doing sth.** nichts dagegen haben, daß jmd. etw. tut

objectionable [əb'dʒekʃənəbl] *adj.* unangenehm ‹*Anblick, Geruch*›; anstößig ‹*Bemerkung, Wort, Benehmen*›; unausstehlich ‹*Kind*›

objectionably [əb'dʒekʃənəblɪ] *adv.* unerträglich ‹*überheblich, aufdringlich*›; anstößig ‹*sich benehmen*›

objective [əb'dʒektɪv] **1.** *adj.* **a)** *(unbiased)* objektiv; sachlich; **b)** *(esp. Philos.: real)* objektiv. **2.** *n. (goal)* Ziel, *das;* **establish one's ~:** sich *(Dat.)* ein Ziel setzen

objective: ~ case *n. (Ling.)* **be in the ~ case** Objekt sein; **~ 'genitive** *n. (Ling.)* Genitivus obiectivus, *der*

objectively [əb'dʒektɪvlɪ] *adv.* **a)** objektiv; **b)** *(Ling.)* als Objekt ‹*gebrauchen*›

objectiveness [əb'dʒektɪvnɪs], **objectivity** [ɒbdʒɪk'tɪvɪtɪ] *ns., no pl.* Objektivität, *die;* **maintain ~:** objektiv bleiben

'object-lesson *n. (warning)* Denkzettel, *der; (very clear example)* Musterbeispiel, *das* **(in, on** für); **it was an ~ to him** es war ihm eine Lehre; **an ~ in** *or* **on how to do sth.**

ein Musterbeispiel dafür, wie man etw. macht

objector [əb'dʒektə(r)] *n.* Gegner, *der*/Gegnerin, *die* (**to** *Gen.*); *see also* **conscientious**

objet d'art [ɒbʒeɪ 'dɑ:(r)] *n., pl.* **objets d'art** [ɒbʒeɪ 'dɑ:(r)] Kunstgegenstand, *der*

obligate ['ɒblɪgeɪt] *v. t., usu. in p.p.* verpflichten

obligation [ɒblɪ'geɪʃn] *n.* **a)** Verpflichtung, *die; (constraint)* Zwang, *der;* **be under** *or* **have an/no ~ to do sth.** verpflichtet/nicht verpflichtet sein, etw. zu tun; **have an/no ~ to[wards] sb.** jmdm. gegenüber eine/keine Verpflichtung haben; **there's no ~ to buy** es besteht kein Kaufzwang; **b)** *(indebtedness)* Dankesschuld, *die (geh.);* **put** *or* **place sb. under an ~:** jmdm. eine Dankespflicht auferlegen; **be under an ~ to sb.** in jmds. Schuld stehen *(geh.);* jmdm. verpflichtet sein; **be under no ~ to sb.** jmdm. nicht verpflichtet sein

obligatory [ə'blɪgətərɪ] *adj.* obligatorisch; **make sth. ~ for sb.** etw. für jmdn. vorschreiben; **it has become ~ to do sth.** es ist zur Pflicht geworden, etw. zu tun

oblige [ə'blaɪdʒ] **1.** *v. t.* **a)** *(be binding on)* **~ sb. to do sth.** jmdm. vorschreiben, etw. zu tun; **one is ~d by law to do sth.** etw. ist gesetzlich vorgeschrieben; **b)** *(constrain, compel)* zwingen; nötigen; **be ~d to do sth.** gezwungen *od.* genötigt sein, etw. zu tun; **you are not ~d to answer these questions** Sie sind nicht verpflichtet, diese Fragen zu beantworten; **feel ~d to do sth.** sich verpflichtet fühlen, etw. zu tun; **c)** *(be kind to)* **~ sb. by doing sth.** jmdm. den Gefallen tun und etw. tun; **would you please ~ me by doing it?** würden Sie bitte so gut sein und es tun?; **~ sb. with sth.** *(help out)* jmdm. mit etw. aushelfen; **could you ~ me with a lift?** könnten Sie mich freundlicherweise mitnehmen?; **d) ~d** *(bound by gratitude)* **be much/greatly ~d to sb. [for sth.]** jmdm. [für etw.] sehr verbunden sein; **much ~d** besten Dank! **2.** *v. i.* **be always ready to ~:** immer sehr gefällig sein; **anything to ~** *(as answer)* stets zu Diensten; **~ with a song** *etc. (coll.)* ein Lied *usw.* zum besten geben

obliging [ə'blaɪdʒɪŋ] *adj.* entgegenkommend

obligingly [ə'blaɪdʒɪŋlɪ] *adv.* entgegenkommenderweise

oblique [ə'bli:k] **1.** *adj.* **a)** *(slanting)* schief ⟨*Gerade, Winkel*⟩; **b)** *(fig.: indirect)* indirekt ⟨*Bemerkung, Hinweis, Frage*⟩; versteckt ⟨*Hinweis*⟩. **2.** *n.* Schrägstrich, *der*

obliquely [ə'bli:klɪ] *adv.* **a)** *(in a slanting direction)* schräg ⟨*einfallen, abzweigen*⟩; **b)** *(fig.: indirectly)* indirekt ⟨*sich beziehen, antworten*⟩

obliterate [ə'blɪtəreɪt] *v. t.* **a)** auslöschen; *(cancel)* entwerten ⟨*Briefmarke*⟩; **b)** *(fig.)* verschleiern ⟨*Wahrheit*⟩; auslöschen ⟨*Erinnerung*⟩; zerstreuen ⟨*Bedenken*⟩; vernichtend schlagen ⟨*Gegner*⟩

obliteration [əblɪtə'reɪʃn] *n. see* **obliterate:** Auslöschung, *die;* Verschleierung, *die;* Zerstreuung, *die*

oblivion [ə'blɪvɪən] *n., no pl.* **a)** *(being forgotten)* Vergessenheit, *die;* **sink** *or* **fall into ~:** in Vergessenheit geraten; **rescued from ~:** der Vergessenheit *(Dat.)* entrissen; **b)** *(forgetting)* Vergessen, *das*

oblivious [ə'blɪvɪəs] *adj.* **be ~ to** *or* **of sth.** *(be unconscious of)* sich *(Dat.)* einer Sache *(Gen.)* nicht bewußt sein; *(not notice)* etw. nicht bemerken *od.* wahrnehmen

oblong ['ɒblɒŋ] **1.** *adj.* rechteckig. **2.** *n.* Rechteck, *das*

obloquy ['ɒbləkwɪ] *n. (literary)* **a)** *(abuse)* Beschimpfungen; **b)** *(disgrace)* Schande, *die*

obnoxious [əb'nɒkʃəs] *adj.*, **obnoxiously** [əb'nɒkʃəslɪ] *adv.* widerlich *(abwertend)*

oboe ['əʊbəʊ] *n. (Mus.)* Oboe, *die*

oboist ['əʊbəʊɪst] *n. (Mus.)* Oboist, *der*/Oboistin, *die*

obscene [əb'si:n] *adj.* obszön; *(coll.: offensive)* widerlich *(abwertend);* unanständig ⟨*Profit*⟩

obscenely [əb'si:nlɪ] *adv.* obszön; *(coll.: offensively)* widerlich *(abwertend);* unanständig ⟨*reich*⟩

obscenity [əb'senɪtɪ] *n.* Obszönität, *die; (coll.: offensive nature)* Widerlichkeit, *die (abwertend)*

obscurantism [ɒbskjʊə'ræntɪzm] *n.* Obskurantismus, *der*

obscurantist [ɒbskjʊə'ræntɪst] **1.** *n.* Obskurant, *der*/Obskurantin, *die (geh.).* **2.** *adj.* **~ doctrine/argument** Obskurantentum, *das (geh.)*

obscure [əb'skjʊə(r)] **1.** *adj.* **a)** *(unexplained)* dunkel; **for some ~ reason** aus irgendeinem unerfindlichen *(geh.) od.* verborgenen Grund; **b)** *(hard to understand)* schwer verständlich ⟨*Argument, Dichtung, Autor, Stil*⟩; unklar ⟨*Hinweis, Textstelle*⟩; **c)** *(unknown)* unbekannt ⟨*Herkunft, Schriftsteller*⟩; *(undistinguished)* unbedeutend; **d)** *(indistinct, vague)* undeutlich ⟨*Spur, Gemurmel*⟩; vage ⟨*Anhaltspunkt*⟩; **e)** *(remote)* abgelegen, entlegen ⟨*Ort*⟩; **f)** *(dark, dim)* dunkel. **2.** *v. t.* **a)** *(make indistinct)* verdunkeln; *(block)* versperren ⟨*Aussicht*⟩; *(conceal)* ⟨*Nebel:*⟩ verhüllen; **b)** *(fig.: make unintelligible)* unverständlich machen; **be ~d** unverständlich werden; **c)** *(fig.: outshine)* in den Schatten stellen

obscurely [əb'skjʊəlɪ] *adv.* **a)** *(indirectly)* vage; **b)** *(in obscurity)* im Verborgenen

obscurity [əb'skjʊərɪtɪ] *n.* **a)** *no pl. (being unknown or inconspicuous)* Unbekanntheit, *die;* **rise out of ~:** bekannt werden; **sink into ~:** in Vergessenheit geraten; **in ~:** unbeachtet, unauffällig ⟨*leben*⟩; **b)** *no pl. (being not clearly known or understood)* **be lost in [the mists of] ~:** im dunkeln liegen; **c)** *(unintelligibleness, unintelligible thing)* Unverständlichkeit, *die;* **d)** *no pl. (darkness)* Dunkelheit, *die*

obsequies ['ɒbsɪkwɪz] *n. pl. (funeral rites)* Beisetzungsfeierlichkeiten *(geh.)*

obsequious [əb'si:kwɪəs] *adj.*, **obsequiously** [əb'si:kwɪəslɪ] *adv.* unterwürfig *(abwertend)*

observable [əb'zɜ:vəbl] *adj.* erkennbar; spürbar ⟨*Mangel, Zunahme, Übergewicht*⟩

observance [əb'zɜ:vəns] *n.* **a)** *no pl. (observing, keeping)* Beachtung, *die;* Befolgung, *die; (of prescribed times)* Einhaltung, *die;* **b)** *(esp. Relig.: practice, rite)* Regel, *die;* **c)** *(rule)* Ordensregel, *die*

observant [əb'zɜ:vənt] *adj.* **a)** aufmerksam; **be ~ of sth.** ein Auge für etw. haben; **how very ~ of you!** sehr scharf beobachtet!; **b)** *(mindful, regardful)* **be ~ of** beachten, sich halten an (+ *Akk.*) ⟨*Gesetz, Regel*⟩

observation [ɒbzə'veɪʃn] *n.* **a)** *no pl.* Beobachtung, *die;* **escape ~:** unbeobachtet bleiben; **powers of ~:** Beobachtungsgabe, *die;* **stay in hospital for ~:** zur Beobachtung im Krankenhaus bleiben; **be [kept] under ~:** beobachtet werden; *(by police, detectives)* observiert *od.* überwacht werden; **b)** *(remark)* Bemerkung, *die* (**on** über + *Akk.*); **make an ~ on sth.** sich zu etw. äußern

observational [ɒbzə'veɪʃənl] *adj.* Beobachtungs⟨*gabe, -methode*⟩

observation: ~ car *n. (Railw.)* Aussichtswagen, *der;* **~ post** *n. (Mil.)* Beobachtungsposten, *der*

observatory [əb'zɜ:vətərɪ] *n.* Observatorium, *das; (Astron. also)* Sternwarte, *die; (Meteorol. also)* Wetterstation, *die*

observe [əb'zɜ:v] *v. t.* **a)** *(watch)* beobachten; ⟨*Polizei, Detektiv:*⟩ observieren, überwachen; *abs.* aufpassen; *(perceive)* bemerken; **b)** *(abide by, keep)* einhalten; feiern ⟨*Weihnachten, Jahrestag*⟩; einlegen ⟨*Schweigeminute*⟩; halten ⟨*Gelübde*⟩; nachkommen *(geh.)* (+ *Dat.*) ⟨*Bitte*⟩; **c)** *(say)* bemerken

observer [əb'zɜ:və(r)] *n.* Beobachter, *der*/Beobachterin, *die*

obsess [əb'ses] *v. t.* **~ sb.** von jmdm. Besitz ergreifen *(fig.);* **be/become ~ed with** *or* **by sb./sth.** von jmdm./etw. besessen sein/werden; **don't let yourself become ~ed by her** versuch in deiner Beziehung zu ihr einen kühlen Kopf zu behalten

obsession [əb'seʃn] *n.* **a)** *(persistent idea)* Zwangsvorstellung, *die;* **be/become an ~ with sb.** für jmdn. zur Sucht geworden sein/werden; **have an ~ with sb.** von jmdm. besessen sein; **b)** *no pl. (Psych.: condition)* Obsession, *die (fachspr.);* Besessenheit, *die;* **develop an ~ about washing** einen Waschzwang entwickeln

obsessional [əb'seʃənl] *adj.* zwanghaft; obsessiv *(Psych.)*

obsessive [əb'sesɪv] *adj.* zwanghaft; obsessiv *(Psych.);* **be ~ about sth.** von etw. besessen sein; **be an ~ eater/gambler** unter Eßzwang leiden/dem Spiel verfallen sein

obsessively [əb'sesɪvlɪ] *adv.* zwanghaft

obsolescence [ɒbsə'lesəns] *n., no pl.* Veralten, *das;* **fall into ~:** veralten; **built-in** *or* **planned ~:** geplanter Verschleiß

obsolescent [ɒbsə'lesənt] *adj.* veraltend; **become/have become** *or* **be ~:** allmählich veralten/nahezu veraltet sein

obsolete ['ɒbsəli:t] *adj.* veraltet; obsolet *(geh.);* **become/have become ~:** veralten/veraltet sein

obstacle ['ɒbstəkl] *n.* Hindernis, *das* (**to** für); **put ~s in sb.'s path** *(fig.)* jmdm. Hindernisse *od.* Steine in den Weg legen; **give rise to ~s** Schwierigkeiten verursachen

'obstacle-race *n.* Hindernisrennen, *das*

obstetric [ɒb'stetrɪk], **obstetrical** [ɒb'stetrɪkl] *adj. (Med.)* Geburts⟨*schock, -kanal*⟩; **~ ward** Entbindungsstation, *die*

obstetrician [ɒbstə'trɪʃn] *n. (Med.)* Geburtshelfer, *der*/-helferin, *die*

obstetrics [ɒb'stetrɪks] *n., no pl. (Med.)* Obstetrik, *die (fachspr.);* Geburtshilfe, *die*

obstinacy ['ɒbstɪnəsɪ] *n., no pl. see* **obstinate:** Starrsinn, *der;* Hartnäckigkeit, *die;* Sturheit, *die (ugs.)*

obstinate ['ɒbstɪnət] *adj.* starrsinnig; *(adhering to particular course of action)* hartnäckig; stur *(ugs.);* **an ~ cold** eine hartnäckige Erkältung; **be as ~ as a mule** ein sturer Bock sein *(ugs. abwertend)*

obstinately ['ɒbstɪnətlɪ] *adv. see* **obstinate:** starrsinnig; hartnäckig; stur *(ugs.)*

obstreperous [əb'strepərəs] *adj.* **a)** randalierend; **be/become ~:** randalieren/zu randalieren beginnen; **b)** *(protesting)* widerspenstig; **stop being so ~!** mach nicht so ein Geschrei! *(ugs.)*

obstruct [əb'strʌkt] *v. t.* **a)** *(block)* versperren; blockieren; *(Med.)* verstopfen; behindern ⟨*Verkehr*⟩; versperren ⟨*Sicht*⟩; **~ sb.'s view** jmdm. die Sicht versperren; **b)** *(fig.: impede; also Sport)* behindern; **c)** *(Parl.)* obstruieren

obstruction [əb'strʌkʃn] *n.* **a)** *no pl. (blocking)* Blockierung, *die; (Med.)* Verstopfung, *die;* Obstruktion, *die (Med.); (of progress; also Sport)* Behinderung, *die; (to success)* Hindernis, *das* (**to** für); **b)** *(Parl.)* Obstruktion, *die;* **c)** *(obstacle)* Hindernis, *das;* Hemmnis, *das*

obstructionism [əb'strʌkʃənɪzm] *n., no pl. (Polit.)* **[policy of] ~:** Obstruktionspolitik, *die*

obstructionist [əb'strʌkʃənɪst] *n. (Polit.)* Obstruktionspolitiker, *der*/-politikerin, *die*

obstructive [əb'strʌktɪv] *adj.* hinderlich; obstruktiv ⟨*Politik, Taktik*⟩; **be ~** ⟨*Person:*⟩ sich querlegen *(ugs.)*

obtain [əb'teɪn] **1.** *v. t.* bekommen ⟨*Ware, Information, Hilfe*⟩; erreichen, erzielen

⟨*Resultat, Wirkung*⟩; erwerben, erlangen ⟨*akademischen Grad*⟩; **~ a divorce** geschieden werden. **2.** *v.i.* Geltung haben; ⟨*Ansicht, Brauch:*⟩ herrschen, verbreitet sein; ⟨*Regelung:*⟩ in Kraft sein

obtainable [əb'teɪnəbl] *adj.* erhältlich ⟨*Ware, Eintrittskarte*⟩; erzielbar ⟨*Wirkung*⟩

obtrude [əb'tru:d] **1.** *v.t.* **~ one's beliefs/opinions on sb.** jmdm. seine Überzeugung/Meinung aufdrängen; **~ oneself [up]on sb./into sth.** sich jmdm. aufdrängen/sich in etw. *(Akk.)* hineindrängen. **2.** *v.i.* sich aufdrängen (**upon** *Dat.*); **~ upon sb.'s grief** jmdn. in seinem Kummer stören

obtrusive [əb'tru:sɪv] *adj.* aufdringlich; *(conspicuous)* auffällig

obtrusively [əb'tru:sɪvlɪ] *adv.* in aufdringlicher Weise

obtrusiveness [əb'tru:sɪvnɪs] *n., no pl.* Aufdringlichkeit, *die; (conspicuousness)* Auffälligkeit, *die*

obtuse [əb'tju:s] *adj.* **a)** *(blunt; also Geom.)* stumpf ⟨*Winkel, Messer*⟩; **b)** *(stupid)* einfältig; **he's being deliberately ~:** er stellt sich dumm

obtusely [əb'tju:slɪ] *adv.* einfältig

obverse ['ɒbvɜ:s] *n.* **a)** *(of coin or medal)* Vorderseite, *die;* Avers, *der (Münzk.);* **b)** *(front)* Schauseite, *die;* **c)** *(fig.: counterpart)* Gegenstück, *das* (**of** zu)

obviate ['ɒbvɪeɪt] *v.t.* begegnen (+ *Dat.*) ⟨*Gefahr, Risiko, Einwand*⟩; **~ the necessity of sth.** etw. unnötig machen

obvious ['ɒbvɪəs] *adj.* offenkundig; eindeutig ⟨*Sieger*⟩; *(easily seen)* augenfällig; sichtlich ⟨*Empfindung, innerer Zustand*⟩; plump ⟨*Trick, Mittel*⟩; **she was the ~ choice** es lag nahe, daß die Wahl auf sie fiel; **the answer is ~:** die Antwort liegt auf der Hand; **the ~ thing to do is ...:** das Naheliegende ist ...; **it's not ~ what we should do next** es ist nicht ersichtlich, was wir als nächstes tun sollten; **with the ~ exception of ...:** natürlich mit Ausnahme von ...; **be ~ [to sb.] that ...:** [jmdm.] klar sein, daß ...; **that's stating the ~:** das ist nichts Neues

obviously ['ɒbvɪəslɪ] *adv.* offenkundig; sichtlich ⟨*enttäuschen, überraschen usw.*⟩; **~, we can't expect any help** es ist klar, daß wir keine Hilfe erwarten können

ocarina [ɒkə'ri:nə] *n. (Mus.)* Okarina, *die*

Occam's razor [ɒkəmz 'reɪzə(r)] *n. (Philos.)* Ökonomieprinzip, *das;* Ockham's razor, *der*

occasion [ə'keɪʒn] **1.** *n.* **a)** *(opportunity)* Gelegenheit, *die;* **rise to the ~:** sich der Situation gewachsen zeigen; **b)** *(reason)* Grund, *der* (**for** zu); *(cause)* Anlaß, *der;* **should the ~ arise** falls sich die Gelegenheit ergibt; **there is no ~ for alarm** es besteht kein Grund zur Sorge; **be [an] ~ for celebration** ein Grund zum Feiern sein; **have ~ to do sth.** [eine] Gelegenheit haben, etw. zu tun; **I had ~ to be in Rome** ich hatte in Rom zu tun; **c)** *(point in time)* Gelegenheit, *die;* **on several ~s** bei mehreren Gelegenheiten; **on that ~:** bei der Gelegenheit; damals; **[up]on ~[s]** gelegentlich; **d)** *(special occurrence)* Anlaß, *der;* **on state ~s** bei offiziellen Anlässen; **it was quite an ~:** es war ein Ereignis; **on the ~ of** anläßlich (+ *Gen.*). **2.** *v.t.* verursachen; erregen, Anlaß geben zu ⟨*Besorgnis*⟩; geben ⟨*Denkanstoß, Anregung*⟩; **~ sb. to do sth.** jmdn. veranlassen, etw. zu tun

occasional [ə'keɪʒənl] *adj.* **a)** *(happening irregularly)* gelegentlich; vereinzelt ⟨*Regenschauer*⟩; **take an** *or* **the ~ break** gelegentlich eine Pause machen; **b)** *(specially written)* Gelegenheits⟨*musik, -dichtung*⟩

occasionally [ə'keɪʒənəlɪ] *adv.* gelegentlich; **[only] very ~:** gelegentlich einmal

oc'casional table *n.* Beistelltisch, *der*

Occident ['ɒksɪdənt] *n. (poet./rhet.)* **the ~** *(the west, European civilization)* der Okzident; das Abendland

occidental [ɒksɪ'dentl] **1.** *adj.* **a)** abendländisch; **b)** *(Polit.)* westlich. **2. O~** *n.* Abendländer, *der*/Abendländerin, *die*

occlude [ə'klu:d] *v.t.* **a)** *(Med.)* verschließen; **b)** *(Chem.)* okkludieren ⟨*Gas*⟩; **c)** *(Meteorol.)* **~d front** Okklusion, *die*

occlusion [ə'klu:ʒn] *n.* **a)** *(Med.)* Okklusion, *die (fachspr.);* Verschluß, *der;* **b)** *(Chem., Meteorol., Dent.)* Okklusion, *die*

occult [ɒ'kʌlt, ə'kʌlt] *adj.* **a)** *(mystical)* okkult ⟨*Kunst, Wissenschaft*⟩; **the ~:** das Okkulte; **b)** *(mysterious)* unergründlich, dunkel ⟨*Rätsel, Geheimnis*⟩; **c)** *(secret)* verborgen

occultism [ɒ'kʌltɪzm, ə'kʌltɪzm] *n.* Okkultismus, *der*

occultist [ɒ'kʌltɪst, ə'kʌltɪst] *n.* Okkultist, *der*/Okkultistin, *die*

occupancy ['ɒkjʊpənsɪ] *n. (residence in a place)* Bewohnung, *die; (moving into property)* Einzug, *der*

occupant ['ɒkjʊpənt] *n.* **a)** *(resident)* Bewohner, *der*/Bewohnerin, *die; (of post)* Inhaber, *der*/Inhaberin, *die; (of car, bus, etc.)* Insasse, *der*/Insassin, *die; (of room)* [Zimmer]bewohner, *der*/-bewohnerin, *die;* **b)** *(Law)* Besitzer, *der*/Besitzerin, *die*

occupation [ɒkjʊ'peɪʃn] *n.* **a)** *(of property) (tenure)* Besitz, *der; (occupancy)* Bewohnung, *die;* **take over the ~ of** in Besitz nehmen; einziehen in (+ *Akk.*) ⟨*Haus, Wohnung, Zimmer*⟩; **the owners of the house are [still]/the new tenants are already in ~:** die Hausbesitzer sind noch nicht ausgezogen/die neuen Mieter sind schon eingezogen; **b)** *(Mil.)* Okkupation, *die;* Besetzung, *die; (period)* Besatzungszeit, *die;* **army of ~:** Besatzungsarmee, *die;* **c)** *(activity)* Beschäftigung, *die; (pastime)* Zeitvertreib, *der;* **d)** *(profession)* Beruf, *der;* **his ~ is civil engineering** er ist Bauingenieur [von Beruf]; **what's her ~?** was ist sie von Beruf?

occupational [ɒkjʊ'peɪʃənl] *adj.* Berufs⟨*beratung, -risiko*⟩; betrieblich ⟨*Altersversorgung*⟩

occupational: ~ di'sease *n. (also joc.)* Berufskrankheit, *die;* **~ 'therapist** *n.* Beschäftigungstherapeut, *der*/-therapeutin, *die;* **~ 'therapy** *n.* Beschäftigungstherapie, *die*

occupier ['ɒkjʊpaɪə(r)] *n. (Brit.)* Besitzer, *der*/Besitzerin, *die; (tenant)* Bewohner, *der*/Bewohnerin, *die*

occupy ['ɒkjʊpaɪ] *v.t.* **a)** *(Mil.; Polit. as demonstration)* besetzen; **the terrorists are ~ing the building** die Terroristen halten das Gebäude besetzt; **b)** *(reside in, be a tenant of)* bewohnen; **~ a flat on a one-year lease** eine Wohnung für ein Jahr gemietet haben; **c)** *(take up, fill)* einnehmen; liegen in (+ *Dat.*) ⟨*Bett*⟩; besetzen ⟨*Sitzplatz, Tisch*⟩; belegen ⟨*Zimmer*⟩; in Anspruch nehmen ⟨*Zeit, Aufmerksamkeit*⟩; **how did you ~ your time?** wie hast du die Zeit verbracht?; **the hotel occupies an attractive site** das Hotel ist schön gelegen; **~ a special place in sb.'s affections** einen besonderen Platz in jmds. Herzen haben; **d)** *(hold)* innehaben ⟨*Stellung, Amt*⟩; **e)** *(busy, employ)* beschäftigen; **~ oneself [with doing sth.]** sich [mit etw.] beschäftigen; **be occupied with** *or* **in doing sth.** damit beschäftigt sein, etw. zu tun; **keep sb.['s mind] occupied** jmdn. [geistig] beschäftigen

occur [ə'kɜ:(r)] *v.i.,* **-rr- a)** *(be met with)* vorkommen; ⟨*Gelegenheit, Schwierigkeit, Problem:*⟩ sich ergeben; ⟨*Gelegenheit:*⟩ sich bieten; ⟨*Krankheit, Problem, Schwierigkeit:*⟩ auftreten; **if the case should ~ that ...:** sollte der Fall eintreten, daß ...; **b)** *(happen)* ⟨*Veränderung:*⟩ eintreten; ⟨*Unfall, Vorfall, Zwischenfall:*⟩ sich ereignen; ⟨*Olympiade:*⟩ stattfinden; ⟨*Todesfall:*⟩ auftreten; **how did your injuries ~?** wie kam es zu deinen Verletzungen?; **this must not ~ again** das darf nicht wieder vorkommen; **c) ~ to sb.** *(be thought of)* jmdm. einfallen *od.* in den Sinn kommen; ⟨*Idee:*⟩ jmdm. kommen; **it ~red to me that she was looking rather pale** mir fiel auf, daß sie ziemlich blaß aussah; **it never ~red to me** auf den Gedanken *od.* darauf bin ich nie gekommen

occurrence [ə'kʌrəns] *n.* **a)** *(incident)* Ereignis, *das;* Begebenheit, *die;* **b)** *(occurring)* Vorkommen, *das; (of disease)* Vorkommen, *das;* Auftreten, *das;* **be of frequent ~:** häufig vorkommen

ocean ['əʊʃn] *n.* **a)** Ozean, *der;* Meer, *das; attrib.* Meeres⟨*strömung, -boden*⟩; **b)** *in pl. (fig. coll.)* **~s of time** massenhaft Zeit *(ugs.);* **he's got ~s of money** er hat Geld wie Heu *(ugs.);* **weep ~s of tears** Ströme von Tränen vergießen

'ocean-going *adj.* Übersee⟨*handel, -dampfer, -schiff*⟩

Oceania [əʊʃɪ'ɑ:nɪə, əʊsɪ'ɑ:nɪə] *pr. n.* Ozeanien *(das)*

oceanic [əʊʃɪ'ænɪk, əʊsɪ'ænɪk] *adj.* ozeanisch; Meeres⟨*tier, -klima, -tiefe, -strömung*⟩; See⟨*vogel, -klima*⟩; *(fig.)* gewaltig

oceanography [əʊʃə'nɒgrəfɪ] *n.* Ozeanographie, *die;* Meereskunde, *die*

ocelot ['ɒsɪlɒt] *n. (Zool.)* Ozelot, *der*

och [ɒx] *int. (Scot., Ir.)* ach

ochre *(Amer.:* **ocher**) ['əʊkə(r)] *n.* Ocker, *der od. das*

ocker ['ɒkə(r)] *n. (Austral. sl.) ungehobelter, rüpelhafter Australier*

o'clock [ə'klɒk] *adv.* **a) it is two/six ~:** es ist zwei/sechs Uhr; **at two/six ~:** um zwei/sechs Uhr; **six ~** *attrib.* Sechs-Uhr-⟨*Zug, Maschine, Nachrichten*⟩; **b)** *indicating direction or position* **see a plane at 3/6/9/12 ~:** ein Flugzeug rechts/genau unter sich *(Dat.)*/links/genau über sich *(Dat.)* sehen; *(horizontally)* ein Flugzeug rechts/genau hinter sich *(Dat.)*/links/genau vor sich *(Dat.)* sehen

Oct. *abbr.* **October** Okt.

octagon ['ɒktəgən] *n. (Geom.)* Achteck, *das;* Oktogon, *das (fachspr.)*

octagonal [ɒk'tægənl] *adj. (Geom.)* achteckig; oktogonal *(fachspr.)*

octahedron [ɒktə'hi:drən] *n., pl.* **~s** *or* **octahedra** [ɒktə'hi:drə] *(Geom.)* Oktaeder, *das (fachspr.);* Achtflächner, *der*

octane ['ɒkteɪn] *n.* Oktan, *das*

octave ['ɒktɪv] *n. (Mus.)* Oktave, *die*

octavo [ɒk'tɑ:vəʊ] *n., pl.* **~s a)** *(book)* Oktavband, *der; (page)* Oktavseite, *die;* **b)** *(size)* Oktav[format], *das*

octet, octette [ɒk'tet] *n. (Mus.)* Oktett, *das;* **string ~:** Streichoktett, *das*

October [ɒk'təʊbə(r)] *n.* Oktober, *der;* **the ~ Revolution** *(Hist.)* die Oktoberrevolution; *see also* **August**

octogenarian [ɒktədʒɪ'neərɪən] **1.** *adj.* achtzigjährig; *(more than 80 years old)* in den Achtzigern *nachgestellt.* **2.** *n.* Achtziger, *der*/Achtzigerin, *die*

octopus ['ɒktəpəs] *n. (lit. or fig.)* Krake, *der;* Octopus, *der (Zool.)*

ocular ['ɒkjʊlə(r)] *adj.* Augen⟨*maß, -krankheit, -täuschung*⟩

oculist ['ɒkjʊlɪst] *n.* Augenarzt, *der*/Augenärztin, *die*

odd [ɒd] *adj.* **a)** *(surplus, spare)* übrig ⟨*Stück*⟩; überzählig ⟨*Spieler*⟩; restlich, übrig ⟨*Silbergeld*⟩; **b)** *(additional)* **£25 and a few ~ pence** 25 Pfund und ein paar Pence; **1,000 and ~ pounds** etwas über 1 000 Pfund; **c)** *(occasional, random)* gelegentlich; **use the occasional ~ moment to do sth.** etw. tun, wenn sich die Gelegenheit ergibt; **I like the ~ whisky** gelegentlich trinke ich gern einen Whisky; **the ~ bit of translating** gelegentliche kleine Übersetzungen; **~ job/~-job man** Gelegenheitsarbeit, *die*/-arbeiter, *der;* **do ~ jobs** Gelegenheitsarbeiten verrichten; *(about the house)* anfallende Arbeiten erledigen; **d)** *(one of pair or group)* einzeln; ~ **socks/gloves** *etc.* nicht zusammengehörende Socken/Handschuhe *usw.*; ~ **numbers/volumes** Einzelnummern/Einzelbände; **e)** *(uneven)* ungerade ‹*Zahl, Seite, Hausnummer*›; **f)** *(plus something)* **she must be forty ~**: sie muß etwas über vierzig sein; **sixty thousand ~**: etwas über sechzigtausend; **twelve pounds ~**: etwas mehr als zwölf Pfund; **g)** *(extraordinary)* merkwürdig; *(strange, eccentric)* seltsam

odd: ~ball, ~ 'fish *ns. (coll.)* komischer Kauz *(ugs.)*

oddity ['ɒdɪtɪ] *n.* **a)** *(strangeness, peculiar trait)* Eigentümlichkeit, *die;* **b)** *(odd person)* Sonderling, *der;* **c)** *(fantastic object, strange event)* Kuriosität, *die*

oddly ['ɒdlɪ] *adv.* seltsam; merkwürdig; ~ **enough** seltsamer- *od.* merkwürdigerweise

odd 'man *n.* **be the ~**: die entscheidende Stimme haben; ~ **out** Außenseiter, *der*/Außenseiterin, *die;* **be the ~ out** *(extra person)* überzählig sein; *(thing)* zu etw. nicht passen; **find the ~ out** das finden, was überzählig ist/nicht paßt

oddment ['ɒdmənt] *n.* **a)** *(left over)* [Über]rest, *der;* *(in sales)* Reststück, *das;* **b)** *in pl. (odds and ends)* Kleinigkeiten; **~s of furniture** einzelne Möbelstücke

oddness ['ɒdnɪs] *n., no pl.* Merkwürdigkeit, *die;* *(strangeness)* Seltsamkeit, *die*

odd: ~numbered *adj.* ungerade; ~ **one** *see* **odd man**

odds [ɒdz] *n. pl.* **a)** *(Betting)* Odds *pl.*; **the ~ were on Black Bess** Black Bess hatte die besten Chancen; **lay** *or* **give/take ~ of six to one in favour of/against sb./a horse** eine 6:1-Wette auf/gegen jmdn./ein Pferd anbieten/annehmen; **I'll lay ~ that ...** *(fig.)* ich wette, daß ...; **take ~ on sth.** auf etw. *(Akk.)* wetten; **over the ~** *(fig.)* zuviel; **pay over the ~ for sth.** einen überhöhten Preis für etw. bezahlen; **be/go over the ~** *(more than is reasonable)* zu weit gehen; *see also* **long odds; short odds; b)** *(chances for or against)* Möglichkeit, *die;* *(chance for)* Aussicht, *die;* Chance, *die;* **[the] ~ are that she did it** wahrscheinlich hat sie es getan; **the ~ are against/in favour of sb./sth.** jmds. Aussichten *od.* Chancen/die Aussichten *od.* Chancen für etw. sind gering/gut; **the ~ are against/in favour of sth. happening** es besteht kaum/durchaus die Möglichkeit, daß etw. geschieht; **struggle against considerable/impossible ~**: mit ziemlich geringen Chancen/völlig chancenlos kämpfen; **by all ~**: bei weitem; **c)** *(balance of advantage)* **against [all] the ~**: allen Widrigkeiten zum Trotz; **d)** *(difference)* Unterschied, *der;* **make no/little ~ [whether ...]** es ist völlig/ziemlich gleichgültig[, ob ...]; **what's the ~?** was macht das schon?; **e)** *(variance)* **be at ~ [with sb./sth.]** sich nicht [mit jmdm./etw.] vertragen; **be at ~ with sb. over sth.** mit jmdm. in etw. *(Dat.)* uneinig sein; **f) ~ and ends,** *(coll.)* **~ and bobs** Kleinigkeiten; *(of food)* Reste; **~ and sods** *(sl.) (things)* Krempel, *der (ugs. abwertend); (persons)* Figuren *(salopp)*

'odds-on 1. *adj.* gut ‹*Chance, Aussicht*›; hoch, klar ‹*Favorit*›; **be ~ [favourite] to win/for sth.** klarer *od.* hoher Favorit/Favorit für etw. sein. **2.** *adv.* wahrscheinlich; **it's ~ that he is alive** die Chancen stehen gut, daß er am Leben ist

ode [əʊd] *n.* Ode, *die* (to an + *Akk.*)

odious ['əʊdɪəs] *adj.*, **odiously** ['əʊdɪəslɪ] *adv.* widerwärtig

odium ['əʊdɪəm] *n. (hatred)* Haß, *der;* **be held in ~ by sb.** bei jmdm. verhaßt sein

odometer [ə'dɒmɪtə(r)] *n.* Hodometer, *das;* Wegmesser, *der*

odor *etc. (Amer.) see* **odour** *etc.*

odoriferous [əʊdə'rɪfərəs] *adj.* wohlriechend *(geh.)*; duftend

odorous ['əʊdərəs] *adj.* **a)** *(fragrant)* wohlriechend *(geh.)*; duftend; **b)** *(malodorous)* übelriechend; übel ‹*Geruch*›

odour ['əʊdə(r)] *n.* **a)** *(smell)* Geruch, *der;* *(fragrance)* Duft, *der;* **~ of cats** Katzengeruch, *der; see also* **body odour; b)** *(fig.)* Note, *die;* **be in/fall** *or* **get into good/bad ~ with sb.** bei jmdm. in gutem/schlechtem Geruch stehen/in guten/schlechten Geruch kommen

odourless ['əʊdəlɪs] *adj.* geruchlos

Odysseus [ə'dɪsjuːs] *pr. n.* Odysseus *(der)*

odyssey ['ɒdɪsɪ] *n.* abenteuerliche Reise; Odyssee, *die (geh.)*; **the O~** *(Myth.)* die Odyssee

OECD *abbr.* **Organization for Economic Cooperation and Development** OECD, *die*

oedema [ɪ'diːmə] *n. (Med.)* Ödem, *das;* Gewebewassersucht, *die*

Oedipus complex ['iːdɪpəs kɒmpleks] *n. (Psych.)* Ödipuskomplex, *der*

o'er [ɔː(r)] *(poet.) see* **over 1, 2**

oesophagus [iː'sɒfəgəs] *n., pl.* **oesophagi** [iː'sɒfədʒaɪ] *or* **~es** *(Anat.)* Ösophagus, *der (fachspr.)*

oestrogen ['iːstrədʒən] *n. (Biochem.)* Östrogen, *das*

œuvre [ɜːvr] *n.* Œuvre, *das (geh.)*; Werk, *das*

of [əv, *stressed* ɒv] *prep.* **a)** *indicating belonging, connection, possession* **articles of clothing** Kleidungsstücke; **be a thing of the past** der Vergangenheit *(Dat.)* angehören; **topic of conversation** Gesprächsthema, *das;* **the brother of her father** der Bruder ihres Vaters; **a friend of mine/the vicar's** ein Freund von mir/des Pfarrers; **that dog of yours** Ihr Hund da; **it's no business of theirs** es geht sie nichts an; **where's that pencil of mine?** wo ist mein Bleistift?; **b)** *indicating starting-point* von; **within a mile of the centre** nicht weiter als eine Meile vom Zentrum entfernt; **for upwards of 10 years** seit mehr als 10 Jahren; **c)** *indicating origin, cause, agency* **have a taste of garlic** nach Knoblauch schmecken; **it was clever of you to do that** es war klug von dir, das zu tun; **the approval of sb.** jmds. Zustimmung; **be of a good family** aus guter Familie sein; **the works of Shakespeare** Shakespeares Werke; **R. T. Smith, of Oxford** R. T. Smith, Oxford; **Lord Morrison of Lambeth** Lord Morrison von Lambeth; **d)** *indicating material, substance* aus; **a dress of cotton** ein Kleid aus Baumwolle; **be made of ...**: aus ... [hergestellt] sein; **e)** *indicating closer definition, identity, or contents* **a pound of apples** ein Pfund Äpfel; **a glass of wine** ein Glas Wein; **a painting of the queen** ein Gemälde der Königin; **the city of Chicago** die Stadt Chicago; **the Republic of Ireland** die Republik Irland; **Professor of Chemistry** Professor der Chemie; **the Gospel of St Mark** das Markusevangelium; das Evangelium des Markus; **family of eight** achtköpfige Familie; **increase of 10%** Zuwachs/Erhöhung von zehn Prozent; **battle of Hastings** Schlacht von *od.* bei Hastings; **University of Oxford** Universität [von] Oxford; **President of the Philippines** Präsident[in] der Philippinen; **the Queen of Spades** die Pikdame; **the love of God** die Liebe Gottes; **the fifth of January** der fünfte Januar; **your letter of 2 January** Ihr Brief vom 2. Januar; **that fool of a personnel manager** dieser Idiot von Personalleiter; **a fool of a woman** eine törichte Frau; **the worst liar of any man I know** der gemeinste Lügner, den ich kenne; **be of value/interest to** von Nutzen/von Interesse *od.* interessant sein für; **the whole of ...**: der/die/das ganze ...; **tales of adventure** Abenteuergeschichten; **f)** *indicating concern, reference, respect* **do not speak of such things** sprich nicht von solchen Dingen; **inform sb. of sth.** jmdn. über etw. *(Akk.)* informieren; **well, what of it?** *(asked as reply)* na und?; **g)** *indicating objective relation* **love of virtue** Tugendliebe, *die;* **his love of his father** seine Liebe zu seinem Vater; **h)** *indicating description, quality, condition* **a frown of disapproval** ein mißbilligendes Stirnrunzeln; **person of extreme views** Mensch mit extremen Ansichten; **work of authority** maßgebendes Werk; **a boy of 14 years** ein vierzehnjähriger *od.* ein 14 Jahre alter Junge; **a city of wide boulevards** eine Stadt mit breiten Alleen; **i)** *indicating partition, classification, inclusion, selection* von; **of these, three ...**: drei von ihnen ...; *(inanimate)* drei davon; **the five of us** wir fünf; **the five of us went there** wir sind zu fünft hingegangen; **some/five of us** einige/fünf von uns; **there are five of us waiting to see the doctor** wir sind fünf, die auf den Doktor warten; **the most dangerous of enemies** ein sehr gefährlicher Feind; **be too much of a gentleman to do sth.** zu sehr Gentleman sein, um etw. zu tun; **he of all men** *(most unsuitably)* ausgerechnet er; *(especially)* gerade er; **of all the impudence!** das ist doch die Höhe!; **here of all places** ausgerechnet hier; **on this night of nights** in solch einer herrlichen Nacht; **of an evening** *(coll.)* abends; des Abends; **of an evening in June** an einem Juniabend; **j)** *(Amer.: before the hour of)* **a quarter of two** Viertel vor zwei; **k)** *(arch.: by)* von; **beloved of all** von allen geliebt

off [ɒf] **1.** *adv.* **a)** *(away, at or to a distance)* **be a few miles ~**: wenige Meilen entfernt sein; **the lake is not far ~**: der See ist nicht weit [weg *od.* entfernt]; **Christmas is not far ~**: es ist nicht mehr lang bis Weihnachten; **some way ~**: in einiger Entfernung; **where are you ~ to?** wohin gehst du?; **I must be ~**: ich muß fort *od.* weg *od.* los; **I'm ~ now** ich gehe jetzt; **~ with you!** geh/geht!; los jetzt!; **~ with his head!** schlagt ihm den Kopf ab!; **~ we go!** *(we are starting)* los *od.* ab geht's!; *(let us start)* gehen/fahren wir!; **they're ~!** *(coll.)* sie sind gestartet!; *see also* **make off; put off; straight off; b)** *(not on or attached or supported)* **get the lid ~**: den Deckel abbekommen; **c)** *(not in good condition)* mitgenommen; **the meat** *etc.* **is ~**: das Fleisch *usw.* ist schlecht [geworden]; **be a bit ~** *(Brit. fig.)* ein starkes Stück sein *(ugs.)*; **d) be ~** *(switched or turned ~)* ‹*Wasser, Gas, Strom:*› abgestellt sein; **the light/radio** *etc.* **is ~**: das Licht/Radio *usw.* ist aus; **put the light ~**: das Licht ausmachen; **leave the bathroom tap ~**: den Hahn im Badezimmer zulassen; **is the gas tap ~?** ist der Gashahn zu?; **neither the water nor the electricity was ~**: weder Wasser noch Strom waren abgestellt; **e) be ~** *(cancelled)* abgesagt sein; ‹*Verlobung:*› [auf]gelöst sein; **the strike is ~**: der Streik ist abgeblasen *(ugs.)*; **is Sunday's picnic ~?** fällt das Picknick am Sonntag aus?; **~ and on** immer mal wieder *(ugs.)*; **f)** *(not at work)* frei; **on my day ~**: an meinem freien Tag; **take/get/have a week** *etc.* **~**: eine Woche *usw.* Urlaub nehmen/bekommen/haben; **be given a day ~ from school** einen Tag schulfrei haben; **be ~ sick** wegen Krankheit fehlen; **g)** *(no longer available)* **soup** *etc.* **is ~**: es gibt keine Suppe *usw.* mehr; **h)** *(entirely, to the end)* **drink ~**: austrinken; **i)** *(situated as regards money etc.)* **he is badly** *etc.* **~**: er ist schlecht *usw.* gestellt; ihm geht es [finanziell] schlecht *usw.*; **we'd be better ~ without him** ohne ihn wären wir besser dran; **there are many people worse ~ than you** vielen geht es schlechter als dir; **he left her comfortably ~**: er hinterließ ihr genug, um gut zu leben; **how are you ~ for food?** wieviel Eßbares hast du noch?; **be badly ~ for sth.** mit etw. knapp sein; *see also* **well off; j)** *(Theatre)* **take place ~**: hinter der Bühne stattfinden; *see also* **noise 1 b. 2.** *prep.* **a)** *(from)* von; **take a little ~ the**

price ein bißchen vom Preis nachlassen; **cut a couple of slices ~ the loaf** einige Scheiben Brot abschneiden; **be a few inches ~ the finish** ein paar Zentimeter vor dem Ziel entfernt sein; **be ~ school/work** in der Schule/am Arbeitsplatz fehlen; **b)** *(diverging from)* **get ~ the subject, talk ~ the point** [vom Thema] abschweifen; **be ~ the point** nicht zur Sache gehören; **c)** *(designed not to cover)* **~-the-shoulder** schulterfrei ⟨*Kleid*⟩; **an ~-the-face hat** ein Hut, der das Gesicht nicht verdeckt; **d)** *(having lost interest in)* **be ~ sth.** etw. leid sein *od.* haben *(ugs.)*; **be ~ one's food** keinen Appetit haben; **be quite ~ sth.** von etw. vollkommen abgekommen sein; **e)** *(no longer obliged to use)* **be ~ drugs** vom Rauschgift losgekommen sein; clean sein *(ugs.)*; **be ~ one's diet** seine Diät abgesetzt haben; **be ~ the tablets** ohne Tabletten auskommen; **f)** *(leading from, not far from)* **just ~ the square** ganz in der Nähe des Platzes; **a street ~ the main road** eine Straße, die von der Hauptstraße abgeht; **take a turning ~ the main road** von der Hauptstraße abbiegen; **g)** *(to seaward of)* vor (+ *Dat.*); **h)** *(Golf)* **play ~ three** mit Vorgabe drei spielen. *See also* **offside. 3.** *adj.* **a) the ~ side** *(Brit.) (when travelling on the left/right)* die rechte/linke Seite; **b)** *(Cricket)* ⟨*Seite, Torstab:*⟩ links vom Werfer, *(if batsman is left-handed)* rechts vom Werfer; **~ drive** Treibschlag nach rechts; *(by left-handed batsman)* Treibschlag nach links; **~ side** *see* **4 a. 4.** *n.* **a)** *(Cricket) Spielfeldhälfte rechts vom rechtshändigen bzw. links vom linkshändigen Schlagmann*; **b)** *(start of race)* Start, *der*

offal ['ɒfl] *n., no pl.* **a)** *(parts of animal's carcass)* Innereien *Pl.*; **b)** *(carrion)* Aas, *das;* **c)** *(refuse)* Abfall, *der;* **d)** *(fig.: dregs, scum)* Abschaum, *der*

off: ~-beat 1. *n. (Mus.)* unbetonter Taktteil; Off-Beat, *der (fachspr.)*; **2.** *adj.* **a)** *(Mus.)* Off-Beat-; **b)** *(fig.: eccentric)* unkonventionell ⟨*Mensch, Lebensweise*⟩; außergewöhnlich ⟨*Vorlesung, Kursus*⟩; **~-'centre 1.** *adj.* nicht zentriert; **2.** *adv.* nicht [genau] in der Mitte; **~ chance** *see* **chance 1 c**; **~'colour** *adj.* **a)** *(not in good health)* unwohl; **be** *or* **feel ~ colour** sich unwohl *od.* schlecht fühlen; **b)** *(Amer.: somewhat indecent)* schlüpfrig; **~-cut** *n.* Rest, *der;* **~-day** *n.* schlechter Tag; **~-duty** *attrib. adj.* Freizeit-; dienstfrei ⟨*Zeit*⟩; ⟨*Polizist usw.*,⟩ der dienstfrei hat

offence [ə'fens] *n. (Brit.)* **a)** *(hurting of sb.'s feelings)* Kränkung, *die;* **I meant** *or* **intended no ~**: ich wollte Sie/ihn *usw.* nicht kränken; **your behaviour caused [great] ~**: Ihr Benehmen war [sehr] kränkend *od.* verletzend; **b)** *(annoyance)* **give ~**: Mißfallen erregen; **take ~**: beleidigt *od.* verärgert sein; **don't take ~, but ...**: nimm es mir nicht übel, aber ...; **no ~** *(coll.)* nichts für ungut; **no ~ to you, but ...** *(coll.)* nichts gegen dich, aber ... *(ugs.)*; **c)** *(transgression)* Verstoß, *der; (crime)* Delikt, *das;* Straftat, *die;* **an ~ against good taste** eine Beleidigung des guten Geschmacks; **criminal/petty ~**: strafbare Handlung/geringfügiges Vergehen; **d)** *(attacking)* Angriff, *der*

offend [ə'fend] **1.** *v. i.* verstoßen (**against** gegen). **2.** *v. t.* **~ sb.** bei jmdm. Anstoß erregen; *(hurt feelings of)* jmdn. kränken; **she was ~ed with him** sie war ihm böse; **~ the eye** das Auge beleidigen; **her delicacy was ~ed** ihr Zartgefühl war verletzt; *abs.* **a refusal often ~s** eine Ablehnung wird oft als Kränkung empfunden

offender [ə'fendə(r)] *n. (against law)* Straffällige, *der/die;* Täter, *der*/Täterin, *die; (against rule)* Zuwiderhandelnde, *der/die; see also* **first offender**

offending [ə'fendɪŋ] *attrib. adj.* **a)** *(that outrages)* anstößig; Anstoß erregend; **he removed the ~ object** er beseitigte den Stein des Anstoßes; **b)** *(that transgresses)* zuwiderhandelnd; **there are penalties for ~ persons** Zuwiderhandlungen werden bestraft

offense *(Amer.) see* **offence**

offensive [ə'fensɪv] **1.** *adj.* **a)** *(aggressive)* offensiv; Angriffs⟨*waffe, -krieg*⟩; **b)** *(giving offence, insulting)* ungehörig; *(indecent)* anstößig; **~ language** Beschimpfungen; **c)** *(repulsive)* widerlich; **be ~ to sb.** jmdm. zuwider sein; auf jmdn. abstoßend wirken. **2.** *n.* **a)** *(attitude of assailant)* offensive Haltung; **take the** *or* **go on the ~**: in die *od.* zur Offensive übergehen; **be on the ~**: aggressiv sein; **b)** *(attack)* Offensive, *die;* Angriff, *der;* **c)** *(fig.: forceful action)* Offensive, *die*

offensively [ə'fensɪvlɪ] *adv.* **a)** *(aggressively)* offensiv; **b)** *(insultingly)* auf beleidigende Weise; *(indecently)* unverschämt; **c)** *(repulsively)* widerlich; abstoßend

offer ['ɒfə(r)] **1.** *v. t.* **a)** anbieten; vorbringen ⟨*Entschuldigung*⟩; bieten ⟨*Chance*⟩; aussprechen ⟨*Beileid*⟩; sagen ⟨*Meinung*⟩; unterbreiten, machen ⟨*Vorschläge*⟩; bieten, spenden ⟨*Schatten*⟩; **have something to ~**: etwas zu bieten haben; **the job ~s good prospects** der Arbeitsplatz hat Zukunft; **b)** *(present to deity etc.)* **~ [up]** opfern; **~ up a sacrifice** ein Opfer darbringen *(geh.)*; **~ prayers for the dead** für die Toten beten; **c)** *(have for sale)* anbieten; **d)** *(show readiness for)* **~ resistance** Widerstand leisten; **~ violence** gewalttätig werden; **~ peace** für den Frieden eintreten; **~ to do sth.** anbieten, etw. zu tun; **~ to help** seine Hilfe anbieten; **e)** *(present to sight or notice)* bieten; **f)** *(Sch., Univ.)* belegen ⟨*Fach*⟩. **2.** *v. i.* ⟨*Gelegenheit, Chance:*⟩ sich bieten. **3.** *n.* **a)** Angebot, *das; (in auction)* Gebot, *das;* **all ~s of help** alle Hilfeangebote; **[have/be] on ~**: im Angebot [haben/sein]; **b)** *(marriage proposal)* Antrag, *der*

offering ['ɒfərɪŋ] *n.* **a)** *no pl. (act)* Anbieten, *das; (to deity)* Opfern, *das;* **b)** *(thing)* Angebot, *das; (to a deity)* Opfer, *das;* **the latest ~ from the publishers** *(joc.)* was die Verleger als Neuestes anbieten

offertory ['ɒfətərɪ] *n. (Eccl.)* **a)** *(part of Mass)* Offertorium, *das;* **b)** *(collection of money)* Kollekte, *die*

off: ~'hand 1. *adv.* **a)** *(without preparation)* auf Anhieb, aus der Hand *(ugs.)* ⟨*sagen, wissen*⟩; spontan ⟨*beschließen, entscheiden*⟩; **b)** *(casually)* leichthin; **2.** *adj.* **a)** *(without preparation)* impulsiv; spontan; **b)** *(casual)* beiläufig; **be ~hand with sb.** zu jmdm. kurz angebunden sein; **he was very ~hand about the whole business** er war, was die ganze Geschichte betrifft, sehr kurz angebunden; **~handed** [ɒf'hændɪd] *see* **~hand 2 b**

office ['ɒfɪs] *n.* **a)** Büro, *das;* **goods ~**: Güterabfertigung, *die;* **b)** *(branch of organization)* Zweigstelle, *die;* Geschäftsstelle, *die;* **c)** *(position with duties)* Amt, *das;* **be in/out of ~**: im/nicht mehr im Amt sein; ⟨*Partei:*⟩ an der/nicht mehr an der Regierung sein; **resign ~**: sein Amt niederlegen; **hold ~**: amtieren; **d)** *(government department)* **Home O~** *(Brit.)* ≈ Innenministerium, *das;* **the Passport O~**: das Paßamt; **e) the usual ~s** *(Brit.: of house)* ≈ Küche, Bad, WC *usw.*; **f)** *(Eccl.) (service)* Gottesdienst, *der; (mass)* Messe, *die (kath. Kirche)*; **O~ for Baptism** Taufbekenntnis *od.* -versprechen, *das;* **O~ for the Dead** Trauergottesdienst, *der;* Totenmesse, *die (kath. Kirche)*; **g) the Holy O~** *(RC Ch.)* das Heilige Officium; **h)** *(kindness)* **[good] ~s** Hilfe, *die;* Unterstützung, *die;* **use one's good ~s to help sb.** jmdm. mit Rat und Tat zur Seite stehen; **i)** *(Amer.: consulting-room)* Büro, *das; (of lawyer)* Kanzlei, *die;* Büro, *das; (of physician)* Sprechzimmer, *das*

office: ~-bearer *n.* Amtsinhaber, *der/*-inhaberin, *die;* **~-block** *n.* Bürogebäude, *das;* **~-boy** *n.* Bürogehilfe, *der;* **~-girl** *n.* Bürogehilfin, *die;* **~ hours** *n. pl.* Dienststunden *Pl.*; Dienstzeit, *die;* **after ~ hours** nach Dienstschluß; **~ job** *n.* Bürotätigkeit, *die;* Bürojob, *der (ugs.)*

officer ['ɒfɪsə(r)] *n.* **a)** *(Army etc.)* Offizier, *der;* **~ of the day** Offizier vom Dienst; **b)** *(holder of office)* Beamte, *der/*Beamtin, *die;* **~ of arms** *(Her.)* Mitglied des Heroldskollegiums; **c)** *(of club etc.)* Funktionär, *der*/Funktionärin, *die;* **d)** *(constable)* Polizeibeamte, *der/*-beamtin, *die;* **yes, ~**: jawohl, Herr Wachtmeister/Frau Wachtmeisterin; **e)** *(bailiff)* **[sheriff's] ~**: Vollstreckungsbeamte, *der/*-beamtin, *die;* **f)** *(member of honorary Order)* **O~ of the Order of the British Empire** Träger des britischen Verdienstordens; **O~ of the Legion of Honour** Ritter der Ehrenlegion

'office-worker *n.* Büroangestellte, *der/die*

official [ə'fɪʃl] **1.** *adj.* **a)** Amts⟨*pflicht, -robe, -person*⟩; **b)** *(derived from authority, formal)* offiziell; amtlich ⟨*Verlautbarung*⟩; regulär ⟨*Streik*⟩; **he is here on ~ business** er ist dienstlich hier; **~ secret** Staatsgeheimnis, *das;* **O~ Secrets Act** *(Brit.)* Gesetz über Landesverrat und Gefährdung der äußeren Sicherheit; **is it ~ yet?** *(coll.)* ist das schon amtlich? **2.** *n.* Beamte, *der/*Beamtin, *die; (party, union, or sports ~)* Funktionär, *der*/Funktionärin, *die*

officialdom [ə'fɪʃldəm] *n., no pl., no art.* Beamtentum, *das;* Bürokratie, *die*

officialese [əfɪʃə'li:z] *n., no pl. (derog.)* Behördensprache, *die;* *(German)* Amtsdeutsch, *das*

officially [ə'fɪʃəlɪ] *adv.* offiziell

officiate [ə'fɪʃɪeɪt] *v. i.* **a) ~ as ...**: fungieren als ...; **she ~d as hostess** sie übernahm die Rolle der Gastgeberin; **b)** *(perform religious ceremony)* **~ at the service** den Gottesdienst abhalten; **~ at a wedding** eine Trauung vornehmen

officious [ə'fɪʃəs] *adj.*, **officiously** [ə'fɪʃəslɪ] *adv.* übereifrig

officiousness [ə'fɪʃəsnɪs] *n., no pl.* Übereifer, *der*

offing ['ɒfɪŋ] *n.* **be in the ~** *(fig.)* bevorstehen; ⟨*Gewitter:*⟩ aufziehen

off: ~-'key 1. *adj.* verstimmt; *(fig.: incongruous)* falsch; **2.** *adv.* falsch ⟨*singen, spielen*⟩; **~-licence** *n. (Brit.)* **a)** *(premises)* ≈ Wein- und Spirituosenladen, *der;* **b)** *(licence)* Konzession für den Verkauf alkoholischer Getränke über die Straße; **~-line** *(Computing)* **1.** ['--] *adj.* Off-line-⟨*Gerät, Betrieb*⟩; **2.** [-'-] *adv.* off line; **~-load** *v. t.* abladen; **~-load sth. on to sb.** *(fig.: get rid of)* etw. bei jmdm. loswerden; **~-peak** *attrib. adj.* **during ~-peak hours** außerhalb der Spitzenlastzeiten; *(of traffic)* außerhalb der Stoßzeiten; **at ~-peak times** *(Telev.)* außerhalb der Haupteinschaltzeit; **~-peak power** *or* **electricity** Nachtstrom, *der;* **~-peak storage heating** Nachtspeicherheizung, *die;* **~print** *n.* Sonderdruck, *der;* **~-putting** ['ɒfpʊtɪŋ] *adj. (Brit. coll.)* abstoßend ⟨*Gesicht, Äußeres, Weg*⟩; abschreckend ⟨*Umfang*⟩; deprimierend ⟨*Anblick*⟩; **~-season** *n.* Nebensaison, *die;* **~set 1.** *n.* **a)** *(compensation)* Ausgleich, *der;* **act as an ~set to sth., be an ~set for sth.** etw. ausgleichen *od.* aufwiegen; **b)** *(Printing: unwanted transfer of ink)* Schmutzen, *das;* Abliegen, *das;* **c) ~set [process]** *(Printing)* Offsetdruck, *der;* **d)** *(Archit.)* Vorsprung, *der;* **2.** ['--, -'-] *v. t., forms as* **set**: **a)** *(counterbalance)* ausgleichen; **b)** *(place out of line)* versetzen; **c)** *(Printing)* im Offsetverfahren drucken; **~shoot** *n.* **a)** *(of plant)* Sproß, *der; (of mountain range)* Ausläufer, *der;* **b)** *(fig.: descendant)* Sproß, *der (geh.)*; Nachkomme, *der;* **c)** *(derivative)* Ableger, *der (fig.)*; *(of religion, philosophy, etc.)* Nebenströmung, *die;* **~shore** *adj.* **a)** *(situated at sea)* küstennah; off shore *(Energiewirtsch.)*; **~shore island** küstennahe Insel; **b)** *(made or registered abroad)* Auslands-; **~shore order** Off-shore-Auftrag, *der;* **c)** *(blowing seawards)* ablandig *(Seemannsspr.)*; **~'side** *adj. (Sport)* Abseits-; **be ~side** abseits *od.* im Abseits sein; **~side trap** Abseitsfalle, *die;* **~spring** *n., pl. same (progeny) (human)* Nachkommenschaft, *die; (of animal)* Junge; **~-'stage 1.** *adj.* in den Kulissen *nachgestellt;* **2.** *adv.* in den Kulissen; **go ~-stage** abgehen; **~-street** *adj.* außerhalb des Straßenbereiches *nachgestellt;* **~-street parking** Stellplatz, *der; (for several cars)* Stellplätze; **~-the-peg** *attrib. adj.* Konfektions-; von der Stange *nachgestellt;* **~-time** *n.* ruhige Zeit; **~ 'white** *adj.* gebrochen weiß; *(yellowish)* vergilbt; **~-year** *n. (Amer.)* Wahljahr, in dem kein Präsident gewählt wird

oft [ɒft] *adv. (arch./literary)* oft; **the ~-told tales** die immer wieder erzählten Geschichten; **~-repeated/-recurring** häufig wiederholt/wiederkehrend; **many a time and ~:** oft genug

often ['ɒfn, 'ɒftn] *adv.* oft; **more ~:** häufiger; **do sth. as ~ as not** etw. genauso oft tun wie man es nicht tut; **more ~ than not** meistens; **every so ~:** gelegentlich; hin und wieder; **once too ~:** einmal zuviel

ogee ['əʊdʒi:, əʊ'dʒi:] **1.** *n.* Karnies, *das (Archit.); (line)* S-Kurve, *die.* **2.** *adj.* S-förmig; **~ arch** *(Archit.)* Eselsrücken, *der*

ogle ['əʊgl] **1.** *v. i.* gaffen *(ugs. abwertend);* **~ at sb.** jmdn. angaffen *(ugs. abwertend).* **2.** *v. t.* **~ sb.** jmdn. angaffen *(ugs. abwertend)*

ogre ['əʊgə(r)] *n.* **a)** *(giant)* Oger, *der;* [menschenfressender] Riese; **b)** *(terrifying person)* Ungeheuer, *das; (terrifying thing)* Schreckbild, *das*

[1]**oh** [əʊ] *int.* oh; *expr. pain* au; **'oh no [you don't]!** auf keinen Fall!; **oh 'no!** o nein!; oje!; **oh 'well** na ja *(ugs.);* tja *(ugs.);* **'oh yes** oh ja; **oh 'yes?** ach ja?; **oh, 'him/'that!** *(coll.)* ach, der/das!; *see also* **boy 2**

[2]**oh** *n. (zero)* Null, *die*

ohm [əʊm] *n. (Electr.)* Ohm, *das;* **Ohm's law** das Ohmsche Gesetz

OHMS *abbr.* **on Her/His Majesty's service** *see* **service 1 m**

oho [əʊ'həʊ] *int.* he

'oh-so- *pref. (coll. derog.)* ach so ⟨*schlau, schick*⟩

oil [ɔɪl] **1.** *n.* **a)** Öl, *das;* **burn the midnight ~** *(fig.)* bis spät in die Nacht arbeiten; **strike ~** *(lit.)* auf Öl stoßen; *(fig.)* das große Los ziehen; *see also* **mineral oil; pour 1 a; b)** *in pl. (paints)* Ölfarben; **paint in ~s** in Öl malen; **c)** *(coll.: picture)* Ölbild, *das.* **2.** *v. t.* **a)** *(apply ~ to)* ölen; **~ the wheels** *(fig.)* den Karren schmieren; **b)** *(supply with ~)* [mit Öl] betanken ⟨*Schiff usw.*⟩; **c)** *(impregnate with ~)* mit Öl behandeln; **~ed silk** Ölseide, *die;* **d) well ~ed** *(fig. sl.: drunk)* abgefüllt

oil: ~-burner *n.* **a)** *(steamship/locomotive)* Dampfschiff/Lokomotive mit Ölfeuerung; **b)** *(device)* Ölbrenner, *der;* **~-burning** *adj.* ölbetrieben; ölgeheizt ⟨*Ofen*⟩; ölgefeuert ⟨*Lokomotive, Schiff*⟩; Ölfeuerungs⟨*anlage, -kessel*⟩; Öl⟨*ofen, -heizung, -lampe*⟩; **~cake** *n., no pl. (Agric.)* Ölkuchen, *der;* **~can** *n.* Ölkanne, *die;* **~-change** *n. (Motor Veh.)* Ölwechsel, *der;* **~cloth** *n.* **a)** *no pl. (waterproofed fabric)* Öltuch, *das;* **b)** *(covering for tables or shelves)* Wachstuch, *das;* Öltuch, *das; (covering for floor)* ≈ Linoleum, *das;* **~-colour** *n., usu. in pl.* Ölfarbe, *die;* **[painted] in ~-colours** in Öl [gemalt]; **~ drum** *n.* Ölfaß, *das;* **~field** *n.* Ölfeld, *das;* **~-fired** *adj.* ölgefeuert; ölbetrieben ⟨*Zentralheizung*⟩; **~-gauge** *n. (Mech. Engin.)* Ölstandsanzeiger, *der;* **~-heater** *n.* Ölofen, *der;* **~ industry** *n.* Mineralölindustrie, *die;* **~-lamp** *n.* Öllampe, *die;* Petroleumlampe, *die;* **~ level** *n.* Ölstand, *der;* **~man** *n.* **a)** *(seller of ~)* Ölhändler, *der/-*händlerin, *die;* **b)** *(industrialist)* Unternehmer in der Ölbranche; *(worker)* Ölarbeiter, *der;* **~-paint** *see* **~-colour; ~-painting** *n.* **a)** *(activity)* Ölmalerei, *die;* **b)** *(picture)* Ölgemälde, *das;* **he/she is no ~-painting** *(coll.)* er/sie ist keine [strahlende] Schönheit; **~-producing** *attrib. adj.* Öl⟨*pflanze, -saat, -schiefer, -sand, -schicht*⟩; [erd]ölfördernd ⟨*Land*⟩; **~-rag** *n.* Öllappen, *der;* **~ refinery** *n.* [Erd]ölraffinerie, *die;* **~-rich** *adj.* ⟨*Land, Gebiet*⟩ mit großem [Erd]ölvorkommen; ölhaltig ⟨*Schiefer, Sand usw.*⟩; **~ rig** *see* [1]**rig 1 b; ~-shale** *n. (Geol.)* Ölschiefer, *der;* **~skin** *n.* **a)** *(material)* Öltuch, *das; attrib.* aus Öltuch *nachgestellt;* **~skin jacket** Öljacke, *die;* **b)** *(garment)* **put on ~skins/an ~skin** Ölzeug anziehen; **~-slick** *see* **slick 2; ~-soluble** *adj.* öllöslich; **~-stove** *n.* Ölofen, *der;* **~-tanker** *n.* Öltanker, *der;* **~ well** *n.* Ölquelle, *die*

oily ['ɔɪlɪ] *adj.* **a)** ölig ⟨*Oberfläche, Hände, Lappen, Flüssigkeit, Geschmack*⟩; Öl⟨*lache, -fleck*⟩; ölverschmiert ⟨*Gesicht, Hände*⟩; verölt ⟨*Motor*⟩; *(containing oil)* viel Öl enthaltend ⟨*Soße*⟩; fettig ⟨*Haut, Haar*⟩; **the food is very ~:** das Essen schwimmt in Öl *(ugs.);* **b)** *(fig.: unctuous, fawning)* schmierig *(abwertend)* ⟨*Kerl, Art*⟩; ölig ⟨*Lächeln, Stimme*⟩

ointment ['ɔɪntmənt] *n.* Salbe, *die; see also* [1]**fly a**

OK [əʊ'keɪ] *(coll.)* **1.** *adj.* in Ordnung; okay *(ugs.);* **[it's] OK by me** mir ist es recht. **2.** *adv.* gut; **be doing OK** seine Sache gut machen. **3.** *int.* okay *(ugs.);* **OK?** [ist das] klar?; okay?. **4.** *n.* Zustimmung, *die;* Okay, *das (ugs.).* **5.** *v. t. (approve)* zustimmen (+ *Dat.*); sein Okay geben (+ *Dat.*) *(ugs.);* **be OK'd by sb.** von jmdm. das Okay bekommen *(ugs.)*

okay [əʊ'keɪ] *see* **OK**

okey-doke [əʊkɪ'dəʊk] *(sl.),* **okey-dokey** [əʊkɪ'dəʊkɪ] *(sl.) see* **OK 3**

old [əʊld] **1.** *adj.* **a)** alt; **[not] be ~ enough to do sth.** [noch nicht] alt genug sein, um etw. zu tun; **he is ~ enough to know better** aus diesem Alter ist er heraus; **he/she is ~ enough to be your father/mother** er/sie könnte dein Vater/deine Mutter sein; **be/get too ~ for doing sth.** *or* **to do sth.** zu alt sein/langsam zu alt sein, um etw. zu tun; **be ~ beyond one's years** seinem Alter voraus sein; **if I live to be that ~:** wenn ich je so alt werde; **grow ~ [gracefully]** [mit Würde] alt werden; **that dress/that new hair-style makes you look ~:** dieses Kleid/diese neue Frisur macht dich alt; **make/get/be/seem ~ before one's time** frühzeitig altern lassen/altern/gealtert sein/gealtert wirken; **be [more than] 30 years ~:** [über] 30 Jahre alt sein; **at ten years ~:** im Alter von 10 Jahren; mit 10 Jahren; *see also* [2]**buffer; fogy;** [1]**fool 1 a; shoulder 1 b; b)** *(experienced)* **be an ~ hand** *or (Brit.)* **stager** ein alter Hase sein *(ugs.);* **an ~ offender** ein mehrfach Vorbestrafter; *see also* **campaigner b; contemptible;** [2]**lag; retainer a; salt 1 d; c)** *(long in use, matured with keeping, long familiar)* alt; **~ iron** Alteisen, *das;* **be still working for one's** *or* **the same ~ firm** noch immer in seiner alten *od.* derselben Firma arbeiten; **you see the same ~ people/faces wherever you go** man sieht immer dieselben Leute/Gesichter, wohin man auch geht; **keep quarrelling over the same ~ thing** immer wieder über dasselbe leidige Thema streiten; **Old Pals Act** *(Brit. joc.)* ≈ Vitamin B *(ugs. scherzh.);* **the ~ firm** *(fig. coll.)* das altbewährte Team; **of the ~ school** *(fig.)* der alten Schule; **that's an '~ one!** *(joke)* der ist [doch] alt!; *(excuse)* das kennen wir schon!; **[as] ~ as the hills** uralt; **that joke is [as] ~ as the hills** dieser Witz hat so einen Bart *(ugs.);* **be as ~ as time** seit Urzeiten bestehen; *see also* **brigade a; score 1 f;** [1]**story a; world d; d)** *in playful or friendly mention* alt *(ugs.);* **you lucky ~ so-and-so!** du bist vielleicht ein alter Glückspilz!; **I saw ~ George today** ich habe heute unsern Freund George getroffen; **I pulled out the ~ cigarette-lighter** ich holte mein Feuerzeug raus; **~ chap/fellow/son** alter Junge *(fam.);* **~ bean/stick/thing** *(coll.)* altes Haus *(ugs. scherzh.);* **[such] a dear ~ thing** [so] ein lieber Mensch; **Old Bill** *(Brit. sl.) (police force)* die Polente *(salopp); (policeman)* Polyp, *der (salopp);* **Old Harry** *or* **Nick** der Teufel; der Leibhaftige *(verhüll.);* **good/dear ~ Harry/London** *(coll.)* der gute alte Harry/das gute alte London; **that car needs a good ~ clean** *or* **wash** *(coll.)* das Auto muß einmal ordentlich gewaschen werden; **have a fine** *or* **good ~ time** *(sl.)* sich köstlich amüsieren; **a fair ~ wind** *(coll.)* ein ganz schöner Wind; **poor ~ Jim/my poor ~ arm** armer Jim/mein armer Arm *(ugs.);* **there was little ~ me, not knowing what to do** *(Amer.)* da war ich nun und wußte nicht, was ich tun sollte; **your silly** *or* **stupid ~ camera** deine blöde *(ugs.)* Kamera; **you silly ~ thing** du dummer Kerl/*(woman)* dummes Ding *(ugs.);* **a load of ~ rubbish** *(coll.)* nichts als blanker Unsinn; **any ~ thing** *(sl.)* irgendwas *(ugs.);* irgendetwas; **any ~ how** *(sl.)* irgendwie; **he just pulls his hat on any ~ how** er setzt sich den Hut auf, wie's grad kommt *(ugs.);* **any ~ place** *or* **where** *(coll.)* irgendwo; **any ~ place will do for me** mir ist alles *od.* jeder Ort recht; **any ~ time** *(coll.)* jederzeit; **any ~ piece of paper** *(coll.)* irgendein Blatt Papier; *see also* **high 1 n; e)** *(belonging to past times)* alt; **in the ~ days** früher; *see also* **bad 1 a; good 1 d, h; f)** *(former)* alt ⟨*Wohnung, Firma, Arbeit, Name*⟩; **at 'my ~ school** in meiner Schule; **~ school tie** *Krawatte mit den Farben der Public School; (fig.) Begünstigung von Absolventen der Public Schools;* ≈ Vitamin B *(ugs. scherzh.);* **the ~ year** das alte Jahr; *see also* **flame 1 c; g)** *(Ling.)* alt⟨*englisch, -lateinisch*⟩. **2.** *n.* **a) the ~** *constr. as pl. (~ people)* alte Menschen; *constr. as sing. (~ things)* Altes; das Alte; **young and ~, ~ and young** jung und alt; alt und jung; **b) the customs/knights of ~:** die Sitten/Ritter früherer Zeiten; die alten Sitten/Ritter; **in [the] days of ~:** in [den] alten Zeiten; **of ~** *(formerly)* einst; *(since the ~ days)* seit jeher; **I know him of ~:** ich kenne ihn von früher; **as of ~:** wie eh und je; wie seit jeher; **from of ~:** von alters her *(geh.)*

old: ~ 'age *n., no pl.* [fortgeschrittenes] Alter; **it must be the effect of ~ age** das muß das Alter bewirken; **die of ~ age** an Altersschwäche sterben; **in ~ age** im [fortgeschrittenen] Alter; **in my** *etc.* **~ age** auf meine *usw.* alten Tage; **you've become quite sensible in your ~ age** *(joc.)* du bist ja doch noch ein ganz vernünftiger Mensch geworden; **live to a ripe ~ age/to the ripe ~ age of ...** *(coll.)* ein hohes Alter/das hohe Alter von ... erreichen; **~-age** *attrib. adj.* Alters⟨*rente, -ruhegeld, -versicherung*⟩; **~-age pensioner** Rentner, *der/*Rentnerin, *die;* **Old 'Bailey** *see* **bailey; ~ boy** *n.* **a)** ehemaliger Schüler; Ehemalige, *der;* **~ boys' reunion** Ehemaligentreffen, *das;* **b)** *(coll.: elderly man or male animal)* alter Knabe *(ugs.);* **c)** *as voc.* alter Junge *od.* Knabe *(ugs.);* Alter *(ugs.);* **~-boy network** *n.* *Filzokratie (ugs.) der Absolventen britischer Eliteschulen und -universitäten;* **~ 'clothes** *n. pl. (worn, shabby clothes)* alte Kleidung *od. (ugs.)* Klamotten; *(discarded clothes)* getragene Kleidung *od.* Kleider; Altkleider *Pl.;* **~ 'country** *n.* **the ~ country** das Heimatland; die Heimat; **~ 'dear** *n. (woman)* ältere Frau; *(iron.)* Alte, *die (ugs.)*

olden ['əʊldn] *adj. (literary)* alt; **in [the] ~**

days *or* **times** in alten Zeiten; **people** *etc.* **of ~ times** Menschen *usw.* früherer Zeiten
Old 'English 1. *n. (Ling.) see* **English 2 a. 2.** *adj.* altenglisch; **~ marmalade** englische Marmelade nach altem Rezept; *see also* **sheep-dog**
old-es'tablished *adj.* alt ‹*Tradition, Brauch*›; alteingesessen ‹*Firma, Geschäft, Familie*›
olde-worlde [əʊldɪ'wɜ:ldɪ] *adj. (coll. joc.)* altertümlich
old: ~-fashioned [əʊld'fæʃnd] **1.** *adj.* altmodisch; ‹*Weihnachtsfest*› nach altem Brauch; **an ~-fashioned look** ein mißbilligender Blick; **2.** *n. (Amer.)* Old Fashioned, *der;* **~ 'folk's home** *see* **~ people's home; Old 'French** *(Ling.)* **1.** *n.* Altfranzösisch, *das;* **2.** *adj.* altfranzösisch; **~ 'girl** *n.* **a)** ehemalige Schülerin; Ehemalige, *die;* **b)** *(coll.: elderly woman or female animal)* altes Mädchen *(ugs.);* alte Dame; **c) the/one's ~ girl** *(coll.) (mother)* die/seine Alte Dame *(ugs.); (mother, wife)* die/seine Alte *(ugs.); (car)* die/seine alte Kutsche *(ugs.);* **d)** *as voc.* altes Mädchen; **Old 'Glory** *n., no pl., no art. (Amer.)* das Sternenbanner; **~ 'gold 1.** *n.* Altgold, *das;* **2.** *adj.* altgolden; **~ guard** *n.* alte Garde; **a man** *or* **one of the ~ guard** einer von der alten Garde; **~ 'hat** *pred. adj. see* **hat b; Old High 'German** *(Ling.)* **1.** *n.* Althochdeutsch, *das;* **2.** *adj.* althochdeutsch; **Old 'Hundredth** *see* **hundredth 2 b**
oldie ['əʊldɪ] *n. (coll.) (person)* Oldie, *der (ugs.);* Oldtimer, *der (scherzh.); (song, record, etc.)* Oldie, *der (ugs.); (film)* alter Streifen *(ugs.); (joke)* olle *od.* alte Kamelle *(ugs.);* **golden ~:** guter Oldie
oldish ['əʊldɪʃ] *adj.* älter
old: ~ 'lady *n.* **a)** alte *od.* ältere Dame; **quite an ~ lady** eine recht alte Dame; **b) the/one's ~ lady** *(coll.) see* **~ girl c; the Old Lady of Threadneedle Street** *(Brit.)* die Bank von England; **~-line** *adj. (Amer.) (established, experienced)* alterfahren ‹*Personen*›; alteingeführt ‹*Unternehmen, Institution*›; *(conservative)* konservativ; *(traditional)* ‹*Diplomat*› alter Schule; **~ 'maid** *n.* **a)** *(elderly spinster)* alte Jungfer *(abwertend);* **b)** *(fig.: precise, fussy, prim person)* altjüngferliche Person; **~-maidish** [əʊld'meɪdɪʃ] *adj.* altjüngferlich; **~ 'man** *n.* **a)** *(aged man)* alter Mann; **b)** *(sl.: superior)* **the ~ man** der Alte *(ugs.);* **c)** *(coll.: father, husband)* **the/one's ~ man** der Alte/sein Alter *(ugs.);* **d)** *as voc.* alter Junge *od.* Knabe *(ugs. oft scherzh.);* Alter *(ugs.);* **~ man's 'beard** *n. (Bot.)* Waldrebe, *die;* **~ 'master** *n. (Art)* alter Meister; **~ 'people's home** *n.* Altenheim, *das;* Altersheim, *das;* **Old Pre'tender** *see* **pretender; ~ 'soldier** *n.* alt[gedient]er Soldat; *(fig.)* alter Hase *(ugs.);* **come the ~ soldier over sb.** *(fig.)* sich jmdm. gegenüber als der Erfahrenere aufspielen; **~ soldiers never die** ein alter Soldat ist nicht so leicht unterzukriegen *(ugs.)*
oldster ['əʊldstə(r)] *n.* alter Mensch; **the/we ~s** die/wir Alten
old: ~-style *attrib. adj.* alten Stils *nachgestellt;* alt ‹*Geldschein, Münze*›; **Old 'Testament** *see* **testament a; ~-time** *adj.* früherer Zeiten *nachgestellt;* von Anno dazumal *nachgestellt;* **~-time dancing** alte Tänze; **~-'timer** *n.* **a)** *(person with long experience)* alter Hase *(ugs.);* Oldtimer, *der (scherzh.);* **b)** *(Amer.) (~ person)* Alte, *der/die; (~ or antique thing)* Oldtimer, *der;* **~ 'wives' tale** *n.* Ammenmärchen, *das;* Altweibermärchen, *das;* **~ 'woman** *n.* **a)** alte Frau; *(fig.: fussy or timid person)* altes Weib *(abwertend);* **b)** *(coll.: mother, wife)* **the/one's ~ woman** *see* **~ girl c; ~-'womanish** *adj.* altweiberhaft; **~-world** *adj. (belonging to ~ times, quaint)* altertümlich; altväterisch ‹*Höflichkeit, Benehmen*›

oleaginous [əʊlɪ'ædʒɪnəs] *adj.* **a)** *(oily, greasy)* ölig; **b)** *(producing oil)* ölhaltig
oleander [əʊlɪ'ændə(r)] *n. (Bot.)* Oleander, *der*
O level ['əʊ levl] *n. (Brit. Sch. Hist.) Abschluß der Mittelstufe (auch in der Erwachsenenbildung als Qualifikation);* **he has five ~s** er hat die 'O'-level-Prüfung in fünf Fächern bestanden
olfactory [ɒl'fæktərɪ] *adj.* olfaktorisch *(geh.);* Geruchs‹*nerv, -sinn*›
oligarchic[al] [ɒlɪ'gɑ:kɪk(l)] *adj. (Polit.)* oligarchisch
oligarchy ['ɒlɪgɑ:kɪ] *n. (Polit.)* Oligarchie, *die*
olive ['ɒlɪv] **1.** *n.* **a)** *(tree)* Ölbaum, *der;* Olivenbaum, *der;* **b)** *(fruit)* Olive, *die;* **c)** *(emblem of peace)* Ölzweig, *der;* **d) ~[-wood]** Olivenholz, *das;* **e)** *(Cookery)* **[beef] ~:** [Rinds]roulade, *die;* **f)** *(colour)* Olivgrün, *das.* **2.** *adj.* **a)** olivgrün; **b)** *(in complexion)* oliv[farben]; olivbraun
olive: ~-branch *n. (fig.)* Friedensangebot, *das;* **offer the ~-branch** ein Versöhnungs- *od.* Friedensangebot machen; **~ 'drab** *n.* Olivgrau, *das;* **~-green 1.** ['---] *adj.* olivgrün; **2.** [--'-] *n.* Olivgrün, *das;* **~ 'oil** *n.* Olivenöl, *das*
Olympiad [ə'lɪmpɪæd] *n.* Olympiade, *die*
Olympian [ə'lɪmpɪən] **1.** *adj.* **a)** *(Greek Mythol.)* olympisch; **the ~ gods** die Götter des Olymp; **b)** *(superior)* olympisch *(geh.);* **c)** *see* **Olympic. 2.** *n.* **a)** *(Greek Mythol.)* Olympier, *der*/Olympierin, *die;* **b)** *(competitor in modern Olympics)* olympischer [Wett]kämpfer/olympische [Wett]kämpferin; Olympionike, *der*/Olympionikin, *die*
Olympic [ə'lɪmpɪk] *adj.* olympisch; **~ Games** Olympische Spiele; **~ champion** Olympiasieger, *der*/-siegerin, *die*
Olympics [ə'lɪmpɪks] *n. pl.* Olympiade, *die;* **Winter ~:** Winterolympiade, *die*
Olympus [ə'lɪmpəs] *(Greek Ant.)* Olymp, *der*
OM *abbr. (Brit.)* **Order of Merit**
ombudsman ['ɒmbʊdzmən] *n., pl.* **ombudsmen** ['ɒmbʊdzmən] Ombudsmann, *der*
omega ['əʊmɪgə] *n. (letter)* Omega, *das; see also* **alpha a**
omelette (omelet) ['ɒmlɪt] *n. (Gastr.)* Omelett, *das;* **one cannot make an ~ without breaking eggs** wo gehobelt wird, [da] fallen Späne *(Spr.)*
omen ['əʊmən] *n.* Omen, *das;* Vorzeichen, *das*
ominous ['ɒmɪnəs] *adj. (of evil omen)* ominös; *(worrying)* beunruhigend; **seem ~:** Schlimmes ahnen lassen
ominously ['ɒmɪnəslɪ] *adv.* bedrohlich; beunruhigend ‹*still*›
omissible [ə'mɪsɪbl] *adj.* weglaßbar; **that is ~:** das kann man weglassen
omission [ə'mɪʃn] *n.* **a)** Auslassung, *die;* **b)** *(non-performance)* Unterlassung, *die;* **sins of ~ and commission** Unterlassungs- und Begehungssünden
omit [ə'mɪt] *v. t.,* **-tt-** **a)** *(leave out)* weglassen; **b)** *(not perform)* versäumen; **~ to do sth.** es versäumen, etw. zu tun
omnibus ['ɒmnɪbəs] **1.** *n.* **a)** *(arch.) see* **bus 1 a; Clapham; b)** *(book)* Sammelband, *der.* **2.** *adj.* Sammel‹*band, -ausgabe*›
omnidirectional [ɒmnɪdɪ'rekʃənl, ɒmnɪdaɪ'rekʃənl] *adj.* allseitig empfindlich ‹*Mikrophon*›; allseitig abstrahlend ‹*Lautsprecher*›; **~ aerial** Rundstrahler, *der*
omnipotence [ɒm'nɪpətəns] *n., no pl.* Allmacht, *die (geh.);* Omnipotenz, *die (geh.)*
omnipotent [ɒm'nɪpətənt] *adj.* allmächtig; omnipotent *(geh.);* **be made ~:** unbeschränkte Machtbefugnisse erhalten
omniscience [ɒm'nɪsɪəns, ɒm'nɪʃjəns] *n., no pl.* Allwissenheit, *die*
omniscient [ɒm'nɪsɪənt, ɒm'nɪʃjənt] *adj.* allwissend

omnivorous [ɒm'nɪvərəs] *adj.* **a)** omnivor *(Zool.);* **~ animal** Allesfresser, *der;* **b)** *(fig.)* unstillbar ‹*Appetit, Neugier, Wißbegier*›
on [ɒn] **1.** *prep.* **a)** *(position)* auf (+ *Dat.*); *(direction)* auf (+ *Akk.*); *(attached to)* an (+ *Dat./Akk.*); **put sth. on the table** etw. auf den Tisch legen *od.* stellen; **be on the table** auf dem Tisch sein; **put/keep a dog on a lead** den Hund an die Leine nehmen/an der Leine halten; **write sth. on the wall** etw. an die Wand schreiben; **be hanging on the wall** an der Wand hängen; **have sth. on one** etw. bei sich *(Dat.)* haben; **on the mountain[-side]** am Berghang; **on the bus/train** im Bus/Zug; **on the shore** am Ufer; **be on the board/committee** im Vorstand/Ausschuß sein; **be on the team** *(Amer.)***/staff** zum Team/zur Belegschaft gehören; **on Oxford 56767** unter der Nummer Oxford 56767; **b)** *(with basis, motive, etc. of)* **on the evidence** auf Grund des Beweismaterials; **borrow money on one's house** eine Grundschuld auf sein Haus aufnehmen; **on the assumption/hypothesis that ...:** angenommen, ...; **c)** *(close to)* an ‹*einer Straße*›; *(in the direction of)* auf ‹*eine Stadt*› zu; **d)** *(coll.: in a position to get)* **the player is on a hat-trick** der Spieler steht vor einem Hattrick; **e)** *in expressions of time* an ‹*einem Abend, Tag usw.*›; **on Sundays** sonntags; **it's just on nine** es ist gerade 9; **on [his] arrival** bei seiner Ankunft; **on entering the room ...:** beim Betreten des Zimmers ...; **on time** *or* **schedule** pünktlich; **f)** *expr. state etc.* **be on heroin** heroinabhängig sein; **be on beer** *(coll.)* Bier trinken; **Armstrong on trumpet** Armstrong, Trompete; **the drinks are on me** *(coll.)* die Getränke gehen auf mich; **the fire went out on me** *(coll.)* mir ist das Feuer ausgegangen; **there is a lot of money on that horse** auf das Pferd ist viel gesetzt worden; **g)** *(added to)* **failure on failure** Fehlschlag auf Fehlschlag; **trouble on trouble** nichts als Ärger; **loss on loss** anhaltende Verluste; **h)** *(concerning, about)* über (+ *Akk.*). **2.** *adv.* **a) have a hat on** einen Hut aufhaben; **your hat is on crooked** dein Hut sitzt schief; **the potatoes are on** die Kartoffeln sind aufgesetzt; **b)** *(in some direction)* **face on** mit dem Gesicht voran; **on and on** immer weiter; **speak/wait/work** *etc.* **on** *(in time)* weiterreden/-warten/-arbeiten *usw.;* **wait on until ...:** solange warten, bis ...; **c)** *(switched or turned on)* **the light/radio etc. is on** das Licht/Radio *usw.* ist an; **put the light on** das Licht anmachen; **leave the bathroom tap on** das Wasser im Badezimmer laufen lassen; **is there a gas tap on?** ist ein Gashahn aufgedreht?; **neither the water nor the electricity was on** es gab weder Wasser noch Strom; **d)** *(arranged)* **the strike is still on** der Streik wird [weiterhin] fortgesetzt; **is Sunday's picnic on?** findet das Picknick am Sonntag statt?; **I have nothing of importance on** ich habe nichts Wichtiges vor; **e)** *ellipt.* (= **go on** *etc.*) weiter; **on with the show!** weitermachen!; **f)** *(being performed)* **what's on at the cinema?** was gibt es *od.* läuft im Kino?; **his play is currently on in London** sein Stück wird zur Zeit in London aufgeführt *od.* gespielt; **the race is on** *(fig.)* das Wettrennen hat begonnen; **g) be on** *(on the stage)* auftreten; *(on the playing-field)* spielen; **h)** *(on duty)* **come/be on** seinen Dienst antreten/Dienst haben; **i) sth. is on** *(feasible)***/not on** etw. ist möglich/ausgeschlossen; **are you on?** *(coll.: will you agree?)* machst du mit?; **you're on!** *(coll.: I agree)* abgemacht!; *(making bet)* die Wette gilt!; **be on about sb./sth.** *(coll.)* [dauernd] über jmdn./etw. sprechen; es von jmdm./etw. haben *(ugs.);* **what is he on about?** was will er [sagen]?; **be on at/keep on and on at sb.** *(coll.)* jmdm. in den Ohren/dauernd in den Ohren liegen *(ugs.);* **on to, onto** auf (+ *Akk.*); **be on to sb.** *(be aware of sb.'s in-*

tentions etc.) jmdn. *od.* jmds. Absichten durchschauen; *(nag sb., suspect sb.)* jmdn. auf dem Kieker haben *(ugs.)*; **be on to sb. to do sth.** jmdn. bearbeiten, etw. zu tun; **be on to sth.** *(have discovered sth.)* etw. ausfindig gemacht haben; *(realize importance of sth.)* etw. [klar] erkennen; **the police/researchers are on to something** die Polizei hat/die Forscher haben eine heiße Spur; **on and off** = **off and on** *see* **off 1c.** *See also* **right 4d. 3.** *adj. (Cricket)* rechts vom Werfer; *(if batsman is left-handed)* links vom Werfer; **on drive** Treibschlag nach links; *(by left-handed batsman)* Treibschlag nach rechts; **on side** *see* **4. 4.** *n. (Cricket) Spielfeldhälfte links vom rechtshändigen bzw. rechts vom linkshändigen Schlagmann*

once [wʌns] **1.** *adv.* **a)** einmal; ~ **a week/month** einmal die Woche/im Monat; ~ **or twice** ein paarmal; einigemal; ~ **again** *or* **more** noch einmal; ~ **[and] for all** ein für allemal; **[every]** ~ **in a while** *or (Brit.)* **way** von Zeit zu Zeit; hin und wieder; **for** ~ **in a way** *(Brit.)* [wenigstens] dieses eine Mal; ausnahmsweise einmal; ~ **an X always an X** X bleibt X; ~ **seen never forgotten** jmd./etw. ist unvergeßlich; *see also* **for 1o; b)** *(multiplied by one)* ein mal; **c)** *(even for one or the first time)* je[mals]; **never/not** ~: nicht ein einziges Mal; **d)** *(formerly)* früher einmal; einst *(geh.)*; ~ **upon a time there lived a king** es war einmal ein König; **e) at** ~ *(immediately)* sofort; sogleich; *(at the same time)* gleichzeitig; **all at** ~ *(all together)* alle auf einmal; *(without warning)* mit einem Mal; **they were all shouting at** ~: sie schrien alle durcheinander. **2.** *conj.* sobald; ~ **past the fence we are safe** wenn wir [nur] den Zaun hinter uns bringen, sind wir in Sicherheit; **will you get it,** ~ **he finds out how valuable it is?** wirst du es auch bekommen, wenn er [einmal] herausfindet, wie wertvoll es ist? **3.** *n.* **[just** *or* **only] this** ~, **for [this/that]** ~: [nur] dieses eine Mal; ~ **was enough for her** sie hatte nach dem ersten Mal schon genug

'once-over *n.* **give sb./sth. a/the** ~: jmdn./etw. kurz in Augenschein nehmen; **sth. needs a** ~ **every month** etw. muß einmal im Monat kurz überprüft/*(cleaning)* gereinigt werden

oncology [ɒŋ'kɒlədʒɪ] *n., no pl., no art. (Med.)* Onkologie, *die*

'oncoming *adj.* [heran]nahend ⟨*Person*⟩; entgegenkommend ⟨*Fahrzeug, Verkehr*⟩; aufkommend ⟨*Sturm*⟩; **'caution:** ~ **vehicles'** „Vorsicht! Gegenverkehr"

one [wʌn] **1.** *adj.* **a)** *attrib.* ein; ~ **thing I must say/admit** ein[e]s muß ich sagen/zugeben; ~ **man,** ~ **vote** ≈ gleiches Wahlrecht für alle; ~ **or two** *(fig.: a few)* ein paar; ~ **more ...:** noch ein ...; ~ **more time** noch einmal; **Act One** *(Theatre)* erster Akt; **from day** ~: vom ersten Tag an; **it's** ~ **[o'clock]** es ist eins *od.* ein Uhr; *see also* **eight 1; half 1a, 3a; many 1a; quarter 1a; b)** *attrib. (single, only)* einzig; **the** ~ **thing** das einzige; **any** ~: irgendein; **in any** ~ **day/year** an einem Tag/in einem Jahr; **at any** ~ **time** zu jeder Zeit; **no** ~: kein; **not** ~ **[little] bit** überhaupt nicht; **not** *or* **never for** ~ **[single] moment** *or* **minute** nicht einen Augenblick *od.* eine Minute [lang]; *see also* **only 1, 2a; thing a, c, f, g; c)** *(identical, same)* ein; **the writer and his principal character are** ~: der Autor und sein Protagonist sind identisch; ~ **and the same person/thing** ein und dieselbe Person/Sache; **it's** ~ **and the same thing** das ist ein und dasselbe; **at** ~ **and the same time** gleichzeitig; *see also* **all 2a; d)** *pred. (united, unified)* **be** ~: eine Einheit bilden; **we are** ~: wir sind uns einig; **be** ~ **as a family/nation** eine einige Familie/Nation sein; **become** ~: sich vereinigen; **be made** ~ *(married)* getraut werden; *see also* **with; e)** *attrib. (a particular but undefined)* **at** ~ **time** einmal; einst *(geh.)*; ~ **morning/evening/night** eines Morgens/Abends/Nachts; ~ **day** *(on day specified)* einmal; *(at unspecified future date)* eines Tages; ~ **day soon** bald einmal; ~ **day next week** irgendwann nächste Woche; ~ **Sunday/weekend/afternoon** an einem Sonntag/Wochenende/Nachmittag; **f)** *attrib. contrasted with 'other'/'another'* ein; **for** ~ **thing** zum einen; ~ **book** *etc.* **after another** *or* **the other** ein Buch *usw.* nach dem anderen; **deal with** ~ **thing after the other** eins nach dem andern machen; **what with** ~ **thing and another** wie das so ist *od.* geht, wenn viel zusammenkommt; **neither** ~ **thing nor the other** weder das eine noch das andere; **for** ~ **reason or another** aus irgendeinem Grund; **at** ~ **time or another** irgendwann einmal; zu irgendeinem Zeitpunkt; *see also* **hand 1n; way 1c, j; g)** *qualifying implied n.* ein...; *(Brit.: ~-pound coin or note)* Pfundnote, *die; (Amer.: ~-dollar bill)* Dollarnote, *die;* **three to** ~, **three-**~ *(Sport)* drei zu eins; ~**-nil** *(Sport)* eins zu null; **in** ~ *(coll.: at first attempt)* auf Anhieb; **got it in** ~! *(coll.)* [du hast es] erraten!; *see also* **every a; hole 1e. 2.** *n.* **a)** eins; ~, **two, three ...!** eins, zwei, drei ...!; **b)** *(number, symbol)* Eins, *die;* **a Roman/arabic** ~: eine römische/arabische Eins; *see also* **eight 2a; c)** *(unit)* **in** ~**s** einzeln; **in** *or* **by** ~**s and twos** *(fig.)* kleckerweise *(ugs.)*; **two for the price of** ~: zwei zum Preis von einem; *see also* **number 1a; ten 2c. 3.** *pron.* **a)** ~ **of ...:** ein... (+ *Gen.*); ~ **of the boys/books** einer der Jungen/eins der Bücher; ~ **of them/us** *etc.* einer von ihnen/uns *usw.*; **any** ~ **of them** jeder/jede/jedes von ihnen; **every** ~ **of them** jeder/jede/jedes [einzelne] von ihnen; **not** ~ **of them** keiner/keine/keines von ihnen; *see also* **thing g; b)** *replacing n. implied or mentioned* ein...; **red** ~**s and yellow** ~**s, big** ~**s and little** ~**s** rote und gelbe, große und kleine; **the jacket is an old** ~: die Jacke ist [schon] alt; **the older/younger** ~: der/die/das ältere/jüngere; **the problem is** ~ **of great complexity/is not** ~ **that will simply go away** das Problem ist sehr komplex/wird sich nicht von selbst lösen; **not that book – the** ~ **on the table** nicht das Buch – das auf dem Tisch; **who is that man, the** ~ **in the blue suit?** wer ist dieser Mann, der im blauen Anzug?; **of the three books, this is the** ~ **which appealed to me most** von den drei Büchern hat mir dieses am besten gefallen; **this is the** ~ **I like** den/die/das mag ich; **my husband is the tall** ~ **over there** mein Mann ist der große da; **you are** *or* **were the** ~ **who insisted on going to Scotland** du warst der-/diejenige, der/die unbedingt nach Schottland wollte; **this** ~: dieser/diese/dieses [da]; **that** ~: der/die/das [da]; **these** ~**s** *or* **those** ~**s?** *(coll.)* die [da] oder die [da]?; **these/those blue** *etc.* ~**s** diese/die blauen *usw.*; **which** ~? welcher/welche/welches?; **which** ~**s?** welche?; **not** ~: keiner/keine/keines; *emphatic* nicht einer/eine/eines; **never a** ~: kein einziger; **many a** ~: viele; **all but** ~: alle außer einem/einer/einem; **the last house but** ~: das vorletzte Haus; **[all] in** ~: in einem; *(in a person)* in einer Person; **I for** ~: ich für mein[en] Teil; ~ **by** ~, ~ **after another** *or* **the other** einzeln; **love/like/hate** ~ **another** sich *od. (geh.)* einander lieben/mögen/hassen; **be kind to** ~ **another** nett zueinander sein; *see also* **all 2a; better 2e; many 1a; c)** *(contrasted with 'other'/'another')* **[the]** ~ **... the other** der/die/das eine ... der/die/das andere; **d)** *(person or creature of specified kind)* **the little** ~: der/die/das Kleine; **dear** *or* **loved** ~: lieber Mensch; **our dear** *or* **loved** ~**s** unsere Lieben; **my sweet** ~: mein Liebling *od.* Schatz; **young** ~ *(youngster)* Kind, *das; (young animal)* Junge, *das;* **the Holy One, the One above** Gott; der Vater im Himmel; **like** ~ **dead** wie ein Toter; **as** ~ **enchanted/bewitched** wie verzaubert/verhext; ~ **John Smith** ein John Smith; **e) [not]** ~ **who does** *or* **to do** *or* **for doing sth.** [nicht] der Typ, der etw. tut; **[not] be** ~ **for parties** *or* **for going to parties** [k]ein Partytyp sein; **be a great** ~ **for tennis** ein begeisterter Tennisspieler; **be a great** ~ **for playing practical jokes** gerne anderen einen Streich spielen; ein großer Witzbold sein; **not be much of a** ~ **for sth./doing sth.** nicht sehr für etw. sein/etw. nicht gern tun; **you 'are a** ~ *(coll.)* du bist [mir] vielleicht einer/eine; **f)** *(representing people in general; also coll.: I, we)* man; *as indirect object* einem; *as direct object* einen; ~**'s** sein; **lose** ~**'s job** seinen Arbeitsplatz verlieren; **wash** ~**'s hands** sich *(Dat.)* die Hände waschen; **g)** *(coll.: joke, story)* **a good/naughty** ~: ein guter/unanständiger Witz; **have you heard the** ~ **about the Irishman who ...?** kennst du den von dem Iren, der ...?; *see also* **good 1h; h)** *(coll.: drink)* **I'll have just a little** ~: ich trinke nur einen Kleinen *(ugs.)*; **this** ~**'s on me/the house** der geht auf mich/auf Kosten des Hauses; **have** ~ **on me** ich geb dir einen aus; **have** ~ **too many** einen über den Durst trinken *(ugs.)*; *see also* **quick one; road a; i)** *(coll.: blow)* **give sb.** ~ **on the head/nose** jmdm. eins über den Kopf/auf die Nase geben *(ugs.)*; **he hit me** ~ **between the eyes** er verpaßte mir einen zwischen die Augen *(ugs.)*; **j)** *(Knitting, Crochet: stitch)* eine Masche; **knit** ~, **purl** ~: eins rechts, eins links; **make** ~: eine Masche zunehmen

one: ~**-armed** *adj.* einarmig; ~**-armed bandit** *(sl.)* einarmiger Bandit *(ugs.)*; ~**-day** *attrib. adj.* eintägig; [für] einen Tag gültig ⟨*Karte, Genehmigung*⟩; ~**-eyed** *adj.* einäugig; **in the land of the blind the** ~**-eyed [man] is king** *(prov.)* unter [den] Blinden ist der Einäugige König *(Spr.)*; ~**-handed** [wʌnhændɪd] **1.** ['---] *adj.* einhändig; **2.** [-'--] *adv.* mit einer Hand; ~**-horse** *attrib. adj.* **a)** *(drawn by only* ~ *horse)* einspännig; *(having only* ~ *horse)* mit nur einem Pferd *nachgestellt;* **it's a** ~**-horse race** *(fig.)* das Rennen ist schon so gut wie gelaufen; **b)** *(fig. sl.: second-rate)* ~**-horse firm** *or* **outfit** kleine Klitsche *(ugs.)*; ~**-horse town** [verschlafenes] Nest *(ugs.)*; ~**-legged** *adj.* einbeinig; ~**-line** *attrib. adj.* einzeilig; ~**-'liner** *n.* Einzeiler, *der;* ~**-man** *attrib. adj.* Einmann⟨*boot, -betrieb usw.*⟩; **a** ~**-man fight/war against sth.** ein einsamer Kampf/Krieg gegen etw.; ~**-man band** Einmannkapelle, *die; (fig.: firm etc.)* Einmannbetrieb, *der;* ~**-man show** *(exhibition)* Einzelausstellung, *die; (play etc.)* Einmannstück, *das; (fig.: firm etc.)* Einmannbetrieb, *der*

oneness ['wʌnnɪs] *n., no pl.* **a)** *(singleness)* ~ **of purpose** Zielstrebigkeit, *die;* **b)** *(unity, harmony)* Übereinstimmung, *die;* Einklang, *der (geh.)*

one: ~**-night 'stand** *n. (coll.)* **a)** *(single performance)* Einzelauftritt, *der;* **b)** *(sexual)* [sexuelles] Abenteuer für eine Nacht; *(partner)* Bettgenosse/-genossin für eine Nacht; ~**-off** *(Brit.)* **1.** *n. (article)* Einzelstück, *das;* Einzelexemplar, *das; (operation)* einmalige Sache; **2.** *adj.* einmalig ⟨*Zahlung, Angebot, Produktion, Verkauf*⟩; Einzel⟨*stück, -modell, -anfertigung, -auftritt, -arbeit*⟩; ~**-parent family** *n.* Einelternfamilie, *die;* ~**-party** *adj. (Polit.)* Einparteien⟨*system, -staat*⟩; ~**-piece** *adj.* einteilig; ~**-'quarter** *attrib. adj.* Viertel-; ⟨*Anteil*⟩ von einem Viertel; ⟨*Anstieg*⟩ um ein Viertel; ~**-room[ed]** ['wʌnru:m(d)] *adj.* Einzimmer⟨*wohnung, -appartement*⟩

onerous ['ɒnərəs, 'əʊnərəs] *adj.* schwer; **find sth. increasingly** ~: etw. zunehmend als Belastung empfinden

onerously ['ɒnərəslɪ, 'əʊnərəslɪ] *adv.* schwer

one: ~'**self** *pron.* **a)** *emphat.* selbst; **as old/rich as ~self** so alt/reich wie man selbst; **older/richer than ~self** älter/reicher als man selbst; **be ~self** man selbst sein; **b)** *refl.* sich; *see also* **herself; ~-shot** *adj. (coll.)* einmalig; Einzel‹*auftritt, -anfertigung*›; ‹*Medikament, Verfahren*› zur einmaligen Anwendung; **a ~-shot solution to a problem** eine auf Anhieb wirksame Lösung eines Problems; **~-sided** *adj.* einseitig; **~step** *n.* Onestep, *der;* **~-storey** *adj.* eingeschossig; **~-'third** *attrib. adj.* Drittel-; ‹*Anteil*› von einem Drittel; ‹*Anstieg*› um ein Drittel; **~-time** *adj.* **a)** *(former)* ehemalig; **b)** *(used once only)* einmalig; **~-to-'~** *adj.* **~-to-~ relation/correspondence** hundertprozentige Parallelität; **~-to-~ translation** Wort-für-Wort-Übersetzung; **~-to-~ teaching** Einzelunterricht, *der;* **~-track** *adj.* eingleisig; **have a ~-track mind** *(lack flexibility)* eingleisig denken; *(be obsessed by one subject)* [immer] nur eins im Kopf haben; **~-'two** *n. (coll.) (Boxing)* Eins-zwei-Schlag, *der; (Sport)* Doppelpaß, *der;* **~-'up** *pred. adj. (coll.)* **be ~-up [on** *or* **over sb.]** *(Sport)* [vor jmdm.] mit einem Punkt/Tor in Führung liegen; *(fig.)* [jmdm.] um eine Nasenlänge voraus sein; **it is ~-up for** *or* **to sb.** jmd. ist im Vorteil; **~-up for** *or* **to you** *(fig.)* eins zu null für dich; **~-upmanship** [wʌn-'ʌpmənʃɪp] *n., no pl., no indef. art.* die Kunst, den anderen immer um eine Nasenlänge voraus zu sein; **~-way** *adj.* **a)** in einer Richtung *nachgestellt;* Einbahn‹*straße, -verkehr*›; Einweg‹*spiegel, -scheibe*›; **~-way radio** Funkempfänger, *der;* **~-way switch** *(Electr.)* einfacher Schalter; **b)** *(single)* einfach ‹*Fahrpreis, Fahrkarte, Flug usw.*›; **c)** *(fig.: ~-sided)* einseitig; **~-woman** *attrib. adj.* Einfrau‹*betrieb, -job, -firma*›; **a ~-woman fight/war against sth.** ein einsamer Kampf/Krieg gegen etw.; **~-woman show** *(exhibition)* Einzelausstellung [einer Künstlerin]; *(play etc.)* Einfraustück, *das; (fig.: firm etc.)* Einfraubetrieb, *der*

'ongoing *adj.* aktuell ‹*Problem, Aktivitäten, Debatte*›; laufend ‹*Forschung, Projekt*›; andauernd ‹*Situation*›

onion ['ʌnjən] *n.* Zwiebel, *die;* **know one's ~s** *(fig. sl.)* sein Geschäft verstehen

onion: ~ dome *n. (Archit.)* Zwiebelkuppel, *die;* **~-skin** *n.* **a)** Zwiebelschale, *die;* **b)** *(paper)* Florpost, *die;* **~ 'soup** *n.* Zwiebelsuppe, *die*

oniony ['ʌnjənɪ] *adj.* Zwiebel‹*geruch, -geschmack*›

on-line *(Computing)* **1.** ['--] *adj.* On-line-‹*Computer, Betrieb*›. **2.** [-'-] *adv.* on line

'onlooker *n.* Zuschauer, *der*/Zuschauerin, *die; (at scene of accident)* Schaulustige, *der/die*

only ['əʊnlɪ] **1.** *attrib. adj.* **a)** einzig...; **the ~ person** der/die einzige; **my ~ regret is that ...:** ich bedaure nur, daß ...; **for the first and ~ time** zum ersten und einzigen Mal; **an ~ child** ein Einzelkind; **the ~ one/ones** der/die/das einzige/die einzigen; **the ~ thing** das einzige; **one and ~** *(sole)* einzig...; *(incomparable)* einzigartig; *see also* **pebble; thing b, c; b)** *(best by far)* **the ~:** der/die/das einzig wahre; **he/she is the ~ one for me** es gibt nur ihn/sie für mich; **the ~ thing** das einzig Wahre. **2.** *adv.* **a)** nur; **we had been waiting ~ 5 minutes when ...:** wir hatten erst 5 Minuten gewartet, als ...; **it's ~/~ just 6 o'clock** es ist erst 6 Uhr/gerade erst 6 Uhr vorbei; **the meat is ~ half done** das Fleisch ist erst halb durch; **I ~ wish I had known** wenn ich es doch nur gewußt hätte; **you ~ have** *or* **you have ~ to ask** *etc.* du brauchst nur zu fragen *usw.;* **you may each take one and one ~:** ihr dürft euch jeder einen/eine/eins nehmen, aber [wirklich] nur einen/eine/eins; **you ~ live once** man lebt nur einmal; **you're ~ young once** man ist nur einmal jung; **~ ever** *(coll.: never more than)* lediglich; **~ if** nur [dann] ..., wenn; **~ if the weather is fine** nur bei gutem Wetter; **he ~ just managed it/made it** er hat es gerade so/gerade noch geschafft; **not ~ ... but also** nicht nur ... sondern auch; *see also* **if 1 d; b)** *(no longer ago than)* erst; **~ the other day/week** erst neulich *od.* kürzlich; **~ the other evening** erst neulich abends; **~ just** gerade erst; **it is ~ now I realize ...:** erst jetzt wird mir klar ...; **c)** *(with no better result than)* **~ to find/discover that ...:** nur, um zu entdecken, daß ...; **d) ~ too ...** *in context of desirable circumstances* [sogar] ausgesprochen ‹*froh, begierig, bereitwillig*›; *in context of undesirable circumstances* viel zu; **be ~ too aware of sth.** sich *(Dat.)* einer Sache *(Gen.)* voll bewußt sein; **it's ~ too true** es ist nur zu wahr; **~ too well** nur zu gut ‹*wissen, kennen, sich erinnern*›; gerne ‹*mögen*›; nur zu genau ‹*hören, aufpassen auf*›. **3.** *conj.* **a)** *(but then)* nur; **b)** *(were it not for the fact that)* **~ [that] I am/he is** *etc.* **...:** ich bin/er ist *usw.* nur ...

only-be'gotten *adj. (Relig.)* **Jesus Christ, the ~ Son of the Father** Jesus Christus, Gottes eingeborener Sohn

o.n.o. [əʊ en 'əʊ] *abbr. (Brit.)* **or near offer** ≈ VHB

'on-off *adj.* **~ switch** Ein-aus-Schalter

onomatopoeia [ɒnəmætə'pi:ə] *n. (Ling.)* Onomatopöie, *die*

onomatopoeic [ɒnəmætə'pi:ɪk] *adj. (Ling.)* onomatopoetisch

'onrush *n.* Ansturm, *der*

'onset *n.* **a)** *(attack)* [Sturm]angriff, *der;* **b)** *(beginning) (of storm)* Einsetzen, *das; (of winter)* Einbruch, *der; (of disease)* Ausbruch, *der*

'onshore *adj.* auflandig *(Seemannsspr.)*

on'side *adj. (Footb.)* nicht abseits

onslaught ['ɒnslɔ:t] *n.* [heftige] Attacke *(fig.)*

on-'stage 1. *adj.* auf der Bühne *nachgestellt.* **2.** *adv.* auf die Bühne ‹*gehen*›; auf der Bühne ‹*stehen*›

'on-street *adj.* auf der Straße *nachgestellt*

'on-the-job *adj.* **~ training** Ausbildung an der Arbeitsstelle

on-the-'spot *adj.* vor Ort *nachgestellt*

onto *see* **on 2 i**

ontological [ɒntə'lɒdʒɪkl] *adj. (Philos.)* ontologisch

ontology [ɒn'tɒlədʒɪ] *n. (Philos.)* Ontologie, *die*

onus ['əʊnəs] *n.* Last, *die;* **the ~ [of proof]** die Beweislast; **the ~ is on him to do it** es ist seine Sache, es zu tun

onward ['ɒnwəd] **1.** *adv.* **a)** *(in space)* vorwärts; **from X ~:** von X an; **they moved ~ into the forest** sie gingen *od.* zogen weiter in den Wald [hinein]; **b)** *(in time)* **from that day ~:** von diesem Tag an; **history from the 12th century ~:** Geschichte vom 12. Jahrhundert an. **2.** *adj.* nach vorn *nachgestellt;* **~ movement** Vorwärtsbewegung, *die;* **~ march** Vormarsch, *der*

onwards ['ɒnwədz] *see* **onward 1**

onyx ['ɒnɪks] *n. (Min.)* Onyx, *der;* **~ marble** Onyxmarmor, *der*

oodles ['u:dlz] *n. pl., constr. as sing. or pl. (coll.)* **~ of** haufenweise *(ugs.);* jede Menge *(ugs.)*

ooh [u:] **1.** *n.* Oh, *das;* Ah, *das;* **the ~s [and ahs] of the audience** die Ohs und Ahs der Zuschauer. **2.** *int. expr. disapproval or delight* oh; *expr. pain* au

oojah ['u:dʒɑ:] *n. (sl.)* Ding, *das (ugs.)*

oompah ['u:mpɑ:] *n.* Humpta, *das*

oomph [ʊmf] *n. (sl.)* **a)** *(attractiveness)* Sex-Appeal, *der;* **b)** *(energy)* Elan, *der*

oops [u:ps] *int. (coll.) expr. surprise* huch; *expr. apology* oh[je]; *expr. apology for a faux pas* oh

ooze [u:z] **1.** *v.i.* **a)** *(percolate, exude)* sickern **(from** aus); *(more thickly)* quellen **(from** aus); **the juice ~s out** der Saft trieft heraus; **b)** *(become moistened)* triefen **(with** von, vor + *Dat.*). **2.** *v.t.* **a) ~ [out]** triefen von *od.* vor (+ *Dat.*); **b)** *(fig.: radiate)* ausstrahlen ‹*Charme, Optimismus*›; ausströmen ‹*Sarkasmus*›. **3.** *n.* **a)** *(mud)* Schlick, *der;* **b)** *(sluggish flow)* Sickern, *das; (sluggish stream)* Rinnsal, *das* **(of** von + *Dat.*)

op [ɒp] *n. (coll.)* **a)** *(Med.)* Operation, *die;* **b)** *(Mil., Navy, Air Force)* Einsatz, *der;* **c)** *(radio operator)* Funker, *der*/Funkerin, *die; (telegraph operator)* Telegrafist, *der*/Telegrafistin, *die*

op. [ɒp] *abbr. (Mus.)* **opus** op.

opacity [ə'pæsɪtɪ] *n., no pl.* **a)** *(not transmitting light)* Opazität, *die (Optik);* Lichtundurchlässigkeit, *die;* **b)** *(obscurity)* Undurchsichtigkeit, *die*

opal ['əʊpl] *n. (Min.)* Opal, *der*

opalescence [əʊpə'lesəns] *n.* Schillern, *das;* Opaleszenz, *die (Optik)*

opalescent [əʊpə'lesənt] *adj.* schillernd; opalisierend; opaleszierend *(Optik)*

'opal glass *n.* Opalglas, *das*

opaque [əʊ'peɪk] *adj.* **a)** *(not transmitting light)* lichtundurchlässig; opak *(fachspr.);* **b)** *(obscure)* dunkel; unverständlich

opaqueness [əʊ'peɪknɪs] *see* **opacity**

'op art *n., no pl., no indef. art.* Op-art, *die*

op. cit. [ɒp 'sɪt] *abbr.* **in the work already quoted** op. cit.

OPEC ['əʊpek] *abbr.* **Organization of Petroleum Exporting Countries** OPEC, *die*

open ['əʊpn] **1.** *adj.* **a)** offen; **with the window ~:** bei geöffnetem Fenster; **~ goal** *(Sport)* leeres Tor; **wear an ~ shirt** sein Hemd offen tragen; **be [wide/half] ~:** [weit/halb] offenstehen; **stand ~:** offenstehen; **swing ~:** aufschwingen; **come ~:** aufgehen; **get sth. ~:** etw. aufbekommen; **hold the door ~ [for sb.]** [jmdm.] die Tür aufhalten; **push/pull/kick the door ~:** die Tür aufstoßen/aufziehen/eintreten; **force sth. ~:** etw. mit Gewalt öffnen; **fling** *or* **throw a door/window [wide] ~:** eine Tür/ein Fenster [weit] aufreißen; **tear** *or* **rip sth. ~:** etw. aufreißen; **with one's mouth ~:** mit offenem Mund; **have one's eyes ~:** die Augen geöffnet haben; **[not] be able to keep one's eyes ~:** [nicht mehr] die Augen offenhalten können; **with ~ eyes** *(attentive, surprised)* mit großen Augen; *see also* **eye 1 a; b)** *(unconfined)* offen ‹*Gelände, Feuer*›; frei ‹*Feld, Blick*›; **~ country** *(with wide views)* weites Land; *(without buildings)* offenes Land; **on the ~ road** auf freier Strecke; **the ~ road lay before me** vor mir lag die freie Landstraße; **the ~ sea** die offene See; **in the ~ air** im Freien; *see also* **sky 1 a; c)** *(not blocked or obstructed)* frei; offen, eisfrei ‹*Hafen, Fluß, Wasser*›; frostfrei ‹*Winter, Wetter*›; **d)** *(ready for business or use)* **be ~** ‹*Laden, Museum, Bank usw.:*› geöffnet sein; **'~'/'~ on Sundays'/'~ 24 hours'** „geöffnet"/„Sonntags geöffnet"/„24 Stunden geöffnet"; **declare a building/an exhibition ~:** ein Gebäude/eine Ausstellung für eröffnet erklären; **e)** *(accessible)* offen; öffentlich ‹*Treffen, Rennen*›; *(available)* frei ‹*Stelle*›; freibleibend ‹*Angebot*›; **it is ~ to you to refuse** es steht dir frei abzulehnen; **lay ~:** offenlegen ‹*Plan*›; **be ~ to the public** für die Öffentlichkeit zugänglich sein; **the competition is ~ to children under 16** [nur] Kinder unter 16 Jahren sind zum Wettbewerb zugelassen; **the job/offer is ~ to men over 25 years of age** die Stelle ist für/das Angebot gilt für Männer über 25 Jahren; **the offer remains** *or* **will be kept ~ until the end of the month** das Angebot bleibt bestehen *od.* gilt noch bis Ende des Monats; **keep a position ~ for sb.** jmdm. eine Stelle freihalten; **keep an account ~:** ein Konto [weiterhin] bestehen lassen; **~ champion** Sieger einer offenen Meisterschaft; ~ **cheque** *(Brit.)* Barscheck, *der;* **in ~ court** in öffentlicher Sitzung *od.* Verhandlung; ~ **ward** offene Station; *see also* **house 1 a; f) be ~ to** *(exposed to)* ausgesetzt sein (+ *Dat.*) ⟨*Wind, Sturm*⟩; *(receptive to)* offen sein für ⟨*Ratschlag, andere Meinung, Vorschlag*⟩; ~ **to infection** infektionsgefährdet *od.* -anfällig; **be ~ to criticism** kritisierbar sein; ~ **to attack by dry rot** anfällig für Trockenfäule; **be ~ to attack from the air** aus der Luft angreifbar sein; **sth. may be ~ to misinterpretation** etw. kann [leicht] falsch ausgelegt werden; **be ~ to sb.'s influence** sich leicht von jmdm. beeinflussen lassen; **I hope to sell it for £ 1,000, but I am ~ to offers** ich möchte es für 1 000 Pfund verkaufen, aber ich lasse mit mir handeln; **lay sb. wide ~** *(fig.)* jmdn. bloßstellen; **lay oneself [wide] ~ to ridicule/attack/criticism** *etc.* sich der Lächerlichkeit preisgeben/sich Angriffen/der Kritik *usw.* aussetzen; **lay oneself [wide] ~ to blackmail/a charge** sich der Gefahr der Erpressung/einer Anklage aussetzen; **be ~ to question/doubt/argument** fraglich/zweifelhaft/umstritten sein; **I am ~ to correction** ich lasse mich gern korrigieren; **g)** *(undecided)* offen; ~ **invitation** Einladung, gelegentlich einmal zu Besuch zu kommen; ~ **return ticket** nicht termingebundene Rückfahrkarte; **have an ~ mind about** *or* **on sth.** einer Sache gegenüber aufgeschlossen *od.* unvoreingenommen sein; **with an ~ mind** aufgeschlossen; **have/keep an ~ mind on a question** in einer Sache unvoreingenommen sein/bleiben; **be [wide] ~:** [völlig] offen sein; **leave sth. ~:** etw. offenlassen; *see also* **verdict a; h)** *(undisguised, manifest)* unverhohlen ⟨*Bewunderung, Haß, Verachtung*⟩; offen ⟨*Verachtung, Empörung, Bruch, Widerstand*⟩; offensichtlich ⟨*Spaltung, Zwiespalt*⟩; ~ **war/warfare** offener Krieg/Kampf; *see also* **secret 2 a; i)** *(frank, communicative)* offen ⟨*Wesen, Streit, Abstimmung, Gesicht, Regierungsstil*⟩; *(not secret)* öffentlich ⟨*Wahl*⟩; **be ~ [about sth./with sb.]** [in bezug auf etw. *(Akk.)*/gegenüber jmdm.] offen sein; **j)** *(not close)* grob ⟨*Muster, Gewebe, Maserung*⟩; offen ⟨*Anordnung*⟩; ~ **order** *(Mil., Navy)* offene Ordnung; **k)** *(expanded, unfolded)* offen, geöffnet ⟨*Pore, Regenschirm*⟩; aufgeblüht ⟨*Blume, Knospe*⟩; aufgeschlagen ⟨*Zeitung, Landkarte, Stadtplan*⟩; ~ **book** offenes *od.* aufgeschlagenes Buch; **sb./sth. is an ~ book [to sb.]** *(fig.)* jmd./etw. ist ein aufgeschlagenes *od.* offenes Buch [für jmdn.]; **an ~ hand** eine aufgehaltene Hand; *(fig.)* eine milde *od.* offene Hand; **with an ~ hand, with ~ hands** *(fig.)* mit einer milden *od.* offenen Hand; **with [an] ~ heart** *(frankly)* offenherzig; *(kindly)* herzlich; *see also* **[1]arm a; open-heart; l)** *(Mus.)* ~ **string** leere Saite; ~ **pipe** offene Pfeife; ~ **note** Naturton, *der;* **m)** *(Ling.)* offen ⟨*Vokal, Silbe*⟩. **2.** *n.* **a) the ~:** das offene Land; **in the ~** *(outdoors)* unter freiem Himmel; *(in an ~ space)* auf offenem Gelände; *(in ~ water)* auf offener *od.* hoher See; **[out] in the ~** *(fig.)* [öffentlich] bekannt; **come [out] into the ~** *(fig.) (become obvious)* herauskommen *(ugs.);* an den Tag kommen; *(speak out)* offen sprechen; **bring sth. [out] into the ~** *(fig.)* etw. an die Öffentlichkeit bringen; **b)** *(Sport)* offene Meisterschaft; Open, *das (fachspr.).* **3.** *v. t.* **a)** öffnen; aufmachen *(ugs.);* ~ **sth. with a key** etw. aufschließen; ~ **sth. wide** etw. weit aufmachen *(ugs.) od.* öffnen; **half ~ sth.** etw. halb aufmachen *(ugs.) od.* öffnen; **[not] ~ one's mouth** *or* **lips** *(fig.)* den Mund [nicht] aufmachen *od.* auftun *(ugs.);* ~ **one's big mouth [to sb. about sth.]** *(fig.)* [etw. jmdm. aus]plaudern; ~ **the** *or* **one's bowels** den Darm entleeren; *see also* **eye 1 a; floodgate; b)** *(allow access to)* ~ **sth. [to sb./sth.]** etw. öffnen [für jmdn./etw.]; *(fig.)* [jmdm./einer Sache] etw. öffnen; ~ **a road to traffic** eine Straße für den Verkehr freigeben; ~ **sth. to the public** etw. der Öffentlichkeit *(Dat.)* zugänglich machen; *see also* **door b; c)** *(establish)* eröffnen ⟨*Konferenz, Kampagne, Diskussion, Laden*⟩; aufmachen *(ugs.)* ⟨*Laden*⟩; beginnen ⟨*Verhandlungen, Krieg, Spiel*⟩; *(declare ~)* eröffnen ⟨*Gebäude usw.*⟩; ~ **the scoring** *(Sport)* den ersten Treffer erzielen; *(Cricket)* den ersten Lauf machen; *(Rugby)* die ersten Punkte machen; ~ **the betting with a £5 stake** das Spiel mit einem Einsatz von 5 Pfund eröffnen; ~ **the bidding** *(in auction)* das erste Gebot abgeben; *(Bridge)* eröffnen; ~ **an account** ein Konto eröffnen; ~ **fire [on sb./sth.]** das Feuer [auf jmdn./etw.] eröffnen; *see also* **[2]ball; parliament; d)** *(unfold, spread out)* aufschlagen ⟨*Zeitung, Landkarte, Stadtplan, Buch*⟩; aufspannen, öffnen ⟨*Schirm*⟩; öffnen ⟨*Fallschirm, Poren*⟩; ~ **one's hand** die *od.* seine Hand öffnen; ~ **one's arms [wide]** die *od.* seine Arme [weit] ausbreiten; ~ **one's legs** die *od.* seine Beine spreizen; **e)** *(reveal, expose)* ~ **a view** *or* **prospect of sth. [to sb.]** [jmdm.] den Blick auf etw. freigeben; **sth. ~s new prospects/horizons/a new world to sb.** *(fig.)* etw. eröffnet jmdm. neue Aussichten/Horizonte/eine neue Welt; ~ **one's heart to sb.** *(fig.)* sich jmdm. öffnen; **f)** *(make more receptive)* ~ **one's mind** aufgeschlossener werden; ~ **one's heart** *or* **mind to sb./sth.** sich jmdm./einer Sache öffnen; ~ **sb.'s mind to sth.** jmdm. etw. nahebringen; **g)** *(cut)* graben ⟨*Stollen, Brunnen, Loch, Gang*⟩; bauen ⟨*Straße durch Berge/Wald*⟩; *(break up)* bearbeiten ⟨*Boden*⟩; ~ **a hole in the wall** ein Loch in die Wand machen. **4.** *v. i.* **a)** sich öffnen; aufgehen; ⟨*Spalt, Kluft:*⟩ sich auftun; **'Doors ~ at 7 p.m.'** „Einlaß ab 19 Uhr"; **the safe ~s with a special key** der Tresor läßt sich mit einem Spezialschlüssel öffnen; ~ **inwards/outwards** nach innen/außen aufgehen; **the door would not ~:** die Tür ging nicht auf *od.* ließ sich nicht öffnen; **his mouth ~ed in a big yawn** sein Mund öffnete sich zu einem ausgiebigen Gähnen; **his eyes ~ed wide** er riß die Augen weit auf; ~ **into/on to sth.** zu etw. führen; sich zu etw. hin öffnen; **the kitchen ~s into the living-room** die Küche hat eine Tür zum Wohnzimmer; **the road ~s into a square** die Straße öffnet sich zu einem Platz; *see also* **heaven b; b)** *(become ~ to customers)* öffnen; aufmachen *(ugs.);* *(start trading etc.)* eröffnet werden; **the shop does not ~ on Sundays** der Laden ist sonntags geschlossen; **c)** *(make a start)* beginnen; ⟨*Ausstellung:*⟩ eröffnet werden; ⟨*Theaterstück:*⟩ Premiere haben; **shares ~ed steady** *or* **firm** *(St. Exch.)* die Aktien eröffneten fest; ~ **for the prosecution** *(Law)* das Eröffnungsplädoyer [in der Hauptverhandlung] halten; **d)** *(become visible)* ~ **before sb./sb.'s eyes** sich jmdm./jmds. Augen bieten; *(fig.)* sich jmdm. eröffnen

~ **'out 1.** *v. t.* **a)** *(unfold)* auseinanderfalten; **b)** *(enlarge, widen)* erweitern; **c)** *(develop)* erweitern. **2.** *v. i.* **a)** *(unfold)* ⟨*Landkarte:*⟩ sich auseinanderfalten lassen; ⟨*Knospe:*⟩ sich öffnen; *(fig.)* ⟨*Person:*⟩ auftauen; **b)** *(widen, expand)* ~ **out into sth.** sich zu etw. erweitern *od.* verbreitern; **c)** *(be revealed)* ~ **out before sb./sb.'s eyes** vor jmdm./jmds. Augen liegen

~ **'up 1.** *v. t.* **a)** aufmachen *(ugs.);* öffnen; aufschlagen ⟨*Buch*⟩; aufspannen, öffnen ⟨*Schirm*⟩; ~ **up a room/house** ein Zimmer/ein Haus öffnen *od.* zugänglich machen; **b)** *(form or make by cutting etc.)* machen ⟨*Loch, Riß*⟩; ~ **up a path through the jungle** einen Weg durch den Urwald schlagen; **the frost has ~ed up big cracks** durch den Frost sind große Risse entstanden; ~ **up a lead** *or* **gap of ten metres/points** einen Vorsprung von zehn Metern/Punkten gewinnen; **c)** *(establish, make more accessible)* eröffnen ⟨*Laden, Filiale*⟩; erschließen ⟨*neue Märkte usw.*⟩; ~ **up a region to trade/tourism** ein Gebiet für den Handel/Tourismus erschließen; ~ **up a new world to sb.** jmdm. eine neue Welt erschließen; ~ **up new opportunities for sb.** jmdm. neue Möglichkeiten eröffnen; **d)** *(make more lively, accelerate)* aufdrehen *(ugs.).* **2.** *v. i.* **a)** *(~ a door)* aufmachen; **b)** ⟨*Blüte, Knospe:*⟩ sich öffnen; **c)** *(be established)* ⟨*Filiale:*⟩ eröffnet werden; ⟨*Firma:*⟩ sich niederlassen; **d)** *(appear, be revealed)* entstehen; ⟨*Aussichten, Möglichkeiten:*⟩ sich eröffnen; ~ **up before sb.** ⟨*Blick, Aussicht:*⟩ sich jmdm. bieten; ⟨*neue Welt:*⟩ sich vor jmdm. auftun; **e)** *(talk freely)* gesprächig werden; ~ **up to sb.** sich jmdm. anvertrauen; sich jmdm. eröffnen *(geh.);* **f)** *(begin shooting)* das Feuer eröffnen; *(begin sounding)* ertönen; **g)** *(become more lively or active)* ⟨*Spiel, Handel:*⟩ sich beleben; *(accelerate)* aufdrehen *(ugs.)*

open: ~-'access library *n.* Freihandbibliothek, *die;* **~-air** *attrib. adj.* Open-air-⟨*Konzert*⟩; Freiluft⟨*restaurant, -aktivitäten*⟩; Freilicht⟨*kino, -aufführung*⟩; ⟨*Ausstellung, Markt, Versammlung*⟩ im Freien *od.* unter freiem Himmel; **~-air [swimming-] pool** Freibad, *das;* **~-and-'shut case** *n. (coll.)* klarer Fall; **~-armed** *adj.* herzlich; **receive** *or* **welcome sb. ~-armed** jmdn. mit offenen Armen aufnehmen *od.* empfangen; **~cast** *adj. (Mining)* **~cast mining/coal/method** Tagebau, *der*/Kohle aus dem Tagebau/Methode des Tagebaus; ~ **day** *n.* Tag der offenen Tür; **~-'door** *attrib. adj.* **~-door policy** Politik der offenen Tür; **~-ended** [əʊpən'endɪd] *adj.* [am Ende] offen; *(fig.: with no predetermined limit)* unbefristet ⟨*Aufenthalt, Vertrag*⟩; uneingeschränkt ⟨*Verpflichtung*⟩; unbegrenzt ⟨*Unterstützung, Kredit*⟩; Open-end-⟨*Diskussion, Debatte*⟩; offen ⟨*Frage*⟩; unerschöpflich ⟨*Thema*⟩; **~-ended spanner** Gabelschlüssel, *der*

opener ['əʊpnə(r)] *n.* **a)** Öffner, *der;* **b)** *(opening item or event) (of entertainment)* Eröffnungsnummer, *die; (of a serial)* erste Folge; *(Sport)* Eröffnungsspiel, *das;* **c)** *(Cricket)* eröffnender Schlagmann; **d) for ~s** *(coll.)* zu Beginn; zunächst einmal

open: ~-eyed *adj.* **a)** mit offenen Augen *nachgestellt;* **in ~-eyed amazement** mit großen Augen; **gaze/stare ~-eyed at sb./sth.** jmdn./etw. mit großen Augen ansehen/anstarren; **gaze/stare ~-eyed** große Augen machen; **b)** *(watchful, alert)* **do sth. ~-eyed** etw. bewußt tun; **~-'field system** *n. (Agric.)* alte Dreifelderwirtschaft; **~-'fronted** *adj.* vorne offen; **~-'handed** *adj.* freigebig; **~-'heart** *attrib. adj. (Med.)* am offenen Herzen *nachgestellt;* **~-'hearted** *adj.* aufrichtig ⟨*Person, Mitgefühl*⟩; herzlich ⟨*Empfang*⟩

opening ['əʊpnɪŋ] **1.** *n.* **a)** Öffnen, *das; (becoming open)* Sichöffnen, *das; (of crack, gap, etc.)* Entstehen, *das; (of exhibition, new centre)* Eröffnen, *das; (of road to traffic)* Freigabe, *die* **(to** für**)**; **hours** *or* **times of ~:** Öffnungszeiten; **it's late ~:** heute haben die Läden länger geöffnet; **'late ~ Thursday'** „donnerstags auch abends geöffnet"; **b)** *(establishment, inauguration, ceremony)* Eröffnung, die; ~ **of Parliament** Parlamentseröffnung, *die;* **c)** *(first performance)* Premiere, *die;* **d)** *(initial part)* Anfang, *der; (Chess)* Eröffnung, *die;* **e)** *(gap, aperture)* Öffnung, *die;* **f)** *(opportunity)* Möglichkeit, *die; (for goods)* Absatzmöglichkeit, *die; (vacancy)* freie *od.* offene Stelle; **wait for an ~:** auf eine günstige Gelegenheit warten; **give sb. an ~:** jmdm. eine Gelegenheit geben; **give sb. an ~ into sth.** ⟨*Person:*⟩ jmdm.

den Einstieg in etw. *(Akk.)* ermöglichen; ⟨*Job:*⟩ für jmdn. ein Einstieg in etw. *(Akk.)* sein; **g)** *(facing pages of book etc.)* Seitenpaar, *das.* **2.** *adj.* einleitend; **the ~ lines** *(of play, poem, etc.)* die ersten Zeilen; **~ night** *(Theatre)* Premiere, *die;* **~ speech/address** Eröffnungsrede/-ansprache, *die;* **~ move** *(Chess)* Eröffnung, *die; (fig.)* erster Schachzug; **~ bid** *(at auction; also Bridge)* erstes Gebot; **~ batsman** *(Cricket)* eröffnender Schlagmann

opening: ~ ceremony *n.* feierliche Eröffnung **(for** *Gen.*); **~ hours** *n. pl.* Öffnungszeiten *Pl.;* **~ time** *n.* **a)** Öffnungszeit, *die;* **wait for ~ time** darauf warten, daß geöffnet wird; **b) ~ times** *see* **~ hours**

open 'letter *n.* offener Brief

openly ['əʊpnlɪ] *adv.* **a)** *(publicly)* in der Öffentlichkeit; öffentlich ⟨*zugeben, verurteilen, abstreiten*⟩; **quite ~:** in aller Öffentlichkeit; **b)** *(frankly)* offen

open: ~ 'market *n.* offener *od.* freier Markt; **~-'minded** *adj.* aufgeschlossen **(about** für); **~-mindedness** [əʊpn'maɪndɪdnɪs] *n., no pl.* Aufgeschlossenheit, *die;* **~-mouthed** [əʊpn'maʊðd] *adj.* mit offenem Mund; **gape in ~-mouthed amazement** mit offenem Munde staunen; **~-necked** *adj.* ⟨*Hemd, Bluse*⟩ mit offenem Kragen; ausgeschnitten ⟨*Kleid, Pullover*⟩

openness ['əʊpnnɪs] *n., no pl.* **a)** *(of countryside etc.)* Weite, *die;* **b)** *(susceptibility)* Empfindlichkeit, *die* **(to** gegen); **c)** *(receptiveness)* Empfänglichkeit, *die;* **~ of mind** Aufgeschlossenheit, *die;* **d)** *(manifestness)* Offenheit, *die;* **I was surprised by the ~ of the people's resistance** ich war überrascht, wie offen die Leute Widerstand leisteten; **e)** *(frankness)* Offenheit, *die;* **f)** *(being spread out)* Grobheit, *die; (of arrangement)* Offenheit, *die*

open: ~-plan *adj.* mit ineinander übergehenden Räumen *nachgestellt;* offen angelegt ⟨*Haus*⟩; **~-plan office** Großraumbüro, *das;* **~ 'prison** *n.* offene Anstalt; **~ 'sandwich** *n.* belegtes Brot; **~ season** *n. (Brit.)* Jagdzeit, *die; (for fish)* Fangzeit, *die;* **it is [the] ~ season for** *or* **on sth.** *(fig.)* etw. ist an der Tagesordnung; **~ 'sesame** *see* **sesame c; ~ 'shelf library** *(Amer.) see* **~-access library; ~ 'shelves** *n. pl.* **these books are on ~ shelves** diese Bücher sind in der Freihandzone [aufgestellt]; **~ 'shop** *n.* Open Shop, *der;* nicht gewerkschaftspflichtiger Betrieb; **~ so'ciety** *n. (Sociol.)* offene Gesellschaft; **~-toe[d]** [əʊpn'təʊ(d)] *adj.* vorn offen ⟨*Schuh, Sandale*⟩; **~-top** *attrib. adj.* offen; oben offen ⟨*Bus*⟩; **O~ Uni'versity** *pr. n. (Brit.)* **the O~ University** die Open University *(britische Fernuniversität); attrib.* ⟨*Kurs*⟩ an der Fernuniversität; ⟨*akademischer Grad*⟩ der Fernuniversität; **~ 'weave** *n. (Textiles)* loses *od.* grobes Gewebe; *attrib.* locker *od.* grob gewebt ⟨*Stoff, Struktur*⟩; **~-work** *n.* durchbrochene Struktur; *(Sewing)* Durchbrucharbeit, *die; attrib.* durchbrochen

¹opera ['ɒpərə] *n.* **a)** Oper, *die;* **b)** *no pl. (branch of art)* **[the] ~:** die Oper; **c) light ~:** Operette, *die*

²opera *pl. of* **opus**

operable ['ɒpərəbl] *adj. (Med.)* operabel

opera: ~-glasses *n. pl.* Opernglas, *das;* **~-hat** *n.* Chapeau claque, *der;* **~-house** *n.* Opernhaus, *das;* **~-singer** *n.* Opernsänger, *der*/-sängerin, *die*

operate ['ɒpəreɪt] **1.** *v. i.* **a)** *(be in action)* in Betrieb sein; ⟨*Bus, Zug usw.:*⟩ verkehren; *(have an effect)* sich auswirken; **the system ~s against our interests/in our favour** das System, wie es derzeit funktioniert, bringt uns Nachteile/Vorteile; **the hospital is operating normally again** im Krankenhaus herrscht wieder normaler Betrieb; **b)** *(function)* arbeiten; **the torch ~s on batteries** die Taschenlampe arbeitet mit Batterien; **c)** *(perform operation)* operieren; arbeiten; **~ on sth.** etw. bearbeiten; **~ [on sb.]** *(Med.)* [jmdn.] operieren; **d)** *(exercise influence)* **~ [up]on sb./sth.** auf jmdn./etw. einwirken; **e)** *(follow course of conduct)* agieren; **the gang ~d by posing as workmen** die Methode der Bande bestand darin, daß sie sich als Arbeiter ausgaben; **f)** *(produce effect)* wirken; **g)** *(Mil.)* operieren. **2.** *v. t.* **a)** *(accomplish)* herbeiführen; **b)** *(cause to work)* bedienen ⟨*Maschine*⟩; fahren ⟨*Auto*⟩; betreiben ⟨*Unternehmen*⟩; unterhalten ⟨*Werk, Post, Busverbindung, Telefondienst*⟩

operatic [ɒpə'rætɪk] *adj.* **a)** Opern⟨*sänger, -musik*⟩; **b)** *(like opera)* opernhaft

operating: ~-room *n. (Med.)* Operationssaal, *der;* **~-table** *n. (Med.)* Operationstisch, *der;* **~-theatre** *n. (Brit. Med.)* Operationssaal, *der*

operation [ɒpə'reɪʃn] *n.* **a)** *(causing to work) (of machine)* Bedienung, *die; (of factory, mine, etc.)* Betrieb, *der; (of bus service, telephone service, etc.)* Unterhaltung, *die;* **ease of ~:** leichte Bedienbarkeit; **b)** *(way sth. works)* Arbeitsweise, *die;* **the engine is noted for its quiet ~** *or* **quietness in ~:** der Motor ist für seinen leisen Lauf bekannt; **c)** *(being operative)* **come into ~** ⟨*Maschine, Gerät:*⟩ zu arbeiten beginnen; ⟨*Gesetz, Gebühr usw.:*⟩ in Kraft treten; **be in ~** ⟨*Maschine, Gerät usw.:*⟩ in Betrieb sein; ⟨*Service:*⟩ zur Verfügung stehen; ⟨*Gesetz:*⟩ in Kraft sein; **be out of ~** ⟨*Maschine, Gerät usw.:*⟩ außer Betrieb sein; ⟨*Service:*⟩ nicht zur Verfügung stehen; **d)** *(active process)* Vorgang, *der;* **drilling ~s** Bohrarbeiten; **~[s] research** *see* **operational research; e)** *(performance)* Tätigkeit, *die;* **repeat the ~:** das Ganze [noch einmal] wiederholen; **f)** *(Med.)* Operation, *die;* **have an ~ [on one's foot]** [am Fuß] operiert werden; **an ~ for appendicitis** eine Blinddarmoperation; **g)** *(Air Force, Mil., Navy)* Einsatz, *der;* Operation, *die;* **night ~s** Nachteinsätze; **~s room** Befehlsstelle, *die; see also* **combined; h)** *(financial transaction)* [Geschäfts]tätigkeit, *die;* **i)** *(Math., Computing)* Operation, *die*

operational [ɒpə'reɪʃənl] *adj.* **a)** *(concerned with operations)* Einsatz⟨*flugzeug, -breite*⟩; Betriebs⟨*wirtschaftlichkeit, -personal*⟩; *(Mil.)* Einsatz-; **b)** *(esp. Mil.: ready to function)* einsatzbereit

operational re'search *n. (Brit.)* Unternehmensforschung, *die*

operative ['ɒpərətɪv] **1.** *adj.* **a)** *(in operation)* **the law became ~:** das Gesetz trat in Kraft; **the scheme is fully ~:** das Programm läuft; **b)** *(effective)* wirksam; **c)** *(most relevant)* **the ~ word is 'quietly'** die Betonung liegt auf „leise"; **d)** *(Med.)* operativ. **2.** *n.* [Fach]arbeiter, *der*/-arbeiterin, *die;* **machine ~:** Maschinist, *der*/Maschinistin, *die*

operator ['ɒpəreɪtə(r)] *n.* **a)** *(worker)* [Maschinen]bediener, *der*/-bedienerin, *die;* Bedienungskraft, *die; (of crane, excavator, etc.)* Führer, *der;* **b)** *(Teleph.) (at exchange)* Vermittlung, *die; (at switchboard)* Telefonist, *der*/Telefonistin, *die;* **c)** *(person engaged in business)* Unternehmer, *der*/Unternehmerin, *die;* *(coll.: shrewd person)* Schlitzohr, *das (ugs.);* **a sly ~** *(coll.)* ein gewiefter Bursche *(ugs.);* **d)** *(Math., Computing)* Operator, *der*

operetta [ɒpə'retə] *n. (Mus.)* Operette, *die*

ophthalmic [ɒf'θælmɪk] *adj.* Augen⟨*arterie, -krankheit, -chirurg, -salbe*⟩

ophthalmic op'tician *n. (Brit.)* Augenoptiker, *der*/-optikerin, *die*

ophthalmology [ɒfθæl'mɒlədʒɪ] *n. (Med.)* Ophthalmologie, *die (fachspr.);* Augenheilkunde, *die*

opiate ['əʊpɪət] *n.* **a)** *(Med.)* Opiat, *das;* **b)** *(fig.)* Betäubungsmittel, *das; (causing addiction)* Droge, *die*

opine [ə'paɪn] *v. t.* **a)** *(express as one's opinion)* meinen; **b)** *(hold as opinion)* denken

opinion [ə'pɪnjən] *n.* **a)** *(belief, judgement)* Meinung, *die* **(on** über + *Akk.*, zu); Ansicht, *die* **(on** von, zu, über + *Akk.*); **his [political] ~s** seine [politische] Einstellung; **his ~s on the matter/on religion** seine Meinung dazu/seine Einstellung zur Religion; **in my ~:** meiner Meinung nach; **be of [the] ~ that ...:** der Ansicht sein, daß ...; **be a matter of ~:** Ansichtssache sein; *see also* **difference a; b)** *no pl., no art. (beliefs etc. of group)* Meinung, *die* **(on** über + *Akk.*); **~ is swinging in his favour** es gibt einen Meinungsumschwung zu seinen Gunsten; **public ~:** die öffentliche Meinung; **c)** *(estimate)* **have a high ~ of sb.** eine hohe Meinung von jmdm. haben; **I formed a better ~ of the place** ich bekam einen besseren Eindruck von dem Ort; **have a great ~ of oneself** sehr von sich überzeugt sein; **have no ~ of sth./sb.** von etw./jmdm. nicht sehr überzeugt sein; **d)** *(formal statement of expert)* Gutachten, *das;* **[get** *or* **secure a] solicitor's/expert's ~:** [ein] Rechts-/Sachverständigengutachten [einholen]; **another** *or* **a second ~:** die Meinung eines weiteren *od.* zweiten Sachverständigen; **e)** *(Law) (expression of reasons for decision)* Urteilsbegründung, *die; (judgement, decision)* Entscheidung, *die;* Urteil, *das*

opinionated [ə'pɪnjəneɪtɪd] *adj.* **a)** *(obstinate)* rechthaberisch; **b)** *(self-willed)* eigensinnig

o'pinion poll *n.* Meinungsumfrage, *die*

opium ['əʊpɪəm] *n.* Opium, *das*

opium: ~ den *n.* Opiumhöhle, *die (abwertend);* **~-pipe** *n.* Opiumpfeife, *die*

opossum [ə'pɒsəm] *n. (Zool.)* **a)** Opossum, *das;* **b)** *(Austral., NZ) see* **possum c**

oppo ['ɒpəʊ] *n., pl.* **~s** *(Brit. sl.)* Kumpel, *der (salopp)*

opponent [ə'pəʊnənt] *n.* Gegner, *der*/Gegnerin, *die*

opportune ['ɒpətju:n] *adj.* **a)** *(favourable)* günstig; **b)** *(well-timed)* zur rechten Zeit *nachgestellt;* **be ~:** zur rechten Zeit kommen

opportunely ['ɒpətju:nlɪ] *adv. see* **opportune:** günstig; zur rechten Zeit; **be ~ timed** zeitlich günstig liegen

opportunism [ɒpə'tju:nɪzm] *n., no pl.* Opportunismus, *der*

opportunist [ɒpə'tju:nɪst] *n.* Opportunist, *der*/Opportunistin, *die*

opportunity [ɒpə'tju:nɪtɪ] *n.* Gelegenheit, *die;* **have plenty of/little ~ for doing** *or* **to do sth.** reichlich/wenig Gelegenheit haben, etw. zu tun; **~ knocks for sb.** eine Gelegenheit bietet sich jmdm.; *see also* **equal opportunity; take 1e**

opposable [ə'pəʊzəbl] *adj. (Anat., Zool.)* opponierbar

oppose [ə'pəʊz] **1.** *v. t.* **a)** *(set oneself against)* sich wenden gegen; opponieren gegen; **b)** *(place as obstacle)* entgegenstellen **(to** *Dat.*); **c)** *(set as contrast)* gegenüberstellen **(to, against** *Dat.*); **d)** *(Anat., Zool.)* opponieren. **2.** *v. i.* ⟨*Opposition:*⟩ opponieren; **the opposing team** die gegnerische Mannschaft

opposed [ə'pəʊzd] *adj.* **a)** *(contrary, opposite)* gegensätzlich; entgegengesetzt; **X and Y are diametrically ~:** X und Y sind einander diametral entgegengesetzt; **as ~ to** im Gegensatz zu; **b)** *(hostile)* **be ~** ⟨*Personen:*⟩ Gegner sein; **be ~ to sth.** gegen etw. sein

opposite ['ɒpəzɪt] **1.** *adj.* **a)** *(on other or farther side)* gegenüberliegend ⟨*Straßenseite, Ufer*⟩; entgegengesetzt ⟨*Ende*⟩; **b)** *(contrary)* entgegengesetzt ⟨*Weg, Richtung*⟩; **c)** *(very different in character)* entgegengesetzt, gegensätzlich ⟨*Beschreibungen, Aussagen*⟩; **be ~ to sth.** das Gegenteil von etw. sein; **be of an ~ kind from ...:** von einer ganz anderen Art sein als ...; **d) the ~ sex** das andere Geschlecht. **2.** *n.* Gegenteil, *das* **(of** von); **be the extreme ~ of sth.** das genaue Gegenteil von etw. sein; **be ~s** einen Gegensatz bilden. **3.** *adv.* gegenüber; **sit ~:** auf der gegenüberliegenden Seite sitzen. **4.** *prep.* gegenüber; **~ each other** einander gegenüber; **play ~ sb.** *(Theatre)* neben jmdm. spielen

opposite 'number *n. (fig.)* Pendant, *das*

opposition [ɒpəˈzɪʃn] *n.* **a)** *no pl. (antagonism)* Opposition, *die; (resistance)* Widerstand, *der* **(to** gegen); **in ~ to** entgegen; **offer ~ to sth.** einer Sache *(Dat.)* Widerstand entgegensetzen; **without ~:** ohne Widerstand; **b)** *(Brit. Polit.)* **the O~, Her Majesty's O~:** die Opposition; **Leader of the O~:** Oppositionsführer, *der*/-führerin, *die;* **[be] in ~:** in der Opposition [sein]; **c)** *(body of opponents or competitors)* Gegner *Pl.;* **d)** *(contrast, antithesis)* Gegensatz, *der* **(to** zu); **e)** *(placing or being placed opposite)* Plazierung an gegenüberliegenden Stellen; **by the ~ of sth. to sth.** indem man etw. gegenüber einer Sache *(Dat.)* plaziert; **f)** *(Astron., Astrol.)* **be in ~:** in Opposition stehen **(with** zu); *abs.* in Opposition zur Sonne stehen

oppress [əˈpres] *v.t.* **a)** *(govern cruelly)* unterdrücken; **b)** *(fig.: weigh down)* ‹*Gefühl:*› bedrücken; ‹*Hitze:*› schwer zu schaffen machen (+ *Dat.*)

oppression [əˈpreʃn] *n.* Unterdrückung, *die*

oppressive [əˈpresɪv] *adj.* **a)** *(tyrannical)* repressiv; **b)** *(fig.: hard to endure)* bedrückend ‹*Ängste, Atmosphäre*› **(to** für); **c)** *(fig.: hot and close)* drückend ‹*Wetter, Klima, Tag*›; **d)** *(fig.: burdensome)* drückend ‹*Steuer*›; repressiv ‹*Gesetz, Beschränkung*›

oppressively [əˈpresɪvlɪ] *adv.* **a)** *(tyrannically)* mit unterdrückerischen Methoden; repressiv ‹*regieren*›; **b)** *(fig.: so as to weigh down)* drückend ‹*heiß*›; **weigh ~ on sb.** schwer auf jmdm. lasten

oppressor [əˈpresə(r)] *n.* Unterdrücker, *der*

opprobrious [əˈprəʊbrɪəs] *adj.* **a)** *(abusive)* verächtlich; **b)** *(shameful)* schändlich

opprobrium [əˈprəʊbrɪəm] *n.* Schande, *die*

opt [ɒpt] *v.i.* sich entscheiden **(for** für); **~ to do sth.** sich dafür entscheiden, etw. zu tun; **~ out** *(not join in)* nicht mitmachen; *(cease taking part)* nicht länger mitmachen; **~ out of** nicht/nicht länger mitmachen bei; *(give up membership of)* austreten aus; *(not take up invitation to)* sich entschließen, doch nicht teilzunehmen an (+ *Dat.*)

optic [ˈɒptɪk] **1.** *adj. (Anat.)* Seh‹*nerv, -hügel, -bahn*›; *(Med.)* Sehnerven‹*entzündung, -atrophie*›. **2.** *n.* **a)** *(in optical instrument)* optisches Element; **b)** *(arch./joc.: eye)* Auge, *das;* **c)** *or* **O~ (P)** *(Brit.: for measuring out spirits)* Portionierer, *der*

optical [ˈɒptɪkl] *adj.* optisch ‹*Zielvorrichtung, Täuschung, Gerät, Fernrohr*›; **~ microscope** Lichtmikroskop, *das;* **~ aid** Sehhilfe, *die*

optical: ~ 'character reader *n. (Computing)* Klarschriftleser, *der;* **~ 'fibre** *n.* Lichtleitfaser, *die*

optically [ˈɒptɪkəlɪ] *adv.* optisch

optician [ɒpˈtɪʃn] *n.* **a)** *(maker or seller of spectacles etc.)* Optiker, *der*/Optikerin, *die;* **b)** *see* **ophthalmic optician**

optics [ˈɒptɪks] *n., no pl.* Optik, *die*

optima *pl. of* **optimum**

optimal [ˈɒptɪml] *see* **optimum 2**

optimise *see* **optimize**

optimism [ˈɒptɪmɪzm] *n., no pl.* Optimismus, *der*

optimist [ˈɒptɪmɪst] *n.* Optimist, *der*/Optimistin, *die*

optimistic [ɒptɪˈmɪstɪk] *adj.* optimistisch

optimistically [ɒptɪˈmɪstɪkəlɪ] *adv.* optimistisch; **~ speaking, ...:** mit etwas Optimismus kann man sagen, daß ...

optimize [ˈɒptɪmaɪz] *v.t.* **a)** *(make optimum)* optimieren; **b)** *(make the most of)* das Beste machen aus

optimum [ˈɒptɪməm] **1.** *n., pl.* **optima** [ˈɒptɪmə] **a)** *(most favourable conditions)* Optimum, *das;* **b)** *(best compromise)* goldener Mittelweg. **2.** *adj.* optimal

option [ˈɒpʃn] *n.* **a)** *(choice)* Wahl, *die; (thing that may be chosen)* Wahlmöglichkeit, *die; (Brit. Univ., Sch.)* Wahlfach, *das;* **I have no ~ but to do sth.** mir bleibt nichts [anderes] übrig, als etw. zu tun; **keep** *or* **leave one's ~s open** sich *(Dat.)* alle Möglichkeiten offenhalten; *see also* **soft option; b)** *no pl. (freedom of choice)* Entscheidungsfreiheit, *die;* **she had no ~ about accepting ...:** sie hatte keine andere Wahl, als ... anzunehmen; **that leaves us no ~ [but to ...]** dann bleibt uns keine andere Wahl[, als zu ...]; **c)** *(St. Exch.)* Option, *die*

optional [ˈɒpʃənl] *adj.* nicht zwingend; fakultativ; **~ subject** Wahlfach, *das;* **formal dress is ~:** Gesellschaftskleidung ist nicht vorgeschrieben; **~ extra** Extra, *das;* **take an ~ paper** eine freiwillige Klausur schreiben

optionally [ˈɒpʃənəlɪ] *adv.* freiwillig

opulence [ˈɒpjʊləns] *n., no pl.* Wohlstand, *der*

opulent [ˈɒpjʊlənt] *adj. (rich)* wohlhabend ‹*Person, Aussehen*›; *(luxurious)* feudal ‹*Auto, Haus, Hotel usw.*›

opulently [ˈɒpjʊləntlɪ] *adv.* im Luxus ‹*leben*›; feudal ‹*möbliert, eingerichtet*›

opus [ˈəʊpəs, ˈɒpəs] *n., pl.* **opera** [ˈɒpərə] **a)** *(Mus.)* Opus, *das;* **b) magnum ~, ~ [magnum]** *(great work)* großes Werk; *(greatest work)* Hauptwerk, *das*

OR *abbr.* **operational research** OR

[1]or [ə(r), *stressed* ɔː(r)] *conj.* **a)** oder; **he cannot read or write** er kann weder lesen noch schreiben; **without food or water** ohne Essen und Wasser; **[either] ... or [else] ...:** entweder ... oder [aber] ...; **b)** *introducing synonym* oder [auch]; *introducing explanation* das heißt; **or rather** beziehungsweise; [oder] genauer gesagt; **c)** *indicating uncertainty* oder; **15 or 20 minutes** 15 bis 20 Minuten; **in a day or two** in ein, zwei Tagen; **a doctor or something** ein Arzt oder so [was] *(ugs.);* **he must be ill or something** vielleicht ist er krank oder so *(ugs.);* **have you gone out of your mind or something?** bist du übergeschnappt, oder was? *(ugs.);* **he or somebody else** er oder sonst jemand; **in Leeds or somewhere** in Leeds oder irgendwo da; *see also* **[1]so 2; d)** *expr. significant afterthought* oder; **he was obviously lying – or was he?** er hat ganz offensichtlich gelogen – oder [doch nicht]?; **they cannot throw you out – or can they?** sie können dich doch nicht hinauswerfen – oder [etwa doch]?

[2]or [ɔː(r)] *(Her.)* **1.** *n.* Gold, *das.* **2.** *adj.* golden

oracle [ˈɒrəkl] *n.* **a)** *(infallible guide or indicator)* Orakel, *das (fig.);* **b)** *(very wise person)* Koryphäe, *die;* Autorität, *die;* **c)** *(place or response of deity)* Orakel, *das;* **d) work the ~** *(Brit. fig.)* [ein wenig] nachhelfen

oracular [əˈrækjʊlə(r)] *adj.* **a)** *(of oracle[s])* Orakel‹*stätte, -priester*›; **b)** *(infallible)* über alle Zweifel erhaben ‹*Äußerung, Buch*›; **c)** *(derog.: obscure or ambiguous)* orakelhaft

oral [ˈɔːrl] **1.** *adj.* **a)** *(spoken)* mündlich ‹*Prüfung, Vereinbarung*›; mündlich überliefert ‹*Tradition*›; **the agreement was only ~:** die Vereinbarung war nur mündlich getroffen worden; **b)** *(done or taken by the mouth)* oral; **~ sex** Oralverkehr, *der;* **c)** *(Anat.)* Mund‹*höhle, -schleimhaut*›. **2.** *n. (coll.: examination)* **the ~[s]** das Mündliche

orally [ˈɔːrəlɪ] *adv.* **a)** *(in speech)* mündlich; **b)** *(by the mouth)* oral; **take ~:** einnehmen

orange [ˈɒrɪndʒ] **1.** *n.* **a)** *(fruit)* Orange, *die;* Apfelsine, *die;* **b)** *(tree)* Orangenbaum, *der;* **mock ~** *(Bot.)* Falscher Jasmin; Blasser Pfeifenstrauch; **c)** *(colour)* **~[-colour]** Orange, *das.* **2.** *adj.* orange[farben]; Orangen‹*geschmack*›; **~ drink** Getränk mit Orangengeschmack

orange: ~-blossom *n.* Orangenblüte, *die;* **~-box** *n.* Apfelsinenkiste, *die;* **~-juice** *n.* Orangensaft, *der;* **O~man** [ˈɒrɪndʒmən] *n., pl.* **O~men** [ˈɒrɪndʒmən] *(Polit.)* Orangeman, *der;* Mitglied der Orange Society; **~-peel** *n.* Orangenschale, *die*

orangery [ˈɒrɪndʒərɪ] *n.* Orangerie, *die*

orange: ~ 'squash *see* **[1]squash 3a; ~-stick** *n.* Maniküreстäbchen, *das*

orang-utan [ɔːræŋʊˈtæn] *n. (Zool.)* Orang-Utan, *der*

orate [əˈreɪt] *v.i. (joc.)* Reden schwingen *(ugs.); (derog.)* salbadern *(ugs. abwertend)*

oration [əˈreɪʃn] *n.* Rede, *die*

orator [ˈɒrətə(r)] *n.* Redner, *der*/Rednerin, *die; (eloquent speaker)* Rhetoriker, *der*/Rhetorikerin, *die*

oratorical [ɒrəˈtɒrɪkl] *adj.* ausdrucksstark

oratorio [ɒrəˈtɔːrɪəʊ] *n., pl.* **~s** *(Mus.)* Oratorium, *das*

oratory [ˈɒrətərɪ] *n.* **a)** *no pl. (art of public speaking)* Redekunst, *die;* Rhetorik, *die;* **b)** *no pl. (rhetorical language)* Rhetorik, *die;* **c)** *(small chapel)* Oratorium, *das*

orb [ɔːb] *n.* **a)** *(sphere)* Kugel, *die;* **b)** *(part of regalia)* Reichsapfel, *der*

orbit [ˈɔːbɪt] **1.** *n.* **a)** *(Astron.)* [Umlauf]bahn, *die;* **b)** *(Astronaut.)* Umlaufbahn, *die;* Orbit, *der; (single circuit)* Umkreisung, *die;* **be in/go into ~ [around the moon]** in der [Mond]umlaufbahn sein/in die [Mond]umlaufbahn eintreten; **put/send into ~:** in die Umlaufbahn bringen/schießen; **c)** *(fig.)* Sphäre, *die;* **d)** *(Anat.)* Augenhöhle, *die;* Orbita, *die (fachspr.);* **e)** *(Phys.: of electron)* Orbital, *das.* **2.** *v.i.* kreisen. **3.** *v.t.* umkreisen

orbital [ˈɔːbɪtl] *adj.* **a)** *(Anat.)* Orbital-; **b)** *(Astron., Phys.)* Bahn-; **c)** Ring‹*straße, -linie*›; **north ~ route** Nordring, *der*

Orcadian [ɔːˈkeɪdɪən] **1.** *adj.* Orkney-; der Orkneyinseln *nachgestellt.* **2.** *n.* Bewohner/Bewohnerin der Orkneyinseln

orchard [ˈɔːtʃəd] *n.* Obstgarten, *der; (commercial)* Obstplantage, *die;* **cherry ~:** Kirschgarten, *der*

orchestra [ˈɔːkɪstrə] *n.* **a)** *(Mus.)* Orchester, *das;* **b)** *see* **orchestra pit**

orchestral [ɔːˈkestrl] *adj.* Orchester-; *(suggestive of orchestra)* orchestral

orchestra: ~ pit *n.* Orchestergraben, *der;* **~ stalls** *n.pl.* Parkett, *das;* **seat in the ~ stalls** Sperrsitz, *der*

orchestrate [ˈɔːkɪstreɪt] *v.t. (Mus.; also fig.)* orchestrieren

orchestration [ɔːkɪˈstreɪʃn] *n.* **a)** *(Mus.)* Orchesterbearbeitung, *die;* Orchestrierung, *die;* **b)** *(fig.)* Orchestrierung, *die*

orchid [ˈɔːkɪd] *n.* Orchidee, *die*

orchis [ˈɔːkɪs] *n. (Bot.)* Knabenkraut, *das;* Orchis, *die (fachspr.)*

ordain [ɔːˈdeɪn] *v.t.* **a)** *(Eccl.)* ordinieren; **be ~ed priest** ordiniert werden; **b)** *(destine)* bestimmen; **if fate should so ~ it** wenn es das Schicksal so will *od.* fügt; **c)** *(decree)* verfügen

ordeal [ɔːˈdiːl] *n.* **a)** Qual, *die; (geh.)* Tortur, *die* **(by** durch); **b)** *(Hist.)* Ordal, *das (fachspr.);* Gottesurteil, *das;* **~ by fire/water** Feuer-/Wasserprobe, *die*

order [ˈɔːdə(r)] **1.** *n.* **a)** *(sequence)* Reihenfolge, *die;* **~ of words, word ~:** Wortstellung, *die;* **~ of play** *(Tennis etc.)* Spielfolge, *die;* **in ~ of importance/size/age** nach Wichtigkeit/Größe/Alter; **be in subject ~** *or* **~ of subject** nach Gebieten geordnet sein; **put sth. in ~:** etw. [in der richtigen Reihenfolge] ordnen; **keep sth. in ~:** etw. in der richtigen Reihenfolge halten; **answer the questions in ~:** die Fragen der Reihe nach beantworten; **out of ~:** nicht in der richtigen Reihenfolge; durcheinander; **the cards get out of ~:** die Karten geraten in Unordnung *od.* durcheinander; **put sth. back out of ~:** etw. nicht an den richtigen Platz zurückstellen/-legen; **b)** *(regular array, normal state)* Ordnung, *die;* **put** *or* **set sth./one's affairs in ~:** Ordnung in etw. bringen/seine Angelegenheiten ordnen; **be/not be in ~:** in Ordnung/nicht in Ordnung sein *(ugs.);* **put sth. in ~** *(repair)* etw. in Ordnung bringen *(ugs.);* **be out of/in ~** *(not in/in working condition)* nicht funktionieren/funktionieren; **'out of ~'** „außer Betrieb"; **the engine is now in running ~:** der Motor läuft jetzt wieder *od.* ist jetzt wieder betriebsbereit; **in good/bad ~:** in gutem/schlechtem Zustand; **in working ~:** betriebsfähig; *see also* **house 1 a; c)** *in sing. and pl. (command)* Anweisung, *die;* Anordnung, *die;* Weisung, *die (geh.); (Mil.)* Befehl, *der; (Law)* Beschluß, *der;* Verfügung, *die;* **my ~s are to ..., I have ~s to ...:** ich habe Anweisung zu ...; **while following ~s** bei Befolgung der Anweisung/bei der Befehlsausführung; **act on ~s** auf Befehl handeln; **be the one who gives the ~s** das Sagen haben; **I don't take ~s from anyone!** ich lasse mir von keinem etwas befehlen!; **~s are ~s** Befehl ist Befehl; **court ~:** Gerichtsbeschluß, *der;* **by ~ of** auf Anordnung (+ *Gen.*); *see also* **doctor 1 a; further 1 b; starter a; d) in ~ to do sth.** um etw. zu tun; **in ~ that sb. should do sth.** damit jmd. etw. tut; **e)** *(Commerc.)* Auftrag, *der* **(for** über + *Akk.*); Bestellung, *die* **(for** *Gen.*); Order, *die (Kaufmannsspr.); (to waiter, ~ed goods)* Bestellung, *die;* **place an ~ [with sb.]** [jmdm.] einen Auftrag erteilen; **have sth. on ~:** etw. bestellt haben; **put goods on ~:** Waren in Bestellung geben; **to ~:** auf Bestellung; **she could cry to ~** *(fig.)* sie konnte auf Befehl weinen; **made to ~:** nach Maß angefertigt, maßgeschneidert ⟨*Kleidung*⟩; **a suit made to ~:** ein Maßanzug; **last ~s please** *(Brit.)* die letzten Bestellungen *(vor der Sperrstunde),* bitte!; *see also* **tall 1 b; f)** *(law-abiding state)* [öffentliche] Ordnung; **forces of ~:** Ordnungsmächte; **keep ~:** Ordnung [be]wahren; *see also* **law b; g)** *(Eccl.: fraternity)* Orden, *der;* **h)** *(Eccl.: grade of ministry)* Weihestufe, *die;* **holy ~s** heilige Weihen; **be in [holy] ~s** dem geistlichen Stand angehören; **take [holy] ~s** die [heiligen] Weihen empfangen; **i)** *(social class)* [Gesellschafts]schicht, *die; (clerical ~, ~ of baronets, etc.)* Stand, *der; see also* **[2]lower 1 b; j)** *(principles of decorum and rules of procedure)* [Geschäfts]ordnung, *die;* **O~! O~!** zur Ordnung!; Ruhe bitte!; **~ in court** *(Brit.) or (Amer.)* **the courtroom** Ruhe im Gerichtssaal; **call sb./the meeting to ~:** jmdn./die Versammlung zur Ordnung rufen; **call a meeting to ~** *(open the proceedings)* eine Versammlung für eröffnet erklären; **point of ~:** Verfahrensfrage, *die;* **[on a] point of ~, Mr Chairman** Antrag zur Geschäftsordnung, Herr Vorsitzender; **be in ~:** zulässig sein; *(fig.)* ⟨*Forderung:*⟩ berechtigt sein; ⟨*Drink, Erklärung:*⟩ angebracht sein; **the speaker is in ~:** der Redner hält sich an die Geschäftsordnung; **it is in ~ for him to do that** es ist in Ordnung, wenn er das tut; **be out of ~:** gegen die Geschäftsordnung verstoßen; ⟨*Verhalten, Handlung:*⟩ unzulässig sein; **that's out of ~, mate** *(coll.)* so [geht's] nicht, Kumpel *(ugs.);* **~ of the day** *(lit. or fig.)* Tagesordnung, *die;* **be the ~ of the day** auf der Tagesordnung stehen; *(fig.)* an der Tagesordnung sein; **~ of business** Geschäftsordnung, *die; (sequence of matters)* Tagesordnung, *die; see also* **standing orders b; k)** *(constitution of things)* Ordnung, *die;* **a new ~ of literary criticism** eine neue Art *od.* Gattung von Literaturkritik; **l)** *(kind, degree)* Klasse, *die;* Art, *die;* **intelligence of a high ~:** hochgradige Intelligenz; **his work is usually of a high ~:** seine Arbeit ist gewöhnlich erstklassig; **m)** *(Archit.)* Säulenordnung, *die;* **n)** *(company of distinguished persons, badge or insignia)* Orden, *der;* **O~ of Merit** *(Brit.)* Verdienstorden, *der;* **Masonic O~:** Freimaurerloge, *die;* **o)** *(Finance)* Order, *die;* Zahlungsanweisung, *die;* **[banker's] ~:** [Bank]anweisung, *die;* **'pay to the ~ of ...'** „zahlbar an ..." (+ *Akk.*); *see also* **money order; standing order a; p)** *(Mil.)* Ordnung, *die;* **marching ~:** Marschordnung, *die;* **in close ~:** in geschlossener Formation; **in battle ~:** in Kampfaufstellung; **q)** *(Math.)* Ordnung, *die;* **~ [of magnitude]** Größenordnung, *die;* **of** *or* **in the ~ of ...:** in der Größenordnung von ...; **of the first ~** ⟨*Gleichung*⟩ ersten Grades; **a scoundrel of the first ~** *(fig. coll.)* ein Schurke ersten Ranges; **r)** *(Eccl.: form of service)* Ritual, *das;* **s)** *(Biol.)* Ordnung, *die; see also* **natural order. 2.** *v. t.* **a)** *(command)* befehlen; anordnen; ⟨*Gott, Schicksal:*⟩ bestimmen; ⟨*Richter:*⟩ verfügen; verordnen ⟨*Arznei, Ruhe usw.*⟩; **~ sb. to do sth.** jmdn. anweisen/*(Milit.)* jmdm. befehlen, etw. zu tun; **~ sth. [to be] done** anordnen, daß etw. getan wird; **the dog was ~ed to be destroyed** es wurde die Tötung des Hundes verfügt *od.* angeordnet; *see also* **doctor 1 a; b)** *(direct the supply of)* bestellen **(from** bei); ordern ⟨*Kaufmannsspr.*⟩; **~ in advance** vorbestellen; **c)** *(arrange)* ordnen; **~ed** geordnet *od.* geregelt ⟨*Leben*⟩; **~ arms** *(Mil.)* Gewehr bei Fuß stehen; **d)** *(command to go)* schicken; *(Mil.)* beordern; **~ sb. [to go] to Spain** jmdn. nach Spanien schicken/beordern; **~ sb. [to come] home** jmdn. befehlen, nach Hause zu kommen; **~ sb. out of the house** jmdn. aus dem Haus weisen; **~ back** zurückbeordern; **e)** *(ordain)* bestimmen

~ a'bout, ~ a'round *v. t. (coll.)* herumkommandieren

~ 'off *v. t. (Sport)* **~ sb. off [the pitch/field]** jmdn. vom Platz stellen

~ 'out *v. t.* hinausschicken; ausschicken, einsetzen ⟨*Truppen usw.*⟩

order: ~-book *n.* **a)** *(Commerc.)* Auftragsbuch, *das;* **b) O~ Book** *(Brit. Parl.)* Buch mit Eintragungen der angemeldeten Anträge; **~-form** *n.* Bestellformular, *das;* Bestellschein, *der;* **O~ in 'Council** *n. (Brit.)* Regierungserlaß, *der*

orderly ['ɔ:dəlɪ] **1.** *adj.* **a)** friedlich ⟨*Demonstration usw.*⟩; diszipliniert ⟨*Menge*⟩; *(conforming to order)* ordnungsgemäß; *(methodical)* methodisch; geordnet ⟨*Linie, Leben*⟩; geregelt ⟨*Leben, Gewohnheiten*⟩; ordentlich ⟨*Mensch*⟩; *(tidy)* ordentlich; **b)** *(Mil.)* diensthabend *od.* -tuend. **2.** *n. (Mil.)* [Offiziers]bursche, *der*

orderly: ~ officer *n. (Brit.)* Offizier vom Dienst, *der;* **~ room** *n.* Schreibstube, *die*

order: ~ pad *n.* Bestellblock, *der;* **~-paper** *n. (Brit. Parl.)* Tagesordnung, *die*

ordinal ['ɔ:dɪnl] *(Math.)* **1.** *adj.* **~ number** *see* **2. 2.** *n.* Ordnungs-, Ordinalzahl, *die*

ordinance ['ɔ:dɪnəns] *n.* **a)** *(order, decree)* Verordnung, *die;* **divine ~:** göttliche Bestimmung; **b)** *(enactment by local authority)* Verfügung, *die;* Bestimmung, *die;* **c)** *(religious rite)* Ritus, *der*

ordinand ['ɔ:dɪnænd] *n. (Eccl.)* Weihekandidat, *der*

ordinarily ['ɔ:dɪnərɪlɪ] *adv.* normalerweise; gewöhnlich; in der Regel; *(unexceptionally)* gewöhnlich

ordinary ['ɔ:dɪnərɪ] *adj.* **a)** *(regular, normal)* normal ⟨*Gebrauch*⟩; üblich ⟨*Verfahren*⟩; *(not exceptional)* gewöhnlich; *(average)* durchschnittlich; **very ~** *(derog.)* ziemlich mittelmäßig; **in the ~ way** *(usually)* normalerweise; **better/worse than ~:** besser/schlechter als sonst; **~ tap-water** normales *od.* gewöhnliches Leitungswasser; **in ~ life** im Alltagsleben; **be no ~ thing** kein gewöhnliches Ding sein; **~ people** *or* **folk** einfache Leute; *see also* **course 1 a; b)** *(Brit. St. Exch.)* **~ share** Stammaktie, *die;* **~ stock** Stammaktien; **c) above the ~:** über dem Durchschnitt; überdurchschnittlich ⟨*Intelligenz usw.*⟩; **out of the ~:** außergewöhnlich; ungewöhnlich; **something/nothing out of the ~:** etwas/nichts Außergewöhnliches

ordinary: ~ level *see* **O level; ~ 'seaman** *n.* Leichtmatrose, *der*

ordination [ɔ:dɪ'neɪʃn] *n.* **a)** *(Eccl.)* Ordination, *die;* Ordinierung, *die;* **b)** *(decreeing)* Bestimmung, *die;* **God's ~:** Gottes Wille

ordnance ['ɔ:dnəns] *n.* **a)** *(guns)* Artillerie, *die;* Geschütze *Pl.;* **~ factory** Waffenfabrik, *die;* **piece of ~:** Geschütz, *das;* **b)** *(service)* Feldzeugwesen, *das;* Feldzeugmeisterei, *die; attrib.* Feldzeug-; **O~ Corps** Technische Truppe

ordnance: ~ map = ~ survey map; ~ 'survey *n. (Brit.)* amtliche Landesvermessung; **~ survey map** amtliche topographische Karte

ore [ɔ:(r)] *n.* Erz, *das*

oregano [ɒrɪ'gɑ:nəʊ, ə'regənəʊ] *n., no pl. (Cookery)* Oregano, *der;* Origano, *der*

organ ['ɔ:gən] *n.* **a)** *(Mus.)* Orgel, *die; (harmonium)* Harmonium, *das; see also* **American organ; b)** *(Biol.)* Organ, *das;* **speech ~s** Sprechwerkzeuge; **the male ~** *(euphem.)* das männliche Glied; **c)** *(medium of communication)* Sprachrohr, *das; (of political party etc.)* Organ, *das*

organdie *(Amer.:* **organdy)** ['ɔ:gəndɪ, ɔ:'gændɪ] *n. (Textiles)* Organdy, *der*

'organ-grinder *n.* Drehorgelspieler, *der/* -spielerin, *die;* Leierkastenmann, *der*

organic [ɔ:'gænɪk] *adj.* **a)** *(also Chem. Physiol.)* organisch; **b)** *(constitutional, inherent, structural)* konstitutionell; *(fundamental, vital)* konstitutiv *(geh.)* ⟨*Teile*⟩; **c)** *(without chemicals)* biologisch, biodynamisch ⟨*Nahrungsmittel*⟩; biologisch-dynamisch ⟨*Ackerbau usw.*⟩; **d)** *(Med.)* organisch, körperlich ⟨*Leiden*⟩

organically [ɔ:'gænɪkəlɪ] *adv.* **a)** *(also Med.)* organisch; **b)** *(without chemicals)* biologisch; biodynamisch

organic 'chemist *n.* Organiker, *der*/Organikerin, *die*

organisation, organise, organised, organiser *see* **organiz-**

organism ['ɔ:gənɪzm] *n.* **a)** *(organized body)* Organismus, *der;* **b)** *(Biol.)* Organismus, *der; (structure)* Aufbau, *der*

organist ['ɔ:gənɪst] *n.* Organist, *der*/Organistin, *die*

organization [ɔ:gənaɪ'zeɪʃn] *n.* **a)** *(organizing, systematic arrangement)* Organisation, *die; (of material)* Ordnung, *die; (of library)* Anordnung, *die;* **~ of time/work** Zeit-/Arbeitseinteilung, *die;* **b)** *(organized body, system)* Organisation, *die*

organizational [ɔ:gənaɪ'zeɪʃənl] *adj.* organisatorisch

organi'zation man *n., Mensch, der die Belange der Organisation, der er dient, über alles stellt*

organize ['ɔ:gənaɪz] *v. t.* **a)** *(give orderly structure to)* ordnen; planen ⟨*Leben*⟩; einteilen ⟨*Arbeit, Zeit*⟩; *(frame, establish)* organisieren ⟨*Verein, Partei, Firma, Institution*⟩; **organizing ability** Organisationstalent, *das;* **I must get ~d** *(get ready)* ich muß fertig werden; **~ sb.** jmdn. an die Hand nehmen *(fig.);* **as soon as I've got myself ~d** sobald ich soweit bin; **b)** *(arrange)* organisieren; **can you ~ the catering?** kümmerst du dich um die Verpflegung?; **c) ~ into groups/teams** in Gruppen/Mannschaften einteilen

organized ['ɔ:gənaɪzd] *adj. (systematic, structured)* organisiert; geregelt ⟨*Leben*⟩; **be well ~ for a trip** für eine Reise gut vorbereitet sein

organizer ['ɔ:gənaɪzə(r)] *n.* **a)** Organisator,

der/Organisatorin, *die; (of event, festival)* Veranstalter, *der*/Veranstalterin, *die;* **b)** *(bag)* Aktentasche, *die*

organ: ~-loft *n.* Orgelempore, *die;* **~-music** *n.* Orgelmusik, *die;* **~-pipe** *n. (Mus.)* Orgelpfeife, *die;* **~-stop** *n. (Mus.)* Orgelregister, *das; (handle)* Registerzug, *der*

orgasm ['ɔ:gæzəm] *n.* Orgasmus, *der;* Höhepunkt, *der (auch fig.)*

orgiastic [ɔ:dʒɪ'æstɪk] *adj.* orgiastisch

orgy ['ɔ:dʒɪ] *n.* Orgie, *die;* **drunken ~:** Orgie unter Alkoholeinfluß; **an ~ of spending** eine Kauforgie; Kaufexzesse; **an ~ of killing** eine Orgie des Tötens; ein Blutrausch

oriel ['ɔ:rɪəl] *n.* Erkerfenster, *das*

orient 1. ['ɔ:rɪənt] *n.* **the O~:** der Orient; *(East Asia)* der Ferne Osten. **2.** ['ɔ:rɪent, 'ɒrɪent] *v. t.* **a)** *(set or determine position of)* ausrichten (**towards** nach); **b)** *(fig.)* einweisen (**in** in + *Akk.*); ausrichten, abstellen (**towards** auf + *Akk.*) ⟨*Programm*⟩; **~ oneself** sich orientieren *od.* zurechtfinden; **-~ed** -orientiert; **money-~ed** materiell orientiert; **career-~ed** berufsbezogen; praxisorientiert

oriental [ɔ:rɪ'entl, ɒrɪ'entl] **1.** *adj.* orientalisch; Orient⟨*teppich*⟩; asiatisch ⟨*Unergründlichkeit*⟩; **the O~ Church** die Ostkirche; die orientalische Kirche; **O~ studies** Orientalistik, *die;* **~ trade/travel** Orienthandel, *der*/Orientreisen. **2.** *n.* Asiat, *der*/Asiatin, *die*

orientalist [ɔ:rɪ'entəlɪst, ɒrɪ'entəlɪst] *n.* Orientalist, *der*/Orientalistin, *die*

orientate ['ɒrɪənteɪt, 'ɔ:rɪənteɪt] *see* **orient 2**

orientation [ɒrɪən'teɪʃn, ɔ:rɪən'teɪʃn] *n.* **a)** *(orienting)* Orientierung, *die; (of new employees etc.)* Einweisung, *die;* **sense of ~:** Orientierungssinn, *der;* **b)** *(relative position)* Ausrichtung, *die; (fig.)* Orientierung, *die;* **what is the ~ of ...?** wie ist ... ausgerichtet?; **my ~ was always towards ...:** ich war immer auf ... ausgerichtet

orien'tation course *n.* Einführungsveranstaltung, *die*

orienteering [ɔ:rɪən'tɪərɪŋ, ɒrɪən'tɪərɪŋ] *n. (Brit.)* Orientierungsrennen, *das*

orifice ['ɒrɪfɪs] *n.* Öffnung, *die; (of tube)* Mündung, *die;* **nasal ~:** Nasenloch, *das*

origami [ɒrɪ'gɑ:mɪ] *n.* Origami, *das*

origin ['ɒrɪdʒɪn] *n. (derivation)* Abstammung, *die;* Herkunft, *die; (beginnings)* Anfänge *Pl.; (of world etc.)* Entstehung, *die; (source)* Ursprung, *der; (of belief, rumour)* Quelle, *die;* **be of humble ~, have humble ~s** bescheidener Herkunft sein; **be Irish by ~:** irischer Herkunft sein; **the ~ of species** die Entstehung der Arten; **country of ~:** Herkunftsland, *das;* **words which are of French ~** *or* **are French in ~:** Wörter französischen Ursprungs; **have its ~ in sth.** seinen Ursprung in etw. *(Dat.)* haben; einer Sache *(Dat.)* seinen Ursprung verdanken

original [ə'rɪdʒɪnl] **1.** *adj.* **a)** *(first, earliest)* ursprünglich; **~ edition** Originalausgabe, *die;* **the ~ inhabitants** die Ureinwohner; **~ sin** *(Theol.)* Erbsünde, *die;* **b)** *(primary)* original; Original-; Ur⟨*text, -fassung*⟩; eigenständig ⟨*Forschung*⟩; *(inventive)* originell; *(creative)* schöpferisch; **an ~ painting** ein Original; **from the ~ German** aus der deutschen Urfassung. **2.** *n.* **a)** Original, *das;* **b)** *(eccentric person)* Original, *das (ugs.)*

originality [ərɪdʒɪ'nælɪtɪ] *n.* Originalität, *die*

originally [ə'rɪdʒɪnəlɪ] *adv.* **a)** ursprünglich; **be ~ from ...:** [ursprünglich] aus ... stammen; **b)** *(in an original way)* originell ⟨*schreiben usw.*⟩; **think ~:** originelle Gedanken haben

originate [ə'rɪdʒɪneɪt] **1.** *v. i.* **~ from** entstehen aus; **~ in** seinen Ursprung haben in (+ *Dat.*); **~ with sb.** von jmdm. stammen. **2.** *v. t.* schaffen; hervorbringen; kreieren ⟨*neue Mode*⟩; *(discover)* erfinden; **who ~d the idea?** von wem stammt die Idee?

origination [ərɪdʒɪ'neɪʃn] *n.* Entstehung, *die*

originator [ə'rɪdʒɪneɪtə(r)] *n.* Urheber, *der*/Urheberin, *die; (inventor)* Erfinder, *der*/Erfinderin, *die;* **who was the ~ of that idea?** von wem stammt diese Idee?

Orkney [Islands] ['ɔ:knɪ (aɪləndz)] *pr. n. [pl.],* **Orkneys** ['ɔ:knɪz] *pr. n. pl.* Orkneyinseln *Pl.;* Orkneys *Pl.*

ornament 1. ['ɔ:nəmənt] *n.* **a)** *(decorative object)* Schmuck-, Ziergegenstand, *der; (on pillar etc.)* Ornament, *das; (person)* Zierde, *die;* **b)** *no pl. (decorating)* Verzierungen *Pl.;* Zierat, *der (geh.);* **for** *or* **by way of ~:** zum Schmuck *od.* zur Zierde; **an altar rich in ~:** ein reichverzierter Altar; **c)** *usu. in pl. (Eccl.)* Kirchengerät, *das;* liturgisches Gerät; **d)** *in pl. (Mus.)* Verzierungen *Pl.;* Ornamente *Pl.* **2.** ['ɔ:nəment] *v. t.* verzieren

ornamental [ɔ:nə'mentl] **1.** *adj.* dekorativ; ornamental *(bes. Kunst);* Zier⟨*pflanze, -naht usw.*⟩; **purely ~:** nur zum Schmuck *od.* zur Zierde; rein dekorativ; **an ~ lake** ein Zierteich. **2.** *n. (plant)* Zierpflanze, *die*

ornamentally [ɔ:nə'mentəlɪ] *adv.* dekorativ

ornamentation [ɔ:nəmen'teɪʃn] *n., no pl.* **a)** *(ornamenting)* Ausschmückung, *die;* **b)** *(embellishment[s])* Verzierung, *die*

ornate [ɔ:'neɪt] *adj.* **a)** *(elaborately adorned)* reich verziert; prunkvoll ⟨*Dekoration*⟩; **heavily ~:** überladen; **b)** *(style)* blumig *(abwertend);* reich ausgeschmückt ⟨*Prosa*⟩

ornery ['ɔ:nərɪ] *adj. (Amer. coll.)* **a)** *(of poor quality)* primitiv *(abwertend);* **b)** *(cantankerous)* aggressiv; streitlustig

ornithological [ɔ:nɪθə'lɒdʒɪkl] *adj.* ornithologisch; vogelkundlich

ornithologist [ɔ:nɪ'θɒlədʒɪst] *n..* Ornithologe, *der*/Ornithologin, *die;* Vogelkundler, *der*/Vogelkundlerin, *die*

ornithology [ɔ:nɪ'θɒlədʒɪ] *n.* Ornithologie, *die;* Vogelkunde, *die*

orphan ['ɔ:fn] **1.** *n.* Waise, *die;* Waisenkind, *das;* **be left an ~:** [zur] Waise werden. **2.** *attrib. adj.* Waisen-. **3.** *v. t.* zur Waise machen; **be ~ed** [zur] Waise werden

orphanage ['ɔ:fənɪdʒ] *n.* Waisenhaus, *das*

orthodontics [ɔ:θə'dɒntɪks] *n., no pl.* Kieferorthopädie, *die*

orthodontist [ɔ:θə'dɒntɪst] *n.* Kieferorthopäde, *der*/Kieferorthopädin, *die*

orthodox ['ɔ:θədɒks] *adj.* orthodox; *(conservative)* konventionell

Orthodox 'Church *n.* orthodoxe Kirche

orthodoxy ['ɔ:θədɒksɪ] *n.* Orthodoxie, *die*

orthography [ɔ:'θɒgrəfɪ] *n.* Orthographie, *die;* Rechtschreibung, *die*

orthopaedic [ɔ:θə'pi:dɪk] *adj.* orthopädisch

orthopaedics [ɔ:θə'pi:dɪks] *n., no pl. (Med.)* Orthopädie, *die*

orthopaedist [ɔ:θə'pi:dɪst] *n. (Med.)* Orthopäde, *der*/Orthopädin, *die*

orthopedic, orthopedics, orthopedist *(Amer.) see* **orthopaed-**

Orwellian [ɔ:'welɪən] *adj.* Orwellsch

OS *abbr.* **a)** *(Brit.)* **Ordnance Survey; b)** **outsize** übergr.

Oscar ['ɒskə(r)] *n. (Cinemat.)* Oscar, *der*

oscillate ['ɒsɪleɪt] *v. i.* **a)** *(swing like a pendulum)* schwingen; oszillieren *(fachspr.);* **b)** *(move to and fro between points)* pendeln; **c)** *(fig.)* schwanken; *(vary between extremes of condition or action)* hin und her gerissen sein; **d)** *(Radio)* schwingen

oscillation [ɒsɪ'leɪʃn] *n.* **a)** *(action) see* **oscillate:** Schwingen, *das;* Oszillieren, *das;* Pendeln, *das;* Schwanken, *das;* Hinund-hergerissensein, *das;* Schwingung, *die;* **b)** *(single ~)* Schwingung, *die; (of pendulum)* Pendelausschlag, *der*

oscillator ['ɒsɪleɪtə(r)] *n. (Electr.)* Oszillator, *der*

oscillograph [ə'sɪləgrɑ:f] *n. (Electr.)* Oszillograph, *der*

oscilloscope [ə'sɪləskəʊp] *n. (Electr.)* Oszilloskop, *das*

osier ['əʊzɪə(r)] *n.* **a)** *(Bot.)* Korbweide, *die;* **b)** *attrib.* Weiden⟨*korb, -rute*⟩; Korb⟨*sessel, -möbel*⟩

osmosis [ɒz'məʊsɪs] *n., pl.* **osmoses** [ɒz'məʊsi:z] Osmose, *die*

osmotic [ɒz'mɒtɪk] *adj.* osmotisch

osprey ['ɒspreɪ] *n. (Ornith.)* Fischadler, *der*

Ossie *see* **Aussie**

ossify ['ɒsɪfaɪ] **1.** *v. i.* ossifizieren *(fachspr.);* verknöchern *(auch fig.).* **2.** *v. t. (turn into bone)* ossifizieren *(fachspr.) od.* verknöchern lassen

Ostend [ɒ'stend] *pr. n.* Ostende *(das)*

ostensible [ɒ'stensɪbl] *adj.* vorgeschoben; Schein-; **~ excuse/reason** Ausrede, *die (abwertend)*/Vorwand, *der*

ostensibly [ɒ'stensɪblɪ] *adv.* vorgeblich

ostentation [ɒsten'teɪʃn] *n.* Ostentation, *die (geh.);* Prahlerei, *die (abwertend); (showiness)* Prunk, *der*

ostentatious [ɒsten'teɪʃəs] *adj.* prunkhaft ⟨*Kleidung, Schmuck*⟩; prahlerisch ⟨*Art*⟩; auffällig großzügig ⟨*Spende*⟩; **be ~ about sth.** mit etw. prunken *od. (ugs.)* protzen

ostentatiously [ɒsten'teɪʃəslɪ] *adv.* ostentativ *(geh.),* demonstrativ ⟨*fehlen, schweigen*⟩; prunkhaft ⟨*leben*⟩; prahlerisch ⟨*bemerken*⟩; auffällig ⟨*sich kleiden, sich benehmen*⟩

osteopath ['ɒstɪəpæθ] *n. (Med.)* Spezialist für Knochenleiden

ostler ['ɒslə(r)] *n. (Brit. Hist.)* Pferdeknecht, *der (veralt.);* Reitknecht, *der (früher)*

ostracise *see* **ostracize**

ostracism ['ɒstrəsɪzm] *n.* Ächtung, *die*

ostracize ['ɒstrəsaɪz] *v. t.* ächten; **~ from sth.** ausschließen von etw.

ostrich ['ɒstrɪtʃ] *n.* **a)** Strauß, *der;* **b)** *attrib.* Straußen⟨*ei*⟩; **~ attitude** Vogel-Strauß-Einstellung, *die*

ostrich: ~-feather *n.* Straußenfeder, *die;* **~-like** *adj.* Vogel-Strauß-⟨*Reaktion, Einstellung*⟩; **~-plume** *n.* Straußenfedern *Pl.*

Ostrogoth ['ɒstrəgɒθ] *n. (Hist.)* Ostgote, *der*/Ostgotin, *die*

OT *abbr.* **Old Testament** A. T.

other ['ʌðə(r)] **1.** *adj.* **a)** *(not the same)* ander...; **the ~ two/three** *etc. (the remaining)* die beiden/drei *usw.* anderen; **the ~ way round** *or* **about** gerade umgekehrt; **~ people's property** fremdes Eigentum; **the ~ one** der/die/das andere; **the ~ thing** *(coll.)* das Gegenteil; **there is no ~ way** es geht nicht anders; **I know of no ~ way of doing it** ich weiß nicht, wie ich es sonst machen soll; **some ~ time** ein andermal; **b)** *(further)* **two ~ people/questions** noch zwei [andere *od.* weitere] Leute/Fragen; **one ~ thing** noch eins; **there's just one ~ thing I need to do** ich muß nur noch eines tun; **have you any ~ news/questions?** hast du noch weitere *od.* sonst noch Neuigkeiten/Fragen?; **some/six ~ people** noch ein paar/noch sechs [andere *od.* weitere] Leute; **no ~ questions** keine weiteren Fragen; **do you know of any ~ person who ...?** weißt du noch jemand anderen *od.* sonst noch jemanden, der ...?; **c)** **~ than** *(different from)* anders als; *(except)* außer; **never ~ than charming** immer charmant; **any person ~ than yourself** jeder außer dir; **d)** **some writer/charity or ~:** irgendein Schriftsteller/Wohltätigkeitsverein; **some time/way or ~:** irgendwann/-wie; **something/somehow/somewhere/somebody or ~:** irgend etwas/-wie/-wo/-wer. *See also* **another 1 d; every c; half 1 a; none 1; place 2 b; side 1 g; this 2 c; woman a; world a. 2.** *n.* **a)** *(~ person or thing)* anderer/andere/anderes; **there are six ~s** es sind noch sechs andere da; **are there any ~s who ...?** ist noch jemand da, der ...?; **tell one from the ~:** sie auseinanderhalten; **one or ~ of you/them** irgendwer *od.* -einer/-eine von euch/ihnen; **any ~:** irgendein anderer/-eine andere/-ein anderes; **not any ~:** kein anderer/ keine andere/kein anderes; **one after the ~:** einer/ eine/eins nach dem/der/dem anderen; *see also* **each 2 b; b)** *(arch.)* **no ~** *(person)* kein anderer/keine andere; **he could do no ~ than come** er konnte nichts anderes tun als kommen. **3.** *adv.* anders; **I've never seen her ~ than with him** ich habe sie immer nur mit ihm zusammen gesehen; **~ than that, no real news** abgesehen davon, keine echten Neuigkeiten

otherwise ['ʌðəwaɪz] **1.** *adv.* **a)** *(in a different way)* anders; **think ~:** anders darüber denken; anderer Meinung sein; **it cannot be ~:** es kann nicht anders sein; **be ~ engaged** anderweitige Verpflichtungen haben; **except where ~ stated** sofern nicht anders angegeben; **..., ~ [known as] Barbarossa** ..., auch als Rotbart bekannt; **b)** *(or else)* sonst; anderenfalls; **he would have let me know ~:** sonst *od.* anderenfalls hätte er mich benachrichtigt; **c)** *(in other respects)* ansonsten *(ugs.)*; im übrigen; **the merits, or ~, of his paintings** die Vorzüge oder Mängel seiner Gemälde; **the probability or ~ of sth.** die Wahrscheinlichkeit oder Unwahrscheinlichkeit einer Sache; **workers enjoyed (or ~) an enforced holiday** die Arbeiter genossen einen erzwungenen Urlaub (oder auch nicht). **2.** *pred. adj.* anders

otiose ['əʊtɪəʊs] *adj. (literary: not required)* überflüssig

otter ['ɒtə(r)] *n.* [Fisch]otter, *der; (fur)* [Fisch]otterpelz, *der*

otter: ~-dog, ~-hound *ns. (Zool., Hunting)* Otterhund, *der*

Ottoman ['ɒtəmən] *adj.* osmanisch ‹*Reich*›

ottoman *n.* **a)** *(seat)* Ottomane, *die;* **b)** *(footstool)* Polsterschemel, *der*

OU *abbr. (Brit.)* **Open University**

oubliette [u:blɪ'et] *n. (Hist.)* Oubliette, *die;* Burgverlies, *das*

ouch [aʊtʃ] *int.* autsch

¹ought [ɔ:t] *v. aux. only in pres. and past* **ought,** *neg. (coll.)* **oughtn't** ['ɔ:tnt] **a) I ~ to do/have done it** *expr. moral duty* ich müßte es tun/hätte es tun müssen; *expr. desirability* ich sollte es tun/hätte es tun sollen; **he tries to tell me what I ~ to think** er will mir vorschreiben, was ich zu denken habe; **behave as one ~:** sich richtig verhalten *od.* korrekt benehmen; **you ~ to see that film** diesen Film solltest du sehen; **she ~ to have been a teacher** sie hätte Lehrerin werden sollen; **~ not** *or* **~n't you to have left by now?** müßtest du nicht schon weg sein?; hättest du nicht schon gehen müssen?; **one ~ not to do it** man sollte es nicht tun; **he ~ to be hanged/in hospital** er gehört an den Galgen/ins Krankenhaus; **b)** *expr. probability* **that ~ to be enough** das dürfte reichen; **there ~ to be a signpost soon** jetzt müßte bald ein Wegweiser kommen; **he ~ to win** er müßte [eigentlich] gewinnen; **he ~ to have reached Paris by now** er müßte *od.* dürfte inzwischen in Paris [angekommen] sein

²ought *n. (coll.)* Null, *die*

oughtn't ['ɔ:tnt] *(coll.)* = **ought not**

Ouija [board] (P), ouija [board] ['wi:dʒə (bɔ:d)] *n. Tafel mit Buchstaben und anderen Zeichen für spiritistische Sitzungen;* Oui-ja-board, *das (Parapsych.)*

ounce [aʊns] *n.* **a)** *(measure)* Unze, *die;* **fluid ~** *(Brit.)* ≈ *0,0284 l; (Amer.)* ≈ *0,0296 l;* **b)** *(fig.)* **not an ~ of common sense** kein Fünkchen Verstand; **there is not an ~ of truth in it** daran ist kein Körnchen Wahrheit; **not have an ~ of sympathy** nicht für fünf Pfennige Mitgefühl haben *(ugs.)*

our ['aʊə(r)] *poss. pron. attrib.* **a)** unser; **we bumped ~ heads** wir stießen uns *(Dat.)* den Kopf *od.* die Köpfe an; **as soon as we've made ~ minds up** sobald wir uns *(Akk.)* entschieden haben; **we have done ~ share** wir haben unseren Teil *od. (geh.)* das Unsere getan; **~ Joe** *etc. (coll.)* unser *od. (ugs.)* uns Joe *usw.;* **b)** *(of all people)* unser; *see also* **father 1 e; lady e; lord 1 b; saviour b.** *See also* **²her**

ours ['aʊəz] *poss. pron. pred.* unserer/unsere/unseres; **that car is ~:** das ist unser Wagen; **~ is a different system** wir haben ein anderes System; unser System ist anders; **in this country of ~:** hierzulande [bei uns]; in diesem unserem Lande *(geh.)*; *see also* **hers**

ourselves [aʊə'selvz] *pron.* **a)** *emphat.* selbst; **b)** *refl.* uns. *See also* **between 1 b; herself**

oust [aʊst] *v. t.* **a)** *(expel, force out)* **~ sb. from his job** jmdn. von seinem Arbeitsplatz vertreiben; **~ sb. from office/his position** jmdn. aus dem Amt/seiner Stellung vertreiben; **~ the president/king/government from power** den Präsidenten/den König /die Regierung entmachten *od.* stürzen; **b)** *(force out and take place of)* verdrängen; ablösen ‹*Regierung*›; **c)** *(Law: deprive)* berauben **(of, from** *Gen.*)

ouster ['aʊstə(r)] *n. (Amer.: dismissal)* Entlassung, *die*

out [aʊt] **1.** *adv.* **a)** *(away from place)* **~ here/there** hier/da draußen; **'Out'** „Ausfahrt"/ „Ausgang" *od.* „Aus"; **that book is ~** *(from library)* das Buch ist ausgeliehen; **~ from under sth.** unter etw. *(Dat.)* hervor; **~ with him!** raus *(ugs.) od.* hinaus mit ihm!; **please keep the dog ~:** lassen Sie bitte den Hund nicht herein; **put the cat ~:** die Katze hinauslassen; **be ~ in the garden** draußen im Garten sein; **what's it like ~?** wie ist es draußen?; **shut the door to keep the wind ~:** die Tür schließen, damit es nicht zieht; **go ~ shopping** *etc.* einkaufen *usw.* gehen; **be ~** *(not at home, not in one's office, etc.)* nicht dasein; **go ~ in the evenings** abends aus- *od.* weggehen; **she was/stayed ~ all night** sie war/blieb eine/die ganze Nacht weg; **have a day ~ in London/at the beach** einen Tag in London/am Strand verbringen; **would you come ~ with me?** würdest du mit mir ausgehen?; **row ~ to ...:** hinaus-/herausrudern zu ...; **ten miles ~ from the harbour** 10 Meilen vom Hafen entfernt; **be ~ at sea** auf See sein; **anchor some way ~:** weit draußen ankern; **the journey ~:** die Hinfahrt; **the goods were damaged on the journey ~:** die Waren wurden auf dem Transport beschädigt; **missionaries were going ~ to India** Missionare gingen nach Indien; **he is ~ in Africa** er ist in Afrika; **~ in the fields** [draußen] auf dem Feld; **how long have you been living ~ here in Australia?** wie lange lebst du schon hier in Australien?; **the Socialist Party is ~:** die Sozialisten sind nicht mehr an der Regierung *od. (ugs.)* am Ruder; **that idea/proposal is ~:** die Idee/der Vorschlag ist indiskutabel; **Tell him that you're married – No, that's ~:** Sag ihm, daß du verheiratet bist. – Nein, das kommt nicht in Frage; **b)** *(Sport, Games)* **be ~** ‹*Ball:*› aus *od.* im Aus sein; ‹*Mitspieler:*› ausscheiden; ‹*Schlagmann:*› aus[geschlagen] sein; **not ~:** nicht aus; **give sb. ~** ‹*Schiedsrichter:*› jmdn. für „Aus" erklären; **c) be ~** *(asleep)* weg sein *(ugs.)*; *(drunk)* hinübersein *(ugs.)*; *(unconscious)* bewußtlos sein; *(Boxing)* aus sein; **~ on one's feet** *(Boxing)* stehend k. o.; *(fig.)* total erschlagen; *see also* **¹count 1 d; d)** *(no longer burning)* aus[gegangen]; **e)** *(no longer visible)* **rub** *etc.* **~:** ausradieren *usw.;* **f)** *(in error)* **be 3 % ~ in one's calculations** sich um 3 % verrechnet *od.* vertan haben; **his reckoning was ~:** seine Berechnung war falsch; **you're a long way ~:** du hast dich gewaltig geirrt; **this is £5 ~:** das stimmt um 5 Pfund nicht *od.* ist um 5 Pfund verkehrt; **my watch is 5 minutes ~:** meine Uhr geht 5 Minuten falsch *od.* verkehrt; *see also* **far 1 d; g)** *(not in fashion)* passé *(ugs.)*; out *(ugs.)*; **h)** *(so as to be seen or heard)* heraus; raus *(ugs.)*; **there is a warrant ~ for his arrest** es liegt ein Haftbefehl gegen ihn vor; **say it ~ loud** es laut sagen; **tell sb. sth. right ~:** jmdm. etw. geradeheraus *od.* ohne Umschweife sagen; **with the waterproof side ~:** mit der wasserdichten Seite nach außen; **[come] ~ with it!** heraus *od. (ugs.)* raus damit *od.* mit der Sprache; **their secret is ~:** ihr Geheimnis ist herausgekommen *od.* bekannt geworden; **[the] truth will ~:** die Wahrheit wird herauskommen *od.* an den Tag kommen; **the moon is ~:** der Mond ist zu sehen; **just ~ – the third volume** soeben erschienen – der dritte Band; **is the evening paper ~ yet?** ist die Abendausgabe schon erschienen?; **the roses are just ~:** die Rosen fangen gerade an zu blühen; **the apple-blossom is ~:** die Apfelbäume stehen in Blüte; **i)** *(known to exist)* **that is the best car ~:** das ist das beste Auto auf dem Markt; **j) be ~ for sth./to do sth.** auf etw. *(Akk.)* aussein/darauf aussein, etw. zu tun; **be ~ for all one can get** alles haben wollen, was man bekommen kann; **be ~ for trouble** Streit suchen; **he's ~ for your money** er hat es auf dein Geld abgesehen; **be ~ to pass the exam/capture the market** entschlossen sein, die Prüfung zu bestehen/den Markt zu erobern; **she's ~ to get him/find a husband** sie ist hinter ihm her/sucht einen Mann; **they're just ~ to make money** sie sind nur aufs Geld aus; ihnen geht es nur ums Geld; **k)** *(to or at an end)* **he had it finished before the day/month was ~:** er war noch am selben Tag/vor Ende des Monats damit fertig; **please hear me ~:** laß mich bitte ausreden; **Eggs? I'm afraid we're ~:** Eier? Die sind leider ausgegangen *od. (ugs.)* alle; **school is ~** *(Amer.)* die Schule ist aus; **l)** *(to a solution or result)* **work ~:** ausrechnen; ausarbeiten ‹*Plan, Strategie*›; **m)** *(in finished form)* **type ~ a thesis** eine Dissertation [ins reine] tippen; **do it ~ in rough first** sich *(Dat.)* erst ein Konzept machen; **n)** *(in radio communication)* Ende; **o) ~ and away** mit Abstand; bei weitem; **a scoundrel ~ and ~, an ~ and ~ scoundrel** ein Schurke durch und durch; **an ~ and ~ disgrace** eine ungeheure *od. (ugs.)* bodenlose Schande. *See also* **about 1 d; luck b; out of; tide 1 a. 2.** *prep.* aus; **go ~ the door** zur Tür hinausgehen; **throw sth. ~ the window** etw. aus dem Fenster werfen. **3.** *n. (way of escape)* Ausweg, *der (fig.)*; *(excuse)* Alibi, *das*

out: ~-act *v. t.* an die Wand spielen; **~back** *n. (esp. Austral.)* Hinterland, *das;* **an ~back farm** eine Farm im Hinterland; **~'bid** *v. t.,* **outbid a)** überbieten; **~bid sb. for sth.** für etw. mehr bieten *od.* ein besseres Angebot machen als jmd.; **b)** *(surpass)* übertrumpfen; **~board** *(Naut., Aeronaut., Motor Veh.)* **1.** *adj.* **a)** Außenbord-; **~board motor** Außenbordmotor, *der;* Außenborder, *der (ugs.)*; **~board motor boat** Boot mit Außenbordmotor; **b)** *(on outside)* sich außenbords befindend; Außenbord-; **2.** *n.* Außenborder, *der (ugs.)*; **~bound** *adj.* auslaufend ‹*Schiff*›; **~break** *n.* Ausbruch, *der;* **a recent ~break of fire caused ...:** ein Brand verursachte kürzlich ...; **at the ~break of war** bei Kriegsausbruch *od.* Ausbruch des Krieges; **an ~break of flu/smallpox** eine Grippe-/Pockenepidemie; **there will be ~breaks of rain during the afternoon** am Nachmittag wird es zu Regenfällen kommen; **~building** *n.* Nebengebäude, *das;* **~burst** *n.* Ausbruch, *der;* **an ~burst of weeping/laughter** ein Weinkrampf/Lachanfall *od.* -krampf; **an ~burst of anger/temper** ein Zornesausbruch *(geh.) od.* Wutanfall; **apologize for one's ~burst** sich für seinen Gefühlsausbruch entschuldigen; **there**

was an ~burst of applause Beifall brach los; ~bursts of flame Auflodern von Flammen; an ~burst of energy ein Anfall von Energie; his ~bursts of violence seine Anfälle von Gewalttätigkeit; ~cast 1. *n.* Ausgestoßene, *der/die;* a social ~cast, an ~cast of society ein Geächteter/eine Geächtete; ein Outcast *(Soziol.);* 2. *adj.* ausgestoßen; verstoßen ‹*Familienmitglied*›; ~'class *v.t.* a) *(belong to higher class than)* überlegen sein (+ *Dat.*); b) *(defeat easily)* in den Schatten stellen; he was ~classed in that race er wurde in diesem Rennen deklassiert; ~come *n.* Ergebnis, *das;* Resultat, *das;* what was the ~come of your meeting? was ist bei eurer Versammlung herausgekommen?; ~crop 1. *n.* a) *(Geol.: stratum)* Ausgehende, *das;* Ausstreichende, *das;* a rock ~crop ausstreichendes Gestein; b) *(fig.)* Auftreten, *das;* 2. *v.i.* a) *(Geol.)* ausstreichen *(fachspr.);* b) *(fig.)* auftauchen; ~cry *n.* a) *no pl. (clamour)* [Aufschrei der] Empörung; [Sturm der] Entrüstung; a public/general ~cry about/against sth. allgemeine Empörung *od.* Entrüstung über etw. *(Akk.);* the ~cry in the press die heftigen Proteste in der Presse; raise an ~cry about sth. lautstarken Protest gegen etw. erheben; b) *(crying out)* Aufschrei, *der;* ~'dated *adj.* veraltet; überholt; antiquiert *(abwertend)* ‹*Ausdrucksweise*›; altmodisch ‹*Vorstellung, Kleidung*›; ~'distance *v.t.* [weit] hinter sich *(Dat.)* lassen; überflügeln; John was ~distanced by his brother in the race John fiel in dem Rennen [weit] hinter seinem Bruder zurück; ~'do *v.t.*, outdoing [aʊt'du:ɪŋ], outdid [aʊt'dɪd], outdone [aʊt'dʌn] übertreffen, überbieten (in an + *Dat.*); not to be outdone [by sb.] um nicht zurückzustehen [hinter jmdm.]; ~door *adj.* ~door shoes/things Straßenschuhe/-kleidung, *die;* be an ~door type gern und oft im Freien sein; lead an ~door life viel im Freien sein; ~door games/pursuits Spiele/Beschäftigungen im Freien; ~door shots *(Photog.)* Außenaufnahmen; ~door swimming-pool Freibad, *das;* ~door ice-rink nicht überdachte Eisbahn; ~'doors 1. *adv.* draußen; sleep ~doors draußen *od.* im Freien schlafen; go ~doors nach draußen gehen; 2. *n.* the [great] ~doors die freie Natur

outer ['aʊtə(r)] *adj.* a) äußer...; Außen‹*fläche, -seite, -wand, -tür, -hafen*›; sb.'s ~ appearance jmds. äußere Erscheinung; jmds. Äußeres; ~ garments Oberbekleidung, *die;* b) *(objective, physical)* äußerlich; the ~ world die Außenwelt. *See also* ¹bar 1i

outermost ['aʊtəməʊst] *adj.* äußerst...

outer 'space *n.* Weltraum, *der;* All, *das;* come from ~ *(fig. coll.)* von einem anderen Stern sein

out: ~'face *v.t.* [durch Blicke] einschüchtern; zum Schweigen bringen ‹*Kritiker*›; ~fall *n.* Ausfluß, *der; (in river engineering)* Vorfluter, *der;* ~fall pipe Abflußrohr, *das;* ~field *n. (Cricket, Baseball)* Außenfeld, *das;* ~fit *n.* a) *(person's clothes)* Kleider *Pl.; (for fancy-dress party)* Kostüm, *das;* wear the same ~fit dasselbe tragen *od.* anhaben; I do like your ~fit! du bist sehr gut angezogen; b) *(complete equipment)* Ausrüstung, *die;* Ausstattung, *die;* c) *(coll.: group of persons)* Haufen, *der (ugs.);* Clique, *die (abwertend); (Mil.)* Haufen, *der (Soldatenspr.);* Trupp, *der; (jazz band)* Ensemble, *das;* d) *(coll.: organization)* Laden, *der (ugs.);* a publishing/manufacturing ~fit ein Verlag/ein Produktionsbetrieb; ~fitter *n.* Ausrüster, *der*/Ausrüsterin, *die;* Ausstatter, *der*/Ausstatterin, *die;* camping/sports ~fitter Camping-/Sportgeschäft, *das;* a gents' ~fitter's ein Herrenausstatter; ~'flank *v.t.* a) *(Mil.: ~manœuvre; also fig.)* überlisten; ausmanövrieren; b) *(Mil.: extend beyond flank of)* umgehen, umfassen ‹*Armee*›; ~flanking movement Umfassungsbewegung, *die;* ~flow *n.* a) *(~ward flow)* Austritt, *der; (fig.: of gold, capital, etc.)* Abfluß, *der;* b) *(amount)* Ausfluß, *der;* Abflußmenge, *die;* c) ~flow [pipe *or* channel] Abfluß, *der;* ~'fox *v.t. (coll.)* austricksen *(ugs.);* ~going 1. *adj.* a) *(retiring from office)* [aus dem Amt] scheidend ‹*Regierung, Präsident, Ausschuß*›; b) *(friendly)* kontaktfreudig ‹*Mensch*›; you should be more ~going du solltest mehr aus dir herausgehen; c) *(going out)* abgehend ‹*Zug, Schiff*›; ausziehend ‹*Mieter*›; ~going flights will be delayed bei den Abflügen wird es zu Verzögerungen kommen; the ~going post *or* mail die ausgehende Post; der Postausgang *(Bürow.);* 2. *n. in pl. (expenditure)* Ausgaben *Pl.;* ~'grow *v.t., forms as* grow: a) *(leave behind)* entwachsen (+ *Dat.*); hinauswachsen über (+ *Akk.*); ablegen ‹*Interesse, Schüchternheit, Vorliebe*›; überwinden ‹*Ansicht, Schüchternheit*›; we've ~grown all that das alles haben wir hinter uns; b) *(become taller than)* größer werden als; über den Kopf wachsen (+ *Dat.*) ‹*älterem Bruder usw.*›; *(grow too big for)* herauswachsen aus ‹*Kleidung*›; ~growth *n.* Auswuchs, *der;* ~'guess *v.t.* gedanklich voraus sein (+ *Dat.*); ausrechnen *(Sportjargon);* ~'gun *v.t. (fig.)* be ~gunned an Feuerkraft unterlegen sein; ~house *n.* a) *(building)* Nebengebäude, *das;* b) *(Amer.: privy)* Außentoilette, *die*

outing ['aʊtɪŋ] *n.* a) *(pleasure-trip)* Ausflug, *der;* school/day's ~: Schul-/Tagesausflug, *der;* firm's/works ~: Betriebsausflug, *der;* go on an ~: einen Ausflug machen; go for an ~ in the car eine Spazierfahrt machen; b) *(appearance) (in athletic contest)* Wettkampf, *der; (in race)* Rennen, *das; (in game)* Spiel, *das*

out: ~landish [aʊt'lændɪʃ] *adj.* a) *(looking or sounding foreign)* fremdländisch; b) *(bizarre)* ausgefallen; seltsam, sonderbar ‹*Benehmen*›; verschroben ‹*Ansichten*›; ~'last *v.t.* überdauern; überleben ‹*Person, Jahrhundert*›; ~law 1. *n.* a) *(lawless violent person)* Bandit, *der*/Banditin, *die;* b) *(person deprived of protection of law)* Geächtete, *der/die (hist.);* 2. *v.t.* a) *(deprive of the protection of law)* ächten *(hist.);* für vogelfrei erklären *(hist.);* b) *(make illegal)* verbieten ‹*Zeitung, Handlung*›; ~lay *n.* an ~lay Ausgaben *Pl.* (on für); initial ~lay Anschaffungskosten *Pl.;* ~lay of capital Kapitalaufwand, *der;* recover the ~lay seine Auslagen zurückbekommen; ~let ['aʊtlet, 'aʊtlɪt] a) *(means of exit)* Ablauf, -fluß, *der;* Auslauf, -laß, *der; (of lake)* Abfluß, *der;* ~let valve Ablaßventil, *das;* b) *(fig.: vent)* Ventil, *das;* c) *(Commerc.) (market)* Absatzmarkt, *der; (shop)* Verkaufsstelle, *die;* d) *(Electr.)* Steckdose, *die; (connection)* Stromanschluß, *der;* ~line 1. *n.* a) *in sing. or pl. (line[s])* Umriß, *der;* Kontur, *die;* Silhouette, *die;* the ~lines of the trees/drawing die Umrisse der Bäume/Zeichnung; visible only in ~line nur in Umrissen sichtbar; b) *(short account)* Grundriß, *der;* Grundzüge *Pl.; (of topic)* Übersicht, die (of über + *Akk.*); *(rough draft for essay, book, play, etc.)* Entwurf, *der* (of, for *Gen. od.* zu); Konzept, *das* (of, for *Gen.*); trace the development in ~line die Entwicklung im Grundriß *od.* in ihren Grundzügen verfolgen; ~line plan Übersichtsplan, *der;* c) *in pl. (main features)* Grundzüge *Pl.;* d) *(sketch)* Skizze, *die;* sketch/draw sth. in ~line etw. in Umrissen skizzieren/zeichnen; ~line map Umrißkarte, *die;* 2. *v.t.* a) *(draw ~line of)* ~line sth. die Umrisse *od.* Konturen einer Sache zeichnen; b) *(define ~line of)* ~line sth. die Umrisse *od.* Konturen einer Sache hervorheben; the mountain was ~lined against the sky die Silhouette/Umrisse *od.* Konturen des Berges zeichnete/zeichneten sich gegen den Himmel ab; c) *(trace or ascertain ~line of)* ~line the limits/boundaries of sth. den Verlauf der Grenzen von etw. ermitteln; d) *(describe in general terms)* skizzieren, umreißen ‹*Programm, Plan, Projekt*›; ~live [aʊt'lɪv] *v.t.* überleben; it's ~lived its usefulness es ist unbrauchbar geworden; es hat ausgedient; ~look *n.* a) *(prospect)* Aussicht, *die* (over über + *Akk.*, on to auf + *Akk.*); *(fig., Meteorol.)* Aussichten *Pl.;* the house has a wonderful ~look over ...: vom Haus aus hat man eine herrliche Aussicht über ... *(Akk.);* what's the ~look? wie sind die Aussichten?; business ~look Geschäftsaussichten *Pl.;* b) *(mental attitude)* Haltung, *die* (on gegenüber); Einstellung, *die* (on zu); Auffassung, *die* (on von); ~look on life Lebensauffassung, *die;* his whole ~look seine ganze Einstellung; adopt a narrow ~look on things in seinen Anschauungen beschränkt sein; die Dinge zu eng sehen; c) *(looking out)* Hinaussehen, *das;* ~lying *adj.* abgelegen, entlegen ‹*Gegend, Vorort, Dorf*›; the ~lying suburbs of Tokyo die Außenbezirke von Tokio; ~ma'nœuvre *v.t.* überlisten ‹*Truppen*›; ausstechen, ausmanövrieren ‹*Rivalen*›; ~moded [aʊt'məʊdɪd] *adj.* a) *(no longer in fashion)* altmodisch; b) *(obsolete)* veraltet; antiquiert *(abwertend)* ‹*Ausdrucksweise*›; ~'number *v.t.* zahlenmäßig überlegen sein (+ *Dat.*); they were ~numbered five to one die anderen waren fünfmal so viele wie sie; be [vastly] ~numbered [by sb.] [jmdm.] zahlenmäßig [weit] unterlegen sein

'out of *prep.* a) *(from within)* aus; go ~ the door zur Tür hinausgehen; fall ~ sth. aus etw. [heraus]fallen; b) *(not within)* be ~ the country im Ausland sein; außer Landes sein *(geh.);* be ~ town/the room nicht in der Stadt/im Zimmer sein; feel ~ it *or* things sich ausgeschlossen *od.* nicht dazu gehörig fühlen; I'm glad to be ~ it ich bin froh, daß ich die Sache hinter mir habe; c) *(outside the limits of)* marry ~ one's faith einen Anhänger/eine Anhängerin eines anderen Glaubens heiraten; born ~ wedlock unehelich geboren; be ~ the tournament aus dem Turnier ausgeschieden sein; *see also* order 1a, b; d) *(from among)* one ~ every three smokers jeder dritte Raucher; 58 ~ every 100 58 von hundert; pick one ~ the pile einen/eine/eins aus dem Stapel herausgreifen; eighth ~ ten als Achter von zehn Teilnehmern *usw.;* choose ~ what is there unter dem auswählen, was vorhanden ist; only one instance ~ several nur einer von mehreren Fällen; e) *(beyond range of)* außer ‹*Reich-/Hörweite, Sicht, Kontrolle*›; f) *(from)* aus; get money ~ sb. Geld aus jmdm. herausholen; do well ~ sb./sth. von jmdm./etw. profitieren; g) *(owing to)* aus ‹*Mitleid, Trotz, Furcht, Verehrung, Neugier usw.*›; h) *(no longer in)* ~ danger außer Gefahr; i) *(without)* be ~ luck kein Glück haben; ~ money ohne Geld; ~ work ohne Arbeit; arbeitslos; we're ~ tea der Tee ist uns ausgegangen; wir haben keinen Tee mehr; be ~ a suit *(Cards)* keine Karten einer Farbe haben; *see also* out-of-work; j) *(by use of)* aus; make a profit ~ sth. mit etw. ein Geschäft machen; made ~ silver aus Silber; what did you make it ~? woraus hast du es gemacht?; k) *(away from)* von ... entfernt; three days ~ port drei Tage nach dem Auslaufen aus dem Hafen; ten miles ~ London 10 Meilen außerhalb von London; l) *(beyond)* see depth d; ordinary c

out: ~-of-date *attrib. adj. (old, not relevant)* veraltet; *(old-fashioned)* altmodisch; unmodern; antiquiert *(abwertend)* ‹*Ausdrucksweise*›; *(expired)* ungültig, verfallen ‹*Karte*›; ~-of-'pocket *attrib. adj.* Bar‹*auslagen*›; ~-of-print *attrib. adj.* vergriffen; **~-of-the-way** *attrib. adj. (remote)* abgelegen; entlegen; *(unusual, seldom met with)* ausgefallen; entlegen; **~-of-town** *attrib. adj.* außerhalb der Stadt gelegen ⟨*Einkaufszentrum*⟩; *(fig.: unsophisticated)* Provinz- *(abwertend)*; **~-of-work** *attrib. adj.* arbeitslos; **~'pace** *v.t.* ausstechen ⟨*Konkurrenten*⟩; *(Sport)* besiegen ⟨*Läufer*⟩; **be ~paced** ⟨*Sportler:*⟩ überholt werden; **~-patient** *n.* ambulanter *od.* poliklinischer Patient/ambulante *od.* poliklinische Patientin; **~-patients['] department]** Poliklinik, *die;* **have sth. done as an ~-patient** etw. ambulant *od.* in der Ambulanz machen lassen; **be an ~-patient** ambulant behandelt werden; **~per'form** *v.t.* überbieten; **~'play** *v.t. (Sport)* besser spielen als; **we can ~play them** wir sind ihnen spielerisch überlegen; **be ~played [by sb.]** [jmdm.] unterlegen sein; **~'point** *v.t. (Sport, esp. Boxing)* auspunkten; **~post** *n.* Außenposten, *der; (of civilization etc.; also Mil.)* Vorposten, *der;* **~pouring** *n., usu. in pl. (expression of emotion)* Gefühlsäußerung, *die; (impetuous, passionate)* Erguß, *der (geh. abwertend);* **~put 1.** *n.* **a)** *(amount)* Output, *der (fachspr.);* Produktion, *die; (of liquid, electricity, etc.)* Leistung, *die; (of coal-mine etc.)* Förderung, *die;* Fördermenge, *die;* **total/daily/average/literary ~put** Gesamt-/Tages-/Durchschnitts-/literarische Produktion; **the factory has a daily ~put of 200 pairs** in der Fabrik werden pro Tag 200 Paar hergestellt; **b)** *(Computing)* Ausgabe, *die;* Output, *der (fachspr.);* **~put capacity/terminal** Ausgabekapazität, *die*/-terminal, *das;* **c)** *(Electr.) (energy)* [Ausgangs]leistung, *die;* Output, *der (fachspr.); (signal)* Ausgangssignal, *das;* **~put circuit/current** Ausgangsschaltung, *die*/-strom, *der;* **d)** *(place)* Ausgang, *der; (recording or printing device)* Ausgabegerät, *das;* **2.** *v.t.*, **-tt-**, **~put** *or* **~putted** ['aʊtpʊtɪd] *(Computing)* ausgeben ⟨*Information*⟩

outrage 1. ['aʊtreɪdʒ] *n.* **a)** *(deed of violence, violation of rights)* Verbrechen, *das; (during war)* Greueltat, *die; (against good taste or decency)* grober *od.* krasser Verstoß; *(upon dignity)* krasse *od.* grobe Verletzung **(upon** *Gen.*); **be an ~ against good taste/decency/upon dignity** den guten Geschmack/Anstand/die Würde in grober *od.* krasser Weise verletzen; **an ~ against humanity** ein Verbrechen gegen die Menschheit; **an ~ upon decency/justice** eine Verhöhnung des Anstands/der Gerechtigkeit; **a bomb ~:** ein verbrecherischer Bombenanschlag; **b)** *(strong resentment)* Empörung, *die* **(at** *gegen*); **react with a sense of ~:** empört sein. **2.** ['aʊtreɪdʒ, aʊt'reɪdʒ] *v.t.* **a)** *(cause to feel resentment, insult)* empören; **be ~d at** *or* **by sth.** über etw. *(Akk.)* empört sein; **b)** *(infringe)* in grober *od.* krasser Weise verstoßen gegen ⟨*Anstand, Moral*⟩

outrageous [aʊt'reɪdʒəs] *adj.* **a)** *(immoderate)* unverschämt *(ugs.)* ⟨*Forderung*⟩; unverschämt hoch ⟨*Preis, Summe*⟩; grell, schreiend ⟨*Farbe*⟩; zu auffällig ⟨*Kleidung*⟩; maßlos ⟨*Übertreibung*⟩; **it's ~!** das ist unverschämt *od.* eine Unverschämtheit!; **b)** *(grossly cruel, offensive)* ungeheuer ⟨*Grausamkeit*⟩; haarsträubend, *(ugs.)* katastrophal ⟨*Behandlung, Bedienung*⟩; unverschämt ⟨*Lüge, Benehmen, Unterstellung*⟩; wüst ⟨*Schmähung*⟩; geschmacklos ⟨*Witz*⟩; ungeheuerlich ⟨*Anklage*⟩; unerhört ⟨*Frechheit, Unhöflichkeit, Skandal*⟩; unflätig ⟨*Sprache*⟩; **c)** *(violent)* grausam ⟨*Rache*⟩; **~ deeds** Untaten; Grausamkeiten

outrageously [aʊt'reɪdʒəslɪ] *adv.* **a)** *(to an immoderate degree)* zu auffällig, aufdringlich ⟨*sich kleiden, schminken*⟩; maßlos ⟨*übertreiben*⟩; **an ~ low neckline** ein herausfordernd tiefer Ausschnitt; **b)** *(atrociously, flagrantly)* unverschämt, schamlos ⟨*lügen, sich benehmen*⟩; fürchterlich ⟨*fluchen*⟩; **~ bad service** haarsträubend schlechte Bedienung; **he suggested quite ~ that ...:** er war so unverschämt vorzuschlagen, daß ...

out'rank *v.t. (Mil.)* einen höheren Rang einnehmen als; rangmäßig stehen über (+ *Dat.*); **be ~ed by sb.** einen niedrigeren Rang als jmd. haben; rangmäßig unter jmdm. stehen

outré ['u:treɪ] *adj.* outriert *(geh. veralt.);* überspannt ⟨*Vorstellung, Geschmack*⟩; absurd ⟨*Kleidung*⟩

out: ~rider *n.* **a)** *(mounted attendant)* berittener Begleiter/berittene Begleiterin; **b)** *(motor-cyclist)* **[motor-cycle] ~rider** Kradbegleiter, *der*/-begleiterin, *die;* **c)** *(Amer.: herdsman)* berittener Viehhirte; **~rigger** *n. (Naut.) (beam, spar, framework)* Maststütze, *die; (log fixed to canoe)* Schwimmbalken, *der;* Ausleger, *der; (iron bracket)* Ausleger, *der; (boat)* Auslegerboot, *das;* **~right 1.** [-'-] *adv.* **a)** *(altogether, entirely)* ganz, komplett ⟨*kaufen, verkaufen*⟩; *(instantaneously, on the spot)* auf der Stelle; **pay for/purchase/buy sth. ~right** sofort den ganzen Preis für etw. bezahlen; **b)** *(openly)* geradeheraus *(ugs.)*, freiheraus, rundheraus ⟨*erzählen, sagen, lachen*⟩; **2.** ['--] *adj.* ausgemacht ⟨*Unsinn, Schlechtigkeit, Unehrlichkeit*⟩; offen, direkt ⟨*Wesensart*⟩; rein, pur *(ugs.)* ⟨*Arroganz, Unverschämtheit, Irrtum, Egoismus, Unsinn*⟩; glatt *(ugs.)* ⟨*Ablehnung, Absage, Lüge*⟩; klar ⟨*Sieg, Niederlage, Sieger*⟩; **~right sale** Verkauf in Bausch und Bogen; **~'run** *v.t., forms as* **run 3: a)** *(run faster than)* schneller laufen *od.* sein als; **b)** *(escape)* entkommen (+ *Dat.*); **~'sell** *v.t., forms as* **sell 1: a)** *(be sold in greater quantities than)* sich besser verkaufen als; **be ~sold by ...:** sich schlechter verkaufen als ...; **b)** *(sell more than)* mehr verkaufen als; **~sell sb. by two to one** zweimal soviel wie jmd. verkaufen; **~set** *n.* Anfang, *der;* Beginn, *der;* **at the ~set** zu Beginn *od.* Anfang; am Anfang; **from the ~set** von Anfang an; **~'shine** *v.t.*, **~shone** [aʊt'ʃɒn] **a)** *(shine brighter than)* heller leuchten als; **b)** *(fig.)* in den Schatten stellen

outside 1. [-'-, '--] *n.* **a)** *(external side)* Außenseite, *die;* **the ~ of the car is red** das Auto ist außen rot; **on the ~:** außen; **on the ~ of the door** außen an der Tür; **overtake sb. on the ~** *(in driving)* jmdn. außen überholen; **b)** *(position on outer side)* **to/from the ~:** nach/von außen; **see a problem from the ~:** ein Problem als Außenstehender/Außenstehende sehen; **be kept on the ~:** ausgeschlossen bleiben; **c)** *(external appearance)* Äußere, *das;* äußere Erscheinung; **d)** *(of path etc.)* Rand, *der;* **e) at the [very] ~** *(coll.)* äußerstenfalls; höchstens. **2.** ['--] *adj.* **a)** *(of, on, nearer the ~)* äußer...; Außen⟨*wand, -mauer, -antenne, -reparatur, -belag, -kajüte, -toilette, -ansicht, -durchmesser*⟩; **b)** *(remote)* **have only an ~ chance** nur eine sehr geringe Chance *od.* eine Außenseiterchance haben; **c)** *(not coming from or belonging within)* fremd ⟨*Hilfe*⟩; äußer... ⟨*Einfluß*⟩; Freizeit⟨*aktivitäten, -interessen*⟩; **~ pressure** Druck von außen; **some ~ help** *(extra workers)* zusätzliche Arbeitskräfte; **~ investment** Investitionen von außen; **an ~ opinion** die Meinung eines Außenstehenden; **the ex-convict had to adjust to the ~ world** der ehemalige Sträfling mußte sich an das Leben draußen gewöhnen; **d)** *(greatest possible)* maximal, höchst ⟨*Schätzung*⟩; **at an ~ estimate** maximal *od.* höchstens *od.* im Höchstfall. **3.** [-'-] *adv.* **a)** *(on the ~)* draußen; *(to the ~)* nach draußen; **the world ~:** die Außenwelt; **come from ~:** von draußen kommen; **seen from ~ it looks ...:** von [dr]außen sieht es ... aus; **come** *or* **step ~** *(as challenge to fight)* komm mal mit nach draußen *od.* vor die Tür; **who's that ~?** wer ist das da draußen?; **b) ~ of** *see* **4; c)** *(sl.: not in prison)* draußen *(ugs.)*. **4.** [-'-] *prep.* **a)** *(on outer side of)* außerhalb (+ *Gen.*); **~ the door** vor der Tür; draußen; **prowl about/park ~ the house** ums Haus herumstreichen/vor dem Haus parken; **b)** *(beyond)* außerhalb (+ *Gen.*) ⟨*Reichweite, Festival, Familie*⟩; **it's ~ the terms of the agreement** es gehört nicht zu den Bedingungen der Abmachung; **this falls ~ the scope of ...:** das geht über den Rahmen von ... hinaus; **c)** *(to the ~ of)* aus ... hinaus; **go ~ the house** nach draußen gehen

outside: ~ 'broadcast *n. (Brit.)* Außenübertragung, *die;* **~ 'edge** *n. (Skating, Cricket)* Außenkante, *die;* **~ 'forward** *n. (Footb., Hockey)* Außenstürmer, *der;* **~ 'half** *n. (Rugby)* Flügelhalbspieler, *der;* **~ 'left** *n. (Footb., Hockey)* Linksaußen, *der*

outsider [aʊt'saɪdə(r)] *n.* **a)** *(non-member, person without special knowledge)* Außenstehende, *der/die;* **b)** *(Sport; also fig.)* Außenseiter, *der;* Outsider, *der*

outside: ~ 'right *n. (Footb., Hockey)* Rechtsaußen, *der;* **~ seat** *n.* Platz am Rand; **~ 'track** *n. (Racing)* Außenbahn, *die*

out: ~size *adj.* überdimensional; **~size person/clothes** Person mit/Kleidung in Übergröße; **~size shop/department** Geschäft/Abteilung für Übergrößen; **~skirts** *n. pl.* Stadtrand, *der;* **on the ~skirts [of Paris]** am Stadtrand [von Paris]; **the ~skirts of the city** die Außenbezirke der Stadt; **~'smart** *v.t. (coll.)* ausschmieren *(ugs.);* reinlegen *(ugs.);* **~'spoken** *adj.* freimütig ⟨*Person, Kritik, Bemerkung, Kommentar*⟩; **the book was ~spoken on the subject** in dem Buch wurde das Thema freimütig *od.* offenherzig *od. (ugs.)* unverblümt behandelt; **~spread** *adj.* ['--, *pred.* -'-] ausgebreitet; **he stood there, [with] arms ~spread** er stand mit ausgebreiteten Armen da; **~-'standing** *adj.* **a)** *(conspicuous)* hervorstechend ⟨*Merkmal*⟩; **b)** *(exceptional)* hervorragend ⟨*Leistung, Redner, Künstler, Dienst*⟩; überragend ⟨*Bedeutung*⟩; außergewöhnlich ⟨*Person, Mut, Fähigkeit, Geschick*⟩; **not be ~standing** nicht überragend sein; **~standing in courage and skill** außergewöhnlich mutig und geschickt; **of ~standing ability/skill** außergewöhnlich fähig/geschickt; **be ~-standing at skating** hervorragend Schlittschuh laufen können; **work of ~standing excellence** ganz hervorragende Arbeit; **c)** *(not yet settled)* ausstehend ⟨*Schuld, Verbindlichkeit, Geldsumme*⟩; offen, unbezahlt ⟨*Rechnung*⟩; unerledigt ⟨*Arbeit*⟩; ungelöst ⟨*Problem*⟩; **there's £5 still ~standing** es stehen noch 5 Pfund aus; **have work still ~standing** noch etwas zu erledigen haben; **~standingly** [aʊt'stændɪŋlɪ] *adv.* außergewöhnlich ⟨*intelligent, gut, begabt*⟩; **not ~standingly** nicht besonders; **be ~standingly good at tennis/Latin** hervorragend Tennis spielen/Latein können; **~station** *n.* Außenposten, *der;* **~'stay** *v.t.* **a)** *(stay beyond)* überziehen ⟨*Urlaub*⟩; **b)** *(stay longer than)* länger bleiben als; *(surpass in staying power, endurance)* mehr Stehvermögen haben als; *see also* **welcome 2a; ~'step** *v.t.* hinausgehen über (+ *Akk.*); **~stretched** *adj.* ausgestreckt; *(spread out)* ausgebreitet; **~'strip** *v.t.* **a)** *(pass in running)* überholen; **b)** *(surpass in competition)* überflügeln; übersteigen ⟨*Einsicht, Ressourcen, Ersparnisse*⟩; **~-takes** *n. pl. (Cinemat. etc.)* Ausschuß, *der;* **~-tray** *n.* Ablage für Ausgänge; **~'vote** *v.t.* überstimmen

outward ['aʊtwəd] **1.** *adj.* **a)** *(external, apparent)* [rein] äußerlich; äußere ⟨*Erscheinung, Bedingung*⟩; **sb.'s ~ self** jmds. äußere Erscheinung; **with an ~ show of confidence** mit einem Anstrich von Selbstsicherheit; **an ~ display of fear** eine Demonstration der

Angst; ~ **form** Erscheinungsform, *die;* äußere Form; **b)** *(directed towards outside)* nach außen gerichtet ⟨*Neigung, Bewegung*⟩; *(going out)* Hin⟨*reise, -fracht*⟩; ~ **flow of money/traffic** Kapitalabfluß, *der*/abfließender Verkehr; **the ~ half of a return ticket** der Hinfahrtabschnitt einer Fahrkarte. **2.** *adv.* nach außen ⟨*aufgehen, richten*⟩; **be ~ bound [for New York]** ⟨*Schiff:*⟩ [mit Kurs auf New York *(Akk.)*] auslaufen; ⟨*Person:*⟩ [in Richtung New York] abreisen

outward-'bound *attrib. adj.* auslaufend **(for** nach) ⟨*Schiff*⟩; abreisend ⟨*Passagier*⟩

outwardly ['aʊtwədlɪ] *adv.* nach außen hin ⟨*Gefühle zeigen*⟩; öffentlich ⟨*Loyalität erklären*⟩

outwards *see* **outward 2**

out: ~'weigh *v.t.* schwerer wiegen als; überwiegen ⟨*Nachteile*⟩; [mehr als] wettmachen ⟨*Verluste*⟩; **~'wit** *v.t.*, **-tt-** überlisten; **~work** *n.* **a)** *(part of fortification)* **~work[s]** Vorfestung, *die;* Vorwerk, *das;* Außenbefestigung, *die;* **b)** *(work)* Arbeit außerhalb des Betriebs; Heimarbeit, *die;* **~worker** *n. jmd., der außerhalb des Betriebs arbeitet;* Heimarbeiter, *der*/-arbeiterin, *die;* **~'worn** *adj. (obsolete)* veraltet ⟨*Brauch, Ansicht, Lehre, Theorie*⟩

ova *pl. of* **ovum**

oval ['əʊvl] **1.** *adj.* **a)** länglichrund ⟨*Form*⟩; eiförmig ⟨*Ball*⟩; **b)** *(having outline of egg)* oval; **O~ Office** *Büro des US-Präsidenten im Weißen Haus.* **2.** *n.* Oval, *das*

ovary ['əʊvərɪ] *n. (Anat.)* Ovarium, *das;* Eierstock, *der; (Bot.)* Ovarium, *das;* Fruchtknoten, *der*

ovation [əʊ'veɪʃn] *n.* Ovation, *die;* begeisterter Beifall; **get an ~ for sth.** Ovationen *od.* begeisterten Beifall für etw. bekommen; **a standing ~:** stehende Ovationen

oven ['ʌvn] *n.* [Back]ofen, *der;* **put sth. in the ~ for 40 minutes** etw. 40 Minuten backen; **cook in a hot/moderate/slow ~:** bei starker/mäßiger/schwacher Hitze backen/braten/schmoren; **it's like an ~ in here** hier ist es warm wie in einem Backofen; **have a bun in the ~** *(sl.)* ein Kind kriegen *(ugs.)*

oven: ~-cloth *n.* Topflappen, *der;* **~-fresh** *adj.* ofenfrisch; **~-glove** *n.* Topfhandschuh, *der;* **~-proof** *adj.* feuerfest; **~-ready** *adj.* backfertig ⟨*Pommes frites, Pastete*⟩; bratfertig ⟨*Geflügel*⟩; **~-to-table** *adj.* feuerfest ⟨*Geschirr*⟩; **~ware** *n., no pl.* feuerfestes Geschirr

over ['əʊvə(r)] **1.** *adv.* **a)** *(outward and downward)* hinüber; **kick ~:** umstoßen; **b)** *(so as to cover surface)* **draw/board/cover ~:** zuziehen/-nageln/-decken; **paint ~:** [an]streichen ⟨*Raum, Wand*⟩; überstreichen ⟨*Inschrift*⟩; **c)** *(with motion above sth.)* **climb/look/jump ~:** hinüber- *od. (ugs.)* rüberklettern/-sehen/-springen; **boil ~:** überkochen; **this goes under and that goes ~:** dies kommt darunter und das darüber; **d)** *(so as to reverse position etc.)* herum; **change ~:** umschalten ⟨*Programm, Sender*⟩; austauschen ⟨*Bilder, Format*⟩; **switch ~:** umschalten ⟨*Programm, Sender*⟩; **it rolled ~ and ~:** es rollte und rollte; **e)** *(across a space)* hinüber; *(towards speaker)* herüber; **row ~ to a place** an einen Ort hinüberrudern; **he swam ~ to us/the other side** er schwamm zu uns herüber/hinüber zur anderen Seite; **fly ~:** vorüberfliegen; **drive sb. ~ to the other side of town** jmdn. ans andere Ende der Stadt fahren; **be ~** *(have arrived)* drüben [angekommen] sein; **~ here/there** *(direction)* hier herüber/dort hinüber; *(location)* hier/dort; **they are ~ [here] for the day** sie sind einen Tag hier; **ask sb. ~ [for dinner]** jmdn. [zum Essen] einladen; **~ against** *(opposite)* gegenüber; *(in contrast to)* im Gegensatz zu; **f)** *(with change from one to another)* **[come in, please,] ~** *(Radio)* übernehmen Sie bitte; **~ and out** *(Radio)* Ende; **and now, ~ to ...** *(Radio)* wir schalten jetzt um nach ...; **and it's ~ to you** jetzt bist du dran; *(Radio)* ich übergebe an Sie; **g)** *(in excess etc.)* **children of 12 and ~:** Kinder im Alter von zwölf Jahren und darüber; **there are two cakes each and one ~:** es sind zwei Kuchen für jeden da und einer übrig; **be [left] ~:** übrig[geblieben] sein; **have ~:** übrig haben ⟨*Geld*⟩; zuviel haben ⟨*Spielkarte*⟩; **9 into 28 goes 3 and 1 ~:** 28 geteilt durch neun ist gleich 3, Rest 1; **it's a bit ~** *(in weight)* es ist ein bißchen mehr; **do you want it ~ or under?** darf es mehr oder soll es weniger sein?; **run three minutes ~:** drei Minuten über die Zeit laufen; **£50 ~ and above** obendrein noch *od.* überdies noch 50 Pfund; **h)** *(from beginning to end)* von Anfang bis Ende; **say sth. twice ~:** etw. wiederholen *od.* zweimal sagen; **[all] ~ again,** *(Amer.)* **~:** noch einmal [ganz von vorn]; **~ and ~ [again]** immer wieder; wieder und wieder *(geh.);* **several times ~:** mehrmals; **i)** *(at an end)* vorbei; vorüber; **be ~:** vorbei sein; ⟨*Aufführung:*⟩ zu Ende sein; **the rain is ~:** der Regen hat aufgehört; **get sth. ~ with** etw. hinter sich *(Akk.)* bringen; **be ~ and done with** erledigt sein; **j) all ~** *(completely finished)* aus [und vorbei]; *(in or on one's whole body etc.)* überall; *(in characteristic attitude)* typisch; **it is all ~ with him** es ist aus mit ihm *(ugs.);* **I ache all ~:** mir tut alles weh; **be shaking all ~:** am ganzen Körper zittern; **be wet all ~:** völlig naß sein; **the dog licked her all ~:** der Hund leckte sie von oben bis unten ab; **I feel stiff all ~:** ich bin ganz steif; **embroidered all ~ with flowers** ganz mit Blumen bestickt; **it happens all ~** *(Amer.: everywhere)* das kommt überall vor; **that is him/sth. all ~:** das ist typisch für ihn/etw.; **k)** *(overleaf)* umseitig; rückseitig; auf der Rückseite; **see ~:** siehe Rückseite. **2.** *prep.* **a)** *(above) (indicating position)* über (+ *Dat.*); *(indicating motion)* über (+ *Akk.*); **bent ~ his books** über seine Bücher gebeugt; **his crime will hang ~ him until he dies** sein Verbrechen wird ihn bis zu seinem Tode verfolgen; **b)** *(on) (indicating position)* über (+ *Dat.*); *(indicating motion)* über (+ *Akk.*); **hit sb. ~ the head** jmdm. auf den Kopf schlagen; **carry a coat ~ one's arm** einen Mantel über dem Arm tragen; **tie a piece of paper ~ a jar** ein Stück Papier auf einem Glas befestigen; **c)** *(in or across every part of)* [überall] in (+ *Dat.*); *(to and fro upon)* über (+ *Akk.*); *(all through)* durch; **all ~** *(in or on all parts of)* überall in (+ *Dat.*); **sell sth./travel all ~ the country** etw. im ganzen Land verkaufen/das ganze Land bereisen; **all ~ Spain** überall in Spanien; in ganz Spanien; **all ~ everything** überall; **you've got jam all ~ your face** du hast überall im Gesicht Marmelade *od.* dein Gesicht ist ganz voller Marmelade; **she spilt wine all ~ her skirt** sie hat sich *(Dat.)* Wein über den ganzen Rock geschüttet; **all ~ the world** in der ganzen Welt; **be all ~ sb.** *(sl.: be very attentive to)* sich an jmdn. ranschmeißen *(salopp);* **show sb. ~ the house** jmdm. das Haus zeigen; **~ all** *see* **overall 3; d)** *(round about) (indicating position)* über (+ *Dat.*); *(indicating motion)* über (+ *Akk.*); **a sense of gloom hung ~ him** ihn umgab eine gedrückte Stimmung; **doubt hangs ~ the authenticity of the diaries** es besteht *od.* bestehen Zweifel an der Echtheit der Tagebücher; **e)** *(on account of)* wegen; **laugh ~ sth.** über etw. *(Akk.)* lachen; **f)** *(engaged with)* bei; **take trouble ~ sth.** sich *(Dat.)* mit etw. Mühe geben; **be a long time ~ sth.** lange für etw. brauchen; **fall asleep ~ one's work** bei der Arbeit einschlafen; **~ work/dinner/a cup of tea/a bottle** bei der Arbeit/beim Essen/bei einer Tasse Tee/einer guten Flasche; **~ the telephone** am Telefon; **g)** *(superior to, in charge of)* über (+ *Akk.*); **have command/authority ~ sb.** Befehlsgewalt über jmdn./Weisungsbefugnis gegenüber jmdm. haben; **be ~ sb.** *(in rank)* über jmdm. stehen; **h)** *(beyond, more than)* über (+ *Akk.*); **an increase ~ last year's total** eine Zunahme gegenüber der letztjährigen Gesamtmenge; **it's been ~ a month since ...:** es ist über einen Monat her, daß ...; **~ and above** zusätzlich zu; **i)** *(in comparison with)* **a decrease ~ last year** eine Abnahme gegenüber dem letzten Jahr; **j)** *(out and down from etc.)* über (+ *Akk.*); **look ~ a wall** über eine Mauer sehen; **the window looks ~ the street** das Fenster geht zur Straße hinaus *od.* liegt zur Straße; **fall ~ a cliff** von einem Felsen stürzen; **jump ~ a precipice** in einen Abgrund springen; **k)** *(across)* über (+ *Akk.*); **the pub ~ the road** die Wirtschaft auf der anderen Straßenseite *od.* gegenüber; **~ sea and land/hill and dale** über Meer und Land/Berg und Tal; **climb ~ the wall** über die Mauer steigen *od.* klettern; **be safely ~ an obstacle** sicher über ein Hindernis gekommen sein; **be ~ the worst** das Schlimmste hinter sich *(Dat.) od.* überstanden haben; **come from ~ the wall** ⟨*Lärm:*⟩ von der anderen Seite der Mauer kommen; **be ~ an illness** eine Krankheit überstanden haben; **l)** *(throughout, during)* über (+ *Akk.*); **stay ~ Christmas/the weekend/Wednesday** über Weihnachten/das Wochenende/bis Donnerstag bleiben; **~ the summer** den Sommer über; **~ the past years** in den letzten Jahren; **mellow ~ the years** ⟨*Person:*⟩ mit den Jahren abgeklärter werden; **m)** *(Math.: divided by)* [geteilt] durch. **3.** *n. (Cricket)* Over, *das;* [Anzahl von] 6/*(esp. in Australia)* 8 Würfel[n]; *see also* **maiden over**

over: ~-a'bundant *adj.* überreichlich; **~a'chieve** *v.i. (Psych.)* einen Leistungsüberschuß haben; **~'act 1.** *v.t.* übertrieben spielen ⟨*Rolle, Theaterstück*⟩; chargieren ⟨*Nebenrolle*⟩; **2.** *v.i.* übertreiben; **~-'active** *adj.* hyperaktiv; **have an ~-active thyroid** an Schilddrüsenüberfunktion leiden; **~-'age** *adj.* zu alt; **~all 1.** *n.* **a)** *(Brit.: garment)* Arbeitsmantel, *der;* Arbeitskittel, *der;* **b)** *in pl.* **[pair of] ~alls** Overall, *der; (with a bib and strap top)* Latzhose, *die;* **2.** *adj.* **a)** *(from end to end; total)* Gesamt⟨*breite, -einsparung, -klassement, -abmessung*⟩; **have an ~all majority** die absolute Mehrheit haben; **b)** *(general)* allgemein ⟨*Verbesserung, Wirkung*⟩; **3.** ['---, --'-] *adv.* **a)** *(in all parts)* insgesamt; **a ship dressed ~all** ein über die Toppen geflaggtes Schiff; **b)** *(taken as a whole)* im großen und ganzen; **come fourth ~all** *(Sport)* Vierter/Vierte der Gesamtwertung werden; **~-am'bitious** *adj.* allzu ehrgeizig ⟨*Projekt, Plan*⟩; **~-an'xiety** *n.* Überängstlichkeit, *die;* übergroße Sorge **(about** um); **~-'anxious** *adj.* **be ~-anxious to do sth.** etw. unbedingt tun wollen; **be ~-anxious about making mistakes** übermäßig besorgt sein, Fehler zu machen; **~arm 1.** *adj.* **a)** *(Cricket)* **~arm bowling** Werfen mit über die Schulter erhobenem Arm; **b)** *(Swimming)* **~arm stroke** Zug, bei dem ein Arm/beide Arme aus dem Wasser gehoben wird/werden; **c)** *(Tennis)* **~arm service** Aufschlag von oben; **2.** *adv.* mit über die Schulter erhobenem Arm ⟨*werfen, aufschlagen*⟩; **~'awe** *v.t.* Ehrfurcht einflößen (+ *Dat.*); ⟨*Waffe, Anzahl:*⟩ einschüchtern; **they were ~awed by the splendour** die Pracht flößte ihnen Ehrfurcht ein; **~'balance 1.** *v.i.* **a)** ⟨*Person:*⟩ das Gleichgewicht verlieren, aus dem Gleichgewicht kommen; **b)** *(capsize)* ⟨*Gegenstand:*⟩ umkippen; ⟨*Boot:*⟩ kentern; **2.** *v.t.* **a)** aus dem Gleichgewicht bringen ⟨*Person*⟩; **b)** *(capsize)* umkippen ⟨*Gegenstand*⟩; zum Kentern bringen ⟨*Boot*⟩; **~'bearing** *adj.*, **~bearingly** [əʊvə'beərɪŋlɪ] *adv.* herrisch; **~bid 1.** [--'-] *v.t., forms as* **bid 1 b** überbieten ⟨*Händler, Geg-*

ner, Gebot›; **2.** [--'-] *v.i., forms as* **bid 2** *(Bridge)* überrufen; **3.** ['---] *n.* höheres Angebot; Übergebot, *das; (higher than justified)* überhöhtes Angebot; **~blouse** *n.* Überziehbluse, *die;* **~'blown** *adj.* **a)** *(past its prime, lit. or fig.)* verblühend; **be ~-blown** [fast] verblüht sein; **b)** *(inflated or pretentious)* geschraubt, gestelzt, gespreizt ‹*Stil, Prosa*›; **~board** *adv.* über Bord; **fall ~board** über Bord gehen; **go ~board** *(fig. coll.)* ausflippen *(ugs.)* **(about** wegen); **~'book** *v.t.* überbuchen; **~boot** *n.* Überschuh, *der;* **~'burden** *v.t. (fig.)* überlasten ‹*System, Person*› **(by** mit); **I don't want to ~burden you** ich möchte Sie nicht überbeanspruchen; **be ~burdened with care/grief** zuviele Sorgen/zuviel Kummer haben; **~call** *(Bridge)* **1.** [--'-] *v.t.* überbieten ‹*Gegner, Gebot*›; **2.** [--'-] *v.i. (Brit.)* überrufen; ein Übergebot *od.* höheres Gebot machen *od.* abgeben; **3.** ['---] *n.* Übergebot, *das;* höheres Gebot; **~-'careful** *adj.* übervorsichtig; **~cast** *adj.* **a)** trübe ‹*Wetter, Himmel, Tag*›; bewölkt ‹*Himmel, Nacht*›; bedeckt, bezogen ‹*Himmel*›; **b)** *(Sewing)* überwendlich ‹*Naht*›; **~-'cautious** *adj.* übervorsichtig; **~-'charge 1.** *v.t.* **a)** *(charge beyond reasonable price)* zuviel abnehmen *od.* abverlangen (+ *Dat.*); **we were ~charged for the eggs** wir haben für die Eier zuviel *od.* einen überhöhten Preis bezahlt; **b)** *(charge beyond right price)* zuviel berechnen (+ *Dat.*); **~charge sb. by 25p** jmdm. 25 Pence zuviel berechnen; **c)** *(put too much charge into)* überladen ‹*Batterie*›; über[be]lasten ‹*Elektrogerät*›; **2.** *v.i.* zuviel berechnen; **~coat** *n.* **a)** *(coat)* Mantel, *der;* **b)** *(of paint)* Anstrich, *der;* **~'come 1.** *v.t., forms as* **come 1: a)** *(prevail over)* überwinden; bezwingen ‹*Feind*›; ablegen ‹*Angewohnheit*›; widerstehen (+ *Dat.*) ‹*Versuchung*›; ‹*Schlaf:*› überkommen, übermannen; ‹*Dämpfe:*› betäuben; **b)** *in p.p. (exhausted, affected)* **he was ~come by grief/with emotion** Kummer/Rührung übermannte *od.* überwältigte ihn; **she was ~come by fear/shyness** Angst/Schüchternheit überkam *od.* überwältigte sie; **they were too ~come with fatigue** sie waren zu müde; **~come with loneliness** von Einsamkeit übermannt; **they were ~come with remorse** Reue befiel sie; **I'm quite ~come** ich bin ganz überwältigt; **2.** *v.i., forms as* **come** siegen; siegreich sein; **~-compen'sation** *n. (Psych.)* Überkompensation, *die;* **~-'confidence** *n.* übersteigertes Selbstvertrauen; **~-'confident** *adj.* übertrieben zuversichtlich; **be ~-confident of success** sich *(Dat.)* des Erfolges allzu sicher sein; **~-'confidently** *adv.* übertrieben zuversichtlich; **~-'cooked** *adj.* verkocht; **~-'critical** *adj.* zu kritisch; überkritisch; **be ~-critical of sth.** etw. zu sehr kritisieren; **~'crowded** *adj.* überfüllt ‹*Zug, Bus, Raum*›; übervölkert ‹*Stadt*›; **~'crowding** *n. (of room, bus, train)* Überfüllung, *die; (of city)* Übervölkerung, *die;* **~de'velop** *v.t. (Photog.)* überentwickeln; **~de'veloped** *adj.* überentwickelt; frühreif ‹*Kind, Jugendliche*›; **~'do** *v.t.,* **~'doing** [əʊvə'du:ɪŋ], **~'did** [əʊvə'dɪd], **~'done** [əʊvə'dʌn] **a)** *(carry to excess)* übertreiben; überladen ‹*Geschichte*›; übertrieben spielen ‹*Rolle, Szene*›; **~do one's gratitude/the sympathy** es mit der Dankbarkeit/dem Mitleid übertreiben; **~do the salt** zu großzügig mit dem Salz umgehen; **b) ~do it** *or* **things** *(work too hard)* sich übernehmen; *(exaggerate)* es übertreiben; **~'done** *adj.* **a)** *(exaggerated)* übertrieben; **b)** *(cooked too much)* verkocht; verbraten ‹*Fleisch*›; **~dose 1.** ['---] *n.* Überdosis, *die;* **2.** [--'-] *v.t.* eine Überdosis geben (+ *Dat.*); **3.** *v.i.* eine Überdosis nehmen; **~draft** *n.* Kontoüberziehung, *die;* **have an ~draft of £50 at the bank** sein Konto um 50 Pfund überzogen haben; **get/pay off an ~draft** einen Überziehungskredit erhalten/abbezahlen; **~'draw** *v.t., forms as* **draw 1** *(Banking)* überziehen ‹*Konto*›; **~'drawn** *adj.* überzogen ‹*Konto*›; **I am ~drawn [at the bank]** mein Konto ist überzogen; **~'dress** *v.i.* sich zu fein anziehen; **~'dressed** *adj.* zu fein angezogen; overdressed *(geh.);* **~drive** *n. (Motor Veh.)* Overdrive, *der;* Schongang, *der;* **~'due** *adj.* überfällig; **the train is 15 minutes ~due** der Zug hat schon 15 Minuten Verspätung; **your rent is ~due** Ihre Miete steht noch aus; **~-'eager** *adj.* übereifrig; **be ~-eager to do sth.** sich übereifrig bemühen, etw. zu tun; **we weren't ~-eager to go back** wir waren nicht gerade wild darauf, zurückzukehren *(ugs.);* **~'eat** *v.i., forms as* **eat** zuviel essen; **~eating** übermäßiges Essen; **~-e'laborate** *adj.* allzu *od.* übertrieben kunstvoll ‹*Konstruktion, Frisur, Stil*›; allzu ausgefeilt ‹*Plan*›; allzu ausgeklügelt ‹*Plan, Entschuldigung*›; **~-'emphasis** *n.* Überbetonung, *die;* **~-'emphasize** *v.t.* überbetonen; **one cannot ~-emphasize the importance of this** man kann nicht genug betonen, wie wichtig das ist; **~-enthusi'astic** *adj.* übertrieben begeistert **(at, about** von); **~estimate 1.** [əʊvər'estɪmeɪt] *v.t.* überschätzen; **~estimate one's own importance** sich zu wichtig nehmen *(ugs.);* **2.** [əʊvər'estɪmət] *n.* zu hohe Schätzung; **~-ex'cite** *v.t.* zu sehr aufregen ‹*Patient*›; **~-excited** überreizt ‹*Zustand, Gemüt*›; **become ~-excited** ganz aufgeregt werden; **~-ex'citement** *n.* Überreizung, *die;* **~ex'ert** *v. refl.* sich überanstrengen; **~-ex'pose** *v.t.* **a)** *(Photog.)* überbelichten; **b) be ~-exposed to sth.** einer Sache *(Dat.)* im Übermaß ausgesetzt sein; **he is becoming ~-exposed** *(on TV)* man sieht sich *(Dat.)* ihn über *(ugs.);* **~-ex'posure** *n.* **a)** *(Photog.)* Überbelichtung, *die;* **b)** *(to radiation)* übermäßige Belastung **(to** durch); *(by the media)* zu häufige Präsentation **(by** durch); **~'feed** *v.t., forms as* **feed 1** überfüttern ‹*Tier, (fam.) Kind*›; **~'fill** *v.t.* zu voll machen; **~'fish** *v.t.* überfischen; **~fishing** Überfischung, *die;* **~flight** *n.* Überflug, *der;* **~flow 1.** [--'-] *v.t.* **a)** *(flow over)* laufen über (+ *Akk.*) ‹*Rand*›; **b)** *(flow over brim of)* überlaufen aus ‹*Tank*›; **a river ~flowing its banks** ein Fluß, der über die Ufer tritt; **c)** *(extend beyond limits of)* ‹*Menge, Personen:*› nicht genug Platz finden in (+ *Dat.*); **d)** *(flood)* überschwemmen ‹*Feld*›; **2.** *v.i.* **a)** *(flow over edge or limit)* überlaufen; **be filled/full to ~flowing** ‹*Raum:*› überfüllt sein; ‹*Flüssigkeitsbehälter:*› zum Überlaufen voll sein; ‹*Schublade:*› fast überquellen; **~flow into the street** ‹*Menge:*› bis auf die Straße stehen; **b)** *(fig.)* ‹*Herz, Person:*› überfließen *(geh.),* überströmen **(with** vor + *Dat.*); **3.** ['---] *n.* **a)** *(what flows over, lit. or fig.)* **the ~flow** was übergelaufen ist; das Übergelaufene; **the ~flow from the cities** die Menschen, für die in den Städten kein Platz ist; **~flow of population** Bevölkerungsüberschuß, *der;* **b)** *(outlet)* **~flow [pipe]** Überlauf, *der;* **~flow meeting** *n.* Parallelversammlung, *die;* **~'fly** *v.t., forms as* [2]**fly 2: a)** *(fly over)* überfliegen; **b)** *(fly beyond)* hinausschießen über (+ *Akk.*) ‹*Landebahn*›; **~'fond** *adj.* **be/not be ~fond of sb./sth.** jmdn./etw. nur zu gern/nicht sonderlich mögen; **be/not be ~fond of doing sth.** etw. nur zu gern/nicht sonderlich gern tun; **~'fondness** *n., no pl.* übertriebene Vorliebe **(for** für); **~ful'fil** *(Amer.:* **~ful'fill)** *v.t.* übererfüllen ‹*[Plan]soll, Plan*›; **~ful'filment** *(Amer.:* **~ful'fillment)** *n.* Überfüllung, *die;* **~'full** *adj.* zu voll; übervoll; **~'generous** *adj.* zu *od.* übertrieben großzügig ‹*Person*›; reichlich groß ‹*Portion*›; **you weren't ~-generous with the butter** mit der Butter bist du ja nicht gerade verschwenderisch umgegangen; **~ground** *adj.* oberirdisch ‹*Krypta, Pflanzenteil*›; oberirdisch verkehrend ‹*Bahn*›; **~'grow** *v.t., forms as* **grow 2** überwachsen, überwuchern ‹*Beet*›; **~grown** *adj.* **a)** überwachsen, überwuchert ‹*Beet*› **(with** von); **b) he acts like an ~grown schoolboy** er führt sich auf wie ein großes Kind; **~hand knot** *n.* einfacher Knoten; **~hang 1.** [--'-] *v.t.,* **~hung** [əʊvə'hʌŋ] ‹*Felsen, Stockwerk:*› hinausragen über (+ *Akk.*); **2.** [--'-] *v.i.,* **~hung** ‹*Fels, Klippe:*› überhängen; **3.** ['---] *n.* Überhang, *der;* **rock ~hang** Felsvorsprung, *der;* Überhang, *der;* **~'hanging** *adj.* überhängend; **~-'hasty** *adj.* vorschnell, übereilt ‹*Urteil, Verurteilung, Entschluß, Schluß, Antwort*›; **be ~-hasty in doing sth.** etw. vorschnell *od.* übereilt tun; **~haul 1.** [--'-] *v.t.* **a)** *(examine and adjust)* überholen ‹*Auto, Schiff, Maschine, Motor*›; überprüfen ‹*System*›; **b)** *(overtake)* überholen ‹*Fahrzeug, Person*›; **2.** ['---] *n.* Überholung, *die;* **need an ~haul** ‹*Maschine:*› überholt werden müssen; ‹*System:*› überarbeitet werden müssen; **give sth. an ~haul** etw. überholen; **~head 1.** [--'-] *adv.* **high ~head** hoch oben; **the sky ~head** der Himmel darüber; *(above me/him/us etc.)* der Himmel über mir/ihm/uns *usw.;* **the clouds ~head** die Wolken am Himmel; **hear a sound ~head** ein Geräusch über sich *(Dat.)* hören; **2.** ['---] *adj.* **a) ~head wires** Hochleitung, *die;* **~head cable** Luftkabel, *das;* Freileitung, *die;* **~head railway** Hochbahn, *die;* **~head lighting** Deckenbeleuchtung, *die;* **~head projector** Overheadprojektor, *der;* **b) ~head expenses/charges/costs** *(Commerc.)* Gemeinkosten *Pl.;* **3.** ['---] *n.* **a) ~heads,** *(Amer.)* **~head** *(Commerc.)* Gemeinkosten *Pl.;* **b)** *(Sport)* Überkopfball, *der;* **~'hear** *v.t., forms as* **hear 1** *(accidentally)* zufällig [mit]hören, mitbekommen ‹*Unterhaltung, Bemerkung*›; *(intentionally)* belauschen ‹*Gespräch, Personen*›; **speak quietly, so that we can't be ~heard** sprich leise, damit niemand etwas mitbekommt; *abs.* **not want sb. to ~hear** nicht wollen, daß jmd. mithört; **~'heat 1.** *v.t.* überhitzen ‹*Motor, Metall usw.*›; **~heated imagination** überdrehte Phantasie; **~heated economy** überhitzte Konjunktur; **2.** *v.i.* zu heiß werden; ‹*Maschine, Lager:*› heißlaufen; *(fig.)* ‹*Konjunktur:*› sich überhitzen; **~-in'dulge 1.** *v.t.* zu sehr frönen *(geh.)* (+ *Dat.*) ‹*Appetit*›; **~-indulge a child** einem Kind gegenüber zu nachgiebig sein; **~-indulge oneself** sich allzusehr gehen lassen; **2.** *v.i.* es übertreiben; **~-indulge in food and drink** sich an Essen und Trinken mehr als gütlich tun; **~-in'dulgence** *n.* übermäßiger Genuß **(in** von); *(towards a person)* zu große Nachgiebigkeit; **~-indulgence in drink/drugs/sex** übermäßiges Trinken/übermäßiger Drogengenuß/zuviel Sex; **~-in'dulgent** *adj.* unmäßig; *(towards a person)* zu nachgiebig; **~-in'sured** *adj.* zu hoch versichert

overjoyed [əʊvə'dʒɔɪd] *adj.* überglücklich **(at** über + *Akk.*)

over: ~kill *n. (Mil.)* Overkill, *das od. der;* **~land 1.** [--'-] *adv.* auf dem Landweg; **2.** ['---] *adj.* **by the ~land route** auf dem Landweg; **~land transport/journey** Beförderung/Reise auf dem Landweg; **~lap 1.** [--'-] *v.t.* überlappen ‹*Fläche, Dachziegel*›; teilweise überdecken ‹*Farbe*›; sich überschneiden mit ‹*Aufgabe, Datum*›; **2.** [--'-] *v.i.* ‹*Flächen, Dachziegel:*› sich überlappen; ‹*Aufgaben, Daten, Zuständigkeitsbereiche:*› sich überschneiden; ‹*Farben:*› sich teilweise überdecken; ‹*Bretter:*› teilweise übereinanderliegen; **3.** ['---] *n.* **a)** Überlappung, *die; (of colours)* teilweise Überdeckung; *(of dates or tasks; between subjects, periods, etc.)* Überschneidung, *die;* **have an ~lap of 4 cm** ‹*Bretter usw.:*› sich auf einer Breite von

4 cm überdecken; **b)** *(~lapping part)* Überlappung, *die; (between map-sheets)* sich überschneidende Teile; **~-'large** *adj.* übergroß; **~-large for sth.** zu groß für etw.; **~lay 1.** [--'-] *v. t., forms as* **²lay 1: a)** *(cover)* bedecken; *(with film, veneer)* überziehen; **b)** *see* **~lie; 2.** ['---] *n.* **a)** *(cover)* Überzug, *der;* **b)** *(transparent sheet)* Auflegefolie, *die;* **~'leaf** *adv.* auf der Rückseite; **see diagram ~leaf** siehe das umseitige Diagramm; **see ~leaf for details** Details siehe Rückseite; **~'lie** *v. t., forms as* **²lie 2** überlagern; **~load 1.** [--'-] *v. t.* überladen *(auch fig.),* überlasten ⟨*Stromkreis, Lautsprecher usw.*⟩; überbelasten ⟨*Maschine, Motor, Mechanismus usw.*⟩; **2.** *v. i.* überbelastet werden; **3.** ['---] *n. (Electr.)* Überlastung, *die;* **~-'long** *adj.* überlang; **~'look** *v. t.* **a)** *(have view of)* ⟨*Hotel, Zimmer, Haus:*⟩ Aussicht haben *od.* bieten auf (+ *Akk.*); **house ~looking the lake** Haus mit Blick auf den See; **b)** *(be higher than)* überragen; **c)** *(not see, ignore)* übersehen; *(allow to go unpunished)* hinwegsehen über (+ *Akk.*) ⟨*Vergehen, Beleidigung*⟩; **~lord** *n.* Oberherr, *der*

overly ['əʊvəlɪ] *adv.* allzu

over: ~'man *v. t.* überbesetzen; **~mantel** *n.* Kaminaufsatz, *der;* **~-'modest** *adj.* zu bescheiden; **~-'much 1.** *adj.* allzu viel; **2.** *adv.* allzusehr

overnight 1. [--'-] *adv. (also fig.: suddenly)* über Nacht; **stay ~ in a hotel** in einem Hotel übernachten; **2.** ['---] *adj.* **a) ~ train/bus** Nachtzug, *der*/Nachtbus, *der;* **~ stay** Übernachtung, *die;* **make an ~ stay** übernachten; **b)** *(fig.: sudden)* **be an ~ success** über Nacht Erfolg haben

overnight: ~ bag *n.* [kleine] Reisetasche; **~ case** *n.* Handköfferchen, *das*

over: ~pass *see* **flyover; ~'pay** *v. t., forms as* **pay 2** überbezahlen; **~'payment** *n.* Überbezahlung, *die;* **receive an ~payment of £20** 20 Pfund zuviel bekommen; **~'play** *v. t.* **a)** *(overact)* übertrieben spielen ⟨*Rolle*⟩; **b)** *(exaggerate)* hochspielen ⟨*Faktor, Bedeutung*⟩; **~play one's hand** *(Cards)* sich überreizen; *(fig.)* den Bogen überspannen; **~-'populated** *adj.* überbevölkert; **~-popu'lation** *n.* Übervölkerung, *die;* **~'power** *v. t.* **a)** *(subdue, overwhelm)* überwältigen; *(wrestling)* bezwingen; **b)** *(render imperceptible)* überdecken *(fig.);* **~'powered** *adj. (Motor Veh.)* übermotorisiert; **~powering** [əʊvə'paʊərɪŋ] *adj.* überwältigend; durchdringend ⟨*Geruch*⟩; **the heat was ~powering** die Hitze war unerträglich; **I find him a bit ~powering** seine Art ist mir manchmal zu viel; **~'praise** *v. t.* zu sehr loben; **~-priced** [əʊvə'praɪst] *adj.* zu teuer; **~print 1.** *v. t.* **a)** [--'-] *(print too many/extra copies of)* **~print sth. by 100 copies** 100 Exemplare zuviel/mehr von etw. drucken; **b)** ['---] *(print further matter on, print over)* überdrucken **(with** mit); **2.** ['---] *n.* [zusätzlicher] Aufdruck; *(on stamp also)* Überdruck, *der;* **~-pro'duce** *v. t.* **~-produce milk/steel** *etc.* zuviel Milch/Stahl *usw.* produzieren; **~-pro'duction** *n., no pl., no indef. art.* Überproduktion, *die;* **~pro'tective** *adj.* überfürsorglich **(towards** gegenüber); **~-'qualified** *adj.* überqualifiziert; **~'rate** *v. t.* überschätzen; **be ~rated** überschätzt werden; ⟨*Buch, Film:*⟩ überbewertet werden; **~'reach** *v. refl.* sich übernehmen; **~-re'act** *v. i.* unangemessen heftig reagieren **(to** auf + *Akk.*); **~-re'action** *n.* Überreaktion, *die* **(to** auf + *Akk.*); **~ride 1.** [--'-] *v. t., forms as* **ride 3** sich hinwegsetzen über (+ *Akk.*); **be ~ridden** mißachtet werden; **2.** ['---] *n. (control)* **[manual] ~ride** Automatikabschaltung, *die;* **~'riding** *adj.* vorrangig; **be of ~riding importance** wichtiger als alles andere sein; **~ripe** *adj.* überreif; **~'rule** *v. t.* **a)** *(set aside)* aufheben ⟨*Entscheidung*⟩; zurückweisen ⟨*Einwand, Appell, Forderung, Argument*⟩; **b)** *(reject proposal of)* **~rule sb.** jmds. Vorschlag ablehnen; **be ~ruled by the majority** von der Mehrheit überstimmt werden; **objection ~ruled!** Einspruch abgelehnt!; **~run** [--'-] *v. t., forms as* **run 3: a) be ~run with** überlaufen sein von ⟨*Touristen*⟩; überwuchert sein von ⟨*Unkraut*⟩; wimmeln von ⟨*Mäusen, Schädlingen*⟩; **b)** *(Mil.)* einfallen in (+ *Akk.*) ⟨*Land*⟩; überrennen ⟨*Stellungen*⟩; **c)** *(exceed)* **~run its allotted time** ⟨*Programm, Treffen, Diskussion:*⟩ länger als vorgesehen dauern; **~run [one's time]** ⟨*Dozent, Redner:*⟩ überziehen; *abs.* **the programme ~ran by five minutes** die vorgesehene Sendezeit wurde um fünf Minuten überzogen; **~-'scrupulous** *adj.* übertrieben gewissenhaft; **he is not ~-scrupulous about that** damit nimmt er es nicht allzu genau; **~seas 1.** [--'-] *adv.* in Übersee ⟨*leben, sein, sich niederlassen*⟩; nach Übersee ⟨*gehen*⟩; **colonies ~seas** überseeische Kolonien; Überseekolonien; **2.** ['---] *adj.* **a)** *(across the sea)* Übersee⟨*postgebühren, -handel, -telefonat*⟩; **~seas broadcasting** Sendungen für Hörer in Übersee; **b)** *(foreign)* Auslands⟨*hilfe, -zulage, -ausgabe, -nachrichten*⟩; ausländisch ⟨*Student*⟩; **~seas visitors/ambassadors** Besucher/Botschafter aus dem Ausland; **~'see** *v. t., forms as* **¹see 1** überwachen; *(manage)* leiten ⟨*Abteilung*⟩; **~seer** *see* **supervisor; ~'sell** *v. t.* **a)** *(overpraise)* zu sehr anpreisen; **b)** *(sell too much of)* **~sell one's goods** mehr Waren verkaufen, als man liefern kann; **~-'sensitive** *adj.* überempfindlich; übersensibel; **~sew** *v. t., forms as* **sew 1** überwendlich nähen; **~-sexed** [əʊvə'sekst] *adj.* sexbesessen; **~'shadow** *v. t. (lit. or fig.)* überschatten; *(fig.: make seem minor)* in den Schatten stellen ⟨*Leistung, Person*⟩; **~shoe** *n.* Überschuh, *der;* **~'shoot** *v. t., forms as* **shoot 2** hinausschießen über (+ *Akk.*); vorbeifahren an (+ *Akk.*) ⟨*Abzweigung*⟩; **~shoot the mark** *(fig.)* über das Ziel hinausschießen; **~shoot [the runway]** ⟨*Pilot, Flugzeug:*⟩ zu weit kommen; **~sight** *n.* **a)** Versehen, *das;* **by or through an ~sight** versehentlich; aus Versehen; **b)** *see* **supervision; ~-simplifi'cation** *n.* zu starke Vereinfachung; **~-'simplify** *v. t.* zu stark vereinfachen; **~size, ~sized** *see* **outsize; ~'sleep** *v. i., forms as* **sleep 2** verschlafen; **~sleep by half an hour** eine halbe Stunde zu lange schlafen; **~-so'licitous** *adj.* übermäßig *od.* allzu besorgt; **~'spend 1.** *v. i., forms as* **spend** zuviel [Geld] ausgeben; **~spending** zu hohe Ausgaben; **~spend by £100** 100 Pfund zuviel ausgeben; **2.** *v. t.* überschreiten, überziehen ⟨*Etat, Budget, Einkommen*⟩; **~spill** *n.* **a)** *(surplus population)* Bevölkerungsüberschuß, *der; attrib.* Satelliten⟨*stadt, -siedlung*⟩; **b)** *(overflow)* **the ~spill** [das,] was übergelaufen ist/überläuft; **~'staff** *v. t.* überbesetzen; **~'staffing** *n.* Überbesetzung, *die;* **~'state** *v. t.* übertrieben darstellen; überbetonen ⟨*Argument*⟩; **~'statement** *n.* Übertreibung, *die; (of case, problem)* übertriebene Darstellung; **~'stay** *v. t.* überziehen ⟨*Urlaub*⟩; **~stay one's time [by three days]** [drei Tage] länger als vorgesehen bleiben; *see also* **welcome 2 a; ~steer** *(Motor Veh.)* **1.** [--'-] *v. i.* übersteuern; **2.** ['---] *n.* Übersteuern, *das;* **~'step** *v. t.* überschreiten; **~step the mark** *(fig.)* zu weit gehen; **~'stock** *v. t.* überbestücken ⟨*Lager*⟩; zu stark besetzen *(Fischereiw.)* ⟨*Teich*⟩; **~'strain 1.** *n.* Überforderung, die; **2.** *v. t.* überfordern; **~'stretch** *v. t.* überdehnen; *(fig.)* überfordern; **~strung** *adj.* kreuzsaitig ⟨*Klavier*⟩; *(fig.)* überreizt; **~-sub'scribed** *adj. (Finance)* überzeichnet

overt ['əʊvət, əʊ'vɜːt] *adj.* unverhohlen; **their actions were ~:** sie haben mit offenen Karten gespielt *od.* nichts verborgen

over: ~'take *v. t.* **a)** *(esp. Brit.: pass)* überholen; **'no ~taking'** *(Brit.)* „Überholen verboten"; **b)** *(catch up)* einholen; **c)** *(fig.)* **be ~taken by events** ⟨*Plan:*⟩ von den Ereignissen überholt werden; **d)** *(exceed)* **supply will ~take demand** das Angebot wird die Nachfrage übersteigen; **e)** *(befall)* hereinbrechen über (+ *Akk.*); ⟨*Schicksal:*⟩ ereilen *(geh.);* **~'tax** *v. t.* **a)** *(demand too much tax from)* überbesteuern; **b)** *(~strain)* überstrapazieren, überfordern ⟨*Verstand, Geduld*⟩; überanstrengen ⟨*Verstand*⟩; **~tax one's strength** sich übernehmen; **don't ~tax my patience!** stell meine Geduld nicht auf die Probe!; **~throw 1.** [--'-] *v. t., forms as* **throw 1: a)** stürzen ⟨*Regierung, Regime usw.*⟩; aus dem Weg räumen ⟨*Gegner*⟩; *(defeat)* schlagen, besiegen ⟨*Feind*⟩; **b)** *(subvert)* umstoßen, *(ugs.)* über den Haufen werfen ⟨*Verfassung, Theorie, Überzeugung*⟩; **2.** ['---] *n.* **a)** *(removal from power)* Sturz, *der;* **b)** *(subversion)* Umsturz, *der; (of ideas)* Umwälzung, *die;* **~time 1.** *n.* Überstunden; **work ten hours'/put in a lot of ~time** zehn/eine Menge Überstunden machen; **be on ~time** Überstunden machen; **~time ban/payment** Überstundenstopp, *der*/-zuschlag, *der;* **2.** *adv.* **work ~time** Überstunden machen; *(fig. coll.)* ⟨*Apparat:*⟩ auf Hochtouren laufen; **his brain/imagination was working ~time** er dachte fieberhaft nach/er hatte eine überspannte Phantasie; **~'tire** *v. t.* übermüden; **~tire oneself** sich übernehmen *od.* überanstrengen

overtly ['əʊvətlɪ, əʊ'vɜːtlɪ] *adv.* unverhohlen

over: ~tone *n.* **a)** *(fig.: implication)* Unterton, *der;* **the crime had political ~tones** das Verbrechen hatte auch politische Implikationen; **b)** *(Mus.)* Oberton, *der;* **~'train** *(Sport)* **1.** *v. t.* übertrainieren; **2.** *v. i.* zuviel trainieren; **~trick** *n. (Bridge)* Überstich, *der;* **~'trump** *v. t. (Cards)* übertrumpfen

overture ['əʊvətjʊə(r)] *n.* **a)** *(Mus.)* Ouvertüre, *die;* **b)** *(formal proposal or offer)* Angebot, *das;* **~s of peace** Friedensangebot, *das;* **make ~s [to sb.]** [jmdm.] ein Angebot machen; *(to woman)* [bei jmdm.] Annäherungsversuche machen

over: ~'turn 1. *v. t.* **a)** *(upset)* umstoßen; **b)** *(overthrow)* umstürzen ⟨*bestehende Ordnung, Vorstellung, Prinzip*⟩; stürzen ⟨*Regierung*⟩; beseitigen ⟨*Institution*⟩; *(reverse)* aufheben ⟨*Urteil, Entscheid[ung]*⟩; **2.** *v. i.* ⟨*Auto, Boot, Kutsche:*⟩ umkippen; ⟨*Boot:*⟩ kentern; ⟨*Auto:*⟩ sich überschlagen; **~-use 1.** [əʊvə'juːz] *v. t.* zu oft verwenden; **2.** [əʊvə'juːs] *n.* zu häufiger Gebrauch; **~'value** *v. t.* überbewerten ⟨*Währung*⟩; **his contribution cannot be ~valued** sein Beitrag kann gar nicht hoch genug bewertet werden; **~view** *n.* Überblick, *der* **(of** über + *Akk.*)

overweening [əʊvə'wiːnɪŋ] *adj.* maßlos ⟨*Ehrgeiz, Gier, Stolz*⟩

'overweight 1. *adj.* **a)** *(obese)* übergewichtig ⟨*Person*⟩; **be [12 pounds] ~:** [12 Pfund] Übergewicht haben; **b)** *(weighing in excess)* zu schwer; *(very heavy)* bleischwer. **2.** *n.* Übergewicht, *das*

overwhelm [əʊvə'welm] *v. t.* **a)** *(overpower)* überwältigen; **b)** *(crush, destroy)* **be ~ed by the enemy** vom übermächtigen Feind völlig aufgerieben werden; **c)** *(bury)* verschütten; ⟨*Wasser:*⟩ überschwemmen, überfluten

overwhelming [əʊvə'welmɪŋ] *adj.* überwältigend; unbändig ⟨*Wut, Kraft, Verlangen, Zorn*⟩; unermeßlich ⟨*Leid, Kummer*⟩; **against ~ odds** entgegen aller Wahrscheinlichkeit

over: ~wind [əʊvə'waɪnd] *v. t., forms as* **²wind 1, 2** überdrehen; **~'work 1.** *v. t.* **a)** *(make work too hard)* mit Arbeit überlasten; **~work oneself** sich überarbeiten; **b)** *(fig.)* überstrapazieren ⟨*Metapher, Wort usw.*⟩; **2.** *v. i.* sich überarbeiten; **3.** *n.* [Arbeits]überlastung, *die;* **become ill from ~work** sich krank arbeiten; ~'**wrought** *adj.* überreizt; ~-'**zealous** *adj.* übereifrig

oviduct ['əʊvɪdʌkt] *n. (Anat., Zool.)* Ovidukt, *der (fachspr.)*; Eileiter, *der*

oviparous [əʊ'vɪpərəs] *adj. (Zool.)* ovipar

ovulate ['ɒvjʊleɪt, 'əʊvjʊleɪt] *v.i. (Physiol.)* ovulieren *(fachspr.)*; reife *od.* befruchtungsfähige Eizellen abstoßen

ovulation [ɒvjʊ'leɪʃn, əʊvjʊ'leɪʃn] *n.* Ovulation, *die (fachspr.)*; Eisprung, *der*

ovum ['əʊvəm] *n., pl.* **ova** ['əʊvə] Ovum, *das (fachspr.)*; *(Biol.)* Ei, *das*

ow [aʊ] *int.* au

owe [əʊ] *v.t.*, **owing** ['əʊɪŋ] **a)** schulden; ~ **sb. sth.**, ~ **sth. to sb.** jmdm. etw. schulden; ~ **it to sb. to do sth.** es jmdm. schuldig sein, etw. zu tun; **I ~ you an explanation** ich bin dir eine Erklärung schuldig; **you ~ it to yourself to take a break** du mußt dir einfach eine Pause gönnen; **can I ~ you the rest?** kann ich dir den Rest schuldig bleiben?; **money was ~d to them** sie hatten Außenstände; **I hate owing money** ich hasse es, Schulden zu haben; ~ **[sb.] for sth.** [jmdm.] etw. bezahlen müssen; **I [still] ~ you for the ticket** du kriegst von mir noch das Geld für die Karte *(ugs.)*; **b)** *(feel gratitude for, be indebted for)* verdanken; ~ **sth. to sb.** jmdm. etw. verdanken *od.* zu verdanken haben

owing ['əʊɪŋ] *pred. adj.* ausstehend; **be ~:** ausstehen; **money is ~ to them** sie haben noch Außenstände; **£10 is ~ on the furniture** für die Möbel müssen noch 10 Pfund bezahlt werden

'**owing to** *prep.* wegen; ~ **his foresight** dank seinem Weitblick; ~ **unfortunate circumstances** auf Grund unglücklicher Umstände

owl [aʊl] *n.* **a)** Eule, *die*; **b)** *(fig. person)* **he's a wise ~:** er ist weise wie eine Eule

owlet ['aʊlɪt] *n.* Eulenjunge, *das*

owlish ['aʊlɪʃ] *adj.* eulenhaft

own [əʊn] **1.** *adj.* eigen; **with one's ~ eyes** mit eigenen Augen; **be sb.'s ~ [property]** jmds. Eigentum sein; jmdm. selbst gehören; **look after one's ~ affairs** sich selbst um seine Angelegenheiten kümmern; **this is your ~ responsibility** dafür bist du selbst verantwortlich; **speak from one's ~ experience** aus eigener Erfahrung sprechen; **this is all my ~ work** das habe ich alles selbst *od.* ganz allein gemacht; **reserve sth. for one's ~ use** etw. für sich selbst reservieren; **have one's ~ room** [s]ein eigenes Zimmer haben; **one's ~ brother** der eigene Bruder; **sb.'s ~ country** jmds. Heimatland; **do one's ~ cooking/housework** selbst kochen/die Hausarbeit selbst machen; **make one's ~ clothes** seine Kleidung selbst schneidern; **virtue is its ~ reward** die Tugend trägt ihren Lohn in sich selbst; **have a charm all [of] its ~:** einen ganz eigenen Reiz haben; **a house/ideas** *etc.* **of one's ~:** ein eigenes Haus/eigene Ideen *usw.*; **have nothing of one's ~:** kein persönliches Eigentum haben; **have enough problems of one's ~:** selbst genug Probleme haben; **have [got] one of one's ~:** selbst einen/eine/eins haben; **for reasons of his ~...:** aus nur ihm selbst bekannten Gründen ...; **come into one's ~** *(Law.: inherit property)* sein Erbe antreten; **that's where he/it comes into his/its ~** *(fig.)* da kommt er/es voll zur Geltung; **on one's/its ~** *(alone)* allein; **drink whisky on its ~:** Whisky pur trinken; **get better on its ~:** von selbst besser werden; **start up on one's ~:** sich selbständig machen; **he's on his ~** *or* **in a class of his ~** *(fig.)* er ist eine Klasse für sich; **be on one's ~** *(without outside help)* auf sich *(Akk.)* selbst gestellt sein; *see also* **business c; call 2j; flesh 1a; get back 2b; ²hold 1k; man 1b; master 1a; right 3a. 2.** *v.t.* **a)** *(possess)* besitzen; **be ~ed by sb.** jmdm. gehören; **who ~s that house?** wem gehört das Haus?; **be privately ~ed** sich in Privatbesitz befinden; **they behaved as if they ~ed the place** sie benahmen sich, als ob der Laden ihnen gehörte *(ugs.)*; **b)** *(acknowledge)* anerkennen; **c)** *see* **admit 1c. 3.** *v.i.* ~ **to** eingestehen; ~ **to doing sth./to being ashamed** [ein]gestehen *od.* zugeben, daß man etw. tut/daß man sich schämt

~ '**up** *v.i. (coll.)* ⟨*Schuldiger, Täter:*⟩ gestehen; ~ **up to sth.** etw. [ein]gestehen *od.* zugeben; ~ **up to having done sth.** [ein]gestehen *od.* zugeben, daß man etw. getan hat; **Come on, ~ up! Who did it?** Na los, raus mit der Sprache! Wer ist es gewesen?

'**own brand** *n.* Hausmarke, *die*

owned [əʊnd] *adj.* **publicly ~:** gemeinde-/staatseigen; **company-~:** firmeneigen; **privately ~:** in Privatbesitz *nachgestellt;* **English/American-~:** in englischem/amerikanischem Besitz befindlich ⟨*Firma, Bank*⟩

owner ['əʊnə(r)] *n.* Besitzer, *der*/Besitzerin, *die*; Eigentümer, *der*/Eigentümerin, *die*; *(of car also)* Halter, *der*/Halterin, *die*; *(of shop, hotel, firm, etc.)* Inhaber, *der*/Inhaberin, *die*; **at ~'s risk** auf eigene Gefahr; **dog-/property-~s** Hunde-/Grundbesitzer

owner-'driver *n. (Brit.) Halter/Halterin eines Autos, der/die das Auto selbst fährt*

ownerless ['əʊnəlɪs] *adj.* herrenlos

owner-'occupier *n. (Brit.)* Eigenheimbesitzer, *der*/-besitzerin, *die*

ownership ['əʊnəʃɪp] *n., no pl.* Besitz, *der*; ~ **is disputed** die Besitzverhältnisse sind umstritten; **the ~ of the land was disputed** es war umstritten, wem das Land gehörte; **be under new ~** ⟨*Firma, Laden, Restaurant:*⟩ einen neuen Inhaber/eine neue Inhaberin haben

own 'goal *n. (lit. or fig.)* Eigentor, *das*

ox [ɒks] *n., pl.* **oxen** ['ɒksn] Ochse, *der*; *see also* **strong 1b**

oxalic acid [ɒksælɪk 'æsɪd] *n. (Chem.)* Oxalsäure, *die (fachspr.)*; Kleesäure, *die*

'**ox-bow** *n.* **a)** *(of yoke)* Brustholz, *das*; **b)** *(Geog.: river bend)* Flußschleife, *die*; *(one of several)* Mäander, *der*

ox-bow 'lake *n. (Geog.)* Altwasser, *das*

Oxbridge ['ɒksbrɪdʒ] *n. (Brit.)* die Universitäten Oxford und Cambridge; *attrib.* ~ **graduate/education** Absolvent[in] der/Ausbildung an der Universität Oxford oder Cambridge

Oxfam ['ɒksfæm] *pr. n.* Oxforder Hungerhilfekomitee

Oxford ['ɒksfəd] *see* **Oxford shoe**

Oxford: ~ '**accent** *n.* Oxford-Akzent, *der*; ~ '**blue** *n.* Dunkelblau, *das*; ~ **shoe** *n.* Schnürhalbschuh, *der*

'**oxhide** *n. (skin)* Rindshaut, *die*; *(leather)* Rindsleder, *das*

oxidant ['ɒksɪdənt] *n. (Chem.)* Oxydationsmittel, *das*

oxidation [ɒksɪ'deɪʃn] *n. (Chem.)* Oxydation, *die*; Oxidation, *die (fachspr.)*

oxide ['ɒksaɪd] *n. (Chem.)* Oxyd, *das*; Oxid, *das (fachspr.)*

oxidize (oxidise) ['ɒksɪdaɪz] *v.t. & i. (Chem.)* oxydieren; oxidieren *(fachspr.)*

oxlip *n.* Primel, *die*; Schlüsselblume, *die*

Oxon. ['ɒksn] *abbr.* **a) Oxfordshire; b) of Oxford University**

Oxonian [ɒk'səʊnɪən] **1.** *adj.* der Universität Oxford *nachgestellt.* **2.** *n.* Mitglied der Universität Oxford

'**oxtail** *n.* Ochsenschwanz, *der*

oxtail 'soup *n. (Gastr.)* Ochsenschwanzsuppe, *die*

'**ox-tongue** *n. (Gastr.)* Ochsenzunge, *die*

oxy-acetylene [ɒksɪə'setɪli:n] *adj.* ~ **welding** Autogenschweißen, *das*; ~ **torch** *or* **blowpipe** *or* **burner** Schweißbrenner, *der*

oxygen ['ɒksɪdʒən] *n. (Chem.)* Sauerstoff, *der*

oxygenate ['ɒksɪdʒəneɪt] *v.t. (Chem., Physiol.)* oxygenieren *(fachspr.)*

oxygenation [ɒksɪdʒə'neɪʃn] *n. (Chem., Physiol.)* Oxygenation, *die (fachspr.)*

oxygen: ~ **bottle,** ~ **cylinder** *ns.* Sauerstoffflasche, *die*; ~ **mask** *n.* Sauerstoffmaske, *die*; ~ **tent** *n. (Med.)* Sauerstoffzelt, *das*

oxymoron [ɒksɪ'mɔ:rɒn] *n. (Rhet.)* Oxymoron, *das*

oyez (oyes) [əʊ'jez, əʊ'jes] *int.* Achtung *(Ruf eines Ausrufers)*

oyster ['ɔɪstə(r)] *n.* Auster, *die*; **the world's his ~** *(fig.)* ihm liegt die Welt zu Füßen

oyster: ~-**bed** *n.* Austernbank, *die*; ~-**catcher** *n. (Ornith.)* Austernfischer, *der*; ~-**farm** *n.* Austernpark, *der*; ~ **knife** *n.* Austernmesser, *das*

Oz [ɒz] *n. (sl.)* Australien *(das)*

oz. *abbr.* **ounce[s]**

ozone ['əʊzəʊn, əʊ'zəʊn] *n.* Ozon, *das*

ozone: ~-**friendly** *adj.* ozonsicher; *(not using CFCs)* FCKW-frei; ~ **hole** *n.* Ozonloch, *das (ugs.)* ~ **layer** *n.* Ozonschicht, *die*; **the hole in the ~ layer** das Ozonloch *(ugs.)*

P

¹P, p [pi:] *n., pl.* **Ps** *or* **P's** P, p, *das*; *see also* **mind 2b**

²P *abbr. (Chess)* **pawn** B

p. *abbr.* **a) page** S.; **b)** [pi:] *(Brit.)* **penny/pence** p; **c)** *(Mus.)* **piano** p; **d)** *(Phys.)* **pico-** p

PA *abbr.* **a) personal assistant** pers. Ass.; **b) public address: PA [system]** LS-Anlage, *die*

Pa *abbr. (Phys.)* **pascal** Pa

pa [pɑ:] *n. (coll.)* Papa, *der (fam.)*

p.a. *abbr.* **per annum** p.a.

pabulum ['pæbjʊləm] *n. (lit. or fig.)* Nahrung, *die*

¹pace [peɪs] **1.** *n.* **a)** *(step, distance)* Schritt, *der*; **b)** *(speed)* Tempo, *das*; **slacken/quicken one's ~** *(walking)* seinen Schritt verlangsamen/beschleunigen; **at a steady/good ~:** in gleichmäßigem/zügigem Tempo; **at a snail's ~:** im Schneckentempo *(ugs.)*; **set the ~:** das Tempo angeben *od.* bestimmen; *(act as ~-maker)* Schrittmacher sein; **keep ~ [with sb./sth.]** [mit jmdm./etw.] Schritt halten; **stay** *or* **stand the ~, stay** *or* **keep with the ~** *(Sport)* das Tempo durchhalten; **be off the ~** *(Sport)* zurückliegen; **he couldn't stand the ~ of life** *(fig.)* ihm war das Leben zu hektisch; **c)** *(of horse)* Paßgang, *der*; **put sb./a horse through his/its ~s** *(fig.)* jmdn./ein Pferd zeigen lassen, was er/es kann; **show one's ~s** zeigen, was man kann. **2.** *v.i.* **a)** schreiten *(geh.)*; [gemessenen Schrittes] gehen; ~ **up and down [the platform/room]** [auf dem Bahnsteig/im Zimmer] auf und ab gehen *od.* marschieren; **b)** *(amble)* ⟨*Pferd:*⟩ im Paß[gang] gehen. **3.** *v.t.* **a)** auf- und abgehen in (+ *Dat.*); **b)** *(set the ~ for)* Schrittmacher sein für

~ '**out** *v.t.* abschreiten ⟨*Entfernung, Weg*⟩

²pace ['peɪsɪ,'pɑ:tʃeɪ] *prep. (formal)* ~ **Mr Smith ...:** ohne Mr. Smith *(Dat.)* zu nahe treten zu wollen ...

pace 'bowler *see* **fast bowler**

-paced [peɪst] *adj. in comb.* **a well-~ performance** eine [rhythmisch] ausgewogene Aufführung; **be even-~:** ein gleichförmiges Tempo haben

'pace-maker *n.* **a)** *(Sport)* Schrittmacher, *der*/-macherin, *die;* **b)** *(Med.)* [Herz]schrittmacher, *der*

'pace-setter *n.* Schrittmacher, *der*/-macherin, *die*

pachyderm ['pækɪdɛ:m] *n.* *(Zool.)* Dickhäuter, *der*

pacific [pə'sɪfɪk] **1.** *adj.* **a)** *(conciliatory, peaceable)* versöhnlich; **b)** *(tranquil)* friedlich; **c)** *(Geog.)* Pazifik⟨*küste, -insel*⟩; **P~ Ocean** Pazifischer *od.* Stiller Ozean. **2.** *n.* **the P~:** der Pazifik

pacification [pæsɪfɪ'keɪʃn] *n.* Befriedung, *die*

pacifier ['pæsɪfaɪə(r)] *n.* **a)** *(person)* Friedensstifter, *der*/-stifterin, *die;* **b)** *(Amer.: baby's dummy)* Schnuller, *der*

pacifism ['pæsɪfɪzm] *n., no pl., no art.* Pazifismus, *der*

pacifist ['pæsɪfɪst] **1.** *n.* Pazifist, *der*/Pazifistin, *die.* **2.** *adj.* pazifistisch

pacify ['pæsɪfaɪ] *v. t.* **a)** besänftigen; beruhigen ⟨*weinendes Kind*⟩; **b)** *(bring peace to)* befrieden ⟨*Land, Provinz*⟩

pack [pæk] **1.** *n.* **a)** *(bundle)* Bündel, *das;* *(Mil.)* Tornister, *der;* *(rucksack)* Rucksack, *der;* **b)** *(derog.: lot)* *(people)* Bande, *die;* **a ~ of lies/nonsense** ein Sack voll Lügen/eine Menge Unsinn; **what a ~ of lies!** alles erlogen!; **c)** *(Brit.)* **~ [of cards]** [Karten]spiel, *das;* **d)** *(wolves, wild dogs)* Rudel, *das;* *(grouse)* Schwarm, *der;* *(hounds, beagles)* Meute, *die;* **e)** *(Cub Scouts, Brownies)* Gruppe, *die;* **f)** *(packet, set)* Schachtel, *die;* Packung, *die;* **~ of ten** Zehnerpackung, *die;* Zehnerpack, *der;* **disc ~** *(Computing)* [Magnet]plattenstapel, *der;* **g)** *see* **ice-pack c; h)** *(Med.)* Packung, *die;* Kompresse, *die;* *(compress)* Tampon, *der;* Kompresse, *die;* *see also* **ice-pack a; i)** *(cosmetic)* Packung, *die;* *(for face)* [Gesichts]maske, *die;* **j)** *(Rugby)* *die Stürmer einer Mannschaft, die die eine Hälfte des Gedränges bilden;* *(scrum)* Gedränge, *das;* **k)** *(Sport: runners)* Feld, *das.* **2.** *v. t.* **a)** *(put into container)* einpacken; **~ sth. into sth.** etw. in etw. *(Akk.)* packen; **b)** *(fill)* packen; **~ one's bags** seine Koffer packen; **c)** *(cram)* vollstopfen *(ugs.);* *(fill with a crowd)* füllen ⟨*Raum, Stadion usw.*⟩; **he ~ed the jury** er sorgte dafür, daß als Geschworene nur ihm genehme Leute berufen wurden; **d)** *(wrap)* verpacken **(in** in + *Dat. od. Akk.*); **~ed in** verpackt in (+ *Dat.*); **e)** *(Med.)* tamponieren; **f)** *(sl.: carry)* tragen, dabeihaben ⟨*Waffe*⟩; **g) ~ [quite] a punch** *(sl.)* ganz schön zuschlagen können *(ugs.);* ⟨*Getränk:*⟩ ganz schön reinhauen *(salopp).* **3.** *v. i.* packen; **send sb. ~ing** *(fig.)* jmdn. rausschmeißen *(ugs.)*

~ a'way *v. t.* wegpacken

~ 'in *v. t.* **a)** *(coll.: give up)* aufstecken *(ugs.);* aufhören mit ⟨*Arbeit, Spiel*⟩; **~ it in!** hör [doch] auf damit!; **b)** *(Theatre sl.)* in Scharen anziehen ⟨*Publikum*⟩; **the new play is ~ing them in** das neue Stück ist ein Zuschauer- *od.* Publikumsmagnet

~ into *v. t.* sich drängen in (+ *Akk.*); **we all ~ed into the car** wir quetschten uns alle in das Auto *(ugs.)*

~ 'off *v. t.* *(send away)* fortschicken

~ 'up 1. *v. t.* **a)** *(package)* zusammenpacken ⟨*Sachen, Werkzeug*⟩; packen ⟨*Paket*⟩; **~ up one's luggage** packen; **b)** *(coll.: stop)* aufhören *od. (ugs.)* Schluß machen mit; **~ up work** Feierabend machen; *(permanently)* aufhören zu arbeiten; **~ it up!** *(sl.)* hör [doch] auf damit! **2.** *v. i.* *(coll.)* **a)** *(give up)* aufhören; Schluß machen *(ugs.);* **b)** *(break down)* den Geist aufgeben *(ugs.);* **the car ~ed up on me** das Auto ist mir verreckt *(ugs.)*

package ['pækɪdʒ] **1.** *n.* **a)** *(bundle; fig. coll.: transaction)* Paket, *das;* **b)** *(container)* Verpackung, *die.* **2.** *v. t.* *(lit. or fig.)* verpacken; **~d into 1 lb. bags** in 1-Pfund-Tüten abgepackt

package: ~ deal *n.* Paket, *das;* **~ holiday, ~ tour** *ns.* Pauschalreise, *die*

packaging ['pækɪdʒɪŋ] *n.* **a)** *(material)* Verpackung, *die;* **b)** *(action)* Verpacken, *das*

'pack-drill *n.* *(Mil.)* Strafexerzieren in voller Marschausrüstung

packed [pækt] *adj.* **a)** gepackt ⟨*Kiste, Koffer*⟩; **~ meal/lunch** Eßpaket, *das*/Lunchpaket, *das;* **b)** *(crowded)* [über]voll ⟨*Theater, Kino, Halle*⟩; **~ to overflowing** völlig überfüllt **(with** von); **~ out** *(coll.)* gerammelt voll *(ugs.)*

packer ['pækə(r)] *n.* Packer, *der*/Packerin, *die;* *(in factory)* Abpacker, *der*/Abpackerin, *die*

packet ['pækɪt] *n.* **a)** *(package)* Päckchen, *das;* *(box)* Schachtel, *die;* **a ~ of cigarettes** eine Schachtel/ein Päckchen Zigaretten; *see also* **pay-packet; b)** *(coll.: large sum of money)* Haufen Geld *(ugs.);* **c)** *(Naut.)* **[steam] ~:** *see* **packet-steamer**

packet: ~ 'soup *n.* Instantsuppe, *die;* Tütensuppe, *die (ugs.);* **~-steamer** *n.* Postschiff, *das*

pack: ~-horse *n.* Packpferd, *das;* **~-ice** *n.* Packeis, *das*

packing ['pækɪŋ] *n.* **a)** *(packaging)* *(material)* Verpackungsmaterial, *das;* *(action)* Verpacken, *das;* **including postage and ~:** einschließlich Porto und Verpackung; **b)** *(to seal joint)* Dichtungsmaterial, *das;* **c) do one's ~:** packen

'packing-case *n.* [Pack]kiste, *die*

pact [pækt] *n.* Pakt, *der;* **make a ~ with sb.** einen Pakt mit jmdm. schließen

¹pad [pæd] **1.** *n.* **a)** *(cushioning material)* Polster, *das;* *(to protect wound)* Kompresse, *die;* *(Sport)* *(on leg)* Beinschützer, *der;* *(on shoulder)* Schulterschützer, *der;* *(on knee)* Knieschützer, *der;* **b)** *(block of paper)* Block, *der;* **a ~ of notepaper, a [writing-]~:** ein Schreibblock; **c)** *(launching surface)* Abschußrampe, *die;* **[helicopter] ~:** [Hubschrauber-]Start-und-Lande-Platz, *der;* **d)** *(coll.: house, flat)* Bude, *die (ugs.);* **e)** *(Zool.)* *(sole)* Ballen, *der;* *(paw)* Pfote, *die;* **f)** *(of brake)* Belag, *der.* **2.** *v. t.,* **-dd- a)** polstern ⟨*Jacke, Schulter, Stuhl*⟩; **b)** *(fig.: lengthen unnecessarily)* auswalzen *(ugs.)* ⟨*Brief, Aufsatz usw.*⟩ **(with** durch)

~ 'out *see* **¹pad 2**

²pad *v. t. & i.,* **-dd-** *(walk softly)* *(in socks, slippers, etc.)* tappen; *(along path etc.)* trotten

padded ['pædɪd] *adj.* gepolstert; **~ 'cell** Gummizelle, *die*

padding ['pædɪŋ] *n.* **a)** Polsterung, *die;* **be filled/covered with ~:** gepolstert sein; **b)** *(fig. superfluous matter)* Füllsel, *das*

¹paddle ['pædl] **1.** *n.* **a)** *(oar)* [Stech]paddel, *das;* **b)** *(paddling)* *(in canoe)* Fahrt im Paddelboot; *(in rowing-boat)* Ruderpartie, *die;* **go for a ~:** paddeln/rudern gehen; **c)** *(stirring implement)* Paddel, *das;* **d)** *(wheel)* Schaufelrad, *das;* *(blade)* Schaufel, *die;* **e)** *(on lock-gate)* Schütz, *das;* **f)** *(Zool.: fin)* Flosse, *die.* **2.** *v. t. & i.* *(in canoe)* paddeln; *(in rowing-boat)* gemächlich rudern; **~ one's own canoe** *(fig. coll.)* auf eigenen Beinen stehen

²paddle 1. *v. i.* *(with feet)* planschen. **2.** *n.* **have a/go for a ~:** ein bißchen planschen/planschen gehen

paddle: ~-boat, ~-steamer *ns.* [Schaufel]raddampfer, *der;* **~-wheel** *n.* Schaufelrad, *das*

paddling-pool ['pædlɪŋpu:l] *n.* Planschbecken, *das*

paddock ['pædək] *n.* **a)** Koppel, *die;* **b)** *(Horse-racing)* Sattelplatz, *der;* *(Motor-racing)* Fahrerlager, *das*

Paddy ['pædɪ] *n.* *(coll.)* Ire, *der;* Paddy, *der*

¹paddy *n.* *(Brit. coll.: bad temper)* Koller, *der (ugs.);* **be in a ~:** einen Koller haben

²paddy, 'paddy-field *ns.* Reisfeld, *das*

'padlock 1. *n.* Vorhängeschloß, *das.* **2.** *v. t.* [mit einem Vorhängeschloß] verschließen

padre ['pɑ:drɪ, 'pɑ:dreɪ] *n.* *(coll.)* Feldgeistliche, *der; as voc.* Herr Pfarrer

paean ['pi:ən] *n.* **~ [of praise]** Preislied, *das;* *(fig.)* Lobeshymne, *die*

paediatric [pi:dɪ'ætrɪk] *adj.* *(Med.)* pädiatrisch; Kinder⟨*schwester, -station*⟩

paediatrician [pi:dɪə'trɪʃn] *n.* *(Med.)* Kinderarzt, *der*/-ärztin, *die*

paediatrics [pi:dɪ'ætrɪks] *n., no pl.* *(Med.)* Pädiatrie, *die (fachspr.);* Kinderheilkunde, *die*

paella [pɑ:'elə] *n.* *(Gastr.)* Paella, *die*

pagan ['peɪgən] **1.** *n.* **a)** *(heathen)* Heide, *der*/Heidin, *die;* **b)** *(fig.: irreligious person)* Ungläubige, *der/die;* gottloser Mensch. **2.** *adj.* **a)** *(heathen)* heidnisch; ungläubig ⟨*Person*⟩; **b)** *(fig.: irreligious)* gottlos

paganism ['peɪgənɪzm] *n.* Heidentum, *das;* Paganismus, *der*

¹page [peɪdʒ] **1.** *n.* Page, *der.* **2.** *v. t. & i.* **~ [for] sb.** *(over loudspeaker)* jmdn. ausrufen; *(by paging-device)* jmdn. anpiepen *(ugs.);* **paging Mr Miller** Herr Miller, bitte!

²page 1. *n.* **a)** Seite, *die;* *(leaf, sheet of paper)* Blatt, *das;* **front/sports/fashion ~:** erste Seite/Sport-/Modeseite, *die;* **~ three girl** Pin-up-Girl, *das;* **write on one side of the ~ only** beschreiben Sie das Blatt nur auf einer Seite; **turn to the next ~:** umblättern; *attrib.* **three-/double-~:** drei-/doppelseitig ⟨*Artikel, Brief*⟩; **b)** *(fig.: episode)* Kapitel, *das;* **go down in the ~s of history** in die Annalen der Geschichte eingehen. **2.** *v. t. see* **paginate**

pageant ['pædʒənt] *n.* **a)** *(spectacle)* Schauspiel, *das;* **b)** *(procession)* [Fest]umzug, *der;* *(play)* **historical ~:** Historienspiel, *das*

pageantry ['pædʒəntrɪ] *n.* Prachtentfaltung, *die;* Prunk, *der;* **empty ~:** eitler Pomp

'page-boy *n.* **a)** *see* **¹page 1; b)** *(hair-style)* Pagenkopf, der

'page proof *n.* *(Printing)* Umbruch, *der*

pager ['peɪdʒə(r)] *n.* Piepser, *der (ugs.)*

paginate ['pædʒɪneɪt] *v. t.* paginieren

pagination [pædʒɪ'neɪʃn] *n.* Paginierung, *die*

'paging-device *see* **pager**

pagoda [pə'gəʊdə] *n.* Pagode, *die*

pah [pɑ:] *int. expr. disgust* bah; *expr. contempt* pa

paid [peɪd] **1.** *see* **pay 2, 3. 2.** *adj.* bezahlt ⟨*Urlaub, Arbeit*⟩; **put ~ to** *(Brit. fig. coll.)* *(terminate)* zunichte machen ⟨*Hoffnung, Plan, Aussichten*⟩; *(deal with)* kurzen Prozeß machen mit *(ugs.)* ⟨*Person*⟩

'paid-up *adj.* bezahlt; **[fully] ~ member** Mitglied, das alle Beträge bezahlt hat; *(fig.)* überzeugtes Mitglied

pail [peɪl] *n.* Eimer, *der*

pailful ['peɪlfʊl] *n.* Eimer, *der;* **a ~ of water** ein Eimer [voll] Wasser

pain [peɪn] **1.** *n.* **a)** *no indef. art.* *(suffering)* Schmerzen; *(mental ~)* Qualen; **feel [some] ~, be in ~:** Schmerzen haben; **cause sb. ~** *(lit. or fig.)* jmdm. wehtun; **b)** *(instance of suffering)* Schmerz, *der;* **I have a ~ in my shoulder/knee/stomach** meine Schulter/mein Knie/Magen tut weh; ich habe Schmerzen in der Schulter/im Knie/habe Magenschmerzen; *(fig.)* **be a ~ in the arse** *(coarse)* einem auf die Eier gehen *(derb);* **be a ~ in the neck** *see* **neck 1 a; c)** *(coll.: nuisance)* Plage, *die;* *(sb./sth. getting on one's nerves)* Nervensäge, *die (ugs.);* **this job/he is a real ~:** diese Arbeit/er kann einem wirklich auf die Nerven *od. (ugs.)* den Wecker gehen; **d)** *in pl.* *(trouble taken)* Mühe, *die;* Anstrengung, *die;* **spare no ~s** keine Mühe *od.* Anstrengung scheuen; **take ~s** sich

(Dat.) Mühe geben (**over** mit, bei); **be at ~s to do sth.** sich sehr bemühen *od.* sich *(Dat.)* große Mühe geben, etw. zu tun; **he got nothing for all his ~s** seine ganze Mühe war umsonst; **e)** *(Law)* **on** *or* **under ~ of death/imprisonment** bei Todesstrafe/unter Androhung *(Dat.)* einer Gefängnisstrafe. **2.** *v. t.* schmerzen

pained [peɪnd] *adj.* gequält

painful ['peɪnfl] *adj.* **a)** *(causing pain)* schmerzhaft ⟨*Krankheit, Operation, Wunde*⟩; **be/become ~** ⟨*Körperteil:*⟩ weh tun *od.* schmerzen/anfangen, weh zu tun; **the glare was ~ to the eyes** das grelle Licht tat in den Augen weh; **suffer from a ~ shoulder** Schmerzen in der Schulter haben; **b)** *(distressing)* schmerzlich ⟨*Gedanke, Erinnerung*⟩; traurig ⟨*Pflicht*⟩; **it was ~ to watch him** es tat weh, ihm zuzusehen; **c)** *(troublesome)* schwierig ⟨*Problem*⟩; *(laborious)* beschwerlich ⟨*Aufstieg*⟩; **make only ~ progress** nur mühsam weiterkommen

painfully ['peɪnfəlɪ] *adv.* **a)** *(with great pain)* unter großen Schmerzen; **my shoes are ~ tight** meine Schuhe drücken fürchterlich *(ugs.)*; **b)** *(fig.)* *(excessively)* über die Maßen *(geh.)*; *(laboriously)* quälend ⟨*langsam*⟩; **~ obvious** nur zu offensichtlich

'**pain-killer** *n.* schmerzstillendes Mittel; Schmerzmittel, *das (ugs.)*

painless ['peɪnlɪs] *adj.* **a)** *(not causing pain)* schmerzlos; **b)** *(fig.: free of trouble, not causing problems)* unproblematisch

painlessly ['peɪnlɪslɪ] *adv.* **a)** schmerzlos ⟨*behandeln*⟩; **b)** *(fig.)* mühelos ⟨*Problem lösen*⟩; problemlos ⟨*verlaufen*⟩

painstaking ['peɪnzteɪkɪŋ] *adj.* gewissenhaft; **it is ~ work** es ist eine mühsame Arbeit; **with ~ care** mit äußerster Sorgfalt

paint [peɪnt] **1.** *n.* **a)** Farbe, *die; (on car)* Lack, *der;* **'wet ~'** „Frisch gestrichen!"; **as clever** *or* **smart as ~:** äußerst intelligent; *see also* **fresh 1 a; luminous a; wet 1 c; b)** *(joc.: cosmetic)* Schminke, *die;* **put one's ~ on** sich anmalen *(ugs.)*. **2.** *v. t.* **a)** *(cover, colour)* [an]streichen; **~ one's body** seinen Körper bemalen; **~ the town red** *(fig. sl.)* auf die Pauke hauen *(ugs.)*; **~ oneself into a corner** *(fig. coll.)* sich selbst in die Bredouille bringen *(ugs.)*; *see also* **black 1 f; b)** *(make picture of, make by ~ing)* malen; *abs.* **~ for a living** Maler/Malerin sein; **the picture was ~ed by R.** das Bild ist von R.; **c)** *(adorn with ~ing)* bemalen ⟨*Wand, Vase, Decke*⟩; **d)** *(fig.: describe)* zeichnen ⟨*Bild*⟩; **~ sth. in glowing/gloomy colours, ~ a glowing/gloomy picture of sth.** etw. in leuchtenden/düsteren Farben malen *od.* schildern; **e)** *(apply cosmetic to)* schminken ⟨*Augen, Gesicht, Lippen*⟩; lackieren ⟨*Nägel*⟩; **f)** *(Med.)* pinseln ⟨*Hals*⟩; bepinseln ⟨*Verletzung*⟩

~ 'in *v. t.* hineinmalen

~ 'on *v. t.* aufmalen

~ 'out *v. t.* übermalen; **~ sb. out of a picture** jmdn. auf einem Bild übermalen

paint: ~box *n.* Malkasten, *der;* Farb[en]kasten, *der;* **~brush** *n.* Pinsel, *der*

painted ['peɪntɪd]: **~ 'lady** *n. (Zool.)* Distelfalter, *der;* **~ 'woman** *n.* Dirne, *die*

[1]**painter** ['peɪntə(r)] *n.* **a)** *(artist)* Maler, *der*/Malerin, *die;* **b)** **[house-]~:** Maler, *der*/Malerin, *die;* Anstreicher, *der*/Anstreicherin, *die*

[2]**painter** *n. (Naut.: rope)* Fangleine, *die*

painting ['peɪntɪŋ] *n.* **a)** *no pl., no indef. art. (art)* Malerei, *die;* **b)** *(picture)* Gemälde, *das;* Bild, *das*

'**painting-book** *n.* Malbuch, *das*

'**paint-stripper** *n.* Abbeizer, *der*

'**paintwork** *n.* **a)** *(action)* Streichen, *das;* **b)** *(painted surface)* Anstrich, *der; (of car)* Lack, *der;* **the ~ in the house** die Innenanstriche des Hauses

pair [peə(r)] **1.** *n.* **a)** *(set of two)* Paar, *das;* **a ~ of gloves/socks/shoes** *etc.* ein Paar Handschuhe/Socken/Schuhe *usw.;* **a** *or* **one ~ of hands/eyes** zwei Hände/Augen; **in ~s** paarweise; **the ~ of them** die beiden; **fine ~ [of rascals]** *(iron.)* feines [Gauner]pärchen *od.* [Gauner]gespann; **b)** *(single article)* **a ~ of pyjamas/scissors** *etc.* ein Schlafanzug/eine Schere *usw.;* **a ~ of trousers/jeans** eine Hose/Jeans; ein Paar Hosen/Jeans; **c)** *(married couple)* [Ehe]paar, *das; (mated animals)* Paar, *das;* Pärchen, *das;* **d)** *(Cards)* Pärchen, *das;* **a ~ of tens** zwei Zehnen; **e)** **~ [of horses]** Zweiergespann [Pferde], *das;* **carriage** *or* **coach and ~:** Zweispänner, *der;* **f)** *(Parl.) zwei Abgeordnete gegnerischer Parteien, die vereinbaren, sich bei einer Abstimmung zu enthalten;* **g)** *(Rowing) (crew)* Zweiermannschaft, *die;* **~s** *(race)* Zweierrennen, *das.* **2.** *v. t.* **a)** *(arrange in couples)* paaren; [paarweise] zusammenstellen; **b)** *(marry)* verheiraten (**with** an + *Akk.,* mit). **3.** *v. i.* ⟨*Tiere:*⟩ sich paaren

~ 'off 1. *v. t.* zu Paaren *od.* paarweise zusammenstellen; **she was ~ed off with Alan** sie bekam Alan als Partner. **2.** *v. i.* Zweiergruppen bilden

~ 'up *see* **~ off 2**

~ with *v. t. (Parl.)* **~ with sb.** ⟨*Abgeordneter:*⟩ *mit jmdm. von der gegnerischen Fraktion vereinbaren, sich bei einer Abstimmung zu enthalten*

pairing ['peərɪŋ] *n. (Parl.)* **~ [arrangement]** *Absprache zwischen Abgeordneten gegnerischer Parteien, sich bei einer Abstimmung zu enthalten*

Paisley ['peɪzlɪ] *adj. (Textiles)* Paisley⟨*schal, -kleid, -samt usw.*⟩; **~ pattern** Paisleymuster, *das*

pajamas [pə'dʒɑːməz] *(Amer.) see* **pyjamas**

Pak [pæk], **Paki** ['pækɪ] *n. (Brit. sl. derog.: Pakistani)* Pakistaner, *der*/Pakistanerin, *die;* **Paki-bashing** Zusammenschlagen von Pakistanern

Pakistan [pɑːkɪ'stɑːn] *pr. n.* Pakistan *(das)*

Pakistani [pɑːkɪ'stɑːnɪ] **1.** *adj.* pakistanisch; **sb. is ~:** jmd. ist Pakistani. **2.** *n.* Pakistani, *der/die;* Pakistaner, *der*/Pakistanerin, *die*

pal [pæl] *(coll.)* **1.** *n.* Kumpel, *der (ugs.); (derog.)* Kumpan, *der (ugs. abwertend);* **be a ~ and ...:** sei so nett und ...; *see also* **old 1 c. 2.** *v. i.,* **-ll-: ~ up with sb.** sich mit jmdm. anfreunden

palace ['pælɪs] *n.* Palast, *der; (of bishop or aristocrat also)* Palais, *das; (stately mansion)* Schloß, *das; attrib.* Schloß⟨*garten, -park*⟩; Palast⟨*wache, -truppe usw.*⟩

palace revo'lution *n. (lit. or fig.)* Palastrevolution, *die*

paladin ['pælədɪn] *n.* **a)** *(Hist.: knight errant)* fahrender Ritter; **b)** *(knightly hero)* Recke, *der*

Palaeocene ['pælɪəsiːn, 'peɪlɪəsiːn] *(Geol.)* **1.** *adj.* paläozän. **2.** *n.* Paläozän, *das*

palaeography [pælɪ'ɒgrəfɪ, peɪlɪ'ɒgrəfɪ] *n.* Paläographie, *die*

palaeolithic [pælɪə'lɪθɪk, peɪlɪə'lɪθɪk] *adj. (Archaeol.)* paläolithisch *(fachspr.)*; altsteinzeitlich; **~ man** Paläolithiker, *der*

palaeontology [pælɪɒn'tɒlədʒɪ, peɪlɪɒn'tɒlədʒɪ] *n.* Paläontologie, *die*

Palaeozoic [pælɪə'zəʊɪk, peɪlɪə'zəʊɪk] *(Geol.)* **1.** *adj.* paläozoisch. **2.** *n.* Paläozoikum, *das*

palatable ['pælətəbl] *adj.* **a)** *(acceptable in taste)* genießbar; trinkbar ⟨*Wein*⟩; *(pleasant)* wohlschmeckend ⟨*Speise*⟩; **b)** *(fig.)* annehmbar, akzeptabel ⟨*Gesetz, Erhöhung, Aufführung*⟩; **make sth. ~ to sb.** jmdm. etw. schmackhaft machen *(ugs.)*; **not be ~ to sb.** jmdm. nicht schmecken *(ugs.)*

palatal ['pælətəl] **1.** *adj.* **a)** *(Anat.)* Gaumen-; **b)** *(Phonet.)* palatal. **2.** *n. (Phonet.)* Palatal, *der*

palate ['pælət] *n.* **a)** *(Anat.)* Gaumen, *der;* **hard/soft ~:** harter/weicher Gaumen; *see also* [2]**cleft 2; b)** *(taste)* Gaumen, *der (geh.)*; **be sharp on the ~:** ⟨*Wein:*⟩ sauer schmecken; **not be to sb.'s ~** *(fig.)* nicht [nach] jmds. Geschmack sein

palatial [pə'leɪʃl] *adj.* palastartig; **built in ~ style** wie ein Palast gebaut

Palatinate [pə'lætɪnət] *pr.n.* **the ~** *(in Germany)* die Pfalz

Palatine ['pælətaɪn] *adj.* palatinisch

palaver [pə'lɑːvə(r)] *n.* **a)** *(coll.: fuss)* Umstand, *der;* Theater, *das (ugs.)*; **b)** *(conference; derog.: idle talk)* Palaver, *das*

[1]**pale** [peɪl] *n.* **a) be beyond the ~** ⟨*Verhalten, Benehmen:*⟩ unmöglich sein; **regard sb. as beyond the ~:** jmdn. indiskutabel finden; **b)** *(stake)* Pfahl, *der; (slat)* [Zaun]latte, *die*

[2]**pale** [peɪl] **1.** *adj.* **a)** blaß, *(esp. in illness)* fahl, *(nearly white)* bleich ⟨*Gesichtsfarbe, Haut, Gesicht, Aussehen*⟩; **go ~:** blaß/bleich werden; **his face was ~:** er war blaß/bleich; **b)** *(light in colour)* von blasser Farbe *nachgestellt;* blaß ⟨*Farbe*⟩; hell ⟨*Sherry*⟩; **a ~ blue/red dress** ein blaßblaues/-rotes Kleid; **~ ale** Pale Ale, *das;* **c)** *(faint)* fahl ⟨*Licht*⟩; **d)** *(fig.: poor)* **~ imitation/reflection** schlechte Nachahmung/schwacher Abglanz. **2.** *v. i.* bleich *od.* blaß werden (**at** bei); **his face ~d** er wurde bleich *od.* blaß; **~ into insignificance** völlig bedeutungslos werden; **~ in comparison with sth.** neben etw. *(Dat.)* verblassen

'**pale-face** *n.* Bleichgesicht, *das*

'**pale-faced** *adj.* blaß

palely ['peɪllɪ] *adv.* fahl, bleich ⟨*scheinen*⟩; matt, schwach ⟨*erleuchten*⟩

paleness ['peɪlnɪs] *n., no pl. (of person)* Blässe, *die*

paleo- *(Amer.) see* **palaeo-**

Palestine ['pælɪstaɪn] *pr. n.* Palästina *(das)*

Palestinian [pælɪ'stɪnɪən] **1.** *adj.* palästinensisch; **sb. is ~:** jmd. ist Palästinenser/Palästinenserin. **2.** *n.* Palästinenser, *der*/Palästinenserin, *die*

palette ['pælɪt] *n.* Palette, *die*

'**palette-knife** *n. (Art)* Palettenmesser, *das*

palfrey ['pɔːlfrɪ] *n. (Hist.)* Zelter, *der*

palimpsest ['pælɪmpsest] *n.* Palimpsest, *der od. das*

palindrome ['pælɪndrəʊm] *n.* Palindrom, *das*

paling ['peɪlɪŋ] *n.* **a)** *(stake)* [Zaun]pfahl, *der; (slat)* [Zaun]latte, *die;* **b)** *(fence)* Lattenzaun, *der*

palisade [pælɪ'seɪd] *n.* **a)** *(fence)* Palisade, *die;* Palisadenzaun, *der;* **b)** *in pl. (Amer.: cliffs) steile, bes. säulenähnliche Formationen aufweisende Felswand*

palish ['peɪlɪʃ] *adj.* bläßlich

[1]**pall** [pɔːl] *n.* **a)** *(over coffin)* Sargtuch, *das;* **b)** *(fig.)* Schleier, *der;* **cast a ~ of gloom over sb.** jmdn. in gedrückte Stimmung versetzen

[2]**pall** *v. i.* **~ [on sb.]** [jmdm.] langweilig werden

Palladian [pə'leɪdɪən] *adj. (Archit.)* palladianisch

'**pall-bearer** *n.* Sargträger, *der*/-trägerin, *die*

[1]**pallet** ['pælɪt] *n.* **a)** *(bed)* Pritsche, *die;* **b)** *(mattress)* Strohsack, *der*

[2]**pallet** *n. (platform)* Palette, *die*

palliasse ['pælɪæs, pælɪ'æs] *n.* Strohsack, *der*

palliate ['pælɪeɪt] *v. t.* **a)** *(alleviate)* lindern, erträglicher machen ⟨*Krankheit*⟩; **b)** *(excuse)* entschuldigen; *(gloss over)* beschönigen

palliative ['pælɪətɪv] *(Med.)* **1.** *adj.* palliativ *(fachspr.)*; lindernd; **~ drug** Palliativ[um], *das (fachspr.)*; Linderungsmittel, *das.* **2.** *n.* Palliativ[um], *das (fachspr.)*; Linderungsmittel, *das*

pallid ['pælɪd] *adj.* **a)** *see* [2]**pale 1 a; b)** matt, blaß ⟨*Farbe*⟩

pallor ['pælə(r)] *n.* Blässe, *die;* Fahlheit, *die*

pally ['pælɪ] *adj. (coll.)* **they are very ~ [with**

each other] sie sind dicke Freunde *(ugs.)*; **be ~ or on ~ terms with sb.** mit jmdm. dick befreundet sein *(ugs.)*; **his ~ manner** seine kumpelhafte Art

¹palm [pɑ:m] *n.* **a)** *(tree)* Palme, *die; attrib.* **~ leaf/oil/kernel/frond** Palmblatt, *das*/-öl, *das*/-kern, *der*/-wedel, *der*; **~ [branch]** *(also Eccl.)* Palmzweig, *der*; **b)** *(symbol of victory)* Siegespalme *die; (Bibl.)* Palme, *die;* **bear or take the ~** *(fig.)* die Siegespalme davontragen *(geh.)*

²palm 1. *n.* **a)** *(of hand)* Handteller, *der;* Handfläche, *die;* **hold/weigh sth. in one's ~ or the ~ of one's hand** etw. in der Hand halten/wiegen; **have sth. in the ~ of one's hand** *(fig.)* etw. in der Hand haben; **on the ~s of one's hands** auf den Handtellern *od.* -flächen; **the ~ of one's right hand** der rechte Handteller; die rechte Handfläche; *see also* **cross 2 a; grease 2; b)** *(of glove)* Innenfläche, *die.* **2.** *v. t.* in der [hohlen] Hand verschwinden lassen

~ 'off *v. t.* **~ sth. off on sb., ~ sb. off with sth.** jmdm. etw. andrehen *(ugs.)*; **~ sb. off on sb. else** jmdn. zu jmd. anderem abschieben *(ugs.)*; **~ sth. off as sth.** etw. als etw. verkaufen; **~ sb. off with promises** jmdn. mit Versprechungen abspeisen *(ugs.)*

palm-'court *adj.* **~ music/orchestra** ≈ Kaffeehausmusik, *die*/-orchester, *das*

palmist ['pɑ:mɪst] *n.* Handleser, *der*/-leserin, *die;* Handliniendeuter, *der*/-deuterin, *die*

palmistry ['pɑ:mɪstrɪ] *n., no pl.* Handlesekunst, *die;* Handliniendeutung, *die*

palm: P~ 'Sunday *n. (Eccl.)* Palmsonntag, *der;* **~-tree** *n.* Palme, *die*

palomino [pælə'mi:nəʊ] *n., pl.* **~s** *(Zool.)* Isabelle, *die*

palpable ['pælpəbl] *adj.* **a)** *(tangible)* fühlbar; tastbar; **b)** *(perceptible)* spürbar ⟨*Unterschied*⟩; eindeutig ⟨*Zeichen*⟩; *(obvious)* offenkundig ⟨*Lüge, Unwissenheit, Absurdität*⟩

palpably ['pælpəblɪ] *adv.* offenkundig

palpitate ['pælpɪteɪt] *v. i.* **a)** *(pulsate)* ⟨*Herz:*⟩ palpitieren *(fachspr.),* pochen, hämmern; **b)** *(throb)* beben; zucken; *(tremble)* zittern (**with** vor + *Dat.*)

palpitation [pælpɪ'teɪʃn] *n.* **a)** *(throbbing)* Beben, *das;* Zucken, *das; (trembling)* Zittern, *das;* **b)** *in pl. (Med.: of heart)* Palpitation, *die (fachspr.)*; Herzklopfen, *das;* **suffer from ~s** Herzklopfen haben

palsy ['pɔ:lzɪ, 'pɒlzɪ] *n. (Med. dated)* Lähmung, *die;* Paralyse, *die (fachspr.)*; *see also* **cerebral palsy**

paltry ['pɔ:ltrɪ, 'pɒltrɪ] *adj.* schäbig; armselig ⟨*Auswahl*⟩; *(trivial)* belanglos; **~ matters** Belanglosigkeiten; **a ~ £5** schäbige 5 Pfund

pampas ['pæmpəz, 'pæmpəs] *n. pl. (Geog.)* Pampas *Pl.*

'pampas-grass *n.* Pampasgras, *das*

pamper ['pæmpə(r)] *v. t.* verhätscheln; **~ oneself** sich verwöhnen

pamphlet ['pæmflɪt] *n. (leaflet)* Prospekt, *der; (esp. Polit.)* Flugblatt, *das; (booklet)* Broschüre, *die; (Polit., Relig.: tract)* Streitschrift, *die*

pamphleteer [pæmflɪ'tɪə(r)] *n.* Verfasser/Verfasserin des Flugblatts/der Streitschrift/der Flugblätter/der Streitschriften

¹pan [pæn] **1.** *n.* **a)** [Koch]topf, *der; (for frying)* Pfanne, *die;* **pots and ~s** Kochtöpfe; **a ~ of milk** ein Topf Milch; *see also* **saucepan; b)** *(of scales)* Schale, *die;* **c)** *(Brit.: of WC)* **[lavatory] ~:** Toilettenschüssel, *die;* **d)** *(Amer. sl.: face)* Visage, *die (ugs. abwertend). See also* **flash 1 a. 2.** *v. t.,* **-nn-** *(coll.)* verreißen ⟨*Theaterstück, Buch, Film usw.*⟩; harte Kritik üben an (+ *Dat.*) ⟨*Person*⟩

~ 'out *v. i. (progress)* sich entwickeln

²pan 1. *v. t.,* **-nn-** *(Cinemat., Telev.)* schwenken; *(Photog.)* mitziehen. **2.** *v. i.,* **-nn-** *(Cinemat., Telev.)* schwenken (**to** auf + *Akk.*); *(Photog.)* [die Kamera] mitziehen; **~ning shot** [Kamera]schwenk, *der.* **3.** *n. (Cinemat., Telev.)* Schwenk, *der*

pan- [pæn] *in comb.* pan⟨*amerikanisch, -slawistisch, -islamisch, -germanisch usw.*⟩; Pan⟨*afrikanismus, -slawist usw.*⟩

panacea [pænə'si:ə] *n.* Allheilmittel, *das*

panache [pə'næʃ] *n.* Schwung, *der;* Elan, *der*

Panama [pænə'mɑ:] **1.** *pr. n.* Panama *(das).* **2.** *n.* **p~ [hat]** Panamahut, *der*

Panama Ca'nal *pr. n.* Panamakanal, *der*

Panamanian [pænə'meɪnɪən] **1.** *adj.* panamaisch; **sb. is ~:** jmd. ist Panamaer/Panamaerin. **2.** *n.* Panamaer, *der*/Panamaerin, *die*

panatella [pænə'telə] *n.* Panatela, *die*

pancake ['pænkeɪk] *n.* Pfannkuchen, *der;* **be flat as a ~:** platt wie ein Pfannkuchen sein; ⟨*Gelände:*⟩ topfeben sein; *(squashed)* platt wie eine Briefmarke sein; ⟨*Reifen:*⟩ völlig platt sein

pancake: P~ Day *n. (Brit.)* Fasnachtsdienstag, *der;* **~ 'landing** *n. (Aeronaut.)* Bauchlandung, *die;* **~ roll** *n.* gerollter Pfannkuchen mit Füllung

panchromatic [pænkrə'mætɪk] *adj. (Photog.)* panchromatisch

pancreas ['pæŋkrɪəs] *n. (Anat.)* Bauchspeicheldrüse, *die;* Pankreas, *das (fachspr.)*

pancreatic [pæŋkrɪ'ætɪk] *adj. (Anat., Physiol.)* Pankreas-; **~ duct** Ausführungsgang des Pankreas

panda ['pændə] *n. (Zool.)* **a)** *see* **giant panda; b) red ~:** Kleiner Panda; Kleiner Bambusbär

'panda car *n. (Brit. Police)* Streifenwagen, *der*

pandemonium [pændɪ'məʊnɪəm] *n.* Chaos, *das; (uproar)* Tumult, *der;* **there was ~ in the stadium** das Stadion war ein Hexenkessel; **~ reigned** es herrschte ein einziges Chaos

pander ['pændə(r)] **1.** *n. (go-between)* Kuppler, *der*/Kupplerin, *die; (procurer)* Zuhälter, *der.* **2.** *v. i.* **~ to** allzu sehr entgegenkommen (+ *Dat.*) ⟨*Person, Geschmack, Instinkt*⟩; frönen (+ *Dat.*) ⟨*Laster*⟩

Pandora's box [pændɔ:rəz 'bɒks] *n. (Mythol.; also fig.)* Büchse der Pandora

p. & p. *abbr. (Brit.)* **postage and packing** Porto und Verpackung

pane [peɪn] *n. (glass)* Scheibe, *die;* **window-~/~ of glass** Fenster-/Glasscheibe, *die*

panegyric [pænɪ'dʒɪrɪk] **1.** *n.* Lobrede, *die* (**on** auf + *Akk.*). **2.** *adj.* panegyrisch *(geh.)*

panel ['pænl] **1.** *n.* **a)** *(of door, wall, etc.)* Paneel, *das; (of fence)* Bretterzaunelement, *das; (of screen, triptych)* Flügel, *der;* **b)** *(esp. Telev., Radio, etc.) (quiz team)* Rateteam, *das; (in public discussion)* Podium, *das;* **~ discussion** Podiumsdiskussion, *die;* **c)** *(advisory body)* Gremium, *das;* Kommission, *die;* **~ of experts** Expertengremium, *das;* **d)** *(Dressmaking)* Einsatz, *der. See also* **control panel; instrument panel. 2.** *v. t., (Brit.)* **-ll-** paneelieren ⟨*Tür, Zimmer, Wand*⟩; täfeln ⟨*Zimmer, Wand*⟩

panel: ~-beater *n.* Autospengler, *der*/-spenglerin, *die;* **~ game** *n.* Ratespiel, *das;* Quiz, *das; (Telev., Radio)* Rate-, Quizsendung, *die*

paneling, panelist *(Amer.) see* **panell-**

panelling ['pænəlɪŋ] *n.* Täfelung, *die*

panellist ['pænəlɪst] *n. (Telev., Radio) (on quiz programme)* Mitglied des Rateteams; *(on discussion panel)* Diskussionsteilnehmer, *der*/-teilnehmerin, *die*

panel: ~-pin *n.* Tapeziernagel, *der;* **~ truck** *n.* Lieferwagen, *der*

panful ['pænfʊl] *n.* Topf, *der;* **a ~ of water** ein Topf [voll] Wasser

pang [pæŋ] *n.* **a)** *(of pain)* Stich, *der; see also* **hunger 1; b)** *(of distress)* **feel ~s of conscience/guilt** Gewissensbisse haben; **feel ~s of remorse** bittere Reue empfinden

'panhandle 1. *n.* **a)** Topfstiel, *der; (of frying-pan)* Pfannenstiel, *der;* **b)** *(of land)* schmaler Landstreifen; *(in US)* Panhandle, *der.* **2.** *v. t. (sl.)* anschnorren *(ugs.)* (**for** um). **3.** *v. i. (sl.)* schnorren *(ugs.)*

panic ['pænɪk] **1.** *n.* Panik, *die;* **be in a [state of] ~ [over or at having done sth.]** von Panik erfaßt *od.* ergriffen sein[, weil man etw. getan hat]; **there was ~ on the stock-market** es kam zu einer Börsenpanik. **2.** *v. i.,* **-ck-** in Panik *(Akk.)* geraten; **don't ~!** nur keine Panik! **3.** *v. t.,* **-ck-** in Panik versetzen; **~ sb. into doing sth.** jmdn. so in Panik versetzen, daß er etw. tut. **4.** *attrib. adj. (overhasty)* übereilt, überstürzt ⟨*Maßnahmen*⟩; wild, atemlos ⟨*Hast*⟩; **~ buying** Hamsterkäufe; **~ selling** Panikverkäufe

panic: ~ bolt *n.* Panikverschluß, *der;* **~ button** *n.* Alarmknopf, *der;* **hit the ~ button** *(fig. coll.)* Alarm schlagen; *(panic)* durchdrehen *(ugs.)*; die Panik kriegen *(ugs.)*

panicky ['pænɪkɪ] *adj.* von Panik bestimmt ⟨*Verhalten, Handeln, Rede*⟩; **be ~:** in Panik sein

panicle ['pænɪkl] *n. (Bot.)* Rispe, *die*

panic: ~-monger *n.* Panikmacher, *der*/-macherin, *die;* **~ stations** *n. pl. (fig. coll.)* **be at ~ stations** am Rotieren sein *(ugs.)* (**about** wegen); **it was ~ stations** alles war am Rotieren *(ugs.)*; **~-stricken, ~-struck** *adjs.* von Panik erfaßt *od.* ergriffen

pannier ['pænɪə(r)] *n.* **a)** *(basket)* Lastkorb, *der;* **b)** *(bag)* Packtasche, *die*

panoply ['pænəplɪ] *n.* Palette, *die (fig.)*; **the full ~ of a state burial** ein Staatsbegräbnis mit allem, was dazu gehört; **a wonderful ~ of colours** eine herrliche Farbenpracht

panorama [pænə'rɑ:mə] *n.* Panorama, *das; (fig.: survey)* Überblick, *der* (**of** über + *Akk.*); **aerial ~:** Luftaufnahme, *die*

panoramic [pænə'ræmɪk] *adj.* Panorama-; **~ survey** *(fig.)* umfassender Überblick (**of** über + *Akk.*)

'pan-pipes *n. pl. (Mus.)* Panflöte, *die*

pansy ['pænzɪ] *n.* **a)** *(Bot.)* Stiefmütterchen, *das;* **b)** *(coll.: effeminate man)* Schwuchtel, *die (ugs.)*; Tunte, *die (ugs.)*

pant [pænt] **1.** *v. i.* keuchen; ⟨*Hund:*⟩ hecheln. **2.** *v. t.* **~ [out]** keuchend hervorstoßen ⟨*Nachricht, Worte*⟩

~ for *v. t.* ringen nach ⟨*Luft, Atem*⟩; schnappen nach ⟨*Luft*⟩; lechzen nach ⟨*Getränk*⟩

pantechnicon [pæn'teknɪkən] *n.* **~ [van]** *(Brit.)* Möbelwagen, *der*

pantheism ['pænθɪɪzm] *n., no art. (Relig.)* Pantheismus, *der*

pantheist ['pænθɪɪst] *n. (Relig.)* Pantheist, *der*/Pantheistin, *die*

pantheistic [pænθɪ'ɪstɪk], **pantheistical** [pænθɪ'ɪstɪkl] *adj. (Relig.)* pantheistisch

pantheon ['pænθɪən, pæn'θi:ən] *n.* Pantheon, *das*

panther ['pænθə(r)] *n. (Zool.)* **a)** Panther, *der;* **b)** *(Amer.: puma)* Puma, *der;* Berglöwe, *der*

pantie-girdle ['pæntɪgɜ:dl] *n. (coll.)* Miederhose, *die*

panties ['pæntɪz] *n. pl. (coll.)* **[pair of] ~:** Schlüpfer, *der*

pantihose ['pæntɪhəʊz] *see* **tights 3 a**

pantile ['pæntaɪl] *n. (Building)* Hohlpfanne, *die*

panto ['pæntəʊ] *n., pl.* **~s** *(Brit. coll.) see* **pantomime a**

pantograph ['pæntəgrɑ:f] *n.* **a)** *(for copying)* Pantograph, *der;* Storchschnabel, *der;* **b)** *(Electr.)* Scherenstromabnehmer, *der*

pantomime ['pæntəmaɪm] *n.* **a)** *(Brit.) Märchenspiel im Varietéstil, das um Weihnachten aufgeführt wird;* **b)** *(gestures)* Pantomime, *die*

pantry ['pæntrɪ] *n.* Speisekammer, *die;* **[butler's] ~:** Anrichtezimmer, *das*

pants [pænts] *n. pl.* **a)** *(esp. Amer. coll.: trousers)* **[pair of]** ~: Hose, *die;* **bore/scare the ~ off sb.** *(fig. coll.)* jmdn. zu Tode langweilen/erschrecken; **talk the ~ off sb.** *(fig. sl.)* jmdn. vollabern *od.* vollquatschen *(ugs.);* **catch sb. with his ~ down** *(fig. sl.)* jmdn. unvorbereitet treffen; *see also* **kick 1a; b)** *(Brit. coll.: underpants)* Unterhose, *die*
'pant suit *n.* Hosenanzug, *der*
panzer ['pæntsə(r)] *adj. (Mil.)* Panzer-
pap [pæp] *n. (food)* Brei, *der; (fig. derog.)* Schmarren, *der (ugs. abwertend)*
papa [pə'pɑ:] *n. (arch. child lang.)* Papa, *der (fam.)*
papacy ['peɪpəsɪ] *n.* **a)** *no pl. (office)* Papat, *der;* **be elected to the ~:** zum Papst gewählt werden; **b)** *(tenure)* Amtszeit als Papst; **c)** *no pl. (papal system)* Papsttum, *das*
papal ['peɪpl] *adj.* päpstlich; *see also* **infallibility**
paparazzo [pæpæ'rɑ:tsəʊ] *n., pl.* **paparazzi** [pæpæ'rɑ:tsi:] Paparazzo, *der*
papaw [pə'pɔ:], **papaya** [pə'paɪə] *n. (Bot.)* **a)** *(tree)* ~ **[tree]** Papaya- *od.* Melonenbaum, *der;* **b)** *(fruit)* Papaya[frucht], *die*
paper ['peɪpə(r)] **1.** *n.* **a)** *(material)* Papier, *das;* **put sth. down on ~:** etw. schriftlich festhalten *od.* niederlegen; **it looks all right on ~** *(in theory)* auf dem Papier sieht es ganz gut aus; **put pen to ~:** zur Feder greifen; **the treaty** *etc.* **isn't worth the ~ it's written on** *(coll.)* der Vertrag *usw.* ist nicht das Papier wert, auf dem er geschrieben steht; **b)** *in pl. (documents)* Dokumente; Unterlagen *Pl.; (to prove identity etc.)* Papiere *Pl.;* **c)** *(in examination) (Univ.)* Klausur, *die; (Sch.)* Arbeit, *die;* **d)** *(newspaper)* Zeitung, *die;* **daily/weekly ~:** Tages-/Wochenzeitung, *die;* **e)** *(wallpaper)* Tapete, *die;* **f)** *(wrapper)* Stück Papier; **don't scatter the ~s all over the floor** wirf das Papier nicht überall auf den Boden; **g)** *(learned article)* Referat, *das; (shorter)* Paper, *das;* **h)** *no pl., no indef. art. (Commerc.: bills of exchange etc.)* [Wert]papiere. **2.** *adj.* **a)** *(made of ~)* aus Papier *nachgestellt;* Papier⟨*mütze, -taschentuch*⟩; **b)** *(theoretical)* nominell ⟨*zahlenmäßige Stärke, Profit*⟩. **3.** *v. t.* tapezieren
~ **'over** *v. t.* [mit Tapete] überkleben; ~ **over the cracks** *(fig.: cover up mistakes/differences)* die Fehler/Differenzen übertünchen
paper: ~**back 1.** *n.* Paperback, *das; (pocket-size)* Taschenbuch, *das;* **available in ~back** als Paperback/Taschenbuch erhältlich; **2.** *adj.* ~**back edition** Paperback-/Taschenbuchausgabe, *die;* ~**back book** Paperback, *das*/Taschenbuch, *das;* ~ **'bag** *n.* Papiertüte, *die;* ~**-boy** *n.* Zeitungsjunge, *der;* ~ **chain** *n.* Papiergirlande, *die;* ~**-chase** *n.* Schnitzeljagd, *die;* ~**-clip** *n.* Büroklammer, *die; (larger)* Aktenklammer, *die;* ~ **'cup** *n.* Pappbecher, *der;* ~ **currency** *see* ~ **money;** ~**-girl** *see* **news-girl;** ~ **'handkerchief** *n.* Papiertaschentuch, *das;* ~**-hanger** *n.* Tapezierer, *der*/Tapeziererin, *die;* ~**-hanging** *n.* Tapezieren, *das;* ~ **'hanky** *n. (coll.)* Papiertaschentuch, *das;* ~**-knife** *n.* Brieföffner, *der;* ~**-making** *n., no pl.* Papierherstellung, *die;* ~**-mill** *n.* Papierfabrik *od.* -mühle, *die;* ~ **money** *n.* Papiergeld, *das;* ~ **'napkin** *n.* Papierserviette, *die;* ~ **'plate** *n.* Pappteller, *der;* ~ **qualification** *n.* Zeugnis, *das;* ~**-round** *n.* Zeitungenaustragen, *das;* **on one's ~-round** beim Zeitungenaustragen; **have/do a ~-round** Zeitungen austragen; ~ **servi'ette** *see* ~ **napkin;** ~**-shop** *n.* Zeitungsgeschäft, *das;* ~**-thin** *adj. (lit. or fig.)* hauchdünn; ~ **'tiger** *see* **tiger a;** ~ **'towel** *n.* Papierhandtuch, *das;* ~**weight** *n.* Briefbeschwerer, *der;* ~**work** *n.* **a)** Schreibarbeit, *die;* Papierkram, *der (abwertend);* **b)** *(documents)* Unterlagen *Pl.*
papery ['peɪpərɪ] *adj.* papierartig; **be ~:** wie Papier sein

papier mâché [pæpjeɪ 'mæʃeɪ, pæpjeɪ 'mɑ:ʃeɪ] *n.* Papiermaché, *das;* Pappmaché, *das*
papist ['peɪpɪst] *n. (Relig. derog.)* Papist, *der*/Papistin, *die (abwertend)*
papoose [pə'pu:s] *n.* Kleinkind, *das (bei den nordamerikanischen Indianern)*
paprika ['pæprɪkə, pə'pri:kə] *n.* **a)** *see* **pepper 1b; b)** *(Cookery: condiment)* Paprika, *der*
Papua New Guinea [pɑ:pʊə nju: 'gɪnɪ] *pr. n.* Papua-Neuguinea *(das)*
papyrus [pə'paɪrəs] *n., pl.* **papyri** [pə'paɪraɪ] Papyrus, *der*
par [pɑ:(r)] *n.* **a)** *(average)* **above/below ~:** über/unter dem Durchschnitt; **the work is [well] below ~:** die Arbeit liegt [weit] unter dem üblichen Niveau; **feel rather below ~, not feel up to ~** *(fig.)* nicht ganz auf dem Posten *od.* Damm sein *(ugs.);* **b)** *(equality)* **be on a ~:** vergleichbar sein; **be on a ~ with sb./sth.** jmdm./einer Sache gleichkommen; **c)** *(Golf)* Par, *das;* **that's about ~ for the course** *(fig. coll.)* das ist so das Übliche; **d)** *(Commerc.: nominal value)* ~ **[of exchange]** Wechselkurs, *der;* **be at/above/below ~** ⟨*Aktie, Wert:*⟩ al/über/unter pari stehen
para ['pærə] *n. (coll.)* **a)** *(paratrooper)* Para, *der;* **b)** *(paragraph)* Absatz, der
para. *abbr.* **paragraph** Abs.; *(in contract or law)* Paragr.
parable ['pærəbl] *n.* Gleichnis, *das;* Parabel, *die (bes. Literaturw.)*
parabola [pə'ræbələ] *n. (Geom.)* Parabel, *die*
parabolic [pærə'bɒlɪk] *adj. (Geom.)* parabolisch; ~ **mirror** Parabolspiegel, *der*
parachute ['pærəʃu:t] **1.** *n.* **a)** Fallschirm, *der;* **b)** *(to brake aircraft etc.)* Bremsfallschirm, *der.* **2.** *v. t.* [mit dem Fallschirm] absetzen ⟨*Person*⟩ **(into** über + *Dat.*); mit dem Fallschirm abwerfen ⟨*Vorräte*⟩. **3.** *v. i.* ⟨*Truppen:*⟩ [mit dem Fallschirm] abspringen **(into** über + *Dat.*). **4.** *adj.* Fallschirm⟨*absprung, -abwurf*⟩; *(Mil.)* Fallschirmjäger-⟨*truppen, -regiment*⟩
parachutist ['pærəʃu:tɪst] *n.* **a) [sports] ~:** Fallschirmspringer, *der*/-springerin, *die;* **b)** *(Mil.)* Fallschirmjäger, *der*
parade [pə'reɪd] **1.** *n.* **a)** *(display)* Zurschaustellung, *die;* **make a ~ of** zur Schau stellen ⟨*Tugend, Eigenschaft*⟩; **make a ~ of one's knowledge** mit seinem Wissen paradieren *(geh.);* **b)** *(Mil.: muster)* Appell, *der;* **on ~:** beim Appell; **c)** *(procession)* Umzug, *der; (of troops)* Parade, *die;* **d)** *(succession)* Reihe, *die;* **e)** *(promenade, street)* Promenade, *die;* **a ~ of shops** eine Reihe Läden. **2.** *v. t.* **a)** *(display)* zur Schau stellen; vorzeigen ⟨*Person*⟩ **(before** bei); **b)** *(march through)* ~ **the streets** durch die Straßen marschieren; **c)** *(Mil.: muster)* antreten lassen. **3.** *v. i.* paradieren; **the national teams ~d round the stadium** die Nationalmannschaften marschierten durch das Stadion
pa'rade-ground *n.* Exerzierplatz, *der*
paradigm ['pærədaɪm] *n. (esp. Ling.)* Paradigma, *das*
paradise ['pærədaɪs] *n.* Paradies, *das;* **children's/gourmet's ~:** Paradies für Kinder/Gourmets; **an earthly ~:** ein Paradies auf Erden; **this is ~!** himmlisch! *See also* **bird of paradise; fool's paradise**
paradox ['pærədɒks] *n.* **a)** Paradox[on], *das;* **b)** *no pl., no indef. art. (quality)* Paradoxie, *die;* Widersprüchlichkeit, *die*
paradoxical [pærə'dɒksɪkl] *adj.* paradox
paradoxically [pærə'dɒksɪkəlɪ] *adv.* paradox; *as sentence-modifier* paradoxerweise
paraffin ['pærəfɪn] *n.* **a)** *(Chem.)* Paraffin, *das;* **b)** *(Brit.: fuel)* Petroleum, *das; attrib.* Petroleum⟨*lampe, -kocher*⟩; **c) liquid ~** *(Brit.: laxative)* Paraffinöl, *das*
paraffin: ~ **'oil** *(Brit.) see* **paraffin b;** ~ **'stove** *n.* Petroleumkocher, *der; (for heating)* Petroleumofen, *der;* ~ **'wax** *n.* Paraffin[wachs], *das*
paragon ['pærəgən] Muster, *das* **(of** an + *Dat.*); **a ~ of beauty** der Inbegriff der Schönheit; ~ **of virtue** Tugendheld, *der*
paragraph ['pærəgrɑ:f] *n.* **a)** *(section of text)* Absatz, *der;* **b)** *(subsection of law etc.)* Paragraph, *der;* **c)** *(Journ.: news item)* Notiz, *die;* **d)** *(symbol)* Absatzzeichen, *das*
Paraguay ['pærəgwaɪ] *pr. n.* Paraguay *(das)*
Paraguayan [pærə'gwaɪən] **1.** *adj.* paraguayisch; **sb. is ~:** jmd. ist Paraguayer/Paraguayerin. **2.** *n.* Paraguayer, *der*/Paraguayerin, *die*
parakeet ['pærəki:t] *n. (Ornith.)* Sittich, *der*
parallax ['pærəlæks] *n. (Astron., Phys.)* Parallaxe, *die*
parallel ['pærəlel] **1.** *adj.* **a)** parallel; **line A is ~ to line B** *(Geom.)* Gerade A ist der Geraden B parallel; **the railway ran ~ to the river** die Bahnlinie verlief parallel zum Fluß; ~ **bars** *(Gymnastics)* Barren, *der;* **b)** *(fig.: similar)* vergleichbar; **be ~:** sich *(Dat.)* [genau] entsprechen; *(share common features)* Parallelen aufweisen; **there is nothing ~ to this in history** dazu gibt es in der Geschichte keine Parallele. **2.** *n.* **a)** Parallele, *die;* **this has no ~** *or* **is without ~:** dazu gibt es keine Parallele; **there is a ~ between x and y** es gibt eine Parallelität zwischen x und y; **the two societies are ~s** die beiden Gesellschaften gleichen sich; **b)** *(Electr.)* **be connected in ~:** parallelgeschaltet sein; **c)** *(Geog.)* ~ **[of latitude]** Breitenkreis, *der;* **the 42nd ~:** der 42. Breitengrad; **d)** *(Astron.)* Deklinationskreis, *der.* **3.** *v. t.* **a)** *(match)* gleichkommen (+ *Dat.*); **his arrogance cannot be ~ed** seine Arroganz ist beispiellos; **b)** *(find sth. similar to)* **this behaviour may be ~ed in human life** eine Parallele zu diesem Verhalten läßt sich beim Menschen feststellen; **c)** *(compare)* vergleichen
parallelism ['pærəlelɪzm] *n. (lit. or fig.)* Parallelität, *die* **(in** *Gen.*); Übereinstimmung, *die* **(in** *Gen.*)
parallelogram [pærə'leləgræm] *n. (Geom.)* Parallelogramm, *das*
paralyse ['pærəlaɪz] *v. t.* **a)** lähmen; paralysieren *(Med.);* **he is ~d in both legs** seine beiden Beine sind gelähmt; **b)** *(fig.)* lahmlegen ⟨*Verkehr, Industrie*⟩; zum Erliegen bringen ⟨*Verkehr*⟩; **be ~d with fright** vor Schreck wie gelähmt sein; **be ~d** ⟨*Verkehr:*⟩ zum Erliegen gekommen sein
paralysis [pə'rælɪsɪs] *n., pl.* **paralyses** [pə'rælɪsi:z] Lähmung, *die;* Paralyse, *die (Med.); (fig., of industry, traffic)* Lahmlegung, *die*
paralytic [pærə'lɪtɪk] **1.** *adj.* **a)** gelähmt; paralytisch *(Med.);* **b)** *(Brit. sl.: very drunk)* [stock-, sternhagel]voll *(salopp).* **2.** *n.* Gelähmte, *der/die;* Paralytiker, *der*/Paralytikerin, *die (Med.)*
paralyze *(Amer.) see* **paralyse**
paramedic [pærə'medɪk] *n.* medizinische Hilfskraft
paramedical [pærə'medɪkl] *adj.* ~ **personnel/staff** medizinisches Hilfspersonal; *(in hospital)* nichtärztliches Personal; ~ **training** Ausbildung zur medizinischen Hilfskraft
parameter [pə'ræmɪtə(r)] **a)** *(defining feature)* Faktor, *der;* **b)** *(Math.)* Parameter, *der*
paramilitary [pærə'mɪlɪtərɪ] *adj.* paramilitärisch; halbmilitärisch
paramount ['pærəmaʊnt] *adj.* **a)** *(supreme)* höchst... ⟨*Macht, Autorität*⟩; oberst... ⟨*Herrscher, Souverän*⟩; **b)** *(pre-eminent)* größt..., höchst... ⟨*Wichtigkeit*⟩; Haupt⟨*gesichtspunkt, -überlegung*⟩; **be ~** ⟨*Wunsch:*⟩ Vorrang haben
paramour ['pærəmʊə(r)] *n. (arch./rhet.)* Buhle, *der/die (dichter. veralt.)*
paranoia [pærə'nɔɪə] *n.* **a)** *(disorder)* Para-

noia, *die (Med.)*; **b)** *(tendency)* **[feeling of] ~**: krankhaftes Mißtrauen; Verfolgungswahn, *der*
paranoiac [pærə'nɔɪæk], **paranoic** [pærə'nəʊɪk] **1.** *n.* *(Med.)* Paranoiker, *der*/Paranoikerin, *die*; **be a ~** *(fig.)* an Verfolgungswahn leiden. **2.** *adj.* *(Med.)* paranoisch; *(fig.)* krankhaft [gesteigert] ⟨*Mißtrauen*⟩
paranoid ['pærənɔɪd] **1.** *adj.* *(Med.)* paranoid *(fachspr.)*; *(fig.)* wahnhaft; krankhaft [gesteigert] ⟨*Mißtrauen, Abneigung, Angst*⟩; **be ~**: an Verfolgungswahn leiden; **he's ~ about his boss** er bildet sich ein, daß sein Chef ihn schikanieren will. **2.** *n.* *(Med.)* Paranoiker, *der*/Paranoikerin, *die*; **be a ~**: paranoid sein; an Verfolgungswahn leiden
paranormal [pærə'nɔ:ml] *adj.* paranormal; übersinnlich
parapet ['pærəpɪt, 'pærəpet] *n.* **a)** *(low wall or barrier)* Brüstung, *die*; **b)** *(Mil.)* Parapett, *das (hist.)*; Brustwehr, *die*
paraphernalia [pærəfə'neɪlɪə] *n. sing.* **a)** *(personal belongings)* Utensilien *Pl.*; **b)** *(equipment) (of justice, power)* Instrumentarium, *das (geh.)*; Apparat, *der*; *(of war)* Material, *das*; **equestrian/sporting/photographic ~**: Reit-/Sport-/Fotoausrüstung, *die*; **the whole ~** *(coll.)* alles, was so dazugehört *(ugs.)*
paraphrase ['pærəfreɪz] **1.** *n.* Umschreibung, *die*; Paraphrase, *die (fachspr.)*. **2.** *v. t.* umschreiben; paraphrasieren *(fachspr.)*
paraplegia [pærə'pli:dʒɪə] *n.* *(Med.)* Paraplegie, *die (fachspr.)*; ≈ Querschnittslähmung, *die*
paraplegic [pærə'pli:dʒɪk] *(Med.)* **1.** *adj.* doppelseitig gelähmt; paraplegisch *(fachspr.)*. **2.** *n.* doppelseitig Gelähmter/Gelähmte; Paraplegiker, *der*/Paraplegikerin, *die (fachspr.)*
parapsychology [pærəsaɪ'kɒlədʒɪ] *n.* Parapsychologie, *die*
paraquat ['pærəkwɒt] *n.* *(Agric.)* Paraquat, *das (ein Kontaktherbizid)*
parasite ['pærəsaɪt] *n.* **a)** *(Biol.)* Schmarotzer, *der*; Parasit, *der (fachspr.)*; **b)** *(fig. derog.: person)* Schmarotzer, *der*; Parasit, *der*; **be a total ~**: nur schmarotzen
parasitic [pærə'sɪtɪk] *adj.* **a)** *(Biol.)* parasitisch; parasitär ⟨*Pilz*⟩; **be ~ on** schmarotzen in (+ *Dat.*); ⟨*Pflanze*:⟩ schmarotzen auf *od.* an (+ *Dat.*); **b)** *(fig.)* schmarotzerisch; schmarotzerhaft; **be ~ on** als Schmarotzer leben von
parasitism ['pærəsaɪtɪzm] *n.*, *no pl.* **a)** *(Biol.)* Parasitismus, *der*; **b)** *(fig.)* Schmarotzertum, *das*
parasol ['pærəsɒl] *n.* Sonnenschirm, *der*; Parasol, *der od. das (veralt.)*
parasympathetic [pærəsɪmpə'θetɪk] *adj.* *(Anat.)* parasympathisch; **~ nerve** Parasympathikus, *der*
paratrooper ['pærətru:pə(r)] *n.* *(Mil.)* Fallschirmjäger, *der*
paratroops ['pærətru:ps] *n. pl.* *(Mil.)* Fallschirmjägertruppe, *die*; Fallschirmjäger *Pl.*
paratyphoid [pærə'taɪfɔɪd] *(Med.)* *n.* Paratyphus, *der*
parboil ['pɑ:bɔɪl] *v. t.* *(Cookery)* ankochen
parcel ['pɑ:sl] **1.** *n.* **a)** *(package)* Paket, *das*; **send/receive sth. by ~ post** etw. mit der Paketpost *od.* als Postpaket schicken/bekommen; **b) a ~ of land** ein Stück Land; *see also* **part 1 a. 2.** *v. t.*, *(Brit.)* **-ll-** [zu Paketen] verpacken
~ 'out *v. t.* aufteilen ⟨*Land*⟩
~ 'up *v. t.* einwickeln
'parcel bomb *n.* Paketbombe, *die*
parch [pɑ:tʃ] **1.** *v. t.* **a)** *(dry out)* ausdörren, austrocknen ⟨*Land, Boden*⟩; **b)** *(toast)* rösten ⟨*Kerne*⟩. **2.** *v. i.* ⟨*Haut*:⟩ austrocknen
parched [pɑ:tʃt] *adj.* ausgedörrt ⟨*Kehle, Land, Boden*⟩; trocken ⟨*Lippen*⟩; **I am [absolutely] ~ [with thirst]** meine Kehle ist wie ausgetrocknet
parchment ['pɑ:tʃmənt] *n.* **a)** *(skin)* Pergament, *das*; **b)** *(manuscript)* Pergament, *das*; *(document)* Urkunde, *die*
pardon ['pɑ:dn] **1.** *n.* **a)** *(forgiveness)* Vergebung, *die (geh.)*; Verzeihung, *die*; **ask sb.'s ~ for sth.** jmdn. wegen etw. um Verzeihung bitten; **no ~ will be given** es gibt kein Pardon; Pardon wird nicht gegeben; **b) beg sb.'s ~**: jmdn. um Entschuldigung *od.* *(geh.)* Verzeihung bitten; **I beg your ~**: entschuldigen *od.* verzeihen Sie bitte; *(please repeat)* wie bitte? *(auch iron.)*; **I do beg your ~**: entschuldigen Sie bitte vielmals; **beg ~** *(coll.)* Entschuldigung; Verzeihung; **~?** *(coll.)* bitte?; **~!** *(coll.)* Entschuldigung!; **c)** *(Law)* **[free] ~**: Begnadigung, *die*; **grant sb. a ~**: jmdn. begnadigen. **2.** *v. t.* **a)** *(forgive)* **~ sb.'s infidelity** jmdm. seine Untreue verzeihen; **~ sb. [for] sth.** jmdm. etw. verzeihen; **b)** *(excuse)* entschuldigen; **~ my saying so, but ...**: entschuldigen Sie bitte, daß ich es so ausdrücke, aber...; **one could be ~ed for thinking ...** es wäre zu entschuldigen, wenn man dächte, ...; **~ 'me!** Entschuldigung!; **c)** *(Law)* begnadigen
pardonable ['pɑ:dənəbl] *adj.* verzeihlich; entschuldbar; verständlich ⟨*Sorge*⟩
pardonably ['pɑ:dənəblɪ] *adv.* verständlicherweise
pare [peə(r)] *v. t.* **a)** *(trim)* schneiden ⟨*Finger-, Zehennägel*⟩; zurichten, beschneiden ⟨*Hufe*⟩; **b)** *(peel)* schälen ⟨*Apfel, Kartoffel*⟩
~ a'way *v. t.* abschälen ⟨*Rinde*⟩; *(fig.)* beschneiden, schmälern ⟨*Privileg, Profit usw.*⟩
~ 'down *v. t.* *(fig.: reduce)* reduzieren, kürzen ⟨*Ausgaben, Kosten, Zuschuß*⟩
parent ['peərənt] *n.* **a)** Elternteil, *der*; **~s** Eltern *Pl.*; **duties as a ~**: elterliche Pflichten; **b)** *(Bot., Zool.)* Elter, *der od. das (fachspr.)*; *(Bot. also)* Mutterpflanze, *die*; *(Zool. also)* Elterntier, *das*; **c)** *(fig.: source)* Quelle, *die*; **d)** *attrib.* Mutter⟨*pflanze, -baum, -zelle, -gesellschaft*⟩; Stamm⟨*firma, -organisation, -organismus*⟩; **~ ship** *(Naut.)* Mutterschiff, *das*
parentage ['peərəntɪdʒ] *n.* *(lit. or fig.)* Herkunft, *die*; *(fig. also)* Ursprung, *der*
parental [pə'rentl] *adj.* elterlich ⟨*Gewalt*⟩; Eltern⟨*pflicht, -haus, -liebe*⟩; ⟨*Abweisung*⟩ durch die Eltern; **~ approval/discipline** Zustimmung/disziplinierende Maßnahmen der Eltern
parenthesis [pə'renθɪsɪs] *n.*, *pl.* **parentheses** [pə'renθɪsi:z] **a)** *(bracket)* runde Klammer; Parenthese, *die (fachspr.)*; **b)** *(word, clause, sentence)* Parenthese, *die (geh.)*; Einschub, *der*; **in ~**: als Parenthese *od.* Einschub; *(fig.)* nebenbei; am Rande
parenthetic [pærən'θetɪk], **parenthetical** [pærən'θetɪkl] *adj.* eingeschoben; parenthetisch *(fachspr.)*
parenthetically [pærən'θetɪkəlɪ] *adv.* parenthetisch; in Parenthese *(geh.)*; *(fig.)* nebenbei, am Rande ⟨*hinzufügen, erwähnen, sagen*⟩
parenthood ['peərənthʊd] *n.*, *no pl.* Elternschaft, *die*; **joys of ~**: Elternfreuden *Pl.*
parent-'teacher association *n.* Eltern-Lehrer-Vertretung, *die*
parer ['peərə(r)] *n.* Küchenmesser, *das*; **potato-~**: Kartoffelschälmesser, *das*
par excellence [pɑ:r 'eksəlãs] *adv.* par excellence *(geh.)*; schlechthin
pariah [pə'raɪə] **[social] ~**: Paria, *der (geh.)*; Ausgestoßene, *der/die*
parietal [pə'raɪətl] *adj.* *(Anat.)* parietal *(fachspr.)*; seitlich; **~ bone** Scheitelbein, *das*
paring ['peərɪŋ] *n.* **a)** *(action) (of fruit, vegetables)* Schälen, *das*; *(of nails)* Schneiden, *das*; *(of hoofs)* Zurichten, *das*; Beschneiden, *das*; **b)** *usu. in pl. (peel, shaving, etc.)* Schalen, *die*; **nail ~s** abgeschnittene Nägel
'paring-knife *see* **parer**
Paris ['pærɪs] *pr. n.* Paris *(das)*
parish ['pærɪʃ] *n.* Gemeinde, *die*
parish: ~ 'church *n.* Pfarrkirche, *die*; **~ 'council** *n.* *(Brit.)* Gemeinderat, *der*; **~ 'councillor** *n.* *(Brit.)* Gemeinderat, *der*/Gemeinderätin, *die*
parishioner [pə'rɪʃənə(r)] *n.* Gemeinde[mit]glied, *das*; **the ~s** die Gemeinde
parish: ~ 'priest *n.* Gemeindepfarrer, *der*; **~-'pump** *adj.* *(Brit.)* krähwinklig *(abwertend)*, provinziell *(abwertend)* ⟨*Angelegenheit*⟩; **~-pump politics** Kirchturmpolitik, *die*; **~ 'register** *n.* Kirchenbuch, *das*
Parisian [pə'rɪzɪən] **1.** *n.* Pariser, *der*/Pariserin, *die*. **2.** *adj.* Pariser ⟨*Mode*⟩; **be ~** ⟨*Person*:⟩ Pariser/Pariserin sein
parity ['pærɪtɪ] *n.* **a)** *(equality)* Parität, *die (geh.)*; Gleichheit, *die*; **have ~ in voting rights** das gleiche Stimmrecht haben; **~ of pay** gleiche Bezahlung; **b)** *(Commerc.)* Parität, *die*; **the ~ of sterling against the dollar** die Pfund-Dollar-Parität
park [pɑ:k] **1.** *n.* **a)** Park, *der*; *(land kept in natural state)* Natur[schutz]park, *der*; **b)** *(sports ground)* Sportplatz, *der*; *(stadium)* Stadion, *das*; *(Baseball, Footb.)* Spielfeld, *das*; **c) amusement ~**: Vergnügungspark, *der*; **business ~**: Betriebsgelände, *das*. *See also* **industrial park**; **science park**; **theme park**. **2.** *v. i.* parken; **find somewhere to ~**: einen Parkplatz finden; **there's nowhere to ~**: da kann man nicht parken; *(all spaces are occupied)* da ist kein Parkplatz frei. **3.** *v. t.* **a)** *(place, leave)* abstellen ⟨*Fahrzeug*⟩; parken ⟨*Kfz*⟩; **the car was ~ed right in front of the house** das Auto parkte genau vor dem Haus; **a ~ed car** ein geparktes *od.* parkendes Auto; **b)** *(coll.: leave, put)* deponieren ⟨*scherzh.*⟩; **~ oneself [down]** *(sl.)* sich [hin]pflanzen *(ugs.)*; **~ oneself on sb.** *(sl.)* sich bei jmdm. häuslich niederlassen *(ugs.)*
parka ['pɑ:kə] *n.* Parka, *der*
park-and-'ride *n.* Park-and-ride-System, *das*; *(place)* Park-and-ride-Parkplatz, *der*
parking ['pɑ:kɪŋ] *n.*, *no pl.*, *no indef. art.* Parken, *das*; **'No ~'** „Parken verboten"; **there is no ~ in the main street** auf der Hauptstraße ist Parkverbot; **'P~ for 500 cars'** „500 Parkplätze"
parking: ~ attendant *n.* Parkplatzwächter, *der*/-wächterin, *die*; **~-disc** *n.* Parkscheibe, *die*; **~ fine** *n.* Geldbuße für falsches Parken; **~-light** *n.* Parklicht, *das*; Parkleuchte, *die*; **~-lot** *n.* *(Amer.)* Parkplatz, *der*; **~-meter** *n.* Parkuhr, *die*; Parkometer, *das od. der*; **~ offence** *n.* Verstoß gegen das Parkverbot; **~-space** *n.* **a)** *no pl.* Parkraum, *der*; **b)** *(single space)* Platz zum Parken; Parkplatz, *der*; *(between other vehicles)* Parklücke, *die*; **~-ticket** *n.* Strafzettel [für falsches Parken]
Parkinson's ['pɑ:kɪnsənz]: **~ disease** *n.* *(Med.)* Parkinson-Krankheit, *die*; **~ law** *n.* *(joc.)* das Parkinsonsche Gesetz
park: ~keeper *n.* Parkwärter, *der*/-wärterin, *die*; **~land** *n.* Parklandschaft, *die*; **~way** *n.* *(Amer.)* *[für Lkw gesperrte]* Allee
parky ['pɑ:kɪ] *adj.* *(Brit. sl.)* frisch *(ugs.)*; kühl
parlance ['pɑ:ləns] *n.* Ausdrucksweise, *die*; Sprache, *die*; **in common/legal/modern ~**: im allgemeinen/juristischen/modernen Sprachgebrauch
parley ['pɑ:lɪ] **1.** *n.* Verhandlungen. **2.** *v. i.* verhandeln; **meet to ~**: sich zu Verhandlungen treffen
parliament ['pɑ:ləmənt] *n.* Parlament, *das*; **[Houses of] P~** *(Brit.)* Parlament, *das*; **in P~**: im Parlament; **be before P~** ⟨*Antrag*:⟩ im Parlament beraten werden; **open P~**: das parlamentarische Sitzungsjahr eröffnen; *see also* **member b**
parliamentarian [pɑ:ləmən'teərɪən] *n.* Parlamentarier, *der*/Parlamentarierin, *die*
parliamentary [pɑ:lə'mentərɪ] *adj.* parlamentarisch; Parlaments⟨*geschäfte, -wahlen,*

-reform›; P~ **approval** Zustimmung des Parlaments; *see also* **privilege 1 a; secretary b**

'**parlor car** *n. (Amer. Railw.)* Salonwagen, *der*

parlour (*Brit.; Amer.:* **parlor**) ['pɑ:lə(r)] *n.* **a)** *(dated: sitting-room)* Wohnzimmer, *das;* gute Stube *(veralt.);* **b)** *(in mansion, convent, inn)* Salon, *der;* **c) ice-cream ~:** Eisdiele, *die;* **beauty/massage ~:** Schönheits-/Massagesalon, *der*

parlour: ~ game *n.* Gesellschaftsspiel, *das;* **~maid** *n. (Hist.)* Hausangestellte *od.* -gehilfin, *die;* **~ tricks** *n. pl.* gesellschaftliche Spielchen

parlous ['pɑ:ləs] *adj. (arch./joc.)* kritisch, bedenklich, besorgniserregend ‹*Zustand*›; kritisch ‹*Zeit*›

Parmesan ['pɑ:mɪzæn, pɑ:mɪ'zæn] *adj., n.* **~ [cheese]** Parmesan[käse], *der*

parochial [pə'rəʊkɪəl] *adj.* **a)** *(narrow)* krähwinklig *(abwertend);* eng ‹*Horizont*›; **be ~ in one's outlook** einen engen Horizont haben; **b)** *(Eccl.)* Gemeinde-; parochial *(fachspr.)*

parochialism [pə'rəʊkɪəlɪzm] *n.* Provinzialismus, *der (abwertend);* Engstirnigkeit, *die (abwertend)*

parodist ['pærədɪst] *n.* Parodist, *der*/Parodistin, *die;* **be a ~ of sth.** etw. parodieren

parody ['pærədɪ] **1.** *n.* **a)** *(humorous imitation)* Parodie, *die, (geh.)* Persiflage, *die* (**of** auf + *Akk.*); **b)** *(feeble imitation)* Abklatsch, *der (abwertend); (of justice)* Verhöhnung, *die.* **2.** *v. t.* parodieren; persiflieren *(geh.)*

parole [pə'rəʊl] **1.** *n. (conditional release)* bedingter Straferlaß *(Rechtsw.); (word of honour)* Ehrenwort, *das;* **he was released** *or* **let out on ~/he is on ~:** er wurde auf Bewährung entlassen; **he's on three months' ~:** er hat drei Monate Bewährung. **2.** *v. t. (Law)* **~ sb.** jmdm. seine Strafe bedingt erlassen

paroxysm ['pærəksɪzm] *n.* Krampf, *der; (fit, convulsion)* Anfall, *der* (**of** von); Paroxysmus, *der (Med., Geol.);* **~ of rage/laughter** Wut-/Lachanfall, *der;* **burst into ~s of laughter** einen Lachkrampf bekommen; **in a ~ of grief** außer sich vor Trauer

parquet ['pɑ:kɪ, 'pɑ:keɪ] *n.* **~ [floor/flooring]** Parkett, *das*

parricide ['pærɪsaɪd] *see* **patricide**

parrot ['pærət] **1.** *n.* **a)** Papagei, *der;* **b)** *(fig.: person)* Nachplapperer, *der*/-plapperin, *die (abwertend).* **2.** *v. t.* nachplappern *(abwertend);* **~ sb.** jmdm. alles nachplappern

'**parrot-fashion** *adv.* papageienhaft, wie ein Papagei ‹*wiederholen*›; stur, mechanisch ‹*lernen*›; **repeat things ~:** [papageienhaft *od.* wie ein Papagei] nachplappern *od.* nachschwatzen

parry ['pærɪ] **1.** *v. t. (Boxing)* abwehren ‹*Faustschlag*›; *(Fencing; also fig.)* parieren ‹*Fechthieb, Frage*›. **2.** *n. (Boxing)* Abwehr, *die; (Fencing)* Parade, *die;* **make a ~** *(Boxing)* abwehren; *(Fencing)* parieren

parse [pɑ:z] *v. t. (Ling.)* grammatisch beschreiben ‹*Wort*›; grammatisch analysieren ‹*Satz*›

parsimonious [pɑ:sɪ'məʊnɪəs] *adj.* sparsam; *(niggardly)* geizig; *(sparing)* sparsam; **be ~ with sth.** mit etw. geizen

parsimony ['pɑ:sɪmənɪ] *n. (meanness)* Geiz, *der; (carefulness)* Sparsamkeit, *die*

parsley ['pɑ:slɪ] *n., no pl., no indef. art.* Petersilie, *die*

parsley: ~ butter *n.* Petersilienbutter, *die;* **~ 'sauce** *n.* Petersiliensauce, *die*

parsnip ['pɑ:snɪp] *n.* Gemeiner Pastinak, *der;* Pastinake, *die; see also* **butter 2**

parson ['pɑ:sn] *n. (vicar, rector)* Pfarrer, *der; (coll.: any clergyman)* Geistliche, *der;* Pfaffe, *der (abwertend); see also* **nose 1 a**

parsonage ['pɑ:sənɪdʒ] *n.* Pfarrhaus, *das*

part [pɑ:t] **1.** *n.* **a)** Teil, *der; (element of history, family, character)* Bestandteil, *der;* **~ of the cake/newspaper** *etc.* ein Teil des Kuchens/der Zeitung *usw.;* **the greater ~:** der größte Teil; der Großteil; **four-~:** vierteilig ‹*Serie*›; **the hottest ~ of the day** die heißesten Stunden des Tages; **accept ~ of the blame** die Schuld teilweise mit übernehmen; **he deserves no small ~ of the credit for this achievement** an diesem Erfolg hat er keinen geringen Anteil; **for the most ~:** größtenteils; zum größten Teil; **in ~:** teilweise; **in large ~:** groß[en]teils; **in ~s** zum Teil; **~ and parcel** wesentlicher Bestandteil; **the funny ~ of it was that he ...:** das Komische daran war, daß er ...; **it's [all] ~ of the fun/job** *etc.* das gehört [mit] dazu; **be** *or* **form ~ of sth.** zu etw. gehören; **be very much a ~ of sth.** wesentlicher Bestandteil von etw. sein; **the affected ~:** die befallene Partie; *see also* **better 1; b)** *(of machine or other apparatus)* [Einzel]teil, *das;* **spare/machine ~:** Ersatz-/Maschinenteil, *das;* **c)** *(share)* Anteil, *der;* **I want no ~ in this** ich möchte damit nichts zu tun haben; **what's your ~ in all this?** was hast du mit all dem zu tun?; **d)** *(duty)* Aufgabe, *die;* **do one's ~:** seinen Teil *od.* seine Pflicht *od.* das Seine tun; **e)** *(Theatre: character, words)* Rolle, *die;* Part, *der (geh.); (copy)* Rollentext, *der; (fig.)* **dress the ~:** die angemessene Kleidung tragen; **play a noble ~:** nobel handeln; **play a [great/considerable] ~** *(contribute)* eine [wichtige] Rolle spielen; **play a ~** *(act deceitfully)* schauspielern *(abwertend);* sich verstellen; *see also* **act 2 b; look 1 e; f)** *(Mus.)* Part, *der;* Partie, *die;* Stimme, *die;* **six-~** sechsstimmig ‹*Fuge, Harmonie*›; **g)** *usu. in pl. (region)* Gegend, *die; (of continent, world)* Teil, *der;* **be in foreign ~s** im Ausland sein; **I am a stranger in these ~s** ich kenne mich hier nicht aus; **in this** *or* **our/your ~ of the world** hierzulande/bei Ihnen; **h)** *(side)* Partei, *die;* **take sb.'s ~:** jmds. *od.* für jmdn. Partei ergreifen; **for my ~:** für mein[en] Teil; **on the ~ of** seitens (+ *Gen.*) *(Papierdt.);* von seiten (+ *Gen.*); **on my/your** *etc.* **~:** meiner-/deinerseits *usw.;* **i)** *pl. (abilities)* **a man of [many] ~s** ein [vielseitig] begabter *od.* befähigter Mann; **j)** *(Ling.)* **~ of speech** Wortart *od.* -klasse, *die; see also* **principal parts; k) take [no] ~ [in sth.]** sich [an etw. *(Dat.)*] [nicht] beteiligen; [bei etw.] [nicht] mitmachen; **those taking ~ were ...:** teilgenommen haben ...; **l) take sth. in good ~:** etw. nicht übelnehmen; **m)** *(Amer.) see* **parting 1 b. 2.** *adv.* teils; **an alloy which is ~ copper, ~ zinc** eine Legierung aus Kupfer und Zink; **~ ... [and] ~ ...:** teils ..., teils ... **3.** *v. t.* **a)** *(divide into parts)* teilen; scheiteln ‹*Haar*›; **b)** *(separate)* trennen; **a fool and his money are soon ~ed** *(prov.)* wer nicht aufpaßt, dem rinnt das Geld durch die Finger; **till death us do ~** *(in marriage vow)* bis daß der Tod uns scheidet; *see also* **company a. 4.** *v. i.* **a)** *(divide into parts)* ‹*Menge:*› eine Gasse bilden; ‹*Wolken:*› sich teilen; ‹*Vorhang:*› sich öffnen; *(become divided or broken)* ‹*Seil, Tau, Kette:*› reißen; ‹*Lippen:*› sich öffnen; **b)** *(separate)* ‹*Wege, Personen:*› sich trennen; **~ from sb./sth.** sich von jmdm./etw. trennen; **let us ~ friends** wir wollen als Freunde auseinandergehen; **~ with** sich trennen von ‹*Besitz, Geld*›; verzichten auf ‹*Kontrolle*›

partake [pɑ:'teɪk] *v. i., forms as* **take 2** *(formal)* **a) ~ of** *(eat)* zu sich nehmen, einnehmen *(geh.)* ‹*Kost, Mahlzeit*›; *(joc.)* sich einverleiben *(scherzh.);* **b)** *(share)* **~ in** sich *(Dat.)* teilen ‹*Beute*›; teilhaben an (+ *Dat.*), teilen ‹*jmds. Schicksal, Freuden*›

partaken *see* **partake**

parterre [pɑ:'teə(r)] *n.* **a)** *(Hort.)* Parterreanlage, *die;* **b)** *(Amer. Theatre)* Parterre, *das*

part-ex'change 1. *n.* **accept sth. in ~ for sth.** etw. für etw. in Zahlung nehmen; **sell sth. in ~:** etw. in Zahlung geben. **2.** *v. t.* in Zahlung geben

parthenogenesis [pɑ:θɪnə'dʒenɪsɪs] *n., no pl. (Biol.)* Parthenogenese, *die (fachspr.);* Jungfernzeugung, *die*

Parthian shot [pɑ:θɪən 'ʃɒt] *n. (remark)* spitze Schlußbemerkung; *(action)* Abschiedsgeste, *die*

partial ['pɑ:ʃl] *adj.* **a)** *(biased, unfair)* voreingenommen; parteiisch ‹*Urteil*›; **b) be/not be ~ to sb./sth.** *(like/dislike)* eine Schwäche/keine besondere Vorliebe für jmdn./etw. haben; **c)** *(incomplete)* partiell ‹*Lähmung, Sonnen-, Mondfinsternis*›; teilweise ‹*Verlust, Mißerfolg*›; Mit‹*verantwortung, -eigentümer usw.*›; **a ~ success** ein Teilerfolg

partiality [pɑ:ʃɪ'ælɪtɪ] *n.* **a)** *(fondness)* Vorliebe, *die; (for alcohol etc.)* Schwäche, *die;* **b)** *(bias)* Voreingenommenheit, *die;* Parteilichkeit, *die;* **show ~:** parteiisch *od.* voreingenommen sein

partially ['pɑ:ʃəlɪ] *adv.* zum Teil; teilweise

participant [pɑ:'tɪsɪpənt] *n. (actively involved)* Beteiligte, *der/die* (**in** an + *Dat.*); *(in arranged event)* Teilnehmer, *der*/Teilnehmerin, *die* (**in** an + *Dat.*)

participate [pɑ:'tɪsɪpeɪt] *v. i. (be actively involved)* sich beteiligen (**in** an + *Dat.*); *(in arranged event)* teilnehmen (**in** an + *Dat.*); *(have part or share)* partizipieren *(geh.),* teilhaben (**in** an + *Dat.*)

participation [pɑ:tɪsɪ'peɪʃn] *n. (active involvement)* Beteiligung, *die* (**in** an + *Dat.*); *(in arranged event)* Teilnahme, *die* (**in** bei, an + *Dat.*); **worker ~:** industrielle Mitbestimmung; **audience ~:** Publikumsbeteiligung, *die*

participator [pɑ:'tɪsɪpeɪtə(r)] *n.* Beteiligte, *der/die;* **be a ~ in sth.** sich an etw. *(Dat.)* beteiligen

participatory [pɑ:'tɪsɪpeɪtərɪ] *adj.* ‹*Fernsehsendung, Theaterstück*› mit Zuschauerbeteiligung; ‹*Radiosendung*› mit Hörerbeteiligung; *(Polit.)* mit Bürgerbeteiligung *nachgestellt*

participial [pɑ:tɪ'sɪpɪəl] *adj. (Ling.)* partizipial; Partizipial-

participle ['pɑ:tɪsɪpl] *n. (Ling.)* Partizip, *das;* Mittelwort, *das;* **present/past ~:** Partizip Präsens/Perfekt; Mittelwort der Gegenwart/Vergangenheit

particle ['pɑ:tɪkl] *n.* **a)** *(tiny portion; also Phys.)* Teilchen, *das; (of sand)* Körnchen, *das;* **b)** *(fig.)* Quentchen, *das (geh.); (of sense, truth)* Fünkchen, *das; (of truth also)* Körnchen, *das;* **c)** *(Ling.)* Partikel, *die*

particoloured (*Brit.; Amer.:* **particolored**) [pɑ:tɪ'kʌləd] *adj.* bunt

particular [pə'tɪkjʊlə(r)] **1.** *adj.* **a)** *(special; more than ordinary)* besonder...; **which ~ place do you have in mind?** an welchen Ort denkst du speziell?; **here in ~:** besonders hier; **nothing/anything [in] ~:** nichts/irgend etwas Besonderes; **what in ~ made you so angry?** was genau hat dich so geärgert?; **b)** *(individual)* **each ~ hair** jedes [einzelne] Haar; **in his ~ case** in seinem [besonderen] Fall; **one ~ example of each type** ein Beispiel für jede Sorte; **c)** *(fussy, fastidious)* genau; eigen *(landsch.);* **I am not ~:** es ist mir gleich; **be ~ about sth.** es mit etw. genau nehmen; in etw. *(Dat.)* eigen sein *(landsch.);* **be ~ in one's habits** in allem genau *od. (landsch.)* eigen sein; **be ~ about what one eats** wählerisch im Essen sein; **d)** *(detailed)* detailliert, ausführlich ‹*Bericht*›; eingehend, genau, gründlich ‹*Kenntnis*›. **2.** *n.* **a)** *in pl. (details)* Einzelheiten; Details; *(of person)* Personalien *Pl.; (of incident)* nähere Umstände; **b)** *(detail)* Einzelheit, *die;* Detail, *das;* **describe sth. in every ~:** etw. in allen Einzelheiten beschreiben

particularize (particularise) [pə'tɪkjʊləraız] **1.** *v. t.* spezifizieren. **2.** *v. i.* ins Detail gehen

particularly [pəˈtıkjʊləlı] *adv.* **a)** *(especially)* besonders; **b)** *(specifically)* speziell; insbesondere

parting [ˈpɑːtıŋ] **1.** *n.* **a)** *(leave-taking)* **[final] ~:** Trennung, *die;* Abschied, *der;* **b)** *(Brit.: in hair)* Scheitel, *der;* **side ~:** Seitenscheitel, *der;* **c) ~ of the ways** *(of road)* Gabelung, *die; (fig.: critical point)* Scheideweg, *der;* **we came to a ~ of the ways** *(fig.)* unsere Wege trennten sich. **2.** *attrib. adj.* Abschieds-; **~ shot** Schlußbemerkung, *die;* **~ glance/advice** Blick/Ratschlag zum Abschied

partisan [pɑːtıˈzæn, ˈpɑːtızæn] **1.** *n.* **a)** *(adherent)* Anhänger, *der*/Anhängerin, *die; (of party also)* Parteigänger, *der*/-gängerin, *die (oft abwertend); (of cause also)* Befürworter, *der*/Befürworterin, *die;* **b)** *(Mil.)* Partisan, *der*/Partisanin, *die.* **2.** *adj.* **a)** *(often derog.: biased)* voreingenommen, parteiisch ⟨*Ansatz, Urteil, Versuch*⟩; Partei⟨*politik, -geist*⟩; **b)** *(Mil.)* Partisanen⟨*gruppe, -krieg, -aktivität*⟩

partisanship [pɑːtıˈzænʃıp, ˈpɑːtızænʃıp] *n., no pl.* Parteinahme, *die;* Parteilichkeit, *die;* Voreingenommenheit, *die*

partita [pɑːˈtiːtə] *n. (Mus.)* Partita, *die;* Suite, *die*

partition [pɑːˈtıʃn] **1.** *n.* **a)** *(division) (of text etc.)* Unterteilung, *die* (**into** in + *Akk.*); *(between subjects)* Trennung, *die;* **b)** *(Polit.)* Teilung, *die;* **c)** *(room-divider)* Trennwand, *die;* **d)** *(section of hall or library)* Abteilung, *die;* Bereich, *der;* **e)** *(Law: of estate etc.)* Aufteilung, *die.* **2.** *v. t.* **a)** *(divide)* aufteilen ⟨*Land, Zimmer*⟩; [unter]teilen ⟨*Zimmer*⟩; **b)** *(Polit.)* teilen ⟨*Land*⟩

~ ˈoff *v. t.* abteilen ⟨*Teil, Raum*⟩

partitive [ˈpɑːtıtıv] *(Ling.) adj.* partitiv ⟨*Wort, Nomen*⟩

partly [ˈpɑːtlı] *adv.* zum Teil; teilweise; **he was ~ responsible for the accident** er war mitschuldig an dem Unglück; **~ ... [and] ~ ...:** teils ..., teils ...

partner [ˈpɑːtnə(r)] **1.** *n.* Partner, *der*/Partnerin, *die;* **~ in crime** Komplize, *der*/Komplizin, *die (abwertend);* **business ~:** Geschäftspartner, *der*/-partnerin, *die;* **be a ~ in a firm** Teilhaber/-haberin einer Firma sein; **junior/senior ~:** Junior, *der*/Senior, *der;* **[dancing] ~:** Tanzpartner, *der*/-partnerin, *die;* **take your ~s** bitte Aufstellung nehmen; **tennis/croquet ~:** Tennis-/Krocketpartner, *der*/-partnerin, *die;* **~ [in marriage]** Ehepartner, *der*/-partnerin, *die; see also* **sleeping partner. 2.** *v. t.* **a)** *(make a ~)* **~ sb. with sb.** jmdn. mit jmdm. zusammenbringen; **be ~ed with sb.** jmds. Partner/Partnerin sein; **b)** *(be ~ of)* **~ sb.** jmds. Partner/Partnerin sein; **~ sb. at tennis/in the dance** mit jmdm. Tennis spielen/tanzen

partnership [ˈpɑːtnəʃıp] *n.* **a)** *(association)* Partnerschaft, *die;* **they were a marvellous ~:** sie waren großartige Partner; **b)** *(Commerc.)* **business ~:** [Personen]gesellschaft, *die;* **go** *or* **enter into ~ with sb.** in jmds. Gesellschaft *(Akk.)* eintreten; **leave the ~:** aus der Gesellschaft ausscheiden

partook *see* **partake**

part: ~-owner *n.* Mitbesitzer, *der*/-besitzerin, *die;* **~ ˈpayment** *n.* **a)** *see* **part-exchange 1; b)** *(sum)* Anzahlung, *die*

partridge [ˈpɑːtrıdʒ] *n., pl. same or* **~s** Rebhuhn, *das*

part: ~-song *n.* mehrstimmiges Lied; **~ ˈtime** *n.* **some employees were put on ~ time** einige Beschäftigte mußten kurzarbeiten; **~-time 1.** [ˈ--] *adj.* Teilzeit⟨*arbeit, -arbeiter*⟩; **be engaged on a ~-time basis to teach French** als Teilzeitlehrer/-lehrerin für Französisch eingestellt sein; **he is only ~-time** er ist nur eine Teilzeitkraft; **2.** [-ˈ-] *adv.* stundenweise, halbtags ⟨*arbeiten, studieren*⟩; **work ~-time** als Teilzeitkraft beschäftigt sein; **~-ˈtimer** *n.* Teilzeitkraft, *die;* **study as a ~-timer** halbtags *od.* stundenweise studieren

parturition [pɑːtjʊˈrıʃn] *n. (Physiol.)* Partus, *der (fachspr.);* Geburt, *die*

part: ~-way *adv.* **~-way down the slope he slipped** nachdem er ein Stück des Hangs bewältigt hatte, rutschte er aus; **we were ~-way through the tunnel** wir hatten ein Stück des Tunnels hinter uns; **go ~-way towards meeting sb.'s demands** jmds. Forderungen *(Dat.)* teilweise *od.* halbwegs entsprechen; **~-way through her speech** mitten in ihrer Rede; **~-work** *n. (Publishing)* Lieferungswerk, *das;* Partwork, *das*

party [ˈpɑːtı] *n.* **a)** *(group united in a cause etc.; Polit., Law)* Partei, *die; attrib.* Partei⟨*apparat, -versammlung, -mitglied, -politik, -politiker usw.*⟩; **opposing ~:** Gegenpartei, *die;* gegnerische Partei; **the P~:** die Partei; **~ loyalty** Treue zur Partei; **b)** *(group)* Gruppe, *die;* **a ~ of tourists** eine Touristengruppe; **hunting ~:** Jagdgesellschaft, *die;* **tennis ~:** Gruppe von Tennisspielern; **c)** *(social gathering)* Party, *die;* Fete, *die (ugs.); (more formal)* Gesellschaft, *die;* **office ~:** Betriebsfest, *das; see also* **birthday; dinner-party; tea-party; d)** *(participator)* Beteiligte, *der/die;* **be [a] ~ in** *or* **to sth.** sich an etw. *(Dat.)* beteiligen; **parties to an agreement/a dispute** Parteien bei einem Abkommen/streitende Parteien; **the guilty ~:** der/die Schuldige; *see also* **third party; e)** *(coll.: person)* Figur, *die (salopp);* **he's a funny old ~:** er ist ein komischer Kauz *(ugs.)*

party: ~-coloured *see* **particoloured; ~ game** *n.* Gesellschaftsspiel, *das;* **~ line** *n.* **a)** [ˈ---] *(Teleph.)* Gemeinschafts-, Sammelanschluß, *der;* **b)** [--ˈ-] *(Polit.)* Parteilinie, *die;* **what is the ~ line on this problem?** welche Linie verfolgt die Partei bei diesem Problem?; **~-ˈliner** *n. (Polit.)* linientreues Parteimitglied; **~ piece** *n.* **this song was my ~ piece** dieses Lied mußte ich auf jeder Gesellschaft zum besten geben; **~ ˈpolitics** *n.* Parteipolitik, *die;* **~ pooper** [ˈpɑːtıpuːpə(r)] *n. (Amer. sl.)* Partymuffel, *der;* **~ spirit** *n.* **a)** [--ˈ--] *(Polit.)* Parteigeist, *der;* **b)** [ˈ----] *(festive atmosphere)* Partystimmung, *die;* **get the ~ spirit going** die Party in Schwung *od.* Schwung in die Party bringen *(ugs.);* **~ trick** *n.* Trick, der auf Partys Stimmung erzeugt; **~-wall** *n.* Mauer zum Nachbargrundstück/-gebäude; Kommunmauer, *die (Rechtsspr.)*

parvenu [ˈpɑːvənuː] **1.** *n.* Parvenü, *der (geh.);* Emporkömmling, *der.* **2.** *adj.* arriviert; neureich; parvenühaft ⟨*Dreistigkeit*⟩

pascal [ˈpæskl] *n. (Phys.)* Pascal, *das*

paschal [ˈpæskl] *adj.* **a)** *(of Jewish Passover)* Passah-; **~ lamb** Passah[lamm], *das; (fig.)* Lamm Gottes; Agnus Dei *(fachspr.);* **b)** *(of Easter)* Oster-

pash [pæʃ] *n. (sl.)* Schulmädchenschwärmerei, *die; (person)* Schwarm, *der (ugs.);* **have a ~ for sb.** für jmdn. schwärmen

pasha [ˈpɑːʃə] *n. (Hist.)* Pascha, *der*

paso doble [pɑːsəʊ ˈdəʊbleı] *n. (Dancing)* Paso doble, *der*

pasque-flower *n.* Kuhschelle, *die*

pass [pɑːs] **1.** *n.* **a)** *(passing of an examination)* bestandene Prüfung; **be awarded a ~ with distinction** ein Examen mit Auszeichnung bestehen; **get a ~ in maths** die Mathematikprüfung bestehen; **'~'** *(mark or grade)* Ausreichend, *das;* [Note] Vier, *die;* **b)** *(written permission)* Ausweis, *der;* Erlaubnisschein, *der; (for going into or out of a place also)* Passierschein, *der; (Mil.: for leave)* Urlaubsschein, *der; (for free transportation)* Freifahrschein, *der; (for free admission)* Freikarte, *die;* **c)** *(critical position)* Notlage, *die;* kritische Lage; **things have come to a pretty ~ [when ...]** es muß schon weit gekommen sein[, wenn ...]; **d)** *(Football)* Paß, *der (fachspr.);* Ballabgabe, *die; (Tennis) see* **passing shot;** *(Fencing)* Ausfall, *der;* **make a ~ to a player** [den Ball] zu einem Spieler passen *(fachspr.) od.* abgeben; **make a ~ over** *(Aeronaut.)* überfliegen; **e)** *(by conjuror, hypnotist)* **~ [of the hands]** Handbewegung, *die;* **f) make a ~ at sb.** *(fig. coll.: amorously)* jmdm. gegenüber Annäherungsversuche machen; jmdn. anmachen *(ugs.);* **g)** *(in mountains)* Paß, *der;* **h)** *(strategic entrance into a country)* strategisch wichtiger Zugang; Schlüsselstellung, *die;* **i)** *(Cards)* Passen, *das.* **2.** *v. i.* **a)** *(move onward)* ⟨*Prozession:*⟩ ziehen; ⟨*Wasser:*⟩ fließen; ⟨*Gas:*⟩ strömen; *(fig.)* ⟨*Redner:*⟩ übergehen (**to** zu); **~ further along** *or* **down the bus, please!** bitte weiter durchgehen!; **b)** *(go)* passieren; **~ through** ⟨*Blut:*⟩ fließen durch ⟨*Organ*⟩; ⟨*Zug, Reisender:*⟩ fahren durch ⟨*Land*⟩; ⟨*Faden:*⟩ gehen durch ⟨*Nadelöhr*⟩; **~ over** *(in plane)* überfliegen ⟨*Ort*⟩; **a cloud ~ed over the sun** eine Wolke schob sich vor die Sonne; **let sb. ~:** jmdn. durchlassen *od.* passieren lassen; **c)** *(be transported, lit. or fig.)* kommen; **~ into history/oblivion** in die Geschichte eingehen/in Vergessenheit geraten; **messages ~ed between them** Nachrichten wurden zwischen ihnen ausgetauscht; **the title/property ~es to sb.** der Titel/Besitz geht auf jmdn. über; **d)** *(change)* wechseln; **~ from one state/stage to another** von einem Zustand in einen anderen/von einem Stadium in ein anderes übergehen; **e)** *(go by)* ⟨*Fußgänger:*⟩ vorbeigehen; ⟨*Fahrer, Fahrzeug:*⟩ vorbeifahren; ⟨*Prozession:*⟩ vorbeiziehen; ⟨*Zeit, Sekunde:*⟩ vergehen; *(by chance)* ⟨*Person, Fahrzeug:*⟩ vorbeikommen; **let sb./a car ~:** jmdn./ein Auto vorbeilassen *(ugs.);* **make it impossible for sb./sth. to ~:** jmdm./einer Sache den Weg versperren; **he said hello as he ~ed** er grüßte im Vorbeigehen; **~ unheeded** ⟨*Bemerkung:*⟩ keine Beachtung finden; **she would not let this ~ without comment** das wollte sie nicht unkommentiert [im Raum stehen] lassen; **f)** *(be accepted as adequate)* durchgehen; hingehen; **let that/it/the matter ~:** das/es/die Sache durch- *od.* hingehen lassen; **g)** *(come to an end)* vorbeigehen; ⟨*Fieber:*⟩ zurückgehen, [ab]sinken; ⟨*Ärger, Zorn, Sturm:*⟩ sich legen; ⟨*Gewitter, Unwetter:*⟩ vorüberziehen; ⟨*Königreich, Volk:*⟩ untergehen; **h)** *(formal/arch. euphem.: die)* ableben *(veralt. geh.);* **~ out of this world** aus dieser Welt gehen *od.* scheiden *(geh. verhüll.);* **i)** *(happen)* passieren; *(between persons)* vorfallen; **bring/come to ~** *(arch.)* bewirken/sich zutragen *od.* begeben *(geh.);* **j)** *(be known)* **~ by** *or* **under the name of White** unter dem Namen White bekannt sein; **k)** *(be accepted)* durchgehen (**as** als, **for** für); **~ as currency** als Währung akzeptiert werden; **l)** *(be sanctioned)* ⟨*Gesetzentwurf:*⟩ angenommen werden, durchgehen; **m)** *(satisfy examiner)* bestehen; **let ~** ⟨*Zensor:*⟩ freigeben ⟨*Film, Buch, Theaterstück*⟩; **n)** *(circulate, be current)* im Umlauf sein; **o)** *(Chess)* **~ed pawn** Freibauer, *der;* **p)** *(Cards)* passen; **[I] ~!** [ich] passe! *See also* **crowd 1 a; ship 1 a. 3.** *v. t.* **a)** *(move past)* ⟨*Fußgänger:*⟩ vorbeigehen an (+ *Dat.*); ⟨*Fahrer, Fahrzeug:*⟩ vorbeifahren an (+ *Dat.*); ⟨*Prozession:*⟩ vorbeiziehen an (+ *Dat.*); *(by chance)* ⟨*Person, Fahrzeug:*⟩ vorbeikommen an (+ *Dat.*); **b)** *(overtake)* vorbeifahren an (+ *Dat.*) ⟨*Fahrzeug, Person*⟩; **c)** *(cross)* überschreiten ⟨*Schwelle, feindliche Linien, Grenze, Marke*⟩; nehmen, überwinden ⟨*Hindernis*⟩; **d)** *(be approved by)* ⟨*Film:*⟩ passieren ⟨*Zensur*⟩; ⟨*Gesetzentwurf:*⟩ verabschiedet werden von ⟨*Parlament*⟩; *(reach standard in)* bestehen ⟨*Prüfung*⟩; *(satisfy requirements of)* kommen durch ⟨*Kontrolle*⟩; **e)** *(approve)* verabschieden ⟨*Gesetzentwurf*⟩; annehmen

⟨*Vorschlag*⟩; ⟨*Zoll:*⟩ abfertigen ⟨*Gepäck*⟩; ⟨*Zensor:*⟩ freigeben ⟨*Film, Buch, Theaterstück*⟩; bestehen lassen ⟨*Prüfungskandidaten*⟩; ~ **sb. as fit** ⟨*Arzt:*⟩ jmdn. für gesund erklären; **f)** *(be too great for)* überschreiten, übersteigen ⟨*Auffassungsgabe, Verständnis*⟩; **g)** *(move)* bringen; ~ **one's hand across one's face** sich mit der Hand über das Gesicht streichen; ~ **a rope/thread through a ring/the eye of a needle** ein Seil/einen Faden durch einen Ring/ein Nadelöhr ziehen *od.* führen; ~ **a duster over the furniture** mit einem Staubtuch über die Möbel wischen; ~ **meat through a mincer/tomatoes through a sieve** Fleisch durch einen Fleischwolf drehen/Tomaten durch ein Sieb streichen; ~ **one's eye over a letter** *etc.* einen Brief *usw.* überfliegen; **h)** *(Footb. etc.)* passen *(fachspr.)* (to zu); abgeben (to an + *Akk.*); zuspielen (to *Dat.*); **i)** *(spend)* verbringen ⟨*Leben, Zeit, Tag*⟩; **j)** *(hand)* ~ **sb. sth.** jmdm. etw. reichen *od.* geben; **would you ~ the salt, please?** gibst *od.* reichst du mir bitte das Salz?; ~ **sth. to another department** etw. an eine andere Abteilung weitergeben; *see also* **around 1 b**; **k)** *(cause to circulate)* in Umlauf bringen ⟨*Geld*⟩; **l)** *(Mil.)* ~ **in review** defilieren *od.* vorbeimarschieren lassen ⟨*Truppen*⟩; *(fig.)* Revue passieren lassen; **m)** *(utter)* fällen, verkünden ⟨*Urteil*⟩; machen ⟨*Bemerkung*⟩; ~ **censure on sth.** etw. tadeln; **n)** *(discharge)* lassen ⟨*Wasser*⟩; ~ **blood** *(from the bowels)* Blut im Stuhl haben; *(by spitting)* Blut spucken; *(by coughing)* Blut husten; *(in urine)* Blut im Urin haben. *See also* **²buck; hat b; muster 1 a; time 1 b**

~ **a'way 1.** *v. i.* **a)** *(cease to exist)* ⟨*Reich:*⟩ untergehen; **b)** *(euphem.: die)* die Augen schließen *od.* zumachen *(verhüll.)*; ~ **away in one's sleep** im Schlaf dahingehen *(geh. verhüll.)*. **2.** *v. t.* verbringen ⟨*Zeit[raum], Abend*⟩

~ **by 1.** ['--] *v. t.* **a)** *(go past)* ⟨*Fußgänger:*⟩ vorbeigehen an (+ *Dat.*); ⟨*Fahrer, Fahrzeug:*⟩ vorbeifahren an (+ *Dat.*); ⟨*Prozession:*⟩ vorbeiziehen an (+ *Dat.*); *(by chance)* ⟨*Person, Fahrzeug:*⟩ vorbeikommen an (+ *Dat.*); **b)** *(omit, disregard)* übergehen. **2.** [-'-] *v. i.* ⟨*Fußgänger:*⟩ vorbeigehen; ⟨*Fahrer, Fahrzeug:*⟩ vorbeifahren; ⟨*Prozession:*⟩ vorbeiziehen; *(by chance)* ⟨*Person, Fahrzeug:*⟩ vorbeikommen; *see also* **side 1 e**

~ **'down** *see* **hand down a, c**

~ **for** *v. t.* durchgehen für; gehalten werden für

~ **'off 1.** *v. t.* **a)** *(represent falsely)* ausgeben (as, for als); als echt ausgeben ⟨*Fälschung*⟩; **b)** *(turn attention away from)* hinweggehen über (+ *Akk.*). **2.** *v. i.* **a)** *(disappear gradually)* ⟨*Schock, Schmerz, Hochstimmung:*⟩ abklingen, sich legen; **b)** *(take place, be carried through)* verlaufen

~ **'on 1.** *v. i.* **a)** *(proceed)* fortfahren; weitermachen; ~ **on to sth.** zu etw. übergehen; **b)** *(euphem.: die)* die Augen schließen *od.* zumachen *(verhüll.)*. **2.** *v. t.* weitergeben (to an + *Akk.*)

~ **out 1.** [-'-] *v. i.* **a)** *(faint)* umkippen *(ugs.)*; aus den Latschen kippen *(salopp)* (with vor + *Dat.*); **b)** *(complete military training)* seine militärische Ausbildung abschließen. **2.** ['--] *v. t.* bekanntgeben, -machen ⟨*Informationen*⟩

~ **'over 1.** *v. t.* übergehen; überschreiten ⟨*Grenze, Schwelle*⟩; ~ **sth. over in silence** etw. stillschweigend übergehen; *see also* ~ **2 b. 2.** *v. i.* *(euphem.: die)* die Augen schließen *od.* zumachen *(verhüll.)*

~ **through 1.** ['--] *v. t.* durchmachen ⟨*schwierige Zeit, Krankheit*⟩; durchleben ⟨*Augenblick*⟩; ⟨*Buch:*⟩ gehen durch ⟨*Hände*⟩; **it ~ed through my mind** es ging mir durch den Sinn; *see also* ~ **2 b. 2.** [-'-] *v. i.* durchreisen; **be just ~ing through** nur auf der Durchreise sein

~ **'up** *v. t.* sich *(Dat.)* entgehen lassen, ungenutzt vorübergehen lassen ⟨*Gelegenheit*⟩; ablehnen, ausschlagen ⟨*Angebot, Einladung*⟩

passable ['pɑ:səbl] *adj.* **a)** *(acceptable)* passabel, annehmbar ⟨*Versuch, Arbeit, Essen, Porträt*⟩; **b)** *(in condition to be crossed, traversed)* passierbar, befahrbar ⟨*Straße*⟩

passably ['pɑ:səblɪ] *adv.* passabel; annehmbar; einigermaßen ⟨*höflich, angenehm, gutaussehend*⟩

passage ['pæsɪdʒ] *n.* **a)** *(going by, through, etc.)* *(of river)* Überquerung, *die; (of time)* [Ab-, Ver]lauf, *der;* Verstreichen, *das; (of seasons)* Wechsel, *der;* **erased by the ~ of time** ausgelöscht vom Strom der Zeit; **their ~ was halted by an obstruction** ein Hindernis hemmte ihren Weg; **b)** *(transition)* Übergang, *der;* **c)** *(voyage)* Überfahrt, *die;* **d)** *(way)* Durchgang, *der;* Weg, *der; (corridor)* Korridor, *der; (for ship, boat, car)* Durchfahrt, *die;* **several ~s ran from the entrance** mehrere Gänge führten vom Eingang weg; **an underground ~:** ein unterirdischer Gang; **I heard a noise in the ~:** ich hörte ein Geräusch auf dem Gang; **e)** *no art., no pl.* *(liberty or right to pass through)* Durchreise, *die;* **guarantee sb. rights of ~ through a territory** jmdm. die Durchreise durch ein Gebiet genehmigen; **f)** *(right to travel)* Passage, *die;* **work one's ~:** seine Überfahrt abarbeiten; **g)** *(part of book etc.)* Passage, *die;* Textstelle, *die;* **h)** *(Mus.)* Passage, *die;* Stelle, *die;* **i)** *(of a bill into law)* parlamentarische Behandlung; *(final)* Annahme, *die;* Verabschiedung, *die;* **j)** *(duct)* **urinary ~:** Harntrakt, *der;* **ear ~:** Gehörgang, *der;* **air ~s** Luft- *od.* Atemwege. *See also* **back passage; bird of passage; front passage; purple passage; rite**

'passage-way *see* **passage d**

pass: ~book *n.* **a)** *(bank-book)* Bankbuch, *das;* Kontobuch, *das;* **b)** *(S. Afr.)* *Ausweispapier für Farbige;* ~ **degree** *n.* *(Brit. Univ.)* **get a ~ degree** ein Examen ohne Prädikat bestehen

passé *adj. masc.*, **passée** *adj. fem.* ['pæseɪ] **a)** *(past prime)* angekratzt *(salopp)*; verblüht ⟨*Frau*⟩; **b)** *(outmoded)* überholt; passé *nicht attr.*

passel ['pæsl] *n.* *(Amer. coll.)* Schar, *die*

passenger ['pæsɪndʒə(r)] *n.* **a)** *(traveller)* *(on ship)* Passagier, *der; (on plane)* Passagier, *der;* Fluggast, *der; (on train)* Reisende, *der/die; (on bus, in taxi)* Fahrgast, *der; (in car, on motor cycle)* Mitfahrer, *der*/Mitfahrerin, *die; (in front seat of car)* Beifahrer, *der*/Beifahrerin, *die;* **b)** *(coll.: ineffective member)* *Mensch, der/Tier, das von den anderen mit durchgeschleppt wird (ugs.)*; **feel like a mere ~ in an enterprise** sich bei einem Unternehmen wie das fünfte Rad am Wagen fühlen; **we cannot afford to have ~s in our team** Leute, die nichts leisten, können wir in unserem Team nicht gebrauchen

passenger: ~ aircraft *n.* Passagierflugzeug, *das;* ~ **elevator** *(Amer.)*, ~ **lift** *(Brit.)* *ns.* Personenaufzug, *der;* ~ **list** *n.* Passagierliste, *die;* ~ **lounge** *n.* Warteraum, *der;* **~-'mile** *n.* Personenmeile, *die;* Passagiermeile, *die (Flugw.)*; ~ **plane** *n.* Passagierflugzeug, *das;* ~ **seat** *n.* Beifahrersitz, *der;* ~ **train** *n.* Zug im Personenverkehr

passer-by [pɑ:sə'baɪ] *n.* Passant, *der*/Passantin, *die*

passim ['pæsɪm] *adv.* *(literary)* passim

passing ['pɑ:sɪŋ] **1.** *n.* **a)** *(going by)* *(of time, years)* Lauf, *der; (of winter)* Vorübergehen, *das; (of old year)* Ausklang, *der; (death)* Ende, *das;* Hinscheiden, *das (geh. verhüll.)*; **in ~:** beiläufig ⟨*bemerken usw.*⟩; flüchtig ⟨*begrüßen*⟩; **b)** *see* **passage i. 2.** *adj.* **a)** *(going past)* vorbeifahrend ⟨*Zug, Auto*⟩; vorbeikommend ⟨*Person*⟩; vorbeiziehend ⟨*Schatten*⟩; **they depend on the ~ trade** sie sind von der Laufkundschaft abhängig; **with every ~ moment** von Minute zu Minute; **b)** *(fleeting)* flüchtig ⟨*Blick*⟩; vorübergehend ⟨*Mode, Laune, Interesse*⟩; **c)** *(superficial)* flüchtig ⟨*Bekanntschaft*⟩; oberflächlich ⟨*Kenntnisse*⟩; *(cursory)* beiläufig ⟨*Bemerkung*⟩; schnell vorübergehend ⟨*Empfindung*⟩. **3.** *adv.* *(arch.)* überaus

passing: ~-note *n.* *(Mus.)* Durchgangston, *der;* Durchgangsdissonanz, *die;* **~-'out [ceremony]** *n.* *(Mil. etc.)* Abschlußfeier, *die;* **~-place** *n.* Ausweichstelle, *die;* ~ **shot** *n.* *(Tennis)* Passierschlag, *der;* Passierschuß, *der;* **~-tone** *(Amer.)* *see* **~-note**

passion ['pæʃn] *n.* **a)** *(emotion)* Leidenschaft, *die;* Leidenschaftlichkeit, *die;* **b)** *(outburst)* Gefühlsausbruch, *der; (of anger)* Wutanfall, *der;* **fly into a ~:** einen Wutanfall bekommen; **c)** *(sexual love)* Leidenschaft, *die; (lust)* Begierde, *die; (desire)* Verlangen, *das;* **d)** *(enthusiasm)* leidenschaftliche Begeisterung; *(object arousing enthusiasm)* Leidenschaft, *die;* **he has a ~ for steam engines** Dampfloks sind seine Leidenschaft; er hat eine Passion für Dampfloks; **have a ~ for lobster/interfering in people's lives** leidenschaftlich gern Hummer essen/sich mit Begeisterung in anderer Leute Angelegenheiten einmischen; **sth. is sb.'s ~/sb.'s ~ is doing sth.** etw./etw. tun ist jmds. Leidenschaft *od.* ist bei jmdm. eine Leidenschaft; **e) P~** *(Relig., Mus.)* Passion, *die;* Leiden Christi *Pl.*; *(narrative)* Leidens- *od.* Passionsgeschichte, *die;* **Bach's 'St Matthew P~':** die Matthäuspassion von Bach

passionate ['pæʃənət] *adj.* **a)** *(quick-tempered)* hitzig; leidenschaftlich; heftig; **a ~ young man** ein Hitzkopf; **b)** *(ardent)* leidenschaftlich ⟨*Person*⟩; heftig ⟨*Verlangen*⟩; **have a ~ faith in sb.** mit glühender Begeisterung an jmdn. glauben; **have a ~ belief in sth.** mit unbeirrbarem Eifer von etw. überzeugt sein; **c)** *(expressing violent or intense feeling)* leidenschaftlich ⟨*Rede*⟩; *(unrestrained)* leidenschaftlich; hemmungslos; **make a ~ plea for mercy** inständig um Gnade bitten *od.* flehen

passionately ['pæʃənətlɪ] *adv.* leidenschaftlich; mit Leidenschaft; hemmungslos ⟨*weinen*⟩; inständig ⟨*bitten*⟩; **be ~ fond of lobster/cricket** leidenschaftlich gerne Hummer essen/Cricket mögen

passion: ~-flower *n.* *(Bot.)* Passionsblume, *die;* **~-fruit** *n.* Passionsfrucht, *die;* Maracuja, *die;* **~-play** *n.* Passionsspiel, *das;* **P~ 'Sunday** *n.* Passionssonntag, *der;* **P~ Week** *n.* **a)** *(before Palm Sunday)* die Woche nach dem ersten Passionssonntag; **b)** *(after Palm Sunday)* die Karwoche

passive ['pæsɪv] **1.** *adj.* **a)** *(suffering action, acted upon)* passiv; **b)** *(without opposition)* passiv; teilnahmslos; widerstandslos; widerspruchslos ⟨*Hinnahme, Annahme*⟩; **remain ~:** unbeteiligt bleiben; ~ **smoking** passives Rauchen; ~ **resistance** passiver Widerstand; **c)** *(inert)* regungslos ⟨*Gestalt, Körper, Wasserfläche*⟩; unbewegt ⟨*Wasserfläche*⟩; passiv ⟨*Rolle*⟩; **your son is too ~:** Ihr Sohn ist zu passiv *od.* hat zuwenig Initiative; **d)** *(not expressed)* unausgesprochen; **e)** *(Metallurgy: unreactive)* passiv; **f)** *(Ling.)* Passiv-; passivisch; ~ **voice** Passiv, *das;* ~ **vocabulary** passiver Wortschatz. **2.** *n.* *(Ling.)* Passiv, *das*

passively ['pæsɪvlɪ] *adv.* teilnahmslos, unbeteiligt ⟨*dasitzen, lächeln, hinnehmen*⟩; tatenlos ⟨*zusehen*⟩; **be ~ involved in sth.** bei etw. eine passive Rolle spielen

passiveness ['pæsɪvnɪs], **passivity** [pæ'sɪvɪtɪ] *ns., no pl.* Passivität, *die;* Teilnahmslosigkeit, *die*

pass: ~-key *n.* **a)** *(master-key)* Hauptschlüssel, *der;* **b)** *(private key)* Hausschlüssel, *der;* **~-mark** *n.* Mindestpunktzahl, *die;* **the ~-mark was 40 %** zum Bestehen [der Klausur *etc.*] mußten mindestens 40% der Punkte erreicht werden; **P~over** *n.* Passah, *das;* **the feast of P~over** das Passahfest; **~port** *n.* **a)** [Reise]paß, *der; attrib.* Paß-; **b)** *(fig.)* Schlüssel, *der* **(to** zu); **~word** *n.* **a)** Parole, *die;* Losung, *die;* **b)** *(Computing)* Paßwort, *das*

past [pɑ:st] **1.** *adj.* **a)** *pred. (over)* vorbei; vorüber; **b)** *attrib. (previous)* früher; vergangen; verflossen *(geh.)* ‹*Jahre*›; früher, ehemalig ‹*Präsident, Vorsitzende usw.*›; **~ history** Vorleben, *das;* **she has a ~ history of violence** sie hat ein gewalttätiges Vorleben; **this is all ~ history** das ist alles Vergangenheit; **her ~ behaviour** *or* **conduct** ihr Verhalten in der Vergangenheit; **in centuries ~:** in vergangenen *od.* früheren Jahrhunderten; **c)** *(just gone by)* letzt...; vergangen; **for weeks ~:** während der letzten Wochen; **in the ~ few days** während der letzten Tage; **the ~ hour/decade** die letzte *od.* vergangene Stunde/das letzte *od.* vorige Jahrzehnt; **d)** *(Ling.)* **~ tense** Vergangenheit, *die;* Präteritum, *das;* **~ definite, ~ historic** historisches Perfekt; **~ perfect** *see* **pluperfect;** *see also* **participle. 2.** *n.* **a)** Vergangenheit, *die; (that which happened in the ~)* Vergangene, *das;* Gewesene, *das;* **in the ~:** früher; in der Vergangenheit ‹*leben*›; **be a thing of the ~:** der Vergangenheit *(Dat.)* angehören; **b)** *(previous history)* Vergangenheit, *die;* **a woman with a ~:** eine Frau mit Vergangenheit; **c)** *(Ling.)* Vergangenheit, *die;* **be/put in the ~:** in der Vergangenheit stehen/in die Vergangenheit setzen. **3.** *prep.* **a)** *(beyond in time)* nach; *(beyond in place)* hinter (+ *Dat.*); **half ~ three** halb vier; **five [minutes] ~ two** fünf [Minuten] nach zwei; **it's ~ midnight** es ist schon nach Mitternacht *od.* Mitternacht vorbei; **it's ~ the time he said he'd arrive** um diese Zeit wollte er eigentlich schon hier sein; **he is ~ sixty** er ist über sechzig; **she's ~ the age for having children** sie ist schon zu alt, um Kinder zu bekommen; **gaze/walk ~ sb./sth.** an jmdm./etw. vorbeiblicken/vorüber- *od.* vorbeigehen; **b)** *(not capable of)* **~ repair/all comprehension** nicht mehr zu reparieren/völlig unverständlich; **he is ~ help/caring** ihm ist nicht mehr zu helfen/es kümmert ihn nicht mehr; **be/be getting ~ it** *(coll.)* [ein bißchen] zu alt sein/allmählich zu alt werden; **I wouldn't put it ~ her to do that** ich würde es ihr schon zutrauen, daß sie das tut; **I wouldn't put anything ~ him** ihm ist alles zuzutrauen. **4.** *adv.* vorbei; vorüber; **hurry ~:** vorüber- *od.* vorbeieilen

pasta ['pæstə, 'pɑ:stə] *n.* Nudeln *Pl.;* Teigwaren *Pl.*

paste [peɪst] **1.** *n.* **a)** Brei, *der; (for cakes)* Teig, *der;* **mix into a smooth/thick ~:** zu einem lockeren/dicken Brei anrühren; zu einem glatten/festen Teig anrühren ‹*Backmischung*›; **b)** *(glue)* Kleister, *der;* **c)** *(of meat, fish, etc.)* Paste, *die; (sweet doughy confection)* Masse, *die;* **anchovy ~:** Sardellenpaste, *die;* **almond ~:** Marzipanmasse, *die;* **d)** *no pl., no indef. art. (imitation gems)* Straß, *der;* Similisteine *Pl.;* **e)** *(Pottery)* Brei, *der.* **2.** *v. t.* **a)** *(fasten with glue)* kleben; **~ sth. down/into sth.** etw. ankleben/in etw. *(Akk.)* einkleben; **b)** *(sl.: beat, thrash, bomb)* in die Pfanne hauen *(ugs.)*

~ 'over *v. t.* überkleben

~ 'up *v. t.* ankleben **(on** an + *Akk.*); *see also* **paste-up**

'pasteboard 1. *n.* Pappe, *die;* Karton, *der;* **2.** *adj.* Papp-; *(fig.)* hohl ‹*Glanz*›; billig ‹*Konstruktion*›

pastel ['pæstl] **1.** *n.* **a)** *(crayon)* Pastellstift, *der;* Pastellkreide, *die;* **b)** *(drawing)* Pastellzeichnung, *die;* **c)** *(art)* Pastellmalerei, *die;* Pastell, *das.* **2.** *adj.* pastellen; pastellfarben; Pastell‹*farben, -töne, -zeichnung, -bild*›; **~ green** Pastellgrün, *das*

'paste-up *n.* Klebeumbruch, *der;* Montage, *die*

pasteurisation, pasteurise *see* **pasteuriz-**

pasteurization [pæstʃəraɪ'zeɪʃn, pɑ:stʃəraɪ'zeɪʃn] *n.* Pasteurisation, *die;* Pasteurisierung, *die*

pasteurize ['pæstʃəraɪz, 'pɑ:stʃəraɪz] *v. t.* pasteurisieren

pastille ['pæstɪl] *n.* Pastille, *die*

pastime ['pɑ:staɪm] *n.* Zeitvertreib, *der; (person's specific ~)* Hobby, *das;* **my ~s are tennis and cricket** in meiner Freizeit spiele ich Tennis und Cricket; **amuse oneself/while away the time with various ~s** sich *(Dat.)* die Zeit mit verschiedenen Beschäftigungen vertreiben; **national ~:** Nationalsport, *der (auch iron.);* **favourite ~:** Lieblingsbeschäftigung, *die*

pasting ['peɪstɪŋ] *n. (sl.)* **give sb. a ~:** jmdm. eins überbraten *(salopp);* **take a ~:** eins übergebraten kriegen *(salopp); (from critics)* verrissen werden *(ugs.)*

past 'master *n. (fig.)* Meister, *der*

pastor ['pɑ:stə(r)] *n.* Pfarrer, *der*/Pfarrerin, *die;* Pastor, *der*/Pastorin, *die*

pastoral ['pɑ:stərl] **1.** *adj.* **a)** Weide-; ländlich ‹*Reiz, Idylle, Umgebung*›; **b)** *(Lit., Art, Mus.)* pastoral; **~ poetry** Hirten-, Schäferdichtung, *die; (ancient)* Bukolik, *die;* **~ drama** Schäferspiel, *das;* **~ theme** ländliches Motiv; **c)** *(Eccl.)* pastoral; des Pfarrers *nachgestellt;* Hirten‹*amt, -brief*›; seelsorgerisch ‹*Pflicht, Aufgabe, Leitung, Aktivitäten*›; **~ care** Seelsorge, *die;* **d)** *(relating to shepherds)* **~ economy** Weidewirtschaft, *die;* **a ~ people** ein Hirtenvolk. **2.** *n. (Lit., Art, Mus.)* Pastorale, *das od. die*

pastorale [pæstə'rɑ:l] *see* **pastoral 2**

pastrami [pæ'strɑ:mɪ] *n. (Amer.) geräuchertes, stark gewürztes Schulterstück vom Rind*

pastry ['peɪstrɪ] *n.* **a)** *(flour-paste)* Teig, *der;* **b)** *(article of food)* Gebäckstück, *das;* **c) pastries** *collect.* [Fein]gebäck, *das*

pastry: ~-board *n.* Backbrett, *das;* **~-cook** *n.* Konditor, *der*/Konditorin, *die;* **~-cutter** *n.* Ausstechform, *die;* **~-wheel** *n.* Kuchenrad, *das*

pasturage ['pɑ:stʃərɪdʒ, 'pɑ:stjʊərɪdʒ] *n.* **a)** *(grazing)* Weide, *die;* **rights of ~:** Weiderecht, *das;* **b)** *(grass)* Futter, *das;* Gras, *das;* **c)** *(land)* Weideland, *das*

pasture ['pɑ:stʃə(r)] **1.** *n.* **a)** *(grass)* Futter, *das;* Gras, *das;* **~ for cattle** Viehfutter, *das;* **b)** *(land)* Weideland, *das; (piece of land)* Weide, *die;* **c)** *(fig.)* **home ~s** heimatliche Gefilde *Pl. (scherzh.);* **in search of ~s new** auf der Suche nach etwas Neuem. **2.** *v. t. (lead or put to ~)* weiden [lassen]. **3.** *v. i.* weiden; grasen

'pasture land *n.* Weideland, *das*

¹pasty ['pæstɪ] *n.* Pastete, *die*

²pasty ['peɪstɪ] *adj.* **a)** teigig; zähflüssig; **b)** *see* **pasty-faced**

pasty-faced ['peɪstɪfeɪst] *adj.* mit teigigem Gesicht *nachgestellt;* **be ~:** ein teigiges Gesicht haben

¹pat [pæt] **1.** *n.* **a)** *(stroke, tap)* Klaps, *der;* leichter Schlag; **give sb./a dog a ~:** jmdn./einen Hund tätscheln; *(once)* jmdm./einem Hund einen Klaps geben; **give sb./a dog a ~ on the head** jmdm./einem Hund den Kopf tätscheln; **give sb. a ~ on the shoulder** jmdm. auf die Schulter klopfen; **a ~ on the back** *(fig.)* eine Anerkennung; **she deserves a ~ on the back** *(fig.)* sie verdient Anerkennung *od.* ein Lob; **give oneself/sb. a ~ on the back** *(fig.)* sich *(Dat.)* [selbst] auf die Schulter klopfen/jmdm. einige anerkennende Worte sagen; **b)** *(of butter)* Stückchen, *das; (of mud, clay)* Klümpchen, *das; see also* **cow-pat. 2.** *v. t.*, **-tt- a)** *(strike gently)* leicht klopfen auf (+ *Akk.*); tätscheln, *(once)* einen Klaps geben (+ *Dat.*) ‹*Person, Hund, Pferd*›; **~ sb. on the arm/head/cheek** jmdm. den Arm/Kopf/die Wange tätscheln; **~ oneself/sb. on the back** *(fig.)* sich *(Dat.)* [selbst]/jmdm. auf die Schulter klopfen; **~ one's face dry** sein Gesicht trockentupfen; **b)** *(flatten)* festklopfen ‹*Sand*›; andrücken ‹*Haare*›; **~ flat** flach klopfen; **~ one's hair into place** sich *(Dat.)* das Haar zurechtlegen

²pat 1. *adv. (ready, prepared)* **have sth. off ~:** etw. parat haben; **know sth. off ~:** etw. aus dem Effeff können *od.* beherrschen *(ugs.);* etw. in- und auswendig können; **come ~** ‹*Antwort:*› wie aus der Pistole geschossen kommen; *(opportunely)* ‹*Geschichte:*› wie gerufen kommen; **stand ~** *(fig.)* keinen Zollbreit nachgeben; unbeirrbar sein. **2.** *adj. (ready)* allzu schlagfertig ‹*Antwort*›; *(opportune)* passend; treffend; **he has some ~ phrases for every occasion** er hat für jede Gelegenheit einen Spruch parat *(ugs.)*

patch [pætʃ] **1.** *n.* **a)** Stelle, *die;* **inflamed ~es of skin** entzündete [Haut]stellen; **a ~ of blue sky** ein Stückchen blauer Himmel; **there were still ~es of snow** es lag vereinzelt *od.* hier und da noch Schnee; **the dog had a black ~ on its ear** der Hund hatte einen schwarzen Fleck am Ohr; **there were ~es of black ice on the roads** auf den Straßen war stellenweise Glatteis; **there were ~es of sunshine** auf einige Stellen schien die Sonne; **~es of rain** *(during period of time)* ab und zu Regen; *(in several places)* stellenweise Regen; **fog ~es** Nebelfelder; **we went through one or two rough ~es on our crossing** während der Überfahrt hatten wir ein- oder zweimal rauhe See; **in ~es** stellenweise; **go through** *or* **strike a bad/good ~** *(Brit.)* eine Pech-/Glückssträhne haben; **a sticky ~ in her life** eine schwierige Phase in ihrem Leben; **b)** *(on worn garment)* Flicken, *der;* **be not a ~ on sth.** *(fig. coll.)* nichts gegen etw. sein; nicht an etw. *(Akk.)* heranreichen; **c)** *(on eye)* Augenklappe, *die;* **wear a ~ on one eye** eine Augenklappe tragen; **d)** *(piece of ground)* Stück Land, *das;* **every ~ of ground** jeder Zentimeter Boden; **potato ~:** Kartoffelacker, *der; (in garden)* Kartoffelbeet, *das;* **e)** *(area patrolled by police; also fig.)* Revier, *das;* **keep off our ~** *(fig.)* komm uns ja nicht ins Gehege; **f)** *(Mil.: badge)* Schulterklappe, *die;* Schulterstück, *das;* **g)** *(Hist.: beauty spot)* Schönheitspflästerchen, *das;* Mouche, *die (geh.).* **2.** *v. t. (apply ~ to)* flicken

~ to'gether *v. t.* zusammenstücke[l]n; *(fig.)* zusammenflicken, zusammenstoppeln *(ugs. abwertend)* ‹*Buch, Artikel*›; zusammenschustern *(ugs. abwertend)* ‹*Grundsatzprogramm, Vereinbarung*›

~ 'up *v. t.* reparieren; zusammenflicken ‹*Segel, Buch*›; notdürftig verbinden ‹*Wunde*›; zusammenflicken *(scherzh.)* ‹*Verletzten*›; *(fig.)* beilegen ‹*Streit, Differenzen*›; kitten ‹*Ehe, Freundschaft*›; **try to ~ the matter up** versuchen, die Sache wieder ins Lot zu bringen

patch: ~-pocket *n.* aufgesetzte Tasche; **~work** *n.* Patchwork, *das;* **a ~work quilt** eine Patchwork-Decke; *(fig.)* **a ~work of fields** ein bunter Teppich von Feldern

patchy ['pætʃɪ] *adj.* uneinheitlich ‹*Qualität*›; ungleichmäßig, unterschiedlich ‹*Arbeit, Aufführung, Ausstoß*›; unausgewogen ‹*Darbietung*›; fleckig ‹*Anstrich*›; stellenweise spärlich ‹*Ernte*›; sehr lückenhaft ‹*Wissen*›; in der Qualität unterschiedlich ‹*Film, Buch, Theaterstück*›

pate [peɪt] *n. (arch.)* Haupt, *das (geh.); (coll.)* Birne, *die (salopp);* Rübe, *die (salopp);* **bald ~:** Glatze, *die*

pâté ['pæteɪ] *n.* Pastete, *die;* **~ de foie gras** ['pæteɪ/'pɑ:teɪ də fwɑ 'grɑ:] Gänseleberpastete, *die*

patella [pəˈtelə] *n., pl.* ~e [pəˈteliː] *(Anat.)* Kniescheibe, *die;* Patella, *die (fachspr.)*
paten [ˈpætn] *n. (Eccl.)* Patene, *die;* Hostienteller, *der*
patent [ˈpeɪtənt, ˈpætənt] **1.** *adj.* **a)** patentiert; patentrechtlich geschützt; gesetzlich geschützt; *(fig.: characteristic)* ureigen; ~ **medicine** Markenmedizin, *die;* patentrechtlich geschütztes Arzneimittel; ~ **article** Markenartikel, *der;* ~ **remedy** Spezial- *od.* Patentrezept, *das;* Patentlösung, *die;* **b)** *(obvious)* offenkundig; offensichtlich. **2.** *n.* **a)** *(licence)* Patent, *das;* ~ **applied for** *or* **pending** Patent angemeldet; **take out a ~ for** *or* **on sth.** sich *(Dat.)* etw. patentieren lassen; **b)** *(invention or process)* Patent, *das;* **c)** *(fig.: exclusive property or claim)* Patent, *das* (**on** auf + *Akk.*). **3.** *v. t.* patentieren lassen; **sth. has been ~ed** etw. ist patentrechtlich geschützt
patentable [ˈpeɪtəntəbl, ˈpætəntəbl] *adj.* patentfähig
patent: ~ **agent** *(Brit.),* ~ **attorney** *(Amer.) ns.* Patentanwalt, *der/*-anwältin, *die*
patentee [peɪtənˈtiː, pætənˈtiː] *n.* Patentinhaber, *der/*-inhaberin, *die*
patent ˈleather *n.* Lackleder, *das;* ~ **shoes** Lackschuhe
patently [ˈpeɪtəntlɪ, ˈpætəntlɪ] *adv.* offenkundig; offensichtlich; ~ **obvious** ganz offenkundig *od.* offensichtlich
patent: ~ **office** *n.* Patentamt, *das;* ~ **rights** *n. pl.* Erfinderrecht, *das*
paterfamilias [peɪtəfəˈmɪlɪæs, pætəfəˈmɪlɪæs] *n. (often joc.)* Familienoberhaupt, *das;* Paterfamilias, *der (geh. scherzh.)*
paternal [pəˈtɜːnl] *adj.* **a)** *(fatherly)* väterlich; **b)** *(related)* ⟨*Großeltern, Onkel, Tante*⟩ väterlicherseits
paternalism [pəˈtɜːnəlɪzm] *n.* Bevormundung, *die*
paternalistic [pətɜːnəˈlɪstɪk] *adj.* patriarchalisch; paternalistisch
paternally [pəˈtɜːnəlɪ] *adv.* väterlich
paternity [pəˈtɜːnɪtɪ] *n.* **a)** *(fatherhood)* Vaterschaft, *die;* **deny ~ of a child** die Vaterschaft an einem Kind bestreiten *od.* leugnen; **b)** *(origin)* Abstammung väterlicherseits, *die*
paternity: ~ **leave** *n.* Vaterschaftsurlaub, *der;* ~ **suit** *n.* Vaterschaftsklage, *die;* Vaterschaftsprozeß, *der;* ~ **test** *n.* Vaterschaftsuntersuchung, *die*
paternoster [pætəˈnɒstə(r)] *n.* **a)** *(prayer)* Vaterunser, *das;* Paternoster, *das;* **b)** *(lift)* Paternoster, *der*
path [pɑːθ] *n., pl.* ~s [pɑːðz] **a)** *(way)* Weg, *der;* Pfad, *der; (merely made by walking)* Trampelpfad, *der;* **keep to the ~:** auf dem Weg bleiben; **b)** *(line of motion)* Bahn, *die; (of tornado, caravan, etc.)* Weg, *der;* **his ~ led across fields and meadows** sein Weg führte ihn über Felder und Wiesen; **into the ~ of a moving vehicle** vor ein Fahrzeug; *see also* **flight path; c)** *(fig.: course of action)* Weg, *der;* **the middle ~:** der Mittelweg; **our ~s crossed/diverged** unsere Wege kreuzten/trennten sich; **the ~ to salvation/of virtue** der Weg des Heils/der Pfad der Tugend
pathetic [pəˈθetɪk] *adj.* **a)** *(pitiful)* mitleiderregend; herzergreifend; **be a ~ sight** ein Bild des Jammers bieten; **b)** *(full of pathos)* pathetisch; **c)** *(contemptible)* armselig ⟨*Entschuldigung*⟩; erbärmlich ⟨*Darbietung, Rede, Person, Leistung*⟩; **are these ~ scribbles meant to be art?** soll dieses jämmerliche Gekritzel vielleicht Kunst sein?; **d)** ~ **fallacy** Vermenschlichung der Natur, *die*
pathetically [pəˈθetɪkəlɪ] *adv.* **a)** *(pitifully)* mitleiderregend ⟨*stöhnen*⟩; herzergreifend ⟨*flehen*⟩; **b)** *(contemptibly)* erbärmlich; erschreckend ⟨*wenig*⟩; ~ **bad** miserabel
ˈpathfinder *n.* **a)** *(person)* jmd., der jmdm. den Weg findet/zeigt; *(fig.)* Wegbereiter, *der/*-bereiterin, *die;* Bahnbrecher, *der/*Bahnbrecherin, *die;* **b)** *(aircraft)* Pfadfinder, *der (Milit.)*
pathless [ˈpɑːθlɪs] *adj.* weglos
pathogen [ˈpæθədʒən] *n. (Med.)* [Krankheits]erreger, *der*
pathogenic [pæθəˈdʒenɪk] *adj. (Med.)* pathogen *(fachspr.);* krankheitserregend
pathological [pæθəˈlɒdʒɪkl] *adj.* **a)** pathologisch; Pathologie-; **b)** *(morbid)* pathologisch; krankhaft; **c)** *(fig.: obsessive)* krankhaft; pathologisch
pathologically [pæθəˈlɒdʒɪkəlɪ] *adv.* pathologisch; *(fig.: obsessively)* krankhaft
pathologist [pəˈθɒlədʒɪst] *n.* Pathologe, *der/*Pathologin, *die*
pathology [pəˈθɒlədʒɪ] *n.* **a)** *(science)* Pathologie, *die;* **b)** *(symptoms)* Symptomatik, *die;* **the ~ of a disease** das Krankheitsbild
pathos [ˈpeɪθɒs] *n.* Pathos, *das*
ˈpathway *n.* **a)** *see* **path a; b)** *(Physiol.)* Bahn, *die;* Leitung, *die;* **optical ~:** Sehbahn, *die*
patience [ˈpeɪʃəns] *n.* **a)** *no pl., no art.* Geduld, *die; (perseverance)* Ausdauer, *die;* Beharrlichkeit, *die; (forbearance)* Langmut, *die;* **with ~:** geduldig; **have endless ~:** eine Engelsgeduld haben; **my ~ is finally exhausted** meine Geduld ist jetzt am Ende *od.* erschöpft; **lose [one's] ~ [with sth./sb.]** [mit etw./jmdm.] die Geduld verlieren; **I lost my ~:** mir riß der Geduldsfaden *(ugs.) od.* die Geduld; **it is enough to try the ~ of a saint** das ist eine harte Geduldsprobe; **have the ~ of a saint** eine Engelsgeduld haben; **b)** *(Brit. Cards)* Patience, *die. See also* **Job**
patient [ˈpeɪʃənt] **1.** *adj.* geduldig; *(forbearing)* langmütig; *(persevering)* beharrlich; **please be ~:** bitte hab Geduld; gedulde dich bitte; **remain ~:** sich in Geduld fassen. **2.** *n.* Patient, *der/*Patientin, *die*
patiently [ˈpeɪʃəntlɪ] *adv. (with composure)* geduldig; mit Geduld; *(with forbearance)* geduldig; nachsichtig; *(with calm)* geduldig; *(with perseverance)* beharrlich; ausdauernd
patina [ˈpætɪnə] *n. (on bronze)* Patina, *die; (on woodwork)* Altersglanz, *der; (fig.)* Patina, *die*
patio [ˈpætɪəʊ] *n., pl.* ~s **a)** *(paved area)* Veranda, *die;* Terrasse, *die;* **b)** *(inner court)* Innenhof, *der;* Patio, *der*
patio ˈdoor *n.* große Glasschiebetür *(zum Garten)*
patisserie [pəˈtɪsərɪ] *n.* **a)** *(shop)* Konditorei, *die;* **b)** *(cakes and pastries)* Feingebäck, *das*
Patna rice [ˈpætnə raɪs] *n.* Patnareis, *der*
patois [ˈpætwɑː] *n., pl. same* **a)** *(dialect)* Mundart, *die;* Dialekt, *der;* **b)** *(jargon)* Jargon, *der*
patriarch [ˈpeɪtrɪɑːk] *n.* **a)** *(of family)* Familienoberhaupt, *das;* Patriarch, *der; (of tribe)* Stammesoberhaupt, *das;* Häuptling, *der;* **b)** *(Relig.) (in early and Orthodox Church)* Patriarch, *der; (RC Ch.)* Bischof von Rom, *der;* **c)** *(founder)* Begründer, *der;* **d)** *(old man)* ehrwürdiger Greis
patriarchal [peɪtrɪˈɑːkl] *adj.* **a)** patriarchalisch; **b)** *(old, venerable)* [alt]ehrwürdig
patriarchy [ˈpeɪtrɪɑːkɪ] *n.* Patriarchat, *das*
patrician [pəˈtrɪʃn] **1.** *n. (Hist.)* Patrizier, *der/*Patrizierin, *die.* **2.** *adj.* **a)** *(noble)* vornehm; edel; **b)** *(Hist.)* patrizisch; Patrizier-; ~ **family** Patrizierfamilie, *die;* Patriziergeschlecht, *das*
patricide [ˈpætrɪsaɪd] *n.* **a)** *(murder)* Vatermord, *der;* **b)** *(murderer)* Vatermörder, *der/*Vatermörderin, *die*
patrimony [ˈpætrɪmənɪ] *n.* Patrimonium, *das;* väterliches Erbe; *(fig.)* Erbe, *das; (endowment)* Vermögen, *das*
patriot [ˈpætrɪət, ˈpeɪtrɪət] *n.* Patriot, *der/*Patriotin, *die*
patriotic [pætrɪˈɒtɪk, peɪtrɪˈɒtɪk] *adj.* patriotisch
patriotism [ˈpætrɪətɪzm, ˈpeɪtrɪətɪzm] *n.* Patriotismus, *der;* vaterländische Gesinnung
patrol [pəˈtrəʊl] **1.** *n.* **a)** *(of police)* Streife, *die; (of watchman)* Runde, *die;* Rundgang, *der; (of aircraft, ship)* Patrouille, *die; (Mil.)* Patrouille, *die;* **put sb. on ~:** jmdn. auf Streife *od. (Milit.)* Patrouille schicken; **policeman on ~:** Streifenpolizist, *der;* **be on** *or* **keep ~** ⟨*Soldat, Wächter:*⟩ patrouillieren; **b)** *(person, group) (Police)* Streife, *die; (Mil.)* Patrouille, *die;* **coast ~:** Küstenwache, *die;* Küstenwacht, *die;* **police ~:** Polizeistreife, *die;* **army ~:** Militärpatrouille, *die;* Militärstreife, *die;* **fire ~:** Brandwache, *die;* **c)** *(troops)* Spähtrupp, *der;* Spähpatrouille, *die;* **d)** *(unit) (of Scouts)* Fähnlein, *das; (of Guides)* Gilde, *die.* **2.** *v. i.,* **-ll-** patrouillieren; ⟨*Polizei:*⟩ Streife laufen/fahren; ⟨*Wachmann:*⟩ seine Runde[n] machen; ⟨*Flugzeug:*⟩ Patrouille fliegen. **3.** *v. t.,* **-ll-** patrouillieren durch (+ *Akk.*); abpatrouillieren ⟨*Straßen, Mauer, Gegend, Lager*⟩; patrouillieren vor (+ *Dat.*) ⟨*Küste, Grenze*⟩; ⟨*Polizei:*⟩ Streife laufen/fahren in (+ *Dat.*) ⟨*Straßen, Stadtteil*⟩; ⟨*Wachmann:*⟩ seine Runde[n] machen in (+ *Dat.*)
patrol: ~ **boat** *n.* Patrouillenboot, *das;* ~ **car** *n.* Streifenwagen, *der;* **~man** [pəˈtrəʊlmən] *n., pl.* ~men [pəˈtrəʊlmən] *(Amer.)* [Streifen]polizist, *der;* ~ **wagon** *n. (Amer.)* Gefangenenwagen, *der*
patron [ˈpeɪtrən] *n.* **a)** *(supporter)* Gönner, *der/*Gönnerin, *die; (of institution, campaign)* Schirmherr, *der/*Schirmherrin, *die;* ~ **of the arts** Kunstmäzen, *der;* **b)** *(customer) (of shop)* Kunde, *der/*Kundin, *die; (of restaurant, hotel)* Gast, *der; (of theatre, cinema)* Besucher, *der/*Besucherin, *die;* **'~s only'** „nur für Kunden/Gäste"; **c)** ~ **[saint]** Schutzheilige, *der/die;* Schutzpatron, *der/*Schutzpatronin, *die;* **d)** *(Brit. Eccl.)* Pfründner, *der/*Pfründnerin, *die*
patronage [ˈpætrənɪdʒ] *n.* **a)** *(support)* Gönnerschaft, *die;* Unterstützung, *die; (for campaign, institution)* Schirmherrschaft, *die;* **b)** *(customer's support)* Kundschaft, *die;* **we thank our customers for their ~:** wir danken unseren Kunden für ihr *od.* das in uns gesetzte Vertrauen; **withdraw one's ~:** ein Geschäft *usw.* nicht mehr betreten; **c)** *(dated: condescension)* Gönnerhaftigkeit, *die;* **with an air of ~:** mit Gönnermiene *od.* gönnerhafter Miene; **d)** *(Polit.)* Recht der Ämterbesetzung
patroness [ˈpeɪtrənes] *n.* **a)** *(supporter)* Gönnerin, *die; (of campaign, institution)* Schirmherrin, *die;* **b)** *(saint)* Schutzheilige, *die;* Schutzpatronin, *die*
patronise, patronising, patronisingly *see* **patroniz-**
patronize [ˈpætrənaɪz] *v. t.* **a)** *(frequent)* besuchen; **we hope you will continue to ~ our services** bitte beehren Sie uns bald wieder; bitte schenken Sie uns auch weiterhin Ihr Vertrauen; **b)** *(support)* fördern; unterstützen; **c)** *(condescend to)* ~ **sb.** jmdn. gönnerhaft *od.* von oben herab *od.* herablassend behandeln
patronizing [ˈpætrənaɪzɪŋ] *adj.,* **patronizingly** [ˈpætrənaɪzɪŋlɪ] *adv.* gönnerhaft; herablassend
patronymic [pætrəˈnɪmɪk] **1.** *n.* Patronymikon, *das;* Vater[s]name, *der.* **2.** *adj.* patronymisch
patsy [ˈpætsɪ] *n. (Amer. sl.)* Einfaltspinsel, *der (ugs.)*
patter [ˈpætə(r)] **1.** *n.* **a)** *(of rain)* Prasseln, *das; (of feet, footsteps)* Trappeln, *das;* Getrappel, *das;* **the ~ of tiny feet** *(fig.)* fröhliches Kindertreiben; **b)** *(language of salesman or comedian)* Sprüche *Pl.;* **sales ~:** Vertretersprüche *Pl.;* **keep up a ~:** ohne Unterbrechung reden; **c)** *(jargon)* Fachjar-

gon, *der.* **2.** *v. i.* **a)** *(make tapping sounds)* ‹*Regen, Hagel:*› prasseln; ‹*Schritte:*› trappeln; **b)** *(run)* trippeln

pattern ['pætən] **1.** *n.* **a)** *(design)* Muster, *das; (on carpet, wallpaper, cloth, etc. also)* Dessin, *das;* **frost ~s** Eisblumen; **a ~ of footprints** Fußspuren *Pl.;* **b)** *(form, order)* Muster, *das;* Schema, *das;* **follow a ~:** einem regelmäßigen Muster *od.* Schema folgen; **behaviour ~:** Verhaltensmuster, *das;* **~ of development** Entwicklungsschema, *das;* **~ of thought** Denkmuster, *das;* Denkschema, *das;* **~ of life** Lebensweise, *die;* **~ of events** Ereignisfolge; **c)** *(model)* Vorlage, *die; (for sewing)* Schnittmuster, *das;* Schnitt, *der; (for knitting)* Strickanleitung, *die;* Strickmuster, *das;* **follow a ~:** nach einer Vorlage arbeiten; *(knitting)* nach einem Strickmuster stricken; **a democracy on the British ~:** eine Demokratie nach britischem Muster; **d)** *(sample)* Muster, *das;* **e)** *(on target)* [Treffer]bild, *das.* **2.** *v. t.* **a)** *(model)* gestalten; **~ sth. after/on sth.** etw. einer Sache *(Dat.)* nachbilden; **she ~ed her behaviour on her father's** sie richtete sich in ihrem Verhalten nach dem Vorbild ihres Vaters; **b)** *(decorate)* mustern; **~ sth. with intricate designs** etw. mit verschlungenen Mustern verzieren

'**pattern-book** *n.* Musterbuch, *das*

patty ['pætɪ] *n.* **a)** *(pie, pastry)* Pastetchen, *das;* **b)** *(Amer.: of meat)* Frikadelle, *die*

paucity ['pɔ:sɪtɪ] *n. (formal)* Mangel, *der* **(of** an + *Dat.*); **~ of support** geringe *od.* mangelnde Unterstützung; **a growing ~ of ...:** immer weniger ...

Paul [pɔ:l] *pr. n. (Hist., as name) (of ruler etc.)* Paul; *(of saint)* Paulus

Pauline ['pɔ:laɪn] *adj. (Bibl.)* Paulinisch

paunch [pɔ:ntʃ] *n.* Bauch, *der;* Wanst, *der (salopp abwertend);* **develop a ~:** einen Bauch ansetzen

paunchy ['pɔ:ntʃɪ] *adj.* dickbäuchig; **become ~:** einen Bauch ansetzen

pauper ['pɔ:pə(r)] *n.* **a)** Arme, *der/die;* **they were ~s** sie waren arm; **live like ~s** leben wie arme Leute; **b)** *(Hist.)* Unterstützungsempfänger, *der/*-empfängerin, *die;* **~'s grave** Armengrab, *das*

pauperism ['pɔ:pərɪzm] *n., no pl.* Armut, *die;* **be reduced to ~:** völlig verarmen

pauperize ['pɔ:pəraɪz] *v. t.* arm machen; **be ~d** verarmt sein

pause [pɔ:z] **1.** *n.* **a)** Pause, *die;* **without [a] ~:** ohne Pause; **an anxious ~:** ängstliches Schweigen; **a ~ in the fighting** eine Kampfpause; **give sb. ~:** jmdm. zu denken geben; **b)** *(Mus.)* Fermate, *die.* **2.** *v. i.* **a)** *(wait)* eine Pause machen; eine Pause einlegen; ‹*Redner:*› innehalten; *(hesitate)* zögern; **~ for reflection/thought** in Ruhe überlegen; **he ~d to consider his next move** er hielt ein und überlegte, wie er weiter vorgehen solle; **~ for a rest** eine Erholungspause *od.* Ruhepause einlegen; **b)** *(linger)* verweilen **(upon, over** bei)

pavan ['pævən], **pavane** [pə'vɑ:n] *n. (Hist./Mus.)* Pavane, *die*

pave [peɪv] *v. t.* **a)** *(cover, lit. or fig.)* befestigen; *(with stones)* pflastern; **b)** *(fig.: prepare)* **~ the way for** *or* **to sth.** einer Sache *(Dat.)* den Weg ebnen; für etw. den Weg ebnen

pavement ['peɪvmənt] *n.* **a)** *(Brit.: footway)* Bürgersteig, *der;* Gehsteig, *der;* **b)** *(paved surface)* Belag, *der;* Pflaster, *das;* **c)** *(Amer.: roadway)* Fahrbahn, *die*

pavilion [pə'vɪljən] *n.* **a)** *(tent)* Festzelt, *das;* Pavillon, *der;* **b)** *(ornamental building)* Pavillon, *der;* **c)** *(Brit. Sport)* Klubhaus, *das;* **d)** *(stand at exhibition)* [Messe]pavillon, *der*

paving ['peɪvɪŋ] *n.* **a)** *(action)* Pflastern, *das;* **b)** *(paced surface)* Pflaster, *das*

'**paving-stone** *n.* Platte, *die;* Pflasterstein, *der*

paw [pɔ:] **1.** *n.* **a)** Pfote, *die; (of bear, lion, tiger)* Pranke, *die;* **b)** *(coll. derog.: hand)* Pfote, *die (ugs. abwertend);* **keep your ~s off [me]/off my car!** Pfoten weg!/Pfoten weg von meinem Auto! **2.** *v. t.* **a)** ‹*Hund, Wolf:*› mit der Pfote/den Pfoten berühren; ‹*Bär, Löwe, Tiger:*› mit der Pranke/den Pranken berühren; *(playfully)* tätscheln; **~ the ground** scharren; **b)** *(coll. derog.: fondle)* befummeln *(ugs.).* **3.** *v. i.* **a)** scharren; **~ at** mit der Pfote/den Pfoten *usw.* berühren; **b) ~ at sb./sth.** *(coll. derog.)* jmdn./etw. befummeln *(ugs.)*

pawl [pɔ:l] *n. (Mech. Engin.)* Sperre, *die;* Sperrklinke, *die*

[1]**pawn** [pɔ:n] *n.* **a)** *(Chess)* Bauer, *der;* **b)** *(fig.)* Schachfigur, *die;* **a ~ in the hands of Fate** ein Spielball des Schicksals

[2]**pawn** **1.** *n.* Pfand, *das;* **in ~:** verpfändet; versetzt; **put sth. in ~:** etw. verpfänden *od.* versetzen; **take sth. out of ~:** etw. einlösen. **2.** *v. t.* **a)** verpfänden; versetzen; **b)** *(fig.)* verpfänden ‹*Leben, Ehre, Wort, Seele*›

pawn: ~broker *n.* Pfandleiher, *der/*-leiherin, *die;* **~broking** *n., no art.* Pfandleihgeschäft, *das;* **~shop** *n.* Leihhaus, *das;* Pfandleihe, *die*

pawpaw [pɔ:'pɔ:] *see* **papaw**

pay [peɪ] **1.** *n., no pl., no indef. art. (wages)* Lohn, *der; (salary)* Gehalt, *das; (of soldier)* Sold, *der;* **the ~ is good** die Bezahlung ist gut; **be in the ~ of sb./sth.** für jmdn./etw. arbeiten; in jmds. Sold/im Sold einer Sache stehen *(abwertend); see also* **equal 1 a. 2.** *v. t.,* **paid** [peɪd] **a)** *(give money to)* bezahlen; *(fig.)* belohnen; **I paid him for the tickets** ich habe ihm das Geld für die Karten gegeben; **~ sb. to do sth.** jmdn. dafür bezahlen, daß er etw. tut; *see also* **coin 1; b)** *(hand over)* zahlen; *(so as to discharge an obligation)* bezahlen; **I paid what I owed him** ich habe meine Schulden bei ihm bezahlt; **~ the bill** die Rechnung bezahlen; **~ sb.'s expenses** *(reimburse)* jmds. Auslagen erstatten; **~ sb. £10** jmdm. 10 Pfund zahlen; **~ £10 for sth.** 10 Pfund für etw. [be]zahlen; **you ~s your money and you takes your choice** *(Brit. fig. coll.)* die Wahl steht bei Ihnen; **~ sth. into a bank account** etw. auf ein Konto ein[be]zahlen; **c)** *(bestow)* **~ sb. a visit** jmdm. einen Besuch abstatten *(geh.); see also* **attention 1 a; compliment 1 a; heed 2; regard 2 a; respect 1 b, e; tribute a; d)** *(yield)* einbringen, abwerfen ‹*Dividende usw.*›; **this job ~s very little** diese Arbeit bringt sehr wenig ein; **e)** *(be profitable to)* **it ~s him to live overseas** er steht sich finanziell besser *(ugs.),* seit er im Ausland lebt; **it would ~ her to do that** *(fig.)* es würde ihr nichts schaden *od.* es würde sich für sie bezahlt machen, das zu tun; **f) ~ the price** den Preis zahlen; **it's too high a price to ~:** das ist ein zu hoher Preis. *See also* **court 1 f; devil 1 c; piper a. 3.** *v. i.,* **paid a)** zahlen; **~ for sth./sb.** etw./für jmdn. bezahlen; **I'll ~ for you as well** ich bezahle für dich mit; **sth. ~s for itself** etw. macht sich bezahlt; **has this been paid for?** ist das schon bezahlt?; **I'd like to know what I'm ~ing for** ich wüßte gern, wofür ich eigentlich mein Geld ausgebe; **b)** *(yield)* sich lohnen; sich auszahlen; ‹*Geschäft:*› rentabel sein; **it ~s to be careful** es lohnt sich, vorsichtig zu sein; **c)** *(fig.: suffer)* büßen müssen; **if you do this you'll have to ~ for it later** wenn du das tust, wirst du später dafür büßen müssen. *See also* **crime b; nose 1 a; paid**

~ a'way *see* **~ out 1 b**

~ 'back *v. t.* **a)** zurückzahlen; **I'll ~ you back later** ich gebe dir das Geld später zurück; **b)** *(fig.)* erwidern ‹*Kompliment*›; sich revanchieren für ‹*Beleidigung, Untreue*›; **I'll ~ him back** ich werde es ihm heimzahlen; **I'll ~ him back with interest** ich werde es ihm mit Zins und Zinseszins zurückzahlen

~ 'in *v. t. & i.* einzahlen

~ 'off 1. *v. t.* **a)** auszahlen ‹*Arbeiter*›; abmustern ‹*Schiffsbesatzung*›; abbezahlen ‹*Schulden*›; ablösen ‹*Hypothek*›; befriedigen ‹*Gläubiger*›; *(fig.)* abgelten ‹*Verpflichtung*›; **b)** *(coll.: bribe)* schmieren *(salopp abwertend); (pay hush-money to)* Schweigegeld zahlen (+ *Dat.*). **2.** *v. i.* **a)** *(coll.)* sich auszahlen; sich bezahlt machen; **b)** *(Naut.)* leewärts steuern. *See also* **pay-off**

~ 'out 1. *v. t.* **a)** auszahlen; *(spend)* ausgeben; **we've already paid out a fortune to these people** wir haben schon ein Vermögen an diese Leute bezahlt *od.* für diese Leute ausgegeben; **~ out large sums on sth.** hohe Beträge für etw. ausgeben; **b)** *(Naut.)* ablaufen lassen ‹*Seil, Tau*›; **c)** *(coll.: punish)* **~ sb. out** es jmdm. heimzahlen; **~ sb. out for sth.** jmdm. etw. heimzahlen. *See also* **payout. 2.** *v. i.* bezahlen

~ 'up 1. *v. t.* zurückzahlen ‹*Schulden*›. **2.** *v. i.* zahlen. *See also* **paid-up**

payable ['peɪəbl] *adj.* **a)** *(due)* zahlbar; **be ~ to sb.** jmdm. *od.* an jmdn. zu zahlen sein; **b)** *(that may be paid)* zahlbar; **make a cheque ~ to the Post Office/to sb.** einen Scheck auf die Post/auf jmds. Namen ausstellen

pay: ~-as-you-'earn *attrib. adj. (Brit.)* **~-as-you-earn system/method** Quellenabzugsverfahren, *das;* **~-as-you-earn tax system** *Steuersystem, bei dem die Lohnsteuer direkt einbehalten wird;* **~-as-you-'enter** *attrib. adj.* ‹*Bus*› *in dem man das Fahrgeld beim Einsteigen bezahlt;* **~ award** *n.* Gehaltserhöhung, *die;* **~-bed** *n.* Privatbett, *das;* **~ cheque** *n.* Lohn-/Gehaltsscheck, *der;* **~-claim** *n.* Lohn-/Gehaltsforderung, *die;* **~-day** *n.* Zahltag, *der;* **~ dirt** *n. (Amer.)* abbauwürdiges Erzlager; **hit ~ dirt** *(fig.)* einen Volltreffer landen *(fig. ugs.)*

PAYE *abbr. (Brit.)* pay-as-you-earn

payee [peɪ'i:] *n.* Zahlungsempfänger, *der/*-empfängerin, *die*

pay envelope *(Amer.) see* **pay-packet**

payer ['peɪə(r)] *n.* Zahler, *der/*Zahlerin, *die;* **bad ~:** unzuverlässiger Zahler

'**pay-increase** *see* **pay-rise**

paying ['peɪɪŋ]: **~ 'guest** *n.* zahlender Gast; **~-'in book** *n. (Brit. Banking) Heft mit Einzahlungsscheinen;* **~-'in slip** *n. (Brit. Banking)* Einzahlungsschein, *der;* **~ patient** *n.* Privatpatient, *der/*-patientin, *die*

pay: ~load *n.* Nutzlast, *die;* **~master** *n.* Zahlmeister, *der; (fig.)* Geldgeber, *der;* **P~master 'General** *n. (Brit. Admin.)* Generalzahlmeister des englischen Schatzamts

payment ['peɪmənt] *n.* **a)** *(act) (of sum, bill, debt)* Begleichung, *die; (of interest, instalment)* Zahlung, *die; (of fine)* Bezahlung, *die; (of tax, fee)* Entrichtung, *die;* Zahlung, *die; (of debt, mortgage)* Abzahlung, *die;* Abtragung, *die;* **in ~ [for sth.]** als Bezahlung [für etw.]; **~ on account** Akontozahlung, *die;* **stop ~** ‹*Bank:*› die Zahlungen einstellen; **stop ~ on a cheque** einen Scheck sperren; **on ~ of ...:** gegen Zahlung von ...; **b)** *(amount)* Zahlung, *die;* **make a ~:** eine Zahlung leisten; **by monthly ~s** auf Monatsraten; **c)** *(fig.)* Belohnung, *die;* Lohn, *der;* **be fitting ~ for sth.** der gerechte Lohn für etw. sein

pay: ~ negotiations *n. pl.* Tarifverhandlungen; **~-off** *n. (sl.) (return)* Lohn, *der; (punishment)* Quittung, *die; (climax)* Clou, *der (ugs.); (bribe)* Bestechungsgeld, *das;* Schmiergeld, *das (ugs. abwertend)*

payola [peɪ'əʊlə] *n. (bribery)* Bestechung, *die; (bribe)* Bestechungsgeld, *das;* Schmiergeld, *das (ugs. abwertend)*

pay: ~-out *n.* Auszahlung, *die;* **~-packet** *n. (Brit.)* Lohntüte, *die;* **~ phone** *n.* Münzfernsprecher, *der;* **~-rise** *n.* Lohn-/Gehaltserhöhung, *die;* **~-roll** *n.* Lohnliste, *die;* **have 200 workers/people on the ~-roll** 200 Arbeiter beschäftigen/Beschäftigte haben; **be on sb.'s ~-roll** für jmdn. *od.* bei jmdm. arbeiten; **a ~-roll of about a hundred** etwa hundert Arbeitsplätze; **reduce the ~-roll** die Lohn- und Gehaltssumme senken; ~ **round** *n.* Tarifrunde, *die;* ~**-slip** *n.* Lohnstreifen, *der*/Gehaltszettel, *der;* ~ **station** *(Amer.) see* ~ **phone;** ~ **talks** *n. pl.* Tarifverhandlungen; ~ **television** *n.* Münzfernsehen, *das*

PC *abbr.* **a)** *(Brit.)* **police constable** Wachtm.; **b)** *(Brit.)* **Privy Counsellor** Geh. R.; Geh. Rat; **c) personal computer** PC

p.c. *abbr.* **per cent** v. H.

pct. *abbr. (Amer.)* **per cent** v. H.

pd. *abbr.* **paid** bez.

p.d.q. [pi:di:'kju:] *abbr. (sl.)* **pretty damn quick** verdammt schnell *(ugs.)*

PE *abbr.* **physical education**

pea [pi:] *n.* Erbse, *die; (plant)* Erbse[npflanze], *die;* **they are as like as two ~s [in a pod]** sie gleichen sich *(Dat.) od.* einander wie ein Ei dem anderen; *see also* **chick-pea; split pea; sweet pea**

peace [pi:s] *n.* **a)** *(freedom from war)* Frieden, *der;* Friede, *der (geh.); (treaty)* Frieden, *der;* Friedensschluß, *der;* **these countries are now at ~:** zwischen diesen Ländern herrscht jetzt Frieden; **maintain/restore ~:** den Frieden bewahren/wiederherstellen; ~**talks/treaty** Friedensgespräche *Pl.*/Friedensvertrag, *der;* **make ~ [with sb.]** [mit jmdm.] Frieden schließen; **the P~ of Utrecht** *(Hist.)* der Friede von Utrecht; **b)** *(freedom from civil disorder)* Ruhe und Ordnung; öffentliche Ordnung; *(absence of discord)* Frieden, *der;* **in ~ [and harmony]** in [Frieden und] Eintracht; **restore ~:** Ruhe und Ordnung wiederherstellen; **the [King's/Queen's] ~:** die öffentliche Ordnung; **bind sb. over to keep the ~:** jmdn. verwarnen *od.* rechtlich verpflichten, die öffentliche Ordnung zu wahren; **be at ~ [with sb./sth.]** mit jmdm./etw. in Frieden leben; **be at ~ with oneself** mit sich selbst im reinen sein; **make [one's] ~ [with sb.]** sich [mit jmdm.] aussöhnen *od.* versöhnen; **make one's ~ with God/the world** seinen Frieden mit Gott/der Welt machen; **hold one's ~:** schweigen; ruhig sein; **c)** *(tranquillity)* Ruhe, *die; (stillness)* Stille, *die;* Ruhe, *die;* **in ~:** in Ruhe; **leave sb. in ~:** jmdn. in Frieden *od.* in Ruhe lassen; **I get no ~:** ich habe keine ruhige Minute; **give sb. no ~:** jmdm. keine Ruhe lassen; **~ and quiet** Ruhe und Frieden; **the ~ and quiet of the countryside** die friedvolle Ruhe der Landschaft; **d)** *(mental state)* Ruhe, *die;* **find ~:** Frieden finden; **~ of mind** Seelenfrieden, *der;* innere Ruhe; **I shall have no ~ of mind until I know it** ich werde keine ruhige Minute haben, bis ich es weiß; **e)** *(in or following biblical use)* **~ be with** *or* **unto you** Friede sei mit dir/euch; **go in ~:** gehe/gehet hin in Frieden; **may his soul rest in ~:** er ruhe in Frieden; **he is at ~** *(literary: is dead)* er ruht in Frieden *(geh.). See also* **breach 1 a; justice c**

peaceable ['pi:səbl] *adj.* **a)** *(not quarrelsome)* friedfertig; friedliebend ⟨*Volk*⟩; *(calm)* friedlich; **b)** *(quiet, undisturbed)* friedlich

peaceably ['pi:səblı] *adv.* **a)** *(amicably)* friedlich; **b)** *(quietly, in peace)* friedlich; **go ~ about one's business** in Ruhe seinen Geschäften nachgehen

'**Peace Corps** *n. (Amer.)* Friedenskorps, *das*

peaceful ['pi:sfl] *adj.* friedlich; friedfertig ⟨*Person, Volk*⟩; ruhig ⟨*Augenblick*⟩; *see also* **coexistence**

peacefully ['pi:sfəlı] *adv.* friedlich; **die ~:** sanft entschlafen

peace: ~keeper *n.* Friedenswächter, *der;* **~-keeping 1.** *adj.* ⟨*Maßnahmen, Operationen*⟩ zur Friedenssicherung; **~-keeping force** Friedenstruppe, *die;* **2.** *n.* Friedenssicherung, *die;* **~-loving** *adj.* friedliebend; **~maker** *n.* Friedensstifter, *der*/-stifterin, *die;* **blessed are the ~makers** *(Bibl.)* selig sind die Friedfertigen; **~-offer** *n.* Friedensangebot, *das;* **~-offering** *n.* Friedensangebot, *das; (fig.)* Versöhnungsgeschenk, *das;* **~-pipe** *n.* Friedenspfeife, *die;* **~ plan** *n.* Friedensplan, *der;* **~time** *n.* Friedenszeiten *Pl.; attrib.* Friedens⟨*produktion, -wirtschaft, -stärke*⟩; in Friedenszeiten *nachgestellt*

peach [pi:tʃ] *n.* **a)** Pfirsich, *der;* **~es-and-cream complexion** Pfirsichhaut, *die;* **b)** *see* **peach-tree; c)** *(coll.)* **sb./sth. is a ~:** jmd./etw. ist spitze *od.* klasse *(ugs.);* **a ~ of a woman/man/house** eine klasse Frau/ein klasse Kerl *od.* Typ/ein klasse Haus *(ugs.);* **d)** *(colour)* Pfirsichton, *der*

peach: ~-blossom *n.* Pfirsichblüte, *die;* **~ 'brandy** *n.* Pfirsichbrandy, *der;* Pfirsichlikör, *der;* **~-coloured** *adj.* pfirsichfarben

'**pea-chick** *n.* Pfauküken, *das*

peach: ~ 'Melba *n.* Pfirsich Melba, *der;* **~-tree** *n.* Pfirsichbaum, *der*

'**peacock** *n.* Pfau, *der;* Pfauhahn, *der;* **strut like a ~:** wie ein Pfau einherstolzieren; **proud/vain as a ~:** stolz/eitel wie ein Pfau; **be proud as a ~ of sth.** vor Stolz auf etw. *(Akk.)* fast bersten

peacock: ~ 'blue 1. *adj.* pfauenblau; **2.** *n.* Pfauenblau, *das;* **~ butterfly** *n.* Tagpfauenauge, *das*

'**peafowl** *n.* Pfau, *der*

'**pea-green** *adj.* erbsengrün; maigrün

'**peahen** *n.* Pfauhenne, *die*

'**pea-jacket** *n.* Kolani, *der;* Pijacke, *die (Seew. veralt.)*

peak [pi:k] **1.** *n.* **a)** *(of cap)* Schirm, *der;* Schild, *der;* **b)** *(of mountain)* Gipfel, *der; (of waves)* Kamm, *der;* Krone, *die;* **c)** *(highest point)* Höhepunkt, *der;* **reach/be at/be past its ~:** seinen Höhepunkt erreichen/den Höhepunkt erreicht haben/den Höhepunkt überschritten haben; **his career was at its ~:** er stand auf dem Höhepunkt seiner Laufbahn; **d)** *(Naut.)* Piek, *die.* **2.** *attrib. adj.* Höchst-, Spitzen⟨*preise, -werte*⟩; **~ listening/viewing audience** höchste Einschaltquote; **~ listening/viewing period** Hauptsendezeit, *die.* **3.** *v. i.* seinen Höhepunkt erreichen; **~ too soon** *(Sport)* vorzeitig in Höchstform sein

[1]**peaked** [pi:kt] *adj.* **~ cap** Schirmmütze, *die*

[2]**peaked** *adj. (pinched)* spitz ⟨*Gesicht*⟩; abgehärmt, verhärmt ⟨*Person, Gesicht, Aussehen*⟩

peak: ~-hour *attrib. adj.* **~-hour travel** Fahren während der Hauptverkehrszeit; **~-hour traffic** Stoßverkehr, *der;* **~-hour listening period** Hauptsendezeit, *die;* **~ load** *n.* Spitzenlast, *die;* **the ~ load of traffic** der Stoßverkehr

peaky ['pi:kı] *adj.* kränklich; **look ~:** nicht gut aussehen; angeschlagen aussehen

peal [pi:l] **1.** *n.* **a)** *(ringing)* Geläut[e], *das;* Läuten, *das;* **~ of bells** Glockengeläut[e], *das;* Glockenläuten, *das;* **b)** *(set of bells)* Glockenspiel, *das;* **c)** *(loud sound)* **a ~ of laughter** schallendes Gelächter; **a ~ of thunder** ein Donnerschlag. **2.** *v. i.* ⟨*Glocken:*⟩ läuten; ⟨*Donner:*⟩ rollen; ⟨*Trompete:*⟩ schmettern. **3.** *v. t.* **a)** erschallen lassen; **b)** *(ring)* läuten ⟨*Glocken*⟩

~ 'out *v. i.* tönen

peanut ['pi:nʌt] *n.* Erdnuß, *die;* **~ butter** Erdnußbutter, *die;* **~s** *(coll.) (trivial thing)* ein Klacks *(ugs.);* kleine Fische *Pl.; (money)* ein paar Kröten *(salopp);* **this is ~s compared to ...:** das ist ein Klacks gegen ...; **work for ~s** für ein Butterbrot arbeiten *(ugs.);* **sell sth. for ~s** etw. für ein Butterbrot *od.* für einen Apfel und ein Ei verkaufen *(ugs.);* **this costs ~s compared to ...:** das ist [fast] geschenkt im Vergleich zu ... *(ugs.);* **be worth ~s** kaum etw. wert sein

pear [peə(r)] *n.* **a)** *(fruit)* Birne, *die;* **b)** *see* **pear-tree.** *See also* **anchovy pear; avocado pear; prickly pear**

'**pear-drop** *n. hartes Bonbon in Birnenform [mit Birnengeschmack]*

pearl [pɜ:l] *n.* **a)** Perle, *die;* **[string of] ~s** *(necklace)* Perlenkette, *die;* **b)** *(fig.)* Juwel, *das;* Kleinod, *das;* Perle, *die;* **be a ~ of architecture** ein Juwel der Baukunst sein; **~ of wisdom** *(often iron.)* Weisheit, *die;* **cast ~s before swine** *(fig.)* Perlen vor die Säue werfen *(salopp);* **c)** *(~-like thing)* Perle, *die;* **~s of dew** Tautropfen. *See also* **mother-of-pearl; seed-pearl**

pearl: ~ 'barley *n.* Perlengraupen *Pl.;* **~ 'bulb** *n.* matte Glühbirne; **~ 'button** *n.* Perlmutt[er]knopf, *der;* **~-diver** *n.* Perlentaucher, *der*/-taucherin, *die;* **~-fisher** *n.* Perlenfischer, *der*/-fischerin, *die;* **~-grey** *adj.* perlgrau; **~-oyster** *n.* Perlmuschel, *die*

pearly ['pɜ:lı] *adj.* **a)** perlmuttern, perlenähnlich, *(geh.)* perlengleich ⟨*Glanz, Schimmer*⟩; perl[en]förmig ⟨*Regen-, Tautropfen*⟩; **b)** *(set with pearls)* perlenbesetzt; **P~ Gates** Himmelstür, *die;* **~ king/queen** *(Brit.) Straßenverkäufer/-verkäuferin in London mit perlenbestickter Kleidung*

'**pear-shaped** *adj.* birnenförmig

peart [pɜ:t] *adj. (Amer.)* fröhlich

'**pear-tree** *n.* Birnbaum, *der;* Birne, *die*

peasant ['pezənt] *n.* **a)** [armer] Bauer, *der;* Landarbeiter, *der;* **~ farmer** Bauer, *der;* **~ uprising** Bauernaufstand, *der;* **~ economy** Agrarwirtschaft, *die;* **~ woman** Bauersfrau, *die;* **b)** *(coll. derog.) (ignorant or stupid person)* Bauer, *der (ugs. abwertend); (lower-class person)* Plebejer, *der (abwertend)*

peasantry ['pezəntrı] *n.* Bauernschaft, *die*

pease-pudding [pi:z'pʊdıŋ] *n.* Erbsenpudding, *der*

pea: ~-shooter *n.* Pusterohr, *das;* **~ 'soup** *n.* Erbsensuppe, *die;* **~-stick** *n.* Bohnenstange, *die*

peat [pi:t] *n.* **a)** *(substance)* Torf, *der;* **b)** *(piece)* Torfstück, *das;* Torfsode, *die;* **cut ~:** Torf stechen

peat: ~bog, *(Brit.)* **~moor** *ns.* Torfmoor, *das*

peaty ['pi:tı] *adj.* torfig

pebble ['pebl] *n.* Kiesel[stein], *der;* **he is/you are not the only ~ on the beach** es gibt noch andere

pebble: ~dash *n.* Kieselrauhputz, *der; attrib.* mit Kieselrauhputz *nachgestellt;* **~ glasses** *n. pl.* [dicke] Brille; **~ lens** *n.* [dickes] Brillenglas

pebbly ['peblı] *adj.* steinig

pecan [pı'kæn] *n.* **a)** *(nut)* Pekannuß, *die;* **b)** *(tree)* Pekannußbaum, *der*

peccadillo [pekə'dıləʊ] *n., pl.* **~es** *or* **~s** *(small sin)* leichte Verfehlung; *(small fault)* kleiner Fehler

peccary ['pekərı] *n. (Zool.)* Pekari, *das;* Nabelschwein, *das*

[1]**peck** [pek] **1.** *v. t.* **a)** hacken; picken ⟨*Körner*⟩; **the bird ~ed my finger/was ~ing the bark** der Vogel pickte mir *od.* mich in den Finger/pickte an der Rinde; **b)** *(kiss)* flüchtig küssen. **2.** *v. i.* picken **(at** nach); **~ at one's food** in seinem Essen herumstochern. **3.** *n.* **a) the hen gave its chick a ~:** die Henne pickte *od.* hackte nach ihrem Küken; **b)** *(kiss)* flüchtiger Kuß; Küßchen, *das*

~ 'out *v. t.* aushacken; auspicken

~ 'up *v. t.* aufpicken

[2]**peck** *n. (measure)* Viertelscheffel, *der;* **a ~ of trouble/dirt** *(fig.)* ein gerütteltes Maß an Sorgen/eine Menge Schmutz

pecker ['pekə(r)] *n.* **a)** *(Amer. sl.: penis)* Schwanz, *der (salopp);* **b) keep your ~ up** *(Brit. coll.)* halt die Ohren steif *(ugs.)*

pecking order ['pekıŋ ɔ:də(r)] *n.* Hackordnung, *die*

peckish ['pekıʃ] *adj.* **a)** *(coll.: hungry)* hungrig; **feel/get ~:** Hunger haben/bekommen; **b)** *(Amer. coll.: irritable)* gereizt

pectin ['pektɪn] *n. (Chem.)* Pektin, *das*

pectoral ['pektərl] **1.** *n.* **a)** *(Med.)* Hustenmittel, *das;* **b)** *in pl. (often joc.)* Brustmuskeln. **2.** *adj. (Anat.)* pektoral *(fachspr.);* Brust⟨*höhle, -atmung*⟩

pectoral: ~ 'cross *n. (Eccl.)* Pektorale, *das;* **~ fin** *n. (Zool.)* Brustflosse, *die;* **~ muscle** *n. (Anat.)* Brustmuskel, *der*

peculiar [pɪ'kju:lɪə(r)] *adj.* **a)** *(strange)* seltsam; eigenartig; sonderbar; **what a ~ person he is!** was ist er doch für ein komischer Kauz! *(ugs.);* **I feel [slightly] ~:** mir ist [etwas] komisch; **a ~ incident occurred** es passierte etwas Seltsames; **b)** *(especial)* besonder...; **be of ~ interest [to sb.]** [für jmdn.] von besonderem Interesse sein; **c)** *(belonging exclusively)* eigentümlich **(to** *Dat.***)**; **this bird is ~ to South Africa** dieser Vogel kommt nur in Südafrika vor; **she has a ~ style of acting, all her own** sie hat einen ganz eigenen Stil, zu spielen

peculiarity [pɪkju:lɪ'ærɪtɪ] *n.* **a)** *no pl., no indef. art. (unusualness)* Ausgefallenheit, *die; (of behaviour, speech)* Sonderbarkeit, *die;* Merkwürdigkeit, *die;* **b)** *(odd trait)* Eigentümlichkeit, *die;* **behavioural peculiarities** seltsame Verhaltensweisen; **c)** *(distinguishing characteristic)* [charakteristisches] Merkmal; Kennzeichen, *das; (special characteristic)* Besonderheit, *die*

peculiarly [pɪ'kju:lɪəlɪ] *adv.* **a)** *(strangely)* seltsam; eigenartig; sonderbar; **b)** *(especially)* besonders; **c)** *(in a way that is one's own)* **be something ~ British** etwas rein Britisches sein; **a treatment ~ his own** eine ganz eigene Behandlung

pecuniary [pɪ'kju:nɪərɪ] *adj. (of money)* finanziell, *(geh.)* pekuniär ⟨*Hilfe, Überlegungen*⟩; **~ award** Geldpreis, *der*

pedagog *(Amer.) see* **pedagogue**

pedagogic[al] [pedə'gɒgɪk(l), pedə'gɒdʒɪk(l)] *adj.* **a)** *(arch./derog.: of a pedagogue)* belehrend; schulmeisterlich *(abwertend);* **b)** *(of pedagogy)* pädagogisch

pedagogue ['pedəgɒg] *n.* **a)** *(arch.: teacher)* Pädagoge, *der*/Pädagogin, *die;* **b)** *(derog.: pedantic teacher)* Schulmeister, *der (abwertend)*

pedagogy ['pedəgɒdʒɪ] *n.* Pädagogik, *die*

pedal ['pedl] **1.** *n.* **a)** *(Mus.) (organ-key, on piano)* Pedal, *das; (organ-stop control)* Fußtritt, *der;* Fußhebel, *der;* **loud ~:** rechtes Pedal; Fortepedal, *das;* **soft ~:** linkes Pedal; Pianopedal, *das;* **b)** *(of bicycle; Mech. Engin., Motor Veh.)* Pedal, *das.* **2.** *v. i., (Brit.)* **-ll- a)** *(work cycle ~s)* **~ [away]** in die Pedale treten; strampeln *(ugs.);* **b)** *(ride)* [mit dem Fahrrad] fahren; radeln *(ugs.);* **~ by/off** vorbeiradeln/losradeln *(ugs.);* **c)** *(Mus.) (on organ)* das Pedal spielen; *(on piano)* die Pedale benutzen. **3.** *v. t., (Brit.)* **-ll-** *(propel)* fahren mit ⟨*Fahrrad, Dreirad*⟩; **~ one's bike** radfahren; radeln *(ugs.)*

pedal: ~-bin *n.* Treteimer, *der;* **~-car** *n.* Tretauto, *das*

pedalo ['pedələʊ] *n., pl.* **~s** Tretboot, *das*

'pedal-pushers *n. pl.* *dreiviertellange Damen-/Mädchenhose*

pedant ['pedənt] *n.* **a)** *(one who overrates learning)* Stubengelehrte, *der/die;* **b)** *(stickler for formal detail)* Pedant, *der*/Pedantin, *die (abwertend);* Kleinigkeitskrämer, *der*/-krämerin, *die (abwertend)*

pedantic [pɪ'dæntɪk] *adj.* **a)** *(ostentatiously learned)* schulmeisterlich *(abwertend);* **b)** *(unduly concerned with formal detail)* pedantisch *(abwertend)*

pedantry ['pedəntrɪ] *n.* Pedanterie, *die;* Kleinlichkeit, *die (abwertend)*

peddle ['pedl] *v. t.* **a)** auf der Straße verkaufen; *(from door to door)* hausieren mit; handeln mit, *(ugs.)* dealen mit ⟨*Drogen, Rauschgift*⟩; **b)** *(fig.: disseminate)* hausieren [gehen] mit ⟨*Theorie, Vorschlag*⟩; verbreiten ⟨*Neuigkeiten, Klatsch, Gerücht*⟩

peddler ['pedlə(r)] *see* **pedlar**

pederast ['pedəræst] *n.* Päderast, *der*

pederasty ['pedəræstɪ] *n.; no pl., no indef. art.* Päderastie, *die*

pedestal ['pedɪstl] *n.* Sockel, *der;* **knock sb. off his ~** *(fig.)* jmdn. von seinem Sockel stoßen; **put** *or* **set sb./sth. on a ~** *(fig.)* jmdn./etw. in den Himmel heben *(ugs.)*

pedestrian [pɪ'destrɪən] **1.** *adj. (uninspired)* trocken; langweilig. **2.** *n.* Fußgänger, *der*/-gängerin, *die;* **~-controlled** *or* **~-operated lights** Bedarfsampel, *die*

pedestrian 'crossing *n.* Fußgängerüberweg, *der*

pedestrianism [pɪ'destrɪənɪzm] *n., no pl. (of style)* Trockenheit, *die;* Langweiligkeit, *die*

pedestrianize [pɪ'destrɪənaɪz] *v. t.* zur Fußgängerzone machen

pedestrian 'precinct *see* **precinct a**

pediatri- *(Amer.) see* **paediatri-**

pedicel ['pedɪsl], **pedicle** ['pedɪkl] *n. (Biol.)* Stiel, *der; (of flower)* [Blüten]stengel, *der*

pedicure ['pedɪkjʊə(r)] **1.** *n. no pl., no art.* Pediküre, *die;* Fußpflege, *die;* **give sb. a ~:** jmdn. pediküren

pedigree ['pedɪgri:] **1.** *n.* **a)** *(genealogical table)* Stammbaum, *der;* Ahnentafel, *die (geh.);* **b)** *(ancestral line)* Stammbaum, *der;* Ahnenreihe, *die; (of animal)* Stammbaum, *der;* **c)** *(derivation)* Herkunft, *die;* **d)** *no pl., no art. (ancient descent)* **have ~, be a man/woman of ~:** von berühmten Ahnen abstammen. **2.** *adj. (with recorded line of descent)* mit Stammbaum *nachgestellt*

pedigreed ['pedɪgri:d] *see* **pedigree 2**

pediment ['pedɪmənt] *n. (Archit.) (in Grecian style)* Giebeldreieck, *das; (in Roman or Renaissance style)* Ziergiebel, *der*

pedlar ['pedlə(r)] *n.* **a)** Straßenhändler, *der*/-händlerin, *die; (from door to door)* Hausierer, *der*/Hausiererin, *die; (selling drugs)* Rauschgifthändler, *der*/-händlerin, *die;* Dealer, *der*/Dealerin, *die (ugs.);* **b)** *(fig.: disseminator)* **be a ~ of gossip/scandal** *etc.* Klatsch/Skandalgeschichten *usw.* verbreiten

pedometer [pɪ'dɒmɪtə(r)] *n.* Pedometer, *das (fachspr.);* Schrittzähler, *der*

peduncle [pɪ'dʌŋkl] *n. (Bot., Zool.)* Stiel, *der*

pee [pi:] *(coll.)* **1.** *v. i.* pinkeln *(salopp);* Pipi machen *(Kinderspr.).* **2.** *n.* **a)** *(urination)* **need/have a ~:** pinkeln müssen/pinkeln *(salopp);* **I must go for a ~:** ich muß mal eben pinkeln *(salopp);* **b)** *(urine)* Pipi, *das (Kinderspr.)*

peek [pi:k] **1.** *v. i.* gucken *(ugs.);* **no ~ing!** nicht gucken!; **~ at sb./sth.** zu jmdm./etw. hingucken; **~ in at sb.** zu jmdm. hereingucken. **2.** *n. (quick)* kurzer Blick; *(sly)* verstohlener Blick; **take a quick ~ round** sich schnell umgucken; **have a ~ through the keyhole** durch das Schlüsselloch gucken *(ugs.);* **take a quick ~ at sb.** kurz zu jmdm. hingucken; **give sb. a ~ at sth.** jmdn. einen Blick auf etw. *(Akk.)* werfen lassen

peekaboo ['pi:kəbu:] **1.** *n. (Amer.) see* **peep-bo. 2.** *adj.* durchsichtig; *(with pattern of small holes)* mit Lochmuster *nachgestellt;* **~ design** Lochmuster, *das*

peel [pi:l] **1.** *v.t.* schälen; **~ the shell off an egg/the skin off a banana** ein Ei/eine Banane schälen; *see also* **eye 1a. 2.** *v. i.* **a)** ⟨*Person, Haut:*⟩ sich schälen *od. (bes. nordd.)* pellen; ⟨*Rinde, Borke:*⟩ sich lösen; ⟨*Farbe:*⟩ abblättern; **b)** *(sl.: undress)* sich ausziehen. **3.** *n.* Schale, *die; see also* **candy 2**

~ a'way 1. *v. t.* abschälen. **2.** *v. i.* **a)** ⟨*Haut:*⟩ sich schälen *od. (bes. nordd.)* pellen; ⟨*Rinde, Borke:*⟩ sich lösen; ⟨*Farbe:*⟩ abblättern; **b)** *(veer away)* ausscheren

~ 'back *v. t.* halb abziehen ⟨*Kabelmantel, Bananenschale*⟩; zurückziehen ⟨*Bettdecke*⟩; umschlagen ⟨*Stoffmuster*⟩

~ 'off 1. *v. t.* abschälen; abstreifen, ausziehen ⟨*Kleider*⟩. **2.** *v. i.* **a)** *see* **~ away 2a; b)** *(veer away)* ausscheren; **c)** *see* **~ 2b**

peeler ['pi:lə(r)] *n.* Schäler, *der;* Schälmesser, *das*

peeling ['pi:lɪŋ] *n.* Stück Schale; **~s** Schalen

[1]peep [pi:p] **1.** *v. i.* ⟨*Maus, Vogel:*⟩ piep[s]en; *(squeal)* quieken. **2.** *n. (shrill sound)* Piepsen, *das; (coll.: slight utterance)* Piep[s], *der (ugs.);* **one ~ out of you and ...:** ein Pieps [von dir], und ...

[2]peep 1. *v. i.* **a)** *(look through narrow aperture)* gucken *(ugs.);* spähen *(geh., veralt., noch landsch.);* **b)** *(look furtively)* verstohlen gucken; linsen *(ugs.);* **~ round** sich umgucken; **no ~ing!** nicht gucken!; **c)** *(come into view)* **~ out** [he]rausgucken; hervorgucken; *(fig.: show itself)* zum Vorschein kommen; durchscheinen. **2.** *n.* kurzer Blick; **steal a ~ at sb.** verstohlen zu jmdm. hingucken; **take a ~ through the curtain** durch die Gardine spähen *od. (ugs.)* linsen

peep-bo ['pi:pbəʊ] **1.** *n.* Guck-guck-Spiel, *das.* **2.** *int.* guck, guck; kuckuck

'peep-hole *n.* Guckloch, *das*

peeping Tom [pi:pɪŋ 'tɒm] *n.* Spanner, *der (ugs.);* Voyeur, *der; attrib.* voyeuristisch

'peep-show *n.* **a)** *(exhibition of small pictures in box)* Guckkastenschau, *die;* **b)** *(erotic spectacle)* Peep-Show, *die*

peep-toe[d] ['pi:ptəʊ(d)] *adj.* vorn offen ⟨*Schuh*⟩; zehenfrei ⟨*Sandale*⟩; **the shoes had a ~ design** die Schuhe waren vorn offen

[1]peer [pɪə(r)] *n.* **a)** *(Brit.: member of nobility)* **~ [of the realm]** Peer, *der; see also* **life peer; b)** *(noble of any country)* hoher Adliger; **the ~s of France** der Hochadel Frankreichs; **c)** *(equal in standing)* Gleichgestellte, *der/die;* **be judged by a jury of one's ~s** von seinesgleichen gerichtet werden; **among her social ~s** unter ihresgleichen; **d)** *(equal in attainment)* Ebenbürtige, *der/die;* **find sb.'s ~:** jemanden finden, der jmdm. ebenbürtig ist

[2]peer *v. i.* *(look searchingly)* forschend schauen; *(look with difficulty)* angestrengt schauen; **~ at sth./sb.** *(searchingly)* [sich *(Dat.)*] etw. genau ansehen/jmdn. forschend *od.* prüfend ansehen; *(with difficulty)* [sich *(Dat.)*] etw. angestrengt ansehen/jmdn. angestrengt ansehen; **~ into a cave/the distance** in eine Höhle/die Ferne spähen; **~ down at sb.** zu jmdm. hinunter-/herunterspähen

peerage ['pɪərɪdʒ] *n.* **a)** *no pl. (Brit.: body of peers)* **the ~:** die Peers; **be raised to the ~:** in den Adelsstand erhoben werden; **b)** *(Brit.: rank of peer)* Peerswürde, *die; see also* **life peerage; c)** *(nobility of any country)* Adel, *der;* **d)** *(book)* Peerskalender, *der; britisches Adelsverzeichnis*

peeress ['pɪəres] *n.* Peereß, *die*

'peer group *n.* Peer-group, *die (Psych., Soziol.)*

peerless ['pɪəlɪs] *adj.* beispiellos

peeve [pi:v] *(coll.)* **1.** *n.* **a)** *(cause of annoyance)* **it was a bit of a ~:** es war ganz schön ärgerlich; **it was one of his ~s that ...:** es wurmte ihn, daß ... *(ugs.); see also* **[1]pet 2c; b)** *(mood)* **be in a [real] ~:** [stock]sauer sein *(ugs.).* **2.** *v. t. (irritate)* nerven *(salopp);* **it ~d me that ...:** es wurmte *od.* fuchste mich, daß ... *(ugs.)*

peeved [pi:vd] *adj. (coll.)* sauer *(ugs.);* **be/get ~ with sb.** auf jmdn. sauer sein/werden; **be ~ at/get ~ about sth.** über etw. *(Akk.)* sauer sein/wegen etw. sauer werden

peevish ['pi:vɪʃ] *adj. (querulous)* nörgelig *(abwertend);* quengelig *(ugs.)* ⟨*Kind*⟩; *(showing vexation)* gereizt

peevishly ['pi:vɪʃlɪ] *adv.* mißmutig; *(in vexation)* **do sth. ~:** etw. gereizt tun

peewit ['pi:wɪt] *n.* **a)** *(Ornith.)* Kiebitz, *der;* **b)** *(cry)* Kiwitt, *das*

peg [peg] **1.** *n. (pin, bolt) (for holding together parts of framework)* Stift, *der; (for tying things to)* Pflock, *der; (for hanging things on)* Haken, *der; (clothes ~)* Wäscheklammer, *die; (for holding tent-ropes)* Hering, *der; (for marking cribbage scores etc.)* Stift, *der; (Mus.: for adjusting strings)* Wirbel, *der;* **off the ~** *(Brit.: ready-made)* von der Stange *(ugs.);* **take sb. down a ~ [or two]** *(fig.)* jmdm. einen Dämpfer aufsetzen *od.* geben; **be taken down a ~ or two** *(fig.)* einen Dämpfer bekommen; **a ~ to hang sth. on** *(fig.)* ein Aufhänger für etw.; *see also* **hole 1 a. 2.** *v. t.,* **-gg- a)** *(fix with ~)* mit Stiften/Pflöcken befestigen; **b)** *(Econ.: stabilize)* stabilisieren; *(support)* stützen; *(freeze)* einfrieren; **~ wages/prices/exchange rates** Löhne/Preise/Wechselkurse stabil halten; **c)** *(Cribbage)* durch eingesteckte Holzstifte anzeigen ⟨*Spielstand*⟩; **~ two holes** den Holzstift zwei Löcher weiter einstecken; **they are level ~ging at school** *(fig.)* sie sind gleich gut in der Schule. **3.** *v. i.,* **-gg-: keep ~ging along** bei der Stange bleiben; **she's still ~ging at her writing** sie schreibt immer noch unverdrossen weiter

~ a'way *v. i.* schuften *(ugs.);* **~ away for four hours** vier Stunden lang ununterbrochen schuften; **[keep] ~[ging] away with sth.** nicht lockerlassen mit etw. *(ugs.)*

~ 'down *v. t.* **a)** *(secure with ~s)* festpflocken; **b)** *see* **pin down a**

~ 'out 1. *v. t.* **a)** *(spread out and secure)* ausspannen ⟨*Felle etc.*⟩; *(Brit.: attach to line)* [draußen] aufhängen ⟨*Wäsche*⟩; **b)** *(mark)* abstecken ⟨*Gebiet, Fläche*⟩. **2.** *v. i.* **a)** *(sl.) (faint)* zusammenklappen *(ugs.); (die)* den Löffel abgeben *(salopp); (cease to function)* den Geist aufgeben *(ugs.);* **b)** *(Croquet)* den Zielpflock treffen; **c)** *(Cribbage)* gewinnen

peg: ~-board *n.* **a)** *(for games)* Lochbrett, *das;* **b)** *(board holding hooks)* gelochte Platte; **~-leg** *n.* **a)** *(artificial leg)* Holzbein, *das;* **b)** *(person)* Stelzfuß, *der (ugs.)*

peignoir ['peɪnwɑ:(r)] *n.* Négligé, *das*

pejorative [pɪ'dʒɒrətɪv] **1.** *adj.* pejorativ *(Sprachw.);* abwertend; **~ word** Pejorativum, *das (Sprachw.).* **2.** *n.* Pejorativum, *das (Sprachw.)*

pejoratively [pɪ'dʒɒrətɪvlɪ] *adv.* abwertend

pekan ['pekən] *n. (Zool.)* Fischermarder, *der*

peke [pi:k] *(coll.) see* **Pekingese 1 a**

Pekingese [pi:kɪŋ'i:z] **(Pekinese** [pi:kɪ'ni:z]**) 1.** *n., pl. same* **a) ~ [dog]** Pekinese, *der;* **b)** *(person)* Pekinger, *der*/Pekingerin, *die.* **2.** *attrib. adj.* Pekinger; **~ man/woman** Pekinger, *der*/Pekingerin, *die*

pelican ['pelɪkən] *n. (Ornith.)* Pelikan, *der*

'pelican crossing *n. (Brit.)* Ampelübergang, *der*

pellagra [pɪ'lægrə, pɪ'leɪgrə] *n. (Med.)* Pellagra, *das*

pellet ['pelɪt] *n.* **a)** *(small ball)* Kügelchen, *das; (mass of food)* Pellet, *das (fachspr.);* **b)** *(pill)* Pille, *die;* **c)** *(regurgitated mass)* Gewölle, *das (Zool., Jägerspr.); (excreted mass)* Kötel, *der (nordd.);* **d)** *(small shot)* Schrot, *der od. das;* **peppered with shotgun ~s** mit Schrot[kugeln] gespickt

pell-mell [pel'mel] **1.** *adv.* **a)** *(in disorder)* durcheinander; *(without discrimination)* wahllos; **everything was heaped together ~:** alles wurde durcheinander auf einen Haufen geworfen; **b)** *(headlong)* Hals über Kopf. **2.** *adj.* [kunter]bunt; chaotisch

pellucid [pɪ'lu:sɪd, pɪ'lju:sɪd] *adj.* **a)** *(transparent)* durchsichtig; [glas]klar ⟨*Wasser*⟩; **b)** *(clear in style)* klar; in einem klaren Stil gehalten ⟨*Schriften*⟩; **c)** *(mentally clear)* klar ⟨*Verstand, Kopf*⟩

pelmet ['pelmɪt] *n. (of wood)* Blende, *die; (of fabric)* Schabracke, *die*

Peloponnese ['peləpəni:s] *pr. n.* **the ~:** der *od.* die Peloponnes

pelota [pɪ'ləʊtə] *n. (Sport)* Pelota, *die;* Pelotaspiel, *das*

[1]pelt [pelt] *n.* **a)** *(of sheep or goat)* Fell, *das; (of fur-bearing animal)* [Roh]fell, *das;* **sheep's ~:** Schaffell, *das;* **b)** *(Tanning: raw skin)* enthaartes Fell

[2]pelt 1. *v. t.* **a)** *(assail with missiles, lit. or fig.)* **~ sb. with sth.** jmdn. mit etw. bewerfen *od. (ugs.)* bombardieren; **~ sb. with questions** jmdn. mit Fragen überschütten *od. (ugs.)* bombardieren; **b)** *(throw a stream of)* **~ sth. at sb.** jmdn. mit etw. bewerfen *od. (ugs.)* bombardieren; **they ~ed abuse at each other** *(fig.)* sie warfen sich [gegenseitig] Beschimpfungen an den Kopf. **2.** *v. i.* **a)** ⟨*Regen:*⟩ prasseln; **it was ~ing down [with rain]** es goß wie aus Kübeln *(ugs.);* **b)** *(run fast)* rasen *(ugs.);* pesen *(ugs.);* **he set off as fast as he could ~:** so schnell er konnte, raste *od.* peste er los *(ugs.).* **3.** *n., no pl., no indef. art.* **[at] full ~:** mit Karacho *(ugs.);* volle Pulle *(salopp)*

pelvic ['pelvɪk] *adj. (Anat.)* Becken-

pelvis ['pelvɪs] *n., pl.* **pelves** ['pelvi:z] *or* **~es** *(Anat.)* Becken, *das;* **renal ~:** Nierenbecken, *das*

[1]pen [pen] **1.** *n.* **a)** *(enclosure)* Pferch, *der;* **b)** *(Navy)* Bunker, *der.* **2.** *v. t.,* **-nn- a)** *(shut up in ~)* einpferchen; **b)** *(confine)* **~ sb. in a corner** jmdn. in eine Ecke drängen

~ 'in *v. t.* **a)** einpferchen; **b)** *(fig.: restrict)* einengen; **feel ~ned in by one's life** sein Leben sehr beengend finden

~ 'up *v. t. see* **~ in b**

[2]pen 1. *n.* **a)** *(for writing)* Federhalter, *der;* **make one's living by the ~:** vom Schreiben leben; **the ~ is mightier than the sword** *(prov.)* die Feder ist mächtiger als das Schwert; *see also* **ball-pen; fountain-pen; paper 1 a; b)** *(quill-feather)* Feder, *die; see also* **quill-pen. 2.** *v. t.,* **-nn-** niederschreiben; **~ a letter to/a note for sb.** jmdm. einen Brief/ein paar Worte schreiben

[3]pen *n. (female swan)* weiblicher Schwan

[4]pen *n. (Amer. sl.: penitentiary)* Knast, *der (ugs.);* **do eight years in the ~:** acht Jahre [Knast] abreißen *(salopp) od. (ugs.)* absitzen

penal ['pi:nl] *adj.* **a)** *(of punishment)* Straf⟨*vollzug, -gesetzbuch*⟩; *(concerned with inflicting punishment)* strafrechtlich ⟨*Bestimmungen, Klauseln*⟩; Straf⟨*gesetze, -gesetzgebung, -maßnahme*⟩; **~ reform** Strafvollzugsreform, *die;* **b)** *(punishable)* strafbar ⟨*Handlung, Tat*⟩; **~ offence** Straftat, *die;* **c) ~ colony** *or* **settlement** Strafkolonie, *die*

penalize (penalise) ['pi:nəlaɪz] *v. t.* **a)** *(subject to penalty)* bestrafen; pönalisieren *(geh.); (Sport)* eine Strafe verhängen gegen; **b)** unter Strafe stellen ⟨*Handlung, Tat*⟩

penal 'servitude *n., no pl., no indef. art. (Brit. Law. Hist.)* Zwangsarbeit, *die*

penalty ['penltɪ] *n.* **a)** *(punishment)* Strafe, *die;* **the ~ for this offence is imprisonment/a fine** auf dieses Delikt steht Gefängnis/eine Geldstrafe; **pay/have paid the ~/the ~ for** *or* **of sth.** *(lit. or fig.)* dafür/für etw. büßen [müssen]/gebüßt haben; **his ~ was a £50 fine** er erhielt eine [Geld]strafe von 50 Pfund; **on** *or* **under ~ of £200/of instant dismissal** bei einer Geldstrafe von 200 Pfund/unter Androhung *(Dat.)* der sofortigen Entlassung; **b)** *(disadvantage)* Preis, *der;* **c)** *(Sport: disadvantage imposed) (Horse-racing)* Pönalität, *die; (Golf)* **~ [stroke]** Strafschlag, *der; (Footb., Rugby) see* **penalty kick;** *(Hockey) see* **penalty bully; penalty corner; penalty shot; d)** *(Bridge)* Strafpunkte

penalty: ~ area *n. (Footb.)* Strafraum, *der;* **~ box** *n. (Footb.)* Strafraum, *der; (Ice Hockey)* Strafbank, *die;* **~ bully** *n. (Hockey)* Siebenmeterball, *der;* **~ clause** *n.* Strafklausel, *die;* **~ corner** *n. (Hockey)* Strafecke, *die;* **~ goal** *n. (Hockey)* Siebenmetertor, *das; (Rugby)* durch einen Straftritt erzieltes Tor; **~ kick** *n. (Footb.)* Strafstoß, *der;* Elfmeter, *der; (Rugby)* Straftritt, *der;* **~ shot** *n. (Hockey)* Strafschlag, *der;* **~ spot** *n. (Footb.)* Strafstoßmarke, *die;* Elfmeterpunkt, *der; (Hockey)* Siebenmeterpunkt, *der*

penance ['penəns] *n., no pl., no art.* Buße, *die;* **act of ~:** Bußübung, *die;* Bußwerk, *das;* **undergo/do ~:** büßen/Buße tun

'pen-and-ink *adj.* Feder⟨*zeichnung, -skizze*⟩

pence *see* **penny**

penchant ['pɑ̃fɑ̃] *n.* Schwäche, *die;* Vorliebe, *die* **(for** für); **have a ~ for doing sth.** dazu neigen, etw. zu tun

pencil ['pensɪl] **1.** *n.* **a)** Bleistift, *der;* **red/coloured ~:** Rot-/Bunt- *od.* Farbstift, *der;* **write in ~:** mit Bleistift schreiben; **a ~ drawing, a drawing in ~:** eine Bleistiftzeichnung; *see also* **lead pencil; b)** *(cosmetic)* Stift, *der;* **eyebrow ~:** Augenbrauenstift, *der.* **2.** *v. t., (Brit.)* **-ll- a)** *(mark)* mit Bleistift/Farbstift markieren; **b)** *(sketch)* mit Bleistift zeichnen *od.* skizzieren; **c)** *(write with ~)* mit einem Bleistift/Farbstift schreiben; **d)** *(write tentatively)* entwerfen; skizzieren; *see also* **~ in b**

~ 'in *v. t.* **a)** *(shade with ~)* mit Bleistift [aus]schraffieren; **b)** *(note or arrange provisionally)* vorläufig notieren

'pencil-case *n.* Griffelkasten, *der; (made of a soft material)* Federmäppchen, *das;* Schreibmäppchen, *das*

pencilled *(Amer.:* **penciled)** ['pensɪld] *adj.* mit Bleistift geschrieben; nachgezogen ⟨*Augenbrauen*⟩

'pencil-sharpener *n.* Bleistiftspitzer, *der*

pendant ['pendənt] **1.** *n.* **a)** *(hanging ornament)* Anhänger, *der; (light)* Hängelampe, *die;* **b)** *(companion)* Pendant, *das (geh.);* **c)** *see* **pennant a. 2.** *adj. see* **pendent**

pendent ['pendənt] **1.** *adj.* **a)** *(hanging)* herabhängend; **b)** *(overhanging)* überhängend

pending ['pendɪŋ] **1.** *adj.* **a)** *(undecided)* unentschieden ⟨*Angelegenheit, Sache*⟩; anhängig *(Rechtsspr.),* schwebend ⟨*Verfahren*⟩; laufend ⟨*Verhandlungen*⟩; **be ~** ⟨*Verfahren:*⟩ noch anhängig sein *(Rechtsspr.),* noch schweben; ⟨*Sache, Angelegenheit:*⟩ noch unentschieden sein *od.* in der Schwebe sein; ⟨*Entscheidung, Probleme:*⟩ noch anstehen; ⟨*Debatte, Verhandlungen:*⟩ noch im Gang sein; **a treaty was ~:** es wurde über einen Vertrag verhandelt; **b)** *(about to come into existence)* bevorstehend ⟨*Krieg*⟩; **patent ~:** Patent angemeldet. **2.** *prep. (until)* **~ his return** bis zu seiner Rückkehr; **~ the final settlement** bis zur endgültigen Regelung; **~ full discussion of the matter** bis die Angelegenheit ausdiskutiert ist

'pending-tray *n.* Ablage für noch Unerledigtes

pendulous ['pendjʊləs] *adj.* **a)** *(suspended, hanging down)* herabhängend; Hänge⟨*backen, -brüste, -ohren*⟩; **b)** *(oscillating)* pendelnd

pendulum ['pendjʊləm] *n.* Pendel, *das;* **the swing of the ~** *(fig.)* der Umschwung; **according to the swing of the ~:** je nachdem, nach welcher Seite das Pendel ausschlägt *(fig.)*

penetrable ['penɪtrəbl] *adj.* **a)** *(capable of being entered)* durchdringlich; **scarcely ~:** fast undurchdringlich; **b)** *(fig.: capable of being found out)* ergründbar; **be ~:** sich ergründen lassen; **c)** *(permeable)* durchlässig

penetrate ['penɪtreɪt] **1.** *v. t.* **a)** *(find access into)* eindringen in (+ *Akk.*); vordringen in (+ *Akk.*) ⟨*unbekannte Regionen*⟩; aufbrechen ⟨*Safe*⟩; *(pass through)* durchdringen; **get sth. to ~ sb.'s mind** etw. in jmds. Kopf reinkriegen *(ugs.);* **~ sb.'s disguise** *(fig.)* hinter jmds. Maske *(Akk.)* schauen; **b)** *(fig.: find out)* ergründen ⟨*Geheimnis*⟩; durchschauen ⟨*Plan, Absicht, Gedanken*⟩; herausfinden ‹*Wahrheit*›; **c)** *(permeate)* dringen in (+ *Akk.*); *(fig.)* durchdringen; *(infiltrate)* infiltrieren; unterwandern; ‹*Spion:*› sich einschleusen in (+ *Akk.*); **d)** *(see into)* ‹*Augen:*› durchdringen ‹*Dunkelheit, Nebel*›; **e)** *(sexually)* eindringen in (+ *Akk.*); penetrieren *(geh.)*. **2.** *v.i.* **a)** *(make a way)* ~ **into/to sth.** in etw. *(Akk.)* eindringen/zu etw. vordringen; ~ **through sth.** durch etw. hindurch dringen; **the cold ~d through the whole house** die Kälte durchdrang das ganze Haus; **b)** *(be understood or realized)* **my hint did not ~:** mein Wink wurde nicht verstanden; **something's finally ~d!** der Groschen ist endlich gefallen *(ugs.)*

penetrating ['penɪtreɪtɪŋ] *adj.* **a)** *(easily heard)* durchdringend; **b)** *(gifted with insight)* scharf ‹*Verstand*›; *(showing insight)* scharfsinnig ‹*Bemerkung, Kommentar, Studie*›; scharf ‹*Beobachtung*›; verstehend ‹*Blick*›

penetration [penɪ'treɪʃn] *n.* **a)** *(finding of access into)* Eindringen, *das* (**of** in + *Akk.*); *(of safe)* Aufbrechen, *das; (act of passing through)* Durchdringen, *das; (passage through)* Durchdringung, *die;* **b)** *no pl. (fig.: discernment)* Scharfsinn, *der;* Scharfsinnigkeit, *die;* **c)** *(act of permeating)* Durchdringen, *das;* Durchdringung, *die; (infiltration)* Infiltration, *die;* Unterwanderung, *die;* **d)** *(seeing into sth.)* Durchdringen, *das;* **e)** *(sexual)* Eindringen des Gliedes [in die Scheide]; Penetration, *die (geh.)*

penetrative ['penɪtrətɪv] *adj.* **a)** *(acute)* scharf ‹*Verstand, Beobachtung*›; **b)** *(permeating)* eindringend

'pen-friend *n.* Brieffreund, *der*/-freundin, *die*

penguin ['peŋgwɪn] *n.* Pinguin, *der*

'penholder *n.* Federhalter, *der*

penicillin [penɪ'sɪlɪn] *n. (Med.)* Penizillin, *das*

peninsula [pɪ'nɪnsjʊlə] *n.* Halbinsel, *die;* **the Lleyn ~:** die Halbinsel Lleyn

peninsular [pɪ'nɪnsjʊlə(r)] *adj.* **a)** *(of a peninsula)* peninsular[isch]; Halbinsel-; *(like a peninsula)* halbinselartig; **b)** *(Hist.: of Spain and Portugal)* **the P~ War** der Spanische Unabhängigkeitskrieg

penis ['pi:nɪs] *n., pl.* **~es** *or* **penes** ['pi:ni:z] *(Anat.)* Penis, *der;* männliches Glied

'penis envy *n. (Psych.)* Penisneid, *der*

penitence ['penɪtəns] *n., no pl.* Reue, *die*

penitent ['penɪtənt] **1.** *adj.* reuevoll *(geh.)*; reuig *(geh.)* ‹*Sünder*›; **be ~:** bereuen; **feel [sincerely] ~:** [echte] Reue empfinden; **be deeply ~ about sth.** tiefe Reue über etw. *(Akk.)* empfinden. **2.** *n. (repentant sinner)* reuiger Sünder/reuige Sünderin; *(person doing penance)* Büßer, *der*/Büßerin, *die (Rel.)*

penitential [penɪ'tenʃl] *adj.* reuevoll; reuig *(geh.)*; Buß‹*tag, -gebet*›; **the ~ psalms** *(Relig.)* die Bußpsalmen

penitentiary [penɪ'tenʃərɪ] **1.** *n. (Amer.)* Straf[vollzugs]anstalt, *die;* [Justiz]vollzugsanstalt, *die.* **2.** *adj.* **a)** *(of penance)* ~ **pilgrimage** Bußpilgerfahrt, *die;* **b)** *(of reformatory treatment)* ~ **system** Strafvollzug, *der*

penitently ['penɪtəntlɪ] *adv.* reuevoll *(geh.)*; reumütig *(öfter scherzh.)* ‹*zurückkehren*›; **behave ~:** Reue zeigen

pen: ~knife *n.* Taschenmesser, *das;* **~-light** *n.* [Mini]stablampe, *die*

penmanship ['penmənʃɪp] *n., no pl.* **a)** *(skill in handwriting)* Schönschreiben, *das;* **a piece of good/bad ~:** ein schön/schlecht geschriebener Text; **b)** *(style of writing)* Schrift, *die*

'pen-name *n.* Schriftstellername, *der*

pennant ['penənt] *n.* **a)** *(Naut.: tapering flag)* Stander, *der;* **broad ~:** Doppelstander, *der;* **b)** *(Amer.: flag symbolizing championship)* Meisterschaftswimpel, *der;* **c)** *see* **pennon**

penniless ['penɪlɪs] *adj. (having no money)* **be ~:** keinen Pfennig Geld haben; *(fig.: be poor)* mittellos sein; **be left ~:** völlig mittellos *od.* ohne einen Pfennig Geld dastehen

pennon ['penən] *n.* **a)** Wimpel, *der;* **b)** *(Mil.: long narrow flag)* Fähnchen, *das;* Fähnlein, *das*

penn'orth ['penəθ] *see* **pennyworth**

Pennsylvania Dutch [pensɪlveɪnɪə 'dʌtʃ] *n.* **a)** *no pl., no indef. art. (dialect)* Pennsylvaniadeutsch, *das;* Pennsilfaanisch, *das;* **b)** *constr. as pl.* **the ~:** die Pennsylvaniendeutschen

penny ['penɪ] *n., pl. usu.* **pennies** ['penɪz] *(for separate coins),* **pence** [pens] *(for sum of money)* **a)** *(British coin, monetary unit)* Penny, *der;* **fifty pence** fünfzig Pence; **two/five/ten/twenty/fifty pence [piece]** Zwei-/Fünf-/Zehn-/Zwanzig-/Fünfzigpencestück, *das od.* -münze, *die; see also* **halfpenny; b)** *(Amer. coll.: one-cent coin)* Cent, *der;* Centstück, *das;* **c) keep turning up like a bad ~** *(coll.)* immer wieder auftauchen; **the ~ has dropped** *(fig. coll.)* der Groschen ist gefallen *(ugs.)*; **pennies from heaven** *(coll.)* ein warmer Regen *(fig. ugs.)*; **in for a ~, in for a pound** *(prov.)* wennschon, dennschon *(ugs.)*; **a pretty ~** *(coll.)* eine hübsche *od.* schöne Stange Geld *(ugs.)*; ein hübsches Sümmchen *(ugs.)*; **I was not a ~ the worse** *(fig.)* es hat mich nichts gekostet *(fig.)*; **take care of the pence** *or* **pennies** im Kleinen sparen; **take care of the pence** *or* **pennies, and the pounds will look after themselves** spare im Kleinen, dann hast du im Großen; **not have two pennies to rub together** ohne einen Pfennig sein; keinen Pfennig haben; **look twice at every ~:** jeden Pfennig dreimal umdrehen; **a ~ for your thoughts** *(coll.)* woran denkst du [gerade]?; **sth. is two** *or* **ten a ~:** etw. gibt es wie Sand am Meer *(ugs.)*; **be ~ wise** im Kleinen sparsam sein; **be ~ wise and pound foolish** im Kleinen sparsam und im Großen verschwenderisch sein; am falschen Ende sparen. *See also* **¹count 2a; honest e; name 1a; spend a**

penny: ~ 'dreadful *n. (Brit.) (cheap storybook)* Groschenheft, *das (abwertend); (cheap novel)* Groschenroman, *der (abwertend);* **~ 'farthing [bicycle]** *n. (Brit. coll)* Hochrad, *das;* **~-pincher** ['penɪpɪnʃə(r)] *n.* Pfennigfuchser, *der*/-fuchserin, *die (ugs.)*; **~-pinching** ['penɪpɪnʃɪŋ] **1.** *n., no pl., no indef. art.* Pfennigfuchserei, *die (ugs.)*; Knauserei, *die (ugs. abwertend)*; **2.** *adj.* knaus[e]rig *(ugs. abwertend)*; **~weight** *n.* Pennyweight, *das;* **~ 'whistle** *see* **whistle 3b**

pennyworth ['pen(ɪw)əθ] *n.* **a)** *pl. same* **a ~ of bread/six ~ of sweets** für einen Penny Brot/für sechs Pence Bonbons; **not a ~ [of]** *(fig.: not even a small amount)* nicht für fünf Pfennig *(ugs.)*; **b)** *(bargain)* **a good/bad ~:** ein guter/schlechter Kauf

penology [pi:'nɒlədʒɪ] *n.* Pönologie, *die*

pen: ~-pal *n. (coll.) see* **pen-friend; ~ portrait** *n.* Charakterbild, *das;* **~-pusher** *n. (coll.)* Büromensch, *der; (male)* Bürohengst, *der (ugs. abwertend);* **~-pushing** *n., no pl., no indef. art. (coll.)* Schreibkram, *der (ugs. abwertend)*

pension ['penʃn] **1.** *n.* **a)** *(given by employer)* Rente, *die; (payment to retired civil servant also)* Pension, *die;* Ruhegehalt, *das (Amtsspr.)*; **retire on a ~:** in *od.* auf Rente gehen *(ugs.)*; ‹*Beamter:*› in Pension gehen; **be on a ~ [from one's company]** eine Rente [von seiner Firma] beziehen; **~ fund** Rentenfonds, *der;* Pensionfonds, *der;* **~ scheme** Rentenversicherung, *die;* **the company has** *or* **operates a ~ fund/scheme for its employees** die Firma hat eine Pensionskasse/betriebliche Altersversorgung für ihre Beschäftigten; **b)** *(given by State)* Rente, *die;* **disability** *or* **disablement ~:** Erwerbsunfähigkeitsrente, *die;* Invalidenrente, *die (ugs.)*; **widow's ~:** Witwenrente, *die;* **war ~:** Kriegsopferrente, *die;* **~ book** ≈ Rentenausweis, *der;* **~ day** Rentenzahltag, *der; see also* **old-age; c)** ['pɑ̃sjɔ̃] *(European boarding-house)* Pension, *die.* **2.** *v.t.* eine Rente zahlen (+ *Dat.*); **be ~ed** eine Rente bekommen

~ 'off *v.t.* **a)** *(discharge)* berenten *(Amtsspr.)*; auf Rente setzen *(ugs.)*; pensionieren ‹*Lehrer, Beamten*›; **b)** *(fig.: cease to use)* ausmustern; ausrangieren *(ugs.)*

pensionable ['penʃənəbl] *adj.* **a)** *(entitled to a pension)* rentenberechtigt; pensionsberechtigt ‹*Beamter*›; **b)** *(entitling to a pension)* zu einer Rente berechtigend; **reach ~ age** das Rentenalter erreichen; *(as civil servant)* das Pensionsalter erreichen; **~ salary/earnings** rentenfähiges Gehalt/rentenfähiger Verdienst

pensioned-off [penʃnd'ɒf] *adj. (fig.)* ausrangiert *(ugs.)*

pensioner ['penʃənə(r)] *n.* Rentner, *der*/Rentnerin, *die; (retired civil servant)* Pensionär, *der*/Pensionärin, *die;* Ruhegehaltsempfänger, *der*/-empfängerin, *die*

pensive ['pensɪv] *adj.* **a)** *(plunged in thought)* nachdenklich; **b)** *(sorrowfully thoughtful)* schwermütig

pensively ['pensɪvlɪ] *adv. see* **pensive:** nachdenklich; schwermütig

pent [pent] *adj.* **a)** *(literary)* eingedämmt; unterdrückt ‹*Atem*›; **b)** ~ **in** *or* **up** eingedämmt ‹*Fluß*›; angestaut ‹*Wut, Ärger*›; *see also* **pent-up**

pentagon ['pentəgən] *n.* **a)** *(Geom.)* Fünfeck, *das;* Pentagon, *das (fachspr.)*; **b) the P~** *(Amer. Polit.)* das Pentagon

pentagonal [pen'tægənl] *adj. (Geom.)* fünfeckig; pentagonal *(fachspr.)*; fünfseitig ‹*Pyramide, Prisma*›

pentagram ['pentəgræm] *n.* Pentagramm, *das;* Drudenfuß, *der*

pentameter [pen'tæmɪtə(r)] *n. (Pros.)* Pentameter, *der*

pentane ['penteɪn] *n. (Chem.)* Pentan, *das*

pentaprism ['pentəprɪzm] *n.* Penta[dachkant]prisma, *das;* **~ viewfinder** *(Photog.)* Prismensucher, *der*

Pentateuch ['pentətju:k] *n. (Bibl.)* **the ~:** die fünf Bücher Mose; der Pentateuch *(fachspr.)*

pentathlete [pen'tæθli:t] *n.* Fünfkämpfer, *der*/-kämpferin, *die*

pentathlon [pen'tæθlən] *n. (Sport)* Fünfkampf, *der*

penta'tonic *adj. (Mus.)* pentatonisch; Fünfton-; **~ scale** fünfstufige Tonleiter

Pentecost ['pentɪkɒst] *n. (Relig.)* Pfingsten, *das;* Pfingstfest, *das; (Jewish harvest festival)* Ernte[dank]fest, *das*

pentecostal [pentɪ'kɒstl] *attrib. adj. (Relig.)* pfingstlich; Pfingst‹*gottesdienst, -hymne, -bewegung*›

Pentecostal 'Church *n. (Relig.)* Pfingstkirche, *die*

pent: ~house *n.* **a)** *(house, flat)* Penthaus, *das;* Penthouse, *das;* **b)** *(sloping roof)* Schleppdach, *das;* **~-up** *attrib. adj.* angestaut ‹*Ärger, Wut*›; verhalten ‹*Freude*›; unterdrückt ‹*Sehnsucht, Gefühle*›

penultimate [pe'nʌltɪmət] *adj.* vorletzt...

penumbra [pɪ'nʌmbrə] *n., pl.* **~e** [pɪ'nʌmbri:] *or* **~s a)** Halbschatten, *der;* **b)** *(Astron.: of sunspot)* Penumbra, *die*

penurious [pɪ'njʊərɪəs] *adj.* **a)** *(poor)* arm ‹*Person*›; entbehrungsreich ‹*Zeit*›; armselig, kümmerlich ‹*Verhältnisse*›; **b)** *(stingy)* geizig; knauserig *(ugs. abwertend)*

penury ['penjʊərɪ] *n., no pl.* Armut, *die;* Not, *die*

peon ['pi:ən, pju:n] *n.* **a)** *(in Latin America: day-labourer)* Tagelöhner, *der;* Peon, *der;* **~ labour** Peonenarbeit, *die;* **b)** *(in India and Pakistan: messenger, attendant)* Bote, *der;* Laufbursche, *der*

peony ['pi:ənɪ] *n. (Bot.)* Pfingstrose, *die;* Päonie, *die;* ~ **red** päonienrot; tiefrot

people ['pi:pl] **1.** *n.* **a)** *(persons composing nation, community, etc.)* Volk, *das;* **b)** *constr. as pl. (persons forming class etc.)* Leute *Pl.;* Menschen; **city/country** ~ *(inhabitants)* Stadt-/Landbewohner; *(who prefer the city/the country)* Stadt-/Landmenschen; **village** ~: Dorfbewohner; **local** ~: Einheimische; **working** ~: arbeitende Menschen; Werktätige *(bes. DDR);* **coloured/white** ~: Farbige/Weiße; ~ **of wealth** reiche *od.* begüterte Leute *Pl.;* **her [own] sort/kind of** ~: ihresgleichen; *see also* **choose 1 a; c)** *constr. as pl. (subjects of ruler)* Volk, *das; (congregation)* Gemeinde, *die;* **d)** *constr. as pl. (persons not of nobility)* **the** ~: das [gemeine] Volk; **e)** *constr. as sing. or pl. (voters)* Volk, *das;* **will of the** ~: Volkswille, *der (Polit.);* **go to the** ~: Wahlen ausschreiben; **f)** *constr. as pl. (persons in general)* Menschen; Leute *Pl.; (as opposed to animals)* Menschen; ~ **say he's very rich** die Leute sagen *od.* man sagt *od.* es heißt, daß er sehr reich sei; er soll sehr reich sein; **that is quite enough to alarm** ~: das reicht zur Genüge, um einen in Alarm zu versetzen; **a crowd of** ~: eine Menschenmenge; **don't tell** ~ **about this** erzähle niemandem davon; ~ **are like that** so sind die Menschen; **I don't understand** ~ **any more** ich verstehe die Welt nicht mehr; **'some** ~ *(certain persons, usu. with whom the speaker disagrees)* gewisse Leute; *(you)* manche Leute; **some '**~! Leute gibt es!; **honestly, some '**~! also wirklich!; **listen, you** ~! hört mal [zu]!; **what do you** ~ **think?** was denkt ihr [denn]?; **you of 'all** ~ **ought ...:** gerade du solltest ...; **who do you think I saw at the party? 'Bill, of all** ~! wen, glaubst du, habe ich auf der Party getroffen? Ausgerechnet Bill!; **no sign of any** ~: keine Menschenseele; **g)** *constr. as pl. (relatives)* Familie, *die.* **2.** *v. t.* **a)** *(fill with* ~ *or animals)* bevölkern; **b)** *(inhabit)* bevölkern; *(become inhabitant of)* besiedeln

peopled ['pi:pld] *adj.* bevölkert

People's Re'public *n. (Polit.)* Volksrepublik, *die;* **the** ~ **of China** die Volksrepublik China

pep [pep] *(coll.)* **1.** *n., no pl., no indef. art.* Schwung, *der;* Pep, *der (salopp);* **be full of** ~: viel Schwung *od. (salopp)* Pep haben. **2.** *v. t.,* **-pp-:** ~ **[up]** aufpeppen *(ugs.)*

peplum ['pepləm] *n. (Fashion)* Schößchen, *das*

pepper ['pepə(r)] **1.** *n.* **a)** Pfeffer, *der;* **black/white** ~: schwarzer/weißer Pfeffer; **b)** *(capsicum plant)* Paprika, *der; (fruit)* Paprikaschote, *die;* **red/yellow/green** ~: roter/gelber/grüner Paprika; **sweet** ~: Gemüsepaprika, *der. See also* **cayenne. 2.** *v. t.* **a)** *(sprinkle with* ~*)* pfeffern; **b)** *(besprinkle)* übersäen; **c)** *(pelt with missiles)* bombardieren *(ugs., auch fig.);* ~ **the target with shot** das Ziel mit Schrot spicken

pepper: ~**-and-'salt** *n. (Textiles)* Pfeffer und Salz; *attrib.* pfeffer- und salzfarben; ~**corn** *n.* Pfefferkorn, *das;* ~**corn rent** symbolischer Pachtzins; ~**-mill** *n.* Pfeffermühle, *die;* ~**mint** *n.* **a)** *(plant)* Pfefferminze, *die;* **b)** *(sweet)* Pfefferminz, *das; attrib.* Pfefferminz⟨*bonbon, -drops, -pastille*⟩; **c)** *(oil)* Pfefferminzöl, *das;* ~**-pot** *n.* Pfefferstreuer, *der*

peppery ['pepərɪ] *adj.* pfeff[e]rig; *(spicy)* scharf; *(fig.: pungent)* scharf; *(fig.: hot-tempered)* jähzornig; **the soup is rather** ~: die Suppe schmeckt ziemlich stark nach Pfeffer/die Suppe ist ziemlich scharf

'pep pill *n. (coll.)* Peppille, *die (ugs.);* Aufputschtablette, *die*

peppy ['pepɪ] *adj. (sl.)* lebhaft, quirlig *(ugs.);* schwungvoll ⟨*Tanz*⟩

pepsin ['pepsɪn] *n. (Chem.)* Pepsin, *das*

'pep talk *n. (coll.)* Aufmunterung, *die;* **give sb. a** ~: jmdm. ein paar aufmunternde Worte sagen

peptic ['peptɪk] *adj. (Physiol.)* peptisch *(fachspr.);* Verdauungs-

peptic 'ulcer *n. (Med.)* peptisches Ulkus *(fachspr.);* Magengeschwür, *das*

peptide ['peptaɪd] *n. (Chem.)* Peptid, *das*

per [pə(r), *stressed* pɜ:(r)] *prep.* **a)** *(by means of)* per ⟨*Post, Bahn, Schiff, Bote*⟩; durch ⟨*Spediteur, Herrn X.*⟩; **b)** *(according to)* **[as]** ~ **sth.** wie in etw. *(Dat.)* angegeben; laut ⟨*Anweisung, Preisliste*⟩; **as** ~ **usual** *(joc.)* wie üblich; **c)** *(for each)* pro; **£50** ~ **week** 50 Pfund in der Woche *od.* pro Woche; **fifty kilometres** ~ **hour** fünfzig Kilometer in der *od.* pro Stunde; **get 11 francs** ~ **pound** 11 Francs für ein Pfund bekommen

peradventure [pərəd'ventʃə(r), perəd'ventʃə(r)] *(arch.) adv.* vielleicht; **lest** ~ **...:** für den Fall, daß ...; **if** ~: im Fall[e], daß ...

perambulator [pə'ræmbjʊleɪtə(r)] *(Brit. formal) see* **pram**

per annum [pər 'ænəm] *adv.* im Jahr; pro Jahr *(bes. Kaufmannsspr., ugs.)*

per capita [pə 'kæpɪtə] **1.** *adv.* pro Kopf; pro Person; **earnings** ~: Pro-Kopf-Einkommen, *das.* **2.** *adj.* Pro-Kopf-⟨*Einkommen, Verbrauch usw.*⟩; ~ **tax** Kopfsteuer, *die*

perceivable [pə'si:vəbl] *see* **perceptible**

perceive [pə'si:v] *v. t.* **a)** *(with the mind)* spüren; bemerken; ⟨*menschlicher Geist:*⟩ wahrnehmen; ~ **sb.'s thoughts** jmds. Gedanken erraten; **b)** *(through the senses)* wahrnehmen; **we** ~**d a figure in the distance** wir erblickten in der Ferne eine Gestalt; **c)** *(regard mentally in a certain way)* wahrnehmen; ~**d** vermeintlich ⟨*Bedrohung, Gefahr, Wert*⟩

per cent *(Brit.; Amer.:* **percent***)* [pə 'sent] **1.** *adv.* **ninety** ~ **effective** zu 90 Prozent wirksam; *see also* **hundred 1 c. 2.** *adj.* **a 5** ~ **increase** ein Zuwachs von 5 Prozent; ein fünfprozentiger Zuwachs. **3.** *n.* **a)** *see* **percentage; b)** *(hundredth)* Prozent, *das*

percentage [pə'sentɪdʒ] *n.* **a)** *(rate or proportion per cent)* Prozentsatz, *der;* **a high** ~ **of alcohol** ein hoher Alkoholgehalt; **what** ~ **of 48 is 11?** wieviel Prozent von 48 sind 11?; ~ **lead/improvement** prozentualer Vorsprung/prozentuale Verbesserung; **b)** *(proportion)* [prozentualer] Anteil

per'centage sign *n.* Prozentzeichen, *das*

perceptible [pə'septɪbl] *adj.* wahrnehmbar; **be quite** ~: ganz offensichtlich sein

perceptibly [pə'septɪblɪ] *adv.* sichtlich; sichtbar, merklich ⟨*schrumpfen, welken*⟩

perception [pə'sepʃn] *n.* **a)** *(act)* Wahrnehmung, *die; (result)* Erkenntnis, *die;* **have keen** ~**s** ein stark ausgeprägtes Wahrnehmungsvermögen haben; **b)** *no pl. (faculty)* Wahrnehmungsvermögen, *das;* **colour** ~: Farbensinn, *der;* **depth** ~: Tiefensehen, *das (Med.);* ~ **of sounds** Gehör, *das;* ~ **of objects** gegenständliche Wahrnehmung; **c)** *(intuitive recognition)* Gespür, *das* **(of** für); *(instance)* Erfassen, *das;* **the direct** ~ **of truth** das unmittelbare Erfassen der Wahrheit; **have no clear** ~ **of sth.** keine klare Vorstellung von etw. haben

perceptive [pə'septɪv] *adj.* **a)** *(discerning)* scharf ⟨*Auge*⟩; fein ⟨*Gehör, Nase, Geruchssinn*⟩; scharfsinnig ⟨*Person*⟩; **b)** *(having intuitive recognition or insight)* einfühlsam ⟨*Person, Zeitungsartikel, Bemerkung*⟩

perceptively [pə'septɪvlɪ] *adv.* **a)** *(discerningly)* mit scharfer Wahrnehmung; **b)** *(with intuitive recognition or insight)* einfühlsam

perceptiveness [pə'septɪvnɪs], **perceptivity** [pɜ:sep'tɪvɪtɪ] *ns., no pl.* **a)** *(discernment)* ~ **of the senses** scharfes Wahrnehmungsvermögen; **b)** *(intuitive recognition, insight)* Einfühlsamkeit, *die*

¹perch [pɜ:tʃ] *n., pl. same or* ~**es** *(Zool.)* Flußbarsch, *der*

²perch 1. *n.* **a)** *(horizontal bar)* Sitzstange, *die; (for hens)* Hühnerstange, *die;* **b)** *(place to sit)* Sitzplatz, *der;* **c)** *(fig.: elevated or secure position)* guter Posten; **knock sb. off his** ~: jmdn. von seinem hohen Roß herunterholen; **come off one's** ~: von seinem hohen Roß herunterkommen *od.* steigen; **d)** *(Brit.: measure) (of length)* Perch, *das;* $5\frac{1}{2}$ Yards; *(of area)* **[square]** ~ *(Brit.)* Quadratperch, *das.* **2.** *v. i.* **a)** sich niederlassen; **b)** *(be supported)* sitzen. **3.** *v. t.* setzen/stellen/legen

perchance [pə'tʃɑ:ns] *adv. (arch.)* **a)** *(possibly)* möglicherweise; vielleicht; **b)** *see* **peradventure**

perched [pɜ:tʃt] *adj.* **be** ~ ⟨*Vogel:*⟩ sitzen; **stand** ~ **on a cliff** hoch auf einer Klippe stehen; **a village** ~ **on a hill** ein hoch oben auf einem Berg gelegenes Dorf; **with his hat** ~ **on the back of his head** mit hinten auf dem Kopf sitzendem Hut

percipient [pə'sɪpɪənt] *adj.* **a)** *(conscious)* wahrnehmend; **be** ~ **of sth.** in der Lage sein, etw. zu erkennen; **b)** *(discerning)* scharf ⟨*Augen*⟩; fein ⟨*Gehör*⟩; scharfsichtig ⟨*Kritiker*⟩

percolate ['pɜ:kəleɪt] **1.** *v. i.* **a)** *(ooze)* ~ **through sth.** durch etw. [durch]sickern; **b)** *(fig.: spread gradually)* vordringen; **c)** *(be brewed in percolator)* ⟨*Kaffee:*⟩ durchlaufen. **2.** *v. t.* **a)** *(permeate)* sickern durch ⟨*Gestein*⟩; **b)** *(fig.: penetrate)* dringen in (+ *Akk.*) ⟨*Bewußtsein*⟩; **c)** *(brew in percolator)* [mit der Kaffeemaschine] machen ⟨*Kaffee*⟩

percolation [pɜ:kə'leɪʃn] *n.* **a)** *(passage of liquid through filter)* [Durch]sickern, *das;* **b)** *(fig.: diffusion by spreading)* Vordringen, *das;* **c)** *(of coffee)* Filtern, *das*

percolator ['pɜ:kəleɪtə(r)] *n.* Kaffeemaschine, *die*

percussion [pə'kʌʃn] *n.* **a)** *(Mus.) (playing by striking)* Anschlag, *der; (group of instruments)* Schlagzeug, *das; attrib.* Schlagzeug⟨*gruppe, -band, -begleitung*⟩; ~ **instrument** Schlaginstrument, *das;* ~ **section** Schlagzeug, *das;* **b)** *(forcible striking)* **explode by** ~: bei Erschütterung explodieren; **c)** *(Med.)* Perkussion, *die; (massage)* Klopfmassage, *die*

per'cussion cap *n. (Arms)* Zündhütchen, *das; (in toy)* Zündblättchen, *das*

percussionist [pə'kʌʃənɪst] *n. (Mus.)* Schlagzeuger, *der/*-zeugerin, *die*

per diem [pɜ: 'di:em] **1.** *adv.* pro Tag; täglich. **2.** *adj.* täglich; **on a** ~ **basis** tageweise. **3.** *n. (allowance)* Tagegeld, *das; (payment)* Entgelt, *das*

perdition [pə'dɪʃn] *n., no pl., no art. (literary: eternal death)* Verdammnis, *die;* **escape** ~: der [ewigen] Verdammnis entkommen; **damn you to** ~! sei auf ewig verdammt!

peregrination [perɪgrɪ'neɪʃn] *n. (arch./joc.)* **a)** *no pl. (travelling)* Reise, *die; (joc.)* Umherreisen, *das;* **b)** *in pl. (travels)* Reisen; **during your** ~**s** *(joc.)* auf deinen Streifzügen

peregrine ['perɪgrɪn] *n.* ~ **[falcon]** *(Ornith.)* Wanderfalke, *der*

peremptorily [pə'remptərɪlɪ, 'perɪmptərɪlɪ] *adv.* **a)** *(so as to admit no contradiction)* kategorisch; *(imperiously)* herrisch; gebieterisch *(geh.);* **b)** *(dogmatically)* beharrlich, hartnäckig ⟨*leugnen*⟩; **speak** ~ **on sth.** sich dogmatisch zu etw. äußern

peremptory [pə'remptərɪ, 'perɪmptərɪ] *adj.* **a)** *(admitting no contradiction)* kategorisch; *(imperious)* herrisch; gebieterisch *(geh.);* **b)** *(essential)* unbedingt; unerläßlich ⟨*Vorschrift*⟩; **c)** *(dogmatic)* beharrlich; hartnäckig; **d)** *(Law)* ~ **writ** gerichtliche Verfügung; ~ **challenge** Ablehnung [eines Geschworenen] ohne Angabe der Gründe

perennial [pə'renjəl] **1.** *adj.* **a)** *(lasting all year)* ganzjährig; perennierend *(fachspr.)* ⟨*Quelle, Brunnen, Bach*⟩; **b)** *(lasting indefinitely)* immerwährend; ewig ⟨*Jugend, Mythos, Suche*⟩; ungelöst ⟨*Problem*⟩; **c)**

(Bot.) ausdauernd; perennierend *(fachspr.).* **2.** *n. (Bot.)* ausdauernde *od. (fachspr.)* perennierende Pflanze

perennially [pə'renjəlɪ] *adv.* **a)** *(throughout the year)* **flow ~** ‹*Fluß:*› das ganze Jahr Wasser führen; **b)** *(perpetually)* ständig; ewig ‹*ungelöst*›

perestroika [perɪ'strɔɪkə] *n.* Perestroika, *die*

perfect 1. ['pɜ:fɪkt] *adj.* **a)** *(complete)* vollkommen; umfassend ‹*Kenntnisse, Wissen*›; **b)** *(faultless)* vollkommen; perfekt ‹*Englisch, Technik, Timing*›; tadellos ‹*Zustand*›; [absolut] gelungen ‹*Aufführung*›; lupenrein ‹*Diamant*›; *(conforming to an abstract concept)* perfekt; **get a technique ~:** eine Technik vollkommen *od.* absolut beherrschen lernen; **~ gas** *(Phys.)* ideales Gas; **c)** *(trained, skilled)* **be ~ in the performance of one's duties** seine Aufgaben tadellos erfüllen; **practice makes ~:** Übung macht den Meister; **d)** *(coll.: exceedingly satisfactory)* herrlich; wunderbar; **e)** *(exact)* perfekt; getreu ‹*Ebenbild, Abbild*›; *(fully what the name implies)* perfekt ‹*Gentleman, Dame, Ehemann, Gastgeberin*›; *see also* **square 1g; f)** *(absolute)* **a ~ stranger** ein völlig Fremder; ein Wildfremder *(ugs.)*; **he is a ~ stranger to me** er ist mir völlig unbekannt; **he is a ~ scream** *(sl.)***/angel** *(coll.)***/charmer** er ist wirklich zum Schreien [komisch]/ein Engel/charmant; **she looks a ~ little angel** sie sieht wie ein richtiger kleiner Engel aus; **I have a ~ right to stay** ich habe eindeutig *od.* durchaus das Recht zu bleiben; **have ~ freedom to make one's own decision** völlig frei entscheiden können; **g)** *(coll.: unmitigated)* absolut; **look a ~ fright/mess** wirklich zum Weglaufen/absolut verboten aussehen *(ugs.)*; **a ~ tantrum** ein regelrechter Wutanfall; **h)** *(Ling.)* Perfekt-; **the ~ tense** das Perfekt; **future ~ tense** Futur II, *das;* vollendetes Futur; **past ~** *see* **pluperfect 2; present ~** *see* **¹present 1d; i)** *(Mus.)* **~ interval** reines Intervall. **2.** *n. (Ling.)* Perfekt, *das.* **3.** [pə'fekt] *v.t.* vervollkommnen; perfektionieren

perfection [pə'fekʃn] *n.* **a)** *no pl. (making perfect)* Vervollkommnung, *die;* Perfektionierung, *die;* **b)** *no pl. (faultlessness)* Vollkommenheit, *die;* Perfektion, *die;* **~ of detail** Vollkommenheit *od.* Perfektion im Detail; **~ of technique** technische Perfektion; **to ~:** perfekt; **it/he succeeded to ~:** es war ein voller Erfolg/er war absolut erfolgreich; **you cook to ~:** du bist eine perfekte Köchin/ein perfekter Koch; **c)** *no pl. (perfect person or thing)* **be ~:** perfekt sein; **d)** *no pl., no indef. art. (most perfect degree)* Inbegriff, *der;* **sth. has reached its ~:** etw. hat seine höchste Vollkommenheit erreicht

perfectionism [pə'fekʃənɪzm] *n., no pl.* Perfektionismus, *der*

perfectionist [pə'fekʃənɪst] *n.* Perfektionist, *der*/Perfektionistin, *die*

perfectly ['pɜ:fɪktlɪ] *adv.* **a)** *(completely)* vollkommen; völlig; **I understand that ~:** ich verstehe das vollkommen *od.* völlig; **be ~ entitled to do sth.** durchaus berechtigt sein, etw. zu tun; **b)** *(faultlessly)* perfekt; tadellos ‹*sich verhalten*›; fehlerlos ‹*singen*›; **c)** *(exactly)* vollkommen; exakt, genau ‹*vorhersagbar*›; **d)** *(coll.: to an unmitigated extent)* furchtbar *(ugs.)* ‹*schrecklich, schlimm, ekelhaft*›

perfect 'pitch *n. (Mus.)* absolutes Gehör

perfidious [pə:fɪdɪəs] *adj.* perfid *(geh.)*; *see also* **Albion**

perfidy ['pɜ:fɪdɪ] *n.* Perfidie, *die (geh.)*

perforate ['pɜ:fəreɪt] *v.t.* **a)** *(make hole[s] through)* perforieren; **suffer from a ~d eardrum/ulcer** ein Loch im Trommelfell/ein durchgebrochenes Magengeschwür haben; **b)** *(make an opening into)* durchlöchern

perforation [pɜ:fə'reɪʃn] *n.* **a)** *(action of perforating)* Perforierung, *die;* **b)** *(hole)* Loch, *das;* **~s** *(line of holes esp. in paper)* Perforation, *die;* *(in sheets of stamps)* Zähnung, *die;* Perforation, *die*

perforator ['pɜ:fəreɪtə(r)] *n.* Perforiermaschine, *die;* *(rock-drill)* Bohrer, *der;* *(used in stripping wallpaper)* Tapetenperforator, *der*

perforce [pə'fɔ:s] *adv. (arch./formal)* notgedrungen

perform [pə'fɔ:m] **1.** *v.t.* **a)** *(fulfil)* ausführen ‹*Befehl, Arbeit, Operation*›; erfüllen ‹*Bitte, Wunsch, Pflicht, Vertrag, Versprechen, Bedingung, Aufgabe*›; nachkommen (+ *Dat.*) ‹*Verpflichtung*›; vollbringen ‹*[Helden]tat, Leistung*›; durchführen ‹*Operation*›; einhalten ‹*Versprechen, Vertrag*›; **b)** *(carry out)* ausfüllen ‹*Funktion*›; vollbringen ‹*Wunder*›; anstellen ‹*Berechnungen*›; durchführen ‹*Experiment, Sektion*›; vornehmen ‹*Sektion*›; vorführen, zeigen ‹*Trick*›; *(in formal manner or according to prescribed ritual)* vollziehen ‹*Trauung, Taufe, Riten, Rituale, Opfer*›; [ab]halten ‹*Gottesdienst*›; *(render)* aufführen ‹*Theaterstück, Scharade*›; vortragen, vorsingen ‹*Lied*›; vorspielen, vortragen ‹*Sonate usw.*›. **2.** *v.i.* **a)** eine Vorführung geben; *(sing)* singen; *(play)* spielen; ‹*Jongleur:*› Kunststücke zeigen *od.* vorführen; ‹*Zauberer:*› Zaubertricks ausführen *od.* vorführen; **he ~ed very well** seine Darbietung war sehr gut; **she ~s as soloist** sie ist Solistin; *(occasionally)* sie tritt als Solistin auf; **she ~ed skilfully on the flute/piano** sie spielte mit großer Könnerschaft Flöte/Klavier; **b)** *(Theatre)* auftreten; **he ~ed very well** sein Auftritt war sehr gut; **c)** *(execute tricks)* ‹*Tier:*› Kunststücke zeigen *od.* vorführen; **train an animal to ~:** einem Tier Kunststücke beibringen; **d)** *(work, function)* ‹*Auto:*› laufen, fahren; **he ~ed all right/well [in the exam]** er machte seine Sache [in der Prüfung] ordentlich/gut; **e)** *(coll. euphem.) (accomplish sexual intercourse)* es machen *(ugs. verhüll.)*; *(excrete, urinate)* ‹*Kind, Haustier:*› machen *(ugs. verhüll.)*

performance [pə'fɔ:məns] *n.* **a)** *(fulfilment) (of promise, duty, task)* Erfüllung, *die;* *(of command)* Ausführung, *die;* **b)** *(carrying out)* Durchführung, *die;* **c)** *(notable feat)* Leistung, *die;* **put up a good ~:** eine gute Leistung zeigen; seine Sache gut machen; **d)** *(performing of play etc.)* Vorstellung, *die;* **the ~s of the gymnasts** die Turnveranstaltungen; **her ~ in the play** ihre [schauspielerische] Leistung in dem Theaterstück; **her ~ as Desdemona** ihre Darstellung *od.* Interpretation der Desdemona; **the ~ of a play/opera** die Aufführung eines Theaterstücks/einer Oper; **give a ~ of a symphony/play** eine Sinfonie/ein Stück spielen *od.* aufführen; **e)** *(achievement under test)* Leistung, *die;* **athletic ~:** die Leistung eines Sportlers; **the car has good ~:** der Wagen bringt viel Leistung; **give an engine more ~:** die Leistung eines Motors erhöhen; **are you satisfied with the ~ of your new car?** sind sie mit ihrem neuen Auto zufrieden?; **the ~ of the equipment, in tests, was somewhat variable** die Anlage hat in Tests nicht immer gleich abgeschnitten; **f)** *(coll.: display of anger etc.)* Auftritt, *der;* **g)** *(coll.: difficult procedure)* Theater, *das (ugs., abwertend)*; Umstand, *der;* **it was a hell of a ~ getting my passport** das war vielleicht ein Umstand *od.* Theater, bis ich meinen Paß hatte

performer [pə'fɔ:mə(r)] *n.* Künstler, *der*/Künstlerin, *die;* **as a ~ of tricks he was unsurpassed** im Vorführen von Tricks war er unübertroffen

performing [pə'fɔ:mɪŋ] *adj.* **a)** *(acting, singing, etc.)* auftretend ‹*Künstler*›; **~ arts** darstellende Künste; **~ rights** Aufführungsrechte *Pl.*; **b)** *(executing tricks)* dressiert ‹*Tier*›

perfume 1. ['pɜ:fju:m] *n.* **a)** *(sweet smell)* Duft, *der;* **b)** *(fluid)* Parfüm, *das;* **~ atomizer** *or* **spray** Parfümzerstäuber, *der.* **2.** [pə'fju:m, 'pɜ:fju:m] *v.t. (impart sweet scent to)* mit Wohlgeruch erfüllen; *(impregnate with sweet smell)* parfümieren

perfumer [pə'fju:mə(r)] *n. (maker of perfume)* Parfümeur, *der*/Parfümeuse, *die;* *(seller of perfume)* Parfümhändler, *der*/Parfümhändlerin, *die*

perfumery [pə'fju:mərɪ] *n.* **a)** *no pl. (preparation of perfumes)* Parfümherstellung, *die;* **b)** *(perfumes)* Parfümeriewaren *Pl.*; *attrib.* Parfümerie-; **c)** *(shop)* Parfümerie, *die*

perfunctorily [pə'fʌŋktərɪlɪ] *adv.* pflichtschuldig; oberflächlich, mechanisch ‹*arbeiten*›

perfunctory [pə'fʌŋktərɪ] *adj.* *(done for duty's sake only)* pflichtschuldig; flüchtig ‹*Erkundigung, Bemerkung*›; *(superficial)* oberflächlich ‹*Arbeit, Überprüfung*›; **his tidying of his bedroom had been very ~:** er hatte sein Zimmer nur sehr oberflächlich aufgeräumt; **put in a ~ appearance** sich, um seiner Pflicht zu genügen, kurz zeigen

pergola ['pɜ:gələ] *n. (Hort.)* Pergola, *die;* Laubengang, *der*

perhaps [pə'hæps, præps] *adv.* vielleicht; **I'll go out, ~:** ich gehe vielleicht aus; **~ so** [das] mag [ja] sein; **~ not** *(maybe this is or will not be the case)* vielleicht auch nicht; *(it might be best not to do this)* vielleicht lieber nicht

perianth ['perɪænθ] *n. (Bot.)* Perianth[ium], *das (fachspr.)*; Blütenhülle, *die*

pericardium [perɪ'kɑ:dɪəm] *n., pl.* **pericardia** [perɪ'kɑ:dɪə] *(Anat.)* Perikard[ium], *das (fachspr.)*; Herzbeutel, *der*

pericarp ['perɪkɑ:p] *n. (Bot.)* Perikarp, *das (fachspr.)*; Fruchtwand, *die*

perigee ['perɪdʒi:] *n. (Astron.)* Perigäum, *das (fachspr.)*; Erdnähe, *die*

peril ['perl] *n.* Gefahr, *die;* **they were in constant ~ from their enemies** sie waren ständig von ihren Feinden bedroht; **be in deadly ~, be in ~ of death** *or* **one's life** in Lebensgefahr sein *od.* schweben; **be in ~ of doing sth.** Gefahr laufen, etw. zu tun; **do sth. at one's ~** *(accepting risk of injury)* etw. auf eigene Gefahr tun

perilous ['perələs] *adj.* **a)** *(full of danger)* gefahrvoll; **be ~:** gefährlich sein; **b)** *(exposed to imminent risk)* gefährdet; anfällig ‹*Beziehung*›; **a ~ pile of chairs** ein gefährlich hoher Turm aus Stühlen

perilously ['perələslɪ] *adv.* gefährlich; **~ ill** todkrank

perimeter [pə'rɪmɪtə(r)] *n.* **a)** *(outer boundary)* [äußere] Begrenzung; Grenze, *die;* **troops were stationed all around the ~ to guard the camp** Truppen waren rundherum postiert, um das Lager zu bewachen; **at the ~ of the race-track** am Rande der Rennbahn; **b)** *(outline of figure)* Umriß, *der;* *(length of outline)* Umfang, *der*

perinatal [perɪ'neɪtl] *adj. (Med.)* perinatal

perineum [perɪ'ni:əm] *n., pl.* **~s** *or* **perinea** [perɪ'ni:ə] *(Anat.)* Damm, *der*

period ['pɪərɪəd] **1.** *n.* **a)** *(distinct portion of history or life)* Periode, *die;* Zeit, *die;* **~s of history** geschichtliche Perioden; **the modern ~:** die Moderne; das Zeitalter der Moderne; **the Reformation/Tudor/Victorian ~:** die Reformationszeit/die Tudorzeit/die viktorianische Zeit; **during the ~ of his youth** in seiner Jugend[zeit]; **at a later ~ of her life** zu einem späteren Zeitpunkt ihres Lebens *od.* in ihrem Leben; **a ~ of literature/art** eine literarische/kunstgeschichtliche Epoche; **the Classical/Romantic/Renaissance ~:** die Klassik/Romantik/Renaissance; **of the ~** *(of the time under discussion)* der damaligen Zeit; **b)** *(any portion of time)* Zeitraum, *der;* Zeitspanne, *die;* **over a ~ [of time]** über einen längeren Zeitraum; **within the agreed ~:** innerhalb der vereinbarten Frist; **showers and bright ~s** *(Meteorol.)* Schauer und Aufheiterungen; **over a longer ~ I changed my mind** im Laufe der Zeit änderte ich meine Meinung; **I've had ~s of anxiety** es gab Zeiten der Angst für mich; **c)** *(Sch.: time allocated for lesson)* Stunde, *die;* **teaching/lesson ~:** Unterrichtsstunde, *die;* **geography/chemistry/English ~:** Geographie-/Chemie-/Englischstunde, *die;* **have five ~s a week for French** fünf Stunden Französisch[unterricht] in der Woche haben; **have two chemistry ~s** zwei Stunden Chemie haben; **a detention ~, a ~ of detention** eine Stunde Arrest; **a free ~:** eine Freistunde; **d)** *(occurrence of menstruation)* Periode, *die;* Regel[blutung], *die;* **have her/a ~:** ihre Periode *od.* Regel *od. (ugs. verhüll.)* Tage haben; **miss one's ~:** ihre Periode nicht bekommen; **~ pains** Menstruationsschmerzen; **e)** *(punctuation mark)* Punkt, *der;* **f)** *(pause in speech)* Pause, *die; (fig.)* Stillstand, *der;* **g)** *(appended to statement)* [und damit] basta! *(ugs.);* **h)** *(time taken by recurring process)* Periode, *die; (Astron.: time of revolution)* Umlaufzeit, *die;* **i)** *(Geol.)* Periode, *die;* **j)** *(complete sentence)* Satz, *der;* Satzgefüge, *das (Sprachw.);* **k)** *(Math.) (set of figures)* [Ziffern]gruppe, *die; (set of recurring figures)* Periode, *die;* **l)** *(Chem.)* Periode, *die.* **2.** *adj.* zeitgenössisch ⟨*Tracht, Kostüm*⟩; Zeit⟨*roman, -stück*⟩; antik ⟨*Möbel*⟩; ⟨*Zimmer*⟩ im Zeitstil; **~ piece** *(play)* Zeitstück, *das; (novel)* Zeitroman, *der;* **this Georgian cabinet is a true ~ piece** dieser georgianische Schrank ist ein für die Zeit ausgesprochen typisches Stück

periodic [pɪərɪˈɒdɪk] *adj.* **a)** *(recurring at regular intervals)* periodisch *od.* regelmäßig [auftretend *od.* wiederkehrend]; *(intermittent)* gelegentlich [auftretend]; vereinzelt ⟨*Regenschauer*⟩; **make ~ good resolutions** von Zeit zu Zeit *od.* immer mal wieder gute Vorsätze fassen; **b)** *(Astron.)* periodisch; **the ~ time of a planet** die Umlaufzeit eines Planeten

periodical [pɪərɪˈɒdɪkl] **1.** *adj.* **a)** *see* **periodic; b)** *(published at regular intervals)* regelmäßig erscheinend; **~ journal/magazine** Zeitschrift, *die.* **2.** *n.* Zeitschrift, *die; attrib.* Zeitschriften-; **weekly/monthly/quarterly ~:** Wochenzeitschrift/Monatsschrift/Vierteljahresschrift, *die*

periodically [pɪərɪˈɒdɪkəlɪ] *adv. (at regular intervals)* regelmäßig; *(intermittently)* gelegentlich

periodic 'table *n. (Chem.)* Periodensystem, *das*

peripatetic [perɪpəˈtetɪk] *adj.* **~ teacher** Lehrer, der/Lehrerin, die an mehreren Schulen unterrichtet; **~ teaching** Unterricht durch Lehrer, die an mehreren Schulen arbeiten; **~ life-style** Wanderleben, *das*

peripheral [pəˈrɪfərl] **1.** *adj.* **a)** *(of the periphery)* ⟨*Parkraum*⟩ in Randlage; **~ road** Ringstraße, *die;* **~ speed** Umfangsgeschwindigkeit, *die;* **b)** *(of minor importance)* peripher *(geh.);* marginal *(geh.);* Rand⟨*problem, -kultur, -erscheinung, -figur, -gebiet, -bemerkung, -lage*⟩; **be merely ~ or of merely ~ importance to sth.** für etw. von nur marginaler *(geh.) od.* untergeordneter Bedeutung sein; **c)** *(Anat.)* peripher; **d)** *(Computing)* peripher. **2.** *n. (Computing)* Peripheriegerät, *das*

peripherally [pəˈrɪfərəlɪ] *adv.* **a)** *(at the periphery)* außen; **b)** *(marginally)* am Rande; peripher *(geh.);* marginal *(geh.)*

periphery [pəˈrɪfərɪ] *n.* **a)** *see* **circumference; b)** *(external boundary)* Begrenzung, *die; (of surface)* Außenfläche, *die;* **c)** *(outer region)* Peripherie, *die (geh.);* Rand, *der*

periphrasis [pəˈrɪfrəsɪs] *n., pl.* **periphrases** [pəˈrɪfrəsi:z] **a)** *no pl. (roundabout way of speaking)* periphrastischer *(Rhet.) od.* umschreibender Stil; **b)** *(roundabout phrase)* Periphrase, *die (Rhet.);* Umschreibung, *die*

periphrastic [perɪˈfræstɪk] *adj.* periphrastisch *(Rhet.);* umschreibend

periscope [ˈperɪskəʊp] *n.* Periskop, *das*

periscopic [perɪˈskɒpɪk] *adj.* periskopisch

perish [ˈperɪʃ] **1.** *v. i.* **a)** *(suffer destruction)* umkommen; ⟨*Volk, Rasse, Kultur:*⟩ untergehen; ⟨*Kraft, Energie:*⟩ versiegen; ⟨*Pflanze:*⟩ eingehen; **his name will never ~:** sein Name wird für alle Zeiten fortleben; **~ by the sword/at the hand of the enemy** durch das Schwert/durch Feindes Hand umkommen; **he ~ed from the cold** er erfror; **... or ~ in the attempt** *(joc.)* ..., koste es, was es wolle; **~ the thought!** Gott behüte *od.* bewahre!; **b)** *(rot)* verderben; ⟨*Fresken, Gemälde:*⟩ verblassen; ⟨*Gummi:*⟩ altern. **2.** *v. t.* **a)** *(reduce to distress)* **we were ~ed [with cold]** wir waren ganz durchgefroren; **b)** *(cause to rot)* [schneller] altern lassen ⟨*Gummi*⟩; angreifen ⟨*Reifen*⟩

perishable [ˈperɪʃəbl] **1.** *adj. (liable to perish)* vergänglich; *(subject to speedy decay)* [leicht] verderblich. **2.** *n. in pl.* leicht verderbliche Güter *od.* Waren

perisher [ˈperɪʃə(r)] *n. (Brit. sl.) (annoying person)* Ekel, *das (ugs.);* Miststück, *das (salopp); (unfortunate person)* **poor ~:** armer Hund *(ugs.);* armes Schwein *(ugs.)*

perishing [ˈperɪʃɪŋ] **1.** *adj.* **a)** *(causing distress)* mörderisch ⟨*Wind, Kälte*⟩; *(very cold)* eiskalt; **b)** *(Brit. sl.: confounded)* elend; **that child is a ~ nuisance** das Kind kann einem den Nerv töten *(ugs.).* **2.** *adv. (Brit. sl.: confoundedly)* fürchterlich *(ugs.)*

peristaltic [perɪˈstæltɪk] *adj. (Physiol.)* peristaltisch

peritoneum [perɪtəˈni:əm] *n., pl.* **~s** *or* **peritonea** [perɪtəˈni:ə] *(Anat.)* Bauchfell, *das*

peritonitis [perɪtəˈnaɪtɪs] *n. (Med.)* Peritonitis, *die (fachspr.);* Bauchfellentzündung, *die*

periwig [ˈperɪwɪg] *n. (Hist.)* Perücke, *die*

¹periwinkle [ˈperɪwɪŋkl] *n.* **a)** *(Bot.)* Immergrün, *das;* **b)** *(colour)* **~ [blue]** Veilchenblau, *das*

²periwinkle *see* **winkle 1**

perjure [ˈpɜ:dʒə(r)] *v. refl. (swear to false statement)* einen Meineid leisten; *(Law: give false evidence under oath)* [unter Eid] falsch aussagen

perjured [ˈpɜ:dʒəd] *adj.* **~ testimony** falsche Aussage unter Eid; **be ~:** [unter Eid] falsch ausgesagt haben; meineidig sein

perjurer [ˈpɜ:dʒərə(r)] *n.* Meineidige, *der/die*

perjury [ˈpɜ:dʒərɪ] *n.* **a)** *(swearing to false statement)* Meineid, *der; (Law: giving false evidence while under oath)* eidliche Falschaussage; **commit ~:** einen Meineid leisten/sich der eidlichen Falschaussage schuldig machen; **b)** *(breach of oath)* Eidesverletzung, *die;* Eidbruch, *der*

¹perk [pɜ:k] *(coll.)* **1.** *v. i.* **~ up** munter werden; ⟨*Wirtschaft:*⟩ in Gang kommen *(ugs.); (cheer up)* aufleben; **life had ~ed up again** das Leben machte wieder Spaß. **2.** *v. t.* **a) ~ up** *(restore liveliness of)* aufmuntern; **I need a drink to ~ me up** ich muß jetzt erst mal zur Aufmunterung was trinken *(ugs.);* **~ up sb.'s spirits** jmdn. aufmuntern; **take pills to ~ oneself up** sich mit Pillen aufputschen; **b) ~ up** *(raise briskly)* aufstellen ⟨*Schwanz, Ohren*⟩; heben ⟨*Kopf*⟩; **c)** *(smarten)* **~ oneself/sth. up** sich feinmachen/etw. verschönern

²perk *n. (Brit. coll.: perquisite)* [Sonder]vergünstigung, *die*

³perk *(coll.)* **1.** *v. i.* ⟨*Kaffee:*⟩ durchlaufen; ⟨*Kaffeemaschine:*⟩ in Gang sein. **2.** *v. t.* machen ⟨*Kaffee*⟩

perkily [ˈpɜ:kɪlɪ] *adv. see* **perky:** lebhaft; munter; keck; selbstbewußt

perky [ˈpɜ:kɪ] *adj.* **a)** *(lively)* lebhaft; munter; **b)** *(self-assertive)* keck; selbstbewußt

perlite [ˈpɜ:laɪt] *n.* Perlit, *der*

¹perm [pɜ:m] **1.** *n. (permanent wave)* Dauerwelle, *die.* **2.** *v. t.* **~ sb.'s hair** jmdm. eine Dauerwelle machen; **have one's hair ~ed** sich *(Dat.)* eine Dauerwelle machen lassen; **have ~ed hair** eine Dauerwelle haben

²perm *(Brit. coll.)* **1.** *n. (permutation)* Tippreihe, *die.* **2.** *v. t.* als Tippreihe ankreuzen

permafrost [ˈpɜ:məfrɒst] *n. (Geog.)* Permafrost, *der;* Dauerfrostboden, *der*

permanence [ˈpɜ:mənəns] *n., no pl.* Dauerhaftigkeit, *die;* **the place had an air of ~:** die Stätte umgab eine Aura von Unvergänglichkeit

permanency [ˈpɜ:mənənsɪ] *n.* **a)** *no pl. see* **permanence; b)** *(condition)* Dauerzustand, *der; (job)* Dauerstellung, *die*

permanent [ˈpɜ:mənənt] *adj.* fest ⟨*Sitz, Bestandteil, Mitglied*⟩; beständig, ewig ⟨*Werte*⟩; treu ⟨*Freund*⟩; ständig ⟨*Plage, Meckern, Wohnsitz, Adresse, Kampf*⟩; Dauer⟨*gast, -stellung, -visum*⟩; bleibend ⟨*Folge, Zahn, Gebiß, Schaden*⟩; **be in ~ residence here** ständig hier wohnen; **of ~ value** von bleibendem Wert; **this time it's ~:** diesmal ist es für immer; **sb./sth. is a ~ fixture** jmd./etw. gehört zum Inventar; **be employed on a ~ basis** fest angestellt sein; **~ magnet** Permanentmagnet, *der*

permanently [ˈpɜ:mənəntlɪ] *adv.* dauernd; auf Dauer ⟨*verhindern, bleiben*⟩; fest ⟨*anstellen, einstellen*⟩; *(repeatedly)* ständig; dauernd; **they live in France ~ now** sie leben jetzt ganz *(ugs.) od.* ständig in Frankreich; **she was ~ disabled in the accident** sie hat bei dem Unfall eine bleibende Behinderung davongetragen; **she was ~ affected by the shock** der Schock hatte für sie bleibende Folgen

permanent: ~ 'wave *n.* Dauerwelle, *die;* **~ 'way** *n. (Brit. Railw.)* Oberbau, *der*

permeable [ˈpɜ:mɪəbl] *adj.* durchlässig; **~ by water** wasserdurchlässig; **be ~ to sth.** etw. durchlassen

permeate [ˈpɜ:mɪeɪt] **1.** *v. t. (get into)* dringen in (+ *Akk.*); *(pass through)* dringen durch; *(saturate)* erfüllen; **~ sb.'s consciousness** jmdm. ins Bewußtsein dringen; **be ~d with** *or* **by sth.** *(fig.)* von etw. durchdrungen sein. **2.** *v. i.* **~ through sth.** etw. durchdringen; **~ through to sb.** zu jmdm. durchdringen

permissible [pəˈmɪsɪbl] *adj.* zulässig; **be ~ to** *or* **for sb.** jmdm. erlaubt sein; **~ under the law** nicht gesetzeswidrig; **~ dose** *(Med.)* zulässige Dosis; *(of radiation)* zulässige Belastung

permission [pəˈmɪʃn] *n., no indef. art.* Erlaubnis, *die; (given by official body)* Genehmigung, *die;* **ask [sb.'s] ~:** [jmdn.] um Erlaubnis bitten; **who gave you ~ to do this?** wer hat dir erlaubt, das zu tun?; **by whose ~?** mit wessen Erlaubnis?; **with your ~:** wenn Sie gestatten; mit Ihrer Erlaubnis; **written ~:** eine schriftliche Genehmigung

permissive [pəˈmɪsɪv] *adj.* **a)** *(giving permission)* **~ legislation** permissive Gesetzgebung; **b)** *(tolerant)* tolerant; großzügig; *(in relation to moral matters)* freizügig; permissiv *(geh.);* **the ~ society** die permissive Gesellschaft

permissiveness [pəˈmɪsɪvnɪs] *n., no pl.* Freizügigkeit, *die;* Toleranz, *die*

permit 1. [pəˈmɪt] *v. t.,* **-tt-** zulassen ⟨*Berufung, Einspruch usw.*⟩; **~ sb. sth.** jmdm. etw. erlauben *od. (geh.)* gestatten; **~ me to offer my congratulations** *(formal)* gestatten Sie mir, Ihnen meine Glückwünsche auszusprechen *(geh.);* **sb. is ~ted to do sth.** es ist jmdm. erlaubt *od. (geh.)* gestattet, etw. zu tun. **2.** *v. i.,* **-tt- a)** *(give opportunity)* es zulassen; **weather ~ting** bei entsprechendem Wetter; wenn das Wetter mitspielt *(ugs.);*

b) *(admit)* ~ **of sth.** etw. erlauben *od.* gestatten; **not ~ of sth.** etw. verbieten. **3.** ['pɜ:mɪt] *n. (written order)* Genehmigung, *die; (for entering premises)* Passierschein, *der; (for using car-park)* Parkausweis, *der;* **fishing ~:** Fischereischein, *der;* Angelschein, *der;* **be a ~-holder** einen Passierschein/Parkausweis/Angelschein *usw.* haben

permutation [pɜ:mjʊ'teɪʃn] *n.* **a)** *(varying of order)* Umstellung, *die;* **b)** *(result of variation of order)* Anordnung, *die; (of series of items)* Reihenfolge, *die;* Permutation, *die (Math.);* **c)** *(selection of items)* Auswahl, *die; (Brit.: in football pools)* Tipreihe, *die;* **make a ~:** eine Auswahl treffen/eine Tipreihe ankreuzen

permute [pə'mju:t] *v. t.* umstellen; *(Math.)* permutieren

pernicious [pə'nɪʃəs] *adj.* verderblich; bösartig ⟨*Krankheit, Person*⟩; schlimm, übel ⟨*Angewohnheit*⟩; *(fatal)* fatal; **be a ~ influence on sb.** einen schlimmen *od.* üblen Einfluß auf jmdn. ausüben; **be ~ to sb./sth.** jmdm./einer Sache abträglich sein *(geh.) od.* schaden; ~ **anaemia** *(Med.)* perniziöse Anämie

pernickety [pə'nɪkɪtɪ] *adj. (coll.)* **a)** *(fastidious, meticulous)* pingelig *(ugs.)* **(about** in bezug auf + *Akk.*); **b)** *(tricky)* heikel ⟨*Frage, Thema*⟩; kitzelig ⟨*Aufgabe, Job*⟩; fummelig *(ugs.)* ⟨*Arbeitsvorgang*⟩

peroration [perə'reɪʃn] *n.* Schlußwort, *das*

peroxide [pə'rɒksaɪd] **1.** *n.* **a)** *(Chem.)* Peroxyd, *das;* **b) [hydrogen] ~:** Wasserstoffperoxyd, *das;* ~ **blonde** Wasserstoffblondine, *die.* **2.** *v. t.* [mit Wasserstoffperoxyd] bleichen

perpendicular [pɜ:pən'dɪkjʊlə(r)] **1.** *adj.* **a)** senkrecht; lotrecht; **b)** *(very steep)* [fast] senkrecht ⟨*Aufstieg, Abstieg*⟩; senkrecht abfallend/aufragend ⟨*Kliff, Felswand usw.*⟩; ~ **drop/slope/rock-face** Steilabfall, *der/*-hang, *der/*-wand, *die;* **c)** *(erect, upright)* aufrecht; *(joc.: standing)* stehend; **be/remain ~** *(joc.)* stehen/stehen bleiben; **d)** *(Geom.)* senkrecht **(to** zu); **two ~ planes/lines** zwei zueinander senkrechte Ebenen/Linien; **e)** *(Archit.)* ⟨*Bauwerk, Fenster*⟩ im Perpendikularstil; **P~ style** Perpendikularstil, *der.* **2.** *n.* **a)** *(line)* Senkrechte, *die* **(to** zu); Lot, *das* **(to** auf + *Dat.*); **b)** *(position)* **the ~:** die Senkrechte; das Lot; **be [slightly] out of [the] ~:** [etwas] aus dem Lot sein; nicht [ganz] senkrecht sein; **c)** *(instrument)* Lot, *das*

perpendicularly [pɜ:pən'dɪkjʊləlɪ] *adv.* **a)** *(vertically)* senkrecht; lotrecht; **b)** *(steeply)* [beinahe] senkrecht; **c)** *(Geom.)* senkrecht

perpetrate ['pɜ:pɪtreɪt] *v. t.* begehen; anrichten ⟨*Blutbad, Schaden*⟩; verüben ⟨*Gemetzel, Greuel*⟩; ausführen ⟨*Streich*⟩; *(joc.)* zum besten geben *(ugs.)* ⟨*Witz, Lied*⟩

perpetration [pɜ:pɪ'treɪʃn] *n. (of crime, blunder)* Begehen, *das; (of atrocity, outrage)* Verübung, *die*

perpetrator ['pɜ:pɪtreɪtə(r)] *n.* [Übel]täter, *der/*-täterin, *die;* **be the ~ of a crime/fraud/atrocity/massacre** ein Verbrechen/einen Betrug begangen haben/eine Greueltat verübt haben/ein Blutbad angerichtet haben

perpetual [pə'petjʊəl] *adj.* **a)** *(eternal)* ewig; **b)** *(continuous)* ständig; **c)** *(coll.: repeated)* ständig; [an]dauernd; **she has ~ crises** sie hat [an]dauernd *od.* ständig Krisen; **d)** *(applicable or valid for ever)* immerwährend; ewig

perpetual 'calendar *n.* **a)** *(table)* ewiger *od.* immerwährender Kalender; **b)** *(device)* Dauerkalender, *der*

perpetually [pə'petjʊəlɪ] *adv.* **a)** *(eternally)* ewig; **b)** *(continuously)* ständig; **c)** *(coll.: repeatedly)* ständig; [an]dauernd

perpetual: ~ 'motion *n., no pl., no art.* ewige Bewegung; **~-'motion machine** *n.* Perpetuum mobile, *das*

perpetuate [pə'petjʊeɪt] *v. t.* **a)** *(preserve from oblivion)* lebendig erhalten ⟨*Andenken*⟩; unsterblich machen ⟨*Namen*⟩; aufrechterhalten ⟨*Tradition*⟩; **b)** *(make perpetual)* aufrechterhalten; erhalten ⟨*Art, Macht*⟩

perpetuation [pəpetjʊ'eɪʃn] *n.* **a)** *(preservation from oblivion)* ~ **of sb.'s memory** Bewahrung jmds. Andenkens; **in ~ of sb.'s memory** zu jmds. Gedächtnis; **b)** *(action of making perpetual)* Aufrechterhaltung, *die; (of species, power)* Erhaltung, *die*

perpetuity [pɜ:pɪ'tju:ɪtɪ] *n., no pl., no indef. art.* ewiger Bestand; **in** *or* **to** *or* **for ~:** für alle Ewigkeit *od.* alle Zeiten

perplex [pə'pleks] *v. t.* **a)** *(bewilder)* verwirren; ~ **sb.'s mind** jmdn verwirren; **such questions have ~ed men since time began** solche Fragen haben die Menschheit seit Anbeginn *(geh.)* beunruhigt; **b)** *(make [more] complicated)* [noch] verwickelter machen; komplizieren

perplexed [pə'plekst] *adj.* **a)** *(bewildered)* verwirrt; *(puzzled)* ratlos; **b)** *(complicated)* kompliziert

perplexedly [pə'pleksɪdlɪ] *adv. see* **perplexed a:** verwirrt; ratlos

perplexity [pə'pleksɪtɪ] *n. no pl.* **a)** *(bewilderment)* Verwirrung, *die; (puzzlement)* Ratlosigkeit, *die;* **look at sb. in ~:** jmdn. voller Verwirrung ansehen; **cause sb. ~:** jmdn. verwirren

perquisite ['pɜ:kwɪzɪt] *n.* **a)** *(incidental benefit)* Vergünstigung, *die;* **b)** *(customary gratuity)* Trinkgeld, *das;* **c)** *(fig.: thing to which person has sole right)* Vorrecht, *das;* Privileg, *das*

Perrier, (P) ['perɪeɪ] *n.* ~ **[water]** Perrier[wasser], *das*

perry ['perɪ] *n. (Brit.)* Birnenmost, *der*

per se [pɜ: 'seɪ] *adv.* an sich; per se *(geh.);* **considered ~:** für sich genommen

persecute ['pɜ:sɪkju:t] *v. t.* **a)** verfolgen; **b)** *(harass, worry)* plagen; zusetzen (+ *Dat.*); **~ sb. with sth.** jmdm. mit etw. zusetzen; **stop persecuting me** laß mich in Ruhe

persecution [pɜ:sɪ'kju:ʃn] *n.* **a)** Verfolgung, *die;* **suffer ~:** verfolgt werden; **b)** *(harassment)* Plagerei, *die*

persecution: ~ complex, ~ mania *ns. (Psych.)* Verfolgungswahn, *der*

persecutor ['pɜ:sɪkju:tə(r)] *n.* **a)** Verfolger, *der/*Verfolgerin, *die;* **b)** *(who harasses)* Peiniger, *der/*Peinigerin, *die*

perseverance [pɜ:sɪ'vɪərəns] *n.* Beharrlichkeit, *die;* Ausdauer, *die*

persevere [pɜ:sɪ'vɪə(r)] *v. i.* ausharren; ~ **with** *or* **at** *or* **in sth.** bei etw. dabeibleiben; ~ **in doing sth.** darauf beharren, etw. zu tun

Persia ['pɜ:ʃə] *pr. n. (Hist.)* Persien *(das)*

Persian ['pɜ:ʃn] **1.** *adj.* persisch; *see also* **English 1. 2.** *n.* **a)** *(person)* Perser, *der/*Perserin, *die;* **b)** *(language)* Persisch, *das; see also* **English 2 a; c)** *see* **Persian cat**

Persian: ~ 'carpet *n.* Perser[teppich], *der;* **~ 'cat** *n.* Perserkatze, *die;* **~ 'lamb** *n.* Persianer, *der;* **~ lamb coat** Persianermantel, *der*

persiflage ['pɜ:sɪflɑ:ʒ] *n.* **[piece of] ~:** Spöttelei, *die;* Persiflage, *die*

persimmon [pə'sɪmən] *n.* Persimone, *die*

persist [pə'sɪst] *v. i.* **a)** *(continue firmly)* beharrlich sein Ziel verfolgen; nicht nachgeben; **~ in sth.** an etw. *(Dat.)* [beharrlich] festhalten; **~ in doing sth.** etw. weiterhin [beharrlich] tun; **~ in one's efforts to do sth.** in seinen Anstrengungen, etw. zu tun, nicht nachlassen; **b)** *(continue in existence)* anhalten

persistence [pə'sɪstəns] *n., no pl.* **a)** *(continuance in particular course)* Hartnäckigkeit, *die;* Beharrlichkeit, *die;* **~ in a habit/a course of action** hartnäckiges *od.* beharrliches Festhalten an einer Gewohnheit/Vorgehensweise; **b)** *(quality of perseverance)* Ausdauer, *die;* Zähigkeit, *die;* **c)** *(continued existence)* Fortbestehen, *das*

persistency [pə'sɪstənsɪ] *see* **persistence**

persistent [pə'sɪstənt] *adj.* **a)** *(continuing firmly or obstinately)* hartnäckig; **be ~ in one's beliefs** hartnäckig an seinen Überzeugungen festhalten; **be ~ in continuing to do sth.** etw. hartnäckig weiterhin tun; **she was ~ in her efforts to ...:** sie gab ihre Versuche, ... zu ..., nicht auf; **b)** *(constantly repeated)* dauernd; hartnäckig ⟨*Gerüchte*⟩; nicht nachlassend ⟨*Anstrengung, Bemühung*⟩; ~ **showers** anhaltende Schauertätigkeit; **suffer ~ attacks of nausea** dauernd *od.* immer wieder Anfälle von Übelkeit haben; **c)** *(enduring)* anhaltend

persistently [pə'sɪstəntlɪ] *adv.* **a)** *(so as to continue firmly or obstinately)* hartnäckig; beharrlich; **b)** *(repeatedly)* hartnäckig ⟨*sich weigern*⟩; **c)** *(enduringly)* ständig; **she has ~ made a nuisance of herself** sie hat die ganze Zeit Ärger gemacht

persnickety [pə'snɪkɪtɪ] *(Amer. coll.) see* **pernickety**

person ['pɜ:sn] *n.* **a)** Mensch, *der;* Person, *die (oft abwertend);* **a rich/sick/unemployed ~:** ein Reicher/Kranker/Arbeitsloser/eine Reiche *usw.;* **the first ~ to leave was ...:** der/die erste, der/die wegging, war ...; **if any ~ ...:** wenn jemand ...; **what sort of ~ do you think I am?** wofür halten Sie mich eigentlich?; **in the ~ of sb.** in jmdm. *od.* jmds. Person; **in ~** *(personally)* persönlich; selbst; **b)** *(living body)* Körper, *der; (appearance)* [äußere] Erscheinung; Äußere, *das;* **c)** *(euphem.: genitals)* **expose one's ~:** sich entblößen; **d)** *(Ling.)* Person, *die;* **first/second/third ~:** erste/zweite/dritte Person; **e)** *(Law)* Person, *die;* **natural/artificial ~:** natürliche/juristische Person

persona [pə'səʊnə] *n., pl.* **~e** [pə'səʊni:] **a)** *(character assumed by author)* Person, *die;* **b)** *(aspect of personality shown to others)* Rolle, *die*

personable ['pɜ:sənəbl] *adj.* sympathisch

personage ['pɜ:sənɪdʒ] *n.* **a)** *(person of rank)* Persönlichkeit, *die;* **b)** *(person not known to speaker)* Person, *die*

persona grata [pəsəʊnə 'grɑ:tə] *n., pl.* **personae gratae** [pəsəʊni: 'grɑ:ti:] Persona grata, *die*

personal ['pɜ:sənl] *adj.* **a)** *(one's own)* persönlich; Privat⟨*angelegenheit, -leben*⟩; **be ~ to sb.** an jmds. Person gebunden sein; ⟨*Sache:*⟩ jmdm. persönlich gehören; *see also* **touch 3 f; b)** *(of the body)* persönlich; **~ appearance** äußere Erscheinung; **~ hygiene** Körperpflege, *die;* **~ contact** *(Sport)* Körperkontakt, *der;* **~ foul** *(Sport)* persönliches Foul; **c)** *(done in person)* persönlich; **~ audience** Privataudienz, *die;* **he gave us a ~ tour of his estate** er zeigte uns persönlich seinen Besitz; **d)** *(directed or referring to the individual)* persönlich; **~ call** *(Brit. Teleph.)* Anruf mit Voranmeldung; **~ computer** Personalcomputer, *der;* **~ stereo** Walkman, *der;* **pay sb. a ~ call** jmdn. privat aufsuchen; **a letter marked 'P~'** ein Brief mit der Aufschrift „Persönlich"; **do you have to make ~ remarks?** mußt du unbedingt persönlich *od.* anzüglich werden?; **it's nothing ~, but ...:** nimm es bitte nicht persönlich, aber ...; **e)** *(given to or making ~ remarks)* persönlich; anzüglich; **f)** *(of a person as opposed to an abstraction)* persönlich; menschlich; *(existing as a person)* persönlich; personal; **g)** *(Ling.)* persönlich; Personal⟨*endung, -pronomen*⟩

personal: ~ as'sistant *n.* persönlicher Referent/persönliche Referentin; **~ column** *n.* Rubrik für private [Klein]anzeigen; **~ es'tate** *n. (Law)* bewegliches Vermögen; **~ identifi'cation number** *n.* persönliche Identifikationsnummer; Geheimcode, *der*

personalise *see* **personalize**

personality [pɜːsəˈnælɪtɪ] *n.* **a)** *(distinctive personal character)* Persönlichkeit, *die;* Wesen, *das; (of inanimate objects)* spezifischer Charakter; **have a strong ~,** *(coll.)* **have lots of ~:** eine starke Persönlichkeit sein *od.* haben; **be lacking in ~:** keine [starke] Persönlichkeit sein; **there was a [strong] ~ clash between them** sie paßten [absolut] nicht zusammen; **b)** *(noted person)* Persönlichkeit, *die;* **she's quite a ~ in the theatre world** sie ist jemand *od.* hat einen Namen in der Welt des Theaters; **c)** *usu. in pl. (personal remark)* persönlicher Angriff; Anzüglichkeit, *die. See also* **split personality**

persoˈnality cult *n.* Personenkult, *der;* Persönlichkeitskult, *der*

personalize [ˈpɜːsənəlaɪz] *v. t.* **a)** *(make personal)* persönlich gestalten; eine persönliche Note geben (+ *Dat.*); *(mark with owner's name etc.)* als persönliches Eigentum kennzeichnen; **~d writing-paper** persönliches Briefpapier; **b)** *(personify)* personifizieren

personally [ˈpɜːsənəlɪ] *adv.* persönlich; **~, I see no objection** ich persönlich sehe keine Einwände

personal: ~ ˈorganizer *n.* Terminplaner, *der;* **~ ˈproperty** *n.* **a)** persönliches Eigentum; **abolish ~ property** das Privateigentum abschaffen; **b)** *see* **personal estate; ~ ˈservice** *n.* individueller Service; **get ~ service** individuell *od.* persönlich bedient werden

personalty [ˈpɜːsənltɪ] *n. (Law)* bewegliches Vermögen

persona non grata [pəsəʊnə nɒn ˈgrɑːtə] *n., pl.* **personae non gratae** [pəsəʊniː nɒn ˈgrɑːtiː] Persona non grata, *die;* unerwünschte Person

personification [pəsɒnɪfɪˈkeɪʃn] *n.* Verkörperung, *die;* **be the [very] ~ of kindness** die Freundlichkeit selbst *od.* in Person sein

personify [pəˈsɒnɪfaɪ] *v.t.* **be kindness personified, ~ kindness** die Freundlichkeit in Person sein

personnel [pɜːsəˈnel] *n.* **a)** *constr. as sing. or pl.* Belegschaft, *die; (of shop, restaurant, etc.)* Personal, *das;* **military ~:** Militärangehörige; *attrib.* Personal-; **~ carrier** *(Mil.)* Schützenpanzer, *der;* **~ manager** Personalchef, *der/*-chefin, *die;* **~ office** Personalbüro, *das;* **~ officer** Personalsachbearbeiter, *der/* -sachbearbeiterin, *die;* **b)** *no pl. no art. (department of firm)* Personalabteilung, *die*

person-to-ˈperson *adj. (Amer. Teleph.)* **~ call** Anruf mit Voranmeldung

perspective [pəˈspektɪv] **1.** *n.* **a)** Perspektive, *die; (picture drawn)* perspektivische Zeichnung; **in ~:** perspektivisch richtig; **b)** *(fig.)* Blickwinkel, *der;* **throw sth. into ~:** etw. ins rechte Licht rücken; **put a different ~ on events** ein neues Licht auf die Ereignisse werfen; **in/out of ~, in the** *or* **its right/wrong ~:** unter dem/nicht unter dem richtigen Blickwinkel; **c)** *(view)* Aussicht, *die; (fig.: mental view)* Ausblick, *der.* **2.** *adj.* perspektivisch

Perspex, (P) [ˈpɜːspeks] *n.* Plexiglas ⓦᶻ, *das*

perspicacious [pɜːspɪˈkeɪʃəs] *adj.* scharfsinnig

perspicacity [pɜːspɪˈkæsɪtɪ] *n., no pl.* Scharfsinnigkeit, *die*

perspicuity [pɜːspɪˈkjuːɪtɪ] *n., no pl.* Klarheit, *die;* Verständlichkeit, *die*

perspicuous [pəˈspɪkjʊəs] *adj.* **a)** *(easily understood)* [klar] verständlich; leicht zu verstehen; **b)** *(expressing things clearly)* sich klar ausdrückend; **be ~:** sich klar ausdrücken

perspiration [pɜːspɪˈreɪʃn] *n.* **a)** Schweiß, *der;* **b)** *(action of perspiring)* Schwitzen, *das;* Transpiration, *die (geh.)*

perspire [pəˈspaɪə(r)] *v. i.* schwitzen; transpirieren *(geh.)*

persuadable [pəˈsweɪdəbl] *adj.* leicht zu überreden; **be easily ~:** sich leicht überreden lassen; **he might be ~:** vielleicht läßt er sich überreden

persuade [pəˈsweɪd] *v. t.* **a)** *(cause to have belief)* überzeugen **(of** von); **~ oneself of sth.** sich *(Dat.)* etw. einreden; **~ oneself [that] ...:** sich *(Dat.)* einreden, daß ...; **~ sb. into believing otherwise** jmdm. etwas anderes einreden *od. (ugs.)* weismachen; **b)** *(induce)* überreden; **~ sb. into/out of doing sth.** jmdn. [dazu] überreden, etw. zu tun/nicht zu tun

persuaded [pəˈsweɪdɪd] *adj.* überzeugt **(of** von)

persuader [pəˈsweɪdə(r)] *n. (sl.: gun)* Kanone, *die (salopp)*

persuasible [pəˈsweɪzɪbl] *see* **persuadable**

persuasion [pəˈsweɪʒn] *n.* **a)** *(action of persuading)* Überzeugung, die; *(persuasiveness)* Überzeugungskraft, *die;* **it didn't take much ~:** es brauchte nicht viel Überredungskunst; **he didn't need much ~ [to have another drink]** man brauchte ihn nicht lange dazu überreden[, noch etwas zu trinken]; **convince sb. by ~:** jmdn. überzeugen; **have considerable powers of ~, be good at ~:** große Überzeugungskraft haben; **b)** *(belief)* Überzeugung, *die;* **c)** *(religious belief)* Glaubensrichtung, *die;* Glaube, *der; (sect)* Glaubensgemeinschaft, *die*

persuasive [pəˈsweɪsɪv] *adj.,* **persuasively** [pəˈsweɪsɪvlɪ] *adv.* überzeugend

persuasiveness [pəˈsweɪsɪvnɪs] *n., no pl.* Überzeugungskraft, *die*

pert [pɜːt] *adj.* **a)** *(saucy, impudent)* unverschämt; frech; **b)** *(neat)* keck ⟨*Hut, Anzug usw.*⟩; hübsch ⟨*Körper, Nase, Hinterteil*⟩; **c)** *(Amer.) see* **peart**

pertain [pəˈteɪn] *v. i.* **a)** *(belong as part)* **~ to** [dazu]gehören zu; verbunden sein mit, einhergehen mit ⟨*Ereignis, Katastrophe*⟩; **b)** *(be relevant)* ⟨*Kriterien usw.:*⟩ gelten; **~ to** von Bedeutung sein für; ⟨*Verhalten:*⟩ anstehen *(geh.)* (+ *Dat.*); ⟨*Begeisterung:*⟩ typisch sein für; **c)** *(have reference)* **~ to sth.** etw. betreffen; mit etw. zu tun haben

pertinacious [pɜːtɪˈneɪʃəs] *adj.* *(resolute)* unbeirrbar; *(stubbornly inflexible)* starrsinnig ⟨*Person*⟩; starr ⟨*Ansichten*⟩; hartnäckig ⟨*Weigerung, Beharren*⟩; unüberwindlich ⟨*Abneigung*⟩

pertinacity [pɜːtɪˈnæsɪtɪ] *n., no pl. see* **pertinacious:** Starrsinnigkeit, *die;* Hartnäckigkeit, *die*

pertinence [ˈpɜːtɪnəns] *n., no pl.* Relevanz, *die;* **of/of no** *or* **without ~:** von/ohne Bedeutung *od.* Belang

pertinent [ˈpɜːtɪnənt] *adj.* relevant **(to** für); **there are some ~ notes in the appendix** im Anhang stehen einige diesbezügliche Bemerkungen *od.* Bemerkungen hierzu

pertinently [ˈpɜːtɪnəntlɪ] *adv.* *(relevantly)* zum passenden Zeitpunkt; *(so as to be to the point)* sachbezogen

pertly [ˈpɜːtlɪ] *adv.* **a)** *(saucily, impudently)* unverschämt; frech; herausfordernd ⟨*gehen, blicken*⟩; **b)** *(neatly)* keck

perturb [pəˈtɜːb] *v. t.* **a)** *(throw into confusion)* stören; durchkreuzen ⟨*Plan*⟩; **b)** *(disturb mentally)* beunruhigen; **get ~ed** unruhig werden; **c)** *(Astron., Phys.)* stören

perturbation [pɜːtəˈbeɪʃn] *n.* **a)** *(throwing into confusion)* Störung, *die; (of plans)* Durchkreuzung, *die;* **b)** *(agitation)* Beunruhigung, *die;* **c)** *(Astron., Phys.)* Störung, *die;* Perturbation, *die (fachspr.)*

Peru [pəˈruː] *pr. n.* Peru *(das)*

perusal [pəˈruːzl] *n.* Lektüre, *die; (of documents)* sorgfältiges Studium; *(fig.: action of examining) (of documents)* sorgfältige Durchsicht; **give sth. a careful ~:** etw. genau durchlesen *od.* studieren

peruse [pəˈruːz] *v. t.* genau durchlesen; *(fig.: examine)* untersuchen; unter die Lupe nehmen *(ugs.)*

Peruvian [pəˈruːvɪən] **1.** *adj.* peruanisch; **sb. is ~:** jmd. ist Peruaner/Peruanerin. **2.** *n.* Peruaner, *der/*Peruanerin, *die*

pervade [pəˈveɪd] *v. t.* **a)** *(spread throughout)* durchdringen; ⟨*Licht:*⟩ durchfluten; **be ~d with** *or* **by** durchdrungen sein von; **b)** *(be rife among)* ⟨*Seuche:*⟩ wüten in (+ *Dat.*); ⟨*Ansicht:*⟩ weit verbreitet sein in (+ *Dat.*)

pervasion [pəˈveɪʒn] *n. (action of spreading throughout sth.)* Durchdringung, *die*

pervasive [pəˈveɪsɪv] *adj.* *(pervading)* durchdringend ⟨*Geruch, Feuchtigkeit, Kälte*⟩; weit verbreitet ⟨*Ansicht*⟩; sich ausbreitend ⟨*Gefühl*⟩; *(able to pervade)* alles durchdringend

pervasively [pəˈveɪsɪvlɪ] *adv.* alles durchdringend; **spread ~:** um sich greifen

perverse [pəˈvɜːs] *adj.* **a)** *(persistent in error)* uneinsichtig, verstockt ⟨*Person*⟩; borniert ⟨*Person, Argument*⟩; **b)** *(different from what is reasonable)* verrückt; **c)** *(peevish)* grimmig; bockig ⟨*Kind*⟩; **d)** *(perverted, wicked)* schlecht, verdorben; **e)** *(Law: contrary to evidence or judge's direction)* abweichend

perversely [pəˈvɜːslɪ] *adv.* **a)** *(with persistence in error)* uneinsichtig; verstockt; **b)** *(contrary to what is reasonable)* verrückt; **c)** *(peevishly)* grimmig; *(of child's behaviour)* bockig

perverseness [pəˈvɜːsnɪs] *see* **perversity**

perversion [pəˈvɜːʃn] *n.* **a)** *(turning aside from proper use)* Mißbrauch, *der; (misconstruction)* Pervertierung, *die; (of words, statement)* Verdrehung, *die; (leading astray)* Verführung, *die;* **~ of justice** Rechtsbeugung, *die;* **b)** *(perverted form of sth.)* Pervertierung, *die;* **c)** *(sexual)* Perversion, *die*

perversity [pəˈvɜːsɪtɪ] *n.* **a)** *(persistence in error)* Uneinsichtigkeit, *die;* Verstocktheit, *die;* **b)** *(difference from what is reasonable)* Verrücktheit, *die*

pervert 1. [pəˈvɜːt] *v. t.* **a)** *(turn aside from proper use or nature)* pervertieren *(geh.)*; beugen ⟨*Recht*⟩; untergraben ⟨*Staatsform, Demokratie*⟩; vereiteln ⟨*Absicht*⟩; **~ [the course of] justice** die Justiz behindern; **b)** *(misconstrue)* verfälschen; **c)** *(lead astray)* verderben. **2.** [ˈpɜːvɜːt] *n.* **a)** *(sexual)* Perverse, *der/die;* perverser Mensch; **he must be a ~:** er muß pervers sein; **b)** *(apostate)* Renegat, *der/*Renegatin, *die*

perverted [pəˈvɜːtɪd] *adj.* **a)** *(turned aside from proper use)* pervertiert *(geh.)*; **b)** *(misconstrued)* verdreht; **c)** *(led astray)* schlecht; verdorben; **d)** *(sexually)* pervers

peseta [pəˈseɪtə] *n.* Peseta, *die*

pesky [ˈpeskɪ] *adj. (Amer. coll.)* verdammt *(ugs.)*

peso [ˈpeɪsəʊ] *n., pl.* **~s** Peso, *der*

pessary [ˈpesərɪ] *n. (Med.)* **a)** Pessar, *das;* **b)** *(vaginal suppository)* Vaginalzäpfchen, *das;* Vaginatorium, *das (fachspr.)*

pessimism [ˈpesɪmɪzm] *n., no pl.* Pessimismus, *der*

pessimist [ˈpesɪmɪst] *n.* Pessimist, *der/*Pessimistin, *die*

pessimistic [pesɪˈmɪstɪk] *adj.,* **pessimistically** [pesɪˈmɪstɪkəlɪ] *adv.* pessimistisch

pest [pest] *n.* **a)** *(troublesome thing)* Ärgernis, *das;* Plage, *die; (troublesome person)* Nervensäge, *die (ugs.)*; *(destructive or annoying animal)* Schädling, *der;* **~s** *(insects)* Schädlinge; Ungeziefer, *das;* **I know it's a ~, but ...** *(a nuisance)* ich weiß, es ist lästig, aber ...; **he's a real ~:** er ist einfach unausstehlich; **~ officer** Schädlingsbekämpfer, *der;* Kammerjäger, *der (veralt.)*; **~ control** Schädlingsbekämpfung, *die;* **b)** *(arch.) (disease)* Seuche, *die; (plague)* Pest, *die*

pester ['pestə(r)] *v.t.* belästigen; nerven *(ugs.)*; ~ **sb. for sth.** jmdm. wegen etw. in den Ohren liegen; ~ **sb. to do sth.** jmdm. in den Ohren liegen, etw. zu tun; ~ **sb. for money** jmdn. [um Geld] anbetteln; ~ **sb. for an interview** jmdn. wegen eines Interviews bedrängen *od. (ugs.)* nerven

pesticide ['pestɪsaɪd] *n.* Pestizid, *das*

pestilence ['pestɪləns] *n.* Pestilenz, *die;* Seuche, *die; (bubonic plague)* Pest, *die*

pestilent ['pestɪlənt] *adj.* **a)** tödlich; todbringend; **b)** *(fig. coll.: troublesome)* unausstehlich; lästig ‹*Ansinnen*›; **c)** *(pernicious)* verderblich; zersetzend ‹*Lehre*›

pestilential [pestɪ'lenʃl] *adj.* **a)** pestilenzartig; **b)** *(fig. coll.: troublesome)* unausstehlich; **he's a ~ nuisance** er ist unausstehlich; **these ~ flies** diese elenden Fliegen; **c)** *(pernicious)* verderblich; zersetzend ‹*Lehre*›

pestle ['pesl] *n.* Stößel, *der;* Pistill, *das (fachspr.)*

[1]pet [pet] **1.** *n.* **a)** *(tame animal)* Haustier, *das;* **b)** *(darling, favourite)* Liebling, *der; (sweet person; also as term of endearment)* Schatz, *der;* **make a ~ of sb.** jmdn. verhätscheln; **mother's** *or* **mummy's ~** *(derog.)* Mamas Liebling; *(male)* Muttersöhnchen, *das (abwertend);* **teacher's ~** *(derog.)* Liebling des Lehrers/der Lehrerin; **you have been a ~:** du bist ein Schatz; **[do] be a ~ and do sth.** sei so lieb und tue etw. **2.** *adj.* **a)** *(kept as ~)* zahm; **b)** *(of or for ~ animals)* Haustier-; **~ accessories** Zoobedarf, *der;* **c)** *(favourite)* Lieblings-; **sth./sb. is sb.'s ~ aversion** *or* **hate** jmd. kann etw./jmdn. auf den Tod nicht ausstehen *(ugs.);* **be sb.'s ~ peeve** jmdm. ein Dorn im Auge sein; **d)** *(expressing fondness)* Kose‹*form, -name*›. **3.** *v.t.*, **-tt- a)** *(treat as favourite)* bevorzugen; verwöhnen; *(indulge)* verhätscheln; **b)** *(fondle)* streicheln; liebkosen. **4.** *v.i.*, **-tt-** knutschen *(ugs.);* zärtlich sein *(verhüll.)*

[2]pet *n. (bad temper)* **in a ~:** verstimmt; beleidigt; eingeschnappt *(ugs.);* **she is in one of her ~s** sie hat mal wieder schlechte Laune

petal ['petl] *n.* Blütenblatt, *das*

-petal[l]ed ['petld] *adj. in comb.* -blättrig ‹*Blüte*›

petard [pɪ'tɑ:d] *n. (Hist.)* Petarde, *die; see also* **hoist 3**

Pete [pi:t] *n.* **for ~'s sake** ≈ **for Heaven's sake** *see* **[1]sake**

Peter ['pi:tə(r)] *pr. n.* Peter; Petrus *(hist., im MA. u. früher);* **Saint ~:** Sankt Petrus *od.* Peter; **rob ~ to pay Paul** ein Loch mit etwas stopfen, was dann woanders fehlt *(fig.); see also* **Blue Peter**

peter *v.i.* ~ **out** [allmählich] zu Ende gehen; ‹*Wasserlauf:*› versickern; ‹*Weg:*› sich verlieren; ‹*Briefwechsel:*› versanden; ‹*Angriff:*› sich totlaufen

Peter 'Pan *n.* Peter Pan; **be a ~:** ein Kindskopf sein; **~ collar** Bubikragen, *der*

petersham ['pi:təʃəm] *n.* Gurtband, *das*

'pet food *n.* Tierfutter, *das*

petiole ['petɪəʊl] *n. (Bot.)* Blattstengel, *der*

petit ['petɪ] *(Law) see* **petty d**

petit bourgeois [pəti: 'bʊəʒwɑ:] *n., pl.* **petits bourgeois** [pəti: 'bʊəʒwɑ:] *(usu. derog.)* Kleinbürger, *der; attrib.* Kleinbürger-; kleinbürgerlich

petite [pə'ti:t] *adj. fem.* zierlich

petite bourgeoisie [pəti:t bʊəʒwɑ:'zi:] *n., no pl., no indef. art.* Kleinbürgertum, *das*

petit four [pəti: 'fʊə(r)] *n., pl.* **petits fours** [pəti: 'fʊə(r)] Petit four, *das*

petition [pə'tɪʃn] **1.** *n.* **a)** *(formal written supplication)* Petition, *die;* Eingabe, *die;* **get together** *or* **up a ~ for/against sth.** Unterschriften für/gegen etw. sammeln; **b)** *(Law: application for writ etc.)* [förmlicher] Antrag; *(for divorce)* Klage, *die.* **2.** *v.t.* eine Eingabe richten an (+ *Akk.*); eine Eingabe machen bei; **~ sb. for sth.** jmdn. um etw. ersuchen. **3.** *v.i.* ~ **for** ersuchen um *(geh.);* nachsuchen um *(geh.); (present ~ for)* eine Unterschriftenliste einreichen für; einkommen um *(geh.);* **~ against** eine Eingabe machen gegen

petitioner [pə'tɪʃənə(r)] *n.* Antragsteller, *der*/Antragstellerin, *die; (for divorce)* Kläger, *der*/Klägerin, *die*

petit point [pəti: 'pwæ̃] *n.* **a)** *(embroidery)* Petit point, *das;* **b)** *(stitch)* Perlstich, *der*

petits pois [pəti: 'pwɑ] *n. pl.* feine Erbsen

Petrarch ['petrɑ:k] *pr. n.* Petrarca *(der)*

petrel ['petrl] *n. (Ornith.)* Sturmvogel, *der*

petrifaction [petrɪ'fækʃn] *n.* Versteinerung, *die*

petrify ['petrɪfaɪ] **1.** *v.t.* **a)** *(change into stone)* petrifizieren *(geh.);* versteinern lassen; **become petrified** versteinern; petrifizieren *(geh.);* **b)** *(fig.: cause to become inert)* erstarren lassen; **be petrified with fear/shock** starr vor Angst/Schrecken sein; vor Angst/Schrecken [wie] versteinert sein *(geh.);* **be petrified by sb./sth.** vor jmdm./etw. erstarren; sich vor jmdm. panisch fürchten; **she looked quite petrified** sie schien entsetzliche Angst zu haben. **2.** *v.i.* *(turn to stone)* versteinern; *(fig.: become inert)* erstarren

petrochemical [petrəʊ'kemɪkl] **1.** *n.* Petrochemikalie, *die.* **2.** *adj.* **a)** *(of chemistry of rocks)* petrochemisch; **b)** *(of chemistry of petroleum)* petro[l]chemisch

petrochemistry [petrəʊ'kemɪstrɪ] *n.* **a)** *(chemistry of rocks)* Petrochemie, *die;* **b)** *(chemistry of petroleum)* Petro[l]chemie, *die*

petrol ['petrl] *n. (Brit.)* Benzin, *das;* **fill up with ~:** tanken

petrolatum [petrə'leɪtəm] *n. (Amer.) see* **petroleum jelly**

petrol: ~ bomb *n. (Brit.)* Benzinbombe, *die;* **~-can** *n. (Brit.)* Benzinkanister, *der;* **~-cap** *n. (Brit.)* Tankverschluß, *der*

petroleum [pɪ'trəʊlɪəm] *n.* Erdöl, *das*

petroleum 'jelly *n.* Vaseline, *die*

'petrol-gauge *n. (Brit.)* Benzinuhr, *die;* Kraftstoffanzeiger, *der (Technik)*

petrology [pɪ'trɒlədʒɪ] *n.* Petrologie, *die*

petrol: ~-pump *n. (Brit.)* **a)** *(in ~-station)* Zapfsäule, *die;* Tanksäule, *die;* **~-pump attendant** Tankwart, *der*/Tankwartin, *die;* **b)** *(in car, aircraft, etc.)* Benzin- *od.* Kraftstoffpumpe, *die;* **~-station** *n. (Brit.)* Tankstelle, *die;* **~-tank** *n. (Brit.) (in car, aircraft, etc.)* Benzintank, *der;* **~-tanker** *n. (Brit.)* Benzintankwagen, *der*

'pet shop *n.* Tierhandlung, *die;* Zoohandlung, *die*

petticoat ['petɪkəʊt] **1.** *n.* Unterrock, *der.* **2.** *adj.* weiblich; Frauen-; **~ government** Frauenherrschaft, *die;* Weiberregiment, *das (abwertend)*

pettifogging ['petɪfɒgɪŋ] *adj.* kleinkariert, kleinlich ‹*Person*›; belanglos ‹*Detail*›; kleinlich ‹*Einwand*›; **his ~ mind** seine Kleinkariertheit

petting ['petɪŋ] *n.* Petting, *das*

pettish ['petɪʃ] *adj.*, **pettishly** ['petɪʃlɪ] *adv.* übellaunig; grantig *(ugs.)*

petty ['petɪ] *adj.* **a)** *(trivial)* belanglos ‹*Detail, Sorgen*›; kleinlich ‹*Einwand, Vorschrift*›; **b)** *(minor)* Klein‹*staat, -unternehmer, -landwirt*›; klein ‹*Geschäftsmann*›; Duodez‹*fürst, -fürstentum, -staat*›; **c)** *(small-minded)* kleinlich; kleinkariert; **d)** *(Law)* geringfügig; Bagatell-; *see also* **session g**

petty: ~ 'cash *n.* kleine Kasse; Portokasse, *die;* **~ 'officer** *n. (Navy)* ≈ [Ober]maat, *der*

petulance ['petjʊləns] *n., no pl.* Bockigkeit, *die*

petulant ['petjʊlənt] *adj.*, **petulantly** ['petjʊləntlɪ] *adv.* bockig

petunia [pɪ'tju:nɪə] *n. (Bot.)* Petunie, *die*

pew [pju:] *n.* **a)** *(Eccl.)* Kirchenbank, *die;* **b)** *(coll.: seat)* [Sitz]platz, *der;* **have** *or* **take a ~:** sich platzen *(ugs. scherzh.)*

pewit *see* **peewit**

pewter ['pju:tə(r)] **1.** *n., no pl., no indef. art.* *(substance, vessels)* Pewter, *der;* [Hart]zinn, *das.* **2.** *attrib. adj.* Zinn‹*becher, -geschirr*›

PG *abbr. (Brit. Cinemat.)* **Parental Guidance** ≈ bedingt jugendfrei

pH [pi:'eɪtʃ] *n. (Chem.)* pH-Wert, *der*

phalanx ['fælæŋks] *n., pl.* **~es** *or* **phalanges** [fæ'lændʒi:z] **a)** *(of troops, police, etc.)* Phalanx, *die;* **b)** *(Anat.)* Phalanx, *die; (of finger)* Fingerglied, *das; (of toe)* Zehenglied, *das*

phallic ['fælɪk] *adj.* phallisch; **~ symbol** Phallussymbol, *das*

phallus ['fæləs] *n., pl.* **~es** *or* **phalli** ['fælaɪ] Phallus, *der*

phantasmagoria [fæntæzmə'gɔ:rɪə] *n.* Trugbild, *das;* Phantasmagorie, *die (geh.)*

phantasy *see* **fantasy a, b**

phantom ['fæntəm] **1.** *n.* **a)** *(spectre)* Phantom, *das; (image)* Phantom, *das;* Trugbild, *das;* **b)** *(mental illusion)* Phantasiegebilde, *das.* **2.** *adj.* Phantom-

phantom: ~ 'limb *n. (Med.)* Phantomglied, *das;* **~ 'pregnancy** *n. (Med.)* Scheinschwangerschaft, *die*

Pharaoh ['feərəʊ] *n.* Pharao, *der*

Pharisaic[al] [færɪ'seɪɪk(l)] *adj.* pharisäerhaft

Pharisee ['færɪsi:] *n.* **a)** Pharisäer, *der;* **b)** **p~** *(self-righteous person)* Pharisäer, *der*

pharmaceutical [fɑ:mə'sju:tɪkl] **1.** *adj.* pharmazeutisch; Arzneimittel-, Pharma‹*industrie, -konzern, -hersteller*›; **~ chemist** Arzneimittelchemiker, *der*/*-chemikerin, die.* **2.** *n. in pl.* Pharmaka

pharmacist ['fɑ:məsɪst] *n.* Apotheker, *der*/Apothekerin, *die; (in research)* Pharmazeut, *der*/Pharmazeutin, *die*

pharmacological [fɑ:məkə'lɒdʒɪkl] *adj.* pharmakologisch

pharmacologist [fɑ:mə'kɒlədʒɪst] *n.* Pharmakologe, *der*/Pharmakologin, *die*

pharmacology [fɑ:mə'kɒlədʒɪ] *n.* Pharmakologie, *die*

pharmacopoeia [fɑ:məkə'pi:ə] *n.* Pharmakopöe, *die;* amtliches Arzneibuch

pharmacy ['fɑ:məsɪ] *n.* **a)** *no pl., no art.* *(preparation of drugs)* Pharmazie, *die;* Arzneimittelkunde, *die;* **b)** *(dispensary)* Apotheke, *die*

pharyngeal [fæ'rɪndʒɪəl] *adj. (Anat., Med.)* Rachen‹*katarrh, -entzündung, -mandel, -höhle usw.*›; Schlund‹*tasche, -krampf*›

pharyngitis [færɪn'dʒaɪtɪs] *n. (Med.)* Rachenkatarrh, *der;* Pharyngitis, *die (fachspr.)*

pharynx ['færɪŋks] *n., pl.* **pharynges** [fə'rɪndʒi:z] *(Anat.)* Schlund, *der;* Rachen, *der;* Pharynx, *der (fachspr.)*

phase [feɪz] **1.** *n.* **a)** Phase, *die; (of project, construction, history also)* Abschnitt, *der; (of illness, development also)* Stadium, *das;* **it's only** *or* **just a ~ [he's/she's going through]** das gibt sich [mit der Zeit] wieder *(ugs.);* **b)** *(Phys., Astron., Chem.)* Phase, *die;* **in ~:** phasengleich; in [gleicher] Phase; **out of ~:** phasenverschoben; **have got out of ~** *(fig.)* nicht mehr koordiniert sein. **2.** *v.t.* stufenweise durchführen

~ **'in** *v.t.* stufenweise einführen

~ **'out** *v.t.* **a)** *(eliminate gradually)* nach und nach auflösen ‹*Abteilung*›; allmählich abschaffen ‹*Verfahrensweise, Methode*›; **b)** *(discontinue production of)* [langsam] auslaufen lassen

Ph.D. [pi:eɪtʃ'di:] *abbr.* **Doctor of Philosophy** Dr. phil.; **he/she is studying for a ~:** er ist Doktorand/sie ist Doktorandin; er/sie promoviert; **John Clarke ~:** Dr. phil. John Clarke; **do one's ~:** seinen Doktor machen; **~ thesis** Doktorarbeit, *die;* Dissertation, *die*

pheasant ['fezənt] *n.* Fasan, *der*

phenobarbitone [fi:nəʊ'bɑ:bɪtəʊn] *(Brit.; Amer.:* **phenobarbital** [fi:nəʊ'bɑ:bɪtl]) *n. (Med.)* Phenobarbital, *das*

phenol ['fi:nɒl] *n. (Chem.)* Phenol, *das;* Karbolsäure, *die*

phenomenal [fɪ'nɒmɪnl] *adj.* **a)** *(remarkable)* phänomenal; sagenhaft *(ugs.);* unwahrscheinlich *(ugs.)* ‹*Spektakel, Radau*›; **b)** *(Philos.)* phänomenal; wahrnehmbar

phenomenalism [fɪ'nɒmɪnəlɪzm] *n. (Philos.)* Phänomenalismus, *der*

phenomenally [fɪ'nɒmɪnəlɪ] *adj.* phänomenal; unglaublich; unwahrscheinlich *(ugs.)* ‹*schlecht, langweilig, laut*›

phenomenon [fɪ'nɒmɪnən] *n., pl.* **phenomena** [fɪ'nɒmɪnə] Phänomen, *das*

phew [fju:] *int.* puh

phial ['faɪəl] *n.* [Medizin]fläschchen, *das;* Phiole, *die*

philander [fɪ'lændə(r)] *v. i. (flirt)* schäkern; flirten; *(with heavier sexual overtones)* nachstellen (**with** *Dat.*)

philanderer [fɪ'lændərə(r)] *n.* Schürzenjäger, *der (spött.)*

philanthropic [fɪlən'θrɒpɪk] *adj.* philanthropisch *(geh.);* menschenfreundlich; Wohltätigkeits‹*organisation, -verein usw.*›

philanthropically [fɪlən'θrɒpɪkəlɪ] *adv.* philanthropisch *(geh.)*

philanthropist [fɪ'lænθrəpɪst] *n.* Philanthrop, *der*/Philanthropin, *die (geh.);* Menschenfreund, *der*/Menschenfreundin, *die*

philanthropy [fɪ'lænθrəpɪ] *n.* Philanthropie, *die (geh.); (love of mankind also)* Menschenliebe, *die;* Menschenfreundlichkeit, *die*

philatelic [fɪlə'telɪk] *adv.* philatelistisch

philatelist [fɪ'lætəlɪst] *n.* Philatelist, *der*/Philatelistin, *die; (collector also)* Briefmarkensammler, *der*/-sammlerin, *die*

philately [fɪ'lætəlɪ] *n.* Philatelie, *die;* Briefmarkenkunde, *die*

philharmonic [fɪlhɑ:'mɒnɪk, fɪlɑ:'mɒnɪk] **1.** *adj.* philharmonisch. **2.** *n.* Philharmonie, *die*

Philip ['fɪlɪp] *pr. n.* Philipp; *(Bibl.)* Philippus

philippic [fɪ'lɪpɪk] *n.* Philippika, *die (geh.)*

Philippine ['fɪlɪpi:n] *adj.* **a)** *(Geog.)* philippinisch; **b)** *see* **Filipino**

Philippines ['fɪlɪpi:nz] *pr. n. pl.* Philippinen *Pl.*

philistine ['fɪlɪstaɪn] **1.** *n.* **a)** *(uncultured person)* [Kultur]banause, *der*/-banausin, *die;* **b)** **P~** *(native of ancient Philistia)* Philister, *der.* **2.** *adj.* banausisch; kulturlos

philistinism ['fɪlɪstɪnɪzm] *n., no pl.* Banausentum, *das; (bourgeois narrow-mindedness)* Philistertum, *das (geh.)*

Phillips ['fɪlɪps] *n.* ~ **screw, (P)** Kreuz[schlitz]schraube, *die;* ~ **screwdriver, (P)** Kreuz[schlitz]schraubenzieher, *der*

philological [fɪlə'lɒdʒɪkl] *adj.* philologisch

philologist [fɪ'lɒlədʒɪst] *n.* Philologe, *der*/Philologin, *die*

philology [fɪ'lɒlədʒɪ] *n.* **a)** *(science of language)* [historische] Sprachwissenschaft; **b)** *(Amer.: study of literature)* Philologie, *die;* Literaturwissenschaft, *die*

philosopher [fɪ'lɒsəfə(r)] *n.* Philosoph, *der*/Philosophin, *die*

philosopher: ~'s stone, ~s' stone *n.* Stein der Weisen

philosophic [fɪlə'sɒfɪk], **philosophical** [fɪlə'sɒfɪkl] *adj.* **a)** philosophisch; philosophisch gebildet *od.* geschult ‹*Person*›; **b)** *(resigned, calm)* abgeklärt; gelassen

philosophically [fɪlə'sɒfɪkəlɪ] *adv.* **a)** ~ **[speaking]** philosophisch betrachtet; vom philosophischen Standpunkt gesehen; **b)** *(calmly)* gelassen

philosophize (philosophise) [fɪ'lɒsəfaɪz] *v. i.* philosophieren (**about, on** über + *Akk.*)

philosophy [fɪ'lɒsəfɪ] *n.* Philosophie, *die;* ~ **of life** Lebensphilosophie, *die;* ~ **of education** Erziehungsphilosophie, *die*

phlebitis [flɪ'baɪtɪs] *n. (Med.)* Venenentzündung, *die;* Phlebitis, *die (fachspr.)*

phlegm [flem] *n., no pl., no indef. art.* **a)** *(Physiol.)* Schleim, *der;* Mucus, *der (Med.);* **b)** *(coolness)* stoische Ruhe; Gleichmut, *der;* **c)** *(stolidness)* Phlegma, *das*

phlegmatic [fleg'mætɪk] *adj.* **a)** *(cool)* gleichmütig; **b)** *(stolid)* phlegmatisch

phlegmatically [fleg'mætɪkəlɪ] *adv. see* **phlegmatic:** gleichmütig; phlegmatisch

phloem ['fləʊem] *n. (Bot.)* Phloem, *das*

phlox [flɒks] *n. (Bot.)* Phlox, *der;* Flammenblume, *die*

phobia ['fəʊbɪə] *n.* Phobie, *die (Psychol.);* [krankhafte] Angst

-phobia ['fəʊbɪə] *n. in comb.* -phobie, *die*

-phobic ['fəʊbɪk] *adj. in comb.* -phob

Phoenician [fə'ni:ʃn] **1.** *adj.* phönizisch; phönikisch. **2.** *n.* Phönizier, *der*/Phönizierin, *die;* Phöniker, *der*/Phönikerin, *die*

phoenix ['fi:nɪks] *n. (Mythol.)* Phönix, *der;* ~**-like** wie ein Phönix

phone [fəʊn] *(coll.)* **1.** *n.* Telefon, *das;* **pick up/put down the ~:** [den Hörer] abnehmen/auflegen; **by ~:** telefonisch; **speak to sb. by ~** *or* **on the ~:** mit jmdm. telefonieren; **be on the ~ for hours** stundenlang telefonieren; **I'm not on the ~:** ich habe kein Telefon. **2.** *v. i.* anrufen; **can we ~ from here?** können wir von hier aus telefonieren? **3.** *v. t.* anrufen; **~ the office/home** im Büro/zu Hause anrufen; **~ a message through to sb.** jmdm. eine Nachricht telefonisch übermitteln *od.* durchgeben. *See also* **telephone**

~ **a'round 1.** *v. i.* herumtelefonieren. **2.** *v. t.* [nacheinander] anrufen

~ **'back** *v. t. & i. (make a return ~ call [to])* zurückrufen; *(make a further ~ call [to])* wieder *od.* nochmals anrufen

~ **'in 1.** *v. i.* anrufen. **2.** *v. t.* telefonisch mitteilen *od.* durchgeben. *See also* **phone-in**

~ **'up** *v. t. & i.* anrufen

phone: ~ **book** *n.* Telefonbuch, *das;* ~ **box** *n.* Telefonzelle, *die;* ~ **call** *n.* Anruf, *der; see also* **telephone call;** ~ **card** *n.* Telefonkarte, *die;* ~**-in** *n.* ~**-in [programme]** *(Radio)* Hörersendung, *die; (Telev.)* Phone-in-Sendung, *die (Jargon);* Sendung mit Zuschaueranrufen

phoneme ['fəʊni:m] *n. (Phonet.)* Phonem, *das*

phone: ~ **number** *n.* Telefonnummer, *die;* ~**-tapping** *n.* Anzapfen von Telefonleitungen

phonetic [fə'netɪk] *adj.* phonetisch; *see also* **alphabet**

phonetically [fə'netɪkəlɪ] *adv.* phonetisch

phonetician [fəʊnɪ'tɪʃn] *n.* Phonetiker, *der*/Phonetikerin, *die*

phonetics [fə'netɪks] *n.* **a)** *no pl.* Phonetik, *die;* **b)** *no pl. (phonetic script)* phonetische Umschrift; **c)** *constr. as pl. (phonetic transcription)* phonetische Angaben

phoney ['fəʊnɪ] *(coll.)* **1.** *adj.*, **phonier** ['fəʊnɪə(r)], **phoniest** ['fəʊnɪɪst] **a)** *(sham)* falsch; gefälscht ‹*Brief, Dokument*›; **there's something a bit ~ about the whole thing** irgend etwas an der ganzen Sache ist faul *(ugs.);* **b)** *(fictitious)* falsch ‹*Name*›; erfunden ‹*Geschichte*›; **c)** *(fraudulent)* Schein‹*firma, -geschäft, -krieg*›; falsch, scheinbar ‹*Doktor, Diplomat, Geschäftsmann*›. **2.** *n.* **a)** *(person)* Blender, *der*/Blenderin, *die;* **this doctor is just a ~:** dieser Arzt ist ein Scharlatan; **b)** *(sham)* Fälschung, *die*

phonograph ['fəʊnəgrɑ:f] *n. (Amer.) see* **gramophone**

phonology [fə'nɒlədʒɪ] *n.* Phonologie, *die*

phony *see* **phoney**

phooey ['fu:ɪ] *int.* pah

phosphate ['fɒsfeɪt] *n. (Chem.)* Phosphat, *das*

phosphor ['fɒsfə(r)] *n.* Phosphor, *der*

phosphorescence [fɒsfə'resəns] *n.* Phosphoreszenz, *die*

phosphorescent [fɒsfə'resənt] *adj.* phosphoreszierend

phosphorus ['fɒsfərəs] *n. (Chem.)* Phosphor, *der*

photo ['fəʊtəʊ] *n., pl.* ~**s** Foto, *das; see also* **photograph 1**

photo- [fəʊtəʊ] *in comb.* **a)** *(light)* photo-/Photo-; **b)** *(photography)* foto-/Foto-

photo: ~ **album** *n.* Fotoalbum, *das;* ~**-call** *n.* Fototermin, *der;* ~**cell** *n.* Photozelle, *die;* ~**'chemical** *adj.* photochemisch; ~**'chemistry** *n.* Photochemie, *die;* ~**composition** *see* **filmsetting;** ~**copier** *n.* Fotokopiergerät, *das;* ~**copy 1.** *n.* Fotokopie, *die;* **2.** *v. t.* fotokopieren; ~**electric** *adj.* photoelektrisch; ~**electric cell** Photozelle, *die;* ~ **finish** *n.* Fotofinish, *das; (fig.)* Kopf-an-Kopf-Rennen, *das;* ~**fit** *n.* Phantombild, *das;* Phantomfoto, *das;* ~**genic** [fəʊtə'dʒenɪk, fəʊtə'dʒi:nɪk] *adj.* fotogen

photograph ['fəʊtəgrɑ:f] **1.** *n.* Fotografie, *die;* Foto, *das;* **take a ~ [of sb./sth.]** [jmdn./etw.] fotografieren; ein Foto [von jmdm./etw.] machen. **2.** *v. t. & i.* fotografieren; **he ~s well/badly** *(as subject)* er läßt sich gut/schlecht fotografieren

'photograph album *n.* Fotoalbum, *das*

photographer [fə'tɒgrəfə(r)] *n.* Fotograf, *der*/Fotografin, *die*

photographic [fəʊtə'græfɪk] *adj.* fotografisch; Foto‹*ausrüstung, -club, -papier, -apparat, -ausstellung, -zeitschrift*›; ~ **memory** *(fig.)* fotografisches Gedächtnis

photographically [fəʊtə'græfɪkəlɪ] *adv.* fotographisch

photography [fə'tɒgrəfɪ] *n., no pl., no indef. art.* Fotografie, *die*

photogravure [fəʊtəgrə'vjʊə(r)] *n.* Photogravüre, *die*

photometer [fəʊ'tɒmɪtə(r)] *n.* Photometer, *der*

photomon'tage *n.* Fotomontage, *die*

photon ['fəʊtɒn] *n. (Phys.)* Photon, *das*

photo: ~**-opportunity** *see* ~**-call;** ~**'sensitive** *adj.* lichtempfindlich; ~**sensi'tivity** *n.* Lichtempfindlichkeit, *die;* ~**setting** *see* **filmsetting; P~stat, (P)** ['fəʊtəstæt] *(Brit.)* **1.** *n. see* **photocopy 1; 2.** *v. t.,* **-tt-** *see* **photocopy 2;** ~**'synthesis** *n. (Bot.)* Photosynthese, *die;* ~**voltaic** *adj. (Phys.)* photovoltaisch

phrasal 'verb *n. (Ling.)* mehrgliedriges Verb

phrase [freɪz] **1.** *n.* **a)** *(Ling.)* Phrase, *die (fachspr.); (idiomatic expression)* idiomatische Wendung; [Rede]wendung, *die;* **set ~:** feste [Rede]wendung; **noun/verb ~:** Nominal-/Verbalphrase, *die;* **b)** *(brief expression)* kurze Formel; **be good at turning a ~:** ausgezeichnet formulieren können; **hackneyed ~:** abgegriffene *od. (ugs.)* abgedroschene Phrase; *see also* **turn 1 j; c)** *(Mus.)* Phrase, *die.* **2.** *v. t.* **a)** *(express in words)* formulieren; ~ **one's idea** seinen Gedanken in Worte fassen; **b)** *(Mus.)* phrasieren

'phrase-book *n.* Sprachführer, *der*

phraseology [freɪzɪ'ɒlədʒɪ] *n.* Ausdrucksweise, *die; (technical terms)* Terminologie, *die*

phrasing ['freɪzɪŋ] *n.* **a)** *(style of expression)* Ausdrucksweise, *die;* **b)** *(Mus.)* Phrasierung, *die*

phrenetic *see* **frenetic**

phrenology [frɪ'nɒlədʒɪ] *n.* Phrenologie, *die*

phut [fʌt] **1.** *adv. (coll.)* **go ~:** kaputtgehen *(ugs.); (fig.)* ‹*Plan, Projekt:*› in die Binsen gehen *(ugs.);* ‹*Geschäft, Firma:*› kaputtgehen *(ugs.).* **2.** *n.* Knall, *der;* ~! peng!

phylloxera [fɪ'lɒksərə] *n. (Zool.)* Reblaus, *die*

phylum ['faɪləm] *n., pl.* **phyla** ['faɪlə] *(Biol.)* [Tier-/Pflanzen]stamm, *der;* Phylum, *das (fachspr.)*

physic ['fɪzɪk] *(arch.)* **1.** *n.* **a)** *(art of healing)* Heilkunde, *die;* **b)** *(medicine)* Arznei, *die* (veralt.); Heilmittel, das. 2. v.t., -ck- mit Arzneimitteln behandeln

physical ['fızıkl] 1. adj. a) (material) physisch ⟨Gewalt⟩; stofflich, dinglich ⟨Welt, Universum⟩; b) (of physics) physikalisch; **it's a ~ impossibility** (fig.) es ist absolut unmöglich; c) (bodily) körperlich; physisch; **you need to take more ~ exercise** du brauchst mehr Bewegung; **~ check-up** or **examination** ärztliche Untersuchung; **get/be ~** (coll.) rabiat werden/sein; d) (carnal, sensual) körperlich ⟨Liebe⟩; sinnlich ⟨Person, Ausstrahlung⟩. 2. n. ärztliche [Vorsorge]untersuchung; (for joining the army) Musterung, die

physical: ~ 'chemistry n. physikalische Chemie; Physikochemie, die; **~ edu'cation** n. Sport, der; Leibesübungen Pl. (Amtsspr.); **~ ge'ography** n. physische Geographie; **~ 'jerks** n. pl. (coll.) Gymnastikübungen

physically ['fızıkəlı] adv. a) (in accordance with physical laws) physikalisch; **~ impossible** (fig.) absolut unmöglich; b) (relating to the body) körperlich; physisch; **they had to be ~ removed** sie mußten mit [physischer] Gewalt entfernt werden; **be ~ sick** einen physischen Ekel empfinden; **~ disabled** körperbehindert

physical: ~ 'science n. exakte Naturwissenschaften; **~ 'training** n. Sport, der; (in school) Sport[unterricht], der

'physic garden n. (arch.) [Heil]kräutergarten, der

physician [fı'zıʃn] n. Arzt, der/Ärztin, die

physicist ['fızısıst] n. Physiker, der/Physikerin, die

physics ['fızıks] n., no pl. Physik, die

physio ['fızıəʊ] n., pl. ~s (coll.) Physiotherapeut, der/Physiotherapeutin, die

physiognomy [fızı'ɒnəmı] n. Physiognomie, die; Gesichtszüge; (study) Physiognomik, die; (fig.: of mountain, country, city, etc.) Physiognomie, die (geh.); Gestalt, die

physiological [fızıə'lɒdʒıkl] adj. physiologisch

physiologist [fızı'ɒlədʒıst] n. Physiologe, der/Physiologin, die

physiology [fızı'ɒlədʒı] n. Physiologie, die

physiotherapist [fızıəʊ'θerəpıst] n. Physiotherapeut, der/-therapeutin, die

physiotherapy [fızıəʊ'θerəpı] n. Physiotherapie, die

physique [fı'zi:k] n. Körperbau, der; **be small in ~**: von geringer Körpergröße od. kleinem Wuchs sein

pi [paı] n. (Math., Greek letter) Pi, das

pianissimo [pıə'nısıməʊ] (Mus.). 1. adj. pianissimo nicht attr.; Pianissimo-. 2. adv. pianissimo. 3. n., pl. ~s or **pianissimi** [pıə'nısımi:] Pianissimo, das

pianist ['pi:ənıst] n. Pianist, der/Pianistin, die

¹piano [pı'ænəʊ] n., pl. ~s (Mus.) (upright) Klavier, das; (grand) Flügel, der; attrib. Klavier-; **play the ~**: Klavier spielen; see also **grand piano; player-piano; upright 1 a**

²piano [pı'ɑ:nəʊ] (Mus.) 1. adj. piano nicht attr.; piano gespielt/gesungen; Piano-. 2. adv. piano. 3. n., pl. ~s or **piani** [pı'ɑ:ni:] (passage) Piano, das

piano-ac'cordion n. Akkordeon, das

pianoforte [pıænə'fɔ:tı] n. (Mus. formal/arch.) Pianoforte, das (veralt.)

Pianola, (P) [pi:ə'nəʊlə] n. Pianola, das

piano [pı'ænəʊ]: **~ music** n. Klaviermusik, die; (score) Klaviernoten Pl.; **~-player** n. Klavierspieler, der/-spielerin, die; **~-stool** n. Klavierschemel, der; **~-tuner** n. Klavierstimmer, der/-stimmerin, die

piazza [pı'ætsə] n. a) pl. **piazze** [pı'ætseı] (public square) Piazza, die; b) pl. ~s (Amer.: veranda) Veranda, die

picador ['pıkədɔ:(r)] n. Picador, der; Lanzenreiter, der

picaresque [pıkə'resk] adj. pikaresk; pikarisch; **~ novel** Schelmenroman, der

picayune [pıkə'ju:n] adj. (Amer. coll.) a) (petty) kleinlich; b) (paltry) unbedeutend; unerheblich

piccalilli [pıkə'lılı] n. Piccalilli, das; scharf gewürztes eingelegtes Senfgemüse

piccaninny ['pıkənını] (Brit.) n. [kleines] Negerkind

piccolo ['pıkələʊ] n., pl. ~s (Mus.) Pikkoloflöte, die; Pikkolo, das

¹pick [pık] n. a) (for breaking up hard ground, rocks, etc.) Spitzhacke, die; (for breaking up ice) [Eis]pickel, der; b) see **toothpick**; c) (Mus.) Plektrum, das

²pick 1. n. a) (choice) Wahl, die; **take your ~**: du hast die Wahl; **you can take your ~ of the rooms** du kannst dir ein Zimmer aussuchen; **she had the ~ of several jobs** sie konnte zwischen mehreren Jobs [aus]wählen; **have [the] first ~ of sth.** als erster aus etw. auswählen dürfen; b) (best part) Elite, die; **the ~ of the herd/fruit** etc. die besten Tiere aus der Herde/die besten Früchte usw.; see also **bunch 1 b**. 2. v.t. a) pflücken ⟨Blumen⟩; [ab]ernten, [ab]pflücken ⟨Äpfel, Trauben usw.⟩; **'~ your own strawberries'** „Erdbeeren zum Selbstpflücken"; b) (select) auswählen; aufstellen ⟨Mannschaft⟩; **~ the** or **a winner/the winning horse** auf den Sieger/das richtige od. siegreiche Pferd setzen; **~ a winner** (fig.) eine gute Wahl treffen; das Große Los ziehen; **~ one's words** seine Worte mit Bedacht wählen; **~ one's way** or **steps** sich (Dat.) vorsichtig [s]einen Weg suchen; **~ one's way through the rules and regulations** sich (Dat.) seinen Weg durch das Dickicht der Vorschriften und Bestimmungen suchen; **~ and choose** sich (Dat.) aussuchen; **you can't ~ and choose which laws to obey** du kannst dir nicht aussuchen, welche Gesetze du befolgen willst [und welche nicht]; **~ one's time [for sth.]** den Zeitpunkt [für etw.] festlegen; **you certainly ~ your times!** (iron.) du suchst dir aber auch immer die unmöglichsten Zeiten aus!; **~ sides [for the game]** abwechselnd einen Spieler/eine Spielerin [für das Spiel] auswählen; c) (clear of flesh) **~ the bones [clean]** ⟨Hund:⟩ die Knochen [sauber] abnagen; **~ the carcass** ⟨Geier, Hyäne usw.:⟩ den Kadaver abfressen; d) **~ sb.'s brains [about sth.]** jmdn. [über etw. (Akk.)] ausfragen od. (ugs.) ausquetschen; e) **~ one's nose/teeth** in der Nase bohren/in den Zähnen [herum]stochern; f) **~ sb.'s pocket** jmdn. bestehlen; **he had his pocket ~ed** er wurde von einem Taschendieb bestohlen; g) **~ a lock** ein Schloß knacken (salopp); h) **~ to pieces** (fig.: criticize) kein gutes Haar lassen an (+ Dat.) (ugs.); i) (Amer. Mus.) zupfen ⟨Saiten⟩; **~ a banjo/guitar** Banjo/Gitarre spielen. See also **bone 1 d; hole 1 a; quarrel 1 a**. 3. v.i. **~ and choose [too much]** [zu] wählerisch sein

~ at v.t. a) (eat without interest) herumstochern in (+ Dat.) ⟨Essen⟩; b) (criticize) herumhacken auf (+ Dat.) (ugs.); c) herumspielen an, (landsch.) knaupeln an (+ Dat.) ⟨Pickel⟩

~ off v.t. a) ['--] (pluck off) abrupfen ⟨Blüten, Blumen⟩; abzupfen, ablesen ⟨Haare, Fusseln⟩; **the helicopter ~ed him off his boat** der Hubschrauber holte ihn aus seinem Boot heraus; b) [-'-] (shoot one by one) [einzeln] abschießen od. (ugs.) abknallen

~ on v.t. a) (victimize) es abgesehen haben auf (+ Akk.); **he's constantly being ~ed on to do the dirty jobs** ihm wird immer die Dreckarbeit aufgehalst; **why ~ on me every time?** warum immer gerade od. ausgerechnet ich?; **~ on someone your own size!** leg dich doch wenigstens mit einem Gleichstarken an! (ugs.); b) (select) sich (Dat.) aussuchen

~ 'out v.t. a) (choose) auswählen; (for oneself) sich (Dat.) aussuchen ⟨Kleid, Blume⟩; heraussuchen, [her]aussortieren ⟨rote Kugeln, kleine Bälle, defekte Ware, [un]reife Früchte⟩; (from text) herausgreifen ⟨Beispiel, Passage⟩; b) (distinguish) ausmachen, entdecken ⟨Detail, jmds. Gesicht in der Menge⟩; **the spotlight ~ed out a child in the audience** der Scheinwerfer erfaßte ein Kind im Publikum; **~ out sth. from sth.** etw. von etw. unterscheiden; c) (highlight) hervorheben ⟨Buchstaben, Inschrift⟩; d) (play by ear etc.) sich (Dat.) zusammensuchen ⟨Melodie⟩

~ 'over v.t. durchstöbern; **the tomatoes have been well ~ed over** die besten Tomaten sind schon herausgesucht worden

~ up 1. ['--] v.t. a) (take up) [in die Hand] nehmen ⟨Brief, Buch usw.⟩; hochnehmen ⟨Baby⟩; [wieder] aufnehmen ⟨Handarbeit⟩; aufnehmen ⟨Masche⟩; auffinden ⟨Fehler⟩; (after dropping) aufheben; **~ sth. up from the table** etw. vom Tisch nehmen; **~ a child up in one's arms** ein Kind auf den Arm nehmen; **~ up the telephone** den [Telefon]hörer abnehmen; **~ up the pieces** (lit. or fig.) die Scherben aufsammeln; **~ up your feet** heb die Füße hoch; see also **thread 1 b**; b) (collect) mitnehmen; (by arrangement) abholen **(at, from** von); (obtain) holen; **~ up sth. on the way home** etw. auf dem Nachhauseweg abholen; c) (become infected by) sich (Dat.) einfangen od. holen (ugs.) ⟨Virus, Grippe⟩; d) (take on board) ⟨Bus, Autofahrer:⟩ mitnehmen; **~ sb. up at** or **from the station** jmdn. vom Bahnhof abholen; e) (rescue from the sea) [aus Seenot] bergen; f) (coll.: earn) einstreichen (ugs.); g) (coll.: make acquaintance of) aufreißen (ugs.); h) (find and arrest) festnehmen; i) (receive) empfangen ⟨Signal, Funkspruch usw.⟩; j) (hear) aufschnappen (ugs.); **he'd ~ed up some tale that ...**: er hatte etwas läuten gehört, daß ...; k) (obtain casually) sich (Dat.) aneignen; bekommen ⟨Sache⟩; **things we ~ed up on our holidays/journeys** Dinge, die wir aus dem Urlaub/von unseren Reisen mitgebracht haben; **~ up languages easily** mühelos Sprachen lernen; **~ up odd habits** seltsame Gewohnheiten annehmen; **where do you ~ up such expressions?** wo hast du denn diese Ausdrücke her?; l) (obtain) auftreiben (ugs.); m) (resume) wieder aufnehmen ⟨Erzählung, Gespräch⟩; n) (succeed in seeing) ausmachen; o) (regain) wiederfinden ⟨Spur, Fährte⟩; wieder aufnehmen ⟨Witterung⟩; **you cross the field and ~ up the path on the other side** du überquerst das Feld und stößt od. kommst auf der anderen Seite wieder auf den Weg; p) (pay) **~ up the bill** etc. **for sth.** die Kosten od. die Rechnung usw. für etw. übernehmen. See also **pick-me-up; pick-up; speed 1 a**. 2. [-'-] v.i. a) (improve, recover) ⟨Gesundheitszustand, Befinden, Stimmung, Laune, Wetter:⟩ sich bessern; ⟨Person:⟩ sich erholen, wieder auf die Beine kommen; ⟨Markt, Geschäft:⟩ sich erholen od. beleben; ⟨Gewinne:⟩ steigen, zunehmen; b) (gain speed) beschleunigen; ⟨Wind:⟩ auffrischen. 3. v. refl. **~ oneself up** wieder aufstehen; (with difficulty) sich wieder aufrappeln (ugs.); (fig.) sich aufrappeln (ugs.)

~ 'up with v.t. (coll.: make the acquaintance of) kennenlernen

pick-a-back ['pıkəbæk] see **piggyback**

pickaninny (Amer.) see **piccaninny**

'pickaxe (Amer.: **'pickax**) see **¹pick a**

picker ['pıkə(r)] n. (of fruit, hops, cotton, etc.) Pflücker, der/Pflückerin, die

picket ['pıkıt] 1. n. a) (Industry) Streikposten, der; **mount a ~ [at** or **on a gate]** [an einem Tor] Streikposten aufstellen; see also **flying picket**; b) (pointed stake) Pfahl, der; c) (Mil.: small body of troops) Feldposten, *der;* **advanced ~:** vorgeschobener Posten; Vorposten, *der;* **d)** *(Mil.: camp-policeman)* Feldjäger, *der.* **2.** *v.t.* Streikposten aufstellen vor (+ *Dat.*) ‹*Fabrik, Büro usw.*›. **3.** *v.i.* Streikposten stehen

'picket duty *n.* **be on/do ~:** Streikposten stehen

picketer ['pɪkɪtə(r)] *n.* Streikposten, *der*

'picket fence *n.* Palisadenzaun, *der*

picketing ['pɪkɪtɪŋ] *n.* Aufstellen von Streikposten; **secondary ~:** *Streikpostenstehen bei einem Betrieb, dem man selbst nicht angehört*

'picket line *n.* Streikpostenkette, *die;* **be on the ~:** Streikposten stehen; in der Streikpostenkette stehen

picking ['pɪkɪŋ] *n.* **a)** Ernten, *das; (of fruit, hops, cotton also)* Pflücken, *das; (of grapes also)* Lesen, *das;* **b)** *(fruit picked)* Ernte, *die;* [Ernte]ertrag, *der;* **a large ~ of apples** eine reiche Apfelernte; **c)** *in pl. (gleanings)* Reste *Pl.; (things stolen)* [Aus]beute, *die; (things allowed)* zusätzliche Vergünstigungen; *(yield)* Ausbeute, *die;* **it's easy ~s** das ist ein einträgliches Geschäft; *see also* **slim 1 b**

pickle ['pɪkl] **1.** *n.* **a)** *(preservative) Konservierungsmittel enthaltende Flüssigkeit; (brine)* Salzlake, *die; (vinegar solution)* Marinade, *die;* **b)** *usu. in pl. (food)* [Mixed] Pickles *Pl.;* Essiggemüse, *das;* **c)** *(coll.: predicament)* **be in a ~:** in der Klemme sitzen *(ugs.);* **get into a ~:** in die Klemme geraten *(ugs.);* **be in a sorry** *or (iron.)* **nice** *etc.* **~:** ganz schön in der Klemme sitzen *(ugs.);* **d)** *(acid solution)* Beize, *die.* **2.** *v.t.* **a)** *(preserve)* [in Essig *od.* sauer] einlegen ‹*Gurken, Zwiebeln, Eier*›; marinieren ‹*Hering*›; **b)** *(treat)* beizen ‹*Leder, Metall*›

pickled ['pɪkld] *adj.* **a)** *(sl.: drunk)* betrunken; besoffen *(derb);* **get [thoroughly] ~:** sich [richtig] vollaufen lassen *(ugs.);* **b)** *(preserved)* eingelegt ‹*Eier usw.*›; mariniert ‹*Hering*›; *(in brine)* gepökelt ‹*Fleisch*›; **~ onions/gherkins** eingelegte Zwiebeln/saure Gurken

pick: ~lock *n.* **a)** *(person)* Einbrecher, *der*/Einbrecherin, *die;* **b)** *(tool)* Dietrich, *der;* **~-me-up** *n.* Stärkungsmittel, *das;* **the holiday/hearing that good news was a real ~-me-up** der Urlaub/diese gute Nachricht hat mir richtig gut getan; **~pocket** *n.* Taschendieb, *der*/-diebin, *die;* **~-up** *n.* **a)** *(of goods)* Laden, *das; attrib.* **~-up [point]** *(for bus passengers etc.)* Haltepunkt, *der;* **b)** *(improvement)* Anstieg, *der;* **a ~-up in sales/quality** ein Anstieg der Verkaufszahlen/eine Verbesserung der Qualität; **c)** *(coll.: person)* Zufallsbekanntschaft, *die;* **is that his latest ~-up?** ist das seine neueste Errungenschaft? *(ugs.);* **d)** *(truck)* **~-up [truck/van]** Kleinlastwagen, *der;* **e)** *(of record-player, guitar)* Tonabnehmer, *der;* Pick-up, *der*

picky ['pɪkɪ] *adj. (Amer. coll.)* pingelig *(ugs.)*

picnic ['pɪknɪk] **1.** *n.* **a)** Picknick, *das;* **go for** *or* **on a ~:** ein Picknick machen; picknicken gehen; **have a ~:** ein Picknick machen; picknicken; **b)** *(coll.: easy task, pleasant experience)* Kinderspiel, *das;* **be no ~:** kein Zuckerlecken *od.* Honig[schl]ecken sein; **the Korean War was a ~ in comparison** der Koreakrieg war dagegen ein Spaziergang. **2.** *v.i.,* **-ck-** picknicken; Picknick machen

'picnic-basket *n.* Picknickkorb, *der*

picnicker ['pɪknɪkə(r)] *n.* **there were a lot of ~s on the beach** viele Menschen machten Picknick am Strand; **the ~s cleared up their litter** die Ausflügler räumten nach dem Picknick ihre Abfälle weg

picnic: ~ 'lunch *n.* **a)** Picknick, *das (als Mittagessen);* **b)** *(packed up)* Lunchpaket, *das;* **~ site** *n.* Picknickplatz, *der*

Pict [pɪkt] *n. (Hist.)* Pikte, *der*/Piktin, *die*

pictogram ['pɪktəgræm], **pictograph** ['pɪktəgrɑ:f] *ns.* Piktogramm, *das*

pictorial [pɪk'tɔ:rɪəl] **1.** *adj.* illustriert ‹*Bericht, Zeitschrift, Wochenmagazin*›; bildlich ‹*Darstellung*›; Bild‹*journalismus, -band, -bericht*›; **give a ~ record of sth.** etw. im Bild festhalten. **2.** *n. (magazine, newspaper, etc.)* Illustrierte, *die*

pictorially [pɪk'tɔ:rɪəlɪ] *adv.* in illustrierter Form; bildhaft ‹*darstellen*›

picture ['pɪktʃə(r)] **1.** *n.* **a)** Bild, *das; see also* **pretty 1 a; tell 1 b; b)** *(portrait)* Porträt, *das; (photograph)* Porträtfoto, *das;* **have one's ~ painted** sich malen *od.* portraitieren lassen; **c)** *(mental image)* Vorstellung, *die;* Bild, *das;* **get a ~ of sth.** sich *(Dat.)* von etw. ein Bild machen; von etw. eine Vorstellung bekommen; **give a ~ of sth.** von etw. einen Eindruck vermitteln; **the employment ~** *(fig.)* das Bild der Arbeitsmarktlage; **present a sorry ~** *(fig.)* ein trauriges *od.* jämmerliches Bild abgeben; **look the [very] ~ of health/misery/innocence** wie das blühende Leben aussehen/ein Bild des Jammers sein/wie die Unschuld in Person aussehen; **be the ~ of delight** die Freude in Person sein; **get the ~** *(coll.)* verstehen[, worum es geht]; **I'm beginning to get the ~:** langsam *od.* allmählich verstehe *od. (ugs.)* kapiere ich; **[do you] get the ~?** verstehst du?; **get the whole ~:** den Gesamtzusammenhang erkennen; **put sb. in the ~** jmdn. ins Bild setzen; **be in the ~** *(be aware)* im Bilde sein; **keep out of the ~:** sich raushalten; **keep sb. in the ~:** jmdn. auf dem laufenden halten; **come** *or* **enter into the ~:** [dabei] eine Rolle spielen; **d)** *(film)* Film, *der;* **e)** *in pl. (Brit.: cinema)* Kino, *das;* **go to the ~s** ins Kino gehen; **what's on at the ~s?** was gibt's *od.* läuft im Kino?; **is there anything on at the ~s?** läuft etwas [Interessantes] im Kino?; **f)** *(delightful object)* **be a ~:** wunderschön *od. (ugs.)* ein Gedicht sein; **her face was a ~:** ihr Gesicht sprach Bände; **she looked a ~:** sie sah bildschön aus. **2.** *v.t.* **a)** *(represent)* abbilden; **b)** *(imagine)* **~ [to oneself]** sich *(Dat.)* vorstellen; **c)** *(describe graphically)* anschaulich schildern

picture: ~-book 1. *n.* Bilderbuch, *das;* **2.** *adj.* Bilderbuch-; **~-card** *n.* Figurenkarte, *die;* Bild, *das;* **~-frame** *n.* Bilderrahmen, *der;* **~-framer** *see* **framer; ~-gallery** *n.* Gemäldegalerie, *die;* **~-hook** *n.* Bilderhaken, *der;* **~ palace** *n. (dated)* Filmpalast, *der (veralt.);* **~ 'postcard** *n.* Ansichtskarte, *die;* **~-rail** *n.* Bilderleiste, *die*

picturesque [pɪktʃə'resk] *adj.* malerisch; pittoresk *(geh.); (vivid)* anschaulich, bildhaft ‹*Beschreibung, Erzählung*›

picturesquely [pɪktʃə'resklɪ] *adv.* malerisch; *(graphically)* anschaulich

picture: ~ window *n.* Panoramafenster, *das;* **~-writing** *n.* Bilderschrift, *die*

piddle ['pɪdl] *(coll.)* **1.** *v.i.* **a)** *(act in trifling way)* **~ about** *or* **around** herummachen *(ugs.);* **b)** *(urinate)* Pipi machen *(Kinderspr.);* pinkeln *(ugs.).* **2.** *n.* **a) have a/do one's ~:** Pipi machen *(Kinderspr.);* pinkeln *(ugs.);* **he needs to have a ~:** er muß mal *(ugs.);* **b)** *(urine)* Pipi, *das (Kinderspr.)*

piddling ['pɪdlɪŋ] *adj. (coll.)* lächerlich *(abwertend)*

pidgin ['pɪdʒɪn] *n.* Pidgin, *das*

pidgin 'English *n.* Pidgin-Englisch, *das*

pie [paɪ] *n. (of meat, fish, etc.)* Pastete, *die; (of fruit etc.)* ≈ Obstkuchen, *der;* **as sweet/nice** *etc.* **as ~** *(coll.)* superfreundlich *(ugs.);* scheißfreundlich *(salopp);* **as easy as ~** *(coll.)* kinderleicht *(ugs.);* **have a finger in every ~** *(coll.)* überall die Finger drin haben *(ugs.);* **that's all just ~ in the sky** *(coll.)* das sind alles nur Luftschlösser; das ist alles völlig unrealistisch

piebald ['paɪbɔ:ld] **1.** *adj.* gescheckt, scheckig ‹*Pferd, Kuh, Pony*›. **2.** *n.* Schecke, *die/der*

piece [pi:s] **1.** *n.* **a)** Stück, *das; (of broken glass or pottery)* Scherbe, *die; (of jigsaw puzzle, crashed aircraft, etc.)* Teil, *der; (Amer.: distance)* [kleines] Stück; **a ~ of meat** ein Stück Fleisch; **[all] in one ~:** unbeschädigt; *(fig.)* heil; wohlbehalten; **in ~s** *(broken)* kaputt *(ugs.);* zerbrochen; *(taken apart)* [in Einzelteile] zerlegt; **break into ~s, fall to ~s** zerbrechen; kaputtgehen *(ugs.);* **break sth. to ~s** etw. zerbrechen *od. (ugs.)* kaputtmachen; **go [all] to ~s** *(fig.)* [völlig] die Fassung verlieren; **[all] of a ~:** aus einem Guß; **be [all] of a ~ with sth.** [ganz] genau zu etw. passen; **say one's ~** *(fig.)* sagen, was man zu sagen hat; **b)** *(part of set)* **~ of furniture/clothing/luggage** Möbel-/Kleidungs-/Gepäckstück, *das;* **a 21-~ tea-set** ein 21teiliges Teeservice; **a five-~ band** eine fünfköpfige Band *od.* Kapelle; **a three-/four-~ suite** eine drei-/vierteilige Sitzgarnitur; **a three-~ suit** ein dreiteiliger Anzug; **c)** *(enclosed area)* **a ~ of land/property** ein Stück Land/Grundstück; **a ~ of water** ein kleines Gewässer; **d)** *(example)* **a ~ of impudence [like that]** eine [solche] Unverschämtheit; **~ of luck** Glücksfall, *der;* **by a ~ of good luck** durch eine glückliche Fügung; **a fine ~ of pottery/Victorian literature** eine sehr schöne Töpferarbeit/ein hervorragendes Werk der viktorianischen Literatur; **fine ~ of work** hervorragende Arbeit; **he's an unpleasant ~ of work** *(fig.)* er ist ein unangenehmer Vertreter *(ugs.); see also* **nasty 1 a; e)** *(item)* **~ of news/gossip/information** Nachricht, *die*/Klatsch, *der*/Information, *die;* **be paid by the ~** ‹*Arbeiter:*› Akkord- *od.* Stücklohn erhalten; **the work is paid by the ~:** für die Arbeit wird Akkord- *od.* Stücklohn gezahlt; *see also* **advice a; f)** *(Chess)* Figur, *die; (Draughts, Backgammon, etc.)* Stein, *der;* **g)** *(coin)* **gold ~:** Goldstück, *das;* **~ of silver** Silbermünze, *die;* **a 10p ~:** ein 10-Pence-Stück; eine 10-Pence-Münze; **~ of eight** mexikanischer *od.* spanischer Dollar; Achterstück, *das (veralt.);* **h)** *(article in newspaper, magazine, etc.)* Beitrag, *der;* **i)** *(literary or musical composition)* Stück, *das;* **~ of music** Musikstück, *das; see also* **villain b; j)** *(coll.: woman)* Mieze, *die (ugs.);* **k)** *(Mil.: weapon) (firearm)* Schußwaffe, *die; (of artillery)* Geschütz, *das;* **l)** *(picture)* Stück, *das;* Werk, *das.* **2.** *v.t.* **~ together** *(lit. or fig.)* zusammenfügen **(from** aus); **~ together what happened** rekonstruieren, was passiert ist

pièce de résistance [pi:eɪs də reɪzɪ'stɑ̃s] *n., pl.* **pièces de résistance** [pi:eɪs də reɪzɪ'stɑ̃s] **a)** *(dish)* Hauptgericht, *das;* Pièce de résistance, *das (veralt.);* **b)** *(item)* Krönung, *die;* **and now for my ~!** und nun die Krönung!

'piecemeal *adv., adj.* stückweise

piece: ~-rate *n.* Akkordsatz, *der;* **be paid at** *or* **be on ~-rates** ‹*Arbeiter:*› Akkord- *od.* Stücklohn erhalten; **the work is paid at ~-rates** für die Arbeit wird Akkord- *od.* Stücklohn gezahlt; **~-work** *n., no pl.* Akkordarbeit, *die;* **put sb. on ~-work** jmdn. im Akkord beschäftigen; **be on ~-work** im Akkord arbeiten; **~-work system** Akkordlohnsystem, *das;* **~-worker** *n.* Akkordarbeiter, *der*/-arbeiterin, *die*

pie: ~ chart *n.* Kreisdiagramm, *das;* **~crust** *n.* Teigmantel, *der*

pied [paɪd] *adj.* gescheckt ‹*Pferd, Kuh usw.*›; [bunt]gefleckt ‹*Schmetterling, Vogel*›

pied-à-terre [pjeɪdɑ:'teə(r)] *n., pl.* **pieds-à-terre** [pjeɪdɑ:'teə(r)] Zweitwohnung, *die*

'pie-dish *n.* Pastetenform, *die*

Pied 'Piper *n.* Rattenfänger, *der;* **the ~ of Hamelin** der Rattenfänger von Hameln

pie: ~-eyed *adj. (sl.)* sternhagelvoll *(ugs.);* **~man** ['paɪmən] *n., pl.* **~men** ['paɪmən] *(arch.)* Pastetenverkäufer, *der*

pier [pɪə(r)] *n.* **a)** *(for landing-place, as promenade)* Pier, *der od. (Seemannsspr.) die;* **b)**

(to protect or form harbour) [Hafen]mole, *die;* Hafendamm, *der;* **c)** *(support of bridge)* Pfeiler, *der;* **d)** *(Archit.)* Trumeau, *der*

pierce [pɪəs] *v. t.* **a)** *(prick)* durchbohren, durchstechen ‹*Hülle, Verkleidung, Ohrläppchen*›; *(penetrate)* sich bohren in, [ein]dringen in (+ *Akk.*) ‹*Körper, Fleisch, Herz*›; **have one's ears ~d** sich *(Dat.)* Löcher in die Ohrläppchen machen *od.* stechen lassen; **b)** *(fig.)* **the cold ~d him to the bone** die Kälte drang ihm bis ins Mark; **a scream ~d the night/silence** ein Schrei gellte durch die Nacht/zerriß die Stille; **c)** *(force one's way through)* durchbrechen ‹*feindliche Linien*›; *(fig.)* erschüttern ‹*Gleichgültigkeit*›

piercing ['pɪəsɪŋ] *adj.* durchdringend ‹*Stimme, Schrei, Blick*›; schneidend ‹*Sarkasmus, Kälte*›

pierrot ['pɪərəʊ] *n.* Pierrot, *der*

pietà [pjeɪ'tɑ:] *n. (Art)* Pieta, *die*

piety ['paɪətɪ] *n.* **a)** *no pl. (quality)* Frömmigkeit, *die;* **b)** *(act)* fromme Handlung

piffle ['pɪfl] *(coll.) n.* **a)** *(nonsense)* Quatsch, *der (ugs.);* **b)** *(empty talk)* Geschwafel, *das (ugs.);* Blabla, *das (ugs.)*

piffling ['pɪflɪŋ] *adj. (coll.)* lächerlich

pig [pɪg] **1.** *n.* **a)** Schwein, *das;* **the sow is in ~:** die Sau ist trächtig; **bleed like a [stuck] ~:** wie ein Schwein bluten *(derb);* heftig bluten; **~s might fly** *(iron.)* da müßte schon ein Wunder geschehen; **buy a ~ in a poke** *(fig.)* die Katze im Sack kaufen; **~ in the middle** *(coll.) Ballspiel, bei dem ein in der Mitte stehender Spieler den Ball, den sich die anderen zuwerfen, fangen muß;* **b)** *(coll.) (greedy person)* Vielfraß, *der (ugs.);* Freßsack, *der (salopp); (obstinate person)* Dickschädel, *der (ugs.); (dirty person)* Ferkel, *das (ugs.);* [Dreck]schwein, *das (derb); (unpleasant thing)* Scheißding, *das (salopp); (unpleasant person)* Ekel, *das (ugs.);* Schwein, *das (derb);* **make a ~ of oneself** *(overeat)* sich *(Dat.)* den Bauch *od.* Wanst vollschlagen *(salopp);* **live like ~s** hausen wie die Schweine *(ugs.);* **c)** *(sl. derog.: policeman)* Bulle, *der (salopp abwertend);* **d)** *(metal)* Massel, *die (Metall.);* **e)** *(Amer.: young swine)* Ferkel, *das. See also* **chauvinist. 2.** *v. t.,* **-gg-:** **~ it** *(coll.)* hausen *(ugs.)*

[1]**pigeon** ['pɪdʒɪn] *n.* Taube, *die;* **cock ~:** Tauber, *der;* Täuber[ich], *der*

[2]**pigeon** *n.* **a)** *see* **pidgin; b)** *(coll.: business)* **be sb.'s ~:** jmdn. angehen; **that's not my ~:** das ist nicht mein Bier *(ugs.)*

pigeon: ~-fancier *n.* Taubenfreund, *der*/-freundin, *die;* **~-hole 1.** *n.* **a)** *(in cabinet etc.)* [Ablage]fach, *das; (for letters)* Postfach, *das;* **put people in ~-holes** *(fig.)* Menschen in Schubladen einordnen *od.* stecken; **b)** *(for pigeon)* [Tauben]flugloch, *das;* **2.** *v. t.* **a)** *(deposit)* [in die Fächer] sortieren; **b)** *(put aside)* auf Eis legen; **get ~-holed** in die Schublade wandern; auf Eis gelegt werden; **c)** *(categorize)* einordnen; in eine Schublade/in Schubladen stecken; **~-loft** *n.* Taubenschlag, *der;* **~-toed 1.** *adj.* **a ~-toed man** ein Mann, der mit einwärts gerichteten Füßen geht; **be ~-toed** mit einwärts gerichteten Füßen *od. (ugs.)* über den großen Onkel gehen; **2.** *adv.* mit einwärts gerichteten Füßen; über den großen Onkel *(ugs.)*

piggery ['pɪgərɪ] *n.* **a)** *(pig-breeding establishment)* Schweinezucht, *die;* **b)** *see* **pigsty; c)** *(coll.: gluttony)* Gefräßigkeit, *die (ugs.)*

piggish ['pɪgɪʃ] *adj. (coll.)* **a)** *(gluttonous)* gefräßig *(ugs.);* verfressen *(salopp);* **b)** *(dirty)* schmuddelig *(ugs.);* dreckig *(ugs.);* **c)** *(stubborn)* dickschädelig; stur

piggy ['pɪgɪ] *(coll.)* **1.** *n.* Schweinchen, *das;* Ferkel, *das.* **2.** *adj.* **~ face** Schweinchengesicht, *das;* **~ eyes** Schweinsäuglein *Pl.*

piggy: ~back 1. *n.* **ask for a ~back** huckepack getragen werden wollen; **give sb. a ~back** jmdn. huckepack nehmen *od.* tragen; **2.** *adv.* huckepack; **3.** *adj.* **give a child a ~back ride** ein Kind huckepack tragen; **~ bank** *n.* Sparschwein[chen], *das*

pig: ~'headed *adj.* dickschädelig *(ugs.);* stur; **~headedness** [pɪg'hedɪdnɪs] *n., no pl.* Dickschädeligkeit, *die (ugs.);* Sturheit, *die;* **~-iron** *n.* Roheisen, *das;* Masseleisen, *das (Metall.)*

piglet ['pɪglɪt] *n.* Ferkel, *das*

'**pig-meat** *n.* Schweinefleisch, *das*

pigment ['pɪgmənt] **1.** *n.* Pigment, *das.* **2.** *v. t.* pigmentieren

pigmentation [pɪgmən'teɪʃn] *n.* Pigmentierung, *die;* Pigmentation, *die*

pigmy *see* **pygmy**

pig: ~pen *(Amer.) see* **pigsty; ~'s 'ear** *n. (Brit. coll.)* **make a ~'s ear of sth.** etw. verpfuschen *od. (ugs.)* vermurksen; **~skin** *n.* **a)** Schweinehaut, *die;* **b)** *(leather)* Schweinsleder, *das; attrib.* schweinsledern; Schweinsleder-; **c)** *(Amer. sl.: football)* Leder, *das (ugs.);* **~sty** *n. (lit. or fig.)* Schweinestall, *der;* **~swill** *n.* Schweinefutter, *das; (fig. coll.) (food)* Schweinefraß, *der (derb); (drink, soup, etc.)* Spülwasser, *das (salopp);* **~tail** *n. (plaited)* Zopf, *der;* **~tails** *(worn loose, at either side of head)* Rattenschwänzchen *Pl. (ugs.)*

[1]**pike** [paɪk] *n., pl. same (Zool.)* Hecht, *der*

[2]**pike** *n. (Arms Hist.)* Pike, *die;* Spieß, *der*

[3]**pike** *n. (Brit. Hist., Amer.)* **a)** *(toll-bar)* Zahlstelle, *die;* Mautstelle, *die (bes. südd. u. österr.);* **b)** *(road)* gebührenpflichtige Straße; Mautstraße, *die (bes. südd. u. österr.)*

pike: ~-perch *n. (Zool.)* Zander, *der;* **~staff** *n.* **plain as a ~staff** sonnenklar *(ugs.)*

pilaff [pɪ'læf] *n.* Pilaw, *der (Kochk.)*

pilaster [pɪ'læstə(r)] *n. (Archit.)* Pilaster, *der*

pilchard ['pɪltʃəd] *n.* Sardine, *die*

[1]**pile** [paɪl] **1.** *n.* **a)** *(heap) (of dishes, plates)* Stapel, *der; (of paper, books, letters)* Stoß, *der; (of clothes)* Haufen, *der;* **b)** *(coll.: large quantity)* Masse, *die (ugs.);* Haufen, *der (ugs.);* **a ~ of troubles/letters/people** eine *od. (ugs.)* jede Menge Sorgen/Briefe/Leute; **a great ~ of work/problems** eine Unmenge Arbeit/Probleme; **a ~ of difficult problems awaited her** eine Menge schwierige Probleme erwartete sie; **c)** *(coll.: fortune)* **make a** *or* **one's ~:** ein Vermögen machen; **he's made his ~:** er hat sein Schäfchen im Trockenen *(ugs.);* **d)** *(large building)* Bauwerk, *das;* **e)** *(Electr.)* Voltasche Säule. **2.** *v. t.* **a)** *(load)* [voll] beladen; **~ a table with dishes** einen Tisch mit [Stapeln von] Geschirr vollstellen; **b)** *(heap up)* aufstapeln ‹*Holz, Steine*›; aufhäufen ‹*Abfall, Schnee*›; **c) ~ furniture into a van/lorry** *etc.* Möbel in einen Liefer-/Lastwagen *usw.* laden

~ 'in 1. *v. i.* **a)** *(get in) (seen from outside)* hineindrängen; *(seen from inside)* hereindrängen; **~ in!** [kommt] nur *od.* immer herein!; quetscht euch rein! *(ugs.);* **b)** *(coll.: begin) (to eat)* reinhauen *(ugs.);* zulangen *(ugs.); (to work)* mit anpacken; *(to fight)* mitmischen *(ugs.);* mit von der Partie sein *(ugs.).* **2.** *v. t.* hineinquetschen *(ugs.)*

~ into *v. t.* drängen in (+ *Akk.*) ‹*Stadion, Halle*›; drängen auf (+ *Akk.*) ‹*Platz, Wiese*›; sich zwängen in (+ *Akk.*) ‹*Auto, Zimmer, Zugabteil, Telefonzelle*›

~ off *(coll.)* **1.** [-'-] *v. i. (seen from inside)* hinausdrängen; *(seen from outside)* herausdrängen. **2.** ['--] *v. t.* drängen *od.* strömen aus ‹*Bus usw.*›

~ 'on 1. *v. i. see* **pile in a. 2.** *v. t. (fig.)* **~ on the work/praise** massiv mit Arbeit/Lob kommen; **~ on the pressure** Druck machen; **~ on the agony, ~ it on** *(coll.)* dick auftragen *(ugs.)*

~ on to *v. t.* **a)** *(heap on to)* **~ logs on to the fire** Holzscheite auf das Feuer legen; **he ~d food on to my plate** er häufte mir Essen auf den Teller; **~ work on to sb.** *(fig.)* jmdm. Arbeit aufbürden *od.* aufladen; **b)** *(enter)* drängen in (+ *Akk.*) ‹*Bus usw.*›

~ 'out *v. i.* nach draußen strömen *od.* drängen

~ 'out of *v. t.* strömen *od.* drängen aus

~ 'up 1. *v. i.* **a)** *(accumulate)* ‹*Waren, Post, Aufträge, Arbeit, Schnee:*› sich auftürmen; ‹*Verkehr:*› sich stauen; ‹*Schulden:*› sich vermehren; ‹*Verdacht, Eindruck, Beweise:*› sich verdichten; **b)** *(crash)* aufeinander auffahren. **2.** *v. t.* aufstapeln ‹*Steine, Bücher usw.*›; auftürmen ‹*Haar, Frisur*›; aufhäufen ‹*Abfall, Schnee*›; *(fig.)* zusammentragen ‹*Beweise usw.*›; **~ up debts** sich immer mehr verschulden. *See also* **pile-up**

[2]**pile** *n.* **a)** *(soft surface)* Flor, *der;* **b)** *(soft hair, down)* Flaum, *der*

[3]**pile** *n. (stake)* Pfahl, *der*

pile: ~-driver *n.* [Pfahl]ramme, *die;* **~-dwelling** *n.* Pfahlbau, *der*

piles [paɪlz] *n. pl. (Med.)* Hämorrhoiden *Pl.*

'**pile-up** *n.* Massenkarambolage, *die*

pilfer ['pɪlfə(r)] *v. t.* stehlen; klauen *(ugs.)*

pilferage ['pɪlfərɪdʒ] *n.* Diebstahl, *der*

pilferer ['pɪlfərə(r)] *n.* Dieb, *der*/Diebin, *die;* Langfinger, *der (oft scherzh.)*

'**pilfer-proof** *adj.* einbruch-/diebstahlsicher

pilgrim ['pɪlgrɪm] *n.* Pilger, *der*/Pilgerin, *die;* Wallfahrer, *der*/Wallfahrerin, *die*

pilgrimage ['pɪlgrɪmɪdʒ] *n.* Pilgerfahrt, *die;* Wallfahrt, *die*

Pilgrim 'Fathers *n. pl. (Hist.)* Pilgerväter *Pl.*

pill [pɪl] *n.* **a)** Tablette, *die;* Pille, *die (ugs.);* **be on ~s** Tabletten einnehmen müssen; **b)** *(coll.: contraceptive)* **the ~** *or* **P~** die Pille *(ugs.);* **be on the ~:** die Pille nehmen *(ugs.);* **come off the ~:** die Pille absetzen *od.* nicht mehr nehmen *(ugs.);* **go on the ~:** mit der Pille anfangen *(ugs.);* **c)** *(fig.: unpleasant thing)* **swallow the ~:** die [bittere] Pille schlucken *(ugs.);* **sweeten the ~:** die bittere Pille versüßen *(ugs.);* **be a bitter ~ [to swallow]** eine bittere Pille *od.* bitter sein; **d)** *(sl./joc.: ball)* Pille, *die (salopp)*

pillage ['pɪlɪdʒ] **1.** *n.* Plünderung, *die.* **2.** *v. t.* [aus]plündern; **the abbey was ~d of its treasures** die Schätze der Abtei wurden geraubt. **3.** *v. i.* plündern

pillar ['pɪlə(r)] *n.* **a)** *(vertical support)* Säule, *die; (with angular cross-section)* Pfeiler, *der; (of bed, door)* Pfosten, *der;* **a ~ of strength** *(fig.)* eine Stütze; **from ~ to post** *(fig.)* hin und her; **b)** *(fig.: supporter) (of church, family, party, society, etc.)* Stütze, *die; (of science, alliance, faith, etc.)* Säule, *die;* **c)** *(upright mass)* **~ of dust/cloud/water** Staub-/Wolken-/Wassersäule, *die;* **d)** *(Mining)* [Abbau]pfeiler, *der*

'**pillar-box** *n. (Brit.)* Briefkasten, *der; attrib.* **~ red** knallrot *(ugs.)*

'**pillbox** *n.* **a)** Pillenschachtel, *die;* **b) ~ [hat]** Pillbox, *die; flacher runder Hut ohne Krempe; (of bell-boy)* Pagenkappe, *die;* **c)** *(Mil.)* MG-Unterstand, *der*

pillion ['pɪljən] *n.* Soziussitz, *der;* Beifahrersitz, *der;* **ride ~:** als Beifahrer/Beifahrerin *od.* auf dem Soziussitz mitfahren

pillock ['pɪlək] *n. (sl.)* Schwachkopf, *der (ugs.)*

pillory ['pɪlərɪ] **1.** *v. t. (lit. or fig.)* an den Pranger stellen. **2.** *n. (Hist.)* Pranger, *der*

pillow ['pɪləʊ] **1.** *n.* [Kopf]kissen, *das.* **2.** *v. t.* **her arm ~ed the sleeping child** das schlafende Kind lag in ihren Arm gebettet; **he was like a baby, ~ed in her arms** wie ein Baby lag er in ihren Armen

pillow: ~case *n.* [Kopf]kissenbezug, *der;* **~-fight** *n.* Kissenschlacht, *die;* **~-lace** *n.* Klöppelspitze, *die;* **~ lava** *n. (Geol.)* Kissenlava, *die;* Pillowlava, *die;* **~slip** *see* **~case; ~ talk** *n.* Bettgeflüster, *das*

'**pill-popping** *n. (sl.)* Pillenschluckerei, *die (ugs.)*

pilot ['paɪlət] **1.** *n.* **a)** *(Aeronaut.)* Pilot, *der*/Pilotin, *die;* Flugzeugführer, *der*/-führerin, *die;* **~'s licence** Flug- *od.* Pilotenschein, *der;* **b)** *(Naut.; also fig.: guide)* Lotse, *der.* **2.** *adj.* Pilot‹*programm, -studie, -projekt usw.*›. **3.** *v. t.* **a)** (Aeronaut.) fliegen; **b)** *(Naut.)* lotsen; **~ sb. into/out of the harbour** jmdn. einlotsen *od.* in den Hafen lotsen/auslotsen *od.* aus dem Hafen lotsen; **c)** *(fig.: guide)* lotsen; **~ a bill through the House** *(Parl.)* einen Gesetzentwurf durch das Parlament bringen
pilot: ~ boat *n.* Lotsenboot, *das;* **~-fish** *n.* Lotsenfisch, *der;* Pilotfisch, *der*
pilotless ['paɪlətlɪs] *adj.* unbemannt; führerlos
pilot: ~-light *n.* **a)** *(gas-burner)* Zündflamme, *die;* **b)** *(electric light)* Kontrollampe, *die od.* -lämpchen, *das;* **~ officer** *n.* *(Brit. Air Force)* ≈ [Flieger]leutnant, *der*
pimento [pɪ'mentəʊ] *n., pl.* **~s** *(berry)* Piment, *der od. das;* Nelkenpfeffer, *der;* *(tree)* Pimentbaum, *der;* Nelkenpfefferbaum, *der*
pimp [pɪmp] **1.** *n.* Zuhälter, *der.* **2.** *v. i.* Zuhälterei betreiben; **~ for sb.** jmds. Zuhälter sein
pimpernel ['pɪmpənel] *n.* *(Bot.)* **[scarlet] ~:** Ackergauchheil, *der;* Roter Gauchheil
pimple ['pɪmpl] *n.* **a)** *(spot)* Pickel, *der;* Pustel, *die;* **he/his face had come out in ~s** er hat Pickel/Pickel im Gesicht bekommen; **b)** *(slight swelling)* Erhebung, *die;* *(on table-tennis bat)* Noppe, *die*
pimpled ['pɪmpld] *adj.* pick[e]lig; genoppt ‹*Tischtennisschläger*›
pimply ['pɪmplɪ] *adj.* pick[e]lig
PIN [pɪn] *abbr.* **~ [number]** *see* **personal identification number**
pin 1. *n.* **a)** Stecknadel, *die;* **you could have heard a ~ drop** man hätte eine Stecknadel fallen hören können; **as clean as a new ~:** blitzblank *(ugs.);* **~s and needles** *(fig.)* Kribbeln, *das;* **I had ~s and needles in my legs** *(fig.)* meine Beine kribbelten *od.* waren eingeschlafen; **b)** *(peg)* Stift, *der;* **split ~:** Splint, *der;* **c)** *(Electr.)* Kontaktstift, *der;* **a two-/three-~ plug** ein zwei-/dreipoliger Stecker; **d) I don't give** *or* **care a ~:** es ist mir völlig egal; **for two ~s I'd resign** es fehlt nicht mehr viel, dann kündige ich; **e)** *(Golf)* Flaggenstock, *der;* **f)** *(Mus.: for string of instrument)* Wirbel, *der;* **g)** *(half-firkin cask)* ≈ Zwanzigliterfaß, *das;* **h)** *(in grenade)* Zündring, *der;* **i)** *in pl. (coll.: legs)* Stelzen *(salopp);* **j)** *(skittle)* Kegel, *der;* *(scoring point)* Punkt, *der;* Pin, *der (Kegelsport);* **k)** *(Amer.: brooch)* Anstecknadel, *die;* **[lapel] ~** *(of society, club, etc.)* Abzeichen, *das;* **l)** *(Med.)* Stift, *der;* Pin, *der (fachspr.).* **2.** *v. t.*, **-nn- a)** nageln ‹*Knochen, Bein, Hüfte*›; **~ a badge to one's lapel** sich *(Dat.)* ein Abzeichen ans Revers heften *od.* stecken; **~ a notice on the board** einen Zettel ans Schwarze Brett hängen *od. (ugs.)* pinnen; **~ together** mit einer Stecknadel zusammenhalten; *(Dressm.)* zusammenstecken; **b)** *(fig.)* **~ one's ears back** die Ohren spitzen *(ugs.);* **~ one's hopes on sb./sth.** seine [ganze] Hoffnung auf jmdn./etw. setzen; **~ the blame/responsibility for sth. on sb.** jmdm. die Schuld an etw. *(Dat.)*/die Verantwortung für etw. zuschieben; **you won't ~ it on him** das wirst du ihm nicht unterschieben *od. (ugs.)* anhängen können; *see also* **faith a; c)** *(seize and hold fast)* **~ sb. against the wall** jmdn. an *od.* gegen die Wand drängen *od.* drücken; **~ sb.'s arms to his sides** jmdm. die Arme an den Körper pressen; **~ sb. to the ground** jmdn. auf den Boden drücken; **~ sb.'s arm behind his back** jmdm. den Arm auf den Rücken drehen
~ 'down *v. t.* **a)** *(fig.: bind)* festlegen, festnageln **(to** *or* **on** auf + *Akk.*); **he's a difficult man to ~ down** man kann ihn nur schwer dazu bringen, sich [auf etwas] festzulegen; **he's difficult to ~ down on policies** es ist schwer, ihn auf eine konkrete Politik festzulegen; **b)** *(trap)* festhalten; **~ sb. down [to the ground]** jmdn. auf den Boden drücken; **c)** *(define exactly)* **~ sth. down in words** etw. in Worte fassen; **I can't quite ~ it down** ich kann es nicht richtig ausmachen; **~ the fault down to the carburettor** feststellen, daß der Fehler im Vergaser liegt; **~ down the exact meaning of a word** die Bedeutung eines Wortes genau bestimmen
~ 'up *v. t.* aufhängen ‹*Bild, Foto*›; anschlagen ‹*Bekanntmachung, Hinweis, Liste*›; aufstecken, hochstecken ‹*Haar, Frisur*›; heften ‹*Saum, Naht*›; *see also* **pin-up**
pinafore ['pɪnəfɔ:(r)] *n.* Schürze, *die (mit Oberteil)*
'**pinafore dress** *n.* Trägerrock, *der;* Trägerkleid, *das*
'**pin-ball** *n.* Flippern, *das;* *attrib.* Flipper‹*spiel, -automat*›; **play ~:** flippern; **have a game of ~:** [eine Runde] flippern
pince-nez ['pænsneɪ] *n., pl. same* Kneifer, *der;* Pincenez, *das (veralt.)*
'**pincer movement** ['pɪnsə mu:vmənt] *n.* *(Mil.)* Zangenbewegung, *die*
pincers ['pɪnsəz] *n. pl.* **a) [pair of] ~:** Beißod. Kneifzange, *die;* **b)** *(of crab etc.)* Schere, *die;* Zange, *die (ugs.)*
pinch [pɪnʃ] **1.** *n.* **a)** *(squeezing)* Kniff, *der;* **give sb. a ~:** jmdn. kneifen *od. (bes. südd., österr.)* zwicken; **give sb. a ~ on the arm/cheek** *etc.* jmdn. *od.* jmdm. in den Arm/die Backe *usw.* kneifen *od. (bes. südd., österr.)* zwicken; **b)** *(fig.)* **feel the ~:** knapp bei Kasse sein *(ugs.);* **the firm is feeling the ~:** der Firma geht es finanziell nicht gut; **at a ~:** zur Not; wenn es [unbedingt] sein muß; **if it comes to a** *or* **the ~:** wenn es zum Äußersten *od.* Schlimmsten kommt; **c)** *(small amount)* Prise, *die;* *see also* **salt 1 a. 2.** *v. t.* **a)** *(grip tightly)* kneifen; zwicken *(bes. südd., österr.);* **~ sb.'s cheek/bottom** jmdn. in die Wange/den Hintern *(ugs.)* kneifen; **I had to ~ myself** ich mußte mich erst mal in den Arm kneifen *(ugs.);* **~ed with cold** *(fig.)* [völlig] durchgefroren; starr vor Kälte; **b)** *(coll.: steal)* klauen *(salopp);* **c)** *(coll.: arrest)* sich *(Dat.)* schnappen *(ugs.);* **get ~ed** geschnappt werden *(ugs.);* **d)** *(Hort.)* **~ back** *or* **down** *or* **out** abzwicken; abknipsen *(ugs.).* **3.** *v. i.* **a)** ‹*Schuh:*› drücken; **that's where the shoe ~es** *(fig.)* da liegt der Hase im Pfeffer *od.* der Hund begraben *(ugs.);* **b)** *(be niggardly)* knapsen *(ugs.),* knausern *(ugs. abwertend)* **(on mit)**
pinchbeck ['pɪntʃbek] **1.** *n.* Tombak, *der.* **2.** *adj.* **a)** aus Tombak *nachgestellt;* **b)** *(fig.: counterfeit)* **be ~:** Talmi sein
'**pinch-hitter** *n.* *(Baseball)* Ersatzspieler, *der*/-spielerin, *die*
'**pincushion** *n.* Nadelkissen, *das*
[1]**pine** [paɪn] *n.* **a)** *(tree)* Kiefer, *die;* *attrib.* Kiefern-; **b)** *(wood)* Kiefernholz, *das;* Kiefer, *die;* *attrib.* Kiefer[nholz]-; **a kitchen in ~:** eine Küche aus Kiefer[nholz]
[2]**pine** *v. i.* **a)** *(languish)* **(over, about** wegen) sich [vor Kummer] verzehren *(geh.);* **b)** *(long eagerly)* **~ for sb./sth.** sich nach jmdm./etw. sehnen *od. (geh.)* verzehren
~ a'way *v. i.* dahinkümmern
pineal ['pɪnɪəl] *adj.* *(Anat.)* **~ body** *or* **gland** Zirbeldrüse, *die;* Epiphyse, *die*
pineapple ['paɪnæpl] *n.* Ananas, *die;* **~ juice** Ananassaft, *der;* **~ rings/chunks** Ananasringe *od.* -scheiben/-stücke
pine: ~-cone *n.* *(Bot.)* Kiefernzapfen, *der;* **~ marten** *n.* *(Zool.)* *(American)* Fichtenmarder, *der;* *(European)* Edelmarder, *der;* **~-needle** *n.* Kiefernnadel, *die*
pinetum [paɪ'ni:təm] *n., pl.* **pineta** [paɪ'ni:tə] Kiefernarboretum, *das*
'**pine-wood** *n.* **a)** *(material)* Kiefernholz, *das;* **b)** *(forest)* Kiefernwald, *der*
ping [pɪŋ] **1.** *n.* *(of bullet)* Pfeifen, *das;* *(of bell)* Klingeln, *das;* **the stone made a ~ as it hit the glass** es machte klick, als der Stein gegen das Glas flog. **2.** *v. i.* ‹*Kugel:*› pfeifen, peitschen; ‹*Glocke, Schreibmaschine:*› klingeln
pinger ['pɪŋə(r)] *n.* Kurzzeitwecker, *der;* *(in kitchen)* Küchenwecker, *der*
ping-pong (*Amer.:* **Ping-Pong,** P) ['pɪŋpɒŋ] *n.* Tischtennis, *das;* Pingpong, *das (ugs. veralt.)*
ping-pong: ~ ball *n.* Tischtennisball, *der;* Pingpongball, *der (ugs. veralt.);* **~ table** *n.* Tischtennisplatte, *die*
pin: ~-head *n.* **a)** Stecknadelkopf, *der;* *attrib. (fig.)* winzig; stecknadelkopfgroß; **b)** *(coll.: fool)* Dummkopf, *der;* Strohkopf, *der (ugs.);* **~-headed** *adj.* blöd *(ugs.);* dämlich *(ugs.);* **~-'high** *adj.* *(Golf)* auf Flaggenstockhöhe *nachgestellt;* **~-hole** *n.* [nadelfeines] Loch; **~-hole camera** *n.* *(Photog.)* Lochkamera, *die;* Camera obscura, *die*
[1]**pinion** ['pɪnjən] *n.* *(cog-wheel)* Ritzel, *das (Technik);* kleines Zahnrad
[2]**pinion 1.** *v. t.* **~ sb., ~ sb.'s arms** jmdm. die Arme [an den Körper] fesseln *od.* binden; **~ sb. to sth.** jmdn. an etw. *(Dat.)* festbinden. **2.** *n.* **a)** *(Ornith.)* *(terminal segment of wing)* Hand[schwinge], *die;* *(flight-feather)* Schwungfeder, *die;* **b)** *(poet.: wing)* Schwinge, *die (geh.);* Fittich, *der (dichter.)*
[1]**pink** [pɪŋk] **1.** *n.* **a)** Pink, *das;* Rosa, *das;* **b) in the ~ of condition** in hervorragendem Zustand; **be in the ~** *(sl.)* kerngesund sein; **c)** *(Bot.)* [Garten]nelke, *die;* **d)** *see* **hunting-pink. 2.** *adj.* **a)** pinkfarben, rosa ‹*Kleid, Wand*›; rosig, rosarot ‹*Himmel, Gesicht, Haut, Wangen*›; **b)** *(Polit. sl.)* rosa[rot]; rot angehaucht. *See also* **elephant;** [1]**gin; rose-pink; salmon-pink; tickle 1 b**
[2]**pink** *v. i.* *(Motor Veh.)* klingeln
[3]**pink** *v. t.* **a)** *(pierce slightly)* piksen; **b)** *(Sewing)* auszacken
pinkie ['pɪŋkɪ] *n.* *(Amer., Scot.)* kleiner Finger
pinking ['pɪŋkɪŋ]: **~ scissors, ~ shears** *ns. pl.* **[pair of] ~ scissors** *or* **shears** Zackenschere, *die*
pinko ['pɪŋkəʊ] *n., pl.* **~s** *(Polit. sl.)* Rosarote, *der/die*
'**pin-money** *n.* *(for private expenditure)* Taschengeld, *das;* *(for dress expenses)* Nadelgeld, *das (veralt.);* *(coll.: small sum)* Taschen- *od.* Trinkgeld, *das (ugs.)*
pinnace ['pɪnəs] *n.* *(Naut.)* Pinasse, *die;* Beiboot, *das*
pinnacle ['pɪnəkl] *n.* **a)** *(Archit.)* Fiale, *die;* **b)** *(natural peak)* Gipfel, *der;* **c)** *(fig.: climax)* Höhepunkt, *der;* Gipfel, *der;* **at the ~ of his fame** auf dem Gipfel *od.* Höhepunkt seines Ruhmes
pinnate ['pɪnət] *adj.* *(Bot.)* gefiedert
pinny ['pɪnɪ] *n.* *(child lang./coll.)* Schürze, *die*
pin: ~-point 1. *v. t.* *(locate, define)* genau bestimmen; *(determine)* genau festlegen; **2.** *n.* [Steck]nadelspitze, *die;* **~-points of light** winzige Lichter; **3.** *adj.* **~-point accuracy** höchste Genauigkeit; **~prick** *n.* Nadelstich, *der;* *(fig.)* [harmlose] Stichelei; **~-stripe** *n.* Nadelstreifen, *der;* *(suit)* Nadelstreifenanzug, *der;* *attrib.* Nadelstreifen‹*anzug, -kostüm*›
pint [paɪnt] *n.* **a)** *(one-eighth of a gallon)* Pint, *das;* ≈ halber Liter; **b)** *(Brit.: quantity of liquid)* Pint, *das;* **a ~ of milk/beer** ≈ ein halbe. Liter Milch/Bier; **have a ~:** ein Bier trinken; **go to the pub for a couple of ~s** auf ein paar Bier[chen] in die Kneipe gehen; **he likes his ~:** er trinkt gern ein Bier[chen]
pinta ['paɪntə] *n.* *(Brit. coll.)* ≈ halber Liter [Milch/Bier *usw.*]; **drink one's daily ~:** täglich seine Milch/sein Bier *usw.* trinken
pin: ~-table *n.* Flipper[automat], *der;* **~tail** *n.* *(Ornith.)* Spießente, *die*

pint 'mug *n.* ≈ Halbliterglas, *das od.* -humpen, *der*

pinto ['pɪntəʊ] *adj., n., pl.* ~s *(Amer.) see* **piebald**

pint: ~-**pot** *n.* ≈ Halbliterhumpen, *der; see also* **quart a**; ~**size[d]** *adj. (fig. coll.)* winzig; mick[e]rig *(ugs.)* ‹*Person*›

pin: ~-**tuck** *n. (Sewing)* Biese, *die;* ~-**up** *(coll.)* **1.** *n.* **a)** *(picture) (of beautiful girl)* Pin-up[-Foto], *das; (of famous person)* Prominentenfoto, *das; (esp. of sports, film or pop star)* Starfoto, *das;* **b)** *(beautiful girl)* Schönheit, *die; (in photograph)* Pin-up-Girl, *das;* **2.** *adj.* Pin-up-‹*Foto, Girl*›; ~-**up-girl/**~-**up-man** Fotomodell, *das;* ~-**wheel** *n.* **a)** *(firework)* Feuerrad, *das;* **b)** *(Amer.: toy)* Windrädchen, *das*

pioneer [paɪə'nɪə(r)] **1.** *n.* Pionier, *der; (fig. also)* Wegbereiter, *der*/Wegbereiterin, *die.* **2.** *v.i.* Pionierarbeit leisten; bahnbrechend sein; ~**ing settlers/studies/work** Pioniere *od.* erste Siedler/bahnbrechende Untersuchungen/Pionierarbeit, *die.* **3.** *v.t.* **a)** *(originate)* Pionierarbeit leisten für ‹*Entwicklung, Technologie, Nutzung*›; **b)** *(open up as ~)* erkunden

pious ['paɪəs] *adj.* **a)** *(devout)* fromm; **a ~ hope** *(lit. or fig.)* ein frommer Wunsch; **b)** *(hypocritically virtuous)* heuchlerisch; scheinheilig; **c)** *(dutiful)* ehrfurchtsvoll; heilig ‹*Pflicht*›. *See also* **fraud b**

piously ['paɪəslɪ] *adv.* **a)** *(devoutly)* **kneel ~:** in frommer Andacht knien; **b)** *(marked by sham)* scheinheilig; **c)** *(dutifully)* ehrfurchtsvoll

[1]**pip** [pɪp] **1.** *n. (seed)* Kern, *der.* **2.** *v.t.*, **-pp-** entkernen

[2]**pip** *n.* **a)** *(on cards, dominoes, etc.)* Auge, *das;* Punkt, *der;* **b)** *(Brit. Mil.)* Stern, *der;* **c)** *(on radar screen)* Echosignal, *das; (spot of light also)* Leuchtpunkt, *der;* Echosignal, *das*

[3]**pip** *n. (Brit.: sound)* [kurzer] Piepston; *(time signal also)* Zeitzeichen, *das;* **when the ~s go** *(during telephone call)* wenn die Piepstöne anzeigen, daß eine neue Münze eingeworfen werden muß

[4]**pip** *n. (coll.)* **give sb. the ~:** jmdm. auf den Wecker gehen *(ugs.);* **sb. has [got] the ~:** jmd. ist sauer *(ugs.)*

[5]**pip** *v.t.*, **-pp-** *(Brit.) (defeat)* besiegen; schlagen; **~ sb. at the post** *(coll.)* jmdn. im Ziel abfangen; *(fig.)* jmdn. im letzten Moment ausbooten *(ugs.)*

pipe [paɪp] **1.** *n.* **a)** *(tube)* Rohr, *das;* **b)** *(Mus.)* Pfeife, *die; (flute)* Flöte, *die; (in organ)* [Orgel]pfeife, *die;* **c)** *in pl. (bagpipes)* Dudelsack, *der;* **d)** **[tobacco-]~:** [Tabaks]pfeife, *die;* **light/smoke a ~:** eine Pfeife anzünden/rauchen; **put that in your ~ and smoke it** *(fig. coll.)* laß dir das gesagt sein; schreib dir das hinter die Ohren *(ugs.); see also* **clay pipe; peace-pipe; e)** *(cask)* Pipe, *das od. die;* 105-Gallonen-Faß, *das;* **f)** *(Geol.)* Schlot, *der.* **2.** *v.t.* **a)** *(convey by ~)* [durch ein Rohr/durch Rohre] leiten; **be ~d** ‹*Öl, Wasser:*› [durch eine Rohrleitung] fließen; ‹*Gas:*› [durch eine Rohrleitung] strömen; **b)** *(transmit by wire etc.)* leiten ‹*Strom*›; übertragen ‹*Sendung*›; [ab]spielen ‹*[Tonband-, Schallplatten]musik*›; **~d music** Hintergrundmusik, *die;* Musikberieselung, *die;* **c)** *(Mus.)* [auf der Flöte/dem Dudelsack] spielen ‹*Melodie, Lied*›; mit Pfeifenklang geleiten *od.* führen ‹*Soldaten*›; **d)** *(utter shrilly)* ‹*Vogel:*› piepsen, pfeifen; ‹*Kind:*› piepsen; **e)** *(Sewing)* paspel[iere]n; **f)** *(Cookery)* spritzen; **g)** *(Naut.)* **~ sb. aboard** jmdn. mit Pfeifenklängen an Bord empfangen. **3.** *v.i.* **a)** *(whistle)* pfeifen; **b)** ‹*Stimme:*› hell klingen, schrillen; ‹*Person:*› piepsen, mit heller *od.* schriller Stimme sprechen; ‹*Vogel:*› pfeifen, piepsen; ‹*kleiner, junger Vogel:*› piepsen; **c)** *(Mus.)* [Flöte/Pfeife] spielen

~ **'down** *v.i. (coll.: be less noisy)* ruhig sein; **~ down, will you!** sei/seid doch mal ruhig! ~ **'up** *v.i. (begin to speak)* sich vernehmen lassen

pipe: ~ **band** *n.* Pfeifer; ~**clay** *n.* Pfeifenton, *der;* ~-**cleaner** *n.* Pfeifenreiniger, *der;* ~-**dream** *n.* Wunschtraum, *der;* Hirngespinst, *das (abwertend);* ~**line** *n.* Pipeline, *die;* **in the ~line** *(fig.)* in Vorbereitung; **pay rises are in the ~line** *(fig.)* Gehaltserhöhungen stehen bevor; **have some ideas in the ~line** *(fig.)* ein paar Ideen auf Lager haben *(ugs.);* ~-**organ** *n. (Mus.)* [Pfeifen]orgel, *die*

piper ['paɪpə(r)] *n.* **a)** Pfeifer, *der*/Pfeiferin, *die; (flautist)* Flötenspieler, *der*/-spielerin, *die;* **pay the ~** *(fig.)* die Kosten tragen; **he who pays the ~ calls the tune** *(prov.)* wes Brot ich ess', des Lied ich sing' *(Spr.);* **b)** *(bagpiper)* Dudelsackspieler, *der*/-spielerin, *die*

pipe: ~-**rack** *n.* Pfeifenständer, *der;* ~-**smoker** *n.* Pfeifenraucher, *der*/-raucherin, *die;* ~ **tobacco** *n.* Pfeifentabak, *der*

pipette [pɪ'pet] *n. (Chem.)* Pipette, *die*

piping ['paɪpɪŋ] **1.** *n.* **a)** *(system of pipes)* Rohrleitungssystem, *das;* **b)** *(quantity of pipes)* Rohrmaterial, *das;* **c)** *(Sewing)* Paspel, *die; (on furniture)* Kordel, *die;* **d)** *(Cookery)* Spritzgußverzierung, *die;* **e)** *(Mus.)* Pfeifen, *das; (of flute)* Flöten, *das;* **f)** *(shrill sound)* Pfeifen, *das.* **2.** *adj.* piepsend

piping 'hot *adj.* kochendheiß

pipistrelle [pɪpɪ'strel] *n. (Zool.)* Zwergfledermaus, *die*

pipit ['pɪpɪt] *n. (Ornith.)* Pieper, *der*

pippin ['pɪpɪn] *n.* Tafelapfel, *der*

'pipsqueak *n. (sl. derog.)* Würstchen, *das (ugs.)*

piquancy ['pi:kənsɪ] *n.* **a)** *(sharpness)* Würze, *die;* pikanter Geschmack; **b)** *(fig.)* Pikanterie, *die (geh.)*

piquant ['pi:kənt, 'pi:kɑ:nt] *adj.*, **piquantly** ['pi:kəntlɪ, 'pi:kɑ:ntlɪ] *adv. (lit. or fig.)* pikant

pique [pi:k] **1.** *v.t.* **a)** *(irritate)* verärgern; **be ~d at sb./sth.** über jmdn./etw. verärgert sein; **b)** *(wound the pride of)* kränken; **be ~d at sth.** wegen etw. gekränkt sein. **2.** *n.* **in a [fit of] ~:** verstimmt; eingeschnappt *(ugs.)*

piqué ['pi:keɪ] *n. (Textiles)* Pikee, *der*

piracy ['paɪrəsɪ] *n.* Seeräuberei, *die;* Piraterie, *die; (fig.)* Piraterie, *die;* **the ~ of books/records/video tapes** der illegale Nachdruck von Büchern/die illegale Pressung von Schallplatten/die illegale Vervielfältigung von Videobändern

piranha [pɪ'rɑ:nə, pɪ'rɑ:njə] *n. (Zool.)* Piranha, *der*

pirate ['paɪrət] **1.** *n.* **a)** Pirat, *der;* Seeräuber, *der; (fig.)* Schwindler, *der; (of book etc.)* Raubdrucker, *der*/-druckerin, *die; (of record)* Raubpresser, *der*/Raubpresserin, *die;* Hersteller/Herstellerin von Raubpressungen; *(of video)* Hersteller/Herstellerin von unerlaubten Kopien; **b)** *(Radio)* [Rundfunk]pirat, *der; attrib.* **~ radio station** Piratensender, *der;* **~ broadcast[ing]** Piratensendung, *die;* **c)** *(ship)* Piratenschiff, *das;* Seeräuberschiff, *das.* **2.** *v.t.* ausplündern ‹*Schiff*›; rauben ‹*Waren usw.*›; *(fig.)* illegal nachdrucken ‹*Buch*›; illegal pressen ‹*Schallplatte*›; illegal vervielfältigen ‹*Videoband*›; **~d edition** Raubdruck, *der*

piratical [paɪ'rætɪkl] *adj.* Piraten-; Seeräuber-; seeräuberisch ‹*Praktiken, Umtriebe*›

pirouette [pɪrʊ'et] **1.** *n.* Pirouette, *die.* **2.** *v.i.* pirouettieren; Pirouetten/eine Pirouette ausführen *od.* drehen

Piscean ['paɪsɪən] *(Astrol.) n.* Fisch, *der;* Fischemann, *der*/-frau, *die*

Pisces ['paɪsi:z, 'pɪski:z] *n., pl. same (Astrol., Astron.)* Fische *Pl.;* Pisces *Pl.; see also* **Aries**

piss [pɪs] *(coarse)* **1.** *n.* **a)** *(urine)* Pisse, *die (derb);* **b)** *(act)* Pissen, *das (derb);* **need a ~:** pissen müssen *(derb);* **have a/go for a ~:** pissen/pissen gehen *(derb);* **c) take the ~ out of sb.** jmdn. verarschen *(salopp);* **stop taking the ~!** laß die Verarscherei! *(salopp).* **2.** *v.i.* **a)** *(urinate)* pissen *(derb);* **b)** *see* **piss down. 3.** *v.t.* pissen *(derb);* **~ oneself** in die Hose pissen *(derb)*

~ **a'bout,** ~ **a'round** *(sl.)* **1.** *v.i.* **a)** *(spend time lazily)* rumhängen *(ugs.);* **b)** *(behave in foolish way)* rummachen *(ugs.);* **c)** *(work in disorganized way)* sich *(Dat.)* einen abbrechen *(salopp);* **~ around with sth.** mit etw. rummachen *(ugs.).* **2.** *v.t.* **~ sb. about** *or* **around** jmdn. wie [den letzten] Dreck behandeln *(salopp)*

~ **down** *v.i. (sl.)* **~ down [with rain]** schiffen *(salopp)*

~ **'off** *(Brit. sl.)* **1.** *v.i.* sich verpissen *(salopp).* **2.** *v.t.* ankotzen *(derb); see also* **pissed off**

'piss artist *n. (sl.)* Suffkopp, *der (salopp)*

pissed [pɪst] *adj. (sl.)* **a)** *(drunk)* voll *(salopp);* besoffen *(derb);* **~ as a lord** *or* **newt** voll wie eine Strandhaubitze *(ugs.);* **~ out of one's mind** *or* **head** *or* **brain** sturzbesoffen *(derb);* hackevoll *(salopp);* **b)** *(Amer.: angry)* [stock]sauer **(with** auf + *Akk.*) *(salopp)*

pissed 'off *adj. (sl.)* stocksauer **(with** auf + *Akk.*) *(salopp);* **get ~ [with sb./sth.]** langsam die Schnauze voll haben [von jmdm./etw.] *(salopp)*

'piss-up *n. (sl.)* Besäufnis, *das (salopp)*

pistachio [pɪ'stɑ:ʃɪəʊ] *n., pl.* ~s **a)** Pistazie, *die;* **b)** *(colour)* Pistaziengrün, *das*

piste [pi:st] *n.* Piste, *die*

pistil ['pɪstɪl] *n. (Bot.)* Stempel, *der*

pistol ['pɪstl] *n. (small firearm)* Pistole, *die;* **hold a ~ to sb.'s head** jmdm. die Pistole an die Schläfe *od.* den Kopf setzen; *(fig.)* jmdm. die Pistole auf die Brust setzen

pistol: ~-**grip** *n.* Pistolengriff, *der;* ~-**shot** *n.* Pistolenschuß, *der;* ~-**whip** *v.t.* mit der Pistole schlagen

piston ['pɪstən] *n.* Kolben, *der*

piston: ~ **engine** *n.* Kolbenmotor, *der;* ~-**ring** *n.* Kolbenring, *der;* ~-**rod** *n.* Kolbenstange, *die;* Pleuelstange, *die*

[1]**pit** [pɪt] **1.** *n.* **a)** *(hole, mine)* Grube, *die; (natural)* Vertiefung, *die; (as trap)* Fallgrube, *die; (for cock-fighting)* Kampfplatz, *der;* **[work] down the ~:** unter Tage [arbeiten] *(Bergmannsspr.);* **dig a ~ for sb.** *(fig.)* jmdm. eine Falle stellen; **this really is the ~s** *(sl.)* das ist wirklich das letzte *(ugs.);* **b) ~ of the stomach** Magengrube, *die;* **c)** *(scar)* [vertiefte] Narbe; *(after smallpox)* Pockennarbe, *die;* **d)** *(Brit. Theatre) (for audience)* Parkett, *das; (for orchestra)* Orchestergraben, *der;* **e)** *(in garage)* Grube, *die; (Motor-racing)* Box, *die;* **f)** *(Amer. St. Exch.)* Maklerstand, *der.* **2.** *v.t.*, **-tt-** **a)** *(set to fight)* kämpfen lassen; **b)** *(fig.: match)* **~ sth. against sth.** etw. gegen etw. einsetzen; **~ one's wits/skill** *etc.* **against sth.** seinen Verstand/sein Können *usw.* an etw. *(Dat.)* messen; **c) be ~ted** *(have ~s)* voller Vertiefungen sein; **the ~ted surface of the moon** die mit Kratern bedeckte Mondoberfläche

[2]**pit** *(Amer.)* **1.** *n. (stone in fruit)* Kern, *der.* **2.** *v.t.*, **-tt-** *(remove ~s from)* entkernen

pit-a-pat ['pɪtəpæt] **1.** *adv.* **go ~** ‹*Herz:*› schneller schlagen; ‹*Regen:*› [sanft] klopfen. **2.** *n. (of heart)* Pochen, *das; (of hoofs, feet)* Getrappel, *das; (of rain etc.)* Klopfen, *das*

[1]**pitch** [pɪtʃ] **1.** *n.* **a)** *(Brit.: usual place)* [Stand]platz, *der; (stand)* Stand, *der; (Sport: playing-area)* Feld, *das;* Platz, *der;* **artificial ~:** Spielfeld mit künstlichem Rasen; *see also* **queer 3; b)** *(Mus.)* Tonhöhe, *die; (of voice)* Stimmlage, *die; (of instrument)* Tonlage, *die;* **have perfect ~:** absolutes Gehör haben; *see also* **concert pitch; c)** *(slope)* Nei-

gung, die; the ~ of the roof die Dachneigung; d) (fig.: degree, intensity) the children were at a high ~ of excitement die Kinder waren wahnsinnig aufgedreht (ugs.); reach such a ~ that ...: sich so zuspitzen, daß...; see also fever pitch; e) see pitching; f) (Baseball: delivery) Pitch, der; Wurf, der; (Golf) see pitch shot; g) (Mech.: distance) (between cog-wheel teeth or screw ridges) Steigung, die; (in one turn of propeller) Steigung, die; h) (Mountaineering) Seillänge, die; i) (sales talk) Verkaufsargumentation, die; make one's ~ (lit. or fig.) seine Vorstellung geben; get one's ~ in early (fig.) seine Sache frühzeitig vorbringen. 2. v. t. a) (erect) aufschlagen; ~ camp ein/das Lager aufschlagen; b) (throw) werfen; the horse ~ed its rider over its head das Pferd warf den Reiter vornüber; the car overturned and the driver was ~ed out der Wagen überschlug sich, und der Fahrer wurde herausgeschleudert; ~ sb. out of sth. jmdn. aus etw. hinauswerfen; c) (Mus.) anstimmen ⟨Melodie⟩; stimmen ⟨Instrument⟩; ~ one's voice too high/at the right level eine zu hohe/die richtige Stimmlage wählen; d) (fig.) ~ a programme at a particular level ein Programm auf ein bestimmtes Niveau abstimmen; our expectations were ~ed too high unsere Erwartungen waren zu hoch gesteckt; e) ~ed battle offene [Feld]schlacht; the debate became a ~ed battle (fig.) aus der Debatte wurde eine Redeschlacht. 3. v. i. (fall) [kopfüber] stürzen; ⟨Schiff, Fahrzeug, Flugzeug:⟩ mit einem Ruck nach vorn kippen; (Cricket) ⟨Ball:⟩ aufschlagen; (repeatedly) ⟨Schiff:⟩ stampfen; ⟨Fahrzeug, Flugzeug:⟩ ruckartig schwingen; ~ forward vornüberstürzen; ⟨Fahrzeug:⟩ ruckartig anfahren

~ 'in v. i. (coll.) loslegen (ugs.); (begin) sich daranmachen (ugs.); ~ in [and or to help] zupacken (ugs.) [und helfen]; mit anpacken

~ into v. t. (coll.) herfallen über (+ Akk.); sich hermachen über (+ Akk.) (ugs.) ⟨Essen⟩

[2]pitch n. (substance) Pech, das; as black as ~: pechschwarz

pitch: ~-'black adj. pechschwarz; stockdunkel (ugs.), pechfinster ⟨Nacht, Raum⟩; **~blende** ['pɪtʃblend] n. (Min.) Pechblende, die; **~-'dark** adj. stockdunkel (ugs.); pechfinster; **~-'darkness** n. tiefste Finsternis

pitched 'roof n. schräges Dach

[1]pitcher ['pɪtʃə(r)] n. a) (vessel) [Henkel]krug, der; (in bedroom etc.) Wasserkanne, die; b) (Bot.) Kanne, die

[2]pitcher n. (Baseball) Werfer, der; Pitcher, der

'pitcher-plant n. (Bot.) Kannenpflanze, die

'pitchfork 1. n. (for hay) Heugabel, die; (for manure) Mistgabel, die. 2. v. t. gabeln; ~ sb. into sth. (fig.) jmdn. in etw. ⟨Akk.⟩ katapultieren

pitching ['pɪtʃɪŋ] n. (of ship) Stampfen, das; (of vehicle, aircraft) ruckartiges Schwingen

pitch: ~-pine n. Pechkiefer, die; (wood) Pitchpine, das; Pechkiefernholz, das; **~-pipe** n. (Mus.) Stimmpfeife, die; **~ shot** n. (Golf) kurzer Annäherungsschlag; Pitchshot, der

piteous ['pɪtɪəs] adj. erbärmlich; (causing pity) mitleiderregend; kläglich ⟨Schrei⟩

piteously ['pɪtɪəslɪ] adv. erbärmlich

'pitfall n. a) Fallstrick, der; (risk) Gefahr, die; avoid all ~s alle Klippen umgehen; b) (animal trap) Fallgrube, die

pith [pɪθ] n. a) (in plant) Mark, das; (of orange etc.) weiße Haut; Albedo, die (Bot.); b) (fig.: essential part) Kern, der; c) (fig.) (strength) Kraft, die; (force of words etc.) Überzeugungskraft, die; men of ~: starke Männer; of ~ and moment gewichtig

'pit-head n. ≈ Zechengelände, das; at the ~: am Schachteingang; ~ baths Waschkauen (Bergmannsspr.); ~ ballot Abstimmung der Bergleute auf der Zeche

'pith helmet n. Tropenhelm, der

pithily ['pɪθɪlɪ] adv. prägnant

pithy ['pɪθɪ] adj. a) markhaltig; reich an Mark nicht attr.; ⟨Orange usw.⟩ mit dicker weißer Haut; b) (fig.) (full of meaning) prägnant; (vigorous) markig

pitiable ['pɪtɪəbl] see pitiful

pitiably ['pɪtɪəblɪ] adv. jämmerlich

pitiful ['pɪtɪfl] adj. a) mitleiderregend; (with strong emotional appeal) erbärmlich; jämmerlich; kläglich ⟨Versuch⟩; b) (contemptible) jämmerlich (abwertend)

pitifully ['pɪtɪfəlɪ] adv. erbärmlich; jämmerlich

pitiless ['pɪtɪlɪs] adj., **pitilessly** ['pɪtɪlɪslɪ] adv. unbarmherzig (auch fig.); erbarmungslos

pitman ['pɪtmən] n. a) pl. pitmen ['pɪtmən] (miner) Bergmann, der; b) pl. ~s (Amer.: connecting-rod) Pleuelstange, die

piton ['pi:tɒn] n. (for rock) Felshaken, der; (for ice) Eishaken, der

pit: ~ pony n. (Brit.) Grubenpferd, das; **~-prop** n. [Gruben]stempel, der; (of wood also) Grubenholz, das; **~-saw** n. Schrotod. Zugsäge, die; **~ stop** n. (Motor-racing) Boxenstopp, der

pitta ['pɪtə] n. ~ [bread] Pittabrot, das; Fladenbrot, das

pittance ['pɪtəns] n. a) Hungerlohn, der (abwertend); (small allowance) [magere] Beihilfe; b) (small amount of money) a ~: ein paar Pfennige

pitter-patter [pɪtə'pætə(r)] see pit-a-pat

pituitary [pɪ'tju:ɪtərɪ] n. ~ [body or gland] (Anat., Zool.) Hirnanhangdrüse, die; Hypophyse, die (fachspr.)

'pit viper n. Grubenotter, die

pity ['pɪtɪ] 1. n. a) (sorrow) Mitleid, das; Mitgefühl, das; feel ~ for sb. Mitgefühl für jmdn. od. mit jmdm. empfinden; have you no ~? hast du [denn] kein Mitleid?; be moved to ~: Mitleid empfinden; have/take ~ on sb./an animal Erbarmen mit jmdm./einem Tier haben; for ~'s sake! um Gottes od. Himmels willen!; b) (cause for regret) [what a] ~! [wie] schade!; it's a ~ about sb./sth. es ist ein Jammer mit jmdm./etw. (ugs.); it's a [great] ~/a thousand pities [that] ...: es ist [sehr od. zu] schade/jammerschade (ugs.) od. ein Jammer (ugs.), daß ...; the ~ of it is [that] ...: das Traurige daran ist, daß ...; more's the ~ (coll.) leider! 2. v. t. bedauern; bemitleiden; I ~ you (also contemptuously) du tust mir leid

pitying ['pɪtɪɪŋ] adj., **pityingly** ['pɪtɪɪŋlɪ] adv. mitleidig

pivot ['pɪvət] 1. n. a) [Dreh]zapfen, der; (of a hinge) Angelzapfen, der; b) (fig.) [Dreh- und] Angelpunkt, der; (crucial point) springender Punkt. 2. v. t. (provide with ~[s]) mit Zapfen/mit einem Zapfen versehen; (mount on ~[s]) drehbar lagern. 3. v. i. sich drehen; the guns ~ easily die Geschütze lassen sich leicht schwenken; ~ on sth. (fig.) von etw. abhängen

pivotal ['pɪvətl] adj. (fig.: crucial) zentral; ~ figure/position Schlüsselfigur, die/Schlüsselstellung, die

pix [pɪks] n. pl. (coll.) Bilder

pixel ['pɪksel] n. (Computing etc.) Bildpunkt, der; Pixel, das

pixie ['pɪksɪ] n. Kobold, der

pixie: ~ hat, ~ hood ns. spitz zulaufendes Käppchen

pixy see pixie

pizza ['pi:tsə] n. Pizza, die

pizzazz [pɪ'zæz] n. Klasse, die; (showiness) Glamour, der

pizzeria [pi:tsə'ri:ə] n. Pizzeria, die

pizzicato [pɪtsɪ'kɑ:təʊ] (Mus.) 1. adj. ~ accompaniment Pizzicatobegleitung; a series of ~ notes eine pizzicato gespielte Tonfolge. 2. adv. pizzicato. 3. n., pl. ~s or pizzicati [pɪtsɪ'kɑ:ti:] Pizzicato, das

pl. abbr. a) plate 1 g; b) plural Pl.

placard ['plækɑ:d] 1. n. Plakat, das; a ~ announcing the date of the next meeting ein Anschlag od. Aushang mit dem nächsten Sitzungstermin. 2. v. t. a) (post up ~s on) mit Plakaten bekleben ⟨Wand usw.⟩; the town is ~ed with posters überall in der Stadt kleben Plakate; b) (advertise) plakatieren

placate [plə'keɪt] v. t. beschwichtigen, besänftigen ⟨Person⟩

placatory [plə'keɪtərɪ] adj. beschwichtigend; besänftigend; Versöhnungs⟨opfer, -gabe⟩

place [pleɪs] 1. n. a) Ort, der; (spot) Stelle, die; Platz, der; put it in a ~ where you can find it tun Sie es an einen Platz, wo Sie es wiederfinden; I left it in a safe ~: ich habe es an einem sicheren Ort gelassen; it was still in the same ~: es war noch an derselben Stelle od. am selben Platz; the [exact] ~ where ...: die [genaue] Stelle, wo od. an der ...; this was the 'last ~ I expected to find you hier hätte ich dich am allerwenigsten erwartet; a ~ in the queue ein Platz in der Schlange; all over the ~: überall; (coll.: in a mess) ganz durcheinander (ugs.); I can't be in two ~s at once ich kann nicht an zwei Orten gleichzeitig sein od. (ugs.) alles auf einmal machen; from ~ to ~: von Ort zu Ort; in ~s hier und da; (in parts) stellenweise; the animal does still exist in ~s das Tier kommt noch vereinzelt vor; find a ~ in sth. (be included) in etw. (Akk.) eingehen; see also take 1 d; b) (fig.: rank, position) Stellung, die; as a critic, his ~ is in the front rank als Kritiker rangiert er ganz vorn; keep/put sb. in his/her ~: jmdn. immer wieder/jmdn. in seine/ihre Schranken weisen; jmdm. immer wieder/jmdm. einen Dämpfer aufsetzen (ugs.); know one's ~: wissen, was sich für einen gehört; it's not my ~ to do that es kommt mir nicht zu, das zu tun; c) (building or area for specific purpose) a [good] ~ to park/to stop ein [guter] Platz zum Parken/eine [gute] Stelle zum Halten; do you know a good/cheap ~ to eat? weißt du, wo man gut/billig essen kann?; We couldn't get into the café. The ~ was full Wir kamen gar nicht erst in das Café. Es war alles voll od. besetzt; ~ of residence or domicile Wohnort, der; ~ of work Arbeitsplatz, der; Arbeitsstätte, die; ~ of worship Andachtsort, der; ~ of amusement Vergnügungsstätte, die; see also another 2 c; d) (country, town) Ort, der; the best hotel in the ~: das beste Hotel am Platz; Paris/Italy is a great ~: Paris ist eine tolle Stadt/Italien ist ein tolles Land (ugs.); ~ of birth Geburtsort, der; know the ~: sich [hier/dort] auskennen; 'go ~s (coll.) herumkommen (ugs.); (fig.) es [im Leben] zu was bringen (ugs.); e) (coll.: premises) Bude, die (ugs.); (hotel, restaurant, etc.) Laden, der (ugs.); liven the ~ up Leben in die Bude bringen (ugs.); she is at his/John's ~: sie ist bei ihm/John; [shall we go to] your ~ or mine? [gehen wir] zu dir oder zu mir?; I called at your ~: ich bin bei dir [zu Hause] vorbeigegangen; a ~ in the country ein Haus auf dem Lande; f) (seat etc.) [Sitz]platz, der; change ~s [with sb.] [mit jmdm.] die Plätze tauschen; (fig.) [mit jmdm.] tauschen; lay a/another ~: ein/noch ein Gedeck auflegen; take one's ~ at table am Tisch Platz nehmen; is this anyone's ~? ist dieser Platz noch frei?; g) (particular spot on surface) Stelle, die; h) (in book etc.) Stelle, die; lose one's ~: die Seite verschlagen od. verblättern; (on page) nicht mehr wissen, an welcher Stelle man ist; keep one's ~: die Stelle markieren, an der man ist/war; find one's ~: die Stelle wiederfinden; **i)** *(step, stage)* **in the first ~:** zuerst; **why didn't you say so in the first ~?** warum hast du das nicht gleich gesagt?; **they should never have got married in the first ~:** sie hätten von vornherein nicht heiraten sollen; **I objected to it in the first ~:** ich war von Anfang an dagegen; **in the first/second/third** *etc.* **~:** erstens/zweitens/drittens *usw.*; **j)** *(proper ~)* Platz, *der;* **everything fell into ~** *(fig.)* alles wurde klar; **take your ~s for the next dance** stellen Sie sich zum nächsten Tanz auf; **he likes to have everything in [its] ~:** bei ihm muß alles an seinem Platz sein; **a woman's ~ is in the home** eine Frau gehört ins Haus; **this is no ~ for a child** das ist kein Ort für ein Kind; **give ~ to sb./sth.** jmdm./einer Sache Platz machen; **winter gave ~ to spring** der Winter räumte dem Frühling das Feld; **the clamp is properly in ~:** die Klammer sitzt richtig; **her hat was held in ~ by a hatpin** ihr Hut wurde von einer Hutnadel festgehalten; **into ~:** fest‹*nageln, -schrauben, -kleben*›; **out of ~:** nicht am richtigen Platz; *(several things)* in Unordnung; *(fig.)* fehl am Platz; **your suggestion is rather out of ~** *(fig.)* dein Vorschlag ist nicht ganz angebracht *od.* passend; **with not a hair out of ~:** makellos frisiert; **in ~ of sb./sth.** an Stelle *od.* anstelle (+ *Gen.*); **I'll go in ~ of you/in your ~:** ich werde an deiner Stelle gehen; **take the ~ of sb./sth.** jmds. Platz *od.* den Platz von jmdm./den Platz von etw. einnehmen; *see also* **sun 1**; **k)** *(position in competition)* Platz, *der;* **drop/go up two ~s in the charts** [um] zwei Plätze in der Hitparade fallen/steigen; **first ~ went to ...:** der erste Platz ging an ... (+ *Akk.*); **take first/second** *etc.* **~:** den ersten/zweiten *usw.* Platz belegen; *(fig.: have priority)* an erster/zweiter *usw.* Stelle kommen; **in second ~:** auf dem zweiten Platz; **beat sb. into second ~:** jmdn. auf den zweiten Platz verweisen; **get a ~** *(Racing)* eine Plazierung erreichen; *(Amer.: second ~)* den zweiten Platz belegen; **l)** *(Math.: position of figure in series)* Stelle, *die; see also* **decimal place; m)** *(job, position, etc.)* Stelle, *die; (as pupil; in team, crew)* Platz, *der;* **university ~:** Studienplatz, *der;* **n)** *(personal situation)* **what would you do in my ~?** was würden Sie an meiner Stelle tun?; **put yourself in my ~:** versetzen Sie sich in meine Lage. **2.** *v. t.* **a)** *(put) (vertically)* stellen; *(horizontally)* legen; **he ~d himself where ...:** er stellte sich dahin, wo ...; **~ a foot on a chair** einen Fuß auf einen Stuhl setzen; **~ the ball on the penalty spot** den Ball auf den Elfmeterpunkt legen; **~ in position** richtig hinstellen/hinlegen; **~ an announcement/advertisement in a paper** eine Anzeige/ein Inserat in eine Zeitung setzen; **~ a bet/~ money on a horse** auf ein Pferd wetten/Geld auf ein Pferd setzen; **b)** *(fig.)* **~ one's trust in sb./sth.** sein Vertrauen auf *od.* in jmdn./etw. setzen; **he ~s happiness above all other things** Glück steht für ihn an erster Stelle; *see also* **emphasis a, c; c)** *in p.p. (situated)* gelegen; **a badly ~d window** ein Fenster an einer ungünstigen Stelle; **be well ~d to watch sth.** einen guten Platz *od.* Standort haben, um bei etw. zuzusehen; **he was not well ~d to return the shot** *(Tennis)* er stand ungünstig zum Ball; **we are well ~d for buses/shops** *etc.* wir haben es nicht weit zur Bushaltestelle/zum Einkaufen *usw.*; **how are you ~d for time/money?** *(coll.)* wie steht's mit deiner Zeit/deinem Geld?; **how are you ~d [for lending me a fiver]?** *(coll.)* wie sieht's bei dir aus[, kannst du mir einen Fünfer leihen]? *(ugs.)*; **be well ~d financially** sich [finanziell] gut stehen *(ugs.)*; **d)** *(find situation or home for)* unterbringen (with bei); **~ sb. in command of a company** jmdm. das Kommando über eine Kompanie erteilen; **~ sb. under sb.'s care** jmdn. in jmds. Obhut geben; **e)** *(invest)* anlegen ‹*Geld*›; *(Commerc.)* absetzen ‹*Waren*›; **~ an order with a firm** einer Firma *(Dat.)* einen Auftrag erteilen; **f)** *(class, identify)* einordnen; einstufen; **~ sb. among the greatest statesmen** jmdn. zu den größten Staatsmännern zählen; **~ an artefact in the Neolithic period** ein Artefakt der Jungsteinzeit zuordnen; **I've seen him before but I can't ~ him** ich habe ihn schon einmal gesehen, aber ich weiß nicht, wo ich ihn unterbringen *od.* *(ugs.)* hintun soll; **g)** *(Sports etc.)* **be ~d** sich plazieren; *(Brit.: in first three)* unter den ersten drei sein; *(Amer.: second)* zweiter sein; **be ~d second in the race/charts** im Rennen/in der Hitliste den zweiten Platz belegen

'place-bet *n.* Platzwette, *die*

placebo [plə'si:bəʊ] *n., pl.* **~s** *(Med.)* Placebo, *das*

place: **~ card** *n.* Tischkarte, *die;* **~-kick** *n.* *(Footb.)* Platztritt, *der;* **~-mat** *n.* Set, *der od. das*

placement ['pleɪsmənt] *n.* Plazierung, *die*

'place-name *n.* Ortsname, *der*

placenta [plə'sentə] *n., pl.* **~e** [plə'senti:] *or* **~s** *(Anat., Zool.)* Plazenta, *die (fachspr.)*; Mutterkuchen, *der*

placer ['pleɪsə(r), 'plæsə(r)] *n.* *(Geol.)* Seife, *die; (place)* [Seifen]lagerstätte, *die*

'place-setting *n.* Gedeck, *das*

placid ['plæsɪd] *adj.* ruhig, gelassen ‹*Person*›; ruhig ‹*Wasser, Wesensart*›; *(peaceable)* friedlich, friedfertig ‹*Person*›

placidity [plə'sɪdɪtɪ] *n., no pl. see* **placid:** Ruhe, *die;* Gelassenheit, *die;* Friedfertigkeit, *die*

placidly ['plæsɪdlɪ] *adv. see* **placid:** ruhig; gelassen; friedlich

placket ['plækɪt] *n.* *(Dressm.)* Schlitz, *der*

plagiarism ['pleɪdʒərɪzm] *n.* Plagiat, *das*

plagiarist ['pleɪdʒərɪst] *n.* Plagiator, *der*

plagiarize (plagiarise) ['pleɪdʒəraɪz] *v. t.* plagiieren

plague [pleɪg] **1.** *n.* **a)** *(esp. Hist.: epidemic)* Seuche, *die;* **the ~** *(bubonic)* die Pest; **spread like the ~:** sich wie eine Seuche ausbreiten; **avoid/hate sb./sth. like the ~:** jmdn./etw. wie die Pest meiden/hassen; **a ~ on it/you!** *(arch.)* hol's/hol dich die Pest!; **a ~ on both your houses!** *(fig. arch.)* hol euch beide die Pest! ; **b)** *(esp. Bibl.: punishment; coll.: nuisance)* Plage, *die;* **c)** *(infestation)* **~ of rats/insects** Ratten-/Insektenplage, *die.* **2.** *v. t.* **a)** *(afflict)* plagen; quälen; **~d with** *or* **by sth.** von etw. geplagt; **a disease that ~s mankind** eine Krankheit, die die Menschheit heimsucht; **b)** *(bother)* **~ sb. [with sth.]** jmdm. [mit etw.] auf die Nerven gehen *(ugs.)*; **be ~d with sth.** von etw. geplagt werden; **be ~d by bad weather** unter schlechtem Wetter zu leiden haben

plaice [pleɪs] *n., pl. same* **a)** Scholle, *die;* **b)** *(Amer.: summer flounder)* Sommerflunder, *die*

plaid [plæd] **1.** *n.* Plaid, *das od. der.* **2.** *adj.* [bunt]kariert; **~ blanket** Plaid, *das od. der*

plain [pleɪn] **1.** *adj.* **a)** *(clear)* klar; *(obvious)* offensichtlich; **He didn't like us. That was ~ enough** Er mochte uns nicht. Das war ganz klar *od.* offenkundig; **make sth. ~ [to sb.]** [jmdm.] etw. klarmachen; **make it ~ that ...:** klarstellen, daß ...; **make oneself/one's meaning ~:** sich verständlich machen; sich klar ausdrücken; **make one's views/intentions ~:** seine Ansichten/Absichten klar zum Ausdruck bringen; **do I make myself ~?** ist das klar?; habe ich mich klar ausgedrückt?; **the reason is ~ [to see]** der Grund liegt auf der Hand; **the consequences of the act were not ~ at the time** die Folgen dieses Schrittes waren zu dieser Zeit nicht absehbar *od.* klar zu erkennen; *see also* **English 2a; pikestaff; b)** *(frank, straightforward)* ehrlich; offen; schlicht ‹*Wahrheit*›; **be ~ with sb.** mit jmdm. *od.* jmdm. gegenüber offen sein; **there was some ~ speaking** es fielen einige offene Worte; **be [all] ~ sailing** *(fig.)* [ganz] einfach sein; **~ dealing** Redlichkeit, *die;* **c)** *(unsophisticated)* einfach; schlicht ‹*Kleidung, Frisur*›; klar ‹*Wasser*›; einfach, bescheiden ‹*Lebensstil*›; *(not lined)* unliniert ‹*Papier*›; *(not patterned)* ‹*Stoff*› ohne Muster; **she is a ~ cook** sie kocht einfach; **~ cooking** gutbürgerliche Küche; **~ stitch** rechte Masche; **~ text** *(without notes)* [unkommentierter] Originaltext; *(decoded)* Klartext, *der; see also* **cover 1c; plain clothes; d)** *(unattractive)* wenig attraktiv ‹*Mädchen*›; **she's rather a ~ Jane** *(coll.)* sie ist nicht gerade eine Schönheit; **e)** *(sheer)* rein; **that's ~ bad manners** das ist einfach schlechtes Benehmen; **that's just ~ common sense** das sagt einem doch der gesunde Menschenverstand. **2.** *adv.* **a)** *(clearly)* deutlich; **b)** *(simply)* einfach; **I'm just ~ tired** ich bin einfach nur müde. **3.** *n.* **a)** Ebene, *die;* **the P~s** *(of North America)* die Prärie; **b)** *(Knitting)* rechte Masche; **two ~, two purl** zwei rechts, zwei links

plain: **~chant** *see* **plainsong; ~ 'chocolate** *n.* halbbittere Schokolade; *(without any sweetness)* bittere Schokolade; **~ 'clothes** *n. pl.* **in ~ clothes** in Zivil; **~-clothes detective** *etc.* Kriminalbeamter *usw.* in Zivil

plainly ['pleɪnlɪ] *adv.* **a)** *(clearly)* deutlich; verständlich ‹*erklären*›; **b)** *(obviously)* offensichtlich; *(undoubtedly)* eindeutig; **c)** *(frankly)* offen; **d)** *(simply, unpretentiously)* einfach; schlicht; bescheiden ‹*leben*›

plainness ['pleɪnnɪs] *n., no pl.* **a)** *(clearness)* Klarheit, *die;* **b)** *(frankness)* Offenheit, *die;* **his ~ of speech** seine Offenheit; **c)** *(simplicity)* Schlichtheit, *die;* **d)** *(ugliness)* Unattraktivität, *die;* Unansehnlichkeit, *die*

plainsman ['pleɪnzmən] *n., pl.* **plainsmen** ['pleɪnzmən] Flachländer, *der; (in North America)* Präriebewohner, *der*

plain: **~song** *n.* *(Mus., Eccl.)* Cantus planus, *der (fachspr.)*; Gregorianischer Gesang; **~-'spoken** *adj.* freimütig

plaint [pleɪnt] *n.* **a)** *(literary: lamentation)* [Weh]klage, *die;* **b)** *(Brit. Law)* Klage, *die*

plaintiff ['pleɪntɪf] *n.* *(Law)* Kläger, *der*/Klägerin, *die*

plaintive ['pleɪntɪv] *adj.* klagend; traurig, leidend ‹*Blick*›

plaintively ['pleɪntɪvlɪ] *adv.* klagend; in klagendem Ton ‹*sprechen usw.*›; traurig, leidend ‹*blicken*›

plain: **~ weave** *n.* Leinwandbindung, *die;* **~ weaving** *n.* Gewebe in Leinwandbindung

plait [plæt] **1.** *n.* *(of hair)* Zopf, *der;* Flechte, *die (geh.)*; *(of straw, ribbon, etc.)* geflochtenes Band. **2.** *v. t.* flechten

plan [plæn] **1.** *n.* Plan, *der; (for story etc.)* Konzept, *das;* Entwurf, *der; (intention)* Absicht, *die;* **~ of action** Aktionsprogramm, *das;* **what is your ~ of action?** wie willst du vorgehen?; **have great ~s for sb.** große Pläne mit jmdm. haben; **~ of campaign** Strategie, *die;* **make ~s for sth.** Pläne für etw. machen *od.* schmieden; **what are your ~s for tomorrow?** was hast du morgen vor?; **your best ~ is to stay on at school** am besten bleibst du auf der Schule; **[go] according to ~:** nach Plan [gehen]; planmäßig [verlaufen *od.* laufen]; *see also* **five-year plan. 2.** *v. t.,* **-nn- a)** planen; *(design)* entwerfen ‹*Gebäude, Maschine*›; **~ to do sth.** planen *od.* vorhaben, etw. zu tun; **as ~ned** plangemäß; wie geplant; *see also* **obsolescence; b)** *(make plan of)* **~ sth.** einen [Lage]plan einer Sache *(Gen.)* *od.* von etw. anfertigen. **3.** *v. i.,* **-nn-** planen; **~ [weeks] ahead** [Wochen] im voraus planen *od.* vorausplanen; **~ for sth.** Pläne für etw. machen; **we hadn't ~ned on that** damit hatten wir nicht gerechnet; **~ on doing sth.** *(coll.)* vorhaben, etw. zu tun;

what do you ~ on doing today? was hast du heute vor?
planchette [plæn'ʃet] *n.* Planchette, *die*
[1]**plane** [pleɪn] *n.* ~**[-tree]** Platane, *die*
[2]**plane 1.** *n. (tool)* Hobel, *der.* **2.** *v.t.* hobeln
[3]**plane 1.** *n.* **a)** *(Geom.)* Ebene, *die; (flat surface)* Fläche, *die; see also* **inclined plane; b)** *(fig.)* Ebene, *die; (moral, intellectual)* Niveau, *das;* ~ **of thought/attainment/knowledge** Denk-/Leistungs-/Wissensniveau, *das;* **c)** *(aircraft)* Flugzeug, *das;* Maschine, die *(ugs.); (Aeronaut.: supporting surface)* Tragfläche, *die.* **2.** *v.i.* gleiten
'**plane-load** *n.* Flugzeugladung, *die*
planet ['plænɪt] *n.* Planet, *der;* **major ~:** Riesenplanet, *der;* **minor ~:** kleiner Planet
planetarium [plænɪ'teərɪəm] *n., pl.* **~s** *or* **planetaria** [plænɪ'teərɪə] Planetarium, *das*
planetary ['plænɪtərɪ] *adj.* planetarisch; Planeten⟨*forscher, -system, -bewegung*⟩
planetoid ['plænətɔɪd] *n. (Astron.)* Planetoid, *der*
plangent ['plændʒənt] *adj.* **a)** *(resounding)* klangvoll; **b)** *(plaintive)* schwermütig und ergreifend; getragen ⟨*Melodie usw.*⟩
planish ['plænɪʃ] *v.t.* glätten; glatthämmern ⟨*Blech*⟩
plank [plæŋk] **1.** *n.* **a)** *(piece of timber)* Brett, *das; (thicker)* Bohle, *die; (on ship)* Planke, *die;* **be as thick as two [short] ~s** *(coll.)* dumm wie Bohnenstroh sein *(ugs.);* **be made to walk the ~** *(Hist.)* über die Planke laufen müssen *(fig.);* **b)** *(fig.: item of political programme)* Programmpunkt, *der.* **2.** *v.t.* **a)** mit Brettern/Bohlen/Planken versehen; beplanken ⟨*Schiff*⟩; ~ **sth. over** etw. mit Brettern abdecken; **b)** *(coll.: put down)* knallen *(ugs.);* **c)** *(Amer.) auf einem Holzbrett garen und servieren;* **~ed steak** Steak auf dem Holzbrett
planking ['plæŋkɪŋ] *n. (planks) see* **plank 1a:** Bretter; Bohlen; Planken; *(of ship)* Beplankung, *die*
plankton ['plæŋktn] *n. (Biol.)* Plankton, *das*
planned e'conomy *n. (Econ.)* Planwirtschaft, *die*
planner ['plænə(r)] *n.* Planer, *der*/Planerin, *die*
planning ['plænɪŋ] *n.* Planen, *das;* Planung, *die;* **at the ~ stage** im Planungsstadium; ~ **permission** Baugenehmigung, *die*
plant [plɑ:nt] **1.** *n.* **a)** *(Bot.)* Pflanze, *die;* **b)** *(machinery) no indef. art.* Maschinen; *(single complex)* Anlage, *die;* **earth-moving ~** *no indef. art.* Maschinen für Erdarbeiten; **generating ~** *no indef. art.* Generatoren; **a generating ~:** eine Generatorenanlage; **c)** *(factory)* Fabrik, *die;* Werk, *das;* **d)** *(sl.: undercover agent)* Spitzel, *der;* **e)** *(sl.: thing concealed)* Untergeschobene, *das;* **he said the heroin was a ~:** er sagte, das Heroin sei ihm untergeschoben worden. **2.** *v.t.* **a)** *(put in ground)* pflanzen; aussäen ⟨*Samen*⟩; anlegen ⟨*Garten usw.*⟩; anpflanzen ⟨*Beet*⟩; bepflanzen ⟨*Land*⟩; ~ **a field with barley** auf einem Feld Gerste anpflanzen; **b)** *(fix)* setzen; ~ **stakes [in the ground]** Pfähle setzen; **he ~ed his feet wide apart** er stellte seine Füße weit auseinander; ~ **oneself** sich hinstellen *od. (ugs.)* aufpflanzen; **c)** *(in mind)* ~ **an idea** *etc.* **in sb.'s mind/in sb.** jmdm. eine Idee *usw.* einimpfen *(ugs.) od. (geh.)* einpflanzen; **d)** *(deliver etc.)* ~ **a blow** *etc.* **on sb.'s nose** *etc.* jmdm. einen Schlag *usw.* auf die Nase *usw.* verpassen; ~ **a kiss on sb.'s forehead** *etc.* jmdm. einen Kuß auf die Stirn *usw.* drücken; **e)** *(sl.: conceal)* schmuggeln *(ugs.);* anbringen ⟨*Wanze*⟩; legen ⟨*Bombe*⟩; ~ **sth. on sb.** jmdm. etw. unterschieben; **f)** *(station as spy etc.)* einschmuggeln
~ '**out** *v.t.* auspflanzen ⟨*Setzlinge*⟩
Plantagenet [plæn'tædʒɪnɪt] *(Brit. Hist.)* **1.** *n.* Plantagenet, *der/die.* **2.** *attrib. adj.* Plantagenet-
[1]**plantain** ['plæntɪn] *n. (Bot.: in temperate regions, Plantago)* Wegerich, *der*
[2]**plantain** *(Bot.: in tropics, Musa)* Kochbanane, *die;* Mehlbanane *die;* Plante, *die (fachspr.)*
plantain 'lily *n. (Bot.)* Funkie, *die*
plantation [plæn'teɪʃn, plɑ:n'teɪʃn] *n.* **a)** *(estate)* Pflanzung, *die;* Plantage, *die;* **b)** *(group of plants)* Anpflanzung, *die*
'**plant-breeding** *n.* Pflanzenzucht, *die*
planter ['plɑ:ntə(r)] *n.* **a)** Pflanzer, *der*/Pflanzerin, *die;* **b)** *(machine)* Pflanzmaschine, *die; (for seeds)* Sämaschine, *die;* **c)** *(container)* Pflanzgefäß, *das*
plant: ~-hire *n.* Baumaschinenverleih, *der;* ~ **kingdom** *n.* Pflanzenreich, *das;* **~-louse** *n. (Zool.)* Pflanzenlaus, *die*
plaque [plɑ:k, plæk] *n.* **a)** *(ornamental tablet)* [Schmuck]platte, *die; (commemorating sb.)* [Gedenk]tafel, *die;* Plakette, *die (Kunstwiss.);* **b)** *(Dent.)* Plaque, *die (fachspr.);* [weißer] Zahnbelag
plasma ['plæzmə] *n.* **a)** *(Anat., Zool., Phys.)* Plasma, *das;* **b)** *(Biol.) see* **protoplasm**
plaster ['plɑ:stə(r)] **1.** *n.* **a)** *(for walls etc.)* [Ver]putz, *der;* **b)** ~ **[of Paris]** Gips, *der;* **have one's leg in ~:** ein Gipsbein *od.* sein Bein in Gips haben; **put sb.'s leg in ~:** jmds. Bein in Gips legen; **c)** *see* **sticking-plaster. 2.** *v.t.* **a)** verputzen ⟨*Wand*⟩; vergipsen, zugipsen ⟨*Loch, Riß*⟩; **b)** *(daub)* ~ **sth. on sth.** etw. dick auf etw. *(Akk.)* auftragen; ~ **make-up on one's face,** ~ **one's face with make-up** sich *(Dat.)* Make-up ins Gesicht kleistern *(ugs.);* **~ed with mud** mit Schlamm bedeckt; **c)** *(stick on)* kleistern *(ugs.)* ⟨*Plakate, Briefmarken*⟩ **(on** auf + *Akk.*); ~ **posters all over the wall/the wall with posters** die Wand mit Plakaten zukleistern *(salopp);* **d)** *(sl.: shell, bomb)* bepflastern *(Soldatenspr.)*
~ '**down** *v.t.* ~ **sb.'s/one's hair down** jmdm./sich das Haar anklatschen
~ '**over** *v.t.* vergipsen ⟨*Loch, Riß*⟩
plaster: ~board *n.* Gipsplatte, *die;* ~ **cast** *n.* **a)** *(model in plaster)* Gipsabguß *od.* -abdruck, *der;* **b)** *(Med.)* Gipsverband, *der*
plastered ['plɑ:stəd] *pred. adj. (sl.: drunk)* voll *(salopp);* **get ~:** sich vollaufen lassen *(salopp)*
plasterer ['plɑ:stərə(r)] *n.* Gipser, *der*
plaster 'saint *n.* Heiligenfigur aus Gips; *(fig., usu. iron.)* Heilige, *der/die (ugs.)*
plastic ['plæstɪk] **1.** *n.* Plastik, *das;* Kunststoff, *der;* Plast, *der (DDR); in pl., attrib.* Plastik-; Kunststoff-; Plast- *(DDR).* **2.** *adj.* **a)** *(made of plastic)* Plastik-; Kunststoff-; Plast- *(DDR);* aus Plastik/Kunststoff/Plast *nachgestellt; (coll. derog.: synthetic)* Plastik-; ~ **bag** Plastiktüte, *die;* ~ **money** *(joc.)* Kreditkarten; **b)** *(produced by moulding)* plastisch; ~ **figure** Plastik, *die;* **c)** *(malleable, lit. or fig.)* formbar; bildbar; **the ~ qualities of wax** die plastischen Eigenschaften von Wachs; **d) the ~ arts** die Plastik; *(including painting etc.)* die bildende Kunst; ~ **surgeon** Facharzt für plastische Chirurgie; ~ **surgery** plastische Chirurgie; **undergo** *or* **have ~ surgery** sich einer plastischen *od.* kosmetischen Operation unterziehen
plastic 'bullet *n.* Plastikgeschoß, *das*
Plasticine, (P) ['plæstɪsi:n] *n.* Plastilin, *das*
plasticise *see* **plasticize**
plasticity [plæ'stɪsɪtɪ] *n., no pl. (lit. or fig.)* Formbarkeit, *die;* Plastizität, *die*
plasticize ['plæstɪsaɪz] *v.t.* geschmeidig machen; plasti[fi]zieren *(fachspr.)*
plasticizer ['plæstɪsaɪzə(r)] *n.* Weichmacher, *der;* Plasti[fi]kator, *der (Chemie)*
plasticky ['plæstɪkɪ] *adj. (coll. derog.)* plastikartig; **be very ~:** billiges Plastikzeug sein
plate [pleɪt] **1.** *n.* **a)** *(for food)* Teller, *der; (large ~ for serving food)* Platte, *die; (Amer.: main course on one ~)* Tellergericht, *das; (Amer.: food for one person)* Gedeck, *das;* **a ~ of soup/sandwiches** ein Teller Suppe/belegte Brote *od.* mit belegten Broten; **have sth. handed to one on a ~** *(fig. coll.)* etw. auf silbernem Tablett serviert bekommen *(fig.);* **have a lot** *etc.* **on one's ~** *(fig. coll.)* viel *usw.* am Hals *od.* um die Ohren haben *(ugs.);* **b)** *(for collection in church)* Teller für die Kollekte; **c)** *(sheet of metal etc.)* Platte, *die;* **d)** *(metal ~ with name etc.)* Schild, *das;* **[number-]~:** Nummernschild, *das;* **put up one's ~** *(fig.)* seine eigene Praxis eröffnen; **e)** *(Photog.)* [photographische] Platte; **f)** *no pl., no indef. art. (Brit.: tableware)* [Tafel]silber, *das; (gold)* Gold[geschirr], *das; (pewter)* Zinn, *das;* Silber-/Gold-/Zinnsachen *Pl.; (plated)* **[made of] real silver, not ~:** aus echtem Silber, nicht nur versilbert; **g)** *(for engraving, printing)* Platte, *die; (impression)* Stich, *der; (illustration)* [Bild]tafel, *die (Druckw.);* **printing ~:** Druckplatte, *die;* **h)** *(Sport) (trophy)* Pokal, *der; (race)* Pokal[wettbewerb], *der;* **i)** *(Dent.)* Gaumenplatte, *die; (coll.: denture)* [Zahn]prothese, *die;* Gebiß, *das;* **j)** *(Amer. Electronics)* Anode, *die;* **k)** *(Geol.)* Platte, *die;* **l)** *(Baseball)* Wurfmal, *das;* **home ~:** Schlagmal, *das. See also* **tracery a. 2.** *v.t.* **a)** *(coat)* plattieren; ~ **sth. [with gold/silver/chromium]** etw. vergolden/versilbern/verchromen; **b)** panzern ⟨*Schiff*⟩
plateau ['plætəʊ] *n., pl.* **~x** ['plætəʊz] *or* **~s a)** Hochebene, *die;* Plateau, *das;* **b)** *(fig.)* **a price ~:** eine Stabilisierung der Preise; **reach/be on a ~** ⟨*Preise, Produktion usw.:*⟩ sich einpendeln/sich eingependelt haben
plated ['pleɪtɪd] *adj.* plattiert; **[gold-]~:** dubliert; vergoldet; **[silver-/chromium-/nickel-]~:** versilbert/verchromt/vernickelt
plateful ['pleɪtfʊl] *n.* Teller, *der;* **a ~ of rice** ein Teller [voll] Reis; **I've already had two ~s** ich habe schon zwei Teller voll gegessen; **I've had a ~** *(fig. coll.)* ich habe die Nase voll davon *(ugs.)*
plate: ~ 'glass *n.* Flachglas, *das;* **~-holder** *n. (Photogr.)* [Platten]kassette, *die;* **~layer** *n. (Brit. Railw.)* Streckenarbeiter, *der*
platelet ['pleɪtlət] *n. (Physiol.)* Blutplättchen, *das*
platen ['plætn] *n. (Printing)* Drucktiegel, *der; (on typewriter)* [Schreib]walze, *die*
plate: ~-rack *n. (Brit.)* Abtropfständer, *der;* Geschirrablage, *die;* **~-warmer** *n.* Tellerwärmer, *der*
platform ['plætfɔ:m] *n.* **a)** *(Brit. Railw.)* Bahnsteig, *der;* **the train leaves from/will arrive at ~ 4** der Zug fährt von Gleis 4 ab/in Gleis 4 ein; **edge of the ~:** Bahnsteigkante, *die;* **b)** *(stage)* Podium, *das;* **c)** *(Polit.)* Wahlplattform, *die;* **d)** *(Geol.)* Strandterrasse, *die;* **e)** *(in bus etc.)* Plattform, *die;* **f)** *(of shoe)* Plateausohle, *die; attrib.* Plateau⟨*schuh, -sohle*⟩
'**platform ticket** *n. (Brit.)* Bahnsteigkarte, *die*
plating ['pleɪtɪŋ] *n. (process)* Plattierung, *die; (coat)* Plattierung, *die;* Auflage, *die;* **gold/silver/chromium ~:** Vergoldung/Versilberung/Verchromung, *die*
platinum ['plætɪnəm] *n.* Platin, *das*
platinum 'blonde 1. *n.* Platinblonde, *die.* **2.** *adj.* platinblond
platitude ['plætɪtju:d] *n.* **a)** *(trite remark)* Platitüde, *die (geh.);* Gemeinplatz, *der;* **b)** *no pl. (triteness)* Banalität, *die*
platitudinous [plætɪ'tju:dɪnəs] *adj.* banal; platt *(abwertend)*
Plato ['pleɪtəʊ] *pr. n.* Plato[n] *(der)*
Platonic [plə'tɒnɪk] *adj.* **a)** *(of Plato)* Platonisch; **b) p~** *(not sexual)* platonisch ⟨*Liebe, Freundschaft*⟩
platonically [plə'tɒnɪkəlɪ] *adv.* platonisch
Platonist ['pleɪtənɪst] *n.* Platoniker, *der*

platoon [plə'tu:n] *n. (Mil.)* Zug, *der*

platter ['plætə(r)] *n. (Amer./arch.)* Platte, *die; (arch.: plate)* Teller, *der;* **have sth. handed to one on a ~** *(fig. coll.)* etw. auf silbernem Tablett serviert bekommen *(fig.)*

platypus ['plætɪpəs] *n. (Zool.)* Schnabeltier, *das*

plaudits ['plɔ:dɪts] *n. pl.* Beifall, *der*

plausibility [plɔ:zɪ'bɪlɪtɪ] *n., no pl.* Plausibilität, *die;* Glaubwürdigkeit, *die; (of person)* Glaubwürdigkeit, *die;* **this version has more ~:** diese Version ist glaubwürdiger *od.* plausibler

plausible ['plɔ:zɪbl] *adj.* plausibel; einleuchtend; glaubwürdig ‹*Person*›

plausibly ['plɔ:zɪblɪ] *adv.* plausibel; einleuchtend; **as long as she ~ could** so lange es sich vertreten ließ

play [pleɪ] **1.** *n.* **a)** *(Theatre)* [Theater]stück, *das;* **television ~:** Fernsehspiel, *das;* **put on a ~:** ein Stück aufführen; **go to [see] a ~:** ins Theater gehen; **a ~ within a ~:** ein Spiel im Spiel; **it was as good as a ~:** dafür hätte man Eintrittsgeld verlangen können; **b)** *(recreation)* Spielen, *das;* Spiel, *das;* **time for ~:** Zeit zum Spielen; **at ~:** beim Spielen; **say/do sth. in ~:** etw. aus *od.* im *od.* zum Spaß sagen/tun; **~ [up]on words** Wortspiel, *das;* **c)** *(Sport)* Spiel, *das; (Amer.: manœuvre)* Spielzug, *der;* **abandon ~:** das Spiel abbrechen; **~ is impossible because of the weather** wegen des Wetters kann nicht gespielt werden; **start/close of ~:** Spielbeginn, *der*/-ende, *das;* **in the last minute of ~:** in der letzten Spielminute; **forward ~:** Angriffsspiel, *das;* **a good piece of ~:** ein guter Spielzug; **be in/out of ~** ‹*Ball:*› im Spiel/aus [dem Spiel] sein; **keep the ball in ~:** den Ball im Spiel halten; **make a ~ for sb./sth.** *(fig. sl.)* hinter jmdm./etw. her sein *(ugs.);* es auf jmdn./etw. abgesehen haben; *see also* **child's play; [2]fair 1 a; foul 1 e; d)** *(gambling)* Spiel, *das;* **e) sb.'s imagination is brought** *or* **called into ~:** jmds. Phantasie wird angeregt; **come into ~, be brought** *or* **called into ~:** ins Spiel kommen; **put into ~:** ins Spiel bringen; **make great ~ of sth.** etw. demonstrativ zur Schau stellen; **make [great] ~ with sth.** viel Wesen um etw. machen; **f)** *(freedom of movement)* Spiel, *das (Technik); (fig.)* Spielraum, *der;* **some/2 mm of/too much ~:** etwas/2 mm/zu viel Spiel; **the knot has too much ~:** der Knoten ist zu locker; **give the rope more ~:** das Seil lockern; **give full ~ to one's emotions/imagination** *etc.*, **allow one's emotions/imagination** *etc.* **full ~** *(fig.)* seinen Gefühlen/seiner Phantasie *usw.* freien Lauf lassen; **g)** *(rapid movement)* **the ~ of light on water** das Spiel des Lichts auf Wasser; **h)** *(turn, move)* **it's your ~:** du bist dran *od.* an der Reihe *(ugs.); (in board-game)* du bist am Zug. **2.** *v. i.* **a)** spielen; **~ for money** um Geld spielen; **~ with sb./sth.** *(lit. or fig.)* mit jmdm./etw. spielen; **have no one to ~ with** niemanden zum Spielen haben; **he won't ~** *(sl.: won't do what sb. wants)* er will nicht mitspielen; **~ with oneself** *(euphem.: sexually)* an sich *(Dat.)* herumspielen *(ugs. verhüll.);* **~ [up]on words** Wortspiele/ein Wortspiel machen; **~ fair [with sb.]** fair [gegen jmdn.] spielen; *(fig.)* [jmdm. gegenüber] fair sein; sich [jmdm. gegenüber] fair verhalten; **not have much time** *etc.* **to ~ with** *(coll.)* zeitlich *usw.* nicht viel Spielraum haben; **~ into sb.'s hands** *(fig.)* jmdm. in die Hand *od.* Hände arbeiten; **~ safe** sichergehen; auf Nummer Sicher gehen *(ugs.);* **~ing safe, she took an umbrella** sicherheits- *od.* vorsichtshalber nahm sie einen Schirm mit; **~ for time** Zeit gewinnen wollen; [ver]suchen, Zeit zu gewinnen; *see also* **fire 1 b; b)** *(be suitable for ~)* **the pitch is ~ing well/badly** auf dem Platz spielt es sich gut/schlecht; **c)** *(Mus.)* spielen (**on** auf + *Dat.*); **~ by ear** nach dem Gehör spielen; **d)** *(Theatre)* spielen; **what is ~ing at the theatre?** was wird im Theater gespielt *od.* gegeben?; *see also* **gallery b; e)** *(move about)* spielen; **a smile ~ed on/about her lips** ein Lächeln spielte um ihre Lippen; **f)** ‹*Springbrunnen:*› in Betrieb sein; **g)** *(fiddle about)* spielen; herumspielen *(ugs.)* (**with** mit, an + *Dat.*). **3.** *v. t.* **a)** *(Mus.: perform on)* spielen; **~ the violin** *etc.* Geige *usw.* spielen; **~ sth. on the piano** *etc.* etw. auf dem Klavier *usw.* spielen; **~ sb. in/out** jmdn. musikalisch begrüßen/verabschieden; **~ sth. by ear** etw. nach dem Gehör spielen; **~ it by ear** *(fig.)* es dem Augenblick/der Situation überlassen; **b)** spielen ‹*Grammophon, Tonbandgerät*›; abspielen ‹*Schallplatte, Tonband*›; spielen lassen ‹*Radio*›; **~ sb. a record** jmdm. eine [Schall]platte vorspielen; **c)** *(Theatre; also fig.)* spielen; **~ a town** in einer Stadt spielen; **~ a theatre** an einem Theater spielen; **~ the fool/innocent** den Clown/Unschuldigen spielen; *see also* **man 1 b; d)** *(execute, practise)* **~ a trick/joke on sb.** jmdn. hereinlegen *(ugs.)*/jmdm. einen Streich spielen; **e)** *(Sport, Cards)* spielen ‹*Fußball, Karten, Schach usw.*›; spielen *od.* antreten gegen ‹*Mannschaft, Gegner*›; *(include in team)* einsetzen, aufstellen ‹*Stürmer, Verteidiger*›; **~ a match** einen Wettkampf bestreiten; *(in team games)* ein Spiel machen; **he ~ed me at chess/squash** er war im Schach/Squash mein Gegner; **~ it cool** *(fig. coll.)* auf cool machen *(salopp);* **~ it right/safe/straight** es geschickt anstellen/auf Nummer Sicher gehen/es sachlich behandeln; **~ oneself in** *(esp. Cricket)* sich einspielen; *(fig.)* sich einarbeiten; *see also* **[1]ball 1 b; [1]duck 1 a; [2]fast 1 a; [1]game 1 a, b, d; hand 1 p; hell b; hookey; f)** *(Sport: execute)* ausführen ‹*Schlag*›; *(Cricket etc.)* schlagen ‹*Ball*›; **g)** *(Chess etc.: move)* ziehen; *(Cards)* spielen; **~ one's last card** *(fig.)* alle seine Karten ausspielen; **have ~ed all one's cards** *(fig.)* seinen letzten Trumpf ausgespielt haben; **~ one's cards right** *(fig.)* es richtig anfassen *(fig.); see also* **[1]trump 1; h)** *(Angling)* drillen; **i)** *(coll.: gamble on)* **~ the market** spekulieren (**in** mit *od. Wirtsch.* in + *Dat.*); **~ the stock market** an der Börse spekulieren

~ a'bout *see* **~ around**

~ a'long *v. i.* mitspielen; **~ along with sb./sth.** sich mit jmdm./etw. arrangieren

~ a'round *v. i. (coll.)* spielen; **~ around with sb./sb.'s affections/sth.** mit jmdm./jmds. Zuneigung spielen/mit etw. herumspielen *(ugs.);* **stop ~ing around!** hör [doch] auf mit dem Blödsinn!

~ at *v. t.* spielen; **what do you think you're ~ing at?** was soll denn das?; **~ at being sb.** jmdn. spielen

~ 'back *v. t.* abspielen ‹*Tonband, Aufnahme*›; **he ~ed part of the discussion back to them** er spielte ihnen einen Teil der Diskussion vor; *see also* **play-back**

~ 'down *v. t.* herunterspielen

~ 'off 1. *v. i.* zum Entscheidungsspiel antreten; *see also* **play-off. 2.** *v. t.* ausspielen; **~ one person/firm** *etc.* **off against another** eine Person/Firma *usw.* gegen eine andere ausspielen

~ on 1. ['--] *v. t. see* **~ upon. 2.** [-'-] *v. i. (Cricket)* auf das eigene Mal schlagen

~ 'up 1. *v. i.* **a)** *(play vigorously)* **~ up!** los, vorwärts!; **b)** *(coll.: behave annoyingly, cause pain)* Schwierigkeiten *od.* Ärger machen. **2.** *v. t.* **a)** *(coll.: annoy, torment)* ärgern; ‹*Krankheit:*› zu schaffen machen (+ *Dat.*); **b)** *(exploit)* hochspielen; Wesen machen von *(ugs.)* ‹*Krankheit*›; hervor-, herauskehren ‹*Eigenschaft usw.*›

~ upon *v. t.* sich *(Dat.)* zunutze machen ‹*Gefühle, Ängste usw.*›; **~ upon sb.'s sympathies** auf jmds. Mitgefühl *(Akk.)* spekulieren *(ugs.)*

~ 'up to *v. t.* **a)** *(Theatre sl.)* gut in Szene setzen ‹*Schauspieler*›; **b)** *(fig.: flatter)* **~ up to sb.** sich bei jmdm. beliebt machen

playable ['pleɪəbl] *adj.* **a)** *(able to be played)* spielbar; **b)** *(Sport: able to be played on)* bespielbar ‹*Spielfeld*›

play: ~-acting *n.* Schauspielkunst, *die;* Schauspielerei, *die (ugs.); (fig.)* Theater, *das (ugs.);* **~-actor** *n. (fig., usu. derog.)* **he's just a ~-actor** er spielt immer nur Theater *(ugs.);* **~ area** *n.* Spielplatz, *der;* **~-back** *n.* Wiedergabe, *die;* **listen to the ~-back** die Aufnahme anhören; **~bill** *n.* **a)** *(poster)* Theaterplakat, *das;* **b)** *(Amer.: theatre programme)* Theaterprogramm, *das;* **~boy** *n.* Playboy, *der*

played 'out *adj.* verbraucht; erschöpft ‹*Person, Tier*›; **this idea is ~:** diese Idee hat sich überlebt

player ['pleɪə(r)] *n.* **a)** Spieler, *der*/Spielerin, *die;* **amateur/professional ~:** Amateur, *der*/Profi[spieler], *der;* **b)** *(Mus.)* Musiker, *der*/Musikerin, *die;* Spieler, *der*/Spielerin, *die;* **orchestral ~:** Orchestermusiker, *der*/-musikerin, *die;* **organ-~:** Orgelspieler, *der*/-spielerin, *die;* **c)** *(actor)* Schauspieler, *der*/Schauspielerin, *die;* **d)** *see* **record-player**

'player-piano *n.* automatisches Klavier; Pianola, *das*

'playfellow *n.* Spielkamerad, *der*/Spielkameradin, *die*

playful ['pleɪfl] *adj.* **a)** *(fond of playing)* spielerisch; *(frolicsome)* verspielt; **b)** *(teasing)* neckisch; *(joking)* scherzhaft

playfully ['pleɪfəlɪ] *adv.* **a)** *(gaily)* spielerisch; ausgelassen; **b)** *(teasingly)* neckisch; *(jokingly)* aus *od.* im *od.* zum Scherz

play: ~goer *n.* Theaterbesucher, *der*/-besucherin, *die;* **be a regular ~goer** regelmäßig ins Theater gehen; **~ground** *n.* Spielplatz, *der; (Sch.)* Schulhof, *der;* **the ~ground of the rich** *(fig.)* der Tummelplatz der Reichen; **~ group** *n.* Spielgruppe, *die;* **~house** *n.* **a)** *(theatre)* Schauspielhaus, *das;* **b)** *(toy house)* Spielhaus, *das*

playing ['pleɪɪŋ] *n.* Spiel, *das*

playing: ~-card *n.* Spielkarte, *die;* **~-field** *n.* Sportplatz, *der;* **~-time** *n.* Spieldauer, *die;* Spielzeit, *die*

playlet ['pleɪlɪt] *n.* Dramolett, *das*

play: ~mate *n.* Spielkamerad, *der*/Spielkameradin, *die;* **~-off** *n.* Entscheidungsspiel, *das;* **~-pen** *n.* Laufgitter, *das;* Laufstall, *der;* **~ school** *n.* Kindergarten, *der;* **~-suit** *n.* Spielanzug, *der;* **~thing** *n. (lit. or fig.)* Spielzeug, *das;* **~things** Spielzeug, *das;* Spielsachen *Pl.;* **~time** *n.* Zeit zum Spielen; **during ~time** *(Sch.)* in der [großen] Pause; **~wright** ['pleɪraɪt] *n.* Dramatiker, *der*/Dramatikerin, *die;* Stückeschreiber, *der*/-schreiberin, *die*

plaza ['plɑ:zə] *n.* Piazza, *die*

PLC, plc *abbr. (Brit.)* **public limited company** ≈ GmbH

plea [pli:] *n.* **a)** *(appeal, entreaty)* Appell, *der* (**for** zu); **make a ~ for sth.** zu etw. aufrufen; **b)** *(pleading)* Begründung, *die; (excuse)* Entschuldigung, *die;* **excuse oneself on the ~ of sth.** sich mit etw. entschuldigen; **c)** *(Law)* Verteidigungsrede, *die;* **special ~:** besondere Einrede; **~ bargaining** *Praktik, bei der Verteidigung und Anklage übereinkommen, daß der Angeklagte ein [Teil]geständnis ablegt und dafür bestimmte Zusicherungen (milderes Strafmaß o. ä.) erhält*

plead [pli:d] **1.** *v. i.*, **~ed** *or (esp. Amer., Scot., dial.)* **pled** [pled] **a)** *(make appeal)* inständig bitten (**for** um); *(imploringly)* flehen (**for** um); **~ with sb. for sth./to do sth.** jmdn. inständig um etw. bitten/jmdn. inständig [darum] bitten, etw. zu tun; *(imploringly)* jmdn. um etw. anflehen/jmdn. anflehen, etw. zu tun; **b)** *(Law: put forward plea; also fig.)* plädieren; **I'd get a lawyer to ~ for me**

ich würde mich von einem Anwalt vertreten lassen; **c)** *(Law)* **how do you ~?** bekennen Sie sich schuldig? **2.** *v.t.*, **~ed** *or (esp. Amer., Scot., dial.)* **pled a)** *(beg)* inständig bitten; *(imploringly)* flehen; **b)** *(Law: offer in mitigation)* sich berufen auf (+ *Akk.*); geltend machen; *(as excuse)* sich entschuldigen mit; **he ~ed insanity** er plädierte auf Unzurechnungsfähigkeit; **~ guilty/not guilty** *(lit. or fig.)* sich schuldig/nicht schuldig bekennen; **~ guilty to [having committed] the crime** sich des Verbrechens schuldig bekennen; **c)** *(present in court)* **~ sb.'s case** *or* **~ the case for sb.** jmds. Sache vor Gericht vertreten

pleading ['pli:dɪŋ] **1.** *adj.* flehend. **2.** *n.* **a)** Bitten, *das; (imploring)* Flehen, *das;* **b)** *usu. in pl. (Law)* Plädoyer, *das;* Vortrag, *der; (written)* Schriftsatz, *der; see also* **special pleading**

pleadingly ['pli:dɪŋlɪ] *adv.* flehentlich

pleasant ['plezənt] *adj.*, **~er** ['plezəntə(r)], **~est** ['plezəntɪst] *(agreeable)* angenehm; schön ⟨*Tag, Zeit*⟩; nett ⟨*Gesicht, Lächeln*⟩; **be ~ with** *or* **to sb.** nett zu jmdm. sein

pleasantly ['plezəntlɪ] *adv.* angenehm; schön ⟨*singen*⟩; freundlich ⟨*sprechen, lächeln usw.*⟩

pleasantry ['plezəntrɪ] *n.* **a)** *(agreeable remark)* Nettigkeit, *die; (humorous remark)* Scherz, *der;* **b)** *(jocularity)* Humor, *der*

please [pli:z] **1.** *v.t.* **a)** *(give pleasure to)* gefallen (+ *Dat.*); Freude machen (+ *Dat.*); **there's no pleasing her** man kann ihr nichts *od.* es ihr nicht recht machen; **she's easy to ~** *or* **easily ~d/hard to ~:** sie ist leicht/nicht leicht zufriedenzustellen; **[just] to ~ you** [nur] dir zu Gefallen; **one can't ~ everybody** man kann es nicht allen recht machen; **~ the eye** das Auge erfreuen; **~ oneself** tun, was man will; **~ yourself** ganz wie du willst; **b)** *([may it] be the will of)* gefallen; **~ God** das gebe Gott; so Gott will; **may it ~ your Honour** *(to a judge)* mit Ihrer Erlaubnis, Hohes Gericht. **2.** *v.i.* **a)** *(think fit)* **what he ~s** was ihm gefällt; was er will; **they come and go as they ~:** sie kommen und gehen, wie es ihnen gefällt; **do as one ~s** tun, was man will; **take as much as you ~:** nimm, soviel[, wie] du willst *od.* möchtest; **b)** *(give pleasure)* gefallen; **anxious** *or* **eager to ~:** bemüht, gefällig zu sein; **the poem is sure to ~:** das Gedicht kommt garantiert gut an *(ugs.) od.* wird bestimmt gefallen; **c)** *in requests* bitte; **may I have the bill, ~?** kann ich bitte zahlen?; **~ do!** aber bitte *od.* gern!; **~ don't** bitte nicht; **d) if you ~:** bitte schön; *(iron.: believe it or not)* stell dir vor

pleased [pli:zd] *adj.* *(satisfied)* zufrieden (**by** mit); *(glad, happy)* erfreut (**by** über + *Akk.*); **he'll be ~ when he sees that** *(iron.)* er wird seine Freude haben, wenn er das sieht; **be ~ at** *or* **about sth.** sich über etw. *(Akk.)* freuen; **be ~ with sth./sb.** mit etw./jmdm. zufrieden sein; **~ with oneself** mit sich selbst zufrieden; **don't look so ~ with yourself** guck nicht so selbstzufrieden *od.* selbstgefällig *(ugs.)*; **be ~ to do sth.** sich freuen, etw. zu tun; *(formal/iron.: with condescension)* belieben, etw. zu tun *(geh./iron.)*; **I am [only too] ~ to be of assistance** es ist mir [wirklich] eine Freude, Ihnen zu helfen; **I shall be ~ to [come]** [ich komme] gerne; *see also* **¹meet 1 c**

pleasing ['pli:zɪŋ] *adj.* gefällig; ansprechend; nett ⟨*Person, Ausblick*⟩; **it is ~ to see how well ...:** es ist eine Freude zu sehen, wie gut ...; **be ~ to the eye/ear** *etc.* das Auge/Ohr *usw.* erfreuen

pleasurable ['pleʒərəbl] *adj.*, **pleasurably** ['pleʒərəblɪ] *adv.* angenehm

pleasure ['pleʒə(r)] **1.** *n.* **a)** *(feeling of joy)* Freude, *die; (usu. derog.: sensuous enjoyment)* Vergnügen, *das;* **sth. gives sb. ~:** etw. macht jmdm. Freude; **for ~:** zum Vergnügen; **it's no ~ to do sth.** es macht keinen Spaß, etw. zu tun; **get a lot of ~ from** *or* **out of sb./sth.** viel Freude *od.* Spaß an jmdm./etw. haben; **b)** *(gratification)* **have the ~ of doing sth.** das Vergnügen haben, etw. zu tun; **it's a ~ to talk to him** es ist ein Vergnügen, mit ihm zu reden; **may I have the ~ [of the next dance]?** darf ich [Sie um den nächsten Tanz] bitten?; **do me the ~ of dining with me** machen Sie mir das Vergnügen *od.* die Freude, mit mir zu speisen; **he had the ~ of knowing that he was always welcome** er war in der glücklichen Lage zu wissen, daß er immer willkommen war; **I don't think I've had the ~:** wir kennen uns noch nicht; **take [a] ~ in** Vergnügen finden *od.* Spaß haben an (+ *Dat.*); **he takes ~ in teasing me** es macht ihm Spaß *od.* bereitet ihm Vergnügen, mich zu necken; **my ~, it's a ~:** gern geschehen; es war mir ein Vergnügen; **the ~ is all mine** das Vergnügen ist ganz meinerseits *od.* auf meiner Seite; **it gives me great ~ to inform you that ..., I have much ~ in informing you that ...** *(formal)* ich freue mich, Ihnen mitteilen zu können, daß ...; **Mrs P. requests the ~ of your company** *(formal)* Frau P. gibt sich *(Dat.)* die Ehre, Sie einzuladen; **Mr F. has great ~ in accepting the invitation** *(formal)* Herr F. nimmt die Einladung mit dem größten Vergnügen an; **with ~:** mit Vergnügen; gern[e]; **with the greatest of ~:** mit dem größten Vergnügen; **c)** *(will, desire)* **what is your ~?** *(formal)* Sie wünschen?; **at ~:** nach Wunsch *od.* Belieben; **come and go at one's ~:** kommen und gehen, wie es einem beliebt *(geh.) od.* wann immer man will; **consult sb.'s ~** *(formal)* fragen, was jmdm. genehm ist *(geh.)*; **we await your ~** *(formal)* wir warten auf Ihren Bescheid; **be detained during Her Majesty's ~:** eine Haftstrafe auf unbestimmte Zeit verbüßen. **2.** *v.t. (give pleasure to)* erfreuen; *(sexually)* beglücken *(scherzh.)*

pleasure: ~-boat *n.* Vergnügungsboot, *das;* **~-craft** *n., pl. same* Vergnügungsboot, *das;* **~ cruise** *n.* Vergnügungsfahrt, *die;* **~-ground** *n.* Vergnügungspark, *der;* **~-loving** *adj.* lebenslustig; *(~-seeking)* vergnügungssüchtig; **~ principle** *n. (Psych.)* Lustprinzip, *das;* **~-seeking 1.** *adj.* vergnügungssüchtig; **2.** *n.* Vergnügungssucht, *die*

pleat [pli:t] **1.** *n.* Falte, *die;* **inverted ~:** Kellerfalte, *die; see also* **box-pleat; knife-pleat. 2.** *v.t.* in Falten legen; fälteln

pleated ['pli:tɪd] *adj.* gefältelt; Falten⟨*rock*⟩

pleb [pleb] *n. (sl.)* Prolet, *der (ugs.)*

plebby ['plebɪ] *adj. (sl.)* primitiv *(abwertend)*

plebeian [plɪ'bi:ən] **1.** *adj.* **a)** proletarisch; **b)** *(coarse)* plebejisch; gewöhnlich. **2.** *n.* **a)** *(in ancient Rome)* Plebejer, *der*/Plebejerin, *die;* **b)** *(commoner)* Bürgerliche, *der/die;* **the ~s** das [einfache] Volk

plebiscite ['plebɪsɪt, 'plebɪsaɪt] *n.* Plebiszit, *das*

plectrum ['plektrəm] *n., pl.* **plectra** ['plektrə] *or* **~s** *(Mus.)* Plektrum, *das*

pled *see* **plead**

pledge [pledʒ] **1.** *n.* **a)** *(promise, vow)* Versprechen, *das;* Gelöbnis, *das (geh.)*; **under the ~ of secrecy** unter dem Siegel der Geheimhaltung; **take** *or* **sign the ~** *(coll.)* sich zur Abstinenz verpflichten; dem Alkohol abschwören; **b)** *(as security)* Pfand, *das;* Sicherheit, *die;* **c)** *(token)* [Unter]pfand, *das (geh.)*; **d)** *(state of being pledged)* Verpfändung, *die;* **put sth. in ~:** etw. verpfänden; **take sth. out of ~:** etw. auslösen. **2.** *v.t.* **a)** *(promise solemnly)* versprechen; geloben ⟨*Treue*⟩; **~ one's word/honour** sein Wort/seine Ehre verpfänden *(geh.)*; **~ one's service[s]** seine Dienste zusichern; **b)** *(bind by promise)* verpflichten; **c)** *(deposit, pawn)* verpfänden (**to** *Dat.*); **d)** *(drink to health of)* einen Trinkspruch *od.* Toast ausbringen auf (+ *Akk.*); **they ~d each other** sie tranken auf ihr gegenseitiges Wohl

Pleiades ['plaɪədi:z] *n. pl. (Astron.)* Plejaden *Pl.*

plein air [plen 'eə(r)] *adj. (Art)* Pleinair-

Pleistocene ['plaɪstəsi:n] *(Geol.)* **1.** *adj.* pleistozän; Pleistozän-. **2.** *n.* Pleistozän, *das*

plenary ['pli:nərɪ] *adj.* **a)** *(entire, absolute)* uneingeschränkt; **~ powers** uneingeschränkte Vollmacht; **b)** *(of all members)* Plenar⟨*sitzung*⟩; Voll⟨*versammlung*⟩

plenipotentiary [plenɪpə'tenʃərɪ] **1.** *adj.* **a)** *(invested with full power)* [general]bevollmächtigt ⟨*Gesandte*⟩; absolut ⟨*Herrscher*⟩; allmächtig ⟨*Parlament*⟩; **b)** *(absolute)* uneingeschränkt. **2.** *n.* [General]bevollmächtigte, *der*

plenitude ['plenɪtju:d] *n., no pl. (abundance)* Fülle, *die* (**of** von)

plenteous ['plentɪəs] *adj. (rhet.)* reichlich; reich ⟨*Ernte*⟩

plentiful ['plentɪfl] *adj.* **a)** *(abundant, copious)* reichlich; häufig ⟨*Element, Rohstoff*⟩; **be ~** *or* **in ~ supply** reichlich vorhanden sein; **there was a ~ supply of food** es gab reichlich zu essen; **b)** *(yielding abundance)* fruchtbar ⟨*Land*⟩; ertragreich ⟨*Jahr*⟩

plentifully ['plentɪfəlɪ] *adv.* reichlich

plenty ['plentɪ] **1.** *n., no pl.* **~ of** viel; eine Menge; *(coll.: enough)* genug; **have you all got ~ of meat?** habt ihr alle reichlich Fleisch?; **take ~ of exercise** sich viel bewegen; **time[s] of ~:** Zeit[en] des Überflusses; **that's ~** *(coll.)* das ist genug *od.* reichlich; das reicht; **take ~!** nimm dir reichlich *od. (ugs.)* ordentlich!; **we gave him ~ of warning** wir haben ihn früh genug gewarnt; *see also* **horn 1 f. 2.** *adj. (coll.)* reichlich vorhanden. **3.** *adv. (coll.)* **it's ~ large enough** es ist groß genug; **there's ~ more where this/those** *etc.* **came from** es ist noch genug da *(ugs.)*

pleonasm ['pli:ənæzm] *n. (Ling.)* Pleonasmus, *der*

pleonastic [pli:ə'næstɪk] *adj. (Ling.)* pleonastisch

plethora ['pleθərə] *n.* **a)** *(fig.: excess)* Unmenge, *die* (**of** von); **b)** *(Med.)* Plethora, *die (fachspr.)*; Blutandrang, *der*

plethoric [plɪ'θɒrɪk] *adj. (Med.)* vollblütig; plethorisch *(fachspr.)*

pleura ['plʊərə] *n., pl.* **~e** ['plʊəri:] *(Anat.)* Pleura, *die (fachspr.)*; Brustfell, *das*

pleural ['plʊərl] *adj. (Anat.)* pleural; **~ cavity** Brusthöhle, *die;* **~ inflammation** Brustfellentzündung, *die*

pleurisy ['plʊərɪsɪ] *n. (Med.)* Pleuritis, *die (fachspr.)*; Brustfellentzündung, *die*

Plexiglas *(Amer.* **P***)*, **plexiglass** ['pleksɪglɑ:s] *n. (Amer.)* Plexiglas, *das* ⓦⓩ

plexus ['pleksəs] *n. (Anat.)* Plexus, *der; see also* **solar plexus**

pliability [plaɪə'bɪlɪtɪ] *n., no pl.* Biegsamkeit, *die; (of leather etc.)* Geschmeidigkeit, *die; (fig.: of person, disposition)* Fügsamkeit, *die;* Nachgiebigkeit, *die*

pliable ['plaɪəbl] *adj.* *(flexible, yielding)* biegsam; geschmeidig ⟨*Ton, Leder*⟩; *(fig.)* nachgiebig ⟨*Charakter*⟩; **be ~ to sb.'s wishes** jmds. Wünschen nachgeben

pliant ['plaɪənt] *adj.* biegsam ⟨*Ast, Körper*⟩; geschmeidig ⟨*Körper*⟩; *(fig.)* formbar

pliers ['plaɪəz] *n. pl.* **[pair of] ~:** Zange, *die*

¹plight [plaɪt] *n.* Notlage, *die;* **hopeless/miserable ~:** trostloser/jämmerlicher Zustand; **what a ~ to find yourself in** was für eine verzweifelte Lage!

²plight *v.t., esp. in p.p. (arch.)* geloben *(geh.)* ⟨*Treue*⟩; schwören ⟨*Eid*⟩; **~ one's word [that ...]** sein Wort [dafür] verpfänden[, daß ...]; *see also* **troth b**

plimsoll ['plɪmsl] *n. (Brit.)* Turnschuh, *der*

Plimsoll: ~ line, ~ mark *ns. (Naut.)* Freibordmarke, *die;* Plimsoll-Marke, *die*

plinth [plɪnθ] *n.* **a)** *(for vase, statue, etc.; of* *wall)* Sockel, *der;* **b)** *(of column)* Plinthe, *die (fachspr.)*

Pliocene ['plaɪəsi:n] *(Geol.)* **1.** *adj.* pliozän; Pliozän-. **2.** *n.* Pliozän, *das*

PLO *abbr.* **Palestine Liberation Organization** PLO, *die*

plod [plɒd] **1.** *v.i.*, **-dd-** trotten; ~ **along** dahintrotten; ~ **[on] through the snow** [weiter] durch den Schnee stapfen; ~ **through a book/one's work** *(fig.)* sich durch ein Buch kämpfen/sich mit seiner Arbeit abplagen. **2.** *v.t.*, **-dd-** entlangtrotten; ~ **one's way home** nach Hause trotten. **3.** *n. (laborious walk)* Stapfen, *das; (laborious work)* Plackerei, *die (ugs.)*

~ **a'way** *v.i. (fig.)* sich abmühen; ~ **away at sth.** sich mit etw. abmühen

~ **'on** *v.i. (fig.)* sich weiterkämpfen; ~ **on with sth.** sich weiter durch etw. kämpfen

plodder ['plɒdə(r)] *n. (worker)* Arbeitstier, *das; (walker)* Fußlahme, *der/die (ugs.);* **he is a ~:** er arbeitet schwerfällig/hat einen schwerfälligen Gang; *(Sch.)* er ist ein bißchen langsam

[1]**plonk** [plɒŋk] *v.t. (coll.)* ~ **sth. [down]** etw. hinknallen *(ugs.) od.* hinwerfen; ~ **sth. down in a corner** etw. in eine Ecke knallen *(ugs.);* ~ **oneself [down] in an armchair** sich in einen Sessel knallen *od.* hauen *(ugs.)*

[2]**plonk** *n. (sl.: wine)* [billiger] Wein

plop [plɒp] **1.** *v.i.*, **-pp-** plumpsen *(ugs.);* ‹*Regen:*› klatschen, platschen. **2.** *v.t.*, **-pp-** plumpsen lassen *(ugs.).* **3.** *n.* Plumpsen, *das;* **with a ~:** mit einem Plumps. **4.** *adv.* plumps

plosive ['pləʊsɪv] *(Ling.)* **1.** *adj.* plosiv; Verschluß-. **2.** *n.* Plosiv, *der;* Verschlußlaut, *der*

plot [plɒt] **1.** *n.* **a)** *(conspiracy)* Komplott, *das;* Verschwörung, *die;* **b)** *(of play, film, novel)* Handlung, *die;* Fabel, *die;* Plot, *der (Literaturw.);* **c)** *(of ground)* Stück Land; **vegetable ~:** Gemüsebeet, *das;* **building ~:** Baugrundstück, *das;* Bauplatz, *der;* **d)** *(curve etc.)* Diagramm, *das;* **e)** *(Amer.: ground plan)* Plan, *der.* **2.** *v.t.*, **-tt-: a)** *(plan secretly)* [heimlich] planen; ~ **treason** auf Verrat sinnen *(geh.);* ~ **to do sth.** [heimlich] planen, etw. zu tun; **b)** *(make plan or map of)* kartieren, kartographieren ‹*Gebiet usw.*›; einen Plan zeichnen (+ *Gen.*) ‹*Gebäude usw.*›; *(make by ~ing)* zeichnen ‹*Karte, Plan*›; *(fig.)* entwerfen ‹*Roman*›; **c)** *(mark on map, diagram)* ~ **[down]** eintragen; einzeichnen. **3.** *v.i.*, **-tt-:** ~ **against sb.** sich gegen jmdn. verschwören; ein Komplott gegen jmdn. schmieden

plotter ['plɒtə(r)] *n.* **a)** *(conspirator)* Verschwörer, *der*/Verschwörerin, *die;* **b)** *(instrument)* Plotter, *der;* Planzeichner, *der*

plough [plaʊ] **1.** *n. (Agric.)* Pflug, *der;* **put one's hand to the ~** *(fig.)* eine Sache in Angriff nehmen; **the P~** *(Astron.)* der Große Wagen *od.* Bär. **2.** *v.t.* **a)** pflügen; ~ **the sand[s]** *(fig.)* Wasser mit einem Sieb schöpfen; **b)** *(cut furrows in)* zerpflügen; **c)** ~ **furrows** Furchen ziehen *od.* pflügen; ~ **a lonely furrow** *(fig.)* allein auf weiter Flur sein *od.* stehen *(geh.);* **d)** *(fig.)* ‹*Schiff:*› [durch]pflügen ‹*Wasserfläche*›; **e)** *(Brit. sl.: reject in examination)* durchrasseln lassen *(salopp).* **3.** *v.i. (Brit. sl.: fail in examination)* durchrasseln *(salopp)*

~ **'back** *v.t.* **a)** unterpflügen; **b)** *(Finance)* reinvestieren; ~ **profits** *etc.* **back into the business** *etc.* Gewinne *usw.* wieder in die Firma *usw.* stecken

~ **'in** *v.t.* unterpflügen

~ **into** *v.t. (move violently)* rasen *od. (salopp)* rasseln in (+ *Akk.*)

~ **through** *v.t. (advance laboriously in)* sich kämpfen durch; ‹*Schiff:*› sich pflügen durch; *(move violently through)* rasen durch

~ **'up** *v.t.* auspflügen ‹*Kartoffeln, Rüben usw.*›; zerpflügen ‹*Boden*›

plough: ~man ['plaʊmən] *n., pl.* **~men** ['plaʊmən] Pflüger, *der;* **~man's [lunch]** *(Brit.) Imbiß aus Käse, Brot und Mixed Pickles;* **~share** *n.* Pflugschar, *die*

plover ['plʌvə(r)] *n. (Ornith.)* Regenpfeifer, *der*

plow *(Amer./arch.) see* **plough 1, 2 a, b, c, d**

ploy [plɔɪ] *n.* Trick, *der; (tactical approach)* Taktik, *die; (gambit)* Manöver, *das; (method)* Masche, *die (ugs.)*

PLR *abbr. (Brit.)* **Public Lending Right**

pluck [plʌk] **1.** *v.t.* **a)** *(pull off, pick)* pflücken ‹*Blumen, Obst*›; ~ **[out]** auszupfen ‹*Federn, Haare*›; **b)** *(pull at, twitch)* zupfen an (+ *Dat.*); zupfen ‹*Saite, Gitarre*›; **he ~ed his mother's skirt** er zupfte seiner Mutter am Rock; **c)** *(strip of feathers)* rupfen. **2.** *v.i.* ~ **at sth.** an etw. *(Dat.)* zupfen; **he ~ed at his mother's skirt** er zupfte seiner Mutter am Rock. **3.** *n.* **a)** *(courage)* Mut, *der;* Schneid, *der (ugs.);* **b)** *(heart, liver, lungs of animal as food)* Innereien *Pl.*

~ **'up** *v.t.* ~ **up [one's] courage** all seinen Mut zusammennehmen; ~ **up courage to do sth.** den Mut finden, etw. zu tun; **he ~ed up [enough] courage to ask her out** er faßte sich *(Dat.)* ein Herz und bat sie, mit ihm auszugehen

pluckily ['plʌkɪlɪ] *adv.*, **plucky** ['plʌkɪ] *adj.* tapfer

plug [plʌg] **1.** *n.* **a)** *(filling hole)* Pfropfen, *der; (in cask)* Spund, *der;* Zapfen, *der; (stopper for basin, vessel, etc.)* Stöpsel, *der; (of wax etc.)* Pfropf, *der;* **b)** *(Electr.)* Stecker, *der; (coll.: socket)* Stecker, *der (ugs.);* **pull the ~ on sb./sth.** *(coll.)* jmdn./einer Sache den Hahn zudrehen *(ugs.); see also* **sparking-plug; c)** *(coll.: of water-closet)* Stöpsel, *der;* **pull the ~:** [ab]ziehen; **d)** *(of tobacco)* Plug, *der (fachspr.); (piece of chewing tobacco)* Priem, *der;* **e)** *(coll.: piece of good publicity)* **give sth. a ~:** Werbung für etw. machen; **give sb. a ~:** jmdm. [etwas] Publicity verschaffen. **2.** *v.t.*, **-gg-: a)** ~ **[up]** zustopfen, verstopfen ‹*Loch usw.*›; **b)** *(coll.: advertise)* Schleichwerbung machen für; *(by presenting sth. repeatedly)* pushen *(ugs.)*

~ **a'way** *v.i. (coll.)* vor sich hin schuften *(ugs.);* ~ **away at sth.** sich mit etw. abschuften *(ugs.)*

~ **'in** *v.t.* anschließen; **is it ~ged in?** ist der Stecker in der Steckdose *od. (ugs.)* drin?; *see also* **plug-in**

plug: ~-hat *n. (Amer. coll.)* Angströhre, *die (ugs. scherzh.);* **~-hole** *n.* Abfluß, *der;* **go down the ~-hole** *(fig. coll.)* im Eimer sein *(salopp);* **~-in** *adj.* anschließbar

plum [plʌm] *n.* **a)** *(tree)* Pflaumenbaum, *der;* Pflaume, *die; (fruit)* Pflaume, *die;* **speak with a ~ in one's mouth** *(Brit. coll.)* affektiert sprechen; **b)** *(fig.)* Leckerbissen, *der;* **a ~ job/position** ein Traumjob *(ugs.);* **his job is a real ~:** sein Job ist einfach traumhaft; **c)** *(colour)* Pflaumenblau, *das*

plumage ['plu:mɪdʒ] *n.* Gefieder, *das*

[1]**plumb** [plʌm] **1.** *v.t. (sound, measure)* [aus]loten; *(fig.)* ergründen ‹*Geheimnis*›; ~ **the depths of loneliness/sorrow** die tiefsten Tiefen der Einsamkeit/Trauer erleben. **2.** *adv.* **a)** *(vertically)* senkrecht; lotrecht; **b)** *(fig.: exactly)* genau; **c)** *(Amer. sl.: utterly)* total *(ugs.);* **you get ~ out of here!** raus hier, aber 'n bißchen plötzlich! *(ugs.).* **3.** *adj.* **a)** *(vertical)* senkrecht; lotrecht; **b)** *(fig.: downright, sheer)* völlig; absolut. **4.** *n.* Lot, *das;* Senkblei, *das;* **off** *or* **out of ~:** außer *od.* nicht im Lot

[2]**plumb** *v.t.* ~ **in** *(connect)* fest anschließen

plumbago [plʌm'beɪgəʊ] *n., pl.* **~s a)** *(Min.)* Graphit, *der;* **b)** *(Bot.)* Bleiwurz, *die*

plumber ['plʌmə(r)] *n.* Klempner, *der;* Installateur, *der*

plumbing ['plʌmɪŋ] *n.* **a)** *(plumber's work)* Klempnerarbeiten *Pl.;* Installationsarbeiten *Pl.;* **b)** *(water-pipes)* Wasserrohre; Wasserleitungen; **a cottage without ~:** ein Häuschen ohne Wasseranschluß; **c)** *(coll.: lavatory)* Klo, *das (ugs.);* **go and inspect the ~:** die Örtlichkeit aufsuchen

'plumb-line *n.* **a)** *(for measuring)* Lot, *das;* **b)** *(fig.)* Maßstab, *der*

'plum-cake *n.* Rosinenkuchen, *der*

plume [plu:m] **1.** *n.* **a)** *(feather)* Feder, *die; (ornamental bunch)* Federbusch, *der;* ~ **of white feathers** weißer Federbusch; **borrowed ~s** *(fig.)* fremde Federn; **b)** ~ **of smoke/steam/snow** Rauchwolke *od.* -fahne/Dampfwolke/Schneefahne, *die.* **2.** *v.t.* **a)** *(furnish, decorate with ~s)* mit Federn schmücken; befiedern ‹*Pfeil*›; **b)** ~ **oneself on sth.** sich mit etw. brüsten; **c)** *(preen etc.)* ‹*Vogel:*› ordnen ‹*Federn*›; **the swan ~d itself** der Schwan ordnete sein Gefieder

plummet ['plʌmɪt] **1.** *v.i.* stürzen. **2.** *n.* **a)** *(weight)* Lotblei, *das; (plumb-line)* Lot, *das;* **b)** *(sounding-lead)* Lot, *das;* Senkblei, *das;* **c)** *(Angling)* Bleigewicht, *das;* Blei, *das*

plummy ['plʌmɪ] *adj.* **a)** *(coll.)* sonor ‹*Stimme*›; *(derog.: affected)* affektiert; **b)** *(coll.: desirable, good)* bombig *(ugs.);* Bomben‹*stelle, -job*› *(ugs.)*

[1]**plump** [plʌmp] *adj.* mollig; rundlich; stämmig ‹*Arme, Beine*›; fleischig ‹*Brathuhn usw.*›; ~ **cheeks** Pausbacken *Pl. (fam.);* runde *od.* volle Backen

~ **'out 1.** *v.i.* sich runden; rund werden. **2.** *v.t.* runden; rund werden lassen

~ **'up 1.** *v.t.* aufschütteln ‹*Kissen*›; *(fatten up)* mästen. **2.** *v.i.* Fett ansetzen

[2]**plump 1.** *v.t.* ~ **sb./oneself/sth. down** jmdn./sich/etw. fallen lassen; **he ~ed the cases in the hall** er setzte die Koffer schwungvoll in der Halle ab. **2.** *v.i.* **a)** *(drop)* fallen; **b)** *(Amer.: move abruptly)* stürmen; stürzen

~ **for** *v.t.* **a)** *(Brit.: vote for)* stimmen für; **b)** *(choose)* sich entscheiden für

plumpness ['plʌmpnɪs] *n., no pl. see* [1]**plump:** Molligkeit, *die;* Rundlichkeit, *die;* Stämmigkeit, *die;* Fleischigkeit, *die*

plum: ~ 'pudding *n.* Plumpudding, *der; (suet pudding) mit Nierenfett zubereiteter Pudding mit Rosinen;* ≈ Rosinenpudding, *der;* **~-tree** *n.* Pflaumenbaum, *der*

plunder ['plʌndə(r)] **1.** *v.t.* [aus]plündern ‹*Gebäude, Gebiet*›; ausplündern ‹*Person*›; rauben ‹*Sache*›; **the church was ~ed of its holy relics** die heiligen Reliquien wurden aus der Kirche geraubt. **2.** *n.* **a)** *(action)* Plünderung, *die; (spoil, booty)* Beute, *die;* **b)** *(sl.: profit)* Profit, *der*

plunderer ['plʌndərə(r)] *n.* Plünd[e]rer, *der*

plunge [plʌndʒ] **1.** *v.t.* **a)** *(thrust violently)* stecken; *(into liquid)* tauchen; ~ **a knife into sb.'s back** jmdm. ein Messer in den Rücken stoßen; **b)** *(fig.)* **~d in thought** in Gedanken versunken; **be ~d into sth.** in etw. *(Akk.)* gestürzt werden; ~ **oneself into sth.** sich in etw. *(Akk.)* stürzen; **be ~d into darkness** in Dunkelheit getaucht sein *(geh.).* **2.** *v.i.* **a)** ~ **into sth.** *(lit. or fig.)* in etw. *(Akk.)* stürzen; **he ~d into the crowd** er tauchte in die Menge ein; ~ **in** sich hineinstürzen; **they ~d into a political discussion** sie stürzten sich in eine politische Diskussion; **b)** *(descend suddenly)* ‹*Straße usw.:*› steil abfallen; **plunging neckline** tiefer Ausschnitt; [tiefes] Dekolleté; ~ **down the stairs** die Treppe hinunterstürzen; **c)** *(enter impetuously)* stürzen; **d)** *(start violently forward)* ‹*Pferd:*› durchgehen; *(pitch)* ‹*Schiff:*› eintauchen; **e)** *(sl.: gamble)* spielen. **3.** *n.* Sprung, *der;* **take the ~** *(fig. coll.)* den Sprung wagen; **they have decided to take the ~ and do it** sie haben sich dazu durchgerungen, es zu tun

plunger ['plʌndʒə(r)] *n.* **a)** *(part of mechanism)* [Tauch]kolben, *der;* Plunger[kolben], *der;* **b)** *(rubber suction cup)* Stampfer, *der*

plunk [plʌŋk] *see* [1]**plonk**

pluperfect [plu:'pɜ:fɪkt] *(Ling.)* **1.** *n.* Plus-

quamperfekt, *das.* **2.** *adj.* ~ **tense** Plusquamperfekt, *das*
plural ['plʊərl] *(Ling.)* **1.** *adj.* pluralisch; Plural-; ~ **noun** Substantiv im Plural; ~ **form** Pluralform, *die;* **third person** ~: dritte Person Plural. **2.** *n.* Mehrzahl, *die;* Plural, *der*
pluralise *see* **pluralize**
pluralism ['plʊərəlɪzm] *n.* **a)** *(holding of more than one office)* Ämterhäufung, *die;* **b)** *(Polit., Sociol.)* Pluralismus, *der*
pluralist ['plʊərəlɪst] *n.* **a)** *(holder of more than one office)* Inhaber mehrerer [Kirchen]ämter; **b)** *(Polit., Sociol.)* Pluralist, *der*
pluralistic [plʊərə'lɪstɪk] *adj.* pluralistisch
plurality [plʊə'rælɪtɪ] *n.* **a)** *(being plural)* Pluralität, *die;* **b)** *(large number)* Vielzahl, *die;* **c)** *(majority)* Majorität, *die;* Mehrheit, *die;* ~ **of sth.** Mehrheit einer Sache *(Gen.);* **d)** *(Amer. Polit.)* [Stimmen]vorsprung, *der* (**over** vor + *Dat.*)
pluralize ['plʊərəlaɪz] *v. t.* pluralisieren *(Sprachw.);* in den Plural setzen
plural: ~ **'number** *see* **plural 2;** ~ **so'ciety** *n.* plurale Gesellschaft; ~ **'vote** *n.* Mehrstimmenrecht, *das;* ~ **'voting** *n.* Pluralwahlrecht, *das*
plus [plʌs] **1.** *prep.* **a)** *(with the addition of)* plus (+ *Dat.*); *(and also)* und [zusätzlich]; **b)** *(above zero)* plus; ~ **ten degrees** plus zehn Grad; zehn Grad plus; **c)** *(coll.);* **he returned from America** ~ **a wife and child** er kam aus Amerika zurück – mit Frau und Kind; **a** ~ **one** *etc.* **player** *(Golf)* ein Spieler mit einer Vorgabe von eins *usw.* **2.** *adj.* **a)** *(additional, extra)* zusätzlich; **b)** *(at least)* **fifteen** *etc.* ~: über fünfzehn *usw.;* **alpha** *etc.* ~ Eins *usw.* plus; **c)** *(Math.: positive)* positiv ‹*Wert, Menge, Größe*›; **d)** *(Electr.)* ~ **pole/terminal** Pluspol, *der.* **3.** *n.* **a)** *(symbol)* Plus[zeichen], *das;* **b)** *(additional quantity)* Plus, *das;* **c)** *(advantage)* Pluspunkt, *der.* **4.** *conj. (sl.)* und außerdem
plus-'fours *n. pl.* Überfallhose, *die*
plush [plʌʃ] **1.** *n.* Plüsch, *der.* **2.** *adj.* **a)** *(made of plush)* Plüsch-; plüschen; **b)** *(covered in plush)* mit Plüsch bezogen; **c)** *(coll.: luxurious)* feudal *(ugs.)*
plushy ['plʌʃɪ] *adj.* **a)** *(of, like plush)* plüschig; **b)** *see* **plush 2 c**
Pluto ['plu:təʊ] *pr. n.* **a)** *(Astron.)* Pluto, *der;* **b)** *(Roman Mythol.)* Pluto *(der)*
plutocracy [plu:'tɒkrəsɪ] *n.* **a)** *(rule by the rich; state)* Plutokratie, *die;* **b)** *(rich ruling class)* Plutokraten *Pl.*
plutocrat ['plu:təkræt] *n.* Plutokrat, *der*
plutocratic [plu:tə'krætɪk] *adj.* plutokratisch
plutonic [plu:'tɒnɪk] *adj.* *(Geol.)* plutonisch; ~ **theory** Plutonismus, *der*
plutonium [plu:'təʊnɪəm] *n.* *(Chem.)* Plutonium, *das*
pluvial ['plu:vɪəl] *adj.* Regen-
¹ply [plaɪ] **1.** *v. t.* **a)** *(use, wield)* gebrauchen; führen; **they plied their oars** sie legten sich in die Ruder; **b)** *(work at)* nachgehen (+ *Dat.*) ‹*Handwerk, Arbeit*›; **c)** *(sell)* verkaufen; **d)** *(supply)* ~ **sb. with sth.** jmdn. mit etw. versorgen; **e)** *(assail)* überhäufen; ~ **sb. with questions** jmdn. mit Fragen überschütten; **f)** *(sail over)* befahren. **2.** *v. i.* **a)** *(go to and fro)* ~ **between** zwischen ‹*Orten*› [hin- und her]pendeln; *(operate on regular services)* zwischen ‹*Orten*› verkehren; **b)** *(attend regularly for custom)* seine Dienste anbieten; ~ **for customers** auf Kunden *od.* Kundschaft warten; **a taxi** ~**ing for hire** ein auf Kundschaft wartendes Taxi
²ply *n.* **a)** *(of yarn, wool, etc.)* [Einzel]faden, *der;* *(of rope, cord, etc.)* Strang, *der;* *(of plywood, cloth, etc.)* Lage, *die;* Schicht, *die;* *see also* **three-ply; two-ply; b)** *see* **plywood**
'plywood *n.* Sperrholz, *das*
PM *abbr.* **a) post-mortem; b) Prime Minister**
p.m. [pi:'em] **1.** *adv.* nachmittags; **one** ~: ein Uhr mittags; **two/five** ~: zwei/fünf Uhr nachmittags; **six/eleven** ~: sechs/elf Uhr abends. **2.** *n.* Nachmittag, *der;* **Monday/this** ~: Montag/heute nachmittag
PMT *abbr.* **premenstrual tension**
pneumatic [nju:'mætɪk] *adj.* pneumatisch; mit Druckluft betrieben *od.* arbeitend ‹*Maschine*›; Druckluft‹*werkzeug, -hammer*›
pneumatically [nju:'mætɪkəlɪ] *adv.* pneumatisch; mit Druckluft *nachgestellt*
pneumatic: ~ **'blonde** *n.* *(joc.)* üppige Blondine; ~ **'drill** *n.* Preßluftbohrer, *der;* ~ **'tyre** *n.* Luftreifen, *der;* Pneumatik, *der*
pneumoconiosis [nju:məʊkɒnɪ'əʊsɪs] *n., no pl.* *(Med.)* Pneumokoniose, *die (fachspr.);* Staublunge, *die*
pneumonia [nju:'məʊnɪə] *n.* Lungenentzündung, *die;* Pneumonie, *die (Med.);* **double/single** ~: doppelseitige/einseitige Lungenentzündung
PO *abbr.* **a) postal order** PA; **b) Post Office** PA; **c)** *(Brit. Navy)* **Petty Officer; d)** *(Brit. Air Force)* **Pilot Officer** LT
po [pəʊ] *n., pl.* **pos** *(coll.)* [Nacht]topf, *der;* Pott, *der (ugs., bes. nordd.)*
¹poach [pəʊtʃ] **1.** *v. t.* **a)** *(catch illegally)* wildern; illegal fangen ‹*Fische*›; ~ **pupils away from other teachers** anderen Lehrern die Schüler abspenstig machen; **b)** *(obtain unfairly)* stehlen, *(ugs.)* klauen ‹*Idee*›; sich *(Dat.)* erschleichen ‹*Vorteil*›. **2.** *v. i.* **a)** *(catch animals illegally)* wildern; **b)** *(encroach)* ~ **[on sb.'s territory]** jmdm. ins Handwerk pfuschen; *(Sport)* dazwischengehen
²poach *v. t.* *(Cookery)* pochieren ‹*Ei*›; dünsten, pochieren ‹*Fisch, Fleisch, Gemüse*›; ~**ed eggs** pochierte *od.* verlorene Eier
¹poacher ['pəʊtʃə(r)] *n.* Wilderer, *der;* Wilddieb, *der;* **the** ~ **turns gamekeeper** aus einem Saulus wird ein Paulus
²poacher *n.* *(Cookery)* Dünster, *der;* **[egg-]**~: Eierkocher für pochierte Eier
pochard ['pəʊtʃəd] *n.* *(Ornith.)* Tafelente, *die*
pock [pɒk] *n.* Pickel, *der;* Pustel, *die (Med.);* *(of smallpox)* Pocke, *die*
pocked [pɒkt] *adj.* durchlöchert (**with** von)
pocket ['pɒkɪt] **1.** *n.* **a)** Tasche, *die;* *(in suitcase etc.)* Seitentasche, *die;* *(in handbag)* [Seiten]fach, *das;* *(on rucksack etc.)* [Außen]tasche, *die;* *(Billiards etc.)* Loch, *das;* Tasche, *die;* **be in sb.'s** ~ *(fig.)* von jmdm. abhängig sein; **the business is virtually in his** ~: in der Firma ist er praktisch der Boss *(ugs.);* **have [got] sb. in one's** ~: jmdn. in der Tasche haben *(ugs.);* **make a hole in sb.'s** ~ *(fig.)* ein Loch in jmds. Geldbeutel *(Akk.)* reißen; **b)** *(fig.: financial resources)* **with an empty** ~, **with empty** ~**s** mit leeren Taschen; **pay for sth. out of one's own** ~: etw. aus eigener *od.* der eigenen Tasche bezahlen; **it is beyond my** ~: es übersteigt meine finanziellen Möglichkeiten; **put one's hand in one's** ~: in die Tasche greifen *(ugs.);* **be in** ~: Geld verdient haben; **be £100 in** ~: 100 Pfund gutgemacht haben; **be out of** ~ *(have lost money)* draufgelegt haben *(ugs.);* zugesetzt haben; **I don't want you to be out of** ~ **because of me** ich möchte nicht, daß du meinetwegen drauflegst *(ugs.) od.* zusetzt; *see also* **out-of-pocket; c)** *(Mil.) (area)* Kessel, *der;* **enemy** ~: [versprengte] feindliche Einheit; ~ **of resistance** Widerstandsnest, *das;* **d)** *(isolated group)* ≈ Schwerpunkt, *der;* ~ **of unemployment** schwerpunktmäßiges Auftreten von Arbeitslosigkeit; **e)** *(Mining, Geol.)* Nest, *das. See also* **²line. 2.** *adj.* Taschen‹*rechner, -uhr, -ausgabe*›. **3.** *v. t.* **a)** *(put in one's pocket)* einstecken; **b)** *(steal)* in die eigene Tasche stecken *(ugs.);* **c)** *(fig.: submit to)* wegstecken; einstecken; **d)** *(fig.: conceal)* verbergen, hinunterschlucken *(ugs.)* ‹*Zorn, Gefühlsregung*›; **e)** *(Billiards etc.)* einlochen
'pocket-book *n.* **a)** *(wallet)* Brieftasche, *die;* **b)** *(notebook)* Notizbuch, *das;* **c)** *(Amer.: paperback)* Taschenbuch, *das;* **in** ~: als Taschenbuch; **d)** *(Amer.: handbag)* Handtasche, *die*
pocketful ['pɒkɪtfʊl] *n.* **a** ~ **of loose change** eine Tasche voll Kleingeld
pocket: ~ **'handkerchief** *n.* **a)** Taschentuch, *das;* **b)** *(fig.: very small area)* **a** ~ **handkerchief of a garden** ein winziger Garten; ~**-knife** *n.* Taschenmesser, *das;* ~**-money** *n.* Taschengeld, *das;* ~**-size[d]** *adj.* **a)** im Taschenformat *nachgestellt;* ~**-sized edition** Taschenausgabe, *die;* **b)** *(fig.: small scale)* Westentaschen- *(ugs. scherzh.);* im [Westen]taschenformat *nachgestellt (ugs. scherzh.);* ~ **'veto** *n.* *(Amer. Polit.) durch Nichtunterzeichnung einer Gesetzesvorlage ausgeübtes Veto*
pock: ~**-mark** *n.* **a)** *(Med.)* Pockennarbe, *die;* **b)** Delle, *die;* *(from bullet)* Einschuß, *der;* ~**-marked** *adj.* **a)** pockennarbig ‹*Gesicht, Haut*›; **b) a wall** ~**-marked with bullets** eine mit Einschüssen übersäte Wand
pod [pɒd] **1.** *n.* **a)** *(seed-case)* Hülse, *die;* *(of pea)* Schote, *die;* Hülse, *die;* **b)** *(in aircraft etc.)* *(for engine)* Gondel, *die;* *(for fuel)* Außentank, *der;* *(for missile etc.)* Behälter, *der;* Pod, *der;* *(radome)* Radom, *das.* **2.** *v. t.*, **-dd-** aus- *od.* enthülsen. **3.** *v. i.*, **-dd-** *(form pods)* [Früchte] ansetzen; *(bear pods)* [Früchte] tragen
podge [pɒdʒ] *n.* *(coll.)* Pummel, *der (ugs.)*
podgy ['pɒdʒɪ] *adj.* dicklich; pummelig *(ugs.),* rundlich *(fam.),* mollig ‹*Frau*›; pausbäckig, *(fam.)* rundlich ‹*Gesicht*›; ~ **cheek** Pausbacke, *die (fam.);* ~ **fingers** Wurstfinger *(ugs.)*
podium ['pəʊdɪəm] *n., pl.* **podia** ['pəʊdɪə] *or* **-s** Podium, *das*
podzol ['pɒdzɒl] *n.* *(Soil Sci.)* Podsol, *der*
poem ['pəʊɪm] *n.* Gedicht, *das;* **symphonic** ~ *(Mus.)* sinfonische Dichtung
poesy ['pəʊɪsɪ, 'pəʊɪzɪ] *n.* *(arch./poet.)* *(poetry)* Poesie, *die;* *(art)* Dichtkunst, *die;* *(poems collectively)* Dichtung, *die*
poet ['pəʊɪt] *n.* *(writer of poems)* Dichter, *der;* Poet, *der (geh.);* *(sb. with great creativity)* Künstler, *der;* **P~s' Corner** die Dichterecke *od.* der Dichterwinkel *(in der Westminsterabtei); see also* **laureate**
poetaster [pəʊɪ'tæstə(r)] *n.* *(dated derog.)* Dichterling, *der (abwertend);* Poetaster, *der (geh. abwertend)*
poetess ['pəʊɪtes] *n.* Dichterin, *die;* Poetin, *die (geh.)*
poetic [pəʊ'etɪk] *adj.* dichterisch; poetisch *(geh.);* anmutig ‹*Bewegung*›; ‹*Bild, Anblick*› voller Poesie; **in** ~ **form** in Versen; *see also* **justice a; licence 1 d**
poetical [pəʊ'etɪkl] *adj.* **a)** *see* **poetic; b)** *(written in verse)* in Gedichtform *nachgestellt;* ~ **drama** Versdrama, *das;* **his** ~ **works** seine Gedichte
poetically [pəʊ'etɪkəlɪ] *adv.* dichterisch; poetisch *(geh.)*
poetry ['pəʊɪtrɪ] *n.* [Vers]dichtung, *die;* Lyrik, *die;* *(fig.)* Poesie, *die (geh.);* **prose** ~: Prosadichtung, *die;* ~ **reading** ≈ Dichterlesung, *die*
'po-faced ['pəʊfeɪst] *adj.* mit unbewegter Miene *nachgestellt;* *(smug, priggish)* blasiert *(abwertend);* *(narrow-minded)* borniert; **sound** ~: abweisend klingen
pogo ['pəʊgəʊ] *n., pl.* ~**s:** ~ **[stick]** Springstab, *der*
pogrom ['pɒgrəm] *n.* Pogrom, *das od. der*
poignancy ['pɔɪnjənsɪ] *n., no pl.* [schmerzliche] Intensität; *(of words, wit, etc.)* Schärfe, *die*
poignant ['pɔɪnjənt] *adj.* tief ‹*Bedauern, Trauer, Schmerz, Verzweiflung*›; überwältigend ‹*Schönheit*›; quälend ‹*Hunger*›; *(causing sympathy)* ergreifend, herzzerreißend ‹*Anblick, Geschichte*›

poignantly ['pɔɪnjəntlɪ] *adv.* *(touchingly)* ergreifend; in bewegenden Worten ‹*sprechen, schreiben*›; *(regretfully)* wehmütig; *(pungently)* beißend

poinsettia [pɔɪn'setɪə] *n.* *(Bot.)* Weihnachtsstern, *der*

point [pɔɪnt] **1.** *n.* **a)** *(tiny mark, dot)* Punkt, *der;* **nought ~ two** Null Komma zwei; *see also* **decimal point; full point; b)** *(sharp end of tool, weapon, pencil, etc.)* Spitze, *die;* **come to a [sharp] ~:** spitz zulaufen; **at gun-~/knife-~:** mit vorgehaltener [Schuß]waffe/vorgehaltenem Messer; **hold sb. at gun-~/knife-~:** jmdn. mit vorgehaltener Pistole/vorgehaltenem Messer bedrohen; **not to put too fine a ~ on it** *(fig.)* um nichts zu beschönigen; **c)** *(single item)* Punkt, *der;* **the ~ under dispute** der strittige Punkt; die strittige Frage; **~ of conscience** Gewissensfrage, *die;* **agree on a ~:** in einem Punkt *od.* einer Frage übereinstimmen; **Are you an experienced cook? – No, in ~ of fact I've never cooked a meal before** Sind Sie ein erfahrener Koch? – Nein, ganz im Gegenteil. Ich habe [bisher] noch nie gekocht; **You haven't met him, have you? – Yes, in ~ of fact, I have** Du kennst ihn nicht, oder? – Doch, wir kennen uns; **be a ~ of honour with sb.** für jmdn. [eine] Ehrensache sein; **possession is nine ~s of the law** das Gesetz ist meistens auf der Seite des Besitzers; *see also* **law a; order 1 j; stretch 1 d; d)** *(unit of scoring)* Punkt, *der;* **win by 100 ~s** mit 100 Punkten Vorsprung gewinnen; **give ~s to sb.** jmdm. eine Vorgabe geben; **score ~s off sb.** *(fig.)* jmdn. an die Wand spielen; **win on ~s** *(Boxing; also fig.)* nach Punkten gewinnen; **a win on ~s** ein Sieg nach Punkten; ein Punktsieg; **e)** *(stage, degree)* **things have reached a ~ where** *or* **come to such a ~ that ...:** die Sache ist dahin *od.* so weit gediehen, daß ...; *(negatively)* es ist so weit gekommen, daß ...; **the shares reached their highest ~:** die Aktien erreichten ihren höchsten Stand *od.* Höchststand; **up to a ~:** bis zu einem gewissen Grad; **beyond a certain ~:** über einen bestimmten Punkt hinaus; **he gave up at this ~:** an diesem Punkt gab er auf; **she was abrupt to the ~ of rudeness** sie war in einer Weise barsch, die schon an Unverschämtheit grenzte; *see also* **boiling-point; freezing-point; melting-point; f)** *(moment)* Zeitpunkt, *der;* **when it comes/came to the ~:** wenn es soweit ist/als es soweit war; wenn es ernst wird/als es ernst wurde; **be at/on the ~ of sth.** kurz vor etw. *(Dat.)* sein; einer Sache *(Dat.)* nahe sein; **be at the ~ of death** im Sterben liegen; **be on the ~ of doing sth.** im Begriff sein, etw. zu tun; etw. gerade tun wollen; **g)** *(distinctive trait)* Seite, *die;* *(feature in animal)* [Rassen]merkmal, *das;* **best/strong ~:** starke Seite; Stärke, *die;* **good/bad ~:** gute/schlechte Seite; **getting up early has its ~s** frühes Aufstehen hat auch seine Vorzüge; **the ~** *(essential thing)* das Entscheidende; **the ~ is, what am I to do if I can't get a job?** fragt sich nur: was mache ich, wenn ich keinen Job finde?; *(thing to be discussed)* **that is just the ~** *or* **the whole ~:** das ist genau der springende Punkt; **come to** *or* **get to the ~:** zur Sache *od.* zum Thema kommen; **keep** *or* **stick to the ~:** beim Thema bleiben; **keep sb. to the ~:** verhindern, daß jmd. [vom Thema] abschweift; **be beside the ~:** unerheblich sein; keine Rolle spielen; **that's beside the ~:** darum geht es nicht; **~ taken** habe verstanden; **carry** *or* **make one's ~:** sich durchsetzen; sein Ziel erreichen; **right, I agree with you, you've made your ~:** also gut, ich gebe dir recht, ich habe verstanden; **in ~:** relevant *(geh.);* **not in ~:** irrelevant *(geh.);* **a case in ~:** ein typisches Beispiel; **that's not in ~:** das gehört nicht zur Sache *od.* hierher; **make a ~ of doing sth.** [großen] Wert darauf legen, etw. zu tun; **... and I shall make a ~ of telling him so** ... und ich werde ihm das jetzt auch mal sagen; **make a ~ of it** Wert darauf legen; **make** *or* **prove a ~:** etw. beweisen; **make** *or* **prove a ~ against sth.** ein Argument gegen etw. anführen *od.* *(geh.)* ins Feld führen; **be always making** *or* **proving a ~ of some kind** ständig etwas beweisen wollen; **to the ~:** sachbezogen; **more to the ~:** wichtiger; **a topic that is not strictly to the ~:** ein Punkt, der nicht direkt zum Thema gehört; **he was very brief and to the ~:** seine Ausführungen waren sehr knapp und sachbezogen; **you have a ~ there** da hast du recht; da ist [et]was dran *(ugs.);* *see also* **take 1 t; h)** *(tip)* Spitze, *die;* *(Boxing)* Kinnspitze, *die;* Kinn, *das;* *(Ballet)* Spitze, *die;* *in pl.* *(of horse, dog, etc.)* *(extremities)* Extremitäten *Pl.;* *(area of contrasting colour in an animal's fur)* Abzeichen *Pl.;* **the ~ of his jaw** seine Kinnspitze; **the ~s of his ears** seine Ohrläppchen; **dance on the ~s of one's toes** auf den Zehen- *od.* Fußspitzen tanzen; **on ~, on one's ~s, on the ~s** *(Ballet)* auf Spitzen; **a ~ [of land]** eine Landspitze *od.* -zunge; **i)** *(of story, joke, remark)* Pointe, *die;* *(pungency, effect)* *(of literary work)* Eindringlichkeit, *die;* *(of remark)* Durchschlagskraft, *die;* Überzeugungskraft, *die;* **see** *or* **get/miss the ~:** die Pointe verstehen/nicht verstehen; **miss the ~ of a joke** die Pointe eines Witzes nicht verstehen *od.* *(ugs.)* mitkriegen; **j)** *(purpose, value)* Zweck, *der;* Sinn, *der;* **what's the ~ of worrying?** was für einen Sinn *od.* Zweck hat es, sich *(Dat.)* Sorgen zu machen?; wozu sich *(Dat.)* Sorgen machen? *(ugs.);* **there's no ~ in protesting** es hat keinen Sinn *od.* Zweck zu protestieren; es ist sinnlos *od.* zwecklos zu protestieren; **k)** *(precise place, spot)* Punkt, *der;* Stelle, *die;* *(Geom.)* Punkt, *der;* **fire broke out at several ~s** an mehreren Punkten *od.* Stellen brach Feuer aus; **Bombay and ~s east** Bombay und Orte östlich davon; **~ of contact** Berührungspunkt, *der;* **~ of no return** Punkt, an dem es kein Zurück mehr gibt; **~ of view** *(fig.)* Standpunkt, *der;* **from my/a money/an atheistic ~ of view** *(fig.)* aus meiner/finanzieller/atheistischer Sicht; von meinem/von einem finanziellen/atheistischen Standpunkt aus; *see also* **departure d; l)** *(Brit.)* **[power** *or* **electric] ~:** Steckdose, *die;* **m)** *(Brit. Railw.)* *usu in pl.* Weiche, *die;* **n)** *(sharp-pointed tool)* spitzes Werkzeug; *(in engraving, etching, etc.)* Grabstichel, *der;* *(in masonry)* Grabmeißel, *der;* Punktiereisen, *das;* **o)** *(of deer)* Ende, *das (Jägerspr.);* Sprosse, *die (Jägerspr.);* **p)** *usu in pl.* *(Motor Veh.: contact device)* Kontakt, *der;* **contact breaker ~:** Unterbrecherkontakt, *der;* **q)** *(unit in Bridge, competition, rationing, stocks, shares, etc.)* Punkt, *der;* *(unit of weight for precious stones)* ein Hundertstel Karat; 0,01 Karat; **prices/the cost of living went up three ~s** die Preise/Lebenshaltungskosten sind um drei [Prozent]punkte gestiegen; **r)** *(on compass)* Strich, *der;* *see also* **cardinal points; s)** *(Printing)* Punkt, *der;* **eight-~** Achtpunkt, *der;* **t)** *(Cricket)* *Feldspieler, der einige Meter seitlich vom Torwächter steht;* *(Lacrosse)* *dem Torwart am nächsten stehender Verteidiger.* **2.** *v. i.* **a)** zeigen, weisen, ‹*Person auch:*› deuten **(to, at** auf + *Akk.*); **it's rude to ~:** es gehört sich nicht, mit dem Finger auf jemanden zu zeigen; **she ~ed through the window** sie zeigte aus dem Fenster; **the compass needle ~ed to the north** die Kompaßnadel zeigte *od.* wies nach Norden; **b) ~ towards** *or* **to** *(fig.)* [hin]deuten *od.* hinweisen auf (+ *Akk.*). **3.** *v. t.* **a)** *(direct)* richten ‹*Waffe, Kamera*› **(at** auf + *Akk.*); **~ one's finger at sth./sb.** mit dem Finger auf etw./jmdn. deuten *od.* zeigen *od.* weisen; **~ me in the right direction** zeige mir den richtigen Weg; **b)** *(Building)* aus-, verfugen ‹*Mauer, Steine*›; ausfüllen ‹*Fugen*›; **c)** *(give force to)* Nachdruck verleihen (+ *Dat.*), unterstreichen ‹*Bemerkung*›; würzen ‹*Erzählung, Rede*›; verstärken ‹*Gefühl*›; **d)** *(sharpen)* [an]spitzen ‹*Bleistift*›; **e)** *(show presence of)* ‹*Hund:*› vorstehen *(Jägerspr.);* **f)** *(punctuate)* mit Satzzeichen versehen; mit Deklamationszeichen versehen ‹*Psalm usw.*›; *(in Hebrew etc.)* mit diakritischen Zeichen versehen

~ 'out *v. t.* hinweisen auf (+ *Akk.*); **~ sth./sb. out to sb.** jmdn. auf etw./jmdn. hinweisen *od.* aufmerksam machen; **I ~ed him out to the others** ich zeigte ihn den anderen; **he ~ed out the house** er zeigte das Haus; **he ~ed out my mistake** er zeigte meinen Fehler auf

~ 'up *v. t.* *(emphasize)* herausstellen; *(make clear)* verdeutlichen

point-'blank 1. *adj.* *(direct, flat)* direkt; *(fig.)* direkt ‹*Frage, Art*›; glatt ‹*Weigerung*›; **~ shot** Schuß aus kürzester Entfernung; Kern- *od.* Fleckschuß, *der (Jägerspr.);* **~ distance** *or* **range** kürzeste Entfernung; Kernschußweite, *die (Jägerspr.);* **give a ~ denial** alles leugnen. **2.** *adv.* **a)** *(at very close range)* aus kürzester Entfernung ‹*schießen*›; **b)** *(in direct line)* direkt; *(fig.: directly)* rundheraus, *(ugs.)* geradeheraus ‹*fragen, sagen*›; **tell sb. ~ that ...:** jmdm. direkt ins Gesicht *od.* unverblümt *od.* *(ugs.)* geradeheraus sagen, daß ...

'point-by-point *adj.* Punkt für Punkt *nachgestellt*

'point-duty *n.* *(Brit.)* *Einsatz zur Verkehrsregelung;* **policeman on ~:** Verkehrspolizist, *der*

pointed ['pɔɪntɪd] *adj.* **a)** spitz; **~ arch** Spitzbogen, *der;* **b)** *(fig.: sharply expressed)* unmißverständlich; deutlich; **c)** *(emphasized)* ostentativ *(geh.);* betont ‹*Interesse, Aufmerksamkeit*›

pointedly ['pɔɪntɪdlɪ] *adv.* *(explicitly, significantly)* demonstrativ; ostentativ *(geh.)*

pointer ['pɔɪntə(r)] *n.* **a)** *(indicator)* Zeiger, *der;* *(rod)* Zeigestock, *der;* **b) ~ [dog]** Pointer, *der;* englischer Vorstehhund; **c)** *(coll.)* *(hint)* Fingerzeig, *der;* Tip, *der (ugs.);* *(indication)* Hinweis, *der* **(to** auf + *Akk.*); **d)** *in pl.* *(Astron.)* *(in Great Bear)* *die vorderen Kastensterne (des Großen Wagens);* *(in Southern Cross)* *die beiden die Längsachse des Kreuzes markierenden Sterne (im Kreuz des Südens)*

pointillism ['pwæntɪlɪzm] *n.* *(Art)* Pointillismus, *der*

pointing ['pɔɪntɪŋ] *n.* *(of brickwork)* Fugung, *die;* *(action)* Ausfugen, *das;* Verfugen, *das;* *(material)* [Fugen]mörtel, *der*

pointless ['pɔɪntlɪs] *adj.* *(without purpose or meaning, useless)* sinnlos; *(without force, meaningless)* belanglos ‹*Bemerkung, Geschichte*›

pointlessly ['pɔɪntlɪslɪ] *adv.* sinnlos; unnötig ‹*sich Sorgen machen*›; unmotiviert ‹*lachen*›; ohne Zweck und Ziel ‹*herumlungern*›

point-to-'point [race] *n.* *(Horse-racing)* Kirchturmrennen, *das*

poise [pɔɪz] **1.** *n.* **a)** *(composure)* Haltung, *die;* *(self-confidence)* Selbstsicherheit, *die;* Selbstvertrauen, *das;* **have ~:** beherrscht sein/selbstsicher sein; **keep one's ~:** Haltung/Selbstsicherheit behalten; **lose one's ~:** die Haltung *od.* Beherrschung *od.* Fassung/sein Selbstvertrauen verlieren; **b)** *(good carriage)* Haltung, *die;* *(of body)* Körperhaltung, *die.* **2.** *v. t.* **a)** *in p.p.* *(in readiness)* **sit ~d on the edge of one's chair** auf der Stuhlkante balancieren; **be ~d for action** einsatzbereit sein; **hang ~d** ‹*Vogel, Insekt:*› schweben; *see also* **poised; b)** *(balance)* balancieren; **c)** *(hold suspended, carry in a particular way)* **~ the spear ready to hurl**

it den Speer wurfbereit in der Hand halten; **~ oneself on one's toes** auf den Zehen stehen
poised [pɔɪzd] *adj.* selbstsicher; *see also* **poise 2 a**
poison ['pɔɪzn] **1.** *n. (harmful substance; lit. or fig.)* Gift, *das;* **slow ~:** langsam wirkendes Gift; **hate sb./sth. like ~:** jmdn./etw. wie die Pest hassen; **what's your ~?** *(coll.)* was trinkst du? **2.** *v. t.* **a)** vergiften; *(cause disease in)* infizieren; *(contaminate)* verseuchen ‹*Boden, Luft, Wasser*›; verpesten *(abwertend)* ‹*Luft*›; *(smear with poison)* vergiften ‹*Pfeil*›; **die of ~ing** an einer Vergiftung sterben; **~ed hand** infizierte Hand; **~ed arrow** Giftpfeil, *der;* **b)** *(fig.) (corrupt)* vergiften ‹*Gedanken, Seele*›; *(injure, destroy)* zerstören, ruinieren ‹*Ehe, Leben*›; vergällen ‹*Freude*›; verderben ‹*Speisen, Feldfrüchte usw.*›; **~ sb.'s mind** jmdn. verderben *od. (geh.)* korrumpieren; **she ~ed his mind** *or* **caused his thoughts to be ~ed against me** sie hat ihn gegen mich aufgebracht
poisoner ['pɔɪzənə(r)] *n.* Giftmörder, *der*/Giftmörderin, *die*
poison 'gas *n.* Giftgas, *das*
poisoning ['pɔɪzənɪŋ] *n.* Vergiftung, *die; (contamination)* Verseuchung, *die*
poison 'ivy *n.* Gifteteu, *der;* Kletternder Giftsumach *(Bot.)*
poisonous ['pɔɪzənəs] *adj.* **a)** giftig; tödlich ‹*Dosis*›; **~ snake/mushroom/substance** Giftschlange, *die*/-pilz, *der*/-stoff, *der;* **b)** *(fig.)* verderblich ‹*Lehre, Wirkung*›; giftig ‹*Blick, Zunge*›
¹poke [pəʊk] *n. (dial.: bag)* Beutel, *der;* Sack, *der; see also* **pig 1 a**
²poke 1. *v. t.* **a) ~ sth. [with sth.]** [mit etw.] gegen etw. stoßen; **she ~d the hedgehog to see if it was dead** sie stieß den Igel an, um zu sehen, ob er tot war; **~ sth. into sth.** etw. in etw. *(Akk.)* stoßen; **~ one's finger up one's nose** den Finger in die Nase stecken; **~ the fire** das Feuer schüren; **he accidentally ~d me in the eye** er stieß mir versehentlich ins Auge; **~ sb. in the ribs** jmdm. einen Rippenstoß geben *od.* versetzen; *see also* **fun 1; b)** *(thrust forward)* stecken ‹*Kopf*›; **~ one's head in through the window** den Kopf zum Fenster hin-/hereinstecken; **~ one's head round the corner/door** um die Ecke gucken *(ugs.)*/den Kopf in die Türöffnung stecken; **~ one's head in** reingucken *(ugs.)*; **~ one's finger at sb.** mit dem Finger nach jmdm. stoßen; **c)** *(pierce)* bohren; **d)** *(coarse: have sexual intercourse with)* stoßen *(derb).* **2.** *v. i.* **a)** *(in pond, at food, among rubbish)* [herum]stochern **(at, in, among** in + *Dat.*); **~ at sth. with a stick** *etc.* mit einem Stock *usw.* nach etw. stoßen; **b)** *(thrust itself)* sich schieben; **his elbows were poking through the sleeves** seine Ärmel hatten Löcher, aus denen die Ellbogen hervorguckten; **c)** *(pry)* schnüffeln *(ugs. abwertend)*; **~ into things that don't concern one** seine Nase in Dinge stecken, die einen nichts angehen *(ugs.).* **3.** *n.* **a)** *(thrust)* Stoß, *der;* **give sb. a ~ [in the ribs]** jmdm. einen [Rippen]stoß versetzen *od.* geben; **give sb. a ~ in the eye** jmdn. ins Auge stoßen; **give the fire a ~:** das Feuer [an]schüren; **better than a ~ in the eye [with a pointed stick]** *(coll.)* besser als gar nichts *od. (derb)* als in die hohle Hand geschissen; **b) have a ~ around a shop** *etc.* in einem Laden *usw.* herumstöbern; **have a ~ around in sb.'s writing-desk** in jmds. Schreibtisch herumstöbern *od.* -wühlen; **c)** *(coarse: sexual intercourse)* Fick, *der (vulg.)*; **have a ~:** stoßen *(derb)*
~ a'bout, ~ a'round *v. i.* **a)** herumschnüffeln *(ugs. abwertend)*; **b)** *(rummage)* herumsuchen *(ugs.)*; herumkramen *(ugs.)*; **~ about in sth. for sth.** etw. nach etw. durchwühlen
~ 'out 1. *v. t.* rausstrecken; **you nearly ~d my eye out** du hast mir fast das Auge ausgestochen; **~ the dirt out of sth.** den Schmutz aus etw. kratzen; **~ one's head out** rausgucken *(ugs.).* **2.** *v. i.* rausgucken *(ugs.)*
'poke-bonnet *n.* Schutenhut, *der*
¹poker ['pəʊkə(r)] *n. (for fire)* Schürstange, *die;* Schüreisen, *das;* **as stiff as a ~:** stocksteif *(ugs.)*
²poker *n. (Cards)* Poker, *das od. der;* **have a game of ~:** eine Runde pokern
poker: ~ dice *n. pl. Würfel mit Spielkartensymbolen;* ≈ Skatwürfel; **~-face** *n.* Pokerface, *das;* Pokergesicht, *das;* **~-faced** *adj.* mit unbewegter Miene *nachgestellt;* **remain ~-faced** keine Miene verziehen
poky ['pəʊkɪ] *adj.* winzig; **~ little** winzig klein; **it's so ~ in here** es ist so eng hier drinnen
Poland ['pəʊlənd] *pr. n.* Polen *(das)*
polar ['pəʊlə(r)] *adj.* **a)** *(of pole)* polar ‹*Kaltluft, Kälte, Fauna, Klima, Gewässer*›; Polar‹*eis, -gebiet, -luft, -meer, -nacht, -fuchs, -hase*›; **b)** *(Magn.)* polar; **c)** *(fig.: central)* zentral; **d)** *(directly opposite)* [diametral] entgegengesetzt; polar *(geh.)*; äußerst ‹*Extrem*›; grundlegend ‹*Unterschied*›
polar: ~ bear *n.* Eisbär, *der;* **~ 'cap** *n. (Geog.)* Polkappe, *die;* **~ 'circles** *n. pl. (Geog.)* Polarkreise; **~ 'front** *n. (Meteorol.)* Polarfront, *die*
Polaris [pə'lɑ:rɪs] *pr. n.* **a)** *(missile)* Polaris, *die;* **b)** *(Astron.)* Polaris *(die)*
polarisation, polarise *see* **polariz-**
polarity [pə'lærɪtɪ] *n.* **a)** *(Magn.)* Polung, *die;* Polarität, *die;* **b)** *(direction of axis; having two poles)* Polarität, *die;* **c)** *(fig.: contrary qualities)* Gegensatz, *der;* Polarität, *die (geh.)*; **d)** *(Electr.)* Polung, *die;* **change of ~:** Polwechsel, *der*
polarization [pəʊləraɪ'zeɪʃn] *n. (Phys.)* Polarisation, *die; (fig.)* Polarisierung, *die;* Polarisation, *die*
polarize ['pəʊləraɪz] **1.** *v. t.* **a)** *(Phys.)* polarisieren; **b)** *(fig.: divide)* spalten; polarisieren *(geh.)*; **~ political life** eine Polarisierung des politischen Lebens bewirken. **2.** *v. i.* sich [auf]spalten; sich polarisieren *(geh.)*
Polaroid, (P) ['pəʊlərɔɪd] *n.* **a)** *(material)* Polaroidfolie, *die* Ⓦ; **b) ~s** *(sun-glasses)* Polaroidbrille, *die* Ⓦ; **c) ~ [camera]** Polaroidkamera, *die* Ⓦ
polar 'star *see* **pole-star**
polder ['pəʊldə(r)] *n.* Polder, *der*
Pole [pəʊl] *n.* Pole, *der*/Polin, *die*
¹pole *n.* **a)** *(support)* Stange, *die; (for pole-vaulter)* Stab, *der; (for large tent, house in lake)* Pfahl, *der;* **be up the ~** *(Brit. sl.) (in difficulty)* in der Klemme sitzen *(ugs.)*; *(crazy)* nicht ganz dicht sein *(ugs. abwertend)*; **drive sb. up the ~** *(Brit. sl.)* jmdn. zum Wahnsinn treiben *(ugs.)*; **b)** *(for propelling boat)* Stake, *die (nordd.)*; **c)** *(of horse-drawn vehicle)* Deichsel, *die;* **~s** [Gabel]deichsel, *die;* **d)** *(measure)* Rute, *die*
²pole *n.* **a)** *(Astron., Geog., Magn., Electr., Geom., Biol.)* Pol, *der;* **positive/negative ~:** positiver/negativer Pol; Plus-/Minuspol, *der;* **they are ~s apart** *(coll.)* zwischen ihnen liegen Welten; *see also* **magnetic pole; North Pole; South Pole; b)** *(fig.)* Pol, *der;* **be at opposite ~s** sich *(Dat.)* als Pol und Gegenpol gegenüberstehen; einander entgegengesetzte Pole bilden
pole-axed ['pəʊlækst] *adj.* **as if ~:** wie vor den Kopf geschlagen
'polecat *n. (Zool.)* **a)** *(Brit.)* Iltis, *der;* **b)** *(Amer.) see* **skunk a**
polemic [pə'lemɪk] **1.** *adj.* polemisch. **2.** *n.* **a)** *(discussion)* Polemik, *die; (written also)* Streitschrift, *die;* **b)** *in pl. (practice)* Polemik, *die*
polemical [pə'lemɪkl] *adj.*, **polemically** [pə'lemɪkəlɪ] *adv.* polemisch
pole: ~ position *n. (Motor-racing)* Poleposition, *die;* **~-star** *n. (Astron.)* Polarstern, *der;* **~-vault** *n.* Stabhochsprung, *der;* **~-vaulter** *n.* Stabhochspringer, *der*/-springerin, *die;* **~-vaulting** *n.* Stabhochsprung, *der;* Stabhochspringen, *das*
police [pə'li:s] **1.** *n. pl.* **a)** Polizei, *die;* **be in the ~:** bei der Polizei sein; **river ~:** Wasserschutzpolizei, *die; attrib.* Polizei‹*wagen, -hund, -schutz, -eskorte, -staat*›; **b)** *(members)* Polizisten *Pl.;* Polizeibeamte *Pl.; attrib.* Polizei-; **whole squads of ~:** ein gewaltiges Polizeiaufgebot; **the ~ are on his trail** die Polizei ist ihm auf der Spur; **extra ~ were called in** zusätzliche Polizeikräfte wurden hinzugezogen; **help the ~ with their enquiries** von der Polizei vernommen werden. **2.** *v. t.* **a)** [polizeilich] überwachen ‹*Gebiet, Verkehr, Fußballspiel*›; kontrollieren ‹*Gebiet, Grenze, Gewässer*›; **b)** *(fig.: check on)* überwachen; kontrollieren; **c)** *(provide with ~)* Polizeibeamte einsetzen in (+ *Dat.*) ‹*Gebiet, Stadt usw.*›; **the inadequate policing of the district** die unzureichende Polizeipräsenz in dem Bezirk
police: ~ constable *n.* Polizist, *der*/Polizistin, *die; (rank)* Polizeihauptwachtmeister, *der;* **~ force** *n.* Polizeitruppe, *die;* **the ~ force** die Polizei; **~man** [pə'li:smən] *n., pl.* **-men** [pə'li:smən] Polizist, *der;* Polizeibeamte, *der; see also* **sleeping policeman; ~ notice** *n.* polizeilicher Hinweis; **'P~ Notice: No Parking'** „Parken polizeilich verboten"; **~-officer** *n.* Polizeibeamte, *der*/-beamtin, *die;* **~ record** *see* **record 3 e; ~ station** *n.* Polizeiwache, *die;* Polizeirevier, *das;* **~woman** *n.* Polizistin, *die;* Polizeibeamtin, *die*
¹policy ['pɒlɪsɪ] *n.* **a)** *(method)* Handlungsweise, *die;* Vorgehensweise, *die; (overall plan)* Politik, *die;* **it is company ~ to ...:** es ist Firmenpolitik, ... zu ...; **adopt** *or* **pursue a wise/cautious/foolish ~:** klug/vorsichtig/töricht vorgehen; **it is the store's ~ to prosecute shoplifters** der Laden erstattet grundsätzlich Anzeige gegen Ladendiebe; **it is not our ~ to do that, our ~ is not to do that** wir machen das grundsätzlich nicht; **government ~:** Regierungspolitik, *die;* **~ on immigration** Einwanderungspolitik, *die;* **party ~:** Parteikurs, *der;* **the firm's policies** die Politik der Firma; **~ decision/document** Grundsatzentscheidung, *die*/-papier, *das;* **~ statement** programmatische Erklärung; Grundsatzerklärung, *die;* **it's bad ~ to ...:** es ist unvernünftig, ... zu ...; *see also* **honesty b; b)** *no pl., no art. (prudent conduct)* **~ demands occasional compromise** manchmal sind Kompromisse das einzig Vernünftige
²policy *n. (Insurance)* Police, *die;* Versicherungsschein, *der;* **take out a ~ on sth.** eine Versicherung für etw. abschließen; **the ~ on my car** meine Autoversicherung
'policy: ~-holder *n.* Versicherte, *der/die;* Versicherungsnehmer, *der*/-nehmerin, *die (fachspr.)*; **~-making** *attrib. adj.* richtungsweisend
polio ['pəʊlɪəʊ] *n., no pl., no art.* Polio, *die;* [spinale] Kinderlähmung; *attrib.* Polio-; **~ vaccine** Polioimpfstoff, *der*
poliomyelitis [pəʊlɪəʊmaɪə'laɪtɪs] *n. (Med.)* Poliomyelitis, *die;* [spinale] Kinderlähmung
Polish ['pəʊlɪʃ] **1.** *adj.* polnisch; **sb. is ~:** jmd. ist Pole/Polin; *see also* **English 1. 2.** *n.* Polnisch, *das; see also* **English 2 a**
polish ['pɒlɪʃ] **1.** *v. t.* **a)** *(make smooth)* polieren; bohnern ‹*Fußboden*›; putzen ‹*Schuhe*›; **highly ~ed** auf Hochglanz poliert; **b)** *(fig.)* ausfeilen ‹*Text, Theorie, Technik, Stil*›; polieren ‹*Text*›; Schliff beibringen (+ *Dat.*) ‹*Person*›; **~ed** geschliffen ‹*Stil, Manieren, Sprache, Auftreten, Weltmann*›; ausgefeilt ‹*Technik, Taktik, Plan, Satz*›; **a highly ~ed piece of prose** ein bis ins kleinste ausgefeiltes Stück Prosa. **2.** *n.* **a)**

(smoothness) Glanz, *der;* **put a ~ on** polieren; **a table with a high ~:** ein auf Hochglanz polierter Tisch; **take off** *or* **spoil the ~** ‹*Person:*› die Politur beschädigen; ‹*Substanz:*› die Politur angreifen; **b)** *(substance)* Poliermittel, *das;* Politur, *die;* **c)** *(fig.)* Geschliffenheit, *die;* Schliff, *der;* **d)** *(action)* **my shoes could do with a ~:** meine Schuhe müßten mal geputzt werden; **give sth. a ~:** etw. polieren; **give the floor a ~:** den Fußboden bohnern; **give the shoes a ~:** die Schuhe putzen; *see also* **¹spit 3 b**

~ 'off *v.t. (coll.)* **a)** *(consume)* verdrücken *(ugs.);* wegputzen *(ugs.)* ‹*Essen*›; aussüffeln *(ugs.)* ‹*Getränk*›; **b)** *(complete quickly)* durchziehen *(ugs.);* **c)** *(defeat)* erledigen; abservieren *(salopp, bes. Sport)*

~ 'up *v.t.* **a)** *(make shiny)* polieren; **b)** *(improve)* ausfeilen ‹*Stil, Technik*›; aufpolieren ‹*[Sprach]kenntnisse*›

polisher ['pɒlɪʃə(r)] *n.* **a)** *(person)* Polierer, *der*/Poliererin, *die;* **b)** *(tool)* Poliergerät, *das; (for floors)* Bohnerklotz, *der; (machine)* Poliermaschine, *die; (for floors)* Bohnermaschine, *die; (cloth)* Poliertuch, *das*

politburo ['pɒlɪtbjʊərəʊ] *n., pl.* **~s** Politbüro, *das*

polite [pə'laɪt] *adj.,* **~r** [pə'laɪtə(r)], **~st** [pə'laɪtɪst] **a)** *(courteous)* höflich; **the ~ form of address** die höfliche Anredeform; **be ~ about her dress** mach ihr ein paar Komplimente zu ihrem Kleid; **he was just being ~:** er wollte nur höflich sein; **b)** *(cultured)* kultiviert; **c)** *(well-mannered)* schicklich *(geh.)* ‹*Verhalten*›; wohlerzogen, artig ‹*Kind*›; **it's not [considered] ~:** es gehört sich *od. (geh.)* schickt sich nicht; **in some circles it is considered ~ to ...** in manchen Kreisen gehört es zum guten Ton, zu ...

politely [pə'laɪtlɪ] *adv.* höflich

politeness [pə'laɪtnɪs] *n., no pl.* Höflichkeit, *die*

politic ['pɒlɪtɪk] **1.** *adj.* **a)** *(prudent)* klug ‹*Person, Handlung*›; opportun *(geh.)* ‹*Handlung*›; **it would be ~ to make some changes** es wäre klug *od. (geh.)* opportun, einiges zu ändern; **it's not ~ to do sth.** es ist unklug *od.* nicht ratsam, etw. zu tun; **b) body ~** *(State)* das Staatswesen. **2.** *v.i.,* **-ck-** sich politisch betätigen *od.* engagieren

political [pə'lɪtɪkl] *adj.* politisch; **~ animal** politischer *od.* politisch engagierter Mensch

political: ~ a'sylum *see* **asylum; ~ economy** *n.* politische Ökonomie; **~ ge'ography** *n.* politische Geographie; **a map of the ~ geography of Britain** eine politische Karte von Großbritannien

politically [pə'lɪtɪkəlɪ] *adv.* politisch; **be ~ aware** *or* **conscious** politisches Bewußtsein haben; **~ speaking** politisch gesehen; vom politischen Standpunkt betrachtet

political: ~ 'prisoner *n.* politischer Gefangener/politische Gefangene; **~ 'science** *n.* Politologie, *die*

politician [pɒlɪ'tɪʃn] *n.* **a)** Politiker, *der*/Politikerin, *die;* **b)** *(Amer. derog.: one seeking gain)* Politiker/Politikerin aus Eigennutz

politicize (politicise) [pə'lɪtɪsaɪz] *v.t.* politisieren

politicking ['pɒlɪtɪkɪŋ] *n. (derog.)* politischer Aktionismus *(abwertend)*

politico [pə'lɪtɪkəʊ] *n., pl.* **~s** *(coll.)* Politiker, *der*/Politikerin, *die*

politics ['pɒlɪtɪks] *n., no pl.* **a)** *no art. (political administration)* Politik, *die; (Univ.: subject)* Politik[wissenschaft], *die;* Politologie, *die;* **b)** *no art., constr. as sing. or pl. (political affairs)* Politik, *die;* **~ is a dirty business** die Politik ist ein schmutziges Geschäft; **interested/involved in ~:** politisch interessiert/engagiert; **enter ~:** in die Politik gehen; **c)** *as pl. (political principles)* Politik, *die; (of individual)* politische Einstellung; **world ~ are complex** die Weltpolitik ist eine komplizierte Angelegenheit; **what are his ~?** wo steht er politisch?; **the ~ of the decision** der politische Hintergrund der Entscheidung; **it is not good ~ to do sth.** es ist politisch unklug, etw. zu tun; **practical ~:** Realpolitik, *die*

polity ['pɒlɪtɪ] *n.* **a)** *(form of government)* politisches System; politische Ordnung; **b)** *(formal/arch.: State)* Staat, *der;* Gemeinwesen, *das*

polka ['pɒlkə, 'pəʊlkə] *n.* Polka, *die*

'polka dot *n.* [großer] Tupfen; **the blouse is patterned with ~s** die Bluse hat ein Muster aus großen Tupfen; **a polka-dot scarf** ein Halstuch mit großen Tupfen

poll [pəʊl] **1.** *n.* **a)** *(voting)* Abstimmung, *die; (to elect sb.)* Wahl, *die; (result of vote)* Abstimmungsergebnis, *das*/Wahlergebnis, *das; (number of votes)* Wahlbeteiligung, *die;* **take a ~:** abstimmen lassen; eine Abstimmung durchführen; **day of the ~:** Wahltag, *der;* **at the ~[s]** bei den Wahlen; **the result of the ~:** das Abstimmungsergebnis/Wahlergebnis; **a defeat at the ~s** eine Wahlniederlage; **go to the ~:** seine Stimme abgeben; zur Wahl gehen; wählen [gehen]; **Britain goes to the ~s** Großbritannien wählt; in Großbritannien wird gewählt; **be at the head of the ~:** die meisten Stimmen erhalten [haben]; **the declaration of the ~:** die Bekanntgabe des Wahlergebnisses; **a heavy/light** *or* **low ~:** eine starke/geringe *od.* niedrige Wahlbeteiligung; **b)** *(survey of opinion)* Umfrage, *die;* **~ findings** Umfrageergebnis, *das;* **c)** *(human head)* Kopf, *der;* Schädel, *der; (part of head)* [Hinter]kopf, *der.* **2.** *v.t.* **a)** *(take vote[s] of)* abstimmen/wählen lassen; **be ~ed** seine Stimme abgeben; **b)** *(take opinion of)* befragen; *(take survey of)* [demoskopisch] erforschen; **those ~ed** die Befragten; **c)** *(obtain in poll)* erhalten ‹*Stimmen*›; **d)** *(cut off top of)* kappen ‹*Baum, Baumkrone*›. **3.** *v.i.* wählen; seine Stimme abgeben

pollack ['pɒlək] *n. (Zool.)* Köhler, *der; (Commerc.)* Seelachs, *der*

pollard ['pɒləd] **1.** *n. (Bot.)* gekappter Baum. **2.** *v.t. (Bot.)* kappen

pollen ['pɒlən] *n. (Bot.)* Pollen, *der;* Blütenstaub, *der*

pollen: ~ analysis *n.* Pollenanalyse, *die;* **~ count** *n.* Pollenmenge, *die;* **~ sac** *n.* Pollensack, *der*

pollinate ['pɒlɪneɪt] *v.t. (Bot.)* bestäuben

pollination [pɒlɪ'neɪʃn] *n. (Bot.)* Bestäubung, *die;* Pollination, *die (fachspr.)*

polling ['pəʊlɪŋ]: **~-booth** *n.* Wahlkabine, *die;* **~-day** *n.* Wahltag, *der;* **~ district** *n.* Wahlbezirk, *der;* **~-station** *n. (Brit.)* Wahllokal, *das*

pollock *see* **pollack**

pollster ['pəʊlstə(r)] *n.* Meinungsforscher, *der*/Meinungsforscherin, *die;* Demoskop, *der*/Demoskopin, *die*

'poll-tax *n.* Kopfsteuer, *die*

pollutant [pə'lu:tənt] **1.** *n. (substance)* [Umwelt]schadstoff, *der.* **2.** *adj.* [umwelt]schädlich; **~ substance** [Umwelt]schadstoff, *der*

pollute [pə'lu:t] *v.t.* **a)** *(contaminate)* verschmutzen, verunreinigen ‹*Luft, Boden, Wasser*›; verpesten *(abwertend)* ‹*Luft*›; **the most ~d cities** die am stärksten mit [Umwelt]schadstoffen belasteten Städte; **b)** *(make foul)* verseuchen; **c)** *(fig.)* verderben ‹*Jugend, Menschen, Charakter*›

pollution [pə'lu:ʃn] *n.* **a)** *(contamination)* [Umwelt]verschmutzung, *die;* **atmospheric ~:** atmosphärische Verschmutzung; Verschmutzung der Atmosphäre; **water ~:** Gewässerverschmutzung, *die;* **noise ~:** Lärmbelästigung, *die;* **b)** *(polluting substance[s])* Verunreinigungen; Schadstoffe; **c)** *(fig.)* Verderben, *das*

Pollyanna [pɒlɪ'ænə] *n. (Amer. derog.)* unverbesserlicher Optimist/unverbesserliche Optimistin; *attrib.* [übertrieben *od.* grundlos] optimistisch

polo ['pəʊləʊ] *n., no pl.* Polo, *das*

polonaise [pɒlə'neɪz] *n. (dance, music)* Polonaise, *die;* Polonäse, *die*

'polo-neck *n.* Rollkragen, *der;* **~[ed]** *attrib.* Rollkragen-; **~ [jumper]** Rollkragenpulli, *der (ugs.);* Rolli, *der (Mode Jargon)*

polo: ~ shirt *n.* Polohemd, *das;* **~-stick** *n.* Polostock, *der*

poltergeist ['pɒltəgaɪst] *n.* Klopfgeist, *der;* Poltergeist, *der*

poltroon [pɒl'tru:n] *n. (derog.)* Angsthase, *der (ugs. abwertend)*

poly ['pɒlɪ] *n., pl.* **~s** *(coll.)* Polytechnikum, *das;* ≈ TH, *die*

polyanthus [pɒlɪ'ænθəs] *n. (Bot.)* [Garten]primel, *die*

polychromatic [pɒlɪkrə'mætɪk] *adj.* **a)** *(many-coloured)* vielfarbig; polychrom *(fachspr.);* **b)** *(Phys.)* polychromatisch

polyclinic ['pɒlɪklɪnɪk] *n.* Poliklinik, *die*

polyester [pɒlɪ'estə(r)] *n.* Polyester, *der*

polyethylene [pɒlɪ'eθɪli:n] *(Amer.) see* **polythene**

polygamist [pə'lɪgəmɪst] *n.* Polygamist, *der (geh.);* **be a ~:** polygam leben *(geh.); (in disposition)* polygam sein *(geh.)*

polygamous [pə'lɪgəməs] *adj.* polygam *(geh., fachspr.)*

polygamy [pə'lɪgəmɪ] *n.* Polygamie, *die (geh., fachspr.);* Mehrehe, *die;* Vielehe, *die*

polyglot ['pɒlɪglɒt] **1.** *adj.* **a)** polyglott *(geh., fachspr.);* mehrsprachig; **b)** *(speaking several languages)* polyglott *(geh.).* **2.** *n.* Polyglotte, *der/die (geh.)*

polygon ['pɒlɪgən] *n. (Geom.)* Vieleck, *das;* Polygon, *das (fachspr.)*

polygraph ['pɒlɪgrɑ:f] *n. (lie-detector)* Lügendetektor, *der;* Polygraph, *der (fachspr.)*

polyhedron [pɒlɪ'hi:drən] *n., pl.* **~s** *or* **polyhedra** [pɒlɪ'hi:drə] *(Geom.)* Polyeder, *das (fachspr.);* Vielflächner, *der*

polymath ['pɒlɪmæθ] *n.* universell Gebildeter/Gebildete

polymer ['pɒlɪmə(r)] *n. (Chem.)* Polymer[e], *das*

polymeric [pɒlɪ'merɪk] *adj. (Chem.)* polymer

polymerisation, polymerise *see* **polymeriz-**

polymerization [pɒlɪməraɪ'zeɪʃn] *n. (Chem.)* Polymerisation, *die*

polymerize ['pɒlɪməraɪz] *v.t. & i. (Chem.)* polymerisieren

Polynesia [pɒlɪ'ni:ʒə] *pr. n.* Polynesien *(das)*

Polynesian [pɒlɪ'ni:ʒən] **1.** *adj.* polynesisch. **2.** *n.* Polynesier, *der*/Polynesierin, *die*

polynomial [pɒlɪ'nəʊmɪəl] *n. (Math.)* Polynom, *das*

polyp ['pɒlɪp] *n. (Zool., Med.)* Polyp, *der*

polyphonic [pɒlɪ'fɒnɪk], **polyphonous** [pə'lɪfənəs] *adj. (Mus.)* polyphon

polyphony [pə'lɪfənɪ] *n. (Mus.)* Polyphonie, *die*

polystyrene [pɒlɪ'staɪri:n] *n.* Polystyrol, *das;* **~ foam** Styropor Ⓦᶻ, *das*

polysyllabic [pɒlɪsɪ'læbɪk] *adj.* vielsilbig

polytechnic [pɒlɪ'teknɪk] *n. (Brit.)* ≈ technische Hochschule *od.* Universität; **~ student/teacher/term** Student/Lehrer/Semester am Polytechnikum

polytheism ['pɒlɪθi:ɪzm] *n.* Polytheismus, *der*

polythene ['pɒlɪθi:n] *n.* Polyäthylen, *das;* Polyethylen, *das (fachspr.); (coll.: plastic)* Plastik, *das;* **~ bag/sheet** Plastikbeutel, *der*/-folie, *die*

polyunsaturated [pɒlɪʌn'sætʃəreɪtɪd] *adj.* mehrfach ungesättigt

polyurethane [pɒlɪ'jʊərɪθeɪn] *n.* Polyurethan, *das*

polyvinyl chloride [pɒlɪvaɪnɪl 'klɔ:raɪd] *n.* Polyvinylchlorid, *das*
pom [pɒm] *n.* **a)** *(dog)* Spitz, *der;* **b)** *(Austral. and NZ sl.: Briton)* Brite, *der*/Britin, *die*
pomade [pə'mɑ:d] *n.* Pomade, *die*
pomaded [pə'meɪdɪd] *adj.* pomadig ⟨*Haar*⟩
pomander [pə'mændə(r)] *n.* Duftkugel, *die*
pome [pəʊm] *n. (Bot.)* Sammelbalgfrucht, *die*
pomegranate ['pɒmɪgrænɪt] *n.* **a)** *(fruit)* Granatapfel, *der;* **b)** *(tree)* Granatapfel[baum], *der;* Granatbaum, *der*
Pomerania [pɒmə'reɪnɪə] *pr. n.* Pommern *(das)*
Pomeranian [pɒmə'reɪnɪən] *n. (dog)* Spitz, *der*
pommel ['pʌml, 'pɒml] **1.** *n.* **a)** *(on sword)* [Schwert]knauf, *der;* **b)** *(on saddle)* Sattelknopf, *der;* **c)** *(Gymnastics)* Pausche, *die.* **2.** *v. t., (Brit.)* **-ll-** *see* **pummel**
'pommel-horse *n.* Seitpferd, *das*
pommy (pommie) ['pɒmɪ] *n. (Austral. and NZ sl. derog.)* Brite, *der*/Britin, *die;* ~ **bastard** Scheißbrite, *der*/-britin, *die (salopp abwertend)*
pomp [pɒmp] *n.* Pomp, *der (abwertend);* Prunk, *der;* Gepränge, *das (geh.);* ~ **and circumstance** festliches Gepränge *(geh.)*
Pompeii [pɒm'peɪi:] *pr. n.* Pompeji *(das)*
¹pom-pom ['pɒmpɒm] *n. (Arms)* Maschinenkanone, *die*
²pom-pom ['pɒmpɒm], **pompon** ['pɒmpɒn] *n.* **a)** *(tuft)* Pompon, *der;* Troddel, *die;* ~ **hat** Pudelmütze, *die;* **b)** *(Bot.)* ~ **[dahlia]** Pompondahlie, *die*
pomposity [pɒm'pɒsɪtɪ] *n., no pl.* Großspurigkeit, *die;* Aufgeblasenheit, *die;* ~ **of language** geschwollene *od.* gespreizte Sprache
pompous ['pɒmpəs] *adj. (self-important)* großspurig; aufgeblasen; geschwollen *(abwertend);* gespreizt *(abwertend)* ⟨*Sprache*⟩; **don't be so ~!** blas dich nicht so auf!
pompously ['pɒmpəslɪ] *adv.* großspurig, aufgeblasen ⟨*auftreten, sich benehmen*⟩; geschwollen *(abwertend),* gespreizt *(abwertend)* ⟨*schreiben, reden*⟩
'pon [pɒn] *(poet./arch.) see* **upon**
ponce [pɒns] *(Brit. sl.)* **1.** *n.* **a)** *(pimp)* Zuhälter, *der;* **b)** *(derog.: homosexual)* Schwule, *der (ugs.);* Homo, *der (ugs.);* **be a ~:** schwul sein. **2.** *v. i.* Zuhälterei betreiben; ~ **for sb.** jmds. Zuhälter sein
~ **a'bout,** ~ **a'round** *v. i. (derog.)* herumtänzeln *(ugs.)*
~ **'up** *v. t. (derog.)* [tuntenhaft] auftakeln *(ugs. abwertend);* **what are you all ~d up for?** wozu hast du dich denn so aufgedonnert? *(salopp)*
poncho ['pɒntʃəʊ] *n., pl.* **~s** Poncho, *der;* Umhang, *der*
pond [pɒnd] *n.* Teich, *der;* **the [big] ~** *(joc.: Atlantic)* der große Teich *(ugs. scherzh.);* **a big fish in a small ~** *(fig.)* eine Lokalgröße; ein Lokalmatador *(ugs.)*
ponder ['pɒndə(r)] **1.** *v. t.* nachdenken über (+ *Akk.*) ⟨*Frage, Problem, Ereignis*⟩; bedenken ⟨*Folgen*⟩; abwägen ⟨*Vorteile, Worte*⟩; ~ **whether/how to do sth.** sich *(Dat.)* überlegen, ob man etw. tun soll/wie man etw. tun kann. **2.** *v. i.* nachdenken **(over, on** über + *Akk.***)**; **careful ~ing** sorgfältige Überlegung; sorgfältiges Nachdenken
ponderous ['pɒndərəs] *adj.* **a)** *(heavy)* schwer; **b)** *(unwieldy, laborious)* schwerfällig; umständlich ⟨*Ausdrucksweise*⟩; **c)** *(dull)* ermüdend
ponderously ['pɒndərəslɪ] *adv.* schwerfällig; umständlich ⟨*sich ausdrücken*⟩
pond: **~-life** *n. (Zool.)* Teichfauna, *die;* **~-skater** *n. (Zool.)* Wasserläufer, *der;* **~weed** *n. (Bot.)* Laichkraut, *das*
pong [pɒŋ] *(Brit. coll.)* **1.** *n.* Gestank, *der (abwertend);* Mief, *der (ugs. abwertend).* **2.** *v. i.* stinken *(abwertend);* miefen *(ugs. abwertend)*
pontiff ['pɒntɪf] *n.* Papst, *der*
pontifical [pɒn'tɪfɪkl] *adj.* **a)** *(of pontiff)* päpstlich; **b)** *(fig.: dogmatic)* pastoral
pontificate [pɒn'tɪfɪkeɪt] *v. i.* dozieren; in dozierendem Ton sprechen
¹pontoon [pɒn'tu:n] *n.* **a)** *(boat)* Ponton, *der;* Prahm, *der;* **b)** *(support)* Ponton, *der*
²pontoon *n. (Brit. Cards)* Siebzehnundvier, *das*
pontoon 'bridge *n.* Pontonbrücke, *die*
pony ['pəʊnɪ] **1.** *n.* **a)** Pony, *das; see also* **shank a; b)** *(Amer. sl.: small glass)* kleines Glas; *(of beer)* Kleine, *das;* **c)** *(Amer. sl.: dancer)* kleine Tänzerin; **d)** *(Amer. sl.: crib)* Klatsche, *die (Schülerspr. landsch.);* Schmierer, *der (österr.);* **e)** *(Brit. sl.: £25)* 25 Pfund. **2.** *v. t. (Amer. sl.)* ~ **up** löhnen *(salopp);* blechen *(ugs.)*
pony: ~ **ex'press** *n.* Ponyexpreß, *der;* **~-tail** *n.* Pferdeschwanz, *der;* **wear one's hair in a ~-tail** einen Pferdeschwanz tragen *od.* haben; **~-trekking** ['pəʊnɪtrekɪŋ] *n. (Brit.)* Ponyreiten, *das*
pooch [pu:tʃ] *n. (Amer. sl.)* Köter, *der (abwertend)*
poodle ['pu:dl] *n.* Pudel, *der;* **be sb.'s ~** *(fig.)* immer nach jmds. Pfeife tanzen
poof [pʊf] *n. (Brit. coll. derog.),* **poofter** [pʊftə(r)] *n. (Austral. coll. derog.)* Schwule, *der (ugs.);* Schwuchtel, *die (salopp abwertend);* Tunte, *die (salopp abwertend)*
pooh [pu:] *int.* **a)** *expr. disgust* bah; bäh; pfui [Teufel]; **b)** *expr. disdain* pah
pooh-'pooh *v. t.* [als läppisch] abtun
¹pool [pu:l] *n.* **a)** *(permanent)* Tümpel, *der;* Wasserloch, *das;* **b)** *(temporary)* Pfütze, *die;* Lache, *die;* ~ **of blood** Blutlache, *die;* ~ **of sunlight/shade** *(fig.)* sonnige/schattige Stelle; **c)** *(swimming-~)* Schwimmbecken, *das; (public swimming-~)* Schwimmbad, *das; (in house or garden)* [Swimming]pool, *der;* **sit at the edge of the ~:** am Beckenrand sitzen; **go to the ~:** ins Schwimmbad gehen; **d)** *(in river)* tiefe Stelle *(in einem Fluß od. Bach);* Kolk, *der (fachspr.);* **the P~ [of London]** *(Brit.) Themseabschnitt unterhalb der London Bridge*
²pool **1.** *n.* **a)** *(Gambling)* [gemeinsame Spiel]kasse; **the ~s** *(Brit.)* das Toto; **do the ~s** Toto spielen; **win the ~s** im Toto gewinnen; **have a big win on the ~s** einen großen Gewinn im Toto haben; **b)** *(common supply)* Fonds, *der;* Topf, *der;* **that goes into the common ~:** das kommt in den großen Topf *(ugs.);* **a [great] ~ of experience** ein [großer] Fundus von *od.* an Erfahrung; ein [umfangreicher] Erfahrungsschatz; **c)** *(group of people)* Reservoir, *das;* Potential, *das;* **typing** *or* **typists' ~:** Schreibzentrale, *die;* **d)** *(Commerc.)* Kartell, *das;* **e)** *(Amer.: game)* Pool[billard], *das.* **2.** *v. t.* zusammenlegen ⟨*Geld, Ersparnisse, Mittel, Besitz*⟩; bündeln ⟨*Anstrengungen*⟩; **they ~ed their experience** sie nutzten ihre Erfahrung gemeinsam
pool: **~-hall,** **~room** *ns. (Amer.)* Billardzimmer, *das;* **~side** *n.* [Schwimm]beckenrand, *der; attrib.* ⟨*Bar, Tisch*⟩ am [Schwimm]beckenrand; ~ **table** *n.* Pool[billard]tisch, *der*
¹poop [pu:p] *n. (Naut.)* **a)** *(stern)* Heck, *das;* Hinterschiff, *das;* **b)** ~ **[deck]** Poop, *die (fachspr.);* Hütte, *die (fachspr.)*
²poop *(coll.)* **1.** *v. t.* schlauchen *(ugs.).* **2.** *v. i.* ~ **out** schlappmachen *(ugs.);* ⟨*Maschine usw.:*⟩ streiken *(ugs.)*
poor [pʊə(r)] **1.** *adj.* **a)** arm; **I am the ~er by £10** *or* **£10 the ~er** ich bin um 10 Pfund ärmer; *see also* **church mouse; b)** *(inadequate)* schlecht; schwach ⟨*Rede, Spiel, Gedächtnis, Beteiligung, Besuch, Leistung, Witz, Gesundheit*⟩; dürftig ⟨*Essen, Kleidung, Unterkunft, Ausrede, Entschuldigung*⟩; **of ~ quality** minderer Qualität; **he's a ~ speller** er ist schlecht in Rechtschreibung; **I'm a ~ traveller** ich vertrage das Reisen nicht gut; **be ~ at maths** *etc.* schlecht *od.* schwach in Mathematik *usw.* sein; **sb. is ~ at games** Ballspiele liegen jmdm. nicht; **have a ~ sense of responsibility** zu wenig Verantwortungsgefühl haben; **have a ~ grasp of sth.** etw. nur unzureichend beherrschen; **I only came a ~ second** bei mir hat es nur für einen schlechten zweiten Platz gereicht; **compared with Joe he comes a ~ second** gegen Joe hat er absolut nichts drin *(ugs.);* **c)** *(paltry)* schwach ⟨*Trost*⟩; schlecht ⟨*Aussichten, Situation*⟩; *(disgusting)* mies *(ugs. abwertend);* **it's very ~ of them not to have replied** es ist sehr schäbig von ihnen *od. (ugs.)* es ist ein schwaches Bild, daß sie nicht geantwortet haben; **have** *or* **stand a ~ chance of success** kaum Aussicht auf Erfolg haben; **that's pretty ~!** das ist reichlich dürftig *od. (ugs.)* ganz schön schwach; *see also* **show 1 e; d)** *(unfortunate)* arm *(auch iron.);* **~ you!** du Armer/Arme!; du Ärmster/Ärmste!; **~ thing/creature!** armes Ding!; das arme Ding!; **~ things!** die Armen *od.* Ärmsten!; **she's all alone, ~ woman** die Ärmste ist ganz allein; sie ist ganz allein, die arme Frau; **~ old Joe** der arme Joe; **~ Joe** *(dead)* der gute Joe; **e)** *(infertile)* karg, schlecht ⟨*Boden, Land*⟩; **f)** *(spiritless, pathetic)* arm ⟨*Teufel, Dummkopf*⟩; armselig, *(abwertend)* elend ⟨*Kreatur, Stümper*⟩; **cut a ~ figure** eine schlechte *od.* klägliche Figur abgeben; **g)** *(iron./joc.: humble)* **in my ~ opinion** nach meiner unmaßgeblichen Meinung; **my ~ self** meine Wenigkeit *(scherzh.);* **h)** *(deficient)* arm **(in an** + *Dat.***)**; **~ in content/ideas/vitamins** inhalts-/ideen-/vitaminarm; **~ in minerals** ⟨*Land*⟩ arm an Bodenschätzen; **i) take a ~ view of** nicht [sehr] viel halten von; für gering halten ⟨*Aussichten, Chancen*⟩; **have a ~ opinion of** eine schlechte *od.* keine [sehr] hohe Meinung haben von ⟨*Person*⟩; gering einschätzen ⟨*jmds. Fähigkeit*⟩. **2.** *n. pl.* **the ~:** die Armen; **respected by both rich and ~:** geachtet von *od.* bei arm und reich
poor: **~-box** *n.* Almosenbüchse, *die;* **~-house** *n. (Hist.)* Armenhaus, *das;* **~-law** *n. (Hist.)* Armengesetz, *das*
poorly ['pʊəlɪ] **1.** *adv.* **a)** *(scantily)* schlecht; unzureichend; **they're ~ off** es geht ihnen [finanziell] schlecht; **sb. is ~ off for sth.** es fehlt *od.* mangelt jmdm. an etw. *(Dat.);* **b)** *(badly)* schlecht; unbeholfen ⟨*schreiben, sprechen*⟩; **he did ~ in his exams** er war in seinen Prüfungen schlecht; **the team is doing ~:** die Mannschaft spielt schlecht; **exports are doing ~:** das Exportgeschäft geht schlecht; **c)** *(meanly)* schlecht ⟨*leben*⟩. **2.** *pred. adj.* schlecht ⟨*aussehen, sich fühlen*⟩; **he has been ~ lately** ihm geht es in letzter Zeit schlecht
'poor: ~ **man's** *adj. (coll.)* des kleinen Mannes *nachgestellt;* **a kind of ~ man's Marlon Brando** ein Marlon-Brando-Verschnitt; ein Westentaschen-Marlon-Brando; ~ **re'lation** *n.* arme Verwandte, *der/die; (fig.)* Stiefkind, *das;* **be the ~ relation** *(fig.)* im Vergleich zu etw. schlecht abschneiden; **feel like a ~ relation** sich *(Dat.)* wie ein Stiefkind vorkommen; **~-relief** *n. (Hist.)* Armenpflege, *die;* ~ **'white** *n. (Amer. Black derog.)* armer Weißer/arme Weiße; **~ white trash** weißer Pöbel *(abwertend);* weißes Gesindel *(abwertend)*
poove [pu:v] *see* **poof**
¹pop [pɒp] **1.** *v. i.,* **-pp-: a)** *(make sound)* ⟨*Korken:*⟩ knallen; ⟨*Schote, Samenkapsel:*⟩ aufplatzen, aufspringen; **a faint ~ping sound** ein leises Knacken; **his buttons ~ped open** seine Knöpfe sprangen auf; *(fig.)* **his eyes ~ped with amazement** er guckte wie ein Auto *(ugs.);* **prices that would make your eyes ~:** Preise, bei denen Sie staunen würden; **b)** *(coll.: move, go quickly)* **let's ~ round to Fred's** komm, wir gehen mal eben *od.*

schnell *od.* kurz bei Fred vorbei *(ugs.)*; **I'll just ~ upstairs and see granny** ich gehe *od. (ugs.)* springe nur mal eben hoch zu Oma; **~ down to London** mal eben *od.* schnell nach London fahren; **you must ~ round and see us** du mußt mal vorbeikommen und uns besuchen *od.* mußt mal bei uns reingucken *(ugs.)*; **she ~ped back for her book** sie lief *od. (ugs.)* flitzte noch mal zurück, um ihr Buch zu holen; **c)** *(fire gun)* ballern *(ugs.)* (**at** auf + *Akk.*). **2.** *v.t.*, **-pp-**: **a)** *(coll.: put)* **~ the meat in the fridge** das Fleisch in den Kühlschrank tun; **~ a cake into the oven** einen Kuchen in den Ofen schieben; **~ a peanut into one's mouth** [sich *(Dat.)*] eine Erdnuß in den Mund stecken; **~ one's head in at the door** den Kopf zur Tür reinstecken; mal eben hereinschauen; **~ one's head out [of the window]** den Kopf [zum Fenster] rausstrecken; **~ the kettle on** den Kessel aufsetzen; **~ a letter in the post** einen Brief einwerfen; einen Brief in den Briefkasten werfen; **~ sth. into a bag** etw. in eine Tasche tun *od.* stecken; **b)** *(cause to burst)* enthülsen ‹*Erbsen, Bohnen*›; platzen *od. (ugs.)* knallen lassen ‹*Luftballon*›; zerknallen ‹*Papiertüte*›; **c)** *(sl.: take as drug)* nehmen; schlucken, *(Jargon)* schmeißen ‹*Pillen, Trips*›; *(by injection)* schießen *(Jargon)*; drücken *(Jargon)*; **d)** *(Amer.: cause to burst)* puffen; **~ corn** Popcorn machen; **e) ~ the question [to sb.]** *(coll.)* jmdm. einen [Heirats]antrag machen. **3.** *n.* **a)** *(sound)* Knall, *der;* Knallen, *das;* **b)** *(coll.: drink)* Sprudel, *der; (flavoured)* Brause, *die (ugs.)*; **soda ~:** Selter[s], *das.* **4.** *adv.* **go ~:** knallen; peng machen *(ugs.)*

~ 'off *v.i.* **a)** *(coll.: die)* abnibbeln *(ugs., bes. nordd.)*; den Löffel weglegen *od.* abgeben *(salopp)*; **b)** *(move or go away)* ‹*Person:*› verschwinden, *(ugs.)* abdampfen

~ 'out *v.i.* hervorschießen aus; **~ one's head out of the window** den Kopf zum Fenster herausstrecken; **~ out from behind a bush** hinter einem Busch hervorspringen; **~ out for a newspaper/to the shops** schnell *od.* eben mal eine Zeitung holen gehen/einkaufen gehen *(ugs.)*; **~ out for a beer** eben mal ein Bier[chen] trinken gehen *(ugs.)*; **he's just ~ped out for a moment** er ist nur mal kurz weggegangen *(ugs.)*

~ 'out of *v.t.* hervorschieben aus; **~ one's head out of the window** den Kopf zum Fenster herausstrecken; **sb.'s eyes nearly** *or* **almost ~ out of his head** *or* **skull** *(coll.) (with surprise)* jmdm. fallen fast die Augen aus dem Kopf; *(with excitement)* jmd. *(bes. Kind)* macht große Augen

~ 'up *v.i.* **a)** *(fig.: appear)* auftauchen; **sb./sth. keeps ~ping up** *(fig.)* jmd./etw. begegnet einem immer wieder *(fig.)*; **b)** *(rise up)* sich aufstellen; *see also* **pop-up**

²pop *(coll.)* **1.** *n. (popular music)* Popmusik, *die;* Pop, *der;* **be top of the ~s** an der Spitze der Charts *od.* Hitlisten stehen. **2.** *adj.* Pop‹*star, -musik usw.*›

³pop *n. (Amer. coll.: father)* Pa[pa], *der (fam.)*

pop. *abbr.* **population** Einw.

pop: ~ art *n., no pl., no indef. art.* Pop-art, *die; attrib.* Pop-art-; **~ concert** *n.* Popkonzert, *das;* **~corn** *n.* Popcorn, *das*

pope [pəʊp] *n.* **a)** *(RC Ch.; also fig.)* Papst, *der*/Päpstin, *die;* **b)** *(Coptic Ch.)* Patriarch, *der;* **c)** *(Orthodox Ch.)* Pope, *der. See also* **nose 1 a**

popery ['pəʊpərɪ] *n., no pl., no art. (derog.)* Pfaffentum, *das (abwertend)*; Papismus, *der (abwertend)*

pop: ~-eyed ['pɒpaɪd] *adj. (coll.)* **a)** *(wide-eyed)* großäugig; **they were ~-eyed with amazement** sie staunten Bauklötze *(salopp)*; **b)** *(having bulging eyes)* glotzäugig; glupschäugig *(nordd.)*; **~ festival** *n.* Popfestival, *das;* **~ group** *n.* Popgruppe, *die;* **~gun** *n.* Spielzeuggewehr, *das*/Spielzeugpistole, *die*

popish ['pəʊpɪʃ] *adj. (arch./derog.)* papistisch *(abwertend)*; **the ~ religion** der Papismus *(abwertend)*

poplar ['pɒplə(r)] *n.* Pappel, *die*

poplin ['pɒplɪn] *n. (Textiles)* Popelin, *der;* Popeline, *der od. die*

pop: ~ music *n.* Popmusik, *die;* **~over** *n. (Amer.)* **a)** *stark aufgehendes Backwerk aus Eiern, Milch, Mehl und Butter;* **b)** *(garment)* weites Kleidungsstück *(das über den Kopf gezogen wird)*

poppadam, poppadum ['pɒpədəm] *n. (Ind. Gastr.) knuspriger, hauchdünner fritierter Fladen*

popper ['pɒpə(r)] *n. (Brit. coll.)* Druckknopf, *der*

poppet ['pɒpɪt] *n. (Brit. coll.)* Schätzchen, *das;* Schatz, *der*

poppy ['pɒpɪ] *n.* **a)** *(Bot.)* Mohn, *der;* **a field of poppies** ein Mohnfeld; **Californian ~:** Goldmohn, *der;* **opium ~:** Schlafmohn, *der;* **Welsh ~:** Scheinmohn, *der;* **b)** *(Brit.: emblem)* [künstliche] Mohnblume *(als Zeichen des Gedenkens am 'Poppy Day')*

poppycock ['pɒpɪkɒk] *n., no pl., no art. (sl.)* Mumpitz, *der (ugs. abwertend)*

poppy: P~ Day *(Brit.) see* **Remembrance Sunday; ~-head** *n.* Mohnkapsel, *die;* **~-seed** *n.* Mohnsamen, *der;* **~ seeds** *(Cookery)* Mohn, *der*

Popsicle, (P) ['pɒpsɪkl] *n. (Amer.)* [Wasser]eis am Stiel

pop: ~ singer *n.* Popsänger, *der*/-sängerin, *die;* Schlagersänger, *der*/-sängerin, *die;* **~ song** *n.* Popsong, *der;* Schlager, *der;* **~ star** *n.* Popstar, *der;* Schlagerstar, *der*

popsy (popsie) ['pɒpsɪ] *n. (coll.) (young woman)* Mieze, *die (salopp)*; *(young girl)* Maus, *die; (as form of address)* Schätzchen, *das*

populace ['pɒpjʊləs] *n., no pl.* **a)** *(common people)* [breite] Masse; Volk, *das;* **the Roman ~:** das Volk von Rom; **b)** *(derog.: rabble)* Pöbel, *der (abwertend)*

popular ['pɒpjʊlə(r)] *adj.* **a)** *(well liked)* beliebt; populär ‹*Entscheidung, Maßnahme*›; **I know I shan't be ~ if I suggest that** ich weiß, daß ich mich mit diesem Vorschlag nicht gerade beliebt mache; **he was a very ~ choice** mit ihm hatte man sich für einen sehr beliebten *od.* populären Mann entschieden; **be ~ with sb.** bei jmdm. beliebt sein; **he's ~ with the girls** die Mädchen mögen ihn; **I'm not very ~ in the office just now** im Büro ist man zur Zeit nicht gut auf mich zu sprechen; **prove ~:** gut ankommen; **b)** *(suited to the public)* volkstümlich; populär *(geh.)*; **at ~ prices** zu günstigen Preisen; **~ edition** Volksausgabe, *die;* **~ journal/newspaper** Massenblatt, *das;* **a ~ romance** ein Liebesroman; **~ science** die Populärwissenschaft; **c)** *(prevalent)* landläufig; allgemein ‹*Unzufriedenheit*›; **~ etymology** Volksetymologie, *die;* **d)** *(of the people)* Volks-; verbreitet ‹*Aberglaube, Irrtum, Meinung*›; allgemein ‹*Wahl, Zustimmung, Unterstützung*›; **~ remedy** Hausmittel, *das;* **by ~ request** auf allgemeinen Wunsch

popular: ~ 'art *n.* Volkskunst, *die;* **~ 'front** *n. (Polit.)* Volksfront, *die*

popularise *see* **popularize**

popularity [pɒpjʊ'lærɪtɪ] *n., no pl.* Popularität, *die;* Beliebtheit, *die; (of decision, measure)* Popularität, *die;* **that won her ~ with her classmates** das machte sie bei ihren Klassenkameradinnen beliebt

popularize ['pɒpjʊləraɪz] *v.t.* **a)** *(make popular)* populär machen; **~ sth.** einer Sache *(Dat.)* Popularität verschaffen; **b)** *(make known)* bekannt machen; **c)** *(make understandable)* breiteren Kreisen zugänglich machen; popularisieren *(geh.)*

popularly ['pɒpjʊləlɪ] *adv.* **a)** *(generally)* allgemein; landläufig; **it is ~ believed that ...:** es ist ein im Volk verbreiteter Glaube, daß ...; **b)** *(for the people)* volkstümlich; [all]gemeinverständlich

popular 'music *n.* Unterhaltungsmusik, *die;* Populärmusik, *die (fachspr.)*

populate ['pɒpjʊleɪt] *v.t.* bevölkern ‹*Land, Gebiet*›; bewohnen ‹*Insel, Gebiet*›; **the characters that ~ his novel** die Charaktere, die seinen Roman bevölkern; **thickly** *or* **heavily** *or* **densely/sparsely ~d** dicht/dünn besiedelt ‹*Land, Gebiet usw.*›; dicht/dünn bevölkert ‹*Stadt*›

population [pɒpjʊ'leɪʃn] *n.* **a)** Bevölkerung, *die;* **Britain has a ~ of 56 million** Großbritannien hat 56 Millionen Einwohner; **the growing immigrant ~ of London** der wachsende Einwandereranteil an der Londoner Bevölkerung; **the seal ~ of Greenland** der Seehundbestand *od. (fachspr.)* die Seehundpopulation Grönlands; **b)** *(Statistics)* Grundgesamtheit, *die*

popu'lation explosion *n.* Bevölkerungsexplosion, *die*

populism ['pɒpjʊlɪzm] *n.* Populismus, *der*

populist ['pɒpjʊlɪst] **1.** *n.* Populist, *der*/Populistin, *die.* **2.** *adj.* populistisch

populous ['pɒpjʊləs] *adj.* dicht bevölkert

'pop-up *adj.* Stehauf‹*buch, -illustration*›; **~-up toaster** Toaster mit Auswerfmechanismus

porcelain ['pɔːslɪn] *n.* **a)** Porzellan, *das;* **Meissen ~:** Meißner Porzellan; *attrib.* Porzellan-; **b)** *(article)* Porzellangegenstand, *der;* **~s** Porzellan, *das*

porch [pɔːtʃ] *n.* **a)** *(Archit.)* Vordach, *das; (with side walls)* Vorbau, *der; (enclosed)* Windfang, *der; (of church etc.)* Vorhalle, *die;* **b)** *(Amer.: veranda)* [offene] Veranda

porcine ['pɔːsaɪn] *adj.* Schweine-; *(fig.)* schweineähnlich; wie ein Schwein *nachgestellt*

porcupine ['pɔːkjʊpaɪn] *n. (Zool.)* **a)** *(Brit.: Hystricidae)* Stachelschwein, *das;* **b)** *(Amer.: Erethizontidae)* Baumstachler, *der*

¹pore [pɔː(r)] *n.* Pore, *die*

²pore *v.i.* **~ over sth.** etw. [genau] studieren; *(think deeply)* **~ over** *or* **on sth.** über etw. *(Akk.)* [gründlich] nachdenken

pork [pɔːk] *n.* Schweinefleisch, *das; attrib.* Schweine-; Schweins- *(bes. südd.)*; **a leg of ~:** eine Schweinekeule

pork: ~-barrel *n. (Amer. coll.) aus politischen Gründen bewilligte staatliche Zuschüsse;* **~-butcher** *n.* Schweinemetzger, *der (bes. südd.)*; Schweineschlachter, *der (bes. nordd.)*; **~ 'chop** *n.* Schweinekotelett, *das*

porker ['pɔːkə(r)] *n.* Mastschwein, *das; (young pig)* Mastferkel, *das*

pork: ~ 'pie *n.* Schweinepastete, *die;* **~-pie 'hat** *n.* flacher [Herren]hut; **~ 'sausage** *n.* Schweinswürstchen, *das*

porn [pɔːn] *n., no pl. (coll.)* Pornographie, *die;* Pornos *(ugs.)*; **write ~:** Pornos schreiben *(ugs.)*; **~ film** Pornofilm, *der (ugs.)*

porno ['pɔːnəʊ] *(coll.)* **1.** *n., no pl. see* **porn. 2.** *adj.* Porno- *(ugs.)*

pornographic [pɔːnə'græfɪk] *adj.* pornographisch; Porno- *(ugs.)*

pornography [pɔː'nɒgrəfɪ] *n.* Pornographie, *die*

porosity [pɔː'rɒsɪtɪ] *n., no pl.* Porosität, *die*

porous ['pɔːrəs] *adj.* porös ‹*Fels, Gestein, Stoff*›; porenreich ‹*Haut, Holz*›

porpoise ['pɔːpəs] *n. (Zool.)* Schweinswal, *der*

porridge ['pɒrɪdʒ] *n., no pl.* **a)** *(food)* Porridge, *der;* [Hafer]brei, *der;* **b)** *(sl.: imprisonment)* Knast, *der (ugs.)*; **do ~:** Knast schieben *(salopp)*; im Knast sitzen *(ugs.)*

porridge 'oats *n. pl.* Haferflocken *Pl.*

¹port [pɔːt] **1.** *n.* **a)** *(harbour)* Hafen, *der;* **come** *or* **put into ~:** [in den Hafen] einlaufen; **leave ~:** [aus dem Hafen] auslaufen;

reach ~: den Hafen erreichen; ankommen; **out of ~**: auf See; **naval ~**: Kriegshafen, *der;* **any ~ in a storm** *(fig. coll.)* manchmal kann man sich's eben nicht aussuchen *(ugs.);* ≈ in der Not frißt der Teufel Fliegen *(ugs.);* **~ of call** Anlaufhafen, *der; (fig.)* Ziel, *das;* **where's your next ~ of call?** *(fig.)* wo willst du als nächstes hin?; **~ of entry** Zoll[abfertigungs]hafen, *der; (for goods)* Einfuhrhafen, *der; (for persons)* Einreisehafen, *der; see also* **free port; b)** *(town)* Hafenstadt, *die;* Hafen, *der;* **c)** *(Naut., Aeronaut.: left side)* Backbord, *das;* **land to ~!** Land an Backbord!; **turn** *or* **put the helm to ~**: nach Backbord drehen. **2.** *adj. (Naut., Aeronaut.: left)* Backbord-; backbordseitig; **on the ~ bow/quarter** Backbord voraus/Backbord achteraus; *see also* **beam 1 e; [1]tack 1 c; watch 1 c**

[2]port *n.* **a)** *(Naut.: opening)* Pforte, *die;* **b)** *(Naut.: porthole)* Seitenfenster, *das; (circular)* Bullauge, *das;* **c)** *(aperture)* Öffnung, *die;* **d)** *(gun aperture)* Schießscharte, *die; (on ship)* Geschützpforte, *die*

[3]port *n. (wine)* Portwein, *der;* Port, *der (ugs.)*

portable ['pɔ:təbl] **1.** *adj.* tragbar; portabel *(Werbespr.).* **2.** *n. (television)* Portable, *der; (radio)* Portable, *der;* Koffergerät, *das; (typewriter)* Portable, *die;* Koffermaschine, *die*

portage ['pɔ:tɪdʒ] *n.* **a)** *(carrying)* Transport über Land; **b)** *(place)* Portage, *die*

Portakabin, (P) ['pɔ:təkæbɪn] *n.* [Bau]container, *der*

portal ['pɔ:tl] *n.* Eingang, *der;* Pforte, *die (geh.); (of church, palace, etc.)* Portal, *das;* **pass through the ~s of a place** *(fig.)* einen Ort besuchen; **the ~s of heaven** die Pforten des Himmels *od.* Himmelspforten *(dichter.)*

port au'thority *n.* Hafenbehörde, *die*

portcullis [pɔ:t'kʌlɪs] *n. (Archit.)* Fallgitter, *das;* Fallgatter, *das*

portend [pɔ:'tend] *v. t.* hindeuten auf (+ *Akk.*); **what does this ~?** was hat das zu bedeuten?

portent ['pɔ:tent] *n. (literary)* Vorzeichen, *das;* Omen, *das;* **a ~ of doom** ein schlimmes [Vor]zeichen; ein böses Omen; **~s of war** Vorzeichen *od.* Vorboten des Krieges; **a ~ of the project's success** ein gutes Omen für den Erfolg des Vorhabens

portentous [pɔ:'tentəs] *adj.* bedeutungsvoll; schicksalhaft ⟨*Bedeutung*⟩; *(ominous)* unheilvoll

[1]porter ['pɔ:tə(r)] *n. (Brit.: doorman)* Pförtner, *der; (of hotel etc.)* Portier, *der*

[2]porter *n.* **a)** *(luggage-handler)* [Gepäck]träger, *der/*-trägerin, *die; (in hotel)* Hausdiener, *der;* **b)** *(Amer., Ir./Hist.: beer)* Porter, *der od. das;* **c)** *(Amer. Railw.)* Schlafwagenschaffner, *der/*-schaffnerin, *die*

porterage ['pɔ:tərɪdʒ] *n. (charge)* Trägerlohn, *der*

porterhouse 'steak *n.* Porterhousesteak, *das*

porter's 'lodge *see* **lodge 1 b**

portfolio [pɔ:t'fəʊlɪəʊ] *n., pl.* **~s a)** *(list)* Portefeuille, *das;* **b)** *(Polit.)* Geschäftsbereich, *der;* Portefeuille, *das (geh.);* **c)** *(case, contents)* Mappe, *die*

'porthole *see* **[2]port b**

portico ['pɔ:tɪkəʊ] *n., pl.* **~es** *or* **~s** *(Archit.)* Säulenvorbau, *der;* Portikus, *der (fachspr.)*

portière [pɔ:'tjeə(r)] *n.* [schwerer] Türvorhang; Portiere, *die*

portion ['pɔ:ʃn] **1.** *n.* **a)** *(part)* Teil, *der; (of ticket)* Abschnitt, *der; (of inheritance)* Anteil, *der;* **b)** *(amount of food)* Portion, *die;* **c)** *(arch./literary: destiny)* Los, *das;* Schicksal, *das;* **d)** *(quantity)* gewisses Maß **(of** an + *Dat.*). **2.** *v. t.* aufteilen **(among** unter + *Akk.*, **into** in + *Akk.*)

~ 'out *v. t.* aufteilen **(among, between** unter + *Akk.*); **she ~ed out the food** sie verteilte das Essen

Portland ['pɔ:tlənd]: **~ ce'ment** *n.* Portlandzement, *der;* **~ 'stone** *n.* Portland[kalk]stein, *der*

portly ['pɔ:tlɪ] *adj.* beleibt; korpulent; **have a ~ frame** beleibt *od.* korpulent sein

portmanteau [pɔ:t'mæntəʊ] *n., pl.* **~s** *or* **~x** [pɔ:t'mæntəʊz] Reisekoffer, *der*

port'manteau word *n.* Port[e]manteauform, *die (fachspr.); (fig.: generalized term)* weiter Begriff

portrait ['pɔ:trɪt] *n.* **a)** *(picture)* Porträt, *das;* Bildnis, *das (geh.); attrib.* Porträt-; **sit for one's ~ [to sb.]** [jmdm.] Porträt sitzen; sich [von jmdm.] porträtieren lassen; **have one's ~ painted** sich porträtieren lassen; **full-length ~**: Ganzporträt, *das;* **b)** *(description)* Porträt, *das;* Bild, *das;* **give/convey an unflattering ~ of sb./sth.** ein wenig schmeichelhaftes Bild von jmdm./etw. zeichnen

portraitist ['pɔ:trɪtɪst] *n.* Porträtist, *der/* Porträtistin, *die; (painter also)* Porträtmaler, *der/*-malerin, *die; (photographer also)* Porträtfotograf, *der/*-fotografin, *die*

portraiture ['pɔ:trɪtʃə(r)] *n.* Porträtieren, *das; (painting also)* Porträtmalerei, *die; (photographing also)* Porträtfotografie, *die;* **he is known for his ~**: er ist für *od.* durch seine Porträts bekannt

portray [pɔ:'treɪ] *v. t.* **a)** *(describe)* darstellen; schildern; **b)** *(make likeness of)* porträtieren ⟨*Person*⟩; darstellen, wiedergeben ⟨*Atmosphäre usw.*⟩; ⟨*Schauspieler:*⟩ darstellen ⟨*Rolle, Person*⟩

portrayal [pɔ:'treɪəl] *n.* **a)** *(description)* Darstellung, *die;* Schilderung, *die; (esp. of person)* Porträt, *das;* **b)** *(acting)* Darstellung, *die;* **c)** *(portrait)* Darstellung, *die;* Porträt, *das*

Portugal ['pɔ:tjʊgl] *pr. n.* Portugal *(das)*

Portuguese [pɔ:tjʊ'gi:z] **1.** *adj.* portugiesisch; **sb. is ~**: jmd. ist Portugiese/Portugiesin; *see also* **English 1. 2.** *n., pl. same* **a)** *(person)* Portugiese, *der/*Portugiesin, *die;* **b)** *(language)* Portugiesisch, *das; see also* **English 2 a**

Portuguese man-of-'war *n. (Zool.)* Portugiesische Galeere

pose [pəʊz] **1.** *v. t.* **a)** *(be cause of)* aufwerfen ⟨*Frage, Problem*⟩; darstellen ⟨*Bedrohung, Problem*⟩; bedeuten ⟨*Bedrohung*⟩; mit sich bringen ⟨*Schwierigkeiten*⟩; **b)** *(propound)* vorbringen; aufstellen ⟨*Theorie*⟩; **c)** *(place)* Aufstellung nehmen lassen, sich aufstellen lassen ⟨*Gruppe, Kinder, Mannschaft, Gesellschaft*⟩; Positur einnehmen lassen, posieren lassen ⟨*Modell*⟩. **2.** *v. i.* **a)** *(assume attitude)* posieren; *(fig.)* sich geziert benehmen *od.* geben *(abwertend);* **~ [in the] nude** für einen Akt posieren; **b) ~ as** sich geben als; **he likes to ~ as an expert** er spielt gern den Experten. **3.** *n.* Haltung, *die;* Pose, *die; (fig.)* Pose, *die;* Gehabe, *das (abwertend);* **strike a ~**: eine Pose einnehmen; **she's always striking ~s** *(fig.)* sie benimmt sich immer so geziert; **hold a ~**: eine Pose beibehalten; in einer Haltung verharren *(geh.);* **hold that ~!** bleib so!; **it's just a [big] ~** *(fig.)* es ist reine Pose

poser ['pəʊzə(r)] *n.* *(question)* knifflige Frage; *(problem)* schwieriges Problem; **that's a real ~**: das ist eine harte Nuß *(ugs.);* **set some ~s for sb.** jmdm. manche harte Nuß zu knacken geben *(ugs.)*

poseur [pəʊ'zɜ:(r)] *n.* Blender, *der (abwertend);* Poseur, *der (geh. abwertend)*

poseuse [pəʊ'zɜ:z] *n. fem.* Blenderin, *die (abwertend)*

posh [pɒʃ] **1.** *adj. (coll.)* vornehm; nobel *(spött.);* stinkvornehm *(salopp);* **~ hotel/newspaper** Nobelhotel, *das/*Nobelgazette, *die (spött.);* **the ~ people** die Schickeria *(ugs.).* **2.** *adv.* **talk ~**: hochgestochen reden/mit vornehmem Akzent sprechen. **3.** *v. t.* **~ up** aufmotzen *(ugs.)*

posit ['pɒzɪt] *v. t.* postulieren *(geh.)*

position [pə'zɪʃn] **1.** *n.* **a)** *(place occupied)* Platz, *der; (of player in team or line-up, of actor, of plane, ship, etc.)* Position, *die; (of hands of clock, words, stars)* Stellung, *die; (of building etc., of organ in body)* Lage, *die; (of river)* [Ver]lauf, *der;* **find one's ~ on a map** seinen Standort auf einer Karte finden; **take [up] one's ~**: seinen Platz einnehmen; **they took their ~ at the end of the queue** sie stellten sich ans Ende der Schlange; **after the second lap he was in fourth ~**: nach der zweiten Runde lag er an vierter Stelle; **he finished in second ~**: er belegte den zweiten Platz; **what ~ do you play [in]?** *(Sport)* in welcher Position spielst du?; **in the starting ~**: auf Startposition; **b)** *(proper place)* **be in/out of ~**: an seinem Platz/nicht an seinem Platz sein; **put sth. into ~**: etw. an seinen Platz stellen; **c)** *(Mil.)* Stellung, *die;* **d)** *(Chess)* Position, *die;* Stellung, *die;* **~ play** Positionsspiel, *das;* Stellungsspiel, *das;* **leave the pieces in ~**: die Figuren aufgestellt *od.* stehen lassen; **e)** *(fig.: mental attitude)* Standpunkt, *der;* Haltung, *die;* **take up a ~ on sth.** einen Standpunkt *od.* eine Haltung zu etw. einnehmen; **take the ~ that ...**: auf dem Standpunkt stehen *od.* sich auf den Standpunkt stellen, daß ...; **f)** *(fig.: situation)* **be in a good ~ [financially]** [finanziell] gut gestellt sein *od.* dastehen; **be in a ~ of strength** eine starke Position haben; **negotiate from a ~ of strength** aus einer Position der Stärke heraus verhandeln; **what's the ~?** wie stehen *od.* liegen die Dinge?; **what would you do if you were in my ~?** was würdest du in meiner Lage tun?; **put yourself in my ~!** versetz dich [einmal] in meine Lage!; **be in a/no ~ to do sth.** in der Lage/nicht in der Lage sein, etw. zu tun; **he's in no ~ to criticize us** es steht ihm nicht zu, uns zu kritisieren; *see also* **jockey 2; g)** *(rank)* Stellung, *die;* Position, *die;* **a person of ~**: eine hochgestellte Persönlichkeit; **a high ~ in society** eine hohe gesellschaftliche Stellung; **a pupil's ~ in class** die Stellung eines Schülers innerhalb der Klasse; **social ~**: gesellschaftliche *od.* soziale Stellung; **h)** *(employment)* [Arbeits]stelle, *die;* Stellung, *die;* **the ~ of ambassador in Bogotá** die Position des Botschafters in Bogotá; **permanent ~**: Dauerstellung, *die;* **the ~ of assistant manager** die Stelle *od.* Position des stellvertretenden Geschäftsführers; **rise to a ~ of responsibility** in eine verantwortliche Stellung aufsteigen; **~ of trust** Vertrauensstellung, *die;* Vertrauensposten, *der;* **i)** *(posture)* Haltung, *die; (during sexual intercourse)* Stellung, *die;* Position, *die; (ballet)* Position, *die; (yoga)* Stellung, *die;* **in a reclining ~**: zurückgelehnt; **in a sitting ~**: in sitzender Position *od.* Stellung; sitzend; **in an uncomfortable ~**: in unbequemer Stellung *od.* Haltung. **2.** *v. t.* **a)** plazieren; positionieren ⟨*Lautsprecherboxen, Leuchten usw.*⟩; aufstellen, postieren ⟨*Polizisten, Wachen*⟩; **~ oneself near the exit** sich in die Nähe des Ausgangs stellen/setzen; ⟨*Wache, Posten usw.:*⟩ sich in der Nähe des Ausgangs aufstellen; **b)** *(Mil.: station)* stationieren

positional [pə'zɪʃənl] *adj.* **a)** *(Ling.)* isolierend ⟨*Sprache*⟩; **b)** *(Sport)* positionell *(fachspr.);* **~ play** Stellungsspiel, *das;* **c)** *(Mil.)* **~ war** Stellungskrieg, *der*

positive ['pɒzɪtɪv] **1.** *adj.* **a)** *(definite)* eindeutig; entschieden ⟨*Weigerung*⟩; positiv ⟨*Recht*⟩; **in a ~ tone of voice** in bestimmtem *od.* entschiedenem Ton; **to my ~ knowledge ...**: wie ich ganz sicher weiß, ...; **b)** *(convinced)* sicher; **Are you sure? – P~! Bist** du sicher? – Absolut [sicher]!; **he is ~ that he is right** er ist sich *(Dat.)* völlig sicher, daß er recht hat; **I'm ~ of it** ich bin [mir] [dessen] ganz sicher; **c)** *(affirmative)* positiv; **d)** *(optimistic)* positiv; **regard sth. in a ~ light** etw.

in positivem Licht sehen; **e)** *(showing presence of sth.)* positiv ‹*Ergebnis, Befund, Test*›; **f)** *(constructive)* konstruktiv ‹*Kritik, Vorschlag, Anregung, Rat, Hilfe*›; positiv ‹*Philosophie, Erfahrung, Denken*›; **she's the most ~ of the group** sie hat von allen in der Gruppe die positivste Einstellung; **g)** *(Math.)* positiv; **h)** *(Ling.)* ungesteigert; **i)** *(Electr.)* positiv ‹*Elektrode, Platte, Ladung, Ion*›; Plus‹*platte, -leiter*›; *see also* **feedback b; j)** *as intensifier (coll.)* echt; **it would be a ~ miracle** es wäre ein echtes Wunder *od. (ugs.)* echt ein Wunder; **k)** *(Photog.)* positiv; Positiv-. **2.** *n.* **a)** *(Ling.)* Positiv, *der;* Grundstufe [des Adjektivs], *die;* **b)** *(Photog.)* Positiv, *das;* Positivbild, *das*

positive discrimi'nation *n.* positive Diskriminierung *(fachspr.);* Bevorzugung, *die*

positively ['pɒzɪtɪvlɪ] *adv.* **a)** *(constructively)* konstruktiv ‹*kritisieren*›; positiv ‹*denken*›; **b)** *(Electr.)* positiv; **c)** *(definitely)* eindeutig, entschieden ‹*sich weigern*›; **d)** *as intensifier (coll.)* echt *(ugs.);* **it's ~ marvellous that ...:** es ist echt spitze, daß ...

'positive sign *n. (Math.)* positives Vorzeichen; *(symbol)* Pluszeichen, *das*

positivism ['pɒzɪtɪvɪzm] *n. (Philos., Relig.)* Positivismus, *der; see also* **logical positivism**

positivist ['pɒzɪtɪvɪst] **1.** *n.* Positivist, *der*/Positivistin, *die.* **2.** *adj.* positivistisch

positron ['pɒzɪtrɒn] *n. (Phys.)* Positron, *das*

posse ['pɒsɪ] *n.* **a)** *(Amer.: force with legal authority)* [Polizei]trupp, *der;* [Polizei]aufgebot, *das;* **b)** *(crowd)* Schar, *die;* **~ of advisers** Beraterstab, *der*

possess [pə'zes] *v. t.* **a)** *(own)* besitzen; verfügen über (+ *Akk.*) *(geh.);* **be ~ed of** gesegnet sein mit *(geh.);* **~ed of money/wealth** bemittelt/begütert; **~ed of reason** vernunftbegabt; **b)** *(have as faculty or quality)* haben; **~ great passion** sehr leidenschaftlich sein; **c)** *(dominate)* ‹*Furcht usw.:*› ergreifen, Besitz nehmen von ‹*Person*›; **what ~ed you/him?** *(coll.)* was ist in dich/ihn gefahren?; was für ein Teufel hat dich/ihn geritten? *(ugs.);* **d)** *(dated: copulate with)* besitzen *(geh. verhüll.);* **e)** *(arch./formal)* **~ oneself of sth.** sich einer Sache *(Gen.)* bemächtigen; sich *(Dat.)* etw. aneignen

possessed [pə'zest] *adj. (dominated)* besessen; **he's a man ~:** er ist ein Besessener; **~ by the devil/by** *or* **with an idea** vom Teufel/von einer Idee besessen; **be ~ by** *or* **with fear/horror** von Angst/Schrecken ergriffen sein; **be ~ by** *or* **with greed/ambition** von Gier/Ehrgeiz besessen sein; **be ~ by** *or* **with envy/rage** von Neid erfüllt sein/rasen; **like one ~:** wie ein Besessener/eine Besessene

possession [pə'zeʃn] *n.* **a)** *(thing possessed)* Besitz, *der;* **some of my ~s** einige meiner Sachen; **b)** *in pl. (property)* Besitz, *der; (territory)* Besitzungen; **worldly ~s** irdische Güter; **all his ~s** sein ganzer Besitz; all seine Habe; **c)** *(controlling)* **take ~ of** *(Mil.)* einnehmen ‹*Festung, Stadt usw.*›; besetzen ‹*Gebiet*›; **the enemy's ~ of the town** die feindliche Herrschaft *od.* Herrschaft des Feindes über die Stadt; **~ by the devil** Besessensein vom Teufel; **d)** *(possessing)* Besitz, *der;* **~ of land/firearms** Landbesitz, *der*/Waffenbesitz, *der;* **be in ~ of sth.** im Besitz einer Sache *(Gen.)* sein; **come into** *or* **get ~ of sth.** in den Besitz einer Sache *(Gen.)* gelangen; **regain** *or* **resume ~ of sth.** wieder in den Besitz einer Sache *(Gen.)* gelangen; **be in ~ of a high income** über ein hohes Einkommen verfügen; **put sb. in ~ of sth./of the facts** jmdn. in den Besitz einer Sache *(Gen.)* bringen/jmdn. ins Bild setzen; **in full ~ of one's senses** im Vollbesitz seiner geistigen Kräfte; **be in full ~ of the facts** voll im Bilde sein; **the information in my ~:** die mir vorliegenden Informationen; **have sth. in one's ~:** im Besitz einer Sache *(Gen.)* sein; **take ~ of** in Besitz nehmen; beziehen ‹*Haus, Wohnung*›; **e)** *(Sport)* **win ~ of the ball** in Ballbesitz gelangen; **lose ~:** den Ball verlieren; **in ~:** im Ballbesitz; **f)** *(Law)* Besitz, *der;* **enter into ~ of sth.** etw. in Besitz nehmen; *see also* **point 1 c; vacant a**

possessive [pə'zesɪv] **1.** *adj.* **a)** *(jealously retaining possession)* besitzergreifend; **be ~ about sth.** etw. eifersüchtig hüten; **be ~ about** *or* **towards sb.** an jmdn. Besitzansprüche stellen; **b)** *(Ling.)* possessiv; **~ adjective** Possessivadjektiv, *das; see also* **pronoun. 2.** *n. (Ling.)* Possessivum, *das*

pos'sessive case *n.* Possessiv[us], *der*

possessively [pə'zesɪvlɪ] *adv.* besitzergreifend

possessor [pə'zesə(r)] *n.* Besitzer, *der*/Besitzerin, *die;* **be the ~ of a fine singing voice** eine schöne Singstimme besitzen

posset ['pɒsɪt] *n. (Hist.) heiße Milch mit Bier od. Wein und Gewürzen*

possibility [pɒsɪ'bɪlɪtɪ] *n.* **a)** Möglichkeit, *die;* **be within the range** *or* **bounds of ~:** im Bereich des Möglichen liegen; **there's no ~ of his coming/agreeing** es ist ausgeschlossen, daß er kommt/zustimmt; **there's not much ~ of success** die Erfolgschancen sind nicht groß; **the constant ~ of failure** die ständige Gefahr des Scheiterns; **if by any ~ ...:** falls tatsächlich ...; *(if without taking any trouble)* falls zufällig ...; **is there any ~ of our being able to do it?** gibt es für uns irgendeine Möglichkeit, es zu tun?; **it's a distinct ~ that ...:** es ist gut möglich, daß ...; **accept that sth. is a ~:** es akzeptieren, daß etw. möglich ist *od.* nicht auszuschließen ist; **he is a ~ for the job** er ist ein möglicher Anwärter auf die Stelle; er kommt für die Stelle in Betracht; **what are the possibilities?** welche Möglichkeiten gibt es?; **b)** *in pl. (potential)* Möglichkeiten *Pl.;* **the house/subject has possibilities** aus dem Haus/Thema läßt sich etwas machen; **the scheme has possibilities** in dem Plan stecken Möglichkeiten

possible ['pɒsɪbl] **1.** *adj.* **a)** möglich; **if ~:** wenn *od.* falls möglich; wenn es geht; **as ... as ~:** so ... wie möglich; möglichst ...; **the greatest ~ assistance** die größtmögliche Unterstützung; **all the assistance ~:** alle denkbare Unterstützung; **anything is ~:** alles ist möglich; es ist alles möglich; **at the earliest ~ time** so früh wie möglich; *(formal)* zum frühestmöglichen Termin/Zeitpunkt; **they made it ~ for me to be here** sie haben es mir ermöglicht, hier zu sein; **the worst ~ solution** die denkbar schlechteste Lösung; die schlechteste der möglichen Lösungen; **if it's at all ~:** wenn es irgend geht *od.* möglich ist; **would it be ~ for me to ...?** könnte ich vielleicht ...?; **it is not ~ to do more** mehr kann man unmöglich tun; **for ~ emergencies** für eventuelle Notfälle; **all ~ risks** alle denkbaren Risiken; **I'll do everything ~ to help you** ich werde mein möglichstes *od.* alles nur Erdenkliche tun, um dir zu helfen; **be as kind to her as ~:** sei so nett zu ihr, wie [nur irgend] möglich; **we will help as far as ~:** wir werden helfen, soweit wir können; **b)** *(likely)* [durchaus *od.* gut] möglich; **few thought his election was ~:** nur wenige glaubten an seine Wahl; **c)** *(acceptable)* möglich; **there's no ~ excuse for it** dafür gibt es keine Entschuldigung; **the only ~ man for the position** der einzige Mann, der für die Stellung in Frage kommt. **2.** *n.* Anwärter, *der*/Anwärterin, *die;* Kandidat, *der*/Kandidatin, *die;* **presidential ~:** Präsidentschaftsanwärter, *der*

possibly ['pɒsɪblɪ] *adv.* **a)** *(by possible means)* **I cannot ~ commit myself** ich kann mich unmöglich festlegen; **how can I ~?** wie könnte ich?; **how could I ~ have come?** wie hätte ich denn kommen können?; **can that ~ be true?** kann das überhaupt wahr sein *od.* stimmen?; **they did all they ~ could** sie haben alles Menschenmögliche *od.* alles in ihrer Macht stehende getan; **if I ~ can** wenn es mir irgendwie möglich ist; **as often as I ~ can** sooft ich irgend kann; **I'll come as soon as I ~ can** ich komme so früh, wie es nur irgend geht; **can you ~ lend me £10?** kannst du mir vielleicht *od.* wohl 10 Pfund leihen?; **b)** *(perhaps)* möglicherweise; vielleicht; **he might ~ be related to them** er ist vielleicht *od.* möglicherweise mit ihnen verwandt; **Do you think ...? – P~:** Glaubst du ...? – Möglich[erweise] *od.* Vielleicht

possum ['pɒsəm] *n. (coll.)* **a)** *see* **opossum a; b) play ~** *(pretend to be asleep)* sich schlafend stellen; *(pretend to be dead)* sich tot stellen; **c)** *(Austral., NZ)* Fuchskusu, *der*

¹post [pəʊst] **1.** *n.* **a)** *(as support)* Pfosten, *der;* **b)** *(stake)* Pfahl, *der;* **deaf as a ~** *(coll.)* stocktaub *(ugs.); see also* **pillar a; c)** *(Racing)* **(starting/finishing ~)** Start-/Zielpfosten, *der;* **be left at the ~:** [hoffnungslos] abgehängt werden *(ugs.);* weit zurückbleiben; *(fig.)* von Anfang an keine Chancen haben; **be first past the ~:** als erster durchs Ziel gehen; **the 'first past the ~' system** das Mehrheitswahlsystem; **be beaten at the ~** *(lit. or fig.)* im letzten Moment noch geschlagen werden; *see also* **⁵pip; d)** *(Sport: of goal)* Pfosten, *der.* **2.** *v. t.* **a)** *(stick up)* anschlagen, ankleben ‹*Plakat, Aufruf, Notiz, Zettel*›; **~ something on the notice-board** einen Anschlag am Schwarzen Brett machen; **'~ no bills'** „Plakate ankleben verboten"; **b)** *(make known)* [öffentlich] anschlagen *od.* bekanntgeben; ausschreiben ‹*Belohnung*›; ausweisen ‹*Ansteigen, Gewinn, Verlust*›; öffentlich ankündigen, bekanntmachen ‹*Veranstaltung*›; **~ [as] missing** als vermißt melden; **c)** *(Amer.: achieve)* erreichen; schaffen; erringen ‹*Sieg*›

~ 'up *v. t.* anschlagen; ankleben; **~ up a notice** einen Anschlag machen

²post 1. *n.* **a)** *(Brit.: one dispatch of letters)* Postausgang, *der;* **by the same ~:** mit gleicher Post; **by return of ~:** postwendend; **sort the ~:** die Postausgänge sortieren; **b)** *(Brit.: one collection of letters)* [Briefkasten]leerung, *die;* **c)** *(Brit.: one delivery of letters)* Post[zustellung], *die;* **in the ~:** bei der Post (*see also* **d**); **the ~ has come** die Post ist da *od.* ist schon gekommen; **the arrival of the ~:** das Eintreffen der Briefpost; **sort the ~:** die Posteingänge sortieren; **is there a second ~ in this area?** gibt es hier eine zweite Postzustellung?; **there is no ~ on Sundays** sonntags kommt keine Post; **there has been no ~ today** heute ist keine Post gekommen; **is there any ~ for me?** habe ich Post?; **have a heavy ~:** viel Post bekommen; **the morning's ~:** die Morgenpost; **you'll get it in tomorrow's ~:** du bekommst es mit der morgigen Post; **d)** *no pl., no indef. art. (Brit.: official conveying)* Post, *die;* **by ~:** mit der Post; per Post; **in the ~:** in der Post (*see also* **c**); **e)** *(~ office)* Post, *die; (~-box)* Briefkasten, *der;* **take sth. to the ~:** etw. zur Post bringen/*(to ~-box)* etw. einwerfen *od.* in den Briefkasten werfen; **drop sth. in the ~:** etw. einwerfen *od.* in den Briefkasten werfen. **2.** *v. t.* **a)** *(dispatch)* abschicken; *(take to ~ office)* zur Post bringen; *(put in ~-box)* einwerfen; **~ sb. sth.** jmdm. etw. schicken; **~ sth. off** etw. abschicken; **b)** *(Bookk.)* übertragen; **~ up** auf den letzten Stand bringen ‹*Bücher*›; verbuchen ‹*Verkäufe, Abschlüsse*›; **c)** *(fig. coll.)* **keep sb. ~ed [about** *or* **on sth.]** jmdn. [über etw. *(Akk.)*] auf dem laufenden halten

³post 1. *n.* **a)** *(job)* Stelle, *die;* Posten, *der;* **in ~:** im Amt; **a teaching ~:** eine Stelle als Lehrer *od.* Lehrerstelle; **a ~ as director** ein Posten als Direktor *od.* Direktorenposten; **the ~ of driver** die Stelle des Fahrers; **a diplomatic ~:** ein diplomatischer Posten; **b)** *(Mil.: place of duty)* Posten, *der; (fig.)* Platz, *der;* Posten, *der;* **the sentries are at/took up their ~s** die Wachen sind auf ihren/bezogen ihre Posten; **take up one's ~** *(fig.)* seinen Platz einnehmen; **all workers must be at their ~s by 8.30** alle Arbeiter müssen um 8.30 Uhr an ihren Arbeitsplätzen sein; **last/first ~** *(Brit. Mil.)* letzter/erster Zapfenstreich; **c)** *(Mil.: position of unit)* Garnison, *die;* Standort, *der;* **d)** *(Mil.: fort)* Fort, *das;* **e)** *(trading-~)* Niederlassung, *die.* **2.** *v. t.* **a)** *(place)* postieren; aufstellen; **b)** *(appoint)* einsetzen; **~ sb. overseas/to Abu Dhabi/to a ship** jmdn. in Übersee/in Abu Dhabi/auf einem Schiff einsetzen; **be ~ed to an embassy** an eine Botschaft versetzt werden; **~ an officer to a unit** einen Offizier einer Einheit *(Dat.)* zuweisen; **be ~ed away** versetzt *od. (Mil.)* abkommandiert werden; **where's he being ~ed to?** wo wird er eingesetzt?; *(to new place)* wohin wird er versetzt?

post- [pəʊst] *pref.* nach-/Nach-; post-/Post- *(mit Fremdwörtern)*

postage ['pəʊstɪdʒ] *n.* Porto, *das*

postage: ~ 'due *n.* Nachgebühr, *die;* **~-due stamp** Portomarke, *die;* **~ meter** *n. (Amer.)* Frankiermaschine, *die;* [Post]freistempler, *der;* **~ stamp** *n.* Briefmarke, *die;* Postwertzeichen, *das (Postw.)*

postal ['pəʊstl] *adj.* **a)** *(of the post)* Post-; postalisch ⟨*Aufgabe, Einrichtung*⟩; **b)** *(by post)* per Post *nachgestellt;* **~ tuition** Fernunterricht, *der*

postal: ~ card *(Amer.) see* **postcard; ~ code** *see* **postcode; ~ district** *n.* Zustellbezirk, *der;* **~ meter** *n. (Amer.) see* **postage meter; ~ order** *n.* ≈ Postanweisung, *die;* **~ rate** *n.* Postgebühr, *die;* **P~ Union** *n.* Postverein, *der;* **~ vote** *n.* Briefwahl, *die*

post: ~-bag *(Brit.) see* **mail-bag; ~-box** *n. (Brit.)* Briefkasten, *der;* **~card** *n.* Postkarte, *die;* **~-chaise** *n. (Hist.)* Postchaise, *die*

post-'classic[al] *adj.* nachklassisch

'postcode *n. (Brit.)* Postleitzahl, *die*

post-'date *v. t.* **a)** *(give later date to)* vordatieren; **b)** *(belong to later date than)* später *od.* jüngeren Datums sein als (+ *Nom.*); von einem späteren Zeitpunkt/aus einer späteren Zeit datieren als (+ *Nom.*)

post-'doctoral *adj.* **~ thesis/grant** Habilitationsschrift, *die*/-stipendium, *das;* **~ research** *Forschungen im Anschluß an die Promotion*

poster ['pəʊstə(r)] *n.* **a)** *(placard)* Plakat, *das; (notice)* Anschlag, *der;* **b)** *(printed picture)* Plakat, *das;* Poster, *das*

'poster colour *see* **poster paint**

poste restante [pəʊst re'stɑ̃t] *n.* Abteilung/Schalter für postlagernde Sendungen; **write to sb. [at the] ~ in Rome** jmdm. postlagernd nach Rom schreiben

posterior [pɒ'stɪərɪə(r)] **1.** *adj.* **a)** *(formal: later)* später; **~ to** nach; **b)** *(placed behind)* hinter... **2.** *n. (joc.)* Hinterteil, *das (ugs.)*

posterity [pɒ'sterɪtɪ] *n., no pl., no art. (future generations)* die Nachwelt; **go down to ~ [as sth.]** [als etw.] in die Geschichte eingehen

'poster paint *n.* Plakatfarbe, *die*

post: ~ exchange *n. (Amer. Mil.)* PX, *das; Kaufhaus für Angehörige der amerikanischen Truppen;* **~-'free** *(Brit.)* **1.** *adj.* **a)** *(free of charge)* portofrei; **b)** *(with postage prepaid)* freigemacht; frankiert; **2.** *adv.* portofrei

post-grad [pəʊst'græd] *(coll.),* **post-'graduate 1.** *adj.* Graduierten-; ⟨*College, Studiengang*⟩ für Graduierte; postgraduell *(fachspr.);* **~ study** ≈ Aufbaustudium, *das;* ≈ *weiterführendes Studium;* **~ student** Graduierte, *der/die;* **~ degree** höherer akademischer Grad. **2.** *n.* Graduierte, *der/die*

post: ~-'haste *adv.* schnellstens; **~-horn** *n. (Hist.)* Posthorn, *das;* **~-horse** *n. (Hist.)* Postpferd, *das;* **~ house** *n. (Hist.)* Poststation, *die*

posthumous ['pɒstjʊməs] *adj.* **a)** nachgelassen, *(geh.)* postum ⟨*Buch usw.*⟩; **b)** *(occurring after death)* nachträglich; post[h]um *(geh.);* **~ fame** Nachruhm, *der;* **c)** nach dem Tode des Vaters geboren, post[h]um *(geh.)* ⟨*Kind*⟩

posthumously ['pɒstjʊməslɪ] *adv.* postum *(geh.),* nach dem Tode ⟨*veröffentlicht werden*⟩; postum *(geh.),* nachträglich ⟨*rehabilitieren, verleihen*⟩; nach dem Tode des Vaters ⟨*geboren*⟩

postil[l]ion [pə'stɪljən] *n. (Hist.)* Postillion, *der*

post-im'pressionism *n.* Nachimpressionismus, *der*

post-im'pressionist *n.* Nachimpressionist, *der*/Nachimpressionistin, *die*

post-impression'istic *adj.* nachimpressionistisch

post-in'dustrial *adj.* postindustriell

posting ['pəʊstɪŋ] *n. (appointment)* Versetzung, *die; (post)* Stelle, *die;* Posten, *der;* **he's got a new ~:** er ist versetzt worden

post: ~man ['pəʊstmən], *pl.* **~men** ['pəʊstmən] *n.* Briefträger, *der;* Postbote, *der (ugs.);* **~man's 'knock** *n. (Brit.) Gesellschaftsspiel, bei dem der 'Postbote' Briefe gegen einen Kuß aushändigt;* **~mark 1.** *n.* Poststempel, *der;* **'date as ~mark'** „Datum des Poststempels"; **2.** *v. t.* abstempeln; **the letter was ~marked 'Brighton'** der Brief war in Brighton abgestempelt; **~master** *n.* Postamtvorsteher, *der;* Postmeister, *der (veralt.);* **P~master 'General** *n., pl.* **P~masters General** *(Hist.)* Postminister, *der*/-ministerin, *die;* **~-mill** *n.* Bockmühle, *die;* **~mistress** *n.* Postamtvorsteherin, *die;* Postmeisterin, *die (veralt.)*

post-'modernism *n.* Postmoderne, *die*

post-mortem [pəʊst'mɔːtəm] **1.** *adv.* nach dem Tode; post mortem *(fachspr.).* **2.** *adj.* **a)** *(after death)* nach dem Tode eintretend, *(fachspr., geh.)* postmortal ⟨*Veränderung*⟩; **~ examination** Leichenschau, *die; (with dissection)* Obduktion, *die;* **b)** *(fig.: after an event)* nachträglich. **3.** *n.* **a)** *(examination)* Obduktion, *die;* **b)** *(fig.)* nachträgliche Bewertung *od.* Analyse; Manöverkritik, *die (fig.);* **hold** *or* **have a ~ on sth.** etw. einer nachträglichen Bewertung *od.* Analyse unterziehen; **hold a ~ on the election** eine Wahlanalyse durchführen; das Wahlergebnis einer Analyse *(Dat.)* unterziehen

post-'natal *adj.* nach der Geburt *nachgestellt;* nachgeburtlich *(fachspr.);* postnatal *(fachspr.)*

post: ~ office *n.* **a)** *(organization)* **the P~ Office** die Post; *attrib.* **P~ Office** Post-; **work for the P~ Office** bei der Post arbeiten; **b)** *(place)* Postamt, *das;* Post, *die;* **c)** *(Amer.) see* **~man's knock; ~-office box** *n.* Postfach, *das;* **~-paid 1.** ['--] *adj.* frankiert; freigemacht; **~-paid envelope** Freiumschlag, *der;* **2.** [-'-] *adv.* portofrei; franko *(fachspr. veralt.);* **£6.50 ~-paid** 6,50 Pfund einschließlich Porto; **reply ~-paid** mit vorfrankiertem Umschlag/mit vorfrankierter Postkarte antworten

postpone [pəʊst'pəʊn, pə'spəʊn] *v. t.* verschieben; *(for an indefinite period)* aufschieben; **~ sth. until next week** etw. auf nächste Woche verschieben; **~ sth. for a year** etw. um ein Jahr verschieben; **~ further discussion of a matter** die weitere Diskussion einer Angelegenheit zurückstellen

postponement [pəʊst'pəʊnmənt, pə'spəʊnmənt] *n.* Verschiebung, *die; (for an indefinite period)* Aufschub, *der;* **a 30-day ~:** eine Verschiebung um 30 Tage

postpositive [pəʊst'pɒzɪtɪv] *adj. (Ling.)* nachgestellt; postpositiv *(fachspr.)*

postprandial [pəʊst'prændɪəl] *adj. (formal/joc.)* Verdauungs⟨*schläfchen, -spaziergang, -schnaps*⟩ *(ugs.);* ⟨*Rede, Gespräch, Schwatz*⟩ nach dem Essen, nach Tisch

'post-room *n.* Poststelle, *die*

postscript ['pəʊstskrɪpt, 'pəʊskrɪpt] *n.* Nachschrift, *die;* Postskript, *das; (fig.)* Nachtrag, *der;* **the ~ was that ...** *(fig.)* das Ende vom Lied war, daß ... *(ugs.);* **add a ~** *(fig.)* einen Nachtrag machen, etwas nachtragen **(to zu)**

post-'tax *adj.* nach Abzug der Steuern *(nachgestellt)*

'post-town *n.* Postort, *der*

postulate 1. ['pɒstjʊleɪt] *v. t. (claim as true, existent, necessary)* postulieren; ausgehen von; *(depend on)* voraussetzen; *(put forward)* aufstellen ⟨*Theorie*⟩. **2.** ['pɒstjʊlət] *n. (fundamental condition)* Postulat, *das (geh.); (prerequisite)* Voraussetzung, *die;* Postulat, *das (geh.); (Math.)* Axiom, *das*

posture ['pɒstʃə(r)] **1.** *n. (relative position)* [Körper]haltung, *die; (fig.: mental, political, military)* Haltung, *die;* **have poor/good ~:** eine schlechte/gute Haltung haben; **put the country in a ~ of defence** das Land in Verteidigungsbereitschaft versetzen. **2.** *v. i.* posieren; *(strike a pose)* sich in Positur werfen *(ugs., leicht spött.)*

'post-war *adj.* Nachkriegs-; der Nachkriegszeit *nachgestellt;* **~ credits** Kriegsanleihen

'postwoman *n.* Briefträgerin, *die;* Postbotin, *die (ugs.)*

posy ['pəʊzɪ] *n.* Sträußchen, *das*

¹pot [pɒt] **1.** *n.* **a)** *(cooking-vessel)* [Koch]topf, *der;* **it's [a case of] the ~ calling the kettle black** *(coll.)* ein Esel schimpft *od. (geh.)* schilt den andern Langohr; der soll/die soll/die sollen sich an die eigene Nase fassen *(ugs.);* **go to ~** *(coll.)* den Bach runtergehen *(ugs.);* **let oneself go to ~** *(coll.)* sich hängen lassen [und den Bach runtergehen] *(ugs.); see also* **¹boil 1a; ¹pan 1a; b)** *(container, contents)* Topf, *der; (teapot, coffee-pot)* Kanne, *die;* **a ~ of tea** eine Kanne Tee; *(in café etc.)* ein Kännchen Tee; *see also* **gold 1b; c)** *(drinking-vessel)* Becher, *der; (with handle)* Krug, *der;* **d)** *(coll.: as prize)* Pott, *der (ugs.);* **e)** *(sl.: prize)* Preis, *der;* **f)** *(coll.: pot-belly)* Schmerbauch, *der (ugs.);* Wampe, *die (ugs. abwertend);* **g)** *(coll.: large sum)* **a ~ of/~s of** massenweise; jede Menge; **h)** *(amount bet)* [Gesamt]einsatz, *der;* Pot, *der;* **contribute to the ~:** [ein]setzen. **2.** *v. t.,* **-tt-: a)** *(put in container[s])* in einen Topf/in Töpfe füllen; **b)** *(put in plant-~)* **~ [up]** eintopfen; **~ out** austopfen; **c)** *(kill)* abschießen; abknallen *(ugs. abwertend);* **d)** *(Brit. Billiards, Snooker)* einlochen. *See also* **potted. 3.** *v. i.,* **-tt-** ballern *(ugs.)* **(at** auf + *Akk.*)

²pot *n. (sl.: marijuana)* Pot, *das (Jargon)*

potable ['pəʊtəbl] *adj. (formal)* trinkbar

potash ['pɒtæʃ] *n.* Kaliumkarbonat, *das;* Pottasche, *die (veralt.);* **~ fertilizer** Kalidünger, *der*

potassium [pə'tæsɪəm] *n. (Chem.)* Kalium, *das*

potato [pə'teɪtəʊ] *n., pl.* **~es a)** Kartoffel, *die;* **a hot ~** *(fig. coll.)* ein heißes Eisen *(ugs.);* **drop sb./sth. like a hot ~** *(coll.)* jmdn./etw. fallen lassen wie eine heiße Kartoffel; *see also* **bake 1a; boil 2a; chip 2b; crisp 2a; ¹fry 2; mash 1d, 2; b)** *(plant)* Kartoffel[pflanze], *die*

potato 'salad *n.* Kartoffelsalat, *der*

pot: ~-belly *n.* **a)** *(bulging belly)* Schmerbauch, *der (ugs.);* Wampe, *die (ugs. abwertend); (from malnutrition)* Blähbauch, *der;* **b)** *(person)* Dickbauch, *der (scherzh.);* Dickwanst, *der (salopp abwertend);* **~-boiler** *n. (derog.) (novel etc.)* Fließbandprodukt, *das (abwertend); (film, theatre production)* Fließbandproduktion, *die (abwertend)*

potency ['pəʊtənsɪ] *n.* **a)** *(of drug)* Wirksamkeit, *die; (of alcoholic drink)* Stärke, *die; (Mil.)* Schlagkraft, *die; (of reason, argument)* Gewichtigkeit, *die; (influence)* Einfluß, *der;* Potenz, *die (geh.);* **the ~ to do sth.** die Fähigkeit, etw. zu tun; **b)** *(of male)* **[sexual]** ~: [sexuelle] Potenz

potent ['pəʊtənt] *adj.* **a)** [hoch]wirksam ⟨*Droge, Medizin*⟩; stark ⟨*Schnaps, Kaffee, Tee usw.*⟩; schlagkräftig ⟨*Mannschaft, Truppe, Waffe*⟩; gewichtig, schwerwiegend ⟨*Grund, Argument*⟩; wichtig, entscheidend ⟨*Faktor*⟩; stark ⟨*Motiv*⟩; *(influential)* einflußreich; potent *(geh.);* **b)** *(sexually)* potent ⟨*Mann*⟩

potentate ['pəʊtənteɪt] *n.* Herrscher, *der*/Herrscherin, *die;* Potentat, *der*/Potentatin, *die (geh. abwertend)*

potential [pə'tenʃl] **1.** *adj.* potentiell *(geh.);* möglich; ~ **energy** potentielle Energie. **2.** *n.* **a)** *(possibility)* Potential, *das (geh.);* Möglichkeiten; ~ **for growth/development** Wachstums-/Entwicklungspotential, *das;* **acting** ~: schauspielerisches Talent; **leadership** ~: Führungsqualitäten; **realize/reach one's** ~: seine Möglichkeiten ausschöpfen; **develop one's** ~: seine Fähigkeiten [weiter]entwickeln; **b)** *(Phys.)* Potential, *das*

potentiality [pətenʃɪ'ælɪtɪ] *n.* **a)** *(capacity)* Möglichkeiten; **have great growth** ~: ein großes Wachstumspotential haben; **b)** *(possibility)* Möglichkeit, *die*

potentially [pə'tenʃəlɪ] *adv.* potentiell *(geh.);* **he's ~ dangerous** er kann gefährlich werden; **a ~ useful invention** eine Erfindung mit Anwendungsmöglichkeiten; **he's ~ capable of it** er wäre dazu fähig; **a ~ rich country** ein Land, das reich sein könnte

potentilla [pəʊtən'tɪlə] *n. (Bot.)* Fingerkraut, *das*

pot: ~-head *n. (sl.)* Kiffer, *der*/Kifferin, *die (ugs.);* **~-herb** *n.* Küchenkraut, *das;* **~-hole 1.** *n.* **a)** *(in road)* Schlagloch, *das;* **b)** *(deep cave)* [tiefe] Höhle; **2.** *v. i.* Höhlen erkunden; **~-holer** ['pɒthəʊlə(r)] *n.* [Hobby]höhlenforscher, *der*/-forscherin, *die;* **~-holing** ['pɒthəʊlɪŋ] *n.* Erkundung von Höhlen; **go ~-holing** Höhlen erkunden gehen; Höhlenfahrten/eine Höhlenfahrt machen *(fachspr.);* **~-hunter** *n.* **a)** *(hunter)* Jäger, der alles abschießt[, was ihm vor die Flinte kommt] *(abwertend);* **b)** *(athlete)* Pokalsammler, *der*/-sammlerin, *die*

potion ['pəʊʃn] *n.* Trank, *der*

pot: ~ 'luck *n.* **take ~ luck [with sb.]** sich überraschen lassen; **there are so many to choose from; I'll just take ~ luck** die Auswahl ist so groß; ich greife einfach mal aufs Geratewohl *od.* blind einen/eine/eins raus; **~ plant** *n.* Topfpflanze, *die*

pot-pourri [pəʊpʊə'ri:, pəʊ'pʊərɪ] *n.* **a)** Duftmischung, *die;* **b)** *(fig.) (of music)* Potpourri, *das; (of literary writings)* Sammlung, *die;* Anthologie, *die (Literaturw.); (mixture)* Sammelsurium, *das;* buntes Allerlei

pot: ~-roast 1. *n.* Schmorbraten, *der;* **2.** *v. t.* schmoren; **~sherd** ['pɒtʃɜ:d] *n. (Archaeol.)* [Ton]scherbe, *die;* **~-shot** *n.* **a)** *(random shot)* Schuß aufs Geratewohl; **take a ~-shot [at sb./sth.]** aufs Geratewohl [auf jmdn./etw.] schießen; **b)** *(fig.: critical remark)* Attacke, *die;* **take a ~-shot at sth.** etw. attackieren; **c)** *(fig.: random attempt)* Versuch auf gut Glück; Schuß ins Blaue [hinein]

pottage ['pɒtɪdʒ] *see* **mess 1 e**

potted ['pɒtɪd] *adj.* **a)** *(preserved)* eingemacht; ~ **meat/fish** Fleisch-/Fischkonserven; **b)** *(planted)* Topf-; **c)** kurzgefaßt; *(derog.: easily assimilated)* für schlichtere Gemüter *nachgestellt;* **a ~ biography/history of England** eine Kurzbiographie/ein Abriß der Geschichte Englands

¹potter ['pɒtə(r)] *n.* Töpfer, *der*/Töpferin, *die*

²potter *v. i.* [he]rumwerkeln *(ugs.);* **~ round the shops** durch die Geschäfte bummeln; **~ along the road** ⟨*Autofahrer:*⟩ gemütlich die Straße entlangzuckeln; **~ [about] in the garden** sich *(Dat.)* im Garten zu schaffen machen

~ a'bout, ~ a'round *v. i.* herumwerkeln *(ugs.)* **(with** an + *Dat.*); **~ about in a canoe** in einem Kanu herumpaddeln; **~ about in the garden** *see* ²~

potter's 'wheel *n.* Töpferscheibe, *die*

pottery ['pɒtərɪ] *n.* **a)** *no pl., no indef. art. (vessels)* Töpferware, *die;* Keramik, *die; attrib.* Ton-; Keramik-; **b)** *(workshop)* Töpferei, *die;* **c)** *no pl., no indef. art. (craft)* Töpferei, *die*

potting-shed ['pɒtɪŋʃed] *n. (Brit.)* Gewächshaus [zum Vorziehen von Pflanzen]

¹potty ['pɒtɪ] *adj. (Brit. sl.: crazy)* verrückt *(ugs.)* **(about,** on nach); **he's driving me ~:** er macht mich wahnsinnig *(ugs.);* **they've gone ~:** sie sind [völlig] übergeschnappt *(ugs.)*

²potty *n. (Brit. coll.)* Töpfchen, *das;* **be ~-trained** aufs Töpfchen gehen

pouch [paʊtʃ] *n.* **a)** *(small bag)* Tasche, *die;* Täschchen, *das; (worn on belt)* Gürteltasche, *die; (draw-string bag)* Beutel, *der;* **b)** *(under eye)* [Tränen]sack, *der;* **c)** *(ammunition-bag)* [Patronen]tasche, *die;* **d)** *(mail-bag)* Postsack, *der;* Postbeutel, *der; (diplomatic bag)* Kuriertasche, *die;* **e)** *(Zool.) (of marsupial)* Beutel, *der; (of pelican)* Kehlsack, *der*

pouffe [pu:f] *n. (cushion)* Sitzpolster, *das;* Puff, *der*

poulterer ['pəʊltərə(r)] *n.* Geflügelhändler, *der*/-händlerin, *die; see also* **baker**

poultice ['pəʊltɪs] **1.** *n.* Breiumschlag, *der;* Breipackung, *die.* **2.** *v. t.* einen Breiumschlag auflegen auf (+ *Akk.*)

poultry ['pəʊltrɪ] *n.* **a)** *constr. as pl. (birds)* Geflügel, *das;* **b)** *no pl., no indef. art. (as food)* Geflügel, *das. See also* **farm 1 a; farmer**

pounce [paʊns] **1.** *v. i.* **a)** sich auf sein Opfer stürzen; **~ [up]on** sich stürzen auf (+ *Akk.*); ⟨*Raubvogel:*⟩ herabstoßen auf (+ *Akk.*); **be ~d upon by sb.** von jmdm. angefallen werden; **b)** *(fig.)* **~ [up]on/at** sich stürzen auf (+ *Akk.*); **then we'll ~!** dann schlagen wir zu!. **2.** *n.* Sprung, *der;* Satz, *der;* **make a ~ on sb.** sich auf jmdn. stürzen

¹pound [paʊnd] *n.* **a)** *(unit of weight)* [britisches] Pfund *(453,6 Gramm);* **two ~s of apples** 2 Pfund Äpfel; **by the ~:** pfundweise; **it's 20 pence a ~:** es kostet 20 Pence das Pfund; **two-~:** Zwei-Pfund-⟨*Dose, Brot, Packung*⟩; zweipfündig, zwei Pfund schwer ⟨*Kugel, Kohlkopf*⟩; **exact** *or* **demand one's ~ of flesh** *(fig.)* sein Recht rücksichtslos verlangen; **b)** *(unit of currency)* Pfund, *das;* **five-~ note** Fünfpfundnote, *die;* Fünfpfundschein, *der;* **it must have cost ~s** das muß eine schöne Stange Geld gekostet haben *(ugs.);* **[it's] a ~ to a penny** *(fig. coll.)* es ist so gut wie sicher; ich wette hundert zu eins

²pound *n. (enclosure)* Pferch, *der; (for stray dogs)* Zwinger [für eingefangene Hunde]; *(for cars)* Abstellplatz [für polizeilich abgeschleppte Fahrzeuge]

³pound 1. *v. t.* **a)** *(crush)* zerstoßen; zerdrücken ⟨*Tomaten*⟩; **b)** *(thump)* einschlagen auf (+ *Akk.*) ⟨*Person*⟩; herumhämmern auf (+ *Dat.*) *(ugs.)* ⟨*Klavier, Tisch, Schreibmaschine*⟩; klopfen ⟨*Fleisch*⟩; ⟨*Sturm:*⟩ heimsuchen ⟨*Gebiet, Insel*⟩; ⟨*Wellen:*⟩ klatschen auf (+ *Akk.*) ⟨*Strand, Ufer*⟩, gegen *od.* an (+ *Akk.*) ⟨*Felsen, Schiff*⟩; ⟨*Geschütz:*⟩ unter Beschuß *(Akk.)* nehmen ⟨*Ziel*⟩; ⟨*Bombenflugzeug:*⟩ bombardieren ⟨*Ziel*⟩; **~ sb./sth. with one's fists** jmdn./etw. mit den Fäusten bearbeiten *od.* traktieren; **the ship was ~ed by the waves** die Wellen klatschten gegen das Schiff; **~ the beat** *(coll.)* ⟨*Polizist:*⟩ zu Fuß seine Runde machen; **c)** *(knock)* **~ to pieces** ⟨*Wellen:*⟩ zertrümmern, zerschmettern ⟨*Schiff*⟩; ⟨*Geschütz, Bomben:*⟩ in Trümmer legen ⟨*Stadt, Mauern*⟩; **d)** *(compress)* **~ [down]** feststampfen ⟨*Erde, Boden*⟩; *(by treading)* festtreten. **2.** *v. i.* **a)** *(make one's way heavily)* stampfen; **b)** *(beat rapidly)* ⟨*Herz:*⟩ heftig schlagen *od.* klopfen *od. (geh.)* pochen; **c)** *(strike)* ⟨*See, Brandung:*⟩ donnern; **~ away** ⟨*Artillerie:*⟩ donnern; **~ at/on** herumhämmern auf (+ *Dat.*) *(ugs.)* ⟨*Klavier, Tisch, Schreibmaschine*⟩

~ a'way at *v. t.* unter schweren [ständigen] Beschuß nehmen ⟨*Feind, Stadt*⟩; *(fig.)* herumhämmern auf (+ *Dat.*) *(ugs.)* ⟨*Klavier, Schreibmaschine usw.*⟩; *(work at)* ackern an (+ *Dat.*) *(ugs.)*

~ 'out *v. t. (on typewriter)* herunterhämmern *(ugs.)* ⟨*Brief, Aufsatz*⟩; *(on piano)* hämmern *(ugs.)* ⟨*Lied, Stück*⟩; **~ out sth. on the typewriter** etw. in die [Schreib]maschine hämmern

poundage ['paʊndɪdʒ] *n.* **a)** *(per pound of weight)* Gebühr [pro Pfund]; **b)** *(per pound sterling) (charge, fee)* Gebühr, *die; (commission)* Provision [pro Pfund]

-pounder ['paʊndə(r)] *n. in comb.* -pfünder, *der*

pounding ['paʊndɪŋ] *n.* **a)** *(striking) (of hammer etc.)* Schlagen, *das;* Klopfen, *das; (of artillery)* [schwerer] Beschuß; *(of waves)* Klatschen, *das;* **the ship took a ~ from the waves** das Schiff wurde von den Wellen kräftig durchgeschüttelt; **our team took a ~:** unsere Mannschaft mußte eine Schlappe einstecken *(ugs.);* **his play took a ~ from the critics** sein Stück wurde von den Kritikern verrissen; **b)** *(of hooves, footsteps)* Stampfen, *das; (of train)* Rumpeln, *das;* **c)** *(beating) (of heart)* Klopfen, *das;* Pochen, *das (geh.); (of music, drums)* Dröhnen, *das*

pound 'note *n. (Hist.)* Pfundnote, *die;* Pfundschein, *der*

'pound[s] sign *n.* Pfundzeichen, *das*

pour [pɔ:(r)] **1.** *v. t.* **a)** gießen, schütten ⟨*Flüssigkeit*⟩; schütten ⟨*Sand, Kies, Getreide usw.*⟩; *(into drinking-vessel)* einschenken; eingießen; **~ a bucket of water over sb.'s head** jmdm. einen Eimer Wasser über den Kopf gießen *od.* schütten; **~ water over the flowers** die Blumen wässern *od.* [mit Wasser] gießen; **they ~ed beer all over him** sie übergossen ihn mit Bier; **~ scorn** *or* **ridicule on sb./sth.** jmdn. mit Spott übergießen *od.* überschütten/über etw. *(Akk.)* spotten; **~ oil on the flames** *(fig.)* Öl ins Feuer gießen; **~ oil on troubled waters** *or* **the water** *(fig.)* Öl auf die Wogen gießen; *see also* **water 1 a; b)** *(discharge)* ⟨*Fluß:*⟩ ergießen *(geh.)* ⟨*Wasser*⟩; *(fig.)* pumpen ⟨*Geld, Geschosse*⟩. **2.** *v. i.* **a)** *(flow)* strömen; ⟨*Rauch:*⟩ hervorquellen **(from** aus); **sweat was ~ing off the runners** den Läufern lief der Schweiß in Strömen herunter; **~ [with rain]** in Strömen regnen; [in Strömen] gießen *(ugs.);* **it never rains but it ~s** *(fig.)* da kommt aber auch alles zusammen; **b)** *(fig.)* strömen; **~ in** herein-/hineinströmen; **~ out** heraus-/hinausströmen; **tourists/refugees ~ into the city** Touristen/Flüchtlinge strömen in Scharen in die Stadt; **~ out of** strömen aus; *(fig.)* ⟨*Menge, Personen:*⟩ strömen aus ⟨*Gebäude, Halle*⟩; ⟨*Musik:*⟩ schallen aus ⟨*Musikbox*⟩; ⟨*Propaganda:*⟩ tönen aus ⟨*Lautsprecher*⟩; **the crowd ~ed out of the doors** die Menge strömte durch die Türen hinaus; **cars ~ed along the road** ein [endloser] Strom von Autos flutete über die Straße; **letters/protests ~ed in** eine Flut von Briefen/Protesten brach herein

~ 'down *v. i.* **it's ~ing down** es gießt [in Strömen] *(ugs.);* **the rain ~ed down** es regnete in Strömen

~ 'forth 1. *v. t.* von sich geben; erklingen lassen ⟨*Lied*⟩; ausschütten ⟨*Kummer*⟩; erzählen ‹*Geschichte*›. **2.** *v. i.* ‹*Gesang, Musik usw.*:› ertönen, erklingen; ‹*Menge, Personen*:› herausströmen

~ **'off** *v. t.* abgießen

~ **'out 1.** *v. t.* eingießen, einschenken ‹*Getränk*›; ‹*Fabrik*:› ausstoßen ‹*Produkte*›; ‹*Sender*:› in den Äther schicken ‹*Musik usw.*›; **the chimney was ~ing out smoke** aus dem Schornstein quoll Rauch; **~ out one's thanks** sich überschwenglich bedanken; **~ out a torrent of words** eine Flut von Worten von sich geben *od.* hervorsprudeln lassen; **~ out one's woes** *or* **troubles/heart to sb.** jmdm. seinen Kummer/sein Herz ausschütten; **~ out one's feelings** seinen Gefühlen Luft machen *od.* Ausdruck geben; **~ out one's story to sb.** [jmdm.] seine Geschichte erzählen. **2.** *v. i. see* ~ **2 b**

pouring ['pɔ:rɪŋ] *adj.* **a)** strömend ‹*Regen*›; **a ~ wet day** ein völlig verregneter Tag; **b)** *(for dispensing)* Gieß-; *(for being poured)* flüssig

pout [paʊt] **1.** *v. i.* **a)** einen Schmollmund machen *od.* ziehen; **~ing lips** Schmollippen *Pl.*; **his mouth ~ed** er zog einen Schmollmund; **b)** *(sulk)* schmollen. **2.** *v. t.* **a)** *(protrude)* aufwerfen, schürzen ‹*Lippen*›; **b)** *(say)* schmollend sagen; schmollen. **3.** *n.* Schmollmund, *der;* **have the** *or* **be in the ~s** schmollen; im Schmollwinkel sitzen *(ugs.)*

poverty ['pɒvətɪ] *n.* **a)** Armut, *die;* **plead ~:** behaupten, kein Geld zu haben; **fall into ~:** in Armut *(Akk.)* geraten; **be reduced to ~:** verarmt sein; **b)** *(Relig.)* Armut, *die;* **c)** *(fig.: deficiency)* Armut, *die* **(in** an + *Dat.***)**; **~ of ideas** Ideenarmut, *die;* gedankliche Armut; **~ of the soil/the region** Kargheit des Bodens/der Gegend; **spiritual ~:** seelische Verelendung; **d)** *(inferiority) (of language, vocabulary)* Armut, *die;* **~ of imagination/intellect** Phantasielosigkeit, *die*/geistige Unzulänglichkeit

poverty: ~ line *n.* Armutsgrenze, *die;* **be on the ~ line** an der Armutsgrenze liegen; **~-stricken** *adj.* notleidend; verarmt; *(fig.)* armselig; kümmerlich; **~ trap** *n. soziale Situation, die dadurch gekennzeichnet ist, daß die Aufnahme einer Erwerbstätigkeit für den Betroffenen zu einer Verschlechterung seiner wirtschaftlichen Lage führen kann, weil er durch sie seinen Anspruch auf staatliche Sozialhilfe verlieren würde*

POW *abbr.* **prisoner of war**

pow [paʊ] *int.* peng

powder ['paʊdə(r)] **1.** *n.* **a)** Pulver, *das;* **b)** *(cosmetic)* Puder, *der;* **put ~ on one's face** sich *(Dat.)* das Gesicht pudern; **c)** *(medicine)* Pulver, *das;* **take a ~** *(Amer. fig. sl.)* die Flatter machen *(salopp)*; **d)** *(gun~)* Pulver, *das;* **keep one's ~ dry** *(fig. coll.)* sein Pulver trocken halten; **he/it is not worth ~ and shot** *(fig.)* er ist keinen Schuß Pulver wert *(ugs.)*/es ist die Mühe nicht wert. **2.** *v. t.* **a)** pudern; **I'll just go and ~ my nose** *(euphem.)* ich muß [nur] mal verschwinden *(ugs. verhüll.)*; **b)** *(reduce to ~)* pulverisieren; zu Pulver verarbeiten ‹*Milch, Eier*›; **~ed milk** Milchpulver, *das;* Trockenmilch, *die;* **~ed eggs** Eipulver, *das;* Trockenei, *das;* **~ed sugar** Puderzucker, *der*

powder: ~ 'blue *n.* **a)** *(for laundry)* Waschblau, *das;* **b)** *(colour)* Himmelblau, *das;* **~ compact** *see* [2]**compact a**

powdering ['paʊdərɪŋ] *n.* **a)** *(act)* [Ein]pudern, *das;* **b) a ~ of snow** eine dünne Schicht Schnee

powder: ~-keg *n. (lit. or fig.)* Pulverfaß, *das;* **~-magazine** *n.* Pulvermagazin, *das;* **~-puff** *n.* Puderquaste, *die;* **~-room** *n.* [Damen]toilette, *die;* **~ snow** *n.* Pulverschnee, *der*

powdery ['paʊdərɪ] *adj.* **a)** *(like powder)* pulv[e]rig; *(in powder form)* pulverförmig; *(finer)* pud[e]rig/puderförmig; **b)** *(crumbly)* bröckelig; bröselig

power [paʊə(r)] **1.** *n.* **a)** *(ability)* Kraft, *die;* **if they had the ~:** wenn sie könnten *od.* die Möglichkeit hätten; **do all in one's ~ to help sb.** alles in seiner Macht *od.* seinen Kräften Stehende tun, um jmdm. zu helfen; **be beyond** *or* **outside** *or* **not be within sb.'s ~:** nicht in jmds. Macht *(Dat.)* liegen; **b)** *(faculty)* Fähigkeit, *die;* Vermögen, *das (geh.)*; *(talent)* Begabung, *die;* Talent, *das;* **~ of smell** Riechvermögen, *das;* Geruchssinn, *der;* **tax sb.'s ~s to the utmost** ‹*Arbeit, Aufgabe*:› jmdn. bis an die Grenzen seiner Leistungsfähigkeit beanspruchen; **psychic ~s** übersinnliche Kräfte; **~s of observation** Beobachtungsgabe, *die;* **~s of persuasion** Überredungskünste; **c)** *(vigour, intensity) (of sun's rays)* Kraft, *die; (of sermon, performance)* Eindringlichkeit, *die; (solidity, physical strength)* Kraft, *die; (of a blow)* Wucht, *die;* **more ~ to you** *or* **your elbow!** viel Erfolg!; **have no ~** ‹*Schuß, Schlag*:› schwach *od.* kraftlos sein; **d)** *(authority)* Macht, *die,* Herrschaft, *die* **(over** über + *Akk.***)**; **have sth. in one's ~** ‹*Diktator*:› etw. in seiner Gewalt haben; die Herrschaft über etw. *(Akk.)* haben; **she was in his ~:** sie war in seiner Gewalt; er hatte sie in seiner Gewalt; **~ corrupts** Macht korrumpiert; **e)** *(personal ascendancy)* **[exercise/get] ~:** Einfluß [ausüben/gewinnen] **(over** auf + *Akk.***)**; **f)** *(political or social ascendancy)* Macht, *die;* **student/worker ~:** ≈ Mitbestimmung der Studenten/Arbeiter; **hold ~:** an der Macht sein; **fall from ~:** die Macht verlieren; ‹*Präsident*:› gestürzt werden; **come into ~:** an die Macht kommen; **the party in ~:** die herrschende Partei; die Partei an der Macht; **~ politics** Machtpolitik, *die;* **balance of ~:** Kräftegleichgewicht, *das;* **hold the balance of ~:** das Zünglein an der Waage sein; **g)** *(authorization)* Vollmacht, *die;* Befugnis, *die;* **~ to negotiate** Verhandlungsvollmacht, *die;* **exceed one's ~s** seine Kompetenzen *od.* Befugnisse überschreiten; *see also* **attorney a; h)** *(influential person)* Autorität, *die; (influential thing)* Machtfaktor, *der;* **be a real ~ in these circles** in diesen Kreisen großen Einfluß haben; **a ~ in the land** eine einflußreiche Macht; **be the ~ behind the throne** *(Polit.)* die graue Eminenz sein; **the ~s that be** die maßgeblichen Stellen; die da oben *(ugs.)*; **i)** *(State)* Macht, *die;* **four-~ conference** Viermächtekonferenz, *die;* **a sea/world ~:** eine See-/Weltmacht; *see also* **Great Power; j)** *(coll.: large amount)* Menge, *die (ugs.)*; **do sb. a ~ of good** jmdm. außerordentlich guttun; **k)** *(Math.)* Potenz, *die;* **3 to the ~ of 4** 3 hoch 4; **l)** *(mechanical, electrical)* Kraft, *die; (electric current)* Strom, *der; (of loudspeaker, transmitter)* Leistung, *die;* **under one's/its own ~:** mit eigener Kraft; **steam-~:** Dampfkraft, *die;* **turn off the ~:** den Strom ausschalten *od.* abstellen; **m)** *(capacity for force)* Leistung, *die; see also* **horsepower; n)** *(Optics)* **[magnifying] ~:** Vergrößerungskraft, *die;* [Brenn]stärke, *die;* **o)** *(deity)* Macht, *die;* **the ~s of darkness** die Mächte der Finsternis; **p)** *(of drug)* Wirkung, *die.* **2.** *v. t.* ‹*Treibstoff, Dampf, Strom, Gas*:› antreiben; ‹*Person*:› betreiben ‹*Maschine*›; ‹*Batterie*:› mit Energie versehen *od.* versorgen; **he ~ed the ball past the goalkeeper** *(fig.)* er hämmerte den Ball ins Netz. **3.** *v. i. (coll.)* rasen

power: ~ base *n.* **the unions are the party's ~ base** die Gewerkschaften sind die Stützen der Partei; **have one's ~ base in the Middle West** seine treueste Anhängerschaft im Mittelwesten haben; **~-boat** *n.* Motorboot, *das;* **~ brakes** *n. pl.* Servobremsen; **~ cable** *n.* Hochspannungsleitung, *die;* **~ cut** *n.* Stromsperre, *die;* Stromabschaltung, *die; (failure)* Stromausfall, *der;* **~-dive 1.** *n.* Sturzflug mit Vollgas, *der;* **2.** *v. i.* einen Sturzflug machen, ohne den Motor zu drosseln; **~ drill** *n.* elektrische Bohrmaschine; **~-driven** *adj.* motorbetrieben; **~ failure** *n.* Stromausfall, *der*

powerful ['paʊəfl] *adj.* **a)** *(strong)* stark; kräftig ‹*Tritt, Schlag, Tier, Geruch, Körperbau, Statur*›; heftig ‹*Gefühl, Empfindung*›; hell, strahlend ‹*Licht*›; scharf ‹*Verstand, Geist*›; überzeugend ‹*Redner, Schauspieler*›; eindringlich ‹*Buch, Rede*›; beeindruckend ‹*Film, Darstellung*›; **b)** *(influential)* mächtig ‹*Clique, Person, Stadt, Herrscher*›; wesentlich ‹*Faktor*›

powerfully ['paʊəfəlɪ] *adv.* kräftig ‹*gebaut*›; eindringlich ‹*predigen*›; **he was ~ attracted to her** sie übte eine starke Anziehungskraft auf ihn aus

power: ~-house *n.* **a)** *see* **power-station; b)** *(fig.)* treibende Kraft; **be an intellectual ~-house** intellektuell stets produktiv sein; **be a ~-house of ideas and energy** ‹*Person*:› ein einfallsreiches Energiebündel sein

powerless ['paʊəlɪs] *adj.* **a)** *(wholly unable)* machtlos; **be ~ to do sth.** nicht die Macht haben, etw. zu tun; **be ~ to help** nicht helfen können; **b)** *(without power)* machtlos; **~ in the hands of the enemy** hilflos in den Händen des Feindes; **leave sb. ~ against sth.** ‹*Gesetz*:› jmdn. machtlos gegen etw. machen; **leave sb. ~ to do sth.** ‹*Gesetz*:› jmdn. daran hindern *od.* es jmdm. unmöglich machen, etw. zu tun

powerlessly ['paʊəlɪslɪ] *adv.* machtlos ‹*zusehen, den Kopf schütteln*›

power: ~ pack *n.* Netzteil, *das;* Netzgerät, *das; (for camera flash)* Generatorteil, *das od. der;* **~ point** *n. (Brit.)* Steckdose, *die;* **~ saw** *n.* Motorsäge, *die;* **~-station** *n.* Kraftwerk, *das;* Elektrizitätswerk, *das;* **~ steering** *n.* Servolenkung, *die;* **~ stroke** *n.* Arbeitstakt, *der;* Arbeitshub, *der;* **~ supply** *n.* Energieversorgung, *die* **(to** *Gen.***)**

powwow ['paʊwaʊ] **1.** *n.* Pow-Wow, *das (Völkerk.)*; *(fig.)* Besprechung, *die.* **2.** *v. i. (fig.)* sich beraten

pox [pɒks] *n.* **a)** *(disease with pocks)* Pocken *Pl.*; Blattern *Pl. (veralt.)*; **a ~ on him!** *(arch.)* daß ihn die Pest hole! *(veralt.)*; **b)** *(coll.: syphilis)* Syphilis, *die;* Syph, *die od. der (salopp)*

p.p. [pi:'pi:] *abbr.* **by proxy** pp[a].

pp *abbr.* **pianissimo** pp

pp. *abbr.* **pages**

p.p.m. *abbr.* **parts per million** *(by volume)* mm^3/l; *(by weight)* mg/kg

PPS *abbr.* **second postscript** PPS

PR *abbr.* **a) proportional representation; b) public relations** PR; Public Relations; **~ man** Werbefachmann, *der;* PR-Mann, *der*

pr. *abbr.* **pair** P.

practicable ['præktɪkəbl] *adj.* **a)** *(feasible)* durchführbar ‹*Projekt, Idee, Plan*›; praktikabel ‹*Lösung, Vorschlag, Plan, Methode*›; **b)** *(usable)* befahrbar, passierbar ‹*Straße, Gelände*›

practical ['præktɪkl] **1.** *adj.* **a)** praktisch; **for all ~ purposes** praktisch; **be true for all ~ purposes** in der Praxis Gültigkeit haben; **b)** *(inclined to action)* praktisch veranlagt ‹*Person*›; praktisch ‹*Denkweise, Veranlagung, Einstellung*›; **~ man** Praktiker, *der;* **have a ~ approach/mind** praktisch an die Dinge herangehen; **c)** *(virtual)* tatsächlich ‹*Freiheit, Organisator*›; **d)** *(feasible)* möglich ‹*Alternative*›; praktikabel ‹*Alternative, Möglichkeit*›; *see also* **politics c. 2.** *n.* praktische Prüfung

practicality [præktɪ'kælɪtɪ] *n.* **a)** *no pl. (of plan)* Durchführbarkeit, *die; (of person)* praktische Veranlagung; **b)** *in pl. (practical details)* **the practicalities of the situation are that ...:** die Situation sieht praktisch so aus, daß ...; **deal in practicalities** sich mit praktischen Dingen befassen

practical: ~ **'joke** *n.* Streich, *der;* **play ~ jokes on sb.** jmdm. Streiche spielen; ~ **'joker** *n.* Witzbold, *der;* **be a ~ joker** anderen gern Streiche spielen
practically ['præktɪkəlɪ] *adv.* **a)** *(almost)* praktisch *(ugs.);* so gut wie; beinahe; **b)** *(in a practical manner)* praktisch; ~ **orientated course** praxisbezogener Kurs; ~ **speaking, I see no way out** ich sehe praktisch keinen Ausweg
'practical nurse *n. (Amer.)* praktisch ausgebildete, nicht examinierte Krankenschwester; Hilfsschwester, *die*
¹practice ['præktɪs] *n.* **a)** *(repeated exercise)* Praxis, *die;* Übung, *die;* **years of ~:** Jahre der Praxis; jahrelange Übung; **put in** *or* **do some/a lot of ~:** üben/viel üben; **after all the ~ he has had, he should ...:** nach so viel Übung sollte er ...; **it's all good ~** *(means of improving)* es ist alles Übung; ~ **makes perfect** *(prov.)* Übung macht den Meister; **be out of ~, not be in ~:** außer Übung sein; **be in ~:** in der Übung sein; **b)** *(spell)* Übungen *Pl.;* **piano ~:** Klavierüben, *das;* **do one's piano ~:** Klavier üben; **c)** *(work or business of doctor, lawyer, etc.)* Praxis, *die; see also* **general practice; d)** *(habitual action)* übliche Praxis; Gewohnheit, *die;* ~ **shows that ...:** die Erfahrung zeigt *od.* lehrt, daß ...; **make a ~ of doing sth.** es sich *(Dat.)* zur [An]gewohnheit machen, etw. zu tun; **good ~** *(satisfactory procedure)* gutes Vorgehen; gute Vorgehensweise; **e)** *(action)* Praxis, *die;* **the ~ tends to be different** in der Praxis sieht es gewöhnlich *od.* die Praxis sieht gewöhnlich anders aus; **actual ~:** Praxis, *die;* **in ~:** in der Praxis; in Wirklichkeit; **be quite useless in ~:** in der Praxis nutzlos sein; praktisch nutzlos sein; **put sth. into ~:** etw. in die Praxis umsetzen; **f)** *(custom)* Gewohnheit, *die;* **don't make a ~ of it** laß es nicht zur Gewohnheit werden; **regular ~:** Brauch, *der;* **it is the regular ~ to do sth.** es ist Brauch *od.* üblich, etw. zu tun; **g)** *(legal procedures)* **[legal] ~:** Gerichtspraxis, *die. See also* **sharp 1 f**
²practice, practiced, practicing *(Amer.) see* **practis-**
practise ['præktɪs] **1.** *v.t.* **a)** *(apply)* anwenden; praktizieren; **b)** *(be engaged in)* ausüben ‹*Beruf, Tätigkeit, Religion*›; ~ **gymnastics** Gymnastik treiben; ~ **medicine** [als Arzt] praktizieren; **c)** *(exercise oneself in)* trainieren in (+ *Dat.*) ‹*Sportart*›; ~ **the bicycle kick** den Fallrückzieher trainieren; ~ **the piano/flute** Klavier/Flöte üben; ~ **one's running** Lauftraining machen. **2.** *v.i.* üben
practised ['præktɪst] *adj.* geübt ‹*Person, Auge, Blick*›; erfahren, versiert, routiniert ‹*Person*›; **with [a] ~ eye** mit geübtem Blick; **with ~ skill** routiniert
practising ['præktɪsɪŋ] *adj.* praktizierend ‹*Arzt, Katholik, Anglikaner usw.*›; ~ **homosexual** aktiv Homosexueller; ~ **barrister** niedergelassener Anwalt
practitioner [præk'tɪʃənə(r)] *n.* Fachmann, *der;* Praktiker, *der*/Praktikerin, *die;* ~ **of the law, legal ~:** Anwalt, *der*/Anwältin, *die; see also* **general practitioner; medical practitioner**
praesidium [praɪ'sɪdɪəm] *see* **presidium**
pragmatic [præg'mætɪk] *adj.* pragmatisch
pragmatically [præg'mætɪkəlɪ] *adv.* pragmatisch; *as sentence-modifier* pragmatisch betrachtet
pragmatism ['prægmətɪzm] *n.* Pragmatismus, *der*
pragmatist ['prægmətɪst] *n.* Pragmatiker, *der*/Pragmatikerin, *die*
Prague [prɑːg] *pr. n.* Prag *(das)*
prairie ['preərɪ] *n.* Grasland, *das;* Grassteppe, *die; (in North America)* Prärie, *die;* **animal of the ~s** Steppentier, *das;* **out on the ~:** in der Grassteppe
prairie: ~ **'chicken** *n.* Präriehuhn, *das;* ~ **dog** *n.* Präriehund, *der;* ~ **fire** *n. (fig.)* Lauffeuer, *das;* ~ **'hen** *see* ~ **chicken;** ~ **'oyster** *n.* Prärieauster, *die;* ~ **'schooner** *n. (Amer. Hist.)* Planwagen, *der;* ~ **'wolf** *n.* Kojote, *der;* Präriewolf, *der*
praise [preɪz] **1.** *v.t.* **a)** *(commend)* loben; *(more strongly)* rühmen; ~ **sb. for sth.** jmdn. für *od.* wegen etw. loben; *(more strongly)* jmdn. wegen etw. rühmen; ~ **sb. for doing sth.** jmdn. dafür loben, daß er etw. tut/getan hat; **b)** *(glorify)* preisen *(geh.), (dichter.)* lobpreisen ‹*Gott*›. **2.** *n.* **a)** *(approval)* Lob, *das;* **win high ~:** großes *od.* hohes Lob erhalten *od.* ernten; **be loud in one's ~s of sth.** des Lobes voll sein über etw. *(geh.);* **a speech in ~ of sb.** eine Lobrede auf jmdn.; **sing one's own/sb.'s ~s** ein Loblied auf sich/jmdn. singen; **b)** *(worship)* Lobpreisung, *die (dichter.);* **offer ~ to God for sth.** Gott für etw. preisen *(geh.) od. (dichter.)* lobpreisen; ~ **be!** Gott dem Herrn sei Lob und Preis! *See also* **damn 1 a**
praiseworthy ['preɪzwɜːðɪ] *adj.* lobenswert; löblich *(oft iron.)*
praline ['prɑːliːn] *n.* gebrannte Nuß; gebrannte Mandel
pram [præm] *n. (Brit.)* Kinderwagen, *der; (for dolls)* Puppenwagen, *der*
prance [prɑːns] *v.i.* **a)** ‹*Pferd:*› tänzeln; **b)** *(fig.)* stolzieren; ‹*Tänzer:*› tänzeln; ~ **about** *or* **around** ‹*Kind, Tänzer:*› herumhüpfen
prang [præŋ] *(Brit. sl.)* **1.** *v.t.* **a)** *(bomb)* bombardieren; bepflastern *(Soldatenspr.);* **b)** *(crash)* zu Bruch fahren ‹*Fahrzeug*›; bruchlanden mit ‹*Flugzeug*›; kaputtfahren *(ugs.)* ‹*Auto*›; **c)** *(damage)* ramponieren *(ugs.).* **2.** *n. (of aircraft)* Absturz, *der; (of vehicle)* Unfall, *der;* **have a ~:** Bruch machen *(Fliegerspr.);* einen Unfall bauen *(ugs.)*
prank [præŋk] *n.* Streich, *der;* Schabernack, *der;* **play a ~ on sb.** jmdm. einen Streich *od.* Schabernack spielen
prankster ['præŋkstə(r)] *n.* Witzbold, *der (ugs. abwertend)*
prat [præt] *n. (sl.)* Trottel, *der (ugs. abwertend)*
prate [preɪt] *v.i.* **a)** *(chatter)* daherreden *(abwertend);* sabbeln *(salopp abwertend);* ~ **about sth.** sich lang und breit über etw. *(Akk.)* auslassen; **b)** *(talk foolishly)* dumm daherreden; schwafeln *(ugs. abwertend);* labern *(ugs. abwertend)*
prating ['preɪtɪŋ] *adj.* geschwätzig *(abwertend);* schwatzhaft *(abwertend)*
prattle ['prætl] **1.** *v. i.* ‹*Kleinkind:*› plappern *(ugs.);* schwafeln *(ugs. abwertend);* ~ **on about sth.** ohne Pause über etw. *(Akk.)* plappern; ~ **away to sb.** zu jmdm. drauflosplappern. **2.** *n.* Geplapper, *das (ugs. abwertend);* Geschwafel, *das (ugs. abwertend)*
prawn [prɔːn] *n.* Garnele, *die*
prawn 'cocktail *n.* Krabbencocktail, *der*
pray [preɪ] **1.** *v.i.* beten **(for** um); **let us ~:** lasset uns beten; ~ **[to God] for sb.** für jmdn. beten; ~ **to God for help** Gott um Hilfe anflehen; ~ **to God to do sth.** zu Gott beten, daß er etw. tue; **he is past ~ing for** ihm ist nicht mehr zu helfen. **2.** *v. t.* **a)** *(beseech)* anflehen, flehen zu ‹*Gott, Heiligen, Jungfrau Maria*› **(for** um); ~ **God for sth.** etw. von Gott erflehen; **b)** *(~ to)* beten zu; ~ **God she is safe** bitte, lieber Gott, laß sie in Sicherheit sein; **c)** *(ellipt.: I ask)* bitte; ~ **consider what ...:** überlegen Sie doch bitte, was ...; **what is the use of that, ~?** wozu, bitte [schön], soll das gut sein? *See also* **mantis**
prayer [preə(r)] *n.* **a)** Gebet, *das;* **make/offer up a ~ for sb.** für jmdn. beten; ein Gebet für jmdn. sprechen; **offer ~s for** beten für; **offer up a quick ~:** schnell ein Gebet sprechen; **say one's ~s** beten; **say your ~s!** *(iron.)* jetzt hast du Grund zum Beten *(iron.);* **lead the ~s** die Gebete vorsprechen; *see also* **lord 1 b; b)** *no pl., no art. (praying)* Beten, *das;* **gather in ~:** sich zum Gebet versammeln; **what's the use of ~?** was nützt es zu beten?; **c)** *(service)* Andacht, *die;* **family ~s** Familienandacht, *die;* **d)** *(entreaty)* inständige *od.* eindringliche Bitte; **e)** *(Amer. coll.: slight chance of success)* Hauch einer Chance; **without a ~ of doing sth.** ohne die geringste Chance *od.* Aussicht, etw. erfolgreich zu tun
prayer: ~**-book** *n.* **a)** Gebetbuch, *das;* **b) the ~ book = the Book of Common Prayer** *see* **Common Prayer;** ~**-mat** *n.* Gebetsteppich, *der;* ~ **meeting** *n.* Gebetsversammlung, *die;* ~**-wheel** *n.* Gebetsmühle, *die*
preach [priːtʃ] **1.** *v.i.* **a)** *(deliver sermon)* predigen **(to** zu, vor + *Dat.;* **on** über + *Akk.*); **b)** *(fig.: give moral advice)* eine Predigt halten *(ugs.); (abwertend)* Moralpredigten halten **(at,** to *Dat.*). **2.** *v. t.* **a)** *(deliver)* halten ‹*Predigt, Ansprache*›; **b)** *(proclaim)* predigen ‹*Evangelium, Botschaft*›; verkündigen ‹*Glauben, Lehre, Evangelium, Botschaft*›; **c)** *(advocate)* predigen *(ugs.)*
preacher ['priːtʃə(r)] *n.* **a)** Prediger, *der*/Predigerin, *die;* **b)** *(fig.)* **be a ~ of privatization** die Privatisierung predigen *(ugs.)*
preachify ['priːtʃɪfaɪ] *v. i.* predigen
preachy ['priːtʃɪ] *adj. (coll.)* predigerhaft
preamble [priː'æmbl] *n.* **a)** *(preliminary statement)* Vorbemerkung, *die;* Einleitung, *die; (to a book)* Geleitwort, *das;* **b)** *(Law)* Präambel, *die*
pre-arrange [priːə'reɪndʒ] *v. t.* vorher absprechen; vorher ausmachen *od.* verabreden ‹*Treffpunkt, Zeichen*›
pre-arrangement [priːə'reɪndʒmənt] *n.* vorherige Absprache; **by ~:** nach vorheriger Absprache
prebend ['prebənd] *n.* Pfründe, *die*
prebendary ['prebəndərɪ] *n.* **a)** *(honorary canon)* ehrenamtlicher Pfründner/ehrenamtliche Pfründnerin; **b)** *(holder of prebend)* Pfründner, *der*/Pfründnerin, *die*
precarious [prɪ'keərɪəs] *adj.* **a)** *(uncertain)* labil, prekär ‹*Gleichgewicht, Situation*›; gefährdet ‹*Friede, Ernte*›; **make a ~ living** eine unsichere Existenz haben; **b)** *(insecure)* gefährlich ‹*Weg, Pfad*›; riskant, gefährlich ‹*Politik, Leben, Balanceakt*›; instabil *(geh.)* ‹*Bauwerk*›; kritisch, bedenklich ‹*Gesundheitszustand*›; unsicher ‹*Koalition*›
precariously [prɪ'keərɪəslɪ] *adv.* **live ~:** eine unsichere Existenz haben; **be perched ~ on the edge of a steep slope** ‹*Haus:*› gefährlich nahe am Rand eines Steilhangs stehen
pre-cast ['priːkɑːst] **1.** *v. t.,* **pre-cast** vorfabrizieren, vorfertigen ‹*Beton*›. **2.** *adj.* vorgefertigt; vorfabriziert
precaution [prɪ'kɔːʃn] *n.* **a)** *(action)* Vorsichts-, Schutzmaßnahme, *die;* **take ~s against sth.** Vorsichts- *od.* Schutzmaßnahmen gegen etw. treffen; **do sth. as a ~:** vorsichts- *od.* sicherheitshalber etw. tun; **do you take ~s?** *(euphem.)* nimmst du Verhütungsmittel?; **b)** *no pl. (foresight)* Vorsicht, *die*
precautionary [prɪ'kɔːʃənərɪ] *adj.* vorsorglich; vorbeugend; prophylaktisch *(geh., Med.);* präventiv *(geh.);* ~ **measure** Vorsichts- *od.* Schutzmaßnahme, *die;* **as a ~ measure** vorsichts- *od.* sicherheitshalber
precede [prɪ'siːd] *v. t.* **a)** *(in rank)* rangieren vor (+ *Dat.*); *(in importance)* wichtiger sein als; Vorrang haben vor (+ *Dat.*); **be ~d by sth.** hinter etw. *(Dat.)* rangieren; **b)** *(in order or time)* vorangehen (+ *Dat.*); *(in vehicle)* voranfahren (+ *Dat.*); *(in time also)* vorausgehen (+ *Dat.*); **the words that ~ [this paragraph]** die [diesem Absatz] vorangehenden Worte; **c)** *(preface, introduce)* ~ **X with Y** X *(Dat.)* Y vorausschicken *od.* voranstellen; ~ **an address with a welcome** einer Ansprache einen Willkommensgruß vorausschicken *od.* voranstellen

precedence ['presɪdəns], **precedency** ['presɪdənsɪ] *n., no pl.* **a)** *(in rank)* Priorität, *die (geh.)* (**over** vor + *Dat.*, gegenüber); Vorrang, *der* (**over** vor + *Dat.*); **b)** *(in time)* Priorität, *die (geh.)* (**over** vor + *Dat.*, gegenüber); zeitliches Vorhergehen; **have [the] ~ over all the others** Priorität vor *od.* gegenüber allen anderen haben; **c)** *(in ceremonies)* Rangordnung, *die*

precedent 1. ['presɪdənt] *n.* **a)** *(example)* Präzedenzfall, *der;* [vorangegangenes] exemplarisches Beispiel; **there is no ~ for this** so ein Fall ist noch nicht vorgekommen; **it is without ~ [that ...]** es ist noch nie dagewesen[, daß ...]; **set** *or* **create** *or* **establish a ~:** einen Präzedenzfall schaffen; **b)** *(Law)* Präzedenzfall, *der;* Präjudiz, *das (fachspr.).* **2.** [prɪ'si:dənt] *adj.* **a)** *(in order)* vorangestellt; vorangehend; **b)** *(in time)* voran-, vorausgehend; vorhergehend

precept ['pri:sept] *n.* **a)** *(command)* Grundsatz, *der;* Prinzip, *das;* **b)** *(moral instruction)* moralischer Grundsatz; Moralprinzip, -gesetz, *das*

precession [prɪ'seʃn] *n. (Phys.)* Präzession, *die;* **~ of the equinoxes** *(Astron.)* Präzession, *die*

pre-Christian [pri:'krɪstjən] *adj.* vorchristlich

precinct ['pri:sɪŋkt] *n.* **a)** *(traffic-free area)* **[pedestrian] ~:** Fußgängerzone, *die;* **[shopping] ~:** für den Verkehr weitgehend gesperrtes Einkaufsviertel; **b)** *(enclosed area)* Areal, *das;* Bereich, *der;* Bezirk, *der;* **temple/cathedral ~:** Tempel-/Dombereich, *der;* **in the hospital ~s** auf dem Krankenhausgelände; **c)** *(boundary)* Grenze, *die;* **within the ~s of the school** auf dem Schulgelände; **d)** *(Amer.: police or electoral district)* Bezirk, *der*

preciosity [preʃɪ'ɒsɪtɪ] *n., no pl.* Affektiertheit, *die*

precious ['preʃəs] **1.** *adj.* **a)** *(costly)* wertvoll, kostbar ‹*Schmuckstück*›; Edel‹*metall, -stein*›; **b)** *(highly valued)* wertvoll, kostbar ‹*Zeit, Eigenschaft, Trostwort, Privileg*›; **be ~ to sb.** jmdm. lieb und wert sein; **c)** *(beloved)* teuer *(geh.),* lieb ‹*Freund*›; **my ~ one!** mein Schatz; **d)** *(affected)* affektiert; **e)** *(coll.: considerable)* beträchtlich; erheblich; **do a ~ sight more work/cost a ~ sight more than ...:** beträchtlich *od.* erheblich mehr tun/kosten als ... **2.** *adv. (coll.)* herzlich ‹*wenig*›; **~ few of them** herzlich wenige von ihnen

precipice ['presɪpɪs] *n.* Abgrund, *der;* **we are on the edge of a ~** *(fig.)* wir stehen am Rande einer Katastrophe

precipitant [prɪ'sɪpɪtənt] *see* **precipitate 1**

precipitate 1. [prɪ'sɪpɪtət] *adj.* **a)** *(hurried)* eilig ‹*Flucht, Entbindung*›; hastig ‹*Abreise*›; **make a ~ exit** hastig *od.* eilig hinausgehen; **b)** *(rash)* übereilt, überstürzt ‹*Tat, Entschluß, Maßnahme*›; groß, fliegend ‹*Eile*›; **be ~ in doing sth.** etw. übereilt tun; **do nothing ~:** nichts übereilt tun. **2.** [prɪ'sɪpɪteɪt] *v. t.* **a)** *(throw down)* hinunterschleudern; **be ~d into a chasm** in eine Spalte stürzen; **~ a nation into war** ‹*Nachricht, Aggression:*› ein Volk in einen Krieg stürzen; **b)** *(hasten)* beschleunigen; *(trigger)* auslösen; **c)** *(Chem.)* ‹*Säure:*› ausfällen; **d)** *(Phys.)* kondensieren. **3.** [prɪ'sɪpɪtət] *n.* **a)** *(Chem.)* Niederschlag, *der;* **b)** *(Phys.)* Niederschlag, *der;* Kondensat, *das*

precipitately [prɪ'sɪpɪtətlɪ] *adv.* übereilt, überstürzt ‹*fliehen, flüchten*›; unüberlegt, voreilig ‹*handeln, sich in etw. stürzen*›; hastig ‹*hetzen, eilen, stürzen*›

precipitation [prɪsɪpɪ'teɪʃn] *n.* **a)** *(Meteorol.)* Niederschlag, *der;* **b)** Voreiligkeit, *die;* Unüberlegtheit, *die*

precipitous [prɪ'sɪpɪtəs] *adj.* **a)** *(very steep)* sehr steil ‹*Schlucht, Abhang, Treppe, Weg*›; schroff ‹*Abhang, Felswand*›; abschüssig ‹*Straße*›; steilwandig ‹*Cañon*›; **~ slope/drop** Steilhang, *der*/[steiler] Absturz; **b)** *see* **precipitate 1**

precipitously [prɪ'sɪpɪtəslɪ] *adv.* **a)** sehr steil ‹*[an]steigen sich erheben, abfallen*›; schroff ‹*ansteigen, abfallen*›; jäh *(geh.)* ‹*abfallen*›; **b)** *see* **precipitately**

précis ['preɪsi:] **1.** *n., pl. same* [preɪsi:z] Inhaltsangabe, *die;* Zusammenfassung, *die;* Précis, *der (fachspr.);* **~ of German history** Abriß der deutschen Geschichte; **do** *or* **make a ~ of sth.** eine Inhaltsangabe einer Sache *(Gen.)* anfertigen. **2.** *v. t.* zusammenfassen

precise [prɪ'saɪs] *adj.* genau; präzise; fein ‹*Instrument*›; groß ‹*Genauigkeit*›; förmlich ‹*Art*›; **be very ~ about sth.** es mit etw. sehr genau nehmen; **put sth. in more ~ terms** etw. präzisieren *od.* präziser ausdrücken; **be [more] ~:** sich präzise[r] ausdrücken; **what are your ~ intentions?** was genau hast du vor?; **..., to be ~:** ..., um genau zu sein; ..., genauer gesagt; **be the ~ opposite of sth.** genau das Gegenteil von etw. sein; **this is the ~ design/colour/shade that ...:** das ist genau das Muster/die Farbe/der Ton, das/die/der ...; **the ~ moment at which ...:** genau der Augenblick, in dem ...; **at that ~ moment** genau in dem Augenblick

precisely [prɪ'saɪslɪ] *adv.* genau; präzise ‹*antworten*›; **speak ~:** sich präzise ausdrücken; **the date is not ~ known** das genaue Datum ist nicht bekannt; **that is ~ what/why ...:** genau das/deswegen ...; **what ~ do you want/mean?** was willst/meinst du eigentlich genau?; **do ~ the opposite** genau das Gegenteil tun; **it is ~ because ...:** gerade weil ...; **it will be 5.21 ~:** es wird genau 5 Uhr 21; **at ~ 1.30, at 1.30 ~:** Punkt 1 Uhr 30; genau um 1 Uhr 30

precision [prɪ'sɪʒn] *n., no pl.* Genauigkeit, *die;* **with[out] a great deal of ~:** [nicht] sehr präzise ‹*sich ausdrücken*›; *attrib.* **a ~ landing** eine Präzisionslandung

precision: ~ 'bombing *n. (Mil.)* Punktzielbombardement, *das;* **~ 'instrument** *n.* Präzisions[meß]gerät, *das;* Feinmeßgerät, *das;* **~ 'tool** *n.* Präzisionswerkzeug, *das*

pre-classical [pri:'klæsɪkl] *adj.* vorklassisch

preclude [prɪ'klu:d] *v. t.* ausschließen ‹*Zweifel*›; **~ sb. from a duty/taking part** jmdn. von einer Pflicht/der Teilnahme entbinden; **so as to ~ all doubt** um jeden Zweifel auszuschließen

precocious [prɪ'kəʊʃəs] *adj.* frühreif ‹*Kind, Jugendlicher, Genie*›; altklug ‹*Äußerung*›; verfrüht ‹*Wachstum, Erfolg*›; **at the ~ age of 25** schon mit 25 Jahren; **a ~ interest in sth.** frühzeitiges Interesse an etw. *(Dat.)*

precociously [prɪ'kəʊʃəslɪ] *adv.* frühreif ‹*sich benehmen*›; altklug ‹*reden*›

precognition [pri:kɒg'nɪʃn] *n.* vorherige Kenntnis (**of** von); *(Parapsych.)* Präkognition, *die*

preconceived [pri:kən'si:vd] *adj.* vorgefaßt ‹*Ansicht, Vorstellung*›

preconception [pri:kən'sepʃn] *n.* vorgefaßte Meinung (**of** über + *Akk.*); **with too many ~s** allzu voreingenommen

precondition [pri:kən'dɪʃn] *n.* Vorbedingung, *die* (**of** für)

pre-cook [pri:'kʊk] *v. t.* vorkochen

pre-cooked [pri:'kʊkt] *adj.* vorgekocht

precursor [pri:'kɜ:sə(r)] *n.* **a)** *(of revolution, movement, etc.)* Wegbereiter, *der*/-bereiterin, *die;* *(of illness)* Vorbote, *der*/Vorbotin, *die;* **b)** *(predecessor)* Vorgänger, *der*/-gängerin, *die*

pre-date [pri:'deɪt] *v. t.* **a)** *(precede in date)* **~ sth.** ‹*Ereignis:*› einer Sache vorausgehen; ‹*Sache:*› aus der Zeit vor etw. *(Dat.)* stammen; **b)** *(give earlier date to)* zurückdatieren ‹*Brief, Scheck*›

pre-dated [pri:'deɪtɪd] *adj.* zurückdatiert ‹*Brief, Scheck*›

predator ['predətə(r)] *n.* Raubtier, *das;* *(fish)* Raubfisch, *der*

predatory ['predətərɪ] *adj.* **a)** *(plundering, robbing)* räuberisch; Raub‹*instinkte, -krieg*›; beutegierig ‹*Gesellschaftsschicht, Charakter*›; **b)** *(preying upon others)* räuberisch; **~ animal** Raubtier, *das*

predecease [pri:dɪ'si:s] *v. t.* **~ sb.** vor jmdm. sterben

predecessor ['pri:dɪsesə(r)] *n.* **a)** *(former holder of position)* Vorgänger, *der*/-gängerin, *die;* **~ in office/title** Amts-/Rechtsvorgänger, *der;* **b)** *(preceding thing)* Vorläufer, *der;* **his second novel is better than its ~:** sein zweiter Roman ist besser als sein erster; **c)** *(ancestor)* Vorfahr[e], *der*/-fahrin, *die;* Ahn, *der (geh.)*/Ahne, *die (geh.)*

predestination [prɪdestɪ'neɪʃn] *n., no pl.* Vorherbestimmung, *die;* Prädestination, *die (geh.)*

predestine [prɪ'destɪn] *v. t.* von vornherein bestimmen (**to** zu); prädestinieren (**to** zu) *(geh.)*

predetermination [pri:dɪtɜ:mɪ'neɪʃn] *n., no pl.* **a)** *(predestination)* Vorherbestimmung, *die;* Prädestination, *die (geh.);* **b)** *(intention)* Vorsatz, *der;* Absicht, *die;* **with a ~ to do sth.** mit dem Vorsatz *od.* in der Absicht, etw. zu tun

predetermine [pri:dɪ'tɜ:mɪn] *v. t.* **a)** im voraus *od.* von vornherein bestimmen; ‹*Gott, Schicksal:*› vorherbestimmen; **b)** *(impel)* zwingen (**to** zu)

predicament [prɪ'dɪkəmənt] *n.* Dilemma, *das;* Zwangslage, *die;* **he found himself in a ~:** er befand sich in einem Dilemma

predicate 1. ['predɪkət] *n.* **a)** *(Ling.)* Prädikat, *das;* **b)** *(Logic)* Prädikat, *das;* Prädikator, *der.* **2.** ['predɪkeɪt] *v. t.* **a)** *(affirm)* **~ sth. of sb./sth.** jmdm./einer Sache etw. zuschreiben; **~ of sb./sth. that ...:** von jmdm./etw. behaupten *od.* sagen, daß ...; **b)** *(found, base)* gründen (**on** auf + *Dat.*); **be ~d on** basieren *(geh.) od.* sich gründen auf (+ *Dat.*); **c)** *(Logic)* zusprechen (**of** *Dat.*)

predicative [prɪ'dɪkətɪv] *adj.* **a)** *(making a predication)* eine Aussage beinhaltend (**of, about** über + *Akk.*); **b)** *(Ling.)* prädikativ

predicatively [prɪ'dɪkətɪvlɪ] *adv. (Ling.)* prädikativ

predict [prɪ'dɪkt] *v. t.* voraus-, vorhersagen; prophezeien; voraus-, vorhersehen ‹*Folgen*›; **what do you ~ will be the result?** wie glaubst du, wird das Ergebnis aussehen?

predictable [prɪ'dɪktəbl] *adj.* voraus-, vorhersagbar; voraus-, vorhersehbar ‹*Folgen, Reaktion, Ereignis*›; berechenbar ‹*Person*›

predictably [prɪ'dɪktəblɪ] *adv.* wie vorauszusehen war; **he was ~ annoyed** wie voraus- *od.* vorherzusehen [war], war er verärgert

prediction [prɪ'dɪkʃn] *n.* Voraus-, Vorhersage, *die*

predigest [pri:dɪ'dʒest, pri:daɪ'dʒest] *v. t.* vorverdauen

predilection [pri:dɪ'lekʃn] *n.* Vorliebe, *die*

predispose [pri:dɪ'spəʊz] *v. t.* **~ sb. to do sth.** jmdn. etw. tun lassen; **be ~d to do sth.** *(be willing to do sth.)* geneigt sein, etw. zu tun; *(tend to do sth.)* dazu neigen, etw. zu tun; **~ sb. to sth.** jmdn. zu etw. neigen lassen; **~ sb. to an illness** jmdn. für eine Krankheit anfällig machen; **~ sb. in favour of sb./sth.** jmdn. für jmdn./etw. einnehmen

predisposition [pri:dɪspə'zɪʃn] *n.* Neigung, *die* (**to** zu); *(Med.)* Anfälligkeit, *die* (**to** für); Prädisposition, *die (fachspr.)*

predominance [prɪ'dɒmɪnəns] *n.* **a)** *(control) (of country)* Vorherrschaft, *die* (**over** über + *Akk.*); Vorrangstellung, *die* (**over** gegenüber); *(of person)* Überlegenheit, *die* (**over** gegenüber); **b)** *(majority)* Überzahl, *die* (**of** von); **there is a ~ of newcomers** die Neulinge sind in der Überzahl

predominant [prɪ'dɒmɪnənt] *adj.* **a)** *(hav-*

ing more power) dominierend ‹*Interesse, Partei, Macht, Persönlichkeit*›; **b)** *(prevailing)* vorherrschend; **the ~ desire expressed by them** der von ihnen über- *od.* vorwiegend zum Ausdruck gebrachte Wunsch
predominantly [prɪ'dɒmɪnəntlɪ] *adv.* überwiegend
predominate [prɪ'dɒmɪneɪt] *v.i.* *(be more powerful)* dominierend sein; *(be more important)* vorherrschen; überwiegen; *(be more numerous)* in der Überzahl sein
pre-eminence [pri:'emɪnəns] *n., no pl.* Vorrangstellung, *die;* **achieve ~:** eine herausragende Stellung erlangen; **her ~ in this field** ihre herausragende Stellung auf diesem Gebiet
pre-eminent [pri:'emɪnənt] *adj.* herausragend; **be ~:** eine herausragende Stellung einnehmen
pre-eminently [pri:'emɪnəntlɪ] *adv.* herausragend; überaus ‹*gelehrt*›; *(mainly)* vor allem; in erster Linie; **figure ~:** an herausragender Stelle stehen
pre-empt [pri:'empt] *v.t.* *(forestall)* zuvorkommen (+ *Dat.*) (**on** bei); **she had been ~ed** man war ihr zuvorgekommen
pre-emptive [pri:'emptɪv] *adj.* **a)** Vorkaufs‹*preis, -recht*›; **~ right** *(of shareholder)* Bezugsrecht, *das;* **he made a ~ bid to gain power** er machte im Vorfeld seine Machtansprüche geltend; **b)** *(Mil.)* Präventiv‹*krieg, -maßnahme, -schlag*›; **c)** *(Bridge)* **~ bid** Sperrgebot, *das*
preen [pri:n] **1.** *v.t.* ‹*Vogel:*› putzen ‹*Federn, Gefieder*›. **2.** *v. refl.* ‹*Vogel:*› sich putzen; ‹*Person:*› sich herausputzen; **~ oneself on sth.** sich *(Dat.)* etwas auf etw. *(Akk.)* einbilden; **he is always ~ing himself on ...:** er brüstet sich dauernd mit ...
prefab ['pri:fæb] *n. (coll.)* *(house)* Fertighaus, *das;* *(building)* Gebäude aus Fertigteilen; Fertigbau, *der*
prefabricate [pri:'fæbrɪkeɪt] *v.t.* vorfertigen ‹*Produkt, Teil, Gebäude usw.*›
prefabricated *adj.* [pri:'fæbrɪkeɪtɪd] **~ house/building** Fertighaus, *das*/Fertigbau, *der;* **a ~ garage** eine in Fertigbauweise errichtete Garage; **a ~ system/scheme** *(fig.)* ein vorfabriziertes System/Schema
prefabrication [pri:fæbrɪ'keɪʃn] *n.* Vorfabrikation, *die;* Vorfertigung, *die*
preface ['prefəs] **1.** *n.* **a)** *(of book)* Vorwort, *das* (**to** *Gen.*); Vorbemerkung, *die* (**to** zu); **b)** *(of speech)* Vorrede, *die;* Einleitung, *die.* **2.** *v.t.* **a)** *(introduce)* einleiten; **b)** *(furnish with a ~)* mit einem Vorwort *od.* einer Vorbemerkung versehen
prefatory ['prefətərɪ] *adj.* einleitend ‹*Hinweise, Worte*›; **be ~ to sth.** etw. einleiten
prefect ['pri:fekt] *n. (Sch.)* *die Aufsicht führender älterer Schüler/führende ältere Schülerin;* **form ~:** *Schüler/Schülerin einer Klasse, der/die die Aufsicht führt*
prefer [prɪ'fɜ:(r)] *v.t.,* **-rr- a)** *(like better)* vorziehen; **~ to do sth.** etw. lieber tun; es vorziehen, etw. zu tun; **~ sth. to sth.** etw. einer Sache *(Dat.)* vorziehen; **I ~ skiing to skating** ich fahre lieber Ski als Schlittschuh; **I ~ not to talk about it** darüber möchte ich lieber nicht sprechen; **I should ~ to wait** ich würde lieber warten; **I'd ~ it if ...:** mir wäre es lieb, wenn ...; **~ to go to prison rather than pay** eher *od.* lieber ins Gefängnis gehen als zu bezahlen; **I ~ that we should wait rather than act now** ich meine, wir sollten lieber warten, als jetzt handeln; **this plant ~s cool conditions** diese Pflanze bevorzugt einen kühlen Standort; **they ~ blondes** sie bevorzugen Blondinen; **I ~ water to wine** ich trinke lieber Wasser als Wein; **which of them do you ~, John or Peter?** wer ist dir lieber, John oder Peter?; **there is tea or coffee, which do you ~?** es gibt Tee oder Kaffee, was ist Ihnen lieber?; **I should ~ something more elegant** ich hätte gerne etwas Eleganteres; **b)** *(submit)* erheben ‹*Anklage, Anschuldigungen*› (**against** gegen, **for** wegen); vorbringen ‹*Beschwerde*›; **c)** *(promote)* befördern; **be ~red to a post** auf einen Posten berufen werden; **he was ~red to the See of Chichester** er wurde zum Bischof von Chichester ernannt
preferable ['prefərəbl] *adj.* vorzuziehen *präd.;* vorzuziehend *attr.;* besser (**to** als); **which do you think ~, x or y?** was ist Ihrer Meinung nach vorzuziehen, x oder y?; **he felt it ~ to be silent** er fand, daß es besser war zu schweigen; **the cold was ~ to the smoke** die Kälte war noch erträglicher als der Rauch
preferably ['prefərəblɪ] *adv.* am besten; *(as best liked)* am liebsten; **a piano, ~ not too expensive** ein möglichst nicht zu teures Klavier; **Wine or beer? – Wine, ~!** Wein oder Bier? - Lieber Wein!
preference ['prefərəns] *n.* **a)** *(greater liking)* Vorliebe, *die;* **for ~** *see* **preferably; have a ~ for sth. [over sth.]** etw. [einer Sache *(Dat.)*] vorziehen; **he has a ~ for tea over coffee** er mag *od.* trinkt lieber Tee als Kaffee; **do sth. in ~ to sth. else** etw. lieber als etw. anderes tun; **b)** *(thing preferred)* **of the three skirts the blue one is my ~:** von den drei Röcken gefällt mir der blaue am besten; **his ~ is a holiday abroad** ein Urlaub im Ausland ist ihm am liebsten; **what are your ~s?** was wäre dir am liebsten?; **I have no ~:** mir ist alles gleich recht; **have you any ~ among his novels?** magst du einen seiner Romane besonders?; **c)** *(prior right)* Vorrecht, *das* (**for** auf + *Akk.*); **give a creditor ~ over sb.** einen Gläubiger gegenüber jmdm. begünstigen; **d)** *(favouring of one person or country)* Präferenzbehandlung, *die;* *(Econ.)* Präferenz, *die;* **give [one's] ~ to sb.** jmdn. bevorzugen; **give sb. ~ over others** jmdm. anderen gegenüber Vergünstigungen einräumen; **e)** *attrib. (Brit. Finance)* Vorzugs-, Prioritäts‹*obligation, -aktie*›
preferential [prefə'renʃl] *adj.* bevorzugt ‹*Behandlung*›; bevorrechtigt ‹*Ansprache, Stellung*›; **[a] ~ status** eine Vorzugsstellung; **give sb. ~ treatment** jmdn. bevorzugt behandeln; **~ customs duties** Präferenz- *od.* Vorzugszölle
preferentially [prefə'renʃəlɪ] *adv.* **a)** bevorzugt ‹*behandeln*›; **b)** *(to a greater extent)* vorwiegend
preferment [prɪ'fɜ:mənt] *n.* **a)** *(promotion)* Beförderung, *die;* *(advancement)* Voran-, Vorwärtskommen, *das;* **receive ~:** befördert werden; **b)** *(post)* höhere *od.* gehobene Stellung; *(Eccl.)* höheres Amt; **c)** *(Law)* **~ of charges** Anklageerhebung, *die*
preferred [prɪ'fɜ:d] *adj.* **a)** bevorzugt; **my ~ conclusion/solution** *etc.* die Schlußfolgerung/Lösung *usw.*, der ich den Vorzug gebe; **b) ~ share** *etc.* = **preference share** *etc. see* **preference e**
prefigure [pri:'fɪgə(r)] *v.t.* **a)** *(represent beforehand)* ankünd[ig]en; hindeuten auf (+ *Akk.*); **b)** *(picture to oneself)* sich *(Dat.)* [vorher] vorstellen; sich *(Dat.)* ausmalen
prefix 1. ['pri:fɪks, prɪ:'fɪks] *v.t.* **a)** *(add)* voranstellen (**to** *Dat.*); **~ a title to a name** einen Titel vor einen Namen setzen; **b)** *(Ling.)* als Präfix setzen (**to** vor + *Akk.*); **~ the definite article to sth.** den bestimmten Artikel vor etw. *(Akk.)* setzen. **2.** ['pri:fɪks] *n.* **a)** *(Ling.)* Präfix, *das;* Vorsilbe, *die;* **b)** *(title)* [Namens]zusatz, *der;* **the ~ 'Mr' before a name** der Zusatz „Mr." vor einem Namen
preflight ['pri:flaɪt] *attrib. adj.* ‹*Informationen, Kontrollen*› vor dem Flug
preform [pri:'fɔ:m] *v.t.* vorbilden; **~ed ideas** vorgeformte Ideen
preggers ['pregəz] *(Brit.),* **preggy** ['pregɪ] *adj. (sl.)* dick *(derb);* schwanger
pregnancy ['pregnənsɪ] *n.* **a)** *(of woman)* Schwangerschaft, *die;* *(of animal)* Trächtigkeit, *die;* **her advanced state of ~:** ihre fortgeschrittene Schwangerschaft; **in the fourth week of ~:** in der vierten Woche der Schwangerschaft *od.* Schwangerschaftswoche; **b)** *(fig.: of speech, words)* Bedeutungsgehalt, *der;* Bedeutungsschwere, *die (geh.)*
'pregnancy test *n.* Schwangerschaftstest, *der*
pregnant ['pregnənt] *adj.* **a)** schwanger ‹*Frau*›; trächtig ‹*Tier*›; **she is ~ with her second child** sie erwartet ihr zweites Kind; **heavily** *or (coll.)* **very ~:** hoch schwanger; **b)** *(fig.: momentous)* bedeutungsschwer *(geh.);* **~ with consequences/meaning** folgenschwer/bedeutungsschwanger
pre-heat [pri:'hi:t] *v.t.* vorheizen ‹*Backofen*›; vorwärmen ‹*Geschirr, Essen*›; vorher erwärmen ‹*Gas, Werkzeug*›
prehensile [prɪ'hensaɪl] *adj. (Zool.)* Greif‹*vermögen, -fuß, -schwanz*›
prehistoric [pri:hɪ'stɒrɪk] *adj.* **a)** vorgeschichtlich; prähistorisch; **tools dating from ~ times** vorgeschichtliche *od.* prähistorische Werkzeuge; **b)** *(coll.) (ancient)* uralt *(ugs.);* *(out of date)* vorsintflutlich *(ugs.)*
prehistory [pri:'hɪstərɪ] *n.* **a)** Vorgeschichte, *die;* Prähistorie, *die;* **b)** *(of a situation etc.)* Vorgeschichte, *die*
pre-ignition [pri:ɪg'nɪʃn] *n. (Motor Veh.)* Frühzündung, *die*
pre-industrial [pri:ɪn'dʌstrɪəl] *adj.* vorindustriell
prejudge [pri:'dʒʌdʒ] *v.t.* **a)** *(form premature opinion about)* vorschnell *od.* voreilig urteilen über (+ *Akk.*); **b)** *(judge before trial)* im voraus beurteilen, vorverurteilen ‹*Person*›; im voraus entscheiden ‹*Fall*›
prejudg[e]ment [pri:'dʒʌdʒmənt] *n.* vorschnelles Urteil (**of** über + *Akk.*); **we must avoid any ~ of the case/accused** wir dürfen den Fall nicht im voraus entscheiden/den Angeklagten nicht vorverurteilen
prejudice ['predʒʊdɪs] **1.** *n.* **a)** *(bias)* Vorurteil, *das;* **colour ~:** Vorurteil aufgrund der Hautfarbe; **overcome ~:** Vorurteile ablegen; **this is mere ~!** das sind bloße Vorurteile!; **b)** *(injury)* Schaden, *der;* Nachteil, *der;* **to sb.'s ~:** zu jmds. Nachteil *od.* Schaden; **without ~ [to court action]** *(Law)* ohne Schaden für die eigenen Rechte [bei gerichtlichem Vorgehen]; **without ~ to sth.** unbeschadet einer Sache *(Gen.);* **be without ~ to sth.** etw. unberührt lassen. **2.** *v.t.* **a)** *(bias)* beeinflussen; **~ sb.** *or* **sb.'s mind in sb.'s favour/against sb.** jmdn. für/gegen jmdn. einnehmen; jmdn. zu jmds. Gunsten/Ungunsten beeinflussen; **b)** *(injure)* beeinträchtigen
prejudiced ['predʒʊdɪst] *adj.* voreingenommen (**about** gegenüber, **against** gegen); **the most ~ passages in this book** die einseitigsten Passagen dieses Buches; **~ opinion** Vorurteil, *das;* **be racially ~:** Rassenvorurteile haben; **be totally ~ against women** Frauen gegenüber völlig voreingenommen *od.* voller Vorurteile sein
prejudicial [predʒʊ'dɪʃl] *adj.* abträglich *(geh.)* (**to** *Dat.*); nachteilig (**to** für); **be ~ to** beeinträchtigen ‹*Anspruch, Chance, Recht*›; schaden (+ *Dat.*) ‹*Interesse*›
prejudicially [predʒʊ'dɪʃəlɪ] *adv.* nachteilig; **affect ~:** beeinträchtigen ‹*Anspruch, Recht*›; schaden (+ *Dat.*) ‹*Interesse*›
prelate ['prelət] *n.* Prälat, *der*
prelim ['pri:lɪm] *n.* **a)** *(coll.: exam)* Vorprüfung, *die;* **b)** *in pl. (Printing)* Titelei, *die*
preliminarily [prɪ'lɪmɪnərɪlɪ] *adv.* vorher
preliminary [prɪ'lɪmɪnərɪ] **1.** *adj.* Vor-; vorbereitend ‹*Forschung, Schritt, Maßnahme*›; einleitend ‹*Kapitel, Vertragsbestimmungen*›; **~ inquiry/request/search** erste Nachforschung/Bitte/Suche; **~ draft** Rohentwurf, *der.* **2.** *n., usu. in pl.* **preliminaries** Präliminarien *Pl.;* *(Sports)* Ausscheidungs-

kämpfe; **as a ~ to sth.** *(as a preparation)* als Vorbereitung auf etw. *(Akk.)*; **just a ~:** nur ein Vorspiel (**to** zu); **we have now completed the preliminaries** wir haben die Vorbereitungen jetzt abgeschlossen; **dispense with the preliminaries** ohne Umschweife *od.* direkt zur Sache kommen; in medias res gehen *(geh.)*; **without any further preliminaries** ohne [weitere] Umschweife. **3.** *adv. see* **preparatory 2**

prelude ['prelju:d] **1.** *n.* **a)** *(introduction)* Anfang, *der* (**to** *Gen.*); Auftakt, *der* (**to** zu); **b)** *(of play)* Vorspiel, *das* (**to** zu); *(of poem)* Einleitung, *die* (**to** zu *od. Gen.*); **c)** *(Mus.)* Präludium, *das;* Vorspiel, *das.* **2.** *v.t.* **a)** *(foreshadow)* ankündigen; **b)** *(start)* **~ sth. by** *or* **with sth.** etw. mit etw. einleiten

pre-marital [pri:'mærɪtl] *adj.* vorehelich; **~ sex** Geschlechtsverkehr vor der Ehe; voreheIicher Geschlechtsverkehr

premature ['premətjʊə(r)] *adj.* **a)** *(hasty)* voreilig, übereilt ⟨*Entscheidung, Handeln*⟩; **b)** *(early)* früh-, vorzeitig ⟨*Altern, Ankunft, Haarausfall*⟩; verfrüht ⟨*Bericht, Eile, Furcht*⟩; **~ baby** Frühgeburt, *die;* **the baby was five weeks ~:** das Baby wurde fünf Wochen zu früh geboren

prematurely ['premətjʊəlɪ] *adv. (early)* vorzeitig; zu früh ⟨*geboren werden*⟩; *(hastily)* voreilig, übereilt ⟨*entscheiden, handeln*⟩

premedical [prɪ:'medɪkl] *adj. (Amer.)* auf das Medizinstudium vorbereitend

premedication [pri:medɪ'keɪʃn] *n. (Med.)* Prämedikation, *die*

premeditated [pri:'medɪteɪtɪd] *adj.* vorsätzlich

premeditation [pri:medɪ'teɪʃn] *n.* Vorsatz, *der;* **with ~:** nach vorheriger Planung; vorsätzlich ⟨*ermorden, ein Verbrechen begehen*⟩

premenstrual [pri:'menstrʊəl] *adj. (Med.)* prämenstruell; **~ tension** prämenstruelle Spannung

premier ['premɪə(r)] **1.** *adj. (first)* erst...; *(best)* best... ⟨*Qualität*⟩; *(most important)* bedeutendst..., wichtigst... ⟨*Position, Stellung*⟩. **2.** *n.* Premier[minister], *der*/Premierministerin, *die*

première ['premjeə(r)] **1.** *n. (of production)* Premiere, *die;* Erstaufführung, *die; (of work)* Uraufführung, *die.* **2.** *v.t.* erst-/uraufführen

premiership ['premɪəʃɪp] *n.* Amtsperiode als Premierminister/-ministerin; *(office)* Amt des Premier[minister]s/der Premierministerin

premise ['premɪs] *n.* **a)** *in pl. (building)* Gebäude, *das; (buildings and land of factory or school)* Gelände, *das; (rooms)* Räumlichkeiten *Pl.;* **on the ~s** hier/dort; *(of public house, restaurant, etc.)* im Lokal; **all repairs are done on the ~s** alle Reparaturen werden an Ort und Stelle erledigt; **b)** *see* **premiss**

premiss ['premɪs] *n. (Logic)* Prämisse, *die*

premium ['pri:mɪəm] *n.* **a)** *(Insurance)* Prämie, *die;* **b)** *(reward)* Preis, *der;* Prämie, *die;* **put a ~ on sth.** *(make advantageous)* etw. belohnen; *(attach special value to)* etw. [hoch ein]schätzen; großen Wert auf etw. *(Akk.)* legen; **c)** *(bonus)* Zusatzzahlung, *die; (additional to fixed price/wage)* Aufgeld, *das*/Prämie, *die;* **d)** *(Amer.: charge for loan)* Kreditgebühr, *die;* **e)** *(St. Exch.)* Agio, *das;* Aufgeld, *das;* **be at a ~:** über pari stehen; *(fig.: be highly valued)* sehr gefragt sein; hoch im Kurs stehen; **those shares are on offer at a ~:** diese Aktien werden über pari *od.* mit einem Agio angeboten

'Premium [Savings] Bond *n. (Brit.)* Prämienanleihe, *die;* Losanleihe, *die*

premolar [pri:'məʊlə(r)] *n. (Anat.)* vorderer Backenzahn; Prämolar, *der (fachspr.)*

premonition [pri:mə'nɪʃn] *n.* **a)** *(forewarning)* Vorwarnung, *die;* **falling leaves gave a ~ of coming winter** fallendes Laub gemahnte an den kommenden Winter; **b)** *(presentiment)* Vorahnung, *die;* **feel/have a ~ of sth.** eine Vorahnung von etw. haben

premonitory [prɪ'mɒnɪtərɪ] *adj.* warnend ⟨*An-, Vorzeichen*⟩; ungut ⟨*Gefühl*⟩

pre-natal [pri:'neɪtl] *adj. (Med.)* pränatal *(fachspr.)*; vor der Geburt *nachgestellt;* **~ care** Schwangerschaftsfürsorge, *die*

preoccupation [prɪɒkjʊ'peɪʃn] *n.* Sorge, *die* (**with** um); **his ~ with his work left little time for his family** er war so sehr mit seiner Arbeit beschäftigt, daß wenig Zeit für die Familie blieb; **first** *or* **greatest** *or* **main ~:** Hauptanliegen, *das;* Hauptsorge, *die*

preoccupied [prɪ'ɒkjʊpaɪd] *adj. (lost in thought)* gedankenverloren; *(concerned)* besorgt (**with** um); *(absorbed)* beschäftigt (**with** mit)

preoccupy [prɪ'ɒkjʊpaɪ] *v.t.* beschäftigen; **my mind is preoccupied** meine Gedanken sind beschäftigt

pre-ordain [pri:ɔ:'deɪn] *v.t.* vorherbestimmen

prep [prep] *n. (Brit. Sch. coll.)* **a)** *(homework)* [Haus-, Schul]aufgaben *Pl.;* Schularbeiten *Pl.;* **b)** *(homework period)* Hausaufgabenvorbereitung, *die*

pre-packaged [pri:'pækɪdʒd], **pre-packed** [pri:'pækt] *adjs.* abgepackt; *(fig.)* vorgefertigt ⟨*Ideen, Meinung*⟩

prepaid *see* **prepay**

preparation [prepə'reɪʃn] *n.* **a)** Vorbereitung, *die;* **be in a state of ~ for combat** kampfbereit sein; **be in ~** ⟨*Publikation:*⟩ in Vorbereitung sein; **be in ~ for sth.** der Vorbereitung einer Sache *(Gen.)* dienen; **in ~ for the new baby/term** als Vorbereitung auf das neue Baby/Semester; **b)** *in pl. (things done to get ready)* Vorbereitungen *Pl.* (**for** für); **~s for war/the funeral/the voyage/the wedding** Kriegs-/Begräbnis-/Reise-/Hochzeitsvorbereitungen; **make ~s for sth.** Vorbereitungen für etw. treffen; **c)** *(Chem., Med., Pharm.)* Präparat, *das;* **herbal ~:** Kräuterpräparat, *das; (Cookery)* Kräutermischung, *die;* **d)** *(Brit. Sch.)* [Haus-, Schul]aufgaben *Pl.;* Schularbeiten *Pl.*

preparative [prɪ'pærətɪv] *see* **preparatory 1 a**

preparatory [prɪ'pærətərɪ] **1.** *adj.* **a)** *(introductory)* vorbereitend, einleitend ⟨*Maßnahme, Schritt*⟩; einleitend ⟨*Ermittlung, Geste, Untersuchung*⟩; Vor⟨*ermittlung, -untersuchung*⟩; **~ work** Vorarbeiten *Pl.;* **b)** *(Sch., Univ.)* für die Aufnahme an einer Public School/einem College vorbereitend; ⟨*Ausbildung, Stunden, Unterricht*⟩ an einer privaten Vorbereitungsschule. **2.** *adv.* **~ to sth.** vor etw. *(Dat.)*; **~ to doing sth.** bevor man etw. tut; **I am packing ~ to departure** *or* **departing** ich packe vor meiner Abreise

pre'paratory school *n.* **a)** *(Brit. Sch.) für die Aufnahme an einer Public School vorbereitende Privatschule;* **b)** *(Amer. Univ.) meist private, für die Aufnahme an einem College vorbereitende Schule*

prepare [prɪ'peə(r)] **1.** *v.t.* **a)** *(make ready)* vorbereiten; entwerfen, ausarbeiten ⟨*Plan, Rede*⟩; herrichten *(ugs.)*, fertigmachen ⟨*Gästezimmer*⟩; *(make mentally ready, equip with necessary knowledge)* vorbereiten ⟨*Person*⟩ (**for** auf + *Akk.*); **~ the ground** *or* **way for sb./sth.** *(fig.)* für jmdn./etw. die nötige Vorarbeit leisten; jmdm. die Steine aus dem Weg räumen; **~ oneself for a shock/the worst** sich auf einen Schock/das Schlimmste gefaßt machen; **be ~d for anything** auf alles gefaßt sein; **be ~d to do sth.** *(be willing)* bereit sein, etw. zu tun; **b)** *(make)* herstellen ⟨*Chemikalie, Metall usw.*⟩; zubereiten ⟨*Essen*⟩. **2.** *v.i.* sich vorbereiten (**for** auf + *Akk.*); **~ for battle/war** ⟨*Land:*⟩ zum Kampf/Krieg rüsten; **~ to do sth.** sich bereit machen *od. (geh.)* anschicken, etw. zu tun; **~ to advance/retreat** sich zum Vorstoß/Rückzug bereit machen

preparedness [prɪ'peərɪdnɪs] *n., no pl. (willingness)* Bereitschaft, *die* (**for** zu); **[state of] ~** *(readiness)* Vorbereitetsein, *das* (**for** für, auf + *Akk.*); **be in a state of ~ for action** *(Amer.)* sich in Alarmbereitschaft befinden

prepay [pri:'peɪ] *v.t.,* **prepaid** [pri:'peɪd] im voraus [be]zahlen; *(pay postage of)* frankieren, freimachen ⟨*Brief, Paket usw.*⟩; **send a parcel carriage prepaid** ein Paket frachtfrei versenden; **prepaid envelope** frankierter Umschlag; Freiumschlag, *der*

prepayment [prɪ:'peɪmənt] *n.* [Be]zahlung im voraus; Voraus[be]zahlung, *die; (of letters, parcels, etc.)* Frankierung, *die;* Freimachung, *die*

preponderance [prɪ'pɒndərəns] *n.* Überlegenheit, *die* (**over** über + *Akk.*, gegenüber); Übergewicht, *das;* **[numerical] ~, ~ in numbers** zahlenmäßige Überlegenheit; zahlenmäßiges Übergewicht

preponderant [prɪ'pɒndərənt] *adj.* überlegen; **~ in numbers** zahlenmäßig überlegen

preponderantly [prɪ'pɒndərəntlɪ] *adv.* überwiegend

preponderate [prɪ'pɒndəreɪt] *v.i.* überwiegen (**over** gegenüber)

preposition [prepə'zɪʃn] *n. (Ling.)* Präposition, *die;* Verhältniswort, *das*

prepositional [prepə'zɪʃənl] *adj. (Ling.)* präpositional; Präpositional⟨*attribut, -fall, -objekt*⟩

prepossess [pri:pə'zes] *v.t.* **a)** *(preoccupy mentally)* erfüllen; beherrschen; **b)** *(prejudice)* beeinflussen; **~ sb. in sb.'s favour/against sb.** jmdn. zu jmds. Gunsten/Ungunsten beeinflussen

prepossessing [pri:pə'zesɪŋ] *adj.* einnehmend, anziehend ⟨*Äußeres, Erscheinung, Person, Lächeln usw.*⟩

preposterous [prɪ'pɒstərəs] *adj.* absurd; grotesk ⟨*Äußeres, Kleidung*⟩

preposterously [prɪ'pɒstərəslɪ] *adv.* absurd; absurderweise ⟨*etw. tun*⟩; **suggest, quite ~, that ...:** absurderweise vorschlagen, daß ...

preppy ['prepɪ] *(Amer.)* **1.** *n. Schüler/Schülerin einer „preparatory school“, der/die sich teuer und gepflegt kleidet, aus wohlhabendem Elternhaus stammt, eher konservativ eingestellt ist.* **2.** *adj.* für einen „Preppy“ typisch ⟨*Kleidung, Meinung usw.*⟩

preprandial [pri:'prændɪəl] *adj. (formal/joc.)* ⟨*Drink usw.*⟩ vor dem Essen, vor Tisch

preprint ['pri:prɪnt] *n.* Vorabdruck, *der*

'prep school *(coll.) see* **preparatory school**

prepuce ['pri:pju:s] *n. (Anat.)* Vorhaut, *die*

Pre-Raphaelite [pri:'ræfəlaɪt] *(Art)* **1.** *n.* Präraffaelit, *der*/-raffaelitin, *die.* **2.** *adj.* präraffaelitisch

pre-record [pri:rɪ'kɔ:d] *v.t.* vorher aufnehmen; **~ed tape** bespieltes Band

prerequisite [pri:'rekwɪzɪt] **1.** *n.* [Grund]voraussetzung, *die.* **2.** *adj.* unbedingt erforderlich

prerogative [prɪ'rɒgətɪv] *n.* **a)** Privileg, *das;* Vorrecht, *das;* **the ~ of mercy** das Begnadigungsrecht; **b)** *(of sovereign)* **[royal] ~:** [königliche] Prärogative

Pres. *abbr.* **President** Präs.

presage 1. ['presɪdʒ] *n.* **a)** *(omen)* Vorzeichen, *das;* **a ~ of worse to come** ein schlechtes Omen; **b)** *(foreboding)* Vorahnung, *die.* **2.** ['presɪdʒ, prɪ'seɪdʒ] *v.t. (foreshadow)* ankündigen; *(give warning of)* ankünden

Presbyterian [prezbɪ'tɪərɪən, presbɪ'tɪərɪən] **1.** *adj.* presbyterianisch. **2.** *n.* Presbyterianer, *der*/Presbyterianerin, *die*

Presbyterianism [prezbɪ'tɪərɪənɪzm, presbɪ'tɪərɪənɪzm] *n.* Presbyterianismus, *der*

presbytery ['prezbɪtərɪ, 'presbɪtərɪ] *n.* Presbyterium, *das*

pre-school ['pri:sku:l] *adj.* Vorschul-; **~ years** Vorschulalter, *das*

prescience ['presɪəns] *n.* Vorausschau, *die*

prescient ['presɪənt] *adj.* weitblickend

pre-scientific [priːsaɪən'tɪfɪk] *adj.* vorwissenschaftlich

prescribe [prɪ'skraɪb] **1.** *v. t.* **a)** *(impose)* vorschreiben; **~d book** *see* **set 4 b; b)** *(Med.; also fig.)* verschreiben; verordnen. **2.** *v. i.* Vorschriften machen

prescript ['priːskrɪpt] *n.* Vorschrift, *die*

prescription [prɪ'skrɪpʃn] *n.* **a)** *(prescribing)* Anordnung, *die;* Vorschreiben, *das;* **b)** *(Med.)* Rezept, *das;* Verschreibung, *die; (medicine)* [verordnete *od.* verschriebene] Medizin; Verordnung, *die (fachspr.);* **be available only on ~:** nur auf Rezept *od.* Verschreibung erhältlich sein; rezept- *od.* verschreibungspflichtig sein

pre'scription charge *n.* Rezeptgebühr, *die*

prescriptive [prɪ'skrɪptɪv] *adj. (Ling.)* präskriptiv

pre-select [priːsɪ'lekt] *v. t.* vorwählen

presence ['prezəns] *n.* **a)** *(being present) (of person)* Gegenwart, *die;* Anwesenheit, *die; (of things)* Vorhandensein, *das;* **in the ~ of his friends** in Gegenwart *od.* Anwesenheit seiner Freunde; **in the ~ of danger** angesichts von Gefahren; **make one's ~ felt** sich bemerkbar machen; **be admitted to/be banished from the King's ~:** zum König vorgelassen werden/aus der Umgebung des Königs verbannt werden; **b)** *(appearance)* Äußere, *das; (bearing)* Auftreten, *das;* **[stage] ~:** Ausstrahlung [auf der Bühne]; **she has ~:** sie stellt etwas dar *od.* strahlt etwas aus; **c)** *(being represented)* Präsenz, *die;* **police ~:** Polizeipräsenz, *die;* **the British ~ east of Suez** die britische Präsenz östlich von Suez; **d)** *(person or thing)* Erscheinung, *die;* **feel an invisible ~ in the room** die Anwesenheit von etwas Unsichtbarem im Zimmer spüren; **e) ~ of mind** Geistesgegenwart, *die*

¹present ['prezənt] **1.** *adj.* **a)** anwesend, *(geh.)* zugegen (**at** bei); **be ~ in the air/water/in large amounts** in der Luft/im Wasser/in großen Mengen vorhanden sein; **all ~ and correct** *(joc.)* alle sind da; **all those ~:** alle Anwesenden; **~ company excepted** Anwesende ausgenommen; **be ~ to sb.** *or* **sb.'s mind** jmdm. gegenwärtig sein; **b)** *(being dealt with)* betreffend; **it's not relevant to the ~ matter** es ist für diese Angelegenheit nicht von Bedeutung; **in the ~ connection** in diesem Zusammenhang; **in the ~ case** im vorliegenden Fall; **c)** *(existing now)* gegenwärtig; jetzig, derzeitig ‹*Dekan, Bischof, Chef usw.*›; **during the ~ month** im laufenden Monat; **the ~ writer/author** *etc.* der Autor des vorliegenden Textes; **d)** *(Ling.)* **~ tense** Präsens, *das;* Gegenwart, *die;* **~ perfect** Perfekt, *das;* vollendete Gegenwart; *see also* **participle; e) a very ~ help in trouble** *(arch.)* eine allgegenwärtige Hilfe in der Not. **2.** *n.* **a) the ~:** die Gegenwart; **up to the ~:** bis jetzt; bisher; **at ~:** zur Zeit; **I can't help you/say more at ~:** im Augenblick kann ich dir nicht helfen/kann ich nicht mehr sagen; **for the ~:** vorläufig; **[there is] no time like the ~:** die Gelegenheit ist günstig; jetzt ist der beste Augenblick; **b)** *(Ling.)* Präsens, *das;* Gegenwart, *die*

²present 1. ['prezənt] *n. (gift)* Geschenk, *das;* Präsent, *das (geh.);* **parting ~:** Abschiedsgeschenk, *das;* **make a ~ of sth. to sb., make sb. a ~ of sth.** jmdm. etw. zum Geschenk machen; *see also* **give 1 a. 2.** [prɪ'zent] *v. t.* **a)** schenken; überreichen ‹*Preis, Medaille*›; **~ sth. to sb.** *or* **sb. with sth.** jmdm. etw. schenken *od.* zum Geschenk machen; **~ sb. with gifts** jmdm. Geschenke machen; **~ sb. with difficulties/a problem** jmdn. vor Schwierigkeiten/ein Problem stellen; **he was ~ed with an opportunity that ...:** ihm bot sich eine Gelegenheit, die ...; **b)** *(express)* **~ one's compliments to sb.** sich jmdm. empfehlen; **~ one's regards to sb.** jmdm. Grüße bestellen *od.* ausrichten; jmdm. seine Grüße entbieten *(geh.);* **c)** *(deliver)* überreichen ‹*Gesuch*› (**to** bei); vorlegen ‹*Scheck, Bericht, Rechnung*› (**to** *Dat.*); **~ one's case** seinen Fall darlegen; **d)** *(exhibit)* zeigen; bereiten ‹*Schwierigkeit*›; aufweisen ‹*Aspekt*›; **~ a ragged appearance** einen zerlumpten Anblick bieten; **~ a bold front** *or* **brave face to the world** sich nach außen hin unerschrocken geben; **e)** *(introduce)* vorstellen (**to** *Dat.*); **f)** *(to the public)* geben, aufführen ‹*Theaterstück*›; zeigen ‹*Film*›; moderieren ‹*Sendung*›; bringen ‹*Fernsehserie, Schauspieler in einer Rolle*›; vorstellen ‹*Produkt usw.*›; vorlegen ‹*Abhandlung*›; darlegen ‹*Theorie usw.*›; **g)** *(Parl.)* vorlegen ‹*Gesetzentwurf*›; **h) ~ arms** *(Mil.)* präsentiert das Gewehr!; **i)** *(aim, hold horizontally)* anlegen ‹*Gewehr usw.*›; **he ~ed his weapon** er legte an. **3.** *v. refl.* ‹*Problem:*› auftreten; ‹*Möglichkeit:*› sich ergeben; **~ itself to sb.** ‹*Möglichkeit:*› jmdm. vor Augen stehen; ‹*Erinnerung usw.:*› sich bei jmdm. einstellen; ‹*Gedanke:*› jmdm. kommen; **~ oneself to sb.** sich jmdm. vorstellen; **~ oneself for interview/an examination** zu einem Gespräch/einer Prüfung erscheinen

presentable [prɪ'zentəbl] *adj.* ansehnlich; **she is quite a ~ young lady** man kann sie gut vorzeigen *od.* sich gut mit ihr sehen lassen; **the flat is not very ~ at the moment** die Wohnung ist im Augenblick nicht besonders präsentabel; **make oneself/sth. ~:** sich/etw. zurechtmachen; **his most ~ jacket** sein bestes Jackett

presentably [prɪ'zentəblɪ] *adv.* ansehnlich; angemessen ‹*sich kleiden*›; ganz ordentlich ‹*Klavier spielen, malen usw.*›

presentation [prezən'teɪʃn] *n.* **a)** *(giving)* Schenkung, *die; (of prize, medal, gift)* Überreichung, *die;* **make sb. a ~ of sth.** jmdm. etw. schenken/überreichen; **b)** *(ceremony)* Verleihung, *die;* **~ of the awards/medals** Preis-/Ordensverleihung, *die;* **c)** *(delivering) (of petition)* Überreichung, *die; (of cheque, report, account)* Vorlage, *die; (of case, position, thesis)* Darlegung, *die; (manner of putting forward, presenting)* Präsentation, *die (geh.);* Darbietung, *die;* **on ~ of** gegen Vorlage (+ *Gen.*); **d)** *(exhibition)* Darstellung, *die;* **e)** *(Theatre, Radio, Telev.)* Darbietung, *die; (Theatre also)* Inszenierung, *die; (Radio, Telev. also)* Moderation, *die;* **f)** *(introduction)* Vorstellung, *die;* **g)** *(Med.)* Lage, *die;* **head/breech ~:** Kopf-/Steißlage, *die*

presen'tation copy *n.* Dedikationsexemplar, *das*

present-'day *adj.* heutig; zeitgemäß ‹*Einstellungen, Ansichten*›; **by ~ standards** nach heutigen *od.* gegenwärtigen Maßstäben

presenter [prɪ'zentə(r)] *n.* **a)** *(of cheque)* Überbringer, *der*/Überbringerin, *die;* **be the ~ of a petition/report** eine Petition überreichen/einen Bericht vorlegen; **b)** *(Radio, Telev.)* Moderator, *der*/Moderatorin, *die*

presentiment [prɪ'zentɪmənt] *n.* Vorahnung, *die;* **I have a ~ about the opening night** ich habe das Gefühl, daß bei der Premiere irgend etwas passiert; **have a ~ that ...:** vorausahnen, daß ...

presently ['prezəntlɪ] *adv.* **a)** *(soon)* bald; **see you ~:** bis gleich; **b)** *(Amer., Scot.: now)* zur Zeit; derzeit

present: ~ 'value, ~ 'worth *ns. (Econ.)* jetziger Wert; Tageswert, *der*

preservation [prezə'veɪʃn] *n., no pl.* **a)** *(action)* Erhaltung, *die; (of leather, wood, etc.)* Konservierung, *die;* **the ~ of peace** die Erhaltung des Friedens; **b)** *(state)* Erhaltungszustand, *der;* **be in an excellent state of ~:** außerordentlich gut erhalten sein; ‹*Person:*› sich außerordentlich gut gehalten haben

preser'vation order *n. Verordnung, die etw. unter Denkmalschutz stellt;* **put a ~ on sth.** etw. unter Denkmalschutz stellen

preservative [prɪ'zɜːvətɪv] **1.** *n.* Konservierungsmittel, *das.* **2.** *adj.* konservierend; Konservierungs-; konservativ ‹*Lösung*›

preserve [prɪ'zɜːv] **1.** *n.* **a)** *in sing. or pl. (fruit)* Eingemachte, *das;* **strawberry/quince ~s** eingemachte Erdbeeren/Quitten; **b)** *(jam)* Konfitüre, *die;* **c)** *(fig.: special sphere)* Domäne, *die (geh.); (of political power)* Einflußbereich, *der;* **d)** *(for wildlife)* [Natur]schutzgebiet, *das;* Reservat, *das; (water)* [Fisch]gehege, *das;* **wildlife/game ~:** Tierschutzgebiet, *das*/Wildpark *der.* **2.** *v. t.* **a)** *(keep safe)* schützen (**from** vor + *Dat.*); **~ sth. from destruction** etw. vor der Zerstörung bewahren; **b)** *(maintain)* aufrechterhalten ‹*Disziplin*›; bewahren ‹*Sehfähigkeit, Brauch, Würde*›; behalten ‹*Stellung*›; wahren ‹*Anschein, Reputation*›; **~ the peace** den Frieden bewahren *od.* erhalten; **c)** *(retain)* speichern ‹*Hitze*›; bewahren ‹*Haltung, Distanz, Humor*›; **d)** *(prepare, keep from decay)* konservieren; präparieren ‹*Leiche, Kadaver*›; **e)** *(keep alive)* erhalten; *(fig.)* bewahren ‹*Erinnerung, Andenken*›; **Heaven ~ us!** [Gott] bewahre!; **f)** *(care for and protect)* hegen ‹*Tierart, Wald*›; unter Schutz stellen ‹*Gewässer, Gebiet*›

pre-set [priː'set] *v. t., forms as* **set 1** vorher einstellen

pre-shrink [priː'ʃrɪŋk] *v. t., forms as* **shrink 2** *(Textiles)* vorschrumpfen; vorwaschen ‹*Jeans*›

pre-shrunk [priː'ʃrʌŋk] *adj. (Textiles)* vorgeschrumpft, vorgewaschen ‹*Jeans*›

preside [prɪ'zaɪd] *v. i.* **a)** *(at meeting etc.)* den Vorsitz haben (**at** bei); präsidieren, vorsitzen (**over** *Dat.*); **b)** *(at meal)* den Vorsitz haben; **~ at dinner** bei Tisch vorsitzen; **c)** *(exercise control)* **~ over** leiten ‹*Abteilung, Organisation, Programm*›; lenken ‹*Geschick*›; vorstehen (+ *Dat.*) ‹*Familie*›; bestimmen ‹*Bildung, Gründung*›

presidency ['prezɪdənsɪ] *n.* **a)** Präsidentschaft, *die;* **b)** *(of legislative body)* Vorsitz, *der;* **c)** *(Univ., esp. Amer.)* Präsidentschaft, *die;* Rektorat, *das;* **d)** *(of society etc.)* Vorsitz, *der;* Präsidentschaft, *die;* **e)** *(of council, board, etc.)* Vorsitz, *der;* **f)** *(Amer.: of bank or company)* Vorstandsvorsitz, *der*

president ['prezɪdənt] *n.* **a)** Präsident, *der*/Präsidentin, *die;* **b)** *(of legislative body)* Vorsitzende, *der/die;* **c)** *(Univ., esp. Amer.)* Präsident, *der*/Präsidentin, *die;* Rektor, *der*/Rektorin, *die;* **d)** *(of society etc.)* Vorsitzende, *der/die;* Präsident, *der*/Präsidentin, *die;* **e)** *(of council, board, etc.)* Vorstand, *der;* Vorsitzende, *der/die;* **Lord P~ of the Council** *(Brit.) Titel des dem Privy Council präsidierenden Kabinettsmitglieds;* **f)** *(Amer.: of bank or company)* Vorstandvorsitzende, *der/die;* Generaldirektor, *der*/-direktorin, *die*

presidential [prezɪ'denʃl] *adj.* Präsidenten-; **~ campaign** Präsidentschaftswahlkampf, *der;* **~ address** Ansprache des Präsidenten; **~ ambitions** Streben nach der Präsidentschaft

presidium [prɪ'sɪdɪəm, prɪ'zɪdɪəm] *n.* Präsidium, *das*

¹press [pres] **1.** *n.* **a)** *(newspapers etc.)* Presse, *die; attrib.* Presse-; **der Presse** *nachgestellt;* **get/have a good/bad ~** *(fig.)* eine gute/schlechte Presse bekommen/haben; *see also* **freedom a; b)** *see* **printing-press; c)** *(printing-house)* Druckerei, *die;* **at** *or* **in [the] ~:** im Druck; **send to [the] ~:** in Druck geben; **go to [the] ~:** in Druck gehen; **d)** *(publishing firm)* Verlag, *der;* **e)** *(for flattening, compressing, etc.)* Presse, *die; (for sports racket)* Spanner, *der;* **f)** *(crowding)* Gedränge, *das;* **g)** *(crowd)* Menge, *die;* **a ~ of people** eine Menschenmenge, *die;* **h)** *(in* *battle)* Getümmel, *das;* Gewühl, *das;* **i)** *(pressing)* Druck, *der;* **give sth. a ~:** etw. drücken; **your trousers could do with a ~:** deine Hosen sollten wieder einmal gebügelt werden; **with a ~ of the button** mit einem Knopfdruck *od.* Druck auf den Knopf; **j)** *(Weightlifting)* Drücken, *das.* **2.** *v. t.* **a)** drücken; pressen; drücken auf (+ *Akk.*) ‹*Klingel, Knopf*›; treten auf (+ *Akk.*) ‹*Gas-, Brems-, Kupplungspedal usw.*›; **~ the trigger** abdrücken; den Abzug betätigen; **b)** *(urge)* drängen ‹*Person*›; *(force)* aufdrängen (**[up]on** *Dat.*); *(insist on)* nachdrücklich vorbringen ‹*Forderung, Argument, Vorschlag*›; verfechten ‹*Standpunkt*›; **~ sb. for an answer** jmdn. zu einer Antwort drängen; **he did not ~ the point** er ließ die Sache auf sich beruhen; **~ the analogy too far** die Analogie zu weit treiben; **c)** *(exert force on)* drücken; pressen; **d)** *(squeeze)* drücken; **~ sb.'s hand** jmdm. die Hand drücken; **e)** *(compress)* pressen; auspressen ‹*Orangen, Saft*›; keltern ‹*Trauben, Äpfel*›; **f)** *(iron)* bügeln; **g)** *(bear heavily on)* bedrängen; **be hard ~ed** *(by enemy)* hart bedrängt werden; *(experience great difficulty)* unter großem Druck stehen; **h) be ~ed for space/time/money** *(have barely enough)* zuwenig Platz/Zeit/Geld haben; **i)** *(Weightlifting)* drücken; **j)** *(make)* pressen ‹*Schallplatte*›. **3.** *v. i.* **a)** *(exert pressure)* drücken; **the child ~ed against the railings** das Kind drückte sich gegen das Geländer; **b)** *(weigh)* **~ [up]on sb.'s mind/heart** jmdn. bedrücken; **c)** *(be urgent)* drängen; **time/sth. ~es** die Zeit drängt/etw. eilt *od.* ist dringend; **d)** *(make demand)* **~ for sth.** auf etw. *(Akk.)* drängen; **e)** *(crowd)* [sich] drängen; **~ up** sich herandrängen; **~ in upon sb.** ‹*Gedanken:*› auf jmdn. eindringen

~ a'head, ~ 'forward, ~ 'on *v. i. (continue)* sich ranhalten *(ugs.);* ‹*Truppen usw.:*› vorpreschen; **~ ahead as soon as possible** so schnell wie möglich weitermachen/-fahren *usw.;* **~ on with one's work/forward with one's initiative** sich mit der Arbeit ranhalten *(ugs.)*/seine Initiative energisch betreiben

~ 'out *v. t.* auspressen; *(out of cardboard)* herausdrücken

²press *v. t.* **~ into service/use** in Dienst nehmen; einsetzen

press: ~ agent *n.* Presseagent, *der*/-agentin, *die;* **~ attaché** *see* **attaché; ~-box** *n.* Pressekabine, *die;* **~-button** *see* **push-button; ~ campaign** *n.* Pressefeldzug, *der;* Pressekampagne, *die;* **~ card** *n.* Presseausweis, *der;* **~-clipping** *(Amer.) see* **~ cutting; ~ conference** *n.* Pressekonferenz, *die;* **~ coverage** *n.* Berichterstattung in der Presse; **~ cutting** *n. (Brit.)* Zeitungsausschnitt, *der;* **~-gallery** *n.* Pressetribüne, *die;* **~-gang 1.** *n. (Hist.)* Preßgang, *der (veralt.);* **2.** *v. t. (Hist.)* pressen; zwangsrekrutieren; *(fig.)* zwingen, pressen **(into** zu)

pressing ['presɪŋ] **1.** *adj.* **a)** *(urgent)* dringend; **the danger was ~:** Gefahr war im Verzug; **b)** *(persistent)* dringlich; nachdrücklich. **2.** *n.* **a)** *(exertion of pressure)* Drücken, *das; (of apples, grapes)* Keltern, *das; (of cheese, olives)* Pressen, *das; (of clothes)* Bügeln, *das;* **b)** *(product, esp. record)* Pressung, *die*

pressingly ['presɪŋlɪ] *adv.* dringend

press: ~man *n. (Brit.: journalist)* Journalist, *der;* Pressemann, *der (ugs.);* **~ office** *n.* Pressebüro, *das;* **~ officer** *n.* Pressereferent, *der*/-referentin, *die;* Pressesprecher, *der*/-sprecherin, *die;* **~ photographer** *n.* Pressephotograph, *der*/-photographin, *die;* **~ release** *n.* Presseinformation, *die;* **~ report** *n.* Pressebericht, *der;* **~-stud** *n. (Brit.)* Druckknopf, *der;* **~-up** *n.* Liegestütz, *der*

pressure ['preʃə(r)] **1.** *n.* **a)** *(exertion of force, amount)* Druck, *der;* **apply firm ~ to the joint** die Verbindung fest zusammendrücken; **atmospheric ~:** Luftdruck, *der;* **b)** *(oppression)* Last, *die;* Belastung, *die;* **mental ~:** psychische Belastung; **c)** *(trouble)* Druck, *der;* **under financial ~:** finanziell unter Druck; **~s at [one's] work** berufliche Belastungen; **the finances of the company were under ~:** die Firma stand [finanziell] unter Druck; **d)** *(urgency)* Druck, *der; (of affairs)* Dringlichkeit, *die;* **the ~ was on him** er stand unter Zeitdruck; **he [positively] thrives under ~:** er braucht den Druck [geradezu]; **e)** *(constraint)* Druck, *der;* Zwang, *der;* **put ~ on sb.** jmdn. unter Druck setzen; **be under a lot of ~ to do sth.** stark unter Druck gesetzt werden, etw. zu tun; **put the ~ on** die Daumenschrauben anlegen *od.* -setzen. *See also* **high pressure; low pressure. 2.** *v. t.* **a)** *(coerce)* **~ sb. into doing sth.** jmdn. [dazu] drängen, etw. zu tun; **b)** *(fig.: apply ~ to)* unter Druck setzen

pressure: ~-cooker *n.* Schnellkochtopf, *der;* **~ gauge** *n. (Motor Veh.)* Druckluftmesser, *der;* Manometer, *das; (Railw.)* Druckanzeige, *die;* **~ group** *n.* Pressure-group, *die;* **~ point** *n. (Med.)* **a)** *(where sore may develop)* Druckstelle, *die;* **b)** *(where bleeding can be stopped)* Druckpunkt, *der;* **~ suit** *n. (Astronaut.)* Druckanzug, *der*

pressurize (pressurise) ['preʃəraɪz] *v. t.* **a)** *see* **pressure 2 a; b)** *(raise to high pressure)* unter Druck setzen; **c)** *(maintain normal pressure in)* druckfest machen, auf Normaldruck halten ‹*Flugzeugkabine*›; **~d cabin/suit** Druckkabine, *die*/-anzug, *der*

prestige [pre'sti:ʒ] **1.** *n.* Prestige, *das;* Renommee, *das.* **2.** *adj.* renommiert; Nobel- ‹*hotel, -gegend*›; **~ value** Prestigewert, *der*

prestigious [pre'stɪdʒəs] *adj.* angesehen

presto ['prestəʊ] *see* **hey**

pre-stressed [pri:'strest] *adj. (Building)* vorgespannt; **~ concrete** Spannbeton, *der*

presumable [prɪ'zju:məbl] *adj.* mutmaßlich

presumably [prɪ'zju:məblɪ] *adv.* vermutlich; **~ he knows what he is doing** er wird schon wissen, was er tut; **~ something must have delayed them** etwas muß sie aufgehalten haben

presume [prɪ'zju:m] **1.** *v. t.* **a)** *(venture)* **~ to do sth.** sich *(Dat.)* anmaßen, etw. zu tun; *(take the liberty)* sich *(Dat.)* erlauben, etw. zu tun; **b)** *(suppose)* annehmen; **be ~d innocent** als unschuldig gelten *od.* angesehen werden; **missing ~d dead** vermißt, wahrscheinlich *od.* mutmaßlich tot. **2.** *v. i.* sich *(Dat.)* anmaßen; **~ [up]on sth.** etw. ausnützen

presumption [prɪ'zʌmpʃn] *n.* **a)** *(arrogance)* Anmaßung, *die;* Vermessenheit, *die;* **have the ~ to do sth.** die Vermessenheit besitzen, etw. zu tun; sich *(Dat.)* anmaßen, etw. zu tun; **b)** *(assumption)* Annahme, *die;* Vermutung, *die;* **the ~ is that he lost it** vermutlich hat er es verloren; es ist zu vermuten, daß er es verloren hat; **we are working on the ~ that ...:** wir gehen von der Annahme aus, daß ...; **the ~ of innocence** die Unschuldsvermutung; **c)** *(ground for belief)* **there is a strong ~ against its truth** es besteht hinreichend Grund zu der Annahme, daß es nicht stimmt

presumptive [prɪ'zʌmptɪv] *adj.* **~ evidence** Indizienbeweis, *der;* **heir ~:** mutmaßlicher Erbe/mutmaßliche Erbin

presumptuous [prɪ'zʌmptjʊəs] *adj.* anmaßend; überheblich; *(impertinent)* aufdringlich

presumptuously [prɪ'zʌmptjʊəslɪ] *adv.* überheblich; *(impertinently)* aufdringlich

presuppose [pri:sə'pəʊz] *v. t.* **a)** *(assume)* voraussetzen; **b)** *(imply)* voraussetzen; zur Voraussetzung haben

presupposition [pri:sʌpə'zɪʃn] *n.* **a)** *(presupposing)* Annahme, *die;* Voraussetzung, *die;* **b)** *(thing assumed)* Prämisse, *die (bes. Philos., Rechtsw.);* Voraussetzung, *die;* **work on a ~:** von einer Prämisse/Voraussetzung ausgehen

pre-tax ['pri:tæks] *adj.* vor Steuern *nachgestellt;* **~ profits** Gewinn vor Steuern

pretence [prɪ'tens] *n. (Brit.)* **a)** *(pretext)* Vorwand, *der;* **under [the] ~ of helping** unter dem Vorwand zu helfen; *see also* **false pretences; b)** *no art. (make-believe, insincere behaviour)* Verstellung, *die;* **c)** *(piece of insincere behaviour)* **it is all** *or* **just a ~:** das ist alles nicht echt; **d)** *(affectation)* Affektiertheit, *die (abwertend);* Unnatürlichkeit, *die;* **e)** *(claim)* Anspruch, *der;* **make the/no ~ of** *or* **to sth.** Anspruch/keinen Anspruch auf etw. *(Akk.)* erheben

pretend [prɪ'tend] **1.** *v. t.* **a)** vorgeben; **she ~ed to be asleep** sie tat, als ob sie schlief[e]; **b)** *(imagine in play)* **~ to be sth.** so tun, als ob man etw. sei; **let's ~ that we are king and queen** laß uns König und Königin spielen; **c)** *(profess falsely)* vortäuschen; simulieren, vorschützen ‹*Krankheit*›; *(say falsely)* vorgeben, fälschlich beteuern **(to** gegenüber); **~ illness** krank spielen *(ugs.);* **d)** *(claim)* **not ~ to do sth.** nicht behaupten wollen, etw. zu tun. **2.** *v. i.* **a)** sich verstellen; **she's only ~ing** sie tut nur so; **~ to sb.** jmdm. etwas vormachen; **b)** *(presume)* sich unterfangen *(geh.);* wagen; **c) ~ to** *(claim)* für sich in Anspruch nehmen; Anspruch erheben auf (+ *Akk.*) *(Titel, Amt)*

pretender [prɪ'tendə(r)] *n.* Prätendent, *der (geh.)*/Prätendentin, *die (geh.)* **(to** auf + *Akk.*); **~ to the throne** Thronanwärter *od.* -prätendent, *der*/Thronanwärterin *od.* -prätendentin, *die;* **Old/Young P~:** *Sohn/Enkel von Jakob II. als britischer Thronanwärter*

pretense *(Amer.) see* **pretence**

pretension [prɪ'tenʃn] *n.* **a)** *(claim)* Anspruch, *der;* **have/make ~s to great wisdom** vorgeben *od.* den Anspruch erheben, sehr klug zu sein; **b)** *(justifiable claim)* Anspruch, *der* **(to** auf + *Akk.*); **a country estate of some ~s** ein Landsitz, der sich sehen lassen kann; **people with ~s to taste and culture** Menschen, die Geschmack und Kultur für sich in Anspruch nehmen können; **c)** *(pretentiousness)* Überheblichkeit, *die;* Anmaßung, *die; (of things: ostentation)* Protzigkeit, *die*

pretentious [prɪ'tenʃəs] *adj.* **a)** prätentiös *(geh.);* hochgestochen; wichtigtuerisch ‹*Person*›; **b)** *(ostentatious)* protzig *(abwertend);* großspurig *(abwertend)* ‹*Person, Verhalten, Art*›

pretentiously [prɪ'tenʃəslɪ] *adv.* **a)** prätentiös *(geh.);* hochgestochen; **speak ~:** wichtigtuerische Reden führen; **b)** *(ostentatiously)* protzig *(abwertend);* großspurig *(abwertend)* ‹*sich benehmen*›

preterite *(Amer.:* **preterit)** ['pretərɪt] *(Ling.)* **1.** *adj.* Präteritums-; **~ tense** Präteritum, *das.* **2.** *n.* Präteritum, *das*

preternatural [pri:tə'nætʃərl] *adj.* **a)** *(nonnatural)* außergewöhnlich; **b)** *(supernatural)* übernatürlich; übersinnlich

pretext ['pri:tekst] *n.* Vorwand, *der;* Ausrede, *die;* **make illness the ~ for staying at home** Krankheit vorschützen, um zu Hause zu bleiben; **[up]on** *or* **under the ~ of doing sth./being ill** unter dem Vorwand *od.* mit der Entschuldigung, etw. tun zu wollen/krank zu sein; **on the slightest ~:** mit *od.* unter dem fadenscheinigsten Vorwand

prettify ['prɪtɪfaɪ] *v. t.* verschönern; *(in an insipid way)* verkitschen

prettily ['prɪtɪlɪ] *adv.* hübsch; sehr schön ‹*singen, tanzen*›; **curtsy ~:** einen graziösen Knicks machen; **thank sb. ~:** sich [bei jmdm.] sehr nett bedanken

pretty ['prɪtɪ] **1.** *adj.* **a)** *(attractive)* hübsch; nett ⟨*Art*⟩; niedlich ⟨*Geschichte, Liedchen*⟩; **she's not just a ~ face!** sie ist nicht nur hübsch[, sie kann auch was]!; **as ~ as a picture** bildhübsch; **not a ~ sight** *(iron.)* kein schöner Anblick; **b)** *(iron.)* hübsch, schön *(ugs. iron.)*; **a ~ state of affairs** eine schöne Geschichte; **a ~ mess** eine schöne Bescherung. **2.** *adv.* ziemlich; **I am ~ well** es geht mir ganz gut; **~ much** *or* **well as ...:** so ziemlich wie ...; **we have ~ nearly finished** wir sind so gut wie fertig; **be ~ well over/exhausted** so gut wie vorbei/erschöpft sein; **~ much the same** ziemlich unverändert; **~ much the same thing** so ziemlich *od.* fast das gleiche; **be sitting ~** *(coll.)* sein Schäfchen im trockenen haben *(ugs.)*; ausgesorgt haben; **~-pretty** *(coll.)* kitschig *(abwertend)*

pretzel ['pretsl] *n.* Brezel, *die*

prevail [prɪ'veɪl] *v. i.* **a)** *(gain mastery)* siegen, die Oberhand gewinnen (**against, over** über + *Akk.*); **~ [up]on sb.** auf jmdn. einwirken; jmdn. überreden; **be ~ed [up]on to do sth.** sich bewegen *od.* überreden lassen, etw. zu tun; **b)** *(predominate)* ⟨*Zustand, Bedingung:*⟩ vorherrschen; **c)** *(be current)* herrschen; **this type of approach ~ed for many years** dieser Ansatz war jahrelang gängig *od.* üblich

prevailing [prɪ'veɪlɪŋ] *adj.* **a)** *(common)* [vor]herrschend; aktuell ⟨*Mode*⟩; **b)** *(frequent)* **the ~ wind is from the West** der Wind kommt vorwiegend von Westen

prevalence ['prevələns] *n., no pl.* Vorherrschen, *das; (of crime, corruption, etc.)* Überhandnehmen, *das; (of disease, malnutrition, etc.)* weite Verbreitung; **gain ~** ⟨*Standpunkt:*⟩ sich durchsetzen

prevalent ['prevələnt] *adj.* **a)** *(existing)* herrschend; gängig, geläufig ⟨*Schreibweise*⟩; weit verbreitet ⟨*Krankheit*⟩; aktuell ⟨*Trend*⟩; **b)** *(predominant)* vorherrschend; **be/become ~:** vorherrschen/sich durchsetzen

prevaricate [prɪ'værɪkeɪt] *v. i.* Ausflüchte machen (**over** wegen)

prevarication [prɪværɪ'keɪʃn] *n.* **a)** *(prevaricating)* Ausflüchte *Pl.*; **b)** *(statement)* Ausflucht, *die*

prevent [prɪ'vent] *v. t. (hinder)* verhindern; **~ sb. from doing sth., ~ sb.'s doing sth.,** *(coll.)* **~ sb. doing sth.** jmdn. daran hindern *od.* davon abhalten, etw. zu tun; **there is nothing to ~ me** nichts hindert mich daran; **~ sb. from coming** jmdn. am Kommen hindern; **catch sb.'s arm to ~ him [from] falling** jmdn. am Arm fassen, damit er nicht fällt; **do everything to ~ it from happening** *or* **~ its happening** alles tun, um es zu verhindern *od.* damit es nicht geschieht

preventable [prɪ'ventəbl] *adj.* vermeidbar

preventative [prɪ'ventətɪv] *see* **preventive**

prevention [prɪ'venʃn] *n.* Verhinderung, *die;* Verhütung, *die;* **~ of crime** Verbrechensverhütung, *die;* **society for the ~ of cruelty to children/animals** Kinderschutzbund/Tierschutzverein, *der;* **~ is better than cure** *(prov.)* Vorbeugen ist besser als Heilen *(Spr.)*

preventive [prɪ'ventɪv] **1.** *adj.* vorbeugend; präventiv *(geh.)*; Präventiv⟨*maßnahme, -krieg*⟩; **~ treatment** *(Med.)* Präventivbehandlung, *die.* **2.** *n.* Vorbeugungsmaßnahme, *die;* Präventivmittel, *das (Med.)*; **as a ~:** zur/als Vorbeugung

preventive: ~ de'tention *n. (Brit. Law)* Sicherungsverwahrung, *die;* **~ 'medicine** *n.* Präventivmedizin, *die*

preview ['pri:vju:] **1.** *n.* **a)** *(of film, play)* Voraufführung, *die; (of exhibition)* Vernissage, *die (geh.); (of book)* Vorbesprechung, *die;* **give a ~:** eine Voraufführung geben/Vernissage veranstalten/Vorbesprechung geben; **b)** *(Amer.: trailer of film)* Vorschau, *die.* **2.** *v. t.* eine Vorschau sehen von ⟨*Film*⟩

previous ['pri:vɪəs] **1.** *adj.* **a)** *(coming before)* früher ⟨*Anstellung, Gelegenheit*⟩; vorherig ⟨*Abend*⟩; vorig ⟨*Besitzer, Wohnsitz*⟩; **the ~ page** die Seite davor; **no ~ experience necessary** keine Berufserfahrung nötig; **no ~ convictions** keine Vorstrafen; **b)** *(prior)* **~ to** vor (+ *Dat.*); **c)** *(hasty)* verfrüht; voreilig. **2.** *adv.* **~ to** vor (+ *Dat.*); **~ to being a nurse, she was ...:** bevor sie Krankenschwester wurde, war sie ...

previously ['pri:vɪəslɪ] *adv.* vorher; **two years ~:** zwei Jahre zuvor

pre-war ['pri:wɔ:(r)] *adj.* Vorkriegs-; **these houses are all ~:** diese Häuser stammen alle aus der Zeit vor dem Krieg

prey [preɪ] **1.** *n., pl. same* **a)** *(animal[s])* Beute, *die;* Beutetier, *das;* **beast/bird of ~:** Raubtier, *das*/-vogel, *der;* **easy ~** *(lit. or fig.)* leichte Beute; **b)** *(victim)* Beute, *die (geh.)*; Opfer, *das;* **fall [a] ~ to sth.** einer Sache *(Dat.)* zum Opfer fallen; **be a ~ to sth.** eine Beute *od.* ein Opfer von etw. werden. **2.** *v.i.* **~ [up]on** ⟨*Raubtier, Raubvogel:*⟩ schlagen; *(take as prey)* erbeuten; *(plunder)* ausplündern ⟨*Person*⟩; *(exploit)* ausnutzen; **~ [up]on sb.'s mind** jmdm. keine Ruhe lassen; ⟨*Krankheit:*⟩ jmdm. sehr zusetzen; ⟨*Kummer, Angst:*⟩ an jmdm. nagen

prezzie ['prezɪ] *n. (coll.)* Geschenk, *das*

price [praɪs] **1.** *n.* **a)** *(money etc.)* Preis, *der;* **the ~ of wheat/a pint** der Weizenpreis/der Preis für ein Bier; **what is the ~ of this?** was kostet das?; **at a ~ of** zum Preis von; **for the ~ of a few drinks** für ein paar Drinks; **~s and incomes policy** Preis- und Einkommenspolitik, *die;* Lohn-Preis-Politik, *die;* **sth. goes up/down in ~:** der Preis von etw. steigt/fällt; etw. steigt/fällt im Preis; **what sort of ~ do they charge for a meal?** was verlangen *od.* berechnen sie für eine Mahlzeit?; **at a ~:** zum entsprechenden Preis; **set a ~ on sth.** einen Preis für etw. festsetzen; **set a ~ on sb.'s head** *or* **life** einen Preis *od.* eine Belohnung auf jmds. Kopf *(Akk.)* aussetzen; **b)** *(betting odds)* Eventualquote, *die;* **c)** *(value)* **be without/beyond ~:** [mit Geld] nicht zu bezahlen sein; **d)** *(fig.)* Preis, *der;* **be achieved at a ~:** seinen Preis haben; **he succeeded, but at a great ~:** er hatte Erfolg, mußte aber einen hohen Preis dafür bezahlen; **every man has his ~:** jeder Mensch hat seinen Preis *od.* ist käuflich; **at/not at any ~:** um jeden/keinen Preis; **at the ~ of ruining his marriage/health** auf Kosten seiner Ehe/Gesundheit; **what ~ ...?** *(Brit. sl.) (what is the chance of ...)* wie wär's mit ...?; *(... has failed)* wie steht's jetzt mit ...? *See also* **pay 2 f. 2.** *v. t. (fix ~ of)* kalkulieren ⟨*Ware*⟩; *(label with ~)* auszeichnen; **modestly ~d** preislich *od.* im Preis gering; **favourably ~d** preisgünstig

price: ~-bracket *see* **price-range; ~-control** *n.* Preiskontrolle, *die;* **~-cut** *n.* Preissenkung, *die;* **~-fixing** *n.* Preisabsprache, *die;* **~ freeze** *n.* Preisstopp, *der*

priceless ['praɪslɪs] *adj.* **a)** *(invaluable)* unbezahlbar; unschätzbar ⟨*Gut*⟩; **b)** *(coll.: amusing)* köstlich

price: ~-list *n.* Preisliste, *die;* **~-range** *n.* Preisspanne, *die;* **it's within/outside my ~-range** das kann ich mir leisten/nicht leisten; **~-ring** *n. (Econ.)* Preiskartell, *das;* **~-rise** *n.* Preisanstieg, *der* (**on** bei); **constant ~-rises** ständig steigende Preise; ständige Preiserhöhungen; **~-tag** *n.* Preisschild, *das; (fig.)* Kosten *Pl.*; **~ war** *n.* Preiskrieg, *der*

pricey ['praɪsɪ] *adj.*, **pricier** ['praɪsɪə(r)], **priciest** ['praɪsɪɪst] *(Brit. coll.)* teuer

prick [prɪk] **1.** *v. t.* **a)** *(pierce)* stechen; stechen in ⟨*Ballon*⟩; aufstechen ⟨*Blase*⟩; **he ~ed his finger with the needle** er stach sich *(Dat.)* mit der Nadel in den Finger; **~ the bubble** *(fig.)* die Illusion zerstören; **~ out** auspflanzen ⟨*Setzlinge*⟩; **b)** *(fig.)* quälen; plagen; **my conscience ~ed me** ich hatte Gewissensbisse; **c)** *(mark)* **~ [off** *or* **out]** vorstechen ⟨*Stickmuster, Linie usw.*⟩; **d)** *(mark off)* markieren. **2.** *v. i.* **a)** *(hurt)* stechen; **b)** *(thrust)* stechen; **~ at sb.'s conscience** jmdm. Gewissensbisse verursachen. **3.** *n.* **a) I felt a little ~:** ich fühlte einen leichten Stich; **give sb.'s finger a ~ with the needle** jmdm. mit der Nadel in den Finger stechen; **~s of conscience** Gewissensbisse *Pl.*; **b)** *(mark)* Punkt, *der;* **c)** *(coarse: penis)* Pimmel, *der (fam.)*; Schwanz, *der (derb)*; **d)** *(coarse, derog.: man)* Wichser, *der (derb)*; **e)** *(arch.: goad)* Stachel, *der;* **kick against the ~s** *(fig.)* wider den Stachel löcken *(geh.)*

~ up 1. *v. t.* aufrichten ⟨*Ohren*⟩; **~ up one's/its ears** *(listen)* die Ohren spitzen. **2.** *v. i.* ⟨*Ohren:*⟩ sich aufrichten

prickle ['prɪkl] **1.** *n.* **a)** *(thorn)* Dorn, *der;* **b)** *(Zool., Bot.)* Stachel, *der.* **2.** *v. t.* stechen; ⟨*Wolle:*⟩ kratzen auf (+ *Dat.*), ⟨*Hitze, Wind:*⟩ prickeln auf (+ *Dat.*) ⟨*Haut*⟩. **3.** *v. i.* kratzen

prickly ['prɪklɪ] *adj.* **a)** *(with prickles)* dornig; stachelig; **be ~** ⟨*Pflanze:*⟩ Stacheln/Dornen haben; **b)** *(fig.)* empfindlich; **c)** *(tingling)* kratzig; **a ~ sensation in the limbs** ein Kribbeln *od.* Prickeln in den Gliedern

prickly: ~ 'heat *n. (Med.)* rote Frieseln; **~ 'pear** *n.* **a)** *(cactus)* Feigenkaktus, *der;* **b)** *(fruit)* Kaktusfeige, *die*

pricy *see* **pricey**

pride [praɪd] **1.** *n.* **a)** Stolz, *der; (arrogance)* Hochmut, *der (abwertend)*; **~ goes before a fall** *(prov.)* Hochmut kommt vor dem Fall *(Spr.)*; **take** *or* **have ~ of place** die Spitzenstellung einnehmen *od.* innehaben; *(in collection etc.)* das Glanzstück sein; **proper ~:** gesunder Stolz; **a proper ~ in oneself** ein gesundes Selbstwertgefühl; **she has a lot of ~:** sie ist sehr stolz; **his own ~ prevented him from doing that** sein Ehrgefühl verbot ihm, das zu tun; **false ~:** falscher Stolz; **take [a] ~ in sb./sth.** auf jmdn./etw. stolz sein; **b)** *(object, best one)* Stolz, *der;* **sb.'s ~ and joy** jmds. ganzer Stolz; **c)** *(of lions)* Rudel, *das.* **2.** *v. refl.* **~ oneself [up]on sth.** *(congratulate oneself)* auf etw. *(Akk.)* stolz sein; *(plume oneself)* sich mit etw. brüsten *(abwertend)*

priest [pri:st] *n.* Priester, *der; see also* **high priest**

priestess ['pri:stɪs] *n.* Priesterin, *die*

priesthood ['pri:sthʊd] *n. (office)* geistliches Amt; *(order of priests; priests)* Geistlichkeit, *die;* **go into the ~:** Priester werden

priestlike ['pri:stlaɪk] *adv.* priesterlich

priestly ['pri:stlɪ] *adj.* priesterlich; Priester⟨*kaste, -rolle*⟩

prig [prɪg] *n. (didactic)* Besserwisser, *der*/-wisserin, *die (abwertend)*; *(smug)* selbstgefälliger Mensch; *(self-righteous)* Tugendbold, *der (ugs., iron.)*

priggish ['prɪgɪʃ] *adj. (didactic)* besserwisserisch *(abwertend)*; *(smug)* selbstgefällig *(abwertend)*; *(self-righteous)* übertrieben tugendhaft

prim [prɪm] *adj.* **a)** spröde, steif ⟨*Person*⟩; streng ⟨*Kleidung*⟩; **~ and proper** etepetete *(ugs.)*; **b)** *(prudish)* zimperlich; prüde

prima ballerina [pri:mə bælə'ri:nə] *n.* Primaballerina, *die*

primacy ['praɪməsɪ] *n.* **a)** *(pre-eminence)* Vorrang, *der;* Primat, *der od. das (geh.)*; **position of ~:** Vorrangstellung, *die;* **b)** *(Eccl.: office)* Primat, *der od. das*

prima donna [pri:mə 'dɒnə] *n. (Theatre; also fig.)* Primadonna, *die*

primaeval *see* **primeval**

prima facie [praɪmə 'feɪʃi:] **1.** *adv.* auf den ersten Blick. **2.** *adj.* glaubhaft klingend; **~ evidence** *(Law)* Anscheinsbeweis, *der;* **I don't see a ~ reason for it** ich sehe keinen einleuchtenden Grund dafür

primal ['praɪml] *adj.* ursprünglich; primitiv; **~ forces** Urkräfte *Pl.*

primarily ['praɪmərɪlɪ] *adv.* in erster Linie
primary ['praɪmərɪ] **1.** *adj.* **a)** *(first in sequence)* primär *(geh.)*; grundlegend; **the ~ meaning of a word** die Grundbedeutung eines Wortes; **~ source** Primärquelle, *die (geh.)*; **b)** *(chief)* Haupt⟨*rolle, -sorge, -ziel, -zweck*⟩; **of ~ importance** von höchster Bedeutung. **2.** *n. (Amer.: election)* Vorwahl, *die*
primary: ~ 'battery *n. (Electr.)* Primärbatterie, *die*; **~ 'cell** *n. (Electr.)* Primärelement, *das*; **~ 'coil** *n. (Electr.)* Primärspule, *die*; **~ 'colour** *see* **colour 1 a**; **~ edu'cation** *n.* Grundschulerziehung, *die*; **~ e'lection** *n. (Amer.)* Vorwahl, *die*; **~ 'feather** *n. (Ornith.)* Schwungfeder, *die*; **~ 'planet** *n. (Astron.)* Hauptplanet, *der*; **~ school** *n.* Grundschule, *die*; *attrib.* **~-school teacher** Grundschullehrer, *der*/-lehrerin, *die*; **~ stress** *n. (Ling.)* Hauptakzent, *der*
primate ['praɪmət, 'praɪmeɪt] *n.* **a)** *(Eccl.)* Primas, *der*; **P~ of England** Primas von England; *Titel des Erzbischofs von York*; **P~ of all England** Primas von ganz England; *Titel des Erzbischofs von Canterbury*; **b)** *(Zool.)* Primat, *der*
[1]**prime** [praɪm] **1.** *n.* **a)** *(perfection)* Höhepunkt, *der*; Krönung, *die*; **in the ~ of life/youth/manhood** in der Blüte seiner/ihrer Jahre/der Jugend *(geh.)*/im besten Mannesalter; **be in/past one's ~**: in den besten Jahren sein/die besten Jahre überschritten haben; **b)** *(best part)* Beste, *das*; **c)** *(Math.)* Primzahl, *die*. **2.** *adj.* **a)** *(chief)* Haupt-; hauptsächlich; **~ motive** Hauptmotiv, *das*; **be of ~ importance** von höchster Wichtigkeit sein; **b)** *(excellent)* erstklassig; vortrefflich ⟨*Beispiel*⟩; **~ ham/lamb/pork** Schinken/Lamm/Schweinefleisch erster Güteklasse; **in ~ condition** ⟨*Sportler, Tier*⟩ in bester Verfassung; voll ausgereift ⟨*Obst*⟩
[2]**prime** *v. t.* **a)** *(equip)* vorbereiten; **~ sb. with sth.** jmdn. mit etw. vertraut machen; **~ sb. with information/advice** jmdn. instruieren/jmdm. Ratschläge erteilen; **well ~d** gut vorbereitet; **b)** *(ply with liquor)* betrunken machen; abfüllen *(ugs.)*; **be well ~d** voll sein *(salopp)*; **c)** grundieren ⟨*Wand, Decke*⟩; **d)** füllen ⟨*Pumpe*⟩; **e)** *(inject petrol into)* Anlaßkraftstoff einspritzen in (+ *Akk.*) ⟨*Motor, Zylinder*⟩; **f)** schärfen ⟨*Sprengkörper*⟩
prime: ~ 'cost *n. (Econ.)* Selbstkosten *Pl.*; **~ me'ridian** *n. (Geog.)* Nullmeridian, *der*; **~ 'minister** *n.* Premierminister, *der*/-ministerin, *die*; **~ 'number** *n. (Math.)* Primzahl, *die*
[1]**primer** ['praɪmə(r)] *n. (book)* Fibel, *die*
[2]**primer** *n.* **a)** *(explosive)* Zündvorrichtung, *die*; **b)** *(paint etc.)* Grundierlack, *der*
prime: ~ rate *n. (Econ.)* Prime rate, *die*; **~ 'ribs** *n. pl.* Hochrippen *Pl.*; **~ time** *n.* Hauptsendezeit, *die*; **~-time TV** Hauptsendezeit im Fernsehen
primeval [praɪ'mi:vl] *adj.* urzeitlich; **~ times/forests** Urzeiten/Urwälder
priming ['praɪmɪŋ] *n. (paint)* Grundanstrich, *der*; Grundierung, *die*
primitive ['prɪmɪtɪv] **1.** *adj.* **a)** primitiv; *(original)* ursprünglich; *(prehistoric)* urzeitlich ⟨*Mensch*⟩; frühzeitlich ⟨*Ackerbau, Technik*⟩; **b)** *(Ling.)* **~ word** Stammwort, *das*; Primitivum, *das (fachspr.)*. **2.** *n. (painter) Maler der Zeit vor der Renaissance*; *(in modern art)* Primitive, *der/die*
primitively ['prɪmɪtɪvlɪ] *adv.* primitiv
primly ['prɪmlɪ] *adv.* steif; streng ⟨*sich kleiden*⟩
primness ['prɪmnɪs] *n. no pl.* Steifheit, *die*; *(of dress)* Strenge, *die*
primogeniture [praɪmə'dʒenɪtʃə(r)] *n. (Law)* **[right of] ~**: Primogenitur, *die*; **rights of ~**: Erstgeburtsrechte *Pl.*
primordial [praɪ'mɔ:dɪəl] *adj.* ursprünglich; Ur⟨*masse, -zustand, -zeiten*⟩; primordial *(bes. Philos.)*; **~ soup** Urschleim, *der*
primp [prɪmp] *v. t.* zurechtstreichen, zurechtzupfen ⟨*Haar, Kleid*⟩; **~ oneself** sich zurecht- *od.* schönmachen *(ugs.)*
primrose ['prɪmrəʊz] *n.* **a)** *(plant, flower)* gelbe Schlüsselblume; Himmelsschlüsselchen, *das*; **the ~ path** *(fig.)* der Pfad des Vergnügens; *(path of least resistance)* der Weg des geringsten Widerstandes; *see also* **evening primrose**; **b)** *(colour)* schlüsselblumengelb
primula ['prɪmjʊlə] *n. (Bot.)* Primel, *die*
Primus, (P) ['praɪməs] *n.* **~ [stove]** Primuskocher, *der*
prince [prɪns] *n.* **a)** *(ruler)* Fürst, *der*; **b)** *(member of royal family)* **~ [of the blood]** Prinz [von Geblüt]; **P~ of Wales** Prinz von Wales; **c)** *(rhet.: sovereign ruler)* Fürst, *der*; Monarch, *der*; **the P~ of Peace** der Friedensfürst; **the P~ of Darkness** der Fürst der Finsternis *od.* der Hölle; **d)** *(fig.: greatest one)* König, *der* (of unter + *Dat.*); **a ~ among men** ein Fürst unter den Sterblichen *(geh.)*
Prince: ~ Albert [prɪns 'ælbət] *n. (Amer. coll.)* Gehrock, *der*; Bratenrock, *der (veralt., scherzh.)*; **~ 'Charming** *n. (fig.)* Märchenprinz, *der*; **p~ 'consort** *n.* Prinzgemahl, *der*
princely ['prɪnslɪ] *adj. (lit. or fig.)* fürstlich; **~ houses** Fürstenhäuser
Prince 'Regent *n.* Prinzregent, *der*
princess ['prɪnses, prɪn'ses] *n.* **a)** Prinzessin, *die*; **~ [of the blood]** Prinzessin [von Geblüt]; **b)** *(wife of prince)* Fürstin, *die*
princess: ~ dress *n.* Prinzeßkleid, *das*; **~ line** *n.* Prinzeßform, *die*; **~ 'royal** *n. [Titel für] älteste Tochter eines Monarchen*
principal ['prɪnsɪpl] **1.** *adj.* **a)** Haupt-; *(most important)* wichtigst...; bedeutendst...; **the ~ cause of lung cancer** die häufigste Ursache für Lungenkrebs; **b)** *(Mus.)* **~ horn/bassoon** *etc.* erstes Horn/Fagott *usw.* **2.** *n.* **a)** *(head of school or college)* Rektor, *der*/Rektorin, *die*; **b)** *(performer)* Hauptdarsteller, *der*/-darstellerin, *die (Theater, Film)*; **c)** *(leader)* Vorsitzende, *der/die*; **d)** *(employer of agent)* Auftraggeber, *der*/-geberin, *die*; **e)** *(in duel)* Duellant, *der*; **f)** *(Finance) (invested)* Kapitalbetrag, *der*; *(lent)* Kreditsumme, *die*; **g)** *(Law) (for whom another is surety)* Hauptschuldner, *der*/-schuldnerin, *die*; *(directly responsible for crime)* Hauptschuldige, *der/die*
principal: ~ 'boy *n. (Brit. Theatre) [gewöhnlich von einer Frau gespielte] männliche Hauptrolle im britischen Weihnachtsmärchen*; **~ clause** *n. (Ling.)* Hauptsatz, *der*; **~ 'girl** *n. (Brit. Theatre) weibliche Hauptrolle im britischen Weihnachtsmärchen*
principality [prɪnsɪ'pælɪtɪ] *n.* Fürstentum, *das*; **the P~** *(Brit.)* Wales
principally ['prɪnsɪpəlɪ] *adv.* in erster Linie
principal 'parts *n. pl. (Ling.)* Stammformen
principle ['prɪnsɪpl] *n.* **a)** Prinzip, *das*; **on the ~ that ...**: nach dem Grundsatz, daß ...; **be based on the ~ that ...**: auf dem Grundsatz basieren, daß ...; **basic ~**: Grundprinzip, *das*; **go back to first ~s** zu den Grundlagen zurückgehen; **in ~**: im Prinzip; **it's the ~ [of the thing]** es geht [dabei] ums Prinzip; **make it a ~ to do sth.** es sich *(Dat.)* zum Prinzip machen, etw. zu tun; **a man of high ~** *or* **strong ~s** ein Mann von *od.* mit hohen Prinzipien; **a matter of ~**: eine Prinzipfrage; **do sth. on ~** *or* **as a matter of ~**: etw. prinzipiell *od.* aus Prinzip tun; **operate by** *or* **work on the same ~**: nach demselben Prinzip funktionieren; **work on the ~ of 'first come, first served'** nach dem Prinzip „wer zuerst kommt, mahlt zuerst" vorgehen; **b)** *(Phys.)* Lehrsatz, *der*; **c)** *(Chem.)* Komponente, *die*
principled ['prɪnsɪpld] *adj.* von Prinzipien geleitet
prink [prɪŋk] *v. t. (coll.)* zurechtmachen *(ugs.)* ⟨*Person, Haar*⟩; schmücken ⟨*Kleid, Haus*⟩; **~ oneself [up]** sich herausputzen; sich zurechtmachen *(ugs.)*
print [prɪnt] **1.** *n.* **a)** *(impression)* Abdruck, *der*; *(finger~)* Fingerabdruck, *der*; *(foot~)* Fußabdruck, *der*; **b)** *(~ed lettering)* Gedruckte, *das*; *(type-face)* Druck, *der*; **clear/large ~**: deutlicher/großer Druck; **this ~ is too small** das ist zu klein gedruckt; **editions in large ~**: Großdruckbücher; *see also* **small print**; **c)** *(handwriting)* **write [sth.] in ~**: [etw.] in Druckschrift schreiben; **d)** *(published or ~ed state)* **be in/out of ~** ⟨*Buch*⟩: erhältlich/vergriffen sein; **appear in/get into ~**: gedruckt werden; *see also* **rush into a**; **e)** *(~ed picture or design)* Druck, *der*; **f)** *(Photog.)* Abzug, *der*; *(Cinemat.)* Kopie, *die*; **black and white/colour ~**: Schwarzweiß-/Farbabdruck, *der*/-kopie, *die*; **g)** *(Textiles) (cloth with design)* bedruckter Stoff; *(design)* Druckmuster, *das*; **h)** *(~ed publication)* Publikation, *die*; **~s** *(Amer. Post)* Druckschriften; **the ~s** *(Amer. Journ.)* die Presse. **2.** *v. t.* **a)** drucken ⟨*Buch, Zeitschrift, Geldschein usw.*⟩; **b)** *(write)* in Druckschrift schreiben; **c)** *(cause to be published)* veröffentlichen ⟨*Artikel, Roman, Ansichten usw.*⟩; **d)** *(Photog.)* abziehen; *(Cinemat.)* kopieren; **e)** *(Textiles)* bedrucken ⟨*Stoff*⟩; **f)** *(impress)* eindrücken; **~ sth. with sth.** etw. mit etw. bedrucken; **~ sth. on** etw. drücken in (+ *Akk.*) ⟨*Haut*⟩; etw. aufdrucken auf (+ *Akk.*) ⟨*Papier, Holz*⟩. **3.** *v. i.* **a)** *(Printing)* drucken; **b)** *(write)* in Druckschrift schreiben
~ 'out *v. t. (Computing)* ausdrucken; *see also* **print-out**
printable ['prɪntəbl] *adj.* druckbar; **be ~** *(Photog.)* einen guten Abzug ermöglichen; **what he replied is not ~** *(fig.)* was er geantwortet hat, zu wiederholen, verbietet sich
printed ['prɪntɪd] *adj.* **a)** *(Printing)* gedruckt; **~ characters** *or* **letters** Druckbuchstaben; **on the ~ page** gedruckt; **b)** *(written like print)* in Druckschrift; **c)** *(published)* veröffentlicht ⟨*Artikel, Roman, Ansichten usw.*⟩; **d)** *(Textiles)* bedruckt ⟨*Stoff*⟩; **~ design** Druckmuster, *das*
printed: ~ 'circuit *n. (Electronics)* gedruckte Schaltung; **~ matter** *n., no pl., no indef. art.* **a)** Gedruckte, *das*; *(Post)* Drucksachen *Pl.*; **[item of] ~ matter** Drucksache, *die*; **~ 'paper** *(Brit. Post) see* **~ matter**
printer ['prɪntə(r)] *n.* **a)** *(Printing) (worker)* Drucker, *der*/Druckerin, *die*; *(owner of business)* Druckereibesitzer, *der*; **firm of ~s** Druckerei, *die*; **send sth. off to the ~'s** etw. in die Druckerei schicken; **at the ~'s** in der Druckerei; **b)** *(Computing)* Drucker, *der*
printer: ~'s 'devil *n. (Hist.)* Setzerjunge, *der*; **~'s 'error** *n.* Druckfehler, *der*; **~'s 'ink** *n.* Druckfarbe, *die*
printing ['prɪntɪŋ] *n.* **a)** Drucken, *das*; **[the] ~ [trade]** das Druckgewerbe; **b)** *(writing like print)* Druckschrift, *die*; **c)** *(edition)* Auflage, *die*; **d)** *(Photog.)* Abziehen, *das*; **e)** *(Textiles)* Bedrucken, *das*
printing: ~ error *n.* Druckfehler, *der*; **~-house** *n.* Druckerei, *die*; **~-ink** *n.* Druckfarbe, *die*; **~-machine** *n. (Brit.)* Druckmaschine, *die*; **~-press** *n.* Druckerpresse, *die*
print: ~maker *n. (Graph. Arts)* Grafiker, *der*/Grafikerin, *die*; **~-out** *n. (Computing)* Ausdruck, *der*; **~-run** *n. (Publishing)* Auflage, die; **what is the ~-run?** wie hoch ist die Auflage?; **~-seller** *n.* Grafikhändler, *der*/-händlerin, *die*; **~-shop** *n.* **a)** *(shop)* Grafikhandlung, *die*; **b)** *(~ing establishment)* [kleinere] Druckerei
prior ['praɪə(r)] **1.** *adj.* vorherig ⟨*Warnung, Zustimmung, Vereinbarung usw.*⟩; früher ⟨*Verabredung, Ehe*⟩; vorrangig ⟨*Bedeutung, Interesse*⟩; Vor⟨*geschichte, -kenntnis, -war-*

nung⟩; **give a matter ~ consideration** eine Angelegenheit vorher überdenken *od.* überprüfen; **have a** *or* **the ~ claim to sth.** ältere Rechte an etw. *(Dat.) od.* auf etw. *(Akk.)* haben. **2.** *adv.* **~ to** vor (+ *Dat.*); **~ to doing sth.** bevor man etw. tut/tat; **~ to that** vorher. **3.** *n. (Eccl.)* Prior, *der*

prioritize (prioritise) [praɪˈɒrɪtaɪz] *v. t.* nach Vordringlichkeit ordnen

priority [praɪˈɒrɪtɪ] *n.* **a)** *(precedence)* Vorrang, *der; attrib.* vorrangig; **have** *or* **take ~:** Vorrang haben (**over** vor + *Dat.*); *(on road)* Vorfahrt haben; **give ~ to sb./sth.** jmdm./einer Sache den Vorrang geben; **give top ~ to sth.** einer Sache *(Dat.)* höchste Priorität einräumen; **what is the order of ~ for those jobs?** in welcher Reihenfolge sollen die Arbeiten erledigt werden?; **be listed in order of ~:** der Vorrangigkeit nach aufgeführt sein; **according to ~:** der Vorrangigkeit nach; **b)** *(matter)* vordringliche Angelegenheit; **our first ~ is to ...:** zuallererst müssen wir ...; **be high/low on the list of priorities** oben/unten auf der Prioritätenliste stehen; **get one's priorities right/wrong** seine Prioritäten richtig/falsch setzen; **it depends on one's** *or* **your priorities** es kommt darauf an, was einem wichtig ist

priory [ˈpraɪərɪ] *n. (Eccl.)* Priorat, *das*

prise *see* ²**prize**

prism [ˈprɪzm] *n. (Optics, Geom.)* Prisma, *das*

prismatic [prɪzˈmætɪk] *adj.* **a)** *(in shape)* prismenförmig; **b) ~ colours** Spektralfarben

prismatic: ~ biˈnoculars *n. pl.* Prismenglas, *das;* **~ ˈcompass** *n. (Surv.)* Patentbussole, *die*

prison [ˈprɪzn] *n.* **a)** *(lit. or fig.)* Gefängnis, *das; attrib.* Gefängnis-; **~ without bars** offene [Vollzugs]anstalt; **stone walls do not a ~ make [nor iron bars a cage]** *(prov.)* ≈ die Gedanken sind frei; **b)** *no pl., no art. (custody)* Haft, *die;* **10 years' ~:** eine zehnjährige Gefängnisstrafe; **in ~:** im Gefängnis; **go to ~:** ins Gefängnis gehen *od. (ugs.)* wandern; **send sb. to ~:** jmdn. ins Gefängnis schicken; **escape/be released from ~:** aus dem Gefängnis ausbrechen/entlassen werden; **put sb. in ~:** jmdn. verhaften *od. (ugs.)* einsperren; **let sb. out of ~:** jmdn. aus der Haft entlassen

ˈprison camp *n.* Gefangenenlager, *das*

prisoner [ˈprɪznə(r)] *n. (lit. or fig.)* Gefangene, *der/die;* **~ [at the bar]** *(accused person)* Angeklagte, *der/die;* **~ of conscience** *aus politischen od. religiösen Gründen Inhaftierter/Inhaftierte;* **a ~ of circumstance** *(fig.)* ein Opfer der Umstände; **hold** *or* **keep sb. ~** *(lit. or fig.)* jmdn. gefangenhalten; **take sb. ~:** jmdn. gefangennehmen

prisoner of ˈwar *n.* Kriegsgefangene, *der/die;* **prisoner-of-war camp** [Kriegs]gefangenenlager, *das*

prison: ~ ˈguard *n.* Gefängniswärter, *der/*-wärterin, *die;* **~ life** *n., no art.* Gefängnisleben, *das;* **~ ˈvisitor** *n.* ≈ Gefangenenfürsorger, *der/*-fürsorgerin, *die*

prissy [ˈprɪsɪ] *adj. (coll.)* zickig *(ugs.);* piepsig *(ugs.)* ⟨*Stimme*⟩

pristine [ˈprɪstiːn, ˈprɪstaɪn] *adj.* unberührt; ursprünglich ⟨*Glanz, Weiße, Schönheit*⟩; **in ~ condition** in tadellosem Zustand

privacy [ˈprɪvəsɪ, ˈpraɪvəsɪ] *n.* **a)** *(seclusion)* Zurückgezogenheit, *die;* **guard one's ~:** seine Privatsphäre abschirmen; **in the ~ of one's [own] home/living-room** in den eigenen vier Wänden *(ugs.);* **invasion of ~/sb.'s ~:** Eindringen in die/jmds. Privatsphäre; **I have** *or* **get no ~ in this house** ich habe keine Ruhe in diesem Haus; **allow sb. no ~:** jmdm. kein Privatleben erlauben; **b)** *(confidentiality)* **in the strictest ~:** unter strengster Geheimhaltung

private [ˈpraɪvət] **1.** *adj.* **a)** *(outside State system)* privat; Privat⟨*unterricht, -schule, -industrie, -klinik, -patient, -station usw.*⟩; **a doctor working in ~ medicine** ein Arzt, der Privatpatienten hat; **have a ~ education** auf eine Privatschule gehen; **b)** *(belonging to individual, not public, not business)* persönlich ⟨*Dinge*⟩; nichtöffentlich ⟨*Versammlung, Sitzung*⟩; privat ⟨*Telefongespräch, Schriftverkehr*⟩; Privat⟨*flugzeug, -strand, -parkplatz, -leben, -konto*⟩; '~' *(on door)* „Privat"; *(in public building)* „kein Zutritt"; *(on ~ land)* „Betreten verboten"; **for [one's own] ~ use** für den persönlichen Gebrauch; **do some ~ studying in the holidays** in den Ferien allein lernen; **the funeral was ~:** die Beisetzung hat in aller Stille stattgefunden; **they were married in a ~ ceremony** ihre Hochzeit wurde im engen Familien- und Freundeskreis gefeiert; **in a ~ capacity** als Privatperson; **c)** *(personal, affecting individual)* persönlich ⟨*Meinung, Interesse, Überzeugung, Rache*⟩; privat ⟨*Vereinbarung, Zweck*⟩; **~ joke** Witz, den nur Eingeweihte verstehen; **~ war** Privatkrieg, *der;* **d)** *(not for public disclosure)* geheim ⟨*Verhandlung, Geschäft, Tränen*⟩; still ⟨*Gebet, Nachdenken, Grübeln*⟩; persönlich ⟨*Gründe*⟩; *(confidential)* vertraulich; **have a ~ word with sb.** jmdn. unter vier Augen sprechen; **e)** *(secluded)* still ⟨*Ort*⟩; *(undisturbed)* ungestört; **we can be ~ here** hier sind wir ungestört; **f)** *(not in public office)* nicht beamtet *(Amtsspr.);* **~ citizen** *or* **individual** Privatperson, *die.* **2.** *n.* **a)** *(Brit. Mil.)* einfacher Soldat; *(Amer. Mil.)* Gefreite, *der;* **~ first ˈclass** *(Amer.)* Obergefreite, *der;* **P~ X** Soldat/Gefreiter X; **b) in ~:** privat; in kleinem Kreis ⟨*feiern*⟩; *(confidentially)* ganz im Vertrauen; **speak to sb. in ~:** jmdn. unter vier Augen sprechen; **make a deal in ~:** ein privates Geschäft abschließen; **you should do it in ~:** du solltest das nicht in der Öffentlichkeit tun; **c)** *in pl. (coll.: genitals)* Geschlechtsteile *Pl.*

private: ~ ˈarmy *n.* Privatarmee, *die;* **~ ˈbed** *n.* Bett für Privatpatienten; **~ ˈcar** *n.* Privatwagen, *der;* **~ ˈcompany** *n. (Brit. Commerc.)* Privatgesellschaft, *die;* **~ ˈenterprise** *n. (Commerc.)* das freie *od.* private Unternehmertum; **[spirit of] ~ enterprise** *(fig.)* Unternehmungsgeist, *der*

privateer [praɪvəˈtɪə(r)] *n.* **a)** Kaperschiff, *das;* **b)** *(person)* Kaper, *der*

private: ~ ˈeye *n. (coll.)* [Privat]detektiv, *der/*-detektivin, *die;* **~ hoˈtel** *n.* Pension, *die;* **~ ˈincome** *n.* private Einkünfte; **~ inˈvestigator** *n.* Privatdetektiv, *der/*-detektivin, *die*

privately [ˈpraɪvətlɪ] *adv.* privat ⟨*erziehen, zugeben, korrespondieren*⟩; vertraulich ⟨*jmdn. sprechen*⟩; insgeheim ⟨*denken, glauben, verhandeln*⟩; **study ~:** private Studien betreiben; **~ owned** in Privatbesitz; **~ held opinion** persönliche Meinung

private: ~ ˈmeans *n. pl. see* **private income; ~ ˈmember** *n. (Brit. Parl.) nicht der Regierung angehörender/angehörende Abgeordnete;* **~ ˈmember's bill** *n. (Brit. Parl.) Gesetzesvorlage eines/einer nicht der Regierung angehörenden Abgeordneten;* **~ ˈparts** *n. pl.* Geschlechtsteile *Pl.;* **~ ˈpractice** *n.* **a)** *(Med.)* Privatpraxis, *die; (patients)* Stamm von Privatpatienten; **he is now in ~ practice** er hat jetzt eine Privatpraxis; **b)** *(of architect/lawyer)* eigenes Büro/eigene Kanzlei; **be in ~ practice** ein eigenes Büro/eine eigene Kanzlei haben; **~ ˈpress** *n.* Privatdruckerei, *die;* **~ ˈproperty** *n.* Privateigentum, *das;* **~ ˈsecretary** *n.* Privatsekretär, *der/*-sekretärin, *die;* **~ ˈsector** *n.* **the ~ sector [of industry]** die Privatwirtschaft; **~ ˈsoldier** *n.* **a)** *(Brit. Mil.)* einfacher Soldat; **b)** *(Amer. Mil.)* Gefreite, *der;* **~ ˈtreaty** *n.* privater Vertrag; **sold by ~ treaty** auf privater Basis verkauft; **~ ˈview[ing]** *n. (Art)* Vernissage, *die; (Cinemat.) Aufführung eines Films für geladene Zuschauer vor der öffentlichen Erstaufführung*

privation [praɪˈveɪʃn] *n. (lack of comforts)* Not, *die;* **suffer many ~s** viele Entbehrungen erleiden

privatisation, privatise *see* **privatiz-**

privatization [praɪvətaɪˈzeɪʃn] *n. (Econ.)* Privatisierung, *die*

privatize [ˈpraɪvətaɪz] *v. t. (Econ.)* privatisieren

privet [ˈprɪvɪt] *n. (Bot.)* Liguster, *der*

privilege [ˈprɪvɪlɪdʒ] **1.** *n.* **a)** *(right, immunity)* Privileg, *das; collect.* Privilegien *Pl.;* **tax ~s** Steuervorteile *Pl.;* **that's a lady's ~:** das ist das Vorrecht einer Dame; **Parliamentary ~:** Immunität des Abgeordneten; **b)** *(special benefit)* Sonderrecht, *das; (honour)* Ehre, *die;* **it was a ~ to listen to him** es war ein besonderes Vergnügen, ihm zuzuhören; **we were expected to pay for the ~** *(iron.)* wir hatten auch noch die Ehre, dafür bezahlen zu dürfen; **c)** *(monopoly)* Vorrecht, *das; (sole right of selling sth.)* Alleinverkaufsrecht, *das;* **d)** *(Amer. St. Exch.)* Termingeschäft, *das;* **buy ~s** Optionsrechte erwerben. **2.** *v. t.* **~ sb. to do sth.** jmdm. das Recht einräumen, etw. zu tun

privileged [ˈprɪvɪlɪdʒd] *adj.* privilegiert; **the ~ classes** die privilegierten Schichten; **a/the ~ few** einige wenige Privilegierte/die kleine Gruppe von Privilegierten; **sb. is ~ to do sth.** jmd. hat die Ehre, etw. zu tun; **I am [greatly] ~ to introduce sb./sth.** es ist mir eine [große] Ehre, Ihnen jmdn./etw. vorstellen zu können; **have a** *or* **be in a ~ position** eine bevorzugte Position innehaben

privy [ˈprɪvɪ] **1.** *adj.* **be ~ to sth.** in etw. *(Akk.)* eingeweiht sein. **2.** *n. (arch./Amer.)* Abtritt, *der (veralt.);* Häuschen, *das (ugs.)*

privy: P~ ˈCouncil *n. (Brit.)* Geheimer [Staats]rat; **~ ˈcounsellor (~ ˈcouncillor)** *n. (Brit.: member of P~ Council)* Geheimer Rat; **~ ˈseal** *n. (Brit.)* Geheimsiegel, *das;* Kleines Siegel; **Lord P~ Seal** Lordsiegelbewahrer, *der*

¹**prize** [praɪz] **1.** *n.* **a)** *(reward, money)* Preis, *der;* **win** *or* **take first/second/third ~:** den ersten/zweiten/dritten Preis gewinnen; **for sheer impudence he takes the ~!** *(fig.)* für seine Frechheit müßte er einen Preis bekommen *(iron.);* **there are no ~s for doing sth.** *(iron.)* es ist kinderleicht, etw. zu tun; **cash** *or* **money ~:** Geldpreis, *der;* **b)** *(in lottery)* Gewinn, *der; (got by buying goods)* Werbegeschenk, *das;* **win sth. as a ~:** etw. gewinnen; **I won a ~ of £1,000** ich habe 1000 Pfund gewonnen; **c)** *(fig.: something worth striving for)* Lohn, *der;* **glittering ~s** verlockender Lohn. **2.** *v. t.* **~ sth. [highly]** etw. hoch schätzen; **gold is one of the most ~d [of] metals** Gold ist eines der begehrtesten Metalle; **we ~ liberty more than life** wir lieben die Freiheit mehr als das Leben; **sb.'s most ~d possessions** jmds. wertvollster Besitz. **3.** *attrib. adj.* **a)** *(~-winning)* preisgekrönt; **b)** *(awarded as ~)* **~ medal/trophy** Siegesmedaille, *die*/Siegestrophäe, *die;* **c)** *(iron.)* **~ idiot** Vollidiot, *der/*-idiotin, *die (ugs.);* **~ muddle** Durcheinander erster Güte; **~ example** Musterbeispiel, *das (iron.)*

²**prize** *v. t. (force)* **~ [open]** aufstemmen; **~ up** abheben ⟨*Diele*⟩; **~ the lid off a crate** eine Kiste aufstemmen; **~ sth. out of sth.** etw. aus etw. herausbekommen; **~ information/a secret out of sb.** Informationen/ein Geheimnis aus jmdm. herauspressen

~ aˈpart *v. t.* auseinanderstemmen

~ ˈout *v. t.* herausbrechen

³**prize** *n.* **a)** *(captured ship)* Prise, *die;* **b)** *(chance find)* [zufälliger] Fund; **this is a rare ~!** das ist ein seltener Fund!

prize: ~-day *n. (Sch.)* Tag der Preisverleihung; **~-day speech** Rede zur Preisverleihung; **~-fight** *n. (Boxing)* Preisboxkampf, *der;* **enter a ~-fight** an einem Preisboxen teilnehmen; **~-fighter** *n. (Boxing)* Preisboxer, *der;* **~-fighting** *n. (Boxing)* Preisboxen, *das;* **~-giving** *n. (Sch.)* Preisverleihung, *die;* **~-money** *n.* Geldpreis, *der; (Sport)* Preisgeld, *das;* **offer £5,000 in ~-money** Geldpreise in Höhe von insgesamt 5 000 Pfund anbieten; **~-winner** *n.* Preisträger, *der/*-trägerin, *die; (in lottery)* Gewinner, *der/*Gewinnerin, *die;* **~-winning** *adj.* preisgekrönt; *(in lottery)* Gewinner-

PRO *abbr.* **a) public relations officer** PR-Manager, *der/*-Managerin, *die;* **b) public relations office** PR-Abteilung, *die*

¹pro [prəʊ] **1.** *n. in pl.* **the ~s and cons** das Pro und Kontra; **there are more ~s than cons** die Sache hat mehr Vorteile als Nachteile. **2.** *adv.* **~ and con** pro und kontra. **3.** *prep.* **~ and con** für und gegen

²pro 1. *n. (coll.)* **a)** *(Sport, Theatre)* Profi, *der;* **b)** *(prostitute)* Nutte, *die (derb).* **2.** *adj.* Profi-

³pro- *pref.* pro-; **~-Communist** prokommunistisch; **be ~-hanging** für die Todesstrafe [durch den Strang] sein

pro-am [prəʊ'æm] *adj. (Sport)* **~ competition** Wettbewerb der Profis und Amateure

probability [prɒbə'bɪlɪtɪ] *n.* **a)** *(likelihood; also Math.)* Wahrscheinlichkeit, *die;* **exceed the bounds of ~:** die Grenzen des Wahrscheinlichen übersteigen; **against all ~:** entgegen aller Wahrscheinlichkeit; **in all ~:** aller Wahrscheinlichkeit nach; **there is little/a strong ~ that ...:** die Wahrscheinlichkeit, daß ..., ist gering/groß; **there's every ~ of a victory** höchstwahrscheinlich wird es zu einem Sieg kommen; **b)** *(likely event)* **the ~ is that ...:** es ist zu erwarten, daß ...; **war is becoming a ~:** der Ausbruch eines Krieges wird immer wahrscheinlicher; **it is more than a possibility, it is a ~:** es ist nicht nur möglich, es ist wahrscheinlich

probable ['prɒbəbl] **1.** *adj.* wahrscheinlich; **highly ~:** höchstwahrscheinlich; **his explanation did not sound very ~:** seine Erklärung klang nicht sehr glaubhaft; **another wet summer looks ~:** es sieht ganz nach einem weiteren verregneten Sommer aus; **he seems the most ~ winner** er scheint die besten Aussichten auf einen Sieg zu haben. **2.** *n. (participant)* wahrscheinlicher Teilnehmer/wahrscheinliche Teilnehmerin (**for** an + *Dat.*); *(candidate)* wahrscheinlicher Kandidat/wahrscheinliche Kandidatin (**for** für)

probably ['prɒbəblɪ] *adv.* wahrscheinlich

probate ['prəʊbeɪt, 'prəʊbət] *n. (Law)* **a)** gerichtliche Testamentsbestätigung; **b)** *(copy)* beglaubigte Testamentsabschrift

probation [prə'beɪʃn] *n.* **a)** Probezeit, *die;* **a year's ~:** eine einjährige Probezeit; **[be put] on ~:** auf Probe [eingestellt werden]; **be on ~:** Probezeit haben; **while on ~:** während der Probezeit; **b)** *(Law)* Bewährung, *die;* **give sb. [two years'] ~, put sb. on ~ [for two years]** jmdm. [zwei Jahre] Bewährung geben; **be on ~:** auf Bewährung sein

probationary [prə'beɪʃənərɪ] *adj.* Probe-; **~ period** Probezeit, *die;* **~ appointment** Einstellung auf Probe

probationer [prə'beɪʃənə(r)] *n.* **a)** *(employee)* Angestellter/Angestellte auf Probe; *(nurse)* Lernschwester, *die/*-pfleger, *der; (candidate)* Probekandidat, *der/*-kandidatin, *die;* **b)** *(Law: offender)* auf Bewährung Freigelassener/Freigelassene

pro'bation officer *n.* Bewährungshelfer, *der/*-helferin, *die*

probe [prəʊb] **1.** *n.* **a)** *(investigation)* Untersuchung, *die* (**into** *Gen.*); **a ~ is being conducted** Nachforschungen werden angestellt; **b)** *(Med., Electronics, Astron.)* Sonde, *die;* **c)** *(pointed instrument)* Tastgerät, *das.* **2.** *v. t.* **a)** *(investigate)* erforschen; untersuchen; **b)** *(with pointed instrument)* stechen in (+ *Akk.*); sondieren *(Med.);* **c)** *(reach deeply into)* gründlich untersuchen ‹*Tasche usw.*›; gründlich erforschen ‹*Kontinent, Weltall*›. **3.** *v. i.* **a)** *(make investigation)* forschen; **he kept probing** er bohrte weiter *(ugs.);* **~ into a matter** einer Angelegenheit *(Dat.)* auf den Grund gehen; **b)** *(with pointed instrument)* herumstochern; *(Med.)* sondieren; **c)** *(reach deeply)* vordringen (**into** in + *Akk.*)

probing ['prəʊbɪŋ] *adj. (penetrating)* gründlich; durchdringend ‹*Blick*›; **~ question** Testfrage, *die*

probity ['prəʊbɪtɪ] *n., no pl.* Rechtschaffenheit, *die*

problem ['prɒbləm] *n.* **a)** *(difficult matter)* Problem, *das; attrib.* Problem‹*gebiet, -fall, -familie, -stück*›; **~ child** Problemkind, *das; (fig.: cause of difficulties)* Sorgenkind, *das;* **I find it a ~ to start** *or* **have a ~ [in] starting the car** ich habe Probleme, das Auto anzulassen; **[I see] no ~** *(coll.)* kein Problem; **what's the ~?** *(coll.)* wo fehlt's denn?; **the ~ about** *or* **with sb./sth.** das Problem mit jmdm./bei etw.; **the ~ of how to do sth.** das Problem *od.* die Frage, wie man etw. tun soll; **the Northern Ireland ~:** die Nordirlandfrage; **he has a drink ~:** er hat ein Alkoholproblem; **that presents a ~:** das ist ein Problem; **the least of her ~s** ihre geringste Sorge; **you think 'you've got ~s!** *(coll. iron.)* deine Sorgen möchte ich haben! *(ugs. iron.);* **b)** *(puzzle)* Rätsel, *das;* **c)** *(Chess, Bridge, Math., Phys., Geom.)* Problem, *das*

problematic [prɒblə'mætɪk], **problematical** [prɒblə'mætɪkl] *adj.* problematisch; *(doubtful)* fragwürdig

problematically [prɒblə'mætɪkəlɪ] *adv.* auf problematische Weise

proboscis [prə'bɒsɪs] *n., pl.* **~es** *or* **probocides** [prə'bɒsɪdi:z] *(Zool.)* Rüssel, *der; (of monkey)* Nase, *die*

procedural [prə'si:djʊrl] *adj.* verfahrensmäßig; *(Law)* verfahrensrechtlich

procedure [prə'si:djə(r)] *n.* **a)** *(particular course of action)* Verfahren, das; Prozedur, *die (meist abwertend);* **~s are under way** es sind Maßnahmen im Gange; **b)** *(way of doing sth.)* Verfahrensweise, *die; (Parl.)* [parlamentarisches] Verfahren; *(Law)* Verfahrensordnung, *die;* **according to democratic ~s** gemäß den Spielregeln der Demokratie; **what is the regular ~?** wie wird das normalerweise gehandhabt?

proceed [prə'si:d] *v. i. (formal)* **a)** *(advance) (on foot)* gehen; *(as or by vehicle)* fahren; *(on horseback)* reiten; *(after interruption)* weitergehen/-fahren/-reiten; **~ somewhere** sich irgendwohin begeben; **~ on one's way** seinen Weg fortsetzen; **as the evening ~ed** im [weiteren] Verlauf des Abends; **~ to business** sich geschäftlichen Dingen zuwenden; **~ to the next item on the agenda** zum nächsten Punkt der Tagesordnung übergehen; **~ [from Rome] to Venice** *(continue)* [von Rom] nach Venedig weiterreisen; **b)** *(begin and carry on)* beginnen; *(after interruption)* fortfahren; **~ to talk/eat** *etc. (begin and carry on)* beginnen, zu sprechen/essen *usw.; (after interruption)* weitersprechen/-essen *usw.;* **~ in** *or* **with sth.** *(begin)* [mit] etw. beginnen; *(continue)* etw. fortsetzen; **c)** *(adopt course)* vorgehen; **we must ~ carefully in this case** wir müssen in diesem Fall umsichtig vorgehen; **~ harshly** *etc.* **with sb.** hart *usw.* mit jmdm. umgehen; **~ discreetly with sth.** etw. diskret behandeln; **d)** *(be carried on)* ‹*Rennen:*› verlaufen; *(be under way)* ‹*Verfahren:*› laufen; *(be continued after interruption)* fortgesetzt werden; **how is the project ~ing?** wie geht das Projekt voran?; **e)** *(go on to say)* fortfahren; **f)** *(originate)* **~ from** *(issue from)* kommen von; *(be caused by)* herrühren von

~ against *v. t. (Law)* gerichtlich vorgehen gegen

proceeding [prə'si:dɪŋ] *n.* **a)** *(action)* Vorgehensweise, *die;* **b)** *in pl. (events)* Vorgänge; **lose control of the ~s** nicht mehr Herr der Lage sein; **I'll go along to watch the ~s** ich geh mal gucken, was da läuft; **be involved in questionable ~s** in eine fragwürdige Sache verwickelt sein; **c)** *in pl. (Law)* Verfahren, *das;* **court ~s** Gerichtsverhandlung, *die;* **court ~s can be lengthy** eine Gerichtsverhandlung kann sich in die Länge ziehen; **legal ~s** Gerichtsverfahren, *das;* **start/take [legal] ~s [against sb.]** gerichtlich [gegen jmdn.] vorgehen; **civil/criminal ~s** Zivil-/Strafprozeß, *der;* **take criminal/divorce ~s against sb.** ein Strafverfahren gegen jmdn. einleiten/einen Scheidungsprozeß gegen jmdn. anstrengen; **d)** *in pl. (report)* Tätigkeitsbericht, *der; (of single meeting)* Protokoll, *das*

proceeds ['prəʊsi:dz] *n. pl.* Erlös, *der* (**from** aus)

pro-ce'lebrity *adj. (Sport)* Schau‹*wettkampf, -turnier*› *(mit Prominenten und Profis)*

¹process ['prəʊses] **1.** *n.* **a)** *(of time or history)* Lauf, *der;* **he learnt a lot in the ~:** er lernte eine Menge dabei; **in the ~ of the operation** *or* **being operated on** im Verlauf der Operation; **in the ~ of teaching his children** bei der Erziehung seiner Kinder; **be in the ~ of doing sth.** gerade etw. tun; **be in ~:** in Gang sein; **sth. is in ~ of formation** etw. wird gerade gebildet; **b)** *(proceeding)* Vorgang, *der;* Prozedur, *die;* **undergo** *or* **be subjected to a ~ of interrogation** mehrfach verhört werden; **by due ~ of law** nach rechtsmäßigem Verfahren; **the democratic ~:** das demokratische Verfahren; **c)** *(method)* Verfahren, *das;* **~es of communication** Kommunikationsprozesse; **by a ~ of elimination** durch Eliminierung; **d)** *(natural operation)* Prozeß, *der;* Vorgang, *der;* **~ of evolution/natural selection** Evolutionsprozeß, *der/*natürliche Auslese; **e)** *(Anat., Bot., Zool.: protuberance)* Fortsatz, *der.* **2.** *v. t.* verarbeiten ‹*Rohstoff, Signal, Daten*›; bearbeiten ‹*Antrag, Akte, Darlehen*›; aufbereiten ‹*Abwasser, Abfall*›; *(for conservation)* behandeln ‹*Leder, Lebensmittel*›; *(Photog.)* entwickeln ‹*Film*›

²process [prə'ses] *v. i.* marschieren

'process cheese *(Amer.),* **'processed cheese** *ns.* Schmelzkäse, *der*

processer *see* **processor**

procession [prə'seʃn] *n.* **a)** Zug, *der; (religious)* Prozession, *die; (festive)* Umzug, *der;* **go/march/move** *etc.* **in ~:** ziehen; **funeral ~:** Trauerzug, *der;* **b)** *(fig.: series)* Reihe, *die;* **his life was an endless ~ of parties** sein Leben war eine endlose Folge von Partys; **there has been a ~ of people in and out of my office all day** heute war in meinem Büro ein ständiges Kommen und Gehen

processional [prə'seʃənl] **1.** *adj.* Prozessions-; **at a ~ pace** im Schrittempo. **2.** *n. (hymn)* Prozessionshymne, *die*

processor ['prəʊsesə(r)] *n. (machine)* Prozessor, *der;* **central ~** *(Computing)* Zentralprozessor, *der*

proclaim [prə'kleɪm] *v. t.* **a)** erklären ‹*Absicht*›; bekanntgeben ‹*Fakten, Einzelheiten*›; beteuern ‹*Unschuld*›; geltend machen ‹*Recht, Anspruch*›; *(declare officially)* verkünden ‹*Amnestie*›; ausrufen ‹*Republik*›; **~ sb./oneself King/Queen** jmdn./sich zum König/zur Königin ausrufen; **~ a country [to be] a republic** in einem Land die Republik ausrufen; **~ 1 January a public holiday** den 1. Januar zum Feiertag erklären; **~ sb./oneself heir to the throne** jmdn./sich zum Thronfolger ernennen; **b)** *(reveal)* verraten; **~ sb./sth. [to be] sth.** verraten, daß jmd./etw. etw. ist

proclamation [prɒklə'meɪʃn] *n.* **a)** *(act of proclaiming)* Verkündung, *die;* Proklamation, *die (geh.);* **the ~ of a new sovereign** die Ausrufung *od.* Proklamation eines neuen Herrschers; **by ~:** durch Bekanntmachung; **b)** *(notice)* Bekanntmachung, *die; (edict, decree)* Erlaß, *der;* **issue** *or* **make a ~:** eine Bekanntmachung/einen Erlaß herausgeben

proclivity [prə'klɪvɪtɪ] *n.* Neigung, *die;* **have/show a ~** *or* **proclivities for** *or* **towards sth.** einen Hang zu etw. haben/zeigen

procrastinate [prə'kræstɪneɪt] *v. i.* zaudern *(geh.);* **~ in doing sth.** es hinauszögern, etw. zu tun; **I ought to start but I keep procrastinating** ich müßte anfangen, aber ich schiebe es immer vor mir her

procrastination [prəkræstɪ'neɪʃn] *n.* Saumseligkeit, *die (geh.);* **there is no time for ~:** die Sache duldet keinen Aufschub; **~ is the thief of time** *(prov.)* ≈ was du heute kannst besorgen, das verschiebe nicht auf morgen *(Spr.)*

procreate ['prəʊkrɪeɪt] **1.** *v. t.* **a) ~ children** Kinder bekommen; **b)** *(fig.: produce)* hervorbringen. **2.** *v. i.* sich fortpflanzen

procreation [prəʊkrɪ'eɪʃn] *n.* Fortpflanzung, *die; (fig.: production)* Erzeugung, *die*

Procrustean [prə'krʌstɪən] *adj.* starr ⟨*Gesetze, Regeln, Prinzipien, Einstellung*⟩; unnachgiebig ⟨*Strenge, Entschlossenheit*⟩

proctor ['prɒktə(r)] *n.* **a)** *(Brit. Univ.) Aufsichtsbeamter der Universität;* **b)** *(Amer. Univ.) see* **invigilator**

procurator ['prɒkjʊəreɪtə(r)] *n.* Stellvertreter, *der*/Stellvertreterin, *die;* Bevollmächtigte, *der/die*

procurator 'fiscal *n. (Scot. Law)* Staatsanwalt, *der*

procure [prə'kjʊə(r)] **1.** *v. t.* **a)** *(obtain)* beschaffen; **~ for sb./oneself** jmdm./sich verschaffen ⟨*Arbeit, Unterkunft, Respekt, Reichtum*⟩; jmdm./sich beschaffen ⟨*Arbeit, Ware*⟩; **b)** *(bring about)* herbeiführen ⟨*Ergebnis, Wechsel, Frieden*⟩; bewirken ⟨*Freilassung*⟩; **c)** *(for sexual gratification)* beschaffen. **2.** *v. i.* Kuppelei betreiben; **procuring** Kuppelei, *die;* **~ for a prostitute** einer Prostituierten *(Dat.)* Kunden beschaffen

procurement [prə'kjʊəmənt] *n. see* **procure 1:** Beschaffung, *die;* Herbeiführung, *die;* Bewirkung, *die*

procurer [prə'kjʊərə(r)] *n. (for sexual purposes)* Kuppler, *der;* **act as a ~ of girls/boys for sb.** jmdm. Mädchen/Jungen besorgen

procuress [prə'kjʊrɪs] *n.* Kupplerin, *die*

Prod [prɒd] *n. (Ir. coll.)* Protestant, *der*/Protestantin, *die;* Evangele, *der (ugs.)*

prod 1. *v. t.,* **-dd- a)** *(poke)* stupsen *(ugs.);* stoßen mit ⟨*Stock, Finger usw.*⟩; **he ~ded the map with his finger** er stieß mit dem Finger auf die Karte; **~ sb. gently** jmdn. anstupsen *od.* leicht anstoßen; **~ the fire/pile of leaves** im Feuer stochern/im Blätterhaufen herumstochern; **~ sb. in the ribs** jmdm. einen Rippenstoß versetzen; jmdn. in die Rippen stoßen; **b)** *(fig.: rouse)* antreiben; nachhelfen (+ *Dat.*) ⟨*Gedächtnis*⟩; **he needs ~ding before he will do anything** man muß ihn zu allem erst antreiben; **~ sb. to do sth.** *or* **into doing sth.** jmdn. drängen, etw. zu tun. **2.** *v. i.,* **-dd-** stochern. **3.** *n.* Stupser, *der;* **a ~ in the/my** *etc.* **ribs** ein Rippenstoß; **give sb. a ~:** jmdm. einen Stupser geben; *(fig.)* jmdn. auf Touren bringen; **this sight gave my memory a ~** *(fig.)* dieser Anblick half meinem Gedächtnis auf die Sprünge

~ a'bout, ~ a'round *v. i. (lit. or fig.)* herumstochern

~ at *v. t.* anstupsen

prodigal ['prɒdɪgl] **1.** *adj.* verschwenderisch; **be ~ with sth.** verschwenderisch mit etw. umgehen; **be ~ of sth.** *(literary)* freigebig mit etw. sein. **2.** *n.* Verschwender, *der*/Verschwenderin, *die*

prodigality [prɒdɪ'gælɪtɪ] *n., no pl.* **a)** *(extravagance)* Verschwendungssucht, *die;* **b)** *(liberality)* Großzügigkeit, *die*

prodigal 'son *n. (Bibl.; also fig. iron.)* verlorener Sohn; **the return of the ~:** die Heimkehr des verlorenen Sohnes

prodigious [prə'dɪdʒəs] *adj.* ungeheuer; unglaublich ⟨*Lügner, Dummkopf*⟩; wunderbar ⟨*Ereignis, Anblick, Taten*⟩; außerordentlich ⟨*Begabung, Können*⟩; gewaltig ⟨*Fortschritt, Kraft, Energie*⟩; **to a ~ degree** über alle Maßen

prodigiously [prə'dɪdʒəslɪ] *adv.* ungeheuer; außerordentlich ⟨*begabt, dumm*⟩

prodigy ['prɒdɪdʒɪ] *n.* **a)** *(gifted person)* [außergewöhnliches] Talent; **musical ~:** musikalisches Wunderkind; *see also* **child prodigy; infant prodigy; b)** *(marvel)* Wunder, *das;* **c) be a ~ of sth.** ein Wunder/*(derog.)* ein Ausbund an etw. *(Dat.)* sein

produce 1. ['prɒdju:s] *n.* **a)** *(things produced)* Produkte *Pl.;* Erzeugnisse *Pl.;* **b)** *(yield)* Ertrag, *der; (Mining)* Ausbeute, *die.* **2.** [prə'dju:s] *v. t.* **a)** *(bring forward)* erbringen ⟨*Beweis*⟩; vorlegen ⟨*Beweismaterial*⟩; beibringen ⟨*Zeugen*⟩; angeben ⟨*Grund*⟩; geben ⟨*Erklärung*⟩; vorzeigen ⟨*Paß, Fahrkarte, Papiere*⟩; **he ~d a splendid shot** ihm gelang ein großartiger Schuß; **~ a rabbit out of a hat** ein Kaninchen aus einem Zylinder hervorzaubern; **he ~d a few coins from his pocket** er holte einige Münzen aus seiner Tasche; **she ~d a gun from her pocket** sie zog einen Revolver aus ihrer Tasche; **b)** produzieren ⟨*Show, Film*⟩; inszenieren ⟨*Theaterstück, Hörspiel, Fernsehspiel*⟩; herausgeben ⟨*Schallplatte, Buch*⟩; **well-~d** gut gemacht ⟨*Film, Theaterstück, Programm*⟩; **c)** *(manufacture)* herstellen; *(in nature; Agric.)* produzieren; zubereiten ⟨*Mahlzeit*⟩; **d)** *(create)* schreiben ⟨*Roman, Gedichte, Artikel, Aufsatz, Symphonie*⟩; schaffen ⟨*Gemälde, Skulptur, Meisterwerk*⟩; aufstellen ⟨*Theorie*⟩; **e)** *(cause)* hervorrufen; bewirken ⟨*Änderung*⟩; herbeiführen ⟨*Reformen*⟩; **f)** *(bring into being)* erzeugen; führen zu ⟨*Situation, Lage, Zustände*⟩; **chemical reactions producing poisonous gases** chemische Reaktionen, bei denen giftige Gase entstehen; **g)** *(yield)* erzeugen ⟨*Ware, Produkt*⟩; geben ⟨*Milch*⟩; tragen ⟨*Wolle*⟩; legen ⟨*Eier*⟩; liefern ⟨*Ernte*⟩; fördern ⟨*Metall, Kohle*⟩; abwerfen ⟨*Ertrag, Gewinn*⟩; hervorbringen ⟨*Dichter, Denker, Künstler*⟩; führen zu ⟨*Resultat*⟩; **h)** *(bear)* gebären; ⟨*Säugetier:*⟩ werfen; ⟨*Vogel, Reptil:*⟩ legen ⟨*Eier*⟩; ⟨*Fisch, Insekt:*⟩ ablegen ⟨*Eier*⟩; ⟨*Bäume, Blumen:*⟩ tragen ⟨*Früchte, Blüten*⟩; entwickeln ⟨*Triebe*⟩; bilden ⟨*Keime*⟩; **~ offspring** Nachwuchs bekommen *(fam.).* **3.** *v. i.* **a)** *(manufacture goods)* produzieren; **producing nation** Erzeugerland, *das;* **b)** *(Brit. Theatre/Radio/Telev.)* Stücke/Hörspiele/Fernsehspiele inszenieren; *(Cinemat.)* Filme produzieren; **c)** *(yield)* Ertrag bringen; **the mine has stopped producing** das Bergwerk fördert nicht mehr *od.* hat die Förderung eingestellt; **d)** *(joc.: bear offspring)* ein Kind/Kinder kriegen *(ugs.)*

producer [prə'dju:sə(r)] *n.* **a)** *(Cinemat., Theatre, Radio, Telev.)* Produzent, *der*/Produzentin, *die;* **b)** *(Brit. Theatre/Radio/Telev.)* Regisseur, *der*/Regisseurin, *die;* **c)** *(Econ.)* Produzent, *der*/Produzentin, *die*

product ['prɒdʌkt] *n.* **a)** *(thing produced)* Produkt, *das; (of industrial process)* Erzeugnis, *das; (of art or intellect)* Werk, *das;* **beauty ~s** Kosmetika; **food ~:** Nahrungsmittelprodukt, *das;* **what is your company's ~?** was stellt Ihre Firma her?; **the ~ of a fertile imagination** das Produkt einer lebhaften Phantasie; **carbon dioxide is a ~ of respiration** Kohlendioxyd entsteht bei der Atmung; **b)** *(result)* Folge, *die;* **be the ~ of one's age** ein Kind seiner Zeit sein; **c)** *(Math.)* Produkt, *das* (**of** aus); **d)** *(total produced)* Produktion, *die;* **the national ~:** das Sozialprodukt; *see also* **'gross 1 d**

production [prə'dʌkʃn] *n.* **a)** *(bringing forward) (of evidence)* Erbringung, *die; (in physical form)* Vorlage, *die; (of witness)* Beibringung, *die; (of reason)* Angabe, *die; (of explanation)* Abgabe, *die; (of passport etc.)* Vorzeigen, *das;* **on ~ of your passport** gegen Vorlage Ihres Passes; **b)** *(public presentation) (Cinemat.)* Produktion, *die; (Theatre)* Inszenierung, *die; (of record, book)* Herausgabe, *die;* **c)** *(action of making)* Produktion, *die; (manufacturing)* Herstellung, *die; (thing produced)* Produkt, *das;* **cease ~:** die Produktion einstellen; **be in/go into ~:** in Produktion sein/gehen; **be** *or* **have gone out of ~:** nicht mehr hergestellt werden; **have a play in ~** ⟨*Theater:*⟩ ein Stück inszenieren; *see also* **mass production; d)** *(thing created)* Werk, *das; (Brit. Theatre: show produced)* Inszenierung, *die;* **e)** *(causing)* Hervorrufen, *das;* **f)** *(bringing into being)* Hervorbringung, *die;* **the ~ of crystals/toxic gases** die Kristallbildung/die Bildung giftiger Gase; **g)** *(process of yielding)* Produktion, *die; (Mining)* Förderung, *die;* **the mine has ceased ~:** das Bergwerk hat die Förderung eingestellt; **h)** *(yield)* Ertrag, *der;* **~ of eggs, egg ~:** Legeleistung, *die;* **[the] annual/total ~ from the mine** die jährliche/gesamte Förderleistung des Bergwerks

production: ~ control *n.* Produktionssteuerung, *die;* **~ cost** *n.* Herstellungskosten *Pl.;* **~ engineer** *n.* Betriebsingenieur, *der;* **~ line** *n.* Fertigungsstraße, *die;* **~ manager** *n.* Produktionsleiter, *der*/-leiterin, *die*

productive [prə'dʌktɪv] *adj.* **a)** *(producing)* **be ~** ⟨*Fabrik:*⟩ produzieren; **the writer's ~ period** die produktive *od.* schöpferische Periode des Schriftstellers; **be ~ of** produzieren ⟨*Ware, Getreide*⟩; hervorbringen ⟨*Ideen, Kunstwerke*⟩; zutage bringen ⟨*Ergebnis, Information*⟩; **b)** *(producing abundantly)* ertragreich ⟨*Land, Boden, Obstbaum, Mine*⟩; leistungsfähig ⟨*Betrieb, Bauernhof*⟩; produktiv ⟨*Künstler, Komponist, Schriftsteller, Geist*⟩; **c)** *(yielding favourable results)* fruchtbar ⟨*Gespräch, Verhandlungen, Forschungsarbeit*⟩; ergiebig ⟨*Nachforschungen*⟩; **it's not very ~ arguing about it** es bringt nichts, darüber zu streiten

productivity [prɒdʌk'tɪvɪtɪ] *n.* Produktivität, *die;* **~ agreement** *or* **deal** Produktivitätsvereinbarung, *die;* **~ bonus** Leistungszulage, *die*

Prof. [prɒf] *abbr.* **Professor** Prof.

prof *n. (coll.)* Prof, *der (ugs.)*

profanation [prɒfə'neɪʃn] *n.* **a)** *(desecration)* Entweihung, *die;* Profanierung, *die (geh.);* **b)** *(disrespectful treatment)* Verunglimpfung, *die (geh.)*

profane [prə'feɪn] **1.** *adj.* **a)** *(irreligious)* gotteslästerlich; **b)** *(irreverent)* respektlos ⟨*Bemerkung, Person*⟩; profan ⟨*Humor, Sprache*⟩; **c)** *(secular)* weltlich; profan. **2.** *v. t.* entweihen

profanity [prə'fænɪtɪ] *n.* **a)** *(irreligiousness, irreligious act)* Gotteslästerung, *die;* **b)** *(irreverent behaviour, act, or utterance)* Respektlosigkeit, *die;* **c)** *(indecent remark)* Fluch, *der*

profess [prə'fes] *v. t.* **a)** *(declare openly)* bekunden ⟨*Vorliebe, Abneigung, Interesse*⟩; **~ to be/do sth.** erklären, etw. zu sein/tun; **~ oneself satisfied** sich zufrieden erklären; **b)** *(claim)* vorgeben; geltend machen ⟨*Recht, Anspruch*⟩; **~ to be/do sth.** behaupten, etw. zu sein/tun; **he ~ed regret that ...:** er behauptete, es tue ihm leid, daß ...; **c)** *(affirm faith in)* sich bekennen zu

professed [prə'fest] *adj.* **a)** *(self-acknowledged)* erklärt ⟨*Marxist, Bewunderer, Absicht*⟩; ausdrücklich ⟨*Zweck*⟩; **be a**

~ **Christian** ein bekennender Christ sein; **b)** *(alleged)* angeblich; **c)** *(Relig.)* **be ~**: die [Ordens]gelübde *od. (fachspr.)* die Profeß abgelegt haben; ~ **monk/nun** Mönch, der/Nonne, die die [Ordens]gelübde abgelegt hat

professedly [prəˈfesɪdlɪ] *adv.* **a)** *(avowedly)* erklärtermaßen; **b)** *(allegedly)* angeblich

profession [prəˈfeʃn] *n.* **a)** Beruf, *der;* **what is your ~?** was sind Sie von Beruf?; **medicine/teaching/the law is a ~ requiring great dedication** der Beruf des Mediziners/Lehrers/Juristen erfordert große Hingabe; **he is training** *or* **studying for the ~ of doctor/banker** er wird Arzt/geht ins Bankfach; **take up/go into** *or* **enter a ~**: einen Beruf ergreifen/in einen Beruf gehen; **be in a ~**: einen Beruf ausüben; **she is in the legal ~**: sie ist Juristin; **be a pilot by ~**: von Beruf Pilot sein; **the [learned] ~s** Theologie, Jura und Medizin; **the oldest ~** *(joc. euphem.)* das älteste Gewerbe der Welt *(verhüll. scherzh.);* **b)** *(body of people)* Berufsstand, *der;* **the ~** *(Theatre sl.)* die Bühne; **c)** *(declaration)* ~ **of faith/love/loyalty** Glaubensbekenntnis, *das*/Liebeserklärung, *die*/Treuegelöbnis, *das;* ~ **of friendship/sympathy** Freundschafts-/Sympathiebekundung, *die;* **make a ~ of, make ~s of** erklären ‹*Liebe*›; geloben ‹*Treue*›; **d)** *(Relig.: affirmation of faith)* Bekenntnis, *das* (of zu); *(faith affirmed)* Glaube, *der;* **make ~ of a faith** sich zu einem Glauben bekennen; **e)** *(Relig.) (vow)* [Ordens]gelübde, *das; (entrance into order)* Profeß, *die (fachspr.);* **make one's ~**: die Gelübde ablegen

professional [prəˈfeʃənl] **1.** *adj.* **a)** *(of profession)* Berufs‹*ausbildung, -leben*›; beruflich ‹*Qualifikation, Laufbahn, Tätigkeit, Stolz, Ansehen*›; ~ **body** Berufsorganisation, *die;* **on ~ business/for ~ reasons/on a ~ matter** geschäftlich; ~ **advice** fachmännischer Rat; ~ **jealousy** Konkurrenzneid, *der;* ~ **standards** Leistungsniveau, *das;* **b)** *(worthy of profession) (in technical expertise)* fachmännisch; *(in attitude)* professionell; *(in experience)* routiniert; **make a ~ job of sth.** etw. fachmännisch erledigen; **c)** *(engaged in profession)* ~ **people** Angehörige hochqualifizierter Berufe; **'apartment to let to ~ woman'** „Wohnung an berufstätige Dame zu vermieten"; **the ~ class[es]** die gehobenen Berufe; **d)** *(by profession)* gelernt; mit abgeschlossener Berufsausbildung *nachgestellt; (not amateur)* Berufs‹*musiker, -sportler, -soldat, -fotograf*›; Profi‹*sportler*›; *(fig.)* notorisch ‹*Unruhestifter, Schnorrer*›; **a ~ killer/spy** *(derog.)* ein professioneller Killer/Agent; **e)** *(paid)* Profi‹*sport, -boxen, -fußball, -tennis*›; **be in the ~ army** Berufssoldat sein; **be in the ~ theatre/on the ~ stage** beruflich am Theater/als Schauspieler arbeiten; **make a career in ~ dancing** Berufstänzer werden. **2.** *n. (trained person, lit. or fig.)* Fachmann, *der*/Fachfrau, *die; (paid worker)* Berufstätige, *der/die; (non-amateur; also Sport, Theatre)* Profi, *der;* **better leave it to a ~/the ~s** überlaß das lieber einem Fachmann/den Fachleuten

professional 'foul *n. (Footb.)* absichtliches Foul

professionalism [prəˈfeʃənəlɪzm] *n., no pl.* **a)** *(of work)* fachmännische Ausführung; *(of person)* fachliche Qualifikation; *(in artistic field)* technisches Können; *(attitude)* professionelle Einstellung; *(ethical quality)* Berufsethos, *das;* **b)** *(paid participation)* Professionalismus, *der;* Profitum, *das;* ~ **in one's attitude to the game** eine profihafte Einstellung zum Spiel

professionally [prəˈfeʃənəlɪ] *adv.* **a)** *(in professional capacity)* geschäftlich ‹*beraten, besuchen, konsultieren*›; beruflich ‹*erfolgreich*›; *(in manner worthy of profession)* professionell; *(ethically)* dem Berufsethos entsprechend; **I'm here ~**: ich bin geschäftlich hier; **be ~ trained/qualified** eine Berufsausbildung/abgeschlossene Berufsausbildung haben; **b)** *(as paid work)* berufsmäßig; **she plays tennis/the piano ~**: sie ist Tennisprofi/von Beruf Pianistin; **she acts ~**: sie ist Berufsschauspielerin; **c)** *(by professional)* fachmännisch ‹*leiten, betreiben*›; von einem Fachmann/von Fachleuten ‹*erledigen lassen*›; **the play was performed ~**: das Stück wurde an einem professionellen Theater aufgeführt

professor [prəˈfesə(r)] *n.* **a)** *(Univ.: holder of chair)* Professor, *der*/Professorin, *die;* **the mathematics ~**: der Professor/die Professorin für Mathematik; ~ **of ...** *(title)* Professor/Professorin für ...; **P~ Smith** Herr/Frau Professor Smith; **how do you do, P~?** guten Tag, Herr/Frau Professor!; **b)** *(Amer.: teacher at university)* Dozent, *der*/Dozentin, *die;* **c)** *(one who professes a religion)* Bekenner, *der*/Bekennerin, *die;* **be a ~ of sth.** sich zu etw. bekennen

professorial [prɒfɪˈsɔːrɪəl] *adj.* **a)** *(Univ.)* professoral; **his ~ duties** seine Pflichten als Professor; ~ **chair** Professur, *die;* **b)** *(characteristic of professor)* ‹*Wissen, Autorität, Art*› eines Professors; *(pedagogic, dogmatic)* professoral *(abwertend)* ‹*Stil, Ton*›; *(fig.)* professorhaft ‹*Aussehen*›

professorship [prəˈfesəʃɪp] *n.* Professur, *die;* **she has been appointed to a ~**: sie ist auf einen Lehrstuhl berufen worden; **hold the P~ of History** den Lehrstuhl für Geschichte innehaben

proffer [ˈprɒfə(r)] *v. t. (literary)* darbieten ‹*Hand, Krone, Geschenk*›; anbieten ‹*Frieden, Hilfe, Dienstleistung, Arm, Freundschaft*›; aussprechen ‹*Dank*›; vorbringen ‹*Vorschlag*›

proficiency [prəˈfɪʃənsɪ] *n.* Können, *das;* **degree** *or* **standard of ~**: Fertigkeit, *die;* **his ~ in mathematics/horsemanship** seine Mathematikkenntnisse/sein reiterliches Können; **achieve great ~ in sth.** große Fertigkeiten in etw. *(Dat.)* erlangen

proficiency: ~ certificate *n.* Leistungsnachweis, *der;* ~ **test** *n.* Leistungstest, *der*

proficient [prəˈfɪʃənt] *adj.* fähig; gut ‹*Pianist, Reiter, Skiläufer usw.*›; geschickt ‹*Radfahrer, Handwerker, Lügner*›; *(in field of knowledge)* bewandert (at, in in + *Dat.*); **be ~ at** *or* **in cooking/maths** gut kochen können/viel von Mathematik verstehen; **he soon became ~**: er beherrschte die Sache bald

profile [ˈprəʊfaɪl] **1.** *n.* **a)** *(side aspect)* Profil, *das;* **in ~**: im Profil; **a drawing in ~**: eine Profilzeichnung; **b)** *(representation)* Profilbild, *das; (outline)* Umriß, *der;* **c)** *(biographical sketch)* Porträt, *das* (of, on *Gen.*); **d)** *(personal record)* [Personal]akte, *die;* **interest ~**: Interessenprofil, *das;* **e)** *(vertical cross-section)* Längsschnitt, *der; (Archit., Geol., Palaeont.)* Profil, *das; (Archaeol.)* Schnitt, *der;* **f)** *(graph, curve)* Kurve, *die;* **g)** *(fig.)* **low ~ [attitude]** Zurückhaltung, *die;* **keep** *or* **maintain a low ~**: sich zurückhalten; **adopt a low ~ approach [to sth.]** sich [in einer Sache] zurückhalten; **high ~ [tactics]** starkes Engagement. **2.** *v. t.* **a)** *(represent from side)* im Profil darstellen; **b)** *(outline)* im Umriß abbilden; **c)** *(sketch biographically)* porträtieren

profit [ˈprɒfɪt] **1.** *n.* **a)** *(Commerc.)* Gewinn, *der;* Profit, *der;* **at a ~**: mit Gewinn ‹*verkaufen*›; **at a 10% ~**: mit einem Gewinn von 10%; **run sth. at a ~**: mit etw. Gewinne erzielen; **run at a ~** ‹*Geschäft:*› Gewinn abwerfen; **make a ~ from** *or* **out of sth.** mit etw. Geld verdienen; **make [a few pence] ~ on sth.** [ein paar Pfennige] an etw. *(Dat.)* verdienen; **show a ~**: einen Gewinn verzeichnen; **yield a ~**: Gewinn abwerfen; ~ **and loss** Gewinn und Verlust; **~-and-loss account** Gewinn-und-Verlust-Rechnung, *die;* **b)** *(advantage)* Nutzen, *der;* **there is no ~ in sth.** etw. ist zwecklos; **be to sb.'s ~**: von Nutzen für jmdn. sein; **find ~ in sth./doing sth.** von etw. profitieren/davon profitieren, daß man etw. tut. **2.** *v. t.* ~ **sb.** für jmdn. von Nutzen sein; **it ~s me nothing to do that** es nützt mir nichts, das zu tun; **it did not ~ them in the end** es hat ihnen letzten Endes gar nichts gebracht. **3.** *v. i. (derive benefit)* profitieren

~ **by** *v. t.* profitieren von; Nutzen ziehen aus ‹*Fehler, Erfahrung*›; ausnützen ‹*Verwirrung*›

~ **from** *v. t.* profitieren von ‹*Reise, Studium, Ratschlag*›; nutzen ‹*Gelegenheit*›

profitability [prɒfɪtəˈbɪlɪtɪ] *n., no pl.* Rentabilität, *die*

profitable [ˈprɒfɪtəbl] *adj.* **a)** *(lucrative)* rentabel; einträglich; **b)** *(beneficial)* lohnend ‹*Unternehmung, Zeitvertreib, Kauf*›; nützlich ‹*Studium, Diskussion, Verhandlung, Nachforschungen*›

profitably [ˈprɒfɪtəblɪ] *adv.* **a)** *(lucratively)* gewinnbringend; **run ~** ‹*Geschäft:*› Gewinn abwerfen; **b)** *(beneficially)* nutzbringend

profiteer [prɒfɪˈtɪə(r)] **1.** *n.* Profitmacher, *der*/-macherin, *die.* **2.** *v. i.* sich bereichern

profiterole [prəˈfɪtərəʊl] *n. (Gastr.)* Profiterole, *die (Kochk.)*

profitless [ˈprɒfɪtlɪs] *adj.* **a)** *(useless)* nutzlos; **b)** *(yielding no profit)* unrentabel

profit: ~-making *adj.* gewinnorientiert; **it was intended to be ~-making** es sollte Gewinn bringen; ~ **margin** *n.* Gewinnspanne, *die;* **~-sharing** *n.* Gewinnbeteiligung, *die; attrib.* Gewinnbeteiligungs-; **~-taking** *n. (St. Exch.)* Gewinnmitnahme, *die*

profligacy [ˈprɒflɪgəsɪ] *n., no pl.* **a)** *(extravagance)* Verschwendung, *die* (with von); **b)** *(dissipation)* Sittenlosigkeit, *die;* **a life of ~**: ein ausschweifendes Leben

profligate [ˈprɒflɪgət] **1.** *adj.* **a)** *(extravagant)* verschwenderisch; **be ~ in spending money** das Geld mit vollen Händen ausgeben; **be ~ of** *or* **with sth.** verschwenderisch umgehen mit etw.; ~ **squandering of sth.** allzu bereitwillige Vergeudung von etw.; **b)** *(dissipated)* hemmungslos ‹*Lust, Trunkenheit, Gier*›; ausschweifend ‹*Person*›. **2.** *n.* **a)** *(spendthrift)* Verschwender, *der*/Verschwenderin, *die;* **b)** *(rake)* Wüstling, *der (abwertend)*

pro forma [prəʊ ˈfɔːmə] **1.** *adv.* pro forma. **2.** *adj.* **a)** *(as formality)* Pro-Forma-; **b)** *(Commerc.)* Muster-. **3.** *n. see* **pro forma invoice**

pro forma 'invoice *n. (Commerc.)* Pro-Forma-Rechnung, *die*

profound [prəˈfaʊnd] *adj.,* **~er** [prəˈfaʊndə(r)], **~est** [prəˈfaʊndɪst] **a)** *(extreme)* tief; heftig ‹*Erregung, Verlangen*›; nachhaltig ‹*Wirkung, Einfluß, Eindruck*›; tiefgreifend ‹*Wandel, Veränderung*›; lebhaft ‹*Interesse*›; tiefempfunden ‹*Beileid, Mitgefühl*›; tiefsitzend ‹*Angst, Mißtrauen*›; völlig ‹*Unwissenheit*›; gespannt ‹*Aufmerksamkeit*›; verborgen ‹*Geheimnis, Tiefe*›; tödlich ‹*Langeweile*›; hochgradig ‹*Schwerhörigkeit*›; **it is a matter of ~ indifference to me** es ist mir völlig gleichgültig; **b)** *(penetrating)* tief; profund *(geh.)* ‹*Wissen, Erkenntnis, Werk, Kenner*›; tiefgründig ‹*Untersuchung, Abhandlung, Betrachtung*›; tiefschürfend ‹*Essay, Vortrag, Analyse, Forscher*›; tiefsinnig ‹*Gedicht, Buch, Schriftsteller*›; scharfsinnig ‹*Politiker, Denker, Forscher*›; **that's a very ~ remark** *(also iron.)* das ist sehr tiefsinnig; **c)** *(demanding thought)* tief ‹*Geheimnis, Bedeutung, Sinn*›; unergründlich ‹*Rätsel, Geheimnis*›; schwierig ‹*Lektüre, Problem, Theorie*›; inhaltsschwer ‹*Symbolik, Worte*›; **d)** *(rhet./fig.: deep)* tief

profoundly [prəˈfaʊndlɪ] *adv.* **a)** *(ex-*

tremely) zutiefst; tief ⟨*schlafen*⟩; stark ⟨*interessiert, beeinflußt, mitgenommen*⟩; überaus ⟨*friedlich, verschlossen, geheimnisvoll*⟩; völlig ⟨*unbedarft, gleichgültig, versunken, rätselhaft*⟩; hochgradig ⟨*schwerhörig*⟩; **I am ~ indifferent about it** es ist mir völlig gleichgültig; **b)** *(penetratingly)* ungemein ⟨*scharfsinnig, beschlagen, feinfühlig*⟩; hoch⟨*intelligent, -gelehrt, -gebildet*⟩; **a ~ wise man** ein Mann von tiefer Weisheit; **..., she said ~:** ..., sagte sie tiefsinnig

profundity [prəˈfʌndɪtɪ] *n.* **a)** *no pl. (extremeness) (of feelings, silence, sleep, respect)* Tiefe, *die; (of joy, sorrow, concern, change)* [großes] Ausmaß; **b)** *no pl. (depth of intellect)* Tiefsinnigkeit, *die; (of analysis, book)* Tiefe, *die;* **c)** *(depth of meaning)* Tiefgründigkeit, *die; in pl.* tiefgründige Gedanken

profuse [prəˈfjuːs] *adj.* **a)** *(giving freely)* überschwenglich; großzügig ⟨*Schenkender, Gebender*⟩; **be ~ in one's thanks/praise** überschwenglich danken/loben; **be ~ in one's apologies** sich wieder und wieder entschuldigen; **b)** *(abundant)* verschwenderisch ⟨*Fülle, Üppigkeit, Vielfalt*⟩; reichlich ⟨*Beifall*⟩; reich ⟨*Ernte*⟩; massenhaft ⟨*Wachstum, Vorkommen*⟩; groß ⟨*Dankbarkeit*⟩; überschwenglich ⟨*Entschuldigung, Lob*⟩; **~ bleeding** starke Blutung

profusely [prəˈfjuːslɪ] *adv.* **a)** *(liberally)* großzügig ⟨*spenden, schenken*⟩; übermäßig ⟨*loben*⟩; **b)** *(abundantly)* massenhaft ⟨*wachsen, vorkommen*⟩; heftig ⟨*bluten, erröten, schwitzen*⟩; überaus ⟨*dankbar*⟩; üppig ⟨*beladen, gedeihen*⟩; überschwenglich ⟨*sich entschuldigen*⟩

profusion [prəˈfjuːʒn] *n.* **a)** *(abundance)* ungeheure *od.* überwältigende Menge; **a ~ of choice** *or* **in the choice offered** eine überreiche Auswahl; **in ~:** in Hülle und Fülle; **in gay/chaotic ~:** in bunter/chaotischer Vielfalt; **b)** *(large amount)* [Über]fülle, *die;* **a ~ of flowers/debts** eine verschwenderische Fülle von Blumen/große Menge Schulden

progenitor [prəˈdʒenɪtə(r)] *n.* **a)** *(ancestor)* Vorfahr[e], *der*/Vorfahrin, *die;* **b)** *(fig.: predecessor)* Vorläufer, *der*/Vorläuferin, *die; (intellectual ancestor)* geistiger Vater

progeny [ˈprɒdʒənɪ] *n., no pl.* Nachkommenschaft, *die;* **they are the ~ of transported convicts** sie sind die Nachkommen deportierter Sträflinge

progesterone [prəˈdʒestərəʊn] *n. (Physiol., Pharm.)* Gelbkörperhormon, *das;* Progesteron, *das (fachspr.)*

prognosis [prɒgˈnəʊsɪs] *n., pl.* **prognoses** [prɒgˈnəʊsiːz] **a)** *(Med.) (forecast)* Prognose, *die;* **what is the doctor's ~?** welche Prognose stellt der Arzt?; **make a ~ of sth.** eine Prognose über etw. *(Akk.)* stellen; **b)** *(prediction)* Vorhersage, *die;* Prognose, *die;* **give** *or* **make a ~ of sth.** einen Ausblick auf etw. *(Akk.)* geben

prognostic [prɒgˈnɒstɪk] *adj. (also Med.)* prognostisch

prognosticate [prɒgˈnɒstɪkeɪt] **1.** *v.t.* **a)** *(foretell; also Med.)* prognostizieren; **b)** *(indicate)* deuten auf (+ *Akk.*). **2.** *v.i.* eine Prognose stellen

prognostication [prɒgnɒstɪˈkeɪʃn] *n.* **a)** *(predicting, forecast)* Prognose, *die;* **make a ~ [about sth.]** [über etw. *(Akk.)*] eine Prognose stellen; **b)** *(indication)* Vorzeichen, *das* **(of** für)

program [ˈprəʊgræm] **1.** *n.* **a)** *(Amer.) see* **programme 1; b)** *(Computing, Electronics)* Programm, *das.* **2.** *v.t.,* **-mm-: a)** *(Amer.) see* **programme 2; b)** *(Computing, Electronics)* programmieren; **~ a computer to do sth.** einen Computer so programmieren, daß er etw. tut; **~ming language** Programmiersprache, *die*

programer *(Amer.) see* **programmer**

programmatic [prəʊgrəˈmætɪk] *adj.* **a)** programmatisch ⟨*Politik, Ansatz, Werk, Autor*⟩; klar umrissen ⟨*Plan, System, Stufen, Projekt*⟩; genau festgelegt ⟨*Zeitplan*⟩; **b)** *(Mus.)* programmatisch ⟨*Komposition, Trend*⟩

programme [ˈprəʊgræm] **1.** *n.* **a)** *([notice of] events)* Programm, *das;* **the evening's ~:** das Abendprogramm; **a ~ of Schubert songs** ein Programm mit *od.* aus Schubertliedern; eine Darbietung von Schubertliedern; **what is the ~ for today?** was steht heute auf dem Programm?; **my ~ for today** mein [heutiges] Tagesprogramm; **b)** *(Radio, Telev.) (presentation)* Sendung, *die; (Radio: service)* Sender, *der;* Programm, *das;* **the ~ is on at 6 o'clock** die Sendung läuft um 6 Uhr; **c)** *(plan, instructions for machine)* Programm, *das;* **a five-year ~:** ein Fünfjahresprogramm; **a ~ of study** ein Studienprogramm. **2.** *v.t.* **a)** *(make ~ for)* ein Programm zusammenstellen für; **b)** *(plan)* festlegen ⟨*Soll*⟩; planen, vorbereiten ⟨*Maßnahmen*⟩; durchplanen ⟨*Leben, Tagesablauf*⟩; **the tumble-drier can be ~d to operate for between 10 and 60 minutes** der Trockner kann auf 10–60 Minuten Betriebszeit eingestellt werden; **c)** *(print in ~)* **be ~d** auf dem Programm stehen; **an event not officially ~d** ein Ereignis, das nicht offiziell angekündigt war/ist; **d)** *(fig.)* **~ sb. to do sth.** jmdn. darauf drillen, etw. zu tun *(ugs.)*

programme: ~ music *n. (Mus.)* Programmusik, *die;* **~ note** *n.* Erläuterung zum Programm

programmer [ˈprəʊgræmə(r)] *n. (Computing, Electronics)* **a)** *(operator)* Programmierer, *der*/Programmiererin, *die;* **b)** *(component)* Programmiergerät, *das;* Programmspeicher, *der*

progress 1. [ˈprəʊgres] *n.* **a)** *no pl., no indef. art. (onward movement)* [Vorwärts]bewegung, *die;* **our ~ has been slow** wir sind nur langsam vorangekommen; **he continued his ~ across the fields** er setzte seinen Weg durch die Felder fort; **make ~:** vorankommen; **I saw how much ~ I had made** ich sah, wie weit ich vorangekommen war; **in ~:** im Gange; **b)** *no pl., no indef. art. (advance)* Fortschritt, *der;* **~ of science/civilization** wissenschaftlicher/kultureller Fortschritt; **there has been some ~ towards peace** man ist dem Frieden etwas nähergekommen; **make ~:** vorankommen; ⟨*Student, Patient:*⟩ Fortschritte machen; **make good ~ [towards recovery]** ⟨*Patient:*⟩ sich gut erholen; **some ~ was made** es wurden einige Fortschritte erzielt; **that's ~ [for you]** *(iron.)* [und] das nennt man nun Fortschritt!; **you can't stand in the way of ~:** man kann den Fortschritt nicht aufhalten; **c)** *(Brit. Hist.) (royal journey)* Rundreise, *die; (state procession)* prunkvolle Prozession. **2.** [prəˈgres] *v.i.* **a)** *(move forward)* vorankommen; **the concert had not ~ed very far** das Konzert war noch nicht weit fortgeschritten; **~ to the next point of discussion** zum nächsten Diskussionspunkt übergehen; **b)** *(be carried on, develop)* Fortschritte machen; ⟨*Krankheit:*⟩ fortschreiten; **my novel is ~ing nicely** ich komme mit meinem Roman gut voran; **~ towards sth.** einer Sache *(Dat.)* näherkommen. **3.** [ˈprəʊgres] *v.t.* vorantreiben

progress [ˈprəʊgres]: **~ chart** *n.* Arbeitsdiagramm, *das;* **~-chaser** *n.* ≈ Kontrolleur, *der*/Kontrolleurin, *die (verantwortlich für die Einhaltung von Produktionszeitplänen)*

progression [prəˈgreʃn] *n.* **a)** *(progressing)* Fortbewegung, *die; (of career)* Verlauf, *der;* **his ~ through life** sein Lebensweg; **his ~ from office clerk to head of department** sein Aufstieg vom Büroangestellten zum Abteilungsleiter; **b)** *(development)* Fortschritt, *der* **(in** bei); **c)** *(succession)* Folge, *die;* **d)** *(Mus.)* Fortschreitung, *die;* Progression, *die;* **e)** *(Math.)* Reihe, *die; see also* **arithmetical; geometrical**

progressive [prəˈgresɪv] **1.** *adj.* **a)** *(moving forward)* fortschreitend; **~ motion** *or* **movement** Vorwärtsbewegung, *die;* **b)** *(gradual)* fortschreitend ⟨*Verbesserung, Verschlechterung*⟩; schrittweise ⟨*Reform*⟩; aufeinanderfolgend ⟨*Ereignisse*⟩; allmählich ⟨*Veränderung, Herannahen, Fortschreiten, Prozeß, Besserung*⟩; **in ~ stages** Schritt für Schritt; **c)** *(improving)* sich [weiter] entwickelnd; **d)** *(worsening)* schlimmer werdend; *(Med.)* progressiv; **e)** *(favouring reform; in culture)* fortschrittlich; progressiv; **~ music** progressive Musik; **f)** *(informal; also Educ.)* progressiv; **g)** *(Taxation)* gestaffelt; progressiv *(fachspr.)*; **~ tax** Progressivsteuer, *die;* **h)** *(Ling.)* **~ tense** Verlaufsform, *die.* **2.** *n.* Progressive, *der/die;* **the ~s** die fortschrittlichen Kräfte

progressively [prəˈgresɪvlɪ] *adv.* **a)** *(continuously)* immer ⟨*weiter, schlechter*⟩; *(gradually)* stetig; Schritt für Schritt ⟨*reformieren*⟩; *(successively)* [chronologisch] fortschreitend; **move ~ towards sth.** sich immer weiter auf etw. zubewegen; **~ approach bankruptcy** sich Schritt für Schritt auf den Bankrott zubewegen; **b)** *(with progressive views, informally; also Educ., Taxation)* progressiv

ˈ**progress report** *n.* Tätigkeitsbericht, *der; (fig.: news)* Lagebericht, *der*

prohibit [prəˈhɪbɪt] *v.t.* **a)** *(forbid)* verbieten; **~ sb.'s doing sth., ~ sb. from doing sth.** jmdm. verbieten, etw. zu tun; **it is ~ed to do sth.** es ist verboten, etw. zu tun; **b)** *(prevent)* verhindern; **~ sb.'s doing sth., ~ sb. from doing sth.** jmdn. daran hindern, etw. zu tun

prohibition [prəʊhɪˈbɪʃn, prəʊɪˈbɪʃn] *n.* **a)** *(forbidding)* Verbot, *das;* **b)** *(edict)* [gesetzliches] Verbot **(against** *Gen.*); **c)** *no pl., no art. (Amer. Hist.)* [gesetzliches] Alkoholverbot; **P~** *(1920–33)* die Prohibition; *attrib.* Prohibitions-

prohibitionist [prəʊhɪˈbɪʃənɪst, prəʊɪˈbɪʃənɪst] *n. (Amer. Hist.: person supporting prohibition) (19th century)* Mitglied der Prohibitionspartei; *(20th century)* **P~:** Prohibitionist, *der*/Prohibitionistin, *die*

prohibitive [prəˈhɪbɪtɪv] *adj.* **a)** *(prohibiting)* prohibitiv *(geh.)*; Verbots⟨*zeichen, -gesetz*⟩; **b)** *(too high)* unerschwinglich ⟨*Preis, Miete*⟩; untragbar ⟨*Kosten*⟩

prohibitively [prəˈhɪbɪtɪvlɪ] *adv. (excessively)* unerschwinglich ⟨*hoch, teuer*⟩

prohibitory [prəˈhɪbɪtərɪ] *see* **prohibitive**

project 1. [prəˈdʒekt] *v.t.* **a)** *(throw)* schleudern; abfeuern ⟨*Kugel, Geschoß*⟩; abschießen ⟨*Rakete*⟩; **~ one's voice to the very back of the auditorium** seine Stimme so erheben, daß sie auch ganz hinten im Zuschauerraum zu hören ist; **b)** werfen ⟨*Schatten, Schein, Licht*⟩; senden ⟨*Strahl*⟩; *(Cinemat.)* projizieren; **~ against** *or* **on to sth.** gegen *od.* auf etw. *(Akk.)* projizieren ⟨*Schatten, Umriß*⟩; **c)** *(make known)* vermitteln; **~ the product more favourably** ein positiveres Bild des Produkts vermitteln; **~ one's own personality** seine eigene Person in den Vordergrund stellen; **d)** *(plan)* planen; **e)** *(extrapolate)* übertragen **(to** auf + *Akk.*); **f)** *(Psych.)* projizieren; **~ sth. [on] to** *or* **on sb./sth.** etw. auf jmdn./etw. projizieren; **g)** *(Geom., Cartography)* projizieren. **2.** *v.i.* **a)** *(jut out)* ⟨*Felsen:*⟩ vorspringen; ⟨*Zähne, Brauen:*⟩ vorstehen; **~ into the sea** ⟨*Felsen:*⟩ ins Meer hinausragen; **~ over the street** ⟨*Balkon:*⟩ über die Straße ragen; **b)** *(Theatre)* laut und deutlich sprechen. **3.** *v. refl. (transport oneself)* **~ oneself into sth.** sich in etw. *(Akk.)* [hinein]versetzen; **~ oneself back in time** sich in eine frühere Zeit/in frühere Zeiten zurückversetzen. **4.** [ˈprɒdʒekt] *n.* **a)** *(plan)* Plan, *der;* **b)** *(enterprise)* Projekt, *das*

projectile [prəˈdʒektaɪl] *n.* Geschoß, *das;* Projektil, *das (Waffent.)*
projection [prəˈdʒekʃn] *n.* **a)** *(throwing)* Schleudern, *das; (of missile)* Abschuß, *der; (of bullet, shell)* Abfeuern, *das;* **b)** *(protruding)* Vorstehen, *das; (protruding thing)* Vorsprung, *der;* **c)** *(making of visible image)* Projektion, *die; (of film)* Vorführung, *die;* **d)** *(making known) (of image or character)* Darstellung, *die; (of product or invention)* Präsentation, *die;* **the ~ of his own personality** seine Selbstdarstellung; **e)** *(planning)* Planung, *die; (thing planned)* Plan, *der;* **make a ~ [for sth.]** einen Plan [für etw.] machen *od.* aufstellen; **f)** *(extrapolation)* Übertragung, *die;* Hochrechnung, *die (Statistik); (estimate of future possibilities)* Voraussage, *die* **(of** über + *Akk.*); **g)** *(Psych.)* Projektion, *die;* **~ of sth. on [to] sb./sth.** Projektion einer Sache *(Gen.)* auf jmdn./etw.; **h)** *(Geom.)* Projektion, *die;* **i)** *(Cartography)* [Karten]projektion, *die;* **conical ~:** Kegelprojektion, *die;* **cylindrical ~:** Zylinderprojektion, *die; see also* **Mercator**
projectionist [prəˈdʒekʃənɪst] *n. (Cinemat.)* Filmvorführer, *der*/-vorführerin, *die*
proˈjection-room *n. (Cinemat.)* Vorführraum, *der*
projector [prəˈdʒektə(r)] *n.* Projektor, *der; (for slides)* Diaprojektor, *der*
prolapse *(Med.)* **1.** [prəʊˈlæps] *v.i.* prolabieren *(fachspr.);* vorfallen. **2.** [ˈprəʊlæps] *n.* Prolaps[us], *der (fachspr.);* Vorfall, *der*
prole [prəʊl] *(Brit. coll. derog.) n.* Prolet, *der*/Proletin, *die (abwertend)*
proletarian [prəʊlɪˈteərɪən] **1.** *adj.* proletarisch. **2.** *n.* Proletarier, *der*/Proletarierin, *die*
proletarianism [prəʊlɪˈteərɪənɪzm] *n., no pl.* Proletariertum, *das*
proletariat, proletariate [prəʊlɪˈteərɪət] *n.* **a)** *(Roman Hist.)* Proletariat, *das;* **b)** *(derog.: lowest class)* Proleten *Pl. (abwertend);* **c)** *(Econ., Polit.)* Proletariat, *das*
proliferate [prəˈlɪfəreɪt] *v.i.* **a)** *(Biol.)* sich stark vermehren; *(Med.)* proliferieren *(fachspr.);* wuchern; **b)** *(increase, lit. or fig.)* sich ausbreiten
proliferation [prəlɪfəˈreɪʃn] *n.* **a)** *(Biol.)* starke Vermehrung; *(Med.)* Proliferation, *die (fachspr.);* Wucherung, *die;* **b)** *(increase, lit. or fig.)* starke Zunahme; *(of nuclear weapons)* Proliferation, *die; (abundance, lit. or fig.)* Unmenge, *die*
prolific [prəˈlɪfɪk] *adj.* **a)** *(fertile)* fruchtbar; **b)** *(productive)* produktiv; **be ~ in sth.** reich an etw. *(Dat.)* sein; **be ~ of sth.** etw. in großen Mengen hervorbringen; **c)** *(abundant)* reich
prolifically [prəˈlɪfɪkəlɪ] *adv.* **a)** *(productively)* reichlich; **b)** *(abundantly)* in Hülle und Fülle
prolix [ˈprəʊlɪks, prəˈlɪks] *adj.* weitschweifig
prolixity [prəˈlɪksɪtɪ] *n., no pl.* Weitschweifigkeit, *die*
prologue *(Amer.:* **prolog)** [ˈprəʊlɒg] *n.* **a)** *(introduction)* Prolog, *der* **(to** zu); **b)** *(fig.)* Vorspiel, *das* **(to** zu)
prolong [prəˈlɒŋ] *v.t.* **a)** *(extend in duration or length)* verlängern; **~ the agony** *(fig. coll.)* die Qual [unnötig] in die Länge ziehen; **don't ~ the agony!** *(fig. coll.)* mach es nicht so spannend! *(ugs.);* **b)** *(Phonet.)* dehnen
prolongation [prəʊlɒŋˈgeɪʃn] *n.* **a)** Verlängerung, *die; (fig.)* Weiterführung, *die;* **b)** *(Phonet.)* Dehnung, *die;* **c)** *(Mus.)* Aushalten, *das*
prolonged [prəˈlɒŋd] *adj.* lang; lang anhaltend ‹*Beifall*›; langgezogen ‹*Schrei*›
prom [prɒm] *n. (coll.)* **a)** *(Brit.: seaside walkway)* [Strand]promenade, *die;* **b)** *(Brit.: concert)* Promenadenkonzert, *das;* **the P~s** *Konzerte, die alljährlich im Sommer in der Royal Albert Hall in London stattfinden;* **c)** *(Amer.: dance)* **school/college ~:** Schul-/Studentenball, *der*
promenade [prɒməˈnɑːd] **1.** *n.* **a)** *(walkway)* Promenade, *die; (Brit.: at seaside)* [Strand]promenade, *die;* **b)** *(leisured walk)* Spaziergang, *der;* Promenade, *die (veralt.);* **go for** *or* **make** *or* **take a ~:** einen Spaziergang machen; **c)** *(Amer.: dance) see* **prom c. 2.** *v.i.* promenieren *(geh.).* **3.** *v.t. (lead)* führen
promenade: ~ concert *n.* Promenadenkonzert, *das;* **~ deck** *n. (Naut.)* Promenadendeck, *das*
promenader [prɒməˈnɑːdə(r)] *n.* **a)** *(one who promenades)* Spaziergänger, *der*/Spaziergängerin, *die;* **b)** *(Brit.: concert-goer)* Konzertbesucher, *der*/-besucherin, *die (auf Stehplätzen bei einem Promenadenkonzert)*
Promethean [prəˈmiːθɪən] *adj.* prometheisch *(geh.)*
prominence [ˈprɒmɪnəns] *n.* **a)** *(conspicuousness)* Auffälligkeit, *die;* **the continual ~ of his name in the newspapers** das ständige [auffällige] Auftauchen seines Namens in den Zeitungen; **b)** *(distinction)* Bekanntheit, *die;* **come into** *or* **rise to ~:** bekannt werden; **fade from ~:** in Vergessenheit geraten; **give ~ to sth.** etw. in den Vordergrund stellen; **c)** *(projecting part)* Vorsprung, *der*
prominent [ˈprɒmɪnənt] *adj.* **a)** *(conspicuous)* auffallend; **b)** *(foremost)* herausragend; **become very ~ as a singer** als Sänger/Sängerin sehr bekannt werden; **he was ~ in politics** er war ein prominenter Politiker; **a ~ topic of discussion** ein vieldiskutiertes Thema; **c)** *(projecting)* vorspringend; vorstehend ‹*Backenknochen, Brauen*›
prominently [ˈprɒmɪnəntlɪ] *adv.* **a)** *(conspicuously)* auffallend; **b)** *(in forefront)* in einer führenden Rolle; **he figured ~ in the case** er spielte in dem Fall eine wichtige Rolle
promiscuity [prɒmɪˈskjuːɪtɪ] *n., no pl.* **a)** *(in sexual relations)* Promiskuität, *die (geh.);* **b)** *(indiscriminate action)* Wahllosigkeit, *die*
promiscuous [prəˈmɪskjʊəs] *adj.* **a)** *(in sexual relations)* promiskuitiv *(geh.);* promisk; **a ~ man** ein Mann, der häufig die Partnerin wechselt; **~ behaviour** häufige Partnerwechsel; **b)** *(mixed)* bunt gemischt; **c)** *(indiscriminate)* wahllos; **d)** *(coll.: casual)* nachlässig
promiscuously [prəˈmɪskjʊəslɪ] *adv.* **a)** *(in sexual relations)* promiskuitiv *(geh.);* promisk; **b)** *(indiscriminately)* wahllos
promise [ˈprɒmɪs] **1.** *n.* **a)** *(assurance)* Versprechen, *das;* **sb.'s ~s** jmds. Versprechungen; **give** *or* **make a ~ [to sb.]** [jmdm.] ein Versprechen geben; **give** *or* **make a ~ [to sb.] to do sth.** [jmdm.] versprechen, etw. zu tun; **I'm not making any ~s** ich kann nichts versprechen; **give** *or* **make a ~ [to sb.] that sth. will happen** [jmdm.] versprechen, daß etw. geschehen wird; **you have my ~:** ich verspreche es dir; **give** *or* **make a ~ of sth. [to sb.]** [jmdm.] etw. versprechen; **~s of love/reform** Liebes-/Reformversprechungen; **it's a ~:** ganz bestimmt; **~s, ~s!** *(coll. iron.)* Versprechungen, nichts als Versprechungen!; **is that a threat or a ~?** *(coll. iron.)* soll das eine Drohung oder ein Versprechen sein?; **b)** *(guarantee)* Zusicherung, *die;* **they gave me a ~ that the work would be ready on time** sie sicherten mir zu, daß die Arbeit rechtzeitig fertig sein werde; **c)** *(fig.: reason for expectation)* Hoffnung, *die;* **he never fulfilled his early ~:** er enttäuschte die Erwartungen, die man zunächst in ihn gesetzt hatte; **land of ~:** Land der Verheißung *(geh.);* **a painter of** *or* **with ~:** ein vielversprechender Maler; **~ of sth.** Aussicht auf etw. *(Akk.).* *See also* **breach 1 a. 2.** *v.t.* **a)** *(give assurance of)* versprechen; **~ sth. to sb., ~ sb. sth.** jmdm. etw. versprechen; **~ revenge** Rache schwören; **b)** *(fig.: give reason for expectation of)* verheißen *(geh.);* **~ sb. sth.** jmdm. etw. in Aussicht stellen; **~ to do/be sth.** versprechen, etw. zu tun/zu sein; **c) ~ oneself sth./that one will do sth.** sich *(Dat.)* etw. vornehmen/sich vornehmen, etw. zu tun; **d)** *(coll.: assure)* **I ~ you** das sage ich dir; **I ~** *or* **let me ~ you this/that** das verspreche ich dir. **3.** *v.i.* **a) ~ well** *or* **favourably [for the future]** vielversprechend [für die Zukunft] sein; **he ~s well as a teacher** er ist ein vielversprechender Lehrer; **b)** *(give assurances)* Versprechungen machen; **I can't ~:** ich kann es nicht versprechen
promised land [prɒmɪst ˈlænd] *n.* **a) the ~** *(Bibl.)* das Gelobte Land; **b)** *(fig.: ideal state)* Paradies, *das*
promising [ˈprɒmɪsɪŋ] *adj.,* **promisingly** [ˈprɒmɪsɪŋlɪ] *adv.* vielversprechend
ˈpromissory note *n. (Finance)* Schuldschein, *der*
promontory [ˈprɒməntərɪ] *n.* Vorgebirge, *das*
promote [prəˈməʊt] *v.t.* **a)** *(advance)* befördern; **b)** *(encourage)* fördern; **a life-style which does not ~ health** ein Lebensstil, der der Gesundheit nicht förderlich ist; **~ the success of the firm** der Firma zu mehr Erfolg verhelfen; **c)** *(publicize)* Werbung machen für; **d)** *(initiate)* in Angriff nehmen ‹*Projekt*›; gründen ‹*Tochtergesellschaft*›; **~ a bill** *(Parl.)* einen Gesetzentwurf einbringen; **e)** *(Chess)* umwandeln; **f)** *(Footb.)* **be ~d** aufsteigen
promoter [prəˈməʊtə(r)] *n.* **a)** *(who organizes and finances event)* Veranstalter, *der*/Veranstalterin, *die; (of ballet tour, pop festival, boxing-match, cycle-race also)* Promoter, *der;* **b)** *(furtherer)* Förderer, *der*/Förderin, *die;* **c)** *(publicizer)* Promoter, *der*/Promoterin, *die;* **d)** *(initiator)* Begründer, *der*/Begründerin, *die; (Parl.) jmd., der einen Gesetzentwurf einbringt und unterstützt;* **[company] ~:** Firmengründer, *der*/-gründerin, *die*
promotion [prəˈməʊʃn] *n.* **a)** *(advancement)* Beförderung, *die;* **win** *or* **gain ~:** befördert werden; **he is due for ~:** er dürfte bald befördert werden; **~ to [the rank of] sergeant** *etc.* Beförderung zum Unteroffizier *usw.;* **b)** *(furtherance)* Förderung, *die;* **c)** *(Sport, Theatre: event)* Veranstaltung, *die;* **d)** *(publicization)* Werbung, *die; (instance)* Werbekampagne, *die;* **sales ~:** Werbung, *die;* **e)** *(initiation)* Begründung, *die; (Parl.: of bill)* Einbringung, *die;* **f)** *(of a company)* Gründung, *die;* **g)** *(Chess)* Umwandlung, *die;* **h)** *(Footb.)* Aufstieg, *der;* **be sure of ~:** mit Sicherheit aufsteigen
promotional [prəˈməʊʃənl] *adj.* **a)** *(of advancement)* Beförderungs‹*aussichten, -möglichkeiten*›; **b)** *(of publicity)* Werbe‹*kampagne, -broschüre, -strategie usw.*›
prompt [prɒmpt] **1.** *adj.* **a)** *(ready to act)* bereitwillig; **be a ~ helper/volunteer** bereitwillig helfen/sich bereitwillig zur Verfügung stellen; **be ~ in doing sth.** *or* **to do sth.** etw. unverzüglich tun; **he was ~ in his reply** er antwortete prompt; **b)** *(done readily)* sofortig; **her ~ answer/reaction** ihre prompte Antwort/Reaktion; **take ~ action** sofort handeln; **make a ~ decision** sich sofort entschließen; **c)** *(punctual)* pünktlich. **2.** *adv.* pünktlich; **at 6 o'clock ~:** Punkt 6 Uhr. **3.** *v.t.* **a)** *(incite)* veranlassen; **~ sb. to sth./to do sth.** jmdn. zu etw. veranlassen/dazu veranlassen, etw. zu tun; **b)** *(supply with words; also Theatre)* soufflieren (+ *Dat.*); *(supply with answers)* vorsagen (+ *Dat.*); *(give suggestion to)* weiterhelfen (+ *Dat.*); **~ sb. with sth.** jmdm. etw. soufflieren/vorsagen/jmdm. mit etw. weiterhelfen; **he had to be ~ed** man mußte ihm soufflieren/vorsagen/weiterhelfen; **c)** *(inspire)* hervorrufen

‹*Kritik, Eifersucht usw.*›; provozieren ‹*Antwort*›; **this ~s the question ...:** hierbei drängt sich die Frage auf: ... **4.** *v. i.* soufflieren. **5.** *n.* Soufflieren, *das;* **give a ~:** soufflieren; **I'll give you a ~ if you need one** *(a suggestion)* wenn nötig, werde ich dir weiterhelfen

prompt: ~-box *n. (Theatre)* Souffleurkasten, *der;* **~ copy** *n. (Theatre)* Rollenheft, *das*

prompter ['prɒmptə(r)] *n. (Theatre)* Souffleur, *der*/Souffleuse, *die*

prompting ['prɒmptɪŋ] *n.* **a) the ~s of his heart/conscience** die Stimme seines Herzens/Gewissens; **b) he never needs ~:** man muß ihn nicht zweimal bitten; **c)** *(Theatre)* Soufflieren, *das*

promptitude ['prɒmptɪtju:d] *see* **promptness**

promptly ['prɒmptlɪ] *adv.* **a)** *(quickly)* prompt; **he ~ went and did the opposite** *(iron.)* er hat natürlich prompt [genau] das Gegenteil getan; **b)** *(punctually)* pünktlich; **at 8 o'clock ~, ~ at 8 o'clock** Punkt 8 Uhr; pünktlich um 8 Uhr

promptness ['prɒmptnɪs] *n., no pl.* Promptheit, *die;* **be carried out with ~:** prompt durchgeführt werden; **the public's ~ in responding to the appeal** die Geschwindigkeit, mit der die Öffentlichkeit auf den Aufruf reagierte

'prompt side *n. (Brit. Theatre) Bühnenseite links vom Schauspieler; (Amer. Theatre) Bühnenseite rechts vom Schauspieler*

promulgate ['prɒməlgeɪt] *v. t.* **a)** *(disseminate)* verbreiten; **b)** *(announce officially)* verkünden

promulgation [prɒməl'geɪʃn] *n. see* **promulgate:** Verbreitung, *die;* Verkündung, *die*

prone [prəʊn] *adj.* **a)** *(liable)* **be ~ to** anfällig sein für ‹*Krankheiten, Depressionen*›; neigen zu ‹*Faulheit, Meditation*›; **be ~ to do sth.** dazu neigen, etw. zu tun; *in comb.* **strike-~:** streikanfällig; **a disaster-~ country** ein Land, in dem es häufig zu Katastrophen kommt; *see also* **accident-prone; b)** *(down-facing)* **assume a ~ position on the floor** sich in Bauchlage auf den Boden legen; **fall/throw oneself ~ to** *or* **on the ground** sich flach auf den Boden fallen lassen/werfen; **slumped ~ over her typewriter** vornüber über ihre Schreibmaschine gesunken; **c)** *(prostrate)* langgestreckt

prong [prɒŋ] **1.** *n.* **a)** *(of fork)* Zinke, *die;* **b)** *(of antler)* Ende, *das.* **2.** *v. t.* aufspießen

-pronged [prɒŋd] *adj. in comb.* -zinkig; **three-~ attack** *(Mil.; also fig.)* Angriff von drei Seiten

pronominal [prə'nɒmɪnl] *adj. (Ling.)* pronominal; Pronominal‹*adjektiv, -adverb*›

pronoun ['prəʊnaʊn] *n. (Ling.) (word replacing noun)* Pronomen, *das;* Fürwort, *das; (pronominal adjective)* Pronominaladjektiv, *das;* **demonstrative ~:** Demonstrativpronomen, *das;* **distributive ~:** Distributivum, *das;* **impersonal** *or* **indefinite ~:** Indefinitpronomen, *das;* **possessive ~:** Possessivpronomen, *das;* besitzanzeigendes Fürwort; **reflexive ~:** Reflexivpronomen, *das*

pronounce [prə'naʊns] **1.** *v. t.* **a)** *(declare formally)* verkünden; **~ a curse [up]on sb.** jmdn. verfluchen; **~ excommunication [up]on sb.** die Exkommunikation über jmdn. verhängen; **~ judgement** das Urteil verkünden; **~ judgement on sb./sth.** über jmdn./etw. das Urteil sprechen; **~ sb./sth. [to be] sth.** jmdn./etw. für etw. erklären; **he was ~d [to be] a traitor** er wurde zum Verräter erklärt; **b)** *(declare as opinion)* erklären für; **he has been ~d an excellent actor** es heißt, er sei ein ausgezeichneter Schauspieler; **he ~d himself [to be]** *or* **~d that he was disgusted with it** er erklärte, er sei empört darüber; **c)** *(speak)* aussprechen ‹*Wort, Buchstaben usw.*›. **2.** *v. i.* **~ on sth.** zu etw. Stellung nehmen; **~ for** *or* **in favour of/against sth.** sich für/gegen etw. aussprechen

pronounceable [prə'naʊnsəbl] *adj.* aussprechbar

pronounced [prə'naʊnst] *adj.* **a)** *(declared)* erklärt; ausgesprochen ‹*Gegner, Autorität*›; **b)** *(spoken)* ausgesprochen; **the h is not ~:** das h wird nicht gesprochen; **c)** *(marked)* ausgeprägt; **walk with a ~ limp** stark hinken

pronouncement [prə'naʊnsmənt] *n.* Erklärung, *die;* **make a ~ [about sth.]** eine Erklärung [zu etw.] abgeben; **make the ~ that ...:** erklären, daß ...

pro'nouncing dictionary *n.* Aussprachewörterbuch, *das*

pronto ['prɒntəʊ] *adv. (sl.)* dalli *(ugs.);* **and [do it] ~!** aber fix! *(ugs.);* aber [ein bißchen] dalli! *(ugs.)*

pronunciation [prənʌnsɪ'eɪʃn] *n.* Aussprache, *die;* **error of ~:** Aussprachefehler, *der;* **what is the ~ of this word?** wie wird dieses Wort ausgesprochen?; **this word has two ~s** dieses Wort kann auf zwei Arten ausgesprochen werden

proof [pru:f] **1.** *n.* **a)** *(fact, evidence)* Beweis, *der;* **very good ~:** sehr gute Beweise; **~ positive** eindeutige Beweise; *see also* **burden 1 a; b)** *no pl., no indef. art. (Law)* Beweismaterial, *das;* **c)** *no pl. (proving)* **in ~ of** zum Beweis (+ *Gen.*); **be capable of experimental ~:** sich experimentell beweisen lassen; **d)** *no pl. (test, trial)* Beweis, *der;* **put a theory to the ~:** eine Theorie unter Beweis stellen; **the ~ of the pudding is in the eating** *(prov.)* Probieren geht über Studieren *(Spr.);* **e)** *no pl., no art. (standard of strength)* Proof *o. Art.;* **100 ~** *(Brit.),* **128 ~** *(Amer.)* 64 Vol.-% Alkohol; **above/below ~:** über/unter 57,27 Vol.-% Alkohol; **f)** *(Printing)* Abzug, *der;* **first ~:** Erstsatz, *der; see also* **galley c; page proof; read 1 a; g)** *(Photog., Art)* [Probe]abzug, *der.* **2.** *adj.* **a)** *(impervious)* **be ~ against sth.** unempfindlich gegen etw. sein; *(fig.)* gegen etw. immun sein; **~ against wind/bullets/the weather** windundurchlässig/kugelsicher/wetterfest; **b)** *in comb. (resistant to)* ‹*kugel-, bruch-, einbruch-, diebes-, idioten*›sicher; ‹*schall-, wasser*›dicht; **flame-~:** nicht brennbar; **c)** hochprozentig ‹*Alkohol*›; **this liqueur is 67.4°** *(Brit.) or (Amer.)* **76.8° ~:** dieser Likör hat 38,4 Vol.-% Alkohol. **3.** *v. t.* **a)** *(Printing) (take ~ of)* andrucken; *(proof-read)* Korrektur lesen; **b)** *(Photog., Art)* einen [Probe]abzug herstellen von; **c)** *(make resistant)* **~ [against sth.]** [gegen etw.] imprägnieren ‹*Stoff, Gewebe*›; [gegen etw.] abdichten ‹*Wand*›; *in comb.* **sound-/water-~:** schall-/wasserdicht machen; **flame-~ sth.** etw. nicht brennbar machen; **d)** *(in baking)* gehen lassen

proof: ~-read *v. t. (Printing)* Korrektur lesen; **~-reader** *n. (Printing)* Korrektor, *der*/Korrektorin, *die;* **~-reading** *n. (Printing)* Korrekturlesen, *das;* **~-sheet** *n. (Printing)* Korrekturfahne, *die;* **~ 'spirit** *n. Alkohol-Wasser-Gemisch mit einem bestimmten Alkoholanteil;* Proof spirit, *der*

[1]prop [prɒp] **1.** *n.* **a)** *(support, lit. or fig.)* Stütze, *die; (Mining)* Strebe, *die;* **b)** *(Rugby) Spieler außen in der vorderen Reihe des Gedränges.* **2.** *v. t.,* **-pp-: a)** *(support)* stützen; **the ladder was ~ped against the house** die Leiter war gegen das Haus gelehnt; **the door was ~ped open with a brick** die Tür wurde von einem Ziegelstein offengehalten; **b)** *(fig.) see* **~ up b**

~ 'up *v. t.* **a)** *(support)* stützen; **~ oneself up on one's elbows** sich auf die Ellbogen stützen; **sit ~ped up against the wall** [mit dem Rücken] an die Wand gelehnt sitzen; **~ up the bar** *(joc./iron.)* an der Theke rumhängen *(ugs.);* **b)** *(fig.)* aufrichten ‹*Person*›; vor dem Konkurs bewahren ‹*Firma*›; stützen ‹*Regierung, Währung*›

[2]prop *n. (coll.)* **a)** *(Theatre, Cinemat.: also fig.)* Requisit, *das;* **b)** *in pl. see* **propertyman**

[3]prop *n. (Aeronaut. coll.)* Propeller, *der*

propaganda [prɒpə'gændə] *n., no pl., no indef. art.* Propaganda, *die*

propagandist [prɒpə'gændɪst] **1.** *n.* Propagandist, *der*/Propagandistin, *die* **(of, for** *Gen.*). **2.** *adj.* propagandistisch; Propaganda‹*schrift, -blatt*›

propagate ['prɒpəgeɪt] **1.** *v. t.* **a)** *(Hort., Bacteriol.)* vermehren **(from, by** durch); *(Breeding, Zool.)* züchten; **b)** *(hand down)* vererben ‹*Eigenschaft, Merkmal*› (to auf + *Akk.*); **c)** *(spread)* verbreiten; **d)** *(Phys.)* **be ~d** sich fortpflanzen. **2.** *v. i.* **a)** *(Bot., Zool., Bacteriol.)* sich vermehren; **b)** *(spread, extend, travel)* sich ausbreiten. **3.** *v. refl. (Bot., Zool., Bacteriol.)* sich vermehren

propagation [prɒpə'geɪʃn] *n.* **a)** *(Hort., Breeding, Bacteriol.: causing to propagate)* Züchtung, *die;* **b)** *(Bot., Zool., Bacteriol.: reproduction)* Vermehrung, *die;* **c)** *(handing down)* Vererbung, *die* (to auf + *Akk.*); **d)** *(spreading)* Verbreitung, *die;* **e)** *(Phys.)* Fortpflanzung, *die*

propagative ['prɒpəgeɪtɪv] *adj.* **a)** *(Hort.)* Vermehrungs-; **b)** *(reproductive)* Fortpflanzungs-

propagator ['prɒpəgeɪtə(r)] *n.* **a)** *(Hort.) (person)* Züchter, *der*/Züchterin, *die; (device)* [beheizbare] Saatkiste; **b)** *(disseminator)* Propagator, *der*/Propagatorin, *die (geh.)*

propane ['prəʊpeɪn] *n. (Chem.)* Propan, *das*

propel [prə'pel] *v. t.,* **-ll-** *(lit. or fig.)* antreiben; **the boat was ~led through the water by the oarsmen** die Ruderer trieben das Boot durchs Wasser; **the rider was ~led over the horse's head** der Reiter wurde über den Kopf des Pferdes geschleudert

propellant [prə'pelənt] *n.* **a)** Treibstoff, *der;* **b)** *(of aerosol spray)* Treibgas, *das;* **c)** *(explosive charge)* Treibladung, *die*

-propelled [prə'peld] *adj. in comb.* -getrieben

propellent [prə'pelənt] *adj.* Antriebs‹*kraft, -energie, -leistung, -mittel, -system*›

propeller [prə'pelə(r)] *n.* Propeller, *der*

propeller: ~ shaft *n. (Aeronaut.)* Propellerwelle, *die; (Motor Veh.)* Kardanwelle, *die;* **~ turbine** *n. (Aeronaut.)* Propellerturbine, *die*

propelling 'pencil *n. (Brit.)* Drehbleistift, *der*

propensity [prə'pensɪtɪ] *n.* Neigung, *die;* **[have] a ~ to** *or* **towards sth.** einen Hang zu etw. [haben]; **have a ~ to do sth.** *or* **for doing sth.** dazu neigen, etw. zu tun

proper ['prɒpə(r)] **1.** *adj.* **a)** *(accurate)* richtig; wahrheitsgetreu ‹*Bericht*›; zutreffend ‹*Beschreibung*›; eigentlich ‹*Wortbedeutung*›; ursprünglich ‹*Fassung*›; **in the ~ sense** im wahrsten Sinne des Wortes; **b)** *postpos. (strictly so called)* im engeren Sinn *nachgestellt;* **within the sphere of architecture ~:** auf dem Gebiet der Architektur an sich; **in London ~:** in London selbst; **c)** *(genuine)* echt; richtig ‹*Wirbelsturm, Schauspieler*›; **d)** *(satisfactory)* richtig; zufriedenstellend ‹*Antwort*›; hinreichend ‹*Grund*›; **e)** *(suitable)* angemessen; *(morally fitting)* gebührend; **do sth. the ~ way** etw. richtig machen; **we must do the ~ thing by him** wir müssen ihn fair behandeln; **he did not know which was the ~ knife to use** er wußte nicht, welches Messer er benutzen sollte; **do as you think ~:** tu, was du für richtig hältst; **that's not a ~ attitude to take towards ...:** so verhält man sich nicht gegenüber ...; **f)** *(conventionally acceptable)* gehörig; **have no notion of what is ~:** nicht wissen, was sich gehört; **language not ~ for a lady's ears** eine Ausdrucksweise, die nicht für die Ohren einer Dame bestimmt ist; **it**

would not be ~ for me to ...: es gehört sich nicht, daß ich ...; **the conduct ~ to a gentleman** das Benehmen, das sich für einen Gentleman gehört; **g)** *(conventional, prim)* förmlich; **h)** *attrib. (coll.: thorough)* richtig; **she gave him a ~ hiding** sie gab ihm eine ordentliche Tracht Prügel; **you gave me a ~ turn** du hast mir einen ganz schönen Schrecken eingejagt. **2.** *adv. (coll.)* **good and ~:** gehörig; nach Strich und Faden *(ugs.)*

proper 'fraction *n. (Math.)* echter Bruch

properly ['prɒpəlɪ] *adv.* **a)** richtig; *(rightly)* zu Recht; *(with decency)* anständig; **~ speaking** genaugenommen; **he is ~ considered to be a great artist** er wird mit Recht als ein großer Künstler angesehen; **he is not ~ a captain at all** er ist eigentlich gar kein Kapitän; **I'm not ~ authorized to do it** ich bin eigentlich nicht dazu berechtigt; **he very ~ went to see the doctor** er tat das einzig Richtige und ging zum Arzt; **b)** *(primly)* förmlich; **c)** *(coll.: thoroughly)* total *(ugs.)*

proper: ~ 'motion *n. (Astron.)* Eigenbewegung, *die*, **~ 'name, ~ 'noun** *ns. (Ling.)* Eigenname, *der*

propertied ['prɒpətɪd] *adj.* begütert; **the ~ class[es]** die besitzende[n] Klasse[n]

property ['prɒpətɪ] *n.* **a)** *(possession[s], ownership)* Eigentum, *das;* **the ~-owning classes** die besitzenden Klassen; **~ speculator/dealer** Immobilienspekulant, *der/*-händler, *der* ; **make sth. sb.'s ~:** jmdm. etw. übereignen; **lost ~:** Fundsachen *Pl.;* **lost ~ [department** *or* **office]** Fundbüro, *das;* **man of ~:** begüterter Mann; **common ~:** Gemeingut, *das; (fig.) see* **common knowledge; b)** *(estate)* Besitz, *der;* Immobilie, *die (fachspr.);* **~ in London is expensive** die Immobilienpreise in London sind hoch; *see also* **personal property a; real property; c)** *(attribute)* Eigenschaft, *die; (effect, special power)* Wirkung, *die;* **d)** *(Cinemat., Theatre)* Requisit, *das*

property: ~ developer *n.* ≈ Bauunternehmer, *der/*-unternehmerin, *die;* **~-man** *n. (Cinemat., Theatre)* Requisiteur, *der;* **~ market** *n.* Immobilienmarkt, *der;* **~ master** *see* **~-man; ~ owner** *n.* Grundbesitzer, *der/*-besitzerin, *die;* **~ qualification** *n. Eigentumsnachweis als Voraussetzung für ein Amt od. Recht;* **~ tax** *n.* Vermögenssteuer, *die*

prop 'forward *see* ¹**prop 1 b**

prophecy ['prɒfɪsɪ] *n.* **a)** *(prediction)* Vorhersage, *die;* **make the ~ that ...:** vorhersagen, daß ...; **b)** *(prophetic utterance)* Prophezeiung, *die;* **c)** *(prophetic faculty)* **[the power** *or* **gift of] ~:** die Gabe der Prophetie *(geh.)*

prophesy ['prɒfɪsaɪ] **1.** *v. t. (predict)* vorhersagen; *(fig.)* prophezeien ‹*Unglück*›; *(as fortune-teller)* weissagen; **what do you ~ will happen?** was wird deiner Vorhersage nach geschehen? **2.** *v. i.* **a)** *(foretell future)* Vorhersagen machen; **~ of sth.** *(lit. or fig.)* etw. ankündigen; **b)** *(speak as prophet)* Prophezeiungen machen

prophet ['prɒfɪt] *n.* **a)** *(lit. or fig.)* Prophet, *der;* **be the ~ of sth.** etw. prophezeien; **~ of doom** Schwarzseher, *der;* **b)** *(advocate)* Vorkämpfer, *der*

prophetess ['prɒfɪtɪs] *n.* **a)** Prophetin, *die;* **b)** *(advocate)* Vorkämpferin, *die*

prophetic [prə'fetɪk] *adj.* prophetisch; **be ~ of sth.** ein Vorzeichen für etw. sein

prophetically [prə'fetɪkəlɪ] *adv.* prophetisch

prophylactic [prɒfɪ'læktɪk] **1.** *adj.* prophylaktisch *(Med., geh.);* vorbeugend. **2.** *n.* **a)** Prophylaxe, *die (Med.);* Vorbeugung, *die; (preventive measure)* Vorbeugungsmaßnahme, *die;* **b)** *(contraceptive)* Verhütungsmittel, *das*

prophylaxis [prɒfɪ'læksɪs] *n., pl.* **prophylaxes** [prɒfɪ'læksi:z] *(Med.)* Prophylaxe, *die*

propinquity [prə'pɪŋkwɪtɪ] *n., no pl. (formal)* **a)** *(nearness)* Nähe, *die* **(to** zu); **in close ~ [to each other]** nah beieinander; **b)** *(kinship)* **[nahe]** Verwandtschaft **(to mit, between** zwischen)

propitiate [prə'pɪʃɪeɪt] *v. t. (formal) (appease)* besänftigen; *(make favourably inclined)* günstig stimmen

propitiation [prəpɪʃɪ'eɪʃn] *n. (formal)* Besänftigung, *die*

propitiatory [prə'pɪʃɪətərɪ] *adj. (formal) (of propitiation)* Besänftigungs-; besänftigend ‹*Wort, Lächeln, Geste*›

propitious [prə'pɪʃəs] *adj.* **a)** *(auspicious)* verheißungsvoll; **b)** *(favouring, benevolent)* günstig; **~ for** *or* **to sth.** günstig für etw.; **~ for** *or* **to doing sth.** dafür geeignet, etw. zu tun; **be hardly ~ to sth.** einer Sache *(Dat.)* kaum förderlich sein

propitiously [prə'pɪʃəslɪ] *adv. (auspiciously, favourably)* günstig

'prop-jet *n. (Aeronaut.) (aircraft)* Turbo-Prop-Flugzeug, *das; (engine)* Turbo-Prop-Triebwerk, *das*

proponent [prə'pəʊnənt] *n.* Befürworter, *der/*Befürworterin, *die*

proportion [prə'pɔ:ʃn] **1.** *n.* **a)** *(portion)* Teil, *der; (in recipe)* Menge, *die;* **the ~ of deaths is high** der Anteil der Todesfälle ist hoch; **what ~ of candidates pass the exam?** wie groß ist der Anteil der erfolgreichen Prüfungskandidaten?; **b)** *(ratio)* Verhältnis, *das;* **the ~ of sth. to sth.** das Verhältnis von etw. zu etw.; **the high ~ of imports to exports** der hohe Anteil der Importe im Vergleich zu den Exporten; **in ~ [to sth.]** [einer Sache *(Dat.)*] entsprechend; **our excitement grew in ~ as the ship came closer** je näher das Schiff kam, desto aufgeregter wurden wir; **c)** *(correct relation)* Proportion, *die; (fig.)* Ausgewogenheit, *die;* **the design lacks ~:** der Entwurf ist schlecht proportioniert; **sense of ~:** Sinn für Proportionen; **be in ~ [to** *or* **with sth.]** *(lit. or fig.)* im richtigen Verhältnis [zu *od.* mit etw.] stehen; **try to keep things in ~** *(fig.)* versuchen Sie, die Dinge im richtigen Licht zu sehen; **be out of ~/all** *or* **any ~ [to** *or* **with sth.]** *(lit. or fig.)* in keinem/keinerlei Verhältnis zu etw. stehen; **get things out of ~** *(fig.)* die Dinge zu wichtig nehmen; *(worry unnecessarily)* sich *(Dat.)* zu viele Sorgen machen; **d)** *in pl. (size)* Dimension, *die;* **the ~s of each room were modest** die Räume waren von bescheidener Größe; **of mountainous ~s** riesenhaften Ausmaßes; **e)** *(Math.)* **[geometric] ~:** Proportion, *die;* **rule of ~ = rule of three** *see* **rule 1 a.** *See also* **direct proportion; inverse proportion. 2.** *v. t. (make proportionate)* proportionieren; *(harmonize)* aufeinander abstimmen; **~ sth. to sth.** etw. einer Sache *(Dat.)* anpassen; **the architect has ~ed the whole building** der Architekt hat das ganze Gebäude ausgewogen gestaltet; *see also* **proportioned**

proportional [prə'pɔ:ʃənl] *adj.* **a)** *(in proportion)* entsprechend; **be ~ to sth.** einer Sache *(Dat.)* entsprechen; **b)** *(in correct relation)* ausgewogen; **be ~ to sth.** *(lit. or fig.)* einer Sache *(Dat.)* entsprechen; **c)** *(Math.)* **~ [to sth.]** proportional [zu etw.]; **d)** *(of proportions)* proportional

proportionality [prəpɔ:ʃə'nælɪtɪ] *n., no pl.* **a)** *(being in proportion)* Verhältnismäßigkeit, *die;* **there is a ~ between A and B** A und B verhalten sich proportional zueinander; **b)** *(harmony)* Ausgewogenheit, *die;* **~ to sth.** ausgewogenes Verhältnis zu etw.

proportionally [prə'pɔ:ʃənəlɪ] *adv.* **a)** *(in proportion)* [dem]entsprechend; **b)** *(in correct relation)* proportional gesehen; **correspond/not correspond ~ to sth.** im richtigen/in keinem Verhältnis zu etw. stehen

proportional: ~ represen'tation *n. (Polit.)* Verhältniswahlsystem, *das;* **~ tax** *n.* Proportionalsteuer, *die*

proportionate [prə'pɔ:ʃənət] *adj.* **a)** *(in proportion)* entsprechend; **~ to sth.** proportional zu etw.; **b)** *(in correct relation)* ausgewogen; **~ to sth.** einer Sache *(Dat.)* entsprechend; **the length of the room is not ~ to its breadth** die Länge des Zimmers steht in keinem Verhältnis zu seiner Breite

proportionately [prə'pɔ:ʃənətlɪ] *adv.* **a)** *(in proportion)* entsprechend; **b)** *(in correct relation)* angemessen

proportioned [prə'pɔ:ʃnd] *adj.* proportioniert; **well-/ill-~:** wohlproportioniert/schlecht proportioniert

proposal [prə'pəʊzl] *n.* **a)** *(thing proposed)* Vorschlag, *der; (offer)* Angebot, *das;* **make ~s for peace** Friedensvorschläge unterbreiten; **make a ~ for doing sth.** *or* **to do sth.** einen Vorschlag machen, etw. zu tun; **his ~ for improving the system** sein Vorschlag zur Verbesserung des Systems; **draw up ~s/a ~:** Pläne/einen Plan aufstellen; **b) ~ [of marriage]** [Heirats]antrag, *der;* **c)** *(act of proposing)* Unterbreitung, *die;* **he was interrupted in the middle of his ~ to her/the committee** er wurde unterbrochen, während er ihr einen Heiratsantrag machte/dem Ausschuß seinen Vorschlag unterbreitete

propose [prə'pəʊz] **1.** *v. t.* **a)** *(put forward for consideration)* vorschlagen; **~ sth. to sb.** jmdm. etw. vorschlagen; **~ marriage [to sb.]** [jmdm.] einen Heiratsantrag machen; **~ a truce** einen Waffenstillstand anbieten *od.* vorschlagen; **b)** *(nominate)* **~ sb. as/for sth.** jmdn. als/für etw. vorschlagen; **c)** *(for drinking of toast)* **~ a toast to sb./sth.** einen Trinkspruch auf jmdn./etw. ausbringen; **~ sb.'s health** sein Glas erheben, um auf jmds. Gesundheit zu trinken; **I [should like to] ~: 'The bride and groom!'** trinken wir auf Braut und Bräutigam!; **d)** *(intend)* **~ doing** *or* **to do sth.** beabsichtigen, etw. zu tun; **e)** *(set up as aim)* planen; **~ sth. to oneself** sich *(Dat.)* etw. vornehmen; **he ~s their destruction** sein Ziel ist ihre Vernichtung. **2.** *v. i.* **a)** *(offer marriage)* **~ [to sb.]** jmdm. einen Heiratsantrag machen; **b)** *see* **dispose 2**

proposer [prə'pəʊzə(r)] *n. (of motion)* Antragsteller, *der/*-stellerin, *die; (of candidate)* Vorschlagende, *der/die*

proposition [prɒpə'zɪʃn] **1.** *n.* **a)** *(proposal)* Vorschlag, *der;* **make** *or* **put a ~ to sb.** jmdm. einen Vorschlag machen; **b)** *(statement)* Aussage, *die;* **Galileo's ~ that the Earth revolves around the Sun** Galileis These, daß die Erde sich um die Sonne dreht; **c)** *(sl.: undertaking, problem)* Sache, *die (ugs.);* **paying ~:** lohnendes Geschäft; **it's not a ~:** das kommt nicht in Frage; **the project is no longer a practical/viable ~:** das Projekt ist nicht mehr durchführbar/rentabel; **he looks a tough/nasty ~:** er scheint ein zäher/widerlicher Typ zu sein *(ugs.);* **d)** *(Logic)* Satz, *der;* Proposition, *die (fachspr.);* **e)** *(Math.)* Satz, *der.* **2.** *v. t. (coll.)* jmdn. anmachen *(ugs.)*

propositional [prɒpə'zɪʃənl] *adj.* **a)** *(Logic)* propositional; **b)** *(Math.)* lehrsatzartig

propound [prə'paʊnd] *v. t.* darlegen; **~ a question** eine Frage aufwerfen; **~ sth. to sb.** jmdm. etw. vortragen

proprietary [prə'praɪətərɪ] *adj.* **a)** *(belonging to private owner)* Eigentums-; ‹*Pflichten*› als Eigentümer; **~ rights/claims** Eigentumsrechte/-ansprüche; **b)** *(characteristic of a proprietor)* **have a ~ attitude to sb.** jmdn. als seinen Besitz betrachten; **c)** *(holding property)* Eigentümer-; **~ owner** Eigenbesitzer, *der/*-besitzerin, *die (Wirtsch.);* **d)** *(privately owned)* privat; **e)** *(patented)* Marken-; **~ brand** *or* **make of washing-powder** Markenwaschmittel, *das*

proprietary: ~ 'company *n. (Brit. Commerc.)* Privatfirma, *die;* **~ 'medicine** *n.* Markenmedikament, *das;* **~ 'name, ~ 'term** *ns. (Commerc.)* Markenname, *der*

proprietor [prəˈpraɪətə(r)] *n.* Inhaber, *der*/Inhaberin, *die; (of newspaper)* Besitzer, *der*/Besitzerin, *die*

proprietorial [prəpraɪəˈtɔːrɪəl] *adj.* **a)** *(of proprietor)* Inhaber-; ‹*Pflichten*› als Inhaber; **b)** *(characteristic of proprietor)* **have a ~ attitude to sb.** jmdn. als seinen Besitz betrachten; **~ pride** Besitzerstolz, *der*

proprietorship [prəˈpraɪətəʃɪp] *n. (ownership)* Eigentum, *das; (of newspaper)* Besitz, *der;* **under sb.'s ~:** während jmd. Inhaber ist/war

proprietress [prəˈpraɪətrɪs] *n.* Inhaberin, *die; (of newspaper)* Besitzerin, *die*

propriety [prəˈpraɪətɪ] *n.* **a)** *no pl. (decency)* Anstand, *der;* **with ~:** anständig; **breach of ~:** Verstoß gegen die guten Sitten; **b)** *in pl.* **the proprieties** die Regeln des Anstands; **observe the proprieties** Anstand und Sitte bewahren; **c)** *no pl. (fitness)* Angemessenheit, *die;* **d)** *no pl. (accuracy)* Richtigkeit, *die;* **with perfect ~:** völlig zu Recht

propulsion [prəˈpʌlʃn] *n.* Antrieb, *der; (driving force, lit. or fig.)* Antriebskraft, *die; see also* **jet propulsion**

propulsive [prəˈpʌlsɪv] *adj.* Antriebs-; *(fig.)* mobilisierend

pro rata [prəʊ ˈrɑːtə] **1.** *adv.* anteilmäßig. **2.** *adj.* anteilmäßig; **be paid on a ~ basis** anteilmäßig bezahlt werden

prorogation [prəʊrəˈgeɪʃn] *n.* Vertagung, *die* **(to** auf + *Akk.*); *(Parl.: interval between sessions)* Parlamentsferien *Pl.*

prorogue [prəˈrəʊg] **1.** *v.t. (also Parl.)* vertagen. **2.** *v.i. (also Parl.)* sich vertagen

prosaic [prəˈzeɪɪk, prəʊˈzeɪɪk] *adj.*, **prosaically** [prəˈzeɪɪkəlɪ, prəʊˈzeɪɪkəlɪ] *adv.* prosaisch *(geh.);* nüchtern

proscenium [prəˈsiːnɪəm] *n., pl.* **~s** *or* **proscenia** [prəˈsiːnɪə] *(Theatre) (front of stage)* Proszenium, *das; (framework)* Bühnenrahmen, *der*

proscenium 'arch *n. (Theatre)* Bühnenrahmen, *der*

proscribe [prəˈskraɪb] *v.t.* **a)** *(Hist.: outlaw)* für vogelfrei erklären; **b)** *(exile)* verbannen; *(fig.)* ächten; **c)** *(prohibit)* verbieten

proscription [prəˈskrɪpʃn] *n.* **a)** *(Hist.: outlawing)* Ächtung, *die;* **b)** *(exile)* Verbannung, *die;* **issue a ~ against sb.** jmdn. in die Verbannung schicken; **c)** *(prohibition)* Verbot, *das*

prose [prəʊz] *n.* **a)** *(form of language)* Prosa, *die; attrib.* Prosa‹*werk, -stil*›; **b)** *(Sch., Univ.)* **~ [translation]** Übersetzung in die Fremdsprache; **a ~ passage for translation** ein Text zur Übersetzung in die Fremdsprache. *See also* **idyll a; poetry**

prosecute [ˈprɒsɪkjuːt] **1.** *v.t.* **a)** *(Law)* strafrechtlich verfolgen; **~ sb. for sth./doing sth.** jmdn. wegen etw. strafrechtlich verfolgen/jmdn. strafrechtlich verfolgen, weil er etw. tut/getan hat; **b)** *(pursue)* verfolgen; **c)** *(carry on)* ausüben. **2.** *v.i.* Anzeige erstatten; **as a barrister, he preferred defending to prosecuting** als Rechtsanwalt zog er die Verteidigung der Anklage vor

prosecuting [ˈprɒsɪkjuːtɪŋ]: **~ at'torney** *n. (Amer. Law),* **~ 'counsel** *n. (Brit. Law)* Staatsanwalt, *der*/-anwältin, *die*

prosecution [prɒsɪˈkjuːʃn] *n.* **a)** *(Law) (bringing to trial)* [strafrechtliche] Verfolgung; *(court procedure)* Anklage, *die;* **start a ~ against sb.** Anklage gegen jmdn. erheben; **b)** *(Law: prosecuting party)* Anklage[vertretung], *die;* **the [case for the] ~:** die Anklage; **witness for the ~, ~ witness** Zeuge/Zeugin der Anklage; **~ lawyer** Staatsanwalt, *der*/-anwältin, *die;* **c)** *(pursuing)* Verfolgung, *die;* **d)** *(carrying on)* Ausübung, *die*

prosecutor [ˈprɒsɪkjuːtə(r)] *n. (Law)* Ankläger, *der*/Anklägerin, *die;* **public ~** ≈ Generalstaatsanwalt, *der*/-anwältin, *die*

proselyte [ˈprɒsɪlaɪt] *n. (convert; also Jewish Relig.)* Proselyt, *der*/Proselytin, *die*

proselytize (proselytise) [ˈprɒsɪlɪtaɪz] *v.i.* missionieren

prose: **~-writer** *n.* Prosaschriftsteller, *der*/-schriftstellerin, *die;* **~-writing** *n.* Prosa, *die*

prosodic [prəˈsɒdɪk] *adj.* prosodisch

prosodist [ˈprɒsədɪst] *n.* Prosodiker, *der*/Prosodikerin, *die*

prosody [ˈprɒsədɪ] *n.* **a)** Verslehre, *die;* **b)** *(Ling.)* Prosodie, *die*

prospect **1.** [ˈprɒspekt] *n.* **a)** *(extensive view)* Aussicht, *die* **(of** auf + *Akk.*); *(spectacle)* Anblick, *der; (mental view)* Einsicht, *die* **(of** in + *Akk.*); **open [up] new ~s to sb.'s mind** jmds. geistigen Horizont erweitern; **b)** *(expectation)* Erwartung, *die* **(of** hinsichtlich); **[at the] ~ of sth./doing sth.** *(mental picture, likelihood)* [bei der] Aussicht auf etw.*(Akk.)*/[darauf], etw. zu tun; **what are the ~s of your coming?** wie sind die Aussichten, daß du kommst?; **have the ~ of sth., have sth. in ~:** etw. in Aussicht haben; **c)** *in pl. (hope of success)* Zukunftsaussichten; **a man with [good] ~s** ein Mann mit Zukunft; **a job with no ~s** eine Stelle ohne Zukunft; **sb.'s ~s of sth./doing sth.** jmds. Chancen auf etw. *(Akk.)*/darauf, etw. zu tun; **what are his ~s of being accepted?** wie stehen seine Chancen, angenommen zu werden?; **~s of survival** Überlebenschancen; **the ~s for sb./sth.** die Aussichten für jmdn./etw.; **d)** *(possible customer)* [möglicher] Kunde/[mögliche] Kundin; *(possible candidate)* Anwärter, *der*/Anwärterin, *die; (possible winner)* Kandidat, *der*/Kandidatin, *die;* **be a good ~ for a race/the job** bei einem Rennen gute Chancen haben/ein aussichtsreicher Kandidat für den Job sein. **2.** [prəˈspekt] *v.i. (explore for mineral)* prospektieren *(Bergw.);* nach Bodenschätzen suchen; *(fig.)* Ausschau halten **(for** nach); **~ for gold** nach Gold suchen. **3.** [prəˈspekt] *v.t.* **a)** *(Mining)* erkunden; prospektieren *(fachspr.);* **~ sth. for sth.** in etw. *(Dat.)* nach etw. suchen; **b)** *(investigate)* untersuchen

prospective [prəˈspektɪv] *adj.* **a)** *(expected)* voraussichtlich; zukünftig ‹*Erbe, Braut*›; potentiell ‹*Käufer, Kandidat*›; **b)** *(referring to the future)* zukünftig; **make ~ enquiries** sich vorab informieren; **take a ~ view of sth.** etw. vorausschauend betrachten

prospectively [prəˈspektɪvlɪ] *adv.* **a)** *(with foresight)* vorsorglich; **b)** *(with future effectiveness)* in der Zukunft

prospector [prəˈspektə(r)] *n.* Prospektor, *der (Bergw.); (for gold)* Goldsucher, *der*

prospectus [prəˈspektəs] *n.* **a)** *(of enterprise)* Prospekt, *der (Wirtsch.);* **b)** *(of book)* Prospekt, *der;* **c)** *(Brit. Sch.)* Lehrprogramm, *das; (Brit. Univ.)* Studienführer, *der*

prosper [ˈprɒspə(r)] *v.i.* gedeihen; ‹*Geschäft:*› florieren; ‹*Kunst usw.:*› eine Blütezeit erleben; ‹*Berufstätiger:*› Erfolg haben; **how is he ~ing in that business of his/in his career?** läuft sein Geschäft gut?/was macht seine Karriere?; **cheats never ~:** ≈ unrecht Gut gedeihet nicht *(Spr.)*

prosperity [prɒˈsperɪtɪ] *n., no pl.* Wohlstand, *der*

prosperous [ˈprɒspərəs] *adj.* **a)** *(flourishing)* wohlhabend; gutgehend, florierend ‹*Unternehmen*›; *(blessed with good fortune)* erfolgreich; **~ years/time** Jahre/Zeit des Wohlstands; **b)** *(auspicious)* günstig

prostate [ˈprɒsteɪt] *n.* **~ [gland]** *(Anat., Zool.)* Prostata, *die;* Vorsteherdrüse, *die*

prosthesis [prɒsˈθiːsɪs] *n., pl.* **prostheses** [prɒsˈθiːsiːz] **a)** *(Med.) (artificial part)* Prothese, *die; (branch of surgery)* Prothetik, *die;* **b)** *(Ling., Pros.)* Prothese, *die*

prosthetic [prɒsˈθetɪk] *adj. (Med., Ling., Pros.)* prothetisch; **~ leg** Beinprothese, *die;* **~ surgery** Prothetik, *die*

prosthetics [prɒsˈθetɪks] *n., no pl. (Med.)* Prothetik, *die*

prostitute [ˈprɒstɪtjuːt] **1.** *n.* **a)** *(woman)* Prostituierte, *die;* **b)** *(man)* Strichjunge, *der (salopp).* **2.** *v.t.* zur Prostitution anbieten; *(fig.)* prostituieren ‹*Talent, Integrität*›; **~ oneself** *(lit. or fig.)* sich prostituieren

prostitution [prɒstɪˈtjuːʃn] *n. (lit. or fig.)* Prostitution, *die*

prostrate **1.** [ˈprɒstreɪt] *adj.* **a)** [auf dem Bauch] ausgestreckt; **she lay ~ before him** sie lag ihm zu Füßen; **~ with grief/shame** von Schmerz/Trauer übermannt; **b)** *(exhausted)* erschöpft; **be ~ with fever** vom Fieber geschwächt sein; **c)** *(Bot.)* kriechend. **2.** [prɒˈstreɪt, prəˈstreɪt] *v.t.* **a)** *(lay flat)* zu Boden werfen ‹*Person*›; **b)** *(make submissive, lay low)* zermürben; *(overcome emotionally)* übermannen; **c)** *(exhaust)* erschöpfen; **be ~d by exhaustion** vor Erschöpfung ganz kraftlos sein. **3.** *v. refl. (throw oneself down)* **~ oneself [at sth./before sb.]** sich [vor etw./jmdm.] niederwerfen; **~ oneself at sb.'s feet** sich jmdm. zu Füßen werfen; **~ oneself [before sb.]** *(humble oneself)* sich [vor jmdm.] demütigen

prostration [prɒˈstreɪʃn, prəˈstreɪʃn] *n.* **a)** *(prostrating oneself)* Fußfall, *der;* **in ~:** [demütig] ausgestreckt; **b)** *(submission)* Unterwürfigkeit, *die; (subjugation)* Unterdrückung, *die;* **c)** *(being emotionally overcome)* Erschütterung, *die;* **d)** *(reduction to powerlessness) (of country or party)* Entmachtung, *die; (of business)* Ruin, *der;* **reduce a country to economic ~:** ein Land wirtschaftlich ruinieren; **e)** *(exhaustion)* Erschöpfung, *die*

prosy [ˈprəʊzɪ] *adj.* langatmig

Prot [prɒt] *see* **Prod**

protagonist [prəʊˈtægənɪst] *n.* **a)** *(advocate)* Vorkämpfer, *der*/Vorkämpferin, *die; (spokesperson)* Wortführer, *der*/-führerin, *die;* **b)** *(Lit./Theatre: chief character)* Protagonist, *der*/Protagonistin, *die; (fig.)* Hauptakteur, *der*/-akteurin, *die*

protean [ˈprəʊtɪən, prəʊˈtiːən] *adj.* proteisch *(geh.)*

protect [prəˈtekt] *v.t.* **a)** *(defend)* schützen **(from** vor + *Dat.*, **against** gegen); **~ed by law** gesetzlich geschützt; **they led happy ~ed lives** sie führten ein glückliches, behütetes Leben; **~ sb. against** *or* **from himself/herself** jmdn. vor sich *(Dat.)* selbst schützen; **~ one's/sb.'s interests** seine/jmds. Interessen wahren; **~ the peace** den Frieden sichern; **b)** *(preserve)* unter [Natur]schutz stellen ‹*Pflanze, Tier, Gebiet*›; **~ed plants/animals** geschützte Pflanzen/Tiere; **the golden eagle is a ~ed bird** der Steinadler steht unter Naturschutz; **c)** *(give legal immunity to)* schützen; **the law ~s foreign diplomats** ausländische Diplomaten genießen den Schutz der Immunität; **be a ~ed tenant** mietrechtlich geschützt sein; **d)** *(Econ.)* durch Protektionismus schützen; **e)** *(render safe)* sichern ‹*Gerät, Leitung*›

protected [prəˈtektɪd]: **~ 'species** *n.* geschützte Art; **~ 'state** *n. (Polit.)* Schutzstaat, *der*

protection [prəˈtekʃn] *n.* **a)** *(defence)* Schutz, *der* **(from** vor + *Dat.*, **against** gegen); **under the ~ of sb./sth.** unter jmds. Schutz/dem Schutz einer Sache *(Gen.);* **[under] police ~:** [unter] Polizeischutz; **b)** *(immunity from molestation)* Schutz, *der; (money paid)* Schutzgeld, *das;* **c)** *(of wildlife etc.)* Schutz, *der;* **d)** *(legal immunity)* Immunität, *die;* **e)** *(Econ.)* Schutz, *der; (system)* Protektionismus, *der;* **f)** *(protective agent)* Schutz, *der;* **as a ~ against** zum *od.* als Schutz gegen

protectionism [prəˈtekʃənɪzm] *n. (Econ.)* Protektionismus, *der*

protectionist [prəˈtekʃənɪst] *(Econ.)* **1.** *n.* Protektionist, *der*/Protektionistin, *die.* **2.** *adj.* protektionistisch

protection: ~ money *n.* Schutzgeld, *das;* **~ racket** *n.* Erpresserorganisation, *die;* **run a ~ racket** die Erpressung von Schutzgeldern organisieren

protective [prəˈtektɪv] *adj.* **a)** *(protecting)* schützend; Schutz‹*hülle, -anstrich, -vorrichtung, -maske*›; **be ~ towards sb.** fürsorglich gegenüber jmdm. sein; **~ instinct** Beschützerinstinkt, *der;* **be ~ against sth.** vor etw. *(Dat.)* schützen; **butterflies/tigers have ~ camouflage/colouring** Schmetterlinge/Tiger haben eine Tarntracht/Tarn- *od.* Schutzfärbung; **the soldiers wore ~ camouflage** die Soldaten trugen Tarnanzüge; **~ clothing** Schutzkleidung, *die;* **b)** *(Econ.)* protektionistisch; Schutz‹*zoll*›

protective: ~ arˈrest, ~ ˈcustody *ns.* Schutzgewahrsam, *der (Amtsspr.);* Schutzhaft, *die*

protectively [prəˈtektɪvlɪ] *adv.* schützend; **she brought up her children too ~:** sie hat ihre Kinder zu behütet aufgezogen; **these insects are ~ coloured** diese Insekten haben eine Schutz- *od.* Tarnfärbung; **a vaccine acts** *or* **works ~:** ein Impfstoff hat eine Schutzwirkung

protector [prəˈtektə(r)] *n.* **a)** *(person)* Beschützer, *der*/Beschützerin, *die;* **b)** *(thing)* Schutz, *der; in comb.* -schutz, *der;* **c)** *(regent)* Regent, *der;* **P~ of the Realm** *(Brit. Hist.)* Regent des Königreiches

protectorate [prəˈtektərət] *n.* *(Int. Law, Brit. Hist.)* Protektorat, *das*

protégé [ˈprɒteʒeɪ] *n.* Protegé, *der (geh.);* Schützling, *der*

protégée [ˈprɒteʒeɪ] *n.* Schützling, *der*

protein [ˈprəʊtiːn] *n.* *(Chem.)* Protein, *das (fachspr.);* Eiweiß, *das;* **a high-~ diet** eine eiweißreiche Kost

pro tem [prəʊ ˈtem] *(coll.)* **1.** *adj.* befristet; ‹*Vorsitzender*› auf Zeit. **2.** *adv.* vorübergehend

pro tempore [prəʊ ˈtempərɪ] **1.** *adj.* befristet; *(temporary)* vorübergehend. **2.** *adv.* vorübergehend

protest 1. [ˈprəʊtest] *n.* **a)** *(remonstrance)* Beschwerde, *die; (Sport)* Protest, *der;* **make** *or* **lodge a ~ [against sb./sth.]** eine Beschwerde [gegen jmdn./etw.] einreichen; **b)** *(show of unwillingness, gesture of disapproval)* **~[s]** Protest, *der;* **under ~:** unter Protest; **in ~ [against sth.]** aus Protest [gegen etw.]; **c)** *no pl., no art. (dissent)* Protest, *der;* **the right of ~:** das Recht zu protestieren; **literature/song of ~:** Protestliteratur, *die*/Protestsong, *der;* **d)** *(Brit. Commerc.: written declaration)* Protest, *der.* **2.** [prəˈtest] *v. t.* **a)** *(affirm)* beteuern; **I ~, I have never seen you before** ich versichere, daß ich Sie noch niemals zuvor gesehen habe; **b)** *(Amer.: object to)* protestieren gegen; **c)** *(Commerc.)* protestieren; zu Protest gehen lassen; **be ~ed** zu Protest gehen. **3.** [prəˈtest] *v. i.* protestieren; *(make written or formal ~)* Protest einlegen **(to** bei); **~ about sb./sth.** gegen jmdn./etw. protestieren; **~ against being/doing sth.** dagegen protestieren, daß man etw. ist/tut

Protestant [ˈprɒtɪstənt] *(Relig.)* **1.** *n.* Protestant, *der*/Protestantin, *die;* Evangelische, *der/die.* **2.** *adj.* protestantisch; evangelisch

Protestantism [ˈprɒtɪstəntɪzm] *n., no pl., no art. (Relig.)* Protestantismus, *der*

protestation [prɒtɪˈsteɪʃn] *n.* **a)** *(affirmation)* Beteuerung, *die;* **a formal ~ that ...:** eine formelle Erklärung, daß ...; **~s of innocence** Unschuldsbeteuerungen; **b)** *(protest)* Protest, *der*

protester [prəˈtestə(r)] *n.* *(dissenter)* Protestierende, *der/die; (at demonstration)* Demonstrant, *der*/Demonstrantin, *die*

protest [ˈprəʊtest]: **~ march** *n.* Protestmarsch, *der;* **~ marcher** *see* **marcher; ~ song** *n.* Protestsong, *der;* **~ vote** *n.* Proteststimme, *die*

proto- [prəʊtə] *in comb.* proto-/Proto-; **~-Germanic** urgermanisch

protocol [ˈprəʊtəkɒl] *n.* Protokoll, *das;* **observe/defy ~:** das Protokoll befolgen/sich über das Protokoll hinwegsetzen

proton [ˈprəʊtɒn] *n.* *(Phys.)* Proton, *das*

protoplasm [ˈprəʊtəplæzəm] *n.* *(Biol.)* Protoplasma, *das*

prototype [ˈprəʊtətaɪp] *n.* Prototyp, *der;* **a ~ aeroplane/machine** der Prototyp eines Flugzeugs/einer Maschine

protozoa [prəʊtəˈzəʊə] *n. pl.* *(Zool.)* Protozoen

protozoan [prəʊtəˈzəʊən] *(Zool.)* **1.** *adj.* protozoisch. **2.** *n.* Protozoon, *das*

protract [prəˈtrækt] *v. t.* verlängern; **a ~ed argument/visit/period of idleness** ein langwieriger Streit/ein längerer Besuch/längere Untätigkeit; **delays became more and more ~ed** die Verzögerungen wurden immer gravierender

protraction [prəˈtrækʃn] *n.* Verlängerung, *die*

protractor [prəˈtræktə(r)] *n.* *(Geom.)* Winkelmesser, *der*

protrude [prəˈtruːd] **1.** *v. i.* herausragen **(from** aus); ‹*Zähne:*› vorstehen; **~ above/beneath/from behind sth.** etw. überragen/unter/hinter etw. *(Dat.)* hervorragen; **~ beyond sth.** über etw. *(Akk.)* hinausragen. **2.** *v. t.* ausstrecken ‹*Fühler*›; vorstülpen ‹*Lippen*›

protrusion [prəˈtruːʒn] *n.* **a)** *(projection) (of jaw or teeth)* Vorstehen, *das;* **b)** *(projecting thing)* Vorsprung, *der*

protuberance [prəˈtjuːbərəns] *n.* **a)** *(state)* Vorstehen, *das;* **b)** *(thing)* Auswuchs, *der*

protuberant [prəˈtjuːbərənt] *adj.* vorstehend; hervortretend ‹*Augen*›

proud [praʊd] **1.** *adj.* **a)** stolz; **it made me [feel] really ~:** es erfüllte mich mit Stolz; **I'm ~ to say I'm never late** ich kann mit Stolz behaupten, nie zu spät zu kommen; **~ to do sth.** *or* **to be doing sth.** stolz darauf, etw. zu tun; **~ of sb./sth./doing sth.** stolz auf jmdn./etw./darauf, etw. zu tun; **he is far too ~ of himself/his house** er bildet sich *(Dat.)* zu viel ein/zu viel auf sein Haus ein; **she answered his offer with a ~ refusal** sie lehnte sein Angebot stolz ab; **b)** *(arrogant)* hochmütig; stolz ‹*Tier*›; **I'm not too ~ to scrub floors** ich bin mir nicht zu gut zum Fußbodenschrubben; **c)** *(Brit.: projecting)* herausstehend; **stand** *or* **be ~ of sth.** *(vertically)* über etw. *(Akk.)* herausragen; **stand out too ~:** zu weit herausragen; **d) ~ flesh** *(Med.)* wildes Fleisch. **2.** *adv. (Brit. coll.)* **do sb. ~** *(treat generously)* jmdn. verwöhnen; *(honour greatly)* jmdm. eine Ehrung bereiten; **do oneself ~:** sich *(Dat.)* etwas Gutes tun

proud-hearted [praʊdˈhɑːtɪd] *adj.* stolz

proudly [ˈpraʊdlɪ] *adv.* **a)** stolz; **remain ~ silent/loyal** stolz schweigen/seine Loyalität bewahren; **b)** *(arrogantly)* hochmütig

provable [ˈpruːvəbl] *adj.* beweisbar; nachweisbar

prove [pruːv] **1.** *v. t., p.p.* **~d** *or (esp. Amer., Scot., literary)* **~n** [ˈpruːvn] **a)** beweisen; nachweisen ‹*Identität*›; **~ one's ability** sein Können unter Beweis stellen; **an expert of ~n ability** ein ausgewiesener Fachmann; **his guilt/innocence was ~d, he was ~d [to be] guilty/innocent** er wurde überführt/seine Unschuld wurde bewiesen; **~ sb. right/wrong** ‹*Ereignis:*› jmdm. recht/unrecht geben; **be ~d wrong** *or* **to be false** ‹*Theorie, System:*› widerlegt werden; **~ sth. to be true** beweisen, daß etw. wahr ist; **~ one's/sb.'s case** *or* **point** beweisen, daß man recht hat/jmdm. recht geben; **it was ~d that ...:** es stellte sich heraus *od.* erwies *od.* zeigte sich, daß ...; *see also* **exception a; point 1 g; b)** *(establish validity of)* beglaubigen ‹*Testament*›; **c)** *(Cookery: cause to rise)* ‹*Hefe:*› gehen lassen ‹*Teig*›. **2.** *v. refl.* **~ oneself** sich bewähren; **~ oneself intelligent/a good player** sich als intelligent/als [ein] guter Spieler erweisen. **3.** *v. i.* **a)** *(be found to be)* sich erweisen als; **~ [to be] unnecessary/interesting/a failure** sich als unnötig/interessant/[ein] Fehlschlag erweisen; **b)** *(Cookery: rise)* [auf]gehen

proven [ˈpruːvn] *adj.* **not ~** *(Scot. Law)* Schuldbeweis nicht erbracht

provenance [ˈprɒvɪnəns] *n.* Herkunft, *die*

Provençal [prɒvɑ̃ˈsɑːl] **1.** *adj.* provenzalisch; *see also* **English 1. 2.** *n.* **a)** *(language)* Provenzalisch, *das;* **b)** *(person)* Provenzale, *der*/Provenzalin, *die. See also* **English 2 a**

Provence [prɒˈvɑ̃s] *pr. n.* die Provence

provender [ˈprɒvɪndə(r)] *n.* Futter, *das; (joc.: food for humans)* Futter, *das (salopp)*

proverb [ˈprɒvɜːb] *n.* Sprichwort, *das;* **be a ~** *(fig.)* ‹*Eigenschaft:*› sprichwörtlich sein; **[Book of] P~s** *sing. (Bibl.)* [Buch der] Sprüche; Sprüche Salomos

proverbial [prəˈvɜːbɪəl] *adj.*, **proverbially** [prəˈvɜːbɪəlɪ] *adv.* sprichwörtlich

provide [prəˈvaɪd] *v. t.* **a)** *(supply)* besorgen; sorgen für; liefern ‹*Beweis*›; bereitstellen ‹*Dienst, Geld*›; **instructions are ~d with every machine** mit jeder Maschine wird eine Anleitung mitgeliefert; **~ homes/materials/a car for sb.** jmdm. Unterkünfte/Materialien/ein Auto [zur Verfügung] stellen; **~ shade for sb.** ‹*Baum usw.:*› jmdm. Schatten spenden; **~ sb. with money** jmdn. unterhalten; *(for journey etc.)* jmdm. Geld zur Verfügung stellen; **be [well] ~d with sth.** mit etw. [wohl]versorgt *od.* [wohl]versehen sein; **~ oneself with sth.** sich *(Dat.)* etw. besorgen; **b)** *(stipulate)* ‹*Vertrag, Gesetz:*› vorsehen; **c) providing that** *see* **provided**

~ against *v. t.* sich wappnen gegen; **have ~d against sth.** gegen etw. gewappnet sein

~ for *v. t.* **a)** *(make provision for)* vorsorgen für; Vorsorge treffen für; ‹*Plan, Gesetz:*› vorsehen ‹*Maßnahmen, Steuern*›; ‹*Schätzung:*› berücksichtigen ‹*Inflation*›; **has everybody been ~d for?** sind alle versorgt?; **b)** *(maintain)* sorgen für, versorgen ‹*Familie, Kind*›

provided [prəˈvaɪdɪd] *conj.* **~ [that] ...:** vorausgesetzt, [daß] ...

providence [ˈprɒvɪdəns] *n.* **a)** *(care of God etc.)* Vorsehung, *die;* **[divine] ~:** die [göttliche] Vorsehung; **a special ~:** eine besondere Fügung [des Schicksals]; **b) P~** *(God)* der Himmel; **c)** *(foresight)* Weitblick, *der;* **have the ~ to do sth.** so vorausschauend sein, etw. zu tun; **d)** *(thrift)* Sparsamkeit, *die*

provident [ˈprɒvɪdənt] *adj.* **a)** *(having foresight)* weitblickend; vorausschauend; **b)** *(thrifty)* sparsam; haushälterisch; **P~ Society** *(Brit.) see* **Friendly Society**

providential [prɒvɪˈdenʃl] *adj.* **a)** *(opportune)* **it was ~ that ...:** es war ein Glück, daß ...; **your arrival was quite ~:** es war wirklich ein Glück, daß du [dazu] kamst; **b)** *(of divine providence)* durch die [göttliche] Vorsehung bewirkt ‹*Befreiung, Rettung*›

providentially [prɒvɪˈdenʃəlɪ] *adv.* **a)** *(opportunely)* durch einen glücklichen Zufall; **help came quite ~:** die Hilfe kam wie eine glückliche Fügung; **work out ~:** sich glücklich fügen; **b)** *(by divine providence)* durch die [göttliche] Vorsehung

providently [ˈprɒvɪdəntlɪ] *adv.* **a)** *(with foresight)* vorausschauend ‹*handeln*›; **he had ~ equipped himself with ...:** er hatte sich vorsorglich mit ... ausgestattet; **b)** *(thriftily)* sparsam, haushälterisch ‹*mit etw. umgehen*›

provider [prəˈvaɪdə(r)] *n.* **a) he was the chief ~ of money/work** er war der Hauptgeldgeber/der größte Arbeitgeber; **the principal ~ of subsidies** der Hauptsubventionsträger; **b)** *(breadwinner)* Ernährer, *der*/Ernährerin, *die;* Versorger, *der*/Versorgerin, *die;* **be the ~ for sb.** jmdn. ernähren *od.* versorgen

province ['prɒvɪns] *n.* **a)** *(administrative area)* Provinz, *die;* **b) the ~s** *(regions outside capital)* die Provinz *(oft abwertend);* **c)** *(sphere of action)* [Arbeits-, Tätigkeits-, Wirkungs]bereich, *der;* [Arbeits-, Tätigkeits]gebiet, *das; (area of responsibility)* Zuständigkeitsbereich, *der;* **that is not my ~:** da kenne ich mich nicht aus; *(not my responsibility)* dafür bin ich nicht zuständig
provincial [prə'vɪnʃl] **1.** *adj.* Provinz-; *(of the provinces)* Provinz-; *(typical of the provinces)* provinziell. **2.** *n.* Provinzbewohner, *der*/-bewohnerin, *die (oft abwertend); (of the provinces also)* Provinzler, *der*/Provinzlerin, *die (abwertend)*
provincialism [prə'vɪnʃəlɪzm] *n.* **a)** *(mode of thought)* Provinzialismus, *der (abwertend);* **b)** *(Ling.)* Provinzialismus, *der*
provincially [prə'vɪnʃəlɪ] *adv.* provinziell; **~ narrow-minded** provinziell und engstirnig
proving-ground ['pru:vɪŋgraʊnd] *n.* Versuchsgelände, *das*
provision [prə'vɪʒn] *n.* **a)** *(providing)* Bereitstellung, *die;* **as a** *or* **by way of ~ against ...:** zum Schutz gegen ...; **~ of medical care** medizinische Versorgung; **make ~ for** vorsorgen *od.* Vorsorge treffen für ‹*Notfall*›; berücksichtigen ‹*Inflation*›; **make ~ for sb. in one's will** jmdn. in seinem Testament bedenken; **make ~ against sth.** Vorkehrungen zum Schutz gegen etw. treffen; **b)** *(amount available)* Vorrat, *der;* **c)** *in pl. (food)* Lebensmittel; *(for expedition also)* Proviant, *der;* **stock up with ~s** Lebensmittelvorräte anlegen; **d)** *(legal statement)* Verordnung, *die; (clause)* Bestimmung, *die*
provisional [prə'vɪʒənl] **1.** *adj.* vorläufig; provisorisch; **~ government** provisorische Regierung; **~ arrangement** Provisorium, *das.* **2.** *n. in pl.* **the P~s** die provisorische IRA
provisional: P~ IR'A *n.* provisorische IRA; **~ licence** *n.* vorläufige Fahrerlaubnis
provisionally [prə'vɪʒənəlɪ] *adv.* vorläufig; provisorisch
proviso [prə'vaɪzəʊ] *n., pl.* **~s** Vorbehalt, *der*
provisory [prə'vaɪzərɪ] *adj.* **a)** *(conditional)* vorbehaltlich; **~ clause** Vorbehaltsklausel, *die;* **b)** *(provisional)* vorläufig; provisorisch
provocation [prɒvə'keɪʃn] *n.* Provokation, *die;* Herausforderung, *die;* **be under severe ~:** stark provoziert werden; **he hit him without ~:** er hat ihn ohne jeden Anlaß geschlagen; **he loses his temper at** *or* **on the slightest** *or* **smallest ~:** er verliert die Beherrschung beim geringsten Anlaß
provocative [prə'vɒkətɪv] *adj.* provozierend; herausfordernd; *(sexually)* aufreizend; **his actions were felt to be ~:** seine Aktionen wurden als Provokation empfunden; **be ~ of** hervorrufen; provozieren; **be ~** *(be intentionally annoying)* provozieren
provoke [prə'vəʊk] *v.t.* **a)** *(annoy, incite)* provozieren ‹*Person*›; reizen ‹*Person, Tier*›; *(sexually)* aufreizen; **be easily ~d** leicht reizbar sein; sich leicht provozieren lassen; **~ sb. to anger/fury** jmdn. in Wut *(Akk.)*/zur Raserei bringen; **~ sb. into doing sth.** jmdn. so sehr provozieren *od.* reizen, daß er etw. tut; **he was finally ~d into taking action** er ließ sich schließlich dazu hinreißen *od.* provozieren, etwas zu unternehmen; **b)** *(give rise to)* hervorrufen; erregen ‹*Ärger, Neugier, Zorn*›; auslösen ‹*Kontroverse, Krise*›; herausfordern ‹*Widerstand*›; verursachen ‹*Zwischenfall*›; Anlaß geben zu ‹*Klagen, Kritik*›; **what ~d the incident?** wie kam es zu dem Zwischenfall?
provoking [prə'vəʊkɪŋ] *adj.* provozierend; herausfordernd; **his behaviour/refusal was [very] ~:** sein Benehmen/seine Weigerung war eine [große] Provokation
provost ['prɒvəst] *n.* **a)** *(Scot.: mayor)* Bürgermeister, *der*/-meisterin, *die;* **Lord P~:** Oberbürgermeister, *der;* **b)** *(Eccl.)* Propst, *der*/Pröpstin, *die;* **c)** *(Univ.)* Provost, *der;* **d)** [prə'vəʊ] *see* **~ marshal**
provost [prə'vəʊ]: **~ guard** *n. (Amer. Mil.) Sondertrupp der Militärpolizei;* **~ 'marshal** *n. (Mil.) Kommandeur der Militärpolizei*
prow [praʊ] *n. (Naut.)* Bug, *der*
prowess ['praʊɪs] *n.* **a)** *(valour)* Tapferkeit, *die;* **b)** *(skill)* Fähigkeiten; Können, *das;* **~ at sports** [große] Sportlichkeit; **sexual ~:** sexuelle Leistungsfähigkeit
prowl [praʊl] **1.** *v.i.* streifen; **~ about/around sth.** etw. durchstreifen; **~ about** *or* **around** herumschleichen *(ugs.).* **2.** *v.t.* durchstreifen. **3.** *n.* Streifzug, *der;* **be on the ~:** auf einem Streifzug sein; *(fig. in search of sexual contact)* was zum Vernaschen suchen *(salopp)*
'prowl car *n. (Amer.)* Streifenwagen, *der*
prowler ['praʊlə(r)] *n.* **the police have warned of ~s in the area** die Polizei warnt vor verdächtigen Personen, die in der Gegend herumstreifen; **see a ~ in the back yard** sehen, wie jmd. im Hinterhof herumschleicht *(ugs.)*
prox. [prɒks] *abbr.* **proximo** n. M.
proximate ['prɒksɪmət] *adj.* unmittelbar ‹*Ursache, Zukunft*›; nächst... ‹*Zukunft*›
proximity [prɒk'sɪmɪtɪ] *n., no pl.* Nähe, *die* (to zu); **a house with equal ~ to the shops and to the beach** ein Haus, das gleichermaßen nah zu den Geschäften und zum Strand liegt
prox'imity fuse *n. (Mil.)* [An]näherungszünder, *der*
proximo ['prɒksɪməʊ] *adj. (Commerc.)* [des] nächsten Monats
proxy ['prɒksɪ] *n.* **a)** *(agency, document)* Vollmacht, *die;* Bevollmächtigung, *die;* **by ~:** durch einen Bevollmächtigten/eine Bevollmächtigte; **give one's ~ to sb.** jmdn. bevollmächtigen; **marriage by ~** ≈ Ferntrauung, *die; see also* **stand 1 g; b)** *(person)* Bevollmächtigte, *der/die; (vote)* durch einen Bevollmächtigten/eine Bevollmächtigte abgegebene Stimme; **make sb. one's ~:** jmdn. bevollmächtigen
prude [pru:d] *n.* prüder Mensch
prudence ['pru:dəns] *n., no pl.* Besonnenheit, *die;* Überlegtheit, *die;* **act with ~:** besonnen *od.* überlegt handeln
prudent ['pru:dənt] *adj.* **a)** *(careful)* besonnen ‹*Person*›; besonnen, überlegt ‹*Verhalten*›; **b)** *(circumspect)* vorsichtig; **think it more ~ to do sth.** es für klüger halten, etw. zu tun
prudently ['pru:dəntlɪ] *adv.* **a)** *(in a prudent manner)* besonnen, überlegt ‹*handeln, sich verhalten*›; **they ~ waited for more information before acting** sie warteten klugerweise ab, bis sie mehr wußten, ehe sie handelten; **b)** *(circumspectly)* vorsichtig
prudery ['pru:dərɪ] *n., no pl.* Prüderie, *die*
prudish ['pru:dɪʃ] *adj.* prüde
[1]**prune** [pru:n] *n.* **a)** *(fruit)* **[dried] ~:** Backod. Dörrpflaume, *die;* **b)** *(coll.: simpleton)* Trottel, *der (ugs. abwertend)*
[2]**prune** *v.t.* **a)** *(trim)* [be]schneiden; **~ back** zurückschneiden; **b)** *(lop off)* **~ [away/off]** ab- *od.* wegschneiden; **~ [out]** herausschneiden; **c)** *(fig.: reduce)* reduzieren; **~ back** Abstriche machen an (+ *Dat.*) ‹*Projekt*›
pruning-shears ['pru:nɪŋʃɪəz] *n. pl.* Gartenschere, *die;* Rosenschere, *die*
prurience ['prʊərɪəns] *n., no pl.* Lüsternheit, *die*
prurient ['prʊərɪənt] *adj.* lüstern
pruritus [prʊə'raɪtəs] *n. (Med.)* Pruritus, *der (fachspr.);* Hautjucken, *das*
Prussia ['prʌʃə] *pr. n. (Hist.)* Preußen *(das)*
Prussian ['prʌʃən] **1.** *adj.* preußisch. **2.** *n.* **a)** *(person)* Preuße, *der*/Preußin, *die;* **b)** *(language)* **Old ~:** Altpreußisch, *das*
Prussian 'blue 1. *n.* Preußischblau, *das.* **2.** *adj.* preußischblau
prussic ['prʌsɪk] *adj. (Chem.)* **~ acid** Blausäure, *die*
[1]**pry** [praɪ] *v.i.* neugierig sein
~ a'bout *v.i.* herumschnüffeln *(ugs. abwertend) od.* -spionieren
~ into *v.t.* seine Nase stecken in (+ *Akk.*) *(ugs.)* ‹*Angelegenheit*›; herumschnüffeln in (+ *Dat.*) *(ugs. abwertend)* ‹*Buch, Brief*›
[2]**pry** *v.t. (Amer.)* **a)** *(get with effort)* **~ sth. open** etw. aufbrechen; **~ a secret** *etc.* **out of sb.** jmdm. ein Geheimnis *usw.* abringen; **b)** *see* [2]**prize**
prying ['praɪɪŋ] *adj.* neugierig
PS *abbr.* **postscript** PS
psalm [sɑ:m] *n. (Eccl.)* Psalm, *der;* **the Book of P~s** *(Bibl.)* das Buch der Psalmen; **the P~s** *(Bibl.)* die Psalmen
'psalm-book *n. (Eccl.)* Psalter, *der*
psalter ['sɔ:ltə(r), 'sɒltə(r)] *n.* Psalter, *der*
psaltery ['sɔ:ltərɪ, 'sɒltərɪ] *n. (Mus.)* Psalterium, *das*
PSBR *abbr. (Brit.)* **public sector borrowing requirement** *see* **public sector**
psephologist [se'fɒlədʒɪst] *n.* Psephologe, *der*/Psephologin, *die (fachspr.);* Wahlanalytiker, *der*/-analytikerin, *die*
psephology [se'fɒlədʒɪ] *n, no pl., no art. (Polit.)* Psephologie, *die (fachspr.);* Wahlanalytik, *die*
pseud [sju:d] *(coll.)* **1.** *adj.* **a)** *(pretentious)* pseudointellektuell; **b)** *see* **pseudo 1 a. 2.** *n. see* **pseudo 2**
pseudo ['sju:dəʊ] **1.** *adj.* **a)** *(sham, spurious)* unecht; **intellectuals, real or ~:** Intellektuelle, seien es richtige oder solche, die gern welche wären; **b)** *(insincere)* verlogen. **2.** *n., pl.* **~s a)** *(pretentious person)* Möchtegern, *der (ugs. spött.);* **b)** *(insincere person)* Heuchler, *der*/Heuchlerin, *die*
pseudo- [sju:dəʊ] *in comb.* pseudo-/Pseudo- *(fachspr., geh.)*
pseudonym ['sju:dənɪm] *n.* Pseudonym, *das*
pshaw [pʃɔ:, ʃɔ:] *int. (arch.) expr. contempt* pah; *expr. impatience* heieiei
psoriasis [sə'raɪəsɪs] *n., pl.* **psoriases** [sə'raɪəsi:z] *(Med.)* Psoriasis, *die (fachspr.);* Schuppenflechte, *die*
psst, pst [pst] *int.* st
PST *abbr.* **Pacific Standard Time** pazifische Standardzeit
psych [saɪk] *v.t. (coll.)* **~ sb. out** jmdn. durchschauen; **~ sb./oneself up** jmdn./sich einstimmen
psyche ['saɪkɪ] *n.* Psyche, *die*
psychedelic [saɪkɪ'delɪk] **1.** *adj.* psychedelisch. **2.** *n.* Psychedelikum, *das;* psychedelische Substanz
psychiatric [saɪkɪ'ætrɪk] *adj.* psychiatrisch
psychiatrist [saɪ'kaɪətrɪst] *n.* Psychiater, *der*/Psychiaterin, *die; see also* [1]**couch 1 b**
psychiatry [saɪ'kaɪətrɪ] *n.* Psychiatrie, *die*
psychic ['saɪkɪk] **1.** *adj.* **a)** *see* **psychical a; b)** *see* **psychical b; c)** *(having occult powers)* **be ~:** übernatürliche Fähigkeiten haben; **you must be ~** *(fig.)* du kannst wohl Gedanken lesen. **2.** *n.* *(medium)* Medium, *das; (clairvoyant)* Hellseher, *der*/-seherin, *die*
psychical ['saɪkɪkl] *adj.* **a)** *(of the soul)* psychisch; seelisch; **~ life** Seelenleben, *das;* **b)** *(of paranormal phenomena)* parapsychisch; **~ research** Parapsychologie, *die*
psycho ['saɪkəʊ] *(coll.)* **1.** *adj.* verrückt *(ugs.).* **2.** *n., pl.* **~s** Verrückte, *der/die (ugs.)*
psycho'analyse *v.t.* psychoanalysieren *(fachspr.);* psychoanalytisch behandeln
psychoa'nalysis *n.* Psychoanalyse, *die*
psycho'analyst *n.* Psychoanalytiker, *der*/-analytikerin, *die*
psychoana'lytic, psychoana'lytical *adj.* psychoanalytisch
psychological [saɪkə'lɒdʒɪkl] *adj.* **a)** *(of the mind)* psychisch ‹*Problem*›; psychologisch

‹*Wirkung, Druck*›; *see also* **block 11; b)** *(of psychology)* psychologisch
psychologically [saɪkəˈlɒdʒɪkəlɪ] *adv.* **a)** *(mentally)* psychisch; **b)** *(in relation to psychology)* psychologisch
psychological ˈwarfare *n.* psychologische Kriegführung
psychologist [saɪˈkɒlədʒɪst] *n. (also fig.)* Psychologe, *der*/Psychologin, *die*
psychology [saɪˈkɒlədʒɪ] *n.* **a)** Psychologie, *die;* **b)** *(coll.: characteristics)* Psychologie, *die (ugs.);* **I can't make out his ~:** ich werde aus ihm nicht schlau *(ugs.)*
psychopath [ˈsaɪkəpæθ] *n.* Psychopath, *der*/Psychopathin, *die*
psychopathic [saɪkəˈpæθɪk] *adj.* psychopathisch
psychopathology [saɪkəʊpəˈθɒlədʒɪ] *n.* Psychopathologie, *die*
psychosis [saɪˈkəʊsɪs] *n., pl.* **psychoses** [saɪˈkəʊsiːz] Psychose, *die*
psychosomatic [saɪkəʊsəˈmætɪk] *adj.* *(Med.)* psychosomatisch
psychoˈtherapy *n., no pl. (Med.)* Psychotherapie, *die;* **treat sth. by ~:** etw. psychotherapeutisch behandeln
psychotic [saɪˈkɒtɪk] **1.** *adj.* psychotisch; **~ illness** Psychose, *die.* **2.** *n.* Psychotiker, *der*/Psychotikerin, *die*
PT *abbr.* **physical training**
pt. *abbr.* **a) part** T.; **b) pint** pt.; **c) point** Pkt.; **pts.** Pkte.
PTA *abbr.* **parent-teacher association**
ptarmigan [ˈtɑːmɪgən] *n. (Ornith.)* Schneehuhn, *das*
Pte. *abbr. (Mil.)* **Private**
pterodactyl [terəˈdæktɪl] *n. (Palaeont.)* Pterodaktylus, *der;* Flugfinger, *der*
PTO *abbr.* **please turn over** b. w.
pub [pʌb] *n. (Brit. coll.)* Kneipe, *die (ugs.); (esp. in British Isles)* Pub, *das; attrib.* Kneipen-; **go to the ~:** in die Kneipe gehen
ˈpub-crawl *n. (Brit. coll.)* Zechtour, *die;* Bierreise, *die (ugs. scherzh.);* Zug durch die Gemeinde *(ugs. scherzh.)*
puberty [ˈpjuːbətɪ] *n., no pl., no art.* Pubertät, *die;* **at ~:** in *od.* während der Pubertät; **age of ~:** Pubertätsalter, *das*
pubescent [pjuːˈbesənt] *adj.* heranreifend
pubic [ˈpjuːbɪk] *adj. (Anat.)* Scham-
pubis [ˈpjuːbɪs] *n., pl.* **pubes** [ˈpjuːbiːz] *(Anat.)* Schambein, *das*
public [ˈpʌblɪk] **1.** *adj.* öffentlich; **~ assembly** Volksversammlung, *die;* **~ confidence** das Vertrauen der Öffentlichkeit; **a ~ danger/service** eine Gefahr für die/ein Dienst an der Allgemeinheit; **the ~ good** das allgemeine Wohl; **be a matter of ~ knowledge** allgemein bekannt sein; **in the ~ eye** im Blickpunkt der Öffentlichkeit; **make a ~ announcement of sth.** etw. öffentlich bekanntgeben *od.* -machen; **make a ~ protest** öffentlich protestieren; **make sth. ~:** etw. publik *(geh.)* od. bekannt machen; **go ~** *(Econ.)* in eine Aktiengesellschaft umgewandelt werden; *(fig.)* an die Öffentlichkeit treten; *see also* **image f. 2.** *n., no pl.; constr. as sing. or pl.* **a)** *(the people)* Öffentlichkeit, *die;* Allgemeinheit, *die;* **the general ~:** die Allgemeinheit; die breite Öffentlichkeit; **member of the ~:** Bürger, *der*/Bürgerin, *die;* **be open to the ~:** für den Publikumsverkehr geöffnet sein; **b)** *(section of community)* Publikum, *das; (author's readers also)* Leserschaft, *die;* **the reading ~:** das Lesepublikum; **c) in ~** *(publicly)* öffentlich; *(openly)* offen; **behave oneself in ~:** sich in der Öffentlichkeit benehmen; **make a fool of oneself in ~:** sich in aller Öffentlichkeit lächerlich machen
public-adˈdress system *n.* Lautsprecheranlage, *die*
publican [ˈpʌblɪkən] *n.* **a)** *(Brit.)* [Gast]wirt, *der*/-wirtin, *die;* **b)** *(Roman Hist., Bibl.)* Zöllner, *der*/Zöllnerin, *die*
public asˈsistance *n. (Amer.)* staatliche Fürsorge
publication [pʌblɪˈkeɪʃn] *n.* **a)** *(making known)* Bekanntmachung, *die;* Bekanntgabe, *die;* **b)** *(issuing of book etc.; book etc. issued)* Veröffentlichung, *die;* Publikation, *die;* **the magazine ceased ~:** das Magazin hat sein Erscheinen eingestellt; **the magazine is a weekly ~:** die Zeitschrift erscheint wöchentlich
public: ~ ˈbar *n. (Brit.)* ≈ Ausschank, *der;* **~ ˈbuilding** *n.* öffentliches Gebäude; **~ ˈcompany** *n. (Brit. Econ.)* Aktiengesellschaft, *die;* **~ convenience** *see* **convenience e; ~ doˈmain** *n.* **in the ~ domain** gemeinfrei ‹*Werk*›; **be in the ~ domain** Allgemeingut sein; frei sein; *(not protected by patent/copyright)* patentrechtlich/urheberrechtlich nicht [mehr] geschützt sein; **~ ˈenemy** *n.* Staatsfeind, *der;* **~ ˈfigure** *n.* Persönlichkeit des öffentlichen Lebens; **~ ˈfootpath** *n.* öffentlicher Fußweg; **~ ˈhealth** *n., no pl., no art.* [öffentliches] Gesundheitswesen; **~ ˈholiday** *n.* gesetzlicher Feiertag; **~ ˈhouse** *n. (Brit.)* Gastwirtschaft, *die;* Gaststätte, *die;* **the 'Lion' ~ house** die Gaststätte „The Lion"; **~ inˈquiry** *n.* öffentliche Untersuchung; **~ ˈinterest** *n.* Interesse der Allgemeinheit
publicise *see* **publicize**
publicist [ˈpʌblɪsɪst] *n.* **a)** *(writer)* Publizist, *der*/Publizistin, *die;* **b)** *(publicity agent)* Publicitymanager, *der*/-managerin, *die*
publicity [pʌbˈlɪsɪtɪ] *n., no pl., no indef. art.* **a)** Publicity, *die; (advertising)* Werbung, *die;* **~ campaign** Werbekampagne, *die;* **~ material** Werbematerial, *das;* **get ~ for sth.** [es] erreichen, daß etw. in der Öffentlichkeit bekannt wird; **b)** *(being public)* Öffentlichkeit, *die;* **c)** *(attention)* Publicity, *die;* Publizität, *die (geh.);* **in the full glare of ~:** im grellen Licht der Öffentlichkeit; **attract ~** ‹*Vorfall:*› Aufsehen erregen
pubˈlicity agent *n.* Publicitymanager, *der*/-managerin, *die*
publicize [ˈpʌblɪsaɪz] *v. t.* publik machen ‹*Ungerechtigkeit*›; werben für, Reklame machen für ‹*Produkt, Veranstaltung*›; **well-~d** ausreichend publik gemacht
public: ~ ˈlaw *n., no pl. (branch of law)* öffentliches Recht; **~ ˈlending right** *n.* Anspruch *(der Autoren u. Verleger)* auf eine Bibliotheksabgabe; **~ ˈlibel** *see* **libel 1 a; ~ ˈlibrary** *n.* öffentliche Bücherei; **~ limited company** *n. (Brit.)* ≈ Aktiengesellschaft, *die*
publicly [ˈpʌblɪklɪ] *adv.* **a)** *(in public)* öffentlich; **b)** *(by the public)* mit öffentlichen Geldern ‹*finanzieren, subventionieren*›; **~ owned** staatseigen; staatlich
public: ~ ˈnuisance *n.* **a)** *(Law)* Störung der öffentlichen [Sicherheit und] Ordnung; **b)** *(coll.)* **make a ~ nuisance of oneself** sich danebenbenehmen *(ugs.);* **be a ~ nuisance** ein allgemeines Ärgernis sein; **~ oˈpinion** *see* **opinion b; ~ ˈorder offence** *n.* Störung der öffentlichen Sicherheit und Ordnung; **~ ˈownership** *n., no pl.* Staatseigentum, *das* (**of** an + *Dat.*); Gemeineigentum, *das* (**of** an + *Dat.*); **be taken into ~ ownership** verstaatlicht werden; **~ property** *n.* Staatsbesitz, *der;* **sth. is ~ property** *(fig.)* etw. ist allgemein bekannt; **~ ˈprosecutor** *n. (Law)* Staatsanwalt, *der*/-anwältin, *die;* **~ ˈpurse** *see* **purse 1 a; P~ ˈRecord Office** *n.* ≈ Bundesarchiv, *das (Bundesrepublik Deutschland);* ≈ Deutsches Zentralarchiv *(DDR);* **~ reˈlations** *n. pl., constr. as sing. or pl.* Public Relations *Pl.;* Öffentlichkeitsarbeit, *die; attrib.* Public-Relations-‹*Abteilung, Berater*›; **~ relations officer** Öffentlichkeitsreferent, *der*/-referentin, *die;* **~ school** *n.* **a)** *(Brit.)* Privatschule, *die; attrib.* Privatschul-; **b)** *(Scot., Amer.: school run by public authorities)* staatliche *od.* öffentliche Schule; **~ ˈsector** *n.* **the ~ sector** der öffentliche *od.* staatliche Sektor; **~ sector borrowing requirement** Kreditbedarf der öffentlichen Hand; **~ ˈservant** *n.* Inhaber/Inhaberin eines öffentlichen Amtes; **~ ˈservice industry** *n.* öffentlicher Dienstleistungsbetrieb; **~ ˈservice vehicle** *n.* öffentliches Verkehrsmittel; **~ ˈspeaking** *n.* Sprechen vor einem [größeren] Publikum; **take lessons in ~ speaking** Rhetorikunterricht nehmen; **~ ˈspirit** *n.* Gemeinsinn, *der;* **~-ˈspirited** *adj.* von Gemeinsinn zeugend ‹*Verhalten*›; **be a ~-spirited person** Gemeinsinn haben; **it was ~-spirited of him to ...:** es zeugt von Gemeinsinn, daß er ...; **~ ˈtransport** *n.* öffentlicher Personenverkehr; **travel by ~ transport** mit öffentlichen Verkehrsmitteln fahren; **~ uˈtility** *n.* öffentlicher Versorgungsbetrieb; **~ ˈworks** *n. pl.* staatliche Bauvorhaben *od.* -projekte
publish [ˈpʌblɪʃ] *v. t.* **a)** *(issue)* ‹*Verleger, Verlag:*› verlegen ‹*Buch, Zeitschrift, Musik usw.*›; ‹*Autor:*› publizieren, veröffentlichen ‹*Text*›; **we will ~ his novel** wir werden seinen Roman verlegen *od.* herausbringen; **be ~ed** erscheinen; **the book has been ~ed by a British company** das Buch ist in *od.* bei einem britischen Verlag erschienen; **he has had a novel ~ed** von ihm ist ein Roman erschienen; **b)** *(announce publicly)* verkünden; *(read out)* verlesen ‹*Aufgebot*›; **c)** *(make generally known)* publik machen ‹*Ergebnisse, Einzelheiten*›
publishable [ˈpʌblɪʃəbl] *adj.* zur Veröffentlichung geeignet
publisher [ˈpʌblɪʃə(r)] *n.* Verleger, *der*/Verlegerin, *die;* **~[s]** *(company)* Verlag, *der;* **who are the ~s of this book?** in welchem Verlag ist dieses Buch erschienen?; **~s of children's books** Kinderbuchverlag, *der;* **music/scientific/magazine ~s** Musikverlag, *der*/wissenschaftlicher Verlag/Zeitschriftenverlag, *der*
publishing [ˈpʌblɪʃɪŋ] *n., no pl., no art.* Verlagswesen, *das; attrib.* Verlags-; **be in ~:** im Verlagswesen [tätig] sein; **~ firm/company** Verlag, *der;* **the ~ business** das Verlagswesen
ˈpublishing-house *n.* Verlag, *der*
puce [pjuːs] **1.** *n.* Flohbraun, *das.* **2.** *adj.* flohbraun; **go ~ in the face** puterrot werden
puck [pʌk] *n. (Ice Hockey)* Puck, *der*
pucker [ˈpʌkə(r)] **1.** *v. t.* **~ [up]** runzeln ‹*Brauen, Stirn*›; krausen, krausziehen ‹*Stirn*›; kräuseln ‹*Lippen*›; *(sewing)* kräuseln ‹*Stoff*›; **~ed** runzlig, faltig ‹*Haut*›. **2.** *v. i.* **~ [up]** ‹*Gesicht:*› sich in Falten legen; ‹*Stoff:*› sich kräuseln. **3.** *n.* Knitter, *der; (in face)* Falte, *die*
puckish [ˈpʌkɪʃ] *adj.* koboldhaft
pud [pʊd] *(coll.) see* **pudding a, b**
pudding [ˈpʊdɪŋ] *n.* **a)** Pudding, *der;* **b)** *(dessert)* süße Nachspeise; **c)** *(person or thing like ~)* Kloß, *der (ugs.)*
pudding: ~-basin, ~-bowl *ns.* Puddingform, *die;* **~ club** *n. (sl.)* **be in the ~ club** 'n dicken Bauch haben *(ugs.);* **~ face** *n.* [Voll]mondgesicht, *das (ugs.);* **~-head** *n.* Gipskopf, *der (ugs. abwertend)*
puddle [ˈpʌdl] *n.* Pfütze, *die*
pudendum [pjuːˈdendəm] *n., pl.* **pudenda** [pjuːˈdendə] *in sing. or pl.* Scham, *die*
pudge [pʌdʒ] *see* **podge**
pudgy [ˈpʌdʒɪ] *see* **podgy**
puerile [ˈpjʊəraɪl] *adj.* kindisch *(abwertend);* infantil *(abwertend)*
puerility [pjʊəˈrɪlɪtɪ] *n., no pl.* Infantilität, *die (abwertend)*
puerperal [pjuːˈɜːpərl] *adj. (Med.)* puerperal *(fachspr.);* **~ fever** Kindbettfieber, *das*
Puerto Rican [pwɜːtəʊ ˈriːkən] **1.** *adj.* puertoricanisch; **sb. is ~:** jmd. ist Puertoricaner/Puertoricanerin. **2.** *n.* Puertoricaner, *der*/Puertoricanerin, *die*

Puerto Rico [pwɜːtəʊ: 'riːkəʊ] *pr. n.* Puerto Rico *(das)*

puff [pʌf] **1.** *n.* **a)** Stoß, *der;* ~ **of breath/wind** Atem-/Windstoß, *der;* **b)** *(sound of escaping vapour)* Zischen, *das;* **c)** *(quantity)* ~ **of smoke** Rauchstoß, *der;* ~ **of steam** Dampfwolke, *die;* **d)** *(in dress etc.)* Bausch, *der;* Puff, *der (veralt.);* **e)** *(pastry)* Blätterteigteilchen, *das; see also* **cream puff; f)** *(advertisement)* Reklame, *die;* **give sth. a ~:** Reklame für etw. machen; **g)** *see* **powder-puff; h) sb. runs out of ~** *(lit. or fig. coll.)* jmdm. geht die Puste aus *(ugs.).* **2.** *v. i.* **a)** ⟨*Blasebalg:*⟩ blasen; ~ **[and blow]** pusten *(ugs.) od.* schnaufen [und keuchen]; **b)** *(~ cigarette smoke etc.)* paffen *(ugs.)* **(at** an + *Dat.*); **c)** *(move with ~ing)* ⟨*Person:*⟩ keuchen; ⟨*Zug, Lokomotive, Dampfer:*⟩ schnaufend fahren; **d)** *(be emitted)* ⟨*Dampf, Luft, Rauch:*⟩ stoßweise entweichen, *(ugs.)* puffen; **e)** *(swell)* ~ **up** ⟨*Frosch:*⟩ sich aufblähen; ~ **out** ⟨*Finger:*⟩ [an]schwellen. **3.** *v. t.* **a)** *(blow)* pusten *(ugs.),* blasen ⟨*Rauch*⟩; stäuben ⟨*Puder*⟩; **b)** *(smoke in ~s)* paffen *(ugs.);* **c)** *(put out of breath) see* ~ **out 1 b; d)** *(utter pantingly)* keuchen; **e)** *(advertise)* hochjubeln *(ugs.);* **f) ~ed sleeve** *see* **puff sleeve**

~ **'out 1.** *v. t.* **a)** *(inflate)* ⟨*Wind:*⟩ blähen, bauschen ⟨*Segel*⟩; **he ~ed out his chest** er blähte seine Brust; **b)** *(put out of breath)* außer Puste *(salopp) od.* Atem bringen ⟨*Person*⟩; **be ~ed out** außer Puste *(salopp) od.* Atem sein; **c)** *(utter pantingly)* heraus-, hervorstoßen; **d)** *(extinguish)* ausblasen; auspusten *(ugs.).* **2.** *v. i.* ⟨*Segel, Fahne:*⟩ sich bauschen, sich [auf]blähen

~ **'up 1.** *v. t.* **a)** *(inflate)* aufblasen; aufpusten *(ugs.);* **b) be ~ed up** *(proud)* aufgeblasen sein **(by** infolge). **2.** *v. i.* sich [auf]blähen

puff: ~-adder *n. (Zool.)* Puffotter, *die;* **~-ball** *n. (Bot.)* Bofist, *der*

'puffer [train] *see* **puff-puff**

puffin ['pʌfɪn] *n. (Ornith.)* Papageientaucher, *der*

puff: ~ 'pastry *n. (Cookery)* Blätterteig, *der;* **~-puff** *n. (Brit. child. lang.)* Puffzug, *der (Kinderspr.);* **~ 'sleeve** *n.* Puffärmel, *der*

puffy ['pʌfɪ] *adj.* verschwollen

pug [pʌg] *n.* **~[-dog]** Mops, *der*

pugilism ['pjuːdʒɪlɪzm] *n., no pl., no art. (formal)* Pugilismus, *der (veralt.);* Faustkampf, *der (geh.)*

pugilist ['pjuːdʒlɪst] *n. (formal)* Pugilist, *der (veralt.);* Faustkämpfer, *der (geh.)*

pugilistic [pjuːdʒɪ'lɪstɪk] *adj. (formal)* pugilistisch *(veralt.)*

pugnacious [pʌg'neɪʃəs] *adj. (literary)* kampflustig

pugnaciously [pʌg'neɪʃəslɪ] *adv. (literary)* mit großem Einsatz ⟨*kämpfen*⟩

pugnacity [pʌg'næsɪtɪ] *n., no pl.* Kampflust, *die*

pug: ~-nose *n.* Stumpfnase, *die;* **~-nosed** *adj.* stumpfnasig

puissance ['pjuːɪsəns, pwɪsəns] *n. (Show-jumping)* Mächtigkeitsspringen, *das*

puke [pjuːk] *(coarse)* **1.** *v. i.* kotzen *(salopp);* **the smell nearly made me ~:** von dem Geruch mußte ich beinahe kotzen. **2.** *v. t.* ~ **up** auskotzen *(salopp);* ausspucken *(ugs.);* ~ **one's guts up** *(sl.)* kotzen wie ein Reiher *(derb).* **3.** *n.* Kotze, *die (salopp);* Ausgespuckte, *das (ugs.)*

pukka ['pʌkə] *adj. (Anglo-Ind.)* richtig; **it's ~ information** es ist Tatsache

pulchritude ['pʌlkrɪtjuːd] *n. (literary)* Lieblichkeit, *die (geh.)*

pull [pʊl] **1.** *v. t.* **a)** *(draw, tug)* ziehen an (+ *Dat.*); ziehen ⟨*Hebel*⟩; ~ **aside** beiseite ziehen; ~ **sb.'s** *or* **sb. by the hair/ears/sleeve** jmdn. an den Haaren/Ohren/am Ärmel ziehen; ~ **shut** zuziehen ⟨*Tür*⟩; ~ **sth. over one's ears/head** sich *(Dat.)* etw. über die Ohren/den Kopf ziehen; ~ **the other one** *or* **leg[, it's got bells on]** *(fig. coll.)* das kannst du einem anderen erzählen; ~ **sth. out of the fire** *(fig.)* etw. [doch] noch retten; ~ **to pieces** in Stücke reißen; *(fig.: criticize severely)* zerpflücken ⟨*Argument, Artikel*⟩; **b)** *(extract)* [her]ausziehen; [heraus]ziehen ⟨*Zahn*⟩; zapfen ⟨*Bier*⟩; **c)** *(coll.: accomplish)* bringen *(ugs.);* ~ **a stunt** *or* **trick** etwas Wahnsinniges tun; ~ **a dirty trick** ein linkes Ding drehen *(ugs.); see also* **²fast 1 d; d)** *(strain)* sich *(Dat.)* zerren ⟨*Muskel, Sehne, Band*⟩; **e)** ~ **a long/wry** *etc.* **face** ein langes/ironisches *usw.* Gesicht machen; *see also* **face 1 a; f)** *(draw from sheath etc.)* ziehen ⟨*Waffe*⟩; ~ **a knife/gun on sb.** ein Messer/eine Pistole ziehen und jmdn. damit bedrohen; **g)** *(Rowing)* pullen *(Seemannsspr.);* rudern; ~ **one's weight** *(do one's fair share)* sich voll einsetzen; **h)** *(hold back)* parieren, verhalten ⟨*Pferd*⟩; ~ **one's punches** ⟨*Boxer:*⟩ verhalten schlagen; *(fig.: be gentle or lenient)* sich zurückhalten; **not ~ one's punches** *(fig.)* nicht zimperlich sein; **i)** *(Printing)* machen ⟨*Abzug*⟩. **2.** *v. i.* **a)** ziehen; **'P~'** „Ziehen"; **b)** ~ **[to the left/right]** ⟨*Auto, Boot:*⟩ [nach links/rechts] ziehen; **c)** *(move with effort)* sich schleppen; **d)** *(pluck)* ~ **at** ziehen an (+ *Dat.*); ~ **at sb.'s sleeve** jmdn. am Ärmel ziehen; **e)** *(draw)* ~ **at** ziehen an (+ *Dat.*) ⟨*Pfeife*⟩. **3.** *n.* **a)** Zug, *der;* Ziehen, *das; (of the moon, sun, etc.)* Anziehungskraft, *die; (of tide)* Sog, *der; (of conflicting emotions)* Widerstreit, *der;* **give a ~ at sth.** an etw. *(Dat.)* ziehen; **feel a ~ on** *or* **at sth.** ein Ziehen an etw. *(Dat.)* spüren; **b)** *no pl. (influence)* Einfluß, *der* **(with** auf + *Akk.,* bei); **c)** *see* **bell-pull; d)** *(drink)* Zug, *der* **(at** aus); **e)** *(Rowing)* Ruderfahrt, *die;* **f)** *(Printing)* Abzug, *der*

~ **a'bout** *v. t. (treat roughly)* zurichten

~ **a'head** *v. i.* in Führung gehen; sich an die Spitze setzen; ~ **ahead of** sich setzen vor (+ *Akk.*); ~ **ahead by a few metres** mit einigen Metern Vorsprung in Führung gehen; **the firm is beginning to ~ ahead of its competitors** die Firma überholt die Konkurrenz allmählich

~ **a'part** *v. t.* **a)** *(take to pieces)* auseinandernehmen; zerlegen; **b)** *(fig.: criticize severely)* zerpflücken ⟨*Interpretation, Argumentation usw.*⟩; verreißen ⟨*Buch, [literarisches] Werk*⟩

~ **a'way 1.** *v. t.* wegziehen. **2.** *v. i.* anfahren; *(with effort)* anziehen; ~ **away from the kerb/platform** anfahren

~ **'back 1.** *v. i.* **a)** *(retreat)* zurücktreten; ⟨*Truppen:*⟩ sich zurückziehen; **b)** *(Sport)* [wieder]aufholen **(to** bis auf + *Akk.*). **2.** *v. t.* **a)** zurückziehen; **b)** *(Sport)* aufholen. *See also* **pull-back**

~ **'down** *v. t.* **a)** herunterziehen; **b)** *(demolish)* abreißen; **c)** *(make less)* drücken ⟨*Preis*⟩; *(weaken)* mitnehmen ⟨*Person*⟩; **d)** *(in exam)* ~ **sb. down** jmds. [Gesamt]note drücken

~ **'in 1.** *v. t.* **a)** hereinziehen; zurückziehen ⟨*Beine*⟩; **b)** *(earn)* kriegen *(ugs.);* **c)** *(attract)* anziehen; **d)** *(coll.: detain in custody)* einkassieren *(salopp):* kassieren *(ugs.).* **2.** *v. i.* **a)** ⟨*Zug:*⟩ einfahren; **b)** *(move to side of road)* an die Seite fahren; *(stop)* anhalten; ~ **in to the side of the road** an den Straßenrand fahren; **a good place to ~ in** eine gute Stelle zum [An]halten; **c)** ~ **in to the bank** ⟨*Boot:*⟩ ans Ufer fahren. *See also* **pull-in**

~ **into** *v. t.* **a)** ⟨*Zug:*⟩ einfahren in (+ *Akk.*); **b)** *(move off road into)* fahren in (+ *Akk.*)

~ **'off** *v. t.* **a)** *(remove)* abziehen; *(violently)* abreißen; ausziehen ⟨*Kleidungsstück*⟩; ausziehen, abstreifen ⟨*Handschuhe*⟩; **b)** *(accomplish)* an Land ziehen *(ugs.)* ⟨*Geschäft, Knüller*⟩; einfahren *(ugs.)* ⟨*Sieg*⟩; abziehen *(salopp)* ⟨*Raubüberfall*⟩

~ **'on** *v. t.* [sich *(Dat.)*] an- *od.* überziehen; *(in a hurry)* sich werfen in (+ *Akk.*)

~ **'out 1.** *v. t.* **a)** *(extract)* herausziehen; [heraus]ziehen ⟨*Zahn*⟩; **b)** *(take out of pocket etc.)* aus der Tasche ziehen; herausziehen ⟨*Messer, Pistole*⟩; [heraus]ziehen, *(scherzh.)* zücken ⟨*Brieftasche*⟩; **c)** *(detach)* heraustrennen ⟨*Zeitungsbeilage, Foto*⟩; **d)** *(withdraw)* abziehen ⟨*Truppen*⟩; herausnehmen ⟨*Spieler, Mannschaft*⟩. *See also* **stop 3 e. 2.** *v. i.* **a)** *(depart)* ⟨*Zug:*⟩ abfahren; ~ **out of the station** aus dem Bahnhof ausfahren; **b)** *(away from roadside)* ausscheren; **c)** *(withdraw)* ⟨*Truppen:*⟩ abziehen **(of** aus); *(from deal, project, competition, etc.)* aussteigen *(ugs.)* **(of** aus); **the first country to ~ out of the negotiations** das erste Land, das seine Teilnahme an den Verhandlungen eingestellt hat; **d)** ~ **out of a dive** ⟨*Flugzeug:*⟩ aus dem Sturzflug abgefangen werden; ⟨*Pilot:*⟩ die Maschine aus dem Sturzflug abfangen. *See also* **pull-out**

~ **'over 1.** *v. i. see* ~ **in 2 b. 2.** *v. t.* ~ **one's car over to the side of the road** seinen Wagen an den Straßenrand *od.* an die Seite fahren

~ **'round 1.** *v. i. (regain health)* wieder auf die Beine kommen; *(regain former success)* wieder Tritt fassen. **2.** *v. t.* wieder auf die Beine bringen ⟨*Patienten*⟩; *(fig.: put into a better condition)* herausreißen *(ugs.)*

~ **'through 1.** *v. t.* durchziehen; ~ **sb. through** *(cause to recover or succeed)* jmdn. durchbringen; ~ **through sth.** etw. überstehen. **2.** *v. i.* ⟨*Patient:*⟩ durchkommen; ⟨*Firma:*⟩ überleben

~ **to'gether 1.** *v. i.* an einem *od.* am selben Strang ziehen. **2.** *v. t.* näher zusammenziehen; zusammenschweißen ⟨*Partei, Allianz*⟩; in Schuß bringen *(ugs.)* ⟨*Firma*⟩; ~ **sb. together** jmdn. auf die Beine helfen. **3.** *v. refl.* sich zusammennehmen

~ **'up 1.** *v. t.* **a)** hochziehen; **b)** ~ **up a chair** einen Stuhl heranziehen; **c)** [he]rausziehen ⟨*Unkraut, Pflanze usw.*⟩; *(violently)* [he]rausreißen; **d)** *(stop)* anhalten, zum Stehen bringen ⟨*Auto*⟩; **e)** *(reprimand)* zurechtweisen; rügen. **2.** *v. i.* **a)** *(stop)* anhalten; **b)** *(improve)* sich verbessern *od.* vorarbeiten. **3.** *v. refl.* sich hocharbeiten. *See also* **bootstraps; pull-up; 'sock a**

'pull-back *n. (withdrawal)* Abzug, *der*

pullet ['pʊlɪt] *n.* Junghenne, *die*

pulley ['pʊlɪ] *n.* Rolle, *die; (for drive-belt)* Riemenscheibe, *die;* **set of ~s** *(tackle)* Flaschenzug, *der*

'pull-in *n.* **a)** *(place at the side of the road for vehicles)* Haltebucht, *die;* **b)** *(Brit.: transport café)* Fernfahrerlokal, *das*

Pullman ['pʊlmən] *n.* ~ **[car or coach]** Pullman[wagen], *der*

'pull-out *n.* **a)** *(folding portion of book etc.)* ausfaltbarer Teil; *(map)* Faltkarte, *die; (detachable section)* heraustrennbarer Teil; **b)** *(withdrawal)* Abzug, *der;* ~ **of troops** Truppenabzug, *der*

pullover ['pʊləʊvə(r)] *n.* Pullover, *der;* Pulli, *der (ugs.)*

'pull-up *n.* **a)** *(stopping-place)* Platz zum Haltmachen; **b)** *(Gymnastics)* Klimmzug, *der*

pulmonary ['pʌlmənərɪ] *adj. (Anat., Physiol.)* Lungen-

pulp [pʌlp] **1.** *n.* **a)** *(of fruit)* Fruchtfleisch, *das;* **b)** *(soft mass)* Brei, *der;* **beat sb. to a ~:** jmdn. zu Brei schlagen *(salopp);* **c)** *(Anat., Zool.: fleshy or soft part)* Mark, *das;* **d)** *(ore)* Trübe, *die.* **2.** *v. t.* zerdrücken, zerstampfen ⟨*Rübe*⟩; einstampfen ⟨*Druckerzeugnis*⟩

pulpit ['pʊlpɪt] *n. (Eccl.)* Kanzel, *die*

pulp: ~ magazine *n.* Groschenheft, *das;* **~wood** *n. (Paper-making etc.)* Industrieholz, *das*

pulpy ['pʌlpɪ] *adj.* **a)** *(soft and moist)* fleischig ⟨*Frucht*⟩; **b)** *(consisting of a soft mass)* breiig

pulsar ['pʌlsɑː(r)] *n. (Astron.)* Pulsar, *der*

pulsate [pʌl'seɪt, 'pʌlseɪt] *v. i.* **a)** *(beat, throb)* pulsieren; ⟨*Herz:*⟩ schlagen; *(fig.*

literary) pulsieren; b) (fig.: vibrate) schwingen; ⟨Land:⟩ pulsieren
pulsation [pʌl'seɪʃn] n. a) (beating, throbbing) Schlagen, das; (of artery; also fig.) Pulsieren, das; b) (fig.: vibration) Schwingen, das
[1]**pulse** [pʌls] 1. n. a) (lit. or fig.) Puls, der; (single beat) Pulsschlag, der; **have/keep one's finger on the ~ of sth.** die Hand am Puls einer Sache (Gen.) haben/auf dem laufenden über etw. (Akk.) bleiben; see also **feel 1a**; b) (rhythmical recurrence) Rhythmus, der; c) (single vibration) Schwingung, die; (Mus.) Betonung, die; (Electronics) Impuls, der. 2. v.i. see **pulsate a, b**
[2]**pulse** n. a) no pl., constr. as sing. or pl. (seeds) Hülsenfrüchte Pl.; b) (variety of edible seed) Hülsenfrucht, die
pulverize (pulverise) ['pʌlvəraɪz] v.t. a) (to powder or dust) pulverisieren; b) (into spray) zerstäuben; c) (fig.: crush) aufreiben ⟨Truppen⟩; abservieren (Sport) ⟨Gegner⟩; **I'll ~ you!** ich schlag' dich zu Brei! (derb)
puma ['pju:mə] n. (Zool.) Puma, der
pumice ['pʌmɪs] 1. n. (Min.) **~[-stone]** Bimsstein, der. 2. v.t. bimsen; mit Bimsstein abreiben
pummel ['pʌml] v.t., (Brit.) **-ll-** einschlagen auf (+ Akk.)
[1]**pump** [pʌmp] 1. n. (machine; also fig.) Pumpe, die. 2. v.i. pumpen. 3. v.t. a) pumpen; **~ sb. full of lead** jmdn. mit Blei vollpumpen (salopp); **~ bullets into sth.** Kugeln in etw. (Akk.) jagen (ugs.); **~ information into sb.** jmdn. mit Wissen vollstopfen (ugs.); b) **~ sth. dry** etw. leerpumpen od. auspumpen od. (Seemannsspr.) lenzen; **~ sb. for information** Auskünfte aus jmdm. herausholen; c) **~ up** (inflate) aufpumpen ⟨Reifen, Fahrrad⟩
[2]**pump** n. a) (shoe) Turn-, Sportschuh, der; **[dancing] ~:** Tanzschuh, der; b) (Amer.: court shoe) Pumps, der
pumpernickel ['pʌmpənɪkl, 'pʊmpənɪkl] n. Pumpernickel, der
pumping-station ['pʌmpɪŋsteɪʃn] n. Pumpwerk, das
pumpkin ['pʌmpkɪn] n. (Bot.) Kürbis, der; attrib. Kürbis-
'**pump-room** n. Pumpenhaus, das; (in spa) Brunnenhaus, das
pun [pʌn] 1. n. Wortspiel, das; **the sentence is a ~ on the words 'bread' and 'bred'** in dem Satz wird mit den Worten „bread" und „bred" gespielt. 2. v.i., **-nn-** ein Wortspiel/Wortspiele Pl. machen **(on mit)**
Punch [pʌntʃ] n. Punch, der; Hanswurst, der; **~ and Judy show** Kasperletheater, das; **be as proud/pleased as ~:** stolz wie ein Pfau od. Spanier sein/(ugs.) sich freuen wie ein Schneekönig
[1]**punch** 1. v.t. a) (strike with fist) boxen; mit der Faust schlagen; **the boxer ~ed his opponent with his left fist** der Boxer traf seinen Gegner mit der Linken; b) (pierce, open up) lochen; **~ a hole** ein Loch stanzen; **~ a hole/holes in sth.** etw. lochen; c) (prod) stoßen; d) (Amer.: drive) vorwärtstreiben ⟨Vieh⟩. 2. n. a) (blow) Faustschlag, der; **a ~ on the head/chin/chest** ein Faustschlag an den Kopf/an das Kinn/vor die Brust; **give sb. a ~ on the jaw/in the ribs** jmdm. einen Kinnhaken/Rippenstoß versetzen; **a ~ with the left fist** ein Schlag mit der linken Faust; b) no pl. (ability to deliver blow) Punch, der (Boxen); Schlagkraft, die; **have a good/strong ~** ⟨Boxer:⟩ einen guten/harten Schlag haben; c) (coll.: vigour) Pep, der (ugs.); **have [a] ~:** Pep haben; **put ~ into sth.** einer Sache (Dat.) Pep geben; d) (device for making holes) (in leather, tickets) Lochzange, die; (in paper) Locher, der; (in leather) Locheisen, das; (Printing) Stempel, der. See also **pack 2g**; **pull 1h**
[2]**punch** n. (drink) Punsch, der

punch: ~-ball n. (Brit.) (ball) Punchingball, der; (bag) Sandsack, der; **~-bowl** n. Bowlengefäß, das; Bowle, die; **~ card** n. (Computing) Lochkarte, die; **~-drunk** adj. a) an einem Boxersyndrom leidend; **be ~-drunk** ein Boxersyndrom haben; punchdrunk sein (Boxen); b) (fig.) benommen; **the troops were ~-drunk** die Truppen waren schwer angeschlagen
punched [pʌntʃt]: **~ card/tape** see **punch card/tape**
punching bag ['pʌntʃɪŋ bæg] (Amer.) see **punch-ball**
punch: ~ line n. Pointe, die; **~ tape** n. (Computing) Lochstreifen, der; **~-up** n. (Brit. coll.) (fist-fight, brawl) Prügelei, die
punchy ['pʌntʃɪ] adj. (forceful) ausdrucksstark ⟨Sprache⟩; zündend ⟨Rede⟩; schwungvoll ⟨Handlung⟩
punctilious [pʌŋk'tɪlɪəs] adj. [peinlich] korrekt; peinlich ⟨Genauigkeit⟩
punctiliously [pʌŋk'tɪlɪəslɪ] adv. [peinlich] korrekt ⟨arbeiten⟩; peinlich ⟨genau⟩
punctual ['pʌŋktʃʊəl] adj. pünktlich
punctuality [pʌŋktʃʊ'ælɪtɪ] n., no pl. Pünktlichkeit, die
punctually ['pʌŋktʃʊəlɪ] adv. pünktlich
punctuate ['pʌŋktʃʊeɪt] v.t. interpunktieren (fachspr.); mit Satzzeichen versehen; (fig.: interrupt) unterbrechen **(with** durch)
punctuation [pʌŋktʃʊ'eɪʃn] n., no pl. Interpunktion, die (fachspr.); Zeichensetzung, die
punctu'ation mark n. Satzzeichen, das
puncture ['pʌŋktʃə(r)] 1. n. a) (flat tyre) Reifenpanne, die; Platte, der (ugs.); b) (hole) Loch, das; (in skin) Einstich, der; see also **lumbar**. 2. v.t. durchstechen; (fig.) verletzen ⟨Würde⟩; kratzen an (+ Dat.) ⟨Mythos⟩; lädieren ⟨Ruf⟩; **be ~d** ⟨Reifen:⟩ ein Loch haben, platt sein; ⟨Haut:⟩ einen Einstich aufweisen. 3. v.i. ⟨Reifen:⟩ ein Loch bekommen, platt werden
pundit ['pʌndɪt] n. a) (expert) Experte, der/Expertin, die; (iron.) Augur, der; b) (learned Hindu) Pandit, der
punditry ['pʌndɪtrɪ] n. Expertentum, das
pungency ['pʌndʒənsɪ] n., no pl. (lit. or fig.) [beißende od. ätzende] Schärfe
pungent ['pʌndʒənt] adj. a) beißend, ätzend ⟨Rauch, Dämpfe⟩; scharf ⟨Soße, Gewürz usw.⟩; stechend riechend ⟨Gas⟩; b) (fig.: biting) beißend; ätzend
punish ['pʌnɪʃ] v.t. a) bestrafen ⟨Person, Tat⟩; strafen (geh.) ⟨Person⟩; **he has been ~ed enough** (fig.) er ist gestraft genug; b) (Boxing coll.: inflict severe blows on) schwer zusetzen (+ Dat.); c) (Sport coll.: take advantage of) kein Pardon kennen bei ⟨schwachen Würfen, Schlägen des Gegners⟩; **the bowlers were ~ed by the batsmen** die Werfer bekamen ihre Quittung von den Schlagmännern; d) (coll.: tax) auf eine harte Probe stellen; e) (coll.: put under stress) strapazieren ⟨Nerven, Bauwerk⟩
punishable ['pʌnɪʃəbl] adj. strafbar; **it is a ~ offence to ...:** es ist strafbar, ... zu ...; **be ~ by sth.** mit etw. bestraft werden
punishing ['pʌnɪʃɪŋ] adj. a) (Boxing coll.) mörderisch ⟨Haken⟩; b) (Sport coll.) tödlich (Sportjargon) ⟨Schuß, Schlag, Volley⟩; **he is a ~ hitter** wenn der Gegner ihm eine Blöße bietet, schlägt er gnadenlos zu; c) (coll.: taxing) mörderisch (ugs.) ⟨Rennen, Zeitplan, Kurs⟩; aufreibend ⟨Wahlkampf⟩
punishment ['pʌnɪʃmənt] n. a) no pl. (punishing) Bestrafung, die; **inflict ~ on sb.** jmdn. bestrafen; **undergo ~:** bestraft werden; eine Strafe erhalten; **deserve ~:** [eine] Strafe verdient haben; **crime and ~:** Verbrechen und Strafe; b) (penalty) Strafe, die; **the ~ for cheating is disqualification** Betrug wird mit Disqualifikation bestraft; **make the ~ fit the crime** (lit. or fig.) Gleiches mit Gleichem vergelten; **as a ~ for sth.** zur Strafe für etw.; c) (coll.: rough treatment) **take a lot of ~:** ganz schön getriezt od. gezwiebelt werden (ugs.). See also **take 1w**
punitive ['pju:nɪtɪv] adj. a) (penal) Straf-; b) (severe) [allzu] rigoros ⟨finanzielle Maßnahmen, Besteuerung⟩; unzumutbar ⟨Steuersatz⟩; c) (Law) **~ damages** verschärfter Schadenersatz
Punjab [pʌn'dʒɑ:b] pr. n. **the ~:** das Pandschab
punk [pʌŋk] 1. n. a) (Amer. sl.: worthless person) Dreckskerl, der (salopp); b) (Amer. coll.: young ruffian) Rabauke, der (ugs.); c) (admirer of ~ rock) Punk, der; (performer of ~ rock) Punk[rock]er, der/-rockerin, die; d) (music) see **~ rock**. 2. adj. a) (coll.: worthless) mies (abwertend); b) (of or playing punk rock) Punk-
punk 'rock n. Punkrock, der
punnet ['pʌnɪt] n. (Brit.) Körbchen, das
[1]**punt** [pʌnt] 1. n. Stechkahn, der. 2. v.t. a) (propel) staken ⟨Boot⟩; (convey) in einem Stechkahn fahren ⟨Person⟩. 3. v.i. staken
[2]**punt** (Footb.) 1. v.t. aus der Hand schießen; ⟨Torwart:⟩ abschlagen. 2. n. Schuß aus der Hand; (by goalkeeper) Abschlag, der
[3]**punt** v.i. (Brit. coll.: bet) wetten; (speculate) spekulieren
[4]**punt** [pʊnt] n. (Finance) Irisches Pfund
[1]**punter** ['pʌntə(r)] n. (coll.) a) (gambler) Zocker, der/Zockerin, die (salopp); b) (client of prostitute) Freier, der (verhüll.); c) **the ~s** (customers) die Leutchen (ugs.)
[2]**punter** n. (in ¹punt) Stechkahnfahrer, der/-fahrerin, die
puny ['pju:nɪ] adj. a) (undersized) zu klein ⟨Baby, Junge⟩; b) (feeble) gering ⟨Kraft⟩; schwach ⟨Waffe, Person⟩; c) (petty) belanglos, unerheblich ⟨Leistung, Einwand⟩
pup [pʌp] 1. n. a) (young dog or wolf) Welpe, der; **be in ~** ⟨Hündin:⟩ trächtig sein; b) (young animal) Junge, das; c) (objectionable young man) Schnösel, der (ugs. abwertend). 2. v.i., **-pp-** ⟨Hündin:⟩ werfen
pupa ['pju:pə] n., pl. **~e** ['pju:pi:] (Zool.) Puppe, die
pupal ['pju:pl] adj. (Zool.) Puppen-
pupate [pju:'peɪt] v.i. (Zool.) sich verpuppen
pupil ['pju:pɪl] n. a) (schoolchild, disciple) Schüler, der/Schülerin, die; b) (Anat.) Pupille, die
puppet ['pʌpɪt] n. a) Puppe, die; (marionette) Marionette, die; see also **glove puppet**; b) (person) Marionette, die; attrib. Marionetten⟨regime, -regierung⟩
puppetry ['pʌpɪtrɪ] n., no pl., no art. (making of puppets) Puppenmachen, das; (production of puppet-shows) Puppenspiel, das
'**puppet-show** n. Puppenspiel, das; (with marionettes) Marionettenspiel, das
puppy ['pʌpɪ] n. Hundejunge, das; Welpe, der; **the dog is still only a ~:** der Hund ist noch ganz jung
'**puppy-dog** n. (child lang.) Hündchen, das; kleiner Hund
puppy: ~ fat n., no pl. (Brit.) Babyspeck, der; **~ love** n. Jugendschwärmerei, die
purblind ['pɜ:blaɪnd] adj. (literary) halbblind nicht präd.; halb blind; (fig.) kurzsichtig
purchasable ['pɜ:tʃəsəbl] adj. käuflich; (available on the market) [im Handel] erhältlich
purchase ['pɜ:tʃəs] 1. n. a) (buying) Kauf, der; **make several ~s/a ~:** verschiedenes/etwas kaufen; b) (thing bought) Kauf, der; **carry one's ~s home** seine Einkäufe nach Hause tragen od. bringen; c) no pl. (hold) Halt, der; (leverage) Hebelwirkung, die; Hebelkraft, die; **get a ~:** guten od. festen Halt finden. 2. v.t. a) kaufen; erwerben (geh.); **purchasing power** Kaufkraft, die; b) (acquire) erkaufen
'**purchase price** n. Kaufpreis, der

purchaser ['pɜ:tʃəsə(r)] *n.* Käufer, *der*/Käuferin, *die*
'**purchase tax** *n. (Brit. Hist.)* ≈ Verbrauchssteuer, *die*
purdah ['pɜ:də] *n. (seclusion of women)* Absonderung der Frauen; **they were kept in ~:** sie durften nicht in Erscheinung treten; *(fig.)* sie wurden kaltgestellt *(ugs.)*
pure [pjʊə(r)] **1.** *adj.* **a)** *(unmixed)* rein; rein, pur ‹*Gold, Silber*›; *(not discordant)* rein ‹*Ton, Note*›; **b)** *(of unmixed descent)* reinblütig ‹*Mensch*›; rein ‹*Blut*›; **c)** *(mere)* pur; rein; **it is madness ~ and simple** es ist schlicht *od.* ganz einfach Wahnsinn; **d)** *(Phonet.)* einfach ‹*Vokal*›; **e)** *(not corrupt)* rein; **blessed are the ~ in heart** *(Bibl.)* selig sind, die reinen Herzens sind; **f)** *(chaste)* rein. *See also* **mathematics a; science a. 2.** *adv.* **a ~ blue sky** ein klarer blauer Himmel
pure: ~-blooded *adj.* reinblütig; **~-bred** *adj.* reinrassig
purée ['pjʊəreɪ] **1.** *n.* Püree, *das;* **tomato ~:** Tomatenmark, *das.* **2.** *v. t.* pürieren
purely ['pjʊəlɪ] *adv.* **a)** *(solely)* rein; **b)** *(merely)* lediglich
pureness ['pjʊənɪs] *see* **purity**
purgative ['pɜ:gətɪv] **1.** *adj.* **a)** *(laxative)* [stark] abführend; Abführ‹*mittel, -tablette*›; purgativ *(fachspr.)*; **b)** *(purifying)* läuternd *(geh.)*. **2.** *n. (medicine)* [starkes] Abführmittel; Purgativum, *das (fachspr.)*
purgatory ['pɜ:gətərɪ] *n. (Relig.)* Fegefeuer, *das;* Purgatorium, das *(fachspr.)*; **undergo ~:** durchs Fegefeuer gehen; **it was ~** *(fig.)* es war eine Strafe *od.* die Hölle
purge [pɜ:dʒ] **1.** *v. t.* **a)** *(cleanse)* reinigen (**of** von); **~ me from my sin** *(Relig.)* reinige mich von meiner Sünde; **b)** *(remove)* entfernen; **~ away** *or* **out** beseitigen; **c)** *(rid)* säubern ‹*Partei*› (**of** von); *(remove)* entfernen ‹*Person*›; **d)** *(Med.)* abführen lassen ‹*Patienten*›; **use sth. to ~ the bowels** etw. zum Abführen verwenden; **e)** *(Law: atone for)* sühnen [für]. **2.** *n.* **a)** *(clearance)* Säuberung[saktion], *die; (Polit.)* Säuberung, *die;* **a ~ of writers** eine gegen Schriftsteller gerichtete Säuberung[saktion]; **b)** *(Med.)* [starkes] Abführmittel
purification [pjʊərɪfɪ'keɪʃn] *n.* **a)** Reinigung, *die;* **b)** *(spiritual cleansing)* Läuterung, *die;* **c)** *(ceremonial cleansing)* Reinigung, *die;* **the P~ [of Our Lady** *or* **the Virgin Mary]** *(Relig.)* Mariä Reinigung; *(feast)* [Mariä] Lichtmeß; Mariä Reinigung
purifier ['pjʊərɪfaɪə(r)] *n.* Reiniger, *der;* Reinigungsmittel, *das; (machine)* Reinigungsapparat, *der;* Reinigungsanlage, *die*
purify ['pjʊərɪfaɪ] *v. t.* **a)** *(make pure or clear)* reinigen; **b)** *(spiritually)* reinigen; läutern; **c)** *(ceremonially)* reinigen
purism ['pjʊərɪzm] *n., no pl.* Purismus, *der*
purist ['pjʊərɪst] *n.* Purist, *der*/Puristin, *die*
puritan ['pjʊərɪtn] **1.** *n.* **a)** Puritaner, *der*/Puritanerin, *die;* **b) P~** *(Hist.)* Puritaner, *der*/Puritanerin, *die.* **2.** *adj.* **a)** puritanisch; **b) P~** *(Hist.)* puritanisch
puritanic [pjʊərɪ'tænɪk], **puritanical** [pjʊərɪ'tænɪkl] *adj.* puritanisch; moralinsauer *(abwertend)*
puritanism ['pjʊərɪtənɪzm] *n., no pl.* **a)** Puritanismus, *der;* puritanische Einstellung; **b) P~** *(Hist.)* Puritanismus, *der*
purity ['pjʊərɪtɪ] *n., no pl.* **a)** Reinheit, *die;* **b)** *(chastity)* Keuschheit, *die*
purl [pɜ:l] **1.** *n.* linke Masche. **2.** *v. t.* links stricken; **~ three stitches** drei linke Maschen stricken
purler ['pɜ:lə(r)] *n. (Brit. coll.)*; **come** *or* **take a ~:** längelang hinknallen *(ugs.)*
purlieus ['pɜ:lju:z] *n. pl.* Außenbezirke *Pl.*; Weichbild, *das;* **within the ~ of A** innerhalb des Stadtgebietes *od.* Weichbildes von A
purlin ['pɜ:lɪn] *n. (Building)* Pfette, *die*
purloin [pə'lɔɪn] *v. t. (literary)* entwenden *(geh.)*
purple ['pɜ:pl] **1.** *adj.* lila; violett; *(crimson)* purpurn; *(fig.)* überfrachtet, überladen ‹*Prosa*›; **his face went ~ with rage** vor Zorn bekam er ein hochrotes Gesicht. **2.** *n.* **a)** Lila, *das;* Violett, *das; (crimson)* Purpur, *das;* **b)** *(dress of cardinal)* Purpur, *der;* **the ~** *(fig.)* das Kardinalskollegium. **3.** *v. i.* ‹*Gesicht:*› dunkelrot anlaufen
purple: ~ 'heart *n. (Brit.)* Purple Heart, *das (Drogenjargon)*; **P~ 'Heart** *n. (Amer. Mil.) US-amerikanisches Verwundetenabzeichen;* **~ passage, ~ patch** *ns.* [über]reich ausgeschmückte Passage
purplish ['pɜ:plɪʃ] *adj.* ins Violette spielend; **be ~:** ins Violette spielen
purport 1. [pə'pɔ:t] *v. t.* **a) ~ to do sth.** *(profess)* [von sich] behaupten, etw. zu tun; *(be intended to seem)* den Anschein erwecken sollen, etw. zu tun; **the ~ed intention/object** die angebliche Absicht/der angebliche Zweck; **a letter ~ing to be written by the president** ein angeblich vom Präsidenten geschriebener Brief; **the document ~s to be official** die Urkunde soll angeblich amtlich sein; **the law ~s to protect morality** das Gesetz soll angeblich die Moral schützen; **b)** *(convey)* beinhalten; **~ that ...:** besagen, daß .... **2.** ['pɜ:pɔ:t] *n.* Inhalt, *der*
purportedly [pə'pɔ:tɪdlɪ] *adv.* angeblich
purpose ['pɜ:pəs] **1.** *n.* **a)** *(object)* Zweck, *der; (intention)* Absicht, *die;* **what is the ~ of doing that?** was hat es für einen Zweck, das zu tun?; **he never did anything without a ~:** er tat nie etwas ohne eine bestimmte Absicht; **you must have had some ~ in mind** du mußt irgend etwas damit bezweckt haben; **wander around with no particular ~:** ziellos *od.* ohne Ziel umherwandern; **answer** *or* **suit sb.'s ~:** jmds. Zwecken dienen *od.* entsprechen; **for a ~:** zu einem bestimmten Zweck; **I did it for a ~:** ich habe damit einen bestimmten Zweck verfolgt; **for the ~ of discussing sth.** um etw. zu besprechen; **on ~:** mit Absicht; absichtlich; **for ~s of** zum Zwecke (+ *Gen.*); *see also* **cross purposes; serve 1 c; b)** *(effect)* **to no ~:** ohne Erfolg; **to some/little/good ~:** mit einigem/wenig/gutem Erfolg; **c)** *(determination)* Entschlossenheit, *die;* **have a ~ in life** in seinem Leben einen Sinn sehen; **give sb. a ~ in life** jmds. Leben *(Dat.)* einen Sinn geben; **d)** *(intention to act)* Absicht, *die.* **2.** *v. t.* beabsichtigen
'**purpose-built** *adj.* [eigens] zu diesem Zweck errichtet ‹*Gebäude*›; [eigens] zu diesem Zweck hergestellt, speziell angefertigt ‹*Gerät, Bauteil*›
purposeful ['pɜ:pəsfl] *adj.* **a)** zielstrebig; *(with specific aim)* entschlossen; **b)** *(with intention)* absichtsvoll
purposefully ['pɜ:pəsfəlɪ] *adv.* **a)** entschlossen; **b)** *(intentionally)* absichtsvoll
purposeless ['pɜ:pəslɪs] *adj.* sinnlos
purposely ['pɜ:pəslɪ] *adv.* absichtlich; mit Absicht
'**purpose-made** *adj.* spezialgefertigt; eigens angelegt ‹*Straße*›
purposive ['pɜ:pəsɪv] *adj. see* **purposeful a**
purr [pɜ:(r)] **1.** *v. i.* schnurren; *(fig.: be in satisfied mood)* strahlen. **2.** *v. t.* durch Schnurren zum Ausdruck bringen; *(fig.)* säuseln; **the cat ~ed her contentment** die Katze schnurrte zufrieden. **3.** *n.* Schnurren, *das*
purse [pɜ:s] **1.** *n.* **a)** *(lit. or fig.)* Portemonnaie, *das;* Geldbeutel, *der (bes. südd.)*; **the public ~:** die Staatskasse; **light ~** *(fig.)* kleiner Geldbeutel *(fig.)*; *see also* **silk 2; b)** *(prize)* Geldpreis *der;* Börse, *die (Boxen)*; **c)** *(Amer.: handbag)* Handtasche, *die.* **2.** *v. t.* kräuseln, schürzen ‹*Lippen*›
purser ['pɜ:sə(r)] *n.* Zahlmeister, *der*/-meisterin, *die*
'**purse-strings** *n. pl.* Schnüre *od.* Bänder [zum Verschließen des Geldbeutels]; **hold the ~** *(fig.)* über das Geld bestimmen; **tighten/loosen the ~** *(fig.)* sparen/mehr ausgeben
pursuance [pə'sju:əns] *n., no pl.* **in ~ of [one's] duties/instructions** pflichtgemäß/auftragsgemäß; **in [the] ~ of his ends** bei der Verfolgung seiner Ziele; **in ~ of the act/decree** gemäß dem Gesetz/der Verfügung
pursuant [pə'sju:ənt] *adv.* **~ to sth.** gemäß einer Sache
pursue [pə'sju:] *v. t.* **a)** *(literary: chase, lit. or fig.)* verfolgen; **bad luck ~d him** er war vom Pech verfolgt; **b)** *(seek after)* streben nach; suchen nach; verfolgen ‹*Ziel*›; **c)** *(look into)* nachgehen (+ *Dat.*); **d)** *(engage in)* betreiben; **~ a career as an accountant** als Buchhalter tätig sein; **~ one's studies** seinem Studium nachgehen; **e)** *(carry out)* durchführen ‹*Plan*›
pursuer [pə'sju:ə(r)] *n.* Verfolger, *der*/Verfolgerin, *die*
pursuit [pə'sju:t, pə'su:t] *n.* **a)** *(pursuing) (of person, animal, aim)* Verfolgung, *die; (of knowledge, truth, etc.)* Streben, *das* (**of** nach); *(of pleasure)*; Jagd, *die* (**of** nach); **the ~ of his studies** die Beschäftigung mit seinen Studien; **in ~ of** auf der Jagd nach ‹*Wild, Dieb usw.*›; in Ausführung (+ *Gen.*) ‹*Beschäftigung, Tätigkeit, Hobby*›; **with the police in [full] ~:** mit der Polizei [dicht] auf den Fersen; *see also* **hot 1 j; b)** *(pastime)* Beschäftigung, *die;* Betätigung, *die*
pursuit: ~ plane *(Amer.) see* **fighter b; ~ race** *n. (Cycling)* Verfolgungsrennen, *das*
purulent ['pjʊərʊlənt] *adj. (Med.) (consisting of pus, full of pus)* eitrig; *(discharging pus)* eiternd; **be ~:** eitern
purvey [pə'veɪ] *v. t. (lit. or fig.)* liefern
purveyor [pə'veɪə(r)] *n.* Lieferant, *der*/Lieferantin, *die;* **a ~ of [wild] rumours** ein Kolporteur [wilder Gerüchte]
purview ['pɜ:vju:] *n. (of act, document)* Geltungsbereich, *der; (of scheme, book, occupation)* Rahmen, *der;* **fall within sb.'s ~:** in jmds. Aufgaben- *od.* Zuständigkeitsbereich fallen
pus [pʌs] *n., no indef. art. (Med.)* Eiter, *der*
push [pʊʃ] **1.** *v. t.* **a)** schieben; *(make fall)* stoßen; schubsen *(ugs.)*; **don't ~ me like that!** schieb *od.* drängel [doch] nicht so!; **~ a car** *(to start the engine)* ein Auto anschieben; **she ~ed the door instead of pulling** sie drückte gegen die Tür, statt zu ziehen; **did he/you** *etc.* **fall** *or* **jump or was he/were you** *etc.* **~ed?** *(fig.)* freiwillig oder unfreiwillig?; **~ sb. about in a wheelchair** jmdn. im Rollstuhl herumfahren; **~ one's hair back** sich *(Dat.)* das Haar zurückstreichen; **the policemen ~ed the crowd back** die Polizisten drängten die Menge zurück; **~ sth. between sth.** etw. zwischen etw. *(Akk.)* schieben; *(to pass right through)* etw. zwischen etw. *(Dat.)* hindurchschieben; **~ sth. under the bottom of the door** etw. unter der Tür [hin]durchschieben; **~ sth. up the hill** etw. den Berg hinaufschieben; **~ one's way through/into/on to** *etc.* **sth.** sich *(Dat.)* einen Weg durch/in/auf *usw.* etw. *(Akk.)* bahnen; **b)** *(fig.: impel)* drängen; **~ sb. into doing sth.** jmdn. dahin bringen, daß er etw. tut; **c)** *(tax)* **~ sb. [hard]** jmdn. [stark] fordern; **~ sb. too hard/too far** jmdn. überfordern; **he ~es himself very hard** er verlangt sich *(Dat.)* sehr viel ab; **be ~ed for sth.** *(coll.: find it difficult to provide sth.)* mit etw. knapp sein; **be ~ed for money** *or* **cash** knapp bei Kasse sein *(ugs.)*; **be ~ed to do sth.** *(coll.)* Mühe haben, etw. zu tun; **~ one's luck** *(coll.)* übermütig werden; **~ one's luck with sth.** sich mit etw. auf ein gefährliches Spiel einlassen; **d)** *(press for sale of)* die Werbetrommel rühren für; pushen *(Werbejargon)*; **e)** *(sell illegally, esp. drugs)* dealen; pushen *(Drogenjargon)*; **f)** *(advance)* **~ sth. a step/stage further** etw. einen Schritt vorantreiben; **not ~ the point** die Sache auf

sich beruhen lassen; ~ **sth. too far** mit etw. zu weit gehen; es mit etw. zu weit treiben; ~ **things to extremes** die Dinge *od.* es zum Äußersten *od.* auf die Spitze treiben; ~ **one's claims** auf seine Ansprüche pochen. **2.** *v. i.* **a)** schieben; *(in queue)* drängeln; *(at door)* drücken; **'P~'** *(on door etc.)* „Drücken"; ~ **and shove** schubsen und drängeln; ~ **at sth.** gegen etw. drücken; **b)** *(make demands)* ~ **for sth.** etw. fordern; **c)** *(make one's way)* **he ~ed between us** er drängte sich zwischen uns; ~ **through the crowd** sich durch die Menge drängeln; ~ **past** *or* **by sb.** sich an jmdm. vorbeidrängeln *od.* -drücken; ~ **by** *(not stop)* weiterrennen *(ugs.)*; **d)** *(assert oneself for one's advancement)* sich in den Vordergrund spielen. **3.** *n.* **a)** Stoß, *der;* Schubs, *der (ugs.)*; **give sth. a ~:** etw. schieben *od.* stoßen; **give sb. a ~:** jmdm. einen Schubs geben *(ugs.)*; jmdm. einen Stoß versetzen; **My car won't start; can you give me a ~?** Mein Auto springt nicht an. Kannst du mich anschieben?; **give sth. a gentle ~:** etw. leicht anstoßen; **we gave a great ~:** wir haben gewaltig gedrückt; **b)** *(effort)* Anstrengungen *Pl.*; *(Mil.: attack)* Vorstoß, *der;* Offensive, *die;* **a ~ forward** *(Mil.)* ein Vorstoß; **make a ~:** sich ins Zeug legen *(ugs.)*; *(Mil.)* einen Vorstoß unternehmen; eine Offensive durchführen; **c)** *(determination)* Tatkraft, *die;* Initiative, *die;* **d)** *(crisis)* **when it comes/came to the ~,** *(Amer. coll.)* **when ~ comes/came to shove** wenn es ernst wird/als es ernst wurde; **at a ~:** wenn es sein muß; **e)** *(Brit. sl.: dismissal)* **get the ~:** rausfliegen *(ugs.)*; **give sb. the ~:** jmdn. rausschmeißen *(ugs.)*; **f)** *(influence)* Förderung, *die;* Protektion, *die;* **g)** *see* **push-button**

~ **a'bout** *v. t.* herumschieben; *(bully)* herumkommandieren

~ **a'head** *v. i.* ‹*Armee:*› [weiter] vorstoßen *od.* -rücken; *(with [regard to] plans etc.)* weitermachen; ~ **ahead with sth.** etw. vorantreiben

~ **a'long 1.** *v. t.* [vor sich *(Dat.)* her]schieben. **2.** *v. i. (coll.)* sich [wieder] auf den Weg machen

~ **a'round** *see* ~ **about**

~ **a'side** *v. t. (lit. or fig.)* beiseite schieben

~ **a'way** *v. t.* wegschieben

~ **'forward 1.** *v. i. see* ~ **ahead. 2.** *v. t.* vorschieben; *(Mil.)* vorstoßen; ~ **oneself forward** sich in den Vordergrund schieben

~ **'in** *v. t.* eindrücken; *(make fall into the water)* hineinstoßen *od (ugs.)* -schubsen

~ **'off 1.** *v. i.* **a)** *(Boating)* abstoßen; **b)** *(sl.: leave)* abhauen *(salopp)*; abschieben *(salopp)*. **2.** *v. t. (Boating)* abstoßen

~ **'on** *see* ~ **ahead**

~ **'out 1.** *v. t.* hinausschieben; ‹*Pflanzen:*› [aus]treiben ‹*Wurzeln*›; *see also* **boat 1 a. 2.** *v. i.* hinausragen

~ **'out of** *v. t. (force to leave)* hinausdrängen aus

~ **'over** *v. t. (make fall)* umstoßen; *see also* **push-over**

~ **'through** *v. t. (fig.)* durchpeitschen *(ugs.)* ‹*Gesetzesvorlage*›; durchdrücken *(ugs.)* ‹*Vorschlag*›; **we ~ed it through successfully** wir haben es durchgekriegt *(ugs.)*

~ **'up** *v. t.* hochschieben; *(fig.)* hochtreiben; *see also* **daisy; push-up**

push: ~-ball *n. (game, ball)* Pushball, *der;* **~-bike** *n. (Brit. coll.)* Fahrrad, *das;* **~-button 1.** *adj.* Drucktasten‹*telefon, -radio*›; **~-button warfare** Krieg per Knopfdruck; automatisierte Kriegführung; **2.** *n.* [Druck]knopf, *der;* Drucktaste, *die;* **~-cart** *n.* **a)** *see* **handcart; b)** *(Amer.: trolley)* Einkaufswagen, *der;* **~-chair** *n. (Brit.)* Sportwagen, *der*

pusher ['pʊʃə(r)] *n.* **a)** *(seller of drugs)* Dealer, *der (Drogenjargon)*; Pusher, *der (Drogenjargon)*; **b)** *(pushy person)* Streber, *der*/Streberin, *die (abwertend)*; Ehrgeizling, *der (ugs. abwertend)*

pushing ['pʊʃɪŋ] *adj.* **a)** [übermäßig] ehrgeizig; **b)** *(coll.)* **be ~ sixty** auf die Sechzig zugehen

push: ~-over *n. (coll.)* Kinderspiel, *das;* **she'll be a ~-over for him** die schafft er mit links *(ugs.)*; die hat gegen ihn nichts drin *(ugs.)*; **the match should be a ~-over for Leeds** das Spiel dürfte für Leeds ein Spaziergang werden *(Sportjargon)*; **~-start 1.** *n.* Schubstart, *der;* **give sb. a ~-start** jmdn. *od.* jmds. Auto anschieben; **2.** *v. t.* anschieben

'push-up *(Amer.) see* **press-up**

pushy ['pʊʃɪ] *adj. (coll.)* [übermäßig] ehrgeizig ‹*Person*›

pusillanimity [pju:sɪlə'nɪmɪtɪ] *n., no pl.* Ängstlichkeit, *die;* Zaghaftigkeit, *die;* *(lack of courage)* Feigheit, *die*

pusillanimous [pju:sɪ'lænɪməs] *adj.,* **pusillanimously** [pju:sɪ'lænɪməslɪ] *adv.* ängstlich; zaghaft; *(without courage)* feige

puss [pʊs] *n.* Mieze, *die (fam.)*; **~, ~, ~!** Miez, Miez, Miez!; **P~ in Boots** der Gestiefelte Kater

pussy ['pʊsɪ] *n.* **a)** *(child lang.: cat)* Miezekatze, *die (fam.)*; Muschi, *die (Kinderspr.)*; **b)** *(coarse) (vulva)* Kätzchen, *das (salopp)*; Muschi, *die (vulg.)*; *(sexual intercourse)* Sex, *der*

pussy: ~-cat *see* **pussy a; ~foot** *v. i.* [herum]schleichen; *(act cautiously)* überängstlich sein; **stop ~footing!** hör auf, wie die Katze um den heißen Brei zu schleichen!; **~ willow** *n.* Salweide, *die;* Palmweide, *die*

pustule ['pʌstju:l] *n. (Med.) (pimple)* Pustel, *die*

'put [pʊt] **1.** *v. t.,* **-tt-, put a)** *(place)* tun; *(vertically)* stellen; *(horizontally)* legen; *(through or into narrow opening)* stecken; ~ **plates on the table** Teller auf den Tisch stellen; ~ **books on the shelf/on top of the pile** Bücher ins Regal stellen/auf den Stapel legen; ~ **clean sheets on the bed** das Bett frisch beziehen; **don't ~ your elbows on the table** laß deine Ellbogen vom Tisch; **I ~ my hand on his shoulder** ich legte meine Hand auf seine Schulter; ~ **a stamp on the letter** eine Briefmarke auf den Brief kleben; ~ **salt on one's food** Salz auf sein Essen tun *od.* streuen; ~ **some more coal on the fire** Kohle nachlegen; ~ **antiseptic on one's finger** sich *(Dat.)* Antiseptikum auf den Finger tun; ~ **the letter in an envelope/the letter-box** den Brief in einen Umschlag/in den Briefkasten stecken; ~ **sth. in one's pocket** etw. in die Tasche stecken; etw. einstecken; ~ **the shopping in the car** die Einkäufe ins Auto tun *od.* legen; ~ **one's hands in one's pockets** die Hände in die Taschen stecken; ~ **sugar in one's tea** sich *(Dat.)* Zucker in den Tee tun; ~ **petrol in the tank** Benzin in den Tank tun *od.* füllen; ~ **the car in[to] the garage** das Auto in die Garage stellen; ~ **rubbish in the waste-paper basket** Abfall in den Papierkorb tun *od.* werfen; ~ **the cork in the bottle** den Korken in die Flasche stecken; ~ **the plug in the socket** den Stecker in die Steckdose stecken; ~ **paper in the typewriter** Papier in die Schreibmaschine tun *od.* einspannen; ~ **tobacco in the pipe** Tabak in die Pfeife tun; die Pfeife stopfen; ~ **a new pane of glass in the window** eine neue Glasscheibe in das Fenster [ein]setzen; ~ **a new engine in the car** einen neuen Motor in das Auto einbauen; ~ **the letters in the file** die Briefe in den Ordner tun *od.* [ein]heften; ~ **documents in the safe** Urkunden in den Safe tun *od.* legen; ~ **fish into a pond** Fische in einen Teich setzen; ~ **the cat into a basket** die Katze in einen Korb setzen *od.* stecken; ~ **the ball into the net/over the bar** den Ball ins Netz befördern *od.* setzen/über die Latte befördern; ~ **one's arm round sb.'s waist** den Arm um jmds. Taille legen; ~ **a bandage round one's wrist** sich *(Dat.)* einen Verband ums Handgelenk legen; ~ **one's hands over one's eyes** sich *(Dat.)* die Hände auf die Augen legen; ~ **one's finger to one's lips** den *od.* seinen Finger auf die Lippen legen; ~ **one's foot through the rotten floorboards/on a chair** den Fuß durch die morschen Dielen stecken/auf einen Stuhl setzen; ~ **the letter at the bottom of the pile** den Brief unter den Stapel legen; ~ **the boxes one on top of the other** die Kisten übereinanderstellen; ~ **the jacket on its hanger** die Jacke auf den Bügel tun *od.* hängen; **where shall I ~ it?** wohin soll ich es tun *(ugs.)*/stellen/legen *usw.?*; wo soll ich es hintun *(ugs.)*/-stellen/-legen *usw.?*; ~ **sb. into a taxi** jmdn. in ein Taxi setzen; ~ **a child on a swing** ein Kind auf eine Schaukel setzen; **we ~ our guest in Peter's room** wir haben unseren Gast in Peters Zimmer *(Dat.)* untergebracht; ~ **the baby in the pram** das Baby in den Kinderwagen legen *od. (ugs.)* stecken; **not know where to ~ oneself** *(fig.)* sehr verlegen sein/werden; ~ **it there!** *(coll.)* laß mich deine Hand schütteln!; **b)** *(cause to enter)* stoßen; ~ **a knife into sb.** jmdm. ein Messer in den Leib stoßen; ~ **a satellite into orbit** einen Satelliten in eine Umlaufbahn bringen; ~ **a bullet** *etc.* **through sb./sth.** *(coll.)* jmdm. eine Kugel verpassen/etw. zerballern *(ugs.)*; **c)** *(bring into specified state)* setzen; ~ **through Parliament** im Parlament durchbringen ‹*Gesetzentwurf usw.*›; ~ **one's proposals through the committee** seine Vorschläge im Ausschuß durchbringen; ~ **sb. in a difficult** *etc.* **position** jmdn. in eine schwierige *usw.* Lage bringen; **be ~ in a difficult** *etc.* **position** in eine schwierige *usw.* Lage geraten; **be ~ in a position of trust** eine Vertrauensstellung erhalten; ~ **sb. in[to] a job** jmdm. eine Arbeit[sstellung] *od. (ugs.)* einen Job geben; **be ~ into power** an die Macht kommen; ~ **sb. on the committee** jmdn. in den Ausschuß schicken; ~ **sth. above** *or* **before sth.** *(fig.)* einer Sache *(Dat.)* den Vorrang vor etw. *(Dat.)* geben; ~ **sth. out of order** etw. kaputtmachen *(ugs.)*; etw. funktionsuntüchtig machen; **be ~ out of order** kaputtgehen *(ugs.)*; defekt werden; ~ **sb. on to sth.** *(fig.)* jmdn. auf etw. *(Akk.)* hinweisen *od.* aufmerksam machen; jmdm. etw. zeigen; ~ **sb. on to a job** *(assign)* jmdm. eine Arbeit zuweisen; **d)** *(impose)* ~ **a limit/an interpretation on sth.** etw. begrenzen *od.* beschränken/interpretieren; *see also* **end 1 a; stop 3 a; veto 1 b; e)** *(submit)* unterbreiten **(to** *Dat.***)** ‹*Vorschlag, Plan usw.*›; ~ **the situation to sb.** jmdm. die Situation darstellen; ~ **sth. to the vote** über etw. *(Akk.)* abstimmen lassen; etw. zur Abstimmung bringen *(Papierdt.)*; **I ~ it to you that you never saw him** ich behaupte *od.* sage, daß Sie ihn nie gesehen haben; **f)** *(cause to go or do)* ~ **sb. to work** jmdn. arbeiten lassen; ~ **sb. on the job** jmdn. damit *od.* mit der Arbeit beauftragen; ~ **sb. out of contention for sth.** jmdn. aus dem Rennen um etw. werfen; jmdm. sämtliche Chancen auf etw. nehmen; **be ~ out of the game by an injury** wegen einer Verletzung nicht mehr spielen können; ~ **sb. out of the championship** jmdm. den Titel abnehmen; **they were ~ out of the cup by Liverpool** sie scheiterten an Liverpool und mußten aus dem Cupwettbewerb ausscheiden; ~ **the troops on full alert** die Streitkräfte in volle Alarm- *od.* Gefechtsbereitschaft versetzen; ~ **sb. on antibiotics** jmdn. auf Antibiotika setzen; ~ **sb. on the stage** jmdn. zur Bühne schicken; *see also* **'pace 1 c; g)** *(impose)* ~ **taxes** *etc.* **upon sth.** etw. mit Steuern *usw.* belegen; Steuern *usw.* für etw. erheben; **h)** *(express)* ausdrücken; **let's ~ it like this: ...:** sagen wir so: ...; **that's one way of ~ting it** *(also iron.)* so kann man es [natürlich] auch ausdrücken; **I don't quite know how to ~ this, but ...**: ich weiß nicht recht, wie ich es sagen sollte, aber ...; **i)** *(render)* **~ sth. into English** *etc.* etw. ins Englische übertragen *od.* übersetzen; **~ sth. into words** etw. in Worte fassen; **~ sth. into one's own words** etw. mit seinen eigenen Worten sagen; **j)** *(write)* schreiben; **~ one's name on the list** seinen Namen auf die Liste setzen; **~ a tick in the box** ein Häkchen in das Kästchen machen; **~ a cross against sth.** etw. ankreuzen; **~ one's signature to sth.** seine Unterschrift unter etw. setzen; **~ a black mark against a name** einen Namen schwarz markieren *od.* anstreichen; **~ sth. on the bill** etw. auf die Rechnung setzen; **~ sth. on the list** *(fig.)* sich *(Dat.)* etw. [fest] vornehmen; etw. vormerken; **k)** *(imagine)* **~ oneself in sb.'s place** *or* **situation** sich in jmdn. *od.* in jmds. Lage versetzen; **l)** *(substitute)* setzen; **m)** *(invest)* **~ money** *etc.* **into sth.** Geld *usw.* in etw. *(Akk.)* stecken; **~ work/time/effort into sth.** Arbeit/Zeit/Energie in etw. *(Akk.)* stecken *od.* auf etw. *(Akk.)* verwenden; **n)** *(stake)* setzen (**on** auf + *Akk.*); **~ money on a horse/on sth. happening** auf ein Pferd setzen/darauf wetten, daß etw. passiert; **o)** *(estimate)* **~ sb./sth. at** jmdn./etw. schätzen auf (+ *Akk.*); **to ~ it no higher** um das Wenigste zu sagen; *see also* **past 3 b**; **p)** *(subject)* **~ sb. to** jmdm. ⟨*Unkosten, Mühe, Umstände*⟩ verursachen *od.* machen; *see also* **shame 1 b; test 1 a; q)** *(drive)* **~ sb. to sth.** jmdn. zu etw. treiben *od.* zwingen; *see also* **²flight a; hard 2 d; ¹rout 1 a; r)** *(harness)* **~ to sth.** vor etw. *(Akk.)* spannen; **s)** *(Athletics: throw)* stoßen ⟨*Kugel*⟩; **~ the shot** kugelstoßen. **2.** *v. i.*, **-tt-, put** *(Naut.)* **~ [out] to sea** in See stechen; auslaufen; **~ into port** [in den Hafen] einlaufen; **~ across/over to** übersetzen nach; **~ out from England** von England aus in See stechen; England verlassen; **~ off** ablegen; **they had to ~ in at Valetta** sie mußten Valetta anlaufen. **3.** *n. (Sport)* Stoß, *der*

~ a'bout 1. *v. t.* **a)** *(circulate)* verbreiten; in Umlauf bringen; **it was ~ about that ...**: man munkelte *(ugs.) od.* es hieß, daß ...; **b)** *(Naut.)* **~ the ship** *etc.* **about** den Kurs [des Schiffes *usw.*] ändern; *(cause to change tack)* [das Schiff *usw.*] wenden; **c)** *(cause to turn about)* wenden ⟨*Pferd usw.*⟩; **d)** *(Scot., N. Engl.) (disconcert)* beunruhigen; *(upset)* verärgern; **don't ~ yourself about** *(inconvenience)* mach keine Umstände. **2.** *v. i. (Naut.)* den Kurs ändern

~ a'cross *v. t.* **a)** *(communicate)* vermitteln (**to** *Dat.*); **b)** *(make acceptable)* ankommen mit; *(make effective)* durchsetzen; **~ sth. across to sb.** mit etw. bei jmdm. ankommen/etw. bei jmdm. durchsetzen; **c)** *(Amer.)* **sb. ~s across a fraud** jmdm. gelingt ein Betrug; **he ~ that tale across them** sie haben ihm diese Geschichte abgenommen; **d) ~ one across sb.** *(sl.) (get the better of)* es jmdm. zeigen; *(deceive)* jmdn. reinlegen *(ugs.) od. (salopp)* linken. *See also* **~ 2**

~ a'side *v. t.* **a)** *(disregard)* absehen von; **~ting aside the fact that ...**: wenn man von der Tatsache *od.* davon absieht, daß ...; von der Tatsache *od.* davon abgesehen, daß ...; **b)** *(save)* beiseite *od.* auf die Seite legen

~ a'sunder *v. t. (arch.)* scheiden

~ a'way *v. t.* **a)** wegräumen; reinstellen ⟨*Auto*⟩; *(in file)* wegheften; abheften; **b)** *(abandon)* ablegen, aufgeben ⟨*Gewohnheiten, Vorurteile*⟩; **c)** *(save)* beiseite *od.* auf die Seite legen; **d)** *(coll.) (eat)* verdrücken *(ugs.)*; *(drink)* runterkippen *(ugs.)*; **e)** *(coll.: confine)* einsperren *(ugs.)*; in eine Anstalt stecken *(ugs.)*; **f)** *(coll.: kill)* einschläfern ⟨*Tier*⟩; um die Ecke bringen *(ugs.)* ⟨*Person*⟩

~ 'back *v. t.* **a) ~ the book back** das Buch zurücktun; **~ the book back on the shelf** das Buch wieder ins Regal stellen *od.* ins Regal zurückstellen; **b) ~ the clock back [one hour]** die Uhr [eine Stunde] zurückstellen; *see also* **clock 1 a**; **c)** *(delay)* zurückwerfen; verzögern ⟨*Ernte, Lieferung*⟩; **d)** *(postpone)* verschieben

~ 'by *v. t.* beiseite *od.* auf die Seite legen; **I've got a few hundred pounds ~ by** ich habe ein paar hundert Pfund auf der hohen Kante *(ugs.)*

~ 'down 1. *v. t.* **a)** *(set down) (vertically)* hinstellen; *(horizontally)* hinlegen; auflegen ⟨*Hörer*⟩; **~ sth. down on sth.** etw. auf etw. *(Akk.)* stellen/legen; **~ down a deposit** eine Anzahlung machen; **b)** *(suppress)* niederwerfen, -schlagen ⟨*Revolte, Rebellion, Aufruhr*⟩; **c)** *(humiliate)* herabsetzen; *(snub)* eine Abfuhr erteilen (+ *Dat.*); abfahren lassen *(salopp)*; *see also* **put-down**; **d)** *(kill painlessly)* töten; **e)** *(write)* notieren; aufschreiben; **~ sth. down in writing** etw. schriftlich niederlegen; **he ~ it all down on paper** er schrieb alles auf; **~ sb.'s name down on a list** jmdn. *od.* jmds. Namen auf eine Liste setzen; **~ sb. down for** für jmdn. reservieren ⟨*Lose*⟩; jmdn. notieren für ⟨*Dienst, Arbeit*⟩; jmdn. anmelden bei ⟨*Schule, Verein usw.*⟩; **I ~ him down for a £5 subscription** ich habe ihn mit einem Beitrag von 5 Pfund notiert; **f)** *(Parl.)* einbringen; stellen ⟨*Antrag*⟩; **g)** *(allow to alight)* aussteigen lassen; absetzen; **h) ~ sb. down as ...**: jmdn. eintragen als ...; **~ sth. down as ...**: etw. angeben als ...; **he ~ himself down as 'unemployed'** er gab als Beschäftigung „arbeitslos“ an; *(fig.: classify)* **~ sb./sth. down as ...**: jmdn./etw. halten für *od.* einschätzen als ...; **i)** *(attribute)* **~ sth. down to sth.** etw. auf etw. *(Akk.)* zurückführen; **j)** *(store)* einlagern; *(in cellar)* einkellern; **k)** *(to bed)* hinlegen ⟨*Baby*⟩; **l)** *(cease to read)* weglegen, aus der Hand legen ⟨*Buch*⟩; **m)** *(land)* aufsetzen. *See also* **³down 1 f. 2.** *v. i. (land)* niedergehen; **look for a place to ~ down** nach einem geeigneten Landeplatz suchen

~ 'forth *v. t. (sprout)* hervorbringen ⟨*neue Triebe, Knospen*⟩; treiben ⟨*Knospen*⟩

~ 'forward *v. t.* **a)** *(propose)* aufwarten mit; **the explanation ~ forward by him** die Erklärung, mit der er aufwartete; **several theories have been ~ forward to account for this** darüber gibt es verschiedene Theorien; **b)** *(nominate)* vorschlagen; **c) ~ the clock forward [one hour]** die Uhr [eine Stunde] vorstellen

~ 'in 1. *v. t.* **a)** *(install)* einbauen; einstellen ⟨*Arbeiter, Hausmeister, Leiter usw.*⟩; **b)** *(elect)* an die Regierung *od.* Macht bringen; **be ~ in** an die Regierung *od.* Macht kommen; **c)** *(enter)* melden ⟨*Person*⟩; **d)** *(submit)* stellen ⟨*Forderung, Antrag*⟩; einreichen ⟨*Bewerbung, Antrag*⟩; **~ in a claim for damages** eine Schadensersatzforderung stellen; **~ in a plea of not guilty** sich nicht schuldig bekennen; **e)** *(devote)* aufwenden ⟨*Mühe, Kraft*⟩; *(perform)* einlegen ⟨*Sonderschicht, Überstunden*⟩; *(coll.: spend)* einschieben ⟨*eine Stunde usw.*⟩; **f)** *(interpose)* einwerfen ⟨*Bemerkung*⟩; **I ~ in a word of warning** ich mischte mich ein und warnte sie/ihn *usw.*; **~ in a blow** zuschlagen; **g)** *(plant)* einpflanzen ⟨*Setzlinge, Stecklinge*⟩; setzen ⟨*Salat, Tomaten, Saatpflanzen*⟩; stecken ⟨*Bohnen, Kartoffeln, Zwiebeln*⟩; [ein]säen ⟨*Samen*⟩; **h)** *(Cricket)* schlagen lassen ⟨*gegnerische Mannschaft*⟩; spielen lassen, einsetzen ⟨*eigenen Spieler*⟩; **they ~ us in [to bat]** sie ließen uns schlagen. *See also* **~ 2. 2.** *v. i.* **~ in for** sich bewerben um ⟨*Stellung, Posten, Vorsitz*⟩; beantragen ⟨*Urlaub, Versetzung*⟩

~ in'side *v. t. (sl.: imprison)* einlochen *(salopp)*

~ 'off *v. t.* **a)** *(postpone)* verschieben (**until** auf + *Akk.*); *(postpone engagement with)* vertrösten (**until** auf + *Akk.*); **can't you ~ her off?** kannst du ihr nicht [erst einmal] absagen?; **b)** *(switch off)* ausmachen; **c)** *(repel)* abstoßen; **don't be ~ off by his rudeness** laß dich von seiner Grobheit nicht abschrecken; **~ sb. off sth.** jmdm. etw. verleiden; **d)** *(distract)* stören; **the noise ~ him off his game** bei dem Lärm konnte er sich nicht mehr auf sein Spiel konzentrieren; **e)** *(fob off)* abspeisen; **f)** *(dissuade)* **~ sb. off doing sth.** jmdn. davon abbringen *od.* jmdm. ausreden, etw. zu tun; **g)** *(remove)* ausziehen, ablegen ⟨*Kleidungsstücke*⟩. *See also* **~ 2**

~ 'on *v. t.* **a)** anziehen ⟨*Kleidung, Hose usw.*⟩; aufsetzen ⟨*Hut, Brille*⟩; *(fig.: assume)* aufsetzen ⟨*Miene, Lächeln, Gesicht*⟩; **~ on a disguise** sich verkleiden; **~ sb.'s clothes on [for him]** jmdn. anziehen, **~ sb.'s shoes on [for him]** jmdm. die Schuhe anziehen; **~ it on** *(coll.)* [nur] Schau machen *(ugs.)*; **he does ~ it on, doesn't he?** er übertreibt doch, oder?; **his modesty is all ~ on** seine Bescheidenheit ist nur gespielt *od. (ugs.)* ist reine Schau; **the town had ~ on a holiday look** die Stadt gab sich festlich; **b)** *(switch or turn on)* anmachen ⟨*Radio, Motor, Heizung, Licht usw.*⟩; aufmachen ⟨*Hahn*⟩; *(cause to heat up)* aufsetzen ⟨*Wasser, Essen, Kessel, Topf*⟩; *(fig.: apply)* ausüben ⟨*Druck*⟩; *see also* **screw 1 a**; **c)** *(gain)* **~ on weight/two pounds** zunehmen/zwei Pfund zunehmen; **~ it on** *(coll.: gain weight)* Speck ansetzen *(ugs.)*; **d)** *(add)* **~ on speed** beschleunigen; **~ 8p on [to] the price** den Preis um 8 Pence erhöhen; 8 Pence auf den Preis aufschlagen; **e)** *(stage)* spielen ⟨*Stück*⟩; zeigen ⟨*Show, Film*⟩; veranstalten ⟨*Ausstellung*⟩; *see also* **act 1 e**; **f)** *(arrange)* einsetzen ⟨*Sonderzug, -bus*⟩; **g)** *see* **~ forward c**; **h)** *(coll.: tease)* veräppeln *(ugs.)*; verarschen *(salopp)*; *see also* **put-on**; **i)** *(Cricket)* die Punktzahl erhöhen um ⟨*Läufe*⟩; [als Werfer] einsetzen ⟨*Spieler*⟩; **be ~ on [to bowl]** als Werfer eingesetzt werden. *See also* **~ 1 a**

~ 'out *v. t.* **a)** rausbringen; auslegen ⟨*Futter*⟩; **~ one's hand out** die Hand ausstrecken; *see also* **tongue a**; **b)** *(extinguish)* ausmachen ⟨*Licht, Lampe*⟩; löschen ⟨*Feuer, Brand*⟩; **c)** *(issue)* [he]rausgeben ⟨*Buch, Zeitschrift, Broschüre, Anweisung, Erlaß*⟩; abgeben ⟨*Stellungnahme, Erklärung*⟩; *(broadcast)* senden; bringen; **d)** *(produce)* produzieren; ausstoßen ⟨*Warenmenge*⟩; **e)** *(annoy)* verärgern; **be ~ out** verärgert *od.* entrüstet sein; **f)** *(inconvenience)* in Verlegenheit bringen; **~ oneself out to do sth.** die Mühe auf sich nehmen, etw. zu tun; **g)** *(make inaccurate)* verfälschen ⟨*Ergebnis, Berechnung*⟩; **h)** *(dislocate)* verrenken; ausrenken ⟨*Schulter*⟩; **~ one's thumb/ankle out** sich *(Dat.)* den Daumen/Knöchel verrenken; **i)** *(give to outside worker)* außer Haus geben; **~ sth. out to sb.** jmdn. mit etw. beauftragen; **j)** *(sprout)* hervorbringen; [aus]treiben; **k)** ausstechen ⟨*Augen*⟩. *See also* **~ 2**

~ 'over *see* **~ across**

~ 'through *v. t.* **a)** *(carry out)* durchführen ⟨*Plan, Programm, Kampagne, Sanierung*⟩; durchbringen ⟨*Gesetz, Vorschlag*⟩; *(complete)* zum Abschluß bringen, abschließen ⟨*Geschäft usw.*⟩; **b)** *(Teleph.)* verbinden (**to** mit); durchstellen ⟨*Gespräch*⟩ (**to** zu); **~ a call through to New York** nach New York telefonieren. *See also* **~ 1 c**

~ to'gether *v. t.* zusammensetzen ⟨*Bauteile, Scherben, Steine, Einzelteile, Maschine usw.*⟩; ordnen ⟨*Gedanken*⟩; erstellen, ausarbeiten ⟨*Begründung, Argumentation, Beweisführung*⟩; *see also* **head 1 a; two 2**

~ 'under *v. t. (make unconscious)* betäuben

~ 'up 1. *v. t.* **a)** heben ⟨*Hand*⟩; *(erect)* errichten ⟨*Gebäude, Denkmal, Gerüst, Zaun*

usw.⟩; bauen ⟨*Haus*⟩; aufstellen ⟨*Denkmal, Gerüst, Verkehrsschilder, Leinwand, Zelt*⟩; aufbauen ⟨*Zelt, Verteidigungsanlagen*⟩; anbringen ⟨*Schild, Notiz usw.*⟩ (**on** an + *Dat.*); ⟨*Igel:*⟩ aufstellen ⟨*Stacheln*⟩; *(fig.)* aufbauen ⟨*Fassade*⟩; abziehen ⟨*Schau*⟩; *see also* **put-up; b)** *(display)* anschlagen; aushängen; **c)** *(offer as defence)* hochnehmen ⟨*Fäuste*⟩; leisten ⟨*Widerstand, Gegenwehr*⟩; **~ up a struggle** sich wehren *od.* zur Wehr setzen; **~ up a bold front** sich tapfer wehren; tapfer Widerstand leisten; **~ up a defence** sich verteidigen; **d)** *(present for consideration)* einreichen ⟨*Petition, Gesuch, Vorschlag*⟩; sprechen ⟨*Gebet*⟩; *(propose)* vorschlagen; *(nominate)* aufstellen; **~ sb. up for election** jmdn. als Kandidaten aufstellen; **~ sb. up for secretary** jmdn. für das Amt des Sekretärs vorschlagen; **e)** *(incite)* **~ sb. up to sth.** jmdn. zu etw. anstiften; **f)** *(accommodate)* unterbringen; **g)** *(increase)* [he]raufsetzen, anheben ⟨*Preis, Miete, Steuer, Zins*⟩; **h)** *(provide)* zur Verfügung stellen; *abs.* **~ up or shut up** *(coll.)* steh zu deinem Wort, oder halt gefälligst den Mund!; **i) ~ sth. up for sale** etw. zum Verkauf anbieten; **~ sth. up for auction** etw. versteigern lassen; **~ sth. up for competition** etw. [öffentlich] ausschreiben; **j)** *(Hunting)* aufscheuchen; auftun *(fachspr.)*; **k)** *(arch.: sheathe)* in die Scheide stecken. *See also* **back 1 a; fight 3 a. 2.** *v. i.* **a)** *(be candidate)* kandidieren; sich aufstellen lassen; **b)** *(lodge)* übernachten; sich einquartieren

~ upon *v. t.* ausnutzen; **let oneself be ~ upon by sb.** sich von jmdm. ausnutzen lassen

~ 'up with *v. t.* sich *(Dat.)* gefallen *od.* bieten lassen ⟨*Beleidigung, Benehmen, Unhöflichkeit*⟩; sich abfinden mit ⟨*Lärm, Elend, Ärger, Bedingungen*⟩; sich abgeben mit ⟨*Person*⟩

[2]put *see* **putt**

putative ['pju:tətɪv] *adj.* mutmaßlich; *(erroneously)* vermeintlich

put: ~-down *n.* Herabsetzung, *die; (snub)* Abfuhr, *die;* **~-on** *n. (coll.)* Veräppelung, *die (ugs.);* Verarschung, *die (salopp)*

put-put ['pʌtpʌt] **1.** *n.* Tuckern, *das.* **2.** *v. i.,* **-tt-** tuckern

putrefaction [pju:trɪ'fækʃn] *n., no pl., no indef. art.* Zersetzung, *die*

putrefy ['pju:trɪfaɪ] *v. i.* sich zersetzen

putrid ['pju:trɪd] *adj.* **a)** *(rotten)* faul; **become ~:** sich zersetzen; **b)** *(of putrefaction)* faulig; **~ smell** Fäulnisgeruch, *der;* **c)** *(fig.: corrupt)* verdorben; verworfen *(geh.);* **d)** *(sl.) (dreadful)* scheußlich; *(stupid)* blödsinnig ⟨*Ansichten*⟩

putsch [pʊtʃ] *n.* Putsch, *der;* **army ~:** Militärputsch, *der*

putt [pʌt] *(Golf)* **1.** *v. i. & t.* putten. **2.** *n.* Putt, *der*

puttee ['pʌtɪ] *n.* **a)** Wickelgamasche, *die;* **b)** *(Amer.: leather legging)* Ledergamasche, *die*

putter ['pʌtə(r)] *(Golf)* Putter, *der*

putting-green ['pʌtɪŋgri:n] *n. (Golf)* **a)** Grün, *das;* **b)** *(miniature-golf course) kleiner Golfplatz nur zum Putten*

putty ['pʌtɪ] **1.** *n.* **a)** Kitt, *der;* **glaziers' ~:** Fensterkitt, *der;* Glaserkitt, *der;* **b) [jewellers'] ~:** Zinnasche, *die;* Polierasche, *die.* **2.** *v. t.* **a)** *(fix with glaziers' ~)* einkitten ⟨*Fensterscheibe*⟩; *(fill with ~)* auskitten ⟨*Risse*⟩; **b)** *(cover with plasterers' ~)* verputzen ⟨*Wand*⟩; ausgipsen ⟨*Fugen*⟩

'putty-knife *n.* Kittmesser, *das*

'put-up *adj.* **a ~ thing/job** eine abgekartete Sache/ein abgekartetes Spiel

puzzle ['pʌzl] **1.** *n.* **a)** *(problem)* Rätsel, *das; (brainteaser)* Denksportaufgabe, *die; (toy)* Geduldsspiel, *das;* **b)** *(enigma)* Rätsel, *das;* **be a ~ to sb.** jmdm. ein Rätsel sein; **be a ~:** rätselhaft sein. **2.** *v. t.* rätselhaft *od.* ein Rätsel sein (+ *Dat.*); vor ein Rätsel stellen; **he would have been ~d to explain it** er hätte nicht gewußt, wie er es hätte erklären sollen; **he was ~d what to do** er wußte nicht, was er tun sollte. **3.** *v. i.* **~ over** *or* **about sth.** sich *(Dat.)* über etw. den Kopf zerbrechen; über etw. rätseln; **we ~d over what had happened** wir rätselten, was wohl passiert war

~ 'out *v. t.* herausfinden; **~ out an answer to a question** eine Antwort auf eine Frage finden

puzzled ['pʌzld] *adj.* ratlos

puzzlement ['pʌzlmənt] *n., no pl.* Verwirrung, *die*

puzzling ['pʌzlɪŋ] *adj.* rätselhaft

PVC *abbr.* **polyvinyl chloride** PVC, *das*

PX *abbr. (Amer.)* **Post Exchange**

pygmy ['pɪgmɪ] **1.** *n.* **a)** Pygmäe, *der;* **b)** *(dwarf; also fig.)* Zwerg, *der*/Zwergin, *die.* **2.** *attrib. adj.* **a)** pygmäisch; **the ~ people** die Pygmäen; **b)** *(dwarf)* Zwerg-

pyjama [pɪ'dʒɑ:mə] *adj.* Pyjama-; Schlafanzug-; **~ suit** Pyjama, *der;* Schlafanzug, *der*

pyjamas [pɪ'dʒɑ:məz] *n. pl.* **[pair of] ~:** Schlafanzug, *der;* Pyjama, *der*

pylon ['paɪlən] *n.* Mast, *der*

pyramid ['pɪrəmɪd] *n.* Pyramide, *die*

pyramidal [pɪ'ræmɪdl] *adj.* pyramidenförmig

'pyramid selling *n., no pl., no indef. art. Verkauf von Vertriebsrechten nach dem Schneeballsystem*

pyre [paɪə(r)] *n.* Scheiterhaufen, *der*

Pyrenean [pɪrə'ni:ən] *adj.* pyrenäisch; **~ mountain dog** Pyrenäenhund, *der*

Pyrenees [pɪrə'ni:z] *pr. n. pl.* **the ~:** die Pyrenäen

pyrethrum [paɪ'ri:θrəm] *n.* **a)** *(flower)* Chrysantheme, *die;* Pyrethrum, *das (veralt.);* **b)** *(insecticide)* Pyrethrum, *das*

Pyrex, (P) ['paɪreks] *n.* ≈ Jenaer Glas, *das* Ⓦz; *attrib.* **~ dish** feuerfeste Glasschüssel

pyrites [paɪ'raɪti:z] *n., no pl. (Min.)* **[iron] ~:** Pyrit, *der;* Eisenkies, *der*

pyrotechnic [paɪrəʊ'teknɪk] **1.** *adj.* pyrotechnisch; Feuerwerks-; *(fig.: brilliant)* brillant. **2.** *n. in pl.* Feuerwerk, *das; (fig.)* Brillanz, *die*

Pyrrhic ['pɪrɪk] *adj.* **~ victory** Pyrrhussieg, *der*

Pythagoras [paɪ'θægərəs] *pr. n.* Pythagoras, *der;* **~' theorem** *(Geom.)* der Satz des Pythagoras

python ['paɪθən] *n.* Python[schlange], *die*

Q

[1]Q, q [kju:] *n., pl.* **Qs** *or* **Q's** Q, q, *das; see also* **mind 2 b**

[2]Q *abbr.* **question** F

Q. *abbr.* **a) Queen** Kgn.; **b) Queen's** kgl.; **c)** *(Chess)* **queen** D

QC *abbr. (Brit.)* **Queen's Counsel**

QED *abbr.* **quod erat demonstrandum** q. e. d.; w. z. b. w.

qr. *abbr.* **quarter[s]** qr.

qt. *abbr.* **quart[s]** qt

qua [kweɪ, kwɑ:] *conj. (literary)* qua *(geh.)*

[1]quack [kwæk] **1.** *v. i.* ⟨*Ente:*⟩ quaken. **2.** *n.* Quaken, *das*

[2]quack *(derog.)* **1.** *n.* Quacksalber, *der (abwertend).* **2.** *attrib. adj.* **a) ~ doctor** Quacksalber, *der;* **b)** Quacksalber⟨*kur, -tropfen, -pillen*⟩ *(abwertend);* **~ remedy** Mittelchen, *das (ugs. abwertend)*

'quack-quack *n. (child lang.)* Quakente, *die (Kinderspr.)*

quad [kwɒd] *n. (coll.)* **a)** *(quadrangle)* Innenhof, *der;* **b)** *(quadraphonic)* **~ [sound system]** Quadro-Anlage, *die;* **c)** *(quadruplet)* Vierling, *der;* **d)** *(Print.: quadrat)* **[em] ~/en ~:** Geviert/Halbgeviert, *das*

quadrangle ['kwɒdræŋgl] *n.* **a)** *(enclosed court)* viereckiger Innenhof; *(with buildings)* Block, *der;* Karree, *das;* **b)** *(Geom.)* Viereck, *das*

quadrant ['kwɒdrənt] *n.* **a)** *(Geom., Astron., Naut.)* Quadrant, *der; (of sphere)* Viertelkugel, *die;* **b)** *(object shaped like quarter-circle)* viertelkreisförmiger Gegenstand

quadraphonic [kwɒdrə'fɒnɪk] *adj.* quadrophon; Quadro⟨*anlage, -sound usw.*⟩

quadratic [kwə'drætɪk] *adj. (Math.)* quadratisch; zweiten Grades *nachgestellt*

quadrilateral [kwɒdrɪ'lætərl] *n. (Geom.)* Viereck, *das*

quadrille [kwə'drɪl] *n.* Quadrille, *die*

quadriplegia [kwɒdrɪ'pli:dʒɪə] *n. (Med.)* Quadri-, Tetraplegie, *die (fachspr.);* gleichzeitige Lähmung aller vier Gliedmaßen

quadriplegic [kwɒdrɪ'pli:dʒɪk] *(Med.)* **1.** *n.* Quadri-, Tetraplegiker, *der*/-plegikerin, *die.* **2.** *adj.* quadri-, tetraplegisch; **be ~:** an allen vier Gliedmaßen gelähmt sein

quadruped ['kwɒdrʊped] *n.* Vierfüßler, *der*

quadruple ['kwɒdrʊpl] **1.** *adj.* **a)** vierfach; **b)** *(four times)* viermal; **be ~ today's value** viermal so hoch sein wie der heutige Wert; **~ the amount** die vierfache Menge; **c)** *(Mus.)* **~ time** Viertertakt, *der.* **2.** *v. t.* mit vier malnehmen ⟨*Zahl*⟩; vervierfachen ⟨*Einkommen, Produktion, Profit*⟩. **3.** *v. i.* sich vervierfachen

quadruplet ['kwɒdrʊplɪt, kwɒ'dru:plɪt] *n.* Vierling, *der*

quadruplicate [kwɒ'dru:plɪkət] *n.* vierfache Ausfertigung; **in ~:** in vierfacher Ausfertigung *nachgestellt*

quaff [kwɑ:f, kwɒf] *(literary)* **1.** *v. i.* zechen *(veralt., scherzh.);* pokulieren *(veralt., scherzh.).* **2.** *v. t.* [mit langen, kräftigen Schlucken] leeren *od.* austrinken ⟨*Glas*⟩; [mit langen, kräftigen Schlucken] trinken ⟨*Getränk*⟩

quag [kwæg, kwɒg] *n. (marshy spot)* sumpfige *od.* morastige Stelle; *(quaking bog)* Schwingmoor, *das*

quagmire ['kwægmaɪə(r), kwɒgmaɪə(r)] *n.* Sumpf, *der;* Morast, *der; (quaking bog)* Schwingmoor, *das; (fig.: complex or difficult situation)* Sumpf, *der;* **be in a ~** *(lit. or fig.)* in einem Sumpf stecken; **a ~ of details/problems** ein Wust von Einzelheiten/Problemen

[1]quail [kweɪl] *n., pl. same or* **~s** *(Ornith.)* Wachtel, *die*

[2]quail *v. i.* ⟨*Person:*⟩ [ver]zagen, den Mut sinken lassen; ⟨*Blick, Mut, Hoffnung, Vertrauen:*⟩ sinken; **make sb.'s courage/spirit ~:** jmdn. entmutigen; **~ at the prospect of sth.** bei der Aussicht auf etw. *(Akk.)* verzagen

quaint [kweɪnt] *adj.* drollig; putzig *(ugs.)* ⟨*Häuschen, Einrichtung*⟩; malerisch, pittoresk ⟨*Ort*⟩; *(odd, strange)* kurios, seltsam ⟨*Bräuche, Anblick, Begebenheit*⟩; schnurrig ⟨*alter Kauz*⟩

quaintly ['kweɪntlɪ] *adv.* putzig *(ugs.);* drollig ⟨*bemerken*⟩

quake [kweɪk] **1.** *n. (coll.)* [Erd]beben, *das.* **2.** *v. i.* beben; ⟨*Sumpfboden:*⟩ schwingen; **~ with fear/fright** vor Angst/Schreck zittern *od.* beben

Quaker ['kweɪkə(r)] *n.* Quäker, *der*/Quäkerin, *die*

quaking ['kweɪkɪŋ]: ~ **bog** *n.* Schwingmoor, *das;* ~**-grass** *n. (Bot.)* Zittergras, *das*

qualification [kwɒlɪfɪ'keɪʃn] *n.* **a)** *(ability)* Qualifikation, *die; (condition to be fulfilled)* Voraussetzung, *die;* **secretarial ~s** Ausbildung als Sekretärin; **b)** *(on paper)* Zeugnis, *das;* **c)** *(limitation)* Vorbehalt, *der;* **without ~:** vorbehaltlos; ohne Vorbehalt; **the offer was subject to one ~:** das Angebot hatte eine Einschränkung

qualified ['kwɒlɪfaɪd] *adj.* **a)** qualifiziert; *(by training)* ausgebildet; *(entitled, having right to)* berechtigt; **be ~ for a job/to vote** die Qualifikation für eine Stelle besitzen/wahlberechtigt sein; **you are better ~ to judge that** du kannst das besser beurteilen; **I am not ~ to speak on that** ich kann darüber nichts sagen; **be ~ to vote** wahlberechtigt sein; **b)** *(restricted)* nicht uneingeschränkt; **a ~ success** kein voller Erfolg; **~ approval/reply** Zustimmung/Antwort unter Vorbehalt; **~ acceptance** bedingte Annahme

qualifier ['kwɒlɪfaɪə(r)] *n.* **a)** *(restriction)* Einschränkung, *die* **(of, on** *Gen.*); **b)** *(person)* **be among the ~s** zu denen gehören, die sich qualifiziert haben; **c)** *(Sport: match)* Qualifikationsspiel, *das*

qualify ['kwɒlɪfaɪ] **1.** *v. t.* **a)** *(make competent, make officially entitled)* berechtigen **(for** zu); **b)** *(modify)* einschränken; modifizieren ‹*Meinung, Feststellung*›; **c)** *(describe)* bewerten; bezeichnen; **d)** *(moderate)* abschwächen; **~ justice with mercy** Gnade vor Recht ergehen lassen; **e)** *(Ling.)* näher bestimmen. **2.** *v. i.* **a) ~ in law/medicine/education/chemistry** seinen [Studien]abschluß in Jura/Medizin/Pädagogik/Chemie machen; **~ as a doctor/lawyer/teacher/chemist** sein Examen als Arzt/Anwalt/Lehrer/Chemiker machen; **b)** *(fulfil a condition)* in Frage kommen **(for** für); **~ for the vote/a pension** wahl-/rentenberechtigt sein; **~ for admission to a university/club** die Aufnahmebedingungen einer Universität/eines Vereins erfüllen; **~ for a post** für eine Stelle qualifiziert sein; **~ for membership** die Bedingungen für die Mitgliedschaft erfüllen; **c)** *(Sport)* sich qualifizieren

qualifying ['kwɒlɪfaɪɪŋ] *adj.* **a) ~ statement** einschränkende Aussage; **b)** *(Sport)* **~ match** Qualifikationsspiel, *das;* **~ round/heat** Ausscheidungs- *od.* Qualifikationsrunde, *die;* **c) ~ examination** Zulassungsprüfung, *die*

qualitative ['kwɒlɪtətɪv] *adj.*, **qualitatively** ['kwɒlɪtətɪvlɪ] *adv.* qualitativ

quality ['kwɒlɪtɪ] **1.** *n.* **a)** Qualität, *die;* **of good/poor** *etc.* **~:** von guter/schlechter *usw.* Qualität; **of the best ~:** bester Qualität; **~ rather than quantity** Qualität, nicht Quantität; **clothes of ~:** Qualitätskleidung, *die;* **the ~ of her writing/craftsmanship** ihre schriftstellerischen Leistungen/handwerklichen Fähigkeiten; **b)** *(characteristic)* Eigenschaft, *die;* **the melodious ~ of her voice** die Melodie ihrer Stimme; **possess the qualities of a ruler/leader** eine Führernatur sein; **have the ~ of inspiring others with confidence** die Gabe haben, andere mit Zuversicht zu erfüllen; *see also* **defect 1 b; c)** *(of sound, voice)* Klang, *der;* **d)** *(arch.: rank)* Rang, *der;* **people of ~:** Leute von Rang [und Namen]. **2.** *adj.* **a)** *(excellent)* Qualitäts-; **b)** *(maintaining ~)* Qualitäts‹*prüfung, -kontrolle*›; *(denoting ~)* Güte‹*grad, -klasse, -zeichen*›

qualm [kwɑːm, kwɔːm] *n.* **a)** *(sudden misgiving)* ungutes Gefühl; **b)** *(scruple)* Bedenken, *das (meist Pl.)* **(over, about** gegen); **he had no ~s about borrowing money** er hatte keine Bedenken, sich *(Dat.)* Geld zu leihen; **c)** *(sick feeling)* Übelkeit, *die*

quandary ['kwɒndərɪ] *n.* Dilemma, *das;* **this demand put him in a ~:** diese Forderung brachte ihn in eine verzwickte Lage; **he was in a ~ about what to do next** er wußte nicht, was er als nächstes tun sollte

quango ['kwæŋgəʊ] *n., pl.* **~s** *(Brit.) halböffentliche Verwaltungseinrichtung*

quanta *pl. of* **quantum**

quantifiable ['kwɒntɪfaɪəbl] *adj.* quantifizierbar

quantify ['kwɒntɪfaɪ] *v. t.* quantifizieren

quantitative ['kwɒntɪtətɪv] *adj.*, **quantitatively** ['kwɒntɪtətɪvlɪ] *adv.* quantitativ

quantity ['kwɒntɪtɪ] *n.* **a)** Quantität, *die;* **b)** *(amount, sum)* Menge, *die;* **what ~ of flour do you need for this recipe?** wieviel Mehl braucht man für dieses Rezept?; **~ of heat** Wärmemenge, *die;* **c)** *(large amount)* [Un]menge, *die;* **coal/gold in quantities** Kohle/Gold in Unmengen *od. (ugs.)* rauhen Mengen; **buy in quantities** in großen Mengen einkaufen; *see also* **³bill 1 h; d)** *(Math.)* Größe, *die;* **e)** *(fig.)* **negligible ~:** Quantité négligeable, *die (geh.);* **he is a negligible ~:** er ist völlig unwichtig; **an unknown ~:** eine unbekannte Größe; **f)** *(Phonet., Pros.)* Quantität, *die*

quantity: ~-mark *n. (Pros.)* Quantitätszeichen, *das;* **~ surveyor** *n.* Baukostenkalkulator, *der*/-kalkulatorin, *die*

quantum ['kwɒntəm] *n., pl.* **quanta** ['kwɒntə] **a)** *(literary) (amount)* Menge, *die; (share, portion)* Anteil, *der; (required, desired, or allowed amount)* Quantum, *das;* **b)** *(Phys.)* Quant, *das*

quantum: ~ jump, ~ leap *ns. (Phys.; also fig.)* Quantensprung, *der;* **~ me'chanics** *n. (Phys.)* Quantenmechanik, *die;* **~ theory** *n. (Phys.)* Quantentheorie, *die*

quarantine ['kwɒrəntiːn] **1.** *n.* Quarantäne, *die; attrib.* Quarantäne‹*bestimmungen, -zeit, -flagge*›; **put under ~:** unter Quarantäne stellen; **be in ~:** unter Quarantäne stehen. **2.** *v. t.* unter Quarantäne stellen

quark [kwɑːk, kwɔːk] *n. (Phys.)* Quark, *das*

quarrel ['kwɒrl] **1.** *n.* **a)** Streit, *der;* **have a ~ with sb. [about/over sth.]** sich mit jmdm. [über etw. *(Akk.) od.* wegen etw./um etw.] streiten; **let's not have a ~ about it** wir wollen uns nicht darüber streiten; **I don't want to have a ~ with you** ich will mich mit dir nicht streiten *od.* will keinen Streit mit dir; **pick a ~ [with sb. over sth.]** [mit jmdm. wegen etw.] Streit anfangen; **b)** *(cause of complaint)* Einwand, *der* **(with** gegen); **I have no ~ with you** ich habe nichts gegen dich. **2.** *v. i., (Brit.)* **-ll-: a)** [sich] streiten **(over** um, **about** über + *Akk.*, wegen); **~ with each other** [sich] [miteinander] streiten; *(fall out, dispute)* sich [zer]streiten **(over** um, **about** über + *Akk.*, wegen); **b)** *(find fault)* etwas auszusetzen haben **(with** an + *Dat.*); **I really can't ~ with that** daran habe ich wirklich nichts auszusetzen

quarrelsome ['kwɒrlsəm] *adj.* streitsüchtig; **his ~ nature** seine Streitsucht

¹quarry ['kwɒrɪ] **1.** *n.* Steinbruch, *der;* **marble/slate ~:** Marmor-/Schieferbruch, *der; (fig.)* Fundgrube, *die* **(of** für); **~ of information** Informationsquelle, *die.* **2.** *v. t.* brechen ‹*Steine, Marmor*›; *(fig.)* zutage fördern. **3.** *v. i. (fig.)* herumstöbern

²quarry *n. (prey)* Beute, *die; (fig.)* Opfer, *das*

quarry: ~man ['kwɒrɪmən] *n., pl.* **~men** ['kwɒrɪmən] Steinbrucharbeiter, *der;* Brecher, *der (fachspr.);* **~ tile** *n.* unglasierte Steinfliese

quart [kwɔːt] *n.* **a)** Quart, *das;* **try to put a ~ into a pint pot** *(fig.)* mehr in etwas unterbringen wollen als hineinpaßt; **b)** *(vessel)* Quartgefäß, *das*

'quart bottle *n.* Quartflasche, *die*

quarter ['kwɔːtə(r)] **1.** *n.* **a)** Viertel, *das;* **a** *or* **one ~ of** ein Viertel (+ *Gen.*); **a ~ [of] the price** ein Viertel des Preises; **divide/cut sth. into ~s** etw. in vier Teile teilen/schneiden; etw. vierteln; **six and a ~:** sechseinviertel; **an hour and a ~:** eineinviertel Stunden; **a ~ [of a pound] of cheese** ein Viertel[pfund] Käse; **~ of lamb/beef** Lamm-/Rinderviertel, *das;* **a ~ of a mile/an hour/a century** eine Viertelmeile/-stunde/ein Vierteljahrhundert; **three ~s of an hour** eine Dreiviertelstunde; **b)** *(of year)* Quartal, *das;* Vierteljahr, *das;* **c)** *(point of time)* **[a] ~ to/past six** Viertel vor/nach sechs; drei Viertel sechs/Viertel sieben *(landsch.);* **there are buses at ~ to and ~ past [the hour]** es fahren Busse um Viertel vor und Viertel nach jeder vollen Stunde *od. (ugs.)* eine Viertelstunde vor und nach voll; **d)** *(direction)* Richtung, *die;* **blow from all ~s** ‹*Wind:*› aus allen Richtungen wehen; **flock in from all ~s** aus allen Himmelsrichtungen zusammenströmen; **from every ~ of the globe** von überall her; **e)** *(source of supply or help)* Seite, *die;* **from this ~:** von dieser Stelle; **secret information from a high ~:** Geheiminformationen von höchster Stelle; **turn for support to other ~s** sich woanders *od.* anderweitig um Unterstützung bemühen; **f)** *(area of town)* [Stadt]viertel, *das;* Quartier, *das;* **in some ~s** *(fig.)* in gewissen Kreisen; **g)** *in pl. (lodgings)* Quartier, *das (bes. Milit.);* Unterkunft, *die;* **take up [one's] ~s** Quartier beziehen; *see also* **close 1 a; h)** *(Brit.: measure) (of volume)* Quarter, *der; (of weight)* ≈ Viertelzentner, *der;* **i)** *(Amer.) (school term)* Vierteischuljahr, *das; (university term)* halbes Semester; **j)** *(Astron.)* Viertel, *das;* **the moon is in its last ~:** der Mond steht im letzten Viertel; **k)** *(mercy)* Schonung, *die;* **give/receive ~:** Schonung *od. (veralt.)* Pardon gewähren/gewährt bekommen; **give no ~ to sb.** jmdm. keinen Pardon *(veralt.)* gewähren *od.* geben; **l)** *(Amer., Can.: amount, coin)* Vierteldollar, *der;* 25-Cent-Stück, *das;* **the bus fare was a ~:** die Busfahrt hat 25 Cent *od.* einen Vierteldollar gekostet; **m)** *(Naut.)* Achterschiff, *das;* Hinterschiff, *das;* **n)** *(in shoemaking)* Seitenteil, *das;* Quartier, *das (fachspr.).* **2.** *v. t.* **a)** *(divide)* vierteln ‹*Apfel, Tomate usw.*›; in vier Teile teilen ‹*Stück Fleisch*›; durch vier teilen ‹*Zahl, Summe*›; **b)** *(lodge)* einquartieren ‹*Soldaten*›; **c)** *(Hist.)* vierteilen ‹*Verbrecher*›

quarter: ~-back *n. (Amer. Football)* Quarterback, *der;* **~-binding** *n. (Bookbinding)* Halbfranz, *das;* **~-day** *n.* Quartalsende, *das;* **~-deck** *n. (Naut.)* **a)** *(of ship)* Quarterdeck, *das;* **b)** *(officers)* Marineoffiziere *Pl.;* **~-'final** *n.* Viertelfinale, *das;* **in the ~-finals** im Viertelfinale; **~-'finalist** *n.* Viertelfinalist, *der*/-finalistin, *die;* **~-'hour** *n.* **a)** Viertelstunde, *die;* **b) on the ~-hour** *(fifteen minutes before)* um Viertel vor; *(fifteen minutes after)* um Viertel nach

quartering ['kwɔːtərɪŋ] *n.* **a)** *(dividing)* Vierteln, *das;* **b)** *(lodging)* Einquartierung, *die*

'quarter-light *n. (Brit. Motor Veh.) (bes. ausstellbares)* Teil des Fond-/Türfensters

quarterly ['kwɔːtəlɪ] **1.** *adj.* vierteljährlich. **2.** *n.* Vierteljahr[e]sschrift, *die.* **3.** *adv.* vierteljährlich; alle Vierteljahre

quarter: ~master *n.* **a)** *(Naut.)* Quartermeister, *der;* **b)** *(Mil.)* Quartiermeister, *der (veralt.);* **~ 'mile** *n.* Viertelmeile, *die;* **~-note** *(Amer. Mus.) see* **crotchet; ~ 'sessions** *n. pl. (Brit. Hist.) vierteljährliche Gerichtssitzungen*

quartet, quartette [kwɔː'tet] *n. (also Mus.)* Quartett, *das;* **piano/string ~:** Klavier-/Streichquartett, *das*

quarto ['kwɔːtəʊ] *n., pl.* **~s a)** *(book)* Quartband, *der;* **b)** *(size)* Quart[format], *das;* **~ paper** Papier im Quartformat

quartz [kwɔːts] *n.* Quarz, *der*

quartz: ~ clock *n.* Quarzuhr, *die;* **~ lamp** *n.* Quarzlampe, *die;* **~ watch** *n.* Quarzuhr, *die*

quasar ['kweɪsɑː(r), 'kweɪzɑː(r)] *n. (Astron.)* Quasar, *der*

quash [kwɒʃ] *v. t.* **a)** *(annul, make void)* aufheben ‹*Urteil, Entscheidung*›; zurückweisen ‹*Einspruch, Klage*›; **b)** *(suppress, crush)* unterdrücken ‹*Opposition*›; niederschlagen ‹*Aufstand, Generalstreik*›

quasi ['kweɪzaɪ, 'kwɑ:zɪ] *adv.* quasi

quasi- *pref.* **a)** *(not real, seeming)* Schein-; **b)** *(half-)* Quasi-; quasi; **~-official** halbamtlich

Quaternary [kwə'tɜ:nərɪ] *(Geol.)* **1.** *adj.* quartär. **2.** *n.* Quartär, *das*

quatrain ['kwɒtreɪn] *n.* *(Pros.)* Vierzeiler, *der;* Quatrain, *das od. der (fachspr.)*

quatrefoil ['kætrəfɔɪl] *n.* *(Archit.)* Vierpaß, *der*

quaver ['kweɪvə(r)] **1.** *n.* **a)** *(Brit. Mus.)* Achtelnote, *die;* **b)** *(Mus.: trill)* Tremolo, *das;* **c)** *(in speech)* Zittern, *das;* Beben, *das (geh.);* **admit with a ~ [in one's voice] that ...:** mit zitternder Stimme zugeben, daß ... **2.** *v. i.* *(vibrate, tremble)* zittern; beben *(geh.)*

quavering ['kweɪvərɪŋ], **quavery** ['kweɪvərɪ] *adjs.* zitternd, bebend ‹*Stimme*›

quay [ki:], **'quayside** *ns.* Kai, *der;* Kaje, *die (nordd.)*

queasiness ['kwi:zɪnɪs] *n., no pl.* Übelkeit, *die*

queasy ['kwi:zɪ] *adj.* unwohl; *(uneasy)* mulmig *(ugs.);* **a ~ feeling** ein Gefühl der Übelkeit; **just the thought of it makes me [feel] ~:** schon beim Gedanken daran wird mir ganz schlecht *od.* übel; **my stomach is in such a ~ state** mir ist so komisch im Magen

queen [kwi:n] *n.* **a)** Königin, *die;* **Q~ of [the] May** Maikönigin, *die;* **b)** *(bee, ant, wasp)* Königin, *die;* **c)** *(personified best example of sth.)* Juwel, *das;* Perle, *die;* **d)** *(Chess, Cards)* Dame, *die;* **~'s bishop/knight/pawn/rook** Damenläufer/-springer/-bauer/-turm, *der;* **~ of hearts** Herzdame, *die;* **e)** *(sl.: male homosexual)* Tunte, *die (salopp). See also* **bench d; colour 1 j; counsel 1 c; English 2 a; evidence 1 b; guide 1 e; highway a; messenger b; peace b; save 1 c; scout 1 a; shilling**

queen: ~ **'bee** *n.* Bienenkönigin, *die;* ~ **'consort** *n.* Königin, *die;* Gemahlin des Königs

queenly ['kwi:nlɪ] *adj.* königlich; *(majestic)* majestätisch

queen 'mother *n.* Königinmutter, *die*

queer [kwɪə(r)] **1.** *adj.* **a)** *(strange)* sonderbar; seltsam; *(eccentric)* komisch; verschroben; **a ~ feeling** ein komisches Gefühl; *see also* **fish 1 c; b)** *(shady, suspect)* merkwürdig; seltsam; **there's something ~ about this whole business** die ganze Sache ist nicht ganz hasenrein; **c)** *(out of sorts, faint)* unwohl; **I feel ~:** mir ist komisch *od. (ugs.)* flau; **you are looking a bit ~:** du siehst ein bißchen angegriffen aus; **d)** *(coll.: mad, insane)* verrückt *(salopp);* **~ in the head** plemplem *(salopp);* **e)** *(sl. derog.: homosexual)* schwul *(ugs.).* **2.** *n.* *(sl. derog.: homosexual)* Schwule, *der (ugs.).* **3.** *v. t.* *(sl.: spoil)* vermasseln *(salopp);* **~ the pitch for sb., ~ sb.'s pitch** jmdm. einen Strich durch die Rechnung machen

queerly ['kwɪəlɪ] *adv.* sonderbar; seltsam

'Queer Street *n.* **be in ~** *(in difficulties, trouble, debt)* in der Tinte sitzen *(ugs.);* in Schwulitäten sein *(ugs.)*

quell [kwel] *v. t.* *(literary)* niederschlagen ‹*Aufstand, Rebellion*›; bezwingen; zügeln ‹*Leidenschaft, Furcht*›; überwinden ‹*Ängste, Befürchtungen*›

quench [kwentʃ] *v. t.* **a)** *(extinguish)* löschen; *(fig.)* auslöschen *(geh.);* **b)** *(satisfy)* **~ one's thirst** seinen Durst löschen *od.* stillen; **c)** *(cool)* löschen ‹*Koks*›; abschrecken ‹*Metall*›; **d)** *(stifle, suppress)* unterdrücken; dämpfen ‹*Begeisterung*›

quern [kwɜ:n] *n.* Handmühle, *die*

querulous ['kwerʊləs] *adj.* gereizt; *(by nature)* reizbar

querulously ['kwerʊləslɪ] *adv.* gereizt; **discuss sth. ~:** in gereiztem Ton über etw. *(Akk.)* diskutieren

query ['kwɪərɪ] **1.** *n.* **a)** *(question)* Frage, *die;* **put/raise a ~:** eine Frage stellen/aufwerfen; **that raises the ~ whether we ...:** das wirft die Frage auf *od.* damit stellt sich die Frage, ob wir ...; **b)** *(question mark)* Fragezeichen, *das.* **2.** *v. t.* **a)** *(call in question)* in Frage stellen ‹*Anweisung, Glaubwürdigkeit, Ergebnis usw.*›; beanstanden ‹*Rechnung, Kontoauszug*›; **b)** *(ask, inquire)* **~ whether/if ...:** fragen, ob ...

quest [kwest] *n.* Suche, *die* **(for** nach); *(for happiness, riches, knowledge, etc.)* Streben, *das* **(for** nach); **in ~ of sth.** auf der Suche nach etw.; **man's ~ for happiness** das menschliche Glücksstreben

question ['kwestʃn] **1.** *n.* **a)** Frage, *die;* **ask sb. a ~:** jmdm. eine Frage stellen; **put a ~ to sb.** an jmdn. eine Frage richten; **don't ask so many ~s!** frag nicht soviel!; **ask ~s** Fragen stellen; **ask me no ~s and I'll tell you no lies** wenn du nicht willst, daß ich lüge, stell mir keine Fragen; **ask a silly ~ and you get a silly answer** *(prov.)* wie die Frage, so die Antwort *(Spr.);* **and no ~s asked** ohne daß groß gefragt wird/worden ist *(ugs.);* **[that's a] good ~!** [das ist eine] gute Frage!; *see also* **leading question; 'pop 2 e; b)** *(doubt, objection)* Zweifel, *der* **(about** an + *Dat.*); **there is no ~ about sth.** es besteht kein Zweifel an *(Dat.)* etw.; **there is no ~ [but] that ...:** es besteht kein Zweifel, daß ...; **accept/follow sth. without ~:** etwas kritiklos akzeptieren/befolgen; **not be in ~:** außer [allem] Zweifel stehen; außer Frage sein *od.* stehen; **your honesty is/is not in ~:** man zweifelt/niemand zweifelt an deiner Ehrlichkeit; **beyond all** *or* **without ~:** zweifellos; ohne Frage *od.* Zweifel; **be beyond all** *or* **be without ~:** außer allem Zweifel stehen; außer Frage sein *od.* stehen; *see also* **call 1 c; c)** *(problem, concern, subject)* Frage, *die;* **sth./it is only a ~ of time** etw./es ist [nur] eine Frage der Zeit; **it is [only] a ~ of doing sth.** es geht [nur] darum, etw. zu tun; **a ~ of money** eine Geldfrage; **there is no/some ~ of his doing that** es kann keine Rede davon sein/es ist die Rede davon, daß er das tut; **the ~ of sth. arises** es erhebt sich die Frage von etw.; **the person/thing in ~:** die fragliche *od.* betreffende Person/Sache; **sth./it is out of the ~:** etw./es ist ausgeschlossen; etw./es kommt nicht in Frage *(ugs.);* **the ~ is whether ...:** es geht darum, ob ...; **that is not the ~:** darum geht es nicht; **beside the ~:** belanglos; **put the ~:** zur Abstimmung aufrufen **(to** *Akk.*); **come into ~:** in Frage kommen; *see also* **beg 1 d; hour e; open 1 f, g; previous question. 2.** *v. t.* **a)** befragen; ‹*Polizei, Gericht usw.*:› vernehmen; **he started ~ing me about where I had been** er fing an, mich danach auszufragen, wo ich gewesen war; **b)** *(throw doubt upon, raise objections to)* bezweifeln; **her goodwill cannot be ~ed** an ihrem guten Willen kann nicht gezweifelt werden

questionable ['kwestʃənəbl] *adj.* fragwürdig

questionably ['kwestʃənəblɪ] *adv.* fragwürdig ‹*sich benehmen*›; auf fragwürdige Weise ‹*erwerben*›

questioner ['kwestʃənə(r)] *n.* Fragesteller, *der*/Fragestellerin, *die*

questioning ['kwestʃənɪŋ] **1.** *adj.* fragend; forschend ‹*Geist*›. **2.** *n.* Fragen, *das;* *(at examination)* Befragung, *die;* *(by police etc.)* Vernehmung, *die;* **brought in for ~:** ins Verhör genommen

questioningly ['kwestʃənɪŋlɪ] *adv.* fragend

question: ~ **mark** *n.* *(lit. or fig.)* Fragezeichen, *das;* **a ~ mark hangs over sth.** etw. muß mit einem [großen] Fragezeichen versehen werden; **~-master** *n.* Quizmaster, *der*

questionnaire [kwestʃə'neə(r)] *n.* Fragebogen, *der*

'question time *n.* Diskussionszeit, *die;* *(Parl.)* Fragestunde, *die;* **at ~ time** während der Diskussionszeit/Fragestunde

queue [kju:] **1.** *n.* **a)** *(line)* Schlange, *die;* **a ~ of people/cars** eine Menschen-/Autoschlange; **a long ~ of people** eine lange Schlange; **stand** *or* **wait in a ~:** Schlange stehen; anstehen; **join the ~:** sich anstellen; **take one's place in a ~:** sich in eine Schlange einreihen; *see also* **jump 3 g; b)** *(of hair)* Zopf, *der.* **2.** *v. i.* **~ [up]** Schlange stehen; anstehen; *(join ~)* sich anstellen; **~ to buy admission tickets** nach Eintrittskarten anstehen; **~ for a bus** an der Bushaltestelle Schlange stehen; **~ for vegetables** nach Gemüse anstehen

queue: **~-jumper** *n.* *(Brit.)* jmd., *der sich vordrängt;* **~-jumping** *n.* *(Brit.)* Vordrängen, *das;* Vordrängeln, *das (ugs.)*

quibble ['kwɪbl] **1.** *n.* **a)** *(argument)* spitzfindiges Argument; **b)** *(petty objection)* Spitzfindigkeit, *die.* **2.** *v. i.* streiten; **~ over** *or* **about sth.** über etw. *(Akk.)* streiten; **~ about the quality of sb.'s work** die Qualität von jmds. Arbeit bekritteln

quibbler ['kwɪblə(r)] *n.* Kritt[e]ler, *der;* Nörgler, *der*

quibbling ['kwɪblɪŋ] *adj.* spitzfindig

quiche [ki:ʃ] *n.* Quiche, *die;* **bacon ~:** Speckkuchen, *der*

quick [kwɪk] **1.** *adj.* **a)** schnell; kurz ‹*Rede, Zusammenfassung, Pause*›; flüchtig ‹*Kuß, Blick usw.*›; **it's ~er by train** mit dem Zug geht es schneller; **'that was/'you were ~!** das ging aber schnell!; **could I have a ~ word with you?** kann ich Sie kurz einmal sprechen?; **he had a ~ bite to eat** er hat schnell etwas gegessen; **how about a ~ drink?** wollen wir kurz einen trinken gehen? *(ugs.);* **write sb. a ~ note** jmdm. schnell ein paar Zeilen schreiben; **be ~!** mach schnell! *(ugs.);* beeil[e] dich!; **be ~ about it!** mach ein bißchen dalli! *(ugs.);* **please try to be ~ [about it]** *(in discussion, on telephone)* bitte fassen Sie sich kurz; **b)** *(ready, sensitive, prompt to act or understand)* schnell ‹*Person*›; wach ‹*Verstand*›; aufgeweckt ‹*Kind*›; **he is very ~:** er ist sehr schnell von Begriff *(ugs.);* **be ~ to do sth.** etw. schnell tun; **be ~ to take offence** schnell *od.* leicht beleidigt sein; **she is ~ to criticise** mit Kritik ist sie schnell bei der Hand; **be ~ at figures/repartee** schnell rechnen können/schlagfertig sein; **he's too ~ for me** mit ihm komme ich nicht mit; **have a ~ ear/eye** ein feines Ohr/scharfes Auge haben; **he has a ~ eye/ear for ...:** er hat ein Auge/Ohr für ...; **[have] a ~ temper** ein aufbrausendes Wesen [haben]; **have ~ wits** Köpfchen haben *(ugs.);* **c)** *(arch.: living, alive)* lebendig; **the ~ and the dead** die Lebenden und die Toten. **2.** *adv.* schnell; **~! [mach] schnell! 3.** *n.* empfindliches Fleisch; **bite one's nails to the ~:** die Nägel bis zum Fleisch abkauen; **be cut** *or* **hurt** *or* **stung** *etc.* **to the ~** *(fig.)* tief getroffen *od.* verletzt sein

quick: **~-acting** *attrib. adj.* schnell wirkend; **~-change** *attrib. adj.* *(Theatre)* Verwandlungs‹*künstler, -nummer*›

quicken ['kwɪkn] **1.** *v. t.* **a)** *(make quicker)* beschleunigen; **b)** *(animate)* lebendig machen; erwecken; **c)** *(stimulate, rouse, inspire)* beflügeln ‹*Phantasie, Begeisterung*›. **2.** *v. i.* **a)** *(become quicker)* sich beschleunigen; schneller werden; ‹*Herz*:› schneller schlagen; **her breath/steps ~ed** sie atmete/ging schneller; **b)** *(be stimulated, roused)* ‹*Hoffnung*:› sich regen *(geh.)*

quick: ~ **fire** *n.* *(Mil.)* Schnellfeuer, *das;* **~-fire questions** *(fig.)* Fragen wie aus dem Maschinengewehr; **~-firing** *adj.* *(Mil.)* Schnellfeuer-; **~-freeze** *v. t.* schnellgefrieren

quickie ['kwɪkɪ] *n. (coll.)* im Schnellverfahren hergestellte Sache; *(drink)* Schluck auf die Schnelle *(ugs.); (sexual intercourse)* eine Nummer auf die Schnelle *(salopp);* **be a ~:** im Schnellverfahren hergestellt sein

'**quicklime** *n.* ungelöschter Kalk

quickly ['kwɪklɪ] *adv.* schnell

'**quick march** *n. (Mil.)* Eilmarsch, *der*

quickness ['kwɪknɪs] *n., no pl.* **a)** *(speed)* Schnelligkeit, *die;* **the ~ of the hand deceives the eye** die Geschicklichkeit der Hand täuscht das Auge; **~ of action** schnelles Handeln; **b)** *(acuteness of perception)* Schärfe, *die;* **~ of the mind** schnelle Auffassungsgabe; **c)** *(hastiness)* **~ of temper** Hitzigkeit, *die;* aufbrausendes Wesen

quick: ~ one *n. (coll.)* Schluck auf die Schnelle *(ugs.);* **have a ~ one** schnell einen trinken [gehen]; *(sexually)* eine schnelle Nummer machen *(salopp);* **~sand** *n.* Treibsand, *der;* Mahlsand, *der (Seemannsspr.);* **~set** *n.* Heckenpflanze, *die; (hedge)* Hecke, *die;* **~-setting** *adj.* schnell trocknend ‹*Klebstoff*›; schnell bindend ‹*Zement*›; schnell gelierend ‹*Konfitüre usw.*›; **~silver** *n.* **a)** Quecksilber, *das;* **b)** *attrib. (fig.)* lebhaft; quecksilbrig; **have a ~silver temperament** Quecksilber im Leib haben *(ugs.);* **~ step** *n.* **a)** *(Mil.)* Eilschritt, *der;* **b)** *(Dancing)* Quickstep, *der;* **~-tempered** *adj.* hitzig; **be ~-tempered** leicht aufbrausen; **~thorn** *n. (Bot.)* Weißdorn, *der;* **~-witted** *adj.* geistesgegenwärtig; schlagfertig ‹*Antwort*›; **~-wittedness** [kwɪk'wɪtɪdnɪs] *n., no pl.* Geistesgegenwart, *die; (of answer)* Schlagfertigkeit, *die*

[1]**quid** [kwɪd] *n. (Brit. sl.)* **a)** *pl. same (one pound)* Pfund, *das;* **a few ~:** ein paar Möpse *od.* Flöhe *(salopp);* **fifty ~:** fünfzig Kugeln *(salopp);* **b) be ~s in** auf sein Geld kommen *(ugs.)*

[2]**quid** *n. (tobacco)* Priem, *der*

quid pro quo [kwɪd prəʊ 'kwəʊ] *n.* Gegenleistung, *die;* Quidproquo, *das (geh.)*

quiescence [kwɪ'esəns] *n.* Ruhe, *die*

quiescent [kwɪ'esənt] *adj.* still; untätig ‹*Vulkan*›

quiet ['kwaɪət] **1.** *adj.*, **~er** ['kwaɪətə(r)], **~est** ['kwaɪətɪst] **a)** *(silent)* still; *(not loud)* leise ‹*Schritte, Musik, Stimme, Motor, Fahrzeug*›; **be ~!** *(coll.)* sei still *od.* ruhig!; **~!** Ruhe!; **keep ~:** still sein; **keep sth. ~, keep ~ about sth.** *(fig.)* etw. geheimhalten; **I want the matter to be kept ~:** ich möchte, daß darüber Stillschweigen bewahrt wird; **keep sb./a child ~:** dafür sorgen, daß jmd. schweigt/ein Kind ruhig ist; **go ~:** still werden; **b)** *(peaceful, not busy)* ruhig; **a ~ evening at home** ein geruhsamer Abend zu Hause; **let's go for a ~ drink** gehen wir in aller Ruhe einen trinken; **have a ~ mind** beruhigt sein; **all was ~ on the border** an der Grenze herrschte Ruhe *od.* war alles ruhig; **c)** *(gentle)* sanft; ruhig ‹*Kind, Person*›; **d)** *(not overt, disguised)* versteckt; heimlich ‹*Groll*›; **have a ~ word with sb.** mit jmdm. unter vier Augen reden; **have a ~ laugh about sth.** im stillen über etw. *(Akk.)* lachen; **on the ~:** still und heimlich; **e)** *(not formal)* zwanglos; klein ‹*Feier*›; **f)** *(not showy)* dezent ‹*Farben, Muster*›; schlicht ‹*Eleganz, Stil*›. **2.** *n.* Ruhe, *die; (silence, stillness)* Stille, *die;* **in the ~ of the night** in der Stille der Nacht; *see also* **peace c. 3.** *v. t. see* **quieten 1**

quieten ['kwaɪətn] *(Brit.)* **1.** *v. t.* **a)** beruhigen; zur Ruhe bringen ‹*Kind, Schulklasse*›; **b)** zerstreuen ‹*Bedenken, Angst, Verdacht*›. **2.** *v. i.* sich beruhigen

~ 'down 1. *v. t. see* **~ 1 a. 2.** *v. i.* sich beruhigen; **since her marriage she has ~ed down** seit sie geheiratet hat, ist sie viel ruhiger geworden

quietism ['kwaɪətɪzm] *n.* Quietismus, *der*

quietly ['kwaɪətlɪ] *adv.* **a)** *(silently)* still; *(not loudly)* leise; **die ~:** eines sanften Todes sterben *(geh.);* **b)** *(peacefully, tranquilly)* ruhig; **be ~ drinking one's tea** in [aller] Ruhe seinen Tee trinken; **I'll come ~** *(said by person being arrested)* ich werde ohne Widerstand mitkommen; **c)** *(gently)* sanft; **a ~ spoken young man** ein ruhiger *od.* stiller junger Mann; **d)** *(not overtly)* insgeheim; **they settled the affair ~:** sie haben die Angelegenheit unter sich *(Dat.)* ausgemacht; **e)** *(not formally)* zwanglos; **get married ~:** im kleinen Rahmen heiraten; **f)** *(not showily)* dezent; schlicht

quietness ['kwaɪətnɪs] *n., no pl.* **a)** *(absence of noise or motion)* Stille, *die; (of reply)* Ruhe, *die; (of car, engine)* Geräuscharmut, *die; (of footsteps)* Geräusch-, Lautlosigkeit, *die;* **b)** *(peacefulness, gentleness)* Ruhe, *die*

quietude ['kwaɪətju:d] *n. (literary)* Stille, *die;* Frieden, *der (geh.)*

quiff [kwɪf] *n. (Brit.)* **a)** *(curl)* Stirnlocke, *die;* Schmachtlocke, *die (ugs.);* **b)** *(tuft of hair)* [Haar]tolle, *die (ugs.)*

quill [kwɪl] *n.* **a)** *see* **quill-feather; b)** *see* **quill-pen; c)** *(stem of feather)* [Feder]kiel, *der;* **d)** *(of porcupine)* Stachel, *der*

quill: ~-feather *n.* Kielfeder, *die;* **~-pen** *n.* [Feder]kiel, *der*

quilt [kwɪlt] **1.** *n.* **a)** *(padded bed-coverlet)* Schlafdecke, *die;* **continental ~:** Steppdecke, *die;* **b)** *(bedspread)* Tagesdecke, *die; see also* **crazy d; patchwork. 2.** *v. t.* **a)** *(cover or line with padded material)* wattieren; **b)** *(make or join like ~)* steppen

quilting ['kwɪltɪŋ] *n.* **a)** *(process)* Steppen, *das;* **b)** *(material)* gesteppter Stoff

quin [kwɪn] *n. (coll.)* Fünfling, *der*

quince [kwɪns] *n.* **a)** *(fruit)* Quitte, *die;* **b)** *(tree)* Quittenbaum, *der; see also* **Japanese quince**

quince 'jelly *n.* Quittengelee, *das*

quinine ['kwɪni:n, kwɪ'ni:n] *n.* Chinin, *das*

quinquennial [kwɪŋ'kwenɪəl] *adj. (lasting five years)* fünfjährig; *(once every five years)* fünfjährlich

quinquennium [kwɪŋ'kwenɪəm] *n., pl.* **~s** *or* **quinquennia** [kwɪŋ'kwenɪə] Jahrfünft, *das*

quinsy ['kwɪnzɪ] *n. (Med.)* Mandelentzündung, *die*

quintessence [kwɪn'tesəns] *n.* **a)** *(most perfect form)* Quintessenz, *die; (embodiment)* Inbegriff, *der;* **b)** *(essence, extract of substance)* Extrakt, *der*

quintessential [kwɪntɪ'senʃl] *adj.* typisch; wesentlich

quintet, quintette [kwɪn'tet] *n. (also Mus.)* Quintett, *das;* **piano/clarinet ~:** Klavier-/Klarinettenquintett, *das*

quintuple ['kwɪntjʊpl] **1.** *adj.* fünffach. **2.** *n.* Fünffache, *das.* **3.** *v. t.* verfünffachen. **4.** *v. i.* sich verfünffachen

quintuplet ['kwɪntjʊplɪt, kwɪn'tju:plɪt] *n.* Fünfling, *der*

quip [kwɪp] **1.** *n.* **a)** *(clever saying)* Witzelei, *die;* Geistreichelei, *die (scherzh. abwertend);* **b)** *(sarcastic remark)* Bissigkeit, *die.* **2.** *v. i.*, **-pp-** *(make quips)* witzeln (**at** über + *Akk.*); geistreicheln *(scherzh. abwertend)*

quire [kwaɪə(r)] *n. (Bookbinding: collection of sheets)* Lage, *die; (24/25 sheets)* 24/25 Bögen Papier; *(4 sheets) 4 zu 8 Blättern gefaltete Bögen;* **in ~s** ungebunden

quirk [kw3:k] *n.* Marotte, *die;* Schrulle, *die (ugs.);* **[by a] ~ of nature/fate/history** *etc.* [durch eine] Laune der Natur/des Schicksals/der Geschichte *usw.*

quirky ['kw3:kɪ] *adj.* schrullig *(ugs.)*

quisling ['kwɪzlɪŋ] *n.* Quisling, *der (abwertend)*

quit [kwɪt] **1.** *pred. adj.* **be ~ of sb./sth.** jmds./einer Sache ledig sein *(geh.).* **2.** *v. t.*, **-tt-**, *(Amer.)* **quit a)** *(give up)* aufgeben; *(cease, stop)* aufhören mit; **~ doing sth.** aufhören, etw. zu tun; **b)** *(depart from)* verlassen; *(leave occupied premises)* ausziehen aus; *abs.* ausziehen; **give notice to ~ [the flat** *etc.***]** [die Wohnung *usw.*] kündigen; **they had** *or* **were given notice to ~ [the flat** *etc.***]** ihnen wurde [die Wohnung *usw.*] gekündigt; **~ hold of sth.** etw. loslassen; **c)** *also abs. (from job)* kündigen

quitch-[grass] ['kwɪtʃ (grɑ:s)] *see* [2]**couch**

quite [kwaɪt] *adv.* **a)** *(entirely)* ganz; völlig; vollkommen; gänzlich ‹*unnötig*›; fest ‹*entschlossen*›; **not ~** *(almost)* nicht ganz; *(noticeably not)* nicht gerade; **I'm sorry – That's ~ all right** Entschuldigung – Schon gut *od.* in Ordnung; **not ~ five o'clock** noch nicht ganz 5 Uhr; **I don't need any help; I'm ~ all right, thank you** danke, es geht schon, ich komme allein zurecht; **I've had ~ enough of it** jetzt habe ich aber genug davon; **how can you be ~ so sure?** wie kannst du so sicher sein?; **I've never known anyone who was ~ so stubborn** ich kenne niemanden, der so stur wie er/sie ist; **I ~ agree/understand** ganz meine Meinung/ich verstehe schon; **~ [so]!** [ja,] genau *od.* richtig!; **be ~ a hero** wirklich ein Idol sein; **that is ~ a different matter** das ist etwas ganz anderes *od.* schon etwas anderes; **we drove at ~ a speed** wir sind vielleicht schnell gefahren *(ugs.);* **they had ~ a party** sie haben vielleicht gefeiert *(ugs.);* **be ~ other than sth.** ‹*Wahrheit, Ansicht:*› sich deutlich von etw. unterscheiden; **~ another story/case** eine ganz andere Geschichte/ein ganz anderer Fall; **b)** *(somewhat, to some extent)* ziemlich; recht; ganz ‹*gern*›; **it was ~ an effort** es war ziemlich *od.* recht anstrengend; **that is ~ a shock/surprise** das ist ein ziemlicher Schock/eine ziemliche Überraschung; **I'd ~ like to talk to him** ich würde ganz gern mit ihm sprechen; **~ a few** ziemlich viele *od.* eine ganze Menge ‹*Bücher, Preise, Urteile*›; **they had ~ a lot of applicants/a run of success** sie hatten eine ziemlich große Anzahl von Kandidaten/sie waren ziemlich lange [Zeit] erfolgreich

quits [kwɪts] *pred. adj.* **be ~ [with sb.]** [mit jmdm.] quitt sein *(ugs.);* **call it ~:** ‹*Einzelperson:*› zustimmen *od.* Ruhe geben; ‹*mehrere Personen:*› sich vertragen; **let's call it ~!** wollen wir die Sache auf sich beruhen lassen!; *(nothing owed)* sagen wir, wir sind quitt; *see also* **double 3 c**

quitter ['kwɪtə(r)] *n.* Drückeberger, *der*/Drückebergerin, *die (ugs. abwertend)*

[1]**quiver** ['kwɪvə(r)] **1.** *v. i.* zittern (**with** vor + *Dat.*); ‹*Stimme, Lippen:*› beben *(geh.);* ‹*Lid:*› zucken; ‹*Stimme:*› vibrieren; **her legs ~ed** ihr zitterten die Beine; ihre Beine zitterten. **2.** *n.* Zittern, *das; (of lips, voice also)* Beben, *das (geh.); (of eyelid)* Zucken, *das;* **there was a ~ in her voice** ihre Stimme zitterte *od. (geh.)* bebte; **be all in a ~:** am ganzen Körper zittern

[2]**quiver** *n. (for arrows)* Köcher, *der*

qui vive [ki: 'vi:v] *n.* **be on the ~:** auf dem Quivive sein *(ugs.);* wachsam sein

quixotic [kwɪk'sɒtɪk] *adj.* lebensfremd ‹*Person, Ideal*›; idealistisch ‹*Verhalten*›; **a ~ act** eine Donquichotterie; **a ~ person** ein Don Quichotte *od.* Quixote *od.* Quijote

quiz [kwɪz] **1.** *n., pl.* **~zes a)** *(Radio, Telev., etc.)* Quiz, *das;* Ratespiel, *das;* **contestants in/guests on the ~:** Quizteilnehmer *Pl.;* **b)** *(interrogation, questionnaire, test)* Prüfung, *die; (for pupils)* Aufgabe, *die.* **2.** *v. t.*, **-zz-** ausfragen (**about sth.** nach etw., **about sb.** über jmdn.), fragen (**about** nach); ‹*Polizei:*› verhören, vernehmen ‹*Verdächtige*›

quiz: ~-master *n. (Radio, Telev.)* Quizmaster, *der;* Spielleiter, *der;* **~ programme, ~ show** *ns. (Radio, Telev.)* Quizsendung, *die*

quizzical ['kwɪzɪkl] *adj.* fragend ‹*Blick, Miene*›; *(mocking)* spöttisch ‹*Lächeln*›

quizzically ['kwɪzɪkəlɪ] *adv.* fragend ‹*blicken*›; *(mocking)* spöttisch ‹*lächeln*›

quoin [kɔɪn] *n.* **a)** *(angle)* Ecke, *die;* **b)** *(corner-stone)* Eckstein, *der*
quoit [kɔɪt] *n. (Games)* [Gummi]ring, *der*
quoits [kɔɪts] *n., no pl. (Games)* Ringtennis, *das*
quorate ['kwɔ:reɪt] *adj.* beschlußfähig
quorum ['kwɔ:rəm] *n.* Quorum, *das*
quota ['kwəʊtə] *n.* **a)** *(share)* Anteil, *der;* **b)** *(maximum quantity)* Höchstquote, *die; (of goods to be produced/imported)* maximale Produktions-/Einfuhrquote; *(quantity of goods to be produced)* Produktionsmindestquote, *die; (of work)* [Arbeits]pensum, *das;* **c)** *(maximum number)* Höchstquote, *die; (of immigrants/students permitted)* maximale Einwanderungs-/Zulassungsquote
quotation [kwəʊ'teɪʃn] *n.* **a)** Zitieren, *das;* Zitate *Pl.; (passage)* Zitat, *das;* **dictionary of ~s** Zitatenlexikon, *das;* **b)** *(amount stated as current price)* [Börsen]kurs, *der;* Quotation, *die (fachspr.);* [Börsen-, Kurs]notierung, *die;* **c)** *(contractor's estimate)* Kosten[vor]anschlag, *der;* Kalkulation, *die*
quo'tation-marks *n. pl.* Anführungszeichen *Pl.*
quote [kwəʊt] **1.** *v. t.* **a)** *also abs.* zitieren **(from** aus); zitieren aus ⟨*Buch, Text, Klassiker, Übersetzung*⟩; *(appeal to)* sich berufen auf (+ *Akk.*) ⟨*Person, Buch, Text, Quelle*⟩; *(mention)* anführen ⟨*Vorkommnis, Beispiel*⟩; **he is ~d as saying that ...:** er soll gesagt haben, daß ...; **don't ~ me on it** sagen Sie nicht, daß Sie das von mir haben; **~ an earlier case to sb.** jmdm. einen früheren Fall nennen; **~ sth. as the reason/an example** etw. als Grund/Beispiel anführen; **..., and I ~, ...:** ... ich zitiere, ...; **b)** *(state price of)* angeben, nennen ⟨*Preis*⟩; quotieren *(fachspr.);* **wheat/the £ is ~d at ...:** der Weizenpreis/Pfundkurs wird mit ... angegeben; **~ sb. a price** jmdm. einen Preis nennen; **c)** *(St. Exch.)* notieren ⟨*Aktie*⟩; **be ~d at a lower price** niedriger notiert werden; **d)** *(enclose in quotation-marks)* in Anführungszeichen *(Akk.)* setzen; **..., ~, ...:** ..., Zitat, ... **2.** *n. (coll.)* **a)** *(passage)* Zitat, *das;* **b)** *(commercial quotation)* Kosten[vor]anschlag, *der;* Kalkulation, *die;* **c)** *usu. in pl. (quotation-mark)* Anführungszeichen, *das;* Gänsefüßchen, *das (ugs.)*
quoth [kwəʊθ] *v. t. 1st & 3rd pers. p. t. (arch.) in sing./pl.* sprach/sprachen *(geh.)*
quotient ['kwəʊʃnt] *n. (Math.)* Quotient, *der; see also* **intelligence quotient**
q.v. [kju:'vi:] *abbr.* **quod vide** s. d.

R

R, r [ɑ:(r)] *n., pl.* **Rs** *or* **R's** **a)** *(letter)* R, r, *das;* **b) the three Rs** Lesen, Schreiben und Rechnen; **c) the R months** die Monate mit r
R. *abbr.* **a) River** Fl.; **R. Thames** die Themse; **b) Regina/Rex** Königin, *die*/König, *der;* **in the case R. v. Smith** in der Sache der Königin/des Königs gegen Smith; **c)** ® **registered as trademark** ®; ⓦ; **d)** *(Amer.)* **Republican; e)** *(Chess)* **rook** T
r. *abbr.* **right** re.
RA *abbr.* **a) Royal Academician** Mitglied der „Royal Academy"; **b) Royal Academy** *see* **academy a; c) Royal Artillery** Königl. Art.
rabbet ['ræbɪt] *n. (groove)* Falz, *der; (to receive edge of door or window)* Anschlag, *der*
rabbi ['ræbaɪ] *n.* Rabbi[ner], *der; (as title)* Rabbi, *der;* **Chief R~:** Oberrabbiner, *der*
rabbit ['ræbɪt] **1.** *n.* **a)** Kaninchen, *das;* **b)** *(Brit. coll.: poor player)* Flasche, *die (ugs.);* Niete, *die (ugs.);* **c)** *(Amer.: hare)* Hase, *der. See also* **breed 2 a; Welsh rabbit. 2.** *v. i. (Brit. coll.: talk)* ~ **[on]** sülzen *(salopp);* quatschen *(salopp)*
rabbit: ~-burrow *n.* Kaninchenbau, *der;* Kaninchenhöhle, *die;* **~-food** *n.* Kaninchenfutter, *das; (fig. joc.)* Grünzeug, *das;* Kaninchenfutter, *das (scherzh.);* **~-fur** *n.* Kaninchenfell, *das;* Kanin, *das (fachspr.); (coat)* Kaninmantel, *der;* **~-hole** *see* **~-burrow; ~-hutch** *n. (lit. or fig. joc.)* Kaninchenstall, *der;* **~ punch** *n.* Rabbitpunch, *der (Boxen);* Genickschlag, *der;* **~-warren** *n.* Kaninchengehege, *das;* **this building is a ~-warren** dieses Gebäude ist das reinste Labyrinth
rabble ['ræbl] *n.* Mob, *der (abwertend);* Pöbel, *der (abwertend)*
rabble: ~-rouser ['ræblraʊzə(r)] *n.* Aufwiegler, *der*/Aufwieglerin, *die;* [Auf]hetzer, *der*/[Auf]hetzerin, *die;* **~-rousing 1.** *adj.* aufwieglerisch, [auf]hetzerisch ⟨*Rede, Wort*⟩; **2.** *n.* [Auf]hetzerei, *die;* Aufwiegelei, *die*
Rabelaisian [ræbə'leɪzjən] *adj.* Rabelaisisch ⟨*Stil, Sprachreichtum*⟩
rabid ['ræbɪd] *adj.* **a)** *([Vet.] Med.)* tollwütig ⟨*Tier, Person*⟩; Tollwut⟨*symptom, -erreger, -virus*⟩; **b)** *(furious, violent)* wild ⟨*Haß, Wut*⟩; *(unreasoning, extreme)* fanatisch ⟨*Demokrat, Reformer, Anhänger, Befürworter, Antisemitismus*⟩
rabies ['reɪbi:z] *n. ([Vet.] Med.)* Tollwut, *die;* Rabies, *die (fachspr.)*
RAC *abbr. (Brit.)* **Royal Automobile Club** Königlicher Britischer Automobilklub
raccoon *see* **racoon**
[1]**race** [reɪs] **1.** *n.* **a)** Rennen, *das; (Swimming)* Turnier, *das;* **have a ~ [with** *or* **against sb.]** mit jmdm. um die Wette laufen/schwimmen/reiten *usw.;* **100 metres ~:** 100-m-Rennen/-Schwimmen, *das;* **be in the ~** *(lit. or fig.)* gut im Rennen liegen; **be out of the ~** ⟨*Läufer, Schwimmer, Reiter usw.:*⟩ ausgeschieden sein; *(fig.)* ⟨*Bewerber:*⟩ nicht mehr im Rennen sein; **b)** *in pl. (series) (for horses)* Pferderennen, *das; (for dogs)* Hunderennen, *das;* **go to the ~s** zum Rennen gehen; **a day at the ~s** ein Tag auf der Rennbahn; **c)** *(fig.)* **a ~ against time** ein Wettlauf mit der Zeit; **sb.'s** *or* **the ~ is [nearly] run** *(after pursuit)* jmd. ist verloren; *(after severe illness, euphem.)* jmds. Zeit ist gekommen *(geh. verhüll.);* **the ~ for governor/nomination** das Rennen um den Gouverneursposten/die Nominierung; **it will be a mad ~ to get the work finished in time** es wird eine wahnsinnige Hetze werden, die Arbeit rechtzeitig fertig zu bekommen; **d)** *(channel of stream)* Gerinne, *das (veralt.); see also* **mill-race; e)** *(Mech. Engin.: of ball-bearing)* Ring, *der.* **2.** *v. i.* **a)** *(in swimming, running, walking, sailing, etc.)* um die Wette schwimmen/laufen/gehen/segeln *usw.* **(with, against** mit); **~ against time** ⟨*Läufer:*⟩ gegen die Uhr laufen; *(fig.)* gegen die Uhr *od.* Zeit arbeiten; **b)** *(indulge in horse-racing)* dem Pferderennsport frönen; *(Sports: in car)* Autorennen fahren; **~ at a meeting** *(own or train horses for it)* bei einem Rennen Pferde laufen lassen; **c)** *(go at full or excessive speed)* ⟨*Motor:*⟩ durchdrehen; ⟨*Puls:*⟩ jagen, rasen; **d)** *(rush)* sich sehr beeilen; hetzen; ⟨*Wolken:*⟩ jagen; *(on foot also)* rennen; jagen; **~ after sb.** jmdm. hinterherhetzen; **~ [a]round** *or* **about** herumhetzen; hin und her hetzen; **~ to finish sth.** sich beeilen, um etw. fertigzukriegen *(ugs.);* **~ ahead with sth.** *(hurry)* etw. im Eiltempo vorantreiben *(ugs.); (make rapid progress)* bei etw. mit Riesenschritten vorankommen *(ugs.).* **3.** *v. t.* **a)** *(have ~ with) (in swimming, riding, walking, running, etc.)* um die Wette schwimmen/reiten/gehen/laufen *usw.* mit; **I'll ~ you** ich mache mit dir einen Wettlauf; **b)** *(cause to ~)* ⟨*Fahrer:*⟩ rasen mit *(ugs.)* ⟨*Auto, Kajak usw.*⟩; ⟨*Steuermann:*⟩ sehr schnell fahren mit ⟨*Schiff*⟩; **c)** hochjagen *(salopp)* ⟨*Motor*⟩; **~ sb. along** jmdn. vorwärts hetzen *(ugs.)*
[2]**race** *n.* **a)** *(Anthrop., Biol.)* Rasse, *die;* **be of mixed ~:** gemischtrassig *od.* -rassisch sein; **b)** *(class of persons)* Klasse, *die; (esp. Relig.)* Kaste, *die;* **c)** *(group with common descent)* Geschlecht, *das;* Sippe, *die; (nation)* Volk, *das; (tribe)* Volk, *das;* Stamm, *der;* **the human ~:** die Menschheit; die Menschen; **be of noble ~:** vornehmer Abkunft *(geh.) od.* Abstammung sein
race: ~card *n.* Rennprogramm, *das;* **~course** *n.* Rennbahn, *die;* **~goer** *n.* Rennbesucher, *der*/-besucherin, *die;* **~ hatred** *n.* Rassenhaß, *der;* **~horse** *n.* Rennpferd, *das*
raceme [rə'si:m] *n. (Bot.)* Blütentraube, *die*
'race-meeting *n. (Sport)* Renntag, *der; (on successive days)* Renntage *Pl.*
racer ['reɪsə(r)] *n. (person)* Läufer, *der*/Läuferin, *die; (horse)* Rennpferd, *das;* Renner, *der; (yacht)* Rennjacht, *die; (bicycle)* Rennrad, *das;* Rennmaschine, *die; (car)* Rennwagen, *der; (plane)* Sportflugzeug, *das*
race: ~ relations *n. pl.* Beziehung zwischen den Rassen; **R~ Relations Act** *(Brit.)* Gesetz gegen Rassendiskriminierung; **~-riot** *n.* Rassenkrawall, *der;* **~-track** *n.* Rennbahn, *die;* **~way** *n. (Amer.)* Trabrennbahn, *die*
rachitic [rə'kɪtɪk] *adj. (Med.)* rachitisch
rachitis [rə'kaɪtɪs] *n. (Med.)* Rachitis, *die*
racial ['reɪʃl] *adj.* Rassen⟨*diskriminierung, -konflikt, -gleichheit, -vorurteil, -unruhen, -stolz*⟩; rassisch ⟨*Gruppe, Minderheit*⟩; **~ attack/assault** rassistischer Angriff/Überfall; **~ harmony** Eintracht unter den Rassen; **Commission for R~ Equality** *(Brit.)* Kommission für Rassengleichheit
racialism ['reɪʃəlɪzm] *n., no pl.* Rassismus, *der*
racialist ['reɪʃəlɪst] **1.** *n.* Rassist, *der*/Rassistin, *die.* **2.** *adj.* rassistisch
racially ['reɪʃəlɪ] *adv.* rassisch; **be ~ prejudiced** Rassenvorurteile haben
racily ['reɪsɪlɪ] *adv.* **a)** flott ⟨*erzählen, schreiben*⟩; pikant ⟨*gewürzt*⟩; kraftvoll ⟨*gestaltet*⟩; **b)** *(Amer.: in a risqué manner)* gewagt ⟨*erzählen, sich kleiden*⟩
racing ['reɪsɪŋ] *n., no pl., no indef. art.* **a)** *(profession, sport)* Rennsport, *der; (with horses)* Pferdesport, *der;* **b)** *(races)* Rennen *Pl.;* **go ~** *(attend horse/motor races)* zum Rennen gehen; **it is a ~ certainty that he will ...:** mit größter Wahrscheinlichkeit wird er ...
racing: ~-bicycle *n.* Rennrad, *das;* Rennmaschine, *die;* **~-car** *n.* Rennwagen, *der;* **~ colours** *n. pl.* Rennfarben *Pl.;* **~ driver** *n.* Rennfahrer, *der*/-fahrerin, *die;* **~-track** *n.* Rennbahn, *die*
racism ['reɪsɪzm] *n.* Rassismus, *der*
racist ['reɪsɪst] **1.** *n.* Rassist, *der*/Rassistin, *die.* **2.** *adj.* rassistisch
[1]**rack** [ræk] **1.** *n.* **a)** *(for luggage in bus, train, etc.)* Ablage, *die; (for pipes, hats, spectacles, toast, plates)* Ständer, *der; (for tools)* Regal, *das; (on bicycle, motor cycle)* Gepäckträger, *der; (on car)* Dachgepäckträger, *der;* **b)** *(for fodder)* Raufe, *die;* **c)** *(instrument of torture)* Folter[bank], *die;* **put sb. on the ~:** jmdn. auf die Folter legen; *(fig.)* ⟨*Problem, Ungewißheit:*⟩ jmdn. quälen; **be on the ~** *(lit. or*

fig.) Folterqualen leiden; **d)** *(Mech. Engin.)* Zahnstange, *die;* ~ **and pinion** Zahntrieb, *der.* **2.** *v. t.* **a)** *(lit. or fig.: torture)* quälen, plagen; **be ~ed by** *or* **with pain** *etc.* von Schmerzen *usw.* gequält und geplagt werden; **b)** *(shake violently)* ‹*Husten, Vibration:*› erschüttern, heftig schütteln ‹*Körper*›; **c)** ~ **one's brain[s]** *(fig.)* sich *(Dat.)* den Kopf zerbrechen *od.* das Hirn zermartern *(ugs.)* **(for** über + *Akk.*)

~ **'up** *v. t. (Amer.: achieve)* machen *(ugs.)*, erzielen ‹*Punkte*›; kriegen *(ugs.)* ‹*Preis*›

[2]rack *n. (joint of lamb etc.)* vorderes Rippenstück [vom Lamm *usw.*]

[3]rack *see* **ruin 1 a**

[4]rack *v. t.* ~ **[off]** abziehen ‹*Wein, Bier*› **(into** auf + *Akk.*)

[1]racket ['rækɪt] *n.* **a)** *(Sport)* Schläger, *der; (Tennis also)* Racket, *das;* **b)** *in pl., usu. constr. as sing. (ball game)* Raquets, *das;* Racquetball, *der*

[2]racket *n.* **a)** *(disturbance, uproar)* Lärm, *der;* Krach, *der;* **make a ~:** Krach *od.* Lärm machen; **they kicked up no end of a ~** *(coll.)* sie machten einen Höllenlärm *(ugs.);* **b)** *(dishonest scheme)* Schwindelgeschäft, *das (ugs.);* **a narcotics** *or* **drug ~:** krimineller Drogenhandel; **c)** *(sl.: line of business)* Job, *der (ugs.);* **I'm in the insurance ~:** ich mache in Versicherungen *(salopp)*

racketeer [rækɪ'tɪə(r)] *n.* Ganove, *der; (profiteer)* Wucherer, *der;* **drug ~:** Drogenhändler, *der*/-händlerin, *die;* Dealer, *der*/Dealerin, *die (ugs.)*

racketeering [rækɪ'tɪərɪŋ] *n.* kriminelle Geschäfte *Pl.;* Schwindel, *der; (profiteering)* Wucher, *der*

'racket-press *n. (Sport)* Spanner, *der*

racking ['rækɪŋ] *attrib. adj.* quälend

rack: ~-railway *n.* Zahnrad-, Zahnstangenbahn, *die;* **~-rent** *n. (excessive rent)* überhöhte Miete; Wuchermiete, *die (abwertend)*

raconteur [rækɒn'tɜ:(r)] *n.* Geschichten-, Anekdotenerzähler, *der*/-erzählerin, *die*

racoon [rə'ku:n] *n. (Zool.)* Waschbär, *der*

racquet *see* **[1]racket**

racy ['reɪsɪ] *adj.* **a)** flott *(ugs.)*, schwungvoll ‹*Erzählweise, Stil, Sprache*›; schwungvoll ‹*Rede*›; pikant ‹*Aroma*›; saftig *(ugs.)* ‹*Humor*›; rassig ‹*Traubensorte, Wein*›; **b)** *(Amer.: risqué)* gewagt, pikant ‹*Geschichte, Anekdote*›

rad [ræd] *n. (Phys.)* Rad, *das*

RADA [ɑ:reɪdi:'eɪ, *(coll.)* 'rɑ:də] *abbr. (Brit.)* **Royal Academy of Dramatic Art** RADA; Königliche Schauspielakademie

radar ['reɪdɑ:(r)] *n.* Radar, *das od. der*

radar: ~ operator *n.* Radartechniker, *der*/-technikerin, *die;* ~ **scanner** *n.* Radarantenne, *die;* ~ **screen** *n.* Radarschirm, *der;* ~ **trap** *n.* Radarfalle, *die (ugs.)*

radial ['reɪdɪəl] **1.** *adj.* **a)** *(arranged like rays or radii)* strahlenförmig angeordnet; radiär *(fachspr.);* strahlig, strahlenförmig ‹*Muster*›; **b)** *(acting or moving from centre)* radial ‹*Durchfluß, Dispersion, Bahn*›; Radial‹*bohrmaschine, -beschleunigung*›; **c)** *(having spokes or radiating lines)* strahlenförmig ‹*Bauform*›; ~ **wheel** Radialrad, *das;* **d)** *(Anat.)* Speichen‹*nerv, -vene*›; ~ **artery** Speichenarterie, *die;* Puls[schlag]ader, *die (volkst.).* **2.** *n.* Radial-, Gürtelreifen, *der*

'radial engine *n.* Sternmotor, *der*

radially ['reɪdɪəlɪ] *adv.* strahlenförmig; radial *(fachspr.)*

radial: ~[-ply] tyre *n.* Radial-, Gürtelreifen, *der*

radian ['reɪdɪən] *n. (Geom.)* Radiant, *der*

radiance ['reɪdɪəns], **radiancy** ['reɪdɪənsɪ] *n.* **a)** *(emission of light rays etc.)* Leuchten, *das; (of sun, stars, lamp also)* Strahlen, *das;* **b)** *(joyful, hopeful, etc. appearance)* Strahlen, *das;* ~ **of joy/hope** freudiges/hoffnungsvolles Strahlen

radiant ['reɪdɪənt] **1.** *adj.* **a)** strahlend, leuchtend ‹*Himmelskörper, Dämmerung*›; leuchtend ‹*Lichtstrahl*›; ~ **colours** leuchtende Farben; **b)** *(fig.)* strahlend; fröhlich ‹*Stimmung*›; **be ~** ‹*Person, Augen:*› strahlen **(with** vor + *Dat.*). **2.** *n.* **a)** *(on electric or gas heater)* Heizfläche, *die;* **b)** *(Astron.)* Radiant, *der*

radiant: ~ heat *n.* Strahlungswärme, *die;* ~ **heater** *n.* Heizstrahler, *der*

radiantly ['reɪdɪəntlɪ] *adv.* **a)** leuchtend; strahlend; **shine ~** ‹*Sonne, Sterne:*› leuchten; ‹*Lichtquelle:*› strahlen; **b)** *(fig.)* strahlend; **be ~ beautiful** von strahlender Schönheit sein

radiate ['reɪdɪeɪt] **1.** *v. i.* **a)** ‹*Sonne, Sterne:*› scheinen, strahlen; ‹*Glas, Metall:*› leuchten, glänzen; ‹*Kerze:*› scheinen; ‹*Hitze, Wärme:*› ausstrahlen, sich verbreiten; ‹*Schein, Radiowellen:*› ausgesendet werden, ausgehen **(from** von); ‹*Lichtstrahl:*› leuchten; **b)** *(diverge or spread from central point)* strahlenförmig ausgehen **(from** von). **2.** *v. t.* **a)** verbreiten, ausstrahlen ‹*Licht, Wärme, Klang*›; aussenden ‹*Strahlen, Wellen*›; **b)** ausstrahlen ‹*Glück, Liebe, Hoffnung, Gesundheit, Fröhlichkeit*›; *(spread as from centre)* verbreiten ‹*Liebe, Heiterkeit usw.*› **(around** um ... herum)

radiation [reɪdɪ'eɪʃn] *n.* **a)** *(emission of energy)* Emission, *die; (of signals)* Ausstrahlung, *die;* **b)** *(energy transmitted)* Strahlung, *die;* Strahlenemission, *die;* **solar ~:** Sonneneinstrahlung, *die;* ~ **from a coal fire** Wärmestrahlung eines Kohleofens; **contaminated by ~:** strahlenverseucht; **c)** *attrib.* Strahlen‹*behandlung, -therapie, -krankheit, -belastung, -dosis, -verseuchung, -zählrohr, -chemie*›; Strahlungs‹*intensität, -leistung, -meßgerät, -energie, -verbrennung, -niveau*›; ~ **leak[age]** Leckstrahlung, *die*

radiator ['reɪdɪeɪtə(r)] *n.* **a)** *(for heating a room)* [Rippen]heizkörper, *der;* Radiator, *der; (portable)* Heizgerät, *das;* Heizstrahler, *der;* **b)** *(for cooling engine)* Kühler, *der*

radiator: ~ cap *n.* Kühlverschraubung, *die;* Kühlerverschlußdeckel, *der;* ~ **grille** *n.* Kühlergrill, *der;* Kühlerschutzgitter, *das;* ~ **mascot** *n.* Kühlerfigur, *die*

radical ['rædɪkl] **1.** *adj.* **a)** *(thorough, drastic; also Polit.)* radikal; drastisch, radikal ‹*Maßnahme*›; umwälzend ‹*Auswirkungen*›; durchgreifend ‹*Umstrukturierung, Veränderung usw.*›; *(Brit. Hist.)* radikal; extrem liberal; *(Amer. Hist.)* radikal [republikanisch]; **a ~ cure** eine Radikalkur; **b)** *(progressive, unorthodox)* radikal; revolutionär ‹*Stil, Design, Sprachgebrauch*›; **c)** *(inherent, fundamental)* grundlegend ‹*Fehler, Unterschied*›; **d)** *(Med.)* ~ **surgery** Radikaloperation, *die;* **e)** *(Bot., Ling., Math.)* Wurzel-. **2.** *n.* **a)** *(Polit.)* Radikale, *der/die;* **b)** *(Math.) (quantity)* Wurzelausdruck, *der;* Radikal, *das (fachspr.); (radical sign)* Wurzelzeichen, *das;* **c)** *(Chem.)* Radikal, *das*

radical 'chic *n.* linke Schickeria

radicalism ['rædɪkəlɪzm] *n., no pl. (Polit.)* Radikalismus, *der*

radically ['rædɪkəlɪ] *adv.* **a)** *(thoroughly, drastically)* radikal; von Grund auf; **b)** *(Polit.)* radikal; **c)** *(originally, basically)* prinzipiell; **d)** *(inherently, fundamentally)* von Grund auf

radicchio [rə'dɪkjəʊ] *n., no pl.* Radicchio, *der*

radicle ['rædɪkl] *n. (Bot.) (part of embryo)* Keimwurzel, *die;* Radicula, *die (fachspr.); (rootlet)* Würzelchen, *das*

radio ['reɪdɪəʊ] **1.** *n., pl.* **~s a)** *no pl., no indef. art.* Funk, *der; (for private communication)* Sprechfunk, *der;* **over the/by ~:** über/per Funk; **b)** *no pl., no indef. art. (Broadcasting)* Rundfunk, *der;* Hörfunk, *der;* **listen to the ~:** Radio hören; **on the ~:** im Radio *od.* Rundfunk; **commercial ~:** Werbefunk, *der;* **work in ~:** beim Rundfunk arbeiten; **c)** *(apparatus)* Radio, *das;* ~ **[equipment]** Funk[sprech]gerät, *das;* **d)** *(broadcasting station)* Rundfunk- *od.* Radiosender, *der;* **R~ Luxembourg** Radio Luxemburg; **R~ One** Erstes [Rundfunk]programm. **2.** *attrib. adj.* **a)** *(Broadcasting)* Rundfunk‹*antenne, -gerät, -empfänger, -sender, -sendung, -sprecher, -interview, -programm, -übertragung, -techniker, -technik*›; Radio‹*gerät, -sendung, -programm, -welle*›; Sende‹*antenne, -mast, -erlaubnis*›; Funk‹*mast, -turm, -frequenz, -verbindung, -verkehr, -netz, -taxi, -gerät, -wagen*›; ~ **beam** Leitfunkstrahl, *der;* Richtstrahl, *der;* ~ **frequency** Hochfrequenz, *die;* ~ **drama** *or* **play** Hörspiel, *das;* **b)** *(Astron.)* Radio‹*astronomie, -galaxis, -teleskop*›. *See also* **fix 4 b; ham 1 c. 3.** *v. t.* funken ‹*Meldung, Nachricht*›; durch *od.* per Funk übermitteln; ~ **sb. for sth.** von jmdm. über Funk etw. anfordern. **4.** *v. i.* funken; eine Funkmeldung *od.* einen Funkspruch übermitteln *od.* durchgeben; **the ship ~ed for help** das Schiff bat über Funk um Hilfe

radio: ~'active *adj.* radioaktiv; **~ac'tivity** *n.* Radioaktivität, *die;* ~ **beacon** *n.* Funkfeuer, *das;* **~-bi'ology** *n.* Strahlenbiologie, *die;* Radiobiologie, *die;* **~-'carbon** *n.* Radiokohlenstoff, *der;* Karbon-14, *das;* **~-carbon dating** *n.* Radiokarbondatierung, *die;* **~-'chemistry** *n.* Radiochemie, *die;* Strahlenchemie, *die;* ~ **control** *n.* Funk[fern]steuerung, *die;* **~-controlled** *adj.* funkgesteuert; ferngesteuert; **~-frequency 1.** *n.* Hochfrequenz, *die;* **2.** *adj.* Hochfrequenz-

radiogram ['reɪdɪəʊgræm] *n.* **a)** *(Brit.)* ≈ Musiktruhe, *die;* **b)** *see* **radiograph 1**

radiograph ['reɪdɪəgrɑ:f] **1.** *n.* Röntgenaufnahme, *die;* Radiogramm, *das (fachspr.).* **2.** *v. t.* eine Röntgenaufnahme/ein Radiogramm machen von

radiographer [reɪdɪ'ɒgrəfə(r)] *n.* Röntgenologe, *der*/Röntgenologin, *die; (instrument-operator)* Röntgenassistent, *der*/-assistentin, *die*

radiographic [reɪdɪə'græfɪk] *adj.* röntgenographisch; radiographisch

radiography [reɪdɪ'ɒgrəfɪ] *n.* Radiographie, *die;* Röntgenographie, *die*

radio: ~'isotope *n.* Radioisotop, *das;* radioaktives Isotop; ~ **lo'cation** *n.* Funkortung, *die;* Radar, *der od. das*

radiological [reɪdɪə'lɒdʒɪkl] *adj.* radiologisch; röntgenologisch

radiologist [reɪdɪ'ɒlədʒɪst] *n.* Radiologe, *der*/Radiologin, *die;* Röntgenologe, *der*/Röntgenologin, *die*

radiology [reɪdɪ'ɒlədʒɪ] *n., no pl.* Radiologie, *die;* Röntgenologie, *die*

radiometer [reɪdɪ'ɒmɪtə(r)] *n.* Radiometer, *das;* Strahlungsmesser, *der*

radio: ~ star *n. (Astron.)* [punktförmige] Radioquelle; ~ **station** *n.* Rundfunkstation, *die;* Rundfunk- *od.* Radiosender, *der;* **~-telegram** *n.* Funktelegramm, *das;* Radiotelegramm, *das;* **~-te'legraphy** *n.* Funktelegraphie, *die;* **~-'telephone** *n.* Funktelefon, *das;* ~ **'telescope** *n.* Radioteleskop, *das;* **~-'therapy** *n.* Strahlentherapie, *die;* Radiotherapie, *die (fachspr.)*

radish ['rædɪʃ] *n.* Rettich, *der; (small, red)* Radieschen, *das*

radium ['reɪdɪəm] *n. (Chem.)* Radium, *das*

radius ['reɪdɪəs] *n., pl.* **radii** ['reɪdɪaɪ] *or* **~es a)** *(Math.)* Radius, *der;* Halbmesser, *der;* ~ **of action** [Aktions]radius, *der;* Wirkungsbereich, *der; (of missile)* Reichweite, *die; (fig.)* Umkreis, *der;* **within a ~ of 20 miles** im Umkreis von 20 Meilen; **b)** *(Anat.)* Speiche, *die;* **c)** *(line from centre)* Strahl, *der; (spoke of wheel)* Speiche, *die;* **d)** *(Bot.)* [Blüten-, Dolden]strahl, *der*

radome ['reɪdəʊm] *n.* Radom, *das*

radon ['reɪdɒn] *n. (Chem.)* Radon, *das*

RAF [ɑ:reɪ'ef, *(coll.)* ræf] *abbr.* **Royal Air Force**

raffia ['ræfɪə] *n.* **a)** *(fibre)* Raphia-, Raffiabast, *der;* ~ **mat** Bastmatte, *die;* **b)** *(tree)* Raphia[palme], *die*

raffish ['ræfɪʃ] *adj.* **a)** liederlich; verkommen; **b)** *(unconventional)* flott

raffle ['ræfl] **1.** *n.* Tombola, *die;* ~ **ticket** Los, *das.* **2.** *v.t.* ~ **[off]** verlosen

raft [rɑ:ft] **1.** *n.* **a)** Floß, *das;* **b)** *(floating trees, ice, etc.)* Drift, *die.* **2.** *v.t. (transport)* flößen; mit dem Floß befördern

rafter ['rɑ:ftə(r)] *n. (Building)* Sparren, *der*

¹rag [ræg] *n.* **a)** [Stoff]fetzen, *der;* [Stoff]lappen, *der;* **[all] in ~s** [ganz] zerrissen; **feel like a wet ~** *(coll.)* wie ausgelaugt sein; **sb. loses his ~** *(sl.)* jmdm. reißt die Geduld; **b)** *in pl. (old and torn clothes)* Lumpen *Pl.;* **[dressed] in ~s [and tatters]** abgerissen; in Lumpen *nachgestellt;* **go from ~s to riches** vom armen Schlucker zum Millionär/zur Millionärin werden; *see also* **chew 1; glad rags; c)** *(derog.: newspaper)* Käseblatt, *das (salopp abwertend);* **d)** *(material for paper)* Lumpen, *der;* Hader, *der (fachspr.);* ~ **paper/fibres** Hadernpapier, *das*/Haderstoff, *der (fachspr.)*

²rag 1. *v.t.*, **-gg-** *(tease, play jokes on)* aufziehen; necken. **2.** *v.i.*, **-gg-** **a)** *(Brit.: engage in rough play)* herumtoben; **b)** *(be noisy and riotous)* Radau *od.* Rabatz machen *(ugs.).* **3.** *n.* **a)** *(Brit. Univ.)* spaßige studentische [Wohltätigkeits]veranstaltung; **the university's Rag Week** *die alljährliche Wohltätigkeitswoche der Universität [mit komischen Darbietungen];* **b)** *(prank)* Ulk, *der;* Streich, *der; in pl.* Ulkerei, *die*

³rag *n. (Mus.)* Rag, *der*

ragamuffin ['rægəmʌfɪn] *n.* [zerlumptes] Gassenkind; **look a proper ~:** ziemlich abgerissen aussehen

rag: ~-and-'bone man *n. (Brit.)* Lumpensammler, *der;* **~-bag** *n.* **a)** Lumpen-, Flickensack, *der;* **b)** *(fig.: collection)* Sammelsurium, *das (abwertend);* **c)** *(fig. sl.: sloppily-dressed woman)* Schlampe, *die (ugs. abwertend);* ~ **book** *n.* Kinderbuch aus unzerreißbarem Material; ~ **doll** *n.* Stoffpuppe, *die*

rage [reɪdʒ] **1.** *n.* **a)** *(violent anger)* Wut, *die; (fit of anger)* Wutausbruch, *der;* **be in/fly into a ~:** in Wut *od. (ugs.)* Rage sein/geraten; **in a fit of ~:** in einem Anfall von Wut; in einem plötzlichen Wutausbruch; **b)** *(vehement desire or passion)* Besessenheit, *die;* **sth. is [all] the ~:** etw. ist [ganz] groß in Mode *od. (ugs.)* ist der letzte Schrei. **2.** *v.i.* **a)** *(rave)* toben; ~ **at** *or* **against sth./sb.** gegen etw./jmdn. wüten *od. (ugs.)* wettern; **b)** *(be violent, operate unchecked)* toben; ‹*Krankheit:*› wüten; ‹*Fieber:*› rasen

ragged ['rægɪd] *adj.* **a)** zerrissen; kaputt *(ugs.);* ausgefranst ‹*Saum, Manschetten, Wundränder*›; **b)** *(rough, shaggy)* zottig ‹*Pferd, Schaf, Haar, Bart*›; **c)** *(jagged)* zerklüftet ‹*Felsen, Küste, Klippe, Landschaft*›; zerzaust ‹*Baum, Strauch*›; *(in tattered clothes)* abgerissen; zerlumpt; **d)** *(imperfect, lacking finish)* stümperhaft *(abwertend)* ‹*Arbeit, Ausführung*›; holprig ‹*Reim, Rhythmus*›; **e)** *(tired)* ermattet; ausgelaugt; **they were run ~:** sie waren völlig erledigt *(ugs.) od.* total groggy *(salopp)*

raggedly ['rægɪdlɪ] *adv.* **a)** abgerissen ‹*gekleidet*›; **b)** *(shaggily)* zottig ‹*wachsen*›; **c)** *(jaggedly)* zerklüftet ‹*verlaufen*›; **d)** *(imperfectly)* stümperhaft *(abwertend)* ‹*musizieren, arbeiten*›

ragged 'robin *n. (Bot.)* Kuckuckslichtnelke, *die*

raglan sleeve [ræglən 'sli:v] *n.* Raglanärmel, *der*

ragout ['rægu:] *n. (Gastr.)* Ragout, *das*

rag: ~ paper *n.* Hadernpapier, *das (fachspr.);* **~stone** *n.* [Kalk-, Kiesel]sandstein, *der;* **~tag [and bobtail]** *n.* Pöbel, *der (abwertend);* Plebs, *der (abwertend);* **~time** *n.* Ragtime, *der; attrib.* Ragtime‹*band, -musik, -sänger*›; ~ **trade** *n. (coll.)* Modebranche, *die (ugs.);* **~weed** *n. (Bot.)* **a)** *see* **ragwort; b)** *(Amer.: Ambrosia)* Ambrosienkraut, *das;* **~wort** *n. (Bot.)* Greiskraut, *das;* Kreuzkraut, *das*

raid [reɪd] **1.** *n.* **a)** Einfall, *der;* Überfall, *der; (Mil.)* Überraschungsangriff *der;* ~ **on a bank** Banküberfall, *der;* **make a ~ on sb.'s orchard/the larder** *(joc.)* jmds. Obstgarten heimsuchen/die Speisekammer plündern *(scherzh.); see also* **air raid; b)** *(by police)* Razzia, *die* **(on** in + *Dat.*); **c)** *(St. Exch.)* ≈ aggressive Unternehmensaufkäufe. **2.** *v.t.* ‹*Polizei:*› eine Razzia machen auf (+ *Akk.*); ‹*Bande/Räuber/Soldaten:*› überfallen ‹*Bank/Viehherde/Land*›; ‹*Trupp, Kommando:*› stürmen ‹*feindliche Stellung*›; ‹*Kinder:*› heimsuchen, plündern *(scherzh.)* ‹*Obstgarten*›; ~ **the larder** *(joc.)* die Speisekammer plündern *(scherzh.)*

raider ['reɪdə(r)] *n. (on bank, farm)* Räuber, *der*/Räuberin, *die; (looter)* Plünderer, *der*/Plünderin, *die; (burglar)* Einbrecher, *der*/Einbrecherin, *die*

¹rail [reɪl] **1.** *n.* **a)** ‹*Kleider-, Gardinen*›stange, *die; (as part of fence) (wooden)* Latte, *die; (metal)* Stange, *die; (on ship)* Reling, *die; (as protection against contact)* Barriere, *die;* **the ~s** *(Horse-racing)* die Innenumzäunung; die Bande; **b)** *(Railw.: of track)* Schiene, *die;* **go off the ~s** *(lit.)* entgleisen; *(fig.) (depart from what is accepted)* auf die schiefe Bahn geraten; *(go mad)* durchdrehen *(ugs.); (get out of control or order)* aus dem Ruder laufen; **c)** *(~way)* [Eisen]bahn, *die; attrib.* Bahn-; **by ~:** mit der Bahn; mit dem Zug; ~ **union** Eisenbahnergewerkschaft, *die.* **2.** *v.t.* ~ **in** einzäunen ‹*Grundstück, Gebäudeteil*›; mit einem Geländer *od.* einer Absperrung umgeben ‹*Altar, Denkmal*›; ~ **off** abzäunen; mit einem [Schutz]geländer versehen

²rail *n. (Ornith.)* Ralle, *die*

³rail *v.i.* ~ **at/against sb./sth.** auf/über jmdn./etw. schimpfen; ~ **at fate** mit dem Schicksal hadern

rail: ~car *n.* Triebwagen, *der;* Schienenbus, *der;* ~ **card** *n.* Berechtigungsausweis, *der; (for senior citizens)* ≈ Seniorenpaß, *der;* ~ **fence** *n. (Amer.) (wooden)* Lattenzaun, *der; (metal)* Stangenzaun, *der;* **~head** *n.* **a)** *(farthest point during construction)* Ende einer im Bau befindlichen Bahnstrecke; Baustellenende, *das;* **b)** *(terminal)* Ausladebahnhof, *der;* Verladebahnhof, *der*

railing ['reɪlɪŋ] *n. (round garden, park)* Zaun, *der; (on sides of staircase)* Geländer, *das*

raillery ['reɪlərɪ] *n.* Neckerei, *die;* Spöttelei, *die*

rail: ~-link *n.* Bahn[strecke], *die;* **~road 1.** *n. (Amer.) see* **railway; 2.** *v.t.* **a)** *(send or push through in haste)* **~road sb. into doing sth.** jmdn. dazu antreiben, etw. zu tun; **~road a bill through parliament** einen Gesetzentwurf im Parlament durchpeitschen *(ugs.);* **b)** *(send to prison by fraud)* unrechtmäßig einsperren *(ugs.);* ~ **strike** *n.* Eisenbahnerstreik, *der*

railway ['reɪlweɪ] *n.* **a)** *(track)* Bahnlinie, *die;* Bahnstrecke, *die;* **b)** *(system)* [Eisen]bahn, *die;* **work on the ~:** bei der Bahn arbeiten; **what a way to run a ~!** *(fig.)* komisches Verfahren!; *see also* **cable railway**

railway: ~ carriage *n.* Eisenbahnwagen, *der;* Reisezugwagen, *der (fachspr.);* ~ **crossing** *n.* Bahnübergang, *der;* ~ **engine** *n.* Lokomotive, *die;* ~ **engineer** *n.* Eisenbahningenieur, *der;* ~ **guide** *n.* Fahrplan, *der; (book)* Kursbuch, *das;* ~ **line** *n.* [Eisen]bahnlinie, *die;* [Eisen]bahnstrecke, *die;* **~man** ['reɪlweɪmən] *n., pl.* **~men** ['reɪlweɪmən] Eisenbahner, *der;* ~ **network** *n.* [Eisen]bahnnetz, *das;* ~ **station** *n.* Bahnhof, *der; (smaller)* [Eisen]bahnstation, *die;* ~ **worker** *n.* Bahnarbeiter, *der;* **~-yard** *n.* Abstellbahnhof, *der;* Rangierbahnhof, *der*

raiment ['reɪmənt] *n. (arch./literary)* Gewand, *das (geh.)*

rain [reɪn] **1.** *n.* **a)** Regen, *der;* **it looks like ~:** es sieht nach Regen aus; **out in the ~:** draußen im Regen ‹*sein, lassen*›; hinaus in den Regen ‹*gehen*›; **come ~ or shine** bei jedem Wetter; *(fig.)* unter allen Umständen; *see also* **right 1 d; b)** *(fig.: of arrows, blows, etc.)* Hagel, *der;* **c)** *in pl. (falls of ~)* **the ~s** die Regenzeit. **2.** *v.i.* **a)** *impers.* **it ~s** *or* **is ~ing** es regnet; **it starts ~ing** *or* **to ~:** es fängt an zu regnen; *see also* **cat a; pour 2 a; b)** ‹*Tränen:*› strömen; ‹*Konfetti, Reis:*› regnen, niedergehen **(on** auf + *Akk.*); ‹*Schläge:*› niederprasseln **(on** auf + *Akk.*); **bombs ~ed on many cities** auf viele Städte regnete es Bomben. **3.** *v.t.* prasseln *od.* hageln lassen ‹*Schläge, Hiebe*›; regnen lassen ‹*Reis, Konfetti*›; ~ **abuse on sb.** eine Schimpfkanonade gegen jmdn. loslassen *(ugs.)*

~ **'down** *v.i.* ‹*Schläge, Steine, Flüche usw.:*› niederprasseln; ‹*Schüsse, Kugeln usw.:*› niederhageln

~ **'off,** *(Amer.)* ~ **'out** *v.t.* **be ~ed off** *or* **out** *(be terminated)* wegen Regen abgebrochen werden; *(be cancelled)* wegen Regen ausfallen; ins Wasser fallen *(ugs. scherzh.)*

rainbow ['reɪnbəʊ] **1.** *n.* Regenbogen, *der;* **secondary ~:** Nebenregenbogen, *der;* **all the colours of the ~:** alle Regenbogenfarben; *see also* **gold 1 b. 2.** *adj.* Regenbogen‹*farben, -streifen*›; regenbogenfarbig, -farben ‹*Kleid, Blumen, Federkleid*›

rainbow 'trout *n.* Regenbogenforelle, *die*

rain: ~-check *n. (Amer.)* Eintrittskarte für Ersatzveranstaltung; **take a ~-check on sth.** *(fig.)* auf etw. *(Akk.)* später wieder zurückkommen; **~-cloud** *n.* Regenwolke, *die;* **~coat** *n.* Regenmantel, *der;* **~drop** *n.* Regentropfen, *der;* **~fall** *n. (shower)* [Regen]schauer, *der; (quantity)* Niederschlag, *der;* ~ **forest** *n.* Regenwald, *der;* **~-gauge** *n.* Regenmesser, *der;* **~-making** *n.* Erzeugung von künstlichem Regen *od.* Niederschlag; künstliche Niederschlagsauslösung; **~proof 1.** *adj.* regendicht; wasserdicht; **2.** *v.t.* appretieren; **~-shower** *n.* Regenschauer, *der;* **~-storm** *n.* stürmisches Regenwetter; heftiger Regenguß; **~-water** *n.* Regenwasser, *das;* **~wear** *n.* Regenkleidung, *die*

rainy ['reɪnɪ] *adj.* regnerisch ‹*Tag, Wetter*›; regenreich ‹*Klima, Gebiet, Sommer, Winter*›; regenverhangen ‹*Himmel*›; ~ **season** Regenzeit, *die;* **keep sth. for a ~ day** *(fig.)* sich *(Dat.)* etw. für schlechte Zeiten aufheben

raise [reɪz] **1.** *v.t.* **a)** *(lift up)* heben; erhöhen ‹*Note, Pulsfrequenz, Temperatur, Steuern, Miete, Lohn, Gehalt, Kosten*›; hochziehen ‹*Rolladen, Fahne, Schultern*›; aufziehen ‹*Vorhang,*›; hochheben ‹*Koffer, Arm, Hand*›; hochschieben ‹*Schiebefenster*›; höher machen, aufhöhen *(fachspr.)* ‹*Mauer usw.*› **(by** um); *(Cookery)* gehen lassen ‹*Brot, Teig*›; ~ **one's eyes** den Blick *od.* die Augen heben; hinaufblicken **(to** zu); aufblicken **(from** von); ~ **one's eyes to heaven** die Augen zum Himmel erheben *(geh.);* ~ **one's glass to sb.** das Glas auf jmdn. erheben; auf jmdn. anstoßen; ~ **one's hand/fist to sb.** die Hand/Faust gegen jmdn. erheben; ~ **one's voice** die Stimme heben; **they ~d their voices** *(in anger)* sie *od.* ihre Stimmen wurden lauter; **don't you ~ your voice at me** schrei mich nicht an!; **war ~d its [ugly] head** der Krieg erhob sein [häßliches] Haupt; **be ~d to the peerage/priesthood** in den Stand eines Peers/in den Priesterstand erhoben werden; *see also* **finger 1a; hat a; roof 1a; b)** *(set upright, cause to stand up)* aufrichten; erheben ⟨*Banner*⟩; aufstellen ⟨*Fahnenstange, Zaun, Gerüst*⟩; ~ **the people to revolt** das Volk zum Aufstand mobilisieren; ~ **the country against an invader** den Widerstand der Bevölkerung gegen einen Eindringling mobilisieren; **be ~d from the dead** von den Toten [auf]erweckt werden; ~ **the dust** *(fig.: cause turmoil)* Ärger machen; ~ **sb.'s spirits** jmds. Stimmung heben; **c)** *(build up, construct)* errichten ⟨*Gebäude, Statue*⟩; verursachen ⟨*Blutblase usw.*⟩; *(create, start)* auslösen ⟨*Kontroverse*⟩; schaffen ⟨*Probleme*⟩; erheben ⟨*Forderungen, Einwände, Ansprüche, Bedenken, Protest*⟩; entstehen lassen ⟨*Vorurteile*⟩; *(introduce)* aufwerfen ⟨*Frage*⟩; zur Sprache bringen, anschneiden ⟨*Angelegenheit, Thema, Problem*⟩; *(utter)* erschallen lassen ⟨*Ruf, Schrei, Beifallgeschrei, Jubel*⟩; **d)** *(grow, produce, breed, rear)* anbauen ⟨*Gemüse, Getreide*⟩; aufziehen ⟨*Vieh, [Haus]tiere*⟩; großziehen ⟨*Familie, Kinder*⟩; **[be born and] ~d in** ... *(Amer.)* [geboren und] aufgewachsen [sein] in ... *(Dat.)*; **e)** *(bring together, procure)* aufbringen ⟨*Geld, Betrag, Summe*⟩; aufstellen ⟨*Armee, Flotte, Truppen*⟩; aufnehmen ⟨*Hypothek, Kredit, Darlehen*⟩; **f)** *(end, cause to end)* aufheben, beenden ⟨*Belagerung, Blockade*⟩; *(remove)* aufheben ⟨*Aufnahme-, Einstellungsstopp, Embargo, Verfügung, Anordnung, Verbot*⟩; **g)** *(cause to appear)* [herbei]rufen, beschwören ⟨*Geist, Verstorbenen, Teufel*⟩; ~ **[merry] hell** *(coll.)* Krach schlagen *(ugs.)* (**over** wegen); **h)** *(Math.)* ~ **to the fourth power** in die 4. Potenz erheben; mit 4 potenzieren; **i)** *(Cards)* erhöhen (**to** auf); ~ **sb.** jmdn. überbieten; ~ **[one's] partner** seinen Mitspieler mit derselben Farbe überbieten *od.* überrufen; **j)** *(coll.: find)* ~ **sb.** jmdn. aufstöbern *od. (ugs.)* auftreiben. **2.** *n.* **a)** *(Cards)* Erhöhen, *das;* **b)** *(Amer.) (in wages)* Lohnerhöhung, *die; (in salary)* Gehaltserhöhung, *die*

~ **'up a)** *(cause to stand up)* aufstellen; **b)** *(build up)* errichten ⟨*Mauer, Gebäude*⟩; aufstapeln ⟨*Haufen*⟩; aufbauen, gestalten ⟨*Struktur*⟩

raised [reɪzd] *adj.* **a)** erhoben ⟨*Arm, Augen, Blick, Stimme*⟩; **b)** *(Amer. Cookery)* aufgegangen ⟨*Teig, Brot, Kuchen*⟩; **c)** [auf]gerauht ⟨*Gewebe, Stoff*⟩; **d)** *(having pattern or design in relief)* erhaben

raisin ['reɪzn] *n.* Rosine, *die*

raison d'être [reɪzɔ̃ 'detr] *n., pl.* **raisons d'être** [reɪzɔ̃ 'detr] Existenzberechtigung, *die;* **his happiness was her ~:** sie lebte nur für sein Wohlergehen

raj [rɑːdʒ] *n. (Ind. Hist.)* Herrschaft, *die;* **the British ~:** die britische Oberherrschaft *(in Indien vor 1947)*

raja[h] ['rɑːdʒə] *n. (Hist.)* Radscha, *der*

[1]rake [reɪk] **1.** *n.* **a)** *(Hort.)* Rechen, *der (bes. südd. u. md.)*; Harke, *die (bes. nordd.)*; **b)** *(Agric.: wheeled implement)* Rechwender, *der;* **c)** *(croupier's)* Rateau, *das;* Geldharke, *die. See also* **thin 1b. 2.** *v. t.* **a)** harken ⟨*Laub, Erde, Fußboden, Kies, Oberfläche*⟩; ~ **together** *(fig.)* zusammentragen ⟨*Beweise, Hinweise, Anklagepunkte*⟩; **b)** ~ **the fire** die Asche entfernen; **c)** *(sweep) (with eyes)* bestreichen; *(with shots)* bestreichen; beharken *(Soldatenspr.)*. **3.** *v. i.* ~ **among** *or* **into** *or* **[around] in** herumstöbern in (+ *Dat.*)

~ **'in** *v. t. (coll.)* scheffeln *(ugs.)* ⟨*Geld*⟩; ~ **in the money,** ~ **it in** Geld scheffeln *(ugs.)*

~ **over** *v. t.* **a)** harken; **b)** *(fig.)* wieder ausgraben; ~ **over old ashes** *(fig.)* alte Geschichten wieder ausgraben

~ **'up** *v. t.* **a)** zusammenharken; **b)** *(fig.)* wieder ausgraben ⟨*Vergangenes*⟩

[2]rake *n.* **a)** *(sloping position, [amount of] slope)* Neigung, *die;* **b)** *(in theatre)* Schräge, *die;* **there is a ~ on this stage** diese Bühne hat eine Schräge

[3]rake *n. (person)* Lebemann, *der*

raked [reɪkt] *adj.* ⟨*Bühne, Zuschauerraum*⟩ mit einer Schräge

'rake-off *n. (coll.)* [Gewinn]anteil, *der*

[1]rakish ['reɪkɪʃ] *adj.* **a)** *(dissolute)* ausschweifend; **b)** *(jaunty)* flott; keß; **wear one's hat at a ~ angle** seinen Hut frech *od.* keck aufgesetzt haben

[2]rakish *adj. (smartly designed)* schnittig

rakishly ['reɪkɪʃlɪ] *adv.* **a)** *(dissolutely)* wie ein Lebemann; **b)** *(jauntily)* keß; keck

[1]rally ['rælɪ] **1.** *v. i.* **a)** *(come together)* sich versammeln; ~ **to the support of** *or* **the defence of,** ~ **behind** *or* **to sb.** *(fig.)* sich hinter jmdn. stellen; **the banks rallied to the support of the pound** die Banken versuchten gemeinsam, das Pfund zu stützen; ~ **round** sich zusammentun; **b)** *(regain health)* sich wieder [ein wenig] erholen; **c)** *(reassemble)* sich [wieder] sammeln; **d)** *(increase in value after fall)* ⟨*Aktie, Kurs:*⟩ wieder anziehen, sich wieder erholen. **2.** *v. t.* **a)** *(reassemble)* wieder zusammenrufen; **b)** *(bring together)* einigen ⟨*Partei, Kräfte*⟩; sammeln ⟨*Anhänger*⟩; **c)** *(rouse)* aufmuntern; *(revive)* ~ **one's strength** seine [ganze] Kraft zusammennehmen; ~ **support for sb./sth.** um Unterstützung für jmdn./etw. werben. **3.** *n.* **a)** *(mass meeting)* Versammlung, *die;* **Scout ~:** [großes] Pfadfindertreffen; **peace ~:** Friedenskundgebung, *die;* **b)** *(competition)* **[motor] ~:** Rallye, *die;* **Monte Carlo R~/Isle of Man TT R~:** Rallye Monte Carlo/Tourist Trophy, *die;* **c)** *(Tennis)* Ballwechsel, *der;* **d) a ~ in prices/shares** ein Anziehen der Preise/Aktienkurse

[2]rally *v. t. (tease)* aufziehen *(ugs.)*; necken

'rally-cross *n. (Sport)* Rallye-Cross, *das*

RAM [ræm] *abbr. (Computing)* **random access memory** RAM; ~ **facility** Randomspeicher, *der*

ram [ræm] **1.** *n.* **a)** *(Zool.)* Schafbock, *der;* Widder, *der;* **b) the Ram** *(Astrol.)* der Widder; *see also* **archer b; c)** *see* **battering ram; d)** *(Naut.: projecting beak)* Rammsporn, *der;* **e)** *(hydraulic lifting-machine)* hydraulischer Widder; **f)** *(weight)* Rammklotz, *der;* Bär, *der;* **g)** *(tool)* Stampfer, *der;* **h)** *(piston)* Plunger, *der.* **2.** *v. t.,* **-mm-: a)** *(force)* stopfen; ~ **a post into the ground** einen Pfosten in die Erde rammen; ~ **in in** etw. *(Akk.)* rammen; **he ~med his hat down on his head** er knallte sich *(Dat.)* seinen Hut auf den Kopf *(ugs.)*; ~ **sth. into sb.** *or* **sb.'s head** *(fig.)* jmdm. etw. einhämmern; ~ **sth. home to sb.** jmdm. etw. deutlich vor Augen führen; *see also* **throat a; b)** *(collide with)* rammen ⟨*Fahrzeug, Pfosten*⟩; **c)** ~ **[down]** *(beat down)* feststampfen ⟨*Erde, Ton, Kies*⟩

Ramadan [ræmə'dɑːn] *n. (Muslim Relig.)* **[month of] ~:** Ramadan, *der*

ramble ['ræmbl] **1.** *n.* **[nature] ~:** Wanderung, *die.* **2.** *v. i.* **a)** *(walk)* umherstreifen (**through, in** in + *Dat.*); **b)** *(wander in discourse)* zusammenhangloses Zeug reden *(abwertend)*; **keep rambling on about sth.** sich endlos über etw. *(Akk.)* auslassen

rambler ['ræmblə(r)] *n.* **a)** Wanderer, *der/* Wanderin, *die;* **b)** *(Bot.)* Kletterrose, *die*

rambling ['ræmblɪŋ] **1.** *n.* Wandern, *das;* ~ **club** Wanderverein, *der.* **2.** *adj.* **a)** *(irregularly arranged)* verschachtelt; verwinkelt ⟨*Straßen*⟩; **b)** *(incoherent)* unzusammenhängend ⟨*Erklärung, Brief*⟩; zerstreut ⟨*Professor*⟩; **c)** *(Bot.)* ~ **rose** Kletterrose, *die*

rambunctious [ræm'bʌŋkʃəs] *adj. (Amer. coll.)* nicht zu bändigend; **be ~:** nicht zu bändigen sein

ramekin ['ræmɪkɪn] **a)** *(Gastr.)* Käsewindbeutel, *der;* Ramequin, *der (fachspr.)*; **b)** *see* ~ **case**

ramekin: ~ case, ~ dish *ns.* kleine Auflaufform

ramification [ræmɪfɪ'keɪʃn] *n.* **a)** *(of river, railway, business; Bot., Anat.)* Verzweigung, *die;* **b)** *usu. in pl. (consequence)* Auswirkungen; **what would be the ~s of this?** wie würde sich das auswirken?

ramify ['ræmɪfaɪ] *v. i.* sich verzweigen; **~ing network** verzweigtes Netz

'ram-jet *n. (Aeronaut.)* ~ **[engine]** Staustrahltriebwerk, *das*

rammer ['ræmə(r)] *n.* Stampfer, *der*

ramp [ræmp] **1.** *n.* **a)** *(slope)* Rampe, *die;* **'beware** *or* **caution, ~!'** „Vorsicht, unebene Fahrbahn!"; **b)** *(Aeronaut.)* Gangway, *die.* **2.** *v. t.* mit einer Rampe versehen

rampage 1. ['ræmpeɪdʒ, ræm'peɪdʒ] *n.* Randale, *die (ugs.)*; **be/go on the ~** *(coll.)* ⟨*Rowdies:*⟩ randalieren; ⟨*verärgerte Person:*⟩ toben. **2.** [ræm'peɪdʒ] *v. i.* ⟨*Rowdies:*⟩ randalieren; ~ **about** ⟨*verärgerte Person:*⟩ toben

rampant ['ræmpənt] *adj.* **a)** *(unchecked)* zügellos ⟨*Gewalt, Rassismus, Randalieren*⟩; schreiend ⟨*soziale Ungerechtigkeit*⟩; steil ansteigend ⟨*Verbrechensrate, Inflation*⟩; üppig ⟨*Wachstum*⟩; **cholera was ~:** die Cholera grassierte; **b)** *postpos. (Her.)* zum Grimmen geschickt ⟨*Löwe*⟩; **c)** *(rank)* **make too ~, cause the ~ growth of** wuchern lassen ⟨*Pflanzen*⟩

rampart ['ræmpɑːt] *n.* **a)** *(walk)* Wehrgang, *der;* **b)** *(protective barrier)* Wall, *der; (fig.)* Schutzschild, *der*

rampion ['ræmpɪən] *n. (Bot.)* Rapunzelglockenblume, *die*

'ramrod *n.* Ladestock, *der;* **[with one's back] as straight** *or* **stiff as a ~** *(fig. coll.)* so steif, als ob man einen Besenstiel verschluckt hätte; stocksteif

'ramshackle *adj.* klapprig ⟨*Auto*⟩; verkommen ⟨*Gebäude*⟩

ran *see* **run 2, 3**

ranch [rɑːntʃ] **1.** *n.* Ranch, *die;* **[mink/ poultry] ~:** [Nerz-/Geflügel]farm, *die;* **livestock ~:** Viehbetrieb, *der;* **meanwhile, back at the ~** *(joc. coll.)* inzwischen ... zu Hause; *see also* **dude ranch. 2.** *v. i.* Viehwirtschaft treiben

rancher ['rɑːntʃə(r)] *n.* *(owner, operator)* Rancher, *der*/Rancherin, *die;* *(employee)* Farmarbeiter, *der/*-arbeiterin, *die;* **be a ~:** eine Ranch haben/auf einer Ranch arbeiten

ranch: ~-hand *n.* Farmarbeiter, *der/*-arbeiterin, *die;* **~-house** *n.* Wohnhaus auf einer/der Ranch

rancid ['rænsɪd] *adj.* ranzig

rancor *(Amer.) see* **rancour**

rancorous ['ræŋkərəs] *adj.* bitter; **feel ~ towards sb.** über jmdn. verbittert sein

rancour ['ræŋkə(r)] *n. (Brit.)* [tiefe] Verbitterung; **she bore him no ~:** sie hegte keinen Groll gegen ihn *(geh.)*

rand [rænd, rɑːnt] *n. (S. Afr. monetary unit)* Rand, *der*

randiness ['rændɪnɪs] *n., no pl.* Lüsternheit, *die (geh.)*; Geilheit, *die*

random ['rændəm] **1.** *n.* **at ~:** wahllos; willkürlich; *(aimlessly)* ziellos; **speak/choose at ~:** ins Blaue hinein reden/aufs Geratewohl wählen. **2.** *adj.* **a)** *(unsystematic)* willkürlich ⟨*Auswahl*⟩; **make a ~ guess** raten aufs Geratewohl; **b)** *(Statistics)* Zufalls-

random: ~ 'access memory *n. (Computing)* Schreib-Lese-Speicher, *der;* ~ **distribution** *n. (Statistics)* Zufallsverteilung, *die*

randomize (randomise) ['rændəmaɪz] *v. t.* randomisieren *(fachspr.)*; willkürlich anordnen

random: ~ 'sample *n. (Statistics)* [Zufalls]stichprobe, *die;* ~ **'variable** *n. (Statistics)* Zufallsvariable, *die*

randy ['rændɪ] *adj.* geil; scharf *(ugs.)*; **feel ~:** geil sein

rang *see* **[2]ring 2, 3**

range [reɪndʒ] **1.** *n.* **a)** *(row)* ~ **of mountains/**

cliffs Berg-/Felsenkette, *die;* **b)** *(of subjects, interests, topics)* Palette, *die; (of musical instrument)* Tonumfang, *der; (of knowledge, voice)* Umfang, *der; (of income, department, possibility)* Bereich, *der;* **~ of influence** Einflußbereich, *der;* **a ~ of options** verschiedene Möglichkeiten; **the annual ~ of temperature** die Temperaturunterschiede im Verlauf des Jahres; **be outside the ~ of a department** nicht in ein Ressort gehören; **sth. is out of** *or* **beyond sb's ~** *(lit. or fig.)* etw. ist außerhalb jmds. Reichweite; **c)** *(Bot., Zool.: area of distribution)* Verbreitungsgebiet, *das;* **d)** *(of telescope, missile, aircraft, etc.)* Reichweite, *die; (distance between gun and target)* Schußweite, *die;* **flying ~:** Flugbereich, *der;* **at a ~ of 200 metres** auf eine Entfernung von 200 Metern; **up to a ~ of 5 miles** bis zu einem Umkreis von 5 Meilen; **shoot at close** *or* **short/long ~:** aus kurzer/großer Entfernung schießen; **[with]in/out of** *or* **beyond [firing] ~:** in/außer Schußweite; **within ~ of a sound** in Hörweite eines Geräuschs; **experience sth. at close ~:** etw. in unmittelbarer Nähe erleben; **e)** *(series, selection)* Kollektion, *die;* **f) [shooting] ~:** Schießstand, *der; (at fun-fair)* Schießbude, *die;* **g)** *(testing-site)* Versuchsgelände, *das;* **h)** *(grazing-ground)* Weide[fläche], *die;* **cattle ~:** Viehweide, *die;* **i) give free ~ to** *(freedom to roam)* frei herumlaufen lassen ‹*Tier*›; umherschweifen lassen ‹*Gedanken*›; **j)** *(direction)* Verlauf, *der;* **k)** *(cooking-stove)* Herd, *der.* **2.** *v. i.* **a)** *(vary within limits)* ‹*Preise, Temperaturen:*› schwanken, sich bewegen **(from ... to** zwischen [+ *Dat.*] ... und); **they ~ in age from 3 to 12** sie sind zwischen 3 und 12 Jahre alt; **b)** *(extend)* ‹*Klippen, Gipfel, Häuser:*› sich hinziehen; **her hobbies ~ from x to y** die Palette ihrer Hobbies reicht von x bis y; **c)** *(Bot., Zool.: occur over wide area)* **the plant/animal ~s from ... to ...:** das Verbreitungsgebiet der Pflanze/des Tieres erstreckt sich von ... bis ...; **d)** *(roam)* umherziehen **(around, about** in + *Dat.*); *(fig.)* ‹*Gedanken:*› umherschweifen; **the discussion ~d over ...:** die Diskussion erstreckte sich auf (+ *Akk.*) ...; **the speaker ~d far and wide** der Redner sprach viele verschiedene Themen an. **3.** *v. t.* **a)** *(arrange)* aufreihen ‹*Bücher, Tische*›; antreten lassen ‹*Soldaten*›; **they ~d themselves in lines** sie stellten sich in Reih und Glied auf; **several enemy platoons were ~d against us** wir standen einer Reihe feindlicher Züge gegenüber; **~ oneself with sb.** *(fig.)* sich auf jmds. Seite schlagen; **~ oneself against sb./sth.** *(fig.)* sich gegen jmdn./etw. zusammenschließen; **~ oneself behind sth.** *(fig.)* sich hinter etw. *(Akk.)* stellen; **b)** richten ‹*Teleskop, Geschütz*› **(on** auf + *Akk.*); **c)** *(roam)* umherstreifen in (+ *Dat.*); durchstreifen ‹*Landschaft, Berge, Wälder*›; befahren ‹*Meere*›

'range-finder *n.* Entfernungsmesser, *der*

ranger ['reɪndʒə(r)] *n.* **a)** *(keeper)* Aufseher, *der*/Aufseherin, *die; (of forest)* Förster, *der*/Försterin, *die;* **b)** *(Amer.: law officer)* Ranger, *der; Angehöriger der berittenen Polizeitruppe;* **c)** *(Brit.: Girl Guide)* Pfadfinderin *(zwischen 14 und 18 Jahren);* **d)** *(Amer. Mil.)* Ranger, *der*

ranging ['reɪndʒɪŋ]: **~-pole, ~-rod** *ns.* *(Surv.)* Bake, *die*

rangy ['reɪndʒɪ] *adj.* langgliedrig

¹rank [ræŋk] **1.** *n.* **a)** *(position in hierarchy)* Rang, *der; (Mil. also)* Dienstgrad, *der;* **be above/below sb. in ~:** einen höheren/niedrigeren Rang/Dienstgrad haben als jmd.; **pull ~** *(coll.)* den Vorgesetzten herauskehren **(on** gegenüber); **of high ~:** hochrangig; **be in the front** *or* **top ~ of performers** ein Künstler der Spitzenklasse sein; **of the first ~:** erstklassig; **b)** *(social position)* [soziale] Stellung; **people of all ~s** Menschen aus allen [Gesellschafts]schichten; **persons of ~:** hochgestellte Persönlichkeiten; **belong to a high ~ of society** zur oberen Gesellschaftsschicht gehören; **c)** *(row)* Reihe, *die;* **d)** *(Brit.: taxi-stand)* [Taxen]stand, *der;* **e)** *(line of soldiers)* Reihe, *die;* **step forward from the ~:** vortreten; **the ~s** *(enlisted men)* die Mannschaften und Unteroffiziere; **the ~ and file** die Mannschaften und Unteroffiziere; *(fig.)* die breite Masse; **close [our/their] ~s** die Reihen schließen; *(fig.)* sich zusammenschließen; **other ~s** Mannschaften und Unteroffiziere; **rise from the ~s** [sich aus dem Mannschaftsstand] zum Offizier hochdienen; *(fig.)* sich hocharbeiten; **f)** *(order)* **keep/break ~[s]** in Reih und Glied stehen/aus dem Glied treten. **2.** *v. t.* **a)** *(classify)* **~ among** *or* **with** zählen *od.* rechnen zu; **his achievement was ~ed with hers** seine Leistung wurde mit ihrer auf eine Stufe gestellt; **be ~ed second in the world** an zweiter Stelle in der Welt stehen; **~ sth. highly** etw. hoch einstufen; **b)** *(arrange)* aufstellen ‹*Schachfiguren*›; in Reih und Glied antreten lassen ‹*Kompanie*›; **c)** *(Amer.: take precedence of)* rangmäßig stehen über (+ *Dat.*); **who ~s whom?** wie ist die Rangordnung? **3.** *v. i.* **a)** *(have position)* **~ among** *or* **with** gehören *od.* zählen zu; **~ above/next to sb.** rangmäßig über/direkt unter jmdm. stehen; **~ high/low** eine hohe/niedere Stellung einnehmen; viel/nicht viel gelten; **it ~s as his best book** es gilt als sein bestes Buch; **b)** *(Amer.: have senior position)* **~ing executive** übergeordneter Manager

²rank *adj.* **a)** *(complete)* blank ‹*Unsinn, Frechheit*›; kraß ‹*Außenseiter, Illoyalität*›; **b)** *(foul-smelling)* stinkend; **~ odour** Gestank, *der;* **smell ~:** stinken; **c)** *(vile)* ordinär; unflätig; **d)** *(rampant)* überwuchert ‹*Garten*›; **~ weeds** [wild] wucherndes Unkraut

'rank-and-file *adj.* einfach ‹*Mitglied, Mann usw.*›

ranker ['ræŋkə(r)] *n.* *(Mil.)* **a)** *(commissioned officer)* aus dem Mannschaftsstand aufgestiegener Offizier; **b)** *(soldier)* einfacher *od.* gemeiner Soldat

rankings ['ræŋkɪŋz] *n. pl.* *(Sport)* Rangliste, *die;* **the team has fallen in the ~:** die Mannschaft ist in der Tabelle nach unten gerutscht

rankle ['ræŋkl] **1.** *v. i.* **it/sb.'s success** *etc.* **~s [with sb.]** es/jmds. Erfolg *usw.* wurmt jmdn. *(ugs.).* **2.** *v. t.* wurmen *(ugs.)*

ransack ['rænsæk] *v. t.* **a)** *(search)* durchsuchen **(for** nach); *(fig.)* kramen in (+ *Dat.*) *(ugs.)* ‹*Erinnerung, Gedächtnis*›; erforschen ‹*Gewissen*›; **b)** *(pillage)* plündern

ransom ['rænsəm] **1.** *n.* **~ [money]** Lösegeld, *das;* **hold to ~:** als Geisel festhalten; *(fig.)* erpressen, unter Druck *(Akk.)* setzen ‹*Regierung*›; **jewels worth a king's ~:** Juwelen, die ein Vermögen wert sind. **2.** *v. t.* **a)** *(redeem)* Lösegeld bezahlen für; auslösen; **b)** *(hold to ransom)* als Geisel festhalten

'ransom note *n.* Erpresserbrief, *der*

rant [rænt] **1.** *v. i.* wettern *(ugs.);* **~ at** anschnauzen *(ugs.);* **~ on about** herumzetern wegen *(ugs.);* **~ and rave about sth.** über etw. *(Akk.)* wettern *(ugs.).* **2.** *n.* **a)** *(tirade)* Tirade, *die (abwertend);* Redeschwall, *der;* **b)** *no pl.* *(empty talk)* Schwulst, *der;* leeres Geschwätz *(ugs.)*

ranunculus [rə'nʌŋkjʊləs] *n., pl.* **~es** *or* **ranunculi** [rə'nʌŋkjʊlaɪ] *(Bot.)* Hahnenfußgewächs, *das*

¹rap [ræp] **1.** *n.* **a)** *(sharp knock)* [energisches] Klopfen; **there was a ~ on** *or* **at the door** es klopfte [laut]; **I heard a ~ on** *or* **at the door** ich hörte es [laut] klopfen; **give sb. a ~ on** *or* **over the knuckles** jmdm. auf die Finger schlagen; *(fig.)* jmdm. auf die Finger klopfen; **get a ~ on** *or* **over the knuckles** *(lit. or fig.)* eins auf die Finger bekommen; **b)** *(sl.: blame)* **take the ~ [for sth.]** [für etw.] den Kopf hinhalten *(ugs.);* **leave sb. behind to take the ~:** jmdn. die Suppe auslöffeln lassen *(ugs.);* **c)** *(Amer. sl.: prison sentence)* Kittchen, *das (ugs.);* Knast, *der (ugs.);* **d)** *(Amer. sl.: criminal charge)* Anklage, *die;* **e)** *(Amer. sl.) (conversation)* Unterhaltung, *die; (discussion)* Palaver, *das (ugs.); (in pop music)* rhythmischer Sprechgesang; Rap, *der.* **2.** *v. t.,* **-pp-** **a)** *(strike smartly)* klopfen; **~ sb. on the knuckles** jmdm. auf die Finger klopfen; **~ sth. on sth.** mit etw. gegen etw. klopfen; **b)** *(criticize)* attackieren. **3.** *v. i.,* **-pp-** **a)** *(make sound)* klopfen **(on an** + *Akk.*); **~ on the table** auf den Tisch klopfen; **b)** *(Amer. sl.: talk)* quatschen *(ugs.)*

~ 'out *v. t.* ausstoßen ‹*Befehl, Fluch*›; **~ out a message** melden

²rap *n.* **I don't care** *or* **give a ~:** es ist mir völlig egal *(ugs.)*

rapacious [rə'peɪʃəs] *adj.* *(greedy)* habgierig; *(predatory)* räuberisch

rapaciously [rə'peɪʃəslɪ] *adv.* *(greedily)* habgierig; *(in predatory manner)* raublustig

rapacity [rə'pæsɪtɪ] *n., no pl.* Habgier, *die; (being predatory)* Raublust, *die*

¹rape [reɪp] **1.** *n.* Vergewaltigung, *die (auch fig.);* Notzucht, *die (Rechtsspr.);* **statutory ~** *(Amer.)* Geschlechtsverkehr mit einer Minderjährigen; **homosexual ~:** Vergewaltigung einer gleichgeschlechtlichen Person. **2.** *v. t.* vergewaltigen; notzüchtigen *(Rechtsspr.); (fig.: despoil)* vergewaltigen ‹*Landschaft*›

²rape *n.* *(Bot., Agric.)* Raps, *der*

rape: ~-cake *n.* Rapskuchen, *der;* **~ oil** *see* **~-seed oil; ~-seed** *n.* Rapssamen, *der;* **~-seed oil** *n.* Rapsöl, *das*

Raphael ['ræfeɪəl] *pr. n.* **a)** *(archangel)* Raphael *(der);* **b)** *(artist)* Raffael *(der)*

rapid ['ræpɪd] **1.** *adj.* schnell ‹*Bewegung, Wachstum, Puls*›; rasch ‹*Folge, Bewegung, Fortschritt, Ausbreitung, Änderung*›; rapide ‹*Niedergang*›; steil ‹*Abstieg*›; reißend ‹*Gewässer, Strömung*›; stark ‹*Gefälle, Strömung*›; **give ~ results** schnell Ergebnisse bringen; **there has been a ~ decline** es ging rapide abwärts. **2.** *n. in pl.* Stromschnellen

rapid-'fire *adj.* Schnellfeuer‹*waffe, -schießen*›; *(fig.)* schnell aufeinanderfolgend ‹*Wiederholung*›; Schnellfeuer‹*witze, -fragen*›

rapidity [rə'pɪdɪtɪ] *n., no pl.* Schnelligkeit, *die*

rapidly ['ræpɪdlɪ] *adv.* schnell; **descend ~** ‹*Hang:*› steil abfallen

rapid 'transit *(Amer.) n.* Schnellverkehr, *der*

rapier ['reɪpɪə(r)] *n.* *(Fencing)* Rapier, *das*

rapine ['ræpaɪn, 'ræpɪn] *n.* *(rhet.)* Plünderung, *die*

rapist ['reɪpɪst] *n.* Vergewaltiger, *der*

rapport [ræ'pɔ:(r)] *n.* [harmonisches] Verhältnis; **have a great ~ with sb.** ein ausgezeichnetes Verhältnis zu jmdm. haben; **establish a ~ with sb.** eine Beziehung zu jmdm. aufbauen; **lack of ~:** fehlende Übereinstimmung

rapprochement [ræ'prɒʃmɑ̃] *n.* *(Polit., Diplom.)* Rapprochement, *das (fachspr.);* Wiederannäherung, *die*

rapscallion [ræp'skæljən] *n.* *(joc.)* Spitzbube, *der (scherzh.);* Schlingel, *der (scherzh.)*

rapt [ræpt] *adj.* gespannt ‹*Aufmerksamkeit, Miene*›; **in ~ contemplation** in Betrachtungen versunken

raptly ['ræptlɪ] *adv.* gespannt ‹*zuhören*›

rapture ['ræptʃə(r)] *n.* **a)** *(ecstatic delight)* **[state of] ~:** Verzückung, *die;* **b)** *in pl.* *(enthusiasm)* **be in ~s** entzückt sein **(over, about** über + *Akk.*); **go into ~s** [überschwenglich] schwärmen **(over, about** von); **be sent into ~s by sth.** über etw. *(Akk.)* in Verzückung geraten

rapturous ['ræptʃərəs] *adj.* begeistert ‹*Applaus, Menge, Willkommen*›; verzückt ‹*Miene*›
[1]**rare** [reə(r)] *adj.* **a)** *(uncommon)* selten; ~ **occurrence** Seltenheit, *die;* **it's ~ for him to do that** es kommt selten vor, daß er etw. tut; **b)** *(thin)* dünn ‹*Luft, Atmosphäre*›; **c)** *(extreme)* **have ~ fun with sb.** mit jmdm. einen Heidenspaß haben; **have a ~ old time** sich köstlich amüsieren
[2]**rare** *adj. (Cookery)* englisch gebraten; nur schwach gebraten; **medium ~:** halb durchgebraten
rarebit ['reəbɪt] *see* **Welsh rarebit**
rare: ~ **'book** *n.* Rarität, *die;* Rarum, *das (Buchw.);* ~ **'earth** *(Chem.) n.* seltene Erde
rarefaction [reərɪ'fækʃn] *n.* Verdünnung, *die*
rarefied ['reərɪfaɪd] *adj.* dünn ‹*Luft*›; *(fig.)* exklusiv
rarefy ['reərɪfaɪ] *v.t.* **a)** verdünnen ‹*Feuchtigkeit, Luft*›; **b)** *(make subtle)* verfeinern
rare 'gas *see* **noble gas**
rarely ['reəlɪ] *adv.* **a)** selten; **b)** *(to an unusual degree)* außergewöhnlich
raring ['reərɪŋ] *adj. (coll.)* **be ~ to go** kaum abwarten können, bis es losgeht
rarity ['reərɪtɪ] *n.* **a)** Seltenheit, *die;* Rarität, *die;* **a collection of rarities** eine Sammlung von Raritäten; **be an object of great ~:** eine große Seltenheit sein; **such people are a ~:** solche Leute sind rar; **b) the ~ of the atmosphere** die dünne Luft
'rarity value *n.* Seltenheitswert, *der*
rascal ['rɑ:skl] *n.* **a)** *(dishonest person)* Halunke, *der;* Schuft, *der;* **b)** *(joc.: mischievous person)* Schlingel, *der (scherzh.);* Spitzbube, *der (scherzh.)*
rascally ['rɑ:skəlɪ] *adj.* **a)** *(dishonest)* schurkisch; **b)** *(joc.: mischievous)* schlimm ‹*Junge, Streich*›
rase *see* **raze**
[1]**rash** [ræʃ] *n. (Med.)* [Haut]ausschlag, *der;* **develop a** *or* **break out** *or* **come out in a ~:** einen Ausschlag bekommen; **bring sb. out in a ~:** einen Ausschlag bei jmdm. hervorrufen; **a ~ of burglaries/strikes** *(fig.)* eine Serie von Einbrüchen/Streiks
[2]**rash** *adj.* voreilig ‹*Urteil, Entscheidung, Entschluß*›; überstürzt ‹*Versprechungen, Handlung, Erklärung*›; *(impetuous)* ungestüm ‹*Person*›
rasher ['ræʃə(r)] *n.* ~ **[of bacon]** Speckscheibe, *die;* **bacon sliced into ~s** in [dünne] Scheiben geschnittener Speck
rashly ['ræʃlɪ] *adv.* voreilig ‹*handeln, etw. versprechen, zustimmen*›
rashness ['ræʃnɪs] *n., no pl.* Voreiligkeit, *die;* **regret one's ~ in doing sth.** bedauern, daß man etw. voreilig getan hat
rasp [rɑ:sp] **1.** *n.* **a)** *(tool)* Raspel, *die;* **b)** *(sound) (of metal on wood)* schneidendes Geräusch; *(of a cricket)* Zirpen, *das; (of breathing)* Rasseln, *das.* **2.** *v.i.* kratzen. **3.** *v.t.* **a)** *(scrape with ~)* raspeln ‹*Blech, Kante*›; **b)** *(say gratingly)* schnarren
raspberry ['rɑ:zbərɪ] *n.* **a)** Himbeere, *die; (plant also)* Himbeerstrauch, *der; attrib.* Himbeer‹*marmelade, -torte, -rosa, -eis*›; **b)** *(sl.: rude noise)* **blow a ~:** verächtlich prusten
'raspberry-cane *n.* Himbeerrute, *die;* Himbeerstrauch, *der*
rasping ['rɑ:spɪŋ] *adj.* krächzend ‹*Husten, Stimme*›; rasselnd ‹*Geräusch*›
Rasta ['ræstə] *n.* Rasta, *der;* **the ~ people** die Rastas
Rastafarian [ræstə'feərɪən] *(Relig.)* **1.** *n.* Rastafari, *der.* **2.** *adj.* Rasta-
raster ['ræstə(r)] *n. (Telev.)* Raster, *das*
rat [ræt] **1.** *n.* **a)** Ratte, *die;* **brown** *or* **sewer ~:** Wanderratte, *die;* **look like a drowned ~** *(coll.)* wie eine gebadete Maus aussehen *(ugs.);* **~s!** *(sl.) (drat it!)* verflixt! *(ugs.);* verdammt! *(salopp); (nonsense!)* Quatsch! *(ugs.);* **smell a ~** *(fig. coll.)* Lunte *od.* den Braten riechen *(ugs.);* **~s leaving** *or* **deserting the [sinking] ship** *(fig.)* Ratten, die das sinkende Schiff verlassen; *see also* **muskrat; water-rat; b)** *(coll. derog.: unpleasant person)* Ratte, *die (derb);* **c)** *(Polit.)* Abtrünnige, *der/die.* **2.** *v.i.,* **-tt-** Ratten jagen; **be out ~ting** auf Rattenfang sein
~ **on** *v.t. (sl.)* **a)** *(inform on)* verpfeifen *(ugs.);* **b)** *(go back on)* nicht halten ‹*Versprechen*›; Verrat üben an (+ *Dat.*) ‹*Politik*›; sitzenlassen *(ugs.)* ‹*Person*›
ratatouille [rætə'tu:ɪ] *n. (Gastr.)* Ratatouille, *die*
rat: **~bag** *n. (sl.)* Knallkopf, *der*/[dumme] Kuh *(ugs.);* **~-catcher** *n.* Rattenfänger, *der*/-fängerin, *die*
ratchet ['rætʃɪt] *n. (Mech. Engin.)* **a)** *(set of teeth)* Zahnkranz, *der;* **b)** ~ **[wheel]** Klinkenrad, *das*
[1]**rate** [reɪt] **1.** *n.* **a)** *(proportion)* Rate, *die;* **increase at a ~ of 50 a week** [um] 50 pro Woche anwachsen; **lose at the ~ of two minutes a day** ‹*Uhr:*› zwei Minuten pro Tag nachgehen; **~ of inflation/absentee ~:** Inflations-/Abwesenheitsrate, *die;* **b)** *(tariff)* Satz, *der;* **interest/taxation ~, ~ of interest/taxation** Zins-/Steuersatz, *der;* **lending/premium ~s** Lombardsatz, *der*/Prämientarif, *der; see also* **bank rate; exchange 3 d; water-rate; c)** *(amount of money)* Gebühr, *die;* ~ **[of pay]** Lohnsatz, *der;* **the ~ for the job** die festgelegte Vergütung für diese Arbeit; **letter/parcel ~:** Briefporto, *das*/Paketgebühr, *die;* **at reduced ~:** gebührenermäßigt ‹*Drucksache*›; **d)** *(speed)* Geschwindigkeit, *die;* Tempo, *das;* **at a** *or* **the ~ of 50 mph** mit [einer Geschwindigkeit von] 80 km/h; **at a good/fast/moderate/dangerous ~:** zügig/mit hoher/mäßiger Geschwindigkeit/gefährlich schnell; **e)** *(Brit.: local authority levy)* Gemeindeabgabe, *die;* Realsteuer, *die;* **county/district ~:** Grafschafts-/Bezirksabgabe, *die;* **[local** *or* **council] ~s** Gemeindeabgaben; **f)** *(coll.)* **at any ~** *(at least)* zumindest; wenigstens; *(whatever happens)* auf jeden Fall; **at this ~ we won't get any work done** so kommen wir zu nichts; **at the ~ you're going, ...** *(fig.)* wenn du so weitermachst, ...; **we can't afford to spend money at this ~:** wir können es uns *(Dat.)* nicht leisten, so mit unserem Geld umzugehen; **you'll always be hard up at that ~:** so wirst du immer knapp bei Kasse sein. *See also* [1]**knot 1 f. 2.** *v.t.* **a)** *(estimate worth of)* schätzen ‹*Vermögen*›; einschätzen ‹*Intelligenz, Leistung, Fähigkeit*›; ~ **sb./sth. highly** jmdn./etw. hoch einschätzen; **b)** *(consider)* betrachten; rechnen **(among** zu); **be ~d the top tennis-player in Europe** als der beste Tennisspieler Europas gelten; **c)** *(assign value to)* beurteilen, bewerten ‹*schulische Leistung, Lesefertigkeit*›; angeben ‹*Lebensdauer, Schubkraft*› **(at** mit); **d)** *(Brit.: subject to payment of local authority levy)* Gemeindeabgaben auferlegen (+ *Dat.*); **e)** *(Brit.: value)* **the house is ~d at £100 a year** die Grundlage für die Berechnung der Gemeindeabgaben für das Haus beträgt 100 Pfund pro Jahr; **f)** *(merit)* verdienen ‹*Auszeichnung, Erwähnung*›; **does his work ~ a pass?** soll man ihn mit dieser Arbeit bestehen lassen?; **he didn't ~ an invitation** *(coll.)* er war nicht wichtig genug, [um] eingeladen zu werden; **g)** *(coll.: think much of)* viel halten von ‹*Person*›; **~/not ~ one's chances** sich *(Dat.)* große/keine großen Chancen ausrechnen. **3.** *v.i.* zählen **(among** zu); ~ **as** gelten als; ~ **high in a team/low on a test** in einer Mannschaft viel gelten/bei einem Test schlecht abschneiden
[2]**rate** *v.t. (scold)* beschimpfen
rateable ['reɪtəbl] *adj. (Brit.)* [real]steuerpflichtig ‹*Eigentum, Gebäude*›; ~ **value** steuerbarer Wert
rate-capping ['reɪtkæpɪŋ] *n. (Brit.) gesetzliches Recht der Regierung, durch Entzug den Etat einer Kommunalverwaltung zu kürzen, wenn diese zu hohe Abgaben erhebt oder im vorangegangenen Haushaltsjahr zuviel Geld ausgegeben hat*
'ratepayer *n. (Brit.)* Realsteuerpflichtige, *der/die;* ≈ Steuerzahler, *der*/-zahlerin, *die*
rather ['rɑ:ðə(r)] *adv.* **a)** *(by preference)* lieber; **he wanted to appear witty ~ than brainy** er wollte lieber geistreich als klug erscheinen; **~ than accept bribes, he decided to resign** ehe er sich bestechen ließ, trat er lieber zurück; **I had ~ die than ...:** ich würde lieber sterben als ...; **no, thanks, I'd ~ not** nein danke, lieber nicht; **I would ~ you ...:** es wäre mir lieber, wenn du ...; **b)** *(somewhat)* ziemlich ‹*gut, gelangweilt, unvorsichtig, nett, warm*›; **I ~ think that ...:** ich bin ziemlich sicher, daß ...; **be a ~ good one** ziemlich gut sein; **be ~ better/more complicated than expected** um einiges besser/komplizierter sein als erwartet; **fall ~ flat** ein ziemlicher Reinfall sein; **be ~ a nice person** ziemlich nett sein; **it is ~ too early** ich fürchte, es ist zu früh; **it looks ~ like a banana** es sieht ungefähr wie eine Banane aus; **I ~ like beans/him** ich esse Bohnen ganz gern/ich mag ihn recht gern; **c)** *(more truly)* vielmehr; **or ~:** beziehungsweise; [oder] genauer gesagt; **he was careless ~ than wicked** er war eher nachlässig als böswillig; **d)** *(Brit. dated coll.: certainly)* aber gewiß doch; na klar *(ugs.)*
rathskeller ['rɑ:tskelə(r)] *n. (Amer.)* Kellerlokal, *das*
ratification [rætɪfɪ'keɪʃn] *n. see* **ratify:** Ratifizierung, *die;* Bestätigung, *die;* Sanktionierung, *die*
ratify ['rætɪfaɪ] *v.t.* ratifizieren ‹*völkerrechtlichen Vertrag*›; bestätigen ‹*Ernennung*›: sanktionieren ‹*Vertrag, Gesetzentwurf*›
[1]**rating** ['reɪtɪŋ] *n.* **a)** *(estimated standing)* Einschätzung, *die;* **security ~:** Geheimhaltungsstufe, *die;* **have a high/low ~:** hoch/niedrig eingeschätzt werden; **b)** *(Radio, Telev.)* **[popularity] ~:** Einschaltquote, *die;* **be high/low in the ~s** eine hohe/niedrige Einschaltquote haben; **c)** *(Navy: rank)* Dienstgrad, *der;* **d)** *(Brit. Navy: sailor)* **[naval] ~:** Mannschaftsdienstgrad, *der;* **deck ~s** Angehörige der Decksmannschaften; **e)** *(of racing-yacht)* Rennwert, *der*
[2]**rating** *n. (scolding)* Schimpfe, *die (ugs.);* **get a ~:** Schimpfe bekommen *(ugs.);* ausgeschimpft werden; **give sb. a ~:** jmdn. ausschimpfen
ratio ['reɪʃɪəʊ] *n., pl.* **~s** Verhältnis, *das;* **in a** *or* **the ~ of 1 to 5** im Verhältnis 1 : 5; **in direct ~ to** *or* **with** im gleichen Verhältnis wie; **the teacher-student ~:** das Verhältnis von Lehrern zu Schülern; **what is the ~ of men to women?** wie hoch ist der Männeranteil im Vergleich zu dem der Frauen?
ratiocination [rætɪɒsɪ'neɪʃn, ræʃɪɒsɪ'neɪʃn] *n.* Reflexion, *die* **(on** über + *Akk.)*
ration ['ræʃn] **1.** *n.* **a)** *(daily food allowance)* [Tages]ration, *die;* **put sb. on short ~s** jmdn. auf halbe Ration setzen *(ugs.);* **b)** *(fixed allowance of food etc. for civilians)* **~[s]** Ration, *die* **(of** an + *Dat.*); **sugar/petrol/meat/sweet ~:** Zucker-/Benzin-/Fleisch-/Süßigkeitenration, *die;* **c)** *(single portion)* Ration, *die;* **be given [out] with the ~s** *(fig. sl.)* automatisch vergeben werden *(ugs.).* **2.** *v.t.* rationieren ‹*Benzin, Autos*›; Rationen zuteilen (+ *Dat.*) ‹*Person*›; *(allocate systematically)* einteilen ‹*Zeit*›; **be ~ed to one glass of spirits per day** nur ein Glas Alkohol pro Tag trinken dürfen; ~ **oneself to ten cigarettes a day** sich *(Dat.)* nur zehn Zigaretten pro Tag erlauben
~ **'out** *v.t.* zuteilen **(to** *Dat.*); in Rationen austeilen **(to** an + *Akk.*)
rational ['ræʃənl] *adj.* **a)** *(having reason)* ra-

tional, vernunftbegabt ⟨*Wesen*⟩; *(sensible)* vernünftig ⟨*Person, Art, Politik usw.*⟩; **b)** *(based on reason; also Math.)* rational ⟨*Erklärung, Analyse, Zahl*⟩
rationale [ræʃə'nɑ:l] *n.* **a)** *(statement of reasons)* rationale Erklärung **(of** für); **b)** *(fundamental reason)* logische Grundlage
rationalisation, rationalise *see* **rationaliz-**
rationalism ['ræʃənəlɪzm] *n.* *(Theol., Philos.)* Rationalismus, *der*
rationalist ['ræʃənəlɪst] *n.* *(Theol., Philos.)* Rationalist, *der*/Rationalistin, *die*
rationalistic [ræʃənə'lɪstɪk] *adj.* rationalistisch
rationality [ræʃə'nælɪtɪ] *n., no pl.* **a)** *see* **rational a:** Rationalität, *die;* Vernunftbegabtheit, *die;* Vernünftigkeit, *die;* Vernunft, *die;* **b)** *(of explanation, analysis, etc.)* Rationalität, *die*
rationalization [ræʃənəlaɪ'zeɪʃn] *n.* *(Econ., Psych.)* Rationalisierung, *die*
rationalize ['ræʃənəlaɪz] **1.** *v. t.* **a)** *(Econ., Psych.)* rationalisieren; **b)** *(explain by rationalism)* ~ **away** rationalistisch erklären. **2.** *v. i.* **a)** Scheinbegründungen finden; **b)** *(be a rationalist)* rational denken/handeln
rationally ['ræʃənəlɪ] *adv.* rational; *(sensibly)* vernünftig
ration: ~ book *n.* Bezugsscheinheft, *das;* **~ card, ~ coupon** *ns.* Bezugsschein, *der*
rationing ['ræʃənɪŋ] *n.* Rationierung, *die*
ratline (ratlin) ['rætlɪn], **ratling** ['rætlɪŋ] *n.* *(Naut.)* Webeleine, *die*
rat: ~ poison *n.* Rattengift, *das;* **~ race** *n.* erbarmungsloser Konkurrenzkampf; **~-run** *n.* hektisches Chaos; **~'s-tail** *n.* Rattenschwanz, *der*
rattan [rə'tæn] *n.* **a)** *(cane)* Peddigrohr, *das;* Rattan, *das; attrib.* Rattan⟨*möbel, -matte, -tau*⟩; **b)** *(Bot.)* Rotangpalme, *die*
rat-tat [ræt'tæt], **rat-tat-tat** [rætæ'tæt] *ns.* Klopfen, *das*
ratter ['rætə(r)] *n.* Rattenjäger, *der*
rattle ['rætl] **1.** *v. i.* **a)** *(clatter)* ⟨*Fenster, Maschinenteil, Schlüssel:*⟩ klappern; ⟨*Hagel:*⟩ prasseln; ⟨*Flaschen:*⟩ klirren; ⟨*Kette:*⟩ rasseln; ⟨*Münzen:*⟩ klingen; **~ at the door** an der Tür rütteln; **b)** *(move)* ⟨*Zug, Bus:*⟩ rattern; ⟨*Kutsche:*⟩ rumpeln. **2.** *v. t.* **a)** *(make ~)* klappern mit ⟨*Würfel, Geschirr, Dose, Münzen, Schlüsselbund*⟩; klirren lassen ⟨*Fenster[scheiben]*⟩; rasseln mit ⟨*Kette*⟩; **b)** *(sl.: disconcert)* **~ sb., get sb. ~d** jmdn. durcheinanderbringen; **don't get ~d!** reg dich nicht auf!; **they tried to ~ the performer** sie versuchten, den Künstler aus dem Konzept zu bringen. *See also* **sabre. 3.** *n.* **a)** *(of baby, musician)* Rassel, *die;* *(of sports fan)* Ratsche, *die;* Klapper, *die;* **b)** *(sound)* Klappern, *das;* *(of hail)* Prasseln, *das;* *(of drums)* Schnarren, *das;* *(of machine-gun)* Rattern, *das;* *(of chains)* Rasseln, *das;* *(of bottles)* Klirren, *das;* **c)** *(of rattlesnake)* Rassel, *die;* Klapper, *die*
~ a'way *v. i.* *(coll.)* *(talk)* schnattern *(ugs.);* *(on typewriter)* klappern *(ugs.);* **~ away at** *or* **on** klappern auf (+ *Dat.*) ⟨*Schreibmaschine*⟩
~ 'off *v. t.* *(coll.)* herunterrasseln *(ugs.);* **~ sth. off like a machine-gun** etw. herunterrattern wie ein Maschinengewehr
~ 'on *v. i.* *(coll.)* plappern *(ugs.)*
~ through *v. t.* *(fig.)* herunterrasseln
rattler ['rætlə(r)] *n.* *(Amer. coll.)* Klapperschlange, *die*
rattle: ~snake *n.* Klapperschlange, *die;* **~trap** *n.* *(coll.)* Klapperkasten, *der (ugs.)*
rattling ['rætlɪŋ] **1.** *adj.* flott ⟨*Tempo*⟩. **2.** *adv.* *(coll.)* verdammt *(ugs.)* ⟨*gut*⟩
'rat-trap *n.* Rattenfalle, *die*
ratty ['rætɪ] *adj.* *(sl.: irritable)* gereizt; **don't get ~ with me!** laß deinen Ärger nicht an mir aus!
raucous ['rɔ:kəs] *adj.* **a)** rauh ⟨*Stimme, Lachen*⟩; **b)** *(boisterous, disorderly)* wild ⟨*Benehmen*⟩; wüst ⟨*Gesänge*⟩; roh ⟨*Zuruf*⟩
raucously ['rɔ:kəslɪ] *adv.* **a)** mit rauher Stimme; **b)** *(boisterously)* **they sang/laughed/shouted ~:** sie sangen wüste Gesänge/lachten roh/stießen wilde Rufe aus
raunchy ['rɔ:ntʃɪ] *adj.* *(lewd)* vulgär; *(suggestive)* scharf *(salopp)*
ravage ['rævɪdʒ] **1.** *v. t.* heimsuchen ⟨*Gebiet, Stadt*⟩; so gut wie vernichten ⟨*Ernte*⟩; schwer zeichnen ⟨*Gesichtszüge*⟩. **2.** *n. in pl.* verheerende Wirkung; **the ~s of time/war** die Zeichen der Zeit/die Wunden des Krieges; **be marked by the ~s of famine** vom Hunger schwer gezeichnet sein
rave [reɪv] **1.** *v. i.* **a)** *(talk wildly)* irrereden; **he's just raving** er redet nur irres Zeug *(ugs.);* **~ at** [wüst] beschimpfen; *see also* **rant 1; b)** *(speak with admiration)* schwärmen **(about, over** von); **c)** *(howl)* ⟨*Wind, Sturm, Meer:*⟩ brausen. **2.** *adj.* *(coll.)* [hellauf] begeistert ⟨*Kritik*⟩. **3.** *n.* *(Brit. sl.: fad, fashion)* **the latest ~:** der letzte Schrei; **it's all the ~:** es ist der letzte Schrei
ravel ['rævl] **1.** *v. t.,* *(Brit.)* **-ll- a)** *(entangle)* verheddern ⟨*Wollstrang*⟩; **~ into knots** verwickeln und verknoten; **b)** *see* **unravel 1. 2.** *v. i.,* *(Brit.)* **-ll- a)** *(become entangled)* sich verwickeln; **b)** *see* **unravel 2**
~ 'out *see* **unravel 1**
raven ['reɪvn] **1.** *n.* Rabe, *der;* Kolkrabe, *der* *(Zool.).* **2.** *adj.* **~-black** [kohl]rabenschwarz ⟨*Haar*⟩; **~-haired** mit kohlrabenschwarzem Haar *nachgestellt*
ravening ['rævənɪŋ] *adj.* beutegierig
ravenous ['rævənəs] *adj.* **a)** ausgehungert; **I'm ~:** ich habe einen Bärenhunger *(ugs.);* **have a ~ hunger/appetite** einen richtigen Heißhunger haben; **b)** *(greedy)* räuberisch
ravenously ['rævənəslɪ] *adv.* heißhungrig; **be ~ hungry** einen Riesenhunger haben *(ugs.);* ausgehungert sein
'rave-up *n.* *(Brit. sl.)* [wilde] Fete *(ugs.)*
ravine [rə'vi:n] *n.* Schlucht, *die;* *(produced by river also)* Klamm, *die*
raving ['reɪvɪŋ] **1.** *n. in pl.* irres Gerede. **2.** *adj.* **a)** *(talking madly)* irreredend ⟨*Wahnsinniger, Idiot*⟩; **b)** *(outstanding)* *(ugs.)* phantastisch ⟨*Erfolg*⟩; **be a ~ beauty** hinreißend schön sein. **3.** *adv.* **be ~ mad** *(insane)* hochgradig schwachsinnig sein; *(stupid)* völlig verrückt sein *(ugs.)*
ravioli [rævɪ'əʊlɪ] *n.* *(Gastr.)* Ravioli *Pl.*
ravish ['rævɪʃ] *v. t.* **a)** *(charm)* entzücken; bezaubern; **be ~ed** hingerissen *od.* bezaubert sein **(by, with** von); **b)** *(rape)* schänden *(veralt.);* Gewalt antun *(geh.* + *Dat.)*
ravishing ['rævɪʃɪŋ] *adj.* bildschön ⟨*Anblick, Person*⟩; hinreißend ⟨*Schönheit*⟩; **~ sight** Augenweide, *die*
raw [rɔ:] **1.** *adj.* **a)** *(uncooked)* roh; **b)** *(inexperienced)* unerfahren; frischgebacken ⟨*Akademiker*⟩; blutig ⟨*Anfänger*⟩; *see also* **recruit 1 a, d; c)** *(unbound)* ungesäumt ⟨*Kante, Stoff*⟩; **d)** *(stripped of skin)* blutig ⟨*Fleisch*⟩; offen ⟨*Wunde*⟩; *(sore)* wund ⟨*Füße*⟩; **e)** *(chilly)* naßkalt; **f)** *(untreated)* Roh⟨*haut, -holz, -seide, -zucker, -erz, -leder*⟩; *(undiluted)* rein ⟨*Alkohol*⟩; **g)** *(fig.: unpolished)* grob; **h)** *(Statistics)* unaufbereitet. *See also* **¹deal 3 a; sienna; umber. 2.** *n.* **nature in the ~:** unverfälschte Natur; **life in the ~:** das Leben, wie es wirklich ist; **in the ~** *(fig.)* unbekleidet ⟨*schlafen*⟩; **touch sb. on the ~** *(Brit. coll.)* jmdn. an [s]einer verwundbaren Stelle treffen
raw: ~-boned ['rɔ:bəʊnd] *adj.* knochig; **~hide** *n.* **a)** *(leather)* Rohleder, *das;* **b)** *(whip)* Peitsche aus Rohleder
Rawlplug, (P) ['rɔ:lplʌg] *n.* Dübel, *der*
raw ma'terial *n.* Rohstoff, *der*
¹ray [reɪ] *n.* **a)** *(lit. or fig.)* Strahl, *der;* **~ of sunshine/light** Sonnen-/Lichtstrahl, *der;* **~ of sunshine** *(fig.)* Sonnenschein, *der;* **~ of hope** Hoffnungsstrahl, *der;* **give sb. a ~ of hope** jmdm. Hoffnung machen; **provide a ~ of comfort** etwas Trost spenden; **b)** *in pl.* *(radiation)* Strahlen; Strahlung, *die; see also* **cosmic; gamma rays; X-ray 1; c)** *(Zool.)* *(of fish's fin)* Flossenstrahl, *der;* Radius, *der (fachspr.);* *(of starfish)* Arm, *der*
²ray *n.* *(fish)* Rochen, *der*
³ray *n.* *(Mus.)* re
'ray gun *n.* *(Science Fiction)* Strahlenpistole, *die*
rayon ['reɪɒn] *n.* *(Textiles)* Reyon, *das od. der; attrib.* Reyon⟨*kleid, -hemd*⟩
raze [reɪz] *v. t.* *(completely destroy)* völlig zerstören; *(pull down)* abreißen; **~ to the ground** dem Erdboden gleichmachen
razor ['reɪzə(r)] *n.* Rasiermesser, *das;* **[electric] ~:** [elektrischer] Rasierapparat; [Elektro- *od.* Trocken]rasierer, *der (ugs.); see also* **safety razor**
razor: ~-bill *n.* *(Ornith.)* Tordalk, *der;* **~-blade** *n.* Rasierklinge, *die;* **~-edge** *n.* Rasierschneide, *die;* **sharpen to a ~-edge** rasiermesserscharf machen; **be** *or* **stand on a ~-edge** *or* **~'s edge** *(fig. coll.)* sich auf einer Gratwanderung befinden; **~-fish** *n.* *(Zool.)* Scheidenmuschel, *die;* **~-sharp** *adj.* sehr scharf ⟨*Messer*⟩; *(fig.)* messerscharf ⟨*Verstand, Intellekt*⟩; scharfsinnig ⟨*Person*⟩; **~-shell** *see* **~-fish; ~-wire** *n.* *wie Stacheldraht verwendeter, dünner, scharfkantiger Draht*
razzamatazz ['ræzəmətæz] *see* **razzmatazz**
razzle ['ræzl] *n.* *(sl.)* **be/go on the ~:** einen draufmachen *(ugs.)*
razzle-dazzle ['ræzldæzl], **razzmatazz** ['ræzmətæz] *ns.* *(sl.)* **a)** *(excitement)* Trubel, *der;* **add ~ to sth.** etwas aufmotzen *(salopp);* **b)** *(extravagant show)* Rummel, *der (ugs.)*
RC *abbr.* **Roman Catholic** r.-k.; röm.-kath.
Rd. *abbr.* **road** Str.
RE *abbr.* *(Brit.)* **a) Royal Engineers** Pionierkorps der britischen Armee; **b) Religious Education** Religionslehre, *die*
¹re *see* **³ray**
²re [ri:] *prep.* **a)** *(coll.)* über (+ *Akk.*); **b)** *(Law)* in Sachen; **c)** *(Commerc.)* betreffs
're [ə(r)] *(coll.)* = **are;** *see* **be**
reach [ri:tʃ] **1.** *v. t.* **a)** *(arrive at)* erreichen; ankommen *od.* eintreffen in (+ *Dat.*) ⟨*Stadt, Land*⟩; ankommen an (+ *Dat.*) ⟨*Reiseziel*⟩; erzielen ⟨*Übereinstimmung, Übereinkunft*⟩; kommen zu ⟨*Entscheidung, Entschluß; Ausgang, Eingang*⟩; **be easily ~ed** leicht erreichbar *od.* zu erreichen sein **(by** mit); **not a sound ~ed our ears** kein Laut drang an unsere Ohren; **your letter ~ed me today** dein Brief hat mich heute erreicht; **have you ~ed page 45 yet?** bist du schon auf Seite 45 [angelangt]?; **you can ~ her at this number/by radio** du kannst sie unter dieser Nummer/über Funk erreichen; **b)** *(extend to)* ⟨*Straße:*⟩ führen bis zu; ⟨*Leiter, Haar:*⟩ reichen bis zu; **c)** *(pass)* **~ me that book** reich mir das Buch herüber. **2.** *v. i.* **a)** *(stretch out hand)* **~ for sth.** nach etw. greifen; **~ across the table/through the window** über den Tisch/durchs Fenster langen; **how high can you ~?** wie hoch kannst du langen?; **b)** *(be long/tall enough)* **sth. will/won't ~:** etw. ist/ist nicht lang genug; **he can't ~ up to the top shelf** er kann das oberste Regal nicht [mit der Hand] erreichen; **will it ~ as far as ...?** wird es bis zu ... reichen? **can you ~?** kannst *od.* kommst du dran? *(ugs.);* **c)** *(go as far as)* ⟨*Wasser, Gebäude, Besitz:*⟩ reichen (**[up]** to bis [hinauf] zu); ⟨*Betrag:*⟩ erreichen **(to** *Akk.*); ⟨*Stimme:*⟩ zu hören sein **(to** bis); **his influence ~es beyond the limits of the town** sein Einfluß reicht über die Stadtgrenzen hinaus. **3.** *n.* **a)** *(extent of reaching)* Reichweite, *die;* **be within easy ~ [of a place]** [von einem Ort aus] leicht erreichbar sein; **live within ~ of sb.** in jmds. Nähe leben; **be out of ~ [of a place]** [von einem Ort aus] nicht erreichbar sein; **be above sb.'s ~:** zu

hoch für jmdn. sein; **keep sth. out of ~ of sb.** etw. unerreichbar für jmdn. aufbewahren; **keep sth. within easy ~:** etw. in greifbarer Nähe aufbewahren; **move sth. beyond sb.'s ~:** etw. aus jmds. Reichweite entfernen; **be within/beyond the ~ of sb.** in/außer jmds. Reichweite sein; *(fig.)* für jmdn. im/nicht im Bereich des Möglichen liegen; *(financially)* für jmdn. erschwinglich/unerschwinglich sein; **b)** *(act of stretching out hand)* **make a ~ for sth.** nach etw. greifen; **it was a long ~ from the bed to the light-switch** der Lichtschalter war vom Bett aus schwer zu erreichen; **c)** *(expanse)* Abschnitt, *der;* **a ~ of woodland** ein Waldgebiet; **the upper/lower ~es [of the river]** die oberen/unteren [Fluß]abschnitte; **d)** *(Naut.)* Segelstrecke zwischen zwei Wendungen; **be on a ~:** raumen Kurs segeln

~ a'cross *v. i.* die Hand ausstrecken

~ 'back *v. i.* zurückreichen **(over** *Akk.;* **to** bis in + *Akk.*)

~ 'down 1. *v. i.* den Arm nach unten ausstrecken; **~ down to sth.** *(be long enough)* bis zu etw. [hinunter]reichen. **2.** *v. t.* hinunterholen; *(to receiving speaker)* herunterreichen

~ 'out 1. *v. t. (stretch out)* ausstrecken ⟨*Fuß, Bein, Hand, Arm*⟩ **(for** nach). **2.** *v. i.* die Hand ausstrecken **(for** nach); **~ out for, ~ out to grasp** ⟨*Person, Hand:*⟩ greifen nach; **~ out to sb.** *(fig.)* jmdn. zu erreichen versuchen

~ 'over *v. i.* die Hand ausstrecken

reachable [ˈriːtʃəbl] *adj.* erreichbar

'reach-me-down *(Brit. coll.) see* **hand-me-down 1 b**

react [rɪˈækt] **1.** *v. i.* **a)** *(respond)* reagieren **(to** auf + *Akk.*); **be quick to ~ to sth.** auf etw. schnell reagieren; **b)** *(act in opposition)* sich widersetzen **(against** *Dat.*); **c)** *(produce reciprocal effect)* zurückwirken **(upon** auf + *Akk.*); seine Wirkung haben **(upon** auf + *Akk.*); **d)** *(Chem., Phys.)* reagieren. **2.** *v. t. (Chem.)* reagieren lassen

reaction [rɪˈækʃn] *n.* **a)** Reaktion, *die* **(to** auf + *Akk.*); **~ against sth.** Widerstand gegen etw.; **action and ~** Wirkung und Gegenwirkung; **what was his ~?** wie hat er reagiert?; **there was a favourable ~ to the proposal** der Vorschlag ist positiv aufgenommen worden; **chemical/nuclear ~:** chemische Reaktion/Kernreaktion, *die;* **I had a bad ~ after the injection** mein Körper hat die Injektion schlecht vertragen; **b)** *(opposite physical action)* Gegenreaktion, *die;* **c)** *(Polit.)* Reaktion, *die;* **forces of ~:** reaktionäre Kräfte

reactionary [rɪˈækʃənərɪ] *(Polit.)* **1.** *adj.* reaktionär. **2.** *n.* Reaktionär, *der*/Reaktionärin, *die*

reactivate [rɪˈæktɪveɪt] *v. t.* reaktivieren; wieder in Gang bringen ⟨*Motor, Generator*⟩; wieder einrichten ⟨*Stützpunkt*⟩

reactive [rɪˈæktɪv] *adj.* **a)** *(showing reaction)* auf eine Reaktion hindeutend ⟨*Symptom*⟩; **~ response** Gegenreaktion, *die;* **b)** *(Chem., Phys.)* reaktiv

reactivity [rɪækˈtɪvɪtɪ] *n. (Chem., Phys.)* Reaktionsfähigkeit, *die*

reactor [rɪˈæktə(r)] *n.* **a) [nuclear] ~:** Kernreaktor, *der;* **pressurized-water ~:** Druckwasserreaktor, *der;* **b)** *(Chem.)* Reaktor, *der;* Reaktionsapparat, *der*

read [riːd] **1.** *v. t.*, **read** [red] **a)** lesen; **~ sb. sth., ~ sth. to sb.** jmdm. etwas vorlesen; **~ a Bill for the first/second/third time** *(Parl.)* einen Gesetzentwurf in erster/zweiter/dritter Lesung beraten; **for 'white' ~ 'black'** statt „weiß" muß es „schwarz" heißen; **~ proof[s]** *(Print.)* Korrektur[en] lesen; **~ the electricity/gas meter** den Strom/das Gas ablesen; **~ all about it!** lesen Sie selbst!; **b)** *(show a reading of)* anzeigen; **c)** *(interpret)* deuten; **~ terror in sb.'s eyes** Schrecken an jmds. Augen *(Dat.)* ablesen können; **~ sb. like a book** *(fig. coll.)* in jmdm. lesen können wie in einem Buch; **~ the cards/ sb.'s hand** Karten lesen/jmdm. aus der Hand lesen; **~ sb.'s mind** *or* **thoughts** jmds. Gedanken lesen; **~ sth. into sth.** etw. in etw. *(Akk.)* hineinlesen; **~ between the lines** zwischen den Zeilen lesen; **d)** *(understand)* hören; **do you ~ me?** können Sie mich hören?; **e)** *(Brit. Univ.: study)* studieren; **f)** *(Computing)* abtasten ⟨*Lochkarte*⟩; lesen ⟨*Band, Information*⟩; **~ into** einlesen in (+ *Akk.*); **~ out of** entnehmen aus. *See also* **take 1 u. 2.** *v. i.*, **read a)** lesen; **~ to sb.** jmdm. vorlesen; **~ [a]round a subject** Hintergrundmaterial zu einem Thema lesen; **b)** *(convey meaning)* lauten; **the contract ~s as follows** der Vertrag hat folgenden Wortlaut; **Arabic ~s from right to left** die arabische Schrift wird von rechts nach links gelesen; **c)** *(affect reader)* sich lesen; **the play ~s better than it acts** das Stück wirkt besser beim Lesen als auf der Bühne. **3.** *n.* **a)** *(time spent in reading)* **have a quiet ~:** in Ruhe lesen; **have a ~ of sth.** *(coll.)* mal in etw. *(Akk.)* gucken *(ugs.)*; **b)** *(Brit. coll.: reading matter)* **be a good ~:** sich gut lesen. **4.** [red] *adj.* **widely** *or* **deeply ~:** sehr belesen ⟨*Person*⟩; **a widely ~/little-~ book/author** ein viel/wenig gelesenes Buch/gelesener Autor; **the most widely ~ book/author** das meistgelesene Buch/der meistgelesene Autor

~ 'back *v. t.* wiederholen; noch einmal vorlesen

~ 'in *v. t. (Computing)* einlesen; *see also* **read-in**

~ 'off *v. t.* durchlesen; *(from meter, board)* ablesen ⟨*Zahl, Stand*⟩

~ 'out *v. t.* **a)** *(aloud)* laut vorlesen; **b)** *(Computing)* ausgeben; *see also* **read-out; c)** *(Amer.: expel)* ausschließen **(of** aus)

~ 'over, ~ 'through *v. t.* durchlesen

~ 'up *v. t.* sich informieren **(on** über + *Akk.*)

readability [riːdəˈbɪlɪtɪ] *n., no pl.* Lesbarkeit, *die;* **improve the ~ of sth.** etwas lesbarer machen

readable [ˈriːdəbl] *adj.* **a)** *(pleasant to read)* lesenswert; **b)** *(legible)* leserlich

readdress [riːəˈdres] *v. t.* umadressieren

reader [ˈriːdə(r)] *n.* **a)** Leser, *der*/Leserin, *die;* **be a slow/good/great ~ [of sth.]** [etw.] langsam/gut/gern lesen; **b)** *(who reads aloud)* Vorlesende, *der/die;* **c)** *(Publishing)* **[publisher's] ~:** [Verlags]lektor, *der*/-lektorin, *die;* **d)** *(textbook)* Lehrbuch, *das;* *(to learn to read, containing original texts)* Lesebuch, *das;* **Latin/poetry ~:** Latein[lehr]buch, *das*/Gedichtbuch, *das;* **e)** *(Printing) see* **proof-reader; f)** *(Brit. Univ.)* ≈ Assistenzprofessor, *der*/-professorin, *die* **(in** für); **g)** *(machine)* Lesegerät, *das*

readership [ˈriːdəʃɪp] *n.* **a)** *(number or type of readers)* Leserschaft, *die;* Leserkreis, *der;* **what is the ~ of the paper?** wie groß ist die Leserschaft der Zeitung?; **b)** *(Brit. Univ.)* ≈ Assistenzprofessur, *die* **(in** für)

readies [ˈredɪz] *n. pl. (sl.)* Knete, *die (ugs.)*; **short of the ~:** knapp bei Kasse *(ugs.)*

readily [ˈredɪlɪ] *adv.* **a)** *(willingly)* bereitwillig; **b)** *(without difficulty)* ohne weiteres

read-in [ˈriːdɪn] *n. (Computing)* Eingabe, *die; attrib.* Eingabe-

readiness [ˈredɪnɪs] *n., no pl.* **a)** Bereitschaft, *die;* **show [a] ~ to do sth.** Bereitschaft zeigen, etw. zu tun; **~ to learn** Lernbereitschaft, *die;* **have/be in ~ [for sth.]** [für etw.] bereithalten/bereit sein; **b)** *(quickness)* Schnelligkeit, *die;* **~ of wit** Schlagfertigkeit, *die*

reading [ˈriːdɪŋ] *n.* **a)** Lesen, *das;* **help sb. with his ~:** jmdm. beim Lesen helfen; **do some ~:** [ein wenig] lesen; **on [a] second ~:** beim zweiten Lesen; **a man of vast** *or* **wide/little ~:** ein sehr/wenig belesener Mann; **b)** *(matter to be read)* Lektüre, *die;* **plenty of ~:** viel zu lesen; **make interesting/be good/dull ~:** interessant/gut/langweilig zu lesen sein; **a book of ~s from the Bible** ein Buch mit ausgewählten Bibeltexten *od.* Auszügen aus der Bibel; **c)** *(figure shown)* Anzeige, *die;* **the temperature ~s for last month** die Temperaturwerte des letzten Monats; **d)** *(recital)* Lesung, *die* **(from** aus); **give a poetry ~:** Gedichte vorlesen; **give a ~ from** lesen aus; **e)** *(interpretation)* [Aus]deutung, *die;* **my ~ of the sentence was ...:** ich habe den Satz so verstanden: ...; **our ~ of the law is that ...:** wir legen das Recht so aus, daß ...; **f)** *(particular form)* Version, *die;* Fassung, *die;* **g)** *(Parl.)* **[first/second/third] ~:** [erste/zweite/dritte] Lesung; **have its first ~:** in erster Lesung beraten werden; **be thrown out on the second ~** *(Brit.)* in zweiter Lesung verworfen werden; **give the bill its second ~** *(Amer.)* den Gesetzentwurf in zweiter Lesung beraten

reading: ~ age *n.* **a child with a ~ age of 10** ein Kind mit der Lesefertigkeit eines Zehnjährigen; **have a ~ age of 10** wie ein zehnjähriges Kind lesen können; **~-desk** *n.* Lesepult, *das;* **~-glasses** *n. pl.* Lesebrille, *die;* **~ knowledge** *n.* **have a ~ knowledge of a language** Texte in einer Sprache lesen können; **~-lamp, ~-light** *ns.* Leselampe, *die;* **~-list** *n.* Literaturliste, *die;* **~ matter** *n., no pl., no indef. art.* Lesestoff, *der;* Lektüre, *die;* **~-room** *n.* Lesesaal, *der*

readjust [riːəˈdʒʌst] **1.** *v. t.* neu einstellen; neu anpassen ⟨*Gehalt, Zinssatz*⟩. **2.** *v. refl.* & *i.* **~ [oneself] to** sich wieder gewöhnen an (+ *Akk.*) ⟨*Leben*⟩

readjustment [riːəˈdʒʌstmənt] *n.* Änderung, *die;* **period of ~:** Zeit der Neuorientierung

read [riːd]: **~-'only memory** *n. (Computing)* Fest[wert]speicher, *der;* **~-out** *n. (Computing)* Ausgabe, *die*

ready [ˈredɪ] **1.** *adj.* **a)** *(prepared)* fertig; **be ~ for the fight** *or* **to fight** kampfbereit sein; **be ~ to do sth.** bereit sein, etw. zu tun; **the troops are ~ to march/for battle** die Truppen sind marsch-/gefechtsbereit; **be ~ for work/school** zur Arbeit/für die Schule bereit sein; *(about to leave)* für die Arbeit/Schule fertig sein; **be ~ to leave** aufbruchsbereit sein; **be ~ for sb.** bereit sein, sich jmdm. zu stellen; **be ~ for anything** auf alles vorbereitet sein; **make ~:** Vorbereitungen treffen **(for** für); **make ~ to go** sich zum Aufbruch bereit machen; **b)** *(willing)* bereit; **I'm ~ to believe it** ich glaube es gerne; **c)** *(prompt)* schnell; **have ~, be ~ with** parat haben, nicht verlegen sein um ⟨*Antwort, Ausrede, Vorschlag*⟩; **be too ~ to suspect others** allzu schnell bereit sein, andere zu verdächtigen; **d)** *(likely)* im Begriff; **be ~ to burst** ⟨*Knospe:*⟩ kurz vor dem Aufbrechen sein; **be ~ to cry** den Tränen nahe sein; **e)** *(within reach)* griffbereit ⟨*Waffe, Fahrkarte, Taschenlampe*⟩; **have your tickets ~!** halten Sie Ihre Fahrkarten bitte bereit!; **a ~ source of supplies** eine sofort zugängliche Bezugsquelle; **f)** *(not reluctant)* bereitwillig ⟨*Zustimmung, Anerkennung*⟩; willig ⟨*Arbeiter*⟩; **g)** *(easy)* leicht ⟨*Löslichkeit, Zugänglichkeit*⟩; **she has a ~ smile** sie lächelt gern. **2.** *adv.* fertig; **~ cooked** vorgekocht. **3.** *n.* **a) at the ~:** schußbereit, im Anschlag ⟨*Schußwaffe*⟩; **b)** *see* **readies**

ready: ~ 'cash *see* **~ money; ~-'made** *adj.* **a)** Konfektions⟨*anzug, -kleidung*⟩; **~-made curtains** Fertiggardinen; **b)** *(fig.)* vorgefertigt; **~ 'money** *n.* **a)** *(cash)* Bargeld, *das;* **b)** *(immediate payment)* **for ~ money** gegen bar; **~ 'reckoner** *n.* Berechnungstabelle, *die; (for conversion)* Umrechnungstabelle, *die;* **~, set** *or* **steady, 'go!** *int.* Achtung, fertig, los!; **~-to-eat** *adj.* Fertig⟨*mahlzeit, -dessert*⟩; **~-to-'wear** *adj.* Konfektions⟨*anzug, -kleidung*⟩

reaffirm [ri:ə'fɜ:m] *v.t.* [erneut] bekräftigen

reaffirmation [ri:æfə'meɪʃn] *n.* [erneute] Bekräftigung

reafforestation [ri:əfɒrɪ'steɪʃn] *n.* Wiederaufforstung, *die*

reagent [ri:'eɪdʒənt] *n.* *(Chem.)* Reagens, *das;* Reagenz, *das*

real [rɪəl] **1.** *adj.* **a)** *(actually existing)* real ⟨*Gestalt, Ereignis, Lebewesen*⟩; wirklich ⟨*Macht*⟩; **b)** *(genuine)* echt ⟨*Interesse, Gold, Seide*⟩; **very ~** *(coll.)* wirklich groß ⟨*Vergnügen, Ehre*⟩; **c)** *(complete)* total *(ugs.)* ⟨*Desaster, Bauernfängerei, Wucher, Enttäuschung*⟩; **d)** *(true)* wahr ⟨*Grund, Freund, Name, Glück*⟩; echt ⟨*Mitleid, Vergnügen, Sieg*⟩; **the ~ thing** *(genuine article)* der/die/das Echte; *(fig.: true love)* [die] wahre Liebe; **look like the ~ thing** wie echt aussehen; **be [not] the ~ thing** [un]echt sein; **have experienced the ~ thing** das Echte kennen; **feel a ~ fool** sich *(Dat.)* wie ein richtiger Idiot vorkommen; **e)** *(Econ.)* real; Real-; **in ~ terms** real ⟨*sinken, steigen*⟩; **salaries decreased in ~ terms** die Realgehälter sind gesunken; **f) be for ~** *(sl.)* echt sein; ⟨*Angebot, Drohung:*⟩ ernst gemeint sein; ⟨*Person:*⟩ aufrichtig sein; **fight for ~:** richtig kämpfen; **g)** *(Philos.)* real; **h)** *(Math., Optics)* reell ⟨*Zahl, Bild, Analyse*⟩. *See also* **tennis. 2.** *adv. (Scot. and Amer. coll. as intensifier)* echt *(ugs.)* ⟨*gut, schön, usw.*⟩; recht ⟨*bald*⟩

real: ~ 'ale *n. (Brit.)* echtes Ale; **~ 'coffee** *n.* Bohnenkaffee, *der;* **~ e'state** *n. (Law)* Immobilien *Pl.;* **be in ~ estate** Immobilienhandel betreiben; **~-estate** *adj.* Immobilien⟨*büro, -makler*⟩

realign [ri:ə'laɪn] *v.t.* neu ordnen ⟨*Text, Daten*⟩; neu aufeinander abstimmen ⟨*Währungen*⟩

realignment [ri:ə'laɪnmənt] *n.* Neuordnung, *die; (of currency)* Realignment, *das (Finanzw.)*

realisable, realisation, realise *see* **realiz-**

realism ['rɪəlɪzm] *n.* Realismus, *der;* **[sense of] ~:** Wirklichkeitssinn, *der*

realist ['rɪəlɪst] *n.* Realist, *der*/Realistin, *die*

realistic [rɪə'lɪstɪk] *adj.* realistisch; **be ~ about sth.** etw. realistisch sehen

realistically [rɪə'lɪstɪkəlɪ] *adv.* realistisch

reality [rɪ'ælɪtɪ] *n.* **a)** *no pl.* Realität, *die;* **appearance and ~:** Schein und Sein; **bring sb. back to ~:** jmdn. in die Realität zurückholen; **in ~:** in Wirklichkeit; **b)** *no pl. (resemblance to original)* Naturtreue, *die;* **with [startling] ~:** [erstaunlich] naturgetreu; **c)** *(real fact)* Gegebenheit, *die;* **the realities of the situation** die tatsächliche Situation

realizable ['rɪəlaɪzəbl] *adj.* realisierbar

realization [rɪəlaɪ'zeɪʃn] *n.* **a)** *(understanding)* Erkenntnis, *die;* **b)** *(becoming real)* Verwirklichung, *die;* **c)** *(Finance: act of selling)* Realisierung, *die*

realize ['rɪəlaɪz] *v.t.* **a)** *(be aware of)* bemerken; realisieren; erkennen ⟨*Fehler*⟩; **they've ~d the importance of tact** sie merkten, wie wichtig Taktgefühl ist; **I never ~d how much I depend on him** erst jetzt wird mir bewußt, wie sehr ich auf ihn angewiesen bin; **~ [that] ...:** merken, daß ...; **I hardly ~d what was happening** ich habe kaum mitbekommen, was da vor sich ging; **I didn't ~** *(abs.)* ich habe es nicht gewußt/*(had not noticed)* bemerkt; **b)** *(make happen)* verwirklichen; **be ~d** wahr werden; **c)** *(Finance: sell for cash)* realisieren *(fachspr.);* in Geld *(Akk.)* umsetzen; **d)** *(fetch as price or profit)* erbringen ⟨*Summe, Gewinn, Preis*⟩; **e)** *(gain)* erwerben ⟨*Vermögen*⟩; machen ⟨*Gewinn*⟩

real: ~ 'life *n* das wirkliche Leben; die Realität; **~-life** *attrib. adj.* real

really ['rɪəlɪ] *adv.* wirklich; **it's a ~ good film** es ist ein wirklich guter Film; **I don't ~/~ don't know what to do now** ich weiß eigentlich/wirklich nicht, was ich jetzt tun soll; **I ~ think you ought to apologize** ich finde wirklich, daß du dich entschuldigen solltest; **not ~:** eigentlich nicht; **that's not ~ a problem** das ist eigentlich kein Problem; **he didn't ~ mean it** er hat es nicht so gemeint; **I ~ don't know** ich weiß es wirklich nicht; **[well,] ~!** [also] so was!; **~, I would never have expected that of you** also wirklich, das hätte ich nie von dir erwartet; **~?** wirklich?; tatsächlich?; **~ and truly** wirklich

realm [relm] *n.* [König]reich, *das;* **be in the ~[s] of fancy** ins Reich der Phantasie gehören; **be within/beyond the ~s of possibility** *or* **the possible** im/nicht im Bereich des Möglichen liegen

real: ~ 'man *n.* richtiger Mann; **~ 'money** *n.* Bargeld, *das;* **pay in ~ money** bar bezahlen; **~ 'property** *n. (Law)* Grundvermögen, *das;* **~ time** *n. (Computing)* Realzeit, *die;* Echtzeit, *die*

realtor ['ri:əltə(r)] *(Amer.) see* **estate agent a**

real 'world *n. (beyond school)* Arbeitswelt, *die; (as opposed to film etc.)* Realität, *die;* **the ~ outside** die [reale] Außenwelt

ream [ri:m] *n.* **a)** *(quantity)* 500 Blatt; halbes [Neu]ries; **three ~s** 1 500 Blatt; anderthalb [Neu]ries; **b)** *in pl. (fig.)* ein ganzer Roman; **write ~s [and ~s] of poetry** ganze Bände von Gedichten schreiben

reanimate [rɪ'ænɪmeɪt] *v.t.* wiederbeleben

reap [ri:p] *v.t.* **a)** *(cut)* schneiden ⟨*Getreide*⟩; **b)** *(gather in)* einfahren ⟨*Getreide, Ernte*⟩; **c)** *(harvest)* abernten ⟨*Feld*⟩; **d)** *(fig.)* ernten ⟨*Ruhm, Lob*⟩; erhalten ⟨*Belohnung*⟩; erzielen ⟨*Gewinn*⟩; **~ what one has sown** ernten, was man gesät hat; **~ the benefits of sth.** die Früchte einer Sache ernten; *see also* **whirlwind a**

reaper ['ri:pə(r)] *n.* **a)** *see* **harvester; b) the [grim] R~** *(fig.)* der Sensenmann *(verhüll.);* der Schnitter [Tod]

reaping ['ri:pɪŋ]: **~-hook** *n.* Sichel, *die;* **~-machine** *see* **harvester a**

reappear [ri:ə'pɪə(r)] *v.i.* wieder auftauchen; *(come back)* [wieder] zurückkommen; ⟨*Sonne:*⟩ wieder zum Vorschein kommen

reappearance [ri:ə'pɪərəns] *n.* Wiederauftauchen, *das*

reapply [ri:ə'plaɪ] **1.** *v.i.* sich erneut bewerben **(for** um). **2.** *v.t.* noch einmal auftragen ⟨*Kleister*⟩

reappoint [ri:ə'pɔɪnt] *v.t.* wieder einstellen

reappointment [ri:ə'pɔɪntmənt] *n.* Wiedereinstellung, *die*

reappraisal [ri:ə'preɪzl] *n.* Neubewertung, *die*

reappraise [ri:ə'preɪz] *v.t.* neu bewerten

[1]**rear** [rɪə(r)] **1.** *n.* **a)** *(back part)* hinterer Teil; **at** *or* *(Amer.)* **in the ~ of** im hinteren Teil (+ *Gen.*); **please move to the ~:** bitte nach hinten durchgehen; **b)** *(back)* Rückseite, *die;* **bring up the ~, be in the ~:** den Schluß bilden; **to the ~ of the house there is ...:** hinter dem Haus ist ...; **go round to the ~ of the house** hinter das Haus gehen; **in the ~ of the procession** am Schluß der Prozession; **the spectators at the ~:** die hinten sitzenden/stehenden Zuschauer; **c)** *(Mil.)* Rücken, *der;* rückwärtiger Teil; **attack in the ~:** von hinten angreifen; **d)** *(coll.: buttocks)* Hintern, *der (ugs.).* **2.** *adj.* hinter ... ⟨*Eingang, Tür, Blinklicht*⟩; **~ axle** Hinterachse, *die*

[2]**rear 1.** *v.t.* **a)** *(bring up)* großziehen ⟨*Kind, Familie*⟩; halten ⟨*Vieh*⟩; hegen ⟨*Wild*⟩; **b)** *(lift up)* heben ⟨*Kopf*⟩; aufrichten ⟨*Leiter*⟩; **~ its ugly head** *(fig.)* seine häßliche Fratze zeigen. **2.** *v.i.* **a)** *(raise itself on hind legs)* **~ [up]** ⟨*Pferd:*⟩ sich aufbäumen; **b)** *(extend to great height)* ⟨*Gebäude, Berg:*⟩ sich erheben **(over, above** über + *Akk.*)

rear: ~-'admiral *n. (Navy)* Konteradmiral, *der;* **~ 'door** *n. (Motor Veh.)* Fondtür, *die;* Hintertür, *die; (to boot)* Hecktür, *die;* **~ 'end** *n. (sl.: buttocks)* Hinterteil, *das (ugs.);* **~-engined** *adj. (Motor Veh.)* mit Heckantrieb *nachgestellt;* **be ~-engined** Heckantrieb haben; **~guard** *n. (Mil.)* Nachhut, *die;* **~guard action** *n. (Mil.)* Nachhutgefecht, *das; (fig.)* Rückzugsgefecht, *das;* **~-lamp, ~-light** *ns.* Rücklicht, *das*

rearm [ri'ɑ:m] **1.** *v.i.* wiederaufrüsten. **2.** *v.t.* wiederaufrüsten ⟨*Land*⟩; wiederbewaffnen ⟨*Truppen*⟩; *(give more modern arms to)* neu bewaffnen *od.* ausrüsten ⟨*Truppen*⟩; **~ sb./oneself** jmdn./sich wiederbewaffnen

rearmament [ri:'ɑ:məmənt] *n.* Wiederbewaffnung, *die; (of country also)* Wiederaufrüstung, *die*

rearmost ['rɪəməʊst] *adj.* hinterst ...

rearrange [ri:ə'reɪndʒ] *v.t.* *(alter plan of)* umräumen ⟨*Möbel, Zimmer*⟩; verlegen ⟨*Treffen, Spiel*⟩ **(for** auf + *Akk.*); ändern ⟨*Anordnung, Programm*⟩

rearrangement [ri:ə'reɪndʒmənt] *n. see* **rearrange:** Umräumen, *das;* Verlegung, *die;* Änderung, *die*

rear: ~-view 'mirror *n.* Rückspiegel, *der;* **~ward** ['rɪəwəd] **1.** *n.* **be to ~ of the troops** sich im Rücken der Truppen befinden; **2.** *adj.* hinter ... ⟨*Teil*⟩; nach hinten gerichtet ⟨*Bewegung*⟩; **in a ~ direction** nach hinten; **3.** *adv.* nach hinten; **~-wheel drive** *n.* Hinterradantrieb, *der*

reason ['ri:zn] **1.** *n.* **a)** *(cause)* Grund, *der;* **what is your ~ for doing that?** aus welchem Grund tust du das/hast du das getan?; **there is [no/every] ~ to assume** *or* **believe that ...:** es besteht [kein/ein guter] Grund zu der Annahme, daß ...; **have every ~ to suppose that ...:** allen Grund zu der Annahme haben, daß ...; **have no ~ to complain** *or* **for complaint** sich nicht beklagen können; **for that [very] ~:** aus [eben] diesem Grund; **for no ~:** grundlos; **no particular ~** *(as answer)* einfach so; **see ~ to do sth.** es für gerechtfertigt halten, etw. zu tun; **all the more ~ for doing sth.** ein Grund mehr, etw. zu tun; **for ~s best known to himself** aus Gründen, die er allein kennt; **for some ~, for one ~ or another** aus irgendeinem Grund; **for ~s of health** aus gesundheitlichen Gründen; **for obvious ~s** aus gutem Grund; **for no obvious ~:** aus keinem ersichtlichen Grund; **for the [simple] ~ that ...:** [einfach,] weil ...; **by ~ of** wegen; aufgrund; **with ~:** aus gutem Grund; **b)** *no pl., no art. (power to understand; sense; Philos.)* Vernunft, *die; (sanity)* gesunder Verstand; **lose one's ~:** den Verstand verlieren; **regain one's ~:** wieder normal werden; *(fig.)* wieder zur Vernunft kommen; **contrary to ~:** unsinnig; absurd; **be out of all ~:** völlig unsinnig sein; **be** *or* **go beyond all ~:** völlig überzogen sein; **I can't see the ~ of it** ich sehe keinen Sinn darin; **in** *or* **within ~:** innerhalb eines vernünftigen Rahmens; **you can have anything within ~:** du kannst alles haben, solange es im Rahmen bleibt; **stand to ~:** unzweifelhaft sein; **not listen to ~:** sich *(Dat.)* nichts sagen lassen; **see ~:** zur Einsicht kommen; **make sb. see ~, bring sb. to ~:** jmdn. zur Einsicht bringen; **Age of R~** *(Hist.)* Zeitalter der Aufklärung *od.* Vernunft; **for ~s of State** aus Gründen der Staatsräson. **2.** *v.i.* **a)** schlußfolgern **(from** aus); **ability to ~:** logisches Denkvermögen; **he can ~ clearly** er hat einen klaren Verstand; **b) ~ with** diskutieren mit **(about, on** über + *Akk.*); **you can't ~ with her** mit ihr kann man nicht vernünftig reden. **3.** *v.t.* **a)** *(conclude)* schlußfolgern; **b)** *(persuade)* **~ sb. into doing sth.** jmdn. dazu überreden, etw. zu tun; **~ sb. out of sth.** jmdm. etw. ausreden; **c)** *(question)* **ours not to ~ why** es ist nicht unsere Sache, nach dem Warum zu fragen

~ 'out *v.t.* sich *(Dat.)* überlegen; **he could ~ out the result** *(knew in advance)* er konnte sich *(Dat.)* das Ergebnis schon denken; **it's easy to ~ out what ...:** man kann sich leicht denken, was ...

reasonable ['ri:zənəbl] *adj.* **a)** vernünftig; angemessen, vernünftig ‹*Forderung*›; **be ~!** sei [doch] vernünftig!; **not be ~ in one's demands** überzogene Forderungen stellen; **beyond ~ doubt** unzweifelhaft; **b)** *(inexpensive)* günstig; **it's a ~ price** das ist ein vernünftiger Preis; **c)** *(fair)* passabel ‹*Leistung, Wein*›; **with a ~ amount of luck** mit ein bißchen Glück; **d)** *(within limits)* realistisch ‹*Chancen, Angebot*›

reasonably ['ri:zənəblı] *adv.* **a)** *(within reason)* vernünftig; **no one could ~ believe that ...:** niemand kann ernsthaft glauben, daß ...; **b)** *(moderately)* **~ priced** preisgünstig; **c)** *(fairly)* ganz ‹*gut*›; ziemlich ‹*gesund*›

reasoned ['ri:znd] *adj.* durchdacht

reasoner ['ri:zənə(r)] *n.* **skilful** *or* **clever ~:** kluger *od.* heller Kopf

reasoning ['ri:zənıŋ] *n.* logisches Denken; *(argumentation)* Argumentation, *die;* **a brilliant piece of ~:** eine brillante Argumentation; **power of ~:** logisches Denkvermögen; **there's no ~ with her** mit ihr kann man nicht vernünftig reden

reassemble [ri:ə'sembl] **1.** *v.i.* sich wieder versammeln; ‹*Streitkräfte, Truppen:*› sich wieder sammeln. **2.** *v.t.* **a)** *(bring together again)* wieder versammeln ‹*Anhänger*›; [wieder] sammeln ‹*Truppen*›; **b)** *(put together again)* wieder zusammenbauen

reassert [ri:ə'sɜ:t] *v.t.* [erneut] bekräftigen

reassertion [ri:ə'sɜ:ʃn] *n.* [erneute] Bekräftigung

reassess [ri:ə'ses] *v.t.* neu bewerten ‹*Situation*›; überdenken ‹*Vorschlag*›; überprüfen ‹*Argument, Beweis, Anspruch*›; *(for taxation)* neu veranlagen ‹*Besitz*›

reassessment [ri:ə'sesmənt] *n.* *(of evidence, argument, claim)* Überprüfung, *die;* *(of proposal)* Überdenken, *das;* *(of situation)* Neubewertung, *die;* *(for taxation)* Neuveranlagung, *die*

reassign [ri:ə'saın] *v.t.* neu zuweisen

reassignment [ri:ə'saınmənt] *n.* *(of personnel)* Versetzung, *die;* *(of resources, money)* Übertragung, *die*

reassurance [ri:ə'ʃʊərəns] *n.* **a)** *(calming)* **give sb. ~:** jmdn. beruhigen; **b)** *(confirmation in opinion)* Bestätigung, *die; in pl.* [wiederholte] Versicherungen

reassure [ri:ə'ʃʊə(r)] *v.t.* **a)** *(calm fears of)* beruhigen; **b)** *(confirm in opinion)* bestätigen; **he needs to be constantly ~d that ...:** man muß ihm dauernd aufs neue bestätigen *od.* versichern, daß ...; **~ sb. about his health** jmdm. versichern, daß er gesund ist

reassuring [ri:ə'ʃʊərıŋ] *adj.*, **reassuringly** [ri:ə'ʃʊərıŋlı] *adv.* beruhigend

reawaken [ri:ə'weıkn] **1.** *v.t.* *(lit. or fig.)* wiedererwecken. **2.** *v.i.* *(lit. or fig.)* wiedererwachen

reawakening [ri:ə'weıknıŋ] *n.* *(fig.)* Wiedererwachen, *das*

[1]**rebate** ['ri:beıt] *n.* **a)** *(refund)* Rückzahlung, *die;* **~ on tax** Steuerrückzahlung, *die;* **get a ~ on the gas-bill** Geld von den Gaswerken zurückbekommen; **b)** *(discount)* Preisnachlaß, *der* (**on** auf + *Akk.*); Rabatt, *der* (**on** auf + *Akk.*); **rate ~** *(Brit.)* Ermäßigung der Gemeindeabgaben

[2]**rebate** ['ræbıt] *see* **rabbet**

rebel 1. ['rebl] *n.* Rebell, *der*/Rebellin, *die.* **2.** *attrib. adj.* **a)** *(of rebels)* Rebellen-; **b)** *(refusing obedience to ruler)* rebellisch; aufständisch. **3.** [rı'bel] *v.i.*, **-ll-** rebellieren

rebellion [rı'beljən] *n.* Rebellion, *die;* **rise [up] in ~:** sich erheben; rebellieren

rebellious [rı'beljəs] *adj.* **a)** *(defiant)* rebellisch; aufsässig; **b)** *(in rebellion)* rebellierend ‹*Sklave, Untertan*›

rebind [ri:'baınd] *v.t.*, **rebound** [ri:'baʊnd] neu [ein]binden

rebirth [ri:'bɜ:θ] *n.* **a)** Wiedergeburt, *die;* **b)** *(revival)* Wiederaufleben, *das*

reborn [ri:'bɔ:n] *adj.* wiedergeboren; **feel ~:** sich wie neugeboren fühlen; **be ~:** wiedergeboren werden

[1]**rebound 1.** [rı'baʊnd] *v.i.* **a)** *(spring back)* abprallen (**from** von); **b)** *(have reactive effect)* zurückfallen (**upon** auf + *Akk.*); **the plan ~ed on her** *or* **on her head** der Plan schadete ihr nur selbst. **2.** ['ri:baʊnd] *n.* **a)** *(recoil)* Abprall, *der;* Rebound, *der (Basketball);* **catch the ball on the ~:** den Abpraller *od. (Basketball)* Rebound fangen; **b)** *(fig.: emotional reaction)* **marry/turn to sb. on the ~:** in seiner Enttäuschung jmdn. heiraten/sich jmdm. zuwenden

[2]**rebound** *see* **rebind**

rebroadcast [ri:'brɔ:dkɑ:st] **1.** *n.* Wiederholung, *die.* **2.** *v.t., forms as* **broadcast 2** wiederholen

rebuff [rı'bʌf] **1.** *n.* [schroffe] Abweisung; **be met with a ~:** auf Ablehnung stoßen; **suffer a ~:** abgelehnt werden. **2.** *v.t.* [schroff] zurückweisen

rebuild [ri:'bıld] *v.t.*, **rebuilt** [ri:'bılt] *(lit. or fig.)* wieder aufbauen; *(make extensive changes to)* umbauen

rebuke [rı'bju:k] **1.** *v.t.* tadeln, rügen (**for** wegen); **~ sb. for doing sth.** jmdn. zurechtweisen, weil er etwas tut/getan hat. **2.** *n.* Rüge, *die;* Zurechtweisung, *die*

rebus ['ri:bəs] *n.* Bilderrätsel, *das*

rebut [rı'bʌt] *v.t.*, **-tt-** *(formal)* widerlegen

rebuttal [rı'bʌtl] *n.* *(Law)* Widerlegung, *die;* **call evidence in ~ of it** den Gegenbeweis dafür antreten

recalcitrant [rı'kælsıtrənt] **1.** *adj.* aufsässig ‹*Person*›; schwergängig ‹*Hebel, Mechanismus*›. **2.** *n.* Unruhestifter, *der*/-stifterin, *die*

recall 1. [rı'kɔ:l] *v.t.* **a)** *(remember)* sich erinnern an (+ *Akk.*); **~ what/how ...:** sich daran erinnern, was/wie ...; **b)** *(serve as reminder of)* erinnern an (+ *Akk.*); **~ sth. to sb.** jmdn. an etw. *(Akk.)* erinnern; **c)** *(summon back)* zurückrufen ‹*Soldat, fehlerhaftes Produkt*›; zurückfordern ‹*Buch*›; **the noise ~ed her to the present** der Lärm brachte sie in die Wirklichkeit zurück; **d)** *(suspend appointment of)* abberufen ‹*Botschafter, Delegation*› (**from** aus). **2.** [rı'kɔ:l, 'ri:kɔ:l] *n.* **a)** *(ability to remember)* **[powers of] ~:** Erinnerungsvermögen, *das;* Gedächtnis, *das; see also* **total recall; b)** *(possibility of annulling)* **beyond** *or* **past ~:** unwiderruflich; **c)** *(summons back)* Rückruf, *der;* *(to active duty)* Wiedereinberufung, *die;* **d)** *(suspension of appointment abroad)* Abberufung, *die*

recant [rı'kænt] **1.** *v.i.* [öffentlich] widerrufen. **2.** *v.t.* widerrufen

recantation [ri:kæn'teıʃn] *n.* Widerruf, *der;* **make a ~ of sth.** etw. widerrufen

[1]**recap** [ri:'kæp] *v.t.*, **-pp-** *(Amer.)* **a)** *(replace cap on)* wieder verschließen ‹*Flasche*›; **b)** *(retread)* runderneuern ‹*Reifen*›

[2]**recap** ['ri:kæp] *(coll.)* **1.** *v.t. & i.*, **-pp-** rekapitulieren; kurz zusammenfassen. **2.** *n.* Zusammenfassung, *die;* **let's just have a quick ~:** fassen wir kurz zusammen

recapitulate [ri:kə'pıtjʊleıt] *v.t. & i.* rekapitulieren; kurz zusammenfassen

recapitulation [ri:kəpıtjʊ'leıʃn] *n.* **a)** *(summing up)* Zusammenfassung, *die;* Rekapitulation, *die;* **b)** *(Mus.)* Reprise, *die*

recapture [ri:'kæptʃə(r)] **1.** *v.t.* **a)** *(capture again)* wieder ergreifen ‹*Gefangenen*›; wieder einfangen ‹*Tier*›; zurückerobern ‹*Stadt*›; **b)** *(re-create)* wieder lebendig werden lassen ‹*Atmosphäre*›; *(experience again)* noch einmal durchleben ‹*Aufregung, Vergangenheit, Jugend, Glück*›. **2.** *n.* *(retaking)* Rückeroberung, *die*

recast [ri:'kɑ:st] *v.t.*, **recast a)** *(remould)* neu gießen; **b)** *(refashion)* revidieren ‹*Vorstellung, Einstellung*›; **c)** *(rewrite)* umschreiben

recce ['rekı] *(Brit. sl.)* *n.* Erkundung, *die;* **make a ~:** die Lage peilen *(ugs.)*

recede [rı'si:d] *v.i.* **a)** ‹*Hochwasser, Flut:*› zurückgehen; ‹*Küste:*› zurückweichen; **his hair is beginning to ~:** er bekommt eine Stirnglatze; **b)** *(be left at increasing distance)* **~ [into the distance]** in der Ferne verschwinden; **c)** *(decline)* ‹*Preis:*› fallen; **~ in importance** an Bedeutung verlieren

receding [rı'si:dıŋ] *adj.* fliehend ‹*Kinn, Stirn*›; zurückweichend ‹*Küste*›; zurückgehend ‹*Flut, Hochwasser*›; *see also* **hairline a**

receipt [rı'si:t] **1.** *n.* **a)** Empfang, *der;* **please acknowledge ~ of this letter/order** bestätigen Sie bitte den Empfang dieses Briefes/dieser Bestellung; **be in ~ of** *(formal)* erhalten haben ‹*Brief*›; **those in ~ of a pension** Rentenempfänger; **[up]on ~ of the news/your remittance** *(formal)* nach Eingang der Nachricht/Ihrer Überweisung; **b)** *(written acknowledgement)* Empfangsbestätigung, *die;* Quittung, *die;* **~ for payment** Quittung, *die;* **c)** *in pl.* *(amount received)* Einnahmen (**from** aus). **2.** *v.t.* quittieren

receivable [rı'si:vəbl] *adj.* *(Commerc.)* offen; ausstehend

receive [rı'si:v] *v.t.* **a)** *(get)* erhalten; beziehen ‹*Gehalt, Rente*›; verliehen bekommen ‹*akademischer Grad*›; **~ a cordial welcome** herzlich begrüßt werden; **~ one's education at a private school** eine Privatschule besuchen; **she ~d a lot of attention/sympathy [from him]** es wurde ihr [von ihm] viel Aufmerksamkeit/Verständnis entgegengebracht; **~ [fatal] injuries** [tödlich] verletzt werden; **'payment ~d with thanks'** „Betrag dankend erhalten"; **your letter will ~ our immediate attention** wir werden Ihren Brief umgehend bearbeiten; **~ insults/praise** beschimpft/gelobt werden; **~ much unfavourable comment** stark kritisiert werden; **~ 30 days [imprisonment]** 30 Tage Gefängnis bekommen; **~ the sacraments/holy communion** *(Relig.)* das Abendmahl/die heilige Kommunion empfangen; **b)** *(accept)* entgegennehmen ‹*Bukett, Lieferung*›; *(submit to)* über sich *(Akk.)* ergehen lassen; **be convicted for receiving [stolen goods]** *(Law)* der Hehlerei überführt werden; **c)** *(serve as receptacle for)* aufnehmen; **d)** *(greet)* reagieren auf *(Akk.)*, aufnehmen ‹*Angebot, Nachricht, Theaterstück, Roman*›; empfangen ‹*Person*›; **e)** *(entertain)* empfangen ‹*Botschafter, Delegation, Nachbarn, Gast*›; **f)** *(consent to hear)* abnehmen ‹*Beichte, Eid*›; entgegennehmen ‹*Gesuch*› (**from** *Gen.*); **~ sb.'s confession/oath** jmdm. die Beichte/den Eid abnehmen; **g)** *(Radio, Telev.)* empfangen ‹*Sender, Signal*›; **are you receiving me?** können Sie mich hören?; **h)** tragen ‹*Last, Gewicht*›; **i)** *(accept as true)* anerkennen ‹*Theorie, Lehre*›; **j)** *(Tennis)* **~ the serve** den Aufschlag nehmen; **Lendl to ~** Lendl nimmt den Aufschlag. *See also* **end 1 d**

~ into *v.t.* aufnehmen in (+ *Akk.*)

received [rı'si:vd] *adj.* landläufig ‹*Vorstellung, Weisheit, Meinung*›; gültig ‹*Version, Text*›

received pronunci'ation (*Amer.:* **Received 'Standard**) *n.* *(Ling.)* englische Standardaussprache

receiver [rı'si:və(r)] *n.* **a)** Empfänger, *der*/Empfängerin, *die;* **b)** *([Table]Tennis)* Rückschläger, *der*/-schlägerin, *die;* **c)** *(Teleph.)* [Telefon]hörer, *der;* **d)** *(Radio, Telev.)* Empfänger, *der;* Receiver, *der (Technik);* **e) [official] ~** *(Law)* *(for property of bankrupt)* [gerichtlich bestellter/bestellte] Konkursverwalter/-verwalterin; *(for insane person)* Pfleger, *der*/Pflegerin, *die;* **f)** *(who receives stolen goods)* Hehler, *der*/Hehlerin, *die;* **g)** *(Chem.: vessel)* Vorlage, *die*

receivership [rı'si:vəʃıp] *n.* *(Law: being in hands of receiver)* Konkursverwaltung, *die;* **put sth. in** *or* **into ~:** etw. unter Konkursverwaltung stellen

recension [rɪ'senʃn] *n.* Überarbeitung, *die;* Rezension, *die (fachspr.)*

recent ['ri:sənt] *adj.* **a)** *(not long past)* jüngst ‹*Ereignisse, Wahlen, Vergangenheit usw.*›; **the ~ closure of the factory** die kürzlich erfolgte Schließung der Fabrik; **at our ~ meeting** als wir uns kürzlich *od.* vor kurzem trafen; **a ~/more ~ survey** eine neuere Untersuchung; **the most ~ survey** die neueste Untersuchung; **at our most ~ meeting** bei unserer letzten Begegnung; **b)** *(not long established)* Neu‹*auflage, -anschaffung, -erscheinung*›; **~ additions to the library's holdings** Neuerwerbungen der Bibliothek; **c) R~** *(Geol.)* Holozän, *das*

recently ['ri:səntlɪ] *adv.* *(a short time ago)* neulich; kürzlich; vor kurzem; *(in the recent past)* in der letzten Zeit; **until ~/until quite ~:** bis vor kurzem/bis vor ganz kurzer Zeit; **~ we've been following a different policy** seit kurzem verfolgen wir eine andere Politik; **as ~ as last year** noch letztes Jahr; **one morning ~:** neulich morgens; **I haven't seen him ~:** ich habe ihn in letzter Zeit nicht gesehen

receptacle [rɪ:septəkl] *n.* **a)** *(container)* Behälter, *der;* Gefäß, *das;* **b)** *(Bot.)* Blütenboden, *der;* Receptaculum, *das (fachspr.)*

reception [rɪ'sepʃn] *n.* **a)** *(welcome) (of person)* Empfang, *der;* Aufnahme, *die; (of play, speech)* Aufnahme, *die;* **meet with a cool ~:** kühl aufgenommen werden; **give sb. a warm ~:** jmdn. herzlich empfangen; **give a favourable ~ to** positiv aufnehmen ‹*Theaterstück, Rede*›; **b)** *(formal party, welcome)* Empfang, *der;* **hold** *or* **give a ~:** einen Empfang geben; **c)** *no art. (Brit.: foyer)* die Rezeption; **d)** *no art. (Radio, Telev.)* der Empfang; **get good ~:** guten Empfang haben

re'ception desk *n.* Rezeption, *die*

receptionist [rɪ'sepʃənɪst] *n.* *(in hotel)* Empfangschef, *der*/-dame, *die; (at doctor's, dentist's)* Sprechstundenhilfe, *die; (at hairdresser's, solarium, etc.) Angestellter, der/Angestellte, die die Kunden empfängt und mit ihnen die Termine vereinbart; (with firm)* Empfangssekretärin, *die*

reception: ~ office *(Amer.) see* **reception c; ~room** *n.* Empfangsraum, *der*

receptive [rɪ'septɪv] *adj.* **a)** aufgeschlossen, empfänglich (**to** für); paarungsbereit ‹*Tier*›; **have a ~ mind** aufgeschlossen sein; **b)** *(Biol.)* Rezeptor-; rezeptorisch

receptively [rɪ'septɪvlɪ] *adv.* rezeptiv

receptor [rɪ'septə(r)] *n.* *(Biol.)* Rezeptor, *der;* **~ organ** Rezeptionsorgan, *das*

recess [rɪ'ses, 'ri:ses] **1.** *n.* **a)** *(alcove)* Nische, *die;* **b)** *(Brit. Parl.; Amer.: short vacation)* Ferien *Pl.; (Amer. Sch.: between classes)* Pause, *die;* **be in ~** ‹*Parlament:*› in den Ferien sein; **adjourn for summer ~** *(Amer.)* sich bis nach der Sommerpause vertagen; **c)** *(lit. or fig.: remote place)* Winkel, *der.* **2.** *v. t.* **a)** *(set back)* [in die Wand] einlassen ‹*Schrank, Fenster*›; **b)** *(provide with ~)* eine Nische aussparen in (+ *Dat.*) ‹*Wand, Mauer*›; **c)** *(Amer.: end sitting of)* unterbrechen ‹*Verhandlung, Sitzung*›. **3.** *v. i. (Amer.: end a sitting)* sich vertagen

recession [rɪ'seʃn] *n.* **a)** *(Econ.: decline)* Rezession, *die (fachspr.);* Konjunkturrückgang, *der;* **period of ~:** Rezession[sphase], *die;* **b)** *(receding)* Zurückgehen, *das*

recessional [rɪ'seʃənl] *(Eccl.)* **1.** *adj.* Schluß‹*hymne, -musik*›. **2.** *n.* [*während des Auszugs der Geistlichen und des Chors gesungene*] Schlußhymne, *die*

recessive [rɪ'sesɪv] *adj.* *(Genetics, Phonet.)* rezessiv

recharge 1. [ri:'tʃɑ:dʒ] *v. t.* aufladen ‹*Batterie*›; nachladen ‹*Waffe*›; **~ one's batteries** *(fig.)* neue Kräfte auftanken. **2.** ['ri:tʃɑ:dʒ] *n.* Nachfüllen, *das;* **the battery needs a ~:** die Batterie muß aufgeladen werden

rechargeable [ri:'tʃɑ:dʒəbl] *adj.* wiederaufladbar

recherché [rə'ʃeəʃeɪ] *adj.* ausgefallen ‹*Vorstellungen, Ansichten*›; gesucht ‹*Ausdruck, Formulierung*›

rechristen [ri:'krɪsn] *v. t.* **a)** *(christen again)* noch einmal taufen; **b)** *see* **rename**

recidivism [rɪ'sɪdɪvɪzm] *n.* Rückfälligkeit, *die*

recidivist [rɪ'sɪdɪvɪst] **1.** *n.* Rückfällige, *der/die; (habitual criminal)* Rückfalltäter, *der/*-täterin, *die.* **2.** *adj.* rückfällig

recipe ['resɪpɪ] *n. (lit. or fig.)* Rezept, *das;* **~ for success** Erfolgsrezept, *das;* **it's a ~ for disaster** damit ist die Katastrophe vorprogrammiert

recipient [rɪ'sɪpɪənt] *n.* Empfänger, *der/*Empfängerin, *die;* **she was the unwilling ~ of his attention** sie war das unfreiwillige Opfer seiner Aufmerksamkeit

reciprocal [rɪ'sɪprəkl] **1.** *adj.* **a)** gegenseitig ‹*Abkommen, Zuneigung, Hilfe*›; **b)** *(Ling.)* reziprok ‹*Pronomen*›. **2.** *n.* *(Math.)* Kehrwert, *der*

reciprocally [rɪ'sɪprəkəlɪ] *adv.* gegenseitig

reciprocate [rɪ'sɪprəkeɪt] **1.** *v. t.* **a)** austauschen ‹*Versprechen*›; erwidern ‹*Gruß, Lächeln, Abneigung, Annäherungsversuch*›; sich revanchieren für ‹*Hilfe*›; **b)** *(Mech. Engin.)* hin- und herbewegen. **2.** *v. i.* **a)** *(respond)* sich revanchieren; **b)** *(Mech. Engin.)* sich hin- und herbewegen; **reciprocating engine/saw** Kolbenmaschine, *die*/Gattersäge, *die;* **reciprocating motion** Hin- und Herbewegung, *die*

reciprocity [resɪ'prɒsɪtɪ] *n.* **a)** *(mutual action)* **there is deep ~ of feeling** es besteht eine innige wechselseitige Gefühlsbindung; **~ of influence** gegen- *od.* wechselseitige Beeinflussung; **b)** *(interchange of privileges)* Wechselseitigkeit, *die;* Reziprozität, *die (fachspr.);* **~ in trade** Handelsreziprozität, *die*

recital [rɪ'saɪtl] *n.* **a)** *(performance)* [Solisten]konzert, *das; (of literature also)* Rezitation, *die;* **piano/poetry ~:** Klavierkonzert, *das*/Gedichtrezitation, *die;* **give one's first solo ~:** seinen ersten Soloauftritt haben; **b)** *(detailed account)* Schilderung, *die;* **give a ~ of sth.** etw. eingehend schildern

recitation [resɪ'teɪʃn] *n.* Rezitation, *die;* **give ~s from Shakespeare** Shakespeare rezitieren; **a ~ of her grievances/my faults** eine detaillierte Aufzählung ihrer Probleme/meiner Fehler

recitative [resɪtə'ti:v] *n.* *(Mus.)* Rezitativ, *das*

recite [rɪ'saɪt] **1.** *v. t.* **a)** *(speak from memory)* rezitieren ‹*Passage, Gedicht*›; **b)** *(give list of)* aufzählen. **2.** *v. i.* rezitieren

reckless ['reklɪs] *adj.* unbesonnen; rücksichtslos ‹*Fahrweise*›; tollkühn ‹*Fluchtversuch*›; **~ of the dangers/consequences** ungeachtet der Gefahren/Folgen

recklessly ['reklɪslɪ] *adv.* unbesonnen; *(without concern for others)* rücksichtslos

reckon ['rekn] **1.** *v. t.* **a)** *(work out)* ausrechnen ‹*Kosten, Lohn, Ausgaben*›; bestimmen ‹*Position*›; **b)** *(conclude)* schätzen; **what do you ~ are his chances?** wie beurteilst du seine Chancen?; **I ~ you're lucky to be alive** ich glaube, du kannst von Glück sagen, daß du noch lebst!; **I ~ to arrive** *or* **I shall arrive there by 8.30** ich nehme an, daß ich [spätestens] halb neun dort bin; **I usually ~ to arrive there by 8.30** in der Regel bin ich [spätestens] halb neun dort; **c)** *(consider)* halten (**as** für); **be ~ed as** *or* **to be sth.** als etw. gelten; **~ sb./sth. [to be] among the best** jmdn./etw. zu den Besten zählen *od.* rechnen; **be ~ed among sth.** zu etw. zählen; **d)** *(arrive at as total)* kommen auf (+ *Akk.*); **I ~ 53 of them** ich komme auf 53. **2.** *v. i.* rechnen; **~ from 1 April** vom 1. April an rechnen

~ 'in *v. t.* [mit] einrechnen

~ on *see* **~ upon**

~ 'up 1. *v. t.* zusammenzählen; **~ up the bill** die Rechnungsposten zusammenzählen. **2.** *v. i.* **~ up with sb.** mit jmdm. abrechnen

~ upon *v. t.* **a)** *(rely on)* zählen auf (+ *Akk.*); **I was ~ing upon doing that this morning** ich hatte gedacht, ich könnte das heute früh tun; **b)** *(expect)* rechnen mit

~ with *v. i.* **a)** *(take into account)* rechnen mit ‹*Hindernis, Möglichkeit*›; **he is a man to be ~ed with** er ist ein Mann, den man nicht unterschätzen sollte; **b)** *(deal with)* abrechnen mit; **you'll have me/the police to ~ with** du bekommst es mit mir/der Polizei zu tun

~ without *v. i.* nicht rechnen mit; **we had ~ed without the weather** das Wetter hat uns einen Strich durch die Rechnung gemacht

reckoner ['rekənə(r)] *see* **ready reckoner**

reckoning ['reknɪŋ] *n.* **a)** *(calculation)* Berechnung, *die;* **by my ~:** nach meiner Rechnung; **day of ~** *(fig.)* Tag der Abrechnung; *(moment of truth)* Stunde der Wahrheit; **be [wildly] out in one's ~:** sich [gehörig] verrechnet haben; **b)** *(bill)* Rechnung, *die. See also* **dead**

reclaim [rɪ'kleɪm] **1.** *v. t.* **a)** urbar machen ‹*Land, Wüste*›; **~ land from the sea** dem Meer Land abgewinnen; **b)** *(recover possession of)* zurückbekommen ‹*Steuern*›; zurückerlangen ‹*Recht*›; **c)** *(for reuse)* zur Wiederverwertung sammeln; wiederverwenden ‹*Rohstoff*›; regenerieren *(Technik).* **2.** *n.* **be past** *or* **beyond ~:** unwiederbringlich verloren sein; **baggage ~:** Gepäckausgabe, *die*

reclamation [reklə'meɪʃn] *n.* Urbarmachung, *die;* **land ~:** Landgewinnung, *die*

recline [rɪ'klaɪn] **1.** *v. i.* **a)** *(lean back)* sich zurücklehnen; **the chair ~s** die Rückenlehne des Sessels läßt sich [nach hinten] verstellen; **reclining seat** *(in car)* Liegesitz, *der;* **b)** *(be lying down)* liegen. **2.** *v. t.* [nach hinten] lehnen; **~ the seat** die Rückenlehne des Sitzes nach hinten verstellen

recliner [rɪ'klaɪnə(r)] *n.* Lehnsessel, *der;* **~ seat** Liegesitz, *der*

recluse [rɪ'klu:s] *n.* Einsiedler, *der*/Einsiedlerin, *die*

reclusive [rɪ'klu:sɪv] *adj.* einsiedlerisch

recognisability, recognisable, recognisably, recognisance, recognise *see* **recogniz-**

recognition [rekəg'nɪʃn] *n.* **a)** *no pl., no art.* Wiedererkennen, *das;* **he's changed beyond all ~:** er ist nicht mehr wiederzuerkennen; **escape ~:** unerkannt bleiben; **b)** *(acceptance, acknowledgement)* Anerkennung, *die;* **achieve/receive ~:** Anerkennung finden; **in ~ of** als Anerkennung für

recognizability [rekəgnaɪzə'bɪlɪtɪ] *n., no pl.* Erkennbarkeit, *die*

recognizable ['rekəgnaɪzəbl] *adj.* erkennbar; deutlich ‹*Unterschied*›; **be ~:** wiederzuerkennen sein

recognizably ['rekəgnaɪzəblɪ] *adv.* erkennbar; **be not ~ different from sth.** sich kaum von etw. unterscheiden

recognizance [rɪ'kɒgnɪzəns] *n.* **a)** *(bond)* Verpflichtung, *die;* **enter into ~s to do sth.** *(Law)* sich vor Gericht dazu verpflichten, etw. zu tun; **b)** *(sum)* Kaution, *die*

recognize ['rekəgnaɪz] *v. t.* **a)** *(know again)* wiedererkennen (**by** an + *Dat.*, **from** durch); **b)** *(acknowledge)* erkennen; anerkennen ‹*Gültigkeit, Land, Methode, Leistung, Bedeutung, Dienst*›; **be ~d as** angesehen werden *od.* gelten als; **c)** *(admit)* zugeben; **~ sth. as valid** etw. als gültig anerkennen; **~ sb. as heir** jmdn. als Erben anerkennen; **~ sb. to be cleverer** *or* **that sb. is cleverer** zugeben, daß jmd. klüger ist; **d)** *(identify nature of)* erkennen; **~ sb. to be a fraud** erkennen, daß jmd. ein Betrüger ist; **e)** *(Amer.: allow to speak)* das Wort erteilen (+ *Dat.*)

recoil 1. [rɪ'kɔɪl] *v. i.* **a)** *(shrink back)* zurückfahren; **he ~ed visibly** er zuckte sichtbar zurück; **~ from an idea** vor einem Gedanken zurückschrecken; **b)** ‹*Waffe:*› einen Rückstoß haben. **2.** ['ri:kɔɪl, rɪ'kɔɪl] *n. (of gun)* Rückstoß, *der* **(from** *Gen.*)
~ [up]on *v. i.* zurückfallen auf (+ *Akk.*); **~ upon sb.'s [own] head** *or* **upon sb.** auf jmdn. [selbst] zurückfallen
recollect [rekə'lekt] **1.** *v. t.* **a)** sich erinnern an (+ *Akk.*); **~ meeting sb.** sich daran erinnern, jmdn. getroffen zu haben; **b) ~ oneself** wieder zu sich selbst finden. **2.** *v. i.* sich erinnern
recollection [rekə'lekʃn] *n.* Erinnerung, *die;* **to the best of my ~ ...:** soweit ich mich erinnern kann, ...; **have a/no ~ of sth.** sich an etw. *(Akk.)* erinnern/nicht erinnern können
recombinant [ri:'kɒmbɪnənt] *adj. (Genetics)* rekombinant
recombination [ri:kɒmbɪ'neɪʃn] *n. (Phys., Genetics)* Rekombination, *die*
recombine [ri:kəm'baɪn] **1.** *v. t.* neu kombinieren. **2.** *v. i.* sich neu kombinieren
recommence [ri:kə'mens] **1.** *v. i.* wieder beginnen. **2.** *v. t.* wieder beginnen mit
recommencement [ri:kə'mensmənt] *n.* Wiederbeginn, *der*
recommend [rekə'mend] *v. t.* **a)** empfehlen; **~ sb. to do sth.** jmdm. empfehlen, etw. zu tun; **b)** *(make acceptable)* sprechen für; **the plan has little/nothing to ~ it** es spricht wenig/nichts für den Plan
recommendable [rekə'mendəbl] *adj.* empfehlenswert; **it is [not] ~ to do sth.** es empfiehlt sich [nicht], etw. zu tun
recommendation [rekəmen'deɪʃn] *n.* Empfehlung, *die;* **speak in ~ of sth./sb.** etw./jmdn. empfehlen; **on sb.'s ~:** auf jmds. Empfehlung *(Akk.);* **letter of ~:** Empfehlungsschreiben, *das;* **make ~s to sb.** jmdn. beraten; **be a ~ for sth.** für etw. sprechen
recompense ['rekəmpens] *(formal)* **1.** *v. t.* **a)** *(reward)* belohnen; **b)** *(make amends to)* entschädigen. **2.** *n., no art., no pl.* **a)** *(reward)* Lohn, *der;* Anerkennung, *die;* **in ~ for** als Dank für; **work without ~:** unentgeltlich arbeiten; **b)** *(compensation)* Entschädigung, *die*
reconcilable ['rekənsaɪləbl] *adj.* versöhnbar ‹*Personen*›; überbrückbar ‹*Differenzen*›; miteinander vereinbar ‹*Unterschiede, Standpunkte*›
reconcile ['rekənsaɪl] *v. t.* **a)** *(restore to friendship)* versöhnen; **become ~d** sich versöhnen; **b)** *(resign oneself)* **~ oneself** *or* **become/be ~d to sth.** sich mit etw. versöhnen; **c)** *(make compatible)* in Einklang bringen ‹*Vorstellungen, Überzeugungen*›; *(show to be compatible)* miteinander vereinen; **one cannot ~ dictatorship and freedom of speech** Diktatur und Redefreiheit sind miteinander unvereinbar; **d)** *(settle)* beilegen ‹*Meinungsverschiedenheit*›
reconciliation [rekənsɪlɪ'eɪʃn] *n.* **a)** *(restoring to friendship)* Versöhnung, *die;* **bring about a ~ between persons** Personen miteinander versöhnen; **try for a ~:** einen Versöhnungsversuch unternehmen; **b)** *(making compatible)* Harmonisierung, *die*
recondite ['rekəndaɪt, rɪ'kɒndaɪt] *adj. (formal)* abstrus
recondition [ri:kən'dɪʃn] *v. t.* [general]überholen; **~ed engine** Austauschmotor, *der*
reconnaissance [rɪ'kɒnɪsəns] *n., no pl., no def. art. (Mil.)* Aufklärung, *die; (of area)* Erkundung, *die;* **after ~:** nach Erkundung der Lage; **the plane was on ~:** das Flugzeug war auf einem Aufklärungsflug; **make a ~ [of the area]** *(lit. or fig.)* das Terrain sondieren; *attrib.* **~ aircraft** Aufklärungsflugzeug, *das;* **~ party** Spähtrupp, *der*
reconnoitre *(Brit.; Amer.:* **reconnoiter**) [rekə'nɔɪtə(r)] **1.** *v. t. (esp. Mil.)* auskundschaften; erkunden ‹*Gelände*›; *(fig.)* erkunden; in Augenschein nehmen ‹*Hotel, Restaurant*›. **2.** *v. i. (esp. Mil.)* auf Erkundung [aus]gehen; *(fig.)* sich umsehen
reconquer [ri:'kɒŋkə(r)] *v. t.* zurückerobern
reconsider [ri:kən'sɪdə(r)] *v. t.* [noch einmal] überdenken; **~ a case** einen Fall von neuem aufrollen; *abs.* **there is still time to ~:** du kannst es dir/wir können es uns *usw.* immer noch überlegen
reconsideration [ri:kənsɪdə'reɪʃn] *n.* Überdenken, *das;* **put a case before the court for ~:** einen Fall zur neuerlichen Beratung vor ein Gericht bringen
reconstitute [ri:'kɒnstɪtju:t] *v. t.* **a)** *(build up again)* wieder aufbauen; rekonstruieren; **b)** *(restore to natural state)* **~ [with water]** [mit Wasser] anrühren; [in Wasser] einweichen ‹*Trockenobst*›; **c)** *(piece together)* rekonstruieren ‹*Ereignisse*›; **d)** *(reorganize)* umbauen ‹*Anlage*›; umbilden ‹*Komitee, Kabinett*›; **e)** *(bring back into existence)* wieder einrichten
reconstitution [ri:kɒnstɪ'tju:ʃn] *n.* **a)** *(building up again)* Rekonstruktion, *die;* **b)** *(restoration to natural state)* Anrühren, *das; (of dried fruit)* Einweichen, *das;* **c)** *(reorganization)* Umbildung, *die;* **d)** *(bringing back into existence)* Wiedereinrichtung, *die*
reconstruct [ri:kən'strʌkt] *v. t.* **a)** *(build again)* wieder aufbauen ‹*Stadt, Gebäude*›; neu errichten ‹*Gerüst*›; rekonstruieren ‹*Anlage*›; *(fig.)* rekonstruieren; **b)** *(reorganize)* umstrukturieren
reconstruction [ri:kən'strʌkʃn] *n.* **a)** *(process)* Wiederaufbau, *der; (reorganization)* Umstrukturierung, *die;* **b)** *(thing reconstructed)* Rekonstruktion, *die*
record 1. [rɪ'kɔ:d] *v. t.* **a)** aufzeichnen; **~ a new LP** eine neue LP aufnehmen; **~ sth. in a book/painting** etw. in einem Buch/auf einem Gemälde festhalten; **be ~ed for ever in sb.'s memory** auf ewig in jmds. Gedächtnis eingegraben sein; **history ~s that ...:** es ist geschichtlich belegt, daß ...; **b)** *(register officially)* dokumentieren; protokollieren ‹*Verhandlung*›; **~ one's vote** seine Stimme abgeben; **count and ~ the votes** die Stimmen auszählen [und das Ergebnis schriftlich festhalten]. **2.** *v. i.* aufzeichnen; *(on tape)* Tonbandaufnahmen/eine Tonbandaufnahme machen; **the tape recorder isn't ~ing properly** das Tonbandgerät nimmt nicht richtig auf. **3.** ['rekɔ:d] *n.* **a) be on ~** ‹*Prozeß, Verhandlung, Besprechung:*› protokolliert sein; **there is no such case on ~:** ein solcher Fall ist nicht dokumentiert; **it is on ~ that ...:** es ist dokumentiert, daß ...; **have sth. on ~:** etw. dokumentiert haben; **there is nothing on ~ to prove that ...:** es gibt keine Aufzeichnungen, die beweisen, daß ...; **put sth. on ~:** etw. schriftlich festhalten; **I am quite happy to go on ~ as having said that** man kann ruhig festhalten, daß ich das gesagt habe; **it is a matter of ~ that ...:** es ist eine verbürgte Tatsache, daß ...; **b)** *(report)* Protokoll, *das; (Law: official report)* [Gerichts]akte, *die;* **c)** *(document)* Dokument, *das; (piece of evidence)* Zeugnis, *das;* Beleg, *der;* **medical ~s** medizinische Unterlagen; **criminal ~s** Strafregister, *das;* **~ of attendance** Anwesenheitsliste, *die;* **keep a ~ of sth.** über etw. *(Akk.)* Buch führen; *(listing persons)* eine Liste von etw. führen; **for the ~:** für das Protokoll; **just for the ~:** der Vollständigkeit halber; *(iron.)* nur der Ordnung halber; **[strictly] off the ~:** [ganz] inoffiziell; **get** *or* **keep** *or* **put** *or* **set the ~ straight** keine Mißverständnisse aufkommen lassen; **let me put the ~ straight** ich möchte es einmal ganz unmißverständlich sagen; **d)** *(disc for gramophone)* [Schall]platte, *die;* **make a ~:** eine Platte machen *(ugs.);* **e)** *(facts of sb.'s/sth.'s past)* Ruf, *der;* **have a good ~ [of achievements]** gute Leistungen vorweisen können; **the aircraft has an excellent ~ for reliability/a good safety ~:** das Flugzeug hat sich als höchst zuverlässig/sehr sicher erwiesen; **have a [criminal/police] ~:** vorbestraft sein; **keep a clean ~:** sich *(Dat.)* nichts zuschulden kommen lassen; **f)** *(best performance)* Rekord, *der;* **set a ~:** einen Rekord aufstellen; **break** *or* **beat the ~:** den Rekord brechen. **4.** *attrib. adj.* Rekord-
record ['rekɔ:d]: **~ album** *n.* [Schall]plattenalbum, *das;* **~-breaking** *adj.* Rekord-
recorded [rɪ'kɔ:dɪd] *adj.* aufgezeichnet ‹*Film, Konzert, Rede*›; überliefert ‹*Ereignis, Geschichte*›; bespielt ‹*Band*›; **~ music** Musikaufnahmen
recorded de'livery *n. (Brit. Post)* eingeschriebene Sendung *(ohne Versicherung);* **send sth. by ~ delivery** etw. per Einschreiben schicken
recorder [rɪ'kɔ:də(r)] *n.* **a)** *(instrument/apparatus)* Aufzeichnungsgerät, *das;* **earthquake ~:** Seismograph, *der;* **b)** *see* **tape recorder; c)** *(Mus.)* Blockflöte, *die;* **d)** *(Brit. Law)* nebenamtlicher Richter *(beim Crown Court usw.)*
'record-holder *n. (Sport)* Rekordhalter, *der*/-halterin, *die*
recording [rɪ'kɔ:dɪŋ] *n.* **a)** *(process)* Aufzeichnung, *die;* **b)** *(what is recorded)* Aufnahme, *die; (to be heard or seen later)* Aufzeichnung, *die*
recording: **~ 'angel** *n. (Theol.)* Engel der Gerechtigkeit; **~ head** *n.* Aufnahmekopf, *der;* **~ session** *n.* Aufnahme, *die;* **~ studio** *n.* Tonstudio, *das;* **~ van** *n.* Aufnahmewagen, *der*
recordist [rɪ'kɔ:dɪst] *n.* **[sound] ~:** Tonmeister, *der*/-meisterin, *die*
record ['rekɔ:d]: **~ library** *n.* Phonothek, *die;* **R~ Office** *see* **Public R~ Office; ~-player** *n.* Plattenspieler, *der;* **~ shop** *n.* [Schall]plattengeschäft, *das;* **~ sleeve** *n.* Plattenhülle, *die;* Plattencover, *das;* **~ token** *n.* [Schall]plattengutschein, *der*
recount [rɪ'kaʊnt] *v. t. (tell)* erzählen
re-count 1. [ri:'kaʊnt] *v. t. (count again)* [noch einmal] nachzählen. **2.** ['ri:kaʊnt] *n.* Nachzählung, *die;* **have a ~:** nachzählen
recoup [rɪ'ku:p] *v. t.* **a)** *(regain)* ausgleichen ‹*Verlust*›; [wieder] hereinbekommen ‹*[Geld]einsatz*›; wiedergewinnen ‹*Stärke, Gesundheit*›; **b)** *(reimburse)* wieder einbringen ‹*Auslagen*›; **~ oneself** seine Ausgaben ausgleichen
recourse [rɪ'kɔ:s] *n.* **a)** *(resort)* Zufluchtnahme, *die;* **have ~ to sb./sth.** bei jmdm./zu etw. Zuflucht nehmen; **b)** *(person or thing resorted to)* Zuflucht, *die;* **your only ~ is legal action** das einzige, was dir bleibt, ist vor Gericht zu gehen; **c)** *(Finance)* Regreß, *der;* Rückgriff, *der*
recover [rɪ'kʌvə(r)] **1.** *v. t.* **a)** *(regain)* zurückerobern; **b)** *(find again)* wiederfinden ‹*Verlorenes, Fährte, Spur*›; **c)** *(retrieve)* zurückbekommen; bergen ‹*Wrack*›; **d)** *(make up for)* aufholen ‹*verlorene Zeit*›; **e)** *(acquire again)* wiedergewinnen ‹*Vertrauen*›; wiederfinden ‹*Gleichgewicht, innere Ruhe usw.*›; **have ~ed one's lost appetite/normal colour** wieder Appetit/Farbe haben; **~ consciousness** das Bewußtsein wiedererlangen; **~ one's senses** *(lit. or fig.)* wieder zur Besinnung kommen; **~ the use of one's hands/feet** seine Hände/Füße wieder gebrauchen können; **~ one's sight** sein Sehvermögen wiedergewinnen; **~ one's voice** seine Stimme wiederfinden; **~ one's breath** wieder zu Atem kommen; **~ oneself** sich fangen; **f)** *(reclaim)* **~ land from the sea** dem Meer Land abgewinnen; **~ metal from scrap** Metall aus Schrott gewinnen; **g)** *(Law)* erheben ‹*Steuer, Abgabe*›; erhalten ‹*Schadenersatz, Schmerzensgeld*›; *abs.* Schadenersatz

erhalten. **2.** *v.i.* ~ **from sth.** sich von etw. [wieder] erholen; **how long will it take him to ~?** wann wird er wieder gesund sein?; **be [completely** *or* **totally** *or* **fully** *or* **quite] ~ed** [völlig] wiederhergestellt sein

re-cover [ri:ˈkʌvə(r)] *v.t.* neu beziehen ‹*Sessel, Schirm usw.*›

recoverable [rɪˈkʌvərəbl] *adj.* **a)** *(capable of being regained)* erstattungsfähig ‹*Unkosten*›; ersetzbar ‹*Schaden, Verlust*›; rückzahlbar ‹*Kaution, Geldeinlage*›; **the cost was ~ through his insurance policy** die Kosten konnten durch seine Versicherung ersetzt werden; **b)** *(capable of being restored)* wiederherstellbar; wiedergewinnbar ‹*Brauchwasser*›; **c)** *(Law)* eintreibbar ‹*Geldstrafe, Schulden usw.*›; **d)** *(extractable)* abbaufähig; abbaubar; förderbar ‹*Öl-, Gasreserven*›

recovery [rɪˈkʌvərɪ] *n.* **a)** *(restoration)* Erholung, *die;* **be on the road to ~:** auf dem Wege der Besserung sein; **make a quick/good ~:** sich schnell/gut erholen; **he is past ~:** für ihn gibt es keine Hoffnung mehr; **b)** *(regaining of sth. lost)* Wiederfinden, *das;* Fund, *der;* **c)** *(Law) (of debts)* Eintreibung, *die;* ~ **of damages** Erfüllung des Anspruchs auf Schadenersatz; **d)** *(Swimming, Rowing)* Rückkehr in die Grundstellung; **e)** *(extraction, reclamation)* Rückgewinnung, *die*

reˈcovery room *n. (Med.)* Aufwachraum, *der*

recreant [ˈrekrɪənt] *(literary)* **1.** *adj.* **a)** *(cowardly)* kleinmütig *(geh.);* verzagt *(geh.);* **b)** *(treacherous)* verräterisch; *(apostate)* abtrünnig. **2.** *n.* **a)** *(coward)* Feigling, *der;* **b)** *(betrayer)* Verräter, *der*/Verräterin, *die; (apostate)* Abtrünnige, *der/die*

recreation [rekrɪˈeɪʃn] *n.* **a)** *(act of relaxing)* Ausruhen, *das;* **b)** *(means of entertainment)* Freizeitbeschäftigung, *die;* Hobby, *das;* **for** *or* **as a ~:** zur Freizeitbeschäftigung *od.* Entspannung; **he enjoys driving as a ~:** Fahren bedeutet für ihn Entspannung

recreational [rekrɪˈeɪʃənl] *adj.* Freizeit‹*wert, -möglichkeiten, -gelände*›; Erholungs‹*gebiet*›

recreation: ~ **centre** *n.* Freizeitzentrum, *das;* ~ **ground** *n.* Freizeitgelände, *das; (for children)* Spielplatz, *der;* ~ **period** *n.* Pause, *die;* ~ **room** *n.* **a)** *(playroom)* Spielzimmer, *das; (hobbyroom)* Hobbyraum, *der;* **b)** *(public room)* Aufenthaltsraum, *der;* ~ **time** *n.* Freizeit, *die; (in school)* Pause, *die*

recriminate [rɪˈkrɪmɪneɪt] *v.i.* Gegenbeschuldigungen erheben

recrimination [rɪkrɪmɪˈneɪʃn] *n.* Gegenbeschuldigung, *die; (counter-accusation)* **[mutual] ~s** [gegenseitige] Beschuldigungen

recrudescence [ri:kru:ˈdesəns] *n. (of symptoms, disease)* erneutes Auftreten; *(of epidemic, aggression, violence)* Wiederaufflackern, *das*

recruit [rɪˈkru:t] **1.** *n.* **a)** *(Mil.)* Rekrut, *der;* **a raw ~:** ein frisch Eingezogener; **b)** *(Amer.) (soldier of lowest rank)* einfacher Soldat; *(sailor of lowest rank)* Matrose, *der;* **c)** *(new member)* neues Mitglied; **d) [raw]** ~ *(fig.: novice)* blutiger Anfänger. **2.** *v.t.* **a)** *(Mil.: enlist)* anwerben; *(into society, party, etc.)* werben ‹*Mitglied*›; **b)** *(select for appointment)* neu einstellen; **staff were ~ed once a year** einmal im Jahr wurden neue Mitarbeiter eingestellt. **3.** *v.i.* **a)** *(Mil.: enlist)* Rekruten anwerben; ‹*Partei, Klub:*› neue Mitglieder finden; **b)** *(select for appointment)* Neueinstellungen vornehmen; ~ **for staff** neue Mitarbeiter einstellen; ~ **from one's own staff** freie Stellen aus den eigenen Reihen besetzen

recruitment [rɪˈkru:tmənt] *n.* **a)** *(Mil.)* Anwerbung, *die; (for membership)* ~ **of members** Mitgliederwerbung, *die;* ~ **has been good this year** die Mitgliederwerbung war dieses Jahr sehr erfolgreich; ~ **for evening classes** Werbung für Abendkurse; **b)** *(process of selecting for appointment)* Neueinstellung, *die*

recta *pl. of* **rectum**

rectal [ˈrektl] *adj. (Anat.)* rektal

rectangle [ˈrektæŋgl] *n.* Rechteck, *das*

rectangular [rekˈtæŋgjʊlə(r)] *adj.* **a)** ~**[-shaped]** rechteckig; **b)** *(placed at right angles)* rechtwinklig

rectifiable [ˈrektɪfaɪəbl] *adj.* korrigierbar ‹*Fehler*›; **do you think the situation is ~?** glauben Sie, daß noch etwas zu machen ist?

rectification [rektɪfɪˈkeɪʃn] *n.* **a)** *(correction of error)* Berichtigung, *die;* Korrektur, *die;* **b)** *(Electr.)* Gleichrichtung, *die*

rectifier [ˈrektɪfaɪə(r)] *n. (Electr.)* Gleichrichter, *der*

rectify [ˈrektɪfaɪ] *v.t.* **a)** korrigieren ‹*Fehler, Berechnung, Kurs*›; richtigstellen ‹*Bemerkung, Sachverhalt*›; Abhilfe schaffen (+ *Dat.*) ‹*Mangel, Mißstand*›; ~ **the situation** die Sache wieder ins Lot bringen; **b)** *(Electr.)* gleichrichten

rectilineal [rektɪˈlɪnɪəl], **rectilinear** [rectɪˈlɪnɪə(r)] *adj.* geradlinig ‹*Bewegung, Strecke, Anordnung*›; aus Geraden gebildet ‹*Winkel*›; geradlinig begrenzt ‹*Figur, Garten*›

rectitude [ˈrektɪtju:d] *n.* **a)** *(with regard to morality)* Rechtschaffenheit, *die;* **a life of ~:** ein rechtschaffenes Leben; **b)** *(with regard to correctness)* Richtigkeit, *die*

recto [ˈrektəʊ] *n., pl.* **~s** *(Printing, Bibliog.)* **a)** *(right-hand page)* rechte Seite; **b)** *(front of leaf)* Rekto, *das (fachspr.);* Vorderseite, *die*

rector [ˈrektə(r)] *n.* **a)** Pfarrer, *der;* **b)** *(Univ.)* Rektor, *der*/Rektorin, *die*

rectory [ˈrektərɪ] *n.* Pfarrhaus, *das*

rectum [ˈrektəm] *n., pl.* **~s** *or* **recta** [ˈrektə] *(Anat.)* Mastdarm, *der;* Rektum, *das (fachspr.)*

recumbent [rɪˈkʌmbənt] *adj.* ruhend; liegend ‹*Skulptur*›; **be [lying] ~:** ruhen

recuperate [rɪˈkju:pəreɪt] **1.** *v.i.* sich erholen. **2.** *v.t.* wiederherstellen ‹*Gesundheit*›; ~ **one's strength/health** wieder zu Kräften kommen/gesund werden

recuperation [rɪkju:pəˈreɪʃn] *n.* Erholung, *die;* **in rest and ~:** in Ruhe und Entspannung

recuperative [rɪˈkju:pərətɪv] *adj.* stärkend; ~ **remedies/powers** Heilmittel/-kräfte

recur [rɪˈkɜ:(r)] *v.i.,* **-rr- a)** sich wiederholen; ‹*Beschwerden, Krankheit usw.:*› wiederkehren; ‹*Problem, Symptom:*› wieder auftreten; **b)** *(return to one's mind)* ‹*Gedanke, Furcht, Gefühl:*› wiederkehren; **c)** *(Math.)* **~ring decimal** periodischer Dezimalbruch; **2.3 ~ring** 2 Komma 3 Periode

recurrence [rɪˈkʌrəns] *n.* **a)** Wiederholung, *die; (of illness, complaint)* Wiederkehr, *die; (of problem, symptom)* Wiederauftreten, *das;* **there's to be no ~ of this type of behaviour** dieses Verhalten darf sich nicht wiederholen; **b)** *(to mind)* Wiederkehr, *die*

recurrent [rɪˈkʌrənt] *adj.* immer wiederkehrend; wiederholt ‹*Hinweis, Bezugnahme*›; **have ~ problems with sth.** häufig Probleme mit etw. haben

recycle [ri:ˈsaɪkl] *v.t. (reuse)* wiederverwerten ‹*Papier, Glas, Abfall*›; *(convert)* wiederaufbereiten ‹*Metall, Brauchwasser, Abfall*›

recycling [ri:ˈsaɪklɪŋ] *n.* Recycling, *das;* Wiederaufbereitung, *die*

red [red] **1.** *adj.* **a)** rot; Rot‹*wild, -buche*›; rotglühend ‹*Feuer, Lava usw.*›; **the ~ colour of the setting sun** das Rot der untergehenden Sonne; **go ~ with shame** rot vor Scham werden; **go ~ in the face** rot werden; **as ~ as a beetroot** puterrot; rot wie eine Tomate *(ugs. scherzh.)*; **her eyes were ~ with crying** sie hatte rotgeweinte Augen; *see also* **paint 2a;** ˈ**see 2a; b)** *(anarchistic)* rot; **c) Red** *(Soviet Russian)* rot, kommunistisch ‹*Soldat, Propaganda*›; **the Red Army** die Rote Armee; **better Red than dead** lieber rot als tot. **2.** *n.* **a)** *(colour)* Rot, *das; (in roulette)* Rouge, *das; (redness)* Röte, *die;* **the ~s** die Rottöne; **b)** *(debt)* **get out of the ~:** aus den roten Zahlen kommen; **[be] in the ~:** in den roten Zahlen [sein]; **c) Red** *(communist)* Rote, *der/die;* **Reds under the bed scare** Angst vor kommunistischer Unterwanderung; **d)** *(ball)* rote Kugel; **e)** *(~ clothes)* **dressed in ~:** rot gekleidet; **f)** *(traffic-light)* Rot, *das;* **the traffic-light is at ~:** die Ampel steht auf Rot; **we drove straight through the ~:** wir fuhren bei Rot durch *(ugs.)*

red: ~ **admiral** *see* **admiral b;** ~ **alert** *n.* [höchste] Alarmbereitschaft; **be on ~ alert** sich in Alarmzustand befinden; ~**-blooded** [ˈredblʌdɪd] *adj.* heißblütig; ~**breast** *n. (Ornith.)* Rotkehlchen, *das;* ~**brick** *adj. (Brit.)* weniger traditionsreich ‹*Universität*›; ~**cap** *n.* **a)** *(Brit.: military policeman)* Militärpolizist, *der;* **b)** *(Amer.: railway porter)* Gepäckträger, *der;* ~ ˈ**carpet** *n. (lit. or fig.)* roter Teppich; ~**-carpet** *adj.;* **give sb. the ~-carpet treatment** *or* **a ~-carpet reception** jmdn. mit großem Bahnhof *(ugs.) od.* mit allen Ehren empfangen; ~ **cell** *n. (Anat., Zool.)* rotes Blutkörperchen; ~ ˈ**cent** *n. (Amer.)* roter Heller; ~**-cheeked** *adj.* rotwangig *(geh.);* **Red** ˈ**China** *n.* Rotchina, *das;* ~**coat** *n. (Brit. Hist.)* Rotrock, *der; britischer Soldat;* ~ **corpuscle** *see* ~ **cell; Red** ˈ**Crescent** *n.* Roter Halbmond; **Red** ˈ**Cross** *n.* Rotes Kreuz; ~ ˈ**currant** *n.* [rote] Johannisbeere

redden [ˈredn] **1.** *v.i.* ‹*Gesicht, Himmel:*› sich röten; ‹*Person:*› rot werden, erröten; ‹*Blätter, Wasser:*› sich rot färben; **his face ~ed [with shame** *etc.*] er lief rot an *od.* bekam einen roten Kopf [vor Scham *usw.*]. **2.** *v.t.* rot färben; röten *(geh.)*

reddish [ˈredɪʃ] *adj.* rötlich; ~ **brown** rotbraun

redecorate [ri:ˈdekəreɪt] *v.t.* renovieren; *(with wallpaper)* neu tapezieren; *(with paint)* neu streichen

redecoration [ri:dekəˈreɪʃn] *n.* Renovierung, *die; (with wallpaper)* Neutapezieren, *das; (with paint)* Neuanstrich, *der*

redeem [rɪˈdi:m] *v.t.* **a)** *(regain)* wiederherstellen ‹*Ehre, Gesundheit*›; wiedergewinnen ‹*Position*›; **b)** *(buy back)* tilgen ‹*Hypothek*›; [wieder] einlösen ‹*Pfand*›; abzahlen ‹*Grundstück*›; **c)** *(convert)* einlösen ‹*Gutschein, Coupon*›; **d)** *(make amends for)* ausgleichen, wettmachen ‹*Fehler, Schuld usw.*›; **he has one ~ing feature** man muß ihm eins zugute halten; **e)** *(repay)* abzahlen ‹*Schuld, Kredit*›; ~ **one's obligation to sb.** seine Schuld jmdm. gegenüber begleichen; **f)** *(fulfil)* einlösen, halten ‹*Versprechen*›; **g)** *(save)* retten; ~ **sb. from his sins/from hell** jmdn. von seinen Sünden/aus der Hölle erlösen; **h)** *(make less bad)* retten ‹*Situation, Beziehung, Party usw.*›; ~ **oneself** sich freikaufen; **he ~ed himself in their eyes by apologizing** er fand Gnade vor ihren Augen, indem er sich entschuldigte

redeemable [rɪˈdi:məbl] *adj.* einlösbar ‹*Gutschein, Pfand, Aktien usw.*›; tilgbar ‹*Schuld*›; kündbar ‹*Obligation*›

redeemer [rɪˈdi:mə(r)] *n.* **a)** Retter, *der;* **b) R~** *(Relig.)* Erlöser, *der;* Heiland, *der*

redefine [ri:dɪˈfaɪn] *v.t.* neu bestimmen *od.* festlegen ‹*Aufgaben, Bedingungen*›; neu formulieren ‹*These, Vertrag[spunkte]*›

redemption [rɪˈdempʃn] *n.* **a)** *(of pawned goods)* Einlösen, *das;* Rückkauf, *der;* **b)** *(of tokens, trading stamps, stocks, etc.)* Einlösen, *das;* **c)** *(of mortgage, debt)* Tilgung, *die; (of land)* Abzahlung, *die;* **d)** *(of promise, pledge)* Erfüllung, *die;* **e)** *(of person, country)* Befreiung, *die;* **he's past** *or* **beyond ~:** für ihn gibt es keine Rettung mehr; **the situation is beyond ~:** die Lage ist hoffnungslos verfahren *od.* völlig ausweglos; **f)** *(deliverance from sin)* Erlösung, *die;* **g)** *(thing that redeems)* Rettung, *die*

redeploy [riːdɪˈplɔɪ] *v.t.* umstationieren ‹*Truppen, Raketen*›; woanders einsetzen ‹*Arbeitskräfte*›; ~ **from ... to ...**: von ... nach ... verlegen
redeployment [riːdɪˈplɔɪmənt] *n.* *(of troops, missiles)* Umstationierung, *die;* *(of labour force, workers, staff)* Einsatz an anderer Stelle; ~ **from ... to ...**: Verlegung von ... nach ...
redesign [riːdɪˈzaɪn] *v.t.* umgestalten ‹*Raum, Mechanismus, Verpackung, Modell*›; überarbeiten ‹*Plan, Design*›
red: ~-eyed *adj.* **be ~-eyed** rote Augen haben; **~-faced** *adj.* rotgesichtig; **be ~-faced** *(with rage/embarrassment)* ein [hoch]rotes Gesicht haben/vor Verlegenheit rot werden; **go ~-faced with rage** vor Wut rot anlaufen; **~ ˈflag** *see* [1]**flag 1; Red ˈGuard** *n.* Rote Garde; *(member)* Rotgardist, *der/*-gardistin, *die;* **~-haired** *adj.* rothaarig; **~-handed** [redˈhændɪd] *adj.* **catch sb. ~-handed** jmdn. auf frischer Tat ertappen; **~head** *n.* Rotschopf, *der (ugs.);* Rothaarige, *der/die;* **~-headed** [ˈredhedɪd] *adj.* rothaarig; **be ~-headed** rote Haare haben; **~ heat** *n.* Rotglut, *die; (fig.)* Glut, *die;* **bring to a ~ heat** auf Rotglut erhitzen; **~ ˈherring** *n.* **a)** *(fish)* Räucherhering, *der;* **b)** *(fig.)* Ablenkungsmanöver, *das; (in thriller, historical research)* falsche Fährte; **~-hot** *adj.* **a)** [rot]glühend; **b)** *(fig.)* glühend ‹*Anhänger, Gläubiger, Liebhaber, Zorn*›; heiß ‹*Blondine, Thema, Musik*›; brandaktuell ‹*Nachricht*›; **this new film is ~-hot stuff** dieser neue Film ist heiß
redid *see* **redo**
Red ˈIndian *(Brit.)* **1.** *n.* Indianer, *der*/Indianerin, *die.* **2.** *adj.* Indianer-
redirect [riːdaɪˈrekt, riːdɪˈrekt] *v.t.* nachsenden ‹*Post, Brief usw.*›; umleiten ‹*Verkehr*›; weiterleiten **(to** an + *Akk.*) ‹*Anfrage*›; richten **(to** auf + *Akk.*) ‹*Aufmerksamkeit*›
redirection [riːdaɪˈrekʃn, riːdɪˈrekʃn] *n.* *(of mail)* Nachsendung, *die; (of traffic)* Umleitung, *die; (of question)* Weiterleitung, *die* **(to** an + *Akk.*)
rediscover [riːdɪˈskʌvə(r)] *v.t.* wiederentdecken
rediscovery [riːdɪˈskʌvərɪ] *n.* Wiederentdeckung, *die*
redistribute [riːdɪˈstrɪbjuːt] *v.t.* umverteilen ‹*Besitz, Einkommen*›; versetzen ‹*Arbeitskräfte*›; *(reorganize)* neu aufteilen
redistribution [riːdɪstrɪˈbjuːʃn] *n.* *(of land, wealth)* Umverteilung, *die; (of labour etc.)* Versetzung, *die, (reorganization)* Neuaufteilung, die
red: ~ lead [red ˈled] *n.* Mennige, *die;* **~-ˈletter day** *n.* **a)** *(memorable day)* im Kalender rot anzustreichender Tag; großer Tag; **b)** *(Relig.)* Feiertag, *der;* **~ ˈlight** *n.* **a)** [rotes] Warnlicht; *(of traffic-lights)* rote [Verkehrs]ampel; **drive straight through the ~ light** bei Rot über die Ampel fahren; **b)** *(fig.)* Warnzeichen, *das;* **they saw the** *or* **a ~ light** bei ihnen leuchtete ein [rotes] Warnsignal auf; **~-ˈlight district** *n.* Amüsierviertel, *das;* Strich, *der (salopp);* **~ meat** *n.* dunkles Fleisch *(z. B. vom Rind);* **~neck** *n.* *(Amer.)* armer weißer Landbewohner aus den Südstaaten; *(derog.)* weißer Rassist *od.* Reaktionär
redness [ˈrednɪs] *n., no pl. (of face, skin, eyes, sky)* Röte, *die; (of blood, fire, rose, dress, light)* rote Farbe
redo [riːˈduː] *v.t.*, **redoes** [riːˈdʌz], **redoing** [riːˈduːɪŋ], **redid** [riːˈdɪd], **redone** [riːˈdʌn] **a)** *(do again)* wiederholen ‹*Prüfung, Spiel, Test*›; neu frisieren ‹*Haare*›; erneuern ‹*Make-up, Lidschatten*›; noch einmal machen ‹*Bett, Hausaufgabe*›; überarbeiten ‹*Aufsatz, Übersetzung, Komposition*›; **~ one's face** sein Make-up erneuern; **b)** *(redecorate)* [gründlich] renovieren; *(repaper)* neu tapezieren; *(repaint)* neu streichen
redolent [ˈredələnt] *adj.* **a)** duftend; **~ odours** Düfte *Pl.;* **~ of** *or* **with sth.** nach etw. duftend; **b)** *(fig.)* **be ~ of sth.** stark an etw. *(Akk.)* erinnern
redone *see* **redo**
redouble [riːˈdʌbl] **1.** *v.t.* **a)** verdoppeln; **b)** *(Bridge)* rekontrieren. **2.** *v.i.* sich verdoppeln. **3.** *n.* *(Bridge)* Rekontra, *das*
redoubt [rɪˈdaʊt] *n.* *(Mil.)* Redoute, *die*
redoubtable [rɪˈdaʊtəbl] *adj.* ehrfurchtgebietend ‹*Person*›; gewaltig, enorm ‹*Aufgabe, Pflicht usw.*›; gefürchtet ‹*Gegner, Krieger*›; glänzend ‹*Anwalt*›
redound [rɪˈdaʊnd] *v.i.* **~ to sb.'s advantage/disadvantage/honour** *or* **credit/fame** jmdm. Vorteile/Nachteile/Ehre/Ruhm einbringen; **~ to sb.'s reputation/good name** zu jmds. Ruf/gutem Namen beitragen
red ˈpepper *n.* **a)** *see* **cayenne; b)** *(vegetable)* rote Paprika[schote]
redraft [riːˈdrɑːft] *v.t.* neu entwerfen; neu aufsetzen ‹*Vertrag*›; neu abfassen ‹*Schriftstück*›
red ˈrag *n. (fig.)* rotes Tuch **(to** für); **be like a ~ to a bull [to sb.]** wie ein rotes Tuch [auf jmdn.] wirken
redraw [riːˈdrɔː] *v.t., forms as* **draw** neu zeichnen
redress [rɪˈdres] **1.** *n.* *(reparation, correction)* Entschädigung, *die;* **seek ~ for sth.** eine Entschädigung für etw. verlangen; **seek [legal] ~**: auf Schadenersatz klagen; **have no ~**: keine Entschädigung erhalten; *(Law)* keinen Rechtsanspruch auf Entschädigung haben. **2.** *v.t.* **a)** *(adjust again)* ins Gleichgewicht bringen; **~ the balance** das Gleichgewicht wiederherstellen; **b)** *(set right, rectify)* wiedergutmachen ‹*Unrecht*›; ausgleichen ‹*Ungerechtigkeiten*›; beseitigen ‹*Mißstand, Übel, Despotie*›; abhelfen (+ *Dat.*) ‹*Beschwerden, Mißbrauch*›
Red: ~ ˈRiding Hood *pr. n.* Rotkäppchen, *das;* **~ ˈSea** *pr. n.* Rote Meer, *das*
red: ~shank *n.* *(Ornith.)* Rotschenkel, *der;* **~-shift** *n.* *(Astron.)* Rotverschiebung, *die;* **~skin** *see* **Red Indian 1; ~ ˈsquirrel** *n.* Eichhörnchen, *das;* **Red ˈStar** *n.* Roter Stern; **~start** *n.* *(Ornith.)* Rotschwanz, *der;* **~ ˈtape** *n.* *(fig.)* [unnötige] Bürokratie; **cut through the ~ tape** die Bürokratie umgehen; **Red Terror** *see* **terror a**
reduce [rɪˈdjuːs] **1.** *v.t.* **a)** *(diminish)* senken ‹*Preis, Gebühr, Fieber, Aufwendungen, Blutdruck usw.*›; verbilligen ‹*Ware*›; reduzieren ‹*Geschwindigkeit, Gewicht, Anzahl, Menge, Preis*›; **at ~d prices** zu herabgesetzten Preisen; **~ one's weight** abnehmen; **b) ~ to order/despair/silence/tears/submission** auf Vordermann bringen *(ugs.)*/in Verzweiflung stürzen/verstummen lassen/zum Weinen bringen/ zum Aufgeben zwingen; **~ sb. to begging** jmdn. an den Bettelstab bringen; **be ~d to starvation** hungern müssen; **be ~d to borrowing money/pawning sth.** sich *(Dat.)* Geld leihen müssen/etw. versetzen müssen; **live in ~d circumstances** in verarmten Verhältnissen leben; **~ sb. to the ranks** jmdn. in den Mannschaftsstand degradieren; **c)** *(convert to other form)* **~ wood to pulp** Holz zu einem Brei verarbeiten; **~ yards to inches** Yards in Inches umwandeln; **d)** *(Photog.)* abschwächen; **e)** *(Med.)* einrenken ‹*Gliedmaße, Gelenk*›; einrichten ‹*Bruch*›; **f)** *(Chem.)* reduzieren. **2.** *v.i.* abnehmen
reducer [rɪˈdjuːsə(r)] *n.* **a)** *(Photog.)* Abschwächer, *der;* **b)** *(Chem.)* Reduktionsmittel, *das*
reducible [rɪˈdjuːsɪbl] *adj.* **a)** reduzierbar **(to** auf + *Akk.*); **be ~**: reduziert werden können **(to** auf + *Akk.*); **b)** *(Chem.)* reduzierbar
reducing [rɪˈdjuːsɪŋ]: **~ agent** *n.* *(Chem.)* Reduktionsmittel, *das;* **~ diet** *n.* Schlankheitskur, *die*
reductio ad absurdum [rɪdʌktɪəʊ æd əbˈsɜːdəm] *n., no pl.* Reductio ad absurdum, *die (geh.)*
reduction [rɪˈdʌkʃn] *n.* **a)** *(amount, process) (in price, costs, wages, rates, speed, etc.)* Senkung, *die* **(in** *Gen.*); *(in numbers, output, etc.)* Verringerung, *die* **(in** *Gen.*); **~ in prices/wages/weight** Preis-/Lohnsenkung, *die*/Gewichtsabnahme, *die;* **there is a ~ on all furniture** alle Möbel sind im Preis heruntergesetzt; **a ~ of £10** ein Preisnachlaß von 10 Pfund; **b)** *(smaller copy)* Verkleinerung, *die;* **c)** *(conversion to other form)* Verarbeitung, *die;* **~ of yards to metres** Umwandlung von Yards in Meter; **d)** *(Photog.)* Abschwächung, *die;* **e)** *(Chem.)* Reduktion, *die*
reductionism [rɪˈdʌkʃənɪzm] *n.* *(Philos.)* Reduktionismus, *der*
reductive [rɪˈdʌktɪv] *adj.* *(Philos.)* reduktiv
redundancy [rɪˈdʌndənsɪ] *n.* **a)** *(Brit.)* Arbeitslosigkeit, *die;* **redundancies** Entlassungen; **b)** *(being more than needed)* Überfluß, *der; (of materials, capital)* Überschuß, *der; (being more than suitable)* Redundanz, *die; (of style)* Überladenheit, *die*
reˈdundancy payment *n.* Abfindung, *die*
redundant [rɪˈdʌndənt] *adj.* **a)** *(Brit.: now unemployed)* arbeitslos; **be made** *or* **become ~**: den Arbeitsplatz verlieren; **make ~**: entlassen; **b)** *(more than needed)* überflüssig; überschüssig ‹*Kapital, Material*›; *(more than suitable)* redundant; überflüssig ‹*Absatz, Kapitel, Wort*›; überladen ‹*Stil*›
reduplicate [rɪˈdjuːplɪkeɪt] **1.** *v.t.* **a)** verdoppeln; *(repeat)* wiederholen; **b)** *(Ling.)* verdoppeln. **2.** *v.i.* *(Ling.)* reduplizieren
reduplication [rɪdjuːplɪˈkeɪʃn] *n.* **a)** *(act of doubling)* Verdopplung, *die; (repetition)* Wiederholung, *die;* **b)** *(Ling.)* Reduplikation, *die*
red: ~ ˈwine *n.* Rotwein, *der;* **~wood** *n.* *(Bot.)* Mammutbaum, *der*
re-echo [riːˈekəʊ] *v.i.* **a)** widerhallen **(with** von); **the cry echoed and ~ed round the cave** der Ruf wurde in dem Gewölbe wieder und wieder zurückgeworfen; **b)** *(fig.)* **these words ~ through the book** an diese Worte wird man in dem Buch immer wieder erinnert
reed [riːd] *n.* **a)** *(Bot.)* Schilf[rohr], *das;* Ried, *das;* **the tall ~s by the river's edge** das hohe Schilf *od.* Ried am Flußufer; **prove to be a broken ~** *(fig.)* sich als unzuverlässig erweisen; **b)** *(Mus.) (part of instrument)* Rohrblatt, *das; (instrument)* Rohrblattinstrument, *das*
reed: ~-bunting *n.* *(Ornith.)* Rohrammer, *die;* **~ instrument** *n.* *(Mus.)* Rohrblattinstrument, *das;* **~-mace** *n.* *(Bot.)* Breitblättriger Rohrkolben; **~-organ** *n.* *(Mus.)* Harmonium, *das;* **~-warbler, ~-wren** *ns.* *(Ornith.)* Teichrohrsänger, *der*
reedy [ˈriːdɪ] *adj.* **a)** schnarrend ‹*Musik, Singen*›; dünn ‹*Stimme*›; **b)** *(full of reeds)* schilfig
[1]**reef** [riːf] *(Naut.)* **1.** *n.* *(on sail)* Reff, *das (Seemannsspr.);* **take in a ~**: die Segel reffen. **2.** *v.t.* reffen *(Seemannsspr.)*
[2]**reef** *n.* **a)** *(ridge)* Riff, *das;* **~ of sand/rocks/coral** Sand-/Fels-/Korallenriff, *das;* **b)** *(fig.)* Klippe, *die;* **c)** *(lode)* Erzgang, *der*
reefer [ˈriːfə(r)] *n.* *(sl.: marijuana cigarette)* Joint, *der (Drogenjargon)*
ˈreef-knot *n.* Kreuzknoten, *der*
reek [riːk] **1.** *n.* Geruch, *der;* Gestank, *der (abwertend).* **2.** *v.i.* **a)** riechen, *(abwertend)* stinken **(of** nach); **b)** *(fig.)* riechen *(ugs.)* **(of, with** nach)
reel [riːl] **1.** *n.* **a)** *(roller, cylinder)* ‹*Papier-, Schlauch-, Garn-, Angel*›rolle, *die;* ‹*Film-, Tonband-, Garn*›spule, *die;* **b)** *(quantity)* Rolle, *die;* **steel rope in ~s of 1800 feet** Stahlseil auf Rollen zu 1800 Fuß; **~ of film** Filmrolle, *die;* **c)** *(dance, music)* Reel, *der.*

2. *v.t.* ~ [up] *(wind on)* aufspulen. 3. *v.i.* a) *(be in a whirl)* sich drehen; **his head was ~ing** in seinem Kopf drehte sich alles; **her mind ~ed with all the facts** ihr schwirrte der Kopf von all den Daten; b) *(sway)* torkeln; *(fig.: be shaken)* taumeln; **begin to ~:** ins Wanken geraten; **his mind ~ed when he heard the news** als er die Nachricht hörte, drehte sich ihm alles

~ **'in** *v.t.* an Land ziehen ⟨*Fisch*⟩

~ **'off** *v.t.* a) *(say rapidly)* herunterleiern *(ugs. abwertend)*, hersagen ⟨*Geschichte*⟩; *(without apparent effort)* abspulen *(ugs.)* ⟨*Gedicht, Namen, Einzelheiten*⟩; b) *(take off)* abwickeln

re-elect [ri:ɪ'lekt] *v.t.* wiederwählen

re-election [ri:ɪ'lekʃn] *n.* Wiederwahl, *die*

re-eligible [ri:'elɪdʒɪbl] *adj.* wiederwählbar; **be ~:** wiedergewählt werden können

re-embark [ri:ɪm'bɑ:k] 1. *v.t.* wieder einschiffen ⟨*Ladung, Passagiere*⟩. 2. *v.i.* sich wieder einschiffen (**for** nach); ~ **on sth.** *(fig.)* bei etw. wieder einsteigen

re-emerge [ri:ɪ'mɜ:dʒ] *v.i.* a) *(out of liquid)* wieder auftauchen; b) *(into view; crop up)* wiederauftauchen; ⟨*Mond, Sonne usw.:*⟩ wieder hervorkommen; c) *(return)* zurückkehren (**in** nach, **from** aus)

re-emergent [ri:ɪ'mɜ:dʒənt] *adj.* wiederauftauchend ⟨*Frage, Idee*⟩; wiederkehrend ⟨*Glaube*⟩; wiedererstehend *(geh.)*⟨*Nation*⟩

re-enact [ri:ɪ'nækt] *v.t.* a) wieder in Kraft setzen ⟨*Gesetz, Erlaß usw.*⟩; b) *(perform)* wiederholen ⟨*Tatsachen, Einzelheiten*⟩; nachstellen ⟨*Szene, Schlacht*⟩; ~ **a role** noch einmal in einer Rolle auftreten

re-enlist *(Mil.)* 1. *v.i.* wieder [in die Armee/Marine] eintreten. 2. *v.t.* wieder anwerben

re-enter [ri:'entə(r)] 1. *v.i.* a) wieder eintreten; *(come on stage)* die Bühne [wieder] betreten; *(as stage direction)* ~ **Hamlet from left** Auftritt Hamlet von links; b) *(for race, exam, etc.)* wieder antreten; c) *(penetrate)* wieder eindringen. 2. *v.t.* wieder betreten ⟨*Raum, Gebäude*⟩; wieder eintreffen in (+ *Dat.*) ⟨*Ortschaft*⟩; wieder einreisen in (+ *Akk.*) ⟨*Land*⟩; wiedereintreten in (+ *Akk.*) ⟨*Erdatmosphäre*⟩

re-entry [ri:'entrɪ] *n.* a) Wiedereintreten, *das; (into country)* Wiedereinreise, *die; (for exam)* Wiederantreten, *das;* nochmaliges Antreten (**for** zu); *(of spacecraft)* **[atmospheric] ~:** Wiedereintritt [in die Erdatmosphäre]; b) *(Law: taking possession again)* Wiederinbesitznahme, *die*

re-erect [ri:ɪ'rekt] *v.t.* wieder aufbauen

re-establish [ri:ɪ'stæblɪʃ] *v.t.* wiederherstellen ⟨*Kontakt, Demokratie, Beziehungen, Frieden, Ordnung*⟩; wiederbeleben ⟨*Brauch, Mode*⟩; wiederaufbauen ⟨*Organisation, Stützpunkt*⟩; wieder einsetzen ⟨*Regierung*⟩; beweisen ⟨*Unschuld usw.*⟩; ~ **sb. as ruler** jmdn. als Herrscher wiedereinsetzen; ~ **oneself as sth./in a position** sich erneut als etw./in einer Position etablieren

¹reeve [ri:v] *n.* a) *(Hist.) (magistrate)* Vogt, *der; (manorial supervisor)* Aufseher, *der;* b) *(minor official)* Gemeindebeamter, *der/*-beamtin, *die*

²reeve *v.t.*, **rove** [rəʊv] *or* **~d** *(Naut.)* scheren ⟨*Tau*⟩; *(fasten)* festzurren

re-examination [ri:ɪgzæmɪ'neɪʃn] *n.* a) *(Law)* erneute [Zeugen]vernehmung; b) *(investigation)* erneute Untersuchung; c) *(act of testing knowledge or ability)* Wiederholungsprüfung, *die;* d) *(act of scrutinizing again)* nochmalige [Über]prüfung

re-examine [ri:ɪg'zæmɪn] *v.t.* a) *(Law)* erneut vernehmen; b) *(investigate)* [erneut] untersuchen; c) *(test knowledge or ability of)* von neuem *od.* wieder prüfen; d) *(scrutinize)* erneut überprüfen

re-export [ri:ɪk'spɔ:t] *v.t.* reexportieren; wieder ausführen

ref [ref] *n. (Sport coll.)* Schiri, *der (Sportjargon); (Boxing)* Ringrichter, *der*

ref. *abbr.* **reference** Verw.; **with ref.** to mit Bz. *od.* unter Bezugn. auf (+ *Akk.*); **your/our ref.** Ihr/unser Zeichen

reface [ri:'feɪs] *v.t.* ~ **sth.** die Fassade einer Sache *(Gen.)* restaurieren

refashion [ri:'fæʃn] *v.t.* umgestalten

refectory [rɪ'fektərɪ] *n. (in college, university)* Mensa, *die; (in convent, monastery)* Refektorium, *das*

refer [rɪ'fɜ:(r)] 1. *v.i.*, **-rr-** a) ~ **to** *(allude to)* sich beziehen auf (+ *Akk.*) ⟨*Buch, Person usw.*⟩; *(speak of)* sprechen von ⟨*Person, Problem, Ereignis usw.*⟩; b) ~ **to** *(apply to, relate to)* betreffen; ⟨*Beschreibung:*⟩ sich beziehen auf (+ *Akk.*); **does that remark ~ to me?** gilt diese Bemerkung mir?; c) ~ **to** *(consult, cite as proof)* konsultieren *(geh.);* nachsehen in (+ *Dat.*); ~ **to sb./a case** sich auf jmdn./einen Fall berufen. 2. *v.t.*, **-rr-** a) *(send on to)* ~ **sb./sth. to sb./sth.** jmdn./etw. an jmdn./auf etw. *(Akk.)* verweisen; ~ **a patient to a specialist** einen Patienten an einen Facharzt überweisen; **the dispute was ~red to the UN** der Streitfall wurde vor die UNO gebracht; ~ **sb. to a paragraph/an article** jmdn. auf einen Abstaz/Artikel aufmerksam machen; ~ **to drawer** *(Banking)* zurück an Aussteller; b) ~ **to** *(assign to)* zurückführen auf (+ *Akk.*); ~ **sth. to sb.** jmdm. etw. zuschreiben; **~red pain** *(Med.)* ausstrahlender Schmerz; c) *(after examination)* zurückstellen ⟨*Prüfling*⟩; [zur Überarbeitung] zurückgeben ⟨*Dissertation*⟩

~ **'back** 1. *v.t.* ~ **back** to zurückverweisen an (+ *Akk.*). 2. *v.i.* a) *(to past event)* ~ **back to** sich beziehen auf (+ *Akk.*); b) *(to source of information)* ~ **back to sb./sth.** Rücksprache halten mit jmdm./auf etw. *(Akk.)* zurückgreifen

referee [refə'ri:] 1. *n.* a) *(Sport: umpire)* Schiedsrichter, *der/*-richterin, *die; (Boxing)* Ringrichter, *der; (Wrestling)* Kampfrichter, *der;* b) *(Brit.: person willing to testify)* Referenz, *die;* c) *(arbitrator)* Schlichter, *der;* d) *(person who assesses)* Gutachter, *der/*Gutachterin, *die.* 2. *v.t.* a) *(Sport: umpire)* als Schiedsrichter/-richterin leiten; ~ **a football game** ein Fußballspiel pfeifen *od.* leiten; b) *(arbitrate)* schlichten; c) *(assess, evaluate)* begutachten. 3. *v.i.* a) *(Sport: umpire)* Schiedsrichter/-richterin sein; b) *(arbitrate)* schlichten; Schlichter sein; c) *(assess or evaluate work)* als Gutachter/Gutachterin tätig sein

reference ['refrəns] *n.* a) *(allusion)* Hinweis, *der* (**to** auf + *Akk.*); **make [several] ~[s] to sth.** sich [mehrfach] auf etw. *(Akk.)* beziehen; **make no ~ to sth.** etw. nicht ansprechen; **omit all ~ to sth.** etw. völlig verschweigen; **put a ~ to sth. in the introduction of the book** in der Einleitung des Buches auf etw. *(Akk.)* hinweisen; b) *(note directing reader)* Verweis, *der* (**to** auf + *Akk.*); c) *(cited book, passage)* Quellenangabe, *die;* d) *(testimonial)* Zeugnis, *das;* Referenz, *die;* **character ~:** persönliche Referenzen; **give sb. a good ~:** jmdm. ein gutes Zeugnis ausstellen; e) *(person willing to testify)* Referenz, *die;* **quote sb. as one's ~:** jmdn. als Referenz angeben; f) *(act of referring)* Konsultation, *die* (**to** *Gen.*) *(geh.);* ~ **to a dictionary/a map** Nachschlagen in einem Wörterbuch/Nachsehen auf einer Karte; **work of ~:** Nachschlagewerk, *das;* **without ~ to sb.** ohne jmdn. zu fragen; **speak without ~ to one's notes** sprechen, ohne seine Aufzeichnungen zu Hilfe zu nehmen; g) *(relation, correspondence)* **have ~ to sth.** in Beziehung zu etw. stehen; **in or with ~ to sth.** mit Bezug auf etw. *(Akk.);* unter Bezugnahme auf etw. *(Akk.);* **with ~ to your suggestion** was deinen Vorschlag anbetrifft. See also **cross-reference; library a; term 1 b**

reference: ~ book *n.* Nachschlagewerk, *das;* **~ mark** *n.* Verweiszeichen, *das*

referendum [refə'rendəm] *n., pl.* **~s** *or* **referenda** [refə'rendə] Volksentscheid, *der;* Referendum, *das*

referral [rɪ'fɜ:rl] *n.* a) *(for advice)* Überweisung, *die* (**to** an + *Akk.*); b) *(for action)* Weiterleitung, *die* (**to** an + *Akk.*)

refill 1. [ri:'fɪl] *v.t.* nachfüllen ⟨*Glas, Feuerzeug*⟩; neu füllen ⟨*Kissen*⟩; mit einer neuen Füllung versehen ⟨*Zahn*⟩; ~ **the glasses** nachschenken; ~ **a pen with ink** einen Füller mit Tinte füllen. 2. ['ri:fɪl] *n.* a) *(cartridge)* [Nachfüll]patrone, *die; (for ball-pen)* Ersatzmine, *die; (pad of paper)* Nachfüllpackung, *die;* b) *(with drink)* Nachgießen, *das;* **can I have a ~?** *(coll.)* gießt du mir noch einmal nach?

refine [rɪ'faɪn] 1. *v.t.* a) *(purify)* raffinieren; b) *(make cultured)* kultivieren; verfeinern ⟨*Stil, Ausdrucksweise*⟩; stilistisch verbessern ⟨*Rede, Aufsatz*⟩; c) *(improve)* verbessern; verfeinern ⟨*Stil, Technik*⟩. 2. *v.i.* a) *(become pure)* rein werden; b) *(become more cultured)* sich verfeinern

~ **[up]on** *v.t.* [weiter] verfeinern; weiterentwickeln

refined [rɪ'faɪnd] *adj.* a) *(purified)* raffiniert; Fein⟨*kupfer, -silber usw.*⟩; ~ **sugar** [Zucker]raffinade, *die;* b) *(cultured)* kultiviert; c) *(precise)* scharfsinnig, differenziert ⟨*Argumentation*⟩; ausgeklügelt ⟨*Technik, Maschine[rie]*⟩; kompliziert ⟨*Rechnung*⟩

refinement [rɪ'faɪnmənt] *n.* a) *(purifying)* Raffination, *die;* b) *(fineness of feeling, elegance)* Kultiviertheit, *die;* **person of ~:** kultivierter Mensch; ~ **of feeling** verfeinertes Gefühl; c) *(subtle manifestation)* Verfeinerung, *die;* d) *(improvement)* Verbesserung, *die;* Weiterentwicklung, *die* ([**up]on** *Gen.*); **introduce ~s into a machine** eine Maschine weiterentwickeln; e) *(piece of reasoning)* Spitzfindigkeit, *die (abwertend)*

refinery [rɪ'faɪnərɪ] *n.* Raffinerie, *die*

refit 1. [ri:'fɪt] *v.t.*, **-tt-** überholen; reparieren; *(equip with new things)* neu ausstatten. 2. *v.i.*, **-tt-** überholt werden; repariert werden; *(renew supplies or equipment)* sich neu ausrüsten. 3. ['ri:fɪt] *n.* Überholung, *die; (with supplies or equipment)* Neuausstattung, *die*

refitment [ri:'fɪtmənt] *see* **refit 3**

reflate [ri:'fleɪt] *v.t. (Econ.)* ankurbeln ⟨*Wirtschaft, Konjunktur*⟩

reflation [ri:'fleɪʃn] *n. (Econ.)* Reflation, *die*

reflationary [ri:'fleɪʃənərɪ] *adj. (Econ.)* reflationär

reflect [rɪ'flekt] 1. *v.t.* a) *(throw back)* reflektieren; **bask in sb.'s ~ed glory** sich in jmds. Ruhm sonnen; b) *(reproduce)* spiegeln; *(fig.)* widerspiegeln ⟨*Ansichten, Gefühle, Werte*⟩; **be ~ed** sich spiegeln; c) *(contemplate)* nachdenken über (+ *Akk.*); ~ **what/how ...:** überlegen, was/wie .... 2. *v.i.* *(meditate)* nachdenken

~ **[up]on** *v.t.* a) *(consider, contemplate)* nachdenken über (+ *Akk.*); abwägen ⟨*Konsequenzen*⟩; b) ~ **credit/discredit [up]on sb./sth.** ein gutes/schlechtes Licht auf jmdn./etw. werfen; c) *(bring discredit on)* diskreditieren; ~ **[up]on sb.'s sincerity** an jmds. Aufrichtigkeit *(Dat.)* zweifeln lassen; ~ **badly [up]on sb./sth.** auf jmdn./etw. ein schlechtes Licht werfen; d) *(bring credit on)* ~ **well [up]on sb./sth.** jmdn./etw. in einem guten Licht erscheinen lassen; e) *(cast doubt or reproach on)* in Zweifel ziehen

re'flecting telescope *see* **reflector b**

reflection [rɪ'flekʃn] *n.* a) *(of light etc.)* Reflexion, *die; (by surface of water etc.)* Spiegelung, *die;* **angle of ~:** Reflexionswinkel, *der;* b) *(reflected light, heat, or colour)* Reflexion, *die; (image; lit. or fig.)* Spiegelbild, *das;* c) *(meditation, consideration)* Nachdenken, *das* (**upon** über + *Akk.*); **be lost in**

~: in Gedanken versunken sein; **on ~: bei** weiterem Nachdenken; **on ~, I think ...:** wenn ich mir das recht überlege, [so] glaube ich ...; **d)** *(censure)* ~ **on** Kritik an (+ *Dat.*); **be a ~ [up]on sb./sth.** an jmdm./etw. zweifeln lassen; **cast ~s on sth.** etw. in Zweifel ziehen; **e)** *(idea)* Vorstellung, *die;* **f)** *(remark)* Reflexion, die *(geh.),* Betrachtung, *die* (**on** über + *Akk.*); **g)** *(Philos.)* Nachdenken, *das;* Reflexion, *die (fachspr.)*

reflective [rɪˈflektɪv] *adj.* **a)** reflektierend; **be ~:** reflektieren; ~ **power** Reflexionsvermögen, *das;* **b)** *(thoughtful)* nachdenklich; **c)** *(reflected)* reflektiert; **d)** *(concerned in reflection)* gedanklich ⟨*Fähigkeiten, Kraft*⟩

reflectively [rɪˈflektɪvlɪ] *adv.* nachdenklich

reflector [rɪˈflektə(r)] *n.* **a)** Rückstrahler, *der;* **b)** *(telescope)* Reflektor, *der*

reflex [ˈri:fleks] **1.** *n. (Physiol.)* Reflex, *der;* **conditioned ~:** bedingter Reflex. **2.** *adj. (by reflection)* Reflex-

reflex: ~ action *n. (Physiol.)* Reflexhandlung, *die;* ~ **angle** *n.* überstumpfer Winkel; ~ **camera** *n. (Photog.)* Spiegelreflexkamera, *die*

reflexion *(Brit.) see* **reflection**

reflexive [rɪˈfleksɪv] *(Ling.) adj.* reflexiv; *see also* **pronoun**

reflexively [rɪˈfleksɪvlɪ] *adv. (Ling.)* reflexiv

reflex reˈaction *n. (Physiol.; also fig.)* Reflexreaktion, *die*

refloat [ri:ˈfləʊt] *v. t.* [wieder] flottmachen ⟨*Schiff*⟩; *(fig.)* wieder flüssig machen *(ugs.)*

reflux [ˈri:flʌks] *n.* **a)** Rückfluß, *der;* **b)** *(Chem.)* Rückfluß, *der*

reform [rɪˈfɔ:m] **1.** *v. t.* **a)** *(make better)* reformieren ⟨*Institution*⟩; bessern ⟨*Person*⟩; **b)** *(abolish)* ~ **sth.** mit etw. aufräumen. **2.** *v.i.* sich bessern. **3.** *n.* **a)** *(of person)* Besserung, *die; (in a system)* Reform, *die* (**in** *Gen.*); **b)** *(removal)* Beseitigung, *die;* **R~ Bill** *(Hist.)* Reformgesetz, *das*

re-form [ri:ˈfɔ:m] **1.** *v. t.* **a)** neu gründen ⟨*Gesellschaft usw.*⟩; **b)** *(Mil.)* neu formieren. **2.** *v. i.* **a)** sich neu bilden; ⟨*Band, Gesellschaft:*⟩ neu gegründet werden; **b)** *(Mil.)* sich neu formieren

reformation [refəˈmeɪʃn] *n. (of attitude)* Änderung, *die* (**in** *Gen.*); *(of society, procedure, practice)* Neugestaltung, *die* (**in** *Gen.*); *(of person, character)* Wandlung, *die* (**in** *Gen.*); **the R~** *(Hist.)* die Reformation

re-formation [ri:fɔ:ˈmeɪʃn] *n.* **a)** Wiederaufbau, *der;* **b)** *(Mil.)* Neuformierung, *die*

reformatory [rɪˈfɔ:mətərɪ] **1.** *adj.* reformatorisch; ~ **measures** Reformmaßnahmen. **2.** *n. (Hist./Amer.)* Besserungsanstalt, *die (veralt.)*

reformed [rɪˈfɔ:md] *adj.* gewandelt; **he's a ~ character** *or* **man** er hat sich positiv verändert; **R~ Church** Reformierte Kirche

reformer [rɪˈfɔ:mə(r)] *n.* **[political] ~:** Reformpolitiker, *der*/-politikerin, *die*

reformism [rɪˈfɔ:mɪzm] *n.* Reformismus, *der*

reformist [rɪˈfɔ:mɪst] **1.** *n.* Reformist, *der*/Reformistin, *die.* **2.** *adj.* reformistisch

reˈform school *n.* Fürsorge[erziehungs]heim, *das*

refract [rɪˈfrækt] *v. t. (Phys.)* brechen

reˈfracting telescope *n.* Linsenfernrohr, *das;* Refraktor, *der (fachspr.)*

refraction [rɪˈfrækʃn] *n. (Phys.)* Brechung, *die;* Refraktion, *die (fachspr.)*; **angle of ~:** Brechungswinkel, *der*

refractive [rɪˈfræktɪv] *adj. (Phys.)* brechend; *see also* **index 1 b**

refractor [rɪˈfræktə(r)] *n. (telescope)* Refraktor, *der*

refractory [rɪˈfræktərɪ] **1.** *adj.* **a)** *(stubborn)* störrisch; widerspenstig; **b)** *(Med.)* hartnäckig; **c)** *(heat-resistant)* hitzebeständig; schwer schmelzbar ⟨*Metalle usw.*⟩. **2.** *n.* hitzebeständiges Material

¹refrain [rɪˈfreɪn] *n.* Refrain, *der*

²refrain *v.i.* ~ **from doing sth.** es unterlassen, etw. zu tun; **could you kindly ~?** würden Sie das bitte unterlassen?; **I think I'd better ~:** ich glaube, ich lasse das besser [sein]; **'please ~ from smoking'** „bitte nicht rauchen"; **he ~ed from comment** er enthielt sich jeden Kommentars *(geh.)*

refresh [rɪˈfreʃ] *v. t.* **a)** *(reanimate)* erquicken *(geh.)*; erfrischen; *(with food and/or drink)* stärken; ~ **oneself** *(with rest)* sich ausruhen; *(with food and/or drink)* sich stärken; **b)** *(freshen up)* auffrischen ⟨*Wissen*⟩; **let me ~ your memory** lassen Sie mich Ihrem Gedächtnis nachhelfen

refresher [rɪˈfreʃə(r)] *n.* **a)** *(Brit. Law)* Sonderhonorar, *das;* **b)** *(coll.)* Erfrischung, *die;* **have a ~:** etwas trinken

reˈfresher course *n.* Auffrischungskurs, *der*

refreshing [rɪˈfreʃɪŋ] *adj.* **a)** wohltuend ⟨*Ruhe*⟩; erfrischend ⟨*Brise, Getränk, Schlaf*⟩; **b)** *(interesting)* erfrischend

refreshment [rɪˈfreʃmənt] *n.* Erfrischung, *die*

refreshment: ~ room *n.* Imbißstube, *die;* ~ **stall** *n.* Erfrischungsstand, *der*

refrigerant [ri:ˈfrɪdʒərənt] *n.* Kühlmittel, *das*

refrigerate [rɪˈfrɪdʒəreɪt] *v. t.* **a)** kühl lagern ⟨*Lebensmittel*⟩; **b)** *(chill)* kühlen; *(freeze)* einfrieren; **c)** *(make cool)* abkühlen ⟨*Luft*⟩

refrigeration [rɪfrɪdʒəˈreɪʃn] *n.* kühle Lagerung; *(chilling)* Kühlung, *die; (freezing)* Einfrieren, *das*

refrigerator [rɪˈfrɪdʒəreɪtə(r)] *n.* Kühlschrank, *der*

refuel [ri:ˈfju:əl], *(Brit.)* **-ll- 1.** *v. t.* auftanken. **2.** *v. i.* [auf]tanken

refuge [ˈrefju:dʒ] *n.* **a)** Zuflucht, *die;* **find [a] ~ from the storm** Schutz vor dem Sturm finden; **take ~ in** Schutz *od.* Zuflucht suchen in (+ *Dat.*) (**from** vor + *Dat.*); *(fig.)* Zuflucht nehmen zu ⟨*Alkohol, Religion, Lüge*⟩; **be a ~ to sb.** jmds. Zuflucht sein; **women's ~:** Frauenhaus, *das;* **b)** *(traffic island)* Verkehrsinsel, *die*

refugee [refjʊˈdʒi:] *n.* Flüchtling, *der;* **~s from the earthquake** Menschen, die Schutz vor dem Erdbeben suchen

refuˈgee camp *n.* Flüchtlingslager, *das*

refulgent [rɪˈfʌldʒənt] *adj. (literary)* strahlend ⟨*Licht, Tag*⟩; leuchtend ⟨*Farbe, Sonnenuntergang*⟩

refund 1. [ri:ˈfʌnd] *v. t.* **a)** *(pay back)* zurückzahlen ⟨*Geld, Schulden*⟩; erstatten ⟨*Kosten*⟩; *abs.* die Schulden zurückzahlen; **your satisfaction guaranteed or your money ~ed** bei Nichtgefallen [bekommen Sie Ihr] Geld zurück; **b)** *(reimburse)* das Geld zurückzahlen (+ *Dat.*); ~ **sb. for** jmdm. [zurück]erstatten ⟨*Kosten*⟩; jmdm. ersetzen ⟨*Verlust, Schaden*⟩. **2.** [ˈri:fʌnd] *n.* Rückzahlung, *die; (of expenses)* [Rück]erstattung, *die;* **get a ~ of five pence on a bottle** fünf Pence [Pfand] für eine Flasche zurückbekommen; **obtain a ~ of sth.** etw. zurückbekommen

refundable [ri:ˈfʌndəbl] *adj.* **be ~:** zurückerstattet werden

refurbish [ri:ˈfɜ:bɪʃ] *v.t.* renovieren ⟨*Haus*⟩; aufarbeiten ⟨*Kleidung*⟩; aufpolieren ⟨*Möbel*⟩

refurnish [ri:ˈfɜ:nɪʃ] *v. t.* neu einrichten

refusal [rɪˈfju:zl] *n.* Ablehnung, *die; (after a period of time)* Absage, *die; (of admittance, entry, permission)* Verweigerung, *die;* ~ **to do sth.** Weigerung, etw. zu tun; **her ~ of food** ihre Weigerung, etwas zu essen; **have/get [the] first ~ on sth.** das Vorkaufsrecht für etw. haben/eingeräumt bekommen; **give sb. [the] first ~:** jmdm. das Vorkaufsrecht einräumen

¹refuse [rɪˈfju:z] **1.** *v.t.* **a)** ablehnen; abweisen ⟨*Heiratsantrag*⟩; verweigern ⟨*Nahrung, Befehl, Bewilligung, Zutritt, Einreise, Erlaubnis*⟩; ~ **sb. admittance/entry/permission** jmdm. den Zutritt/die Einreise/die Erlaubnis verweigern; ~ **to do sth.** sich weigern, etw. zu tun; **b)** *(not oblige)* abweisen ⟨*Person*⟩; **c)** ⟨*Pferd:*⟩ verweigern ⟨*Hindernis*⟩. **2.** *v. i.* **a)** ablehnen; *(after request)* sich weigern; **b)** ⟨*Pferd:*⟩ verweigern

²refuse [ˈrefju:s] **1.** *n.* Abfall, *der;* Müll, *der;* **the ~ is collected once a week** einmal in der Woche ist Müllabfuhr. **2.** *adj.* ~ **chemicals/water** Chemieabfälle/Abwasser, *das*

refuse [ˈrefju:s]: ~ **collection** *n.* Müllabfuhr, *die;* ~ **collector** *n.* Müllwerker, *der;* ~ **disposal** *n.* Abfallbeseitigung, *die;* ~ **heap** *n.* Müllhaufen, *der*

refusenik [rɪˈfju:znɪk] *n. sowjetischer Jude, dem die Ausreise [nach Israel] verweigert wurde*

refutation [refjʊˈteɪʃn] *n.* Widerlegung, *die;* **the book was a ~ of the theory** in dem Buch wurde die Theorie widerlegt

refute [rɪˈfju:t] *v. t.* widerlegen

regain [rɪˈgeɪn] *v. t.* **a)** *(recover possession of)* zurückgewinnen ⟨*Zuversicht, Vertrauen, Achtung, Augenlicht*⟩; zurückerobern ⟨*Gebiet*⟩; ~ **one's health/strength** wieder gesund werden/zu Kräften kommen; ~ **control of sth.** etw. wieder unter Kontrolle bringen; *see also* **consciousness a; b)** *(reach)* wieder erreichen ⟨*Küste, Land*⟩; wieder bekommen ⟨*Platz*⟩; ~ **firm ground again** wieder festen Boden unter den Füßen haben; **c)** *(recover)* ~ **one's balance/footing** das Gleichgewicht/den Halt wiedergewinnen; ~ **one's feet** wieder auf die Beine kommen

regal [ˈri:gl] *adj.* **a)** *(magnificent, stately)* majestätisch ⟨*Person, Baum, Art, Tier, Würde*⟩; prachtvoll ⟨*Villa, Zustand*⟩; groß ⟨*Luxus*⟩; **b)** *(royal)* königlich; ~ **office/power** Amt/Macht des Königs/der Königin

regale [rɪˈgeɪl] *v.t.* **a)** verwöhnen (**with, on** mit); ~ **sb. with stories** jmdn. mit Geschichten unterhalten; **b)** *(give delight to)* erfreuen ⟨*Auge, Ohr, Sinne, Person*⟩; **be ~d** ⟨*Auge, Ohr, Sinne:*⟩ sich laben *(geh.)*; ⟨*Person:*⟩ sich erquicken *(geh.)* (**by** an + *Dat.*)

regalia [rɪˈgeɪlɪə] *n.pl.* **a)** *(of royalty)* Krönungsinsignien; **b)** *(of order)* Ordensinsignien

regally [ˈri:gəlɪ] *adv.* wie ein König/eine Königin

regard [rɪˈgɑ:d] **1.** *v. t.* **a)** *(gaze upon)* betrachten; ~ **sb. fixedly** jmdn. anstarren; **b)** *(give heed to)* beachten ⟨*jmds. Worte, Rat*⟩; Rücksicht nehmen auf (+ *Akk.*) ⟨*Wunsch, Gesundheit, jmds. Recht*⟩; **c)** *(fig.: look upon, contemplate)* betrachten; ~ **sb. kindly/warmly** jmdm. freundlich gesinnt/herzlich zugetan sein; ~ **sb. unfavourably** jmdm. ablehnend gegenüberstehen; ~ **sth. with suspicion/horror** mißtrauisch gegen/entsetzt über etw. *(Akk.)* sein; ~ **sb. with envy/scorn** neidisch auf jmdn. sein/jmdn. verachten; ~ **sb. with respect/dislike** Respekt vor jmdm./eine Abneigung gegen jmdn. haben; ~ **sb. as a friend/fool/genius** jmdn. als Freund betrachten/für einen Dummkopf/ein Genie halten; **be ~ed as** gelten als; ~ **sth. as wrong** etw. für falsch halten; **d)** *(concern, have relation to)* betreffen; berücksichtigen ⟨*Tatsachen*⟩; **as ~s sb./sth., ~ing sb./sth.** was jmdn./etw. angeht *od.* betrifft. **2.** *n.* **a)** *(attention)* Beachtung, *die;* **pay ~ to/have ~ to** *or* **for sb./sth.** jmdm./etw. Beachtung schenken; **pay due ~ to sb.** jmdm. die nötige Beachtung erweisen; **having ~ to these facts ...:** unter Berücksichtigung dieser Tatsachen ...; **without ~ to** ohne Rücksicht auf (+ *Akk.*); **b)** *(esteem, kindly feeling)* Achtung, *die;* **hold sb./sth. in high/low ~, have** *or* **show a high/low ~ for sb./sth.** jmdn./etw. sehr schätzen/geringschätzen; **show one's high ~ for sth.** seine Wertschätzung für etw. zum Ausdruck bringen; **c)** *in pl.* Grüße; **send one's ~s** grüßen lassen; **give her my ~s** grüße sie von mir; **with kind[est] ~s** mit herzlich[st]en Grüßen; **d)** *(relation, respect)* Beziehung, *die;* **in this ~:** in dieser Beziehung *od.* Hinsicht; **in** *or* **with ~ to sb./sth.** in bezug auf jmdn./etw.; **e)** *(gaze)* Blick, *der*

regardful [rɪ'gɑ:dfl] *adj.* aufmerksam; **be ~ of** im Auge behalten ‹*Gefahr, Schwierigkeit*›; Beachtung schenken (+ *Dat.*) ‹*Interesse, Problem, Gefühl*›

regarding [rɪ'gɑ:dɪŋ] *see* **regard 1 d**

regardless [rɪ'gɑ:dlɪs] **1.** *adj.* **~ of sth.** ungeachtet *od.* trotz einer Sache *(Gen.);* **~ of the consequences/cost** ohne Rücksicht auf die Folgen/Kosten. **2.** *adv.* trotzdem; **carry on ~:** trotzdem weitermachen

regatta [rɪ'gætə] *n.* Regatta, *die;* **sailing ~:** Segelregatta, *die*

regd. *abbr.* **registered** *(Law)* ges. gesch.

regency ['ri:dʒənsɪ] *n.* **a)** Regentschaft, *die* **(of** über + *Akk.*); **b)** *(commission)* Regentschaftsrat, *der;* *(fig.)* [stellvertretendes] Führungsgremium; **c) the R~** *(in England)* die Regentschaft Georgs IV (1810–20); **R~:** *attrib.* Regency‹*möbel, -stil*›

regenerate 1. [rɪ'dʒenəreɪt] *v. t.* **a)** *(generate again, re-create)* regenerieren *(bes. Chemie, Biol.);* neu beleben ‹*Haß, Angst, Liebe*›; **b)** *(improve, reform)* erneuern ‹*Kirche, Gesellschaft*›; **~ sb.** aus jmdm. einen neuen Menschen machen; **feel ~d** sich wie neugeboren fühlen; **c)** *(Biol.: form afresh)* regenerieren *(fachspr.),* neu bilden ‹*Gewebe, verlorenen Körperteil*›. **2.** [rɪ'dʒenərət] *adj.* **a)** *(Relig.: reborn)* wiedergeboren; **b)** *(improved)* gewandelt ‹*Person*›; *(reformed)* umgestaltet ‹*Gesellschaft, Institution*›

regeneration [rɪdʒenə'reɪʃn] *n.* **a)** *(recreation, re-formation)* Neuentstehung, *die;* *(fig.: revival, renaissance)* Wiederbelebung, *die;* *(of church, society)* Erneuerung, *die;* **b)** *(Relig.: spiritual rebirth)* Wiedergeburt, *die;* **c)** *(Biol.: regrowth)* Regeneration, *die (fachspr.);* Neubildung, *die*

regenerative [rɪ'dʒenərətɪv] *adj.* regenerativ

regent ['ri:dʒənt] **1.** *n.* **a)** Regent, *der*/Regentin, *die;* **b)** *(Amer. Univ.)* Mitglied des Verwaltungsrates; **the R~s** der Verwaltungsrat. **2.** *adj.* **Prince R~:** Prinzregent, *der*

reggae ['regeɪ] *n. (Mus.)* Reggae, *der*

regicide ['redʒɪsaɪd] *n.* **a)** *(murder)* Königsmord, *der;* **b)** *(murderer)* Königsmörder, *der/*-mörderin, *die*

regime, régime [reɪ'ʒi:m] *n.* **a)** *(system)* [Regierungs]system, *das;* *(derog.)* Regime, *das;* *(fig.)* bestehende Ordnung; *see also* **ancien régime; b)** *(process)* Methode, *die;* **working ~:** Funktionsweise, *die;* **c)** *(Med.) see* **regimen**

regimen ['redʒɪmən] *n. (Med.)* Heilprogramm, *das;* *(diet)* Diätplan, *der*

regiment 1. ['redʒɪmənt], 'redʒmənt] *n.* **a)** *(Mil.: organizational unit)* Regiment, *das;* **parachute/Highland ~:** Luftlande-/Hochlandregiment, *das;* **b)** *(Mil.: operational unit)* Abteilung, *die;* **artillery/tank ~:** Artillerie-/Panzerabteilung, *die;* **Royal R~ [of Artillery]** *(Brit.)* Königliche Artillerie; **c)** *(fig.: large number) (of persons, animals)* Heer, *das;* *(of books etc.)* Masse, *die.* **2.** ['redʒɪment, 'redʒment] *v. t. (organize)* reglementieren

regimental [redʒɪ'mentl] *(Mil.)* **1.** *adj.* Regiments‹*kleidung, -vorräte*›; **the ~ officers** die Offiziere des Regiments; *see also* **colour 1 j. 2.** *n. in pl.* [Militär]uniform, *die;* *(of particular regiment)* Regimentsuniform, *die*

regimentation [redʒɪmən'teɪʃn, redʒɪmen'teɪʃn] *n.* Reglementierung, *die*

Regina [rɪ'dʒaɪnə] *n. (Law)* **~ v. Jones** die Königin gegen Jones

region ['ri:dʒn] *n.* **a)** *(area)* Gebiet, *das;* **the north-western ~:** der Nordwesten; **b)** *(administrative division)* Bezirk, *der;* *(Brit. Radio)* Sendegebiet, *das;* **administrative ~:** Verwaltungsbezirk, *der;* **Strathclyde/North-West R~:** Bezirk Strathclyde/Nordwest; **c)** *(fig.: sphere)* Bereich, *der;* Gebiet, *das;* **in the ~ of two tons** ungefähr zwei Tonnen; **d)** *(layer)* Schicht, *die;* Region, *die;* **e)** *(Anat.)* Region, *die;* **~ of the eyes/mouth** Augen-/Mundpartie, *die;* *see also* **lower regions**

regional ['ri:dʒənl] *adj.* regional ‹*System, Akzent, Förderung*›; Regional‹*planung, -fernsehen, -programm, -ausschuß*›; **~ dialect** Regiolekt, *der (Sprachw.);* regionaler Dialekt; **~ wines of France** Weine aus französischen Anbaugebieten

regionalism ['ri:dʒənəlɪzm] *n.* *(Polit., Ling.)* Regionalismus, *der*

regionalize ['ri:dʒənəlaɪz] *v. t.* regionalisieren

register ['redʒɪstə(r)] **1.** *n.* **a)** *(book, list)* Register, *das;* *(at school)* Klassenbuch, *das;* **parish/hotel/marriage ~:** Kirchen-/Fremden-/Heiratsbuch, *das;* **~ of births, deaths and marriages** Personenstandsbuch, *das;* **medical ~:** Ärzteregister, *das;* **electoral** *or* **parliamentary ~, ~ of voters** Wählerliste, *die;* Wählerverzeichnis, *das;* **~ of members/patients** Mitgliederverzeichnis, *das*/Patientenkartei, *die;* **civil service ~:** Verzeichnis der Beamten; **call** *or* **mark the ~** *(at school)* die Anwesenheit der Schüler überprüfen; **b)** *(Mus.) (in organ)* Registerzug, *der;* *(in harpsichord)* Rechen, *der;* *(set of pipes)* Register, *das;* **c)** *(Mus.: range of tones)* Tonumfang, *der;* *(part of voice-compass)* Register, *das (fachspr.);* Tonlage, *die;* **middle ~:** Mittellage, *die;* **head/chest ~:** Kopf-/Brustregister, *das;* **d)** *(Mech.)* Klappe, *die;* Schieber, *der;* **e)** *(recording device)* Zählwerk, *das;* *see also* **cash register; f)** *(Printing)* Register, *das;* **be in ~:** Register halten; **g)** *(Photog.)* Register, *das;* Passer, *der;* **h)** *(Ling.)* Register, *das.* **2.** *v. t.* **a)** *(set down)* schriftlich festhalten ‹*Name, Zahl, Experiment, Detail*›; *(on file; fig.: make mental note of)* registrieren **(on** in + *Dat.*) ‹*Name, Faktum, Rat*›; **b)** *(enter)* registrieren ‹*Geburt, Heirat, Todesfall, Patent*›; *(cause to be entered)* registrieren lassen; eintragen ‹*Warenzeichen, Firma, Verein*›; anmelden ‹*Auto, Patent*›; *(at airport)* einchecken ‹*Gepäck*›; *abs. (at hotel)* sich ins Fremdenbuch eintragen; **~ [oneself] with the police** sich polizeilich anmelden; **c)** *(enrol)* anmelden; *(Univ.)* einschreiben, immatrikulieren; *(as voter)* eintragen **(on** in + *Akk.*) ‹*Person*›; *abs. (as student)* sich einschreiben *od.* immatrikulieren; *(in list of voters)* sich ins Wählerverzeichnis eintragen lassen; **~ [oneself] with a doctor** sich bei einem praktischen Arzt eintragen lassen; **d)** *(record)* anzeigen, registrieren ‹*Temperatur*›; **e)** *(Post)* eingeschrieben versenden; **have sth. ~ed** etw. einschreiben lassen; **f)** *(express)* zeigen ‹*Gefühlsregung, Freude*›; widerspiegeln ‹*Angst*›; zum Ausdruck bringen ‹*Entsetzen, Überraschung*›; **~ a protest** Protest anmelden. **3.** *v. i. (make impression)* einen Eindruck machen **(on, with** auf + *Akk.*); **it didn't ~ with him** er hat das nicht registriert

registered ['redʒɪstəd] *adj.* [ins Standesregister] eingetragen ‹*Taufe, Heirat*›; [ins Handelsregister] eingetragen ‹*Firma*›; eingeschrieben, immatrikuliert ‹*Student*›; schriftlich festgehalten ‹*Fakten, Zahlen*›; eingeschrieben ‹*Brief, Post, Päckchen*›; **~ disabled** ≈ Behinderter/Behinderte mit Schwerbehindertenausweis; **State R~ Nurse** *(Brit.)* staatlich geprüfte Krankenschwester/staatlich geprüfter Krankenpfleger; **~ trade mark** eingetragenes Warenzeichen; **by ~ post** per Einschreiben

'register office *n. (Brit.)* Standesamt, *das*

registrar ['redʒɪstrɑ:(r), redʒɪ'strɑ:(r)] *n.* **a)** *(official recorder) (at university)* ≈ Kanzler, *der*/Kanzlerin, *die;* *(local official)* Standesbeamte, *der*/-beamtin, *die;* **b)** *(Brit.: in court of law)* ≈ Rechtspfleger, *der*/-pflegerin, *die;* **c)** *(Med.) Arzt/Ärztin in der klinischen Fachausbildung*

Registrar 'General *n. Leiter/Leiterin des Amtes für Bevölkerungsstatistik*

registration [redʒɪ'streɪʃn] *n.* **a)** *(act of registering)* Registrierung, *die;* *(enrolment)* Anmeldung, *die;* *(of students)* Einschreibung, *die;* Immatrikulation, *die;* *(of voters)* Eintragung ins Wählerverzeichnis; *(Post)* Einschreiben, *das;* **cost of ~** *(of letter, parcel)* Einschreibegebühr, *die;* **b)** *(entry)* [Register]eintrag, *der;* **make a ~ of** registrieren; **~ fee** Anmeldegebühr, *die;* *(for educational course)* Kursgebühr, *die*

registration: ~ document *n. (Brit.)* Kraftfahrzeugbrief, *der;* **~ mark, ~ number** *ns. (Motor Veh.)* amtliches *od.* polizeiliches Kennzeichen; **~ plate** *n. (Motor Veh.)* Nummernschild, *das*

registry ['redʒɪstrɪ] *n.* **a) ~ [office]** Standesamt, *das;* *attrib.* standesamtlich ‹*Trauung*›; **be married in a ~ [office]** sich standesamtlich trauen lassen; **b)** *(place for registers)* Registratur, *die;* **c)** *(registration)* Registrierung, *die;* Eintragung, *die;* *(of students)* Einschreibung, *die;* Immatrikulation, *die*

Regius ['ri:dʒɪəs] *adj.* **~ professor** *(Brit. Univ.) Inhaber/Inhaberin eines von einem Monarchen errichteten od. durch Berufung der Krone besetzten Lehrstuhls*

regress [rɪ'gres] *v. i.* **a)** *(in development)* sich zurückentwickeln; *(in career)* Rückschritte machen; **a sign of society ~ing** ein Zeichen gesellschaftlichen Rückschritts; **b)** *(Psych.)* regredieren **(to** in + *Akk.*)

regression [rɪ'greʃn] *n.* **a)** *(return to previous state)* rückläufige Entwicklung; **a ~ to less civilized standards** ein Rückfall in weniger zivilisierte Normen; **b)** *(Psych.)* Regression, *die;* **c)** *(Med.: decline)* Rückbildung, *die;* **d)** *(backward movement)* Rückkehr, *die*

re'gression curve *n. (Statistics)* Regressionskurve, *die*

regressive [rɪ'gresɪv] *adj.* **a)** *(Psych., Med., Logic)* regressiv; **b)** *(tending to go back in development)* rückschrittlich

regret [rɪ'gret] **1.** *v. t.*, **-tt- a)** *(feel sorrow for loss of)* nachtrauern (+ *Dat.*); **b)** *(be sorry for)* bedauern; **~ having done sth.** es bedauern, daß man etw. getan hat; **~ being unable to do sth.** *or* **that one cannot do sth.** es bedauern, daß man etw. nicht tun kann; **it is to be ~ted that ...:** es ist bedauerlich, daß ...; **I ~ to say that ...:** ich muß leider sagen, daß ...; **we ~ to hear that ...:** wir hören mit Bedauern, daß ... **2.** *n.* Bedauern, *das;* **feel ~ at sb.'s doing sth.** bedauern, daß jmd. etw. tut; **feel ~ for having done sth.** es bedauern, daß man etw. getan hat; **there's no point in having ~s** es hat keinen Sinn, sich jetzt noch darüber Gedanken zu machen; **much to my ~:** zu meinem großen Bedauern; **send one's ~s** *(polite refusal)* sich entschuldigen lassen; **please accept my ~s at having to refuse** seien Sie mir bitte nicht böse, aber ich muß leider ablehnen

regretful [rɪ'gretfl] *adj.* bedauernd ‹*Blick*›; **be ~ that one has done sth.** bedauern, daß man etw. getan hat

regretfully [rɪ'gretfəlɪ] *adv.* mit Bedauern

regrettable [rɪ'gretəbl] adj. bedauerlich

regrettably [rɪ'gretəblɪ] *adv.* bedauerlicherweise; bedauerlich ‹*teuer*›

regroup [ri:'gru:p] **1.** *v. t.* **a)** umgruppieren; *(into classes)* neu einteilen **(into** in + *Akk.*); **b)** *(Mil.: reorganize)* neu formieren ‹*Truppen*›. **2.** *v. i.* **a)** *(form a new group)* sich neu gruppieren; *(meet again)* wieder zusammenkommen; **b)** *(Mil.)* sich neu formieren

regular ['regjʊlə(r)] **1.** *adj.* **a)** *(recurring uniformly, habitual, orderly)* regelmäßig; geregelt ⟨*Arbeit*⟩; fest ⟨*Anstellung, Reihenfolge*⟩; ~ **customer** Stammkunde, *der*/-kundin, *die;* ~ **staff** Stammpersonal, *das;* ~ **doctor** Hausarzt, *der;* **our** ~ **postman** unser [gewohnter] Briefträger; **get** ~ **work** ⟨*Freiberufler:*⟩ regelmäßig Aufträge bekommen; **my bowels are** ~, **I am** ~: ich habe regelmäßig Stuhlgang; **what's the** ~ **procedure for opening a deposit account?** wie richtet man normalerweise ein Sparkonto ein?; **her periods are always** ~: sie bekommt ihre Periode immer regelmäßig; **have** *or* **lead a** ~ **life** ein geregeltes Leben führen; *see also* **hour c; b)** *(evenly arranged, symmetrical)* regelmäßig; **c)** *(correct)* angemessen ⟨*Verhalten, Verfahren*⟩; **d)** *(properly qualified)* ausgebildet; ~ **army** reguläre Armee; ~ **soldiers** Berufssoldaten; **e)** *(Ling.)* regelmäßig; **f)** *(coll.: thorough)* richtig *(ugs.);* **g)** *(Geom.)* regelmäßig; regulär *(fachspr.);* **h)** *(Eccl.)* Regular⟨*kleriker, -geistlicher*⟩. **2.** *n.* **a)** *(coll.: ~ customer, visitor, etc.)* Stammkunde, *der*/-kundin, *die; (in pub)* Stammgast, *der;* **b)** *(coll.: permanently employed person)* Festangestellte, *der/die;* **c)** *(soldier)* Berufssoldat, *der;* **d)** *(Amer.: gasoline)* Normal, *das (ugs.);* **e)** *(Eccl.)* Regularkleriker, *der*

regularise *see* **regularize**

regularity [regjʊ'lærɪtɪ] *n.* **a)** Regelmäßigkeit, *die;* **b)** *(Ling.)* regelmäßige Flexion

regularize ['regjʊləraɪz] *v. t.* **a)** *(make regular)* regeln; *(by law)* gesetzlich regeln *od.* festlegen; ~ **the proceedings** vorschriftsmäßig verfahren; **b)** *(make steady)* stabilisieren ⟨*Atmung, Puls, Spannung*⟩

regularly ['regjʊləlɪ] *adv.* **a)** *(at fixed times)* regelmäßig; *(constantly)* ständig; **b)** *(steadily)* gleichmäßig; **c)** *(symmetrically)* regelmäßig ⟨*bauen, anlegen*⟩; **d)** *(in an orderly manner)* korrekt

regulate ['regjʊleɪt] *v. t.* **a)** *(control)* regeln; *(subject to restriction)* begrenzen; **b)** *(adjust)* regulieren; einstellen ⟨*Apparat, Maschine, Zeit*⟩; [richtig ein]stellen ⟨*Uhr*⟩; **she** ~**s her hours to fit in with his** sie paßt sich ihm in ihrer Zeiteinteilung an; **c)** *(moderate)* senken ⟨*Ausgaben*⟩; *(adapt)* anpassen ⟨*Lebensstil, Verhalten, Gewohnheit*⟩; ~ **one's lifestyle to fit in with sth.** seinen Lebensstil an etw. *(Akk.)* anpassen

regulation [regʊ'leɪʃn] *n.* **a)** *(regulating)* Regelung, *die; (of quantity, speed)* Regulierung, *die; (of machine)* Einstellen, *das; (of life-style, conduct, habit, mind)* Anpassung, *die; (of expenses)* Senkung, *die;* **b)** *(rule)* Vorschrift, *die;* **be against** ~**s** vorschriftswidrig sein; **school/safety/fire** ~**s** Schulordnung, *die*/Sicherheits-/Brandschutzvorschriften; **c)** *attrib. (according to rule)* vorgeschrieben ⟨*Geschwindigkeit*⟩; vorschriftsmäßig ⟨*Kleidung*⟩; *(usual)* üblich ⟨*Größe, Kleidung, Frisur*⟩

regulative ['regjʊlətɪv] *adj.* regulativ; ~ **mechanism** Regelmechanismus, *der*

regulator ['regjʊleɪtə(r)] *n.* **a)** *(device)* Regler, *der; (of clock, watch)* Gangregler, *der;* **b)** *(clock)* Normaluhr, *die;* Regulator, *der (veralt.)*

regurgitate [ri:'gɜ:dʒɪteɪt] *v. t.* **a)** ⟨*Person:*⟩ erbrechen ⟨*Essen*⟩; ⟨*Tier:*⟩ herauswürgen ⟨*Beute*⟩; *(Med.)* zurückpumpen ⟨*Blut*⟩; **b)** *(fig.)* ausspucken

rehabilitate [ri:hə'bɪlɪteɪt] *v. t.* rehabilitieren; renovieren, wiederherrichten ⟨*altes Gebäude*⟩; ~ **[back into society]** wieder [in die Gesellschaft] eingliedern

rehabilitation [ri:həbɪlɪ'teɪʃn] *n.* Rehabilitation, *die; (of building)* Renovierung, *die;* Instandsetzung, *die;* ~ **[in society]** Wiedereingliederung [in die Gesellschaft]

rehash 1. [ri:'hæʃ] *v. t.* aufwärmen; **just** ~ **a text** einen Text ein bißchen aufpolieren *(ugs.).* **2.** ['ri:hæʃ] *n.* **a)** *(restatement)* Aufguß, *der (abwertend);* **b)** *(act or process of restating) (of old arguments)* Aufwärmen, *das;* **do a** ~ **of the text** den Text ein bißchen aufpolieren *(ugs.)*

rehearsal [rɪ'hɜ:sl] *n.* **a)** *(Theatre, Mus., etc.)* Probe, *die;* **have a** ~/~**s** proben *(of Akk.);* **the play is now in** ~: das Stück wird jetzt geprobt; *see also* **dress rehearsal; b)** *(recounting)* Aufzählung, *die; (recital)* Vortrag, *der;* **give a** ~ **of** aufzählen ⟨*Ereignisse*⟩

rehearse [rɪ'hɜ:s] *v. t.* **a)** *(Theatre, Mus., etc.)* proben; **b)** *(recite)* sprechen ⟨*Gebet*⟩; rezitieren ⟨*Gedicht, Stück*⟩; *(repeat)* wiederholen; ~ **sth. again to sb.** jmdm. etw. noch einmal erzählen; **c)** *(enumerate)* aufzählen; **d)** *(train)* proben mit ⟨*Schauspieler, Musiker*⟩; **be** ~**d in the correct use of sth.** in den korrekten Gebrauch von etw. eingeübt werden

re-heat [ri:'hi:t] *v. t.* wieder erwärmen; aufwärmen ⟨*Essen*⟩

rehouse [ri:'haʊz] *v. t.* umquartieren

rehousing [ri:'haʊzɪŋ] *n.* Umquartierung, *die*

Reich [raɪk, raɪx] *n. (Hist.)* [Deutsches] Reich; **the First/Second** ~: das Heilige Römische/Deutsche Reich; **the Third** ~: das Dritte Reich

reign [reɪn] **1.** *n.* Herrschaft, *die; (of monarch also)* Regentschaft, *die;* **in the** ~ **of King Charles** während der Regentschaft König Karls; *see also* **terror a. 2.** *v. i.* **a)** *(hold office)* herrschen **(over** über + *Akk.*); ~**ing champion** amtierender Meister/amtierende Meisterin; *see also* **supreme 1 b; b)** *(prevail)* herrschen; **silence** ~**s** es herrscht Ruhe

reignite [ri:ɪg'naɪt] **1.** *v. t.* wieder anzünden; wieder entzünden ⟨*Gas*⟩. **2.** *v. i.* sich wieder entzünden

Reilly *see* **Riley**

reimburse [ri:ɪm'bɜ:s] *v. t.* [zurück]erstatten ⟨[*Un*]*kosten, Spesen*⟩; entschädigen ⟨*Person*⟩; ~ **sb. for** jmdm. [zurück]erstatten ⟨[*Un*]*kosten, Spesen*⟩; jmdm. ersetzen ⟨*Verlust*⟩

reimbursement [ri:ɪm'bɜ:smənt] *n.* Rückzahlung, *die; (of expenses)* Erstattung, *die*

reimport [ri:ɪm'pɔ:t] *v. t.* reimportieren **(into** nach)

reimpose [ri:ɪm'pəʊz] *v. t.* erneuern; wieder erheben ⟨*Zoll, Steuer*⟩; erneut verhängen ⟨*Kriegsrecht, Sanktionen*⟩; wieder anordnen ⟨*Rationierung*⟩

rein [reɪn] **1.** *n.* **a)** Zügel, *der;* **keep a child on** ~**s** ein Kind am Laufgurt führen; **draw** ~: die Zügel anziehen; **give one's horse the** ~**[s]** [seinem Pferd] die Zügel schießen lassen; **b)** *(fig.)* Zügel, *der;* **hold the** ~**s** die Zügel in der Hand haben; **give [full]** ~ **to sth.** einer Sache *(Dat.)* die Zügel schießen lassen; **keep a tight** ~ **on** an der Kandare halten ⟨*Person*⟩; im Zaum halten ⟨*Gefühle*⟩; in Schranken halten ⟨*Ausgaben*⟩; **assume/drop the** ~**s of government/power** die Amtsgeschäfte/Macht übernehmen/abgeben; *see also* **free 1 c. 2.** *v. t.* **a)** *(check, guide)* lenken ⟨*Pferd*⟩; ~ **to a halt** zum Stehen bringen ⟨*Pferd*⟩; **b)** *(restrain)* im Zaum halten ⟨*Zunge*⟩

~ **'back 1.** *v. t.* zügeln ⟨*Pferd*⟩. **2.** *v. i.* die Zügel anziehen

~ **'in 1.** *v. t. (check, lit. or fig.)* zügeln. **2.** *v. i.* haltmachen

~ **'up 1.** *v. t.* zügeln ⟨*Pferd*⟩. **2.** *v. i.* die Zügel anziehen

reincarnate [ri:ɪn'kɑ:neɪt] *v. t. (Relig.)* reinkarnieren; **be** ~**d** wiedergeboren werden

reincarnation [ri:ɪnkɑ:'neɪʃn] *n. (Relig.)* Reinkarnation, *die;* Wiedergeburt, *die*

reindeer ['reɪndɪə(r)] *n., pl. same* Ren[tier], *das*

'reindeer moss *n. (Bot.)* Rentierflechte, *die*

reinforce [ri:ɪn'fɔ:s] *v. t.* verstärken ⟨*Truppen, Mauer, Festung, Stoff*⟩; aufstocken ⟨*Vorräte*⟩; stärken ⟨*Partei, Gesundheit*⟩; erhöhen ⟨*Anzahl*⟩; untermauern ⟨*Argument*⟩; bestätigen ⟨*Behauptung*⟩; ~ **sb.'s opinion/determination** jmdn. in seiner Meinung/Entschlossenheit bestärken; ~**d concrete** Stahlbeton, *der;* ~ **the message** was man zu verstehen geben wollte, unterstreichen *od.* bekräftigen

reinforcement [ri:ɪn'fɔ:smənt] *n.* **a)** *(of bridge etc.)* Verstärkung, *die; (of provisions)* Aufstockung, *die; (of numbers)* Zunahme, *die; (of argument)* Untermauerung, *die; (of determination)* Bestärkung, *die;* **b)** ~**[s]** *(additional men etc.)* Verstärkung, *die;* **c)** *(on punch-holes)* Verstärkungsring, *der; (for elbow of garment)* Schoner, *der; (for buckled girder)* Armierung, *die*

reinsert [ri:ɪn'sɜ:t] *v. t.* noch einmal einwerfen ⟨*Münze*⟩; ⟨*Arzt:*⟩ noch einmal einstechen ⟨*Nadel*⟩; noch einmal setzen ⟨*Inserat*⟩

reinstate [ri:ɪn'steɪt] *v. t.* wiederherstellen ⟨*Recht und Ordnung*⟩; wieder einstellen ⟨*Arbeiter*⟩; *(in position)* wieder einsetzen; **be** ~**d in sb.'s favour** jmds. Gunst wiedergewonnen haben; **be** ~**d on the throne** wieder auf den Thron gehoben werden

reinstatement [ri:ɪn'steɪtmənt] *n. (of law and order)* Wiederherstellung, *die;* **his** ~ **in the job** seine Wiedereinstellung

reinsurance [ri:ɪn'ʃʊərəns] Rückversicherung, *die; (extension)* Verlängerung der Versicherung

reinsure [ri:ɪn'ʃʊə(r)] *v. t.* rückversichern; *(extend)* die Versicherung verlängern für

reinter [ri:ɪn'tɜ:(r)] *v. t.,* **-rr-** wieder begraben

reinterpret [ri:ɪn'tɜ:prɪt] *v. t.* *(interpret afresh)* noch einmal interpretieren; *(give different interpretation)* neu interpretieren

reinvent [ri:ɪn'vent] *v. t. see* **wheel 1 a**

reinvest [ri:ɪn'vest] *v. t.* reinvestieren *(fachspr.);* wieder anlegen ⟨*Kapital*⟩

reinvestment [ri:ɪn'vestmənt] *n. (fresh investment)* Reinvestition, *die (fachspr.);* Wiederanlage, *die*

reinvigorate [ri:ɪn'vɪgəreɪt] *v. t.* neu beleben; **feel** ~**d** sich gestärkt fühlen

reissue [ri:'ɪʃu:, ri:'ɪsju:] **1.** *v. t.* neu herausbringen. **2.** *n.* Neuauflage, *die; (of film)* Wiederveröffentlichung, *die*

reiterate [ri:'ɪtəreɪt] *v. t.* wiederholen

reiteration [ri:ɪtə'reɪʃn] *n.* Wiederholung, *die*

reject 1. [rɪ'dʒekt] *v. t.* **a)** ablehnen; abweisen ⟨*Freier*⟩; verweigern ⟨*Nahrung*⟩; zurückweisen ⟨*Bitte, Annäherungsversuch*⟩; **b)** *(Med.)* nicht vertragen ⟨*Bluttransfusion, Nahrung, Medizin*⟩; abstoßen ⟨*Transplantat*⟩. **2.** ['ri:dʒekt] *n. (person)* Ausgestoßene, *der/die; (Mil.)* Untaugliche, *der/die; (thing)* Ausschuß, *der*

rejection [rɪ'dʒekʃn] *n.* **a)** *see* **reject 1 a:** Ablehnung, *die;* Abweisung, *die;* Verweigerung, *die;* Zurückweisung, *die;* **parental** ~: Ablehnung durch die Eltern; **b)** *(Med.)* Abstoßung, *die;* ~ **of food indicates that ...:** daß der Körper Nahrung nicht verträgt, läßt erkennen, daß ...

re'jection slip *n.* Absage, *die*

rejig [ri:'dʒɪg] *v. t.,* **-gg-** umrüsten **(with** auf + *Akk.*); *(coll.: rearrange)* ummodeln

rejoice [rɪ'dʒɔɪs] *v. i.* **a)** *(feel great joy)* sich freuen **(over, at** über + *Akk.*); ~ **in the Lord!** freut Euch im Herrn!; **b)** *(make merry)* feiern

~ **in** *v. i.* **a)** *(joc.: be called by)* ~ **in a name/title** sich mit einem Namen/Titel schmücken *(scherzh.);* **b)** *(joc.: have)* sich erfreuen (+ *Gen.*); gesegnet sein mit *(oft spött.)*

rejoicing [rɪ'dʒɔɪsɪŋ] *n.* **a) [sounds of]** ~: Jubel, *der;* **b)** *in pl. (celebrations)* Feier, *die*

[1]rejoin [rɪ'dʒɔɪn] *v. t. (reply)* erwidern **(to** auf + *Akk.*)

[2]rejoin [riːˈdʒɔɪn] **1.** *v. t.* **a)** *(join again)* wieder stoßen zu ⟨*Regiment*⟩; wieder eintreten in (+ *Akk.*) ⟨*Partei, Verein*⟩; **~ each other** sich wieder treffen; **~ one's ship** wieder an Bord gehen; **b)** *(reunite)* wieder zusammenfügen ⟨*Bruchstücke*⟩; ⟨*Verkehrsteilnehmer:*⟩ wieder kommen auf (+ *Akk.*) ⟨*Straße, Autobahn*⟩; ⟨*Straße:*⟩ wieder [ein]münden in (+ *Akk.*) ⟨*Straße, Autobahn*⟩. **2.** *v. i.* ⟨*Personen:*⟩ sich wieder treffen; ⟨*Straßen:*⟩ wieder zusammentreffen

rejoinder [rɪˈdʒɔɪndə(r)] *n.* Erwiderung, *die* **(to** auf + *Akk.***)**

rejuvenate [rɪˈdʒuːvəneɪt] *v. t.* verjüngen ⟨*Person, Haut*⟩; neu beleben ⟨*Institution, wirtschaftliches/gesellschaftliches Leben*⟩

rejuvenation [rɪdʒuːvəˈneɪʃn] *n.* Verjüngung, *die; (of institutions, economic life, social life)* Neubelebung, *die*

rekindle [riːˈkɪndl] **1.** *v. t.* **a)** *(relight)* wieder anfachen; **b)** *(fig.: reawaken)* wieder entfachen ⟨*Liebe, Leidenschaft*⟩; wieder aufleben lassen ⟨*Sehnsucht, Verlangen, Hoffnung*⟩. **2.** *v. i.* sich wieder entzünden; *(fig.)* wieder aufflammen

relapse [rɪˈlæps] **1.** *v. i.* ⟨*Kranker:*⟩ einen Rückfall bekommen; **~ into** zurückfallen in (+ *Akk.*) ⟨*Götzendienst, Barbarei*⟩; **~ into drug-taking/shop-lifting** rückfällig werden [und wieder Drogen nehmen/Ladendiebstähle begehen]; **~ into silence/lethargy** wieder in Schweigen/Lethargie verfallen. **2.** *n.* Rückfall, *der* **(into** in + *Akk.***)**

relate [rɪˈleɪt] **1.** *v. t.* **a)** *(tell)* erzählen ⟨*Geschichte*⟩; erzählen von ⟨*Abenteuer*⟩; **b)** *(bring into relation)* in Zusammenhang bringen **(to, with** mit**)**; **~ two things** eine Verbindung zwischen zwei Dingen herstellen; **c)** *(establish relation or connection between)* einen Zusammenhang herstellen zwischen. **2.** *v. i.* **a) ~ to** *(have reference)* ⟨*Vorlesung:*⟩ handeln von; ⟨*Behauptung, Frage, Angelegenheit:*⟩ in Zusammenhang stehen mit; betreffen ⟨*Person*⟩; **b) ~ to** *(feel involved or connected with)* eine Beziehung haben zu

related [rɪˈleɪtɪd] *adj.* **a)** *(by kinship or marriage)* verwandt **(to** mit**)**; **~ by marriage** verschwägert; **they are all ~ [to one another]** sie sind alle miteinander verwandt; **b)** *(connected)* miteinander in Zusammenhang stehend; verwandt ⟨*Sprache, Begriff, Art, Spezies, Fach*⟩

relation [rɪˈleɪʃn] *n.* **a)** *(connection)* Beziehung, *die* **(of ... and** zwischen ... und); Zusammenhang, *der* **(of ... and** zwischen ... und); **be out of all ~ to** in keinem Verhältnis stehen zu ⟨*Kosten, geleisteter Arbeit*⟩; **have some ~ to** in einem gewissen Zusammenhang stehen zu; **in** *or* **with ~ to** in bezug auf (+ *Akk.*); **the ~s expressed by prepositions** die durch Präpositionen ausgedrückten Bezüge; *see also* [2]**bear 1 c**; **b)** *in pl. (dealings) (with parents, police)* Verhältnis, *das* **(with** zu); *(with country)* Beziehungen **(with** zu, mit); *(sexual intercourse)* intime Beziehungen **(with** zu); **trading ~s** Handelsbeziehungen; **c)** *(kin, relative)* Verwandte, *der/die;* **what ~ is he to you?** wie ist er mit dir verwandt?; **is she any ~ [to you]?** ist sie mit dir verwandt?; **d)** *(narrative, account)* Erzählung, *die; (of details)* Aufzählung, *die;* **e)** *(Law)* Anzeige, *die;* **at the** *or* **by ~ of** auf Anzeige *(Akk.)* von

relationship [rɪˈleɪʃnʃɪp] *n.* **a)** *(mutual tie)* Beziehung, *die* **(with** zu**)**; **have a good/bad ~ with sb.** zu jmdm. ein gutes/schlechtes Verhältnis haben; **doctor-patient ~:** Verhältnis zwischen Arzt und Patient; **b)** *(kinship)* Verwandtschaftsverhältnis, *das;* **what is your ~ to him?** in welchem Verwandtschaftsverhältnis stehst du zu ihm?; **c)** *(connection)* Beziehung, *die; (between cause and effect)* Zusammenhang, *der;* **d)** *(sexual)* Verhältnis, *das*

relative [ˈrelətɪv] **1.** *n.* **a)** *(family connection)* Verwandte, *der/die;* **have many ~s** eine große Verwandtschaft haben; **b)** *(related species)* Verwandte, *der/die;* **c)** *(Ling.)* Relativ[um], *das.* **2.** *adj.* **a)** *(corresponding)* relativ; **the ~ value of British and German currency is ...:** das Wertverhältnis von der englischen zur deutschen Währung beträgt ...; **b)** *(comparative)* jeweilig; **the ~ costs of a and b** die Kostenrelation zwischen a und b; **with ~ calmness** relativ gelassen; **c)** *(defined in relation to sth. else)* relativ ⟨*Dichte, Feuchtigkeit*⟩; **~ positions of troops** Truppenkonstellation, *die;* **~ densities/heights** Dichte-/Höhenrelation, *die;* **~ majority** *(Brit. Polit.)* relative Mehrheit; **d)** *(proportioned to sth. else)* **be ~ to sth.** sich nach etw. richten; **a large population ~ to the town's size** eine im Verhältnis zur Größe der Stadt beachtliche Einwohnerzahl; **e)** *(implying comparison with sth. else)* relativ ⟨*Begriff*⟩; **f)** *(conditioned by relation to sth. else)* abhängig **(to** von); **be ~ to sth./sb.** ⟨*Geschmack, Größe:*⟩ durch etw./jmdn. relativiert werden; **g)** *(correlative)* sich gegenseitig bedingend; **'parents' and 'children' are ~ terms** die Begriffe „Eltern" und „Kinder" bedingen sich gegenseitig; **h)** *(having reference to sth.)* **~ to** in Zusammenhang mit; **give me the grid references ~ to your location** geben Sie mir die Koordinaten Ihres Standorts; **i)** *(Mus.)* parallel ⟨*Dur-, Molltonart*⟩

relative: ~ 'adjective *n. (Ling.)* Relativadjektiv, *das;* **~ 'adverb** *n. (Ling.)* Relativadverb, *das;* **~ 'clause** *n. (Ling.)* Relativsatz, *der*

relatively [ˈrelətɪvlɪ] *adv.* relativ; verhältnismäßig

relative 'pronoun *n.* Relativpronomen, *das*

relativise *see* **relativize**

relativism [ˈrelətɪvɪzm] *n. (Philos.)* Relativismus, *der*

relativist [ˈrelətɪvɪst] *n. (Philos.)* Relativist, *der*/Relativistin, *die*

relativistic [relətɪˈvɪstɪk] *adj.* **a)** relativistisch; **b)** *(Phys.)* Relativitäts⟨*theorie, -korrektion*⟩

relativity [reləˈtɪvɪtɪ] *n.* **a)** *(fact of being relative)* Abhängigkeit, *die* **(to** von); **b)** *(Phys.)* Relativität, *die;* **~ theory, the theory of ~:** die Relativitätstheorie; **c)** *(Econ.) (of posts)* Stellenstaffelung, *die; (of salaries)* Gehaltsstaffelung, *die;* **campaign for ~ in pay with men** ⟨*Frauen:*⟩ sich für die tarifliche Gleichstellung mit den Männern einsetzen

relativize [ˈrelətɪvaɪz] *v. t.* relativieren

relax [rɪˈlæks] **1.** *v. t.* **a)** *(make less tense)* entspannen ⟨*Muskel, Körper[teil]*⟩; lockern ⟨*Muskel, Feder, Griff*⟩; *(fig.)* lockern; **winter ~ed its grip on the landscape** *(fig.)* der Winter ließ die Landschaft aus seiner Umklammerung; **b)** *(make less strict)* lockern ⟨*Gesetz, Disziplin, Sitten*⟩; **c)** *(slacken)* nachlassen in (+ *Dat.*) ⟨*Bemühungen, Aufmerksamkeit*⟩; verlangsamen ⟨*Tempo*⟩; **he began to ~ his attention** seine Aufmerksamkeit ließ allmählich nach. **2.** *v. i.* **a)** *(become less tense)* sich entspannen; **his face** *or* **features ~ed into a smile** sein Gesicht entspannte sich zu einem Lächeln; **b)** *(slacken)* nachlassen **(in** in + *Dat.*); **c)** *(become less stern)* sich mäßigen **(in** in + *Dat.*); **d)** *(cease effort)* sich entspannen; ausspannen; *(stop worrying, calm down)* sich beruhigen; **let's just ~!** *(stop worrying!)* nur ruhig Blut!

relaxant [rɪˈlæksənt] *n. (Med.)* Relaxans, *das*

relaxation [riːlækˈseɪʃn] *n.* **a)** *(recreation)* Freizeitbeschäftigung, *die;* **play tennis as a ~:** zur Entspannung Tennis spielen; **b)** *(cessation of effort)* Erholung, *die* **(from** von); **find time for ~:** Zeit für Muße finden; **c)** *(reduction of physical tension; also fig.)* Lockerung, *die;* **d)** *(Phys.)* Relaxation, *die*

relaxed [rɪˈlækst] *adj.* **a)** *(informal, not anxious)* entspannt, gelöst ⟨*Atmosphäre, Lächeln, Gefühl, Person*⟩; **she's a very ~ person** sie ist ein sehr gelassener Mensch *od.* die Gelassenheit in Person; **at a ~ pace** gemächlich; **b)** *(not strict or exact)* gelockert ⟨*Regel, Beschränkung*⟩; locker ⟨*Moral*⟩

relaxing [rɪˈlæksɪŋ] *adj.* entspannend; erholsam; **have a ~ bath** zur Entspannung ein Bad nehmen

relay 1. [ˈriːleɪ] *n.* **a)** *(gang)* Schicht, *die;* **work in ~s** schichtweise arbeiten; **b)** *(race)* Staffel, *die;* **c)** *(vehicles)* **~ [of cars]** [Fahrzeug]stafette, *die;* **d)** *(driving operation)* Fahrzeugstafette, *die;* **e)** *(Electr.)* Relais, *das;* **protective ~:** Schutzrelais, *das;* **f)** *(Radio, Telev.)* **radio ~:** Richtfunkverbindung, *die;* **~ station** Relaisstation, *die;* **g)** *(transmission)* Übertragung, *die;* **direct ~:** Direktübertragung, *die.* **2.** [riːˈleɪ, ˈriːleɪ] *v. t.* **a)** *(pass on)* weiterleiten; **~ a message to sb. that ...:** jmdm. ausrichten *od.* mitteilen, daß ...; **b)** *(Radio, Telev., Teleph.)* übertragen; **c)** *(transport)* [in einer Stafette] befördern; **form a chain to ~ water to the scene of the fire** eine Kette bilden, um Wasser zur Brandstelle durchzureichen

re-lay [riːˈleɪ] *v. t.*, **re-laid** [riːˈleɪd] wieder verlegen ⟨*Teppich, Fliesen*⟩; neu belegen ⟨*Fußboden, Straße*⟩; *(after damage)* neu [ver]legen ⟨*Rohr, Leitung*⟩

'relay race *n. (Running, Hurdling)* Staffellauf, *der; (Swimming)* Staffelschwimmen, *das;* **the 4 × 100 metres ~:** die 4 × 100-Meter-Staffel; **hurdles ~:** Hürdenstaffel, *die*

release [rɪˈliːs] **1.** *v. t.* **a)** *(free)* freilassen ⟨*Tier, Häftling, Sklaven*⟩; *(from imprisonment, jail)* entlassen **(from** aus); *(from bondage, trap)* befreien **(from** aus); *(from pain)* erlösen **(from** von); *(from promise, obligation, vow)* entbinden **(from** von); *(from work)* freistellen **(from** von); **b)** *(let go, let fall)* loslassen; lösen ⟨*Handbremse, Sprungfeder*⟩; ausklinken ⟨*Bombe*⟩; **~ one's hold or grip on sth.** etw. loslassen; **~ the shutter** *(Photog.)* den Verschluß auslösen; **~ the pressure** den Druck verringern; **c)** *(make known)* veröffentlichen ⟨*Erklärung, Nachricht*⟩; *(issue)* herausbringen ⟨*Film, Schallplatte, Produkt*⟩; **d)** *(emit)* ablassen ⟨*Dampf*⟩; freisetzen ⟨*Energie, Strahlung*⟩. **2.** *n.* **a)** *(act of freeing) see* **1 a:** Freilassung, *die;* Entlassung, *die;* Befreiung, *die;* Erlösung, *die;* Entbindung, *die;* Freistellung, *die;* **b)** *(of published item)* Veröffentlichung, *die;* **when does the film go out on general ~?** wann kommt der Film in die Kinos?; **the film/record is scheduled for ~ in the autumn** der Film/die Schallplatte soll im Herbst herausgebracht werden *od.* herauskommen; **a new ~ by Bob Dylan** eine neue Platte *od.* eine Neuveröffentlichung von Bob Dylan; **the film is a recent ~:** der Film ist erst vor kurzem herausgekommen; **c)** *(handle, lever, button)* Auslöser, *der;* **carriage ~:** Wagenrücklauf, *der;* **d)** *(of steam)* Ablassen, *das; (of pressure)* Verringerung, *die; (of energy, radiation)* Freisetzung, *die*

relegate [ˈrelɪgeɪt] *v. t.* **a)** *(dismiss, consign)* **~ sb. to the position or status of ...:** jmdn. zu ... degradieren; **~ sth. to the rubbish-bin** etw. in den Mülleimer wandern lassen; **b)** *(Sport)* absteigen lassen; **be ~d** absteigen **(to** in + *Akk.*); **c)** *(hand over)* weiterleiten **(to** an + *Akk.*); **d)** *(banish)* verbannen

relegation [relɪˈgeɪʃn] *n.* **a)** *(action of dismissing, consigning)* Degradierung, *die;* **her ~ to the position of ...:** ihre Degradierung zu ...; **b)** *(Sport)* Abstieg, *der;* **c)** *(action or state of banishment)* Verbannung, *die*

relent [rɪˈlent] *v. i.* sich erweichen lassen; *(yield to compassion)* Mitleid zeigen; ⟨*Wetter:*⟩ besser werden

relentless [rɪˈlentlɪs] *adj.* unerbittlich; erbarmungslos ⟨*Necken*⟩; schonungslos ⟨*Kritik, Heftigkeit*⟩

relentlessly [rɪˈlentlɪslɪ] *adv.* unerbittlich; erbarmungslos ⟨*necken*⟩; schonungslos ⟨*kritisieren*⟩

relevance [ˈrelɪvəns], **relevancy** [ˈrelɪvənsɪ] *n.* Relevanz, die (**to** für); **what ~ does it have to this?** inwiefern ist es dafür relevant?; **be of ~ to sth.** für etw. relevant sein

relevant [ˈrelɪvənt] *adj.* relevant (**to** für); wichtig ⟨*Information, Dokument*⟩; entsprechend ⟨*Formular*⟩; zuständig ⟨*Person*⟩; **~ to the case** sachdienlich *(Amtsspr.)*; **is this question ~ to the argument?** tut diese Frage etwas zur Sache?

reliability [rɪlaɪəˈbɪlɪtɪ] *n., no pl.* Zuverlässigkeit, *die*

reliable [rɪˈlaɪəbl] *adj.* zuverlässig

reliableness [rɪˈlaɪəblnɪs] *see* **reliability**

reliably [rɪˈlaɪəblɪ] *adv.* zuverlässig; **I am ~ informed that ...:** ich habe aus zuverlässiger Quelle erfahren, daß ...

reliance [rɪˈlaɪəns] *n. (trust, confidence)* Vertrauen, *das* (**in** zu, **on** auf + *Akk.*); *(dependence)* Abhängigkeit, *die* (**on** von); **she resented her ~ on his money** es ärgerte sie, daß sie auf sein Geld angewiesen war; **have ~ on** *or* **in sb./sth.** zu jmdm./etw. Vertrauen haben; **place much ~ [up]on sb.** großes Vertrauen in jmdn. setzen; **there is little ~ to be placed on sth./sb.** auf etw./jmdn. ist kaum Verlaß

reliant [rɪˈlaɪənt] *adj. (dependent)* **be ~ on sb./sth.** von jmdm./etw. abhängig sein; *(for help also)* auf jmdn./etw. angewiesen sein

relic [ˈrelɪk] *n.* **a)** *(Relig.)* Reliquie, *die;* **b)** *(surviving trace or memorial)* Überbleibsel, *das (ugs.)*; Relikt, *das;* **c)** *(remains, residue)* Überrest, *der;* **d)** *(derog./joc.: old or old-fashioned person or thing)* Fossil, *das (fig.)*; **he is a ~ from the Sixties** er ist noch aus den sechziger Jahren übriggeblieben

relict [ˈrelɪkt] *n.* **a)** *(arch.: widow)* Witib, *die (veralt.)*; **b)** *(Biol., Geog., Geol.)* Relikt, *das*

[1]**relief** [rɪˈliːf] *n.* **a)** *(alleviation, deliverance)* Erleichterung, *die;* **give** *or* **bring [sb.] ~ [from pain]** [jmdm.] [Schmerz]linderung verschaffen *od.* bringen; **it was with great ~ that I heard the news of ...:** mit großer Erleichterung habe ich die Nachricht vom ... vernommen; **breathe** *or* **heave a sigh of ~:** erleichtert aufatmen; **it was a ~ to take off his tight shoes/to bump into somebody he knew** es war eine Wohltat für ihn, die engen Schuhe auszuziehen/daß ihm ein Bekannter über den Weg lief; **what a ~!, that's a ~!** da bin ich aber erleichtert!; **b)** *(that which makes a change from monotony)* Abwechslung, *die;* ; *see also* **comic 1 c; [2]light 1 a; c)** *(assistance)* Hilfe, *die; (financial state assistance)* Sozialhilfe, *die; attrib.* Hilfs⟨*fond, -organisation, -komitee*⟩; **~ party** *or* **team** Rettungsmannschaft, *die;* **~ worker** Rettungshelfer, *der*/-helferin, *die; (in disaster)* Katastrophenhelfer, *der*/-helferin, *die;* **go/live on ~:** Fürsorge beantragen/von der Fürsorge leben; **go** *or* **come to sb.'s ~:** jmdm. zu Hilfe eilen *od.* kommen; **d)** *(Brit. Hist.: assistance)* Fürsorge, *die;* **e)** *(replacement of person)* Ablösung, *die; attrib.* **~ watchman/driver/troops** ablösender Wachmann/Fahrer/ablösende Truppen; **~ sentry** Wachablösung, *die;* **f)** *(Mil.) (reinforcement)* Verstärkung, *die; (raising of siege)* Entsatz, *der;* **g)** *(Law: redress)* Entschädigung, *die*

[2]**relief** *n.* **a)** *(Art)* **works in ~:** Reliefarbeiten; **high/low ~:** Hoch-/Flachrelief, *das;* **b)** *(piece of sculpture)* Relief, *das;* **c)** *(appearance of being done in ~)* reliefartiges Aussehen; **stand out in strong ~ against sth.** sich scharf gegen etw. abheben; *(fig.)* in krassem Gegensatz zu etw. stehen; **bring out in [full] ~** *(lit. or fig.)* deutlich herausarbeiten

relief: ~ bus, ~ coach *ns. (additional)* Entlastungsbus, *der; (as replacement)* Ersatzbus, *der;* **~ map** *n.* Reliefkarte, *die;* **~ road** *n.* Entlastungsstraße, *die*

relieve [rɪˈliːv] *v. t.* **a)** *(lessen, mitigate)* lindern; helfen (+ *Dat.*) ⟨*Notleidenden*⟩; verringern ⟨*Dampfdruck, Anspannung*⟩; unterbrechen ⟨*Eintönigkeit*⟩; erleichtern ⟨*Gewissen*⟩; *(remove)* abbauen ⟨*Anspannung*⟩; stillen ⟨*Schmerzen*⟩; *(remove or lessen monotony of)* auflockern; **I am** *or* **feel ~d to hear that ...:** es erleichtert mich zu hören, daß ...; **b)** *(release from duty)* ablösen ⟨*Wache, Truppen*⟩; **c) ~ sb.** *(of task, duty)* jmdn. entbinden (**of** von); *(of responsibility, load)* jmdm. abnehmen (**of** *Akk.*); *(from debt)* jmdm. erlassen (**from** *Akk.*); *(of burden, duty, from sorrow, worry)* jmdn. befreien (**of, from** von); **~ sb.'s mind of doubt** jmdm. die Zweifel nehmen; **d) ~ sb. of sth.** *(joc.: steal from)* jmdn. um etw. erleichtern *(scherzh.)*; **e) ~ one's feelings** seinen Gefühlen Luft machen; **f) ~ oneself** *(empty the bladder or bowels)* sich erleichtern *(verhüll.)*; **g)** *(release from a post)* entbinden (**of, from** von); *(dismiss)* entheben *(geh.)* (**of, from** *Gen.*); **~ sb. from duty** *or* **of his post** *or* **office** *or* **duties** jmdn. ablösen; **h)** *(Mil.: free from siege)* entsetzen *(bes. Mil.)*; befreien

religion [rɪˈlɪdʒn] *n.* **a)** Religion, *die;* **freedom of ~:** Glaubensfreiheit, *die;* **what is your ~?** welcher Religion gehörst du an?; **that's against my ~:** das verstößt gegen meinen Glauben; **no thanks, I won't have a cigarette; it's against my ~** *(joc.)* nein danke, ich möchte keine Zigarette, ich bin überzeugter Nichtraucher; *see also* **established c; b)** *(recognition of God)* Glaube, *der;* **get ~** *(sl./joc.)* fromm werden; **c)** *(object of devotion or obligation)* **he makes a ~ of snooker** Snooker ist ihm heilig; **she makes a ~ of keeping her house clean** es ist ihr eine heilige Pflicht, ihr Haus sauberzuhalten *(iron.)*

religious [rɪˈlɪdʒəs] **1.** *adj.* **a)** *(pious)* religiös; fromm; **b)** *(concerned with religion)* Glaubens⟨*freiheit, -eifer*⟩; Religions⟨*freiheit, -unterricht, -kenntnisse*⟩; religiös ⟨*Überzeugung, Zentrum*⟩; **c)** *(of monastic order)* religiös ⟨*Orden*⟩; **~ community** Ordensgemeinschaft, *die;* **~ house** Kloster, *das;* **d)** *(scrupulous)* peinlich ⟨*Sorgfalt, Genauigkeit, Ordnung*⟩; **with ~ care** *or* **exactitude** sehr gewissenhaft ⟨*arbeiten*⟩; **pay ~ attention to details** peinlich genau auf Details achten. **2.** *n., pl. same* Ordensmitglied, *das*

religiously [rɪˈlɪdʒəslɪ] *adv.* **a)** *(piously, reverently)* inbrünstig ⟨*beten*⟩; ehrfürchtig ⟨*verehren, niederknien*⟩; **b)** *(conscientiously, scrupulously)* gewissenhaft ⟨*beachten, durchsehen, verbessern*⟩; peinlich genau ⟨*saubermachen, verbessern*⟩

reline [riːˈlaɪn] *v. t.* neu [aus]füttern ⟨*Kleidungsstück*⟩; neu belegen ⟨*Bremse*⟩; doublieren ⟨*Gemälde*⟩; **~ a hat with a silk lining** einen Hut mit Seide neu ausfüttern

relinquish [rɪˈlɪŋkwɪʃ] *v. t.* **a)** *(give up, abandon)* aufgeben; ablassen von ⟨*Gewohnheit, Glaube*⟩; zurückziehen ⟨*Klage*⟩; verzichten auf (+ *Akk.*) ⟨*Recht, Anspruch, Macht*⟩; aufgeben ⟨*Anspruch, Stelle, Arbeit, Besitz*⟩; **~ the right/one's claim to sth.** auf sein Recht/seinen Anspruch auf etw. verzichten; **~ sth. to sb.** etw. an jmdn. abtreten; zugunsten von jmdm. auf etw. *(Akk.)* verzichten; **b) ~ one's hold** *or* **grip on sb./sth.** jmdn./etw. loslassen; **c)** *(fig.)* **~ one's hold on reality** den Bezug zur Realität verlieren; **he has ~ed his hold over** *or* **on her** er hat aufgehört, sie zu bevormunden

relinquishment [rɪˈlɪŋkwɪʃmənt] *n.* Aufgabe, *die; (of belief)* Ablassen, *das* (**of** von); *(of right, power, claim, territory)* Verzicht, *der* (**of** auf + *Akk.*)

reliquary [ˈrelɪkwərɪ] *n.* Reliquiar, *das*

relish [ˈrelɪʃ] **1.** *n.* **a)** *(liking)* Vorliebe, *die;* **show a real ~ for doing sth.** etw. mit Vorliebe tun; **have a great/no ~ for sth.** viel/nichts für eine Sache übrig haben; **do sth. with [great] ~:** etw. mit [großem] Genuß tun; **he takes [great] ~ in doing sth.** es bereitet ihm [große] Freude, etw. zu tun; **b)** *(condiment)* Relish, *das (Kochk.)*; **c)** *(attractive quality)* Reiz, *der;* **have no/great ~:** reizlos/sehr verlockend sein; **meat has no ~ when one is ill** man hat keine Lust auf Fleisch, wenn man krank ist. **2.** *v. t.* genießen; reizvoll finden ⟨*Gedanke, Vorstellung*⟩; **I should ~ a lobster and a bottle of wine** was ich jetzt gern hätte, wäre ein Hummer und eine Flasche Wein

relive [riːˈlɪv] *n.* noch einmal durchleben; **~ one's life** noch einmal leben

reload [riːˈləʊd] *v. t.* nachladen ⟨*Schußwaffe*⟩; wieder beladen ⟨*Lastwagen*⟩; wieder aufladen ⟨*Waren*⟩; **~ the camera** einen neuen Film einlegen

relocate [riːləˈkeɪt] **1.** *v. t.* **a)** *(move to another place)* verlegen ⟨*Fabrik, Büro*⟩; versetzen ⟨*Angestellten, Fenster, Ventil*⟩; **b)** *(find again)* wieder ausfindig machen ⟨*Aufenthaltsort*⟩; wiederfinden ⟨*Eingang, Gleise*⟩. **2.** *v. i. (settle)* sich niederlassen

relocation [riːləˈkeɪʃn] *n. (of factory, office)* Verlegung, *die; (of employee)* Versetzung, *die;* **~ expenses** Umzugskosten *Pl.*

reluctance [rɪˈlʌktəns] *n., no pl.* Widerwille, *der;* Abneigung, *die;* **have a [great] ~ to do sth.** etw. nur mit Widerwillen tun; **show some ~ at doing sth.** etw. nur ungern tun

reluctant [rɪˈlʌktənt] *adj.* unwillig; **be ~ to do sth.** etw. nur ungern *od.* widerstrebend tun; **give sb. ~ assistance** jmdm. nur widerstrebend helfen

reluctantly [rɪˈlʌktəntlɪ] *adv.* nur ungern; widerstrebend

rely [rɪˈlaɪ] *v. i.* **a)** *(have trust)* sich verlassen (**[up]on** auf + *Akk.*); **you can always ~ on him to turn up too early** *(iron.)* du kannst dich darauf verlassen, daß er immer zu früh kommt; **b)** *(be dependent)* angewiesen sein (**[up]on** auf + *Akk.*); **[have to] ~ on sb. to help** darauf angewiesen sein, daß jmd. hilft

remade *see* **remake 1**

remain [rɪˈmeɪn] *v. i.* **a)** *(be left over)* übrigbleiben; **all that ~ed for me to do was to ...:** ich mußte *od.* brauchte nur noch ...; **nothing ~s but to thank you all** es bleibt mir nur, Ihnen allen zu danken; **only one match still ~s to be played** es muß nur noch ein Spiel ausgetragen werden; **the few pleasures that ~ to an old man** die wenigen Freuden, die einem alten Mann [noch] bleiben; **b)** *(stay)* bleiben; **~ behind** noch dableiben; **~ in sb.'s memory** jmdm. im Gedächtnis bleiben; **c)** *(continue to be)* bleiben; **~ true to sb.'s memory** jmdm. ein treues Andenken bewahren; **that** *or* **it ~s to be seen** das bleibt abzuwarten *od.* wird sich zeigen; **the fact ~s that ...:** das ändert nichts an der Tatsache *od.* daran, daß ...; **I ~, yours faithfully, J. Smith** ich verbleibe mit freundlichen Grüßen Ihr J. Smith

remainder [rɪˈmeɪndə(r)] **1.** *n.* **a)** *(sb. or sth. left over; also Math.)* Rest, *der;* **the ~ of the guests** die übrigen Gäste; **b)** *(remaining stock)* Restposten, *der;* **[publisher's] ~:** Restauflage, *die;* **c)** *(Law)* Anwartschaft auf die Nacherbschaft; **d)** *(right to succeed to a title or position)* Anwartschaft auf die Nachfolge. **2.** *v. t. (Publishing)* [als Restauflage] zu herabgesetztem Preis verkaufen

remaining [rɪˈmeɪnɪŋ] *adj.* restlich; übrig; **spend one's ~ years ...:** seinen Lebensabend ... verbringen

remains [rɪˈmeɪnz] *n. pl.* **a)** *(left-over part)* Reste; **b)** *(corpse)* sterbliche [Über]reste *(verhüll.)*; **c)** *(relics)* Relikte; Reste; **Roman ~:** Relikte aus der Römerzeit

remake 1. [riːˈmeɪk] *v. t.*, **remade** [riːˈmeɪd] wieder machen ⟨*Bett*⟩; neu vereinbaren ⟨*Verabredung*⟩; wieder herrichten ⟨*Klei-*

dung›; ~ **the booking** neu buchen. **2.** ['ri:meɪk] *n. (Cinemat.)* Remake, *das (fachspr.);* Neuverfilmung, *die;* **do a ~ of sth.** etw. neu verfilmen

remand [rɪ'mɑ:nd] **1.** *v. t.* ~ **sb. [in** *or* **into custody]** jmdn. in Untersuchungshaft behalten; **be ~ed in custody/on bail** in Untersuchungshaft bleiben müssen/gegen Kaution aus der Untersuchungshaft entlassen werden. **2.** *n.* **[period of]** ~**:** Untersuchungshaft, *die;* **place sb. on ~:** jmdn. in Untersuchungshaft nehmen; **be held on ~:** in Untersuchungshaft bleiben müssen

remand: ~ centre *n. (Brit.) Untersuchungsgefängnis für jugendliche Straftäter zwischen 14 und 21 Jahren;* ~ **home** *n. (Brit. Hist.) Untersuchungsgefängnis für jugendliche Straftäter unter 17 Jahren*

remark [rɪ'mɑ:k] **1.** *v. t.* **a)** *(say)* bemerken **(to** gegenüber); **b)** *(arch.: observe)* gewahr werden. **2.** *v. i.* eine Bemerkung machen **([up]on** zu, über + *Akk.*). **3.** *n.* **a)** *(comment)* Bemerkung, *die* **(on** über + *Akk.*); **make a ~:** eine Bemerkung machen **(about, at** über + *Akk.*); **I have a few ~s to make about that** ich habe dazu einiges zu sagen; **b)** *no art. (commenting)* Kommentar, *der;* **without ~:** kommentarlos; **be worthy of special ~** *(formal)* besondere Beachtung verdienen; **nothing worthy of ~** *(formal)* nichts Bemerkenswertes

remarkable [rɪ'mɑ:kəbl] *adj.* **a)** *(notable)* bemerkenswert; **b)** *(extraordinary)* außergewöhnlich; **a boy who is ~ for his stupidity** ein Junge von ganz außergewöhnlicher Dummheit

remarkably [rɪ'mɑ:kəblɪ] *adv.* **a)** *(notably)* bemerkenswert; **b)** *(exceptionally)* außergewöhnlich

remarriage [ri:'mærɪdʒ] *n.* Wiederverheiratung, *die*

remarry [ri:'mærɪ] *v. i. & t.* wieder heiraten

rematch [ri:'mætʃ] *n.* Rückkampf, *der*

remediable [rɪ'mi:dɪəbl] *adj.* behebbar; **be ~:** beseitigt werden können; **is the situation ~?** gibt es einen Ausweg aus der Situation?

remedial [rɪ'mi:dɪəl] *adj.* **a)** *(affording a remedy)* Heil‹*behandlung, -wirkung*›; *(intended to remedy deficiency etc.)* rehabilitierend ‹*Maßnahme*›; **take ~ action** Hilfsmaßnahmen ergreifen; **be ~ rather than preventive** eher therapeutischer als vorbeugender Natur sein; **b)** *(Educ.)* Förder-; **classes in ~ reading** Förderunterricht im Lesen; ~ **education** Förderunterricht, *der*

remedy ['remɪdɪ] **1.** *n.* **a)** *(cure)* [Heil]mittel, *das* **(for** gegen); **cough/herbal ~:** Husten-/Kräutermittel, *das;* **cold/flu ~:** Mittel gegen Erkältung/Grippe; **be past** *or* **beyond ~:** unheilbar sein; **b)** *(means of counteracting)* [Gegen]mittel, *das* **(for** gegen); **c)** *(Law: redress) (through civil proceedings)* Rechtsbehelf, *der; (through self-help)* Entschädigung, *die.* **2.** *v. t.* beheben ‹*Sprachfehler, Problem*›; ausgleichen ‹*Kurzsichtigkeit*›; retten ‹*Situation*›; **the problem/situation cannot be remedied** das Problem kann nicht behoben werden/die Situation ist nicht zu retten

remember [rɪ'membə(r)] *v. t.* **a)** *(keep in memory)* denken an (+ *Akk.*); *(bring to mind)* sich erinnern an (+ *Akk.*); **I've just ~ed what I wanted to tell you** mir ist gerade [wieder] eingefallen, was ich dir sagen wollte; **don't you ~ me?** erinnern Sie sich nicht an mich?; ~ **who/where you are!** vergiß nicht, wer/wo du bist; **I can't ~ the word I want** das Wort, das ich brauche, fällt mir gerade nicht ein; **she gave him something to ~ her by** sie gab ihm etwas, das ihn an sie erinnern sollte; *(fig.)* sie gab ihm einen Denkzettel; **I ~ed to bring the book** ich habe daran gedacht, das Buch mitzubringen; **I can't ~ how to put it back together** ich weiß nicht mehr, wie es wieder zusammengesetzt wird; **do you ~ when the bus leaves?** weißt du noch, wann der Bus abfährt?; **I can never ~ her name** ich kann mir ihren Namen einfach nicht merken; **I distinctly ~ posting the letter** ich erinnere mich genau, daß ich den Brief eingeworfen habe; **if I ~ correctly** *(abs.)* wenn ich mich recht erinnere; **an evening to ~:** ein unvergeßlicher Abend; **b)** *(convey greetings from)* grüßen; ~ **me to them** grüße sie von mir; **she asked to be ~ed to you** sie läßt dich grüßen; **c)** ~ **oneself** sich zusammennehmen; **d)** ~ **sb. in one's will/prayers** jmdn. in seinem Testament bedenken/in sein Gebet einschließen

remembrance [rɪ'membrəns] *n.* Gedenken, *das;* **in ~ of sb.** zu jmds. Gedächtnis; zum Gedenken an jmdn.

Remembrance: ~ Day *n. (Brit.)* **a)** *(Hist.: 11 Nov.)* Gedenktag für die Gefallenen der beiden Weltkriege; **b)** *see* ~ **Sunday;** ~ **Sunday** *n. (Brit.)* ≈ Volkstrauertag, *der*

remind [rɪ'maɪnd] *v. t.* erinnern **(of** an + *Akk.*); ~ **sb. to do sth.** jmdn. daran erinnern, etw. zu tun; **can you ~ me how to do it?** kannst du mal meinem Gedächtnis nachhelfen, wie man das macht?; **that ~s me, ...:** dabei fällt mir ein, ...; **you are ~ed that ...:** beachten Sie bitte, daß ...; **travellers are ~ed that ...:** Reisende werden darauf hingewiesen, daß ...

reminder [rɪ'maɪndə(r)] *n.* Erinnerung, *die* **(of** an + *Akk.*); *(mnemonic)* Gedächtnishilfe *od.* -stütze, *die; (photo etc.)* Andenken, *das* **(of** an + *Akk.*); **give sb. a ~ that ...:** jmdn. daran erinnern, daß ...; **serve as/be a ~ of sth.** an etw. *(Akk.)* erinnern; ~ **[letter]** Mahnung, *die;* Mahnbrief, *der;* **a gentle ~:** ein zarter Wink

reminisce [remɪ'nɪs] *v. i.* sich in Erinnerungen *(Dat.)* ergehen **(about** an + *Akk.*)

reminiscence [remɪ'nɪsəns] *n.* **a)** Erinnerung, *die* **(of** an + *Akk.*); **b)** *in pl. (memoirs)* [Lebens]erinnerungen *Pl.;* Memoiren *Pl.*

reminiscent [remɪ'nɪsənt] *adj.* **a)** ~ **of sth.** an etw. *(Akk.)* erinnernd; **be ~ of sth.** an etw. *(Akk.)* erinnern; **b)** *(nostalgic)* ~ **mood** nostalgische Stimmung

remiss [rɪ'mɪs] *adj.* nachlässig **(of** von)

remission [rɪ'mɪʃn] *n.* **a)** *(of sins)* Vergebung, *die;* **b)** *(of debt, punishment)* Erlaß, *der;* **c)** *(prison sentence)* Straferlaß, *der;* **he gained one year's ~:** ihm ist ein Jahr erlassen worden; **d)** *(Med.)* Remission, *die;* **go into ~:** remittieren

remit 1. [rɪ'mɪt] *v. t.,* **-tt- a)** *(pardon)* vergeben ‹*Sünde, Beleidigung usw.*›; **b)** *(cancel)* erlassen ‹*Steuer, Gebühr usw.*›; ~ **sb.'s punishment** jmdm. seine Strafe erlassen; **c)** *(refer)* weiterleiten ‹*Frage, Angelegenheit*› **(to** an + *Akk.*); *(Law)* zurückverweisen ‹*Fall, Bericht*›; **d)** *(postpone)* verschieben, vertagen **(until** bis, **to** auf + *Akk.*); **e)** *(send)* überweisen ‹*Geld*›. **2.** ['ri:mɪt, rɪ'mɪt] *n.* Aufgabe, *die;* Auftrag, *der*

remittance [rɪ'mɪtəns] *n.* Überweisung, *die*

remnant ['remnənt] *n.* **a)** Rest, *der;* **only a ~ of the family survives** nur noch wenige Mitglieder der Familie leben; **~s of carpet/wood** Teppich-/Holzreste *Pl.;* **sale of ~s** Resteverkauf, *der;* **b)** *(trace)* Überrest, *der;* **salvage the ~s of sth.** retten, was von etw. übriggeblieben ist

remodel [ri:'mɒdl] *v. t., (Brit.)* **-ll-** *(lit. or fig.)* umgestalten

remold *(Amer.) see* **remould**

remonstrance [rɪ'mɒnstrəns] *n.* Protest, *der* **(with, against** gegen)

remonstrate ['remənstreɪt, rɪ'mɒnstreɪt] *v. i.* protestieren **(against** gegen); ~ **with sb.** jmdm. Vorhaltungen machen **(on** wegen)

remonstration *see* **remonstrance**

remonstrative ['remənstreɪtɪv, rɪ'mɒnstrətɪv] *adv.* protestierend; Protest‹*brief usw.*›

remorse [rɪ'mɔ:s] *n.* Reue, *die* **(for, about** über + *Akk.*); **without ~:** erbarmungslos

remorseful [rɪ'mɔ:sfl] *adj.* reuig, reuevoll *(geh.);* reumütig *(öfter scherzh.);* Reue‹*gefühl*›; **feel ~:** Reue empfinden

remorseless [rɪ'mɔ:slɪs] *adj.* **a)** *(merciless)* erbarmungslos ‹*Grausamkeit, Barbarei*›; **b)** *(relentless)* unerbittlich ‹*Schicksal, Logik*›

remorselessly [rɪ'mɔ:slɪslɪ] *adv. see* **remorseless:** erbarmungslos; unerbittlich

remote [rɪ'məʊt] *adj.,* **~r** [rɪ'məʊtə(r)], **~st** [rɪ'məʊtɪst] **a)** *(far apart)* entfernt; **be very ~ from each other** sehr weit voneinander entfernt sein; **nations as ~ in culture as X and Y** Völker mit so verschiedenen *od.* unterschiedlichen Kulturen wie X und Y; **b)** *(far off)* fern ‹*Vergangenheit, Zukunft, Zeit*›; früh ‹*Altertum*›; abgelegen, *(geh.)* entlegen ‹*Ort, Gebiet*›; ~ **from** *(lit. or fig.)* weit entfernt von; ~ **from the road** weitab von der Straße; **c)** *(not closely related)* entfernt, weitläufig ‹*Vorfahr, Nachkomme, Verwandte*›; **d)** *(aloof)* unnahbar, distanziert ‹*Person, Art*›; **e)** *(slight)* gering ‹*Auswirkung, Chance, Möglichkeit, Vorstellung*›; **I don't have the ~st idea what you're talking about** ich habe nicht die geringste *od.* leiseste Ahnung, wovon du sprichst

remote: ~ con'trol *n. (of vehicle)* Fernlenkung, *die;* Fernsteuerung, *die; (of apparatus)* Fernbedienung, *die;* **~-con'trol[led]** *adj.* ferngesteuert; ferngelenkt; fernbedient ‹*Anlage*›

remotely [rɪ'məʊtlɪ] *adv.* **a)** *(distantly)* entfernt, weitläufig ‹*verwandt*›; ~ **controlled** *see* **remote-control[led]; b)** *(aloofly)* distanziert, unnahbar ‹*lächeln, antworten*›; **c)** *(slightly)* **they are not [even] ~ alike** sie haben [aber auch] nicht die entfernteste Ähnlichkeit [miteinander]; **it is not [even] ~ possible that ...:** es besteht [aber auch] nicht die geringste Möglichkeit, daß ...

remoteness [rɪ'məʊtnɪs] *n., no pl.* **a)** *(seclusion)* Abgeschiedenheit, *die;* Abgelegenheit, *die; (distance)* große Entfernung **(from** von); **b)** *(of relationship)* Weitläufigkeit, *die;* **c)** *(separateness)* fehlender Zusammenhang **(of ... from** zwischen ... und); ~ **from everyday life** Lebensfremdheit, *die*

remould 1. [ri:'məʊld] *v. t.* *(refashion)* ummodeln, umgestalten **(into** zu); *(Motor Veh.)* runderneuern ‹*Reifen*›. **2.** ['ri:məʊld] *n. (Motor Veh.)* runderneuerter Reifen

remount [ri:'maʊnt] **1.** *v. t.* **a)** *(ascend again)* wieder hinaufsteigen ‹*Leiter*›; ~ **one's horse/bicycle** wieder aufs Pferd/Fahrrad steigen; **b)** *(put in fresh mount)* wieder aufziehen ‹*Bild*›. **2.** *v. i. (on horse)* wieder aufsitzen; *(on bicycle)* wieder aufs Fahrrad steigen

removable [rɪ'mu:vəbl] *adj.* abnehmbar; entfernbar ‹*Fleck, Trennwand*›; herausnehmbar ‹*Futter*›; **be ~:** sich entfernen lassen

removal [rɪ'mu:vl] *n.* **a)** *(taking away)* Entfernung, *die; (of passage from book)* Streichung, *die* **(from** aus); *(of traces)* Beseitigung, *die; (taking off)* **the ~ of the valve from the tyre proved difficult** es war schwierig, das Ventil aus dem Reifen herauszunehmen; **b)** *(dismissal)* Entlassung, *die;* **the minister's ~ from office** die Entfernung des Ministers aus dem Amt; **c)** *see* **remove 1 c:** Beseitigung, *die;* Vertreibung, *die;* Zerstreuung, *die;* **d)** *(transfer)* **his ~ to another school** seine Umschulung; **the ~ of the books to the next room** die Umräumung *od.* das Umräumen der Bücher in das andere Zimmer; **his ~ to another department** seine Versetzung in eine andere Abteilung; **his ~ to hospital** seine Einlieferung ins Krankenhaus; **e)** *(transfer of furniture)* Umzug, *der;* **'Smith & Co., R~s'** „Smith & Co., Spedition"; **office/factory ~:** Büro-/Werksverlegung, *die*

removal: ~ expenses *n. pl.* Umzugskosten *Pl.;* ~ **firm** *n.* Spedition, *die;* ~ **man**

n. Möbelpacker, *der;* ~ **van** *n.* Möbelwagen, *der*

remove [rɪ'mu:v] **1.** *v. t.* **a)** *(take away)* entfernen; streichen ‹*Buchpassage*›; wegnehmen, wegräumen ‹*Papiere, Ordner usw.*›; abräumen ‹*Geschirr*›; beseitigen ‹*Spur*›; *(take off)* abnehmen; ausziehen ‹*Kleidungsstück*›; **she ~d her/the child's coat** sie legte ihren Mantel ab/sie zog dem Kind den Mantel aus; ~ **a book from the shelf/the valve from a tyre** ein Buch vom Regal nehmen/das Ventil aus einem Reifen [heraus]nehmen; ~ **one's make-up** sich abschminken; ~ **the papers/dishes from the table** die Papiere/das Geschirr vom Tisch räumen; **the parents ~d the child from the school** die Eltern nahmen das Kind von der Schule; **b)** *(dismiss)* entlassen; ~ **sb. from office/his post** jmdn. aus dem Amt/von seinem Posten entfernen; **c)** *(eradicate)* beseitigen ‹*Gefahr, Hindernis, Problem, Zweifel*›; vertreiben ‹*Angst*›; zerstreuen ‹*Verdacht, Befürchtungen*›; **d)** *(transfer)* ~ **a pupil to another school** einen Schüler auf eine andere Schule schicken; **we ~d the books to another room** wir haben die Bücher in ein anderes Zimmer umgeräumt; ~ **an employee to another department** einen Angestellten in eine andere Abteilung versetzen; **e)** *(euphem.: kill)* beseitigen *(verhüll.)*; **f)** *in p.p. see* **cousin**; **g)** *in p.p. (remote)* **be entirely ~d from politics/everyday life** gar nichts mit Politik zu tun haben/völlig lebensfremd sein. **2.** *v. i.* [um]ziehen; ~ **to the country** aufs Land ziehen; **they ~d from here** sie sind [von hier] weggezogen. **3.** *n.* **a)** *(degree)* Schritt, *der;* **be only a few ~s/but one ~ from** nicht mehr weit/nur noch einen Schritt entfernt sein von; **at one ~**: auf Distanz **(from** gegenüber); **b)** *(distance)* Abstand, *der* **(from zu)**; **be a far ~ from sth.** weit entfernt von etw. sein

remover [rɪ'mu:və(r)] *n.* **a)** *(of paint/varnish/hair/rust)* Farb-/Lack-/Haar-/Rostentferner, *der;* **b)** *(removal man)* Möbelpacker, *der;* **[firm of] ~s** Spedition[sfirma], *die*

remunerate [rɪ'mju:nəreɪt] *v. t.* bezahlen; entlohnen; *(recompense)* belohnen

remuneration [rɪmju:nə'reɪʃn] *n.* Bezahlung, *die;* Entlohnung, *die; (reward)* Belohnung, *die*

remunerative [rɪ'mju:nərətɪv] *adj.* lohnend; einträglich

Renaissance [rə'neɪsəns, rə'neɪsɑ̃s, rɪ'neɪsəns] *n.* **a)** *no pl. (Hist.)* Renaissance, *die;* ~ **man** der Renaissancemensch; **b) r~** *(rebirth)* Renaissance, *die;* Wiedergeburt, *die (geh.)*

renal ['ri:nl] *adj. (Anat., Med.)* Nieren-

rename [ri:'neɪm] *v. t.* umbenennen; umtaufen ‹*Schiff*›

renascence *see* **Renaissance b**

rend [rend] **rent** [rent] *v. t. (literary)* **a)** *(tear)* reißen **(from aus)**; **b)** *(split)* spalten ‹*Baum, Gruppe, Land*›; ‹*Schrei:*› zerreißen ‹*Stille*›

render ['rendə(r)] *v. t.* **a)** *(make)* machen; **the tone ~ed the statement an insult** der Ton machte die Feststellung zu einer Beleidigung; **b)** *(show, give)* leisten ‹*Gehorsam, Hilfe*›; erweisen ‹*Ehre, Achtung, Respekt, Dienst*›; bieten, gewähren ‹*Schutz*›; ~ **a service to sb.**, ~ **sb. a service** jmdm. einen Dienst erweisen; ~ **thanks [un]to God** Gott Dank sagen; ~ **[un]to Caesar the things that are Caesar's** *(Bibl.)* gebet dem Kaiser, was des Kaisers ist; **c)** *(pay)* entrichten ‹*Tribut, Steuern, Abgaben*›; **d)** *(represent, reproduce)* wiedergeben, spielen ‹*Musik, Szene, Rolle*›; *(translate)* übersetzen **(by** mit); ~ **a text into another language** einen Text in eine andere Sprache übertragen; **e)** *(present)* ~ **a report to sb.** jmdm. Bericht erstatten; ~ **an annual account [to sb.]** [jmdm.] einen Jahresbericht vorlegen; **account ~ed** *(Commerc.)* ausgestellte Rechnung; **f)** *(Building: plaster)* berappen *(fachspr.)*, verputzen ‹*Mauer*›; **g)** ~ **[down]** auslassen ‹*Fett*›

~ **'up** *v. t. (formal)* übergeben **(to** *Dat.*) ‹*Festung, Fort, Stadt*›

rendering ['rendərɪŋ] *n.* **a)** Wiedergabe, *die; (translation)* Übersetzung, *die* **(into** in + *Akk.*); *(of play also)* Aufführung, *die; (of musical piece, poem also)* Vortrag, *der; (of historical events also)* Darstellung, *die;* **give a [superb]** ~ **of sth.** etw. [meisterhaft] wiedergeben/aufführen/vortragen/darstellen; **b)** *(Building: plastering)* Berapp, *der (fachspr.)*; Putz, *der*

rendezvous ['rɒndɪvu:, 'rɒndeɪvu:] **1.** *n., pl. same* ['rɒndɪvu:z, 'rɒndeɪvu:z] **a)** *(meeting-place)* Treffpunkt, *der;* **b)** *(meeting)* Rendezvous, *das (veralt., meist noch scherzh.)*; Verabredung, *die;* **c)** *(Astronaut.)* Rendezvous, *das.* **2.** *v. i., pres.* **~es** ['rɒndɪvu:z, 'rɒndeɪvu:z], *p.t. & p.p.* **~ed** ['rɒndɪvu:d, 'rɒndeɪvu:d], *pres. p.* **~ing** ['rɒndɪvu:ɪŋ, 'rɒndeɪvu:ɪŋ] sich treffen

rendition [ren'dɪʃn] *see* **rendering a**

renegade ['renɪgeɪd] **1.** *n.* Abtrünnige, *der/die;* Renegat, *der*/Renegatin, *die (abwertend).* **2.** *adj.* abtrünnig

renege, renegue [rɪ'ni:g, rɪ'neɪg] *v. i.* **a)** *(Amer. Cards)* nicht bedienen; **b)** ~ **[on an agreement/a promise]** [eine Vereinbarung/ein Versprechen] nicht einhalten

renegotiate [ri:nɪ'gəʊʃɪeɪt] *v. t.* neu aushandeln; erneut verhandeln über (+ *Akk.*)

renew [rɪ'nju:] *v. t.* **a)** *(restore, regenerate, recover)* erneuern; wieder wecken *od.* wachrufen ‹*Gefühle*›; wiederherstellen ‹*Kraft*›; ~ **sb.'s energy** jmdm. neue Energie geben; **feel spiritually ~ed** sich wie neugeboren fühlen; **b)** *(replace)* erneuern; auffüllen ‹*Vorrat*›; ausbessern ‹*Kleidungsstück*›; **c)** *(begin again)* erneuern ‹*Bekanntschaft*›; wiederaufnehmen ‹*Kampf, Korrespondenz*›; fortsetzen ‹*Angriff, Bemühungen*›; **~ed exhortations/outbreaks of rioting** erneute Ermahnungen/Krawalle; **d)** *(repeat)* wiederholen ‹*Aussage, Beschuldigung*›; **e)** *(extend)* erneuern, verlängern ‹*Vertrag, Genehmigung, Ausweis etc.*›; ~ **a library book** ‹*Bibliothekar/Benutzer:*› ein Buch [aus der Bücherei] verlängern/verlängern lassen

renewable [rɪ'nju:əbl] *adj.* regenerationsfähig ‹*Energiequelle*›; verlängerbar ‹*Vertrag, Genehmigung, Ausweis*›

renewal [rɪ'nju:əl] *n.* **a)** Erneuerung, *die; (of contract, passport etc. also)* Verlängerung, *die; (of attack)* Wiederaufnahme, *die; (of library book)* Verlängerung der Leihfrist; **b) [urban]** ~: [Stadt]sanierung, *die*

rennet ['renɪt] *n.* Lab, *das*

renounce [rɪ'naʊns] **1.** *v. t.* **a)** *(abandon)* verzichten auf (+ *Akk.*); **b)** *(refuse to recognize)* aufkündigen ‹*Vertrag, Freundschaft*›; aufgeben ‹*Grundsatz, Plan, Versuch*›; leugnen ‹*jmds. Autorität*›; verstoßen ‹*Person*›; ~ **the world** der Welt *(Dat.)* entsagen *(geh.)*; ~ **the devil/one's faith** dem Teufel/seinem Glauben abschwören. **2.** *v. i.* **a)** *(Law)* offiziell seinen Verzicht erklären; **b)** *(Cards)* nicht bedienen

renouncement [rɪ'naʊnsmənt] *see* **renunciation a**

renovate ['renəveɪt] *v. t.* renovieren ‹*Gebäude*›; restaurieren ‹*Möbel, Gemälde*›

renovation [renə'veɪʃn] *n.* Renovierung, *die; (of furniture etc.)* Restaurierung, *die*

renown [rɪ'naʊn] Renommee, *das;* Ansehen, *das;* **of [great]** ~: von hohem Ansehen; sehr berühmt ‹*Stadt*›

renowned [rɪ'naʊnd] *adj.* berühmt **(for** wegen, für); **he is ~ as a portrait-painter** er hat als Porträtmaler einen großen Namen

[1]**rent** *see* **rend**

[2]**rent** [rent] *n. (tear, cleft)* Riß, *der (auch fig.)*; *(cleft also)* Spalte, *die;* ~ **in the clouds** Wolkenspalt, *der*

[3]**rent** [rent] **1.** *n. (for house, flat, etc.)* Miete, *die; (for land)* Pacht, *die;* **have a house free of ~**: ein Haus mietfrei bewohnen; **for ~** *(Amer.)*‹*Haus, Wohnung etc.*› zu vermieten; ‹*Land*› zu verpachten; ‹*Kostüme*› zu verleihen. **2.** *v. t.* **a)** *(use)* mieten ‹*Haus, Wohnung usw.*›; pachten ‹*Land*›; mieten ‹*Auto, Gerät*›; **b)** *(let)* vermieten ‹*Haus, Wohnung, Auto etc.*› **(to** *Dat.*, an + *Akk.*); verpachten ‹*Land*› **(to** *Dat.*, an + *Akk.*). **3.** *v. i.* ‹*Haus, Wohnung, Auto usw.:*› vermietet werden; ‹*Land:*› verpachtet werden

~ **'out** *v. t. see* [3]**rent 2 b**

rentable ['rentəbl] *adj. see* [3]**rent 2:** zu [ver]mieten/[ver]pachten *präd.*; zu [ver]mietend/[ver]pachtend *attr.*

rent: ~-a-car *attrib. adj.* **~-a-car business/company/service** Autoverleih, *der;* **~-a-crowd** *n.* bestellter Haufen; *(claque)* Claque, *die*

rental ['rentl] *n.* **a)** *(from houses etc.)* Miete, *die; (from land)* Pacht, *die;* **b)** *see* [3]**rent 2:** Mietung, *die;* Pachtung, *die; (letting)* Vermietung, *die;* Verpachtung, *die;* **car ~**: Autoverleih, *der;* **the property is on ~**: der Besitz ist verpachtet *od.* in Pacht; **c)** *(Amer.: thing rented)* Mietgegenstand, *der;* Mietsache, *die (Rechtsw.)*

'rental library *n. (Amer.) (kommerzielle)* Leihbücherei

rent: ~-a-mob *n.* bestellter Haufen von Randalierern; **~-a-van** *attrib. adj.* **~-a-van business/company/service** Transportermietung, *die;* **~-boy** *n. (coll.)* Strichjunge, *der (salopp)*; **~-collector** *n. jmd., der für den Hausbesitzer die Miete kassiert;* ~ **control** *n.* ≈ Mietpreisbindung, *die;* **~-controlled** *adj.* mietpreisgebunden; **~-free** *adj.* mietfrei; ~ **officer** *n. Beamter/Beamtin der kommunalen Beratungsstelle für mietrechtliche Fragen;* ~ **rebate** *n.* Mietermäßigung, *die;* ~ **tribunal** *n.* Mietgericht, *das*

renumber [ri:'nʌmbə(r)] *v. t.* umnumerieren; neu beziffern *od.* benummern

renunciation [rɪnʌnsɪ'eɪʃn] *n.* **a)** *see* **renounce 1 a, b:** Verzicht, *der;* Aufkündigung, *die;* Aufgabe, *die;* Leugnung, *die;* Verstoßung, *die;* **b)** *(self-denial)* Selbstverleugnung, *die*

reoccupation [ri:ɒkjʊ'peɪʃn] *n.* Wiederbesetzung, *die; (of house etc.)* Wiederübernahme, *die*

reoccupy [ri:'ɒkjʊpaɪ] *v. t.* wiederbesetzen *(Milit.)*‹*Ort, Stellung*›; wieder übernehmen ‹*Haus, Wohnung*›

reopen [ri:'əʊpn] **1.** *v. t.* **a)** *(open again)* wieder öffnen; wieder aufmachen; wiedereröffnen ‹*Geschäft, Lokal usw.*›; **b)** *(return to)* wiederaufnehmen ‹*Diskussion, Verhandlung, Feindseligkeiten*›; wiederaufnehmen, wieder aufrollen ‹*Fall*›; zurückkommen auf (+ *Akk.*) ‹*Angelegenheit*›. **2.** *v. i.* ‹*Geschäft, Lokal usw.:*› wieder öffnen; wiedereröffnet werden; ‹*Verhandlungen, Unterricht:*› wieder beginnen

reorder [ri:'ɔ:də(r)] **1.** *v. t.* **a)** *(Commerc.: order again)* nachbestellen ‹*Ware*›; *(after theft, loss)* neu bestellen; **b)** *(rearrange)* umordnen; neu ordnen; *(on list)* umstellen ‹*Namen*›; neu festlegen ‹*Reihenfolge*›. **2.** *n.* *(Commerc.)* Nachbestellung, *die*

reorganisation, reorganise *see* **reorganiz-**

reorganization [ri:ɔ:gənaɪ'zeɪʃn] *n.* Umorganisation, *die; (of text)* Neugliederung, *die; (of time, work)* Neueinteilung, *die*

reorganize [ri:'ɔ:gənaɪz] *v. t.* umorganisieren; neu einteilen ‹*Zeit, Arbeit*›; neu gliedern ‹*Aufsatz, Referat*›

reorient [ri:'ɔ:rɪent, ri:'ɒrɪent], **reorientate** [ri:'ɒrɪənteɪt, ri:'ɔ:rɪənteɪt] *v. t.* neu ausrichten ‹*Programm, Politik, Denken, Handeln*›; ~ **a person** einem Menschen eine neue Orientierung geben

reorientation [riːɒrɪən'teɪʃn, riːɔːrɪən'teɪʃn] *n.* Neuorientierung, *die*

[1]rep [rep] *n. (Textiles)* Rips, *der*

[2]rep *n. (coll.: representative)* Vertreter, *der*/Vertreterin, *die*

[3]rep *n. (Theatre coll.)* Repertoiretheater, *das;* **be in ~:** an einem Repertoiretheater spielen

Rep. *abbr. (Amer.)* **a) Representative** Abg.; **b) Republican** Rep.

repaid *see* **repay**

repaint 1. [riː'peɪnt] *v.t.* neu streichen ‹*Gebäude, Wand, Tür usw.*›; neu lackieren ‹*Auto*›. **2.** ['riːpeɪnt] *n.* **the door needs a ~:** die Tür braucht einen neuen Anstrich; **give sth. a ~:** etw. neu streichen/lackieren

[1]repair [rɪ'peə(r)] **1.** *v.t.* **a)** *(restore, mend)* reparieren; ausbessern ‹*Kleidung, Straße*›; **b)** *(remedy)* wiedergutmachen ‹*Schaden, Fehler*›; beheben ‹*Schaden, Mangel*›. **2.** *n.* **a)** *(restoring, renovation)* Reparatur, *die;* **be beyond ~:** sich nicht mehr reparieren lassen; **be in need of ~:** reparaturbedürftig sein; ‹*Schuhe:*› repariert werden müssen; **be under ~:** ‹*Maschine, Gerät, Fahrzeug:*› in Reparatur sein; **the road is under ~:** an der Straße werden gerade Bauarbeiten ausgeführt; **closed for ~s** wegen Reparaturarbeiten geschlossen; **'~s [done] while you wait'** „Reparaturschnelldienst"; **b)** *no pl., no art. (condition)* **be in good/bad ~** *or* **in a good/bad state of ~:** in gutem/schlechtem Zustand sein

[2]repair *v.i. (formal: go)* sich begeben **(to** nach/zu/in + *Akk.*) *(Papierdt.)*

repairable [rɪ'peərəbl] *adj.* reparabel; **be ~** *or* **in a ~ state** zu reparieren sein

repairer [rɪ'peərə(r)] *n. (of watches/shoes)* Uhr-/Schuhmacher, *der;* **take sth. to the ~'s** etw. zur Reparatur bringen

repair: ~man *n. (of mechanism)* Mechaniker, *der; (in house)* Handwerker, *der;* **~ shop** *n.* Reparaturwerkstatt, *die*

repaper [riː'peɪpə(r)] *v.t.* neu tapezieren

reparation [repə'reɪʃn] *n.* **a)** *(making amends)* Wiedergutmachung, *die;* **b)** *(compensation)* Entschädigung, *die;* **~s** *(for war damage)* Reparationen; **make ~ [for sth.]** [für etw.] Ersatz leisten

repartee [repɑː'tiː] *n.* **a)** *(witty retort)* schlagfertige Antwort; **b)** *(making of retorts)* Schlagfertigkeit, *die;* **be good at ~:** schlagfertig sein

repast [rɪ'pɑːst] *n. (formal)* Mahl, *das (geh.)*

repatriate [riː'pætrɪeɪt] *v.t.* repatriieren

repatriation [riːpætrɪ'eɪʃn] *n.* Repatriierung, *die*

repay [riː'peɪ] **1.** *v.t.,* **repaid** [riː'peɪd] **a)** *(pay back)* zurückzahlen ‹*Schulden usw.*›; erstatten ‹*Spesen*›; **if you'll lend me £1, I'll ~ you next week** wenn du mir ein Pfund leihst, zahle *od.* gebe ich es dir nächste Woche zurück; **b)** *(return)* erwidern ‹*Besuch, Gruß, Freundlichkeit*›; **c)** *(give in recompense)* **~ sb. for sth.** jmdm. etw. vergelten; **d)** *(requite)* **~ efforts** *etc.* für Bemühungen *usw.* entschädigen. **2.** *v.i.,* **repaid** Rückzahlungen leisten

repayable [riː'peɪəbl] *adj.* rückzahlbar; **~ at the end of the year** zum Jahresende zurückgezahlt werden müssen

repayment [riː'peɪmənt] *n.* **a)** *(paying back)* Rückzahlung, *die;* **she's having trouble with the ~s** sie hat Schwierigkeiten mit der Rückzahlung; **b)** *(reward)* Lohn, *der* **(for** für)

re'payment mortgage *n.* Tilgungshypothek, *die*

repeal [rɪ'piːl] **1.** *v.t.* aufheben ‹*Gesetz, Erlaß usw.*›. **2.** *n.* Aufhebung, *die*

repeat [rɪ'piːt] **1.** *n.* **a)** Wiederholung, *die; (Radio, TV also)* Wiederholungssendung, *die;* **do a ~ of sth.** etw. wiederholen; **there will be a ~ of this programme** diese Sendung wird wiederholt; **b)** *(Commerc.)* Nachbestellung, *die;* **c)** *(Mus.) (passage)* Wiederholung, *die; (sign)* Wiederholungszeichen, *das;* **d)** *(repeated pattern)* Rapport, *der (bes. Kunstwiss.).* **2.** *v.t.* **a)** *(say, do, broadcast again)* wiederholen; **'not, ~ 'not** auf [gar] keinen Fall; unter [gar] keinen Umständen; **'nobody, [I] ~ 'nobody** niemand, ich betone, niemand; *(Radio)* niemand, ich wiederhole, niemand; **please ~ after me: ...:** sprich/sprecht/sprechen Sie mir bitte nach: ...; **b)** *(recite)* aufsagen ‹*Gedicht, Strophe, Text*›; **c)** *(report)* weitererzählen **(to** *Dat.*); **do you want me to ~ the conversation?** soll ich dir das Gespräch wiedergeben?. **3.** *v.i.* **a)** *(Math.: recur)* ‹*Zahl:*› periodisch sein; **b)** *(Amer.: vote more than once)* seine Stimme mehrmals abgeben. **4.** *v. refl.* **~ oneself/itself** sich wiederholen

repeater [rɪ'piːtə(r)] *n.* **a)** *(Horol.)* Repetieruhr, *die;* **b)** *(Arms)* Repetiergewehr, *das;* Mehrlader, *der*

repeating 'decimal *n. (Math.)* periodische Dezimalzahl

repeat: ~ 'order *n. (Commerc.)* Nachbestellung, *die;* **~ per'formance** *n.* Wiederholungsvorstellung, *die (Theater); (of music)* Wiederholungskonzert, *das*

repêchage ['repəʃɑːʒ] *n. (esp. Rowing)* Hoffnungslauf, *der; (Fencing)* Trostrunde, *die*

repel [rɪ'pel] *v.t.,* **-ll- a)** *(drive back)* abwehren ‹*Feind, Angriff, Annäherungsversuch, Schlag usw.*›; widerstehen (+ *Dat.*) ‹*Versuchung*›; abstoßen ‹*Feuchtigkeit, elektrische Ladung, Magnetpol*›; **b)** *(be repulsive to)* abstoßen

repellent [rɪ'pelənt] **1.** *adj.* **a)** *(repugnant)* abstoßend; **b)** *(repelling)* **water-~:** wasserabstoßend *od. (seltener)* -abweisend; **mosquito-~:** Mückenschutz‹*mittel usw.*›. **2.** *n.* **[insect-]~:** Insektenschutzmittel, *das*

repent [rɪ'pent] **1.** *v.i.* bereuen **(of** *Akk.*). **2.** *v.t.* bereuen

repentance [rɪ'pentəns] *n.* Reue, *die*

repentant [rɪ'pentənt] *adj.* reuig, reuevoll *(geh.);* reumütig *(öfter scherzh.);* **a ~ sinner** ein reuiger Sünder

repercussion [riːpə'kʌʃn] *n. usu. in pl.* Auswirkung, *die* **([up]on** auf + *Akk.*)

repertoire ['repətwɑː(r)] *n.* **a)** *(Mus., Theatre)* Repertoire, *das* **(of** an + *Dat.*, von); **b)** *(complete list)* Spektrum, *das*

repertory ['repətərɪ] *n.* **a)** *see* **repertoire; b)** *(Theatre)* Repertoiretheater, *das;* **play/be in ~:** an einem Repertoiretheater spielen

'repertory company *n.* Repertoiretheater, *das*

répétiteur [repetɪ'tɜː(r)] *n. (Mus., Theatre)* [Kor]repetitor, *der*

repetition [repɪ'tɪʃn] *n.* Wiederholung, *die*

repetitious [repɪ'tɪʃəs] *adj.* sich immer wiederholend *attr.;* **his style is ~:** er wiederholt sich immer

repetitive [rɪ'petɪtɪv] *adj.* eintönig; **sth. is ~:** etw. bietet keine Abwechslung

rephrase [riː'freɪz] *v.t.* umformulieren; **I'll rephrase that** ich will es anders ausdrücken

repine [rɪ'paɪn] *v.i. (literary)* hadern *(geh.)* **(at** mit)

replace [rɪ'pleɪs] *v.t.* **a)** *(put back in place) (vertically)* zurückstellen; wieder einordnen ‹*Karteikarte*›; *(horizontally)* zurücklegen; [wieder] auflegen ‹*Telefonhörer*›; **I ~d the key in the lock** ich steckte den Schlüssel wieder ins Schloß; **he ~d the fish in the tank** er setzte den Fisch wieder in den Tank; **b)** *(take place of, provide substitute for)* ersetzen; **~ A with** *or* **by B** A durch B ersetzen; **c)** *(renew)* ersetzen ‹*Gestohlenes usw.*›; austauschen, auswechseln ‹*Maschinen[teile] usw.*›; auswechseln ‹*Glühbirne*›; auffüllen ‹*Vorrat*›

replaceable [rɪ'pleɪsəbl] *adj.* ersetzbar ‹*Person, Verlorenes usw.*›; austauschbar, auswechselbar ‹*Maschinenteil usw.*›

replacement [rɪ'pleɪsmənt] *n.* **a)** *(putting back) see* **replace a:** Zurückstellen, *das;* Zurücklegen, *das;* Wiedereinordnen, *das;* Auflegen, *das;* **b)** *(provision of substitute for)* Ersatz, *der;* Ersetzen, *das; attrib.* Ersatz-; **the ~ of the blood loss** der Ausgleich des Blutverlusts; **c)** *(substitute)* Ersatz, *der;* **~ [part]** Ersatzteil, *das;* **~s** *(staff, troops)* Ersatz, *der;* **my ~:** mein Nachfolger/meine Nachfolgerin

replant [riː'plɑːnt] *v.t.* **a)** *(plant again)* umpflanzen; **b)** *(provide with new plants)* neu bepflanzen

replay 1. [riː'pleɪ] *v.t.* wiederholen ‹*Spiel*›; nochmals abspielen ‹*Tonband usw.*›. **2.** ['riːpleɪ] *n.* Wiederholung, *die; (match)* Wiederholungsspiel, *das*

replenish [rɪ'plenɪʃ] *v.t.* [wieder] auffüllen

replenishment [rɪ'plenɪʃmənt] *n.* **a)** *(renewing) (of supplies)* Auffüllung, *die;* Wiederauffüllen, *das; (of stocks)* Ergänzung, *die;* **b)** *(fresh supply)* **~s** Nachschub, *der*

replete [rɪ'pliːt] *adj.* **a)** *(filled)* reich **(with** an + *Dat.*); **a story ~ with drama** eine Geschichte voller Dramatik; **b)** *(gorged)* satt

repleteness [rɪ'pliːtnɪs] *n., no pl.* Sattheit, *die;* **feeling of ~:** Völlegefühl, *das*

repletion [rɪ'pliːʃn] *n.* Sättigung, *die;* **eat to ~:** sich satt essen

replica ['replɪkə] *n.* Nachbildung, *die; (of work of art)* Kopie, *die; (by original artist)* Replik, *die; (esp. on smaller scale)* Modell, *das;* **he is a ~ of his brother** er ist das Ebenbild *(geh.)* seines Bruders

replicate ['replɪkeɪt] **1.** *v.t.* nachbilden; replizieren *(Kunstwiss.); (Biol.)* replizieren. **2.** *v.i. (Biol.)* sich reproduzieren

replication [replɪ'keɪʃn] *n.* **a)** Nachbildung, *die;* **b)** *(Biol.)* Replikation, *die*

reply [rɪ'plaɪ] **1.** *v.i.* **~ [to sb./sth.]** [jmdm./auf etw. (*Akk.*)] antworten; **~ [to the gunfire]** das Feuer erwidern. **2.** *v.t.* **~ that ...:** antworten, daß ... **3.** *n.* **a)** Antwort, *die* **(to** auf + *Akk.*); **my ~ to him** die Antwort, die ich ihm gegeben habe/geben werde *usw.;* **in/by way of ~:** als Antwort; **in ~ to your letter** in Beantwortung Ihres Schreibens *(Amtsspr.);* **what did he say in ~?** was hat er darauf geantwortet?; **make [a] ~** *(formal)* [eine] Antwort geben; **b)** *(Law)* Replik, *die*

reply: ~ coupon *n. (Post)* internationaler Antwortschein; **~-paid** *adj.* **~-paid telegram** RP-Telegramm, *das;* **~-paid envelope** Freiumschlag, *der*

repoint [riː'pɔɪnt] *v.t. (Building)* neu ausfugen *od.* verfugen

repopulate [riː'pɒpjʊleɪt] *v.t.* neu besiedeln

report [rɪ'pɔːt] **1.** *v.t.* **a)** *(relate)* berichten/ *(in writing)* einen Bericht schreiben über (+ *Akk.*) ‹*Ereignis usw.*›; *(state formally also)* melden; **sb. is/was ~ed to be ...:** jmd. soll ... sein/gewesen sein; **she ~ed all the details to me** sie berichtete mir [über] alle Einzelheiten; **it is ~ed from Buckingham Palace that ...:** aus dem Buckingham-Palast wird gemeldet *od.* berichtet, daß ...; **nothing to ~:** keine besonderen Vorkommnisse; **~ sb. missing** jmdn. als vermißt melden; **the papers ~ed him [as] dead** laut Zeitungsberichten war er tot; **~ progress on** *(Brit.)* einen Tätigkeitsbericht abgeben über (+ *Akk.*); **b)** *(repeat)* übermitteln **(to** *Dat.*) ‹*Botschaft*›; wiedergeben **(to** *Dat.*) ‹*Worte, Sinn*›; **he is ~ed as having said that ...:** er soll gesagt haben, daß ...; **c)** *(name or notify to authorities)* melden **(to** *Dat.*); *(for prosecution)* anzeigen **(to** bei); **d)** *(present)* **~ oneself [to sb.]** sich [bei jmdm.] melden; **~ oneself present** *(Mil.)* sich zur Stelle melden. **2.** *v.i.* **a)** Bericht erstatten **(on** über + *Akk.*); berichten **(on** über + *Akk.*); **he ~s on financial affairs for the 'Guardian'** er schreibt für den Wirtschaftsteil des „Guardian"; **b)** *(present oneself)* sich melden **(to**

bei); ~ **for duty** sich zum Dienst melden; ~ **sick** sich krank melden; **c)** *(be responsible)* ~ **to sb.** jmdm. unterstehen; **d)** *(give report)* ~ **well/badly of sb./sth.** Gutes/Schlechtes *od.* nichts Gutes über jmdn./etw. berichten; *(Radio/Telev.)* **Mark Tally ~ing [from Delhi]** Mark Tally berichtet [aus Delhi]. **3.** *n.* **a)** *(account)* Bericht, *der* **(on, about** über + *Akk.*); *(in newspaper etc. also)* Reportage, *die* **(on** über + *Akk.*); **make a ~:** einen Bericht abfassen; **an official ~ on price trends** ein Gutachten über die Preisentwickling; **b)** *(Sch.)* Zeugnis, *das;* **c)** *(sound)* Knall, *der;* **d)** *(rumour)* Gerücht, *das;* **the ~ goes that ...:** man sagt, daß ...; **know sth. only by ~:** etw. nur vom Hörensagen kennen/wissen

~ **'back** *v.i.* **a)** *(present oneself again)* sich zurückmelden **(for** zu); **b)** *(give a report)* Bericht erstatten **(to** *Dat.*)

reportage [repɔːˈtɑːʒ] *n.* Reportage, *die*

reportedly [rɪˈpɔːtɪdlɪ] *adv.* wie verlautet; **they have ~ made huge profits** sie sollen sehr große Gewinne gemacht haben

reported 'speech *n. (Ling.)* indirekte Rede

reporter [rɪˈpɔːtə(r)] *n. (Radio, Telev., Journ.)* Reporter, *der*/Reporterin, *die;* Berichterstatter, *der*/-erstatterin, *die*

re'port stage *n. (Brit. Parl.) Unterhausdebatte über Gesetzentwurf nach dessen Beratung im Ausschuß*

repose [rɪˈpəʊz] *(literary)* **1.** *n.* **a)** *(rest, respite)* Ruhe, *die;* **in ~:** ruhend; **b)** *(composure)* Gelassenheit, *die.* **2.** *v.i.* **a)** *(lie)* ruhen; *(joc.: be situated)* liegen; sich befinden; **b)** *(be supported)* beruhen **([up]on** auf + *Dat.*). **3.** *v.t. (rest)* ausruhen

reposition [riːpəˈzɪʃn] *v.t.* umstellen; verstellen ‹*Teil*›

repository [rɪˈpɒzɪtərɪ] *n.* **a)** *(receptacle)* Behälter, *der;* **b)** *(store)* Lager, *das;* *(fig.)* *(book etc.)* Fundgrube, *die* **(of** für); *(person)* Quelle, *die* **(of** für)

repossess [riːpəˈzes] *v.t.* wiedergewinnen ‹*Gebiet usw.*›; wieder in Besitz nehmen ‹*Waren*›; ‹*Bausparkasse:*› beschlagnahmen lassen ‹*Haus*›

repossession [riːpəˈzeʃn] *n. (of territories etc.)* Wiedergewinnung, *die; (of goods)* Wiederinbesitznahme, *die; (of house)* Erwirkung der Beschlagnahme

repot [riːˈpɒt] *v.t.,* **-tt-** umtopfen

repp *see* **'rep**

reprehend [reprɪˈhend] *v.t.* tadeln; rügen

reprehensible [reprɪˈhensɪbl] *adj.* tadelnswert; sträflich; **be morally ~:** moralisch zu verurteilen sein

reprehensibly [reprɪˈhensɪblɪ] *adv.* tadelnswert; sträflich

represent [reprɪˈzent] *v.t.* **a)** *(symbolize)* verkörpern; **b)** *(denote, depict, present)* darstellen **(as** als); *(Theatre also)* spielen; **the symbol x ~s guttural sounds** das Zeichen x steht für Gutturallaute; **I am not what you ~ me as** *or* **to be** ich bin nicht so, wie du mich hinstellst; **c)** *(correspond to)* entsprechen (+ *Dat.*); **d)** *(be specimen of, act for)* vertreten

re-present [riːprɪˈzent] *v.t.* erneut vorlegen

representation [reprɪzenˈteɪʃn] *n.* **a)** *(depicting, image)* Darstellung, *die;* **b)** *(acting for sb.)* Vertretung, *die;* **c)** *(protest)* Protest, *der;* **make ~s to sb.** bei jmdm. Protest einlegen

representational [reprɪzenˈteɪʃənl] *adj.* **a)** gegenständlich ‹*Kunst*›; **b)** *see* **representative 2c**

representative [reprɪˈzentətɪv] **1.** *n.* **a)** *(member, successor, agent, deputy)* Vertreter, *der*/Vertreterin, *die; (firm's agent, deputy also)* Repräsentant, *der*/Repräsentantin, *die;* **there were no ~s of the family at the funeral** die Familie war bei der Beerdigung nicht vertreten; **b) R~** *(Amer. Polit.)* Abgeordneter/Abgeordnete im Repräsentantenhaus; **House of R~s** Repräsentantenhaus, *das.* **2.** *adj.* **a)** *(typical)* repräsentativ **(of** für); **a ~ modern building** ein typisches modernes Gebäude; **Charles II was fully ~ of his age** Charles II war ein typischer Vertreter seiner Zeit; **b)** *(consisting of deputies)* Abgeordneten‹*versammlung, -kammer usw.*›; **c)** *(Polit.: based on representation)* repräsentativ; Repräsentativ‹*system, -verfassung*›; **~ government/institutions** parlamentarische Regierung/Institution; **d) be ~ of** *(portray)* darstellen; *(symbolize)* symbolisieren; ‹*Person:*› verkörpern; **e)** *(that presents sth. to the mind)* **~ faculty/power** Vorstellungsvermögen, *das*/-kraft, *die*

representatively [reprɪˈzentətɪvlɪ] *adv.* repräsentativ

representativeness [reprɪˈzentətɪvnɪs] *n., no pl.* Repräsentanz, *die*

repress [rɪˈpres] *v.t.* **a)** unterdrücken ‹*Aufruhr, Gefühle, Lachen usw.*›; **b)** *(Psych.)* verdrängen ‹*Gefühle*› **(from** aus)

repressed [rɪˈprest] *adj.* unterdrückt; *(Psych.)* verdrängt

repression [rɪˈpreʃn] *n.* Unterdrückung, *die; (Psych.)* Verdrängung, *die*

repressive [rɪˈpresɪv] *adj.* repressiv; **~ measures** Repressivmaßnahmen

reprieve [rɪˈpriːv] **1.** *v.t.* **~ sb.** *(postpone execution)* jmdm. Strafaufschub gewähren; *(remit execution)* jmdn. begnadigen; *(fig.)* verschonen. **2.** *n.* Strafaufschub, *der* **(of** für); Begnadigung, *die; (fig.)* Gnadenfrist, *die*

reprimand [ˈreprɪmɑːnd] **1.** *n.* Tadel, *der;* Verweis, *der.* **2.** *v.t.* tadeln; einen Verweis erteilen (+ *Dat.*)

reprint 1. [riːˈprɪnt] *v.t.* **a)** *(print again)* wieder abdrucken; **b)** *(make reprint of)* nachdrucken. **2.** [ˈriːprɪnt] *n.* **a)** *(book reprinted)* Nachdruck, *der;* **b) how big was the ~?** wieviel Exemplare wurden nachgedruckt?; **it has had ten ~s** es ist zehnmal nachgedruckt worden; **c)** *(article printed separately)* Sonderdruck, *der*

reprisal [rɪˈpraɪzl] *n.* Vergeltungsakt, *der* **(for** gegen)

reprise [rəˈpriːz] *n. (Mus.)* Reprise, *die*

repro [ˈriːprəʊ] **1.** *n. (Printing)* Repro, *das;* **~ [proof]** Reproabzug, *der.* **2.** *adj.* **it's only ~:** es ist nur eine Reproduktion

reproach [rɪˈprəʊtʃ] **1.** *v.t.* **~ sb.** jmdm. Vorwürfe machen; **~ sb. with** *or* **for sth.** jmdm. etw. vorwerfen *od.* zum Vorwurf machen; **~ sb. bitterly for having done sth.** jmdm. bittere Vorwürfe machen, daß er etw. getan hat; **have nothing to ~ oneself for** *or* **with** sich *(Dat.)* nichts vorzuwerfen haben. **2.** *n.* **a)** *(rebuke)* Vorwurf, *der;* **be above** *or* **beyond ~:** über jeden Vorwurf erhaben sein; **be used as a term of ~:** abwertend gebraucht werden; **look of ~:** vorwurfsvoller Blick; **b)** *(disgrace)* Schande, *die* **(to** für)

reproachful [rɪˈprəʊtʃfl] *adj.,* **reproachfully** [rɪˈprəʊtʃfəlɪ] *adv.* vorwurfsvoll

reprobate [ˈreprəbeɪt] **1.** *n.* Halunke, *der.* **2.** *adj.* verkommen

reprocess [riːˈprəʊses] *v.t.* wiederaufbereiten; **~ing plant** Wiederaufbereitungsanlage, *die*

reproduce [riːprəˈdjuːs] **1.** *v.t.* **a)** wiedergeben; reproduzieren *(Druckw.)*‹*Bilder usw.*›; **b) ~ oneself** sich fortpflanzen; sich vermehren; **c)** *(Biol.: form afresh)* neu bilden ‹*Organe, Gliedmaßen usw.*›. **2.** *v.i.* **a)** *(multiply)* sich fortpflanzen; sich vermehren; **b)** *(give copy)* sich reproduzieren lassen

reproducible [riːprəˈdjuːsɪbl] *adj.* reproduzierbar; **be ~:** sich reproduzieren lassen

reproduction [riːprəˈdʌkʃn] *n.* **a)** Wiedergabe, *die;* Reproduktion, *die (Druckw.);* **~ of sound** Tonwiedergabe, *die;* **b)** *(producing offspring)* Fortpflanzung, *die;* **c)** *(copy)* Reproduktion, *die;* **printed ~:** Druck, *der;* *attrib.* **~ furniture** Stilmöbel *Pl.;* **a ~ Chippendale chair** ein Stuhl im Chippendalestil; **d)** *(Biol.: forming afresh)* Regeneration, *die*

reproductive [riːprəˈdʌktɪv] *adj.* Fortpflanzungs-

reprographic [riːprəˈgræfɪk] *adj.* reprographisch *(Druckw.)*

reproof [rɪˈpruːf] *n.* Tadel, *der;* **a glance/word of ~:** ein tadelnder Blick/ein tadelndes Wort; **deserving of ~:** tadelnswert

reprove [rɪˈpruːv] *v.t.* tadeln ‹*Verhalten usw.*›; tadeln, zurechtweisen ‹*Person*›

reproving [rɪˈpruːvɪŋ] *adj.* tadelnd

reprovingly [rɪˈpruːvɪŋlɪ] *adv.* tadelnd

reptile [ˈreptaɪl] *n.* Reptil, *das;* Kriechtier, *das; (fig. derog.)* Ekel, *das (ugs. abwertend)*

reptilian [repˈtɪljən] **1.** *adj.* reptilartig; *(of the Reptilia)* Reptilien‹*knochen, -schädel*›. **2.** *n.* Reptil, *das;* Kriechtier, *das*

republic [rɪˈpʌblɪk] *n.* Republik, *die*

republican [rɪˈpʌblɪkən] **1.** *adj.* **a)** republikanisch; **b)** *(Amer. Polit.)* **R~ Party** Republikanische Partei. **2.** *n.* **R~** *(Amer. Polit.)* Republikaner, *der*/Republikanerin, *die*

republicanism [rɪˈpʌblɪkənɪzm] *n.* Republikanismus, *der*

republication [riːpʌblɪˈkeɪʃn] *n.* Wiederveröffentlichung, *die*

republish [riːˈpʌblɪʃ] *v.t.* wieder veröffentlichen

repudiate [rɪˈpjuːdɪeɪt] *v.t.* **a)** *(deny)* zurückweisen ‹*Anschuldigung usw.*›; *(reject)* nicht anerkennen ‹*Autorität, Vertrag usw.*›; **b)** *(disown)* verstoßen ‹*Person*›

repudiation [rɪpjuːdɪˈeɪʃn] *n. see* **repudiate:** Zurückweisung, *die;* Nichtanerkennung, *die;* Verstoßung, *die*

repugnance [rɪˈpʌgnəns] *n. (strong dislike)* [starke] Abneigung **(to[wards]** gegen); Abscheu, *der* **(to[wards]** vor + *Dat.*)

repugnant [rɪˈpʌgnənt] *adj. (distasteful)* widerlich; abstoßend; **be ~ to sb.** jmdm. widerlich sein

repulse [rɪˈpʌls] **1.** *v.t.* abwehren *(auch fig.);* zurückweisen ‹*Unterstellung*›. **2.** *n.* Abwehr, *die;* **suffer a ~:** eine Niederlage erleiden

repulsion [rɪˈpʌlʃn] *n.* **a)** *(disgust)* Widerwille, *der* **(towards** gegen); **b)** *(Phys.)* Repulsion, *die*

repulsive [rɪˈpʌlsɪv] *adj.* **a)** *(disgusting)* abstoßend; widerwärtig; **b)** *(Phys.)* repulsiv

repulsively [rɪˈpʌlsɪvlɪ] *adv.* abstoßend

repurchase [riːˈpɜːtʃɪs] **1.** *v.t.* zurückkaufen. **2.** *n.* Rückkauf, *der*

reputable [ˈrepjʊtəbl] *adj.* angesehen ‹*Person, Familie, Beruf, Zeitung usw.*›; anständig ‹*Verhalten*›; seriös ‹*Firma*›

reputably [ˈrepjʊtəblɪ] *adv.* anständig

reputation [repjʊˈteɪʃn] *n.* **a)** Ruf, *der;* **have a ~ for** *or* **of doing/being sth.** in dem Ruf stehen, etw. zu tun/sein; **he has a ~ for integrity/stealing** er gilt als integer/man sagt, daß er stiehlt; **what sort of ~ do they have?** wie ist ihr Ruf?; **b)** *(good name)* Name, *der;* Renommee, *das;* **men with a ~ as scientists** Männer, die sich als Wissenschaftler einen Namen gemacht haben; **make one's** *or* **gain a ~:** sich *(Dat.)* einen Namen machen **(as** als); **c)** *(bad name)* schlechter Ruf; **get oneself** *or* **acquire quite a ~:** sich in Verruf bringen

repute [rɪˈpjuːt] **1.** *v.t. in pass.* **be ~d [to be] sth.** als etw. gelten; **she is ~d to have/make ...:** man sagt, daß sie ... hat/macht; **be very highly ~d [as a doctor]** einen sehr guten Ruf [als Arzt] haben. **2.** *n.* Ruf, *der;* Ansehen, *das;* **hold sb./sth. in high ~:** von jmdm./etw. eine hohe Meinung haben; jmdn./etw. hochschätzen *(geh.);* **of ill ~:** von schlechtem Ruf; **a house of ill ~:** ein Haus von zweifelhaftem Ruf; **know sb. by ~:** von jmdm. schon viel gehört haben; **a philosopher of ~:** ein angesehener Philosoph

reputed [rɪ'pju:tɪd] *adj.* angeblich; **the ~ father** der mutmaßliche Vater

reputedly [rɪ'pju:tɪdlɪ] *adv.* angeblich; vermeintlich

request [rɪ'kwest] **1.** *v. t.* bitten; **~ sth. of** *or* **from sb.** jmdn. um etw. bitten; **~ sb.'s presence** um jmds. Anwesenheit bitten; **~ silence** um Ruhe bitten; **~ a record** einen Plattenwunsch äußern; **~ that ...:** darum bitten, daß ...; **~ sb. to do sth.** jmdn. [darum] bitten, etw. zu tun; **the essay I am ~ed to write** der Essay, den ich schreiben soll; **'You are ~ed not to smoke'** „Bitte nicht rauchen". **2.** *n.* Bitte, *die* (**for** um); **at sb.'s ~:** auf jmds. Bitte *od.* Wunsch *(Akk.)* [hin]; **make a ~ for sth.** um etw. bitten; **I have one ~ to make of** *or* **to you** ich habe eine Bitte an Sie; **by** *or* **on ~:** auf Wunsch; **have one's ~:** seine Bitte *od.* seinen Wunsch erfüllt bekommen; **record ~s** *(Radio)* Plattenwünsche *Pl.*; **we do not receive many ~s for it** dafür haben wir keine große Nachfrage; **c)** *no art., no pl. (demand)* **be in great ~, be much in ~:** sehr gefragt sein

request: ~ programme *n. (Radio)* Wunschkonzert, *das;* **~ stop** *n. (Brit.)* Bedarfshaltestelle, *die*

requiem ['rekwɪem] *n.* Requiem, *das*

requiem 'mass *n. (Eccl.)* Requiem, *das (kath. Kirche);* Totenmesse, *die*

require [rɪ'kwaɪə(r)] *v. t.* **a)** *(need, wish to have)* brauchen; benötigen; erfordern ⟨*Tun, Verhalten*⟩; **a catalogue/guide is available if ~d** bei Bedarf ist ein Katalog erhältlich/auf Wunsch steht ein Führer zur Verfügung; **is there anything else you ~?** brauchen/*(want)* wünschen Sie außerdem noch etwas?; **I have all I ~:** ich habe alles, was ich brauche; **it ~d all his authority ...:** es bedurfte seiner ganzen Autorität ... *(geh.)*; **b)** *(order, demand)* verlangen (**of** von); **~ sb. to do sth., ~ of sb. that he does sth.** von jmdm. verlangen, daß er etw. tut; **be ~d to do sth.** etw. tun müssen *od.* sollen; **~d reading** Pflichtlektüre, *die*

requirement [rɪ'kwaɪəmənt] *n.* **a)** *(need)* Bedarf, *der;* **meet the ~s** den Bedarf decken; **meet sb.'s ~s** jmds. Wünschen entsprechen; **what are your ~s?** was brauchen Sie?; **borrowing ~:** Kreditbedarf, *der;* **b)** *(condition)* Erfordernis, *das; (for a job)* Voraussetzung, *die;* **fulfil sb.'s ~s** jmds. Anforderungen *(Dat.)* genügen; **there are certain language ~s for this job** diese Stelle setzt [bestimmte] Sprachkenntnisse voraus

requisite ['rekwɪzɪt] **1.** *adj.* notwendig (**to, for** für); erforderlich ⟨*Voraussetzung, Kenntnisse*⟩. **2.** *n.* Erfordernis, *das* (**for** für); **be a ~ for sth.** für etw. erforderlich sein; **toilet/travel ~s** Toiletten-/Reiseartikel *Pl.*

requisition [rekwɪ'zɪʃn] **1.** *n.* **a)** *(esp. Law: demand)* Aufforderung, *die;* **b)** *(order for sth.)* Anforderung, *die* (**for** *Gen.*); *(by force if necessary)* Beschlagnahmung, *die* (**for** *Gen.*); **make a ~ on sb. for sth.** etw. bei jmdm. anfordern; **be put under ~:** beschlagnahmt werden. **2.** *v. t.* anfordern; *(by force if necessary)* beschlagnahmen

requital [rɪ'kwaɪtl] *n.* Vergeltung, *die*

requite [rɪ'kwaɪt] *v. t.* vergelten; **~ sb. for sth.** jmdm. etw. vergelten; *(avenge)* jmdm. etw. heimzahlen

reran *see* **rerun 1**

reread [ri:'ri:d] *v. t.*, **reread** [ri:'red] wieder *od.* nochmals lesen; **~ sth. several times** etw. mehrmals *od.* wiederholt lesen

reredos ['rɪədɒs] *n. (Eccl.)* Altaraufsatz, *der;* Retabel, *das*

re-route [ri:'ru:t] *v. t.*, **~ing** umleiten

rerun 1. [ri:'rʌn] *v. t., forms as* **run** wiederholen ⟨*Rennen*⟩; wieder auf- *od.* vorführen ⟨*Film*⟩; wieder abspielen ⟨*Tonband*⟩. **2.** ['ri:rʌn] *n. see* **1:** Wiederholung, *die;* Wiederaufführung, *die;* Wiederabspielen, *das*

resale [ri:'seɪl] *n.* Weiterverkauf, *der (Wirtsch.)* (**to** an + *Akk.*); **'not for ~'** „nicht zum Wiederverkauf bestimmt"; *(on free samples)* „unverkäufliches Muster"; **~ price maintenance** Preisbindung, *die*

resat *see* **resit 1, 2**

reschedule [ri:'ʃedju:l] *v. t.* **a)** zeitlich neu festlegen ⟨*Veranstaltung, Flug, Programm usw.*⟩; **the flight will be ~d for 5 o'clock** der Flug wird auf 5 Uhr verlegt; **b)** *(Fin.)* umschulden, refinanzieren ⟨*Kredit, Darlehen*⟩; refinanzieren ⟨*Schulden*⟩

rescind [rɪ'sɪnd] *v. t.* für ungültig erklären

rescue ['reskju:] **1.** *v. t.* retten (**from** aus); *(set free)* befreien (**from** aus); **~ sb. from drowning** jmdn. vorm Ertrinken retten. **2.** *n. see* **1:** Rettung, *die;* Befreiung, *die; attrib.* Rettungs⟨*dienst, -versuch, -mannschaft, -aktion*⟩; **go/come to the/sb.'s ~:** jmdm. zu Hilfe kommen; **once again it was Margaret to the ~:** es war wieder mal Margaret, die die Situation gerettet hat

rescuer ['reskju:ə(r)] *n.* Retter, *der*/Retterin, *die*

research [rɪ'sɜ:tʃ, 'ri:sɜ:tʃ] **1.** *n.* **a)** *(scientific study)* Forschung, *die* (**into, on** über + *Akk.*); **do ~ in biochemistry** auf dem Gebiet der Biochemie forschen; **carry out/be engaged in ~ into sth.** wissenschaftliche Untersuchungen über etw. *(Akk.)* durchführen/sich in seiner Forschungsarbeit mit etw. befassen; **piece of ~:** Forschungsarbeit, *die; (investigation)* Untersuchung, *die;* **b)** *(inquiry)* Nachforschung, *die* (**into** über + *Akk.*). **2.** *v. i.* forschen; **~ into sth.** etw. erforschen *od.* untersuchen; *(esp. Univ.)* über etw. *(Akk.)* forschen. **3.** *v. t.* erforschen; untersuchen; recherchieren ⟨*Buch usw.*⟩

research assistant [-'- ---, '-- ---] *n.* wissenschaftlicher Assistent/wissenschaftliche Assistentin

researcher [rɪ'sɜ:tʃə(r), 'ri:sɜ:tʃə(r)] *n.* Forscher, *der*/Forscherin, *die*

research: ~ fellow *n.* Forschungsstipendiat, *der*/-stipendiatin, *die;* **~ fellowship** *n.* Forschungsstipendium, *das*

resection [rɪ'sekʃn] *(Med.)* Resektion, *die*

reselect [ri:sɪ'lekt] *v. t. (Parl.)* wieder aufstellen ⟨*Abgeordneten*⟩

reselection [ri:sɪ'lekʃn] *n. (Parl.)* Wiederaufstellung, *die*

resell [ri:'sel] *v. t.*, **resold** [ri:'səʊld] weiterverkaufen (**to** an + *Akk.*)

resemblance [rɪ'zembləns] *n.* Ähnlichkeit, *die* (**to** mit, **between** zwischen + *Dat.*); **bear a faint/strong/no ~ to ...:** eine geringe/starke/keine Ähnlichkeit mit ... haben

resemble [rɪ'zembl] *v. t.* ähneln, gleichen (+ *Dat.*); **they ~ each other** sie ähneln *od.* gleichen sich *(Dat.)* *od.* einander

resent [rɪ'zent] *v. t.* übelnehmen; **she ~ed his familiarity/success** sie nahm ihm seine Vertraulichkeit übel/mißgönnte ihm seinen Erfolg; **I ~ the way you take my help for granted** es gefällt mir nicht, wie du meine Hilfe als selbstverständlich hinnimmst; **she ~ed his having won** sie ärgerte sich darüber, daß er gewonnen hatte

resentful [rɪ'zentfl] *adj.* übelnehmerisch, nachtragend ⟨*Person, Art, Verhalten*⟩; grollend *(geh.)* ⟨*Blick*⟩; **be ~ of** *or* **feel ~ about sth.** etw. übelnehmen; **be ~ of sb.'s criticism/success** jmdm. seine Kritik übelnehmen/seinen Erfolg mißgönnen

resentfully [rɪ'zentfəlɪ] *adv.* grollend *(geh.)*; voller Groll *nachgestellt (geh.)*

resentment [rɪ'zentmənt] *n., no pl.* Groll, *der (geh.);* **feel ~ towards** *or* **against sb.** einen Groll auf jmdn. haben

reservation [rezə'veɪʃn] *n.* **a)** Reservierung, *die;* **[seat] ~:** [Platz]reservierung, *die;* **have a ~ [for a room]** ein Zimmer reserviert haben; **b)** *(doubt, objection)* Vorbehalt, *der* (**about** gegen); Bedenken (**about** bezüglich + *Gen.*); **without ~:** ohne Vorbehalt; vorbehaltlos; **with ~s** mit [gewissen] Vorbehalten; *see also* **mental reservation; c) central ~** *(Brit. Road Constr.)* Mittelstreifen, *der;* **d)** *(Amer.: land reserved for Indians)* Reservat, *das;* Reservation, *die*

reserve [rɪ'zɜ:v] **1.** *v. t.* **a)** *(secure)* reservieren lassen ⟨*Zimmer, Tisch, Platz*⟩; *(set aside)* reservieren; **~ the right to do sth.** sich *(Dat.)* [das Recht] vorbehalten, etw. zu tun; **all seats ~d** Plätze nur auf Vorbestellung; **all rights ~d** alle Rechte vorbehalten; **b)** *in pass. (be kept)* **be ~d for sb.** ⟨*Funktion, Tätigkeit:*⟩ jmdm. vorbehalten sein; **c)** *(postpone)* aufheben ⟨*Überraschung, Neuigkeit*⟩; **~ judgement** sein Urteil aufschieben; **~ oneself for sth.** sich für etw. schonen; **~ one's strength** seine Kräfte schonen. **2.** *n.* **a)** *(extra amount)* Reserve, *die* (**of** an + *Dat.*) *(Banking also)* Rücklage, *die;* **~s of energy/strength** Energie-/Kraftreserven; **hidden ~:** stille Reserve; **have/hold** *or* **keep sth. in ~:** etw. in Reserve haben/halten; **b)** *in sing. or pl. (Mil.) (troops)* Reserve, *die;* **the ~s** die Reservetruppen *od.* -einheiten; **c)** *see* **reservist; d)** *(Sport)* Reservespieler, *der*/-spielerin, *die;* **the R~s** die Reserve; **e)** *(place set apart)* Reservat, *das;* **f)** *(restriction)* Vorbehalt, *der;* **without ~:** ohne Vorbehalt; vorbehaltlos; **g)** *see* **reserve price; h)** *(self-restraint, reticence)* Reserve, *die;* Zurückhaltung, *die*

reserve 'currency *n.* Reservewährung, *die*

reserved [rɪ'zɜ:vd] *adj.* **a)** *(reticent)* reserviert; zurückhaltend; **b)** *(booked)* reserviert

reserve: ~ list *n. (Mil.)* **be on the ~ list** Reservist sein; **~ player** *n.* Reservespieler, *der*/-spielerin, *die;* **~ price** *n.* Mindestgebot, *das*

reservist [rɪ'zɜ:vɪst] *n. (Mil.)* Reservist, *der*

reservoir ['rezəvwɑ:(r)] *n.* **a)** *([artificial] lake)* Reservoir, *das;* **b)** *(container)* Behälter, *der;* Speicher, *der; (of fountain-pen)* Tintenraum, *der;* **c)** *(reserve supply)* Vorrat, *der* (**of** an + *Dat.*); *(fig.)* Reservoir, *das*

reset [ri:'set] *v. t.*, **-tt-, reset a)** neu [ein]fassen ⟨*Schmuck-, Edelstein*⟩; neu stellen ⟨*Uhr, Timer*⟩; umstellen ⟨*Uhr*⟩ (**for, to** auf + *Akk.*); **b)** *(Med.)* wieder einrichten ⟨*Gliedmaße, Knochen*⟩; wieder einrenken ⟨*ausgerenktes Gelenk*⟩; **c)** *(Printing)* neu setzen

resettle [ri:'setl] *v. t.* **a)** umsiedeln ⟨*Flüchtlinge usw.*⟩ (**in** in + *Akk.*); **b)** *(repopulate)* wieder besiedeln ⟨*Gebiet*⟩

resettlement [ri:'setlmənt] *n.* **a)** *(of refugees)* Umsiedlung, *die;* **b)** *(repopulating)* Neubesiedlung, *die*

reshape [ri:'ʃeɪp] *v. t.* **a)** *(give new form to)* umgestalten; umstellen ⟨*Politik*⟩; **b)** *(remould)* umformen

reshuffle [ri:'ʃʌfl] **1.** *v. t.* **a)** *(reorganize)* umbilden ⟨*Kabinett usw.*⟩; **b)** *(Cards)* neu mischen. **2.** *n.* Umbildung, *die;* **Cabinet ~:** Kabinettsumbildung, *die*

reside [rɪ'zaɪd] *v. i. (formal)* **a)** *(dwell)* wohnen; wohnhaft sein *(Amtsspr.)*; ⟨*Monarch, Präsident usw.:*⟩ residieren; **b)** *(be vested, present, inherent)* liegen (**in** bei)

residence ['rezɪdəns] *n.* **a)** *(abode)* Wohnsitz, *der; (house)* Wohnhaus, *das; (mansion)* Villa, *die; (of a head of state or church, an ambassador)* Residenz, *die;* **the President's official ~:** der offizielle Wohnsitz des Präsidenten; **have one's ~ in London/in Victoria Street** seinen Wohnsitz in London haben/seine Privatwohnung in der Victoria Street haben; **b)** *(residing)* Aufenthalt, *der;* **take up [one's] ~ in Rome** seinen Wohnsitz in Rom nehmen; **be in ~** ⟨*König, Präsident usw.:*⟩ [an seinem offiziellen Wohnsitz] anwesend sein; ⟨*Student:*⟩ im College sein; **we have a doctor in ~:** wir haben einen Arzt im Hause; **writer** *etc.* **in ~:** *von einer Gemeinde od. einer Institution geförderter, am Ort lebender Schriftsteller usw.*

'residence permit *n.* Aufenthaltsgenehmigung, *die*
residency ['rezɪdənsɪ] *n. (Amer. Med.)* Zeit als Assistenzarzt/-ärztin im Krankenhaus
resident ['rezɪdənt] **1.** *adj.* **a)** *(residing)* wohnhaft; ~ **population** [orts]ansässige Bevölkerung; **he is ~ in England** er hat seinen Wohnsitz in England; **b)** *(living in)* im Haus wohnend ‹*Haushälterin*›; Anstalts‹*arzt, -geistlicher*›; ~ **tutor** Hauslehrer, *der.* **2.** *n.* **a)** *(inhabitant)* Bewohner, *der*/Bewohnerin, *die; (in a town etc. also)* Einwohner, *der*/Einwohnerin, *die; (at hotel)* Hotelgast, *der;* **'access/parking for ~s only'** „Anlieger frei"/„Parken nur für Anlieger"; **local ~:** Anwohner, *der*/Anwohnerin, *die;* **~s association** *Interessengemeinschaft von [benachbarten] Anwohnern eines bestimmten Gebiets;* **b)** *(Amer. Med.)* ≈ Assistenzarzt, *der*/-ärztin, *die*
residential [rezɪ'denʃl] *adj.* **a)** Wohn‹*gebiet, -siedlung, -straße*›; **for ~ purposes** zu Wohnzwecken; ~ **hotel** Hotel für Dauergäste; **b)** ~ **course** *Kurs, dessen Teilnehmer am Ort wohnen;* **the ~ qualification for voters** *Nachweis des Wohnsitzes als Voraussetzung zur Ausübung des Wahlrechts*
residential 'care *n.* stationäre Pflege
resident 'parking *n.* Parken nur für Anlieger
residual [rɪ'zɪdjʊəl] *adj.* zurückgeblieben; noch vorhanden; ungeklärt ‹*Problem, Frage*›
residue ['rezɪdju:] *n.* **a)** *(remainder)* Rest, *der;* **b)** *(Law)* restlicher Nachlaß *(nach Abzug aller Nachlaßverbindlichkeiten);* **c)** *(Chem.)* Rückstand, *der*
residuum [rɪ'zɪdjʊəm] *n., pl.* **residua** [rɪ'zɪdjʊə] *(Chem.)* Rückstand, *der*
resign [rɪ'zaɪn] **1.** *v. t. (hand over)* zurücktreten von ‹*Amt*›; verzichten auf (+ *Akk.*) ‹*Recht, Anspruch*›; ~ **the leadership to sb.** jmdm. die Führung überlassen *od.* -geben; ~ **one's commission** *(Mil.)* seinen Abschied nehmen; ~ **one's job/post** seine Stelle/Stellung kündigen. **2.** *v. refl.* ~ **oneself to sth./to doing sth.** sich mit etw. abfinden/sich damit abfinden, etw. zu tun. **3.** *v. i.* **a)** ‹*Arbeitnehmer:*› kündigen; ‹*Regierungsbeamter:*› zurücktreten (**from** von); ‹*Geistlicher, Richter:*› sein Amt niederlegen; ‹*Vorsitzender:*› zurücktreten, sein Amt niederlegen; ~ **from one's post** ‹*Beamter:*› seine Stellung kündigen; **b)** *(Chess)* aufgeben
resignation [rezɪg'neɪʃn] *n.* **a)** *see* **resign 3a:** Kündigung, *die;* Verzicht, *der* (**of** auf + *Akk.*); Rücktritt, *der;* Amtsniederlegung, *die;* **give** *or* **send in** *or* **tender one's ~:** seinen Rücktritt/seine Kündigung einreichen/sein Amt niederlegen; **b)** *(being resigned)* Ergebenheit, *die* (**to** in + *Akk.*)
resigned [rɪ'zaɪnd] *adj.* resigniert; **become/be ~ to sth.** sich mit etw. abfinden/abgefunden haben
resignedly [rɪ'zaɪnɪdlɪ] *adv.* resigniert
resilience [rɪ'zɪlɪəns], **resiliency** [rɪ'zɪlɪənsɪ] *n., no pl.* **a)** *(elasticity)* Elastizität, *die;* **b)** *(fig.)* Unverwüstlichkeit, *die*
resilient [rɪ'zɪlɪənt] *adj.* **a)** *(elastic)* elastisch; **b)** *(fig.)* unverwüstlich; **be ~:** sich nicht [so leicht] unterkriegen lassen
resin ['rezɪn] *n.* **a)** *(Bot.)* Harz, *das;* **b) [synthetic] ~:** Kunstharz, *das*
resinous ['rezɪnəs] *adj. (like resin)* harzartig; *(containing resin)* harzig; harzhaltig
resist [rɪ'zɪst] **1.** *v. t.* **a)** *(withstand action of)* standhalten (+ *Dat.*) ‹*Frost, Hitze, Feuchtigkeit usw.*›; **be unable to ~ an infection/disease** keine Abwehrkräfte gegen eine Infektion/Krankheit haben; **b)** *(oppose, repel)* sich widersetzen (+ *Dat.*) ‹*Maßnahme, Festnahme, Plan usw.*›; widerstehen (+ *Dat.*) ‹*Versuchung, jmds. Charme*›; Widerstand leisten gegen ‹*Angriff, Feind*›; sich wehren gegen ‹*Veränderung, Einfluß*›. **2.** *v. i. see* **1b:** sich widersetzen; widerstehen; Widerstand leisten; sich wehren
resistance [rɪ'zɪstəns] *n.* **a)** *(resisting, opposing force; also Phys., Electr.)* Widerstand, *der* (**to** gegen); **make** *or* **offer no ~ [to sb./sth.]** [jmdm./einer Sache] keinen Widerstand leisten; **take the line of least ~** *(fig.)* den Weg des geringsten Widerstandes gehen; *see also* **passive 1b; b)** *(power of resisting)* Widerstandsfähigkeit, *die* (**to** gegen); ~ **to wear and tear** Strapazierfähigkeit, *die;* ~ **to heat/cold** Hitze-/Kältebeständigkeit, *die;* **c)** *(Biol., Med.)* Widerstandskraft, *die* (**to** gegen); **d)** *(against occupation)* Widerstand, *der;* **the French R~:** die Résistance
resistance: ~ fighter *n.* Widerstandskämpfer, *der*/-kämpferin, *die;* ~ **movement** *n.* Widerstandsbewegung, *die*
resistant [rɪ'zɪstənt] *adj.* **a)** *(opposed)* **be ~ to** sich widersetzen (+ *Dat.*); sich entgegenstellen (+ *Dat.*); **b)** *(having power to resist)* widerstandsfähig (**to** gegen); **highly ~ to wear and tear** sehr strapazierfähig; **heat-/water-/rust-~:** hitze-/wasser-/rostbeständig; **c)** *(Med., Biol.)* resistent (**to** gegen)
resistor [rɪ'zɪstə(r)] *n. (Electr.)* Widerstand, *der*
resit 1. [ri:'sɪt] *v. t.*, **-tt-**, **resat** [ri:'sæt] wiederholen ‹*Prüfung*›. **2.** *v. i.*, **-tt-**, **resat** die Prüfung wiederholen. **3.** ['ri:sɪt] *n.* Wiederholungsprüfung, *die*
resold *see* **resell**
resole [ri:'səʊl] *v. t.* neu besohlen
resolute ['rezəlu:t] *adj.* resolut, energisch ‹*Person*›; entschlossen ‹*Tat*›; entschieden ‹*Antwort, Weigerung*›
resolutely ['rezəlu:tlɪ] *adv.* entschlossen
resolution [rezə'lu:ʃn] *n.* **a)** *(decision)* Entschließung, *die; (Polit. also)* Resolution, *die;* **a ~ of sympathy/solidarity** eine Sympathie-/Solidaritätserklärung; **b)** *(resolve)* Vorsatz, *der;* **make a ~:** einen Vorsatz fassen; **make a ~ to do sth.** den Vorsatz fassen, etw. zu tun; **break one's ~:** seinem Vorsatz untreu werden; **good ~s** gute Vorsätze; **New Year['s] ~s** gute Vorsätze fürs neue Jahr; **c)** *no pl. (firmness)* Entschlossenheit, *die;* **d)** *no pl. (solving) see* **resolve 1a, b:** Beseitigung, *die;* Ausräumung, *die;* Lösung, *die;* **e)** *(separation; also Phys., Mus.)* Auflösung, *die*
resolve [rɪ'zɒlv] **1.** *v. t.* **a)** *(dispel)* beseitigen, ausräumen ‹*Schwierigkeit, Zweifel, Unklarheit*›; **b)** *(explain)* lösen ‹*Problem, Rätsel*›; **c)** *(decide)* beschließen; **they ~d that they must part** sie beschlossen, sich zu trennen; **this discovery made me ~ to leave** diese Entdeckung hat mich zu dem Entschluß gebracht, fortzugehen; **d)** *(settle)* beilegen ‹*Streit*›; klären ‹*Streitpunkt*›; regeln ‹*Angelegenheit*›; **e)** *(separate; also Phys., Mus.)* auflösen (**into** in + *Akk.*); **f)** *(analyse, divide; also Mech.)* zerlegen (**into** in + *Akk.*). **2.** *v. i.* **a)** *(decide)* ~ **[up]on sth./doing sth.** sich zu etw. entschließen/sich [dazu] entschließen, etw. zu tun; **b)** *(dissolve)* sich auflösen (**into** in + *Akk.*). **3.** *n.* **a)** Vorsatz, *der;* **make a/keep one's ~:** einen Vorsatz fassen/bei seinem Vorsatz bleiben; **make a ~ to do sth.** den Vorsatz fassen, etw. zu tun; **b)** *(Amer.) see* **resolution a; c)** *(resoluteness)* Entschlossenheit, *die*
resolved [rɪ'zɒlvd] *pred. adj.* ~ **[to do sth.]** entschlossen[, etw. zu tun]; **he was ~ that ...:** es stand für ihn fest, daß ...
re'solving power *n. (Phys.)* Auflösungsvermögen, *das*
resonance ['rezənəns] *n.* Resonanz, *die; (of voice)* voller Klang; *(fig.)* Widerhall, *der*
resonant ['rezənənt] *adj.* **a)** *(resounding)* hallend ‹*Echo, Ton, Klang*›; volltönend ‹*Stimme*›; **b)** *(tending to reinforce sounds)* ‹*Raum, Körper:*› mit viel Resonanz
resonate ['rezəneɪt] *v. i.* mitschwingen; resonieren *(Physik, Musik)*
resonator ['rezəneɪtə(r)] *n. (Phys., Mus.)* Resonator, *der*
resorption [rɪ'sɔ:pʃn] *n. (Biol., Med.)* Resorption, *die*
resort [rɪ'zɔ:t] **1.** *n.* **a)** *(resource, recourse)* Ausweg, *der* ; **have ~ to force** Gewalt anwenden; **without ~ to force** ohne Gewaltanwendung; **you were my last ~:** du warst meine letzte Rettung *(ugs.);* **as a** *or* **in the last ~:** als letzter Ausweg; **in the last ~** *(in the end)* letzten Endes; **b)** *(place frequented)* Aufenthalt[sort], *der;* **[holiday] ~:** Urlaubsort, *der;* Ferienort, *der;* **ski/health ~:** Skiurlaubs-/Kurort, *der;* **mountain/coastal ~:** Ferienort im Gebirge/an der Küste; **seaside ~:** Seebad, *das;* **c)** *(frequenting)* häufiger Besuch. **2.** *v. i.* ~ **to sth./sb.** zu etw. greifen/sich an jmdn. wenden (**for** um); ~ **to violence** *or* **force** Gewalt anwenden; ~ **to stealing/shouting** *etc.* sich aufs Stehlen/Schreien *usw.* verlegen; ~ **to crime** kriminell werden
resound [rɪ'zaʊnd] *v. i.* **a)** *(ring)* widerhallen (**with** von); **b)** *(produce echo)* hallen; **his fame ~ed through Greece** *(fig.)* sein Ruhm hallte durch [ganz] Griechenland
resounding [rɪ'zaʊndɪŋ] *adj.* hallend ‹*Lärm, Schreie, Schritte*›; schallend ‹*Gelächter, Stimme*›; überwältigend ‹*Mehrheit, Sieg, Erfolg*›; gewaltig ‹*Niederlage, Mißerfolg*›
resoundingly [rɪ'zaʊndɪŋlɪ] *adv.* schallend ‹*ertönen, erklingen*›; **be ~ successful** ein durchschlagender Erfolg sein
resource [rɪ'sɔ:s, rɪ'zɔ:s] *n.* **a)** *usu. in pl. (stock)* Mittel *Pl.;* Ressource, *die;* **have no inner ~s** keine inneren Reserven haben; **financial/mineral ~s** Geldmittel *Pl.*/Bodenschätze *Pl.;* **~s in** *or* **of men and money** Reserven an Menschen und Geldmitteln; **b)** *usu. pl. (Amer.: asset)* Aktivposten, *der;* **c)** *(expedient)* Ausweg, *der;* **be at the end of one's ~s** am Ende seiner Möglichkeiten sein; **be left to one's own ~s** sich *(Dat.)* selbst überlassen sein; **as a last ~:** als letzter Ausweg; **d)** *no art., no pl. (ingenuity)* Findigkeit, *die;* **be full of ~:** sich *(Dat.)* immer zu helfen wissen
resourceful [rɪ'sɔ:sfl, rɪ'zɔ:sfl] *adj.* findig ‹*Person*›; einfallsreich ‹*Plan*›
resourcefully [rɪ'sɔ:sfəlɪ, rɪ'zɔ:sfəlɪ] *adv.* findig
resourcefulness [rɪ'sɔ:sflnɪs, rɪ'zɔ:sflnɪs] *n., no pl. (of person)* Findigkeit, *die; (of plan etc.)* Einfallsreichtum, *der*
respect [rɪ'spekt] **1.** *n.* **a)** *(esteem)* Respekt, *der* (**for** vor + *Dat.*); Achtung, *die* (**for** vor + *Dat.*); **show ~ for sb./sth.** Respekt vor jmdm./etw. zeigen; **hold sb. in [high** *or* **great] ~:** jmdn. [sehr] achten; **command ~:** Respekt einflößen; **treat sb./sth. with ~:** jmdm./etw. mit Respekt *od.* Achtung begegnen/etw. mit Vorsicht behandeln; **with [all due] ~, ...:** bei allem Respekt, ...; mit Verlaub, ... *(geh.);* **b)** *(consideration)* Rücksicht, *die* (**for** auf + *Akk.*); **have** *or* **pay [no] ~ to sth.** etw. [nicht] berücksichtigen; **c)** *(aspect)* Beziehung, *die;* Hinsicht, *die;* **in ~ of style** hinsichtlich des Stils; in stilistischer Hinsicht; **in all/many/some ~s** in jeder/vieler/mancher Beziehung *od.* Hinsicht; **d)** *(reference)* Bezug, *der;* **with ~ to ...:** in bezug auf ... *(Akk.);* was ... [an]betrifft; **have ~ to sth.** etw. betreffen; sich auf etw. *(Akk.)* beziehen; **e)** *in pl.* **give him my ~s** grüße ihn von mir; **pay one's ~s to sb.** *(formal)* jmdm. seine Aufwartung machen *(veralt.);* **pay one's last ~s** jmdm. die letzte Ehre erweisen *(geh.).* **2.** *v. t.* respektieren; achten; **he doesn't ~ his teachers much** er hat nicht viel Respekt vor seinen Lehrern; **much ~ed** sehr angesehen ‹*Politiker, Firma*›; ~ **sb.'s feelings** auf jmds. Gefühle Rücksicht nehmen; ~ **the rules of the road** die Verkehrsregeln beachten

respectability [rɪspektəˈbɪlɪtɪ] *n., no pl. see* **respectable a:** Ansehen, *das;* Ehrbarkeit, *die (geh.);* **I do not doubt the ~ of his motives** ich zweifle nicht daran, daß seine Motive ehrenwert sind

respectable [rɪˈspektəbl] *adj.* **a)** *(of good character)* angesehen ⟨*Bürger usw.*⟩; ehrenwert ⟨*Motive*⟩; *(decent)* ehrbar *(geh.)* ⟨*Leute, Kaufmann, Hausfrau*⟩; **b)** *(presentable)* anständig, respektabel ⟨*Beschäftigung usw.*⟩; vornehm, gut ⟨*Adresse*⟩; ordentlich, *(that one can be seen in)* vorzeigbar *(ugs.)* ⟨*Kleidung*⟩; **are you ~?** *(joc.)* hast du was an? *(ugs.);* **c)** *(considerable)* beachtlich ⟨*Summe*⟩; **d)** *(passable)* passabel

respectably [rɪˈspektəblɪ] *adv.* **a)** anständig ⟨*sich benehmen*⟩; ordentlich ⟨*gekleidet*⟩; **be ~ employed** eine anständige Beschäftigung haben; **b)** *(passably)* passabel

respecter [rɪˈspektə(r)] *n.* **be no ~ of persons** alle ohne Ansehen der Person gleich behandeln

respectful [rɪˈspektfl] *adj.* respektvoll **(to[wards]** gegenüber)

respectfully [rɪˈspektfəlɪ] *adv.* respektvoll; **~ yours, X** *(formal)* Ihr sehr ergebener X

respecting [rɪˈspektɪŋ] *prep.* bezüglich; hinsichtlich

respective [rɪˈspektɪv] *adj.* jeweilig; **you must go to your ~ places** jeder von euch muß auf seinen Platz gehen; **he and I contributed ~ amounts of £10 and £1** er und ich steuerten Beträge von 10 bzw. 1 Pfund bei

respectively [rɪˈspektɪvlɪ] *adv.* beziehungsweise; **the two cars were red and white ~:** die beiden Autos waren rot bzw. weiß; **he and I contributed £10 and £1 ~:** er und ich steuerten 10 bzw. 1 Pfund bei

respell [ri:ˈspel] *v. t.,* **respelt** *(Brit.)* [ri:ˈspelt] *or* **respelled** noch einmal buchstabieren

respiration [resprˈreɪʃn] *n.* *(one breath)* Atemzug, *der; (breathing)* Atmung, *die;* **she was finding ~ difficult** das Atmen fiel ihr schwer

respirator [ˈrespɪreɪtə(r)] *n.* **a)** *(protecting device)* Atemschutzgerät, *das;* **b)** *(Med.)* Respirator, *der*

respiratory [ˈrespərətərɪ, rɪˈspɪrətərɪ] *adj.* Atem⟨*geräusch, -wege*⟩; Atmungs⟨*system, -organ, -funktion*⟩; **~ infection** Infektion der Atemwege

respire [rɪˈspaɪə(r)] *v. t. & i.* atmen; respirieren *(Med.)*

respite [ˈrespaɪt] *n.* **a)** *(delay)* Aufschub, *der;* **b)** *(interval of relief)* Ruhepause, *die;* **~ from sth.** Erholung von etw.; **without ~:** ohne Pause *od.* Unterbrechung

resplendent [rɪˈsplendənt] *adj.* prächtig; **~ in his uniform** in der vollen Pracht seiner Uniform

resplendently [rɪˈsplendəntlɪ] *adv.* prächtig

respond [rɪˈspɒnd] **1.** *v. i.* **a)** *(answer)* antworten **(to** auf + *Akk.*); **~ to sb.'s greeting** jmds. Gruß erwidern; **b)** *(react)* reagieren **(to** auf + *Akk.*); ⟨*Patient, Bremsen, Lenkung usw.:*⟩ ansprechen **(to** auf + *Akk.*); **[not] ~ to kindness** [nicht] empfänglich für Freundlichkeit sein; **they ~ed very generously to this appeal** der Aufruf fand bei ihnen ein großes Echo; **the illness ~s to treatment** die Krankheit läßt sich behandeln. **2.** *v. t.* antworten; erwidern. **3.** *n. (Archit.)* Wandpfeiler, *der;* Pilaster, *der (fachspr.)*

respondent [rɪˈspɒndənt] *n. (Law)* Beklagte, *der/die; (in divorce case)* Scheidungsbeklagte, *der/die*

response [rɪˈspɒns] *n.* **a)** *(answer)* Antwort, *die* **(to** auf + *Akk.*); **in ~ [to]** als Antwort [auf (+ *Akk.*)]; **in ~ to your letter** in Beantwortung Ihres Schreibens *(Papierdt.);* **make no ~:** nicht antworten; **b)** *(reaction)* Reaktion, *die;* **make no ~ to sth.** auf etw. *(Akk.)* nicht reagieren; **his ~ was to resign** er reagierte mit seinem Rücktritt; **meet with no/a large ~:** kein Echo/großes Echo finden; **£20,000 was raised in ~ to the appeal** der Aufruf brachte Spenden in Höhe von 20 000 Pfund ein; **c)** *(Eccl.)* Responsorium, *das*

responsibility [rɪspɒnsɪˈbɪlɪtɪ] *n.* **a)** *no pl., no indef. art. (being responsible)* Verantwortung, *die;* **take** *or* **bear** *or* **accept** *or* **assume/claim [full] ~ [for sth.]** die [volle] Verantwortung [für etw.] übernehmen; **'the management accepts no ~ for garments left here'** „die Geschäftsleitung übernimmt keine Haftung für die Garderobe"; **lay** *or* **put** *or* **place the ~ for sth. on sb.['s shoulders]** jmdn. für etw. verantwortlich machen; **claim ~ for a bombing** sich zu einem Bombenanschlag bekennen; **do sth. on one's own ~:** etw. in eigener Verantwortung tun; *(at one's own risk)* etw. auf eigene Verantwortung tun; **b)** *(duty)* Verpflichtung, *die;* **the responsibilities of office** die Dienstpflicht; **that's 'your ~:** dafür bist du verantwortlich

responsible [rɪˈspɒnsɪbl] *adj.* **a)** verantwortlich **(for** für); **hold sb. ~ for sth.** jmdn. für etw. verantwortlich machen; **be ~ to sb. [for sth.]** jmdm. gegenüber [für etw.] verantwortlich sein; **be ~ for sth.** ⟨*Person:*⟩ für etw. verantwortlich sein; ⟨*Sache:*⟩ die Ursache für etw. sein; **what's ~ for the breakdown?** woran liegt die Betriebsstörung?; **I've made you ~ for the travel arrangements** ich habe dir die Verantwortung für die Reisevorbereitungen übertragen; **b)** verantwortlich, verantwortungsvoll ⟨*Stellung, Tätigkeit, Aufgabe*⟩; **c)** *(trustworthy)* verantwortungsvoll, verantwortungsbewußt ⟨*Person*⟩

responsibly [rɪˈspɒnsɪblɪ] *adv.* verantwortungsbewußt ⟨*handeln, sich verhalten*⟩

responsive [rɪˈspɒnsɪv] *adj. (reacting positively)* aufgeschlossen ⟨*Person*⟩; gut ansprechend ⟨*Bremsen, Motor usw.*⟩; **the audience was very ~, it was a very ~ audience** das Publikum ging sehr gut mit; **be ~ to sth.** auf etw. *(Akk.)* reagieren *od.* eingehen

respray 1. [ri:ˈspreɪ] *v. t.* neu spritzen ⟨*Auto*⟩. **2.** [ˈri:spreɪ] *n.* neue Lackierung; **give the car a ~:** den Wagen neu spritzen

¹rest [rest] **1.** *v. i.* **a)** *(lie, lit. or fig.)* ruhen; **~ on** ruhen auf (+ *Dat.*); ⟨*Schatten, Licht:*⟩ liegen auf (+ *Dat.*); *(fig.)* ⟨*Argumentation:*⟩ sich stützen auf (+ *Akk.*); ⟨*Ruf:*⟩ beruhen auf (+ *Dat.*); **~ against sth.** an etw. *(Dat.)* lehnen; **sit with one's back ~ing against sth.** mit dem Rücken an etw. *(Akk.)* gelehnt sitzen; **her head is ~ing against his shoulder** ihr Kopf liegt an seiner Schulter; **b)** *(take repose)* ruhen; sich ausruhen **(from** von); *(pause)* eine Pause machen *od.* einlegen; **never let one's enemy ~:** seinem Feind keine Ruhepause gönnen; **she never ~s** ihre Hände ruhen nie; **I won't ~ until ...:** ich werde nicht ruhen noch rasten, bis ...; **tell sb. to ~** ⟨*Arzt:*⟩ jmdm. Ruhe verordnen; **be ~ing** *(Brit. Theatre)* ⟨*Schauspieler:*⟩ ohne Engagement sein; **c)** *(euphem.: lie in death)* ruhen *(geh.);* **let her/may she ~ in peace** laß sie/möge sie in Frieden ruhen; **d)** *(be left)* **let the matter ~:** die Sache ruhenlassen; **... and there the matter ~ed** ... und dabei blieb es; **~ assured that ...:** seien Sie versichert, daß ...; **e) ~ with sb.** ⟨*Verantwortung, Entscheidung, Schuld:*⟩ bei jmdm. liegen; **f)** *(Agric.: lie fallow)* ruhen; brachliegen; **g)** *(Amer. Law)* ⟨*Verteidigung:*⟩ die Beweiserhebung abschließen. *See also* **laurel a; oar a. 2.** *v. t.* **a)** *(place for support)* **~ sth. against sth.** etw. an etw. *(Akk.)* lehnen; **~ sth. on sth.** *(lit. or fig.)* etw. auf etw. *(Akk.)* stützen; **she was ~ing all her hopes on her son** sie setzte ihre ganze Hoffnung auf ihren Sohn; **he ~ed the load on the ground [for a moment]** er setzte die Last [für einen Augenblick] ab; **b)** *(give relief to)* ausruhen lassen ⟨*Pferd, Person*⟩; ausruhen ⟨*Augen*⟩; schonen ⟨*Stimme, Körperteil*⟩; **~ oneself** sich ausruhen; **c)** *(Agric.: allow to lie fallow)* brachlegen *(fachspr.);* ruhen lassen; **d)** *(Law)* **~ one's case** sein Plädoyer beschließen; **e) [may] God ~ his soul!** Gott hab ihn selig! **3.** *n.* **a)** *(repose)* Ruhe, *die;* **need nine hours' ~:** neun Stunden Schlaf brauchen; **go** *or* **retire to ~:** sich zur Ruhe legen *od.* begeben *(geh.);* **get a good night's ~:** sich ordentlich ausschlafen; **be at ~** *(euphem.: be dead)* ruhen *(geh.);* **go to one's ~** *(euphem.: die)* zur ewigen Ruhe eingehen *(geh. verhüll.);* **lay to ~** *(euphem.: bury)* zur letzten Ruhe betten *(geh. verhüll.);* **b)** *(freedom from exertion)* Ruhe[pause], *die;* Erholung, *die* **(from** von); **take a ~:** sich ausruhen **(from** von); **tell sb. to take a ~:** ⟨*Arzt:*⟩ jmdm. Ruhe verordnen; **set sb.'s mind at ~:** jmdn. beruhigen **(about** hinsichtlich); **c)** *(pause)* **~ period** [Ruhe]pause, *die;* **have** *or* **take a ~:** [eine] Pause machen; **give sb./sth. a ~:** ausruhen lassen ⟨*Person, Nutztier*⟩; ruhen lassen ⟨*Maschine*⟩; *(fig.)* ruhenlassen ⟨*Thema, Angelegenheit*⟩; **d)** *(stationary position)* **at ~:** in Ruhe; **come to ~:** zum Stehen kommen; *(have final position)* landen; **bring to ~:** zum Stehen bringen; **e)** *(support) (for telephone receiver)* Gabel, *die; (for billiard-cue, telescope, firearm)* Auflage, *die; (for neck)* Stütze, *die;* **f)** *(Mus.)* Pause, *die*

~ 'up *v. i.* sich ausruhen

²rest *n. (remainder)* **the ~:** der Rest; **we'll do the ~:** alles Übrige erledigen wir; **the ~ of her clothes** ihre übrigen Kleider; **the ~ of the butter** die restliche *od.* übrige Butter; **she's no different from the ~:** sie ist nicht besser als die anderen; **and [all] the ~ of it** und so weiter; **for the ~:** im übrigen; sonst

restart 1. [ri:ˈstɑ:t] *v. t.* **a)** *(start again)* wieder anstellen ⟨*Maschine*⟩; wieder anlassen ⟨*Auto, Motor*⟩; **b)** *(resume)* wiederaufnehmen ⟨*Verhandlungen, Berufstätigkeit*⟩; fortsetzen ⟨*Spiel*⟩; neu starten ⟨*Rennen*⟩; **~ work** wieder anfangen zu arbeiten. **2.** [ri:ˈstɑ:t] *v. i.* **a)** ⟨*Motor:*⟩ wieder anspringen; **b)** *(resume)* wieder anfangen; ⟨*Verhandlungen:*⟩ wieder aufgenommen werden. **3.** [ˈri:stɑ:t] *n. see* **1 b:** Wiederaufnahme, *die;* Fortsetzung, *die*

restate [ri:ˈsteɪt] *v. t. (express again)* noch einmal darlegen; *(express differently)* anders darlegen; *(Mus.: repeat)* wiederaufnehmen ⟨*Thema*⟩

restatement [ri:ˈsteɪtmənt] *n.* *(repetition)* nochmalige Darlegung; nochmalige Feststellung; *(reformulation)* Neuformulierung, *die; (Mus.)* Wiederaufnahme, *die*

restaurant [ˈrestərɔ̃, ˈrestərɒnt] *n.* Restaurant, *das*

'restaurant car *n. (Brit. Railw.)* Speisewagen, *der*

restaurateur [restərəˈtɜ:(r)] *n.* Gastwirt, *der*

rest: ~-cure *n. (Med.)* Erholungskur, *die;* **~-day** *n.* Ruhetag, *der*

rested [ˈrestɪd] *adj.* ausgeruht

restful [ˈrestfl] *adj.* **a)** *(free from disturbance)* ruhig ⟨*Tag, Woche, Ort*⟩; **b)** *(conducive to rest)* beruhigend; **be a ~ person to be with** Ruhe ausstrahlen

restfully [ˈrestfəlɪ] *adv.* ruhig ⟨*schlafen*⟩; geruhsam ⟨*Zeit verbringen*⟩

restfulness [ˈrestflnɪs] *n., no pl.* Entspanntheit, *die;* Gelöstheit, *die*

'rest-home *n.* Pflegeheim, *das*

'resting-place *n.* Rastplatz, *der;* **last ~** *(euphem.)* letzte Ruhestätte *(geh.)*

restitution [restɪˈtju:ʃn] *n.* Rückgabe, *die; (of sth. lost)* Erstattung, *die;* Ersatz, *der;* **make ~:** Ersatz leisten; **make ~ of sth. to sb.** jmdm. etw. zurückgeben/erstatten

restive [ˈrestɪv] *adj.* **a)** *(stubborn)* störrisch ⟨*Pferd, Person*⟩; **become ~** ⟨*Pferd:*⟩ bocken; **b)** *(unmanageable)* aufsässig ⟨*Einwohner, Bevölkerung*⟩; **c)** *(restless)* unruhig

restively [ˈrestɪvlɪ] *adv.* **a)** *(stubbornly)* störrisch; **b)** *(in fidgety manner)* unruhig

restless ['restlıs] *adj.* **a)** *(affording no rest)* unruhig ‹*Nacht, Schlaf, Bewegung*›; **b)** *(uneasy)* ruhelos ‹*Person, Sehnsucht*›; **c)** *(taking no rest)* rastlos ‹*Person, Lebensstil*›

restlessly ['restlıslı] *adv. see* **restless a, b:** unruhig; ruhelos

restlessness ['restlısnıs] *n., no pl. see* **restless b, c:** Ruhelosigkeit, *die;* Rastlosigkeit, *die*

restock [ri:'stɒk] **1.** *v. t.* **a)** ~ **a shop** das Lager eines Geschäfts wieder auffüllen; **b)** wieder besetzen ‹*Fluß, Teich*›; wieder aufforsten ‹*Wald*›; ~ **a farm** einen [landwirtschaftlichen] Betrieb wieder mit Vieh besetzen. **2.** *v. i. (Commerc.)* das Lager auffüllen

restoration [restə'reıʃn] *n.* **a)** *(restoring) (of peace, health)* Wiederherstellung, *die; (of a work of art, building, etc.)* Restaurierung, *die;* Restauration, *die (fachspr.);* **her ~ to health** ihre [gesundheitliche] Wiederherstellung; **b)** *(giving back)* Rückgabe, *die;* **c)** *(re-establishment)* Wiedereinführung, *die;* **the R~** *(Brit. Hist.)* die Restauration

restorative [rı'stɒrətıv, rı'stɔ:rətıv] **1.** *adj.* stärkend; aufbauend; Stärkungs-, Aufbau‹*mittel*›; Aufbau-, Kräftigungs‹*kost*›. **2.** *n.* Stärkungs- *od.* Aufbaumittel, *das*

restore [rı'stɔ:(r)] *v. t.* **a)** *(give back)* zurückgeben; **b)** *(bring to original state)* restaurieren ‹*Bauwerk, Kunstwerk usw.*›; konjizieren ‹*Text, Satz*› *(Literaturw.);* ~ **sb. to health, ~ sb.'s health** jmds. Gesundheit *od.* jmdn. wiederherstellen; **his strength was ~d** er kam wieder zu Kräften; ~ **sb. to better spirits** jmdn. aufheitern; **c)** *(reinstate)* wiedereinsetzen **(to** in + *Akk.*); ~ **sb. to the throne/to power** jmdn. als König/Königin wiedereinsetzen/jmdn. wieder an die Macht bringen; **her success ~d her to her place as leading actress** der Erfolg hat sie wieder zur führenden Schauspielerin gemacht; **d)** *(re-establish)* wiederherstellen ‹*Ordnung, Ruhe, Vertrauen*›; **e)** *(put back)* ~ **the book to its place [on the shelf]** das Buch wieder an seinen Platz [im Regal] zurückstellen

restorer [rı'stɔ:rə(r)] *n.* **a)** *(Art, Archit.: person)* Restaurator, *der*/Restauratorin, *die;* **b)** *(agent)* ≈ Pflegemittel, *das; see also* **hair-restorer**

restrain [rı'streın] *v. t.* zurückhalten ‹*Gefühl, Lachen, Drang, Person*›; bändigen ‹*unartiges Kind, Tier*›; ~ **sb./oneself from doing sth.** jmdn. davon abhalten/sich zurückhalten, etw. zu tun; ~ **yourself!** beherrsch dich!

restrained [rı'streınd] *adj.* zurückhaltend ‹*Wesen, Kritik*›; verhalten ‹*Blick, Geste, Gefühl*›; beherrscht ‹*Reaktion, Worte*›; unaufdringlich ‹*Stil*›

restraint [rı'streınt] *n.* **a)** *(restriction)* Einschränkung, *die;* **without ~:** ungehindert; **b)** *(reserve)* Zurückhaltung, *die;* **c)** *(moderation)* Unaufdringlichkeit, *die; (self-control)* Selbstbeherrschung, *die;* **with ~:** unaufdringlich; **without ~:** ungehemmt; **his style shows a lack of ~:** er hat einen aufdringlichen Stil

restrict [rı'strıkt] *v. t.* beschränken **(to** auf + *Akk.*); ‹*Kleidung:*› be-, einengen; **the trees ~ed our view** die Bäume nahmen uns die freie Sicht

restricted [rı'strıktıd] *adj.* **a)** *(limited)* beschränkt; begrenzt; ~ **diet** Diät, *die;* **I feel ~ in these clothes** ich fühle mich in dieser Kleidung beengt *od.* eingeengt; **b)** *(subject to restriction)* Sperr‹*gebiet*›; begrenzt ‹*Zulassung, Aufnahme, Anwendbarkeit*›; **be ~ to 30 m.p.h.** nicht schneller als 30 Meilen in der Stunde fahren dürfen; **be ~ to doing sth.** sich darauf beschränken müssen, etw. zu tun; **be ~ within narrow limits** ‹*Freiheit:*› stark eingeschränkt sein; **c)** *(not for disclosure)* geheim ‹*Dokument, Information*›

restricted 'area *n.* **a)** Sperrgebiet, *das;* **b)** *(Brit.: with speed limit)* Gebiet mit Geschwindigkeitsbeschränkung

restriction [rı'strıkʃn] *n.* Be-, Einschränkung, *die* **(on** *Gen.*); *(of persons)* Einengung, *die;* **without ~:** ohne Einschränkung; uneingeschränkt; **put** *or* **place** *or* **impose ~s on sth.** etw. einschränken *od.* Einschränkungen *(Dat.)* unterwerfen; **speed/weight/price ~:** Geschwindigkeits-/Gewichts-/Preisbeschränkung, *die*

restrictive [rı'strıktıv] *adj.* restriktiv; einschränkend *nicht präd.;* beengend ‹*Kleidung*›

restrictively [rı'strıktıvlı] *adv.* restriktiv; einschränkend

restrictive 'practice *n. (Commerc.)* wettbewerbsbeschränkende Geschäftspraktik

'rest-room *n. (esp. Amer.)* Toilette, *die*

restructure [ri:'strʌktʃə(r)] *v. t.* umstrukturieren

'rest stop *n. (Amer.)* Raststätte, *die*

restyle [ri:'staıl] *v. t.* neu stylen; ~ **sb.'s hair** jmdm. eine neue Frisur machen

result [rı'zʌlt] **1.** *v. i.* **a)** *(follow)* ~ **from sth.** die Folge einer Sache *(Gen.)* sein; von etw. herrühren; *(future)* aus etw. resultieren; **b)** *(end)* ~ **in sth.** in etw. *(Dat.)* resultieren; zu etw. führen; **the game ~ed in a draw** das Spiel endete mit einem Unentschieden; ~ **in sb.'s doing sth.** zur Folge haben, daß jmd. etw. tut. **2.** *n.* Ergebnis, *das;* Resultat, *das;* **be the ~ of sth.** die Folge einer Sache *(Gen.)* sein; **as a ~ [of this]** infolgedessen; **he knows how to get ~s** er weiß, wie man Ergebnisse *od.* Erfolg erzielt; **without ~:** ergebnislos; **What was the ~? – Leeds won 3–2** Wie ist es ausgegangen? – Leeds hat 3 : 2 gewonnen; **when you add up the figures, what is the ~?** was kommt heraus, wenn du die Zahlen zusammenzählst?

resultant [rı'zʌltənt] **1.** *adj.* daraus resultierend; sich daraus ergebend. **2.** *n. (Phys.)* Resultante, *die;* Resultierende, *die*

resume [rı'zju:m] **1.** *v. t.* **a)** *(begin again)* wiederaufnehmen; fortsetzen ‹*Reise*›; wieder annehmen ‹*Gewohnheit*›; **b)** *(get back)* wieder-, zurückgewinnen; wieder übernehmen ‹*Kommando*›; ~ **possession of sth.** etw. wieder in Besitz nehmen; *see also* **seat 1b.** **2.** *v. i.* weitermachen; ‹*Parlament:*› die Sitzung fortsetzen; ‹*Unterricht:*› wieder beginnen

résumé ['rezʊmeı] *n.* **a)** *(summary)* Zusammenfassung, *die;* **b)** *(Amer.: curriculum vitae)* Lebenslauf, *der*

resumption [rı'zʌmpʃn] *n.* **a)** *see* **resume 1a:** Wiederaufnahme, *die;* Fortsetzung, *die;* Wiederannahme, *die;* **b)** *see* **resume 1b:** Wieder-, Zurückgewinnung, *die;* Wiederübernahme, *die;* Wiedereinnahme, *die*

resurface [ri:'sɜ:fıs] **1.** *v. t.* ~ **a road** den Belag einer Straße erneuern. **2.** *v. i. (lit. or fig.)* wieder auftauchen

resurgence [rı'sɜ:dʒəns] *n.* Wiederaufleben, *das*

resurgent [rı'sɜ:dʒənt] *adj.* wieder auflebend; wieder erwachend ‹*Leben*›; **be ~:** wieder aufleben

resurrect [rezə'rekt] *v. t.* **a)** *(raise from the dead)* wieder zum Leben erwecken; **b)** *(revive)* wiederbeleben; wieder aufleben lassen ‹*Vorstellungen, Bräuche*›; *(coll.: dig out)* wieder ausgraben ‹*alte Kleider usw.*›

resurrection [rezə'rekʃn] *n.* **a)** *(Relig.)* Auferstehung, *die;* **the R~:** die Auferstehung Christi; **b)** *(revival)* Wiederbelebung, *die;* Wiederaufleben, *das*

resuscitate [rı'sʌsıteıt] *v. t. (lit. or fig.)* wiederbeleben

resuscitation [rısʌsı'teıʃn] *n. (lit. or fig.)* Wiederbelebung, *die*

ret. *abbr.* **retired** a. D.; i. R.

retail 1. ['ri:teıl] *n.* Einzelhandel, *der.* **2.** *adj.* Einzel‹*handel*›; Einzelhandels‹*geschäft, -preis*›; [End]verkaufs‹*preis*›. **3.** *adv.* **buy/sell ~:** en détail kaufen/verkaufen *(Kaufmannsspr.).* **4.** *v. t.* **a)** ['ri:teıl, rı'teıl] *(sell)* [im Einzelhandel] verkaufen; **b)** [rı'teıl] *(relate)* weitererzählen ‹*Klatsch*›; ~ **a conversation to sb.** jmdm. ein Gespräch wiedererzählen. **5.** ['ri:teıl, rı'teıl] *v. i.* im Einzelhandel verkauft werden **(at, for** für)

retailer ['ri:teılə(r), rı'teılə(r)] *n.* Einzelhändler, *der/*-händlerin, *die*

retail 'price index *n. (Brit.)* Preisindex des Einzelhandels

retain [rı'teın] *v. t.* **a)** *(keep)* behalten; sich *(Dat.)* bewahren ‹*Witz, Einfallsreichtum, Fähigkeit*›; ein-, zurückbehalten ‹*Gelder*›; gespeichert lassen ‹*Information*›; ~ **power** ‹*Partei:*› an der Macht bleiben; ~ **possession of sth.** etw. im Besitz behalten; ~ **control [of sth.]** die Kontrolle [über etw. *(Akk.)*] behalten; **b)** *(continue to practise)* festhalten an *(Dat.),* beibehalten ‹*Gewohnheit, Tradition, Brauch*›; **c)** *(keep in place)* ‹*Damm:*› stauen/‹*Deich:*› zurückhalten/‹*Boden:*› speichern/‹*Gefäß:*› halten ‹*Wasser*›; ~ **sth. in position** etw. in der richtigen Position halten; **d)** *(secure services of)* beauftragen ‹*Anwalt*›; **e)** *(not forget)* behalten, sich *(Dat.)* merken ‹*Gedanke, Tatsache*›

retainer [rı'teınə(r)] *n.* **a)** *(Hist.: follower)* Trabant, *der;* **old ~** *(joc.)* altes Faktotum; **b)** *(fee)* Honorarvorschuß, *der*

retaining: ~ fee *n.* Honorarvorschuß, *der;* **~ wall** *n.* Böschungsmauer, *die*

retake 1. [ri:'teık] *v. t., forms as* **take 1, 2: a)** *(recapture)* wieder einnehmen ‹*Stadt, Festung*›; **b)** *(take again)* wiederholen ‹*Prüfung, Strafstoß*›; **c)** *(Cinemat.)* nachdrehen ‹*Szene*›. **2.** ['ri:teık] *n.* **a)** *(of exam)* Wiederholung, *die;* **b)** *(Cinemat.)* Retake, *das;* Neuaufnahme, *die*

retaliate [rı'tælıeıt] *v. i.* Vergeltung üben **(against** an + *Dat.*); sich revanchieren *(ugs.);* ‹*Truppen:*› zurückschlagen; kontern **(against** *Akk.*) ‹*Maßnahme, Kritik*›; ~ **by doing sth.** sich revanchieren, indem man etw. tut

retaliation [rıtælı'eıʃn] *n.* *(in war, fight)* Vergeltung, *die;* Gegenschlag, *der; (in argument etc.)* Konter, *der (ugs.);* Konterschlag, *der;* **in ~ for** als Vergeltung für; **she did that in ~ for his cruelty** sie revanchierte sich damit für seine Grausamkeit

retaliatory [rı'tæljətərı] *adj.* Vergeltungs‹*maßnahme, -angriff*›

retard [rı'tɑ:d] *v. t.* verzögern; retardieren *(bes. Physiol., Psych.)*

retardant [rı'tɑ:dənt] **1.** *adj.* hemmend; **flame-/rust-~:** feuer-/rosthemmend. **2.** *n.* Hemmstoff, *der*

retardation [ri:tɑ:'deıʃn] *n.* Verzögerung, *die;* Retardation, *die (bes. Physiol., Psych.); (braking)* Bremswirkung, *die*

retarded [rı'tɑ:dıd] *adj.* **a)** *(Psychol.)* **[mentally] ~:** [geistig] zurückgeblieben; **b)** *(Motor Veh.)* ~ **ignition** Spätzündung, *die*

retarder [rı'tɑ:də(r)] *n. (Motor Veh.)* Dauerbremse, *die*

retch [retʃ, ri:tʃ] **1.** *v. i.* würgen. **2.** *n.* Würgen, *das*

retd. *abbr.* **retired** a. D.; i. R.

retell [ri:'tel] *v. t.,* **retold** [ri:'təʊld] nacherzählen; *(tell again)* noch einmal erzählen

retention [rı'tenʃn] *n.* **a)** *(keeping) (of power)* Erhaltung, *die; (of money)* Einbehaltung, *die;* **b)** *see* **retain b:** Festhalten, *das* **(of** an + *Dat.*); Beibehaltung, *die;* **c)** ~ **of water** *(by soil, plant)* Speicherung von Wasser; **d)** *see* **retain d:** Beauftragung, *die;* **e)** *(Med.)* Retention, *die; (of urine)* Verhaltung, *die;* **f) powers of ~:** Merkfähigkeit, *die*

retentive [rı'tentıv] *adj.* **a)** gut ‹*Gedächtnis*›; **a memory ~ of details** ein gutes Gedächtnis für Details; **b)** *(holding moisture)* Feuchtigkeit speichernd *nicht präd.* ‹*Boden*›; **soil ~ of moisture** Boden, der Feuchtigkeit speichert

rethink [ri:ˈθɪŋk] **1.** *v.t.*, **rethought** [ri:ˈθɔ:t] noch einmal überdenken. **2.** *n.* **have a ~ about sth.** etw. noch einmal überdenken

reticence [ˈretɪsəns] *n., no pl.* Zurückhaltung, *die* (**on** in bezug auf + *Akk.*)

reticent [ˈretɪsənt] *adj.* **a)** *(reserved)* zurückhaltend (**on, about** in bezug auf + *Akk.*); **b)** *(restrained)* schlicht ⟨*Stil*⟩

retina [ˈretɪnə] *n., pl.* **~s** *or* **~e** [ˈretɪni:] *(Anat.)* Retina, *die (fachspr.)*; Netzhaut, *die*

retinitis [retɪˈnaɪtɪs] *n. (Med.)* Netzhautentzündung, *die;* Retinitis, *die (fachspr.)*

retinue [ˈretɪnju:] *n.* Gefolge, *das*

retiracy [rɪˈtaɪərəsɪ] *n., no pl. (Amer.)* Abgeschiedenheit, *die*

retiral [rɪˈtaɪərl] *n. (Scot.)* Rücktritt, *der* (**from** von); Ausscheiden, *das* (**from** aus)

retire [rɪˈtaɪə(r)] **1.** *v.i.* **a)** *(give up work or position)* ausscheiden (**from** aus); aufhören [zu arbeiten]; ⟨*Angestellter, Arbeiter:*⟩ in Rente *(Akk.)* gehen; ⟨*Beamter, Militär:*⟩ in Pension *od.* den Ruhestand gehen; ⟨*Selbständiger:*⟩ sich zur Ruhe setzen; **~ on a pension** ⟨*Angestellter, Arbeiter:*⟩ auf *od.* in Rente *(Akk.)* gehen; ⟨*Beamter, Militär:*⟩ in Pension *(Akk.)* gehen; **b)** *(withdraw)* sich zurückziehen (**to** in + *Akk.*); *(Sport)* aufgeben; **~ [to bed]** sich [zum Schlafen] zurückziehen; **~ from the world/into oneself** sich von der Welt/in sich *(Akk.)* selbst zurückziehen. **2.** *v.t. (compel to leave)* aus Altersgründen entlassen; pensionieren, in den Ruhestand versetzen ⟨*Beamten, Militär*⟩; **be ~d early** in den vorzeitigen Ruhestand versetzt werden

retired [rɪˈtaɪəd] *adj.* **a)** *(no longer working)* aus dem Berufsleben ausgeschieden ⟨*Angestellter, Arbeiter, Selbständiger*⟩; ⟨*Beamter, Soldat:*⟩ im Ruhestand, pensioniert; **be ~:** nicht mehr arbeiten; ⟨*Angestellter, Arbeiter:*⟩ Rentner/Rentnerin *od.* in Rente *(Akk.)* sein; ⟨*Beamter, Soldat:*⟩ im Ruhestand *od.* pensioniert sein; **b)** *(withdrawn)* zurückgezogen ⟨*Leben*⟩

retired list *n. (Mil.)* Liste der aus dem aktiven Dienst Ausgeschiedenen

retiree [rɪtaɪəˈri:] *n. (Amer.)* Ruheständler, *der*/-ständlerin, *die;* *(ex-employee also)* Rentner, *der*/Rentnerin, *die;* *(ex-civil servant/serviceman also)* Pensionär, *der*/Pensionärin, *die*

retirement [rɪˈtaɪəmənt] *n.* **a)** *(leaving work)* Ausscheiden aus dem Arbeitsleben; **b)** *no art. (period)* Ruhestand, *der;* **go into ~** ⟨*Selbständiger:*⟩ sich zur Ruhe setzen; ⟨*Angestellter, Arbeiter:*⟩ in Rente *(Akk.)* gehen; ⟨*Beamter, Militär:*⟩ in Pension *od.* den Ruhestand gehen; **take early ~:** ⟨*Selbständiger:*⟩ sich vorzeitig zur Ruhe setzen; ⟨*Angestellter, Arbeiter:*⟩ vorzeitig in Rente *(Akk.)* gehen; ⟨*Beamter, Militär:*⟩ sich vorzeitig pensionieren lassen; **how will you spend your ~?** was machen Sie, wenn Sie einmal nicht mehr arbeiten/in Rente/im Ruhestand sind?; **c)** *(withdrawing)* Rückzug, *der* (**to, into** in + *Akk.*); **d)** *(seclusion)* Zurückgezogenheit, *die;* **live in ~:** zurückgezogen leben

retirement: **~ age** *n.* Altersgrenze, *die; (of employees also)* Rentenalter, *das; (of civil servants, servicemen also)* Pensionsalter, *das;* **~ pay, ~ pension** *ns. (for employees)* [Alters]rente, *die; (for civil servants, servicemen)* Pension, *die*

retiring [rɪˈtaɪərɪŋ] *adj. (shy)* zurückhaltend

retiring: **~ age** *see* **retirement age**; **~ collection** *n. (at church service)* Kollekte, *die; (at concert)* Spendensammlung, *die*

retold *see* **retell**

retook *see* **retake 1**

retool [ri:ˈtu:l] *v.t.* umrüsten (**for** auf + *Akk.*)

¹retort [rɪˈtɔ:t] **1.** *n.* Entgegnung, *die,* Erwiderung, *die* (**to** auf + *Akk.*). **2.** *v.t.* entgegnen. **3.** *v.i.* scharf antworten

²retort *n. (Chem., Industry)* Retorte, *die*

retouch [ri:ˈtʌtʃ] *v.t. (Art, Photog., Printing)* retuschieren

retrace [rɪˈtreɪs] *v.t.* **a)** *(trace back)* zurückverfolgen; **b)** *(trace again)* nachvollziehen ⟨*Entwicklung*⟩; **c)** *(go back over)* zurückgehen; **~ one's steps/path** denselben Weg noch einmal zurückgehen

retract [rɪˈtrækt] **1.** *v.t.* **a)** *(withdraw)* zurücknehmen; *abs.* **he refused to ~:** er weigerte sich, es zurückzunehmen; **b)** *(Aeronaut.)* einziehen, einfahren ⟨*Fahrgestell*⟩; **c)** *(draw back)* zurückziehen; einziehen ⟨*Fühler, Krallen*⟩. **2.** *v.i.* **a)** *(Aeronaut.)* ⟨*Fahrgestell:*⟩ einziehbar *od.* einfahrbar sein; **b)** *(be drawn back)* ⟨*Fühler, Krallen:*⟩ eingezogen werden

retractable [rɪˈtræktəbl] *adj. (Aeronaut.)* einziehbar, einfahrbar ⟨*Fahrgestell*⟩

retraction [rɪˈtrækʃn] *n.* **a)** *(withdrawing)* Zurücknahme, *die;* **make a ~ of sth.** etw. zurücknehmen; **b)** *(drawing-back of undercarriage, claws, etc.)* Einziehen, *das*

retrain [ri:ˈtreɪn] **1.** *v.i.* [sich] umschulen [lassen]. **2.** *v.t.* umschulen ⟨*Person*⟩

retraining [ri:ˈtreɪnɪŋ] *n.* Umschulung, *die; attrib.* Umschulungs⟨*programm*⟩

retranslate [ri:trænsˈleɪt] *v.t.* [zu]rückübersetzen

retranslation [ri:trænsˈleɪʃn] *n.* Rückübersetzung, *die*

retransmit [ri:trænsˈmɪt] *v.t.,* **-tt-** **a)** *(transmit again)* noch einmal übermitteln ⟨*Nachricht*⟩; noch einmal senden ⟨*Signal*⟩; **b)** *(transmit further)* weiterübermitteln ⟨*Nachricht*⟩; weitersenden ⟨*Signal*⟩

retread *(Motor Veh.)* **1.** [ˈri:tred] *n.* runderneuerter Reifen. **2.** [ri:ˈtred] *v.t.* runderneuern ⟨*Reifen*⟩

retreat [rɪˈtri:t] **1.** *n.* **a)** *(withdrawal; also Mil. or fig.)* Rückzug, *der;* **their ~ from the territory/position** ihr Rückzug aus dem Gebiet/von der Stellung; **beat a ~:** den Rückzug antreten; *(fig.)* das Feld räumen; **make good one's ~:** sich in Sicherheit *(Akk.)* bringen; *(fig.)* sich aus dem Staub machen *(ugs.); see also* **hasty**; **b)** *(place of seclusion)* Zuflucht, *die;* Zufluchtsort, *der; (hiding-place also)* Unterschlupf, *der;* **country ~:** Refugium auf dem Lande; **c)** *(Relig.: for prayer)* Exerzitien *Pl.;* **d)** *(Mil.: bugle-call) (for return to barracks)* Zapfenstreich, *der; (for withdrawal)* **sound/give the ~:** zum Rückzug blasen. **2.** *v.i.* **a)** *(withdraw; also Mil. or fig.)* sich zurückziehen; *(in fear)* zurückweichen; **~ within oneself** sich in sich *(Akk.)* selbst zurückziehen; **~ from a territory/position** sich aus einem Gebiet/von einer Stellung zurückziehen; **~ from an aggressive stance** eine aggressive Haltung aufgeben; **b)** *(recede)* ⟨*Überschwemmung, Gletscher usw.:*⟩ zurückgehen

retrench [rɪˈtrenʃ] **1.** *v.t.* senken ⟨*Ausgaben, Lohn*⟩. **2.** *v.i.* sich einschränken

retrenchment [rɪˈtrenʃmənt] *n.* Senkung, *die;* **policy of ~:** Sparpolitik, *die*

retrial [ri:ˈtraɪəl] *n. (Law)* Wiederaufnahmeverfahren, *das;* **he asked for a ~:** er verlangte eine Wiederaufnahme des Verfahrens

retribution [retrɪˈbju:ʃn] *n.* Vergeltung, *die;* **in ~ for** zur Vergeltung für

retributive [rɪˈtrɪbjʊtɪv] *adj.* vergeltend; ausgleichend ⟨*Gerechtigkeit*⟩

retrievable [rɪˈtri:vəbl] *adj.* **a)** *(able to be set right)* noch nicht ausweglos *od.* völlig verfahren ⟨*Situation*⟩; wiedergutzumachend *nicht präd.* ⟨*Fehler*⟩; **be ~** ⟨*Situation:*⟩ zu retten sein; ⟨*Fehler:*⟩ wiedergutzumachen sein; **b)** *(able to be rescued)* zu rettend/*(from wreckage)* zu bergend *nicht präd.*; **be ~:** zu retten/bergen sein; **c)** *(able to be recovered)* **the ball/money is ~:** den Ball/das Geld kann man wiederholen/-bekommen; **d)** *(Computing)* wiederauffindbar ⟨*Information*⟩

retrieval [rɪˈtri:vl] *n.* **a)** *(setting right) (of situation)* Rettung, *die; (of mistake)* Wiedergutmachung, *die;* **beyond** *or* **past ~:** hoffnungslos; **b)** *(rescue)* Rettung, *die; (from wreckage)* Bergung, *die* (**from** aus); **c)** *(recovery) see* **retrieve 1c**: Zurückholen, *das;* Wiederholen, *das;* Wiedergewinnung, *die;* **the ~ of the money was difficult** es war schwierig, das Geld wiederzubekommen; **the money/chance was lost beyond ~:** das Geld/die Gelegenheit war unwiederbringlich verloren; **d)** *(Computing)* Wiederauffinden, *das*

retrieve [rɪˈtri:v] *v.t.* **a)** *(set right)* wiedergutmachen ⟨*Fehler*⟩; retten ⟨*Situation*⟩; **b)** *(rescue)* retten (**from** aus); *(from wreckage)* bergen (**from** aus); **timber ~d from the beach** als Strandgut aufgelesenes Holz; **c)** *(recover)* zurückholen ⟨*Brief*⟩; wiederholen ⟨*Ball*⟩; wiedergewinnen ⟨*Ansehen, Würde*⟩; wiederbekommen ⟨*Geld*⟩; **~ sth. from the depths of one's subconscious** etw. aus den Tiefen seines Unterbewußtseins hervorholen; **d)** *(Computing)* wiederauffinden ⟨*Information*⟩; **e)** *(fetch)* ⟨*Hund:*⟩ apportieren

retriever [rɪˈtri:və(r)] *n.* Apportierhund, *der; (breed)* Retriever, *der*

retroactive [retrəʊˈæktɪv] *adj.* rückwirkend; **~ effect** Rückwirkung, *die*

retrochoir [ˈretrəʊkwaɪə(r)] *n. (Eccl. Archit.)* Retrochor, *der*

retrograde [ˈretrəgreɪd] *adj.* **a)** *(retreating)* **~ motion** Rückwärtsbewegung, *die;* **~ step** *(fig.)* Rückschritt, *der;* **b)** *(reverting to the past)* rückschrittlich ⟨*Idee, Politik, Maßnahme*⟩; **c)** *(inverse)* umgekehrt ⟨*Reihenfolge*⟩

retrogress [retrəˈgres] *v.i.* **a)** sich zurückbewegen; **b)** *(fig.: deteriorate)* ⟨*Gesundheitszustand:*⟩ sich verschlechtern

retrogression [retrəˈgreʃn] *n.* **a)** Rückwärtsbewegung, *die;* **b)** *(Biol.)* Rückentwicklung, *die*

retrogressive [retrəˈgresɪv] *adj.* **a)** *see* **retrograde a, b**; **b)** *(Biol.)* rückläufig ⟨*Entwicklung*⟩

retro-rocket [ˈretrəʊrɒkɪt] *n. (Astronaut.)* Bremsrakete, *die*

retrospect [ˈretrəspekt] *n.* **in ~:** im nachhinein; **in ~, I think ...:** rückblickend *od.* im nachhinein glaube ich, ...

retrospection [retrəˈspekʃn] *n.* Rückschau, *die*

retrospective [retrəˈspektɪv] **1.** *adj.* **a)** retrospektiv *(geh.)*; **~ exhibition** Retrospektive, *die (geh.)*; **take a ~ look at sth.** Rückschau auf etw. *(Akk.)* halten *(geh.)*; **b)** *(applying to the past)* rückwirkend ⟨*Lohnerhöhung, Gesetz, Vertragsänderung*⟩; **be ~:** Rückwirkung haben. **2.** *n. (Art)* Retrospektive, *die (geh.)*

retrospectively [retrəˈspektɪvlɪ] *adv.* **a)** *(by retrospection)* im nachhinein, rückblickend ⟨*betrachten*⟩; **b)** *(so as to apply to the past)* rückwirkend; **a law operating ~:** ein rückwirkendes Gesetz; ein Gesetz mit Rückwirkung

retroussé [rəˈtru:seɪ] *adj.* **~ nose** Stupsnase, *die*

retry [ri:ˈtraɪ] *v.t. (Law)* neu verhandeln ⟨*Fall*⟩; neu verhandeln gegen ⟨*Person*⟩

retsina [reˈtsi:nə] *n.* Retsina, *der*

retune [ri:ˈtju:n] *v.t.* **a)** neu stimmen ⟨*Musikinstrument*⟩; **b)** neu einstellen ⟨*Radio*⟩

returf [ri:ˈtɜ:f] *v.t.* neuen Rasen verlegen auf (+ *Dat.*) ⟨*Platz, Spielfeld usw.*⟩

return [rɪˈtɜ:n] **1.** *v.i.* **a)** *(come back)* zurückkommen; zurückkehren *(geh.)*; ⟨*Jahreszeit:*⟩ wiederkehren; *(go back)* zurückgehen; zurückkehren *(geh.)*; *(go back by vehicle)* zurückfahren; zurückkehren *(geh.)*; **~ home** wieder nach Hause kommen/gehen/fahren/zurückkehren; **~ to work** *(after holiday or strike)* die Arbeit wieder aufnehmen; **she had gone never to ~:** sie war für immer gegangen; ~ **to health** wieder gesund werden; **his good spirits quickly ~ed** seine gute Laune stellte sich rasch wieder ein; **b)** *(revert)* ~ **to a subject/one's old habits** auf ein Thema zurückkommen/in seine alten Gewohnheiten zurückfallen; **unto dust thou shalt ~** *(Relig.)* zu Staub sollst du wieder werden. **2.** *v. t.* **a)** *(bring back)* zurückbringen; zurückgeben ‹*geliehenen/gestohlenen Gegenstand, gekaufte Ware*›; [wieder] zurückschicken ‹*unzustellbaren Brief*›; *(to original position)* zurückstellen ‹*Hebel*›; *(hand back, refuse)* zurückweisen ‹*Scheck*›; *(put back) (vertically)* [wieder] zurückstellen ‹*Buch, Ordner*›; *(horizontally)* [wieder] zurücklegen ‹*Geld, Buch, Ordner*›; *(to file)* wieder einheften ‹*Brief*›; **~ed with thanks** mit Dank zurück; **'~ to sender'** *(on letter)* „zurück an Absender"; **he ~ed his purse to his pocket** er steckte sein Portemonnaie wieder ein; **he ~ed the fish to the water** er setzte den Fisch wieder ins Wasser; **b)** *(restore)* ~ **sth. to its original state** *or* **condition** etw. wieder in seinen ursprünglichen Zustand versetzen; **c)** *(yield)* abwerfen ‹*Gewinn*›; **d)** *(give back sth. similar)* erwidern ‹*Besuch, Gruß, Liebe, Gewehrfeuer*›; sich revanchieren für *(ugs.)* ‹*Freundlichkeit, Gefallen*›; zurückgeben ‹*Schlag*›; **e)** *(elect)* wählen ‹*Kandidaten*›; ~ **sb. to Parliament** jmdn. ins Parlament wählen; **f)** *(Sport)* zurückschlagen ‹*Ball*›; *(throw back)* zurückwerfen; **g)** *(answer)* erwidern; entgegnen; **h)** *(declare)* ~ **a verdict of guilty/not guilty** ‹*Geschworene:*› auf „schuldig"/„nicht schuldig" erkennen; ~ **sb. guilty** jmdn. schuldig sprechen. **3.** *n.* **a)** *(coming back)* Rückkehr, *die; (to home)* Heimkehr, *die; (of illness)* Wiederauftreten, *das;* **his ~ to work/school had to be delayed** er mußte die Wiederaufnahme seiner *od.* der Arbeit verschieben/er konnte erst später [als vorgesehen] wieder zur Schule gehen; **point of no ~** *see* **point 1 k**; ~ **to health** Genesung, *die (geh.);* **many happy ~s [of the day]!** herzlichen Glückwunsch [zum Geburtstag]!; **wish sb. many happy ~s [of the day]** jmdm. [zum Geburtstag] alles Gute wünschen; **b) by ~ [of post]** postwendend; **c)** *(ticket)* Rückfahrkarte, *die; (for flight)* Rückflugschein, *der;* **single or ~?** einfach oder hin und zurück?; **d)** *(proceeds)* **~[s]** Ertrag, Gewinn, *der* **(on, from** aus); ~ **on capital** Kapitalgewinn, *der; see also* **diminishing; e)** *(bringing back)* Zurückbringen, *das; (of property, goods, book)* Rückgabe, *die* **(to** an + *Akk.*); *(of cheque)* Zurückweisung, *die; (of loan)* Rückzahlung, *die;* **f)** *(giving back of sth. similar)* Erwiderung, *die;* **receive/get sth. in ~ [for sth.]** etw. [für etw.] bekommen; **g)** *(Sport: striking back)* Rückschlag, *der; (throw back)* Rückwurf, *der;* **pick up the ~** *(Footb. etc.)* den zurückgespielten Ball annehmen; **h)** *(report)* Bericht, *der; (set of statistics)* statistischer Bericht; Statistik, *die;* **income-tax ~**: Einkommenssteuererklärung, *die;* **election ~s** Wahlergebnisse; **i)** *(Brit. Parl.: electing)* Wahl, *die;* **j)** *attrib. (Archit.)* Flügel‹*mauer, -wand*›

returnable [rɪ'tɜ:nəbl] *adj.* Mehrweg‹*behälter, -flasche usw.*›; rückzahlbar ‹*Gebühr, Kaution*›; ~ **bottle** Pfandflasche, *die;* ~ **deposit** Pfand, *der*

returned [rɪ'tɜ:nd] *adj.* heimgekehrt; ~ **emigrant** Rückwanderer, *der*

return: ~ **'fare** *n.* Preis für eine Rückfahrkarte/*(for flight)* einen Rückflugschein; **what is the ~ fare?** wieviel kostet eine Rückfahrkarte/ein Rückflugschein?; ~ **'flight** *n.* Rückflug, *der; (both ways)* Hin- und Rückflug, *der;* ~ **'game** *n.* Rückspiel, *das*

re'turning officer *n. (Brit. Parl.)* Wahlleiter, *der/-leiterin, die*

return: ~ **'journey** *n.* Rückreise, *die;* Rückfahrt, *die; (both ways)* Hin- und Rückfahrt, *die;* ~ **'match** *n.* Rückspiel, *das;* ~ **'ticket** *n. (Brit.)* Rückfahrkarte, *die; (for flight)* Rückflugschein, *der*

retype [ri:'taɪp] *v. t.* neu tippen

reunification [ri:ju:nɪfɪ'keɪʃn] *n.* Wiedervereinigung, *die*

reunion [ri:'ju:njən] *n.* **a)** *(gathering)* Treffen, *das;* **b)** *(reuniting)* Wiedersehen, *das;* **c)** *(reunited state)* Wiedervereinigung, *die*

reunite [ri:jʊ'naɪt] **1.** *v. t.* wieder zusammenführen; **a ~d Germany** ein wiedervereinigtes Deutschland. **2.** *v. i.* sich wieder zusammenschließen; ‹*Kirchen:*› sich wieder vereinigen

reusable [ri:'ju:zəbl] *adj.* wiederverwendbar

reuse 1. [ri:'ju:z] *v. t.* wiederverwenden. **2.** [ri:'ju:s] *n.* Wiederverwendung, *die*

Rev. ['revərənd, *(coll.)* rev] *abbr.* **Reverend** Rev.

rev [rev] *(coll.)* **1.** *n., usu. in pl.* Umdrehung, *die;* Tour, *die (Technikjargon);* ~ **counter** *(Brit.)* Tourenzähler, *der (ugs.).* **2.** *v. i.*, **-vv-** mit hoher Drehzahl *od.* hochtourig laufen. **3.** *v. t.*, **-vv-** hochdrehen *(Technikjargon); (noisily)* aufheulen lassen ‹*Motor*›

~ **'up 1.** *v. i.* ‹*Motor:*› hochgejagt werden *(Technikjargon);* **I heard [the sound of] a car ~ving up** ich hörte den Motor eines Autos aufheulen. **2.** *v. t.* hochjagen *(Technikjargon);* aufheulen lassen ‹*Motor[rad]*›

revaluation [ri:væljʊ'eɪʃn] *n.* **a)** *(of object)* Neubewertung, *die;* **b)** *(Econ.: of currency)* Aufwertung, *die*

revalue [ri:'vælju:] *v. t.* **a)** neu bewerten; **b)** *(Econ.)* aufwerten ‹*Währung*›

revamp [ri:'væmp] *(coll.) v. t.* renovieren ‹*Zimmer, Gebäude*›; [wieder] aufmöbeln *od.* aufpolieren ‹*Schrank, Auto usw.*›; neu bearbeiten ‹*Stück, Musical usw.*›; auf Vordermann bringen *(ugs.)* ‹*Firma*›

Revd. ['revərənd, *(coll.)* rev] *abbr.* **Reverend** Rev.

reveal [rɪ'vi:l] **1.** *v. t.* enthüllen *(geh.);* verraten; offenbaren *(geh., Theol.),* [offen] zeigen ‹*Gefühle*›; **be ~ed** ‹*Wahrheit:*› ans Licht kommen; **all will be ~ed** *(joc.)* es kommt alles ans Licht *(scherzh.);* ~ **one's identity** seine Identität preisgeben *(geh.);* ~ **oneself/itself to be** *or* **as being sth.** sich als etw. erweisen; ~ **sb. to be sth.** jmdn. als etw. enthüllen *(geh.);* **the rising curtain ~ed a street scene** der sich hebende Vorhang gab den Blick auf eine Straßenszene frei; **there was not much that the dress did not ~**: das Kleid verhüllte nur wenig. **2.** *n. (Archit.)* Laibung, *die*

revealed religion [rɪvi:ld rɪ'lɪdʒn] *n.* Offenbarungsreligion, *die*

revealing [rɪ'vi:lɪŋ] *adj.* aufschlußreich ‹*Darstellung, Dokument*›; verräterisch ‹*Bemerkung, Versprecher*›; offenherzig *(scherzh.)* ‹*Kleid, Bluse usw.*›; **be ~ about sth.** etwas *od.* einiges über etw. *(Akk.)* verraten

reveille [rɪ'vælɪ, rɪ'velɪ] *n. (Mil.)* Reveille, *die (fachspr. veralt.);* Wecksignal, *das;* **sound [the] ~**: das Wecksignal geben; **~ was at 6 a. m.** Wecken war um sechs Uhr morgens

revel ['revl] **1.** *v. i., (Brit.)* **-ll- a)** *(take delight)* genießen **(in** *Akk.*); ~ **in doing sth.** es [richtig] genießen, etw. zu tun; **b)** *(carouse)* feiern; ~ **the night away,** ~ **till dawn** die Nacht durchfeiern *(ugs.).* **2.** *n. usu pl.* Feiern, *das;* Feierei, *die (ugs.)*

revelation [revə'leɪʃn] *n.* **a)** Enthüllung, *die;* **be a ~**: einem die Augen öffnen; **the dessert/concert was a ~**: das Dessert/Konzert war eine Offenbarung *(scherzh.);* **what a ~!** unglaublich!; **be a ~ to sb.** jmdm. die Augen öffnen; **b)** *(Relig.)* Offenbarung, *die;* **[the** *or* **the Book of] R~[s]** die Offenbarung [des Johannes]; **R~[s] 3:14** Offenbarung 3,14

reveller ['revələ(r)] *n.* Feiernde, *der/die*

revelry ['revəlrɪ] *n.* Feiern, *das;* Feierei, *die (ugs.);* **spend the whole night in ~**: die ganze Nacht durchfeiern *(ugs.);* **hear sounds of ~**: hören, wie gefeiert wird

revenge [rɪ'vendʒ] **1.** *v. t.* rächen ‹*Person, Tat*›; sich rächen für ‹*Tat*›; ~ **oneself** *or* **be ~d [on sb.] [for sth.]** sich [für etw.] [an jmdm.] rächen. **2.** *n.* **a)** *(action)* Rache, *die;* **[desire for] ~**: Rachsucht, *die (geh.);* **take ~** *or* **have** *or (literary)* **exact one's ~ [on sb.] [for sth.]** Rache [an jmdm.] [für etw.] nehmen *od. (geh.)* üben; **~ is sweet** Rache ist süß; **in ~ for sth.** als Rache für etw.; **b)** *(Sport, Games)* Revanche, *die;* **give sb. his ~**: jmdm. Revanche geben

revengeful [rɪ'vendʒfl] *adj.* rachsüchtig *(geh.);* ~ **act** Racheakt, *der*

revenue ['revənju:] *n.* **a)** *(State's income)* **[national/state] ~**: Staatseinnahmen; öffentliche Einnahmen; **b) ~[s]** *(income)* Einnahmen; Einkünfte *Pl.;* **source of ~**: Einnahmequelle, *die;* **c) R~** *(department) oberste Finanzbehörde*

revenue: ~ **officer** *n.* ≈ Zollbeamter, *der/-beamtin, die;* ~ **stamp** *n.* Steuerzeichen, *das; (paper strip on cigarette-packet etc.);* [Steuer]banderole, *die*

reverberate [rɪ'vɜ:bəreɪt] **1.** *v. i.* ‹*Geräusch, Musik:*› widerhallen. **2.** *v. t.* zurückwerfen; reflektieren

reverberation [rɪvɜ:bə'reɪʃn] *n.* **~[s]** Widerhall, *der;* ~ **of sound** Schallreflexion, *die;* **the ~s of that episode** *(fig.)* der Nachhall dieser Begebenheit

revere [rɪ'vɪə(r)] *v. t.* verehren

reverence ['revərəns] *n.* **a)** *(revering)* Verehrung, *die;* Ehrfurcht, *die;* **hold sb. in** *or* **regard sb. with ~**: jmdn. verehren; **hold sth. in ~**: etw. heilig halten; **pay ~ to sb.** jmdm. Verehrung entgegenbringen; **have/show ~ for sth./sb.** vor etw./jmdm. Ehrfurcht haben/zeigen; **b) Your/His R~** *(arch./Ir./joc.)* Euer/Seine Hochwürden

reverend ['revərənd] **1.** *adj.* ehrwürdig; **the R~ John Wilson, the R~ Mr Wilson** Hochwürden [John] Wilson; **the Very/Right R~ Donald Todd** Hochwürden [Donald] Todd; **the Most R~ Archbishop of York** Seine Exzellenz der Hochwürdigste Erzbischof von York; **the R~ Father [O'Higgins]** Hochwürden [O'Higgins]; **the ~ gentleman** Hochwürden; **R~ Mother** Ehrwürdige Schwester Oberin *od.* Frau Oberin. **2.** *n. (coll.)* Pfarrer, *der; (form of address)* Hochwürden

reverent ['revərənt] *adj.* ehrfürchtig; **have a ~ attitude to sb., be ~ towards sb.** Ehrfurcht vor jmdm. haben; **in hushed and ~ tones** mit ehrfurchtsvoll gedämpfter Stimme

reverential [revə'renʃl] *adj.* ehrfürchtig

reverently ['revərəntlɪ] *adv.* ehrfürchtig; ehrerbietig ‹*sich verneigen*›

reverie ['revərɪ] *n.* Träumerei, *die;* **be deep** *or* **lost** *or* **sunk in [a] ~**: in Träumereien *(Akk.)* versunken sein; **fall into a ~**: in Träumereien *(Akk.)* versinken

reversal [rɪ'vɜ:sl] *n.* **a)** Umkehrung, *die;* ~ **[colour] film** Umkehrfilm, *der;* **b)** *(Law)* Aufhebung, *die*

reverse [rɪ'vɜ:s] **1.** *adj.* entgegengesetzt ‹*Richtung*›; Rück‹*seite*›; umgekehrt ‹*Reihenfolge*›; **the ~ side of the coin** *(fig.)* die Kehrseite der Medaille. **2.** *n.* **a)** *(contrary)* Gegenteil, *das;* **quite the ~!** ganz im Gegenteil!; **in ~**: rückwärts ‹*schreiben, drucken*›; **b)** *(Motor Veh.)* Rückwärtsgang, *der;* **in ~**: im Rückwärtsgang; **put the car into ~, go into ~**: den Rückwärtsgang einlegen; **c)** *(defeat)* Rückschlag, *der;* **~s of fortune** Schicksalsschläge *Pl.;* **d)** *(back side of coin etc.)* Rückseite, *die;* Revers, *der (Münzk.); (design)* Rückseitenbild, *das;* **e)** *(back of page)* Rückseite, *die;* Verso, *das (Buchw.).* **3.** *v. t.* **a)** *(turn around)* umkehren ‹*Reihenfolge, Wortstellung, Bewegung, Rich-*

tung〉; grundlegend revidieren 〈*Politik*〉; ~ **the charge[s]** *(Brit.)* ein R-Gespräch anmelden; **make a ~d-charge call** *(Brit.)* ein R-Gespräch führen; ~ **arms** *(Mil.)* die Gewehre mit dem Kolben nach oben halten; **b)** *(cause to move backwards)* zurücksetzen; ~ **a car into sth.** ein Auto rückwärts in etw. *(Akk.)* fahren; **c)** *(revoke)* aufheben 〈*Urteil, Anordnung*〉; kassieren *(Rechtsspr.)* 〈*Urteil*〉; rückgängig machen 〈*Maßnahme*〉. **4.** *v. i.* zurücksetzen; rückwärts fahren; ~ **into sth.** rückwärts in etw. *(Akk.)* fahren

reverse 'gear *n. (Motor Veh.)* Rückwärtsgang, *der; see also* **gear 1 a**

reversible [rɪ'vɜ:sɪbl] *adj.* **a)** umkehrbar, *(fachspr.)* reversibel 〈*Vorgang*〉; *(capable of being revoked)* aufhebbar 〈*Entscheidung, Anordnung*〉; **b)** *(having two usable sides)* beidseitig verwendbar, *(Textilw.)* beidrecht 〈*Stoff*〉; beidseitig tragbar 〈*Kleidungsstück*〉; Wende〈*mantel, -jacke*〉

re'versing light *n.* Rückfahrscheinwerfer, *der*

reversion [rɪ'vɜ:ʃn] *n.* **a)** *(return)* Rückkehr, *die* **(to** zu); ~ **to type** *(Biol.)* Rückschlag auf eine frühere Ahnenform; *(fig.)* atavistischer Rückfall; **b)** *(Law: return of estate)* Rückfall, *der;* Heimfall, *der (Rechtsspr.)*

revert [rɪ'vɜ:t] *v. i.* **a)** *(recur, return)* zurückkommen **(to** auf + *Akk.*), wieder aufgreifen **(to** *Akk.*) 〈*Thema, Angelegenheit, Frage*〉; 〈*Gedanken:*〉 zurückkehren *(geh.)* **(to** zu); **to ~ to ...:** um wieder auf ... *(Akk.)* zurückzukommen; **she has ~ed to using her maiden name** sie hat wieder ihren Mädchennamen angenommen; ~ **to type** *(Biol.)* auf eine frühere Ahnenform zurückschlagen; **he has ~ed to type** *(fig.)* er geht jetzt wieder seinen alten Gewohnheiten nach; ~ **to its natural state** in den Naturzustand zurückkehren; ~ **to savagery** 〈*Menschen:*〉 in den Zustand der Wildheit zurückfallen; ~ **to desert** *etc.* 〈*Land:*〉 wieder verwüsten *usw.*; **b)** *(Law)* 〈*Eigentum:*〉 zurückfallen, *(Rechtsspr.)* heimfallen **(to** an + *Akk.*)

revetment [rɪ'vetmənt] *n.* Futtermauer, *die (Archit.)*

review [rɪ'vju:] **1.** *n.* **a)** *(survey)* Übersicht, *die* **(of** über + *Akk.*); Überblick, *der* **(of** über + *Akk.*); *(of past events)* Rückschau, *die* **(of** auf + *Akk.*); **be a ~ of sth.** einen Überblick *od.* eine Übersicht über etw. *(Akk.)* geben; **b)** *(re-examination)* [nochmalige] Überprüfung; nochmalige Prüfung; *(of salary)* Revision, *die;* **be under** ~ 〈*Vereinbarung, Lage:*〉 nochmals geprüft werden; **c)** *(account)* Besprechung, *die;* Kritik, *die;* Rezension, *die;* ~ **copy** *(Publishing)* Rezensionsexemplar, *das;* **d)** *(periodical)* Zeitschrift, *die;* **e)** *(Mil.)* Inspektion, *die;* *(march)* Parade, *die;* **naval ~:** Flottenparade, *die;* **pass in ~:** [vorbei]defilieren; **pass sth. in ~** *(fig.)* etw. Revue passieren lassen. **2.** *v. t.* **a)** *(survey)* untersuchen; prüfen; **b)** *(re-examine)* überprüfen; **c)** *(Mil.)* inspizieren; mustern; **d)** *(write a criticism of)* besprechen; rezensieren; **e)** *(Law)* überprüfen

reviewer [rɪ'vju:ə(r)] *n.* Rezensent, *der*/Rezensentin, *die;* Kritiker, *der*/Kritikerin, *die*

revile [rɪ'vaɪl] *v. t.* schmähen *(geh.)*

revise [rɪ'vaɪz] **1.** *v. t.* **a)** *(amend)* revidieren 〈*Urteil, Gesetz, Vorschlag*〉; **R~d Version** *(Brit.) revidierte Fassung der „Authorized Version" der Bibel (im 19. Jh.)*; **b)** *(check over)* durchsehen 〈*Manuskript, Text, Notizen*〉; **c)** *(reread)* noch einmal durchlesen 〈*Notizen*〉; *abs.* lernen; ~ **one's maths** Mathe *(ugs.)* wiederholen. **2.** *n. (Printing)* Revisionsbogen, *der*

reviser [rɪ'vaɪzə(r)] *n.* Bearbeiter, *der*/Bearbeiterin, *die;* *(of printer's proof)* Korrektor, *der*/Korrektorin, *die*

revision [rɪ'vɪʒn] *n.* **a)** *(amending)* Revision, *die;* **in need of ~:** revisionsbedürftig; **b)** *(checking over)* Durchsicht, *die;* **c)** *(amended version)* [Neu]bearbeitung, *die;* überarbeitete *od.* revidierte Fassung; **d)** *(rereading)* Wiederholung, *die;* ~ **exercises** Wiederholungsübungen

revisionism ['rɪ'vɪʒənɪzm] *n.* Revisionismus, *der*

revisionist [rɪ'vɪʒənɪst] **1.** *n.* Revisionist, *der*/Revisionistin, *die.* **2.** *adj.* revisionistisch

revisit [ri:'vɪzɪt] *v. t.* wieder besuchen

revitalize (revitalise) [ri:'vaɪtəlaɪz] *v. t.* neu beleben

revival [rɪ'vaɪvl] *n.* **a)** *(making active again, bringing back into use)* Wieder- *od.* Neubelebung, *die;* ~ **of learning/letters** neue geistige/literarische Blüte; **b)** *(Theatre)* Wiederaufführung, *die;* Revival, *das;* **c)** *(Relig.: awakening)* Erweckung, *die;* ~ **meeting** Erweckungsversammlung, *die;* **d)** *(restoration)* Wiederherstellung, *die;* Regenerierung, *die (geh.)*; *(to consciousness or life; also fig.)* Wiederbelebung, *die*

revivalism [rɪ'vaɪvəlɪzm] *n.* Erweckungsglaube, *der;* Revivalism, *der*

revivalist [rɪ'vaɪvəlɪst] *n.* Erwecker, *der*/Erweckerin, *die;* *(evangelist)* Erweckungsprediger, *der*

revive [rɪ'vaɪv] **1.** *v. i.* **a)** *(come back to consciousness)* wieder zu sich kommen; **b)** *(be reinvigorated)* wieder aufleben; zu neuem Leben erwachen; 〈*Geschäft:*〉 sich wieder beleben; **his spirits/hopes ~d** er lebte wieder auf/schöpfte neue Hoffnung. **2.** *v. t.* **a)** *(restore to consciousness)* wiederbeleben; **b)** *(restore to healthy state)* wieder auf die Beine bringen 〈*Person*〉; wieder aufleben lassen 〈*Blume*〉; *(strengthen, reawaken)* wieder wecken 〈*Lebensgeister, Ehrgeiz, Interesse, Wunsch*〉; ~ **sb.'s hopes** jmdn. neue Hoffnung schöpfen lassen; **c)** *(make active again, bring back into use)* wieder aufleben lassen; **the mini-skirt was ~d** der Minirock kam wieder in Mode *(Akk.)*; **d)** *(Theatre)* wieder auf die Bühne bringen; **e)** *(renew memory of)* wieder lebendig werden lassen

revocable ['revəkəbl] *adj.* widerrufbar

revocation [revə'keɪʃn] *n. see* **revoke 1:** Aufhebung, *die;* Widerrufung, *die;* Zurückziehen, *das;* Zurücknahme, *die*

revoke [rɪ'vəʊk] **1.** *v. t.* **a)** *(cancel)* aufheben 〈*Erlaß, Privileg, Entscheidung*〉; widerrufen 〈*Befehl*〉; zurückziehen 〈*Auftrag*〉; **b)** *(withdraw)* widerrufen 〈*Erlaubnis, Genehmigung*〉; zurücknehmen 〈*Versprechen*〉. **2.** *v. i.* *(Cards)* [unzulässigerweise] nicht bedienen. **3.** *n. (Cards)* Revoke, *die*

revolt [rɪ'vəʊlt] **1.** *v. i.* **a)** *(rebel)* revoltieren, aufbegehren *(geh.)* **(against** gegen); **b)** *(feel revulsion)* sich sträuben **(at, against, from** gegen); 〈*Magen:*〉 revoltieren, rebellieren **(from** bei). **2.** *v. t.* mit Abscheu erfüllen; **she was ~ed by their brutality** ihre Brutalität erfüllte sie mit Abscheu. **3.** *n. (rebelling)* Aufruhr, *der;* Rebellion, *die;* *(rising)* Revolte, *die (auch fig.)*; Aufstand, *der;* **a spirit of ~:** eine rebellische Stimmung; **be** *or* **rise in ~:** revoltieren; aufbegehren *(geh.)*

revolting [rɪ'vəʊltɪŋ] *adj.* *(repulsive)* abscheulich; scheußlich 〈*Gedanke, Wetter*〉; widerlich 〈*Person*〉; **be ~ to sb.'s sense of decency** jmds. Anstandsgefühl verletzen

revoltingly [rɪ'vəʊltɪŋlɪ] *adv.* abstoßend 〈*häßlich, grausam*〉

revolution [revə'lu:ʃn] *n.* **a)** *(lit. or fig.)* Revolution, *die;* **the American R~:** die Amerikanische Revolution; der Nordamerikanische Unabhängigkeitskrieg; **b)** *(single turn)* Umdrehung, *die;* **number of ~s** Drehzahl, *die;* **c)** *(Astron.: movement in orbit)* Umlauf, *der*

revolutionary [revə'lu:ʃənərɪ] **1.** *adj.* **a)** *(Polit.)* revolutionär; **b)** *(involving great changes)* revolutionär; umwälzend; *(pioneering)* bahnbrechend; **c) R~** *(Amer. Hist.)* des Nordamerikanischen Unabhängigkeitskrieges *nachgestellt;* der Amerikanischen Revolution *nachgestellt.* **2.** *n.* Revolutionär, *der*/Revolutionärin, *die*

revo'lution counter *n.* Drehzahlmesser, *der*

revolutionize (revolutionise) [revə'lu:ʃənaɪz] *v. t.* grundlegend verändern; revolutionieren 〈*Gesellschaft, Technik*〉

revolve [rɪ'vɒlv] **1.** *v. t.* **a)** *(turn round)* drehen; **b) ~ sth. in one's mind** *(ponder)* etw. erwägen. **2.** *v. i.* sich drehen **(round, about, on** um); **everything ~s around her** sie ist der Mittelpunkt[, um den sich alles dreht]

revolver [rɪ'vɒlvə(r)] *n.* [Trommel]revolver, *der*

revolving [rɪ'vɒlvɪŋ] *attrib. adj.* drehbar; Dreh〈*stuhl, -tür, -bühne*〉; ~ **credit** *(Finance)* Revolvingkredit, *der*

revue [rɪ'vju:] *n.* Kabarett, *das;* *(musical show)* Revue, *die*

revulsion [rɪ'vʌlʃn] *n.* **a)** *(feeling)* Abscheu, *der* **(at** vor + *Dat.*, gegen); **have a sense of ~ about sth.** von etw. angewidert sein; **b)** *(recoiling)* Distanzierung, *die* **(from** von)

reward [rɪ'wɔ:d] **1.** *n.* Belohnung, *die;* *(for kindness)* Dank, *der;* Lohn, *der;* *(recognition of merit etc.)* Auszeichnung, *die;* **get very little ~:** kaum belohnt werden; **offer a ~ of £100** 100 Pfund Belohnung aussetzen. **2.** *v. t.* belohnen; **is that how you ~ me for my help?** ist das der Dank für meine Hilfe?

rewarding [rɪ'wɔ:dɪŋ] *adj.* lohnend 〈*Zeitvertreib, Beschäftigung*〉; **be ~/financially ~:** sich lohnen/einträglich sein; **bringing up a child can be very ~:** das Großziehen eines Kindes kann einem sehr viel geben

rewind [ri:'waɪnd] *v. t.*, **rewound** [ri:'waʊnd] **a)** *(wind again)* wieder aufziehen 〈*Uhr*〉; **b)** *(wind back)* zurückspulen 〈*Film, Band*〉

rewire [ri:'waɪə(r)] *v. t.* mit neuen Leitungen versehen; ~ **a house/car** in einem Haus/Auto die Leitungen erneuern

reword [ri:'wɜ:d] *v. t.* umformulieren; neu formulieren

rework [ri:'wɜ:k] *v. t.* neu bearbeiten 〈*Theaterstück, Szene usw.*〉; neu formulieren 〈*Satz, Absatz, Text*〉

rewound *see* **rewind**

rewrite 1. [ri:'raɪt] *v. t.*, **rewrote** [ri:'rəʊt], **rewritten** [ri:'rɪtn] *(write again)* noch einmal [neu] schreiben; *(write differently)* umschreiben. **2.** ['ri:raɪt] *n.* Neufassung, *die;* **a complete ~:** eine völlig neue Fassung

'rewrite man *n. (Amer.)* Rewriter, *der (fachspr.)*; Bearbeiter, *der*

Reynard ['renəd, 'reɪnəd] **~[, the fox]** Reineke [Fuchs]

r. h. *abbr.* **right hand** r.

rhapsodic [ræp'sɒdɪk] *adj.* **a)** *(Mus.)* rhapsodisch; **b)** *(fig.: ecstatic)* ekstatisch

rhapsodize (rhapsodise) ['ræpsədaɪz] *v. i.* schwärmen **(about, on** von; **over** über + *Akk.*)

rhapsody ['ræpsədɪ] *n.* **a)** *(Mus.)* Rhapsodie, *die;* **b)** *(ecstatic utterance)* Schwärmerei, *die;* **go into rhapsodies over sth.** über etw. *(Akk.)* in Ekstase geraten

rhea ['ri:ə] *n. (Ornith.)* Nandu, *der*

Rhenish ['ri:nɪʃ, 'renɪʃ] *(arch.) adj.* rheinisch; ~ **wine** Rheinwein, *der;* ~ **Confederation** *(Hist.)* Rheinbund, *der*

rheostat ['ri:əstæt] *n. (Electr.)* Rheostat, *der*

rhesus ['ri:səs]: ~ **baby** *n. (Med.)* Rh-geschädigtes Baby; ~ **factor** *n. (Med.)* Rhesusfaktor, *der;* ~ **monkey** *n.* Rhesusaffe, *der;* ~-'**negative** *n. (Med.)* Rhesusfaktor negativ; ~-'**positive** *n. (Med.)* Rhesusfaktor positiv

rhetoric ['retərɪk] *n.* **a)** *(art of discourse)* **[art of] ~:** Redekunst, *die;* Rhetorik, *die;* **b)** *(derog.)* Phrasen *(abwertend)*

rhetorical [rɪ'tɒrɪkl] *adj.* **a)** rhetorisch 〈*Frage, Diskurs*〉; **b)** *(derog.: designed to impress)* phrasenhaft *(abwertend)*

rheumatic [ru:'mætɪk] **1.** *adj.* rheumatisch.

2. n. a) in pl. (coll.) Rheuma, das (ugs.); b) (person) Rheumatiker, der/Rheumatikerin, die; Rheumakranke, der/die
rheumatism ['ru:mətɪzm] n. (Med.) Rheumatismus, der; Rheuma, das (ugs.)
rheumatoid arthritis [ru:mətɔɪd ɑ:'θraɪtɪs] n. (Med.) chronischer Gelenkrheumatismus
Rhine [raɪn] pr. n. Rhein, der
'Rhineland pr. n. Rheinland, das
Rhineland-Pa'latinate [raɪnlænd pə'lætɪnət] pr. n. Rheinland-Pfalz (das)
Rhine 'wine n. Rheinwein, der
rhino ['raɪnəʊ] n., pl. same or ~s (coll.), **rhinoceros** [raɪ'nɒsərəs] n., pl. same or ~es Nashorn, das; Rhinozeros, das
rhizome ['raɪzəʊm] n. (Bot.) Rhizom, das (fachspr.); Wurzelstock, der
Rhodes [rəʊdz] pr. n. Rhodos (das)
Rhodesia [rəʊ'di:ʒə] pr. n. (Hist.) Rhodesien (das)
Rhodesian [rəʊ'di:ʒən] (Hist.) **1.** adj. rhodesisch. **2.** n. Rhodesier, der/Rhodesierin, die
rhododendron [rəʊdə'dendrən] n. (Bot.) Rhododendron, der; Alpenrose, die
rhombic ['rɒmbɪk] adj. rhombisch
rhombus ['rɒmbəs] n., pl. **~es** or **rhombi** ['rɒmbaɪ] (Geom.) Rhombus, der; Raute, die
rhubarb ['ru:bɑ:b] n. **a)** Rhabarber, der; (root, purgative) Rhabarberwurzel, die; **b)** (Theatre coll.) ~, ~, ~ ...: Rhabarber, Rhabarber, Rhabarber ...
rhyme [raɪm] **1.** n. **a)** Reim, der; **find no ~ or reason in sth.** sich (Dat.) auf etw. (Akk.) keinen Reim machen können; **without ~ or reason** ohne Sinn und Verstand; **b)** (short poem) Reim, der; (rhyming verse) gereimte Verse; **put sth. into ~:** etw. in Reime setzen; **c)** (rhyming word) Reimwort, das; **'honey' is a ~ for** or **to 'money'** „honey" reimt sich auf „money". **2.** v. i. **a)** sich reimen (**with** auf + Akk.); **b)** (versify) reimen. **3.** v. t. reimen
'rhyme-scheme n. (Pros.) Reimschema, das
rhyming ['raɪmɪŋ]: **~ 'couplet** n. (Pros.) Reimpaar, das; **~ dictionary** n. Reimwörterbuch, das; **~ slang** n. Rhyming Slang, der; Slang, bei dem das eigentliche Wort durch eine sich darauf reimende Phrase oder einen Teil einer solchen ersetzt wird
rhythm [rɪðm] n. Rhythmus, der; **~ and blues** (Mus.) Rhythm and Blues, der
rhythmic ['rɪðmɪk], **rhythmical** ['rɪðmɪkl] adj. rhythmisch; gleichmäßig
rhythm: ~ method n. Rhythmusmethode, die; **~ section** n. Rhythmusgruppe, die
RI abbr. (Sch.) **religious instruction**
rib [rɪb] **1.** n. **a)** (Anat.) Rippe, die; **bruised ~s** Rippenprellung, die; **dig in the ~s** Rippenstoß, der; **b) ~[s]** (joint of meat) Rippenstück, das; **c)** (supporting piece) (of insect's wing) Ader, die; (of feather) Kiel, der; Schaft, der; (of boat, ship) Spant, das; (of bridge, leaf, ceiling, in knitting, fabric) Rippe, die; (of umbrella) Speiche, die; **d)** (Amer. coll.: joke) Witz, der; Flachs, der (ugs.). **2.** v. t., **-bb-** (coll.) aufziehen (ugs.)
ribald ['rɪbəld] adj. zotig; schmutzig ⟨Lachen⟩; unanständig ⟨Ausdrücke⟩; (irreverent) anzüglich; rüde ⟨Gesellschaft⟩
ribaldry ['rɪbəldrɪ] n. Derbheit, die; Zotigkeit, die; (irreverence) Anzüglichkeit, die
riband ['rɪbənd] see **ribbon a**
ribbed [rɪbd] adj. gerippt
ribbon [rɪbn] n. **a)** (band for hair, dress, etc.) Band, das; (on typewriter) [Farb]band, das; (on medal) [Ordens]band, das; **campaign/service ~:** Kriegs-/Dienstauszeichnung, die; see also **blue ribbon**; **b)** (fig.: strip) Streifen, der; **~ of light** Lichtstreifen, der; **c)** in pl. (ragged strips) Fetzen Pl.; **tear to ~s** zerfetzen; (fig.: condemn) fertigmachen (ugs.); in der Luft zerreißen ⟨Buch, Stück usw.⟩
ribbon: ~ building, ~ development ns., no pl. Bandbebauung, die
'rib-cage n. (Anat.) Brustkorb, der
ribonucleic acid [raɪbənju:kli:ɪk 'æsɪd] n. (Biol.) Ribonukleinsäure, die
rice [raɪs] n. Reis, der
rice: ~-field n. Reisfeld, das; **~-paper** n. Reispapier, das; **~ 'pudding** n. Reispudding, der
ricer ['raɪsə(r)] n. (Amer.) ≈ Kartoffelpresse, die
'rice wine n. Reiswein, der
rich [rɪtʃ] **1.** adj. **a)** reich; see also **get-rich-quick**; **b)** (having great resources) reich (**in** an + Dat.); (fertile) fruchtbar ⟨Land, Boden⟩; **oil-~:** ölreich; **~ in vitamins/lime/forests** vitamin-/kalk-/waldreich; **a play ~ in new ideas** ein Stück voll neuer Ideen; **strike it ~:** das große Geld machen; **c)** (splendid) prachtvoll; prächtig; reich ⟨Ausstattung⟩; **d)** (containing much fat, oil, eggs, etc.) gehaltvoll; (indigestible) schwer ⟨Essen⟩; **e)** (deep, full) voll[tönend] ⟨Stimme⟩; voll ⟨Ton⟩; satt ⟨Farbe, Farbton⟩; schwer ⟨Geruch⟩; voll ⟨Geschmack⟩; **f)** (ample) reichlich; **g)** (valuable) wertvoll; reich (geh.) ⟨Geschenke, Opfergaben⟩; **h)** (amusing) köstlich; **that's ~!** köstlich!; (iron.) das ist stark! (ugs.); **i)** (Motor Veh.) fett ⟨Gemisch⟩. **2.** n. pl. **the ~:** die Reichen; **~ and poor** Arm und Reich
riches ['rɪtʃɪz] n. pl. Reichtum, der
richly ['rɪtʃlɪ] adv. **a)** (splendidly) reich; üppig ⟨ausgestattet⟩; prächtig ⟨gekleidet⟩; **~ ornamented** reichverziert; reichgeschmückt; **~ coloured** farbenprächtig; **~ endowed** reichlich ausgestattet; **b)** (fully) voll und ganz; **~ deserved** wohlverdient
richness ['rɪtʃnɪs] n., no pl. **a)** (elaborateness) Pracht, die; Prächtigkeit, die; **the ~ of ornamentation** der Reichtum der Ornamentik; die reiche Ornamentik; **b)** (of food) Reichhaltigkeit, die; (indigestibility) Schwere, die; **c)** (fullness) (of voice) voller Klang; Vollheit, die; (of colour) Sattheit, die; **d)** (great resources) Reichtum, der (**in** an + Dat.); (of soil) Fruchtbarkeit, die
Richter scale ['rɪktə skeɪl] n. (Geol.) Richter-Skala, die
¹rick [rɪk] n. (stack of hay) Dieme, die (bes. nordd.); Schober, der (bes. südd., österr.)
²rick (Brit.) **1.** n. (slight sprain or strain) Verrenkung, die; **have a ~ in one's neck** einen verrenkten Hals haben. **2.** v. t. verrenken; **~ one's neck** sich (Dat.) den Hals verrenken
rickets ['rɪkɪts] n. constr. as sing. or pl. (Med.) Rachitis, die
rickety ['rɪkɪtɪ] adj. **a)** (shaky) wack[e]lig; **b)** (feeble) hinfällig, gebrechlich, (ugs.) wack[e]lig ⟨alter Mensch⟩
rickshaw ['rɪkʃɔ:] n. Rikscha, die
ricochet ['rɪkəʃeɪ] **1.** n. **a)** Abprallen, das; **b)** (hit) Abpraller, der. **2.** v.i., **~[t]ing** ['rɪkəʃeɪɪŋ], **~[t]ed** ['rɪkəʃeɪd] abprallen (**off** von)
rictus ['rɪktəs] n. **a)** (Anat., Zool.) Mund-/Maul-/Schnabelöffnung, die; **b)** (fig.) weit aufgerissener Mund
rid [rɪd] v. t., **-dd-, rid: ~ sth. of sth.** etw. von etw. befreien; **~ oneself of sb./sth.** sich von jmdm./etw. befreien; sich jmds./einer Sache entledigen (geh.); **be ~ of sb./sth.** jmdn./etw. los sein (ugs.); **get ~ of sb./sth.** jmdn./etw. loswerden; **we are well ~ of him** wir sind froh, daß wir ihn los sind (ugs.)
riddance ['rɪdəns] n. **good ~ [to bad rubbish]** zum Glück od. Gott sei Dank ist er/es usw. weg!; **he's left at last – and good ~ to him!** er ist endlich gegangen – Gott sei Dank!
ridden see **ride 2, 3**
¹riddle ['rɪdl] n. Rätsel, das; **talk** or **speak in ~s** in Rätseln sprechen; **tell sb. a ~:** jmdm. ein Rätsel aufgeben
²riddle 1. n. (sieve) [Schüttel]sieb, das. **2.** v. t. **a)** (fill with holes) durchlöchern; **~d with bullets** von Kugeln durchsiebt od. durchlöchert; **~d with corruption/mistakes** (fig.) von Korruption durchsetzt/mit od. von Fehlern übersät; **b)** (sift) sieben
ride [raɪd] **1.** n. **a)** (journey) (on horseback) [Aus]ritt, der; (in vehicle, at fair) Fahrt, die; **~ in a train/coach** Zug-/Busfahrt, die; **go for a ~:** ausreiten; **go for a [bi]cycle ~:** radfahren; (longer distance) eine Radtour machen; **go for a ~ [in the car]** [mit dem Auto] wegfahren; **have a ~ in a train/taxi/on the merry-go-round** mit dem Zug/Taxi/Karussell fahren; **can I have a ~ on your bike/pony?** darf ich mal mit deinem Rad fahren/auf deinem Pony reiten?; **give sb. a ~:** jmdn. mitnehmen; **give sb. a ~ on one's back** jmdn. auf seinen Schultern reiten lassen; **be/come along for the ~** (coll.) nur so (ugs.) od. nur aus Interesse dabei sein/mitkommen; **take sb. for a ~:** jmdn. spazierenfahren; (fig. sl.: deceive) jmdn. reinlegen (ugs.); **b)** (quality of ~) Fahrkomfort, der; **the car gives [you] a bumpy/smooth etc. ~:** das Auto fährt holprig/sanft usw.; **give sb. a rough/an easy ~** (fig.) es jmdm. schwer-/leichtmachen; **have a rough/an easy ~:** es schwer/leicht haben; **c)** (path) Reitweg, der. **2.** v. i., **rode** [rəʊd], **ridden** ['rɪdn] **a)** (travel) (on horse) reiten; (on bicycle, in vehicle; Amer.: in elevator) fahren; **~ to town on one's bike/in one's car/on the train** mit dem Rad/Auto/Zug in die Stadt fahren; **b)** (float) **~ at anchor** vor Anker liegen od. (Seemannsspr.) reiten; **~ high [in the sky]** (fig.) ⟨Mond:⟩ hoch am Himmel schweben; **c)** (be carried) reiten; rittlings sitzen; **'X ~s again'** (fig.) „X ist wieder da"; **be riding on sth.** (fig.) von etw. abhängen; **be riding for a fall** halsbrecherisch reiten; (fig.) in sein Unglück rennen (ugs.); **be riding high** (fig.) Oberwasser haben (ugs.); **let sth. ~** (fig.) etw. auf sich beruhen lassen; see also **forth c; hound 1 a; roughshod. 3.** v. t., **rode, ridden a)** (ride on) reiten ⟨Pferd usw.⟩; fahren mit ⟨Fahrrad⟩; **learn to ~ a bicycle** radfahren lernen; **~ the waves** sich auf den Wellen wiegen; **b)** (oppress) plagen; **ridden by fears/guilt** von Ängsten/von Schuldgefühlen geplagt od. heimgesucht; **c)** (traverse) (on horseback) reiten; (on cycle) fahren; **d)** (yield to) reiten (Boxsport), ausweichen (+ Dat.) ⟨Schlag⟩; **e)** (Amer. coll.: harass) fertigmachen (ugs.); **I guess I've been riding you pretty hard** ich hab' dir wohl ziemlich zugesetzt
~ a'way v. i. wegreiten/wegfahren
~ 'down v. t. umreiten
~ 'off see **~ away**
~ 'out v. t. abreiten (Seemannsspr.) ⟨Sturm⟩; (fig.) überstehen
~ 'up v. i. **a) ~ up [to sth.]** ⟨Reiter:⟩ an etw. (Akk.) heranreiten; ⟨Fahrer:⟩ an etw. (Akk.) heranfahren; **b) the skirt rode up over her knees** (fig.) der Rock rutschte über ihr Knie
rider ['raɪdə(r)] n. **a)** Reiter, der/Reiterin, die; (of cycle) Fahrer, der/Fahrerin, die; **b)** (addition) Zusatz, der; **add a ~:** einen Zusatz machen; (Brit. Law) eine zusätzliche Erklärung od. Feststellung abgeben
riderless ['raɪdəlɪs] adj. reiterlos
ridge [rɪdʒ] **1.** n. **a)** (of roof) First, der; (of nose) Rücken, der; **b)** (long hilltop) Grat, der; Kamm, der; **~ of hills** Höhenrücken, der; **~ of mountains** Gebirgskamm, der; **c)** (Agric.) Kamm, der; Rücken, der; **d)** (Meteorol.) **~ [of high pressure]** langgestrecktes Hoch; (connecting two highs) Hochdruckbrücke, die. **2.** v. t. häufeln
ridge: ~-piece n. Firstbalken, der; **~-pole** n. Firststange, die; **~ tent** n. Hauszelt, das; **~-tile** n. Firstziegel, der; **~way** n. Gratweg, der
ridicule ['rɪdɪkju:l] **1.** n. Spott, der; **object of ~:** Zielscheibe des Spotts; Gespött, das; **hold sb./sth. up to ~:** jmdn./etw. der Lä-

cherlichkeit preisgeben; **lay oneself open to ~**: sich dem Gespött aussetzen. **2.** *v. t.* verspotten; spotten über (+ *Akk.*)

ridiculous [rɪ'dɪkjʊləs] *adj.* lächerlich; **don't be ~!** sei nicht albern!; **make oneself [look] ~**: sich lächerlich machen

ridiculously [rɪ'dɪkjʊləslɪ] *adv.* lächerlich

riding ['raɪdɪŋ] *n.* Reiten, *das*

riding: ~-breeches *n. pl.* Reithose, *die;* **~-crop** *n.* Reitgerte, *die;* **~ habit** *n.* Reitkleid, *das;* **~-lamp** *n. (Naut.)* Ankerlaterne, *die;* **~ lesson** *n.* Reitstunde, *die;* **~-light** *see* **~-lamp; ~-school** *n.* Reitschule, *die*

Riesling ['ri:zlɪŋ, 'ri:slɪŋ] *n.* Riesling, *der*

rife [raɪf] *pred. adj.* **a)** *(widespread)* weit verbreitet; **rumours were ~**: es gingen Gerüchte um; **b) ~ with** *(full of)* voller; voll von; **the country was ~ with rumours of war** im ganzen Land gab es Kriegsgerüchte

riff-raff ['rɪfræf] *n.* Gesindel, *das*

rifle ['raɪfl] **1.** *n. (firearm)* Gewehr, *das; (hunting-~)* Büchse, *die.* **2.** *v. t.* **a)** *(ransack)* durchwühlen; *(pillage)* plündern; **~ sth. of its contents** etw. ausplündern, **b)** *(make grooves in)* ziehen *(fachspr.)* ⟨*Gewehrlauf*⟩. **3.** *v. i.* **~ through sth.** etw. durchwühlen

rifle: ~-barrel *n.* Gewehrlauf, *der; (of hunting-~)* Büchsenlauf, *der;* **~-butt** *n.* Gewehrkolben, *der;* **~man** ['raɪflmən] *n., pl.* **~men** ['raɪflmən] Schütze, *der;* **~-range** *n.* Schießstand, *der;* Schießplatz, *der;* **~-shot** *n.* Gewehrschuß, *der*

rift [rɪft] *n.* **a)** *(dispute)* Unstimmigkeit, *die;* **b)** *(cleft)* Spalte, *die; (in cloud)* Riß, *der*

'rift-valley *n. (Geog.)* Graben[bruch], *der*

[1]rig [rɪg] **1.** *n.* **a)** *(Naut.)* Takelung, *die;* **b)** *(for oil-well)* [Öl]förderturm, *der; (off shore)* Förderinsel, *die;* **drilling ~**: Bohrturm, *der; (off shore)* Bohrinsel, *die;* **c)** *(outfit)* Kluft, *die;* **in full ~**: in Schale *(ugs.);* **in full climbing ~**: in voller Klettermontur *(ugs.).* **2.** *v. t.,* **-gg- a)** *(Naut.)* auftakeln; **b)** *(Aeronaut.) (assemble)* montieren; *(fit out)* ausrüsten ⟨*Flugzeug*⟩

~ 'out *v. t.* ausstaffieren

~ 'up *v. t.* aufbauen

[2]rig *v. t.,* **-gg-** *(falsify)* fälschen ⟨*Wahl*⟩; verfälschen, *(geh.)* manipulieren ⟨*[Wahl]ergebnis*⟩; **~ the market** die Preise/*(St. Exch.)* die Kurse manipulieren *(geh.) od.* künstlich beeinflussen; **the whole thing was ~ged** das war alles Schiebung *(ugs.)*

rigger ['rɪgə(r)] *n.* **a)** *(Naut.)* Takler, *der*/Taklerin, *die;* **b)** *(Aeronaut.)* [Rüst]mechaniker, *der*/[Rüst]mechanikerin, *die*

[1]rigging ['rɪgɪŋ] *n.* **a)** *(Naut.)* Takelung, *die; (ropes and chains also)* Gut, *das;* Takelage, *die;* **b)** *(Aeronaut.)* Ausrüstung, *die*

[2]rigging *n. (illicit manipulation)* Manipulation, *die (geh.);* Schiebung, *die (ugs.)*

right [raɪt] **1.** *adj.* **a)** *(just, morally good)* richtig; **it's not ~ for sb. to do sth.** es ist nicht richtig *od.* recht von jmdm., daß er etw. tut; **it is only ~ [and proper] to do sth./that sb. should do sth.** es ist nur recht und billig, etw. zu tun/daß jmd. etw. tut; **do the ~ thing by sb.** sich jmdm. gegenüber anständig verhalten; **b)** *(correct, true)* richtig; **~ enough** völlig richtig; **~ enough!** in Ordnung!; okay! *(ugs.);* **you're [quite] ~**: du hast [völlig] recht; **too ~** *(coll.)* allerdings!; **how ~ you are!** wie recht du hast!; **you are ~ to do** *or* **in doing it** du tust recht daran, es zu tun; **be ~ in sth.** recht mit etw. haben; **let's get it ~ this time!** machen wir es diesmal besser!; **let's get this ~!** das wollen wir doch mal klarstellen!; **is that clock ~?** geht die Uhr da richtig?; **have you got the ~ fare?** haben Sie das Fahrgeld passend?; **put** *or* **set ~**: richtigstellen ⟨*Irrtum, Behauptung*⟩; wiedergutmachen ⟨*Unrecht*⟩; berichtigen ⟨*Fehler*⟩; bereinigen ⟨*Mißverständnis, Angelegenheit*⟩; beheben ⟨*Mißstand, Mangel*⟩; wieder in Ordnung bringen ⟨*Situation, Angelegenheit, Maschine, Gerät*⟩; richtig stellen ⟨*Uhr*⟩; **put** *or* **set sb. ~**: jmdn. berichtigen *od.* korrigieren; **~ [you are]!,** *(Brit.)* **~ oh!** *(coll.)* ja, gut!; okay! *(ugs.);* **that's ~**: ja[wohl]; so ist es; **that's ~, smash the place up!** *(iron.)* recht so, hau nur immer auf den Putz *(ugs. iron.);* **is that ~?** stimmt das?; *(indeed?)* aha!; **[am I] ~?** nicht [wahr]?; oder [nicht]? *(ugs.); see also* **all 3; road b; track 1 a; c)** *(preferable, most suitable)* richtig; recht; **the ~ man for the job** der richtige Mann [dafür]; **do sth. the ~ way** etw. richtig machen; **say/do the ~ thing** das Richtige sagen/tun; **know how to say the ~ thing** die richtigen *od.* passenden Worte finden; **I did the ~ thing when I ...**: es war richtig, daß ich ...; *see also* **Mr; whale a; d)** *(sound, sane)* richtig; **all's ~ with the world** die Welt *od.* alles ist in Ordnung; **not be quite ~ in the head** nicht ganz bei Verstand sein; nicht ganz richtig [im Kopf] sein; **as ~ as rain** *(coll.) (in health)* gesund wie ein Fisch im Wasser; *(satisfactory)* in bester Ordnung; **put** *or* **set sb. ~** *(restore to health)* jmdn. [wieder] in Ordnung *od.* auf die Beine bringen; **she'll be ~** *(Austral. coll.)* das geht [schon] in Ordnung *(ugs.);* **I'll/we'll** *etc.* **see you ~**: es soll dein Schaden nicht sein; *see also* **mind 1 g; e)** *(coll./arch.: real, properly so called)* richtig; recht *(veralt.);* **you're a ~ one!** du bist mir der/die Richtige!; **your room's in a ~ mess** in deinem Zimmer sieht es wüst aus; **he made a ~ mess of that job/of it** er hat die Sache/es total vermurkst *(ugs.);* **f)** *(opposite of left)* recht...; *see also* **turn 1 c; be sb.'s ~ arm** *(fig.)* jmds. rechte Hand sein; **g) R~** *(Polit.)* recht... *See also* **right side. 2.** *v. t.* **a)** *(avenge)* aus der Welt schaffen ⟨*Unrecht*⟩; **b)** *(correct)* berichtigen; richtigstellen; **c)** *(restore to upright position)* [wieder] aufrichten; ⟨*Boot usw.:*⟩ **~ itself** sich [von selbst] [wieder] aufrichten; *(fig.: come to proper state)* ⟨*Mangel:*⟩ sich [von selbst] geben; ⟨*Körper, Organismus:*⟩ *(ugs.)* von selbst in Ordnung kommen. **3.** *n.* **a)** *(fair claim, authority)* Recht, *das;* Anrecht, *das;* **have a/no ~ to sth.** ein/kein Anrecht *od.* Recht auf etw. *(Akk.)* haben; **have a** *or* **the/no ~ to do sth.** das/kein Recht haben, etw. zu tun; **as of ~**: kraft Gesetzes; **by ~ of** auf Grund (+ *Gen.*); **belong to sb. as of** *or* **by ~**: jmds. rechtmäßiges Eigentum sein; **what ~ has he [got] to do that?** mit welchem Recht tut er das?; **in one's own ~**: aus eigenem Recht; **an authoress in her own ~**: eine eigenständige Autorin; **the ~ to work/life** das Recht auf Arbeit/Leben; **~-to-work** *attrib. (Amer.)* gegen Gewerkschaftszwang gerichtet ⟨*Gesetz, Politik*⟩; **~-to-work state** Staat ohne Gewerkschaftszwang; **the ~ to life** das Recht auf Leben *(des ungeborenen Kindes);* **~-to-life** *attrib.* auf den Schutz ungeborenen Lebens gerichtet; **grazing ~s** Weiderechte *Pl.;* **~ of way** *(~ to pass across)* Wegerecht, *das; (path)* öffentlicher Weg; *(precedence)* Vorfahrtsrecht, *das;* **who has the ~ of way?** wer hat Vorfahrt?; **Bill of R~s** Bill of Rights, *die;* **Black R~s** Rechte der Schwarzen; **be within one's ~s to do sth.** etw. mit [Fug und] Recht tun können; **b)** *(what is just)* Recht, *das;* **~ is on our side** das Recht ist auf unserer Seite; **understand the ~s and wrongs of a situation** beurteilen können, was [bei einer Sache] richtig und was falsch ist; **by ~[s]** von Rechts wegen; **do ~ by sb.** jmdn. anständig behandeln; **do ~**: sich richtig verhalten; richtig handeln; **do ~ to do sth.** recht daran tun, etw. zu tun; **in the ~**: im Recht; **c)** *(~-hand side)* rechte Seite; **move to the ~**: nach rechts rücken; **on** *or* **to the ~ [of the door]** rechts [von der Tür]; **on** *or* **to my ~, to the ~ of me** rechts von mir; zu meiner Rechten; **from ~ and left** von rechts und links; **d)** *(Polit.)* **the R~**: die Rechte; *(radicals)* die Rechten; **be on the R~ of the party** dem rechten Flügel der Partei angehören; **e)** *in pl. (proper state)* **set** *or* **put sth. to ~s** etw. in Ordnung bringen; **set** *or* **put the world to ~s** die Welt verbessern; **f)** *(Boxing)* Rechte, *die;* **g) get sb. bang to ~s** *(Brit. sl.) or (Amer. sl.)* **dead to ~s** jmdn. auf frischer Tat ertappen; **h)** *(Theatre)* [stage] **~**: linke Bühnenseite; **i)** *(in marching) see* **[2]left 3 e. 4.** *adv.* **a)** *(properly, correctly, justly)* richtig ⟨*machen, raten, halten*⟩; **go ~** *(succeed)* klappen *(ugs.);* **nothing is going ~ for** *or* **with me today** bei mir klappt heute nichts *(ugs.);* **if I remember ~**: wenn ich mich recht *od.* richtig erinnere; **b)** *(to the side opposite left)* nach rechts; **~ of the road** rechts von der Straße; **~, left, and centre, left, ~, and centre** *(fig. coll.)* überall; *(repeatedly)* immer wieder; **c)** *(all the way)* bis ganz; *(completely)* ganz; völlig; **windows coming ~ down to the floor** Fenster, die bis ganz auf den Fußboden herunterreichen; **~ through the summer** den ganzen Sommer hindurch; **turn ~ round** sich ganz umdrehen; ⟨*Zeiger:*⟩ eine ganze Umdrehung machen; **~ round the house** ums ganze Haus [herum]; **rotten ~ through** durch und durch verfault; **d)** *(exactly)* genau; **~ in the middle of sth.** mitten in etw. *(Dat./Akk.);* **~ now** im Moment; jetzt sofort, gleich ⟨*handeln*⟩; **~ on the chin** direkt *od.* genau am/ans Kinn; **he was '~ next to me** *(coll.)* er war direkt *od.* genau neben mir; **~ at the beginning** gleich am Anfang; **~ on!** *(coll.) (approving)* recht so!; so ist's recht!; *(agreeing)* genau!; ganz recht!; **e)** *(straight)* direkt; genau; **go ~ on [the way one is going]** [weiter] geradeaus gehen *od.* fahren; **I'm going ~ home now** ich gehe jetzt direkt nach Hause; **f)** *(coll.: immediately)* **~ [away/off]** sofort; gleich; **I'll be ~ 'with you** ich bin gleich [wieder] da; **things went wrong ~ at** *or* **from the beginning** es ging schon am Anfang *od.* von Anfang an schief; **g)** *(very)* sehr; **~ royal** [wahrhaft] fürstlich ⟨*Mahl, Empfang*⟩; **a ~ royal dressing down** eine Standpauke, die sich gewaschen hat *(ugs.); see also* **honourable d; reverend 1**

right: ~ a'bout ['turn *or (Amer.)* **'face]** *n. (Mil.)* Rechtsummachen, *das;* Kehrtwendung nach rechts; *(as command)* rechtsum!; *(fig.)* Kehrtwendung, *die;* **~ angle** *n.* rechter Winkel; **at ~ angles to ...**: rechtwinklig zu ...; im rechten Winkel zu ...; **~-angled** *adj.* rechtwinklig; **~ 'back** *n. (Footb.)* rechter Verteidiger/rechte Verteidigerin

righteous ['raɪtʃəs] **1.** *adj.* **a)** *(upright)* rechtschaffen, *(bibl.)* gerecht ⟨*Person*⟩; gerecht ⟨*Gott, Staat, Herr*⟩; **b)** *(morally justifiable)* gerecht ⟨*Zorn, Sache*⟩; gerechtfertigt ⟨*Maßnahme, Tat*⟩. **2.** *n. pl.* **the ~**: die Gerechten

'right-footed *adj.* mit dem rechten Fuß geschickter; rechtsfüßig ⟨*Fußballspieler*⟩

rightful ['raɪtfl] *adj.* **a)** *(fair)* gerecht ⟨*Sache, Strafe*⟩; berechtigt ⟨*Forderung, Anspruch*⟩; **b)** *(entitled)* rechtmäßig ⟨*Besitzer, Eigentümer, Herrscher, Erbe, Anteil*⟩

rightfully ['raɪtfəlɪ] *adv.* **a)** *(fairly)* rechtmäßig; **b)** *(correctly)* mit *od.* zu Recht

right: ~ 'hand *n.* **a)** rechte Hand; Rechte, *die;* **b)** *(right side)* **on** *or* **at sb.'s ~ hand** zu jmds. Rechten; rechts von jmdm.; **c)** *(fig.: chief assistant)* rechte Hand; **~-hand** *adj.* recht...; rechtsgängig, rechtsdrehend ⟨*Schraube, Gewinde*⟩; **~-hand bend** Rechtskurve, *die;* **on the/your ~-hand side** rechts; auf der rechten Seite; *see also* **drive 1 i; ~-handed** [raɪt'hændɪd] **1.** *adj.* **a)** rechtshändig; ⟨*Schlag*⟩ mit der Rechten; ⟨*Werkzeug*⟩ für Rechtshänder; **be ~-handed** Rechtshänder/Rechtshänderin sein; **b)** *(turning to right)* rechts angeschlagen ⟨*Tür*⟩; Rechts⟨*gewinde, -drehung*⟩; rechtsgängig, rechtsdrehend ⟨*Schraube, Gewinde*⟩;

2. *adv.* rechtshändig; mit der rechten Hand; ~**-handedness** [raɪt'hændɪdnɪs] *n.* Rechtshändigkeit, *die;* ~**-hander** [raɪt'hændə(r)] *n.* **a)** *(person)* Rechtshänder, *der*/-händerin, *die;* **b)** *(blow)* Schlag mit der Rechten; *(Boxing)* Rechte, *die;* ~**-hand 'man** *n.* *(chief assistant)* rechte Hand
rightism ['raɪtɪzm] *n., no pl. (Polit.)* Konservativismus, *der*
rightist ['raɪtɪst] *(Polit.)* **1.** *adj.* rechtsorientiert. **2.** *n.* Rechte, *der/die*
rightly ['raɪtlɪ] *adv.* **a)** *(fairly, correctly)* richtig; **do** ~: richtig handeln; **..., and** ~ **so:** ..., und zwar zu Recht; ~ **or wrongly, ...:** ob es nun richtig ist/war oder nicht, ...; **b)** *(fitly)* zu Recht
right-'minded *adj.* gerecht denkend
rightness ['raɪtnɪs] *n., no pl.* Richtigkeit, *die*
righto ['raɪtəʊ, raɪ'təʊ] *int.* *(Brit.)* okay *(ugs.);* alles klar *(ugs.)*
'right side *n.* **a)** *(of fabric)* Oberseite, *die;* **b)** **be on the** ~ **of fifty** noch keine fünfzig sein; **[the]** ~ **out/up** richtig herum; **get on the** ~ **of sb.** *(fig.)* sich mit jmdm. gut stellen
'rights issue *n. (Finance)* Bezugsangebot, *das*
'right-thinking *adj.* gerecht denkend
rightward ['raɪtwəd] **1.** *adv.* [nach] rechts ⟨*abbiegen*⟩; nach rechts ⟨*blicken, sich wenden*⟩; **lie** ~ **of sth.** rechts von etw. liegen. **2.** *adj.* rechter Hand *nachgestellt*
rightwards ['raɪtwədz] *see* **rightward 1**
right: ~**-wing** *adj.* **a)** *(Sport)* Rechtsaußen-⟨*spieler, -position*⟩; **b)** *(Polit.)* recht...; rechtsgerichtet; Rechts⟨*intellektueller, -extremist, -radikalismus*⟩; ~**-winger** *n.* **a)** *(Sport)* Rechtsaußen, *der;* **b)** *(Polit.)* Angehöriger/Angehörige des rechten Flügels; **extreme** ~**-winger** Rechtsaußen, *der/die (Jargon);* Rechtsradikale, *der/die*
rigid ['rɪdʒɪd] *adj.* **a)** starr; *(stiff)* steif; *(hard)* hart; *(firm)* fest; ~ **airship** Starrluftschiff, *das;* **b)** *(fig.: harsh, inflexible)* streng ⟨*Person*⟩; unbeugsam ⟨*Haltung, System*⟩
rigidity [rɪ'dʒɪdɪtɪ] *n., no pl. see* **rigid: a)** Starrheit, *die;* Steifheit, *die;* Härte, *die;* Festigkeit, *die;* **b)** Strenge, *die*
rigidly ['rɪdʒɪdlɪ] *adv.* **a)** starr; **b)** *(harshly, inflexibly)* [allzu] streng; peinlich ⟨*korrekt*⟩; rigoros ⟨*vernichten, beschränken*⟩
rigmarole ['rɪgmərəʊl] *n. (derog.)* **a)** *(long story)* langatmiges Geschwafel *(ugs. abwertend);* **b)** *(complex procedure)* Zirkus, *der (ugs. abwertend)*
rigor ['rɪgə(r)] *(Amer.) see* **rigour**
rigor mortis [rɪgə 'mɔːtɪs] *n. (Med.)* Totenstarre, *die;* Rigor mortis, *der (fachspr.)*
rigorous ['rɪgərəs] *adj.* **a)** *(strict)* streng; rigoros ⟨*Methode, Maßnahme, Beschränkung, Strenge*⟩; ~ **tests** strenge Prüfungen; **b)** *(marked by extremes)* hart ⟨*Leben, Bedingungen, Winter*⟩; extrem ⟨*Klima*⟩; **c)** *(precise)* peinlich ⟨*Genauigkeit, Beachtung*⟩; exakt ⟨*Analyse*⟩; streng ⟨*Beurteilung, Maßstab*⟩; scharf ⟨*Auge*⟩; genau ⟨*Arbeit*⟩
rigorously ['rɪgərəslɪ] *adv.* **a)** *(strictly)* streng; rigoros ⟨*durchführen, ausschließen*⟩; **b)** *(precisely)* exakt ⟨*berechnen*⟩
rigour ['rɪgə(r)] *n. (Brit.)* **a)** *(strictness)* Strenge, *die;* **b)** *(extremeness)* Härte, *die;* Strenge, *die;* **the** ~**s of sth.** die Unbilden *(geh.)* einer Sache *(Gen.);* **c)** *(precision)* Stringenz, *die (geh.);* *(of argument)* Schlüssigkeit, *die*
rile [raɪl] *v.t. (coll.)* ärgern; **get/feel** ~**d** sich ärgern; **it** ~**s me when ...:** es fuchst mich, wenn ... *(ugs.)*
Riley ['raɪlɪ] *n.* **live** *or* **lead the life of** ~ *(sl.)* wie die Made im Speck leben *(ugs.)*
rill [rɪl] *n.* Bächlein, *das*
rim [rɪm] *n.* Rand, *der;* *(of wheel)* Felge, *die*
rime [raɪm] *n. (frost)* [Rauh]reif, *der*
rimless ['rɪmlɪs] *adj.* randlos
-rimmed [rɪmd] *adj. in comb.* -randig
rind [raɪnd] *n. (of fruit)* Schale, *die;* *(of cheese)* Rinde, *die;* *(of bacon)* Schwarte, *die*

¹ring [rɪŋ] **1.** *n.* **a)** Ring, *der;* **b)** *(Horse-racing, Boxing)* Ring, *der;* *(bull~)* Arena, *die;* *(in circus)* Manege, *die;* **the** ~ *(bookmakers)* der Ring; die Buchmacher; **c)** *(group)* Ring, *der;* *(gang)* Bande, *die;* *(controlling prices)* Kartell, *das;* **d)** *(circle)* Kreis, *der;* **make** *or* **run** ~**s [a]round sb.** *(fig.)* jmdn. in die Tasche stecken *(ugs.);* **e)** *(halo round moon)* Hof, *der;* **f)** *(Chem.)* Ring, *der.* **2.** *v.t.* **a)** *(surround)* umringen; einkreisen ⟨*Wort, Buchstaben usw.*⟩; **b)** *(Brit.: put* ~ *on leg of)* beringen ⟨*Vogel*⟩
²ring 1. *n.* **a)** *(act of sounding bell)* Läuten, *das;* Klingeln, *das;* **there's a** ~ **at the door** es hat geklingelt; **give two** ~**s** zweimal läuten *od.* klingeln; **b)** *(Brit. coll.: telephone call)* Anruf, *der;* **give sb. a** ~: jmdn. anrufen; **c)** *(resonance; fig.: impression)* Klang, *der;* *(fig.)* **have the** ~ **of plausibility/truth** einleuchtend/glaubhaft klingen; *(fig.)* **a** ~ **of insistence in her tone** ein nachdrücklicher Ton in ihrer Stimme. **2.** *v.i.,* **rang** [ræŋ], **rung** [rʌŋ] **a)** *(sound clearly)* [er]schallen; ⟨*Hammer:*⟩ [er]dröhnen; **oaths rang across the yard** Flüche hallten über den Hof; **b)** *(be sounded)* ⟨*Glocke, Klingel, Telefon:*⟩ läuten; ⟨*Wecker, Telefon, Kasse:*⟩ klingeln; **the doorbell rang** die Türklingel ging; es klingelte; **c)** *(~ bell)* läuten **(for nach)**; **please** ~ **for attention** bitte läuten; **d)** *(Brit.: make telephone call)* anrufen; **e)** *(resound)* ⟨*Wald, Raum, Halle:*⟩ [wider]hallen **(with von)**; ~ **in sb.'s ears** jmdm. in den Ohren klingen; ~ **true/false** ⟨*Münze:*⟩ echt/falsch klingen; *(fig.)* glaubhaft/unglaubhaft klingen; **f)** *(hum)* summen; *(loudly)* dröhnen; **my ears are** ~**ing** mir dröhnen die Ohren. **3.** *v.t.,* **rang, rung a)** läuten ⟨*Glocke*⟩; ~ **the [door]-bell** läuten; klingeln; ~ **a peal** die Glocken läuten; **it** ~**s a bell** *(fig. coll.)* es kommt mir [irgendwie] bekannt vor; ~ **the bell [with sb.]** *(fig.)* [bei jmdm.] ankommen *(ugs.); see also* **change 1 h; knell b; b)** *(Brit.: telephone)* anrufen
~ **'back** *v.t. & i. (Brit.)* **a)** *(again)* wieder anrufen; **b)** *(in return)* zurückrufen
~ **down** *v.t. (Theatre)* fallen lassen, herunterlassen ⟨*Vorhang*⟩; ~ **the curtain down on a project/a love affair** *(fig.)* unter ein Vorhaben/Liebesverhältnis einen Schlußstrich ziehen
~ **'in 1.** *v.i. (Brit.)* anrufen. **2.** *v.t.* einläuten
~ **'off** *v.i. (Brit.)* auflegen; abhängen
~ **'out 1.** *v.i.* ertönen. **2.** *v.t.* ausläuten
~ **round** *(Brit.)* **1.** [-'-] *v.i.* herumtelefonieren. **2.** ['--] *v.t.* herumtelefonieren bei
~ **'up** *v.t.* **a)** *(Brit.: telephone)* anrufen; **b)** *(record on cash register)* [ein]tippen; bongen *(ugs.);* **c)** *(Theatre)* ~ **up the curtain** den Vorhang hochziehen
ring: ~**-a-~-o'-'roses** *n.* Ringelreihen, *der;* ~ **binder** *n.* Ringbuch, *das;* ~ **circuit** *n. (Electr.)* Ringschaltung, *die;* ~**-dove** *n.* Ringeltaube, *die*
ringed [rɪŋd] *adj.* beringt; **the** ~ **planet** der Ringplanet
ringer ['rɪŋə(r)] *n.* **a)** *(bell-~)* [Glocken]läuter, *der;* **b) be a [dead]** ~ **for sb./sth.** *(sl.: very similar)* für jmdn. durchgehen [können]/einer Sache *(Dat.)* [aufs Haar] gleichen
ring: ~**-fence** *n.* Umzäunung, *die;* ~**-finger** *n.* Ringfinger, *der*
ringing ['rɪŋɪŋ] **1.** *adj.* **a)** *(clear and full)* schallend ⟨*Stimme, Gelächter*⟩; *(sonorous)* klangvoll, volltönend ⟨*Stimme, Lachen, Lied*⟩; *(resounding)* dröhnend ⟨*Schlag*⟩; **b)** *(decisive)* eindringlich ⟨*Appell*⟩. **2.** *n.* **a)** *(sounding, sound)* Läuten, *das;* **b)** *(Brit. Teleph.)* ~ **tone** Freiton, *der;* **c)** *(sensation)* ~ **in the** *or* **one's ears** Ohrensausen, *das*
'ringleader *n.* Rädelsführer, *der (abwertend);* Anführer, *der*/Anführerin, *die*
ringlet ['rɪŋlɪt] *n.* [Ringel]löckchen, *das*
ring: ~ **main** *n. (Electr.)* Ringnetz, *das;* ~**master** *n.* Dresseur, *der;* ~**-pull** *adj.* ~**-pull can** Aufreißdose, *die;* Ring-Pull-Dose, *die;* ~ **road** *n.* Ringstraße, *die;* ~**side 1.** *n.* **at the** ~**side** [direkt] am Ring; **2.** *adj.* ~**side seat** *(Boxing)* Ringplatz, *der;* *(in circus)* Manegenplatz, *der;* Logenplatz, *der (auch fig.);* ~**sider** ['rɪŋsaɪdə(r)] *n.* Zuschauer mit Ring-/Manegenplatz; ~**way** *n.* Ringstraße, *die;* ~**worm** *n.* *(Med.)* Kopfgrind, *der;* Flechtengrind, *der*
rink [rɪŋk] *n.* *(for ice-skating)* Eisbahn, *die;* *(for curling)* Eisschießbahn, *die;* *(for roller-skating)* Rollschuhbahn, *die;* *(bowling-green)* Bowlingfläche, *die*
rinse [rɪns] **1.** *v.t.* **a)** *(wash out)* ausspülen ⟨*Mund, Gefäß usw.*⟩; *abs.* **please** ~ *(said by dentist)* bitte mal [aus]spülen; **b)** *(wash lightly)* durchspülen ⟨*Wäsche*⟩; **c)** *(put through water)* [aus]spülen ⟨*Wäsche usw.*⟩; abspülen ⟨*Hände, Geschirr*⟩. **2.** *n.* **a)** *(rinsing)* Spülen, *das;* Spülung, *die;* **give sth. a [good/quick]** ~: etw. [gut/schnell] abspülen/ausspülen/spülen; **after several** ~**s** nach mehrmaligem Spülen; **have a** ~ *(said by dentist)* bitte [aus]spülen; **b)** *(solution)* [Haar]tönung, *die;* [Haar]töner, *der*
~ **a'way** *v.t.* wegspülen
~ **'out** *v.t.* **a)** *(wash with clean water)* ausspülen ⟨*Wäsche, Mund, Behälter*⟩; **b)** *(remove by washing)* [her]ausspülen
riot ['raɪət] **1.** *n.* **a)** *(violent disturbance)* Aufruhr, *der;* ~**s** Unruhen *Pl.;* Aufstand, *der;* **there'll be a** ~ *(fig.)* es wird Ärger *od.* einen Aufstand geben *(ugs.);* **b)** *(noisy or uncontrolled behaviour)* Krawall, *der;* Tumult, *der;* **run** ~: randalieren; *(in protest)* auf die Barrikaden gehen *(ugs.);* **run** ~ **[all over sth.]** ⟨*Pflanze:*⟩ [etw. völlig über]wuchern; **let one's imagination run** ~: seiner Phantasie freien Lauf lassen; **c)** *(unrestrained indulgence)* Orgie, *die;* **d)** *(coll.: amusing thing or person)* **be a** ~: zum Piepen sein *(ugs.).* **2.** *v.i.* einen Aufstand machen; **the mob had been** ~**ing all night** der Mob hatte während der ganzen Nacht gewütet; **the** ~**ing** der Aufruhr; die Unruhen
'Riot Act *n. (Hist.)* Aufruhrgesetz, *das;* **read sb. the** ~ *(fig. coll.)* jmdm. die Leviten lesen
rioter ['raɪətə(r)] *n.* Aufrührer, *der*
riotous ['raɪətəs] *adj.* **a)** *(turbulent)* aufrührerisch ⟨*Menge*⟩; tumultartig ⟨*Vorgang*⟩; **b)** *(dissolute)* ausschweifend; **c)** *(unrestrained)* wild; schallend ⟨*Gelächter*⟩; **a** ~ **display of colour** eine reiche Farbenpracht
riotously ['raɪətəslɪ] *adv.* **a)** *(dissolutely)* ausschweifend; **b)** ~ **funny** *(coll.)* urkomisch; zum Schreien *präd. (ugs.)*
riot: ~ **police** *n.* Bereitschaftspolizei, *die;* ~ **shield** *n.* Schutzschild, *der*
¹rip [rɪp] **1.** *n.* **a)** *(tear)* Riß, *der;* **b)** *(act of ripping)* Reißen, *das.* **2.** *v.t.,* **-pp- a)** *(make tear in)* zerreißen; ~ **open** aufreißen; *(with knife)* aufschlitzen; ~ **one's skirt on sth.** sich *(Dat.)* an etw. *(Dat.)* das Kleid einreißen *od.* zerreißen; ~ **sth. down the middle/to pieces** etw. in der Mitte *od.* etw. mitten durchreißen/in Stücke zerreißen; **b)** *(make by tearing)* reißen ⟨*Loch*⟩. **3.** *v.i.,* **-pp- a)** *(split)* [ein]reißen; **b)** *(coll.)* **let** ~: loslegen *(ugs.);* **he let** ~ **down the motorway** er bretterte volles Rohr über die Autobahn *(ugs.);* **let** ~ **at sb.** jmdn. zur Minna machen *(ugs.)*
~ **a'part** *v.t. (tear apart)* auseinanderreißen; zerreißen; *(destroy)* demolieren
~ **a'way** *v.t.* abreißen; ~ **sth. away from sth.** etw. von etw. reißen
~ **'down** *v.t.* abreißen; herunterreißen
~ **into** *v.t.* ~ **into sb.** *(attack)* über jmdn. herfallen; *(fig.: attack verbally)* jmdm. ins Gesicht springen *(ugs.)*
~ **'off** *v.t.* **a)** *(remove from)* reißen von; *(remove)* abreißen; herunterreißen ⟨*Maske, Kleidungsstück*⟩; **b)** *(sl.: defraud)* übers Ohr hauen *(ugs.);* bescheißen *(derb);* **c)** *(sl.: steal)* klauen *(salopp). See also* **rip-off**

~ **'out** *v.t.* herausreißen (**of** aus)

~ **'up** *v.t.* zerreißen; kaputtreißen *(ugs.)*; ~ **up an agreement** *(fig.)* aus einer Vereinbarung einfach wieder aussteigen *(ugs.)*

²rip *n.* **a)** *(roué)* Windhund, *der (abwertend)*; **b)** *(rascal)* Halunke, *der (scherzh.)*

RIP *abbr.* **rest in peace** R.I.P.

'rip-cord *n.* Reißleine, *die*

ripe [raɪp] *adj.* reif (**for** zu); ausgereift ‹*Käse, Wein, Plan*›; vollkommen, vollendet ‹*Gelehrsamkeit*›; reich ‹*Erfahrung*›; groß ‹*Verständnis*›; **the time is ~ for doing sth.** es ist an der Zeit, etw. zu tun; **be ~ for development** ‹*Land*:› entwicklungsreif sein; ~ **old age** hohes Alter

ripen ['raɪpn] **1.** *v.t.* zur Reife bringen; *(fig.)* reifen lassen *(geh.)*. **2.** *v.i.* *(lit. or fig.)* reifen; ~ **into sth.** *(fig.)* zu etw. reifen *(geh.)*

ripeness ['raɪpnɪs] *n., no pl. (lit. or fig.)* Reife, *die*

rip-off *n. (sl.)* Nepp, *der (ugs. abwertend)*; **that place is a ~**: das ist ein Neppladen *(ugs. abwertend)*

riposte [rɪ'pɒst] **1.** *n.* **a)** *(retort)* [rasche] Entgegnung *od. (geh.)* Replik; **b)** *(Fencing)* Riposte, *die.* **2.** *v.i.* **a)** *(retort)* [rasch] antworten; **b)** *(Fencing)* ripostieren

ripper ['rɪpə(r)] *n.* Lustmörder, *der;* **the Yorkshire R~**: der Ripper von Yorkshire

ripping ['rɪpɪŋ] *adj. (Brit. dated sl.)* famos *(ugs. veralt.)*

ripple ['rɪpl] **1.** *n.* **a)** *(small wave)* kleine Welle; **the breeze sent ~s along the surface** die Brise kräuselte die Oberfläche; **b)** *(sound)* **a ~ of applause/laughter** kurzer Beifall/ein perlendes Lachen; **c)** *(Electr.)* leichte [Strom]schwankung. **2.** *v.i.* **a)** *(form ~s)* ‹*See*:› sich kräuseln; ‹*Muskeln*:› spielen; **b)** *(flow)* ‹*Welle*:› plätschern; ‹*Bach*:› in kleinen Wellen fließen; **c)** *(sound)* erklingen. **3.** *v.t.* kräuseln

'ripple-mark *n.* Rippelmarke, *die*

rip: ~-roaring *adj.* wahnsinnig *(ugs.)*; Wahnsinns- *(ugs.)*; **~-saw** *n.* Längsschnittsäge, *die;* **~-snorter** ['rɪpsnɔ:tə(r)] *n. (sl.)* *(person)* Teufelskerl, *der (ugs.)*; *(thing)* **a ~-snorter of a storm/match** *etc.* ein mordsmäßiger Sturm/mordsmäßiges Spiel *usw.*; ~ **tide** *n.* *(turbulence)* Kabbelung, *die; (current)* Brandungsrückströmung, *die*

rise [raɪz] **1.** *n.* **a)** *(going up) (of sun etc.)* Aufgang, *der; (Theatre: of curtain)* Aufgehen, *das; (advancement)* Aufstieg, *der;* ~ **and** ~ *(joc.)* unaufhaltsamer Aufstieg; **b)** *(emergence)* Aufkommen, *das;* **c)** *(increase) (in value, price, cost)* Steigerung, *die; (St. Exch.: in shares)* Hausse, *die; (in population, temperature)* Zunahme, *die;* **be on the ~**: steigen; zunehmen; **d)** *(Brit.)* **[pay]** ~ *(in wages)* Lohnerhöhung, *die; (in salary)* Gehaltserhöhung, *die;* **e)** *(hill)* Anhöhe, *die;* Erhebung, *die;* **a ~ in the road** eine Steigung; **f)** *(origin)* Ursprung, *der;* **give ~ to** führen zu; ‹*Ereignis*:› Anlaß geben zu ‹*Spekulation*›; **what has given ~ to this bizarre idea?** wie kommt denn diese seltsame Idee?; **g)** *(Angling)* Steigen, *das; (fish)* steigender Fisch; **h) get** *or* **take a ~ out of sb.** *(fig.) (make fun of)* sich über jmdn. lustig machen; *(annoy, provoke)* jmdn. reizen; **i)** *(height of step)* [Stufen]höhe, *die.* **2.** *v.i.*, **rose** [rəʊz], **risen** ['rɪzn] **a)** *(go up)* aufsteigen; ~ **[up] into the air** ‹*Rauch*:› aufsteigen, in die Höhe steigen; ‹*Ballon, Vogel, Flugzeug*:› sich in die Luft erheben; **b)** *(come up)* ‹*Sonne, Mond*:› aufgehen; ‹*Blase*:› aufsteigen; **indignation rose in him** Unmut stieg in ihm hoch; **c)** *(reach higher level)* steigen; ‹*Stimme*:› höher werden; **her pleading rose to heights of passionate eloquence** ihr inständiges Bitten steigerte sich zu leidenschaftlicher Beredtheit; **d)** *(extend upward)* aufragen; sich erheben; ‹*Weg, Straße*:› ansteigen; ~ **to 2,000 metres** ‹*Berg*:› 2 000 m hoch aufragen; ~ **[a storey] higher than sth.** etw. [um ein Stockwerk] überragen; **e)** *(advance)* ‹*Person*:› aufsteigen, aufrücken; ~ **to a rank/to be the director** in einen Rang/zum Direktor aufsteigen; ~ **in one's profession** in seinem Beruf voran- *od.* vorwärts- *od.* weiterkommen; ~ **in the world** voran- *od.* weiterkommen; *see also* **fame; ¹rank 1 e; f)** *(increase)* steigen; ‹*Interesse*:› wachsen; ‹*Stimme*:› lauter werden; *(blow more strongly)* ‹*Wind, Sturm*:› auffrischen, stärker werden; ~ **to a gale** zum Sturm werden; **g)** *(Cookery)* ‹*Teig, Kuchen*:› aufgehen; **h)** *(become more cheerful)* ‹*Stimmung, Moral*:› steigen; **i)** *(come to surface)* ‹*Fisch*:› steigen; ~ **to the bait** *(fig.)* sich ködern lassen *(ugs.)*; ~ **to sb.'s taunts** sich von jmdm. herausfordern lassen; **j)** *(Theatre)* ‹*Vorhang*:› aufgehen, sich heben; ~ **on a scene** *or* **to reveal a scene** [aufgehen *od.* sich heben und] den Blick auf eine Szene freigeben; **k)** *(rebel, cease to be quiet)* ‹*Person*:› aufbegehren *(geh.)*, sich erheben; ~ **as one man** wie ein Mann aufstehen; ~ **in arms** einen bewaffneten Aufstand machen; **my whole soul ~s against it** mein ganzes Inneres sträubt sich dagegen; *see also* **gorge 1 b; l)** *(get up)* ~ **[to one's feet]** aufstehen; *(from sitting or lying also; after accolade)* sich erheben; **he fell, never to ~ again** er stürzte und kam nicht wieder auf die Beine; ~ **on its hind legs** ‹*Pferd*:› steigen; ~ **and shine!** *(coll.)* aufstehen!; raus aus den Federn! *(ugs.)*; *see also* **sun 1; m)** *(adjourn)* ‹*Parlament*:› in die Ferien gehen, die Sitzungsperiode beenden; *(end a session)* die Sitzung beenden; **n)** *(come to life again)* auferstehen; **Christ is ~n** Christus ist auferstanden *od. (geh.)* erstanden; ~ **from the ashes** *(fig.)* ‹*Industrie*:› aus den Trümmern wiedererstehen; **look as though one had ~n from the grave** wie eine lebende Leiche aussehen *(salopp)*; **o)** *(have origin)* ‹*Fluß*:› entspringen

~ **above** *v.t.* überragen; *(fig.)* hinauskommen über (+ *Akk.*) ‹*Niveau*›; *(morally)* erhaben sein über (+ *Akk.*)

~ **to** *v.t. see* **challenge 1 b; occasion 1 a**

~ **'up** *v.i.* **a)** *(get up)* aufstehen; sich erheben; **b)** *(advance)* aufsteigen; *(in level)* ansteigen; **c)** *(rebel)* ~ **up [in revolt]** aufbegehren *(geh.)*; sich erheben; **d)** *(extend upward)* ‹*Berg*:› aufragen; ~ **up to 2,000 metres** 2 000 m hoch aufragen

riser ['raɪzə(r)] *n.* **a)** *(one who gets up)* **early ~**: Frühaufsteher, *der*/Frühaufsteherin, *die;* **late ~**: Spätaufsteher, *der*/Spätaufsteherin, *die;* **b)** *(of stair, step)* Setzstufe, *die;* **c)** *(vertical pipe)* Steigrohr, *das;* Steigleitung, *die*

risible ['rɪzɪbl] *adj. (literary)* lächerlich

rising ['raɪzɪŋ] **1.** *n.* **a)** *(appearance above the horizon)* Aufgang, *der;* **b)** *(increase in height)* Steigen, *das;* **he waited for the ~ of the tide** er wartete auf die Flut; **c)** *(getting up)* Aufstehen, *das;* **d)** *(revolt)* Aufstand, *der;* **e)** *(resurrection)* Auferstehung, *die.* **2.** *adj.* **a)** *(appearing above the horizon)* aufgehend; **b)** *(increasing)* steigend ‹*Kosten, Temperatur*›; *(fig.)* wachsend ‹*Entrüstung, Wut, Ärger, Bedeutung*›; **c)** *(mounting)* steigend ‹*Wasser, Flut*›; hochgehend ‹*Welle*›; **d) the ~ generation** die heranwachsende Generation; **e)** *(advancing in standing)* aufstrebend; **f)** *(sloping upwards)* ansteigend; **g)** *(approaching the age of)* **be ~ forty** auf die Vierzig zugehen; **be ~ sixteen** sechzehn werden; **the ~ fives** die fast fünfjährigen Kinder

rising: ~ butt *see* ~ **hinge;** ~ **'damp** *n.* aufsteigende Feuchtigkeit; ~ **hinge** *n.* Hebescharnier, *das*

risk [rɪsk] **1.** *n.* **a)** *(hazard)* Gefahr, *die;* *(chance taken)* Risiko, *das;* ~ **of infection/loss** Ansteckungsgefahr, *die*/Verlustrisiko, *das;* **there is a/no ~ of sb.'s doing sth.** *or* **that sb. will do sth.** es besteht die/keine Gefahr, daß jmd. etw. tut; **at the ~ of one's life** unter Lebensgefahr; **be at ~** ‹*Zukunft, Plan*:› in Gefahr sein, gefährdet sein; **at one's own ~**: auf eigene Gefahr *od.* eigenes Risiko; **at owner's ~**: auf Gefahr *od.* Risiko des Eigentümers; **'coats/luggage** *etc.* **left at owner's ~'** „keine Haftung für Garderobe/Gepäck *usw.*"; **put at ~**: gefährden; in Gefahr bringen; **run** *or* **take a ~**: ein Risiko *od.* Wagnis eingehen *od.* auf sich *(Akk.)* nehmen; **run** *or* **take ~s/a lot of ~s** etwas/viel riskieren; **take ~s with one's life** sein Leben in Gefahr bringen *od.* riskieren; **run the ~ of doing sth.** Gefahr laufen, etw. zu tun; *(knowingly)* es riskieren, etw. zu tun; **take the ~ of doing sth.** es riskieren, etw. zu tun; das Risiko eingehen *od.* in Kauf nehmen, etw. zu tun; **b)** *(Insurance)* **he is a poor/good ~**: bei ihm ist das Risiko groß/gering. **2.** *v.t.* riskieren; wagen ‹*Sprung, Kampf*›; **you'll ~ losing your job** du riskierst es, deinen Job zu verlieren; **I'll ~ it!** ich lasse es drauf ankommen; ich riskiere es; ~ **one's life/neck** sein Leben/seinen Hals riskieren; *(thoughtlessly)* sein Leben aufs Spiel setzen

riskily ['rɪskɪlɪ] *adv.* riskant; gewagt

'risk-money *n.* Fehlgeld, *das*

risky ['rɪskɪ] *adj.* gefährlich; riskant, gewagt ‹*Experiment, Unternehmen, Projekt*›

risotto [rɪ'zɒtəʊ] *n., pl.* **~s** *(Cookery)* Risotto, *der od. das*

risqué ['rɪskeɪ] *adj.* gewagt; nicht ganz salonfähig

rissole ['rɪsəʊl] *n. (Cookery)* Rissole, *die*

rite [raɪt] *n.* Ritus, *der;* ~ **of passage** Rite de passage *(Völkerk.)*; Übergangsritus, *der*

ritual ['rɪtʃʊəl] **1.** *adj. (of ritual)* rituell; Ritual‹*mord, -tötung*›; *(done as ritual)* ritualisiert; ~ **object** Kultgegenstand, *der.* **2.** *n.* **a)** *(act)* Ritual, *das;* **b)** *no pl. (prescribed procedure)* Ritus, *der;* Ritual, *das;* **he likes ~**: er mag Rituale

ritualistic [rɪtʃʊə'lɪstɪk] *adj.* ritualistisch

ritually ['rɪtʃʊəlɪ] *adv.* rituell; in einem rituellen Akt ‹*töten*›

ritzy ['rɪtsɪ] *adj. (coll.)* **a)** *(high-class)* feudal, nobel ‹*Hotel, Restaurant, Wohnung usw.*›; smart ‹*Mann, Kleidung*›; **b)** *(derog.: ostentatiously smart)* stinkfein ‹*Vorort, Schule*›; *(pretentious-looking)* protzig *(ugs. abwertend)*

rival ['raɪvl] **1.** *n.* **a)** *(competitor)* Rivale, *der*/Rivalin, *die;* **they were ~s for her affection** sie rivalisierten um ihre Zuneigung; **~s in love** Nebenbuhler; **business ~s** Konkurrenten; **b)** *(equal)* **have no ~/~s** seines-/ihresgleichen suchen; **without ~s** konkurrenzlos. **2.** *v.t.*, *(Brit.)* **-ll-** gleichkommen (+ *Dat.*); nicht nachstehen (+ *Dat.*); **he can't ~ that** da kann er nicht mithalten; **I cannot ~ him for speed** an Geschwindigkeit kann ich es nicht mit ihm aufnehmen. **3.** *adj.* rivalisierend ‹*Gruppen*›; konkurrierend ‹*Forderungen*›; Konkurrenz‹*unternehmen usw.*›; ~ **applicant** Mitbewerber, *der*/-bewerberin, *die*

rivalry ['raɪvlrɪ] *n.* Rivalität, *die (geh.)*; **business ~**: Wettbewerb, *der;* **friendly ~**: freundschaftlicher Wettstreit

riven ['rɪvn] *adj. (dated, literary)* zerrissen; ~ **by grief** vom Gram zerfressen

river ['rɪvə(r)] **1.** *n.* **a)** Fluß, *der; (large)* Strom, *der;* **the ~ Thames** *(Brit.)*, **the Thames ~** *(Amer.)* die Themse; **sell sb. down the ~** *(fig. coll.)* jmdn. verschaukeln *(ugs.)*; **go up the ~** *(Amer. fig. coll.)* ins Kittchen wandern *(ugs.)*; **b)** *(fig.)* Strom, *der;* ~ **of lava** Lavastrom, *der;* **~s of tears/blood** Ströme von Tränen/Blut. **2.** *attrib. adj.* **a)** *(Biol.)* Fluß‹*delphin, -aal, -krebs*›; **b)** *(of ~)* Fluß‹*tal, -ufer, -gott usw.*›

river: ~ basin *n.* Stromgebiet, *das;* Einzugsgebiet [eines Flusses]; **~-bed** *n.* Flußbett, *das;* ~ **bottom** *n. (Amer.)* Flußebene, die; ~-**head** *n.* Flußquelle, *die;* ~**side 1.** *n.* Flußufer, *das;* **on** *or* **by the ~side** am Fluß; **2.** *attrib. adj.* am Fluß gelegen; am Fluß *nachgestellt*

rivet ['rɪvɪt] **1.** *n.* Niete, *die;* Niet, *der od. das (Technik).* **2.** *v.t.* **a)** [ver]nieten; ~ **sth. down/together** etw. annieten *od.* festnieten/zusammennieten; **b)** *(fig.: hold firmly)* fesseln ‹*Person, Aufmerksamkeit, Blick*›; **be ~ed to the spot** wie angenagelt [da]stehen *(ugs.);* **be ~ed on sth.** ‹*Aufmerksamkeit:*› durch etw. gefesselt werden; **his eyes were ~ed on** *or* **to the screen** seine Augen waren auf den Bildschirm geheftet *(geh.)*

riveter ['rɪvɪtə(r)] *n.* Nieter, *der*/Nieterin, *die; (machine)* Nietmaschine, *die*

riveting ['rɪvɪtɪŋ] *adj.* fesselnd

Riviera [rɪvɪ'eərə] *n.* Riviera, *die*

rivulet ['rɪvjʊlɪt] *n. (lit. or fig.)* Bach, *der*

rly. *abbr.* **railway** Eisenb.

RM *abbr. (Brit.)* **a) Royal Mail; b) Royal Marines**

rm. *abbr.* **room** Zi.

RN *abbr. (Brit.)* **Royal Navy** Königl. Mar.

RNA *abbr.* **ribonucleic acid** RNS

RNIB *abbr. (Brit.)* **Royal National Institute for the Blind** *Königliches Blindeninstitut*

RNLI *abbr. (Brit.)* **Royal National Lifeboat Institution** *Königliches Institut für Rettungsboote*

RNR, RNVR *abbrs. (Brit. Hist.)* **Royal Navy [Volunteer] Reserve** *[Freiwillige] Reserve der Königlichen Marine*

[1]**roach** [rəʊtʃ] *n., pl. same (fish)* Plötze, *die;* Rotauge, *das*

[2]**roach** *(Amer.) see* **cockroach**

road [rəʊd] *n.* **a)** Straße, *die;* **the Birmingham/London ~:** die Straße nach Birmingham/London; *(name of ~/street)* **London/Shelley R~:** Londoner Straße/Shelleystraße; **'~ up'** „Straßenarbeiten"; **'~ narrows'** „Fahrbahnverengung"; **across** *or* **over the ~ [from us]** [bei uns *od. (geh.)* uns *(Dat.)*] gegenüber; **by ~** *(by car/bus)* per Auto/Bus; *(by lorry/truck)* per LKW; **off the ~** *(on the verge etc.)* neben der Straße *od.* Fahrbahn; *(across country)* im Gelände ‹*ein Fahrzeug benutzen*›; durchs Gelände ‹*fahren*›; *(being repaired)* in der Werkstatt; in Reparatur; **take a vehicle off the ~** *(no longer use it)* ein Fahrzeug stillegen; **one for the ~** *(coll.)* ein Glas zum Abschied; **be a danger on the ~:** eine Gefahr für den Straßenverkehr sein; **be on the ~:** auf Reisen *od.* unterwegs sein; ‹*Theaterensemble usw.:*› auf Tournee *od. (ugs.)* Tour *(Dat.)* sein; **put a vehicle on the ~:** ein Fahrzeug in Betrieb nehmen; **take the ~:** sich auf den Weg machen; aufbrechen; *(become tramp)* ein Tramp werden; **the rule of the ~:** die Verkehrsregeln; **b)** *(means of access)* Weg, *der;* **set sb. on the ~ to ruin** jmdn. ins Verderben führen; **be on the right ~:** auf dem richtigen Weg sein; **be on the ~ to success/ruin** auf dem Weg zum Erfolg sein/in sein Verderben rennen; **change one's mind somewhere along the ~** *(fig.)* es sich *(Dat.)* irgendwo unterwegs anders überlegen; **end of the ~** *(destination)* Ziel, *das; (limit)* Ende, *das;* **it's the end of the ~ for us** *(fig.)* mit uns ist es jetzt vorbei; **c)** *(one's way)* Weg, *der;* **get in sb.'s ~** *(coll.)* jmdm. in die Quere kommen *(ugs.);* **get out of my ~!** *(coll.)* geh mir aus dem Weg!; **d)** *(Amer.) see* **railway; e)** *(Mining)* Strecke, *die;* **f)** *usu. in pl. (Naut.)* Reede, *die;* **lie in the ~s** auf der Reede liegen

road: ~ accident *n.* Verkehrsunfall, *der;* **~-accident victims** Verkehrsopfer; ~ **atlas** *n.* Autoatlas, *der;* ~**-bed** *n.* **a)** *(foundation of ~, railway)* Unterbau, *der;* **b)** *(Amer.: part of ~ on which vehicles travel)* Fahrbahn, *die;* ~**-block** *n.* Straßensperre, *die;* ~**-book** *n.* Autoreiseführer, *der;* ~ **bridge** *n.* Straßenbrücke, *die;* ~ **fund licence** *n. (Brit.)* Kfz-Steuerbeleg, *der;* ~**-hog** *n.* Verkehrsrowdy, *der (abwertend);* ~**-holding** *n. (Brit. Motor Veh.)* Straßenlage, *die;* ~**-house** *n.* Rasthaus, *das*

roadie ['rəʊdɪ] *n. (coll.)* Roadie, *der*

road: ~ manager *n.* Roadmanager, *der;* ~**-map** *n.* Straßenkarte, *die;* ~**-mender** *n.* Straßen[bau]arbeiter, *der*/-arbeiterin, *die;* ~**-metal** *n.* Schotter, *der; (smaller pieces)* Splitt, *der;* ~ **roller** *n.* Straßenwalze, *die;* ~**runner** *n. (Ornith.) (Geococcyx californianus)* Erdkuckuck, *der; (G. velox)* Rennkuckuck, *der;* ~ **safety** *n.* Verkehrssicherheit, *die;* ~ **sense** *n.* Gespür für Verkehrssituationen; ~ **show** *n. (lit. or fig.)* Tournee, *die;* Tour, *die (ugs.);* ~**side 1.** *n.* Straßenrand, *der;* **at** *or* **by/along the ~side** am Straßenrand; an/entlang der Straße; **2.** *adj.* ‹*Gasthaus usw.*› am Straßenrand, an der Straße; **~side inn** Rasthaus, *das;* ~ **sign** *n.* Straßenschild, *das (ugs.);* Verkehrszeichen, *das*

roadster ['rəʊdstə(r)] *n.* **a)** *(open car)* Roadster, *der;* Sportkabrio[lett], *das;* **b)** *(bicycle)* Tourenrad, *das*

road: ~-sweeper *n.* **a)** *(person)* Straßenkehrer, *der*/-kehrerin, *die (bes. südd.);* Straßenfeger, *der*/-fegerin, *die (bes. nordd.);* **b)** *(machine)* [Straßen]kehrmaschine, *die;* ~ **test** *n.* Fahrtest, *der;* ~**-test** *v.t.* einem Fahrtest unterziehen; ~ **transport** *n.* **a) form of ~ transport** Verkehrsmittel der Straße; **b)** *(process)* Personen- und Güterbeförderung auf der Straße; ~**-user** *n.* Verkehrsteilnehmer, *der*/-teilnehmerin, *die;* ~**way** *n.* **a)** *(road)* Straße, *die;* **b)** *(central part of road)* Fahrbahn, *die;* ~**-works** *n. pl.* Straßenbauarbeiten *Pl.;* '**~-works**' „Baustelle"; ~**worthy** *adj.* fahrtüchtig ‹*Fahrzeug*›

roam [rəʊm] **1.** *v.i.* umherstreifen; herumstreifen *(ugs.);* ‹*Nomade:*› wandern; *(stray)* ‹*Tier:*› streunen; ~ **through the town** durch die Stadt streifen; **be free to ~** ‹*Tier:*› frei herumlaufen dürfen; **tendency to ~:** Hang zum Streunen. **2.** *v.t.* streifen durch; durchstreifen *(geh.).* **3.** *n.* Streifzug, *der*

~ **a'bout,** ~ **a'round 1.** *v.i.* herumstreifen *(ugs.);* umherstreifen; **he ~s about all over the place** er zieht überall in der Gegend herum *(ugs.).* **2.** *v.t.* herumstreifen in (+ *Dat.*) *(ugs.);* durchstreifen *(geh.)*

roamer ['rəʊmə(r)] *n. (person)* Herumtreiber, *der (ugs.); (animal)* streunendes Tier

roaming ['rəʊmɪŋ] *adj.* wandernd ‹*Herde*›; *(fig.)* schweifend, wandernd ‹*Gedanke*›

[1]**roan** [rəʊn] **1.** *adj.* stichelhaarig ‹*Fell, Tier*›. **2.** *n. (horse)* stichelhaariges Pferd; *(cow)* stichelhaarige Kuh; **be a ~:** stichelhaarig sein

[2]**roan** *n. (Bookbinding)* Schafleder, *das*

roar [rɔ:(r)] **1.** *n. (of wild beast)* Brüllen, *das;* Gebrüll, *das; (of water)* Tosen, *das;* Getose, *das; (of avalanche, guns)* Donner, *der; (of applause)* Tosen, *das; (of machine, traffic)* Dröhnen, *das;* Getöse, *das;* **a ~ of applause** tosender Beifall; **~s/a ~ [of laughter]** dröhnendes *od.* brüllendes Gelächter. **2.** *v.i.* **a)** *(cry loudly)* brüllen (**with** vor + *Dat.*); ~ **[with laughter]** [vor Lachen] brüllen; **b)** *(make loud noise)* ‹*Motor:*› dröhnen; ‹*Artillerie:*› donnern; *(blaze up)* ‹*Feuer:*› bullern *(ugs.);* **c)** *(travel fast)* ‹*Fahrzeug:*› donnern. **3.** *v.t.* brüllen; ~ **[one's] approval [of sth.]** [einer Sache *(Dat.)*] lautstark zustimmen

roaring ['rɔ:rɪŋ] **1.** *adj.* **a)** *(making loud noise)* dröhnend ‹*Motor, Donner*›; tosend ‹*Meer*›; brüllend ‹*Löwe*›; **b)** *(blazing loudly)* bullernd *(ugs.)* ‹*Feuer*›; **a ~ inferno** ein tosendes Inferno; **c)** *(riotous)* **a ~ success** ein Bombenerfolg *(ugs.);* **the ~ twenties** die wilden zwanziger Jahre; die Roaring Twenties; **d)** *(brisk)* **do a ~ business** *or* **trade** ein Bombengeschäft machen; *see also* **forty 2. 2.** *adv.* ~ **drunk** sternhagelvoll *(salopp)*

roast [rəʊst] **1.** *v.t.* **a)** *(cook by radiant heat)* braten; *(prepare by heating)* rösten ‹*Kaffeebohnen, Erdnüsse, Mandeln, Kastanien*›; **b)** *(expose to heat)* ~ **oneself in front of the fire/in the sun** sich am Feuer rösten lassen/in der Sonne braten lassen *(scherzh.);* **c)** *(Metallurgy)* rösten ‹*Erz*›; **d)** *(coll.) (tell off)* zusammenstauchen *(ugs.)* ‹*Person*›; *(esp. Amer.: criticize)* abqualifizieren; heruntermachen *(salopp);* geißeln, anprangern ‹*Vorgehensweise*›; verreißen ‹*Buch usw.*›. **2.** *attrib. adj.* gebraten ‹*Fleisch, Ente usw.*›; Brat‹*hähnchen, -kartoffeln*›; Röst‹*kastanien*›; **eat ~ duck/pork/beef** Enten-/Schweine-/Rinderbraten essen; ~ **[sirloin of] beef** Roastbeef, *das.* **3.** *n.* **a)** *(~ meat, meat for ~ing)* Braten, *der;* **b)** *see* **1 a:** Braten, *das;* Rösten, *das;* **give sth. a ~:** etw. braten/rösten; **c)** *(Amer.: social gathering)* Grillparty, *die;* Grillfest, *das.* **4.** *v.i.* **a)** ‹*Fleisch:*› braten; **b)** *(bask in warmth of sun/fire)* sich braten/rösten lassen *(scherzh.)*

roaster ['rəʊstə(r)] *n.* **a)** *(oven)* Bratofen, *der; (dish)* Bratentopf, *der; (for coffee)* Röstmaschine, *die;* **b)** *(chicken)* Brathähnchen, *das;* **c)** *(Metallurgy: furnace)* Röstofen, *der;* **d)** *(coll.: hot day)* knallheißer Tag *(ugs.)*

roasting ['rəʊstɪŋ] **1.** *n.* **a)** *(cooking)* Braten, *das; (of coffee, ore)* Rösten, *das; attrib.* ‹*Fleisch, Huhn*› zum Braten; Brat‹*spieß, -zeit*›; Braten‹*wender, -gabel*›; **b)** *(severe criticism) (by parent, boss, etc.)* Standpauke, *die (ugs.); (by critic)* Verriß, *der (ugs.);* **get a ~:** eins auf den Deckel kriegen *(ugs.);* **give sb. a ~:** jmdn zusammenstauchen *(ugs.);* **give sth. a ~** ‹*Kritiker:*› etw. verreißen *(ugs.).* **2.** *adj. (coll.: hot)* knallheiß *(ugs.);* **I am ~:** ich komme um vor Hitze

rob [rɒb] *v.t.,* **-bb-** ausrauben ‹*Bank, Safe, Kasse*›; berauben ‹*Person*›; *abs.* rauben; ~ **sth. of sth.** einer Sache *(Dat.)* etw. nehmen; ~ **sb. of sth.** jmdm. etw. rauben *od.* stehlen; *(deprive of what is due)* jmdn. um etw. bringen *od.* betrügen; *(withhold sth. from)* jmdm. etw. vorenthalten; ~ **a bird of its eggs** einem Vogel die Eier wegnehmen; **be ~bed** bestohlen werden; *(by force)* beraubt werden; **we wuz ~bed** *(Sport sl.)* das war Schiebung! *(ugs.); see also* **Peter**

robber ['rɒbə(r)] *n.* Räuber, *der*/Räuberin, *die;* **band of ~s** Räuberbande, *die*

robbery ['rɒbərɪ] *n.* Raub, *der;* **robberies** Raubüberfälle; **it's sheer ~!** das ist ja die reinste Halsabschneiderei *(ugs. abwertend)*

robe [rəʊb] **1.** *n.* **a)** *(ceremonial garment)* Gewand, *das (geh.); (of judge, vicar)* Talar, *der;* **coronation ~s** Krönungsornat, *der;* ~ **of office** Amtstracht, *die;* **b)** *(long garment)* [langes Über]gewand; **c)** *(dressing-gown)* Morgenrock, *der;* **beach ~:** Bademantel, *der;* **d) christening ~:** Taufkleid, *das;* **e)** *(Amer.: blanket)* [Reise]decke, *die;* **f)** *(Amer.: wardrobe)* [Kleider]schrank, *der.* **2.** *v.t. (formal)* ~ **sb. in sth.** jmdn. in etw. *(Akk.)* kleiden; jmdm. etw. anlegen *(geh.);* **the vicar/judge ~d himself** der Pfarrer/Richter legte *(geh.) od.* zog einen/seinen/den Talar an. **3.** *v.i. (formal)* sich ankleiden *(geh.)*

robin ['rɒbɪn] *n. (Ornith.)* **a)** ~ **[redbreast]** Rotkehlchen, *das;* **b)** *(Amer.: thrush)* Wanderdrossel, *die*

robing-room ['rəʊbɪŋru:m, 'rəʊbɪŋrʊm] *n.* Ankleideraum, *der*

Robin 'Hood *n.* Robin Hood *(der)*

robinia [rə'bɪnɪə] *n. (Bot.)* Robinie, *die;* falsche Akazie

robot ['rəʊbɒt] *n.* Roboter, *der*

robotics [rəʊ'bɒtɪks] *n., no pl.* Robotertechnik, *die;* Robotik, *die*

robust [rəʊ'bʌst] *adj.* **a)** *(strong)* robust ‹*Person, Gesundheit, Nervenkostüm*›; kräftig ‹*Person, Wein*›; *(not delicate)* unempfindlich, widerstandsfähig ‹*Pflanze*›; **b)** *(strongly built)* kräftig ‹*Gestalt, Körperbau*›; robust ‹*Fahrzeug, Maschine, Konstruktion, Möbel*›; stabil ‹*Haus*›; **c)** *(fig.: straightfor-*

ward) unerschütterlich ⟨*Skepsis*⟩; nüchtern ⟨*Verstand*⟩; fest ⟨*Glaube*⟩

robustly [rəʊˈbʌstlɪ] *adv.* stabil, solide ⟨*bauen*⟩; energisch ⟨*sich entgegenstellen*⟩

[1]**rock** [rɒk] *n.* **a)** *(piece of ~)* Fels, *der;* **come to grief on the ~s** ⟨*Schiff:*⟩ auf Felsen *od.* Klippen auflaufen; **be as solid as a ~** *(fig.)* absolut zuverlässig sein; **be as steady as a ~:** bombenfest sein; *(fig.)* durch nichts zu erschüttern sein; **b)** *(large ~, hill)* Felsen, *der;* Fels, *der (geh.);* **the R~ [of Gibraltar]** [der Felsen von] Gibraltar; **c)** *(substance)* Fels, *der; (esp. Geol.)* Gestein, *das;* **mass of ~:** Felsmasse, *die;* **d)** *(boulder)* Felsbrocken, *der; (Amer.: stone)* Stein, *der;* Steinbrocken, *der;* **'danger, falling ~s'** „Achtung *od.* Vorsicht, Steinschlag!"; „Steinschlaggefahr!"; **e)** *no pl., no indef. art. (hard sweet)* **stick of ~:** Zuckerstange, *die;* **sell ~:** Zuckerstangen verkaufen; **f)** *(fig.: support)* Stütze, *die;* Rückhalt, *der; (of society)* Fundament, *das;* **g)** *(fig.: source of danger or destruction)* **a ~ on which others have foundered** eine Klippe, an der schon andere gescheitert sind; **be heading for the ~s** ⟨*Ehe:*⟩ zu scheitern drohen; **be on the ~s** *(fig. coll.) (be short of/without money)* knapp bei Kasse/pleite sein *(ugs.); (have failed)* ⟨*Ehe, Firma:*⟩ kaputt sein *(ugs.);* **h) on the ~s** *(with ice cubes)* mit Eis *od.* on the rocks; **i)** *in pl. (Amer. sl.: money)* Kies, *der (salopp);* **j)** *(sl.: gem)* Klunker, *der (ugs.)*

[2]**rock 1.** *v. t.* **a)** *(move to and fro)* wiegen; *(in cradle)* schaukeln; wiegen; **~ oneself** *(in chair)* schaukeln; sich wiegen; **b)** *(shake)* erschüttern; *(fig.)* erschüttern ⟨*Person*⟩; **~ sth. to its foundations** *(fig.)* etw. in seinen Grundfesten erschüttern; **~ the boat** *(fig. coll.)* Trouble machen *(ugs.).* **2.** *v. i.* **a)** *(move to and fro)* sich wiegen; schaukeln; **b)** *(sway)* schwanken; wanken; **~ with laughter** sich vor Lachen *(Dat.)* schütteln; **c)** *(dance)* rocken; Rock tanzen; **~ and roll** Rock and Roll tanzen. **3.** *n.* **a)** *(~ing motion, spell of ~ing)* Schaukeln, *das;* **give the cradle a ~:** die Wiege schaukeln; **b)** *(beat music or dance)* Rock, *der; attrib.* Rock-; **~ and** *or* **'n' roll [music]** Rock and Roll, *der;* Rock 'n' Roll, *der;* **do the ~ and roll** Rock and Roll tanzen

rock: ~-'bottom *(coll.)* **1.** *adj.* **~-bottom prices** Schleuderpreise *(ugs.);* **at a ~-bottom price/rent** spottbillig *(ugs.);* **2.** *n.* **reach** *or* **hit** *or* **touch ~-bottom** ⟨*Handel, Währung, Nachfrage, Preis usw.:*⟩ in den Keller fallen *od.* sinken *(ugs.);* **her spirits reached ~-bottom** ihre Stimmung war auf dem Tiefpunkt [angelangt]; **~-cake** *n. Rosinengebäck mit rauher Oberfläche;* **~-climbing** *n.* [Fels]klettern, *das*

rocker [ˈrɒkə(r)] *n.* **a)** *(Brit.: gang member)* Rocker, *der;* **b)** *(curved bar of chair, cradle, etc.)* Kufe, *die;* **be/go off one's ~** *(fig. sl.)* übergeschnappt *od.* durchgedreht sein *(ugs.)*/überschnappen *(ugs.) od.* durchdrehen *(ugs.);* **c)** *(rocking-chair)* Schaukelstuhl, *der;* **d)** *(Electr.)* **~ [switch]** Wippschalter, *der;* **e)** *(Mech. Engin.)* Kipphebel, *der*

rockery [ˈrɒkərɪ] *n.* Steingarten, *der*

[1]**rocket** [ˈrɒkɪt] **1.** *n.* **a)** Rakete, *die;* **~ range** *(place)* Raketenversuchsgelände, *das;* **b)** *(Brit. sl.: reprimand)* **give sb. a ~:** jmdm. eine Zigarre verpassen *(ugs.);* **get a ~:** eine Zigarre bekommen *(ugs.).* **2.** *v. i.* **a)** ⟨*Preise:*⟩ in die Höhe schnellen; **b) ~ into the air** wie eine Rakete in die Luft schießen

[2]**rocket** *n. (Bot.)* **a) [sweet] ~:** Nachtviole, *die;* **b)** *(used in salad)* [Öl]ranke, *die*

rocket: ~-base *n. (Mil.)* Raketen[abschuß]basis, *die;* **~-bomb** *n.* **a)** *(air-to-ground)* [Flieger]rakete, *die;* Luft-Boden-Rakete, *die;* **b)** *(ground-to-ground)* [Artillerie]rakete, *die;* Boden-Boden-Rakete, *die;* **~ engine** *n.* Raketentriebwerk, *das;* **~-firing** *adj.* mit Raketen bewaffnet *nachgestellt;* **~ flight** *n.* Raketenflug, *der;* **~-launcher** *n.* Raketenwerfer, *der;* **~ plane** *n.* Raketenflugzeug, *das;* **~-powered, ~-propelled** *adjs.* raketengetrieben; **~ propulsion** *n.* Raketenantrieb, *der;* **~ range** *n.* Raketenversuchsgelände, *das*

rocketry [ˈrɒkɪtrɪ] *n., no pl.* Raketentechnik, *die*

rock: ~ face *n.* Felswand, *die;* **~fall** *n.* Steinschlag, *der;* **~-garden** *n.* Steingarten, *der;* **~-hard** *adj.* steinhart

Rockies [ˈrɒkɪz] *pr. n. pl.* **the ~:** die Rocky Mountains

rocking [ˈrɒkɪŋ]: **~-chair** *n.* Schaukelstuhl, *der;* **~-horse** *n.* Schaukelpferd, *das*

rock: ~like *adj.* felsartig; felsenfest ⟨*Glaube usw.*⟩; **~-plant** *n.* Felsenpflanze, *die; (Hort.)* Steingartengewächs, *das;* **~ salmon** *n.* **a)** *(Brit.: dogfish)* Katzenhai, *der;* **b)** *(Amer.: Seriola)* Gelbschwanzmakrele, *die;* **~-salt** *n.* Steinsalz, *das*

rocky [ˈrɒkɪ] *adj.* **a)** *(coll.: unsteady)* wackelig *(ugs.);* **b)** *(full or consisting of rocks)* felsig; **c) the R~ Mountains** *see* **Rockies**

rococo [rəˈkəʊkəʊ] **1.** *adj.* Rokoko-; *(florid)* schwülstig. **2.** *n., pl.* **~s** Rokoko, *das*

rod [rɒd] *n.* **a)** Stange, *die;* **ride the ~s** *(Amer. sl.)* [im Gestänge unter Eisenbahnwaggons] schwarzfahren; **b)** *(shorter)* Stab, *der;* **~ of office** Amtsstab, *der;* **c)** *(for punishing)* Stock, *der;* Rute, *die;* **the ~** *(punishment)* die Prügelstrafe; **make a ~ for one's own back** *(fig.)* sich *(Dat.)* selbst eine Rute aufbinden *(veralt.);* **a ~ to beat sb. with** *(fig.)* Sanktionen gegen jmdn.; **rule with a ~ of iron** *(fig.)* mit eiserner Faust *od.* Rute regieren; **spare the ~ and spoil the child** wer die Rute schont, verdirbt das Kind; **d)** *(for fishing)* [Angel]rute, *die;* **e)** *(measure)* Rute, *die (veralt.);* **f)** *(Amer. sl.: gun)* Schießeisen, *das (ugs.);* **g)** *(Anat.)* Stäbchen, *das*

rode *see* **ride 2, 3**

rodent [ˈrəʊdənt] *n.* Nagetier, *das*

ˈ**rodent officer** *n. (Brit.)* Rattenfänger, *der*

rodeo [ˈrəʊdɪəʊ, rəʊˈdeɪəʊ] *n., pl.* **~s** Rodeo, *der od. das*

[1]**roe** [rəʊ] *n. (of fish)* **[hard] ~:** Rogen, *der;* **[soft] ~:** Milch, *die*

[2]**roe** *n. (deer)* Reh, *das*

roe: ~buck *n.* Rehbock, *der;* **~-deer** *n.* Reh, *das*

roentgen [ˈrʌntjən] *n. (Phys.)* Röntgen, *das*

rogation [rəˈgeɪʃn] *n. (Eccl.)* Bittlitanei, *die;* **R~ Days** Bittage *Pl.;* **R~ Sunday** [der Sonntag] Rogate; **R~ Week** Bittwoche, *die*

roger [ˈrɒdʒə(r)] *int.* **a)** *(message received)* verstanden; **b)** *(sl.: I agree)* okay *(ugs.)*

rogue [rəʊg] **1.** *n.* **a)** Gauner, *der (abwertend);* **~s' gallery** *(Police)* Verbrecheralbum, *das;* **b)** *(joc.: mischievous child)* Spitzbube, *der (scherzh.);* **c)** *(dangerous animal)* **~ [buffalo/elephant** *etc.*] bösartiger Einzelgänger. **2.** *attrib. adj.* defekt; fehlerhaft; **~ car** Montagsauto, *das;* **~ result** Ausreißer, *der;* **~ firms** schwarze Schafe unter den Firmen

roguery [ˈrəʊgərɪ] *n., no pl., no indef. art.* Gaunerei, *die; (mischief)* Spitzbüberei, *die*

roguish [ˈrəʊgɪʃ] *adj.* **a)** gaunerhaft; **b)** *(mischievous)* spitzbübisch

roguishly [ˈrəʊgɪʃlɪ] *adv. see* **roguish:** gaunerhaft; spitzbübisch

roisterer [ˈrɔɪstərə(r)] *n.* Krakeeler, *der (ugs. abwertend)*

role, rôle [rəʊl] *n.* Rolle, *die*

role: ~-playing *n.* Rollenspiel, *das;* Rollenverhalten, *das;* **~ reversal** *n.* Rollentausch, *der*

[1]**roll** [rəʊl] *n.* **a)** Rolle, *die; (of cloth, tobacco, etc.)* Ballen, *der; (of fat on body)* Wulst, *der;* **~ of film** Rolle Film; **b)** *(of bread etc.)* **[bread] ~:** Brötchen, *das;* **egg/ham ~:** Eier-/Schinkenbrötchen, *das;* **jam ~:** [Biskuit]rolle mit Marmelade; **c)** *(document)* [Schrift]rolle, *die;* **d)** *(register, catalogue)* Liste, *die;* Verzeichnis, *das;* **~ of honour** Gedenktafel [für die Gefallenen]; **e)** *(Brit.: list of solicitors)* Anwaltsliste, *die;* **strike sb. off the ~s** jmdm. die Zulassung entziehen; **f)** *(Mil., Sch.: list of names)* Liste, *die;* **schools with falling ~s** Schulen mit sinkenden Schülerzahlen; **call the ~:** die Anwesenheit feststellen; **g)** *(Amer.: of paper money)* Geldbündel, *das*

[2]**roll 1.** *n.* **a)** *(of drum)* Wirbel, *der; (of thunder)* Rollen, *das;* **b)** *(motion)* Rollen, *das;* **c)** *(single movement)* Rolle, *die; (of dice)* Wurf, *der;* **d)** *(gait)* wiegender Gang. **2.** *v. t.* **a)** *(move, send)* rollen; *(between surfaces)* drehen; **b)** *(shape by ~ing)* rollen; **~ a cigarette** eine Zigarette rollen *od.* drehen; **~ one's own** [selbst] drehen; **~ snow/wool into a ball** einen Schneeball formen/Wolle zu einem Knäuel aufwickeln; **[all] ~ed into one** *(fig.)* in einem; **~ oneself/itself into a ball** sich zusammenrollen; **~ed in blankets** in Decken eingewickelt; **c)** *(flatten)* walzen ⟨*Rasen, Metall usw.*⟩; ausrollen ⟨*Teig*⟩; **d) ~ one's eyes** die Augen rollen; **~ one's eyes at sb.** *(amorously)* jmdm. schöne Augen machen; **~ one's shoulders/head** die Schultern/den Kopf kreisen; **e) ~ one's r's** das r rollen; **f)** *(Amer.)* **~ dice** würfeln; **g)** *(Amer. sl.: rob)* ausrauben. **3.** *v. i.* **a)** *(move by turning over)* rollen; **heads will ~** *(fig.)* es werden Köpfe rollen; **b)** *(operate)* ⟨*Maschine:*⟩ laufen; ⟨*Presse:*⟩ sich drehen; rotieren; *(on wheels)* rollen; **let it ~** *(start the machine etc.)* laß laufen; **be ready to ~** ⟨*Kamera:*⟩ aufnahmebereit sein; **get sth. ~ing** *(fig.)* etw. ins Rollen bringen; **keep things ~ing** *(fig.)* die Dinge am Laufen halten; *see also* **aisle; [1]ball 1 a, b; c)** *(wallow, sway, walk)* sich wälzen; *(walk also)* schwanken; **the way he ~s along** sein wiegender Gang; **d)** *(Naut.)* ⟨*Schiff:*⟩ rollen, schlingern; **e)** *(revolve)* ⟨*Augen:*⟩ sich [ver]drehen; **f)** *(flow, go forward)* sich wälzen *(fig.);* ⟨*Wolken:*⟩ ziehen; ⟨*Tränen:*⟩ rollen; **~ off** *or* **from sb.'s tongue** *(fig.)* ⟨*Worte:*⟩ jmdm. von den Lippen fließen; **g)** *(make deep sound)* ⟨*Donner:*⟩ rollen; ⟨*Trommel:*⟩ dröhnen

~ aˈbout *v. i.* herumrollen; ⟨*Schiff:*⟩ schlingern, rollen; ⟨*Kind, Hund usw.:*⟩ sich wälzen; **be ~ing about with laughter** sich vor Lachen wälzen

~ aˈlong 1. *v. i.* **a)** [dahin]rollen; ⟨*Fahrzeug:*⟩ [dahin]rollen, [dahin]fahren; **things are ~ing along nicely** *(fig.)* die Dinge laufen gut; **b)** *(coll.: turn up)* eintrudeln *(ugs.);* aufkreuzen *(salopp).* **2.** *v. t.* entlangrollen

~ aˈway 1. *v. i.* ⟨*Ball:*⟩ wegrollen; ⟨*Nebel, Wolken:*⟩ sich verziehen. **2.** *v. t.* wegrollen

~ ˈback 1. *v. t.* **a)** zurückrollen; **b)** *(cause to retreat)* zurückschlagen ⟨*Feinde, Truppen*⟩; **c) ~ back the years/centuries** das Rad der Zeit [um Jahre/Jahrhunderte] zurückdrehen. **2.** *v. i.* ⟨*Wagen, Wellen:*⟩ zurückrollen

~ ˈby *v. i.* vorbeirollen; ⟨*Zeit:*⟩ vergehen; **the years ~ed by** die Jahre zogen ins Land

~ ˈin 1. *v. i. (coll.)* ⟨*Briefe, Geschenke, Geldbeträge:*⟩ eingehen; ⟨*Personen, Kunden:*⟩ hereinströmen; **~ in an hour late** mit einer Stunde Verspätung aufkreuzen *(salopp).* **2.** *v. t.* herein-/hineinrollen

~ ˈoff *v. i.* **a)** *(fall off)* herunterrollen; **b)** *(start)* sich in Bewegung setzen

~ ˈon 1. *v. t.* mit einer Rolle auftragen ⟨*Farbe*⟩. **2.** *v. i.* **a)** *(pass by)* ⟨*Jahre:*⟩ vergehen; **b)** *(Brit. coll.)* **~ on Saturday!** wenn doch schon Samstag wäre! *See also* **roll-on**

~ ˈout 1. *v. t.* **a)** *(make flat and smooth)* auswalzen ⟨*Metall*⟩; ausrollen ⟨*Teig, Teppich*⟩; **b)** *(bring out)* herausbringen; **~ out the barrel** *(fig. coll.)* ein paar Flaschen den Hals brechen *(ugs.).* **2.** *v. i.* heraus-/hinausrollen

~ ˈover 1. *v. i.* ⟨*Person:*⟩ sich umdrehen, *(to make room)* sich zur Seite rollen; **~ over [and over]** ⟨*Auto:*⟩ sich [immer wieder] überschlagen; **the dog ~ed over on to its back** der Hund rollte sich auf den Rücken. **2.** *v. t.* herumdrehen; *(with effort)* herumwälzen

~ **'past** *see* ~ **by**

~ **'up 1.** *v. t.* **a)** aufrollen ⟨*Teppich, Maßband*⟩; zusammenrollen ⟨*Regenschirm, Landkarte, Dokument usw.*⟩; hochkrempeln ⟨*Hose*⟩; *see also* **sleeve a; b)** *(Mil.)* aufrollen ⟨*feindliche Stellung*⟩. **2.** *v. i.* **a)** *(curl up)* sich zusammenrollen; **b)** *(arrive)* aufkreuzen *(salopp)*; ~ **up!** ~ **up!** hereinspaziert!; **they ~ed up in their new car** sie fuhren in ihrem neuen Auto vor

roll: ~away [bed] *n.* Raumsparbett auf Rollen; **~-bar** *n. (Motor Veh.)* Überrollbügel, *der;* **~-call** *n.* Aufrufen aller Namen; *(Mil.)* Zählappell, *der*

rolled [rəʊld]: ~ **'gold** *n.* Goldauflage, *die;* ~ **'oats** *n. pl.* Haferflocken *Pl.*

roller ['rəʊlə(r)] *n.* **a)** *(heavy, for pressing, smoothing road, lawn, etc.)* Walze, *die; (smaller, for towel, painting, pastry)* Rolle, *die;* **b)** *(Med.)* ~ **[bandage]** Binde, *die;* **c)** *(for hair)* Lockenwickler, *der;* **put one's hair in ~s** sich *(Dat.)* die Haare aufdrehen; **d)** *(wave)* Roller, *der (Meeresk.)*

roller: ~ **bearing** *n.* Rollenlager, *das (Technik);* ~ **blind** *n.* Rouleau, *das;* Rollo, *das;* **~-coaster** *n.* Achterbahn, *die;* **~-skate 1.** *n.* Rollschuh, *der;* **2.** *v. i.* Rollschuh laufen; **~-skater** *n.* Rollschuhläufer, *der*/-läuferin, *die;* **~-skating** *n.* Rollschuhlaufen, *das;* **~-skating rink** Rollschuhbahn, *die;* ~ **towel** *n. auf einer Rolle hängendes endloses Handtuch*

'roll film *n.* Rollfilm, *der*

rollick ['rɒlɪk] *v. i.* ausgelassen spielen; ~ **[about]** [herum]tollen

rollicking ['rɒlɪkɪŋ] **1.** *adj. (unrestrained)* ausgelassen. **2.** *n.* **give sb. a** ~ *(coll.)* jmdm. den Marsch blasen *(salopp)*

rolling ['rəʊlɪŋ] *adj.* **a)** *(moving from side to side)* rollend ⟨*Augen*⟩; schwankend ⟨*Gang*⟩; schlingernd ⟨*Schiff*⟩; **b)** *(undulating)* wogend ⟨*See*⟩; wellig ⟨*Gelände*⟩; ~ **hills** sanfte Hügel; **c)** *(resounding)* rollend ⟨*Donner*⟩; hochtrabend *(abwertend)* ⟨*Phrasen*⟩; **d)** *(coll.: rich)* **be ~ [in it** *or* **in money]** im Geld schwimmen *(ugs.)*

rolling: ~-mill *n.* Walzwerk, *das;* **~-pin** *n. (Cookery)* Teigrolle, *die;* Nudelholz, *das;* **~-stock** *n.* **a)** *(Brit. Railw.)* Fahrzeugbestand, *der;* rollendes Material *(fachspr.);* **b)** *(Amer.: road vehicles)* Fahrzeugpark, *der;* ~ **'stone** *n. (fig.)* unsteter Mensch; **a ~ stone gathers no moss** *(prov.)* wer ein unstetes Leben führt, bringt es zu nichts

roll: ~mop[s] *n. (Gastr.)* Rollmops, *der;* **~-neck 1.** *n.* Rollkragen, *der;* **2.** *adj.* Rollkragen-; **~-on** *n.* **a)** *(corset)* elastischer Hüfthalter; **b)** *(deodorant)* Deoroller, *der;* **~-on ~-off** *adj.* **~-on ~-off ship/ferry** Roll-on-roll-off-Schiff, *das*/-Fähre, *die;* **~-top** *n.* Rollverschluß, *der;* **~-top desk** *n. Schreibtisch mit Rollverschluß*

roly-poly [rəʊlɪ'pəʊlɪ] **1.** *n.* **a)** ~ **[pudding]** ≈ Strudel, *der;* **b)** *(Amer.: toy)* Stehaufmännchen, *das.* **2.** *adj. (coll.)* kugelrund

ROM [rɒm] *abbr. (Computing)* **read-only memory** ROM

Roman ['rəʊmən] **1.** *n.* **a)** Römer, *der*/Römerin, *die;* **b) r~** *(Printing)* Antiqua, *die.* **2.** *adj.* **a)** römisch; ~ **road** Römerstraße, *die;* **b)** *see* **Roman Catholic 1.** *See also* **snail**

roman à clef [rəʊmɑ:n ɑ: 'kleɪ] *n. (Lit.)* Schlüsselroman, *der*

Roman: ~ **'alphabet** *n.* lateinisches Alphabet; ~ **'candle** *n.* ≈ Goldregen, *der;* ~ **'Catholic 1.** *adj.* römisch-katholisch; **2.** *n.* Katholik, *der*/Katholikin, *die;* **sb. is a ~ Catholic** jmd. ist römisch-katholisch; ~ **Ca'tholicism** *n., no pl.* Katholizismus, *der*

romance [rə'mæns] **1.** *n.* **a)** *(love affair)* Romanze, *die;* **b)** *(love-story)* [romantische] Liebesgeschichte; **c)** *(romantic quality)* Romantik, *die;* **there was an air of ~ about the place** der Ort hatte etwas Romantisches; **d)** *(Lit.) (medieval tale)* Romanze, *die; (improbable tale)* phantastische Geschichte; **e)** *(make-believe)* Phantasterei, *die;* **f)** *(Mus.)* Romanze, *die;* **g) R~** *(Ling.)* Romanisch, *das.* **2.** *adj.* **R~** *(Ling.)* romanisch; **R~ languages and literature** *(subject)* Romanistik, *die.* **3.** *v. i.* phantasieren

romancer [rəʊ'mænsə(r)] *n.* Phantast, *der (abwertend)*

Roman 'Empire *n. (Hist.)* Römisches Reich; **Holy ~:** Heiliges Römisches Reich [Deutscher Nation]

Romanesque [rəʊmə'nesk] *n. (Art, Archit.)* Romanik, *die*

Romania [rəʊ'meɪnɪə] *pr. n.* Rumänien *(das)*

Romanian [rəʊ'meɪnɪən] **1.** *adj.* rumänisch; **sb. is ~:** jmd. ist Rumäne/Rumänin; *see also* **English 1. 2.** *n.* **a)** *(person)* Rumäne, *der*/Rumänin, *die;* **b)** *(language)* Rumänisch, *das; see also* **English 2 a**

romanize (romanise) ['rəʊmənaɪz] *v. t.* **a)** *(Hist.)* romanisieren *(veralt.);* **b)** *(Relig.)* katholisieren

Roman: ~ **law** *n.* römisches Recht; ~ **'nose** *n.* Römernase, *die;* ~ **'numeral** *n.* römische Ziffer

Romansh [rə'mænʃ, rə'mɑ:nʃ] **1.** *n.* Romantsch, *das.* **2.** *adj.* Romantsch-

romantic [rəʊ'mæntɪk] **1.** *adj.* **a)** *(emotional, fantastic)* romantisch; ~ **fiction** *(love-stories)* Liebesromane; **b) R~** *(Lit., Art)* romantisch; der Romantik *nachgestellt.* **2.** *n.* **R~** *(Lit., Art, Mus.)* Romantiker, *der*/Romantikerin, *die*

romantically [rəʊ'mæntɪkəlɪ] *adv.* romantisch

Romanticism [rəʊ'mæntɪsɪzm] *n. (Lit., Art, Mus.)* Romantik, *die*

Romanticist [rəʊ'mæntɪsɪst] *n. (Lit., Art, Mus.)* Romantiker, *der*

romanticize [rəʊ'mæntɪsaɪz] *v. t.* romantisieren

'roman type *n. (Printing)* Antiquaschrift, *die*

Romany ['rəʊmənɪ] **1.** *n.* **a)** *(gypsy)* Rom, *der;* **the Romanies** die Roma; **b)** *(language)* Romani, *das.* **2.** *adj.* **a)** Roma-; **b)** *(Ling.)* Romani-

Rome [rəʊm] *pr. n.* Rom *(das);* **all roads lead to ~** *(prov.)* alle Wege führen nach Rom *(Spr.);* **~ was not built in a day** *(prov.)* Rom ist nicht an einem Tag erbaut worden *(Spr.);* **when in ~ do as the Romans [do]** man muß sich den örtlichen Gegebenheiten anpassen

Romeo ['rəʊmɪəʊ] *n., pl.* **~s** Casanova, *der*

romp [rɒmp] **1.** *v. i.* **a)** [herum]tollen; **b)** *(coll.: win, succeed, etc. easily)* ~ **home** *or* **in** spielend gewinnen; ~ **through sth.** etw. spielend schaffen; ~ **along** dahinflitzen *(ugs.).* **2.** *n.* Tollerei, *die;* **have a ~** *see* **1 a**

rompers ['rɒmpəz] *n. pl.* Spielhöschen, *das*

'romper suit *n.* Spielanzug, *der*

rondo ['rɒndəʊ] *n., pl.* **~s** *(Mus.)* Rondo, *das*

roo [ru:] *n. (Austral. coll.)* Känguruh, *das*

rood [ru:d] *n. (crucifix)* Kruzifix, *das*

rood: ~-loft *n.* Empore des Lettners; **~-screen** *n.* Lettner, *der*

roof [ru:f] **1.** *n.* **a)** Dach, *das;* **under one ~:** unter einem Dach; **live under the same ~ [as sb.]** [mit jmdm.] unter einem Dach wohnen *(ugs.);* **have a ~ over one's head** ein Dach über dem Kopf haben; **go through the ~** ⟨*Preise:*⟩ kraß in die Höhe steigen; **sb. goes through** *or* **hits the ~** *(fig. coll.)* jmd. geht an die Decke *(ugs.);* **raise the ~** *(fig. coll.: make much noise)* die Wände zum Beben bringen; **b)** *(Anat.)* ~ **of the mouth** Gaumen, *der.* **2.** *v. t.* bedachen; ~ **in** *or* **over** überdachen

'roof-garden *n.* Dachgarten, *der*

roofing ['ru:fɪŋ] *n.* **a)** *(action)* Bedachung, *die;* **b)** *(material for roof)* Deckung, *die*

'roofing felt *n.* Dachpappe, *die*

roofless ['ru:flɪs] *adj.* dachlos

roof: ~-rack *n.* Dachgepäckträger, *der;* ~ **timbers** *n. pl.* Dachstuhl, *der;* **~-top** *n.* Dach, *das;* **shout sth. from the ~-tops** *(fig.)* etw. in die Welt hinausrufen

[1]**rook** [rʊk] **1.** *n. (Ornith.)* Saatkrähe, *die.* **2.** *v. t.* **a)** *(charge extortionately)* neppen *(ugs. abwertend);* **b)** *(in gambling)* ausnehmen; ~ **sb. of £10** jmdm. 10 Pfund abnehmen

[2]**rook** *n. (Chess)* Turm, *der*

rookery ['rʊkərɪ] *n.* **a)** Saatkrähenkolonie, *die;* **b)** *(of penguins or seals)* Kolonie, *die*

rookie ['rʊkɪ] *n.* **a)** *(Mil. sl.)* Rekrut, *der;* **b)** *(Amer.: new member etc.)* Neuling, *der*

room [ru:m, rʊm] **1.** *n.* **a)** *(in building)* Zimmer, *das; (esp. without furniture)* Raum, *der; (large ~, for function)* Saal, *der;* **leave the ~** *(coll.: go to lavatory)* austreten *(ugs.);* **b)** *no pl., no indef. art. (space)* Platz, *der;* **we have no ~ for idlers** für Müßiggänger ist bei uns kein Platz; **give sb. ~:** jmdm. Platz machen; **give sb. ~ to do sth.** *(fig.)* jmdm. die Freiheit lassen, etw. zu tun; ~ **and to spare** Platz genug; **make ~ [for sb./sth.]** [jmdm./einer Sache] Platz machen; **c)** *(scope)* **there is no ~ for dispute/doubt about that** darüber kann es keine Diskussion/keinen Zweifel geben; **there is still ~ for improvement in his work** seine Arbeit ist noch verbesserungsfähig; **this did not leave us much ~ for manœuvre** das ließ uns wenig Spielraum; **d)** *in pl. (apartments, lodgings)* Wohnung, *die;* **'~s to let'** „Zimmer zu vermieten"; **e)** *(persons in a ~)* Raum, *der;* Zimmer, *das. See also* **cat a. 2.** *v. i. (Amer.: lodge)* wohnen; ~ **with sb.** *(be tenant of)* bei jmdm. wohnen; *(share with)* mit jmdm. zusammenwohnen

'room-divider *n.* Raumteiler, *der*

-roomed [ru:md, rʊmd] *adj. in comb.* **a three-~ flat** eine Dreizimmerwohnung; **a one-~/four-~ building** ein Haus mit einem Zimmer/vier Zimmern

roomette [ru:'met, rʊ'met] *n. (Amer. Railw.)* Schlafwagenkabine, *die*

roomful ['ru:mfʊl, 'rʊmfʊl] *n.* **a ~ of people** *etc.* ein Zimmer voll[er] Leute *usw.*

rooming-house ['ru:mɪŋhaʊs] *n.* Pension, *die*

room: ~-mate *n.* Zimmergenosse, *der*/-genossin, *die;* Stubenkamerad, *der (Milit.);* ~ **service** *n.* Zimmerservice, *der;* ~ **temperature** *n.* Zimmertemperatur, *die*

roomy ['ru:mɪ] *adj.* geräumig

roost [ru:st] **1.** *n.* Schlafplatz, *der; (perch)* [Sitz]stange, *die;* **come home to ~** *(fig.)* jmdm. heimgezahlt werden; *see also* **rule 2 b. 2.** *v. i.* sich [zum Schlafen] niederlassen

rooster ['ru:stə(r)] *n. (Amer.)* Hahn, *der*

[1]**root** [ru:t] **1.** *n.* **a)** Wurzel, *die;* **pull sth. up by the ~/~s** etw. mit der Wurzel/den Wurzeln ausreißen; *(fig.)* etw. mit der Wurzel ausrotten; **put down ~s/strike** *or* **take ~** *(lit. or fig.)* Wurzeln schlagen; *(fig.)* **strike at the ~[s] of sth.** etw. in seinem Lebensnerv treffen; **have ~s** verwurzelt sein; **without ~s** wurzellos; **b)** *(source)* Wurzel, *die; (basis)* Grundlage, *die;* **have its ~s in sth.** einer Sache *(Dat.)* entspringen; **get at** *or* **to the ~[s] of things** den Dingen auf den Grund kommen; **be at the ~ of the matter** der Kern der Sache sein; **the ~ cause** der wirkliche Grund; **c)** *(Ling.)* Wurzel, *die;* **d)** *(Mus.)* Grundton, *der;* **e)** *(Math.: square ~)* [Quadrat]wurzel, *die* (of aus). **2.** *v. t.* ~ **a plant firmly** eine Pflanze fest einpflanzen; **have ~ed itself in sth.** *(fig.)* in etw. *(Dat.)* verwurzelt sein; **stand ~ed to the spot** wie angewurzelt dastehen. **3.** *v. i.* ⟨*Pflanze:*⟩ wurzeln, anwachsen

~ **'out** *v. t.* ausrotten; ausmerzen

~ **'up** *v. t.* mit den Wurzeln ausreißen; ausroden ⟨*Baum[stumpf], Busch*⟩

²root *v.i.* **a)** *(turn up ground)* wühlen **(for** nach); **b)** *(coll.)* ~ **for** *(cheer)* anfeuern; *(wish for success of)* Stimmung machen für
~ **a'bout,** ~ **a'round** *v.i.* herumwühlen
~ **'out** *v.t. (find by search)* zu Tage fördern
root: ~ **and 'branch 1.** *adj.* radikal; ⟨*Reform*⟩ an Haupt und Gliedern; **2.** *adv.* radikal; an Haupt und Gliedern ⟨*reformieren*⟩; ~ **beer** *n. (Amer.)* Rootbeer, *das (schäumendes Getränk aus Wurzeln und Kräutern);* ~ **crop[s]** *n. [pl.]* Hackfrüchte *Pl.*
rooted ['ru:tɪd] *adj.* eingewurzelt
rootless ['ru:tlɪs] *adj.* wurzellos
root: ~**-mean-'square** *n. (Math.)* quadratisches Mittel; ~ **sign** *see* **radical sign 2 b;** ~**-stock** *n.* **a)** *(rhizome)* Wurzelstock, *der;* **b)** *(for grafting)* Unterlage, *die;* ~ **vegetable** *n.* Wurzelgemüse, *das;* ~ **word** *n. (Ling.)* Wurzelwort, *das*
rope [rəʊp] **1.** *n.* **a)** *(cord)* Seil, *das;* Tau, *das;* ~**'s end** *(short piece)* Tauende, *das;* **b)** *(Amer.: lasso)* Lasso, *das;* **c)** *(for hanging sb.)* **the** ~: der Strang; *(fig.: death penalty)* die Todesstrafe; **d)** *in pl. (Boxing)* **the** ~**s** die Seile; **be on the** ~**s** *(lit., or fig.: near defeat)* in den Seilen hängen; **e)** *in pl.* **learn the** ~**s** lernen, sich zurechtzufinden; *(at work)* sich einarbeiten; **know the** ~**s** sich auskennen; **show sb. the** ~**s** jmdn. mit allem vertraut machen; **f) give sb. some** ~ *(fig.)* jmdm. eine gewisse Freiheit lassen; **give him enough** ~ **and he'll hang himself** *(fig.)* laß ihn alleine machen, dann schaufelt er sich sein eigenes Grab; **g)** *(Mount.)* **on the** ~: am Seil. **2.** *v.t.* **a)** festbinden; ~ **sb. to a tree** jmdn. an einen Baum binden; **b)** *(Mount.)* anseilen
~ **'in** *v.t.* **a)** mit einem Seil/mit Seilen absperren ⟨*Gebiet*⟩; **b)** *(fig.)* einspannen *(ugs.); (for membership)* anheuern *(ugs.);* **how did you get** ~**d in to that?** warum hast du dich dazu breitschlagen lassen? *(ugs.)*
~ **'off** *v.t.* [mit einem Seil/mit Seilen] absperren
~ **to'gether** *v.t. (Mount.)* aneinanderseilen
rope: ~**-dancer** *n.* Seiltänzer, *der*/-tänzerin, *die;* ~**-'ladder** *n.* Strickleiter, *die;* ~ **'sole** *n.* Kordelsohle, *die;* ~**-walker** *n.* Seilakrobat, *der*/-akrobatin, *die;* ~**way** *n.* Seilbahn, *die*
ropy ['rəʊpɪ] *adj. (coll.) (poor)* schäbig; *(in a bad state)* mitgenommen; **be a bit** ~: nicht viel taugen; **you look a bit** ~: du siehst ziemlich kaputt aus
Roquefort ['rɒkfɔ:(r)] *n.* Roquefort, *der*
ro-ro ['rəʊrəʊ] *adj.* Ro-Ro- ⟨*Schiff, Fähre*⟩
rorqual ['rɔ:kwəl] *n. (Zool.)* Finnwal, *der*
Rorschach test ['rɔ:ʃɑ:k test] *n. (Psych.)* Rorschachtest, *der*
rosary ['rəʊzərɪ] *n. (Relig.)* Rosenkranz, *der*
¹rose [rəʊz] **1.** *n.* **a)** *(plant, flower)* Rose, *die;* ~ **of Jericho/Sharon** Jerichorose, *die*/Johanniskraut, *das;* **no bed of** ~**s** *(fig.)* kein Honigschlecken; ~**s[,** ~**s,] all the way** *(fig.)* der Himmel auf Erden; **it's not all** ~**s** es ist nicht alles [so] rosig; **everything's [coming up]** ~**s** alles ist bestens; **[there's] no** ~ **without a thorn** *(prov.)* keine Rose ohne Dornen *(Spr.);* **Wars of the R**~**s** *(Brit. Hist.)* Rosenkriege *Pl.;* ~**s in one's cheeks** rosige Wangen; **b)** *(colour)* Rosa, *das;* **c)** *(nozzle)* Brause, *die.* **2.** *adj.* rosa[farben]
²rose *see* **rise 2**
rosé [rəʊ'zeɪ, 'rəʊzeɪ] *n.* Rosé, *der*
roseate ['rəʊzɪət] *adj.* rosenrot
rose: ~**-bed** *n.* Rosenbeet, *das;* ~**-bud** *n.* Rosenknospe, *die;* ~**-bud mouth** Kirschenmund, *der (dichter.);* ~**-bush** *n.* Rosenstrauch, *der;* ~**-coloured** *adj. (lit. or fig.)* rosarot; **see things through** ~**-coloured spectacles** die Dinge durch eine rosarote Brille sehen; ~**-fish** *n.* Rotbarsch, *der;* ~**-garden** *n.* Rosengarten, *der;* ~**-hip** *n. (Bot.)* Hagebutte, *die;* ~**-hip tea** Hagebuttentee, *der;* ~**-leaf** *n.* Rosenblatt, *das*

rosemary ['rəʊzmərɪ] *n. (Bot.)* Rosmarin, *der*
rose: ~**-petal** *n.* Rosen[blüten]blatt, *das;* ~**-pink 1.** *adj.* rosarot; **2.** *n.* Rosarot, *das;* ~**-red 1.** *adj.* rosenrot; **2.** *n.* Rosenrot, *das;* ~**-tinted** *see* **rose-coloured;** ~**-tree** *n.* Rosenstock, *der*
rosette [rəʊ'zet] *n.* Rosette, *die*
rose: ~**-water** *n.* Rosenwasser, *das;* ~**-window** *n. (Archit.)* Fensterrose, *die;* ~**wood** *n.* Rosenholz, *das*
Rosicrucian [rəʊzɪ'kru:ʃn] **1.** *n.* Rosenkreuzer, *der*/-kreuzerin, *die.* **2.** *adj.* Rosenkreuzer-
rosin ['rɒzɪn] *n.* Harz, *das; (for violin bow)* Kolophonium, *das*
RoSPA ['rɒspə] *abbr. (Brit.)* **Royal Society for the Prevention of Accidents**
roster ['rɒstə(r)] **1.** *n.* Dienstplan, *der.* **2.** *v.t.* einteilen ⟨*Arbeitskraft*⟩; **call for flexible** ~**ing** flexible Dienstpläne fordern
rostrum ['rɒstrəm] *n., pl.* **rostra** ['rɒstrə] *or* ~**s** *(platform)* Podium, *das; (desk)* Rednerpult, *das*
rosy ['rəʊzɪ] *adj.* **a)** rosig; **b)** *(fig.)* rosig ⟨*Zukunft, Aussichten*⟩; **paint a** ~ **picture of sth.** etw. in den rosigsten Farben schildern
rot [rɒt] **1.** *n.* **a)** *see* **2 a:** Verrottung, *die;* Fäulnis, *die;* Verwesung, *die;* Vermoderung, *die; (rust)* Rost, *der; (fig.: deterioration)* Verfall, *der;* **stop the** ~ *(fig.)* dem Verfall Einhalt gebieten; **the** ~ **has set in** *(fig.)* der Verfall hat eingesetzt; *see also* **dry rot; b)** *(sl.: nonsense)* Quark, *der (salopp);* ~! Blödsinn! *(ugs.).* **2.** *v.i.,* **-tt- a)** *(decay)* verrotten; ⟨*Fleisch, Gemüse, Obst:*⟩ verfaulen; ⟨*Leiche:*⟩ verwesen; ⟨*Metall:*⟩ verrosten; ⟨*Laub:*⟩ vermodern, verrotten; ⟨*Holz:*⟩ faulen; ⟨*Zähne:*⟩ schlecht werden; **b)** *(fig.: go to ruin)* verrotten; **leave sb. to** ~: jmdn. verrotten lassen *(ugs.).* **3.** *v.t.,* **-tt- a)** *(make rotten)* verrotten lassen; verfaulen lassen ⟨*Fleisch, Gemüse, Obst*⟩; vermodern *od.* verrotten lassen ⟨*Laub*⟩; faulen lassen ⟨*Holz*⟩; verwesen lassen ⟨*Leiche*⟩; zerstören ⟨*Zähne*⟩; **that stuff will** ~ **your guts** *(sl.)* das Zeug bringt dich um *(ugs.);* **b)** *(Brit. sl.: tease)* aufziehen *(ugs.)*
~ **a'way** *v.i.* verfaulen; ⟨*Leiche:*⟩ verwesen; ⟨*Holz:*⟩ faulen; *(moulder away)* vermodern
rota ['rəʊtə] *n. (Brit.)* **a)** *(order of rotation)* Turnus, *der;* **draw up the cleaning** ~: den Putzplan aufstellen; **she has a regular** ~ **of visitors** sie bekommt in regelmäßigem Turnus Besuch; **b)** *(list of persons)* [Arbeits]plan, *der*
Rotarian [rəʊ'teərɪən] **1.** *n.* Rotarier, *der.* **2.** *adj.* rotarisch; Rotarier-
rotary ['rəʊtərɪ] **1.** *adj.* **a)** *(acting by rotation)* rotierend; Rotations-; ~ **engine** Drehkolbenmotor, *der;* ~ **press** *(Printing)* Rotationsmaschine, *die;* ~ **pump** Kreiselpumpe, *die;* ~ **mower** Rasenmäher mit rotierenden Messern; **b) R**~: Rotarier-; **R**~ **Club** Rotary-Club, *der.* **2.** *n.* **a) The R**~, **R**~ **International** der Rotary-Club; Rotary International; **b)** *(Amer.: roundabout)* Verkehrskreisel, *der*
rotate [rəʊ'teɪt] **1.** *v.i.* **a)** *(revolve)* rotieren; sich drehen; ~ **on an axis** sich um eine Achse drehen; **b)** *(alternate)* **these posts** ~ **regularly** diese Stellen werden in einem regelmäßigen Turnus neu besetzt. **2.** *v.t.* **a)** *(cause to revolve)* in Rotation versetzen; **b)** *(alternate)* abwechselnd erledigen ⟨*Aufgaben*⟩; abwechselnd erfüllen ⟨*Pflichten*⟩; ~ **[the] crops** Fruchtwechselwirtschaft betreiben; **change the way one** ~**s the crops** die Fruchtfolge ändern
rotation [rəʊ'teɪʃn] *n.* **a)** Rotation, *die,* Drehung, *die* **(about** um); **b)** *(succession)* turnusmäßiger Wechsel; *(in political office)* Rotation, *die;* ~ **of crops** Fruchtfolge, *die;* **the** ~ **of the seasons** der Wechsel der Jahreszeiten; **by** ~: im Turnus; ~ **in office** turnusmäßiger Amtswechsel; **take office in** *or* **by** ~: ein Amt nach dem Rotationsprinzip ausüben
rotatory ['rəʊtətərɪ] *adj.* Dreh-; drehend
rotavate ['rəʊtəveɪt] *v.t.* mit der Fräse bearbeiten ⟨*Boden*⟩
Rotavator, (P) ['rəʊtəveɪtə(r)] *n.* [Boden]fräse, *die*
rote [rəʊt] *n.* **by** ~: auswendig ⟨*lernen, aufsagen*⟩; **teach sth. by** ~: etw. durch Auswendiglernen einüben
'rote-learning *n.* Auswendiglernen, *das*
'rot-gut *(sl.)* **1.** *n.* Fusel, *der (ugs., abwertend).* **2.** *adj.* fuselig
rotisserie [rəʊ'tɪsərɪ] *n.* **a)** *(restaurant)* Rotisserie, *die;* **b)** *(appliance)* Grill, *der*
rotor ['rəʊtə(r)] *n.* Rotor, *der (Technik)*
rotten ['rɒtn] **1.** *adj.,* ~**er** ['rɒtənə(r)], ~**est** ['rɒtənɪst] **a)** *(decayed)* verrottet; verwest ⟨*Leiche*⟩; vermodert, verrottet ⟨*Laub, Holz*⟩; verfault ⟨*Obst, Gemüse, Fleisch*⟩; faul ⟨*Ei, Zähne*⟩; *(rusted)* verrostet; ~ **to the core** *(fig.)* verdorben bis ins Mark; völlig verrottet ⟨*System, Gesellschaft*⟩; **b)** *(corrupt)* verdorben; verkommen; **c)** *(sl.: bad)* mies *(ugs.);* **feel** ~ *(ill)* sich mies fühlen *(ugs.); (have a bad conscience)* ein schlechtes Gewissen haben; **it's a** ~ **shame** so ein Mist *(ugs.);* ~ **luck** saumäßiges Pech *(salopp).* **2.** *adv. (sl.)* saumäßig *(salopp);* **hurt/stink something** ~: saumäßig weh tun/stinken *(salopp);* **spoilt** ~: ganz schön verwöhnt *(ugs.)*
rottenly ['rɒtnlɪ] *adv. (sl.)* saumäßig *(salopp)*
rotter ['rɒtə(r)] *n. (sl.)* mieser Typ *(salopp abwertend);* Halunke, *der*
rotund [rəʊ'tʌnd] *adj.* **a)** *(round)* rund; **b)** *(plump)* rundlich
rotunda [rə'tʌndə] *n.* Rotunde, *die (Archit.)*
rotundity [rəʊ'tʌndɪtɪ] *n., no pl.* **a)** *(roundness)* Rundheit, *die;* **b)** *(plumpness)* Rundlichkeit, *die*
rouble ['ru:bl] *n.* Rubel, *der*
roué ['ru:eɪ] *n.* Roué, *der (veralt.)*
rouge [ru:ʒ] **1.** *n.* **a)** *(cosmetic powder)* Rouge, *das;* **b)** *(polishing agent)* Englischrot, *das; see also* **jeweller. 2.** *v.t.* ~ **one's cheeks** *or* **face** Rouge auflegen
rough [rʌf] **1.** *adj.* **a)** *(coarse, uneven)* rauh; holp[e]rig ⟨*Straße usw.*⟩; uneben ⟨*Gelände*⟩; aufgewühlt ⟨*Wasser*⟩; *(shaggy)* haarig ⟨*Lebewesen*⟩; stopp[e]lig ⟨*Bart*⟩; **b)** *(violent)* rauh, roh, grob *(abwertend)* ⟨*Person, Worte, Behandlung, Benehmen*⟩; **the** ~ **element [of the population]** die Rowdys [unter der Bevölkerung]; **the remedy was** ~ **but effective** die Behandlung war eine Roßkur, aber sie hat gewirkt; **c)** *(harsh to the senses)* rauh; kratzig ⟨*Geschmack, Getränk*⟩; sauer ⟨*Apfelwein*⟩; **d)** *(trying)* hart; **this is** ~ **on him** das ist hart für ihn; **sth. is** ~ **going** etw. ist nicht einfach; **have a** ~ **time** es schwer haben; **give sb. a** ~ **time** es jmdm. schwer machen; **have a** ~ **tongue** einen rauhen Ton am Leibe haben *(ugs.); see also* **edge 1 a; e)** *(fig.: deficient in polish)* derb; rauh ⟨*Empfang*⟩; unbeholfen ⟨*Stil*⟩; ungeschliffen ⟨*Benehmen, Sprache*⟩; **f)** *(rudimentary)* primitiv ⟨*Unterkunft, Leben*⟩; *(approximate)* grob ⟨*Skizze, Schätzung, Einteilung, Übersetzung*⟩; vag ⟨*Vorstellung*⟩; ~ **notes** stichwortartige Notizen; ~ **attempt** erster Versuch; ~ **draft** Rohentwurf, *der;* **in a somewhat** ~ **state** in einem einigermaßen unfertigen Zustand; **a** ~ **circle** ein ungefährer Kreis; ~ **paper/notebook** Konzeptpapier, *das*/Kladde, *die;* **g)** *(coll.: ill)* angeschlagen *(ugs.). See also* **¹deal 3 a. 2.** *n.* **a)** *(hooligan)* Schläger, *der (abwertend);* Rowdy, *der (abwertend);* **b)** *(Golf)* Rough, *das;* **c) take the** ~ **with the smooth** die Dinge nehmen, wie sie kommen; **d)** *(unfinished state)* **[be] in** ~: [sich] im Rohzustand [befinden]. **3.** *adv.* rauh ⟨*spielen*⟩; scharf ⟨*reiten*⟩; **sleep** ~: im Freien schlafen. **4.** *v.t.* ~ **it** primitiv leben; **he had to** ~ **it for**

a while er mußte eine Zeitlang auf den gewohnten Komfort verzichten
~ 'in *v. t.* skizzenhaft einzeichnen; [mit wenigen Strichen] andeuten
~ 'out *v. t.* [grob] entwerfen
~ 'up *v. t.* **a)** *(sl.: deal roughly with)* anrempeln *(ugs.)*; **b)** *(ruffle)* gegen den Strich streichen ⟨*Haare*⟩
roughage ['rʌfɪdʒ] *n.* **a)** *(for people)* Ballaststoffe *Pl. (Med.)*; **b)** *(for animals)* Rauhfutter, *das (Landw.)*
rough: ~-and-ready *adj.* **a)** *(not elaborate)* provisorisch; skizzenhaft ⟨*Beschreibung*⟩; behelfsmäßig ⟨*Hütte, Methode*⟩; grob ⟨*Schätzung*⟩; **a ~-and-ready method for calculating sth.** eine Faustformel für die Berechnung von etw.; **b)** *(not refined)* rauhbeinig *(ugs.)* ⟨*Person*⟩; **~-and-'tumble 1.** *adj.* wild; turbulent ⟨*Atmosphäre*⟩; **2.** *n.* [wildes] Handgemenge; [wilde] Rauferei; *(fig.: turbulent life)* Catch-as-catch-can, *das (ugs. abwertend)*; **~cast** *(Building)* **1.** *adj.* mit Grobmörtel verputzt; **2.** *n.* Grobmörtel, *der;* **3.** *v. t.* mit Grobmörtel verputzen; **~ 'copy** *n.* **a)** *(original draft)* [erster] Entwurf; Konzept, *das;* **b)** *(simplified copy)* grobe Skizze; **~ 'diamond** *n. (fig.)* ungehobelter, aber guter Mensch; **he's a ~ diamond** er ist rauh, aber herzlich; **~-dry** *v. t.* [nur] trocknen ⟨*Wäsche*⟩; **~ 'edges** *n. pl. (in book)* unbeschnittene Kanten; **he has a few ~ edges** *(fig.)* er ist ein wenig ungeschliffen
roughen ['rʌfn] **1.** *v. t.* aufrauhen ⟨*Oberfläche*⟩; rauh machen ⟨*Hände*⟩. **2.** *v. i.* rauh werden
rough: ~ 'grazing *n. (Brit.)* natürliche Weide; **~ house** *n. (sl.)* Keilerei, *die (ugs.)*; **~ 'justice** *n.* ziemlich willkürliche Urteile; **~ 'luck** *n.* Pech, *das*
roughly ['rʌflɪ] *adv.* **a)** *(violently)* roh; grob; **b)** *(crudely)* leidlich; grob ⟨*skizzieren, bearbeiten, bauen*⟩; **c)** *(approximately)* ungefähr; grob ⟨*geschätzt*⟩; *see also* **speaking 2**
'roughneck *n. (coll.)* **a)** *(Amer.: rowdy)* Raufbold, *der (abwertend)*; **b)** *(driller on oil rig)* Bohrarbeiter, *der*
roughness ['rʌfnɪs] *n.* **a)** *no pl.* Rauheit, *die; (unevenness)* Unebenheit, *die;* **b)** *no pl. (sharpness) (of wine, fruit juice)* Säure, *die; (of voice)* Rauheit, *die;* **c)** *no pl. (violence)* Roheit, *die;* **the ~ of the area** die Häufigkeit von Gewalttaten in der Gegend; **d)** *(rough place or part)* unausgefeilte Stelle
rough: ~ 'passage *n.* **a)** *(Naut.)* rauhe [Über]fahrt; **b)** *(fig.)* **get a ~ passage** ⟨*Gesetzentwurf:*⟩ nur mit Mühe durchkommen; **the interview board gave him a ~ passage** die Prüfungskommission hat es ihm nicht leicht gemacht; **~ 'ride** *n. see* **ride 1 b**; **~-rider** *n.* **a)** *(horse-breaker)* Zureiter, *der;* **b)** *(Mil.)* irregulärer Kavallerist; **~shod** *adj.* **ride ~shod over sb./sth.** jmdn./etw. mit Füßen treten; **~ stuff** *n. (sl.)* Zoff, *der (salopp)*; **~ 'work** *n.* **a)** *(needing force)* Knochenarbeit, *die (ugs.)*; **b)** *(preliminary)* Vorbereitungsarbeit, *die*
roulette [ru:'let] *n.* Roulette, *das*
Roumania [ru'meɪnɪə] *see* **Romania**
Roumanian [ru'meɪnɪən] *see* **Romanian**
round [raʊnd] **1.** *adj.* **a)** rund; rundlich ⟨*Arme*⟩; **~ cheeks** Pausbacken *Pl. (fam.)*; **in ~ figures, it will cost £1,000** rund gerechnet wird es 1 000 Pfund kosten; **a ~ dozen** ein volles *od.* ganzes Dutzend; **b)** *(plain)* **in the ~est manner, in ~ terms** ohne Umschweife; rundheraus; **c)** *(considerable)* stattlich ⟨*Summe, Preis*⟩; **a good ~ sum** eine hübsche Summe; **d)** *(semicircular)* **~ arch** Rundbogen, *der;* **e)** *(Phonet.)* gerundet; **f)** *(full-toned and mellow)* voll ⟨*Ton*⟩; volltönend ⟨*Stimme*⟩. **2.** *n.* **a)** *(recurring series)* Serie, *die;* **~ of talks/negotiations** Gesprächs-/Verhandlungsrunde, *die;* **the daily ~:** der Alltag; **the daily ~ of chores** die täglichen Pflichten; **b)** *(charge of ammunition)* Ladung, *die;* **50 ~s [of ammunition]** 50 Schuß Munition; **put five ~s in a magazine** fünf Kugeln in ein Magazin stecken; **fire five ~s** fünf Schüsse abfeuern; **c)** *(division of game or contest)* Runde, *die;* **d)** *(burst)* **~ of applause** Beifallssturm, *der;* **~s of cheers** Hochrufe; **e) ~ [of drinks]** Runde, *die;* **f)** *(regular calls)* Runde, *die;* Tour, *die;* **be on sb.'s ~:** auf jmds. Tour liegen; **the doctor is on her ~ at present** Frau Doktor macht gerade Hausbesuche; **go [on]** *or* **make one's ~s** ⟨*Posten, Wächter usw.:*⟩ seine Runde machen *od.* gehen; ⟨*Krankenhausarzt:*⟩ Visite machen; **make the ~ of the wards** Visite machen; **do** *or* **go the ~s** ⟨*Person, Gerücht usw.:*⟩ die Runde machen *(ugs.)*; **do the ~s of all the second-hand shops/one's relatives** alle Gebrauchtwarenläden/seine Verwandtschaft abklappern *(ugs.)*; **she is certainly doing the ~s** *(is promiscuous)* sie macht bei den Männern die Runde *(ugs.)*; **g)** *(Golf)* Runde, *die;* **a ~ of golf** eine Runde Golf; **h)** *(Mus.)* Round, *der (fachspr.)*; einfacher Zirkelkanon; **i)** *(slice)* **a ~ of bread/toast** eine Scheibe Brot/Toast; **a ~ of cucumber sandwiches** ein Gurkensandwich *(in 2 od. 4 Stücke geschnitten)*; **j) in the ~** *postpos. (Art)* als Vollplastik; vollplastisch; *(fig.: as a whole)* ganzheitlich; **theatre in the ~:** Arenabühne, *die;* Rundtheater, *das;* **k)** *(Archery)* Runde, *die.* **3.** *adv.* **a) all the year ~:** das ganze Jahr hindurch; **the third time ~:** beim dritten Mal; **have a wall all ~:** von einer Mauer eingeschlossen sein; **have a look ~:** sich umsehen; **b)** *(in girth)* **be [all of] ten feet ~:** einen Umfang von [mindestens] zehn Fuß haben; **c)** *(from one point, place, person, etc. to another)* **tea was handed ~:** es wurde Tee herumgereicht; **he asked ~ among his friends** er fragte seine Freunde; **the room was hung ~ with portraits** in dem Zimmer hingen ringsum Portraits; **for a mile ~:** im Umkreis einer Meile; **d)** *(by indirect way)* herum; **walk ~:** außen herum gehen; **go a/the long way ~:** einen weiten Umweg machen; **e)** *(here)* hier; *(there)* dort; **I'll go ~ tomorrow** ich gehe morgen hin; **call ~ any time!** kommen Sie doch jederzeit vorbei!; **ask sb. ~ [for a drink]** jmdn. [zu einem Gläschen zu sich] einladen; **order a car** *etc.* **~:** nach einem Wagen *usw.* schicken; **send a car ~:** einen Wagen vorbeischicken; *see also* **clock 1 a. 4.** *prep.* **a)** um [... herum]; **a tour ~ the world** eine Weltreise; **travel ~ England** durch England reisen; **she had a blanket ~ her** sie hatte eine Decke um sich geschlungen; **the box had a band ~ it** um die Schachtel war ein Band gebunden; **right ~ the lake** um den ganzen See herum; **be ~ the back of the house** hinter dem Haus sein; **run ~ the back of the house** hinten ums Haus rennen; *(to position there)* hinter das Haus rennen; **run ~ the streets** durch die Straßen rennen; **walk** *etc.* **~ and ~ sth.** immer wieder um etw. herumgehen *usw.*; **she ran ~ and ~ the park** sie lief Runde um Runde durch den Park; **b)** *(with successive visits to)* **he hawks them ~ the cafés** er hausiert mit ihnen in den Cafés; **he sings ~ the pubs** er singt in den Kneipen; **we looked ~ the shops** wir sahen uns in den Geschäften um; **c)** *(in various directions from)* um [... herum]; rund um ⟨*einen Ort*⟩; **look ~ one** um sich schauen; **in Chelsea and ~ it** in und um Chelsea; **do you live ~ here?** wohnst du [hier] in der Nähe?; **if you're ever ~ this way** wenn du hier in der Nähe bist; **d) argue ~ and ~ a matter/problem** *etc.* um eine Sache/ein Problem *usw.* herumreden *(ugs.)*. **5.** *v. t.* **a)** *(give ~ shape to)* rund machen; runden ⟨*Lippen, Rücken*⟩; **b)** *(state as ~ number)* runden **(to** auf + *Akk.*); **c)** *(go ~)* umfahren/umgehen *usw.*; **~ a turn/bend** um eine Kurve fahren/gehen/kommen *usw.*; **~ a cape** um ein Kap fahren; **d)** *(Phonet.)* mit Rundung der Lippen sprechen; labialisieren *(Sprachw.)*
~ 'down *v. t.* abrunden ⟨*Zahl*⟩ **(to** auf + *Akk.*)
~ 'off *v. t. (also fig.: complete)* abrunden
~ on *v. t.* anfahren
~ 'out *v. t.* vervollständigen
~ 'up *v. t.* **a)** *(gather, collect together)* verhaften ⟨*Verdächtige*⟩; zusammentreiben ⟨*Vieh*⟩; beschaffen, *(ugs.)* auftreiben ⟨*Geld*⟩; *see also* **round-up**; **b)** *(to ~ figure)* aufrunden **(to** auf + *Akk.*)
round: ~ a'bout 1. *adv.* **a)** *(on all sides)* ringsum; **the villages ~ about** die umliegenden Dörfer; **b)** *(indirectly)* auf Umwegen; **c)** *(approximately)* rund; **~ about 2,500 people** um die *od.* rund 2 500 Leute; **2.** *prep.* rund um; **~about 1.** *n.* **a)** *(Brit.: road junction)* Verkehrskreisel, *der;* **b)** *(Brit.: merry-go-round)* Karussell, *das;* **what you lose on the swings you gain on the ~abouts** *(prov.)* was man auf der einen Seite verliert, gewinnt man auf der anderen; **it is swings and ~abouts** es gleicht sich aus; **2.** *adj.* **a)** *(meandering)* **a [very] ~about way** *or* **road** *or* **route** *etc.* ein [sehr] umständlicher Weg; **~about journey** Reise mit Umwegen; **the taxi took us/went a ~about way** das Taxi brachte uns auf einem Umweg zum Ziel/machte einen Umweg; **b)** *(fig.: indirect)* umständlich; **a more ~about method** eine weniger direkte Methode; **~ 'brackets** *n. pl.* runde Klammern; **~ dance** *n.* Rundtanz, *der*
rounded ['raʊndɪd] *adj.* **a)** rund; abgerundet ⟨*Kante*⟩; **b)** *(perfected)* abgerundet; harmonisch ⟨*Person*⟩; **c)** *(fig.: polished)* ausgefeilt; **d)** *(sonorous)* voll
roundel ['raʊndl] *n.* **a)** *(disc)* [kleine runde] Scheibe; **b)** *(mark)* Kreiszeichen, *das*
roundelay ['raʊndɪleɪ] *n. (Mus.)* einfaches Liedchen mit Refrain
rounders ['raʊndəz] *n. sing. (Brit.)* Rounders, *das;* Rundball, *das (dem Baseball ähnliches Spiel)*
round: ~-eyed *adj.* mit großen Augen *nachgestellt;* **be ~-eyed with amazement** große Augen machen; **~-faced** *adj.* pausbäckig *(fam.)*; **~ game** *n. Spiel für beliebig viele Mitspieler, bei dem jeder gegen jeden spielt;* **R~head** *n. (Brit. Hist.)* Rundkopf, *der*
roundly ['raʊndlɪ] *adv.* entschieden
'round-neck *adj.* ⟨*Pullover, Bluse usw.*⟩ mit rundem Halsausschnitt
roundness ['raʊndnɪs] *n., no pl.* Rundheit, *die; (of figure)* Rundlichkeit, *die*
round: ~ 'number *n.* runde Zahl; **~ 'robin** *n.* **a)** *(petition)* Petition, *die (mit kreisförmig angeordneten Unterschriften)*; **b)** *(Amer.: tournament)* Round-Robin-Turnier, *das (Sport)*; **~-'shouldered** *adj.* ⟨*Person*⟩ mit einem Rundrücken; **be ~-shouldered** einen Rundrücken haben
roundsman ['raʊndzmən] *n., pl.* **roundsmen** ['raʊndzmən] **a)** *(Brit.)* Austräger, *der;* **milk ~:** Milchmann, *der (ugs.)*; **b)** *(Amer.: police officer)* ≈ Polizeimeister, *der*
round: R~ 'Table *n.* runde Tafel des Königs Artus; **[King Arthur and the] Knights of the R~ Table** [König Artus und die] Ritter der Tafelrunde; **~-table 'conference** *n.* Round-table-Konferenz, *die;* **~-the-'clock** *adj.* rund um die Uhr *nachgestellt; see also* **clock 1 a**; **~ 'trip** *n.* **a)** Rundreise, *die;* **b)** *(Amer.: return trip)* Hin- und Rückfahrt, *die;* **the ~ trip to the island** die Fahrt zu der Insel und zurück; **~ trip ticket** Rückfahrkarte, *die;* **~-up** *n.* **a)** *(gathering-in) (of persons)* Einfangen, *das; (arrest)* Verhaftung, *die; (of animals)* Zusammentreiben, *das;* **b)** *(summary)* Zusammenfassung, *die;* **~worm** *n. (Zool., Med.)* Spulwurm, *der*
rouse [raʊz] **1.** *v. t.* **a)** *(awaken, lit. or fig.)* wecken **(from** aus); **~ oneself** aufwachen;

(overcome indolence) sich aufraffen; ~ **sb./oneself to action** jmdn. zur Tat anstacheln/sich zur Tat aufraffen; **b)** *(provoke)* reizen; **he is terrible when ~d** er ist furchtbar, wenn man ihn reizt; ~ **sb. to anger** jmdn. in Wut bringen; **c)** *(cause)* wecken; hervorrufen, auslösen ⟨*Empörung, Beschuldigungen*⟩; **d)** *(startle from cover)* aufscheuchen. **2.** *v.i.* ~ **[up]** aufwachen

rousing ['raʊzɪŋ] *adj.* mitreißend ⟨*Lied*⟩; leidenschaftlich ⟨*Rede*⟩; stürmisch ⟨*Beifall*⟩

roustabout ['raʊstəbaʊt] *n.* **a)** *(Amer.: labourer)* Hilfsarbeiter, *der;* Handlanger, *der; (dockhand)* Schauermann, *der;* **b)** *(labourer on oil rig)* Bohrarbeiter, *der*

[1]**rout** [raʊt] **1.** *n. (disorderly retreat)* [wilde] Flucht; *(disastrous defeat)* verheerende Niederlage; **put to ~:** in die Flucht schlagen; *(arch., Law: mob)* Horde, *die.* **2.** *v.t.* aufreiben ⟨*Feind, Truppen*⟩; vernichtend schlagen ⟨*Gegner*⟩

[2]**rout** *v.i. (root)* wühlen

~ **'out** *v.t.* herausjagen; ~ **sb. out of sth.** jmdn. aus etw. jagen

route [ru:t, *Mil. also:* raʊt] **1.** *n.* **a)** *(course)* Route, *die;* Weg, *der;* **a [very] circuitous ~** *(lit. or fig.)* ein [großer] Umweg; **shipping ~:** Schiffahrtsstraße, *die;* **bus/air ~:** Bus-/Fluglinie, *die;* **b)** *(Amer.: delivery round)* Bezirk, *der.* **2.** *v.t.,* **~ing** fahren lassen ⟨*Fahrzeug*⟩; führen ⟨*Linie*⟩; **the train is ~d through** *or* **via Crewe** der Zug fährt über Crewe

route: ~man ['ru:tmən] *n., pl.* **~men** ['ru:tmən] *(Amer.) (delivery-man)* Austräger, *der; (salesman)* Vertreter, *der;* ~ **march** *n. (Mil.)* Übungsmarsch, *der*

router ['raʊtə(r)] *n. (tool)* Nuthobel, *der*

routine [ru:'ti:n] **1.** *n.* **a)** *(regular procedure)* Routine, *die;* **strict ~s must be kept to** ein genau festgelegter Ablauf muß eingehalten werden; **creature of ~:** Gewohnheitsmensch, *der;* **establish a new ~ after retirement** nach der Pensionierung einen neuen Lebensrhythmus finden; **b)** *(coll.) (set speech)* Platte, *die (ugs.); (formula)* Spruch, *der;* **c)** *(Theatre)* Nummer, *die; (Dancing, Skating)* Figur, *die; (Gymnastics)* Übung, *die;* **d)** *(Computing)* Routine, *die.* **2.** *adj.* routinemäßig; Routine⟨*arbeit, -untersuchung usw.*⟩; **the investigation was purely ~:** die Untersuchung verlief absolut routinemäßig

routinely [ru:'ti:nlɪ] *adv.* routinemäßig

roux [ru:] *n., pl. same (Cookery)* Mehlschwitze, *die*

[1]**rove** [rəʊv] **1.** *v.i.* ziehen; ⟨*Blick:*⟩ schweifen *(geh.);* ~ **[about]** herumziehen. **2.** *v.t.* streifen durch; durchstreifen *(geh.);* ⟨*Blick:*⟩ durchschweifen ⟨*Raum*⟩

[2]**rove** *see* **reeve**

[1]**rover** ['rəʊvə(r)] *n. (wanderer)* Vagabund, *der (veralt.);* **R~ Scout** *(Hist.)* Rover, *der*

[2]**rover** *n. (pirate)* Pirat, *der*

roving ['rəʊvɪŋ]: ~ **com'mission** *n.* Reiseauftrag, *der;* **have a ~ commission** einen Aufgabenbereich haben, bei dem man viel herumkommt; ~ **'eye** *n.* **have a ~ eye** den Frauen/Männern schöne Augen machen

[1]**row** [raʊ] *(coll.)* **1.** *n.* **a)** *(noise)* Krach, *der;* **make a ~:** Krach machen; *(protest)* Rabatz machen *(ugs.);* **b)** *(quarrel)* Krach, *der (ugs.);* **have/start a ~:** Krach haben/anfangen *(ugs.);* **they're always having** *or* **they keep having ~s** sie streiten dauernd; sie haben ständig Krach *(ugs.);* **c) get into a ~ over sth.** *(be reprimanded)* wegen etw. Ärger kriegen *(ugs.).* **2.** *v.i.* sich streiten

[2]**row** [rəʊ] *n.* **a)** Reihe, *die;* **in a ~:** in einer Reihe; *(coll.: in succession)* nacheinander; hintereinander; **b)** *(line of numbers etc.)* Zeile, *die;* **c)** *(terrace)* ~ **[of houses]** [Häuser]zeile, *die;* [Häuser]reihe, *die*

[3]**row** **1.** *v.i. (move boat with oars etc.)* rudern; ~ **out/back** hinaus-/zurückrudern. **2.** *v.t.* rudern; ~ **sb. across** jmdn. hinüberrudern. **3.** *n.* **go for a ~:** rudern gehen; **after a long ~:** nach langem Rudern

rowan ['rəʊən, 'raʊən] *see* **rowan-tree**

rowan: ~-berry *n.* Vogelbeere, *die;* **~-tree** *n.* **a)** *(Scot., N.Engl.)* Eberesche, *die;* **b)** *(Amer.)* amerikanische Eberesche

row-boat ['rəʊbəʊt] *n.* Ruderboot, *das*

rowdiness ['raʊdɪnɪs] *n., no pl.* Rabaukenhaftigkeit, *die; (behaviour)* rabaukenhaftes Benehmen

rowdy ['raʊdɪ] **1.** *adj.* rowdyhaft *(abwertend);* ~ **adolescents** jugendliche Rowdys *(abwertend);* **the ~ element in the audience** die Rüpel *(abwertend)* unter den Zuhörern; ~ **scenes** tumultartige Szenen; **the party was ~:** auf der Party ging es laut zu. **2.** *n.* Krawallmacher, *der;* Rabauke, *der*

rowdyism ['raʊdɪɪzm] *n., no pl.* Rabaukentum, *das (abwertend)*

rower ['rəʊə(r)] *n.* Ruderer, *der/*Ruderin, *die;* **be a ~:** rudern

row-house ['rəʊhaʊs] *n. (Amer.)* Reihenhaus, *das*

rowing ['rəʊɪŋ] *n., no pl.* Rudern, *das;* **do a lot of/like ~:** viel/gern rudern

rowing: ~-boat *n. (Brit.)* Ruderboot, *das;* **~-club** *n.* Ruderklub, *der;* **~-machine** *n.* Rudergerät, *das*

rowlock ['rɒlək] *n. (Brit.)* Dolle, *die*

royal ['rɔɪəl] **1.** *adj.* königlich; **the ~ plural** der Pluralis majestatis; *see also* **academy a; assent 2; blood 1 c; commission 1 d; duke a; Highness; regiment 1 b; right 4 g; tennis; we. 2.** *n. (coll.)* Mitglied der Königsfamilie; **the ~s** die Königsfamilie

royal: R~ 'Air Force *n. (Brit.)* Königliche Luftwaffe; ~ **'blue** *n. (Brit.)* Königsblau, *das;* ~ **'burgh** *n. (in Schottland)* grafschaftsfreie Stadt; **R~ Engi'neers** *n. pl. Pioniertruppe der britischen Armee;* ~ **'family** *n.* königliche Familie; ~ **'icing** *n. (Cookery)* Zuckerguß, *der*

royalism ['rɔɪəlɪzm] *n.* Royalismus, *der*

royalist ['rɔɪəlɪst] *n.* Royalist, *der/*Royalistin, *die; attrib.* Royalisten-; royalistisch

royal 'jelly *n.* Gelée royale, *das*

royally ['rɔɪəlɪ] *adv.* königlich

royal: R~ Ma'rine *n. (Brit.) britischer Marineinfanterist;* **R~ 'Navy** *n. (Brit.)* Königliche Kriegsmarine; ~ **'oak** *n. Eichenzweig, der zum Gedenken der Wiedereinsetzung Charles II. als König getragen wird;* ~ **stag** *n. (Hunting)* Kapitalhirsch, *der;* ~ **'standard** *n.* königliche Standarte

royalty ['rɔɪəltɪ] *n.* **a)** *(payment)* Tantieme, *die* **(on** für); **b)** *collect. (royal persons)* Mitglieder des Königshauses; **c)** *no pl., no art. (member of royal family)* ein Mitglied der königlichen Familie; **she's ~:** sie gehört zur königlichen Familie

royal 'warrant *n. Recht, den königlichen Hof zu beliefern*

rozzer ['rɒzə(r)] *n. (Brit. sl.)* Polyp, *der (salopp)*

RPI *abbr. (Brit.)* **retail price index**

r.p.m. [ɑ:pi:'em] *abbr.* **a) resale price maintenance; b) revolutions per minute** U.p.M.

RSPCA *abbr. (Brit.)* **Royal Society for the Prevention of Cruelty to Animals** *britischer Tierschutzverein*

RSVP *abbr.* **répondez s'il vous plaît** R.S.V.P.; U.A.w.g.

rt. *abbr.* **right**

Rt. Hon. *abbr. (Brit.)* **Right Honourable**

Rt. Rev[d]. *abbr.* **Right Reverend; the ~:** S./Sr. E[xz].

rub [rʌb] **1.** *v.t.,* **-bb- a)** reiben **(on, against** an + *Dat.*); *(with ointment etc.)* einreiben; *(to remove dirt etc.)* abreiben; *(to dry)* trockenreiben; *(with sandpaper)* [ab]schmirgeln; ~ **sth. off sth.** etw. von etw. reiben; ~ **sth. dry** etw. trocken reiben; ~ **one's hands** sich *(Dat.)* die Hände reiben; ~ **noses** die Nasen aneinanderreiben; ~ **shoulders** *or* **elbows with sb.** *(fig.)* Tuchfühlung mit jmdm. haben; ~ **a hole in sth.** ein Loch in etw. *(Akk.)* scheuern; ~ **one's feet on sth.** sich *(Dat.)* die Füße an etw. *(Dat.)* reiben; ~ **two things together** zwei Dinge aneinanderreiben; ~ **sth. through a sieve** etw. durch ein Sieb streichen; **he ~bed liniment over his chest** er rieb sich *(Dat.)* die Brust mit einem Einreibemittel ein; *see also* **nose 1 a; penny c; b)** *(reproduce by ~bing) kopieren, indem man auf ein Relief Papier legt und mit Malkreide, Bleistift o.ä. darüberreibt.* **2.** *v.i.,* **-bb- a)** *(exercise friction)* reiben **([up]on, against** an + *Dat.*); **b)** *(get frayed)* sich abreiben; ~ **bare** sich blank reiben *od.* scheuern. **3.** *n.* Reiben, *das;* **give it a quick ~:** reib es kurz·ab; **there's the ~** *(fig.)* da liegt der Haken [dabei] *(ugs.)*

~ **a'long** *v.i.* **a)** ~ **along [together]** [gut] miteinander auskommen; **b)** *(financially)* auskommen

~ **a'way** *v.t.* abreiben ⟨*Farbe, Schmutz*⟩; wegmassieren ⟨*Schmerzen*⟩

~ **'down** *v.t.* **a)** *(prepare)* abschmirgeln; **b)** *(dry)* abreiben. *See also* **rub-down**

~ **'in** *v.t.* einreiben; **there's no need to** *or* **don't ~ it in** *(fig.)* reib es mir nicht [dauernd] unter die Nase *(ugs.)*

~ **'off 1.** *v.t.* wegreiben; wegwischen. **2.** *v.i. (lit. or fig.)* abfärben **(on** auf + *Akk.*); **a lot of dirt/oil ~bed off on my hands** ich bekam sehr schmutzige/ölige Hände

~ **'out 1.** *v.t.* ausreiben; *(from paper)* ausradieren. **2.** *v.i.* sich ausreiben/*(from paper)* sich ausradieren lassen

~ **'up 1.** *v.t.* **a)** *(polish)* blank reiben; wienern *(ugs.);* **b)** *(revise)* auffrischen; aufpolieren *(ugs.);* **c)** ~ **sb. up the right/wrong way** *(fig.)* jmdm. um den Bart gehen *(ugs.)*/auf den Schlips treten *(ugs.)*

[1]**rubber** ['rʌbə(r)] *n.* **a)** Gummi, *das od. der; attrib.* Gummi-; **b)** *(eraser)* Radiergummi, *der;* **c)** *(sl.: condom)* Gummi, *der (salopp);* **d)** *in pl. (Amer.: galoshes)* Galoschen *Pl.*

[2]**rubber** *n. (Cards)* Robber, *der*

rubber: ~ 'band *n.* Gummiband, *das;* ~ **'cheque** *n. (coll.)* ungedeckter Scheck; ~ **goods** *n. pl.* Gummiwaren; *(condoms)* Gummis *(ugs.)*

rubberize ['rʌbəraɪz] *v.t.* gummieren

rubber: ~-neck *(Amer.)* **1.** *n.* Gaffer, *der/*Gafferin, *die (abwertend);* **2.** *v.i.* einen langen Hals/lange Hälse machen *(ugs.);* ~ **plant** *n. (Bot.)* Gummibaum, *der;* ~ **solution** *n.* Gummilösung, *die;* ~ **'stamp** *n.* **a)** Gummistempel, *der;* **b)** *(fig.: one who endorses uncritically)* Jasager, *der/*Jasagerin, *die (abwertend);* **the council is a ~ stamp body** die Ratsversammlung sagt zu allem ja und amen *(ugs.);* **~-'stamp** *v.t. (fig.: approve)* absegnen *(ugs. scherzh.)*

rubbery ['rʌbərɪ] *adj.* gummiartig; *(tough)* zäh; **be tough and ~:** zäh wie Gummi sein

rubbing ['rʌbɪŋ] *n.: Kopie, die entsteht, wenn man auf ein Relief Papier legt und mit Malkreide, Bleistift o.ä. darüberreibt*

rubbish ['rʌbɪʃ] **1.** *n., no pl., no indef. art.* **a)** *(refuse)* Abfall, *der;* Abfälle; *(to be collected and dumped)* Müll, *der;* **b)** *(worthless material)* Plunder, *der (ugs. abwertend);* **be ~:** nichts taugen; **c)** *(nonsense)* Quatsch, *der (ugs.);* Blödsinn, *der (ugs.);* **talk a lot of ~:** eine Menge Blödsinn reden; **what ~!** was für ein Quatsch *od.* Schmarren! **2.** *int.* Quatsch *(ugs. abwertend).* **3.** *v.t.* verreißen

rubbish: ~-bin *n.* Abfall-/Mülleimer, *der; (in factory)* Abfall-/Mülltonne, *die;* **~-chute** *n.* Müllschlucker, *der;* **~-dump** *n.* Müllkippe, *die;* **~-heap** *n.* Müllhaufen, *der; (in garden)* Abfallhaufen, *der;* **~-tip** *n.* Müllabladeplatz, *der*

rubbishy ['rʌbɪʃɪ] *adj.* mies *(ugs.);* ~ **newspaper** Käseblatt, *das (salopp abwertend)*

rubble ['rʌbl] *n.* **a)** *(from damaged building)* Trümmer *Pl.; (Geol. also)* Schutt, *der;*

reduce sth. to ~: etw. in Schutt und Asche legen; **b)** *(water-worn stones)* Geröll, *das*
'**rub-down** *n.* **give sb./sth. a [quick] ~:** jmdn./etw. [kurz *od.* schnell] abreiben
rube [ru:b] *n. (Amer. coll.)* Bauer, *der (ugs.)*
rubella [rʊ'belə] *n. (Med.)* Röteln *Pl.*
Rubicon ['ru:bɪkən] *n.* **cross the ~** *(fig.)* den Rubikon überschreiten *(geh.)*
rubicund ['ru:bɪkʌnd] *adj. (literary)* rosig; rotgesichtig ‹*Person*›
Rubik cube [ru:bɪk 'kju:b] *n.* Zauberwürfel, *der;* Rubik-Würfel, *der*
rubric ['ru:brɪk] *n.* **a)** Rubrik, *die;* **b)** *(commentary)* Glosse, *die*
ruby ['ru:bɪ] **1.** *n.* **a)** *(precious stone)* Rubin, *der; (Horol.)* Stein, *der;* **b)** *(colour)* Rubinrot, *das.* **2.** *adj.* **a)** *(red)* rubinfarben; rubinrot; **b)** *(containing stone)* Rubin‹*ring, -brosche usw.*›
ruby: ~-red *adj.* rubinrot; **~ 'wedding** *n.* Rubinhochzeit, *die*
RUC *abbr.* **Royal Ulster Constabulary** *nordirische Polizei*
ruche [ru:ʃ] *n.* Rüsche, *die*
ruched [ru:ʃt] *adj.* Rüschen-
[1]**ruck** [rʌk] *n.* **a)** *(Sport: main body of competitors)* Feld, *das;* **b)** *(fig.: crowd, mass)* Masse, *die;* **c)** *(Rugby)* offenes Gedränge
[2]**ruck,** *(Brit.)* **ruckle** ['rʌkl] **1.** *n. (crease)* Falte, *die.* **2.** *v. i.* **~ up** hochrutschen
rucksack ['rʌksæk, 'rʊksæk] *n.* Rucksack, *der*
ruckus ['rʌkəs] *n.,* **ructions** ['rʌkʃnz] *n. pl. (coll.)* Rabatz, *der (ugs.)*
rudder ['rʌdə(r)] *n.* Ruder, *das*
rudderless ['rʌdəlɪs] *adj.* ruderlos; ohne Ruder *nachgestellt; (fig.)* richtungslos
ruddy ['rʌdɪ] *adj.* **a)** *(reddish)* rötlich; **b)** *(rosy)* rosig; **c)** *(Brit. sl. euphem.: bloody)* verdammt *(salopp)*
rude [ru:d] *adj.* **a)** *(impolite)* unhöflich; *(stronger)* rüde; **say ~ things** *or* **be ~ about sb.** in ungehöriger Weise von jmdm. sprechen; **be ~ to sb.** zu jmdm. grob unhöflich sein; jmdn. rüde behandeln; **be ~ to a teacher** zu einem Lehrer frech *od.* unverschämt sein; **b)** *(abrupt)* unsanft; **~ awakening** böses *od. (geh.)* jähes Erwachen; **c)** *(hearty)* **in ~ health** *(dated)* kerngesund; **d)** *(simple)* primitiv; **e)** *(obscene)* unanständig
rudely ['ru:dlɪ] *adv.* **a)** *(impolitely)* unhöflich; rüde; **b)** *(abruptly)* jäh *(geh.);* **be ~ reminded of sth.** unsanft an etw. *(Akk.)* erinnert werden; **c)** *(roughly)* primitiv; **a ~ constructed hut** eine grob gezimmerte Hütte; **d)** *(obscenely)* unanständig; **gesture ~ at sb.** jmdm. eine unanständige Geste zeigen
rudeness ['ru:dnɪs] *n., no pl. (bad manners)* ungehöriges *od.* rüdes Benehmen
rudiment ['ru:dɪmənt] *n.* **a)** *in pl. (first principles)* Grundzüge *Pl.;* Grundlagen *Pl.;* **know the ~s of law** über juristische Grundkenntnisse verfügen; **b)** *in pl. (imperfect beginning)* [erster] Ansatz
rudimentary [ru:dɪ'mentərɪ] *adj.* **a)** *(elementary)* elementar; primitiv ‹*Gebäude*›; **~ knowledge** Grundkenntnisse *Pl.;* **b)** *(Anat., Zool.)* rudimentär
rue [ru:] *v.t.,* **~ing** *or* **ruing** ['ru:ɪŋ] *(literary: repent of)* bereuen; **you'll live to ~ it** es wird dich noch gereuen *(geh., veralt.);* **~ the day/hour when ...:** den Tag/die Stunde verwünschen, da ...
rueful ['ru:fl] *adj.,* **ruefully** ['ru:fəlɪ] *adv.* reumütig; reuig
[1]**ruff** [rʌf] *n.* Halskrause, *die*
[2]**ruff** *n. (sandpiper)* Kampfläufer, *der*
[3]**ruff** *(Cards)* **1.** *n.* Trumpfen, *das.* **2.** *v.i.* trumpfen. **3.** *v. t.* mit einem Trumpf stechen
ruffian ['rʌfɪən] *n.* Rohling, *der (abwertend);* **gang of ~s** Schlägerbande, *die;* **the little ~** *(joc.)* der kleine Strolch
ruffianly ['rʌfɪənlɪ] *adj.* roh; rauh ‹*Bursche*›
ruffle ['rʌfl] **1.** *v. t.* **a)** *(disturb smoothness of)* kräuseln; **~ sb.'s hair** jmdm. durch die Haare fahren; *see also* **feather 1 a; b)** *(upset)* aus der Fassung bringen; **her composure was not ~d** sie verlor ihre Fassung nicht; **be easily ~d** leicht aus der Fassung geraten; **c)** *(gather)* kräuseln. **2.** *n. (frill)* Rüsche, *die*
~ 'up *v. t.* sträuben ‹*Gefieder*›
rug [rʌg] *n.* **a)** *(for floor)* [kleiner, dicker] Teppich; **Persian ~:** Perserbrücke, *die;* **pull the ~ [out] from under sb.** *(fig.)* jmdm. den Boden unter den Füßen wegziehen; **b)** *(wrap, blanket)* [dicke] Wolldecke
Rugby ['rʌgbɪ] *n.* Rugby, *das; see also* **fives**
Rugby: ~ ball *n.* Rugbyball, *der;* **~ 'football** *n.* **a)** *(game) see* **Rugby; b)** *(ball) see* **~ ball; ~ 'footballer** *n.* Rugbyspieler, *der;* **~ 'League** *n. (Brit.) Profi-Rugby (mit 13 Spielern pro Mannschaft);* **~-player** *see* **~ footballer; ~ tackle** *n.* tiefes Fassen *(Rugby);* **the policeman brought him down with a ~ tackle** der Polizist warf sich auf ihn und riß ihn zu Boden; **~ 'Union** *n. (Brit.) Amateur-Rugby (mit 15 Spielern pro Mannschaft)*
rugged ['rʌgɪd] *adj.* **a)** *(sturdy)* robust; **b)** *(involving hardship)* hart ‹*Test*›; **c)** *(unpolished)* rauh; unverfälscht ‹*Ehrlichkeit, Freundlichkeit usw.*›; **with ~ good looks** gutaussehend mit markanten Gesichtszügen; **d)** *(uneven)* zerklüftet; unwegsam ‹*Land, Anstieg*›; zerfurcht ‹*Gesicht*›
ruggedize ['rʌgɪdaɪz] *v. t. (Amer.)* armieren
ruggedly ['rʌgɪdlɪ] *adv.* **~ constructed** robust gebaut; **~ handsome** gutaussehend mit markanten Gesichtszügen
rugger ['rʌgə(r)] *n. (Brit. coll.)* Rugby, *das*
Ruhr [rʊə(r)] *pr. n.* **the ~:** das Ruhrgebiet
ruin ['ru:ɪn] **1.** *n.* **a)** *no pl., no indef. art. (decay)* Verfall, *der;* **bring about one's own ~:** sich selbst ruinieren; **be reduced to a state of ~:** völlig verfallen sein; **the ~ of his hopes** das Ende seiner Hoffnungen; **go to** *or* **fall into rack and ~** ‹*Gebäude:*› völlig verfallen; ‹*Garten:*› völlig verwahrlosen; ‹*Pläne:*› zunichte werden; **b)** *no pl., no indef. art. (downfall)* Ruin, *der;* **his business was facing ~:** sein Geschäft stand am Rande des Ruins; **~ stared her in the face** sie stand vor dem Ruin; **c)** *in sing. or pl. (remains)* Ruine, *die;* **in ~s** in Trümmern; **he is a ~** *(fig.)* er ist eine Ruine *(ugs.) od.* ein Wrack; **rise from the ~s of sth.** aus den Trümmern einer Sache entstehen; **d)** *(cause of ~)* Ruin, *der;* Untergang, *der;* **you'll be the ~ of me** du ruinierst mich [noch]. **2.** *v. t.* ruinieren; verderben ‹*Urlaub, Abend*›; zunichte machen ‹*Aussichten, Möglichkeiten usw.*›
ruination [ru:ɪ'neɪʃn] *n., no pl. see* **ruin 1 d**
ruined ['ru:ɪnd] *adj.* **a)** *(reduced to ruins)* verfallen; **~ town** Ruinenstadt, *die;* **a ~ castle/palace/church** eine Burg-/Palast-/Kirchenruine; **b)** *(brought to ruin)* ruiniert; **his speculations left him a ~ man** seine Spekulationen ruinierten ihn; **c)** *(spoilt)* verdorben
ruinous ['ru:ɪnəs] *adj.* **a)** *(in ruins)* verfallen; **b)** *(disastrous)* ruinös; katastrophal ‹*Wirkung*›; **be ~ to sb./sth.** jmdn./etw. ruinieren
ruinously ['ru:ɪnəslɪ] *adv.* ruinös; katastrophal ‹*teuer, hoch usw.*›
rule [ru:l] **1.** *n.* **a)** *(principle)* Regel, *die;* **~ of conduct/decorum/cricket/life** Verhaltens-/Anstands-/Kricket-/Lebensregel, *die;* **the ~s of the game** *(lit. or fig.)* die Spielregeln; **stick to** *or* **play by the ~s** *(lit. or fig.)* sich an die Spielregeln halten; **~s and regulations** Regeln und Vorschriften; **[always] make it a ~ to do sth.** *(fig.)* es sich *(Dat.)* zur Regel machen, etw. zu tun; **be against the ~s** regelwidrig sein; *(fig.)* gegen die Spielregeln verstoßen; **bend** *or* **stretch the ~s** *(fig.)* ein Auge zudrücken *(ugs.);* **R~s** *(Austral. Footb.) Fußball nach den australischen Regeln;* **as a ~:** in der Regel; **~ of three** *(Math.)* Dreisatz, *der;* **~ of thumb** Faustregel, *die;* **the usual ~ of thumb is ...:** als Faustregel gilt ...; **~ of thumb estimate** grobe Schätzung; **b)** *(custom)* Regel, *die;* **the ~ of the house is that ...:** in diesem Haus ist es üblich, daß ...; **suits are the ~ on such an occasion** bei einem solchen Anlaß trägt man normalerweise einen Anzug; **c)** *no pl. (government)* Herrschaft, *die* **(over** über + *Akk.*); **the ~ of law** die Autorität des Gesetzes; **d)** *(Eccl.: code)* [Ordens]regel, *die;* **e)** *(graduated measure)* Maß, *das; (tape)* Bandmaß, *das; (folding)* Zollstock, *der;* **f)** *(Printing)* Linie, *die. See also* **road a; work 2 a. 2.** *v. t.* **a)** *(control)* beherrschen; **b)** *(be the ruler of)* regieren; ‹*Monarch, Diktator usw.:*› herrschen über (+ *Akk.*); **~ the roost [in the house]** Herr im Hause sein; *see also* **rod c; c)** *(give as decision)* entscheiden; **he ruled the ball out** er entschied, daß der Ball aus war; **~ a motion out of order** einen Antrag nicht zulassen; **~ sb. out of order** jmdm. [unter Hinweis auf die Geschäftsordnung] das Wort entziehen; **d)** *(draw)* ziehen ‹*Linie*›; *(draw lines on)* linieren ‹*Papier*›. **3.** *v.i.* **a)** *(govern)* herrschen; **~ by fear** eine Schreckensherrschaft führen; **X ~s** *(sl.)* X ist der/die Größte; **b)** *(decide, declare formally)* entscheiden **(against** gegen; **in favour of** für); **~ on a matter** in einer Sache entscheiden
~ 'off 1. *v.t.* mit einem Strich abtrennen; **~ off a margin** am Rand einen Strich ziehen. **2.** *v.i.* einen Schlußstrich ziehen
~ 'out *v. t.* **a)** *(exclude, eliminate)* ausschließen; **b)** *(prevent)* unmöglich machen
'**rule-book** *n. (lit. or fig.)* Regeln; Regelbuch, *das*
ruled [ru:ld] *adj.* liniert ‹*Papier*›
ruler ['ru:lə(r)] *n.* **a)** *(person)* Herrscher, *der*/Herrscherin, *die;* **b)** *(for drawing or measuring)* Lineal, *das*
ruling ['ru:lɪŋ] **1.** *n.* **a)** *(decision)* Entscheidung, *die;* **b)** *(using a ruler)* Linierung, *die.* **2.** *adj.* **a)** *(predominating)* herrschend ‹*Meinung*›; vorherrschend ‹*Charakterzug*›; **sb.'s ~ ambition/passion** jmds. größter Ehrgeiz/größte Leidenschaft; **b)** *(current)* **[the] ~ prices** die geltenden Preise; **c)** *(governing, reigning)* herrschend ‹*Klasse*›; regierend ‹*Partei*›; amtierend ‹*Regierung*›
[1]**rum** [rʌm] *n.* Rum, *der*
[2]**rum** *adj. (Brit. coll.) (odd)* seltsam
Rumania [ru:'meɪnɪə] *see* **Romania**
Rumanian [ru:'meɪnɪən] *see* **Romanian**
rumba ['rʌmbə] **1.** *n.* Rumba, *die, österr. der;* **dance the ~:** Rumba tanzen. **2.** *v. i.,* **~ed** *or* **~'d** ['rʌmbəd] Rumba tanzen
[1]**rumble** ['rʌmbl] **1.** *n.* **a)** *(sound)* Grollen, *das; (of heavy vehicle)* Rumpeln, *das (ugs.);* **b)** *(Amer. sl.: street-fight)* Straßenschlacht, *die;* Schlacht, *die (fig.);* **c)** *(Amer. coll.: rumour)* Gerücht, *das;* **the ~ is that ...:** man munkelt, daß ... **2.** *v. i.* **a)** *(make low, heavy sound)* grollen; ‹*Magen:*› knurren; **b)** *(go with rumbling noise)* rumpeln *(ugs.)*
[2]**rumble** *v. t. (coll.: understand)* spitzkriegen *(ugs.)* ‹*Sache*›; auf die Schliche kommen (+ *Dat.*) ‹*Person*›
'**rumble seat** *n. (Amer. dated)* Notsitz, *der*
rumbustious [rʌm'bʌstʃəs] *adj. (coll.)* wild
ruminant ['ru:mɪnənt] *(Zool.)* **1.** *n.* Wiederkäuer, *der.* **2.** *adj.* wiederkäuend
ruminate ['ru:mɪneɪt] *v. i.* **a) ~ over** *or* **about** *or* **on sth.** über etw. *(Akk.)* nachsinnen *(geh.) od.* grübeln; **she sat ruminating for a moment** sie saß einen Augenblick nachdenklich da; **b)** *(Zool.)* wiederkäuen
rumination [ru:mɪ'neɪʃn] *n.* **a)** Nachsinnen, *das (geh.);* Grübeln, *das;* **his ~s were interrupted** seine Gedanken wurden unterbrochen; **b)** *(Zool.)* Wiederkäuen, *das*
ruminative ['ru:mɪnətɪv] *adj.* beschaulich ‹*Stimmung*›; grüblerisch ‹*Person*›
rummage ['rʌmɪdʒ] **1.** *v. i.* wühlen *(ugs.);* kramen *(ugs.);* **~ among old clothes** in alten

Kleidungsstücken herumwühlen *od.* -stöbern; ~ **through sth.** etw. durchwühlen *(ugs.);* ~ **about** *or* **around** herumkramen *(ugs.).* **2.** *n.* **have a** ~ **through sth.** etw. durchwühlen *od.* durchstöbern; **enjoy a good** ~ **around bookshops** gern in Buchhandlungen herumstöbern *(ugs.)*

~ **'out** *v. t.* hervorkramen *(ugs.)*

'rummage sale *see* **jumble sale**

rummy ['rʌmɪ] *n. (Cards)* Rommé, *das*

rumour *(Brit.; Amer.:* **rumor***)* ['ru:mə(r)] **1.** *n.* **a)** *(unverified story)* Gerücht, *das;* **there is a** ~ **that ...:** es geht das Gerücht, daß ...; **there is a persistent** ~ **that ...:** das Gerücht hält sich hartnäckig, daß ...; **b)** *no pl., no art. (common talk)* Gerücht, *das;* ~ **puts the number of casualties at around 5,000** Gerüchten zufolge liegt die Zahl der Opfer bei 5 000; ~ **has it that ...:** es geht das Gerücht, daß ... **2.** *v. t.* **sb. is ~ed to have done sth., it is ~ed that sb. has done sth.** man munkelt *(ugs.) od.* es geht das Gerücht, daß jmd. etw. getan hat; **the ~ed earthquake** das Erdbeben, das sich [Gerüchten zufolge] ereignet haben soll

rump [rʌmp] *n.* **a)** *(buttocks)* Hinterteil, *das (ugs.);* **meat from the** ~**:** Fleisch aus der Keule; **b)** *(remnant)* Rest, *der;* **sth. is only a** ~**:** von etw. ist nur noch der Rumpf übrig; **the R~** *(Brit. Hist.)* das Rumpfparlament

rumple ['rʌmpl] *v. t.* **a)** *(crease)* zerknittern; **b)** *(tousle)* zerzausen

'rump steak *n.* Rumpsteak, *das*

rumpus ['rʌmpəs] *n., no pl. (coll.)* Krach, *der (ugs.);* Spektakel, *der (ugs.);* **kick up** *or* **make a** ~**:** einen Spektakel veranstalten *(ugs.)*

'rumpus room *n. (Amer.)* Hobbyraum, *der*

run [rʌn] **1.** *n.* **a)** Lauf, *der;* **let the dogs out for a** ~**:** die Hunde hinauslassen, damit sie Auslauf haben; **go for a** ~ **before breakfast** vor dem Frühstück einen Lauf machen; **make a late** ~ *(Sport or fig.)* zum Endspurt ansetzen; **come towards sb./take a hurdle/start off at a** ~**:** jmdm. entgegenlaufen/eine Hürde im Lauf nehmen/losrennen; **I've had a good** ~ **for my money** ich bin auf meine Kosten gekommen; **we'll give our opponents a good** ~ **for their money** wir werden es unseren Gegnern nicht leichtmachen; **on the** ~**:** auf der Flucht; **keep the enemy on the** ~**:** den Feind nicht zur Ruhe kommen lassen; **b)** *(trip in vehicle)* Fahrt, *die; (for pleasure)* Ausflug, *der;* **on the** ~ **down to Cornwall** auf der Fahrt nach Cornwall; **a two-hour/a day's** ~**:** eine Fahrt von zwei Stunden/eine Tagesreise; **go for a** ~ **[in the car]** einen [Auto]ausflug machen; **c)** *(continuous stretch)* Länge, *die;* **a 500 ft.** ~ **of pipe** eine Rohrleitung von 500 Fuß Länge; **d)** *(spell)* **have a** ~ **of fine weather** eine Schönwetterperiode haben; **she has had a long** ~ **of success** sie war lange [Zeit] erfolgreich; **have a long** ~ ⟨*Stück, Show:*⟩ viele Aufführungen erleben; **a successful [West End]** ~**:** eine erfolgreiche Spielzeit [im Westend]; **e)** *(succession)* Serie, *die; (Cards)* Sequenz, *die;* **a** ~ **of victories** eine Siegesserie; **f)** *(tendency)* Ablauf, *der;* ~ **of [the] play** *(Sport)* Spielverlauf, *der;* **the general** ~ **of things/events** der Lauf der Dinge/der Gang der Ereignisse; **g)** *(regular route)* Strecke, *die;* **do a regular** ~ **between London and Edinburgh** regelmäßig die Strecke London–Edinburgh fahren; **he is on** *or* **he does the Glasgow** ~**:** er fährt die Glasgower Strecke; **h)** *(Cricket, Baseball)* Lauf, *der;* Run, *der;* **i)** *see* **ladder 1 b; j)** *(Mus.)* Lauf, *der;* **k)** *(quantity produced) (of book)* Auflage, *die;* **production** ~**:** Ausstoß, *der (Wirtsch.);* **l)** *(demand)* Run, *der* **(on** auf + *Akk.***);** **m)** *(general type)* **the common** *or* **general** ~ **of people** der Durchschnittsmensch; **he's not like the usual** ~ **of disc jockeys** er ist anders als die üblichen Diskjockeys; **n) the ~s** *(sl.: diarrhoea)* Durchmarsch, *der (salopp);* **o)** *(unrestricted use)* **give sb. the** ~ **of sth.** jmdm. etw. zu seiner freien Verfügung überlassen; **have the** ~ **of sth.** etw. zu seiner freien Verfügung haben; **p)** *(animal enclosure)* Auslauf, *der; (regular track of animals)* Wildwechsel, *der. See also* **long 1 c; short 1 a; ski-run. 2.** *v. i.,* **-nn-, ran** [ræn], **run a)** laufen; *(fast also)* rennen; ~ **for all one is worth** rennen so schnell man kann; ~ **for the bus** laufen *od.* rennen, um den Bus zu kriegen *(ugs.);* ~ **to help sb.** jmdm. zu Hilfe eilen; ~ **at sb.** auf jmdn. losstürzen; **the horse ran at the fence** das Pferd lief auf den Zaun zu; **b)** *(compete)* laufen; **he ran sixth/a poor third** er wurde sechster/erreichte einen mäßigen dritten Platz; **c)** *(hurry)* laufen; **don't** ~ **to me when things go wrong** komm mir nicht angelaufen, wenn etwas schiefgeht *(ugs.);* ~ **to meet sb.** jmdm. entgegenlaufen; **he ran to meet her at the gate** er lief ihr bis ans Tor entgegen; **d)** *(roll)* laufen; ⟨*Ball, Kugel:*⟩ rollen, laufen; **the wheels ran into a rut** die Räder gerieten in eine Furche; **e)** *(slide)* laufen; ⟨*Schlitten, [Schiebe]tür:*⟩ gleiten; **f)** *(revolve)* ⟨*Rad, Maschine:*⟩ laufen; **g)** *(Naut.)* ~ **for Plymouth** Plymouth anlaufen; ~ **into port** in den Hafen einlaufen; ~ **aground** auf Grund laufen; *see also* **foul 1 f; h)** *(flee)* davonlaufen; ~ **for it** *(coll.)* sich aus dem Staub machen *(ugs.);* ~ **for cover** schnell in Deckung gehen; *see also* **life a; i)** *(travel)* ~ **over** *or* **across** hinüberfahren; ~ **down/up [to London]** [nach London] runter-/rauffahren *(ugs.);* ~ **into town** in die Stadt fahren; **j)** *(operate on a schedule)* fahren; ~ **between two places** ⟨*Zug, Bus:*⟩ zwischen zwei Orten verkehren; **the train is ~ning late** der Zug hat Verspätung; **we're ~ning late** *(fig.)* wir sind spät dran *(ugs.);* ~ **on time** pünktlich sein; keine Verspätung haben; **the train doesn't** ~ **on Sundays** der Zug verkehrt nicht an Sonntagen; **k)** *(pass cursorily)* ~ **through** überfliegen ⟨*Text*⟩; ~ **through one's head** *or* **mind** ⟨*Gedanken, Ideen:*⟩ einem durch den Kopf gehen; ~ **through the various possibilities** die verschiedenen Möglichkeiten durchspielen; **his eyes ran over the article/photo** er ließ die Augen über den Artikel/das Foto wandern; **her fingers ran over the keys** ihre Finger liefen über die Tasten; **the tune is ~ning in my head** die Melodie geht mir im Kopf herum; **l)** *(flow)* laufen; ⟨*Fluß:*⟩ fließen; ⟨*Augen:*⟩ tränen; **your bath is ~ning** dein Bad läuft ein; **till the blood ran** bis es blutete; **the child's nose was ~ning** dem Kind lief die Nase; **the walls are ~ning with moisture** die Wände triefen vor Nässe *(Dat.);* ~ **dry** ⟨*Fluß*⟩ austrocknen; ⟨*Quelle:*⟩ versiegen; **the taps had** ~ **dry** es lief kein Wasser mehr aus der Leitung; ~ **low** *or* **short** knapp werden; ausgehen; **we ran short of** *or* **low on fruit** unsere Obstvorräte wurden knapp *od.* gingen aus; **m)** *(flow rapidly)* **a heavy sea was ~ning** es herrschte starker Seegang; **the tide ran strong/out** die Flutwellen schlugen hoch/die Flut ging zurück; **n)** *(be current)* ⟨*Vertrag, Theaterstück:*⟩ laufen; **o)** *(be present)* ~ **through sth.** sich durch etw. ziehen; ~ **in the family** ⟨*Eigenschaft, Begabung:*⟩ in der Familie liegen; **p)** *(function)* laufen; **keep/leave the engine ~ning** den Motor laufen lassen/nicht abstellen; **the machine ~s on batteries/oil** *etc.* die Maschine läuft mit Batterien/Öl *usw.;* **things aren't ~ning too smoothly in their marriage** *(fig.)* in ihrer Ehe läuft es [zur Zeit] nicht besonders gut *(ugs.);* **q)** *(have a course)* ⟨*Straße, Bahnlinie:*⟩ verlaufen; **r)** *(have wording)* lauten; ⟨*Geschichte:*⟩ gehen *(fig.);* **s)** *(have tendency)* **my inclination does not** ~ **that way** meine Neigung geht nicht in diese Richtung; **t)** *(have certain level)* **inflation is ~ning at 15 %** die Inflationsrate beläuft sich auf *od.* beträgt 15 %; **interest rates are ~ning at record levels** die Zinsen bewegen sich auf Rekordhöhe; **u)** *(seek election)* kandidieren; ~ **for mayor** für das Amt des Bürgermeisters kandidieren; **v)** *(spread quickly)* **a cheer ran down** *or* **along the lines of soldiers** ein Hurra ging durch die Reihen der Soldaten; **a shiver ran down my spine** ein Schau[d]er *(geh.)* lief mir den Rücken hinunter; **w)** *(spread undesirably)* ⟨*Butter, Eis:*⟩ zerlaufen; ⟨*Farben:*⟩ *(in washing)* auslaufen; *(on painting etc.)* ineinanderlaufen; **x)** *(Cricket)* einen Lauf *od.* Run machen; **y)** *(ladder)* Laufmaschen bekommen; **stockings guaranteed not to** ~**:** garantiert laufmaschensichere Strümpfe. *See also* **also; blood 1 a; cut 2 e; feeling 1 c; riot 1 b; wild 1 c; [1]writ a. 3.** *v. t.,* **-nn-, ran, run a)** *(cause to move)* laufen lassen; *(drive)* fahren; ~ **the ship aground** das Schiff auf Grund laufen lassen *od. (Seemannsspr.)* auflaufen lassen; ~ **the boat into the water** das Boot zu Wasser lassen; ~ **the car into the garage** das Auto in die Garage fahren; ~ **one's hand/fingers through/along** *or* **down** *or* **over sth.** mit der Hand/den Fingern durch etw. fahren/über etw. *(Akk.)* streichen; ~ **an** *or* **one's eye along** *or* **down** *or* **over sth.** *(fig.)* etw. überfliegen; ~ **one's finger down a list** mit dem Finger eine Liste entlangfahren; ~ **a rope through sth.** ein Seil durch etw. führen; **b)** *(cause to flow)* [ein]laufen lassen; ~ **a bath** ein Bad einlaufen lassen; **c)** *(organize, manage)* führen, leiten ⟨*Geschäft usw.*⟩; durchführen ⟨*Experiment*⟩; veranstalten ⟨*Wettbewerb*⟩; führen ⟨*Leben*⟩; **the people who** ~ **things [in this city]** die maßgeblichen Leute [dieser Stadt]; ~ **the show** *(fig. coll.)* das Sagen haben *(ugs.);* **d)** *(operate)* bedienen ⟨*Maschine*⟩; verkehren lassen ⟨*Verkehrsmittel*⟩; einsetzen ⟨*Sonderbus, -zug*⟩; laufen lassen ⟨*Motor*⟩; abspielen ⟨*Tonband*⟩; ~ **a train service** eine Schienenverbindung unterhalten; ~ **a taxi** Taxi fahren; ~ **forward/back** vorwärts-/zurückspulen ⟨*Film, Tonband*⟩; **e)** *(own and use)* sich *(Dat.)* halten ⟨*Auto*⟩; **a Jaguar is expensive to** ~**:** ein Jaguar ist im Unterhalt sehr teuer; **~ning a freezer saves money** mit einer Tiefkühltruhe spart man Geld; ~ **a car with defective brakes** ein Auto mit defekten Bremsen fahren; **f)** *(take for journey)* fahren; **I'll** ~ **you into town** ich fahre *od.* bringe dich in die Stadt; **g)** *(pursue)* jagen; ~ **to earth** in seinen Unterschlupf hetzen ⟨*Tier*⟩; *(fig.)* aufspüren; ~ **sb. hard** *or* **close** jmdm. auf den Fersen sein *od.* sitzen *(ugs.);* **be** ~ **off one's feet** alle Hände voll zu tun haben *(ugs.); (in business)* Hochbetrieb haben *(ugs.);* **h)** *(complete)* laufen ⟨*Rennen, Marathon, Strecke*⟩; ~ **messages/errands** Botengänge machen; **the race will be** ~ **tomorrow** das Rennen wird morgen gelaufen/gefahren; **i)** *(smuggle)* schmuggeln ⟨*Waffen, Drogen, Personen*⟩; schleusen ⟨*Personen*⟩; **j)** *(enter for race or election)* laufen lassen ⟨*Pferd*⟩; aufstellen ⟨*Kandidaten*⟩; **k)** *(publish)* bringen *(ugs.)* ⟨*Bericht, Artikel usw.*⟩; in die Zeitung setzen ⟨*Anzeige*⟩; **l)** ~ **a fever/a temperature** Fieber/erhöhte Temperatur haben. *See also* **course 1 a; [2]fine 1 g; [2]gauntlet; ground 1 b; ragged e; risk 1 a**

~ **a'bout** *v. i.* **a)** *(bustle)* hin- und herlaufen; **b)** *(play without restraint)* herumtollen; herumspringen *(ugs.). See also* **runabout**

~ **a'cross** *v. t.* ~ **across sb.** jmdn. treffen; jmdm. über den Weg laufen; ~ **across sth.** auf etw. *(Akk.)* stoßen

~ **after** *v. t.* **a)** *(~ to catch, follow persistently)* hinterherlaufen (+ *Dat.*); **b)** nachlaufen (+ *Dat.*) ⟨*Mode usw.*⟩

~ **a'long** *v. i. (coll.: depart)* sich trollen *(ugs.)*

~ **a'round 1.** *v. i.* **a)** ~ **around with sb.** sich mit jmdm. herumtreiben; **b)** *see* **run about a; c)** *see* **run about b. 2.** *v. t.* herumfahren

~ a'way *v. i.* **a)** *(flee)* weglaufen; fortlaufen; **b)** *(abscond)* ~ **away [from home/from the children's home]** [von zu Hause/aus dem Kinderheim] weglaufen; **c)** *(elope)* ~ **away with sb./together** mit jmdm./zusammen durchbrennen *(ugs.)*; **d)** *(bolt)* ⟨*Pferd:*⟩ durchgehen; **e)** ⟨*Wasser:*⟩ ablaufen; **f)** *(get ahead)* ~ **away from the rest of the field** dem übrigen Feld davonlaufen. *See also* **runaway**

~ a'way with *v. t.* **a)** *(coll.: steal)* abhauen mit *(salopp)*; **b)** *(fig.: win)* ~ **away with the top prize/all the trophies** den 1. Preis/alle Trophäen erringen; **c)** *(fig.: be misled by)* ~ **away with the idea** *or* **notion that ...**: irrtümlich annehmen, daß ...; **don't ~ away with the idea that ...**: glaub bloß nicht, daß ...; **he let his imagination/enthusiasm ~ away with him** seine Phantasie/Begeisterung ist mit ihm durchgegangen; **d)** *(fig.: consume)* verbrauchen; verschlingen ⟨*Geld*⟩; fressen *(ugs.)* ⟨*Benzin*⟩. *See also* **run away c**

~ 'back over *v. t.* sich *(Dat.)* in Erinnerung rufen; **her thoughts ran back over the past** sie dachte an die vergangenen Zeiten

~ 'down **1.** *v. t.* **a)** *(collide with)* überfahren; **b)** *(find after search)* aufspüren; **c)** *(criticize)* heruntermachen *(ugs.)*; herabsetzen; **don't ~ yourself down all the time** mach dich nicht immer selbst so schlecht; **d)** *(cause to diminish)* abbauen; verringern ⟨*Produktion*⟩; **e)** *(cause to lose power)* leer machen ⟨*Batterie*⟩. **2.** *v. i.* **a)** hin-/herunterlaufen/-rennen/-fahren; **b)** *(decline)* sich verringern; ⟨*Schienennetz:*⟩ schrumpfen; **c)** *(lose power)* ausgehen; ⟨*Batterie:*⟩ leer werden; ⟨*Uhr, Spielzeug:*⟩ ablaufen. *See also* **rundown**

~ 'in **1.** *v. t.* **a)** *(prepare for use)* einfahren ⟨*Auto*⟩; sich einlaufen lassen ⟨*Maschine*⟩; **b)** *(coll.: arrest)* hoppnehmen *(salopp)*. **2.** *v. i.* hin-/hereinlaufen/-rennen

~ into *v. t.* **a)** ~ **into a telegraph-pole/tree** gegen einen Telegrafenmast/Baum fahren; ~ **into a sandbank** auf eine Sandbank geraten *od. (Seemannsspr.)* auflaufen; **b)** *(cause to collide with)* ~ **one's car into a tree** seinen Wagen gegen einen Baum fahren; **c)** *(cause to incur)* ~ **the family into debt** die Familie in Schulden stürzen; **d)** *(fig.: meet)* ~ **into sb.** jmdm. in die Arme laufen *(ugs.)*; **e)** *(be faced with)* stoßen auf (+ *Akk.*) ⟨*Schwierigkeiten, Widerstand, Probleme usw.*⟩; **f)** *(enter)* geraten in (+ *Akk.*) ⟨*Sturm, schlechtes Wetter, Schulden*⟩; **his debts ~ into thousands** seine Schulden gehen in die Tausende; **g)** *(merge with)* ~ **into one another** ⟨*Seen, Tage:*⟩ ineinander übergehen

~ 'off **1.** *v. i. see* ~ **away a, c. 2.** *v. t.* **a)** *(compose rapidly)* hinwerfen ⟨*ein paar Zeilen, Verse, Notizen*⟩; zu Papier bringen ⟨*Brief*⟩; **b)** *(produce on machine)* abziehen ⟨*Kopien, Handzettel usw.*⟩; **c)** *(cause to drain away)* ablaufen lassen; **d)** *(recite fluently) see* **rattle off**; **e)** *(decide by run-off)* durch Stechen entscheiden; *see also* **run-off**

~ 'off with *v. t. (coll.: steal)* abhauen mit *(salopp)*; *see also* ~ **away c**; ~ **away with b**

~ 'on **1.** *v. i.* **a)** *(continue without a break)* weitergehen; ⟨*Krankheit:*⟩ fortschreiten; ⟨*Redner:*⟩ weiterreden; **b)** *(Printing: continue on same line)* **'~ on'** „ohne Absatz"; **c)** *(elapse)* ⟨*Zeit:*⟩ verstreichen; **d)** *(join up)* **let the letters ~ on** *(beim Schreiben)* die Buchstaben miteinander verbinden; **e)** *(talk incessantly)* reden wie ein Wasserfall *(ugs.)*; **her tongue ~s on** ihr Mundwerk steht nicht still *(ugs.)*. **2.** *v. t.* **a)** *(Printing)* als fortlaufenden Text setzen; **b)** ['--] *(be concerned with)* sich befassen mit; **his mind was ~ning on this subject** seine Gedanken kreisten um dieses Thema

~ 'out **1.** *v. i.* **a)** hin-/herauslaufen/-rennen; **he ran out a deserved winner** er ging aus dem Kampf als verdienter Sieger hervor; *see also* **run 2 m**; **b)** *(become exhausted)* ⟨*Vorräte, Bestände:*⟩ zu Ende gehen; ⟨*Geduld:*⟩ sich erschöpfen; **we have ~ out** wir haben keinen/keine/keines mehr; *(sold everything)* wir sind ausverkauft; **c)** *(expire)* ⟨*Vertrag:*⟩ ablaufen; **time is ~ning out** die Zeit wird knapp; **d)** *(jut out)* ⟨*Land:*⟩ vorspringen; ⟨*Pier:*⟩ ins Meer hinausreichen. *See also* **sand 1 c. 2.** *v. t. (Cricket)* ~ **a batsman out** *einen Schlagmann zum Ausscheiden bringen, indem man mit dem Ball das Tor zerstört, bevor er die Schlagmallinie erreicht*

~ 'out of *v. t.* **a)** *(exhaust stock of)* **sb. ~s out of sth.** jmdm. geht etw. aus; **I'm ~ning out of patience** meine Geduld geht zu Ende; **we're ~ning out of time** uns wird die Zeit [allmählich] knapp; **b)** *(flow out of)* auslaufen aus

~ 'out on *v. t. (desert)* im Stich lassen

~ over **1.** ['---] *v. t.* **a)** *see* **go over 2 a**; **b)** *(knock down)* überfahren. *See also* **run 2 k. 2.** [-'--] *v. i.* **a)** *(overflow)* überlaufen; **b)** *(exceed limit)* [die Zeit] überziehen

~ through *v. t.* **a)** *see* **get through 2 h**; **b)** abspielen ⟨*Tonband, Film*⟩; **c)** *(rehearse)* durchspielen ⟨*Theaterstück*⟩; **d)** [-'-] *(pierce right through)* ~ **sb. through with sth.** jmdn. mit etw. durchbohren. *See also* **run 2 k, o; run-through**

~ to *v. t.* **a)** *(amount to)* umfassen; ⟨*Geldsumme, Kosten:*⟩ sich belaufen auf (+ *Akk.*); **b)** *(be sufficient for)* **sth. will ~ to sth.** etw. reicht für etw.; **c)** *(afford)* **sb. can ~ to sth.** jmd. kann sich *(Dat.)* etw. leisten; **d)** *(show inclination towards)* ~ **to fat** [zu] dick werden; **his style ~s too easily to sentiment** sein Stil gleitet allzu leicht ins Sentimentale ab; *see also* **seed 1 b**

~ 'up **1.** *v. i.* **a)** hinlaufen; *(Sport)* Anlauf nehmen; **he ran up to where they were standing** er lief *od.* rannte zu ihnen hin; **come ~ning along** herangelaufen kommen; **b)** *(amount to)* ~ **up to** sich belaufen auf (+ *Akk.*). **2.** *v. t.* **a)** *(hoist)* hissen ⟨*Fahne*⟩; **b)** *(make quickly)* rasch nähen ⟨*Kleidungsstück*⟩; zusammenzimmern ⟨*Schuppen*⟩; hochziehen *(ugs.)* ⟨*Gebäude*⟩; **c)** *(allow to accumulate)* ~ **up debts/a [big] bill** Schulden/eine hohe Rechnung zusammenkommen lassen. *See also* **run-up**

~ 'up against *v. t.* stoßen auf (+ *Akk.*) ⟨*Probleme, Widerstand usw.*⟩

run: ~about *n. (coll.)* **[little] ~about** Kleinwagen, *der*; **~-around** *n. (coll.)* **give sb. the ~-around** jmdn. an der Nase herumführen *(ugs.)*; **~away 1.** *n.* Ausreißer, *der*/Ausreißerin, *die (ugs.)*; **2.** *attrib. adj.* **a)** *(fleeing)* flüchtig; **she was a ~away schoolgirl** sie war aus der Schule weggelaufen; **have a ~away wedding** weglaufen und heiraten; **b)** *(out of control)* durchgegangen ⟨*Pferd*⟩; außer Kontrolle geraten ⟨*Fahrzeug, Preise*⟩; *(fig.)* galoppierend ⟨*Inflation*⟩; **c)** *(outstanding)* überwältigend ⟨*Erfolg*⟩; triumphal ⟨*Sieg*⟩; **~-down 1.** *n.* **a)** *(coll.: briefing)* Übersicht, *die* **(on** über + *Akk.*); **b)** *(reduction)* Abbau, *der*; **2.** *adj.* **a)** *(tired)* mitgenommen; **in a completely ~-down condition** völlig erschöpft; **b)** *(neglected)* heruntergekommen *(ugs.)* ⟨*Gegend, Stadt, Gewerbe*⟩

rune [ru:n] *n.* Rune, *die*

[1]rung [rʌŋ] *n.* **a)** *(of ladder)* Sprosse, *die*; **b)** *(fig.)* **start on the bottom** *or* **lowest/reach the top** *or* **highest ~**: auf der ersten Sprosse beginnen/die oberste Sprosse erreichen

[2]rung *see* **[2]ring 2, 3**

runic ['ru:nɪk] *adj.* Runen-; runisch

runnel ['rʌnl] *n.* **a)** *(brook)* Wasserlauf, *der*; Rinnsal, *das (geh.)*; **b)** *(gutter)* Rinne, *die*

runner ['rʌnə(r)] *n.* **a)** Läufer, *der*/Läuferin, *die*; **b)** *(horse in race)* **eight ~s were in the race** acht Pferde liefen beim Rennen; **c)** *(messenger)* Bote, *der*; Laufbursche, *der*; **d)** *(Bot.: creeping stem)* Ausläufer, *der*; **e)** *(twining plant)* Kletterpflanze, *die*; **f)** **curtain ~**: Gardinenröllchen, *das*; **g)** *(part on which sth. slides)* Kufe, *die*; *(for curtains)* Gardinenleiste, *die*; *(groove)* Laufschiene, *die*; **h)** *(cloth)* Tischläufer, *der*; *(carpet)* Läufer, *der*; **i)** *(who handles illegal goods)* Schieber, *der (ugs.)*; **[drug-]~**: [Drogen]kurier, *der (ugs.)*; **j)** *(who runs a blockade)* Blockadebrecher, *der*; **k)** *(car)* **'good ~'** „fährt *od.* läuft einwandfrei"

runner: ~ bean *n. (Brit.)* Stangenbohne, *die*; **~-'up** *n.* Zweite, *der/die*; **the ~s-up** die Plazierten; **they were joint ~s-up** sie teilten sich den zweiten Platz

running ['rʌnɪŋ] **1.** *n.* **a)** *(management)* Leitung, *die*; **b)** *(action)* Laufen, *das*; *(jogging)* Jogging, *das*; **make the ~** *(in competition)* an der Spitze liegen; *(fig.: have the initiative)* den Ton angeben; **take up the ~**: sich an die Spitze setzen; **in/out of the ~**: im/aus dem Rennen; **be out of the ~ for the Presidency** keine Aussichten [mehr] auf die Präsidentschaft haben; **c)** *(ability to run)* **have a lot of ~ left** noch gute Laufkondition haben; **d)** *(Horse-racing: condition of surface)* **the ~ is good/soft** es läßt sich gut laufen/die Laufbahn ist weich; **e)** *(of engine, machine)* Laufen, *das*. **2.** *adj.* **a)** *(continuous)* ständig; fortlaufend ⟨*Erklärungen*⟩; **have** *or* **fight a ~ battle** *(fig.)* ständig im Streit liegen; *see also* **fire 1 g**; **b)** *(in succession)* hintereinander; **win for the third year ~**: schon drei Jahre hintereinander gewinnen; **c)** *(Motor Veh.)* **in ~ order** in fahrbereitem Zustand

running: ~-board *n.* Trittbrett, *das*; ~ **'commentary** *n. (Broadcasting; also fig.)* Live-Kommentar, *der*; ~ **costs** *n. pl.* Betriebskosten *Pl.*; ~ **dog** *n. (Polit. derog.)* Kettenhund, *der (abwertend)*; ~ **'head-[line]** *n. (Printing)* Kolumnentitel, *der*; ~ **'jump** *n.* **you can [go and] take a ~ jump [at yourself]** *(fig. sl.)* du kannst mir den Buckel runterrutschen *(ugs.)*; ~ **knot** *n.* Knoten einer Schlinge; ~ **mate** *n. (Amer.)* **a)** Mitkandidat, *der*/Mitkandidatin, *die [als Vizepräsidentschaftskandidat]*; **b)** *(horse as pace-setter)* Pacemacher, *der*; ~ **re'pairs** *n. pl.* laufende Reparaturen; **~-shoe** *n.* Rennschuh, *der*; **~-shorts** *n. pl.* Sporthose, *die*; ~ **'sore** *n.* nässende Wunde; *(fig.)* schwärende Wunde; ~ **stitch** *n. (Needlework)* Vorstich, *der*; ~ **'title** *see* ~ **head**; ~ **'total** *n.* fortlaufende Summe; **~-track** *n.* Aschenbahn, *die*; ~ **'water** *n.* **a)** *(in stream)* fließendes Gewässer; **b)** *(available through pipe)* fließendes Wasser; **hot and cold ~ water** fließendes kaltes und warmes Wasser

runny ['rʌnɪ] *adj.* **a)** *(secreting mucus)* laufend ⟨*Nase*⟩; **b)** *(excessively liquid)* zerlaufend; zu dünn ⟨*Farbe, Marmelade*⟩

'run-off *n. (Sport)* Stechen, *das*

run-of-the-'mill *adj.* ganz gewöhnlich

runt [rʌnt] *n.* **a)** *(weakling pig)* Kümmerer, *der (Landw.)*; **b)** *(fig. derog.)* Kümmerling, *der (abwertend)*

run: ~-through *n.* **a)** *(cursory reading)* **give a text a [quick] ~-through, have a [brief] ~-through of a text** einen Text [kurz] überfliegen; **b)** *(rapid summary)* Überblick, *der* **(of** über + *Akk.*); **c)** *(rehearsal)* Durchlaufprobe, *die*; **~-up** *n.* **a)** *(approach to an event)* **during** *or* **in the ~-up to an event** im Vorfeld *(fig.)* eines Ereignisses; **b)** *(Sport)* Anlauf, *der*; **take a ~-up** Anlauf nehmen

runway ['rʌnweɪ] *n. (for take-off)* Startbahn, *die*; *(for landing)* Landebahn, *die*

rupee [ru:'pi:] *n.* Rupie, *die*

rupture ['rʌptʃə(r)] **1.** *n.* **a)** *(lit. or fig.)* Bruch, *der*; **b)** *(Med.)* Ruptur, *die*. **2.** *v. t.* **a)** *(burst)* aufreißen; **a ~d appendix/spleen** ein geplatzter Blinddarm/eine gerissene Milz; **b)** ~ **oneself** sich *(Dat.)* einen Bruch zuziehen *od.* heben; **c)** *(sever)* auseinanderbrechen lassen ⟨*Beziehungen, Einheit*⟩. **3.** *v. i.* reißen; ⟨*Blutgefäß, Blinddarm:*⟩ platzen

rural ['rʊərl] *adj.* ländlich; ~ **life** Landleben, *das*

rural: ~ **'dean** *n. (Eccl.)* ≈ Dekan, *der;* ~ **'district** *n. (Brit. Admin. Hist.)* ≈ Landkreis, *der*

Ruritania [rʊərɪ'teɪnɪə] *n. fiktionales mitteleuropäisches Königreich;* Ruritanien *(das);* ≈ Operettenstaat, *der*

ruse [ru:z] *n.* List, *die*

[1]**rush** [rʌʃ] *n. (Bot.)* Binse, *die*

[2]**rush 1.** *n.* **a)** *(rapid moving forward)* **be swept away by the ~ of the current** von der Gewalt der Strömung mitgerissen werden; **make a ~ for sth.** sich auf etw. *(Akk.)* stürzen; **the ~ to the coast** der Ansturm auf die Küste; **the holiday ~:** der [hektische] Urlaubsverkehr; **b)** *(hurry)* Eile, *die;* **what's all the ~?** wozu diese Hast?; **be in a [great] ~:** in [großer] Eile sein; es [sehr] eilig haben; **everything happened in such a ~:** es ging alles so schnell; **have a ~ to get somewhere** sich abhetzen, um irgendwohin zu kommen; **c)** *(surging)* Anwandlung, *die* **(of** von); **a ~ of blood [to the head]** *(fig. coll.)* eine [plötzliche] Anwandlung; **d)** *(period of great activity)* Hochbetrieb, *der; (~-hour)* Stoßzeit, *die;* **there is a ~ on** es herrscht Hochbetrieb *(ugs.);* **a ~ of new orders** eine Flut von neuen Aufträgen; **e)** *in pl. (Cinemat. coll.)* [Bild]muster; Musterkopien; **f)** *(heavy demand)* Ansturm, *der* **(for, on** auf + *Akk.*); **g)** *(Footb.)* Sturmangriff, *der;* **h)** *(Amer. Footb.)* Durchbruch, *der.* **2.** *v.t.* **a)** *(convey rapidly)* ~ **sb./sth. somewhere** jmdn./etw. auf schnellstem Wege irgendwohin bringen; ~ **sb. supplies** jmdn. schnell mit Vorräten versorgen; ~ **sb. round the sights** jmdn. von einer Sehenswürdigkeit zur anderen hetzen; ~ **through Parliament** im Parlament durchpeitschen *(ugs. abwertend)* ⟨*Gesetz*⟩; ~ **a regiment to the front** ein Regiment an die Front werfen; **be ~ed** *(have to hurry)* in Eile sein; **b)** *(cause to act hastily)* ~ **sb. into doing sth.** jmdn. dazu drängen, etw. zu tun; ~ **sb. into danger/trouble/marriage** jmdn. in Gefahr/Schwierigkeiten bringen/zur Heirat drängen; **she hates to be ~ed** sie kann es nicht ausstehen, wenn sie sich [ab]hetzen muß; **c)** *(perform quickly)* auf die Schnelle erledigen; *(perform too quickly)* ~ **it** zu schnell machen; **d)** *(Mil. or fig.: charge)* stürmen; überrumpeln ⟨*feindliche Gruppe*⟩; ~ **one's fences** *(fig.)* überstürzt handeln; **e)** *(sl.: swindle)* ~ **sb.** jmdn. neppen *(ugs. abwertend);* **how much did they ~ you for that sherry?** wieviel haben sie dir für den Sherry abgeknöpft? *(salopp);* **f)** *(Amer.) (entertain)* keilen *(ugs.);* umwerben; *(date)* umwerben. *See also* **foot 1 a. 3.** *v.i.* **a)** *(move quickly)* eilen; ⟨*Hund, Pferd:*⟩ laufen; **she ~ed into the room** sie stürzte ins Zimmer; ~ **through Customs/the exit** durch den Zoll/Ausgang stürmen; ~ **to help sb.** jmdm. zu Hilfe eilen; **b)** *(hurry unduly)* sich zu sehr beeilen; **don't ~!** nur keine Eile!; **don't be tempted to ~!** laß dir Zeit [dabei]!; **there is no need to ~:** es gibt keinen Grund zur Eile; **c)** *(flow rapidly)* stürzen; ~ **past** vorbeistürzen; ~ **down** hinunterstürzen; **d)** *(surge up rapidly)* **the blood ~ed to his face** das Blut schoß ihm ins Gesicht

~ **a'bout,** ~ **a'round** *v.i.* herumhetzen

~ **at** *v.t.* sich stürzen auf (+ *Akk.*); *(Mil.: charge)* anstürmen gegen ⟨*Stellung usw.*⟩

~ **'in** *v.i.* hin-/hereinstürzen; *(fig.)* ~ **in with new solutions** vorschnell neue Lösungen präsentieren; **fools ~ in [where angels fear to tread]** *(prov.)* blinder Eifer schadet nur *(Spr.)*

~ **into** *v.t.* ~ **into sth.** in etw. *(Akk.)* hin-/hereinstürzen; *(fig.)* sich in etw. *(Akk.)* stürzen/etw. überstürzt tun; ~ **into print with sth.** etw. schnellstens veröffentlichen; **you shouldn't ~ into it** das sollte man nicht übereilen

~ **'up** *v.i.* angestürzt kommen; ~ **up to sb.** zu jmdm. stürzen

rush: ~**-hour** *n.* Stoßzeit, *die;* Hauptverkehrszeit, *die;* ~**-hour traffic** Berufsverkehr, *der;* ~ **job** *n.* eilige Arbeit; ~ **mat** *n.* Binsenmatte, *die;* ~ **order** *n.* Eilauftrag, *der;* dringende Bestellung

rusk [rʌsk] *n.* Zwieback, *der*

russet ['rʌsɪt] **1.** *n.* **a)** *(reddish-brown)* Rotbraun, *das;* **b)** *(apple) Apfel mit rot- od. gelbbrauner od. braun gesprenkelter rauher Schale.* **2.** *adj.* rotbraun

Russia ['rʌʃə] *pr. n.* Rußland *(das)*

Russian ['rʌʃn] **1.** *adj.* russisch; **sb. is ~:** jmd. ist Russe/Russin; *see also* **English 1. 2.** *n.* **a)** *(person)* Russe, *der*/Russin, *die;* **b)** *(language)* Russisch, *das;* **Little ~:** Ukrainisch, *das; see also* **English 2 a**

Russian: ~ **'boot** *n.* Russenstiefel, *der;* ~ **rou'lette** *n.* russisches Roulett[e]; ~ **'salad** *n.* russischer Salat

Russki ['rʌskɪ] *n., pl.* ~**s** *or* ~**es** *(joc./derog.)* Rußki, *der (salopp)*

Russo- [rʌsəʊ] *in comb.* russisch-/Russisch-

rust [rʌst] **1.** *n., no pl., no indef. art.* **a)** Rost, *der;* **protection against ~:** Rostschutz, *der;* **b)** *(Bot.)* Rost, *der.* **2.** *v.i.* **a)** rosten; **b)** *(fig.: become impaired)* ⟨*Fähigkeiten, Gedächtnis:*⟩ einrosten *(fig.).* **3.** *v.t.* [ver]rosten lassen; **badly ~ed** stark verrostet; **~ed up** festgerostet

~ **'through** *v.i.* durchrosten

'rust-coloured *adj.* rostfarben

rustic ['rʌstɪk] **1.** *adj.* **a)** *(of the country)* ländlich; ~ **life** Landleben, *das;* **b)** *(unrefined)* bäurisch *(abwertend);* **c)** *(roughly built)* rustikal ⟨*Mobiliar*⟩; grob gezimmert ⟨*Bank, Brücke usw.*⟩. **2.** *n.* Bauer, *der*/Bäuerin, *die (abwertend)*

rustically ['rʌstɪkəlɪ] *adv.* rustikal

rusticate ['rʌstɪkeɪt] *v.t.* zeitweilig von der Universität relegieren

rusticity [rʌ'stɪsɪtɪ] *n.* Ländlichkeit, *die*

'rustic-work *n. (Archit.)* Rustika, *die*

rustle ['rʌsl] **1.** *n.* Rascheln, *das.* **2.** *v.i.* rascheln. **3.** *v.t.* **a)** rascheln lassen; rascheln mit ⟨*Papieren*⟩; **b)** *(Amer.: steal)* stehlen; **c)** *(Amer. coll.) see* ~ **up**

~ **'up** *v.t. (coll.: produce)* auftreiben *(ugs.);* zusammenzaubern *(fig.)* ⟨*Mahlzeit*⟩

rustler ['rʌslə(r)] *n. (Amer.)* Viehdieb, *der;* **sheep ~:** Schafdieb, *der*

rustless ['rʌstlɪs] *adj.* rostfrei

'rust-proof 1. *adj.* rostfrei. **2.** *v.t.* rostfrei *od.* rostbeständig machen

rusty ['rʌstɪ] *adj.* **a)** *(rusted)* rostig; **b)** *(fig.: impaired by neglect)* eingerostet; **I am a bit ~:** ich bin ein bißchen aus der Übung; **c)** *(rust-coloured)* rostfarben; rostfarbig; rost⟨*braun, -rot*⟩

[1]**rut** [rʌt] **1.** *n.* **a)** *(track)* Spurrille, *die;* **b)** *(fig.: established procedure)* **get into a ~:** in einen gewissen Trott verfallen; **be in a ~:** aus dem [Alltags]trott nicht mehr herauskommen. **2.** *v.t.,* **-tt-** durchfurchen

[2]**rut 1.** *n. (sexual excitement)* Brunst, *die; (of roe-deer, stag, etc.)* Brunft, *die (Jägersprache).* **2.** *v.i.,* **-tt-** in der Brunst sein; ⟨*Schalenwild:*⟩ brunften *(Jägerspr.)*

rutabaga [ru:tə'beɪgə] *see* **swede**

ruthless ['ru:θlɪs] *adj.,* **ruthlessly** ['ru:θlɪslɪ] *adv.* rücksichtslos

ruthlessness ['ru:θlɪsnɪs] *n., no pl.* Rücksichtslosigkeit, *die*

rutted ['rʌtɪd], **rutty** ['rʌtɪ] *adjs.* zerfurcht

Rwanda [rʊ'ændə] *pr. n.* Ruanda *(das)*

rye [raɪ] *n.* **a)** *(cereal)* Roggen, *der;* **b)** ~ **[whisky]** Roggenwhisky, *der;* Rye, *der;* **c)** *(Amer.) see* **rye bread**

rye: ~ **bread** *n.* Roggenbrot, *das;* ~**-grass** *n.* Raigras, *das*

S

S, s [es] *n., pl.* **Ss** *or* **S's** ['esɪs] **a)** *(letter)* S, s, *das;* **b)** *(curve)* **S bend** S-Biegung, *die*

's *(coll.)* = **is, has, does; let's** [lets] = **let us**

S. *abbr.* **a) south** S; **b) southern** s.; **c) Saint** St.

s. *abbr.* **a) second[s]** Sek.; **b) singular** Sg.; **c) son** S.

SA *abbr.* **a) South America; b) South Africa; c) Sturmabteilung** SA

Saar [zɑ:(r)] *pr. n.* Saar, *die*

Saarland ['zɑ:lænd] *pr. n.* Saarland, *das*

Saarlander ['zɑ:lændə(r)] *n.* Saarländer, *der*/-länderin, *die*

sabbath ['sæbəθ] *n.* **a)** *(Jewish)* Sabbat, *der;* **b)** *(Christian)* Sonntag, *der;* **c) witches' ~:** Hexensabbat, *der*

sabbatical [sə'bætɪkl] **1.** *adj.* **a)** *(Jewish Relig.)* ~ **year** Sabbatjahr, *das:* **b)** ~ **term/year** Forschungssemester/-jahr, *das.* **2.** *n.* Forschungsurlaub, *der*

saber *(Amer.) see* **sabre**

sable ['seɪbl] *n.* **a)** *(Zool., also fur)* Zobel, *der;* **b) [American] ~:** Fichtenmarder, *der (Zool.);* Amerikanischer Zobel

sabotage ['sæbətɑ:ʒ] **1.** *n. (lit. or fig.)* Sabotage, *die;* **act of ~:** Sabotageakt, *der;* **industrial ~:** Wirtschaftssabotage, *die.* **2.** *v.t.* einen Sabotageakt verüben auf (+ *Akk.*); *(fig.)* sabotieren ⟨*Pläne usw.*⟩; **vehicles were ~d** es wurden Sabotageakte auf Fahrzeuge verübt

saboteur [sæbə'tɜ:(r)] *n.* Saboteur, *der*

sabre ['seɪbə(r)] *n. (Brit.)* Säbel, *der;* **rattle the ~** *(fig.)* mit dem Säbel rasseln *(abwertend)*

sabre: ~**-cut** *n.* **a)** *(blow)* Säbelhieb, *der;* **b)** *(wound)* Säbelverletzung, *die;* ~**-rattling 1.** *n.* Säbelrasseln, *das (abwertend);* **2.** *adj.* säbelrasselnd *(abwertend)*

sac [sæk] *n. (Biol.)* **air ~:** Luftsack, *der (Zool.);* **foetal ~:** Fruchtblase, *die (Med.)*

saccharin ['sækərɪn] *n.* Saccharin, *das*

saccharine ['sækəri:n] *adj. (lit. or fig.)* süßlich

sacerdotal [sæsə'dəʊtl] *adj. (priestly)* priesterlich; Priester⟨*gewand, -amt*⟩

sachet ['sæʃeɪ] *n.* **a)** *(small packet) (for shampoo etc.)* Beutel, *der; (cushion-shaped)* Kissen, *das;* **a ~ of shampoo** ein Beutel/Kissen Shampoo; **b)** *(bag for scenting clothes)* Duftkissen, *das*

[1]**sack** [sæk] **1.** *n.* **a)** Sack, *der;* **buy sth. by the ~:** etw. sackweise kaufen; **a ~ of potatoes** ein Sack Kartoffeln; **three ~s of mail** drei Säcke mit Post; **b)** *(coll.: dismissal)* Rausschmiß, *der (ugs.);* **threaten sb. with the ~:** jmdm. mit Entlassung drohen; **get the ~:** rausgeschmissen werden *(ugs.);* **give sb. the ~:** jmdn. rausschmeißen *(ugs.);* **c) hit the ~** *(sl.)* sich in die Falle hauen *(salopp).* **2.** *v.t.* **a)** *(coll.: dismiss)* rausschmeißen *(ugs.)* **(for** wegen); **b)** *(put into ~[s])* einsacken

[2]**sack 1.** *v.t. (loot)* plündern. **2.** *n.* Plünderung, *die*

'sackcloth *n.* Sackleinen, *das; (mourning)* Trauergewand, *das; (penitential)* Büßergewand, *das;* **in ~ and ashes** in Sack und Asche *(geh.)*

sackful ['sækfʊl] *n.* Sack, *der;* **three ~s of potatoes/cement** drei Sack Kartoffeln/Zement; **by the ~:** sackweise

[1]**sacking** ['sækɪŋ] *n.* **a)** *(coll.: dismissal)* Rausschmiß, *der (ugs.);* **b)** *(coarse fabric)* Sackleinen, *das*
[2]**sacking** *see* [2]**sack 2**
'**sack race** *n.* Sackhüpfen, *das*
sacral ['seɪkrl] *adj.* **a)** *(Anat.)* Sakral-; **the ~ vertebrae** die Kreuzbeinwirbel; Vertebrae sacrales *(Med.);* **b)** *(Anthrop.)* sakral
sacrament ['sækrəmənt] *n.* Sakrament, *das;* **the last ~s** die Sterbesakramente; **the ~ [of the altar], the Blessed** *or* **Holy S~:** das Altarsakrament; **administer/receive the ~** *(the Eucharist)* das Sakrament austeilen/empfangen; **the Holy S~** *(the Host)* das Allerheiligste
sacramental [sækrə'mentl] *adj.* sakramental; **~ doctrine** Lehre von den Sakramenten
sacred ['seɪkrɪd] *adj.* heilig; geheiligt ⟨*Tradition*⟩; geistlich ⟨*Musik, Dichtung*⟩; **nothing is ~ to him, he holds nothing ~** *(lit. or fig.)* ihm ist nichts heilig; **is nothing ~?** *(iron.)* scheut man denn vor nichts mehr zurück?
sacred: ~ '**cow** *n. (lit. or fig.)* heilige Kuh; **S~ 'Heart** *n.* **the S~ Heart [of Jesus]** das Herz Jesu
sacredness ['seɪkrɪdnɪs] *n., no pl.* Heiligkeit, *die*
sacrifice ['sækrɪfaɪs] **1.** *n.* **a)** *(giving up valued thing)* Opferung, *die; (of principles)* Preisgabe, *die; (of pride, possessions)* Aufgabe, *die;* **make ~s** Opfer bringen; **b)** *(offering to deity)* Opfer, *das;* **~s to the gods** den Göttern dargebrachte Opfer; *(fig.)* **fall a ~ to sth.** einer Sache *(Dat.)* zum Opfer fallen; **c)** *(Games: deliberate incurring of loss)* Opfern, *das; (Baseball) Schlag ins Aus, wobei der Läufer weiterkommt; (Bridge)* Opfer, *das* **(against** für). **2.** *v. t.* **a)** *(give up, offer as ~)* opfern; **~ oneself/sth. to sth.** sich/etw. einer Sache *(Dat.)* opfern; **b)** *(sell at a loss)* zu einem Schleuderpreis verkaufen *(ugs.).* **3.** *v. i.* opfern
sacrificial [sækrɪ'fɪʃl] *adj.* Opfer-; **~ victim** Opfer, *das;* **~ price** *(fig.)* Schleuderpreis, *der*
sacrilege ['sækrɪlɪdʒ] *n., no pl.* **[act of] ~:** Sakrileg, *das;* **be little short of ~:** an ein Sakrileg grenzen
sacrilegious [sækrɪ'lɪdʒəs] *adj.* sakrilegisch; *(fig.)* frevelhaft
sacristan ['sækrɪstən] *n. (Eccl.)* Küster, *der;* Kirchendiener, *der (bes. ev. Kirche);* Sakristan, *der (bes. kath. Kirche)*
sacristy ['sækrɪstɪ] *n. (Eccl.)* Sakristei, *die*
sacrosanct ['sækrəsæŋkt] *adj. (lit. or fig.)* sakrosankt
sacrum ['seɪkrəm] *n. (Anat.)* Kreuzbein, *das;* Sakrum, *das (fachspr.)*
sad [sæd] *adj.* **a)** *(sorrowful)* traurig **(at, about** über + *Akk.*); **he was ~ at** *or* **about not getting the job** er war traurig, weil er die Stelle nicht bekam; **feel ~, be in a ~ mood** traurig sein; **it left him a ~der and a wiser man** er hat dabei viel Lehrgeld zahlen müssen; durch Schaden ist er klug geworden; **b)** *(causing grief)* traurig; schmerzlich ⟨*Tod, Verlust*⟩; **it's ~ about Jim** es ist schade um Jim; **~ to say, ...:** bedauerlicherweise ...; **I am ~ to say that ...:** leider *od.* zu meinem Bedauern muß ich sagen, daß ...; leider ...; **c)** *(derog./joc.: deplorably bad)* traurig
sadden ['sædn] *v. t.* traurig stimmen; **be deeply ~ed** tieftraurig sein; **his old age was ~ed by ...:** sein Alter war überschattet von ...; **I was ~ed to see that ...:** es betrübte mich, zu sehen, daß ...
saddle ['sædl] **1.** *n.* **a)** *(seat for rider)* Sattel, *der;* **be in the ~** *(fig.)* das Heft in der Hand haben *(geh.);* **b)** *(ridge between summits)* [Berg]sattel, *der;* **c)** *(support for cable)* Kabelsattel, *der;* **d)** *(Gastr.)* Rücken, *der;* Rückenstück, *das;* **~ of lamb/mutton** Lamm-/Hammelrücken, *der.* **2.** *v. t.* **a)** satteln ⟨*Pferd usw.*⟩; **b)** *(fig.)* **~ sb. with sth.** jmdm. etw. aufbürden *(geh.);* **~ debts/responsibility [up]on sb.** Schulden/Verantwortung auf jmdn. abwälzen
~ 'up *v. t. & i.* aufsatteln
saddle: **~back** *n.* **a)** *(Archit.)* Satteldach, *das;* **b)** *(hill)* Hügel mit sattelförmigem Rücken; **c)** *(pig)* Sattelschwein, *das;* **~backed** *adj.* sattelförmig; **~-bag** *n.* Satteltasche, *die;* **~-blanket** *n.* Satteldecke, *die;* Woilach, *der;* **~-bow** ['sædlbəʊ] *n.* Zwiesel, *der;* **~-cloth** *see* **~-blanket**
saddler ['sædlə(r)] *n.* Sattler, *der*
saddlery ['sædlərɪ] *n.* **a)** *(work, place)* Sattlerei, *die;* **b)** *(saddles etc.)* Sattlerwaren *Pl.*
saddle: **~-soap** *n.* Sattelseife, *die;* **~ sore** *n.* Sattelwunde, *die;* **~-sore** *adj.* **be ~-sore** wund vom Reiten/Radfahren sein; **~ stitch** *n.* **a)** *(Bookbinding)* Heftstich, *der;* **b)** *(Needlework)* Vorstich, *der*
sadism ['seɪdɪzm] *n.* Sadismus, *der*
sadist ['seɪdɪst] *n.* Sadist, *der*/Sadistin, *die*
sadistic [sə'dɪstɪk] *adj.*, **sadistically** [sə'dɪstɪkəlɪ] *adv.* sadistisch
sadly ['sædlɪ] *adv.* **a)** *(with sorrow)* traurig; **b)** *(unfortunately)* leider; **c)** *(deplorably)* erbärmlich *(abwertend);* **they are ~ lacking in common sense** sie haben erbärmlich wenig [gesunden Menschen]verstand
sadness ['sædnɪs] *n., no pl.* Traurigkeit, *die* **(at, about** über + *Akk.*)
sado-masochism [seɪdəʊ'mæsəkɪzm] *n.* Sadomasochismus, *der*
sado-masochist [seɪdəʊ'mæsəkɪst] *n.* Sadomasochist, *der*/Sadomasochistin, *die*
'**sad sack** *n. (Amer. sl.)* trübe Tasse *(ugs. abwertend)*
s.a.e. [eseɪ'i:] *abbr.* **stamped addressed envelope** adressierter Freiumschlag
safari [sə'fɑ:rɪ] *n.* Safari, *die;* **be/go on ~:** auf Safari sein/gehen
sa'fari park *n.* Safaripark, *der*
safe [seɪf] **1.** *n.* **a)** Safe, *der;* Geldschrank, *der;* **b)** *(Amer. coll.: contraceptive)* Präser, *der (salopp);* **c)** *see* **meat safe. 2.** *adj.* **a)** *(out of danger)* sicher **(from** vor + *Dat.*); **he's ~:** er ist in Sicherheit; **the bullfighter was ~:** der Stierkämpfer war nicht in Gefahr; **make sth. ~ from sth.** etw. gegen etw. sichern; **~ and sound** sicher und wohlbehalten; **b)** *(free from danger)* ungefährlich; sicher ⟨*Ort, Hafen*⟩; **she's a ~ driver** sie fährt sicher; **better ~ than sorry** Vorsicht ist besser als Nachsicht *(ugs.);* **is the water ~ to drink?** kann man das Wasser ohne Risiko trinken?; **wish sb. a ~ journey** jmdm. eine gute Reise wünschen; **is the car ~ to drive?** ist der Wagen verkehrssicher?; **the maximum ~ load** das zulässige Ladegewicht; **a ~ margin** eine Sicherheitsmarge; **the beach is ~ for bathing** es ist ungefährlich, am Strand zu baden; **to be on the ~ side** zur Sicherheit; **we had better be on the ~ side** wir sollten lieber sichergehen; **c)** *(unlikely to produce controversy)* sicher; bewährt *(iron.)* ⟨*Klischee*⟩; **it is ~ to say [that ...]** man kann mit einiger Sicherheit sagen[, daß ...]; **it is not ~ to generalize in such a matter** in einer solchen Frage kann man nicht einfach verallgemeinern; **d)** *(reliable)* sicher ⟨*Methode, Investition, Stelle*⟩; naheliegend ⟨*Vermutung*⟩; **in ~ hands** in guten Händen; **a ~ Conservative seat** *(Polit.)* eine Hochburg der Konservativen Partei; **e)** *(secure)* **be ~ in prison, be in ~ custody** in sicherem Gewahrsam sein; **your secrets will be ~ with me** deine Geheimnisse sind bei mir gut aufgehoben.
safe: ~ '**bet** *n.* **it is a ~ bet he will be there** man kann darauf wetten, daß er dort ist; **he is a ~ bet to win/for Prime Minister** man kann darauf wetten, daß er gewinnt/daß er der nächste Premierminister wird; **~-breaker** *n.* Geldschrankknacker, *der (ugs.);* ~ '**conduct** *n.* **a)** *(privilege)* freies *od.* sicheres Geleit; **b)** *(document)* Schutzbrief, *der (Politik, Dipl.);* **~-cracker** *n. see* **~-breaker;** ~ **de'posit** *n.* Tresor, *der;* **~-deposit box** *(at the bank)* Banksafe, *der;* **~guard 1.** *n.* Schutz, *der;* **as a ~guard against infection** zum Schutz gegen Infektionen; **2.** *v. t.* schützen; **~guard sb.'s future/interests** jmds. Zukunft sichern/Interessen wahren; **~ house** *n.* geheimer Unterschlupf *(von Terroristen, Agenten usw.);* ~ '**keeping** *n.* sichere Obhut *(geh.); (of thing)* [sichere] Aufbewahrung
safely ['seɪflɪ] *adv.* **a)** *(without harm)* sicher; **did the parcel arrive ~?** ist das Paket heil angekommen?; **b)** *(securely)* sicher; **the children are ~ tucked up in bed** die Kinder liegen friedlich im Bett; **be ~ behind bars** [in sicherem Gewahrsam] hinter Schloß und Riegel sein; **c)** *(with certainty)* **one can ~ say [that] she will come** man kann mit ziemlicher Sicherheit sagen, daß sie kommt
safe: ~ **period** *n.* unfruchtbare Tage; ~ '**seat** *n. (Polit.)* Hochburg, *die;* ≈ sicherer Wahlkreis; ~ '**sex** *n.* Safer Sex, *der;* geschützter Sex
safety ['seɪftɪ] *n.* **a)** *(being out of danger)* Sicherheit, *die;* **cross the river in ~:** sicher über den Fluß fahren; **b)** *(lack of danger)* Ungefährlichkeit, *die; (of a machine)* Betriebssicherheit, *die;* **do sth. with ~:** etw. tun, ohne sich einer Gefahr *(Dat.)* auszusetzen; **there is ~ in numbers** zu mehreren ist man sicherer; **a ~ first policy** eine Politik der Vorsicht; **one can say with ~ that ...:** man kann mit Sicherheit behaupten, daß ...; **c)** *attrib.* Sicherheits⟨*netz, -kette, -faktor, -maßnahmen, -vorrichtungen*⟩
safety: **~-belt** *n.* Sicherheitsgurt, *der;* **~-catch** *n. (of door)* Sicherheitsverriegelung, *die; (of gun)* Sicherungshebel, *der;* **~ curtain** *n. (Theatre)* eiserner Vorhang; **~ fuse** *n. (Electr.)* Sicherung, *die;* **~ glass** *n.* Sicherheitsglas, *das;* **~ helmet** *n.* Schutzhelm, *der;* **~ margin** *n.* Spielraum, *der;* **~ match** *n.* Sicherheitszündholz, *das;* **~-pin** *n.* Sicherheitsnadel, *die;* **~ play** *n. (Bridge)* Auf-sicher-Spielen, *das; Spiel, bei dem geringe Verluste hingenommen werden, um größere zu vermeiden;* **~ razor** *n.* Rasierapparat, *der;* **~-valve** *n.* Sicherheitsventil, *das (Technik); (fig.)* Ventil, *das (fig.);* **~ zone** *n. (Amer.: traffic island)* Verkehrsinsel, *die*
saffron ['sæfrən] **1.** *n.* Safran, *der; see also* **meadow saffron. 2.** *adj.* safrangelb
sag [sæg] **1.** *v. i.*, **-gg-** **a)** *(have downward bulge)* durchhängen; **b)** *(sink)* sich senken; absacken *(ugs.);* ⟨*Gebäude:*⟩ [in sich *(Akk.)*] zusammensacken *(ugs.);* ⟨*Schultern:*⟩ herabhängen; ⟨*Brüste:*⟩ hängen; *(fig.: decline)* ⟨*Mut, Stimmung:*⟩ sinken; **the interest/story-line ~s halfway through the book** die Spannung/Geschichte läßt in der Mitte des Buches [spürbar] nach; **~ging breasts** Hängebusen, *der (ugs.);* **c)** *(hang lopsidedly)* **the gate ~ged half off its hinges** das Tor hing schief in den Angeln; **the bridge ~s on one side** die Brücke ist auf einer Seite abgesackt *(ugs.).* **2.** *n.* **a)** *(amount that rope etc. ~s)* Durchhang, *der;* **b)** *(sinking)* **there was a ~ in the seat/mattress** der Sitz war durchgesessen/die Matratze war durchgelegen
saga ['sɑ:gə] *n.* **a)** *(story of adventure)* Heldenepos, *das (fig.); (medieval narrative)* Saga, *die (Literaturw.);* **knightly ~:** ≈ Ritterroman, *der;* **the ~ of a family** die Geschichte einer Familie; **b)** *(coll.: long involved story)* [ganzer] Roman *(fig.);* **the ~ of our holiday in Spain** die Geschichte unseres Spanienurlaubs
sagacious [sə'geɪʃəs] *adj.* klug; **~ mind** scharfer Verstand
sagaciously [sə'geɪʃəslɪ] *adv.* klug
sagacity [sə'gæsɪtɪ] *n., no pl.* Klugheit, *die*
[1]**sage** [seɪdʒ] *n. (Bot.)* Salbei, *der od. die;* **~-and-onion stuffing** Salbei-und-Zwiebel-Füllung, *die*

[2]**sage 1.** *n.* Weise, *der.* **2.** *adj.* weise
sage: ~-brush *n. (Bot.)* Beifuß, *der (in nordamerikanischen Steppen)*; ~ **'cheese,** ~ **'Derby** *ns.* Käse mit Salbeigewürz; **~-'green 1.** *adj.* salbeigrün; **2.** *n.* Salbeigrün, *das*
sagely ['seɪdʒlɪ] *adv.* weise
sage 'tea *n.* Salbeitee, *der*
Sagittarian [sædʒɪ'teərɪən] *n. (Astrol.)* Schütze, *der*
Sagittarius [sædʒɪ'teərɪəs] *n. (Astrol., Astron.)* der Schütze; der Sagittarius; *see also* **Aries**
sago ['seɪgəʊ] *n., pl.* **~s** Sago, *der*
Sahara [sə'hɑ:rə] *pr. n.* **the ~ [Desert]** die [Wüste] Sahara
sahib [sɑ:b, 'sɑ:ɪb] *n.* **a)** *(arch.: title)* Sahib, *der;* **b)** *(coll.: gentleman)* Herr, *der*
said *see* **say 1**
sail [seɪl] **1.** *n.* **a)** *(voyage in sailing vessel)* Segelfahrt, *die;* **go for a ~:** eine Segelfahrt machen; **the island is ten days' ~ from Plymouth** von Plymouth aus erreicht man die Insel [mit dem Segelschiff] in zehn Tagen; **b)** *(piece of canvas)* Segel, *das;* **in** *or* **under full ~:** mit vollen Segeln; **under ~:** unter Segel *(Seemannsspr.)*; **c)** *pl. same (ship)* Segelschiff, *das;* **d)** *(of windmill)* [Windmühlen]flügel, *der. See also* **make 1 s; set 1 l; shorten 2 b; strike 2 t;** [1]**wind 1 a. 2.** *v. i.* **a)** *(travel on water)* fahren; *(in sailing boat)* segeln; **a lovely boat to ~ in** ein schönes Boot zum Segeln; **b)** *(start voyage)* auslaufen **(for** nach); in See stechen; **c)** *(glide in air)* segeln; **d)** *(fig.: be thrown)* segeln *(ugs.)*; **the bottle which ~ed past his ear** die Flasche, die an seinem Ohr vorbeisegelte *(ugs.)*; **e)** *(walk in stately manner)* segeln *(ugs.)*; **~ by** vorübersegeln *(salopp)*; **f)** *(move smoothly)* gleiten; **~ through** hindurchgleiten; **g)** *(fig. coll.: pass easily)* **~ through an examination** eine Prüfung spielend schaffen. *See also* **colour 1 j;** [1]**wind 1 a. 3.** *v. t.* **a)** steuern ⟨*Boot, Schiff*⟩; segeln mit ⟨*Segeljacht, -schiff*⟩; **b)** *(travel across)* durchfahren, befahren ⟨*Meer*⟩; ⟨*Segelschiff:*⟩ durchsegeln
~ 'in *v. i. (coll.: enter)* hereinsegeln *(ugs.)*
~ into *v. t. (coll.)* **a) ~ into a room** in ein Zimmer hereingesegelt kommen *(ugs.)*; **b)** *(attack)* **~ into sb.** über jmdn. herfallen
sail: ~boarding *see* **windsurfing; ~boat** *n. (Amer.)* Segelboot, *das;* **~cloth** *n.* Segeltuch, *das*
sailing ['seɪlɪŋ] *n.* **a)** *(handling a boat)* Segeln, *das;* **weather for ~:** Segelwetter, *das;* **b)** *(departure from a port)* Abfahrt, *die;* **there are regular ~s from here across to the island** von hier fahren regelmäßig Schiffe hinüber zur Insel
sailing: ~ boat *n.* Segelboot, *das;* **~ orders** *n. pl.* Order zum Auslaufen; **~ ship, ~ vessel** *ns.* Segelschiff, *das*
'sail-maker *n.* Segelmacher, *der*
sailor ['seɪlə(r)] *n.* Seemann, *der; (in navy)* Matrose, *der;* **be a good/bad ~** *(not get seasick/get seasick)* seefest/nicht seefest sein
'sailor suit *n.* Matrosenanzug, *der*
sainfoin ['sænfɔɪn, 'seɪnfɔɪn] *n. (Bot.)* Esparsette, *die*
saint 1. [sənt] *adj.* **S~ Michael/Helena** der heilige Michael/die heilige Helena; Sankt Michael/Helena; *as voc.* heiliger Michael/heilige Helena; **~ Michael's [Church]** die Michaelskirche; **~ Andrew's/George's cross** Andreas-/Georgskreuz, *das.* **2.** [seɪnt] *n.* Heilige, *der/die;* **make** *or* **declare sb. a ~** *(RC Ch.)* jmdn. heiligsprechen; **be as patient as a ~:** eine Engelsgeduld haben; *see also* **aunt, patron c**
Saint Bernard [sənt 'bɜ:nəd] *n.* **~ [dog]** Bernhardiner, *der*
sainthood ['seɪnthʊd] *n.* Heiligkeit, *die*
Saint: ~ James [sənt 'dʒeɪmz] *n.* **Court of ~ James** *der britische Hof;* **~ John's wort** [sənt 'dʒɒnz wɜ:t] *n. (Bot.)* Johanniskraut, *das;* **~ Lawrence** [sənt 'lɒrəns] *n. (Geog.)* Sankt-Lorenz-Strom, *der*
saintly ['seɪntlɪ] *adj.* heilig; **~ patience** Engelsgeduld, *die*
Saint: ~ Peter's [sənt 'pi:təz] *pr. n. (in Rome)* die Peterskirche; **s~'s day** *n.* Tag eines/einer Heiligen; *see also* **all 1 b; ~ Swithin's day** [sənt 'swɪðɪnz deɪ] *n. 15. Juli, der nach britischem Volksglauben wetterbestimmend für die folgenden vierzig Tage ist;* ≈ Siebenschläfer, *der;* **~ Vitus's dance** [sənt vaɪtəsɪz 'dɑ:ns] *see* **dance 3 d**
[1]**sake** [seɪk] *n.* **for the ~ of** um ... *(Gen.)* willen; **for my** *etc.* **~:** um meinetwillen *usw.*; mir *usw.* zuliebe; **for all our ~s** uns allen zuliebe; **for your/its own ~:** um deiner/seiner selbst willen; **art for art's ~:** Kunst um ihrer selbst willen; **for the ~ of a few pounds** wegen ein paar Pfund; **for Christ's** *or* **God's** *or* **goodness'** *or* **Heaven's** *or (coll.)* **Pete's** *etc.* **~:** um Gottes *od.* Himmels willen; **for old times' ~:** um der schönen Erinnerung willen; *see also* **appearance b; argument b; ; convenience b**
[2]**sake** ['sɑ:kɪ] *n. (drink)* Sake, *der*
salaam [sə'lɑ:m] *n.* Salam [alaikum] *(veralt., noch scherzh.)*; *in pl. (respects)* Komplimente *(veralt.)*
salable *see* **saleable**
salacious [sə'leɪʃəs] *adj.* **a)** *(lustful)* lüstern; **b)** *(inciting sexual desire)* pornographisch
salaciously [sə'leɪʃəslɪ] *adv.* lüstern
salad ['sæləd] *n.* Salat, *der;* **ham/tomato ~:** Schinken-/Tomatensalat, *der*
salad: ~ cream *n.* ≈ Mayonnaise, *die;* **~ days** *n. pl.* **in my ~ days** als ich noch nicht trocken hinter den Ohren war *(ugs.)*; **~-dressing** *n.* Dressing, *das;* Salatsoße, *die;* **~-oil** *n.* Salatöl, *das;* **~-servers** *n. pl.* Salatbesteck, *das*
salamander ['sæləmændə(r)] *n.* **a)** *(Zool.)* Salamander, *der;* **b)** *(Amer.) see* **gopher a**
salami [sə'lɑ:mɪ] *n.* Salami, *die*
sal ammoniac [sæl ə'məʊnɪæk] *n.* Salmiak, *der od. das*
salaried ['sælərɪd] *adj.* **a)** *(receiving salary)* Gehalt beziehend; **~ employee** Angestellte, *der/die;* **the ~ class** die Gehaltsempfänger; **b)** *(having salary attached to it)* **~ post** Stelle mit festem Gehalt
salary ['sælərɪ] *n.* Gehalt, *das; (Amer.: weekly)* Lohn, *der;* **~ increase** Gehaltserhöhung, *die;* **what is your ~?** wie hoch ist dein Gehalt?; **draw a ~:** ein Gehalt beziehen
sale [seɪl] *n.* **a)** *(selling)* Verkauf, *der;* **[up] for ~:** zu verkaufen; **put up** *or* **offer for ~:** zum Verkauf anbieten; **on ~:** im Handel; **on ~ at your chemist's** in Ihrer Apotheke erhältlich; **go on ~:** in den Handel kommen; **offer** *etc.* **sth. on a ~ or return basis** etw. auf Kommissionsbasis anbieten *usw.*; **b)** *(instance of selling)* Verkauf, *der;* **make a ~:** einen Verkauf tätigen *(Kaufmannsspr.)*; **find a ready ~ for sth.** etw. gut verkaufen; **sth. finds a ready ~:** etw. verkauft sich gut; **c)** *in pl., no art. (amount sold)* Verkaufszahlen *Pl.* **(of** für); Absatz, *der;* **d) [jumble** *or* **rummage] ~:** [Wohltätigkeits]basar, *der;* **~ of work** Wohltätigkeitsbasar mit eigenen Bastel-, Handarbeiten; **e)** *(disposal at reduced prices)* Ausverkauf, *der;* **clearance/end-of-season/summer ~:** Räumungs-/Schluß-/Sommerschlußverkauf, *der;* **at the s~s** im Ausverkauf; **f)** *(public auction)* [Verkauf durch] Versteigerung; **put sth. up for ~ [by auction]** etw. zur Versteigerung anbieten
saleable ['seɪləbl] *adj.* verkäuflich; **be [highly] ~:** sich [gut] verkaufen lassen
sale: ~-ring *n.* Käuferring bei einer Auktion; **~-room** *n. (Brit.)* Auktionsraum, *der*
sales: ~ assistant *(Brit.)*, **~ clerk** *(Amer.) ns.* Verkäufer, *der*/Verkäuferin, *die;* **~ department** *n.* Verkaufsabteilung, *die;* **~ desk** *see* **desk b; ~ force** *n.* Vertreterstab, *der;* **~girl, ~lady** *ns.* Verkäuferin, *die;* **~man** ['seɪlzmən] *n., pl.* **~men** ['seɪlzmən] Verkäufer, *der;* **~ manager** *n.* Verkaufsleiter, *der/*-leiterin, *die;* Sales-manager, *der*
salesmanship ['seɪlzmənʃɪp] *n., no pl., no indef. art.* Kunst des Verkaufens
sales: ~ patter, ~ pitch *ns.* Verkaufsargumentation, *die;* **~ rep** *(coll.)*, **~ representative** *ns.* [Handels]vertreter, *der/*-vertreterin, *die;* **~ resistance** *n.* Kaufunlust, *die;* **~ talk** *see* **~ patter; ~ tax** *n.* Umsatzsteuer, *die;* **~woman** *n.* Verkäuferin, *die*
salient ['seɪlɪənt] **1.** *adj.* **a)** *(striking)* auffallend; ins Auge springend; hervorstechend ⟨*Charakterzug*⟩; **the ~ points of a speech** die herausragenden Punkte einer Rede; **b)** *(pointing outwards)* vorspringend. **2.** *n. (Mil.)* vorgeschobene Stellung
saline ['seɪlaɪn] *adj.* salzig; Salz⟨*ablagerung*⟩; **~ solution** Salzlösung, *die; (Med.)* [physiologische] Kochsalzlösung; **~ drip** *(Med.)* Tropfinfusion, *die*
salinity [sə'lɪnɪtɪ] *n.* Salzgehalt, *der;* **be high in ~:** stark salzhaltig sein
saliva [sə'laɪvə] *n.* Speichel, *der*
salivary ['sælɪvərɪ, sə'laɪvərɪ] *adj. (Anat.)* **~ gland** Speicheldrüse, *die*
salivate ['sælɪveɪt] *v. i.* speicheln
sa'liva test *n.* Speicheltest, *der (bes. Med.)*
[1]**sallow** ['sæləʊ] *adj.* blaßgelb
[2]**sallow** *n. (Bot.)* Salweide, *die*
sallowness ['sæləʊnɪs] *n., no pl.* gelbliche Blässe
Sally ['sælɪ] *see* **aunt**
sally 1. *n.* **a)** *(Mil.: sortie)* Ausfall, *der;* **b)** *(excursion)* Ausflug, *der;* **c)** *(verbal attack)* **his sallies against the authorities** seine Ausfälle gegen die Obrigkeit; **d)** *(witty remark)* Geistesblitz, *der (ugs.).* **2.** *v. i.* **a) ~ out** *(Mil.: make sortie/sorties)* einen Ausfall/Ausfälle machen; **b) ~ forth** aufbrechen, sich aufmachen **(for** zu)
salmon ['sæmən] **1.** *n., pl. same* Lachs, *der.* **2.** *adj. (colour)* lachsfarben; lachsrosa ⟨*Farbton*⟩
'salmon-coloured *adj.* lachsfarben
salmonella [sælmə'nelə] *n.* Salmonelle, *die;* **~ poisoning** Salmonellenvergiftung, *die*
salmon: ~-ladder, ~-leap *ns.* Lachstreppe, *die;* **~-pink 1.** *n.* lachsrosa Farbton; **2.** *adj.* lachsfarben; **~ 'trout** *n.* Lachsforelle, *die*
salon ['sælɔ̃] *n.* Salon, *der*
'salon music *n.* Salonmusik, *die*
saloon [sə'lu:n] *n.* **a)** *(public room in ship, hotel, etc.)* Salon, *der;* **dining ~:** Speisesaal, *der;* **billiard ~** *(Brit.)* Billardraum, *der;* **b)** *(Brit.: motor car)* Limousine, *die;* **c)** *(Amer.: bar)* Saloon, *der*
saloon: ~ 'bar *n. (Brit.) separater Teil eines Pubs mit mehr Komfort;* **~ 'car** *see* **saloon b; ~ deck** *n.* Salondeck, *das*
salsify ['sælsɪfɪ] *n. (Bot.)* Haferwurz, *die*
salt [sɔ:lt, sɒlt] **1.** *n.* **a)** *(for food etc.; also Chem.)* **[common] ~:** [Koch]salz, *das;* **above/below the ~** *(Hist.)* oben/unten an der Tafel; **rub ~ in[to] the wound** *(fig.)* Salz in die Wunde streuen; **take sth. with a grain** *or* **pinch of ~** *(fig.)* etw. cum grano salis *(geh.) od.* nicht ganz wörtlich nehmen; **be the ~ of the earth** *(fig.)* anständig und rechtschaffen sein; das Salz der Erde sein *(bibl.)*; **be worth one's ~:** etwas taugen; *(worth the money one is paid)* sein Geld wert sein; **b)** *in pl. (medicine)* Salz, *das;* **like a dose of ~s** *(sl.)* in Null Komma nichts *(ugs.)*; **he went through the department like a dose of ~s** *(fig.)* er kehrte in der Abteilung mit eisernem Besen [aus]; **c)** *(fig.: zest)* Salz, *das (fig.)*; Würze, *die (fig.)*; **d) [old] ~** *(sailor)* [alter] Seebär *(ugs. scherzh.).* **2.** *adj.* **a)** *(containing or tasting of ~)* salzig; *(preserved with ~)* gepökelt ⟨*Fleisch*⟩; gesalzen ⟨*Butter*⟩; **b)** *(bitter)* salzig ⟨*Tränen*⟩; **c)** *(biting)* scharf, ätzend ⟨*Witz*⟩. **3.** *v. t.* **a)** *(add ~*

to) salzen; *(fig.)* würzen; **b)** *(preserve with ~ or brine)* [ein]pökeln; **~ed beef/pork** gepökeltes Rind-/Schweinefleisch; **c)** *(spread ~ on)* **~ the roads** Salz auf die Straßen streuen

~ a'way, ~ 'down *v. t. (coll.)* auf die hohe Kante legen *(ugs.)*

SALT [sɔ:lt, sɒlt] *abbr.* **Strategic Arms Limitation Talks/Treaty** SALT

salt: ~-cellar *n. (open)* Salzfaß, *das; (sprinkler)* Salzstreuer, *der;* **~ 'lake** *n.* Salzsee, *der;* **~-lick** *n.* Salzlecke, *die (Jägerspr.);* **~-marsh** *n.* Salzwiesengebiet, *das; (formed by evaporation)* Salzsumpf, *der;* **~-mine** *n.* Salzbergwerk, *das;* **~-pan** *n.* Salzpfanne, *die*

saltpetre *(Amer.:* **saltpeter***)* ['sɔ:ltpi:tə(r), 'sɒltpi:tə(r)] *n.* Salpeter, *der*

salt: ~-shaker *n. (Amer.)* Salzstreuer, *der;* **~-spoon** *n.* Salzlöffelchen, *das;* **~-sprinkler** *n.* Salzstreuer, *der;* **~ 'water** *n.* Salzwasser, *das;* **~-water** *adj.* Salzwasser-; **~-works** *n. sing., pl. same* Saline, *die*

salty ['sɔ:ltɪ, 'sɒltɪ] *adj.* salzig; *(fig.)* scharf ‹*Witz*›

salubrious [sə'lu:brɪəs] *adj.* gesund; **not a very ~ area** *(fig.)* ein etwas zweifelhaftes Viertel

saluki [sə'lu:kɪ] *n.* Saluki, *der;* Persischer Windhund

salutary ['sæljʊtərɪ] *adj.* heilsam ‹*Wirkung, Einfluß, Schock*›; heilkräftig ‹*Medizin*›

salutation [sæljʊ'teɪʃn] *n. (formal)* Gruß, *der;* Begrüßung, *die;* **form of ~** Begrüßungsformel, *die;* **raise one's hat [to sb.] in ~:** [vor jmdm.] zum Gruß den Hut ziehen

salute [sə'lu:t] **1.** *v. t.* **a)** *(Mil., Navy)* **~ sb.** jmdn. [militärisch] grüßen; *(fig.: pay tribute to)* sich vor jmdm. verneigen; **b)** *(greet)* grüßen. **2.** *v. i. (Mil., Navy)* [militärisch] grüßen. **3.** *n.* **a)** *(Mil., Navy)* Salut, *der;* militärischer Gruß; **fire a seven-gun ~:** sieben Schuß Salut abfeuern; **give a ~:** militärisch grüßen; **take the ~** ‹*Vorgesetzter:*› den militärischen Gruß entgegennehmen; ‹*Staatsoberhaupt usw.:*› die Parade abnehmen; **b)** *(gesture of greeting)* Gruß, *der;* **c)** *(Fencing)* [Fecht]gruß, *der*

Salvadorean [sælvə'dɔ:rɪən] **1.** *n.* Salvadorianer, *der*/Salvadorianerin, *die.* **2.** *adj.* salvadorianisch

salvage ['sælvɪdʒ] **1.** *n.* **a)** *(rescue of property)* Bergung, *die; attrib.* Bergungs‹*arbeiten, -aktion*›; **b)** *(payment)* Bergelohn, *der (Seew.);* **c)** *(rescued property)* Bergegut, *das; (for recycling)* Sammelgut, *das;* **collect bottles for ~:** Flaschen zur Wiedergewinnung von Glas sammeln. **2.** *v. t.* **a)** *(rescue)* bergen; retten *(auch fig.)* **(from** von); **~ one's valuables from the flames** seine Wertsachen aus den Flammen retten; **b)** *(save for recycling)* für die Wiederverwendung sammeln

'salvage operation *n.* Bergungsaktion, *die*

salvation [sæl'veɪʃn] *n.* **a)** *no art. (Relig.)* Erlösung, *die;* **doctrine of ~:** Heilslehre, *die;* **find ~:** zum Heil gelangen; **work out one's own ~** *(fig.)* auf eigene Weise ans Ziel gelangen; **b)** *(means of preservation)* Rettung, *die;* **those biscuits were my ~** *(joc.)* diese Kekse haben mir das Leben gerettet *(scherzh.)*

Salvation 'Army *n.* Heilsarmee, *die*

Salvationist [sæl'veɪʃənɪst] *n. (member of Salvation Army)* Heilsarmist, *der*/-armistin, *die*

¹salve [sælv] **1.** *n.* Balsam, *der (geh.)* **(to** für); **his apology was merely a ~ for his conscience** mit der Entschuldigung wollte er nur sein Gewissen beruhigen. **2.** *v. t. (soothe)* besänftigen; beruhigen ‹*Gewissen*›

²salve [sælv] *v. t. see* **salvage 2 a**

salver ['sælvə(r)] *n.* Tablett, *das*

salvo ['sælvəʊ] *n., pl.* **~es** *or* **~s a)** *(of guns)* Salve, *die;* **b) ~ of applause/laughter** Beifalls-/Lachsalve, *die*

sal volatile [sæl vɒ'lætɪlɪ] *n.* Riechsalz, *das*

Samaritan [sə'mærɪtən] *n.* **good ~:** [barmherziger] Samariter; **I decided to be a good ~:** ich beschloß, ein gutes Werk zu tun; **the ~s** *(organization)* ≈ die Telefonseelsorge

samba ['sæmbə] *n.* Samba, *der*

Sam Browne [sæm 'braʊn] *n.* **a)** *(von brit. Offizieren getragenes)* Koppel mit Schulterriemen; **b)** *(cyclist's)* Leuchtgurt, *der*

same [seɪm] **1.** *adj.* **the ~:** der/die/das gleiche; **the ~ [thing]** *(identical)* der-/die-/dasselbe; **the ~ afternoon/evening** *(of ~ day)* schon am Nachmittag/Abend; **she seemed just the ~ [as ever] to me** sie schien mir unverändert *od.* immer noch die alte; **my parents are much the ~** *(not much changed)* meine Eltern haben sich kaum geändert; **he was no longer the ~ man** er war nicht mehr derselbe; **one and the ~ person/man** ein und dieselbe Person/ein und derselbe Mann; **the very ~:** genau der/die/das; ebenderselbe/-dieselbe/-dasselbe; **much the ~ as** fast genauso wie; **this/that/these** *or* **those ~:** ebender-/ebendie-/ebendasselbe/ebendieselben; genau der-/die-/dasselbe/dieselben; *see also* **token 1 d. 2.** *pron.* **the ~,** *(coll.)* **~** *(the ~ thing)* der-/die-/dasselbe; **he ran up big bills but was not strong at paying ~** *(coll.)* er machte große Schulden, machte aber keine Anstalten, sie zu bezahlen; **an actual banana or a photo of the ~:** eine echte Banane oder ein Foto davon; **things haven't been the ~ since you left** seit du nicht mehr da bist, haben sich die Dinge geändert; **they look [exactly] the ~:** sie sehen gleich aus; **more of the ~:** noch mehr davon; **and the ~ to you!** *(also iron.)* danke gleichfalls; **[the] ~ again** das gleiche noch einmal; **I feel bored – S~ here** *(coll.)* Ich langweile mich – Dito. **3.** *adv.* **[the] ~ as you do** genau wie du; **the ~ as before** genau wie vorher; **be pronounced the ~:** gleich ausgesprochen werden; **all** *or* **just the ~:** trotzdem; nichtsdestotrotz *(ugs., oft scherzh.);* **think the ~ of/feel the ~ towards** dasselbe halten von/empfinden für

'same-day *adj.* ‹*Dienst*› noch am gleichen Tag

sameness ['seɪmnɪs] *n., no pl.* Gleichheit, *die*

Samoa [sə'məʊə] *pr. n.* Samoa *(das)*

Samoan [sə'məʊən] **1.** *adj.* samoanisch. **2.** *n.* Samoaner, *der*/Samoanerin, *die*

samovar ['sæməvɑ:(r)] *n.* Samowar, *der*

sampan ['sæmpæn] *n.* Sampan, *der*

sample ['sɑ:mpl] **1.** *n.* **a)** *(representative portion)* Auswahl, *die; (in opinion research, statistics)* Querschnitt, *der;* Sample, *das;* **b)** *(example)* [Muster]beispiel, *das; (specimen)* Probe, *die;* **[commercial] ~:** Muster, *das; attrib.* Probe‹*exemplar, -seite*›; **~ of air/blood** Luft-/Blutprobe, *die.* **2.** *v. t.* probieren; **~ the pleasures of country life** die Freuden des Landlebens kosten *(geh.)*

¹sampler ['sɑ:mplə(r)] *n. (piece of needlework)* Stickarbeit, *die;* Stickerei, *die*

²sampler *n. (trial pack)* Probe[packung], *die*

Samson ['sæmsn] *pr. n.* Samson, *der; (fig.: strong man)* Herkules, *der*

samurai ['sæmʊəraɪ] *n., pl. same or* **~s** *(Hist.)* Samurai, *der*

sanatarium [sænə'teərɪəm] *(Amer.) see* **sanatorium**

sanatorium [sænə'tɔ:rɪəm] *n., pl.* **~s** *or* **sanatoria** [sænə'tɔ:rɪə] **a)** *(clinic)* Sanatorium, *das;* **b)** *(sick-bay)* Krankenzimmer, *das*

sanctification [sæŋktɪfɪ'keɪʃn] *n.* Heiligung, *die (geh.)*

sanctify ['sæŋktɪfaɪ] *v. t.* **a)** heiligen; **b)** *(consecrate)* weihen; heiligen *(bes. bibl.)*

sanctimonious [sæŋktɪ'məʊnɪəs] *adj.*, **sanctimoniously** [sæŋktɪ'məʊnɪəslɪ] *adv.* scheinheilig

sanction ['sæŋkʃn] **1.** *n.* **a)** *(official approval)* Sanktion, *die;* **give one's ~ to sth.** seine Erlaubnis für etw. geben; **b)** *(Polit.: penalty; Law: punishment)* Sanktion, *die.* **2.** *v. t.* sanktionieren

sanctity ['sæŋktɪtɪ] *n., no pl.* Heiligkeit, *die*

sanctuary ['sæŋktʃʊərɪ] *n.* **a)** *(holy place)* Heiligtum, *das;* **b)** *(part of church)* Altarraum, *der;* Sanktuarium, *das (kath. Kirche);* **c)** *(place of refuge)* Zufluchtsort, *der; (Hist.: guaranteeing safety)* Freistatt, *die;* **d)** *(for animals or plants)* Naturschutzgebiet, *das;* **bird/animal ~:** Vogel-/Tierschutzgebiet, *das;* **e)** *(asylum)* Asyl, *das;* Freiung, *die (hist.);* **take ~:** Zuflucht suchen

sanctum ['sæŋktəm] *n. (joc.: private retreat)* **[inner] ~:** Allerheiligste, *das (fig.)*

sanctus ['sæŋktəs] *n.* Sanctus, *das (kath. Kirche)*

'sanctus bell *n.* Sakristeiglocke, die

sand [sænd] **1.** *n.* **a)** Sand, *der;* **the beach has four miles of ~:** der Sandstrand ist 4 Meilen lang; **built on ~** *(fig.)* auf Sand gebaut; **have** *or* **keep** *or* **bury one's head in the ~** *(fig.)* den Kopf in den Sand stecken; **b)** *in pl. (expanse)* Sandbank, *die; (beach)* Sandstrand, *der;* **c)** *in pl.* **the ~s [of time] are running out** *(fig.)* die Zeit läuft ab; **d)** *(Amer. coll.: determination)* **have not got ~ enough to do sth.** nicht den Mumm *(ugs.)* haben, etw zu tun; **he loses his ~:** ihm rutscht das Herz in die Hose *(ugs., oft scherzh.). See also* **plough 2 a. 2.** *v. t.* **a)** *(sprinkle)* **~ the road** die Straße mit Sand streuen; **b)** *(bury)* **be ~ed up** *or* **over** versandet sein; **c)** *(polish)* **~ sth. down** etw. [ab]schmirgeln

sandal ['sændl] *n.* Sandale, *die*

sandal: ~-tree *n.* Sandelbaum, *der;* **~wood** *n.* **[red] ~wood** Sandelholz, *das;* **~wood oil** Sandel[holz]öl, *das*

sand: ~bag 1. *n.* Sandsack, *der;* **2.** *v. t.* **a)** *(barricade)* mit Sandsäcken schützen; **b)** *(Amer.: coerce)* **~bag sb. into sth.** jmdn. zu etw. zwingen; **~bag sb. into doing sth.** jmdn. so lange bearbeiten, bis er etw. tut; **~bank** *n.* Sandbank, *die;* **~-bar** *n.* Sandbank, *die (an Flußmündungen, Häfen);* **~-bath** *n. (Chem.)* Sandbad, *das;* **~-blast** *v. t.* sandstrahlen *(Technik);* **~-box** *n. (Amer.)* Sandkasten, *der;* **~boy** *n.* **be happy as a ~boy** glücklich und zufrieden sein; **~-castle** *n.* Sandburg, *die;* **~ dollar** *n. (Amer.: Zool.)* Sanddollar, *der;* **~-dune** *n.* Düne, *die*

sander ['sændə(r)] *n.* Sandpapierschleifmaschine, *die*

sand: ~-glass *n.* Sanduhr, *die;* **~-hill** *n.* Düne, *die;* **~lot** *n. (Amer.)* Spielplatz, *der; (for older children)* Bolzplatz, *der (ugs.);* **~man** ['sændmæn] *n.* Sandmann, *der;* **~-martin** *n. (Brit. Ornith.)* Uferschwalbe, *die;* **~paper 1.** *n.* Sandpapier, *das;* **2.** *v. t.* [mit Sandpapier] [ab]schmirgeln; **~piper** *n. (Ornith.)* Wasserläufer, *der;* **~-pit** *n.* Sandkasten, *der;* **~stone** *n.* Sandstein, *der;* **~storm** *n.* Sandsturm, *der;* **~ trap** *n. (Amer. Golf)* Bunker, *der*

sandwich ['sændwɪdʒ, 'sændwɪtʃ] **1.** *n.* **a)** Sandwich, *der od. das;* ≈ [zusammengeklapptes] belegtes Brot; **cheese ~:** Käsebrot, *das;* **open ~:** belegtes Brot; **b)** *see* **sandwich cake. 2.** *v. t.* einschieben **(between** zwischen + *Akk.*; **into** in + *Akk.*); **be ~ed between other people/cars** zwischen andere Personen gequetscht werden/Autos eingeklemmt sein

sandwich: ~-board *n. von einem Sandwichmann getragenes Reklameplakat;* **~ cake** *n. ein- od. mehrschichtig gefüllter Kuchen;* **~ course** *n. Ausbildung mit abwechselnd theoretischem und praktischem Unterricht;* **~-man** *n.* Sandwichmann, *der;* **~ tin** *n.* Brotbüchse, *die*

sandy ['sændɪ] *adj.* **a)** *(consisting of sand)* sandig; Sand‹*boden, -strand*›; **b)** *(yellowish-red)* rotblond ‹*Haar*›

'sand-yacht *n.* Strandsegler, *der*
sane [seɪn] *adj.* **a)** geistig gesund; **they do not think him entirely ~:** sie halten ihn nicht für ganz normal; **not ~:** geistesgestört; **b)** *(sensible)* vernünftig
sanely ['seɪnlɪ] *adv.* **a)** normal; **b)** *(sensibly)* vernünftig
sang *see* **sing 1, 2**
sang-froid [sɑ̃'frwɑː] *n.* Kaltblütigkeit, *die;* Sang-froid, *das (veralt.)*
sangria [sæŋ'griːə] *n.* Sangria, *die*
sanguinary ['sæŋgwɪnərɪ] *adj.* **a)** *(delighting in bloodshed)* blutrünstig; **b)** *(bloody)* blutig
sanguine ['sæŋgwɪn] *adj.* **a)** *(confident)* zuversichtlich (**about** was ... betrifft); heiter ‹*Temperament*›; **b)** *(florid)* blühend ‹*Gesichtsfarbe*›
sanguinely ['sæŋgwɪnlɪ] *adv.* zuversichtlich
sanitarium [sænɪ'teərɪəm] *(Amer.) see* **sanatorium**
sanitary ['sænɪtərɪ] *adj.* sanitär ‹*Verhältnisse, Anlagen*›; gesundheitlich ‹*Gesichtspunkt, Problem*›; Gesundheits‹*behörde*›; hygienisch ‹*Küche, Krankenhaus, Gewohnheit*›; Sanitär‹*fliesen, -abflußrohr*›
sanitary: ~ engi'neer *n.* Sanitärtechniker, *der*/-technikerin, *die;* **~ engi'neering** *n.* Sanitärtechnik, *die;* **~ inspector** *n.* Gesundheitsinspektor, *der*/-inspektorin, *die;* **~ napkin** *(Amer.),* **~ towel** *(Brit.) ns.* Damenbinde, *die;* **~ ware** *n., no pl.* Sanitärkeramik, *die*
sanitation [sænɪ'teɪʃn] *n., no pl.* **a)** *(drainage, refuse disposal)* Kanalisation und Abfallbeseitigung; **b)** *(hygiene)* Hygiene, *die*
sanitize (sanitise) ['sænɪtaɪz] *v. t.* keimfrei machen ‹*Luft, Toilettensitz, Besteck*›; *(fig.)* entschärfen ‹*Dokument, Protokoll, Film*›
sanity ['sænɪtɪ] *n.* **a)** *(mental health)* geistige Gesundheit; **lose one's ~:** den Verstand verlieren; **cause sb. to lose his ~:** jmdn. um den Verstand bringen; **fear for/doubt sb.'s ~:** um jmds. Zurechnungsfähigkeit fürchten/an jmds. Verstand *(Dat.)* zweifeln; **b)** *(good sense)* Vernünftigkeit, *die;* **restore ~ to the proceedings** die Veranstaltung wieder in vernünftige Bahnen lenken
sank *see* **sink 2, 3**
sans [sænz] *prep. (arch./joc.)* ohne
sanserif [sæn'serɪf] *(Printing)* **1.** *n.* Grotesk[schrift], *die.* **2.** *adj.* serifenlos; Grotesk‹*buchstabe, -ziffer*›
Sanskrit ['sænskrɪt] **1.** *adj.* sanskritisch; Sanskrit‹*text, -inschrift, -literatur*›; ‹*Grammatik*› des Sanskrits; *see also* **English 1. 2.** *n.* Sanskrit, *das; see also* **English 2 a**
Santa ['sæntə] *(coll.),* **Santa Claus** ['sæntə klɔːz] *n.* der Weihnachtsmann
¹sap [sæp] **1.** *n.* **a)** *(Bot.)* Saft, *der; (fig.: vital spirit)* belebende Kraft; **in the spring the ~ rises** im Frühling steigen die Säfte; **b)** *(Amer. sl.: club)* Knüppel, *der.* **2.** *v. t.,* **-pp-** **a)** *(drain)* den Saft entziehen (+ *Dat.*) ‹*Holz*›; *(for sugar, rubber)* anzapfen (**for** zur Gewinnung von); **b)** *(fig.: exhaust vigour of)* zehren an (+ *Dat.*); **~ sb. of [all] his/her strength** jmdn. [völlig] entkräften; **her strength had been ~ped by disease/hunger** Krankheit/Hunger hatte an ihren Kräften gezehrt; **c)** *(Amer. sl.: hit)* mit einem Knüppel/mit Knüppeln schlagen
²sap **1.** *v. t.,* **-pp-** unterhöhlen ‹*Fundament, Mauer*›. **2.** *n. (Mil.) (trench)* Sappe, *die; (under enemy's fortification)* Tunnel, *der*
³sap *n. (sl.: fool)* Trottel, *der (ugs. abwertend);* **find some ~ to do sth.** einen Dummen finden, der etw. tut
sapele [sə'piːlɪ] *n.* **a)** *(tree)* Sapelli[baum], *der;* **b)** *(wood)* Sapelli[holz], *das*
'sap-green **1.** *n.* Saftgrün, *das.* **2.** *adj.* saftgrün
sapling ['sæplɪŋ] *n.* junger Baum
sapper ['sæpə(r)] *n. (Brit. Mil.)* Pionier, *der*
Sapphic ['sæfɪk] *(Pros.)* **1.** *adj.* sapphisch. **2.** *n.* sapphischer Vers
sapphire ['sæfaɪə(r)] *n.* Saphir, *der;* **~ blue** saphirblau; **~ ring** Saphirring, *der;* **~ wedding** 45. Hochzeitstag
sappy ['sæpɪ] *adj.* saftig ‹*Gras*›; *(fig.: full of vitality)* voll Saft und Kraft *nachgestellt*
'sapwood *n. (Bot.)* Splintholz, *das*
saraband[e] ['særəbænd] *n. (Mus., Dancing)* Sarabande, *die*
Saracen ['særəsn] *(Hist., Ethnol.)* **1.** *n.* Sarazene, *der*/Sarazenin, *die (veralt.).* **2.** *adj.* sarazenisch; Sarazenen‹*führer, -frau*›
sarcasm ['sɑːkæzəm] *n.* Sarkasmus, *der; (remark)* sarkastische Bemerkung; **with heavy ~:** mit beißendem Sarkasmus
sarcastic [sɑː'kæstɪk] *adj.,* **sarcastically** [sɑː'kæstɪkəlɪ] *adv.* sarkastisch
sarcoma [sɑː'kəʊmə] *n., pl.* **~ta** [sɑː'kəʊmətə] *(Med.)* Sarkom, *das*
sarcophagus [sɑː'kɒfəgəs] *n., pl.* **sarcophagi** [sɑː'kɒfəgaɪ] Sarkophag, *der*
sardine [sɑː'diːn] *n. (Zool.)* Sardine, *die; (Gastr.)* [Öl]sardine, *die;* **like ~s** *(fig.)* wie die Ölsardinen
Sardinia [sɑː'dɪnɪə] *pr. n.* Sardinien *(das)*
Sardinian [sɑː'dɪnɪən] **1.** *n.* **a)** *(person)* Sarde, *der*/Sardin, *die;* Sardinier, *der*/Sardinierin, *die;* **b)** *(language)* Sardisch, *das.* **2.** *adj.* sardisch
sardonic [sɑː'dɒnɪk] *adj.* höhnisch ‹*Bemerkung*›; sardonisch ‹*Lachen, Lächeln*›; **he can be very ~:** er kann sehr bissig sein
sardonically [sɑː'dɒnɪkəlɪ] *adv.* höhnisch ‹*bemerken*›; sardonisch ‹*lächeln, lachen*›
sarge [sɑːdʒ] *n. (sl.)* Sergeant, *der; (Mil.)* ≈ Hauptfeld, *der (Militärjargon)*
sari ['sɑːrɪ] *n.* Sari, *der*
sarky ['sɑːkɪ] *adj. (Brit. coll.)* ätzend *(ugs.)*
sarnie ['sɑːnɪ] *(Brit. coll.) see* **sandwich 1 a**
sarong [sə'rɒŋ] *n.* Sarong, *der*
sartorial [sɑː'tɔːrɪəl] *adj.* **he has high ~ standards** er stellt hohe Ansprüche, was seine Kleidung betrifft; **~ fashion** Herrenmode, *die;* **he was the height of ~ elegance** er war der Inbegriff des elegant gekleideten Herrn
SAS *abbr. (Brit. Mil.)* **Special Air Service** *auf Geheimoperationen spezialisiertes Regiment der Britischen Armee*
¹sash [sæʃ] *n.* Schärpe, *die*
²sash *n.* **a)** *(of window)* Fensterrahmen, *der;* **b)** *(window)* Schiebefenster, *das*
sashay ['sæʃeɪ] *v. i. (Amer.)* **a)** *(walk casually)* schlendern; **b)** *(ostentatiously)* stolzieren; **c)** *(diagonally)* **~ through a crowd** sich durch eine Menschenmenge schlängeln
sash: ~-cord, ~-line *ns.* Gewichtsschnur, *die;* **~-'window** *n.* Schiebefenster, *das*
sass [sæs] *(Amer. coll.)* **1.** *n.* Frechheit, *die.* **2.** *v. t.* frech sein zu
Sassenach ['sæsənæx, 'sæsənæk] *(Scot., Ir.; usu. derog.)* **1.** *n.* Engländer, *der*/Engländerin, *die.* **2.** *adj.* englisch
sassy ['sæsɪ] *adj. (Amer. coll.)* **a)** *(cheeky)* frech; **b)** *(stylish)* schick
sat *see* **sit**
Sat. *abbr.* **Saturday** Sa.
Satan ['seɪtən] *pr. n.* Satan, *der*
satanic [sə'tænɪk] *adj.* satanisch; teuflisch
Satanism ['seɪtənɪzm] *n., no pl., no art.* Satanismus, *der;* Satanskult, *der*
satchel ['sætʃl] *n.* [Schul]ranzen, *der*
sate [seɪt] *v. t. (literary)* **a)** *(gratify)* stillen ‹*Hunger, Durst, Verlangen, Zorn*›; zufriedenstellen ‹*Person*›; **feel pleasantly ~d** ein angenehmes Sättigungsgefühl empfinden; **~ oneself on sth.** sich an etw. *(Dat.)* sättigen *(geh.);* **b)** *(cloy)* übersättigen ‹*Lust, Verlangen*›; **become ~d with/be ~d by sth.** einer Sache *(Gen.)* überdrüssig werden/sein
sateen [sə'tiːn] *n. (Textiles)* Baumwollsatin, *der*
satellite ['sætəlaɪt] **1.** *n.* **a)** *(Astronaut., Astron.; also country)* Satellit, *der;* **by ~:** über Satellit; **b)** *(fig.) (object associated with another)* Ableger, *der (fig.); (follower)* Trabant, *der (fig.).* **2.** *attrib. adj.* Satelliten‹*film, -bild, -fernsehen, -regierung*›; **~ industries** Zulieferindustrie, *die*
satellite: ~ 'broadcasting *n., no pl., no art.* Satellitenfunk, *der;* **~ dish** *n.* Parabolantenne, *die;* **~ state** *n.* Satellitenstaat, *der;* **~ town** *n.* Satelliten- *od.* Trabantenstadt, *die*
satiate ['seɪʃɪeɪt] *see* **sate**
satiation [seɪʃɪ'eɪʃn] *n.* **a)** *(gratification)* Sättigung, *die;* **b)** *(cloying)* Übersättigung, *die*
satiety [sə'taɪətɪ] *n.* Übersättigung, *die;* **to [the point of] ~:** bis zum Überdruß
satin ['sætɪn] **1.** *n.* Satin, *der.* **2.** *attrib. adj.* **a)** *(made of ~)* Satin-; **b)** *(like ~)* seidig
'satinwood *n. (tree)* [ostindischer] Satinholzbaum; *(wood)* [ostindisches] Satinholz
satiny ['sætɪnɪ] *adj.* seidig
satire ['sætaɪə(r)] *n.* Satire, *die* (**on** auf + *Akk.*); **element/tone of ~:** satirisches Element/satirischer Ton; **gift** *or* **talent for ~:** satirische Begabung
satirical [sə'tɪrɪkl] *adj.,* **satirically** [sə'tɪrɪkəlɪ] *adv.* satirisch
satirise *see* **satirize**
satirist ['sætɪrɪst] *n.* Satiriker, *der*/Satirikerin, *die;* **be a ~ of sb./sth.** jmdn./etw. mit satirischen Mitteln angreifen
satirize ['sætɪraɪz] *v. t.* **a)** *(write satire on)* satirisch darstellen; **b)** *(describe satirically)* ‹*Buch, Film usw.:*› eine Satire sein auf (+ *Akk.*); **be brutally ~d** ‹*Person:*› das Opfer gnadenloser Satire werden
satisfaction [sætɪs'fækʃn] *n.* **a)** *no pl. (act)* Befriedigung, *die;* **we strive for the ~ of our clients** wir bemühen uns, unsere Kunden zufriedenzustellen; **b)** *no pl. (feeling of gratification)* Befriedigung, *die* (**at, with** über + *Akk.*); Genugtuung, *die* (**at, with** über + *Akk.*); **job ~:** Befriedigung in der Arbeit; **it is with [great] ~ that I .../it gives me [great] ~ to ...:** es erfüllt mich mit [großer] Befriedigung, zu ...; **get ~ out of one's work** in seiner Arbeit Befriedigung finden; **there's a lot of ~ [to be had] in doing sth.** es ist sehr befriedigend, etw. zu tun; **what ~ can it give you?** was befriedigt dich daran?; **I can't get any ~ from him** er stellt mich nicht zufrieden; **c)** *no pl. (gratified state)* **meet with sb.'s** *or* **give sb. [complete] ~:** jmdn. [in jeder Weise] zufriedenstellen; **~ guaranteed** Sie werden garantiert zufrieden sein; **fail to give ~** ‹*Arbeit:*› nicht zufriedenstellend ausfallen; ‹*Angestellte:*› nicht zufriedenstellend arbeiten; **to sb.'s ~, to the ~ of sb.** zu jmds. Zufriedenheit; **d)** *(instance of gratification)* Befriedigung, *die;* **it is a great ~ to me that ...:** es erfüllt mich mit großer Befriedigung, daß ...; **give every ~:** in jeder Hinsicht befriedigend sein; **have the ~ of doing sth.** das Vergnügen haben, etw. zu tun; **one of the ~s of the job** eine der Befriedigungen, die die Arbeit gewährt; **e)** *(Hist.: revenge in duel)* Satisfaktion, *die*
satisfactorily [sætɪs'fæktərɪlɪ] *adv.* zufriedenstellend; richtig ‹*passen*›; **progress ~:** befriedigende Fortschritte machen
satisfactory [sætɪs'fæktərɪ] *adj.* zufriedenstellend; angemessen ‹*Bezahlung*›
satisfied ['sætɪsfaɪd] *adj.* **a)** *(contented)* zufrieden; *(replete)* satt; **be ~ with doing sth.** sich damit begnügen, etw. zu tun; **be ~ to do sth.** damit zufrieden sein, etw. zu tun; **b)** *(convinced)* überzeugt (**of** von); **be ~ that ...:** [davon] überzeugt sein, daß ...
satisfy ['sætɪsfaɪ] **1.** *v. t.* **a)** *(content)* befriedigen; zufriedenstellen ‹*Kunden, Publikum*›; entsprechen (+ *Dat.*) ‹*Vorliebe, Empfinden, Meinung, Zeitgeist*›; erfüllen ‹*Hoffnung, Erwartung*›; **~/fail to ~ the examiners** die Prüfung bestehen/nicht bestehen; **b)** *(rid of want)* befriedigen; *(put an end to)* stillen ‹*Hunger, Durst*›; *(make replete)* sättigen; **that meal wouldn't ~ a spar-**

row davon würde nicht einmal ein Spatz satt; **c)** *(convince)* ~ **sb. [of sth.]** jmdn. [von etw.] überzeugen; ~ **sb. that ...:** jmdn. [davon] überzeugen, daß ...; ~ **oneself of** *or* **as to** sich überzeugen von ‹*Wahrheit, Ehrlichkeit*›; sich *(Dat.)* Gewißheit verschaffen über (+ *Akk.*) ‹*Motiv*›; ~ **oneself as to what happened** sich *(Dat.)* Klarheit *od.* Gewißheit darüber verschaffen, was geschehen ist; **d)** *(adequately deal with)* ausräumen ‹*Einwand, Zweifel*›; erfüllen ‹*Bitte, Forderung, Bedingung*›; **e)** *(pay)* begleichen ‹*Schulden*›; befriedigen ‹*Gläubiger, Forderung*›; **f)** *(fulfil)* erfüllen ‹*Vertrag, Verpflichtung, Forderung*›; **g)** *(Math.)* erfüllen ‹*Gleichung*›. **2.** *v. i.* **a)** *(make replete)* sättigen; **b)** *(be convincing)* ‹*Argument:*› überzeugen

satisfying ['sætɪsfaɪɪŋ] *adj.* befriedigend; sättigend ‹*Gericht, Speise*›; zufriedenstellend ‹*Antwort, Lösung, Leistung*›

satsuma [sæt'su:mə] *n.* Satsuma, *die*

saturate ['sætʃəreɪt, 'sætjʊreɪt] *v. t.* **a)** *(soak)* durchnässen; [mit Feuchtigkeit durch]tränken ‹*Boden, Erde*›; **cake ~d in** *or* **with liqueur** mit Likör getränkter Kuchen; **b)** *(fill to capacity)* auslasten; sättigen ‹*Markt*›; **c)** *(Mil.: bomb intensively)* mit einem Bombenteppich belegen; **d)** *(Phys., Chem.)* sättigen

saturated ['sætʃəreɪtɪd, 'sætjʊreɪtɪd] *adj.* **a)** *(soaked)* durchnäßt; völlig naß ‹*Boden*›; **b)** *(imbued)* durchdrungen **(with, in** von); **be ~ with** durchdrungen sein von; ganz erfüllt sein von ‹*Duft*›; **be ~ in history/tradition** sehr geschichtsträchtig/traditionsreich sein; **c)** *(filled to capacity)* ausgelastet; gesättigt ‹*Markt*›; **d)** *(Phys., Chem.)* gesättigt ‹*Lösung, Verbindung, Fett*›; **e)** *(Art)* satt ‹*Farbe, Farbton*›

saturation [sætʃə'reɪʃn, sætjʊ'reɪʃn] *n.* **a)** *(soaking, being soaked)* Durchnässung, *die;* **b)** *(filling to capacity)* Auslastung, *die* **(by, with** mit); *(of market)* Sättigung, *die;* **c)** *(Mil.)* ~ **[bombing]** Flächenbombardierung, *die;* **d)** *(Phys., Chem.)* Sättigung, *die;* **e)** *(colour intensity)* Sattheit, *die*

satu'ration point *n.* **a)** *(limit of capacity)* [Ober]grenze, *die; (of market)* Sättigungspunkt, *der; (limit of response)* Grenze der Aufnahmefähigkeit; *(of harmful effect)* Grenze der Belastbarkeit; **b)** *(Phys.)* Sättigungspunkt, *der*

Saturday ['sætədeɪ, 'sætədɪ] **1.** *n.* Sonnabend, *der;* Samstag, *der.* **2.** *adv. (coll.)* **he comes ~s** er kommt sonnabends *od.* samstags. *See also* **Friday**

Saturn ['sætən] *pr. n.* **a)** *(Astron.)* Saturn, *der;* **b)** *(Roman Mythol.)* Saturn *(der)*

Saturnalia [sætə'neɪlɪə] *n. pl. (Roman Ant.)* Saturnalien *Pl.*

saturnine ['sætənaɪn] *adj.* melancholisch; düster ‹*Einstellung*›; *(sinister)* finster

satyr ['sætə(r)] *n. (Mythol.)* Satyr, *der*

sauce [sɔ:s] **1.** *n.* **a)** Soße, *die;* **be served with the same ~** *(fig.)* es mit *od.* in gleicher Münze heimgezahlt bekommen; *see also* **gander a**; **b)** *(fig.: sth. that adds piquancy)* Würze, *die;* **c)** *(Amer.: stewed fruit)* Kompott, *das;* **d)** *(Amer. coll.)* **the ~:** Alkohol; **in the ~:** alkoholisiert; **e)** *(Amer.: vegetables)* Beilage, *die;* **f)** *(impudence)* Frechheit, *die;* **he's got a lot of ~!** der ist ganz schön frech!; **don't give me any of your ~!** sei nicht so frech! **2.** *v. t. (coll.)* frech sein zu

sauce: ~**-boat** *n.* Sauciere, *die;* ~**-box** *n. (coll.)* Frechdachs, *der (fam.);* ~**pan** ['sɔ:spən] *n.* Kochtopf, *der; (with straight handle)* [Stiel]kasserolle, *die*

saucer ['sɔ:sə(r)] *n.* Untertasse, *die;* **their eyes were like ~s** *(fig.)* sie machten große Augen *(ugs.);* **with eyes like ~s** *(fig.)* mit großen Augen; *see also* **flying saucer**

saucerful ['sɔ:səfʊl] *n.* **a ~ [of milk]** eine Untertasse [Milch *od.* voll Milch]

saucily ['sɔ:sɪlɪ] *adv.* **a)** *(rudely)* frech; **b)** *(pertly)* keck

sauciness ['sɔ:sɪnɪs] *n., no pl.* **a)** *(rudeness)* Frechheit, *die;* **b)** *(pertness, jauntiness)* Keckheit, *die*

saucy ['sɔ:sɪ] *adj.* **a)** *(rude)* frech; **b)** *(pert, jaunty)* keck

Saudi ['saʊdɪ] **1.** *adj.* **a)** *see* **Saudi-Arabian 1; b)** *(of dynasty)* saudisch ‹*Prinz, Palast*›. **2.** *n.* **a)** *see* **Saudi-Arabian 2; b)** *(member of dynasty)* Saudi, *der*

Saudi Arabia [saʊdɪ ə'reɪbɪə] *pr. n.* Saudi-Arabien *(das)*

Saudi-Arabian [saʊdɪə'reɪbɪən] **1.** *adj.* saudiarabisch. **2.** *n.* Saudi[araber], *der*/-araberin, *die*

sauerkraut ['saʊəkraʊt] *n. (Gastr.)* Sauerkraut, *das*

sauna ['sɔ:nə, 'saʊnə] *n.* Sauna, *die;* **have** *or* **take a ~:** saunieren; ein Saunabad nehmen

saunter ['sɔ:ntə(r)] **1.** *v. i.* schlendern; **I think I will ~ [down/over/up] to the village** ich werde wohl ins Dorf runter-/rüber-/raufschlendern *(ugs.).* **2.** *n. (stroll)* Bummel, *der (ugs.); (leisurely pace)* Schlenderschritt, *der;* **at a ~:** im Schlenderschritt; **go for a** *or* **have a ~:** schlendern

saurian ['sɔ:rɪən] **1.** *n. (Zool.)* Echse, *die; (Palaeont.)* Saurier, *der.* **2.** *adj. (Zool.: of the Sauria)* der Echsen *nachgestellt; (lizard-like)* echsenartig; ~ **reptile** Echse, *die*

sausage ['sɒsɪdʒ] *n.* Wurst, *die; (smaller)* Würstchen, *das;* **not a ~** *(fig. sl.)* gar nix *(ugs.)*

sausage: ~**-dog** *n. (Brit. coll.)* Dackel, *der;* ~**-machine** *n.* Wurstfüllmaschine, *die; (Educ. fig.)* Bildungsfabrik, *die (abwertend);* ~**-meat** *n.* Wurstmasse, *die;* ~ **'roll** *n. Blätterteig mit Wurstfüllung*

sauté ['səʊteɪ] *(Cookery)* **1.** *adj.* sautiert *(fachspr.);* kurz [an]gebraten; ~ **potatoes** ≈ Bratkartoffeln. **2.** *n.* Sauté, *das.* **3.** *v. t.,* **~d** *or* **~ed** ['səʊteɪd] sautieren *(fachspr.);* kurz [an]braten

Sauterne[s] [səʊ'tɜ:n] Sauternes[wein], *der*

savage ['sævɪdʒ] **1.** *adj.* **a)** *(uncivilized)* primitiv; wild ‹*Volksstamm*›; unzivilisiert ‹*Land*›; **b)** *(fierce)* brutal; wild ‹*Tier*›; scharf ‹*Hund*›; jähzornig ‹*Temperament*›; schonungslos ‹*Kritiker, Satiriker*›; **have a wild, ~ look in one's eye** wild und brutal aussehen; **make a ~ attack on sb.** brutal über jmdn. herfallen; *(fig.)* jmdn. schonungslos angreifen. **2.** *n.* **a)** *(uncivilized person)* Wilde, *der/die (veralt.);* **behave like ~s** sich wie die Wilden aufführen *(abwertend);* **b)** *(barbarous or uncultivated person)* Barbar, *der*/Barbarin, *die (abwertend).* **3.** *v. t.* **a)** ‹*Hund:*› anfallen ‹*Kind usw.*›; *(lacerate)* zerfleischen; **b)** *(fig.)* ‹*Kritiker, Journalist:*› herfallen über (+ *Akk.*) ‹*Politiker usw.*›; ‹*Kritiker, Zeitung:*› schonungslos verreißen ‹*Theaterstück usw.*›

savagely ['sævɪdʒlɪ] *adv.* *(fiercely)* brutal; wild ‹*brüllen*›; wüst ‹*beschimpfen*›; schonungslos ‹*kritisieren*›

savagery ['sævɪdʒrɪ] *n., no pl.* **a)** *(uncivilized condition)* Unzivilisiertheit, *die;* **b)** *(ferocity)* Brutalität, *die*

savannah (savanna) [sə'vænə] *n. (Geog.)* Savanne, *die*

save [seɪv] **1.** *v. t.* **a)** *(rescue)* retten **(from** vor + *Dat.*); **please, ~ me!** bitte helfen Sie mir!; ~ **sb. from the clutches of the enemy/from making a mistake** jmdn. aus den Klauen des Feindes retten/davor bewahren, daß er einen Fehler macht; **alcoholics must be ~d from themselves** Alkoholiker müssen vor sich *(Dat.)* selbst geschützt werden; **he ~d my reputation** er rettete meinen guten Ruf; ~ **oneself from falling** sich [beim Hinfallen] fangen; **be ~d by the bell** *(fig. coll.)* gerade noch mal davonkommen *(ugs.);* ~ **the day** die Situation retten; *see also* **bacon; face 1 a; life a; skin 1 a; b)** *(keep undamaged)* schonen ‹*Kleidung, Möbelstück*›; **c) God ~ the King/Queen** *etc.* Gott behüte *od.* beschütze den König/die Königin *usw.;* **[God] ~ sb. from sb./sth.** Gott bewahre jmdn. vor jmdm./etw.; **d)** *(Theol.)* retten ‹*Sünder, Seele, Menschen*›; **be past saving** nicht mehr zu retten sein; ~ **oneself** ‹*Sünder:*› seine Seele retten; **Jesus ~s!** Jesus ist der Retter!; **e)** *(put aside)* aufheben; sparen ‹*Geld*›; sammeln ‹*Rabattmarken, Briefmarken*›; *(conserve)* sparsam umgehen mit ‹*Geldmitteln, Kräften, Wasser*›; ~ **money for a rainy day** *(fig.)* einen Notgroschen zurücklegen; ~ **water for the drought** Wasser für die Trockenzeit sammeln; ~ **oneself** sich schonen; seine Kräfte sparen; ~ **one's breath** sich *(Dat.)* seine Worte sparen; **you can ~ your pains** *or* **trouble/apologies** die Mühe/deine Entschuldigungen kannst du dir sparen; ~ **a seat for sb.** jmdm. einen Platz freihalten; **f)** *(make unnecessary)* sparen ‹*Geld, Zeit, Energie*›; ~ **sb./oneself sth.** jmdm./sich etw. ersparen; ~ **oneself money/half the cost** Geld/die Hälfte des Preises [ein]sparen; ~ **sb./oneself doing sth.** *or* **having to do sth.** es jmdm./sich ersparen, etw. tun zu müssen; **a stitch in time ~s nine** *(prov.)* was du heute kannst besorgen ...; Vorsorge ist besser als Nachsorge; **g)** *(avoid losing)* nicht verlieren ‹*Satz, Karte, Stich*›; *(prevent from making a score)* abwehren ‹*Schuß, Ball*›; verhindern ‹*Tor*›; *(Cricket)* ‹*Fänger:*› verhindern ‹*Lauf*›; **his goal ~d the match for his team** sein Tor rettete seine Mannschaft vor der Niederlage. **2.** *v. i.* **a)** *(put money by)* sparen; ~ **with a building society** bei einer Bausparkasse sparen; **b)** *(avoid waste)* sparen **(on** *Akk.*); ~ **on food** am Essen sparen; **c)** *(Sport)* ‹*Torwart:*› halten. **3.** *n. (Sport)* Abwehr, *die;* Parade, *die (fachspr.);* **make a ~** ‹*Torwart:*› halten. **4.** *prep. (arch./poet./rhet.)* mit Ausnahme (+ *Gen.*). **5.** *conj. (arch.)* außer; ~ **for sth.** von etw. abgesehen

~ **'up 1.** *v. t.* sparen; sammeln, sparen ‹*Marken, Gutscheine usw.*›. **2.** *v. i.* sparen **(for** für, auf + *Akk.*)

save-as-you-'earn *n. (Brit.) Sparen durch regelmäßige Abbuchung eines bestimmten Betrages vom Lohn-/Gehaltskonto*

saveloy ['sævəlɔɪ] Zervelatwurst, *die*

saver ['seɪvə(r)] *n.* **a)** *(of money)* Sparer, *der*/Sparerin, *die;* **b)** *in comb. (device)* **sth. is a time-~/labour-~/money-~:** etw. spart Zeit/Arbeit/Geld; **c)** ~ **of souls** Seelenretter, *der*/-retterin, *die*

saving ['seɪvɪŋ] **1.** *n.* **a)** *in pl. (money saved)* Ersparnisse *Pl.;* **have money put by in ~s** Geld zurückgelegt haben; **how much have you got in your ~s?** wieviel Geld hast du [an]gespart?; **b)** *(rescue; also Theol.)* Rettung, *die;* **c)** *(instance of economy)* Ersparnis, *die;* ~ **in** *or* **of** *or* **on time/money/fuel/effort** Zeit-/Geld-/Brennstoff-/Arbeitsersparnis, *die;* **make a ~ in** *or* **of money/on equipment/in** *or* **of time** Geld/Ausrüstung/Zeit [ein]sparen; **there's no ~ at all** es wird überhaupt nichts eingespart; **there are ~s to be made on clothes** man kann beim Kleiderkauf einiges sparen. **2.** *adj.* **a)** *in comb.* ‹*kosten-, benzin*›sparend; **b)** *(redeeming)* **the only ~ feature of the play** das einzig Versöhnliche an dem Stück. **3.** *prep. (except)* bis auf (+ *Akk.*)

saving: ~ **clause** *n.* einschränkende Klausel; Vorbehaltsklausel, *die;* ~ **'grace** *n.* versöhnender Zug; **her only ~ grace was her honesty** das Einzige, was einen mit ihr versöhnte, war ihre Ehrlichkeit

savings: ~ **account** *n.* Sparkonto, *das;* ~ **account and loan association** *(Amer.) see* **building society;** ~ **bank** *n.* Sparkasse, *die;* ~ **certificate** *n. (Brit.)* Staatspapier, *das*

saviour *(Amer.:* **savior)** ['seɪvjə(r)] *n.* **a)** Retter, *der*/Retterin, *die; (thing)* Rettung, *die;* **b)** *(Relig.)* **our/the S~:** unser/der Heiland

savoir-faire [sævwɑ:'feə(r)] *n.* Gewandtheit, *die*

savor *(Amer.) see* **savour**

[1]**savory** *(Amer.) see* **savoury**

[2]**savory** ['seɪvərɪ] *n. (Bot.)* Bohnenkraut, *das*

savour ['seɪvə(r)] *(Brit.)* **1.** *n.* **a)** *(flavour)* Geschmack, *der; (fig.)* Charakter, *der;* **b)** *(trace)* **a ~ of sth.** ein Hauch *od.* Anflug von etw.; **c)** *(enjoyable quality)* Reiz, *der.* **2.** *v. t. (lit. or fig., literary)* genießen; **that is a dish/perfume I particularly ~:** das Gericht/Parfüm ist ein ganz besonderer Genuß für mich. **3.** *v. i.* **sth. ~s of sth.** *(fig.)* etw. schmeckt nach etw. *(fig.)*

savoury ['seɪvərɪ] *(Brit.)* **1.** *adj.* **a)** *(not sweet)* pikant; *(having salt flavour)* salzig; **b)** *(appetizing)* appetitanregend. **2.** *n.* [pikantes] Häppchen

Savoy [sə'vɔɪ] *pr. n.* Savoyen *(das)*

savoy *n.* **~ [cabbage]** Wirsing[kohl], *der*

savvy ['sævɪ] *(sl.)* **1.** *v. t.* kapieren *(ugs.);* **I don't ~ French** Französisch hab' ich nicht drauf *(salopp).* **2.** *v. i.* **..., ~? ...,** kapiert? *(ugs.);* **no ~** *(I don't know)* keine Ahnung *(ugs.); (I don't understand)* nix capito *(salopp).* **3.** *n.* Durchblick, *der (ugs.).* **4.** *adj. (Amer.)* ausgebufft *(salopp)*

[1]**saw** [sɔ:] **1.** *n.* Säge, *die;* **musical ~:** singende Säge. **2.** *v. t., p.p.* **~n** [sɔ:n] *or* **~ed** [zer]sägen; *(make with ~)* sägen; **~ across** *or* **through** durchsägen; **~ in half** in der Mitte durchsägen; **~ the air [with one's hands/arms]** [mit den Händen/Armen] in der Luft herumfuchteln *(ugs.).* **3.** *v. i., p.p.* **~n** *or* **~ed a)** sägen; **~ through sth.** etw. durchsägen; **b)** *(fig.)* **~ away [at the violin]** [auf der Geige] drauflossägen *(ugs.)*

~ 'down *v. t.* umsägen ‹*Baum*›

~ 'off *v. t.* absägen

~ 'up *v. t.* zersägen **(into** in + *Akk.*)

[2]**saw** *n. (saying)* Sprichwort, *das*

[3]**saw** *see* [1]**see**

sawder ['sɔ:də(r)] *n. (coll.)* **soft ~:** Schmus, *der (ugs.);* **give sb. a load of soft ~:** jmdm. ordentlich Honig um den Bart schmieren *(ugs.)*

saw: ~dust *n.* Sägemehl, *das;* **~-edged** *adj.* gezähnt ‹*Klinge*›; **a ~-edged knife** ein Sägemesser

saw: ~fish *n.* Sägerochen, *der;* Sägefisch, *der;* **~mill** *n.* Sägemühle, *die*

'sawn-off *adj. (Brit.)* **a)** abgesägt; ‹*Gewehr*› mit abgesägtem Lauf; **b)** *(coll.: undersized)* mickrig *(ugs. abwertend)*

saw: ~-pit *n.* Sägegrube, *die;* **~tooth[ed]** ['sɔ:tu:θ(t)] *adj.* **a)** gezackt ‹*Berge*›; Säge‹*dach*›; **b)** *(Electr.)* Sägezahn‹*generator, -schwingung, -spannung*›

sawyer ['sɔ:jə(r)] *n.* Säger, *der;* Sägemüller, *der*

sax [sæks] *n. (Mus. coll.)* Saxophon, *das*

saxe [sæks] *n.* **~ [blue]** Sächsischblau, *das*

saxifrage ['sæksɪfrɪdʒ, 'sæksɪfreɪdʒ] *n. (Bot.)* Steinbrech, *der*

Saxon ['sæksn] **1.** *n.* **a)** Sachse, *der*/Sächsin, *die;* **b)** *(Ling.)* Sächsisch, *das;* **[Old] ~:** Westsächsisch, *das.* **2.** *adj.* **a)** sächsisch; **b)** *(Ling.)* sächsisch; *(of Old ~)* westsächsisch

Saxony ['sæksənɪ] *pr. n.* Sachsen *(das)*

saxophone ['sæksəfəʊn] *n. (Mus.)* Saxophon, *das*

saxophonist [sæk'sɒfənɪst, 'sæksəfəʊnɪst] *n.* Saxophonist, *der*/Saxophonistin, *die*

say [seɪ] **1.** *v.t., pres. t.* **he ~s** [sez], *p.t. & p.p.* **said** [sed] **a)** sagen; **~ sth. out loud** etw. aussprechen *od.* laut sagen; **~ sth. to oneself** sich *(Dat.)* etw. sagen; **he said something about going out** er hat etwas von Ausgehen gesagt; **please ~ something** bitte sag doch etwas; *(make a short speech)* sage bitte ein paar Worte; **all I can ~ is ...:** ich kann nur sagen ...; **what more can I ~?** was soll ich da noch [groß] sagen?; **I don't know 'what to ~:** ich weiß nicht, was ich [dazu] sagen soll; **I wouldn't [go so far as to] ~ that, but ...:** das würde ich nicht [unbedingt] sagen, aber ...; **..., not to ~ ...:** ..., um nicht zu sagen ...; **it ~s a lot** *or* **much** *or* **something for sb./sth. that ...:** es spricht sehr für jmdn./etw., daß ...; **have a lot/not much to ~ for oneself** viel reden/nicht viel von sich geben; **~ no 'more!** *(I understand)* schon gut; **we'll** *or* **let's ~ no more about it** reden wir nicht mehr davon; **there is no** *or* **nothing more to be said** es erübrigt sich jedes weitere Wort **(on** zu); **to ~ nothing of** *(quite apart from)* ganz zu schweigen von; mal ganz abgesehen von; **that is to ~:** das heißt; **as much as to ~:** als wollte er/sie *usw.* sagen ...; **as you might ~:** wie man sagen könnte; **having said that, that said** *(nevertheless)* abgesehen davon; **when all is said and done** letzten Endes; **~ what you 'like** du kannst sagen, was du willst; **though I ~ it myself ...:** wenn ich es mal selbst so sagen darf; **you can ~ 'that again, you 'said it** *(coll.)* das kannst du laut sagen *(ugs.);* **you don't '~ [so]** *(coll.)* was du nicht sagst *(ugs.);* **~s** *or* **said he** *etc.***/said I** *or (coll.)* **~s I** sagt er/*(ugs.)* sag' ich; **~s you** *(sl.)* wer's glaubt, wird selig *(ugs. scherzh.);* **~s who?** *(coll.)* wer sagt das?; **I'll ~ [it is]!** *(coll.: it certainly is)* und wie!; **don't let** *or* **never let it be said [that] ...:** niemand soll sagen können, [daß] ...; **they** *or* **people ~** *or* **it is said [that] ...:** man sagt, [daß] ...; **..., they ~:** ..., sagt man *od.* heißt es; **I can't ~ [that] I like cats/the idea** ich kann nicht gerade sagen *od.* behaupten, daß ich Katzen mag/die Idee gut finde; **what I [always] ~ is ...:** also, ich sage immer, ...; **[well,] I 'must ~:** also, ich muß schon sagen; **I should ~ so/not** ich glaube schon/nicht; *(emphatic)* bestimmt/bestimmt nicht; **Is it true that ...? – So she ~s** Stimmt es, daß ...? – Das sagt sie [jedenfalls]; **what have you got to ~ for yourself?** was haben Sie zu Ihren Gunsten zu sagen?; **there's a lot to be said for** *or* **in favour of/against sth.** es spricht viel für/gegen etw.; **there's something to be said on both sides/either side** man kann für beide Seiten/jede Seite Argumente anführen; **who can** *or* **who is to ~?** *(rhet.)* wer weiß das schon *od.* kann das schon sagen?; **I cannot** *or* **could not ~:** das kann ich nicht sagen; **I can't ~ fairer than that** ein besseres Angebot kann ich nicht machen; **he didn't ~:** er hat dazu *od.* darüber nichts gesagt; **I'd rather not ~:** ich möchte es lieber nicht sagen; **and so ~ all of us** der Meinung sind wir auch; **what do** *or* **would you ~ to sb./sth.?** *(think about)* was hältst du von jmdm./etw.?; was würdest du zu jmdm./etw. sagen?; **how ~ you?** *(Law)* wie lautet Ihr Urteil?; **[let us** *or* **shall we] ~:** sagen wir mal; **~ it were true, what then?** angenommen es stimmt, was dann?; *see also* **dare 1 a; hearsay; no 2 b; 'so 2; when 1 a; word 1 b; yes 1; b)** *(recite, repeat, speak words of)* sprechen ‹*Gebet, Text*›; aufsagen ‹*Einmaleins, Gedicht*›; lesen ‹*Messe*›; **c)** *(have specified wording or reading)* sagen; ‹*Zeitung:*› schreiben; ‹*Uhr:*› zeigen ‹*Uhrzeit*›; **the Bible ~s** *or* **it ~s in the Bible [that] ...:** in der Bibel heißt es, daß ...; die Bibel sagt, daß ...; **a sign ~ing ...:** ein Schild mit der Aufschrift ...; **what does it ~ here?** was steht hier?; **d)** *(express, convey information)* sagen; **~ things well/eloquently** sich gut/gewandt ausdrücken; **what I'm trying to ~ is this** was ich sagen will, ist folgendes; **his expression said it all** sein Gesichtsausdruck sagte alles; **a novel that really ~s something** ein Roman, der wirklich eine Aussage hat; **~ nothing to sb.** *(fig.)* ‹*Musik, Kunst:*› jmdm. nichts bedeuten; **which/that is not ~ing much** *or* **a lot** was nicht viel heißen will/das will nicht viel heißen; *see also* **soon b; e)** *(order)* sagen; **do as** *or* **what I ~:** tun Sie, was ich sage; **he said [to us] to be ready at ten** er hat gesagt, wir sollten um zehn fertig sein; **f)** *in pass.* **she is said to be clever/have done it** man sagt, sie sei klug/habe es getan; **a horse is said to be a pony when ...:** man bezeichnet ein Pferd als Pony, wenn ...; **the said Mr Smith** *(Law/joc.)* besagter Mr. Smith *(Papierdt., scherzh.);* **g) 215, ~ two hundred and fifteen** 215, in Worten: zweihundert[und]fünfzehn. **2.** *v. i.* **a)** *(speak)* sagen; **I ~!** *(Brit.) (seeking attention)* Entschuldigung!; *(admiring)* Donnerwetter!; *(dismayed)* ich fürchte; *(reproachful)* ich muß schon sagen!; **b)** *in imper. (poet.: tell)* sag an! *(veralt.);* **c)** *in imper. (Amer.)* Mensch! **3.** *n.* **a)** *(share in decision)* **have a** *or* **some ~:** ein Mitspracherecht haben **(in** bei); **have no ~:** nichts zu sagen haben; **b)** *(power of decision)* **the [final] ~:** das letzte Wort **(in** bei); **c)** *(what one has to say)* **have one's ~:** seine Meinung sagen; *(chance to speak)* **get one's** *or* **have a ~:** zu Wort kommen

SAYE *abbr. (Brit.)* **save-as-you-earn**

saying ['seɪɪŋ] *n.* **a)** *(maxim)* Redensart, *die;* **there is a ~ that ...:** wie es [im Sprichwort/in der Maxime] heißt, ...; **as the ~ goes** wie es so schön heißt; **b)** *(remark)* Ausspruch, *der;* **the ~s of Chairman Mao** die Worte des Vorsitzenden Mao; **c) there is no ~ what/why ...:** man kann nicht sagen, was/warum ...; **go without ~:** sich von selbst verstehen

'say-so *n.* **a)** *(power of decision)* **on/without sb.'s ~:** auf/ohne jmds. Anweisung *(Akk.);* **the final ~:** das letzte Wort; **b)** *(assertion)* **I won't believe it just on your ~:** das glaube ich dir nicht einfach so

sc. ['saɪlɪset] *abbr.* **scilicet** sc.; d. h.

scab [skæb] *n.* **a)** *(over wound, sore)* [Wund]schorf, *der;* **form a ~:** verschorfen; **be covered in ~s** mit Schorf bedeckt sein; **b)** *no pl. (skin-disease)* Räude, *die; (plant-disease)* Schorf, *der;* **c)** *(derog.: strike-breaker)* Streikbrecher, *der*/-brecherin, *die;* **use ~ labour** Streikbrecher einsetzen

scabbard ['skæbəd] *n.* Scheide, *die*

scabies ['skeɪbi:z] *n. (Med.)* Krätze, *die;* Skabies, *die (fachspr.)*

scabious ['skeɪbɪəs] *n. (Bot.)* Krätz[en]kraut, *das;* Skabiose, *die (fachspr.)*

scabrous ['skeɪbrəs] *adj.* **a)** *(requiring tact)* heikel ‹*Thema*›; **b)** *(indecent)* geschmacklos; **c)** *(Bot., Physiol., Zool.)* rauh

scads [skædz] *n. pl. (Amer. coll.)* **~ of money** *etc.* haufenweise Geld *usw. (ugs.)*

scaffold ['skæfəld] *n.* **a)** *(for execution)* Schafott, *das;* **go to the ~:** auf das Schafott kommen; **b)** *(for building)* Gerüst, *das*

scaffolding ['skæfəldɪŋ] *n., no pl.* Gerüst, *das; (materials)* Gerüstmaterial, *das;* **be surrounded by ~:** eingerüstet sein *(Bauw.);* **erect [a] ~ around** einrüsten *(Bauw.)*

'scaffolding-pole *n.* Gerüststange, *die*

scalar ['skeɪlə(r)] *(Math.)* **1.** *n.* Skalar, *der.* **2.** *adj.* skalar; Skalar-

scald [skɔ:ld, skɒld] **1.** *n.* Verbrühung, *die.* **2.** *v. t.* **a)** verbrühen; **~ oneself** *or* **one's skin** sich verbrühen; **be ~ed to death** tödliche Verbrühungen erleiden; **cry ~ing tears** heiße Tränen weinen; **~ing hot** brühheiß; **like a ~ed cat** wie von der Tarantel gestochen; **b)** *(Cookery)* erhitzen ‹*Milch*›; **c)** *(clean with boiling water)* auskochen; **d)** *(remove hair or feathers from)* [ab]brühen ‹*Schwein, Geflügel*›; *(remove skin from)* überbrühen ‹*Gemüse, Obst*›

[1]**scale** [skeɪl] **1.** *n.* **a)** Schuppe, *die; (of rust)* Flocke, *die;* **the ~s fall from sb.'s eyes** *(fig.)* es fällt jmdm. wie Schuppen von den Augen; **b)** *no pl. (deposit in kettles, boilers, etc.)* Kesselstein, *der; (on teeth)* Zahnstein, *der.* **2.** *v. t.* **a)** *(remove scales from)* [ab]schuppen ‹*Fisch*›; **b)** *(remove deposit from)* von Kesselstein befreien ‹*Kessel, Boiler*›; von Zahnstein befreien ‹*Zähne*›

[2]**scale** **1.** *n.* **a)** *in sing. or pl. (weighing-*

instrument) ~[s] Waage, *die;* **a pair** *or* **set of ~s** eine Waage; **bathroom/kitchen/letter ~[s]** Personen-/Küchen-/Briefwaage, *die;* **the ~s are evenly balanced** *(fig.)* die Chancen sind ausgewogen; **b)** *(dish of balance)* Waagschale, *die;* **tip** *or* **turn the ~[s]** *(fig.)* den Ausschlag geben; **tip** *or* **turn the ~[s] at 65 kilos** 65 Kilo wiegen *od.* auf die Waage bringen; **c)** *(Astrol.)* **the S~s** die Waage; *see also* **archer b. 2.** *v. t.* wiegen

[3]**scale 1.** *n.* **a)** *(series of degrees)* Skala, *die;* **the social ~:** die gesellschaftliche Stufenleiter; **b)** *(Mus.)* Tonleiter, *die;* **c)** *(dimensions)* Ausmaß, *das; (standard)* Richtschnur, *die;* **be on a small ~:** bescheidenen Umfang haben; **on a grand ~:** im großen Stil; **on a commercial ~:** gewerbsmäßig; **plan on a large ~:** in großem Rahmen planen; **on an international ~:** auf internationaler Ebene; ‹*Katastrophe*› von internationalem Ausmaß; **economies of ~:** Einsparungen durch Produktionserweiterung; **d)** *(ratio of reduction)* Maßstab, *der; attrib.* maßstab[s]gerecht ‹*Modell, Zeichnung*›; **what is the ~ of the map?** welchen Maßstab hat diese Karte?; **a map with a ~ of 1:250,000** eine Karte im Maßstab 1:250000; **on a large/small ~:** in großem/kleinem Maßstab; **to ~:** maßstab[s]gerecht; **be drawn on** *or* **to a ~ of 1:2** im Maßstab 1:2 gezeichnet sein; **be in ~:** maßstab[s]getreu sein; **be in ~ with sth.** im Maßstab zu etw. passen; **be out of ~:** im Maßstab nicht passen **(with** zu); **e)** *(indication) (on map, plan)* Maßstab, *der; (on thermometer, ruler, exposure meter)* [Anzeige]skala, *die; (instrument)* Meßstab, *der;* **what ~ are these temperatures measured in?** nach welcher [Einheiten]skala werden diese Temperaturen gemessen?; **a ruler marked off in the metric ~:** ein Lineal mit Zentimeterskala; **f)** *(Math.)* **~ [of notation]** Positionssystem, *das;* **decimal ~:** Dezimalsystem, *das;* **binary ~:** Dualsystem, *das;* Binärsystem, *das.* **2.** *v. t.* **a)** *(climb, clamber up)* ersteigen ‹*Festung, Mauer, Leiter, Gipfel*›; erklettern ‹*Felswand, Leiter, Gipfel*›; **b)** *(represent in proportion)* [ab]stufen, staffeln ‹*Fahrpreise*›; maßstab[s]gerecht anfertigen ‹*Zeichnung*›; **~ production/prices to demand** die Produktion/Preise an die Nachfrage anpassen

~ 'down *v. t.* [entsprechend] drosseln ‹*Produktion*›; [entsprechende] Abstriche machen an (+ *Dat.*) ‹*Ideen*›; **a ~d down version** eine kleinere Version

~ 'up *v. t.* [entsprechend] vergrößern ‹*Umfang, Ausmaß*›; **a ~d up version** eine größere Version

scalene ['skeɪli:n] *adj. (Geom.)* ungleichseitig ‹*Dreieck*›

'scale-pan *n.* Waagschale, *die*

scaling-ladder ['skeɪlɪŋlædə(r)] *n.* Sturmleiter, *die; (of fire-engine)* Feuer[wehr]leiter, *die*

scallion ['skæljən] *n. (Bot.)* **a)** *see* **shallot; b)** *(spring onion)* Frühlingszwiebel, *die*

scallop ['skæləp, 'skɒləp] **1.** *n.* **a)** *in pl. (ornamental edging)* Feston, *das;* Bogenkante, *die;* **b)** *(Zool.)* Kammuschel, *die; (Gastr.)* Jakobsmuschel, *die;* **c)** *(Cookery: pan)* muschelförmige Schale. **2.** *v. t.* festonieren

scallop-'edge *n.* Bogenkante, *die*

scalloping ['skæləpɪŋ, 'skɒləpɪŋ] *n.* Feston, *das;* **be decorated with ~:** festoniert sein

'scallop-shell *n.* Kammuschel[schale], *die*

scallywag ['skælɪwæg] *n.* Schlingel, *der (scherzh.);* Tunichtgut, *der*

scalp [skælp] **1.** *n.* **a)** Kopfhaut, *die;* **b)** *(war-trophy)* Skalp, *der; (fig.)* Trophäe, *die;* **be after sb.'s ~** *(fig.)* jmdm. an den Kragen wollen; **the newspapers call for ~s** *(fig.)* die Zeitungen wollen Köpfe rollen sehen. **2.** *v. t.* **a)** skalpieren; **b)** *(criticize)* kein gutes Haar lassen an (+ *Dat.*) *(ugs.)* ‹*Person, Buch*›; **c)** *(Amer.) (defeat)* vernichtend schlagen, fertigmachen *(ugs.)* ‹*Partei, Gegner*›; **d)** *(Amer. coll.: sell)* mit hohem Gewinn weiterverkaufen ‹*Aktien, Eintrittskarte*›; **get ~ed tickets** Karten auf dem Schwarzmarkt bekommen

scalpel ['skælpl] *n. (Med.)* Skalpell, *das*

scalper ['skælpə(r)] *n. (Amer. coll.)* kleiner Spekulant/kleine Spekulantin; *(ticket-tout)* [Karten]schwarzhändler, *der*/-händlerin, *die*

scaly ['skeɪlɪ] *adj.* **a)** schuppig; abblätternd ‹*Farbe, Rost*›; **be ~** ‹*Schlange:*› eine schuppige Haut haben; **b)** *(covered in deposit)* mit Kesselstein überzogen; *(covered in tartar)* mit Zahnstein überzogen; **c)** *(forming deposit)* **~ substance** *or* **incrustation** Kesselstein, *der;* Wasserstein, *der*

scam [skæm] *n. (Amer. sl.)* Masche, *die (ugs.)*

scamp [skæmp] **1.** *n. (derog./joc.)* Spitzbube, *der (abwertend/fam.).* **2.** *v. t. see* **skimp 1**

scamper ['skæmpə(r)] **1.** *v. i.* ‹*Person:*› flitzen; ‹*Tier:*› huschen; *(hop)* hoppeln; **the mice ~ed to and fro** die Mäuse huschten hin und her; **~ down the stairs** die Treppe hinunterflitzen; *(romp)* **~ through the woods/park** durch die Wälder/den Park tollen. **2.** *n.* **have a ~** *(romp)* herumtollen

scampi ['skæmpɪ] *n. pl.* Scampi *Pl.*

scan [skæn] **1.** *v. t.*, **-nn- a)** *(examine intensely)* [genau] studieren; *(search thoroughly, lit. or fig.)* absuchen **(for** nach); **b)** *(look over cursorily)* flüchtig ansehen; überfliegen ‹*Zeitung, Liste usw.*› **(for** auf der Suche nach); **c)** *(examine for radioactivity)* auf Radioaktivität *(Akk.)* untersuchen; **d)** *(examine with beam)* durchleuchten ‹*Gepäck*›; ‹*Radar:*› [mittels Strahlen] abtasten ‹*Luftraum*›; ‹*Flugsicherung:*› [mittels Radar] überwachen ‹*Luftraum*›; **e)** *(Med.)* szintigraphisch untersuchen ‹*Körper, Organ*›; **f)** *(Pros.)* das Metrum bestimmen von ‹*Vers[zeile]*›; **g)** *(Telev.)* abtasten ‹*Ziel, Bild*›. **2.** *v. i.*, **-nn-** ‹*Vers[zeile]:*› das richtige Versmaß haben; **make sth. ~:** etw. in das richtige Versmaß bringen. **3.** *n.* **a)** *(thorough search)* Absuchen, *das;* **b)** *(quick look)* **[cursory] ~:** flüchtiger Blick; **do a quick ~ of** *or* **through** überfliegen, flüchtig durchblättern ‹*Zeitung*›; **c)** *(examination for radioactivity)* Untersuchung auf Radioaktivität *(Akk.)*; **d)** *(examination by beam)* Durchleuchtung, *die;* **check the radar ~ for sth.** den Radarschirm nach etw. absuchen; **e)** *(Med.)* szintigraphische Untersuchung; **body-/brain-~:** Ganzkörper-/Gehirnscan, *der;* **have a ~:** sich szintigraphisch untersuchen lassen

scandal ['skændl] *n.* **a)** Skandal, *der* **(about/of** um); *(story)* Skandalgeschichte, *die;* **b)** *(outrage)* Empörung, *die;* **arouse a feeling** *or* **sense of ~ in sb.** jmdn. mit Empörung erfüllen; **c)** *no art. (damage to reputation)* Schande, *die;* **be untouched by ~:** einen makellosen Ruf haben; **be ruined by ~:** durch einen Skandal ruiniert werden; **d)** *(malicious gossip)* Klatsch, *der (ugs.); (in newspapers etc.)* Skandalgeschichten

scandalize (scandalise) ['skændəlaɪz] *v. t.* schockieren

scandalmonger ['skændlmʌŋgə(r)] *n.* Klatschmaul, *das (salopp abwertend); (in the press)* Schreiber/Schreiberin von Skandalgeschichten

scandalmongering ['skændlmʌŋgərɪŋ] *n.* Verbreitung von Skandalgeschichten

scandalous ['skændələs] *adj.* skandalös; schockierend ‹*Bemerkung*›; Skandal‹*blatt, -presse, -geschichte, -bericht*›; **how ~!** unerhört!; **this is ~:** das ist ein Skandal

'scandal sheet *n. (derog.)* Skandalblatt, *das (abwertend);* Klatschblatt, *das (ugs. abwertend)*

Scandinavia [skændɪ'neɪvɪə] *pr. n.* Skandinavien *(das)*

Scandinavian [skændɪ'neɪvɪən] **1.** *adj.* skandinavisch; **sb. is ~:** jmd. ist Skandinavier/Skandinavierin. **2.** *n.* **a)** *(person)* Skandinavier, *der*/Skandinavierin, *die;* **b)** *(Ling.)* skandinavische Sprachen

scanner ['skænə(r)] *n.* **a)** *(to detect radioactivity)* Geigerzähler, *der;* **b)** *(radar aerial)* Radarantenne, *die;* **c)** *(Med.)* [Szinti]scanner, *der;* **d)** *(Telev.)* Bildabtaster, *der*

scansion ['skænʃn] *n. (Pros.)* metrische Gliederung; *(rhythm analysis)* Bestimmung des Versmaßes

scant [skænt] *adj. (arch./literary)* karg *(geh.)* ‹*Lob, Lohn*›; wenig ‹*Rücksicht*›; **pay sb./sth. ~ attention** jmdn./etw. kaum beachten; **a ~ two hours** knappe zwei Stunden

scantily ['skæntɪlɪ] *adv.* kärglich; spärlich ‹*bekleidet*›

scanty ['skæntɪ] *adj.* spärlich; knapp ‹*Bikini*›; nur wenig ‹*Vergnügen, Spaß*›

scapegoat ['skeɪpgəʊt] *n.* Sündenbock, *der;* **make sb. a ~:** jmdn. zum Sündenbock machen; **act as** *or* **be a ~ for sth.** als Sündenbock für etw. herhalten müssen

scapegrace ['skeɪpgreɪs] *n.* Taugenichts, *der*

scapula ['skæpjʊlə] *n., pl.* **~e** ['skæpjʊli:] *(Anat.)* Schulterblatt, *das*

scar [skɑ:(r)] **1.** *n. (lit. or fig.)* Narbe, *die;* **duelling ~:** Schmiß, *der;* **battle ~:** Kriegsnarbe, *die;* **bear the ~s of sth.** *(fig.)* von etw. gezeichnet sein; **be a ~ on the landscape** *(fig.)* ein Schandfleck in der Landschaft sein. **2.** *v. t.*, **-rr-: ~ sb./sb.'s face** bei jmdm./in jmds. Gesicht *(Dat.)* Narben hinterlassen; **~ sb. for life** *(fig.)* jmdn. für sein ganzes Leben zeichnen; **leave sb. [badly] ~red** *(lit. or fig.)* [schlimme] Narben bei jmdm. hinterlassen. **3.** *v. i.* **~ over** vernarben

scarab ['skærəb] *n. (Zool., gem)* Skarabäus, *der*

scarce [skeəs] **1.** *adj.* **a)** *(insufficient)* knapp; **b)** *(rare)* selten; **make oneself ~** *(coll.)* sich aus dem Staub machen *(ugs.).* **2.** *adv. (arch./literary)* kaum

scarcely ['skeəslɪ] *adv.* kaum; **there was ~ a drop of wine left** es war fast kein Tropfen Wein mehr da; **~ [ever]** kaum [jemals]; **it is ~ likely** es ist wenig wahrscheinlich; **she will ~ be pleased** *(iron.: by no means)* sie wird sich nicht gerade freuen

scarceness ['skeəsnɪs] *n., no pl.* Knappheit, *die* **(of** an + *Dat.*)

scarcity ['skeəsɪtɪ] *n.* **a)** *(short supply)* Knappheit, *die* **(of** an + *Dat.*); **there is a ~ of sugar** es herrscht Zuckerknappheit; **~ of teachers** Lehrermangel, *der;* **food ~:** Lebensmittelknappheit, *die;* **b)** *no pl. (rareness)* Seltenheit, *die;* **have [a] ~ value** Seltenheitswert haben

scare [skeə(r)] **1.** *n.* **a)** *(sensation of fear)* Schreck[en], *der;* **give sb. a ~:** jmdm. einen Schreck[en] einjagen; **I had/it gave me a [nasty] ~:** ich bekam einen [bösen] Schrecken; **b)** *(general alarm; panic)* [allgemeine] Hysterie; **bomb ~:** Bombendrohung, *die;* **food-poisoning ~:** Alarm wegen Lebensmittelvergiftung; **~ story** Schauergeschichte, *die.* **2.** *v. t.* **a)** *(frighten)* Angst machen (+ *Dat.*); *(startle)* erschrecken; **he/hard work/your threat doesn't ~ me** ich habe keine Angst vor ihm/harter Arbeit/deiner Drohung; **~ sb. into doing sth.** jmdn. dazu bringen, etw. [aus Angst] zu tun; **~ sb. out of his mind** *or* **skin** *or* **wits** *(fig.)*, **~ sb. rigid** *or* **silly** *or* **stiff** *(fig.)*, **~ the wits** *or* *(coarse)* **the shit out of sb.** *(fig.)* jmdm. eine wahnsinnige Angst einjagen *(ugs.); (startle)* jmdn. zu Tode erschrecken; **horror films ~ the pants off me** *(coll.)* bei Horrorfilmen habe ich immer eine wahnsinnige Angst *(ugs.)*; **b)** *(drive away)* verscheuchen ‹*Vögel*›. **3.** *v. i.* erschrecken **(at** bei); ‹*Pferd:*› scheuen **(at** vor + *Dat.*); **~ easily** sich leicht erschrecken lassen

~ **a'way** *v. t.* verscheuchen
~ **'off** *v. t.* verscheuchen
~ **'out,** ~ **'up** *v. t. (Amer.: Hunting, fig.)* aufstöbern ‹*Wild, Gegenstand*›; auftreiben *(ugs.)* ‹*etw. zu essen, Informationen*›
scare: ~**-buying** *n. (Amer.)* Hamsterkäufe *Pl.;* ~**crow** *n. (lit. or fig.)* Vogelscheuche, *die*
scared [skeəd] *adj.* verängstigt ‹*Gesicht, Stimme*›; **be/feel [very]** ~: [große] Angst haben; **be** ~ **of sb./sth.** vor jmdm./etw. Angst haben; **be** ~ **of doing/to do sth.** sich nicht [ge]trauen, etw. zu tun; **be** ~ **[that] sth. might happen** befürchten, daß etw. passieren könnte
scaremonger ['skeəmʌŋgə(r)] *n.* Panikmacher, *der*/-macherin, *die (abwertend)*
'scare tactics *n. pl.* ≈ Panikmache, *die (ugs.)*
scarf [skɑ:f] *n., pl.* ~**s** *or* **scarves** [skɑ:vz] Schal, *der; (triangular/square piece of fine material)* Halstuch, *das; (worn over hair)* Kopftuch, *das; (worn over shoulders)* Schultertuch, *das*
scarf: ~**-pin** *n. (Brit.)* Vorstecknadel, *die;* Halstuchnadel, *die;* ~**-ring** *n. (Brit.)* Halstuchring, *der*
[1]**scarify** ['skærɪfaɪ, 'skeərɪfaɪ] *v. t.* **a)** *(Med.)* skarifizieren *(fachspr.);* anritzen; **b)** *(fig.: by criticism)* geißeln; **c)** *(Agric.)* auflockern ‹*Boden*›; *(Constr.)* aufreißen ‹*Straße*›
[2]**scarify** ['skeərɪfaɪ] *v. t. (coll.: frighten)* Angst machen (+ *Dat.*); ~**ing** beängstigend
scarlatina [skɑ:lə'ti:nə] *see* **scarlet fever**
scarlet ['skɑ:lɪt] **1.** *n.* Scharlach, *der;* Scharlachrot, *das.* **2.** *adj.* scharlachrot; **I turned** ~: ich wurde puterrot; *see also* **pimpernel**
scarlet: ~ **'fever** *n. (Med.)* Scharlach, *der;* ~ **'runner** *n. (Bot.)* Feuerbohne, *die*
scarp [skɑ:p] *n.* Steilhang, *der*
scarper ['skɑ:pə(r)] *v. i. (Brit. sl.)* abhauen *(salopp);* sich aus dem Staub machen *(ugs.)*
'scar tissue *n. (Med.)* Narbengewebe, *das*
scarves *pl. of* **scarf**
scary ['skeərɪ] *adj. (coll.)* **a)** *(frightening)* furchterregend ‹*Anblick*›; schaurig ‹*Film, Geschichte*›; angsteinflößend ‹*Person, Gesicht*›; **a** ~ **moment** eine Schrecksekunde; **it was** ~ **to listen to** beim Zuhören konnte man richtig Angst kriegen *(ugs.);* **b)** *(easily frightened)* schreckhaft ‹*Kind, Tier*›; *(timid)* ängstlich
scathing ['skeɪðɪŋ] *adj.* beißend ‹*Spott, Kritik*›; scharf ‹*Angriff*›; bissig ‹*Person, Humor, Bemerkung*›; **be** ~ **about sth.** etw. bissig herabsetzen *od. (ugs.)* heruntermachen
scathingly ['skeɪðɪŋlɪ] *adv.* scharf ‹*kritisieren*›; bissig ‹*sagen, bemerken*›
scatological [skætə'lɒdʒɪkl] *adj.* **a)** *(obscene)* obszön; ~ **language** Fäkalsprache, *die;* **b)** *(Med., Palaeont.)* skatologisch
scatter ['skætə(r)] **1.** *v. t.* **a)** vertreiben; zerstreuen, auseinandertreiben ‹*Menge*›; zunichte machen ‹*Hoffnungen*›; **he slammed his fist on the table,** ~**ing china everywhere** er schlug mit der Faust auf den Tisch, daß das Porzellan in alle Richtungen flog; **b)** *(distribute irregularly)* verstreuen; ausstreuen ‹*Samen*›; **ice-cream with nuts** ~**ed on top** mit Nüssen bestreutes Eis; **c)** *(partly cover)* [be]streuen ‹*Straße*›; ~ **a field with seeds** Samen auf einem Feld ausstreuen. **2.** *v. i.* sich auflösen; ‹*Menge:*› sich zerstreuen; *(in fear)* auseinanderstieben. **3.** *n.* **a)** *see* ~**ing a; b)** *(Arms)* Streuung, *die*
scatter: ~**-brain** *n.* zerstreuter Mensch; Schussel, *der (ugs.);* ~**-brained** *adj.* zerstreut; schusselig *(ugs.);* ~ **cushion** *n.* Sofakissen, *das*
scattered ['skætəd] *adj.* verstreut; vereinzelt ‹*Fälle, Anzeichen, Regenschauer*›; **thinly** ~ **population** verstreut lebende Bevölkerung
scattering ['skætərɪŋ] *n.* **a)** *(small amount)* **a** ~ **of people/customers/letters** ein paar vereinzelte Leute/Kunden/Briefe; **add a** ~ **of nuts to sth.** Nüsse auf etw. *(Akk.)* streuen; **a thin** ~ **of snow** eine dünne Schneedecke; **b)** *(Phys.)* Streuung, *die*
scatter: ~ **rug** *n.* Brücke, *die;* ~**-shot** *(Amer.)* **1.** *n.* Streupatrone, *die;* **2.** *adj.* willkürlich
scatty ['skætɪ] *adj. (Brit. sl.)* dußlig *(salopp);* **drive sb.** ~: jmdn. verrückt machen *(ugs.)*
scavenge ['skævɪndʒ] **1.** *v. t.* **a)** sich *(Dat.)* holen; ~ **sth. from a jumble sale** etw. auf einem Flohmarkt ergattern; **b)** *(search)* durchstöbern **(for** nach); absuchen ‹*Strand*›; fleddern ‹*Leiche*›. **2.** *v. i.* ~ **for sth.** nach etw. suchen; **live by scavenging** ‹*Geier:*› Aasfresser sein; ~ **through** durchstöbern *(ugs.)* ‹*Abfallhaufen*›
scavenger ['skævɪndʒə(r)] *n. (animal)* Aasfresser, *der; (fig. derog.: person)* Aasgeier, *der (ugs. abwertend)*
scenario [sɪ'nɑ:rɪəʊ, sɪ'neərɪəʊ] *n., pl.* ~**s** *(Theatre, Cinemat.; also fig.)* Szenario, *das*
scene [si:n] *n.* **a)** *(place of event)* Schauplatz, *der; (in novel, play, etc.)* Ort der Handlung; **the** ~ **of the novel is set in Venice** der Roman spielt in Venedig; ~ **of the crime** Ort des Verbrechens; Tatort, *der;* **b)** *(portion of play, film, or book)* Szene, *die; (division of act)* Auftritt, *der;* **love/trial** ~: Liebes-/Gerichtsszene, *die;* **steal the** ~ ‹*Schauspieler:*› die Szene beherrschen; *(fig.)* sich in den Vordergrund spielen; **c)** *(display of passion, anger, jealousy)* Szene, *die;* **create** *or* **make a** ~: eine Szene machen; **there were** ~**s of rejoicing** es spielten sich Freudenszenen ab; **end in violent** ~**s** mit Gewalttätigkeiten enden; **d)** *(view)* Anblick, *der; (as depicted)* Aussicht, *die;* **present a** ~ **of horror** ein Bild des Schreckens bieten *(geh.);* **change of** ~: Tapetenwechsel, *der (ugs.);* **e)** *(place of action)* Ort des Geschehens; **arrive** *or* **come on the** ~: auftauchen; **a new political party has appeared on the** ~: eine neue Partei ist auf den Plan getreten; **he got into a bad** ~ *(sl.)* er ist ins Schleudern gekommen *(salopp);* **leave** *or* **quit the** ~: abtreten; **f)** *(field of action)* **the political/drug/artistic** ~: die politische/Drogen-/Kunstszene; **the fashion/sporting** ~: die Modewelt/die Welt des Sports; **the social** ~: das gesellschaftliche Leben; **g)** *(sl.: area of interest)* **what's your** ~**?** worauf stehst du? *(ugs.);* worauf fährst du ab? *(salopp);* **that's not my** ~: das ist nicht mein Fall *(ugs.);* **h)** *(Theatre: set)* Bühnenbild, *das;* **change the** ~: die Kulissen auswechseln; **behind the** ~**s** *(lit. or fig.)* hinter den Kulissen; **behind-the-**~**s investigation** *(fig.)* geheime Untersuchung; **give a behind-the-**~**s glimpse [of sth.]** einen Blick hinter die Kulissen [einer Sache *(Gen.)*] gewähren; **set the** ~ **[for sb.]** *(fig.)* [jmdm.] die Ausgangssituation darlegen
'scene: ~**-change** *n. (Theatre)* Kulissenwechsel, *der;* ~**-painter** *n.* Kulissenmaler, *der*/-malerin, *die*
scenery ['si:nərɪ] *n., no pl.* **a)** *(Theatre)* Bühnenbild, *das;* **b)** *(landscape)* Landschaft, *die; (picturesque)* [malerische] Landschaft; **mountain** ~: Gebirgslandschaft, *die;* **some beautiful** ~: einige schöne Landstriche; **change of** ~: Tapetenwechsel, *der (ugs.)*
scene: ~**-shifter** *n. (Theatre)* Bühnenarbeiter, *der*/-arbeiterin, *die;* ~**-shifting** *n. (Theatre)* Kulissenwechsel, *der*
scenic ['si:nɪk] *adj.* **a)** *(with fine natural scenery)* landschaftlich schön; **a** ~ **drive** eine Fahrt durch schöne Landschaft; ~ **beauty** *or* **qualities** landschaftliche Schönheit; ~ **railway** Berg-und-Tal-Bahn, *die;* **b)** *(Theatre)* Bühnen-; **be a** ~ **designer** Bühnenbildner/-bildnerin sein; **c)** *(Art: in painting etc.)* szenisch
scent [sent] **1.** *n.* **a)** *(smell)* Duft, *der; (fig.)* [Vor]ahnung, *die;* **catch the** ~ **of sth.** den Duft von etw. in die Nase bekommen; **b)** *(Hunting; also fig.: trail)* Fährte, *die;* **get/be on the [right]** ~ *(lit. or fig.)* die richtige Fährte finden/auf der richtigen Fährte sein; **be on the** ~ **of sb./sth.** *(fig.)* jmdm./einer Sache auf der Spur sein; **[lay** *or* **set] a false** ~ *(lit. or fig.)* eine falsche Fährte [legen]; **put the hounds on/off the** ~: die Hunde auf die Fährte setzen/von der Fährte abbringen; **put** *or* **throw sb. off the** ~ *(fig.)* jmdn. auf eine falsche Fährte bringen; **put sb. on the** ~ **of sb./sth.** *(fig.)* jmdn. auf jmds. Spur bringen/einer Sache *(Dat.)* auf die Spur bringen; *see also* **cold 1 k; hot 1 i; c)** *(Brit.: perfume)* Parfüm, *das;* **d)** *(sense of smell)* Geruchssinn, *der; (fig.: power to detect)* Spürsinn, *der.* **2.** *v. t.* **a)** *(lit. or fig.)* wittern; spüren ‹*Heuchelei*›; ‹*Tier:*› beriechen *(ugs.),* beschnuppern ‹*Boden*›; **b)** *(apply perfume to)* parfümieren
~ **'out** *v. t. (lit. or fig.)* aufspüren
'scent-bottle *n. (Brit.)* Parfümfläschchen, *das*
scented ['sentɪd] *adj.* **a)** *(having smell)* duftend; **be** ~ ‹*Blume:*› duften; ~ **air** von Düften erfüllte Luft; **b)** *(perfumed)* parfümiert
'scent-gland *n. (Zool.)* Duftdrüse, *die*
scentless ['sentlɪs] *adj.* geruchlos; ‹*Blume*› ohne Duft; **be** ~: nicht duften
scepsis ['skepsɪs] *n., no pl. (Philos.)* Skepsis, *die*
scepter *(Amer.) see* **sceptre**
sceptic ['skeptɪk] *n.* Skeptiker, *der*/Skeptikerin, *die; (with religious doubts)* [Glaubens]zweifler, *der*/-zweiflerin, *die*
sceptical ['skeptɪkl] *adj.* skeptisch; **be** ~ **about** *or* **of sb./sth.** jmdm./einer Sache skeptisch gegenüberstehen
sceptically ['skeptɪkəlɪ] *adv.* skeptisch
scepticism ['skeptɪsɪzm] *n.* Skepsis, *die; (Philos.)* Skeptizismus, *der; (religious doubt)* Glaubenszweifel *Pl.*
sceptre ['septə(r)] *n. (Brit.; lit. or fig.)* Zepter, *das*
schedule ['ʃedju:l] **1.** *n.* **a)** *(list)* Tabelle, *die; (for event, festival)* Programm, *das;* **b)** *(plan of procedure)* Zeitplan, *der;* **filming** ~: Drehplan, *der;* **we are working to a tight** ~: unsere Termine sind sehr eng; **go** *or* **happen [according] to** ~: nach Plan laufen; **c)** *(set of tasks)* Terminplan, *der;* Programm, *das;* **work/study** ~: Arbeits-/Studienplan, *der;* **a heavy work** ~: ein umfangreiches Arbeitspensum; **d)** *(tabulated statement)* Aufstellung, *die; (appendix)* tabellarischer Anhang; *(blank form)* Formblatt, *das;* **[tax]** ~: Steuertabelle, *die;* **e)** *(timetable)* Fahrplan, *der;* **f)** *(time stated in plan)* **on** ~: programmgemäß; **arrive on** ~: pünktlich ankommen; **flight** ~**s** Ankunfts- und Abflugzeiten; **bus/train** ~**s** Ankunfts- und Abfahrtszeiten der Busse/Züge; *see also* **ahead c; behind 2 e. 2.** *v. t.* **a)** *(make plan of)* zeitlich planen; *(appoint to be done)* anberaumen ‹*Sitzung*›; **be** ~**d for Thursday** für Donnerstag geplant sein; **we are** ~**d to start next week** laut Plan sollen wir nächste Woche anfangen; **they have** ~**d the building for demolition** nach ihren Plänen soll das Gebäude abgerissen werden; **b)** *(make timetable of)* einen Fahrplan aufstellen für; *(include in timetable)* in den Fahrplan aufnehmen; **trains which are** ~**d to run at a given time** Züge, die zu einer bestimmten Zeit fahren sollen; **c)** *(make list of)* auflisten; *(include in list)* aufführen **(in** in + *Dat.*); *(Brit.: to be preserved)* unter Denkmalschutz stellen ‹*Gebäude*›
scheduled ['ʃedju:ld] *adj.* **a)** *(according to timetable)* [fahr]planmäßig ‹*Zug, Halt*›; flugplanmäßig ‹*Zwischenlandung*›; Linien- ‹*flugzeug, -dienst, -maschine*›; ~ **flight** Linienflug, *der;* **make a** ~ **stop** ‹*Flugzeug:*›

planmäßig zwischenlanden; **b)** *(Brit.: in list of protected buildings)* unter Denkmalschutz stehend
schematic [skɪˈmætɪk, skiːˈmætɪk] *adj.*, **schematically** [skɪˈmætɪkəlɪ, skiːˈmætɪkəlɪ] *adv.* schematisch
schematize (schematise) [ˈskiːmətaɪz] *v. t.* schematisieren (**into** zu)
scheme [skiːm] **1.** *n.* **a)** *(arrangement)* Anordnung, *die;* **general ~ of things** allgemeine Gegebenheiten; *see also* **colour scheme; b)** *(table of classification, outline)* Schema, *das;* **~ [of study]** *(syllabus)* Studienprogramm, *das;* **c)** *(plan)* Programm, *das; (project)* Projekt, *das;* **pension ~:** Altersversorgung, *die;* **d)** *(dishonest plan)* Intrige, *die;* **~ of revenge** Racheplan, *der;* **what ~ are you plotting?** was führst du im Schilde? **2.** *v. i.* Pläne schmieden; **~ for sb.'s downfall/to assassinate sb.** jmds. Sturz/ein Attentat auf jmdn. planen. **3.** *v. t.* im Schilde führen
schemer [ˈskiːmə(r)] *n.* Intrigant, *der*/Intrigantin, *die;* **your sister is a real little ~:** deine Schwester ist ein raffiniertes kleines Biest *(ugs.)*
scheming [ˈskiːmɪŋ] **1.** *n., no pl., no indef. art.* Winkelzüge *Pl.;* Machenschaften *Pl.;* **be given to ~:** gern intrigieren. **2.** *adj.* intrigant; **be a ~ person, have a ~ nature** gern intrigieren
scherzo [ˈskeətsəʊ] *n., pl.* **~s** *(Mus.)* Scherzo, *das*
schilling [ˈʃɪlɪŋ] *n.* Schilling, *der*
schism [ˈsɪzm, ˈskɪzm] *n.* **a)** *(Eccl.)* Schisma, *das;* **b)** *(in any group)* Spaltung, *die*
schismatic [sɪzˈmætɪk, skɪzˈmætɪk] *adj. (Eccl.)* schismatisch
schist [ʃɪst] *n. (Geol.)* Schiefer, *der*
schizo [ˈskɪtsəʊ] *(coll.)* **1.** *n., pl.* **~s** Schizophrene, *der/die.* **2.** *adj.* schizophren
schizoid [ˈskɪtsɔɪd] *(Psych.)* **1.** *adj.* schizoid. **2.** *n.* Schizoide, *der/die;* **be a ~:** schizoid sein
schizophrenia [skɪtsəˈfriːnɪə] *n. (Psych.)* Schizophrenie, *die*
schizophrenic [skɪtsəˈfrenɪk, skɪtsəˈfriːnɪk] *(Psych.; also fig. coll.)* **1.** *adj.* schizophren; ⟨*Symptom*⟩ der Schizophrenie. **2.** *n.* Schizophrene, *der/die*
schlock [ʃlɒk] *n. (coll.)* Mist, *der (fig.)*
schmaltz [ʃmɔːlts] *n. (coll.)* Schmalz, *der (ugs. abwertend)*
schmaltzy [ˈʃmɔːltsɪ] *adj. (coll.)* schmalzig *(abwertend)*
schmuck [ʃmʌk] *n. (esp. Amer. sl.)* Schwachkopf, *der (abwertend)*
schnapps [ʃnæps] *n.* Schnaps, *der*
schnauzer [ˈʃnaʊtsə(r)] *n.* Schnauzer, *der*
schnitzel [ˈʃnɪtsl] *n. (Gastr.)* [Kalbs]schnitzel, *das*
schnorkel [ˈʃnɔːkl] *see* **snorkel**
scholar [ˈskɒlə(r)] *n.* **a)** *(learned person)* Gelehrte, *der/die;* **literary/linguistic/musical ~:** Literatur-/Sprach-/Musikwissenschaftler *der*/-wissenschaftlerin, *die;* **Shakespeare[an] ~:** Shakespeare-Forscher, *der*/-Forscherin, *die;* **be a ~ in one's field** Experte/Expertin auf seinem/ihrem Gebiet sein; **b)** *(one who learns)* Schüler, *der*/Schülerin, *die;* **be no ~:** kein guter Schüler/keine gute Schülerin sein; **c)** *(holder of scholarship)* Stipendiat, *der*/Stipendiatin, *die*
scholarly [ˈskɒləlɪ] *adj.* wissenschaftlich; *(having much learning)* gelehrt; **a ~ life** ein Gelehrtenleben; **he has a ~ appearance** er hat das Aussehen eines Gelehrten
scholarship [ˈskɒləʃɪp] *n.* **a)** *(payment for education)* Stipendium, *das;* **closed ~:** *Stipendium, das nur bestimmten Bewerbern gewährt wird;* **open ~:** *Stipendium, um das sich jeder bewerben kann;* **b)** *no pl. (scholarly work)* Gelehrsamkeit, *die (geh.); (methods)* Wissenschaftlichkeit, *die;* **a work full of ~:** ein hochwissenschaftliches Werk; **c)** *no pl. (body of learning)* **literary/linguistic/historical ~:** Literatur-/Sprach-/Geschichtswissenschaft, *die;* **contribute to Shakespearean/Romance ~:** einen Beitrag zur Shakespeare-Forschung/Romanistik leisten
scholastic [skəˈlæstɪk] *adj.* **a)** akademisch; Akademiker⟨*familie, -milieu*⟩; wissenschaftlich ⟨*Buchhandlung, Leistung, Standard*⟩; **b)** *(Philos., Theol.)* scholastisch
scholasticism [skəˈlæstɪsɪzm] *n.* **a)** Scholastizismus, *der;* **b)** *(Philos., Theol.)* Scholastik, *die*
[1]**school** [skuːl] **1.** *n.* **a)** Schule, *die; (Amer.: university, college)* Hochschule, *die; attrib.* Schul-; **what do they teach them in ~s?** was lernen sie in der Schule?; **be at** *or* **in ~:** in der Schule sein; *(attend ~)* zur Schule gehen; **be kept in ~ [late]** nachsitzen müssen; **to/from ~:** zur/von *od.* aus der Schule; **go to ~:** zur Schule gehen; **leave ~:** die Schule verlassen; **have ~:** Schule *od.* Unterricht haben; **have time off ~:** schulfrei haben; **be absent from ~:** in der Schule fehlen; **one hour before/after ~:** eine Stunde vor Unterrichtsbeginn/nach Schulschluß; **there will be no ~ today** heute ist keine Schule; **the ~ of life** *(fig.)* die Schule des Lebens; **~ is fun/boring** Schule macht Spaß/ist langweilig; **my first day of ~, the day I started ~:** mein erster Schultag; **b)** *attrib.* Schul⟨*arzt, -aufsatz, -bus, -bibliothek, -gebäude, -jahr, -orchester, -system*⟩; **~ holidays** Schulferien *Pl.;* **~ exchange** Schüleraustausch, *der;* **the ~ term** die Schulzeit; **take ~ meals** in der Schule [zu Mittag] essen; **the ~ caretaker** der Hausmeister der Schule; **my rusty ~ French** mein eingerostetes Schulfranzösisch; **c)** *(disciples)* Schule, *die;* **~ of thought** Lehrmeinung, *die; see also* **old 1 c, f; d)** *(Brit.: group of gamblers)* Runde, *die;* **e)** *(Univ.: department)* Institut, *das;* **~ of history** Institut für Zeitgeschichte; **law/medical ~:** juristische/medizinische Fakultät. **2.** *v. t.* **a)** *(send to ~)* einschulen; **b)** *(train)* erziehen; dressieren ⟨*Pferd*⟩; **~ sb. in sth.** jmdn. in etw. *(Akk.)* unterweisen *(geh.)*
[2]**school** *n. (of fish)* Schwarm, *der;* Schule, *die (Zool.)*
school: ~ age *n.* Schulalter, *das;* **children of ~ age** Kinder im schulpflichtigen Alter; **~-bag** *n.* Schultasche, *die;* **~-board** *n. (Amer./Hist.)* [örtliche] Schulbehörde; **~-book** *n.* Schulbuch, *das;* **~boy** *n.* Schüler, *der; (with reference to behaviour)* Schuljunge, *der;* **every ~boy knows that** das weiß jeder Schuljunge; **~boyish** *adj.* schuljungenhaft; **~child** *n.* Schulkind, *das;* **~-days** *n. pl.* Schulzeit, *die*
schooled [skuːld] *adj.* geschult ⟨*Pferd*⟩; **be [highly] ~ in sth.** [ausgezeichnet] Bescheid wissen über etw. *(Akk.)*
school: ~ fees *n. pl.* Schulgeld, *das;* **~fellow** *n.* Mitschüler, *der*/-schülerin, *die;* Schulkamerad, *der*/-kameradin, *die;* **~-friend** *n.* Schulfreund, *der*/-freundin, *die;* **~girl** *n.* Schülerin, *die; (with reference to behaviour)* Schulmädchen, *das;* **~girlish** *adj.* schulmädchenhaft; **~house** *n.* Schulhaus, *das*
schooling [ˈskuːlɪŋ] *n.* **a)** Schulbildung, *die;* **he has had little ~:** er hat keine richtige Schulbildung gehabt; **have one's ~:** zur Schule gehen; **I received my ~ at his hands** er war mein Lehrmeister; **b)** *(Horse-riding)* Ausbildung, *die*
school: ~-kid *n. (coll.)* Schulkind, *das;* **~-leaver** *n. (Brit.)* Schulabgänger, *der*/-abgängerin, *die;* **~-ˈleaving age** *n. (Brit.)* Schulabgangsalter, *das;* **~-ma'am** *n. (coll.) see* **~-marm; ~man** [ˈskuːlmən] *n., pl.* **~men** [ˈskuːlmən] **a)** *(medieval teacher)* Magister, *der; (Philos., Theol.)* Scholastiker, *der;* **b)** *(Amer.: teacher)* Lehrer, *der;* **~-marm** [ˈskuːlmɑːm] *n. (coll.)* Gouvernante, *die (ugs.);* **~-marmish** [ˈskuːlmɑːmɪʃ] *adj. (coll.)* gouvernantenhaft; altjüngferlich; **~master** *n.* Lehrer, *der;* **~mastering** [ˈskuːlmɑːstərɪŋ] *n.* Schuldienst, *der;* **~mate** *see* **schoolfellow; ~mistress** *n.* Lehrerin, *die;* **~room** *n.* Schulzimmer, *das;* **~teacher** *n.* Lehrer, *der*/Lehrerin, *die;* **~-time** *n.* **a)** *(lesson-time)* Schule, *die;* Unterricht, *der;* **in** *or* **during ~-time** während des Unterrichts; **b)** *(~-days)* Schulzeit, *die;* **~-work** *n.* Schularbeiten *Pl.*
schooner [ˈskuːnə(r)] *n.* **a)** *(Naut.)* Schoner, *der;* **b)** *(Brit.: sherry glass)* [hohes] Sherryglas; **c)** *(Amer.: beer-glass)* [großes] Bierglas
schottische [ʃɒˈtiːʃ] *n. (Mus.)* Schottisch, *der*
schuss [ʃʊs] *(Skiing)* **1.** *n. (downhill run)* Schuß, *der; (course)* Schußpiste, *die.* **2.** *v. i.* Schuß fahren. **3.** *v. t.* in Schußfahrt *(Dat.)* hinunterfahren
schwa [ʃwɑː] *n. (Phonet.)* Schwa, *das*
sciatic [saɪˈætɪk] *adj. (Med.)* ischiadisch; Ischias⟨*schmerzen, -symptom*⟩; **have a ~ hip** Ischiasbeschwerden in der Hüfte haben
sciatica [saɪˈætɪkə] *n. (Med.)* Ischias, *die (fachspr. der od. das)*
sciatic nerve [saɪætɪk ˈnɜːv] *n. (Anat.)* Ischiadikus, *der (fachspr.);* Ischiasnerv, *der*
science [ˈsaɪəns] *n.* **a)** *no pl., no art.* Wissenschaft, *die;* **applied/pure ~:** angewandte/reine Wissenschaft; **the ~ of medicine, medical ~:** Medizin, *die;* **b)** *(branch of knowledge)* Wissenschaft, *die;* **moral ~:** Sittenlehre, *die;* **c) [natural] ~:** Naturwissenschaften; *attrib.* naturwissenschaftlich ⟨*Buch, Labor*⟩; **d)** *(technique, expert's skill)* Kunst, *die*
science: ~ ˈfiction *n.* Science-fiction, *die;* **~ park** *n.* Technologiepark, *der*
scientific [saɪənˈtɪfɪk] *adj.* **a)** wissenschaftlich; *(of natural science)* naturwissenschaftlich; **b)** *(using technical skill)* technisch gut ⟨*Boxer, Schauspieler, Tennis*⟩
scientifically [saɪənˈtɪfɪkəlɪ] *adv.* **a)** wissenschaftlich; *(with relation to natural science)* naturwissenschaftlich; nach wissenschaftlichen Methoden ⟨*Vieh züchten*⟩; **b)** *(using technical skill)* technisch gut ⟨*boxen*⟩
scientist [ˈsaɪəntɪst] *n.* Wissenschaftler, *der*/Wissenschaftlerin, *die; (in physical or natural science)* Naturwissenschaftler, *der*/-wissenschaftlerin, *die; (student of a science)* Student/Studentin der Naturwissenschaften; **biological/social/computer ~s** Biologen/Soziologen/Informatiker
Scientologist [saɪənˈtɒlədʒɪst] *n.* Anhänger/Anhängerin der Scientology [Kirche]
Scientology [saɪənˈtɒlədʒɪ] *n.* Scientology, *die*
sci-fi [ˈsaɪfaɪ] *n. (coll.)* Science-fiction, *die*
scilla [ˈsɪlə] *n. (Bot.)* Szilla, *die;* Blaustern, *der*
Scillies [ˈsɪlɪz], **Scilly Isles** [ˈsɪlɪ aɪlz] *pr. n. pl.* Scilly-Inseln *Pl.*
scimitar [ˈsɪmɪtə(r)] *n.* Krummsäbel, *der*
scintillate [ˈsɪntɪleɪt] *v. i. (fig.)* vor Geist sprühen
scintillating [ˈsɪntɪleɪtɪŋ] *adj. (fig.)* geistsprühend
scintillation [sɪntɪˈleɪʃn] *n.* **a)** *no pl. (sparkling)* Funkeln, *das;* **b)** *(spark)* Funke, *der;* **c)** *(Astron., Phys.)* Szintillation, *die*
scion [ˈsaɪən] *n.* **a)** *(Hort.)* Schößling, *der; (for grafting)* Edelreis, *das;* **b)** *(descendant)* Sproß, *der*
scissors [ˈsɪzəz] *n. pl.* **[pair of] ~:** Schere, *die;* **any/some ~:** eine Schere; **be a ~-and-paste job** [aus anderen Werken] zusammengeschrieben sein
ˈscissors kick *n. (Swimming)* Scherenschlag, *der*
sclerosis [skləˈrəʊsɪs] *n., pl.* **scleroses** [skləˈrəʊsiːz] **a)** *(Med.)* Sklerose, *die;* **disseminated** *or* **multiple ~:** multiple Sklerose; **b)** *(Bot.)* Verholzung, *die*

sclerotic [sklə'rɒtɪk] *adj.* **a)** *(Med.)* sklerotisch; **be a ~ patient** an Sklerose leiden; **b)** *(Bot.)* verholzt; **c)** *(Anat.)* skleral *(fachspr.)*

¹scoff [skɒf] *v.i. (mock)* spotten; **~ing remarks** spöttische Bemerkungen; **~ at sb./sth.** sich über jmdn./etw. lustig machen; **he ~ed at danger** er spottete der Gefahr *(geh.)*

²scoff *(sl.)* **1.** *v.t. (eat greedily)* verschlingen. **2.** *v.i.* sich [*(Dat.)* den Bauch] vollschlagen *(salopp)*

scoffer ['skɒfə(r)] *n.* Spötter, *der*/Spötterin, *die*

scold [skəʊld] **1.** *v.t.* schelten *(geh.)*; ausschimpfen (**for** wegen); **she ~ed him for coming late** sie schimpfte ihn aus *od.* schalt ihn, weil er zu spät kam. **2.** *v.i.* schimpfen; **~ing wife** zänkische Ehefrau. **3.** *n.* Xanthippe, *die (abwertend)*

scolding ['skəʊldɪŋ] *n.* Schimpfen, *das; (instance)* Schelte, *die (geh.)*; Schimpfe, *die (ugs.)*; **give sb. a ~ [for sth.]** jmdn. [wegen etw.] schelten *od.* ausschimpfen; **get a ~:** ausgeschimpft werden

scollop ['skɒləp] *see* **scallop**

sconce [skɒns] *n.* **a)** *(flat candlestick)* flacher Kerzenständer; *(candlestick fixed to wall)* Wandleuchter, *der;* **b)** *(socket)* [Kerzen]halterung, *die*

scone [skɒn, skəʊn] *n. weicher, oft zum Tee gegessener kleiner Kuchen*

scoop [sku:p] **1.** *n.* **a)** *(shovel)* Schaufel, *die;* **a ~ of coal** eine Schaufel Kohlen; **b)** *(ladle; ladleful)* Schöpflöffel, *der;* [Schöpf]kelle, *die;* **c)** *(for ice-cream, mashed potatoes)* Portionierer, *der; (quantity taken by ~)* Portion, *die; (of ice-cream)* Kugel, *die;* **d) apple-~:** Apfelausschneider, *der;* **cheese-~:** Käsestecher, *der;* **e)** *(large profit)* Fischzug, *der (fig.)*; **make a [considerable] ~:** einen beachtlichen Schnitt machen *(ugs.)*; **f)** *(Journ.)* Knüller, *der (ugs.)*; Scoop, *der (fachspr.)*. **2.** *v.t.* **a)** *(lift)* schaufeln ‹*Kohlen, Zucker*›; *(with ladle)* schöpfen ‹*Flüssigkeit, Schaum*›; *(out of fruit, cheese)* ausstechen ‹*Kerngehäuse, Probe*›; **b)** *(secure)* erzielen ‹*Gewinn*›; hereinholen *(ugs.)* ‹*Auftrag*›; *(in a lottery, bet)* gewinnen ‹*Vermögen*›; **~ the pool** den ganzen Einsatz gewinnen; **c)** *(Journ.)* ausstechen

~ 'out *v.t.* **a)** *(hollow out)* aushöhlen; schaufeln ‹*Loch, Graben*›; **b)** *(remove)* [her]ausschöpfen ‹*Flüssigkeit*›; auslöffeln ‹*Fruchtfleisch*›; schöpfen ‹*Mousse, Brei*›; *(with a knife)* herausschneiden ‹*Fruchtfleisch, Gehäuse*›; *(excavate)* ausbaggern ‹*Erde*›

~ 'up *v.t.* schöpfen ‹*Wasser, Suppe*›; schaufeln ‹*Erde*›; aufschaufeln ‹*Kohlen, Kies*›; **he ~ed the child up in his arms** er hob das Kind in seine Arme

'scoop-neck *n.* U-Ausschnitt, *der;* **a ~ dress** ein Kleid mit U-Ausschnitt

scoot [sku:t] *v.i. (coll.)* rasen; *(to escape)* die Kurve kratzen *(ugs.)*; **off you go, ~!** verschwinde/verschwindet!

scooter ['sku:tə(r)] *n.* **a)** *(toy)* Roller, *der;* **b) [motor] ~:** [Motor]roller, *der*

¹scope [skəʊp] *n., no indef. art.* **a)** Bereich, *der; (of person's activities)* Betätigungsfeld, *das; (of person's job)* Aufgabenbereich, *der; (of law)* Geltungsbereich, *der; (of department etc.)* Zuständigkeitsbereich, *der;* Zuständigkeit, *die; (of discussion, meeting, negotiations, investigations, etc.)* Rahmen, *der;* **that is a subject within my ~:** davon verstehe ich etwas; **that is a subject beyond my ~:** das fällt nicht in meine Sparte; *(beyond my grasp)* das ist mir zu hoch; **that is beyond the ~ of my essay** das sprengt den Rahmen meines Aufsatzes; **b)** *(opportunity)* Entfaltungsmöglichkeiten *Pl.*; **give ample ~ for new ideas** weiten Raum für neue Ideen bieten

²scope *n. (coll.) (telescope)* Fernrohr, *das; (microscope)* Mikroskop, *das*

scorch [skɔ:tʃ] **1.** *v.t.* verbrennen; versengen. **2.** *v.i.* **a)** *(become damaged by heat)* versengt werden; verbrennen; **b)** *(sl.: run or travel quickly)* flitzen. **3.** *n.* versengte Stelle; Brandfleck, *der*

scorched earth policy [skɔ:tʃt 'ɜ:θ pɒlɪsɪ] *n. (Mil.)* Politik der verbrannten Erde

scorcher ['skɔ:tʃə(r)] *n. (Brit. coll.)* **today's a [real] ~:** heute ist [wirklich] eine Affenhitze *(salopp)*; **what a ~!** ist das eine Affenhitze heute!

scorching ['skɔ:tʃɪŋ] **1.** *adj.* **a)** glühend heiß; sengend, glühend ‹*Hitze*›; **b)** *(coll.)* affenartig *(ugs.)* ‹*Geschwindigkeit*›. **2.** *adv.* **~ hot** glühend heiß ‹*Tag, Wetter*›

score [skɔ:(r)] **1.** *n.* **a)** *(points)* [Spiel]stand, *der; (made by one player)* Punktzahl, *die; (Golf)* Score, *der;* **What's the ~? – The ~ was 4–1 at half-time** Wie steht es? – Der Halbzeitstand war 4 : 1; **final ~:** Endstand, *der;* **keep [the] ~:** zählen; *(in written form)* aufschreiben; anschreiben; **know the ~** *(fig. coll.)* wissen, was Sache ist *od.* was läuft *(salopp)*; **b)** *(Mus.)* Partitur, *die; (Film)* [Film]musik, *die;* **in ~:** in Partitur; **c)** *pl.* **~** *or* **~s** *(group of 20)* zwanzig; **a ~ of people** [ungefähr] zwanzig Leute; **three ~ years and ten** siebzig Jahre; **d)** *in pl. (great numbers)* **~s [and ~s] of** zig *(ugs.)*; Dutzende [von]; **~s of times** zigmal *(ugs.)*; **e)** *(notch)* Kerbe, *die; (scratch)* Kratzer, *der;* Schramme, *die; (weal)* Striemen, *der; (crack in skin)* Schrunde, *die;* **make a ~ on the cardboard** die Pappe [ein]ritzen; **f)** *(dated: running account)* Rechnung, *die; (in bar, restaurant also)* Zeche, *die;* **pay off** *or* **settle an old ~** *(fig.)* eine alte Rechnung begleichen; **g)** *(reason)* Grund, *der;* **on one/this ~:** aus einem/diesem Grund; **on the ~ of** wegen; **on that ~:** was das betrifft *od.* angeht; diesbezüglich. **2.** *v.t.* **a)** *(win)* erzielen ‹*Erfolg, Punkt, Treffer usw.*›; **~ a direct hit on sth.** ‹*Person:*› einen Volltreffer landen; ‹*Bombe:*› etw. voll treffen; **the play ~d a success** das Stück war *od.* wurde ein Erfolg; **they ~d a success** sie hatten Erfolg *od.* konnten einen Erfolg [für sich] verbuchen; **you've ~d a success there** das ist ein Erfolg für dich; **~ a goal** ein Tor schießen/werfen; **we ~d 13** wir haben 13 Punkte gemacht/Tore geschossen/Tore geworfen; **~ points off** *(coll.) see* **~ off; b)** *(make notch/notches in)* einkerben; *(carve in)* [ein]ritzen; **~ grooves in sth.** Rillen in etw. *(Akk.)* kratzen; **the wood was deeply ~d** *(with notches/grooves)* in dem Holz waren tiefe Kerben/Rillen; **c)** *(be worth)* zählen; **the ace ~s ten [points]** das As zählt zehn [Punkte]; **d)** *(allot ~ to)* ‹*Punktrichter, Juror:*› Punkte geben (+ *Dat.*); **e)** *(dated: mark up)* ankreiden (**to** *or* **against** *Dat.*) *(veralt.)*; **~ sth. against** *or* **to sb.** *(fig.)* jmdm. etw. negativ anrechnen; **f)** *(Mus.)* setzen; *(orchestrate)* orchestrieren ‹*Musikstück*›; *(compose music for)* die Musik komponieren *od.* schreiben für ‹*Film, Theaterstück*›; **g)** *(make record of)* aufschreiben ‹*Punkte*›; **h)** *(Amer.: criticize severely)* heftig angreifen; schwere Vorwürfe erheben gegen. **3.** *v.i.* **a)** *(make score)* Punkte/einen Punkt erzielen *od. (ugs.)* machen; punkten *(bes. Boxen)*; *(~ goal/goals)* ein Tor/Tore schießen/werfen; **~ high** *or* **well** *(in test etc.)* eine hohe Punktzahl erreichen *od.* erzielen; **do you know how to ~?** weißt du, wie gezählt wird?; **b)** *(keep score)* aufschreiben; anschreiben; **c)** *(secure advantage)* die besseren Karten haben (**over** gegenüber, im Vergleich zu); *(be a hit)* ‹*Schauspieler:*› gut ankommen *(ugs.)*; **d)** *(sl.: obtain drugs)* Stoff auftreiben *(ugs.)*; **e)** *(sl.: have sex)* zum Schuß kommen *(salopp)* (**with** bei); **I'd like to ~ with her** ich würde sie gerne [mal] aufs Kreuz legen *od.* vernaschen *(salopp)*

~ off *v.t. (coll.)* als dumm hinstellen

~ 'out, ~ 'through *v.t.* durchstreichen; ausstreichen

~ 'up *v.t.* anschreiben; verbuchen ‹*Erfolg, Sieg usw.*›; **~ up the amount I owe you for these goods** setzen Sie den Betrag für die Waren auf mein Konto

score: ~-board *n.* Anzeigetafel, *die;* **~-book** *n. (Sport)* Anschreibebögen; **~-card** *n. (Sport)* Anschreibekarte, *die; (Golf)* Scorekarte, *die*

scorer ['skɔ:rə(r)] *n.* **a)** *(recorder of score)* Anschreiber, *der*/Anschreiberin, *die;* **b)** *(Footb.)* Torschütze, *der*/-schützin, *die;* **he was the top** *or* **highest ~:** er hat die meisten Tore/Punkte/Treffer *usw.* erzielt

'score-sheet *n.* Anschreibebogen, *der*

scoring ['skɔ:rɪŋ] *n.* **a)** *(Mus.)* Instrumentierung, *die; (for orchestra)* Orchestrierung, *die;* **b)** *(keeping score)* Aufschreiben, *das;* Anschreiben, *das*

scorn [skɔ:n] **1.** *n., no pl., no indef. art.* Verachtung, *die;* **with ~:** mit *od.* voll[er] Verachtung; verachtungsvoll; **be the ~ of sb.** von jmdm. verachtet werden; *see also* **pour 1 a. 2.** *v.t.* **a)** *(hold in contempt)* verachten; **b)** *(refuse)* in den Wind schlagen ‹*Rat*›; ausschlagen ‹*Angebot*›; verschmähen *(geh.)*; **~ doing** *or* **to do sth.** es für unter seiner Würde halten, etw. zu tun

scornful ['skɔ:nfl] *adj.* verächtlich ‹*Lächeln, Blick*›; **with ~ disdain** voll[er] Verachtung; verachtungsvoll; **be ~ of sth.** für etw. nur Verachtung haben

scornfully ['skɔ:nfəlɪ] *adv.* verächtlich; voll[er] Verachtung

Scorpian ['skɔ:pɪən] *n. (Astrol.)* Skorpion, *der*

Scorpio ['skɔ:pɪəʊ] *n. (Astrol., Astron.)* der Skorpion; der Scorpius; *see also* **Aries**

scorpion ['skɔ:pɪən] *n.* **a)** *(Zool.)* Skorpion, *der;* **b)** *(Astrol.)* **the S~:** der Skorpion; *see also* **archer b**

Scot [skɒt] *n.* Schotte, *der*/Schottin, *die*

Scotch [skɒtʃ] **1.** *adj.* **a)** *(of Scotland) see* **Scottish; b)** *(Ling.) see* **Scots 1 b. 2.** *n.* **a)** *(whisky)* Scotch, *der;* schottischer Whisky; **b)** *(Ling.) see* **Scots 2; c)** *constr. as pl.* **the ~:** die Schotten

scotch *v.t.* **a)** *(frustrate)* zunichte machen ‹*Plan*›; **b)** *(put an end to)* den Boden entziehen (+ *Dat.*) ‹*Gerücht, Darstellung*›

Scotch: ~ 'broth *n. (Gastr.) Hammelfleisch- od. Rindfleischsuppe mit Gemüse und Perlgraupen;* **~ 'egg** *n. (Gastr.) hartgekochtes Ei in Wurstbrät;* **~ 'fir** *n.* [Gemeine] Kiefer; Waldkiefer, *die;* **~man** ['skɒtʃmən] *see* **Scotsman; ~ 'mist** *n.* dichter Nieselregen; **~ 'pine** *see* **~ fir; ~ tape, (P)** *n. (Amer.)* ≈ Tesafilm, *der* Ⓦ; **~ 'terrier** *n.* Scotch[terrier], *der;* **~ 'whisky** *n.* schottischer Whisky; **~woman** *see* **Scotswoman**

scot-'free *pred. adj.* ungeschoren; **get off/go/escape ~:** ungeschoren davonkommen *od.* bleiben

Scotland ['skɒtlənd] *pr. n.* Schottland *(das)*

Scotland 'Yard *n. (Brit.)* Scotland Yard *(der)*

Scots [skɒts] **1.** *adj.* **a)** *(esp. Scot.) see* **Scottish; b)** *(Ling.)* schottisch. **2.** *n. (dialect)* Schottisch, *das*

Scots: ~man ['skɒtsmən] *n., pl.* **~men** ['skɒtsmən] Schotte, *der;* **~woman** *n.* Schottin, *die*

Scottie ['skɒtɪ] *n. (coll.)* **a)** *see* **Scotch terrier; b)** *(man)* Schotte, *der*

Scottish ['skɒtɪʃ] *adj.* schottisch; **sb. is ~:** jmd. ist Schotte/Schottin

scoundrel ['skaʊndrl] *n.* Schuft, *der (abwertend)*; *(villain)* Schurke, *der (abwertend)*

scoundrelly ['skaʊndrəlɪ] *adj.* schurkisch *(abwertend)*; schuftig *(abwertend)*

¹scour [skaʊə(r)] *v.t.* **a)** *(cleanse by friction)* scheuern ‹*Topf, Metall*›; **~ out** ausscheuern ‹*Topf*›; **b)** *(clear out)* **~ [out]** durchspülen ‹*Rohr*›; **c)** *(remove by rubbing)* [ab]scheuern; **~ away/off** ab-/wegscheuern

[2]**scour** *v. t. (search)* durchkämmen **(for** nach)

scourer ['skaʊərə(r)] *n.* Topfreiniger, *der;* Topfkratzer, *der*

scourge [skɜ:dʒ] **1.** *n. (lit. or fig.)* Geißel, *die;* **they were the ~ of the English coast** sie suchten die englische Küste immer wieder heim. **2.** *v. t.* **a)** *(whip)* geißeln; **b)** *(afflict)* heimsuchen

scouse [skaʊs] *(Brit. sl.)* **1.** *n.* **a)** *(dialect)* Liverpooler Dialekt; **b)** *(person)* Liverpooler, *der*/Liverpoolerin, *die.* **2.** *adj.* Liverpooler

[1]**scout** [skaʊt] **1.** *n.* **a) [Boy] S~:** Pfadfinder, *der;* **King's/Queen's S~** *(im Britischen Commonwealth) Pfadfinder der höchsten Rangstufe; see also* **girl scout; b)** *(Mil. etc.: sent to get information)* Späher, *der*/Späherin, *die;* Kundschafter, *der*/Kundschafterin, *die; (aircraft)* Aufklärer, *der;* **c)** *(Brit. Univ.: college servant)* Collegediener, *der;* **d)** *(coll.: helpful person)* **be a good ~:** immer bereit sein zu helfen; **e)** *(act of looking)* Erkundung, *die; (Mil.)* Aufklärung, *die;* **take a ~ around** sich umsehen. **2.** *v. i.* auf Erkundung gehen; **~ for sb./sth.** nach jmdm./etw. Ausschau halten: **be ~ing for talent** auf Talentsuche sein

~ a'bout, ~ a'round *v. i.* sich umsehen **(for** nach); Ausschau halten **(for** nach)

~ 'out *v. t.* auskundschaften; erkunden

[2]**scout** *v. t. (reject)* ablehnen; zurückweisen; aus der Welt schaffen ‹*Gerücht*›

'**scout car** *n. (Mil.)* Panzerspähwagen, *der*

scouting ['skaʊtɪŋ] *n.* **a)** *(reconnaissance)* Erkundung, *die;* Aufklärung, *die (Milit.);* **b) S~:** Pfadfindertum, *das;* Pfadfinderei, *die (ugs.); (Scout movement)* Pfadfinderbewegung, *die*

scout: ~ leader, *(Hist.)* **~master** *ns.* Pfadfinderführer, *der;* **S~ movement** *n.* Pfadfinderbewegung, *die*

scowl [skaʊl] **1.** *v. i.* ein mürrisches *od.* verdrießliches Gesicht machen; **~ at sb.** jmdn. mürrisch *od.* verdrießlich ansehen. **2.** *n.* mürrischer *od.* verdrießlicher [Gesichts]ausdruck

SCR *abbr. (Brit. Univ.)* **a) Senior Common Room; b) Senior Combination Room**

scrabble [skræbl] **1.** *v. i. (scratch)* ‹*Maus, Hund:*› scharren, kratzen; **~ about** ‹*Maus:*› herumkratzen *od.* -scharren; *(for missing object)* ‹*Person:*› wühlen **(for** nach); **the child was scrabbling in the sand** das Kind buddelte *(ugs.)* im Sand. **2.** *n.* **S~, (P)** Scrabble, *das*

scrag[-end] [skræg('end)] *n. (Gastr.)* Hals, *der;* Halsstück, *das*

scraggy ['skrægɪ] *adj. (derog.)* mager ‹*Person, Tier*›; dürr ‹*Arme, Beine*›; hager ‹*Hals*›

scram [skræm] *v. i.,* **-mm-** *(sl.)* abhauen *(salopp);* verschwinden *(ugs.)*

scramble ['skræmbl] **1.** *v. i.* **a)** *(clamber)* klettern; kraxeln *(ugs.);* **~ through a hedge** sich durch eine Hecke zwängen; **b)** *(move hastily)* hasten *(geh.);* rennen *(ugs.);* **~ for sth.** um etw. rangeln; ‹*Kinder:*› sich um etw. balgen; **c)** *(Air Force)* [im Alarmfalle] aufsteigen. **2.** *v. t.* **a)** *(Cookery)* **~ some eggs** Rührei[er] machen; **would you like your eggs ~d?** möchtest du deine Eier als Rührei?; *see also* **scrambled egg; b)** *(Teleph., Radio)* verschlüsseln ‹*Botschaft, Nachricht*›; an ein Verschlüsselungsgerät anschließen ‹*Telefon*›; **c)** *(mix together)* [ver]mischen; **d)** *(deal with hastily)* **~ a bill through Parliament** einen Gesetzentwurf durchs Parlament peitschen *(ugs.);* **~ the ball away** *(Footb.)* den Ball [irgendwie] wegschlagen. **3.** *n.* **a)** *(struggle)* Gerangel, *das* **(for** um); *(on roads)* [Verkehrs]gewühl, *das;* [Verkehrs]chaos, *das;* **b)** *(climb)* Kletterpartie, *die (ugs.)*

scrambled egg [skræmbld 'eg] *n. (Gastr.)* Rührei, *das*

scrambler ['skræmblə(r)] *n. (Teleph., Radio)* [elektronisches] Verschlüsselungsgerät

[1]**scrap** [skræp] **1.** *n.* **a)** *(fragment) (of paper, conversation)* Fetzen, *der; (of food)* Bissen, *der;* **~ of paper** Stück Papier; *(small, torn)* Papierfetzen, *der;* **b)** *(odds and ends) (of food)* Reste *Pl.; (of language)* Brocken *Pl.;* **a few ~s of information/news** ein paar bruchstückhafte Informationen/Nachrichten; **a few ~s of French** ein paar Brocken Französisch; **c)** *(smallest amount)* **not a ~ of** kein bißchen; *(of sympathy, truth also)* nicht ein Fünkchen; *(of truth also)* nicht ein Körnchen; **not a ~ of evidence** nicht die Spur eines Beweises; **d)** *no pl., no indef. art. (waste metal)* Schrott, *der;* **~ metal** Schrott, *der;* Altmetall, *das;* **~ iron** Eisenschrott, *der;* Alteisen, *das;* **e)** *no pl., no indef. art. (rubbish)* Abfall, *der;* **they are ~:** das ist Abfall *od.* sind Abfälle. **2.** *v. t.,* **-pp-** wegwerfen; wegschmeißen *(ugs.); (send for scrap)* verschrotten; *(fig.)* aufgeben ‹*Plan, Projekt usw.*›; **you can ~ that idea right away** die Idee kannst du gleich vergessen *(ugs.)*

[2]**scrap** *(coll.)* **1.** *n. (fight)* Rauferei, *die;* Klopperei, *die (ugs.); (verbal)* Kabbelei, *die (ugs.);* **get into a ~ with sb.** sich mit jmdm. in die Wolle kriegen *(ugs.);* **have a ~:** sich in der Wolle haben *(ugs.).* **2.** *v. i.,* **-pp-** sich raufen **(with** mit); *(verbally)* sich kabbeln

'**scrap-book** *n.* [Sammel]album, *das*

scrape [skreɪp] **1.** *v. t.* **a)** *(make smooth)* schaben ‹*Häute, Möhren, Kartoffeln usw.*›; abziehen ‹*Holz*›; *(damage)* verkratzen, verschrammen ‹*Fußboden, Auto*›; schürfen ‹*Körperteil*›; **~ one's knee/the skin off one's knee** sich *(Dat.)* das Knie schürfen/sich *(Dat.)* am Knie die Haut abschürfen; **b)** *(remove)* [ab]schaben, [ab]kratzen **(off, from** von) ‹*Farbe, Schmutz, Rost*›; **c)** *(draw along)* schleifen; **~ the bow across the fiddle** mit dem Bogen über die Geige kratzen; **d)** *(remove dirt from)* abstreifen ‹*Schuhe, Stiefel*›; **e)** *(draw back)* straff kämmen ‹*Haar*›; **f)** *(excavate)* scharren ‹*Loch*›; **g)** *(accumulate by care with money)* **~ together/up** *(raise)* zusammenkratzen *(ugs.); (save up)* zusammensparen; **h) ~ together/up** *(amass by scraping)* zusammenscharren ‹*Sand, Kies*›; *(rake together)* zusammenharken ‹*Laub usw.*›; *(amass with difficulty)* zusammenkriegen *(ugs.)* ‹*Geld*›; **~ [an] acquaintance with sb.** sich bei jmdm. anbiedern *(abwertend);* **i)** *(leave no food on or in)* abkratzen ‹*Teller*›; auskratzen ‹*Schüssel*›; **j)** *(Naut.)* von Bewuchs befreien *od.* reinigen ‹*Schiff*›. *See also* **barrel a. 2.** *v. i.* **a)** *(pass along with sound)* schleifen; **the chalk ~d along the blackboard** die Kreide kratzte über die Tafel; **b)** *(emit scraping noise)* ein schabendes Geräusch machen; **c)** *(rub)* streifen **(against, over** *Akk.*); **d)** *(very nearly graze or be grazed)* **~ over sth.** ‹*Flugzeug:*› haarscharf über etw. *(Akk.)* hinwegfliegen; **~ past each other** ‹*Autos:*› haarscharf aneinander vorbeifahren; **~ into second place** *(fig.)* mit Hängen und Würgen *(ugs.)* auf den zweiten Platz kommen; **e) bow and ~:** katzbuckeln *(abwertend);* **f)** *(be careful with money)* sein Geld zusammenhalten; *see also* **scrimp. 3.** *n.* **a)** *(act, sound)* Kratzen, *das* **(against** an + *Dat.*); Schaben, das **(against** an + *Dat.*); **give the potatoes a ~:** die Kartoffeln schaben; **b)** *(predicament)* Schwulitäten *Pl. (ugs.);* **be in a/get into a ~:** in Schwulitäten sein/kommen; **get sb. out of a ~:** jmdm. aus der Bredouille *od.* Patsche helfen *(ugs.);* **c)** *(scraped place)* Kratzer, *der (ugs.);* Schramme, *die*

~ a'long *v. i. (fig.)* sich über Wasser halten **(on** mit)

~ a'way *v. t.* abkratzen, abschaben

~ 'by *see* **~ along**

~ 'out *v. t.* **a)** *(excavate)* buddeln *(ugs.);* scharren; **b)** *(clean)* auskratzen, -schaben

~ through 1. ['--] *v. t.* **a)** sich zwängen durch; **b)** *(fig.: just succeed in passing)* mit Hängen und Würgen kommen durch ‹*Prüfung*›. **2.** [-'-] *v. i.* **a)** sich durchzwängen; **b)** *(fig.: just succeed in passing examination)* mit Hängen und Würgen durchkommen

scraper ['skreɪpə(r)] *n.* **a)** *(for shoes)* Kratzeisen, *das; (grid)* Abtreter, *der;* Abstreifer, *der;* **b)** *(hand tool, kitchen utensil)* Schaber, *der; (for clearing snow)* Schneescharre, *die;* Schneeschieber, *der; (for clearing mud or dung)* [Schmutz]kratzer, *der; (decorator's)* Spachtel, *der; (for removing ice from car windows)* [Eis]kratzer, *der*

'**scraperboard** *n. (Art)* Schabpapier, *das*

'**scrap-heap** *n.* Schutthaufen, *der;* Müllhaufen, *der;* **the scheme has been thrown/is on the ~** *(fig.)* der Plan ist zu Makulatur gemacht worden/ist Makulatur; **sb. is on the ~:** jmd. wird nicht mehr gebraucht; *(because of age)* jmd. gehört zum alten Eisen *(fig. ugs.)*

scrapings ['skreɪpɪŋz] *n. pl.* Schabsel; Geschabsel, *das*

scrap: ~ merchant *n.* Schrotthändler, *der*/-händlerin, *die;* **~ 'paper** *n.* Schmierpapier, *das*

scrappily ['skræpɪlɪ] *adv.* unzulänglich; *(without unity)* uneinheitlich; *(unsystematically)* unsystematisch

scrappy ['skræpɪ] *adj.* **a)** *(not complete)* lückenhaft ‹*Bericht, Bildung usw.*›; *(not unified)* uneinheitlich; **b)** *(lacking consistency)* inkonsistent *(geh.),* unausgewogen ‹*Aufsatz, Bericht*›; **c)** *(made up of bits or scraps)* zusammengestoppelt *(abwertend);* **a ~ meal, consisting of left-overs** ein aus Resten zusammengestoppeltes Essen

'**scrap-yard** *n.* Schrottplatz, *der;* **be sent to the ~:** verschrottet werden

scratch [skrætʃ] **1.** *v. t.* **a)** *(score surface of)* zerkratzen; verkratzen; *(score skin of)* kratzen; **~ the surface [of sth.]** ‹*Geschoß usw.:*› [etw.] streifen; **he has only ~ed the surface [of the problem]** er hat das Problem nur oberflächlich gestreift; **~ an A and find a B** *(fig.)* in jedem A steckt ein B; **b)** *(get scratch[es] on)* **~ oneself/one's hands** *etc.* sich schrammen/sich *(Dat.)* die Hände *usw.* zerkratzen *od.* [zer]schrammen *od.* ritzen; **c)** *(scrape without marking)* kratzen; kratzen an (+ *Dat.*) ‹*Insektenstich usw.*›; **~ oneself/one's arm** *etc.* sich kratzen/sich *(Dat.)* den Arm *usw. od.* am Arm *usw.* kratzen; *abs.* ‹*Person:*› sich kratzen; **~ one's head** sich am Kopf kratzen; **~ one's head [over sth.]** *(fig.)* sich *(Dat.)* den Kopf über etw. *(Akk.)* zerbrechen; **you ~ my back and I'll ~ yours** *(fig. coll.)* eine Hand wäscht die andere *(Spr.);* **d)** *(form)* kratzen, ritzen ‹*Buchstaben etc.*›; *(excavate in ground)* kratzen, scharren ‹*Loch*› **(in** in + *Akk.*); *(scribble)* kritzeln ‹*Zeilen*›; **~ a living** sich schlecht und recht ernähren **(from** von); **e)** *(erase from list)* streichen **(from** aus); *(withdraw from competition)* von der Starter- *od.* Teilnehmerliste streichen ‹*Rennpferd, Athleten*›; *(Amer. Polit.)* [von der Kandidatenliste] streichen ‹*Kandidat*›; *abs.* ‹*Rennfahrer:*› [seine Meldung *od.* Nennung] zurückziehen. **2.** *v. i.* **a)** *(make wounds, cause itching, make grating sound)* kratzen; **b)** *(scrape)* ‹*Huhn:*› kratzen, scharren. **3.** *n.* **a)** *(mark, wound; coll.: trifling wound)* Kratzer, *der (ugs.);* Schramme, *die;* **be covered in ~es** zer- *od.* verkratzt sein; zer- *od.* verschrammt sein; **without a ~:** ohne eine Schramme; **b)** *(sound)* Kratzen, *das* **(at** an + *Dat.*); Kratzgeräusch, *das;* **there was a ~ at the door** es kratzte an der Tür; **c)** *(spell of scratching)* **have a [good] ~:** sich [ordentlich] kratzen; **d)** *(Sport) hinterste Startlinie (bei Handikaprennen);* **on ~:** ohne Vorgabe; **e) start from ~** *(fig.)* bei Null anfangen *(ugs.);* **be up to ~** ‹*Arbeit, Leistung:*› nichts zu wünschen übriglassen; ⟨*Person:*⟩ in Form *od. (ugs.)* auf Zack sein; **not be up to ~:** [einiges] zu wünschen übriglassen; ⟨*Mensch:*⟩ nicht in Form *od. (ugs.)* auf Zack sein; **bring sth. up to ~:** etw. auf Vordermann *(scherzh.) od. (ugs.)* auf Zack bringen; **bring sb.'s performance up to ~:** jmdn. in Form *od. (ugs.)* auf Zack bringen; **f)** *no pl., no indef. art. (sl.: money)* Kohle, *die (salopp);* Knete, *die (salopp).* **4.** *adj.* **a)** *(Sport)* ohne Vorgabe *nachgestellt;* **~ player** *(Golf)* Scratchspieler, *der;* **b)** *(collected haphazardly)* bunt zusammengewürfelt; improvisiert ⟨*Mahlzeit*⟩

~ a'bout, ~ a'round *v. i.* scharren; *(fig.: search)* suchen **(for** nach**)**

~ 'off *v. t.* abkratzen; *(delete)* streichen ⟨*Person, Name*⟩

~ 'out *v. t.* **a)** *(score out)* aus-, durchstreichen ⟨*Name, Wort*⟩; **b)** *(gouge out)* auskratzen ⟨*Auge*⟩

~ 'through *see* **~ out a**

~ to'gether, ~ 'up *v. t.* zusammenstoppeln *(ugs.)* ⟨*Mahlzeit*⟩; zusammenkratzen *(ugs.)* ⟨*Geld*⟩

'scratchboard *see* **scraperboard**

scratchily ['skrætʃɪlɪ] *adv.* kratzend

scratchy ['skrætʃɪ] *adj.* **a)** *(making sound of scratching)* kratzig [klingend] ⟨*Schallplatte*⟩; **this is a ~ nib** diese Feder kratzt; **b)** *(causing itching)* kratzig ⟨*Wolle, Kleidungsstück*⟩; **c)** *(careless)* kritzlig *(ugs.)* ⟨*Handschrift, Zeichnung*⟩; **d)** *(irritable)* kratzbürstig; kratzig *(ugs.)*

scrawl [skrɔ:l] **1.** *v. t.* hinkritzeln; **~ sth. on sth.** etw. auf etw. *(Akk.)* kritzeln. **2.** *v. i.* kritzeln. **3.** *n.* **a)** *(piece of writing)* Gekritzel, *das; (handwriting)* Klaue, *die (salopp abwertend);* **b)** *(note)* hingekritzelte Zeilen

~ 'out *v. t.* wegstreichen ⟨*Wort*⟩

~ 'over *v. t.* vollkritzeln, vollschmieren ⟨*Seite, Buch*⟩

scrawny ['skrɔ:nɪ] *adj. (derog.)* hager, dürr ⟨*Hals, Person*⟩; mager ⟨*Vieh*⟩

scream [skri:m] **1.** *v. i.* **a)** *(utter cry)* schreien **(with** vor + *Dat.***)**; **~ at sb.** jmdn. anschreien; **b)** *(give shrill cry)* ⟨*Vogel, Affe:*⟩ schreien; **c)** *(whistle or hoot shrilly)* ⟨*Sirene, Triebwerk:*⟩ heulen; ⟨*Reifen:*⟩ quietschen; ⟨*Säge:*⟩ kreischen; **the car ~ed past** das Auto kam mit heulendem Motor vorbeigerast; **d)** *(laugh)* schreien **(with** vor + *Dat.***)**; **e)** *(speak or write excitedly)* **~ about sth.** um etw. ein großes Geschrei machen *(ugs.);* **the shipyards are ~ing for work** die Werften schreien nach Aufträgen *(geh.);* **f)** *(be blatantly obvious)* ⟨*Schlagzeile:*⟩ in die Augen springen, einem entgegenspringen. **2.** *v. t.* schreien; **~ sth. at sb.** jmdm. etw. ins Gesicht schreien. **3.** *n.* **a)** *(cry)* Schrei, *der; (of siren or jet engine)* Heulen, *das;* **~s of pain/laughter** Schmerzensschreie/gellendes Gelächter; **b)** *(sl.: comical person or thing)* **be a ~:** zum Schreien sein *(ugs.)*

screaming ['skri:mɪŋ] *adj.* **a)** schreiend; quietschend ⟨*Reifen*⟩; heulend ⟨*Sirene, Wind, Triebwerk*⟩; **b)** *(funny)* urkomisch

screamingly [skri:mɪŋlɪ] *adv.* **~ funny** urkomisch

scree [skri:] *n.* **~ [s] a)** *(stones)* Schutt, *der;* Geröll, *das;* Schotter, *der;* **b)** *(mountain slope)* Schutthalde, *die*

screech [skri:tʃ] **1.** *v. i. (utter cry)* ⟨*Kind, Eule:*⟩ kreischen, schreien; *(make sound like cry)* ⟨*Bremsen:*⟩ quietschen, kreischen; **~ to a halt, come to a ~ing halt** ⟨*Auto:*⟩ quietschend *od.* kreischend zum Stehen kommen. **2.** *v. t.* kreischen. **3.** *n. (cry)* Schrei, *der;* Kreischen, *das; (sound like cry)* Quietschen, *das;* Kreischen, *das;* **give a ~ of laughter** gellend auflachen

'screech-owl *n.* **a)** *(Brit.: barn-owl)* Schleiereule, *die;* **b)** *(Amer.: of genus Otus)* Zwergohreule, *die; (Otus asio)* Kreischeule, *die*

screed [skri:d] *n.* **a)** *(lengthy writing)* Roman, *der (ugs.);* **b)** *(harangue)* Strafpredigt, *die;* **c)** *(Building)* Estrich, *der*

screen [skri:n] **1.** *n.* **a)** *(partition)* Trennwand, *die; (piece of furniture)* Wandschirm, *der; (fire-~)* [Ofen]schirm, *der; see also* **rood-screen; b)** *(sth. that conceals from view)* Sichtschutz, *der; (Hunting)* [Jagd]schirm, *der; (of trees, persons, fog)* Wand, *die; (of persons)* Mauer, *die; (expression of face or measure adopted for concealment)* Maske, *die; (of indifference, secrecy also)* Wand, *die;* Mauer, *die;* **c)** *(surface on which pictures are projected)* Leinwand, *die;* Projektionswand, *die; (in cathode-ray tube)* Schirm, *der;* **[TV] ~** [Fernseh]schirm, *der;* Bildschirm, *der;* **the ~** *(Cinemat.)* die Leinwand; **stage and ~:** Bühne und Leinwand; **the small ~:** der Bildschirm; **d)** *(vertical display surface) (for exhibits)* Stellwand, *die; (for notices)* Pinnwand, *die;* Anschlagtafel, *die;* **e)** *(Phys.)* [Schutz]schirm, *der; (Electr.)* Abschirmung, *die;* **f)** *(Motor Veh.) see* **windscreen; g)** *(Amer.: netting to exclude insects)* Fliegendraht, *der;* Fliegengitter, *das;* **h)** *(sieve)* [Wurf]sieb, *das;* Durchwurf, *der;* **i)** *(Cricket) see* **sight-screen; j)** *(Photog.)* Mattscheibe, *die;* **k)** *(Printing)* [Bild]raster, *der.* **2.** *v. t.* **a)** *(shelter)* schützen **(from** vor + *Dat.***)**; *(conceal)* verdecken; **~ one's eyes from the sun** seine Augen vor der Sonne schützen *od. (geh.)* gegen die Sonne beschirmen; **be ~ed from view** vor Einblicken geschützt sein; **~ sth. from sb.** etw. jmds. Blicken entziehen; **b)** *(show)* vorführen, zeigen ⟨*Dias, Film*⟩; **c)** *(test)* durchleuchten **(for** auf ... *[Akk.]* hin**)**; **d)** *(fig.: protect)* decken ⟨*Straftäter*⟩; *(from blame)* in Schutz nehmen **(from** gegen**)**; *(from justice)* bewahren **(from** vor + *Dat.***)**; **e)** *(sieve)* [durch]sieben; **f)** *(Electr. Phys., Nucl. Engin.)* abschirmen

~ 'off *v. t.* abteilen ⟨*Teil eines Raums*⟩; [mit einem Wandschirm] abtrennen ⟨*Bett*⟩

screen: ~-play *n. (Cinemat.)* Drehbuch, *das;* **~-printing** *n. (Textiles)* Gewebefilmdruck, *der;* **~ test** *n. (Cinemat.)* Probeaufnahmen *Pl.;* **~-writer** *n. (Cinemat.)* Filmautor, *der/*-autorin, *die*

screw [skru:] **1.** *n.* **a)** Schraube, *die;* **he has a ~ loose** *(coll. joc.)* bei ihm ist eine Schraube locker *od.* lose *(salopp);* **put the ~[s] on sb.** *(fig. coll.)* jmdm. [die] Daumenschrauben anlegen *(ugs.);* **b)** *(Naut., Aeronaut.)* Schraube, *die;* **c)** *(sl.: prison warder)* Wachtel, *die (salopp);* Schien, *der (Gaunerspr. veralt.);* **d)** *(coarse) (copulation)* Fick, *der (vulg.);* Nummer, *die (derb); (partner in copulation)* Ficker, *der/*Fickerin, *die (vulg.);* **have a ~:** ficken *(vulg.);* vögeln *(vulg.);* **be a good ~:** gut ficken *od.* vögeln *(vulg.);* **e)** *(Brit. sl.: wages)* **they're/he's** *etc.* **paid a good ~:** die Kohlen stimmen [bei ihnen/ihm] *(ugs.);* **f)** *(turn of ~)* [Um]drehung, *die;* **give the bolt another ~:** dreh die Schraube noch eine Umdrehung weiter. **2.** *v. t.* **a)** *(fasten)* schrauben **(to** an + *Akk.***)**; **~ together** zusammenschrauben; verschrauben; **~ down** festschrauben; **have one's head ~ed on [straight** *or* **the right way** *or* **properly]** *(coll.)* ein vernünftiger Mensch sein; **b)** *(turn)* schrauben ⟨*Schraubverschluß usw.*⟩; **~ one's head round** den Kopf verdrehen; **~ a piece of paper into a ball** ein Stück Papier zu einer Kugel zusammendrehen; **c)** *(sl.: extort)* [raus]quetschen *(salopp)* ⟨*Geld, Geständnis*⟩ **(out of** aus**)**; **can't you ~ a bit more money out of your parents?** kannst du deinen Eltern nicht noch ein bißchen mehr Geld aus dem Kreuz leiern? *(salopp);* **~ sb. for a loan/for repayment** ein Darlehen/die Rückzahlung aus jmdm. rausquetschen *(salopp);* **d)** *(coarse: copulate with)* ⟨*Mann:*⟩ ficken *(vulg.),* vögeln *(vulg.);* ⟨*Frau:*⟩ ficken mit *(vulg.),* vögeln mit *(vulg.);* **e)** *(sl.: burgle)* knacken *(salopp)* ⟨*Tresor*⟩; einen Bruch machen bei *(salopp)* ⟨*Bank usw.*⟩. **3.** *v. i.* **a)** *(revolve)* sich schrauben lassen; sich drehen lassen; **~ to the right** ein Rechtsgewinde haben; **~ out/together** sich herausschrauben/zusammenschrauben lassen; **b)** *(coarse: copulate)* ficken *(vulg.);* vögeln *(vulg.)*

~ 'up *v. t.* **a)** *(make tenser)* spannen ⟨*Saite*⟩; **~ up one's courage** sich *(Dat.)* ein Herz fassen; **b)** *(crumple up)* zusammenknüllen ⟨*Blatt Papier*⟩; **c)** *(make grimace with)* verziehen ⟨*Gesicht*⟩; *(contract the outer parts of)* zusammenkneifen ⟨*Augen, Mund*⟩; **d)** *(sl.: bungle)* vermurksen *(ugs.);* vermasseln *(salopp);* **~ it/things up** Mist bauen *(salopp)*

screw: ~ball *(Amer. sl.)* **1.** *n.* Spinner, der/Spinnerin, *die (ugs. abwertend);* **be a ~:** spinnen; **2.** *adj.* spleenig; **~-cap** *n.* Schraubdeckel, *der;* Schraubverschluß, *der;* **~-coupling** *n. (Mech. Engin.)* Gewindemuffe, *die;* **~driver** *n.* **a)** Schraubenzieher, *der;* Schraubendreher, *der (fachspr.);* **b)** *(cocktail)* Wodka-Orange, *der;* Screwdriver, *der*

screwed [skru:d] *adj. (sl.: drunk)* besoffen *(salopp)*

'screwed-up *adj. (fig. coll.)* neurotisch; **get [all] ~ about sth.** wegen etw. ausflippen *(ugs.)*

screw-top *see* **screw-cap**

screwy ['skru:ɪ] *adj. (sl.: eccentric)* spinnig *(ugs. abwertend);* spleenig; *(crazy)* verrückt ⟨*Humor, Idee, Plan*⟩

scribble ['skrɪbl] **1.** *v. t.* **a)** *(write hastily)* hinkritzeln ⟨*Zeilen, Nachricht*⟩; **b)** *(draw carelessly or meaninglessly)* kritzeln ⟨*Skizze, Muster*⟩; **c)** *(joc. derog.: write)* absondern *(salopp abwertend)* ⟨*Gedicht, Artikel*⟩. **2.** *v. i.* **a)** *(write hurriedly, draw carelessly)* kritzeln; **b)** *(joc. derog.: be journalist etc.)* schreiben; **are you still scribbling?** machst du [immer] noch auf Schreiberling? *(ugs. abwertend).* **3.** *n.* Gekritzel, *das (abwertend); (handwriting)* Klaue, *die (salopp abwertend)*

~ 'out, ~ 'over *v. t.* aus-, durchstreichen; überkritzeln

scribbler ['skrɪblə(r)] *n. (joc. derog.)* Schreiberling, *der (abwertend); (of poems also)* Dichterling, *der (abwertend)*

scribbling ['skrɪblɪŋ]: **~-pad** *n. (Brit.)* Notizblock, *der;* **~-paper** *n. (Brit.)* Schmierpapier, *das (ugs.)*

scribe [skraɪb] *n.* **a)** *(producer of manuscripts)* Schreiber, *der;* Skriptor, *der; (copyist)* Abschreiber, *der;* Kopist, *der;* **b)** *(Bibl.: theologian)* Schriftgelehrte, *der*

scrimmage ['skrɪmɪdʒ] **1.** *n.* Gerangel, *das.* **2.** *v. i.* rangeln; ⟨*spielende Kinder:*⟩ sich balgen

scrimp [skrɪmp] *v. i.* knausern *(ugs.);* knapsen *(ugs.);* **~ and save** *or* **scrape** knapsen und knausern *(ugs.);* **~ on sth.** mit etw. knausern

scrip [skrɪp] *n. (Finance)* **a)** *(certificate)* Scrip, *der;* Zwischenschein, *der;* **b)** *(extra share[s])* Gratisaktie, *die/*Gratisaktien *Pl.*

script [skrɪpt] **1.** *n.* **a)** *(handwriting)* Handschrift, *die;* **in ~:** handgeschrieben; handschriftlich; **b)** *(of play)* Regiebuch, *das; (of film)* [Dreh]buch, *das;* Skript, *das (fachspr.);* **c)** *(for broadcaster)* Skript, *das;* Manuskript, *das;* **d)** *(system of writing)* Schrift, *die;* **e)** *(Printing)* Schreibschrift, *die;* **f)** *(Brit. Educ.)* [Prüfungs]arbeit, *die.* **2.** *v. t.* schriftlich ausarbeiten ⟨*Rede*⟩; das [Dreh]buch schreiben zu ⟨*Film, Fernsehspot usw.*⟩; das Storyboard machen zu ⟨*Fernsehspot*⟩

'script girl *n.* Skriptgirl, *das*

scriptorium [skrɪp'tɔ:rɪəm] *n., pl.* **scriptoria** [skrɪp'tɔ:rɪə] *or* **~s** Skriptorium, *das;* [Kloster]schreibstube, *die*

scriptural ['skrɪptʃərl, 'skrɪptʃʊrl] *adj.* **a)** *(of the Bible)* biblisch ⟨*Geschichte*⟩; Bibel-

⟨*kenntnis*⟩; Schrift⟨*lesung*⟩; **b)** *(founded on doctrines of the Bible)* schriftgemäß

scripture ['skrɪptʃə(r)] *n.* **a)** *(Relig.: sacred book)* heilige Schrift; **[Holy] S~, the [Holy] S~s** *(Christian Relig.)* die [Heilige] Schrift; *attrib.* Bibel⟨*text, -stunde*⟩; **b)** *(Christian Relig.: Bible text)* Bibeltext, *der;* **c)** *no pl., no art. (Sch.)* Religion, *die*

'script-writer *n. (of film)* Drehbuchautor, *der/*-autorin, *die; (for radio)* Hörspielautor, *der/*-autorin, *die*

scrofula ['skrɒfjʊlə] *n. (Med.)* Skrofulose, *die;* Skrofeln *Pl.*

scroll [skrəʊl] **1.** *n.* **a)** *(roll)* Rolle, *die;* **b)** *(design) (Archit.)* Volute, *die;* Schnecke, *die; (Mus.: on violin)* Schnecke, *die; (flourish in writing)* Schnörkel, *der.* **2.** *v. t. (Computing)* verschieben; scrollen *(fachspr.);* **~ a few pages** ein paar Seiten durchlaufen lassen

'scrollwork *n., no pl. (Art)* Schneckenverzierung, *die*

Scrooge [skru:dʒ] *n. (coll.: derog.)* Geizkragen, *der (ugs. abwertend);* **don't be such a ~:** sei nicht so geizig

scrotum [skrəʊtəm] *n., pl.* **scrota** ['skrəʊtə] *or* **~s** *(Anat.)* Hodensack, *der;* Skrotum, *das (fachspr.)*

scrounge [skraʊndʒ] *(coll.)* **1.** *v. t.* **a)** *(cadge)* schnorren *(ugs.)* **(off, from** von); **~ things** schnorren; **b)** *(take illicitly)* mitgehen lassen *(ugs.);* sich *(Dat.)* unter den Nagel reißen *(salopp).* **2.** *v. i.* **a)** *(cadge things)* schnorren *(ugs.)* **(from** bei); **b)** *(take things illicitly)* klauen *(salopp);* **c) ~ [around]** herumsuchen; herumstöbern *(ugs.);* **~ for sth.** nach etw. suchen. **3.** *n.* **be on the ~ [for sth.]** [etw.] schnorren wollen *(ugs.)*

scrounger ['skraʊndʒə(r)] *n. (coll.) (cadger)* Schnorrer, *der/*Schnorrerin, *die (ugs. abwertend)*

[1]scrub [skrʌb] **1.** *v. t.,* **-bb- a)** *(rub)* schrubben *(ugs.);* scheuern; **b)** *(coll.: cancel, scrap)* zurücknehmen ⟨*Befehl*⟩; sausenlassen, schießenlassen *(salopp)* ⟨*Plan, Projekt*⟩; wegschmeißen *(ugs.)* ⟨*Brief*⟩; **the project had to be ~bed** das Projekt mußte abgeblasen werden *(ugs.).* **2.** *v. i.,* **-bb- a)** *(use brush)* schrubben *(ugs.);* scheuern; **b)** *see* **~ up. 3.** *n.* **give sth. a ~:** etw. schrubben *(ugs.) od.* scheuern

~ 'out *v. t.* **a)** *(clean thoroughly)* schrubben *(ugs.),* [aus]scheuern ⟨*Pfanne*⟩; schrubben *(ugs.),* scheuern ⟨*Zimmer*⟩; **b)** *(remove)* ausbürsten ⟨*Fleck*⟩; **c)** *see* **~ 1 b**

~ 'up *v. i. (Med.)* sich *(Dat.)* die Hände [und Unterarme] desinfizieren

[2]scrub *n.* **a)** *(brushwood)* Buschwerk, *das;* Strauchwerk, *das;* Gesträuch, *das; (area of brushwood)* Buschland, *das;* **b)** *(stunted person, animal, or plant)* Kümmerling, *der*

scrubber ['skrʌbə(r)] *n.* **a)** *(sl.: immoral woman)* Flittchen, *das (ugs. abwertend);* Nutte, *die (abwertend); (sluttish woman)* Schlampe, *die (ugs. abwertend);* **b)** *(Chem.)* Wascher, *der*

'scrub-brush *(Amer.),* **'scrubbing-brush** *ns.* Scheuerbürste, *die*

scrubby ['skrʌbɪ] *adj.* **a)** *(bristly)* stoppelig ⟨*Kinn*⟩; stachelig, borstig ⟨*Bart*⟩; **b)** *(with stunted bushes)* mit [niedrigem] Busch- *od.* Strauchwerk bewachsen ⟨*Gebiet*⟩; **c)** *(stunted)* krüppelhaft ⟨*Büsche, Sträucher*⟩

[1]scruff [skrʌf] *n.* **by the ~ of the neck** beim *od.* am Genick

[2]scruff *n. (Brit. coll.) (scruffy man)* vergammelter Typ *(ugs.); (scruffy woman, girl)* Schlampe, *die (abwertend)*

scruffily ['skrʌfɪlɪ] *adv. (coll.)* gammelig *(ugs. abwertend)* ⟨*angezogen*⟩

scruffy ['skrʌfɪ] *adj.* vergammelt *(ugs. abwertend);* heruntergekommen ⟨*Haus, Restaurant, Gegend*⟩; ungepflegt ⟨*Haar*⟩

scrum [skrʌm] *n.* **a)** *(Rugby)* Gedränge, *das;* **b)** *(coll.: milling crowd)* Gedränge, *das;* Gewimmel, *das;* **a ~ of press photographers** ein Schwarm von Pressefotografen

scrum-'half *n. (Rugby)* Gedrängehalb[spieler], *der*

scrummage ['skrʌmɪdʒ] *see* **scrum a**

scrump [skrʌmp] *v. t. & i.* stehlen

scrumptious ['skrʌmʃəs] *adj. (coll.)* lecker ⟨*Essen*⟩; **she's/she looks ~:** sie ist zum Anbeißen/sie sieht zum Anbeißen aus *(ugs.)*

scrumpy ['skrʌmpɪ] *n. (esp. dial.)* ≈ saurer Apfelmost *(bes. südd.)*

scrunch [skrʌntʃ] *see* **crunch**

scruple ['skru:pl] **1.** *n.* **a)** *in sing. or pl.* Skrupel, *der;* Bedenken, *das;* **be [totally] without ~:** keine[rlei] Bedenken *od.* Skrupel haben; **a person with no ~s** ein gewissen- *od.* skrupelloser Mensch; **have no ~s about doing sth.** keine Bedenken *od.* Skrupel haben, etw. zu tun; **b)** *(Brit. Hist.: unit of weight)* Skrupel, *das.* **2.** *v. i.* Bedenken *od.* Skrupel haben; **[not] ~ to do sth./about doing sth.** [keine] Bedenken *od.* Skrupel haben, etw. zu tun

scrupulous ['skru:pjʊləs] *adj.* **a)** *(conscientious)* gewissenhaft ⟨*Mensch*⟩; unbedingt ⟨*Ehrlichkeit*⟩; peinlich ⟨*Sorgfalt*⟩; **pay ~ attention to sth.** peinlich auf etw. *(Akk.)* achten; **b)** *(over-attentive to detail)* penibel *(geh.);* pingelig *(ugs.);* [übermäßig] streng ⟨*Eltern*⟩; **be ~ about sth./in sth.** es mit etw. übertrieben genau nehmen

scrupulously ['skru:pjʊləslɪ] *adv.* **a)** *(conscientiously)* peinlich ⟨*sauber, genau*⟩; **~ honest** auf unbedingte Ehrlichkeit bedacht; **b)** *(with undue attention to detail)* penibel *(geh.);* pingelig *(ugs.)*

scrutineer [skru:tɪ'nɪə(r)] *n. (Brit. Admin.)* ≈ Wahlvorstand, *der*

scrutinize (scrutinise) ['skru:tɪnaɪz] *v. t.* [genau] untersuchen ⟨*Gegenstand, Forschungsgegenstand*⟩; [über]prüfen ⟨*Rechnung, Paß, Fahrkarte*⟩; mustern ⟨*Miene, Person*⟩

scrutiny ['skru:tɪnɪ] *n., no pl.* **a)** *(critical gaze)* musternder Blick; prüfender Blick; *(close examination) (of recruit)* Musterung, *die; (of bill, passport, ticket)* [Über]prüfung, *die;* **bear ~:** einer [genauen] Prüfung standhalten; **b)** *(Brit.: examination of votes)* Stimmenauszählung, *die*

scuba ['skju:bə, 'sku:bə] *n. (Sport)* Regenerationstauchgerät, *das; attrib.* Geräte⟨*tauchen*⟩; [Geräte]tauch⟨*ausrüstung*⟩

scud [skʌd] *v. i.,* **-dd- a)** *(skim along)* ⟨*Wolke:*⟩ jagen; **b)** *(Naut.)* **~ before the wind** vor dem Wind laufen *od. (fachspr.)* lenzen

scuff [skʌf] **1.** *v. t.* **a)** *(graze)* streifen; **~ one's shoe against sth.** etw. mit dem Schuh streifen; **b)** *(mark by grazing)* verkratzen, verschrammen ⟨*Schuhe, Fußboden*⟩. **2.** *n.* **a)** Kratzer, *der;* Kratzspur, *die;* Schramme, *die;* **b)** *(slipper)* Pantoffel, *der*

scuffle ['skʌfl] **1.** *n.* Handgreiflichkeiten *Pl.;* Tätlichkeiten *Pl.;* **a ~ broke out** es kam zu Handgreiflichkeiten *od.* Tätlichkeiten. **2.** *v. i.* **a)** handgreiflich *od.* tätlich werden **(with gegen)**; **b)** *(shuffle)* schlurfen; *(scurry)* ⟨*Mäuse:*⟩ rascheln

scull [skʌl] **1.** *n.* **a)** *(oar)* Skull, *das;* **b)** *(boat)* Skullboot, *das.* **2.** *v. t.* skullen; rudern. **3.** *v. i.* skullen

scullery ['skʌlərɪ] *n.* Spülküche, *die*

sculpt [skʌlpt] **1.** *v.t.* bildhauern *(ugs.).* **2.** *v.i. (coll.)* bildhauern *(ugs.);* **make a living from ~ing** vom Bildhauern leben

sculptor ['skʌlptə(r)] *n.* Bildhauer, *der/*-hauerin, *die*

sculptress ['skʌlptrɪs] *n.* Bildhauerin, *die*

sculptural ['skʌlptʃərl] *adj.* **a)** plastisch; **b)** *(resembling sculpture)* skulptural *(geh.)* ⟨*Gesichtszüge, Form*⟩; plastisch

sculpture ['skʌlptʃə(r)] **1.** *n.* **a)** *(art)* Bildhauerei, *die;* **b)** *(piece of work)* Skulptur, *die;* Plastik, *die; (pieces collectively)* Skulpturen; Plastiken. **2.** *v. t.* **a)** *(represent)* skulpt[ur]ieren *(geh.);* bildhauerisch darstellen; **~d in marble/stone/bronze** in Marmor/Stein gehauen/in Bronze gegossen; **b)** *(shape)* formen **(into** zu); **a finely ~d nose** eine schön *od.* fein modellierte Nase. **3.** *v. i.* bildhauern *(ugs.);* skulpt[ur]ieren *(geh.); (in plastic material)* modellieren

scum [skʌm] *n.* **a)** Schmutzschicht, *die; (film)* Schmutzfilm, *der; (on soup etc.)* oben schwimmende Schicht; *(greasy)* Fettschicht, *die;* **a ring of ~ around the bath** ein Schmutzrand in der Badewanne; **b)** *no pl., no indef. art. (fig. derog.)* Abschaum, *der (abwertend);* Auswurf, *der (abwertend);* **the ~ of the earth/of humanity** der Abschaum der Menschheit

[1]scupper ['skʌpə(r)] *n. (Naut.)* Speigatt, *das*

[2]scupper *v. t. (Brit. coll.)* **a)** *(defeat)* über den Haufen werfen *(ugs.)* ⟨*Plan*⟩; **we're ~ed if the police arrive** wenn die Polizei kommt, sind wir erledigt; **b)** *(sink)* versenken ⟨*Schiff, Mannschaft*⟩; **be ~ed** ⟨*Mannschaft:*⟩ absaufen *(salopp)*

scurf [skɜ:f] *n.* Schuppen *Pl.*

scurfy ['skɜ:fɪ] *adj.* schuppig ⟨*Haar, Fell*⟩

scurrilous ['skʌrɪləs] *adj.* **a)** *(abusive)* niederträchtig; **b)** *(gross, obscene)* unflätig

scurrilously ['skʌrɪləslɪ] *adv.* **a)** *(abusively)* in niederträchtiger Weise; **b)** *(grossly, obscenely)* in unflätiger Weise

scurry ['skʌrɪ] **1.** *v. i.* huschen; flitzen *(ugs.).* **2.** *n.* **a)** *(bustle)* Geschäftigkeit, *die;* **b)** *(act)* Hetze, *die;* **a ~ for the best seats** ein Sturm auf die besten Plätze; **c)** *(sound) (of feet)* Getrappel, *das*

scurvy ['skɜ:vɪ] **1.** *n. (Med.)* Skorbut, *der.* **2.** *adj. (arch.)* niederträchtig

'scuse [skju:z] *v. t. (coll.)* **~ me** 'tschuldigung; **~ fingers** 'tschuldigung, daß *od.* wenn ich die Finger nehme

scut [skʌt] *n. (of deer)* Wedel, *der (Jägerspr.); (of rabbit, hare)* Blume, *die (Jägerspr.)*

[1]scuttle ['skʌtl] *n.* **a)** *(coal-box)* Kohlenfüller, *der;* **b)** *(Brit. Motor Veh.) Teil der Karosserie zwischen Motorhaube und unterem Rand der Windschutzscheibe*

[2]scuttle *(Naut.)* **1.** *v. t.* versenken. **2.** *n.* Luke, *die*

[3]scuttle *v. i. (scurry)* rennen; flitzen *(ugs.);* ⟨*Maus, Krabbe:*⟩ huschen; **she ~d off** sie huschte davon

Scylla and Charybdis [sɪlə ənd kə'rɪbdɪs] *n., no pl.* **between ~:** zwischen Szylla und Charybdis

scythe [saɪð] **1.** *n.* Sense, *die.* **2.** *v. t.* [mit der Sense] mähen ⟨*Wiese, Gras, usw.*⟩; [mit der Sense] abmähen ⟨*Gras usw.*⟩

SDI *abbr.* **strategic defence initiative** SDI

SDLP *abbr.* **Social Democratic and Labour Party** sozialistische Partei Nordirlands

SDP *abbr. (Brit. Polit.)* **Social Democratic Party**

SDR *abr. (Econ.)* **special drawing right** SZR

SE *abbr.* **a)** [saʊ'θi:st] **south-east** SO; **b)** [saʊ'θi:stən] **south-eastern** sö.

sea [si:] *n.* **a)** Meer, *das;* **the ~:** das Meer; die See; **by ~:** mit dem Schiff; **by the ~:** am Meer; an der See; **at ~:** auf See *(Dat.);* **be all at ~** *(fig.)* nicht mehr weiter wissen; **when it comes to maths I'm all at ~:** von Mathe hab' ich nicht die geringste Ahnung; **worse things happen at ~** *(joc.)* davon geht die Welt nicht unter *(ugs.);* **beyond [the] ~[s]** *(literary) see* **overseas a; go to ~:** in See stechen; *(become sailor)* zur See gehen *(ugs.);* **on the ~** *(in ship)* auf See *(Dat.); (on coast)* am Meer; an der See; **put [out] to ~:** in See *(Akk.)* gehen *od.* stechen; auslaufen; *see also* **high seas; inland sea; b)** *(specific tract of water)* Meer, *das;* **the seven ~s** *(literary/poet.)* die sieben [Welt]meere; **c)** *(freshwater lake)* See, *der;* **the S~ of Galilee** der See Genezareth; **d)** *in sing. or pl. (state of ~)* See, *die; (wave)* Welle, *die;* Woge, *die* *(geh.)*; See, *die (Seemannsspr.)*; **there was a heavy ~:** es herrschte schwere See *(Seemannsspr.)*; **run into heavy ~s** in schwere See kommen *(Seemannsspr.)*; *see also* **half-seas-over; ship 2d; e)** *(fig.: vast quantity)* Meer, *das; (of drink)* Strom, *der;* **f)** *attrib. (of or on the ~)* See⟨*klima, -wind, -wasser, -schlacht, -karte, -weg*⟩; Meer⟨*gott, -ungeheuer, -wasser, -salz usw.*⟩; Meeres⟨*grund, -küste, -niveau, -spiegel usw.*⟩; *(in names of marine fauna or flora)* See⟨*maus, -gurke, -anemone, -löwe, -schildkröte usw.*⟩; Meer⟨*brasse, -neunauge, -gurke usw.*⟩

sea: ~ 'air *n.* Seeluft, *die;* **~ a'nemone** *n. (Zool.)* Seeanemone, *die;* Seerose, *die;* **~ bass** *n. (Zool.)* [Schwarzer] Sägebarsch; **~-'bed** *n.* Meeresboden *der;* Meeresgrund, *der;* **~-bird** *n.* Seevogel, *der;* **~board** *n.* Küste, *die;* **~boot** *n.* Seestiefel, *der;* **~ breeze** *n. (Meteorol.)* Seewind, *der;* Seebrise, *die;* **~ captain** *n.* [Schiffs]kapitän, *der;* **~ change** *n. (esp. literary: unexpected or notable transformation)* erstaunliche Metamorphose *(geh.)*; **~-chest** *n. (Naut.)* Seekiste, *die;* **~-coast** *n.* Meeresküste, *die;* **~ 'cucumber** *n. (Zool.)* Seegurke, *die;* Meergurke, *die;* **~-dog** *n.* **a)** *(Zool.)* Seehund, *der;* **b)** *(literary/joc.: experienced sailor)* Seebär, *der (ugs. scherzh.)*; **~ eagle** *n.* Seeadler, *der;* **~farer** ['si:feərə(r)] *n. (formal)* Matrose, *der;* **~faring** ['si:feərɪŋ] **1.** *adj.* **~faring man** Seemann, *der;* **~faring nation** Seefahrernation, *die;* seefahrende Nation; **his ~faring days** die Zeit, als er zur See fuhr; **2.** *n., no pl., no indef. art.* Seefahrt, *die;* **~-fish** *n.* Seefisch, *der;* **~ fog** *n.* Seenebel, *der;* **~food** *n.* Meeresfrüchte *Pl.; attrib.* Fisch⟨*restaurant*⟩; **~food cocktail** Cocktail aus Meeresfrüchten; **~-fowl** *see* **~-bird; ~ front** *n. unmittelbar am Meer gelegene Straße[n] einer Seestadt;* **a walk along the ~ front** ein Spaziergang am Wasser *od.* auf der Uferpromenade; **the hotels on the ~ front** die Hotels direkt am Wasser *od.* an der Uferpromenade; **~-god** *n.* Meergott, *der;* **~going** *adj. (for crossing sea)* seegehend; **~going yacht** Hochseejacht, *die;* **~-green 1.** [-'-] *n.* Seegrün, *das;* Meergrün, *das;* **2.** ['--] *adj.* seegrün; meergrün; **~-gull** *n.* [See]möwe, *die;* **~-horse** *n. (Zool.)* Seepferdchen, *das;* **~-kale** *n. (Bot.)* Meerkohl, *der;* Seekohl, *der;* Englischer Kohl

¹seal [si:l] *n.* **a)** *(Zool.)* Robbe, *die;* **[common] ~:** [Gemeiner] Seehund; **b)** *see* **~skin**

²seal 1. *n.* **a)** *(piece of wax, lead, etc., stamp, impression)* Siegel, *das; (lead ~ also)* Plombe, *die; (stamp also)* Siegelstempel, *der;* Petschaft, *das; (impression also)* Siegelabdruck, *der;* **fix a ~ on** versiegeln; *(using lead)* verplomben; plombieren; **put [lead] ~s on** verplomben, plombieren ⟨*Tür*⟩; **~s of office** *(Brit.)* Dienstsiegel; Amtssiegel; **b)** *(adhesive stamp)* Julmarke, *die (Philat.)*; **c) set the ~ on** *(fig.)* zementieren (+ *Akk.*); **set one's ~ to sth.** *(fig.)* grünes Licht für etw. geben; etw. absegnen *(ugs.)*; **d)** *(guarantee)* **gain the ~ of respectability** sich *(Dat.)* großes Ansehen erwerben; **have the ~ of official approval** offiziell gebilligt werden; **e)** *(to close aperture)* Abdichtung, *die; (odour-trap)* Geruchsverschluß, *der. See also* **privy seal. 2.** *v.t.* **a)** *(stamp with ~, affix ~ to)* siegeln ⟨*Dokument*⟩; *(fasten with ~)* verplomben, plombieren ⟨*Tür, Stromzähler*⟩; **b)** *(close securely)* abdichten ⟨*Behälter, Rohr usw.*⟩; zukleben ⟨*Umschlag, Paket*⟩; [zum Verschließen der Poren] kurz anbraten ⟨*Fleisch*⟩; **my lips are ~ed** *(fig.)* meine Lippen sind versiegelt; **be a ~ed book to sb.** *(fig.)* ein Buch mit sieben Siegeln für jmdn. sein; **~ed orders** versiegelte Order; **c)** *(stop up)* verschließen; abdichten ⟨*Leck*⟩; verschmieren ⟨*Riß*⟩; **d)** *(decide)* besiegeln ⟨*Geschäft, Abmachung, jmds. Schicksal*⟩; **e)** *(provide with water-~)* mit einem Geruchsverschluß versehen ⟨*Rohr*⟩; **f)** *(Road Constr.)* befestigen; mit einer [Fahrbahn]decke versehen

~ 'in *v.t.* bewahren ⟨*Geschmack*⟩; am Austreten hindern ⟨*Fleischsaft*⟩

~ 'off *v.t.* abriegeln

~ 'up *see* **~ 2b, c**

'sea lane *n. (Naut.)* See[schiffahrts]straße, *die*

sealant ['si:lənt] *n.* Dichtungsmaterial, *das*

sea: ~-legs *n.pl.* Seebeine *Pl. (Seemannsspr.)*; **get** *or* **find one's ~-legs** sich *(Dat.)* Seebeine wachsen lassen *(Seemannsspr.)*; **~-level** *n.* Meeresspiegel, *der (fachspr.)*; **200 feet above/below ~-level** 200 Fuß über/unter dem Meeresspiegel *od.* über/unter Meereshöhe *od. (fachspr.)* Normalnull; **at ~-level** auf Meereshöhe *(Dat.)*

sealing-wax ['si:lɪŋwæks] *n.* Siegellack, *der;* Siegelwachs, *das*

'sea-lion *n. (Zool.)* Seelöwe, *der*

'Sea Lord *n. (Brit.)* Seelord, *der*

'sealskin *n.* Robbenfell, *das; (garment)* Robbenfelljacke, *die*/Robbenfellmantel, *der usw.*

Sealyham [terrier] ['si:lɪəm (terɪə[r])] *n.* Sealyhamterrier, *der*

seam [si:m] *n.* **a)** *(line of joining)* Naht, *die; (Carpentry)* Verbindung, *die;* **come apart at the ~s** aus den Nähten gehen; *(fig. coll.: fail)* zusammenbrechen; **burst at the ~s** *(fig.)* aus den *od.* allen Nähten platzen *(ugs.)*; *see also* **fall 2t; b)** *(fissure)* Spalt, *der;* Spalte, *die; (in ship)* Naht, *die (fachspr.)*; **c)** *(Mining)* Flöz, *das; (Geol.) (stratum)* Schicht, *die; (line between strata)* [Schicht]fuge, *die;* **d)** *(wrinkle)* Runzel, *die;* Falte, *die*

seaman ['si:mən] *n., pl.* **seamen** ['si:mən] **a)** *(sailor)* Matrose, *der; see also* **able seaman; ordinary seaman; b)** *(expert in navigation etc.)* Seemann, *der*

seamanlike ['si:mənlaɪk] *adj.* seemännisch

seamanship ['si:mənʃɪp] *n., no pl.* seemännisches Geschick; Seemannschaft, *die (fachspr.)*

'sea-mark *n. (Naut.)* Seezeichen, *das*

seamed [si:md] *adj.* **a)** *(having seam)* **~ stockings** Strümpfe mit Naht; **b)** *(wrinkled)* faltig; runzlig; zerfurcht; **c)** *(Geol.: having seams)* geschiefert

sea: ~-mew *n.* [See]möwe, *die;* **~ mile** *see* **nautical mile; ~ mist** *n.* Küstennebel, *der*

seamless ['si:mlɪs] *adj.* nahtlos

sea: ~ monster *n. (Mythol.)* Seeungeheuer, *das;* Meerungeheuer, *das;* **~mount** *n. (Geog.)* Tiefseeberg, *der*

seamstress ['semstrɪs] *n.* Näherin, *die*

seamy ['si:mɪ] *adj.* **a)** *(having wrinkles)* faltig, runzlig; **b)** *(run down)* heruntergekommen ⟨*Stadtteil*⟩; **the ~ side [of life** *etc.*] *(fig.)* die Schattenseite[n] [des Lebens *usw.*]

seance ['seɪɑ̃s], **séance** ['seɪɑ̃s] *n.* Séance, *die (fachspr.)*; spiritistische Sitzung

sea: ~-pink *n. (Bot.)* Grasnelke, *die;* Strandnelke, *die;* **~plane** *n.* Wasserflugzeug, *das;* **~port** *n.* Seehafen, *der;* **~ power** *n.* Seemacht, *die;* **~ quake** *n.* Seebeben, *das*

sear [sɪə(r)] *v.t.* verbrennen, versengen; *(Med.: cauterize)* ausbrennen ⟨*Wunde*⟩

search [sɜ:tʃ] **1.** *v.t.* durchsuchen (**for** nach); absuchen ⟨*Gebiet, Fläche*⟩ (**for** nach); prüfen *od.* musternd blicken in (+ *Akk.*) ⟨*Gesicht*⟩; *(fig.: probe)* erforschen ⟨*Herz, Gewissen*⟩; suchen in (+ *Dat.*), durchstöbern *(ugs.)* ⟨*Gedächtnis*⟩ (**for** nach); **~ me** *(coll.)* keine Ahnung! **2.** *v.i.* suchen; **~ after sth.** etw. *od.* nach etw. suchen. **3.** *n.* Suche, *die* (**for** nach); *(of building, room, etc.)* Durchsuchung, *die;* **make a ~ for** suchen nach ⟨*Waffen, Drogen, Diebesgut*⟩; **in ~ of sb./sth.** auf der Suche nach jmdm./etw.; **go off in ~ of sth.** sich auf die Suche nach etw. machen; **right of ~:** Durchsuchungsrecht, *das*

~ for *v.t.* suchen [nach]

~ 'out *v.t.* heraussuchen; aufspüren ⟨*Person mit unbekanntem Aufenthalt*⟩

~ through *v.t.* durchsuchen; durchsehen ⟨*Buch*⟩

searcher ['sɜ:tʃə(r)] *n.* Sucher, *der*/Sucherin, *die;* Suchende, *der/die;* **the ~s returned with the missing child** die Suchmannschaft kehrte mit dem vermißten Kind zurück

searching ['sɜ:tʃɪŋ] *adj.* prüfend, forschend ⟨*Blick*⟩; bohrend ⟨*Frage*⟩; *(thorough)* eingehend ⟨*Untersuchung*⟩

searchingly ['sɜ:tʃɪŋlɪ] *adv.* prüfend, forschend ⟨*jmdn. ansehen*⟩; eingehend ⟨*befragen*⟩

search: ~light *n.* **a)** *(lamp)* Suchscheinwerfer, *der;* **b)** *(beam of light)* Scheinwerferlicht, *das (auch fig.)*; *(fig.)* Rampenlicht, *das;* **the ~light is on him** *(fig.)* er steht im Scheinwerfer- *od.* Rampenlicht; **~-party** *n.* Suchtrupp, *der;* Suchmannschaft, *die;* **~-warrant** *n. (Law)* Durchsuchungsbefehl, *der*

searing ['sɪərɪŋ] *adj.* sengend ⟨*Hitze*⟩; brennend ⟨*Schmerz*⟩; *(fig.: intense)* bohrend, stechend ⟨*Blick*⟩

sea: ~-salt *n.* Meersalz, *das;* Seesalz, das; **~scape** *n.* **a)** *(Art: picture)* Seestück, *das;* Marine, *die;* **b)** *(view)* Meerespanorama, *das;* **S~ Scout** *n. (Brit.)* Seepfadfinder, *der*/-pfadfinderin, *die;* **~ serpent** *n.* Seeschlange, *die;* **~-shanty** *see* ²**shanty; ~ shell** *n.* Muschel[schale], *die;* **~-shore** *n. (land near ~)* [Meeres]küste, *die; (beach)* Strand, *der;* **walk along the ~-shore** am Meer/Strand entlanggehen; **~sick** *adj.* seekrank; **~sickness** *n., no pl.* Seekrankheit, *die;* **~side** *n., no pl.* [Meeres]küste, *die;* **by/to/at the ~side** am/ans/am Meer; an der/an die/an der See; **~side town** Seestadt, *die;* **the usual ~side attractions** die Vergnügungen, die die Küste gemeinhin bietet

season ['si:zn] **1.** *n.* **a)** *(time of the year)* Jahreszeit, *die;* **dry/rainy ~:** Trocken-/Regenzeit, *die;* **b)** *(time of breeding) (for mammals)* Tragezeit, *die; (for birds)* Brutzeit, *die; (time of flourishing)* Blüte[zeit], *die; (time when animal is hunted)* Jagdzeit, *die;* **blackberry ~:** Brombeerzeit, *die;* **nesting ~:** Nistzeit, *die;* Brut[zeit], *die; see also* **close season; open season; c)** *(time devoted to specified, social activity)* Saison, *die;* **harvest/opera ~:** Erntezeit, die/Opernsaison, *die;* **football ~:** Fußballsaison, *die;* **holiday** *or (Amer.)* **vacation ~:** Urlaubszeit, *die;* Ferienzeit, *die;* **tourist ~:** Touristensaison, *die;* Reisezeit, *die;* **the ~ of goodwill** *(Christmas)* die Zeit der Nächstenliebe; **'compliments of the ~'** *(formal),* **'the ~'s greetings'** „ein frohes Weihnachtsfest und ein glückliches neues Jahr"; **d) raspberries are in/out of** *or* **not in ~:** jetzt ist die/nicht die Saison *od.* Zeit für Himbeeren; **be in ~** *(on heat)* brünstig sein; **a word in ~** *(literary)* ein Rat[schlag] zur rechten Zeit; **in and out of ~:** zu jeder passenden oder unpassenden Zeit; *(again and again)* immer wieder; **e)** *(ticket) see* **season-ticket; f)** *(period of time)* Zeit, *die; (Theatre, Cinemat.)* Spielzeit, *die;* **for a ~** *(dated)* eine Zeitlang; **they are doing a ~ in Oxford** sie gastieren [zur Zeit] in Oxford; **put on a Shakespeare/Russian ~:** ≈ Shakespeare-/russische Wochen veranstalten. *See also* **high season; low season; off-season; silly 1a. 2.** *v.t.* **a)** *(make palatable, lit. or fig.)* würzen ⟨*Fleisch, Rede*⟩; **b)** *(mature)* ablagern lassen ⟨*Holz*⟩; **~ed** erfahren ⟨*Wahlkämpfer, Soldat, Reisender*⟩; **c)** *(temper)* mäßigen *(geh.)* ⟨*Impulsivität*⟩. **3.** *v.i.* ⟨*Holz:*⟩ ablagern; ⟨*Whisky:*⟩ lagern, reifen

seasonable ['si:zənəbl] *adj.* **a)** *(suitable to*

the time of the year) der Jahreszeit gemäß; **b)** *(opportune)* willkommen ‹*Angebot*›; *(meeting needs of occasion)* geboten ‹*Vorsicht*›; passend ‹*Worte*›

seasonably ['si:zənəblı] *adv.* **a)** *(in a way typical of the season)* der Jahreszeit entsprechend; **b)** *(so as to be opportune)* zur rechten Zeit

seasonal ['si:zənl] *adj.* Saison‹*arbeit, -geschäft*›; saisonabhängig ‹*Preise*›

seasonally ['si:zənəlı] *adv.* saisonal, saisonbedingt ‹*schwanken*›; ~ **adjusted** *(Statistics)* saisonbereinigt ‹*Arbeitslosenzahlen*›

seasoning ['si:zənıŋ] *n.* **a)** *(Cookery)* Gewürze *Pl.;* Würze, *die;* **b)** *(fig.)* Würze, *die;* **have a ~ of wit** ‹*Unterhaltung:*› witzig *od.* geistreich *od.* mit Witz gewürzt sein

'**season-ticket** *n.* Dauerkarte, *die; (for one year/month)* Jahres-/Monatskarte, *die*

seat [si:t] **1.** *n.* **a)** *(thing for sitting on)* Sitzgelegenheit, *die; (in vehicle, cinema, etc.)* Sitz, *der; (of toilet)* [Klosett]brille, *die (ugs.);* **use sth. for a ~:** sich auf etw. *(Akk.)* setzen; *(be sitting)* auf etw. *(Dat.)* sitzen; **b)** *(place)* Platz, *der; (in vehicle)* [Sitz]platz, *der;* **have** *or* **take a ~:** sich [hin]setzen; Platz nehmen *(geh.);* **take one's ~ at table** sich zu Tisch setzen; **keep one's ~:** sitzen bleiben; ‹*Reiter:*› im Sattel bleiben, sich im Sattel halten; **resume one's ~:** sich wieder [hin]setzen; *(after the interval etc.)* seinen Platz wieder einnehmen; wieder Platz nehmen *(geh.); see also* **back seat; c)** *(part of chair)* Sitzfläche, *die;* **d)** *(buttocks)* Gesäß, *das; (part of clothing)* Gesäßpartie, *die; (of trousers)* Sitz, *der;* Hosenboden, *der;* **by the ~ of one's pants** *(coll. fig.)* nach Gefühl; **e)** *(site)* Sitz, *der; (of disease also)* Herd, *der (Med.); (of learning)* Stätte, *die (geh.); (of trouble)* Quelle, *die;* **~ of the fire** Brandherd, *der;* **f)** *(right to sit in Parliament etc.)* Sitz, *der;* Mandat, *das;* **be elected to a ~ in Parliament** ins Parlament gewählt werden; **be appointed to a ~ on a committee** in einen Ausschuß berufen werden; **g) [country] ~** *(mansion)* Landsitz, *der;* **h)** *(on horseback)* Sitz, *der;* [Sitz]haltung, *die;* **i)** *(Mech. Engin.)* Sitz, *der;* **valve ~:** Ventilsitz, *der.* **2.** *v. t.* **a)** *(cause to sit)* setzen; *(accommodate at table etc.)* unterbringen; *(ask to sit)* ‹*Platzanweiser:*› einen Platz anweisen (+ *Dat.*); **~ oneself** sich setzen; **b)** *(have seats for)* Sitzplätze bieten (+ *Dat.*); **~ 500 people** 500 Sitzplätze haben; **the car ~s five comfortably** in dem Auto haben fünf Personen bequem Platz; **c)** *(fit with seats)* bestuhlen ‹*Saal usw.*›; **d)** *(Mech. Engin.)* in [die richtige] Position bringen

'**seat-belt** *n. (Motor Veh., Aeronaut.)* Sicherheitsgurt, *der;* **fasten one's ~:** sich anschnallen; den Gurt anlegen; **wear a ~:** angeschnallt sein; *(during journey)* angeschnallt fahren

seated ['si:tıd] *adj.* sitzend; **remain ~:** sitzen bleiben; **take 50 ~ passengers** 50 Sitzplätze haben; **be ~** *(formal)* Platz nehmen *(geh.)*

-seater ['sı:tə(r)] *adj. in comb.* -sitzig; **two-~ [car]** Zweisitzer, *der*

seating ['si:tıŋ] *n., no pl., no indef. art.* **a)** *(seats)* Sitzplätze; Sitzgelegenheiten; **b)** *(act)* Plazierung, *die;* Versorgung mit Sitzplätzen; **c)** *attrib.* Sitz‹*ordnung, -plan*›; **~ accommodation** Sitzgelegenheiten; Sitzplätze; **the ~ arrangements** die Sitzordnung

SEATO ['si:təʊ] *abbr.* **South-East-Asia Treaty Organisation** SEATO, *die*

sea: **~-urchin** *n. (Zool.)* Seeigel, *der;* **~-wall** *n.* Strandmauer, *die; (dike)* Deich, *der*

seaward ['si:wəd] **1.** *adj.* seewärtig ‹*Kurs, Wind*›; **the ~ side** die Seeseite; **the ~ view** die Aussicht aufs Meer *od.* auf die See. **2.** *adv.* seewärts; nach See zu. **3.** *n.* **to [the] ~:** zur Seeseite hin

seawards ['si:wədz] *see* **seaward 2**

sea: **~-water** *n.* Meerwasser, *das;* Seewasser, *das;* **~weed** *n.* [See]tang, *der;* **~worthy** *adj.* seetüchtig

sebaceous [sı'beıʃəs] *adj.* talgig; **~ duct/gland** *(Anat.)* Talgdrüsenausführungsgang, *der*/Talgdrüse, *die*

seborrhoea *(Amer.:* **seborrhea)** [sebə'ri:ə] *n. (Med.)* Seborrhö[e], *die (fachspr.);* Talgfluß, *der*

sec [sek] *(coll.) see* **second 2 b**

Sec. *abbr.* **Secretary** Sekr.

sec. *abbr.* **second[s]** Sek.

secant ['si:kənt, 'sekənt] *n. (Math.)* Sekante, *die; (of angle)* Sekans, *der*

secateurs [sekə'tɜ:z, 'sekətɜ:z] *n. pl. (Brit. Hort.)* Gartenschere, *die;* Rosenschere, *die*

secede [sı'si:d] *v. i. (Polit./Eccl./formal)* sich abspalten **(from** von); ‹*Mitglied:*› austreten **(from** aus)

secession [sı'seʃn] *n. (Polit./Eccl./formal)* Abspaltung, *die; (of member)* Austritt, *der;* **the ~ of some southern states** die Sezession einiger Südstaaten

seclude [sı'klu:d] *v. t.* absondern; **~ oneself** *(from society)* sich abkapseln *od.* absondern; *(into a room)* sich zurückziehen **(into** in + *Akk.*)

secluded [sı'klu:dıd] *adj.* **a)** *(hidden from view)* versteckt; *(somewhat isolated)* abgelegen; **b)** *(solitary)* zurückgezogen ‹*Leben*›

seclusion [sı'klu:ʒn] *n.* **a)** *(keeping from company)* Absonderung, *die; (being kept from company)* Abgesondertheit, *die;* **in ~ from** abgesondert von; **b)** *(privacy) (of life)* Zurückgezogenheit, *die; (of room)* Abgeschiedenheit, *die;* **in ~:** zurückgezogen ‹*leben*›; **c)** *no pl. (remoteness)* Abgelegenheit, *die*

second ['sekənd] **1.** *adj.* zweit...; zweitwichtigst... ‹*Stadt, Hafen usw.*›; **~ largest/highest** *etc.* zweitgrößt.../-höchst... *usw.;* **come in/be ~:** zweiter/zweite werden/sein; **every ~ week** jede zweite Woche; **~ to none** unübertroffen. **2.** *n.* **a)** *(unit of time or angle)* Sekunde, *die;* **b)** *(coll.: moment)* Sekunde, *die (ugs.);* **wait a few ~s** einen Moment warten; **in a ~** *(immediately)* sofort *(ugs.); (very quickly)* im Nu *(ugs.);* **just a ~!** *(coll.)* einen Moment!; **c)** *(additional person or thing)* **a ~:** noch einer/eine/eins; **d) the ~** *(in sequence)* der/die/das zweite; *(in rank)* der/die/das Zweite; **be the ~ to arrive** als zweiter/zweite ankommen; **be a good ~:** einen guten zweiten Platz belegen; **e)** *(in duel, boxing)* Sekundant, *der*/Sekundantin, *die;* **~s out [of the ring]** *(Boxing)* Ring frei!; **f)** *in pl. (helping of food)* zweite Portion; *(~ course)* zweiter Gang; **are there any ~s?** kann man eine zweite Portion bekommen?; **g)** *(day)* **the ~ of May** der zweite Mai; **the ~ [of the month]** der Zweite [des Monats]; **h)** *(~ form)* zweite [Schul]klasse; Zweite, *die (Schuljargon);* **i)** *in pl. (goods of second quality)* Waren zweiter Wahl; **be ~s** zweite Wahl sein; **j)** *(Motor Veh.)* zweiter Gang; **in ~:** im zweiten [Gang]; **change into ~:** in den zweiten [Gang] schalten; **k)** *(Brit. Univ.)* ≈ Gut, *das;* ≈ Zwei, *die;* **she got a ~ in mathematics** sie hat in Mathematik mit [einem] Gut *od.* [einer] Zwei abgeschlossen; **l)** *(Mus.)* Sekunde, *die.* **3.** *v. t.* **a)** *(support in debate)* unterstützen ‹*Antrag, Nominierung*›; sekundieren *(geh.);* **I'll ~ that!** *(coll.)* dem schließe ich mich an!; **b)** [sı'kɒnd] *(transfer)* vorübergehend versetzen; **c)** ['sekənd] *(support)* unterstützen; **d)** [sı'kɒnd] *(Brit. Mil.)* abstellen

secondarily ['sekəndərılı] *adv.* **a)** in zweiter Linie; an zweiter Stelle; **b)** *(indirectly)* mittelbar; indirekt

secondary ['sekəndərı] *adj.* **a)** *(of less importance)* zweitrangig; sekundär *(geh.);* Neben‹*akzent, -sache*›; *(derived from sth. primary)* weiterverarbeitend ‹*Industrie*›; **~ literature** Sekundärliteratur, *die;* **be ~ to sth.** einer Sache *(Dat.)* untergeordnet sein; **b)** *(indirectly caused)* sekundär *(geh., Med., Biol.); see also* **picketing; c)** *(supplementary)* zusätzlich; **d) S~** *(Geol.) see* **Mesozoic 1**

secondary: **~ coil** *n. (Electr.)* Sekundärspule, *die;* **~ colour** *see* **colour 1 a; ~ education** *n.* höhere Schule; *(result)* höhere Schulbildung; **~ 'modern [school]** *n. (Brit. Hist.)* ≈ Mittelschule, *die (veralt.);* Realschule, *die;* **~ school** *n.* höhere *od.* weiterführende Schule

second: **~ 'base** *see* **'base 1 c; ~-best 1.** ['---] *adj.* zweitbest...; **2.** [--'-] *adv.* **come off ~-best** den kürzeren ziehen *(ugs.);* **3.** [--'-] *n., no pl.* Zweitbeste, *der/die/das;* **don't settle for [the] ~-best!** gib dich nicht mit halben Sachen zufrieden; **~ 'chamber** *n. (Parl.)* zweite Kammer; **~ 'childhood** *see* **childhood; ~ 'class** *n.* **a)** *(set ranking after others)* zweite Kategorie; **b)** *(Transport, Post)* zweite Klasse; **travel in the ~ class** zweiter Klasse reisen; **c)** *(Brit. Univ.) see* **second 2 k; ~-class 1.** ['---] *adj.* **a)** *(of lower class)* zweiter Klasse *nachgestellt;* Zweite[r]-Klasse-‹*Post, Passagier, Fahrkarte usw.*›; **get a ~-class degree** *(Brit. Univ.)* mit der Note Zwei *od.* Gut abschließen; **b)** *(of inferior class)* zweitklassig *(abwertend);* **~-class citizen** Bürger zweiter Klasse; **~-class stamp** *Briefmarke für langsamere Postzustellung;* **2.** [--'-] *adv.* zweiter Klasse; **~ 'coming** *n., no pl. (Relig.)* zweite Ankunft; Wiederkunft, *die;* [zweite] Parusie *(fachspr.);* **~ 'cousin** *see* **cousin**

seconder ['sekəndə(r)] *n.* Befürworter, *der*/-worterin, *die;* Sekundant, *der*/Sekundantin, *die (geh.)*

second: **~ 'fiddle** *see* **fiddle 1 a; ~ 'floor** *see* **floor 1 b; ~ form** *see* **form 1 d; ~ 'gear** *n., no pl. (Motor Veh.)* zweiter Gang; *see also* **gear 1 a; ~-generation** *adj.* der zweiten Generation *nachgestellt;* **~-guess** *v. t. (Amer.)* **a)** im Nachhinein kritisieren; **b)** *(anticipate)* voraussehen; **~-guess sb.** voraussehen, was jmd. tun wird; **~ hand** *n. (Horol.)* Sekundenzeiger, *der;* **~-hand 1.** ['---] *adj.* **a)** *(used)* gebraucht ‹*Kleidung, Auto usw.*›; antiquarisch ‹*Buch*›; Secondhand‹*buch, -schallplatte, -kleidung usw.*›; **~-hand car** Gebrauchtwagen, *der;* **b)** *(selling used goods)* Gebrauchtwaren-; Secondhand‹*laden, -shop*›; **c)** *(taken on another's authority)* ‹*Nachrichten, Bericht*› aus zweiter Hand; **2.** [--'-] *adv.* aus zweiter Hand *(auch fig.);* gebraucht; **get a book ~-hand** ein Buch antiquarisch kaufen; **~ 'home** *n.* Zweitwohnung, *die; (holiday house)* Ferienhaus, *das;* **~ in com'mand** *n. (Mil.)* stellvertretender Kommandeur; *(of ship)* stellvertretender Kommandant; *(fig. coll.)* stellvertretender Leiter; **~ lieu'tenant** *n. (Mil.)* ≈ Leutnant, *der*

secondly ['sekəndlı] *adv.* zweitens

secondment [sı'kɒndmənt] *n. (Brit.)* **a)** *(of official)* vorübergehende Versetzung; **be on [a] ~:** vorübergehend versetzt sein; **b)** *(Mil.)* Abstellung, *die*

second: **~ name** *n.* Nachname, *der;* Zuname, *der;* **~ 'nature** *n., no pl., no art. (coll.)* zweite Natur; **become/be ~ nature to sb.** jmdm. zur zweiten Natur werden/geworden sein; jmdm. in Fleisch und Blut *(Akk.)* übergehen/übergegangen sein; **~ 'officer** *n. (Naut.)* zweiter Offizier; **~ 'person** *see* **person d; ~-'rate** *adj.* zweitklassig; **very/rather ~-rate** sehr/ziemlich mittelmäßig; **~-'rater** *n. (coll.)* **be a ~-rater** zweitklassig sein; **~ 'reading** *see* **reading g; ~s hand** *see* **~ hand; ~ sight** *see* **sight 1 a; ~ 'string** *see* **string 1 b; ~ 'thoughts** *n. pl.* **have ~ thoughts** es sich *(Dat.)* anders überlegen **(about** mit); **we've had ~ thoughts about buying the house** wir wollen das Haus nun doch nicht kaufen;

we've had ~ thoughts about the house wir haben uns das mit dem Haus doch noch einmal überlegt; **there's no time for ~ thoughts** es ist zu spät, es sich noch einmal anders zu überlegen; **but on ~ thoughts I think I will** wenn ich mir's [noch mal] überlege, werde ich es doch tun; ~ **wind** *see* ¹**wind 1f**
secrecy ['si:krɪsɪ] *n.* **a)** *(keeping of secret)* Geheimhaltung, *die;* **with great ~:** in aller Heimlichkeit *od.* ganz im geheimen; **b)** *(secretiveness)* Heimlichtuerei, *die (abwertend);* **c)** *(unrevealed state)* Heimlichkeit, *die;* **be shrouded in ~:** geheimgehalten werden; **in ~:** im geheimen
secret ['si:krɪt] **1.** *adj.* **a)** *(kept private, not to be made known)* geheim; Geheim⟨*fach, -tür, -abkommen, -kode*⟩; **keep sth. ~:** etw. geheimhalten **(from** vor + *Dat.*); **b)** *(acting in secret)* heimlich ⟨*Trinker, Liebhaber, Bewunderer*⟩. **2.** *n.* **a)** Geheimnis, *das;* **make no ~ of sth.** kein Geheimnis aus etw. machen; *(not conceal feelings, opinion)* kein[en] Hehl aus etw. machen; **keep the ~:** es für sich behalten; **keep ~s/a ~:** schweigen *(fig.);* den Mund halten *(ugs.);* **can you keep a ~?** kannst du schweigen?; **make sth. a ~:** etw. geheimhalten; **keep ~s from sb.** Geheimnisse vor jmdm. haben; **let sb. in on a ~:** jmdn. in ein Geheimnis einweihen; **be in the ~:** eingeweiht sein; **open ~:** offenes Geheimnis; **the ~ of health/success** *etc.* das Geheimnis der Gesundheit/des Erfolgs *usw.;* der Schlüssel zur Gesundheit/zum Erfolg *usw.;* **b) in ~:** im geheimen; heimlich
secret 'agent *n.* Geheimagent, *der*/-agentin, *die*
secretaire [sekrɪ'teə(r)] *see* **escritoire**
secretarial [sekrə'teərɪəl] *adj.* Sekretariats⟨*personal*⟩; Sekretärinnen⟨*kursus, -tätigkeit*⟩; ⟨*Arbeit*⟩ als Sekretärin; ~ **skills** Steno- und Schreibmaschinenkenntnisse
secretariat [sekrə'teərɪət] *n.* Sekretariat, *das*
secretary ['sekrətərɪ] *n.* **a)** *(official of organization)* Sekretär, *der*/Sekretärin, *die;* *(of company)* Schriftführer, *der*/-führerin, *die;* **honorary ~:** ehrenamtlicher Sekretär; **b)** *(personal assistant)* Sekretär, *der*/Sekretärin, *die;* **Parliamentary [Private] S~** *(Brit. Parl.)* ≈ parlamentarischer Staatssekretär/parlamentarische Staatssekretärin; **Permanent S~** *(Brit. Admin.)* ≈ Staatssekretär, *der*/-sekretärin, *die; see also* **private secretary**
secretary: ~-bird *n.* Sekretär, *der;* **S~-'General** *n., pl.* **Secretaries-General** Generalsekretär, *der*/-sekretärin, *die;* **S~ of 'State** *n.* **a)** *(Brit. Polit.)* Minister, *der*/Ministerin, *die;* **S~ of State for Defence** Verteidigungsminister, *der*/-ministerin, *die;* **b)** *(Amer. Polit.)* Außenminister, *der*/-ministerin, *die;* **c)** *(Amer. Admin.: head of records department) Leiter/Leiterin des Archivs eines Bundesstaates*
secretaryship ['sekrətərɪʃɪp] *n.* **a)** *(office)* Amt des Sekretärs/der Sekretärin; **b)** *(tenure)* Amtszeit als Sekretär/Sekretärin
secret 'ballot *n.* geheime Abstimmung
secrete [sɪ'kri:t] *v.t.* **a)** *(Physiol.)* absondern; sezernieren *(fachspr.);* **b)** *(formal/literary: hide)* verbergen; ~ **oneself** sich verbergen
secretion [sɪ'kri:ʃn] *n.* **a)** *(Physiol.)* Absonderung, *die; (process also)* Sekretion, *die (fachspr.); (substance also)* Sekret, *das (fachspr.);* **b)** *(formal/literary: concealing)* Verbergen, *das*
secretive ['si:krɪtɪv] *adj.* verschlossen ⟨*Person*⟩; geheimnisvoll ⟨*Lächeln*⟩; **be ~:** heimlich tun *(abwertend) od.* geheimnisvoll tun **(about** mit); **she was being very ~ about something** sie versuchte, irgend etwas zu verheimlichen
secretively ['si:krɪtɪvlɪ, sɪ'kri:tɪvlɪ] *adv.* geheimnisvoll ⟨*lächeln*⟩; **behave ~:** geheimnisvoll *od. (abwertend)* heimlich tun
secretly ['si:krɪtlɪ] *adv.* heimlich; insgeheim ⟨*etw. glauben*⟩
secretory [sɪ'kri:tərɪ] *adj. (Physiol.)* sekretorisch
secret: S~ Police *n.* Geheimpolizei, *die;* **S~ 'Service** *n.* Geheimdienst, *der;* ~ **so'ciety** *n.* Geheimbund, *der*
sect [sekt] *n.* **a)** Sekte, *die;* **b)** *(religious denomination)* Religionsgemeinschaft, *die;* **c)** *(followers of school of thought)* Schule, *die*
sectarian [sek'teərɪən] **1.** *adj.* konfessionell; konfessionell motiviert ⟨*Handlungen*⟩; konfessionell ausgerichtet ⟨*Erziehung*⟩; Konfessions⟨*krieg, -streit*⟩. **2.** *n.* Sektenanhänger *der*/-anhängerin, *die;* Sektierer, *der*/Sektiererin, *die*
sectarianism [sek'teərɪənɪzm] *n., no pl.* Sektierertum, *das*
section ['sekʃn] *n.* **a)** *(part cut off)* Abschnitt, *der;* Stück, *das; (part of divided whole)* Teil, *der; (of railway track)* [Strecken]abschnitt, *der;* Teilstück, *das;* **b)** *(of firm)* Abteilung, *die; (of organization etc.)* Sektion, *die; (of orchestra or band)* Gruppe, *die;* **accounts ~** *(Econ.)* Buchhaltung, *die;* **business ~** *(in newspaper)* Wirtschaftsteil, *der;* **c)** *(component part)* [Einzel]teil, *das;* [Bau]element, *das; (of ship, bridge, etc. also)* Sektion, *die (Technik);* **d)** *(of chapter, book)* Abschnitt, *der; (of statute, act)* Paragraph, *der;* **e)** *(part of community)* Gruppe, *die;* **f)** *(Amer.: area of country)* [Landes]teil, *der;* Gebiet, *das;* **g)** *(representation)* Schnitt, *der;* **vertical/horizontal/longitudinal/oblique ~:** Vertikal-/Horizontal-/Längs-/Schrägschnitt, *der;* **h)** *(Amer.: square mile)* Section, *die;* **i)** *(Geom.) (cutting of solid)* Schnitt, *der; ([area of] figure)* Schnitt, *der;* Schnittfläche, *die; (shape or area of cross-section)* Querschnitt, *der; see also* **conic; j)** *(Amer.: district)* Bezirk, *der;* **the business/residential ~:** die City/die Wohngebiete; **k)** *(Med.)* Schnitt, *der;* **abdominal ~:** Bauchdeckenschnitt, *der*
sectional ['sekʃənl] *adj.* **a)** *(pertaining to a representation)* Schnitt-; **b)** *(pertaining to part of community)* Gruppen⟨*interessen*⟩; partikular ⟨*Interessen*⟩; ⟨*Auseinandersetzung*⟩ zwischen den Bevölkerungsgruppen; **c)** *(made in parts)* zum Zusammenbauen *nachgestellt*
sectionalism ['sekʃənəlɪzm] *n.* Partikularismus, *der (meist abwertend)*
sector ['sektə(r)] *n.* **a)** *(of activity)* Sektor, *der;* Bereich, *der;* **the leisure/industrial ~:** der Freizeitsektor/der Bereich der Industrie; *see also* **private sector; public sector; b)** *(Geom.)* Sektor, *der; (of circle also)* Kreisausschnitt, *der;* **c)** *(Mil.) (area)* Kampfabschnitt, *der;* Gefechtsabschnitt, *der*
secular ['sekjʊlə(r)] *adj. (not sacred)* säkular *(geh.);* weltlich ⟨*Angelegenheit, Schule, Musik, Gericht*⟩; profan *(geh.)* ⟨*Musik*⟩; ~ **buildings** Profanbauten *(fachspr.)*
secular 'clergy *n. pl. (Eccl.)* Weltgeistlichkeit, *die;* Weltklerus, *der*
secularism ['sekjʊlərɪzm] *n.* Säkularismus, *der*
secularize (secularise) ['sekjʊləraɪz] *v.t.* säkularisieren; verweltlichen; **become ~d** verweltlichen
secure [sɪ'kjʊə(r)] **1.** *adj.* **a)** *(safe)* sicher; ~ **against burglars/fire** gegen Einbruch/Feuer geschützt; einbruch-/feuersicher; **make sth. ~ from attack/enemies** etw. gegen Angriffe/Feinde sichern; **b)** *(firmly fastened)* fest; **be ~** ⟨*Ladung:*⟩ gesichert sein; ⟨*Riegel, Tür:*⟩ fest zu sein; ⟨*Tür:*⟩ ver- *od.* zugeriegelt sein; ⟨*Schraube:*⟩ fest sein *od.* sitzen; **make sth. ~:** etw. sichern; **c)** *(untroubled)* sicher, gesichert ⟨*Existenz*⟩; **feel ~:** sich sicher *od.* geborgen fühlen; ~ **in the knowledge that ...:** in dem sicheren Bewußtsein, daß ...; **emotionally ~:** emotional stabil. **2.** *v.t.* **a)** *(obtain)* sichern **(for** *Dat.*); beschaffen ⟨*Auftrag*⟩ **(for** *Dat.*); *(for oneself)* sich *(Dat.)* sichern; **b)** *(confine)* fesseln ⟨*Gefangenen*⟩; *(in container)* einschließen ⟨*Wertsachen*⟩; *(fasten firmly)* sichern, fest zumachen ⟨*Fenster, Tür*⟩; festmachen ⟨*Boot*⟩ **(to an** + *Dat.*); **c)** *(guarantee)* absichern ⟨*Darlehen*⟩; ~ **oneself [against sth.]** sich [gegen etw.] absichern; **d)** *(fortify)* sichern
securely [sɪ'kjʊəlɪ] *adv.* **a)** *(firmly)* fest ⟨*verriegeln, zumachen*⟩; sicher ⟨*befestigen*⟩; **b)** *(safely)* sicher ⟨*untergebracht sein*⟩; ~ **locked up** unter sicherem Verschluß
security [sɪ'kjʊərɪtɪ] *n.* **a)** *(safety)* Sicherheit, *die; (of knot)* sicherer Halt; **b)** *(safety of State or organization)* Sicherheit, *die;* ~ **[measures]** Sicherheitsmaßnahmen; Sicherheitsvorkehrungen; ~ **reasons** Sicherheitsgründe; **national ~:** nationale Sicherheit; Staatssicherheit, *die;* **c)** *(thing that guarantees)* Sicherheit, *die;* Gewähr, *die;* Garantie, *die; (object of value)* Pfand, *das;* **as or in ~ for sth.** als Sicherheit/Pfand für etw.; **obtain a loan on [the] ~ of sth.** auf etw. *(Akk.)* ein Darlehen bekommen; **d)** *usu. in pl. (Finance)* Wertpapier, *das;* **securities** Wertpapiere; Effekten *Pl.;* **e) emotional ~:** emotionale Sicherheit; **he needs the ~ of a good home** er braucht die Geborgenheit eines guten Zuhauses; **f)** *(assured freedom from want)* Sicherheit, *die*
security: S~ Council *n. (Polit.)* Sicherheitsrat, *der;* ~ **forces** *n. pl.* Sicherheitskräfte *Pl.;* ~ **guard** *n.* Wächter, *der*/Wächterin, *die;* ~ **man** *n.* Wachmann, *der;* ~ **officer** *n.* Sicherheitsbeauftragte, *der/die;* ~ **risk** *n.* Sicherheitsrisiko, *das*
sedan [sɪ'dæn] *n.* **a)** *(Hist.: chair)* Sänfte, *die;* **b)** *(Amer. Motor Veh.)* Limousine, *die*
se'dan-chair *see* **sedan a**
sedate [sɪ'deɪt] **1.** *adj.* **a)** bedächtig; gesetzt ⟨*alte Dame*⟩; ruhig ⟨*Kind*⟩; gemächlich ⟨*Tempo, Leben, Auto*⟩; **in a ~ manner** in aller Ruhe; **b)** *(fig.)* schlicht; gemächlich ⟨*altes Pferd*⟩. **2.** *v.t. (Med.)* sedieren *(fachspr.);* ruhigstellen
sedately [sɪ'deɪtlɪ] *adv.* bedächtig; gemächlich ⟨*fahren*⟩
sedation [sɪ'deɪʃn] *n. (Med.)* Sedation, *die (fachspr.);* Ruhigstellung, *die;* **be under ~:** sediert sein *(fachspr.);* ruhig gestellt sein
sedative ['sedətɪv] **1.** *n. (Med.)* Sedativum, *das (fachspr.);* Beruhigungsmittel, *das.* **2.** *adj.* **a)** *(Med.)* sedativ *(fachspr.);* ~ **agent** *see* **1; b)** *(fig.: calming)* beruhigend ⟨*Wirkung*⟩
sedentary ['sedəntərɪ] *adj.* sitzend ⟨*Haltung, Lebensweise, Tätigkeit*⟩; **lead a ~ life** eine sitzende Lebensweise haben; viel sitzen
sedge [sedʒ] *n. (Bot.)* **a)** *(plant)* Segge, *die;* **b)** *no pl. (bed)* Seggenried, *das*
'sedge-warbler, 'sedge-wren *ns. (Ornith.)* Schilfrohrsänger, *der*
sediment ['sedɪmənt] *n.* **a)** *(matter)* Ablagerung, *die;* Ablagerungen *Pl.;* **b)** *(lees)* Bodensatz, *der; (of wine also)* Depot, *das (fachspr.);* **c)** *(Geol.)* Sediment, *das*
sedimentary [sedɪ'mentərɪ] *adj. (Geol.)* sedimentär; Sediment⟨*gestein*⟩
sedimentation [sedɪmən'teɪʃn] *n.* Sedimentation, *die (fachspr.);* Bildung von Ablagerungen
sedition [sɪ'dɪʃn] *n.* Aufruhr, *der;* **[incitement to] ~:** Anstiftung zum Aufruhr
seditious [sɪ'dɪʃəs] *adj.* aufrührerisch; staatsgefährdend ⟨*Delikt*⟩
seduce [sɪ'dju:s] *v.t.* **a)** *(sexually)* verführen; **b)** *(lead astray)* verführen; *(distract)* ablenken **(away from** von); ~ **sb. into doing sth.** jmdn. dazu verführen *od.* verleiten, etw. zu tun
seducer [sɪ'dju:sə(r)] *n.* Verführer, *der*

seduction [sɪ'dʌkʃn] *n.* **a)** *(sexual)* Verführung, *die;* **b)** *(leading astray)* Verführung, *die* (into zu); Verleitung, *die* (into zu); **c)** *(thing that tempts)* Verlockung, *die;* Versuchung, *die*
seductive [sɪ'dʌktɪv] *adj.* verführerisch; verlockend ⟨*Angebot*⟩
seductively [sɪ'dʌktɪvlɪ] *adv.* verführerisch
sedulous ['sedʒʊləs] *adj. (formal)* unermüdlich; eifrig ⟨*Sammler*⟩; *(painstaking)* akkurat *(geh.)* ⟨*Sorgfalt, Arbeiter*⟩
sedulously ['sedʒʊləslɪ] *adv. (formal)* unermüdlich; *(painstakingly)* akkurat; geflissentlich ⟨*etw. vermeiden, überhören*⟩
[1]**see** [si:] **1.** *v. t.,* **saw** [sɔ:], **seen** [si:n] **a)** sehen; **let sb. ~ sth.** *(show)* jmdm. etw. zeigen; **let me ~:** laß mich mal sehen; **I saw her fall** *or* **falling** ich habe sie fallen sehen; **he was ~n to fall down the stairs** man hat gesehen, wie er die Treppe hinunterfiel; **he was ~n to leave** *or* **~n leaving the building** er ist beim Verlassen des Gebäudes gesehen worden; **I'll believe it when I ~ it** das will ich erst mal sehen; **they saw it happen** sie haben gesehen, wie es passiert ist; sie haben es gesehen; **can you ~ that house over there?** siehst du das Haus da drüben?; **for all [the world] to ~:** für jedermann sichtbar; *(fig.: in public)* in aller Öffentlichkeit; vor aller Welt; **be worth ~ing** sehenswert sein; sich lohnen *(ugs.);* **~ the light** *(fig.: undergo conversion)* das Licht schauen *(geh.);* **I saw the light** *(I realized my error etc.)* mir ging ein Licht auf *(ugs.);* **he'll ~ the light eventually** *(he'll realize the truth)* ihm werden die Augen noch aufgehen; **~ the light [of day]** *(be born)* das Licht der Welt erblicken *(geh.); (fig.: be published or produced)* herauskommen; '**~ things** Halluzinationen haben; **I must be ~ing things** *(joc.)* ich glaub', ich seh' nicht richtig; **~ stars** Sterne sehen *(ugs.);* **~ the sights/town** sich *(Dat.)* die Sehenswürdigkeiten/Stadt ansehen; **~ visions** Visionen *od.* Gesichte haben; **~ one's way [clear] to do** *or* **to doing sth.** es einrichten, etw. zu tun; **we cannot ~ our way [clear] to do it** es ist uns [zur Zeit] nicht möglich, es zu tun; *see also* **back 1 a; something c, g; world a; b)** *(watch)* sehen; **let's ~ a film** sehen wir uns *(Dat.)* einen Film an!; **c)** *(meet [with])* sehen; treffen; *(meet socially)* zusammenkommen mit; sich treffen mit; **I'll ~ you there/at 5** wir sehen uns dort/um 5; **~ you!** *(coll.),* **[I'll] be ~ing you!** *(coll.)* bis bald *(ugs.);* **~ you on Saturday/soon** bis Samstag/bald; *see also* [1]**long 1 c; d)** *(speak to)* sprechen ⟨*Person*⟩ (about wegen); *(pay visit to)* gehen zu, *(geh.)* aufsuchen ⟨*Arzt, Anwalt usw.*⟩; *(receive)* empfangen; **the doctor will ~ you now** Herr Doktor läßt bitten; **whom would you like to ~?** wen möchten Sie sprechen?; zu wem möchten Sie?; **e)** *(discern mentally)* sehen; **I ~ it all!** jetzt ist mir alles klar; **I can ~ it's difficult for you** ich verstehe, daß es nicht leicht für dich ist; **I ~ what you mean** ich verstehe [was du meinst]; **~ what I mean?** siehst du?; **I saw that it was a mistake** mir war klar, daß es ein Fehler war; **I don't ~ the point of it** ich sehe keinen Sinn darin; **I can't ~ the good/advantage of doing it** ich kann keinen Sinn/Vorteil darin sehen, es zu tun; **he didn't ~ the joke** er fand es [gar] nicht lustig; *(did not understand)* er hat den Witz nicht verstanden; **I can't think what she ~s in him** ich weiß nicht, was sie an ihm findet; **I saw myself [being] obliged to ...:** ich sah mich gezwungen, zu...; **f)** *(consider)* sehen; **let me ~ what I can do** [ich will] mal sehen, was ich tun kann; **g)** *(foresee)* sehen; **I can ~ I'm going to be busy** ich sehe [es] schon [kommen], daß ich beschäftigt sein werde; **I can ~ it won't be easy** ich sehe schon *od.* weiß jetzt schon, daß es nicht einfach sein wird; **h)** *(find out)* feststellen; *(by looking)* nachsehen; **that remains to be ~n** das wird man sehen; **~ if you can read this** guck mal, ob du das hier lesen kannst *(ugs.);* **i)** *(take view of)* sehen; betrachten; **~ things as sb. does** jmds. Ansichten teilen; **try to ~ it my way** versuche es doch mal aus meiner Sicht zu sehen; **as I ~ it** meines Erachtens; meiner Ansicht *od.* Meinung nach; *see also* **eye 1 a;** [2]**fit 1 c; j)** *(learn)* sehen; **I ~ from your letter that ...:** ich entnehme Ihrem Brief, daß ...; **as we have ~n** wie wir schon gesehen haben; **k)** *(make sure)* **~ [that] ...:** zusehen *od.* darauf achten, daß ...; **l)** *usu. in imper. (look at)* einsehen ⟨*Buch*⟩; **~ below/p. 15** siehe unten/S. 15; **m)** *(experience)* erleben; **live to ~ sth.** etw. miterleben; **1936 saw him in India/a revolution in that country** 1936 hielt er sich in Indien auf/kam es in dem Land zu einer Revolution; **I've ~n it all** mir ist nichts unbekannt; **I've ~n it all before** das kenne ich; **now I've ~n everything!** *(iron.)* hat man so etwas schon erlebt *od.* gesehen!; **n)** *(be witness of)* erleben; *(be the scene of)* Schauplatz (+ *Gen.*) sein; **we shall ~:** wir werden [ja/schon] sehen; **~/have ~n life** das Leben kennenlernen/kennen; **he will not** *or* **never ~ 50 again** er ist [bestimmt] über 50; *see also* **day c; service 1 a, p; o)** *(imagine)* sich *(Dat.)* vorstellen; **~ sb./oneself doing sth.** sich vorstellen, daß jmd./man etw. tut; **~ oneself as a star** sich schon als Star sehen; **I can ~ it now – ...:** ich sehe es schon bildhaft vor mir – ...; **p)** *(contemplate)* mit ansehen; zusehen bei; **[stand by and] ~ sb. doing sth.** [tatenlos] zusehen *od.* es [tatenlos] mit ansehen, wie jmd. etw. tut; **I'll ~ him damned** *or* **dead** *or* **hanged** *or* **in hell [first]** das wäre das Letzte[, was ich täte]!; nie im Leben!; **q)** *(escort)* begleiten, bringen (to [bis] zu); **r)** *(supervise)* **~ the doors locked/the book through the press** das Abschließen der Türen/den Druck des Buches überwachen; **I'll stay and ~ you on the bus** ich bleibe noch, bis du im Bus sitzt; **s)** *(consent willingly to)* einsehen; **not ~ [oneself] doing sth.** es nicht einsehen, daß man etw. tut; **he couldn't ~ it** er konnte sich nicht damit anfreunden; **t)** *(Gambling)* mithalten mit. **2.** *v. i.,* **saw, seen a)** *(discern objects)* sehen; **~ for yourself!** sieh doch selbst!; **~ red** rotsehen *(ugs.);* **sth. makes sb. ~ red** jmd. sieht bei etw. rot *(ugs.);* etw. bringt jmdn. zur Weißglut; **b)** *(make sure)* nachsehen; **c)** *(reflect)* überlegen; **let me ~:** laß mich überlegen; warte mal ['n Moment] *(ugs.);* **d) I ~:** ich verstehe; aha *(ugs.);* ach so *(ugs.);* **you ~:** weißt du/wißt ihr/wissen Sie; **there you are, you ~!** Siehst du? Ich hab's doch gesagt!; **well, you ~, ...** *(in apologies)* es tut mir leid, aber ...; **she used to be a nurse, you ~:** sie war nämlich mal Krankenschwester; **~?** *(coll.)* verstanden? *(salopp);* klar? *(salopp);* **as far as I can ~:** soweit ich das *od.* es beurteilen kann; **~ here!** na hör/hören Sie mal!
~ about *v. t.* sich kümmern um; **I'll ~ about getting the car repaired** ich werde mich darum kümmern, daß das Auto repariert wird; **I've come to ~ about the room/cooker** ich komme wegen des Zimmers/des Herdes; **I'll ~ about it** *(consider it)* [ich will] mal sehen *(ugs.);* **we'll ~ about that!** *(you may well be wrong)* das werden wir ja sehen!
~ into *v. t.* **a)** *(gain view into)* [hinein]sehen in (+ *Akk.*); [rein]gucken *(ugs.)* in (+ *Akk.*); **~ into it** hineinsehen; reingucken *(ugs.);* **b)** *(fig.: investigate)* nachgehen, auf den Grund gehen (+ *Dat.*) ⟨*Angelegenheit, Klage*⟩
~ 'off *v. t.* **a)** *(say farewell to)* verabschieden; **b)** *(chase away)* vertreiben; **~ him off, Rover!** mach ihm Beine, Rover! *(ugs.);* **c)** *(defeat)* erledigen; abservieren *(Sportjargon)*
~ 'out 1. *v. i.* hinaussehen; rausgucken *(ugs.).* **2.** *v. t.* **a)** *(remain till end of)* ⟨*Zuschauer:*⟩ sich *(Dat.)* zu Ende ansehen ⟨*Spiel*⟩; ableisten ⟨*Amtsperiode*⟩; ⟨*Patient:*⟩ überleben ⟨*Zeitraum*⟩; **enough fuel to ~ the winter out** genug Heizmaterial, um über den Winter zu kommen; **~ sb. out** *(be present at sb.'s death)* bei jmds. Tod bei ihm/ihr sein; *(live or last until sb.'s death)* ⟨*Person, Gegenstand:*⟩ jmdn. überleben; **b)** *(escort from premises)* hinausbegleiten (of aus); hinausbringen (of aus); **~ oneself out** allein hinausfinden; **c)** *see* **~ through c**
~ over, ~ round *v. t.* besichtigen
~ through *v. t.* **a)** ['--] *(penetrate with vision)* hindurchsehen durch; durchgucken *(ugs.)* durch; *see also* **see-through; b)** ['--] *(fig.: penetrate nature of)* durchschauen; **c)** [-'-] *(not abandon)* zu Ende *od.* zum Abschluß bringen; **~ things through** bei der Stange bleiben; **d)** [-'-] *(be sufficient for)* **~ sb. through** jmdm. reichen; **we have enough food to ~ us through the weekend** wir haben für das Wochenende genug zu essen; **e) ~ sb. through his difficulties** jmdm. über seine Schwierigkeiten hinweghelfen
~ to *v. t.* sich kümmern um; **I'll ~ to that** dafür werde ich sorgen; **~ to it that ...:** dafür sorgen, daß ...; **well, ~ to it you do!** gut, dann sieh mal zu!
[2]**see** *n. (Eccl.)* [erz]bischöflicher Stuhl; **the Holy See** *or* **See of Rome** *(RC Ch.)* der Heilige *od.* Apostolische Stuhl
seed [si:d] **1.** *n.* **a)** *(grain)* Samen, *der;* Samenkorn, *das; (of grape etc.)* Kern, *der; (for birds)* Korn, *das;* **b)** *no pl., no indef. art.* (**~s** *collectively)* Samen[körner] *Pl.; (as collected for sowing)* Saatgut, *das;* Saat, *die; (of various plants also)* Sämereien *Pl.;* **grass-~:** Grassamen *Pl.;* **go** *or* **run to ~:** Samen bilden; ⟨*Salat:*⟩ [in Samen] schießen; *(fig.)* herunterkommen *(ugs.);* **c)** *(fig.: beginning)* Saat, *die;* Samen, *der (geh.);* **sow [the] ~s of doubt/a conflict/discord** für Zweifel/Konflikt sorgen/Zwietracht säen; **d)** *(Sport coll.)* gesetzter Spieler/gesetzte Spielerin; **fourth ~/number one ~:** als Nummer vier/eins gesetzter Spieler/gesetzte Spielerin; **e)** *no pl. (arch.) (semen)* Samen, *der;* **f)** *no pl. (Bibl.: descendants)* Same, *der.* **2.** *v. t.* **a)** *(place* **~s** *in)* besäen; **b)** *(Sport)* setzen ⟨*Spieler*⟩; **be ~ed number one** als Nummer eins gesetzt werden/sein; **c)** *(lit. or fig.: sprinkle [as] with* **~***)* besäen; **d)** *(place crystal[s] in)* impfen ⟨*Wolken, chemische Lösung*⟩. **3.** *v. i.* **a)** *(produce* **~s***)* Samen bilden; **b)** *(go to* **~***)* [in Samen] schießen; **c)** *(sow* **~s***)* säen
seed: ~-bed *n.* **a)** *(Hort.)* [Saat]beet, *das;* **b)** *(fig.: place of development)* Grundlage, *die; (of evil)* Brutstätte, *die;* **prepare the ~-bed of sth.** einer Sache *(Dat.)* den Boden bereiten; **~-cake** *n.* Kümmelkuchen, *der;* **~-corn** *n.* Saatgetreide, *das;* Saatkorn, *das;* **~ crystal** *n. (Chem.)* [Kristallisations]keim, *der;* Impfkristall, *der*
seedless ['si:dlɪs] *adj.* kernlos ⟨*Trauben, Rosinen*⟩
seedling ['si:dlɪŋ] *n.* Sämling, *der*
seed: ~-money *n.* Anfangs-, Startkapital, *das;* **~-packet** *n.* Samentüte, *die;* **~-pearl** *n.* Samenperle, *die;* Saatperle, *die;* **~-potato** *n. (Hort.)* Saatkartoffel, *die;* **~sman** ['si:dzmən] *n., pl.* **~smen** ['si:dzmən] *n.* Samenhändler, *der;* **~-time** *n.* [Aus]saatzeit, *die*
seedy ['si:dɪ] *adj.* **a)** *(coll.: unwell)* **feel ~:** sich [leicht] angeschlagen fühlen; **b)** *(shabby)* schäbig, *(ugs. abwertend)* vergammelt ⟨*Aussehen, Kleidung*⟩; heruntergekommen ⟨*Stadtteil*⟩; **c)** *(disreputable)* zweifelhaft ⟨*Person*⟩
seeing ['si:ɪŋ] **1.** *conj.* **~ [that] ...:** da ...; wo ... *(ugs.).* **2.** *n., no pl., no indef. art. (faculty or power of sight)* Sehvermögen, *das;* **~ is believing** so was glaubt man erst, wenn man es gesehen hat

seeing 'eye *n. (dog)* Blindenhund, *der*
seek [si:k] *v. t.*, **sought** [sɔ:t] **a)** suchen; anstreben ⟨*Posten, Amt*⟩; sich bemühen um ⟨*Anerkennung, Freundschaft, Interview, Einstellung*⟩; *(try to reach)* aufsuchen; ~ **shelter/help/one's fortune/sb.'s advice** Schutz/Hilfe/sein Glück/jmds. Rat suchen; **scientists are ~ing the solution** Wissenschaftler suchen nach der Lösung; **b)** *(literary/formal: attempt)* suchen *(geh.)*; versuchen; ~ **to do sth.** suchen, etw. zu tun *(geh.)*; **I'm only ~ing to establish a fact** es ist mir nur darum zu tun, eine Tatsache festzustellen *(geh.)*; *see also* **level 1 a**
~ **after** *v. t.* suchen nach; **be much sought after** sehr gesucht sein
~ **for** *v. t.* suchen nach; **~ing for information** auf der Suche nach Informationen
~ **'out** *v. t.* ausfindig machen ⟨*Sache, Ort*⟩; aufsuchen, kommen zu ⟨*Menschen*⟩
seeker ['si:kə(r)] *n.* Sucher, *der*/Sucherin, *die;* ~ **after the Truth** Wahrheitssucher, *der*/-sucherin, *die (geh.)*; **bargain-~s** Leute, die Jagd auf günstige Angebote machen/machten *usw.*
seem [si:m] *v. i.* **a)** *(appear [to be])* scheinen; **you ~ tired** du wirkst müde; **she ~s nice** sie scheint nett zu sein; **it's not quite what it ~s** es ist nicht ganz das, was es [zunächst] zu sein scheint; **it ~s like only yesterday** es ist, als wäre es erst gestern gewesen; **he ~s certain to win** es sieht ganz so aus, als würde er gewinnen; **she ~s younger than 45** sie wirkt jünger als 45; **what ~s to be the trouble?** wo fehlt's denn? *(ugs.)*; wo drückt denn der Schuh? *(ugs.)*; **it ~s a pity** es ist doch schade; **I ~ to recall having seen him before** ich glaube mich zu erinnern, ihn schon einmal gesehen zu haben; **it just ~s as if it were** es scheint nur so *od.* kommt einem nur so vor; **doing such a thing just doesn't ~ right somehow** es ist doch irgendwie nicht richtig, so etwas zu tun; **it ~s [that] ...:** anscheinend ...; **it ~s to me that it's silly to do that** ich finde es töricht *od.* es kommt mir töricht vor, das zu tun; **it ~s that we had better decide quickly** wir sollten uns wohl besser schnell entscheiden; **it ~s you were lying** du hast ja wohl gelogen; **it ~s [as if] there will be war** es sieht nach Krieg aus; es sieht so aus, als ob es Krieg geben wird; **it would** *or (arch.)* **should ~ to be ...:** es scheint ja wohl ... zu sein; **you know everything, it would ~:** du scheinst ja wohl alles zu wissen; **it would ~ that he is ...:** er scheint ja wohl ... zu sein; **so it ~s** *or* **would ~:** so will es scheinen; **Dead? – So it would ~:** Tot? – Allem Anschein nach; **so it ~s!** *(iron.)* was Sie nicht sagen! *(iron.)*; **b) sb. can't ~ to do sth.** *(coll.)* jmd. scheint etw. nicht tun zu können; **I just can't ~ to do it** *(coll.)* ich kann es einfach irgendwie nicht [tun] *(ugs.)*; **she doesn't ~ to notice such things** *(coll.)* so was merkt sie irgendwie nicht *(ugs.)*; ~ **good to sb.** jmdm. das beste [zu sein] scheinen
seeming ['si:mɪŋ] *adj.* scheinbar
seemingly ['si:mɪŋlɪ] *adv.* **a)** *(evidently)* offensichtlich; **b)** *(to outward appearance)* scheinbar
seemly ['si:mlɪ] *adj.* anständig; **it isn't ~ to praise oneself** es gehört sich nicht, sich selbst zu loben
seen *see* **¹see**
seep [si:p] *v. i.* ~ **[away]** [ab]sickern; ~ **in through** durch etw. hineinsickern; ~ **out of sth.** aus etw. heraussickern; **[gradually] ~ through to sb.'s consciousness** *(fig.)* jmdm. [langsam] dämmern *(ugs.) od.* bewußt werden
seepage ['si:pɪdʒ] *n.* **a)** Versickern, *das; (into sth.)* Hineinsickern, *das;* **b)** *(quantity)* Lache, *die; (of oil)* Ölausbiß, *der (Geol.)*; *(of gas)* Austritt, *der*
seer [sɪə(r)] *n. (prophet)* Seher, *der*/Seherin, *die*
seersucker ['sɪəsʌkə(r)] *n. (Textiles)* Seersucker, *der; Baumwoll- od. Leinengewebe mit Kreppstreifen; attrib.* ⟨*Kleid, Tagesdecke*⟩ aus Seersucker
'see-saw 1. *n.* **a)** *(plank)* Wippe, *die;* **b)** *no art. (game)* Wippen, *das;* **let's have a game of ~:** komm, wir gehen auf die Wippe *od.* wippen; **c)** *(fig.: contest)* Auf und Ab, *das.* **2.** *v. i.* **a)** *(move up and down)* ⟨*Weg, Straße:*⟩ auf und ab führen; ⟨*Deck:*⟩ [auf und ab] schaukeln; **b)** *(vacillate)* schwanken; **c)** *(play on ~)* wippen
seethe [si:ð] *v. i.* **a)** *(surge)* ⟨*Wellen, Meer:*⟩ branden; ⟨*Straßen usw.:*⟩ wimmeln **(with** von); *(bubble or foam as if boiling)* schäumen; **b)** *(fig.: be agitated)* schäumen; ~ **[with anger/inwardly]** vor Wut/innerlich schäumen
'see-through *adj.* durchsichtig
segment 1. ['segmənt] *n.* **a)** *(of orange, pineapple)* Scheibe, *die;* Schnitz, *der (bes. südd.)*; *(of cake, pear)* Stück, *das; (of worm, skull, limb)* Segment, *das; (of bowel)* Abschnitt, *der;* Segment, *das (Med.)*; *(of economy, market)* Bereich, *der;* **b)** *(Ling., Geom., Sociol.)* Segment, *das;* ~ **of a circle** Kreissegment, *das.* **2.** [seg'ment, 'segmənt] *v. t.* untergliedern; [in Gruppen] aufteilen ⟨*Menschen*⟩. **3.** *v. i. (Biol.)* sich teilen
segmentation [segmən'teɪʃn] *n.* Untergliederung, *die; (Biol.)* Zellteilung, *die*
segregate ['segrɪgeɪt] *v. t.* **a)** trennen; isolieren ⟨*Kranke*⟩; aussondern ⟨*Forschungsgebiet*⟩; **b)** *(racially)* segregieren *(geh.)*; absondern
segregation [segrɪ'geɪʃn] *n., no pl.* **a)** Trennung, *die;* **b) [racial] ~:** Rassentrennung, *die*
segregationist [segrɪ'geɪʃənɪst] *n.* Befürworter/Befürworterin der Rassentrennung
seine [seɪn] *n. (Fishing)* **~[-net]** Treibnetz, *das*
seismic ['saɪzmɪk] *adj.* seismisch; ~ **area** *or* **region** Erdbebengebiet, *das;* **of ~ proportions** *(fig.)* von verheerenden Ausmaßen
seismically ['saɪzmɪkəlɪ] *adv.* seismisch
seismograph ['saɪzməgrɑ:f] *n.* Seismograph, *der;* Seismometer, *das*
seize [si:z] **1.** *v. t.* **a)** ergreifen; ~ **power** die Macht ergreifen; ~ **sb. by the arm/collar/shoulder** jmdn. am Arm/Kragen/an der Schulter packen; ~ **the opportunity** *or* **occasion/moment [to do sth.]** die Gelegenheit ergreifen/den günstigen Augenblick nutzen [und etw. tun]; ~ **any/a** *or* **the chance [to do sth.]** jede/die Gelegenheit nutzen[, um etw. zu tun]; **be ~d with remorse/panic** von Gewissensbissen geplagt/von Panik ergriffen werden; **she ~d it with both hands** *(fig.)* sie griff mit beiden Händen zu *(fig.)*; **b)** *(capture)* gefangennehmen ⟨*Person*⟩; kapern ⟨*Schiff*⟩; mit Gewalt übernehmen ⟨*Flugzeug, Gebäude*⟩; einnehmen ⟨*Festung, Brücke*⟩; **c)** *(understand)* erfassen; **d)** *(confiscate)* beschlagnahmen. **2.** *v. i. see* ~ **up**
~ **on** *v. t.* sich *(Dat.)* vornehmen ⟨*Einzelheit, Aspekt, Schwachpunkt*⟩; aufgreifen ⟨*Idee, Vorschlag*⟩; ergreifen ⟨*Chance*⟩
~ **'up** *v. i.* sich festfressen; ⟨*Verkehr:*⟩ zusammenbrechen, zum Erliegen kommen
~ **upon** *see* ~ **on**
seizure ['si:ʒə(r)] *n.* **a)** *(capturing)* Gefangennahme, *die; (of ship)* Kapern, *das; (of aircraft, building)* Übernahme, *die; (of fortress, bridge)* Einnahme, *die;* ~ **of power** Machtergreifung, *die;* **b)** *(confiscation)* Beschlagnahme, *die;* **c)** *(Med.: attack)* Anfall, *der*
seldom ['seldəm] **1.** *adv.* selten; ~ **or never** so gut wie nie; **~, if ever** fast nie; äußerst selten. **2.** *adj.* selten; **a ~ thing** eine Seltenheit; etwas Seltenes
select [sɪ'lekt] **1.** *adj.* **a)** *(carefully chosen)* ausgewählt; **only the most ~ company** nur eine kleine Gruppe Auserwählter; **b)** *(exclusive)* exklusiv. **2.** *v. t.* auswählen; ~ **one's own apples** sich *(Dat.)* die Äpfel selbst aussuchen
select com'mittee *n.* Sonderkommission, *die*
selectee [sɪlek'ti:] *n. (Amer.)* Einberufene, *der*
selection [sɪ'lekʃn] *n.* **a)** *(what is selected [from])* Auswahl, *die* **(of an** + *Dat.*, **from** aus); *(person)* Wahl, *die;* **a ~ from ...** *(Mus.)* eine Auswahl aus ...; **make a ~** *(one)* eine Wahl treffen; *(several)* eine Auswahl treffen; **~s from the best writers** ausgewählte Werke der besten Schriftsteller; **what is your ~ for the Derby?** was ist dein Tip für das Derby?; **b)** *(act of choosing)* [Aus]wahl, *die;* ~ **committee** Auswahlkomitee, *das;* **c)** *(being chosen)* Wahl, *die;* **his ~ as president** seine Wahl zum Präsidenten; **d)** *(Biol.: in evolution)* Selektion, *die;* Auslese, *die*
selective [sɪ'lektɪv] *adj.* **a)** *(using selection)* selektiv; *(careful in one's choice)* wählerisch; **b)** *(Electr.)* selektiv; trennscharf
selectively [sɪ'lektɪvlɪ] *adv.* selektiv; **not read ~ enough** [viel] zu wahllos lesen; **shop ~:** gezielt einkaufen
selectiveness [sɪ'lektɪvnɪs] *n., no pl.* Eingrenzung, *die*
selectivity [sɪlek'tɪvɪtɪ, selek'tɪvɪtɪ, si:lek'tɪvɪtɪ] *n., no pl.* **have a high degree of ~:** ⟨*Insektizid:*⟩ nur spezifisch wirksam sein; **show ~:** wählerisch sein
selectman [sɪ'lektmən], *pl.* **selectmen** [sɪ'lektmən] *n. (Amer.)* Stadtrat, *der*
selectness [sɪ'lektnɪs] *n., no pl.* Exklusivität, *die*
selector [sɪ'lektə(r)] *n.* **a)** *(person who selects) (of team)* Mannschaftsaufsteller, *der*/-aufstellerin, *die; (of merchandise)* Einkäufer, *der*/Einkäuferin, *die;* **b)** *(device that selects) (knob)* Schaltknopf, *der; (lever)* Schaltgriff, *der; (switch)* Wahlschalter, *der; (for selecting programmes)* Programmtaste, *die; (of computer)* Selektor, *der*
self [self] *n., pl.* **selves** [selvz] **a)** *(person's essence)* Selbst, *das (geh.)*; Ich, *das;* **be one's usual ~:** man selbst sein; **not be one's usual cheerful ~:** nicht so fröhlich wie sonst sein; **be back to one's former** *or* **old ~ [again]** wieder der/die alte sein; **one's better ~:** sein besseres Ich; **my humble ~/your good selves** *(joc.)* meine Wenigkeit/die werten Herrschaften *(scherzh.)*; **how is your good ~?** *(arch.)* wie ist das werte Befinden? *(veralt.)*; **b)** *(one's own interest)* die eigene Person; **she cares for nothing but ~:** sie nimmt nur sich selbst wichtig; **she has no thoughts of ~:** sie ist sehr selbstlos; **c)** *(Commerc.)* **drawn to ~:** auf selbst ausgestellt ⟨*Scheck*⟩; **pay to ~:** zahlbar an Aussteller *od.* selbst
self- *pref.* **a)** *expr. direct reflexive action* selbst⟨*anklagend, -schließend*⟩; Selbst⟨*ankläger, -anzeige*⟩; **stand ~-accused** sich selbst angeklagt haben; **b)** *expr. action or condition* selbst-; **~-acting** automatisch; selbsttätig
self: ~-ad'dressed *adj.* **a ~-addressed envelope** ein adressierter Rückumschlag; **~-ad'hesive** *adj.* selbstklebend; **~-ad'vertisement** *n.* Selbstreklame, *die;* **~-ag'grandizement** *n.* Vergrößerung der eigenen Macht; **~-a'nalysis** *n.* Selbstanalyse, *die;* **~-ap'pointed** *adj.* selbsternannt; **~-as'sertion** *n.* Durchsetzungsvermögen, *das* (over gegenüber); **~-as'sertive** *adj.*, **~-assertively** [selfə'sɜ:tɪvlɪ] *adv.* selbstbewußt; **~-as'sertiveness** *n., no pl.* Durchsetzungsvermögen, *das;* **a ~-assertiveness training course** ein Trainingskurs in Durchsetzungsvermögen; **~-as'surance** *n., no pl.* Selbstbewußtsein, *das;* Selbstsicherheit, *die;* **~-as'sured** *adj.* selbstsicher; selbstbewußt; **~-'catering 1.** *adj.* mit Selbstversorgung *nachgestellt;* **2.** *n.* Selbstversorgung, *die;* **~-'centred** *adj.* egozentrisch;

ichbezogen; **~-'closing** *adj.* selbstschließend; **~-coloured** *adj. (with uniform colouring)* einfarbig; **~-com'mand** *n., no pl.* Selbstbeherrschung, *die;* **~-con'demned** *adj.* **be** *or* **stand ~-condemned** sich selbst überführt haben; **~-con'fessed** *adj.* erklärt; **~-'confidence** *n., no pl.* Selbstvertrauen, *das;* **~-'confident** *adj.*, **~-'confidently** *adv.* selbstsicher; **~-'conscious** *adj.* **a)** *(ill at ease)* unsicher; **b)** *(deliberate)* reflektiert ‹*Prosa, Stil*›; **~-'consciousness** *n.* **a)** Unsicherheit, *die;* **b)** *(deliberateness)* Reflektiertheit, *die;* **~-con'tained** *adj.* **a)** *(not dependent)* selbstgenügsam; *(not communicative)* verschlossen; **b)** *(having no parts in common)* unabhängig ‹*Maschine, Anlage*›; einzeln stehend ‹*Haus*›; **c)** *(Brit.: complete in itself)* abgeschlossen ‹*Wohnung*›; **~-contra'dictory** *adj.* mit sich selbst in Widerspruch; **~-con'trol** *n., no pl.* Selbstbeherrschung, *die;* **~-con'trolled** *adj.* voller Selbstbeherrschung *nachgestellt;* **~-'critical** *adj.* selbstkritisch; **~-de'ception** *n.* Selbsttäuschung, *die;* Selbstbetrug, *der;* **~-de'feating** *adj.* unsinnig; zwecklos; **~-de'fence** *n., no pl., no indef. art.* Notwehr, *die;* Selbstverteidigung, *die;* **in ~-defence** aus Notwehr; **~-defence classes** Selbstverteidigungskurs, *der;* **~-de'nial** *n.* Selbstverleugnung, *die;* **~-de'struct** *v. i.* sich selbst zerstören; **~-de'struction** *n.* Selbstzerstörung, *die;* **~-de'structive** *adj.*, **~-de'structively** *adv.* selbstzerstörerisch; **~-'discipline** *n., no pl.* Selbstdisziplin, *die;* **~-drive** *adj.* **~-drive hire [company]** Autovermietung, *die;* **~-drive vehicle** Mietwagen, *der;* **~-'educated** *adj.* autodidaktisch; **be ~-educated, be a ~-educated person** Autodidakt/Autodidaktin sein; **~-ef'facing** *adj.* zurückhaltend; **~-em'ployed** *adj.* selbständig; **~-employed man/woman** Selbständige, *der/die;* **~-e'steem** *n.* **a)** *(~-respect)* Selbstachtung, *die;* **b)** *(~-conceit)* Selbstgefälligkeit, *die;* **~-'evident** *adj.*, **~-'evidently** *adv.* offenkundig; **~-ex'planatory** *adj.* ohne weiteres verständlich; **be ~-explanatory** für sich selbst sprechen; **~-ex'pression** *n., no pl., no indef. art.* Selbstdarstellung, *die;* **~-fertili'zation** *n. (Biol.)* Selbstbefruchtung, *die;* **~-financing** *adj.* sich selbst tragend; kostenneutral ‹*Tarifvertrag*›; **~-ful'filling** *adj.* zur eigenen Bestätigung mit beitragend; **~-fulfilling prophecy** zur Bestätigung ihrer selbst mit beitragende Voraussage; Self-fulfilling prophecy, *die (Soziol.);* **~-'governing** *adj.* selbstverwaltet; **~-'government** *n., no pl., no indef. art.* Selbstverwaltung, *die;* **~-'help** *n., no pl.* Selbsthilfe, *die;* **~-'image** *n.* Selbstbild, *das;* **~-im'portance** *n., no pl.* Selbstgefälligkeit, *die; (arrogant and pompous bearing)* Selbstherrlichkeit, *die;* **~-im'portant** *adj.* selbstgefällig; *(arrogant and pompous)* selbstherrlich; **~-im'posed** *adj.* selbstauferlegt; **~-im'provement** *n.* selbständige Weiterbildung; **~-in'duced** *adj.* **a)** selbstverursacht; **b)** *(Electr.)* selbstinduziert; **~-in'duction** *n. (Electr.)* Selbstinduktion, *die;* **~-in'dulgence** *n.* Maßlosigkeit, *die;* **a little ~-indulgence never hurt anyone** sich ein bißchen zu verwöhnen, hat noch keinem geschadet; **this novel is a piece of pure ~-indulgence** dieser Roman ist weiter nichts als Selbstbefriedigung des Autors; **~-in'dulgent** *adj.* maßlos; **I've been very ~-indulgent lately** ich habe mich in der letzten Zeit sehr gehenlassen; **~-in'flicted** *adj.* selbst beigebracht ‹*Wunde*›; selbst auferlegt ‹*Strafe*›; **~-'interest** *n.* Eigeninteresse, *das;* **~-in'vited** *adj.* **a ~-invited guest** ein Gast, der sich selbst eingeladen hat

selfish ['selfɪʃ] *adj.* egoistisch; selbstsüchtig

selfishly ['selfɪʃlɪ] *adv.* egoistisch; selbstsüchtig; **do sth. ~:** etw. aus Egoismus tun

selfishness ['selfɪʃnɪs] *n., no pl.* Egoismus, *der;* Selbstsucht, *die*

self: ~-justifi'cation *n.* Rechtfertigung, *die;* **attempt at ~-justification** Versuch, sich zu rechtfertigen; **~-'knowledge** *n.* Selbsterkenntnis, *die*

selfless ['selflɪs] *adj.*, **selflessly** ['selflɪslɪ] *adv.* selbstlos

self: ~-'loading *adj.* mit Selbstladevorrichtung *nachgestellt;* **~-'locking** *adj.* selbstschließend; **~-'love** *n., no pl.* Selbstliebe, *die;* Eigenliebe, *die;* **~-made** *adj.* selbstgemacht; **a ~-made man** ein Selfmademan; **she is a ~-made woman** sie hat sich aus eigener Kraft hochgearbeitet; **~-o'pinionated** *adj.* **a)** *(conceited)* eingebildet; von sich eingenommen; **b)** *(obstinate)* starrköpfig; rechthaberisch; **~-per'petuating** *adj.* sich selbst erhaltend; **be ~-perpetuating** sich selbst erhalten; **~-'pity** *n., no pl.* Selbstmitleid, *das;* **~-'portrait** *n.* Selbstporträt, *das;* **~-pos'sessed** *adj.* selbstbeherrscht; **remain ~-possessed** die Selbstbeherrschung behalten; **be ~-possessed** sich beherrschen *od.* zusammennehmen; **~-pos'session** *n., no pl.* Selbstbeherrschung, *die;* **~-preser'vation** *n., no pl., no indef. art.* Selbsterhaltung, *die;* **~-'propagating** *adj. (Bot.)* selbstbefruchtend; **be ~-propagating** Selbstbefruchter sein; *(fig.)* sich selbst vermehren; **~-pro'pelled** *adj.* mit Eigenantrieb *nachgestellt;* **~-'raising flour** *n. (Brit.)* mit Backpulver versetztes Mehl; **~-re'gard** *n., no pl.* Selbstachtung, *die;* **~-'regulating** *adj.* sich selbst steuernd ‹*Maschine*›; autonom ‹*Institution*›; **~-re'liance** *n., no pl.* Selbstvertrauen, *das;* Selbstsicherheit, *die;* **~-re'liant** *adj.* selbstbewußt; selbstsicher; **~-re'spect** *n., no pl.* Selbstachtung, *die;* **~-re'specting** *adj.* mit Selbstachtung *nachgestellt;* **no ~-respecting person ...:** niemand, der etwas auf sich hält, ...; **~-re'straint** *n., no pl.* Selbstbeherrschung, *die;* **~-'righteous** *adj.* selbstgerecht; **~-'righteousness** *n., no pl.* Selbstgerechtigkeit, *die;* **~-'righting** *adj.* selbstaufrichtend; **~-'rising flour** *(Amer.) see* **~-raising flour; ~-'sacrifice** *n.* Selbstaufopferung, *die;* **~-'sacrificing** *adj.* [sich] aufopfernd ‹*Mutter, Vater*›; aufopfernd ‹*Liebe*›; **~same** *adj.* **the ~same** der-/die-/dasselbe; **~-satis'faction** *n., no pl.* Selbstzufriedenheit, *die; (smugness)* Selbstgefälligkeit, *die;* **~-'satisfied** *adj.* selbstzufrieden; *(smug)* selbstgefällig; **~-'sealing** *adj.* **a)** *(automatically sealing)* selbstdichtend; **b)** *(~-adhesive)* selbstklebend; **~-seeking 1.** *adj.* selbstsüchtig; **2.** *n., no pl.* Selbstsucht, *die;* **~-'service 1.** *n.* **a)** *(operation)* Selbstbedienung, *die; attrib.* Selbstbedienungs-; **b)** *(shop)* Selbstbedienungsladen, *der; (petrol station)* Tankstelle zum Selbsttanken; *(restaurant)* Selbstbedienungsrestaurant, *das;* **2.** *pred. adj.* **the petrol station is/has become ~-service** die Tankstelle hat Selbstbedienung/hat auf Selbstbedienung umgestellt; **~-sown** *adj.* selbstausgesät; **~-'starter** *n. (Motor Veh.)* Selbststarter, *der;* **~-'study** *n.* Selbststudium, *das;* **~-styled** *adj.* selbsternannt; von eigenen Gnaden *nachgestellt;* **~-suf'ficiency** *n.* Unabhängigkeit, *die; (of country)* Autarkie, *die;* **~-suf'ficient** *adj. (independent)* unabhängig; autark ‹*Land*›; selbständig ‹*Person*›; **be ~-sufficient in food** seinen Nahrungsbedarf selbst decken; **~-sup'porting** *adj.* **a)** sich selbst tragend ‹*Unternehmen, Verein*›; finanziell unabhängig ‹*Person*›; **the club/firm is ~-supporting** der Verein/die Firma trägt sich selbst; **b)** *(not requiring support)* freitragend ‹*Konstruktion, Gebäude*›; **~-'tapping** *adj.* selbstschneidend ‹*Schraube*›; **~-'taught** *adj.* autodidaktisch; selbsterlernt ‹*Fertigkeiten*›; **~-taught person** Autodidakt, *der*/Autodidaktin, *die;* **be a ~-taught painter/be ~-taught in German** sich *(Dat.)* das Malen/Deutsch selbst beigebracht haben; **she is ~-taught** sie ist Autodidaktin; **~-'will** *n., no pl.* Eigensinn, *der;* **~-'willed** *adj.* eigensinnig; **~-winding** *adj.* automatisch; **a ~-winding watch** eine Uhr mit Selbstaufzug

sell [sel] **1.** *v. t.*, **sold** [səʊld] **a)** verkaufen; **the shop ~s groceries** in dem Laden gibt es Lebensmittel [zu kaufen]; **~ sth. to sb., ~ sb. sth.** jmdm. etw. verkaufen; **~ one's life** *etc.* **dear** *or* **dearly** *(fig.)* sein Leben *usw.* teuer verkaufen; **it is the advertising that ~s the product** die Werbung sorgt für den Absatz des Produkts; **~ by ...** *(on package)* ≈ mindestens haltbar bis ...; **b)** *(betray)* verraten; **c)** *(offer dishonourably)* verkaufen; verhökern *(ugs. abwertend);* **~ oneself/one's soul** sich/seine Seele verkaufen **(to** *Dat.***)**; **d)** *(sl.: cheat, disappoint)* verraten; anschmieren *(salopp);* **I've been sold!, sold again!** ich bin [wieder] der/die Dumme! *(ugs.);* **e)** *(gain acceptance for)* **~ sb. as ...:** jmdn. als ... verkaufen *(ugs.);* **~ sth. to sb.** jmdn. für etw. gewinnen; **~ sb. the idea of doing sth.** jmdn. für den Gedanken gewinnen, etw. zu tun; **f) ~ sb. on sth.** *(coll.: make enthusiastic)* jmdn. für etw. begeistern *od.* erwärmen; **be sold on sth.** *(coll.)* von etw. begeistert sein. *See also* **dummy 1 e; river 1 a; short 1 i. 2.** *v. i.*, **sold a)** sich verkaufen [lassen]; ‹*Person:*› verkaufen; **the book sold 5,000 copies in a week** in einer Woche wurden 5 000 Exemplare des Buches verkauft; **b) ~ at** *or* **for** kosten. *See also* **cake 1 b. 3.** *n.* **a) be a tough ~:** ein Ladenhüter *(abwertend)* sein; sich schlecht verkaufen; **be an easy ~:** ein Verkaufsschlager sein; sich gut verkaufen; **b)** *(coll.: deception)* Schwindel, *der (abwertend). See also* **hard sell; soft sell**

~ 'off *v. t.* verkaufen; abstoßen ‹*Anteile, Aktien*›

~ 'out 1. *v. t.* **a)** ausverkaufen; restlos verkaufen; **the play/performance was sold out** das Stück/die Aufführung war ausverkauft; **b)** *(coll.: betray)* verpfeifen *(ugs.).* **2.** *v. i.* **a) we have** *or* **are sold out** wir sind ausverkauft; **sth. ~s out quickly** etw. verkauft sich schnell; **~ out to another firm** durch Verkauf in eine andere Firma übergehen; **b)** *(coll.: betray one's cause)* **~ out to sb./sth.** zu jmdm./etw. überlaufen. *See also* **sell-out**

~ 'out of *v. t.* **we have** *or* **are sold out of sth.** etw. ist ausverkauft

~ 'up *v. t. (Brit.)* verkaufen; *abs.* sein Hab und Gut verkaufen

'sell-by date *n.* ≈ Mindesthaltbarkeitsdatum, *das*

seller ['selə(r)] *n.* **a)** Verkäufer, *der*/Verkäuferin, *die;* **be a ~ of sth.** etw. verkaufen; **a ~'s** *or* **~s' market** ein Verkäufermarkt; **b)** *(product)* **be a slow/bad ~:** sich nur langsam/schlecht verkaufen; **be a fast** *or* **strong** *or* **big ~:** ein Renner *od.* Verkaufsschlager sein; **be a good ~:** sich gut verkaufen

selling ['selɪŋ] **1.** *n.* **a)** *(act, occupation)* Verkaufen, *das;* **b)** *(salesmanship)* Verkauf, *der;* **training in ~:** Verkaufsschulung, *die.* **2.** *adj. in comb.* **a fast-** *or* **good-selling book** ein Buch, das sich gut verkauft

selling: ~-point *n.* **a [good] ~-point** ein Verkaufsargument; *(fig.)* ein Pluspunkt; **~ price** *n.* Verkaufspreis, *der*

Sellotape, (P) ['seləʊteɪp] *n., no pl., no indef. art.* ≈ Tesafilm, *der*

sellotape *v. t.* mit Klebeband kleben

'sell-out *n.* **a)** *(event)* **be a ~:** ausverkauft sein; **b)** *(coll.: betrayal)* Verrat, *der*

selvage, selvedge ['selvɪdʒ] *n.* Webkante, *die*

selves *pl. of* **self**
semantic [sɪ'mæntɪk] *adj.* semantisch
semantically [sɪ'mæntɪkəlɪ] *adv.* semantisch
semantics [sɪ'mæntɪks] *n., no pl.* Semantik, *die;* **only argue about ~s** sich um Worte streiten
semaphore ['seməfɔ:(r)] **1.** *n.* **a)** *(apparatus)* Signalmast, *der;* Semaphor, *das od. der;* **b)** *(system)* Winken, *das;* **~ alphabet** Winkeralphabet, *das.* **2.** *v. i.* **~ to sb.** jmdm. ein Winksignal übermitteln. **3.** *v. t.* [durch Winksignale] übermitteln
semblance ['sembləns] *n.* **a)** *(outward appearance)* Anschein, *der;* **without a ~ of regret/a smile** ohne das geringste Zeichen von Bedauern/den Anflug eines Lächelns; **without even the ~ of a trial** ohne auch nur die geringste Verhandlung; **bring some ~ of order to sth.** wenigstens den Anschein von Ordnung in etw. *(Akk.)* bringen; **b)** *(resemblance)* Ähnlichkeit, *die*
semeiology [si:maɪ'ɒlədʒɪ], **semeiotics** [si:maɪ'ɒtɪks] *see* **semiology**
semen ['si:men] *n. (Physiol.)* Samen, *der;* Sperma, *das*
semester [sɪ'mestə(r)] *n. (Univ.)* Semester, *das*
semi ['semɪ] *n. (coll.)* **a)** *(Brit.: house)* Doppelhaushälfte, *die;* **b)** *(Amer.: vehicle)* Sattelanhänger, *der*
semi- *pref.* halb-/Halb-
semi: ~-auto'matic 1. *adj.* halbautomatisch; **2.** *n.* halbautomatische Feuerwaffe; **~-basement** *n.* Halbsouterrain, *das;* **~bold** *adj. (Printing)* halbfett; **~breve** *n. (Brit. Mus.)* ganze Note; **~circle** *n.* Halbkreis, *der;* **~'circular** *adj.* halbkreisförmig; **~-'colon** *n.* Semikolon, *das;* **~con'ductor** *n. (Phys.)* Halbleiter, *der;* **~-'conscious** *adj.* halb bewußtlos; **be only ~-conscious** nicht bei vollem Bewußtsein sein; **~-'darkness** *n.* Halbdunkel, *das;* **in ~-darkness** im Halbdunkel; **~-de'tached 1.** *adj.* **the house is ~-detached** es ist eine Doppelhaushälfte; **a ~-detached house** eine Doppelhaushälfte; **2.** *n. (Brit.: house)* Doppelhaushälfte, *die;* **~'final** *n.* Halbfinale, *das;* Semifinale, *das;* **in the ~finals** im Halbfinale; **~'finalist** *n.* Halbfinalteilnehmer, *der/*-teilnehmerin, *die;* Halbfinalist, *der/*-finalistin, *die;* **~-'finished** *adj.* halbfertig; **~-'invalid** *n.* Teilinvalide, *der/die;* **~-literate** *adj.* **be ~-literate** kaum lesen und schreiben können
seminal ['semɪnl, 'si:mɪnl] *adj.* **a)** *(having originative power)* schöpferisch; *(embryonic)* keimhaft; **b)** *(reproductive)* Samen‹leiter, -flüssigkeit›
seminar ['semɪnɑ:(r)] *n.* **a)** *(small class)* Seminar, *das;* **b)** *(Amer.: conference)* Konferenz, *die;* **c)** *(study-course)* Kurs[us], *der;* Seminar, *das*
seminarian [semɪ'neərɪən], **seminarist** ['semɪnərɪst] *ns.* Seminarist, *der*
seminary ['semɪnərɪ] *n.* Priesterseminar, *das*
semiology [si:mɪ'ɒlədʒɪ], **semiotics** [si:mɪ'ɒtɪks] *ns.* Semiotik, *die;* Semiologie, *die*
semi: ~-'permanent *adj.* fast permanent; **~-'precious** *adj.* **~-precious stone** Halbedelstein, *der;* Schmuckstein, *der;* **be ~-precious** ein Halbedelstein sein; **~quaver** *n. (Brit. Mus.)* Sechzehntelnote, *die;* **~-'skilled** *adj.* angelernt; **~-'sweet** *adj.* halbsüß ‹Sekt, Wein›; [nur] leicht gesüßt ‹Kuchen, Schokolade›
Semite ['si:maɪt, 'semaɪt] **1.** *n.* Semit, *der/*Semitin, *die.* **2.** *adj.* semitisch
Semitic [sɪ'mɪtɪk] *adj.* semitisch
'semitone *n. (Mus.)* Halbton, *der*
'semi-trailer *n.* Sattelanhänger, *der*
semolina [semə'li:nə] *n.* **a)** Grieß, *der;* **b)** *(pudding)* Grießpudding, *der*
sempstress *see* **seamstress**
SEN *abbr. (Brit.)* **State Enrolled Nurse**
Sen. *abbr.* **a)** **Senator** Sen.; **b)** **Senior** sen.
senate ['senət] *n.* Senat, *der*
senator ['senətə(r)] *n.* Senator, *der/*Senatorin, *die*
send [send] **1.** *v. t.,* **sent** [sent] **a)** *(cause to go)* schicken; senden *(geh.);* **~ sb. to Africa** jmdn. nach Afrika schicken; **~ sb. to university/boarding-school** jmdn. auf die Universität/ins Internat schicken; **~ sb. on a course/tour** jmdn. in einen Kurs/auf eine Tour schicken; **~ a dog after sb.** einen Hund auf jmdn. hetzen; **she ~s her best wishes/love** sie läßt grüßen/herzlich grüßen; **~ [sb.] apologies/congratulations** sich [bei jmdm.] entschuldigen lassen/[jmdm.] seine Glückwünsche übermitteln; **she sent him congratulations on ...:** sie schickte ihm Glückwünsche zu ...; **~ sb. home/to bed** jmdn. nach Hause/ins Bett schicken; **~ sb. to his death** jmdn. in den Tod schicken; *see also* **word 1 f; b)** *(grant)* schicken; **~ her victorious!** *(arch.)* [Herr,] laß sie siegreich sein!; **God ~s the rain on the just and the unjust** *(prov.)* Gott läßt regnen über Gerechte und Ungerechte; **c)** *(propel)* **~ a rocket into space** eine Rakete in den Weltraum schießen; **~ a ball over the wall** einen Ball über die Mauer schießen; **~ up clouds of dust** Staubwolken aufwirbeln; **~ sth. to the ground/hurtling through the air** etw. zu Boden werfen/durch die Luft sausen lassen; **~ sb. sprawling/reeling** jmdn. zu Boden strekken/ins Wanken bringen; **~ sb. running for cover** jmdn. schnell Deckung suchen lassen; **~ sth. off course** etw. vom Kurs abkommen lassen; *see also* **²fly 1 d; d)** *(drive into condition)* **~ sb. mad** *or* **crazy** jmdn. verrückt machen *(ugs.);* **~ sb. into raptures/a temper/fits of laughter** jmdn. ins Schwärmen geraten lassen/in Wut bringen/dazu bringen, daß er sich totlacht *(ugs.);* **~ sb. to sleep** jmdn. zum Einschlafen bringen; **that loud music ~s me round the bend** *(fig. coll.)* bei dieser lauten Musik könnte ich verrückt *od.* wahnsinnig werden *(ugs.);* **e)** *(dismiss)* **~ sb. about his/her** *etc.* **business** jmdn. vor die Tür setzen; *see also* **Coventry; pack 3; f)** *(sl.: put into ecstasy)* begeistern; **she really ~s me** sie macht mich total an *(salopp).* **2.** *v. i.,* **sent: ~ to sb. for sth.** *(by letter)* jmdn. um etw. anschreiben; **we'll ~ to Germany for that** wir werden nach Deutschland schreiben, daß sie uns das schicken
~ a'head *v. t.* vorausschicken; **he was sent ahead of the main group** er wurde dem Haupttrupp vorausgeschickt
~ a'way 1. *v. t.* wegschicken; fortschicken *(landsch., geh.);* **we like to ~ our guests away with pleasant memories** wir möchten unseren Gästen angenehme Erinnerungen mitgeben; *see also* **flea. 2.** *v. i.* **~ away [to sb.] for sth.** etw. [bei jmdm.] anfordern
~ 'back *v. t.* **a)** *(return)* zurückschicken; **b)** *(because of dissatisfaction)* zurückgehen lassen ‹Speise, Getränk›; *(by post)* zurückschicken ‹Ware›
~ 'down 1. *v. t.* **a)** [hinunter]schicken; **b)** *(Brit. Univ.)* relegieren *(geh.);* von der Hochschule verweisen; **c)** *(put in prison)* hinter Schloß und Riegel bringen *(ugs.);* **d)** *(Cricket)* werfen ‹Ball›; **e)** nach unten treiben ‹Preis, Kosten, Temperatur›. **2.** *v. i.* **~ down [to the store] for sth.** etw. aus dem Lager holen lassen
~ for *v. t.* **a)** *(tell to come)* holen lassen; rufen ‹Polizei, Arzt, Krankenwagen›; **b)** *(order from elsewhere)* anfordern
~ 'in *v. t.* einschicken
~ 'off 1. *v. t.* **a)** *(dispatch)* abschicken ‹Sache›; losschicken *(ugs.)* ‹Person›; **~ one's children off to boarding-school** seine Kinder ins Internat schicken; **b)** *(bid farewell to)* verabschieden; *see also* **send-off; c)** *(Sport)* vom Platz stellen. **2.** *v. i.* **~ off for sth. [to sb.]** etw. [von jmdm.] anfordern
~ 'on *v. t.* **a)** *(forward)* nachsenden ‹Post›; **they sent me on to you** ich wurde an Sie verwiesen; **b)** *(cause to go ahead)* **~ on [ahead]** vorausschicken; **c)** *(cause to participate)* **~ a player on** einen Spieler einsetzen
~ 'out 1. *v. t.* **a)** *(issue)* verschicken; **b)** *(emit)* aussenden ‹Hilferuf, Nachricht›; abgeben ‹Hitze›; senden ‹Lichtstrahlen›; ausstoßen ‹Rauch›; verströmen ‹Geruch›; **c)** *(dispatch)* schicken; **~ sb. out to Africa** jmdn. nach Afrika schicken; **~ sb. out for sth.** jmdn. schicken, um etw. zu besorgen; **d)** *(order to leave)* hinausschicken. **2.** *v. i.* **~ out for sth.** etw. besorgen *od.* holen lassen
~ 'up *v. t.* **a)** *(Brit. coll.: ridicule) (in play, sketch, song)* parodieren; *(in cartoon)* karikieren; *see also* **send-up; b)** *(Amer. sl.: put in prison)* in den Knast stecken *(ugs.);* einbuchten *(salopp);* **c)** *(transmit to higher authority)* weiterleiten **(to** an + *Akk.*); **d)** *(cause to rise)* steigen lassen ‹Ballon›; hochtreiben ‹Preis, Kosten, Temperatur›; **~ sb.'s temperature up** *(fig. joc.)* jmdn. zum Kochen bringen *(ugs.);* **e)** *(destroy)* in die Luft jagen *(ugs.) od.* sprengen
sender ['sendə(r)] *n. (of goods)* Lieferant, *der/*Lieferantin, *die; (of letter)* Absender, *der/*Absenderin, *die*
send: ~-off *n.* Verabschiedung, *die;* **give sb. a good ~-off** jmdn. groß verabschieden; **~-up** *n. (Brit. coll.: parody)* Parodie, *die; (in cartoon)* Karikatur, *die;* **do a ~-up of sb./sth.** jmdn./etw. parodieren
Senegal [senɪ'gɔ:l] *pr. n.* Senegal *(das) od. der*
Senegalese [senɪgə'li:z] **1.** *adj.* senegalesisch; **sb. is ~:** jmd. ist Senegalese/Senegalesin. **2.** *n., pl. same* Senegalese, *der/*Senegalesin, *die*
senescent [sɪ'nesənt] *adj.* alternd
senile ['si:naɪl] *adj.* senil; *(physically)* altersschwach; *(caused by old age)* altersbedingt ‹Apathie, Schwatzhaftigkeit›; **~ decay** Altersabbau, *der*
senile de'mentia *n. (Med.)* senile Demenz
senility [sɪ'nɪlɪtɪ] *n., no pl.* Senilität, *die; (physical infirmity)* Altersschwäche, *die*
senior ['si:nɪə(r)] **1.** *adj.* **a)** *(older)* älter; **be ~ to sb.** älter als jmd. sein; **~ team** Seniorenmannschaft, *die;* **b)** *(of higher rank)* höher ‹Rang, Beamter, Stellung›; leitend ‹Angestellter, Stellung›; *(longest-serving)* ältest ...; **someone ~:** jemand in höherer Stellung; **~ management** Geschäftsleitung, *die;* **~ consultant/nurse** *(in hospital)* ≈ Oberarzt, *der/*Oberschwester, *die;* **be ~ to sb.** eine höhere Stellung als jmd. haben; **she is ~/not very ~:** sie hat einen/keinen gehobenen Posten; **c)** *appended to name (the elder)* **Mr Smith S~:** Mr. Smith senior; **d)** *(Brit. Sch.)* **~ school** *or* **section** Oberstufe, *die;* **e)** *(Brit. Univ.)* **~ combination** *or* **common room** Gemeinschaftsraum für Dozenten; **f)** *(Amer. Sch., Univ.)* **~ class** Abschlußklasse, *die;* **~ year** letztes Jahr vor der Abschlußprüfung. **2.** *n.* **a)** *(older person)* Ältere, *der/die; (person of higher rank)* Vorgesetzte, *der/die;* **be sb.'s ~ [by six years]** *or* **[six years] sb.'s ~:** [sechs Jahre] älter als jmd. sein; **b)** *(Brit. Sch.)* Schüler/Schülerin einer höheren Schule; *(in the last three years)* Oberstufenschüler, *der/*-schülerin, *die;* **c)** *(Amer.) (Sch.)* Schüler/Schülerin im letzten Schuljahr; *(Univ.)* Student/Studentin im letzten Studienjahr
senior: ~ 'citizen *n.* Senior, *der/*Seniorin, *die;* **~ college** *n. (Amer.)* höhere Schule; ≈ [Gymnasial]oberstufe, *die*
seniority [si:nɪ'ɒrɪtɪ] *n.* **a)** *(superior age)* Alter, *das;* **b)** *(priority in length of service)* höheres Dienstalter; **c)** *(superior rank)* höherer Rang

senior: ~ **'officer** *n.* höherer Beamter/höhere Beamtin; *(Mil.)* ranghöchster Offizier; **sb.'s ~ officer** jmds. Vorgesetzter; ~ **'partner** *n.* Seniorpartner, *der*/-partnerin, *die;* ~ **service** *n. (Brit.)* Marine, *die*

senna ['senə] *n.* **a)** *(Bot.)* Sennespflanze, *die;* Kassie, *die;* **b)** *(drug)* Sennesblätter; Senna, *die*

sensation [sen'seɪʃn] *n.* **a)** *(feeling)* Gefühl, *das;* **~ of hunger/thirst/giddiness** Hunger-/Durst-/Schwindelgefühl, *das;* **have a ~ of falling** das Gefühl haben zu fallen; **b)** *(person, event, etc. causing intense excitement)* Sensation, *die;* **a great ~:** ein großes Ereignis; **c)** *(excitement)* Aufsehen, *das*

sensational [sen'seɪʃənl] *adj.* **a)** *(spectacular)* aufsehenerregend; sensationell; **b)** *(arousing intense response)* reißerisch *(abwertend);* Sensations⟨*blatt, -presse*⟩; **c)** *(phenomenal)* phänomenal

sensationalism [sen'seɪʃənəlɪzm] *n.* Sensationshascherei, *die (abwertend);* **[desire for] ~:** Sensationsgier, *die (abwertend)*

sensationally [sen'seɪʃənəlɪ] *adv.* sensationell

sense [sens] **1.** *n.* **a)** *(faculty of perception)* Sinn, *der;* **~ of smell/touch/taste** Geruchs-/Tast-/Geschmackssinn, *der;* **come to one's ~s** das Bewußtsein wiedererlangen; **b)** *in pl. (normal state of mind)* Verstand, *der;* **in full possession of one's ~s** im Vollbesitz seiner geistigen Kräfte; **no one in his ~s would do that** niemand mit einem Funken Verstand würde so etwas tun; **have taken leave of** *or* **be out of one's ~s** den Verstand verloren haben; **frighten sb. out of his ~s** jmdm. einen furchtbaren Schrecken einjagen; **come to one's ~s** zur Vernunft kommen; **bring sb. to his ~s** jmdn. zur Vernunft *od.* Besinnung bringen; **c)** *(consciousness)* Gefühl, *das;* **~ of responsibility/guilt** Verantwortungs-/Schuldgefühl, *das;* **out of a ~ of duty** aus Pflichtgefühl; **~ of gratitude** Gefühl der Dankbarkeit; **a keen ~ of honour** ein ausgeprägtes Ehrgefühl; **have a ~ of one's own importance** sich sehr wichtig nehmen; *see also* **direction c; humour 1 a; road sense; d)** *(ability to perceive)* Gespür, *das; (instinct)* [instinktives] Gespür; **~ of the absurd** Gespür für das Absurde; **e)** *(practical wisdom)* Verstand, *der;* **there's a lot of ~ in what he's saying** was er sagt, klingt sehr vernünftig; **sound** *or* **good ~:** [gesunder Menschen]verstand; **not have the ~ to do sth.** nicht so schlau sein, etw. zu tun; **there is no ~ in doing that** es hat keinen Sinn, das zu tun; **what is the ~ of** *or* **in doing that?** was hat man davon *od.* wozu soll es gut sein, das zu tun?; **have more ~ than to do sth.** genug Verstand haben, etw. nicht zu tun; **talk ~:** vernünftig reden; **now you are talking ~:** jetzt wirst du vernünftig; **you're just not talking ~:** du redest einfach Unsinn; **see ~:** zur Vernunft kommen; **make sb. see ~:** jmdn. zur Vernunft bringen; **be a man/woman of ~:** wissen, was man tut; **she hasn't the ~ she was born with** sie hat keinen Funken Verstand; *see also* **common sense; f)** *(meaning)* Sinn, *der; (of word)* Bedeutung, *die;* **in the strict** *or* **literal ~:** im strengen *od.* wörtlichen Sinn; **in every ~ [of the word]** in jeder Hinsicht; **there is a ~ in which ...:** man könnte durchaus die Ansicht vertreten, daß ...; **in some ~:** irgendwie; **in a** *or* **one ~:** in gewisser Hinsicht *od.* Weise; **make ~:** einen Sinn ergeben; **her arguments do not make ~ to me** ihre Argumente leuchten mir nicht ein; **it does not make ~ to do that** es ist Unsinn *od.* unvernünftig, das zu tun; **it makes [a lot of] ~** *(is [very] reasonable)* es ist [sehr] sinnvoll; **it makes good** *or* **sound financial ~:** es ist in finanzieller Hinsicht sinnvoll; **it all makes ~ to me now** jetzt verstehe ich alles; **it just doesn't make ~:** es ergibt einfach keinen Sinn; **now you're making ~:** jetzt verstehe ich, was du sagen willst; **make ~ of sth.** etw. verstehen; aus etw. schlau werden; **g)** *(prevailing sentiment)* **take the ~ of the meeting** die Meinung der Versammlung einholen. **2.** *v. t.* spüren; ⟨*Tier:*⟩ wittern; ⟨*Gerät:*⟩ wahrnehmen

senseless ['senslɪs] *adj.* **a)** *(unconscious)* bewußtlos; **b)** *(foolish)* unvernünftig; dumm; **what a ~ thing to do/say!** wie kann man nur so etwas Dummes machen/sagen!; **c)** *(purposeless)* unsinnig ⟨*Argument*⟩; sinnlos ⟨*Diskussion, Vergeudung*⟩

'sense-organ *n.* Sinnesorgan, *das*

sensibility [sensɪ'bɪlɪtɪ] *n.* **a)** *in pl. (susceptibility)* Empfindlichkeit, *die;* **her sensibilities are easily wounded** sie ist sehr schnell verletzt *od.* gekränkt; **b)** *(openness to emotional impressions)* Sensibilität, *die* **(to** in bezug auf + *Akk.*); **~ to pain/beauty** Schmerzempfindlichkeit, *die*/Empfänglichkeit für Schönheit; **c)** *(delicacy of feeling)* Feingefühl, *das* **(to** gegenüber; **of** für); Einfühlungsvermögen, *das* **(of** in + *Akk.*); **d)** *(over-sensitiveness)* Empfindsamkeit, *die*

sensible ['sensɪbl] *adj.* **a)** *(reasonable)* vernünftig; **he was ~ enough to do it** er war so vernünftig, es zu tun; **be ~ [about it]!** sei doch vernünftig!; **b)** *(practical)* praktisch; zweckmäßig; fest ⟨*Schuhe*⟩; **c)** *(appreciable)* gravierend ⟨*Fehler*⟩; beachtlich, merklich ⟨*Anstieg, Rückgang, Unterschied*⟩; **d)** *(literary: aware)* **be ~ of** *or* **to sth.** etw. spüren

sensibly ['sensɪblɪ] *adv.* **a)** *(reasonably)* vernünftig; besonnen; **~ enough, he refused** er war so vernünftig abzulehnen; **b)** *(practically)* zweckmäßig; **c)** *(appreciably)* merklich

sensitisation, sensitise *see* **sensitiz-**

sensitive ['sensɪtɪv] *adj.* **a)** *(recording slight changes)* empfindlich; **be ~ to sth.** empfindlich auf etw. *(Akk.)* reagieren; **~ to light** lichtempfindlich; **b)** *(touchy)* empfindlich **(about** wegen); **be ~ to sth.** empfindlich auf etw. *(Akk.)* reagieren; **c)** heikel ⟨*Thema, Diskussion*⟩; **d)** *(perceptive)* einfühlsam

sensitively ['sensɪtɪvlɪ] *adv.* empfindlich ⟨*reagieren*⟩; einfühlsam ⟨*darstellen*⟩

'sensitive plant *n. (Bot.; also fig.: person)* Mimose, *die*

sensitivity [sensɪ'tɪvɪtɪ] *n.* **a)** *(capacity to respond emotionally)* Sensibilität, *die;* Empfindlichkeit, *die* **(to** gegen); **offend sb.'s sensitivities** jmds. Feingefühl verletzen; **b)** *(responsiveness)* Empfindlichkeit, *die;* **~ to light** Lichtempfindlichkeit, *die*

sensitization [sensɪtaɪ'zeɪʃn] *n.* Sensibilisierung, *die*

sensitize ['sensɪtaɪz] *v. t.* sensibilisieren **(to** für)

sensor ['sensə(r)] *n.* Sensor, *der*

sensory ['sensərɪ] *adj.* sensorisch; Sinnes⟨*wahrnehmung, -organ*⟩

sensual ['sensjʊəl, 'senʃʊəl] *adj.* sinnlich; lustvoll ⟨*Leben*⟩; Sinnen⟨*freude, -genuß*⟩

sensuality [sensjʊ'ælɪtɪ, senʃʊ'ælɪtɪ] *n.* Sinnlichkeit, *die*

sensually ['sensjʊəlɪ, 'senʃʊəlɪ] *adv.* sinnlich; genußvoll ⟨*essen*⟩

sensuous ['sensjʊəs] *adj.* sinnlich

sensuously ['sensjʊəslɪ] *adv.* sinnlich; **~ beautiful** von sinnlicher Schönheit *nachgestellt*

sent *see* **send**

sentence ['sentəns] **1.** *n.* **a)** *(decision of law-court)* [Straf]urteil, *das; (fig.)* Strafe, *die;* **give sb. a three-year ~:** jmdn. zu drei Jahren Haft verurteilen; **pass ~ [on sb.]** [jmdm.] das Urteil verkünden; **be under ~ of death** zum Tode verurteilt sein; *(fig.)* zum Untergang verurteilt sein; **b)** *(Ling.)* Satz, *der; see also* **complex 1 c; 'compound 1 f; simple e. 2.** *v. t. (lit. or fig.)* verurteilen **(to** zu)

'sentence-modifier *n. (Ling.)* Satzpartikel, *die*

sententious [sen'tenʃəs] *adj.* **a)** *(pithy)* prägnant; sentenziös *(geh.);* **b)** *(affectedly formal)* salbungsvoll *(abwertend);* **c)** *(given to pompous moralizing)* moralistisch; schulmeisterhaft

sententiously [sen'tenʃəslɪ] *adv.* **a)** *(pithily)* kurz und prägnant; **b)** *(pompously)* schulmeisterhaft

sentient ['senʃənt] *adj.* empfindungsfähig

sentiment ['sentɪmənt] *n.* **a)** *(mental feeling)* Gefühl, *das;* **noble ~s** edle Gesinnung; **~ unchecked by reason** nicht vernunftgesteuerte Gefühle; **those are** *or* *(sl.)* **them's my ~s** so denke ich darüber; **b)** *(emotion conveyed in art)* Empfindung, *die;* **c)** *no pl. (emotional weakness)* Sentimentalität, *die;* Rührseligkeit, *die;* **d)** *(expression of view)* Gedanke, *der*

sentimental [sentɪ'mentl] *adj.* **a)** *(motivated by feeling)* sentimental; **sth. has ~ value [for sb.]** jmd. hängt an etw. *(Dat.);* **~ attachment to sth.** gefühlsmäßige Bindung an etw. *(Akk.);* **for ~ reasons** aus Sentimentalität; **b)** *(appealing to sentiment)* rührselig; sentimental; **a ~ song** eine Schnulze

sentimentalism [sentɪ'mentəlɪzm] *n., no pl.* Sentimentalität, *die*

sentimentalist [sentɪ'mentəlɪst] *n.* sentimentaler Mensch

sentimentality [sentɪmen'tælɪtɪ] *n.* Sentimentalität, *die*

sentimentalize [sentɪ'mentəlaɪz] **1.** *v. i.* sich sentimentalen Gefühlen hingeben. **2.** *v. t.* sentimental darstellen

sentimentally [sentɪ'mentəlɪ] *adv.* sentimental; gefühlsmäßig ⟨*verbunden*⟩

sentinel ['sentɪnl] *n. (lit. or fig.)* Wache, *die;* **stand ~ over sth.** *(fig.)* über etw. *(Akk.)* wachen

sentry ['sentrɪ] *n. (lit. or fig.)* Wache, *die;* **stand ~ at the door** an der Tür Wache halten

sentry: **~-box** *n.* Wachhäuschen, *das;* **~-duty** *n.* **be on ~-duty** Wachdienst haben

sepal ['sepl, 'si:pl] *n. (Bot.)* Kelchblatt, *das*

separability [sepərə'bɪlɪtɪ] *n., no pl.* Trennbarkeit, *die*

separable ['sepərəbl] *adj.* **a)** trennbar; zerlegbar ⟨*Werkzeug, Gerät*⟩; **b)** *(Ling.)* trennbar ⟨*Vorsilbe, Verb*⟩

separate 1. ['sepərət] *adj.* verschieden ⟨*Fragen, Probleme, Gelegenheiten*⟩; getrennt ⟨*Konten, Betten*⟩; gesondert ⟨*Teil*⟩; separat ⟨*Eingang, Toilette, Blatt Papier, Abteil*⟩; Sonder⟨*vereinbarung*⟩; *(one's own, individual)* eigen ⟨*Zimmer, Identität, Organisation*⟩; **lead ~ lives** getrennt leben; **go ~ ways** getrennte Wege gehen; **the ~ volumes** die einzelnen Bände; **one is quite ~ from the other** das eine ist ganz unabhängig von dem anderen/*(different)* ganz anders als das andere; **keep two things ~:** zwei Dinge auseinanderhalten; **keep issue A ~ from issue B** Frage A und Frage B getrennt behandeln; **keep one's cheque-book ~ from one's bank card** Scheckbuch und Scheckkarte getrennt aufbewahren. **2.** ['sepəreɪt] *v. t.* **a)** trennen; **they are ~d** *(no longer live together)* sie leben getrennt; **b)** *(Amer.: discharge)* entlassen **(from** aus). **3.** *v. i.* **a)** *(disperse)* sich trennen; **b)** ⟨*Ehepaar*⟩ sich trennen; **c)** *(secede)* sich abspalten; **d)** *see* **~ out 1.** *See also* **separates**

~ 'out 1. *v. i.* sich entmischen *(fachspr.);* sich trennen. **2.** *v. t. (distinguish)* auseinanderhalten; *(extract)* trennen

separately ['sepərətlɪ] *adv.* getrennt; **they had, quite ~, reached the same conclusion** sie waren – ganz unabhängig voneinander – zum gleichen Schluß gekommen

separate 'maintenance *n. (Law)* Unterhalt, *der*

separates ['sepərəts] *n. pl. (Fashion)* Separates; einzelne Kleidungsstücke [die man kombinieren kann]

separation [sepə'reɪʃn] *n.* **a)** Trennung, *die;* **judicial** *or* **legal ~:** gerichtliche Tren-

nung; **b)** *(Amer.: resignation, discharge)* Entlassung, *die* (**from** aus)
sepa'ration order *n.* gerichtliche Anordnung des Getrenntlebens
separatism ['sepərətɪzm] *n.* **a)** *(advocacy of separation)* Separatismus, *der;* **b)** *(segregation)* **[racial/class]** ~: [Rassen-/Klassen]trennung, *die*
separatist ['sepərətɪst] *n.* Separatist, *der*/Separatistin, *die; attrib.* ~ **movement** Separatistenbewegung, *die*
separator ['sepəreɪtə(r)] *n.* Separator, *der*
sepia ['si:pɪə] *n.* **a)** *(pigment)* Sepia, *die;* **b)** *(colour)* Sepiabraun, *das;* ~ **photograph/drawing** sepiafarbenes Foto/Sepiazeichnung, *die;* **c)** *(drawing)* Sepiazeichnung, *die*
sepsis ['sepsɪs] *n., pl.* **sepses** ['sepsi:z] *(Med.)* Sepsis, *die (fachspr.);* Blutvergiftung, *die*
Sept. *abbr.* **September** Sept.
septa *pl. of* **septum**
September [sep'tembə(r)] *n.* September, *der; see also* **August**
septet, septette [sep'tet] *n. (Mus.)* Septett, *das*
septic ['septɪk] *adj.* septisch
septicaemia (*Amer.:* **septicemia**) [septɪ'si:mɪə] *n. (Med.)* Sepsis, *die;* Septikämie, *die (fachspr.)*
septic 'tank *n.* Faulraum, *der*
septuagenarian [septjʊədʒɪ'neərɪən] **1.** *adj.* siebzigjährig; *(more than 70 years old)* in den Siebzigern *nachgestellt.* **2.** *n.* Siebziger, *der*/Siebzigerin, *die*
septum ['septəm] *n., pl.* **septa** ['septə] *(Anat., Bot., Zool.)* Septum, *das*
sepulcher *(Amer.) see* **sepulchre**
sepulchral [sɪ'pʌlkrl] *adj.* **a)** *(of burial)* Grab-; Bestattungs⟨*brauch, -ritus*⟩; **b)** *(fig.: funereal)* düster
sepulchre ['seplkə(r)] *n. (Brit.)* Grab, *das;* **the Holy S~:** das Heilige Grab
sequel ['si:kwl] *n.* **a)** *(consequence, result)* Folge, *die* (**to** von); **b)** *(continuation)* Fortsetzung, *die;* **there was a tragic ~:** es gab ein tragisches Nachspiel; **in the ~:** in der Folge
sequence ['si:kwəns] *n.* **a)** *(succession)* Reihenfolge, *die;* **rapid/logical ~:** rasche/logische Abfolge; **a ~ of musicals** eine Reihe von Musicals; **b)** *(part of film; set of poems, also Cards; Mus., Eccl.)* Sequenz, *die;* **c)** *(succession without cause)* Aufeinanderfolge, *die;* **d)** ~ **of tenses** *(Ling.)* Zeitenfolge, *die*
sequential [sɪ'kwenʃl] *adj. (forming a sequence)* aufeinanderfolgend; **be ~ to** *or* **upon sth.** auf etw. *(Akk.)* folgen
sequester [sɪ'kwestə(r)] **1.** *v. t.* **a)** *(set apart)* abtrennen ⟨*Teil*⟩; absondern ⟨*Person*⟩; **b)** *(Law: seize)* sequestrieren; **c)** *(confiscate)* beschlagnahmen. **2.** *v. refl.* sich fernhalten; ~ **oneself from the world** sich von der Welt abkapseln
sequestered [sɪ'kwestəd] *adj.* abgelegen; ⟨*Leben*⟩ in Abgeschiedenheit
sequestrate ['si:kwɪstreɪt] *see* **sequester 1 b, c**
sequestration [si:kwɪ'streɪʃn] *n.* **a)** *(Law: appropriation)* Sequestration, *die;* **b)** *(confiscation)* Beschlagnahme, *die*
sequestrator ['si:kwɪstreɪtə(r)] *n.* Sequester, *der*
sequin ['si:kwɪn] *n.* Paillette, *die*
sequined, sequinned ['si:kwɪnd] *adj.* paillettenbesetzt ⟨*Kleid*⟩
sequoia [sɪ'kwɔɪə] *n. (Bot.)* Mammutbaum, *der;* Sequoia, *die (fachspr.)*
sera *pl. of* **serum**
seraglio [sə'rɑ:ljəʊ] *n., pl.* **~s** Harem, *der;* Serail, *das (veralt.)*
seraph ['serəf] *n., pl.* **seraphim** ['serəfɪm] *or* **~s** Seraph, *der*
seraphic [sə'ræfɪk] *adj.* seraphisch *(geh.)*
Serb [sɜ:b] *see* **Serbian**
Serbia ['sɜ:bɪə] *pr. n.* Serbien, *das*
Serbian ['sɜ:bɪən] **1.** *adj.* serbisch; **sb. is ~:** jmd. ist Serbe/Serbin; *see also* **English 1. 2.** *n.* **a)** *(dialect)* serbischer Dialekt; **b)** *(person)* Serbe, *der*/Serbin, *die. See also* **English 2 a**
Serbo-Croat [sɜ:bəʊ'krəʊæt], **Serbo-Croatian** [sɜ:bəʊkrəʊ'eɪʃn] **1.** *adj.* serbokroatisch; *see also* **English 1. 2.** *n.* Serbokroatisch, *das; see also* **English 2 a**
serenade [serə'neɪd] **1.** *n. (Mus.)* **a)** Ständchen, *das;* **sing** *or* **play sb. a ~:** jmdm. ein Ständchen bringen; **b)** *(cantata)* Serenade, *die.* **2.** *v. t. (Mus.)* ~ **sb.** jmdm. ein Ständchen bringen
serendipity [serən'dɪpɪtɪ] *n.* glücklicher Zufall
serene [sɪ'ri:n, sə'ri:n] *adj.,* **~r** [sɪ'ri:nə(r), sə'ri:nə(r)], **~st** [sɪ'ri:nɪst, sə'ri:nɪst] **a)** *(calm)* klar ⟨*Wetter, Himmel*⟩; **b)** *(unruffled)* unbewegt ⟨*Wasser, See usw.*⟩; **c)** *(placid)* ruhig; gelassen; **calm and ~:** ruhig und gelassen
serenely [sɪ'ri:nlɪ, sə'ri:nlɪ] *adv.* gelassen; ~ **indifferent** gleichmütig und gelassen
serenity [sɪ'renɪtɪ, sə'renɪtɪ] *n., no pl.* **a)** *(placidity)* Gelassenheit, *die;* **b)** *(of clear weather)* Klarheit, *die*
serf [sɜ:f] *n.* **a)** *(villein)* Leibeigene, *der/die;* **b)** *(fig.: drudge)* Sklave, *der*
serfdom ['sɜ:fdəm] *n.* Leibeigenschaft, *die; (fig.)* Sklaverei, *die;* Plackerei, *die (ugs.)*
serge [sɜ:dʒ] *n. (Textiles)* Serge, *die*
sergeant ['sɑ:dʒənt] *n.* **a)** *(Mil.)* Unteroffizier, *der;* **b)** *(police officer)* ≈ Polizeimeister, *der*
sergeant: ~-'major *(Amer.),* **[regimental] ~-major** *(Brit.)* ≈ [Ober]stabsfeldwebel, *der; see also* **company g**
serial ['sɪərɪəl] **1.** *adj.* **a)** *(forming a series)* aufeinanderfolgend; ~ **production** Serienproduktion, *die;* **publish sth. in ~ form** etw. in Serienform veröffentlichen; **b)** *(issued in instalments)* Fortsetzungs⟨*geschichte, -roman*⟩; ~ **radio/TV play** Radio-/Fernsehserie, *die;* **c)** *(periodical)* periodisch erscheinend; **a monthly ~ publication** eine Monatsschrift; **d)** *(Mus., Computing)* seriell. **2.** *n.* **a)** *(story)* Fortsetzungsgeschichte, *die; (on radio, television)* Serie, *die;* **b)** *(periodical)* [periodisch erscheinende] Zeitschrift; Periodikum, *das (geh.)*
serialize ['sɪərɪəlaɪz] *v. t.* in Fortsetzungen veröffentlichen; *(on radio, television)* in Fortsetzungen *od.* als Serie senden
serial 'killer *n.* Serienmörder, *der*
serially ['sɪərɪəlɪ] *adv.* in Fortsetzungen, als Serie ⟨*senden*⟩; ~ **numbered** fortlaufend numeriert
serial: ~ number *n.* Seriennummer, *die;* **~ rights** *n. pl.* Rechte zur Veröffentlichung als Serie
series ['sɪəri:z, 'sɪərɪz] *n., pl. same* **a)** *(sequence)* Reihe, *die;* **a ~ of events/misfortunes** eine Folge von Ereignissen/Mißgeschicken; **b)** *(set of successive issues)* Serie, *die;* **radio/TV ~:** Hörfunkreihe/Fernsehserie, *die;* ~ **of programmes** Sendereihe, *die;* **first ~:** erste Folge; **c)** *(set of books)* Reihe, *die;* **d)** *(group of stamps etc.)* Serie, *die;* **e)** *(group of games etc.)* Serie, *die;* **a lecture ~:** eine Vortragsreihe; **f)** *(Chem.: set of elements)* homologe Reihe; **g)** *(Electr.)* **in ~:** in Reihe; hintereinander; **h)** *(Mus., Math.)* Reihe, *die;* **i)** *(Geol.: set of strata)* Schichtenfolge, *die*
serif ['serɪf] *n. (Printing)* Serife, *die*
serio-comic [sɪərɪəʊ'kɒmɪk] *adj.* tragikomisch
serious ['sɪərɪəs] *adj.* **a)** *(earnest)* ernst; ~ **music** ernste Musik; **a ~ play** ein ernstes Stück; **b)** *(important, grave)* ernst ⟨*Angelegenheit, Lage, Problem, Zustand*⟩; ernsthaft ⟨*Frage, Einwand, Kandidat*⟩; gravierend ⟨*Änderung*⟩; schwer ⟨*Krankheit, Unfall, Fehler, Überschwemmung, Niederlage*⟩; ernstzunehmend ⟨*Rivale*⟩; ernstlich ⟨*Gefahr, Bedrohung*⟩; bedenklich ⟨*Verschlechterung, Mangel*⟩; **things are/sth. is getting ~:** die Lage spitzt sich zu/ etw. nimmt ernste Ausmaße an; **there is a ~ danger that ...:** es besteht ernste Gefahr, daß ...; ~ **charge/offence** schwerwiegender Vorwurf/schwerer Verstoß; **c)** *(in earnest)* **are you ~:** ist das dein Ernst?; **but now to be ~:** aber jetzt mal im Ernst; **you cannot be ~:** das kann doch nicht dein Ernst sein; **he is a ~ worker** er nimmt seine Arbeit ernst; **be ~ about sth./doing sth.** etw. ernst nehmen/ernsthaft tun wollen; **is he ~ about her?** meint er es ernst mit ihr?; **give sth. ~ thought** ernsthaft über etw. *(Akk.)* nachdenken
seriously ['sɪərɪəslɪ] *adv.* **a)** *(earnestly)* ernst[haft]; **speak ~ to sb.** mit jmdm. ein ernstes Wort sprechen; **quite ~, ...:** ganz im Ernst, ...; **take sth./sb. ~:** etw./jmdn. ernst nehmen; **b)** *(severely)* ernstlich; schwer ⟨*verletzt, überflutet*⟩; **go ~ wrong** ⟨*Person:*⟩ sich schwer täuschen; ⟨*Sache:*⟩ völlig mißglücken *od.* fehlschlagen
seriousness ['sɪərɪəsnɪs] *n., no pl.* **a)** *(earnestness)* Ernst, *der;* Ernsthaftigkeit, *die;* **in all ~:** ganz im Ernst; **b)** *(gravity)* Schwere, *die; (of situation)* Ernst, *der*
sermon ['sɜ:mən] *n.* **a)** *(Relig.)* Predigt, *die;* **the S~ on the Mount** die Bergpredigt; **give a ~:** eine Predigt halten; **b)** *(moral reflections)* Mahnrede, *die;* **c)** *(lecture, scolding)* [Moral]predigt, *die*
sermonize ['sɜ:mənaɪz] **1.** *v. t.* ~ **sb.** jmdm. eine [Moral]predigt halten. **2.** *v. i.* **a)** *(lecture)* ⟨*Person:*⟩ dozieren; ⟨*Buch, Film:*⟩ moralisieren; **b)** *(preach)* predigen
serpent ['sɜ:pənt] *n.* **a)** *(snake)* Schlange, *die;* **b)** *(fig.: treacherous person)* falsche Schlange; **c)** *(Mus.)* Serpent, *der*
serpentine ['sɜ:pəntaɪn] **1.** *adj.* **a)** *(tortuous)* Serpentinen-; gewunden ⟨*Fluß*⟩; **b)** *(of serpent)* Schlangen-; *(resembling a snake)* schlangengleich. **2.** *n. (Min.)* Serpentin, *der*
SERPS [sɜ:ps] *abbr. (Brit.)* **State earnings-related pension scheme**
serrated [se'reɪtɪd] *adj.* gezackt; ~ **knife** Sägemesser, *das*
serration [se'reɪʃn] *n.* gezackter Rand; *(one tooth)* Zacke, *die;* **in ~s** gezackt
serried ['serɪd] *adj.* dicht ⟨*Reihen*⟩
serum ['sɪərəm] *n., pl.* **sera** ['sɪərə] *or* **~s** *(Physiol.)* Serum, *das*
servant ['sɜ:vənt] *n.* **a)** *(wage-earning employee)* Angestellte, *der/die;* **a faithful ~ of the company** ein treuer Diener der Firma; **b)** *(domestic attendant)* Diener, *der*/Dienerin, *die; (female also)* Dienstmädchen, *das;* **keep** *or* **have ~s** Bedienstete haben; **c)** *(in letter)* **your humble** *(arch.) or* **obedient ~** *(Brit.)* Ihr ergebenster *od.* untertänigster Diener *(veralt.). See also* **civil servant; domestic 1 a; public servant**
'servant-girl *n.* Dienstmädchen, *das*
'servants' hall *n.* Dienstbotenzimmer, *das*
serve [sɜ:v] **1.** *v. t.* **a)** *(work for)* dienen (+ *Dat.*); **she had ~d the family well for ten years** sie hatte der Familie zehn Jahre lang gute Dienste geleistet; ~ **two masters** *(fig.)* auf beiden Schultern Wasser tragen; **b)** *(be useful to)* dienlich sein (+ *Dat.*); **this car ~d us well** dieses Auto hat uns gute Dienste getan; **if my memory ~s me right** wenn mich mein Gedächtnis nicht täuscht; **c)** *(meet needs of)* nutzen (+ *Dat.*); **in order to ~ some private ends** für Privatzwecke; **that excuse will not ~ you** die Entschuldigung wird dir nichts nützen; **one packet ~s him for a week** eine Packung reicht ihm für eine Woche; ~ **a/no purpose** einen Zweck erfüllen/keinen Zweck haben *od.* zwecklos sein; ~ **sb.'s needs** *or* **purpose[s]** *or* **turn** jmds. Zweck *(Dat.)* genügen; ~ **its purpose** *or* **turn** seinen Zweck erfüllen; ~ **the purpose of doing sth.** den Zweck erfüllen *od.* dem Zweck genügen, etw. zu tun; **d)** *(go through period of)* durchlaufen ⟨*Lehre*⟩; absitzen,

verbüßen ⟨*Haftstrafe*⟩; ~ **a four-year term as Prime Minister** vier Jahre lang Premierminister sein; ~ **one's time** *(hold office)* seine Amtszeit ableisten; ~ **[one's] time** *(undergo apprenticeship)* seine Lehrzeit durchmachen; *(perform military service)* seinen Wehrdienst ableisten; *(undergo imprisonment)* seine Zeit absitzen; **e)** *(dish up)* servieren; *(pour out)* einschenken (**to** *Dat.*); **dinner is ~d** das Essen ist aufgetragen; ~ **tea in china cups** Tee in Porzellantassen reichen; **f)** *(render obedience to)* dienen (+ *Dat.*) ⟨*Gott, König, Land*⟩; **g)** *(attend)* bedienen; **are you being ~d?** werden Sie schon bedient?; **h)** *(supply)* versorgen; **~s three** *(in recipe)* für drei Personen *od.* Portionen; **i)** *(provide with food)* bedienen; **has everyone been ~d?** sind alle bedient?; **j)** *(make legal delivery of)* zustellen; ~ **a summons on sb.** jmdn. vorladen; **he has been ~d notice to quit** ihm ist gekündigt worden; ~ **sb. with a writ,** ~ **a writ on sb.** jmdm. eine Verfügung zustellen; **k)** *(Tennis etc.)* aufschlagen; ~ **many double faults** viele Doppelfehler machen; ~ **an ace** ein As schlagen; **l)** *(arch./literary: treat)* behandeln; ~ **sb. ill/well** jmdm. einen schlechten/guten Dienst erweisen; **m) ~[s]** *or* **it ~s him right!** *(coll.)* [das] geschieht ihm recht!; **n)** *(copulate with)* decken. **2.** *v. i.* **a)** *(do service)* dienen; ~ **as chairman** das Amt des Vorsitzenden innehaben; ~ **as a Member of Parliament** Mitglied des Parlaments sein; ~ **on a jury** Geschworener/Geschworene sein; ~ **on a board** Mitglied des Aufsichtsrates sein; **b)** *(be employed; be soldier etc.)* dienen; Dienst tun; **he ~d against the Russians** er hat gegen die Russen gekämpft; **c)** *(be of use)* ~ **to do sth.** dazu dienen, etw. zu tun; ~ **to show sth.** etw. zeigen; **if memory ~s** wenn mein Gedächtnis mich nicht trügt; **for him nothing would ~ but ...:** er war nur mit ... zufriedenzustellen; ~ **for** *or* **as** dienen als; **it will ~:** das geht schon; das tut's *(ugs.)*; **d)** *(~ food)* **be employed to ~ at table** zum Auftragen eingestellt sein; **shall I ~?** soll ich auftragen?; **e)** *(attend in shop etc.)* bedienen; **f)** *(Eccl.)* ministrieren; **g)** *(Tennis etc.)* aufschlagen; **it's your turn to ~:** du hast Aufschlag. **3.** *n. see* **service 1 h**

~ **'out** *v. t.* **a)** *(distribute)* austeilen; ausgeben; **b)** *(work)* ableisten ⟨*Dienst*⟩; beenden ⟨*Lehrzeit*⟩; **c)** *(punish in return)* ~ **sb. out** es jmdm. heimzahlen

~ **'up** *v. t.* **a)** *(put before eaters)* servieren; **b)** *(offer for consideration)* auftischen *(ugs.)*

service ['sɜ:vɪs] **1.** *n.* **a)** *(doing of work for employer etc.)* Dienst, *der;* **give good ~:** gute Dienste leisten; **do ~ as sth.** als etw. dienen; **see ~** ⟨*Gerät:*⟩ seine Dienste tun; **he has seen ~ in the tropics** er hat in den Tropen Dienst getan; **sth. has seen long ~:** etw. hat lange Zeit gute Dienste geleistet; **he died in the ~ of his country** er starb in Pflichterfüllung für sein Vaterland; **have thirty years' ~ behind one** dreißig Jahre Dienstzeit hinter sich *(Dat.)* haben; **b)** *(sth. done to help others)* **do sb. a ~:** jmdm. einen guten Dienst erweisen; **~s** Dienste; *(Econ.)* Dienstleistungen; **ask for sb.'s ~s** jmdn. um Unterstützung bitten; **do you need the ~s of a doctor?** brauchen Sie einen Arzt?; **[in recognition of her] ~s to the hospital/state** [in Anerkennung ihrer] Verdienste um das Krankenhaus/den Staat; **c)** *(Eccl.)* Gottesdienst, *der;* **d)** *(act of attending to customer)* Service, *der; (in shop, garage, etc.)* Bedienung, *die;* **e)** *(system of transport)* Verbindung, *die;* **airline ~:** Flugverbindung, *die;* **there is no bus ~ on Sundays** sonntags verkehren keine Busse; **the number 325 bus ~:** die Buslinie Nr. 325; **when does the Oxford ~ leave?** wann fährt der Zug/Bus nach Oxford ab?; **f)** *(provision of maintenance)* **[after-sale** *or* **follow-up] ~:** Kundendienst, *der;* **ask for a ~:** den Kundendienst kommen lassen; **take one's car in for a ~:** sein Auto zur Inspektion bringen; **g)** *no pl., no art. (operation)* Betrieb, *der;* **bring into ~:** in Betrieb nehmen; **out of ~:** außer Betrieb; **take out of ~:** außer Betrieb setzen; **go** *or* **come into ~:** in Betrieb genommen werden; **h)** *(Tennis etc.)* Aufschlag, *der;* **whose ~ is it?** wer hat Aufschlag?; **i)** *(crockery set)* Service, *das;* **dessert/tea ~:** Dessert-/Tee-Service, *das;* **j)** *(legal delivery)* Zustellung, *die;* **k)** *(assistance)* **can I be of ~ [to you]?** kann ich Ihnen behilflich sein?; **will it be of ~ to you?** wird es Ihnen helfen?; **l)** *(payment)* Bedienung, *die;* Bedienungsgeld, *das; see also* **service charge; m)** *(person's behalf)* **in his ~:** in seinem Auftrag; **I'm at your ~:** ich stehe zu Ihren Diensten; **'on His/Her Majesty's ~'** *(Brit.)* „[gebührenfreie] Dienstsache"; **n)** *(department of public employ)* **the consular ~:** der Konsulatsdienst; **the railway/telephone ~:** das Eisenbahnwesen/der Telefondienst; **BBC World S~:** BBC Weltsender; **public ~:** öffentlicher Dienst; *see also* **Civil Service; Secret Service; o)** *in pl. (Brit.: public supply)* Versorgungseinrichtungen; **cut off all the ~s** Gas, Wasser und Strom abstellen; **p)** *(Mil.)* **the [armed** *or* **fighting] ~s** die Streitkräfte; **in the ~s** beim Militär; **be on ~:** dienen; **see ~:** im Einsatz sein; **q)** *(being servant)* **be in/go into ~:** in Stellung sein/gehen *(veralt.)* **(with** bei); **r)** *(employ)* Stellung, *die;* **enter the ~ of sb.** bei jmdm. in Stellung gehen *(veralt.)*; **take sb. into one's ~:** jmdn. in seine Dienste nehmen. **2.** *v. t.* **a)** *(provide maintenance for)* warten ⟨*Wagen, Waschmaschine, Heizung*⟩; **take one's car to be ~d** sein Auto zur Inspektion bringen; **b)** *(perform business function for)* versorgen; **c)** *(pay interest on)* Zinsen zahlen für ⟨*Schulden*⟩; **d)** *(copulate with)* ⟨*Tier:*⟩ decken. **3.** *adj.* militärisch; Militär⟨*fahrzeug, -flugzeug*⟩; **a ~ family** die Familie eines Militärangehörigen

serviceable ['sɜ:vɪsəbl] *adj.* **a)** *(useful)* nützlich; **b)** *(durable)* haltbar; **the shoes are ~ rather than fashionable** die Schuhe sind eher praktisch als modisch

service: ~ **area** *n.* **a)** *(for motorists' needs)* Raststätte, *die;* **b)** *(Radio, Telev.)* Sendebereich, *der;* **~-book** *n. (Eccl.)* Gesangbuch, *das;* ~ **charge** *n. (in restaurant)* Bedienungsgeld, *das; (of bank)* Bearbeitungsgebühr, *die;* **~-court** *n. (Tennis etc.)* Aufschlagfeld, *das;* ~ **dress** *n., no pl.* Dienstkleidung, *die;* ~ **engineer** *n.* Servicetechniker, *der*/-technikerin, *die;* ~ **flat** *n. (Brit.)* Wohnung mit Betreuung; ~ **hatch** *n.* Durchreiche, *die;* ~ **industry** *n.* Dienstleistungsbetrieb, *der;* ~ **lift** *n.* Lastenaufzug, *der;* **~man** ['sɜ:vɪsmən] *n., pl.* **~men** ['sɜ:vɪsmən] *(in armed ~s)* Militärangehörige, *der;* ~ **road** *n.* Zufahrtsstraße, *die;* ~ **station** *n.* Tankstelle, *die;* **~woman** *n.* Militärangehörige, *die*

serviette [sɜ:vɪ'et] *n. (Brit.)* Serviette, *die*

servi'ette-ring *n. (Brit.)* Serviettenring, *der*

servile ['sɜ:vaɪl] *adj.* unterwürfig; erbärmlich ⟨*Unterwürfigkeit, Furcht*⟩

servilely ['sɜ:vaɪllɪ] *adv.* unterwürfig

servility [sɜ:'vɪlɪtɪ] *n., no pl.* Unterwürfigkeit, *die*

serving ['sɜ:vɪŋ] **1.** *n. (quantity)* Portion, *die.* **2.** *adj.* dienend

serving: ~ **dish** *n.* Servierschüssel, *die;* ~ **hatch** *n.* Durchreiche, *die;* **~-spoon** *n.* Vorlegelöffel, *der*

servitude ['sɜ:vɪtju:d] *n., no pl. (lit. or fig.)* Knechtschaft, *die; see also* **penal servitude**

servo ['sɜ:vəʊ] *n., pl.* **~s** Servoeinrichtung, *die*

servo: **~-assisted** *adj.* **~-assisted brakes** Servobremsen; **~-mechanism** *n.* Servomechanismus, *der;* **~-motor** *n.* Servomotor, *der*

sesame ['sesəmɪ] *n.* **a)** *(herb)* Sesam, *der;* **b)** *(seed)* ~ **[seed]** Sesamkorn, *das;* **c) open ~!** Sesam, öffne dich!; **an open ~:** ein Sesam-öffne-dich

sessile ['sesaɪl] *adj. (Bot., Zool.)* sessil *(fachspr.)*; festsitzend

'sessile oak *n.* Traubeneiche, *die*

session ['seʃn] *n.* **a)** *(meeting)* Sitzung, *die;* **discussion ~:** Diskussionsrunde, *die;* **be in ~:** tagen; **b)** *(period spent)* Sitzung, *die; (by several people)* Treffen, *das;* **have daily tennis ~s with sb.** mit jmdm. täglich Tennis spielen; **let's have a cleaning ~ tomorrow** laß/laßt uns morgen [mal] groß reinemachen; **recording ~:** Aufnahme, *die;* **have a card ~:** zusammen Karten spielen; **c)** *(Brit.: academic year)* Studienjahr, *das;* **d)** *(Amer.: university term)* Vorlesungsperiode, *die;* **the summer ~:** die Sommervorlesungen; **e)** *(time for meeting)* Sitzung, *die;* **summer ~s** Sommersitzungsperiode, *die;* **f)** *(Eccl.)* Kirchenvorstand, *der;* **g)** *(Law)* **Court of S~** *oberstes schottisches Zivilgericht;* **petty ~s** *summarisches Schnellverfahren vor mehreren Friedensrichtern; see also* **quarter sessions**

sestet [ses'tet] *n.* **a)** *see* **sextet; b)** *(Pros.)* Sextett, *das*

sestina [ses'ti:nə] *n. (Pros.)* Sestine, *die*

set [set] **1.** *v. t.*, **-tt-, set a)** *(put) (horizontally)* legen; *(vertically)* stellen; ~ **sb. ashore** jmdn. an Land setzen; ~ **food before sb.** jmdm. Essen hinstellen; ~ **one brick on another** einen Stein auf den anderen setzen; ~ **the proposals before the board** *(fig.)* dem Vorstand die Vorschläge unterbreiten *od.* vorlegen; ~ **sth. against sth.** *(balance)* etw. einer Sache *(Dat.)* gegenüberstellen; **b)** *(apply)* setzen; ~ **pen to paper** etwas zu Papier bringen; ~ **a match to sth.** ein Streichholz an etw. halten; *see also* **fire 1 a; hand 1 a; 'light 1 e; ²seal 1 c; shoulder 1 a; c)** *(adjust)* einstellen (**at** auf + *Akk.*); aufstellen ⟨*Falle*⟩; stellen ⟨*Uhr*⟩; ~ **your watch by mine** stell deine Uhr nach meiner; ~ **the alarm for 5.30 a.m.** den Wecker auf 5.30 Uhr stellen; **d) be ~** *(have location of action)* ⟨*Buch, Film:*⟩ spielen; ~ **a book/film in Australia/a brothel** ein Buch/einen Film in Australien/in einem Bordell spielen lassen; **e)** *(specify)* festlegen ⟨*Bedingungen*⟩; festsetzen ⟨*Termin, Ort usw.*⟩ (**for** auf + *Akk.*); ~ **the interest rate at 10%** die Zinsen auf 10% festsetzen; ~ **limits** Grenzen setzen; **f)** *(bring into specified state)* ~ **sth./things right** *or* **in order** etw./die Dinge in Ordnung bringen; ~ **sb. laughing** jmdn. zum Lachen bringen; ~ **a dog barking** einen Hund anschlagen lassen; ~ **sb. thinking that ...:** jmdn. auf den Gedanken bringen, daß ...; **the news ~ me thinking** die Nachricht machte mich nachdenklich; *see also* **cap 1 a; defiance; ease 1 a; edge 1 a; fire 1 b; foot 1 a; free 1 a; ¹go 1 f; house 1 a; motion 1 a; ¹rest 3 b; right 1 d, 3 e; g)** *(put forward)* stellen ⟨*Frage, Aufgabe*⟩; aufgeben ⟨*Hausaufgabe*⟩; vorschreiben ⟨*Textbuch, Lektüre*⟩; *(compose)* zusammenstellen ⟨*Rätsel, Fragen, Prüfungsaufgaben*⟩; ~ **sb. an example,** ~ **an example to sb.** jmdm. ein Beispiel geben; ~ **sb. a task/problem** jmdm. eine Aufgabe stellen/jmdn. vor ein Problem stellen; ~ **[sb./oneself] a target** [jmdm./sich] ein Ziel setzen; **h)** *(turn to solid)* fest werden lassen; **is the jelly ~ yet?** ist das Gelee schon fest?; **i)** *(put in ground to grow)* einpflanzen, setzen ⟨*Pflanzen*⟩; säen ⟨*Samen*⟩; **j)** *(lay for meal)* decken ⟨*Tisch*⟩; auflegen ⟨*Gedeck*⟩; **k)** *(place for visitor)* aufstellen ⟨*Stuhl, Tisch*⟩; **l)** ~ **sail** *(hoist sail)* die Segel setzen *od.* hissen; *(begin voyage)* losfahren (**for** nach); **m)** ~ **a watch** *(guard)* eine Wache aufstellen; ~ **the watch** *(Naut.)* die Wache aufstellen; **n)** *(establish)* aufstellen ⟨*Rekord, Richtlinien*⟩; ~ **the fashion for sth.** etw. in Mode bringen; ~

the pace das Tempo bestimmen; **o)** *(Med.: put into place)* [ein]richten; einrenken ⟨*verrenktes Gelenk*⟩; **p)** *(fix)* legen ⟨*Haare*⟩; ~ **eyes on sb./sth.** jmdn./etw. sehen; ~ **one's teeth** *(lit. or fig.)* die Zähne zusammenbeißen; *see also* **face 1 a; heart 1 b; hope 1; mind 1 c; price 1 a; scene h; store 1 f; value 1 a; q)** *(Printing)* setzen; ~ **close/out** *or* **wide** eng/breit setzen; **r)** ~ **sb. to sth./doing sth.** jmdn. zu etw. anhalten/jmdn. veranlassen, etw. zu tun; ~ **sb. wood-chopping** jmdn. Holz hacken schicken; ~ **oneself to sth./do sth.** sich an etw. *(Akk.)* machen/daran machen, etw. zu tun; ~ **sb. in charge of sth.** jmdn. mit etw. betrauen; ~ **a dog on sb.** einen Hund auf jmdn. hetzen; ~ **a dog/the police after sb.** einen Hund/die Polizei auf jmdn. hetzen; **they** ~ **their thugs/detectives on him** sie setzten ihre Schläger/Detektive auf ihn an; ~ **sb. against sb.** jmdn. gegen jmdn. aufbringen; ~ **father against son** Zwietracht säen zwischen Vater und Sohn; *see also* **work 1 a; s)** ~ **sth. to music** *or* **a tune** etw. vertonen; **t)** *(ornament)* besetzen; [ein]fassen ⟨*Edelstein, Ränder*⟩; bepflanzen ⟨*Beet*⟩; **the lid was** ~ **with gems** der Deckel war mit Edelsteinen besetzt; **a sky** ~ **with stars** ein sternenbesetzter Himmel; **u) be** ~ **on a hill** ⟨*Haus:*⟩ auf einem Hügel stehen; **v)** *(make fast)* fixieren ⟨*Farbe, Färbemittel*⟩. **2.** *v. i.*, **-tt-, set a)** *(solidify)* fest werden; **has the jelly** ~ **yet?** ist das Gelee schon fest?; **b)** *(go down)* ⟨*Sonne, Mond:*⟩ untergehen; **sb.'s star** ~**s** *(fig.)* jmds. Stern ist im Sinken begriffen; **c)** *(flow along)* **the current** ~**s eastwards** die Strömung geht nach Osten; ~ **against sth.** *(fig.)* sich gegen etw. richten; **d)** *(Bot.) (form into or develop fruit)* ⟨*Blüte, Pflanze:*⟩ Frucht ansetzen; *(develop out of blossom)* ⟨*Frucht:*⟩ sich entwickeln; **e)** ⟨*Gesicht:*⟩ sich verhärten (**with** vor + *Dat.*); **f)** *(take rigid attitude)* ~ **[rigidly]** ⟨*Jagdhund:*⟩ [fest] vorstehen. **3.** *n.* **a)** *(group)* Satz, *der;* ~ **[of two]** Paar, *das;* **a** ~ **of chairs** eine Sitzgruppe; eine Stuhlgarnitur; **a** ~ **of stamps** ein Satz Briefmarken; **a complete** ~ **of Dickens' novels** eine Gesamtausgabe der Romane von Dickens; **a** ~ **of lectures** eine Vortragsreihe; **chess** ~: Schachspiel, *das;* **b)** *see* **service 1 i; c)** *(section of society)* Kreis, *der;* **racing** ~: Rennsportfreunde *od.* -fans; **the younger** ~: die Jüngeren; **the fast** ~: die Lebewelt; *see also* **jet set; smart 1 c; d)** *(Math.)* Menge, *die;* **theory of** ~**s** Mengenlehre, *die;* **e)** ~ **[of teeth]** Gebiß, *das;* **f)** *(radio or TV receiver)* Gerät, *das;* Apparat, *der;* **g)** *(Tennis)* Satz, *der;* **h)** *(of hair)* Frisieren, *das;* Einlegen, *das;* **have a shampoo and** ~: sich *(Dat.)* die Haare waschen und legen lassen; **i)** *(Theatre: built-up scenery)* Szenenaufbau, *der;* **j)** *(area of performance) (of film)* Drehort, *der; (of play)* Bühne, *die;* **on the** ~ *(for film)* bei den Dreharbeiten; *(for play)* bei den Proben; **k)** *(granite paving-block)* Pflasterstein, *der;* **l)** *(burrow)* Bau, *der;* **m)** *(of dog)* **[dead]** ~: Vorstehen, *das;* **make a dead** ~ **at sb.** *(fig.) (try to win affections of)* sich an jmdn. heranmachen; *(attack)* über jmdn. herfallen; **n)** *(Hort.) (shoot, cutting)* Setzling, *der; (bulb)* Knolle, *die;* Zwiebel, *die;* **o)** *(literary: sunset)* **at** ~ **of sun** bei Sonnenuntergang; **p)** *no pl. (posture)* Haltung, *die;* **the** ~ **of his head** seine Kopfhaltung; **q)** *(way dress etc. sits or flows)* Sitz, *der.* **4.** *adj.* **a)** *(fixed)* starr ⟨*Linie, Gewohnheit, Blick, Lächeln*⟩; fest ⟨*Absichten, Zielvorstellungen, Zeitpunkt*⟩; **be** ~ **in one's ways** *or* **habits** in seinen Gewohnheiten festgefahren sein; **deep-**~ **eyes** tiefliegende Augen; **b)** *(assigned for study or discussion)* vorgeschrieben ⟨*Buch, Text*⟩; bestimmt, festgelegt ⟨*Thema*⟩; **be a** ~ **book** Pflichtlektüre sein; **c)** *(according to fixed menu)* ~ **meal** *or* **menu** Menü, *das;* **d)** *(ready)* **sth. is** ~ **to increase** etw. wird bald steigen; **be/get** ~ **for sth.** zu etw. bereit sein/sich zu etw. fertigmachen; **be/get** ~ **to leave** bereit sein/sich fertigmachen zum Aufbruch; **all** ~**?** *(coll.)* alles klar *od.* fertig?; **be all** ~ **for sth.** zu etw. bereit sein; **be all** ~ **to do sth.** bereit sein, etw. zu tun; **are we all** ~**?** alle startklar? *(ugs.);* **e)** *(determined)* **be** ~ **on sth./doing sth.** zu etw. entschlossen sein/entschlossen sein, etw. zu tun; **be [dead]** ~ **against sth.** [absolut] gegen etw. sein; **of** ~ **purpose** mit Absicht; absichtlich; *see also* **close-set**

~ **about** *v. t.* **a)** *(begin purposefully)* ~ **about sth.** sich an etw. *(Akk.)* machen; etw. in Angriff nehmen; ~ **about doing sth.** sich daranmachen, etw. zu tun; **b)** *(spread)* verbreiten ⟨*Gerücht, Geschichte*⟩; **c)** *(coll.: attack)* herfallen über (+ *Akk.*)

~ **a'part** *v. t.* **a)** *(reserve)* reservieren; einplanen ⟨*Zeit*⟩; **b)** *(make different)* abheben (**from** von); **his strength** ~**s him apart from others** durch seine Kraft zeichnet er sich gegenüber anderen aus

~ **a'side** *v. t.* **a)** *(put to one side)* beiseite legen ⟨*Buch, Zeitung, Strickzeug*⟩; beiseite stellen ⟨*Stuhl, Glas usw.*⟩; unterbrechen ⟨*Arbeit, Tätigkeit*⟩; außer acht lassen ⟨*Frage*⟩; unberücksichtigt lassen ⟨*Angebot*⟩; *(postpone)* aufschieben ⟨*Arbeit*⟩; **b)** *(cancel)* aufheben ⟨*Urteil, Entscheidung*⟩; **c)** *(pay no attention to)* außer acht lassen ⟨*Unterschiede, Formalitäten*⟩; begraben ⟨*Feindschaft*⟩; vergessen ⟨*Bitterkeit, Stolz, Eifersucht*⟩; abschaffen ⟨*Recht*⟩; **d)** *(reserve)* aufheben ⟨*Essen, Zutaten*⟩; einplanen ⟨*Minute, Zeit*⟩; beiseite legen ⟨*Geld*⟩; *(save for customer)* zurücklegen ⟨*Ware*⟩; **why don't you** ~ **aside a day to come and visit me?** halt dir doch [einfach] einen Tag frei, an dem du mich besuchen kommst!

~ **'back** *v. t.* **a)** *(hinder progress of)* behindern ⟨*Fortschritt*⟩; aufhalten ⟨*Entwicklung*⟩; zurückwerfen ⟨*Projekt, Programm*⟩; **b)** *(coll.: be an expense to)* ~ **sb. back a fair amount/sum** jmdn. eine hübsche Summe kosten; **c)** *(place at a distance)* zurücksetzen; **the house is** ~ **back some distance from the road** das Haus steht in einiger Entfernung von der Straße; **d)** *(postpone)* verschieben ⟨*Termin*⟩ (**to** auf + *Akk.*). *See also* **set-back**

~ **'by** *see* ~ **aside a, d**

~ **'down** *v. t.* **a)** *(allow to alight)* absetzen ⟨*Fahrgast, Ladung*⟩; **the bus will** ~ **you down there** der Bus hält dort; du kannst dort aus dem Bus aussteigen; **b)** *(record on paper)* niederschreiben; **c)** *(place on surface)* absetzen; abstellen; **d)** *(fix)* anberaumen ⟨*Sitzung, Treffen, Anhörung, usw.*⟩; **e)** *(attribute)* zuschreiben (**to** *Dat.*); **f)** ~ **down as** *or* **for** *or* **to be** *(judge)* halten für; *(record)* eintragen als

~ **'forth 1.** *v. i. (begin journey)* aufbrechen; ~ **forth on a journey** eine Reise antreten. **2.** *v. t. (present)* darstellen ⟨*Zahlen, Kosten*⟩; darlegen ⟨*Programm, Ziel, Politik*⟩

~ **'forward** *v. t.* **a)** *(move further in front)* weiter nach vorn stellen *od.* setzen; **b)** *(present)* darlegen ⟨*Programm, Plan usw.*⟩; **c)** *(bring forward in time)* voranbringen ⟨*Ernte, Entwicklung usw.*⟩; **d)** vorstellen ⟨*Uhr*⟩

~ **'in 1.** *v. i. (gain a hold)* ⟨*Dunkelheit, Regen, Reaktion, Verfall:*⟩ einsetzen; ⟨*Mode:*⟩ aufkommen. **2.** *v. t. (insert)* einsetzen

~ **'off 1.** *v. i. (begin journey)* aufbrechen; *(start to move)* loslaufen; ⟨*Zug:*⟩ losfahren; ~ **off for work** sich auf den Weg zur Arbeit machen. **2.** *v. t.* **a)** *(show to advantage)* hervorheben; **b)** *(start)* führen zu; auslösen ⟨*Reaktion, Alarmanlage*⟩; einleiten ⟨*Entwicklung*⟩; in Umlauf setzen ⟨*Gerücht*⟩; ~ **sb. off into hysterics** jmdn. hysterisch werden lassen; ~ **sb. off thinking/laughing** jmdn. zum Nachdenken anregen/zum Lachen bringen; **c)** *(cause to explode)* explodieren lassen; abbrennen ⟨*Feuerwerk*⟩; **d)** *(counterbalance)* ausgleichen; ~ **sth. off against sth.** etw. einer Sache *(Dat.)* gegenüberstellen; *(use as compensatory item)* etw. als Ausgleich für etw. nehmen

~ **on** *v. t. (attack)* überfallen

~ **'out 1.** *v. i.* **a)** *(begin journey)* aufbrechen; **b)** *(begin with intention)* ~ **out to do sth.** sich *(Dat.)* vornehmen, etw. zu tun; ~ **out in business** sein eigenes Geschäft aufmachen; ~ **out on a career as ...**: eine Laufbahn als ... einschlagen. **2.** *v. t.* **a)** *(present)* darlegen ⟨*Gedanke, Argument*⟩; auslegen ⟨*Waren*⟩; ausbreiten ⟨*Geschenke*⟩; aufstellen ⟨*Schachfiguren*⟩; setzen ⟨*Pflanzen*⟩; **b)** *(state, specify)* darlegen ⟨*Bedingungen, Einwände, Vorschriften*⟩; **c)** *(mark out)* entwerfen. *See also* **set-out**

~ **over** *v. t.* stellen über (+ *Akk.*)

~ **'to** *v. i.* **a)** *(begin vigorously)* sich daranmachen; *(begin eating hungrily)* es sich *(Dat.)* schmecken lassen; **b)** *(begin to fight)* loslegen *(ugs.); see also* **set-to**

~ **'up 1.** *v. t.* **a)** *(erect)* errichten ⟨*Straßensperre, Denkmal*⟩; aufstellen ⟨*Kamera*⟩; aufbauen ⟨*Zelt, Spieltisch*⟩; ~ **up the type** setzen; ~ **up a column in type** eine Spalte setzen; **b)** *(establish)* bilden ⟨*Regierung usw.*⟩; gründen ⟨*Gesellschaft, Organisation, Orden*⟩; aufbauen ⟨*Kontrollsystem, Verteidigung*⟩; einleiten ⟨*Untersuchung*⟩; einrichten ⟨*Büro*⟩; ~ **oneself up as a dentist/in business** sich als Zahnarzt niederlassen/ein Geschäft aufmachen; ~ **sb. up in business** jmdm. die Gründung eines eigenen Geschäfts ermöglichen; **c)** *(begin to utter)* anstimmen; **the class** ~ **up such a din** die Klasse veranstaltete einen solchen Lärm; **d)** *(cause)* auslösen ⟨*Infektion, Reaktion*⟩; **e)** *(coll.: make stronger)* stärken; **a good breakfast should** ~ **you up for the day** ein gutes Frühstück gibt dir Kraft für den ganzen Tag; **well** ~ **up** kerngesund; kraftstrotzend; **f)** *(achieve)* aufstellen ⟨*Rekord, Zeit*⟩; **g)** *(provide adequately)* ~ **sb. up with sth.** jmdn. mit etw. versorgen *od. (ugs.)* eindecken; **h)** *(place in view)* anbringen ⟨*Schild, Warnung*⟩; hissen ⟨*Flagge*⟩; **i)** *(prepare)* vorbereiten ⟨*Experiment*⟩; betriebsbereit machen ⟨*Maschine*⟩; **j)** *(propound)* aufstellen ⟨*Theorie*⟩; **k)** ~ **sb. up** *(coll.: frame)* jmdm. die Schuld in die Schuhe schieben. *See also* **house 1 a; set-up; shop 1 b. 2.** *v. i.* ~ **up in business/in the fashion trade** ein Geschäft aufmachen/sich in der Modebranche etablieren; ~ **up as a dentist** sich als Zahnarzt niederlassen. **3.** *v. refl.* ~ **oneself up as** *or* **to be sb./sth.** *(coll.)* sich als jmd./etw. aufspielen

set: ~**-back** *n.* **a)** *(checking of progress)* Rückschlag, *der;* **b)** *(defeat)* Niederlage, *die;* ~**-off** *n.* **a)** *(counterbalance)* Ausgleich, *der* (**against** für); **b)** *(Commerc., Law)* Ausgleich, *der* (**to, against** für); **by** ~**-off against other cheques** durch Verrechnung mit anderen Schecks; **c)** *(start)* Aufbruch, *der;* **d)** *(adornment)* Zier, *die;* ~**-out** *n. (commencement)* Start, *der;* ~ **phrase** *n.* feste Wendung; Phrase, *die;* ~ **'piece** *n.* **a)** *(design formed with fireworks)* Bild aus Feuerwerkskörpern; **b)** *(Footb.)* Standardsituation, *die;* ~ **point** *n. (Tennis etc.)* Satzball, *der;* ~ **'screw** *n. (Mech. Engin.)* Stellschraube, *die;* ~ **'scrum** *n. (Rugby)* Gedränge, *das;* ~ **'speech** *n.* fertige Rede; ~ **square** *n.* Zeichendreieck, *das*

sett [set] *see* **set 3 k, l, n**

settee [se'ti:] *n.* Sofa, *das*

setter ['setə(r)] *n. (dog)* Setter, *der*

'set theory *n. (Math.)* Mengenlehre, *die*

setting ['setɪŋ] *n.* **a)** *(Mus.)* Vertonung, *die;* **b)** *(frame for jewel)* Fassung, *die;* **c)** *(surroundings)* Rahmen, *der; (of novel etc.)* Schauplatz, *der;* **a cottage in a pleasant** ~:

ein Häuschen in schöner Umgebung; **d)** *(Theatre)* Bühnendekoration, *die;* **e)** *(plates and cutlery)* Gedeck, *das*

'setting-lotion *n.* Haarfestiger, *der*

settle ['setl] **1.** *v. t.* **a)** *(place) (horizontally)* [sorgfältig] legen; *(vertically)* [sorgfältig] stellen; *(at an angle)* [sorgfältig] lehnen; ~ **a patient in his bed/an armchair** einen Patienten richtig ins Bett legen/im Sessel zurechtsetzen; **he ~d himself comfortably on the couch** er machte es sich *(Dat.)* auf der Couch bequem; **b)** *(establish) (in house or business)* unterbringen; *(in country or colony)* ansiedeln ⟨*Volk*⟩; **we got them ~d in their new house** wir haben ihnen geholfen, sich in ihrem neuen Haus einzurichten; **c)** *(determine, resolve)* aushandeln, sich einigen auf ⟨*Preis*⟩; beilegen ⟨*Streit, Konflikt, Meinungsverschiedenheit*⟩; beseitigen, ausräumen ⟨*Zweifel, Bedenken*⟩; entscheiden ⟨*Frage, Spiel*⟩; regeln, in Ordnung bringen ⟨*Angelegenheit*⟩; entscheiden über (+ *Akk.*) ⟨*Sieger*⟩; festlegen, planen ⟨*Urlaub*⟩; **nothing has been ~d as yet** es ist noch nichts entschieden; **that should ~ the match** damit dürfte das Spiel entschieden sein; ~ **the matter among yourselves!** macht das unter euch aus!; **that ~s it** dann ist ja alles klar *(ugs.); expr. exasperation* jetzt reicht's! *(ugs.);* ~ **a case out of court** sich außergerichtlich vergleichen; ~ **one's affairs** seine Angelegenheiten in Ordnung bringen; seinen Nachlaß regeln; ~ **the day/date/place** den Tag/Termin/Ort festsetzen *od.* festlegen; **is the date ~d yet?** steht der Termin schon fest?; **d)** *(deal with, dispose of)* fertig werden mit; *see also* **'hash 1; e)** *(pay money owed according to)* bezahlen, *(geh.)* begleichen ⟨*Rechnung, Betrag*⟩; erfüllen ⟨*Forderung, Anspruch*⟩; ausgleichen ⟨*Konto*⟩; *see also* **score 1 f; f)** *(cause to sink)* sich absetzen lassen ⟨*Bodensatz, Sand, Sediment*⟩; **a shower will ~ the dust** ein Schauer wird den Staub binden; **g)** *(calm)* beruhigen ⟨*Nerven, Magen*⟩; *(aid digestion of)* verdauen ⟨*Essen*⟩; **h)** *(colonize)* besiedeln; **i)** *(bestow)* ~ **money/property on sb.** jmdm. Geld/Besitz übereignen; ~ **an annuity on sb.** jmdm. eine Rente aussetzen. **2.** *v. i.* **a)** *(become established)* sich niederlassen; *(as colonist)* sich ansiedeln; **b)** *(end dispute)* sich einigen; **c)** *(pay what is owed)* abrechnen; **d)** *(in chair, in front of the fire, etc.)* sich niederlassen; *(to work etc.)* sich konzentrieren (**to** auf + *Akk.*); *(into way of life, retirement, middle age, etc.)* sich gewöhnen (**into** an + *Akk.*); **it took a long time to ~ in our new house** es dauerte lange, bis wir uns in unserem neuen Haus richtig eingelebt hatten; **the cold ~d on her chest** die Erkältung hat sich ihr auf die Bronchien gelegt; **the snow/dust ~d on the ground** der Schnee blieb liegen/der Staub setzte sich [am Boden] ab; **darkness/silence/fog ~d over the village** Dunkelheit/Stille/Nebel legte *od.* senkte sich über das Dorf; *see also* **dust 1 a; e)** *(subside)* ⟨*Haus, Fundament, Boden:*⟩ sich senken; *(sink)* ⟨*Schiff:*⟩ sinken; ⟨*Sediment:*⟩ sich ablagern; ⟨*Kristalle:*⟩ sich absetzen (**at, on** auf + *Dat.*); **f)** *(be digested)* ⟨*Essen:*⟩ sich setzen; *(become calm)* ⟨*Magen:*⟩ sich beruhigen; **g)** *(become clear)* ⟨*Wein, Bier:*⟩ sich klären

~ **'back** *v. i.* **a)** *(relax)* sich zurücklehnen (**in** in + *Dat.*); **b)** ~ **back into one's routine** sich wieder in die Alltagsroutine hineinfinden

~ **'down 1.** *v. i.* **a)** *(make oneself comfortable)* sich niederlassen (**in** in + *Dat.*); ~ **down for the night** sich schlafen *od.* zur Ruhe legen; **b)** *(become established in a place) (in town or house)* seßhaft *od.* heimisch werden; *(in school)* sich eingewöhnen (**in** in + *Akk.*); ~ **down in a job** *(find permanent work)* eine feste Anstellung finden; *(get used to a job)* sich einarbeiten; **c)** *(marry)* **it's about time he ~d down** er sollte allmählich häuslich werden [und heiraten]; ~ **down to married life** ein häusliches Eheleben beginnen; **d)** *(calm down)* ⟨*Person:*⟩ sich beruhigen; ⟨*Lärm, Aufregung:*⟩ sich legen; ~ **down to work** richtig mit der Arbeit anfangen. **2.** *v. t.* **a)** *(make comfortable)* ~ **oneself down** sich [gemütlich] hinsetzen; ~ **oneself down in a chair** sich [gemütlich] auf einen Stuhl setzen; ~ **the baby down for the night/to sleep** das Baby schlafen legen; **b)** *(calm down)* beruhigen

~ **for** *v. t.* **a)** *(agree to)* sich zufriedengeben mit; **b)** *(decide on)* sich entscheiden für

~ **'in 1.** *v. i. (in new home)* sich einleben; *(in new job or school)* sich eingewöhnen. **2.** *v. t.* **we all helped to ~ them in** wir trugen alle dazu bei, daß sie heimisch wurden

~ **on** *v. t.* **a)** *(decide on)* sich entscheiden für; **b)** *(agree on)* sich einigen auf (+ *Akk.*)

~ **'up** *v. i.* abrechnen; ~ **up with the waiter** beim Kellner bezahlen

~ **with** *v. t.* ~ **with sb.** *(pay agreed amount to sb.)* jmdm. eine Abfindung zahlen; *(pay all the money owed to sb.)* bei jmdm. seine Rechnung begleichen; *(fig.)* mit jmdm. abrechnen; **now to ~ with 'you!** jetzt bist du dran! *(ugs.)*

settled ['setld] *adj.* fest ⟨*Meinung, Überzeugung, Grundsätze, Gewohnheit*⟩; festgelegt ⟨*Verfahren*⟩; vorausbestimmt ⟨*Zukunft*⟩; beständig ⟨*Wetter*⟩; geregelt ⟨*Lebensweise*⟩; **I don't feel ~ in this house/job** ich kann mich in diesem Haus nicht heimisch fühlen/in diese Arbeit nicht hineinfinden; **we can now expect ~ weather** jetzt ist eine Wetterberuhigung zu erwarten

settlement ['setlmənt] *n.* **a)** Entscheidung, *die; (in relation to price)* Einigung, *die; (of argument, conflict, dispute, differences, troubles)* Beilegung, *die; (of problem)* Lösung, *die; (of question)* Klärung, *die; (of affairs)* Regelung, *die; (of court case)* Vergleich, *der;* **reach a ~:** zu einer Einigung kommen; **reach a ~ out of court** sich außergerichtlich vergleichen; **terms of ~** *(Law)* Vergleichsbedingungen; **b)** *(of bill, account, etc.)* Bezahlung, *die;* Begleichung, *die;* **a cheque in ~ of a bill** ein Scheck zur Begleichung einer Rechnung; **c)** *(Law: bestowal)* Zuwendung, *die; (in will)* Legat, *das (fachspr.);* Vermächtnis, *das; see also* **marriage settlement; d)** *(colony)* Siedlung, *die; (colonization)* Besiedlung, *die;* **penal ~:** Strafkolonie, *die;* **e)** *(subsidence)* [Ab]senkung, *die*

settler ['setlə(r)] *n.* **a)** *(colonist)* Siedler, *der*/Siedlerin, *die;* **b)** *(sl.: decisive blow or argument)* entscheidender Schlag

settling day ['setlɪŋ deɪ] *n. (Brit. St. Exch.)* Abrechnungstermin, *der*

set: ~-to ['settu:] *n., pl.* **~-tos** Streit, *der;* **~-tos** Streitereien; *(with fists)* Prügeleien; **have a ~-to** Streit haben; *(with fists)* sich prügeln; **~-up** *n. (coll.)* **a)** *(organization)* System, *das; (structure)* Aufbau, *der;* **b)** *(situation)* Zustand, *der;* **isn't it a rather strange ~-up?** ist das nicht ein bißchen seltsam?; **what's the ~-up here?** wie läuft das hier? *(ugs.)*

seven ['sevn] **1.** *adj.* sieben; **the S~ Years War** der Siebenjährige Krieg; *see also* **eight 1; sea b; wonder 1 b. 2.** *n. (number, symbol)* Sieben, *die; see also* **eight 2 a, c, d**

'sevenfold *adj., adv.* siebenfach; *see also* **eightfold**

'seven-league boots *n. pl.* Siebenmeilenstiefel

seventeen [sevn'ti:n] **1.** *adj.* siebzehn; **sweet ~:** süße siebzehn [Jahre alt]; *see also* **eight 1. 2.** *n.* Siebzehn, *die; see also* **eight 2 a; eighteen 2**

seventeenth [sevn'ti:nθ] **1.** *adj.* siebzehnt...; *see also* **eighth 1. 2.** *n. (fraction)* Siebzehntel, *das; see also* **eighth 2**

seventh ['sevnθ] **1.** *adj.* sieb[en]t...; *see also* **eighth 1; heaven a. 2.** *n.* **a)** *(in sequence)* sieb[en]te, *der/die/das; (in rank)* Sieb[en]te, *der/die/das; (fraction)* Sieb[en]tel, *das;* **b)** *(Mus.)* Septime, *die;* **c)** *(day)* **the ~ of May** der sieb[en]te Mai; **the ~ [of the month]** der Sieb[en]te [des Monats]; **S~-day Adventists** Siebenten-Tags-Adventisten

seventieth ['sevntɪɪθ] **1.** *adj.* siebzigst...; *see also* **eighth 1. 2.** *n. (fraction)* Siebzigstel, *das; see also* **eighth 2**

seventy ['sevntɪ] **1.** *adj.* siebzig; **one-and-~** *(arch.) see* **seventy-one 1;** *see also* **eight 1. 2.** *n.* Siebzig, *die;* **one-and-~** *(arch.) see* **seventy-one 2;** *see also* **eight 2 a; eighty 2**

seventy: ~-eight *n. (record)* Achtundsiebziger[platte], *die;* **~-first** *etc. adj.* einundsiebzigst... *usw.; see also* **eighth 1; ~-one** *etc.* **1.** *adj.* einundsiebzig *usw.; see also* **eight 1; 2.** *n.* Einundsiebzig *usw., die; see also* **eight 2 a**

seven-year 'itch *n.* **the ~:** ≈ das verflixte sieb[en]te Jahr

sever ['sevə(r)] **1.** *v. t.* **a)** *(cut)* durchtrennen; *(fig.: break off)* abbrechen ⟨*Beziehungen, Verbindung*⟩; **some cables were ~ed in the storm** einige Kabel sind bei dem Sturm gerissen; **b)** *(separate with force)* abtrennen; *(with axe etc.)* abhacken; **the axe ~ed his head from his body** die Axt trennte seinen Kopf vom Rumpf; **c)** *(divide)* **the sea ~s England and** *or* **from France** das Meer trennt England und *od.* von Frankreich. **2.** *v. i. (tear)* reißen; *(be torn off)* abreißen

several ['sevrl] **1.** *adv.* **a)** *(a few)* mehrere; einige; ~ **times** mehrmals; mehrere *od.* einige Male; ~ **more copies** noch einige Exemplare mehr; **b)** *(separate, diverse)* verschieden; **joint and ~** *(Law)* gesamtschuldnerisch ⟨*Haftung*⟩. **2.** *pron.* einige; ~ **of us** einige von uns; ~ **of the buildings** einige *od.* mehrere [der] Gebäude

severally ['sevrəlɪ] *adv.* gesondert; **jointly and ~** *(Law)* gesamtschuldnerisch

severance ['sevərəns] *n. (of diplomatic relations)* Abbruch, *der; (of communications)* Unterbrechung, *die; (of contract)* Lösung, *die;* ~ **pay** Abfindung, *die*

severe [sɪ'vɪə(r)] *adj.,* **~r** [sɪ'vɪərə(r)], **~st** [sɪ'vɪərɪst] **a)** *(strict)* streng; hart ⟨*Urteil, Strafe, Kritik*⟩; **be ~ on** *or* **with sb.** streng mit jmdm. sein *od.* umgehen; **b)** *(violent, extreme)* streng ⟨*Frost, Winter*⟩; schwer ⟨*Sturm, Dürre, Verlust, Behinderung, Verletzung*⟩; rauh ⟨*Wetter*⟩; heftig ⟨*Anfall, Schmerz*⟩; **c)** *(making great demands)* hart ⟨*Test, Prüfung, Konkurrenz*⟩; scharf ⟨*Tempo*⟩; **d)** *(serious, not slight)* bedrohlich ⟨*Mangel, Knappheit*⟩; heftig, stark ⟨*Blutung*⟩; schwer ⟨*Krankheit*⟩; **e)** *(unadorned)* streng ⟨*Stil, Schönheit, Dekor*⟩

severely [sɪ'vɪəlɪ] *adv.* hart; hart, streng ⟨*bestrafen*⟩; schwer ⟨*verletzt, behindert*⟩; **leave sth. ~ alone** unbedingt die Finger von etw. lassen *(ugs.);* **be ~ critical of sth.** etw. scharf kritisieren

severeness [sɪ'vɪənɪs], **severity** [sɪ'verɪtɪ] *ns.* Strenge, *die; (of drought, shortage)* großes Ausmaß; *(of criticism)* Schärfe, *die;* **with ~:** streng ⟨*bestrafen*⟩; **the severities of army life** die Härte des Soldatenlebens

Seville [sə'vɪl] *pr. n.* Sevilla *(das)*

Seville orange [sevɪl 'ɒrɪndʒ] *n.* Pomeranze, *die;* Sevillaorange, *die*

sew [səʊ] **1.** *v. t., p.p.* **~n** [səʊn] *or* **~ed** [səʊd] nähen ⟨*Kleid, Naht, Wunde*⟩; heften, broschieren ⟨*Buch usw.*⟩; zunähen ⟨*Loch, Riß*⟩; ~ **together** zusammennähen ⟨*Stoff, Leder usw.*⟩; ~ **money into one's coat** Geld in seinen Mantel einnähen. **2.** *v. i., p.p.* **~n** *or* **~ed** nähen

~ **'down** *v. t.* aufnähen

~ **'in** *v. t.* einsetzen ⟨*Flicken*⟩

~ **'on** *v. t.* annähen ⟨*Knopf*⟩; aufnähen ⟨*Abzeichen, Band*⟩

~ **'up** *v.t.* **a)** nähen ⟨*Saum, Naht, Wunde*⟩; **they ~ed me up after the operation** *(coll.)* nach der Operation haben sie mich wieder zugenäht; **b)** *(Brit. fig. coll.: settle, arrange)* **be ~n up** unter Dach und Fach sein; *(completely organized)* durchorganisiert sein; **we've got the match all ~n up** wir haben den Sieg schon in der Tasche *(ugs.)*
sewage ['sju:ɪdʒ, 'su:ɪdʒ] *n.* Abwasser, *das*
sewage: ~ **disposal** *n.* Abwasserbeseitigung, *die;* ~ **farm** *n.*, ~ **works** *n. sing., pl. same* Kläranlage, *die*
[1]**sewer** ['sju:ə(r), 'su:ə(r)] *n. (tunnel)* Abwasserkanal, *der; (pipe)* Abwasserleitung, *die*
[2]**sewer** ['səʊə(r)] *n. (person)* Näher, *der*/Näherin, *die*
sewerage ['sju:ərɪdʒ, 'su:ərɪdʒ] *n.* **a)** *(system of sewers)* Kanalisation, *die;* **b)** *no pl. (removal of sewage)* Abwasserbeseitigung, *die;* **c)** *(sewage)* Abwasser, *das*
sewing ['səʊɪŋ] *n.* Näharbeit, *die*
sewing: **~-basket** *n.* Nähkorb, *der;* **~-machine** *n.* Nähmaschine, *die*
sewn *see* **sew**
sex [seks] **1.** *n.* **a)** Geschlecht, *das;* **what ~ is the baby/puppy?** welches Geschlecht hat das Baby/der Welpe?; **b)** *(sexuality; coll.: intercourse)* Sex, *der (ugs.);* **have ~ with sb.** *(coll.)* mit jmdm. schlafen *(verhüll.);* Sex mit jmdm. haben *(salopp).* **2.** *attrib. adj.* Geschlechts⟨*organ, -trieb*⟩; Sexual⟨*verbrechen, -trieb, -instinkt*⟩. **3.** *v.t.* **a)** *(determine ~ of)* ~ **a rabbit/chicken** das Geschlecht eines Kaninchens/Kükens bestimmen; **b) be highly ~ed** einen starken Sexualtrieb haben
'sex act *n.* Geschlechtsakt, *der*
sexagenarian [seksədʒɪ'neərɪən] **1.** *adj.* sechzigjährig; *(more than 60 years old)* in den Sechzigern *nachgestellt.* **2.** *n.* Sechziger, *der*/Sechzigerin, *die*
sex: ~ **aid** *n.* Mittel zur sexuellen Stimulation; ~ **appeal** *n.* Sex Appeal, *der;* ~ **bomb** *see* ~**pot**; ~ **change** *n.* Geschlechtsumwandlung, *die;* **~-change operation** *n.* operative Geschlechtsumwandlung; ~ **chromosome** *n. (Biol.)* Geschlechtschromosom, *das;* ~ **discrimination** *n.* sexuelle Diskriminierung; ~ **education** *n.* Sexualerziehung, *die*
sexily ['seksɪlɪ] *adv.* aufreizend, *(ugs.)* sexy ⟨*sprechen, lächeln*⟩; **walk ~:** einen aufreizenden *od. (ugs.)* sexy Gang haben
sexism ['seksɪzm] *n., no pl.* Sexismus, *der*
sexist ['seksɪst] **1.** *n.* Sexist, *der*/Sexistin, *die.* **2.** *adj.* sexistisch
'sex kitten *n.* Sexbiene, *die (salopp)*
sexless ['sekslɪs] *adj.* geschlechtslos
sex: ~ **life** *n.* Geschlechtsleben, *das;* Sexualleben, *das;* **~-linked** *adj. (Biol.)* geschlechtsgebunden; ~ **maniac** *n.* Triebverbrecher, *der;* **you ~ maniac!** *(coll.)* du geiler Bock *(ugs.);* **he behaves like a ~ maniac** *(coll.)* er benimmt sich, als habe er nur Sex im Kopf
sexology [sek'sɒlədʒɪ] *n.* Sexologie, *die;* Sexualwissenschaft, *die*
sexploitation [seksplɔɪ'teɪʃn] *n.* [kommerzielle] Ausbeutung der Sexualität; Geschäft mit dem Sex; ~ **film** [kommerzieller] Sexfilm
sex: **~pot** *n. (coll.)* Sexbombe, *die (salopp);* ~ **shop** *n.* Sex-Shop, *der;* **~-starved** *adj.* sexuell ausgehungert; ~ **symbol** *n.* Sexidol, *das*
sextant ['sekstənt] *n.* Sextant, *der*
sextet, sextette [sek'stet] *n. (Mus.)* Sextett, *das*
sexton ['sekstən] *n.* Küster, *der;* Kirchendiener, *der*
'sexton beetle *n. (Zool.)* Totengräber, *der*
sextuplet ['sekstju:plɪt, sek'stju:plɪt] *n.* Sechsling, *der*
sexual ['seksjʊəl, 'sekʃʊəl] *adj.* **a)** sexuell; geschlechtlich, sexuell ⟨*Anziehung, Erregung, Verlangen, Diskriminierung*⟩; ~ **maturity/behaviour** Geschlechtsreife, *die*/Sexualverhalten, *das;* **b)** *(Biol.)* Geschlechts-; geschlechtlich ⟨*Fortpflanzung*⟩
sexual 'intercourse *n., no pl., no indef. art.* Geschlechtsverkehr, *der*
sexuality [seksjʊ'ælɪtɪ, sekʃʊ'ælɪtɪ] *n., no pl.* Sexualität, *die;* Geschlechtlichkeit, *die*
sexually ['seksjʊəlɪ, 'sekʃʊəlɪ] *adv.* **a)** sexuell; ~ **mature** geschlechtsreif; ~ **transmitted disease** durch Geschlechtsverkehr übertragbare Krankheit; Geschlechtskrankheit, *die;* **b)** *(Biol.)* geschlechtlich
sexual 'organs *n. pl.* Geschlechtsorgane
sexy ['seksɪ] *adj.* sexy *(ugs.);* erotisch ⟨*Film, Buch, Gemälde*⟩
Seychelles [seɪ'ʃelz] *pr. n.* Seychellen *Pl.*
sez [sez] *v.i.* ~ **'you = says you** *see* **say 1 a**
SF *abbr.* **science fiction** SF
Sgt. *abbr.* **Sergeant** Uffz.
sh [ʃ] *int.* sch; pst
shabbily ['ʃæbɪlɪ] *adv.*, **shabby** ['ʃæbɪ] *adj.* schäbig
shabby-gen'teel *adj.* von schäbiger Eleganz *nachgestellt*
shack [ʃæk] **1.** *n.* Hütte, *die.* **2.** *v.i. (coll.)* ~ **up with sb.** mit jmdm. zusammenziehen
shackle ['ʃækl] **1.** *n.* **a)** *usu. in pl. (lit. or fig.)* Fessel, *die; (fetter)* Fußfessel, *die;* **b)** *(coupling link)* Schäkel, *der (Technik).* **2.** *v.t. (lit. or fig.)* anketten (**to** an + *Akk.*); **the chain is ~d to the anchor** die Kette ist mit einem Schäkel am Anker befestigt
shade [ʃeɪd] **1.** *n.* **a)** Schatten, *der;* **the ~s of night/evening** *(literary)* die Schatten der Nacht/des Abends *(dichter.);* **put sb./sth. in[to] the ~** *(fig.)* jmdn./etw. in den Schatten stellen; **38[°C] in the ~:** 38° im Schatten; **b)** *(colour)* Ton, *der; (fig.)* Schattierung, *die;* **the newest ~s of lipstick** die neuesten Lippenstiftfarben; **various ~s of purple** verschiedene Violettöne; **~s of meaning** Bedeutungsnuancen *od.* -schattierungen; **all ~s of opinion** Standpunkte der verschiedensten Schattierungen; **c)** *(small amount)* Spur, *die;* **d)** *(ghost)* Geist, *der;* **~s of the past** die Schatten der Vergangenheit; **the ~s** *(Mythol.)* das Schattenreich; das Reich der Schatten; **~s of ...!** das erinnert an ...!; **e)** *(eye-shield)* [Augen]schirm, *der; (lamp~)* [Lampen]schirm, *der; (window-blind)* Jalousie, *die;* **f)** *in pl. (coll.: sun-glasses)* Sonnenbrille, *die.* **2.** *v.t.* **a)** *(screen)* beschatten *(geh.);* Schatten geben (+ *Dat.*); **be ~d from the sun** vor Sonneneinstrahlung geschützt sein; ~ **one's eyes with one's hand** die Hand schützend über die Augen halten; **b)** abdunkeln ⟨*Fenster, Lampe, Licht*⟩; **c)** *(darken with lines)* ~ **[in]** [ab]schattieren; **d)** *(just defeat)* knapp überbieten. **3.** *v.i. (lit. or fig.)* übergehen (**into** in + *Akk.*); ~ **[off] into another** *or* **each other** ineinander übergehen
~ **'in** *v.t.* [ab]schattieren
shading [ʃeɪdɪŋ] *n.* Schattierung, *die; (protection from light)* Lichtschutz, *der*
shadow ['ʃædəʊ] **1.** *n.* **a)** Schatten, *der;* **his life was lived in the ~s** *(fig.)* er lebte sein Leben im Verborgenen; **cast a ~ over** *(lit. or fig.)* einen Schatten werfen auf (+ *Akk.*); **cast a long ~** *(fig.)* großen *od.* nachhaltigen Einfluß haben; **be in sb.'s ~** *(fig.)* in jmds. Schatten stehen; **have deep ~s under one's eyes** tiefe Schatten unter den Augen haben; **be afraid of one's own ~** *(fig.)* sich vor seinem eigenen Schatten fürchten; **be sb.'s ~** *(fig.)* jmds. Schatten sein; **b)** *(slightest trace)* **without a ~ of doubt** ohne den Schatten eines Zweifels; **catch at** *or* **chase after ~s** einem Phantom *od. (geh.)* Schatten nachjagen; **c)** *(ghost, lit. or fig.)* Schatten, *der;* **be worn to a ~** *(fig.)* sich völlig aufgerieben haben; **he is only a ~ of his former self** *(fig.)* er ist nur noch ein *od.* der Schatten seiner selbst; **d) S~** *attrib. (Brit. Polit.)* ⟨*Minister, Kanzler*⟩ im Schattenkabinett; **S~ Cabinet** Schattenkabinett, *das.* **2.** *v.t.* **a)** *(darken)* überschatten; **b)** *(follow secretly)* beschatten
'shadow boxing *n.* Schattenboxen, *das*
shadowy ['ʃædəʊɪ] *adj.* **a)** *(not distinct)* schattenhaft; schemenhaft *(geh.);* **b)** *(full of shade)* schattig
shady ['ʃeɪdɪ] *adj.* **a)** *(giving shade)* schattenspendend *(geh.); (situated in shade)* schattig; **b)** *(disreputable)* zwielichtig
shaft [ʃɑ:ft] *n.* **a)** *(of tool, golf club, feather, spear, lance)* Schaft, *der;* **b)** *(Archit.)* [Säulen]schaft, *der;* **c)** *(Mech. Engin.)* Welle, *die;* **d)** *(of cart or carriage)* Deichsel, *die:* **pair of ~s** Gabeldeichsel, *die;* **e)** *(of mine, blast-furnace, tunnel, drain, lift, etc.)* Schacht, *der;* **f)** *(arrow)* Pfeil, *der; (stem of arrow)* Schaft, *der;* **g)** *(of light or lightning)* Strahl, *der*
[1]**shag** [ʃæg] *n.* **a)** *(tobacco)* Shag[tabak], *der;* Feinschnitt, *der;* **b)** *(Ornith.)* Krähenscharbe, *die*
[2]**shag** *v.t.,* **-gg-** *(sl.)* bumsen *(salopp)*
shagged [ʃægd] *adj. (sl.)* **be ~ [out]** fix und fertig sein *(ugs.)*
shaggy ['ʃægɪ] *adj.* **a)** *(hairy)* zottelig; **b)** *(unkempt)* struppig
shaggy-'dog story *n. endlos langer Witz ohne richtige Pointe*
Shah [ʃɑ:] *n.* Schah, *der*
shake [ʃeɪk] **1.** *n.* **a)** Schütteln, *das;* **give sb./sth. a ~:** jmdn./etw. schütteln; **with a ~ of the head** mit einem Kopfschütteln; **be all of a ~:** am ganzen Körper zittern; **be no great ~s** *(coll.)* nicht gerade umwerfend sein *(ugs.);* **get the ~s** *(coll.) (due to alcoholism)* einen Tatterich kriegen *(ugs.); (with fear)* das große Zittern kriegen *(ugs.);* **b)** *see* **milk shake**; **c)** *(Amer., NZ: earthquake)* Erdbeben, *das;* **d) in [half] a ~, in two** *etc.* **~s [of a lamb's tail], in a brace of ~s** *(coll.)* in einer Sekunde. **2.** *v.t.,* **shook** [ʃʊk], **shaken** ['ʃeɪkn] *or (arch./coll.)* **shook a)** *(move violently)* schütteln; **the dog shook itself** der Hund schüttelte sich; **be ~n to pieces** völlig durchgeschüttelt werden; ~ **one's fist/a stick at sb.** jmdm. mit der Faust/einem Stock drohen; ~ **salt/pepper over one's food** [sich *(Dat.)*] Salz/Pfeffer aufs *od.* über das Essen streuen; **'~ [well] before using'** „vor Gebrauch [gut] schütteln!"; ~ **hands** sich *(Dat.) od.* einander die Hand geben *od.* schütteln; **they shook hands to conclude the deal** sie besiegelten das Geschäft durch Handschlag; **she won't ~ hands with me** sie gibt mir nicht die Hand; **let's ~ hands** gib mir deine Hand; ~ **sb. by the hand** jmdm. die Hand schütteln *od.* drücken; **b)** *(cause to tremble)* erschüttern ⟨*Gebäude usw.*⟩; ~ **one's head [over sth.]** [über etw. *(Akk.)*] den Kopf schütteln; *see also* **leg a**; **c)** *(weaken)* erschüttern; ~ **sb.'s faith in sth./sb.** jmds. Glauben an etw./jmdn. erschüttern; **d)** *(agitate)* erschüttern; **she was badly ~n by the news of his death** die Nachricht von seinem Tod erschütterte sie sehr; **she was not hurt, only badly ~n** sie wurde nicht verletzt, sondern erlitt nur einen schweren Schock; **he failed his exam – that shook him!** er hat die Prüfung nicht bestanden – das war ein Schock für ihn!; ~ **sb.'s composure** jmdn. aus dem Gleichgewicht bringen; ~ **sb. rigid** *(sl.)* jmdn. umhauen *(salopp).* **3.** *v.i.,* **shook, shaken** *or (arch./coll.)* **shook a)** *(tremble)* wackeln; ⟨*Boden, Stimme:*⟩ beben; ⟨*Hand:*⟩ zittern; ⟨*Baum:*⟩ schwanken; ~ **[all over] with cold/fear** [am ganzen Leib] vor Kälte/Angst schlottern; ~ **like a leaf** wie Espenlaub zittern; ~ **with emotion** vor Erregung beben; ~ **in one's shoes** *(coll.)* vor Angst schlottern; **b)** *(coll.: ~ hands)* sich *(Dat.)* die Hand geben; **let's ~ on it!** schlag ein!; Hand drauf!; ~ **on sth.** etw. durch Handschlag besiegeln
~ **'down 1.** *v.t.* **a)** *(get down by shaking)* herunterschütteln; **b)** *(Amer. sl.: extort money*

from) ausnehmen *(salopp);* ~ **sb. down for £50** jmdn. um 50 Pfund erleichtern *(ugs.).* **2.** *v. i.* **a)** *(sleep)* kampieren *(ugs.); see also* **shake-down; b)** *(settle)* ‹*Maschine, Motor:*› sich einlaufen; ‹*Person:*› sich eingewöhnen, sich akklimatisieren

~ **'off** *v. t. (lit. or fig.)* abschütteln; *see also* **dust 1 a**

~ **'out** *v. t.* ausschütteln; *(spread out)* ausbreiten; *see also* **shake-out**

~ **'up** *v. t.* **a)** *(mix)* schütteln; **b)** aufschütteln ‹*Kissen*›; **c)** *(make uncomfortable by shaking)* durchschütteln; **d)** *(discompose)* einen Schrecken einjagen (+ *Dat.*); **she felt pretty ~n up** sie hatte einen ziemlichen Schrecken bekommen; **e)** *(rouse to activity)* aufrütteln; **f)** *(coll.: reorganize)* umkrempeln *(ugs.). See also* **shake-up**

'shake-down *n.* [improvisiertes] Nachtlager

shaken *see* **shake 2, 3**

'shake-out *n.* radikale Umorganisation; *(making workers redundant)* Rationalisierung, *die*

shaker ['ʃeɪkə(r)] *n.* **a)** *(vessel)* Mixbecher, *der;* Shaker, *der;* **b) S~** *(Relig.)* Shaker, *der;* **c)** *(implement)* Streuer, *der*

Shakespe[a]rean, Shakespe[a]rian [ʃeɪk'spɪərɪən] *adj.* Shakespearesch ‹*Sonett, Stil*›; ‹*Zeit, Zeitalter*› Shakespeares

'shake-up *n.* **a)** *(mixing)* **get a [good] ~:** [gut] geschüttelt werden; **b)** *(restoring to shape)* **give the pillows a good ~:** die Kissen tüchtig aufschütteln; **c)** *(coll.: reorganization)* **give sth. a [good] ~:** etw. [total] umkrempeln *(ugs.);* **sth. needs a ~:** etw. muß [mal] umgekrempelt werden *(ugs.);* **government ~:** Regierungsumbildung, *die;* **d)** *(rousing to activity)* Neubelebung, *die*

shakily ['ʃeɪkɪlɪ] *adv.* unsicher ‹*stehen, lachen*›; wack[e]lig *(ugs.)* ‹*gehen, stehen*›; mit zittriger Stimme ‹*sprechen*›; mit zittriger Hand ‹*gießen*›

shaky ['ʃeɪkɪ] *adj.* **a)** *(unsteady)* wack[e]lig ‹*Möbelstück, Leiter, Haus*›; zittrig ‹*Hand, Stimme, Bewegung, Greis*›; **feel ~:** sich zittrig fühlen; **be ~ on one's legs** wacklig auf den Beinen sein *(ugs.);* **b)** *(unreliable)* auf wackligen Füßen stehend *(ugs.);* **his German is rather ~:** sein Deutsch steht auf wackligen Füßen *(ugs.)*

shale [ʃeɪl] *n.* Schiefer, *der*

'shale oil *n.* Schieferöl, *das*

shall [ʃl, *stressed* ʃæl] *v.aux. only in pres.* **shall,** *neg. (coll.)* **shan't** [ʃɑ:nt], *past* **should** [ʃəd, *stressed* ʃʊd], *neg. (coll.)* **shouldn't** ['ʃʊdnt] **a)** *expr. simple future* werden; **b) should** *expr. conditional* würde/würdest/würden/würdet; **he should not have gone if I could have prevented it** er wäre nicht gegangen, wenn ich es hätte verhindern können; **I should have been killed if I had let go** ich wäre getötet worden, wenn ich losgelassen hätte; **c)** *expr. command* **any person found in possession of such weapons ~ be guilty of an offence** *(Law)* jeder, der im Besitz solcher Waffen angetroffen wird, macht sich strafbar *od.* eines Vergehens schuldig; **the committee ~ not be disturbed** der Ausschuß darf nicht gestört werden; **thou shalt not steal** *(Bibl.)* du sollst nicht stehlen; **d)** *expr. will or intention* **what ~ we do?** was sollen wir tun?; **let's go in, ~ we?** gehen wir doch hinein, oder?; **I'll buy six, ~ I?** ich kaufe 6 [Stück], ja?; **you ~ pay for this!** das sollst du mir büßen!; **we should be safe now** jetzt dürften wir in Sicherheit sein; **he shouldn't do things like that!** er sollte so etwas nicht tun!; **oh, you shouldn't have!** das wäre doch nicht nötig gewesen!; **you should be more careful** du solltest vorsichtiger *od.* sorgfältiger sein; *see also* **worry 2; e)** *in conditional clause* **if we should be defeated** falls wir unterliegen [sollten]; **should I be there, I will tell her** sollte ich dort sein, werde ich es ihr sagen; **I should hope so** ich hoffe es; *(indignant)* das möchte ich hoffen!; **f)** *in tentative assertion* **I should like to disagree with you on that point** in dem Punkt *od.* da möchte ich dir widersprechen; **I should say it is time we went home** ich würde sagen *od.* ich glaube, es ist Zeit, daß wir nach Hause gehen; **g)** *forming question* **~ you be going to church?** gehst du in die Kirche?; **h)** *expr. purpose* **in order that he ~** *or* **should be able to go** damit er gehen kann; **I gave him £5 so that he should have enough money for the journey** ich habe ihm 5 Pfund gegeben, so daß er genug Geld für die Reise hat/hatte. *See also* **seem a**

shallot [ʃə'lɒt] *n.* Schalotte, *die*

shallow ['ʃæləʊ] **1.** *adj.* seicht ‹*Wasser, Fluß*›; flach ‹*Schüssel, Teller, Wasser*›; *(fig.)* seicht *(abwertend)* ‹*Unterhaltung, Gerede, Roman*›; flach *(abwertend)* ‹*Person, Denker, Geist*›; platt *(abwertend)* ‹*Argument, Verallgemeinerung*›; **~ breathing** flache Atmung. **2.** *n. in pl.* Flachwasser, *das*

shalom [ʃə'lɒm] **1.** *int.* Schalom. **2.** *n.* Schalom, *das*

sham [ʃæm] **1.** *adj.* unecht; imitiert ‹*Leder, Holz, Pelz, Stein*›. **2.** *n. (pretence)* Heuchelei, *die; (person)* Heuchler, *der*/Heuchlerin, *die;* **it is all a mere ~:** das ist alles bloße Heuchelei; **their marriage is only a ~:** ihre Ehe besteht nur auf dem Papier; **his life is a ~:** sein Leben ist eine einzige Lüge. **3.** *v. t.,* **-mm-** vortäuschen, simulieren; **~ dead/ill/stupid** sich tot/krank/dumm stellen. **4.** *v. i.,* **-mm-** simulieren; sich verstellen

shaman ['ʃæmən] *n.* Schamane, *der*

shamble ['ʃæmbl] **1.** *v. i.* schlurfen; **a shambling gait** ein schlurfender Gang. **2.** *n.* Schlurfen, *das;* **move along at a ~:** sich [schwerfällig] schlurfend vorwärtsbewegen

shambles ['ʃæmblz] *n. sing. (coll.: mess)* Chaos, *das;* **the house/room was a ~:** das Haus/Zimmer glich einem Schlachtfeld; **the economy is in a ~:** in der Wirtschaft herrschen chaotische Zustände; **she made a ~ of her job** sie hat bei ihrer Arbeit ein heilloses Durcheinander angerichtet

shambolic [ʃæm'bɒlɪk] *adj. (coll.)* chaotisch

shame [ʃeɪm] **1.** *n.* **a)** Scham, *die;* **feel ~/no ~ for what one did** sich schämen/sich nicht schämen für das, was man getan hat; **hang one's head in** *or* **for ~:** beschämt den Kopf senken; **blush with ~:** vor Scham erröten; schamrot werden; **be without ~:** schamlos sein; **have no [sense of] ~:** kein[erlei] Schamgefühl besitzen; **have you no ~?** schämst du dich nicht?; **to my ~ I must confess ...:** ich muß zu meiner Schande gestehen ...; **for ~!** du solltest dich/er sollte sich *usw.* schämen!; **b)** *(state of disgrace)* Schande, *die;* **~ on you!** du solltest dich schämen; **put sb./sth. to ~:** jmdn. beschämen/etw. in den Schatten stellen; **bring ~ on the family name, be a ~ to one's family** seiner Familie *(Dat.)* Schande machen; **c) what a ~!** *(disgrace)* es ist eine Schande!; *(bad luck)* so ein Pech!; *(pity)* wie schade!; **it is a crying** *or* **terrible** *or* **great ~:** es ist eine wahre Schande. **2.** *v. t.* beschämen; **~ sb. into doing/out of doing sth.** jmdn. dazu bringen, daß er sich schämt und etw. tut/nicht tut; **~ one's family** seiner Familie *(Dat.)* Schande machen

'shamefaced *adj.* betreten; **have a ~ look, look ~:** betreten dreinblicken

shamefacedly ['ʃeɪmfeɪsɪdlɪ] *adv.* betreten

shameful ['ʃeɪmfl] *adj.* beschämend

shamefully ['ʃeɪmfəlɪ] *adv.* beschämend; **she is ~ ignorant** sie weiß beschämend wenig; es ist eine Schande, wie wenig sie weiß

shameless ['ʃeɪmlɪs] *adj.* schamlos; **are you completely ~?** hast du denn gar kein Schamgefühl?

shamelessly ['ʃeɪmlɪslɪ] *adv.* schamlos

shammy ['ʃæmɪ] *n.* **~ [leather]** *(coll.)* Putzleder *das; (for windows)* Fensterleder, *das*

shampoo [ʃæm'pu:] **1.** *v. t.* schamponieren ‹*Haar, Teppich, Polster, Auto*›; **shall I ~ your hair for you?** soll ich dir die Haare waschen? **2.** *n.* Shampoo[n], *das;* **carpet ~:** Teppichschaum, *der;* **medicated ~:** medizinisches Shampoo; **car ~:** Autoshampoo, *das;* **have a ~ and set** sich *(Dat.)* die Haare waschen und [ein]legen lassen; **give one's hair a ~:** sich *(Dat.)* die Haare [mit Shampoo] waschen *od.* schamponieren

shamrock ['ʃæmrɒk] *n.* Klee, *der; (emblem of Ireland)* Shamrock, *der*

shandy ['ʃændɪ] *n.* Bier mit Limonade; Radlermaß, *die (bes. südd.)*

Shangri-La [ʃæŋgrɪ'lɑ:] *n.* Paradies, *das*

shank [ʃæŋk] *n.* **a)** *(of person)* Unterschenkel, *der;* **[go] on S~s's mare** *or* **pony** auf Schusters Rappen [reisen] *(scherzh.);* **b)** *(of horse)* Vordermittelfuß, *der;* Röhrbein, *das; (cut of meat)* [Hinter]hesse, *die;* **c)** *(Bot.)* Stiel, *der;* **d)** *(of pillar)* [Säulen]schaft, *der; (of key, anchor, nail, fish-hook)* Schaft, *der; (of spoon)* [Löffel]stiel, *der*

shan't [ʃɑ:nt] *(coll.)* = **shall not**

shantung [ʃæn'tʌŋ] *n.* Shantung, *der (Textilw.);* Schantungseide, *die*

[1]shanty ['ʃæntɪ] *n. (hut)* [armselige] Hütte

[2]shanty *n. (song)* Shanty, *das;* Seemannslied, *das*

'shanty town *n.* Elendsviertel, *das*

SHAPE [ʃeɪp] *abbr.* **Supreme Headquarters Allied Powers Europe** oberstes Hauptquartier der Nato-Streitkräfte in Europa

shape [ʃeɪp] **1.** *v. t.* **a)** *(create, form)* formen; bearbeiten ‹*Holz, Stein*› **(into** zu); **~ a dress at the waist** ein Kleid taillieren; **you can ~ plastic when it is hot** erwärmter Kunststoff läßt sich [ver]formen; **b)** *(adapt, direct)* prägen, formen ‹*Charakter, Person*›; nehmen ‹*Kurs*› **(for** auf + *Akk.*); [entscheidend] beeinflussen ‹*Gang der Geschichte, Leben, Zukunft, Gesellschaft*›. **2.** *v. i.* sich entwickeln; **the way things are shaping, we should be able to come** so wie sich die Dinge entwickeln, werden wir wohl kommen können. **3.** *n.* **a)** *(external form, outline)* Form, *die;* **spherical/rectangular in ~:** kugelförmig/rechteckig; **in the ~ of a circle** kreisförmig; in der Form eines Kreises; **she is the right ~ for a dancer** sie hat die richtige Figur für eine Tänzerin; **take ~** ‹*Konstruktion, Skulptur:*› Gestalt annehmen *(see also* **c); b)** *(appearance)* Gestalt, *die;* **a monster in human ~:** ein Ungeheuer in Menschengestalt; **in the ~ of a woman** in Gestalt einer Frau; **a paperweight in the ~ of a lizard** ein Briefbeschwerer in Form einer Eidechse; **c)** *(specific form)* Form, *die;* Gestalt, *die;* **a surprise in the ~ of an invitation/a holiday** eine Überraschung in Form einer Einladung/Ferienreise; **nothing in the ~ of ...:** nichts in der Art ... (+ *Gen.*); **take ~** ‹*Plan, Vorhaben:*› Gestalt *od.* feste Formen annehmen *(see also* **a); get one's ideas into ~:** seine Gedanken sammeln; Ordnung in seine Gedanken bringen; **knock sth. out of ~:** etw. verbeulen *od.* demolieren; **knock sth. into ~:** etw. wieder in Form bringen; **we have knocked the plans into ~:** wir haben die Pläne jetzt im wesentlichen fertig; **in all ~s and sizes, in every ~ and size** in allen Formen und Größen; **the ~ of things to come** die Dinge, die da kommen sollen/sollten; **this may be the ~ of things to come** so könnte das in Zukunft aussehen; *see also* **lick 1 a; d)** *(condition)* Form, *die (bes. Sport);* **do yoga to keep in ~:** Yoga machen, um in Form zu bleiben; **be in good/bad ~:** gut/schlecht in Form sein; **be in poor ~ mentally/physically** geistig/körperlich in schlechter Verfassung sein; **what sort of ~ is the business in?** wie steht es um die Firma?; **be in no ~ to do sth.** nicht in der Lage sein, etw. zu tun; **e)** *(person seen, ghost)* Gestalt, *die;* **f)** *(mould) (for hats)* Hutform, *die; (for puddings, jellies, etc.)* Form, *die*

~ 'up *v. i.* sich entwickeln; **how's the new editor shaping up?** wie macht sich der neue Redakteur?

shaped [ʃeɪpt] *adj.* geformt; **be ~ like a pear** die Form einer Birne haben; **this is an oddly ~ cake** dieser Kuchen hat eine ungewöhnliche *od.* eigentümliche Form

shapeless ['ʃeɪplɪs] *adj.* formlos; unförmig ⟨*Kleid, Person*⟩; unstrukturiert ⟨*Theaterstück*⟩

shapely ['ʃeɪplɪ] *adj.* wohlgeformt ⟨*Beine, Busen*⟩; gut ⟨*Figur*⟩; formschön ⟨*Auto, Design*⟩

shard [ʃɑːd] *see* **sherd**

share [ʃeə(r)] **1.** *n.* **a)** *(portion)* Teil, *der od. das; (part one is entitled to)* **[fair] ~:** Anteil, *der;* **he had a large ~ in bringing it about** er hatte großen Anteil daran, daß es zustande kam; **come in for one's full ~ of criticism** seinen Teil Kritik einstecken müssen *od.* abbekommen; **pay one's ~ of the bill** seinen Teil der Rechnung bezahlen; **have a ~ in the profits** am Gewinn beteiligt sein; **fair ~s** gerechte Teile; **do more than one's [fair] ~ of the work** mehr als seinen Teil zur Arbeit beitragen; **each had his ~ of the cake** jeder bekam seinen Teil vom Kuchen ab; **have more than one's [fair] ~ of the blame/attention** mehr Schuld zugewiesen bekommen/mehr Beachtung finden, als man verdient; **she had her ~ of luck/bad luck** sie hat aber auch Glück/Pech gehabt; **take one's ~ of the responsibility** seinen Teil Verantwortung tragen; **take one's ~ of the blame** seinen Teil Schuld auf sich *(Akk.)* nehmen; **go ~s** teilen; **let me go ~s with you in the taxi fare** ich möchte mich an den Kosten für das Taxi beteiligen; **it was ~ and ~ alike** es wurde brüderlich geteilt; *see also* **lion a; b)** *(part-ownership of property)* [Geschäfts]anteil, *der; (part of company's capital)* Aktie, *die;* **have a ~ in a business** an einem Geschäft beteiligt sein; **hold ~s in a company** *(Brit.)* Anteile *od.* Aktien einer Gesellschaft besitzen; *see also* **¹defer a; ordinary b. 2.** *v. t.* teilen; gemeinsam tragen ⟨*Verantwortung*⟩; **~ the same birthday/surname** am gleichen Tag Geburtstag/den gleichen Nachnamen haben. **3.** *v. i.* **~ in** teilnehmen an (+ *Dat.*); beteiligt sein an (+ *Dat.*) ⟨*Gewinn, Planung*⟩; teilen ⟨*Freude, Erfahrung*⟩; **there are no single rooms left, so I'll have to ~:** es sind keine Einzelzimmer mehr frei, so daß ich mit jemandem ein Zimmer teilen muß

~ 'out *v. t.* aufteilen **(among** unter + *Akk.*); *see also* **share-out**

share: ~ certificate *n.* Aktienurkunde, *die;* Mantel, *der (Finanzw.);* **~-cropper** *n.* *(Amer.)* Teilpächter, *der;* **~holder** *n.* Aktionär, *der*/Aktionärin, *die;* **~ index** *n.* *(Econ.)* Aktienindex, *der;* **~-out** *n.* Aufteilung, *die*

shariah [ʃə'riːə] *n.* *(Islamic Law)* Scharia, *die*

shark [ʃɑːk] *n.* **a)** Hai[fisch], *der;* **b)** *(fig.: swindler)* gerissener Geschäftemacher; **property ~:** Grundstückshai, *der (ugs. abwertend)*

'shark-skin *n.* **a)** *(skin)* Haut des Haifischs; *(tanned)* Haifischleder, *das;* **b)** *(fabric)* Haifischhaut, *die (Textilw.)*

sharp [ʃɑːp] **1.** *adj.* **a)** *(with fine edge)* scharf; *(with fine point)* spitz ⟨*Nadel, Bleistift, Giebel, Gipfel*⟩; **~ sand** scharfer Sand *(Bauw.);* **b)** *(clear-cut)* scharf ⟨*Umriß, Kontrast, Bild, Gesichtszüge, Linie*⟩; deutlich ⟨*Unterscheidung*⟩; präzise ⟨*Eindruck*⟩; scharf umrissen ⟨*Schatten*⟩; **c)** *(abrupt, angular)* scharf ⟨*Kurve, Winkel*⟩; eng, scharf ⟨*Kurve*⟩; spitz ⟨*Winkel*⟩; steil, schroff ⟨*Abhang*⟩; stark ⟨*Gefälle*⟩; **a ~ rise/fall in prices** ein jäher Preisanstieg/Preissturz; **d)** *(intense)* groß ⟨*Appetit, Hunger[gefühl]*⟩; *(acid, pungent)* scharf ⟨*Würze, Geschmack, Sauce, Käse*⟩; sauer ⟨*Apfel*⟩; herb ⟨*Wein*⟩; *(shrill, piercing)* schrill ⟨*Schrei, Pfiff*⟩; *(biting)* scharf ⟨*Wind, Frost, Luft*⟩; *(sudden, severe)* heftig ⟨*Schmerz, Anfall, Krampf, Kampf*⟩; *(harsh, acrimonious)* scharf ⟨*Protest, Tadel, Ton, Stimme, Zunge, Worte*⟩; **a short ~ struggle** ein kurzer, heftiger Kampf; **a short ~ shock** ein kräftiger Schock; **e)** *(acute, quick)* scharf ⟨*Augen, Verstand, Gehör, Ohr, Beobachtungsgabe, Intelligenz, Geruchssinn*⟩; aufgeweckt ⟨*Kind*⟩; scharfsinnig ⟨*Bemerkung*⟩; begabt ⟨*Schüler, Student*⟩; raffiniert ⟨*Schachzug*⟩; **be ~ at maths** gut in Mathe sein *(ugs.);* **be as ~ as a needle** schlagfertig sein; **that was pretty ~!** das war ganz schön clever!; **keep a ~ look-out for the police!** halt die Augen offen, falls die Polizei kommt!; **keep a ~ watch** scharf aufpassen; **her mind is as ~ as a needle** sie hat einen messerscharfen Verstand; **f)** *(derog.: artful, dishonest, quick to take advantage)* gerissen; **~ practice** unlautere Praktiken; **g)** *(vigorous, brisk)* flott *(ugs.);* **that was ~ work** das ging schnell; **~'s the word!, be ~ about it!** mach schnell!; **h)** *(Mus.)* [um einen Halbton] erhöht ⟨*Note*⟩; **F/G/C** *etc.* **~:** fis, Fis/gis, Gis/cis, Cis *usw., das;* **i)** *(sl.: stylish)* scharf *(ugs.);* todschick *(ugs.);* **she is a ~ dresser** sie ist [immer] todschick angezogen *(ugs.).* **2.** *adv.* **a)** *(punctually)* **at six o'clock ~:** Punkt sechs Uhr; **on the hour ~, ~ on the hour** genau zur vollen Stunde; **b)** *(suddenly)* scharf ⟨*bremsen*⟩; plötzlich ⟨*anhalten*⟩; **turn ~ right** scharf nach rechts abbiegen; **c) look ~!** halt dich ran! *(ugs.);* **d)** *(Mus.)* zu hoch ⟨*singen, spielen*⟩. **3.** *n.* *(Mus.)* erhöhter Ton; *(symbol)* Kreuz, *das;* Erhöhungszeichen, *das*

'sharp-edged *adj.* scharfkantig; scharf ⟨*Messer*⟩

sharpen ['ʃɑːpn] *v. t.* schärfen *(auch fig.);* [an]spitzen ⟨*Bleistift*⟩; *(fig.)* anregen ⟨*Appetit*⟩; verstärken ⟨*Schmerz*⟩

'sharp end *n.* *(coll.)* **a)** *(Naut.)* Bug, *der;* **be at the ~:** im vorderen Teil des Schiffes sein; **b)** *(fig.: place of direct action or decision)* vorderste Linie *od.* Front; **at the ~:** in vorderster Front

sharpener ['ʃɑːpnə(r)] *n.* *(for pencil)* Bleistiftspitzer, *der;* Spitzer, *der (ugs.); (for tools)* Abziehstein, *der;* Schleifstein, *der*

sharper ['ʃɑːpə(r)] *n.* *(at cards)* Falschspieler, *der; (swindler)* Betrüger, *der*

sharp: ~-eyed *adj.* scharfäugig; **be ~-eyed** scharfe Augen haben; **be as ~-eyed as a hawk/lynx** Augen wie ein Adler/Luchs haben; **it was ~-eyed of you to spot the fault** daß du den Fehler entdeckt hast, zeigt, daß du ein scharfes Auge hast; **~-featured** *adj.* scharf geschnitten ⟨*Gesicht*⟩; ⟨*Person*⟩ mit scharfen Gesichtszügen

sharpish ['ʃɑːpɪʃ] *adv.* *(coll.) (quickly)* rasch; *(promptly)* unverzüglich; sofort

sharply ['ʃɑːplɪ] *adv.* **a)** *(acutely)* spitz; **~ angled** spitzwinklig; **come ~ to a point** spitz[winklig] zu *od.* in einem Punkt zusammenlaufen; **b)** *(clearly)* scharf ⟨*voneinander unterschieden, kontrastierend, umrissen*⟩; **c)** *(abruptly)* scharf ⟨*bremsen, abbiegen*⟩; steil, schroff ⟨*abfallen*⟩; **d)** *(acidly)* scharf ⟨*gewürzt*⟩; *(harshly)* in scharfem Ton ⟨*antworten*⟩; **~ contested** hart umkämpft; **~ worded letter** Brief in scharfem Ton; **e)** *(quickly)* schnell, rasch ⟨*denken, handeln*⟩

sharpness ['ʃɑːpnɪs] *n., no pl.* Schärfe, *die; (fineness of point)* Spitzheit, *die*

sharp: ~shooter *n.* Scharfschütze, *der;* **~-witted** *adj.* scharfsinnig

shat *see* **shit 1, 2**

shatter ['ʃætə(r)] **1.** *v. t.* **a)** *(smash)* zertrümmern; **b)** *(destroy)* zerschlagen ⟨*Hoffnungen*⟩; ruinieren ⟨*Gesundheit*⟩; **c)** *(coll.: severely discompose)* schwer mitnehmen. **2.** *v. i.* zerbrechen; zerspringen

shattered ['ʃætəd] *adj.* **a)** zerbrochen, zersprungen ⟨*Scheibe, Glas, Fenster*⟩; *(fig.)* zerstört ⟨*Hoffnungen*⟩; zerrüttet ⟨*Nerven, Gesundheit*⟩; **b)** *(coll.: greatly upset)* **she was ~ by the news** die Nachricht hat sie schwer mitgenommen; **I'm ~!** ich bin ganz erschüttert!; **c)** *(Brit. coll.: exhausted)* **I'm ~:** ich bin [völlig] kaputt *(ugs.);* **I feel/she looks ~:** ich bin [völlig] kaputt/sie sieht [ziemlich] kaputt aus *(ugs.)*

shattering ['ʃætərɪŋ] *adj.* **a)** *(ruinously destructive)* verheerend ⟨*Wirkung, Explosion*⟩; vernichtend ⟨*Schlag, Niederlage*⟩; **b)** *(coll.: very upsetting)* erschütternd; **it must have been ~ for you** es muß dich schwer mitgenommen haben; **c)** *(coll.: exhausting)* wahnsinnig anstrengend *(ugs.)*

'shatter-proof *adj.* splitterfrei; **~ glass** Sicherheitsglas, *das*

shave [ʃeɪv] **1.** *v. t.* **a)** rasieren; abrasieren ⟨*Haare*⟩; **he ~d his beard** er hat sich *(Dat.)* den Bart abrasiert; **b)** *(pare surface of)* abhobeln; **c)** *(fig.)* **~ a few hundredths of a second off the record** den Rekord um ein paar Hundertstelsekunden verbessern; **d)** *(graze)* ⟨*Auto:*⟩ streifen. **2.** *v. i.* **a)** sich rasieren; **b)** *(scrape)* **~ past sth.** etw. [leicht] streifen. **3.** *n.* **a)** Rasur, *die;* **have** *or* **get a ~:** sich rasieren; **have** *or* **get a ~ at the barber's** sich beim Friseur rasieren lassen; **this razor gives a good ~:** dieser Rasierapparat rasiert gut; **a clean** *or* **close ~:** eine Glattrasur; **b) close ~** *(fig.) see* **close 1 f; c)** *(tool)* Schabmesser, *das*

~ 'off *v. t.* abrasieren ⟨*Bart, Haare*⟩

shaven ['ʃeɪvn] *adj.* rasiert; [kahl]geschoren ⟨*Kopf*⟩

shaver ['ʃeɪvə(r)] *n.* **a)** Rasierapparat, *der;* Rasierer, *der (ugs.);* **b)** *(dated coll.: lad)* **[young] ~:** junger Spund *(ugs.)*

'shaver point *n.* Anschluß *od.* Steckdose für den Rasierapparat

Shavian ['ʃeɪvɪən] *adj.* Shawsch

shaving ['ʃeɪvɪŋ] *n.* **a)** *(action)* Rasieren, *das;* **b)** *in pl. (of wood, metal, etc.)* Späne

shaving: ~-brush *n.* Rasierpinsel, *der;* **~-cream** *n.* Rasiercreme, *die;* **~-foam** *n.* Rasierschaum, *der;* **~-mug** *n.* Rasierbecken, *das;* **~-soap** *n.* Rasierseife, *die;* **~-stick** *n.* Stangenrasierseife, *die*

shawl [ʃɔːl] *n.* Schultertuch, *das; (light blanket)* Umschlagtuch, *das*

she [ʃɪ, *stressed* ʃiː] **1.** *pron.* sie; *referring to personified things or animals which correspond to German masculines/neuters* er/es; **it was ~** *(formal)* sie war es; *see also* **¹,²her; hers; herself. 2.** *n., pl.* **~s** [ʃiːz] Sie, *die (ugs.);* **is it a he or a ~?** ist es ein Er oder eine Sie?

she- [ʃiː] *pref.* weiblich; **~-ass/-bear** Eselin, *die*/Bärin, *die;* **~-cat, ~-devil** *(fig. derog.: malignant woman)* Drachen, *der (salopp abwertend)*

sheaf [ʃiːf] *n., pl.* **sheaves** [ʃiːvz] *(of corn etc.)* Garbe, *die; (of paper, arrows, etc.)* Bündel, *das*

shear [ʃɪə(r)] **1.** *v. t., p. p.* **shorn** [ʃɔːn] *or* **~ed a)** *(clip)* scheren; **be shorn of sth.** *(fig.)* einer Sache *(Gen.)* beraubt sein/werden; **b)** *(Mech., Geol.: break)* abscheren. **2.** *v. i., p. p.* **shorn** *or* **~ed** ⟨*Bolzen, Metallteil:*⟩ abscheren *(Technik);* **the motor boat ~ed through the water** *(fig.)* das Motorboot durchschnitt das Wasser *(fig.);* **the cutter blades ~ed through the metal** die Schneiden der Schere zerschnitten das Metall. **3.** *n.* *(Mech., Geol.)* Scherung, *die*

~ 'off 1. *v. t.* abtrennen. **2.** *v. i.* abscheren *(Technik)*

shearer ['ʃɪərə(r)] *n.* **a)** *(of sheep)* Scherer, *der;* **b)** *(metal-worker)* Metallschneider, *der;* **c)** *(machine)* Schneidemaschine, *die*

shearing ['ʃɪərɪŋ] *n.* Scheren, *das*

shears [ʃɪəz] *n. pl.* **[pair of]** ~ *(große)* Schere, *die;* garden ~: Heckenschere, *die*
'shearwater *n. (Ornith.)* Sturmtaucher, *der*
sheath [ʃiːθ] *n., pl.* ~s [ʃiːðz, ʃiːθs] **a)** *(for knife, dagger, sword, etc.)* Scheide, *die;* **b)** *(Zool.) (of insect)* Elytron, *das;* Schutzdecke, *die;* **c)** *(Electr.)* Mantel, *der;* **d)** *(condom)* Gummischutz, *der*
sheathe [ʃiːð] *v. t.* **a)** *(put into sheath)* in die Scheide stecken ⟨*Messer, Schwert, Dolch*⟩; **b)** *(protect)* ummanteln **(in, with** mit)
sheathing ['ʃiːðɪŋ] *n.* Ummantelung, *die*
'sheath-knife *n.* Fahrtenmesser, *das*
¹sheave [ʃiːv] *n.* Rolle, *die*
²sheave *v. t.* zu Garben binden ⟨*Getreide*⟩
sheaves *pl. of* **sheaf**
¹shed [ʃed] *v. t.,* **-dd-, shed a)** *(part with)* verlieren; abwerfen, verlieren ⟨*Laub, Geweih*⟩; abstreifen ⟨*Haut, Hülle, Badehose*⟩; ausziehen ⟨*Kleidung*⟩; **a duck's back ~s water** vom Rücken einer Ente läuft das Wasser ab; **the snake is ~ding its skin** die Schlange häutet sich; **dogs/cats ~ hairs** Hunde/Katzen haaren; **you should ~ a few pounds** du solltest ein paar Pfund abspecken *(salopp);* **b)** vergießen ⟨*Blut, Tränen*⟩; **~ tears over sth.** wegen einer Sache Tränen vergießen; **don't ~ any tears over him** seinetwegen solltest du keine Tränen vergießen; **without ~ding blood** ohne Blutvergießen; **c)** *(dispense)* verbreiten ⟨*Wärme, Licht*⟩; *see also* **'light 1 h; d)** *(fig.: cast off)* abschütteln ⟨*Sorgen, Bürde*⟩; ablegen ⟨*Gewohnheit*⟩
²shed *n.* Schuppen, *der;* **wooden ~:** Holzschuppen, *der*
she'd [ʃɪd, *stressed* ʃiːd] **a) = she had; b) = she would**
sheen [ʃiːn] *n.* Glanz, *der*
sheep [ʃiːp] *n., pl. same* **a)** Schaf, *das;* **separate the ~ from the goats** *(fig.)* die Böcke von den Schafen trennen; **count ~** *(fig.)* Schäfchen zählen *(fam.);* **follow sb. like ~:** jmdm. wie eine Schafherde folgen; *see also* **black sheep; eye 1 a; lamb 1 a; wolf 1 a; b)** *(person)* Schäfchen, *das (fam.);* Schäflein, *das (fam.)*
sheep: ~-dip *n.* Desinfektionsbad für Schafe; **~-dog** *n.* Hütehund, *der;* Schäferhund, *der;* **Old English S~-dog** Bobtail, *der;* **~-farm** *n. (Brit.)* Schaffarm, *die;* **~-farmer** *n. (Brit.)* Schafzüchter, *der/* -züchterin, *die;* **~-fold** *n.* **a)** *(pen)* Schafhürde, *die;* Pferch, *der;* **b)** *(shelter)* Schafstall, *der*
sheepish ['ʃiːpɪʃ] *adj. (awkwardly self-conscious)* verlegen; *(embarrassed)* kleinlaut; **he felt a bit ~** *(foolish)* es war ihm ein bißchen peinlich
sheepishly ['ʃiːpɪʃlɪ] *adv. see* **sheepish:** verlegen; kleinlaut
sheep: ~meat *n.* Schaffleisch, *das;* **~-pen** *see* **sheep-fold a; ~shank** *n. (knot)* lange Trompete *(Seemannsspr.);* **~-shearing** *n.* Schafschur, *die;* **~skin** *n.* **a)** Schaffell, *das;* **~skin [jacket]** Schaffelljacke, *die;* **b)** *(leather)* Schafleder, *das;* **~-walk** *n. (Brit.)* Schafweide, *die*
¹sheer [ʃɪə(r)] **1.** *adj.* **a)** *attrib. (mere, absolute)* rein; blank ⟨*Unsinn, Gewalt*⟩; **by ~ chance** rein zufällig; **it is a ~ impossibility to do it** es ist schier unmöglich, es zu tun; **that's ~ robbery!** das ist ja der reinste Wucher!; **the ~ insolence of it!** so eine Frechheit!; **only by ~ hard work** nur durch harte Arbeit; **b)** *(perpendicular)* schroff ⟨*Felsen, Abfall*⟩; steil ⟨*Felsen, Abfall, Aufstieg*⟩; **c)** *(finely woven)* hauchfein. **2.** *adv. (perpendicularly)* schroff; steil
²sheer *v. i. (Naut.)* [aus]scheren
~ **a'way** *v. i* **a)** *(Naut.)* abscheren; **b) ~ away from** *(fig.: avoid)* ausweichen (+ *Dat.*) ⟨*Person, Thema*⟩
¹sheet [ʃiːt] **1.** *n.* **a)** Laken, *das; (for covering mattress)* Bettuch, *das;* Laken, *das;* **put clean ~s on the bed** das Bett frisch beziehen; **between the ~s** *(in bed)* im Bett; *see also* **white 1 b; b)** *(of thin metal, plastic)* Folie, *die; (of iron, tin)* Blech, *das; (of glass, of thicker metal, plastic)* Platte, *die; (of stamps)* Bogen, *der; (of paper)* Bogen, *der;* Blatt, *das;* **a ~ of iron/plastic** ein Eisenblech/eine Plastikfolie; **a ~ of paper** ein Papierbogen; ein Bogen *od.* Blatt Papier; **five ~s of wrapping paper** 5 Bögen Einwickelpapier; **a 250-~ roll of toilet-paper** eine 250-Blatt-Rolle Toilettenpapier; **~ of music** Notenblatt, *das;* **~ glass/metal/iron** Flachglas, *das*/Blech, *das*/Eisenblech, *das; see also* **clean 1 b; c)** *(wide expanse)* ⟨*Eis-, Lava-, Nebel*⟩decke, *die;* **a ~ of water covered the lawn** der Rasen stand unter Wasser; **a huge ~ of flame** ein Flammenmeer; **the rain was coming down in ~s** es regnete in Strömen; **d)** *(Printing)* Druckbogen, *der;* **a book in ~s** ein Rohexemplar. **2.** *v. i.* **the rain was ~ing down** es regnete in Strömen
²sheet *n.* **a)** *(of sail)* Schot, *die;* **b) be three ~s in** *or* **to the wind** *(sl.)* voll wie eine Strandhaubitze sein *(ugs.)*
'sheet-anchor *n. (Naut.)* Notanker, *der; (fig.)* Rettungsanker, *der*
sheeting ['ʃiːtɪŋ] *n.* **a)** *(cloth for making bedsheets)* Bettzeugstoff, *der;* Haustuch, *das;* **b)** *(of thin metal, plastic, etc.)* Folie, *die; (of iron, tin)* Blech, *das; (of thicker metal, plastic)* Platte, *die*
sheet: ~ lightning *n. (Meteorol.)* Flächenblitz, *der;* **~ music** *n.* Notenblätter
sheik, sheikdom *see* **sheikh, sheikhdom**
sheikh [ʃeɪk, ʃiːk] *n.* Scheich, *der*
sheikhdom [ʃeɪkdəm, ʃiːkdəm] *n.* Scheichtum, *das*
sheila ['ʃiːlə] *n. (Austral. and NZ sl.: young woman)* Puppe, *die (salopp)*
shekel ['ʃekl] *n.* **a)** Schekel, *der;* **b)** *in pl. (coll.: money, riches)* Moneten *Pl. (ugs.)*
sheldrake ['ʃeldreɪk] *n., fem. and pl.* **shelduck** *or* **sheld duck** ['ʃeldʌk] *(Ornith.)* Brandente, *die;* Brandgans, *die*
shelf [ʃelf] *n., pl.* **shelves** [ʃelvz] **a)** *(flat board)* Brett, *das;* Bord, *das; (compartment)* Fach, *das; (set of shelves)* Regal, *das;* **~ of books** Bücherbrett, *das;* **be left on the ~** *(fig.)* sitzengeblieben sein *(ugs.);* **be put on the ~** *(fig.)* aufs Abstellgleis geschoben werden *(ugs.);* **b)** *(Geol.)* Riff, *das; see also* **continental shelf**
shelf-ful ['ʃelffʊl] *n.* **a ~ of books** *etc.* ein Bord voll Bücher *usw.*
shelf: ~-life *n.* Lagerfähigkeit, *die;* **~-mark** *n.* Standortnummer, *die;* **~-room, ~-space** *ns.* Stellfläche [im Regal]; **give ~-room** *or* **-space to sth.** sich *(Dat.)* etw. ins Regal stellen
shell [ʃel] **1.** *n.* **a)** *(casing)* Schale, *die; (of turtle, tortoise)* Panzer, *der; (of pupa)* Hülle, *die; (of snail)* Haus, *das; (of pea)* Schote, *die;* Hülse, *die; (of insect's wing)* Flügeldecke, *die;* **collect ~s on the beach** am Strand Muscheln sammeln; **bring sb. out of his ~** *(fig.)* jmdn. aus der Reserve locken *(ugs.);* **come out of one's ~** *(fig.)* aus sich herausgehen; **retire** *or* **go into one's ~** *(fig.)* sich in sein Schneckenhaus zurückziehen *(ugs.);* **b)** *(frame)* Gerippe, das *(fig.); (of unfinished building)* Rohbau, *der; (of building needing to be refurbished)* Außenmauern und Dach; *(of ruinous building)* Ruine, *die;* **c)** *(pastry case)* Teighülle, *die;* **d)** *(racing-boat)* Rennruderboot, *das;* **e)** *(Motor Veh.)* **[body] ~:** Aufbau, *der;* Karosserie, *die; (after fire, at breaker's, etc.)* [Karosserie]gerippe, *das;* **f)** *(Mil.) (bomb)* Granate, *die; (Amer.: cartridge)* Patrone, *die.* **2.** *v. t.* **a)** *(take out of ~)* schälen; knacken, schälen ⟨*Nuß*⟩; öffnen ⟨*Auster*⟩; enthülsen, *(nordd.)* palen ⟨*Erbsen*⟩; **as easy as ~ing peas** kinderleicht; **~ed nuts** Nußkerne; **b)** *(Mil.)* [mit Artillerie] beschießen
~ **'out** *v. t. & i. (sl.)* blechen *(ugs.)* **(on** für)
she'll [ʃɪl, *stressed* ʃiːl] **= she will**
shellac [ʃə'læk] **1.** *n.* Schellack, *der.* **2.** *v. t.,* **-ck- a)** *(varnish)* mit Schellack überziehen; **b)** *(Amer. sl.: defeat, thrash)* vermöbeln *(ugs.);* fertigmachen *(ugs.)*
shell: ~fish *n., pl. same* **a)** Schal[en]tier, *das; (oyster, clam)* Muschel, *die; (crustacean)* Krebstier, *das;* **b)** *in pl. (Gastr.)* Meeresfrüchte *Pl.;* **~-pink** *adj.* muschelrosa; **~proof** *adj.* bombensicher; **~-shock** *n. (Psych.)* Kriegsneurose, *die;* **~-shocked** *adj.* **be ~-shocked** eine Kriegsneurose haben; *(fig.)* niedergeschmettert sein
shelter ['ʃeltə(r)] **1.** *n.* **a)** *(shield)* Schutz, *der* **(against** vor + *Dat.,* gegen); **bomb** *or* **air-raid ~:** Luftschutzraum, *der;* **get under ~:** sich unterstellen; **under the ~ of the rocks/ of night** im Schutz der Felsen/der Nacht; **wooden/mountain ~:** Holz-/Berg- *od.* Schutzhütte, *die;* **b)** *no pl. (place of safety)* Zuflucht, *die;* **we needed food and ~:** wir brauchten etwas zu essen und eine Unterkunft; **look for ~ for the night** eine Unterkunft für die Nacht suchen; **offer** *or* **give sb. ~, provide ~ for sb.** jmdm. Zuflucht gewähren *od.* bieten; **in the ~ of one's home** im Schutz *od.* in der Geborgenheit seines Heims; **take ~ [from a storm]** [vor einem Sturm] Schutz suchen; **seek/reach ~:** Schutz *od.* Zuflucht suchen/finden. **2.** *v. t.* schützen **(from** vor + *Dat.*); Unterschlupf gewähren (+ *Dat.*) ⟨*Flüchtling*⟩; **~ sb. from blame/harm** jmdn. decken/gegen alle Gefahren schützen. **3.** *v. i.* Schutz *od.* Zuflucht suchen **(from** vor + *Dat.*); **this is a good place to ~:** hier ist man gut geschützt
sheltered ['ʃeltəd] *adj.* geschützt ⟨*Platz, Tal*⟩; behütet ⟨*Leben*⟩; **~ workshops** beschützende Werkstätten; **~ employment** Beschäftigung in beschützenden Werkstätten; **live in ~ housing** in einer Altenwohnung/in Altenwohnungen leben
shelve [ʃelv] **1.** *v. t.* **a)** *(put on shelves)* ins Regal stellen; *(fig.) (abandon)* ad acta *od. (ugs.)* zu den Akten legen; *(defer)* auf Eis legen *(ugs.);* **b)** *(fit with shelves)* ein Regal einbauen (+ *Akk.*) ⟨*Nische*⟩; ausfachen *(fachspr.),* mit Fächern versehen ⟨*Schrank*⟩; mit Borden versehen ⟨*Wand*⟩. **2.** *v. i.* **~ away/off/out into** ⟨*Berg, Boden, Ebene:*⟩ abfallen nach
shelves *pl. of* **shelf**
shelving ['ʃelvɪŋ] *n., no pl.* Regale *Pl.*
shemozzle [ʃɪ'mɒzl] *n. (sl.)* **a)** *(rumpus, brawl)* Keilerei, *die (ugs.);* **b)** *(muddle)* Schlamassel, *der (ugs.)*
shenanigans [ʃɪ'nænɪgənz] *n. pl. (coll.) (trickery)* Tricks; *(nonsense)* Fez, *der (ugs.); (high-spirited behaviour)* Klamauk, *der (ugs. abwertend)*
shepherd ['ʃepəd] **1.** *n.* Schäfer, *der;* Schafhirt, *der; (Relig. fig.)* Hirt[e], *der (geh.);* **the Good S~:** der Gute Hirte. **2.** *v. t.* hüten; *(fig.)* führen
'shepherd dog *n.* Hütehund, *der;* Schäferhund, *der; see also* **German shepherd [dog]**
shepherdess ['ʃepədɪs] *n.* Schäferin, *die;* Schafhirtin, *die*
shepherd: ~'s 'crook *n.* Schäferstock, *der;* Hirtenstab, *der (geh.);* **~'s 'pie** *n. (Gastr.) Auflauf aus Hackfleisch mit einer Schicht Kartoffelbrei darüber;* **~'s 'purse** *n. (Bot.)* Hirtentäschelkraut, *das*
sherbet ['ʃɜːbət] n. **a)** *(fruit juice; also Amer.: water-ice)* Sorbet[t], *der od. das;* **b)** *(effervescent drink)* Brauselimonade, *die; (powder)* Brausepulver, *das*
sherd [ʃɜːd] *n.* Scherbe, *die*
sheriff ['ʃerɪf] *n.* Sheriff, *der*
'sheriff court *n. (Scot. Law) Grafschaftsgericht mit Zuständigkeit in Zivil- und Strafsachen*
Sherpa ['ʃɜːpə] *n. (Ethnol.)* Sherpa, *der/* Sherpani, *die*

sherry ['ʃerɪ] *n.* Sherry, *der;* ~ **glass** Sherryglas, *das;* ≈ Südweinglas, *das*

she's [ʃɪz, *stressed* ʃi:z] **a)** = she is; **b)** = she has

Shetland ['ʃetlənd] *pr. n. see* **Shetland Islands**

Shetlander ['ʃetləndə(r)] *n.* Shetländer, *der*/-länderin, *die*

Shetland Islands *pr. n. pl.* Shetlandinseln *Pl.;* Shetlands *Pl.*

Shetland: ~ '**jumper** *n.* Pullover aus Shetlandwolle; ~ '**pony** *n.* Shetlandpony, *das*

Shetlands ['ʃetləndz] *pr. n. pl.* Shetlands *Pl.*

Shetland: ~ '**sheepdog** *n.* Sheltie, *der;* ~ '**wool** *n.* Shetlandwolle, *die*

shew *(arch.) see* **show 2, 3**

shh [ʃ] *int.* pst; sch

Shiah ['ʃi:ə] *n. (Muslim Relig.)* Schia, *die*

shibboleth ['ʃɪbəleθ] *n.* Schibboleth, *das (geh.); (catchword)* Schlagwort, *das*

shield [ʃi:ld] **1.** *n.* **a)** *(piece of armour)* Schild, *der;* **b)** *(in machinery etc.)* Schutz, *der; (protective plate)* Schutzplatte, *die; (protective screen)* Schutzschirm, *der;* **radiation** ~: Strahlenschutz, *der;* **c)** *(fig.: person or thing that protects)* Schild, *der (geh.);* **d)** *(Zool.)* Schild, *der;* **e)** *(Geol.)* Schild, *der;* **f)** *(Her.)* [Wappen]schild, *der;* **g)** *(Sport: trophy)* Trophäe, *die (in Form eines Schildes);* **h)** *(Amer.: policeman's badge)* Dienstmarke, *die.* **2.** *v. t.* **a)** *(protect)* schützen (**from** vor + *Dat.*); **b)** *(conceal)* decken ⟨*Schuldigen*⟩; ~ **sb. from the truth** die Wahrheit von jmdm. fernhalten

shier, shiest *see* [1]**shy 1**

shift [ʃɪft] **1.** *v. t.* **a)** *(move)* verrücken, umstellen ⟨*Möbel*⟩; wegnehmen ⟨*Arm, Hand, Fuß*⟩; wegräumen ⟨*Schutt*⟩; entfernen ⟨*Schmutz, Fleck*⟩; *(to another floor, room, or place)* verlegen ⟨*Büro, Patienten, Schauplatz*⟩; bringen ⟨*Gerümpel*⟩; *(to another town)* versetzen ⟨*Person*⟩; ~ **one's weight to the other foot** sein Gewicht auf den anderen Fuß verlagern; ~ **the responsibility/blame on to sb.** *(fig.)* die Verantwortung/Schuld auf jmdn. schieben; *see also* [1]**ground 1 b; b)** *(Amer. Motor Veh.)* ~ **gears** schalten; **c)** *(sl.: consume)* verkonsumieren *(ugs.);* **d)** *(coll.: sell)* loswerden *(ugs.).* **2.** *v. i.* **a)** ⟨*Wind*:⟩ drehen (**to** nach); ⟨*Ladung*:⟩ verrutschen; *(in drama, novel, etc.)* ⟨*Szene*:⟩ wechseln (**to** nach); ⟨*Schauplatz*:⟩ sich verlagern (**to** nach); ~ **uneasily in one's chair** unruhig auf dem Stuhl hin und her rutschen; **b)** *(manage)* ~ **for oneself** selbst für sich sorgen; **c)** *(sl.: move quickly)* rasen; **this new Porsche really** ~**s** der neue Porsche geht ab wie eine Rakete *(ugs.);* **d)** *(Amer. Motor Veh.: change gear)* schalten; ~ **down into second gear** in den zweiten Gang runterschalten *(ugs.).* **3.** *n.* **a) a** ~ **in emphasis** eine Verlagerung des Akzents; **a** ~ **in values/public opinion** ein Wandel der Wertvorstellungen/ein Umschwung der öffentlichen Meinung; **a** ~ **towards/away from liberalism** eine Hinwendung zum/Abwendung vom Liberalismus; **b)** *(for work)* Schicht, *die;* **eight-hour/late** ~: Achtstunden-/Spätschicht, *die;* **do** *or* **work the late** ~: Spätschicht haben; **work in** ~**s** Schichtarbeit machen; **c)** *(stratagem, dodge)* Kunstgriff, *der;* **d) make** ~ **with/without sth.** sich *(Dat.)* mit/ohne etw. behelfen; **e)** *(of typewriter)* Umschaltung, *die; attrib.* ~ **key** Umschalttaste, *die;* Umschalter, *der;* **f)** *(Amer. Motor Veh.: gear-change)* Schaltung, *die;* **manual/automatic** ~: Hand-/Automatikschaltung, *die;* **g)** *(dress)* Hängekleid, *das;* Hänger, *der;* **h)** *(Phys.)* Verschiebung, *die;* **i)** *(Ling.)* **sound** ~: Lautverschiebung, *die*

shifting 'sands *n. pl. (lit. or fig.)* Flugsand, *der*

shiftless ['ʃɪftlɪs] *adj. (lacking resourcefulness)* unbeholfen; *(incapable)* unfähig

shifty ['ʃɪftɪ] *adj.* verschlagen *(abwertend)*

Shiite ['ʃi:aɪt] *(Muslim Relig.)* **1.** *n.* Schiit, *der*/Schiitin, *die.* **2.** *adj.* schiitisch

shillelagh [ʃɪ'leɪlə, ʃɪ'leɪlɪ] *n.* Knüppel, *der (aus Schlehdorn- oder Eichenholz)*

shilling ['ʃɪlɪŋ] *n.* Shilling, *der;* **take the King's/Queen's** ~ *(arch.)* sich als Rekrut [gegen Handgeld] anwerben lassen; *see also* **cut off f**

shilly-shally ['ʃɪlɪʃælɪ] *v. i.* zaudern; **stop** ~**ing!** entschließ dich endlich!

shimmer ['ʃɪmə(r)] **1.** *v. i.* schimmern. **2.** *n.* Schimmer, *der*

shimmery ['ʃɪmərɪ] *adj.* schimmernd

shin [ʃɪn] **1.** *n.* Schienbein, *das;* ~ **of beef** *(Cookery)* [Vorder]hesse, *die.* **2.** *v. i.*, **-nn-:** ~ **up/down a tree** *etc.* einen Baum *usw.* hinauf-/hinunterklettern

'**shin-bone** *n.* Schienbein, *das*

shindig ['ʃɪndɪg] *n. (coll.)* **a)** *see* **shindy; b)** *(party)* Fete, *die (ugs.)*

shindy ['ʃɪndɪ] *n.* *(brawl)* Rauferei, *die; (row)* Streit, *der; (noise)* Krach, *der; see also* **kick up b**

shine [ʃaɪn] **1.** *v. i.*, **shone** [ʃɒn] **a)** ⟨*Lampe, Licht, Stern*:⟩ leuchten; ⟨*Sonne*:⟩ scheinen; *(reflect light)* glänzen; ⟨*Mond*:⟩ scheinen; **his face shone with happiness/excitement** *(fig.)* er strahlte vor Glück/sein Gesicht glühte vor Aufregung; **a fine morning with the sun shining** ein schöner Morgen mit [strahlendem] Sonnenschein; **b)** *(fig.: be brilliant)* glänzen; **a shining example/light** ein leuchtendes Beispiel/eine Leuchte; ~ **at sport** im Sport glänzen; **he does not exactly** ~ **at maths** er ist nicht gerade eine Leuchte in Mathe *(ugs.).* **2.** *v. t.* **a)** *p. t. & p. p.* **shone** leuchten lassen; ~ **a light on sth./in sb.'s eyes** etw. anleuchten/jmdm. in die Augen leuchten; ~ **the torch this way** leuchte einmal hierher; **b)** *p. t. & p. p.* ~**d** *(clean and polish)* putzen; *(make shiny)* polieren. **3.** *n., no pl.* **a)** *(brightness)* Schein, *der;* Licht, *das; see also* **rain 1 a; b)** *(polish)* Glanz, *der;* **give your shoes a good** ~: bring deine Schuhe auf Hochglanz; **have a** ~ ⟨*Oberfläche*:⟩ glänzen; **put a** ~ **on sth.** etw. zum Glänzen bringen; **take the** ~ **off sth.** *(fig.: spoil sth.)* einen Schatten auf etw. *(Akk.)* werfen; **c) take a** ~ **to sb./sth.** *(coll.)* Gefallen an jmdm./etw. finden

[1]**shingle** ['ʃɪŋgl] **1.** *n.* **a)** *(Building)* Schindel, *die;* **b)** *(Amer.: signboard)* [Praxis]schild, *das;* **c)** *(Hairdressing)* Bubikopf, *der.* **2.** *v. t.* **a)** *(Building)* schindeln; **b)** *(Hairdressing)* zu einem Bubikopf schneiden ⟨*Haar*⟩; ~**d hair** Bubikopf, *der*

[2]**shingle** *n., no pl., no indef. art. (pebbles)* Kies, *der; attrib.* ~ **beach** Kiesstrand, *der*

shingles ['ʃɪŋglz] *n. sing. (Med.)* Gürtelrose, *die*

shingly ['ʃɪŋglɪ] *adj.* kiesig; ~ **beach** Kiesstrand, *der*

shin: ~**-guard,** ~**-pad** *ns.* Schienbeinschutz, *der*

Shinto ['ʃɪntəʊ], **Shintoism** ['ʃɪntəʊɪzm] *ns., no pl., no indef. art. (Relig.)* Schintoismus, *der*

Shintoist ['ʃɪntəʊɪst] *n. (Relig.)* Schintoist, *der*/Schintoistin, *die*

shiny ['ʃaɪnɪ] *adj.* **a)** *(glistening, polished)* glänzend; **b)** *(worn)* blank

ship [ʃɪp] **1.** *n.* **a)** Schiff, *das;* **take** ~: sich einschiffen (**for** nach); **when my** ~ **comes home** *or* **in** *(fig.)* wenn ich zu Geld komme; ~ **of the desert** *(fig.)* Wüstenschiff, *das (geh. scherzh.);* Schiff der Wüste *(geh.);* **we were just** ~**s that pass in the night** *(fig.)* nur einmal kreuzten sich unsere Wege; **the** ~ **of state** das Staatsschiff *(geh.); see also* [1]**break 1 g; company a, h;** [1]**tar 1; b)** *(Amer.: aircraft)* Flugzeug, *das;* Maschine, *die;* **c)** *(coll.: spacecraft)* Raumschiff, *das.* **2.** *v. t.*, **-pp- a)** *(take on board)* einschiffen, an Bord bringen ⟨*Vorräte, Ladung, Passagiere*⟩; *(transport by sea)* verschiffen ⟨*Auto, Truppen*⟩; *(send by train, road, or air)* verschicken, versenden ⟨*Waren*⟩; **b)** *(Naut.: position)* setzen ⟨*Ruderpinne, Mast, Positionslichter*⟩; **c)** ~ **oars** *(bring them into the boat)* die Riemen einlegen *od.* -ziehen; **d)** ~ **water/a sea** Wasser/eine See übernehmen *(Seemannsspr.).* **3.** *v. i.*, **-pp- a)** *(embark)* sich einschiffen; **b)** *(take service on* ~*)* anheuern, anmustern *(Seemannsspr.)*

~ '**off** *v. t.* versenden, verschicken ⟨*Waren*⟩; schicken ⟨*Person*⟩

~ '**out** *v. t.* verschiffen ⟨*Ladung, Güter*⟩

ship: ~**board 1.** *adj.* ⟨*Romanze usw.*⟩ an Bord; **2.** *n., no pl., no art.* **on** ~**board** an Bord; ~**-breaker** *n.* Abwrackfirma, *die;* ~**broker** *n.* Schiffsmakler, *der;* ~**builder** *n.* Schiff[s]bauer, *der;* **firm of** ~**builders** Schiffbaufirma, *die;* ~**building** *n., no pl., no indef. art.* Schiffbau, *der;* ~**-canal** *n.* Schiffahrtskanal, *der;* ~**load** *n.* Schiffsladung, *die;* ~**mate** *n.* Schiffskamerad, *der*

shipment ['ʃɪpmənt] *n.* **a)** Versand, *der; (by sea)* Verschiffung, *die;* **b)** *(amount)* Sendung, *die;* **a** ~ **of bananas** eine Ladung Bananen

'**shipowner** *n.* Schiffseigentümer, *der*/-eigentümerin, *die;* Schiffseigner, *der*/-eignerin, *die; (of several ships)* Reeder, *der*/Reederin, *die*

shipper ['ʃɪpə(r)] *n. (merchant)* Spediteur, *der*/Spediteurin, *die; (company)* Spedition, *die*

shipping ['ʃɪpɪŋ] *n.* **a)** *no pl., no indef. art. (ships)* Schiffe *Pl.; (traffic)* Schiffahrt, *die;* Schiffsverkehr, *der;* **all** ~: alle Schiffe/der ganze Schiffsverkehr; **closed to** ~: für Schiffe/für die Schiffahrt gesperrt; **b)** *(transporting)* Versand, *der*

shipping: ~**-agent** *n.* Schiffsagent, *der;* ~ **forecast** *n.* Seewetterbericht, *der;* ~ **lane** *n.* Schiffahrtsweg, *der; (fairway)* Fahrrinne, *die;* ~ **line** *see* [1]**line 1 i;** ~**-office** *n.* **a)** *(of* ~*-agent)* Schiffsagentur, *die;* **b)** *(hiring seamen)* Heuerbüro, *das*

ship: ~**'s 'biscuit** *n.* Schiffszwieback, *der;* ~**'s chandler** *n.* Schiffsausrüster, *der;* ~**shape** *pred. adj.* in bester Ordnung; **get sth.** ~**shape** etw. in Ordnung bringen; **find everything** ~**shape and Bristol fashion** *(coll.)* alles picobello *od.* tipptopp *(ugs.)* vorfinden; ~**'s 'papers** *n. pl.* Schiffspapiere *Pl.;* ~**-way** *n.* Helling, *die (Schiffbau);* ~**wreck 1.** *n. (lit. or fig.)* Schiffbruch, *der;* **suffer** ~**wreck** Schiffbruch erleiden; **end in** ~**wreck** *(fig.)* scheitern; **2.** *v. t.* **be** ~**wrecked** Schiffbruch erleiden; *(fig.: be ruined)* ⟨*Hoffnung*:⟩ sich zerschlagen haben; ⟨*Karriere*:⟩ gescheitert sein; **be** ~**wrecked on an island** bei einem Schiffbruch auf eine Insel verschlagen werden; ~**wright** *n. (*~*-builder)* Schiff[s]bauer, *der; (*~*'s carpenter)* Schiffszimmermann, *der;* ~**yard** *n.* [Schiffs]werft, *die*

shire ['ʃaɪə(r)] *n.* **a)** *(county)* Grafschaft, *die;* **b) the S**~**s** *(group of counties) die auf -shire endenden englischen Grafschaften; (midland counties)* die Grafschaften in Mittelengland; **c)** *see* **shire-horse**

'**shire-horse** *n. bes. in Mittelengland gezüchtetes schweres Zugpferd*

shirk [ʃɜ:k] *v. t.* sich entziehen (+ *Dat.*) ⟨*Pflicht, Verantwortung*⟩; ausweichen (+ *Dat.*) ⟨*Blick, Kampf*⟩; ~ **one's job/doing sth.** sich vor der Arbeit drücken/sich davor drücken *(ugs.),* etw. zu tun; **you're** ~**ing!** [du bist ein] Drückeberger! *(ugs. abwertend)*

shirker ['ʃɜ:kə(r)] *n.* Drückeberger, *der (ugs. abwertend)*

shirring ['ʃɜ:rɪŋ] *n.* Kräusel[ung], *die*

shirt [ʃɜ:t] *n.* **[man's]** ~: [Herren- *od.* Ober]hemd, *das;* **[woman's** *or* **lady's]** ~: Hemdbluse, *die;* **sports/rugby/football** ~: Trikot/Rugby-/Fußballtrikot, *das;* **keep your** ~ **on!** *(fig. sl.)* [nur] ruhig Blut! *(ugs.);*

have the ~ off sb.'s back *(fig.)* jmdm. das Hemd über den Kopf ziehen *(fig. ugs.)*; **lose the ~ off one's back** alles bis aufs Hemd verlieren *(ugs.)*; **put one's ~ on sth.** *(fig. sl.)* sein letztes Hemd für etw. verwetten *(ugs.)*
shirt: ~ blouse *n.* Hemdbluse, *die;* **~ dress** *n.* Hemdblusenkleid, *das;* **~-front** *n.* Hemdbrust, *die; (separate or detachable)* Vorhemd, *das*
shirting ['ʃɜ:tɪŋ] *n.* Hemdenstoff, *der*
shirt: ~-sleeve 1. *n.* Hemdsärmel, *der;* **work in one's ~-sleeves** in Hemdsärmeln arbeiten; **2.** *adj.* hemdsärmelig; körperlich ⟨*Arbeit*⟩; **it is real ~-sleeve weather** bei diesem Wetter kann man ohne Jacke gehen; **~-tail** *see* **tail 1d**; **~waist** *(Amer.) see* **~ blouse**; **~waister** ['ʃɜ:tweɪstə(r)] *(Brit.) see* **~ dress**
shirty ['ʃɜ:tɪ] *adj. (sl.)* sauer *(salopp)*; **get ~ with sb./about sth.** auf jmdn./wegen etw. sauer werden; **be ~ with sb.** rotzig *(salopp abwertend)* zu jmdm. sein
shish kebab ['ʃɪʃ kɪbæb, 'ʃɪʃ kɪbɑ:b] *n. (Gastr.)* Kebab, *der*
shit [ʃɪt] *(coarse)* **1.** *v.i.*, **-tt-, shitted** *or* **shit** *or* **shat** [ʃæt] scheißen *(derb)*; **~ in one's pants** sich *(Dat.)* in die Hose[n] scheißen. **2.** *v. refl.*, **-tt-, shitted** *or* **shit** *or* **shat** sich *(Dat.)* in die Hose[n] scheißen *(derb)*. **3.** *int.* Scheiße *(derb)*. **4.** *n.* **a)** *(excrement)* Scheiße, *die (derb)*; **have** *(Brit.) or (Amer.)* **take a ~:** scheißen *(derb)*; **have/get the ~s** die Scheißerei *(derb)* haben/kriegen; **when the ~ hits the fan** wenn die Kacke am Dampfen ist *(derb)*; **b)** *(hashish)* Shit, *der od. das (Drogenjargon)*; **c)** *(person)* Scheißkerl, *der; (nonsense)* Scheiß, *der (salopp abwertend)*; **don't give me that ~:** erzähl mir nicht so einen Scheiß! *(salopp)*; **I don't give a ~ [about it]** das ist mir scheißegal *(salopp)*; **who gives a ~!** ist doch scheißegal! *(salopp)*; **it's not worth a ~:** es ist einen Dreck wert *(salopp abwertend)*; **beat** *or* **kick** *or* **knock the ~ out of sb.** *(fig.)* jmdn. gehörig verdreschen *(ugs.)*; **I'll beat the ~ out of you!** ich mach' Hackfleisch aus dir! *(ugs.)*; **be up ~ creek [without a paddle]** *(fig.)* bis zum Hals in der Scheiße stecken *(derb)*; **have/get the ~s** *(fig.)* Schiß haben/kriegen *(salopp)*
shite [ʃaɪt] *(coarse)* **1.** *int.* Scheibenkleister *(ugs. verhüll.)*. **2.** *n.* Scheiß, *der (salopp)*; **not give a ~ for sb./sth.** sich einen [Scheiß]dreck um jmdn./etw. kümmern *(salopp)*
shitless ['ʃɪtlɪs] *adj. (coarse)* **be scared ~:** sich *(Dat.)* vor Angst in die Hose[n] scheißen *(derb)*
'**shit-scared** *pred. adj. (coarse)* **be ~:** Schiß haben *(salopp)*
shitty ['ʃɪtɪ] *adj. (coarse)* beschissen *(derb)*; Scheiß- *(salopp)*
[1]**shiver** ['ʃɪvə(r)] **1.** *v. i. (tremble)* zittern **(with** vor + *Dat.*); **~ all over** am ganzen Leib *od.* Körper zittern; **~ like a leaf** wie Espenlaub zittern *(geh.)*. **2.** *n. (trembling, lit. or fig.)* Schau[d]er, *der (geh.)*; **~ of cold/fear** Kälte-/Angstschauer, *der;* **send ~s** *or* **a ~ up** *or* **[up and] down sb.'s back** *or* **spine** jmdm. [einen] Schauder über den Rücken jagen; **give sb. the ~s** *(fig.)* jmdn. schaudern lassen; **get/have the ~s** *(fig.)* eine Gänsehaut *(fig.) od. (bei Krankheit)* Schüttelfrost bekommen/haben
[2]**shiver 1.** *n. in pl. (fragments)* **break/burst into ~s** in Stücke zerbrechen *od.* zerspringen. **2.** *v. t.* zersplittern lassen; **~ me timbers** potz Blitz! *(veralt.)*. **3.** *v. i.* zerspringen
shivery ['ʃɪvərɪ] *adj.* verfroren ⟨*Person*⟩; **I feel all ~:** mich fröstelt
[1]**shoal** [ʃəʊl] *n.* **a)** *(shallow place)* Untiefe, *die; (sandbank)* Sandbank, *die;* **b)** *in pl. (fig.: hidden danger)* Klippen
[2]**shoal** *n. (of fish)* Schwarm, *der; (fig.)* Schar, *die;* **~s of letters/complaints** Unmengen von Briefen/Beschwerden
[1]**shock** [ʃɒk] **1.** *n.* **a)** Schock, *der;* **I got the ~ of my life** ich erschrak zu Tode; **the general feeling is one of ~:** man ist allgemein erschüttert; **come as a ~ to sb.** ein Schock für jmdn. sein; **give sb. a ~:** jmdm. einen Schock versetzen; **he's in for a [nasty] ~!** er wird eine böse Überraschung erleben!; **~ horror!** *(joc.)* Schreck, laß nach! *(ugs. scherzh.)*; *see also* **sharp 1d**; **b)** *(violent impact)* Erschütterung, *die* **(of** durch); **c)** *(Electr.)* Schlag, *der;* **d)** *(Med.)* Schock, *der;* **die of/be suffering from ~:** an einem Schock sterben/unter Schock[wirkung] stehen; **~ is dangerous** ein Schock kann gefährlich sein; **be in [a state of] ~:** unter Schock[wirkung] stehen; **[electric] ~:** Elektroschock, *der.* **2.** *v. t.* **a) ~ sb. [deeply]** ein [schwerer] Schock für jmdn. sein; **sb. is [terribly] ~ed by/at sth.** etw. ist ein [schwerer] Schock für jmdn.; **b)** *(scandalize)* schockieren; **I'm not easily ~ed** mich schockiert so leicht nichts; **be ~ed by sth.** über etw. *(Akk.)* schockiert sein. **3.** *v. i.* schockieren
[2]**shock** *n. (of corn-sheaves)* Hocke, *die (meist aus zwölf Garben)*
[3]**shock** *n.* **a ~ of red hair** ein roter Haarschopf; **an untidy ~ of thick grey hair** eine dichte graue Mähne *(scherzh.)*
'**shock absorber** *n.* Stoßdämpfer, *der*
shocker ['ʃɒkə(r)] *n. (coll.)* **a) he is a ~ for gambling/drink/the girls** er ist ein hemmungsloser Zocker/Säufer/Weiberheld *(salopp)*; **b)** *(novel etc.)* Schocker, *der (ugs.)*
shock-headed ['ʃɒkhedɪd] *adj.* **be ~:** eine Mähne haben *(ugs.)*; **a ~ little boy/girl** ein kleiner Strubbelkopf *(ugs.)*
shocking ['ʃɒkɪŋ] **1.** *adj.* **a)** schockierend; **b)** *(coll.: very bad)* fürchterlich *(ugs.)*; **what a ~ thing to say** wie kann man nur so etwas sagen! *(ugs.)*. **2.** *adv. (coll.)* **~ bad** fürchterlich *(ugs.)*
shockingly ['ʃɒkɪŋlɪ] *adv.* **a)** *(badly)* schockierend [schlecht] ⟨*behandeln, sich benehmen*⟩; **b)** *(extremely)* sündhaft *(ugs.)* ⟨*teuer*⟩; erbärmlich ⟨*schlecht*⟩
shocking 'pink *adj.* grellrosa
shock: ~proof *adj.* stoßfest ⟨*Uhr, Kiste*⟩; erschütterungsfest ⟨*Gebäude*⟩; **~ tactics** *n. pl. (Mil.) taktischer Einsatz von Stoßtruppen; (fig.)* Überrumpelungstaktik, *die;* **~ therapy, ~ treatment** *ns. (Med.)* Schocktherapie, *die;* Schockbehandlung, *die;* **~ troops** *n. pl. (Mil.)* Stoßtruppen *(veralt.)*; **~ wave** *n.* Druckwelle, *die* **(from** *Gen.*); *(of earthquake)* Erschütterungswelle, *die* **(from** *Gen.*)
shod *see* **shoe 2**
shoddily ['ʃɒdɪlɪ] *adv.* schludrig *(ugs. abwertend)*; **treat sb. ~:** jmdn. schäbig behandeln *(abwertend)*
shoddy ['ʃɒdɪ] **1.** *n.* Shoddy, *das od. der (Textilw.)*; Reißwolle, *die.* **2.** *adj.* schäbig *(abwertend)*; *(poorly done, poor in quality)* minderwertig ⟨*Arbeit, Stoff, Artikel*⟩
shoe [ʃu:] **1.** *n.* **a)** Schuh, *der;* **I shouldn't like to be in his ~s** *(fig.)* ich möchte nicht in seiner Haut stecken *(ugs.)*; **put oneself into sb.'s ~s** *(fig.)* sich in jmds. Lage *(Akk.)* versetzen; **sb. shakes in his ~s** jmdm. schlottern die Knie; **if the ~ fits** *(Amer.)* = **if the cap fits** *see* **cap 1a**; *see also* **pinch 3a**; **b)** *(of horse)* [Huf]eisen, *das;* **c)** *(of brake)* Backe, *die.* **2.** *v. t.*, **~ing** ['ʃu:ɪŋ], **shod** [ʃɒd] beschlagen ⟨*Pferd*⟩; *(protect with iron tip)* beschuhen ⟨*Pfahl*⟩; **be well shod** ⟨*Person:*⟩ gut beschuht sein
shoe: ~ bar *n.* Schnellschusterei, *die;* **~black** *n.* Schuhputzer, *der;* **~-box** *see* [2]**box 1a**; **~-brush** *n.* Schuhbürste, *die;* **~-buckle** *n.* Schuhschnalle, *die;* **~-cream** *n.* Schuhcreme, *die;* **~horn** *n.* Schuhlöffel, *der;* **~-lace** *n.* Schnürsenkel, *der;* Schuhband, *das;* **~-leather** *n.* Schuhleder, *das;* **you can save your ~-leather** den Weg kannst du dir sparen
shoeless ['ʃu:lɪs] *adj.* ohne Schuhe
shoe: ~maker *n.* Schuhmacher, *der;* Schuster, *der;* **~making** *n., no pl.* Schuhmacherei, *die;* **~-polish** *n.* Schuhcreme, *die;* **~-repairer** *n.* Flickschuster, *der (veralt.)*; Schuster, *der;* **~shine** *n. (Amer.)* **have** *or* **get a ~shine** sich *(Dat.)* die Schuhe putzen lassen; **~shine boy** *n. (Amer.)* Schuhputzer, *der;* **~-shop** *n.* Schuhgeschäft, *das;* **~ spray** *n.* Schuhspray, *der od. das;* **~-string** *n.* **a)** *see* **~-lace**; **b)** *(coll.: small amount)* **on a ~-string** mit ganz wenig Geld; **a ~-string budget** ein minimaler Etat; **~-string financing** Finanzierung mit ganz wenig Geld; **~-string 'tie** *n. wie eine Krawatte getragene, durch einen Ring oder eine Schleife gehaltene Schnur;* **~-tree** *n.* Schuhspanner, *der*
shone *see* **shine 1, 2**
shoo [ʃu:] **1.** *int.* sch. **2.** *v. t.* scheuchen; **~ away** fort- *od.* wegscheuchen
shook *see* **shake 2, 3**
shoot [ʃu:t] **1.** *v. i.*, **shot** [ʃɒt] **a)** schießen **(at** auf + *Akk.*); **~ to kill** ⟨*Polizei:*⟩ scharf schießen; **have sth. to ~ at** *(fig.)* ein Ziel vor Augen *od.* eine Zielvorstellung haben; *see also* [1]**hip a**; **b)** *(move rapidly)* schießen *(ugs.)*; **~ past sb./down the stairs** an jmdm. vorbeischießen/die Treppe hinunterschießen *(ugs.)*; **come ~ing in** hereingeschossen kommen *(ugs.)*; **pain shot through/up his arm** ein Schmerz schoß durch seinen Arm/seinen Arm hinauf; **c)** *(Bot.)* austreiben; **d)** *(Sport)* schießen; **e)** *(coll.: speak out)* **~!** schieß los! *(ugs.)*. **2.** *v. t.*, **shot a)** *(wound)* anschießen; *(kill)* erschießen; *(hunt)* schießen; **~ sb. dead** jmdn. erschießen *od. (ugs.)* totschießen; **~ an animal and kill it** ein Tier tödlich treffen; **he was fatally shot in the head** ihn traf ein tödlicher Kopfschuß; **~ oneself in the foot** *(fig. coll.)* sich *(Dat.)* ins eigene Fleisch schneiden; **you'll get shot for this** *(fig.)* du kannst dein Testament machen *(ugs.)*; **he ought to be shot** *(fig.)* der gehört aufgehängt *(ugs.)*; **b)** schießen mit ⟨*Bogen, Munition, Pistole*⟩; abschießen ⟨*Pfeil, Kugel*⟩ **(at** auf + *Akk.*); **c)** *(sl.: inject)* schießen *(Drogenjargon)* ⟨*Heroin, Kokain*⟩; **d)** *(send out)* zuwerfen ⟨*Lächeln, Blick*⟩ **(at** *Dat.*); [aus]treiben ⟨*Knospen, Schößlinge*⟩; **the volcano shot lava high into the air** der Vulkan schleuderte Lava hoch in die Luft; **~ a line** *(fig. sl.)* angeben *(ugs.)* **(about** mit); **~ the moon** *(Brit. sl.)* bei Nacht und Nebel abhauen *(ugs.)*; *see also* [1]**bolt 1c**; **e)** *(Sport)* schießen ⟨*Tor, Ball, Puck*⟩; *(Basketball)* werfen ⟨*Korb*⟩; **~ dice** würfeln; **~ a hole in one** *(Golf)* ein Loch mit einem Schlag spielen; *see also* **craps**; **f)** *(push, slide)* vorschieben ⟨*Riegel*⟩; herausziehen ⟨*Manschetten*⟩; schütten ⟨*Mehl, Kohle*⟩; **g)** *(Cinemat.)* drehen ⟨*Film, Szene*⟩; **h)** *(pass swiftly over)* schießen über (+ *Akk.*) ⟨*Brücke, Stromschnelle, Wasserfall*⟩; **~ the lights** *(sl.)* eine rote Ampel überfahren. **3.** *n.* **a)** *(Bot.)* Trieb, *der;* **b)** *see* **chute a**; **c)** *(~ing-party, -expedition, -practice, -land)* Jagd, *die;* **a duck ~:** eine Entenjagd; **the whole [bang] ~** *(sl.)* der ganze Kram *od.* Krempel *(ugs.)*
~ a'head *v.i.* vorpreschen; **~ ahead of sb.** jmdn. blitzschnell hinter sich *(Dat.)* lassen
~ a'long *v.i.* dahinschießen
~ 'down *v.t.* abschießen ⟨*Flugzeug*⟩; niederschießen ⟨*Person*⟩; *(fig.)* entkräften ⟨*Argument*⟩; **be shot down in flames** ⟨*Flugzeug:*⟩ in Brand geschossen werden und abstürzen; *(fig.)* ⟨*Person, Argument:*⟩ in der Luft zerrissen werden
~ 'off 1. *v.t.* abschießen ⟨*Gewehr*⟩; **~ one's mouth off** *(sl.)* das Maul aufreißen *(derb)*. **2.** *v.i.* losschießen *(ugs.)*
~ 'out 1. *v.i.* hervorschießen; **the dog shot out of the gate** der Hund schoß aus dem Tor heraus *(ugs.)*. **2.** *v. t.* herausschleudern; **~ it out** *(sl.)* sich schießen; *see also* **shoot-out**

~ '**up** **1.** *v.i.* in die Höhe schießen; ‹*Preise, Temperatur, Kosten, Pulsfrequenz:*› in die Höhe schnellen. **2.** *v.t.* herumschießen in (+ *Dat.*) *(ugs.)*; **be badly shot up** schwer beschossen werden
shooter ['ʃu:tə(r)] *n. (coll.: gun)* Ballermann, *der (ugs.)*
shooting ['ʃu:tɪŋ] *n.* **a)** Schießerei, *die;* **new outbreaks of ~ were reported** ein erneutes Aufflammen der Schießereien wurde gemeldet; **two more ~s were reported** Meldungen zufolge wurden erneut zwei Menschen von Schüssen getroffen; **b)** *(Sport)* Schießen, *das;* **rifle ~:** Gewehrschießen, *das;* **c)** *(Hunting)* **go ~:** auf die Jagd gehen; **d)** *(Cinemat.)* Dreharbeiten *Pl.*
shooting: ~-box *n. (Brit. Hunting)* Jagdhütte, *die;* **~-brake, ~-break** *n. (Brit. Motor Veh.)* Kombiwagen, *der;* **~-gallery** *n.* Schießstand, *der; (at fun-fair)* Schießbude, *die;* **~-iron** *n. (sl.)* Schießeisen, *das (ugs.);* Schießprügel, *der (salopp);* **~-match** *n.* **a)** Wettschießen, *das;* **b) the whole ~-match** *(sl.)* der ganze Kram *od.* Krempel *(ugs. abwertend);* **~-party** *n.* Jagdgesellschaft, *die;* **~-range** *n.* Schießstand, *der;* ~ '**star** *n.* Sternschnuppe, *die;* **~-stick** *n.* Jagdstock, *der;* ~ **war** *n.* offener Krieg
'**shoot-out** *n.* Schießerei, *die*
shop [ʃɒp] **1.** *n.* **a)** *(premises)* Laden, *der;* Geschäft, *das;* **go to the ~s** einkaufen gehen; **keep a ~:** einen Laden *od.* ein Geschäft haben; **keep [the] ~ for sb.** jmdn. im Laden *od.* Geschäft vertreten; **all over the ~** *(fig. sl.)* überall; **look for sth. all over the ~** *(fig. sl.)* in jedem Winkel nach etw. suchen; **my books are all over the ~** *(fig. sl.)* meine Bücher liegen wie Kraut und Rüben durcheinander *(ugs.);* **b)** *(business)* **set up ~:** ein Geschäft eröffnen; *(as a lawyer, dentist, etc.)* eine Praxis aufmachen; **shut up ~:** das Geschäft schließen; **talk ~:** fachsimpeln *(ugs.);* **no [talking] ~, please!** keine Fachsimpelei, bitte! *(ugs.);* **c)** *(sl.: institution, establishment)* Laden, *der (ugs.);* **d)** *(workshop)* Werkstatt, *die;* **engineering ~:** Maschinenbauhalle, *die;* **pattern/machine ~:** Modell-/Maschinenwerkstatt, *die;* **e)** *(action)* Einkauf, *der. See also* **closed shop. 2.** *v.i.,* **-pp-** einkaufen; **go ~ping** einkaufen gehen; ~ *or* **go ~ping for shoes** Schuhe kaufen gehen. **3.** *v.t.* **-pp-** *(Brit. sl.)* verpfeifen
~ **a'round** *v.i.* sich umsehen **(for** nach)
shop: ~ **assistant** *n. (Brit.)* Verkäufer, *der*/Verkäuferin, *die;* **~-boy** *n.* Ladenbursche, *der (veralt.);* **~-fitter** *n.* Ladenbauer, *der;* **firm of ~-fitters** Ladenbaufirma, *die;* **~-fittings** *n. pl.* Ladeneinrichtung, *die;* **~-floor** *n.* **a)** *(place)* Produktion, *die (ugs.);* **the worker on the ~-floor** der einfache Arbeiter; **what is the feeling on the ~-floor?** was ist die Meinung der Arbeiter?; **b)** *(workers)* **the ~-floor** die Arbeiter; *attrib.* Arbeiter-; **~-floor democracy** Demokratie am Arbeitsplatz; **~-front** *n.* Schaufensterfront, *die;* **~-girl** *n.* Ladenmädchen, *das (veralt.);* **~keeper** *n.* Ladenbesitzer, *der*/-besitzerin, *die;* **~-lifter** *n.* Ladendieb, *der*/-diebin, *die;* **~-lifting** *n., no pl., no indef. art.* Ladendiebstahl, *der;* **~owner** *see* **~keeper**
shopper ['ʃɒpə(r)] *n.* **a)** *(person)* Käufer, *der*/Käuferin, *die;* **b)** *(wheeled bag)* Einkaufsroller, *der*
shopping ['ʃɒpɪŋ] *n.* **a)** *(buying goods)* Einkaufen, *das;* **do the/one's ~:** einkaufen/[seine] Einkäufe machen; **b)** *(items bought)* Einkäufe *Pl.*
shopping: ~-bag *n.* Einkaufstasche, *die;* **~-basket** *n.* Einkaufskorb, *der;* ~ **centre** *n.* Einkaufszentrum, *das;* ~ **day** *n.* Einkaufstag, *der;* **~-list** *n.* Einkaufszettel, *der; (fig.)* Wunschliste, *die;* ~ **mall** *n. (Amer.)* Einkaufszentrum, *das;* ~ **street** *n.* Geschäftsstraße, *die;* ~ **trolley** *n.* Einkaufswagen, *der*
shop: ~-soiled *adj. (Brit.) (slightly damaged)* leicht beschädigt; *(slightly dirty)* angeschmutzt; **~-steward** *n.* [gewerkschaftlicher] Vertrauensmann; **~-talk** *n., no pl.* Fachsimpelei, *die (ugs.);* **~walker** *n. (Brit.)* ≈ Abteilungsleiter, *der*/-leiterin, *die;* **~-'window** *n.* Schaufenster, *das;* **~-worn** *see* **~-soiled**
[1]**shore** [ʃɔ:(r)] *n.* Ufer, *das; (coast)* Küste, *die; (beach)* Strand, *der;* **on the ~:** am Ufer/an der Küste/am Strand; **on the ~[s] of Lake Garda** am Ufer des Gardasees; **off ~:** vor der Küste; **a mile off [the] ~:** eine Meile vom Ufer entfernt/vor der Küste/vom Strand entfernt; **be on ~** ‹*Seemann:*› an Land sein; **these ~s** dieses Land; diese Gestade *(dichter.)*
[2]**shore 1.** *n. (prop, beam)* Stützbalken, *der;* Stütze, *die.* **2.** *v.t. (support)* abstützen ‹*Tunnel*›
~ '**up** *v.t. (support)* abstützen ‹*Mauer, Haus*›; *(fig.)* stützen ‹*Währung, Wirtschaft*›
shore: ~-based ['ʃɔ:beɪst] *adj.* landgestützt ‹*Rakete*›; ~ **leave** *n. (Naut.)* Landurlaub, *der;* **~-line** *n. (Geog.)* Uferlinie, *die*
shoring ['ʃɔ:rɪŋ] *n.* Abstützung, *die*
shorn *see* **shear 1, 2**
short [ʃɔ:t] **1.** *adj.* **a)** kurz; **a ~ time** *or* **while ago/later** vor kurzem/kurze Zeit später; **for a ~ time** *or* **while** eine kleine Weile; ein [kleines] Weilchen; **a ~ time before he left** kurz bevor er ging; **a ~ time** *or* **while before/after sth.** kurz vor/nach etw. *(Dat.);* **in a ~ time** *or* **while** *(soon)* bald; in Kürze; **within a ~ [space of] time** innerhalb kurzer Zeit; **a few ~ years of happiness** einige wenige Jahre des Glücks; **in the ~ run** *or* **term** kurzfristig; kurzzeitig; **there is only a ~ haul ahead of us** *(fig.)* wir haben es bald geschafft; **wear one's hair/skirts ~:** seine Haare kurz tragen/kurze Röcke tragen; **be ~ in the arm/leg** ‹*Person:*› kurzarmig/kurzbeinig sein; ‹*Kleidungsstück:*› im Arm/Bein kurz sein; **have/get sb. by the ~ hairs** *or (sl.)* **by the ~ and curlies** jmdn. in der Hand haben/in die Hand kriegen *(ugs.);* **~ back and sides** kurzer Haarschnitt; **make ~ work of sb./sth.** mit jmdm./etw. kurzen Prozeß machen *(ugs.);* **he made ~ work of the puzzle** er hatte das Rätsel im Handumdrehen gelöst; *see also* **neck 1 b; notice 1 b; range 1 d; shrift; straw b; b)** *(not tall)* klein ‹*Person, Wuchs*›; niedrig ‹*Gebäude, Baum, Schornstein*›; **c)** *(not far-reaching)* kurz ‹*Wurf, Schuß, Gedächtnis*›; **take a ~ view of things** kurzsichtig sein; **d)** *(deficient, scanty)* knapp; **be in ~ supply** knapp sein; **good doctors are in ~ supply** gute Ärzte sind rar *od. (ugs.)* sind Mangelware; **give sb. ~ weight** jmdn. beim Abwiegen übervorteilen; *(inadvertently)* sich zu jmds. Ungunsten beim Abwiegen versehen; **be [far/not far] ~ of a record** einen Rekord [bei weitem] nicht erreichen/[knapp] verfehlen; **his jump was 4 cm. ~ of the record** sein Sprung verfehlte den Rekord um 4 cm; **sb./sth. is so much/so many ~:** jmdm./einer Sache fehlt soundsoviel/fehlen soundsoviele; **sb. is ~ of sth.** jmdm. fehlt es an etw. *(Dat.);* **he is [rather] ~ on talent** er ist nicht besonders talentiert; **time is getting/is ~:** die Zeit wird/ist knapp; **the poor harvest has left them ~ of food** wegen der schlechten Ernte fehlt es ihnen an Nahrung; **don't leave yourself ~ [of money/food]** paß auf, daß du selbst noch genug [Geld/zu essen] hast; **keep sb. ~ [of sth.]** jmdn. [mit etw.] kurzhalten; **[have to] go ~ [of sth.]** [an etw. *(Dat.)*] Mangel leiden [müssen]; **she is ~ of milk today** sie hat heute nicht genug Milch; **the firm is ~ of staff** die Firma hat zu wenig Arbeitskräfte; **be ~ [of cash]** knapp [bei Kasse] sein *(ugs.);* **be ~ of sth.** ‹*Preis, Temperatur, Leistung usw.:*› unter etw. *(Dat.)* liegen; **he is just ~ of six feet/not far ~ of 60** er ist knapp sechs Fuß [groß]/sechzig [Jahre alt]; **a few inches ~ of the line** nur wenige Zoll vor der Linie; **she is three months ~ of retirement** sie steht 3 Monate vor ihrer Pensionierung; **be still far ~ of one's target** von seinem Ziel noch weit entfernt sein; **his behaviour has been little** *or* **not far ~ of criminal** sein Verhalten war beinahe kriminell; **if it was not fraud, it was not far ~ of it** wenn es auch kein ausgesprochener Betrug war, so war es doch nicht weit davon entfernt; **it is nothing ~ of miraculous** es ist ein ausgesprochenes Wunder; *see also* **hundredweight c; measure 1 a; ration 1 a; run 2 l; ton a; e)** *(brief, concise)* kurz; **a ~ history of Wales** eine kurzgefaßte Geschichte von Wales; **the ~ answer is ...:** um es kurz zu machen: die Antwort ist ...; **~ and sweet** *(iron.)* kurz und schmerzlos *(ugs.);* **~ and to the point** kurz und geradeheraus *(ugs.) od.* direkt; **something ~** *(drink)* ein Schnaps; **in ~, ...:** kurz, ... ; **his name is Robert, [but he is called] Bob for ~:** er heißt Robert, [wird aber] kurz Bob [genannt]; **Dick is ~ for Richard** Dick ist eine Kurzform von Richard *od.* kurz für Richard; **f)** *(curt, uncivil)* kurz angebunden; barsch; **g)** *(Cookery)* mürbe ‹*Teig*›; **h)** *(Pros., Phonet.)* kurz; **i)** *(St. Exch.)* **~ sale** Leerverkauf, *der;* **make a ~ sale** fixen; **sell sth. ~:** etw. leer verkaufen; **sell oneself ~** *(fig.)* sein Licht unter den Scheffel stellen; **sell sb./sth. ~** *(fig.)* jmdn./etw. unterschätzen; **j)** *(Cricket) relativ nahe beim Schlagmann [stehend];* **~ ball** kurzer Ball; **k)** *(cards)* **~ suit** kurze Farbe. **2.** *adv.* **a)** *(abruptly)* plötzlich; **stop ~:** plötzlich abbrechen; ‹*Musik, Gespräch:*› jäh *(geh.)* abbrechen; **stop ~ at sth.** über etw. *(Akk.)* nicht hinausgehen; **stop sb. ~:** jmdm. ins Wort fallen; **pull up ~:** plötzlich anhalten; **bring** *or* **pull sb. up ~:** jmdn. stutzen lassen; *see also* **cut 1 c; b)** *(curtly)* kurz angebunden; barsch; **c)** *(before the expected place or time)* **jump/land ~:** zu kurz springen/zu früh landen *(ugs.);* **~ of sth.** vor etw. *(Dat.);* **stop ~ of the line** vor der Linie stehen-/liegenbleiben; **the bomb dropped/landed ~ [of its target]** die Bombe fiel vor das/landete *(ugs.)* vor dem Ziel; **fall** *or* **come ~** *(fig.)* ‹*Leistung, Vorstellung usw.:*› enttäuschen; **fall** *or* **come [far/considerably] ~ of sth.** etw. [bei weitem] nicht erreichen; **stop ~ of sth.** *(fig.)* vor etw. zurückschrecken; **stop ~ of doing sth.** davor zurückschrecken, etw. zu tun; **be caught** *or* **taken ~** *(at a disadvantage)* in Bedrängnis geraten; *(coll.: need to go to toilet)* plötzlich dringend müssen *(fam.);* **d) nothing ~ of a catastrophe/miracle can ...:** nur eine Katastrophe/ein Wunder kann ...; **~ of locking him in, how can I keep him from going out?** wie kann ich ihn daran hindern auszugehen – es sei denn ich schlösse ihn ein? **3.** *n.* **a)** *(Electr. coll.)* Kurze, *der (ugs.);* **b)** *(coll.: drink)* Schnaps, *der (ugs.);* **c)** *(Cinemat.)* Kurzfilm, *der. See also* [1]**long 2 b; shorts. 4.** *v.t. (Electr. coll.)* kurzschließen. **5.** *v.i. (Electr. coll.)* einen Kurzschluß kriegen *(ugs.)*
shortage ['ʃɔ:tɪdʒ] *n.* Mangel, *der* **(of** an + *Dat.*); **~ of fruit/teachers** Obstknappheit, *die*/Lehrermangel, *der*
short: ~bread *n.* Shortbread, *das; Keks aus Butterteig;* **~cake** *n.* **a)** *see* **~bread; b)** *(cake served with fruit) Obstkuchen mit Mürbeteigboden;* **a strawberry ~cake** ein Erdbeerkuchen aus Mürbeteig; **~-'change** *v.t.* zu wenig [Wechselgeld] herausgeben (+ *Dat.*); *(fig.)* übers Ohr hauen *(ugs.);* prellen; ~ '**circuit** *n. (Electr.)* Kurzschluß, *der;* **~-'circuit** *(Electr.)* **1.** *v.t.* kurzschließen; *(fig.)* umgehen; **2.** *v.i.* einen Kurzschluß bekommen; **~coming** *n., usu. in pl.* Unzulänglichkeit, *die;* **he has only one**

~**coming** er hat nur einen Fehler; ~ '**commons** *n. pl.* **be on ~ commons** zu wenig zu essen haben; ~ '**cut** *n.* Abkürzung, *die;* **take a ~ cut** *(lit. or fig.)* eine Abkürzung machen; **be a ~ cut to sth.** *(fig.)* den Weg zu etw. abkürzen; **there is no ~ cut to success** *(fig.)* der Weg zum Erfolg läßt sich nicht abkürzen; ~ **division** *see* **division g**; ~ '**drink** *n.* hochprozentiges Getränk; **have a ~ drink** etwas Hochprozentiges trinken

shorten ['ʃɔ:tn] **1.** *v. i.* **a)** *(become shorter)* kürzer werden; **b)** *(decrease)* sich verkleinern; ‹*Preis, Gewinnquote:*› sinken. **2.** *v. t.* **a)** *(make shorter)* kürzen; *(curtail)* verkürzen ‹*Besuch, Wartezeit, Inkubationszeit*›; **b)** *(decrease)* senken; reduzieren; ~ **sail** *(Naut.)* die Segel reffen; **c)** *(Cookery)* mürbe machen

shortening ['ʃɔ:tnɪŋ] *n.* **a)** *(making shorter)* [Ver]kürzung, *die; (growing shorter)* Kürzerwerden, *das;* **b)** *(Cookery)* Ziehfett, *das (zum Mürbemachen des Teigs)*

short: ~**fall** *n.* Fehlmenge, *die; (in budget, financial resources)* Defizit, *das;* ~-**haired** *adj.* kurzhaarig; ~**hand** *n.* Kurzschrift, *die;* Stenographie, *die;* **write ~hand** stenographieren; ~**hand writer** Stenograph, *der/* Stenographin, *die;* **that's ~hand for ...** *(fig.)* das ist eine Kurzformel für ...; *see also* **typist**; ~-**handed** [ʃɔ:t'hændɪd] *adj.* zu klein ‹*Team*›; **we are terribly ~-handed** wir haben furchtbar wenig Leute; ~ **haul** *n.* Kurzstreckentransport, *der;* [Güter]nahtransport, *der;* ~-**haul** *adj.* Kurzstrecken‹*flug, -flugzeug*›; ‹*Lastwagen, Bus*› für den Nahverkehr; ~-**haul route** Kurzstrecke, *die;* ~-**haul transport** Güternahverkehr, *der;* ~ '**head** *n. (Brit. Horse-racing)* kurzer Kopf *(fachspr.)*; **win by a ~ head** mit einem kurzen Kopf Vorsprung gewinnen; **win an election by a ~ head** eine Wahl knapp gewinnen; ~**hold** *adj.* kurzzeitig ‹*Mietverhältnis*›; ~**horn** *n. (Agric.)* Shorthornrind, *das; attrib.* Shorthorn-

shortie ['ʃɔ:tɪ] *n. (coll.)* **a)** *see* **shorty a**; **b)** *(garment)* Shorty, *das;* ~ **night-dress/dress** kurzes Nachthemd/kurzes Kleid

shortish ['ʃɔ:tɪʃ] *adj.* ziemlich kurz; ziemlich klein ‹*Person*›

short: ~-**legged** *adj.* kurzbeinig; ~ **list** *n. (Brit.)* engere Auswahl; **be on/put sb. on the ~ list** in der engeren Auswahl sein/jmdn. in die engere Auswahl nehmen; ~-**list** *v. t.* in die engere Auswahl nehmen; ~-**lived** ['ʃɔ:tlɪvd] *adj.* kurzlebig

shortly ['ʃɔ:tlɪ] *adv.* **a)** *(soon)* in Kürze; gleich *(ugs.)*; ~ **before/after sth.** kurz vor/nach etw.; ~ **before/after arriving, he phoned us** kurz vor/nach seiner Ankunft rief er uns an; *(outside cinema, theatre)* **'coming ~'** „demnächst"; „Voranzeige"; **b)** *(briefly)* kurz; **c)** *(curtly)* kurz angebunden; in barschem Ton

shortness ['ʃɔ:tnɪs] *n., no pl.* **a)** *(short extent or duration)* Kürze, *die;* **despite the ~ of his life** trotz seines kurzen Lebens; **b)** *(smallness) (of person)* Kleinheit, *die;* geringe Körpergröße; **c)** *(scarcity, lack)* Knappheit, *die* (**of an** + *Dat.*); ~ **of breath** Kurzatmigkeit; **d)** *(briefness)* Kürze, *die;* **e)** *(curtness)* Barschheit, *die;* **f)** *(of pastry)* Mürbheit, *die*

short: ~ '**odds** *n. pl. (Racing, also fig.)* **it's/I would give you ~ odds on X winning** es ist so gut wie sicher, daß X gewinnt; ~ '**order** *n. (Amer.)* **a)** *(for food)* Schnellgericht, *das;* **b)** **in ~ order** auf der Stelle; ~-**order** *adj. (Amer.)* Schnell-; ~-**order counter** Selbstbedienungsbüffet, *das;* ~ '**pastry** *n. (Cookery)* Mürbeteig, *der;* ~-**range** *adj.* **a)** *(with ~ range)* Kurzstrecken-; **b)** *(relating to ~ future period)* kurzfristig

shorts [ʃɔ:ts] *n. pl.* **a)** *(trousers)* kurze Hose[n]; Shorts *Pl.; (in sports)* Sporthose, *die;* **football ~**: Fußballshorts; **b)** *(Amer.: underpants)* Unterhose, *die*

short: ~ '**sight** *n., no pl., no art.* Kurzsichtigkeit, *die;* **have ~ sight** kurzsichtig sein; ~-**sighted** [ʃɔ:t'saɪtɪd] *adj.*, ~-**sightedly** [ʃɔ:t'saɪtɪdlɪ] *adv. (lit. or fig.)* kurzsichtig; ~-**sightedness** [ʃɔ:t'saɪtɪdnɪs] *n., no pl. (lit. or fig.)* Kurzsichtigkeit, *die;* ~-**sleeved** ['ʃɔ:tsli:vd] *adj.* kurzärm[e]lig; ~ '**sleeves** *n. pl.* kurze Ärmel; ~-**staffed** [ʃɔ:t'stɑ:ft] *adj.* **be [very] ~-staffed** [viel] zu wenig Personal haben; ~ **stop** *n. (Baseball)* **a)** *no pl., no art. (position)* Shortstopposition, *die;* **b)** *(player)* Shortstop, *der;* ~ '**story** *n. (Lit.)* Short story, *die;* Kurzgeschichte, *die;* **short ~ story** Short short story, *die;* ~ '**suit** *n. (Cards)* kurze Farbe; **have a ~ suit in hearts** wenig Herz haben; ~ '**temper** *n.* aufbrausendes *od.* cholerisches Temperament; **have a ~ temper** aufbrausend *od.* cholerisch sein; ~-'**tempered** *adj.* aufbrausend; cholerisch; **be ~-tempered with sb.** ungehalten zu jmdm. sein; ~-**term** *adj.* kurzfristig; *(provisional)* vorläufig ‹*Lösung, Antwort*›; ~ '**time** *n. (Industry)* Kurzarbeit, *die;* **be on** *or* **work ~ time** kurzarbeiten; ~-**time** *adj.* ~-**time working** Kurzarbeit, *die;* ~ '**title** *n.* Kurztitel, *der;* ~ '**trousers** *n. pl.* kurze Hose[n]; ~ '**wave** *n. (Radio)* Kurzwelle, *die;* ~-**wave** *adj. (Radio)* Kurzwellen-; ~-**winded** [ʃɔ:t'wɪndɪd] *adj.* kurzatmig

shorty ['ʃɔ:tɪ] *n. (coll.)* **a)** *(person)* Kleine, *der/die (ugs.)*; **he/she is a ~**: er ist so'n Kleiner/sie ist so'ne Kleine *(ugs.)*; **b)** *see* **shortie b**

shot [ʃɒt] **1.** *n.* **a)** *pl. same (single projectile for cannon or gun)* Geschoß, *das;* Kugel, *die (ugs.); collect.* Munition, *die;* **b)** *(Athletics)* Kugel, *die;* **put the ~**: die Kugel stoßen; kugelstoßen; **[putting] the ~**: Kugelstoßen, *das;* **c)** *pl. same (lead pellet)* [Schrot]kugel, *die; collect.* Schrot, *der od. das; see also* **lead shot**; **d)** *(discharge of gun)* Schuß, *der; (firing of rocket)* Abschuß, *der;* Start, *der;* **the ~ had gone home** *(fig.)* das hatte gesessen *(ugs.)*; **fire a ~ [at sb./sth.]** einen Schuß [auf jmdn./etw.] abgeben; **like a ~** *(fig.)* wie der Blitz *(ugs.)*; **I'd do it like a ~**: ich würde es auf der Stelle tun; **call the ~s** *(fig.)* das Sagen haben *(ugs.)*; **let sb. call the ~s** nach jmds. Pfeife tanzen *(ugs.)*; **have a ~ at sth./at doing sth.** *(fig.)* etw. versuchen/versuchen, etw. zu tun; **the answer is not correct, but it is a good ~**: die Antwort ist nicht richtig, aber es war [für den Anfang] schon ganz gut *(ugs.)*; *see also* **dark 2c**; **long shot**; **Parthian shot**; **parting 2**; **snap shot**; **e)** *(Sport: stroke, kick, throw)* Schuß, *der; (Archery, Shooting)* Schuß, *der;* **f)** *(Photog.)* Aufnahme, *die; (Cinemat.)* Einstellung, *die;* **do** *or* **film interior/exterior/location ~s** *(Cinemat.)* Innenaufnahmen machen/Außenaufnahmen machen/am Originalschauplatz drehen; **out of/in ~** *(Photog.)* außerhalb des Bildes/im Bild; **g)** *(person who shoots in specified way)* Schütze, *der;* **h)** *(injection)* Spritze, *die; (of drug)* Schuß, *der (Jargon)*; **be a ~ in the arm for sb./sth.** *(fig.)* jmdm./einer Sache Aufschwung geben; **i)** *(coll.: dram of spirits)* Schluck, *der (fig.)*; **a ~ of whisky/rum** *etc.* ein Schluck Whisky/Rum *usw.*. **2.** *v. t. & i. see* **shoot 1, 2. 3.** *adj.* **a)** *(iridescent)* durchschossen; ~ **[through] with sth.** mit etw. durchschossen; **hair ~ with grey** graumeliertes Haar; **b) get ~ of sb./sth.** *(sl.)* jmdn./etw. loswerden; **I wish I could get ~ of him** ich würde ihn am liebsten auf den Mond schießen *(salopp)*; **c)** *(sl.)* **be ~** *(exhausted, finished)* im Eimer sein *(salopp)*; **my nerves are ~ [to pieces]** ich bin mit den Nerven [völlig] fertig *(ugs.)*

shot: ~-**blasting** ['ʃɒtblɑ:stɪŋ] *n.* Kugelstrahlen, *das (Technik)*; ~-**firer** ['ʃɒtfaɪərə(r)] *n.* Sprengmeister, *der;* Schießmeister, *der;* ~**gun** *n.* [Schrot]flinte, *die;* ~**gun wedding/marriage** *(fig. coll.)* Mußheirat/Mußehe, *die (ugs.)*; ~-**put** *n., no pl., no indef. art. (Athletics)* Kugelstoßen, *das;* ~-**putter** ['ʃɒtpʊtə(r)] *n. (Athletics)* Kugelstoßer, *der/*-stoßerin, *die*

should *see* **shall**

shoulder ['ʃəʊldə(r)] **1.** *n.* **a)** Schulter, *die;* ~ **to ~** *(lit. or fig.)* Schulter an Schulter; **put** *or* **set one's ~ to the wheel** *(fig.)* sich ins Geschirr legen; **straight from the ~** *(fig.)* unverblümt; **cry on sb.'s ~** *(fig.)* sich bei jmdm. ausweinen; *see also* **chip 1a**; **cold shoulder**; **head 1a**; **rub 1a**; **b)** *in pl. (upper part of back)* Schultern *Pl.; (of garment)* Schulterpartie, *die;* **lie** *or* **rest/fall on sb.'s ~s** *(fig.)* auf jmds. Schultern *(Dat.)* lasten/jmdm. aufgebürdet werden; **he has broad ~s** *(fig.: is able to take responsibility)* er hat einen breiten Rücken; **have** *or* **be an old head on young ~s** *(fig.)* reif für sein Alter sein; **have a good head on one's ~s** *(fig.)* Köpfchen haben *(ugs.)*; **c)** *see* ~-**joint a**; **d)** *(Gastr.)* Bug, *der;* Schulter, *die;* ~ **of lamb/veal** Lamm-/Kalbsschulter, *die;* **e)** *(Road Constr.)* Randstreifen, *der;* Seitenstreifen, *der; see also* **hard shoulder**. **2.** *v. t.* **a)** *(push with ~)* rempeln; ~ **one's way through the crowd** sich rempelnd einen Weg durch die Menge bahnen; **b)** *(take on one's ~s)* schultern; *(fig.)* übernehmen ‹*Verantwortung, Aufgabe*›; auf sich *(Akk.)* nehmen ‹*Schuld, Bürde*›; ~ **arms** *(Mil.)* das Gewehr schultern

~ **a'side** *v. t.* beiseite rempeln; *(fig.)* beiseite schieben

shoulder: ~-**bag** *n.* Umhängetasche, *die;* ~-**belt** *n.* Schulterband, *das;* ~-**blade** *n.* Schulterblatt, *das*

-**shouldered** ['ʃəʊldəd] *adj. in comb.* -schult[e]rig; **square-/straight-~**: mit eckigen/geraden Schultern *nachgestellt*

shoulder: ~-**high 1.** ['---] *adj.* schulterhoch; **2.** [--'-] *adv.* **lift/carry sb. ~-high** jmdn. auf die Schultern heben/auf den Schultern tragen; **they carried him through the streets, ~-high** sie trugen ihn auf den Schultern durch die Straßen; ~-**holster** *n.* Schulterhalfter, *die;* ~-**joint** *n.* **a)** *(Anat.)* Schultergelenk, *das;* **b)** *(Gastr.)* Schulterstück, *das;* Bugstück, *das;* ~-**length** *adj.* schulterlang; ~-**pad** *n.* Schulterpolster, *das;* ~-**strap** *n.* **a)** *(on ~ of garment)* Schulterklappe, *die;* **b)** *(on bag)* Tragriemen, *der; (suspending a garment)* Träger, *der*

shouldn't ['ʃʊdnt] *(coll.)* = **should not**; *see* **shall**

shout [ʃaʊt] **1.** *n.* **a)** Ruf, *der; (inarticulate)* Schrei, *der;* **warning ~, ~ of alarm** Warnruf, *der/*-schrei, *der;* ~ **of joy/rage** Freuden-/Wutschrei, *der;* ~ **of encouragement/approval** Anfeuerungs-/Beifallsruf, *der;* **give sb. a ~**: jmdn. rufen; *(fig. coll.: let sb. know)* jmdm. Bescheid sagen; **b)** *(coll.: turn to pay for drinks)* Runde, *die;* **stand sb. a ~**: jmdm. einen ausgeben *(ugs.)*. **2.** *v. i.* **a)** schreien; ~ **with laughter/pain** vor Lachen/Schmerzen schreien; ~ **with** *or* **for joy** vor Freude schreien; ~ **at sb.** *(be loudly abusive to sb.)* jmdn. anschreien; **you don't have to ~ [at me] – I can hear you** Du brauchst nicht zu schreien. Ich höre dich auch so; **don't ~!** schrei nicht so!; **she ~ed for him to come** sie schrie *od.* rief, er solle kommen; **he ~ed to me to be careful/help him** er schrie *od.* rief mir zu, ich solle vorsichtig sein/ihm helfen; ~ **for sb./sth.** nach jmdm./etw. schreien; ~ **for help** um Hilfe schreien *od.* rufen; **it's nothing to ~ about** *(fig.)* darauf braucht er/sie/man *usw.* sich *(Dat.)* nichts einzubilden; **b)** *(Austral. and NZ coll.: stand drinks etc.)* einen ausgeben *(ugs.)* (**for** *Dat.*). **3.** *v.t.* **a)** schreien; ~ **abuse** pöbeln; ~ **oneself hoarse** sich heiser schreien; **b)** *(Austral. and NZ coll.)* ~ **a drink/a beer for sb., ~ sb. to a drink/a beer** jmdm. einen/ein Bier ausgeben *(ugs.)*

~ 'down v.t. a) runterrufen; b) ~ sb. down (prevent from being heard) jmdn. niederschreien
~ 'out 1. v.i. aufschreien; if you know the answer, don't ~ out – wait till ...: wenn ihr die Antwort wißt, schreit nicht einfach los – wartet, bis ... 2. v.t. [laut] rufen; schreien

shouting ['ʃaʊtɪŋ] 1. adj. schreiend. 2. n. (act of shouting) Schreien, das; Schreierei, die (abwertend); (shouts) Geschrei, das; it's all over but or bar the ~ (fig.) das Rennen ist im Grunde schon gelaufen (ugs.)

shove [ʃʌv] 1. n. Stoß, der; little ~: Schubs, der (ugs.); a ~ with one's foot ein Tritt [mit dem Fuß]; ein Fußtritt; get the ~ (coll.) rausfliegen (ugs.); give sb. the ~ (coll.) jmdn. rausschmeißen (ugs.). 2. v.t. a) stoßen; schubsen (ugs.); b) (use force to propel) schieben; c) (coll.: put) tun. See also throat a. 3. v.i. drängen; drängeln (ugs.); ~ past the vehicles/through the crowd (coll.) sich an den Fahrzeugen vorbei/durch die Menge drängeln (ugs.). See also push 2a, 3d
~ a'bout see ~ around
~ a'long (coll.) 1. v.t. schieben. 2. v.i. sich vorwärtsschieben; (fig. sl.: depart) abschieben (ugs.)
~ a'round v.t. (coll.) herumschieben; (fig.) herumschubsen (ugs.)
~ a'way v.t. (coll.) wegschubsen (ugs.)
~ 'off 1. v.t. (coll.) a) (away) wegschubsen (ugs.); b) (down) runterschubsen (ugs.). 2. v.i. a) (coll.: move boat from shore) abstoßen; b) (sl.: depart) abschieben (ugs.)
~ 'over (coll.) 1. v.t. rüberschieben (ugs.). 2. v.i. rüberrücken (ugs.)
~ 'past v.i. (coll.) sich vorbeidrängeln od. -quetschen (ugs.)

shove-'halfpenny n. Spiel, bei dem Münzen in die Felder des Spielbretts gestoßen werden müssen

shovel ['ʃʌvl] 1. n. a) (implement, part of machine) Schaufel, die; (machine) Bagger, der; see also spade a; b) (quantity) see shovelful. 2. v.t., (Brit.) -ll- a) schaufeln; b) (fig.) ~ food into one's mouth Essen in sich reinschaufeln od. -stopfen (ugs.)

shovelful ['ʃʌvlfʊl] n. a ~ of earth etc. eine Schaufel Erde usw.; ~s of earth schaufelweise Erde

show [ʃəʊ] 1. n. a) (act of making visible) Zeigen, das; without any ~ of anger/emotion/grief ohne jedes Zeichen des Ärgers/von Gefühl/der Trauer; ~ of generosity Geste der Großzügigkeit; ~ of knowledge Zurschaustellung von Wissen; make a ~ of sth. etw. zur Schau stellen; ~ of force/strength etc. Demonstration der Macht/Stärke usw.; b) (display) Pracht, die; (spectacle, pageant) Schauspiel, das (geh.); a ~ of flowers/colour eine Blumen-/Farbenpracht; the trees make a wonderful ~: die Bäume entfalten eine wunderbare Pracht; be on ~: ausgestellt sein; put sth. on ~: etw. ausstellen; c) (exhibition) Ausstellung, die; Schau, die; dog ~: Hundeschau, die; ~ animal ausgestelltes Tier; d) (entertainment, performance) Show, die; (Theatre) Vorstellung, die; (Radio, Telev.) [Unterhaltungs]sendung, die; summer ~: Sommerprogramm, das; the ~ must go on die Show geht weiter; (fig.) das Leben geht weiter; see also steal 1a; stop 1b; e) (coll.: effort) that's a very good ~: das kann sich sehen lassen; it's a poor ~: das ist ein schwaches Bild; put up a good/poor ~: eine gute/schlechte Figur machen; good ~! gut [gemacht]!; bad or poor ~! schwaches Bild!; f) (sl.: undertaking, business) it's his ~: er ist der Boss (ugs.); who is running this ~? wer ist hier der Boss? (ugs.); give the [whole] ~ away alles ausquatschen (salopp); see also run 3c; g) (outward appearance) Anschein, der; make a great ~ of friendliness ungeheuer freundlich tun; make or put on a [great] ~ of doing sth. sich (Dat.) [angestrengt] den Anschein geben, etw. zu tun; she puts on a brave ~ of being able to cope sie gibt sich (Dat.) tapfer den Anschein, als käme sie immer gut zurecht; h) (pomp) the pomp and ~ of great State occasions der Pomp und Prunk großer Staatsakte; be for ~: reine Angeberei sein (ugs.); i) (Med.: discharge) (at onset of labour) leichte Blutung als erstes Anzeichen der beginnenden Geburt; (at beginning of menstrual period) Vorzeichen der beginnenden Menstruation. 2. v.t., p.p. ~n [ʃəʊn] or ~ed a) (allow or cause to be seen) zeigen; (produce) vorzeigen ⟨Paß, Fahrschein usw.⟩; ~ one's cards or hand (Cards) seine Karten aufdecken; (fig.: reveal one's intentions) die Karten auf den Tisch legen; have nothing/something to ~ for it [dabei] nichts/etwas zum Vorzeigen haben; see also cause 1c; face 1a; feather 1a; ¹flag 1; tooth a; b) (reveal, disclose) zeigen; ~ sb. sth., ~ sth. to sb. jmdm. etw. zeigen; ~ me an A and I will ~ you a B jedes A ist ein B; that dress ~s your petticoat bei diesem Kleid sieht man deinen Unterrock; this material does not ~ the dirt auf diesem Material sieht man den Schmutz nicht; ~ oneself sich zeigen; ~ itself (become visible) zum Vorschein kommen; (reveal itself) sich zeigen; erkennbar sein; ~ itself at its best/in all its glory sich von der besten Seite/in all seiner Herrlichkeit zeigen; the task has been ~n to be difficult die Aufgabe hat sich als schwierig erwiesen; this episode ~s him to be honest/a liar dieser Vorfall zeigt, daß er ehrlich/ein Lügner ist; ~ oneself/itself to be sth. sich als etw. erweisen; see also ¹heel 1a; colour 1h; sign 1e; c) (manifest, give evidence of) zeigen; beweisen ⟨Mut, Entschlossenheit, Urteilsvermögen usw.⟩; ~ hesitation zaudern; he is ~ing his age man sieht ihm sein Alter an; see also fight 3c; mettle a; willing 2; d) ~ [sb.] kindness/mercy freundlich [zu jmdm.] sein/Erbarmen [mit jmdm.] haben; ~ mercy on or to sb. Erbarmen mit jmdm. haben; e) (indicate) zeigen ⟨Gefühl, Freude usw.⟩; ⟨Thermometer, Uhr usw.:⟩ anzeigen; as ~n in the illustration wie die Abbildung zeigt; the frontiers are ~n by a blue line/towns are ~n in red die Grenzen sind durch eine blaue Linie/Städte sind rot gekennzeichnet; the accounts ~ a profit die Bücher weisen einen Gewinn aus; the firm ~s a profit/loss die Firma macht Gewinn/Verlust; f) (offer for viewing) zeigen; (exhibit in a show) ausstellen; g) (demonstrate, prove) zeigen; ~ sb. that ...: jmdm. beweisen, daß ...; it all/just goes to ~ that ...: das beweist nur, daß ...; it all goes to ~, doesn't it? das beweist es doch, oder?; I'll ~ you/him etc.! ich werd's dir/ihm usw. schon zeigen!; ~ sb. who's boss jmdm. zeigen, wer das Sagen hat; see also door; h) (conduct) führen; ~ sb. over the house/to his place jmdn. durchs Haus/an seinen Platz führen. 3. v.i., p.p. ~n or ~ed a) (be visible) sichtbar od. zu sehen sein; (come into sight) sich zeigen; zum Vorschein kommen; he was angry/bored, and it ~ed er war wütend/langweilte sich, und man sah es [ihm an]; his age is beginning to ~: man sieht ihm sein Alter allmählich an; your slip is ~ing dein Unterrock guckt raus; b) (coll.: arrive) sich blicken lassen (ugs.); auftauchen; c) (be ~n) ⟨Film:⟩ laufen; ⟨Künstler:⟩ ausstellen; 'Gandhi' – now ~ing in the West End „Gandhi" – Jetzt im West End; d) (make sth. known) time will ~: man wird es [ja] sehen; only time will ~: das wird sich erst im Laufe der Zeit herausstellen; e) (Amer. Horse-racing) sich [unter den ersten drei] plazieren
~ 'in v.t. hineinführen/hereinführen
~ 'off 1. v.t. a) (display) ~ sth./sb. off etw./jmdn. vorführen od. vorzeigen; (in order to impress) mit etw./jmdm. prahlen od. (ugs.) angeben; b) (display to advantage) zur Geltung bringen. 2. v.i. angeben (ugs.); prahlen; see also show-off
~ 'out v.t. hinausführen
~ 'round v.t. herumführen
~ 'through v.i. durchscheinen
~ 'up 1. v.t. a) (conduct upstairs) hinaufführen/heraufführen; b) (make visible) deutlich sichtbar machen; aufdecken ⟨Betrug⟩; this incident has ~n him up as or for a coward or to be a coward dieser Vorfall hat gezeigt, daß er [in Wirklichkeit od. eigentlich] ein Feigling ist; c) (coll.: embarrass) blamieren. 2. v.i. a) (be easily visible) [deutlich] zu sehen od. erkennen sein; (fig.) sich zeigen; it will not ~ up on the photocopy das kommt auf der Photokopie nicht heraus; b) (coll.: arrive) sich blicken lassen (ugs.); auftauchen

show: ~ **biz** (sl.), ~ **business** ns., no pl., no art. Schaugeschäft, das; Showbusineß, das; ~-business personalities/connections Persönlichkeiten aus dem/Verbindungen zum Schaugeschäft od. Showbusineß; ~-**case** n. Vitrine, die; Schaukasten, der; (fig.) Schaufenster, das; ~**down** n. (fig.) Kraftprobe, die; have a ~down [with sb.] sich [mit jmdm.] auseinandersetzen

shower ['ʃaʊə(r)] 1. n. a) Schauer, der; ~ of rain/sleet/hail Regen-/Schneeregen-/Hagelschauer, der; a ~ of confetti/sparks/stones/petals ein Konfettiregen/Funkenregen/Steinhagel/Regen von Blütenblättern; a ~ of letters/curses eine Flut von Briefen/Flüchen; b) (~-bath) Dusche, die; attrib. Dusch-; have or take a [cold/quick/daily] ~: [kalt/schnell/täglich] duschen; be under the ~: unter der Dusche stehen; the ~s der Duschraum; c) (Amer.: party) ~ [party] Geschenkparty, die (für eine Braut, bei der sie Aussteuergegenstände geschenkt bekommt); baby ~: Geschenkparty für eine werdende Mutter, bei der sie Babyartikel geschenkt bekommt; d) (Brit. sl.: contemptible persons) Sauhaufen, der (salopp). 2. v.t. a) ~ sth. over or on sb., ~ sb. with sth. jmdn. mit etw. überschütten; b) (fig.: lavish) ~ sth. [up]on sb., ~ sb. with sth. jmdn. mit etw. überhäufen. 3. v.i. a) (fall in ~s) ~ down [up]on sb. ⟨Wasser, Konfetti:⟩ auf jmdn. herabregnen; ⟨Steine, Verwünschungen:⟩ auf jmdn. niederhageln; b) (have a ~-bath) duschen

shower: ~-**bath** n. Dusche, die; ~-**cap** n. Duschhaube, die; ~-**curtain** n. Duschvorhang, der; ~ **gel** n. Duschgel, das; ~-**proof** adj. [bedingt] regendicht

showery ['ʃaʊərɪ] adj. the weather is ~: es herrscht Schauerwetter; outlook ~: weitere Aussichten: schauerartige Regenfälle; a cold and ~ day ein kalter Tag mit häufigen Schauern

show: ~ **flat** n. (Brit.) Musterwohnung, die; ~**girl** n. Showgirl, das; ~**ground** n. Ausstellungsgelände, das; ~ **house** n. Musterhaus, das

showily ['ʃəʊɪlɪ] adv. angeberisch; behave ~: eine Schau machen (ugs.); angeben

showing ['ʃəʊɪŋ] n. a) (of film) Vorführung, die; (of television programme) Sendung, die; at the film's first ~: bei der Premiere des Films; b) (evidence) on this ~: demnach; on any ~: wie man es auch [dreht und] wendet; on or by sb.'s own ~: nach jmds. eigener Darstellung; on present ~: wie es sich im Augenblick darstellt; c) (quality of performance) Leistung, die; make a good/poor etc. ~: eine gute/schwache usw. Leistung zeigen; on this ~: bei dieser Leistung

show: ~-**jumper** n. (Sport) a) (person) Springreiter, der/-reiterin, die; b) (horse) Springpferd, das; ~-**jumping** n. (Sport) Springreiten, das; ~**man** ['ʃəʊmən] n., pl. ~men ['ʃəʊmən] a) (proprietor of fairground *booth etc.)* Schausteller, *der;* **b)** *(person skilled in showmanship)* Showman, *der*

showmanship ['ʃəʊmənʃɪp] *n., no pl.* schauspielerisches Talent; **it's nothing but ~:** es ist reine Schauspielerei

shown *see* **show 2, 3**

show: ~-off *n.* Aufschneider, *der*/Aufschneiderin, *die;* Angeber, *der*/Angeberin, *die (ugs.);* **don't be such a ~-off** gib nicht so an!; **~-piece** *n.* Renommierstück, *das (geh.); (of exhibition, collection)* Schaustück, *das; (highlight)* Paradestück, *das;* **a real ~-piece** ein richtiges Prachtexemplar *od.* -stück *(ugs.);* **~-place** *n.* Attraktion, *die;* **~room** *n.* Ausstellungsraum, *der;* **~room price** Endverbraucherpreis, *der;* **~-stopper** *n. (coll.)* **be a ~-stopper** Furore machen; **~ trial** *n.* Schauprozeß, *der*

showy ['ʃəʊɪ] *adj.* **a)** *(gaudy, ostentatious)* protzig *(ugs.);* **b)** *(striking)* großartig; prächtig ‹*Farben*›; [farben]prächtig ‹*Blumen, Blüten*›

shrank *see* **shrink 1, 2**

shrapnel ['ʃræpnl] *n. (Mil.)* **a)** *(fragments)* Bomben-/Granatsplitter; **piece of ~:** Bomben-/Granatsplitter, *der;* **b)** *(projectile)* Schrapnell, *das; collect.* Schrapnelle

shred [ʃred] **1.** *n.* Fetzen, *der;* **without a ~ of clothing on him/her** ohne einen Fetzen [Kleidung] am Leib; **not a ~ of evidence/truth** keine Spur eines Beweises/kein Fünkchen Wahrheit; **cut/tear** *etc.* **sth. to ~s** etw. in Fetzen schneiden/reißen *usw.;* **tear sb.'s reputation to ~s** jmds. Ruf ruinieren; **tear sb.['s character] to ~s** kein gutes Haar an jmdm. lassen; **tear a theory/an argument to ~s** eine Theorie/eine Argumentation zerpflücken; **in ~s** in Fetzen; **our clothes were in ~s** unsere Kleidung war zerfetzt; **sb.'s nerves are in ~s** *(fig.)* jmd. ist mit den Nerven am Ende; **sb.'s reputation is in ~s** jmds. guter Ruf ist ruiniert. **2.** *v.t.,* **-dd-** [im Reißwolf] zerkleinern ‹*Papier, Textilien*›; raspeln ‹*Gemüse*›

shredder ['ʃredə(r)] *n. (for paper, clothes)* Reißwolf, *der; (kitchen aid)* Raspel, *die;* **~ [attachment]** Schnitzelwerk, *das*

shrew [ʃru:] *n.* **a)** *(Zool.)* Spitzmaus, *die;* **b)** *(woman)* Beißzange, *die (salopp)*

shrewd [ʃru:d] *adj.* scharfsinnig ‹*Mensch*›; klug ‹*Entscheidung, Investition, Schritt, Geschäftsmann*›; genau ‹*Schätzung, Einschätzung*›; treffsicher ‹*Urteilsvermögen*›; **I had a pretty ~ idea** *or* **suspicion what his next move would be** mir war ziemlich klar, was er als nächstes tun würde; **have a ~ mind** scharfsinnig sein

shrewdly ['ʃru:dlɪ] *adv.* klug; **he ~ decided to take the job** er entschloß sich klugerweise dazu, die Stelle anzunehmen

shrewdness ['ʃru:dnɪs] *n., no pl. see* **shrewd:** Scharfsinnigkeit, *die;* Klugheit, *die;* Genauigkeit, *die* Treffsicherheit, *die*

shrewish ['ʃru:ɪʃ] *adj.,* **shrewishly** ['ʃru:ɪʃlɪ] *adv.* zänkisch

'shrew-mouse *see* **shrew a**

shriek [ʃri:k] **1.** *n.* **a)** *(shrill cry)* [Auf]schrei, *der;* **give a ~:** [auf]schreien; **give a ~ of horror/fear** *etc.* einen Schrei des Entsetzens/der Angst *usw.* ausstoßen; **there were ~s of laughter from the children** die Kinder kreischten vor Lachen; **b)** *(high-pitched sound)* Kreischen, *das.* **2.** *v.i.* **a)** *(give shrill cry)* [auf]schreien; **~ with horror/fear** *etc.* vor Entsetzen/Angst *usw.* [auf]schreien; **~ [with laughter]** vor Lachen kreischen; **b)** *(make high-pitched sound)* kreischen. **3.** *v.t.* schreien

~ 'out 1. *v.i.* aufschreien. **2.** *v.t.* schreien

shrift [ʃrɪft] *n.* **give sb. short ~:** jmdn. kurz abfertigen *(ugs.);* **get short ~ [from sb.]** [von jmdm.] kurz abgefertigt werden *(ugs.)*

shrike [ʃraɪk] *n. (Ornith.)* Würger, *der*

shrill [ʃrɪl] **1.** *adj.* schrill; *(fig.)* lautstark. **2.** *v.i.* schrillen. **3.** *v.t.* gellend schreien

shrillness ['ʃrɪlnɪs] *n., no pl.* Schrillheit, *die*

shrilly ['ʃrɪlɪ] *adv.* schrill; *(fig.)* lautstark ‹*fordern, protestieren*›

shrimp [ʃrɪmp] **1.** *n.* **a)** *pl.* **~s** *or* **~** *(Zool.)* Garnele, *die;* Krabbe, *die (ugs.); (Gastr.)* Krabbe, *die; attrib.* Garnelen-/Krabben-; **b)** *(derog.: small person)* Knirps, *der (abwertend).* **2.** *v.i.* Krabben/Garnelen fangen

shrine [ʃraɪn] *n.* **a)** *(tomb)* Grab, *das; (casket)* Schrein, *der (veralt.); (casket holding sacred relics)* Reliquienschrein, *der;* **be a sacred ~ of Christendom** ‹*Altar, Kapelle:*› eines der größten Heiligtümer der Christenheit sein; **b)** *(fig.: place hallowed by memory)* Gedenkstätte, *die;* **~ to sb./sth.** Gedenkstätte für jmdn./etw.

shrink [ʃrɪŋk] **1.** *v.i.,* **shrank** [ʃræŋk], **shrunk** [ʃrʌŋk] **a)** *(grow smaller)* schrumpfen; ‹*Mensch:*› kleiner werden; ‹*Kleidung, Stoff:*› einlaufen; ‹*Metall, Holz:*› sich zusammenziehen; **~ to nothing** ‹*Handel, Einkünfte:*› einen absoluten Tiefststand erreichen; **b)** *(recoil)* sich zusammenkauern; **~ from sb./sth.** vor jmdm. zurückweichen/vor etw. *(Dat.)* zurückschrecken; **~ from doing sth.** sich scheuen, etw. zu tun; *see also* **violet 1 a. 2.** *v.t.,* **shrank, shrunk** sich zusammenziehen lassen ‹*Metall, Holz*›; einlaufen lassen ‹*Textilien*›. **3.** *n.* **a)** *(act)* Schrumpfen, *das; (of fabric)* Einlaufen, *das;* **b)** *(degree) see* **shrinkage b; c)** *(sl.: psychiatrist)* Seelendoktor, *der*

~ a'way *v.i.* **a)** *(recoil)* zurückweichen **(from** vor **+** *Dat.***); b)** *(grow smaller)* zusammenschrumpfen

~ 'back *v.i.* zurückweichen **(from** vor **+** *Dat.***); ~ back from sth./doing sth.** vor etw. *(Dat.)* zurückschrecken/sich scheuen, etw. zu tun

shrinkage ['ʃrɪŋkɪdʒ] *n.* **a)** *(act) (of clothing, material)* Einlaufen, *das; (of income, trade, etc.)* Rückgang, *der;* **b)** *(degree)* Schrumpfung, *die*

shrink: ~-proof, ~-resistant *adjs.* schrumpffrei; **be ~-proof** nicht einlaufen; **~-wrap** *v.t.* in einer Schrumpffolie verpacken

shrive [ʃraɪv] *v.t.,* **shrove** [ʃrəʊv], **shriven** [ʃrɪvn] *(RC Ch. arch.)* **~ sb.** jmdm. die Beichte abnehmen

shrivel ['ʃrɪvl] **1.** *v.t., (Brit.)* **-ll-: ~ [up]** schrump[e]lig machen; runzlig machen ‹*Haut, Gesicht*›. **2.** *v.i., (Brit.)* **-ll-: ~ [up]** verschrumpeln; ‹*Haut, Gesicht:*› runzlig werden; ‹*Ballon:*› zusammenschrumpfen

~ up 1. *v.t. see* **~ 1. 2.** *v.i.* **a)** *see* **~ 2; b)** *(fig.: from fear or nervousness)* verschüchtert werden; **I just wanted to ~ up when ...:** ich wäre am liebsten in den Erdboden versunken, als ...

shrivelled (*Amer.:* **shriveled**) ['ʃrɪvld] *adj.* schrump[e]lig; verschrumpelt; **a ~ old lady** eine verhutzelte alte Frau

shriven *see* **shrive**

shroud [ʃraʊd] **1.** *n.* **a)** Leichentuch, *das (veralt.);* **b)** *(fig.) (of fog, mystery, etc.)* Schleier, *der; (of snow)* Decke, *die;* **c)** *in pl. (of ship)* Wanten *Pl.; (of parachute)* Fangleine, *die.* **2.** *v.t. (cover and conceal)* einhüllen; **~ sth. in sth.** etw. in etw. *(Akk.)* hüllen; **mystery/uncertainty ~s their fate** ein Geheimnis/Ungewißheit umgibt ihr Schicksal *(geh.)*

shrove *see* **shrive**

Shrove [ʃrəʊv]: **~-tide** *n.* Fastnacht, *die;* **~ 'Tuesday** *n.* Fastnachtsdienstag, *der*

shrub [ʃrʌb] *n.* Strauch, *der*

shrubbery ['ʃrʌbərɪ] *n.* **a)** Gesträuch, *das;* **b)** *(shrubs collectively)* Sträucher

shrubby ['ʃrʌbɪ] *adj.* **a)** *(like a shrub)* strauchartig; **b)** *(covered with shrubs)* mit Strauchwerk bewachsen

shrug [ʃrʌg] **1.** *n.* **~ [of one's** *or* **the shoulders]** Achselzucken, *das;* **give a ~ [of one's** *or* **the shoulders]** die/mit den Achseln zucken; **give a ~ of resignation/indifference** *etc.* resigniert/gleichgültig *usw.* mit den Achseln zucken. **2.** *v.t. & i.* **-gg-: ~ [one's shoulders]** die *od.* mit den Achseln zucken

~ 'off *v.t.* in den Wind schlagen; **~ sth. off as unimportant** etw. als unwichtig abtun

shrunk *see* **shrink 1, 2**

shrunken ['ʃrʌŋkn] *adj.* verhutzelt *(ugs.)* ‹*Mensch*›; schrump[e]lig, verschrumpelt ‹*Äpfel*›; *(fig.)* geschrumpft ‹*Reserven, Gewinn, Resourcen*›; **~ head** Schrumpfkopf, *der*

shuck [ʃʌk] *(Amer.)* **1.** *n.* **a)** Schale, *die; (pea-pod)* Hülse, *die;* **b)** *in pl. (slightest amount)* **I don't care ~s about it** es kümmert mich nicht die Bohne *(ugs.);* **~s!** *expr. annoyance, regret* verdammt! *(salopp).* **2.** *v.t.* ausschälen

shudder ['ʃʌdə(r)] **1.** *v.i.* **a)** *(shiver)* zittern **(with** vor **+** *Dat.***); sb. ~s to think of sth.** jmdn. schaudert bei dem Gedanken an etw. *(Akk.);* **b)** *(vibrate)* zittern; **~ to a halt** zitternd zum Stehen kommen. **2.** *n.* **a)** *(shivering)* Zittern, *das;* Schauder, *der;* **sb. has/gets the ~s** *(coll.)* jmdn. schaudert; **it gives me the ~s to think of it** *(coll.)* mich schaudert, wenn ich daran denke; **b)** *(vibration)* Zittern, *das;* **a ~ went through the building** das Gebäude erzitterte

shuffle ['ʃʌfl] **1.** *n.* **a)** Schlurfen, *das;* **walk with a ~:** schlurfend gehen; schlurfen; **b)** *(Cards)* Mischen, *das;* **give the cards a [good] ~:** die Karten [gut] mischen; **it is his ~:** er ist an der Reihe zu mischen; er muß mischen; **c)** *(fig.: change)* Umbildung, *die;* **cabinet/ministerial ~:** Kabinettsumbildung, *die;* **d)** *(Dancing) (movement)* Schlurfschritt, *der; (dance) schlurfender Tanz;* ≈ Schleifer, *der.* **2.** *v.t.* **a)** *(rearrange)* umbilden ‹*Kabinett*›; umbesetzen ‹*Posten*›; sortieren ‹*Schriftstücke usw.*›; *(mix up)* durcheinanderbringen; **b)** *(Cards)* mischen; **c) ~ one's feet in embarrassment** verlegen von einem Fuß auf den anderen treten; **he ~s his feet when he walks** er schlurft beim Gehen. **3.** *v.i.* **a)** *(Cards)* mischen; **b)** *(move, walk)* schlurfen; **c)** *(shift one's position)* herumrutschen

~ a'long *v.i.* dahinschlurfen

~ 'off 1. *v.t.* abstreifen ‹*Kleidungsstück*›; **~ the responsibility off [on to sb.]** die Verantwortung auf jmdn. abwälzen. **2.** *v.i.* wegschlurfen *(ugs.)*

shuffling ['ʃʌflɪŋ] *adj.* schlurfend

shufti ['ʃʊftɪ, 'ʃʌftɪ] *n. (Brit. sl.)* **have a ~ at sth.** sich *(Dat.)* etw. angucken *(ugs.)*

shun [ʃʌn] *v.t.,* **-nn-** meiden

'shun [ʃʌn] *int. (Brit. Mil.)* stillgestanden!

shunt [ʃʌnt] **1.** *v.t.* **a)** *(Railw.)* rangieren; **~ [off]** *(fig.)* abschieben; **b)** *(Electr.)* shunten. **2.** *v.i. (Brit. Railw.)* rangieren. **3.** *n.* **a)** *(Railw.)* Rangieren, *das;* **b)** *(Electr.)* Neben[schluß]widerstand, *der;* Shunt, *der;* **c)** *(Med.)* Shunt, *der;* **d)** *(sl.: collision)* Karambolage, *die (ugs.);* **have a ~:** eine Karambolage haben *(ugs.)*

shunter ['ʃʌntə(r)] *n. (Railw.)* Rangierer, *der*

shush [ʃʊʃ] **1.** *int. see* **hush 3. 2.** *v.i.* **a)** *(call for silence)* um Ruhe bitten; **b)** *(be silent)* still *od.* ruhig sein. **3.** *v.t.* zum Schweigen bringen

shut [ʃʌt] **1.** *v.t.,* **-tt-, shut a)** zumachen; schließen; **~ sth. to sb./sth.** etw. für jmdn./etw. schließen; **~ a road to traffic** eine Straße für den Verkehr sperren; **the strike ~ the factory for a month** der Streik hat die Fabrik für einen Monat lahmgelegt; **~ the door on sb.** jmdm. die Tür vor der Nase zuschlagen *(ugs.);* **~ the door on sth.** *(fig.)* die Möglichkeit einer Sache *(Gen.)* verbauen; **~ one's eyes to sth.** *(fig.)* seine Augen vor etw. *(Dat.)* verschließen; *(turn a blind eye to sth.)* über etw. *(Akk.)* hinwegsehen; **~ one's ears to sth.** *(fig.)* die Ohren vor etw. *(Dat.)*

verschließen; ~ **one's heart to sb./mind to sth.** *(fig.)* sich jmdm./einer Sache verschließen; ~ **your mouth** *or* **trap** *or* **face** *or* **gob** *or* *(Amer.)* **head!** *(sl.: stop talking)* halt den Mund *(ugs.) od.* die Klappe *(salopp) od.* die Fresse *(derb) od.* Schnauze *(derb)!*; ~ **it!** *(sl.: stop talking)* halt die Klappe! *(salopp)*; **b)** *(confine)* ~ **sb./an animal in[to] sth.** jmdn./ein Tier in etw. *(Akk.)* sperren; ~ **oneself in[to] a room** sich in einem Zimmer einschließen; ~ **sth. in a safe** etw. in einen Safe schließen; **c)** *(exclude)* ~ **sb./an animal out of sth.** jmdn./ein Tier aus etw. aussperren; **d)** *(catch)* ~ **one's finger/coat in a door** sich *(Dat.)* den Finger/den Mantel in einer Tür einklemmen; **e)** *(fold up)* schließen, zumachen ‹*Buch, Hand*›; zusammenklappen ‹*Klappmesser, Fächer*›. **2.** *v. i.*, **-tt-, shut** schließen; ‹*Laden:*› schließen, zumachen; ‹*Blüte:*› sich schließen; **the door/case won't ~:** die Tür/der Koffer geht nicht zu *od.* schließt nicht; **the door ~ on/after him** die Tür schloß sich vor/hinter ihm. **3.** *adj.* zu; geschlossen; **bang/kick sth. ~:** etw. zuknallen/mit einem Fußtritt zuschlagen; **bang/swing ~** ‹*Tür:*› zuknallen/zufallen; **we are ~ for lunch/on Saturdays** wir haben über Mittag/samstags geschlossen *od.* zu; **remain** *or* **stay ~:** geschlossen bleiben; zu bleiben; **keep sth. ~:** etw. geschlossen halten *od.* zu lassen; **be** *or* **get ~ of sb./sth.** *(sl.)* = **get shot of sb./sth.** *see* **shot 3 b**

~ **a'way** *v. t.* wegschließen; **keep sth. ~ away safely** etw. unter sicherem Verschluß halten

~ **'down 1.** *v. t.* **a)** zumachen, schließen ‹*Deckel, Fenster*›; **b)** *(shut off)* absperren; **c)** *(terminate operation of)* stillegen; abschalten ‹*Kernreaktor*›; einstellen ‹*Aktivitäten*›; *(Radio, Telev.)* einstellen ‹*Sendebetrieb*›; **the strike has ~ down the factory/newspaper** der Streik hat die Fabrik lahmgelegt/hat das Erscheinen der Zeitung verhindert. **2.** *v. i.* *(cease working)* ‹*Laden, Fabrik:*› geschlossen werden; ‹*Zeitung, Sendebetrieb:*› eingestellt werden; **the winter resorts/ski-lifts ~ down during the summer** die Einrichtungen der Winterkurorte sind im Sommer geschlossen/die Skilifte sind im Sommer außer Betrieb; **the radio/television ~s down after midnight** der Rundfunk/das Fernsehen stellt den Sendebetrieb nach Mitternacht ein; *see also* **shut-down**

~ **'in** *v. t.* **a)** *(keep in)* einschließen; ‹*Damm:*› zurückhalten ‹*Wasser*›; **b)** *(encircle)* umschließen; **feel ~ in** sich eingeschlossen fühlen

~ **'off 1.** *v. t.* **a)** *(stop)* unterbrechen ‹*Strom, Fluß*›; abstellen ‹*Motor, Maschine, Gerät*›; **b)** *(isolate)* absperren; ~ **sb. off from sb./sth.** jmdn. von jmdm./etw. abschneiden; ~ **sb. off from society** jmdn. aus der Gesellschaft ausschließen; ~ **oneself off from sb./sth.** sich gegen jmdn./etw. abkapseln. **2.** *v. i.* *(stop working)* sich abstellen

~ **'out** *v. t.* **a)** *(keep out)* aussperren; versperren ‹*Aussicht*›; *(exclude from view)* verdecken; *(prevent)* ausschließen ‹*Gefahr, Möglichkeit*›; **the skyscraper/tree ~s out the light** der Wolkenkratzer/Baum nimmt das Licht weg; **b)** *(fig.: exclude)* ~ **sb. out from sth.** jmdn. von etw. ausschließen; ~ **out all thoughts/memories of sb./sth.** alle Gedanken/Erinnerungen an jmdn./etw. beiseite schieben; **c)** *(Amer. Sport)* ~ **sb. out** jmdn. nicht zum Zuge kommen lassen. *See also* **shut-out**

~ **'to 1.** *v. t.* [ganz] schließen. **2.** *v. i.* ‹*Tür:*› zufallen

~ **'up 1.** *v. t.* **a)** *(close)* abschließen; zuschließen; ~ **up [the/one's] house** das/sein Haus [sicher] abschließen; *see also* **shop 1 b**; **b)** *(put away)* einschließen ‹*Dokumente, Wertsachen usw.*›; einsperren ‹*Tier, Menschen*›; ~ **sth. up in sth.** etw. in etw. *(Akk.)* schließen; ~ **sb. up in an asylum/a prison** jmdn. in eine Anstalt/ein Gefängnis sperren; **c)** *(reduce to silence)* zum Schweigen bringen. **2.** *v. i.* **a)** *(coll.: be quiet)* den Mund halten *(ugs.)*; ~ **up!** halt den Mund! *(ugs.)*; **b)** *(lock up premises)* abschließen

shut: ~**-down** *n.* **a)** *(stoppage)* Schließung, *die; (of newspaper, operations)* Einstellung, *die;* **b)** *(Radio, Telev.)* Sendeschluß, *der; (period)* Sendepause, *die;* ~**-eye** *n.* *(coll.)* Nickerchen, *das (fam.)*; **get** *or* **have a bit** *or* **a spot of ~-eye** ein Nickerchen halten; ~**-out** *n.* **a)** *(Amer. Sport)* Zu-null-Spiel, *das;* **b)** *(in industrial dispute) see* **lock-out**

shutter ['ʃʌtə(r)] *n.* **a)** Laden, *der; (of window)* Fensterladen, *der;* **put up the ~s** *(fig.: cease business)* zumachen; schließen; **b)** *(Photog.)* Verschluß, *der;* ~ **release** Auslöser, *der;* ~ **setting** [eingestellte] Verschlußzeit, *die;* ~ **speed** Verschlußzeit, *die*

shuttle ['ʃʌtl] **1.** *n.* **a)** *(in loom)* [Web]schützen, *der;* Schiffchen, *das; (in sewing-machine)* Schiffchen, *das;* **b)** *(Transport) (service)* Pendelverkehr, *der;* Pendelservice, *der; (bus)* Pendelbus, *der; (aircraft)* Pendelmaschine, *die; (train)* Pendelzug, *der; see also* **space ~**; **c)** *see* **shuttlecock. 2.** *v. t.* **a)** *(cause to move to and fro)* ~ **sth. backwards and forwards** etw. hin und her schicken; ~ **passengers about** Passagiere hin und her fahren; **b)** *(transport)* im Pendelverkehr transportieren. **3.** *v. i.* pendeln; ~ **backwards and forwards** *or* **to and fro** *or* **back and forth** hin und her pendeln

shuttle: ~**cock** *n.* Federball, *der;* **be tossed backwards and forwards like a ~cock** wie ein Pingpongball hin- und hergehen; ~ **diplomacy** *n.* ≈ Reisediplomatie, *die;* ~ **service** *n.* Pendelverkehr, *der;* Pendelservice, *der*

¹shy [ʃaɪ] **1.** *adj.*, ~**er** *or* **shier** ['ʃaɪə(r)], ~**est** *or* **shiest** ['ʃaɪɪst] **a)** scheu; *(diffident)* schüchtern; **don't be ~:** sei nicht [so] schüchtern!; **feel ~ about doing sth.** sich genieren, etw. zu tun; **feel ~ in sb.'s presence/with sb.** sich in jmds. Gegenwart/bei jmdm. gehemmt fühlen; **be ~ of strangers** eine Scheu vor Fremden haben; **be ~ of doing sth.** Hemmungen haben, etw. zu tun; *see also* **bite 1**; **fight 1 a**; **b)** *(sl.: short)* **be ~ of sth.** knapp mit etw. sein; **he is six months ~ of his retirement** ihm fehlt noch ein halbes Jahr, bis er pensioniert wird *(ugs.)*. **2.** *v. i.* scheuen (**at** vor + *Dat.*)

~ **a'way** *v. i.* ~ **away from sth.** ‹*Pferd:*› vor etw. *(Dat.)* scheuen; ~ **away from sth./doing sth.** *(fig.)* etw. scheuen/sich scheuen, etw. zu tun

²shy 1. *v. t.* *(throw)* ~ **sth. at sth./sb.** etw. auf etw./jmdn. schmeißen *(ugs.)*. **2.** *v. i.* schmeißen *(ugs.)* (**at** nach). **3.** *n.* Wurf, *der;* **have a ~ at sth.** nach etw. schmeißen *(ugs.)*; *see also* **coconut shy**

shyly ['ʃaɪlɪ] *adv.* scheu; *(diffidently)* schüchtern

shyness ['ʃaɪnɪs] *n., no pl.* Scheuheit, *die; (diffidence)* Schüchternheit, *die*

shyster ['ʃaɪstə(r)] *n.* *(Amer. coll.)* Ganove, *der; (lawyer)* Winkeladvokat, *der (abwertend)*

SI [es'aɪ] *adj.* *(Phys.)* SI-; **SI units** SI-Einheiten

si [si:] *see* **te**

Siamese [saɪə'mi:z] **1.** *adj.* siamesisch. **2.** *n., pl. same* **a)** *(Hist.: native of Siam)* Siamese, *der*/Siamesin, *die;* **b)** *(Ling. Hist.) see* **Thai 2 b**; **c)** *(Zool.)* Siamese, *der*

Siamese: ~ **'cat** *n.* Siamkatze, *die;* ~ **'twins** *n. pl.* siamesische Zwillinge

Siberia [saɪ'bɪərɪə] *pr. n.* Sibirien *(das)*

Siberian [saɪ'bɪərɪən] **1.** *adj.* sibirisch. **2.** *n.* Sibirjake, *der*/Sibirjakin, *die*

sibilant ['sɪbɪlənt] **1.** *adj.* zischend; ~ **sound** *see* **2. 2.** *n.* *(Phonet.)* Zischlaut, *der;* Sibilant, *der (fachspr.)*

sibling ['sɪblɪŋ] *n.* *(male)* Bruder, *der; (female)* Schwester, *die; in pl.* Geschwister *Pl.; attrib.* Geschwister-

sibyl ['sɪbɪl] *n.* Sibylle, *die*

sic [sɪk] *adv.* sic

Sicilian [sɪ'sɪljən, sɪ'sɪlɪən] **1.** *adj.* sizil[ian]isch. **2.** *n.* Sizilianer, *der*/Sizilianerin, *die*

Sicily ['sɪsɪlɪ] *pr. n.* Sizilien *(das)*

sick [sɪk] **1.** *adj.* **a)** *(ill)* krank; **mentally ~:** geisteskrank; **be ~ with** *or (arch.)* **of sth.** an etw. *(Dat.)* erkrankt sein; etw. haben; **go ~, fall** *or (coll.)* **take ~:** krank werden; **be off ~:** krank [gemeldet] sein; *see also* **report 2 b**; **b)** *(Brit.: vomiting or about to vomit)* **be ~:** sich erbrechen; **be ~ over sb./sth.** sich über jmdn./etw. erbrechen; **I think I'm going to be ~:** ich glaube, ich muß mich erbrechen *od.* ich muß brechen; **sb. is ~ at** *or* **to his/her stomach** *(Amer.)* jmdm. ist [es] schlecht *od.* übel; **a ~ feeling** ein Übelkeitsgefühl; **sb. gets/feels ~:** jmdm. wird/ist [es] übel *od.* schlecht; **he felt ~ with fear** ihm war vor Angst [ganz] übel; **[as] ~ as a cat** *or* **dog** *(coll.)* speiübel; kotzübel *(derb)*; **I get ~ in cars** beim Autofahren wird mir immer schlecht; **sth. makes sb. ~:** von etw. wird [es] jmdm. schlecht *od.* übel (*see also* **d**); **c)** *(sickly)* elend ‹*Aussehen*›; leidend ‹*Blick*›; matt ‹*Lächeln*›; ungesund ‹*Blässe*›; **d)** *(fig.)* ~ **at heart** niedergeschlagen; **worried ~:** krank vor Sorgen; **the team was ~ at losing** *(coll.)* es hat der Mannschaft schwer zu schaffen gemacht, daß sie verloren hat; **be ~ for home** Heimweh haben; **[as] ~ as a parrot** *(sl.)* völlig fertig *(ugs.)*; **be/get ~ of sb./sth.** jmdn./etw. nicht mehr/allmählich nicht mehr ausstehen können *od.* satt haben/allmählich satt haben; **be ~ and tired** *or* ~ **to death of sb./sth.** *(coll.)* von jmdm./etw. die Nase [gestrichen] voll haben *(ugs.)*; **be ~ of the sight/sound of sb./sth.** *(coll.)* jmdn./etw. nicht mehr sehen/hören können; **be ~ of doing sth.** es satt haben, etw. zu tun; **make sb. ~** *(disgust)* jmdn. anekeln; *(coll.: make envious)* jmdn. ganz neidisch machen; **look ~** *(sl.) (be discomfited, upset)* dumm dastehen *(ugs.)*; *(be unimpressive)* ‹*Leistung, Ergebnis, Bilanz usw.:*› ein schwaches Bild sein *(ugs.)*; ‹*Aktie, Währung usw.:*› mies stehen *(ugs.)*; ‹*Firma:*› mies dastehen *(ugs.)* (*see also* **b**); *see also* **enough 2**; **e)** *(deranged)* pervers; *(morally corrupt)* krank ‹*Gesellschaft*›; *(morbid)* makaber ‹*Witz, Humor, Phantasie*›. **2.** *n.* **a)** *pl.* **the ~:** die Kranken; **b)** *(Brit. coll.: vomit)* Erbrochene, *das;* Kotze, *die (salopp)*. **3.** *v. t.* *(coll.)* ~ **[up]** erbrechen; ausspucken *(ugs.)*

sick: ~**-bay** *see* **³bay c**; ~**-bed** *n.* Krankenbett, *das;* ~**-benefit** *n.* *(Brit.)* Krankengeld, *das*

sicken ['sɪkn] **1.** *v. i.* **a)** *(become ill)* krank werden; erkranken *(geh.)*; **be ~ing for an illness/the measles** *(Brit.)* krank werden/[die] Masern bekommen; **that child is ~ing for something** *(Brit.)* das Kind wird krank *od. (ugs.)* brütet etwas aus; **b)** *(feel nausea or disgust)* ~ **at sth.** sich vor etw. *(Dat.)* ekeln; ~ **of sth./of doing sth.** einer Sache *(Gen.)* überdrüssig sein/es überdrüssig sein, etw. zu tun. **2.** *v. t.* **a)** *(cause to feel ill)* **sth. ~s sb.** bei etw. wird jmdm. übel; **b)** *(disgust)* **you ~/your behaviour ~s me** du widerst mich an/dein Benehmen widert mich an; **doesn't it ~ you?** findest du es nicht auch widerlich?

sickening ['sɪknɪŋ] *adj.* **a)** ekelerregend; widerlich ‹*Anblick, Geruch*›; **with a ~ thud** mit einem entsetzlichen dumpfen Geräusch; **b)** *(coll.: infuriating)* unerträglich; **it's really ~:** es kann einen krank machen

sickeningly ['sɪknɪŋlɪ] *adv.* **a)** ekelerregend; **his ~ unctuous manner** seine widerliche salbungsvolle Art; **b)** *(coll.: infuriatingly)* unverschämt *(ugs.)*

sick 'headache *n.* Migräne, *die*

sickle ['sɪkl] *n.* Sichel, *die; see also* **hammer 1 a**

'**sick-leave** *n.* Urlaub wegen Krankheit, *der;* Genesungsurlaub, *der (Milit.);* **be on ~:** ≈ krank geschrieben sein

sickle: ~ cell *n. (Med.)* Sichelzelle, *die;* **~-cell anaemia** Sichelzellenanämie, *die;* **~-shaped** *adj.* sichelförmig

'**sick-list** *n.* Liste der Kranken, *die;* **on the ~:** krank [gemeldet/geschrieben]

sickly ['sɪklɪ] *adj.* **a)** *(ailing)* kränklich; **b)** *(weak, faint)* schwach; matt ‹*Lächeln*›; kraftlos ‹*Sonne*›; fahl ‹*Licht*›; blaß ‹*Hautfarbe, Gesicht*›; **a ~ grey dawn/light** eine fahlgraue Dämmerung/ein fahlgraues Licht; **c)** *(nauseating)* ekelhaft; widerlich; *(mawkish)* süßlich; **~-sweet** ekelhaft süßlich; *(fig.: over-sentimental)* zuckersüß *(abwertend)*

'**sick-making** *adj. (coll.)* **a) sth. is ~:** von etw. wird einem schlecht; **b)** *(fig.: annoying)* unverschämt *(ugs.)*

sickness ['sɪknɪs] *n.* **a)** *no art. (being ill)* Krankheit, *die;* **in ~ and in health** in Gesundheit und in Krankheit; *see also* **bed 1 a; benefit 1 b; b)** *(disease; also fig.)* Krankheit, *die;* **childhood ~:** Kinderkrankheit, *die;* **c)** *(nausea)* Übelkeit, *die; (vomiting)* Erbrechen, *das;* **bout of ~:** Anfall von Erbrechen; *see also* **morning sickness**

sick: ~-nurse *see* **nurse 1; ~-pay** *n.* Entgeltfortzahlung im Krankheitsfalle; *(paid by insurance)* Krankengeld, *das;* **~-room** *n.* Krankenzimmer, *das*

side [saɪd] **1.** *n.* **a)** Seite, *die;* **another car rammed the ~ of ours** ein anderer Wagen rammte unseren an der Seite; **this ~ up** oben; **lie on its ~:** auf der Seite liegen; **put** *or* **lay sth. on its ~:** etw. auf die Seite legen; **over the ~** *(over gunwale of ship/boat)* über Bord *(Akk.);* **lean over the ~** *(Naut.)* sich über die Reling lehnen; **b)** *(Math.: boundary of plane figure)* Seite, *die;* **c)** *(of flat object)* Seite, *die;* **on both ~s** auf beiden Seiten; *see also* **bread 1 a; coin 1; right side; wrong side; d)** *(of animal or person)* Seite, *die;* **be hit in the ~:** in die Seite getroffen werden; **sleep on one's right/left ~:** auf der rechten/linken Seite schlafen; **paralysed in/on/down one ~:** halbseitig gelähmt; **~ of mutton/beef/pork** Hammel-/Rinder-/Schweinehälfte, *die;* **~ of bacon** Speckseite, *die;* **split** *(fig.) or* **burst** *(fig.)***/shake one's ~s [laughing** *or* **with laughter]** vor Lachen platzen/sich vor Lachen nicht mehr halten können; **walk/stand ~ by ~:** nebeneinander gehen/stehen; **work/fight** *etc.* **~ by ~ [with sb.]** Seite an Seite [mit jmdm.] arbeiten/kämpfen *usw.;* **live ~ by ~ [with sb.]** in [jmds.] unmittelbarer Nachbarschaft leben; **live ~ by ~ with death/poverty** in der ständigen Gegenwart des Todes/der Armut leben; *see also* **blind side; thorn c; e)** *(part away from the centre)* Seite, *die;* **the eastern ~ of the town** der Ostteil der Stadt; **the ~s of sb.'s mouth** jmds. Mundwinkel; **right[-hand]/left[-hand] ~:** rechte/linke Seite; **on the right[-hand]/left[-hand] ~ of the road** auf der rechten/linken Straßenseite; **from ~ to ~** *(right across)* quer hinüber; *(alternately each way)* von einer Seite auf die andere *od.* zur anderen; **to one ~:** zur Seite; **on one ~:** an der Seite; **on one ~ of his face** auf einer Seite seines Gesichts; **stand on** *or* **to one ~:** an *od.* auf der Seite stehen; **take sb. to** *or* **on one ~:** jmdn. zur Seite nehmen; **leave a question to** *or* **on one ~:** eine Frage beiseite lassen; **put** *or* **set** *or* **place sth. on one ~ [for sb./sth.]** etw. [für jmdn./etw.] beiseite legen; **put sth. on one ~** *(fig.) (postpone dealing with sth.)* etw. beiseite legen; **on the ~** *(fig.) (in addition to regular work or income)* nebenbei; nebenher; *(as a ~-bet)* als zusätzliche Wette; *(secretly)* insgeheim; *(Amer.: as a ~-dish)* als Beilage; **tell sb. sth. on the ~:** jmdm. etw. im Vertrauen erzählen/sagen; **she is his/he has a bit on the ~** *(sl.)* mit ihr treibt er's noch nebenbei *(ugs.)*/er hat nebenbei noch 'ne andere *(ugs.);* **pass by on the other ~** *(fig.)* so tun, als ginge es einen nichts an; *see also* **laugh 2; f)** *(space beside person or thing)* Seite, *die;* **he never left her ~:** er wich nie von ihrer Seite; **at** *or* **by sb.'s ~:** an jmds. Seite; neben jmdm.; **at** *or* **by the ~ of the car** beim *od.* am Auto; **at** *or* **by the ~ of the road/lake/grave** an der Straße/am See/am Grab; **look tiny by the ~ of sb./sth.** neben jmdm./etw. winzig wirken; **on all ~s** *or* **every ~:** von allen Seiten ‹*umzingelt, kritisiert*›; **look on all ~s** sich nach allen Seiten umsehen; **from all ~s** *or* **every ~:** von allen Seiten; **g)** *(in relation to dividing line)* Seite, *die;* **[on] either ~ of** beiderseits, auf beiden Seiten (+ *Gen.*); **[to** *or* **on] one ~ of** neben (+ *Dat.*); **this/the other ~ of** *(with regard to space)* diesseits/jenseits (+ *Gen.*); *(with regard to time)* vor/nach (+ *Dat.*); **he is this ~ of fifty** er ist unter fünfzig; **what he did was only just this ~ of fraud/perfection** was er tat, war hart an der Grenze zum Betrug/war schon fast perfekt; **this ~ [of] the grave** im Diesseits; **on the other ~** *(fig.: after death)* im Jenseits; *see also* **grass 1 a; right side; wrong side; h)** *(aspect)* Seite, *die; (department)* Bereich, *der;* **see both ~s [of the question]** beide Seiten verstehen; **there are two ~s to every question** alles hat seine zwei Seiten; **look on the bright/gloomy ~ [of things]** die Dinge von der angenehmen/düsteren Seite sehen; **see the funny ~ of sth.** etw. von der komischen Seite sehen; **be on the high/flat/expensive** *etc.* **~:** [etwas] hoch/flach/teuer *usw.* sein; *see also* **err; safe 2 b; seamy b; i)** *(opposing group or position)* Seite, *die;* Partei, *die; (Sport: team)* Mannschaft, *die;* **put sb.'s ~:** jmds. Seite vertreten; **be on the winning ~** *(fig.)* auf der Seite der Gewinner stehen; **let the ~ down** *(fig.)* versagen; **change ~s** zur anderen Seite überwechseln; **time is on sb.'s ~:** die Zeit arbeitet für jmdn.; **whose ~ are you/is he on?** auf wessen Seite stehst du/steht er?; **take sb.'s ~:** sich auf jmds. Seite stellen; **take ~s [with/against sb.]** [für/gegen jmdn.] Partei ergreifen; **keep one's ~ of a bargain** seinen Teil einer Abmachung einhalten; *see also* **no side; j)** *(of family)* Seite, *die;* **on one's/sb.'s father's/mother's ~:** väterlicher-/mütterlicherseits; **the Welsh ~ of the family** der walisische Teil der Familie; **k)** *(Brit. Billiards/Snooker)* Effet, *der;* **put ~ on** *or* **apply ~ to the ball** dem Ball Effet geben; **l)** *(Math.: of equation)* Seite, *die.* **2.** *v.i.* **~ with sb.** sich auf jmds. Seite *(Akk.)* stellen; **~ against sb.** sich gegen jmdn. stellen. **3.** *adj.* seitlich; Seiten-

side: ~-arms *n. pl. (Mil.)* Seitengewehre; **~-band** *n. (Radio)* Seitenband, *das;* **~-bet** *n. (Gambling)* zusätzliche Wette; **~board** *n.* Anrichte, *die;* Sideboard, *das;* **~boards** *(coll.),* **~burns** *ns. pl.* **a)** Backenbart, *der;* **b)** *(hair growing down in front of the ears)* Koteletten *Pl.;* **~-car** *n.* Beiwagen, *der*

-sided ['saɪdɪd] *adj. in comb.* -seitig; **a high-~ enclosure/box** eine hohe Einfriedung/Schachtel; **a glass-~ showcase** ein Schaukasten mit gläsernen Seitenwänden; **a steep-~ mountain** ein steiler Berg; **an open-~ structure** eine seitlich offene Konstruktion

side: ~-dish *n.* Beilage, *die;* **~-door** *n.* Seitentür, *die;* **by a ~-door** *(fig.)* durch eine Hintertür; **~-drum** *n. (Mus.)* kleine Trommel; **~-effect** *n.* Nebenwirkung, *die;* **~-entrance** *n.* Seiteneingang, *der;* **~-exit** *n.* Seitenausgang, *der;* **~-glance** *n. (lit. or fig.)* Seitenblick, *der* **(at** auf + *Akk.*); **~-issue** *n.* Randproblem, *das;* **~-kick** *n. (coll.)* Kumpan, *der;* **~light** *n.* **a)** *(Motor Veh.)* Begrenzungsleuchte, *die;* **drive on ~lights** mit Standlicht fahren; **b)** *(Naut.)* Seitenlaterne, *die;* **c)** *(light from the ~)* Seitenlicht, *das;* **d)** *(fig.: incidental information)* Streiflicht, *das;* **~line 1.** *n.* **a)** *(goods)* Nebensortiment, *das;* **b)** *(occupation)* Nebenbeschäftigung, *die;* **c)** *in pl. (Sport)* Begrenzungslinien; **on the ~lines** *(outside play area/track etc.)* am Spielfeldrand/am Rande der Bahn *(usw.);* **be content to sit on the ~lines** *(fig.)* sich mit einer Zuschauerrolle begnügen; **remain on the ~lines** *(fig.)* sich [aus allem] heraushalten; **2.** *v.t. (Amer. Sport)* **be ~-lined because of injury/with a broken arm** wegen einer Verletzung/eines gebrochenen Arms ausfallen; **~-line sb. for foul play** jmdn. wegen eines Fouls vom Platz stellen; **~long 1.** *adj. (directed to one ~)* **a ~long look/glance** ein Seitenblick; **2.** *adv.* seitwärts; **look/glance ~long at sb.** einen Seitenblick auf jmdn. werfen; **~-on 1.** *adj.* seitlich; **2.** *adv.* seitlich; **look at sth. ~-on** etw. von der Seite ansehen; **~-piece** *n.* Seitenteil, *das; (of ladder)* Holm, *der; (of spectacles)* Bügel, *der;* **~-plate** *n.* kleiner Teller *(neben dem Teller für das Hauptgericht)*

sidereal [saɪ'dɪərɪəl] *adj.* siderisch; **~ time** siderische [Umlauf]zeit; *see also* **year a**

side: ~-road *n.* Seitenstraße, *die;* **~-saddle 1.** *n.* Damensattel, *der;* **2.** *adv.* **ride ~-saddle** im Damensattel reiten; **~-salad** *n.* Salat [als Beilage]; **steak with chips and a ~-salad** Steak mit Pommes frites und dazu ein Salat; **~-shoot** *n. (Bot.)* Seitensproß, *der;* **~-show** *n.* Nebenattraktion, *die;* **~-slip 1.** *n.* **a)** *(Aeronaut.)* seitliches Abrutschen; **b)** *(sideways skid)* seitliches Wegrutschen; **2.** *v.i.* **a)** *(Aeronaut.)* seitlich abrutschen; **b)** *(skid sideways)* seitlich wegrutschen; **~sman** ['saɪdzmən] *n., pl.* **~smen** ['saɪdzmən] *(Eccl.)* Kirchendiener, *der;* **~-spin** *see* **~ 1 k; ~-splitting** *adj.* zwerchfellerschütternd; **be ~-splitting** zum Brüllen sein *(ugs.);* **~-splittingly** ['saɪdsplɪtɪŋlɪ] *adv.* **be ~-splittingly funny** zum Brüllen sein *(ugs.);* **~-step 1.** *n.* Schritt zur Seite, *der; (in dancing)* Seitenschritt, *der;* **2.** *v.t. (lit. or fig.)* ausweichen (+ *Dat.*); **3.** *v.i.* zur Seite treten; *(fig.)* ausweichen; **~-street** *n.* Seitenstraße, *die;* **~-swipe** *n.* Seitenhieb, *der;* **take a ~-swipe at sb./sth.** *(fig.)* einen Seitenhieb auf jmdn./etw. austeilen; **~-table** *n.* Beistelltisch, *der;* **~track 1.** *n. (Railw.) see* **siding; 2.** *v.t.* **a)** *(Railw.)* auf ein Nebengleis schieben; **b)** *(fig.)* **get ~-tracked** abgelenkt werden; **~-trip** *n.* kleiner Ausflug; Abstecher, *der;* **~-view** *n.* Seitenansicht, *die;* **~walk** *n. (Amer.) see* **pavement a; ~wall** *n.* Seitenwand, *die;* **~ways** ['saɪdweɪz] **1.** *adv.* seitwärts; **look at sb./sth. ~ways** jmdn./etw. von der Seite ansehen; **look ~ways at sb.** *(fig.)* jmdn. von der Seite ansehen; jmdn. schief ansehen *(ugs.);* **be knocked ~ways** *(fig. coll.) (be devastated)* am Boden zerstört sein *(ugs.)* **(by** von); *(be very amazed)* [ganz] von den Socken sein *(ugs.)* **(by** über + *Akk.*); **~ways on** von der Seite; **~ways on to sth.** quer zu etw.; **2.** *adj.* seitlich; **~ways view/look** *or* **glance** Seitenansicht, *die*/Seitenblick, *der;* **~-whiskers** *n. pl.* Backenbart, *der;* **~ wind** *n.* Seitenwind, *der*

siding ['saɪdɪŋ] *n. (Railw.)* Abstellgleis, *das;* Rangiergleis, *das*

sidle ['saɪdl] *v.i.* schleichen; **~ up to sb.** [sich] zu jmdm. schleichen

siege [si:dʒ] *n. (Mil.)* Belagerung, *die; (by police)* Umstellung, *die;* **be under ~** *(lit. or fig.)* belagert sein; *(by police)* umstellt sein; **lay ~ to sth.** *(lit. or fig.)* etw. belagern

sienna [sɪ'enə] *n. (Art)* **raw/burnt ~:** Siena natur/gebrannte Siena

sierra [sɪ'erə] *n. (Geog.)* Sierra, *die*

siesta [sɪ'estə] *n.* Siesta, *die;* **have** *or* **take a ~:** [eine] Siesta halten *od.* machen

sieve [sɪv] **1.** *n.* Sieb, *das;* **have a head** *or* **memory like a ~** *(coll.)* ein Gedächtnis wie ein Sieb haben *(ugs.).* **2.** *v.t.* sieben; *(fig.: select by examining)* [aus]sieben
~ **'out** *v.t.* aussieben
sift [sɪft] **1.** *v.t.* sieben; *(fig.: examine closely)* unter die Lupe nehmen; **~ together the flour, salt, and baking-powder** Mehl, Salz und Backpulver [zusammen] in ein Gefäß sieben; **~ sth. from sth.** etw. von etw. trennen. **2.** *v.i.* **~ through** durchsehen ‹*Briefe, Dokumente usw.*›; durchsuchen ‹*Trümmer, Asche, Habseligkeiten usw.*›
~ **'out** *v.t. (lit. or fig.)* aussieben; **~ out sth. from sth.** etw. aus etw. heraussieben; *(fig.)* etw. von etw. trennen
sifter ['sɪftə(r)] *n. (Cookery)* Sieb, *das*
sigh [saɪ] **1.** *n.* Seufzer, *der;* **give** *or* **breathe** *or* **utter** *or* **heave a ~:** einen Seufzer ausstoßen *od.* tun; **~ of relief/sadness/contentment** Seufzer der Erleichterung/trauriger Seufzer/Seufzer der Zufriedenheit. **2.** *v.i.* seufzen; **~ with relief/despair/contentment** *etc.* vor Erleichterung/Verzweiflung/Zufriedenheit *usw. od.* erleichtert/verzweifelt/zufrieden *usw.* seufzen; **~ for sth./sb.** *(fig.)* sich nach etw./jmdm. sehnen; nach etw./jmdm. seufzen *(geh.).* **3.** *v.t.* seufzen
sight [saɪt] **1.** *n.* **a)** *(faculty)* Sehvermögens, *das;* **loss of ~:** Verlust des Sehvermögens; **spoil** *or* **ruin one's ~:** sich *(Dat.)* die Augen verderben; **second ~:** das Zweite Gesicht; **near ~** *see* **short sight; by ~:** mit dem Gesichtssinn *od.* den Augen; **know sb. by ~:** jmdn. vom Sehen kennen; *see also* **long sight; short sight; b)** *(act of seeing)* Anblick, *der;* **at [the] ~ of sb./of blood** bei jmds. Anblick/beim Anblick von Blut; **it was our first ~ of the sea** es war das erste Mal, daß wir das Meer sahen; **catch ~ of sb./sth.** *(lit. or fig.)* jmdn./etw. erblicken; **lose ~ of sb./sth.** *(lit. or fig.)* jmdn./etw. aus dem Auge *od.* den Augen verlieren; **be lost to ~:** den Blicken entschwunden sein *(geh.);* **disappear from ~:** [den Blicken] entschwinden *(geh.);* **have** *or* **get a good/quick ~ of sth.** etw. gut/kurz sehen können; **keep ~ of sth.** *(lit. or fig.)* etw. im Auge behalten; **read music at ~:** Noten vom Blatt lesen; **play sth. at ~:** etw. vom Blatt spielen; **translate a text at ~:** einen Text aus dem Stegreif übersetzen; **shoot sb. at** *or* **on ~:** jmdn. gleich [bei seinem Erscheinen] erschießen; **the guards had orders to shoot at** *or* **on ~:** die Wachen hatten Befehl, [auf jeden] sofort zu schießen; ; **buy sth. ~ unseen** etw. unbesehen kaufen; **at first ~:** auf den ersten Blick; **love at first ~:** Liebe auf den ersten Blick; *see also* **'line 1 c; c)** *(opinion)* **in sb.'s ~:** in jmds. Augen *(Dat.);* **in the ~ of God/of the law** vor Gott/vor dem Gesetz; **d)** *(spectacle)* Anblick, *der;* **be a sorry ~:** einen traurigen Anblick *od.* ein trauriges Bild bieten; **it is a ~ to see** *or* **to behold** *or* **worth seeing** das muß man gesehen haben; **a ~ for sore eyes** eine Augenweide; **be/look a [real] ~** *(coll.) (amusing)* [vollkommen] unmöglich aussehen *(ugs.); (horrible)* böse *od.* schlimm aussehen; **e)** *in pl. (noteworthy features)* Sehenswürdigkeiten *Pl.;* **see the ~s** sich *(Dat.)* die Sehenswürdigkeiten ansehen; **f)** *(range)* Sichtweite, *die;* **in ~** *(lit. or fig.)* in Sicht; **in sb.'s ~, in ~ of sb.** vor jmds. Augen *(Dat.);* **come into ~:** in Sicht kommen; **keep sb./sth. in ~** *(lit. or fig.)* jmdn./etw. im Auge behalten; **victory/our goal is now within** *or* **in [our] ~** *(fig.)* der Sieg/unser Ziel ist jetzt in Sicht; **within** *or* **in ~ of sb./sth.** *(able to see)* in jmds. Sichtweite *(Dat.)*/in Sichtweite einer Sache; **come/get within ~ of sb./sth.** in jmds. Sichtweite *(Akk.)*/in Sichtweite einer Sache kommen; **keep** *or* **stay within** *or* **in ~ of sth./sb.** in Sichtweite *(Dat.)* einer Sache/in jmds. Sichtweite *(Dat.)* bleiben; **out of sb.'s ~:** außerhalb jmds. Sichtweite; **be out of ~:** außer Sicht sein; *(sl.: be excellent)* wahnsinnig sein *(ugs.);* **drop out of ~** *(fig.)* aus dem Blickfeld verschwinden; **vanish out of ~:** verschwinden; **keep out of [sb.'s] ~:** sich [von jmdm.] nicht sehen lassen; sich [jmdm.] nicht zeigen; **I thought it best to keep out of his ~:** ich hielt es für das beste, ihm nicht unter die Augen zu kommen; **keep sth./sb. out of sb.'s ~:** jmdn. etw./jmdn. nicht sehen lassen; **put sth. out of [sb.'s] ~:** etw. [vor jmdm.] verstecken; **not let sb./sth. out of one's ~:** jmdn./etw. nicht aus den Augen lassen; **[get] out of my ~!** geh mir aus den Augen!; verschwinde! *(ugs.);* **out of ~, out of mind** *(prov.)* aus den Augen, aus dem Sinn; **g)** *(aim, observation)* **take a ~:** zielen; **take a ~ at sth.** etw. anvisieren; *(with gun)* auf etw. *(Akk.)* zielen; **h)** *(device for aiming)* Visier, *das;* **~s** Visiervorrichtung, *die;* **telescopic ~:** Zielfernrohr, *das;* **line sth./sb. up in one's ~s** auf etw./jmdn. zielen; etw./jmdn. anvisieren; **have sth./sb. [lined up] in one's ~s** etw./jmdn. im Visier haben; *(fig.)* es auf etw./jmdn. abgesehen haben; **have** *or* **set one's ~s on sth.** *(fig.)* etw. anpeilen; **his ~s were set on doing it** er hatte es sich *(Dat.)* zum Ziel gesetzt, es zu tun; **set one's ~s [too] high** *(fig.)* seine Ziele [zu] hoch stecken; **lower/raise one's ~s** *(fig.)* zurückstecken/sich *(Dat.)* ein höheres Ziel setzen; **i)** *no pl., no def. art. (coll.: great deal)* **a ~ too clever/expensive** *etc.* entschieden zu schlau/teuer *usw.;* **a [long** *or* **damn** *or* **damned] ~ better/more expensive** *etc.* entschieden besser/teurer *usw.;* **not by a long ~:** lange *od.* längst nicht. **2.** *v.t.* **a)** sichten ‹*Land, Schiff, Flugzeug, Wrack*›; sehen ‹*Entflohenen, Vermißten*›; antreffen ‹*seltenes Tier, seltene Pflanze*›; **b)** *(take ~ of)* anvisieren
sighted ['saɪtɪd] *adj.* sehend; **partially ~:** [hochgradig] sehbehindert; **the blind and the partially ~** Blinde und [hochgradig] Sehbehinderte
sighting ['saɪtɪŋ] *n.* Beobachtung, *die;* **there have been several ~s of the escaped prisoner** der entflohene Häftling wurde mehrfach gesehen
sightless ['saɪtlɪs] *adj.* blind
sight: ~-read *(Mus.) v.t. & i.* ‹*Pianist usw.:*› vom Blatt spielen; ‹*Sänger:*› vom Blatt singen; **~-reader** *n. (Mus.)* **be a good/poor ~-reader** ‹*Pianist usw.:*› gut/schlecht vom Blatt spielen; ‹*Sänger:*› gut/schlecht vom Blatt singen; **~-reading** *n., no pl. (Mus.)* **be good/bad** *or* **poor at ~-reading** ‹*Pianist usw.:*› gut/schlecht vom Blatt spielen [können]; ‹*Sänger:*› gut/schlecht vom Blatt singen [können]; **~-screen** *n. (Cricket)* Kontrastschirm, *der;* **~seeing** *n.* Sightseeing, *das (Touristikjargon);* **go ~seeing** Besichtigungen machen; **do [a lot of] ~seeing** [viele] Sehenswürdigkeiten besichtigen; **~seeing bus** Sightseeingbus, *der;* **~seeing tour/trip** Besichtigungsfahrt, *die;* Sightseeingtour, *die (Touristikjargon); (in town)* Stadtrundfahrt, *die;* **~seer** *n.* Tourist *(der die Sehenswürdigkeiten besichtigt);* **~-testing** *n.* Durchführung von Sehtests; **~-testing is free** Sehtests sind kostenlos
sigma ['sɪgmə] *n.* Sigma, *das*
sign [saɪn] **1.** *n.* **a)** *(symbol)* Zeichen, *das;* **chemical/mathematical ~:** chemisches/mathematisches Zeichen; **b)** *(Astrol.)* **~ [of the zodiac]** [Tierkreis]zeichen, *das;* Sternzeichen, *das;* **what ~ are you?** welches Tierkreiszeichen *od.* Sternzeichen bist du?; **sb.'s birth ~:** jmds. Tierkreiszeichen; **c)** *(notice)* Schild, *das;* **direction ~:** Wegweiser, *der;* **[advertising] ~:** Reklameschild, *das;* Reklame, *die; (illuminated, flashing)* Leuchtreklame, *die;* **danger ~** *(lit. or fig.)* Gefahrenzeichen, *das;* **d)** *(outside shop etc.) see* **signboard; e)** *(indication)* Zeichen, *das; (of future event)* Anzeichen, *das;* **his behaviour is a ~ that he is unhappy** sein Verhalten ist ein Zeichen dafür, daß er unglücklich ist; **there is little/no/every ~ of a quick settlement of the strike** *or* **that the strike will be settled quickly** wenig/nichts/alles deutet auf eine baldige Beendigung des Streiks hin *od.* deutet darauf hin, daß der Streik bald beendet wird; **this is a ~ of his intelligence** das zeugt von seiner Intelligenz; **she gave** *or* **showed no ~ of having heard** *or* **that she had heard me** *(did not reveal)* sie ließ durch nichts erkennen, daß sie mich gehört hatte; *(there was no indication)* es deutete nichts darauf hin, daß sie mich gehört hatte; **if he was angry, he gave no ~ of it** wenn er ärgerlich war, so zeigte er es doch nicht; **show [no] ~s of fear/fatigue/strain/improvement** *etc.* [keine] Anzeichen der Angst/Müdigkeit/Anstrengung/Besserung *usw.* zeigen *od.* erkennen lassen; **the carpet showed little/some ~[s] of wear** der Teppich wirkte kaum/etwas abgenutzt; **the cave shows ~s of having been inhabited** in der Höhle gibt es Anzeichen dafür, daß sie bewohnt war; **the window shows no ~[s] of having been forced** das Fenster zeigt keine Spuren von Gewaltanwendung; **as a ~ of** als Zeichen (+ *Gen.*); **do sth. as a ~ of sth.** etw. zum Zeichen einer Sache *(Gen.)* tun; **at the first** *or* **slightest ~ of sth.** schon beim geringsten Anzeichen von etw.; **there was no ~ of him/the car anywhere** er/der Wagen war nirgends zu sehen; **there was no ~ of life** keine Menschenseele war zu sehen; **~ of the times** Zeichen der Zeit; **f)** *(gesture, signal)* Zeichen, *das;* **give sb. a ~ to do sth., make a ~ to** *or* **for sb. to do sth.** jmdm. ein Zeichen geben, etw. zu tun; *see also* **V-sign; g)** *(mark)* Zeichen, *das;* **h)** *(Math.)* Vorzeichen, *das.* **2.** *v.t.* **a)** *(write one's name etc. on)* unterzeichnen; unterschreiben; ‹*Künstler, Autor:*› signieren ‹*Werk*›; **~ the guestbook** sich ins Gästebuch eintragen; **a ~ed copy [of a book]** ein [hand]signiertes Exemplar [eines Buches]; **~ed, sealed, and delivered** *(Law)* unterschrieben, gesiegelt und ausgehändigt; *(fig.)* unter Dach und Fach; **b) ~ one's name** [mit seinem Namen] unterzeichnen *od.* unterschreiben; **~ oneself R.A. Smith** mit R.A. Smith unterschreiben; **c)** *see* **~ up 1; d)** *(indicate)* zeigen. **3.** *v.i.* **a)** *(write one's name)* unterschreiben; **~ for sth.** *(acknowledge receipt of sth.)* etw. quittieren; *(~ a contract etc. for sth.)* [einen Vertrag über] etw. *(Akk.)* unterschreiben; **b)** *(signal)* **~ to sb. to do sth.** jmdm. ein Zeichen geben, etw. zu tun; **c)** *see* **~ on 2 a**
~ **a'way** *v.t.* abtreten ‹*Eigentum*›; verzichten auf ‹*Recht, Freiheit usw.*›
~ **'in 1.** *v.t.* **~ sb./sth. in [on arrival]** jmds. Eintreffen/das Eintreffen einer Sache schriftlich vermerken *od.* registrieren. **2.** *v.i.* sich [bei der Ankunft] eintragen
~ **'off 1.** *v.i.* **a)** *(cease employment)* kündigen; ‹*Seemann:*› abheuern, abmustern *(Seemannsspr.);* **b)** *(at end of shift etc.)* sich [zum Feierabend *usw.*] abmelden; **c)** *(Radio)* sich verabschieden; ‹*Pilot:*› die Frequenz verlassen *(Funkw.);* **d)** *(at end of letter)* Schluß machen. **2.** *v.t.* kündigen; abheuern, abmustern ‹*Seemann*› *(Seemannsspr.)*
~ **'on 1.** *v.t.* einstellen ‹*Arbeitskräfte*›; verpflichten ‹*Fußballspieler*›; anwerben ‹*Soldaten*›; anheuern, anmustern ‹*Seeleute*›. **2.** *v.i.* **a)** *(~ an engagement)* sich verpflichten **(with bei); b)** *(at start of shift etc.)* **~ on for the night shift** sich [per Unterschrift] zur Nachtschicht anmelden; **c)** *(Radio)* ‹*Rundfunkstation:*› seine Sendungen aufnehmen; ‹*Funker:*› sich melden; **d) ~ on [for the dole]** *(coll.)* sich arbeitslos melden; stempeln gehen *(ugs. veralt.)*
~ **'out 1.** *v.t.* **~ books out from the library** Bücher als [aus der Bibliothek] entliehen

eintragen. **2.** *v.i.* sich [schriftlich] abmelden; ⟨*Hotelgast:*⟩ abreisen

~ 'over *v.t.* überschreiben ⟨*Immobilien*⟩; übertragen ⟨*Rechte*⟩

~ 'up 1. *v.t. (engage)* [vertraglich] verpflichten; einstellen ⟨*Arbeiter*⟩; aufnehmen ⟨*Mitglied*⟩; einschreiben ⟨*Kursteilnehmer*⟩. **2.** *v.i.* sich [vertraglich] verpflichten **(with** bei); *(join a course etc.)* sich einschreiben

signal ['sɪgnl] **1.** *n.* **a)** Signal, *das;* **a ~ for sth./to sb.** ein Zeichen zu etw./für jmdn.; **at a ~ from the headmaster** auf ein Zeichen des Direktors; **the ~ was for/against us/at red** *(Railw.)* das Signal zeigte „halt"/„freie Fahrt"/stand auf Rot; **alarm** *or* **danger/warning ~:** Gefahr-/Warnsignal, *das;* **hand ~s** *(Motor Veh.)* Handzeichen; **sound/light/flag ~:** akustisches Signal/Lichtsignal, *das*/Flaggensignal, *das;* **radio** *or* **wireless ~:** Funkspruch, *der;* **distress ~:** Notsignal, *das;* **code of ~s** *see* **signal-book; the Royal Corps of S~s,** *(coll.)* **the S~s** *(Brit. Mil.) die Fernmeldetruppe der britischen Armee;* **b)** *(occasion, cause)* Signal, *das;* Zeichen, *das;* **the ~ for rioting/pandemonium** das Zeichen zum Aufruhr/Chaos; **c)** *(Electr., Radio, etc.)* Signal, *das.* **2.** *v.i., (Brit.)* **-ll-** signalisieren; Signale geben; ⟨*Kraftfahrer:*⟩ blinken; *(using hand etc. signals)* anzeigen; **~ for assistance** ein Hilfesignal geben; **~ to sb. [to do sth.]** jmdm. ein Zeichen geben[, etw. zu tun]. **3.** *v.t., (Brit.)* **-ll- a)** *(lit. or fig.)* signalisieren; **~ sb. [to do sth.]** jmdm. ein Zeichen geben[, etw. zu tun]; **the driver ~led a right turn/that he was turning right** der Fahrer zeigte an, daß er [nach] rechts abbiegen wollte; **b)** *(Radio etc.)* funken; [über Funk] durchgeben. **4.** *adj.* außergewöhnlich

signal: ~-book *n. (Mil., Navy)* Signalbuch, *das;* **~-box** *n. (Railw.)* Stellwerk, *das*

signaler *(Amer.) see* **signaller**

'signal-flag *n. (Mil., Navy, Railw.)* Signalflagge, *die*

'signal-lamp *n. (Naut., Railw.)* Signallampe, *die*

signaller ['sɪgnələ(r)] *n. (Mil.)* Blinker, *der;* *(with flags)* Signalgast, *der (Seew.)*

signally ['sɪgnəlɪ] *adv.* ungeheuer; unerhört; **~ ineffective** bemerkenswert ineffektiv; **not ~ successful** nicht übermäßig erfolgreich

signal: ~man ['sɪgnlmən] *n., pl.* **~men** ['sɪgnlmən] **a)** *(Brit. Railw.)* Bahnwärter, *der;* **b)** *see* **signaller; ~-tower** *(Amer.) see* **signal-box**

signatory ['sɪgnətərɪ] **1.** *adj.* unterzeichnend; vertragschließend ⟨*Partei, Land*⟩; Signatar⟨*macht, -staat*⟩ *(Politik).* **2.** *n. (person)* Unterzeichner, *der;* *(party)* vertragschließende Partei; *(state)* Signatarstaat, *der;* **~ to a petition** Unterzeichner einer Petition; **~ to the treaty/agreement** *(state)* Signatarstaat des Abkommens

signature ['sɪgnətʃə(r)] *n.* **a)** Unterschrift, *die;* *(on painting)* Signatur, *die;* **put one's ~ to sth.** seine Unterschrift unter etw. *(Akk.)* setzen; **b)** *(Mus.) see* **key signature; time signature; c)** *(Printing) (figure or letter)* Signatur, *die (Buchw.);* *(folded sheet)* Bogen, *der;* **d)** *(Amer. Med.)* Signatur, *die*

'signature tune *n. (Radio, Telev.)* Erkennungsmelodie, *die*

'signboard *n.* Schild, *das;* *(advertising)* Reklameschild, *das*

signet ['sɪgnɪt] *n.* Petschaft, *das;* Signet, *das (veralt.)*

'signet-ring *n.* Siegelring, *der*

significance [sɪg'nɪfɪkəns] *n.* **a)** *(meaning, importance)* Bedeutung, *die;* **be of [no] ~:** [nicht] von Bedeutung sein; **a matter of great/little/no ~:** eine [sehr] wichtige/ziemlich unwichtige/völlig unwichtige Angelegenheit; **b)** *(meaningfulness)* Bedeutsamkeit, *die*

significant [sɪg'nɪfɪkənt] *adj.* **a)** *(noteworthy, important)* bedeutend; **b)** *(suggestive)* bedeutsam; **be ~ of sth.** etw. verraten; etwas über etw. *(Akk.)* aussagen; **c)** *(having a meaning)* bedeutungstragend *(Sprachw.);* **be ~:** etwas bedeuten; **d)** *(Statistics)* signifikant

significant 'figure *n. (Math.)* signifikante Ziffer

significantly [sɪg'nɪfɪkəntlɪ] *adv.* **a)** *(suggestively)* bedeutungsvoll; *as sentence-modifier* **~ [enough]** bedeutsamerweise; **b)** *(notably)* bedeutend; signifikant *(geh., fachspr.)*

signification [sɪgnɪfɪ'keɪʃn] *n.* Bedeutung, *die*

signify ['sɪgnɪfaɪ] **1.** *v.t.* **a)** *(indicate, mean)* bedeuten; **b)** *(communicate, make known)* kundtun *(geh.);* zum Ausdruck bringen. **2.** *v.i.* **it does not ~:** es hat nichts zu bedeuten *od. (ugs.)* zu sagen

signing ['saɪnɪŋ] *n.* **a)** Unterschreiben, *das;* *(formal)* Unterzeichnung, *die;* **b)** *(~ up)* Verpflichtung, *die*

'sign language *n.* Zeichensprache, *die*

sign: ~-painter *see* **~-writer; ~post 1.** *n. (lit. or fig.)* Wegweiser, *der;* **2.** *v.t.* ausschildern ⟨*Route, Umleitungsstrecke usw.*⟩; mit Wegweisern versehen ⟨*Straße*⟩; **~-writer** *n.* Schildermaler, *der*

Sikh [si:k, sɪk] *n.* Sikh, *der;* **she is a ~:** sie gehört der Sikh-Religion an

Sikhism ['si:kɪzm, 'sɪkɪzm] *n., no pl.* Sikh-Religion, *die*

silage ['saɪlɪdʒ] *(Agric.)* **1.** *n.* Silage, *die;* Gärfutter, *das.* **2.** *v.t.* silieren

silence ['saɪləns] **1.** *n.* Schweigen, *das;* *(keeping a secret)* Verschwiegenheit, *die;* *(taciturnity)* Schweigsamkeit, *die;* *(stillness)* Stille, *die;* **there was ~:** es herrschte Schweigen/Stille; **there was a sudden/** *(iron.)* **deafening ~:** es trat plötzlich Stille ein/es herrschte Totenstille; **an awkward ~/awkward ~s** ein betretenes Schweigen/peinliche [Gesprächs]pausen; **his story was punctuated by long ~s** lange Sprechpausen unterbrachen seine Erzählung; **~!** Ruhe!; **'~ – recording in progress'** „Bitte Ruhe – Aufnahme"; **~ on sth.** Schweigen zu etw.; **in ~:** schweigend; **suffer in ~:** schweigend leiden; **call for ~:** um Ruhe bitten; **keep ~** *(lit. or fig.)* schweigen; **break the ~:** die Stille unterbrechen; *(be the first to speak)* das Schweigen brechen; **break one's ~** *(lit. or fig.)* sein Schweigen brechen; **reduce sb. to ~** *(lit. or fig.)* jmdn. zum Schweigen *od.* Verstummen bringen; **a minute's ~:** eine Schweigeminute; **the [two minutes'] ~** *(Brit.: on Remembrance Sunday)* die zwei Schweigeminuten *(am Heldengedenktag);* **~ is golden** Schweigen ist Gold; *see also* **pass over 1. 2.** *v.t.* **a)** *(make silent)* zum Schweigen *od.* Verstummen bringen; *(fig.)* ersticken ⟨*Zweifel, Ängste, Proteste*⟩; mundtot machen ⟨*Gegner, Zeugen*⟩; *(coll.: kill)* zum Schweigen bringen *(verhüllend);* **b)** *(make quieter)* leiser machen ⟨*Motor, Maschine, Auspuff, Bohrmaschine usw.*⟩

silencer ['saɪlənsə(r)] *n.* *(for door)* Türschließer, *der;* *(Brit. Motor Veh.)* Schalldämpfer, *der;* Auspufftopf, *der;* *(Arms)* Schalldämpfer, *der*

silent ['saɪlənt] *adj.* **a)** stumm; *(noiseless)* unhörbar; *(still)* still; **as ~ as the grave** *or* **tomb** totenstill; **deaf people live in a ~ world** Taube leben in einer lautlosen Welt; **be ~** *(say nothing)* schweigen; *(be still)* still sein; *(not be working)* ⟨*Maschine:*⟩ stillstehen; ⟨*Waffen:*⟩ schweigen; **fall ~:** verstummen; **keep** *or* **remain ~** *(lit. or fig.)* schweigen; *(jmd., der verhört wird:)* beharrlich schweigen; **b)** *(taciturn)* schweigsam; **the strong, ~ type** der starke, tatkräftige Typ, der nicht viel Worte macht; **c)** *(Ling.)* stumm; **d)** *(Cinemat.)* **~ film** Stummfilm, *der;* **the early motion pictures were ~:** die ersten Filme waren Stummfilme *od.* waren ohne Ton

silently ['saɪləntlɪ] *adv.* schweigend; stumm ⟨*weinen, beten*⟩; *(noiselessly)* lautlos

silent: ~ ma'jority *n.* schweigende Mehrheit; **~ 'partner** *(Amer.) see* **sleeping partner**

Silesia [saɪ'li:ʃə] *pr. n.* Schlesien *(das)*

Silesian [saɪ'li:ʃn] **1.** *adj.* schlesisch; **sb. is ~:** jmd. ist Schlesier/Schlesierin. **2.** *n.* **a)** *(person)* Schlesier, *der*/Schlesierin, *die;* **b)** *(dialect)* Schlesisch, *das;* **speak ~:** schlesischen Dialekt sprechen

silhouette [sɪlʊ'et] **1.** *n.* **a)** *(picture)* Schattenriß, *der;* **b)** *(appearance against the light)* Silhouette, *die;* **in ~:** als Silhouette. **2.** *v.t.* **be ~d against sth.** sich als Silhouette gegen etw. abheben

silica ['sɪlɪkə] *n.* Kieselerde, *die*

silicate ['sɪlɪkeɪt] *n. (Chem.)* Silikat, *das*

siliceous [sɪ'lɪsɪəs] *adj.* Kiesel-

silicon ['sɪlɪkən] *n. (Chem.)* Silicium, *das;* Silizium, *das;* **~ chip** Siliciumchip, *der;* Siliziumchip, *der*

silicone ['sɪlɪkəʊn] *n. (Chem.)* Silikon, *das*

silicosis [sɪlɪ'kəʊsɪs] *n., pl.* **silicoses** [sɪlɪ'kəʊsi:z] *(Med.)* Silikose, *die*

silk [sɪlk] **1.** *n.* **a)** Seide, *die;* **sewing/embroidery ~:** Näh-/Stickseide, *die;* **take ~** *(Brit. Law)* Kronanwalt werden; **b)** *in pl. (kinds of ~ material)* Seidenstoffe; *(garments)* seidene Kleider *od.* Kleidungsstücke; *(Horse-racing)* Rennfarben *Pl.;* **c)** *(of spider etc.)* [Spinnen]faden, *der;* **d)** *(Bot.)* Seide, *die;* **e)** *(Brit. Law coll.)* Kronanwalt, *der.* **2.** *attrib. adj.* seiden; Seiden-; **you can't make a ~ purse out of a sow's ear** *(prov.)* aus einem Schweinsohr läßt sich kein seidener Beutel machen

silken ['sɪlkn] *adj.* **a)** seiden; Seiden-; **b)** *(lustrous)* seidig; **c)** *see* **silky b**

silk: ~ 'finish *n.* Seidenglanz, *der;* **~ 'hat** *n.* Zylinder, *der*

silkily ['sɪlkɪlɪ] *adv.* **a)** *(lustrously)* seiden; seidig; **b)** *(suavely)* **speak ~:** mit samtener Stimme sprechen

silk: ~-mill *n.* Seidenspinnerei, *die;* **~-screen printing** *see* **screen-printing; ~worm** *n. (Zool.)* Seidenraupe, *die*

silky ['sɪlkɪ] *adj.* **a)** seidig; **have a ~ feel** sich wie Seide anfühlen; **b)** *(suave)* glatt; samten, samtig ⟨*Stimme*⟩

sill [sɪl] *n.* **a)** *(of door)* [Tür]schwelle, *die;* *(of window)* Fensterbank, *die;* **b)** *(Geol.)* [schichtparalleler] Lagergang; Sill, *der (fachspr.)*

sillabub *see* **syllabub**

silliness ['sɪlɪnɪs] *n.* **a)** *no pl.* Dummheit, *die;* Blödheit, *die (ugs.);* **b)** *usu. in pl. (instance)* Dummheit, *die;* *(piece of childishness)* Albernheit, *die*

silly ['sɪlɪ] **1.** *adj.* dumm; blöd[e] *(ugs.);* *(imprudent, unwise)* töricht; unklug; *(childish)* albern; **only a ~ little cut [in the finger]** bloß ein läppischer *(ugs.)* kleiner Schnitt [im Finger]; **with a ~ little hammer like this one** mit so einem albernen kleinen Hammer wie diesem; **the ~ season** *(Journ.)* die Saure-gurkenzeit; **[you] ~ child/thing!** [du] dummes Kind/dummes Ding!; **the ~ thing** *(inanimate object)* das dumme *od. (ugs.)* blöde Ding; **a ~ thing** *(a foolish action)* etwas Dummes *od. (ugs.)* Blödes; *(a trivial matter)* eine blödsinnige Kleinigkeit *(ugs.);* *(a stupid person)* ein dummes Ding; **it/that was a ~ thing to do** es/das war dumm *od. (ugs.)* blöd; **~ fool** Dummkopf, *der (ugs.);* **not do anything ~** *(lit. or fig.)* keine Dummheit[en] machen; **knock sb. ~:** jmdn. bewußtlos schlagen; **I was scared ~:** mir rutschte das Herz in die Hose *(ugs.);* **laugh oneself ~:** sich halb totlachen; *see also* **'me. 2.** *n. (coll.)* Dummchen, *das;* Dummerchen, *das (fam.)*

'silly-billy *n. (coll.)* Kindskopf, *der;* **be a ~**

[about sth.] sich [bei etw.] dumm *od.* kindisch anstellen

silo ['saɪləʊ] *n., pl.* **~s a)** *(Agric.)* Silo, *der;* **b)** *(Brit.)* **[grain/cement] ~:** [Getreide-/Zement]silo, *der;* **c)** *(Mil.)* **[missile] ~:** [Raketen]silo, *der*

silt [sɪlt] **1.** *n.* Schlamm, *der;* Schlick, *der.* **2.** *v.t.* **~ up** verschlämmen. **3.** *v.i.* **~ up** verschlammen

siltation [sɪl'teɪʃn] *n.* **a)** *(process)* Verschlämmung, *die;* **b)** *(state)* Verschlammung, *die*

Silurian [saɪ'ljʊərɪən, sɪ'ljʊərɪən] *(Geol.)* **1.** *adj.* silurisch. **2.** *n.* Silur, *das*

silver ['sɪlvə(r)] **1.** *n.* **a)** *no pl., no indef. art.* Silber, *das;* **the price of ~:** der Silberpreis; **b)** *(colour)* Silber, *das;* **c)** *no pl., no indef. art. (coins)* Silbermünzen *Pl.;* Silber, *das (ugs.);* **for thirty pieces** *or* **a handful of ~** *(fig.)* für einen Judaslohn; **d)** *(vessels, cutlery)* Silber, *das; (cutlery of other material)* Besteck, *das;* **e)** *(medal)* Silber, *das;* **win two ~s** zweimal Silber gewinnen. **2.** *attrib. adj.* silbern; Silber⟨*pokal, -münze*⟩; **have a ~ tongue** zungenfertig sein; *see also* **¹spoon 1 a; standard 1 h. 3.** *v.t.* **a)** *(coat with ~)* versilbern; *(coat with amalgam)* verspiegeln ⟨*Glas*⟩; **b)** ergrauen lassen ⟨*Haar*⟩. **4.** *v.i.* ergrauen

silver: ~'band *n. (Mus.)* Blaskapelle *(deren Instrumente versilbert sind);* **~ 'birch** *n. (Bot.)* Weißbirke, *die;* **~ collection** *n.* Sammlung, *die (bei der Silbermünzen gespendet werden);* **~-coloured** *adj.* silberfarben; silberfarbig; **~ 'fir** *n. (Bot.)* Weißtanne, *die;* Silbertanne, *die;* **~-fish** *n. (Zool.)* **a)** *(insect)* Silberfischchen, *das;* **b)** *(fish)* Silberfisch, *der; (variety of goldfish)* weißer Goldfisch; **~ 'foil** *n.* **a)** Silberfolie, *die; (aluminium foil)* Alufolie, *die;* **b)** *(tin foil)* Stanniol, *das;* **~ 'fox** *n. (Zool.; also fur)* Silberfuchs, *der;* **~ 'gilt** *n.* **a)** *(gilded ~)* vergoldetes Silber; **~ gilt dish/tray** Teller/Tablett aus vergoldetem Silber; **b)** *(imitation gilt)* Goldimitation, *die;* **~-grey** *adj.* silbergrau; silbriggrau; **~-haired** *adj.* silberhaarig *(geh.);* **~ 'jubilee** *n.* silbernes Jubiläum; **~ 'leaf** *n.* Blattsilber, *das;* **~ 'medal** *n.* Silbermedaille, *die;* **~ 'medallist** *n.* Silbermedaillengewinner, *der/-gewinnerin, die;* **~-mine** *n.* Silbermine, *die;* **~ 'paper** *n.* Silberpapier, *das;* **~ 'plate** *n., no pl., no indef. art.* **a)** versilberte Ware; *(coating)* Silberauflage, *die;* **b)** *(vessels, tableware)* Silbergeschirr, *das;* **be ~ plate** versilbert sein; **~-plate** *v.t.* versilbern; **~-plated** *adj.* versilbert; **~ sand** *n. feiner, reiner Sand;* **~ 'screen** *n.* **the ~ screen** die Leinwand; **~ service** *n.* **a)** *(set of ~ware)* silbernes Service; **b)** *no pl. (method of restaurant service)* englisches Service; Rundservice, *das;* **~side** *n. (Brit. Gastr.)* Schwanzstück, *das;* **~smith** *n.* Silberschmied, *der/-schmiedin, die;* **~-tongued** *adj. (fig.)* zungenfertig; **~ware** *n., no pl.* Silber, *das;* **~ 'wedding** *n.* Silberhochzeit, *die;* silberne Hochzeit

silvery ['sɪlvərɪ] *adj. (silver-coloured)* silbrig; *(clear-sounding)* silbern *(dichter.);* silbrig *(geh.)*

silviculture ['sɪlvɪkʌltʃə(r)] *n.* Waldbau, *der*

simian ['sɪmɪən] **1.** *adj.* **a)** *(apelike)* affenähnlich; **b)** *(Zool.)* ⟨*Gehirn usw.*⟩ des/der Affen. **2.** *n.* **a)** *(ape or monkey)* Affe, *der;* **b)** *(Zool.)* Menschenaffe, *der*

similar ['sɪmɪlə(r)] *adj. (also Geom.)* ähnlich **(to** *Dat.***)**; **some flour and a ~ amount of sugar** etwas Mehl und ungefähr die gleiche Menge Zucker; **our tastes are very ~:** wir haben einen sehr ähnlichen Geschmack; **of ~ size/colour** *etc.* von ähnlicher Größe/Farbe *usw.;* **be ~ in size/appearance** *etc.* **[to sb./sth.]** eine ähnliche Größe/ein ähnliches Aussehen haben [wie jmd./etw.]; **look/taste/smell** *etc.* **~ [to sth.]** ähnlich aussehen/schmecken/riechen *usw.* [wie etw.]; **the two brothers look very ~:** die beiden Brüder sehen sich *(Dat.)* sehr ähnlich

similarity [sɪmɪ'lærɪtɪ] *n.* Ähnlichkeit, *die* **(to** mit**)**; **point of ~:** Ähnlichkeit, *die;* **there the ~ ends** sonst gibt es keine Gemeinsamkeiten

similarly ['sɪmɪləlɪ] *adv.* ähnlich; *(in exactly the same way)* ebenso; **~ effective/costly** *etc.* ähnlich/ebenso effektiv/teuer *usw.*

simile ['sɪmɪlɪ] *n. (Lit.)* Vergleich, *der;* Simile, *das (geh., veralt.)*

similitude [sɪ'mɪlɪtju:d] *n. (literary)* Ähnlichkeit, *die*

simmer ['sɪmə(r)] **1.** *v.i.* **a)** *(Cookery)* ⟨*Flüssigkeit:*⟩ sieden; **put the fish in the water and allow to ~ for ten minutes** den Fisch ins Wasser legen und zehn Minuten ziehen lassen; **b)** *(fig.)* gären; **let things ~:** die Dinge sich entwickeln lassen; **~ with rage/excitement** eine Wut haben/innerlich ganz aufgeregt sein. **2.** *v.t. (Cookery)* köcheln lassen ⟨*Suppe, Soße usw.*⟩; ziehen lassen ⟨*Fisch, Klöße usw.*⟩. **3.** *n. (Cookery)* **keep at a** *or* **on the ~:** sieden lassen ⟨*Wasser*⟩; köcheln lassen ⟨*Suppe, Soße usw.*⟩

~ 'down *v.i.* sich abregen *(ugs.);* **let things/the situation ~ down** abwarten, bis sich die Wogen geglättet haben

simnel cake ['sɪmnl keɪk] *n. (Brit.)* ≈ Rosinenkuchen, *der*

simper ['sɪmpə(r)] **1.** *v.i.* affektiert *od.* gekünstelt lächeln. **2.** *v.t.* mit einem affektierten *od.* gekünstelten Lächeln sagen. **3.** *n.* affektiertes *od.* gekünsteltes Lächeln

simpering ['sɪmpərɪŋ] *adj.* affektiert, gekünstelt ⟨*Lächeln, Art*⟩; affektiert ⟨*Frau*⟩

simple ['sɪmpl] *adj.* **a)** *(not compound, not complicated)* einfach; *(not elaborate)* schlicht ⟨*Mobiliar, Schönheit, Kunstwerk, Kleidung*⟩; **the ~ life** das einfache Leben; *see also* **simple interest; b)** *(unqualified, absolute)* einfach; simpel; **it was a ~ misunderstanding** es war [ganz] einfach ein Mißverständnis; **it is a ~ fact that ...:** es ist [ganz] einfach eine Tatsache, *od.* eine simple Tatsache, daß ...; *see also* **pure 1 c; c)** *(easy)* einfach; **the ~st thing would be** *or* **it would be the ~st if ...:** es wäre das einfachste *od.* am einfachsten, wenn ...; **as ~ as ABC** kinderleicht; **it's/it isn't as ~ as that** so einfach ist das/ist das nicht; **it would make things so ~ if ...:** es wäre alles so einfach, wenn ...; **'Electronics made ~'** „Elektronik leicht gemacht"; **it would make my job/task much ~r** es würde mir meine Arbeit sehr erleichtern/meine Aufgabe sehr vereinfachen; **d)** *(unsophisticated)* schlicht; *(foolish)* dumm; einfältig; *(feeble-minded)* debil; *(humble)* einfach ⟨*Person, Arbeiter, Bauer, Leute*⟩; **the ~ pleasures of life** die kleinen Freuden des Lebens; **e)** *(Ling.)* **~ tense** einfache Zeitform; **~ past** Präteritum, *das;* **~ sentence** einfacher Satz

simple: ~-hearted ['sɪmplhɑ:tɪd] *adj.* schlicht; **~ 'interest** Kapitalzins, *der;* **~-minded** *adj.* **a)** *(unsophisticated)* schlicht; **b)** *(feeble-minded)* debil

'simple time *n. (Mus.)* nicht zusammengesetzte Taktart

simpleton ['sɪmpltən] *n.* Einfaltspinsel, *der (ugs.)*

simplex ['sɪmpleks] *n. (Ling.)* Simplex, *das*

simplicity [sɪm'plɪsɪtɪ] *n., no pl.* Einfachheit, *die; (unpretentiousness, lack of sophistication)* Schlichtheit, *die;* **be ~ itself** ein Kinderspiel sein

simplification [sɪmplɪfɪ'keɪʃn] *n.* **a)** *no pl.* Vereinfachung, *die;* Simplifizierung, *die (geh.);* **b)** *(instance)* Vereinfachung, *die;* Simplifikation, *die (geh.)*

simplify ['sɪmplɪfaɪ] *v.t.* vereinfachen; simplifizieren *(geh.);* **it would ~ matters if ...:** es würde die Sache vereinfachen, wenn ...

simplistic [sɪm'plɪstɪk] *adj.* [all]zu simpel

simply ['sɪmplɪ] *adv.* **a)** *(in an uncomplicated manner)* einfach; *(in an unsophisticated manner)* schlicht; **live/eat ~:** einfach leben/essen; **speak ~:** in schlichten Worten sprechen; **b)** *(absolutely)* einfach; **he's ~ wonderful** er ist einfach großartig; **c)** *(categorically, without good reason, without asking)* einfach; *(merely)* nur; **it ~ isn't true** es ist einfach nicht wahr; **you ~ must see that film** du mußt den Film einfach sehen; **I was ~ trying to help** ich wollte nur helfen; **quite ~:** ganz einfach; **~ because ...:** einfach weil ...; nur weil ...; **he ~ didn't feel like working** er hatte ganz einfach keine Lust zu arbeiten

simulate ['sɪmjʊleɪt] *v.t.* **a)** *(feign)* vortäuschen; heucheln ⟨*Reue, Tugendhaftigkeit, Entrüstung, Begeisterung*⟩; simulieren, vortäuschen ⟨*Krankheit*⟩; **b)** *(mimic)* nachahmen; *(resemble)* aussehen wie (+ *Nom.*); **c)** simulieren ⟨*Bedingungen, Wetter, Umwelt usw.*⟩

simulated ['sɪmjʊleɪtɪd] *adj.* **a)** *(feigned)* geheuchelt; vorgetäuscht; **b)** *(artificial)* imitiert ⟨*Leder, Pelz usw.*⟩; **c)** simuliert ⟨*Bedingungen, Wetter, Umwelt usw.*⟩

simulation [sɪmjʊ'leɪʃn] *n.* **a)** *(feigning)* Vortäuschung, *die; (of illness)* Vortäuschung, *die;* Simulation, *die;* **b)** *(imitation of conditions)* Simulation, *die;* **c)** *(simulated object)* Imitation, *die*

simulator ['sɪmjʊleɪtə(r)] *n.* Simulator, *der*

simultaneity [sɪmltə'ni:ɪtɪ] *n., no pl.* Gleichzeitigkeit, *die*

simultaneous [sɪml'teɪnɪəs] *adj.* gleichzeitig **(with** mit**)**; simultan *(fachspr., geh.);* **be ~:** gleichzeitig/simultan erfolgen

simultaneous: ~ display *n. (Chess)* Simultanvorstellung, *die;* **~ equations** *n. pl. (Math.)* Gleichungssystem, *das;* **~ interpretation** *n.* Simultandolmetschen, *das*

simultaneously [sɪml'teɪnɪəslɪ] *adv.* gleichzeitig; simultan *(fachspr., geh.)*

sin [sɪn] **1.** *n.* Sünde, *die;* **a life of ~:** ein Leben in Sünde; ein sündiges Leben; **live in ~** *(coll.)* in Sünde leben *(veralt., scherzh.);* **[as] miserable as ~:** todunglücklich; **for my ~s** *(joc.)* um meiner Missetaten willen *(scherzh.);* **the ~s of the fathers** die Missetat[en] der Väter; *see also* **beset b; find out b; multitude a; omission b; original 1 a; wage 1. 2.** *v.i.,* **-nn-** sündigen; **~ against sb./God** an jmdm./Gott *od.* gegen jmdn./Gott sündigen; sich an jmdm./Gott versündigen *(geh.);* **~ against the rules** gegen die Regeln verstoßen; **he is more ~ned against than ~ning** man sündigt mehr an ihm, als daß er selbst sündigt

Sinai Peninsula [saɪnaɪ pɪ'nɪnsjʊlə] *pr. n.* Halbinsel Sinai

'sin bin *n. (Sport coll.)* Strafbank, *die*

since [sɪns] **1.** *adv.* seitdem; **he has ~ remarried, he has remarried ~:** er hat danach wieder geheiratet; **she had not eaten anything so delicious before or ~:** sie hatte weder vorher noch nachher je etwas so Köstliches gegessen; **long ~:** vor langer Zeit; **not long ~:** vor nicht allzulanger Zeit; **he is long ~ dead** er ist seit langem tot; **a long time/many years/six weeks ~:** vor langer Zeit/vielen Jahren/sechs Wochen. **2.** *prep.* seit; **~ seeing you ...:** seit ich dich gesehen habe; **~ then/that time** inzwischen; **he joined the firm 16 years ago and has been with them ~ then** er ist vor 16 Jahren in die Firma eingetreten und ist heute noch dort; **~ when?** seit wann?; **her mother died in 1980, ~ when/~ which time she has been looking after her father** ihre Mutter starb 1980, und seitdem/seit dieser Zeit versorgt sie ihren Vater. **3.** *conj.* **a)** seit; **it is a long time/so long/not so long ~ ...:** es ist lange/so lange/gar nicht lange her, daß ...; **how long is it ~ he left you?** wie lange ist es her, daß er dich verlassen hat?; **b)** *(seeing that, as)* da

sincere [sɪn'sɪə(r)] *adj.,* **~r** [sɪn'sɪərə(r)], **~st**

[sɪn'sɪərɪst] aufrichtig; herzlich ‹*Grüße, Glückwünsche usw.*›; wahr ‹*Freund*›

sincerely [sɪn'sɪəlɪ] *adv.* aufrichtig; **I [most] ~ hope so** *(coll.)* das will ich schwer hoffen *(ugs.)*; **yours ~** *(in letter)* mit freundlichen Grüßen

sincerity [sɪn'serɪtɪ] *n., no pl.* Aufrichtigkeit, *die;* **in all ~:** in aller Aufrichtigkeit; **have the ring of ~:** aufrichtig klingen

sine [saɪn] *n. (Math.)* Sinus, *der*

sinecure ['sɪnɪkjʊə(r), 'saɪnɪkjʊə(r)] *n.* Pfründe, *die;* Sinekure, *die;* **this job is no ~:** diese Arbeit ist kein reines Honiglecken *(ugs.)*

sine die [saɪnɪ 'daɪi:, sɪneɪ 'di:eɪ] *adv.* auf unbestimmte Zeit

sine qua non [saɪnɪ kweɪ 'nɒn, sɪneɪ kwɑ: 'nəʊn] *n.* notwendige Bedingung; Conditio sine qua non *(geh.)*

sinew ['sɪnju:] *n.* **a)** *(Anat.)* Sehne, *die;* **strain every nerve and ~ [to do sth.]** *(fig.)* alle Muskeln anspannen[, um etw. zu tun]; **b)** *(strength)* Kraft, *die*

'sine wave *n. (Math.)* Sinuswelle, *die*

sinewy ['sɪnju:ɪ] *adj.* sehnig; *(fig.: vigorous)* kraftvoll; **the ~ vigour/strength of his style** sein kraftvoller Stil

sinfonia [sɪn'fəʊnɪə] *n. (Mus.)* Sinfonia, *die;* *(in name of orchestra)* Sinfonieorchester, *das;* Sinfoniker *Pl.*

sinfonietta [sɪnfəʊnɪ'etə] *n. (Mus.)* **a)** Sinfonietta, *die;* **b)** *(orchestra)* kleines Sinfonieorchester; *(string orchestra)* Streichorchester, *das*

sinful ['sɪnfl] *adj.* sündig; *(reprehensible)* sündhaft; **it is ~ to ...:** es ist eine Sünde, ... zu ...

sing [sɪŋ] **1.** *v. i.,* **sang** [sæŋ], **sung** [sʌŋ] singen; *(fig.)* ‹*Kessel, Wind:*› singen; ‹*Geschoß:*› sirren, pfeifen; *(sl.: turn informer)* singen *(salopp)*; **~ to sb.** jmdm. [etw.] vorsingen; **~ to the guitar/piano** zur Gitarre/zum Klavier singen; **his ears are ~ing** seine Ohren sausen; **~ of sb./sth.** *(celebrate in verse)* jmdn./etw. besingen *(geh.)*; von jmdm./etw. singen *(dichter. veralt.)*. **2.** *v. t.,* **sang, sung** singen; **~ [the] alto** [den] Alt singen; **~ sb. a song** *or* **a song for sb.** jmdm. ein Lied vorsingen; **~ sb. to sleep** jmdn. in den Schlaf singen; *see also* **praise 2 a; tune 1 a, b. 3.** *n. (Amer.)* **have a ~:** [gemeinsam] singen

~ a'long *v. i.* mitsingen

~ 'out 1. *v. i.* **a)** *(~ loudly)* [laut *od.* aus voller Kehle] singen; **~ out merrily** fröhlich singen; **b)** *(call out)* [laut] rufen; **~ out for sb./sth.** nach jmdm./etw. rufen. **2.** *v. t. (shout)* rufen; schreien

~ 'up *v. i.* lauter singen

singable ['sɪŋəbl] *adj.* singbar; *(easily ~)* sangbar; kantabel *(geh.)*

Singapore [sɪŋgə'pɔ:(r)] *pr. n.* Singapur *(das)*

singe [sɪndʒ] **1.** *v. t.,* **~ing** ansengen; versengen; absengen ‹*Geflügel, Schwein*›; **~ sb.'s hair** *(Hairdressing)* jmdm. die Haarspitzen abbrennen. **2.** *v. i.,* **~ing** [ver]sengen. **3.** *n.* Brandfleck, *der*

singer ['sɪŋə(r)] *n.* Sänger, *der*/Sängerin, *die;* **this canary is a good ~:** dieser Kanarienvogel singt schön

singing ['sɪŋɪŋ] *n., no pl.* **a)** Singen, *das;* *(fig.) see* **sing 1:** Singen, *das;* Sirren, *das;* Pfeifen, *das;* **beautiful/loud ~:** schöner/lauter Gesang; **the ~ of the birds** der Gesang der Vögel; **his ~ is terrible** er singt furchtbar; **have a ~ in one's ears** Ohrensausen haben; **b)** *no art. (Art)* Gesang, *der; attrib.* Gesangs-; **~ voice** Singstimme, *die*

single ['sɪŋgl] **1.** *adj.* **a)** einfach; einzig ‹*Ziel, Hoffnung*›; *(for one person)* Einzel‹*bett, -zimmer*›; einfach ‹*Größe*›; *(without the other one of a pair)* einzeln; **~ flower/stem** *etc.* einzelne Blume/einzelner Stamm *usw.*; **speak with a ~ voice** *(fig.)* mit einer Stimme sprechen; **~ sheet/cover** Bettuch/Bettbezug für ein Einzelbett; **~ ticket** *(Brit.)* einfache Fahrkarte; **~ fare** *(Brit.)* Preis für [die] einfache Fahrt; *see also* **combat 1; entry h; ³file 1 a; track 1 b, d; b)** *(one by itself)* einzig; *(isolated)* einzeln; **one ~ ...:** ein einziger/eine einzige/ein einziges ...; **at a** *or* **one ~ blow** *or* **stroke** mit einem Schlag; **two minds with but a ~ thought** zwei Seelen und ein Gedanke; **c)** *(unmarried)* ledig; **a ~ man/woman/~ people** ein Lediger/eine Ledige/Ledige; **~ parent** alleinerziehender Elternteil; **he/she is a ~ parent** er/sie ist alleinerziehend; **d)** *(separate, individual)* einzeln; **can a ~ argument be advanced for it?** läßt sich dafür überhaupt irgendein Argument vorbringen?; **every ~ one** jeder/jede/jedes einzelne; **every ~ time/day** aber auch jedesmal/jeden Tag; **not a ~ one** kein einziger/keine einzige/kein einziges; **not a ~ word/dress/soul** kein einziges Wort/Kleid/keine Menschenseele; **she did not see a ~ thing she liked** sie hat aber auch nichts gesehen, was ihr gefiel; **not/never for a ~ minute** *or* **moment** keinen [einzigen] Augenblick [lang]. **2.** *n.* **a)** *(Brit.: ticket)* einfache Fahrkarte; **[a] ~/two ~s to Manchester, please** einmal/zweimal einfach nach Manchester, bitte; **b)** *(record)* Single, *die;* **c)** *in pl. (Golf)* Single, *das;* *(Tennis)* Einzel, *das;* **women's** *or* **ladies'/men's ~s** Damen-/Herreneinzel, *das;* **d)** *(Brit. Hist.: pound note)* Einpfundschein, *der;* *(Amer.: dollar note)* Eindollarschein, *der;* **e)** *(Cricket) Schlag für einen Lauf.* **3.** *v. t.* **~ out** aussondern; *(be distinctive quality of)* auszeichnen **(from** vor + *Dat.*); **~ sb./sth. out as/for sth.** jmdn./etw. als etw./für etw. auswählen; **~ sb. out for promotion/special attention** jmdn. für eine Beförderung vorsehen/sich mit jmdm. besonders befassen

single: ~-barrelled *(Amer.:* **~-barreled)** ['sɪŋglbærəld] *adj. (Arms)* einläufig; **~-bedded room** ['sɪŋglbedɪd ru:m] *n.* Einzelzimmer, *das;* **~-breasted** ['sɪŋglbrestɪd] *adj. (Tailoring)* einreihig; **~ cream** *n.* [einfache] Sahne; **~-decker 1.** *n.* **be a ~-decker** ‹*Bus, Straßenbahn:*› nur ein Deck haben; **2.** *adj.* **~-decker bus/tram** Bus/Straßenbahn mit [nur] einem Deck; **~-engined** ['sɪŋglendʒɪnd] *adj.* einmotorig; **~ [European] market** *n.* [europäischer] Binnenmarkt; **~-handed 1.** ['----] *adj.* **a)** Einhand‹*segeln, -segler*›; **~-handed attempt to row across the Atlantic** Versuch, allein über den Atlantik zu rudern; **his ~-handed efforts to get a new hospital** seine einsamen Bemühungen um ein neues Krankenhaus; **b)** *(for one hand)* **~-handed weapon/fishing rod** Waffe/Angelrute für eine Hand; **2.** [-'--] *adv.* **a)** allein; **sail round the world ~-handed** als Einhandsegler um die Welt fahren; **root out corruption ~-handed** im Alleingang die Korruption ausrotten; **b)** *(with one hand)* mit einer Hand; einhändig; **~-lens 'reflex camera** *n. (Photog.)* einäugige Spiegelreflexkamera; **~-line** *adj.* einspurig; **~-minded** *adj.* zielstrebig; **be ~-minded in one's aim** unbeirrbar sein Ziel verfolgen; **~-mindedly** [sɪŋgl'maɪndɪdlɪ] *adv.* zielstrebig

singleness ['sɪŋglnɪs] *n., no pl.* **~ of purpose** Zielstrebigkeit, *die*

'single-phase *adj. (Electr.)* einphasig; **~ current** Einphasenstrom, *der*

'singles bar *n.* Singlekneipe, *die*

single: ~-seater *n.* Einsitzer, *der;* **~-seater aircraft** einsitziges Flugzeug; **~-storey** *adj.* eingeschossig

singlet ['sɪŋglɪt] *n. (Brit.: vest)* Unterhemd, *das;* *(Sport)* Trikot, *das*

singleton ['sɪŋgltən] *n. (Cards)* blanke Karte; **a ~ in hearts, a ~ heart** ein blankes Herz

'single-track *adj.* eingleisig ‹*Bahnlinie*›; einspurig ‹*Straße*›

singly ['sɪŋglɪ] *adv.* **a)** einzeln; **b)** *(by oneself)* allein

'singsong 1. *adj.* leiernd *(ugs.)*; **say/recite sth. in a ~ manner/voice** etw. herunterleiern *(ugs.)*; **his ~ accent** sein Singsang. **2.** *n.* **a)** *(monotonous tone or rhythm)* leiernder Ton; **recite sth./say sth. in a ~:** etw. herunterleiern *(ugs.)*; **speak in a ~:** leiernd sprechen; **b)** *(Brit.: singing)* gemeinschaftliches Singen; **have a ~:** gemeinsam singen

singular ['sɪŋgjʊlə(r)] **1.** *adj.* **a)** *(Ling.)* singularisch; Singular-; **~ noun** Substantiv im Singular; **~ form** Singularform, *die;* **first person ~:** erste Person Singular; **~ number** *see* **2; b)** *(individual)* einzeln; *(unique)* einmalig; einzigartig; **c)** *(extraordinary)* einmalig; einzigartig; *(odd)* eigenartig; sonderbar; **how very ~!** wie eigenartig *od.* sonderbar! **2.** *n. (Ling.)* Einzahl, *die;* Singular, *der;* **I said you could have 'an apple – in the ~** *(coll.)* ich habe gesagt, du kannst einen Apfel haben – von Äpfeln war nicht die Rede

singularity [sɪŋgjʊ'lærɪtɪ] *n., no pl.* Eigenartigkeit, *die;* Sonderbarkeit, *die*

singularly ['sɪŋgjʊləlɪ] *adv. (extraordinarily)* außerordentlich; einmalig ‹*schön*›; *(strangely)* seltsam

Sinhalese [sɪnhə'li:z, sɪnə'li:z] **1.** *adj.* singhalesisch; **sb. is ~:** jmd. ist Singhalese/Singhalesin. **2.** *n.* **a)** *pl. same (person)* Singhalese, *der*/Singhalesin, *die;* **b)** *no pl. (language)* Singhalesisch, *das*

sinister ['sɪnɪstə(r)] *adj.* **a)** *(of evil omen)* unheilverkündend; **b)** *(suggestive of malice)* finster; *(wicked)* übel; **c)** *(Her.)* link...; sinister *(fachspr.)*; *see also* **baton e; ²bend b**

sink [sɪŋk] **1.** *n.* **a)** Spülbecken, *das;* Spüle, *die;* **pour sth. down the ~:** etw. in den Ausguß schütten; *see also* **kitchen sink; b)** *(cesspool)* Senkgrube, *die;* Kloake, *die;* *(fig.: place of vice etc.)* Kloake, *die;* Pfuhl, *der;* **c)** *(Geog.: pool)* Senke, *die;* Vertiefung, *die;* **d)** *(Geol.) see* **sink-hole; e)** *(Phys.)* Feldsenke, *die.* **2.** *v. i.,* **sank** [sæŋk] *or* **sunk** [sʌŋk], **sunk a)** sinken; **we shall ~ or swim together** *(fig.)* wir werden gemeinsam untergehen oder gemeinsam überleben; **leave sb. to ~ or swim** *(fig.)* jmdn. seinem Schicksal überlassen; **b) ~ into** *(become immersed in)* sinken in (+ *Akk.*); versinken in (+ *Dat.*); *(penetrate)* eindringen in (+ *Akk.*); *(fig.: be absorbed into)* dringen in (+ *Akk.*) ‹*Bewußtsein*›; **~ into an armchair/the cushions** in einen Sessel/die Kissen sinken; **~ into sb.'s/each other's arms** jmdm./sich in die Arme sinken; **~ into a deep sleep/a coma/trance/reverie** in einen tiefen Schlaf/in ein Koma/in Trance/in Träumerei sinken *(geh.)*; **~ into depression/despair** in Schwermut/Verzweiflung *(Akk.)* versinken; **~ into crime/poverty** *etc.* dem Verbrechen/der Armut *usw.* verfallen; **be sunk in thought/despair** in Gedanken/in Verzweiflung *(Akk.)* versunken sein; *see also* **oblivion; c)** *(come to lower level or pitch)* sinken; *(suffer subsidence)* absinken; *(slope down)* sich senken; *(be turned downwards)* ‹*Augen:*› sich senken; *(shrink inwards)* ‹*Augen, Wangen:*› einfallen; *(subside, abate)* ‹*Flut, Wasser, Fluß:*› sinken; *(fig.: fail)* ‹*Moral, Hoffnung:*› sinken; **the patient is ~ing [fast]** mit dem Patienten geht es zu Ende *(verhüll.)*; **sb.'s heart ~s/spirits ~:** jmds. Stimmung sinkt; **sb.'s heart/courage ~s into his/her boots** *(coll.)* jmdm. rutscht *od.* fällt das Herz in die Hose[n] *(ugs.)*; **~ to one's knees** auf die *od.* seine Knie sinken; **d)** *(fall)* ‹*Preis, Temperatur, Währung, Produktion usw.:*› sinken; **~ in value** im Wert sinken. **3.** *v. t.,* **sank** *or* **sunk, sunk a)** versenken; *(cause failure of)* zunichte machen; **be sunk** *(fig. coll.: have failed)* aufgeschmissen sein *(ugs.)*; **~ one's differences** seine Streitigkeiten begraben; **enough luggage/make-up to ~ a battleship** *(fig. joc.)* tonnenweise *(ugs.)*

Gepäck/pfundweise *(ugs.)* Make-up; **b)** *(lower)* senken; *(Golf)* ins Loch schlagen ⟨*Ball*⟩; **c)** *(dig)* niederbringen; *(inlay)* einlegen; *(recess)* versenken; *(embed)* stoßen ⟨*Messer, Schwert*⟩; graben *(geh.)* ⟨*Zähne, Klauen*⟩; ~ **a pole into the ground** einen Pfahl in den Boden senken; *see also* **fence 1 a**

~ **'back** *v.i.* zurücksinken; ~ **back into crime/poverty** *(fig.)* wieder dem Verbrechen/der Armut verfallen

~ **'down** *v.i.* hinabsinken; niedersinken; ~ **down to the floor/ground** auf den/zu Boden sinken; ~ **down into the mud** im Schlamm versinken; **his head sank down on to his chest** der Kopf sank ihm auf die Brust; **she sank down [on her knees] before him** sie sank vor ihm [auf die Knie] nieder

~ **'in 1.** *v.i.* **a)** *(become immersed)* einsinken; *(penetrate)* eindringen; **b)** *(fig.: be absorbed into the mind)* jmdm. ins Bewußtsein dringen; ⟨*Warnung, Lektion:*⟩ verstanden werden. **2.** *v.t.* einsenken ⟨*Stütze, Pfahl*⟩

sinker ['sɪŋkə(r)] *n. (Fishing)* Senker, *der; (of drift-net)* Grundgewicht, *das; see also* **hook 1 a**

'sink-hole *n. (Geol.)* Schluckloch, *das*

sinking ['sɪŋkɪŋ] **1.** *adj.* **a)** sinkend; **[the] rats desert a ~ ship** die Ratten verlassen das sinkende Schiff; **b)** *(declining)* untergehend ⟨*Sonne*⟩; **c)** *(falling in value)* sinkend; **d)** **with a ~ heart** *(fig.)* beklommen; resigniert. **2.** *n.* **a)** *(of ship) (deliberate)* Versenkung, *die; (accidental)* Sinken, *das;* Untergang, *der; (of well)* Niederbringung, *die;* **b)** ~ **of the heart** *(fig.)* Beklommenheit, *die;* **a ~ feeling** *(fig.)* ein flaues Gefühl [im Magen]

'sinking fund *n. (Finance)* Tilgungsfonds, *der*

'sink unit *n.* Spüle, *die*

sinless ['sɪnlɪs] *adj.* sündenfrei, sündlos ⟨*Mensch, Leben*⟩; untad[e]lig ⟨*Verhalten*⟩

sinner ['sɪnə(r)] *n.* Sünder, *der*/Sünderin, *die*

Sinn Fein [ʃɪn 'feɪn] *n., no pl., no indef. art.* Sinn Fein, *die (nationalistische irische Partei)*

Sino- ['saɪnəʊ] *in comb.* sino-/Sino-; **a ~-Russian war** ein chinesisch-russischer Krieg

sinter ['sɪntə(r)] **1.** *v.t.* sintern *(Technik).* **2.** *v.i.* sintern

sinuous ['sɪnjʊəs] *adj.* gewunden; sich schlängelnd ⟨*Schlange*⟩; *(lithe)* geschmeidig ⟨*Körper, Bewegungen*⟩

sinus ['saɪnəs] *n. (Anat.)* Sinus, *der (fachspr.);* **[paranasal] ~:** Nebenhöhle, *die*

sinusitis [saɪnə'saɪtɪs] *n. (Med.)* Nebenhöhlenentzündung, *die;* Sinusitis, *die (fachspr.)*

Sioux [su:] *n., pl. same (Ethnol.)* Sioux, *der/die; attrib.* Sioux-

sip [sɪp] **1.** *v.t.,* **-pp-:** ~ **[up]** schlürfen. **2.** *v.i.,* **-pp-:** ~ **at/from sth.** an etw. *(Dat.)* nippen. **3.** *n.* Schlückchen, *das;* **have** *or* **take a ~ [of sth.]** ein Schlückchen [von etw.] nehmen; **in ~s** schlückchenweise

siphon ['saɪfn] **1.** *n.* **a)** *(bottle)* Siphon, *der;* **b)** *(pipe)* Saugheber, *der.* **2.** *v.t.* [durch einen Saugheber] laufen lassen; ~ **sth. from a tank** etw. [mit einem Saugheber] aus einem Tank ablassen. **3.** *v.i.* [durch einen Saugheber] laufen; *(fig.: flow as if through a ~)* laufen

~ **'off** *v.t.* [mit einem Saugheber] ablassen; *(fig.: transfer)* abzweigen

~ **'out** *v.t.* [mit einem Saugheber] ablassen

sir [sɜ:(r)] *n.* **a)** *(formal address)* der Herr; *(to teacher)* Herr Meier/Schmidt *usw.;* Herr Lehrer/Studienrat *usw. (veralt.);* **no '~!** keinesfalls!; von wegen! *(ugs.);* **yes '~!** allerdings; **Sir!** *(Mil.)* Herr Oberst/Leutnant *usw.!; (yes)* jawohl, Herr Oberst/Leutnant *usw.!;* **b)** *(in letter)* **Dear Sir** Sehr geehrter Herr; **Dear Sirs** Sehr geehrte [Damen und] Herren; **Dear Sir or Madam** Sehr geehrte Dame/Sehr geehrter Herr; **c) Sir** [sə(r)] *(titular prefix)* Sir; **d)** [sɜ:(r)] *(person addressed as 'Sir')* Sir, *der;* **e)** *no art. (Sch. sl.: teacher)* der [Herr] Lehrer; **I shall tell ~:** das sag' ich *(ugs.)*

sire ['saɪə(r)] **1.** *n.* **a)** Vatertier, *das;* **b)** *(poet.) (father)* Vater, *der; (ancestor)* Ahnherr, *der (geh. veralt.);* **c)** *(arch.)* **yes, ~:** ja, Herr. **2.** *v.t.* zeugen

siren ['saɪrən] **1.** *n.* **a)** Sirene, *die;* **factory/ship's ~:** Fabrik-/Schiffssirene, *die;* **air-raid ~:** Luftschutzsirene, *die;* **b)** *(temptress)* Sirene, *die (geh.);* Circe, *die (geh.);* **c)** *(Greek Mythol.)* Sirene, *die.* **2.** *adj.* sirenenhaft; **~ song** Sirenengesang, *der*

sirloin ['sɜ:lɔɪn] *n.* **a)** *(Brit.: upper part of loin of beef)* Roastbeef, *das;* **a ~ of beef** ein Stück Roastbeef; **~ steak** Rumpsteak, *das;* **b)** *(Amer.)* Rumpsteak, *das*

sirocco [sɪ'rɒkəʊ] *n., pl.* **~s** Schirokko, *der*

sirup *(Amer.) see* **syrup**

sis [sɪs] *n. (coll.)* Schwesterherz, *das (scherzh.)*

sisal ['saɪsl] *n.* **a)** *(fibre)* Sisal, *der; attrib.* Sisal-; **b)** *(Bot.)* Sisalagave, *die; attrib.* Sisal-

siskin ['sɪskɪn] *n. (Ornith.)* [Erlen]zeisig, *der*

sissified ['sɪsɪfaɪd] *adj.* weibisch *(abwertend); (cowardly)* feige *(abwertend)*

sissy ['sɪsɪ] **1.** *n. (effeminate man)* weibischer Typ; *(cowardly person)* Waschlappen, *der (ugs. abwertend).* **2.** *adj.* weibisch *(abwertend); (cowardly)* feige *(abwertend)*

sister ['sɪstə(r)] *n.* **a)** Schwester, *die;* **she has been a ~ to him/her** *(fig.)* sie war für ihn/sie wie eine Schwester; **the Robinson ~s** die Robinson-Schwestern; **b)** *(friend, associate fellow member)* Schwester, *die; (in trade union)* Kollegin, *die;* **~ company** Schwesterfirma, *die;* **c)** *(Relig.)* Schwester, *die;* **S~ of Mercy** Barmherzige Schwester; **d)** *(Brit.: senior nurse)* Oberschwester, *die;* **ward ~:** Stationsschwester, *die;* **theatre ~:** Operationsschwester, *die;* **e)** *(Brit. coll.: nurse)* Schwester, *die*

sisterhood ['sɪstəhʊd] *n.* **a)** *no pl.* Schwesterschaft, *die;* schwesterliches Verhältnis; **b)** *(religious society)* Schwesternschaft, *die*

'sister-in-law *n., pl.* **sisters-in-law** Schwägerin, *die*

sisterly ['sɪstəlɪ] *adj.* schwesterlich; **~ love** Schwesterliebe, *die*

'sister ship *n. (Naut.)* Schwesterschiff, *das*

Sistine Chapel [sɪsti:n 'tʃæpl, sɪstaɪn 'tʃæpl] *n.* **the ~:** die Sixtinische Kapelle

sit [sɪt] **1.** *v.i.,* **-tt-, sat** [sæt] **a)** *(become seated)* sich setzen; **~ on** *or* **in a chair/in an armchair** sich auf einen Stuhl/in einen Sessel setzen; **~!** *(to dog)* sitz!; **~ by** *or* **with sb.** sich zu jmdm. setzen; **~ over there!** setz dich dort drüben hin!; **b)** *(be seated)* sitzen; **don't just ~ there!** sitz nicht einfach rum *(ugs.);* **~ at home** *(fig.)* zu Hause sitzen; **~ in judgement on** *or* **over sb./sth.** über jmdn./etw. zu Gericht sitzen; **~ on one's hands** *(fig.)* sich nicht rühren; **~ still!** sitz ruhig *od.* still!; **~ tight** *(coll.)* ruhig sitzen bleiben; *(fig.: stay in hiding)* sich nicht fortrühren; *(fig.: persevere in a course of action)* sich nicht beirren lassen; **~ well [in the saddle/on one's horse]** einen guten Sitz haben; *see also* **fence 1 a; foot 1 a; pretty 2; c)** **~ for one's portrait/to a painter** *etc.* Porträt sitzen/einem Maler *usw.* Modell sitzen; **d)** *see* **baby-sit; e)** *(take a test)* **~ for sth.** die Prüfung für etw. machen; **f)** *(be in session)* tagen; **g)** *(be on perch or nest)* sitzen; **h)** *(be situated)* sich befinden; **the sewing-machine sat in the attic** die Nähmaschine stand auf dem Dachboden herum; **~ well on sb.** *(fit)* jmdm. gut passen; *(suit)* jmdm. gut stehen; *(fig.)* gut zu jmdm. passen; **i)** *(be member of elected body)* **~ at Westminster** Mitglied des [britischen] Parlaments sein; **~ for** *(Brit. Parl.)* vertreten; Abgeordneter/Abgeordnete sein für. **2.** *v.t.,* **-tt-, sat a)** *(cause to be seated, place)* setzen; **b)** *(Brit.)* **~ an examination** eine Prüfung machen; *(have space for) see* **seat 2 b**

~ a'bout, ~ a'round *v.i.* herumsitzen *(ugs.)*

~ 'back *v.i.* **a)** sich zurücklehnen; **b)** *(fig.: do nothing)* sich im Sessel zurücklehnen *(fig.);* **the government is ~ting back and letting the situation worsen** die Regierung sieht tatenlos zu, wie sich die Lage verschlechtert

~ 'by *v.i.* tatenlos zusehen

~ 'down 1. *v.i.* **a)** *(become seated)* sich setzen **(on/in** auf/in **+** *Akk.);* **~ you down** *(coll.)* setz dich hin; **b)** *(be seated)* sitzen; **take sth. ~ting down** *(fig.)* etw. auf sich *(Dat.)* sitzen lassen. **2.** *v.t. (cause to be seated)* **~ sb. down** *(invite to ~)* jmdn. Platz nehmen lassen; *(help to ~)* jmdm. helfen, sich zu setzen. *See also* **sit-down**

~ 'in *v.i.* **a)** *(occupy place as protest)* ein Sit-in veranstalten; **b)** *(stay in)* zu Hause bleiben; **c)** *(participate)* mitspielen; **~ in on** *(be present at)* teilnehmen an (+ *Dat.);* dabeisein bei; **d)** *see* **stand in a.** *See also* **sit-in**

~ on *v.t.* **a)** *(serve as member of)* sitzen in (+ *Dat.)* ⟨*Ausschuß usw.*⟩; **~ on the jury** *(Law)* Geschworener sein; **b)** *(coll.: delay)* in der Schublade liegen lassen *(fig. ugs.);* auf die lange Bank schieben *(ugs.)* ⟨*Entscheidung*⟩; **c)** *(coll.: repress)* unterdrücken; nicht aufkommen lassen ⟨*Wunsch, Gedanken*⟩; **people like her want ~ting on/ought to be sat on** Leute wie sie muß/sollte man an der kurzen Leine halten *(ugs.);* **d)** *(fig.: hold on to)* festhalten

~ 'out 1. *v.i.* draußen *od.* im Freien sitzen. **2.** *v.t.* **a)** *(take no part in)* aussetzen; **~ out a dance** einen Tanz auslassen; **b)** *(endure)* durchstehen

~ 'through *see* **~ out 2 b**

~ 'up 1. *v.i.* **a)** *(rise)* sich aufsetzen; **b)** *(be sitting erect)* [aufrecht] sitzen; **c)** *(not slouch)* gerade sitzen; **~ up straight!** sitz gerade!; **make sb. ~ up** *(fig. coll.)* jmdn. aufhorchen lassen; **~ up and take notice** *(fig. coll.)* aufhorchen; **d)** *(delay going to bed)* aufbleiben; **~ up [waiting] for sb.** aufbleiben und auf jmdn. warten; **~ up with sb.** bei jmdm. Nachtwache halten. **2.** *v.t.* aufsetzen. *See also* **sit-up**

~ upon *see* **~ on;** *see also* **sit-upon**

sitar ['sɪtɑ:(r), sɪ'tɑ:(r)] *n. (Mus.)* Sitar, *der*

sitcom ['sɪtkɒm] *(coll.) see* **situation comedy**

'sit-down 1. *n.* **have a ~:** sich setzen; **enjoy a ~:** sich gern einmal hinsetzen. **2.** *adj.* **~ demonstration** Sitzblockade, *die;* **~ meal** *(im Sitzen eingenommenes)* Essen; **~ strike** Sitzstreik, *der*

site [saɪt] **1.** *n.* **a)** *(land)* Grundstück, *das;* **archaeological/prehistoric burial ~:** archäologische Grabungsstätte/vorgeschichtliche Grabstätte; **exhibition ~:** Ausstellungsgelände, *das;* **~ of a battle** Kampfplatz, *der;* **b)** *(location)* Sitz, *der; (of new factory etc.)* Standort, *der;* **c)** *see* **building-site. 2.** *v.t. (locate)* stationieren ⟨*Raketen*⟩; **~ a factory in London** London als Standort einer Fabrik wählen; **be ~d** gelegen sein

'sit-in *n.* Sit-in, *das*

siting ['saɪtɪŋ] *n.* Standortwahl, *die* **(of** für); *(position)* Lage, *die; (of missiles)* Stationierung, *die;* **the ~ of the new exhibition centre in Leeds** die Wahl von Leeds als Standort des neuen Ausstellungszentrums

sitter ['sɪtə(r)] *n.* **a)** *(Sport sl.) (easy catch)* leicht zu fangender Ball; *(easy shot)* idiotensichere Vorlage *(ugs. scherzh.);* **b)** *(artist's model)* Modell, *das;* **c)** *(hen)* Glucke, *die;* Bruthenne, *die;* **d)** *see* **baby-sitter**

sitting ['sɪtɪŋ] **1.** *n.* **a)** *(session)* Sitzung, *die;* **lunch is served in two ~s** es wird in zwei Schichten Mittag gegessen; **when is the first ~ [for lunch]?** wann geht der erste Schub [zum Mittagessen]?; **in one** *or* **at a ~** *(fig.)* in einem Zug[e]; **b)** *(Law)* Sitzungsperiode,

die. **2.** *adj.* **a)** *(not flying or running)* sitzend; **b)** *(hatching)* sitzend; brütend; **these are ~ hens** das sind Bruthennen
sitting: ~ **'duck** *n. (fig.)* leichtes Ziel; ~ **'member** *n. (Brit. Parl.)* **she is/was the ~ member** sie ist/war die derzeitige/damalige Abgeordnete; **~-room** *n.* **a)** *(lounge)* Wohnzimmer, *das; (in public buildings)* Aufenthaltsraum, *der;* **b)** *(space)* Sitzplatz, *der;* ~ **'target** *see* ~ **duck;** ~ **'tenant** *n.* **he is/was the ~ tenant** er ist/war der jetzige/damalige Mieter; **there is a ~ tenant** es ist ein Mieter vorhanden
situate 1. ['sɪtjʊeɪt] *v.t.* legen; einrichten ‹Büro›. **2.** ['sɪtjʊət] *adj. (Law) see* **situated**
situated ['sɪtjʊeɪtɪd] *adj.* **a)** gelegen; **be ~:** liegen; **a badly ~ house** ein Haus in schlechter *od.* ungünstiger Lage; **the house is well ~ for the shops** in der Nähe des Hauses gibt es gute Einkaufsmöglichkeiten; **b) be well/badly ~ financially** finanziell gut/schlecht gestellt sein
situation [sɪtjʊ'eɪʃn] *n.* **a)** *(location)* Lage, *die;* **b)** *(circumstances)* Situation, *die;* **a ~ of some delicacy** eine ziemlich heikle Situation; **be in the happy ~ of being able to do sth.** in der glücklichen Lage sein, etw. tun zu können; **his ~ is as follows: ...:** seine Lage stellt sich folgendermaßen dar: ...; **what's the ~?** wie steht's?; **lead to a compromise ~:** zu einem Kompromiß führen; **the firm is in a profit ~:** die Firma schreibt Gewinne; **c)** *(job)* Stelle, *die;* **~s vacant/wanted** Stellenangebote/-gesuche
situational [sɪtjʊ'eɪʃənl] *adj.* Situations-; **~ drama** Handlungsdrama, *das (Literaturw.)*
situation 'comedy *n.* Situationskomödie, *die (Serie von Radio- oder Fernsehkomödien mit unverbundenen Episoden bei gleichbleibenden Rollen)*
sit: ~-up *n. Bewegung aus der Rückenlage in den Langsitz (als gymnastische Übung);* **do twenty ~-ups** sich zwanzigmal aufsetzen; **~-upon** *n. (coll.)* Sitzfläche, *die (ugs. scherzh.)*
six [sɪks] **1.** *adj.* sechs; **be ~ feet** *or* **foot under** *(coll.)* unter der Erde liegen; **it is ~ of one and half-a-dozen of the other** *(coll.)* das ist Jacke wie Hose *(ugs.); see also* **eight 1. 2.** *n.* **a)** *(number, symbol)* Sechs, *die;* **be at ~es and sevens** sich in einem heillosen Durcheinander befinden; *(on an issue or matter)* heillos zerstritten sein **(on** über + *Akk.*); *see also* **best 3 d; eight 2 a, c, d; b)** *(Cricket) Schlag, mit dem man sechs Punkte gewinnt; see also* **hit 1 k**
Six 'Counties *n. pl.* **the ~:** Nordirland *(das) (mit Londonderry, Antrim, Down, Armagh, Tyrone, Fermanagh)*
six: ~fold *adj., adv.* sechsfach; *see also* **eightfold; ~-'footer** *n. (person)* Zwei-Meter-Mann, *der/*-Frau, *die;* **most of them are ~-footers** die meisten sind fast zwei Meter groß; **~-pack** *n.* Sechserpack, *der;* **~pence** ['sɪkspəns] *n. (Brit. Hist.: coin)* Sixpence, *der;* **~penny** ['sɪkspənɪ] *adj. (Brit.)* zu sechs Pennies *nachgestellt; see also* **²bit g; ~-shooter** *n.* sechsschüssiger Revolver
sixteen [sɪks'ti:n] **1.** *adj.* sechzehn; **sweet ~** süße sechzehn [Jahre alt]; *see also* **eight 1. 2.** *n.* Sechzehn, *die; see also* **eight 2 a, d; eighteen 2**
sixteenth [sɪks'ti:nθ] **1.** *adj.* sechzehnt...; *see also* **eighth 1. 2.** *n. (fraction)* Sechzehntel, *das; see also* **eighth 2**
six'teenth-note *n. (Amer. Mus.)* Sechzehntelnote, *die*
sixth [sɪksθ] **1.** *adj.* sechst...; *see also* **eighth 1. 2.** *n.* **a)** *(in sequence)* sechste, *der/die/das; (in rank)* Sechste, *der/die/das; (fraction)* Sechstel, *das;* **b)** *see* **sixth form; c)** *(Mus.)* Sexte, *die;* **d)** *(day)* **the ~ of May** der sechste Mai; **the ~ [of the month]** der Sechste [des Monats]. *See also* **eighth 2**
sixth: ~ **form** *n. (Brit. Sch.)* ≈ zwölfte/dreizehnte Klasse; **~-form college** *n. (Brit. Sch.)* ≈ Oberstufenzentrum, *das; College, das nur Schüler der zwölften/dreizehnten Klasse aufnimmt;* **~-former** *n. (Brit. Sch.)* Schüler/Schülerin der zwölften/dreizehnten Klasse
sixtieth ['sɪkstɪɪθ] **1.** *adj.* sechzigst...; *see also* **eighth 1. 2.** *n. (fraction)* Sechzigstel, *das; see also* **eighth 2**
sixty ['sɪkstɪ] **1.** *adj.* sechzig; *see also* **eight 1; one-and-~** *(arch.) see* **sixty-one 1. 2.** *n.* Sechzig, *die;* **one-and-~** *(arch.) see* **sixty-one 2;** *see also* **eight 2 a; eighty 2**
sixty: ~-'first *etc. adj.* einundsechzigst... *usw.; see also* **eighth 1; ~-'one** *etc.* **1.** *adj.* einundsechzig *usw.; see also* **eight 1; 2.** *n.* Einundsechzig *usw., die; see also* **eight 2 a**
¹size [saɪz] **1.** *n.* **a)** Größe, *die; (fig. of problem, project)* Umfang, *der;* Ausmaß, *das;* **reach full ~:** auswachsen; **be quite a ~:** ziemlich groß sein; **what a ~ he is!** wie groß er ist!; **be twice the ~ of sth.** zweimal so groß wie etw. sein; **who can afford a car that ~?** wer kann sich *(Dat.)* einen so großen Wagen leisten?; **what ~ [of] box do you want?** welche Größe soll die [gewünschte] Schachtel haben?; **take the ~ of sth.** etw. [aus]messen; **be small in ~:** klein sein; **be of great/small ~:** groß/klein sein; **a car of some ~:** ein ziemlich großes Auto; **be of a ~:** gleich groß sein; **be the ~ of sth.** so groß wie etw. sein; **be the ~ of a pea** erbsengroß sein; **a house the ~ of a palace** ein Haus so groß wie ein Palast; **that's [about] the ~ of it** *(fig. coll.)* so sieht die Sache aus *(ugs.);* **try sth. for ~:** etw. [wegen der Größe] anprobieren; *(fig.)* es einmal mit etw. versuchen; **what ~?** wie groß?; *see also* **cut down 1 c; b)** *(graded class)* Größe, *die; (of paper)* Format, *das;* **collar/waist ~:** Kragen-/Taillenweite, *die;* **take a ~ 7 shoe/~ 7 in shoes** Schuhgröße 7 haben; **what ~ is Madam?** welche Größe hat die Dame?; **A 5 ~ paper** A 5-Papier; **E 10 ~:** Größe E 10. **2.** *v.t.* nach der Größe sortieren
~ **'up** *v.t.* taxieren ‹Lage›; **I can't ~ her up** ich werde aus ihr nicht schlau *(ugs.)*
²size 1. *n.* Leim, *der; (for textiles)* Schlichte, *die.* **2.** *v.t.* leimen; schlichten ‹Textilfaser›
-size [saɪz] *adj. in comb.* **average-~:** durchschnittlich groß; **full-~ portrait/bottle** lebensgroßes Porträt *od.* Porträt in Lebensgröße/große Flasche; **small-/medium-/large-~:** klein/mittelgroß/groß
sizeable ['saɪzəbl] *adj.* ziemlich groß; beträchtlich ‹Summe, Schwierigkeiten, Wissen, Einfluß, Unterschied›; ansehnlich ‹Betrag›
-sized [saɪzd] *adj. in comb. see* **-size; good-~** größer
sizzle ['sɪzl] **1.** *v.i.* **a)** zischen; **b)** *(coll.: be hot or excited)* schmoren *(ugs.);* **be sizzling with anger** vor Wut kochen *(ugs.).* **2.** *n.* Zischen, *das*
sizzling ['sɪzlɪŋ] **1.** *adj.* **a)** zischend; **b)** *(very hot)* brütendheiß; **~ heat/weather** Gluthitze, *die;* **c)** *(very fast)* blitzschnell *(ugs.).* **2.** *adv.* **~ hot** brütendheiß ‹Wetter›; zischend heiß ‹Steak›
skat [skæt] *n. (Cards)* Skat, *der*
¹skate [skeɪt] *n. (Zool.)* Rochen, *der*
²skate 1. *n. (ice-~)* Schlittschuh, *der; (roller-~)* Rollschuh, *der;* **get one's ~s on** *(Brit. fig. coll.)* sich sputen. **2.** *v.i. (ice-~)* Schlittschuh laufen; *(roller-~)* Rollschuh laufen; **he ~d over to her/in circles** er lief zu ihr hinüber/drehte Kreise; **the insects ~ on the water** *(fig.)* die Insekten gleiten über das Wasser; **~ on thin ice** *(fig.)* sich auf dünnem Eis bewegen; *(put oneself in danger)* sich auf dünnes Eis begeben
~ over, ~ round *v.t. (fig.) (avoid)* hinweggehen über (+ *Akk.*) ‹Frage, Problem›; *(touch lightly on)* [nur] streifen
³skate *n. (sl.: contemptible person)* **[cheap] ~:** mieser Kerl *(ugs. abwertend);* **you dirty ~:** du Dreckskerl *(derb abwertend)*
skate: ~board 1. *n.* Skateboard, *das;* Rollerbrett, *das;* **2.** *v.i.* Skateboard fahren; **~boarder** *n.* Skateboardfahrer, *der/*-fahrerin, *die;* **~boarding** *n., no pl.* Skateboardfahren, *das*
skater ['skeɪtə(r)] *n. (ice-~)* Eisläufer, *der/*-läuferin, *die; (roller-~)* Rollschuhläufer, *der/*-läuferin, *die*
skating ['skeɪtɪŋ] *n., no pl. (ice-~)* Schlittschuhlaufen, *das; (roller-~)* Rollschuhlaufen, *das*
'skating-rink *n.* **a)** *(ice)* Eisbahn, *die;* Eisfläche, *die;* **b)** *(for roller-skating)* Rollschuhbahn, *die*
skedaddle [skɪ'dædl] *v.i. (coll.)* türmen *(salopp)*
skeet [ski:t] *n. (Sport)* **~ [shooting]** Skeetschießen, *das*
skein [skeɪn] *n.* **a)** *(of wool etc.)* Strang, *der;* Docke, *die;* **b)** *(fig.: tangle)* Knäuel, *das; (of lies)* Netz, *das;* **c) a ~ of wild geese** eine Schar Wildgänse
skeletal ['skelɪtl] *adj.* **a)** *(relating to the skeleton)* Skelett-; **b)** *(emaciated)* knochendürr ‹Körper, Hand›; **have a ~ appearance, look ~:** wie ein Skelett *od.* Gerippe aussehen
skeleton ['skelɪtn] *n.* **a)** Skelett, *das;* Gerippe, *das;* **have a ~ in the cupboard** *(Brit.) or (Amer.)* **closet** *(fig.)* eine Leiche im Keller haben *(ugs.);* **b)** *(framework)* Skelett, *das (Bauw.); (of ship)* Gerippe, *das;* **c)** *(outline)* Gerüst, *das;* **d)** *(fig.: thin person or animal)* Gerippe, *das;* **she was reduced to a ~:** sie magerte fast bis zum Gerippe ab
skeleton: ~ **'crew** *n.* Stammbesatzung, *die;* ~ **'key** *n.* Dietrich, *der;* ~ **'service** *n.* **provide a ~ service** den Betrieb notdürftig aufrechterhalten; **there were buses running, but it was only a ~ service** es fuhren zwar Busse, aber nur einige wenige; ~ **'staff** *n.* Minimalbesetzung, *die*
skepsis, skeptic *(Amer.) see* **scep-**
sketch [sketʃ] **1.** *n.* **a)** *(drawing)* Skizze, *die;* **do** *or* **make a ~:** eine Skizze anfertigen; **b)** *(fig.: outline)* **give** *or* **deliver a ~ of the situation** die Lage skizzieren; **the plan is only a ~ at the moment** der Plan existiert zur Zeit nur in [groben] Umrissen; **c)** *(play)* Sketch, *der;* **d)** *(Lit., Mus.)* Skizze, *die.* **2.** *v.t. (lit. or fig.)* skizzieren. **3.** *v.i.* skizzieren
~ **'in** *v.t.* **a)** *(draw)* einzeichnen; **b)** *(fig.: outline)* skizzieren
~ **'out** *v.t. (lit. or fig.)* [in groben Umrissen] skizzieren
sketch: ~-block *n.* Skizzenblock, *der;* **~-book** *n.* Skizzenbuch, *das*
sketcher ['sketʃə(r)] *n.* Skizzenmaler, *der/*-malerin, *die* **(of** für)
sketchily ['sketʃɪlɪ] *adv.* skizzenhaft; flüchtig ‹vorbereiten, berichten, aufzeichnen›
sketching ['sketʃɪŋ] *n.* Skizzieren, *das*
sketch: ~ **map** *n.* Faustskizze, *die;* **~-pad** *see* **sketch-block**
sketchy ['sketʃɪ] *adj.* **a)** skizzenhaft; **b)** *(incomplete)* lückenhaft ‹Information, Bericht›; **c)** *(inadequate)* unzureichend
skew [skju:] **1.** *adj.* schräg; schief ‹Gesicht›. **2.** *n.* **on the ~:** schräg ‹überqueren›; schief ‹tragen, aufsetzen›; **the picture is [hanging] on the ~:** das Bild hängt schief. **3.** *v.t.* abschrägen; verzerren ‹Gesicht, Gestalt, Sachverhalt›. **4.** *v.i.* **~ round** sich drehen
skewer ['skju:ə(r)] **1.** *n.* [Brat]spieß, *der.* **2.** *v.t.* aufspießen
skew-'whiff *(Brit. coll.) see* **askew**
ski [ski:] **1.** *n.* **a)** Ski, *der;* **b)** *(on vehicle)* Kufe, *die.* **2.** *v.i.* Ski laufen *od.* fahren; **~ down the hill** [auf Skiern] den Berg hinabfahren; **~ cross-country** Skilanglauf machen
ski: ~-bob *n.* Skibob, *der;* **~-bobbing** *n.* Skibobfahren, *das;* ~ **boot** *n.* Skistiefel, *der;* ~ **cap** *n.* Skimütze, *die*

skid [skɪd] **1.** *v.i.*, **-dd- a)** schlittern; *(from one side to the other; spinning round)* schleudern; **~ to a halt** schlitternd/schleudernd zum Stehen kommen; **b)** *(on foot)* rutschen. **2.** *n.* **a)** Schlittern, *das; (from one side to the other; spinning round)* Schleudern, *das;* **go into a ~:** ins Schlittern/Schleudern geraten; **get out of the ~, correct the ~:** das Schlittern/Schleudern abfangen; **steer into the ~:** gegenlenken; **b)** *(Aeronaut.)* Gleitkufe, *die;* **tail/wing ~:** Gleitkufe unter dem Leitwerk/Flügel; **c)** *(braking device)* Radschuh, *der;* Hemmschuh, *der;* **d)** *(support)* Stützbalken, *der;* **e)** *(slideway)* Schrotbaum, *der; (used in pairs or sets)* Schrotleiter, *die; (roller)* Rolle, *die;* **be on the ~s** *(fig. coll.)* auf dem absteigenden Ast sein; **the plan/project is on the ~s** *(fig. coll.)* der Plan/das Projekt droht zu scheitern; **put the ~s under sb./sth.** *(fig. coll.)* jmdn./etw. zu Fall bringen

skid: ~ chains *see* **snow chains; ~ -lid** *n. (sl.)* Sturzhelm, *der;* **~-marks** *n. pl.* Schleuderspur, *die;* **~pad** *n. (Amer.),* **~-pan** *n. (Brit.) Gelände, auf dem ein Schleudertraining durchgeführt wird;* **~ row** [skɪd'rəʊ] *n. (Amer.)* Pennerviertel, *das (salopp abwertend);* **end up on ~ row** *(coll.)* als Penner enden *(salopp abwertend)*

skier ['ski:ə(r)] *n.* Skiläufer, *der*/-läuferin, *die;* Skifahrer, *der*/-fahrerin, *die*

skiff [skɪf] *n.* Skiff, *das; (racing-boat also)* Einer, *der*

skiffle ['skɪfl] *n.* Skiffle, *der od. das; attrib.* Skiffle-

'ski goggles *n. pl.* Skibrille, *die*

skiing ['ski:ɪŋ] *n., no pl.* Skilaufen, *das;* Skifahren, *das; (Sport)* Skisport, *der*

ski: ~-jump *n.* **a)** *(slope)* Sprungschanze, *die;* **b)** *(leap)* Skisprung, *der;* **~-jumper** *n.* Skispringer, *der*/-springerin, *die;* **~-jumping** *n., no pl.* Skispringen, *das*

skilful ['skɪlfl] *adj.* **a)** *(having skill)* geschickt; gewandt ‹*Redner*›; gut ‹*Beobachter, Lehrer*›; **b)** *(well executed)* geschickt; kunstvoll ‹*Gemälde, Plastik, Roman, Komposition*›; *(expert)* fachgerecht ‹*Beurteilung*›; kunstgerecht ausgeführt ‹*Operation*›

skilfully ['skɪlfəlɪ] *adv.* geschickt; kunstvoll ‹*malen, dichten, komponieren*›; fachgerecht ‹*urteilen*›; kunstgerecht ‹*operieren*›

skilfulness ['skɪlflnɪs] *n., no pl. see* **skill a**

'ski-lift *n.* Skilift, *der*

skill [skɪl] *n.* **a)** *(expertness)* Geschick, *das;* Fertigkeit, *die; (of artist)* Können, *das;* **have ~ at** *or* **in sth.** Geschick/Fertigkeit in etw. *(Dat.)* haben; **b)** *(technique)* Fertigkeit, *die; (of weaving, bricklaying)* Technik, *die;* Kunst, *die;* **the ~ of making guests feel at home** die Kunst, Gäste sich wie zu Hause fühlen zu lassen; **c)** *in pl. (abilities)* Fähigkeiten; **office ~s** Büroerfahrung, *die;* **language ~s** Sprachkenntnisse, *die;* **d)** *(dexterity)* Geschicklichkeit, *die; (of speech)* Gewandtheit, *die; (of painting)* Kunstfertigkeit, *die*

skilled [skɪld] *adj.* **a)** *see* **skilful a; b)** *(requiring skill)* qualifiziert ‹*Arbeit, Tätigkeit*›; **~ trade** Ausbildungsberuf, *der;* Lehrberuf, *der (veralt.);* **c)** *(trained)* ausgebildet; *(experienced)* erfahren; **be ~ in diplomacy/sewing** ein guter Diplomat sein/gut nähen können; **~ men** Fachleute *Pl.*

skillet ['skɪlɪt] *n.* **a)** *(Brit.: cooking-pot)* Tiegel, *der (mit Füßen);* **b)** *(Amer.: frying-pan)* Bratpfanne, *die*

skillful, skillfully, skillfulness *(Amer.) see* **skilful** *etc.*

skim [skɪm] **1.** *v.t.*, **-mm- a)** *(remove)* abschöpfen; abrahmen ‹*Milch*›; **b)** *(touch in passing)* streifen; **c)** *(pass closely over)* **~ sth.** dicht über etw. *(Akk.)* fliegen; **d)** *(throw)* segeln lassen; hüpfen lassen ‹*Stein*›; **e)** *(scan briefly) see* **~ through. 2.** *v.i.*, **-mm-** segeln; **a bullet ~med past** *or* **by my arm** eine Kugel schwirrte an meinem Arm vorbei

~ 'off *v.t.* **a)** abschöpfen; **b)** *(fig.) see* **cream off**

~ through *v.t.* überfliegen ‹*Buch, Zeitung*›

skimmed 'milk, skim 'milk *n.* entrahmte Milch

skimp [skɪmp] **1.** *v.t.* sparen an (+ *Dat.*); **he did the work badly, ~ing it** er schluderte bei seiner Arbeit *(ugs.).* **2.** *v.i.* sparen **(with,** on an + *Dat.*); **he had to ~ on food/clothes** er mußte am Essen/an der Kleidung sparen

skimpily ['skɪmpɪlɪ] *adv.* sparsam ‹*bekleidet*›; kärglich ‹*essen*›; knapp ‹*geschneidert*›

skimpy ['skɪmpɪ] *adj.* sparsam; karg ‹*Mahl*›; kärglich ‹*Leben*›; winzig ‹*Badeanzug*›; [zu] knapp ‹*Anzug*›; spärlich ‹*Wissen*›

skin [skɪn] **1.** *n.* **a)** Haut, *die;* **be all** *or* **just ~ and bone** *(fig.)* nur Haut und Knochen sein *(ugs.);* **be soaked** *or* **wet to the ~:** bis auf die Haut durchnäßt sein; **change one's ~** *(fig.)* sich völlig verwandeln; **by** *or* **with the ~ of one's teeth** mit knapper Not; **get under sb.'s ~** *(fig. coll.) (irritate sb.)* jmdm. auf die Nerven gehen *od.* fallen *(ugs.); (fascinate or enchant sb.)* jmdm. unter die Haut gehen *(ugs.);* **have a thick/thin ~** *(fig.)* ein dickes Fell haben *(ugs.)*/dünnhäutig sein; **jump out of one's ~** *(fig.)* aus dem Häuschen geraten *(ugs.);* **save one's ~** *(fig.)* seine Haut retten *(ugs.);* **it's no ~ off my/his** *etc.* **nose** *(coll.)* das braucht mich/ihn *usw.* nicht zu jucken *(ugs.);* **wear sth. next to one's ~:** etw. auf der [bloßen] Haut tragen; **we are all brothers under the ~:** wir sind uns im Grunde alle sehr ähnlich; **b)** *(hide)* Haut, *die;* **c)** *(fur)* Fell, *das;* **d)** *(peel)* Schale, *die; (of onion, peach also)* Haut, *die;* **e)** *(sausage-casing)* Haut, *die;* Pelle, *die (landsch., bes. nordd.);* **f)** *(leather)* Leder, *das;* **g)** *(Brit. sl.) see* **skinhead a; h)** *(vessel)* Schlauch, *der;* **i)** *(Naut., Aeronaut.)* Außenhaut, *die;* **j)** *(stencil)* Matrize, *die.* **2.** *v.t.*, **-nn-** *(remove ~ from)* häuten; schälen ‹*Frucht*›; **~ one's knee** *etc.* sich *(Dat.)* das Knie *usw.* [auf]schürfen **(on** an, auf + *Dat.*, **against** an + *Dat.*); **~ sb. alive** *(fig. coll.)* Hackfleisch aus jmdm. machen *(ugs.); see also* **eye 1 a**

skin: ~-cream *n.* Hautcreme, *die;* **~-'deep** *adj. (fig.)* oberflächlich; *see also* **beauty a; ~ disease** *n.* Hautkrankheit, *die;* **~-dive** *v.i.* tauchen; **~-diver** *n.* Taucher, *der*/Taucherin, *die;* **~-diving** *n., no pl.* Tauchen, *das;* **~-flick** *n. (sl.)* Pornofilm, *der (ugs.);* **~flint** *n.* Geizhals, *der (abwertend);* **~-food** *n.* Nährcreme, *die*

skinful ['skɪnfʊl] *n. (coll.)* **have [got] a ~:** voll sein *(salopp)*

skin: ~ game *n. (Amer. sl.)* [betrügerisches] Glücksspiel; **~-graft** *n.* Hauttransplantation, *die;* **~head** *n.* **a)** *(Brit.)* Skinhead, *der;* **b)** *(Amer. sl.: naval recruit)* Marinerekrut, *der*

-skinned [skɪnd] *adj. in comb.* -häutig

skinny ['skɪnɪ] *adj.* mager

'skinny-dipping *n. (Amer. sl.)* Nacktbaden, *das*

skint [skɪnt] *adj. (Brit. coll.)* bankrott; **be ~:** blank *od.* pleite sein *(ugs.)*

skin: ~ test *n.* Hauttest, *der;* **~-tight** *adj.* hauteng

¹skip [skɪp] **1.** *v.i.*, **-pp- a)** hüpfen; **b)** *(use skipping-rope)* seilspringen; **c)** *(change quickly)* springen *(fig.);* **d)** *(make omissions)* überspringen; **e)** *(coll.: flee)* abhauen *(ugs.).* **2.** *v.t.*, **-pp- a)** *(omit)* überspringen; *(in mentioning names)* übergehen; **~ it!** *(sl.)* vergiß es *(ugs.);* **my heart ~ped a beat** *(fig.)* mir stockte das Herz; **b)** *(coll.: miss)* schwänzen *(ugs.)* ‹*Schule usw.*›; liegenlassen ‹*Hausarbeit*›; **~ breakfast/lunch** *etc.* das Frühstück/Mittagessen *usw.* auslassen; **c)** *(coll.: flee from)* abhauen aus *(ugs.); see also* **'bail 1 a; d) ~ rope** *(Amer.)* seilspringen. **3.** *n.* Hüpfer, *der;* Hopser, *der (ugs.);* **give a ~ of delight** vor Freude hüpfen

~ a'bout *v.i.* **a)** herumhüpfen; **b) he did not stay with his subject but ~ped about** er hielt sich nicht an sein Thema, sondern sprang von einem Gegenstand zum anderen *od.* nächsten

~ a'cross *v.i.* hinüberspringen; rüberspringen *(ugs.);* **~ across to France** *(fig.)* kurz nach Frankreich hinüberfahren *od. (ugs.)* rüberfahren

~ a'round *see* **~ about**

~ 'off *v.i.* **a)** *see* **pop off b; b)** *(flee)* sich absetzen *(ugs.)*

~ over 1. [-'--] *v.i. see* **~ across. 2.** ['---] *v.t. see* **~ 2 a**

~ through *v.t.* **a)** *see* **skim through; b)** *(make short work of)* [rasch] durchziehen *(ugs.);* herunterschnurren *(ugs.)* ‹*Vorlesung*›

²skip *n.* **a)** *(Building)* Container, *der;* **b)** *(Mining)* Skip, *der;* Fördergefäß, *das*

³skip *(Sport coll.) see* **skipper 1 c**

ski: ~-plane *n.* Kufenflugzeug, *das;* **~ pole** *n.* Skistock, *der*

skipper ['skɪpə(r)] **1.** *n.* **a)** *(Naut.)* Kapitän, *der; (of yacht)* Skipper, *der (Seglerjargon);* **b)** *(Aeronaut.)* [Flug]kapitän, *der;* **c)** *(Sport)* [Mannschafts]kapitän, *der.* **2.** *v.t.* **~ a yacht** *etc.* Kapitän einer Jacht *usw.* sein; **~ the team to victory** die Mannschaft zum Sieg führen

skipping-rope ['skɪpɪŋrəʊp] *(Brit.),* **'skip-rope** *(Amer.) ns.* Sprungseil, *das;* Springseil, *das*

'ski resort *n.* Skiurlaubsort, *der*

skirl [skɜ:l] *n.* durchdringendes *od.* gellendes Pfeifen

skirmish ['skɜ:mɪʃ] **1.** *n.* **a)** *(fight)* Rangelei, *die (ugs.); (of troops, armies)* Gefecht, *das (Milit.);* **b)** *(fig.: argument)* Auseinandersetzung, *die.* **2.** *v.i.* **a)** *(fight)* miteinander rangeln *(ugs.);* ‹*Armeen, Truppen:*› sich *(Dat.)* Gefechte *(Milit.)* liefern; **b)** *(fig.: argue)* [sich] streiten

skirt [skɜ:t] **1.** *n.* **a)** Rock, *der;* **b)** *(of coat)* Schoß, *der;* **c)** *(border)* Rand, *der;* Saum, *der (geh.);* **d)** *(on hovercraft)* Schürze, *die;* **e)** *(Riding)* Seitenblatt, *das;* **f)** *(Brit.: cut of meat)* **~ of beef** Rindfleisch vom Unterbauch; **g)** *(sl.: woman)* **[a bit of] ~:** [eine] Mieze *(salopp).* **2.** *v.t.* **a)** *(go past edge of)* herumgehen um; **b)** *(border on)* ‹*Straße, Weg:*› entlangführen an (+ *Dat.*). **3.** *v.i.* **~ along sth.** an etw. *(Dat.)* entlanggehen/-fahren/-reiten *usw.*

~ round *v.t.* herumgehen um; *(fig.)* umgehen; ausweichen (+ *Dat.*)

skirting ['skɜ:tɪŋ] *n.* **~[-board]** *(Brit.)* Fußleiste, *die*

ski: ~-run *n.* Skihang, *der; (prepared)* [Ski]piste, *die;* **~stick** *n.* Skistock, *der;* **~ suit** *n.* Skianzug, *der*

skit [skɪt] *n.* parodistischer Sketch **(on** über + *Akk.*)

'ski tow *n.* Schlepplift, *der*

skittish ['skɪtɪʃ] *adj.* **a)** *(nervous)* nervös ‹*Pferd*›; *(inclined to shy)* schreckhaft ‹*Pferd*›; **b)** *(lively)* ausgelassen; aufgekratzt *(ugs.)*

skittishly ['skɪtɪʃlɪ] *adv. see* **skittish:** nervös; schreckhaft; ausgelassen; aufgekratzt *(ugs.)*

skittle ['skɪtl] *n.* **a)** Kegel, *der;* **b)** *in pl., constr. as sing. (game)* Kegeln, *das;* **play [at] ~s** kegeln; see also **beer**

~ 'out *v.t. (Cricket)* in schneller Folge ausscheiden lassen ‹*die gegnerischen Schlagmänner*›

skive [skaɪv] **1.** *v.t.* **a)** *(pare)* schaben ‹*Leder, Fell*›; **b)** *(Brit. sl.: evade)* sich drücken vor (+ *Dat.*) *(ugs.);* schwänzen *(ugs.)* ‹*Schule usw.*›. **2.** *v.i. (Brit. sl.)* sich drücken *(ugs.)*

~ 'off *(Brit. sl.)* **1.** *v.i.* sich verdrücken *(ugs.).* **2.** *v.t.* schwänzen *(ugs.)*

skiver ['skaɪvə(r)] *n. (Brit. sl.)* Drückeberger, *der*/Drückebergerin, *die*

skivvy ['skɪvɪ] *n. (Brit. coll. derog.)* Dienstmädchen, *das (fig. ugs.);* Dienstbolzen, *der (salopp abwertend)*
skua ['skju:ə] *n. (Ornith.)* Skua[raubmöwe], *die*
skulduggery [skʌl'dʌgərɪ] *n. (joc.)* Hinterlist, *die; (Polit.)* Intrige, *die;* **a piece/an act of ~:** eine Hinterlist/Intrige; **what ~ got you the job?** mit welchen Tricks hast du die Stelle bekommen?
skulk [skʌlk] *v. i.* **a)** *(lurk)* lauern; **b)** *(move stealthily)* schleichen; **c)** *(be cowardly)* sich verkriechen; **d)** *(shirk duty)* krankfeiern *(ugs.)*
~ 'off *v. i.* sich fortschleichen
skull [skʌl] *n.* **a)** *(Anat.)* Schädel, *der;* **b)** *(as object)* Totenschädel, *der; (representation)* Totenkopf, *der;* **c)** *(fig.: seat of intelligence)* Schädel, *der;* **can't you/when will you get it into** *or* **through your thick ~?** *(coll.)* geht das nicht/wann geht das endlich in deinen Schädel [hinein]? *(ugs.)*
skull: ~ and cross-bones [skʌlən'krɒsbəʊnz] *n.* Totenkopf, *der (mit gekreuzten Knochen); (flag)* Totenkopfflagge, *die;* **~-cap** *n.* **a)** *(hat)* Scheitelkäppchen, *das;* **b)** *(Anat.)* Schädeldach, *das*
skullduggery *see* **skulduggery**
-skulled [skʌld] *adj. in comb.* -schädelig
skunk [skʌŋk] *n.* **a)** *(Zool.)* Stinktier, *das;* Skunk, *der;* **b)** *(coll.: contemptible person)* Stinktier, *das (derb);* **c)** *(fur)* Skunk, *der*
'skunk-bear *(Amer.) see* **wolverine**
sky [skaɪ] **1.** *n.* Himmel, *der;* **in the ~:** am Himmel; **out of a clear [blue] ~** *(fig.)* aus heiterem Himmel *(ugs.);* **praise sb./sth. to the skies** jmdn./etw. in den Himmel heben *(ugs.);* **there is not a cloud in the ~** *(lit. or fig.)* es zeigt sich kein Wölkchen am Himmel; **the ~'s the limit** *(fig.)* da gibt es [praktisch] keine Grenze; **for a man with his qualifications the ~'s the limit** *(fig.)* einem so hochqualifizierten Mann stehen alle Möglichkeiten offen; **under the open ~:** unter freiem Himmel. **2.** *v. t. (Sport)* hoch in die Luft schlagen
sky: ~-blue 1. *adj.* himmelblau; **2.** *n.* Himmelblau, *das;* **~-diver** *n.* Fallschirmspringer, *der*/-springerin, *die;* **~-diving** *n.* Fallschirmspringen, *das (als Sport);* Fallschirmsport, *der;* **~-high 1.** *adj.* himmelhoch; astronomisch *(ugs.)* ⟨*Preise usw.*⟩; **2.** *adv.* hoch in die Luft ⟨*werfen, steigen usw.*⟩; **go ~-high** ⟨*Preise usw.:*⟩ in astronomische Höhen klettern *(ugs.);* **blow a building/a theory ~-high** ein Gebäude in die Luft jagen *(ugs.)*/eine Theorie völlig umwerfen; **~jack** *(Journ. coll.)* **1.** *v. t.* entführen; **2.** *n.* Flugzeugentführung, *die;* **~-jacker** ['skaɪdʒækə(r)] *n. (Journ. coll.)* Flugzeugentführer, *der*/-entführerin, *die;* **~lark 1.** *n. (Ornith.)* [Feld]lerche, *die;* **2.** *v. i.* **~lark [about** *or* **around]** herumalbern *(ugs.);* **~light** *n.* Dachfenster, *das;* **~line** *n.* Silhouette, *die; (characteristic of certain town)* Skyline, *die;* **~-rocket 1.** *n.* Rakete, *die;* **2.** *v. i. (fig. coll.)* ⟨*Preise usw.:*⟩ in die Höhe schnellen; ⟨*Beliebtheit:*⟩ ungeheuer *(ugs.)* wachsen; **~sail** ['skaɪseɪl, 'skaɪsl] *n. (Naut.)* Skysegel, *das;* **~scraper** *n.* Wolkenkratzer, *der*
skyward ['skaɪwəd] **1.** *adj.* zum Himmel gerichtet; **in a ~ direction/on a ~ path** himmelwärts *(geh.).* **2.** *adv.* himmelwärts *(geh.);* zum *od. (veralt.)* gen Himmel
skywards *see* **skyward 2**
sky: ~way *n. (Aeronaut.)* Fluglinie, *die;* **~-writing** *n.* Himmelsschrift, *die*
slab [slæb] *n.* **a)** *(flat stone etc.)* Platte, *die;* **mortuary ~:** Totenbank, *die;* **b)** *(thick slice)* [dicke] Scheibe; *(of cake)* [dickes] Stück; *(of chocolate, toffee)* Tafel, *die*
'slab cake *n.* Kastenkuchen, *der*
[1]**slack** [slæk] **1.** *adj.* **a)** *(lax)* nachlässig; schlampig *(ugs. abwertend);* **his ~ attendance** sein unregelmäßiges Erscheinen; **be ~ about** *or* **in** *or* **with sth.** in bezug auf etw. *(Akk.)* nachlässig sein; **not be ~ about** *or* **in** *or* **at doing sth.** nicht lange zögern, etw. zu tun; **b)** *(loose)* schlaff; locker ⟨*Schraube, Verband, Strumpfband*⟩; **c)** *(sluggish)* schlaff; schwach ⟨*Wind, Flut*⟩; **d)** *(Commerc.: not busy)* flau; **a ~ three weeks** eine dreiwöchige Flaute. **2.** *n.* **a)** *(Naut.)* Lose, *die;* **take in** *or* **up the ~ on sth.** die Lose an etw. *(Dat.)* durchholen; **b)** *(lull)* Flaute, *die.* **3.** *v. i. (coll.)* bummeln *(ugs.)*
~ 'off *see* **slacken off**
~ 'up *see* **slacken up**
[2]**slack** *n. (coal-dust)* Grus, *der*
slacken ['slækn] **1.** *v. i.* **a)** *(loosen)* sich lockern; **b)** *(diminish)* nachlassen; ⟨*Geschwindigkeit:*⟩ sich verringern; ⟨*Schritt:*⟩ sich verlangsamen. **2.** *v. t.* **a)** *(loosen)* lockern; **b)** *(diminish)* verringern; verlangsamen ⟨*Schritt*⟩; **~ one's efforts/attempts** in seinen Anstrengungen/Bemühungen nachlassen
~ 'off 1. *v. i.* **a)** *(loosen) see* **~ 1 a; b)** *(diminish) see* **~ 1 b; c)** *(relax)* es etwas langsamer angehen lassen *(ugs.).* **2.** *v. t.* **a)** *(loosen) see* **~ 2 a; b)** *(diminish) see* **~ 2 b**
~ 'up *v. i.* **a)** *(reduce speed)* ⟨*Zug, Auto:*⟩ die Fahrt verlangsamen; ⟨*Schritt:*⟩ sich verlangsamen; **b)** *see* **~ off 1 c**
slacker ['slækə(r)] *n. (derog.)* Faulenzer, *der*
slackly ['slæklɪ] *adv.* **a)** *(negligently)* nachlässig; schlampig *(ugs. abwertend);* **b)** *(loosely)* locker; schlaff ⟨*hängen*⟩
slackness ['slæknɪs] *n., no pl.* **a)** *(negligence)* Nachlässigkeit, *die;* **b)** *(idleness)* Bummelei, *die (ugs.);* **c)** *(looseness)* Schlaffheit, *die;* **d)** *(of market, trade)* Flaute, *die*
slacks [slæks] *n. pl.* **[pair of] ~:** lange Hose; Slacks *Pl. (Mode)*
slack 'water *n.* Stauwasser, *das*
slag [slæg] **1.** *n.* **a)** *(Metallurgy, Geol.)* Schlacke, *die; see also* **basic slag; b)** *(sl.: slattern)* Schlampe, *die (salopp).* **2.** *v. t.* **~ [off]** herziehen über (+ *Akk.*) *(ugs.)*
'slag-heap *n. (Mining)* Schlackenhalde, *die*
slain *see* **slay**
slake [sleɪk] *v. t.* **a)** stillen; löschen, stillen ⟨*Durst*⟩; **b)** *(Chem.)* löschen
slaked lime [sleɪkt 'laɪm] *see* [1]**lime a**
slalom ['slɑ:ləm] *n. (Skiing; Motor-/Canoe-racing)* Slalom, *der; see also* **giant slalom**
[1]**slam** [slæm] **1.** *v. t.,* **-mm- a)** *(shut)* zuschlagen; zuknallen *(ugs.);* **~ the door in sb.'s face** jmdm. die Tür vor der Nase zuschlagen; **b)** *(put violently)* knallen *(ugs.);* **~ sb. in[to] prison** *(coll.)* jmdn. einbuchten *(salopp);* **~ one's foot on the brake** *(coll.)* auf die Bremse steigen *(ugs.);* **c)** *(sl.: criticize) see* **slate 3 a; d)** *(coll.: hit with force)* knallen *(ugs.)* ⟨*Ball*⟩. **2.** *v. i.,* **-mm- a)** zuschlagen; zuknallen *(ugs.);* **b)** *(move violently)* stürmen; **the car ~med against** *or* **into the wall** das Auto knallte *(ugs.)* gegen die Mauer. **3.** *n. (sound)* Knall, *der;* **hear the ~ of the door** die Tür zuknallen hören *(ugs.)*
~ 'down *v. t.* [hin]knallen *(ugs.);* **~ sth. down on sth.** etw. auf etw. *(Akk.)* knallen *(ugs.);* **~ down a window** ein Fenster zuknallen *(ugs.)*
~ 'on *v. t. (coll.)* **~ on the brakes** auf die Bremse latschen *(salopp)*
~ 'to 1. *v. i.* zuschlagen; zuknallen *(ugs.).* **2.** *v. t.* zuschlagen; zuknallen *(ugs.)*
[2]**slam** *n.* **a)** *(Cards)* Schlemm, *der;* **grand/little** *or* **small ~:** großer/kleiner Schlemm; **b)** *(Sport)* **achieve the grand ~:** alle [wichtigen] Meistertitel gewinnen; *(Tennis)* den Grand Slam gewinnen
slam'bang *adv.* mit einem Knall
slammer ['slæmə(r)] *n. (sl.)* Kittchen, *das (ugs.)*
slander ['slɑ:ndə(r)] **1.** *n.* **a)** *(false report, defamation)* Verleumdung, *die* **(on** *Gen.***); b)** *(Law)* [mündliche] Verleumdung. **2.** *v. t.* verleumden; schädigen ⟨*Ruf*⟩
slanderer ['slɑ:ndərə(r)] *n.* Verleumder, *der*/Verleumderin, *die*
slanderous ['slɑ:ndərəs] *adj.* verleumderisch
slang [slæŋ] **1.** *n.* Slang, *der;* ⟨*Theater-, Soldaten-, Juristen*⟩jargon, *der; attrib.* Slang⟨*wort, -ausdruck*⟩. **2.** *v. t.* **~ sb.** jmdn. übel beschimpfen; **~ sth.** etw. zerreißen *(ugs.)*
'slanging-match *n.* gegenseitige [lautstarke] Beschimpfung; **I had a ~ with her** wir warfen uns gegenseitig Beschimpfungen an den Kopf
slangy ['slæŋɪ] *adj.* Slang⟨*ausdruck, -wort*⟩; salopp ⟨*Wortwahl, Redeweise*⟩
slant [slɑ:nt] **1.** *v. i.* ⟨*Fläche:*⟩ sich neigen; ⟨*Linie:*⟩ schräg verlaufen; **the roof ~s at an angle of 45°** das Dach hat eine Neigung von 45°; **green hills ~ing down to the sea** grüne Hügel, die schräg zum Meer abfallen; **his writing ~s from left to right** seine Schrift ist nach rechts geneigt *od.* er schreibt nach rechts; **the desk-top ~s** die Schreibtischplatte ist geneigt. **2.** *v. t.* **a)** abschrägen; schräg zeichnen ⟨*Linie*⟩; **b)** *(fig.: bias)* [so] hinbiegen *(ugs.)* ⟨*Meldung, Bemerkung*⟩. **3.** *n.* **a)** Schräge, *die;* **have a ~ to the right** ⟨*Handschrift:*⟩ nach rechts geneigt sein; **cut sth. with** *or* **on a** *or* **the ~:** etw. schräg abschneiden; **be on a** *or* **the ~:** schräg sein; **write on the ~:** schräg schreiben; **b)** *(fig.: bias)* Tendenz, *die;* Färbung, *die;* **have a left-wing ~** ⟨*Bericht:*⟩ links gefärbt sein; **put a right-wing ~ on sth.** von etw. eine rechts gefärbte Darstellung geben; **give an unfair ~ to events** die Vorfälle schief darstellen
slanted ['slɑ:ntɪd] *adj. (fig.)* gefärbt; **a ~ question** eine Suggestivfrage
'slant-eyed *adj. (also derog.)* schlitzäugig
slanting ['slɑ:ntɪŋ] *adj.* schräg
'slantways ['slɑ:ntweɪz], **slantwise** ['slɑ:ntwaɪz] *adv.* schräg
slap [slæp] **1.** *v. t.,* **-pp- a)** schlagen; **~ sb. on the face/arm/hand** jmdm. ins Gesicht/auf den Arm/auf die Hand schlagen; **~ sb.'s face** *or* **sb. in** *or* **on the face** jmdn. ohrfeigen; **I'll ~ your face!** du bekommst eine Ohrfeige; **~ one's thigh[s]** sich *(Dat.)* auf die Schenkel schlagen; **~ sb. on the back** jmdm. auf die Schulter klopfen; **she deserves to be ~ped on the back** *(fig.)* sie verdient Beifall; Hut ab vor ihr! *(ugs.);* **b)** *(put forcefully)* knallen *(ugs.);* **he ~ped the handcuffs on the prisoner** er ließ die Handschellen an den Armen des Gefangenen zuschnappen; **~ a fine on sb.** *(fig.)* jmdm. eine Geldstrafe aufbrummen *(ugs.);* **~ sb. in jail** *(coll.)* jmdn. ins Gefängnis stecken *(ugs.);* **c)** *(put hastily or carelessly)* klatschen *(ugs.).* **2.** *v. i.,* **-pp-** schlagen; klatschen. **3.** *n.* Schlag, *der;* **give sb. a ~:** jmdn. [mit der flachen Hand] schlagen; **give sth. a ~:** [mit der flachen Hand] auf etw. *(Akk.)* schlagen; **a ~ in the face** *(lit. or fig.)* ein Schlag ins Gesicht; **give sb. a ~ on the back** *(lit. or fig.)* jmdm. auf die Schulter klopfen; **a ~ on the back for sb./sth.** *(fig.)* eine Anerkennung für jmdn./etw.; **the judge gave him more than just a ~ on the wrist** *(fig.)* der Richter verpaßte ihm einen ordentlichen Denkzettel *(ugs.).* **4.** *adv.* voll; **run ~ into sb.** *(lit. or fig.)* mit jmdm. zusammenprallen; **hit sb. ~ in the eye/face** *etc.* jmdn. mit voller Wucht ins Auge/Gesicht treffen; **~ in the middle** genau in der Mitte; **he arrived ~ on time** er kam auf die Minute pünktlich
~ 'down *v. t.* **a)** *(lay forcefully)* hinknallen *(ugs.);* **~ sth. down on sth.** etw. auf etw. *(Akk.)* knallen *(ugs.);* **b)** *(coll.: check, suppress, reprimand)* **~ sb. down** jmdm. eins auf den Deckel geben *(ugs.);* **be ~ped down** eins auf den Deckel kriegen *(ugs.)*
~ 'on *v. t.* **a)** *(coll.: apply hastily)* draufklatschen *(ugs.)* ⟨*Farbe, Tapete, Make-up*⟩; zuschnappen lassen ⟨*Handschellen*⟩; **b)** *(coll.: impose)* draufschlagen *(ugs.)*

slap: ~ **and 'tickle** *n. (Brit. coll.)* Fummelei, *die (salopp);* **~-bang** *adv.* **the table was ~-bang in the middle of the room** der Tisch stand einfach mitten im Zimmer; **~dash 1.** *adv.* ruck, zuck *(ugs.);* **2.** *adj.* **in a ~dash way/fashion/manner** im Schnellverfahren; *(carelessly)* schludrig *(ugs. abwertend);* **her essay is ~dash** ihr Aufsatz ist hingeschludert *(ugs. abwertend);* **he is a ~dash sort** er ist ein schludriger Typ; **be ~dash in one's work** bei seiner Arbeit schludern *(ugs. abwertend);* **~-happy** *adj. (coll.)* **a)** *(punch-drunk, lit. or fig.)* taumelig; **b)** *(cheerfully casual)* unbekümmert; **~stick** *n. (Theatre: comedy style)* Slapstick, *der;* **~stick comedy/humour** Slapstickkomödie, *die*/-humor, *der;* **~-up** *attrib. adj. (sl.)* ⟨*Essen, Diner*⟩ mit allen Schikanen *(ugs.)*

slash [slæʃ] **1.** *v. i.* ~ **with one's sword** sein Schwert schwingen; ~ **at sb./sth. with a knife/stick** auf jmdn./etw. mit einem Messer losgehen/mit einem Stock ausholen. **2.** *v. t.* **a)** *(make gashes in)* aufschlitzen; ~ **one's wrists** sich *(Dat.)* die Pulsadern aufschneiden; ~ **sth. to ribbons** *or* **shreds** etw. zerfetzen; **b)** *(Dressm., Tailoring)* [auf]schlitzen; **c)** *(fig.: reduce sharply)* [drastisch] reduzieren; [drastisch] kürzen ⟨*Etat, Gehalt, Umfang*⟩; ~ **costs by one million** die Kosten um eine Million reduzieren; ~ **a book to half its original length** ein Buch auf die Hälfte der ursprünglichen Länge zusammenstreichen; **he ~ed five seconds off the world record** er hat die Weltrekordmarke um [beachtliche] fünf Sekunden unterboten; **d)** *(clear by ~ing)* **he ~ed his way through the undergrowth** er schlug sich *(Dat.)* einen Weg durch das Unterholz frei. **3.** *n.* **a)** *(slashing stroke)* Hieb, *der;* **b)** *(wound)* Schnitt, *der;* **give sb. a ~ on the arm** jmdm. den Arm aufschlitzen; **c)** *(slit; Dressm., Tailoring)* Schlitz, *der;* **d)** *(Amer.: tree debris)* Holzabfall, *der (nach Waldbränden, Naturkatastrophen oder Holzschlag);* **e)** **go for a** *or* **have a ~** *(sl.: urinate)* sich auspissen gehen *(derb)*

slash-and-'burn *attrib. adj. (Agric.)* ~ **method** Brandrodung, *die*

slashed [slæʃt] *adj. (Dressm., Tailoring)* geschlitzt; ~ **sleeves** Schlitzärmel

slashing ['slæʃɪŋ] *adj.* vernichtend ⟨*Angriff, Kritik*⟩

slat [slæt] *n.* Leiste, *die; (of wood in bedstead, fence)* Latte, *die; (in Venetian blind)* Lamelle, *die*

slate [sleɪt] **1.** *n.* **a)** *(Geol.)* Schiefer, *der;* **b)** *(Building)* Schieferplatte, *die;* **c)** *(writing-surface)* Schiefertafel, *die;* **put sth. on the ~** *(Brit. coll.)* etw. anschreiben *(ugs.);* **wipe the ~ clean** *(fig.)* einen Schlußstrich ziehen; **d)** *(Amer. Polit.: list of candidates)* Kandidatenliste, *die.* **2.** *attrib. adj.* Schiefer-; ~ **roof** Schieferdach, *das.* **3.** *v. t.* **a)** *(Brit. coll.: criticize)* in der Luft zerreißen *(ugs.)* **(for** wegen); **b)** *(Amer.: schedule)* ansetzen ⟨*Treffen, Besprechung*⟩

slate: ~-colour *n.* Schieferfarbe, *die;* **~-coloured** *adj.* schieferfarben; **~-grey 1.** *n.* Schiefergrau, *das;* **2.** *adj.* schiefergrau; **~-pencil** *n.* Schiefergriffel, *der*

slating ['sleɪtɪŋ] *n. (Brit. coll.)* **get** *or* **take a ~:** in der Luft zerrissen werden *(ugs.)* **(for** wegen); **give sb./sth. a ~:** jmdn./etw. in der Luft zerreißen *(ugs.)* **(for** wegen)

slattern ['slætən] *n.* Schlampe, *die (ugs. abwertend)*

slatternly ['slætənlɪ] *adj.* schlampig *(ugs. abwertend)*

slaughter ['slɔ:tə(r)] **1.** *n.* **a)** *(killing for food)* Schlachten, *das;* Schlachtung, *die; see also* **lamb 1 a; b)** *(massacre)* Abschlachten, *das; (in battle, war)* Gemetzel, *das;* **the wholesale ~ of birds** der Vogelmord im großen Stil. **2.** *v. t.* **a)** *(kill for food)* schlachten; **b)** *(massacre)* abschlachten; niedermetzeln *(abwertend);* **c)** *(coll.: defeat utterly)* fertigmachen *(salopp)*

'slaughterhouse *see* **abattoir**

Slav [slɑ:v] **1.** *n.* Slawe, *der*/Slawin, *die.* **2.** *adj.* slawisch

slave [sleɪv] **1.** *n.* **a)** Sklave, *der*/Sklavin, *die; see also* **white slave; b)** *(fig.)* **be a ~ of** *or* **to sth.** Sklave von etw. sein; **be a ~ to sb.** jmdm. verfallen sein; **c)** *(drudge)* Kuli, *der;* **work like a ~:** wie ein Kuli *od.* Brunnenputzer schuften *(ugs.).* **2.** *v. i.* schuften *(ugs.);* ~ **at sth.** sich mit etw. abplagen; ~ **over a hot stove all day** den ganzen Tag am Herd stehen *(ugs.)*

~ **a'way** *v. i.* sich abplagen; sich abrackern *(salopp);* ~ **away at sth.** sich mit etw. abplagen

slave: ~-drive *v. t.* schinden; **~-driver** *n.* **a)** Sklavenaufseher, *der;* **b)** *(fig.: taskmaster)* Sklaventreiber, *der*/-treiberin, *die (abwertend);* ~ **'labour** *n.* Sklavenarbeit, *die; (fig.)* Ausbeutung, *die*

¹slaver ['slævə(r)] **1.** *v. i.* sabbern *(ugs.);* ⟨*Tier:*⟩ geifern; **he was ~ing at the mouth** ihm rann Speichel aus dem Mund; ~ **over sb./sth.** *(fig. derog.)* nach jmdm./etw. gieren. **2.** *n., no indef. art.* Geifer, *der*

²slaver ['sleɪvə(r)] *n.* Sklavenhändler, *der*/-händlerin, *die*

slavery ['sleɪvərɪ] *n., no pl.* **a)** Sklaverei, *die;* **b)** *(drudgery)* Sklavenarbeit, *die;* Sklaverei, *die*

slave: ~-trade *n.* Sklavenhandel, *der;* **~-trader** *n.* Sklavenhändler, *der*/-händlerin, *die*

Slavic ['slɑ:vɪk] **1.** *adj.* slawisch. **2.** *n.* Slawisch, *das*

slavish ['sleɪvɪʃ] *adj.* sklavisch

slavishly ['sleɪvɪʃlɪ] *adv.* sklavisch

Slavonia [slə'vəʊnɪə] *pr. n.* Slawonien *(das)*

Slavonic [slə'vɒnɪk] **1.** *adj.* slawisch. **2.** *n.* Slawisch, *das;* **Church** *or* **Old [Church] ~:** Altkirchenslawisch, *das*

slay [sleɪ] *v.t.,* **slew** [slu:], **slain** [sleɪn] *(see also* **c)** **a)** *(literary)* ermorden; *(with sword, club also)* erschlagen; vernichtend schlagen ⟨*Armee*⟩; **b)** *(coll.: defeat utterly)* in die Pfanne hauen *(ugs.);* **c)** *p.t., p.p.* **~ed** *(coll.: amuse greatly)* **he/his jokes ~ed me** über ihn/seine Witze hätte ich mich totlachen können *(ugs.)*

SLD *abbr. (Brit. Polit.)* **Social and Liberal Democrats** Sozial-Liberaldemokratische Partei

sleazily ['sli:zɪlɪ] *adv.* schäbig *(abwertend);* in schäbigen Verhältnissen ⟨*leben*⟩; **dress ~:** schäbig angezogen gehen

sleazy ['sli:zɪ] *adj. (squalid)* schäbig *(abwertend);* heruntergekommen *(ugs.)* ⟨*Person*⟩; *(disreputable)* anrüchig

sled [sled] *(Amer.)* **1.** *v. i.,* **-dd-** *see* **¹sledge 2. 2.** *n.* Schlitten, *der*

¹sledge [sledʒ] **1.** *n.* Schlitten, *der.* **2.** *v. i.* Schlitten fahren; rodeln. **3.** *v. t.* mit dem Schlitten fahren

²sledge *see* **sledge-hammer**

'sledge-hammer 1. *n.* Vorschlaghammer, *der.* **2.** *adj.* schlagend ⟨*Argument*⟩; wuchtig ⟨*Schlag*⟩; ~ **style** Holzhammermethode, *die (ugs.)*

sleek [sli:k] **1.** *adj.* **a)** *(glossy)* seidig ⟨*Fell, Haar, Pelz*⟩; ⟨*Tier*⟩ mit seidigem Fell; **b)** *(well-fed)* wohlgenährt; **c)** *(polished)* glatt; *(glossy)* seidig glänzend; **the ~ lines of the car** die schnittige Form des Wagens. **2.** *v. t.* glätten

~ **'back** *see* **slick back**

~ **'down** *see* **slick down**

sleep [sli:p] **1.** *n.* Schlaf, *der;* **get some ~:** schlafen; **it's time we got some ~:** es ist Zeit zum Schlafengehen; **get three hours' ~:** drei Stunden schlafen; **get/go to ~:** einschlafen; **go to ~!** schlaf jetzt!; **not lose [any] ~ over sth.** *(fig.)* wegen etw. keine schlaflose Nacht haben; **some cocoa should put him to ~:** etwas Kakao, und er müßte einschlafen; **put an animal to ~** *(euphem.)* ein Tier einschläfern; **he put** *or* **sent me to ~ with his stories** *(coll.)* bei seinen Geschichten bin ich fast eingeschlafen; **talk in one's ~:** im Schlaf sprechen; **one's last ~** *(fig.)* der ewige Schlaf; **walk in one's ~:** schlafwandeln; **I can/could do it in my ~** *(fig.)* ich kann/könnte es im Schlaf; **be in a deep ~:** fest schlafen; **get** *or* **have a good night's ~:** [sich] gründlich ausschlafen; **have a ~:** schlafen; **have a short ~:** ein [kurzes] Schläfchen machen. **2.** *v. i.,* **slept** [slept] **a)** schlafen; ~ **late** lange schlafen; ausschlafen; ~ **like a log** *or* **top** wie ein Stein schlafen *(ugs.);* ~ **tight!** *(coll.)* schlaf gut!; ~ **at sb.'s** bei jmdm. schlafen; *see also* **rough 3; b)** *(fig.: be dormant)* schlafen *(fig.);* ⟨*Vulkan, Haß:*⟩ ruhen, schlafen; **c)** *(fig.: lie in grave)* ruhen *(geh.).* **3.** *v. t.,* **slept a)** ~ **the sleep of the just** *or* **dead** *(joc.)* den Schlaf des Gerechten schlafen *(scherzh.);* **b)** *(accommodate)* schlafen lassen; **the hotel ~s 80** das Hotel hat 80 Betten. *See also* **wink 3 b**

~ **a'round** *v. i. (coll.)* herumschlafen *(ugs.)*

~ **a'way** *v. t.* verschlafen

~ **'in** *v. i.* **a)** *(sleep late)* im Bett bleiben; **b)** *(live in)* im Hause wohnen

~ **'off** *v. t.* ausschlafen; ~ **it off** seinen Rausch ausschlafen; ~ **off one's lunch** [nach dem Mittagessen] einen Verdauungsschlaf halten

~ **on 1.** *v. i.* [-'-] weiterschlafen. **2.** *v. t.* ['--] überschlafen

~ **'out** *v. i.* **a)** *(sleep in the open)* im Freien schlafen; **b)** *(live out)* nicht im Hause wohnen

~ **through** *v. t.* ~ **through the noise/alarm** trotz des Lärms/Weckerklingelns [weiter]schlafen

~ **together** *v. i. (coll. euphem.)* miteinander schlafen

~ **with** *v. t.* ~ **with sb.** *(coll. euphem.)* mit jmdm. schlafen

sleeper ['sli:pə(r)] *n.* **a)** Schläfer, *der;* **be a heavy/light ~:** einen tiefen/leichten Schlaf haben; **b)** *(Brit. Railw.: support)* Schwelle, *die;* **c)** *(Railw.) (coach)* Schlafwagen, *der; (berth)* Schlafwagenplatz, *der; (overnight train)* **[night] ~:** Nachtzug mit Schlafwagen; **d)** *(ear-ring)* [medizinischer] Ohrstecker; **e)** *(slow starter)* **the novel/film was a ~:** dem Roman/Film gelang erst spät der Durchbruch *(fig.);* **f)** *(Amer.) see* **sleepsuit**

sleepily ['sli:pɪlɪ] *adv.* **a)** *(drowsily)* schläfrig; **b)** *(sluggishly)* schwerfällig; *(unobservantly)* schlafmützig *(ugs. abwertend)*

sleepiness ['sli:pɪnɪs] *n., no pl. (drowsiness)* Schläfrigkeit, *die*

sleeping ['sli:pɪŋ] *adj. (lit. or fig.)* schlafend; schlummernd ⟨*Leidenschaft*⟩; **let ~ dogs lie** *(fig.)* keine schlafenden Hunde wecken

sleeping: ~ accommodation *n.* Übernachtungsmöglichkeit, *die;* **the price includes ~ accommodation** im Preis ist die Übernachtung inbegriffen; **~-bag** *n.* Schlafsack, *der;* **S~ 'Beauty** *pr. n.* Dornröschen *(das);* **~-car[riage]** *n. (Railw.)* Schlafwagen, *der;* **~-draught** *n.* Schlaftrunk, *der;* **~-drug** *n.* Schlafmittel, *das;* ~ **'partner** *n. (Commerc.)* stiller Teilhaber; **~-pill** *n.* Schlaftablette, *die;* ~ **po'liceman** *n. (Brit.)* Bodenschwelle, *die;* **~ sickness** *n. (Med.)* Schlafkrankheit, *die;* **~-suit** *see* **sleepsuit; ~-tablet** *see* **~-pill**

sleepless ['sli:plɪs] *adj.* schlaflos

sleeplessness ['sli:plɪsnɪs] *n., no pl.* Schlaflosigkeit, *die*

sleep: ~suit *n.* [Baby]schlafanzug, *der;* **~-walk** *v. i.* schlafwandeln; **~-walker** *n.* Schlafwandler, *der*/-wandlerin, *die;* **~-walking** *n.* Schlafwandeln, *das*

sleepy ['sli:pɪ] *adj.* **a)** *(drowsy)* schläfrig; **b)**

(sluggish) schwerfällig; *(unobservant)* schlafmützig *(ugs. abwertend)*; **c)** *(peaceful)* verschlafen ‹*Dorf, Stadt usw.*›

sleepy: ~head *n.* Schlafmütze, *die (ugs.)*; **~ sickness** *n. (Med.)* Kopfgrippe, *die;* europäische Schlafkrankheit

sleet [sli:t] **1.** *n., no indef. art.* Schneeregen, *der.* **2.** *v.i. impers.* **it was ~ing** es gab Schneeregen

sleeve [sli:v] *n.* **a)** Ärmel, *der;* **have sth. up one's ~** *(fig.)* etw. in petto haben *(ugs.)*; **roll up one's ~s** *(lit. or fig.)* die Ärmel hochkrempeln *(ugs.)*; *see also* **heart 1 b; laugh; b)** *(record-cover)* Hülle, *die;* **c)** *(Mech.)* Muffe, *die (Technik)*; **d)** *(Aeronaut.) (wind-sock)* Windsack, *der*

-sleeved [sli:vd] *adj. in comb.* -ärmelig

sleeveless ['sli:vlɪs] *adj.* ärmellos

'sleeve-note *n.* Covertext, *der*

sleigh [sleɪ] **1.** *n.* Schlitten, *der.* **2.** *v.i. & t.* mit dem Schlitten fahren

sleigh: ~-bell *n.* Schlittenschelle, *die;* **~-ride** *n.* Schlittenfahrt, *die*

sleight of hand [slaɪt əv 'hænd] *n.* Fingerfertigkeit, *die;* **verbal ~:** verbale Taschenspielereien

slender ['slendə(r)] *adj.* **a)** *(slim)* schlank; schmal ‹*Buch, Band*›; **b)** *(meagre)* mager ‹*Einkommen, Kost*›; gering ‹*Chance, Mittel, Vorräte, Hoffnung, Kenntnis*›; schwach ‹*Entschuldigung, Argument, Grund*›; **be a person of ~ means** *or* **resources** wenig Geld haben; einen schmalen *(geh.)* Geldbeutel haben

slenderize ['slendəraɪz] **1.** *v.t.* **~ [the figure]** schlank machen. **2.** *v.i.* abnehmen

slenderly ['slendəlɪ] *adv.* **~ built/made** von schlankem Wuchs *nachgestellt;* **be ~ provided for** schlecht versorgt sein

slept *see* **sleep 2, 3**

sleuth [slu:θ] **1.** *n.* Detektiv, *der.* **2.** *v.i.* **go ~ing** sich detektivisch betätigen

[1]slew [slu:] **1.** *v.i.* **~ to the left/right/side** sich [schnell] nach links/rechts/seitwärts drehen; ‹*Kran:*› nach links/rechts/seitwärts schwenken. **2.** *v.t.* herumschleudern; schwenken ‹*Kran*›

~ [a]'round 1. *v.i.* sich [schnell] drehen; **~ around to the left** ‹*Kran:*› nach links schwenken. **2.** *v.t.* [schnell] drehen; schwenken ‹*Kran*›

[2]slew *see* slay a, b

[3]slew *n. (Amer. coll.)* Haufen, *der (ugs.)*; **a ~ of people/things** ein Haufen *(ugs.)* Leute/Dinge; **~s of spectators/snow** massenhaft *(ugs.)* Zuschauer/Schnee; **~s of work** Berge von Arbeit

slice [slaɪs] **1.** *n.* **a)** *(cut portion)* Scheibe, *die; (of apple, melon, peach, apricot, cake, pie)* Stück, *das;* **a ~ of life** ein Ausschnitt aus dem Leben; *see also* **cake 1 a, b; b)** *(share)* Teil, *der; (allotted part of profits, money)* Anteil, *der;* **a ~ of land** ein Stück Land; **have a ~ of luck** Glück haben; **c)** *(utensil)* [Braten]wender, *der;* **d)** *(Golf, Tennis: stroke)* Slice, *der.* **2.** *v.t.* **a)** *(cut into portions)* in Scheiben schneiden; in Stücke schneiden ‹*Bohnen, Apfel, Pfirsich, Kuchen usw.*›; **~ sth. thick/thin/into pieces** etw. dick/dünn/in Stücke schneiden; **b)** *(Golf)* slicen; *(Tennis)* unterschneiden; slicen. **3.** *v.i.* schneiden; **~ through** durchschneiden; durchpflügen ‹*Wellen, Meer*›

~ 'off *v.t.* abschneiden

~ 'up *v.t.* aufschneiden; *(fig.: divide)* aufteilen

sliced [slaɪst] *adj. (cut into slices)* aufgeschnitten; kleingeschnitten ‹*Gemüse*›; **~ bread** Schnittbrot, *das;* **the greatest thing since ~ bread** *(coll. joc.)* der/die/das Größte seit der Erfindung der Bratkartoffel *(ugs. scherzh.)*

-slicer [slaɪsə(r)] *n. in comb.* -schneidemaschine, *die;* **egg-~:** Eierschneider, *der*

slick [slɪk] **1.** *adj. (coll.)* **a)** *(dextrous)* professionell; **b)** *(pretentiously dextrous)* clever *(ugs.)*; **c)** *(slippery)* glatt ‹*Fußboden*›; rutschig ‹*Straße, Weg*›; **d)** *(glossy)* seidig glänzend; **e)** *(glib)* glatt; glattzüngig *(geh. abwertend)*; **have a ~ tongue** glattzüngig sein *(geh. abwertend).* **2.** *n.* **[oil-]~:** Ölteppich, *der.* **3.** *v.t. see* **sleek 2**

~ 'back *v.t.* **~ back one's hair** sich *(Dat.)* die Haare anklatschen *(salopp)*

~ 'down *v.t.* **~ down one's hair** sich *(Dat.)* die Haare anklatschen *(salopp)*

slicker ['slɪkə(r)] *n. (Amer.)* **a)** *(swindler)* Trickbetrüger, *der*/-betrügerin, *die;* **b)** *see* **city slicker; c)** *(raincoat)* Regenmantel, *der; (oilskin)* [gelbe] Öljacke

slid *see* **slide 1, 2**

slide [slaɪd] **1.** *v.i.,* **slid** [slɪd] **a)** rutschen; ‹*Kolben, Schublade, Feder*› gleiten; **the bolt slid home** der Riegel glitt ins Schloß; **~ down sth.** etw. hinunterrutschen; **b)** *(glide over ice)* schlittern; **c)** *(move smoothly)* gleiten; **everything slid into place** *(fig.)* alles fügte sich zusammen; **d)** *(fig.: take its own course)* **let sth./things ~:** etw./die Dinge schleifen lassen *(fig.)*; **e)** *(fig.: go imperceptibly)* **~ into** hineinschlittern in (+ *Akk.*) *(ugs.)*; **~ from one note to another** ‹*Sänger, Stimme, Musik:*› von einem Ton zum nächsten gleiten. **2.** *v.t.,* **slid a)** schieben; **~ the bolt across on a door** an einer Tür den Riegel vorschieben; **~ the envelope under the door** den Brief unter der Tür durchschieben; **b)** *(place unobtrusively)* gleiten lassen. **3.** *n.* **a)** *(Photog.)* Dia[positiv], *das;* **b)** *(track on ice)* Rutschbahn, *die (ugs.)*; Schlitterbahn, *die (landsch.)*; **c)** *(toboggan slope)* **[toboggan] ~:** Rodelbahn, *die;* **d)** *(chute) (in children's playground)* Rutschbahn, *die; (for goods etc.)* Rutsche, *die;* **e)** *(Mech. Eng.)* Gleitbahn, *die; (moving part)* Gleitstück, *das;* Schieber, *der;* **f)** *see* **hair-slide; g)** *(act of sliding)* Ausrutscher, *der (ugs.)*; **go for** *or* **have a ~** *(on chute)* rutschen [gehen]; *(on ice)* schlittern [gehen]; **h)** *(fig.: decline)* **be on the ~:** auf dem absteigenden Ast sein; **the ~ in the value of the pound** das Abgleiten des Pfundes; **i)** *(Mus.)* Zug, *der;* **j)** *(for microscope)* Objektträger, *der*

slide: ~ control *n.* Flachbahnregler, *der (Technik)*; **~ fastener** *(Amer.) see* **zip 1 a; ~ film** *n. (Photog.)* Diafilm, *der;* **~ lecture** *n.* Diavortrag, *der;* **~ projector** *n.* Diaprojektor, *der;* **~-rule** *n. (Math.)* Rechenschieber, *der;* **~-valve** *n. (Mech. Engin.)* [Absperr]schieber, *der (Technik)*

sliding ['slaɪdɪŋ]: **~ 'door** *n.* Schiebetür, *die;* **~ 'keel** *n. (Naut.)* Schwert, *das;* **~ roof** *n.* Schiebedach, *das;* **~ 'scale** *n.* **~ scale [of fees]** gleitende [Gebühren]skala; **~ seat** *n. (Rowing)* Rollsitz, *der*

slight [slaɪt] **1.** *adj.* **a)** leicht; schwach ‹*Hoffnung, Aussichten, Wirkung*›; gedämpft ‹*Optimismus*›; gering ‹*Bedeutung*›; **have only a ~ acquaintance with sth.** etw. nur oberflächlich kennen; **on the ~est pretext** unter dem geringsten Vorwand; **the ~est thing makes her nervous** die kleinste Kleinigkeit macht sie nervös; **b)** *(scanty)* oberflächlich; **with but ~ inconvenience** ohne größere Unannehmlichkeiten; **pay sb. ~ attention** jmdn. kaum beachten; **c)** *(slender)* zierlich; *(weedy)* schmächtig; *(flimsy)* zerbrechlich; **d) not in the ~est** nicht im geringsten; **not the ~est ...:** nicht der/die/das geringste ...; **I haven't the ~est idea** ich habe nicht die leiseste Ahnung. **2.** *v.t. (disparage)* herabsetzen; *(fail in courtesy or respect to)* brüskieren; *(ignore)* ignorieren. **3.** *n. (on sb.'s character, reputation, good name)* Verunglimpfung, *die* **(on** *Gen.*); *(on sb.'s abilities)* Herabsetzung, *die* **(on** *Gen.*); *(lack of courtesy)* Affront, *der* **(on** gegen); *(neglect)* Nichtachtung, *die*

slightly ['slaɪtlɪ] *adv.* **a)** ein bißchen; leicht ‹*verletzen, riechen nach, gewürzt sein, ansteigen*›; flüchtig ‹*jmdn. kennen*›; oberflächlich ‹*etw. kennen*›; **b) ~ built** *(slender)* zierlich; *(weedy)* schmächtig

slily *see* **slyly**

slim [slɪm] **1.** *adj.* **a)** schlank; schmal ‹*Band, Buch*›; **b)** *(meagre)* mager; schwach ‹*Entschuldigung, Aussicht, Hoffnung*›; gering ‹*Gewinn, Chancen*›; **the profit/the supper was ~ pickings** der Gewinn/das Abendessen war ziemlich mickrig; **there were only ~ pickings left** da war nicht mehr viel zu holen. **2.** *v.i.,* **-mm-** abnehmen. **3.** *v.t.,* **-mm-** schlanker machen; *(fig.: decrease)* kürzen ‹*Budget*›; verschlanken *(Jargon)* ‹*Produktion*›; reduzieren ‹*Nachfrage, Anzahl*›

~ 'down 1. *v.i.* abnehmen; schlanker werden. **2.** *v.t. see* **~ 3**

slime [slaɪm] **1.** *n.* Schlick, *der; (mucus, viscous matter)* Schleim, *der.* **2.** *v.t.* mit Schlick/Schleim bedecken

'slime mould *n. (Bot.)* Schleimpilz, *der*

'slimline *adj.* schlank; schlank geschnitten ‹*Kleid*›; kalorienarm ‹*Lebensmittel*›

slimmer ['slɪmə(r)] *n. (Brit.) jmd., der etwas für die schlanke Linie tut;* **advice/a diet for ~s** Ratschläge/eine Diät zum Abnehmen

slimming ['slɪmɪŋ] **1.** *n.* **a)** Abnehmen, *das; attrib.* Schlankheits-; **be in need of ~:** abnehmen müssen; **b)** *(fig.: reduction) (of budget)* Kürzung, *die; (of number)* Reduzierung, *die.* **2.** *adj.* schlank machend ‹*Lebensmittel*›; **be ~:** schlank machen

slimness ['slɪmnɪs] *n., no pl. (slenderness)* Schlankheit, *die; (of book)* geringer Umfang

slimy ['slaɪmɪ] *adj.* **a)** schleimig; schlickig ‹*Schlamm*›; **b)** *(slippery)* glitschig *(ugs.)*; **c)** *(fig.: obsequious)* schleimig *(abwertend)*; schmierig *(abwertend)*

[1]sling [slɪŋ] **1.** *n.* **a)** *(weapon)* Schleuder, *die;* **b)** *(Med.)* Schlinge, *die;* **c)** *(carrying-belt)* Tragriemen, *der; (for carrying babies)* Tragehöschen, *das;* **d)** *(hoist)* Anschlagseil, *das (Technik); (belt)* Anschlagband, *das (Technik); (chain)* Anschlagkette, *die (Technik).* **2.** *v.t.,* **slung** [slʌŋ] **a)** *(hurl from ~)* schleudern; **b)** *(coll.: throw)* schmeißen *(ugs.)*; **she slung him his coat** sie schmiß ihm seinen Mantel zu *(ugs.)*; *see also* **mud c; c)** *(suspend)* hängen; *(put in ~ ready for hoisting)* anhängen ‹*Last*›; **she slung the bag over her arm** sie hängte sich *(Dat.)* die Tasche über den Arm

~ a'way *v.t. (coll.)* wegschmeißen *(ugs.)*

~ 'out *v.t. (coll.)* **a)** *(throw out)* **~ sb. out** jmdn. rausschmeißen *od.* -werfen *(ugs.)*; **b)** *see* **~ away**

[2]sling *n. (drink)* Sling, *der (Mischgetränk mit Brandy od. Rum); see also* **gin sling**

sling: ~-back *n.* **~-back [shoe]** Slingpumps, *der;* **~shot** *(Amer.) see* **catapult 1**

slink [slɪŋk] *v.i.,* **slunk** [slʌŋk] schleichen

~ a'way, ~ off *v.i.* davonschleichen; sich fortstehlen

slinkily ['slɪŋkɪlɪ] *adv.* aufreizend

slinky ['slɪŋkɪ] *adj.* **a)** aufreizend; **b)** hauteng ‹*Kleidung*›

slip [slɪp] **1.** *v.i.,* **-pp- a)** *(slide)* rutschen; ‹*Messer:*› abrutschen; *(and fall)* ausrutschen; **he ~ped and broke his leg** er rutschte aus und brach sich *(Dat.)* das Bein; **b)** *(escape)* schlüpfen; **money ~s through my fingers like water** Geld zerrinnt mir zwischen den Fingern; **let the reins ~ out of one's hands** *(lit. or fig.)* sich *(Dat.)* die Zügel entgleiten lassen; **let a chance/opportunity ~:** sich *(Dat.)* eine Chance/Gelegenheit entgehen lassen; **let [it] ~ that ...:** verraten, daß ...; **let ~ the dogs of war** *(rhet.)* die Kriegsfurie loslassen; **c)** *(go)* **~ to the butcher's** [rasch] zum Fleischer rüberspringen *(ugs.)*; **~ from the room/~ behind a curtain** aus dem Zimmer/hinter einen Vorhang schlüpfen; **d)** *(move smoothly)* gleiten; **everything ~ped into place** *(fig.)* alles fügte sich zusammen; e) (make mistake) [Flüchtigkeits]fehler machen; f) (deteriorate) nachlassen; ⟨Moral, Niveau, Ansehen:⟩ sinken. 2. v. t., -pp- a) stecken; ~ the dress over one's head das Kleid über den Kopf streifen; ~ sb. sth. jmdm. etw. zustecken; ~ sb. a glance jmdm. einen verstohlenen Blick zuwerfen; b) (escape from) entwischen (+ Dat.); the dog ~ped its collar der Hund streifte sein Halsband ab; the boat ~ped its mooring das Boot löste sich aus seiner Verankerung; ~ sb.'s attention jmds. Aufmerksamkeit (Dat.) entgehen; ~ sb.'s memory or mind jmdm. entfallen; c) (release) loslassen; ~ a dog from its chain einen Hund von der Kette lassen; d) (Naut.) slippen; ~ anchor den Anker lichten; e) (Motor Veh.) schleifen lassen ⟨Kupplung⟩; f) (Knitting) ~ a stitch eine Masche abheben; g) (Med.) ~ a disc einen Bandscheibenvorfall erleiden; see also slipped disc. 3. n. a) (fall) after his ~: nachdem er ausgerutscht [und gestürzt] war; a ~ on these steps could be nasty auf diesen Stufen auszurutschen könnte schlimme Folgen haben; have a [bad] ~: [sehr unglücklich] ausrutschen; b) (mistake) Versehen, das; Ausrutscher, der (ugs.); there's been a ~ in the accounts bei der Berechnung ist ein Fehler unterlaufen; a ~ of the tongue/pen ein Versprecher/Schreibfehler; I'm sorry, it was a ~ of the tongue/pen Entschuldigung, ich habe mich versprochen/verschrieben; make a ~: einen Fehler machen; see also cup 1a; c) (underwear) Unterrock, der; see also show 3a; d) (pillowcase) [Kopf]kissenbezug, der; e) (strip) ~ of metal/plastic Metall-/Plastikstreifen, der; ~ of wood Holzleiste, die; ~ of glass langes, schmales Stück Glas; f) (piece of paper) ⟨Einzahlungs-, Wett⟩schein, der; ~ [of paper] Zettel, der; g) give sb. the ~ (escape) jmdm. entwischen (ugs.); (avoid) jmdm. ausweichen; h) (Naut.: landing-stage) Aufschleppe, die; Slip, der; i) in pl. (Shipb.) Helling, die od. der; j) a ~ of a boy/girl ein zierlicher Junge/ein zierliches Mädchen; eine halbe Portion (ugs.); k) (Cricket) Feldspieler, der seitlich hinter dem Tor aufgestellt ist; he was caught at ~ or in the ~s sein Ball wurde seitlich hinter dem Tor gefangen; l) (Ceramics) geschlämmter Ton. See also gym-slip

~ a'cross v. i. rüberspringen (ugs.)

~ a'way v. i. a) (leave quietly) ⟨Person:⟩ sich fortschleichen; b) (pass quickly) ⟨Zeit, Tage, Wochen usw.:⟩ verfliegen

~ 'back v. i. zurückschleichen; (very quickly) zurücksausen; ~ back into unconsciousness wieder das Bewußtsein verlieren

~ be'hind v. i. zurückfallen; (with one's work) in Rückstand geraten

~ 'by v. i. a) (pass unnoticed) vorbeischleichen; ⟨Fehler:⟩ durchrutschen (ugs.); b) see ~ away b

~ 'down v. i. runterrutschen (ugs.); ⟨Getränk:⟩ die Kehle runterlaufen (ugs.)

~ 'in 1. v. i. sich hineinschleichen; (enter briefly) [kurz] reinkommen (ugs.); (enter unnoticed) ⟨Fehler:⟩ sich einschleichen. 2. v. t. einfließen lassen ⟨Bemerkung⟩

~ into v. t. a) (put on) schlüpfen in (+ Akk.) ⟨Kleidungsstück⟩; b) (lapse into) verfallen in (+ Akk.)

~ 'off 1. v. i. a) (slide down) runterrutschen (ugs.); b) see ~ away a. 2. v. t. abstreifen ⟨Schmuck, Bezug, Handschuh⟩; schlüpfen aus ⟨Kleid, Hose, Schuh⟩; ausziehen ⟨Strumpf, Handschuh⟩

~ 'on v. t. überstreifen ⟨Bezug, Handschuh, Ring⟩; schlüpfen in (+ Akk.) ⟨Kleid, Hose, Schuh⟩; anziehen ⟨Strumpf, Handschuh⟩; anlegen ⟨Schmuck⟩; see also slip-on

~ 'out v. i. a) (leave) sich hinausschleichen; ~ out to the butcher's zum Fleischer rüberspringen (ugs.); ~ out to have a cigarette hinausschlüpfen, um eine Zigarette zu rauchen; b) (be revealed) it ~ped out es ist mir/dir/ihm usw. herausgerutscht

~ 'over v. i. a) (fall) ausrutschen; b) see ~ across

~ 'past see ~ by

~ 'round v. i. rübergehen (ugs.); (towards speaker) rüberkommen (ugs.)

~ 'through v. i. durchschlüpfen; ⟨Fehler:⟩ durchrutschen (ugs.)

~ 'up v. i. (coll.) einen Schnitzer machen (ugs.) (on, over bei); see also slip-up

slip: ~-case n. Schuber, der; ~-cover n. a) (for unused furniture) Schutzüberzug, der; b) (Amer.: loose cover) Überzug, der; c) (protective book-jacket) Schutzhülle, die; Buchhülle, die; d) see ~-case; ~-knot n. a) (easily undone knot) Slipstek, der; b) see running knot; ~-on 1. adj. ~-on shoes Slipper; 2. n. (shoe) Slipper, der; ~-over n. Pullunder, der

slippage ['slɪpɪdʒ] n. a) (Mech.) Schlupf, der; b) (Commerc.) Rückstand, der

slipped 'disc n. (Med.) Bandscheibenvorfall, der

slipper ['slɪpə(r)] n. Hausschuh, der; see also hunt 2b

'slipper-bath n. (Brit.) teilweise abgedeckte Badewanne; (individual bath in public baths) Wannenbad, das

slippered ['slɪpəd] adj. in Hausschuhen nachgestellt

slippery ['slɪpərɪ] adj. a) (causing slipping) schlüpfrig; glitschig; the shoes are ~: die Schuhe haben [sehr] glatte Sohlen; be on a ~ path or slope (fig.) auf einem verhängnisvollen Weg sein; b) (elusive) schlüpfrig; glitschig; wendig ⟨Spieler⟩; (shifty) aalglatt (abwertend); (unreliable) windig (ugs.); he is a ~ customer er ist aalglatt (abwertend); as ~ as an eel aalglatt (abwertend); c) (fig.: delicate) heikel ⟨Thema, Fall⟩

slippy ['slɪpɪ] adj. a) (coll.) see slippery; b) (Brit. coll.) be or look ~: sich sputen (veralt.); sich ranhalten (ugs.)

slip: ~-ring n. (Electr.) Schleifring, der; ~-road n. (Brit.) (for approach) Zufahrtsstraße, die; (to motorway) Auffahrt, die; (to estate) Einfahrt, die; (for leaving) Ausfahrt, die; ~shod adj. schlampig (ugs. abwertend); abgetreten ⟨Schuh⟩; (fig.: careless, unsystematic) schlud[e]rig (ugs. abwertend); ~-stream n. a) (of car, motor cycle) Fahrtwind, der; (Racing) Windschatten, der; b) (of propeller) Propellerwind, der; (of ship; also Brit. fig.) Kielwasser, das; ~-up n. (coll.) Schnitzer, der (ugs.); there's been a ~-up somewhere irgendwo hat jemand einen Schnitzer gemacht (ugs.); ~way see slip 3h, i

slit [slɪt] 1. n. Schlitz, der; the sleeves have ~s in them die Ärmel haben Schlitze od. sind geschlitzt; make ~s in the fat of the pork die Schwarte des Schweinebratens einritzen. 2. v. t., -tt-, slit a) aufschlitzen; ~ sb.'s throat jmdm. die Kehle durchschneiden; b) (Dressmaking) schlitzen ⟨Rock, Ärmel⟩

'slit-eyed adj. schlitzäugig

slither ['slɪðə(r)] v. i. rutschen; (on ice, polished floor also) schlittern

slit: ~-'pocket n. Durchgrifftasche, die; ~ trench n. (Mil.) Schützenloch, das

sliver ['slɪvə(r)] n. a) (slip) (of wood) Span, der; (of paper) Streifen, der; (of food) dünne Scheibe; b) (splinter) Splitter, der; ~ of wood/glass/bone Holz-/Glas-/Knochensplitter, der; c) (Textiles) Kammzug, der

slivovitz ['slɪvəvɪts] n. Slibowitz, der

slob [slɒb] n. (coll.) Schwein, das (derb); lazy ~: fauler Sack (salopp abwertend); fat ~: Fettsack, der (salopp abwertend)

slobber ['slɒbə(r)] 1. v. i. sabbern (ugs.); ~ over sb./sth. jmdn./etw. besabbern; (fig.) von jmdm./etw. schwärmen. 2. v. t. vollsabbern (ugs.). 3. n. see ¹slaver 2

slobbery ['slɒbərɪ] adj. the bib is all ~: das Lätzchen ist ganz vollgesabbert (ugs.); a ~ kiss ein [feuchter] Schmatz (ugs.)

sloe [sləʊ] n. (Bot.) Schlehe, die

sloe: ~-eyed adj. a) (with ~-coloured eyes) mit schwarzblauen Augen nachgestellt; b) (slant-eyed) schlitzäugig; ~-gin n. ≈ Schlehenlikör, der; Sloe-Gin, der

slog [slɒg] 1. v. t., -gg- dreschen (ugs.) ⟨Ball⟩; (in boxing, fight) voll treffen; (with several blows) eindreschen auf (+ Akk.) (ugs.). 2. v. i., -gg- a) (hit) draufschlagen (ugs.); b) (fig.: work doggedly) sich abplagen; schuften (ugs.); (for school, exams) büffeln (ugs.); c) (walk doggedly) sich schleppen; ~ along sich dahinschleppen. 3. n. a) (hit) [wuchtiger] Schlag; give sb./sth. a ~: jmdm./einer Sache einen wuchtigen Schlag versetzen; b) (hard work) Plackerei, die (ugs.); it took me a good two hours' ~: ich mußte mich gut zwei Stunden abplagen; c) (tiring walk, hike) [auf die Knochen gehender] Fußmarsch

~ at v. t. a) (hit) ~ at sb./sth. auf jmdn./etw. eindreschen (ugs.); b) (work hard at) sich abplagen mit

~ a'way v. i. sich abplagen; ~ away at sth. sich mit etw. abplagen; keep ~ging away! streng dich weiter an!

~ 'out v. t. (coll.) ~ it out es [bis zum Ende] durchstehen; ~ one's guts out sich kaputtarbeiten (ugs.)

slogan ['sləʊgən] n. a) (striking phrase) Slogan, der; (advertising ~) Werbeslogan, der; Werbespruch, der; b) (motto) Wahlspruch, der; (in political campaign) [Wahl]slogan, der

slogger ['slɒgə(r)] n. a) (hitter) be a [real] ~: immer nur draufschlagen (ugs.); b) (hard worker) Arbeitstier, das (fig.)

sloop [slu:p] n. (Naut.) Slup, die

'sloop-rigged adj. (Naut.) mit Sluptakelung nachgestellt; be ~: Sluptakelung haben

slop [slɒp] 1. v. i., -pp- schwappen (out of, from aus). 2. v. t., -pp- a) (spill) (unintentionally) schwappen; (intentionally) kippen; klatschen (ugs.) ⟨Farbe an die Wand⟩; b) (make mess on) vollschütten. 3. n. a) (liquid food) Schleim, der; Geschlabber, das (ugs.); b) (spilt liquid) Lache, die; c) (fig. derog.: gush) Geseire, das (ugs.). See also slops a

~ a'bout, ~ a'round v. i. a) (splash about) herumschwappen (ugs.); b) (move in slovenly manner) herumschlurfen (ugs.)

~ 'out v. i. die Toiletteneimer leeren

~ 'over v. i. (splash over) überschwappen

'slop-basin n. (Brit.) Schale für den Bodensatz aus der [Tee]tasse

slope [sləʊp] 1. n. a) (slant) Neigung, die; (of river) Gefälle, das; there is a downward/upward ~ to the garden der Garten fällt ab/steigt an; the house is built on a steep/gentle ~: das Haus steht an einem steilen/sanften Hang; the roof was at a ~ of 45° das Dach hatte eine Neigung von 45°; be on a or the ~: geneigt sein; b) (slanting ground) Hang, der; c) (Skiing) Piste, die. 2. v. i. (slant) sich neigen; ⟨Wand, Mauer:⟩ schief sein; ⟨Boden, Garten:⟩ abschüssig sein; ~ upwards/downwards ⟨Straße:⟩ ansteigen/abfallen. 3. v. t. abschrägen; ~ arms (Mil.) das Gewehr schultern; ~ arms! (Mil.) Gewehr über!

~ a'way v. i. a) (slant) abfallen; b) see ~ off

~ down v. i. sich hinabneigen

~ 'off v. i. (sl.) sich verdrücken (ugs.)

~ 'up v. i. a) (rise) ansteigen; b) (approach casually) daherkommen; ~ up to sb. auf jmdn. zugehen/zukommen

'slop-pail n. Toiletteneimer, der; (for kitchen slops) Abfalleimer, der

sloppily ['slɒpɪlɪ] adv. a) (carelessly) schlud[e]rig (ugs. abwertend); she speaks

English **rather ~:** sie spricht ein ziemlich schlud[e]riges Englisch *(ugs. abwertend)*; **b)** *(untidily)* unordentlich; schlampig *(ugs. abwertend)*; **c)** *(sentimentally)* voller Rührseligkeit

sloppy ['slɒpɪ] *adj.* **a)** *(careless)* schlud[e]rig *(ugs. abwertend)*; **b)** *(untidy)* unordentlich; schlampig *(ugs. abwertend)*; **c)** *(splashed)* vollgeschwappt; **d)** *(sentimental)* rührselig; **it's ~ to kiss Grandma at my age** ich bin schon zu erwachsen, um Großmama einen Kuß zu geben

sloppy Joe [slɒpi 'dʒəʊ] *n. langer, weiter Pullover für Mädchen;* Schlabberpulli, *der (ugs.)*

slops [slɒps] *n. pl.* **a)** Schmutzwasser, *das; (contents of bedroom or prison vessels)* Fäkalien *Pl.*; **empty the ~:** die Nachttöpfe leeren und das Schmutzwasser beseitigen; **b)** *see* **slop 3 a**

slosh [slɒʃ] **1.** *v. i.* platschen *(ugs.)*; ⟨*Flüssigkeit:*⟩ schwappen. **2.** *v. t.* **a)** *(coll.: pour clumsily)* schwappen; **b)** *(coll.: pour liquid on)* übergießen; **c)** *(Brit. sl.: hit)* verdreschen *(ugs.)*. **3.** *n.* **a)** *see* **slush**; **b)** *(Brit. sl.: heavy blow)* [wuchtiger] Schlag

~ a'bout, ~ a'round 1. *v. i.* **a)** *(splash about playfully)* herumspritzen *(ugs.)*; **b)** *(slop about)* herumschwappen *(ugs.)*. **2.** *v. t.* verspritzen

sloshed [slɒʃt] *adj. (Brit. coll.)* blau *(ugs.)*

slot [slɒt] **1.** *n.* **a)** *(hole)* Schlitz, *der;* **b)** *(groove)* Nut, *die;* **the ~ for a tenon** das Zapfenloch *(Technik)*; **c)** *(coll.: position)* Platz, *der;* **d)** *(coll.: in schedule)* Termin, *der; (Radio, Telev.)* Sendezeit, *die;* **the news will go out in its usual ~ at 10 o'clock** die Nachrichten werden wie üblich um 10 Uhr gesendet. **2.** *v. t.*, **-tt- a)** *(provide with holes)* schlitzen; *(provide with grooves)* nuten; **b)** *(insert)* **~ sth. into place/sth.** etw. einfügen/in etw. *(Akk.)* einfügen. **3.** *v. i.*, **-tt-: ~ into place/sth.** *(lit. or fig.)* sich einfügen/in etw. *(Akk.)* einfügen; **everything ~ted into place** *(fig.)* alles fügte sich zusammen

~ 'in 1. *v. t.* einfügen; **can you ~ me in at 10 o'clock?** *(fig.)* können Sie mich um 10 Uhr dazwischenschieben?. **2.** *v. i. (lit. or fig.)* sich einfügen

~ to'gether 1. *v. t.* zusammenfügen. **2.** *v. i. (lit. or fig.)* sich zusammenfügen

sloth [sləʊθ] *n.* **a)** *no pl. (lethargy)* Trägheit, *die;* **b)** *(Zool.)* Faultier, *das*

'sloth-bear *n. (Zool.)* Lippenbär, *der*

slothful ['sləʊθfl] *adj.* träge; schwerfällig ⟨*Anstrengungen, Versuche*⟩; **a life of ~ ease** ein Leben träger Bequemlichkeit; **develop ~ habits** ziemlich träge werden

slot: ~-machine *n.* **a)** *(vending-machine)* Automat, *der;* **b)** *(Amer.) see* **fruit machine; ~-meter** *n.* Münzzähler, *der*

slouch [slaʊtʃ] **1.** *n.* **a)** *(posture)* schlaffe Haltung; **walk with a ~:** einen nachlässigen Gang haben; **b)** *(sl.: lazy person)* Faulpelz, *der;* **be no ~ at sth.** etwas loshaben in etw. *(Dat.)*; **he's no ~ at billiards/at geography** er ist verdammt gut im Billard/in Geographie *(ugs.)*. **2.** *v. i.* **a)** sich schlecht halten; **don't ~!** halte dich gerade!; **b)** *(be ungainly)* sich herumflegeln *(ugs. abwertend)*; **sit ~ed over one's desk** schlaff über seinem Schreibtisch hängen

~ a'bout, ~ a'round *v. i.* herumlungern *(salopp)*

'slouch hat *n.* Schlapphut, *der*

¹slough [slaʊ] *n. (literary)* Sumpf, *der; see also* **despond 2**

²slough [slʌf] **1.** *n.* **a)** *(Zool.)* abgestreifte Haut; *(whole skin of snake)* Natternhemd, *das;* **b)** *(Med.)* Schorf, *der.* **2.** *v. t. (Zool.; fig.: abandon)* abstreifen

~ 'off *see* **²slough 2**

Slovak ['sləʊvæk] **1.** *adj.* slowakisch; **sb. is ~:** jmd. ist Slowake/Slowakin; *see also* **English 1. 2.** *n.* **a)** *(person)* Slowake, *der*/Slowakin, *die;* **b)** *(language)* Slowakisch, *das; see also* **English 2 a**

Slovakia [slə'vɑ:kɪə] *pr. n.* Slowakei, *die*

sloven ['slʌvn] *n. (female)* Schlampe, *die (ugs. abwertend); (male)* Liederjan, *der (ugs. abwertend)*

Slovene ['sləʊvi:n] **1.** *adj.* slowenisch. **2.** *n.* **a)** *(person)* Slowene, *der*/Slowenin, *die;* **b)** *(language)* Slowenisch, *das*

Slovenia [slə'vi:nɪə] *pr. n.* Slowenien *(das)*

Slovenian [slə'vi:nɪən] *see* **Slovene**

slovenliness ['slʌvnlɪnɪs] *n., no pl.* Schlampigkeit, *die (ugs. abwertend)*

slovenly ['slʌvnlɪ] **1.** *adj.* schlampig *(ugs.)*; schlud[e]rig *(ugs.)*; **be a ~ dresser** sich schlampig *od.* schlud[e]rig anziehen *(ugs.)*. **2.** *adv.* schlampig *(ugs.)*; schlud[e]rig *(ugs.)*

slow [sləʊ] **1.** *adj.* **a)** langsam; **~ and steady wins the race, ~ and sure does it** eile mit Weile! *(Spr.)*; **~ but sure** langsam, aber zuverlässig; **b)** *(gradual)* langsam; langwierig ⟨*Suche, Arbeit*⟩; **make a ~ recovery from one's illness** sich nur langsam von seiner Krankheit erholen; **be ~ in doing sth.** etw. langsam tun; **get off to a ~ start** beim Start langsam wegkommen; ⟨*Aufruf, Produkt:*⟩ zunächst nur wenig Anklang finden; **make ~ progress [in** *or* **at** *or* **with sth.]** nur langsam [mit etw.] vorankommen; *see also* **going 1 b**; **c) be ~ [by ten minutes], be [ten minutes] ~** ⟨*Uhr:*⟩ [zehn Minuten] nachgehen; **d)** *(preventing quick motion)* nur langsam befahrbar ⟨*Strecke, Straße, Belag*⟩; **e)** *(tardy)* **[not] be ~ to do sth.** [nicht] zögern, etw. zu tun; **f)** *(not easily roused)* **be ~ to anger/to take offence** sich nicht leicht ärgern/beleidigen lassen; **g)** *(dull-witted)* schwerfällig; langsam; **be ~ at mathematics** sich in Mathematik schwertun *(ugs.)*; **be ~ [to understand]** schwer *od.* langsam von Begriff sein *(ugs.)*; **be ~ of speech** schwerfällig *od.* unbeholfen sprechen; *see also* **uptake**; **h)** *(burning feebly)* schwach; **i)** *(uninteresting)* langweilig; **j)** *(Commerc.)* flau ⟨*Geschäft*⟩; **k)** *(not hot)* **bake in a ~ oven** bei schwacher Hitze backen; **l)** *(Photog.)* niedrigempfindlich ⟨*Film*⟩; lichtschwach ⟨*Objektiv*⟩; **m) ~ court** *(Tennis)*/**~ wicket** *(Cricket)* langsamer Platz. **2.** *adv.* langsam; **'~'** „langsam fahren!"; **go ~:** langsam fahren; *(Brit. Industry)* langsam arbeiten. **3.** *v. i.* langsamer werden; **we ~ed to a gentle walk** wir wurden immer langsamer, bis wir nur noch gemächlich gingen; **~ to a halt** anhalten; ⟨*Zug:*⟩ zum Stehen kommen; ⟨*Produktion:*⟩ zum Erliegen kommen. **4.** *v. t.* **~ a train/car** die Geschwindigkeit eines Zuges/Wagens verringern; **the accident ~ed traffic to a crawl** der Unfall verlangsamte den Verkehr derart, daß er sich nur noch kriechend vorwärtsbewegte

~ 'down 1. *v. i.* **a)** langsamer werden; seine Geschwindigkeit verringern; *(in working/speaking)* langsamer arbeiten/sprechen; ⟨*Produktion, Geburten-/Sterbeziffer, Inflations[rate]:*⟩ sinken; **b)** *(reduce pace of living)* langsamer machen *(ugs.)*; **have to ~ down after a heart attack** nach einem Herzanfall kürzertreten müssen. **2.** *v. t.* verlangsamen; **the driver ~ed the car/train down** der Autofahrer/Lokomotivführer fuhr langsamer; **the accident ~ed traffic down to a crawl** der Unfall verlangsamte den Verkehr derart, daß er sich nur noch kriechend vorwärtsbewegte; **~ down one's pace of living** kürzertreten; **[You can't help me.] You'd only ~ me down** [Du kannst mir nicht helfen.] Du würdest mich nur aufhalten; **his illness has ~ed him down a lot** durch seine Krankheit ist seine Leistungsfähigkeit stark zurückgegangen. *See also* **slow-down**

~ 'up *see* **~ down**

slow: ~ 'bowler *n. (Cricket)* langsamer Werfer; **~coach** *n.* Trödler, *der*/Trödlerin, *die (ugs. abwertend)*; **~-down** *n.* **a)** *(deceleration)* Verlangsamung, *die* (in *Gen.*); *(in birth, death, inflation rate, output, production, number)* Sinken, *das* **(in** *Gen.***)**; **there's been a ~-down in the number of ...:** die Zahl der ... ist gesunken; **b)** *(go-slow)* Bummelstreik, *der;* **~ 'handclap** *n. (Brit.)* müdes Klatschen *(als Ausdruck des Mißfallens)*

slowly ['sləʊlɪ] *adv.* langsam; **~ but surely** langsam, aber sicher

slow: ~ 'march *n. (Mil.)* langsamer Defiliermarsch; **~-match** *n.* Lunte, *die;* **~ 'motion** *n. (Cinemat.)* Zeitlupe, *die;* **in ~-motion** in Zeitlupe; **~ motion replay** *(Sport)* Zeitlupenwiederholung, *die;* **~-moving** *adj.* **a)** sich langsam fortbewegend; **b)** *(Commerc.)* schlecht gehend; **be ~-moving** schlecht gehen

slowness ['sləʊnɪs] *n., no pl.* **a)** Langsamkeit, *die;* **b)** *(gradualness)* Langsamkeit, *die; (of search, work)* Langwierigkeit, *die;* **c)** *(slackness)* Zögern, *das;* **his ~ to react** *or* **in reacting** sein zögerndes Reagieren; **d)** *(stupidity)* Schwerfälligkeit, *die;* **~ [of comprehension/mind/wit]** Begriffsstutzigkeit, *die (abwertend)*; **e)** *(dullness)* Langweiligkeit, *die*

slow: ~ 'poison *see* **poison 1; ~poke** *(Amer.) see* **slowcoach; ~ 'puncture** *n.* winziges Loch *(durch das ein Reifen o.ä. nur langsam die Luft verliert)*; **~-witted** [sləʊ'wɪtɪd] *adj.* [geistig] schwerfällig; **~-worm** *n. (Zool.)* Blindschleiche, *die*

SLR *abbr. (Photog.)* **single-lens reflex**

slub [slʌb] *n. (Textiles)* Noppe, *die*

sludge [slʌdʒ] *n.* **a)** *(mud)* Matsch, *der (ugs.)*; Schlamm, *der;* **b)** *(sediment)* [schlammiger] Bodensatz; **c)** *(Motor Veh.)* Ölschlamm, *der;* **d)** *(sewage)* Klärschlamm, *der*

¹slug [slʌg] *n.* **a)** *(Zool.)* Nacktschnecke, *die;* **b)** *(bullet)* [rohe] Gewehrkugel; Flintenlaufgeschoß, *das (Waffent.)*; **c)** *(for airgun)* Luftgewehrkugel, *die;* **d)** *(lump of metal)* [rundlicher] Metallklumpen; **a ~ of gold/platinum/silver** *etc.* ein Klumpen Gold/Platin/Silber *usw.*; **e)** *(Amer.: tot of liquor)* **a ~ of whisky/rum** *etc.* ein Schluck Whisky/Rum *usw.*; **f)** *(Printing) (bar)* Reglette, *die; (line)* gegossene Zeile

²slug *(Amer.: hit)* **1.** *v. t.*, **-gg-** niederschlagen. **2.** *n.* [harter] Schlag; **give sb. a ~:** jmdn. niederschlagen

~ 'out *v. t.* **~ it out** es [bis zum Ende] austragen; **the boys were ~ging it out to decide who ...:** die Jungen prügelten sich darum, wer ...

sluggard ['slʌgəd] *n.* Faulpelz, *der; (lacking in speed)* lahme Ente *(ugs.)*

sluggish ['slʌgɪʃ] *adj.* träge; schleppend ⟨*Gang, Schritt*⟩; schwerfällig ⟨*Reaktion, Vorstellungskraft*⟩; *(Commerc.)* flau; schleppend ⟨*Nachfrage, Geschäftsgang*⟩

sluggishly ['slʌgɪʃlɪ] *adv.* träge; schleppenden Schrittes ⟨*gehen, sich bewegen*⟩; schwerfällig ⟨*reagieren*⟩; *(Commerc.)* schleppend ⟨*sich verkaufen, vorangehen*⟩

sluice [slu:s] **1.** *n.* **a)** *(Hydraulic Engin.)* Schütz, *das;* **b)** *(water) vom Schütz aufgestautes/durch das Schütz fließendes Wasser;* **c)** *see* **sluice-way; d)** *(rinsing)* **give sb./sth. a ~ [down]** *(with hose)* jmdn./etw. abspritzen; *(with bucket)* jmdn./etw. [mit Wasser] übergießen. **2.** *v. t.* **a)** *(Hydraulic Engin.)* unter Wasser setzen; **b)** *(provide with sluices)* mit Schützen versehen; **c)** *(Mining)* waschen; **d) ~ [down]** *(douse) (with hose)* abspritzen; *(with bucket)* übergießen

~ a'way *v. t.* wegspülen; *(with hose)* wegspritzen

~ 'out *v. t.* ausspülen; *(with hose)* ausspritzen

sluice: ~-gate *n. (Hydraulic Engin.)* Schütz, *das;* **~-valve** *n. (Hydraulic Engin.)* Schieber, *der;* **~-way** *n.* **a)** *(Hydraulic*

Engin.: channel for sluice) Gerinne, *das;* **b)** *(Mining)* Waschrinne, *die*
slum [slʌm] **1.** *n.* Slum, *der; (single house or apartment)* Elendsquartier, *das.* **2.** *v.i.,* **-mm-: go ~ming** in die Slums gehen; *(fig.)* sich unters [gemeine] Volk mischen. **3.** *v.t.,* **-mm-: ~ it** wie arme Leute leben; *(fig.)* sich unters [gemeine] Volk mischen
slumber ['slʌmbə(r)] *(poet./rhet.)* **1.** *n. (lit. or fig.)* **~[s]** Schlummer, *der (geh.);* **fall into a light/long ~:** in leichten/tiefen Schlummer sinken; **be in a ~** *(fig.)* schlummern *(geh.).* **2.** *v.i. (lit. or fig.)* schlummern *(geh.);* ‹*Vulkan:*› ruhen
~ a'way *v.t.* verschlafen
slumberous ['slʌmbərəs] *adj. (poet./rhet.)* **a)** *(sleepy)* schläfrig; **b)** *(sleep-inducing)* einschläfernd
'slumber-wear *n. (Commerc.)* Nachtwäsche, *die*
slumbrous ['slʌmbrəs] *see* **slumberous**
'slum clearance *n.* Slumsanierung, *die*
slummy ['slʌmɪ] *adj.* verslumt
slump [slʌmp] **1.** *n.* Sturz, *der (fig.); (in demand, investment, sales, production)* starker Rückgang **(in** *Gen.***)**; *(economic depression)* Depression, *die (Wirtsch.); (in morale, interest, popularity)* Nachlassen, *das* **(in** *Gen.***)**; **~ in prices** Preissturz, *der.* **2.** *v.i.* **a)** *(Commerc.)* stark zurückgehen; ‹*Preise, Kurse:*› stürzen *(fig.);* **the economy ~ed** die Wirtschaft geriet in eine Depression; **b)** *(be diminished)* ‹*Popularität, Moral, Unterstützung usw.:*› nachlassen; **c)** *(collapse)* fallen; **they found him ~ed over the table/in his chair/on the floor** sie fanden ihn über dem Tisch/auf seinem Stuhl/auf dem Boden zusammengesunken
~ 'down *v.i.* zusammensinken
slung *see* **¹sling 2**
slunk *see* **slink**
slur [slɜ:(r)] **1.** *v.t.,* **-rr-: ~ one's words/speech** undeutlich sprechen; **~red speech** undeutliche Aussprache. **2.** *v.i.,* **-rr-: his speech began to ~:** er begann undeutlich zu sprechen. **3.** *n.* **a)** *(stigma)* Schande, *die* **(on** für); *(imputation)* Verleumdung, *die; (insult)* Beleidigung, *die* **(on** für); **cast a ~ on sb./sth.** jmdn./etw. verunglimpfen *(geh.);* **it's a/no ~ on his reputation** es schmälert seinen Ruf/seinen Ruf nicht; **b)** *(Mus.)* [Legato]bogen, *der*
slurp [slɜ:p] *(coll.)* **1.** *v.t.* **~ [up]** schlürfen. **2.** *n.* Schlürfen, *das;* **drink one's juice in three big ~s** seinen Saft in drei Zügen ausschlürfen; **drink [one's beer] with a ~:** beim [Bier]trinken schlürfen
slurry ['slʌrɪ] *n.* **a)** *(liquid cement)* Zementbrühe, *die;* **b)** *(suspension)* Schlamm, *der;* Suspension, *die (Chemie);* **c)** *(thin mud)* Schlammbrühe, *die;* **d)** *(Mining)* Kohlenschlamm, *der;* **e)** *(Agric.)* Gülle, *die*
slush [slʌʃ] *n.* **a)** *(thawing snow)* Schneematsch, *der;* **b)** *(fig. derog.: sentiment)* sentimentaler Kitsch
'slush fund *n.* Fonds für Bestechungsgelder
slushy ['slʌʃɪ] *adj.* **a)** *(wet)* matschig; **b)** *(derog.: sloppy)* sentimental
slut [slʌt] *n.* Schlampe, *die (ugs. abwertend)*
sluttish ['slʌtɪʃ] *adj.* schlampig *(ugs. abwertend)*
sly [slaɪ] **1.** *adj.* **a)** *(crafty)* schlau; gerissen *(ugs.)* ‹*Geschäftsmann, Schachzug, Trick*›; verschlagen *(abwertend)* ‹*Blick*›; **he is a ~ one** *or* **type** *or* **customer** das ist ein ganz Gerissener *od.* Schlauer *(ugs.);* **b)** *(secretive)* heimlichtuerisch; verschlagen *(abwertend)* ‹*Rivale*›; **what a ~ one he is!** so ein Heimlichtuer!; **a ~ dog** *(fig. coll.)* ein Heimlichtuer/eine Heimlichtuerin; **c)** *(knowing)* vielsagend ‹*Blick, Lächeln*›. **2.** *n.* **on the ~:** heimlich; **he is a womanizer on the ~:** er ist ein heimlicher Schürzenjäger
'slyboots *n. sing. (coll.)* Schlauberger, *der (ugs.); (secretive person)* Heimlichtuer, *der*/Heimlichtuerin, *die*
slyly ['slaɪlɪ] *adv.* **a)** *(craftily)* schlau; arglistig ‹*täuschen*›; **b)** *(secretively]* heimlich; **c)** *(knowingly)* vielsagend ‹*blicken, lächeln*›
¹smack [smæk] **1.** *n.* **a)** *(flavour)* Beigeschmack, *der; (smell)* Duft, *der;* **b)** *(trace)* Spur, *die; (fig.)* Anflug, *der.* **2.** *v.i.* **~ of** *(taste of)* schmecken nach; *(smell of)* riechen nach; *(fig.)* riechen nach *(ugs.)*
²smack 1. *n.* **a)** *(sound)* Klatsch, *der; (of lips)* Schmatzen, *das; (of hand, stick)* Klatschen, *das;* **b)** *(blow)* Schlag, *der; (on child's bottom)* Klaps, *der (ugs.);* **a ~ in the face** eine Ohrfeige; **a ~ in the eye** *or* **face** *(fig.)* ein Schlag ins Gesicht; **c)** *(coll.: attempt)* **have a ~ at sth.** es mit etw. versuchen; **he had a ~ at the world record** er versuchte, den Weltrekord zu verbessern; **have a ~ at doing sth.** versuchen, etw. zu tun; **c)** *(loud kiss)* Schmatz, *der (ugs.).* **2.** *v.t.* **a)** *(slap)* [mit der flachen Hand] schlagen; *(lightly)* einen Klaps *(ugs.)* geben (+ *Dat.*); **~ sb.'s face/bottom/hand** jmdn. ohrfeigen/jmdm. eins hintendrauf geben *(ugs.)*/jmdm. eins auf die Hand geben *(ugs.);* **I'll ~ your bottom!** du kriegst eins hinten drauf! *(ugs.);* **b) ~ one's lips** [mit den Lippen] schmatzen; **c)** *(propel)* knallen *(ugs.).* **3.** *v.i.* **~ into the net/wall** ins Netz/gegen die Mauer knallen *(ugs.);* **I ~ed into him** wir knallten zusammen *(ugs.).* **4.** *adv.* **a)** *(coll.: with a smack)* **go ~ into a lamp-post** gegen einen Laternenpfahl knallen *(ugs.);* **b)** *(exactly)* direkt
³smack *n. (sl.: heroin)* Junk, *der (Drogenjargon)*
⁴smack *n. (Naut.)* Fischkutter, *der*
smacker ['smækə(r)] *n. (sl.)* **a)** *(loud kiss)* Schmatz, *der (ugs.);* **b)** *(blow)* [wuchtiger] Schlag; **give** *or* **deal sb. a ~ on the nose** jmdm. voll auf die Nase hauen *(ugs.);* **c)** *(Brit.: £1)* Pfund, *das;* ≈ Scheinchen, *das (ugs.);* **d)** *(Amer.: $1)* Dollar, *der;* ≈ Scheinchen, *das (ugs.)*
small [smɔ:l] **1.** *adj.* **a)** *(in size)* klein; gering ‹*Wirkung, Appetit, Fähigkeit*›; schmal ‹*Taille, Handgelenk*›; dünn ‹*Stimme*›; **I'm afraid I've nothing ~er** ich habe es leider nicht kleiner *(ugs.);* **it's a ~ world** die Welt ist klein; **they came in ~ numbers** es kamen nur wenige; **the ~est room** *(fig. coll. euphem.)* das Örtchen *(fam. verhüll.); see also* **hour b; still 1 e; b)** *attrib.* **(~-scale)** klein; Klein‹*aktionär, -sparer, -händler, -betrieb, -bauer*›; *see also* **way 1 k; c)** *(young, not fully grown)* klein; *see also* **²fry; d)** *(of the* **~er** *kind)* klein; **~ letter** Kleinbuchstabe, *der;* **spell with a ~ letter** klein schreiben; **feel ~** *(fig.)* sich *(Dat.)* ganz klein vorkommen; **look ~** *(fig.)* [ziemlich] schlecht aussehen *(ugs.);* **make sb. feel/look ~** *(fig.)* jmdn. beschämen/ein schlechtes Licht auf jmdn. werfen; *see also* **²arm 1 a; beer; circle 1 a; intestine; mercy 1 b; ²slam a; e)** *(not much)* wenig; **it's ~ comfort** es ist ein geringer Trost; **demand for/interest in the product was ~:** die Nachfrage nach/das Interesse an dem Produkt war gering; **have ~ cause for sth./to do sth.** wenig Grund zu etw. haben/wenig Grund haben, etw. zu tun; **[it's] ~ wonder** [es ist] kein Wunder; **no ~ excitement/feat** einige Aufregung/keine geringe Leistung; **f)** *(trifling)* klein; **we have a few ~ matters/points/problems to clear up before ...:** es sind noch ein paar Kleinigkeiten zu klären, bevor ...; **g)** *(minor)* unbedeutend; gering ‹*Ruhm, Anerkennung*›; **great and ~:** hoch und niedrig; **h)** *(petty)* kleinlich *(abwertend);* **have a ~ mind** ein Kleinkrämer sein *(abwertend);* **i)** *(fine)* fein ‹*Kies, Schrot*›. **2.** *n. (Anat.)* **~ of the back** Kreuz, *das; see also* **smalls. 3.** *adv.* klein
small: ~ 'ad *n. (coll.)* Kleinanzeige, *die;* **the ~ ads section/pages/column** der Teil/die Seiten/die Rubrik mit den Kleinanzeigen; **~-bore** *adj. (Arms)* kleinkalibrig; Kleinkaliber-; **~ 'capital** *n. (Printing)* Kapitälchen, *das;* **~ 'change** *n., no pl., no indef. art.* **a)** *(coins)* Kleingeld, *das;* **b)** *(remarks)* Trivialitäten; *(business)* Kleinkram, der *(ugs.);* **~ 'claim** *n. (Law)* ≈ Bagatellsache, *die;* **~ 'claims court** *n. (Law) Gericht für Bagatellsachen;* **~ craft** *n. pl. (Naut.)* Boote; **~ goods** *n. pl. (Austral.)* feine Fleisch- und Wurstwaren; **~holder** *n. (Brit. Agric.)* Kleinbauer, *der*/-bäuerin, *die;* **~holding** *n. (Brit. Agric.)* landwirtschaftlicher Kleinbetrieb
smallish ['smɔ:lɪʃ] *adj.* ziemlich klein/gering; ziemlich schmal ‹*Taille*›
small: ~-'minded *adj.* kleinlich; engstirnig, kleingeistig ‹*Einstellung*›; **~-mindedness** [smɔ:l'maɪndɪdnɪs] *n.* kleinliche Art; Krämergeist, *der (abwertend)*
smallness ['smɔ:lnɪs] *n., no pl.* **a)** Kleinheit, *die; (of waist)* Schmalheit, *die; (of income, amount, stock)* Bescheidenheit, *die;* **b)** *(pettiness)* Kleinlichkeit, *die;* **~ of mind** *see* **small-mindedness**
small: ~pox *n. (Med.)* Pocken *Pl.;* **~ 'print** *n. (lit. or fig.)* Kleingedruckte, *das*
smalls [smɔ:lz] *n. pl. (Brit. coll.)* Unterwäsche, *die*
small: ~-scale *attrib. adj.* in kleinem Maßstab *nachgestellt;* klein ‹*Konflikt, Unternehmer*›; Klein‹*betrieb, -bauer, -gärtner*›; **~ 'screen** *n. (Telev.)* Bildschirm, *der;* **~-size** *adj. see* **-size; ~ talk** *n.* leichte Unterhaltung; *(at parties)* Smalltalk, *der;* **engage in** *or* **make ~ talk [with sb.]** [mit jmdm.] Konversation machen; **sb. has no ~ talk** leichte Konversation liegt jmdm. einfach nicht; **~-time** *attrib. adj. (coll.)* Schmalspur- *(ugs. abwertend);* **~-time crook** kleiner Ganove *(ugs. abwertend);* **~-town** *attrib. adj.* Kleinstadt-; kleinstädtisch
smarm [smɑ:m] *v.i. (coll.)* schöntun *(ugs.);* **~ to sb.** jmdm. schöntun *(ugs.);* **~ over sb.** sich bei jmdm. anbiedern *(abwertend)*
~ 'down *v.t.* **~ down one's hair** sein Haar [mit Frisiercreme/Haarwasser] glätten
smarmy ['smɑ:mɪ] *adj.* kriecherisch *(abwertend);* schmeichlerisch ‹*Stimme*›; **her ~ approaches** ihre Anbiederungsversuche; **he's so ~:** er ist solch ein Kriecher *(abwertend)*
smart [smɑ:t] **1.** *adj.* **a)** *(clever)* clever; smart; *(ingenious)* raffiniert; *(accomplished)* hervorragend; **get ~** *(Amer. coll.)* zur Vernunft kommen; **act** *or* **get ~ with sb.** *(Amer. coll.)* zu jmdm. *od.* jmdm. gegenüber frech werden; **~ money** *(Finance)* Geld der klugen Geschäftsleute; **b)** *(neat)* schick; schön ‹*Haus, Garten, Auto*›; **keep sth. ~:** etw. gut in Ordnung halten; **he made a ~ job of it** er hat es schön gemacht; **c)** *attrib. (fashionable)* elegant; smart; **the ~ set** die elegante Welt; die Schickeria; **d)** *(vigorous)* hart ‹*Schlag, Gefecht*›; scharf ‹*Zurechtweisung, Schmerz, Schritt*›; **e)** *(prompt)* flink; **look ~:** sich beeilen; **f)** *attrib. (dishonest)* nicht ganz reell ‹*Geschäft, Handel, Praktiken, Trick*›; **g)** *attrib. (unscrupulous)* clever. **2.** *adv. see* **smartly. 3.** *v.i.* schmerzen; **I/my leg ~ed with pain** ich verspürte einen Schmerz/mein Bein schmerzte; **his vanity/pride ~ed** *(fig.)* er fühlte sich in seiner Eitelkeit/seinem Stolz verletzt; **she ~ed from his remarks** seine Bemerkungen verletzten sie; **~ under sth.** *(fig.)* unter etw. *(Dat.)* leiden. **4.** *n. (lit. or fig.)* Schmerz, *der; (from wound, ointment)* Brennen, *das; (from pain)* Stechen, *das*
smart alec[k], smart alick [smɑ:t 'ælɪk] *(coll. derog.)* **1.** *n.* Besserwisser, *der (abwertend).* **2.** *attrib. adj.* neunmalklug; besserwisserisch *(abwertend)*
'smart-arse, *(Amer.)* **'smart-ass** *(sl.)* **1.** *ns.* Klugscheißer, *der (salopp abwertend).* **2.** *attrib. adjs.* klugscheißerisch *(salopp abwertend)*

'smart card *n.* Chipkarte, *die*

smarten ['smɑːtn] **1.** *v. t.* **a)** *(make spruce)* herrichten; **she ~ed her appearance** sie machte sich zurecht; **he ~ed his hair/clothes** er brachte sein Haar/seine Kleidung in Ordnung *(ugs.)*; **~ oneself** *(tidy up)* sich zurechtmachen; *(dress up)* sich herrichten; *(improve appearance in general)* auf sein Äußeres achten; **b)** *(accelerate)* **~ one's pace** seinen Schritt/seine Schritte beschleunigen. **2.** *v. i.* **the pace ~ed** das Tempo beschleunigte sich

~ 'up 1. *v. t.* **a)** *see* **~ 1 a; b)** *(fig.)* **~ up one's ideas** sich am Riemen reißen *(ugs.)*. **2.** *v. i. (tidy up)* sich zurechtmachen; *(dress up)* sich herrichten; *(improve appearance in general)* auf sein Äußeres achten; **the hotel/town has ~ed up a great deal** das Hotel/die Stadt hat sich sehr gemacht *(ugs.)*

smartish ['smɑːtɪʃ] **1.** *adj. (fairly neat)* ganz schick; *(fairly prompt)* ziemlich flink. **2.** *adv.* **[pretty] ~:** [ganz] schnell

smartly ['smɑːtlɪ] *adv.* **a)** *(cleverly)* clever; *(in a know-all way)* besserwisserisch *(abwertend)*; **that was ~ put** das war gut gesagt; **b)** *(neatly)* schmuck ‹*[an]gestrichen*›; smart, flott ‹*gekleidet, geschnitten*›; **c)** *(fashionably)* vornehm; **d)** *(vigorously)* hart; *(sharply)* scharf ‹*zurechtweisen*›; hart ‹*anpacken*›; **set off ~ down the road** in scharfem Schritt die Straße hinuntergehen; **e)** *(promptly)* sofort; auf der Stelle

smartness ['smɑːtnɪs] *n., no pl.* **a)** *(cleverness)* Cleverneß, *die*; *(attitude of know-all)* Besserwisserei, *die (abwertend)*; **b)** *(neatness)* Gepflegtheit, *die*; **~ [of appearance]** ansprechendes Äußeres; **c)** *(vigour)* Härte, *die*; *(sharpness)* Schärfe, *die*; **~ of pace** Tempo, *das*; **d)** *(promptness)* Flinkheit, *die*

smarty ['smɑːtɪ]: **~-boots, ~-pants** *ns. sing. see* **smart aleck 1**

smash [smæʃ] **1.** *v. t.* **a)** *(break)* zerschlagen; **~ sth. against the wall/down on the floor** etw. an die Wand/auf den Boden schmettern; **~ one's hand/arm/leg** sich *(Dat.)* die Hand/den Arm/das Bein zerschmettern; **~ sth. to pieces** etw. zerschmettern; **b)** *(defeat)* zerschlagen ‹*Rebellion, Revolution, Opposition*›; zerschmettern ‹*Feind*›; *(in games)* vernichtend schlagen; klar verbessern ‹*Rekord*›; **c)** *(hit hard)* **~ sb. in the face/mouth** jmdm. [hart] ins Gesicht/auf den Mund schlagen; **I'll ~ your face** *(sl.)* ich polier' dir die Fresse *(derb)*; **d)** *(Tennis)* schmettern; **e)** *(propel forcefully)* schmettern; **he ~ed the car into a wall/his fist down on the table** er knallte *(ugs.)* mit dem Wagen gegen eine Mauer/schlug mit der Faust auf den Tisch; **he ~ed his way into the house with an iron bar** er schlug sich *(Dat.)* seinen Weg in das Haus mit einer Eisenstange frei. **2.** *v. i.* **a)** *(shatter)* zerbrechen; **b)** *(crash)* krachen; **~ into a wall/lamp-post** an *od.* gegen eine Mauer/einen Laternenpfahl krachen; **the cars ~ed into each other** die Wagen krachten zusammen *(salopp)*; **c)** *(Commerc.) see* **crash 3 d. 3.** *n.* **a)** *(sound)* Krachen, *das*; *(of glass)* Klirren, *das*; **b)** *see* **smash-up; c)** *(coll.) see* **smash hit; d)** *(Tennis)* Schmetterball, *der*; **e)** *(Commerc.) see* **crash 1 c. 4.** *adv.* krach

~ 'down *v. t.* einschlagen ‹*Tür*›

~ 'in *v. t.* zerschmettern; eindrücken ‹*Rippen, Motorhaube, Kotflügel*›; einschlagen ‹*Fenster, Tür, Schädel*›; ‹*Explosion:*› eindrücken ‹*Fenster, Tür*›; **~ sb.'s face in** *(coll.)* jmdm. die Fresse polieren *(derb)*

~ 'up 1. *v. t.* zertrümmern. **2.** *v. i.* zerschellen; ‹*Auto:*› zertrümmert werden; *see also* **smash-up**

smash-and-'grab [raid] *n. (coll.)* Schaufenstereinbruch, *der*

smashed [smæʃt] *adj. (sl.)* **a)** *(drunk)* **get ~ on sth.** von etw. besoffen werden *(derb)*; *(deliberately)* sich mit etw. vollaufen lassen *(salopp)*; **be ~ out of one's head** *or* **mind** *or* **brains** sturzbetrunken *(ugs.) od. (derb)* sturzbesoffen sein; **b)** *(on drugs)* stoned *(Drogenjargon)*

smasher ['smæʃə(r)] *n. (coll.)* **be a ~:** [ganz] große Klasse sein *(ugs.)*; **what a ~ he/she/it is!** er/sie/es ist ganz große Klasse! *(ugs.)*; **a ~ of a girl-friend** eine tolle Freundin

smash 'hit *n. (coll.) (film, play)* Kassenschlager, *der (ugs.)*; *(song, record)* Riesenhit, *der (ugs.)*

smashing ['smæʃɪŋ] *adj. (coll.: excellent)* toll *(ugs.)*; klasse *(ugs.)*; **[how] ~!** toll! *(ugs.)*; klasse! *(ugs.)*; **he/she is ~** *(physically attractive)* er/sie sieht klasse *od.* ganz toll aus *(ugs.)*

'smash-up *n.* schwerer Zusammenstoß; **there has been a ~ between two cars/trains** zwei Autos/Züge sind zusammengekracht *(ugs.)*; **multiple ~:** Massenkarambolage, *die*

smatter ['smætə(r)], **smattering** ['smætərɪŋ] *ns.* oberflächliche Kenntnisse; *(feeble)* Halbwissen, *das (abwertend)*; **have a ~ of German** ein paar Brocken Deutsch können

smear [smɪə(r)] **1.** *v. t.* **a)** *(daub)* beschmieren; *(put on or over)* schmieren; **~ oneself/one's body/face with a cream/lotion/ointment** sich/seinen Körper/sein Gesicht mit einer Creme/Lotion/Salbe einreiben; **~ cream/ointment over one's body/face/hands** sich *(Dat.)* den Körper/das Gesicht/die Hände mit Creme/Salbe einreiben; **~ed with blood** blutbeschmiert *od.* -verschmiert; **he had paint ~ed on his face** sein Gesicht war mit Farbe beschmiert; **ink was ~ed all over the letter** der ganze Brief war mit Tinte verschmiert; **b)** *(smudge)* verwischen; verschmieren; **c)** *(fig.: defame)* in den Schmutz ziehen. **2.** *n.* **a)** *(blotch)* [Schmutz]fleck, *der*; **a ~ of ink/paint/fat** *etc.* ein [verschmierter] Tinten-/Farb-/Fettfleck *usw.*; **b)** *(fig.: defamation)* **a ~ on him/his [good] name/his [good] reputation** eine Beschmutzung seiner Person/seines [guten] Namens/seines Ansehens; **c)** *(Med.)* Abstrich, *der*; **blood ~:** Blutausstrich, *der*

smear: ~ campaign *n.* Schmutzkampagne, *die*; **~ tactics** *n. pl.* schmutzige Mittel; **~ test** *n. (Med.)* Abstrich, *der*; **~ word** *n.* Schmähwort, *das*

smeary ['smɪərɪ] *adj.* **a)** verschmiert ‹*Glas, Tischplatte, Kleid*›; **make sth. ~:** etw. verschmieren; **b)** *(likely to smear)* schmierend; **be very ~:** ‹*Farbe, Tinte:*› leicht schmieren

smegma ['smegmə] *(Physiol.)* Smegma, *das*

smell [smel] **1.** *n.* **a)** *no pl., no art.* **have a good/bad sense of ~:** einen guten/schlechten Geruchssinn haben; **b)** *(odour)* Geruch, *der* (**of** nach); *(pleasant also)* Duft, *der* (**of** nach); **a ~ of burning/gas** ein Brand-/Gasgeruch; **there was a ~ of coffee** es duftete nach Kaffee; **sth. has a nice/strong** *etc.* **~ [to it]** etw. riecht angenehm/stark *usw.*; **c)** *(stink)* Gestank, *der*; **d)** *(act of inhaling)* **one ~ was enough** einmal riechen genügte; **have** *or* **take a ~ at** *or* **of sth.** an etw. *(Dat.)* riechen. **2.** *v. t.*, **smelt** [smelt] *or* **~ed a)** *(perceive)* riechen; *(fig.)* wittern; **I can ~ burning/gas** es riecht brandig/nach Gas; **I could ~ trouble** *(fig.)* es roch nach Ärger; *see also* **rat 1 a; b)** *(inhale ~ of)* riechen an (+ *Dat.*); **just ~ the sea air!** riech [doch] mal nur die Seeluft! **3.** *v. i.*, **smelt** *or* **~ed a)** *(emit ~)* riechen; *(pleasantly also)* duften; **b)** *(recall ~; fig.: suggest)* **~ of sth.** nach etw. riechen; **c)** *(stink)* riechen; **his breath ~s** er riecht aus dem Mund; **d)** *(perceive ~)* riechen; **she can't ~ because of her cold** sie riecht nichts wegen ihrer Erkältung; **~ at sth.** an etw. *(Dat.)* riechen

~ 'out *v. t. (lit. or fig.)* aufspüren

smelling salts ['smelɪŋ sɔːlts, 'smelɪŋ sɒlts] *n. pl.* Riechsalz, *das*

smelly ['smelɪ] *adj.* stinkend *(abwertend)*; **be ~:** stinken *(abwertend)*

¹smelt [smelt] *v. t. (Metallurgy)* **a)** *(melt)* verhütten ‹*Erz*›; **b)** *(refine)* erschmelzen ‹*Metall*›

²smelt *n., pl.* **~s** *or same (Zool.)* Stint, *der*

³smelt *see* **smell 2, 3**

smelter ['smeltə(r)] *n. (Metallurgy)* **a)** *(person)* Schmelzer, *der*; **b)** *(smelting-works)* Schmelzhütte, *die*

smidgen, smidgin ['smɪdʒən] *n. (coll.)* **a ~:** ein klein bißchen

smile [smaɪl] **1.** *n.* Lächeln, *das*; **a ~ of joy/satisfaction** ein freudiges/befriedigtes Lächeln; **be all ~s** über das ganze Gesicht strahlen; **break into a ~:** [plötzlich] zu lächeln beginnen; **give a [little] ~:** [schwach] lächeln; **give sb. a ~:** jmdn. anlächeln; **give me a big ~ now!** jetzt mal schön lächeln!; **raise a ~:** ein Lächeln hervorlocken; *(make oneself ~)* sich *(Dat.)* ein Lächeln abringen; **raise a few ~s** zum Lächeln anregen; **take that ~ off your face!** hör auf zu grinsen!; **this'll put a ~ on your face** das wird dich freuen; **with a ~:** mit einem Lächeln [auf den Lippen]; lächelnd. **2.** *v. i.* lächeln; **make sb. ~:** jmdn. zum Lachen bringen; **keep smiling** *(fig.: not despair)* das Lachen nicht verlernen *(fig.)*; **keep smiling!** Kopf hoch!; keep smiling!; **come up smiling** *(fig. coll.)* sich nicht unterkriegen lassen *(ugs.)*; **~ at sb.** jmdn. anlächeln; **~ at sth.** *(lit. or fig.)* über etw. *(Akk.)* lächeln; **~, please!** bitte recht freundlich! **~ with delight/pleasure** vor Freude strahlen; **Fortune ~d on us/our efforts** das Glück lachte uns *(veralt.)*. **3.** *v. t.* **a) ~ encouragement/one's thanks** aufmunternd/dankend lächeln; **~ a welcome** zur Begrüßung [freundlich] lächeln; **b) ~ a friendly/sad smile** freundlich/traurig lächeln

smirch [smɜːtʃ] *(literary)* **1.** *v. t.* **a)** besudeln *(geh.)*; **b)** *(fig.: disgrace) see* **besmirch. 2.** *n.* **a)** [Schmutz]fleck, *der*; **b)** *(fig.: disgrace)* Schandfleck, *der (fig.)*; **cast a ~ on sb./sth.** ein Schandfleck für jmdn./etw. sein

smirk [smɜːk] **1.** *v. i.* grinsen. **2.** *n.* Grinsen, *das*

smite [smaɪt] *v. t.*, **smote** [sməʊt], **smitten** ['smɪtn] *(arch./literary)* **a)** *(strike)* schlagen (**on** auf, an + *Akk.*); **~ one's breast/forehead** sich *(Dat.)* an die Brust/Stirn schlagen; **b)** *(affect suddenly)* **an idea/his conscience smote him** eine Vorstellung bemächtigte sich seiner *(geh.)*/ihm schlug das Gewissen *(geh.)*; **the light smote our eyes** das Licht blendete unsere Augen; **c)** *(afflict)* **be smitten by** *or* **with desire/terror/the plague** von Verlangen/Schrecken ergriffen/mit der Pest geschlagen sein *(geh.)*; **be smitten by** *or* **with a** *or* **the desire to do sth.** von dem Verlangen ergriffen sein, etw. zu tun; **be smitten by** *or* **with sb./sb.'s charms** jmdm./jmds. Zauber erlegen sein; **d)** *(defeat)* zerschmettern; erschlagen ‹*Person*›

smith [smɪθ] *n.* Schmied, *der*

-smith *n. suf.* **a)** *(metal-worker)* -schmied, *der*; **b)** *(fig.: creator)* **song-~:** versierter Songkomponist; **word-~** *(creator of words)* Wortschöpfer, *der*; **the word-~ John Updike** der versierte Schriftsteller John Updike

smithereens [smɪðə'riːnz] *n. pl.* **blow/smash sth. to ~:** etw. in tausend Stücke sprengen/schlagen; **in ~:** in tausend Stücken

smithy ['smɪðɪ] *n.* Schmiede, *die*

smitten *see* **smite**

smock [smɒk] **1.** *n.* **a)** [Arbeits]kittel, *der*; **painter's ~:** Malerkittel, *der*; **b)** *see* **smock-frock. 2.** *v. t. (Sewing)* smoken

'smock-frock *n.* Bauernkittel, *der (veralt.)*

smocking ['smɒkɪŋ] *n. (Sewing)* Smokarbeit, *die*

smog [smɒg] *n.* Smog, *der*

smoke [sməʊk] **1.** *n.* **a)** Rauch, *der*; **go up in ~:** in Rauch [und Flammen] aufgehen; *(fig.)* in Rauch aufgehen; **like ~** *(sl.)* wie ein geölter Blitz *(ugs.)*⟨*laufen, fahren*⟩; *(without hindrance)* wie geschmiert *(ugs.)* ⟨*zusammenarbeiten, funktionieren*⟩; **[there is] no ~ without fire** *(prov.)* kein Rauch ohne Flamme *(Spr.)*; **b)** *(act of smoking tobacco)* **a ~ would be nice just now** jetzt würde ich gern eine rauchen; **have a [quick] ~:** [schnell eine] rauchen; **I'm dying for a ~:** ich würde schrecklich gern eine rauchen *(ugs.)*; **c)** *(sl.: cigarette)* **a packet of ~s** ein Päckchen Zigaretten; **have you got a ~?** hast du was *(ugs.)* zu rauchen?. **2.** *v.i.* **a)** *(~ tobacco)* rauchen; **do you mind if I ~?** stört es Sie, wenn ich rauche?; **~ like a chimney** rauchen wie ein Schlot *(ugs.)*; **b)** *(emit ~)* rauchen; *(burn imperfectly)* qualmen; *(emit vapour)* dampfen. **3.** *v.t.* **a)** rauchen; *see also* **pipe 1 d**; **b)** *(darken)* schwärzen ⟨*Glas*⟩; ⟨*Petroleumlampe:*⟩ verräuchern ⟨*Wand, Decke*⟩; **c)** räuchern ⟨*Fleisch, Fisch*⟩

~ 'out *v.t.* **a)** *(exterminate, expel)* ausräuchern; **b)** *(fill with ~)* verräuchern; **c)** *(fig.: discover)* aufspüren ⟨*Verbrecher*⟩; auf die Spur kommen (+ *Dat.*) ⟨*Absicht, Plan*⟩

smoke: ~ a'batement *n.* Rauchverringerung, *die*; **~-bomb** *n.* Rauchbombe, *die*

smoked ['sməʊkt] *adj.* *(Cookery)* geräuchert; **~ glass** dunkel getöntes Glas; *(for decorative purposes)* Rauchglas, *das*

'smoke-detector *n.* Rauchmelder, *der*

'smoke-dried *adj.* geräuchert

smokeless ['sməʊklɪs] *adj.* rauchlos; rauchfrei ⟨*Zone*⟩

smoker ['sməʊkə(r)] *n.* **a)** Raucher, *der*/Raucherin, *die*; **be a heavy ~:** ein starker Raucher/eine starke Raucherin sein; **~'s companion** Raucherbesteck, *das*; **~'s cough/heart/throat** *(Med.)* Raucherhusten, *der*/-herz, *das*/-kehle, *die*; **b)** *(Railw.)* *see* **smoking-compartment**

smoke: ~-ring *n.* Rauchring, *der*; **~-room** *n.* *(Brit.)* Rauchsalon, *der*; Rauchzimmer, *das*; **~-screen** *n.* [künstliche] Nebelwand; *(fig.)* Vernebelung, *die* **(for** *Gen.***)**; **throw up a thick ~-screen round a scandal** die Fakten eines Skandals gründlich vernebeln; **~-signal** *n.* Rauchzeichen, *das*; Rauchsignal, *das*; **~-stack** *see* **stack 1 f**

smoking ['sməʊkɪŋ] *n.* **a)** *(act)* Rauchen, *das*; **'no ~'** „Rauchen verboten"; **no-~ compartment** *(Railw.)* Nichtraucherabteil, *das*; **b)** *no art.* *(seating area)* **[do you want to sit in] ~ or non-~?** [möchten Sie für] Raucher oder Nichtraucher?; **the next carriage is ~:** der nächste Wagen ist für Raucher

smoking: ~-compartment *n.* *(Railw.)* Raucherabteil, *das*; **~-jacket** *n.* Rauchjacke, *die*; Hausrock, *der*; **~-room** *(Brit.)* *see* **smoke-room**

smoky ['sməʊkɪ] *adj.* *(emitting smoke)* rauchend; qualmend; *(smoke-filled, smoke-stained)* verräuchert; *(coloured or tasting like smoke)* rauchig; **be too ~** ⟨*Feuer, Kamin, Lampe:*⟩ zu stark rauchen *od.* qualmen; **~ quartz/topaz/glass** Rauchquarz, *der*/-topas/-glas, *das*; **~ grey** rauchgrau

smolder *(Amer.)* *see* **smoulder**

smooch [smu:tʃ] *(coll.)* **1.** *v.i.* [sich] knutschen *(ugs.)*. **2.** *n.* Knutschen, *das* *(ugs.)*; **have a ~:** [sich] knutschen *(ugs.)*

smooth [smu:ð] **1.** *adj.* **a)** *(even)* glatt; eben ⟨*Straße, Weg*⟩; **as ~ as glass/silk/a baby's bottom** spiegelglatt/glatt wie Seide/wie ein Kinderpopo *(ugs.)*; **beat the mixture until ~:** die Mischung glattrühren; **be ~ to the touch** sich glatt anfühlen; **make sth. ~:** etw. glätten; **be worn ~** ⟨*Treppenstufe:*⟩ abgetreten sein; ⟨*Reifen:*⟩ abgefahren sein; ⟨*Fels, Stein:*⟩ glattgeschliffen sein; **this razor gives a ~ shave** dieser Rasierapparat rasiert glatt; **b)** *(mild)* weich; **as ~ as velvet** *(fig.)* samtweich; **c)** *(fluent)* flüssig; geschliffen ⟨*Stil, Diktion*⟩; **d)** *(not jerky)* geschmeidig ⟨*Bewegung*⟩; ruhig ⟨*Fahrt, Flug, Lauf einer Maschine, Bewegung, Atmung*⟩; weich ⟨*Start, Landung, Autofahren, Schalten*⟩; **come to a ~ stop** ⟨*Wagen, Bus, Zug:*⟩ weich zum Stehen kommen; **e)** *(without problems)* reibungslos; **the change-over was fairly ~:** der Wechsel ging ziemlich reibungslos vonstatten; **f)** *(equable)* ruhig ⟨*Art, Wesen*⟩; **g)** *(derog.: suave)* glatt; *(~-tongued)* glattzüngig *(geh. abwertend)*; **he is a ~ operator** er ist gewieft; **h)** *(coll.: elegant)* schick; **i)** *(skilful)* geschickt; souverän. **2.** *adv. see* **smoothly**. **3.** *v.t.* **a)** glätten; glattstreichen, glätten ⟨*Stoff, Tuch, Papier*⟩; glattstreichen ⟨*Haar*⟩; glattschleifen ⟨*Stein*⟩; *(with plane)* glatthobeln ⟨*Holz*⟩; *(with sandpaper)* glattschleifen, glätten ⟨*Holz*⟩; *(fig.: soothe)* besänftigen; **he ~ed the creases/wrinkles from the paper/cloth** er strich die Falten aus dem Papier/Stoff; **b)** *(Statistics)* bereinigen; **c)** *(fig.: free from impediments)* **~ sb.'s/sth.'s path** jmdm./einer Sache den Weg ebnen *od.* die Wege ebnen; **~ the way for sb./sth.** jmdm./einer Sache den Weg *od.* die Wege ebnen. **4.** *v.i.* *(lit. or fig.)* sich glätten

~ a'way *v.t.* glätten, ausstreichen ⟨*Falten*⟩; *(fig.)* vertreiben ⟨*Sorgen, Ängste*⟩; ausräumen ⟨*Differenzen, Schwierigkeiten*⟩

~ 'back *v.t.* [glatt] zurückstreichen ⟨*Haare*⟩; *(with comb)* [glatt] zurückkämmen

~ 'down 1. *v.t.* glattstreichen ⟨*Haar*⟩; *(fig.)* schlichten ⟨*Streit*⟩; besänftigen ⟨*Person*⟩; **~ things down a bit** ein wenig die Wogen glätten. **2.** *v.i. see* **smooth 4**

~ out *v.t.* glattstreichen ⟨*Falte, Tuch*⟩; ausstreichen ⟨*Farbe, Teig*⟩; *(fig.)* ausräumen ⟨*Schwierigkeiten, Hindernisse*⟩

~ 'over *v.t.* *(fig.)* beilegen ⟨*Streit*⟩; ausräumen ⟨*Schwierigkeiten*⟩; **we ~ed things over** wir bereinigten die Angelegenheit

'smooth-bore *n.* *(Arms)* Gewehr mit glattem Lauf

smoothie ['smu:ðɪ] *n.* *(coll. derog.)* aalglatter Typ *(ugs.)*

smoothly ['smu:ðlɪ] *adv.* **a)** *(evenly)* glatt; **b)** *(fluently)* flüssig; **~ flowing** eingängig ⟨*Poesie, Prosa, Musik*⟩; **c)** *(not jerkily)* geschmeidig ⟨*sich bewegen*⟩; reibungslos ⟨*funktionieren*⟩; ruhig ⟨*atmen, fließen, fahren*⟩; weich ⟨*starten, landen, schalten*⟩; **a ~ running engine** *(Motor Veh.)* ein rund laufender Motor; **this pen writes ~:** dieser Füller *(ugs.)* schreibt einwandfrei; **d)** *(without problems)* reibungslos; glatt; **e)** *(derog.: suavely)* aalglatt *(abwertend)*; glattzüngig *(geh. abwertend)* ⟨*sprechen*⟩; **f)** *(coll.: elegantly)* schick; **g)** *(skilfully)* geschickt; souverän

smoothness ['smu:ðnɪs] *n., no pl.* **a)** *(evenness)* Glätte, *die*; **have the ~ of silk** seidig glatt sein; **b)** *(mildness)* Weichheit, *die*; **c)** *(fluency)* Flüssigkeit, *die*; **d)** *(lack of jerkiness)* *(of movement)* Geschmeidigkeit, *die*; *(of machine operation, breathing)* Gleichmäßigkeit, *die*; **the ~ of his driving** sein gefühlvolles Fahren; **e)** *(lack of problems)* Reibungslosigkeit, *die*; **f)** *(equability)* Sanftheit, *die*; **g)** *(derog.: suavity)* Glätte, *die* *(abwertend)*; **h)** *(coll.: elegance)* Schick, *der*; **i)** *(skill)* Geschicklichkeit, *die*; Souveränität, *die*

smooth: ~ 'tongue *n.* *(fig.: suavity)* Glattzüngigkeit, *die* *(geh. abwertend)*; **have a ~:** eine einschmeichelnde Art haben; **~-tongued** *adj.* glattzüngig

smote *see* **smite**

smother ['smʌðə(r)] **1.** *v.t.* **a)** *(stifle)* ersticken; **he was ~ed by the avalanche** er erstickte in der Lawine; **b)** *(overwhelm)* überschütten **(with, in mit)**; **~ sb. with kisses** jmdn. mit seinen Küssen [fast] ersticken; **c)** *(extinguish)* ersticken; **d)** *(fig.: suppress)* unterdrücken ⟨*Kichern, Gähnen, Schluchzen, Tatsachen, Wahrheit*⟩; ersticken ⟨*Kritik, Gerücht, Schluchzen, Gelächter, Schreie*⟩; dämpfen ⟨*Lärm*⟩; **e)** *(Amer.: defeat quickly)* erledigen ⟨*Feind, Gegner*⟩; **f)** *(cover entirely)* **~ sth. in sth.** etw. mit etw. bedecken; **~ed in dust/dirt** voller Staub/Schmutz; **strawberries ~ed in** *or* **with cream** Erdbeeren mit reichlich [flüssiger] Sahne. **2.** *v.i.* ersticken

~ 'up *v.t.* vertuschen ⟨*Verbrechen, Skandal*⟩; unterdrücken ⟨*Gerücht, Wahrheit, Vorschlag*⟩

smothery ['smʌðərɪ] *adj.* stickig; *(overwhelming)* erdrückend

smoulder ['sməʊldə(r)] *v.i.* **a)** schwelen; **b)** *(fig.)* ⟨*Haß, Rebellion:*⟩ schwelen; ⟨*Liebe:*⟩ glimmen *(geh.)*; **she was ~ing with rage** Zorn schwelte in ihr; **she/her eyes ~ed with desire/rage** sie glühte *(geh.)*/ihre Augen glühten vor Verlangen/Zorn; **a ~ing beauty** eine glutvolle Schönheit

¹smudge [smʌdʒ] **1.** *v.t.* **a)** *(blur)* verwischen; **b)** *(smear)* schmieren; **~ sth. on sth.** etw. auf etw. *(Akk.)* schmieren; **c)** *(make smear on)* verschmieren; **d)** *(fig.: disgrace)* beschmutzen. **2.** *v.i.* ⟨*Füller, Tinte, Farbe:*⟩ schmieren; **my hand slipped and the drawing/ink/paint ~d** meine Hand rutschte aus, und die Zeichnung/Tinte/Farbe war verwischt. **3.** *n.* **a)** *(smear)* Fleck, *der*; *(fig.)* Schandfleck, *der*; **b)** *(blur)* Schmierage, *die* *(ugs.)*; **be a mass of ~s** eine einzige Schmiererei sein *(ugs. abwertend)*

²smudge *n.* *(Amer.: fire)* Rauchfeuer, *das* *(zum Schutz vor Insekten od. Kälte)*

'smudge-pot *n.* *(Amer.)* *Kessel mit Brennmaterial für ein Rauchfeuer zur Vertreibung von Insekten od. zum Kälteschutz*

smudgy ['smʌdʒɪ] *adj.* **a)** *(dirty)* schmutzig; verschmutzt; **b)** *(blurred)* verwischt; **c)** *(smudging easily)* schmierend; **be ~** ⟨*Füller, Tinte:*⟩ schmieren

smug [smʌg] *adj.* selbstgefällig *(abwertend)*; **she is very ~ about it/her job/her new house** sie ist darauf/auf ihre Stelle/auf ihr neues Haus sehr eingebildet *(abwertend)*

smuggle ['smʌgl] *v.t.* schmuggeln

~ a'way *v.t.* wegschaffen; **~ sb. away through a back door** jmdn. durch eine Hintertür hinausschmuggeln

~ 'in *v.t.* einschmuggeln; hinein-/hereinschmuggeln ⟨*Person*⟩

~ 'out *v.t.* hinaus-/herausschmuggeln

smuggler ['smʌglə(r)] *n.* Schmuggler, *der*/Schmugglerin, *die*

smuggling ['smʌglɪŋ] *n.* Schmuggel, *der*; Schmuggeln, *das*; **the ~ of dogs into Britain** das Einschmuggeln von Hunden nach Großbritannien

smugly ['smʌglɪ] *adv.* selbstgefällig *(abwertend)*

smugness ['smʌgnɪs] *n., no pl.* Selbstgefälligkeit, *die* *(abwertend)*

smut [smʌt] *n.* **a)** Rußflocke, *die*; *(smudge)* Rußfleck, *der*; **be covered in ~s** voller Ruß sein; **b)** *no art.* *(lewd matter)* Schund, *der* *(abwertend)*; **talk ~:** schweinigeln *(ugs. abwertend)*; **c)** *(Bot.)* *(disease)* Brand, *der*; *(fungus)* Brandpilz, *der*

smutty ['smʌtɪ] *adj.* **a)** *(dirty)* verschmutzt; **b)** *(lewd)* schmutzig *(abwertend)*; **he is ~:** er ist schweinisch *(ugs. abwertend)*

snack [snæk] *n.* Imbiß, *der*; Snack, *der*; **eat many ~s between meals** viel zwischendurch essen; **have a [quick] ~:** [rasch] eine Kleinigkeit essen *(ugs.)*

'snack-bar *n.* Schnellimbiß, *der*; Snackbar, *die*

snaffle ['snæfl] **1.** *n.* *(Riding)* Trense, *die*. **2.** *v.t.* **a)** *(sl.)* mopsen *(fam.)* ⟨*Schokolade, Zeitung*⟩; klauen *(salopp)* ⟨*Diamanten, Geheimdokumente, Geld*⟩; **b)** *(Riding)* die Trense anlegen (+ *Dat.*)

~ 'up *v.t.* [sich *(Dat.)*] schnappen *(ugs.)*

'snaffle-bit *n.* *(Riding)* Trensengebiß, *das*

snafu [snæ'fu:] *(Amer. sl.)* **1.** *pred. adj.* chaotisch. **2.** *n.* Chaos, *das*; **they left us in ~:** sie ließen uns im Schlamassel stecken *(ugs.)*

snag [snæg] **1.** *n.* **a)** *(jagged point)* Zacke, *die;* **b)** *(problem)* Haken, *der;* **what's the ~?** wo klemmt es [denn]? *(ugs.);* **hit a ~, run up against a ~:** auf ein Problem *od.* eine Schwierigkeit stoßen; **there's a ~ in it** die Sache hat einen Haken; **c)** *(tear)* Loch, *das; (pulled thread)* gezogener Faden. **2.** *v. t.,* **-gg- a)** *(catch)* **I've ~ged my coat** mein Mantel hat sich verfangen; ich bin mit dem Mantel hängengeblieben; **b)** *(tear)* einreißen; **c)** *(Amer.: catch quickly)* **~ sth.** sich *(Dat.)* etw. schnappen *(ugs.)*

snail [sneɪl] *n.* Schnecke, *die;* **Roman ~:** Weinbergschnecke, *die;* **at [a] ~'s pace** im Schneckentempo *(ugs.)*

'snail-like *adj.* schneckenartig; schneckenhaft *(ugs.)*

snake [sneɪk] **1.** *n.* **a)** Schlange, *die;* **~s and ladders** *Brettspiel, bei dem je nach Augenzahl beim Würfeln Spielsteine „Leitern" hinauf- und „Schlangen" hinabbewegt werden;* **b)** *(derog.)* **~ [in the grass]** *(woman)* [falsche] Schlange; *(man)* falscher Kerl *od. (ugs.)* Hund; **c)** *(Econ.)* **the ~:** die Währungsschlange *(Jargon).* **2.** *v. i.* sich schlängeln

snake: ~-bite *n.* **a)** Schlangenbiß, *der;* **b)** *(drink) Getränk aus gleichen Teilen Apfelwein und Lagerbier;* **~-charmer** *n.* Schlangenbeschwörer, *der;* **~-skin** *n.* Schlangenleder, *das*

snaky ['sneɪkɪ] *adj.* **a)** *(winding)* gewunden; schlangenartig ‹*Bewegung*›; **b)** *(sly)* hinterhältig

snap [snæp] **1.** *v. t.,* **-pp- a)** *(break)* zerbrechen; **~ sth. in two** *or* **in half** etw. in zwei Stücke brechen; **b) ~ one's fingers** mit den Fingern schnalzen; **~ one's fingers at sth./sb.** *(fig.)* auf etw./jmdn. pfeifen *(ugs.);* **c)** *(move with ~ping sound)* **~ sth. home** *or* **into place** etw. einrasten *od.* einschnappen lassen; **~ shut** zuschnappen lassen ‹*Portemonnaie, Tür, Schloß*›; zuklappen ‹*Buch, Zigarettendose, Etui*›; **~ sth. open** etw. aufschnappen lassen; **d)** *(take photograph of)* knipsen; **e)** *(say in sharp manner)* fauchen; *(speak crisply or curtly)* bellen. **2.** *v. i.,* **-pp- a)** *(break)* brechen; **b)** *(fig.: give way under strain)* ausrasten *(ugs.);* **my patience has finally ~ped** nun ist mir der Geduldsfaden aber gerissen; **something ~ed in me** *(fig.)* da war bei mir das Maß voll; **c)** *(make as if to bite)* [zu]schnappen; **d)** *(move smartly)* **~ into action** loslegen *(ugs.);* **~ into life** aufschrecken; **~ to attention** strammstehen; **~ to it!** *(coll.)* leg/legt los! *(ugs.);* **e)** *(move with ~ping sound)* **~ home** *or* **into place** einrasten; einschnappen; **~ shut** zuschnappen; ‹*Kiefer:*› zusammenklappen; ‹*Mund:*› zuklappen; **~ together** zusammenklappen; **~ open** aufschnappen; **f)** *(speak in sharp manner)* fauchen; **g)** *(take photograph)* knipsen. **3.** *n.* **a)** *(sound)* Knacken, *das; (of whip)* Knallen, *das;* **b)** *(biscuit)* Plätzchen, *das; see also* **brandy-snap; c)** *(Photog.)* Schnappschuß, *der;* **d)** *(Brit. Cards)* Schnippschnapp[schnurr], *das;* **e) cold ~:** kurze Kälteperiode; **f)** *(zest)* Schwung, *der.* **4.** *attrib. adj. (spontaneous)* spontan; **call a ~ election/vote** Knall und Fall *(ugs.)* einen Wahltermin festsetzen/eine Abstimmung herbeiführen. **5.** *int.* **a)** *(Brit. Cards)* schnapp; **b)** *(when two things are seen to match coincidentally)* genau gleich *(ugs.)*

~ at *v. t.* **a)** *(bite)* **~ at sb./sth.** nach jmdm./etw. schnappen; **~ at sb.'s heels** jmdm. auf den Fersen sein; **he ran with a pack of dogs ~ping at his heels** er rannte, dicht gefolgt von einer Hundemeute; **b)** *(speak sharply to)* anfauchen *(ugs.);* **c)** *(Amer.: accept eagerly)* **~ at a chance** eine Gelegenheit beim Schopf[e] ergreifen; **~ at an invitation/a job** bei einer Einladung/einem Job keinesfalls nein sagen *od. (salopp)* gleich zuschlagen

~ 'back 1. *v. i.* **a)** *(return)* zurückschnellen; **b)** *(reply)* **~ back [at sb.]** jmdn. anfauchen *(ugs.);* **c)** *(Amer. fig.: make quick recovery)* sich schnell [wieder] erholen. **2.** *v. t. (say as a retort)* zurückgeben

~ 'off 1. *v. i.* abbrechen; abknicken ‹*Zweig, Antenne*›. **2.** *v. t.* **a)** *(break)* abbrechen; **~ sth. off sth.** etw. von etw. abbrechen; **b)** *(bite)* abbeißen; **~ sb.'s head off** *(fig.)* jmdm. den Kopf abreißen *(fig.);* **c)** *(Amer.: switch off)* ausknipsen *(ugs.);* ausschalten; **d)** aufklappen ‹*Deckel, Verschluß*›

~ 'on 1. *v. i.* zuschnappen; **~ on to sth.** sich an etw. *(Dat.)* festklemmen. **2.** *v. t.* **a)** *(fasten)* festklemmen; zuklappen ‹*Deckel*›; **~ sth. on sth.** etw. auf etw. *(Akk.)* klemmen; **b)** *(Amer.: switch on)* anknipsen *(ugs.). See also* **snap-on**

~ 'out *v. t.* bellen ‹*Befehl, Anweisung*›

~ 'out of *v. t.* abwerfen; sich befreien von ‹*Gefühl, Stimmung, Komplex*›; **~ out of it!** *(coll.)* hör auf damit!; *(wake up)* wach auf!

~ 'up *v. t.* **a)** *(pick up)* [sich *(Dat.)*] schnappen; **b)** *(fig. coll.: seize)* [sich *(Dat.)*] schnappen *(ugs.);* **~ up a bargain/an offer** bei einem Angebot [sofort] zugreifen *od. (salopp)* zuschlagen; **~ sth. up in the sales** etw. beim Ausverkauf ergattern *(ugs.);* **the tickets were ~ped up immediately** die Karten waren sofort weg

snap: ~ bean *n. (Amer.)* Brechbohne, *die;* **~dragon** *n. (Bot.)* Löwenmäulchen, *das;* **~-fastener** *n.* Druckknopf, *der;* **~-on** *attrib. adj.* Klemm-

snappy ['snæpɪ] *adj.* **a)** *(lively)* lebhaft; temperamentvoll ‹*Tanz, Musik*›; **b)** *(smart)* schick; **be a ~ dresser** sich flott *od.* schick kleiden; **c)** *(coll.)* **look ~!, make it ~!** ein bißchen dalli! *(ugs.)*

snap: ~ 'shot *(gunshot)* ungezielter Schuß; **~shot** *(Photog.) n.* Schnappschuß, *der*

snare [sneə(r)] **1.** *n.* **a)** *(trap)* Schlinge, *die;* Falle, *die (auch fig.);* **set a ~ [for sb.]** [jmdm.] eine Falle stellen; **b)** *(temptation)* Fallstrick, *der;* **c)** *(Mus.)* Schnarrsaite, *die;* **d)** *(Mus.) see* **~ drum. 2.** *v. t.* [mit einer Schlinge] fangen ‹*Tier, Vogel*›; **~ sb.** jmdn. in eine Falle locken

'snare drum *n.* Wirbeltrommel, *die;* kleine Trommel

¹snarl [snɑːl] **1.** *v. i.* **a)** *(growl)* ‹*Hund:*› knurren; ‹*Tiger:*› fauchen; **b)** *(speak)* knurren. **2.** *v. t.* knurren. **3.** *n.* Knurren, *das; (of tiger)* Fauchen, *das;* **..., he said to him with a ~:** ..., knurrte er ihn an

~ at *v. t.* anknurren; ‹*Tiger:*› anfauchen

²snarl 1. *n. (tangle)* Knoten, *der.* **2.** *v. t.* verheddern *(ugs.).* **3.** *v. i.* sich verheddern *(ugs.)*

~ 'up 1. *v. t. (confuse)* durcheinanderbringen; *(bring to a halt)* zum Erliegen bringen; **get ~ed up** ‹*Wolle usw.:*› sich verheddern *(ugs.);* **get ~ed up in the traffic** im Verkehr steckenbleiben. **2.** *v. i.* ‹*Verkehr:*› stocken; ‹*Wolle:*› sich verheddern *(ugs.)*

'snarl-up *n.* Stau, *der;* Stockung, *die*

snatch [snætʃ] **1.** *v. t.* **a)** *(grab)* schnappen; **~ a bite to eat** [schnell] einen Bissen zu sich nehmen; **~ a kiss** sich *(Dat.)* einen Kuß stehlen *(scherzh.);* **~ an opportunity** eine Gelegenheit beim Schopf[e] ergreifen; **~ a rest** sich *(Dat.)* eine Ruhepause verschaffen; **~ hold of sb./sth.** jmdn./etw. schnappen; **~ hold of sb. by the collar/ear** jmdn. am Kragen/Ohr packen; **~ some sleep** ein bißchen schlafen; **~ a nap** *(coll.)* ein Nickerchen *(fam.)* halten; **~ the lead** die Führung übernehmen *od.* an sich *(Akk.)* nehmen; **~ sth. from sth.** etw. schnell von etw. nehmen; *(very abruptly)* etw. von etw. reißen; **~ sth. from sb.** jmdm. etw. wegreißen; **~ sth. out of sb.'s hand/pocket** jmdm. etw. aus der Hand reißen/schnell aus der Tasche ziehen; **b)** *(steal)* klauen *(ugs.); (kidnap)* kidnappen. **2.** *v. i.* einfach zugreifen. **3.** *n.* **a) make a ~ at sb./sth.** nach jmdm./etw. greifen; **b)** *(Brit. sl.: robbery)* Raub, *der;* **c)** *(sl.: kidnap)* Kidnapping, *das;* **d)** *(fragment)* **a ~ of a song** ein paar Takte von einem Lied; **~es of talk/conversation** Gesprächsfetzen *od.* -brocken *Pl.;* **e)** *in pl. (spells)* **do sth. in** *or* **by ~es** etw. mit Unterbrechungen tun; **f)** *(weight-lifting)* Reißen, *das*

~ at *v. t.* **a) ~ at sb./sth.** nach jmdm./etw. schnappen; **b)** *(fig.) see* **jump at b**

~ a'way *v. t.* [schnell] wegziehen **(from** *Dat.*); **~ sth. away from sb.** jmdm. etw. wegreißen

~ 'up *v. t.* [sich *(Dat.)*] schnappen

snazzy ['snæzɪ] *adj. (sl.)* [super]schick *(ugs.)*

sneak [sniːk] **1.** *v. t.* **a)** *(take)* stibitzen *(fam.);* **b)** *(fig.)* **~ a look at sb./sth.** nach jmdm./etw. schielen; **c)** *(bring)* **~ sth./sb. into a place** etw./jmdn. in einen Ort schmuggeln; **~ sth. into one's bag** etw. heimlich in die Tasche stecken; **d)** *(sl.: steal)* klauen *(ugs.);* mitgehen lassen *(ugs.).* **2.** *v. i.* **a)** *(Brit. Sch. sl.: tells tales)* petzen *(Schülerspr.);* **~ on sb.** jmdn. verpetzen *(Schülerspr.);* **b)** *(move furtively)* schleichen. **3.** *attrib. adj.* **a)** *(without warning)* **~ attack/raid** Überraschungsangriff, *der;* **b) a ~ preview of the film/play/programme** eine inoffizielle Vorpremiere des Films/Stücks/Programms. **4.** *n.* **a)** *(shifty person)* Fiesling, *der (salopp);* **b)** *(Brit. Sch. sl.: tell-tale)* Petze, *die (Schülerspr.)*

~ a'way *v. i.* [sich] fortschleichen; sich davonmachen

~ 'in 1. *v. i.* **a)** *(enter stealthily)* sich hineinschleichen; *(fig.)* sich einschleichen; **b)** *(win narrowly)* knapp siegen. **2.** *v. t.* **a)** *(bring in)* einschmuggeln *(ugs.);* **b)** *(Amer.: include)* **~ in a mention of sth./a word about sth.** etw. [beiläufig] erwähnen/ein Wort über etw. *(Akk.)* einstreuen

~ 'out *v. i.* [sich] hinausschleichen

~ 'out of *(Amer.: avoid)* **~ out of sth./doing sth.** sich vor etw. *(Dat.)* drücken *(ugs.)*/sich davor drücken *(ugs.),* etw. zu tun

sneaker ['sniːkə(r)] *(Amer.)* Turnschuh, *der*

sneaking ['sniːkɪŋ] *attrib. adj.* heimlich; leise ‹*Verdacht*›

'sneak-thief *n.* Einschleichdieb, *der*

sneaky ['sniːkɪ] **a)** *(underhand)* hinterhältig; **b) have a ~ feeling that ...:** so ein leises Gefühl haben, daß ...

sneer [snɪə(r)] **1.** *v. i.* **a)** *(smile scornfully)* spöttisch *od.* höhnisch lächeln/grinsen; hohnlächeln; **b)** *(speak scornfully)* höhnen *(geh.);* spotten. **2.** *v. t. (say)* höhnen *(geh.);* spotten. **3.** *n.* **a)** *(look)* Hohnlächeln, *das;* **b)** *(remark)* höhnische *od.* spöttische Bemerkung; **a cynical/sarcastic ~:** eine zynische/sarkastische Bemerkung

~ at *v. t.* **a)** *(smile scornfully at)* höhnisch anlächeln/angrinsen; **b)** *(express scorn for)* verhöhnen *(geh.);* spotten über (+ *Akk.*)

sneeze [sniːz] **1.** *v. i.* niesen; **not to be ~d at** *(fig. coll.)* nicht zu verachten *(ugs.).* **2.** *n.* Niesen, *das*

snicker ['snɪkə(r)] *see* **snigger**

snide [snaɪd] *adj.* **a)** *(sneering)* abfällig; **b)** *attrib. (Amer.: mean, underhand)* mies *(ugs.)*

sniff [snɪf] **1.** *n.* **a)** Schnüffeln, *das;* Schnuppern, *das; (with running nose, while crying)* Schniefen, *das; (contemptuous)* Naserümpfen, *das;* **give a disdainful ~:** geringschätzig die Nase rümpfen; **have a ~ at sth.** an etw. *(Dat.)* riechen *od.* schnuppern; **have a ~ at this!** hier, riech *od.* schnupper mal!; **I didn't get a ~ of the food** *(coll.)* ich habe von dem Essen keinen Krümel abbekommen; **not a ~!** leer ausgegangen!; **b)** *(quantity ~ed)* **have a [good] ~ of sea air/of perfume** [ausgiebig] die Seeluft/am Parfüm schnuppern. **2.** *v. i.* schniefen; die Nase hochziehen; *(to detect a smell)* schnuppern; *(to ex-*

press contempt) die Nase rümpfen. **3.** *v. t.* **a)** *(smell)* riechen *od.* schnuppern an (+ *Dat.*) ⟨*Essen, Getränk, Blume, Parfüm, Wein*⟩; **the dog ~ed the air/the lamp-post** der Hund schnupperte/schnupperte am Laternenpfahl [herum]; **~ glue/cocaine** Klebstoff schnüffeln/Kokain sniffen *(Drogenjargon)*; **b)** *(utter with contempt)* naserümpfend sagen

~ **at** *v. t.* **a)** schnuppern *od.* riechen an (+ *Dat.*) ⟨*Blume, Essen*⟩; **b)** *(show contempt for)* die Nase rümpfen über (+ *Akk.*); **not to be ~ed at = not to be sneezed at** *see* **sneeze 1**

~ **'out** *v. t.* aufspüren

sniffer dog ['snɪfə dɒg] *n.* Spürhund, *der*

sniffle ['snɪfl] **1.** *v. i.* schniefen; schnüffeln *(ugs.)*. **2.** *n. (coll.)* **a)** Schniefen, *das;* Schnüffeln, *das (ugs.)*; **b)** *in pl.* **have the ~s** [einen] Schnupfen haben

sniffy ['snɪfɪ] *adj. (coll.)* **a)** *(contemptuous)* hochnäsig *(ugs.)*; **b)** *(sniffing)* **sb. is ~:** jmd. schnüffelt; *(has a cold)* schnieft

snifter ['snɪftə(r)] *n.* **a)** *(sl.: drink)* Kurze, *der (ugs.)*; **b)** *(Amer.: glass)* [Kognak]schwenker, *der*

snigger ['snɪgə(r)] **1.** *v. i.* [boshaft] kichern. **2.** *n.* [boshaftes] Kichern

snip [snɪp] **1.** *v. t.*, **-pp-** schnippeln *(ugs.)*, schneiden ⟨*Loch*⟩; schnippeln *(ugs.) od.* schneiden an (+ *Dat.*) ⟨*Tuch, Haaren, Hecke*⟩; *(cut off)* abschnippeln *(ugs.)*; abschneiden. **2.** *v. i.*, **-pp-** schnippeln *(ugs.)*; schneiden. **3.** *n.* **a)** *(Brit. sl.: certainty)* **be a ~:** idiotensicher sein *(ugs.)*; **b)** *(Brit. sl.: good bargain)* Schnäppchen, *das (ugs.)*; **c)** *(cut)* Schnitt, *der;* Schnipser, *der (ugs.)*; **d)** *(piece)* Schnipsel, *der od. das;* **e)** *in pl. (shears)* [Hand]blechschere, *die*

snipe [snaɪp] **1.** *n., pl. same or ~s (Ornith.)* Schnepfe, *die.* **2.** *v. i. (Mil.)* aus dem Hinterhalt schießen

~ **at** *v. t.* **a)** *(Mil.)* aus dem Hinterhalt beschießen; **b)** *(fig.: make snide comments about)* anschießen *(ugs.)*

sniper ['snaɪpə(r)] *n.* Heckenschütze, *der*

snippet ['snɪpɪt] *n.* **a)** *(piece)* Schnipsel, *der od. das;* **b)** *(of information in newspaper)* Notiz, *die; (of knowledge)* Bruchstück, *das; (from a book)* Passage, *die; (of conversation)* Gesprächsfetzen, *der;* **useful ~s of information** nützliche Hinweise

snipping ['snɪpɪŋ] *n.* Schnipsel, *der od. das*

snit [snɪt] *n. (Amer. sl.)* **be in a ~** *(agitated)* am Rotieren sein *(ugs.)*; *(annoyed)* auf achtzig sein *(ugs.)*

snitch [snɪtʃ] *(sl.)* **1.** *v. t.* klauen *(ugs.)*. **2.** *v. i.* auspacken *(salopp)*; **~ on sb.** jmdn. verpfeifen *(salopp)*

snivel ['snɪvl] *v. i., (Brit.)* **-ll- a)** *(have runny nose)* **stop ~ling, use a handkerchief** hör auf, dauernd die Nase hochzuziehen – nimm ein Taschentuch; **b)** *(sniff, sob)* schniefen; schnüffeln *(ugs.)*

snivelling *(Amer.:* **sniveling**) ['snɪvəlɪŋ] *(fig.)* **1.** *attrib. adj.* heulend; greinend *(ugs.)* ⟨*Opposition*⟩. **2.** *n.* Geheule, *das;* Gegreine, *das (ugs.)*

snob [snɒb] *n.* Snob, *der (abwertend); attrib.* **~ appeal** *or* **value** Snob-Appeal, *der; see also* **inverted snob**

snobbery ['snɒbərɪ] *n.* Snobismus, *der*

snobbish ['snɒbɪʃ] *adj.*, **snobbishly** ['snɒbɪʃlɪ] *adv.* snobistisch

snog [snɒg] *(Brit. sl.)* **1.** *v. i.*, **-gg-** knutschen *(ugs.)*. **2.** *n.* Knutschen, *das (ugs.)*; **have a ~ [with sb.]** [mit jmdm.] knutschen

snood [snu:d] *n.* Haarnetz, *das*

snook [snu:k] *n. (sl.)* **cock a ~ at sb.** jmdm. eine lange Nase drehen *(ugs.)*; *(fig. also)* jmdm. eine Nase drehen *(ugs.)*

snooker ['snu:kə(r)] **1.** *n.* **a)** *no pl., no indef. art.* Snooker [Pool], *das;* Taschenbillard, *das;* **b)** *(tactical position) Situation beim Billardspiel, in der der Spieler die richtige Kugel nicht direkt spielen kann.* **2.** *v. t.* **a)** *in eine Lage bringen, in der die richtige Kugel nicht direkt gespielt werden kann;* **be ~ed** *die richtige Kugel nicht direkt spielen können;* **b)** *(fig. sl.: thwart)* vereiteln; **he was ~ed** ihm wurde ein Strich durch die Rechnung gemacht

snoop [snu:p] *(coll.)* **1.** *v. i.* schnüffeln *(ugs.)*; **~ into sth.** in einer Sache [herum]schnüffeln *(ugs.)*; **~ about** *or* **around** herumschnüffeln *(ugs.)*; **~ around the village** im Dorf herumschnüffeln. **2.** *n.* **have a ~ around** sich [ein bißchen] umsehen

snooper ['snu:pə(r)] *n. (coll.)* Schnüffler, *der*/Schnüfflerin, *die (ugs.)*

snootily ['snu:tɪlɪ] *adv.*, **snooty** ['snu:tɪ] *adj. (coll.)* hochnäsig *(ugs.)*

snooze [snu:z] *(coll.)* **1.** *v. i.* dösen *(ugs.)*. **2.** *n.* Nickerchen, *das (fam.)*; **have a ~:** ein Nickerchen machen

snore [snɔ:(r)] **1.** *v. i.* schnarchen. **2.** *n.* Schnarcher, *der (ugs.)*; **~s** Schnarchen, *das*

snorkel ['snɔ:kl] **1.** *n.* Schnorchel, *der.* **2.** *v. i., (Brit.)* **-ll-** schnorcheln

snort [snɔ:t] **1.** *v. i.* schnauben **(with, in** vor + *Dat.*); **~ with laughter** vor Lachen prusten; **~ in disbelief** ungläubig schnauben. **2.** *v. t.* **a)** schnauben; **~ one's disgust/disbelief/anger** vor Ekel/ungläubig/wütend schnauben; **b)** *(sl.: take)* **~ [coke]** [Koks] sniffen *(Drogenjargon)*. **3.** *n.* **a)** Schnauben, *das;* **give a ~ of indignation/rage** vor Mißbilligung/Wut schnauben; **with a ~ of rage** wutschnaubend; **~s of laughter** prustendes Gelächter; **b)** *(coll.: drink)* Kurze, *der (ugs.)*; **c)** *(sl.: of drug)* Sniff, *der (Jargon)*

snorter ['snɔ:tə(r)] *n. (sl.)* **a)** *(gale)* Orkan, *der;* **b)** *(difficult task)* **a ~ [of a job]** eine Plackerei *(ugs.)*; **the exam was a ~:** die Prüfung war ein Schlauch *(ugs.)*

snot [snɒt] *n. (sl.)* Rotz, *der (derb)*; Schnodder, *der (derb)*

'snot-rag *n. (sl.)* Rotzfahne, *die (salopp)*

snotty ['snɒtɪ] *adj. (sl.)* **a)** *see* **snooty**; **b)** *(running with nasal mucus)* rotznäsig *(salopp)*; **~ child** Rotznase, *die (salopp)*; **~ handkerchief** Rotzfahne, *die (salopp)*; **~ nose** Rotznase, *die (salopp)*

'snotty-nosed *adj. (sl.)* **a)** rotzig; rotznäsig *(salopp)*; **b)** *see* **snooty**

snout [snaʊt] *n.* **a)** *(nose)* Schnauze, *die; (of pig, ant-eater)* Rüssel, *der; (of wild boar)* Gebrech, *das (Jägerspr.)*; **b)** *(nose-piece)* Nase, *die;* **c)** *(derog.: nose)* Rüssel, *der (salopp)*; Zinken, *der (salopp)*; **d)** *(Brit. sl.: tobacco)* Kraut, *das (ugs., oft abwertend)*; *(cigarette)* Kippe, *die (ugs.)*; Lulle, *die (ugs.)*; **e)** *(Brit. sl.: informer)* Schnüffler, *der (ugs. abwertend)*; Spürhund, *der (ugs.)*

snow [snəʊ] **1.** *n., no indef. art.* **a)** Schnee, *der;* **be [as] pure as the driven ~** ⟨*Person:*⟩ unschuldig wie ein/die Engel sein; **b)** *in pl. (areas)* Schnee, *der; (falls)* Schneefälle; **c)** *(sl.: cocaine)* Schnee, *der (Drogenjargon)*; **d)** *(on TV screen etc.)* Schnee, *der.* **2.** *v. i. impers.* **it ~s** *or* **is ~ing** es schneit; **it starts ~ing** *or* **to ~:** es fängt an zu schneien. **3.** *v. t. (Amer. sl.)* **~ sb.** bei jmdm. Eindruck schinden *(ugs.)*

~ **'in** *v. t.* **they are ~ed in** sie sind eingeschneit

~ **'under** *v. t.* **be ~ed under** ⟨*Haus:*⟩ eingeschneit sein; ⟨*Straße:*⟩ zugeschneit sein; *(fig.) (with work)* erdrückt werden; *(with presents, letters)* überschüttet werden

~ **'up** *see* **~ in**

snow: ~ball 1. *n.* Schneeball, *der;* **~ball fight** Schneeballschlacht, *die;* **have a ~ball effect** eine Kettenreaktion auslösen; **not have** *or* **stand a ~ball's chance in hell** *(coll.)* nicht die geringste Chance haben; **2.** *v. t.* mit Schneebällen bewerfen; **3.** *v. i.* **a)** Schneebälle werfen; **b)** *(fig.: increase greatly)* lawinenartig zunehmen; **~-blower** *n.* Schneefräse, *die;* **~-boot** *n.* Schneestiefel, *der;* **~-bound** *adj.* eingeschneit; **~-capped** *adj.* schneebedeckt; schneegekrönt *(dichter.)*; **~ chains** *n. pl.* Schneeketten *Pl.*; **~-covered** *adj.* schneebedeckt; **~-drift** *n.* Schneeverwehung, *die;* Schneewehe, *die;* **~drop** *n.* Schneeglöckchen, *das;* **~fall** *n.* Schneefall, *der;* **~flake** *n.* Schneeflocke, *die;* **~-goose** *n.* Schneegans, *die;* **~ job** *n. (Amer. sl.)* **do a ~ job on sb.** jmdn. beschwatzen *(ugs.)*; **~-leopard** *n.* Schneeleopard, *der;* **~-line** *n.* Schneegrenze, *die;* **~man** *n.* Schneemann, *der; see also* **abominable; ~mobile** ['snəʊməbi:l] *n.* Schneemobil, *das;* **~-plough** *n.* Schneepflug, *der;* **~scape** *n.* Schneelandschaft, *die;* **~-shoe** *n.* Schneeschuh, *der;* **~-shovel** *n.* Schneeschaufel, *die;* **~ shower** *n.* Schneeschauer, *der;* **~-storm** *n.* Schneesturm, *der;* **~-white** *adj.* schneeweiß; **S~ 'White** *pr. n.* Schneewittchen, *das*

snowy ['snəʊɪ] *adj.* **a)** *(having much snow)* schneereich ⟨*Gegend, Monat*⟩; schneebedeckt ⟨*Berge*⟩; **~ weather** Schneewetter, *das;* **b)** *(white)* schneeweiß

snowy 'owl *n.* Schnee-Eule, *die*

SNP *abbr.* **Scottish National Party** *Schottische Nationalpartei*

snub [snʌb] **1.** *v. t.*, **-bb- a)** *(rebuff)* brüskieren; vor den Kopf stoßen; **b)** *(reprove)* zurechtweisen; *(insult)* beleidigen; **c)** *(reject)* ablehnen; **d)** *(Amer.)* **~ out** ausdrücken. **2.** *n.* Abfuhr, *die;* **get** *or* **receive a ~:** eine Abfuhr erhalten; **give sb. a [proper] ~:** jmdm. eine [gehörige] Abfuhr erteilen

snub: ~ 'nose *n.* Stupsnase, *die;* Stupsnäschen, *das (fam.)*; *(of car, aeroplane)* stumpfe Schnauze *(ugs.) od.* Nase; **~-nosed** *adj.* stupsnasig; stumpfnasig ⟨*Auto, Flugzeug*⟩; mit stumpfer Schnauze *(ugs.) nachgestellt*

[1]snuff [snʌf] *n.* **a)** *(tobacco)* Schnupftabak, *der;* **take a pinch of ~:** eine Prise schnupfen; **b) be up to ~** *(Brit. sl.: not easily deceived)* mit allen Wassern gewaschen sein *(ugs.)*; *(in good health or condition)* auf der Höhe sein *(ugs.)*

[2]snuff *v. t.* beschneiden, putzen ⟨*Kerze*⟩; **~ it** *(sl.: die)* ins Gras beißen *(salopp)*

~ **'out 1.** *v. t.* **a)** *(extinguish)* löschen ⟨*Kerze*⟩; **b)** *(fig.: put an end to)* zerstören; zunichte machen ⟨*Hoffnung*⟩; niederschlagen ⟨*Revolte*⟩; *(kill)* töten; umbringen. **2.** *v. i. (sl.)* ins Gras beißen *(salopp)*

'snuff-box *n.* Schnupftabak[s]dose, *die*

snuffer ['snʌfə(r)] *n.* Löschhütchen, *das;* **pair of ~s** Licht[putz]schere, *die*

snuffle ['snʌfl] **1.** *v. i.* **a)** *(sniff)* schnüffeln **(at** an + *Dat.*); *(with cold, after crying)* schniefen; **b)** *(make sniffing sound)* schnüffeln **(at** an + *Dat.*); **c)** *(breathe noisily)* schnaufen. **2.** *n.* **a)** *(sniff)* **~[s]** Schnaufen, *das; (of horses)* Schnauben, *das;* **b)** *in pl.* **have the ~s** [einen] Schnupfen haben

snug [snʌg] **1.** *adj.* **a)** *(cosy)* gemütlich, behaglich ⟨*Haus, Zimmer, Bett*⟩; *(warm)* mollig warm ⟨*Zimmer, Mantel, Bett*⟩; **in bed sb. is as ~ as a bug in a rug** im Bett hat es jmd. urgemütlich *od.* richtig kuschelig; **b)** *(sheltered)* geschützt; **c)** *(close-fitting)* **be a ~ fit** genau passen; ⟨*Kleidung:*⟩ wie angegossen sitzen *od.* passen. **2.** *n. (Brit.: bar-parlour) Nebenzimmer in einer Gastwirtschaft, bes. für Stammgäste*

snuggle ['snʌgl] **1.** *v. i.* **~ together** sich aneinanderschmiegen *od.* -kuscheln; **~ down in bed** sich ins Bett kuscheln; **~ up with a book** es sich *(Dat.)* mit einem Buch gemütlich machen. **2.** *v. t.* **she ~d the crying child to her body** sie drückte das weinende Kind zärtlich an sich

snugly ['snʌglɪ] *adv.* **a)** *(cosily)* gemütlich; behaglich; **be/lie ~ tucked up** behaglich eingemumm[el]t sein/liegen *(fam.)*; **b)** *(close-fitting)* **fit ~:** genau passen; ⟨*Kleidung:*⟩ wie angegossen sitzen *od.* passen

¹so [səʊ] **1.** *adv.* **a)** *(by that amount)* so; **as winter draws near, so it gets darker** je näher der Winter rückt, desto dunkler wird es; **as fast as the water poured in, so we bailed it out** in dem Maße, wie das Wasser eindrang, schöpften wir es heraus; **so ... as** so ... wie; **there is nothing so fine as ...:** es gibt nichts Schöneres als ...; nichts ist so schön wie ...; **not so [very] difficult/easy** *etc.* nicht so schwer/leicht *usw.*; **it's not so easy/big after all** so einfach/groß ist es nun wieder auch nicht; **so beautiful a present** so ein schönes Geschenk; ein so schönes Geschenk; **so great a general as X** ein so großer General wie X; **[it's] not so bad as ...:** [es ist] nicht so schlecht wie ...; **so far** bis hierher; *(until now)* bisher; bis jetzt; *(to such a distance)* so weit; **I trust him only so far** ich traue ihm nur bis zu einem gewissen Grad; **and so on [and so forth]** und so weiter und so fort; und so weiter; und so fort; **so long!** bis dann *od.* gleich *od.* nachher *od.* später! *(ugs.)*; **so many** so viele; *(unspecified number)* soundso viele; **they looked like so many chimney-sweeps** sie sahen alle aus wie die Schornsteinfeger; **so much** so viel; *(unspecified amount)* soundsoviel; **[just] so much/many** *(nothing but)* nichts als; **his books are just so much rubbish** seine Bücher taugen alle nichts; **the villages are all so much alike** die Dörfer gleichen sich alle so sehr; **so much for the agenda** so viel zur Tagesordnung; **so much for him/his plans** das wär's, was ihn/seine Pläne angeht; **so much for my hopes** und ich habe mir solche Hoffnungen gemacht; **so much for that** *(after having dealt with a tricky problem)* das wäre geschafft; das hätten wir; **so much the better** um so besser; **if he doesn't want to stay, so much the worse for him** wenn er nicht bleiben will, ist er selber schuld; **not so much ... as** weniger ... als [eher]; **be not so much angry as disappointed** weniger verärgert als [viel mehr] enttäuscht sein; **not so much as** *(not even)* [noch] nicht einmal; **not so much as glance at sth.** auf etw. *(Akk.)* nicht einmal einen Blick werfen; *see also* **ever f**; **every c**; **far 1 d**; **¹long 3 a, b**; **more 3 h**; **never a**; **b)** *(in that manner)* so; **so be it** einverstanden; so sei es *(geh.)*; **this being so** da dem so ist *(geh.)*; **it so happened that he was not there** er war [zufällig] gerade nicht da; **c)** *(to such a degree)* so; **this answer so provoked him that ...:** diese Antwort provozierte ihn so *od.* derart, daß ...; **I went straight to bed, I was so tired** ich war so müde, daß ich gleich zu Bett ging; **put it so as not to offend him** sag es so, daß es ihn nicht kränkt; **I am not so big a fool as to believe that** ich bin nicht so dumm, das zu glauben; **I got so I could ...** *(Amer.)* ich war soweit, daß ich ... konnte; **so much so that ...:** so sehr, daß ...; das geht/ging so weit, daß ...; **d)** *(with the intent)* **so as to** um ... zu; **run so as not to get wet** rennen, um nicht naß zu werden; so **[that]** damit; **e)** *(emphatically)* so; **I'm so glad/tired!** ich bin ja so froh/müde!; **so kind of you!** wirklich nett von Ihnen!; **so sorry!** *(coll.)* Entschuldigung!; Verzeihung!; **f)** *(indeed)* **It's a rainbow! – So it is!** Es ist ein Regenbogen! – Ja, wirklich!; **'You suggested this trip. – So I did** Du hast diese Reise vorgeschlagen. – Das stimmt; **you said it was good, and so it was** du sagtest, es sei gut, und so war es auch; **is that so?** so? *(ugs.)*; wirklich?; **and so he did** und das machte/tat er [dann] auch; **it 'is so** *expr. certainty* doch!; **it may be so, possibly so** [das ist] möglich; **g)** *(likewise)* **so am/have/would/could/will/do I** ich auch; **as a is to b, so is c to d** a verhält sich zu b wie c zu d; **as in the arts, so in politics, it's true that ...:** in der Politik wie in der Kunst gilt, daß ...; **h)** *(thus)* so; **and so it was that ...:** und so geschah es, daß ...; **not so!** nein, nein! *See also* **how 1**; **if 1 a**; **just 2 a**; **quite a**; **so so. 2.** *pron.* **he suggested that I should take the train, and if I had done so, ...:** er riet mir, den Zug zu nehmen, und wenn ich es getan hätte, ...; **we must consider what would be the result of so doing** wir müssen bedenken, was das für Folgen hätte; **I'm afraid so** leider ja; ich fürchte schon; **the teacher said so** der Lehrer hat es gesagt; **it was self-defence – or so the defendant said** es war Selbstverteidigung – so sagte jedenfalls der Angeklagte; **so saying, he departed** mit diesen Worten ging er; **so say all of us** das sagen wir alle; **Why do I have to go to bed? – Because I say so** Warum muß ich ins Bett? – Weil ich es sage; **I suppose so** ich nehme an *(ugs.)*; *expr. reluctant agreement* wenn es sein muß; *granting grudging permission* von mir aus; **I told you so** ich habe es dir [doch] gesagt; **so I gathered** ich weiß [es]; **so I gathered from the newspaper** ich weiß es aus der Zeitung *od.* habe es aus der Zeitung erfahren; **he is a man of the world, so to say** *or* **speak** es menschelt sozusagen bei ihm; **it will take a week or so** es wird so *(ugs.)* *od.* etwa eine Woche dauern; **there were twenty or so people** es waren so *(ugs.)* um die zwanzig Leute da; **very much so** in der Tat; allerdings; *see also* **say 1 a. 3.** *conj.* *(therefore)* daher; **so 'that's what he meant** das hat er also gemeint; **cigarettes are dangerous, so don't smoke** Zigaretten sind schädlich, also rauch nicht!; **so what is the answer?** wie lautet also die Antwort?; **so you are from Oxford then?** Sie kommen also aus Oxford?; **so 'there you are!** da bist du also!; **so there you 'are!** ich habe also recht!; **so what are you going to do now?** was machen Sie denn jetzt?; **so what's the joke/problem?** was ist denn daran witzig?/was ist denn das Problem?; **so where have you been?** wo warst du denn?; **so that's 'that** *(coll.)* *(it's done)* [al]so, das war's *(ugs.)*; *(it's over)* das war's also *(ugs.)*; *(everything has been taken care of)* das wär's dann *(ugs.)*; **so there!** [und] fertig!; [und damit] basta! *(ugs.)*; **so you see ...:** du siehst also ...; **so?** na und?

²so *see* **soh**

So. *abbr.* *(Amer.)* **South** S

soak [səʊk] **1.** *v. t.* **a)** *(steep)* einweichen ⟨*Wäsche in Lauge*⟩; eintauchen ⟨*Brot in Milch, Tapete in Wasser*⟩; **~ oneself in the sun** sich in der Sonne aalen *(ugs.)*; **b)** *(wet)* naß machen; durchnässen; durchtränken ⟨*Erde*⟩; **~ sb. from head to foot** jmdn. von Kopf bis Fuß durchnässen *od.* *(ugs.)* patschnaß machen; **~ed in sth.** von etw. durchtränkt; mit *od.* von etw. getränkt; **a rag ~ed in petrol** ein mit Benzin getränkter Lappen; **~ed in sweat** schweißgebadet; **~ed with sweat** schweißgetränkt; **this town is ~ed in history** *(fig.)* in dieser Stadt weht der Hauch der Geschichte; **c)** *(absorb)* *see* **~ up**; **d)** *(sl.: obtain money from)* melken *(salopp)*; schröpfen *(ugs.)*. **2.** *v. i.* **a)** *(steep)* **put sth. in sth. to ~:** etw. in etw. *(Dat.)* einweichen; **lie ~ing in the bath** ⟨*Person:*⟩ sich im Bad durchweichen lassen; **the liver was put to ~ in milk** die Leber wurde in Milch eingelegt; **b)** *(drain)* ⟨*Feuchtigkeit, Nässe:*⟩ sickern; **~ away** wegsickern. **3.** *n.* **a)** **give sth. a [good] ~:** etw. [gründlich] einweichen; **give the garden a [good] ~:** den Garten [gut] wässern; **put in ~:** einweichen; **he leaves his dentures in ~ overnight** er legt sein künstliches Gebiß über Nacht in eine Reinigungsflüssigkeit; **b)** *(coll.: drinker)* Säufer, *der*/Säuferin, *die* *(derb, oft abwertend)*; Suffkopp, *der* *(ugs.)*

~ 'in 1. *v. i.* **a)** *(seep in)* einsickern; eindringen; ⟨*Flecken:*⟩ einziehen; **b)** *(fig.)* **let the atmosphere ~ in** die Atmosphäre auf sich *(Akk.)* einwirken lassen. **2.** *v. t.* *see* **~ up**

~ into *v. t.* sickern in (+ *Akk.*); ⟨*Tinte usw.:*⟩ einziehen in (+ *Akk.*)

~ through 1. *v. t.* **a)** ['--] *(penetrate)* ⟨*Flüssigkeit, Strahlen:*⟩ dringen durch; ⟨*Regenwasser, Blut:*⟩ sickern durch; **b)** [-'-] *(drench)* durchnässen. **2.** *v. i.* [-'-] durchdringen

~ 'up *v. t.* **a)** *(absorb)* aufsaugen; **~ up the sunshine** in der Sonne baden; **b)** *(fig.)* auf sich *(Akk.)* einwirken lassen, aufnehmen ⟨*Atmosphäre*⟩; aufnehmen, in sich *(Akk.)* aufsaugen ⟨*Wissen usw.*⟩

'soak-away *n.* *(Brit.)* Abflußgrube, *die*

soaking ['səʊkɪŋ] **1.** *n.* *(drenching)* **need a [good] ~** ⟨*Garten:*⟩ [gut] gewässert werden müssen; ⟨*Tuch:*⟩ [gründlich] eingeweicht werden müssen; **get a ~:** eine Dusche abbekommen; **give sb./sth. a ~:** jmdn./etw. naß machen. **2.** *adv.* **~ wet** völlig durchnäßt; klatsch- *od.* patschnaß *(ugs.)*. **3.** *adj.* **a)** *(drenched)* naß [bis auf die Haut]; patschnaß *(ugs.)*; **be ~** ⟨*Kleidung:*⟩ völlig durchnäßt sein; ⟨*Gras:*⟩ patschnaß sein *(ugs.)*; **b)** *(saturating)* alles durchnässend ⟨*Regen, Strom*⟩

'so-and-so *n.*, *pl.* **~'s a)** *(person not named)* [Herr/Frau] Soundso; *(thing not named)* Dings, *das*; **b)** *(coll.: contemptible person)* Biest, *das* *(ugs.)*; **poor ~:** armes Schwein *(ugs.)*

soap [səʊp] **1.** *n.*, *no indef. art.* **a)** Seife, *die*; **a bar** *or* **tablet of ~:** ein Stück Seife; **with ~ and water** mit Wasser und Seife; **b)** *(coll.)* *see* **soap opera. 2.** *v. t.* **~ [down]** einseifen

soap: ~-box *n.* **a)** *see* **~-dish a**; **b)** *(packing-box)* Seifenschachtel, *die*; **c)** *(stand)* ≈ Apfelsinenkiste, *die*; **get on one's ~-box** *(fig.)* laut seine Meinung äußern; Volksreden halten; **d)** *(cart)* Seifenkiste, *die*; **~-box derby** Seifenkistenrennen, *das*; **~-bubble** *n.* Seifenblase, *die*; **~-dish** *n.* **a)** *(container)* Seifendose, *die*; **b)** *(open dish)* Seifenschale, *die*; **~-flakes** *n. pl.* Seifenflocken *Pl.*; **~ opera** *n.* *(Telev., Radio)* Seifenoper, *die* *(ugs.)*; **~ powder** *n.* Seifenpulver, *das*; **~stone** *n.* *(Min.)* Speckstein, *der*; **~suds** *n. pl.* Seifenschaum, *der*

soapy ['səʊpɪ] *adj.* seifig; **~ water** Seifenwasser, *das*; Seifenlauge, *die*

soar [sɔ:(r)] *v. i.* **a)** *(fly up)* aufsteigen; *(hover in the air)* segeln; **b)** *(extend)* **~ into the sky** in den Himmel ragen; **c)** *(fig.: rise rapidly)* steil ansteigen; ⟨*Preise, Kosten usw.:*⟩ in die Höhe schießen *(ugs.)*; **my hopes have ~ed again** ich schöpfe wieder große Hoffnung; **~ above sb./sth.** jmdn./etw. überrunden *od.* überragen *od.* hinter sich *(Dat.)* lassen

soaring ['sɔ:rɪŋ] *attrib. adj.* **a)** *(flying)* segelnd; [hoch am Himmel] schwebend; **b)** *(fig.: rising rapidly)* sprunghaft ansteigend; galoppierend ⟨*Preise, Inflation, Kosten*⟩; hoch[fliegend, -gesteckt] ⟨*Ideale*⟩; **c)** *(lofty)* hoch aufragend

SOB [esəʊ'bi:] *abbr.* *(Amer.)* **son of a bitch**

sob [sɒb] **1.** *v. i.*, **-bb-** schluchzen (**with** vor + *Dat.*). **2.** *v. t.*, **-bb-** schluchzen. **3.** *n.* Schluchzer, *der*; **~s [of anguish/pain]** [schmerzvolles] Schluchzen

~ 'out *v. t.* schluchzen; **she ~bed out her story** sie erzählte schluchzend *od.* unter Schluchzen ihre Geschichte; **~ one's heart out** bitterlich weinen

sobbing ['sɒbɪŋ] **1.** *n.* Schluchzen, *das*. **2.** *adj.* schluchzend

sober ['səʊbə(r)] *adj.* **a)** *(not drunk)* nüchtern; **as ~ as a judge** stocknüchtern; **b)** *(moderate)* solide; **c)** *(solemn)* ernst; **d)** *(subdued)* schlicht; gedeckt ⟨*Farben*⟩; nüchtern ⟨*Umgebung*⟩; **be a ~ dresser** sich solide kleiden; **e)** *(rational, realistic)* nüchtern; **the ~ truth/fact** die nackte Wahrheit/Tatsache

~ 'down *v. i.* ruhig werden; *(after being excited)* sich abkühlen *(ugs.)*; **he has ~ed down a lot** er ist wesentlich vernünftiger geworden

~ 'up 1. *v. i.* nüchtern werden; ausnüchtern. **2.** *v. t.* ausnüchtern

sobering ['səʊbərɪŋ] *adj.* ernüchternd; **he found it a ~ experience** das Erlebnis ernüchterte ihn *od.* brachte ihn zur Vernunft; **it is a ~ thought that ...:** der Gedanke ist ganz schön ernüchternd, daß ...
soberly ['səʊbəlɪ] *adv.* nüchtern; vernünftig; **dress ~:** sich solide kleiden
sober: ~-minded *adj.* nüchtern; vernünftig; **~-sides** *n., pl. same* Miesepeter, *der (ugs. abwertend)*
sobriety [sə'braɪətɪ] *n., no pl., no indef. art.* **a)** *(not being drunk)* Nüchternheit, *die;* **b)** *(moderation)* Bescheidenheit, *die;* **c)** *(seriousness)* Ernsthaftigkeit, *die;* **~ of mind/judgment** Nüchternheit im Denken/Urteilen
sobriquet ['səʊbrɪkeɪ] *n. (nickname)* Spitzname, *der*
sob: ~-sister *n. (Amer. Journ.) Schreiberin rührseliger Geschichten; (giving advice to readers)* Briefkastentante, *die (ugs.);* **~-story** *n.* rührselige Geschichte; **~-stuff** *n., no indef. art., no pl. (coll.)* Schmalz, *das (ugs.); (book, film, etc.)* Schmachtfetzen, *der (salopp)*
'so-called *adj.* sogenannt; *(alleged)* angeblich
soccer ['sɒkə(r)] *n. (coll.)* Fußball, *der;* **~ ball** Fußball, *der*
sociability [səʊʃə'bɪlɪtɪ] *n., no pl.* Geselligkeit, *die*
sociable ['səʊʃəbl] *adj.* gesellig; **she's not feeling ~ today** ihr ist heute nicht nach Gesellschaft zumute; **he did it just to be ~:** er hat es nur getan, um nicht ungesellig zu sein
sociably ['səʊʃəblɪ] *adv.* gesellig; aufgeschlossen; **they spent the evening ~ together** sie verbrachten den Abend in geselliger Runde
social ['səʊʃl] **1.** *adj.* **a)** sozial; gesellschaftlich; **~ welfare** Fürsorge, *die;* **b)** *(of ~ life)* gesellschaftlich; gesellig ‹*Abend, Beisammensein*›; **~ behaviour** Benehmen in Gesellschaft; **~ engagement** gesellschaftliche Verpflichtung; **c)** *(Zool.)* sozial; gesellig [lebend]. **2.** *n. (gathering)* geselliges Beisammensein
social: ~ anthro'pology *n.* Sozialanthropologie, *die;* **~ 'class** *n.* Gesellschaftsschicht, *die;* [Gesellschafts]klasse, *die;* **~ 'climber** *n.* Emporkömmling, *der (abwertend);* [sozialer] Aufsteiger *(ugs.);* **~ club** *n.* Klub für geselliges Beisammensein; **~ compact, ~ contract** *ns. (Polit.)* Gesellschaftsvertrag, *der;* **S~ 'Democrat** *n. (Polit.)* Sozialdemokrat, *der*/-demokratin, *die;* **S~ Demo'cratic Party** *n. (Brit. Polit.)* Sozialdemokratische Partei; **~ engineering** *n.* Social engineering, *das;* Sozialtechnologie, *die;* **~ 'history** *n.* Sozialgeschichte, *die*
socialisation, socialise *see* **socializ-**
socialism ['səʊʃəlɪzm] *n.* Sozialismus, *der*
socialist ['səʊʃəlɪst] **1.** *n.* Sozialist, *der*/Sozialistin, *die.* **2.** *adj.* sozialistisch
socialite ['səʊʃəlaɪt] *n. bekannte Persönlichkeit des gesellschaftlichen Lebens*
socialization [səʊʃəlaɪ'zeɪʃn] *n.* Sozialisation, *die*
socialize ['səʊʃəlaɪz] **1.** *v.t.* umgänglich machen; **become ~d** umgänglich[er] werden; **~d medicine** *(Amer.)* öffentliche Gesundheitsfürsorge. **2.** *v.i.* geselligen Umgang pflegen; **~ with sb.** *(chat)* sich mit jmdm. unterhalten; **he is out socializing** er ist mit Bekannten *od. (ugs.)* irgendwelchen Leuten unterwegs
social life *n.* gesellschaftliches Leben; **a place with plenty of ~:** ein Ort, wo etwas los ist *(ugs.);* **not have much ~** ‹*Person:*› nicht viel ausgehen
socially ['səʊʃəlɪ] *adv.* **meet ~:** sich privat treffen; **have a good time ~:** viel unter die Leute kommen; **~ acceptable** aus der richtigen Gesellschaftsschicht; **~ deprived** sozial benachteiligt
social: ~ 'order *n.* Gesellschaftsordnung, *die;* **~ 'outcast** *n.* Außenseiter der Gesellschaft; **~ 'policy** *n. (Polit.)* Sozialpolitik, *die;* **~ re'form** *n.* Sozialreform, *die;* **fight for ~ reform** für Sozialreformen *od.* gesellschaftliche Reformen kämpfen; **~ 'science** *n.* Sozialwissenschaften *Pl.;* Gesellschaftswissenschaften *Pl.;* **~ 'scientist** *n.* Sozialwissenschaftler, *der*/-wissenschaftlerin, *die;* **~ se'curity** *n.* **a)** *(Brit.: benefit)* Sozialhilfe, *die;* **b)** *(welfare system)* soziale Sicherheit; **c)** *(Amer.: insurance)* Sozialversicherung, *die;* **~ 'service** *n.* **a)** *(service to society)* soziales Engagement; **b)** *(a service provided by the government)* staatliche Sozialleistung; **~ 'status** *n.* sozialer Status; **~ structure** *n.* Sozialstruktur, *die;* **~ studies** *n. sing. (Educ.)* Gemeinschaftskunde, *die;* **~ system** *n.* Gesellschaftssystem, *das;* **~ work** *n.* Sozialarbeit, *die;* **~ worker** *n.* Sozialarbeiter, *der*/-arbeiterin, *die*
societal [sə'saɪətl] *adj. (formal)* gesellschaftlich
society [sə'saɪətɪ] **1.** *n.* **a)** Gesellschaft, *die;* **be embarrassed in ~:** in Gegenwart anderer verlegen sein; **avoid ~:** gesellschaftlichen Umgang meiden; **high ~:** High-Society, *die;* **b)** *(club, association)* Verein, *der; (Commerc.)* Gesellschaft, *die; (group of persons with common beliefs, aims, interests, etc.)* Gemeinschaft, *die; see also* **friend c; Jesus. 2.** *attrib. adj.* **a)** *(of high ~)* Gesellschafts-; [High-]Society-; **she is a ~ hostess** sie gibt Feste für die [gehobene] Gesellschaft; **~ people** Leute der High-Society; **b)** *(of club or association)* Vereins-, Klub‹*vorsitzender, -treffen, -ausflug, -sekretär usw.*›
socio- [səʊsɪəʊ] *in comb.* sozio-/Sozio-
sociobi'ology *n.* Soziobiologie, *die*
socio'cultural *adj.* soziokulturell
socio-eco'nomic *adj.* sozioökonomisch
sociolingu'istic *adj.* soziolinguistisch
sociolingu'istics *n. sing.* Soziolinguistik, *die*
sociological [səʊsɪə'lɒdʒɪkl] *adj.* soziologisch
sociologist [səʊsɪ'ɒlədʒɪst] *n.* Soziologe, *der*/Soziologin, *die*
sociology [səʊsɪ'ɒlədʒɪ] *n.* Soziologie, *die*
[1]**sock** [sɒk] *n.* **a)** *pl.* **~s** *or (Commerc./coll.)* **sox** [sɒks] Socke, *die;* Socken, *der (südd., österr., schweiz.); (ankle ~, esp. for children also)* Söckchen, *das;* **knee-length ~s** Kniestrümpfe *Pl.;* **pull one's ~s up** *(Brit. fig. coll.)* sich am Riemen reißen *(ugs.);* **put a ~ in it!** *(Brit. sl.)* halt die Klappe! *(salopp); (stop doing sth.)* hör auf [damit]!; **b)** *see* **insole d; c)** *(of horse) see* [1]**stocking b**
[2]**sock** *(coll.)* **1.** *v.t. (hit)* schlagen, hauen *(ugs.);* **~ sb. in the mouth/on the chin/jaw** jmdm. eine reinhauen *(salopp);* jmdn. in die Schnauze hauen *(derb);* **~ it to sb.** *(Amer. sl.)* jmdm. Saures geben *(salopp); (fig.: impress sb.)* es jmdm. zeigen *(ugs.).* **2.** *n.* **give sb. a ~ on the chin/jaw/in the mouth** jmdm. eine reinhauen *(salopp)*
socket ['sɒkɪt] *n.* **a)** *(Anat.) (of eye)* Höhle, *die; (of joint)* Pfanne, *die;* **~ of a tooth** Zahnfach, *das (Anat.);* **b)** *(Electr.)* Steckdose, *die; (receiving a bulb)* Fassung, *die;* **c)** *(for attachment)* Fassung, *die; (of pipe)* Muffe, *die; (of candle-holder)* [Kerzen]tülle, *die*
socket: ~-spanner, *(Amer.)* **~-wrench** *ns.* Steckschlüssel, *der*
sockeye ['sɒkaɪ] *n. (Zool.)* **~ [salmon]** Blaurückenlachs, *der*
Socrates ['sɒkrəti:z] *pr. n.* Sokrates *(der)*
Socratic [sə'krætɪk] *adj.* sokratisch
[1]**sod** [sɒd] *n. (turf)* Sode, *die;* **be/lie under the ~:** unter der Erde liegen
[2]**sod** *(sl.)* **1.** *n. (bastard, swine)* Sau, *die (derb); (fool)* Rindvieh, *das (salopp);* **that's ~'s law, ~'s law was proved right** *(coll.)* es mußte ja so kommen; **the poor old ~:** das arme Schwein *(salopp);* **not give a ~ = not give a damn** *see* **damn 2 b. 2.** *v. t.,* **-dd-: ~ that/you!** verdammter Mist/scher dich zum Teufel! *(ugs.)*
~ 'off *v. i. imper. (sl.)* verpiß dich *(derb)*
soda ['səʊdə] *n.* **a)** *(sodium compound)* Soda, *die od. das; see also* **caustic 1 b; b)** *(drink)* Soda[wasser], *das;* **whisky and ~:** Whisky mit Soda
soda: ~-bread *n. mit Backsoda gebackenes Brot;* **~-fountain** *n. (Amer.)* **a)** *(container)* Mineralwasserbehälter, *der;* **b)** *(shop) Erfrischungshalle bzw. -bar, in der es vor allem Erfrischungsgetränke und Speiseeis gibt;* **~-siphon** *n.* Siphon, *der;* Siphonflasche, *die;* **~-water** *n.* Soda[wasser], *das*
sodden ['sɒdn] *adj.* durchnäßt (**with** von)
sodding ['sɒdɪŋ] *attrib. adj. (sl.)* Scheiß- *(derb)*
sodium ['səʊdɪəm] *n. (Chem.)* Natrium, *das*
sodium: ~ bi'carbonate *n. (Chem.)* doppeltkohlensaures Natrium; Natriumhydrogenkarbonat, *das;* **~ 'carbonate** *n. (Chem.)* Natriumkarbonat, *das;* Soda, *die od. das;* **~ 'chloride** *n. (Chem.)* Natriumchlorid, *das;* **~ hy'droxide** *n. (Chem.)* Ätznatron, *das;* **~ lamp** *n.* Natriumdampflampe, *die;* **~ 'nitrate** *n. (Chem.)* Natriumnitrat, *das*
sodomite ['sɒdəmaɪt] *n.* Sodomit, *der*
sodomize ['sɒdəmaɪz] *v.t.* sodomisieren *(geh.);* anal verkehren mit; Sodomie betreiben mit ‹*Tier*›
sodomy ['sɒdəmɪ] *n.* Analverkehr, *der;* Sodomie, *die (veralt.); (with animal)* Sodomie, *die*
soever *see* **howsoever, whatsoever,** *etc.*
sofa ['səʊfə] *n.* Sofa, *das;* **~ bed** Bettcouch, *die*
soffit ['sɒfɪt] *n. (Archit.)* Windbrett, *das*
soft [sɒft] **1.** *adj.* **a)** weich; zart, weich ‹*Haut*›; **the ground is ~:** der Boden ist aufgeweicht; *(Sport)* der Boden ist schwer; **as ~ as butter** weich wie Butter; butterweich; **~ ice-cream** Soft-Eis, *das;* **~ toys** Stofftiere; **~ water area** Gebiet mit weichem Wasser; **b)** *(mild)* sanft; mild ‹*Klima*›; zart ‹*Duft*›; **c)** *(compassionate)* **have a ~ heart** ein weiches Herz haben; weichherzig sein; **have a ~ spot for sb./sth.** eine Vorliebe *od.* Schwäche für jmdn./etw. haben; **you are too ~!** du bist zu weich[herzig]!; **d)** *(delicate)* sanft ‹*Augen*›; weich ‹*Farbe, Licht*›; **e)** *(quiet)* leise; sanft; **f)** *(gentle)* sanft; *(amorous)* zärtlich ‹*Blicke*›; **be ~ on sb.** *(coll.: be in love with)* in jmdn. verknallt sein *(ugs.);* für jmdn. schwärmen; **be ~ on** *or* **with sb.** *(coll.: be unusually lenient with)* mit jmdm. sanft umgehen; jmdn. [zu] sanft anfassen; *see also* **nothing 1 c; g)** *(sl.: easy)* bequem, *(ugs.)* locker ‹*Job, Leben*›; **have a ~ job** eine ruhige Kugel schieben *(ugs.);* **h)** *(compliant)* nachgiebig; *see also* **touch 3 i; i)** *(too indulgent)* zu nachsichtig; zu lasch *(ugs.);* **be ~ with sb.** sich *(Dat.)* von jmdm. alles bieten lassen; **j)** *(gently curved)* weich ‹*Umriß, Linien, Züge*›; **k)** *(weak)* schlaff ‹*Muskeln*›; weichlich *(abwertend)* ‹*Mann*›; verweichlicht ‹*Volk*›; **l) be/go ~ in the head** *(coll.)* nicht alle Tassen im Schrank haben *(ugs.)*/verrückt werden *(ugs.);* **m)** *(Scot., Ir.: moist)* feucht ‹*Wetter, Tag*›; **n)** *(Phonet.)* weich. **2.** *adv. (quietly)* leise
soft: ~ball *n.* Softball, *der (Variante des Baseballs mit weicherem Ball);* **~-boiled** *adj.* weichgekocht ‹*Ei*›; **~-centred** *adj.* ‹*Praline usw.*› mit weicher Füllung; **~ coal** *n.* Fettkohle, *die;* **~ copy** *n. (Computing)* Softcopy, *die;* **~ cover** *n.* **book with a ~ cover** Buch mit einem Softcover *(Verlagsw.) od.* mit einem flexiblen Einband; **~ currency** *n. (Econ.)* weiche Währung; *attrib.*

⟨*Markt, Land*⟩ mit weicher Währung; ~ **detergent** *n.* biologisch abbaubares Waschmittel; ~ **drink** *n.* alkoholfreies Getränk; ~ **drug** *n.* weiche Droge

soften ['sɒfn] **1.** *v.i.* weicher werden; **~ing of the brain** Gehirnerweichung, *die (Med.); (coll.: stupidity)* Verkalkung, *die (ugs.).* **2.** *v.t.* weich klopfen ⟨*Fleisch*⟩; aufweichen ⟨*Boden*⟩; dämpfen ⟨*Beleuchtung*⟩; mildern ⟨*Farbe, Farbton*⟩; enthärten ⟨*Wasser*⟩; **~ the blow** *(fig.)* den Schock mildern

~ **'up** *v.t.* weichklopfen *(ugs.)* ⟨*Boxgegner*⟩; aufweichen ⟨*Verteidigungsanlagen*⟩; *(verbally)* milder stimmen

softener ['sɒfənə(r)] *n.* **a)** *(for water)* [Wasser]enthärter, *der;* **b)** *(for fabrics)* Weichspülmittel, *das;* Weichspüler, *der*

soft: ~ **'focus** *n. (Photog.)* Weichzeichnung, *die;* ~ **fruit** *n.* Beerenobst, *das;* ~ **'furnishings** *n. pl. (Brit.)* Raumtextilien *Pl.;* ~ **goods** *n. pl. (Brit.)* Textilien *Pl.;* ~**'headed** *adj.* dumm; schwachköpfig; ~**-'hearted** *adj.* weichherzig

softie *see* **softy**

soft 'landing *n. (Astronaut.)* weiche Landung

softly ['sɒftlı] *adv.* **a)** *(quietly)* leise ⟨*sprechen, singen, gehen*⟩; **b)** *(gently)* sanft; **speak ~:** mit sanfter Stimme sprechen; **c)** *(not dazzlingly)* sanft ⟨*scheinen, leuchten*⟩; **d)** *(affectionately)* zärtlich

softness ['sɒftnıs] *n., no pl. see* **soft 1: a)** Weichheit, *die;* Zartheit, *die;* **the silky ~ of her hair** ihr seidenweiches Haar; **b)** Sanftheit, *die;* Milde, *die;* Zartheit, *die;* **there is a ~ in the air** die Luft ist mild *od. (geh.)* lind; **c) ~ of heart** Weichherzigkeit, *die;* **d)** *(delicacy)* Sanftheit, *die;* Weichheit, *die;* **e)** *(of voice, music, etc.)* Gedämpftheit, *die;* **f)** *(gentleness)* Sanftheit, *die;* Zärtlichkeit, *die;* **g)** *(compliance)* Nachgiebigkeit, *die;* **h)** *(leniency)* Nachsichtigkeit, *die;* Laschheit, *die (ugs.);* **i)** *(of lines, features, outline)* Weichheit, *die;* **j)** *(weakness)* Schlaffheit, *die;* Weichlichkeit, *die (abwertend);* **k)** *(coll.: silliness)* **~ in the head** Gehirnerweichung, *die (ugs.)*

soft: ~ **option** *n.* Weg des geringsten Widerstandes; ~ **'palate** *n. (Anat.)* weicher Gaumen; Gaumensegel, *das (fachspr.);* ~ **pedal** *see* **pedal 1a;** ~**-'pedal 1.** *v.i.* **a)** *(Mus.)* mit [dem] Pianopedal spielen; **b)** *(fig.: go easy)* sich zurückhalten; **~-pedal on sth.** etw. herunterspielen; **2.** *v.t.* **a)** *(Mus.)* mit [dem] Pianopedal spielen; **b)** *(fig.: tone down)* herunterspielen; ~ **'porn** *(coll.),* ~ **por'nography** *ns.* Softpornographie, *die;* ~ **roe** *n.* Milch, *die;* ~ **'sell** *n.* **give sb. the ~ sell** jmdn. auf die sanfte Tour *(ugs.)* zum Kauf zu bewegen versuchen; *attrib.* **~ sell salesmanship** sanfte Tour *(ugs.)* beim Verkaufsgespräch; **give sb. the ~ sell treatment** jmdn. auf die sanfte Tour *(ugs.)* zum Kauf zu bewegen versuchen; **~-shell, ~-shelled** *adjs.* **a)** *(Zool.)* mit weicher Schale *nachgestellt;* **b)** *(fig.)* gemäßigt; lasch *(abwertend);* ~ **'soap** *n.* **a)** *(cleanser)* Schmierseife, *die;* **b)** *(fig.: flattery)* Schmeichelei, *die;* **use ~ soap** schmeicheln; schöntun *(ugs.); attrib.* **~-soap tactics/policy/treatment** gezielte Schmeichelei; gezieltes Schöntun *(ugs.);* ~**-'soap** *v.t.* **~-soap sb.** jmdm. Honig um den Bart schmieren *(ugs.);* **~-spoken** *adj.* leise sprechend ⟨*Person*⟩; leise [gesprochen] ⟨*Wort*⟩; **be ~-spoken** leise sprechen; ~ **'tissue** *n. (Anat.)* weiches Körpergewebe; ~ **touch** *see* **touch 3j;** ~ **verge** *n. (Brit.)* Grünstreifen, *der;* ~**ware** *n., no pl., no indef. art. (Computing)* Software, *die;* ~**wood** *n.* Weichholz, *das; attrib.* Weichholz-

softy ['sɒftı] *n.* **a)** *(coll.: weakling)* Weichling, *der;* Waschlappen, *der (ugs.); (boy/girl who easily cries)* Heulpeter, *der/*Heulsuse, *die (ugs.);* **b)** *(sentimental person)* **be a ~:** sentimental sein; **you old ~!** du sentimentales Huhn! *(ugs.)*

soggy ['sɒgı] *adj.* aufgeweicht ⟨*Boden*⟩; durchnäßt ⟨*Kleider*⟩; matschig ⟨*Salat*⟩; nicht durchgebacken, *(landsch.)* glitschig ⟨*Brot, Kuchen*⟩

soh [səʊ] *n. (Mus.)* sol

soi-disant [swɑ'di:zɑ̃] *adj. (calling oneself)* selbsternannt; *(claimed as such)* sogenannt

soigné *(fem.:* **soignée***)* ['swɑnjeı] *adj.* soigniert *(geh.)* ⟨*Person, Restaurant*⟩; elegant ⟨*Kleid*⟩

[1]**soil** [sɔıl] *n.* **a)** *(earth)* Erde, *die;* Boden, *der;* **b)** *(ground)* Boden, *der;* **on British/foreign ~:** auf britischem Boden/im Ausland *od. (geh.)* in der Fremde

[2]**soil 1.** *v.t. (lit. or fig.)* beschmutzen; **~ one's/sb.'s reputation** *(by scandal, criminal activities)* sein/jmds. Ansehen *od.* seinen/jmds. guten Ruf beflecken *(geh.); (by failure)* seinen/jmds. Ruf schmälern; *see also* **hand 1a. 2.** *n.* Schmutz, *der*

'soil conservation *n.* Bodenschutz, *der*

soiled [sɔıld] *adj.* schmutzig ⟨*Wäsche, Windel*⟩; gebraucht ⟨*Damenbinde*⟩

soil: **~-pipe** *n.* senkrechtes Abflußrohr; ~ **science** *n.* Bodenkunde, *die*

soirée ['swɑ:reı] *n.* Soiree, *die*

sojourn ['sɒdʒɜ:n, 'sɒdʒən] *(literary)* **1.** *v.i.* verweilen *(geh.);* weilen *(geh.)* **(at** in + *Dat.*). **2.** *n.* Aufenthalt, *der*

[1]**sol** [sɒl] *n. (Chem.)* Sol, *das*

[2]**sol** *see* **soh**

solace ['sɒləs] **1.** *n.* Trost, *der;* **take** *or* **find ~ in sth.** Trost in etw. *(Dat.)* finden; sich mit etw. trösten; **turn to sb./sth. for ~:** bei jmdm./etw. Trost suchen. **2.** *v.t.* trösten

solar ['səʊlə(r)] *adj. (Astron.)* Sonnen-

solar: ~ **battery** *n.* Sonnenbatterie, *die;* Solarbatterie, *die;* ~ **cell** *n.* Sonnenzelle, *die;* Solarzelle, *die;* ~ **'day** *n. (Astron.)* Sonnentag, *der;* ~ **e'clipse** *n. (Astron.)* Sonnenfinsternis, *die;* ~ **'energy** *n.* Solarenergie, *die;* Sonnenenergie, *die*

solarium [sə'leərıəm] *n., pl.* **solaria** [sə'leərıə] Solarium, *das*

solar: ~ **'panel** *n.* Sonnenkollektor, *der; (on satellite)* Sonnensegel, *das;* ~ **'plexus** *n. (Anat.)* Solarplexus, *der;* Sonnengeflecht, *das;* ~ **'power** *n.* Sonnenenergie, *die;* **~-powered** *adj.* mit Sonnenenergie betrieben; ~ **radiation** *n.* Sonnenstrahlung, *die;* ~ **system** *n. (Astron.)* Sonnensystem, *das*

sold *see* **sell 1, 2**

solder ['sɒldə(r), 'səʊldə(r)] **1.** *n.* Lot, *das (Technik).* **2.** *v.t.* löten

soldering-iron ['sɒldərıŋaıən, 'səʊldərıŋaıən] *n.* Lötkolben, *der*

soldier ['səʊldʒə(r)] **1.** *n.* Soldat, *der;* **[common] ~:** einfacher Soldat; **officers and ~s** Offiziere und Mannschaften; **~ of fortune** Glücksritter, *der (abwertend); (mercenary)* Söldner, *der; see also* **old soldier; private 2a; tin soldier; toy soldier; unknown 1. 2.** *v.i.* als Soldat dienen

~ **'on** *v.i. (coll.)* weitermachen

soldierly ['səʊldʒəlı] **1.** *adj.* soldatisch. **2.** *adv.* wie ein Soldat

soldiery ['səʊldʒərı] *n.* **a)** *constr. as pl. (soldiers)* Militär, *das;* **b)** *(troop)* Soldateska, *die (abwertend)*

[1]**sole** [səʊl] **1.** *n.* **a)** *(Anat.; of shoe)* Sohle, *die;* **inner ~** *see* **insole b; b)** *(of plough)* Pflugsohle, *die; (of plane)* Sohle, *die.* **2.** *v.t.* [be]sohlen

[2]**sole** *n. (fish)* Seezunge, *die; see also* **lemon sole**

[3]**sole** *adj.* einzig; alleinig ⟨*Verantwortung, Erbe, Recht*⟩; Allein⟨*erbe, -eigentümer*⟩; **the operation is the surgeon's ~ responsibility** für die Operation ist allein[e] der Chirurg zuständig; **he is the ~ judge of whether ...:** er allein urteilt darüber, ob .../entscheidet, ob ...

solecism ['sɒlısızm] *n.* **a)** *(blunder)* [sprachlicher] Fehler; **b)** *(social gaffe)* Fauxpas, *der*

soled [səʊld] *adj.* besohlt; **leather-/thick-~** ⟨*Schuhe*⟩ mit Ledersohlen/dicken Sohlen

solely ['səʊllı] *adv.* einzig und allein; ausschließlich; **~ because ...:** nur [deswegen], weil ...; einzig und allein, weil ...

solemn ['sɒləm] *adj.* feierlich; ernst ⟨*Anlaß, Gespräch*⟩; **the ~ truth** die reine Wahrheit

solemnity [sə'lemnıtı] *n.* **a)** *no pl.* Feierlichkeit, *die;* **b)** *(rite)* Feierlichkeit, *die*

solemnization [sɒləmnaı'zeıʃn] *n.* feierlicher Vollzug; *(of mass)* Zelebration, *die;* Feier, *die*

solemnize ['sɒləmnaız] *v.t.* [feierlich] vollziehen; zelebrieren, feiern ⟨*Messe*⟩

solemnly ['sɒləmlı] *adv.* feierlich

solemn 'mass *n.* Hochamt, *das*

solenoid ['səʊlənɔıd] *n.* Zylinderspule, *die; (converting energy)* Magnetspule, *die*

sol-fa [sɒl'fɑ:] *(Mus.)* **1.** *v.t. & i.* solmisieren. **2.** *n.* Solmisation, *die; see also* **tonic sol-fa**

solicit [sə'lısıt] **1.** *v.t.* **a)** *(appeal to)* erregen ⟨*Interesse*⟩; **~ sb. for sth.** jmdn. um etw. bitten; **b)** *(Commerc.)* **~ sb. for sth.** bei jmdm. um etw. werben; **he ~ed [interested people for] investment in his enterprise** er warb um Kapitalanleger für sein Unternehmen; **c)** *(make sexual offer to)* **~ sb.** sich jmdm. anbieten. **2.** *v.i.* **a)** *(make request)* **~ for sth.** um etw. bitten *od. (geh.)* ersuchen; *(in a petition)* etw. [mit einer Eingabe] fordern; **b)** *(Commerc.)* **~ for sth.** um etw. werben; **c)** *(offer illicit sex)* **~ [for custom]** sich anbieten; **be arrested for ~ing** ⟨*Prostituierte:*⟩ wegen öffentlichen Sichanbietens festgenommen werden

solicitation [səlısı'teıʃn] *n. (formal: request)* Drängen, *das*

solicitor [sə'lısıtə(r)] *n.* **a)** *(Brit.: lawyer)* Rechtsanwalt, *der/*-anwältin, *die (der/die nicht vor höheren Gerichten auftritt);* **b)** *(Amer.: canvasser)* Werber, *der*

Solicitor-'General *n., pl.* **Solicitors-General a)** *(Brit. Law) zweiter Kronanwalt;* **b)** *(Amer. Law) ranghöchster [beamteter] Staatssekretär im Justizministerium*

solicitous [sə'lısıtəs] *adj.* **a)** *(eager)* **be ~ of sth.** um etw. bemüht sein; **be ~ to do sth.** [darum] bemüht sein, etw. zu tun; **b)** *(anxious)* besorgt; **~ of** *or* **about** *or* **for sb./sth.** um jmdn./etw. besorgt

solicitously [sə'lısıtəslı] *adv.* **a)** *(eagerly)* eifrig; **b)** *(anxiously)* besorgt

solicitude [sə'lısıtju:d] *n. (anxiety, concern)* Besorgtheit, *die*

solid ['sɒlıd] **1.** *adj.* **a)** *(rigid)* fest; **freeze/be frozen ~:** [fest] gefrieren/gefroren sein; **set ~:** fest werden; **b)** *(of the same substance all through)* massiv; **~ silver** massives Silber; **a ~-silver tea service/watch** *etc.* ein Teeservice/eine Uhr *usw.* aus massivem *od.* reinem Silber; **~ gold** reines Gold; **a ~-gold watch/crown/bar** eine reingoldene Uhr/Krone/ein Barren reines Gold; **~ tyre** Vollgummireifen, *der;* **be packed ~** *(coll.)* gerammelt voll sein *(ugs.);* **c)** *(well-built)* stabil; solide gebaut ⟨*Haus, Mauer usw.*⟩; **have a ~ majority** *(Polit.)* eine solide Mehrheit haben; **d)** *(reliable)* verläßlich, zuverlässig ⟨*Freund, Helfer, Verbündeter*⟩; fest ⟨*Stütze*⟩; **e)** *(complete)* ganz; **a good ~ meal** eine kräftige Mahlzeit; **a ~ day/hour/week** ein ganzer Tag/eine ganze *od.* volle Stunde/eine ganze Woche; **f)** *(sound)* stichhaltig ⟨*Argument, Grund*⟩; solide ⟨*Arbeiter, Finanzlage, Firma*⟩; solide, gediegen ⟨*Komfort, Grundlage*⟩; **g)** *(Geom.: having three dimensions)* dreidimensional; räumlich; **h)** *(Geom.: concerned with solids)* stereometrisch; **~ geometry** Stereometrie, *die;* **i)** *(Printing)* kompreß; kompreß gesetzt ⟨*Seite*⟩; **j)** *(united)* einig; **a ~ vote for ...:** eine einstimmige Entscheidung für ...; **be ~ with sb.** mit jmdm. einig sein; *(Amer. coll.: friendly)* mit jmdm.

auf gutem Fuß stehen; **go** *or* **be ~ for sb./sth.** uneingeschränkt für jmdn./etw. sein; **k)** heftig ⟨*Schlag*⟩. **2.** *n.* **a)** *(substance)* fester Körper; **b)** *in pl. (food)* feste Nahrung; **c)** *(Geom.)* Körper, *der*

solid 'angle *n. (Geom.)* Raumwinkel, *der*

solidarity [sɒlɪ'dærɪtɪ] *n., no pl.* Solidarität, *die;* **show ~ with sb.** sich mit jmdn. solidarisch zeigen

solid: ~ 'fuel *n.* fester Brennstoff; **~-'fuel** *attrib. adj.* Festbrennstoff-; **~-fuel rocket** Feststoffrakete, *die*

solidification [səlɪdɪfɪ'keɪʃn] *n.* Verfestigung, *die;* Verhärtung, *die;* Erstarrung, *die*

solidify [sə'lɪdɪfaɪ] **1.** *v.t.* verfestigen. **2.** *v.i. (become solid)* hart *od.* fest werden; erstarren; ⟨*Flüssigkeit, Lava:*⟩ erstarren

solidity [sə'lɪdɪtɪ] *n., no pl. see* **solid 1: a)** Festigkeit, *die;* **b)** Massivität, *die;* **c)** Stabilität, *die;* **d)** *(of reasons, argument)* Stichhaltigkeit, *die*

solidly ['sɒlɪdlɪ] *adv.* **a)** *(firmly)* stabil; **b)** *(compactly)* **a ~ built person** ein kräftig gebauter Mensch; **c)** *(ceaselessly)* pausenlos; **he wrote ~ for four hours** er schrieb vier Stunden ohne Pause; **d)** *(whole-heartedly)* **be ~ behind sb./sth.** uneingeschränkt hinter jmdm./einer Sache stehen; **e)** *(with sound reasons)* stichhaltig; **argue ~ for sth.** stichhaltige Argumente für etw. vorbringen

solid: ~ so'lution *n. (Chem.)* feste Lösung; **~ 'state** *n. (Phys.)* fester Zustand; **~-state** *adj. (Phys.)* Festkörper⟨*physik, -geräte, -schaltung*⟩

soliloquize [sə'lɪləkwaɪz] *v.i.* monologisieren; *(to oneself)* Selbstgespräche führen

soliloquy [sə'lɪləkwɪ] *n.* Monolog, *der; (talking to oneself)* Selbstgespräch, *das*

solipsism ['sɒlɪpsɪzm, 'səʊlɪpsɪzm] *n. (Philos.)* Solipsismus, *der*

solitaire [sɒlɪ'teə(r)] *n.* **a)** *(gem)* Solitär, *der;* **a ~ diamond/ring** ein [Diamant]solitär/ein Solitärring; **b)** *(ring)* Solitärring, *der;* **c)** *(game)* Solitär, *das;* **d)** *(Amer. Cards)* Patience, *die;* **e)** *(Ornith.)* Einsiedler, *der*

solitary ['sɒlɪtərɪ] **1.** *adj.* **a)** einsam; **a ~ existence/life** ein Einsiedlerdasein/-leben; **~ confinement** Einzelhaft, *die;* **b)** *(sole)* einzig; **c)** *(Zool.)* solitär; **d)** *(Bot.) see* **single 1 a. 2.** *n. (sl.)* Einzelhaft, *die*

solitude ['sɒlɪtju:d] *n.* **a)** *(loneliness, remoteness)* Einsamkeit, *die;* **b)** *(lonely place)* Einöde, *die*

solmization [sɒlmɪ'zeɪʃn] *n. (Mus.)* Solmisation, *die*

solo ['səʊləʊ] **1.** *n., pl.* **~s a)** *(Mus.)* Solo, *das;* **b)** *(Cards)* **~ [whist]** Solo[-whist], *das;* **go ~:** ein Solo spielen; **c)** *(Aeronaut.)* Alleinflug, *der.* **2.** *adj.* **a)** *(Mus.)* Solo⟨*spiel, -part, -tanz, -instrument*⟩; **b)** *(unaccompanied)* **~ flight** Alleinflug, *der;* **~ performance** Solo- *od.* Alleinvorstellung, *die;* **~ achievement/effort** Einzelleistung, *die;* **a ~ act on the trapeze** eine Solonummer auf dem Trapez; **~ motor cycle** Motorrad ohne Beiwagen. **3.** *adv. (unaccompanied)* solo ⟨*singen, spielen, tanzen usw.*⟩; **go/fly ~** *(Aeronaut.)* einen Alleinflug machen

soloist ['səʊləʊɪst] *n. (Mus.)* Solist, *der*/Solistin, *die*

Solomon ['sɒləmən] *pr. n.* Salomo[n] *(der);* **be as wise as ~:** salomonische Weisheit besitzen; **judgment of ~:** salomonisches Urteil; *see also* **song**

Solomon 'Islands *pr. n. pl.* **the ~:** die Salomoninseln; die Salomonen

Solomon's 'seal *n. (figure; also Bot.)* Salomonssiegel, *das*

solstice ['sɒlstɪs] *n.* **a)** *(time of year)* Sonnenwende, *die;* **summer/winter ~:** Sommer-/Wintersonnenwende, *die;* **b)** *(point)* Wendepunkt, *der*

solubility [sɒljʊ'bɪlɪtɪ] *n.* **a)** *(capacity to be dissolved)* Löslichkeit, *die;* **b)** *(of problem etc.)* Lösbarkeit, *die*

soluble ['sɒljʊbl] *adj.* **a)** *(that can be dissolved)* löslich; solubel *(fachspr.);* **~ in water, water-~:** wasserlöslich; **fat-~:** fettlöslich; **b)** *(solvable)* lösbar

solute ['sɒlju:t] *n. (Chem.)* gelöster Stoff

solution [sə'lu:ʃn, sə'lju:ʃn] *n.* **a)** *(Phys., Chem.)* Lösung, *die;* **b)** *([result of] solving)* Lösung, *die* **(to** *Gen.*); **there is/is no ~ to sth.** etw. kann/kann nicht gelöst werden; **find a ~ to sth.** eine Lösung für etw. finden; etw. lösen

solvable ['sɒlvəbl] *adj.* lösbar

solve [sɒlv] *v.t.* lösen

solvency ['sɒlvənsɪ] *n. (Finance)* Solvenz, *die*

solvent ['sɒlvənt] **1.** *adj.* **a)** *(Chem.: dissolving)* lösend: **~ liquid** *or* **fluid** Lösungsmittel, *das;* **b)** *(Finance)* solvent. **2.** *n. (Chem.)* Lösungsmittel, *das* **(of, for** für); **~ abuse** Mißbrauch von Lösungsmitteln als Rauschmittel

Somali [sə'mɑ:lɪ] **1.** *adj.* somalisch. **2.** *n.* **a)** *(person)* Somali, *der/die;* **b)** *(language)* Somali, *das*

Somalia [sə'mɑ:lɪə] *pr. n.* Somalia *(das)*

Somalian [sə'mɑ:lɪən] **1.** *adj.* somalisch. **2.** *n.* Somalier, *der*/Somalierin, *die*

somatic [sə'mætɪk] *adj.* somatisch

sombre (*Amer.:* **somber**) ['sɒmbə(r)] *adj.* dunkel; düster ⟨*Atmosphäre, Stimmung*⟩; ernst ⟨*Anlaß*⟩

sombre: ~-coloured *adj.* düster; **~-looking** *adj.* düster [aussehend]

sombrely ['sɒmbəlɪ] *adv.* düster; dunkel ⟨*gekleidet*⟩; schwach ⟨*leuchten*⟩

sombrero [sɒm'breərəʊ] *n., pl.* **~s** Sombrero, *der*

some [səm, *stressed* sʌm] **1.** *adj.* **a)** *(one or other)* [irgend]ein; **~ fool** irgendein Dummkopf *(ugs.);* **~ day** eines Tages; irgendwann einmal; **~ [experienced] person** [irgend] jemand[, der Erfahrung hat]; **~ shop/book or other** irgendein Laden/Buch; **~ person or other** irgend jemand; irgendwer; **b)** *(a considerable quantity of)* einig...; etlich... *(ugs. verstärkend);* **speak at ~ length/wait for ~ time** ziemlich lang[e] sprechen/warten; **~ time/weeks/days/years ago** vor einiger Zeit/vor einigen Wochen/Tagen/Jahren; **~ time soon** bald [einmal]; **as ~ small token of** als ein kleines Zeichen (+ *Gen.*); **thirty ~ years** *(coll.)* über dreißig Jahre; *see also* **few 1 b; c)** *(a small quantity of)* ein bißchen; **would you like ~ wine?** möchten Sie [etwas] Wein?; **do ~ shopping/reading** einkaufen/lesen; **have ~ sense of decency** ein gewisses Gefühl für Anstand besitzen; **do have ~ sense!** sei doch vernünftig!; **d)** *(to a certain extent)* **~ guide** eine gewisse Orientierungshilfe; **that is ~ proof** das ist [doch] gewissermaßen ein Beweis; **it was ~ help having my sister here** es war mir eine gewisse Hilfe, daß meine Schwester hier war; **you are ~ help!** *(iron.)* du bist [mir] vielleicht eine Hilfe! *(ugs.);* **e)** *(sl.: true)* **this is ~ war/poem/car!** das ist vielleicht ein Krieg/Gedicht/Wagen! *(ugs.);* **he's ~ fool!** er ist vielleicht ein Dummkopf!; **f)** *(approximately)* etwa; ungefähr. **2.** *pron.* einig...; **Do you want any potatoes? – I have ~ already** Möchtest du Kartoffeln? – Ich habe schon welche; **This chocolate is delicious. – Do have ~ more** Diese Schokolade ist köstlich. – Nimm dir doch noch etwas [davon]; **she only ate ~ of it** sie hat es nur teilweise aufgegessen; **I collect stamps – If I find ~, I'll send them** Ich sammle Briefmarken – Wenn ich welche finde, schicke ich sie dir; **~ of her ideas are good** sie hat einige gute Ideen; **~ of the greatest music** einige der größten Werke der Musik; **this country has ~ of the highest mountains in the world** in diesem Land sind mit die höchsten Berge der Welt *(ugs.);* **~ say ...:** manche sagen ...; **~ ..., others ...:** manche ..., andere ...; die einen ..., andere ...; **... and then ~:** und noch einige/einiges mehr. **3.** *adv. (coll.: in ~ degree)* ein bißchen; etwas; **~ more** noch ein bißchen

somebody ['sʌmbədɪ] *n. & pron.* jemand; **~ or other** irgend jemand; *(important person)* **be [a] ~:** jemand *od.* etwas sein; etwas vorstellen

'someday *adv. (Amer.)* eines Tages; irgendwann einmal

'somehow *adv.* **~ [or other]** irgendwie; **we must find money ~ [or other]** wir müssen irgendwie Geld beschaffen

someone ['sʌmwən, *stressed* 'sʌmwʌn] *pron. see* **somebody**

'someplace *(Amer. coll.) see* **somewhere**

somersault ['sʌməsɔ:lt, 'sʌməsɒlt] **1.** *n.* Purzelbaum, *der (ugs.);* Salto, *der (Sport);* **turn a ~:** einen Purzelbaum schlagen *(ugs.);* einen Salto springen *(Sport).* **2.** *v.i.* einen Purzelbaum schlagen *(ugs.);* einen Salto springen *(Sport)*

'something *n. & pron.* **a)** *(some thing)* etwas; **~ new/old/good/bad** etwas Neues/Altes/Gutes/Schlechtes; **~ told me that .../to do sth.** *(coll.)* etwas sagte mir, daß .../befahl mir, etw. zu tun; **b)** *(some unspecified thing)* [irgend] etwas; **~ or other** irgend etwas; **she is a lecturer in ~ or other** sie ist Dozentin für irgendwas *(ugs.);* **c)** *(some quantity of a thing)* etwas; **have ~ before you go** nimm etwas zu dir *od.* iß etwas, bevor du gehst; **will you have a drop of ~?** nimmst du einen Schluck?; **I have seen ~ of his work** ich habe einige seiner Arbeiten *od. (ugs.)* etwas von ihm gesehen; **see ~ of a place/festival** ein bißchen was von einem Ort/Fest sehen *(ugs.);* **there is ~ in what you say** was du sagst, hat etwas für sich; an dem, was du sagst, ist etwas dran *(ugs.);* **he has ~ about him** er hat etwas Besonderes an sich *(Dat.);* **it is ~ to have got so far** es ist schon etwas [Besonderes], so weit gekommen zu sein; **you may have ~ there** *(you have had a good idea)* der Gedanke hat etwas für sich; **d)** *(impressive or important thing, person, etc.)* **the party was quite ~:** die Party war spitze *(ugs.);* **make ~ of oneself** etwas aus sich machen; **to be world champion at that age is quite ~:** in diesem Alter Weltmeister zu sein, das ist schon etwas; **e) or ~** *see* **¹or c; f) ~ like** etwa wie; **he left ~ like a million** er hinterließ etwa eine Million; **it looks ~ like a cross** es sieht [etwa] wie ein Kreuz aus; **that's ~ 'like** *(coll.)* läßt sich hören/sehen! *(ugs.);* **that's ~ like it** das ist schon besser; **g) ~ of an expert/a specialist** so etwas wie ein Fachmann/Spezialist; **see ~ of sb.** jmdn. sehen. *See also* **else a, b**

'sometime 1. *adj.* ehemalig; **he was ~ captain of the team** er war früher Mannschaftskapitän. **2.** *adv.* irgendwann

'sometimes *adv.* manchmal; **~ ..., at other times ...:** manchmal ..., manchmal ...

'somewhat 1. *adv. (rather)* irgendwie; ziemlich; **more than ~ surprised/disappointed** *(coll.)* ganz schön *(ugs.) od.* mehr als [nur] überrascht/enttäuscht. **2.** *pron.* **~ of an expert** so etwas wie ein Fachmann

'somewhere 1. *adv.* **a)** *(in a place)* irgendwo; **~ about** *or* **around thirty [years old]** [so *(ugs.)*] um die dreißig [Jahre alt]; **~ between five and ten** [so *(ugs.)*] zwischen fünf und zehn; **b)** *(to a place)* irgendwohin; **get ~** *(coll.) (in life)* es zu etwas bringen; *(in a task)* weiterkommen. **2.** *n.* **look for ~ to stay** sich nach einer Unterkunft umsehen; **find ~ suitable to do sth.** einen geeigneten Ort finden, [um] etw. zu tun; **she prefers ~ hot for her holidays** in den Ferien fährt sie am liebsten irgendwohin, wo es heiß ist

somnolence ['sɒmnələns] *n.* Schläfrigkeit, *die*

somnolent ['sɒmnələnt] *adj.* **a)** *(sleepy)* schläfrig; **b)** *(sleep-inducing)* einschläfernd; **c)** *(Med.)* somnolent

son [sʌn] *n.* Sohn, *der; (as address)* **[my] ~:** mein Sohn; **adopted ~:** Adoptivsohn, *der;* **~ and heir** Sohn und Erbe; **be a ~ of the soil** mit der Scholle verbunden sein; **the Son of Man** *(Relig.)* der Menschensohn; **the ~s of men** *(Relig.)* die Menschen; **the Son [of God]** *(Relig.)* der Sohn [Gottes]; **~ of a bitch** *(derog.)* Scheißkerl, *der (derb); (thing)* Scheißding, *das (derb); see also* **father 1 a, e; gun 1 a; mother 1 a**
sonar ['səʊnɑ:(r)] *n.* Sonar, *das*
sonata [sə'nɑ:tə] *n. (Mus.)* Sonate, *die;* **~ form** Sonatenform, *die*
sonde [sɒnd] *n. (Meteorol.)* [Raum]sonde, *die*
song [sɒŋ] *n.* **a)** Lied, *das; (esp. political ballad)* Song, *der; (pop ~)* [Pop]song, *der;* **S~ of S~s, S~ of Solomon** *(Bibl.)* Hohelied, *das;* Lied der Lieder, *das;* **b)** *no pl. (singing)* Gesang, *der;* **on ~** *(fig. coll.)* in Spitzenform; **break** *or* **burst forth into ~:** ein Lied anstimmen; **for a ~:** für einen Apfel und ein Ei *(ugs.);* **it is nothing to make a ~ about** *(coll.)* es ist nicht der Rede wert; **~ and dance** *(Brit. coll.: fuss; Amer. coll.: rigmarole)* viel *od.* großes Trara *(ugs.);* **c)** *(bird cry)* Gesang, *der; (of cuckoo)* Ruf, *der*
song: ~bird *n.* Singvogel, *der;* **~-book** *n.* Liederbuch, *das;* **~-cycle** *n. (Mus.)* Liederzyklus, *der*
songster ['sɒŋstə(r)] *n.* **a)** *(singer, poet)* Sänger, *der;* **b)** *(Amer.: song-book)* Liederbuch, *das*
songstress ['sɒŋstrɪs] *n. fem.* Sängerin, *die*
'song-writer *n.* Songschreiber, *der/*-schreiberin, *die*
sonic ['sɒnɪk] *attrib. adj.* Schall-; **~ depth finder** Echolot, *das*
sonic: ~ 'bang *see* **~ boom; ~ barrier** *see* **sound barrier; ~ boom** *n.* Überschallknall, *der;* **~ mine** *n.* Geräuschmine, *die*
'son-in-law *n., pl.* **sons-in-law** Schwiegersohn, *der*
sonnet ['sɒnɪt] *n.* Sonett, *das;* **~ sequence** Sonettenzyklus, *der*
sonny ['sʌnɪ] *n. (coll.)* Kleiner *(der);* kleiner Mann *(ugs.)*
sonority [sə'nɒrɪtɪ] *n. (of voice)* Wohlklang, *der;* Sonorität, *die (geh. selten); (of ship's horn, bell, etc.)* voller Klang
sonorous [sə'nɔ:rəs, 'sɒnərəs] *adj.* volltönend; sonor ⟨*Stimme*⟩; klangvoll ⟨*Instrument, Sprache*⟩
soon [su:n] *adv.* **a)** bald; *(quickly)* schnell; **b)** *(early)* früh; **how ~ will it be ready?** wann ist es denn fertig?; **none too ~:** keinen Augenblick zu früh; **no ~er said than done** gesagt, getan; **~er said than done** leichter gesagt als getan; **no ~er had I arrived than ...:** kaum war ich angekommen, da ...; **~ enough** früh genug; **~er or later** früher oder später; **Which train shall I take? – Whichever arrives the ~er** Welchen Zug soll ich nehmen? – Den, der zuerst ankommt; **the car must be serviced every 12 months or every six thousand miles, whichever is the ~er** der Wagen muß alle 12 Monate bzw. alle sechstausend Meilen gewartet werden, je nachdem [, was früher der Fall ist]; **the ~er [...] the better** *(coll.),* **better ~er than later** je früher *od.* eher [...], desto besser; **c) as ~ as his death was known/he heard of it** sobald sein Tod bekannt wurde/er davon gehört hatte; **we'll set off just as ~ as he arrives** sobald er ankommt, machen wir uns auf den Weg; **as ~ as possible** so bald wie möglich; **d)** *(willingly)* gern; **just as ~ [as ...]** genauso gern [wie ...]; **she would ~er die than ...:** sie würde lieber sterben, als ...; **which would you ~er/~est do?** was würdest du lieber/am liebsten tun?; **they would kill you as ~ as look at you** *(coll.)* sie würden dich sofort *od.* auf der Stelle umbringen; **~er you than me** lieber du als ich
soonish ['su:nɪʃ] *adv. (coll.)* recht bald

soot [sʊt] **1.** *n.* Ruß, *der.* **2.** *v. t.* verrußen; rußig machen
soothe [su:ð] *v. t.* **a)** *(calm)* beruhigen; beschwichtigen ⟨*Gefühle*⟩; **b)** *(make less severe)* mildern; lindern ⟨*Schmerz*⟩; **~ sb.'s cares away** jmds. Sorgen vertreiben
soothing ['su:ðɪŋ] *adj.* beruhigend; wohltuend ⟨*Bad, Creme, Massage*⟩
soothsayer ['su:θseɪə(r)] *n. (arch.)* Wahrsager, *der/*Wahrsagerin, *die*
sooty ['sʊtɪ] *adj.* **a)** *(soot-covered)* verrußt; rußig; **b)** *(black)* schwarz [wie Ruß]
sop [sɒp] **1.** *n.* **a)** *(piece of bread)* Stück eingeweichtes Brot; **b)** *(fig.)* Beschwichtigungsmittel, *das;* **sth. is intended as a ~ to sb., sth. is a ~ given to sb.** etw. soll jmdn. beschwichtigen. **2.** *v. i.,* **-pp-: be ~ping [wet] [with rain]** [vom Regen] völlig durchnäßt sein
~ 'up *v. t.* aufnehmen
sophism ['sɒfɪzm] *n.* Sophismus, *der*
sophist ['sɒfɪst] *n.* Sophist, *der/*Sophistin, *die*
sophistical [sə'fɪstɪkl] *adj.* sophistisch
sophisticate 1. [sə'fɪstɪkeɪt] *v. t.* verbilden. **2.** [sə'fɪstɪkət] *adj. see* **sophisticated a. 3.** *n.* Kultursnob, *der*
sophisticated [sə'fɪstɪkeɪtɪd] *adj.* **a)** *(cultured)* kultiviert; gepflegt ⟨*Restaurant, Küche*⟩; anspruchsvoll ⟨*Roman, Autor, Unterhaltung, Stil*⟩; **b)** *(elaborate)* ausgeklügelt ⟨*Autozubehör*⟩; differenziert, subtil ⟨*Argument, System, Ansatz*⟩; hochentwickelt ⟨*Technik, Elektronik, Software, Geräte*⟩; *(derog.: over-complex)* spitzfindig ⟨*Argument*⟩; **~ in style** stilistisch verfeinert
sophistication [səfɪstɪ'keɪʃn] *n.* **a)** *(refinement)* Kultiviertheit, *die; (of argument)* Differenziertheit, *die; (derog.)* Spitzfindigkeit, *die; (of style, manner)* Subtilität, *die;* **the ~ of French cooking** die Raffinesse der französischen Küche; **b)** *(advanced methods)* hoher Entwicklungsstand [der Technik]; **era of technical ~:** Zeitalter hochentwickelter Technik
sophistry ['sɒfɪstrɪ] *n.* Sophisterei, *die*
sophomore ['sɒfəmɔ:(r)] *n. (Amer. Sch./Univ.)* Student/Studentin einer High-School *bzw.* Universität im zweiten Studienjahr
soporific [sɒpə'rɪfɪk] **1.** *adj.* schläfrig ⟨*Person*⟩; einschläfernd ⟨*Wirkung, Rede*⟩; **~ drug/medicine** Schlafmittel, *das.* **2.** *n.* Schlafmittel, *das*
sopping *see* **sop 2**
soppy ['sɒpɪ] *adj. (Brit. coll.: sentimental)* rührselig; sentimental ⟨*Person*⟩; **be ~ on sb.** in jmdn. verschossen sein *(ugs.)*
soprano [sə'prɑ:nəʊ] *n., pl.* **~s** *or* **soprani** [sə'prɑ:ni:] *(Mus.) (voice, singer, part)* Sopran, *der; (female singer also)* Sopranistin, *die;* **~ flute/clarinet** Sopranflöte, *die/*-klarinette, *die;* **~ clef** Sopranschlüssel, *der*
sorbet ['sɔ:bɪt, 'sɔ:beɪ] *n.* Sorbet, *das*
sorcerer ['sɔ:sərə(r)] *n.* Zauberer, *der*
sorceress ['sɔ:sərɪs] *n.* Zauberin, *die*
sorcery ['sɔ:sərɪ] *n.* Zauberei, *die*
sordid ['sɔ:dɪd] *adj.* **a)** *(base)* dreckig *(abwertend);* unehrenhaft, unlauter ⟨*Motiv*⟩; unerfreulich ⟨*Detail, Geschichte*⟩; **b)** *(greedy)* habgierig ⟨*Person*⟩; schmutzig ⟨*Geschäft*⟩; **c)** *(squalid)* schmutzig; schäbig ⟨*Wohnung, Verhältnisse*⟩; heruntergekommen ⟨*Stadtviertel*⟩
sore [sɔ:(r)] **1.** *adj.* **a)** *(painful)* weh; *(inflamed or injured)* wund; **sb. has a ~ back/foot/arm** *etc.* jmdm. tut der Rücken/Fuß/Arm *usw.* weh; **~ point** *or* **spot** *(fig.)* wunder Punkt; **touch on a ~ point, touch a ~ spot** *(fig.)* an einen wunden Punkt rühren; **a ~ subject** ein heikles Thema; **have ~ feelings about sth.** wegen einer Sache verletzt sein; **b)** *(irritated)* verärgert; sauer *(ugs.);* **feel ~:** sich ärgern *od.* aufregen; **c)** *(Amer.: vexed)* böse; sauer *(ugs.);* **be ~ at sb./about** *or* **over sth.** böse *od. (ugs.)* sauer auf jmdn./über etw. *(Akk.)* sein; **d)** *(severe)* schwer; groß ⟨*Not, Schwierigkeiten*⟩; dringlich ⟨*Problem*⟩. **2.** *n.* **a)** *(abrasion)* wunde Stelle; **b)** *(fig.: painful thought)* Wunde, *die*
sorely ['sɔ:lɪ] *adv.* sehr; arg *(südd.);* **be ~ in need of sth.** etw. dringend brauchen; **~ tempted** stark versucht
soreness ['sɔ:nɪs] *n.* Schmerz, *der; (inflammation)* Wundsein, *das*
sorghum ['sɔ:gəm] *n.* Sorghum, *das*
sorority [sə'rɒrɪtɪ] *n.* **a)** *(sisterhood)* Schwesternorden, *der; (Amer.: female section of church congregation)* Frauen der Gemeinde; **b)** *(Amer.: society)* Studentinnenvereinigung, *die*
[1]sorrel ['sɒrl] *n. (Bot.)* Sauerampfer, *der*
[2]sorrel 1. *adj.* fuchsrot; rotbraun. **2.** *n. (horse)* Fuchs, *der;* rotbraunes Pferd
sorrow ['sɒrəʊ] **1.** *n.* **a)** *(distress)* Kummer, *der;* Leid, *das;* **feel [great] ~ that ...:** es [sehr] bedauern, daß ...; **he felt great ~ at the news** die Nachricht bekümmerte ihn sehr; **cause sb. [great] ~:** jmdm. [großen] Kummer bereiten; **act more in ~ than in anger** mehr aus Kummer *od.* Betrübnis handeln als aus Zorn; **b)** *(misfortune)* Sorge, *die;* **he has had many ~s** er hat viel [Schweres] durchgemacht; **all the ~s of the world** alles *od.* das ganze Leid der Welt; **the Man of S~s** *(Relig.)* der Schmerzensmann; *see also* **drown 2 b. 2.** *v. i.* **a)** *(feel sorrow)* sich grämen *(geh.)* **(at, over, for** über + *Akk.,* um); **b)** *(mourn)* trauern **(for, after** um)
sorrowful ['sɒrəʊfl, 'sɒrəfl] *adj.* **a)** *(sad)* betrübt ⟨*Person*⟩; traurig ⟨*Anlaß, Lächeln, Herz*⟩; **with a ~ heart** mit Kummer im Herzen; **feel ~ at sth.** über etw. *(Akk.)* bekümmert sein; **b)** *(distressing)* traurig; leidvoll ⟨*Dasein*⟩
sorrowing ['sɒrəʊɪŋ] *attrib. adj.* trauernd
sorry ['sɒrɪ] *adj.* **a)** *(regretful)* **sb. is ~ to do sth.** jmdm. tut es leid, etw. tun zu müssen; **I am ~ to disappoint you** ich muß dich leider enttäuschen; **sb. is ~ that ...:** es tut jmdm. leid, daß ...; **sb. is ~ about sth.** jmdm. tut etw. leid; **~ about your accident** es tut mir leid, daß du einen Unfall hattest; **~, but ...** *(coll.)* tut mir leid, aber ...; **I'm ~** *(won't change my mind)* tut mir leid; **~ I'm late** *(coll.)* Entschuldigung, daß ich zu spät komme; **My mother died two months ago. – Oh, I 'am ~!** Meine Mutter ist vor zwei Monaten gestorben. – Herzliches Beileid!; **I'm ~ to say leider; I can't say [that] I'm ~!** ich bin nicht gerade traurig darüber; **sb. is** *or* **feels ~ for sb./sth.** jmd. tut jmdm. leid/jmd. bedauert etw.; **you'll be ~:** das wird dir noch leid tun; **feel ~ for oneself** *(coll.)* sich selbst bemitleiden; sich *(Dat.)* leid tun; **~!** Entschuldigung!; **~?** wie bitte?; **~ about that!** *(coll.)* tut mir leid!; **~ to bother you** Entschuldigung, wenn ich störe; *see also* **safe 2 b; b)** *attrib. (wretched)* traurig; faul, fadenscheinig ⟨*Entschuldigung*⟩
sort [sɔ:t] **1.** *n.* **a)** Art, *die; (type)* Sorte, *die;* **cakes of several ~s** verschiedene Kuchensorten; **a new ~ of bicycle** ein neuartiges Fahrrad; **people of every/that ~:** Menschen jeden/diesen Schlages; **people of every ~ and kind** alle möglichen Leute; **it takes all ~s [to make a world]** *(coll.)* es gibt so'ne und solche *(ugs.); (when referring to eccentric behaviour)* jedem Tierchen sein Pläsierchen *(scherzh.);* **all ~s of ...:** alle möglichen ...; **support sb. in all ~s of ways** jmdn. auf vielerlei Art und Weise unterstützen; **there are all ~s of things to do** es gibt alles mögliche *od.* allerlei zu tun; **she is just/not my ~:** sie ist genau/nicht mein Typ *(ugs.);* **she is not the ~ to do that** es ist nicht ihre Art, das zu tun; **what ~ of [a] person do you think I am?** für wen hältst du mich?; **you'll do nothing of the ~:** das kommt gar nicht in Frage; **he's a ~ of stockbroker, I believe** *(coll.)* er ist [so] eine Art [von] Börsenmakler, glaube ich; ~

of *(coll.)* irgendwie; irgendwo *(salopp); (more or less)* mehr oder weniger; *(to some extent)* ziemlich *(ugs.)*; **it's ~ of difficult for me to explain** *(coll.)* ich kann es irgendwie nicht so gut *od.* leicht erklären; **Have you finished? – Well, ~ of** *(coll.)* Bist du fertig? – Mehr oder weniger; **I ~ of expected it** *(coll.)* ich habe es irgendwie erwartet; **nothing of the ~:** nichts dergleichen; **or something of the ~:** oder so [etwas ähnliches] *(ugs.)*; **a funny ~ of person/day/car** ein komischer Mensch/Tag/Wagen; **it is music of a ~** *(derog.)* es ist so was ähnliches wie Musik; **he is a doctor/footballer of a ~** *or* **of ~s** *(derog.)* er nennt sich Arzt/Fußballspieler; **we don't mix with people of that ~:** mit solchen Leuten wollen wir nichts zu tun haben; **he/she is a good ~** *(coll.)* er/sie ist schon in Ordnung *(ugs.)*; **he is not a bad ~ at all** *(coll.)* er ist nicht der Schlechteste *(ugs.)*; **b) be out of ~s** nicht in Form sein; *(be irritable)* schlecht gelaunt sein; **c)** *(Printing)* Letter, *die.* **2.** *v. t.* sortieren

~ 'out *v. t.* **a)** *(arrange)* sortieren; **~ out material for an essay** Material für einen Aufsatz zusammenstellen; **b)** *(settle)* klären; schlichten ⟨*Streit*⟩; beenden ⟨*Verwirrung*⟩; **it will ~ itself out** es wird schon in Ordnung kommen; **c)** *(organize)* durchorganisieren; auf Vordermann bringen *(ugs.)*; **~ oneself out** ⟨*Neuankömmling usw.:*⟩ sich einrichten; **things have ~ed themselves out** die Dinge haben sich eingerenkt; **d)** *(sl.: punish)* **~ sb. out** jmdm. zeigen, wo's langgeht *(ugs.)*; **e)** *(select)* aussuchen; wählen; **~ out the truth from the lies** die Lügen von der Wahrheit unterscheiden; Lüge und Wahrheit unterscheiden; **~ out the good apples/singers from the bad [ones]** die guten Äpfel/Sänger von den schlechten trennen

'sort code *n. (Banking)* Bankleitzahl, *die*

sorter ['sɔːtə(r)] *n.* **a)** *(arranger)* Sortierer, *der*/Sortiererin, *die;* **b)** *(for punched cards)* Sorter, *der;* Sortiermaschine, *die*

sortie ['sɔːtiː, 'sɔːtɪ] *n. (Mil.; also fig.)* **a)** Ausfall, *der;* **b)** *(flight)* Einsatz, *der*

sorting ['sɔːtɪŋ] *n.* Sortieren, *das*

sorting: ~-machine *n.* Sortiermaschine, *die;* **~-office** *n.* Postverteilstelle, *die*

SOS [esəʊ'es] *n.* **a)** SOS, *das;* **~ appeal** Hilfeaufruf, *der;* **b)** *(Brit.: broadcast)* **~ message** Suchmeldung, *die; (to motorists)* Reiseruf, *der*

'so so, 'so-so *adj., adv.* so lala *(ugs.)*

sot [sɒt] *n.* Trinker, *der*/Trinkerin, *die;* Säufer, *der*/Säuferin, *die (salopp)*

sottish ['sɒtɪʃ] *adj.* versoffen *(salopp)*

sotto voce [sɒtəʊ 'vəʊtʃɪ] *adv.* mit gedämpfter Stimme

sou [suː] *n. (Hist./coll.)* Sou, *der;* **not have a ~:** keinen roten Heller haben

soubrette [suː'bret] *n. (Theatre)* Soubrette, *die*

soufflé ['suːfleɪ] *n. (Gastr.)* Soufflé, *das;* **~ dish** Souffléform, *die*

sough [sʌf, saʊ] *(literary)* **1.** *n.* Rauschen, *das.* **2.** *v. i.* rauschen

sought *see* **seek**

soul [səʊl] *n.* **a)** Seele, *die;* **sell one's ~ for sth.** *(fig.)* seine Seele für etw. verkaufen; **upon my ~!** *(dated)* meiner Treu! *(veralt.)*; **bare one's ~ to sb.** jmdm. sein Herz ausschütten; *see also* **heart 1 b; life b; b)** *(intellect)* Geist, *der;* **not be able to call one's ~ one's own** nicht sein eigener Herr sein; **his whole ~ revolted from it** er sträubte sich mit ganzer Seele dagegen; **c)** *(person)* Seele, *die;* **not a ~:** keine Menschenseele; **be the ~ of discretion** die Verschwiegenheit selbst *od.* in Person sein; **be a good ~ and fetch me a cup of tea** sei ein Schatz *(ugs.)* und hol mir eine Tasse Tee; **the poor little ~:** das arme kleine Ding; **d)** *(Negro Culture) die Kultur der schwarzen US-Amerikaner; (music)* Soul, *der.*

soul: ~ brother *n. schwarzer Nordamerikaner (als [bewußter] Teilhaber der schwarzen Kultur);* ≈ Bruder, *der;* **~-destroying** ['səʊldɪstrɔɪɪŋ] *adj.* **a)** *(boring)* nervtötend; geisttötend; **b)** *(depressing)* deprimierend

'soul food *n. traditionelle Küche der schwarzen Nordamerikaner*

soulful ['səʊlfl] *adj.* gefühlvoll; *(sad)* schwermütig

soulfully ['səʊlfəlɪ] *adv.* mit viel Gefühl; *(sadly)* voll Schwermut

soulless ['səʊllɪs] *adj.* **a)** *(ignoble)* seelenlos *(geh.)*; gefühllos; **b)** *(dull)* öde

soul: ~ mate *n.* Seelenverwandte, *der/die;* **~ music** *n.* Soul, *der;* Soulmusik, *die;* **~-searching** *n.* Gewissenskampf, *der;* **~ sister** *n. schwarze Nordamerikanerin (als [bewußte] Teilhaberin der schwarzen Kultur);* ≈ Schwester, *die;* **~-stirring** *adj.* aufwühlend; *(inspiring)* mitreißend

¹sound [saʊnd] **1.** *adj.* **a)** *(healthy)* gesund; intakt ⟨*Gebäude, Mauerwerk*⟩; gut ⟨*Frucht, Obst, Holz, Boden*⟩; **of ~ mind** im Vollbesitz der geistigen Kräfte; **~ in mind and body** gesund an Geist und Seele; **~ in wind and limb** kerngesund; **the building was structurally ~:** das Gebäude hatte eine gesunde Bausubstanz; *see also* **bell 1 a; b)** *(well-founded)* vernünftig ⟨*Argument, Rat*⟩; klug ⟨*Wahl*⟩; **it makes ~ sense** es ist sehr vernünftig; **make ~ progress** gute Fortschritte machen; **c)** *(Finance: secure)* gesund, solide ⟨*Basis*⟩; klug ⟨*Investition*⟩; **d)** *(competent, reliable)* solide ⟨*Spieler*⟩; **have a ~ character** charakterfest sein; **e)** *(undisturbed)* tief, gesund ⟨*Schlaf*⟩; **be a ~ sleeper** einen gesunden Schlaf haben; **f)** *(thorough)* gehörig *(ugs.)* ⟨*Niederlage, Tracht Prügel*⟩; gekonnt ⟨*Leistung*⟩. **2.** *adv.* fest, tief ⟨*schlafen*⟩; **fall/be ~ asleep** in einen tiefen *od.* festen Schlaf fallen/tief *od.* fest schlafen

²sound 1. *n.* **a)** *(Phys.)* Schall, *der;* **the speed of ~:** die Schallgeschwindigkeit; **b)** *(noise)* Laut, *der; (of wind, sea, car, footsteps, breaking glass or twigs)* Geräusch, *das; (of voices, laughter, bell)* Klang, der; **do sth. without a ~:** etw. lautlos tun; **c)** *(Radio, Telev., Cinemat.)* Ton, *der;* **loss of ~:** Tonausfall, *der;* **d)** *(music)* Klang, *der; (jazz, pop, rock)* Sound, *der;* **the king entered to the ~ of trumpets** von Trompetenstößen begleitet, trat der König ein; **the ~ of drums** Trommellaute *Pl.*; **dance to the ~ of a band** zu den Klängen einer Band tanzen; **e)** *(Phonet.: articulation)* Laut, *der;* **f)** *(fig.: impression)* **I like the ~ of your plan** ich finde, Ihr Plan hört sich gut an; **I like the ~ of him** was du von ihm erzählst, hört sich gut an; **I don't like the ~ of this** das hört sich nicht gut an; **g)** *in pl. (~-waves)* Töne; **h)** *(meaningless noise)* Wortgeklingel, *das;* Wortschwall, *der;* **i)** *(earshot)* **within ~ of sb./sth.** in jmds. Hörweite/in Hörweite einer Sache. **2.** *v. i.* **a)** *(seem)* klingen; **it ~s as if .../like ...:** es klingt, als .../wie ...; **it ~s to me as if .../like ...:** es hört sich für mich an, als .../wie ...; **from his lack of enthusiasm it ~s as if he wanted to give up** nach seinem Mangel an Begeisterung zu urteilen, klingt es so, als wolle er aufgeben; **it ~s to me from what you have said that ...:** was du gesagt hast, klingt für mich so, als ob ...; **that ~s a good idea to me** ich finde, die Idee hört sich gut an; **~s good to me!** klingt gut! *(ugs.)*; gute Idee! *(ugs.)*; **that ~s odd to me** das hört sich seltsam an, finde ich; **b)** *(emit ~)* [er]tönen. **3.** *v. t.* **a)** *(cause to emit ~)* ertönen lassen; **~ the trumpet** trompeten; in die Trompete blasen; **b)** *(utter)* **~ a note of caution** zur Vorsicht mahnen; **his words ~ed a note of alarm in my mind** seine Worte versetzten mich in Alarmstimmung; **c)** *(pronounce)* aussprechen; **d)** *(cause to be heard)* **~ sb.'s praises** ein Loblied auf jmdn. singen; **~ a fanfare** eine Fanfare erklingen lassen

~ 'off *v. i. (coll.: talk pompously)* tönen *(ugs.)*, schwadronieren **(on, about** von)

³sound *n.* **a)** *(strait)* Sund, *der;* Meerenge, *die;* **b)** *(inlet)* Meeresarm, *der;* **Plymouth S~:** die Bucht von Plymouth

⁴sound *v. t.* **a)** *(Naut.: fathom)* ausloten; sondieren; **b)** *(fig.: test) see* **~ out; c)** *(Meteorol.)* untersuchen; erforschen; sondieren; **e)** *(Med.)* abhorchen

~ 'out *v. t.* ausfragen ⟨*Person*⟩; sondieren *(geh.)*, herausbekommen ⟨*Sache*⟩; **~ sb. out on sth.** bei jmdm. wegen etw. vorfühlen

sound: ~ barrier *n.* Schallmauer, *die;* **go through** *or* **break the ~ barrier** die Schallmauer durchbrechen; **~-box** *n. (in violin, guitar, etc.)* Resonanzkörper, *der;* **~ broadcasting** *n.* Hörfunk, *der;* **~ check** *n.* Soundcheck, *der;* Tonprobe, *die;* **~ effect** *n.* Geräuscheffekt, *der;* **~ engineer** *n. (Radio, Telev., Cinemat.)* Toningenieur, *der*/-ingenieurin, *die;* **~-hole** *n. (Mus.)* Schalloch, *das*

¹sounding ['saʊndɪŋ] *adj. in comb.* **strange-/clear-/loud-~:** seltsam/klar/laut [klingend]

²sounding *n.* **a)** *(Naut.: measurement)* Lotung, *die;* **take ~s** Lotungen vornehmen; loten; **b)** *(fig.)* Sondierung, *die (geh.)*; **make ~s in a locality** ein Terrain sondieren; **carry out ~s of public opinion/of interested parties** die öffentliche Meinung sondieren/mit den Beteiligten Sondierungsgespräche führen

sounding: ~-board *n.* **a)** *(canopy)* Schalldeckel, *der;* **b)** *(Mus.)* Decke, *die;* **c)** *(fig.: means of spreading opinions)* Sprachrohr, *das;* **d)** *(fig.: trial audience)* ≈ Testgruppe, *die;* **~-line** *n. (Naut.)* Lotleine, *die;* **~-rod** *n. (Naut.)* Peilstock, *der*

soundless ['saʊndlɪs] *adj.* lautlos; stumm, tonlos ⟨*Sprache, Gebet*⟩

soundly ['saʊndlɪ] *adv.* **a)** *(solidly)* stabil, solide ⟨*bauen*⟩; **b)** *(well)* vernünftig ⟨*argumentieren, urteilen, investieren*⟩; **c)** *(deeply)* tief, fest ⟨*schlafen*⟩; **d)** *(thoroughly)* anständig, ordentlich *(ugs.)* ⟨*verhauen*⟩; vernichtend ⟨*schlagen, besiegen*⟩; **perform ~:** eine gute Leistung zeigen

soundness ['saʊndnɪs] *n., no pl.* **a)** *(of mind, body)* Gesundheit, *die; (of construction, structure)* Solidität, *die;* **b)** *(of argument)* Stichhaltigkeit, *die; (of policy, views)* Vernünftigkeit, *die;* **c)** *(of sleep)* Tiefe, *die;* **d)** *(competence, reliability)* Solidität, *die;* **e)** *(solvency)* wirtschaftliche Gesundheit; Solvenz, *die*

sound: ~-post *n. (Mus.)* Stimmstock, *der;* **~-proof 1.** *adj.* schalldicht; **2.** *v. t.* schalldicht machen; **~-proofing** *n.* Schallisolierung, *die;* **~ recorder** *n.* Tonaufnahmegerät, *das;* **~ shift** *see* **shift 3 i; ~ technician** *see* **~ engineer; ~-track** *n. (Cinemat.)* Soundtrack, *der;* **~ truck** *n. (Amer.)* Lautsprecherwagen, *der;* **~-wave** *n. (Phys.)* Schallwelle, *die*

soup [suːp] *n.* Suppe, *die;* **be/land in the ~** *(fig. sl.)* in der Patsche sitzen/landen *(ugs.)*

~ 'up *v. t. (Motor Veh. coll.)* frisieren *(ugs.)*

soupçon ['suːpsɔ̃] *n.* Spur, *die; (of anger, irony)* Anflug, *der;* **a ~ of garlic/grey** eine Spur Knoblauch/von Grau

souped-up ['suːptʌp] *attrib. adj. (Motor Veh. coll.)* frisiert *(ugs.)*

soup: ~-kitchen *n.* Volksküche, *die;* Suppenküche, *die;* **~-plate** *n.* Suppenteller, *der;* **~-spoon** *n.* Suppenlöffel, *der*

soupy ['suːpɪ] *adj.* **a)** *(thick)* sämig ⟨*Flüssigkeit*⟩; trübe, schlammig ⟨*Wasser*⟩; **b)** *(coll.: sentimental)* rührselig; sentimental

sour [saʊə(r)] **1.** *adj.* **a)** *(having acid taste)* sauer; **b)** *(morose)* griesgrämig *(abwertend)*; säuerlich ⟨*Blick*⟩; **c)** *(unpleasant)* bitter; **when things go ~:** wenn man *od.* einem alles leid wird; **the place has gone ~ on him** der Ort ist ihm verleidet [worden]; **d)** *(rank)* säuerlich ⟨*Geruch*⟩; **e)** *(deficient in lime)* sauer ⟨*Boden*⟩. *See also* **grape. 2.** *v. t.* **a)** versauern lassen; sauer machen; **b)** *(fig.: spoil)* verbauen ⟨*Karriere*⟩; trüben ⟨*Beziehung*⟩; **c)** *(fig.: make gloomy)* verbittern. **3.** *v. i.* **a)** sauer werden; **b)** *(deteriorate)* ⟨*Beziehungen:*⟩ sich trüben. **4.** *n. (Amer.: cocktail)* Sour, *der*

source [sɔ:s] *n.* Quelle, *die;* ~ **of income/infection** Einkommensquelle, *die*/Infektionsherd, *der;* **the** ~ **of all woes** die Wurzel allen Übels; **locate the** ~ **of a leak** *(lit. or fig.)* feststellen, wo eine undichte Stelle ist; **the whole thing is a** ~ **of some embarrassment to us** das Ganze ist für uns ziemlich unangenehm; **at** ~: an der Quelle; **tax deducted at** ~: Quellensteuer, *die;* **my wages are taxed at** ~: die Steuer wird direkt von meinem Lohn abgezogen

source: ~**-book** *n.* Quellensammlung, *die;* ~ **language** *n.* Ausgangssprache, *die*

sour 'cream *n.* saure Sahne; Sauerrahm, *der*

sourly ['saʊəlɪ] *adv.* säuerlich

sour: ~**puss** *n. (sl.) (male)* Miesepeter, der *(ugs.); (female)* miesepetrige Ziege *(ugs.)*

sousaphone ['su:zəfəʊn] *n. (Mus.)* Sousaphon, *das*

souse [saʊs] *v. t.* **a)** *(plunge into liquid)* eintauchen; **b)** *(soak)* **get/be** ~**d** durchnäßt werden/sein; **c)** *(pickle)* einlegen

soutane [su:'tɑ:n] *n. (RC Ch.)* Soutane, *die*

south [saʊθ] **1.** *n.* **a)** Süden, *der;* **the** ~: Süd *(Met., Seew.);* **in/to[wards]/from the** ~: im/nach *od. (geh.)* gen/von Süden; **to the** ~ **of** südlich von; südlich (+ *Gen.*); **b)** *usu.* **S**~ *(part lying to the* ~*)* Süden, *der;* **from the S**~: aus dem Süden; **c)** *(Cards)* Süd. **2.** *adj.* südlich; Süd⟨*küste, -wind, -grenze, -tor*⟩. **3.** *adv.* südwärts; nach Süden; **a** ~**-facing wall** eine nach Süden gelegene Mauer; ~ **of** südlich von; südlich (+ *Gen.*); *see also* **¹by 1 d**

South: ~ **'Africa** *pr. n.* Südafrika *(das);* ~ **'African 1.** *adj.* südafrikanisch; **2.** *n.* Südafrikaner, *der*/-afrikanerin, *die;* ~ **A'merica** *pr. n.* Südamerika *(das);* ~ **A'merican 1.** *adj.* südamerikanisch; **2.** *n.* Südamerikaner, *der*/-amerikanerin, *die*

south: ~**bound** *adj.* ⟨*Zug usw.*⟩ in Richtung Süden; ~**-'east 1.** *n.* Südosten, *der;* **in/to[wards]/from the** ~**-east** im/nach *od. (geh.)* gen/von Südosten; **to the** ~**-east of** südöstlich von, südöstlich (+ *Gen.*); **2.** *adj.* südöstlich; Südost⟨*wind, -fenster, -küste*⟩; **3.** *adv.* südostwärts; nach Südosten; ~**-east of** südöstlich von; südöstlich (+ *Gen.*); ~**'easter** *n.* Südostwind, *der;* ~**-'easterly 1.** *adj.* südöstlich; **2.** *adv. (position)* im Südosten; *(direction)* nach Südosten; ~**-'eastern** *adj.* südöstlich

southerly ['sʌðəlɪ] **1.** *adj.* **a)** *(in position or direction)* südlich; **in a** ~ **direction** nach Süden; **b)** *(from the south)* ⟨*Wind*⟩ aus südlichen Richtungen; **the wind was** ~: der Wind kam aus südlichen Richtungen. **2.** *adv.* **a)** *(in position)* südlich; *(in direction)* südwärts; **b)** *(from the south)* aus *od.* von Süd[en]. **3.** *n.* Süd[wind], *der*

southern ['sʌðən] *adj.* südlich; Süd⟨*grenze, -hälfte, -seite, -fenster, -wind*⟩; südländisch ⟨*Temperament*⟩; ~ **Spain** Südspanien; das südliche Spanien; ~ **Africa** das südliche Afrika; *see also* **cross 1 f; hemisphere a**

southerner ['sʌðənə(r)] *n. (male)* Südengländer/-franzose/-italiener *usw., der; (female)* Südengländerin/-französin/-italienerin *usw., die; (Amer.)* Südstaatler, *der*/-staatlerin, *die;* **he's a** ~: er kommt aus dem Süden

Southern: ~ **'Europe** *pr. n.* Südeuropa *(das);* ~ **European 1.** *adj.* südeuropäisch; **2.** *n.* Südeuropäer, *der*/-europäerin, *die;* ~ **'Ireland** *pr. n.* Südirland *(das);* **s**~ **'lights** *n. pl.* Südlicht, *das*

southernmost ['sʌðənməʊst] *adj.* südlichst ...

South: ~ **'German 1.** *adj.* süddeutsch; **2.** *n.* Süddeutsche, *der/die;* ~ **'Germany** *pr. n.* Süddeutschland *(das);* ~ **Ko'rea** *pr. n.* Südkorea *(das);* ~ **Ko'rean 1.** *adj.* südkoreanisch; **2.** *n.* Südkoreaner, *der*/-koreanerin, *die*

South of 'England *pr. n.* Südengland *(das); attrib.* südenglisch

south: ~**paw** *(Boxing coll.)* **1.** *n.* Linkshänder, *der*/Linkshänderin, *die;* **2.** *adj.* linkshändig; **S**~ **'Pole** *pr. n.* Südpol, *der;* **S**~ **Sea** *adj.* Südsee-; **S**~ **Sea Islander** Südseeinsulaner, *der*/-insulanerin, *die;* **S**~ **'Seas** *pr. n. pl.* Südsee, *die;* ~**-**~**-'east 1.** *n.* Südsüdosten, *der;* **2.** *adj.* südsüdöstlich; Südsüdost-; **3.** *adv.* südsüdostwärts; ~**-**~**-'west 1.** *n.* Südsüdwesten, *der;* **2.** *adj.* südsüdwestlich; Südsüdwest-; **3.** *adv.* südsüdwestwärts

southward ['saʊθwəd] **1.** *adj.* nach Süden gerichtet; *(situated towards the south)* südlich; **in a** ~ **direction** nach Süden; [in] Richtung Süden. **2.** *adv.* südwärts; **they are** ~ **bound** sie fahren nach *od.* [in] Richtung Süden. **3.** *n.* Süden, *der*

southwards ['saʊθwədz] *see* **southward 2**

south: ~**-'west 1.** *n.* Südwesten, *der;* **in/to[wards]/from the** ~**-west** im/nach *od. (geh.)* gen/von Südwesten; **to the** ~**-west of** südwestlich von; südwestlich (+ *Gen.*). **2.** *adj.* südwestlich; Südwest⟨*wind, -fenster, -küste*⟩. **3.** *adv.* südwestwärts; nach Südwesten; ~**-west of** südwestlich von; südwestlich (+ *Gen.*); **S**~**-West 'Africa** *pr. n.* Südwestafrika, *(das);* ~**-wester** [saʊθ'westə(r)] *n.* Südwestwind, *der;* ~**-'westerly 1.** *adj.* südwestlich; **2.** *adv. (position)* im Südwesten; *(direction)* nach Südwesten; ~**-'western** *adj.* südwestlich

souvenir [su:və'nɪə(r)] *n. (of holiday)* Andenken, *das;* Souvenir, *das* **(of** aus); *(of wedding-day, one's youth, etc.)* Andenken, *das* **(of** an + *Akk.*)

sou'wester [saʊ'westə(r)] *n.* **a)** *(hat)* Südwester, *der;* **b)** *(coat)* Ölhaut, *die*

sovereign ['sɒvrɪn] **1.** *n.* **a)** *(ruler)* Souverän, *der;* **b)** *(Brit. Hist.: coin)* Sovereign, *der;* 20-Shilling-Münze, *die.* **2.** *adj.* **a)** *(independent)* souverän ⟨*Staat, Volk*⟩; **b)** *(supreme)* höchst...; **c)** *(arch.: royal)* souverän; **d)** *(very good)* ausgezeichnet ⟨*Medikament*⟩

sovereignty ['sɒvrɪntɪ] *n.* **a)** *(supreme power)* Souveränität, *die;* Oberhoheit, *die;* **b)** *(royal position)* Stellung als Souverän; **c)** *(autonomous state)* souveräner Staat

Soviet ['səʊvɪət, 'sɒvɪət] *(Hist.)* **1.** *adj.* sowjetisch; Sowjet⟨*bürger, -literatur, -kultur, -ideologie*⟩. **2.** *n.* Sowjet, *der;* **Supreme S**~: Oberster Sowjet

Soviet: ~ **'Russia** *pr. n. (Hist.)* Sowjetrußland *(das);* ~ **'Union** *pr. n. (Hist.)* Sowjetunion, *die*

¹sow [səʊ] *v. t., p. p.* **sown** [səʊn] *or* ~**ed** [səʊd] **a)** *(plant)* [aus]säen; *(fig.)* legen ⟨*Minen*⟩; **b)** *(plant with seed)* einsäen, besäen ⟨*Feld, Boden*⟩; **c)** *(cover thickly)* spicken *(ugs.);* **meadows** ~**n with daisies** mit Gänseblümchen bedeckte Wiesen; **d)** *(fig.: initiate)* säen. *See also* **oat b; seed 1 c; whirlwind a**

²sow [saʊ] *n.* **a)** *(female pig)* Sau, *die;* **b)** *(Metallurgy) (trough)* Kokille, *die; (block of iron)* Massel, *die. See also* **silk 2**

sower ['səʊə(r)] *n.* Sämann, *der*/Säerin, *die;* **be a** ~ **of discord** Zwietracht säen

sowing ['səʊɪŋ] *n.* Säen, *das;* Aussaat, *die*

sown *see* **¹sow**

sox [sɒks] *n. pl. (Commerc./coll.) see* **¹sock a**

soya [bean] ['sɔɪə (bi:n)], **soy bean** ['sɔɪ bi:n] *ns.* **a)** *(plant)* Soja[bohne], *die;* **b)** *(seed)* Sojabohne, *die*

soy sauce ['sɔɪ sɔ:s] *n.* Sojasoße, *die*

sozzled ['sɒzld] *adj. (sl.)* voll *(ugs.);* besoffen *(derb);* **get** ~: sich besaufen *(derb)*

spa [spɑ:] *n.* **a)** *(place)* Bad, *das;* Badeort, *der;* **b)** *(spring)* Mineralquelle, *die*

space [speɪs] **1.** *n.* **a)** Raum, *der;* **stare into** ~: in die Luft *od.* ins Leere starren; **b)** *(interval between points)* Platz, *der;* **the houses are separated by a** ~ **of ten feet** die Häuser sind durch einen 10 Fuß breiten Zwischenraum getrennt; **clear a** ~: Platz schaffen; **he needs** ~ *(fig.)* er braucht Bewegungsfreiheit; **c)** *(area on page)* Platz, *der;* **d) the wide open** ~**s** das weite, flache Land; **the vast** ~**s of the prairie/desert** die weite Fläche *od.* die Weite[n] der Prärie/Wüste; **e)** *(Astron.)* Weltraum, *der; see also* **outer space; f)** *(blank between words)* Zwischenraum, *der;* Spatium, *das (Druckw.);* **five** ~**s from the left margin** fünf Anschläge vom linken Rand [entfernt]; **g)** *(interval of time)* Zeitraum, *der;* **in the** ~ **of a minute/an hour** *etc.* innerhalb einer Minute/Stunde *usw.;* **in a short** ~ **of time he was back** nach kurzer Zeit war er zurück. **2.** *v. t.* **the line is/the letters are badly** ~**d** die Zeile ist/die Buchstaben sind schlecht spationiert *(Druckw.);* **the posts are** ~**d at intervals of one metre** die Pfosten sind im Abstand von einem Meter aufgestellt

~ **'out** *v. t.* verteilen; ~ **the figures out clearly** die Zahlen so weit auseinanderschreiben, daß sie deutlich lesbar sind

space: ~ **age** *n.* [Welt]raumzeitalter, *das;* Zeitalter der Raumfahrt, *das;* ~**-bar** *n.* Leertaste, *die;* ~**craft** *n.* Raumfahrzeug, *das; (unmanned)* Raumsonde, *die*

spaced [out] [speɪst ('aʊt)] *adj. (sl.: under influence of drug)* high *(Drogenjargon)*

space: ~ **flight** *n.* **a)** *(a journey through* ~*)* [Welt]raumflug, *der;* **b)** *see* ~ **travel;** ~**-heater** *n.* Heizgerät, *das;* ~**man** *see* ~ **traveller;** ~ **medicine** *n.* Raumfahrtmedizin, *die;* ~ **opera** *n. (esp. Amer.)* Weltraumoper, *die (ugs.);* ~ **probe** *n.* Raumsonde, *die;* ~**-saving** *adj.* platzsparend; raumsparend; ~**ship** *n.* Raumschiff, *das;* ~ **shuttle** *n.* Raumfähre, *die;* Raumtransporter, *der;* ~ **station** *n.* [Welt]raumstation, *die;* ~**suit** *n.* Raumanzug, *der;* ~**-'time** *n. (Phys.)* Raum-Zeit-Welt, *die;* ~ **travel** *n.* Raumfahrt, *die;* ~ **traveller** *n.* Raumfahrer, *der*/-fahrerin, *die;* ~ **vehicle** *see* **spacecraft;** ~ **walk** *n.* Spaziergang im All

spacial, spacially *see* **spatial, spatially**

spacing ['speɪsɪŋ] *n.* Zwischenraum, *der; (Printing)* Sperrungen; Spationierung, *die (Druckw.);* **single/double** ~ *(on typewriter)* einfacher/doppelter Zeilenabstand

spacious ['speɪʃəs] *adj.* **a)** *(vast in area)* weitläufig ⟨*Garten, Park, Ländereien*⟩; **b)** *(roomy)* geräumig ⟨*Raum*⟩; breit ⟨*Straße*⟩

spaciously ['speɪʃəslɪ] *adv.* weitläufig

spade [speɪd] *n.* **a)** *(for digging)* Spaten, *der;* **call a** ~ **a** ~ *or (joc.)* **a bloody shovel** das Kind beim [rechten] Namen nennen *(ugs.);* **she was never afraid to call a** ~ **a** ~: sie nahm nie ein Blatt vor den Mund *(ugs.);* **b)** *(Cards)* Pik, *das; see also* **club 1 d; c)** *(Amer. sl. derog.)* Neger, *der*

spadeful ['speɪdfʊl] *n.* **a** ~**/two** ~**s of soil** ein/zwei Spaten [voll] Erde

'spadework *n. (fig.)* Kleinarbeit, *die; (preliminary work)* Vorarbeit, *die*

spadix ['speɪdɪks] *n., pl.* **spadices** ['speɪdɪsi:z] *(Bot.)* Kolben, *der*

spaghetti [spə'getɪ] *n.* **a)** Spaghetti *Pl.;* **b)** *(joc.: cables)* Kabelsalat, *der (ugs.)*

spaghetti 'Western *n. (Cinemat.)* Italowestern, *der*

Spain [speɪn] *pr. n.* Spanien *(das)*

spall [spɔ:l] **1.** *v. t.* **a)** *(chip)* absplittern; **b)** *(Mining)* mit dem Hammer zerkleinern ⟨*Erz*⟩. **2.** *v. i.* splittern. **3.** *n.* Splitter, *der*

Spam, (P) [spæm] *n.* Frühstücksfleisch, *das*

¹span [spæn] **1.** *n.* **a)** *(full extent)* Spanne, *die;* ~ **of life/time** Lebens-/Zeitspanne, *die;* **throughout the whole** ~ **of Roman history** in der gesamten römischen Geschichte; **b)** *(of* bridge) Spannweite, *die;* **the bridge crosses the river in a single ~:** die Brücke überspannt den Fluß in einem einzigen Bogen; **c)** *(Aeronaut.)* Spannweite, *die;* **d)** *(of hand)* Spanne, *die.* **2.** *v.t.,* **-nn- a)** *(extend across)* überspannen ‹*Fluß*›; umfassen ‹*Zeitraum*›; **b)** *(measure)* nach Spannen messen

²span *see* **spick**

spandrel ['spændrl] *n.* *(Archit.)* [Bogen]zwickel, *der;* Spandrille, *die*

spang [spæŋ] *adv.* *(Amer. coll.)* ganz; ~ **in the middle of the night/the road** mitten in der Nacht/auf der Straße

spangle ['spæŋgl] **1.** *n. see* **sequin. 2.** *v.t.* **~d with stars/buttercups** von glitzernden Sternen/mit leuchtenden Butterblumen übersät; *see also* **star-spangled**

Spaniard ['spænjəd] *n.* Spanier, *der*/Spanierin, *die*

spaniel ['spænjəl] *n.* Spaniel, *der*

Spanish ['spænɪʃ] **1.** *adj.* spanisch; **sb. is ~:** jmd. ist Spanier/Spanierin; *see also* **English 1. 2.** *n.* **a)** *(language)* Spanisch, *das; see also* **English 2 a; b)** *constr. as pl. (people)* Spanier

Spanish: ~ **A'merica** *pr. n. die spanischsprachigen Länder Lateinamerikas;* ~ **'fly** *n.* Spanische Fliege; ~ **'Main** *pr. n.* *(Hist.)* **the ~ Main** *die Nordostküste Südamerikas zwischen dem Orinoko und Panama sowie der angrenzende Teil der Karibik;* ~ **'omelette** *n. Omelette mit Zwiebeln, grünem Paprika und Tomaten;* ≈ Omelette andalusische Art *(Kochk.);* ~ **'onion** *n.* spanische Zwiebel; Bermudazwiebel, *die (Kochk.)*

spank [spæŋk] **1.** *n.* ≈ Klaps, *der (ugs.).* **2.** *v.t.* ~ **sb.** jmdm. den Hintern versohlen *(ugs.);* **get ~ed** den Hintern voll kriegen *(ugs.).* **3.** *v.i.* ‹*Pferd:*› schnell traben

spanking ['spæŋkɪŋ] **1.** *n.* Tracht Prügel, *die (ugs.); (for sexual gratification)* Hinternversohlen, *das (ugs.).* **2.** *adj.* *(coll.)* scharf ‹*Trab, Lauf, Galopp, Tempo*›. **3.** *adv.* *(coll.)* ~ **new** funkelnagelneu *(ugs.)*

spanner ['spænə(r)] *n.* *(Brit.)* Schraubenschlüssel, *der;* **put** *or* **throw a ~ in the works** *(fig.)* Sand ins Getriebe streuen

'span roof *n.* Satteldach, *das*

¹spar [spɑ:(r)] *v.i.,* **-rr- a)** *(Boxing)* sparren; **b)** *(fig.: argue)* [sich] zanken

²spar *n.* **a)** *(pole)* Rundholz, *das;* Spiere, *die (Seemannsspr.);* **b)** *(Aeronaut.)* Holm, *der*

³spar *n.* *(Min.)* Spat, *der*

spare [speə(r)] **1.** *adj.* **a)** *(not in use)* übrig; ~ **time/moment** Freizeit, *die*/freier Augenblick; **not have ~ cash** kein Bargeld [übrig] haben; **have sth. going ~** *(coll.)* etwas übrig haben; **there is one ~ seat** ein Platz ist noch frei; **are there any ~ tickets for Friday?** gibt es noch Karten für Freitag?; **b)** *(for use when needed)* zusätzlich, Extra‹*bett, -tasse*›; ~ **room** Gästezimmer, *das;* **go ~** *(Brit. sl.: be very angry)* durchdrehen *(salopp);* **c)** *(frugal)* karg ‹*Kost, Mahlzeit*›; **d)** *(lean)* schlank ‹*Wuchs, Gestalt*›; **e)** schlicht ‹*Stil*›. **2.** *n.* Ersatzteil, *das*/-reifen, *der usw.;* **I haven't got a pen; have you a ~?** ich hab' keinen Stift, hast du einen übrig? **3.** *v.t.* **a)** *(do without)* entbehren; **can you ~ me a moment?** hast du einen Augenblick Zeit für mich?; **we arrived with ten minutes to ~:** wir kamen zehn Minuten früher an; als wir ankamen, hatten wir noch zehn Minuten Zeit [übrig]; **b)** *(not inflict on)* ~ **sb. sth.** jmdm. etw. ersparen; **c)** *(not hurt)* [ver]schonen; **if I am ~d** wenn ich so lange lebe; **d)** *(not cause)* ~ **sb.'s blushes** jmdm. die Verlegenheit *od.* Peinlichkeit ersparen; **e)** *(fail to use)* **not ~ any expense/pains** *or* **efforts** keine Kosten/Mühe scheuen; **no expense ~d** an nichts gespart; **not ~ oneself in one's efforts to ...:** keine Mühe scheuen ... *See also* **enough 2; rod c**

sparely ['speəlɪ] *adv.* ~ **built** schlank [gebaut]

spare: ~ **'part** *n.* Ersatzteil, *das;* ~**-rib** *n.* **a)** *(cut of meat)* Kamm, *der;* **b)** *(dish)* [Schäl]rippchen, *das;* ~ **'tyre** *n.* **a)** Reserve-, Ersatzreifen, *der;* **b)** *(Brit. fig. coll.)* Rettungsring, *der (ugs.);* ~ **'wheel** *n.* Ersatzrad, *das*

sparing ['speərɪŋ] *adj.* sparsam; **be ~ of sth./in the use of sth.** mit etw. sparsam umgehen

sparingly ['speərɪŋlɪ] *adv.* sparsam

spark [spɑ:k] **1.** *n.* **a)** Funke, *der;* **shower of ~s** Funkenregen, *der;* **the ~s [begin to] fly** *(fig.)* es funkt *(ugs.);* **a ~ of generosity/decency** *(fig.)* ein Funke[n] Großzügigkeit/Anstand; **not a ~ of life remained** *(fig.)* keine Spur von Leben blieb übrig; **b)** *(electrical discharge)* Funkenentladung, *die;* **c)** *(in sparking-plug)* Zündfunke[n], *der (Kfz-W.);* **d) a bright ~** *(clever person; also iron.)* ein schlauer Kopf. **2.** *v.t. see* ~ **off. 3.** *v.i.* **a)** Funken sprühen; **b)** *(Electr.)* funken

~ **'off** *v.t.* **a)** *(cause to explode)* zünden; **b)** *(fig.: start)* auslösen

'spark-gap *n.* *(Electr.)* Funkenstrecke, *die*

sparking-plug ['spɑ:kɪŋplʌg] *n.* *(Brit. Motor Veh.)* Zündkerze, *die*

sparkle ['spɑ:kl] **1.** *v.i.* **a)** *(flash)* ‹*Tautropfen:*› glitzern; ‹*Augen:*› funkeln, sprühen; **b)** *(perform brilliantly)* glänzen; **c)** *(be lively)* sprühen (**with** vor + *Dat.*). **2.** *n.* Glitzern, *das;* Funkeln, *das;* **he lost all his ~** *(fig.)* er hat sein sprühendes Temperament verloren

sparkler ['spɑ:klə(r)] *n.* **a)** *(firework)* Wunderkerze, *die;* **b)** *(sl.: diamond)* Klunker, *der (ugs.)*

sparkling ['spɑ:klɪŋ] *adj.* **a)** *(flashing)* glitzernd ‹*Stein, Diamant*›; **b)** *(bright)* funkelnd ‹*Augen*›; ~ **vivacity** sprühende Lebhaftigkeit; **c)** *(brilliant)* glänzend ‹*Schauspiel, Aufführung, Rede*›

sparkling 'wine *n.* Schaumwein, *der*

'spark-plug *see* **sparking-plug**

'sparring partner *n.* *(Boxing)* Sparringspartner, *der;* **this is my old ~** *(fig.)* dies ist mein alter Freund, mit dem ich oft die Klingen gekreuzt habe *(geh.)*

sparrow ['spærəʊ] *n.* Sperling, *der;* Spatz, *der;* **house ~:** Haussperling, *der;* Hausspatz, *der; see also* **hedge-sparrow**

'sparrow-hawk *n.* Sperber, *der*

sparse [spɑ:s] *adj.* spärlich; dünn ‹*Besiedlung*›

sparsely ['spɑ:slɪ] *adv.* spärlich; dünn ‹*besiedelt*›

sparseness ['spɑ:snɪs], **sparsity** ['spɑ:sɪtɪ] *ns., no pl.* Spärlichkeit, *die*

Spartan ['spɑ:tn] **1.** *adj.* spartanisch. **2.** *n.* Spartaner, *der*/Spartanerin, *die*

spasm ['spæzm] *n.* **a)** Krampf, *der;* Spasmus, *der (Med.);* **b)** *(convulsive movement)* Anfall, *der;* ~ **of coughing** Hustenanfall, *der;* **c)** *(coll.)* **a ~ of activity** plötzliche fieberhafte Aktivität

spasmodic [spæz'mɒdɪk] *adj.* **a)** *(marked by spasms)* krampfartig; spasmodisch *(Med.);* **b)** *(intermittent)* sporadisch ‹*Anwachsen, Bemühungen*›

spasmodically [spæz'mɒdɪkəlɪ] *adv.* **a)** krampfartig, *(Med.)* spasmodisch ‹*zucken*›; **b)** *(intermittently)* sporadisch

spastic ['spæstɪk] *(Med.)* **1.** *n.* Spastiker, *der*/Spastikerin, *die.* **2.** *adj.* spastisch [gelähmt]

¹spat *see* **¹spit 1, 2**

²spat [spæt] *n.* *(gaiter)* Gamasche, *die*

³spat *n.* *(coll.: quarrel)* Krach, *der (ugs.)*

spate [speɪt] *n.* **a)** *(flood)* **the river/waterfall is in [full] ~:** der Fluß/Wasserfall führt Hochwasser; **b)** *(fig.: large amount)* **a ~ of sth.** eine Flut von etw.; **a ~ of burglaries** eine Einbruchsserie

spatial ['speɪʃl] *adj.*, **spatially** ['speɪʃəlɪ] *adv.* räumlich

spatter ['spætə(r)] **1.** *v.t.* spritzen ‹*Lehm, Wasser*›; ~ **sb./sth. with sth.** jmdn./etw. mit etw. bespritzen. **2.** *n.* Spritzer, *der*

spatula ['spætjʊlə] *n.* **a)** Spachtel, *die;* **b)** *(Surg.)* Spatel, *der od. die*

spatulate ['spætjʊlət] *adj.* spatelförmig

spawn [spɔ:n] **1.** *v.t.* **a)** *(produce)* ablegen ‹*Eier*›; *(fig.)* hervorbringen; **b)** *(derog.: breed)* produzieren. **2.** *v.i.* laichen. **3.** *n., constr. as sing. or pl.* **a)** *(Zool.)* Laich, *der;* **b)** *(derog.: offspring)* Brut, *die (salopp abwertend)*

spay [speɪ] *v.t.* sterilisieren ‹*Katze, Hündin*›

speak [spi:k] **1.** *v.i.,* **spoke** [spəʊk], **spoken** ['spəʊkn] **a)** sprechen; **we spoke this morning** wir sprachen heute morgen miteinander; ~ **with sb.** mit jmdm. sprechen; ~ **[with sb.] on** *or* **about sth.** [mit jmdm.] über etwas *(Akk.)* sprechen; ~ **for/against sth.** sich für/gegen etw. aussprechen; **sth. ~s well for sb.** etw. spricht für jmdn.; **~ing as a trade unionist/a European** als Gewerkschafter/Europäer; **the minister rose to ~:** der Minister erhob sich, um das Wort zu ergreifen; **b)** *(on telephone)* **Is Mr Grant there? – S~ing!** Ist Mister Grant da? – Am Apparat!; **Mr Grant ~ing** *(when connected to caller)* Grant hier; hier ist Grant; **who is ~ing, please?** wer ist am Apparat, bitte?; mit wem spreche ich, bitte? *See also* **manner a; ¹so 2. 2.** *v.t.,* **spoke, spoken a)** *(utter)* sprechen ‹*Satz, Wort, Sprache*›; **b)** *(make known)* sagen ‹*Wahrheit*›; ~ **one's opinion/mind** seine Meinung sagen; sagen, was man denkt; **c)** *(convey without words)* **sth. ~s volumes** etw. spricht Bände; **sth. ~s volumes for sth.** etw. spricht sehr für etw.

~ **for** *v.t.* sprechen für; ~ **for oneself** für sich selbst sprechen; **~ing for myself, I prefer tea to coffee** ich selber trinke lieber Tee als Kaffee; ~ **for yourself!** das ist [nur] deine Meinung!; ~ **for itself/themselves** für sich selbst sprechen; **We're all depressed – S~ for yourself!** Wir sind alle deprimiert. – Du vielleicht, ich nicht!; **sth. is spoken for** *(reserved)* etw. ist schon vergeben

~ **of** *v.t.* sprechen von; **~ing of Mary** da wir gerade von Mary sprechen; apropos Mary; **nothing to ~ of** nichts Besonderes *od.* Nennenswertes; **no trees to ~ of** kaum Bäume; **these tyres have no tread to ~ of** bei diesen Reifen kann man kaum noch von Profil sprechen; *see also* **devil 1 c**

~ **'out** *v.i.* seine Meinung sagen; seine Stimme erheben; ~ **out against sth.** seine Stimme gegen etw. erheben; sich gegen etw. aussprechen

~ **to** *v.t.* **a)** *(address)* sprechen mit; reden mit; **I know him to ~ to** ich kenne ihn [nur] flüchtig; ~ **when** *or* **don't ~ until you are spoken to** rede nur, wenn du gefragt wirst; **b)** *(request action from)* ~ **to sb. about sth.** mit jmdm. wegen einer Sache *od.* über etw. *(Akk.)* sprechen; **c)** *(coll.: reprove)* ~ **to sb.** sich mit jmdm. unterhalten *(verhüllend);* **d)** ~ **to a subject** sich zu einem Thema äußern; **e)** *(~ in confirmation of)* **I can ~ to his having been there** ich kann bestätigen *od.* bezeugen, daß er dort war

~ **'up** *v.i.* **a)** *(~ more loudly)* lauter sprechen; **b)** *see* ~ **out**

'speakeasy *n.* *(Amer. Hist. sl.) Lokal, in dem illegal Alkohol ausgeschenkt wurde*

speaker ['spi:kə(r)] *n.* **a)** *(in public)* Redner, *der*/Rednerin, *die;* **be a/the ~ for** *or* **at an event** bei einem Anlaß eine/die Rede halten; **b)** *(of a language)* Sprecher, *der*/Sprecherin, *die;* **be a French ~, be a ~ of French** Französisch sprechen; **c) S~** *(Polit.)* Sprecher, *der;* ≈ Parlamentspräsident, *der;* **Mr S~:** Herr Vorsitzender; *see also* **catch 1 f; d)** *see* **loudspeaker**

speaking ['spi:kɪŋ] **1.** *n.* **a)** *(talking)* Sprechen, *das;* **a good ~ voice** eine gute Sprechstimme; **not be on ~ terms with sb.** nicht [mehr] mit jmdm. reden; **b)** *(speech-making)* Rede, *die; see also* **public speaking. 2.** *adv.* **strictly/roughly/generally/legally ~:** genaugenommen/grob gesagt/im allgemeinen/aus juristischer Sicht; **figuratively ~:** bildlich gesprochen

speaking: ~ acquaintance *n.* [flüchtige] Bekannte, *der/die;* **~ 'clock** *n. (Brit.)* telefonische Zeitansage; **~-tube** *n. Sprechverbindung zwischen zwei Räumen, Gebäuden usw. mittels einer Rohrleitung;* Sprachrohr, *das*

spear [spɪə(r)] **1.** *n.* **a)** Speer, *der;* **b)** *(of plant)* Stange, *die.* **2.** *v. t.* aufspießen

spear: ~head 1. *n. (fig.)* Speerspitze, *die; (Mil.)* Angriffsspitze, *die;* **2.** *v. t. (fig.)* **~head sth.** etw. anführen; die Speerspitze von etw. bilden *(bes. Pol.); (Mil.)* bei etw. die Angriffsspitze bilden; **~mint** *n.* Grüne Minze; **~mint sweet/chewing-gum** Pfefferminzbonbon/-kaugummi, *der od. das*

¹spec [spek] *n. (coll.: speculation)* Spekulation, *die;* **on ~:** auf gut Glück; auf Verdacht *(ugs.)*

²spec [spek] *(coll.) see* **specification a**

special ['speʃl] **1.** *adj.* speziell; besonder...; Sonder⟨*korrespondent, -zug, -mission, -behandlung, -ausgabe, -bedeutung, -auftrag*⟩; **nobody ~:** niemand Besonderer; **her own ~ way** ihre eigene Art; **a ~ occasion** ein besonderer Anlaß; **a very ~ relationship** eine besonders enge Beziehung; **~ friend** besonders enger Freund/enge Freundin. **2.** *n. (newspaper)* Sonderausgabe, *die; (train)* Sonderzug, *der*

special: S~ Branch *n. (Brit. Police) Abteilung der britischen Polizei, deren Aufgabe die Wahrung der inneren Sicherheit ist;* ≈ Sicherheitsdienst, *der;* **~ 'case** *n.* Sonderfall, *der;* **~ 'constable** *n. (Brit. Police)* Hilfspolizist, *der/*-polizistin, *die;* **~ corres'pondent** *n.* Sonderkorrespondent, *der/*-korrespondentin, *die;* Sonderberichterstatter, *der/*-berichterstatterin, *die;* **~ de'livery** *n. (Post)* Eilzustellung, *die;* **~ 'drawing rights** *n. pl. (Finance)* Sonderziehungsrechte *Pl.* [auf den Internationalen Währungsfonds]; **~ e'dition** *n.* Sonderausgabe, *die;* **~ effects** *n. pl. (Cinemat.)* Special effects *Pl. (fachspr.);* Spezialeffekte

specialisation, specialise *see* **specializ-**

specialism ['speʃəlɪzm] *n.* **a)** *see* **specialization; b)** *(field of study)* Spezialgebiet, *das*

specialist ['speʃəlɪst] *n.* **a)** Spezialist, *der/*Spezialistin, *die;* Fachmann, *der/*Fachfrau, *die;* **an eighteenth-century ~:** ein Spezialist für das achtzehnte Jahrhundert; **~ knowledge** Fachwissen, *das;* **b)** *(Med.)* Facharzt, *der/*-ärztin, *die;* **eye/heart/cancer ~:** Augenarzt/Herz-/Krebsspezialist, *der*

speciality [speʃɪ'ælɪtɪ] *n.* **a)** *(activity, skill, product)* Spezialität, *die; (interest)* Spezialgebiet, *das;* **she makes a ~ of her pies** Pasteten sind ihre Spezialität; **b)** *(special feature)* [besonderes] Merkmal *od.* Kennzeichen

specialization [speʃəlaɪ'zeɪʃn] *n.* Spezialisierung, *die*

specialize ['speʃəlaɪz] **1.** *v. i.* sich spezialisieren (**in** auf + *Akk.*). **2.** *v. t. (Biol.: modify)* **become ~d** ⟨*Glied, Organ:*⟩ sich gesondert ausbilden

special 'licence *n. (Brit.) Sondererlaubnis, die die Heirat ohne Aufgebot oder an einem anderen als dem gewöhnlichen Ort zuläßt*

specially ['speʃəlɪ] *adv.* **a)** speziell; **make sth. ~:** etw. speziell *od.* extra anfertigen; **~ made/chosen for me** eigens für mich gemacht/ausgewählt; **a ~ made wheelchair/lift** ein spezieller Rollstuhl/Lift; **a ~ adapted bus** ein spezieller Bus; **b)** *(especially)* besonders

special: ~ 'offer *n.* Sonderangebot, *das;* **have a ~ offer on sth.** etw. im Sonderangebot haben; **on ~ offer** im Sonderangebot; **~ 'pleading** *n.* **a)** *(biased argument)* Rechtsverdrehung, *die (abwertend);* **b)** *(Law) Plädoyer, das die Umstände eines Falles besonders berücksichtigt*

specialty ['speʃltɪ] *(esp. Amer.) see* **speciality a**

speciation [spi:sɪ'eɪʃn, spi:ʃɪ'eɪʃn] *n. (Biol.)* Art[en]bildung, *die*

specie ['spi:ʃi:, 'spi:ʃɪ] *n.* Hartgeld, *das*

species ['spi:ʃi:z, 'spi:ʃɪz] *n., pl. same* **a)** *(Biol.)* Spezies, *die (fachspr.);* Art, *die;* **b)** *(sort)* Art, *die;* **a dangerous ~ of criminal** ein gefährlicher Typ [von] Verbrecher

specific [spɪ'sɪfɪk] **1.** *adj.* **a)** *(definite)* deutlich, klar ⟨*Aussage*⟩; bestimmt ⟨*Ziel, Grund*⟩; **make a ~ request** einen bestimmten Wunsch äußern; **make no ~ preparations** keine besonderen Vorbereitungen treffen; **could you be more ~?** kannst du dich genauer ausdrücken?; **b)** *(of a species)* **the ~ name of a plant** der Name einer Pflanzenart; **c)** *(individual)* eigen (**to** *Dat.*); typisch (**to** für); *see also* **gravity d; heat 1 b. 2.** *n.* **a)** *(arch. Med.: remedy)* Spezifikum, *das;* **b)** *in pl. (details)* Einzelheiten Pl.; Details *Pl.*

specifically [spɪ'sɪfɪkəlɪ] *adv.* ausdrücklich; eigens; extra *(ugs.)*

specification [spesɪfɪ'keɪʃn] *n.* **a)** *often pl. (details)* technische Daten; *(instructions)* Konstruktionsplan, *der; (for building)* Baubeschreibung, *die;* **b)** *(specifying)* Spezifizierung, *die (geh.);* **c) [patent] ~:** Patentschrift, *die*

specificity [spesɪ'fɪsɪtɪ] *n.* Genauigkeit im Detail

specify ['spesɪfaɪ] *v. t. (name expressly)* ausdrücklich sagen; ausdrücklich nennen ⟨*Namen*⟩; *(include in specifications)* [genau] aufführen; **as specified above** wie oben aufgeführt; **unless otherwise specified** wenn nicht anders angegeben; **'other (please specify)'** „andere (bitte genaue Angaben machen)"

specimen ['spesɪmən] *n.* **a)** *(example)* Exemplar, *das;* **a ~ of his handwriting** eine Schriftprobe von ihm; **some ~s of her work** ein paar Arbeitsproben von ihr; **~ signature** Unterschriftsprobe, *die;* **b)** *(sample)* Probe, *die;* **a ~ of his urine was required** es wurde eine Urinprobe von ihm benötigt; **c)** *(coll./derog.: type)* Marke, *die (salopp)*

'specimen page *n.* Probeseite, *die*

specious ['spi:ʃəs] *adj.* **a ~ argument** ein nur scheinbar treffendes Argument; **a ~ pretence/appearance of honesty** ein Anschein von Ehrlichkeit

speck [spek] *n.* **a)** *(spot)* Fleck, *der; (of paint also)* Spritzer, *der;* **b)** *(particle)* Teilchen, *das;* **~ of soot/dust** Rußflocke, *die/*Staubkörnchen, *das;* **a ~ on the horizon** ein Pünktchen am Horizont; **the ore sparkled with ~s of gold** in dem Erz glitzerten Goldsprenkel; **c)** *(blemish)* Fleck, *der;* **have ~s** fleckig sein

specked [spekt] *adj.* fleckig ⟨*Frucht*⟩; **his coat is ~ with paint/mud** auf seinem Mantel sind Farb-/Schlammspritzer

speckle ['spekl] *n.* Tupfen, *der;* Sprenkel, *der*

speckled ['spekld] *adj.* gesprenkelt

specs [speks] *n. pl. (coll.: spectacles)* Brille, *die*

spectacle ['spektəkl] *n.* **a)** *in pl.* **[pair of] ~s** Brille, *die;* **b)** *(public show)* Spektakel, *das;* **c)** *(object of attention)* Anblick, *der;* Schauspiel, *das;* **make a ~ of oneself** sich unmöglich aufführen

spectacled ['spektəkld] *adj.* bebrillt

spectacular [spek'tækjʊlə(r)] **1.** *adj.* spektakulär. **2.** *n.* Spektakel, *das*

spectacularly [spek'tækjʊləlɪ] *adv.* außergewöhnlich; **be ~ successful** [einen] spektakulären Erfolg haben

spectator [spek'teɪtə(r)] *n.* Zuschauer, *der/*Zuschauerin, *die*

spec'tator sport *n.* Publikumssport, *der*

specter *(Amer.) see* **spectre**

spectra *pl. of* **spectrum**

spectral ['spektrl] *adj.* **a)** *(ghostly)* geisterhaft; gespenstisch; **b)** *(Phys.)* spektral

spectre ['spektə(r)] *n. (Brit.)* **a)** *(apparition)* Gespenst, *das;* **b)** *(disturbing image)* Schreckgespenst, *das*

spectrogram ['spektrəgræm] *n. (Phys.)* Spektrogramm, *das*

spectrograph ['spektrəgrɑ:f] *n. (Phys.)* Spektrograph, *der*

spectrometer [spek'trɒmɪtə(r)] *n. (Phys.)* Spektrometer, *das*

spectroscope ['spektrəskəʊp] *n. (Phys.)* Spektroskop, *das*

spectroscopy [spek'trɒskəpɪ] *n. (Phys.)* Spektroskopie, *die*

spectrum ['spektrəm] *n., pl.* **spectra** ['spektrə] *(Phys.; also fig.)* Spektrum, *das;* **~ of opinion** Meinungsspektrum, *das*

specula *pl. of* **speculum**

speculate ['spekjʊleɪt] *v. i.* spekulieren (**about, on** über + *Akk.*); Vermutungen *od.* Spekulationen anstellen (**about, on** über + *Akk.*); **~ as to what .../as to the wisdom of doing sth.** darüber spekulieren, was .../ob es klug sei, etw. zu tun; **~ on the Stock Exchange/in the gold market/in rubber** an der Börse/am Goldmarkt/mit *od. (Wirtsch. Jargon)* in Gummi spekulieren

speculation [spekjʊ'leɪʃn] *n.* Spekulation, *die* (**over** über + *Akk.*); **~ on the Stock Exchange/in the gold market/in rubber** Spekulation an der Börse/am Goldmarkt/mit *od. (Wirtsch. Jargon)* in Gummi; **there has been much ~ that ...:** man hat viel darüber spekuliert, daß ...

speculative ['spekjʊlətɪv] *adj.* spekulativ; **~ transactions** Spekulationsgeschäfte

speculatively ['spekjʊlətɪvlɪ] *adv.* spekulativ

speculator ['spekjʊleɪtə(r)] *n.* Spekulant, *der/*Spekulantin, *die*

speculum ['spekjʊləm] *n., pl.* **specula** ['spekjʊlə] *(Med.)* Spekulum, *das*

sped *see* **speed 2, 3**

speech [spi:tʃ] *n.* **a)** *(public address)* Rede, *die;* **make** *or* **deliver** *or* **give a ~:** eine Rede halten; **~ for the defence** *(Law)* Plädoyer des Verteidigers; **King's/Queen's S~** *(Parl.)* Thronrede, *die;* **b)** *(faculty of speaking)* Sprache, *die;* **lose/recover** *or* **find one's [power of] ~:** die Sprache verlieren/wiederfinden; **c)** *(act of speaking)* Sprechen, *das;* Sprache, *die;* **d)** *(manner of speaking)* Sprache, *die;* Sprechweise, *die;* **his ~ was slurred** er sprach undeutlich; **e)** *(Ling.: utterances)* Sprache, *die;* **children's ~:** Kindersprache, *die. See also* **figure 1 h; part 1 j; set speech**

speech: ~ act *n. (Ling.)* Sprechakt, *der;* **~-day** *n. (Brit. Sch.)* jährliches Schulfest; **~ defect** *n.* Sprachfehler, *der*

speechify ['spi:tʃɪfaɪ] *v. i. (coll.)* eine Rede schwingen *(ugs.)*

speechless ['spi:tʃlɪs] *adj.* **a)** sprachlos (**with** vor + *Dat.*); **~ with rage** sprachlos vor Wut; **b)** *(dumb)* stumm

speech: ~-making *n., no pl.* **be good at ~-making** ein guter Redner/eine gute Rednerin sein; **all the ~-making was over** alle Reden waren gehalten; **~ therapy** *n.* Sprachtherapie, *die;* **have ~ therapy** sprachtherapeutisch behandelt werden; **~-writer** *n.* Redenschreiber, *der/*-schreiberin, *die*

speed [spi:d] **1.** *n.* **a)** Geschwindigkeit, *die;* Schnelligkeit, *die; (of typist)* Schreibgeschwindigkeit, *die;* **at full** *or* **top ~:** mit Höchstgeschwindigkeit; mit Vollgas *(ugs.);* **pick up ~:** schneller werden; **top ~:** Spitzengeschwindigkeit, *die;* **with the ~ of light** mit Lichtgeschwindigkeit; *(fig.)* blitzschnell; **drive at a reckless ~:** rücksichtslos schnell fahren; **at a ~ of eighty miles an hour** mit einer Geschwindigkeit von achtzig Meilen in der Stunde; **at ~:** mit hoher Geschwindigkeit; **b)** *(gear)* Gang, *der;* **a**

five-~ gearbox eine 5-Gang-Schaltung; c) *(Photog.) (of film etc.)* Lichtempfindlichkeit, *die; (of lens)* **[shutter]** ~: Belichtungszeit, *die;* d) *(sl.: drug)* Speed, *das (Jargon). See also* **air speed; 'full 1 d; ground speed. 2.** *v.i.,* **sped** [sped] *or* **~ed** a) *(go fast)* schnell fahren; rasen *(ugs.);* **the hours/days sped by** die Stunden/Tage vergingen wie im Fluge; b) *p.t. & p.p.* **~ed** *(go too fast)* zu schnell fahren; rasen *(ugs.).* **3.** *v.t.,* **sped** *or* **~ed: ~ sb. on his/her way** jmdn. verabschieden; **God ~ you** Gott steh dir/euch bei

~ 'off *v.i.* davonbrausen

~ 'up 1. *v.t.,* **~ed up** beschleunigen; **~ up the work** die Arbeit vorantreiben; *(one's own work)* sich mit der Arbeit beeilen. **2.** *v.i.,* **~ed up** sich beeilen. *See also* **speed-up**

speed: ~boat *n.* Rennboot, *das;* **~ bump, ~ hump** *ns.* Bodenschwelle, *die*

speedily ['spi:dılı] *adv.* a) *(at speed)* schnell; b) *(soon)* umgehend

speeding ['spi:dıŋ] *n. (going too fast)* zu schnelles Fahren; Rasen, *das (ugs. abwertend);* Geschwindigkeitsüberschreitung, *die (Verkehrsw.);* **his third ~ offence** seine dritte Geschwindigkeitsüberschreitung

speed: ~ limit *n.* Tempolimit, *das;* Geschwindigkeitsbeschränkung, *die (Verkehrsw.);* **~ merchant** *n. (coll.)* Raser, *der (ugs. abwertend)*

speedo ['spi:dəʊ] *n., pl.* **~s** *(Brit. coll.)* Tacho, *der (ugs.)*

speedometer [spi:'dɒmıtə(r)] *n.* Tachometer, *der od. das*

speed: ~ ramp *n.* Bodenschwelle, *die;* **~ trap** *n.* Geschwindigkeitskontrolle, *die; (with radar)* Radarfalle, *die (ugs.);* **~-up** *n.* a) *(acceleration)* Beschleunigung, *die;* b) *(increase in work rate)* Steigerung der [Arbeits]produktivität; **~way** *n.* a) *(motorcycle racing)* Speedwayrennen, *das;* **the ~way world champion** der Speedwayweltmeister; b) *(race-track)* Speedwaybahn, *die;* c) *(Amer.: public road)* Schnellstraße, *die*

speedwell ['spi:dwel] *n. (Bot.)* Ehrenpreis, *der*

speedy ['spi:dı] *adj.* schnell; umgehend, prompt ‹*Antwort*›; **the medication is ~ and effective** das Medikament wirkt schnell und gut

speleology [spelı'ɒlədʒı, spi:lı'ɒlədʒı] *n.* Speläologie, *die;* Höhlenkunde, *die*

¹spell [spel] **1.** *v.t.,* **spelt** [spelt] *(Brit.) or* **~ed** a) schreiben; *(aloud)* buchstabieren; b) *(form)* **what do these letters/what does b-a-t ~?** welches Wort ergeben diese Buchstaben/die Buchstaben b-a-t?; c) *(fig.: have as result)* bedeuten; **that ~s trouble** das bedeutet nichts Gutes. **2.** *v.i.,* **spelt** *(Brit.) or* **~ed** *(say)* buchstabieren; *(write)* richtig schreiben; **he can't ~:** er kann keine Rechtschreibung *(ugs.)*

~ 'out, ~ 'over *v.t.* a) *(read letter by letter)* [langsam] buchstabieren; b) *(fig.: explain precisely)* genau erklären; genau darlegen

²spell *n.* a) *(period)* Weile, *die;* **do a ~ of joinery/in prison** eine Weile *od.* Zeitlang als Tischler arbeiten/im Gefängnis sitzen; **a ~ of overseas service** eine Zeitlang Dienst in Übersee; **on Sunday it will be cloudy with some sunny ~s** am Sonntag wolkig mit sonnigen Abschnitten; **a cold ~:** eine Kälteperiode; **return from a ~ in America** von einem Aufenthalt in Amerika zurückkehren; **a long ~ when ...:** eine lange Zeit, während der ...; b) *(Austral.: period of rest)* [Ruhe]pause, *die;* **have a ten minutes' ~:** zehn Minuten Pause machen

³spell *n.* a) *(words used as a charm)* Zauberspruch, *der;* **cast a ~ over** *or* **on sb./sth., put a ~ on sb./sth.** jmdn./etw. verzaubern; b) *(fascination)* Zauber, *der;* **break the ~:** den Bann brechen; **be under a ~:** unter einem Bann stehen

spell: ~bind *v.t.* bezaubern; **~bound** *adj.* verzaubert; **he can hold his readers ~bound** er kann seine Leser in seinem Bann halten

spelling ['spelıŋ] *n.* a) Rechtschreibung, *die;* **the original Shakespearian ~** die ursprüngliche Schreibung nach Shakespeare; b) *(sequence of letters)* Schreibweise, *die*

spelling: ~-bee *n.* Rechtschreib[e]wettbewerb, *der;* **~ checker** *n.* Rechtschreibprogramm, *das;* **~ mistake** *n.* Rechtschreibfehler, *der*

¹spelt *see* **¹spell**

²spelt [spelt] *n. (Agric.)* Dinkel, *der*

spend [spend] *v.t.,* **spent** [spent] a) *(pay out)* ausgeben; **~ money like water** *or (coll.)* **as if it's going out of fashion** sein *od.* das Geld mit beiden Händen ausgeben *od.* hinauswerfen *(ugs.);* **money well spent** sinnvoll ausgegebenes Geld; **it was money well spent** es hat sich ausgezahlt; **~ a penny** *(fig. coll.)* mal verschwinden [müssen] *(ugs.);* b) *(use)* aufwenden **(on** für); **~ one's time/a day** seine Zeit/einen Tag verbringen; **time well spent** sinnvoll verwendete Zeit; **it was effort/time well spent** es hat sich ausgezahlt; c) **~ itself** *(fig.)* ‹*Sturm, Wut:*› sich legen

spendable ['spendəbl] *adj.* verfügbar

spender ['spendə(r)] *n.* **he's a [big] ~:** bei ihm sitzt das Geld locker *(ugs.)*

'spending money *n.* a) *(Amer.) see* **pocket-money;** b) *(Brit.: sum intended for spending)* verfügbares Geld

'spendthrift *n.* Verschwender, *der*/Verschwenderin, *die*

spent 1. *see* **spend. 2.** *adj.* a) *(used up)* verbraucht; **~ cartridge** leere Geschoßhülse; b) *(drained of energy)* erschöpft; ausgelaugt; hinfällig ‹*Kranker, Greis*›; **a ~ force** *(fig.)* eine Kraft, die sich erschöpft hat

sperm ['spɜ:m] *n., pl.* **~s** *or same (Biol.)* a) *(semen)* Sperma, *der;* b) *(spermatozoon)* Samenfaden, *der*

spermatic [spɜ:'mætık] *adj.* Samen-

spermatic 'cord *n.* Samenstrang, *der*

spermatozoon [spɜ:mətə'zəʊɒn] *n., pl.* **spermatozoa** [spɜ:mətə'zəʊə] Spermatozoon, *das;* Spermium, *das*

'sperm bank *n.* Samenbank, *die*

spermicidal ['spɜ:mısaıdl] *adj.* spermizid

spermicide ['spɜ:mısaıd] *n.* Spermizid, *das*

'sperm whale *n.* Pottwal, *der*

spew [spju:] **1.** *v.t.* spucken. **2.** *v.i.* sich ergießen

~ 'out 1. *v.t.* erbrechen, [aus]spucken ‹*Gegessenes*›; ‹*Vulkan:*› spucken, speien ‹*Lava*›; **~ out waste products into the rivers** ‹*Fabriken:*› Abfälle in die Flüsse [aus]speien; **propaganda was ~ed out by the stations** *(fig.)* die Sender spien Propaganda. **2.** *v.i.* sich ergießen **(of, from** aus)

sphagnum ['sfægnəm] *n., pl.* **sphagna** ['sfægnə] *n.* Torf, *der;* **~ moss** Torfmoos, *das*

sphere [sfıə(r)] *n.* a) *(field of action)* Bereich, *der;* Sphäre, *die (geh.);* **be distinguished in many ~s** sich auf vielen Gebieten ausgezeichnet haben; **that's outside my ~:** das gehört nicht zu meinem Tätigkeitsbereich; **~ of life** Lebensbereich, *der;* **~ of influence** Einflußbereich, *der;* b) *(Geom.)* Kugel, *die;* c) *(heavenly body)* Sphäre, *die;* **music/harmony of the ~s** Sphärenmusik/-harmonie, *die*

spherical ['sferıkl] *adj.* a) *(globular)* kugelförmig; b) *(Math.)* sphärisch

sphincter ['sfıŋktə(r)] *n. (Anat.)* Sphinkter, *der (fachspr.);* Schließmuskel, *der*

sphinx [sfıŋks] *n.* Sphinx, *die*

sphinxlike ['sfıŋkslaık] *adj.* sphinxhaft; **she gave a ~ smile** sie lächelte wie eine Sphinx

spica ['spaıkə] *n.* a) *(Bot.)* Ähre, *die;* b) *(Med.)* Spica, *die*

spice [spaıs] **1.** *n.* a) Gewürz, *das; (collectively)* Gewürze *Pl.; attrib.* Gewürz-; **dealer in ~s** Gewürzhändler, *der;* b) *(fig.: excitement);* Würze, *die;* **the ~ of life** die Würze des Lebens. **2.** *v.t.* würzen; **a ~d account** *(fig.)* ein ausgeschmückter Bericht; **a book ~d with humour** *(fig.)* ein mit Humor gewürztes Buch

'spice-rack *n.* Gewürzregal, *das*

spicily ['spaısılı] *adv.* mit Würze

spiciness ['spaısınıs] *n., no pl.* Würze, *die*

spick [spık] *adj.* **~ and span** blitzblank *od.* -sauber *(ugs.)*

spicy ['spaısı] *adj.* a) pikant; würzig; b) *(racy)* pikant; **~ things** Pikanterien *Pl.*

spider ['spaıdə(r)] *n.* Spinne, *die; (~-like creature)* Spinnentier, *das;* **~ and fly** *(fig.)* Raubtier und Beute

spider: ~ crab *n.* See- *od.* Meeresspinne, *die;* **~-man** *n. Bauarbeiter, der auf Gerüsten in großer Höhe arbeitet;* **~ monkey** *n.* Klammeraffe, *der;* **~ plant** *n.* Grünlilie, *die;* **~'s web** *(Amer.:* **~ web)** Spinnennetz, *das; (fig.)* Netz, *das*

spidery ['spaıdərı] *adj.* spinnenförmig; krakelig *(ugs.)* ‹*Schrift*›; **~ legs** Spinnenbeine

spiel [spi:l] *(sl.)* **1.** *n.* Sermon, *der (ugs.); (excuse)* Story, *die;* **don't give me all that ~:** erzähl mir doch nichts! **2.** *v.i. (Amer.)* schwadronieren; labern *(salopp)*

~ 'off *v.t. (Amer. sl.)* **he can ~ off answers to 250 questions** er kann Antworten auf 250 Fragen herunterrasseln *(ugs.)*

spiffing ['spıfıŋ] *adj. (arch. coll.)* ausgezeichnet; famos *(ugs. veralt.)*

spigot ['spıgət] *n.* Zapfen, *der*

¹spike [spaık] **1.** *n.* a) Stachel, *der; (of running-shoe)* Spike, *der;* b) *in pl. (shoes)* Spikes *Pl.;* c) *(large nail)* großer Nagel; *(Railw.)* Schienennagel, *der;* d) *(for holding papers)* Zettelspieß, *der.* **2.** *v.t.* a) mit [großen] Nägeln befestigen ‹*Schiene*›; mit Spikes versehen ‹*Schuhe*›; **~ sb.'s guns** *(fig.)* jmdm. einen Strich durch die Rechnung machen *(ugs.);* b) *(coll.: add spirits or drugs to)* **sb. ~d his drink** jmd. hat ihm etwas in seinen Drink getan; **~ coffee with cognac/spirits with LSD** Cognac in den Kaffee/LSD in den Schnaps tun

²spike *n. (Bot.)* Ähre, *die*

spike 'heel *see* **stiletto b**

spikelet ['spaıklıt] *n. (Bot.)* Ährchen, *das*

spiky ['spaıkı] *adj.* a) *(like a spike)* spitz [zulaufend]; stachelig ‹*Haare*›; b) *(having spikes)* stach[e]lig; c) *(coll.: easily offended) see* **prickly b**

¹spill [spıl] **1.** *v.t.,* **spilt** [spılt] *or* **~ed** a) verschütten ‹*Flüssigkeit*›; **~ sth. on sth.** etw. auf etw. *(Akk.)* schütten; **~ [sb.'s] blood** [jmds.] Blut vergießen; b) *(sl.: divulge)* ausquatschen *(salopp);* **~ the beans [to sb.]** [jmdm. gegenüber] aus der Schule plaudern; **not ~ the beans [to sb.]** [jmdm. gegenüber] dichthalten *(ugs.). See also* **milk 1. 2.** *v.i.,* **spilt** *or* **~ed** überlaufen. **3.** *n. (fall)* Sturz, *der;* **have/take a ~:** stürzen

~ 'over *v.i.* überlaufen; *(fig.)* überquellen; ‹Unruhen:› sich ausbreiten; *(develop into something else)* umschlagen

²spill *n. (for lighting)* Fidibus, *der*

spillage ['spılıdʒ] *n.* a) *(act)* Verschütten, *das;* **~ of oil** *(from tanker)* das Auslaufen von Öl; b) *(quantity)* Verschüttete, *das;* **there was little ~:** es wurde wenig verschüttet; *(from tanker)* es lief wenig Öl aus

spillikins ['spılıkınz] *n. sing.* Mikado, *das*

'spillway *n.* Überfall, *der*

spilt *see* **¹spill 1, 2**

spin [spın] **1.** *v.t.,* **-nn-, spun** [spʌn] a) spinnen; **~ yarn** Garn spinnen; **~ a yarn** *(fig.)* ein Garn spinnen *(bes. Seemannsspr.);* fabulieren; b) *(in washing-machine etc.)* schleudern; c) *(cause to whirl round)* [schnell] drehen; wirbeln [lassen]; **~ a top** kreiseln; **~ a coin** eine Münze kreiseln lassen; *(toss)* eine Münze werfen; d) *(Sport: impart ~ to)* Effet *od.* Spin geben *(+ Dat.)* ‹*Ball*›. **2.** *v.i.,* **-nn-, spun** sich drehen; **my**

head is ~ning *(fig.) (from noise)* mir brummt der Schädel *(ugs.); (from too much work)* ich weiß nicht [mehr], wo mir der Kopf steht; *(from many impressions)* mir schwirrt der Kopf. **3.** *n.* **a)** *(whirl)* **give sth. a ~:** etw. in Drehung versetzen; **give the washing a [short] ~:** die Wäsche [kurz] schleudern; **the decision rested on the ~ of a coin** die Entscheidung sollte durch das Werfen einer Münze herbeigeführt werden; **b)** *(Aeronaut.)* Trudeln, *das; see also* **flat spin; c)** *(Sport: revolving motion)* Effet, *der;* Spin, *der;* **d)** *(outing)* **go for a ~:** einen Ausflug machen; **a ~ in the car** eine Spritztour mit dem Auto; **e)** *(Phys.)* Spin, *der*

~ 'out *v. t.* **a)** *(prolong)* in die Länge ziehen; **b)** *(use sparingly)* **~ one's money out until pay-day** sein Geld bis zum Zahltag strecken; **he spun out his glass of whisky** er trank lange an seinem Glas Whisky

~ 'round 1. *v. i.* sich drehen; ‹*Person:*› sich [schnell] umdrehen. **2.** *v. t.* [schnell] drehen

spina bifida [spaɪnə 'bɪfɪdə] *n. (Med.)* Spina bifida, *die (fachspr.);* Spaltwirbel, *der*

spinach ['spɪnɪdʒ] *n.* **a)** Spinat, *der;* **b)** *(Amer. coll.: inessential decoration)* Schnickschnack, *der (ugs.)*

spinal ['spaɪnl] *adj. (Anat.)* Wirbelsäulen-; Rückgrat[s]-; *see also* **marrow b**

spinal: ~ 'column *n.* Wirbelsäule, *die;* **~ 'cord** *n.* Rückenmark, *das*

'spin bowler *n. (Cricket)* Werfer, der Spins wirft

spindle ['spɪndl] *n.* **a)** Spindel, *die;* **b)** *(pin bearing bobbin)* Spulenhalter, *der*

spindle: ~-shanks *n. sing.* **be a ~-shanks** spindeldürre Beine haben; **~-shaped** *adj.* spindelförmig

spindly ['spɪndlɪ] *adj.* spindeldürr ‹*Person, Beine, Arme*›

spin-'drier *n.* Wäscheschleuder, *die*

'spindrift *n.* Gischt, *der od. die*

spin-'dry *v. t.* schleudern

spine [spaɪn] *n.* **a)** *(backbone)* Wirbelsäule, *die;* **b)** *(Bot., Zool.)* Stachel, *der;* **c)** *(fig.: source of strength)* Rückgrat, *das;* **d)** *(of book)* Buchrücken, *der;* **e)** *(ridge)* [Gebirgs]grat, *der*

spine: ~-chiller *n.* Schocker, *der (ugs.);* **this film is a ~-chiller** bei diesem Film läuft es einem eiskalt den Rücken herunter *(ugs.);* **~-chilling** *adj.* gruselig

spineless ['spaɪnlɪs] *adj.* **a)** *(fig.)* rückgratlos; **b)** *(Zool.: without spines)* ‹*Fisch*› ohne Flossenstrahlen

spinelessly ['spaɪnlɪslɪ] *adv.* **give in/surrender ~:** so rückgratlos sein und nachgeben/ sich ergeben

spinet [spɪ'net, 'spɪnɪt] *n. (Mus. Hist.)* Spinett, *das*

spinnaker ['spɪnəkə(r)] *n. (Naut.)* Spinnaker, *der*

spinner ['spɪnə(r)] *n.* **a)** *(Cricket)* Werfer, der Spins wirft; **b)** *(spin-drier)* Wäscheschleuder, *die;* **c)** *(manufacturer engaged in spinning)* Spinner, *der*/Spinnerin, *die*

spinneret ['spɪnəret] *n.* **a)** *(Zool.)* Spinndrüse, *die;* **b)** *(Textiles)* Spinndüse, *die*

spinney ['spɪnɪ] *n. (Brit.)* Gehölz, *das*

spinning ['spɪnɪŋ] *n.* Spinnen, *das*

spinning: ~ jenny *n.* Jenny-[Spinn]maschine, *die;* **~-top** *n.* Kreisel, *der;* **~-wheel** *n.* Spinnrad, *das*

'spin-off *n.* Nebenprodukt, *das*

spinster ['spɪnstə(r)] *n.* **a)** ledige Frau; Junggesellin, *die;* **remain a ~:** ledig bleiben; **b)** *(derog.: old maid)* alte Jungfer *(abwertend)*

spinsterhood ['spɪnstəhʊd] *n., no pl.* Ledigsein, *das*

spiny ['spaɪnɪ] *adj.* dornig; stachelig

spiny 'lobster *n.* Languste, *die*

spiraea [spaɪə'ri:ə] *n. (Bot.)* Spierstrauch, *der*

spiral ['spaɪrl] **1.** *adj.* spiralförmig; spiralig; **~ spring** Spiralfeder, *die.* **2.** *n.* Spirale, *die;* **the ~ of rising prices and wages** die Lohn-Preis-Spirale. **3.** *v. i. (Brit.)* **-ll-** ‹*Weg:*› sich hochwinden; ‹*Kosten, Profite:*› in die Höhe klettern; ‹*Rauch:*› in einer Spirale aufsteigen

spirally ['spaɪrəlɪ] *adv.* spiralig; spiralförmig

spiral: ~ 'nebula *n. (Astron.)* Spiralnebel, *der;* **~ 'staircase** *n.* Wendeltreppe, *die*

spirant ['spaɪrənt] *(Phonet.)* **1.** *adj.* spirantisch. **2.** *n.* Spirant, *der (fachspr.);* Reibelaut, *der*

spire [spaɪə(r)] *n.* Turmspitze, *die*

spirit ['spɪrɪt] **1.** *n.* **a)** *in pl. (distilled liquor)* Spirituosen *Pl.;* **tax on ~s** Alkoholsteuer, *die;* **b)** *(mental attitude)* Geisteshaltung, *die;* **in the right/wrong ~:** mit der richtigen/ falschen Einstellung; **take sth. in the wrong ~:** etw. falsch auffassen; etw. in den falschen Hals kriegen *(ugs.);* **take sth. in the ~ in which it is meant** etw. so auffassen, wie es gemeint ist; **as the ~ takes/moves one** wie man gerade Lust hat; **do sth. in a ~ of mischief** etw. in böser Absicht tun ; **enter into the ~ of sth.** innerlich bei einer Sache [beteiligt] sein *od.* dabeisein; **'that's the ~!** das ist die richtige Einstellung!; **c)** *(courage)* Mut, *der;* **play with ~:** mit ganzer Seele spielen; **d)** *(vital principle, soul, inner qualities)* Geist, *der;* **the ~ is willing but the flesh is weak** der Geist ist willig, aber das Fleisch ist schwach; **give up one's ~:** seinen Geist *od.* seine Seele aushauchen *(geh. verhüll.);* **in [the] ~:** innerlich; im Geiste; **be with sb. in ~:** in Gedanken od. im Geist[e] bei jmdm. sein; **the poor in ~** *(arch.)* die Armen im Geiste; **e)** *(person supplying energy)* treibende Kraft; Motor, *der (fig.);* **f)** *(real meaning)* Geist, *der;* Sinn, *der;* **follow the ~ of the instructions** die Anweisungen sinngemäß ausführen; **obey the letter but not the ~ of the law** dem Buchstaben, nicht dem Geist[e] des Gesetzes gehorchen; **g)** *(mental tendency)* Geist, *der;* *(mood)* Stimmung, *die;* **the ~ of the age** *or* **times** der Zeitgeist; **h) high ~s** gehobene Stimmung; gute Laune; **in high** *or* **great** *or* **good ~s** in gehobener Stimmung; gut gelaunt; **in poor** *or* **low ~s** niedergedrückt; **i)** *(liquid got by distillation)* Spiritus, *der;* **j)** *(purified alcohol)* reiner Alkohol; **k)** *(solution in alcohol)* Geist, *der;* Spiritus, *der;* **~[s] of wine** *(arch.)* Weingeist, *der.* **2.** *v. t.* **~ away, ~ off** verschwinden lassen; **be ~ed away** *or* **off** verschwinden

spirited ['spɪrɪtɪd] *adj.* **a)** *(lively)* lebendig ‹*Übersetzung, Vortrag*›; beherzt ‹*Angriff, Versuch, Antwort, Verteidigung*›; lebhaft ‹*Antwort*›; **b) low/proud-~:** niedergedrückt/stolz; **high-~:** ausgelassen; temperamentvoll ‹*Pferd*›; **mean-~:** gemein

spiritedly ['spɪrɪtɪdlɪ] *adv.* lebendig ‹*schreiben*›; vehement ‹*ablehnen*›

'spirit lamp *n.* Spirituslampe, *die*

spiritless ['spɪrɪtlɪs] *adj.* dumpf ‹*Person*›; stumpfsinnig ‹*Apathie*›

'spirit-level *n.* Wasserwaage, *die*

spiritual ['spɪrɪtʃʊəl] **1.** *adj.* **a)** spirituell *(geh.);* **a ~ relationship** eine platonische *(geh.)* Beziehung; **his ~ home** seine geistige Heimat; **b)** *(concerned with religion)* geistlich; **lords ~** *(Brit. Parl.) Bischöfe und Erzbischöfe im britischen Oberhaus.* **2.** *n.* **[Negro] ~:** [Negro] Spiritual, *das*

spiritualism ['spɪrɪtʃʊəlɪzm] *n.* **a)** *(belief in contact with spirits)* Spiritismus, *der;* **b)** *(system of doctrines)* Spiritualismus, *der*

spiritualist ['spɪrɪtʃʊəlɪst] *n.* Spiritist, *der*/ Spiritistin, *die*

spirituality [spɪrɪtʃʊ'ælɪtɪ] *n., no pl.* Spiritualität, *die (geh.)*

spiritually ['spɪrɪtʃʊəlɪ] *adv.* spirituell; **~ minded** vergeistigt ‹*Person*›

spirt *see* **[2]spurt**

[1]spit [spɪt] **1.** *v. i.,* **-tt-, spat** [spæt] *or* **spit a)** spucken; **he spat in his enemy's face** er spuckte seinem Feind ins Gesicht; **it makes you [want to] ~:** es kann einen auf die Palme bringen *(ugs.);* **b)** *(make angry noise)* fauchen; **~ at sb.** jmdn. anfauchen; **c)** *(rain lightly)* **~ [down]** tröpfeln *(ugs.);* **d)** *(throw out sparks)* ‹*Feuer:*› Funken sprühen; ‹*Öl:*› spritzen. **2.** *v. t.,* **-tt-, spat** *or* **spit a)** spucken; **~ sth. at sb.** mit etw. nach jmdm. spucken; **b)** *(fig.: utter angrily)* **~ defiance at sb.** jmdn. trotzig anfauchen. **3.** *n.* **a) [dead** *or* **very] ~ [and image]** *(coll.) see* **spitting image; b)** *(spittle)* Spucke, *die;* **~ and polish** *(cleaning work)* Putzen und Reinigen; Wienern, *das;* **all that ~ and polish in the army** das ewige Putzen und Wienern in der Armee

~ 'out *v. t.* **~ sth. out** etw. ausspucken; **~ out curses at sb.** jmdm. die Flüche nur so ins Gesicht spucken; **she spat out the words** sie spuckte die Worte nur so aus; **~ it out!** *(fig. coll.)* spuck es aus! *(ugs.)*

[2]spit 1. *n.* **a)** *(point of land)* Halbinsel, *die;* **b)** *(reef)* Riff, *das;* *(shoal)* Untiefe, *die;* *(sandbank)* Sandbank, *die;* **c)** *(for roasting meat)* Spieß, *der.* **2.** *v. t.,* **-tt-** *(pierce)* [auf]spießen

[3]spit *n. (spade-depth)* Spatentiefe, *die*

'spitball *n. (Amer.: pellet)* [mit Speichel getränktes] Papierkügelchen

spite [spaɪt] **1.** *n.* **a)** *(malice)* Boshaftigkeit, *die;* **do sth. from** *or* **out of ~:** etw. aus Boshaftigkeit tun; **b) in ~ of** trotz; **in ~ of oneself** obwohl man es eigentlich nicht will; wider *od.* gegen seinen [eigenen] Willen. **2.** *v. t.* ärgern; **cut off one's nose to ~ one's face** sich *(Dat. od. Akk.)* ins eigene Fleisch schneiden

spiteful ['spaɪtfl] *adj.,* **spitefully** ['spaɪtfəlɪ] *adv.* boshaft; gehässig *(abwertend)*

'spitfire *n.* Giftspritze, *die (ugs. abwertend)*

spitting 'image *n.* **be the ~ of sb.** jmdm. wie aus dem Gesicht geschnitten sein

spittle ['spɪtl] *n.* Spucke, *die;* Speichel, *der*

spittoon [spɪ'tu:n] *n.* Spucknapf, *der*

spiv [spɪv] *n. (Brit. sl.)* **a)** *(person living by his wits)* smarter kleiner Geschäftemacher; **b)** *(black-market dealer)* Schwarzhändler, *der;* Schieber, *der (ugs.)*

splash [splæʃ] **1.** *v. t.* **a)** spritzen; **~ sb./sth. with sth.** jmdn./etw. mit etw. bespritzen; **~ sth. on [to]** *or* **over sb./sth.** jmdn./etw. mit etw. bespritzen; etw. auf jmdn./etw. spritzen; **~ sth. about** etw. herumspritzen *(ugs.);* **sth. gets ~ed on sth.** etw. spritzt auf etw. *(Akk.);* **b)** *(Journ.: display prominently)* als Aufmacher bringen ‹*Story usw.*›; **be ~ed all over the front page** auf der ersten Seite groß aufgemacht sein *(ugs.);* **c)** *(with scattered colour)* sprenkeln. **2.** *v. i.* **a)** *(fly about in drops)* spritzen; **b)** *(cause liquid to fly about)* [umher]spritzen; **c)** *(move with ~ing)* platschen *(ugs.).* **3.** *n.* **a)** Spritzen, *das;* **hit the water with a ~:** ins Wasser platschen *(ugs.);* **make a [big] ~** *(fig.)* Furore machen; **b)** *(liquid)* Spritzer, *der;* **c)** *(noise)* Plätschern, *das;* **d)** *(prominent display of news etc.)* **get a front-page ~:** der Aufmacher auf der Titelseite sein; **e)** *(coll.: dash)* Schuß [Sodawasser]; **whisky and a ~ of ginger-ale** Whisky mit einem Schuß Ingwerbier; **f)** *(spot of dirt etc.)* Spritzer, *der;* **g)** *(patch of colour)* Tupfer, *der*

~ a'bout *v. i.* herumspritzen *(ugs.);* [herum]planschen

~ 'down *v. i.* wassern; *see also* **splash-down**

~ 'out *v. i. (coll.)* **~ out on sth.** für etw. unbekümmert Geld ausgeben

splash: ~back *n. Wandverkleidung zum Schutz vor Spritzern;* **~-down** *n.* Wasserung, *die*

splatter ['splætə(r)] **1.** *v. i.* ‹*Bach:*› plätschern; ‹*Blut:*› spritzen. **2.** *v. t.* bespritzen. **3.** *n.* Plätschern, *das*

splay [spleɪ] **1.** *v. t.* **a)** *(spread)* **~ [out]** spreizen; **b)** *(construct with divergent sides)* ausschrägen. **2.** *v.i.* ‹*Linien:*› [schräg] auseinanderlaufen; ‹*Tischbeine, Stuhlbeine:*› schräg nach außen gehen; ‹*Finger, Zehen:*› gespreizt sein; ‹*Räder:*› schräg zueinander stehen. **3.** *n.* Ausschrägung, *die.* **4.** *adj.* gespreizt

splay: ~-foot 1. *n.* Spreizfuß, *der;* **2.** *adj. see* **~-footed; ~-footed** *adj.* spreizfüßig

spleen [spli:n] *n.* **a)** *(Anat.)* Milz, *die;* **b)** *(bad mood)* schlechte Laune; Übellaunigkeit, *die; (anger, rage)* Wut, *die;* **vent one's ~ [on sb.]** seine schlechte Laune/Wut [an jmdm.] abreagieren

splendid ['splendɪd] *adj. (excellent, outstanding)* großartig; *(beautiful)* herrlich; *(sumptuous, magnificent)* prächtig; **live in ~ isolation** von der Außenwelt abgeschirmt leben; **cut a ~ figure** imposant aussehen

splendidly ['splendɪdlɪ] *adv. (excellently, outstandingly)* großartig; *(sumptuously, magnificently)* prächtig; **live ~:** prunkvoll leben; **get along ~ with sb.** bestens mit jmdm. auskommen; **this flat will suit you ~:** diese Wohnung ist genau das Richtige für Sie

splendiferous [splen'dɪfərəs] *adj. (coll.)* prachtvoll

splendour *(Brit.; Amer.:* **splendor***)* ['splendə(r)] *n.* **a)** *(magnificence)* Pracht, *die;* **b)** *(brightness)* Glanz, *der*

splenetic [splɪ'netɪk] *adj.* mürrisch; unwirsch

splice [splaɪs] **1.** *v.t.* **a)** *(join ends of by interweaving)* verspleißen *(Seemannsspr.);* **b)** *(join in overlapping position)* [an den Enden überlappend] zusammenfügen; zusammenkleben ‹*Filmstreifen usw.*›; **~ a scene into a film** eine Szene in einen Film einschneiden; **c) get ~d** *(coll.: get married)* sich verehelichen. *See also* **main brace. 2.** *n.* Spleiß, *der (Seemannsspr.)*

splint [splɪnt] **1.** *n.* Schiene, *die;* **put sb.'s arm in a ~:** jmds. Arm schienen. **2.** *v.t.* schienen

splinter ['splɪntə(r)] **1.** *n.* Splitter, *der.* **2.** *v.i.* **a)** *(become split into long pieces)* splittern; **~ away from sth.** von etw. absplittern; **b)** *(fig.: split into factions)* sich aufsplittern. **3.** *v.t. (also fig.: split into factions)* zersplittern

splinter: ~ group *n.* Splittergruppe, *die;* **~ party** *n.* Splitterpartei, *die;* **~-proof** *adj.* splittersicher

splintery ['splɪntərɪ] *adj.* splitterig

split [splɪt] **1.** *n.* **a)** *(tear)* Riß, *der;* **b)** *(division into parts)* [Auf]teilung, *die;* **c)** *(fig.: rift)* Spaltung, *die;* **a ~ between Moscow and her allies** ein Bruch zwischen Moskau und seinen Verbündeten; **d)** *(Gymnastics, Skating)* **the ~s** *or (Amer.)* **~:** Spagat, *der od. das;* **do the ~s** Spagat machen; in den Spagat gehen. *See also* **banana split. 2.** *adj.* gespalten; **~ lip** aufgeplatzte Lippe; **~ decision** *(Boxing)* nicht einstimmige Entscheidung; **be ~ on a question** [sich *(Dat.)*] in einer Frage uneins sein; **be ~ down the middle** in zwei Lager gespalten sein; *see also* **pin 1 b. 3.** *v.t.,* **-tt-, split a)** *(tear)* zerreißen; **b)** *(divide)* teilen; spalten ‹*Holz*›; **let's ~ the money between us** laßt uns das Geld unter uns aufteilen; **~ persons/things into groups** Personen/Dinge in Gruppen *(Akk.)* aufteilen *od.* einteilen; **they ~ a bottle of wine** sie teilen/teilten sich *(Dat.)* eine Flasche Wein; **~ the difference** sich in der Mitte treffen; **~ hairs** *(fig.)* Haare spalten; **c)** *(divide into disagreeing parties)* spalten; **~ the ticket** *or* **one's vote** *(Amer. Polit.)* splitten; **d)** *(remove by breaking)* **~ [off** *or* **away]** abbrechen; **e)** *(Phys.)* spalten ‹*Atom*›. *See also* **side 1 d. 4.** *v.i.,* **-tt-, split a)** *(break into parts)* ‹*Holz:*› splittern; ‹*Stoff, Seil:*› reißen; **b)** *(divide into parts)* sich teilen; ‹*Gruppe:*› sich spalten; ‹*zwei Personen:*› sich trennen; **c)** *(be removed by breaking)* **~ from** absplittern von; **~ apart** zersplittern; **d)** *(sl.: betray secrets)* auspacken *(ugs.);* quatschen *(ugs.);* **e)** *(sl.: depart)* abhauen *(ugs.)*

~ a'way *v.i.* absplittern; **~ away from** absplittern von; ‹*Parteiflügel, Gruppierung:*› sich abspalten von

~ 'off 1. *v.t.* abspalten. **2.** *v.i. see* **~ away**

~ on *v.t. (sl.)* **~ on sb. [to sb.]** jmdn. [bei jmdm.] verpfeifen *(ugs.)*

~ 'open 1. *v.i.* aufbrechen. **2.** *v.t.* öffnen ‹*Nuß, Schote*›; **he ~ his head open** er hat sich *(Dat.)* den Kopf aufgeschlagen

~ 'up 1. *v.t.* aufteilen. **2.** *v.i. (coll.)* sich trennen; **~ up with sb.** sich von jmdm. trennen; mit jmdm. Schluß machen *(ugs.)*

~ with *v.i. (coll.)* brechen mit

split: ~ in'finitive *n. (Ling.) Konstruktion im Englischen, bei der zwischen Infinitivkonjunktion und Infinitiv ein Adverb eingeschoben wird;* **~-level** *adj.* mit Zwischengeschoß; auf zwei Ebenen; **a ~-level lounge** ein Wohnraum auf zwei Ebenen; **~-level cooker** *Einbauherd, bei dem Kochplatten und Backofen getrennt sind;* **~ 'pea** *n.* getrocknete [halbe] Erbse; **~ perso'nality** *n.* gespaltene Persönlichkeit *(Psych.);* **~ pin** *n.* Splint, *der;* **~ ring** *n.* Spaltring, *der;* **~ 'second** *n.* **in a ~ second** im Bruchteil einer Sekunde; **a ~ second from now** in einem Augenblick; **~-second timing** [zeitliche] Abstimmung auf die Sekunde genau; **~ 'shift** *n.* Teilschicht, *die;* **~ 'ticket** *n. (Amer. Polit.) Stimmzettel, auf dem mehrere Kandidaten verschiedener Parteien angekreuzt werden können*

splitting ['splɪtɪŋ] *adj.* **a ~ headache** rasende Kopfschmerzen; **sb.'s head is ~:** jmd. hat rasende Kopfschmerzen

splodge [splɒdʒ] *(Brit.) see* **splotch**

splosh [splɒʃ] *(coll.)* **1.** *n.* Platschen, *das (ugs.);* **there was a great ~:** es platschte *(ugs.)* laut. **2.** *v.i.* platschen *(ugs.).* **3.** *v.t. see* **splash 1 a**

splotch [splɒtʃ] **1.** *n.* Fleck, *der;* Klecks, *der.* **2.** *v.t.* **a)** *(daub)* verschmieren; **b)** *(make ~ on)* beklecksen

splurge [splɜ:dʒ] **1.** *n.* Wirbel, *der;* **go on a ~:** ein paar größere Anschaffungen machen; **~ of activity** Aktivitätsschub, *der.* **2.** *v.i. see* **splash out**

splutter ['splʌtə(r)] **1.** *v.i.* ‹*Feuer, Gaslampe:*› flackern; ‹*Fett:*› spritzen; ‹*Person:*› prusten; ‹*Motor:*› stottern; **~ with rage/indignation** vor Wut/Entrüstung schnauben. **2.** *v.t.* stottern ‹*Worte*›

spoil [spɔɪl] **1.** *v.t.,* **~t** [spɔɪlt] *or* **~ed a)** *(impair)* verderben; ruinieren ‹*Leben*›; **he always ~s a joke in the telling** wenn er einen Witz erzählt, verdirbt er immer die Pointe; **the news ~t his dinner/evening** die Nachricht verdarb ihm das Essen/den Abend; **~t ballot papers** ungültige Stimmzettel; *see also* **¹tar 1; b)** *(injure character of)* verderben *(geh.);* verziehen ‹*Kind*›; **~ sb. for sth.** jmdn. für etw. zu anspruchsvoll machen; *see also* **rod c; c)** *(pamper)* verwöhnen; **be ~t for choice** die Qual der Wahl haben. **2.** *v.i.,* **~t** *or* **~ed a)** *(go bad)* verderben; **b) be ~ing for a fight/for trouble** Streit/Ärger suchen. **3.** *n.* **a)** *(plunder)* **~[s]** Beute, *die;* **~s of war** Kriegsbeute, *die;* **b)** *(Mining etc.: waste material)* Abraum, *der*

spoiler ['spɔɪlə(r)] *n. (of car, aircraft)* Spoiler, *der; (of glider)* Bremsklappe, *die*

spoil: ~-sport *n.* Spielverderber, *der/*-verderberin, *die;* **~s system** *n. (Amer.) vom Gewinner einer Wahl betriebene Ämterpatronage*

spoilt 1. *see* **spoil 1, 2. 2.** *adj.* verzogen ‹*Kind*›

¹spoke [spəʊk] *n.* **a)** *(of wheel)* Speiche, *die;* **put a ~ in sb.'s wheel** *(fig.)* jmdm. einen Knüppel zwischen die Beine werfen; **b)** *see* **¹rung a**

²spoke, spoken *see* **speak**

'spokeshave *n.* Schabhobel, *der*

spokesman ['spəʊksmən] *n., pl.* **spokesmen** ['spəʊksmən] Sprecher, *der*

spokesperson ['spəʊkspɜ:sn] *n.* Sprecher, *der/*Sprecherin, *die*

spokeswoman ['spəʊkswʊmən] *n.* Sprecherin, *die*

spoliation [spəʊlɪ'eɪʃn] *n. (plunder)* Plünderung, *die; (of vessel)* Kaperung, *die*

spondee ['spɒndi:, 'spɒndɪ] *n. (Pros.)* Spondeus, *der*

sponge [spʌndʒ] **1.** *n.* **a)** Schwamm, *der;* **throw in the ~** *(Boxing)* das Handtuch werfen *od.* schmeißen; *(fig.)* das Handtuch werfen *(ugs.);* **b)** *see* **sponge-cake; sponge pudding; c)** *(Surg.)* Tupfer, *der;* **d)** *(porous metal)* Schwamm, *der;* **e) have a ~ down** sich mit dem Schwamm abwaschen; **give the chair a ~ down** den Stuhl [mit dem Schwamm] abwischen. **2.** *v.t.* **a)** *see* **cadge 1; b)** *(wipe)* mit einem Schwamm waschen

~ 'down *v.t.* mit einem Schwamm abwaschen

~ off *v.t.* **a)** [-'-] *(wipe off)* mit einem Schwamm abwischen; *(wash off)* mit einem Schwamm abwaschen; **b)** ['--] *see* **~ on**

~ on *v.t. (coll.)* **~ on sb.** bei *od.* von jmdm. schnorren *(ugs.)*

sponge: ~-bag *n. (Brit.)* Kulturbeutel, *der;* **~ biscuit** *n.* ≈ Biskotte, *die (Kochk.);* **~-cake** *n.* Biskuitkuchen, *der;* **~ 'pudding** *n.* Schwammpudding, *der (Kochk.); leichter, im Wasserbad zubereiteter Pudding*

sponger ['spʌndʒə(r)] *n.* Schmarotzer, *der/*Schmarotzerin, *die;* Schnorrer, *der/*Schnorrerin, *die*

sponge 'rubber *n.* Schaumgummi, *der*

spongy ['spʌndʒɪ] *adj.* schwammig

sponsor ['spɒnsə(r)] **1.** *n.* **a)** *(firm paying for event, one donating to charitable event)* Sponsor, *der;* **b)** *(of legislative proposal)* **the ~s of this Bill are Labour MPs** hinter dieser Gesetzesvorlage stehen Labour-Abgeordnete; **c)** *(group supporting candidate)* **his ~ is a trade union** er wird von einer Gewerkschaft unterstützt; **d)** *(godparent)* Pate, *der/*Patin, *die.* **2.** *v.t.* **a)** *(pay for)* sponsern ‹*Programm, Veranstaltung*›; **b)** *(subscribe to)* finanziell unterstützen, sponsern ‹*Wohlfahrtsverband*›; **c)** *(introduce for legislation)* einbringen ‹*Gesetzesvorlage*›; **d)** *(support)* unterstützen ‹*Kandidaten*›

sponsored ['spɒnsəd] *adj.* gesponsert; finanziell gefördert; **~ run** *als Wohltätigkeitsveranstaltung durchgeführter Dauerlauf mit gesponserten Teilnehmern*

sponsorship ['spɒnsəʃɪp] *n.* **a)** *(financial support)* **take over the ~ of sth.** etw. sponsern; **withdraw from the ~ of sth.** etw. nicht mehr sponsern; **b)** *(introduction of legislation)* Einbringen, *das;* **c)** *(support of candidate)* Unterstützung, *die*

spontaneity [spɒntə'ni:ɪtɪ] *n., no pl.* Spontan[e]ität, *die*

spontaneous [spɒn'teɪnɪəs] *adj.* spontan; **make a ~ offer of sth.** spontan etw. anbieten

spontaneous: ~ com'bustion *n.* Selbstentzündung, *die;* **~ gene'ration** *n.* Urzeugung, *die*

spontaneously [spɒn'teɪnɪəslɪ] spontan; von selbst ‹*passieren*›

spoof [spu:f] *(coll.)* **1.** *n.* Veralberung, *die* **(of, on** von); Parodie, *die* **(of, on** auf + *Akk.).* **2.** *v.t.* durch den Kakao ziehen *(ugs.)*

spook [spu:k] *n. (joc.)* Geist, *der;* Gespenst, *das; (sl.: spy)* Spion, *der;* **it gives me the ~s** es ist mir richtig unheimlich

spooky ['spu:kɪ] *adj.* gespenstisch

spool [spu:l] **1.** *n.* **a)** *(reel)* Spule, *die* ; **b)** *(Angling)* Trommel, *die.* **2.** *v.t.* spulen

¹spoon [spu:n] **1.** *n.* **a)** Löffel, *der;* **fruit-~:** Kompottlöffel, *der;* **be born with a silver ~ in one's mouth** mit einem goldenen *od.* sil-

bernen Löffel im Mund geboren werden; **wooden ~** *(fig.)* Trostpreis *(für den Letzten eines Wettbewerbs, oft in ironischer Weise überreicht)*; **b)** *(amount) see* **spoonful; c)** *(Angling)* Blinker, *der.* **2.** *v. t.* löffeln
~ **'up** *v. t.* auflöffeln
²spoon *v. i. (arch.: be amorous)* schmusen
'spoonbill *n. (Ornith.)* Löffler, *der*
spoonerism ['spu:nərɪzm] *n. witziges Vertauschen der Anfangsbuchstaben o. ä. von zwei oder mehr Wörtern (wie bei „Leichenzehrer" für „Zeichenlehrer")*
'spoon-feed *v. t.* mit dem Löffel füttern; **~ sb.** *(fig.)* jmdm. alles vorkauen *(ugs.)*
spoonful ['spu:nfʊl] *n.* **a ~ of sugar** ein Löffel [voll] Zucker
spoor [spʊə(r)] *n.* Spur, *die;* Fährte, *die*
sporadic [spə'rædɪk] *adj.* sporadisch; vereinzelt ‹*Schauer, Schüsse, Gebäude*›
sporadically [spə'rædɪkəlɪ] *adv.* hin und wieder
spore [spɔ:(r)] *n.* **a)** *(Bot.: cell)* Spore, *die;* **b)** *(Biol.: bacterium)* Spore, *die*
sporran ['spɒrən] *n. (Scot.) mit Fell besetzte Tasche, die von den Bewohnern der Highlands vorne über dem Kilt getragen wird*
sport [spɔ:t] **1.** *n.* **a)** *(pastime)* Sport, *der;* **~s** Sportarten; **team/winter/water/indoor ~:** Mannschafts-/Winter-/Wasser-/Hallensport, *der;* **b)** *no pl., no art. (collectively)* Sport, *der;* **go in for ~, do ~:** Sport treiben; **he likes doing ~ at school** er mag den Sport[unterricht] in der Schule; **have good ~** *(Hunting)* großes Jagdglück haben; **c)** *in pl. (Brit.)* **[athletic] ~s** Athletik, *die;* **S~s Day** *(Sch.)* Sportfest, *das;* **the ~s** der sportliche Wettkampf; **d)** *no pl., no art. (fun)* Spaß, *der;* **do/say sth. in ~:** etw. im *od.* zum Scherz tun/sagen; **make ~ of sb./sth.** sich über jmdn./etw. lustig machen; **e)** *(coll.: good fellow)* netter Kerl *(ugs.)*; *(Austral. as voc.: mate)* Kumpel! *(ugs.)*; Sportsmann! *(ugs.)*; **Aunt Joan is a real ~:** Tante Joan ist echt *(ugs.)* in Ordnung; **be a [good] ~ and help me** sei so nett und hilf mir; **be a good/bad ~** *(in games)* ein guter/schlechter Verlierer sein; **f)** *(Amer.: playboy)* Playboy, *der;* **g)** *(Zool., Bot.)* Variante, *die.* **2.** *v. t.* stolz tragen ‹*Kleidungsstück*›; protzen mit ‹*Neuerwerbung*›. **3.** *v. i.* **a)** *(amuse oneself)* sich tummeln; **b)** *(Biol.: mutate)* variieren
sporting ['spɔ:tɪŋ] *adj.* **a)** *(interested in sport)* sportlich; **b)** *(generous)* großzügig; *(fair)* fair; anständig; **do the ~ thing and do sth.** so anständig sein, etw. zu tun; **give sb. a ~ chance** jmdm. eine [faire] Chance geben; **c)** *(relating to sport)* Sport-; **~ dog/rifle** Jagdhund, *der*/Pirschbüchse, *die;* **~ giant** *or* **hero** Sportgröße, *die*
'sporting house *n. (Amer.)* Bordell, *das*
sportingly ['spɔ:tɪŋlɪ] *adv.* **a)** *(generously)* **~ do sth.** so großzügig sein, etw. zu tun; **b)** *(sportively)* in sportlichem Geist
sportive ['spɔ:tɪv] *adj.* verspielt ‹*junges Tier*›; ausgelassen ‹*Stimmung, Schar*›; **be in a ~ mood** zum Spielen aufgelegt sein
sports: ~ car *n.* Sportwagen, *der;* **~ commentator** *n. (Radio, Telev.)* Sportberichterstatter, *der*/-berichterstatterin, *die;* **~ editor** *n. (Journ.)* Sportredakteur, *der*/-redakteurin, *die;* **~ field** *n.* Sportplatz, *der;* **~ jacket** *n.* sportlicher Sakko; **~man** ['spɔ:tsmən] *n., pl.* **~men** ['spɔ:tsmən] **a)** Sportler, *der;* **b)** *(generous person)* großzügiger Mensch; *(fair-minded person)* anständiger Mensch; **c)** *(Hunting)* Jäger, *der*
sportsmanlike ['spɔ:tsmənlaɪk] *see* **sporting b**
sportsmanship ['spɔ:tsmənʃɪp] *n.* **a)** *(fairness)* [sportliche] Fairneß; **b)** *(skill)* sportliche Leistung
sports: ~ news *n. (Radio, Telev.)* Sportnachrichten; **~ page** *n. (Journ.)* Sportseite, *die;* **~ programme** *n. (Radio, Telev.)* Sportsendung, *die;* **~ section** *n. (Journ.)* Sportteil, *der;* **~wear** *n., no pl.* Sport[be]kleidung, *die;* **~woman** *n.* Sportlerin, *die*
sporty ['spɔ:tɪ] *adj.* **a)** *(coll.: sport-loving)* sportlich; **the whole family is ~:** die ganze Familie ist sportbegeistert; **b)** *(jaunty)* sportlich ‹*Aussehen*›; **wear one's hat at a ~ angle** seinen Hut flott aufgesetzt haben; **be a ~ dresser** sich sportlich kleiden; **c)** *(designed for sport)* Sport‹*boot, -wagen, -rad*›
spot [spɒt] **1.** *n.* **a)** *(precise place)* Stelle, *die;* **this is the precise/exact/very ~ where he landed** genau an dieser Stelle *od.* genau hier ist er gelandet; **on this ~:** an dieser Stelle; **the very same ~:** genau die gleiche Stelle; **in ~s** stellenweise; *(fig.: partly)* teilweise; **run on the ~:** auf der Stelle laufen; **on the ~** *(fig.) (instantly)* auf der Stelle; **be on the ~** *(be present)* zur Stelle sein; **and now over to our man on the ~** *(Radio, Telev.)* und nun schalten wir um zu unserem Mann am Ort des Geschehens; **be in/get into/get out of a [tight] ~** *(fig. coll.)* in der Klemme sitzen/in die Klemme geraten/sich aus einer brenzligen Lage befreien *(ugs.)*; **put sb. on the ~** *(fig. coll.: cause difficulties for sb.)* jmdn. in Verlegenheit bringen; *(Amer. sl.: decide to kill sb.)* jmdn. auf die Abschußliste setzen; **b)** *(inhabited place)* Ort, *der;* **a nice ~ on the Moselle** ein hübscher Flecken an der Mosel; **c)** *(suitable area)* Platz, *der;* **holiday/sun ~:** Ferienort, *der*/Ferienort [mit Sonnengarantie]; **picnic ~:** Picknickplatz, *der;* **a sheltered ~:** ein geschützter Platz; **a nice ~ to live** eine hübsche Wohngegend; **d)** *(dot)* Tupfen, *der;* Tupfer, *der;* *(larger)* Flecken, *der;* **change one's ~s** *(fig.)* aus seiner Haut herauskommen *(fig.)*; **knock ~s off sb.** *(fig. coll.)* jmdn. in die Pfanne hauen *(ugs.)*; **see ~s before one's eyes** Sterne sehen *(ugs.)*; **e)** *(stain)* **~ [of blood/grease/ink]** [Blut-/Fett-/Tinten]fleck, *der;* **f)** *(Brit. coll.: small amount)* **do a ~ of work/sewing** ein bißchen arbeiten/nähen; **how about a ~ of lunch?** wie wär's mit einem Bissen zu Mittag?; **a ~ of whisky** ein Schluck Whisky; **a ~ of culture** ein bißchen Kultur; **have** *or* **be in a ~ of bother** *or* **trouble** etwas Ärger haben; **be in a ~ of trouble with the law** Ärger mit der Polizei haben; **g)** *(drop)* **a ~** *or* **a few ~s of rain** ein paar Regentropfen; **h)** *(establishment)* **eating/drinking/entertainment ~:** Eß-/Trink-/Vergnügungslokal, *das;* **i)** *(area on body)* [Körper]stelle, *die;* **a tender/sore ~** *(lit.)* eine empfindliche/wunde Stelle; **a sore ~ with sb.** *(fig.)* jmds. neuralgischer Punkt; **have a weak ~** *(fig.)* eine Schwachstelle haben; *see also* **sore 1 a; j)** *(fig. coll.: job)* Job, *der (ugs.)*; **k)** *(Telev. coll.: position in programme)* Sendezeit, *die;* **the 7 o'clock ~:** das Siebenuhrprogramm; **l)** *(Med.)* Pickel, *der;* **heat ~:** Hitzebläschen, *das;* **break out in ~s** Ausschlag bekommen; **m)** *(on dice, dominoes)* Punkt, *der;* **n)** *(spotlight)* Spot, *der;* **o)** *(fig.: blemish)* Schandfleck, *der* *(emotional)*; **remain without a ~ on one's reputation** immer eine weiße Weste behalten *(ugs.)*; **p)** *(Sport: dot)* Aufsetzmarke, *die;* **the ~[-ball]** *(Billiards)* der Punktball; **the [penalty] ~:** die Elfmetermarke; der Elfmeterpunkt; **q)** *(Commerc.)* **~s, ~ goods** sofort lieferbare Ware; Lokoware, *die (fachspr.)*; **pay ~ cash** [sofort] bar zahlen. *See also* **blind spot; leopard; soft 1 c; ¹tender b. 2.** *v. t.,* **-tt- a)** *(detect)* entdecken; identifizieren ‹*Verbrecher*›; erkennen ‹*Gefahr*›; **it is easy to ~ an American among a group of tourists** man kann leicht feststellen, wer in einer Gruppe von Touristen Amerikaner ist; **b)** *(take note of)* erkennen ‹*Flugzeugtyp, Vogel, Talent*›; **go train-/plane-~ting** Zug-/Flugzeugtypen bestimmen; **c)** *(coll.: pick out)* tippen auf (+ *Akk.*) *(ugs.)* ‹*Sieger, Gewinner usw.*›; **d)** *(stain)* beflecken; *(with ink or paint)* beklecksen; *(with mud)* beschmutzen; **e)** *(Billiards etc.)* aufstellen; **f)** *(Mil.: locate)* orten. **3.** *v. i.,* **-tt-: it is ~ting with rain** es tröpfelt *(ugs.)*
spot: ~ 'check *n. (test made immediately)* sofortige Überprüfung **(on** *Gen.*); *(test made on randomly selected subject)* Stichprobe, *die;* **make** *or* **carry out a ~ check on sth.** etw. sofort stichprobenweise überprüfen; **~-check** *v. t.* stichprobenweise überprüfen; **~ height** *n. (Geog.)* Höhenangabe, *die;* **~ lamp** *n.* Spotlight, *das;* *(Motor Veh.)* Scheinwerfer, *der*
spotless ['spɒtlɪs] *adj.* **a)** *(unstained)* fleckenlos; **her house is absolutely ~** *(fig.)* ihr Haus ist makellos sauber; **clean sth. until it is ~:** etw. reinigen, bis man kein Stäubchen mehr findet; **b)** *(fig.: blameless)* mustergültig; untadelig ‹*Charakter*›
spotlessly ['spɒtlɪslɪ] *adv.* **~ clean/white** tadellos sauber/makellos weiß
spot: ~light 1. *n.* **a)** *(Theatre)* [Bühnen]scheinwerfer, *der;* **b)** *(Motor Veh.)* Scheinwerfer, *der;* **c)** *(fig.: attention)* **the ~light is on sb.** jmd. steht im Rampenlicht [der Öffentlichkeit]; **be in the ~light** im Rampenlicht [der Öffentlichkeit] stehen; **keep out of the ~light** sich von der Öffentlichkeit fernhalten; **2.** *v. t.,* **~lighted** *or* **~lit a)** *(Theatre)* [mit dem Scheinwerfer] anstrahlen; **b)** *(fig.: highlight)* in den Blickpunkt der Öffentlichkeit bringen; **~ market** *n. (Commerc.)* Spotmarkt, *der;* **~-'on** *(coll.)* **1.** *adj.* goldrichtig *(ugs.)*; **I was ~-on** ich lag genau richtig *(ugs.)*; **your estimate was ~-on** mit deiner Schätzung hast du ins Schwarze getroffen; **2.** *adv.* haargenau *(ugs.)*; **~-remover** *n.* Fleck[en]entferner, *der;* **~ 'survey** *n.* [Blitz]umfrage, *die*
spotted ['spɒtɪd] *adj.* **a)** gepunktet; **a blue dress/tie ~ with white** ein blaues Kleid mit weißen Tupfen/eine blaue Krawatte mit weißen Punkten; **b)** *(Zool.)* **~ woodpecker/hyena** Buntspecht, *der*/Tüpfelhyäne, *die*
spotted: ~ 'Dick *n. (Brit.: pudding)* Pudding mit getrockneten Früchten; **~ 'dog** *n.* **a)** *(coll.: Dalmatian)* Dalmatiner, *der;* **b)** *see* **~ Dick**
spotter ['spɒtə(r)] *n.* **~ [plane]** Erkundungsflugzeug, *das*
spotty ['spɒtɪ] *adj.* **a)** *(spotted)* gefleckt; *(stained)* fleckig; **b)** *(pimply)* picklig; **be ~:** viele Pickel haben; *(have a rash)* einen [starken] Ausschlag haben
spot: ~-weld 1. *v. t.* punktschweißen; **2.** *n.* Punktschweißung, *die;* **~-welding** *n.* Punktschweißen, *das*
spouse [spaʊz] *n.* [Ehe]gatte, *der*/-gattin, *die;* *(joc.)* Angetraute, *der/die;* Gemahl, *der*/Gemahlin, *die*
spout [spaʊt] **1.** *n.* **a)** *(tube)* Schnabel, *der;* *(of water-pump)* [Auslauf]rohr, *das;* *(of overflow)* Überlaufrohr, *das;* *(of tap)* Ausflußrohr, *das;* *(of gargoyle)* Speirohr, *das;* *(of fountain)* Spritzdüse, *die;* **be up the ~** *(sl.: pawned)* im Leihhaus sein; *(sl.: ruined)* im Eimer sein *(ugs.)*; *(Brit. sl.: pregnant)* ein Kind kriegen *(ugs.)*; **b)** *(chute)* Rutsche, *die.* **2.** *v. t.* **a)** *(discharge)* ausstoßen ‹*Wasser, Lava, Öl*›; **the wound ~s blood** aus der Wunde strömt Blut; **b)** *(declaim)* deklamieren ‹*Verse*›; *(rattle off)* herunterrasseln *(ugs.)* ‹*Zahlen, Fakten usw.*›; **~ compliments/remarks** mit Komplimenten/Bemerkungen um sich werfen; **~ nonsense** Unsinn verzapfen *(ugs.)*. **3.** *v. i.* **a)** *(gush)* schießen **(from** aus); **b)** *(declaim)* schwadronieren *(abwertend)*; schwafeln *(ugs. abwertend)*; **~ at sb.** jmdm. etwas vorpredigen *(ugs.)*
~ **'out** *v. i.* herausströmen; **~ out of sth.** aus etw. strömen
sprain [spreɪn] **1.** *v. t.* verstauchen; **~ one's ankle/wrist** sich *(Dat.)* den Knöchel/das Handgelenk verstauchen. **2.** *n.* Verstauchung, *die*
sprang *see* **spring 2, 3**

sprat [spræt] *n.* Sprotte, *die;* **set a ~ to catch a mackerel** *or* **herring** *or* **whale** *(fig.)* mit der Wurst nach dem Schinken *od.* der Speckseite werfen *(ugs.)*

sprawl [sprɔ:l] **1.** *n.* **a)** *(slump)* **lie in a ~:** ausgestreckt [da]liegen; **b)** *(straggle)* verstreute Ansammlung; **the city was one huge ~ over the map** die Stadt dehnte sich auf der Landkarte als riesiger Fleck aus; **the ~ of the handwriting across the page** die quer über die ganze Seite gezogene Handschrift; *see also* **urban. 2.** *v. i.* **a)** *(spread oneself)* sich ausstrecken; **b)** *(fall)* der Länge nach hinfallen; **send sb. ~ing** jmdn. zu Boden strecken *(geh.);* **c)** *(straggle)* sich ausbreiten. **3.** *v. t.* **a)** *(splay out)* ausstrecken; **be** *or* **lie ~ed in/on/over sth.** ausgestreckt in/auf/über etw. *(Dat.)* liegen; **b)** *(spread)* verstreuen; **~ words/letters across the page** Wörter/Buchstaben großzügig über die ganze Seite pinseln

~ a'bout *v. i.* sich herumflegeln *(ugs. abwertend)*

~ 'out *v. i.* **a)** *(stretch out)* sich ausstrecken; **b)** *(straggle)* sich hinziehen

sprawled out [sprɔ:ld 'aʊt] *adj.* ausgestreckt [liegend]

sprawling ['sprɔ:lɪŋ] *attrib. adj.* **a)** *(extended)* ausgestreckt [liegend]; **b)** *(falling)* der Länge nach hinfallend; **c)** *(straggling)* verstreut liegend ⟨*Gebäude*⟩; wuchernd ⟨*Großstadt*⟩; **d)** *(spidery)* ausladend, *(scrawled)* krakelig *(ugs.)* ⟨*Handschrift*⟩

¹spray [spreɪ] *n.* **a)** *(bouquet)* Strauß, *der;* **a ~ of roses** ein Strauß Rosen; **b)** *(branch)* Zweig, *der; (of palm or fern)* Wedel, *der;* **c)** *(brooch) Brosche in der Form eines kleinen Straußes od. Zweigs*

²spray 1. *v. t.* **a)** *(in a stream)* spritzen; *(in a mist)* sprühen ⟨*Parfum, Farbe, Spray*⟩; **they ~ed the general's car with bullets** sie durchsiebten den Wagen des Generals mit Kugeln; **b)** *(treat)* besprühen ⟨*Haar, Haut, Pflanze*⟩; spritzen ⟨*Nutzpflanzen*⟩; **the vandals ~ed the car with paint** die Rabauken besprühten das Auto mit Farbe. **2.** *v. i.* spritzen. **3.** *n.* **a)** *(drops)* Sprühnebel, *der;* **b)** *(liquid)* Spray, *der od. das;* **c)** *(container)* Spraydose, *die; (in gardening)* Spritze, *die;* **hair/throat ~:** Haar-/Rachenspray, *der od. das;* **perfume ~:** Parfümzerstäuber, *der*

~ on [to] *v. t.* **~ sth. on [to] sth.** etw. mit etw. besprühen

~ 'out *v. i.* heraussspritzen

'spray can *see* **aerosol a**

sprayer ['spreɪə(r)] *n.* **a)** *(person)* **[paint] ~:** Spritzlackierer, *der*/-lackiererin, *die;* **b)** *(tool)* Sprühgerät, *das; (in pest control, gardening)* Spritze, *die*

'spray-gun *n.* Spritzpistole, *die*

spread [spred] **1.** *v. t.*, **spread a)** ausbreiten ⟨*Tuch, Landkarte*⟩ **(on** auf + *Dat.***)**; streichen ⟨*Butter, Farbe, Marmelade*⟩; **the peacock ~ its tail** der Pfau schlug ein Rad; **the yacht ~ its sails** die Segel der Jacht blähten sich; **b)** *(cover)* **~ a roll with marmalade/butter** ein Brötchen mit Marmelade/Butter bestreichen; **the sofa was ~ with a blanket** auf dem Sofa lag eine Decke [ausgebreitet]; **c)** *(fig.: display)* **a magnificent view/meal was ~ before us** uns *(Dat.)* bot sich eine herrliche Aussicht/uns *(Dat.)* wurde ein herrliches Mahl aufgetragen; **d)** *(extend range of)* verbreiten; **drought has ~ famine to many areas** durch die Dürre breitete sich in vielen Gebieten eine Hungersnot aus; **e)** *(distribute)* verteilen; *(untidily)* verstreuen; streuen ⟨*Dünger*⟩; verbreiten ⟨*Zerstörung, Angst, Niedergeschlagenheit*⟩; **f)** *(make known)* verbreiten; **~ the word** *(tell news)* es weitersagen; *(coll.: pass on a message)* die Nachricht weitergeben; *(Relig.)* das Wort Gottes verkünden; **g)** *(separate)* ausbreiten ⟨*Arme*⟩; öffnen ⟨*Lippen*⟩; spreizen ⟨*Beine*⟩; *see also* **wing 1 a. 2.** *v. i.*, **spread a)** sich ausbreiten; **a smile/a blush ~ across** *or* **over his face** ein Lächeln breitete sich *(geh.)* über sein Gesicht/er wurde ganz rot im Gesicht; **margarine ~s easily** Margarine läßt sich leicht streichen; **~ing branches/trees** ausladende Äste/Bäume; **~ like wildfire** sich in *od.* mit Windeseile verbreiten; **b)** *(scatter, disperse)* sich verteilen; **the odour ~s through the room** der Geruch breitet sich im ganzen Zimmer aus; **c)** *(circulate)* ⟨*Neuigkeiten, Gerücht, Kenntnis usw.:*⟩ sich verbreiten. **3.** *n.* **a)** *(expanse)* Fläche, *die;* **we could see the whole ~ of the town** wir konnten das ganze Stadtgebiet überblicken; **b)** *(span) (of tree)* Kronendurchmesser, *der; (of wings)* Spann[weite], *die;* **an oak with a magnificent ~ of branches** eine Eiche mit einer prächtigen Baumkrone; **c)** *(breadth)* **have a wide ~** ⟨*Interessen, Ansichten:*⟩ breit gefächert sein; **a wide ~ of responsibility** ein großer Verantwortungsbereich; **d)** *(extension)* Verbreitung, *die; (of city, urbanization, poverty)* Ausbreitung, *die;* **e)** *(diffusion)* Ausbreitung, *die; (of learning, knowledge)* Verbreitung, *die;* Vermittlung, *die;* **f)** *(distribution)* Verteilung, *die;* **g)** *(coll.: meal)* Festessen, *das;* Schmaus, *der (veralt.);* **h)** *(paste)* Brotaufstrich, *der;* ⟨*Rindfleisch-, Lachs*⟩paste, *die;* ⟨*Käse-, Erdnuß-, Schokoladen*⟩krem, *die;* **i)** *(girth) see* **middle-aged; j)** *see* **bedspread; k)** *(Printing)* **the advertisement was a full-page/double-page ~:** die Anzeige war ganzseitig/doppelseitig; **l)** *(Amer. sl.: ranch)* Ranch, *die.* **4.** *v. refl.* **a)** *(stretch out)* sich ausstrecken; **b)** *(talk or write at length)* sich verbreiten

~ a'bout, ~ a'round *v. t.* **a)** *(convey)* verbreiten ⟨*Neuigkeiten, Gerücht usw.*⟩; **b)** *(strew)* verstreuen; ausstreuen ⟨*Samen*⟩

~ 'out 1. *v. t.* **a)** *(extend)* ausbreiten ⟨*Arme*⟩; **b)** *(space out)* verteilen ⟨*Soldaten, Tänzer, Pfosten*⟩; legen ⟨*Karten*⟩; ausbreiten ⟨*Papiere*⟩. **2.** *v. i.* sich verteilen; ⟨*Soldaten:*⟩ ausschwärmen

~ 'over 1. *v. t.* **~ sth. over a certain time** etw. über eine bestimmte Zeit ausdehnen; **the mortgage/repayment is ~ over twenty years** die Hypothek hat eine Laufzeit von zwanzig Jahren/die Rückzahlung wird [ratenweise] innerhalb von zwanzig Jahren geleistet. **2.** *v. i.* sich erstrecken über (+ *Akk.*); **~ over into** hineinreichen in (+ *Akk.*)

spread-'eagle *v. t.* **a)** *(tie)* an den ausgestreckten Armen und Beinen fesseln; **b)** *(flatten)* **the police ~d the suspect against the car** die Polizei ließ den Verdächtigen sich mit ausgestreckten Armen und Beinen gegen das Auto stellen; **lie** *or* **be ~d** ausgestreckt [da]liegen

spreader ['spredə(r)] *n.* Streugerät, *das;* **grit-~:** Splittstreuwagen, *der;* **manure/fertilizer-~:** Stallmist-/Düngerstreuer, *der*

'spreadsheet *n. (Computing)* Arbeitsblatt, *das*

spree [spri:] *n.* **a)** *(spell of spending)* Einkaufsorgie, *die (ugs.);* **go on a shopping ~:** ganz groß einkaufen gehen; **have a ~:** viel Geld ausgeben; **b) be/go out on the ~** *(coll.)* einen draufmachen *(ugs.)*

sprig [sprɪg] *n.* **a)** *(twig)* Zweig, *der;* **b)** *(ornament) Schmuck in der Form eines Zweiges;* **c)** *(young person)* Sproß, *der (scherzh.);* **d)** *(tack)* Stift, *der*

sprightly ['spraɪtlɪ] *adj.* munter

spring [sprɪŋ] **1.** *n.* **a)** *(season)* Frühling, *der;* **in ~ 1969, in the ~ of 1969** im Frühjahr 1969; **in early/late ~:** zu Anfang/Ende des Frühjahrs; **last/next ~:** letzten/nächsten Frühling; **full of the joys of ~** *(iron.)* aufgekratzt *(ugs.);* fröhlich; **~ weather/fashions/flowers** Frühlingswetter, *das*/Frühlingsmoden/-blumen; **in [the] ~:** im Frühling *od.* Frühjahr; **in the ~ of his/her life** *(literary)* im Frühling seines/ihres Lebens *(dichter.);* **b)** *(source, lit. or fig.)* Quelle, *die;* **c)** *(Mech.)* Feder, *die;* **~s** *(vehicle suspension)* Federung, *die;* **d)** *(jump)* Sprung, *der;* **make a ~ at sb./at an animal** sich auf jmdn./ein Tier stürzen; **make a ~ at sth.** auf etw. *(Akk.)* zuspringen; **e)** *(elasticity)* Elastizität, *die;* **the mattresses have no ~ in them** die Matratzen federn nicht; **walk with a ~ in one's step** mit beschwingten Schritten gehen; **put a ~ in[to] sb.'s step** jmds. Schritt beschwingen; **f)** *(recoil)* Zurückschnellen, *das;* **snap back with a ~:** zurückschnellen. **2.** *v. i.*, **sprang** [spræŋ] *or (Amer.)* **sprung** [sprʌŋ], **sprung a)** *(jump)* springen; **~ [up] from sth.** von etw. aufspringen; **~ at sb.'s throat** jmdm. an die Kehle springen; **the blood ~s to sb.'s cheeks** jmdm. schießt das Blut ins Gesicht; **~ to one's feet** aufspringen; **~ to sb.'s assistance/defence** jmdm. beispringen; **~ to life** *(fig.)* [plötzlich] zum Leben erwachen; **b)** *(arise)* entspringen **(from** *Dat.***)**; ⟨*Saat, Hoffnung:*⟩ keimen; ⟨*Bogen:*⟩ aufstreben *(geh.);* **~ to fame** über Nacht bekannt werden; **his actions ~ from a false conviction** seine Handlungen entspringen einer falschen Ansicht; **~ to mind** jmdm. einfallen; **c)** *(recoil)* **~ back into position** zurückschnellen; **~ to** *or* **shut** ⟨*Tür, Falle, Deckel:*⟩ zuschnappen; **d)** *(split)* zerbrechen; *(become warped)* sich verziehen; **~ from sth.** von etw. abbrechen. **3.** *v. t.*, **sprang** *or (Amer.)* **sprung, sprung a)** *(make known suddenly)* **~ a new idea/a proposal/a question on sb.** jmdn. mit einer neuen Idee/einem Vorschlag/einer Frage überfallen; **~ a surprise on sb.** jmdn. überraschen; **b)** *(cause to operate)* zünden ⟨*Mine*⟩; aufspringen lassen ⟨*Schloß*⟩; zuschnappen lassen ⟨*Falle*⟩; **c)** *(sl.: set free)* herausholen **(from** aus**)**; **d)** *(Hunting: rouse)* aufscheuchen **(from** aus**)**; **e)** *(split)* bersten lassen *(geh.);* **I've sprung my racket** mein Schläger ist gesprungen; **f)** *(provide with ~s)* federn; **be well sprung** gut gefedert sein

~ 'back *v. i.* zurückschnellen

~ from *v. t.* **a)** *(appear from)* [plötzlich] herkommen; **where did you ~ from?** wo kommst du so plötzlich her?; **b)** *(originate from)* herrühren von; ⟨*Person:*⟩ abstammen von; **he ~s from a country family** er stammt aus einer ländlichen Familie

~ 'up *v. i.* ⟨*Wind, Zweifel:*⟩ aufkommen; ⟨*Gebäude:*⟩ aus dem Boden wachsen; ⟨*Pflanze:*⟩ aus dem Boden schießen; ⟨*Organisation, Freundschaft:*⟩ entstehen

spring: ~ balance *n.* Federwaage, *die;* **~ bed** *see* **bed 1 a; ~ 'binder** *n.* Klemmappe, *die;* **~board** *n. (Sport; also fig.)* Sprungbrett, *das; (in circus)* Schleuderbrett, *das*

springbok ['sprɪŋbɒk] *n.* **a)** *(Zool.)* Springbock, *der;* **b)** *in pl.* **the S~s** *(Rugby)* die Südafrikaner; *Spitzname für Mitglieder südafrikanischer Rugby-/Cricketmannschaften*

spring: ~ 'cabbage *n.* Frühkohl, *der;* **~ 'chicken** *n.* **a)** *(fowl)* junges Hähnchen; **b)** *(fig.: person)* **be no ~ chicken** nicht mehr der/die Jüngste sein *(ugs.);* **~-'clean 1.** *n.* [großer] Hausputz; *(in spring)* Frühjahrsputz, *der;* **2.** *v. t.* **~-clean [the whole house]** [großen] Hausputz/Frühjahrsputz machen; **~-clip** *n.* Klammer, *die*

springer ['sprɪŋə(r)] *n.* **~ [spaniel]** Springerspaniel, *der*

spring: ~ gun *n. (Hunting)* Legbüchse, *die; (Mil.)* Selbstschuß, *der;* **~-loaded** *adj.* mit Sprungfeder *nachgestellt;* **~ 'mattress** *n.* Sprungfedermatratze, *die;* **~ 'onion** *n.* Frühlingszwiebel, *die;* **~ sus'pension** *n. (Motor Veh.)* federnde Aufhängung; **~ 'tide** *n.* Springflut, *die;* **~tide** *n. (literary)* Frühlingszeit, *die (geh.);* **~time** *n.* Frühling, *der;* **~ water** *n.* Quellwasser, *das*

springy ['sprɪŋɪ] *adj.* elastisch; federnd ⟨*Schritt, Brett, Boden*⟩

sprinkle ['sprɪŋkl] *v. t.* **a)** *(scatter)* streuen; sprengen ⟨*Flüssigkeit*⟩; **~ sth. over/on sth.** etw. über/auf etw. *(Akk.)* streuen/sprengen; ~ **sth. with sth.** etw. mit etw. bestreuen/besprengen; **b)** *(fig.: distribute)* verteilen; **c)** *(fall on)* spritzen auf (+ *Akk.*)

sprinkler ['sprɪŋklə(r)] *n.* **a)** *(Hort.: for watering)* Sprinkler, *der; (Agric.)* Regner, *der;* **b)** *(fire extinguisher)* ~**s**, ~ **system** Sprinkleranlage, *die*

sprinkling ['sprɪŋklɪŋ] *n.* **a ~ of snow/sugar/dust** eine dünne Schneedecke/Zucker-/Staubschicht; **a ~ of gold dust/rain** eine winzige Menge Goldstaub/ein paar Regentropfen; **there was only a ~ of holidaymakers on the beach** nur ein paar vereinzelte Urlauber waren am Strand

sprint [sprɪnt] **1.** *v. t. & i.* rennen; sprinten *(bes. Sport);* spurten *(bes. Sport);* ~ **for the line** *or* **tape** den Endspurt anziehen. **2.** *n.* **a)** *(race)* Sprint, *der (bes. Sport);* **the hundred-metres ~** *(competition)* der Hundertmeterlauf; **b)** *(fig.: short burst of speed)* Sprint, *der (bes. Sport);* Spurt, *der (bes. Sport);* **final ~:** Endspurt, *der*

sprinter ['sprɪntə(r)] *n.* Sprinter, *der*/Sprinterin, *die*

sprit [sprɪt] *n. (Naut.)* Spriet, *das*

sprite [spraɪt] *n.* [Elementar]geist, *der;* **a ~ of the air** ein Luftgeist

spritsail ['sprɪtseɪl, 'sprɪtsl] *n.* *(Naut.)* Sprietsegel, *das*

spritzer ['sprɪtsə(r)] *n. (Amer.)* Schorle, *die*

sprocket ['sprɒkɪt] *n. (Mech. Engin.)* Zahn, *der*

'**sprocket-wheel** *n. (Mech. Engin.)* [Ketten]zahnrad, *das*

sprog [sprɒg] *n. (sl.)* **a)** *(child)* Sprößling, *der;* **b)** *(trainee)* Stift, *der*

sprout [spraʊt] **1.** *n.* **a)** *in pl. (coll.) see* **Brussels sprouts; b)** *(Bot.) see* **shoot 3 a. 2.** *v. i.* **a)** *(lit. or fig.)* sprießen *(geh.);* ~ **into life** ⟨*Pflanzen:*⟩ sprießen [und blühen]; **b)** *(grow)* emporschießen; ⟨*Bart:*⟩ wachsen; **c)** *(fig.)* ⟨*Gebäude:*⟩ wie Pilze aus dem Boden schießen; **the garden is ~ing all over with flowers** im Garten schießen überall die Blumen empor. **3.** *v. t.* [aus]treiben ⟨*Blüten, Knospen*⟩; sich *(Dat.)* wachsen lassen ⟨*Bart*⟩; *(fig.)* aus dem Boden wachsen lassen ⟨*Gebäude*⟩; hervorbringen ⟨*Ideen*⟩; schaffen ⟨*Arbeitsplätze*⟩; **the young deer was ~ing antlers** dem jungen Rehbock wuchs das Geweih; **my chin is sprouting hairs** auf meinem Kinn wachsen [Bart]haare

spruce [spru:s] **1.** *adj.* gepflegt; **look ~:** adrett aussehen. **2.** *n. (Bot.)* Fichte, *die.* **3.** *v. t.* ~ **up** verschönern; ~ **the house up** das [ganze] Haus aufräumen und putzen; ~ **sb./oneself up [for sth.]** jmdn./sich [für etw.] zurechtmachen *(ugs.);* **get ~d up** sich feinmachen *(ugs.)*

sprucely ['spru:slɪ] *adv.* adrett ⟨*sich kleiden*⟩; **be ~ kept** sehr gepflegt sein

sprung [sprʌŋ] **1.** *see* **spring 2, 3. 2.** *attrib. adj.* gefedert

spry [spraɪ] *adj.* rege

spryly ['spraɪlɪ] *adv.* munter; **walk** *or* **move ~:** munteren Schrittes gehen

spud [spʌd] *n.* **a)** *(Brit. sl.: potato)* Kartoffel, *die;* **b)** *(spade)* Unkrautstecher, *der*

spud-bashing ['spʌdbæʃɪŋ] *n. (Brit. Mil. sl.)* Kartoffelschälen, *das*

spue *see* **spew**

spume [spju:m] **1.** *n.* Gischt, *die.* **2.** *v. i.* aufschäumen; gischten *(geh.)*

spun *see* **spin 1, 2**

spunk [spʌŋk] *n.* **a)** *(coll.: courage)* Mumm, *der (ugs.);* **b)** *(Brit. sl.: semen)* Samen, *der;* Soße, *die (vulg.)*

spunky ['spʌŋkɪ] *adj.* mutig; **he is very ~:** er hat viel Mumm in den Knochen *(ugs.)*

spur [spɜ:(r)] **1.** *n.* **a)** Sporn, *der;* **put** *or* **set ~s to one's horse** seinem Pferd die Sporen geben; **win one's ~s** *(Hist./fig.)* sich *(Dat.)* die [ersten] Sporen verdienen; **b)** *(fig.: stimulus)* Ansporn, *der* (to für); **act** *or* **serve as a ~ to sb. in sth.** jmdn. bei etw. anspornen; **on the ~ of the moment** ganz spontan; **c)** *(branch road)* Nebenstraße, *die;* **d)** *(Railw.: branch line)* Nebengleis, *das;* **e)** *(climbing-iron)* Steigeisen, *das;* **f)** *(Bot.: short branch)* Kurztrieb, *der;* kurzer Zweig. **2.** *v. t.,* **-rr- a)** *(prick)* die Sporen geben (+ *Dat.*); spornen *(veralt.);* **b)** *(fig.: incite)* anspornen; ~ **sb. [on] to sth./to do sth.** jmdn. zu etw. anspornen/anspornen, etw. zu tun; **c)** *(fig.: stimulate)* hervorrufen; in Gang setzen ⟨*Aktivität*⟩; erregen ⟨*Interesse*⟩. **3.** *v. i.,* **-rr-** das Pferd/die Pferde antreiben

~ '**on** *v. t.* anspornen; antreiben ⟨*Pferd*⟩; ⟨*Habgier:*⟩ treiben; *see also* ~ **2 b**

spurge [spɜ:dʒ] *n. (Bot.)* Wolfsmilch, *die*

'**spur-gear** *n. (Mech.)* Stirnrad, *das*

spurious ['spjʊərɪəs] *adj.* unaufrichtig ⟨*Charakter, Handlung, Verhalten*⟩; gespielt ⟨*Gefühl, Interesse*⟩; zweifelhaft ⟨*Anspruch, Vergnügen*⟩; falsch ⟨*Name, Münze*⟩; ~ **coins** Falschgeld, *das;* **be of ~ character/descent** einen unaufrichtigen Charakter haben/illegitimer Abstammung sein

spuriously ['spjʊərɪəslɪ] *adv.* fälschlicherweise

spurn [spɜ:n] *v. t. (reject)* zurückweisen; abweisen; ausschlagen ⟨*Angebot, Gelegenheit*⟩; sich entziehen (+ *Dat.*) ⟨*Realität, Umwelt*⟩; von sich weisen ⟨*Ansinnen*⟩

[1]**spurt** [spɜ:t] **1.** *n.* Spurt, *der (bes. Sport);* **final ~:** Endspurt, *der;* **there was a ~ of activity** es brach kurzzeitig lebhafte Aktivität aus; **in a sudden ~ of energy** in einem plötzlichen Anfall von Energie; **put on a ~:** einen Spurt einlegen. **2.** *v. i.* spurten *(bes. Sport)*

[2]**spurt 1.** *v. i.* ~ **out [from** *or* **of]** herausspritzen [aus]; ~ **from** ⟨*Rauch:*⟩ quellen aus; ⟨*Flüssigkeit:*⟩ spritzen aus. **2.** *v. t.* **the wound ~ed blood** aus der Wunde spritzte Blut. **3.** *n.* Strahl, *der*

sputnik ['spʊtnɪk, 'spʌtnɪk] *n.* Sputnik, *der*

sputter ['spʌtə(r)] **1.** *v. t. (utter)* heraussprudeln; *(incoherently)* stottern. **2.** *v. i.* **a)** *(speak) (vehemently)* wettern; *(in hurried fashion)* stammeln; **b)** *(crackle)* zischen; **c)** *see* **splutter 1**

sputum ['spju:təm] *n., pl.* **sputa** ['spju:tə] *(Med.)* **a)** *(saliva)* Speichel, *der;* **b)** *(phlegm)* Sputum, *das*

spy [spaɪ] **1.** *n.* **a)** *(secret agent)* Spion, *der*/Spionin, *die;* **b)** *(watcher)* Spion, *der*/Spionin, *die;* Schnüffler, *der*/Schnüfflerin, *die (abwertend);* **be a ~ for sb./sth.** für jmdn./etw. als Spitzel arbeiten; ~ **in the sky/cab** *(coll.)* Spionagesatellit, *der*/Fahrt[en]schreiber, *der.* **2.** *v. t. (literary)* ausmachen; ~ **a way out of the situation** einen Ausweg aus der Lage finden. **3.** *v. i. (watch closely)* [herum]spionieren; *(practise espionage)* Spionage treiben; ~ **on sb./a country** jmdm. nachspionieren/gegen ein Land spionieren; ~ **on sb.'s movements** jmdm. auf Schritt und Tritt nachspionieren; ~ **on each other** sich gegenseitig argwöhnisch beobachten

~ '**out** *v. t.* aufspüren; ausspionieren ⟨*Feind, feindliche Stellung*⟩; ~ **out the land** *(lit. or fig.)* die Lage erkunden

spy: ~**glass** *n.* Handfernrohr, *das;* Perspektiv, *das;* ~**hole** *n.* Spion, *der;* Guckloch, *das;* ~**master** *n. (coll.)* Chef eines Spionagerings; ~ **ring** *n.* Spionagering, *der;* ~ **satellite** *n.* Spionagesatellit, *der*

sq., Sq. *abbr.* **square, Square**

squab [skwɒb] *n.* **a)** *(Ornith.: fledgeling)* [noch nicht flügger] Jungvogel; *(pigeon)* Jungtaube, *die;* **b)** *(cushion)* Kissen, *das;* *(Brit.: of car seat)* Rücken-/Seitenlehne, *die*

squabble ['skwɒbl] **1.** *n.* Streit, *der;* **petty ~s** kleine Streitereien; **have a ~ [with sb. about sth.]** [mit jmdm. wegen einer Sache] Streit haben *(ugs.);* sich [mit jmdm. wegen einer Sache] streiten. **2.** *v. i.* sich zanken **(over, about** wegen)

squad [skwɒd] *n.* **a)** *(Mil.)* Gruppe, *die;* Trupp, *der;* **b)** *(group)* Mannschaft, *die; see also* **firing-squad; c)** *(Police)* **special ~:** Sonder[einsatz]kommando, *das;* **Drug/Fraud S~:** Rauschgift-/Betrugsdezernat, *das;* ~ **car** *(Amer.)* Einsatzwagen, *der; see also* **flying squad; vice squad**

squaddie, squaddy ['skwɒdɪ] *n. (Brit. Mil. sl.)* Gemeine, *der*

squadron ['skwɒdrən] *n.* **a)** *(Mil.) (of tanks)* Bataillon, *das; (of cavalry)* Schwadron, *die;* **b)** *(Navy)* Geschwader, *das;* **c)** *(Air Force)* Staffel, *die;* ~ **leader** *(Air Force)* Major der Luftwaffe

squalid ['skwɒlɪd] *adj.* **a)** *(dirty)* [abstoßend] schmutzig; **living conditions were ~:** man lebte mitten im Schmutz; **b)** *(poor)* schäbig; armselig; **c)** *(fig.: sordid)* abstoßend

squall [skwɔ:l] **1.** *n. (gust)* Bö, *die;* **look out** *or* **be on the look out for ~s** *(fig.)* auf der Hut sein. **2.** *v. i.* brüllen; ~ **in pain** brüllen *od.* schreien vor Schmerz

squally ['skwɔ:lɪ] *adj.* böig

squalor ['skwɒlə(r)] *n., no pl.* **a)** *(dirtiness)* Schmutz, *der;* **live in ~:** in Schmutz und Elend leben; **a life of ~:** ein Leben in Schmutz und Elend; **b)** *(fig.)* Schmutzigkeit, *die*

squander ['skwɒndə(r)] *v. t.* vergeuden ⟨*Talent, Zeit, Geld*⟩; verschleudern ⟨*Ersparnisse, Vermögen*⟩; nicht nutzen ⟨*Chance, Gelegenheit*⟩; ~ **one's life** sein Leben wegwerfen

square [skweə(r)] **1.** *n.* **a)** *(Geom.)* Quadrat, *das;* **b)** *(object, arrangement)* Quadrat, *das;* **carpet ~:** Teppichfliese, *die;* **cheese ~:** Scheiblette, *die* Ⓦⓩ; **tile ~:** [quadratische] Kachel; **c)** *(on board in game)* Feld, *das;* **be** *or* **go back to ~ one** *(fig. coll.)* wieder von vorn anfangen müssen; **d)** *(open area)* Platz, *der;* **e)** *(scarf)* [quadratisches] Tuch; **silk ~:** Seidentuch, *das;* **f)** *(Mil.: drill area)* **[barrack-]~:** Kasernenhof, *der;* **g)** *(Math.: product)* Quadrat, *das;* **a perfect ~:** eine Quadratzahl; **h)** *(sl.: old-fashioned person)* Spießer, *der*/Spießerin, *die (abwertend);* **i) on the ~ = on the level** *see* **level 1 a; j)** *(instrument)* Winkel, *der;* **L-/T-~:** L-förmiger Meßwinkel/Kreuzwinkel, *der; see also* **set square; try-square; k)** *(Amer.: block of buildings)* Quadrat, *das;* Karree, *das;* **l)** *(Cricket: pitch area)* [Haupt]spielfläche, *die. See also* **inverse square law; magic square; word-square. 2.** *adj.* **a)** quadratisch; *see also* **hole 1 a; b) a ~ foot/mile/metre** *etc.* ein Quadratfuß/eine Quadratmeile/ein Quadratmeter *usw.;* **a foot ~:** ein Fuß im Quadrat; **the S~ Mile** die City von London; **c)** *(right-angled)* rechtwink[e]lig; ~ **with** *or* **to** im rechten Winkel zu; **the wall is not ~ with the ceiling** die Wand ist nicht im Lot mit der Decke; ~ **on to sth.** rechtwinklig zu etw.; **d)** *(stocky)* gedrungen ⟨*Statur, Gestalt*⟩; ⟨*Gegenstand:*⟩ von gedrungenem Format; **be ~ in build** gedrungen gebaut sein; **e)** *(in outline)* rechteckig; eckig ⟨*Schultern, Kinn*⟩; ~**-shouldered** breitschultrig; **f)** *(quits)* quitt *(ugs.);* **be [all] ~:** [völlig] quitt sein *(ugs.);* ⟨*Spieler:*⟩ gleich stehen; ⟨*Spiel:*⟩ unentschieden stehen; **the match finished all ~:** das Spiel ging unentschieden aus; **get ~ with sb.** mit jmdm. quitt werden *(ugs.);* *(get revenge)* es jmdm. heimzahlen; **g)** *(sl.: old-fashioned)* spießig *(abwertend).* **3.** *adv.* **a)** breit ⟨*sitzen*⟩; **put sth. ~ in the middle of sth.** etw. mitten auf etw. *(Akk.)* stellen; **hit sb. ~ on the jaw** jmdm. genau auf die Kinnlade schlagen; **the ball hit him ~ on the head** der Ball traf ihn genau am Kopf; **look sb. ~ in the face** *or* **between the eyes** jmdm. fest in die Augen sehen; **b)** *(fairly)* ehrlich; fair ⟨*behandeln*⟩. *See also* [2]**fair 2 c. 4.** *v. t.* **a)** *(make right-angled)* rechtwinklig machen; vierkantig zuschneiden ⟨*Holz*⟩; **b)** *(place squarely)* ~ **one's shoulders** seine Schultern straffen; **c)** *(divide into ~s)* in Karos einteilen; **~d paper** kariertes Papier; **d)** *(Math.: multiply)* quadrieren; **3 ~d is 9** 3 [im] Quadrat ist 9; 3 hoch 2 ist 9; **e)** *(reconcile)* **~ sth. with sth.** etw. mit etw. in Einklang bringen; **f) ~ it with sb.** *(coll.: get sb.'s approval)* es mit jmdm. klären; **g)** *(coll.: bribe)* schmieren *(salopp)*; **h)** *(settle)* begleichen; **~ one's debt[s]** seine Schuld[en] begleichen; **I have a debt to ~ with him** *(fig.)* mit ihm werde ich [noch] abrechnen; *see also* **account 2 a; i)** *(draw level in)* **~ [the/one's match** *or* **score]** zum Unentschieden verkürzen; gleichziehen; **j) ~ the circle** *(Geom.)* den Kreis quadrieren. **5.** *v. i. (be consistent)* übereinstimmen; **sth. does not ~ with sth.** etw. steht nicht im Einklang mit etw.; **it just does not ~:** hier stimmt doch etwas nicht

~ 'off 1. *v. t. (make ~) see* **~ 4 a. 2.** *v. i. (raise fists)* die Fäuste heben

~ 'up *v. i. (settle up)* abrechnen

~ 'up to *v. t.* **a)** *(raise fists against)* sich mit erhobenen Fäusten aufbauen *(ugs.)* vor (+ *Dat.*); **they ~d up to each other** sie traten sich kampfbereit gegenüber; **b)** *(confront)* **~ up to sb./sth.** jmdm./einer Sache entgegentreten

square: ~-bashing ['skweəbæʃɪŋ] *n. (Brit. Mil. sl.)* Kasernenhofdrill, *der;* **~ 'brackets** *n. pl.* eckige Klammern; **~-built** *adj.* quadratisch ⟨*Gebäude*⟩; gedrungen ⟨*Person*⟩; vierschrötig ⟨*Mann*⟩; **~ dance** *n.* Square dance, *der;* **~ 'deal** *n.* faires Geschäft; **get a ~ deal** *(not be swindled)* kein schlechtes Geschäft machen; *(receive adequate compensation)* fair *od.* anständig behandelt werden; **~ 'leg** *n. (Cricket) Feldspieler, der die Stellung hinter dem Schlagmann innehat*

squarely ['skweəlɪ] *adv.* **a)** *(directly)* fest ⟨*ansehen*⟩; genau ⟨*treffen*⟩; aufrecht ⟨*sitzen*⟩; **his works place him ~ in the Romantic tradition** mit seinem Werk steht er direkt in der romantischen Tradition; **b)** *see* **fairly e**

square: ~ 'meal *n.* anständige Mahlzeit *(ugs.)*; **~ number** *n. (Math.)* Quadratzahl, *die;* **~-rigged** ['skweərɪgd] *adj. (Naut.)* ⟨*Schoner*⟩ mit Rahsegeln; **a ~-rigged sailing ship** ein voll getakelter Rahsegler; **~ 'root** *n. (Math.)* Quadratwurzel, *die;* **~-root sign** [Quadrat]wurzelzeichen, *das;* **~ sail** *n. (Naut.)* Rahsegel, *das;* **~-toed** ['skweətəʊd] *adj.* **~-toed shoes/boots** [an den Zehen] breite Schuhe/Stiefel; **~ wave** *n. (Phys.)* Rechteckwelle, *die*

¹squash [skwɒʃ] **1.** *v. t.* **a)** *(crush)* zerquetschen; **~ sth. flat** etw. platt drücken; **b)** *(compress)* pressen; **~ in/up** eindrücken/zusammendrücken ⟨*Gegenstand*⟩; **~ sb./sth. into sth.** jmdn./etw. in etw. *(Akk.)* [hinein]zwängen; **c)** *(put down)* niederschlagen ⟨*Aufstand*⟩; zunichte machen ⟨*Hoffnung, Traum*⟩; **d)** *(coll.: dismiss)* ablehnen ⟨*Vorschlag, Plan*⟩; **e)** *(coll.: silence)* zum Schweigen bringen. **2.** *v. i.* sich quetschen; **~ in** sich hineinquetschen; **we ~ed up** wir drängten uns zusammen; **~ into the back seat of a car** sich auf den Rücksitz eines Wagens quetschen. **3.** *n.* **a)** *(drink)* Fruchtsaftgetränk, *das;* **orange ~:** Orangensaftgetränk, *das; (concentrated)* Orangensaftkonzentrat, *das;* **b)** *(Sport)* **~ [rackets]** Squash, *das;* **c)** *see* **crush 2 a**

²squash *n. (gourd)* [Speise]kürbis, *der*

squash: ~ ball *n.* Squashball, *der;* **~ court** *n.* Squashfeld, *das;* **~ racket** *n.* Squashschläger, *der;* **~ rackets** *see* **¹squash 3 b**

squashy ['skwɒʃɪ] *adj.* weich ⟨*Kuchen, Obst*⟩

squat [skwɒt] **1.** *v. i.*, **-tt- a)** *(crouch)* hocken; *(crouch down)* sich hocken; **b)** *(coll.: sit)* sitzen; *(sit down)* sich setzen; **c)** *(coll.: occupy property) (house)* eine Hausbesetzung machen; *(land)* eine Landbesetzung machen; **~ in a house/on land** ein Haus besetzen/Land besetzen. **2.** *adj.* rundlich; untersetzt. **3.** *n. (coll.)* **a)** *(occupation) (of house)* Hausbesetzung, *die; (of land)* Landbesetzung, *die;* **b)** *(house)* besetztes Haus; *(land)* besetztes Land

~ 'down *v. i.* sich [nieder]hocken; *(on seat)* sich hinsetzen

squatter ['skwɒtə(r)] *n. (illegal occupier)* Besetzer, *der*/Besetzerin, *die; (of house also)* Hausbesetzer, *der*/-besetzerin, *die*

squaw [skwɔː] *n.* Squaw, *die*

squawk [skwɔːk] **1.** *v. i.* ⟨*Hahn, Krähe, Rabe:*⟩ krähen; ⟨*Huhn:*⟩ kreischen; *(complain)* ⟨*Person:*⟩ keifen *(abwertend)*. **2.** *n.* **a)** *(bird-cry)* **~[s]** *(of crow, cockerel, raven)* Krähen, *das; (of hen)* Kreischen, *das;* **b)** *(complaint)* Gekeif[e], *das (ugs. abwertend);* **utter ~s of complaint** sich keifend beschweren; **~ of anger/indignation** wütendes/entrüstetes Gezeter

squeak [skwiːk] **1.** *n.* **a)** *(of animal)* Quieken, *das;* **b)** *(of hinge, door, brake, shoe, etc.)* Quietschen, *das;* **c)** *(coll.: escape)* **have a narrow ~:** gerade noch [mit dem Leben] davonkommen; **that was a narrow ~!** das war knapp! *(ugs.)*. *See also* **bubble and squeak. 2.** *v. i.* **a)** ⟨*Tier:*⟩ quieken; **b)** ⟨*Scharnier, Tür, Bremse, Schuh usw.:*⟩ quietschen; **c)** *(coll.: pass)* **~ through/past [sth.]** mit Müh und Not [durch etw.] durchkommen/[an etw. *(Dat.)*] vorbeikommen; **d)** *(sl.) see* **squeal 1 d**

squeaky ['skwiːkɪ] *adj.* quietschend; schrill ⟨*Stimme*⟩; **be ~ clean** blitzsauber sein *(ugs.)*; *(fig.)* eine blütenweiße Weste haben *(fig. ugs.)*

squeal [skwiːl] **1.** *v. i.* **a) ~ with pain/in fear** ⟨*Person:*⟩ vor Schmerz/Angst aufschreien; ⟨*Tier:*⟩ vor Schmerz/Angst laut quieken; **~ with laughter/for joy/in excitement** vor Lachen/Freude/Aufregung kreischen; **b)** ⟨*Bremsen, Räder:*⟩ kreischen; ⟨*Reifen:*⟩ quietschen; **c)** *(sl.: protest)* **~ [in protest]** lauthals protestieren; **d)** *(sl.: inform)* singen *(salopp)* (to bei); **~ on sb.** jmdn. verpfeifen *(salopp)*. **2.** *v. t.* kreischen. **3.** *n.* Kreischen, *das; (of tyres)* Quietschen, *das; (of animal)* Quieken, *das;* **give a ~ of fear** ⟨*Person:*⟩ vor Angst laut schreien; ⟨*Tier:*⟩ vor Angst laut quieken; **give a ~ of anger** vor Zorn aufschreien; **give a ~ of delight/excitement/joy** vor Vergnügen/Aufregung/Freude kreischen; **with a ~ of delight** kreischend vor Entzücken

squeamish ['skwiːmɪʃ] *adj.* **a)** *(easily nauseated)* **be ~:** zartbesaitet sein; **this film is not for the ~:** dieser Film ist nichts für zarte Gemüter; **b)** *(fastidious)* zimperlich

squeegee [skwiː'dʒiː] **1.** *n.* **a)** *(for floor)* [Boden]wischer, *der; (for window)* [Fenster]wischer, *der;* **b)** *(Photog.) (roller)* Rollenquetscher, *der; (stripper)* Abstreifer, *der.* **2.** *v. t.* **a)** *(wipe)* mit dem [Boden]wischer putzen ⟨*Fußboden*⟩; mit dem [Fenster]wischer putzen ⟨*Fenster*⟩; **b)** *(Photog.: roll)* mit dem Rollenquetscher/Abstreifer rollen

squeeze [skwiːz] **1.** *n.* **a)** *(pressing)* Druck, *der;* **it only takes a gentle ~:** man braucht nur leicht zu drücken; **give sth. a [small] ~:** etw. [leicht] drücken; **put the ~ on sb.** *(fig. sl.)* jmdm. [die] Daumenschrauben anlegen; jmdn. durch die Mangel drehen *(salopp)*; **b)** *(small quantity)* **a ~ of juice/washing-up liquid** ein Spritzer Saft/Spülmittel; **a ~ of toothpaste/icing** ganz wenig Zahnpasta/Zuckerguß; **c)** *(crush)* Gedränge, *das;* **be in a tight ~** *(fig.)* = **be in a fix** *see* **fix 4 a; d)** *(Econ.: restriction)* Beschränkung, *die* (on *Gen.*); **e)** *(Brit.: embrace)* **give sb. a [big/final] ~:** jmdn. [fest/ein letztes Mal] an sich drücken. **2.** *v. t.* **a)** *(press)* drücken; drücken auf (+ *Akk.*) ⟨*Tube, Plastikflasche*⟩; kneten ⟨*Ton, Knetmasse*⟩; ausdrücken ⟨*Schwamm, Wäsche, Pickel*⟩; *(to get juice)* auspressen ⟨*Früchte, Obst*⟩; **~ sb.'s hand** jmdm. die Hand drücken; **~ the trigger** auf den Abzug drükken; **b)** *(extract)* drücken (**out of** aus); **~ out sth.** etw. herausdrücken; **~ sth. on to sth.** etw. auf etw. *(Akk.)* drücken; **c)** *(force)* zwängen; **~ one's way past/into/out of sth.** sich an etw. *(Dat.)* vorbei-/in etw. *(Akk.)* hinein-/aus etw. herauszwängen; **d)** *(fig. coll.)* **~ sth. from sb.** etw. aus jmdm. herauspressen; **e)** *(emit)* **~ [out]** herauspressen ⟨*Träne*⟩; herausbringen ⟨*Laut, Antwort*⟩; sich abringen ⟨*Lächeln*⟩; **f)** *(fig.: constrain)* unter Druck setzen; **~ sb. into doing sth.** jmdn. dazu bringen, etw. zu tun; **~ sb. out of sth./out** *(fig. coll.)* jmdn. aus etw. drängen/hinausdrängen; **g)** *(Bridge)* zum Abwerfen zwingen; **h)** *(coll.: extort)* **~ money out of sb.** Geld aus jmdm. herauspressen. **3.** *v. i.* **~ past sb./sth.** sich an jmdm./etw. vorbeidrängen; **~ between two persons** sich zwischen zwei Personen *(Dat.)* durchdrängen; **~ under** *or* **underneath sth.** sich unter etw. *(Dat.)* hindurchzwängen; **~ under a bed** sich unter ein Bett zwängen; **~ together** sich zusammendrängen; **~ down a hole** sich in ein Loch zwängen

~ 'in 1. *v. t.* **a)** reinquetschen; **b)** *(fig.: fit in)* einschieben. **2.** *v. i.* sich hineinzwängen

~ 'up *v. i.* sich zusammendrängen; **~ up against sb./sth.** sich [fest] an jmdn./etw. drücken

squeeze: ~ bottle *see* **squeezy bottle; ~-box** *n. (sl.)* Quetschkommode, *die (salopp scherzh.)*

squeezer ['skwiːzə(r)] *n. (device)* Presse, *die*

squeezy bottle ['skwiːzɪ bɒtl] *n.* [elastische] Plastikflasche

squelch [skweltʃ] **1.** *v. t.* **a)** *(stamp on)* stampfen; **b)** *(silence)* zum Schweigen bringen. **2.** *v. i.* **a)** *(make sucking sound)* quatschen *(ugs.)*; **b)** *(go over wet ground)* patschen

squib [skwɪb] *n.* **a)** *(firework)* Knallfrosch, *der;* **damp ~** *(fig.)* Reinfall, *der;* **b)** *(lampoon)* [kurze] Satire

squid [skwɪd] *n. (Zool., Gastr.)* Kalmar, *der*

squidgy ['skwɪdʒɪ] *adj. (Brit. coll.)* durchweicht; matschig *(ugs.)*

squiggle ['skwɪgl] *n.* Schnörkel, *der*

squiggly ['skwɪglɪ] *adj.* schnörk[e]lig; **put a ~ line under sth.** etw. unterschlängeln

squint [skwɪnt] **1.** *n.* **a)** *(Med.)* Schielen, *das;* **have a ~:** schielen; **b)** *(stealthy look)* Schielen, *das (ugs.)*; **c)** *(coll.: glance)* kurzer Blick; **have** *or* **take a ~ at** einen Blick werfen auf (+ *Akk.*); überfliegen ⟨*Text, Zeitung*⟩; **d)** *(Eccl.: opening) schräge Maueröffnung, durch die man den Altar sieht.* **2.** *v. i.* **a)** *(Med.)* schielen; **b)** *(with half-closed eyes)* blinzeln; die Augen zusammenkneifen; **~ at sth.** etw. blinzelnd anschauen; **c)** *(obliquely)* **~ through a gap** durch eine Lücke lugen; **d)** *(coll.: glance)* **~ at** einen [kurzen] Blick werfen auf (+ *Akk.*); überfliegen ⟨*Zeitung, Text*⟩; **I ~ ed through his window as I passed** ich schielte im Vorbeigehen durch sein Fenster. **3.** *v. t.* **~ one's eyes** die Augen zusammenkneifen

squire ['skwaɪə(r)] **1. a)** *(country gentleman)* Squire, *der;* ≈ Gutsherr, *der;* **b)** *(Brit. coll. voc.: sir)* **want to buy any watches, ~?** möchte der Herr Uhren kaufen? *(veralt.)*; wollen Sie Uhren kaufen, Meister? *(ugs.)*; **c)** *(Hist.: attendant)* Knappe, *der.* **2.** *v. t.* begleiten

squirm [skwɜːm] *v. i.* **a)** *see* **wriggle 1; b)** *(fig.: show unease)* sich winden (**with** vor)

squirrel ['skwɪrl] *n.* **a)** *(Zool.)* Eichhörnchen, *das; see also* **grey squirrel; ground-squirrel; red squirrel; b)** *(fur)* Eichhörnchen[fell], *das;* Feh, *das*

squirt [skwɜːt] **1.** *v. t.* spritzen; sprühen ⟨*Spray, Puder*⟩; **~ sth. at sb.** jmdn. mit etw. bespritzen/besprühen; **~ sb. in the eye/face [with sth.]** jmdm. [etw.] ins Auge/Gesicht

spritzen/sprühen; ~ **oneself with water/deodorant** sich mit Wasser bespritzen/mit Deodorant besprühen. **2.** *v.i.* spritzen. **3.** *n.* Spritzer, *der;* **a ~ of juice** ein Spritzer Saft
squishy ['skwɪʃɪ] *adj.* patschend *(ugs.)*
Sr. *abbr.* **a)** Senior sen.; sr.; **b)** Señor; **c)** *(Relig.)* **Sister** Sr.
Sri Lanka [sri: 'læŋkə] *pr. n.* Sri Lanka *(das)*
Sri Lankan [sri: 'læŋkən] **1.** *adj.* srilankisch. **2.** *n.* Srilanker, *der*/Srilankerin, *die;* **sb. is a ~**: jmd. ist aus Sri Lanka
SRN *abbr.* **State Registered Nurse** staatl. gepr. Krankenschwester/-pfleger
SS *abbr.* **a)** [seɪnts] **Saints** St.; **b)** **steamship** D; **c)** *(Nazi élite force)* SS, *die*
SSE [saʊθsaʊθ'i:st] *abbr.* **south-south-east** SSO
SSW [saʊθsaʊθ'west] *abbr.* **south-south-west** SSW
St *abbr.* **Saint** St.
St. *abbr.* **Street** Str.
st. *abbr.* *(Brit.: unit of weight)* **stone**
stab [stæb] **1.** *v.t.*, **-bb- a)** *(pierce)* stechen; **~ the air** in der Luft herumfuchteln; **~ sb. in the chest** jmdm. in die Brust stechen; **~ a piece of meat** in ein Stück Fleisch stechen; **he had been severely ~bed** er hatte gefährliche Stichwunden erhalten; **b)** *(fig.) (hurt)* **~ sb.'s heart** jmdm. ins Herz schneiden *(geh.);* **~ sb.'s conscience** jmds. Gewissen quälen; *(attack)* **~ sb. in the back** *(fig.)* jmdm. in den Rücken fallen. **2.** *v.i.*, **-bb- a)** *(pierce)* stechen; **b)** *(thrust)* zustechen; **~ at sb.** nach jmdm. stechen. **3.** *n.* **a)** *(act)* Stich, *der;* *(fig.)* **that was a real ~ in the back** ich fühlte mich/er fühlte sich *usw.* wirklich verraten und verkauft; **b)** *(coll.: attempt)* **make** *or* **have a ~ [at it]** [es] probieren; **c)** *(blow)* Stich, *der;* *(with beak)* Hieb, *der;* **d)** *(wound)* Stichwunde, *die;* **e)** *(fig.) (pang)* **~ of conscience/guilt** Gewissensbiß, *der*/[quälendes] Schuldbewußtsein
stabbing ['stæbɪŋ] **1.** *n.* Messerstecherei, *die.* **2.** *attrib. adj.* stechend ⟨*Schmerz*⟩
stabilisation *etc. see* **stabiliz-**
stability [stə'bɪlɪtɪ] *n., no pl.* Stabilität, *die;* **his character lacks ~**: er ist charakterlich nicht gefestigt
stabilization [steɪbɪlaɪ'zeɪʃn] *n.* Stabilisierung, *die*
stabilize ['steɪbɪlaɪz] **1.** *v.t.* stabilisieren. **2.** *v.i.* sich stabilisieren
stabilizer ['steɪbɪlaɪzə(r)] *n.* **a)** *(Naut.)* Stabilisator, *der;* **b)** *(Aeronaut.)* **vertical ~** *see* **tail-fin; horizontal ~** *see* **tailplane; c)** *(Cycling)* Stützrad, *das*
[1]**stable** ['steɪbl] *adj.* **a)** *(steady)* stabil; **the patient was in a ~ condition** *or* **was ~**: der Zustand des Patienten *od.* der Patient war stabil; **a ~ family background** geordnete Familienverhältnisse; *see also* **equilibrium; b)** *(resolute)* gefestigt ⟨*Person, Charakter*⟩
[2]**stable 1.** *n.* **a)** *(for horses)* Stall, *der;* **b)** *(Horse-racing: establishment)* [Renn]stall, *der;* **the horses are trained at his ~**: die Pferde werden in seinem Stall trainiert; **c)** *(fig.: origin)* Stall, *der (ugs.);* **the latest model from the X ~**: das jüngste Modell aus dem Hause X; **from the same ~** ⟨*Person*⟩ aus demselben Stall *(ugs.);* ⟨*Produkt*⟩ aus demselben Haus. **2.** *v.t.* *(put in ~)* in den Stall bringen; *(keep in ~)* **the pony was ~d at a nearby farm** das Pony war im Stall eines nahegelegenen Bauernhofes untergebracht
stable: ~-boy *see* **~-lad; ~-door** *n.* *(made in two parts)* quergeteilte Tür; *see also* [2]**lock 2a; ~-lad, ~man** *ns.* Stallbursche, *der*
stabling ['steɪblɪŋ] *n., no indef. art.* Ställe; Stallungen
staccato [stə'kɑ:təʊ] *(Mus.)* **1.** *adj.* staccato gesetzt; *(fig.)* abgehackt ⟨*Sprache*⟩; **speak with a ~ delivery** schnell und abgehackt sprechen; **~ bursts of gun-fire** ein Stakkato von Gewehrfeuer. **2.** *adv.* staccato. **3.** *n.* *(also fig.)* Stakkato, *das*
stac'cato mark *n.* *(Mus.)* Stakkatozeichen, *das*
stack [stæk] **1.** *n.* **a)** *(of hay etc.)* Schober, *der (südd., österr.);* Feim, *der (nordd., md.);* **b)** *(pile)* Stoß, *der;* Stapel, *der;* **place sth. in ~s** etw. [auf]stapeln; **c)** *(coll.: large amount)* Haufen, *der (ugs.);* **a ~ of work/money** ein Haufen Arbeit/Geld; **have a ~ of things to do** einen Haufen zu tun haben *(ugs.);* **have ~s of money** Geld wie Heu haben *(ugs.);* **d)** **[chimney-]~**: Schornstein, *der;* **e)** *(factory chimney)* Fabrikschornstein, *der;* **blow one's ~** *(Amer. fig. coll.)* = **blow one's top** *see* [1]**blow 2h; f)** *(funnel)* **[smoke-]~**: Schornstein, *der;* **g)** *(Aeronaut.)* *übereinander in Warteschleifen kreisende Flugzeuge;* **h)** *(Brit.: rock pillar)* Felssäule, *die;* **i)** *(in library)* Magazin, *das.* **2.** *v.t.* **a)** *(pile)* **~ [up]** [auf]stapeln; **~ logs in a pile** Holz zu einem Stoß aufschichten; **be well ~ed** *(fig. sl.: have large bust)* viel Holz vor der Hütte haben *(ugs. scherzh.);* **~ing** stapelbar ⟨*Stühle usw.*⟩; **b)** *(arrange fraudulently)* **~ the cards** beim Mischen betrügen; **the odds** *or* **cards** *or* **chips are ~ed against sb.** *(fig.)* jmd. hat schlechte Karten *(fig. ugs.);* **c)** *(Aeronaut.)* übereinander Warteschleifen fliegen lassen; **we are ~ed right up to 30,000 feet** der Warteraum ist schon bis in 30 000 Fuß Höhe belegt
~ 'up *see* **~ 2a**
stadium ['steɪdɪəm] *n.* Stadion, *das*
staff [stɑ:f] **1.** *n.* **a)** *(stick)* Stock, *der;* **b)** *constr. as pl. (personnel)* Personal, *das;* **editorial ~**: Redaktion, *die;* **diplomatic ~**: diplomatisches Korps; **the ~ of the firm** die Betriebsangehörigen; die Belegschaft [der Firma]; **~ meeting** Belegschaftsversammlung, *die;* **c)** *constr. as pl. (of school)* Lehrerkollegium, *das;* Lehrkörper, *der (Amtsspr.);* *(of university or college)* Dozentenschaft, *die;* **~-student ratio** Verhältnis zwischen Lehrenden und Studierenden; **~ meeting** *(at school)* Lehrerkonferenz, *die;* *(at university or college)* Dozentenkonferenz, *die;* **d)** *pl.* **staves** [steɪvz] *(Mus.)* Liniensystem, *das;* **~ notation** Notation mit Hilfe des Liniensystems; **e)** *(Mil.: officers)* Stab, *der;* *see also* **chief 1b; f)** *(ceremonial rod)* Stab, *der;* **pastoral ~** *(Eccl.)* Bischofsstab, *der;* **g)** *(fig.: support)* Stütze, *die;* **bread/Christ is the ~ of life** Brot ist die Grundlage des Lebens/Christus ist das Brot des Lebens; **h)** *(Surv.: rod)* Meßlatte, *die. See also* **flagstaff; general staff. 2.** *v.t.* mit Personal ausstatten; **a hospital ~ed by women** ein Krankenhaus, dessen Personal aus Frauen besteht
'staff college *n.* *(Brit. Mil.)* Stabsakademie, *die (Milit.)*
staffed [stɑ:ft] *adj.* mit Personal ausgestattet
staffer ['stɑ:fə(r)] *n.* *(Amer. Journ.)* Redaktionsmitglied, *das*
staff: ~ nurse *n.* *(Brit.)* Zweitschwester, *die/Krankenpfleger in der Stellung einer Zweitschwester;* **~ officer** *n.* *(Mil.)* Stabsoffizier, *der;* **~-room** *n.* Lehrerzimmer, *das;* **~ sergeant** *n.* **a)** *(Brit. Mil.)* ≈ Oberfeldwebel, *der;* **b)** *(Amer. Mil.)* ≈ Feldwebel, *der*
stag [stæg] *n.* **a)** Hirsch, *der;* **b)** *(Amer.: lone man)* Herr ohne Damenbegleitung; **c)** *(Brit. St. Exch. sl.)* Konzertzeichner, *der*
'stag beetle *n.* *(Zool.)* Hirschkäfer, *der*
stage [steɪdʒ] **1.** *n.* **a)** *(Theatre)* Bühne, *die;* **down/up ~** *(position)* vorne/hinten auf der Bühne; *(direction)* nach vorn/nach hinten; **[be/appear] on ~**: auf der Bühne [stehen/erscheinen]; **be appearing on ~ at the Royal** am Royal spielen; **b)** *(fig.)* **the ~**: das Theater; **write for the ~**: für die Bühne schreiben; **go on the ~**: zur Bühne *od.* zum Theater gehen; **c)** *(part of process)* Stadium, *das;* Phase, *die;* **be at a difficult/late/critical ~**: sich in einer schwierigen/späten/kritischen Phase befinden; **negotiations are at an early ~**: die Verhandlungen befinden sich im Anfangsstadium; **at such a late ~**: zu einem so späten Zeitpunkt; **at this ~**: in diesem Stadium; **do sth. in** *or* **by ~s** etw. abschnittsweise *od.* nach und nach tun; **I am past the ~ of caring** das ist mir inzwischen gleich; **in the final ~s** in der Schlußphase; **d)** *(raised platform)* Gerüst, *das;* *see also* **landing-stage; e)** *(of microscope)* Mikroskoptisch, *der;* **f)** *(fig.: scene)* Bühne, *die;* **quit the political ~** *or* **the ~ of politics** von der politischen Bühne abtreten; **hold the ~**: die Szene beherrschen; **set the ~ for sb./sth.** jmdm. den Weg ebnen/etw. in die Wege leiten; **the ~ was set for a bitter argument** damit waren die Voraussetzungen für eine erbitterte Auseinandersetzung gegeben; **g)** *(stopping-place)* Station, *die;* **h)** *(distance)* Etappe, *die;* **the ~ from Paris to Marseilles** die Strecke Paris–Marseille; **travel by [easy] ~s** in [kurzen] Etappen reisen; *see also* **fare-stage; i)** *(Geol., Electr., Astronaut.)* Stufe, *die.* **2.** *v.t.* **a)** *(present)* inszenieren; **b)** *(arrange)* veranstalten ⟨*Wettkampf, Ausstellung*⟩; ausrichten ⟨*Veranstaltung*⟩; organisieren ⟨*Streik*⟩; bewerkstelligen ⟨*Rückzug*⟩; **~ a comeback** ein Comeback schaffen
stage: ~-coach *n.* Postkutsche, *die;* **~craft** *n., no pl., no indef. art.* *(Theatre)* Bühnenkunst, *die;* **~ direction** *n.* *(Theatre)* Bühnenanweisung, *die;* **~ door** *n.* *(Theatre)* Bühneneingang, *der;* **~ effect** *n.* *(Theatre)* Bühneneffekt, *der;* **~ fright** *n.* *(Theatre)* Lampenfieber, *das;* **~-hand** *n.* *(Theatre)* Bühnenarbeiter, *der*/-arbeiterin, *die;* **~ 'left** *see* [2]**left 3c; ~-manage** *v.t.* **a)** *(Theatre)* als Inspizient/Inspizientin mitwirken bei ⟨*Inszenierung*⟩; **b)** *(fig.)* veranstalten; inszenieren ⟨*Revolte usw.*⟩; **~-manager** *n.* *(Theatre)* Inspizient, der/Inspizientin, *die;* **~-name** *n.* *(Theatre)* Künstlername, *der;* **~ play** *n.* *(Theatre)* Bühnenstück, *das*
stager ['steɪdʒə(r)] *see* **old 1b**
stage: ~ right *see* **right 3h; ~ rights** *n. pl.* Aufführungsrechte; **~-struck** *adj.* theaterbesessen; **~ whisper** *n.* Beiseitesprechen, *das;* **in a ~ whisper** beiseite
stagflation [stæg'fleɪʃn] *n.* *(Econ.)* Stagflation, *die*
stagger ['stægə(r)] **1.** *v.i.* schwanken; torkeln *(ugs.).* **2.** *v.t.* **a)** *(cause to totter)* zum Schwanken bringen; **b)** *(astonish)* die Sprache verschlagen (+ *Dat.*); **I was ~ed** es hat mir die Sprache verschlagen; **c)** *(position out of line, arrange alternately)* versetzt anordnen; **~ed junction** versetzt angelegte Kreuzung; **~ed** *(fig.)* gestaffelt ⟨*Ferien, Schichten, Essenszeiten*⟩
~ a'bout, ~ a'round *v.i.* [hin- und her]taumeln; [herum]torkeln *(ugs.)*
staggering ['stægərɪŋ] *adj.* erschütternd ⟨*Schlag, Schock, Verlust*⟩; schwindelerregend ⟨*Menge, Höhe*⟩; folgenschwer ⟨*Auswirkung, Bedeutung*⟩; zutiefst beunruhigend ⟨*Nachricht*⟩; **the ~ fact is that no one really knew who he was** erschütternd ist, daß niemand ihn wirklich kannte
staggeringly ['stægərɪŋlɪ] *adv.* erstaunlich; *as sentence-modifier* erstaunlicherweise
stagily ['steɪdʒɪlɪ] *adv.* betont auffällig ⟨*sich kleiden*⟩; affektiert ⟨*sich benehmen*⟩
staging ['steɪdʒɪŋ] *n., no indef. art.* **a)** Gerüst, *das;* *(used as stage)* Bühne, *die;* **b)** *(Hort.: shelves)* Regale; **c)** *(Theatre: production)* Inszenierung, *die*
staging: ~ area *n.* *(Mil.)* Sammelplatz, *der;* **~ post** *n.* Zwischenstation, *die*
stagnant ['stægnənt] *adj.* **a)** *(motionless)* stehend ⟨*Gewässer*⟩; **the water is ~**: das Wasser steht; **b)** *(fig.: lifeless)* abgestumpft ⟨*Geist, Seele*⟩; stagnierend ⟨*Wirtschaft*⟩; dumpf ⟨*Leben*⟩; **the economy is ~**: die Wirtschaft stagniert

stagnate [stæg'neɪt] *v. i.* **a)** ‹*Wasser usw.:*› abstehen; **b)** *(fig.)* ‹*Wirtschaft, Geschäft:*› stagnieren; ‹*Geist, Künstler:*› in Lethargie verfallen; ‹*Person:*› abstumpfen

stagnation [stæg'neɪʃn] *n., no pl.* **a)** *(of water etc.)* Stehen, *das;* **b)** *(fig.)* Stagnation, *die*

stag: ~ night *n. Zechabend des Bräutigams mit seinen Freunden kurz vor seiner Hochzeit;* **~ party** *n.* Herrenabend, *der; (before wedding) Trinkgelage des Bräutigams mit seinen Freunden kurz vor seiner Hochzeit*

stagy ['steɪdʒɪ] *adj.* theatralisch; **be a ~ dresser** sich betont auffällig kleiden; **they have a ~ manner** sie benehmen sich wie die Schauspieler

staid [steɪd] *adj.* **a)** *(steady, sedate)* gesetzt; **lead a ~ existence** ein gleichförmiges Leben führen; **b)** *(serious)* bieder

staidly ['steɪdlɪ] *adv.* **a)** *(soberly)* bieder; **b)** *(sedately)* ruhig

stain [steɪn] **1.** *v. t.* **a)** *(discolour)* verfärben; *(make ~s on)* Flecken hinterlassen auf (+ *Dat.*); **b)** *(fig.: besmirch)* beflecken; besudeln *(geh. abwertend);* **c)** *(colour)* färben; beizen ‹*Holz*›; **d)** *(Biol.: impregnate)* anfärben. **2.** *v. i.* sich verfärben; *(take ~s)* Flecken bekommen. **3.** *n.* **a)** *(discoloration)* Fleck, *der;* **b)** *(fig.: blemish)* Schandfleck, *der;* **without a ~ on his character** mit einem fleckenlosen Charakter *od. (fig.)* einer fleckenlosen Weste; **c)** *(colouring-material)* Beize, *die;* **d)** *(Biol.)* Farbstoff, *der*

stained 'glass *n.* farbiges Glas; Farbglas, *das;* **the ~ at the church** die farbigen Glasfenster *od.* die Glasmalereien in der Kirche; **~ window** Fenster mit Glasmalerei

stainless ['steɪnlɪs] *adj.* **a)** *(spotless)* fleckenlos; **b)** *(non-rusting)* rostfrei

stainless 'steel *n.* Edelstahl, *der*

'stain-remover *n.* Fleck[en]entferner, *der*

stair [steə(r)] *n.* **a)** *(set of steps)* **~s**, *(arch./Scot.)* **~**: Treppe, *die;* **below ~s** in den Wirtschaftsräumen [im Souterrain]; **b)** *(step)* [Treppen]stufe, *die;* **c)** *in pl. (landing-stage)* Landungssteg, *der. See also* **downstairs; ¹flight 1 d; upstairs**

stair: ~-carpet *see* **carpet 1 a; ~-carpeting** *see* **carpeting a; ~case** *n.* Treppenhaus, *das; (one flight)* Treppe, *die;* **on the ~case** auf der Treppe; *see also* **spiral staircase; winding staircase; ~head** *see* **landing d; ~-rod** *n.* Läuferstange, *die;* **it's raining ~-rods** *(coll.)* es regnet Bindfäden *(ugs.);* **~way** *n.* **a)** *(access via ~s)* Treppenaufgang, *der;* **b)** *(~-case)* Treppe, *die;* **~-well** *n.* Treppenhaus, *das*

stake [steɪk] **1.** *n.* **a)** *(pointed stick)* Pfahl, *der;* **pull up ~s** *(Amer. fig. coll.)* seine Zelte abbrechen; **b)** *(wager)* Einsatz, *der;* **be at ~**: auf dem Spiel stehen; **at ~ is the Gold Medal** es geht um die Goldmedaille; **have a lot of money at ~ on a project** viel Geld in ein Projekt gesteckt haben; **have a ~ in sth.** in etw. *(Akk.)* investiert haben; **have a 50 % ~ in a firm** einen fünfzigprozentigen Anteil an einer Firma halten; **c)** *in pl. (Horse-racing) (prize-money)* Geldpreis, *der; (race)* [Wett]rennen um einen Geldpreis; **d)** *(for execution)* **be burnt at the ~**: auf dem Scheiterhaufen verbrannt werden; **go to the ~ for sth.** *(fig.)* sich für etw. kreuzigen lassen. **2.** *v. t.* **a)** *(secure)* [an einem Pfahl/an Pfählen] anbinden; **~ sth. down** etw. einpflocken; **~ a claim [to sb./sth.]** *see* **claim 3 e; b)** *(wager)* setzen (**on** auf + *Akk.*); **c)** *(risk)* aufs Spiel setzen (**on** für); **I'll ~ my reputation on his innocence** ich verbürge mich mit meinem guten Namen für seine Unschuld; **~ one's life on sth.** seinen Kopf auf etw. *(Akk.)* wetten *(ugs.);* **you can ~ your life on that** darauf kannst du Gift nehmen *(ugs.)* ; **d)** *(Amer. coll.: finance)* **~ sb.** jmdm. finanziell unter die Arme greifen; **~ a business/venture** Geld in ein Geschäft/Unternehmen stecken

~ 'off *v. t.* [mit Pfählen] abstecken

~ 'out *v. t.* **a)** *(mark out)* mit Pfählen begrenzen; eingrenzen; **b)** *(fig.: claim)* beanspruchen; **have ~d out a field of study as one's own** ein Fachgebiet für sich alleine gepachtet haben *(ugs.);* **c)** *(Amer. coll.: observe)* überwachen; *see also* **stake-out**

stake: ~-boat *n. (Rowing) verankertes Boot, das die Rennstrecke bei einem Bootsrennen markiert;* **~-net** *n.* Schockernetz, *das;* **~-out** *n. (Amer. coll.)* Überwachung, *die*

stalactite ['stæləktaɪt] *n. (Geol.)* Stalaktit, *der*

stalagmite ['stæləgmaɪt] *n. (Geol.)* Stalagmit, *der*

stale [steɪl] **1.** *adj.* **a)** alt; muffig; abgestanden ‹*Luft*›; alt[backen] ‹*Brot*›; schal ‹*Bier, Wein usw.*›; *(fig.)* abgedroschen ‹*Witz, Trick*›; überholt ‹*Nachricht*›; **b)** *(jaded)* ausgelaugt. **2.** *v. t.* alt werden lassen ‹*Lebensmittel*›; auslaugen ‹*Sportler, Schauspieler*›

'stalemate 1. *n. (Chess; also fig.)* Patt, *das;* **end in** *or* **reach ~**: mit einem Patt enden. **2.** *v. t.* **a)** *(Chess)* **~ sb.** jmdn. in eine Pattsituation bringen; **b)** *(fig.: halt)* zum Stillstand bringen; aufhalten ‹*Verfahren*›; verhindern ‹*Fortschritte*›

staleness ['steɪlnɪs] *n., no pl.* **a)** *(lack of freshness)* Muffigkeit, *die; (of air)* Abgestandenheit, *die; (of bread)* Altbackenheit, *die; (of beer etc.)* Schalheit, *die; (fig.: lack of novelty)* Abgedroschenheit, *die; (of news)* Überholtheit, *die;* **b)** *(jadedness)* Ausgelaugtheit, *die*

Stalinism ['stɑ:lɪnɪzm] *n. (Polit.)* Stalinismus, *der*

Stalinist ['stɑ:lɪnɪst] *n. (Polit.)* Stalinist, *der/* Stalinistin, *die*

¹stalk [stɔ:k] **1.** *v. i.* **a)** stolzieren; **~ along** einherschreiten/-stolzieren *(geh.);* **b)** *(Hunting)* pirschen; **be ~ing** auf der Pirsch sein. **2.** *v. t.* sich heranpirschen an (+ *Akk.*)

²stalk [stɔ:k] *n.* **a)** *(Bot.) (main stem)* Stengel, *der; (of leaf, flower, fruit)* Stiel, *der; (of cabbage)* Strunk, *der;* **b)** *(Zool.)* Stiel, *der; (of crab etc.)* [Augen]stiel, *der;* **his eyes stood** *or* **were out on ~s** *(fig.)* er machte *od.* bekam Stielaugen *(ugs.)*

stalker ['stɔ:kə(r)] *n.* Pirscher, *der*

¹stall [stɔ:l] **1.** *n.* **a)** Stand, *der;* **b)** *(for horse)* Box, *die; (for cow)* Stand, *der;* **c)** *(Eccl.: seat)* Stuhl, *der;* **the choir ~s** das Chorgestühl; **d)** *in pl. (Brit. Theatre: seats)* **[front] ~s** Parkett, *das;* **in the rear/cheap ~s** auf den hinteren/billigen Parkettplätzen; **e)** *(Brit. Horse-racing)* **the [starting-]~s** die Startboxen; **f)** *(of engine)* Stehenbleiben, *das;* **g)** *(Aeronaut.)* Überziehen, *das;* **go into a ~**: durchsacken. **2.** *v.t.* abwürgen *(ugs.)* ‹*Motor*›. **3.** *v. i.* **a)** ‹*Motor:*› stehenbleiben; **b)** *(Aeronaut.)* durchzusacken beginnen

²stall 1. *v. i.* ausweichen; **~ on a promise** *(delay)* die Einlösung eines Versprechens hinauszögern; **quit ~ing!** *(Amer. coll.)* hör auf, drum herumzureden! *(ugs.).* **2.** *v. t.* blockieren ‹*Gesetz, Fortschritt*›; aufhalten ‹*Feind, Fortschritt*›

'stall-holder *n.* Standinhaber, *der/*-inhaberin, *die*

stallion ['stæljən] *n.* Hengst, *der*

stalwart ['stɔ:lwət] **1.** *adj.* **a)** *(sturdy)* stämmig; **b)** *attrib. (fig.: determined)* entschieden; entschlossen ‹*Kämpfer*›; *(loyal)* treu; getreu *(geh.).* **2.** *n. (loyal supporter)* treuer Anhänger/treue Anhängerin; **Party ~**: treues Parteimitglied

stamen ['steɪmen, 'steɪmən] *n. (Bot.)* Staubblatt, *das*

stamina ['stæmɪnə] *n.* **a)** *(physical staying-power)* Ausdauer, *die;* **b)** *(endurance)* Durchhaltevermögen, *das*

stammer ['stæmə(r)] **1.** *v. i.* stottern. **2.** *v. t.* stammeln; **~ [out] one's thanks/apologies** stammelnd danken/eine Entschuldigung stammeln. **3.** *n.* Stottern, *das;* **have a ~, speak with a ~**: stottern

stammerer ['stæmərə(r)] *n.* Stotterer, *der/* Stotterin, *die*

stamp [stæmp] **1.** *v. t.* **a)** *(impress, imprint sth. on)* [ab]stempeln; **~ sth. on sth.** etw. auf etw. *(Akk.)* [auf]stempeln; **~ envelopes with sth.** etw. auf Umschläge drucken; **b) ~ one's foot/feet** mit dem Fuß/den Füßen stampfen; **~ the snow from one's boots** den Schnee von den Stiefeln stampfen; **~ the floor** *or* **ground [in anger/with rage]** [ärgerlich/wütend] auf den Boden stampfen; **c)** *(put postage ~ on)* frankieren; freimachen *(Postw.);* **~ed addressed envelope** frankierter Rückumschlag; **d)** *(mentally)* **~ oneself/itself** *or* **become** *or* **be ~ed on sb.['s memory** *or* **mind]** sich jmdm. fest einprägen; **e)** *(crush)* zerstampfen; **f)** *(flatten)* **~ flat** platt stampfen *od.* treten ‹*Schachtel, Dose*›; **~ down** feststampfen *od.* -treten ‹*Erde, Schnee, Steine*›; **g)** *(characterize)* kennzeichnen; **~ sb. [as] a genius** zeigen, daß jmd. ein Genie ist. **2.** *v. i.* aufstampfen; **~ up and down** auf und ab stampfen. **3.** *n.* **a)** Marke, *die; (postage ~)* Briefmarke, *die; see also* **first-class 1 a; insurance stamp; second-class 1 b; trading stamp; b)** *(instrument for ~ing, mark)* Stempel, *der;* **c)** *(fig.: characteristic)* **bear the ~ of genius/greatness** Genialität/Größe erkennen lassen; **leave one's ~ on sth.** einer Sache seinen Stempel aufdrücken; **d)** *(fig.: kind)* [Menschen]schlag, *der;* **men of his ~**: Menschen seines Schlages *od.* seiner Prägung

~ on *v. t.* **a)** *(crush)* zertreten ‹*Insekt, Dose*›; zertrampeln ‹*Blumen*›; **~ on sb.'s foot** jmdm. auf den Fuß treten; **b)** *(suppress)* durchgreifen gegen. *See also* **~ 1 a, d**

~ 'out *v. t.* **a)** *(eliminate)* ausmerzen; ersticken ‹*Aufstand, Feuer*›; niederwalzen ‹*Opposition, Widerstand*›; **b)** *(cut out)* [aus]stanzen

stamp: ~-album *n.* Briefmarkenalbum, *das;* **~-book** *n.* Briefmarkenheftchen, *das;* **~-collecting** *n.* Briefmarkensammeln, *das;* **~-collection** *n.* Briefmarkensammlung, *die;* **~-collector** *n.* Briefmarkensammler, *der/*-sammlerin, *die;* **~-duty** *n.* Stempelsteuer, *die*

stampede [stæm'pi:d] **1.** *n.* **a)** Stampede, *die;* **b)** *(rush of people) (due to interest)* Ansturm, *der; (due to panic)* wilde Flucht; **b)** *(Amer. Polit.)* starker Zulauf. **2.** *v. i.* **a)** in Panik fliehen; **b)** *(rush)* ‹*Personen:*› stürmen. **3.** *v. t.* **a) ~ a herd** bei einer Herde eine Stampede auslösen; **b) ~ sb. into doing sth.** jmdn. dazu drängen, etw. zu tun

'stamp-hinge *see* **hinge 1 c**

stamping-ground ['stæmpɪŋgraʊnd] *n.* Revier, *das;* **one's old ~**: der Ort, wo man früher immer zu finden war

'stamp-machine *n.* Briefmarkenautomat, *der*

stance [stæns, stɑ:ns] *n.* **a)** *(Golf, Cricket: position)* Stellung, *die;* **b)** *(posture; fig.: attitude)* Haltung, *die;* **take up a ~ over** *or* **on sth.** *(fig.)* eine Haltung zu etw. einnehmen

stanch [stɑ:nʃ, stɔ:nʃ] *v. t.* **a)** *(stop flow of)* stillen ‹*Blut*›; **b)** *(stop flow from)* abbinden ‹*Wunde*›

stanchion ['stɑ:nʃn] *n.* Stütze, *die; (of flat wagon)* Runge, *die; (of awning)* Sonnensegelstütze, *die*

stand [stænd] **1.** *v. i.,* **stood** [stʊd] **a)** stehen; **all ~!** aufstehen!; **don't just ~ there [, do something]!** steh nicht so herum[, tu doch etwas!]; **~ for the National Anthem/for a minute's silence** zur Nationalhymne/zu einer Schweigeminute aufstehen; **~ in a line** *or* **row** sich in einer Reihe aufstellen; *(be ~ing)* in einer Reihe stehen; **we stood talk-**

ing wir standen da und unterhielten uns; ~ **or fall by sth.** *(fig.)* mit etw. stehen und fallen; ~ **empty** leer stehen; *see also* **standstill; b)** *(have height)* **he ~s six feet tall/the tree ~s 30 feet high** er ist sechs Fuß groß/der Baum ist 30 Fuß hoch; ~ **high above sb./sth.** *(fig.)* [rangmäßig] weit über jmdm. stehen/etw. bei weitem übersteigen; **c)** *(be at level)* ⟨*Aktien, Währung, Thermometer:*⟩ stehen (**at** auf + *Dat.*); ⟨*Fonds:*⟩ sich belaufen (**at** auf + *Akk.*); ⟨*Absatz, Export usw.:*⟩ liegen (**at** bei); **d)** *(hold good)* bestehenbleiben; **my decision still ~s** an meiner Entscheidung hat sich nichts geändert; **my offer/promise still ~s** mein Angebot/Versprechen gilt nach wie vor; **e)** *(find oneself, be)* ~ **first in line for the throne** in der Thronfolge der Erste sein; ~ **convicted of treachery** wegen Verrats verurteilt sein; **as it ~s, as things ~:** wie die Dinge [jetzt] liegen; **the law as it ~s** das bestehende *od.* gültige Recht; **the matter ~s thus** die Sache steht so; ~ **prepared to dispute sth.** bereit sein, über etw. *(Akk.)* zu diskutieren; **as a statesman he ~s alone in contemporary politics** *(fig.)* es gibt in der gegenwärtigen Politik keinen, der ihm als Staatsmann das Wasser reichen könnte; **I'd like to know where I ~** *(fig.)* ich möchte wissen, wo ich dran bin; ~ **in need** Not leiden; ~ **in need of sth.** einer Sache *(Gen.)* dringend bedürfen; **f)** *(be candidate)* kandidieren (**for** für); ~ **in an election** bei einer Wahl kandidieren; ~ **as a candidate/nominee** kandidieren/nominiert sein; ~ **as a Liberal/Conservative** für die Liberalen/Konservativen kandidieren; ~ **for Parliament** *(Brit.)* für einen Parlamentssitz kandidieren; ~ **for office** *(Brit.)* sich um ein Amt bewerben; **g)** ~ **proxy for sb.** jmdn. vertreten; **h)** *(place oneself)* sich stellen; ~ **from under sb.** *or* **sb.'s feet** *(Amer.)* jmdm. nicht ständig vor den Füßen herumlaufen; ~ **in the way of sth.** *(fig.)* einer Sache *(Dat.)* im Weg stehen; **[not]** ~ **in sb.'s way** *(fig.)* jmdm. [keine] Steine in den Weg legen; **i)** *(be likely)* ~ **to win** *or* **gain/lose sth.** etw. gewinnen/verlieren können; **what do I ~ to gain from/by it?** was kann ich dabei gewinnen?; **j)** *(Cricket: be umpire)* schiedsrichtern; **k)** *(Naut.: hold course)* ~ **in for** *or* **towards sth.** Kurs auf etw. *(Akk.)* nehmen; ~ **into danger** auf eine Gefahr zusteuern. *See also* **correct 1 a; deliver d; ease 1 f; easy 2; ²fast 2 a; ²firm 2; foot 1 a; leg 1 a; ¹light 1 a; ²pat a. 2.** *v. t.*, **stood a)** *(set in position)* stellen; ~ **sth. on end/upside down** etw. hochkant/auf den Kopf stellen; **b)** *(endure)* ertragen; vertragen ⟨*Klima*⟩; **I can't ~ the heat/noise** ich halte die Hitze/den Lärm nicht aus; **I cannot ~ [the sight of] him/her** ich kann ihn/sie nicht ausstehen; **he can't ~ the pressure/strain/stress** er ist dem Druck/den Strapazen/dem Streß nicht gewachsen; **I can't ~ it any longer!** ich halte es nicht mehr aus; ~ **closer examination** einer genaueren [Über]prüfung standhalten; ~ **the test of time** sich bewähren; **he can't ~ being told what to do** er kann es nicht leiden *od.* ausstehen, wenn man ihm Vorschriften macht; **c)** *(undergo)* ausgesetzt sein (+ *Dat.*); **the play/player has stood much criticism** das Stück/der Spieler stieß auf viel Kritik; ~ **trial [for sth.]** [wegen einer Sache] vor Gericht stehen; **d)** *(buy)* ~ **sb. sth.** jmdm. etw. ausgeben *od.* spendieren *(ugs.)*; **can I ~ you a lunch?** Gehen wir zusammen was essen? Ich lade dich ein. *See also* **chance 1 c; ¹ground 1 b; ¹pace 1 b; treat 1 c. 3.** *n.* **a)** *(support)* Ständer, *der;* **b)** *(stall; at exhibition)* Stand, *der;* **c)** *(raised structure)* Tribüne, *die;* **d)** *(resistance)* Widerstand, *der;* **put up a brave ~ against sb./sth.** jmdm./einer Sache tapfer Widerstand leisten; **take** *or* **make a ~** *(fig.)* klar Stellung beziehen (**for/against/on** für/gegen/zu); **e)** *(Cricket)* **a ~ of 90 runs** eine gemeinsame Serie von 90 Läufen; **f)** *(~ing-place for taxi, bus, etc.)* Stand, *der;* **g)** *(performance on tour)* Auftritt, *der;* **h)** *(of trees, corn, clover, etc.)* Bestand, *der;* **i)** *(position)* **take one's ~:** sich aufstellen; **take one's ~ on the podium** seinen Platz auf der Tribüne einnehmen; **take a [firm] ~ [on sth.]** [in etw. *(Dat.)*] einen festen Standpunkt vertreten; **what's your ~ [on this matter]?** welchen Standpunkt vertrittst du [in dieser Sache]? **j)** *(Amer.: witness-box)* Zeugenstand, *der;* **take the ~:** in den Zeugenstand treten. *See also* **grandstand; one-night stand**

~ **a'bout,** ~ **a'round** *v. i.* herumstehen

~ **a'side** *v. i.* **a)** *(step aside)* zur Seite treten; Platz machen; **b)** *(fig.: withdraw)* abseits stehen; ~ **aside from sth.** sich an etw. nicht beteiligen

~ **'back** *v. i.* **a)** ~ **[well] back [from sth.]** [ein gutes Stück] [von etw.] entfernt stehen; **b)** *see* ~ **aside a; c)** *(fig.: distance oneself)* zurücktreten; **sometimes one must ~ back from daily affairs** von Zeit zu Zeit muß man von seinen Alltagsgeschäften Abstand gewinnen; **d)** *(fig.: withdraw)* ~ **back from sth.** sich aus einer Sache heraushalten

~ **behind** *v. t.* ~ **behind sb./sth.** *(lit. or fig.)* hinter jmdm./etw. stehen

~ **between** *v. t.* **sth. ~s between sb. and sth.** *(fig.)* etw. steht jmdm. bei etw. im Wege

~ **by 1.** [-'-] *v. i.* **a)** *(remain apart)* abseits stehen; ~ **[idly] by and watch sth. happen** *or* **while sth. happens** untätig zusehen, wie etw. geschieht; ~ **by and do nothing to prevent sth.** sich abseits halten und nicht eingreifen, um etw. zu verhindern; **b)** *(be near)* daneben stehen; **c)** *(be ready)* sich zur Verfügung halten; ~ **by ready to do sth.** Gewehr bei Fuß stehen, um etw. zu tun. **2.** ['--] *v. t.* **a)** *(support)* ~ **by sb./one another** jmdm./sich [gegenseitig] *od. (geh.)* einander beistehen; **b)** *(adhere to)* ~ **by sth.** zu etw. stehen; ~ **by the terms of a contract** einen Vertrag einhalten; ~ **by a promise** ein Versprechen halten; ~ **by a resolution** einen Beschluß [in die Tat] umsetzen; **c)** *(Naut.: prepare to use)* klarmachen. *See also* **stand-by**

~ **'down 1.** *v. i.* **a)** *(withdraw, retire)* verzichten; ~ **down in favour of a person** zugunsten einer Person *(Gen.)* zurücktreten; **b)** *(leave witness-box)* den Zeugenstand verlassen; **c)** *(Brit. Mil.: go off duty)* seinen Posten verlassen; ~ **down from guard duty** seinen Wachdienst beenden; **d)** *(Mil.: disband)* sich auflösen. **2.** *v. t.* **a)** *(Brit. Mil.: relieve from duty)* abziehen; **b)** *(Mil.: disband)* auflösen

~ **for** *v. t.* **a)** *(signify)* bedeuten; **she hates him and all that he ~s for** sie haßt ihn und alles, was mit ihm zusammenhängt; **b)** *(represent)* ~ **for sb./sth.** für jmdn./etw. eintreten; sich für jmdn./etw. einsetzen; **c)** *see* **stand 1 f; d)** *(coll.: tolerate)* sich bieten lassen; **that's one thing I won't ~ for** das ist etwas, was ich nicht haben kann

~ **'in** *v. i.* **a)** *(deputize)* aushelfen; ~ **in for sb.** für jmdn. einspringen; **b)** *(share)* ~ **in with sb. [for sth.]** mit jmdm. die Kosten [für etw.] teilen; **c)** *(Naut.) see* **stand 1 k.** *See also* **stand-in**

~ **'off 1.** *v. i. (move away)* sich entfernen; *(keep away)* sich in einiger Entfernung halten. **2.** *v. t. see* **²lay off 1 a**

~ **'out** *v. i.* **a)** *(persist)* ~ **out for/against sth.** hartnäckig für etw. kämpfen/sich hartnäckig gegen etw. wehren; **b)** *(be prominent)* herausragen; **the reason for the crisis ~s out** der Grund für die Krise ist augenfällig; ~ **out against** *or* **in contrast to sth.** sich gegen etw. abheben; ~ **out a mile** nicht zu übersehen sein; ⟨*Grund, Antwort:*⟩ [klar] auf der Hand liegen; **c)** *(be outstanding)* herausragen (**from** aus); **d)** *(Naut.)* ~ **out to sea** in See gehen

~ **over 1.** *v. t.* **a)** [-'--] *see* **hold over; b)** ['---] *(watch)* beaufsichtigen. **2.** [-'--] *v. i.* **sth. can ~ over** etw. kann warten; **any unfinished business ~s over to the next meeting** alle unerledigten Punkte werden bis zum nächsten Treffen zurückgestellt

~ **to** *see* ~ **by 1 d;** *see also* **reason 1 b**

~ **to'gether** *v. i.* zusammenstehen; *(for a photograph)* sich [gemeinsam] aufstellen; *(fig.)* zusammenhalten

~ **'up 1.** *v. i.* **a)** *(rise)* aufstehen; ~ **up and be counted** *(fig.)* Farbe bekennen; **b)** *(be upright)* stehen; **I have only the clothes I ~ up in** ich besitze nur die Kleider, die ich am Leibe trage; ~ **up straight** sich aufrecht hinstellen; **c)** *(be valid) see* **²hold 2 d; d)** ~ **up well [in comparison with sb./sth.]** [im Vergleich zu jmdm./etw.] gut abschneiden; *(maintain worth or position)* ⟨*Preis, Wert:*⟩ sich [im Vergleich zu etw.] gut halten. **2.** *v. t. (coll.: fail to keep date with)* ~ **sb. up** jmdn. versetzen *(ugs.)*. *See also* **stand-up**

~ **'up for** *v. t.* ~ **up for sb./sth.** für jmdn./etw. Partei ergreifen; sich für jmdn./etw. stark machen; **why didn't you ~ up for me?** warum hast du mich nicht unterstützt?

~ **'up to** *v. t.* **a)** *(face steadfastly)* ~ **up to sb.** sich jmdm. entgegenstellen; jmdm. die Stirn bieten; ~ **up to sth.** sich einer Sache *(Dat.)* stellen; ~ **up to an ordeal well/badly** eine Tortur tapfer/nicht aushalten; ~ **up to criticism** sich von Kritik nicht beirren lassen; **b)** *(survive intact under)* ~ **up to sth.** einer Sache *(Dat.)* standhalten; ~ **up to wear and tear** eine starke Beanspruchung aushalten

stand-alone [stændə'ləʊn] *adj. (Computing)* selbständig

standard ['stændəd] **1.** *n.* **a)** *(norm)* Maßstab, *der;* **safety ~s** Sicherheitsnormen; **above/below/up to ~:** überdurchschnittlich [gut]/unter dem Durchschnitt/der Norm entsprechend; **by anybody's ~s** für jeden; **b)** *(degree)* Niveau, *das;* **of [a] high/low ~:** von hohem/niedrigem Niveau; **a high ~ of competence** ein hohes Maß an Kompetenz; **set a high/low ~ in** *or* **of sth.** hohe/niedrige Ansprüche an etw. *(Akk.)* stellen; **the first competitor set a high ~:** der erste Bewerber setzte einen hohen Maßstab; **this pupil sets himself too low a ~ in his work** dieser Schüler verlangt zu wenig von sich selbst; ~ **of living** Lebensstandard, *der;* **c)** *in pl. (moral principles)* Prinzipien; **~s of sexual behaviour** Maßstäbe für das Sexualverhalten; **d)** *(flag)* Standarte, *die; (fig.: cause)* Banner, *das (geh.)*; **many flocked to the ~** *(fig.)* viele strömten zur Fahne; **e)** *(Hort.)* Hochstamm, *der;* ~ **rose** Hochstammrose, *die;* **f)** *(Bot.)* ~ **[shrub]** natürlich gewachsener Strauch; ~ **[tree]** Baum mit naturgemäßem Kronenaufbau; **g) lamp ~** *see* **lamp-post; h)** *(in currency)* Feingehalt, *der;* Standard, *der;* **the silver/monetary ~:** der Silberstandard/Münzfuß. *See also* **double standard; gold standard; royal standard. 2.** *adj.* **a)** *(conforming to ~, authoritative)* Standard-; *(used as reference)* Normal-; **b)** *(widely used)* normal; **what is the ~ thing to do in such cases?** was macht man normalerweise in solchen Fällen?; **be ~ procedure** Vorschrift sein; **have sth.** *or* **include sth.** *or* **be fitted with sth. as ~:** serienmäßig mit etw. ausgerüstet sein; **sth. is a ~ feature** etw. gehört zur Standardausrüstung; **a ~ letter** ein Schemabrief *(Bürow.)*; **a ~ model** ein Standardmodell; **be ~ practice** allgemein üblich sein; **it is ~ practice for sb. to do sth.** es ist üblich, daß jmd. etw. tut; **follow the ~ pattern** dem üblichen Muster folgen

standard: ~-bearer *n.* **a)** *(Mil.: flagbearer)* Standartenträger, *der;* **b)** *(fig.: leader)* Bannerträger, *der*/-trägerin, *die (geh.)*; Vorkämpfer, *der*/-kämpferin, *die;* **~-bearer for** *or* **in sth.** Vorkämpfer einer Sa-

che *(Gen.)*; **S~-bred** *n. (Amer.)* Amerikanischer Traber; **S~ 'English** *n.* Standardenglisch, *das*
standardisation, standardise *see* **standardiz-**
standardization [stændədaɪ'zeɪʃn] *n.* Standardisierung, *die*
standardize ['stændədaɪz] *v.t.* standardisieren
standard: ~ 'lamp *n. (Brit.)* Stehlampe, *die*; **~ time** *n.* Normalzeit, *die*
'stand-by 1. *n., pl.* **~s a)** *(reserve)* **[act] as a ~:** als Ersatz [bereitstehen]; **be on ~** ⟨*Polizei, Feuerwehr, Truppen:*⟩ einsatzbereit sein; ⟨*Schauspieler:*⟩ sich bereithalten; ⟨*Flugzeug:*⟩ startbereit sein; **the army was put on ~:** die Armee wurde in Einsatzbereitschaft versetzt; **b)** *(resource)* Rückhalt, *der*; **sth. is a good ~:** auf etw. *(Akk.)* kann man jederzeit zurückgreifen; **drink was his only ~:** das Trinken war seine einzige Zuflucht; **have some tins of food/an emergency pack as a ~:** einige Konserven für Notfälle/einen Notvorrat haben; **the generator is a ~:** der Generator dient als Notaggregat. **2.** *attrib. adj.* Ersatz-; **~ safety equipment** zusätzliche Sicherheitsausrüstung; **~ ticket/passenger** Stand-by-Ticket, *das*/-Passagier, *der*
standee [stæn'di:] *n. (Amer. coll.)* stehender Passagier/Zuschauer
'stand-in 1. *n.* Ersatz, *der*; *(in theatre, film)* Ersatzdarsteller, *der*/-darstellerin, *die*; *(Sport)* Ersatzspieler, *der*/-spielerin, *die*. **2.** *attrib. adj.* Ersatz-
standing ['stændɪŋ] **1.** *n.* **a)** *(repute)* Ansehen, *das*; **have some ~:** recht angesehen sein; **be of** *or* **have [a] high ~:** ein hohes Ansehen genießen; **have no ~:** ein Niemand sein; **what is his ~?** welchen Rang bekleidet er?; **be in good ~ with sb.** sich gut mit jmdm. stehen; *see also* **equal 1 a**; **b)** *(service)* **be an MP of twenty years' ~:** seit zwanzig Jahren [ununterbrochen] dem Parlament angehören; **be a member/judge of long/short ~:** seit langem/kurzem Mitglied/Richter sein; **a girl-friend of long ~:** eine langjährige Freundin; *see also* **long-standing**; **c)** *(duration)* **of long/short ~:** von langer/kurzer Dauer; **a feud of long ~:** ein alter Zwist; **d) ~ place** Standplatz, *der*. **2.** *adj.* **a)** *(erect)* stehend; **after the storm there was scarcely a tree still ~:** nach dem Sturm stand kaum mehr ein Baum; **~ corn** stehendes Korn; **~ stone** Menhir, *der*; **leave sb. ~** *(lit. or fig.: progress much faster)* jmdn. weit hinter sich *(Dat.)* lassen; **b)** *attrib. (established)* fest ⟨*Regel, Brauch*⟩; **he has a ~ excuse** er bringt immer die gleiche Entschuldigung; *see also* **joke 1 b**; **c)** *attrib. (permanent)* stehend ⟨*Heer*⟩; feststehend ⟨*Praxis*⟩; **I have a ~ invitation to visit them whenever I want to** sie haben mich eingeladen, sie, wann immer ich will, zu besuchen; **d)** *attrib. (stationary)* **~ jump** Standsprung, *der*; **~ start** Hochstart, *der*
standing: ~ com'mittee *n.* ständiger Ausschuß; **~ 'order** *n.* **a)** *(payment instruction)* Dauerauftrag, *der*; *(for regular supply)* Abonnement, *das*; **b)** *in pl. (rules)* Geschäftsordnung, *die*; **~ o'vation** *n.* stürmischer Beifall; stehende Ovation *(geh.)*; **~-room** *n., no pl., no indef. art.* Stehplätze; **~ 'water** *n.* stehendes Gewässer; *(Golf)* Wassergraben, *der*; **~ wave** *n. (Phys.)* stehende Welle
'stand-off *n.* **a)** *(Amer.: deadlock)* verfahrene Situation; **finish/result in a ~:** in einer Sackgasse enden/in eine Sackgasse geraten; **b) ~ [half]** *(Rugby) see* **fly-half**
stand-offish [stænd'ɒfɪʃ] *adj.* reserviert
stand: ~ 'patter *n. (Amer. Polit.)* strammer Konservativer/stramme Konservative; **~-pipe** *n. (for water-supply)* Standrohr, *das*; **~point** *n.* **a)** *(observation point)* Standort, *der*; **b)** *(fig.: viewpoint)* Standpunkt, *der*; **~still** *n.* Stillstand, *der*; **be at a ~still** stillstehen; ⟨*Fahrzeug, Flugzeug:*⟩ stehen; ⟨*Produktion, Verkehr:*⟩ zum Erliegen gekommen sein; **come to a ~still** zum Stillstand kommen; ⟨*Verhandlungen:*⟩ zum Stillstand kommen; **the traffic/production came to a ~still** der Verkehr/die Produktion kam zum Erliegen; **bring to a ~still** zum Stehen bringen; zum Erliegen bringen ⟨*Produktion*⟩; **~-up** *adj.* **~-up fight** Schlägerei, *die*
stank *see* **stink 1**
stanza ['stænzə] *n. (Pros.)* Strophe, *die*
¹staple ['steɪpl] **1.** *n. (for fastening paper)* [Heft]klammer, *die*; *(for fastening netting)* Krampe, *die*. **2.** *v.t. (with a stapler)* heften **(on to** an + *Akk.*); *(with a hammer)* krampen **(to** an + *Akk.*)
²staple 1. *attrib. adj.* **a)** *(principal)* Grund-; **a ~ diet** *or* **food** ein Grundnahrungsmittel; **b)** *(Commerc.: important)* grundlegend; **~ goods** Haupthandelsartikel; **the ~ export of a country** das Hauptexportgut eines Landes. **2.** *n.* **a)** *(Commerc.: major item)* Haupterzeugnis, *das*; **b)** *(raw material)* Rohstoff, *der*; **c)** *(fig.: fundamental part)* **the ~ of conversation** das zentrale Thema der Unterhaltung; **d)** *(Textiles: fibre)* Faser, *die*
stapler ['steɪplə(r)] *n.* [Draht]hefter, *der*
star [stɑ:(r)] **1.** *n.* **a)** Stern, *der*; **reach for the ~s** *(fig.)* nach hohen Zielen streben; **three-~ general** *(Amer. Mil.)* Drei-Sterne-General, *der*; **three/four ~ hotel** Drei-/Vier-Sterne-Hotel, *das*; **two/four ~ [petrol]** Normal-/Super[benzin], *das*; **the S~s and Stripes** *(Amer.)* das Sternenbanner; **the pupil got a ~ for his work** der Schüler erhielt für seine Arbeit ein Sternchen *(als Auszeichnung)*; **b)** *(prominent person)* Star, *der*; **be a rising ~ [of the tennis world]** ein aufgehender Stern [am Tennishimmel] sein; **c)** *(asterisk)* Stern, *der*; Sternchen, *das*; **d)** *(Astrol.)* Stern, *der*; **read one's/the ~s** sein/das Horoskop lesen; **be born under an unlucky ~:** unter einem ungünstigen Stern geboren sein. *See also*; **double star; evening star; morning star; ¹see 1 a; shooting star. 2.** *attrib. adj.* Star-; **~ pupil** bester Schüler/beste Schülerin; **~ turn** *or* **attraction** Hauptattraktion, *die*; **receive ~ billing** als Star/Stars des Abends auftreten. **3.** *v.t.*, **-rr- a)** *(decorate)* mit Sternen schmücken; **~red pattern** Sternenmuster, *das*; **b)** *(mark with asterisk)* mit einem Stern[chen] versehen; **c)** *(feature as star)* **~ring Humphrey Bogart and Lauren Bacall** mit Humphrey Bogart und Lauren Bacall in den Hauptrollen; **the film ~red Newman and Redford** in dem Film spielten Newman und Redford die Hauptrollen. **4.** *v.i.*, **-rr-: ~ in a film/play/TV series** in einem Film/einem Stück/einer Fernsehserie die Hauptrolle spielen
starboard ['stɑ:bəd] *(Naut., Aeronaut.)* **1.** *n.* Steuerbord, *das*; **land to ~!** Land an Steuerbord!; **turn** *or* **put the helm to ~:** nach Steuerbord drehen. **2.** *adj.* steuerbord-; steuerbordseitig; **on the ~ bow/quarter** Steuerbord voraus/achteraus; *see also* **¹tack 1 c; watch 1 c**
starch [stɑ:tʃ] **1.** *n.* **a)** Stärke, *die*; **b)** *(fig.)* Steifheit, *die*. **2.** *v.t.* stärken
Star 'Chamber *n.* **a)** *(Brit. Hist.)* Sternkammer, *die (Gericht zur Verfolgung von Straftaten gegen die Krone)*; **b)** *(fig.: tribunal)* ≈ Volksgerichtshof, *der (fig.)*
starched [stɑ:tʃt] *adj.* gestärkt; *(fig.)* steif
'starch-reduced *adj.* stärkearm
starchy ['stɑ:tʃɪ] *adj.* **a)** *(containing much starch)* stärkehaltig ⟨*Nahrungsmittel*⟩; **b)** *(fig.: prim)* steif
'star-crossed *adj.* **they were ~ lovers** ihre Liebe stand unter einem schlechten Stern
stardom ['stɑ:dəm] *n.* Starruhm, *der*
stare [steə(r)] **1.** *v.i.* **a)** *(gaze)* starren; **~ in surprise/amazement** überrascht/erstaunt starren; **~ in horror** erschreckt starren; **~ at sb./sth.** jmdn./etw. anstarren; **it is rude to ~ at people** es ist unhöflich, andere [Leute] anzustarren; **b)** *(have fixed gaze)* starr blikken. **2.** *v.t.* **~ sb. into silence** jmdn. durch Anstarren zum Schweigen bringen; **~ sb. in the face** jmdn. [feindselig] fixieren; *(fig.)* jmdm. ins Auge springen; **ruin was staring him in the face** ihm drohte der Ruin; **I looked for my purse for ages and it was staring me in the face all the time** ich suchte eine Ewigkeit mein Portemonnaie, und dabei lag es die ganze Zeit direkt vor meiner Nase *(ugs.)*. **3.** *n.* Starren, *das*; **fix sb. with a [curious/malevolent] ~:** jmdn. [neugierig/böse] anstarren
~ 'down, ~ 'out *v.t.* **~ sb. down** *or* **out** jmds. Blick niederzwingen *(geh.)*; jmdn. so lange anstarren, bis er/sie die Augen abwendet
star: ~fish *n.* Seestern, *der*; **~-gazer** ['stɑ:geɪzə(r)] *n. (coll.)* Sterngucker, *der (ugs. scherzh.)*
staring ['steərɪŋ] *attrib. adj.* starrend ⟨*Augen*⟩; **with ~ eyes** mit starrem Blick; **be stark ~ mad** *(fig. coll.)* völlig verrückt sein *(ugs.)*
stark [stɑ:k] **1.** *adj.* **a)** *(bleak)* öde; spröde ⟨*Schönheit, Dichtung*⟩; **b)** *(obvious)* scharf umrissen; nackt ⟨*Wahrheit*⟩; scharf ⟨*Kontrast, Umriß*⟩; kraß ⟨*Unterschied, Gegensatz, Realismus*⟩; **be in ~ contrast [to sb./sth.]** sich stark unterscheiden [von jmdm./etw.]; **c)** *(extreme)* schier ⟨*Entsetzen, Dummheit*⟩; nackt ⟨*Armut, Angst*⟩. **2.** *adv.* völlig; **~ naked** splitternackt *(ugs.)*; *see also* **staring**
starkers [stɑ:kəz] *pred. adj. (Brit. sl.)* splitternackt *(ugs.)*
starkly ['stɑ:klɪ] *adv.* **a)** *(clearly)* überdeutlich; scharf ⟨*kontrastieren*⟩; **b)** *(harshly)* grell ⟨*erleuchtet*⟩; **state a problem in ~ realistic terms** ein Problem kraß und realistisch darlegen
starless ['stɑ:lɪs] *adj.* stern[en]los
starlet ['stɑ:lɪt] *n. (Cinemat.)* Starlet[t], *das*
'starlight *n., no pl.* Sternenlicht, *das*
starling ['stɑ:lɪŋ] *n. (Ornith.)* **a)** [Gemeiner] Star; **b)** *(of family Sturnidae)* Star, *der*; *(of family Icteridae)* Stärling, *der*
'starlit *adj.* sternhell
Star: ~ of Bethlehem [stɑ:r əv 'beθlɪhem] *n. (Bot.)* Stern von Bethlehem; Milchstern, *der*; **~ of David** [stɑ:r əv 'deɪvɪd] *n.* David[s]stern, *der*
starry ['stɑ:rɪ] *adj.* **a)** sternklar ⟨*Himmel, Nacht*⟩; sternenübersät ⟨*Himmel*⟩; **b)** *(shining)* strahlend, leuchtend ⟨*Augen*⟩
'starry-eyed *adj.* blauäugig *(fig.)*
star: ~ shell *n. (Mil.)* Leuchtgeschoß, *das*; **~ sign** *n.* Sternzeichen, *das*; **~-spangled** *adj.* mit Sternen übersät; sternbesät *(dichter.)*; **the S~-Spangled Banner** das Sternenbanner; **~-studded** *adj.* **a)** mit Sternen übersät; **b)** ⟨*Show, Film, Besetzung*⟩ mit großem Staraufgebot
start [stɑ:t] **1.** *v.i.* **a)** *(begin)* anfangen; beginnen *(oft geh.)*; **when we first ~ed** ganz zu Anfang; **don't 'you ~!** *(coll.)* nun fang du auch noch [damit] an!; **~ on [at] sb.** *(coll.)* auf jmdn. einhacken *(ugs.)*; **don't ~ on at me about that again!** nun fang nicht schon wieder damit an!; **~ on sth.** etw. beginnen; **~ on Latin** mit Latein beginnen; **~ with sth./sb.** bei *od.* mit etw./jmdm. anfangen; **prices ~ at ten dollars** die Preise beginnen bei zehn Dollar; **~ at the beginning** am Anfang beginnen; **to ~ with** zuerst *od.* zunächst einmal; **~ing from next month** ab nächsten Monat; *see also* **get 2 b; scratch 3 a**; **b)** *(set out)* aufbrechen; **c)** *(make sudden movement)* aufschrecken; **~ with pain/surprise** vor Schmerz/Überraschung auffahren; **~ from one's chair** von seinem Stuhl hochfahren; **~ back** zurückfahren; **~ with fright** vor Schreck zurückwei-

chen; **d)** *(begin to function)* anlaufen; ⟨*Auto, Motor usw.:*⟩ anspringen; **e)** *(burst)* **his eyes ~ed from their sockets/his skull** *or* **head** die Augen traten ihm aus den Höhlen/dem Kopf. **2.** *v.t.* **a)** *(begin)* beginnen [mit]; **we ~ed the holiday on Sunday** unser Urlaub begann am Sonntag; **I have just ~ed a book by Böll** ich habe gerade ein Buch von Böll angefangen; **~ life in Australia** *(be born)* seine ersten Lebensjahre in Australien verbringen; **have ~ed life as sth.** *(fig.)* ursprünglich etw. gewesen sein; **~ school** in die Schule kommen; **~ work** mit der Arbeit beginnen **(on** an + *Dat.*); *(after leaving school)* zu arbeiten anfangen; **~ doing** *or* **to do sth.** [damit] anfangen, etw. zu tun; **b)** *(cause)* auslösen; anfangen ⟨*Streit, Schlägerei*⟩; legen ⟨*Brand*⟩; *(accidentally)* verursachen ⟨*Brand*⟩; **you've really ~ed something now!** jetzt hast du aber was angerichtet!; **you trying to ~ something?** *(coll.)* willst du 'ne Schlägerei anfangen?; **c)** *(set up)* ins Leben rufen ⟨*Organisation, Projekt*⟩; aufmachen ⟨*Laden, Geschäft*⟩; herausbringen ⟨*Zeitung*⟩; gründen ⟨*Verein, Firma, Zeitung*⟩; **d)** *(switch on)* einschalten; starten, anlassen ⟨*Motor, Auto*⟩; **e) ~ sb. doing sth.** jmdn. anfangen lassen, etw. zu tun; **~ sb. working on a project** jmdn. mit der Arbeit an einem Projekt anfangen lassen; **they ~ the children writing at an early age** sie bringen den Kindern schon früh das Schreiben bei; **~ sb. drinking/coughing/laughing** jmdn. zum Trinken/Husten/Lachen bringen; **~ sb. on a diet** jmdn. auf Diät *(Akk.)* setzen; **she ~ed the baby on solid foods** sie gab dem Baby erstmals feste Nahrung; **~ sb. in business/a trade** jmdm. die Gründung eines Geschäfts ermöglichen/jmdn. in ein Handwerk einführen; **f)** *(Sport)* **~ a race** ein Rennen starten; **~ a football match** ein Fußballspiel anpfeifen; **g) ~ a family** eine Familie gründen; **they have ~ed a baby** sie erwarten ein Kind; **h)** *(Hunting: rouse)* aufscheuchen **(from** aus). **3.** *n.* **a)** Anfang, *der;* Beginn, *der; (of race)* Start, *der;* **from the ~:** von Anfang an; **from ~ to finish** von Anfang bis Ende; **at the ~:** am Anfang; **at the ~ of the war/day** bei Kriegsbeginn/zum Tagesanfang; **be in at** *or* **in on the ~ of sth.** von Anfang an bei etw. dabei sein; **it could be the ~ of something big** *(coll.)* daraus könnte eine größere Sache werden *(ugs.)*; **make a ~:** anfangen **(on, with** mit); *(on journey)* aufbrechen; **make an early/late ~ [for town/to one's holiday]** früh/spät [in die Stadt/in die Ferien] aufbrechen; **get off to** *or* **make a good/slow/poor ~:** einen guten/langsamen/schlechten Start haben; **for a ~** *(coll.)* zunächst einmal; **b)** *(Sport: ~ing-place)* Start, *der;* **c)** *(Sport: advantage)* Vorsprung, *der;* **give sb. 60 metres ~:** jmdm. eine Vorgabe von 60 Metern geben; **have a ~ over** *or* **on sb./sth.** *(fig.)* einen Vorsprung vor jmdm./etw. haben; *see also* **head start; d)** *(good beginning)* **[good] ~:** guter Start; **get a good ~ in life** einen guten Start ins Leben haben; **e)** *(jump)* **she remembered** *or* **realized with a ~ that ...:** sie schreckte zusammen, als ihr einfiel, daß ...; **give sb. [a] ~:** jmdm. einen Schreck einjagen; **give a ~:** zusammenfahren; **f)** *in pl. (jerks)* **give several ~s** mehrmals rucken; *see also* **¹fit b**

~ for *v.t.* sich auf den Weg machen nach/zu

~ 'in *v.i.* **a)** *(coll.: begin to do)* **~ in to do sth.** sich daranmachen *(ugs.)*, etw. zu tun; **~ in on sth./on doing sth.** *(Amer. coll.)* sich an etw. *(Akk.)* machen *(ugs.)*/sich daranmachen *(ugs.)*, etw. zu tun; **b) ~ in on sb. [for sth.]** *(criticize)* jmdn. [wegen etw.] attackieren

~ 'off 1. *v.i.* **a)** *see* **set off 1; b)** *(coll.: begin action)* **~ off by showing sth.** zu Beginn etw. zeigen; **c) ~ off with** *or* **on sth.** *(begin on)* mit etw. beginnen; **today we ~ed off with Latin** heute hatten wir zuerst Latein. **2.** *v.t.* **a) ~ sb. off working** jmdn. mit der Arbeit anfangen lassen; **~ sb. off on a task/job** jmdn. in eine Aufgabe/Arbeit einweisen; **~ sb. off on a craze** jmdm. einen Floh ins Ohr setzen *(ugs.)*; **b)** *see* **set off 2 b**

~ 'out *v.i.* **a)** *see* **set out 1; b)** *see* **set off 1**

~ 'up 1. *v.i.* **a)** *see* **jump up; b)** *(be set going)* starten; ⟨*Motor:*⟩ anspringen; **c)** *(begin to work)* **~ up in engineering/insurance** als Ingenieur/in der Versicherungsbranche anfangen; **~ up in a trade/as a plumber** sich als Handwerker/als Klempner selbständig machen. **2.** *v.t.* **a)** *(form)* beginnen ⟨*Gespräch*⟩; gründen ⟨*Geschäft, Firma*⟩; schließen ⟨*Freundschaft*⟩; **b)** *(~ [engine of])* starten; anlassen

starter ['stɑ:tə(r)] *n.* **a)** *(Sport: signaller)* Starter, *der;* **be under ~'s orders** *(Horse-racing)* am Start stehen; **b)** *(Sport: entrant)* Starter, *der*/Starterin, *die; (horse)* startendes Pferd; **be a ~ in a race** in einem Rennen starten; **c)** *(Motor Veh.)* **~ [motor]** Anlasser, *der;* **press the ~:** den Starter- *od.* Anlasserknopf drücken; **d)** *(initial action)* Anfang, *der;* **an easy question for a ~:** als erstes eine leichte Frage; **as a ~:** zuerst; **for ~s** *(coll.)* erstens einmal; **e)** *(hors d'œuvre etc.)* Vorspeise, *die;* **for a ~:** als Vorspeise

starting ['stɑ:tɪŋ]: **~-block** *n. (Athletics)* Startblock, *der;* **~-gate** *n. (Horse-racing)* Startmaschine, *die;* **~-grid** *n. (Motor-racing)* Startplatz, *der;* **on the second row of the ~-grid** in der zweiten Startreihe; **~-handle** *n. (Brit.)* [Anlasser]kurbel, *die;* **~-line** *n.* Startlinie, *die;* **~-pistol** *n. (Sport)* Startpistole, *die;* **~-point** *n. (lit. or fig.)* Ausgangspunkt, *der; (for solving a problem)* Ansatzpunkt, *der;* **~-post** *n. (Sport)* Startpfosten, *der;* **~-price** *n. (Horse-racing)* endgültige Quote; **~-stall** *see* **¹stall 1 e; ~ time** *n.* Anfangszeit, *die*

startle ['stɑ:tl] *v.t.* erschrecken; **be ~d by sth.** über etw. *(Akk.)* erschrecken

startling ['stɑ:tlɪŋ] *adj.* erstaunlich; überraschend ⟨*Nachricht*⟩; *(alarming)* bestürzend ⟨*Nachricht, Entdeckung*⟩

startlingly ['stɑ:tlɪŋlɪ] *adv.* erstaunlich; *(alarmingly)* bestürzend

starvation [stɑ:'veɪʃn] *n.* Verhungern, *das;* **die of** *or* **from/suffer from ~:** verhungern/hungern *od.* Hunger leiden; **be** *or* **live on a ~ diet** fast am Verhungern sein; **~ wages** Hungerlohn, *der*

starve [stɑ:v] **1.** *v.i.* **a)** *(die of hunger)* **~ [to death]** verhungern; **b)** *(suffer hunger)* hungern; **c) be starving** *(coll.: feel hungry)* am Verhungern sein *(ugs.)*; **you must be starving!** *(coll.)* du mußt einen Mordshunger haben! *(ugs.)*; **d)** *(fig.: suffer want)* hungern *(geh.)* **(for** nach); **be spiritually ~d** seelisch ausgehungert sein. **2.** *v.t.* **a)** *(kill by starving)* **~ sb. [to death]** jmdn. verhungern lassen; **be ~d [to death]** verhungern; **b)** *(deprive of food)* hungern lassen; **feed a cold, ~ a fever** bei Erkältung soll man essen, bei Fieber hungern; **c)** *(deprive)* **we were ~d of knowledge** uns *(Dat.)* wurde [viel] Wissen vorenthalten; **feel ~d of affection** unter einem Mangel an Zuneigung leiden; *see also* **sex-starved; d)** *(force)* **~ sb. into submission/surrender** jmdn. bis zur Unterwerfung/Kapitulation aushungern

~ 'out *v.t.* aushungern

'star wars *n. pl.* der Krieg der Sterne

stash [stæʃ] *(sl.)* **1.** *v.t.* **~ [away]** verstecken; **he ~ed the sweets in his pocket** er ließ die Bonbons in seiner Tasche verschwinden; **~ money away** Geld beiseite schaffen. **2.** *n.* [geheimes] Lager

stasis ['stæsɪs, 'steɪsɪs] *n., pl.* **stases** ['stæsi:z, 'steɪsi:z] **a)** *(stagnation)* Stillstand, *der; (of economy)* Stagnation, *die;* **b)** *(Biol.: stoppage)* Stase, *die*

state [steɪt] **1.** *n.* **a)** *(condition)* Zustand, *der;* **~ of the economy** Wirtschaftslage, *die;* **the ~ of play** *(Sport)* der Spielstand; **the ~ of play [at the moment] is that X leads** nach dem gegenwärtigen Spielstand führt X; **the ~ of play in the negotiations/debate** *(fig.)* der [gegenwärtige] Stand der Verhandlungen/Debatte; **the ~ of things** der Stand der Dinge; **the ~ of things in general** die allgemeine Lage; **the ~ of the art** der [gegenwärtige] Stand der Technik; *see also* **state-of-the-art; the ~ of the nation** die Lage der Nation; **be in a ~ of war** sich im Kriegszustand befinden; **a ~ of war exists** es herrscht Kriegszustand; **be in a ~ of excitement/sadness/anxiety** aufgeregt/traurig/ängstlich sein; **b)** *(mess)* **what a ~ you're in!** wie siehst du denn aus! **things are in a ~, I can tell you** es herrschen wirklich finstere Zustände, sag' ich dir; **c)** *(anxiety)* **be in a ~** *(be in a panic)* aufgeregt sein; *(be anxious)* sich *(Dat.)* Sorgen machen; *(be excited)* ganz aus dem Häuschen sein *(ugs.)*; **get into a ~** *(coll.)* Zustände kriegen *(ugs.)*; **don't get into a ~!** reg dich nicht auf! *(ugs.)*; **d)** *(nation)* Staat, *der;* **[affairs] of S~:** Staats[geschäfte]; **e)** *(federal ~) (of Germany, Austria)* Land, *das; (of America)* Staat, *der;* **the [United] S~s** *sing.* die [Vereinigten] Staaten; **the Northern/Southern S~s** *(Amer.)* die Nord-/Südstaaten; **S~s' Rights** *(Amer.)* Rechte der einzelnen Bundesstaaten; **f) S~** *(civil government)* Staat, *der;* **g)** *(pomp)* Prunk, *der;* **in ~:** in vollem Staat; **keep ~:** hofhalten; **lie in ~:** aufgebahrt sein; **h)** *(social rank)* soziale Stellung; **i)** *(Bibliog.: variant)* Abdruckszustand, *der;* **j)** *(Bot.: stage)* Stadium, *das;* **the larval ~** *(Zool.)* das Larvenstadium. *See also* **affair b; evidence 1 b; grace 1 e; mind 1 e. 2.** *attrib. adj.* **a)** *(of nation or federal ~)* staatlich; Staats⟨*bank, -sicherheit, -geheimnis, -dienst*⟩; **~ control** staatliche Kontrolle; **~ education** staatliches Erziehungswesen; **S~ university** *(Amer.)* [öffentliche] Universität eines Bundesstaates; **b)** *(ceremonial)* Staats-; **the ~ opening of Parliament** *(Brit.)* die feierliche Eröffnung des Parlaments [nach der Sommerpause]. **3.** *v.t.* **a)** *(express)* erklären; *(fully or clearly)* darlegen; äußern ⟨*Meinung*⟩; angeben ⟨*Alter usw.*⟩; **'please ~ full particulars'** „bitte genaue Angaben machen"; **this condition is ~d in the insurance policy** so steht es ausdrücklich in der Versicherungspolice; **~ one's opinion that ...:** die Überzeugung äußern, daß ...; **b)** *(specify)* festlegen; **can you ~ the year when ...?** kannst du das Jahr nennen, in dem ...?; **at ~d intervals** in genau festgelegten Abständen; **at** *or* **by the ~d time** zur festgesetzten Zeit; **c)** *(Law: set out)* **~ a case** einen Fall vortragen; **d)** *(Mus.: introduce)* einführen

state: ~-aided *adj.* staatlich gefördert; **~-controlled** *adj.* **a)** *(owned)* staatseigen; **b)** *(restricted)* staatlich kontrolliert; **~craft** *n. (statesmanship)* Kunst der Staatsführung; **S~ Department** *n. (Amer. Polit.)* Außenministerium, *das*

statehood ['steɪthʊd] *n.* **a)** *(sovereignty)* Eigenstaatlichkeit, *die;* **b)** *(Amer.: federation)* **be admitted to ~:** als Bundesstaat aufgenommen werden

'state-house *n. (Amer.: legislature building)* Parlamentsgebäude, *das*

stateless ['steɪtlɪs] *adj.* staatenlos; **~ person** Staatenlose, *der/die*

stately ['steɪtlɪ] *adj.* majestätisch; stattlich ⟨*Körperbau, Erscheinung, Gebäude*⟩; hochtrabend ⟨*Stil*⟩; feierlich ⟨*Prozession*⟩; **at a ~ pace** gemessenen Schrittes

stately 'home *n. (Brit.)* Herrensitz, *der; (grander)* Schloß, *das*

statement ['steɪtmənt] *n.* **a)** *(stating, account, thing stated)* Aussage, *die; (declaration)* Erklärung, *die; (allegation)* Behauptung, *die;* **make a ~** ⟨*Zeuge:*⟩ eine Aussage

machen; ⟨*Politiker:*⟩ eine Erklärung abgeben (on zu); **b)** *(Finance: report)* ~ **[of account], [bank]** ~: Kontoauszug, *der*
state: ~-of-the-'art *adj.* auf dem neuesten Stand der Technik *nachgestellt;* **~-owned** *adj.* staatlich; in Staatsbesitz *nachgestellt;* **~room** *n.* **a)** Prunkzimmer, *das;* **b)** *(Naut.)* private [Luxus]kabine; **c)** *(Amer. Railw.)* privates [Luxus]abteil; **S~ school** *n.* *(Brit.)* staatliche Schule; **S~side** *(Amer. coll.)* **1.** *adv.* **be/work/travel/head S~side** in den Staaten *(ugs.)* sein/arbeiten/in die Staaten *(ugs.)* reisen/fahren; **2.** *adj.* ⟨*Szene, Mode*⟩ in den Staaten *(ugs.)*
statesman ['steɪtsmən] *n., pl.* **statesmen** ['steɪtsmən] Staatsmann, *der; see also* **elder statesman**
statesmanlike ['steɪtsmənlaɪk] *adj.* staatsmännisch; diplomatisch ⟨*Lösung*⟩
statesmanship ['steɪtsmənʃɪp] *n., no pl.* **a)** *(Polit.: management)* Staatslenkung, *die;* **b)** *(wise leadership)* staatsmännisches Geschick
'State system *n., no pl. (Brit. Educ.)* staatliches Schulwesen
'statewide *adj.* landesweit; *(in USA)* im ganzen [Bundes]staat *nachgestellt*
static ['stætɪk] **1.** *adj.* **a)** *(Phys.)* statisch; **b)** *(not moving)* statisch; *(not changing)* konstant ⟨*Umweltbedingungen*⟩; **be ~**: stagnieren; **remain ~** ⟨*Zustand:*⟩ unverändert bleiben; ⟨*Preise:*⟩ gleich bleiben; **c)** *(Electr.)* [elektro]statisch. **2.** *n.* **a)** *(atmospherics)* atmosphärische Störungen; **b)** *see* **static electricity**
static elec'tricity *n.* *(Phys.)* statische Elektrizität
statics ['stætɪks] *n., no pl. (Mech.)* Statik, *die*
station ['steɪʃn] **1.** *n.* **a)** *(position)* Position, *die;* **be assigned a ~**: einen [Stand]ort zugewiesen bekommen; **take up one's ~**: seine Position einnehmen; **b)** *(establishment)* Station, *die; (Broadcasting)* Sender, *der;* **radar [tracking] ~** *(Mil.)* Radarstation, *die;* **c)** *see* **railway-station; d)** *(status)* Rang, *der;* **occupy a humble/an exalted ~**: eine niedrige/hohe Position bekleiden; **have ideas above one's ~**: sich für etwas Besseres halten; **marry above/below** *or* **beneath one's ~**: über/unter seinem Stand heiraten; **e)** *(Amer.: post office)* Poststelle, *die;* **f)** *(post) (Mil.)* Posten, *der; (Navy, Air Force)* Stützpunkt, *der; (Police)* Wache, *die;* **g)** *(Austral.: farm)* Farm, *die;* **[sheep-]~**: Schaffarm, *die;* **h) ~ of the Cross** *(Relig.)* Kreuzwegstation, *die (kath. Kirche).* **2.** *v. t.* **a)** *(assign position to)* stationieren; abstellen ⟨*Auto*⟩; aufstellen ⟨*Wache*⟩; **b)** *(place)* stellen; *(Sport)* aufstellen; **~ oneself** sich aufstellen
stationary ['steɪʃənərɪ] *adj.* **a)** *(not moving)* stehend; **be ~**: stehen; **the traffic was ~**: der Verkehr war zum Erliegen gekommen; **b)** *(fixed)* stationär
'station break *n. (Amer. Radio and Telev.)* Pausenzeichen, *das*
stationer ['steɪʃənə(r)] *n.* Schreibwarenhändler, *der/*-händlerin, *die;* **~'s [shop]** Schreibwarengeschäft, *das*
stationery ['steɪʃənərɪ] *n.* **a)** *(writing-materials)* Schreibwaren *Pl.;* **b)** *(writing-paper)* Briefpapier, *das;* **a ~ set** [eine Mappe mit] Briefpapier; eine Briefmappe; **office ~**: Bürobedarf, *der; see also* **continuous stationery**
'Stationery Office *n. (Brit.)* **[Her/His] Majesty's ~** *britischer Staatsverlag, der auch die staatlichen Stellen mit Bürobedarf versorgt*
station: ~-house *n. (Amer.: police station)* [Polizei]wache, *die;* **~-master** *n. (Railw.)* Stationsvorsteher, *der/*-vorsteherin, *die;* **~ sergeant** *n. (Brit. Police) Leiter einer Polizeiwache im Range eines Sergeanten;* **~-wagon** *n. (Amer.)* Kombi[wagen], *der*
statistic [stə'tɪstɪk] *n.* statistische Tatsache; **I disliked being treated as just a ~**: es mißfiel mir, nur als Nummer behandelt zu werden
statistical [stə'tɪstɪkl] *attrib. adj.*, **statistically** [stə'tɪstɪkəlɪ] *adv.* statistisch
statistician [stætɪ'stɪʃn] *n.* Statistiker, *der/* Statistikerin, *die*
statistics [stə'tɪstɪks] *n.* **a)** *as pl. (facts)* Statistik, *die;* **~ of population/crime, population/crime ~**: Bevölkerungs-/Kriminalitätsstatistik, *die;* **according to ~**: nach der Statistik; **~ show that one in three marriages ends in divorce** nach der Statistik endet eine von drei Eheschließungen mit Scheidung; **b)** *no pl. (science)* Statistik, *die*
statue ['stætʃu:, 'stætju:] *n.* Statue, *die;* **as still as a ~**: reglos wie eine Statue; *see also* **liberty**
statuesque [stætjʊ'esk, stætʃʊ'esk] *adj.* statuenhaft; *(imposing)* stattlich
statuette [stætʃʊ'et, stætjʊ'et] *n.* Statuette, *die*
stature ['stætʃə(r)] *n.* **a)** *(body height)* Statur, *die;* **be of short ~, be short in ~**: von kleiner Statur sein; **b)** *(fig.: standing)* Format, *das;* **be of international ~ in one's field** auf seinem Gebiet eine international anerkannte Kapazität sein; **a person of [some] ~**: eine [recht] bedeutende Persönlichkeit; **he was not of the same ~ as Picasso** er hatte nicht das Format *od.* die Größe Picassos
status ['steɪtəs] *n.* **a)** *(position)* Rang, *der;* **have no ~ in society** kein angesehenes Mitglied der Gesellschaft sein; **rise in ~**: an Ansehen gewinnen; **social ~**: [gesellschaftlicher] Status; **the ~ of this information is 'secret'** diese Information ist als „geheim" eingestuft; **be a person of high/low ~ in a firm** in einer Firma eine hohe/niedrige Stellung haben; **her ~ among scientists** ihr wissenschaftlicher Rang; **equality of ~ [with sb.]** Gleichstellung [mit jmdm.]; **financial ~**: finanzielle *od.* wirtschaftliche Lage; **b)** *(superior position)* Status, *der;* **have [some] ~ in the firm** in der Firma einen [ziemlich] hohen Rang bekleiden; **c)** *(Law)* Status, *der;* **have [no] legal ~**: [nicht] rechtsgültig sein; ⟨*Person:*⟩ über keinerlei Rechte verfügen
status: ~ quo [steɪtəs 'kwəʊ] *n.* Status quo, *der;* **~ symbol** *n.* Statussymbol, *das*
statute ['stætju:t] *n.* **a)** *(Law)* Gesetz, *das;* **by ~**: per Gesetz; **b)** *in pl. (rules)* Statut, *das;* Satzung, *die*
statute: ~-barred *adj.* *(Law)* verjährt; **~-book** *n.* *(Law)* Gesetzbuch, *das;* **put an Act** *or* **a law on the ~-book** ein Gesetz durchbringen; **put a measure/provision on the ~-book** einer Maßnahme/Bestimmung Gesetzeskraft *(Dat.)* verleihen; **~ law** *n.* *(Law)* **a)** *(statute)* Gesetz, *das;* **b)** *no pl., no indef. art.* kodifiziertes *od.* schriftlich niedergelegtes Recht; **~ mile** *n.* englische Meile
statutory ['stætjʊtərɪ] *adj.* **a)** *(Law)* gesetzlich ⟨*Feiertag, Bestimmung, Erfordernis, Erbe*⟩; gesetzlich vorgeschrieben ⟨*Strafe*⟩; gesetzlich festgeschrieben ⟨*Löhne, Zinssatz*⟩, gesetzlich festgelegt ⟨*Voraussetzung, Sätze, Zeit*⟩; **~ law** kodifiziertes Recht; **~ rights** [gesetzliche] Rechte; *see also* **¹rape 1; b)** *(relating to the statutes of an institution)* Satzungs⟨*bestimmungen*⟩; von der Satzung vorgesehen ⟨*Geldbuße usw.*⟩; **in accordance with the ~ requirements** *or* **conditions** satzungsgemäß
¹staunch [stɔ:nʃ, stɑ:nʃ] *adj.* treu ⟨*Freund, Anhänger*⟩; streitbar ⟨*Kämpfer, Anhänger*⟩; überzeugt ⟨*Katholik, Demokrat usw.*⟩; unerschütterlich ⟨*Mut, Hingabe, Glaube*⟩; standhaft ⟨*Herz*⟩; **be ~ in one's belief** an seinem Glauben unerschütterlich festhalten; **be ~ in one's support for sb./sth.** jmdn./etw. getreu unterstützen
²staunch *see* **stanch**
staunchly ['stɔ:nʃlɪ, 'stɑ:nʃlɪ] *adv.* standhaft ⟨*beistehen*⟩; unerschrocken ⟨*kämpfen, verteidigen*⟩; treu ⟨*ergeben sein*⟩; unerschütterlich ⟨*an etw. (Dat.) festhalten*⟩
stave [steɪv] **1.** *n.* **a)** *(Mus.) see* **staff 1d; b)** *(of barrel)* Daube, *die;* **c)** *(rung)* Sprosse, *die;* **d)** *(lit.: stanza)* Strophe, *die.* **2.** *v. t.,* **~d** *or* **stove** [stəʊv] ein Loch schlagen in (+ *Akk.*)
~ 'in *v.t.* *(crush)* eindrücken ⟨*Karosserie, Tür, Fenster, Rippen*⟩; einschlagen ⟨*Kopf, Kiste*⟩; *(break hole in)* ein Loch schlagen in (+ *Akk.*); **the boat was ~d in** das Boot schlug leck
~ 'off *v.t.,* **~d off** abwenden; abwehren ⟨*Angriff*⟩; verhindern ⟨*Krankheit*⟩; stillen ⟨*Hunger, Durst*⟩; zurückweisen ⟨*Forderung*⟩
¹stay [steɪ] **1.** *n.* **a)** Aufenthalt, *der; (visit)* Besuch, *der;* **during her ~ with us** während sie bei uns zu Besuch war; **come/go for a short ~ with sb.** jmdn. kurz besuchen; **have a week's ~ in London** eine Woche in London verbringen; **b)** *(Law)* **~ [of execution]** Aussetzung [der Vollstreckung]; *(fig.)* Galgenfrist, *die;* **c)** *(support)* Stütze, *die;* **d)** *in pl. (Hist.) see* **corset 1a. 2.** *v. i.* **a)** *(remain)* bleiben; **he ~ed in the club/army for five years** er war fünf Jahre Klubmitglied/in der Armee; **~ open till 10 o'clock** ⟨*Geschäft:*⟩ bis 10 Uhr geöffnet sein; **be here to ~, have come to ~**: sich fest eingebürgert haben; ⟨*Arbeitslosigkeit, Inflation:*⟩ zum Dauerzustand geworden sein; ⟨*Modeartikel:*⟩ in Mode bleiben; **~ with the leaders** sich an der Spitze halten *od.* behaupten; **~! halt!**; *(to dog)* bleib hier!; **~ for** *or* **to dinner/for the party** zum Essen/zur Party bleiben; **~ put** *(coll.)* ⟨*Ball, Haar:*⟩ liegen bleiben; ⟨*Hut:*⟩ fest sitzen; ⟨*Bild:*⟩ hängen bleiben; ⟨*Person:*⟩ bleiben[, wo man ist]; **I am ~ing put in this armchair** aus diesem Sessel rühre ich mich so schnell nicht weg; **~ sitting** sitzen bleiben; **~ 'with it!** *(coll.)* bleib dran! *(ugs.)*; **~ with me!** bleib bei mir!; **~ around!** bleib in der Nähe!; **b)** *(dwell temporarily)* wohnen; **~ abroad** im Ausland leben; **he ~ed [for] two weeks in London before flying to Brussels** er verbrachte zwei Wochen in London, bevor er nach Brüssel flog; **~ the night in a hotel** die Nacht in einem Hotel verbringen; **~ at sb.'s** *or* **with sb. for the weekend** das Wochenende bei jmdm. verbringen; **c)** *(Sport)* durchhalten; **~ well at a fast pace/over any distance** bei schnellem Tempo/über jede Entfernung gut mithalten. **3.** *v. t.* **a)** *(arch./literary: stop)* aufhalten; **~ one's hand** *(fig.)* sich bedeckt halten; **~ sb.'s hand** *(fig.)* jmdn. zurückhalten; **b)** *(endure)* **~ the course** *or* **distance** die [ganze] Strecke durchhalten; *(fig.)* durchhalten; *see also* **¹pace 1b; c)** *(satisfy)* stillen ⟨*Hunger, Durst*⟩; **d)** *(Law)* aussetzen; **e)** *(literary: support)* stützen
~ a'head *v. i.* die Führung halten
~ a'way *v. i.* **a)** *(not attend)* **~ away [from sth.]** [von etw.] wegbleiben; [einer Sache *(Dat.)*] fernbleiben; **~ away from school/a meeting** nicht zur Schule/zu einem Treffen gehen/kommen; **if the visitors/customers ~ away** wenn die Besucher/Käufer ausbleiben; **b)** *(~ distant)* **~ away from the dog!** komm dem Hund nicht zu nahe!; **he ~ed well away from the wall** er hielt sich ein gutes Stück von der Wand entfernt; **~ away from him!** laß ihn in Ruhe!; **~ away from drugs** die Finger von Drogen lassen *(ugs.)*
~ 'back *v. i.* **a)** *(not approach)* zurückbleiben; **b)** *see* **~ behind; c)** *(remain in place)* **the door won't ~ back** die Tür bleibt nicht offen
~ be'hind *v. i.* zurückbleiben; **have to ~ behind [after school]** nachsitzen müssen; **we ~ed behind after the lecture** wir sind nach der Vorlesung noch dageblieben; **can you ~ behind for a moment?** kannst du einen Augenblick [hier] warten?
~ 'down *v. i.* **a)** *(remain lowered)* unten blei-

ben; **they ~ed down out of sight** sie blieben unten, so daß man sie nicht sehen konnte; **b)** *(not increase)* stabil bleiben; **c)** *(Educ.: not go to higher form)* sitzenbleiben *(ugs.)*

~ 'in *v. i.* **a)** *(remain in position)* halten; **will these creases ~ in?** bleiben diese Falten [drin *(ugs.)*]?; **this passage [of the book] should ~ in** diese Passage sollte nicht gestrichen werden; **b)** *(remain indoors)* im Hause bleiben; *(remain at home)* zu Hause bleiben

~ 'off 1. *v. i.* **a)** wegbleiben *(ugs.)*; **b)** *(away from work, school)* **[have to] ~ off** nicht zur Schule/Arbeit gehen [können]. **2.** *v. t.* **a)** *(not go on to)* nicht betreten ‹*Rasen, Teppich, Beete*›; nicht gehen auf (+ *Akk.*) ‹*Straße usw.*›; **~ off the bottle/off drugs** die Finger vom Alkohol/von Drogen lassen *(ugs.)*; **b)** *(be absent from)* **~ off school/work** nicht zur Schule/Arbeit gehen

~ 'on *v. i.* **a)** *(remain in place)* ‹*Hut, Perücke, Kopftuch:*› sitzen bleiben; ‹*falsche Wimpern, Aufkleber:*› haften; ‹*Deckel, Rad:*› halten; **b)** *(remain in operation)* angeschaltet bleiben; anbleiben *(ugs.)*; **c)** *(remain present)* noch [da]bleiben; **~ on at school** auf der Schule bleiben; **~ on as chairman** Vorsitzender bleiben

~ 'out *v. i.* **a)** *(not go home)* wegbleiben *(ugs.)*; nicht nach Hause kommen/gehen; **don't ~ out late!** komm nicht zu spät nach Hause!; **b)** *(remain outside)* draußen bleiben; **c)** *(fig.)* **~ out of sb.'s way** jmdm. aus dem Wege gehen; **d)** *(remain on strike)* **~ out [on strike]** im Ausstand bleiben

~ 'over *v. i. (coll.)* über Nacht bleiben

~ 'up *v. i.* **a)** *(not go to bed)* aufbleiben; **b)** *(remain in position)* ‹*Pfosten, Gebäude:*› stehenbleiben; ‹*Plakat:*› hängen bleiben; ‹*Flugzeug, Haare:*› oben bleiben; **my socks won't ~ up** meine Socken rutschen [ständig]

²stay 1. *n.* **a)** *(Naut.)* Stag, *das;* **b)** *(guy-rope)* Zeltleine, *die;* *(guy-wire)* Drahtseil, *das;* **c)** *(Aeronaut., Archit.)* Strebe, *die.* **2.** *v. t. (Naut.)* stagen

'stay-at-home 1. *n.* häuslicher Mensch; **be a real ~:** ein richtiger Stubenhocker *(ugs. abwertend)* sein. **2.** *attrib. adj.* häuslich

stayer ['steɪə(r)] *n. (lit. or fig.)* Steher, *der*

staying-power ['steɪɪŋpaʊə(r)] *n.* Durchhaltevermögen, *das*

staysail ['steɪseɪl, 'steɪsl] *n. (Naut.)* Stagsegel, *das*

STD *abbr.* **a)** *(Brit. Teleph.)* **subscriber trunk dialling** Selbstwählfernverkehr, *der;* **~ code** Vorwahl[nummer], *die;* **b)** *(Med.)* **sexually transmitted disease** *see* **sexually a**

stead [sted] *n., no pl., no art.* **a) in sb.'s ~:** an jmds. Stelle *(Dat.)*; **the bishop's deputy went in his ~:** anstelle des Bischofs ging sein Vertreter; **b) stand sb. in good ~:** jmdm. zustatten kommen; **that car has stood her in good ~:** dieser Wagen hat ihr gute Dienste geleistet

steadfast ['stedfəst, 'stedfɑ:st] *adj.* standhaft; zuverlässig ‹*Freund*›; fest ‹*Entschluß*›; unverwandt ‹*Blick*›; unerschütterlich ‹*Glaube*›; unverbrüchlich *(geh.)* ‹*Freundschaft, Treue*›; **be ~ in one's belief that ...:** fest daran glauben, daß ...

steadfastly ['stedfəstlɪ, 'stedfɑ:stlɪ] *adv.* standhaft; fest ‹*glauben*›; unverwandt ‹*[an]blicken*›; **adhere ~ to one's principles/faith** fest zu seinen Grundsätzen/seinem Glauben stehen

steadily ['stedɪlɪ] *adv.* **a)** *(stably)* fest; festen Schrittes ‹*gehen*›; sicher ‹*radfahren*›; **b)** *(without faltering)* fest ‹*[an]blicken*›; **c)** *(continuously)* stetig; ohne Unterbrechung ‹*arbeiten, marschieren*›; **it was raining ~:** es hat ununterbrochen geregnet; **progress ~:** stetige Fortschritte machen; **news flowed in ~ all day** den ganzen Tag gingen pausenlos Nachrichten ein; **d)** *(firmly)* standhaft ‹*sich weigern*›; fest ‹*glauben*›; **e)** *(reliably)* zuverlässig

steady ['stedɪ] **1.** *adj.* **a)** *(stable)* stabil; *(not wobbling)* standfest; **as ~ as a rock** völlig standfest ‹*Leiter, Tisch*›; völlig stabil ‹*Boot*›; ganz ruhig ‹*Hand*›; **in an emergency he is as ~ as a rock** *(lit. or fig.)* in einer Notsituation läßt er sich durch nichts erschüttern; **be ~ on one's feet** *or* **legs/bicycle** sicher auf den Beinen sein/sicher auf seinem Fahrrad fahren; **hold** *or* **keep one's hand ~:** die Hand ruhig halten; **hold** *or* **keep the ladder ~:** die Leiter festhalten; **~ as she goes!** *(coll.)* immer so weiter!; **b)** *(still)* ruhig; **turn a ~ eye** *or* **gaze** *or* **look on sb.** jmdn. fest ansehen; **c)** *(regular, constant)* stetig; gleichmäßig ‹*Arbeit, Tempo*›, stabil ‹*Preis, Lohn*›; gleichbleibend ‹*Temperatur*›; beständig ‹*Klima, Summen, Lärm*›; **we had ~ rain/drizzle** wir hatten Dauerregen/es nieselte [bei uns] ständig; **at a ~ pace** mit gleichmäßiger Geschwindigkeit; **[keep her] ~!** *(Naut.)* Kurs halten!; **prices have remained ~:** die Preise sind stabil geblieben; **~!** Vorsicht!; *(to dog, horse)* ruhig!; **~ on!** langsam! *(ugs.)*; **~ on, or you'll knock the vase over/hurt me** Vorsicht, sonst wirfst du die Vase um/verletzt du mich; **d)** *(invariable)* unerschütterlich; beständig ‹*Wesensart*›; standhaft ‹*Weigerung*›; fest ‹*Charakter, Glaube*›; **have a ~ character** charakterfest sein; **~ purpose** Zielstrebigkeit, *die;* **e)** *(enduring)* **a ~ job** eine feste Stelle; **a ~ boyfriend/girl-friend** ein fester Freund/eine feste Freundin *(ugs.)*; **f)** *(reliable)* zuverlässig. **2.** *v. t.* festhalten ‹*Leiter*›; beruhigen ‹*Pferd, Nerven*›; ruhig halten ‹*Boot, Flugzeug*›; **~ the table/vase** für einen festen Stand des Tisches/der Vase sorgen; **she steadied herself against the table/with a stick** sie hielt sich am Tisch fest/stützte sich mit einem Stock. **3.** *v. i.* ‹*Preise:*› sich stabilisieren; ‹*Geschwindigkeit:*› sich mäßigen; **the boat steadied** das Boot wurde [wieder] ruhiger. **4.** *n. (coll.)* fester Freund/feste Freundin *(ugs.)*. **5.** *adv.* **go ~ with sth.** mit etw. vorsichtig sein; **go ~ with sb.** *(coll.)* mit jmdm. gehen *(ugs.)*; **are you going ~ with anyone?** hast du einen festen Freund/eine feste Freundin? *(ugs.)*

steak [steɪk] *n.* Steak, *das;* *(of ham, bacon, gammon, salmon, etc.)* Scheibe, *die;* **a chicken/turkey/veal ~:** ein Hähnchen-/Puten-/Kalbsschnitzel; **~ and kidney pie/pudding** Rindfleisch-Nieren-Pastete, *die;* **~ au poivre** [steɪk əʊ 'pwɑ:vr] Pfeffersteak, *das;* **~ tartare** Tatarbeefsteak, *das;* **a [fish] ~:** eine Scheibe [Fisch]; *see also* **fillet 1 a; sirloin a**

steak: ~-house *n.* Steakhaus, *das;* **~-knife** *n.* Messer mit Sägezahnung

steal [sti:l] **1.** *v. t.*, **stole** [stəʊl], **stolen** ['stəʊln] **a)** stehlen **(from** *Dat.***)**; **~ a ride** schwarzfahren; **~ sb.'s boy-friend/girl-friend** jmdm. den Freund/die Freundin ausspannen *(ugs.)*; **she was the star of the play, but the little dog stole the show** *(fig.)* sie war der Star des Stückes, aber der kleine Hund stahl ihr die Schau; *see also* **scene b; thunder 1 c; b)** *(get slyly)* rauben *(geh. scherzh.)* ‹*Kuß, Umarmung*›; entlocken ‹*Worte, Interview*›; sich *(Dat.)* genehmigen *(ugs. scherzh.)* ‹*Nickerchen*›; **~ a glance [at sb./sth.]** jmdm. einen verstohlenen Blick zuwerfen/einen verstohlenen Blick auf etw. *(Akk.)* werfen; **c)** *(fig.: win)* **she stole my heart** sie eroberte mein Herz; **~ a march on sb.** jmdm. zuvorkommen. **2.** *v. i.*, **stole, stolen a)** stehlen; **~ from sb.** jmdn. bestehlen; **~ from the till/supermarket** aus der Kasse/im Supermarkt stehlen; **b)** *(move furtively)* sich stehlen; **~ in/out/up** sich hinein-/hinaus-/hinaufstehlen; **mist stole over the valley** beinahe unbemerkt breitete sich Nebel über das Tal aus; **~ up [on sb./sth.]** sich [an jmdn./etw.] heranschleichen; **old age is ~ing up on me** langsam, aber sicher werde ich alt. **3.** *n. (Amer. coll.)* **a)** *(theft)* Diebstahl, *der;* **b)** *(bargain)* **that dress is a ~:** dieses Kleid ist [fast *od.* halb] geschenkt *(ugs.)*

~ a'bout, ~ a'round *v. i.* herumschleichen *(ugs.)*

~ a'way *v. i.* sich fortstehlen

stealth [stelθ] *n.* Heimlichkeit, *die;* **use ~:** heimlich vorgehen; **by ~:** heimlich

stealthily ['stelθɪlɪ] *adv.* heimlich; verstohlen

stealthy ['stelθɪ] *adj.* heimlich; verstohlen ‹*Blick, Bewegung, Tun*›

steam [sti:m] **1.** *n., no pl., no indef. art.* Dampf, *der;* **the window was covered with ~:** das Fenster war beschlagen; **all the ~ has gone out of him/the idea** *(coll.)* er hat seinen ganzen Schwung verloren/aus der Idee ist der Dampf raus *(ugs.)*; **get up ~:** Dampf aufmachen; *(fig.)* in Fahrt kommen; **get up ~ to do sth.** *(fig.)* den nötigen Dampf aufbringen, um etw. zu tun; **let off ~** *(fig.)* Dampf ablassen *(ugs.)*; **run out of ~:** keinen Dampf mehr haben; *(fig.)* den Schwung verlieren; **under its own ~:** mit eigener Kraft; **under one's own ~** *(fig.)* aus eigener Kraft; *see also* **¹full 1 d. 2.** *v. t.* **a)** *(Cookery)* dämpfen; dünsten; **~ed pudding** gedämpfter Pudding; **b) ~ open an envelope** einen Umschlag mit [heißem] Wasserdampf öffnen. **3.** *v. i.* **a)** *(emit steam)* dampfen; **~ing hot** dampfend heiß; **heat the water till ~ing hot** das Wasser erhitzen, bis es dampft; **b)** *(move)* dampfen; **he went ~ing after the thief** *(fig. coll.)* er stürmte mit Volldampf *(ugs.)* hinter dem Dieb her

~ a'head *v. i. (fig. coll.)* rasche Fortschritte machen

~ 'over *v. i.* [sich] beschlagen

~ 'up 1. *v. t.* **a)** beschlagen lassen; **be ~ed up** beschlagen sein; **b)** *(fig. coll.)* **be/get [all] ~ed up** [total] ausrasten *(ugs.)*; **don't get ~ed up about it!** reg dich doch darüber nicht so auf! **2.** *v. i.* beschlagen

steam: ~-bath *n.* Dampfbad, *das;* **~boat** *n.* Dampfschiff, *das;* *(small)* Dampfboot, *das;* **~-boiler** *n.* Dampfkessel, *der;* **~-coal** *n.* Dampfkesselkohle, *die;* **~-driven** *adj.* dampfgetrieben; **a ~-driven boat/train/tractor** ein Dampfboot/eine Dampflok/ein Traktor mit Dampfantrieb; **~-engine** *n.* **a)** *(Railw.)* Dampflok[omotive], *die;* **b)** *(stationary engine)* Dampf[kraft]maschine, *die*

steamer ['sti:mə(r)] *n.* **a)** *(Naut.)* Dampfer, *der;* **b)** *(Cookery)* Dämpfer, *der*

steam: ~-gauge *n.* Dampfdruckmesser, *der;* **~-hammer** *n. (Metallurgy)* Dampfhammer, *der;* **~ iron** *n.* Dampfbügeleisen, *das;* **~ 'radio** *n. (coll. joc.)* Dampfradio, *das (ugs. scherzh.)*; **~roller 1.** *n. (lit. or fig.)* Dampfwalze, *die;* **2.** *v. t.* [mit der Dampfwalze] walzen; *(fig.)* niederwalzen; **~roller a bill through Parliament** ein Gesetz durchpeitschen *(ugs.)*; **~ship** *n.* Dampfschiff, *das;* **~ train** *n. (Railw.)* Dampfzug, *der;* **~ 'turbine** *n.* Dampfturbine, *die;* **~ whistle** Dampfpfeife, *die*

steamy ['sti:mɪ] *adj.* **a)** dunstig; Dunst‹*wolke*›; feucht ‹*Hitze*›; beschlagen ‹*Glas*›; **b)** *(coll.: erotic)* heiß

steed [sti:d] *n. (literary/joc.)* Roß, *das (geh./scherzh.)*

steel [sti:l] **1.** *n.* **a)** Stahl, *der;* **have a heart of ~** *(fig.)* stahlhart sein; **a man of ~:** ein stahlharter Mann; **as hard/true as ~:** stahlhart/treu wie Gold; **cold ~:** blanker Stahl; **pressed ~:** Preßstahl, *der;* **b)** *(knife-sharpener)* Wetzstahl, *der;* **c)** *(literary: sword)* Schwert, *das.* **2.** *attrib. adj.* stählern; Stahl‹*helm, -block, -platte*›. **3.** *v. t.* **~ oneself for/against sth.** sich für/gegen etw. wappnen *(geh.)*; **she ~ed her heart/herself against his pleas** sie verschloß ihr Herz/sich seinen Bitten; **~ oneself to do sth.** allen Mut zusammennehmen, um etw. zu tun

steel: ~ **'band** *n. (Mus.)* Steelband, *die;* ~ **'drum** *n. (Mus.)* Steeldrum, *die;* **~-grey** **1.** *n.* Stahlgrau, *das;* **2.** *adj.* stahlgrau; ~ **gui'tar** *n. (Mus.)* Hawaiigitarre, *die;* **~maker** *n.* Stahlproduzent, *der*/-produzentin, *die;* **~-mill** *n.* Stahlwalzwerk, *das;* ~ **'plate** *n.* Stahlplatte, *die;* **~-plated** ['sti:lpleɪtɪd] *adj. (for protection)* mit Stahlplatten gepanzert; *(for durability)* mit Stahl überzogen; ~ **'wool** *n.* Stahlwolle, *die;* **~worker** *n.* Stahlarbeiter, *der*/-arbeiterin, *die;* **~works** *n. sing., pl. same* Stahlwerk, *das*

steely ['sti:lɪ] *adj.* **a)** *(strong)* stählern; **b)** *(resolute)* eisern; **c)** *(severe)* steinern

'steelyard *n.* Laufgewichtswaage, *die*

[1]**steep** [sti:p] *adj.* **a)** steil; **b)** *(rapid)* stark ⟨*Preissenkung*⟩; steil ⟨*Preisanstieg*⟩; **c)** *(coll.: excessive)* happig *(ugs.)*; **the bill is [a bit] ~:** die Rechnung ist [ziemlich] gesalzen *(ugs.)*; **be a bit ~ = be a bit much** *see* **much 1 b; that's pretty ~[, coming from you/him]** das ist ein starkes Stück *(ugs.)* [von dir/ihm]

[2]**steep** *v. t.* **a)** *(soak)* einweichen; **b)** *(bathe)* baden

steeped [sti:pt] *adj.* durchdrungen **(in** von); **a place ~ in history/tradition** ein geschichtsträchtiger/von der Tradition durchdrungener Ort

steepen ['sti:pn] **1.** *v. i.* steil[er] werden. **2.** *v. t.* steil[er] machen

steeple ['sti:pl] *n.* Kirchturm, *der*

steeple: ~chase *n. (Sport)* **a)** *(horse-race)* Steeplechase, *die;* Hindernisrennen, *das;* **b)** *(Athletics)* Hindernislauf, *der;* **~chaser** *n. (Sport)* **a)** *(rider)* Reiter/Reiterin bei einer Steeplechase; **b)** *(runner)* Hindernisläufer, *der*/-läuferin, *die;* **c)** *(horse)* Steepler, *der;* **~chasing** ['sti:pltʃeɪsɪŋ] *n. (Sport)* Hindernisrennen, *das;* **~jack** *n. Arbeiter, der/Arbeiterin, die Reparaturarbeiten an Kaminen, Kirchtürmen usw. ausführt*

steeply ['sti:plɪ] *adv.* steil ⟨*ansteigen, abfallen*⟩

'steep-sided *see* **-sided**

[1]**steer** [stɪə(r)] **1.** *v. t.* **a)** steuern; lenken; **this car is easy to ~:** dieser Wagen ist leicht lenkbar; **b)** *(direct)* **~ a** *or* **one's way through ...:** steuern durch ...; **~ a** *or* **one's course for a place** auf einen Ort zusteuern; *(in ship, plane, etc.)* Kurs auf einen Ort nehmen; **~ a** *or* **one's course for home** Kurs in Richtung Heimat nehmen; **~ a middle course** *(fig.)* einen Mittelweg einschlagen; **c)** *(guide movement of)* führen, lotsen ⟨*Person*⟩; **~ a bill through Parliament** eine Gesetzesvorlage über die parlamentarischen Hürden bringen; **~ sb./the conversation towards/away from a subject** jmdn./das Gespräch auf ein Thema lenken/von einem Thema ablenken. **2.** *v. i.* steuern; **~ in and out of/~ between the obstacles** zwischen den Hindernissen hindurchsteuern; **~ clear of sb./sth.** *(fig. coll.)* jmdm./einer Sache aus dem Weg[e] gehen; **~ clear of opium/politics** die Finger von Opium/der Politik lassen; **~ for sth.** etw. ansteuern; **~ left/right** nach links/rechts steuern; **~ due north** *(Naut.)* direkt nach Norden steuern

[2]**steer** *n. (Zool.)* junger Ochse

steering ['stɪərɪŋ] *n.* **a)** *(Motor Veh.)* Lenkung, *die;* **b)** *(Naut.)* Ruder, *das;* Steuerung, *die*

steering: ~-column *n. (Motor Veh.)* Lenksäule, *die;* **~ committee** *n.* Lenkungsausschuß, *der;* **~-gear** *n. (Naut.)* Steuervorrichtung, *die;* Ruderanlage, *die;* **~-lock** *n. (Motor Veh.)* Lenkradschloß, *das;* **~-wheel** *n.* **a)** *(Motor Veh.)* Lenkrad, *das;* **b)** *(Naut.)* Steuerrad, *das*

steersman ['stɪəzmən] *n., pl.* **steersmen** ['stɪəzmən] *(Naut.)* Steuermann, *der*

stein [staɪn] *n.* Bierkrug, *der;* Stein, *der (südd.)*

stellar ['stelə(r)] *adj.* stellar

[1]**stem** [stem] **1.** *n.* **a)** *(Bot.) (of tree, shrub)* Stamm, *der; (of flower, leaf, fruit)* Stiel, *der; (of corn)* Halm, *der;* **b)** *(of glass)* Stiel, *der;* **c)** *(Mus.)* Notenhals, *der;* **d)** *(of tobacco-pipe)* Pfeifenrohr, *das;* **e)** *(Ling.)* Stamm, *der;* **f)** *(Naut.)* **from ~ to stern** vom Bug bis zum Heck. **2.** *v. i.,* **-mm-: ~ from sth.** auf etw. *(Akk.)* zurückzuführen sein. **3.** *v. t.,* **-mm-** *(make headway against)* standhalten (+ *Dat.*)

[2]**stem** *v. t.,* **-mm-** *(check, dam up)* aufhalten; eindämmen ⟨*Flut*⟩; stillen ⟨*Blutung, Wunde*⟩; *(fig.)* Einhalt gebieten (+ *Dat.*) *(geh.)*; stoppen ⟨*Redefluß*⟩; **~ the tide of criticism** die Welle[n] der Kritik eindämmen

-stemmed [stemd] *adj. in comb.* -stielig ⟨*Glas, Pfeife, Blume, Frucht*⟩; -stämmig ⟨*Baum, Strauch*⟩

'stem-turn *n. (Skiing)* Stemmbogen, *der*

stench [stentʃ] *n.* Gestank, *der (abwertend)*

stencil ['stensl] **1.** *n.* **a)** ~ **[-plate]** Schablone, *die;* **b)** *(for duplicating)* Matrize, *die;* **c)** *(~led pattern/lettering)* schabloniertes Muster/schablonierte Schrift. **2.** *v. t., (Brit.)* **-ll- a)** *(produce with ~)* mit einer Schablone zeichnen; schablonieren; **b)** *(ornament)* [mittels Schablone] mustern

Sten gun ['sten gʌn] *n. (Arms) Art Maschinenpistole*

stenographer [ste'nɒgrəfə(r)] *n.* Stenograph, *der*/Stenographin, *die*

stentorian [sten'tɔ:rɪən] *adj.* laut [hallend]; **a ~ voice** eine Stentorstimme *(geh.)*

step [step] **1.** *n.* **a)** *(movement, distance)* Schritt, *der;* **at every ~:** mit jedem Schritt; **watch sb.'s every ~** *(fig.)* jmdn. auf Schritt und Tritt überwachen; **take a ~ towards/away from sb.** einen Schritt auf jmdn. zugehen/von jmdm. wegtreten; **take a ~ back/sideways/forward** einen Schritt zurücktreten/zur Seite treten/nach vorn treten; **a ~ forward/back** *(fig.)* ein Schritt nach vorn/zurück; ein Fortschritt/Rückschritt; **a ~ in the right/wrong direction** *(fig.)* ein Schritt in die richtige/falsche Richtung; **mind** *or* **watch your ~!** *(lit. or fig.)* paß auf!; **I can't walk another ~:** ich kann keinen Schritt mehr gehen; **don't move another ~!** keinen Schritt weiter!; **b)** *(stair)* Stufe, *die;* *(on vehicle)* Tritt, *der;* **a flight of ~s** eine Treppe; **mind the ~!** Vorsicht, Stufe!; *(warning by one person to another)* paß auf die Stufe auf!; **[pair of] ~s** *(ladder)* Stehleiter, *die;* *(small)* Trittleiter, *die;* **c) follow** *or* **walk in sb.'s ~s** *(fig.)* in jmds. Fußstapfen treten; **d)** *(short distance)* **it's only a ~ to my house** es sind nur ein paar Schritte bis zu mir; **e) be in ~:** im Schritt sein; *(with music, in dancing)* im Takt sein; **be in/out of ~ with sth.** *(fig.)* mit etw. Schritt/nicht Schritt halten; **he is rarely in ~ with others** er befindet sich selten in Einklang mit anderen; **be out of ~:** aus dem Schritt geraten sein; *(with music, in dancing)* nicht im Takt sein; **he is out of ~ with his colleagues/the official party line** er ist über Kreuz mit seinen Kollegen/weicht von der offiziellen Parteilinie ab; **break ~:** aus dem Tritt geraten *od.* kommen; **change ~:** den Schritt wechseln; **fall into** *or* **get in ~:** in den Gleichschritt fallen; **fall into** *or* **get in ~ with sb./sth.** mit jmdm./etw. im Gleichschritt [mit]marschieren; *(fig.)* sich jmdm./einer Sache fügen; **prices are out of ~ with wage increases** die Preise stehen in keinem Verhältnis zu den Lohnerhöhungen; **keep in ~:** den Schritt halten; *(with music, in dancing)* im Takt bleiben; **keep in ~ with sth./sb.** *(fig.)* mit etw./jmdm. Schritt halten; **f)** *(action)* Schritt, *der;* **take ~s to do sth.** Schritte unternehmen, um etw. zu tun; *see also* **false step; g)** *(stage in process)* Schritt, *der;* **S~ one: ...:** erster Schritt: ...; **keep one ~ ahead [of sb./sth.]** [jmdm./einer Sache] einen Schritt *od.* eine Nasenlänge voraus sein; **~ by ~:** Schritt für Schritt; **the first ~ in sb.'s career** die erste Sprosse auf jmds. Karriereleiter; **what is the next ~?** wie geht es weiter?; **h)** *(grade)* Stufe, *die;* **i)** *(sound of foot, manner of walking)* Schritt, *der;* **know sb. from his ~, know sb.'s ~:** jmdn. an seinem Schritt erkennen; **walk with a skip in one's ~:** hüpfenden Schrittes gehen; **j)** *(Amer. Mus.)* große Sekunde. **2.** *v. i.,* **-pp-** treten; **~ lightly** *or* **softly** leise auftreten; **~ hesitantly/heavily/clumsily** mit zögernden Schritten gehen/einen schweren/unbeholfenen Schritt haben; **~ from the pavement on to the road** vom Bürgersteig auf die Straße treten; **~ across** *or* **over a puddle/gap** einen [großen] Schritt über eine Pfütze/Spalte machen; **don't ~ across the line!** nicht über die Linie treten!; **~ inside** eintreten; **please ~ inside for a moment** kommen Sie bitte auf einen Augenblick herein; **~ into** treten in (+ *Akk.*); steigen in (+ *Akk.*) ⟨*Fahrzeug, Flugzeug, Wanne*⟩; **~ into sb.'s shoes** *(fig.)* an jmds. Stelle treten; **~ into one's dress/trousers** in sein Kleid/seine Hose steigen *(ugs.)*; **~ on sth.** *(on the ground)* auf etw. *(Akk.)* treten; **~ on sb.'s foot/on the dog's tail** jmdm. auf den Fuß/dem Hund auf den Schwanz treten; **~ on a patch of oil/water** in eine Öl-/Wasserpfütze treten; **~ on [to]** steigen auf (+ *Akk.*); steigen in (+ *Akk.*) ⟨*Fahrzeug, Flugzeug*⟩; **~ on it** *(coll.)* auf die Tube drücken *(ugs.)*; **~ on sb.'s toes = tread on sb.'s toes** *see* **tread 2; ~ out of** treten aus; steigen aus ⟨*Fahrzeug, Bad, Fluß*⟩; **~ out of the room for a few minutes** für ein paar Minuten aus dem Zimmer gehen; **~ out of one's dress/trousers** aus seinem Kleid/seiner Hose steigen *(ugs.)*; **~ out of line** *(fig.)* aus der Reihe tanzen *(ugs.)*; **I ~ped outside** ich trat hinaus; **Have you been calling my girl-friend names? I think you'd better ~ outside!** Hast du meine Freundin beschimpft? Komm, wir gehen mal zusammen raus *(ugs.)*; **~ over sb./sth.** über jmdn./etw. steigen; **~ over the starting-line** über die Startlinie treten; **~ this way, please** hier entlang, bitte; **~ through a door/window** durch eine Tür treten/ein Fenster steigen; *see also* **breach 1 c; gas 1 b**

~ a'side *v. i.* **a)** zur Seite treten; **b)** *(fig.: resign)* seine Stellung räumen

~ 'back *v. i.* zurücktreten; **~ back in fright/surprise** vor Schreck/Überraschung [einen Schritt] zurückweichen

~ 'down 1. *v. i.* **a) ~ down into the auditorium** ins Publikum herunterkommen *od.* -steigen; **~ down from the train/into the boat** aus dem Zug/in das Boot steigen; **b)** *(fig.) see* **stand down 1 a. 2.** *v. t. (Electr.)* heruntertransformieren *(ugs.)*; *see also* **step-down**

~ 'forward *v. i.* **a)** [einen Schritt] vortreten; **b)** *(fig.: present oneself)* sich melden; **would somebody like to ~ forward and help me with the trick?** würde jemand gern nach vorn kommen und mir bei dem Trick assistieren?; **he ~ped forward as the new candidate** er präsentierte sich als neuer Kandidat; **several ~ped forward** einige meldeten sich [freiwillig]

~ 'in *v. i.* **a)** eintreten; *(into vehicle)* einsteigen; *(into pool)* hineinsteigen; **would you mind ~ping in for a moment?** würden Sie bitte einen Augenblick hereinkommen?; **b)** *(fig.) (take sb.'s place)* einspringen; *(intervene)* eingreifen

~ 'off 1. *v. i.* **a)** *(get off) (from vehicle)* aussteigen; *(from a height)* hinabspringen; **b)** *(Mil.: begin to march)* abmarschieren. **2.** *v. t.* **a)** *(get off)* steigen aus ⟨*Fahrzeug*⟩; treten von ⟨*Bürgersteig*⟩; springen von ⟨*Klippe, Brücke*⟩; **b)** *(measure by pacing)* abschreiten *(geh.)*

~ 'out 1. *v. i.* **a)** *(leave a place)* hinausgehen; **the car/boat stopped and she ~ped out** der Wagen/das Boot hielt an und sie stieg aus;

b) (lengthen stride) ausschreiten (geh.); c) (dated fig.: be active socially) ausgehen; he has been ~ping out with this girl for a few months now er geht jetzt schon seit ein paar Monaten mit diesem Mädchen (ugs.). 2. v.t. steigen aus ⟨Fahrzeug⟩

~ 'up 1. v.i. a) (ascend) hinaufsteigen; ~ up into [ein]steigen in (+ Akk.) ⟨Fahrzeug⟩; ~ up on to steigen auf (+ Akk.) ⟨Podest, Tisch⟩; b) (approach) ~ up and ask sb.'s name auf jmdn. zugehen und ihn nach seinem Namen fragen; ~ right up! treten Sie näher!; ~ up to sb. zu jmdm. treten; c) (increase) zunehmen. 2. v.t. a) (increase) erhöhen; intensivieren ⟨Wahlkampf⟩; verstärken ⟨Anstrengungen⟩; verschärfen ⟨Sicherheitsmaßnahmen, Streik⟩; b) (Electr.) hinauftransformieren (ugs.); see also step-up 2

step: ~brother n. Stiefbruder, der; **~child** n. Stiefkind, das; **~daughter** n. Stieftochter, die; **~-down** attrib. adj. (Electr.) ~-down converter or transformer Abwärtstransformator, der; **~father** n. Stiefvater, der; **~-ladder** n. Stehleiter, die; **~mother** n. Stiefmutter, die; **~parent** n. Stiefelternteil, der; ~parents Stiefeltern Pl.

steppe [step] n. (Geog.) Steppe, die

stepped [stept] adj. gestuft; terrassiert ⟨Berg, Hang⟩; Stufen⟨pyramide, -giebel⟩

'steppeland n. (Geog.) Steppenland, das

stepping-stone ['stepɪŋstəʊn] n. Trittstein, der; (fig.) Sprungbrett, das (to für, in)

step: ~sister n. Stiefschwester, die; **~son** n. Stiefsohn, der; **~-up** 1. n. Erhöhung, die; a ~-up in output/production/security measures eine Steigerung des Ausstoßes/der Produktion/Verschärfung der Sicherheitsmaßnahmen; 2. attrib. adj. (Electr.) ~-up converter or transformer Aufwärtstransformator, der

stereo ['sterɪəʊ, 'stɪərɪəʊ] 1. n., pl. ~s a) (equipment) Stereoanlage, die; see also personal d; b) (sound reproduction) Stereo, das. 2. adj. a) (sound) stereo; Stereo⟨effekt, -aufnahme, -platte⟩; b) (Optics) stereoskopisch

stereophonic [sterɪə'fɒnɪk, stɪərɪə'fɒnɪk] adj., **stereophonically** [sterɪə'fɒnɪkəlɪ, stɪərɪə'fɒnɪkəlɪ] adv. stereophon

stereoscope ['sterɪəskəʊp, 'stɪərɪəskəʊp] n. Stereoskop, das

stereoscopic [sterɪə'skɒpɪk, stɪərɪə'skɒpɪk] adj. stereoskopisch

stereotype ['sterɪətaɪp, 'stɪərɪətaɪp] 1. n. a) Stereotyp, das (Psych.); Klischee, das; b) (Printing: plate) Stereotyp[ie]platte, die; c) no pl. (Printing: process) (making of ~s) Stereotypie, die; ~ [printing] Drucken mit Stereotyp[ie]platten. 2. v.t. in ein Klischee zwängen; ~ sb. as a villain jmdn. in das Klischee des Schurken zwängen; ~d stereotyp ⟨Redensart, Frage, Vorstellung⟩; klischeehaft ⟨Sprache, Denkweise⟩; the ~d business man das Klischee des Geschäftsmanns

sterile ['steraɪl] adj. a) (germ-free) steril; b) (barren, lit. or fig.) steril; unfruchtbar; (fig.) erfolglos ⟨Geschäftsjahr, Bemühung⟩; nutzlos ⟨Tätigkeit⟩; fruchtlos ⟨Diskussion, Gespräch⟩

sterilisation, sterilise, steriliser see steriliz-

sterility [stə'rɪlɪtɪ] n., no pl. a) (absence of germs) Sterilität, die; b) (barrenness, lit. or fig.) Sterilität, die; Unfruchtbarkeit, die; (fig.: of discussion) Fruchtlosigkeit, die

sterilization [sterɪlaɪ'zeɪʃn] n. Sterilisation, die

sterilize ['sterɪlaɪz] v.t. a) (make germ-free) sterilisieren; b) (make barren) sterilisieren ⟨Tier, Mensch⟩; unfruchtbar machen ⟨Land⟩

sterilizer ['sterɪlaɪzə(r)] n. Sterilisator, der

sterling ['stɜ:lɪŋ] 1. n., no pl., no indef. art. Sterling, der; do they accept or take ~? kann man bei ihnen in Pfund [Sterling] bezahlen?; five pounds ~: fünf Pfund Sterling; in ~: in Pfund [Sterling]; ~ area (Hist.) Sterlingblock, der. 2. attrib. adj. a) ~ silver Sterlingsilber, das; b) (fig.) gediegen; he is a ~ chap! er ist ein zuverlässiger Bursche!; do ~ work erstklassige Arbeit leisten; [this is] ~ stuff! (coll.) tadellos!; erstklassig!

¹stern [stɜ:n] adj. streng; hart ⟨Strafe⟩; ernst ⟨Warnung⟩; made of ~er stuff (fig.) aus härterem Holz [geschnitzt]; be ~ with sb. mit jmdm. streng sein; jmdn. hart anpacken (ugs.)

²stern n. (Naut.) Heck, das; ~ foremost [mit dem] Heck voraus; see also ¹stem 1f

sternly ['stɜ:nlɪ] adv. streng; ernsthaft ⟨warnen⟩; in strengem Ton ⟨sprechen⟩; mit strenger Hand ⟨regieren⟩

'stern-post n. (Naut.) Achtersteven, der

sternum ['stɜ:nəm] n., pl. ~s or sterna ['stɜ:nə] (Anat.) Brustbein, das; Sternum, das (fachspr.)

steroid ['stɪərɔɪd, 'sterɔɪd] n. (Chem.) Steroid, das

stet [stet] (Printing) v.i. imper. bleibt

stethoscope ['steθəskəʊp] n. (Med.) Stethoskop, das

stetson ['stetsn] n. Stetson[hut], der

stevedore ['sti:vədɔ:(r)] n. (Naut.) Schauermann, der

stew [stju:] 1. n. a) (Gastr.) Eintopf, der; Irish ~: Irish-Stew, das; b) (coll.: state) be in/get into a ~: in heller Aufregung sein/völlig aus dem Häuschen geraten (ugs.); be in or get into a ~ about or over sth. sich über etw. (Akk.) [schrecklich (ugs.)] aufregen; don't get into a ~ about nothing! dreh nicht unnötig durch! (ugs.). 2. v.t. (Cookery) schmoren [lassen]; ~ apples/plums Apfel-/Pflaumenkompott kochen. 3. v.i. a) (Cookery) schmoren; ⟨Obst:⟩ gedünstet werden; ~ [in one's own juice] (fig.) [im eigenen Saft] schmoren (ugs.); b) (fig.: fret) ~ over a problem sich (Dat.) über ein Problem den Kopf zerbrechen (ugs.); c) (fig.: swelter) schmoren (ugs.)

steward ['stju:əd] 1. n. a) (on ship, plane) Steward, der; b) (supervising official) (at public meeting, ball, etc.) Ordner, der/Ordnerin, die; ~s (of race) Rennleitung, die; ~s' enquiry (Horse-racing) [Untersuchung und] Beratung der Rennleitung; see also shop-steward; c) (estate manager) Verwalter, der/Verwalterin, die. 2. v.t. verwalten; ~ a meeting bei einer öffentlichen Veranstaltung Ordner/Ordnerin sein

stewardess ['stju:ədɪs] n. Stewardeß, die

stewardship ['stju:ədʃɪp] n. Verwaltung, die; hold the ~ of an estate Verwalter/Verwalterin eines Gutes sein

stewed [stju:d] adj. a) (Cookery) geschmort; ~ apples/plums Apfel-/Pflaumenkompott, das; b) (over-brewed) the tea is ~: der Tee hat zu lange gezogen; c) (sl.: drunk) blau (ugs.); voll (salopp)

stewing steak ['stju:ɪŋ steɪk] n., no pl., no indef. art. [Rinder]schmorfleisch, das

stew: ~-pan n. (Cookery) Schmorpfanne, die; **~-pot** n. (Cookery) Schmortopf, der

stick [stɪk] 1. v.t., stuck [stʌk] a) (thrust point of) stecken; ~ sth. in[to] sth. mit etw. in etw. (Akk.) stechen; she stuck a needle in[to] her finger sie stach sich (Dat.) mit einer Nadel in den Finger; get stuck into sb./sth./a meal (sl.: begin action) jmdm. eine Abreibung verpassen/sich in etw. (Akk.) reinknien/tüchtig reinhauen (salopp); I stuck a knife in[to] him ich stieß od. (ugs.) rammte ihm ein Messer in den Leib; b) (impale) spießen; ~ sth. [up]on sth. etw. auf etw. (Akk.) [auf]spießen; like a stuck pig ⟨bluten⟩ wie ein Schwein; ⟨schreien⟩ wie eine gestochene Sau; c) (coll.: put) stecken; he stuck a feather in his hat/a rose in his buttonhole er steckte sich (Dat.) eine Feder an den Hut/eine Rose in das Knopfloch; ~ a picture on the wall/a vase on the shelf ein Bild an die Wand hängen/eine Vase aufs Regal stellen; ~ 10% on the bill 10% zusätzlich auf die Rechnung setzen; ~ one's hat on one's head sich (Dat.) den Hut auf den Kopf stülpen; ~ one's head out of the window den Kopf aus dem Fenster strecken; ~ sth. in the kitchen etw. in die Küche tun (ugs.); ~ one on sb. (sl.: hit) jmdm. eine langen (ugs.); ~ one's hands in one's pockets die Hände in den Taschen vergraben; you know where you can ~ that!, [you can] ~ it! (sl.) das kannst du dir sonstwohin stecken!; d) (with glue etc.) kleben; e) (make immobile) the car is stuck in the mud das Auto ist im Schlamm steckengeblieben; the door is stuck die Tür klemmt [fest]; she's been stuck indoors all day (fig. coll.) sie hat den ganzen Tag im Haus hocken müssen (ugs.); f) (puzzle) be stuck for an answer/for ideas um eine Antwort/um Ideen verlegen sein; Can you help me with this problem? I'm stuck Kannst du mir bei diesem Problem helfen? Ich komme nicht weiter; be stuck for money (coll.) gerade kein Geld haben; g) (cover) ~ sth. with pins/needles Stecknadeln/Nadeln in etw. (Akk.) stecken; h) (stab) ~ sb. with a knife jmdm. einen Messerstich beibringen; i) (Brit.: paste on wall) kleben; '~ no bills' „Plakate ankleben verboten!"; j) (Brit. coll.: tolerate) ~ it durchhalten; she can't ~ him sie kann ihn nicht riechen (salopp); he can't ~ the book/film er kann das Buch/den Film nicht ausstehen; she can't ~ the heat/such conditions sie kann die Hitze/solche Bedingungen nicht ertragen; I can't ~ it/my job any longer das/mein Job steht mir bis oben od. hier (ugs.); k) (coll.) be stuck with sth. (have to accept) sich mit etw. herumschlagen müssen (ugs.); be stuck with sb. jmdn. am od. auf dem Hals haben (ugs.); if we don't sell our car soon we'll be stuck with it wenn wir unser Auto nicht bald verkaufen, werden wir's überhaupt nicht mehr los (ugs.); l) (sl.) be stuck on sb./sth. (captivated by) auf jmdn./etw. abfahren (salopp); be stuck on an idea eine fixe Idee haben. 2. v.i., stuck a) (be fixed by point) stecken; there's a splinter ~ing in my finger ich habe einen [Holz]splitter im Finger; b) (adhere) kleben; mud ~s (fig.) etwas bleibt immer hängen (fig.); ~ to sth. an etw. (Dat.) kleben; my wet clothes stuck to my body meine nassen Kleider klebten mir am Körper; ~ in the/sb.'s mind (fig.) im/jmdm. im Gedächtnis haftenbleiben; she was called the 'iron lady' and the nickname stuck sie wurde „Eiserne Lady" genannt, und der Spitzname blieb an ihr hängen; c) (become immobile) ⟨Auto, Räder:⟩ steckenbleiben; ⟨Schublade, Tür, Griff, Bremse:⟩ klemmen; ⟨Schlüssel:⟩ feststecken; ~ fast ⟨Auto, Rad:⟩ feststecken; ⟨Reißverschluß, Tür, Schublade:⟩ festklemmen; the words stuck in his throat die Worte blieben ihm in der Kehle stecken; the record is stuck die Platte ist hängengeblieben; see also stick-in-the-mud; d) (protrude) a letter stuck from his pocket ein Brief schaute ihm aus der Tasche; e) (coll.: remain) bleiben; are you going to ~ indoors all day? willst du den ganzen Tag im Hause [herum]hocken? (ugs.); f) (coll.: be considered valid) the accusations will not ~: die Anschuldigungen ziehen nicht (ugs.); make a charge ~: mit einer Anklage durchkommen (ugs.); be made to ~: hieb- und stichfest gemacht werden; g) (Cards) Do you want another card? – No, I'll ~: Willst du noch eine Karte? – Nein, ich behalte mein Blatt. 3. n. a) ([cut] shoot of tree, piece of wood) Stock, der; (staff) [Holz]stab, der; (walking-~) Spazierstock, der; (for handicapped person) Krückstock, der; pick up a large ~ from the ground einen großen Knüppel vom Boden aufheben; gather dry ~s trockene Äste sammeln; see also **big 1 a; b)** *see* **rod c; c)** *(Hockey etc.)* Schläger, *der;* **~s!** hoher Stock!; **d)** *(long piece)* **a ~ of chalk/shaving-soap** ein Stück Kreide/Rasierseife; **a ~ of dynamite/sealing-wax** eine Stange Dynamit/Siegellack; **a ~ of rock/celery/rhubarb** eine Stange Rocks/Sellerie/Rhabarber; **a cinnamon ~:** eine Zimtstange; **e)** *no pl., no art. (coll.: criticism)* **get** *or* **take [some] ~:** viel einstecken müssen; **give sb. [some] ~:** jmdn. zusammenstauchen *(ugs.);* **f) give sb. the ~, take the ~ to sb.** *(cane sb.)* jmdn. den Stock spüren lassen; **g) ~ of furniture** *(coll.)* Möbelstück, *das;* **up ~s** *(sl.)* seine [Sieben]sachen zusammenpacken *(ugs.);* **h)** *(Motor Veh.: gear-lever) see* **gear-stick; i)** *(Mus.) see* **baton c; j)** *(Printing)* Winkelhaken, *der;* **k) the ~s** *(Horse-racing sl.)* die Hürden; die Hindernisse; **the race is over the ~s** das Rennen geht über Hindernisse; **l)** *in pl. (sl.: rural area)* **in the ~s** in der hintersten Provinz; **m)** *(coll.: person)* **a queer ~:** komischer Kauz *(ugs.);* **a funny old ~:** ein komischer alter Kauz *(ugs.);* **n)** *(Mil.: of bombs)* Reihenwurf, *der. See also* **²cleft 2; cross 4 b; dirty 1 h; wrong 1 c**

~ a'bout, ~ a'round *v. i. (coll.)* dableiben; *(wait)* warten

~ at *v. t.* **a)** *(hesitate at)* **~ at sth./nothing** vor etw. *(Dat.)*/nichts zurückschrecken; **b)** *(keep on with)* **~ at one's books/studying** fleißig Bücher wälzen/studieren; **~ 'at it** *(coll.)* dranbleiben *(ugs.)*

~ by *v. t. (fig.)* stehen zu

~ 'down *v. t.* **a)** *(glue down)* festkleben; zukleben ‹*Umschlag*›; **b)** *(coll.: put down)* hinknallen *(ugs.)* ‹*Tisch, Kiste*›; **c)** *(coll.: write down)* schreiben

~ 'in *v. t.* **a)** *(jab in)* hineinstechen ‹*Spritze, Nadel*›; anstecken ‹*Hutnadel*›; **get stuck in** *(sl.) (working)* ranklotzen *(salopp); (eating)* reinhauen *(salopp);* **b)** *(glue in)* einkleben; **c)** *(coll.: put in)* hineinstecken; *see also* **nose 1 a**

~ 'on 1. *v. t.* **a)** *(glue on)* aufkleben ‹*Briefmarke, Etikett*›; ankleben ‹*Tapete*›; **b)** *(attach by pin etc.)* anstecken; **c)** *(coll.: put on)* aufsetzen ‹*Hut, Wasserkessel*›; auflegen ‹*Schallplatte*›; **stick an extra amount on the bill** *(fig.)* einen zusätzlichen Betrag auf die Rechnung setzen. **2.** *v. i.* kleben[bleiben]. *See also* **stick-on**

~ 'out 1. *v. t.* **a)** herausstrecken ‹*Brust, Zunge*›; ausstrecken ‹*Arm, Bein*›; **~ one's tongue out at sb.** jmdm. die Zunge herausstrecken; **would you like to ~ your neck out and predict the winner of the race?** *(fig. coll.)* willst du eine Prognose wagen, wer das Rennen gewinnt?; **he is not one to ~ his chin out** *(fig. coll.)* er verbrennt sich *(Dat.)* nicht gern die Finger *(ugs.);* **b) ~ it out** *(coll.)* = **sweat it out** *see* **sweat 3 d. 2.** *v. i.* **a)** *(project)* ‹*Brust, Bauch:*› vorstehen; ‹*steifes Kleid:*› abstehen; ‹*Nagel, Ast:*› herausstehen; **his ears ~ out** er hat abstehende Ohren; **her hair stuck out from under the hat** ihr Haar schaute unter dem Hut hervor; **she lay in bed with her legs/toes ~ing out** sie lag im Bett, und ihre Beine/Zehen schauten heraus; **b)** *(fig.: be obvious)* sich abheben; **~ out a mile** *(sl.)* [klar] auf der Hand liegen; **it ~s out a mile that he is only after her money** *(sl.)* daß er nur hinter ihrem Geld her ist, ist klar wie dicke Tinte *(ugs.);* **~ out like a sore thumb** *(coll.)* ins Auge springen; **if you don't wear the correct clothes you'll ~ out like a sore thumb** *(coll.)* wenn du nicht korrekt gekleidet bist, fällst du unangenehm auf; **c) ~ out for sth.** *see* **hold out 2 c**

~ to *v. t.* **a)** *(be faithful to)* halten zu ‹*Person*›; halten ‹*Versprechen*›; bleiben bei ‹*Entscheidung, Meinung*›; treu bleiben (+ *Dat.*) ‹*Idealen, Grundsätzen*›; **b)** *(not deviate from)* sich halten an (+ *Akk.*) ‹*Plan, Text, Original*›; bleiben an (+ *Dat.*) ‹*Arbeit*›; bleiben bei ‹*Wahrheit, Thema*›; **~ to business** bei der Sache bleiben; **~ to the point** beim Thema bleiben; **~ to what you are good at** bleibe bei dem, was du [gut] kannst; **thanks, but I'll ~ to beer** danke, ich bleibe beim Bier. *See also* **gun 1 a; ³last; stick-to-it-ive; ¹story a**

~ to'gether 1. *v. t.* zusammenkleben. **2.** *v. i.* **a)** *(adhere together)* zusammenkleben; **b)** *(fig.: remain united)* zusammenhalten

~ 'up 1. *v. t.* **a)** *(seal)* zukleben; **b) be stuck up with sth.** *(coll.: sticky)* von etw. klebrig sein; **c)** *(coll.: put up, raise)* strecken, recken ‹*Kopf, Hals*›; anschlagen ‹*Bekanntmachung, Poster*›; aufschlagen ‹*Zelt*›; hinbauen, -setzen ‹*Häuser*›; raufsetzen *(ugs.)* ‹*Preise*›; anbringen ‹*Regal*›; **he stuck his nose up [in the air]** er streckte seine Nase in die Luft; **~ up one's hand** die Hand heben; **~ sth. up on a shelf** etw. auf ein Regal tun *(ugs.);* **~ 'em up!** *(sl.)* Pfoten hoch! *(salopp);* **d)** *(sl.: rob)* ausrauben; *see also* **stick-up; e) stuck up** *(conceited)* eingebildet; **be stuck up about sth.** sich *(Dat.)* etwas auf etw. *(Akk.)* einbilden. **2.** *v. i.* **a)** ‹*Haar, Kragen:*› hochstehen; ‹*Nagel, Pflasterstein:*› hervorstehen; **b) ~ up for sb./sth.** für jmdn./etw. eintreten; **~ up for yourself!** setz dich zur Wehr!

~ with *v. t. (coll.)* **a)** *(keep contact with)* **~ with the leaders** sich an der Spitze halten *(bes. Sport);* **~ 'with it!** bleib dran! *(ugs.);* **b)** *(remain faithful to)* bleiben bei ‹*Gruppe, Partei*›; halten zu ‹*Freund*›; die Treue halten (+ *Dat.*) ‹*Verein*›

stick de'odorant *n.* Deo[dorant]stift, *der*

sticker ['stɪkə(r)] *n.* Aufkleber, *der; see also* **billsticker**

'stick figure *n.* Strichmännchen, *das*

sticking ['stɪkɪŋ]: **~-place** *see* **~-point; ~-plaster** *n. (Med.)* Heftpflaster, *das;* **~-point** *n. (fig.)* Hürde, *die*

stick: ~-insect *n.* Gespenst[heu]schrecke, *die;* **~-in-the-mud 1.** *n. (person lacking initiative)* Trantüte, *die (ugs. abwertend); (unprogressive person)* Spießer, *der (abwertend);* **2.** *adj. (lacking in initiative)* schlafmützig *(ugs. abwertend); (unprogressive)* spießig *(abwertend)*

stickleback ['stɪklbæk] *n. (Zool.)* Stichling, *der*

stickler ['stɪklə(r)] *n.* **be a ~ for tidiness/authority** es mit der Sauberkeit sehr genau nehmen/in puncto Autorität keinen Spaß verstehen

stick: ~-on *adj.* selbstklebend; **~pin** *n. (Amer.)* Krawattennadel, *die;* **~-to-it-ive** [stɪk'tu:ɪtɪv] *adj. (Amer.)* verbissen; hartnäckig; **~-up** *n. (sl.)* bewaffneter Raubüberfall

sticky ['stɪkɪ] *adj.* **a)** klebrig; feucht ‹*Farbe, gestrichener/gewaschener Gegenstand*›; zäh ‹*Teig, Brei, Mischung*›; **~ label** Aufkleber, *der;* **~ tape** Klebestreifen, *der;* **b)** *(humid)* schwül ‹*Klima, Luft*›; feucht ‹*Haut*›; **be all hot and ~:** ganz verschwitzt sein; **c)** *(coll.: uncooperative)* unnachgiebig; **be ~ about doing sth.** etw. [nur] widerwillig tun; **d)** *(sl.: unpleasant)* vertrackt *(ugs.);* heikel; **a ~ situation** eine brenzlige Lage; *see also* **end 1 h**

sticky 'wicket *n. (Cricket) Spielfeld, das nach einem Regen schlecht zu bespielen ist;* **bat** *or* **be on a ~** *(fig.)* sich auf schlüpfrigem Boden befinden

stiff [stɪf] **1.** *adj.* **a)** *(rigid)* steif; hart ‹*Bürste, Stock*›; **be frozen ~:** steif vor Kälte sein; ‹*Wäsche, Körper[teile]:*› steif gefroren sein; **this brush is ~ with paint** dieser Pinsel ist mit Farbe verklebt; *see also* **lip a; b)** *(intense, severe)* hartnäckig; schroff ‹*Absage*›; kräftig ‹*Standpauke*›; **~ competition** scharfe Konkurrenz; **c)** *(formal)* steif; förmlich ‹*Brief, Stil*›; **d)** *(difficult)* hart ‹*Test*›; schwer ‹*Frage, Prüfung*›; steil ‹*Abstieg, Anstieg*›; **be ~ going** *(fig. coll.)* harte Arbeit sein; **e)** stark, *(Seemannsspr.)* steif ‹*Wind, Brise*›; **f)** *(not bending, not working freely, aching)* steif ‹*Gelenk, Gliedmaßen, Nacken, Person*›; schwergängig ‹*Angel, Kolben, Gelenk*›; **g)** *(coll.: excessive)* saftig *(ugs.)* ‹*Preis, Strafe*›; **h)** *(strong)* steif *(ugs.)* ‹*Drink*›; stark ‹*Dosis, Medizin*›; **a ~ shot of rum** ein Schuß steifen Rum; **i)** *(thick)* zäh[flüssig]; **j)** *(coll.)* **be bored/scared/worried ~:** sich zu Tode langweilen/eine wahnsinnige Angst haben *(ugs.)*/sich *(Dat.)* furchtbare *(ugs.)* Sorgen machen; **bore/scare/worry sb. ~:** jmdn. zu Tode langweilen/jmdm. eine wahnsinnige Angst einjagen *(ugs.)*/jmdm. furchtbare *(ugs.)* Sorgen machen; **k)** *pred.* **the road was ~ with police** auf der Straße wimmelte es von Polizisten. **2.** *n. (sl.)* Leiche, *die*

stiffen ['stɪfn] **1.** *v. t.* **a)** steif machen; stärken ‹*Kragen*›; versteifen ‹*Material*›; zäh[flüssig]er machen ‹*Paste, Teig*›; steif werden lassen ‹*Gliedmaße*›; **b)** *(fig.: bolster)* verstärken ‹*Widerstand*›; stärken ‹*Moral, Entschlossenheit*›. **2.** *v. i.* **a)** ‹*Person:*› erstarren; **b)** ‹*Wind, Brise:*› steifer werden *(Seemannsspr.)*, auffrischen; **c)** *(become thicker)* ‹*Teig:*› steifer werden; ‹*Mischung:*› zäher werden; **d)** *(fig.: become more resolute)* sich verstärken; **his resolve ~ed** er wurde in seinem Entschluß bestärkt

stiffener ['stɪfnə(r)] *n.* **a)** *(for collar, corset)* Stäbchen, *das;* **b)** *(starch)* Stärke, *die;* **c)** *(Building)* Queraussteifung, *die;* **d)** *(coll.: drink)* kleine Stärkung *(scherzh.)*

stiffening ['stɪfnɪŋ] *n.* Versteifung, *die*

stiffly ['stɪflɪ] *adv.* **a)** *(rigidly, formally)* steif; *(fig.)* hartnäckig ‹*Widerstand leisten*›; **b)** *(strongly)* stark, *(Seemannsspr.)* steif ‹*wehen*›; **c)** *(erectly, with restricted movement)* steif ‹*sitzen, gehen*›; kerzengerade ‹*stehen*›

stiff-'necked *adj. (fig.)* starrsinnig

stiffness ['stɪfnɪs] *n., no pl.* **a)** *(rigidity, formality)* Steifheit, *die; (of letter, language)* Förmlichkeit, *die;* **b)** *(intensity)* Härte, *die;* **c)** *(difficulty)* Schwierigkeit, *die;* **d)** *(of wind)* Stärke, *die;* Steifheit, *die (Seemannsspr.);* **e)** *(lack of suppleness)* Steifheit, *die; (of hinge, piston)* geringe Beweglichkeit; **have a ~ in one's limbs** steife Glieder haben; *(due to exercise)* Muskelkater haben; **f)** *(coll.: excessiveness) (of punishment)* Strenge, *die; (of demand, price)* Überzogenheit, *die;* **g)** *(thick consistency)* Zähheit, *die*

stifle ['staɪfl] **1.** *v. t.* ersticken; *(fig.: suppress)* unterdrücken; ersticken ‹*Widerstand, Aufstand, Schrei*›; übergehen ‹*Einwand*›; **we were ~d by the heat** wir erstickten fast vor Hitze. **2.** *v. i.* ersticken; **~ in the bad air/smoke** an der schlechten Luft/vom Rauch fast ersticken

stifling ['staɪflɪŋ] *adj.* stickig; drückend ‹*Hitze*›; *(fig.)* einengend ‹*Atmosphäre*›; erdrückend ‹*Einfluß, Herrschaft*›; **the heat was ~:** es war drückend heiß

stigma ['stɪgmə] *n., pl.* **~s** *or* **~ta** ['stɪgmətə, stɪg'mɑ:tə] **a)** *(mark of shame)* Stigma, *das (geh.);* Makel, *der (geh.);* **the ~ of having been in prison** das Stigma, im Gefängnis gewesen zu sein; **b)** *(Bot.)* Stigma, *das;* Narbe, *die;* **c)** *in pl.* **~ta** *(Relig.)* Stigmata

stigmatize (stigmatise) ['stɪgmətaɪz] *v. t.* stigmatisieren *(geh.);* brandmarken

stile [staɪl] *n.* Zauntritt, *der;* Trittleiter, *die; see also* **dog 1 a**

stiletto [stɪ'letəʊ] *n., pl.* **~s** *or* **~es a)** *(dagger)* Stilett, *das;* **b) ~ [heel]** Stöckelabsatz, *der;* **~[-heeled shoe]** Stöckelschuh, *der*

¹still [stɪl] **1.** *adj.* **a)** *pred.* still; **be ~:** [still] stehen; ‹*Fahne:*› sich nicht bewegen; ‹*Hand:*› ruhig sein; **hold** *or* **keep sth. ~:** etw. ruhig halten; **hold** *or* **keep a ladder/horse ~:** eine Leiter/ein Pferd festhalten; **hold ~!** halt still!; **keep** *or* **stay ~:** stillhalten; *(not change posture)* ruhig bleiben; ‹*Pferd:*› stillstehen; ‹*Gegenstand:*› liegenbleiben; **sit ~:** stillsitzen; **stand ~:** stillstehen; ‹*Uhr:*› stehen; ‹*Arbeit:*› ruhen; *(stop)* stehenbleiben; **my heart stood ~** *(fig.)* mir blieb das Herz stehen; **the country has just stood ~ for the last 20 years** *(fig.)* das Land hat sich die letzten 20 Jahre einfach nicht weiterentwickelt; **time stood ~:** die Zeit schien stillzustehen; *see also* **statue; b)** *(calm)* ruhig; *see also* **deep 2; c)** *(without sound)* still; ruhig; **d)** *(not sparkling)* nicht moussierend ‹*Wein*›; still ‹*Mineralwasser*›; **is this water sparkling or ~?** ist dieses Wasser mit oder ohne Kohlensäure?; **e)** *(hushed)* leise; **a** *or* **the ~ small voice [of conscience]** die [leise] Stimme des Gewissens. **2.** *adv.* **a)** *(without change)* noch; *expr. surprise or annoyance* immer noch; **drink your tea while it is ~ hot** trink deinen Tee, solange er [noch] heiß ist; **b)** *(nevertheless)* trotzdem; **~, we must not forget the opposite standpoint** wir dürfen aber auch den gegensätzlichen Standpunkt nicht außer acht lassen; **~, what can you do about it?** aber was kann man dagegen tun?; **c)** *with comparative (even)* noch; **become fatter ~** *or* **~ fatter** noch *od.* immer dicker werden; **better/worse ~** *as sentence-modifier* besser/schlimmer noch; *see also* **less 2. 3.** *n.* **a)** *(Photog.)* Fotografie *die;* **~s from the film** Filmbilder; **b)** *(silence)* **in the ~ of the night** in der Stille der Nacht. **4.** *v. t. (literary)* beruhigen; glätten ‹*Wogen*›; stillen ‹*Hunger, Durst, Schmerz*›; beschwichtigen ‹*Gefühle*›; befriedigen ‹*Ehrgeiz*›; ausräumen ‹*Zweifel*›; dämpfen ‹*Geräusch*›

[2]still *n.* Destillierapparat, *der*

still: ~ birth *n.* Totgeburt, *die;* **~born** *adj.* **a)** totgeboren; **the child was ~born** das Kind war eine Totgeburt *od.* kam tot zur Welt; **b)** *(fig.) see* **abortive; ~ life** *n., pl.* **~ lifes** *or* **lives** *(Art)* Stilleben, *das*

stillness ['stɪlnɪs] *n., no pl.* **a)** *(motionlessness)* Bewegungslosigkeit, *die;* **b)** *(quietness)* Stille, *die*

still: ~ picture *see* **[1]still 3 a; ~-room** *n. (Brit.)* Destillierraum, *der*

stilt [stɪlt] *n.* **a)** Stelze, *die;* **b)** *(support of building)* Pfahl, *der;* **c)** *(Ornith.)* Stelzenläufer, *der*

stilted ['stɪltɪd] *adj.* gestelzt; gespreizt

Stilton ['stɪltən] *n.* Stilton[käse], *der*

stimulant ['stɪmjʊlənt] **1.** *attrib. adj. (Med.)* stimulierend. **2.** *n. (lit. or fig.)* Stimulans, *das;* Anregungsmittel, *das*

stimulate ['stɪmjʊleɪt] *v. t.* **a)** anregen; stimulieren *(geh.);* beleben ‹*Körper*›; *(sexually)* erregen; **b)** *(fig.)* anregen ‹*Geist, Diskussion, Appetit*›; hervorrufen ‹*Reaktion*›; wecken ‹*Interesse, Neugier*›; beleben ‹*Wirtschaft, Wachstum, Markt, Absatz*›; **~ sb. to sth./to do sth.** jmdn. zu etw. anregen/dazu anregen, etw. zu tun

stimulating ['stɪmjʊleɪtɪŋ] *adj.* **a)** anregend; stimulierend *(geh.);* belebend ‹*Bad*›; *(sexually)* erregend; **b)** *(fig.)* interessant; inspirierend ‹*Prediger, Einfluß, Musik, Buch*›

stimulation [stɪmjʊ'leɪʃn] *n.* **a)** Anregung, *die;* Stimulierung, *die (geh.); (sexual)* Erregung, *die;* **b)** *(fig.)* Anregung, *die; (of reaction)* Hervorrufen, *das; (of interest, curiosity)* Wecken, *das; (of economy, market, growth, sales)* Belebung, *die*

stimulative ['stɪmjʊlətɪv] *adj.* anregend; stimulierend *(geh.);* **the ~ effect of a cold shower** die belebende Wirkung einer kalten Dusche

stimulus ['stɪmjʊləs] *n., pl.* **stimuli** ['stɪmjʊlaɪ] **a)** *(spur)* Ansporn, *der* **(to** zu**); act as a ~ to sb.'s ambition** jmds. Ehrgeiz anspornen; **b)** *(rousing effect)* Anregung, *die;* **give a ~ to sales** den Umsatz beleben; **c)** *(Physiol.)* Stimulus, *der;* Reiz, *der*

sting [stɪŋ] **1.** *n.* **a)** *(wounding)* Stich, *der; (by jellyfish, nettles)* Verbrennung, *die;* **b)** *(pain)* Stechen, *das;* stechender Schmerz; *(from ointment, cane, whip, wind, rash)* Brennen, *das;* **the ~ of his criticism/remark/reproach** der Stachel seiner Kritik/Bemerkung/seines Vorwurfs; **a ~ in the tail** *(fig.)* ein Pferdefuß; **the story/film/letter had a ~ in the tail** am Ende der Geschichte/des Films/Briefs kam es knüppeldick *(ugs.);* **take the ~ out of sth.** *(fig.)* einer Sache *(Dat.)* den Stachel nehmen *(geh.);* **c)** *(Zool.)* [Gift]stachel, *der; (of jellyfish)* Nesselkapsel, *die; (of snake)* Giftzahn, *der;* **d)** *(Bot.)* Brennhaar, *das;* **e)** *(vigour) see* **bite 3 e; f)** *(fraud)* Ding, *das (ugs.); (police operation)* Operation, *die.* **2.** *v. t.,* **stung** [stʌŋ] **a)** *(wound)* stechen; **a bee stung [him on] his arm** eine Biene stach ihm in den Arm; **a jellyfish stung me/my leg** ich habe mich/mein Bein an einer Qualle verbrannt; **b)** *(cause pain to)* **the cane stung the boy's fingers** der Stock brannte dem Jungen auf den Fingern; **the smoke/the wind stung my eyes** der Rauch/der Wind brannte mir in den Augen; **c)** *(hurt mentally)* tief treffen; [zutiefst] verletzen; **his conscience stung him** er hatte Gewissensbisse; **~ing** scharf ‹*Vorwürfe, Anklagen, Kritik*›; **stung by remorse** von Reue gequält; **d)** *(incite)* **~ sb. into sth./doing sth.** jmdn. zu etw. anstacheln/dazu anstacheln, etw. zu tun; **he was stung to anger by their insults** ihre Beleidigungen erregten seinen Zorn; **e)** *(sl.: swindle)* übers Ohr hauen *(ugs.);* **~ sb. for sth.** jmdn. um etw. neppen *(ugs.);* **how much did they ~ you for [it]?** was haben sie dir [dafür] abgeknöpft? *(salopp).* **3.** *v. i.,* **stung a)** *(feel pain)* brennen; **smoke makes my eyes ~:** Rauch brennt mir in den Augen; **the antiseptic made the wound/my skin ~:** das Antiseptikum brannte auf der Wunde/auf meiner Haut; **b)** *(have ~)* stechen; **not all nettles/sorts of jellyfish ~:** nicht alle Nesseln/Quallenarten brennen

stingily ['stɪndʒɪlɪ] *adv.* geizig; **behave ~:** knausern *(ugs.)*

stinging-nettle ['stɪŋɪŋnetl] *n. (Bot.)* Brennessel, *die*

'sting-ray *n. (Zool.)* Stechrochen, *der*

stingy ['stɪndʒɪ] *adj.* geizig; knaus[e]rig *(ugs.);* kümmerlich ‹*Spende, Portion, Mahlzeit*›; **be ~ with sth.** mit etw. geizen

stink [stɪŋk] **1.** *v. i.,* **stank** [stæŋk] *or* **stunk** [stʌŋk], **stunk a)** stinken **(of** nach**); ~ to high heaven** *(coll.)* gottserbärmlich stinken; *(fig.)* ‹*Angelegenheit, Korruption:*› zum Himmel stinken; **he ~s of money** *(sl.)* er stinkt vor Geld *(ugs.);* **something ~s here** *(coll.: is suspicious)* an dieser Sache stinkt etwas *(ugs.);* **b)** *(fig.: be repulsive)* **sth. ~s** an etw. (+ *Dat.*) stinkt etwas *(ugs.);* **the book/film ~s** das Buch/der Film ist widerwärtig. **2.** *n.* **a)** *(bad smell)* Gestank, *der;* **b)** *(coll.: fuss)* Stunk, *der (ugs.);* **the scandal created an almighty ~:** der Skandal führte zu einem Riesenstunk *(ugs.);* **kick up** *or* **raise a ~ about sth.** wegen etw. Stunk machen *(ugs.);* **c)** *(sl.)* **like ~:** wie verrückt *(ugs.);* **run like ~:** wie eine gesengte Sau *(derb)* rennen

'stink-bomb *n.* Stinkbombe, *die*

stinker ['stɪŋkə(r)] *n. (sl.)* **a)** *(offensive person)* Stinker, *der (salopp);* Stinktier, *das (derb);* **b)** *(offensive thing)* Widerlichkeit, *die (abwertend);* **a ~ [of a letter/reply]** ein stinkiger Brief/eine stinkige Antwort *(salopp);* **a ~ [of a cold]** eine saumäßige Erkältung *(derb);* **c)** *(difficult task)* Hammer, *der (ugs.);* harte Nuß *(ugs.)*

stinking ['stɪŋkɪŋ] **1.** *adj.* **a)** stinkend; **b)** *(sl.: objectionable)* widerlich *(abwertend);* **a ~ cold** eine saumäßige Erkältung *(derb).* **2.** *adv. (sl.)* **~ rich/drunk** stinkreich *(salopp)*/stinkbesoffen *(derb)*

stint [stɪnt] **1.** *v. t.* **a)** *(restrict share of)* kurzhalten; **~ oneself [of sth.]** sich [mit etw.] einschränken; **~ sb. of sth.** jmdn. mit etw. kurzhalten; **b)** *(supply stingily)* geizen mit; sparen mit ‹*Worten*›. **2.** *v. i.* **~ on sth.** an etw. *(Dat.)* sparen. **3.** *n.* **a)** *(allotted amount)* [Arbeits]pensum, *das;* **do** *or* **work** *or* **have a long ~:** ein großes Arbeitspensum erledigen; **each of us did our ~ at the wheel** jeder von uns saß eine Zeitlang am Steuer; **b)** *(limitation)* Einschränkung, *die;* **without ~:** uneingeschränkt

stipend ['staɪpend] *n.* Besoldung, *die; (Eccl.)* Gehalt, *das*

stipendiary [staɪ'pendɪərɪ, stɪ'pendɪərɪ] **1.** *attrib. adj.* besoldet; **~ magistrate** *see* **2. 2.** *n. (Brit.)* besoldeter Friedensrichter

stipple ['stɪpl] *v. t.* **a)** *(Art)* punktieren; **b)** *(roughen)* [auf]rauhen ‹*Putz, Farbe*›

stipulate ['stɪpjʊleɪt] *(demand)* fordern; verlangen; *(lay down)* festlegen; *(insist on)* sich *(Dat.)* ausbedingen

stipulation [stɪpjʊ'leɪʃn] *n.* **a)** *(condition)* Bedingung, *die;* **on** *or* **with the ~ that ...:** unter der Bedingung, daß ...; **b)** *(act) see* **stipulate:** Forderung, *die;* Festlegung, *die;* Ausbedingung, *die*

stipule ['stɪpju:l] *n. (Bot.)* Nebenblatt, *das*

[1]stir [stɜ:(r)] **1.** *v. t.,* **-rr- a)** *(mix)* rühren; umrühren ‹*Tee, Kaffee*›; **keep ~ring the soup** die Suppe ständig umrühren; **~ sth. into sth.** etw. in etw. *(Akk.)* [ein]rühren; **b)** *(move)* bewegen; **~ oneself out of bed** sich aus dem Bett bewegen *od. (geh.)* bequemen; **~ one's stumps** *(coll.)* einen Zahn zulegen *(ugs.);* **c)** *(fig.: arouse)* bewegen; wecken ‹*Neugier, Interesse, Gefühle, Phantasie*›; **a story to ~ the heart/blood** eine herzergreifende Geschichte/eine Geschichte, die das Blut in Wallung bringt; **~ sb. to action** jmdn. zum Handeln anstacheln; **~ sb. to greater efforts** jmdn. zu größeren Anstrengungen anspornen. **2.** *v. i.,* **-rr- a)** *(move)* sich rühren; *(in sleep, breeze)* sich bewegen; **without ~ring** regungslos; **[not] ~ from the spot** sich [nicht] vom Fleck rühren; **b)** *(fig.: be aroused)* sich regen *(geh.);* **c)** *(rise from bed)* aufstehen; **nobody was ~ring in the house/village** das ganze Haus/Dorf schlief noch. **3.** *n., no pl.* **a)** *(commotion)* Aufregung, *die; (bustle, activity)* Betriebsamkeit, *die;* **cause** *or* **create** *or* **make a [big** *or* **great] ~:** [großes] Aufsehen erregen; **b)** *(act of ~ring sth.)* **give the coffee/paint a ~:** den Kaffee umrühren/die Farbe rühren

~ 'in *v. t.* einrühren

~ 'up *v. t.* **a)** *(disturb)* aufrühren; **b)** *(fig.: arouse, provoke)* wecken ‹*Neugier, Interesse, Leidenschaft*›; aufrütteln ‹*Anhänger, Gefolgsleute*›; entfachen ‹*Liebe, Haß, Streit, Zorn, Revolution*›; schüren ‹*Haß, Feindseligkeit*›; **~ up the past/ill feelings** die Vergangenheit aufrühren/ungute Gefühle wecken; **~ up public opinion** die öffentliche Meinung aufbringen; **~ it up** *(coll.)* Unfrieden stiften

[2]stir *n. (sl.: prison)* Knast, *der (ugs.);* **be in ~:** Knast schieben *(salopp)*

stir: ~-crazy *adj. (sl.)* **be ~-crazy** eine Gefängnispsychose haben; **~-fry** *v. t. (Cookery)* unter Rühren schnell braten

stirrer ['stɜ:rə(r)] *n.* **a)** *(utensil)* Rührer, *der;* **b)** *(one who provokes)* Aufwiegler, *der*/Aufwieglerin, *die*

stirring ['stɜ:rɪŋ] *adj.* bewegend ‹*Musik, Theaterstück, Poesie*›; spannend ‹*Roman, Geschichte*›; mitreißend ‹*Auftritt, Rede, Marsch*›; bewegt ‹*Zeiten*›

stirringly ['stɜ:rɪŋlɪ] *adv.* bewegend ‹*gespielt*›; spannend ‹*erzählt*›; mitreißend ‹*gespielter Marsch*›

stirrup ['stɪrəp] *n.* **a)** *(Riding)* Steigbügel, *der;* **b)** *(of garment)* Steg, *der;* **c)** *(Anat.)* **~[-bone]** Steigbügel, *der*

stirrup: ~-cup *n.* Abschiedstrunk, *der (geh.);* **~-iron** *n. (Riding)* Steigbügel, *der;* **~-pump** *n.* Handpumpe, *die (mit Fußstütze)*

stitch [stɪtʃ] **1.** *n.* **a)** *(Sewing: pass of needle)* Stich, *der; see also* **save 1 f; b)** *(result of needle movement) (Knitting, Crocheting)* Masche, *die; (Sewing, Embroidery)* Stich, *der;* **drop a ~** *(Knitting)* eine Masche fallenlassen; **undo the ~es** aufziehen; *(in seam, hem)* die Naht auftrennen; **c)** *(kind of ~) (Knitting)* Muster, *das; (Sewing, Embroidery)* Stich, *der;* **d)** *(coll.: piece of clothing)* **not have a ~ on** splitter[faser]nackt *(ugs.)* sein; **the burglars stole every ~ of clothing I had** die Einbrecher stahlen mir sämtliche Klamotten *(salopp);* **e)** *(pain)* **[have] a ~ [in the side]** Seitenstechen [haben]; **f)** *(coll.)* **be in ~es** sich kugeln vor Lachen *(ugs.);* **he/his jokes had me in ~es** ich wäre [beinahe] vor Lachen über ihn/seine Witze gestorben *(ugs.);* **g)** *(Med.: to sew up wound)* Stich, *der;* **~es** Naht, *die;* **he had his ~es taken out** ihm wurden die Fäden gezogen; **need [five] ~es** [mit fünf Stichen] genäht werden müssen; **h)** *(Bookbinding)* Heftung, *die.* **2.** *v.t.* nähen; *(Embroidery)* sticken; *(Bookbinding)* heften. **3.** *v.i.* nähen; *(Embroidery)* sticken; *(Bookbinding)* heften

~ 'down *v.t.* festnähen

~ 'on *v.t.* annähen ‹*Knopf*›; aufnähen ‹*Flicken, Borte*›

~ 'up *v.t.* nähen; zusammennähen ‹*Stoffteile*›; vernähen ‹*Loch, Riß, Wunde*›

stitching ['stɪtʃɪŋ] *n.* **a)** *(series of stitches)* Naht, *die;* **b)** *(ornamental stitches)* Stickerei, *die;* **c)** *(Bookbinding: fastening)* Heftung, *die*

stoat [stəʊt] *n.* Hermelin, *das*

stochastic [stə'kæstɪk] *adj.* stochastisch

stock [stɒk] **1.** *n.* **a)** *(origin, family, breed)* Abstammung, *die;* **a horse of good racing/breeding ~:** ein Renn-/Zuchtpferd mit gutem Stammbaum; **be** *or* **come of farming/French/good ~:** bäuerlicher/französischer Herkunft sein/aus einer guten Familie stammen; **b)** *(supply, store)* Vorrat, *der; (in shop etc.)* Warenbestand, *der;* **our ~ is high/low** wir haben genug/zu wenig vorrätig; **our ~s of food/sherry** unsere Lebensmittelvorräte/unser Vorrat an Sherry *(Dat.);* **have a good ~ of information/knowledge** umfangreiche Informationen/ein umfangreiches Wissen haben; **be in ~/out of ~:** vorrätig/nicht vorrätig sein; **sb. is out of ~ of sth.** jmd. hat etw. nicht vorrätig; **get** *or* **lay in a ~ of coal** sich *(Dat.)* einen Kohlevorrat anlegen; **have sth. in ~:** etw. auf *od. (Kaufmannsspr.)* am Lager haben; **keep sth. in ~** *(have available as a general policy)* etw. führen; **renew** *or* **replenish one's ~ of sth.** seinen Vorrat an etw. *(Dat.)* auffüllen; **take ~:** Inventur machen; *(fig.)* Bilanz ziehen; **take ~ of sb.** *(fig.)* jmdn. mustern; **take ~ of sth.** *(fig.)* über etw. *(Akk.)* Bilanz ziehen; **take ~ of oneself** *(fig.)* sein Leben Revue passieren lassen; **take ~ of one's position/situation/prospects** seinen Standort/seine Situation/seine Zukunftsaussichten bestimmen; *see also* **rolling-stock; c)** *(Cookery)* Brühe, *die;* **d)** *(Finance)* Wertpapiere; *(shares)* Aktien; **sb.'s ~ is high/low** *(fig.)* jmds. Aktien stehen gut/schlecht *(fig.);* **take** *or (Amer.)* **put ~ in sth.** *(fig.)* viel von etw. halten; *see also* **¹defer a; ordinary b; e)** *(Hort.)* Stamm, *der; (for grafting)* Unterlage, *die;* **f)** *(handle)* Griff, *der; (of gun)* Schaft, *der; (of plough)* Sterz, *der; see also* **²lock 1 e; g)** *(Agric.)* [lebendes und totes] Inventar [eines landwirtschaftlichen Betriebes]; *see also* **fatstock; livestock; h)** *(raw material)* [Roh]material, *das;* **[film] ~:** Filmmaterial, *das;* **[paper] ~:** Papierstoff, *der; (for printing on)* Papier, *das;* **i)** *(Bot.)* Levkoje, *die; see also* **night-scented stock; Virginia stock; j)** *in pl. (Hist.: punishment-frame)* Stock, *der;* **k)** *(Naut.: anchor crossbar)* Stock, *der;* **l)** *in pl. (Naut.: construction support)* Helling, *die;* Helgen, *der;* **be on the ~s** auf dem Stapel liegen; *(fig.)* in Vorbereitung sein; **have sth. on the ~s** *(fig.)* an etw. *(Dat.)* arbeiten; **m)** *(tree-stump)* [Baum]stumpf, *der. See also* **laughing-stock. 2.** *v.t.* **a)** *(supply with ~)* beliefern; **~ a pond/river/lake with fish** einen Teich/Fluß/See mit Fischen besetzen; **her larder is ~ed with tins** sie hat einen [großen] Vorrat an Konserven in der Speisekammer; **a cellar ~ed with wine/sherry** ein gut mit Wein/Sherry bestückter Keller; **he has a memory ~ed with useless information** sein Gedächtnis ist mit nutzlosem Wissen vollgepfropft *(ugs.);* **b)** *(Commerc.: keep in ~)* auf *od. (fachspr.)* am Lager haben; führen. **3.** *attrib. adj.* **a)** *(Commerc.)* vorrätig; **a ~ size/model** eine Standardgröße/ein Standardmodell; **b)** *(fig.: trite, unoriginal)* abgedroschen *(ugs.);* **~ character** Standardrolle, *die*

~ 'up 1. *v.i.* **~ up [with sth.]** sich *(Dat.)* einen Vorrat an etw. *(Dat.)* anlegen; **~ up with coal for the winter** sich für den Winter mit Kohlen eindecken; **~ up on sth.** seine Vorräte an etw. auffüllen. **2.** *v.t.* auffüllen; mit Fischen besetzen ‹*Teich, Fluß, See*›; **the library needs ~ing up with new books** die Bibliothek muß ihren Bestand um neue Bücher erweitern

stockade [stɒ'keɪd] **1.** *n.* Palisade, *die.* **2.** *v.t.* mit einer Palisade befestigen

stock: ~-breeder *n.* Viehzüchter, *der/*-züchterin, *die;* **~-breeding** *n.* Viehzucht, *die;* **~broker** *n. (Finance)* Effektenmakler, *der/*-maklerin, *die;* **~broker belt** *Wohngebiet reicher Geschäftsleute in der Umgebung einer Großstadt;* ≈ Speckgürtel, *der (ugs.);* **~broking** ['stɒkbrəʊkɪŋ] *n., no pl. (Finance)* Effektenhandel, *der;* **~broking is a lucrative profession** der Handel mit Wertpapieren ist ein einträglicher Beruf; **~-car** *n.* **a)** *(Amer. Railw.)* Viehwaggon, *der;* **b)** *(racing-car)* Stock-Car, *der;* **~-car racing** *n.* Stock-Car-Rennen, *das;* **~ cube** *n. (Cookery)* Brühwürfel, *der;* **~ exchange** *n. (Finance)* Börse, *die;* **the S~ Exchange** *(Brit.)* die [Londoner] Börse; **~fish** *n. (Cookery)* Stockfisch, *der;* **~holder** *n. (Finance)* Wertpapierbesitzer, *der/*-besitzerin, *die; (of shares)* Aktionär, *der/*Aktionärin, *die;* **be a ~holder in the company** Anteile an der Gesellschaft besitzen

stockily ['stɒkɪlɪ] *adv.* **~ built** stämmig

stockinet[te] [stɒkɪ'net] *n. (Textiles)* Trikot, *der*

¹stocking ['stɒkɪŋ] *n.* **a)** Strumpf, *der;* **in one's ~[ed] feet** in Strümpfen; **hang up one's ~:** den Strumpf für den Weihnachtsmann aufhängen; **b)** *(of horse)* Strumpf, *der*

²stocking *n. see* **stock 2:** Belieferung, *die;* Besatz, *der;* Lagerhaltung, *die*

stockinged ['stɒkɪŋd] *adj. see* **¹stocking a**

stocking: ~-filler *n. (Brit.)* **a)** *kleines Geschenk, das in den für den Weihnachtsmann aufgehängten Strumpf gesteckt wird;* **b)** zusätzliche Kleinigkeit *(als Weihnachtsgeschenk);* **~ mask** *n.* Strumpfmaske, *die;* **~-stitch** *n. (Knitting)* Glattgestrick, *das;* **knit in ~-stitch** glatt rechts stricken; **~-stuffer** *(Amer.) see* **~-filler**

stock-in-'trade *n.* Inventar, *das; (workman's tools)* Handwerkszeug, *das; (fig.: resource)* [festes] Repertoire; **be the ~ of sb.** zu jmds. festem Repertoire gehören

stockist ['stɒkɪst] *n. (Brit. Commerc.)* Fachhändler/-händlerin [mit größerem Warenlager]

stock: ~jobber *n. (Finance)* **a)** *(Brit.: dealer)* Jobber, *der;* **b)** *(Amer. derog.: broker)* [Börsen]spekulant, *der/*-spekulantin, *die;* **~jobbing** *n. (Brit. Finance)* Börsenspekulation, *die;* **~list** *n.* **a)** *(Finance)* Kurszettel, *der;* **b)** *(Commerc.)* Inventarliste, *die;* **~-market** *n. (Finance)* **a)** *see* **stock exchange; b)** *(trading)* Börsengeschäft, *das;* **lose money on the ~-market** Geld an der Börse verlieren; **~pile 1.** *n.* Vorrat, *der; (of weapons)* Arsenal, *das;* **2.** *v.t.* horten; anhäufen ‹*Waffen*›; **~-pot** *n. (Cookery)* Suppentopf, *der;* **~-room** *n.* Lager, *das;* **~-'still** *pred. adj.* bewegungslos; **stand ~-still** regungslos [da]stehen; **~-taking** *n. (Commerc.)* Inventur, *die;* **closed for ~-taking** wegen Inventur geschlossen

stocky ['stɒkɪ] *adj.* stämmig; kräftig ‹*Pflanze, Trieb*›

'stockyard *n.* Viehhof, *der*

stodge [stɒdʒ] *n. (coll.: food)* Brei, *der*

stodgy ['stɒdʒɪ] *adj.* **a)** pappig [und schwerverdaulich] ‹*Essen*›; **b)** *(heavy, uninteresting)* langweilig ‹*Buch*›; schwerfällig ‹*Stil, Poesie*›; **c)** *(dull, drab)* trübselig ‹*Person, Leben usw.*›

stoic ['stəʊɪk] **1.** *n.* **a)** **S~** *(Philos.)* Stoiker, *der;* **b)** *(impassive person)* Stoiker, *der/*Stoikerin, *die.* **2.** *adj.* **a)** **S~** *(Philos.)* stoisch; **the S~ philosophers/school** die Stoiker/die Stoa; **b)** stoisch ‹*Person, Ablehnung, Antwort usw.*›

stoical ['stəʊɪkl] *adj.*, **stoically** ['stəʊɪkəlɪ] *adv.* stoisch

stoicism ['stəʊɪsɪzm] *n., no pl.* **a)** **S~** *(Philos.)* Stoizismus, *der;* **b)** *(impassiveness)* Stoizismus, *der (geh.);* stoische Ruhe; **do sth. with ~:** etw. mit stoischer Gelassenheit tun

stoke [stəʊk] **1.** *v.t.* heizen ‹*Ofen, Kessel*›; unterhalten ‹*Feuer*›; **~ a fire with coal** Kohle nachlegen. **2.** *v.i. see* **~ up 2**

~ 'up 1. *v.t.* aufheizen ‹*Kessel, Ofen, Dampfmaschine*›; **~ a fire up** Brennstoff auf ein Feuer legen. **2.** *v.i. (coll.: feed oneself)* sich vollstopfen *(ugs.)*

stoke: ~hold *n. (Naut.)* Heizraum, *der;* **~hole** *n.* Heizerstand, *der*

stoker ['stəʊkə(r)] *n.* Heizer, *der/*Heizerin, *die (Berufsbez.)*

STOL [stɒl] *abbr. (Aeronaut.)* **short take off and landing** STOL; Kurzstart

¹stole [stəʊl] *n.* Stola, *die*

²stole *see* **steal 1, 2**

stolen ['stəʊln] **1.** *see* **steal 1, 2. 2.** *attrib. adj.* heimlich ‹*Vergnügen, Kuß*›; verstohlen ‹*Blick*›; **~ goods** Diebesgut, *das;* **receiving ~ goods** Hehlerei, *die;* **receiver of ~ goods** Hehler, *der/*Hehlerin, *die*

stolid ['stɒlɪd] *adj.* stur *(ugs.);* wacker *(iron.)* ‹*Arbeiter*›; unbeirrbar ‹*Entschlossenheit*›; hartnäckig ‹*Schweigen, Weigerung, Gleichgültigkeit*›

stolidity [stə'lɪdɪtɪ] *n., no pl.* Sturheit, *die (ugs.); (of refusal, opposition)* Hartnäckigkeit, *die*

stolidly ['stɒlɪdlɪ] *adv.* stur *(ugs.);* wacker *(iron.)* ‹*arbeiten*›; starrsinnig ‹*sich widersetzen, schweigen*›; stumpf ‹*blicken, marschieren*›

stoma ['stəʊmə] *n., pl.* **~s** *or* **~ta** ['stəʊmətə] **a)** *(Zool.)* Körperöffnung, *die;* **b)** *(Bot.)* Spaltöffnung, *die*

stomach ['stʌmək] **1.** *n.* **a)** *(Anat., Zool.)* Magen, *der;* **lie heavy on sb.'s ~:** jmdm. schwer im Magen liegen; **on an empty ~:** mit leerem Magen ‹*arbeiten, fahren, weggehen*›; auf nüchternen Magen ‹*Alkohol trinken, Medizin einnehmen*›; **on a full ~:** mit vollem Magen; **turn sb.'s ~:** jmdm. den Magen umdrehen *(ugs.);* **the smell/sight of food turned her ~:** bei dem Geruch/beim Anblick des Essens drehte sich ihr der Magen um *(ugs.);* **b)** *(abdomen, paunch)* Bauch, *der;* **have a pain in one's ~:** Bauchschmerzen haben; **lie on one's ~:** auf dem Bauch liegen; **develop a ~:** einen Bauch ansetzen; **pull your ~ in!** zieh deinen Bauch ein!; *see also* **¹pit 1 b; c) have the/no ~ [for sth.]** *(wish/not wish to eat)* Appetit/keinen Appetit [auf etw. *(Akk.)*] haben; *(fig.: interest)* Lust/keine Lust [auf etw. *(Akk.)*] haben; *(fig.: courage)* Mut/keinen Mut [zu etw.] haben. **2.** *v.t.* **a)** *(eat, drink)* herunterbekommen *(ugs.); (keep down)* bei sich behalten; **b)** *(fig.: tolerate)* ausstehen; hinnehmen ⟨*Beleidigung*⟩; akzeptieren ⟨*Vorstellung, Vorgehen, Rat*⟩

stomach: ~-ache *n.* Magenschmerzen *Pl.;* **have a ~-ache** Magenschmerzen haben; **~-pump** *n. (Med.)* Magenpumpe, *die;* **~ upset** *n.* Magenverstimmung, *die*

stomp [stɒmp] **1.** *n. (dance)* Stomp, *der.* **2.** *v. i.* **a)** *(tread heavily)* **~ [about** *or* **around]** [umher]stampfen; **b)** *(Amer.: stamp feet)* [mit den Füßen] aufstampfen

stone [stəʊn] **1.** *n.* **a)** Stein, *der;* **[as] hard as [a] ~:** steinhart; **his heart is** *or* **he has a heart of** *or* **[as] hard as [a] ~** *(fig.)* sein Herz ist aus Stein; er hat ein Herz aus Stein; **throw ~s/a ~ at sb.** jmdn. mit Steinen bewerfen/einen Stein auf jmdn. werfen; *(fig.)* jmdm. am Zeug flicken *(ugs.);* **cast** *or* **throw the first ~** *(fig.)* den ersten Stein werfen; **only a ~'s throw [away]** *(fig.)* nur einen Steinwurf weit entfernt; **leave no ~ unturned** *(fig.)* Himmel und Hölle in Bewegung setzen; **leave no ~ unturned to achieve sth.** *(fig.)* alles dransetzen, um etw. zu erreichen; *see also* **bird a; blood 1 a; glass 2; philosopher's stone; Portland stone; rolling stone; b)** *(gem)* [Edel]stein, *der;* **c)** *(Med., Bot.)* Stein, *der;* **d)** *see* **hailstone; e)** *pl. same (Brit.: weight unit) Gewicht von 6,35 kg.* **2.** *adj.* steinern; Stein⟨*hütte, -kreuz, -mauer, -brücke*⟩; **~ jar/urn** Krug/Urne aus Steingut. **3.** *v. t.* **a)** mit Steinen bewerfen; **~ sb. [to death]** jmdn. steinigen; **~ me!, ~ the crows!** *(sl.)* mich laust der Affe! *(ugs.);* **b)** entsteinen ⟨*Obst*⟩

stone: S~ Age *n. (Archaeol.)* Steinzeit, *die; attrib.* Steinzeit-; **~-cold 1.** *adj.* eiskalt; **2.** *adv.* **~-cold sober** stocknüchtern

stoned [stəʊnd] *adj. (sl.)* stoned *(Drogenjargon); (drunk)* voll zu *(salopp);* **get ~ [on drugs]** sich anturnen *(ugs.);* **be ~ out of one's head** *or* **mind** völlig stoned *od.* zugekifft sein *(Drogenjargon); (drunk)* total zu sein *(ugs.)*

stone: ~-'dead *pred. adj.* mausetot *(fam.);* **kill sth. ~-dead** *(fig.)* etw. völlig zunichte machen; **~-'deaf** *adj.* stocktaub *(ugs.);* **~-ground** *adj.* mit Mühlsteinen gemahlen; **~mason** *n.* Steinmetz, *der;* **~-pine** *n. (Bot.)* Pinie, *die;* Nußkiefer, *die;* **~'wall** *(Brit.)* **1.** *v. i.* mauern *(fig.);* **~wall on an issue** in einer Angelegenheit mauern; **2.** *v. t.* **~wall sth.** bei etw. mauern; **~walling** ['stəʊnwɔːlɪŋ] *n. (Brit.)* **~walling [tactics]** Hinhaltetaktik, *die;* **~ware** *n., no pl.* Steingut, *das; attrib.* ⟨*Krug, Vase*⟩ aus Steingut; **~work** *n.* Mauerwerk, *das*

stony ['stəʊnɪ] *adj.* **a)** *(full of stones)* steinig; **fall on ~ ground** *(fig.)* auf unfruchtbaren Boden fallen; **b)** *(like stone)* steinartig; **c)** *(hostile)* steinern *(geh.)* ⟨*Blick, Miene*⟩; frostig ⟨*Person, Empfang, Schweigen*⟩; **d)** *pred. (sl.) see* **stony-broke**

stony-'broke *pred. adj. (sl.)* völlig abgebrannt *(ugs.)*

stood *see* **stand 1, 2**

stooge [stuːdʒ] *(sl.)* **1.** *n.* **a)** *(Theatre: comedian)* Stichwortgeber, *der*/-geberin, *die;* **b)** *(compliant person)* Marionette, *die (fig.).* **2.** *v. i.* **~ for sb.** *(for comedian)* jmdm. die Stichworte liefern; *(as deputy etc.)* jmds. Marionette sein

stool [stuːl] *n.* **a)** Hocker, *der;* **fall between two ~s** *(fig.)* sich zwischen zwei Stühle setzen; **b)** *see* **footstool; c)** *in sing. or pl. (Physiol.: faeces)* Stuhl, *der;* **d)** *(Bot.) (of tree) Baumstumpf mit frisch austreibenden Schößlingen; (of dormant plant)* Wurzelstock, *der; (of cut plant)* Mutterpflanze, *die*

'stool-pigeon *n.* **a)** *(Hunting)* Locktaube, *die;* **b)** *(fig.: decoy)* Lockvogel, *der;* **c)** *(police-informer)* Polizeispitzel, *der*

¹stoop [stuːp] **1.** *v. i.* **~ [down]** sich bücken; **~ over sth.** sich über etw. *(Akk.)* beugen; **he'd ~ to anything to get his way** *(fig.)* ihm ist jedes Mittel recht[, um sein Ziel zu erreichen]; **I wouldn't ~ so low!** *(fig.)* ich würde mich nicht so erniedrigen!; **~ to do sth.** *(fig.)* sich dazu erniedrigen, etw. zu tun; **~ to deceit/a lie** sich für Verrat/eine Lüge hergeben; **b)** *(have ~)* gebeugt gehen; **c)** *see* **swoop 2. 2.** *v. t.* beugen; **~ed with old age** vom Alter gebeugt. **3.** *n.* gebeugte Haltung; **have a/walk with a ~:** einen krummen Rücken haben/gebeugt gehen

²stoop *n. (Amer.) nicht überdachte, über Treppen erreichbare Terrasse vor einem Haus*

stop [stɒp] **1.** *v. t.,* **-pp- a)** *(not let move further)* anhalten ⟨*Person, Fahrzeug*⟩; aufhalten ⟨*Fortschritt, Verkehr, Feind*⟩; verstummen lassen *(geh.)* ⟨*Gerücht, Geschichte, Lüge*⟩; ⟨*Tormann:*⟩ halten ⟨*Ball*⟩; **she ~ped her car** sie hielt an; **~ thief!** haltet den Dieb!; **there's no ~ping sb.** jmd. läßt sich nicht aufhalten; **~ a bullet** *or* **one** *(sl.) (get killed)* umgelegt werden *(salopp); (get wounded)* eine Kugel abkriegen *(ugs.) see also* **track 1 b; b)** *(not let continue)* unterbrechen ⟨*Redner, Spiel, Gespräch, Vorstellung*⟩; beenden ⟨*Krieg, Gespräch, Treffen, Spiel, Versuch, Arbeit*⟩; stillen ⟨*Blutung*⟩; stoppen ⟨*Produktion, Uhr, Streik, Inflation*⟩; einstellen ⟨*Handel, Zahlung, Lieferung, Besuche, Subskriptionen, Bemühungen*⟩; abstellen ⟨*Strom, Gas, Wasser, Mißstände*⟩; beseitigen ⟨*Schmerz*⟩; **~ that/that nonsense/that noise/your threats!** hör damit/mit diesem Unsinn/diesem Lärm/deinen Drohungen auf!; **he had his grant/holidays ~ped** seine Unterstützung wurde/Ferien wurden gestrichen; **bad light ~ped play** *(Sport)* das Spiel wurde wegen schlechter Lichtverhältnisse abgebrochen; **~ the show** *(fig.)* Furore machen; **just you try and ~ me!** versuch doch, mich daran zu hindern!; **~ working** mit der Arbeit aufhören; **~ smoking/crying** aufhören zu rauchen/weinen; **never ~ doing sth.** etw. unaufhörlich tun; **~ 'saying that!** sag das nicht mehr!; **~ being silly!** hör mit diesem Quatsch auf!; **~ it!** hör auf [damit]!; *(in more peremptory tone)* Schluß damit!; **~ oneself** sich zurückhalten; **I couldn't ~ myself** ich konnte nicht anders; see also **rot 1 a; c)** *(not let happen)* verhindern ⟨*Verbrechen, Unfall*⟩; **I managed to ~ myself [from] punching him** ich mußte mich sehr zurückhalten, um ihn nicht zu schlagen; **He was determined to do/say it. We couldn't ~ him** Er war entschlossen, es zu tun/sagen. Wir konnten ihn nicht davon abhalten; **she couldn't ~ herself [from] coughing** sie versuchte vergeblich, ihren Husten zu unterdrücken; **you won't ~ me [from] seeing her** du wirst mich nicht daran hindern, sie zu sehen; **he tried to ~ us parking** er versuchte uns am Parken zu hindern; **he phoned his mother to ~ her [from] worrying** er rief seine Mutter an, damit sie sich keine Sorgen machte; **~ sth. [from] happening** verhindern, daß etw. geschieht; **there's nothing to ~ me/you** *etc.* **[doing sth.]** es gibt nichts, was mich/dich *usw.* daran hindern könnte[, etw. zu tun]; **d)** *(cause to cease working)* abstellen ⟨*Maschine usw.*⟩; ⟨*Streikende:*⟩ stillegen ⟨*Betrieb*⟩; **his/her face is enough to ~ a clock** *(fig. coll.)* wenn man sein/ihr Gesicht sieht, haut es einen um *(ugs.);* **e)** *(block up)* zustopfen ⟨*Loch, Öffnung, Riß, Ohren*⟩; verschließen ⟨*Wasserhahn, Rohr, Schlauch, Flasche*⟩; **~ holes in a wall with concrete/filler** Löcher in einer Wand mit Beton/Spachtelmasse füllen; **~ sb.'s mouth** *(fig.)* jmdm. den Mund stopfen *(ugs.);* **f)** *(withhold)* streichen; **the cost will be ~ped out of** *or* **from his salary** die Kosten werden von seinem Gehalt abgezogen; **~ payment** *(Finance)* die Zahlungen [wegen Insolvenz] einstellen; **~ [payment of] a cheque** einen Scheck sperren lassen; **g)** *(Boxing) (parry)* parieren; *(knock out)* k.o. schlagen; **h)** *(Mus.)* **~ a string** eine Saite greifen; **a ~ped pipe [of an organ]** eine gedackte [Orgel]pfeife. **2.** *v. i.,* **-pp- a)** *(not extend further)* aufhören; ⟨*Straße, Treppe:*⟩ enden; ⟨*Ton:*⟩ verstummen; ⟨*Ärger:*⟩ verfliegen; ⟨*Schmerz:*⟩ abklingen; ⟨*Zahlungen, Lieferungen:*⟩ eingestellt werden; **at this point his knowledge ~s** an diesem Punkt ist sein Wissen erschöpft; **b)** *(not move or operate further)* ⟨*Fahrzeug, Fahrer:*⟩ halten; ⟨*Maschine, Motor:*⟩ stillstehen; ⟨*Uhr, Fußgänger, Herz:*⟩ stehenbleiben; **he ~ped in the middle of the sentence** er unterbrach sich mitten im Satz; **he never ~s to think [before he acts]** er denkt nie nach [bevor er handelt]; **~!** halt!; **~ at nothing** vor nichts zurückschrecken; **~ dead** plötzlich stehenbleiben; ⟨*Redner:*⟩ abbrechen; **you never know when to ~:** du weißt einfach nicht, wann du aufhören mußt; *see also* **short 2 a; track 1 b; c)** *(coll.: stay)* bleiben; **~ at a hotel/at a friend's house/with sb.** in einem Hotel/im Hause eines Freundes/bei jmdm. wohnen; **~ for** *or* **to dinner** zum Essen bleiben; **~ for coffee afterwards** zum Kaffeetrinken [noch] dableiben; **I'm not ~ping** ich kann nicht lange bleiben. **3.** *n.* **a)** *(halt)* Halt, *der;* **there will be two ~s for coffee on the way** es wird unterwegs zweimal zum Kaffeetrinken angehalten; **this train goes to London with only two ~s** dieser Zug fährt mit nur zwei Zwischenhalten nach London; **bring to a ~:** zum Stehen bringen ⟨*Fahrzeug*⟩; zum Erliegen bringen ⟨*Verkehr*⟩; unterbrechen ⟨*Arbeit, Diskussion, Treffen*⟩; **the fire brought the show/performance to a [sudden] ~:** das Feuer setzte der Show/dem Auftritt ein [plötzliches] Ende *(geh.);* **come to a ~:** stehenbleiben; ⟨*Fahrzeug:*⟩ zum Stehen kommen; ⟨*Gespräch:*⟩ abbrechen; ⟨*Arbeit, Verkehr:*⟩ zum Erliegen kommen; ⟨*Vorlesung:*⟩ abgebrochen werden; **make a ~ at** *or* **in a place** in einem Ort haltmachen; **put a ~ to** abstellen ⟨*Mißstände, Unsinn*⟩; unterbinden ⟨*Versuche*⟩; aus der Welt schaffen ⟨*Gerücht*⟩; **put a ~ on a cheque** einen Scheck sperren lassen; **without a ~:** ohne Halt ⟨*fahren, fliegen*⟩; ohne anzuhalten ⟨*gehen, laufen*⟩; ununterbrochen ⟨*arbeiten, reden*⟩; **b)** *(place)* Haltestelle, *die;* **the ship's first ~ is Cairo** der erste Hafen, den das Schiff anläuft, ist Kairo; **the plane's first ~ is Frankfurt** die erste Zwischenlandung des Flugzeuges ist in Frankfurt; **c)** *(Brit.: punctuation-mark)* Satzzeichen, *das; see also* **full stop a; d)** *(in telegram)* stop; **e)** *(Mus.) (row of organ-pipes)* Register, *das; (organ-knob)* Registerzug, *der;* **pull out all the ~s** *(fig.)* alle Register ziehen; **f)** *(to limit movement)* Anschlag, *der;* **g)** *(Photog.)* Blende, *die;* **h)** *(Phonet.)* Verschlußlaut, *der*

~ a'way *(coll.) see* **stay away a**

~ be'hind *(coll.) see* **stay behind**

~ 'by *(Amer.)* **1.** *v. i.* vorbeischauen *(ugs.);* **~ by at the store** im Geschäft vorbeigehen *(ugs.).* **2.** *v. t.* **~ by sb.'s house** *or* **place [and have a drink]** bei jmdm. [auf einen Drink] vorbeischauen *(ugs.);* **we'll ~ by the shop and get some apples** wir gehen schnell im Laden vorbei und kaufen [uns] ein paar Äpfel

~ 'down *v. t. (Photog.)* **~ down to f/16** auf Blende 16 abblenden

~ 'in *(coll.) see* **stay in b**

~ 'off *v. i.* einen Zwischenaufenthalt einlegen; **~ off at the pub for a packet of cigarettes** an der Kneipe kurz anhalten, um Zigaretten zu kaufen; *see also* **stopoff**

~ 'on *(coll.) see* **stay on c**

~ 'out *v. i. (coll.)* **a)** draußen bleiben; **b)** *(remain on strike)* ⟨*Arbeiter:*⟩ weiterstreiken *(ugs.)*

~ 'over *v. i.* einen Zwischenaufenthalt machen; *(remain for the night)* übernachten **(at** bei); *see also* **stopover**

~ **'up 1.** *v. t. see* ~ **1e. 2.** *v. i. (coll.) see* **stay up a**

stop: ~-button *n.* Stopptaste, *die;* **press the ~-button** [auf] die Stopptaste drücken; **~cock** *n.* Abstellhahn, *der;* Absperrhahn, *der (Technik);* **~gap** *n.* Notbehelf, *der; (scheme, measure, plan, person)* Notlösung, *die; attrib.* behelfsmäßig; **a ~gap measure** eine Behelfsmaßnahme; **~-'go** *n. (Brit.)* Hin und Her, *das; (boom and recession)* Auf und Ab, *das; attrib.* **~-go strategy/policies** strategisches/politisches Hin und Her; **~-light** *n.* **a)** *(red traffic-light)* rotes Licht; **if the ~-light shows** wenn die Ampel rot ist; **b)** *(Motor Veh.)* Bremslicht, *das;* ~ **line** *n. (on road)* Haltelinie, *die;* **~off** *see* **~over; ~-order** *n.* **a)** *(Finance)* limitierter Börsenauftrag; **b)** *(Law) gerichtliche Anordnung, daß über bei Gericht hinterlegte Wertpapiere nicht verfügt werden darf;* **~over** *n.* Stopover, *der;* Zwischenaufenthalt, *der; (of aircraft)* Zwischenlandung, *die*

stoppage ['stɒpɪdʒ] *n.* **a)** *(halt)* Stillstand, *der; (strike)* Streik, *der; (in traffic)* Stau, *der; (Sport)* Unterbrechung, *die;* **b)** *(cancellation)* Sperrung, *die; (of delivery)* Einstellung, *die;* **c)** *(deduction)* Abzug, *der*

stopper ['stɒpə(r)] **1.** *n.* Stöpsel, *der;* Pfropfen, *der;* **put a ~** *or* **the ~s on sth./sb.** *(fig.)* einer Sache *(Dat.)* einen Riegel vorschieben/jmdm. einen Strich durch die Rechnung machen. **2.** *v. t.* zustöpseln

stopping ['stɒpɪŋ] *see* **filling 1a**

stopping: ~ distance *n.* Anhalteweg, *der (fachspr.);* **~-place, ~-point** *ns.* Station, *die; (where train must stop)* Haltepunkt, *der; (where one might rest)* Ort zum Rasten; ~ **train** *n. (Brit. Railw.)* Nahverkehrszug, *der*

stop: ~-press *n. (Brit. Journ.)* letzte Meldung/Meldungen; *attrib.* **~-press news** letzte Meldungen; ~ **sign** *n.* Stoppschild, *das;* **~-signal** *n.* Haltesignal, *das;* **~-watch** *n.* Stoppuhr, *die*

storage ['stɔːrɪdʒ] *n.* **a)** *no pl., no indef. art. (storing)* Lagerung, *die; (of furniture)* Einlagerung, *die; (of films, books, documents)* Aufbewahrung, *die; (of data, water, electricity)* Speicherung, *die;* **my furniture is in ~:** meine Möbel sind [bei einer Spedition] eingelagert; **put in[to] ~:** zur Aufbewahrung geben ‹*Möbel*›; *see also* **cold storage; b)** *see* **storage space; c)** *(cost of warehousing)* Lagergebühr, *die*

storage: ~ battery *n. (Electr.)* Akkumulator, *der;* ~ **capacity** *n. (Computing)* Speicherkapazität, *die;* ~ **cell** *n. (Electr.)* Akkumulator, *der;* ~ **heater** *n.* [Nacht]speicherofen, *der;* ~ **space** *n.* Lagerraum, *der; (in house)* Platz [zum Aufbewahren]; **I need ~ space for all my books** ich brauche Platz, um alle meine Bücher aufzubewahren; ~ **tank** *n.* Sammelbehälter, *der;* Lagertank, *der*

store [stɔː(r)] **1.** *n.* **a)** *(Amer.: shop)* Laden, *der;* **b)** *in sing. or pl. (Brit.: large general shop)* Kaufhaus, *das; see also* **department store; c)** *(warehouse)* Lager, *das; (for grain, hay)* Speicher, *der; (for valuables)* Depot, *das; (for arms)* Waffenkammer, *die; (for books, films, documents)* Magazin, *das;* **put sth. in ~:** etw. [bei einer Spedition] einlagern; **d)** *(stock)* Vorrat, *der* **(of an +** *Dat.*); **a great ~ of knowledge** ein großer Wissensschatz; **I don't have an unlimited ~ of patience** meine Geduld ist nicht unerschöpflich; **get in** *or* **lay in a ~ of sth.** einen Vorrat an etw. *(Dat.)* anlegen; **have** *or* **keep coal/food in ~:** einen Kohlenvorrat/einen Vorrat an Lebensmitteln haben; **have enough arms/ammunition in ~:** genug Waffen/Munition in Reserve haben; **be** *or* **lie in ~ for sb.** jmdn. erwarten; **have a surprise in ~ for sb.** eine Überraschung für jmdn. [auf Lager] haben; **there was another surprise in ~ for him** noch eine Überraschung wartete auf ihn; **that's a treat in ~:** das ist eine erfreuliche Aussicht; **there'll be trouble in ~:** es wird Ärger geben; **who knows what the future has in ~?** wer weiß, was die Zukunft mit sich bringt?; **e)** *in pl. (supplies)* Vorräte; **the ~s** *(place)* das [Vorrats]lager; **f) lay** *or* **put** *or* **set [great] ~ by** *or* **on sth.** [großen] Wert auf etw. legen; **g)** *(Brit. Computing)* Speicher, *der.* **2.** *v. t.* **a)** *(put in ~)* einlagern; speichern ‹*Getreide, Energie, Wissen*›; einspeichern ‹*Daten*›; ablegen ‹*Papiere, Dokumente*›; **~ food/nuts/coal/wine** *(collect as reserve)* sich *(Dat.)* einen Vorrat an Lebensmitteln/Nüssen/Kohle/Wein anlegen; **b)** *(leave for storage)* unterbringen; **c)** *(hold)* aufnehmen; speichern ‹*Energie, Daten*›. **3.** *attrib. adj.* **a)** *(Breeding)* Mast-; **b)** *(Amer.: shop-bought)* Konfektions‹*kleidung*›

~ **a'way** *v. t.* lagern; ablegen ‹*Akten*›; **~ food away** sich *(Dat.)* einen Lebensmittelvorrat anlegen; **~ things away in a trunk/at a friend's house** Sachen in einer Truhe verstauen/bei einem Freund aufbewahren; **~ away information** Informationen sammeln und aufbewahren

~ **'up** *v. t.* speichern; **~ up provisions/food/wine/coal/nuts** sich *(Dat.)* Vorräte/Lebensmittel-/Wein-/Kohlenvorräte/einen Vorrat an Nüssen anlegen; **you're only storing up trouble for yourself** du handelst dir nur immer mehr Schwierigkeiten ein

store: ~ detective *n.* Kaufhausdetektiv, *der;* **~house** *n.* Lager[haus], *das;* **sb. is a ~house of knowledge/information [about angling]** jmd. ist ein wandelndes Lexikon[, was das Angeln betrifft]; **the book is a real ~house of facts [about Germany]** das Buch ist eine wahre Fundgrube [für jeden, der sich über Deutschland orientieren will]; **~keeper** *n.* **a)** *(one in charge of ~s)* Lagerist, *der*/Lageristin, *die; (Mil.)* Verwalter der Materialausgabe; **b)** *(Amer.: shopkeeper)* Besitzer eines Einzelhandelsgeschäftes; **~man** ['stɔːmən] *n., pl.* **~men** ['stɔːmən] **a)** *(man in charge of ~s)* Lagerist, *der; (Mil.)* Verwalter der Materialausgabe; **b)** *(handler of ~d goods)* Lagerarbeiter, *der;* **~-room** *n.* Lagerraum, *der; (for food on ship)* Proviantraum, *der; (in restaurant, canteen)* Speisekammer, *die*

storey ['stɔːrɪ] *n.* Stockwerk, *das;* Geschoß, *das;* **a five-~ house** ein fünfgeschossiges Haus; **third-~ window** Fenster im zweiten Stock[werk]

-storeyed ['stɔːrɪd] *adj. in comb.* -geschossig; **three-~ house** dreigeschossiges Haus

storied ['stɔːrɪd] *adj. (literary: legendary)* legendenumwoben

-storied *(Amer.) see* **-storeyed**

stork [stɔːk] *n.* Storch, *der*

storm [stɔːm] **1.** *n.* **a)** Unwetter, *das; (thunder~)* Gewitter, *das;* **the night of the ~:** die Sturmnacht; **cross the Channel in a ~:** den Ärmelkanal bei Sturm überqueren; **a ~ in a teacup** *(fig.)* ein Sturm im Wasserglas; **b)** *(fig.: dispute)* Sturm der Entrüstung; **~ and stress** Sturm und Drang; **c)** *(fig.: outburst) (of applause, protest, indignation, criticism)* Sturm, *der; (of abuse, insults, tears)* Flut, *die; (of missiles, shots, arrows, blows)* Hagel, *der;* **a ~ of blows rained down on his head** Schläge hagelten auf seinen Kopf; **d)** *(Mil.: attack)* Sturm, *der;* **take sb./sth. by ~:** jmdn. überrumpeln/etw. im Sturm nehmen; **e)** *(Meteorol.: wind)* [schwerer] Sturm. **2.** *v. i.* **a)** stürmen; **he ~ed in** er kam hereingestürmt; **~ about** *or* **around in a violent temper** voller Wut herumtoben *(ugs.);* **b)** *(talk violently)* toben; **~ at sb.** jmdn. andonnern *(ugs.);* **~ against sth./sb.** gegen etw. wettern *(ugs.)*/gegen jmdn. vom Leder ziehen. **3.** *v. t. (Mil.)* stürmen

storm: ~-centre *n. (Meteorol.)* Auge *od.* Zentrum eines Wirbelsturms; **~-cloud** *n.* **a)** *(Meteorol.)* Gewitterwolke, *die;* **b)** *(fig.)* **the ~-clouds [of war] are gathering** dunkle Wolken ziehen am Horizont auf [und kündigen Krieg an]; **~-door** *n.* äußere Windfangtür; **~-trooper** *n. (Hist.)* SA-Mann, *der (ns.);* **~-troops** *n. pl.* **a)** *(Mil.)* Sturmtruppen; **b)** *(Hist.)* Sturmabteilung, *die (ns.);* SA, *die (ns.)*

stormy ['stɔːmɪ] *adj.* **a)** stürmisch; wild ‹*Beschimpfung*›; hitzig ‹*Auseinandersetzung*›; **b)** *(indicating storms)* auf Sturm hindeutend; **be** *or* **look ~:** nach Sturm aussehen

¹story ['stɔːrɪ] *n.* **a)** *(account of events)* Geschichte, *die;* **give the ~ of sth.** etw. schildern *od.* darstellen; **the suspects' stories did not coincide** die Aussagen der Verdächtigen stimmten nicht überein; **[that's] a likely ~** *(iron.)* wer's glaubt, wird selig *(ugs. scherzh.);* **it is quite another ~ now** *(fig.)* jetzt sieht alles ganz anders aus; **the [old,] old ~, the same old ~** *(fig.)* das alte Lied *(ugs.);* **tall ~:** unglaubliche Geschichte; **that's [a bit of] a tall ~!** das ist ein bißchen dick aufgetragen! *(ugs.);* **that's a different ~** *(fig.)* das ist etwas ganz anderes; **that's his ~ [and he's sticking to it]** er bleibt bei dem, was er gesagt hat; **that's only 'half the ~:** das ist noch nicht alles; **the bruise told its 'own ~:** der blaue Fleck sprach für sich selbst; **the ~ goes that ...:** man erzählt sich, daß ...; **or so the ~ goes** so erzählt man sich; **the whole ~ came out** alles kam heraus *(ugs.);* **that's not the whole ~:** das ist noch nicht alles; **to cut** *or* **make a long ~ short, ...:** kurz [gesagt], ...; **b)** *(narrative)* Geschichte, *die;* **but that is another ~:** aber das ist eine andere Geschichte; **that's the ~ of my life!** *(fig.)* das ist mein ewiges Problem!; *see also* **short story; c)** *(news item)* Bericht, *der;* Story, *die (ugs.);* **d)** *(past) see* **history a; e)** *(plot)* Story, *die;* **f)** *(set of [interesting] facts)* **the objects in the room have a ~:** die Gegenstände in dem Zimmer haben ihre eigene Geschichte; **there is an interesting ~ behind that sword** um dieses Schwert rankt sich eine interessante Geschichte *(geh.);* **g)** *(coll./child lang.: lie)* Märchen, *das;* **tell stories** Märchen erzählen

²story *(Amer.) see* **storey**

story: ~-book 1. *n.* Geschichtenbuch, *das; (with fairy-tales)* Märchenbuch, *das;* **2.** *attrib. adj.* Bilderbuch-; **~-book world** Märchenwelt, *die;* **~-line** *see* **¹story e; ~-teller** *n.* **a)** *(narrator)* [Geschichten]erzähler, *der*/-erzählerin, *die;* **b)** *(writer)* Erzähler, *der*/Erzählerin, *die;* **c)** *(raconteur)* Anekdotenerzähler, *der*/-erzählerin, *die;* **she's a wonderful ~-teller** sie kann wundervoll erzählen; **d)** *(coll./child lang.: liar)* Lügenbold, *der;* **~-telling** *n.* Geschichtenerzählen, *das; (fig.: lying)* Lügengeschichten- *od.* Märchenerzählen, *das*

stout [staʊt] **1.** *adj.* **a)** *(strong)* fest; stabil ‹*Boot, Werkzeug, Messer, Zaun*›; dick ‹*Tür, Mauer, Damm, Stock, Papier*›; robust ‹*Material, Kleidung*›; stark ‹*Seil, Abwehr*›; kräftig ‹*Pflanze, Pferd, Pfeiler*›; **b)** *(fat)* beleibt; **of ~ build** von gedrungenem Körperbau; **c)** *(brave, staunch)* unverzagt; heftig ‹*Widerstand, Opposition*›; entschieden ‹*Ablehnung*›; stark ‹*Gegner*›; fest ‹*Glaube*›; **a ~ heart** ein festes Herz; **be ~ of heart** sehr beherzt sein; **~ fellow** *(arch./coll.)* wackerer Kerl *(veralt.).* **2.** *n. (drink)* Stout, *der*

stout-hearted ['staʊthɑːtɪd] *adj.* beherzt; unerschrocken

stoutly ['staʊtlɪ] *adv.* **a)** *(strongly)* stabil ‹*gebaut, gezimmert*›; **~ made** solide, robust ‹*Schuhwerk*›; stark ‹*Seil*›; **~ built** stämmig; kräftig ‹*Tier*›; stabil ‹*Haus, Zaun, Tor*›; dick ‹*Tür, Mauer*›; **b)** *(staunchly)* beherzt; hartnäckig ‹*behaupten, ablehnen, widerstehen*›; fest ‹*glauben*›

stoutness ['staʊtnɪs] *n., no pl. (fatness)* Beleibtheit, *die*

[1]**stove** [stəʊv] *n.* Ofen, *der; (for cooking)* Herd, *der;* **electric ~:** Elektroherd, *der*

[2]**stove** *see* **stave 2**

'**stove-pipe** *n. (also hat)* Ofenrohr, *das*

stow [stəʊ] *v.t.* **a)** *(put into place)* packen (**into** in + *Akk.*); verstauen (**into** in + *Dat.*); *(Naut.)* stauen; **she ~ed the letter out of sight/behind some books** sie steckte den Brief weg *(ugs.)*/hinter ein paar Bücher; **b)** *(fill)* vollpacken; vollstopfen *(ugs.); (Naut.)* befrachten; **c)** *(sl.: stop)* aufstecken *(ugs.);* **~ it!** hör auf! *(ugs.); (stop talking)* [halt die] Klappe! *(salopp)*

~ a'way 1. *v.t.* verwahren; **he keeps his savings ~ed away in a sock** er hat seine Ersparnisse in einem Strumpf versteckt. **2.** *v.i.* als blinder Passagier reisen; *see also* **stowaway**

stowage ['stəʊɪdʒ] *n.* **a)** *(space for stowing)* Platz, *der; (Naut.)* Stauraum, *der;* **b)** *(action of stowing)* Aufbewahrung, *die;* Unterbringung, *die; (Naut.)* Stauen, *das;* **c)** *(Naut.: stowed goods)* Ladung, *die*

'**stowaway** *n.* blinder Passagier

straddle ['strædl] *v.t.* **a)** *(be positioned across)* **~** *or* **sit straddling a fence/chair** rittlings auf einem Zaun/Stuhl sitzen; **~** *or* **stand straddling a ditch** mit gespreizten Beinen über einem Graben stehen; **his legs ~d the chair/brook** er saß rittlings auf dem Stuhl/stand mit gespreizten Beinen über dem Bach; **their farm ~s the border** ihre Farm liegt beiderseits der Grenze; **the bridge ~s the river/road** die Brücke überspannt den Fluß/die Straße; **b)** *(part widely)* **sit/stand with legs ~d** *or* **~d legs** mit gespreizten Beinen sitzen/stehen; **~ one's legs** die Beine spreizen; **c)** *(Mil.)* eindecken; **the bombs ~d the target** die Bomben schlugen zu beiden Seiten *od.* beiderseits des Ziels ein

Stradivarius [strædɪ'veərɪəs] *n. (Mus.)* Stradivari, *die*

strafe [strɑːf] *v.t. (Mil.)* beharken *(Soldatenspr.)*

straggle ['strægl] *v.i.* **a)** *(trail)* **~ [along] behind the others** den anderen hinterherzockeln *(ugs.);* **the last few walkers ~ed in** die letzten Geher trotteten ins Ziel; **the procession ~d [out] along the road** der Zug zockelte die Straße entlang *(ugs.);* **b)** *(spread in irregular way)* ‹*Dorf, Stadt:*› sich ausbreiten; ‹*Häuser, Bäume:*› verstreut stehen; **the brook/fence goes straggling through/over the meadow** der Bach zieht sich mit vielen Windungen/der Zaun verläuft kreuz und quer über die Wiese; **c)** *(grow untidily)* ‹*Pflanze:*› wuchern; ‹*Haar, Bart:*› zottig wachsen

straggler ['stræglə(r)] *n.* Nachzügler, *der*

straggling ['stræglɪŋ] *adj.* **a)** *(trailing)* nachzockelnd *(ugs.);* **b)** *(irregular)* verstreut ‹*Häuser*›; ungeordnet ‹*Reihe*›; unregelmäßig ‹*Baumreihe, Schrift*›; ‹*Fluß, Zaun, Straße*› mit vielen Krümmungen; weiträumig angelegt ‹*Stadt, Gebäude*›; **a ~ village** eine Streusiedlung; **c)** *(long and untidy)* wuchernd; zottig ‹*Haar, Bart*›

straggly ['stræglɪ] *see* **straggling c**

straight [streɪt] **1.** *adj.* **a)** gerade; aufrecht ‹*Haltung*›; glatt ‹*Haar*›; **in a ~ line** in gerader Linie; **the ~ and narrow** der Pfad der Tugend; **keep sb. on/keep to the ~ and narrow** jmdn. im Zaum halten/auf dem Pfad der Tugend wandeln *(geh.); see also* **arrow 1**; **b)** *(not having been bent)* ausgestreckt ‹*Arm, Bein*›; durchgedrückt ‹*Knie*›; **c)** *(not misshapen)* gerade ‹*Bein*›; **d)** *(Fashion)* gerade geschnitten; **e)** *(undiluted, unmodified)* unvermischt; **have** *or* **drink whisky/gin ~:** Whisky/Gin pur trinken; **a ~ choice** eine klare Wahl; **make a ~ bet on a horse** auf ein Pferd auf Sieg setzen; **f)** *(successive)* fortlaufend; **win in ~ sets** *(Tennis)* ohne Satzverlust gewinnen; **the team had ten ~ wins** die Mannschaft hat zehn Spiele hintereinander gewonnen; **~ As** *(Amer.)* lauter Einsen; **g)** *(undeviating)* direkt ‹*Blick, Schlag, Schuß, Paß, Ball, Weg*›; **sb. has a ~ aim, sb.'s aim is ~:** jmd. zielt genau; **a ~ hit** *or* **blow** *(Boxing)* eine Gerade; **a ~ left/right** *(Boxing)* eine linke/rechte Gerade; **give sb. a ~ look** jmdn. scharf ansehen; **h)** *(candid)* geradlinig ‹*Mensch*›; ehrlich ‹*Antwort*›; klar ‹*Abfuhr, Weigerung, Verurteilung*›; unmißverständlich ‹*Rat*›; **~ dealings/speaking** direkte Verhandlungen/unverblümte Sprache; **a ~ answer to a ~ question** eine klare Antwort auf eine klare Frage; **he did some ~ talking with her** er sprach sich mit ihr offen aus; **be ~ with sb.** zu jmdm. offen sein; **i)** *(logical)* klar; **her thinking is clear and ~:** ihr Denken ist klar und logisch; **j)** *(Theatre)* ernst; *(not avant-garde)* konventionell; **k)** *(in good order, not askew)* **we/the rooms are ~ now after the move** wir haben uns/die Zimmer nach dem Umzug jetzt eingerichtet; **the accounts are ~:** die Bücher sind in Ordnung; **the picture is ~:** das Bild hängt gerade; **is my hair/tie ~?** sitzt meine Frisur/Krawatte [richtig]?; **is my hat [on] ~?** sitzt mein Hut [richtig]?; **pull sth. ~:** etw. geradeziehen; **put ~:** geradeziehen ‹*Krawatte*›; gerade aufsetzen ‹*Hut*›; gerade hängen ‹*Bild*›; aufräumen ‹*Zimmer, Sachen*›; richtigstellen ‹*Fehler, Mißverständnis*›; **put things ~:** alles in Ordnung bringen; **put things ~ with sb.** mit jmdm. alles klären; **get sth. ~** *(fig.)* etw. genau *od.* richtig verstehen; **let's get it** *or* **the facts** *or* **things ~:** wir sollten alles genau klären; **get this ~!** merk dir das [ein für allemal]!; **put sb. ~:** jmdn. aufklären; **put** *or* **set the record ~:** die Sache *od.* das richtigstellen; *see also* **straight face**; **l)** *(sl.: heterosexual)* hetero *(ugs.);* **m)** *(coll.: conventional)* [spieß]bürgerlich *(abwertend); (Mus.)* konventionell. **2.** *adv.* **a)** *(in a ~ line)* gerade; **she came ~ at me** sie kam geradewegs auf mich zu; **~ opposite** genau gegenüber; **head ~ for the wall** genau auf die Mauer zusteuern; **go ~** *(fig.: give up crime)* ein bürgerliches Leben führen; **b)** *(directly)* geradewegs; **~ after** sofort nach; **the knife went ~ through his hand** das Messer ging mitten durch seine Hand; **the pianist went ~ into the next piece** der Klavierspieler ging sofort zum nächsten Stück über; **come ~ to the point** direkt *od.* gleich zur Sache kommen; **look sb. ~ in the eye** jmdm. direkt in die Augen blicken; **~ ahead** *or* **on** immer geradeaus; **they went ~ ahead and did it** sie taten es sofort; *see also* **horse 1 a**; **shoulder 1 a**; **c)** *(honestly, frankly)* aufrichtig; **give it to me ~:** sei ganz offen zu mir!; **he came ~ out with it** er sagte es ohne Umschweife; **I told him ~ [out] that ...:** ich sagte [es] ihm ins Gesicht, daß ...; **play ~ with sb.** mit jmdm. ein ehrliches Spiel spielen; **d)** *(upright)* gerade ‹*sitzen, stehen, wachsen*›; **e)** *(accurately)* zielsicher; **he can't shoot [very] ~:** er ist nicht [sehr] zielsicher; **f)** *(clearly)* klar ‹*sehen, denken*›. **3.** *n.* **a)** *(~ condition)* **out of the ~ = out of true** *see* **true 2**; **b)** *(~ stretch)* gerade Strecke; *(Sport)* Gerade, *die;* **final** *or* **home** *or* **last ~** *(Sport; also fig.)* Zielgerade, *die;* **c)** *(Cards)* Straße, *die;* Folge, *die*

straight: ~ a'way *adv. (coll.)* sofort; gleich; **~away** *(Amer.) adj.* **a)** *attrib. (straight)* gerade; **b)** *(straightforward)* nüchtern; sachlich; **~ 'bat** *n. (Cricket)* aufrecht gehaltener Schläger; **keep a ~ bat** *(Brit. fig.)* sich anständig benehmen; **~-edge** *n. (for paper-hanging)* Tapezierschiene, *die; (Metalw.)* Haarlineal, *das*

straighten ['streɪtn] **1.** *v.t.* **a)** geradeziehen ‹*Kabel, Teppich, Seil*›; geradebiegen ‹*Draht*›; glätten ‹*Falte, Kleidung, Haare*›; geraderücken ‹*Hut, Krawatte, Brille*›; gerade machen ‹*Tischkante*›; begradigen ‹*Fluß, Straße*›; geradehalten ‹*Rücken*›; strecken ‹*Beine, Arme*›; gerade hängen ‹*Bild*›; **b)** *(put in order)* aufräumen; einrichten ‹*neue Wohnung*›; in Ordnung bringen ‹*Geschäftsbücher, Finanzen*›. **2.** *v.i.* gerade werden; ‹*Haar:*› glatt werden

~ 'out 1. *v.t.* **a)** geradebiegen ‹*Draht*›; geradeziehen ‹*Seil, Kabel*›; glätten ‹*Decke, Teppich*›; begradigen ‹*Fluß, Straße*›; **b)** *(put in order, clear up)* klären; aus der Welt schaffen ‹*Mißverständnis, Meinungsverschiedenheit*›; in Ordnung bringen ‹*Angelegenheit*›; berichtigen ‹*Fehler*›; **~ sb. out** jmdn. zur Einsicht bringen; **~ sb. out on sth.** jmdn. über etw. *(Akk.)* aufklären; **things will ~ themselves out** das wird sich von selbst regeln; **c)** *(sl.: beat up)* jmdn. vermöbeln *(salopp);* **do you want ~ing out?** soll ich dir eine reinhauen? *(salopp).* **2.** *v.i.* gerade werden; ‹*Haar:*› glatt werden; **things will ~ out** das wird sich von selbst regeln

~ 'up 1. *v.t. see* **tidy up 2. 2.** *v.i.* sich aufrichten

straight: ~ 'eye *n.* gute Augen; **~ 'face** *n.* unbewegtes Gesicht; **with a ~ face** ohne eine Miene zu verziehen; **keep a ~ face** keine Miene verziehen; **~-faced** *adj.* mit unbewegter Miene *nachgestellt;* **be ~-faced** keine Miene verziehen; **~ 'fight** *n. (Brit. Polit.) direkter Kampf zwischen zwei Kandidaten;* **~ 'flush** *see* [4]**flush**; **~'forward** *adj.* **a)** *(frank)* freimütig; geradlinig ‹*Politik*›; schlicht ‹*Stil, Sprache, Erzählung, Bericht*›; klar ‹*Anweisung, Vorstellungen*›; **have a ~forward approach to a problem** ein Problem direkt angehen; **be ~forward in one's dealings** offen und gerade sein; **b)** *(simple)* einfach; eindeutig ‹*Lage*›; **~'forwardly** *adv.* **a)** *(frankly)* ehrlich ‹*handeln*›; offen ‹*sprechen, sagen*›; **b)** *(simply)* deutlich ‹*erklären*›; **~ man** *n. (Theatre) Schauspieler, der einem Komiker die Stichwörter für seine Gags liefert*

straightness ['streɪtnɪs] *n., no pl.* **a)** Geradheit, *die; (of hair)* Glattheit, *die; (Fashion)* gerader Schnitt; **b)** *(fig.) (candour) (of answer)* Offenheit, *die; (of purpose)* Geradlinigkeit, *die; (of dealings)* Ehrlichkeit, *die*

straight: ~ 'off *adv. (coll.)* schlankweg *(ugs.);* **~ 'ticket** *n. (Amer. Polit.)* **vote the ~ [Republican/Democratic] ticket** die [republikanische/demokratische] Liste unverändert wählen; **~ 'tip** *n.* Insidertip, *der;* **~ 'up** *adv. (sl.: honestly)* echt *(ugs.);* **Do you mean what you say? – S~ up!** Meinst du auch, was du sagst? – Na klar! *(ugs.);* **he offered me a lot of money, ~ up!** er hat mir einen Haufen Geld angeboten, ehrlich! *(ugs.)*

[1]**strain** [streɪn] **1.** *n.* **a)** *(pull)* Belastung, *die; (on rope)* Spannung, *die;* **put a ~ on sb./sth.** jmdn./etw. belasten; **b)** *(extreme physical or mental tension)* Streß, *der;* **feel the ~:** die Anstrengung spüren; **stand** *or* **take the ~:** die Belastung *od.* den Streß aushalten; **he has a lot of ~ at work** die Arbeit nimmt ihn stark in Anspruch; **place sb. under [a] great ~:** jmdn. einer starken Belastung aussetzen; **be under [a great deal of] ~:** unter großem Streß stehen; **c)** *(person, thing)* **be a ~ on sb./sth.** jmdn./etw. belasten; eine Belastung für jmdn./etw. sein; **be a ~ on sb.'s nerves** an jmds. Nerven zerren; **find sth. a ~:** etw. als Belastung empfinden; **d)** *(injury) (muscular)* Zerrung, *die; (over~ on heart, back, etc.)* Überanstrengung, *die;* **e)** *in sing. or pl. (burst of music)* Klänge; *(burst of poetry)* Vers, *der;* Zeile, *die;* **take up the ~** *(lit. or fig.)* einstimmen; einfallen; **f)** *(tone)* Ton, *der;* **g)** *(Phys.)* Deformation, *die.* **2.** *v.t.* **a)** *(over-exert)* überanstrengen; zerren ‹*Muskel*›; überbeanspruchen ‹*Geduld, Loyalität usw.*›; **~ one's back carrying heavy boxes** sich beim Tragen schwerer Kisten verheben; **~ oneself** *(lit. or fig. iron.)* sich

übernehmen; sich überanstrengen; **b)** *(stretch tightly)* [fest] spannen; **~ed relations** *(fig.)* gespannte Beziehungen; **c)** *(exert to maximum)* **~ oneself/sb./sth.** das Letzte aus sich/jmdm./etw. herausholen; **~ one's ears/ eyes/voice** seine Ohren/Augen/Stimme anstrengen; **~ oneself to do sth.** sich nach Kräften bemühen, etw. zu tun; **d)** *(use beyond proper limits)* verzerren ⟨*Wahrheit, Lehre, Tatsachen*⟩; überbeanspruchen ⟨*Geduld, Wohlwollen*⟩; **e)** *in p.p. (forced)* gezwungen ⟨*Lächeln*⟩; künstlich ⟨*Humor, Witz*⟩; gewagt ⟨*Interpretation*⟩; **f)** *(hug)* **~ sb./sth. to oneself/to sth.** jmdn./etw. an sich/etw. *(Akk.)* drücken; **g)** *(filter)* durchseihen; seihen (**through** durch); **~ [the water from] the vegetables** das Gemüse abgießen; **~ sth. from a liquid** etw. aus einer Flüssigkeit herausfiltern. **3.** *v. i.* **a)** *(strive intensely)* sich anstrengen; *(resist while being close to breaking-point)* ächzen (**under** unter + *Dat.*); **he ~ed to lift the box** er versuchte ächzend *od.* mit aller Kraft, die Kiste hochzuheben; **~ at sth.** an etw. *(Dat.)* zerren; **~ at the leash** an der Leine zerren; *(fig.)* es kaum erwarten können; **~ after sth.** sich mit aller Gewalt um etw. bemühen; **~ after an effect** Effekthascherei betreiben; **b)** *(be filtered)* durchlaufen; *(percolate through sand etc.)* durchsickern; **~ at a gnat [and swallow a camel]** Mücken seihen und Kamele verschlucken *(bibl.)*

~ a'way, ~ 'off *v. t.* abseihen; abgießen ⟨*Wasser*⟩

~ 'out *v. t.* [her]ausfiltern

²strain *n.* **a)** *(breed)* Rasse, *die; (of plants)* Sorte, *die; (of virus)* Art, *die; (human stock)* Familie, *die;* **b)** *no pl. (tendency)* Neigung, *die* (**of** zu); Hang, *der* (**of** zu); **a cruel ~:** ein grausamer Zug

strainer ['streɪnə(r)] *n.* Sieb, *das*

strait [streɪt] **1.** *n.* **a)** *in sing. or pl. (Geog.)* [Wasser]straße, *die;* Meerenge, *die;* **the S~s [of Gibraltar/Malacca]** die Straße von Gibraltar/die Malakkastraße; **b)** *usu. in pl. (distressing situation)* Schwierigkeiten; *see also* **dire c. 2.** *adj. (arch.) (narrow)* schmal ⟨*Weidefläche, Weg*⟩; eng ⟨*Pforte*⟩

straitened ['streɪtnd] *adj.* beschränkt ⟨*Verhältnisse*⟩

strait: ~-jacket 1. *n. (lit. or fig.)* Zwangsjacke, *die;* **2.** *v. t. (lit. or fig.)* in eine Zwangsjacke stecken; **~-laced** [streɪt'leɪst] *adj. (fig.)* puritanisch

Straits of Magellan [streɪts əv mə'gelən] *pr. n.* Magellanstraße, *die*

strake [streɪk] *n. (Naut.)* Planke, *die*

¹strand [strænd] *n. (thread)* Faden, *der; (of wire)* Litze, *die (Elektrot.); (of rope)* Strang, *der; (of beads, pearls, flowers, etc.)* Kette, *die; (of hair)* Strähne, *die; (Biol., Phys.)* Faser, *die; (fig.)* Strang, *der;* **a ~ of beads** eine Perlenkette

²strand 1. *v. t.* **a)** *(leave behind)* trocken setzen; **be [left] ~ed** *(fig.)* seinem Schicksal überlassen sein; *(be stuck)* festsitzen; **leave sb. ~ed** *(fig.)* jmdn. seinem Schicksal überlassen; **the strike left them ~ed in England** wegen des Streiks saßen sie in England fest; **b)** *(wash ashore)* an Land spülen ⟨*Leiche, Wrackteile*⟩; *(run aground)* auf Grund setzen ⟨*Schiff*⟩. **2.** *v. i.* stranden. **3.** *n. (rhet./poet.: foreshore)* Gestade, *das (dichter.)*

strange [streɪndʒ] *adj.* **a)** *(peculiar)* seltsam; sonderbar; merkwürdig; **feel [very] ~, come over [very] ~** *(coll.)* sich [ganz] komisch im Kopf *od. (ugs. scherzh.)* beduselt fühlen; **it feels ~ to do sth.** es ist ein merkwürdiges *od.* komisches Gefühl, wenn man etw. tut; **~ to say** seltsamerweise; **b)** *(alien, unfamiliar)* fremd; **~ to sb.** jmdm. fremd; **c)** *(unaccustomed)* **~ to sth.** nicht vertraut mit etw.; **feel ~:** sich nicht zu Hause fühlen; **I feel ~, suddenly having so much power** es ist [für mich] ganz ungewohnt, plötzlich soviel Macht zu haben; **I am [quite] ~ here** ich bin fremd hier; ich kenne mich hier nicht aus

strangely ['streɪndʒlɪ] *adv.* seltsam; merkwürdig; **~ enough, ...:** seltsamerweise ...; so seltsam es klingt, ...

strangeness ['streɪndʒnɪs] *n., no pl. (oddness)* Seltsamkeit, *die;* Merkwürdigkeit, *die*

stranger ['streɪndʒə(r)] *n.* **a)** *(foreigner, unknown person)* Fremde, *der/die;* **he is a ~ here/to** *or* **in the town** er ist hier/in der Stadt fremd; **he is no ~ to this sort of work** diese Arbeit ist ihm nicht fremd; **she is a /no ~ to the British stage** sie ist auf den britischen Bühnen unbekannt/bekannt; **he is a/no ~ to me** er ist mir nicht bekannt/ist mir bekannt; **you are quite a ~:** man kennt dich ja kaum noch; **hello, ~:** hallo, lange nicht gesehen; **b)** *(one lacking certain experience)* **be a ~ in sth.** in etw. *(Dat.)* unerfahren sein; **be a/no ~ to sth.** etw. nicht gewöhnt/etw. gewöhnt sein; **c)** *(Brit. Parl.)* Besucher, *der*/Besucherin, *die;* **S~s' Gallery** Besuchergalerie, *die*

strangle ['stræŋgl] *v. t.* **a)** *(throttle)* erdrosseln; erwürgen; **b)** *(fig.: suppress)* unterdrücken; **~ at birth** im Keim ersticken

'stranglehold *n. (lit. or fig.)* Würgegriff, *der*

strangulated ['stræŋgjʊleɪtɪd] *adj. (Med.)* **~ hernia** eingeklemmter Bruch

strangulation [stræŋgjʊ'leɪʃn] *n.* Erdrosseln, *das;* Erwürgen, *das; (fig.)* Unterdrückung, *die;* Strangulierung, *die (geh.)*

strap [stræp] **1.** *n.* **a)** *(leather strip)* Riemen, *der; (textile strip)* Band, *das; (shoulder-~)* Träger, *der; (for watch)* Armband, *das;* **the ~** *(punishment)* die Züchtigung mit dem Riemen; **be given [a lick of] the ~:** den Riemen zu schmecken bekommen; **b)** *(to grasp in vehicle)* Halteriemen, *der.* **2.** *v. t.,* **-pp- a)** *(secure with ~)* **~ [into position/down]** festschnallen; **~ oneself in** sich anschnallen; **b)** *see* **~ up b; c) be ~ped for cash** *(coll.)* sehr klamm sein *(ugs.);* **d)** *(punish with ~)* mit dem Riemen züchtigen

~ 'up *v. t.* **a)** *(fasten ~s of)* zuschnallen; **b)** *(bind with adhesive plaster)* verpflastern

strap: ~hanger *n.* stehender Fahrgast; **~ hinge** *n.* Langband, *das (Technik)*

strapless ['stræplɪs] *adj.* trägerlos

strapping ['stræpɪŋ] *adj.* stramm

Strasbourg ['stræzbɜ:g] *pr. n.* Straßburg *(das)*

strata *pl. of* **stratum**

stratagem ['strætədʒəm] *n. (trick)* [Kriegs]list, *die;* Strategem, *das (geh.)*

strategic [strə'ti:dʒɪk], **strategical** [strə'ti:dʒɪkl] *adj.* **a)** strategisch; **a ~ moment** ein strategisch günstiger Zeitpunkt; **b)** *(of great military importance)* strategisch wichtig; *(necessary to plan)* bedeutsam ⟨*Element, Faktor*⟩

strategically [strə'ti:dʒɪkəlɪ] *adv.* strategisch

strategic 'studies *n., no pl.* Strategie, *die*

strategist ['strætɪdʒɪst] *n.* Stratege, *der*/Strategin, *die*

strategy ['strætɪdʒɪ] *n.* Strategie, *die; (fig. also)* Taktik, *die;* **use ~** *(fig.)* taktisch *od.* strategisch vorgehen; **it was bad ~** *(fig.)* es war taktisch *od.* strategisch unklug

stratification [strætɪfɪ'keɪʃn] *n.* **a)** *(Geol., Archaeol.)* Schichtung, *die;* Stratifikation, *die (fachspr.);* **b)** *(Sociol.)* [soziale] Schichtung

stratify ['strætɪfaɪ] *v. t.* **a)** *(Geol., Archaeol.)* stratifizieren; **stratified rock** in Schichten gewachsener Fels; **b)** *(Sociol.)* in Schichten einteilen; Schichten zuordnen; **a stratified society** eine mehrschichtige Gesellschaft

stratosphere ['strætəsfɪə(r)] *n. (Geog.)* Stratosphäre, *die; (fig.)* höhere Regionen

stratospheric [strætə'sferɪk] *adj. (Geog.)* stratosphärisch; Stratosphären⟨*flugzeug, -flug*⟩; *(fig.)* schwindelerregend ⟨*Höhe*⟩

stratum ['strɑ:təm, 'streɪtəm] *n., pl.* **strata** ['strɑ:tə, 'streɪtə] Schicht, *die;* Stratum, *das (fachspr.)*

stratus ['streɪtəs, 'strɑ:təs] *n., pl.* **strati** ['streɪtaɪ, 'strɑ:taɪ] *(Meteorol.)* Schichtwolke, *die;* Stratus, *der (fachspr.); attrib.* **~ clouds** Stratuswolken

straw [strɔ:] *n.* **a)** *no pl. (stalks of grain)* Stroh, *das; attrib.* Stroh-; **b)** *(single stalk)* Strohhalm, *der;* **catch** *or* **clutch** *or* **grasp at ~s** *or* **a ~** *(fig. coll.)* sich an einen Strohhalm klammern; **be the last ~, be the ~ that broke the camel's back** *(coll.)* das Faß zum Überlaufen bringen; **that's the last** *or* **final ~:** jetzt reicht's aber; **draw ~s [for sth.]** Hölzchen [um etw.] ziehen; **draw** *or* **pick the short ~:** das kürzere Hölzchen ziehen; *(fig.)* das schlechtere Los ziehen; **~ in the wind** Vorzeichen, *das;* Vorbote, *der;* **c) [drinking-]~:** Trinkhalm, *der;* Strohhalm, *der;* **d)** *(trifle)* Nichtigkeit, *die;* **it doesn't matter a ~ to me** es kümmert mich keinen Pfifferling *(ugs.);* **I don't give a ~:** ich gebe keinen Pfifferling dafür *(ugs.);* **e)** *(hat)* Strohhut, *der. See also* **cheese straw**

strawberry ['strɔ:bərɪ] *n.* **a)** Erdbeere, *die;* **b)** *(colour)* Erdbeerrot, *das; see also* **crush 1 a**

strawberry: ~ 'blonde 1. *adj.* rotblond; **2.** *n.* Rotblonde, *die;* **~-mark** *n.* [rötliches] Muttermal

straw: ~-board *n.* Strohpapier, *das;* Strohpappe, *die;* **~ boss** *n. (Amer.)* Vorarbeiter, *der;* **~-colour** *n.* Strohgelb, *das;* **~-coloured** *adj.* strohgelb; **~ 'hat** *n.* Strohhut, *der;* **~ poll, ~ vote** *ns.* Testabstimmung, *die*

stray [streɪ] **1.** *v. i.* **a)** *(wander)* streunen; *(fig.: in thought etc.)* abschweifen (**into** in + *Akk.*); **~ [away] from** sich absondern von; **the child had ~ed from his parents** das Kind war seinen Eltern weggelaufen; **~ into enemy territory** sich auf feindliches Gebiet verirren; **b)** *(move in meandering course)* ⟨*Auto:*⟩ schlingern; *(move without deliberate control)* **my gaze kept ~ing to the wart on his nose** mein Blick wanderte immer wieder zu der Warze auf seiner Nase; **he could not control his ~ing hands** er konnte seine Hände einfach nicht bei sich behalten; **c)** *(deviate)* abweichen (**from** von); **have ~ed** sich verirrt haben; **~ from the path of virtue** vom Pfad der Tugend abweichen *(geh.);* **he had ~ed once** einmal war er vom Wege abgekommen *(fig.);* **~ from the point/from** *or* **off the road** vom Thema/von der Straße abkommen; **somehow I ~ed into acting/the theatre** irgendwie habe ich mich aufs Schauspielern verlegt/bin ich am Theater gelandet. **2.** *n.* *(animal)* streunendes Tier; *(without owner)* herrenloses Tier; *(person)* Streuner, *der*/Streunerin, *die (abwertend); see also* **waif. 3.** *adj.* **a)** streunend; *(without owner)* herrenlos; *(out of proper place)* verirrt; **b)** *(occasional, isolated)* vereinzelt; **c)** *(Phys.)* streuend

streak [stri:k] **1.** *n.* **a)** *(narrow line)* Streifen, *der; (in hair)* Strähne, *die;* **~ of lightning** Blitzstrahl, *der;* **like a ~ [of lightning]** [schnell] wie der Blitz *(ugs.);* wie ein geölter Blitz *(ugs.);* **b)** *(fig.: element)* **have a jealous/ cruel ~:** zur Eifersucht/Grausamkeit neigen; **have a ~ of meanness/jealousy** eine geizige/eifersüchtige Ader haben; **c)** *(fig.: spell)* **~ of good/bad luck, lucky/unlucky ~:** Glücks-/Pechsträhne, *die;* **be on a** *or* **have a winning/losing ~:** eine Glücks-/Pechsträhne haben. **2.** *v. t.* streifen; **~ sth. with green** etw. mit grünen Streifen versehen; **hair ~ed with grey** Haar mit grauen Strähnen; **~ed with paint/mud/tears** farbverschmiert/ dreckbeschmiert/tränenverschmiert. **3.** *v. i.* **a)** *(move rapidly)* flitzen *(ugs.);* **b)** *(coll.: run naked)* blitzen *(ugs.);* flitzen *(ugs.)*

streaker ['stri:kə(r)] *n. (coll.)* Blitzer,

der/Blitzerin, *die (ugs.)*; Flitzer, *der*/Flitzerin, *die (ugs.)*
streaking ['stri:kɪŋ] *n. (coll.: running naked)* Blitzen, *das (ugs.)*; Flitzen, *das (ugs.)*
streaky ['stri:kɪ] *adj.* streifig; gestreift ⟨*Muster, Fell*⟩
streaky 'bacon *n.* durchwachsener Speck
stream [stri:m] **1.** *n.* **a)** *(of flowing water)* Wasserlauf, *der; (brook)* Bach, *der;* **b)** *(flow, large quantity)* Strom, *der; (of abuse, excuses, words)* Schwall, *der;* **~s** *or* **a ~ of applications** eine Flut von Bewerbungen; **in ~s** in Strömen; **the children rushed in ~s/in a ~ through the school gates** die Kinder strömten durch die Schultore; **c)** *(current)* Strömung, *die; (fig.)* Trend, *der;* **against/with the ~ of sth.** *(fig.)* gegen den/mit dem Strom einer Sache; **go against/with the ~** ⟨*Person:*⟩ gegen den/mit dem Strom schwimmen; *see also* **Gulf Stream; d)** *(Brit. Educ.)* Parallelzug, *der;* **e) be/go on ~** ⟨*Industry*⟩ in Betrieb sein/den Betrieb aufnehmen. **2.** *v. i.* **a)** *(flow)* strömen; ⟨*Sonnenlicht:*⟩ fluten; **tears ~ed down her face** Tränen strömten ihr über das Gesicht; **b)** *(run with liquid)* **my eyes ~ed** mir tränten die Augen; **the windows/walls were ~ing with condensation** die Fenster/Wände schwitzten; **his back was ~ing with sweat** sein Rücken war schweißnaß *od.* schweißüberströmt; **c)** *(wave)* ⟨*Haare, Fahne:*⟩ flattern, wehen. **3.** *v. t.* **a)** *(emit)* **his nose was ~ing blood** Blut floß ihm aus der Nase; **b)** *(Brit. Educ.)* in Parallelzüge *od.* leistungshomogene Gruppen einteilen
~ 'down *v. i.* ⟨*Sonne:*⟩ vom Himmel strahlen; **the rain is ~ing down** es regnet in Strömen
~ 'in *v. i.* hereinströmen/hineinströmen
~ 'out *v. i.* **a)** *(move out like ~)* herausströmen/hinausströmen; **b)** *(float)* flattern; wehen
~ 'past *v. i.* vorbeiströmen
~ 'through *v. i.* hindurchströmen
streamer ['stri:mə(r)] *n.* **a)** *(ribbon)* Band, *das; (of paper)* Luftschlange, *die;* Papierschlange, *die;* **b)** *(Journ.: headline)* Schlagzeile, *die;* Aufmacher, *der;* **c)** *(pennon)* Wimpel, *der*
streaming ['stri:mɪŋ] **1.** *n. (Brit. Educ.)* Einteilung in Parallelzüge *od.* leistungshomogene Gruppen; Streaming, *das.* **2.** *adj.* *(flowing)* laufend ⟨*Nase*⟩; tränend ⟨*Auge*⟩; schwitzend ⟨*Wand, Fenster*⟩; **have a ~ cold** Schnupfen haben
streamlet ['stri:mlɪt] *n.* Bächlein, *das*
stream: ~line 1. *n.* **a)** *(shape)* Stromlinienform, *die (Physik, Technik);* **b)** *(line of flow)* Stromlinie, *die (Physik);* **2.** *v. t.* **a)** *(give shape to)* [eine] Stromlinienform geben (+ *Dat.*); **be ~lined** eine Stromlinienform haben; **b)** *(simplify)* rationalisieren; *(reduce)* einschränken; **~ of 'consciousness** *n. (Lit.)* *(flow of thoughts)* Bewußtseinsstrom, *der; (literary style)* Stream of consciousness, *der*
street [stri:t] *n.* **a)** Straße, *die;* **in** *(Brit.) or* **on ... Street** in der ...straße; **in the ~:** auf der Straße; *(St. Exch.)* nach Börsenschluß; **I wouldn't cross the ~ to do that** *(fig.)* ich würde mir deswegen kein Bein ausreißen *(ugs.);* **be on the ~[s]** *(be published)* ⟨*Zeitung:*⟩ draußen sein; *(have no place to live)* auf der Straße liegen *(ugs.); (be available to be bought)* im [Straßen]verkauf sein; **be/go on the ~s** *(be/become a prostitute)* auf die Straße gehen *(ugs.);* **take to the ~s** auf die Straße gehen *(ugs.);* **keep the youngsters off the ~s** dafür sorgen, daß sich die Jugendlichen nicht auf der Straße herumtreiben; **it isn't a very interesting job, but at least it keeps me off the ~s** *(iron.)* der Job ist zwar nicht sehr interessant, aber wenigstens stehe ich nicht mehr auf der Straße *(ugs.);* **not in the same ~ [as sb./sth.]** *(fig. coll.)* nicht zu vergleichen [mit jmdm./etw.]; **~s ahead [of sb./sth.]** *(coll.)* um Längen besser [als jmd./etw.] *(ugs.);* **be [right** *or* **just] up sb.'s ~** *(coll.)* jmds. Fall sein *(ugs.);* **the ~s of San Francisco are paved with gold** *(fig.)* in San Francisco liegt das Geld auf der Straße; **b)** *(people in ~)* Straße, *die*
street: ~car *n. (Amer.)* Straßenbahn, *die;* Tram, *die (südd., österr., schweiz.);* **~ cred** ['stri:t kred] *(coll.),* **~ credibility** *ns.* [glaubwürdiges] Image; **~ cries** *n. pl.* *(Brit.)* Straßen- *od.* Händlerrufe; **~ crime** *n., no pl., no indef. art.* Straßenkriminalität, *die;* **~ door** *n.* [vordere] Haustür; **~ enter'tainer** *n.* Straßenkünstler, *der*/-künstlerin, *die;* **~-fight** *n.* Straßenkampf, *der; (heavy fighting)* Straßenschlacht, *die;* **~-fighting** *n.* Straßenkampf, *der;* **sporadic ~-fighting broke out** vereinzelt brachen Straßenkämpfe aus; **~-lamp, ~-light** *ns.* Straßenlaterne, *die;* Straßenlampe, *die;* **~-lighting** *n.* Straßenbeleuchtung, *die;* **~-map** *n.* Stadtplan, *der;* **~-market** *n.* Markt, *der;* **~-party** *n.* Straßenfest, *das;* **~-plan** *see* **~-map;** **~-sweeper** *n.* **a)** *(person)* Straßenfeger, *der*/-fegerin, *die (bes. nordd.);* Straßenkehrer, *der*/-kehrerin, *die (bes. südd.);* **b)** *(machine)* Kehrmaschine, *die; (vehicle)* Straßenkehrmaschine, *die;* **~ theatre** *n.* Straßentheater, *das;* **~ urchin** *n.* Straßenkind, *das;* **~ value** *n.* Straßenverkaufswert, *der;* **~-walker** *n. fem.* Nutte, *die (ugs.);* **~-wise** *adj. (coll.)* **be ~-wise** wissen, wo es langgeht
strength [streŋθ] *n.* **a)** *(power)* Kraft, *die; (strong point, force, intensity, amount of ingredient; also Finance)* Stärke, *die; (of argument)* [Überzeugungs]kraft, *die; (of poison, medicine)* Wirksamkeit, *die; (of legal evidence)* [Beweis]kraft, *die; (resistance of material, building, etc.)* Stabilität, *die; (artistic forcefulness)* [künstlerische/dichterische/musikalische] Kraft; **recover/exhaust one's ~:** seine Kräfte wiedererlangen/erschöpfen; **not know one's own ~:** nicht wissen, wie stark man ist; **give sb. ~:** jmdn. stärken; jmdm. Kraft geben; *see also* **give 1 e; ~ of conviction/feeling** Überzeugungskraft, *die*/Stärke der Emotionen; **~ of character/will/purpose** Charakterstärke, *die*/Willensstärke *od.* -kraft, *die*/Zielstrebigkeit, *die;* **from ~:** aus einer Position der Stärke heraus; **go from ~ to ~:** immer erfolgreicher werden; **on the ~ of sth./that** auf Grund einer Sache *(Gen.)*/dessen; **we can have a drink on the ~ of that** darauf können wir einen trinken; **b)** *(proportion present)* Stärke, *die; (full complement)* **be below ~/up to ~:** weniger als/etwa die volle Stärke haben; **in [full] ~:** in voller Stärke; **the police were there in ~:** ein starkes Polizeiaufgebot war da
strengthen ['streŋθən, 'streŋkθən] **1.** *v. t.* *(give power to)* stärken; *(reinforce, intensify, increase in number)* verstärken; erhöhen ⟨*Anteil*⟩; *(make more effective)* unterstützen; *(increase main ingredient of)* stärker machen ⟨*Getränk*⟩; kräftiger machen ⟨*Farbe, Anstrich*⟩; **~ sb.'s resolve** jmdn. in seinem Entschluß bestärken; **~ sb.'s hand** *(fig.)* jmds. Position stärken. **2.** *v. i.* stärker werden
strenuous ['strenjʊəs] *adj.* **a)** *(energetic)* energisch; gewaltig ⟨*Anstrengung*⟩; **b)** *(requiring exertion)* anstrengend
strenuously ['strenjʊəslɪ] *adv.* mit aller Kraft ⟨*sich anstrengen*⟩; angestrengt ⟨*arbeiten*⟩; heftig ⟨*bestreiten, bekräftigen*⟩
strenuousness ['strenjʊəsnɪs] *n., no pl.* Schwere, *die*
streptococcus [streptə'kɒkəs] *n., pl.* **streptococci** [streptə'kɒkaɪ] *(Bacteriol.)* Streptokokkus, *der*
stress [stres] **1.** *n.* **a)** *(strain)* Streß, *der;* **be [placed] under ~:** unter Streß *(Dat.)* stehen; **b)** *(emphasis)* Betonung, *die;* Nachdruck, *der;* **lay** *or* **place** *or* **put [a] ~ on sth.** auf etw. *(Akk.)* Wert *od.* Gewicht legen; **c)** *(accentuation)* Betonung, *die; (in verse)* Hebung, *die;* **put the/a ~ on sth.** etw. betonen; **which syllable carries the ~?** welche Silbe trägt den Ton?; **d)** *(Mech.)* Belastung, *die;* [elastische] Spannung *(fachspr.). See also* **storm 1 b. 2.** *v. t.* **a)** *(emphasize)* betonen; Wert legen auf (+ *Akk.*) ⟨*richtige Ernährung, gutes Benehmen, Sport usw.*⟩; **~ [the point] that ...:** darauf hinweisen, daß ...; **b)** *(Ling.)* betonen ⟨*Silbe, Vokal usw.*⟩; **c)** *(subject to strain)* überanstrengen; *(Mech.)* belasten; [elastischer] Spannung aussetzen *(fachspr.)*
'stress disease *n.* Streßkrankheit, *die;* Managerkrankheit, *die (volkst.)*
stressful ['stresfl] *adj.* anstrengend; stressig *(ugs.)*
'stress-mark *n.* Betonungszeichen, *das*
stretch [stretʃ] **1.** *v. t.* **a)** *(lengthen, extend)* strecken ⟨*Arm, Hand*⟩; recken ⟨*Hals*⟩; dehnen ⟨*Gummiband*⟩; *(spread)* ausbreiten ⟨*Decke*⟩; *(tighten)* spannen; **he lay ~ed out on the ground** er lag ausgestreckt auf dem Boden; **~ one's legs** *(by walking)* sich *(Dat.)* die Beine vertreten; **b)** *(widen)* dehnen; **~ [out of shape]** ausweiten ⟨*Schuhe, Jacke*⟩; **c)** *(fig.: make the most of)* ausschöpfen ⟨*Reserve*⟩; fordern ⟨*Person, Begabung*⟩; **d)** *(fig.: extend beyond proper limit)* überschreiten ⟨*Befugnis, Grenzen des Anstands*⟩; strapazieren *(ugs.)* ⟨*Geduld*⟩; es nicht so genau nehmen mit ⟨*Gesetz, Bestimmung, Begriff, Grundsätzen*⟩; **~ a point** großzügig sein; **~ credibility** nicht sehr glaubhaft sein; **~ the truth** ⟨*Aussage:*⟩ nicht ganz der Wahrheit entsprechen; **he's certainly ~ing the truth there** er nimmt es hier mit der Wahrheit nicht so genau; **we're a bit ~ed at the moment** wir sind zur Zeit ziemlich überlastet; **~ it/things** den Bogen überspannen; *see also* **wing 1 a. 2.** *v. i.* **a)** *(extend in length)* sich weiten; sich dehnen; ⟨*Person, Tier:*⟩ sich strecken; **b)** *(have specified length)* sich [aus]dehnen; **~ from A to B** sich von A bis B erstrecken; **the traffic jam ~ed all the way back to Junction 9** der Verkehr staute sich bis zur Auffahrt Neun [zurück]; **c) ~ to sth.** *(be sufficient for)* für etw. reichen; **could you ~ to £10?** hast du vielleicht sogar 10 Pfund? **3.** *v. refl.* sich [dehnen und] strecken. **4.** *n.* **a)** *(lengthening, drawing out)* **have a ~, give oneself a ~:** sich strecken; **with a ~, I can reach ...:** wenn ich mich strecke, kann ich bis an ... *(Akk.)* reichen; **give sth. a ~:** etw. dehnen *od.* weiter machen; **b)** *(exertion)* **by no ~ of the imagination** auch mit viel Phantasie nicht; **at a ~** *(fig.)* wenn es sein muß *(see also* **c)**; **at full ~:** auf Hochtouren; **c)** *(expanse, length)* Abschnitt, *der;* **a ~ of road/open country** ein Stück Straße/Land; **at a ~:** ohne Unterbrechung *(see also* **b)**; **d)** *(Amer. Racing)* Gerade, *die;* **e)** *(sl.: length of imprisonment)* **do a [five-year] ~:** [fünf Jahre] im Knast sitzen *(ugs.);* **go down for another ~:** wieder einmal in den Knast wandern *(ugs.);* **f)** *(in fabric)* Elastizität, *die;* **there is a lot of ~ in this material** das Material ist sehr dehnbar. **5.** *adj.* dehnbar; Stretch⟨*hose, -gewebe*⟩
~ 'out 1. *v. t.* **a)** *(extend by straightening)* [aus]strecken ⟨*Arm, Bein*⟩; ausbreiten ⟨*Decke*⟩; auseinanderziehen ⟨*Seil*⟩; **~ oneself out** sich [lang] ausstrecken; **b)** *(eke out)* **~ sth. out** mit etw. reichen. **2.** *v. i.* **a)** *(~ one's hands out) (lit. or fig.)* die Hände ausstrecken (**to** nach); **b)** *(extend)* sich ausdehnen; **c)** *(last for sufficient time)* reichen
stretcher ['stretʃə(r)] **1.** *n.* **a)** *(for carrying a person)* [Trag]bahre, *die;* **b)** *(between chair-legs)* Steg, *der;* **c)** *(for canvas)* Rahmen, *der;* **d)** *(in boat)* Stemmbrett, *das;* **e)** *(Building)* Läufer, *der.* **2.** *v. t.* auf einer Bahre tragen

'stretcher-bearer *n.* [Kranken]träger, *der*

stretch: ~ **marks** *n. pl. (after pregnancy)* Schwangerschaftsstreifen; ~ **pants** *n. pl.* Stretchhose, *die*

stretchy ['stretʃɪ] *adj. (coll.)* dehnbar

strew [stru:] *v. t., p.p.* ~**ed** [stru:d] *or* ~**n** [stru:n] **a)** *(scatter)* streuen ⟨*Blumen, Sand usw.*⟩; **clothes were ~n about the room** Kleider lagen im ganzen Zimmer verstreut herum; **b)** *(cover, lit. or fig.)* bestreuen; **the grass was ~n with litter** [überall] auf dem Gras war Abfall verstreut

stricken ['strɪkn] *adj.* **a)** *(afflicted)* heimgesucht; havariert ⟨*Schiff, Flugzeug*⟩; *(showing affliction)* schmerzerfüllt; **be ~ with fever/a disease** von Fieber geschüttelt/einer Krankheit heimgesucht werden; ~ **with fear/grief/misfortune** angsterfüllt/gramgebeugt/vom Schicksal geschlagen; ~ **in years** *(arch.)* von den Jahren gezeichnet; **b)** *(Amer.: deleted)* ~ **from sth.** aus etw. gestrichen

strict [strɪkt] *adj.* **a)** *(firm)* streng; strenggläubig ⟨*Katholik, Moslem usw.*⟩; **in ~ confidence** streng vertraulich; **he is ~ about what his children wear** er achtet streng darauf, was seine Kinder anziehen; **b)** *(precise)* streng; genau ⟨*Übersetzung*⟩; **keep a ~ watch** genau *od.* scharf aufpassen; **in the ~ sense [of the word]** im strengen Sinn[e] [des Wortes]

strictly ['strɪktlɪ] *adv.* streng; **there is ~ no smoking here** Rauchen ist hier streng[stens] verboten; ~ **between ourselves** ganz im Vertrauen; **this is ~ between ourselves** das muß unter uns bleiben; ~ **[speaking]** strenggenommen; *see also* **bird a**

strictness ['strɪktnɪs] *n., no pl.* **a)** *(firmness)* Strenge, *die;* **b)** *(precision)* Genauigkeit, *die*

stricture ['strɪktʃə(r)] *n.* **a)** *usu. in pl. (critical remark)* ~**[s]** [scharfe *od.* heftige] Kritik; ~**[s] [up]on sth.** Kritik an etw. *(Dat.);* **pass ~s [up]on sb.** jmdn. kritisieren; **b)** *(Med.)* Verengung, *die;* Striktur, *die*

stride [straɪd] **1.** *n.* **a)** Schritt, *der; (of galloping horse)* [Galopp]sprung, *der;* **make ~s [towards sth.]** *(fig.)* [in Richtung auf etw. *(Akk.)*] Fortschritte machen; **make great ~s** *(fig.)* große Fortschritte machen; **get into one's ~:** seinen Rhythmus finden; *(fig.)* in Fahrt *od.* Schwung kommen; **put sb. off his ~, throw sb. out of his ~** *(fig.)* jmdn. aus dem Konzept bringen; **be thrown out of** *or* **lose one's ~** *(lit. or fig.)* aus dem Tritt kommen; **take sth. in one's ~** *(fig.)* mit etw. gut fertig werden; **b)** *in pl. (Brit. and Austral. sl.: trousers)* Hose, *die.* **2.** *v. i.,* **strode** [strəʊd], **stridden** ['strɪdn] [mit großen Schritten] gehen; *(solemnly)* schreiten *(geh.); (take single step)* ~ **across sth.** über etw. *(Akk.)* hinwegschreiten *(geh.).* **3.** *v. t.,* **strode, stridden:** ~ **the streets/moors** durch die Straßen/über die Moore wandern

~ **'out** *v. i.* ausschreiten *(geh.)*

stridency ['straɪdənsɪ] *n., no pl. see* **strident:** Schrillheit, *die;* Grellheit, *die*

strident ['straɪdənt] *adj.* schrill ⟨*Stimme, Blech[bläser]*⟩; *(fig.)* grell ⟨*Farbe, Satire*⟩; schrill ⟨*Protest, Ton*⟩

stridently ['straɪdəntlɪ] *adv.* gellend ⟨*rufen, laut*⟩; *(fig.)* grell ⟨*sich kleiden*⟩; aufdringlich ⟨*vulgär*⟩; in schrillem Ton ⟨*sich beklagen*⟩

strife [straɪf] *n., no pl., no indef. art.* Streit, *der;* Zwist, *der (geh.);* **we live in a world of ~:** wir leben in einer Welt der Zwietracht *(geh.)*

strike [straɪk] **1.** *n.* **a)** *(Industry)* Streik, *der;* Ausstand, *der;* **be on/go [out]** *or* **come out on ~:** in den Streik getreten sein/in den Streik treten; *see also* **hunger-strike; sit-down 2; b)** *(Finance, Mining, Oil Industry)* Treffer, *der (fig. ugs.);* **make a ~:** sein Glück machen; *(Mining)* fündig werden; **make a gold/an oil ~:** auf Gold/Öl *(Akk.)* stoßen; **c)** *(sudden success)* **[lucky] ~:** Glückstreffer, *der;* **make a lucky ~, get one's lucky ~:** Glück haben; **d)** *(act of hitting)* Schlag, *der; (of snake)* Biß, *der;* **e)** *(Mil.)* Angriff, *der* **(at** auf + *Akk.*); **pre-emptive ~:** Präventivschlag, *der;* **f)** *(Bowling)* Abräumen, *das;* **get a ~:** abräumen; **g)** *(Baseball)* Fehlschlag, *der;* **h)** *(Geol.)* Streichen, *das;* **angle of ~:** Streichwinkel, *der.* **2.** *v. t.,* **struck** [strʌk], **struck** *or (arch.)* **stricken** ['strɪkn] **a)** *(hit, send by hitting)* schlagen; ⟨*Schlag, Geschoß:*⟩ treffen ⟨*Ziel*⟩; ⟨*Blitz:*⟩ [ein]schlagen in (+ *Akk.*), treffen; *(afflict)* treffen; ⟨*Epidemie, Seuche, Katastrophe usw.:*⟩ heimsuchen; ⟨*Schmerz:*⟩ durchzucken; ~ **one's head on** *or* **against the wall** mit dem Kopf gegen die Wand schlagen; **his head struck the pavement** er schlug mit dem Kopf auf das Pflaster; **the car struck a pedestrian** das Auto erfaßte einen Fußgänger; **the ship struck the rocks** das Schiff lief auf die Felsen; ~ **sth. in two** etw. entzweischlagen; etw. spalten; ~ **sth. from sb.'s hand** jmdm. etw. aus der Hand schlagen; ~ **sb./sth. aside** jmdn. zur Seite stoßen/etw. zur Seite schlagen; **b)** *(delete)* streichen **(from, off** aus); **c)** *(deliver)* ~ **two punches** zweimal zuschlagen; ~ **sb. a blow** jmdm. einen Schlag versetzen; **who struck [the] first blow?** wer hat zuerst geschlagen?; ~ **a blow against sb./against** *or* **to sth.** *(fig.)* jmdm./einer Sache einen Schlag versetzen; ~ **a blow for sth.** *(fig.)* eine Lanze für etw. brechen; **d)** *(produce by hitting flint)* schlagen ⟨*Funken*⟩; *(ignite)* anzünden ⟨*Streichholz*⟩; ~ **a light!** *(dated sl., expr. disgust)* das darf doch nicht wahr sein! *(ugs.);* **e)** *(chime)* schlagen; **f)** *(Mus.)* anschlagen ⟨*Töne auf dem Klavier*⟩; anzupfen, anreißen ⟨*Töne auf der Gitarre*⟩; *(fig.)* anschlagen ⟨*Ton*⟩; *see also* **'chord a; g)** *(impress)* beeindrucken; ~ **sb.'s notice** jmdm. auffallen; ~ **sb. as [being] silly** jmdm. dumm zu sein scheinen *od.* dumm erscheinen; **it ~s sb. that ...:** es scheint jmdm., daß...; **how does it ~ you?** was hältst du davon?; **h)** *(occur to)* einfallen (+ *Dat.*); **i) struck on sb./sth.** *(coll.: infatuated with)* hingerissen von jmdm./etw.; **j)** *(cause to become)* **a heart attack struck him dead** er erlag einem Herzanfall; **be struck blind/dumb** erblinden/verstummen; **I was struck speechless by the news** die Nachricht verschlug mir die Sprache; ~ **me dead!** *(sl.)* du kannst mich totschlagen *(ugs.);* **k)** *(attack)* überfallen; *(Mil.)* angreifen; *(wound with fangs)* ⟨*Schlange:*⟩ ihre Zähne schlagen in (+ *Akk.*); **l)** *(encounter)* begegnen (+ *Dat.*); ~ **a patch of bad luck** eine Pechsträhne haben; **m)** *(Mining)* stoßen auf (+ *Akk.*); ~ **gold** auf Gold stoßen; *(fig.)* einen Glückstreffer landen *(ugs.)* **(in** mit); *see also* **oil 1 a; n)** *(reach)* stoßen auf (+ *Akk.*) ⟨*Hauptstraße, Weg, Fluß*⟩; **o)** *(achieve)* ~ **success** [plötzlich] Erfolg haben; ~ **a compromise** einen Kompromiß erreichen; *see also* **balance 1 d; bargain 1 a; p)** *([cause to] penetrate)* **the cold struck his very marrow** die Kälte ging ihm durch Mark und Bein; ~ **sb.'s heart/sb. to the quick** jmdn. ins Herz/Mark treffen; ~ **fear into sb.** jmdn. in Angst versetzen; ~ **root** Wurzeln treiben *od.* schlagen; **q)** *(fill)* ~ **sb. with fear/foreboding** jmdn. mit Furcht/Vorahnungen erfüllen; **r)** *(Hort.)* setzen; aus Ablegern ziehen ⟨*Pflanze*⟩; **s)** *(adopt)* einnehmen ⟨*[Geistes]haltung*⟩; **t)** *(take down)* einholen ⟨*Segel, Flagge*⟩; abbrechen ⟨*Zelt, Lager*⟩; ~ **one's flag** *(fig.)* die Flagge streichen; **u)** *(mint)* prägen; schlagen *(veralt.). See also* **happy a; note 1 a; rich 1 b; stricken. 3.** *v. i.,* **struck, struck** *or (arch.)* **stricken a)** *(deliver a blow)* zuschlagen; ⟨*Pfeil:*⟩ treffen; ⟨*Blitz:*⟩ einschlagen; ⟨*Unheil, Katastrophe, Krise, Leid:*⟩ hereinbrechen *(geh.); (collide)* zusammenstoßen; *(hit)* schlagen **(against** gegen, **[up]on** auf + *Akk.*); ⟨*Schiff:*⟩ auflaufen **(on** auf + *Akk.*); **b)** *(ignite)* zünden; **c)** *(chime)* schlagen; **eight o'clock has struck** es hat acht Uhr geschlagen; **hear the hour ~:** den Stundenschlag hören; **d)** *(Industry)* streiken; **e)** *(attack; also Mil.)* zuschlagen *(fig.); (wound with fang)* zubeißen; **f)** *(make a find) (Mining)* fündig werden; *(Hunting)* die Witterung aufnehmen; ~ **lucky** Glück haben; **g)** *(penetrate)* ~ **through sth.** durch etw. dringen; **the wind ~s cold** der kalte Wind geht durch und durch; **his words struck into my heart** seine Worte trafen mich ins Herz; **h)** *(direct course)* ~ **south** *etc.* sich nach Süden *usw.* wenden; ⟨*Straße:*⟩ nach Süden *usw.* verlaufen; ⟨*Schiff:*⟩ Kurs nach Süden *usw.* nehmen; ~ **across the fields/down the hill/through the forest** über die Felder/den Hügel hinunter/durch den Wald gehen; **i)** *(launch)* ~ **into sth.** mit etw. beginnen; **j)** *(Hort.)* Wurzeln treiben *od.* schlagen; **k)** *(Angling) (hook fish)* anschlagen; *(seize bait)* anbeißen. *See also* **iron 1 a**

~ **at** *v. t.* schlagen nach; *(fig.)* einen Schlag versetzen (+ *Dat.*); rütteln an (+ *Dat.*) ⟨*Grundfesten*⟩; *see also* **'root 1 a**

~ **'back** *v. i. (lit. or fig.)* zurückschlagen; ~ **back at sb./sth.** sich gegen jmdn./etw. zur Wehr setzen

~ **'down** *v. t.* niederschlagen; *(fig.)* niederwerfen *(geh.); (Amer. Law: reverse)* aufheben

~ **'off 1.** *v. t.* **a)** *(remove)* abschlagen; **b)** *(remove from membership)* streichen ⟨*Namen*⟩; *(from professional body)* die Zulassung/Approbation entziehen (+ *Dat.*); **c)** *(produce by copying)* abziehen. **2.** *v. i.* aufbrechen

~ **on** *see* ~ **upon**

~ **'out 1.** *v. t.* **a)** *(devise)* ausarbeiten; **b)** *(delete)* streichen; **c)** *(Baseball)* ausmachen. **2.** *v. i.* **a)** *(hit out)* zuschlagen; ~ **out at sb./sth.** nach jmdm./etw. schlagen; *(fig.)* jmdn./etw. scharf angreifen; ~ **out on all sides** um sich schlagen; ~ **out wildly** wild um sich schlagen; **b)** *(swim vigorously)* mit kräftigen Zügen schwimmen; *(fig.)* Anstrengungen unternehmen; ~ **out for sth.** *(fig.)* sich mit aller Kraft um etw. bemühen; **c)** *(set out) (lit. or fig.)* aufbrechen; **d)** *(Baseball)* aussein

~ **through** *v. t.* durchstreichen ⟨*Wort*⟩; *(on list also)* ausstreichen

~ **up 1.** ['--] *v. t.* **a)** *(start)* beginnen ⟨*Unterhaltung*⟩; anknüpfen ⟨*Bekanntschaft*⟩; schließen ⟨*Freundschaft*⟩; ~ **up a friendship with sb.** sich mit jmdm. anfreunden; **b)** *(begin to play)* anstimmen. **2.** [-'-] *v. i.* beginnen

~ **upon** *v. t.* finden ⟨*Lösung, Ausweg*⟩; **I have just struck upon an idea** mir ist gerade eine Idee gekommen

strike: ~ **action** *n.* Streikaktionen; **take ~ action** Streikmaßnahmen ergreifen; ~ **ballot** *n.* Urabstimmung, *die;* ~ **benefit** *see* ~ **pay;** ~**bound** *adj.* bestreikt ⟨*Fabrik*⟩; vom Streik/von Streiks betroffen ⟨*Industrie*⟩; durch einen Streik lahmgelegt ⟨*Zugverkehr, Land*⟩; ~**-breaker** *n.* Streikbrecher, *der*/-brecherin, *die;* ~**-force** *see* **striking-force;** ~ **pay** *n.* Streikgeld, *das*

striker ['straɪkə(r)] *n.* **a)** *(worker on strike)* Streikende, *der/die;* **b)** *(Cricket)* Schläger, *der*/Schlägerin, *die; (Footb.)* Stürmer, *der*/Stürmerin, *die; (Billiards)* Spieler/Spielerin, der/die am Stoß ist; **c)** *(Arms)* Schlagbolzen, *der;* **d)** *(Horol.) (clock)* Schlaguhr, *die; (mechanism)* Schlagwerk, *das*

striking ['straɪkɪŋ] *adj.* **a)** *(arresting)* auffallend; erstaunlich ⟨*Ähnlichkeit, Unterschied*⟩; bemerkenswert ⟨*Idee*⟩; schlagend ⟨*Beispiel*⟩; **b)** *(Horol.)* mit Schlagwerk *nachgestellt;* Schlagwerk-

striking: ~**-distance** *n.* Reichweite, *die; (of [bullet from] gun etc.)* Schußweite, *die;* **the troops had advanced to within ~-distance**

of the capital die Truppen hatten sich der Hauptstadt auf Reichweite genähert; **within easy ~-distance of a town** *(fig.)* in unmittelbarer Nähe einer Stadt; **I'm now [with]in ~-distance of my own car** *(can almost afford it)* ein eigener Wagen ist inzwischen in Reichweite gekommen; **~-force** *n. (Mil., Police)* Einsatzkommando, *das*

strikingly ['straɪkɪŋlɪ] *adv.* auffallend; umwerfend ‹*ähnlich sehen*›; **be ~ obvious** ins Auge springen

Strine [straɪn] *n., no pl., no art.* australisches Englisch; *attrib.* australisch ‹*Akzent usw.*›

string [strɪŋ] **1.** *n.* **a)** *(thin cord)* Schnur, *die; (to tie up parcels etc. also)* Bindfaden, *der; (ribbon)* Band, *das;* **a puppet on ~s/on a ~:** eine Marionette; **how long is a piece of ~?** wie weit ist der Himmel?; **[have/keep sb.] on a ~:** [jmdn.] an der Leine *(ugs.) od.* am Gängelband [haben/halten]; **pull the ~s** *(fig.)* die Fäden in der Hand haben; **pull [a few *or* some] ~s** *(fig.)* seine Beziehungen spielen lassen; **there are ~s attached** *(fig.)* es sind Bedingungen/es ist eine Bedingung damit verknüpft; **..., but there are ~s attached ...,** aber nur unter Bedingungen/einer Bedingung; **without ~s, with no ~s attached** ohne Bedingung[en]; **b)** *(of bow)* Sehne, *die; (of racket, musical instrument)* Saite, *die;* **have another ~ to one's bow** *(fig.)* noch ein Eisen im Feuer haben *(ugs.)*; **first/second ~:** erste/zweite Wahl; **as a second ~:** als zweites Eisen im Feuer *(ugs.)*; **a racket with nylon ~s** ein Schläger mit Nylonbespannung; **a six-~ guitar** eine sechssaitige Gitarre; **c)** *in pl. (Mus.) (instruments)* Streichinstrumente; *(players)* Streicher; **~ quartet/orchestra** Streichquartett/-orchester, *das;* **he plays in the ~s** er spielt bei den Streichern; **d)** *(series, sequence)* Kette, *die; (procession)* Zug, *der; (of onions)* Zopf, *der; (Computing)* String, *der;* Zeichenfolge, *die;* **he owns a ~ of racehorses** ihm gehören etliche Rennpferde; **he has had a ~ of girlfriends** er hat eine Freundin nach der anderen gehabt; **e)** *(in bean)* Faden, *der. See also* **apron a; bowstring; shoe-string. 2.** *v. t.,* **strung** [strʌŋ] **a)** bespannen ‹*Tennisschläger, Bogen, Gitarre usw.*›; **be strung to breaking-point** *(fig.)* ‹*Nerven:*› zum Zerreißen gespannt sein; **b)** *(thread)* auffädeln; aufziehen; **c)** *(arrange in line)* aufreihen; *(stretch out)* spannen; **~ sth. round one's neck** sich *(Dat.)* etw. um den Hals hängen; **d)** *(tie with ~)* verschnüren; **e)** die Fäden abziehen von ‹*Bohnen*›. *See also* **highly-strung**

~ a'long *(coll.)* **1.** *v. i.* sich anschließen; **~ along with sb.** mit jmdm. mitgehen; *(have relationship)* mit jmdm. gehen *(ugs.)*. **2.** *v. t.* **a)** *(deceive)* an der Nase herumführen *(ugs.)*; **b)** *(keep dangling)* hinhalten

~ 'out 1. *v. t.* verstreuen; **~ one's meals out at longer intervals** die Abstände zwischen den Mahlzeiten vergrößern. **2.** *v. i. (in space)* sich verteilen

~ to'gether *v. t. (join on a thread)* auffädeln; aufziehen; *(join by tying)* zusammenbinden; *(join coherently)* miteinander verknüpfen; **he can't ~ two sentences together** er kann keine zwei zusammenhängende Sätze hervorbringen

~ 'up *v. t.* **a)** *(tie with ~)* schnüren; *(hang up)* aufhängen ‹*Lampions, Papiergirlanden*›; **b)** *(coll.: kill by hanging)* aufhängen *(ugs.)*; **c)** *(make tense)* unter Druck setzen; **strung up** angespannt

string: ~ bag *n.* [Einkaufs]netz, *das;* **~ band** *n. (Mus.)* Streichorchester, *das;* **~ bass** [strɪŋ 'beɪs] *n. (Mus.)* Kontrabaß, *der;* **~'bean** *n. (Amer.)* grüne Bohne; *(fig. joc.: tall thin person)* Bohnenstange, *die (ugs. scherzh.)*

stringed [strɪŋd] *attrib. adj. (Mus.)* Saiten-

-stringed *adj. in comb. (Mus.)* -saitig

stringency ['strɪndʒənsɪ] *n., no pl.* **a)** *(strictness)* Strenge, *die;* **b) financial ~:** Geldknappheit, *die*

stringent ['strɪndʒənt] *adj.* **a)** *(strict)* streng ‹*Bestimmung, Gesetz, Maßnahme, Test*›; schlüssig ‹*Argumentation*›; überzeugend ‹*Plan*›; **b)** *(tight)* angespannt ‹*Finanzlage*›

stringently ['strɪndʒəntlɪ] *adv.* **a)** *(strictly)* streng; energisch ‹*durchsetzen*›; stringent ‹*logisch*›; schlüssig ‹*argumentieren*›; **b)** eisern ‹*sparen*›

stringer ['strɪŋə(r)] *n.* **a)** *(in construction)* Stringer, *der (Bauw.)*; **b)** *(Journ.)* Korrespondent, *der*/Korrespondentin, *die (in freier Mitarbeit)*

string 'vest *n.* Netzhemd, *das*

stringy ['strɪŋɪ] *adj.* **a)** *(fibrous)* faserig; **b)** *(resembling string)* dünn ‹*Haar*›; faserig ‹*Gewebe*›; **c)** *(forming threads)* Fäden ziehend; zäh ‹*Konsistenz*›; **be ~:** Fäden ziehen; ‹*Konsistenz:*› zäh sein

[1]strip [strɪp] **1.** *v. t.,* **-pp- a)** *(denude)* ausziehen ‹*Person*›; leerräumen, ausräumen ‹*Haus, Schrank, Regal*›; abziehen ‹*Bett*›; abtakeln *(Seemannsspr.)* ‹*Schiff*›; entrinden ‹*Baum*›; abbeizen ‹*Möbel, Türen*›; ausschlachten, *(dismantle)* auseinandernehmen ‹*Maschine, Auto*›; überdrehen ‹*Schraube, Mutter*›; beschädigen ‹*Getriebe*›; **~ped to the waist** mit nacktem Oberkörper; **~ sb. of sth.** jmdn. einer Sache *(Gen.)* berauben *(geh.)*; **~ sb. of his rank/title/medals/decorations/office** jmdm. seinen Rang/Titel/seine Medaillen/Auszeichnungen aberkennen/jmdn. seines Amtes entkleiden *(geh.)*; **~ sb. of his power** jmdm. die Macht nehmen; **~ A of B** B von A entfernen; **~ the garden of [all its] flowers** alle Blumen im Garten abpflücken; **~ a tree [of fruit]** einen Baum abernten; **~ the trees [of leaves]** die Bäume entlauben; **~ the walls** die Tapeten entfernen; **b)** *(remove)* entfernen **(from, off** von); abziehen ‹*Laken*›; abnehmen ‹*Vorhang, Bild*›; abschälen ‹*Rinde, Schale*›; abstreifen ‹*Hülle*›; **~ the clothes/shirt off sb.'s back *or* off sb.** jmdm. die Kleider/das Hemd vom Leibe reißen; **~ the medals off *or* from sb.'s chest** jmdm. die Orden abreißen; **~ sb.'s property/title from him** *(fig.)* jmdm. seinen Besitz abnehmen/Titel aberkennen. **2.** *v. i.,* **-pp-** sich ausziehen; **~ to the waist/[down] to one's underwear** den Oberkörper freimachen/sich bis auf die Unterwäsche ausziehen. **3.** *n.* **do a ~:** sich ausziehen; *(erotically)* einen Striptease vorführen; *attrib.* **~ act** Striptease, *der*

~ 'down 1. *v. t.* **a)** *(dismantle)* auseinandernehmen; **b)** *(undress)* ausziehen; **c)** *(reduce)* einschränken. **2.** *v. i.* sich ausziehen

~ 'off 1. *v. t.* **a)** abreißen; abschälen ‹*Rinde*›; abziehen ‹*Tapete*›; **~ sth. off sth.** etw. von etw. abreißen/abschälen/abziehen; **he ~ped off the soldier's medals** er riß dem Soldaten die Orden ab; **b)** ausziehen ‹*Kleidung*›. **2.** *v. i.* sich ausziehen

[2]strip *n.* **a)** *(narrow piece)* Streifen, *der;* **the curtains hung in ragged ~s** die Vorhänge hingen in Fetzen; **a ~ of land** ein schmales Stück *od.* Streifen Land; **tear sb. off a ~, tear a ~ off sb.** *(Brit. sl.)* jmdm. den Marsch blasen *(ugs.)*; **b)** *(Metallurgy)* Band, *das;* **c)** *see* **strip cartoon; d)** *(Brit. Sport coll.: clothes)* Trikot, *das*

strip: ~ cartoon *n.* Comic[strip], *der;* **~ club** *n.* Stripteaselokal, *das*

stripe [straɪp] *n.* **a)** Streifen, *der;* **b)** *(Mil.)* [Ärmel]streifen, *der;* **get/lose a ~:** befördert/degradiert werden; **c)** *(Amer.: nature)* Schlag, *der. See also* **star 1a**

striped [straɪpt] *adj.* gestreift; Streifen‹*muster, -hyäne*›

strip: ~ farming *n., no pl., no indef. art.* Streifenflurwirtschaft, *die;* **~ light** *n.* Neonröhre, *die; (Theatre)* Lichtwanne, *die;* **~ lighting** *n.* Neonbeleuchtung, *die;* Neonlicht, *das*

stripling ['strɪplɪŋ] *n.* Jüngelchen, *das*

'strip mine *n. (Amer. Mining)* Tagebau, *der*

stripped pine [strɪpt 'paɪn] *n.* abgebeizte Kiefer

stripper ['strɪpə(r)] *n.* **a)** *(solvent)* Farbentferner, *der; (for wallpaper)* Tapetenlöser, *der; (tool)* Kratzer, *der;* **b)** *(strip-tease performer)* Stripteasetänzer, *der*/-tänzerin, *die;* Stripper, *der*/Stripperin, *die (ugs.)*

strip: ~ 'poker *n. (Cards)* Strippoker, *das;* **~-search 1.** *n. Leibesvisitation, bei der der Durchsuchte sich ausziehen muß;* **do a ~-search on a suspect** *einen Verdächtigen, der sich zuvor ausziehen mußte, durchsuchen;* **2.** *v. t.* **we were ~-searched** wir mußten uns zur Durchsuchung ausziehen; **~-show** *n.* Strip-Show, *die;* **~-'tease 1.** *n.* Striptease, *der;* **2.** *v. i.* strippen *(ugs.)*

stripy ['straɪpɪ] *adj.* gestreift ‹*Fell, Blazer*›; Streifen‹*muster, -stoff*›

strive [straɪv] *v. i.,* **strove** [strəʊv], **striven** ['strɪvn] **a)** *(endeavour)* sich bemühen; **~ to do sth.** bestrebt sein *(geh.) od.* sich bemühen, etw. zu tun; **~ after *or* for sth.** nach etw. streben; **~ after *or* for the right answer** sich bemühen, die richtige Antwort zu finden; **b)** *(contend)* kämpfen **(for** um); **~ together *or* with each other [for sth.]** miteinander [um etw.] ringen

strobe [strəʊb] *(coll.),* **stroboscope** ['strəʊbəskəʊp] *ns.* **a)** *(instrument)* Stroboskop, *das;* **b)** *(lamp)* Stroboskoplicht, *das*

stroboscopic [strəʊbə'skɒpɪk] *adj.* stroboskopisch; **~ lamp/light** Stroboskoplicht, *das*

strode *see* **stride 2, 3**

[1]stroke [strəʊk] **1.** *n.* **a)** *(act of striking)* Hieb, *der;* Schlag, *der; (of sword, axe)* Hieb, *der; (of sword also)* Streich, *der (geh.)*; **finishing ~** *(lit. or fig.)* Todesstoß, *der (see also* **g)**; **b)** *(Med.)* Schlaganfall, *der;* **paralytic/apoplectic ~:** paralytischer/apoplektischer Anfall; **c)** *(sudden impact)* **~ of lightning** Blitzschlag, *der;* **by a ~ of fate/fortune** durch eine Fügung des Schicksals/einen [glücklichen] Zufall; **~ of [good] luck** Glücksfall, *der;* **have a ~ of bad/[good] luck** Pech/Glück haben; **by a ~ of bad/[good] luck, the door was locked/open** das Unglück/Glück wollte es, daß die Tür verschlossen/offen war; **d)** *(single effort)* Streich, *der; (skilful effort)* Schachzug, *der;* **at a *or* one ~:** auf einen Schlag *od.* Streich; **not do a ~ [of work]** keinen [Hand]schlag tun; **~ of genius** genialer Einfall; **e)** *(of pendulum, heart, wings, oar)* Schlag, *der; (in swimming)* Zug, *der; (of piston)* Hub, *der (Technik)*; **f)** *(Billiards etc.)* Stoß, *der; (Tennis, Cricket, Golf, Rowing)* Schlag, *der; (Swimming, Rowing: style)* Stil, *der;* **off one's ~** *(lit. or fig.)* nicht in Form; **put sb. off his/her ~** *(lit. or fig.)* jmdn. aus dem Takt bringen; **g)** *(mark, line)* Strich, *der; (of handwriting; also fig.: detail)* Zug, *der; (symbol /)* Schrägstrich, *der;* **with a ~ of the *or* one's pen** mit einem Federstrich; **finishing ~s** *(lit. or fig.)* letzte Pinselstriche; *(fig.)* letztes Feilen *(see also* **a)**; **h)** *(sound of clock)* Schlag, *der;* **on the ~ of nine** Punkt neun [Uhr]; **it was on the ~ of nine when ...:** es war Schlag neun [Uhr], als ...; **on the ~:** pünktlich; **i)** *(oarsman)* Schlagmann, *der.* **2.** *v. t. (Rowing)* als Schlagmann rudern in (+ *Dat.*)

[2]stroke 1. *v. t.* streicheln; **~ one's chin/beard** sich *(Dat.)* über das Kinn/den Bart streichen; **~ sth. over/across sth.** mit etw. über etw. *(Akk.)* streichen; **~ one's hand across one's brow** sich *(Dat.)* mit der Hand über die Stirn streichen; **~ sth. back** etw. zurückstreichen. **2.** *n.* **give sb./sth. a ~:** jmdn./etw. streicheln; **give the dog's ears a ~:** dem Hund die Ohren streicheln

~ '**down** *v.t.* glattstreichen; *(fig.)* besänftigen

stroke: ~ **oar** *n. (Rowing) (oar)* Schlagriemen, *der; (oarsman)* Schlagmann, *der;* ~-**play** *n. (Cricket) Spiel mit spektakulären, mutigen Schlägen*

stroll [strəʊl] **1.** *v.i.* **a)** *(saunter)* spazierengehen; ~ **into sth.** in etw. *(Akk.)* schlendern; **b)** *(go from place to place)* umherziehen; ~ **from town to town** von Ort zu Ort ziehen. **2.** *n.* Spaziergang, *der;* **at a ~:** in gemächlichem Schritt *od.* Tempo; **go for a ~:** einen Spaziergang machen

~ **a'long 1.** *v.i.* daherspazieren *od.* -schlendern. **2.** *v.t.* ~ **along sth.** an etw. *(Dat.)* entlangspazieren *od.* -schlendern

~'**on** *v.i.* weiterschlendern

stroller ['strəʊlə(r)] *n.* **a)** Spaziergänger, *der;* **b)** *(push-chair)* Sportwagen, *der*

strong [strɒŋ] **1.** *adj.,* ~**er** ['strɒŋgə(r)], ~**est** ['strɒŋgɪst] **a)** *(resistant)* stark; gefestigt ⟨*Ehe*⟩; stabil ⟨*Möbel*⟩; solide, fest ⟨*Fundament, Schuhe*⟩; streng ⟨*Vorschriften, Vorkehrungen*⟩; robust ⟨*Konstitution, Magen, Stoff, Porzellan*⟩; *(Econ.)* stark ⟨*Währung*⟩; **a man of ~ will/resolve** ein willensstarker Mann/Mann von großer Entschlußkraft; **you have to have a ~ stomach** *(fig.)* man muß einiges vertragen können; **have a ~ head [for alcohol]** viel [Alkohol] vertragen können; **be ~ [again]** ⟨*Patient:*⟩ [wieder] gesund sein; **the market [in oil] is ~** *(Commerc.)* die Nachfrage [nach Öl] ist groß; **b)** *(powerful)* stark, kräftig ⟨*Person, Tier*⟩; kräftig ⟨*Arme, Beine, Muskeln, Tritt, Schlag, Zähne*⟩; stark ⟨*Linse, Brille, Strom, Magnet*⟩; gut ⟨*Augen*⟩; **as ~ as a horse** *or* **an ox** *(fig.)* bärenstark *(ugs.);* **the ~ silent man/type** der starke, schweigsame Mann/Typ; **a man of ~ character** ein charakterstarker Mann; **c)** *(effective)* stark ⟨*Regierung, Herrscher, Wille*⟩; streng ⟨*Disziplin, Lehrer*⟩; gut ⟨*Gedächtnis, Schüler*⟩; fähig ⟨*Redner, Mathematiker*⟩; *(formidable)* stark ⟨*Gegner, Kombination*⟩; aussichtsreich ⟨*Kandidat*⟩; *(powerful in resources)* reich ⟨*Nation, Land*⟩; leistungsfähig ⟨*Wirtschaft*⟩; stark ⟨*Besetzung*⟩; *(numerous, of specified number)* stark ⟨*Delegation, Truppe, Kontingent usw.*⟩; *(Cards)* gut ⟨*Blatt*⟩; *(Games, Sport)* spielstark; stark ⟨*Mannschaft*⟩; **she is ~ in Latin** Latein ist ihre Stärke; sie ist gut in Latein; **Latin is her ~est subject** in Latein ist sie am besten; **sb.'s ~ point** jmds. Stärke; **the article is not ~ on facts** in bezug auf Tatsachen steht der Artikel auf schwachen Füßen; **the company is a dozen ~:** die Firma hat ein Dutzend Mitarbeiter; **a 10,000-~ army** eine 10 000 Mann starke Armee; **fate dealt him a ~ hand** *(fig.)* das Schicksal hat es gut mit ihm gemeint; **d)** *(convincing)* gut, handfest ⟨*Grund, Beispiel, Argument*⟩; **there is a ~ possibility that ...:** es ist sehr wahrscheinlich, daß ...; **e)** *(vigorous, moving forcefully)* stark; voll ⟨*Unterstützung*⟩; spannend ⟨*Plot*⟩; fest ⟨*Überzeugung*⟩; kraftvoll ⟨*Stil*⟩; *(fervent)* glühend ⟨*Anhänger, Verfechter einer Sache*⟩; **take ~ measures/action** energisch vorgehen; **be a ~ believer in sth.** fest an etw. *(Akk.)* glauben; **f)** *(affecting the senses)* stark; kräftig, stark ⟨*Geruch, Geschmack, Stimme*⟩; markant ⟨*Gesichtszüge*⟩; *(pungent)* streng ⟨*Geruch, Geschmack*⟩; kräftig ⟨*Käse*⟩; **the fish is rather ~:** der Fisch riecht schon sehr; **g)** *(concentrated)* stark; konzentriert ⟨*Lösung*⟩; hochprozentig ⟨*Alkohol*⟩; kräftig ⟨*Farbe*⟩; **I need a ~ drink** ich muß mir erst mal einen genehmigen *(ugs.);* **h)** *(emphatic)* stark ⟨*Ausdruck, Protest*⟩; heftig ⟨*Worte, Wortwechsel*⟩; *(Phonet., Pros.)* stark betont ⟨*Silbe*⟩; stark ⟨*Reim*⟩; **i)** *(Ling.)* stark ⟨*Verb, Deklination usw.*⟩. **2.** *adv.* stark; **the wind was blowing ~:** es wehte ein starker Wind; **come on ~** *(sl.)* in Fahrt kommen *(ugs.);* **sb. is going ~:** es geht jmdm. gut; **they are still going ~** *(after years of marriage)* mit ihnen geht es noch immer gut; *(after hours of work)* sie sind noch immer eifrig dabei; **the restaurant is still going ~:** das Restaurant geht immer noch gut; *see also* **come o**

strong: ~ '**arm** *n., no pl.* Muskelkraft, *die; attrib.* ~-**arm methods** brutale Methoden; ~-**box** *n.* Kassette, *die;* ~**hold** *n.* Festung, *die; (fig.)* Hochburg, *die;* ~ '**language** *n., no pl., no indef. art.* derbe Ausdrucksweise; **use ~ language** sich derb ausdrücken

strongly ['strɒŋlɪ] *adv.* **a)** stark; fest ⟨*etabliert*⟩; solide ⟨*gearbeitet*⟩; ~ **built** solide gebaut; *(in body)* kräftig gebaut; **b)** *(powerfully)* stark; **c)** *(convincingly)* überzeugend ⟨*darlegen*⟩; **d)** *(vigorously)* energisch ⟨*protestieren, bestreiten*⟩; nachdrücklich ⟨*unterstützen*⟩; dringend ⟨*raten*⟩; fest ⟨*glauben*⟩; **I feel ~ about it** es ist mir sehr ernst damit; es liegt mir sehr am Herzen; **I ~ suspect that ...:** ich habe den starken Verdacht, daß ...

strong: ~ **man** *n.* Muskelmann, *der (ugs.); (fig.) (capable man)* führender Kopf; *(dictator)* starker Mann; ~ '**meat** *n., no pl., no art. (fig.)* starker Tobak *(ugs.);* ~-'**minded** *adj.* [seelisch] robust; *(determined)* willensstark; ~ **point** *n. (fortified position)* Stützpunkt, *der; see also* ~ **1 c;** ~-**room** *n.* Tresorraum, *der;* Stahlkammer, *die;* ~ '**suit** *n. (Cards)* lange Farbe; *(fig.)* Stärke, *die;* ~-'**willed** *adj.* willensstark

strontium ['strɒntɪəm] *n. (Chem.)* Strontium, *das*

strop [strɒp] **1.** *n.* Streichriemen, *der.* **2.** *v.t.,* **-pp-** [auf dem Streichriemen] schärfen

stroppy ['strɒpɪ] *adj. (Brit. sl.)* pampig *(salopp)*

strove *see* **strive**

struck *see* **strike 2, 3**

structural ['strʌktʃərl] *adj.* **a)** baulich; Bau⟨*material*⟩; tragend ⟨*Wand, Säule, Balken*⟩; Konstruktions⟨*fehler*⟩; statisch ⟨*Probleme*⟩; **b)** *(Biol.)* strukturell; Struktur⟨*muster, -merkmal*⟩; **c)** *(Geol.)* tektonisch; **d)** *(Sociol.)* strukturell

structural: ~ **engi'neering** *n.* Hochbau, *der;* ~ **formula** *n. (Chem.)* Strukturformel, *die*

structuralism ['strʌktʃərəlɪzm] *n.* Strukturalismus, *der*

structurally ['strʌktʃərəlɪ] *adv.* strukturell; *(Geol.)* tektonisch ⟨*geformt*⟩; **the building is ~ sound** das Gebäude hat eine gute Bausubstanz; ~, **the building is ...:** baulich gesehen ist das Gebäude ...

structural '**steel** *n. (Building)* Baustahl, *der*

structure ['strʌktʃə(r)] **1.** *n.* **a)** *(manner of construction)* Bauweise, *die; (interrelation of parts; also Anat., Biol., Geol., Ling., Lit., Phys.)* Struktur, *die;* Aufbau, *der; (Mus.)* Kompositionsweise, *die;* Struktur, *die;* **bone/skeletal ~:** Knochenbau, *der*/Knochengerüst, *das;* **sentence ~:** Satzbau, *der;* **price ~:** Preisverhältnis, *das;* **b)** *no pl., no indef. art. (formal arrangement of parts)* Strukturierung, *die;* **people must have ~ in their daily lives** der Mensch braucht eine gewisse Ordnung in seinem Alltag; **c)** *(something constructed)* Konstruktion, *die; (building)* Bauwerk, *das; (complex whole; also Biol.)* Struktur, *die.* **2.** *v.t.* strukturieren; regeln ⟨*Leben*⟩; aufbauen ⟨*literarisches Werk*⟩; *(construct)* konstruieren; bauen

structured ['strʌktʃəd] *adj.* strukturiert; geregelt ⟨*Leben*⟩

strudel ['stru:dl] *n. (Gastr.)* Strudel, *der*

struggle ['strʌgl] **1.** *v.i.* **a)** *(try with difficulty)* kämpfen; ~ **to do sth.** sich abmühen, etw. zu tun; ~ **for a place/a better world** um einen Platz/für eine bessere Welt kämpfen; ~ **for breath** nach Atem ringen; ~ **against** *or* **with sb./sth.** mit jmdm./etw. *od.* gegen jmdn./etw. kämpfen; ~ **with sth.** *(try to cope)* sich mit etw. quälen; mit etw. kämpfen; **b)** *(proceed with difficulty)* sich quälen; *(into tight dress, through narrow opening)* sich zwängen; **I ~d past** ich kämpfte mich vorbei; ~ **to one's feet** unter Schwierigkeiten aufstehen; **c)** *(physically)* kämpfen; *(resist)* sich wehren; ~ **free** freikommen; sich befreien; **d)** *(be in difficulties, have difficulty in life)* kämpfen *(fig.);* **after three laps I was struggling** nach drei Runden hatte ich zu kämpfen. **2.** *n.* **a)** *(exertion)* **with a ~:** mit Mühe; **it was a long ~:** es kostete viel Mühe; **after all our valiant ~s** nach all unserem tapferen Bemühen; **have a [hard] ~ to do sth.** [große] Mühe haben, etw. zu tun; **a life of hardship and ~:** ein hartes und mühseliges Leben; **the ~ for freedom** der Kampf für die Freiheit; **b)** *(physical fight)* Kampf, *der; (confused wrestle)* Handgemenge, *das;* **legal ~:** Rechtsstreit, *der;* **the ~ against** *or* **with sb./sth.** der Kampf gegen *od.* mit jmdm./etw.; **the ~ for influence/power** der Kampf um Einfluß/die Macht; **the ~ for existence** *or* **life** *or* **survival** der Kampf ums Überleben; **surrender without a ~:** kampflos aufgeben

struggling ['strʌglɪŋ] *adj. (in life) ums Überleben und um Anerkennung kämpfend*

strum [strʌm] **1.** *v.i.,* **-mm-** klimpern *(ugs.)* (on auf + *Dat.*). **2.** *v.t.,* **-mm-** klimpern *(ugs.)* auf (+ *Dat.*). **3.** *n.* Klimpern, *das (ugs.);* **have a ~:** klimpern *(ugs.)*

strumpet ['strʌmpɪt] *n. (arch./rhet.)* Dirne, *die (veralt.)*

strung *see* **string 2**

[1]**strut** [strʌt] **1.** *v.i.,* **-tt-** *(walk)* stolzieren. **2.** *n.* stolzierender Gang

[2]**strut 1.** *n. (support)* Strebe, *die.* **2.** *v.t.,* **-tt-** verstreben

'**struth** [stru:θ] *int.* Himmel! *(ugs.)*

strychnine ['strɪkni:n] *n.* Strychnin, *das*

Stuart ['stju:ət] *(Brit. Hist.)* **1.** *n.* Stuart, *der/die.* **2.** *attrib. adj.* **the ~ dynasty** *etc.* die Dynastie *usw.* der Stuarts

stub [stʌb] **1.** *n.* **a)** *(short remaining portion)* Stummel, *der; (of cigarette)* Kippe, *die;* ~ **of pencil** Bleistiftstummel, *der;* **b)** *(counterfoil)* Abschnitt, *der; (of ticket)* Abriß, *der;* **c)** *(of tree, branch, tooth)* Stumpf, *der;* **d)** *(limb, tail, etc.)* Stummel, *der.* **2.** *v.t.,* **-bb- a)** ~ **one's toe [against** *or* **on sth.]** sich *(Dat.)* den Zeh [an etw. *(Dat.)*] stoßen; **b)** ausdrücken ⟨*Zigarette usw.*⟩; *(with one's foot)* austreten ⟨*Zigarette usw.*⟩

~ '**out** *v.t.* ausdrücken

'**stub-axle** *n. (Mech.)* Achsschenkel, *der*

stubble ['stʌbl] *n., no pl.* Stoppeln *Pl.*

stubbly ['stʌblɪ] *adj.* stopp[e]lig; ~ **field/beard** Stoppelfeld, *das*/-bart, *der (ugs.)*

stubborn ['stʌbən] *adj.* **a)** *(obstinate)* starrköpfig *(abwertend);* dickköpfig *(ugs.);* störrisch ⟨*Tier, Gesicht, Haltung*⟩; hartnäckig ⟨*Vorurteil, Streit*⟩; **be ~ in insisting on sth.** stur *(ugs. abwertend)* auf etw. *(Dat.)* beharren; **[as] ~ as a mule** störrisch wie ein Maulesel *(ugs.);* **b)** *(resolute)* hartnäckig; fest ⟨*Mut, Entschlossenheit, Treue*⟩; hart ⟨*Augen, Kinn*⟩; **c)** *(intractable)* störrisch *(fig.);* vertrackt *(ugs.)* ⟨*Problem*⟩; hartnäckig ⟨*Unkraut, Krankheit*⟩

stubbornly ['stʌbənlɪ] *adv.* **a)** *(obstinately)* störrisch; wild ⟨*entschlossen*⟩; **b)** *(resolutely, intractably)* hartnäckig

stubbornness ['stʌbənnɪs] *n., no pl.* **a)** *(obstinacy)* Starrköpfigkeit, *die;* **b)** *(resolution, intractability)* Hartnäckigkeit, *die*

stubby ['stʌbɪ] *adj.* kurz [und dick]; gedrungen, untersetzt ⟨*Person*⟩; ~ **tail** Stummelschwanz, *der*

stucco ['stʌkəʊ] **1.** *n., pl.* ~**es** *(fine plaster)* Stuck, *der; (coarse plaster)* Putz, *der; (work)* Stuckarbeit, *die;* Stukkatur, *die; attrib.* Stuck-. **2.** *v.t. (coat with coarse plaster)* verputzen; *(decorate with fine plaster)* stuckieren

stuck *see* **stick 1, 2**
'stuck up *see* **stick up 1 e**
[1]**stud** [stʌd] **1.** *n.* **a)** *(boss)* Beschlagnagel, *der; (on clothes)* Niete, *die; (on boot)* Stollen, *der; (marker in road)* Nagel, *der (Verkehrsw.);* **b)** *(for shirt)* Knebel, *der; (cufflink)* Manschettenknopf, *der; (for ear)* Ohrstecker, *der.* **2.** *v. t.,* **-dd-** *(set with ~s)* beschlagen; *(be scattered over)* verstreut sein über (+ *Akk.*); **~ded** mit Nägeln beschlagen ‹*Tür, Möbel*›; mit Nieten verziert ‹*Jacke, Gürtel*›; **~ded with flowers/stars** *etc.* mit Blumen/Sternen *usw.* übersät; **a jewel-~ded crown** eine juwelenbesetzte Krone
[2]**stud** *n.* **a)** *(Breeding)* Gestüt, *das;* **put a horse out to ~:** ein Pferd nur noch zur Zucht verwenden; **b)** *(stallion)* Deckhengst, *der;* Zuchthengst, *der;* Beschäler, *der (fachspr.);* **c)** *(sl.: man)* Zuchthengst, *der (derb)*
'stud-book *n.* *(Breeding)* Stutbuch, *das;* Gestütbuch, *das*
student ['stju:dənt] *n.* Student, *der*/Studentin, *die; (in school or training establishment)* Schüler, *der*/Schülerin, *die;* **a good ~:** ein eifriger Student/Schüler/eine eifrige Studentin/Schülerin; **be a ~ of sth.** etw. studieren; **~ of medicine** Student/Studentin der Medizin; Medizinstudent, *der*/-studentin, *die;* **eternal ~:** ewiger Student *(ugs.); attrib.* **~ days** Studenten-/Schulzeit, *die;* **~ demonstration** Studenten-/Schülerdemonstration, *die;* **~ driver** *(Amer.)* Fahrschüler, *der*/-schülerin, *die;* **~ nurse** Lernschwester, *die*/Pflegeschüler, *der;* **be a ~ doctor/teacher** ein medizinisches Praktikum/Schulpraktikum machen
stud: **~-farm** *n.* *(Breeding)* Gestüt, *das;* **~-horse** *see* [2]**stud b**
studied ['stʌdɪd] *adj.* **a)** *(thoughtful)* [wohl]überlegt; **b)** *(intentional)* gewollt; gesucht ‹*Stil, Ausdrucksweise*›; gezielt ‹*Beleidigung*›; **c)** *(well-read)* belesen
studiedly ['stʌdɪdlɪ] *adv.* **a)** *(thoughtfully)* überlegt; **b)** *(intentionally)* **be ~ casual** sich gewollt lässig geben
studio ['stju:dɪəʊ] *n., pl.* **~s** **a)** *(photographer's or painter's workroom)* Atelier, *das; (workshop for the performing arts)* Studio, *das;* **b)** *(Cinemat.) (room)* Studio, *das; (organization)* Filmgesellschaft, *die;* **~s** *(premises)* Studios; **c)** *(Radio, Telev.)* Studio, *das*
studio: **~ apartment** *(Amer.) see* **~ flat;** **~ 'audience** *n.* *(Radio, Telev.)* Publikum im Studio; **~ couch** *n.* Schlafcouch, *die;* Bettcouch, *die;* **~ flat** *n.* *(Brit.)* **a)** Atelier, *das;* **b)** *(one-room flat)* Einzimmerwohnung, *die*
studious ['stju:dɪəs] *adj.* **a)** *(assiduous in study)* lerneifrig; gelehrt ‹*Beschäftigung, Buch, Aussehen, Atmosphäre*›; **~ life** Gelehrtendasein, *das;* **b)** *(earnest)* ernsthaft ‹*Anstrengung*›; *(intentional)* bewußt; **~ to do** *or* **in doing sth.** bemüht, etw. zu tun
studiously ['stju:dɪəslɪ] *adv.* **a)** *(with attention to learning)* **be ~ inclined** gern studieren; lernbegierig sein; **b)** *(diligently)* eifrig; *(intentionally)* bewußt ‹*rücksichtsvoll, kühl*›; geflissentlich ‹*aus dem Weg gehen*›
studiousness ['stju:dɪəsnɪs] *n., no pl.* **a)** *(application to study)* Lerneifer, *der;* **b)** *(careful attention)* Beflissenheit, *die*
study ['stʌdɪ] **1.** *n.* **a)** Studium, *das;* Lernen, *das;* **I enjoy my studies** das Studium macht mir Spaß; **~ does not come naturally to him** das Lernen fällt ihm nicht leicht; **what branch of ~ is he engaged in?** welche Studienrichtung hat er eingeschlagen?; **the ~ of mathematics/law** das Studium der Mathematik/der Rechtswissenschaft; **be still under ~:** noch untersucht *od.* geprüft werden; **[books on] African/Social Studies** *(Educ./Univ.)* [Bücher zur] Afrikanistik/Sozialwissenschaft; **graduate studies** *(Educ./Univ.)* Graduiertenstudium, *das;* **b)** *(piece of work)* **a ~ of** *or* **on sth.** eine Studie über etw. *(Akk.);* **studies are being carried out** zur Zeit werden Untersuchungen durchgeführt; **make a ~ of sth.** über etw. *(Akk.)* [wissenschaftliche] Untersuchungen anstellen; **c)** *(object of examination)* Studienobjekt, *das;* **make sth. one's ~:** sich *(Dat.)* etw. zur Aufgabe machen; **a ~ in sth.** ein Musterbeispiel *(fig.)* für etw.; **his face was a ~!** sein Gesicht war sehenswert!; **d)** *(Art)* Studie, *die; (Mus.)* Etüde, *die;* Übung, *die; (Lit., Theatre)* Studie, *die* **(in, of** über + *Akk.*); **as a ~ in perspective/composition** als perspektivische Studie/Kompositionsstudie; **e)** *(contemplation)* Kontemplation, *die; see also* **brown study; f)** *(room)* Arbeitszimmer, *das.* **2.** *v. t.* **a)** *(seek knowledge of)* studieren; *(at school)* lernen; **~ politics all one's life/~ Goethe** sich sein Leben lang mit Politik/sich mit Goethe beschäftigen; **b)** *(scrutinize)* studieren; **c)** *(read attentively)* studieren ‹*Fahrplan*›; sich *(Dat.)* [sorgfältig] durchlesen ‹*Prüfungsfragen, Bericht*›; **d)** *(learn by heart)* studieren. **3.** *v. i.* lernen; *(at university)* studieren; **~ under sb.** bei jmdm. studieren; **~ to be a doctor/teach French** Medizin studieren/Französisch für das Lehramt studieren; **~ for the medical profession** Medizin studieren
'study group *n.* Arbeitsgruppe, *die;* Arbeitskreis, *der*
stuff [stʌf] **1.** *n.* **a)** *no pl., no indef. art. (material[s])* Zeug, *das (ugs.); (artistic productions)* Sachen *Pl. (ugs.); (coll.: drugs)* Stoff, *der (salopp); (sl.: money)* Kohle, *die (salopp);* **garden ~:** Grünzeug, *das (ugs.);* **have the ~ of a champion** das Zeug zum Champion haben *(ugs.);* **be made of sterner ~:** aus härterem Stoff gemacht sein *(fig.);* **the ~ of fairy stories** der Stoff für Märchen; **the ~ that dreams/heroes are made of** der Stoff, aus dem die Träume sind/Helden gemacht sind *(fig.);* **plastic is useful ~:** Plastik ist eine nützliche Sache; **push [the] ~** *(coll.: deal in drugs)* mit Stoff handeln *(salopp);* **there has been some interesting ~ in the papers/on the radio** es gab ein paar interessante Sachen in den Zeitungen/im Radio *(ugs.);* **that actor has been in some good ~ lately** dieser Schauspieler hat zuletzt ein paar gute Sachen gemacht *(ugs.);* **b)** *no pl., no indef. art. (activity, knowledge)* **do painting or drawing, ~ like that** malen oder zeichnen oder so was *(ugs.);* **do one's ~** *(coll.)* seine Sache machen; **get on and do your ~!** *(coll.)* na los, mach schon! *(ugs.);* **know one's ~** *(coll.: be knowledgeable)* sich auskennen; *(know one's job)* seine Sache verstehen; **that's the ~!** *(coll.)* so ist's richtig!; **that's the ~ to give the troops** *(fig. coll.)* das ist jetzt genau das richtige; **c)** *no pl. (valueless matter)* Zeug, *das (ugs. abwertend);* **~ [and nonsense]!** *(coll.)* dummes Zeug! *(ugs. abwertend);* **d)** *(Textiles)* Wolle, *die;* Wollzeug, *das (veralt.); attrib.* wollen ‹*Hemd*›. *See also* [2]**bit a; hot stuff; kid 1 c; rough stuff. 2.** *v. t.* **a)** stopfen; zustopfen ‹*Loch, Ohren*›; *(in taxidermy)* ausstopfen; *(Cookery)* füllen; *(make eat to repletion)* stopfen, nudeln ‹*Gans*›; *(coarse: copulate with)* stoßen *(vulg.);* **~ envelopes [with letters]** Briefe in Umschläge stecken; **~ sth. with** *or* **full of sth.** etw. mit etw. vollstopfen *(ugs.);* **[go and] get ~ed!** *(sl.)* hau ab! *(ugs.);* **~ oneself** *(sl.)* sich vollstopfen *(ugs.);* **~ one's face** *(sl.)* sich *(Dat.)* den Bauch vollstopfen *(ugs.);* **~ ballot boxes** *(Amer.: insert bogus votes)* Stimmen fälschen; **he ~ed a banknote into my hand** er drückte mir einen Geldschein in die Hand; **b)** *(sl.)* **~ him/the family reputation!** zum Teufel mit ihm/der Familienehre!; **~ it!** Scheiß drauf! *(derb);* **he can ~ it!** er kann mich mal! *(derb).* **3.** *v. i.* sich vollstopfen *(ugs.)*
~ 'up *v. t.* verstopfen
stuffed 'shirt *n.* *(coll. derog.)* Wichtigtuer, *der (ugs. abwertend)*
stuffiness ['stʌfɪnɪs] *n., no pl.* **a)** *(airlessness)* Stickigkeit, *die;* **the ~ of the room** die stickige Luft im Zimmer; **b)** *(congestion)* **the ~ in his nose/head** seine verstopfte Nase/entzündete Stirnhöhle; **c)** *(coll.: ill humour)* Übellaunigkeit, *die;* **d)** *(coll.: primness)* Spießigkeit, *die (abwertend)*
stuffing ['stʌfɪŋ] *n.* **a)** *(material)* Füllmaterial, *das;* **a ~ of horsehair** eine Füllung aus Roßhaar; **knock** *or* **take the ~ out of sb./a theory** *(coll. fig.)* jmdn. umhauen *(ugs.)*/eine Theorie wie ein Kartenhaus in sich zusammenfallen lassen; **b)** *(Cookery)* Füllung, *die*
stuffy ['stʌfɪ] *adj.* **a)** *(stifling)* stickig ‹*Zimmer, Atmosphäre*›; **b)** *(congested)* verstopft; **my head feels very ~:** meine Stirnhöhle ist ganz zu *(ugs.);* **c)** *(coll.: ill-humoured)* sauertöpfisch *(ugs. abwertend);* **he got very ~ about it** er reagierte sehr sauer *(salopp)* [darauf]; **d)** *(coll.: prim)* spießig *(abwertend)* **(about** gegenüber)
stultify ['stʌltɪfaɪ] *v. t.* **a)** *(reduce to absurdity)* der Lächerlichkeit preisgeben; ins Lächerliche ziehen ‹*Entscheidung, Anstrengungen*›; **b)** *(neutralize)* zunichte machen; **c)** *(impair)* lähmen; **have a ~ing effect on sth.** sich lähmend auf etw. *(Akk.)* auswirken; **~ing boredom/monotony** lähmende Langeweile/Monotonie
stumble ['stʌmbl] **1.** *v. i.* **a)** stolpern **(over** über + *Akk.*); **b)** *(falter)* stocken; **~ over sth./through life** über etw. *(Akk.)*/durchs Leben stolpern; **c)** **~ across** *or* **[up]on sb./sth.** *(find by chance)* über jmdn. stolpern *(fig. ugs.)*/auf etw. *(Akk.)* stoßen. **2.** *n.* **a)** *(trip)* Stolpern, *das;* **b)** *(error)* Stocken, *das*
stumbling-block ['stʌmblɪŋblɒk] *n.* Stolperstein, *der*
stump [stʌmp] **1.** *n.* **a)** *(of tree, branch, tooth)* Stumpf, *der; (of cigar, pencil)* Stummel, *der;* **up a ~** *(Amer. sl.)* aufgeschmissen *(salopp);* **b)** *(of limb, tail, etc.)* Stummel, *der; (artificial leg)* Stelze, *die;* **~s** *(joc.: legs)* Stelzen *(salopp); see also* [1]**stir 1 b;** **c)** *(Cricket)* Stab, *der;* **draw ~s** das Ende des Spieltages ansagen; **d)** *(improvised platform)* Rednertribüne, *die;* **on the ~** *(coll.)* im Wahlkampf; **go on** *or* **take the ~** *(lit. or fig.)* sich auf die Bühne begeben. **2.** *v. t.* **a)** *(confound)* verwirren; durcheinanderbringen; **be ~ed** ratlos sein; **be ~ed for an answer** um eine Antwort verlegen sein; **this problem has got me ~ed** bei diesem Problem weiß ich nicht mehr weiter; **b)** *(Cricket)* ausschalten ‹*Schlagmann*›*(, der außerhalb einer bestimmten Zone steht, durch Umwerfen der Stäbchen)*; **c)** *(Amer. Polit.)* als Wahlkämpfer bereisen. **3.** *v. i.* **a)** *(walk stiffly)* stapfen; *(walk noisily)* trampeln; **b)** *(Amer. Polit.: make speeches)* sich aufs Podium stellen; **~ing tour** Wahlkampfreise, *die*
~ 'out *see* **~ 2 b**
~ 'up *(Brit. coll.) v. t. & i.* blechen *(ugs.)*
stumpy ['stʌmpɪ] *adj.* gedrungen; **~ tail** Stummelschwanz, *der;* **~ pencil** Bleistiftstummel, *der*
stun [stʌn] *v. t.,* **-nn-** **a)** *(knock senseless)* betäuben; **be ~ned** *(unconscious)* bewußtlos sein; *(dazed)* benommen sein; **b)** *(fig.)* **be ~ned at** *or* **by sth.** von etw. wie betäubt sein; **a ~ned silence** ein fassungsloses Schweigen; **a superb performance which ~ned the critics and audience alike** eine herausragende Darbietung, die Kritiker und Publikum gleichermaßen in ihren Bann schlug; **c)** *(deafen temporarily)* betäuben; **be ~ned by sth.** von etw. wie betäubt sein
stung *see* **sting 2, 3**
stunk *see* **stink 1**
stunner ['stʌnə(r)] *n.* *(coll.)* **be a ~:** Spitze sein *(ugs.)*
stunning ['stʌnɪŋ] *adj.* *(coll.)* **a)** *(splendid)*

hinreißend; umwerfend *(ugs.)*; **b)** *(causing insensibility)* wuchtig ⟨*Schlag*⟩; **c)** *(shocking)* bestürzend ⟨*Nachricht*⟩; horrend ⟨*Preis*⟩; *(amazing)* sensationell; **d)** *(deafening)* ohrenbetäubend *(ugs.)*

stunningly [ˈstʌnɪŋlɪ] *adv. (coll.)* umwerfend *(ugs.)*; unfaßbar ⟨*langweilig, schrecklich, häßlich*⟩

¹stunt [stʌnt] *v. t.* hemmen, beeinträchtigen ⟨*Wachstum, Entwicklung*⟩; **~ed trees** verkümmerte Bäume; **emotionally ~ed** seelisch verkümmert

²stunt 1. *n.* halsbrecherisches Kunststück; *(Cinemat.)* Stunt, *der; (Advertising)* [Werbe]gag, *der.* **2.** *v. i.* Stunts vollführen

ˈstunt man *n.* Stuntman, *der*

stupefaction [stjuːpɪˈfækʃn] *n., no pl.* **a)** Benommenheit, *die;* **b)** *(astonishment)* Verblüffung, *die*

stupefy [ˈstjuːpɪfaɪ] *v. t.* **a)** *(benumb)* ⟨*Hitze:*⟩ benommen machen; ⟨*Mühsal:*⟩ abstumpfen; **be stupefied with** *or* **by** benommen sein von ⟨*Schlag, Alkohol, Droge*⟩; abgestumpft sein von ⟨*Armut, Kummer*⟩; **b)** *(astound)* die Sprache verschlagen (+ *Dat.*); **be stupefied** wie vor den Kopf geschlagen sein

stupendous [stjuːˈpendəs] *adj.* gewaltig; außergewöhnlich ⟨*Schönheit, Intelligenz, Talent*⟩; großartig ⟨*Urlaub, Schauspieler*⟩

stupendously [stjuːˈpendəslɪ] *adv.* außergewöhnlich; gewaltig ⟨*groß*⟩; großartig ⟨*sich verhalten*⟩

stupid [ˈstjuːpɪd] **1.** *adj.*, **~er** [ˈstjuːpɪdə(r)], **~est** [ˈstjuːpɪdɪst] **a)** *(slow-witted, unintelligent)* dumm; einfältig ⟨*Person, Aussehen*⟩; *(ridiculous)* lächerlich; *(pointless)* dumm *(ugs.)* ⟨*Witz, Geschichte, Gedanke*⟩; *expr. rejection or irritation* blöd *(ugs.)*; **where is that ~ key?** wo ist jetzt der blöde *(ugs.)* Schlüssel?; **it would be ~ to do sth.** es wäre töricht, etw. zu tun; **that was a ~ place to leave the car** es war töricht, das Auto dort abzustellen; **b)** *(in state of stupor)* benommen **(with** von); teilnahmslos, apathisch ⟨*Blick*⟩; **be bored ~:** zu Tode gelangweilt sein. **2.** *n. (coll.)* Dummkopf, *der (ugs.)*

stupidity [stjuːˈpɪdɪtɪ] *n.* Dummheit, *die; (of action also)* Torheit, *die; (of facial expression)* Einfältigkeit, *die*

stupidly [ˈstjuːpɪdlɪ] *adv.* dumm; **~ [enough], I have ...:** dummerweise habe ich ...; **he ~ admitted that ...:** törichterweise hat er zugegeben, daß ...

stupor [ˈstjuːpə(r)] *n.* **a)** *(torpidity)* Benommenheit, *die; (Med.)* Stupor, *der;* **drink oneself into a ~:** sich bis zur Bewußtlosigkeit betrinken; **b)** *(apathy)* Erstarrung, *die;* **c)** *(amazement)* **stand in a ~:** starr vor Staunen stehen

sturdily [ˈstɜːdɪlɪ] *adv. (robustly)* fest ⟨*angeln*⟩; mit festem Schritt ⟨*gehen*⟩; *(resolutely)* fest ⟨*überzeugt*⟩; entschlossen ⟨*sich entgegenstellen*⟩; **~ built** kräftig [gebaut] ⟨*Person, Pferd*⟩; stabil [gebaut] ⟨*Stuhl, Fahrrad*⟩

sturdiness [ˈstɜːdɪnɪs] *n., no pl. (robustness)* Stabilität, *die; (of person)* Stämmigkeit, *die; (resoluteness)* Stärke, *die;* Festigkeit, *die*

sturdy [ˈstɜːdɪ] *adj. (robust)* stabil ⟨*Haus, Stuhl, Schiff*⟩; kräftig ⟨*Rasse, Pflanze, Pferd, Kind*⟩; kräftig [gebaut] ⟨*Person*⟩; *(resistant to disease or rough weather)* robust; *(thickset)* stämmig ⟨*Mensch*⟩; *(strong)* stämmig ⟨*Beine, Arme*⟩; *(sound)* solide; *(resolute)* fest ⟨*Glaube, Grundsätze*⟩; stark ⟨*Gegner, Verfechter, Widerstand*⟩

sturgeon [ˈstɜːdʒən] *n. (Zool.)* Stör, *der*

stutter [ˈstʌtə(r)] **1.** *v. i.* stottern; ⟨*Gewehr:*⟩ tacken. **2.** *v. t.* stottern. **3.** *n.* Stottern, *das; (of gun)* Tacken, *das; (of flame)* Flackern, *das;* **speak with a ~:** stottern; **have a bad ~:** stark stottern

~ ˈout *v. t.* stotternd hervorbringen

stutterer [ˈstʌtərə(r)] *n.* Stotterer, *der*/Stotterin, *die*

¹sty [staɪ] *see* **pigsty**

²sty, stye [staɪ] *n. (Med.)* Gerstenkorn, *das*

Stygian [ˈstɪdʒɪən] *adj. (Mythol.; also fig.)* stygisch

style [staɪl] **1.** *n.* **a)** *(manner)* Stil, *der; (in conversation)* Ton, *der; (in performance)* Art, *die;* **~ of swimming/running** Schwimm-/Laufstil, *der;* **that's the ~!** so ist es richtig!; **be bad** *or* **not good ~:** schlechter *od.* kein guter Stil sein; **b)** *(collective features) (in artistic presentation; also Printing, Publishing)* Stil, *der; (of habitual behaviour)* Art, *die;* **it's not my ~ [to do that]** das ist nicht mein Stil; **dress in the latest/modern ~:** sich nach der neuesten/neuen Mode kleiden; **the costumes were in** *or* **of the ~ of the 1940s** es waren Kostüme im Stil der 40er Jahre; **cook in the French ~:** französisch kochen; *see also* **cramp 2 a; house style; c)** *(superior way of living, behaving, etc.)* Stil, *der;* **in ~:** stilvoll; *(on a grand scale)* im großen Stil; **in the grand ~:** im großen Stil; **she is a woman of ~:** sie hat Stil; **live a life of ~:** ein luxuriöses Leben führen; **have no ~:** keinen Stil haben; **d)** *(sort)* Art, *die;* **~ of music** Musikrichtung, *die;* **she is not his ~:** sie paßt nicht zu ihm; **this house is not my ~:** das Haus ist nichts für mich; **e)** *(pattern)* Art, *die; (of clothes)* Machart, *die; (hair-~)* Frisur, *die;* **she has had her hair cut in a page-boy ~:** sie hat sich *(Dat.)* einen Pagenkopf schneiden lassen; **have one's hair done in a different ~:** sich *(Dat.)* eine andere Frisur machen lassen; **f)** *(descriptive formula)* Titel, *der; (of firm)* Firmenbezeichnung, *die;* **~ [of address]** Anrede, *die;* **g)** *(Bot.)* Griffel, *der.* **2.** *v. t.* **a)** *(design)* entwerfen; stilisieren *(veralt.)*; **~ one's own hair** sich *(Dat.)* seine Frisuren selbst machen; **elegantly ~d clothes** elegant geschnittene Kleidung; **clothes ~d for comfort** bequem geschnittene Kleidung; **b)** *(designate)* nennen; *(address)* anreden; **~ oneself sth.** sich bezeichnen als etw.

-style *in comb.* **a Tudor-~ house** ein Haus im Tudorstil; **a Queen-Anne-~ chair** ein Queen-Anne-Stuhl; **Indian-~ curry** indischer Curry; **French-~ cooking** französische Küche; **peasant-~ skirt** Bauernrock, *der;* **dressed cowboy-~:** wie ein Cowboy gekleidet

ˈstyle-book *n.* Buch mit Modellen; *(of hairdresser)* Frisurenheft, *das; (Printing, Publishing)* Buch mit Satzanweisungen

styling [ˈstaɪlɪŋ] *n.* **a)** *(imparting of style)* Styling, *das;* **that hairdresser is good at ~:** dieser Friseur kann gut [neue] Frisuren entwerfen; **b)** *(Lit., Publishing)* stilistische Überarbeitung; **c)** *(ornamentation)* **intricate ~:** komplizierte Verzierungen

stylise *see* **stylize**

stylish [ˈstaɪlɪʃ] *adj.* stilvoll; elegant ⟨*Kleidung, Auto, Hotel, Person*⟩

stylishly [ˈstaɪlɪʃlɪ] *adv.* stilvoll; elegant ⟨*geschnitten, angezogen*⟩; **~ elegant** vornehm und elegant

stylishness [ˈstaɪlɪʃnɪs] *n., no pl.* Stil, *der; (of clothes)* Eleganz, *die*

stylist [ˈstaɪlɪst] *n.* **a)** *(Lit., Sport)* Stilist, *der*/Stilistin, *die;* **b)** *(designer)* Designer, *der*/Designerin, *die; (hair-~)* Haarstilist, *der*/-stilistin, *die*

stylistic [staɪˈlɪstɪk] *adj.* stilistisch; Stil⟨*mittel, -merkmale*⟩

stylistically [staɪˈlɪstɪkəlɪ] *adv.* stilistisch

stylistics [staɪˈlɪstɪks] *n., no pl.* Stilistik, *die*

stylize [ˈstaɪlaɪz] *v. t.* stilisieren

stylus [ˈstaɪləs] *n., pl.* **styli** [ˈstaɪlaɪ] *or* **~es a)** *(gramophone needle)* [Abtast]nadel, *die;* **sapphire/diamond ~:** Saphir, *der*/Diamant, *der;* **b)** *(writing-tool)* Griffel, *der; (engraving-tool)* Grabstichel, *der*

stymie [ˈstaɪmɪ] **1.** *n. (difficult situation)* Sackgasse, *die (fig.)*. **2.** *v. t. (thwart)* in die Klemme *(ugs.)* geraten lassen; **be ~d** aufgeschmissen sein *(salopp)*; **~ oneself** sich *(Dat.)* selber ein Bein stellen

styptic [ˈstɪptɪk] **1.** *adj.* blutstillend. **2.** *n.* blutstillendes Mittel; Hämostyptikum, *das (Med.)*

Styria [ˈstɪrɪə] *pr. n.* Steiermark, *die*

Styx [stɪks] *pr. n. (Greek Mythol.)* Styx, *der;* **cross the ~** *(fig.)* den Styx überqueren *(geh.)*

suave [swɑːv] *adj.* **a)** *(affable)* verbindlich; **b)** *(agreeable)* sanft ⟨*Farbe, Licht, Musik*⟩; lieblich ⟨*Wein, Geschmack*⟩

suavely [ˈswɑːvlɪ] *adv.* **a)** *(affably)* verbindlich; **he was always ~ polite** er war stets verbindlich und höflich; **b)** *(agreeably)* sanft

suavity [ˈswɑːvɪtɪ] *n.* **a)** *(affability)* Verbindlichkeit, *die;* **b)** *(agreeableness)* [angenehme] Milde; **suavities** Annehmlichkeiten

sub [sʌb] *(coll.)* **1.** *n.* **a)** *(subscription)* Abo, *das (ugs.)*; **b)** *(esp. Sport: substitute)* Ersatz, *der;* **c)** *(submarine)* U-Boot, *das;* **d)** *see* **sub-editor. 2.** *v. i.*, **-bb-** *see* **sub-edit**

sub- *pref.* unter-; *(mit Fremdwörtern meist)* sub-

subˈalpine *adj. (Geog.) (of higher mountain slopes)* subalpin *(fachspr.)*; *(of lower Alpine slopes)* Voralpen-

subaltern [ˈsʌbltən] *n. (Brit. Mil.)* Subalternoffizier, *der*

subaqua [sʌbˈækwə] *adj.* Tauch⟨*sport, -klub*⟩

subaˈtomic *adj. (Phys.)* subatomar

ˈsubcategory *n.* Subkategorie, *die*

ˈsubclass *n. (esp. Biol.)* Unterklasse, *die*

ˈsubcommittee *n.* Unterausschuß, *der*

subˈconscious *(Psych.)* **1.** *adj.* unterbewußt; **~ mind** Unterbewußtsein, *das.* **2.** *n.* Unterbewußtsein, *das*

subˈconsciously *adv. (Psych.)* unterbewußt

subˈcontinent *n. (Geog.)* Subkontinent, *der*

subcontract 1. [sʌbkənˈtrækt] *v. t. (accept under secondary contract)* als Subunternehmer übernehmen; *(offer under secondary contract)* an Subunternehmer/an einen Subunternehmer vergeben; **~ a job to sb.** eine Arbeit an jmdn. [in einem Untervertrag] vergeben. **2.** *v. i. (accept secondary contract)* als Subunternehmer arbeiten; *(offer secondary contract)* Aufträge an Subunternehmer/an einen Subunternehmer vergeben. **3.** [sʌbˈkɒntrækt] *n.* Untervertrag, *der*

subconˈtractor *n.* Subunternehmer, *der*/-unternehmerin, *die*

ˈsubculture *n. (Sociol.)* Subkultur, *die*

subcuˈtaneous *adj. (Anat.)* subkutan

subdivide [ˈsʌbdɪvaɪd, sʌbdɪˈvaɪd] **1.** *v. t. (further divide)* erneut teilen; *(divide into parts)* unterteilen. **2.** *v. i.* **~ into sth.** sich in etw. *(Akk.)* teilen

subdivision [ˈsʌbdɪvɪʒn, sʌbdɪˈvɪʒn] *n. (subdividing)* erneute Teilung; *(subordinate division)* Unterabteilung, *die;* **~ [of sth.] into sth.** Unterteilung [einer Sache *(Gen.)*] in etw. *(Akk.)*

subˈdominant *n. (Mus.)* Subdominante, *die*

subdue [səbˈdjuː] *v. t. (conquer)* besiegen; unterwerfen; *(bring under control)* bändigen ⟨*Kind, Tier*⟩; ruhigstellen ⟨*Patienten*⟩; unter Kontrolle bringen ⟨*Demonstranten usw.*⟩; bezähmen ⟨*Gefühle, zornige Person*⟩; urbar machen ⟨*Land*⟩; *(reduce in intensity)* dämpfen ⟨*Zorn, Heftigkeit, gute Laune, Lärm, Licht*⟩; abkühlen *(fig.)* ⟨*Leidenschaft*⟩; verblassen lassen ⟨*Farben*⟩

subdued [səbˈdjuːd] *adj.* gedämpft; **he seemed rather ~:** er schien ziemlich gedämpfter Stimmung zu sein

sub-ˈedit *v. t. (Journ., Publishing)* **a)** *(be assistant editor of)* mit herausgeben; **b)** *(Brit.: prepare copy for)* redigieren

sub-ˈeditor *n. (Journ., Publishing)* **a)** *(assistant editor)* Mitherausgeber, *der*/Mitherausgeberin, *die;* **b)** *(Brit.: one who prepares ma-*

terial) Redaktionsassistent, *der/*-assistentin, *die*

'subgroup *n.* Untergruppe, *die*

'subhead, 'subheading *ns.* **a)** *(subordinate division)* Unterabschnitt, *der;* **b)** *(subordinate title)* Untertitel, *der*

sub'human *adj.* unmenschlich; *(Zool.)* menschenähnlich; **treat sb. as ~:** jmdn. wie einen Untermenschen behandeln

subject 1. ['sʌbdʒɪkt] *n.* **a)** *(citizen)* Staatsbürger, *der/*-bürgerin, *die; (in relation to monarch)* Untertan, *der/*Untertanin, *die; (under domination)* Sklave, *der/*Sklavin, *die (fig.);* **b)** *(topic)* Thema, *das; (department of study)* Fach, *das; (area of knowledge)* Fach[gebiet], *das; (Art)* Motiv, *das;* Sujet, *das (geh.); (Mus.)* Thema, *das;* **sb. is the ~ of a book** über jmdn. ist ein Buch geschrieben worden; **be the ~ of an investigation** Gegenstand einer Untersuchung sein; **on the ~ of money** über das Thema Geld ‹*reden usw.*›; beim Thema Geld ‹*sein, bleiben*›; **change the ~:** das Thema wechseln; **c) be a ~ for sth.** *(cause sth.)* zu etw. Anlaß geben; **she was a ~ for ridicule** man machte sich über sie lustig; **d)** *(Ling., Logic, Philos.)* Subjekt, *das;* **e)** *(Med.)* Patient, *der; (of scientific research)* Versuchsperson, *die/*-tier, *das/*-objekt, *das. See also* **liberty. 2.** *adj.* **a)** *(conditional)* **be ~ to sth.** von etw. abhängig sein *od.* abhängen; **sth. is ~ to alteration** etw. kann geändert werden; **prices/dates/programme details [are] ~ to alteration without further notice** Preis-/Termin-/Programmänderungen [sind] vorbehalten; **b)** *(prone)* **be ~ to** anfällig sein für ‹*Krankheit*›; neigen zu ‹*Melancholie*›; ausgesetzt sein (+ *Dat.*) ‹*Mißdeutung, Feuchtigkeit*›; **c)** *(dependent)* abhängig; **~ to** *(dependent on)* untertan (+ *Dat.*) ‹*König usw.*›; unterworfen (+ *Dat.*) ‹*Verfassung, Gesetz, Krone*›; untergeben (+ *Dat.*) ‹*Dienstherrn*›. **3.** *adv.* **~ to sth.** vorbehaltlich einer Sache *(Gen.);* **~ to the weather['s] being fine** vorausgesetzt, das Wetter ist gut. **4.** [səb'dʒekt] *v. t.* **a)** *(subjugate, make submissive)* unterwerfen; **~ sb./sth. to sb./sth.** jmdn./etw. jmdm./einer Sache unterwerfen; **b)** *(expose)* **~ sb./sth. to sth.** jmdn./etw. einer Sache *(Dat.)* aussetzen; **~ sb. to torture** jmdn. der Folter unterwerfen; **~ sth. to chemical analysis** etw. einer chemischen Analyse unterziehen

'subject: ~ catalogue *n.* Schlagwortkatalog, *der;* **~ heading** *n.* Stichwort, *das;* **~ index** *n.* Sachregister, *das*

subjection [səb'dʒekʃn] *n.* *(subjugation)* Unterwerfung, *die* **(to** unter + *Akk.*); *(condition of being subject)* Abhängigkeit, *die* **(to** von)

subjective [səb'dʒektɪv] *adj.* **a)** subjektiv; **b)** *(Ling.)* Subjekt-; **be ~:** Subjekt sein

subjectively [səb'dʒektɪvlɪ] *adv.* **a)** subjektiv; **~ speaking, I like him** ich persönlich mag ihn; **b)** *(Ling.)* als Subjekt ‹*gebrauchen*›

subjectiveness [səb'dʒektɪvnɪs], **subjectivity** [sʌbdʒɪk'tɪvɪtɪ] *ns., no pl.* Subjektivität, *die*

'subject-matter *n., no pl., no indef. art.* Gegenstand, *der;* **make good ~ for sth.** ein gutes Thema für etw. abgeben

sub judice [sʌb 'dʒu:dɪsɪ, sʊb'ju:dɪkeɪ] *adj.* *(Law)* anhängig; *(not decided)* [noch] nicht entschieden

subjugate ['sʌbdʒʊgeɪt] *v. t.* **a)** *(conquer)* unterjochen **(to** unter + *Akk.*); **b)** *(subdue)* bezwingen; bändigen ‹*Kind, Pferd*›

subjugation [sʌbdʒʊ'geɪʃn] *n.* **a)** *(conquest)* Unterjochung, *die* **(to** unter + *Akk.*); **b)** *(moral subjection) (action)* Knechtung, *die (geh. abwertend); (result)* Knechtschaft, *die; (of passions etc.)* Bezwingung, *die;* Unterwerfung, *die* **(to** unter + *Akk.*); *(condition)* sklavische Abhängigkeit **(to** von)

subjunctive [səb'dʒʌŋktɪv] *(Ling.)* **1.** *adj.* konjunktivisch; Konjunktiv-. **2.** *n.* Konjunktiv, *der;* **past/present ~:** Konjunktiv II *od.* Präteritum/Konjunktiv I *od.* Präsens

subjunctive 'mood *n.* *(Ling.)* Konjunktiv, *der*

sub'lease *see* **sublet**

sub'let *v. t.*, **-tt-, sublet** untervermieten

sub-lieu'tenant *n.* *(Brit. Navy)* Oberleutnant zur See

sublimate 1. ['sʌblɪmeɪt] *v. t.* *(Chem., Psych.; also fig.)* sublimieren. **2.** ['sʌblɪmət] *n.* *(sublimated substance)* Sublimat, *das (Chemie)*

sublimation [sʌblɪ'meɪʃn] *n.* **a)** *(Chem.) (act)* Sublimierung, *die; (process)* Sublimation, *die; (substance)* Sublimat, *das;* **b)** *(elevation; Psych.: diversion)* Sublimierung, *die* **(to** zu, **into** in + *Akk.*); Sublimation, *die*

sublime [sə'blaɪm] **1.** *adj.*, **~r** [sə'blaɪmə(r)], **~st** [sə'blaɪmɪst] *(exalted)* erhaben; *(iron.)* vollendet *(fig. iron.)* ‹*Chaos*›; unglaublich ‹*Frechheit*›; **sth. goes from the ~ to the ridiculous** *(iron.)* etw. ist ein echter Abstieg [ins Profane]. **2.** *v. t.* *(Chem.)* **a)** *(convert)* sublimieren; **b)** *(release)* freisetzen. **3.** *v. i.* *(Chem.)* sublimieren

sublimely [sə'blaɪmlɪ] *adv.* schlechthin vollkommen ‹*tanzen*›; erhaben ‹*handeln, edel*›; *(iron.)* vollkommen ‹*töricht, betrunken*›; völlig ‹*ohne Ahnung*›; **~ beautiful** von erhabener Schönheit *nachgestellt*

subliminal [sʌb'lɪmɪnl] *adj.* *(Physiol., Psych.)* unterschwellig; subliminal *(fachspr.);* **~ advertising** unterschwellige Werbung

sublimity [sə'blɪmɪtɪ] *n.* *(literary)* Erhabenheit, *die; (high degree)* hoher Grad **(of** an + *Dat.*)

Sub-Lt. *abbr.* *(Brit. Navy)* **Sub-Lieutenant** Olt. zur See

sub-ma'chine-gun *n.* Maschinenpistole, *die*

submarine [sʌbmə'ri:n, 'sʌbməri:n] **1.** *n.* Unterseeboot, *das;* U-Boot, *das.* **2.** *adj.* Unterwasser-; unterseeisch *(Geol.);* submarin *(fachspr.);* **~ warfare** U-Boot-Krieg, *der*

submerge [səb'mɜ:dʒ] **1.** *v. t.* **a)** *(place under water)* **~ sth. [in the water]** etw. eintauchen *od.* ins Wasser tauchen; **be ~d [at high tide]** [bei Flut] unter Wasser stehen; **b)** *(inundate)* ‹*Wasser:*› überschwemmen; **be ~d in water** unter Wasser stehen; **c)** *(fig.: obscure, bury)* **be ~d by** *or* **in sth.** unter etw. *(Dat.)* verborgen sein. **2.** *v. i.* abtauchen *(Seemannsspr.)*

submerged [səb'mɜ:dʒd] *adj.* versunken ‹*Schiff, Stadt*›; überschwemmt ‹*Felder*›; unter Wasser befindlich ‹*Fels, Eisberg*›; **~ in work** *(fig.)* mit Arbeit überhäuft; **~ by debts** *(fig.)* bis über die Ohren verschuldet *(ugs.)*

submersible [səb'mɜ:sɪbl] **1.** *adj.* tauchfähig. **2.** *n.* Tauchboot, *das*

submersion [səb'mɜ:ʃn] *n.* Eintauchen, *das; (in baptism)* Submersion, *die (Theol.);* **the watch will not withstand ~:** die Uhr ist nicht wasserfest

sub'miniature *adj.* Subminiatur-; *(Photog.)* Kleinstbild-

submission [səb'mɪʃn] *n.* **a)** *(surrender)* Unterwerfung, *die* **(to** unter + *Akk.*); **force/frighten sb. into ~:** jmdn. zwingen, sich zu unterwerfen/jmdm. durch Einschüchterung seinen Willen aufzwingen; **b)** *no pl., no art.* *(meekness)* Unterwerfung, *die;* **attitude of ~:** Demutshaltung, *die (Verhaltensf.);* **c)** *(presentation)* Einreichung, *die* **(to** bei); *(thing put forward)* Einsendung, *die; (by witness)* Aussage, *die;* **in my ~:** meiner Meinung nach

submissive [səb'mɪsɪv] *adj.* gehorsam; unterwürfig *(abwertend);* **be ~ to sb./sth.** sich jmdm./einer Sache unterwerfen

submissively [səb'mɪsɪvlɪ] *adv.* gehorsam; unterwürfig *(abwertend)*

submissiveness [səb'mɪsɪvnɪs] *n., no pl.* Gehorsam, *der;* Unterwürfigkeit, *die (abwertend)*

submit [səb'mɪt] **1.** *v. t.*, **-tt- a)** *(present)* einreichen; vorbringen ‹*Vorschlag*›; abgeben ‹*[Doktor]arbeit usw.*›; **~ sth. for sb.'s approval/perusal** jmdm. etw. zur Billigung vorlegen/zu lesen geben; **~ sth. to sb.** jmdm. etw. vorlegen; **~ sth. to scrutiny/investigation** etw. einer Prüfung/Untersuchung unterziehen; **~ sth. to sb.'s examination** jmdm. etw. zur Prüfung vorlegen; **~ one's entry to a competition** seine Teilnehmerkarte *usw.* für ein Preisausschreiben einsenden; **entries must be ~ted by 1 May** Einsendeschluß ist der 1. Mai; **~ that ...** *(urge deferentially)* behaupten, daß ...; **b)** *(surrender)* **~ oneself to sb./sth.** sich jmdm./einer Sache unterwerfen; **~ oneself to Fate** sich in sein Schicksal fügen; **~ oneself to ridicule** sich dem Spott aussetzen; **c)** *(subject)* **~ sth. to heat** etw. der Hitze *(Dat.)* aussetzen; **~ sb. to a treatment** jmdn. einer Behandlung *(Dat.)* unterziehen; **~ oneself to sth.** sich einer Sache *(Dat.)* unterziehen. **2.** *v. i.*, **-tt- a)** *(surrender)* aufgeben; sich unterwerfen **(to** *Dat.*); **~ to sb.'s charms** jmds. Zauber *(Dat.)* erliegen; **~ to sb.'s request** jmds. Bitte *(Dat.)* nachkommen; **b)** *(defer)* **~ to sb./sth.** sich jmdm./einer Sache beugen; **c)** *(agree to undergo)* **~ to sth.** sich einer Sache *(Dat.)* aussetzen

sub'normal *adj.* unterdurchschnittlich; subnormal *(Med.); (in intelligence)* minderbegabt

subordinate 1. [sə'bɔ:dɪnət] *adj.* *(inferior)* untergeordnet; *(lower-ranking)* rangniedriger; *(secondary)* zweitrangig; **be ~ to sb./sth.** jmdm./einer Sache untergeordnet sein; **be of ~ importance** von untergeordneter Bedeutung sein; *see also* **clause b. 2.** *n.* Untergebene, *der/die.* **3.** [sə'bɔ:dɪneɪt] *v. t.* *(place in lower class)* niedriger einstufen **(to** als); *(render subject; also Ling.)* unterordnen **(to** *Dat.*)

suborn [sə'bɔ:n] *v. t.* anstiften; *(by bribery)* bestechen

'sub-plot *n.* Nebenhandlung, *die*

subpoena [səb'pi:nə, sə'pi:nə] *(Law)* **1.** *n.* Vorladung, *die:* **serve a ~ [up]on sb.** jmdm. eine Vorladung persönlich zustellen. **2.** *v. t.*, **~ed** *or* **~'d** [səb'pi:nəd, sə'pi:nəd] vorladen

sub rosa [sʌb 'rəʊzə] *(literary)* **1.** *adj.* Subrosa- *(geh.);* [streng] geheim. **2.** *adv.* sub rosa *(geh.);* in aller Heimlichkeit

'subroutine *n.* *(Computing)* Unterprogramm, *das;* Subroutine, *die*

subscribe [səb'skraɪb] **1.** *v. t.* **a)** *(sign one's name to)* unterzeichnen; **b)** *([promise to] contribute)* **~ sth.** zusichern, etw. zu spenden; **be ~d** als Spende zugesichert worden sein; **have ~d half the costs** sich verpflichtet haben, die Hälfte der Kosten zu übernehmen. **2.** *v. i.* **a)** *(express adhesion)* **~ to sth.** sich einer Sache *(Dat.)* anschließen; **b)** *(sign one's name)* unterzeichnen **(to** *Akk.*); **c)** *([promise to] make contribution)* **~ to** *or* **for sth.** eine Spende für etw. zusichern; **~ to [a newspaper]** [eine Zeitung] abonnieren

subscriber [səb'skraɪbə(r)] *n.* **a)** *(one who signs)* Unterzeichner, *der/*Unterzeichnerin, *die* **(of, to** *Gen.*); Unterzeichnete, *der/die (Amtsdt.);* **b)** *(one who assents)* Befürworter, *der/*Befürworterin, *die* **(to** *Gen.*); **c)** *(contributor)* Spender, *der/*Spenderin, *die* **(of, to** für); *(to a newspaper etc.)* Abonnent, *der/*Abonnentin, *die* **(to** *Gen.*); *(of a society etc.)* Mitglied, *das;* **d)** *(Teleph.)* Fernsprechkunde, *der/*-kundin, *die*

subscriber trunk 'dialling *n.* *(Brit. Teleph.)* Selbstwählferndienst, *der*

'subscript *(Math. etc.)* **1.** *adj.* tiefgestellt. **2.** *n.* [tiefgestellter] Index

subscription [səb'skrɪpʃn] *n.* **a)** *(thing sub-*

scribed) Spendenbeitrag, *der* **(to** für); *(membership fee)* Mitgliedsbeitrag, *der* **(to** für); *(prepayment for newspaper etc.)* Abonnement, *das* **(to** *Gen.*); **[buy] by ~:** im Abonnement [beziehen]; **a year's ~:** ein Jahresabonnement; **b)** *(act of subscribing) (signing)* Unterzeichnung, *die; (subscribing money)* Spende, *die;* **[be built] by ~:** mit Spenden [gebaut werden]; **c)** *(Publishing: offer of lower price)* Subskription, *die*

subscription: ~ concert *n.* Abonnementskonzert, *das;* **~ library** *n. (Mitgliedsbeiträge erhebende)* Leihbücherei

'subsection *n.* Unterabschnitt, *der*

subsequent ['sʌbsɪkwənt] *adj.* folgend; nachfolgend ⟨*Kind*⟩; später ⟨*Gelegenheit*⟩; **~ events** spätere *od.* die folgenden Ereignisse

subservient [səb'sɜːvɪənt] *adj.* **a)** *(merely instrumental)* dienend; **be ~ to sb./sth.** jmdm./einer Sache dienen; **b)** *(subordinate)* untergeordnet **(to** *Dat.*); **c)** *(obsequious)* unterwürfig; servil *(abwertend)*

'subset *n. (Math.)* Teilmenge, *die*

subside [səb'saɪd] *v. i.* **a)** *(sink to lower level)* ⟨*Wasser, Flut, Fluß:*⟩ sinken; ⟨*Boden, Haus:*⟩ sich senken; ⟨*Schwellung:*⟩ zurückgehen; ⟨*schwebende Teile:*⟩ absinken, sich absetzen; **~ in exhaustion** erschöpft zusammensinken; **~ [on] to one's knees/the ground** auf die Knie/zu Boden sinken; **b)** *(abate)* nachlassen; ⟨*Wellen, Wind, Wut, Lärm, Beifall, Aufregung:*⟩ sich legen; ⟨*Fieber, Delirium, Migräne:*⟩ abklingen; *(cease activity)* müde werden; ermatten *(geh.)*; **~ into** verfallen in (+ *Akk.*) ⟨*Untätigkeit, Schweigen usw.*⟩

subsidence [səb'saɪdəns, 'sʌbsɪdəns] *n.* **a)** *(sinking) (of ground, structure)* Senkung, *die; (of liquid)* Sinken, *das; (of swelling)* Zurückgehen, *das; (of suspended matter)* Sichabsetzen, *das;* **b)** *(abatement) see* **subside b**: Nachlassen, *das;* Sichlegen, *das;* Abklingen, *das;* **~ into sth.** Verfallen in etw. *(Akk.)*

subsidiary [səb'sɪdɪərɪ] **1.** *adj.* **a)** *(auxiliary)* unterstützend; subsidiär *(fachspr.)*; untergeordnet ⟨*Funktion, Stellung*⟩; Neben⟨*fach, -fluß, -aspekt*⟩; **~ fund** Hilfsfond, *der;* **~ to sth.** einer Sache *(Dat.)* untergeordnet; *(secondary)* gegenüber einer Sache zweitrangig; **b)** *(Commerc.)* **~ company** *see* **2. 2.** *n. (Commerc.)* Tochtergesellschaft, *die*

subsidisation, subsidise *see* **subsidiz-**

subsidization [sʌbsɪdaɪ'zeɪʃn] *n.* *(act of subsidizing)* Subventionierung, *die; (money given as subsidy)* Subventionen; *(of individual person)* finanzielle Unterstützung

subsidize ['sʌbsɪdaɪz] *v. t.* subventionieren; finanziell unterstützen ⟨*Person*⟩

subsidy ['sʌbsɪdɪ] *n.* Subvention, *die;* **receive a ~:** subventioniert werden; **grant/pay a ~ to sb./sth.** jmdn./etw. subventionieren; jmdn./etw. mit öffentlichen Mitteln fördern

subsist [səb'sɪst] *v. i.* **a)** *([continue to] exist)* existieren; *(remain in force)* bestehen; **b)** *(keep oneself alive)* existieren; subsistieren *(veralt.)*; **~ on sth.** von etw. leben

subsistence [səb'sɪstəns] *n.* **a)** *(subsisting)* [Über]leben, *das;* **be enough for a bare ~:** gerade genug zum [Über]leben sein; ⟨*Einkommen:*⟩ das Existenzminimum sein; **~ is not possible under these conditions** unter diesen Bedingungen kann man nicht leben *od.* existieren; **b) [means of] ~:** Lebensgrundlage, *die;* **millet is their chief means of ~:** sie leben hauptsächlich von Hirse

subsistence: ~ allowance *n.* Außendienstzulage, *die; (abroad)* Auslandszulage, *die;* **~ farming** *n.* Subsistenzwirtschaft, *die (Soziol., Wirtsch.)*; **~ level** *n.* Existenzminimum, *das;* **live at ~ level** gerade genug zum Leben haben; **~ wage** *n.* ≈ Existenzminimum, *das*

'subsoil *n.* Untergrund, *der*

sub'sonic *adj.* Unterschall-

'subspecies *n., pl. same (Biol.)* Unterart, *die*

substance ['sʌbstəns] *n.* **a)** Stoff, *der;* Substanz, *die;* **b)** *no pl. (solidity)* Substanz, *die;* **this is an argument of little ~:** dieses Argument ist ziemlich substanzlos; **the food lacks ~:** das Essen ist nicht sehr gehaltvoll; **a man of ~:** ein begüterter Mann; **c)** *no pl. (content) (of book etc.)* Inhalt, *der;* **there is not enough ~ in the plot** die Handlung gibt nicht genug her; **there is no ~ in his claim/the rumour** seine Behauptung/das Gerücht entbehrt jeder Grundlage; **d)** *no pl. (essence)* Kern, *der;* **in ~:** im wesentlichen

sub'standard *adj.* **a)** unzulänglich; **the printing/recording was ~:** der Druck/die Aufnahme war nicht zufriedenstellend; **b)** *(Ling.)* nicht standardsprachlich

substantial [səb'stænʃl] *adj.* **a)** *(considerable)* beträchtlich; erheblich ⟨*Zugeständnis, Verbesserung*⟩; größer... ⟨*Darlehen*⟩; **'~ price required'** „namhafte Summe erforderlich"; **b)** gehaltvoll ⟨*Essen, Nahrung*⟩; **you need something more ~ [to eat]** du brauchst etwas Gehaltvolleres *od.* Kräftigeres [zu essen]; **c)** *(solid in structure)* solide, stabil ⟨*Möbel*⟩; solide ⟨*Haus*⟩; kräftig ⟨*Körperbau*⟩; wesentlich ⟨*Unterschied, Argument*⟩; **d)** *(having substance)* stofflich; materiell; **e)** *(well-to-do)* begütert ⟨*Person*⟩; zahlungskräftig ⟨*Firma*⟩; **f)** weitgehend ⟨*Übereinstimmung, Zustimmung*⟩; ziemlich sicher ⟨*Beweis*⟩; **be in ~ agreement** sich *(Dat.)* so gut wie *od.* praktisch einig sein

substantially [səb'stænʃəlɪ] *adv.* **a)** *(considerably)* wesentlich; **b)** *(solidly)* **~ built** solide gebaut ⟨*Haus usw.*⟩; kräftig gebaut ⟨*Person*⟩; **c)** *(essentially)* im wesentlichen; **~ free from sth.** weitgehend frei von etw.

substantiate [səb'stænʃɪeɪt] *v. t.* erhärten; untermauern

substantiation [səbstænʃɪ'eɪʃn] *n.* Erhärtung, *die;* Untermauerung, *die;* **in ~ of his claim** zur Erhärtung *od.* Untermauerung seines Anspruchs

substantive 1. [səb'stæntɪv] *adj.* **a)** *(not amended)* in der vorliegenden Form *nachgestellt;* **b)** *(Mil.)* **a ~ rank** der Rang eines Berufssoldaten. **2.** ['sʌbstəntɪv] *n. (Ling.)* Substantiv, *das*

'substation *n. (Electr.)* Hochspannungsverteilungsanlage, *die*

substitutable ['sʌbstɪtjuːtəbl] *adj.* substituierbar

substitute ['sʌbstɪtjuːt] **1.** *n.* **a) ~[s]** Ersatz, *der;* **~s for rubber** Ersatzstoffe für Gummi; **coffee ~:** Kaffee-Ersatz, *der;* **there is no ~ for real ale/hard work** es geht nichts über das echte englische Bier/über harte Arbeit; **b)** *(Sport)* Ersatzspieler, *der/*-spielerin, *die.* **2.** *adj.* Ersatz-; **a ~ teacher/secretary** *etc.* eine Vertretung. **3.** *v. t.* **a) ~ A for B** B durch A ersetzen; **~ oil for butter** statt Butter Öl nehmen; **~ a striker for a midfield player** einen Mittelfeldspieler gegen einen Stürmer auswechseln *od.* austauschen; **he doesn't like potatoes, so we ~d rice** da er keine Kartoffeln mag, gaben wir ihm statt dessen Reis; **b)** *(coll.)* **~ A by** *or* **with B** A durch B ersetzen. **4.** *v. i.* **~ for sb.** jmdn. vertreten; für jmdn. einspringen; *(Sport)* für jmdn. ins Spiel kommen; **Thompson ~d for Clark just after half-time** kurz nach der Halbzeit kam Thompson für Clark ins Spiel *od.* wurde Clark gegen Thompson ausgetauscht

substitution [sʌbstɪ'tjuːʃn] *n.* Ersetzung, *die;* Substitution, *die (geh., fachspr.)*; *(Sport)* Spielerwechsel, *der;* **~ of A for B** Verwendung von A statt B; **make a ~** *(Sport)* [einen Spieler] auswechseln

sub'stratum *n., pl.* **substrata a)** *(Geol.)* **a ~ of rock** ein felsiger Untergrund; **b)** *(Ling., Biol., Chem., fig.)* Substrat, *das (geh., fachspr.)*

'substructure *n.* Unterbau, *der; (of oil rig also)* Stützkonstruktion, *die*

subsume [səb'sjuːm] *v. t.* einordnen **(in, into** in + *Akk.*); **~ an item under a category** einen Punkt einer Kategorie *(Dat.)* zuordnen

'sub-system *n.* Subsystem, *das (geh.)*; Teilsystem, *das*

'subtenancy *n.* Untervermietung, *die; (of land, farm, shop)* Unterverpachtung, *die; (relationship)* Untermiete, *die; (of land, farm, shop)* Unterpacht, *die*

'subtenant *n.* Untermieter, *der/*-mieterin, *die; (of land, farm, shop)* Unterpächter, *der/*-pächterin, *die*

subtend [sʌb'tend] *v. t. (Geom.)* gegenüberliegen (+ *Dat.*) ⟨*Winkel*⟩; schneiden ⟨*Bogen*⟩

subterfuge ['sʌbtəfjuːdʒ] *n.* **a)** *no pl., no art.* Täuschungsmanöver *Pl.;* **b)** *(trick)* Trick, *der*

subterranean [sʌbtə'reɪnɪən] *adj.* unterirdisch; subterran *(fachspr.)*

'subtitle 1. *n. (for film, of book, etc.)* Untertitel, *der.* **2.** *v. t.* untertiteln; **the book is ~d ...:** das Buch hat den Untertitel ...

subtle ['sʌtl] *adj.,* **~r** ['sʌtlə(r)], **~st** ['sʌtlɪst] **a)** *(delicate)* zart ⟨*Duft, Dunst, Parfüm*⟩; fein ⟨*Geschmack, Aroma*⟩; **b)** *(elusive)* subtil *(geh.)*; fein ⟨*Unterschied*⟩; unaufdringlich ⟨*Charme*⟩; **c)** *(refined)* fein ⟨*Ironie, Humor*⟩; zart ⟨*Hinweis*⟩; subtil *(geh.)* ⟨*Scherz*⟩; **d)** *(perceptive)* feinsinnig ⟨*Beobachter, Kritiker*⟩; fein ⟨*Intellekt*⟩; **~ perception** feines Gespür; **e)** *(ingenious)* geschickt; raffiniert ⟨*Plan*⟩; **~ art** hohe Kunst

subtlety ['sʌtltɪ] *n.* **a)** *no pl. see* **subtle:** Zartheit, *die;* Feinheit, *die;* Subtilität, *die (geh.)*; Unaufdringlichkeit, *die;* Feinsinnigkeit, *die;* Geschicklichkeit, *die;* Raffiniertheit, *die;* **b) subtleties** Feinheiten

subtly ['sʌtlɪ] *adv.* auf subtile Weise *(geh.)*; zart ⟨*hinweisen auf, andeuten*⟩; geschickt ⟨*argumentieren*⟩; **~ flavoured/perfumed** von feinem Geschmack *nachgestellt*/zart duftend

'subtotal *n.* Zwischensumme, *die*

subtract [səb'trækt] *v. t.* abziehen **(from** von); subtrahieren **(from** von)

subtraction [səb'trækʃn] *n.* Subtraktion, *die;* Abziehen, *das*

sub'tropical *adj.* subtropisch

suburb ['sʌbɜːb] *n.* Vorort, *der;* **live in the ~s** am Stadtrand leben

suburban [sə'bɜːbən] *adj.* **a)** *(of suburbs)* Vorort-; ⟨*Leben, Haus*⟩ am Stadtrand; **~ spread** *or* **sprawl** eintönige, endlose Vororte; **b)** *(derog.: limited in outlook)* spießig *(abwertend)*

suburbanite [sə'bɜːbənaɪt] *n.* Vorstädter, *der/*Vorstädterin, *die*

suburbia [sə'bɜːbɪə] *n. (derog.)* die [eintönigen] Vororte

subvention [səb'venʃn] *n.* Subvention, *die (Wirtsch.)*

subversion [səb'vɜːʃn] *n.* Subversion, *die; (of government, monarchy, etc.)* [Um]sturz, *der*

subversive [səb'vɜːsɪv] **1.** *adj.* subversiv; **be ~ of sth.** etw. unterminieren. **2.** *n.* Subversive, *der/die*

subversively [səb'vɜːsɪvlɪ] *adv.* subversiv

subvert [səb'vɜːt] *v. t.* stürzen ⟨*Monarchie, Regierung*⟩; unterminieren ⟨*Moral, Loyalität*⟩; [zur Illoyalität] aufstacheln ⟨*Person*⟩

'subway *n.* **a)** *(passage)* Unterführung, *die;* **b)** *(Amer.: railway)* Untergrundbahn, *die;* U-Bahn, *die (ugs.)*

sub'zero *adj.* **~ temperatures/conditions** Temperaturen unter Null

succeed [sək'siːd] **1.** *v. i.* **a)** *(achieve aim)* Erfolg haben; **sb. ~s in sth.** jmdm. gelingt etw.; jmd. schafft etw.; **sb. ~s in doing sth.** es gelingt jmdm., etw. zu tun; jmd. schafft es, etw. zu tun; **~ in business/college** geschäftlich/im Studium erfolgreich sein; **I did not ~ in doing it** ich habe es nicht geschafft; es ist mir nicht gelungen; **I ~ed in passing the test** ich habe die Prüfung mit Erfolg *od.* erfolgreich abgelegt; **he usually ~s in anything he puts his mind to** ihm gelingt gewöhnlich alles, was er sich *(Dat.)* vornimmt; **~ in one's aims** seine Ziele erreichen; **the plan did not ~**: der Plan ist gescheitert; **b)** *(come next)* die Nachfolge antreten; **~ to an office/the throne** die Nachfolge in einem Amt/die Thronfolge antreten; **~ to a title/an estate** einen Titel/ein Gut erben. **2.** *v. t.* **a)** *(take place of)* ablösen ⟨*Monarchen, Beamten*⟩; **~ sb. [in a post]** jmds. Nachfolge [in einem Amt] antreten; **b)** *(follow)* **day ~ed day** ein Tag folgte auf den anderen

succeeding [sək'si:dɪŋ] *adj.* [nach]folgend; *(one after another)* aufeinanderfolgend ⟨*Generationen, Regierungen*⟩

success [sək'ses] *n.* Erfolg, *der;* **meet with ~**: Erfolg haben; erfolgreich sein; **make a ~ of sth.** bei etw. Erfolg haben; **'wishing you every ~'** „ich wünsche/wir wünschen Ihnen viel Erfolg"; **have little/considerable ~ in doing sth.** wenig/beträchtlichen Erfolg dabei haben, etw. zu tun; **I didn't have much ~ with her** ich war bei ihr nicht sonderlich erfolgreich; **~ at last!** endlich hat es geklappt! *(ugs.)*; **nothing succeeds like ~** *(prov.)* nichts ist so erfolgreich wie der Erfolg *(Spr.)*; **he was a great ~ as headmaster/Hamlet** er war als Schulleiter sehr erfolgreich/als Hamlet ein großer Erfolg

successful [sək'sesfl] *adj.* erfolgreich; **be ~ in sth./doing sth.** Erfolg bei etw. haben/dabei haben, etw. zu tun; **he was ~ in his attempts to ...**: es gelang ihm, ... zu ...; **she made a ~ attempt on the record** der Rekordversuch ist ihr gelungen

successfully [sək'sesfəlɪ] *adv.* erfolgreich; **he ~ avoided the question** es gelang ihm, der Frage auszuweichen

succession [sək'seʃn] *n.* **a)** Folge, *die;* **four games/years** *etc.* **in ~**: vier Spiele/Jahre *usw.* hintereinander; **in quick/rapid ~**: in schneller/rascher Folge; **in close ~** *(in space)* dicht hintereinander; *(in time)* kurz hintereinander; **the ~ of the seasons** die Abfolge der Jahreszeiten; **b)** *(series)* Serie, *die;* **a ~ of losses/visitors** eine Verlust-/Besucherserie; **c)** *(right of succeeding to the throne etc.)* Erbfolge, *die;* **he is second in ~**: er ist Zweiter in der Erbfolge; **in ~ to his uncle** als Nachfolger seines Onkels; **the apostolic ~** *(RC Ch.)* die Apostolische Nachfolge *od.* Sukzession

successive [sək'sesɪv] *adj.* aufeinanderfolgend; **five ~ games/jobs** fünf Spiele/Stellungen hintereinander

successively [sək'sesɪvlɪ] *adv.* hintereinander

successor [sək'sesə(r)] *n.* Nachfolger, *der*/Nachfolgerin, *die;* **sb.'s ~, the ~ to sb.** jmds. Nachfolger; **the ~ to the throne** der Nachfolger auf dem Thron

suc'cess story *n.* Erfolgsstory, *die (ugs.)*; **he is a typical American ~**: er hat eine typische amerikanische Erfolgskarriere hinter sich *(Dat.)*

succinct [sək'sɪŋkt] *adj.* *(terse)* knapp; *(clear, to the point)* prägnant

succinctly [sək'sɪŋktlɪ] *adv.* *(tersely)* in knappen Worten; *(clearly)* prägnant

succinctness [sək'sɪŋktnɪs] *n., no pl.* *(terseness)* Knappheit, *die; (clarity)* Prägnanz, *die*

succour *(Amer.:* **succor***)* ['sʌkə(r)] *(literary)* **1.** *v. t.* Beistand leisten (+ *Dat.*). **2.** *n.* Beistand, *der;* Unterstützung, *die;* **bring ~ to the wounded** die Leiden der Verwundeten lindern

succulence ['sʌkjʊləns] *n., no pl.* Saftigkeit, *die*

succulent ['sʌkjʊlənt] **1.** *adj.* **a)** saftig ⟨*Pfirsich, Steak usw.*⟩; **b)** *(Bot.)* sukkulent; fleischig; **~ plants** Sukkulenten. **2.** *n. (Bot.)* Sukkulente, *die;* Fettpflanze, *die*

succulently ['sʌkjʊləntlɪ] *adv.* saftig

succumb [sə'kʌm] *v. i.* **a)** *(be forced to give way)* unterliegen; **~ to sth.** einer Sache *(Dat.)* erliegen; **~ to grief/despair** in Kummer/Verzweiflung verfallen; **~ to temptation** der Versuchung erliegen; **~ to pressure** dem Druck nachgeben; **b)** *(die)* **~ [to one's illness/wounds** *etc.*] seiner Krankheit/seinen Verletzungen *usw.* erliegen

such [sʌtʃ] **1.** *adj., no compar. or superl.* **a)** *(of that kind)* solch ...; **~ a person** solch *od. (ugs.)* so ein Mensch; ein solcher Mensch; **~ a book** solch *od. (ugs.)* so ein Buch; ein solches Buch; **~ people** solche Leute; **~ things** so etwas; **symphonies and other ~ compositions** Sinfonien und andere Kompositionen dieser Art; **shoplifting and ~ crimes** Ladendiebstahl und derartige *od.* ähnliche Vergehen; **there are many ~ cases** so etwas kommt oft vor; **or some ~ thing** oder so etwas; oder etwas in der Art; **some ~ plan** irgend so ein Plan *(ugs.)*; **I said no ~ thing** ich habe nichts dergleichen gesagt; **you'll do no ~ thing** das wirst du nicht tun; **there is no ~ bird** solch einen *od.* einen solchen Vogel gibt es nicht; **experiences ~ as these** solche *od.* derartige Erfahrungen; **there is no ~ thing as a unicorn** Einhörner gibt es gar nicht; **there is no ~ thing as honour among thieves** Diebe kennen keine Ehre; **~ writers as Eliot and Fry** Schriftsteller wie Eliot und Fry; **~ grapes as you never saw** Trauben, wie du sie noch nie gesehen hast; **I will take ~ steps as I think necessary** ich werde die Schritte unternehmen, die ich für notwendig halte; **~ money as I have** das bißchen Geld, das ich habe; **at ~ a time** zu einer solchen Zeit; **at ~ a moment as this** in einem Augenblick wie diesem; *(disapproving)* gerade jetzt; **in ~ a case** in einem solchen *od. (ugs.)* so einem Fall; **for** *or* **on ~ an occasion** zu einem solchen Anlaß; **by all means stay for lunch, ~ as it is** bleib doch zum Mittagessen, aber es gibt nichts Besonderes; **~ a one as he/she is impossible to replace** jemand wie er/sie ist unersetzlich; *see also* **another 1b; luck b; b)** *(so great)* solch ...; derartig; **I got ~ a fright that ...**: ich bekam einen derartigen *od. (ugs.)* so einen Schrecken, daß ...; **your stupidity is ~ as to fill me with despair** deine Dummheit treibt mich noch zur Verzweiflung; **~ was the force of the explosion that ...**: die Explosion war so stark, daß ...; **to ~ an extent** dermaßen; **c)** *(with adj.)* so; **~ a big house** ein so großes Haus; **she has ~ lovely blue eyes** sie hat so schöne blaue Augen; **~ a wonderfully fresh green** so ein herrlich frisches Grün; **~ a long time** so lange. **2.** *pron.* **a)** as **~**: als solcher/solche/solches; *(strictly speaking)* im Grunde genommen; an sich; **this is not a promotion as ~**: dies ist im Grunde genommen *od.* eigentlich keine Beförderung; **~ is not the case** das ist nicht der Fall; **~ is life** so ist das Leben; **~ as** wie [zum Beispiel]; **~ 'as?** zum Beispiel?; **b)** *(people or things of stated kind)* **all ~**: alle seinesgleichen/ihresgleichen; **we do not have any ~**: wir haben nichts dergleichen; **or some ~**: oder so etwas; **I can give you ~ as I have** ich kann dir [das Wenige] geben, was ich habe

such-and-such ['sʌtʃənsʌtʃ] **1.** *adj.* **in ~ a place at ~ a time** an dem und dem Ort um die und die Zeit; **Mr ~**: Herr Sowieso. **2.** *pron.* der und der/die und die/das und das

suchlike ['sʌtʃlaɪk] *(coll.)* **1.** *pron.* derlei. **2.** *attrib. adj.* dergleichen

suck [sʌk] **1.** *v. t.* saugen **(out of** aus); lutschen ⟨*Bonbon*⟩; saugen an (+ *Dat.*) ⟨*Pfeife*⟩; **~ one's thumb** am Daumen lutschen; **~ an orange dry** eine Apfelsine auslutschen; **~ sb. dry** *(extort all sb.'s money)* jmdn. bis aufs Blut aussaugen; *(exhaust sb.)* jmdn. auslaugen. **2.** *v. i.* ⟨*Baby:*⟩ saugen; **~ at sth.** an etw. *(Dat.)* saugen; **~ at a lollipop** an einem Lutscher lecken; einen Lolli lutschen. **3.** *n.* **have a ~ at an ice lolly/at a straw** an einem Eis lutschen/Strohhalm saugen *od.* ziehen

~ 'down *v. t.* hinunterziehen; ⟨*Strudel:*⟩ in die Tiefe ziehen

~ 'in *v. t.* einsaugen; ⟨*Strudel:*⟩ in die Tiefe ziehen

~ 'off *v. t. (coarse)* **~ sb. off** jmdm. einen ablutschen *od.* abkauen *(vulg.)*

~ 'under *v. t.* in die Tiefe ziehen

~ 'up 1. *v. t.* aufsaugen ⟨*Staub, Feuchtigkeit*⟩; *(with a straw)* einsaugen; *(into a pipette)* ansaugen; *(by dredger, tubes, etc.)* verschlucken. **2.** *v. i.* **~ up to sb.** *(sl.)* jmdm. in den Hintern kriechen *(salopp)*

sucker ['sʌkə(r)] *n.* **a)** *(suction pad)* Saugfuß, *der; (Zool.)* Saugnapf, *der; (of leech)* Saugscheibe, *die;* **b)** *(one attracted)* **be a ~ for sb./sth.** eine Schwäche für jmdn./etw. haben; **c)** *(sl.: dupe)* Dumme, *der/die;* **poor ~**: armer Trottel; **he's always being had for a ~**: er fällt immer auf alles herein; **d)** *(Bot.)* unterirdischer Ausläufer; **e)** *(fish)* Sauger, *der;* **f)** *(Amer.) see* **lollipop**

'sucking-pig *n.* Spanferkel, *das*

suckle ['sʌkl] **1.** *v. t.* säugen. **2.** *v. i.* [an der Brust] trinken

suckling ['sʌklɪŋ] *n. (unweaned child)* Säugling, *der;* **these piglets are still ~s** diese Ferkel werden noch gesäugt; *see also* **mouth 1 a**

sucrose ['su:krəʊz, 'sju:krəʊz] *n. (Chem.)* Saccharose, *die*

suction ['sʌkʃn] *n.* **a)** *(sucking)* Absaugen, *das; (force)* Saugwirkung, *die;* **b)** *(of air, currents, etc.)* Sog, *der;* **work by ~**: durch Saugwirkung arbeiten

suction: ~-pad *n.* Saugfuß, *der;* **~ pump** *n.* Saugpumpe, *die*

Sudan [su:'dɑ:n] *pr. n.* **[the] ~**: [der] Sudan

Sudanese [su:də'ni:z] **1.** *adj.* sudanesisch; **sb. is ~**: jmd. ist Sudanese/Sudanesin. **2.** *n., pl. same* Sudanese, *der*/Sudanesin, *die*

sudden ['sʌdn] **1.** *adj.* **a)** *(unexpected)* plötzlich; **I had a ~ thought** auf einmal *od.* plötzlich fiel mir etwas ein; **b)** *(abrupt, without warning)* jäh ⟨*Abgrund, Übergang, Ruck*⟩; **there was a ~ bend in the road** plötzlich machte die Straße eine Biegung. **2.** *n.* **all of a ~**: plötzlich

sudden 'death *attrib. adj. (Sport coll.)* **a ~ play-off** ein Stichentscheid; *(Footb.: using penalties)* ein Elfmeterschießen

suddenly ['sʌdnlɪ] *adv.* plötzlich

suddenness ['sʌdnnɪs] *n., no pl.* Plötzlichkeit, *die*

suds [sʌdz] *n. pl.* **a) [soap-]~** [Seifen]lauge, *die; (froth)* Schaum, *der;* **b)** *(Amer. sl.: beer)* Gerstensaft, *der (scherzh.)*

sudsy ['sʌdzɪ] *adj. (coll.)* seifig; *(frothy)* schaumig

sue [su:, sju:] **1.** *v. t. (Law)* verklagen **(for** auf + *Akk.*). **2.** *v. i.* **a)** *(Law)* klagen **(for** auf + *Akk.*); **b)** *(fig.)* **~ for peace/mercy** um Frieden/Gnade bitten

suede [sweɪd] *n.* Wildleder, *das; (finer)* Veloursleder, *das*

suet ['su:ɪt, 'sju:ɪt] *n.* Talg, *der*

suet 'pudding *n. mit Talg zubereiteter Pudding*

Suez ['sʊɪz, 'sju:ɪz] *pr. n.* Suez *(das);* **~ Canal** Suez-Kanal, *der*

suffer ['sʌfə(r)] **1.** *v. t.* **a)** *(undergo)* erleiden ⟨*Verlust, Unrecht, Schmerz, Niederlage*⟩; durchmachen, erleben ⟨*Schweres, Kummer*⟩; dulden ⟨*Unverschämtheit*⟩; **~ disablement** invalide werden; **the dollar ~ed further losses against the yen** der Dollar mußte weitere Einbußen gegenüber dem Yen hinnehmen; **~ neglect** vernachlässigt werden; **b)** *(tolerate)* dulden; **not ~ fools gladly** mit

dummen Leuten keine Geduld haben; **c)** *(arch.: allow)* lassen; **~ sth. to be done** *(Bibl.)* etw. geschehen lassen; **~ the little children to come unto me** *(Bibl.)* lasset die Kindlein zu mir kommen; **he ~s no one to contradict him** er duldet *od. (veralt.)* leidet keinen Widerspruch. **2.** *v.i.* leiden; **~ for sth.** *(for a cause)* für etw. leiden; *(in expiation)* für etw. büßen; **the engine ~ed severely** der Motor hat sehr gelitten; **if you publish this article, your reputation will ~:** wenn Sie diesen Artikel veröffentlichen, wird das Ihrem Ruf schaden
~ from *v.t.* leiden unter (+ *Dat.*); leiden an (+ *Dat.*) ‹*Krankheit*›; **~ from shock** unter Schock[wirkung] stehen; **~ from faulty planning/bad execution** an falscher Planung/schlechter Durchführung kranken; **the trees have ~ed from the frost** die Bäume haben durch den Frost gelitten
sufferance ['sʌfərəns] *n.* Duldung, *die;* **his behaviour is beyond ~:** sein Benehmen ist unerträglich; **he remains here on ~ only** er ist hier bloß geduldet
sufferer ['sʌfərə(r)] *n.* Betroffene, *der/die; (from disease)* Leidende, *der/die;* **~s from rheumatism/arthritis, rheumatism/arthritis ~s** Rheuma-/Arthritisleidende
suffering ['sʌfərɪŋ] *n.* Leiden, *das;* **he had experienced untold ~ from cancer** als Krebskranker hatte er unsäglich gelitten; **her ~s are now at an end** sie hat jetzt ausgelitten *(geh.)*
suffice [sə'faɪs] **1.** *v.i.* genügen; **~ it to say: ...:** nur soviel sei gesagt: ...; **this ~d to infuriate her** das genügte *od.* reichte schon, um sie wütend zu machen. **2.** *v.t.* genügen (+ *Dat.*); reichen für
sufficiency [sə'fɪʃənsɪ] *n., no pl.* Zulänglichkeit, *die; (sufficient amount)* ausreichende Menge
sufficient [sə'fɪʃənt] *adj.* genug; **~ money/food** genug Geld/genug zu essen; **be ~:** genügen; **~ reason** Grund genug; **I'm not ~ of an expert** ich bin nicht Fachmann genug; **have you had ~?** *(food, drink)* haben Sie schon genug?; **I think you have drunk quite ~:** ich glaube, du hast schon genug getrunken
sufficiently [sə'fɪʃəntlɪ] *adv.* genug; *(adequately)* ausreichend; **~ large** groß genug; **a ~ large number** eine genügend große Zahl
suffix ['sʌfɪks] **1.** *n.* **a)** *(Ling.)* Suffix, *das (fachspr.);* Nachsilbe, *die;* **b)** *(Math.) see* **subscript 2. 2.** *v.t.* suffigieren *(fachspr.);* anhängen ‹*Nachsilbe*›
suffocate ['sʌfəkeɪt] **1.** *v.t.* ersticken; **he was ~d by the smoke** der Rauch erstickte ihn; er erstickte an dem Rauch; **suffocating heat** drückende Hitze; **this dreary existence is suffocating me** *(fig.)* dieses eintönige Leben erdrückt mich. **2.** *v.i.* ersticken; **she was suffocating in the hot little kitchen** sie wäre in der heißen kleinen Küche fast erstickt
suffocation [sʌfə'keɪʃn] *n.* Erstickung, *die;* **a feeling of ~:** das Gefühl, zu ersticken
suffragan ['sʌfrəgən] *(Eccl.)* **1.** *adj.* **~ bishop** Suffraganbischof, *der.* **2.** *n.* **[bishop] ~:** Suffragan, *der*
suffrage ['sʌfrɪdʒ] *n. (right of voting)* Wahlrecht, *das;* **female** *or* **women's ~:** das Frauenwahlrecht
suffragette [sʌfrə'dʒet] *n. (Hist.)* Frauenrechtlerin, *die;* Suffragette, *die*
suffuse [sə'fju:z] *v.t.* **a blush ~d her cheeks** Schamröte stieg ihr ins Gesicht; **the evening sky was ~d with crimson** der Abendhimmel war in purpurnes Licht getaucht
Sufi ['su:fɪ] *n. (Muslim Relig.)* Sufi, *der*
sugar ['ʃʊgə(r)] **1.** *n.* **a)** Zucker, *der;* **two ~s, please** *(spoonfuls)* zwei Löffel Zucker, bitte; *(lumps)* zwei Stück Zucker, bitte; **b)** *(fig.: flattery)* Schöntuerei, *die (abwertend);* **c)** *(Amer. sl.: money)* Kohle, *die (salopp);* **d)** *(Amer. coll.: darling)* Süße, *der/die (fam.).* **2.** *v.t.* zuckern; *(fig.)* versüßen; verzuckern
sugar: ~ basin *see* **~-bowl; ~-beet** *n.* Zuckerrübe, *die;* **~-bowl** *n.* Zuckerschale, *die; (covered)* Zuckerdose, *die;* **~-cane** *n.* Zuckerrohr, *das;* **~-coated** *adj.* gezuckert; mit Zucker überzogen ‹*Dragee usw.*›; **~-daddy** *n. (sl.) spendabler älterer Mann, der ein junges Mädchen aushält;* **~-loaf** *n.* Zuckerhut, *der;* **~-lump** *n.* Zuckerstück, *das; (when counted)* Stück Zucker, *das;* **~-pea** *n.* Zuckererbse, *die;* **~-refinery** *n.* Zuckerraffinerie, *die;* **~-shaker, ~-sifter** *ns.* Zuckerstreuer, *der;* **~-tongs** *n. pl.* Zuckerzange, *die*
sugary ['ʃʊgərɪ] *adj.* süß; *(fig.)* süßlich ‹*Lächeln, Stimme, Musik*›
suggest [sə'dʒest] **1.** *v.t.* **a)** *(propose)* vorschlagen; **~ sth. to sb.** jmdm. etw. vorschlagen; **he ~ed going to the cinema** er schlug vor, ins Kino zu gehen; **b)** *(assert)* **are you trying to ~ that he is lying?** wollen Sie damit sagen, daß er lügt?; **he ~ed that the calculation was incorrect** er sagte, die Rechnung sei falsch; **I ~ that ...** *(Law)* ich unterstelle, daß ...; **c)** *(make one think of)* suggerieren; ‹*Symptome, Tatsachen:*› schließen lassen auf (+ *Akk.*); **what does this music ~ to you?** woran denken Sie bei dieser Musik? **2.** *v. refl.* **~ itself [to sb.]** ‹*Möglichkeiten, Ausweg:*› sich [jmdm.] anbieten; ‹*Gedanke:*› sich [jmdm.] aufdrängen
suggestible [sə'dʒestɪbl] *adj.* beeinflußbar; suggestibel *(geh.)*
suggestion [sə'dʒestʃn] *n.* **a)** Vorschlag, *der;* **at** *or* **on sb.'s ~:** auf jmds. Vorschlag *(Akk.);* **I am open to ~s** ich bin Vorschlägen *od.* Anregungen aufgeschlossen; **b)** *(insinuation)* Andeutungen *Pl.;* **there is no ~ that he co-operated with the kidnappers** niemand unterstellt, daß er mit den Entführern zusammengearbeitet hat; **what a ~!** wie kann man so etwas nur sagen!; **c)** *(fig.: trace)* Spur, *die;* **not a ~ of condescension** nicht die Spur von Herablassung; **she speaks German with a ~ of a Polish accent** sie spricht Deutsch mit einem ganz leichten polnischen Akzent; **there is a ~ of blue in the grey** das Grau hat einen leichten Stich ins Blaue
sug'gestion[s] box *n.* Kummerkasten, *der*
suggestive [sə'dʒestɪv] *adj.* **a)** suggestiv *(geh.);* **be ~ of sth.** auf etw. *(Akk.)* schließen lassen; **~ power** Suggestion, *die;* **b)** *(risqué)* anzüglich; gewagt; zweideutig ‹*Scherze, Lieder*›
suggestively [sə'dʒestɪvlɪ] *adv.* **a)** vielsagend; **b)** *(in a risqué manner)* gewagt
suggestiveness [sə'dʒestɪvnɪs] *n., no pl.* **a)** Suggestion, *die;* **b)** *(sexual undertones)* Anzüglichkeit, *die;* Gewagtheit, *die*
suicidal [su:ɪ'saɪdl, sju:ɪ'saɪdl] *adj.* **a)** *(leading or tending to suicide)* selbstmörderisch ‹*Akt, Absicht*›; suizidal *(fachspr.)* ‹*Verhalten, Patient*›; **~ tendencies** eine Neigung zum Selbstmord; **I felt** *or* **was quite ~:** ich hätte mich am liebsten gleich umgebracht; **b)** *(dangerous)* selbstmörderisch ‹*Fahrweise, Verhalten usw.*›
suicide ['su:ɪsaɪd, 'sju:ɪsaɪd] *n.* **a)** Selbstmord, *der (auch fig.);* Suizid, *der (fachspr.); (viewed more positively)* Freitod, *der (geh.);* **commit ~:** Selbstmord *od. (fachspr.)* Suizid begehen; *(viewed more positively)* den Freitod wählen *(geh.);* **attempt ~:** einen Selbstmordversuch unternehmen; **b)** *(person)* Selbstmörder, *der*/-mörderin, *die;* Suizidant, *der*/Suizidantin, *die (fachspr.)*
suicide: ~ attempt *n.* Selbstmordversuch, *der;* **~ pact** *n.* Selbstmordpakt, *der;* **~ squad** *n.* Selbstmordkommando, *das*
sui generis [sju:aɪ 'dʒenərɪs, su:ɪ 'genərɪs] *adj.* einzigartig; **be ~:** einzig in seiner Art sein
suit [su:t, sju:t] **1.** *n.* **a)** *(for men)* Anzug, *der; (for women)* Kostüm, *das;* **a three-piece-~:** ein dreiteiliger Anzug; ein Dreiteiler; **~ of armour** Harnisch, *der;* **buy [oneself] a new ~ of clothes** sich neu einkleiden; **b)** *(Law)* **~ [at law]** Prozeß, *der;* [Gerichts]verfahren, *das;* **c)** *(Cards)* Farbe, *die;* **follow ~:** Farbe bedienen; *(fig.)* das Gleiche tun; *see also* **'long 1 m; d)** *(courtship)* Werbung, *die (um eine Frau).* **2.** *v.t.* **a)** anpassen **(to** *Dat.***)**; **~ the action to the word** den Worten Taten folgen lassen; **b) be ~ed [to sth./one another]** [zu etw./zueinander] passen; **he is not at all ~ed to marriage** er eignet sich überhaupt nicht für die Ehe; **they are ill/well ~ed** sie passen schlecht/gut zueinander; **c)** *(satisfy needs of)* passen (+ *Dat.*); recht sein (+ *Dat.*); **will Monday ~ you?** ist Montag Ihnen recht?; paßt Ihnen Montag?; **he comes when it ~s him** er kommt, wann es ihm gerade paßt; **does the climate ~ you/your health?** bekommt Ihnen das Klima?; **dried fruit/asparagus does not ~ me** ich vertrage kein Trockenobst/keinen Spargel; **d)** *(go well with)* passen zu; **does this hat ~ me?** steht mir dieser Hut?; **black ~s her** Schwarz steht ihr gut. **3.** *v.i.* **a)** *(be convenient)* ‹*Termin:*› recht sein; **b)** *(go well)* **she'll ~:** sie ist genau richtig; **the job ~s with his abilities** die Stelle entspricht seinen Fähigkeiten. **4.** *v. refl.* **~ oneself** tun, was man will; **~ yourself!** [ganz] wie du willst!; **you can ~ yourself whether you come or not** du kannst kommen oder nicht, ganz wie du willst
suitability [su:tə'bɪlɪtɪ, sju:tə'bɪlɪtɪ] *n., no pl.* Eignung, *die* **(for** für); *(of clothing, remark; for an occasion)* Angemessenheit, *die* **(for** für); **his ~ as a teacher** seine Eignung zum *od.* als Lehrer; **we must check the ~ of the date** wir müssen prüfen, ob der Termin paßt
suitable ['su:təbl, 'sju:təbl] *adj.* geeignet; *(for an occasion)* angemessen ‹*Kleidung*›; angebracht ‹*Bemerkung*›; *(matching; convenient)* passend; **I did not find anything ~ to go with this dress** ich habe nichts gefunden, was zu diesem Kleid paßt; **this girlfriend is not ~ for him** diese Freundin paßt nicht zu ihm; **Monday is the most ~ day [for me]** Montag paßt [mir] am besten
suitableness ['su:təblnɪs, 'sju:təblnɪs] *see* **suitability**
suitably ['su:təblɪ, 'sju:təblɪ] *adv.* angemessen; gehörig ‹*entrüstet*›; gebührend ‹*beeindruckt*›; entsprechend ‹*gekleidet*›; **a ~ treated metal** ein in geeigneter Weise bearbeitetes Metall
'suitcase *n.* Koffer, *der;* **live out of a ~:** aus dem Koffer leben
suite [swi:t] *n.* **a)** *(of furniture)* Garnitur, *die;* **three-piece ~:** Polstergarnitur, *die;* **bedroom ~:** Schlafzimmereinrichtung, *die;* **b)** *(of rooms)* Suite, *die;* **executive/bridal ~:** Chef-/Hochzeitssuite, *die;* **c)** *(Mus.)* Suite, *die*
suitor ['su:tə(r), 'sju:tə(r)] *n.* Freier, *der*
sulfate, sulfide, sulfite, sulfonamide, sulfur, sulfuric *(Amer.) see* **sulph-**
sulk [sʌlk] **1.** *n., usu. in pl.* **have a ~** *or* **the ~s, be in** *or* **have a fit of the ~s** eingeschnappt sein *(ugs.);* schmollen. **2.** *v.i.* schmollen; **he always ~s if he doesn't get his own way** er ist immer gleich eingeschnappt, wenn er seinen Willen nicht kriegt *(ugs.)*
sulkily ['sʌlkɪlɪ] *adv.* eingeschnappt *(ugs.);* schmollend
sulkiness ['sʌlkɪnɪs] *n., no pl.* Schmollen, *das;* **the ~ of her expression/look** ihr schmollender Gesichtsausdruck/Blick
sulky ['sʌlkɪ] **1.** *adj.* schmollend; eingeschnappt *(ugs.).* **2.** *n. (Horse-racing)* Sulky, *das*
sullen ['sʌlən] *adj.* mürrisch; verdrießlich; *(fig.)* düster ‹*Himmel*›
sullenly ['sʌlənlɪ] *adv.* mürrisch; verdrießlich

sullenness ['sʌlənnɪs] *n., no pl.* Verdrießlichkeit, *die*
sully ['sʌlɪ] *v.t. (formal)* besudeln *(geh.)*
sulphate ['sʌlfeɪt] *n.* Sulfat, *das*
sulphide ['sʌlfaɪd] *n.* Sulfid, *das*
sulphite ['sʌlfaɪt] *n.* Sulfit, *das*
sulphonamide [sʌl'fɒnəmaɪd] *n.* Sulfonamid, *das*
sulphur ['sʌlfə(r)] *n.* Schwefel, *der*
sulphuric [sʌl'fjʊərɪk] *adj.* **~ acid** Schwefelsäure, *die*
sultan ['sʌltən] *n.* Sultan, *der*
sultana [sʌl'tɑ:nə] *n.* **a)** *(raisin)* Sultanine, *die;* **b)** *(wife of sultan)* Sultanin, *die*
sultriness ['sʌltrɪnɪs] *n., no pl.* Schwüle, *die; (fig.: sensuality)* Sinnlichkeit, *die*
sultry ['sʌltrɪ] *adj.* schwül ‹*Wetter, Tag, Atmosphäre*›; *(fig.: sensual)* sinnlich; schwül ‹*Schönheit*›
sum [sʌm] **1.** *n.* **a)** *(total amount, lit. or fig.)* Summe, *die* **(of** aus); **~ [total]** Ergebnis, *das;* **that was the ~ total of our achievements** *or* **of what we achieved** das war alles, was wir erreicht haben; **in ~:** summa summarum; **b)** *(amount of money)* Summe, *die;* **a cheque for this ~:** ein Scheck über diesen Betrag; *see also* **lump sum; c)** *(Arithmetic)* Rechenaufgabe, *die;* **do ~s** rechnen; **she is good at ~s** sie kann gut rechnen; sie ist gut im Rechnen. **2.** *v.t.,* **-mm-** addieren
~ 'up 1. *v.t.* **a)** zusammenfassen; **b)** *(Brit.: assess)* einschätzen; **this ~med him up perfectly** damit war er treffend charakterisiert. **2.** *v.i.* ein Fazit ziehen; ‹*Richter:*› resümieren; **in ~ming up, I should like to ...:** zusammenfassend möchte ich ...
sumac[h] ['su:mæk, 'ʃu:mæk, 'sju:mæk] *n.* Sumach, *der*
summarily ['sʌmərɪlɪ] *adv.* **a)** *(shortly)* knapp; **b)** *(without formalities or delay)* summarisch; **~ dismissed** fristlos entlassen; **~ convicted** *(Law)* im summarischen Verfahren verurteilt
summarize ['sʌməraɪz] *v.t.* zusammenfassen
summary ['sʌmərɪ] **1.** *adj.* **a)** *(short)* knapp; **b)** *(without formalities or delay)* summarisch *(geh.);* fristlos ‹*Entlassung*›; *(Law)* **~ justice/jurisdiction** Schnelljustiz, *die;* **~ conviction** Verurteilung im summarischen Verfahren *(Rechtsw.).* **2.** *n.* Zusammenfassung, *die*
summer ['sʌmə(r)] **1.** *n.* **a)** Sommer, *der;* **in [the] ~:** im Sommer; **in early/late ~:** im Früh-/Spätsommer; **last/next ~:** letzten/nächsten Sommer; **a ~'s day/night** ein Sommertag/eine Sommernacht; **in the ~ of 1983, in ~ 1983** im Sommer 1983; **two ~s ago we went to France** im Sommer vor zwei Jahren waren wir in Frankreich; *see also* **Indian summer; solstice a; b)** *in pl. (literary: years)* Lenze *(geh.).* **2.** *attrib. adj.* Sommer-
summer: ~-house *n.* [Garten]laube, *die;* **~ 'lightning** *n.* Wetterleuchten, *das;* **~ 'pudding** *n. (Brit.) Süßspeise aus Kompott und Weißbrot;* **~ school** *n.* Sommerkurs, *der;* **~ term** *n.* Sommerhalbjahr, *das;* **S~ Time** *n. (Brit.: for daylight saving)* die Sommerzeit; **~time** *n. (season)* Sommer, *der;* **~ visitor** *n.* Sommergast, *der;* **~ weight** *adj. (Textiles)* [sommerlich] leicht; Sommer-
summery ['sʌmərɪ] *adj.* sommerlich
summing-up [sʌmɪŋ'ʌp] *n.* Zusammenfassung, *die*
summit ['sʌmɪt] *n.* **a)** *(peak, lit. or fig.)* Gipfel, *der;* **he was at the ~ of his power** er stand auf dem Gipfel[punkt] seiner Macht; **b)** *(discussion)* Gipfel, *der;* **~ conference/meeting** Gipfelkonferenz, *die*/-treffen, *das;* **at ~ level** auf höchster Ebene
summitry ['sʌmɪtrɪ] *n.* Gipfeldiplomatie, *die*
summon ['sʌmən] *v.t.* **a)** *(call upon)* rufen **(to** zu); holen ‹*Hilfe*›; zusammenrufen ‹*Aktionäre*›; **b)** *(call by authority)* zu sich zitieren; einberufen ‹*Parlament*›; **she was ~ed to the presence of the Queen** sie wurde zur Königin befohlen *(veralt.);* **c)** *(Law: to court)* vorladen ‹*Angeklagten, Zeugen*›; **d) ~ sb. to do sth.** jmdn. auffordern, etw. zu tun
~ 'up *v.t.* aufbringen ‹*Mut, Kräfte, Energie, Begeisterung*›
summons ['sʌmənz] **1.** *n.* **a)** Aufforderung, *die;* **receive a ~ from sb. to do sth.** von jmdm. aufgefordert werden, etw. zu tun; **b)** *(Law)* Vorladung, *die;* **serve a ~ on sb.** jmdm. eine Vorladung zustellen. **2.** *v.t. (Law)* **~ sb. to appear in court** jmdn. gerichtlich vorladen *od.* vor Gericht laden
sumo ['su:məʊ] *n., pl.* **~s: ~ [wrestling]** Sumo, *das;* **~ [wrestler]** Sumokämpfer, *der*
sump [sʌmp] *n.* **a)** *(Brit. Motor Veh.)* Ölwanne, *die;* **b)** *(Mining)* Sumpf, *der*
sumptuous ['sʌmptjʊəs] *adj.* üppig; luxuriös ‹*Einband, Möbel, Kleidung*›
sumptuously ['sʌmptjʊəslɪ] *adv.* üppig; luxuriös ‹*eingerichtet*›
sumptuousness ['sʌmptjʊəsnɪs] *n., no pl.* Üppigkeit, *die;* **the ~ of the binding/furnishings** der luxuriöse Einband/die luxuriöse Einrichtung
sun [sʌn] **1.** *n.* Sonne, *die;* **rise with the ~:** in aller Herrgottsfrühe aufstehen; **a place in the ~** *(fig.)* ein Platz an der Sonne; **catch the ~** *(be in a sunny position)* viel Sonne abbekommen; *(get ~burnt)* einen Sonnenbrand bekommen; **a touch of the ~:** ein leichter Sonnenstich; **under the ~** *(fig.)* auf der Welt; **chat about everything under the ~:** über alles Mögliche schwatzen; **there is nothing new under the ~:** es gibt nichts Neues unter der Sonne; *see also* **hay; midnight sun. 2.** *v. refl.,* **-nn-** *(lit. or fig.)* sich sonnen
Sun. *abbr.* **Sunday** So.
sun: ~baked *adj.* an der Sonne getrocknet ‹*Ziegel*›; ausgedörrt ‹*Landschaft, Prärie usw.*›; **~bathe** *v.i.* sonnenbaden; **~bather** *n.* Sonnenbadende, *der/die;* **~bathing** *n.* Sonnenbaden, *das;* **~beam** *n.* Sonnenstrahl, *der;* **~-bed** *n. (with UV lamp)* Sonnenbank, *die; (in garden etc.)* Gartenliege, *die;* **~belt** *n. (Amer.)* Sonnengürtel, *der; die südlichen Staaten der USA;* **~-blind** *n.* Markise, *die;* **~-bonnet** *n.* Sonnenhäubchen, *das;* **~burn 1.** *n.* Sonnenbrand, *der;* **2.** *v.i.* **my skin ~burns/I ~burn very easily** ich kriege sehr leicht einen Sonnenbrand; **~burnt** *adj.* **a)** *(suffering from ~burn)* **be ~burnt** einen Sonnenbrand haben; **have a ~burnt back/face** einen Sonnenbrand auf dem Rücken/im Gesicht haben; **get badly ~burnt** einen schlimmen Sonnenbrand bekommen; **b)** *(tanned)* sonnenverbrannt ‹*Person, Gesicht usw.*›
sundae ['sʌndeɪ, 'sʌndɪ] *n.* **[ice-cream] ~:** Eisbecher, *der*
Sunday ['sʌndeɪ, 'sʌndɪ] **1.** *n.* **a)** Sonntag, *der;* **never in a month of ~s** nie im Leben; **b)** *in pl. (newspapers)* Sonntagszeitungen. **2.** *adv. (coll.)* **she comes ~s** sie kommt sonntags. *See also* **best 3b; Friday**
Sunday: ~ 'driver *n. (derog.)* Sonntagsfahrer, *der*/-fahrerin, *die (abwertend);* **~ painter** *n.* Sonntagsmaler, *der*/-malerin, *die;* **~ school** *n.* Sonntagsschule, *die;* ≈ Kindergottesdienst, *der*
'sun-deck *n.* Sonnendeck, *das*
sunder ['sʌndə(r)] *(arch./literary) v.t.* brechen
sun: ~dew *n. (Bot.)* Sonnentau, *der;* **~dial** *n.* Sonnenuhr, *die;* **~down** *see* **sunset; ~downer** ['sʌndaʊnə(r)] *n. (Austral.)* Pennbruder, *der (ugs.);* **~-drenched** *adj.* sonnenüberflutet *(geh.);* **~-dress** *n.* Strand- *od.* Sonnenkleid, *das;* **~-dried** *adj.* an der Sonne getrocknet
sundry ['sʌndrɪ] **1.** *adj.* verschieden; **~ articles** verschiedene *od.* diverse Artikel. **2.** *n. in pl.* Verschiedenes; Diverses; *see also* **all 2a**
sun: ~fast *adj. (Amer.)* lichtecht ‹*Farben*›; **~fish** *n.* Sonnen-, Mondfisch, *der;* **~flower** *n.* Sonnenblume, *die;* **~flower seeds** Sonnenblumenkerne
sung *see* **sing 1, 2**
sun: ~-glasses *n. pl.* Sonnenbrille, *die;* **~-god** *n.* Sonnengott, *der;* **~-hat** *n.* Sonnenhut, *der;* **~-helmet** *n.* Tropenhelm, *der*
sunk *see* **sink 2, 3**
sunken ['sʌŋkn] *adj.* versunken ‹*Schatz*›; gesunken ‹*Schiff*›; eingefallen ‹*Augen, Wangen*›; tieferliegend ‹*Garten, Zimmer*›; in den Boden eingelassen ‹*Badewanne*›
sun-lamp *n.* Höhensonne, *die*
sunless ['sʌnlɪs] *adj.* ‹*Ecke, Stelle, Tal*› wo die Sonne nie hinkommt; trübe ‹*Tag*›
sun: ~light *n.* Sonnenlicht, *das;* **come into the ~light!** komm in die Sonne!; **~lit** *adj.* sonnenbeschienen ‹*Landschaft*›; sonnig ‹*Zimmer, Garten*›; **~ lounge** *n.* Veranda, *die*
Sunni ['sʌnɪ] *n. (Muslim Relig.)* Sunnit, *der*/Sunnitin, *die; attrib.* sunnitisch
sunnily ['sʌnɪlɪ] *adv.* lustig; freundlich
Sunnite ['sʌnaɪt] *n. (Muslim Relig.)* Sunnit, *der*/Sunnitin, *die*
sunny ['sʌnɪ] **a)** sonnig; **~ intervals** Aufheiterungen; **the ~ side of the house/street** die Sonnenseite des Hauses/der Straße; **~ side up** ‹*Spiegelei*› mit dem Gelben nach oben; **b)** *(cheery)* fröhlich ‹*Wesen, Lächeln*›; **have a ~ disposition** eine Frohnatur sein
sun: ~ray *n.* Sonnenstrahl, *der;* **~ray treatment** *n.* Bestrahlung, *die;* **~rise** *n.* Sonnenaufgang, *der;* **at ~rise** bei Sonnenaufgang; *attrib.* **~rise industry** Zukunftsindustrie, *die;* **~-roof** *n.* Schiebedach, *das;* **~-seeker** *n.* Sonnenhungrige, *der/die;* **~set** *n.* Sonnenuntergang, *der;* **at ~set** bei Sonnenuntergang; **~shade** *n.* Sonnenschirm, *der; (awning)* Markise, *die;* **~shine** *n.* **a)** Sonnenschein, *der;* **sit in the ~shine** in der Sonne sitzen; **b)** *(joc.: as form of address) (to child)* Kleiner/Kleine; *(between men)* Kumpel *(ugs.);* **~shine roof** *see* **sunroof; ~spot** *n.* **a)** *(Astron.)* Sonnenfleck, *der;* **b)** *(place)* Sonnenparadies, *das;* **~stroke** *n.* Sonnenstich, *der;* **suffer from/get ~stroke** einen Sonnenstich haben/bekommen; **~-tan** *n.* [Sonnen]bräune, *die;* **get a ~-tan** braun werden; **~-tan lotion** *n.* Sonnencreme, *die;* **~-tanned** *adj.* braun[gebrannt]; sonnengebräunt *(geh.);* **~-tan oil** *n.* Sonnenöl, *das;* **~-top** *n.* Sonnentop, *das;* **~-trap** *n.* sonniges Plätzchen; **~-up** *(Amer.) see* **~rise; ~ visor** *n.* Blendschirm, *der;* **~-worshipper** *n. (lit./joc.)* Sonnenanbeter, *der*/-anbeterin, *die*
sup [sʌp] *v.t.,* **-pp- a)** *(arch.: have supper)* zu Abend essen; **b)** *(Scot., N. Engl.: drink)* süffeln *(ugs.)*
super ['su:pə(r)] *(coll.)* **1.** *n.* **a)** *(actor)* Statist, *der*/Statistin, *die;* **b)** *(Police) see* **superintendent a. 2.** *adj. (Brit.)* super *(ugs.);* **you've all been really ~ to me** ihr wart wirklich unheimlich nett zu mir
superabundance [su:pərə'bʌndəns] *n.* Überfluß, *der;* **a ~ of wealth** übermäßiger Wohlstand
superabundant [su:pərə'bʌndənt] *adj.* überreichlich
superannuate [su:pə'rænjʊeɪt] *v.t.* pensionieren
superannuated [su:pə'rænjʊeɪtɪd] *adj.* pensioniert; überaltert ‹*Ideen*›
superannuation [su:pərænjʊ'eɪʃn] *n.* **a) ~ [contribution/payment]** Beitrag zur Rentenversicherung; **~ fund** Rentenfonds, *der;* **b)** *(pension)* Rente, *die*
superb [sʊ'pɜ:b, sju:'pɜ:b] *adj.* einzigartig; erstklassig ‹*Essen, Zustand*›; **look ~:** phantastisch aussehen *(ugs.)*

superbly [sʊ'pɜ:blɪ, sju:'pɜ:blɪ] *adv.* erstklassig

supercargo ['su:pəkɑ:gəʊ] *n., pl.* **~es** Superkargo, *der*

supercharge ['su:pətʃɑ:dʒ] *v.t.* aufladen ‹*Motor*›; **~d car/engine** Auto/Motor mit Kompressor

supercharger ['su:pətʃɑ:dʒə(r)] *n.* *(Motor Veh.)* Kompressor, *der*

supercilious [su:pə'sɪlɪəs] *adj.*, **superciliously** [su:pə'sɪlɪəslɪ] *adv.* hochnäsig

superciliousness [su:pə'sɪlɪəsnɪs] *n., no pl.* Hochnäsigkeit, *die*

supercomputer [su:pəkəm'pju:tə(r)] *n.* Supercomputer, *der*

superconductivity [su:pəkɒndʌk'tɪvɪtɪ] *n.* *(Phys.)* Supraleitfähigkeit, *die*

superconductor [su:pəkən'dʌktə(r)] *n.* *(Phys.)* Supraleiter, *der*

supercool ['su:pəku:l] *v.t.* *(Phys.)* unterkühlen

super-duper ['su:pədu:pə(r)] *adj.* *(Brit. coll.)* Superklasse- *(ugs.)*; **be ~:** Superklasse sein *(ugs.)*

superego [su:pər'i:gəʊ, su:pər'egəʊ] *n., pl.* **~s** *(Psych.)* Über-Ich, *das*

superficial [su:pə'fɪʃl] *adj.* *(also fig.)* oberflächlich; leicht ‹*Änderung, Schaden*›; äußerlich ‹*Ähnlichkeit*›

superficiality [su:pəfɪʃɪ'ælɪtɪ] *n.* Oberflächlichkeit, *die*

superficially [su:pə'fɪʃəlɪ] *adv.* an der Oberfläche; ‹*Thema*› oberflächlich ‹*behandeln*›; äußerlich ‹*ähnlich sein*›

superfine ['su:pəfaɪn] *adj.* **a)** *(of extra quality)* hochfein; **b)** *(excessively fine)* hauchdünn ‹*Unterschied*›

superfluity [su:pə'flu:ɪtɪ] *n.* **a)** Überflüssigkeit, *die;* **b)** *(amount)* Überfluß, *der* (**of** an + *Dat.*)

superfluous [sʊ'pɜ:flʊəs, sju:'pɜ:flʊəs] *adj.* überflüssig

superfluously [sʊ'pɜ:flʊəslɪ, sju:'pɜ:flʊəslɪ] *adv.* überflüssigerweise

superfluousness [sʊ'pɜ:flʊəsnɪs, sju:'pɜ:flʊəsnɪs] *n., no pl.* Überflüssigkeit, *die*

superglue ['su:pəglu:] *n.* Sekundenkleber, *der*

supergrass ['su:pəgrɑ:s] *n.* *(Journ.)* Superspitzel, *der (abwertend)*

superheat [su:pə'hi:t] *v.t.* überhitzen

superhighway ['su:pəhaɪweɪ] *n.* *(Amer.)* Autobahn, *die*

superhuman [su:pə'hju:mən] *adj.* übermenschlich

superimpose [su:pərɪm'pəʊz] *v.t.* aufbringen ‹*Schicht usw.*›; aufkopieren ‹*Bild*›; **~ a on b** a auf b legen; *(fig.)* b mit a überlagern; **be ~d on sth.** *(state, lit. or fig.)* etw. überlagern

superintend [su:pərɪn'tend] *v.t.* überwachen; beaufsichtigen

superintendent [su:pərɪn'tendənt] *n.* **a)** *(Brit. Police)* Kommissar, *der*/Kommissarin, *die;* *(Amer. Police)* [Polizei]präsident, *der*/-präsidentin, *die;* **b)** *(of hostel)* Leiter, *der*/Leiterin, *die;* **~ of schools** ≈ Schulrat, *der*/-rätin, *die;* **c)** *(Amer.: caretaker)* Hausverwalter, *der*/-verwalterin, *die*

superior [su:'pɪərɪə(r), sju:'pɪərɪə(r), sʊ'pɪərɪə(r)] **1.** *adj.* **a)** *(of higher quality)* besonders gut ‹*Restaurant, Qualität, Stoff*›; überlegen ‹*handwerkliches Können, Technik, Intelligenz*›; **he thinks he is ~ to us** er hält sich für besser *od.* etwas Besseres als wir; **this car is ~ in speed to mine** dieser Wagen ist meinem an Geschwindigkeit überlegen; **b)** *(having higher rank)* höher... ‹*Stellung, Rang, Gericht*›; **be ~ to sb.** einen höheren Rang als jmd. haben; **c)** *(greater in number)* zahlenmäßig überlegen ‹*Truppen*›; **the enemy's ~ numbers** die zahlenmäßige Überlegenheit des Feindes; **d)** *(supercilious)* überlegen; hochnäsig *(abwertend)*; **e)** *(not influenced)* **be ~ to sth.** über etw. *(Dat.)* stehen; **f)** *(Printing)* hochgestellt ‹*Zahl, Buchstabe*›. **2.** *n.* **a)** *(sb. higher in rank)* Vorgesetzte, *der/die;* **b)** *(sb. better)* Überlegene, *der/die;* **he has no ~ in courage** keiner hat mehr Mut als er

superiority [su:pɪərɪ'ɒrɪtɪ, sju:pɪərɪ'ɒrɪtɪ, sʊpɪərɪ'ɒrɪtɪ] *n.* Überlegenheit, *die* (**to** über + *Akk.*); *(of goods)* besondere Qualität; *(haughtiness)* Hochnäsigkeit, *die;* **his ~ in talent** sein größeres Talent

superlative [su:'pɜ:lətɪv, sju:'pɜ:lətɪv] **1.** *adj.* **a)** unübertrefflich; einmalig gut; **b)** *(Ling.)* superlativisch; **the ~ degree** der Superlativ; die zweite Steigerungsstufe; **a ~ adjective/adverb** ein Adjektiv/Adverb im Superlativ. **2.** *n.* *(Ling.)* Superlativ, *der*

superlatively [su:'pɜ:lətɪvlɪ, sju:'pɜ:lətɪvlɪ] *adv.* einmalig gut

superman ['su:pəmæn] *n., pl.* **supermen** ['su:pəmen] Supermann, *der;* *(Philos., Lit.)* Übermensch, *der*

supermarket ['su:pəmɑ:kɪt] *n.* Supermarkt, *der*

supernatural [su:pə'nætʃərl] *adj.* übernatürlich; **the ~:** das Übernatürliche

supernaturally [su:pə'nætʃərəlɪ] *adv.* auf übernatürliche Weise

supernova [su:pə'nəʊvə] *n., pl.* **~e** [su:pə'nəʊvi:] *or* **~s** *(Astron.)* Supernova, *die*

supernumerary [su:pə'nju:mərərɪ] **1.** *adj.* überzählig. **2.** *n.* zusätzliche Arbeitskraft; *(actor)* Statist, *der*/Statistin, *die*

superpose [su:pə'pəʊz] *see* **superimpose**

superpower ['su:pəpaʊə(r)] *n.* *(Polit.)* Supermacht, *die*

superscript ['su:pəskrɪpt] **1.** *n.* hochgestelltes Zeichen. **2.** *adj.* hochgestellt

supersede [su:pə'si:d] *v.t.* ablösen (**by** durch); **old ~d ideas** alte, überholte Vorstellungen

supersonic [su:pə'sɒnɪk] *adj.* Überschall-; **go ~:** die Schallmauer durchbrechen

superstar ['su:pəstɑ:(r)] *n.* Superstar, *der*

superstition [su:pə'stɪʃn] *n.* *(lit. or fig.)* Aberglaube, *der;* **~s** abergläubische Vorstellungen; *(religious practices)* abergläubische Praktiken

superstitious [su:pə'stɪʃəs] *adj.*, **superstitiously** [su:pə'stɪʃəslɪ] *adv.* abergläubisch

superstore ['su:pəstɔ:(r)] *n.* Großmarkt, *der*

superstructure ['su:pəstrʌktʃə(r)] *n.* **a)** Aufbau, *der;* **b)** *(Sociol.)* Überbau, *der*

supertanker ['su:pətæŋkə(r)] *n.* Supertanker, *der*

supertax ['su:pətæks] *n.* Ergänzungsabgabe *od.* -steuer, *die*

supertonic [su:pə'tɒnɪk] *n.* *(Mus.)* zweite Stufe; Subdominantparallele, *die (fachspr.)*

supervene [su:pə'vi:n] *v.i.* dazwischenkommen

supervise ['su:pəvaɪz] *v.t.* beaufsichtigen

supervision [su:pə'vɪʒn] *n.* Aufsicht, *die*

supervisor ['su:pəvaɪzə(r)] *n.* Aufseher, *der*/Aufseherin, *die;* *(for Ph. D. thesis)* Doktorvater, *der;* *(Amer.: school officer)* Fachbereichsleiter, *der*/-leiterin, *die;* **works ~:** Vorarbeiter, *der*/-arbeiterin, *die;* **office ~:** Bürovorsteher, *der*/-vorsteherin, *die*

supervisory ['su:pəvaɪzərɪ] *adj.* Aufsichts-

supine ['su:paɪn, 'sju:paɪn] *adj.* **he was** *or* **lay ~:** er lag auf dem Rücken; **assume a ~ position** sich auf den Rücken legen; **~ acceptance** *(fig.)* gleichgültige Hinnahme

supper ['sʌpə(r)] *n.* Abendessen, *das;* *(simpler meal)* Abendbrot, *das;* **have** *or* **eat [one's] ~:** zu Abend essen; **be at** *or* **eating** *or* **having [one's] ~:** beim Abendessen/Abendbrot sein; zu Abend essen; **sing for one's ~** *(fig.)* etwas für sein Geld tun *(ugs.)*; **The Last S~:** das [letzte] Abendmahl; *see also* **Lord 1 b**

'supper-time *n.* Abendbrotzeit, *die;* **it's ~:** es ist Zeit zum Abendessen

supplant [sə'plɑ:nt] *v.t.* ablösen, ersetzen (**by** durch); ausstechen ‹*Widersacher, Rivalen*›

supple ['sʌpl] *adj.* geschmeidig

supplement 1. ['sʌplɪmənt] *n.* **a)** Ergänzung, *die* (**to** + *Gen.*); *(addition)* Zusatz, *der;* **vitamin ~:** Vitaminpräparat, *das;* **b)** *(of book)* Nachtrag, *der;* *(separate volume)* Supplement, *das;* Nachtragsband, *der;* *(of newspaper)* Beilage, *die;* **c)** *(to fare etc.)* Zuschlag, *der.* **2.** ['sʌplɪmənt, sʌplɪ'ment] *v.t.* ergänzen

supplementary [sʌplɪ'mentərɪ] *adj.* zusätzlich; Zusatz‹*rente, -frage*›; **~ fare/charge** Zuschlag, *der;* *see also* **benefit 1 b**

suppleness ['sʌplnɪs] *n., no pl.* Geschmeidigkeit, *die*

supplicant ['sʌplɪkənt] *n.* Bittsteller, *der*/stellerin, *die*

supplicate ['sʌplɪkeɪt] **1.** *v.t.* anflehen. **2.** *v.i.* flehen (**for** um)

supplication [sʌplɪ'keɪʃn] *n.* Flehen, *das;* **in ~:** flehentlich

supplier [sə'plaɪə(r)] *n.* *(Commerc.)* Lieferant, *der*/Lieferantin, *die*

supply [sə'plaɪ] **1.** *v.t.* **a)** liefern ‹*Waren usw.*›; sorgen für ‹*Unterkunft*›; zur Verfügung stellen ‹*Lehrmittel, Arbeitskleidung usw.*›; beliefern ‹*Kunden, Geschäft*›; versorgen ‹*System*›; **~ sth. to sb., ~ sb. with sth.** jmdn. mit etw. versorgen/*(Commerc.)* beliefern; **could you ~ me with the tools?** könnten Sie mir das Werkzeug zur Verfügung stellen?; **b)** *(make good)* erfüllen ‹*Nachfrage, Bedarf*›; abhelfen (+ *Dat.*) ‹*Mangel*›. **2.** *n.* **a)** *(stock)* Vorräte *Pl.*; **a large ~ of food** große Lebensmittelvorräte; **a good ~ of reading matter** ausreichende Lektüre; **new supplies of shoes** neue Schuhlieferungen; **military/medical supplies** militärischer/medizinischer Nachschub; **~ and demand** *(Econ.)* Angebot und Nachfrage; *see also* **short 1 d**; **b)** *(provision)* Versorgung, *die* (**of** mit); **the wholesaler has cut off our ~:** der Großhändler beliefert uns nicht mehr; **their gas ~ was cut off** ihnen ist das Gas abgestellt worden; **the blood ~ to the brain** die Versorgung des Gehirns mit Blut; **c)** *(Brit. Parl.)* Haushalt, *der;* **S~ Day** Tag der Verabschiedung des Parlamentshaushalts; **d) ~ [teacher]** Vertretung, *die;* **be/go on ~:** Vertretung sein/als Vertretung gehen. **3.** *attrib.* Versorgungs‹*schiff, -netz, -basis, -lager usw.*›; **~ lines** Nachschubwege

sup'ply-side *adj.* *(Econ.)* angebotsseitig

support [sə'pɔ:t] **1.** *v.t.* **a)** *(hold up)* stützen ‹*Mauer, Verletzten*›; *(bear weight of)* tragen ‹*Dach*›; **b)** *(give strength to)* stärken; **~ sb. in his struggle** jmdn. in seinem Kampf bestärken; **c)** unterstützen ‹*Politik, Verein*›; *(Footb.)* **~ Spurs** Spurs-Fan sein; **d)** *(give money to)* unterstützen; spenden für; **e)** *(provide for)* ernähren ‹*Familie, sich selbst*›; **f)** *(Cinemat., Theatre: take secondary part to)* **~ed by ...:** mit ... in weiteren Rollen; **g)** *(bring facts to confirm)* stützen ‹*Theorie, Anspruch, Behauptung*›; *(speak in favour of)* befürworten ‹*Streik, Maßnahme*›; **h)** *(represent adequately)* verkörpern ‹*Rolle*›; **i)** *(usu. neg.: tolerate)* ertragen; hinnehmen ‹*Dreistigkeit usw.*›. **2.** *n.* **a)** Unterstützung, *die;* **give ~ to sb./sth.** jmdn./etw. unterstützen; **in ~:** zur Unterstützung; **speak in ~ of sb./sth.** jmdn. unterstützen/etw. befürworten; **b)** *(money)* Unterhalt, *der;* **c)** *(sb./sth. that ~s)* Stütze, *die;* **hold on to sb./sth. for ~:** sich an jmdm./etw. festhalten

supportable [sə'pɔ:təbl] *adj.* vertretbar; erträglich ‹*Lärm*›

supporter [sə'pɔ:tə(r)] *n.* **a)** Anhänger, *der*/Anhängerin, *die;* **a football ~:** ein Fußballfan; **~s of a strike** Befürworter eines Streiks; **b)** *(Her.)* Schildhalter, *der*

sup'porters' club *n.* *(Sport)* Fanclub, *der*

supporting [sə'pɔ:tɪŋ] *adj.* *(Cinemat.,*

Theatre) ~ **role** Nebenrolle, *die;* **the** ~ **cast** die Darsteller der Nebenrollen; ~ **actor/actress** Schauspieler/-spielerin in einer Nebenrolle; ~ **film** Vorfilm, *der;* Beifilm, *der*
supportive [səˈpɔːtɪv] *adj.* hilfreich; **be very ~ [to sb.]** [jmdm.] eine große Hilfe *od.* Stütze sein
supˈport price *n. (Finance)* Stützungspreis, *der*
suppose [səˈpəʊz] *v. t.* **a)** *(assume)* annehmen; ~ *or* **supposing [that] he ...:** angenommen, [daß] er ...; **always supposing that ...:** immer vorausgesetzt, daß ...; ~ **we wait until tomorrow/went for a walk** wir könnten eigentlich bis morgen warten/einen Spaziergang machen; ~ **we change the subject** reden wir lieber von etwas anderem; **b)** *(presume)* vermuten; **I ~d she was in Glasgow** ich vermutete sie in Glasgow; **I ~ she will be here by ten** sie wird wohl bis um zehn kommen; **whom do you ~ he meant by that remark?** wen, glaubst du, hat er mit der Bemerkung gemeint?; **I don't ~ you have an onion to spare?** Sie haben wohl nicht zufällig eine Zwiebel übrig?; **we're not going to manage it, are we? – I ~ not** wir werden es wohl nicht schaffen – ich glaube kaum; **I ~ so** ich nehme es an; *(doubtfully)* ja, vermutlich; *(more confidently)* ich glaube schon; **I ~ I shall have to tell you** ich werde es dir wohl sagen müssen; **c) be ~d to do/be sth.** *(be generally believed to do/be sth.)* etw. tun/sein sollen; **cats are ~d to have nine lives** Katzen sollen angeblich neun Leben haben; **that restaurant is ~d to be quite cheap** das Restaurant soll ziemlich billig sein; **d)** *(allow)* **you are not ~d to do that/to kick people** das darfst du nicht/du darfst andere Leute nicht treten!; **I'm not ~d to be here** ich dürfte eigentlich gar nicht hier sein; **e)** *(presuppose)* voraussetzen
supposed [səˈpəʊzd] *attrib. adj.* mutmaßlich
supposedly [səˈpəʊzɪdlɪ] *adv.* angeblich
supposition [sʌpəˈzɪʃn] *n.* Annahme, *die;* Vermutung, *die;* **be based on ~:** auf Annahmen *od.* Vermutungen beruhen
suppository [səˈpɒzɪtərɪ] *n. (Med.)* Zäpfchen, *das;* Suppositorium, *das (fachspr.)*
suppress [səˈpres] *v. t.* **a)** unterdrücken; *(stop)* zum Stillstand bringen ⟨*Blutung*⟩; verbieten ⟨*Zeitung*⟩; **b)** *(Electr.)* entstören ⟨*Zündung, Elektrogerät*⟩; ausschalten ⟨*Störung*⟩
suppression [səˈpreʃn] *n.* **a)** Unterdrückung, *die;* **b)** *(Electr.)* Entstörung, *die; (of interference)* Ausschaltung, *die*
suppressor [səˈpresə(r)] *n. (Electr.)* Entstörgerät, *das*
suppurate [ˈsʌpjʊreɪt] *v. i. (Med.)* eitern
suppuration [sʌpjʊˈreɪʃn] *n. (Med.) (formation of pus)* Eiterung, *die; (discharge of pus)* Eitern, *das*
supremacy [suːˈpreməsɪ, sjuːˈpreməsɪ] *n., no pl.* **a)** *(supreme authority)* Souveränität, *die;* **b)** *(superiority)* Überlegenheit, *die;* **air/naval ~:** Luft-/Seeherrschaft, *die;* **gain ~ over others** Vorherrschaft *od.* eine Vormachtstellung über andere erlangen; *see also* **white supremacy**
supreme [suːˈpriːm, sjuːˈpriːm] **1.** *adj.* **a)** *(highest)* höchst...; **the S~ Being** das Höchste Wesen; **S~ Court** *(Law)* Oberster Gerichtshof; ~ **end** *or* **good** höchstes Gut; *see also* **Soviet 2; b)** *(ultimate)* **the ~ test** die schwierigste Probe; **make the ~ sacrifice** sein Leben zum Opfer bringen; **c)** *(greatest)* höchst...; größt... ⟨*Stunde*⟩; **a ~ moment** ein unvergleichlicher Augenblick; **he is ~ among musicians** er ist der größte aller Musiker; **a ~ artist** ein unübertroffener Künstler; **reign ~:** souverän herrschen; **confusion reigns ~:** es herrscht große Verwirrung. **2.** *n. (Gastr.)* **chicken ~:** Hühnchen in Rahmsoße; ~ **of sole** Seezunge in Rahmsoße
suprême [suːˈprem] *see* **supreme 2**
supremely [suːˈpriːmlɪ, sjuːˈpriːmlɪ] *adv.* äußerst; unvergleichlich ⟨*schön*⟩
supremo [suːˈpriːməʊ, sjuːˈpriːməʊ] *n., pl.* **~s** *(Brit.)* Boß, *der (ugs.)*
Supt. *abbr.* **Superintendent**
sura[h] [ˈsʊərə] *n. (Muslim Relig.)* Sure, *die*
surcharge [ˈsɜːtʃɑːdʒ] **1.** *n.* **a)** *(extra cost)* Zuschlag, *der;* **b)** *(on postage stamp)* [Porto]aufdruck, *der;* **c)** *(fine for false tax return)* Steuerzuschlag, *der.* **2.** *v. t.* **a)** ~ **sb. [10 %]** jmdn. mit einem Zuschlag [von 10 %] belegen; **b)** *(overprint)* überdrucken ⟨*Briefmarke*⟩
surcoat [ˈsɜːkəʊt] *n. (arch.)* Überjacke, *die*
surd [sɜːd] *n. (Math.)* Wurzelausdruck, *der*
sure [ʃʊə(r)] **1.** *adj.* **a)** *(confident)* sicher; **be ~ of sth.** sich *(Dat.)* einer Sache *(Gen.)* sicher sein; **you may be ~ of his honesty** du kannst dich auf seine Ehrlichkeit verlassen; ~ **of oneself** selbstsicher; **he looks very ~ of himself** er macht einen sehr selbstsicheren Eindruck; **I'm not quite ~ why** ich weiß nicht genau, warum; **I can't be ~ about him** ich bin mir über ihn nicht im klaren; **I'm ~ I didn't mean to insult you** ich wollte dich ganz bestimmt nicht beleidigen; **I'm ~ I don't know** ich weiß es ganz bestimmt nicht; **don't be too ~:** da wäre ich mir nicht so sicher; **b)** *(safe)* sicher; **make sth. ~:** etw. sichern; **be on ~r ground** *(lit. or fig.)* sich auf festerem Boden befinden; *see also* **slow 1 a; c)** *(certain)* sicher; **you're ~ to be welcome** Sie werden ganz sicher *od.* bestimmt willkommen sein; **it's ~ to rain** es wird bestimmt regnen; **there is ~ to be a garage** es gibt bestimmt eine Tankstelle; **don't worry, it's ~ to turn out well** keine Sorge, es wird schon alles gutgehen; **he is ~ to ask questions about the incident** er wird auf jeden Fall Fragen zu dem Vorfall stellen; **d)** *(undoubtedly true)* sicher; **to be ~** *expr. concession* natürlich; *expr. surprise* wirklich!; tatsächlich!; **for ~** *(coll.: without doubt)* auf jeden Fall; **e) make ~ [of sth.]** sich [einer Sache] vergewissern; *(check)* [etw.] nachprüfen; **you'd better make ~ of a seat** *or* **that you have a seat** du solltest dir einen Platz sichern; **make** *or* **be ~ you do it, be ~ to do it** *(do not fail to do it)* sieh zu, daß du es tust; *(do not forget)* vergiß nicht, es zu tun; **be ~ to write** vergiß nicht zu schreiben; **make ~ you've got everything you need** sieh zu, daß du alles hast, was du brauchst; **make ~ you don't forget to do it** vergiß auf keinen Fall, es zu tun; **be ~ you finish the work by tomorrow** machen Sie die Arbeit auf jeden Fall bis morgen fertig; **be ~ not to be late** sieh zu, daß du nicht zu spät kommst; **f)** *(reliable)* sicher ⟨*Zeichen*⟩; zuverlässig ⟨*Freund, Bote, Heilmittel*⟩; **a ~ winner** ein todsicherer Tip *(ugs.).* **2.** *adv.* **a) as ~ as can be** *(coll.)* so sicher wie das Amen in der Kirche; **as ~ as I'm standing here** so wahr ich hier stehe; ~ **as hell** todsicher; ~ **enough** tatsächlich; **it's brandy ~ enough!** das ist tatsächlich Weinbrand!; **it's brandy ~ enough, but ...:** es ist wohl Weinbrand, aber ...; *see also* **¹egg; b)** *(Amer. coll.: certainly)* wirklich; echt *(ugs.);* **Can you dance? – I ~ can** Kannst du tanzen? – Und ob!. **3.** *int.* **~!, ~ thing!** *(Amer.)* na klar! *(ugs.)*
sure: ~-fire *attrib. adj. (Amer. coll.)* todsicher; **~-footed** *adj. (lit. or fig.)* trittsicher
surely [ˈʃʊəlɪ] *adv.* **1. a)** *as sentence-modifier* doch; **there is no truth in it, ~!** das kann doch gar nicht stimmen; ~ **we've met before?** wir kennen uns doch, oder?; ~ **you are not going out in this snowstorm?** du willst doch wohl in dem Schneesturm nicht rausgehen?; **b)** *(steadily)* sicher; **slowly but ~:** langsam, aber sicher; **c)** *(certainly)* sicherlich; **the plan will ~ fail** der Plan wird garantiert scheitern. **2.** *int. (Amer.)* natürlich; selbstverständlich
sureness [ˈʃʊənɪs] *n., no pl.* Sicherheit, *die;* ~ **of purpose** Entschlossenheit, *die*
surety [ˈʃʊərətɪ, ˈʃʊətɪ] *n.* Bürge, *der*/Bürgin, *die;* **stand ~ for sb.** für jmdn. bürgen
surf [sɜːf] **1.** *n.* Brandung, *die.* **2.** *v. i.* surfen
surface [ˈsɜːfɪs] **1.** *n.* **a)** *no pl.* Oberfläche, *die;* **outer ~:** Außenfläche, *die;* **the earth's ~:** die Erdoberfläche; **on the ~ of the table** auf der Tischplatte; **the ~ of the road** die Straßendecke; **the ~ of the lake** die Seeoberfläche; **on the ~:** an der Oberfläche; *(Mining)* über Tage; **b)** *(outward appearance)* Oberfläche, *die;* **one never gets below the ~ with him** bei ihm bleibt alles immer oberflächlich; **on the ~:** oberflächlich betrachtet; **she remained calm on the ~:** äußerlich blieb sie ganz ruhig; **come to the ~:** an die Oberfläche kommen; ⟨*Taucher, Unterseeboot:*⟩ auftauchen; *(fig.)* ans Licht kommen *(fig.);* **c)** *(Geom.)* Fläche, *die.* **2.** *attrib. adj. (lacking depth)* oberflächlich. **3.** *v. i.* **a)** auftauchen; *(fig.)* hochkommen; ⟨*Untergrundbahn:*⟩ nach oben kommen; **b)** *(coll.: wake up, get up)* hochkommen *(ugs.).* **4.** *v. t.* mit einem Belag versehen ⟨*Straße*⟩
surface: ~ area *n.* Oberfläche, *die;* **~ mail** *n.* gewöhnliche Post *(die auf dem Land- bzw. Seeweg befördert wird);* **~ noise** *n. (on record)* Kratzen, *das;* **~ soil** *n.* oberste Bodenschicht; **~ ˈtension** *n. (Phys.)* Oberflächenspannung, *die;* **~-to-air** *adj.* **~-to-air missile** Boden-Luft-Rakete, *die;* **~ vessel** *n.* Überwasserfahrzeug, *das;* **~-water** *n.* Oberflächenwasser, *das;* **~ worker** *n. (Min.)* Übertagearbeiter, *der*
ˈsurf-board *n.* Surfbrett, *das*
surfeit [ˈsɜːfɪt] **1.** *n.* Übermaß, *das;* **a ~ of rich food** zuviel schweres Essen. **2.** *v. t.* übersättigen
surfer [ˈsɜːfə(r)] *n.* Surfer, *der*/Surferin, *die*
ˈsurf-riding *n.* Surfen, *das*
surge [sɜːdʒ] **1.** *v. i.* ⟨*Wellen:*⟩ branden; ⟨*Fluten, Menschenmenge:*⟩ sich wälzen; ⟨*elektrischer Strom:*⟩ ansteigen; **anger ~d within him** Zorn wallte in ihm auf; **the crowd ~d forward** die Menschenmenge drängte sich nach vorn. **2.** *n.* **a)** *(of the sea)* Branden, *das;* **b)** *(of crowd)* Sichwälzen, *das; (of electric current)* Anstieg, *der;* **c)** *(fig.: of interest, enthusiasm, anger, pity)* Woge, *die*
~ ˈup *v. i.* aufsteigen; ⟨*Gefühl:*⟩ aufwallen
surgeon [ˈsɜːdʒən] *n.* **a)** Chirurg, *der*/Chirurgin, *die;* **b)** *(Mil., Navy: medical officer)* Stabsarzt, *der*/-ärztin, *die*
surgeon ˈgeneral *n.* **a)** *(Amer. Mil.)* Generalstabsarzt, *der*/-ärztin, *die;* **b)** *(Amer. Admin.)* ≈ Gesundheitsminister, *der*/-ministerin, *die*
surgery [ˈsɜːdʒərɪ] *n.* **a)** *no pl., no indef. art.* Chirurgie, *die;* **need ~:** operiert werden müssen; **undergo ~:** sich einer Operation *(Dat.)* unterziehen; **be saved by ~:** durch eine Operation gerettet werden; **b)** *(Brit.: place)* Praxis, *die;* **doctor's/dental ~:** Arzt-/Zahnarztpraxis, *die;* **c)** *(Brit.: time; session)* Sprechstunde, *die;* **the times of ~:** die Sprechzeiten; **when is his ~?** wann hat er Sprechstunde?; **hold a ~** *(Brit. coll.)* ⟨*Abgeordneter, Anwalt usw.:*⟩ eine Sprechstunde abhalten
surgical [ˈsɜːdʒɪkl] *adj.* chirurgisch; ~ **treatment** Operation, *die*/Operationen; ~ **gauze** Verbandsmull, *der;* ~ **boot/stocking** orthopädischer Schuh/Strumpf; ~ **spirit** *Methylalkohol [zur Hautdesinfektion vor Operationen];* ≈ Alkohol, *der*
surgically [ˈsɜːdʒɪkəlɪ] *adv.* operativ ⟨*behandeln, entfernen*⟩
surliness [ˈsɜːlɪnɪs] *n., no pl.* Verdrießlichkeit, *die;* mürrische Art; **the ~ of his look** sein mürrischer Blick
surly [ˈsɜːlɪ] *adj.* mürrisch; verdrießlich
surmise [səˈmaɪz] **1.** *n.* Vermutung, *die;* Mutmaßung, *die.* **2.** *v. t.* mutmaßen; **she**

had ~d as much das hatte sie schon vermutet. 3. v. i. mutmaßen

surmount [sə'maʊnt] v. t. a) krönen; **a shield ~ed by a crown** ein bekrönter Wappenschild; b) *(overcome)* überwinden ‹*Hindernis, Schwierigkeiten*›

surmountable [sə'maʊntəbl] *adj.* überwindbar

surname ['sɜ:neɪm] 1. n. Nachname, *der;* Zuname, *der.* 2. v. t. **be ~d ...:** den Zunamen ... tragen

surpass [sə'pɑ:s] v. t. übertreffen (in an + *Dat.*); **~ oneself** sich selbst übertreffen; **sth. ~es [sb.'s] comprehension** etw. ist [jmdm.] unbegreiflich

surpassing [sə'pɑ:sɪŋ] *adj.* unvergleichlich ‹*Schönheit, Leistung*›

surplice ['sɜ:plɪs] n. *(Eccl.)* Chorhemd, *das*

surplus ['sɜ:pləs] 1. n. Überschuß, *der* (of an + *Dat.*); **a ~ of coffee** Kaffeeüberschüsse *Pl.*; **army ~:** Restbestände der Armee; **army ~ store/boots** Laden für Restbestände/Schuhe aus Restbeständen der Armee; *see also* **government surplus.** 2. *adj.* überschüssig; **be ~ to sb.'s requirements** von jmdm. nicht benötigt werden; **~ stocks** Überschüsse *Pl.*

surprise [sə'praɪz] 1. n. a) Überraschung, *die;* **take sb. by ~:** jmdn. überrumpeln; **the fort was taken by ~:** die Festung wurde durch Überrumpelungstaktik eingenommen; **to my great ~, much to my ~:** zu meiner großen Überraschung; sehr zu meiner Überraschung; **look up in ~:** überrascht aufblicken; **it came as a ~ to us** es war für uns eine Überraschung; **~, ~!** *(iron.)* sieh mal einer an! *(spött.)*; b) *attrib.* überraschend, unerwartet ‹*Besuch*›; **a ~ attack/defeat** ein Überraschungsangriff/eine überraschende Niederlage; **it's to be a ~ party** die Party soll eine Überraschung sein; **~ packet** *(Brit. fig.)* Wundertüte, *die (scherzh.).* 2. v. t. überraschen; überrumpeln ‹*Feind*›; **I shouldn't be ~d if ...:** es würde mich nicht wundern, wenn ...; **be ~d at sb./sth.** sich über jmdn./etw. wundern; **~ sb. into doing sth.** jmdn. dazu überrumpeln, etw. zu tun

surprising [sə'praɪzɪŋ] *adj.* überraschend; **there's nothing ~ about that** daran ist nichts Überraschendes; **it's hardly ~ that ...:** es ist kaum verwunderlich, daß ...; **~ though it may seem** so erstaunlich es auch klingen mag

surprisingly [sə'praɪzɪŋlɪ] *adv.* überraschend; **~ [enough], he was ...:** überraschenderweise war er ...

surreal [sə'ri:əl] *adj.* surrealistisch

surrealism [sə'ri:əlɪzm] n., *no pl.* Surrealismus, *der*

surrealist [sə'ri:əlɪst] 1. n. Surrealist, *der*/Surrealistin, *die.* 2. *adj.* surrealistisch

surrealistic [səri:ə'lɪstɪk] *adj.* surrealistisch

surrender [sə'rendə(r)] 1. n. a) *(submitting to enemy)* Kapitulation, *die;* b) *(giving up possession)* Aufgabe, *die; (of insurance policy)* Rückkauf, *der; (of firearms)* Abgabe, *die.* 2. v. i. kapitulieren; **~ to sb.** sich jmdm. beugen; **~ to despair/pressure/panic** sich der Verzweiflung überlassen/sich dem Druck beugen/sich zu Panik hinreißen lassen. 3. v. t. a) *(give up possession of)* aufgeben; preisgeben ‹*Freiheit, Privileg*›; niederlegen ‹*Amt*›; abgeben, aushändigen ‹*Wertgegenstände*›; b) zurückkaufen ‹*Versicherungspolice*›. 4. v. *refl.* sich hingeben (to + *Dat.*)

sur'render value n. Rückkaufswert, *der*

surreptitious [sʌrəp'tɪʃəs] *adj.* heimlich; verstohlen ‹*Blick*›

surreptitiously [sʌrəp'tɪʃəslɪ] *adv.* heimlich; verstohlen ‹*blicken*›

surrogate ['sʌrəgət] n. a) *(deputy)* Stellvertreter, *der*/-vertreterin, *die;* b) *(substitute)* Ersatz, *der*

surrogate 'mother n. Leihmutter, *die*

surround [sə'raʊnd] 1. v. t. a) *(come or be all round)* umringen; ‹*Truppen, Heer:*› umzingeln ‹*Stadt, Feind*›; b) *(enclose, encircle)* umgeben; **be ~ed by** *or* **with sth.** von etw. umgeben sein. 2. n. *(Brit.)* Umrandung, *die*

surrounding [sə'raʊndɪŋ] *adj.* umliegend ‹*Dörfer*›; **~ area** Umgebung, *die;* **the ~ countryside** die [Landschaft in der] Umgebung

surroundings [sə'raʊndɪŋz] n. *pl.* Umgebung, *die*

surtax ['sɜ:tæks] n. Ergänzungsabgabe *od.* -steuer, *die*

surveillance [sə'veɪləns] n. Überwachung, *die;* **keep sb. under ~:** jmdn. überwachen; **be under ~:** überwacht werden

survey 1. [sə'veɪ] v. t. a) *(take general view of)* betrachten; *(from high point)* überblicken ‹*Landschaft, Umgebung*›; b) *(examine)* inspizieren ‹*Gebäude usw.*›; c) *(assess)* bewerten ‹*Situation, Problem usw.*›; d) *(Surv.)* vermessen ‹*Grundstück, Land usw.*›. 2. ['sɜ:veɪ] n. a) *(general view, critical inspection)* Überblick, *der* (of über + *Akk.*); *(of landscape)* Betrachtung, *die;* b) *(by opinion poll)* Umfrage, *die; (by research)* Untersuchung, *die;* **conduct a ~ into sth.** eine Umfrage zu etw. veranstalten/etw. untersuchen; **a telephone ~:** eine Telefonbefragung; c) *(Surv.)* Vermessung, *die;* d) *(building inspection)* Inspektion, *die*

surveying [sə'veɪɪŋ] n. a) Landvermessung, *die;* b) *(Constr.)* Abstecken, *das;* c) *(profession)* **go into ~:** Landvermesser/-vermesserin werden

surveyor [sə'veɪə(r)] n. a) *(of building)* Gutachter, *der*/Gutachterin, *die; see also* **quantity surveyor;** b) *(of land)* Landvermesser, *der*/-vermesserin, *die;* Geodät, *der*/Geodätin, *die;* c) *(official inspector)* **S~ of Weights and Measures** Eichmeister, *der*/-meisterin, *die;* d) *(Amer.: customs officer)* Zollbeamte, *der*/-beamtin, *die*

survival [sə'vaɪvl] n. a) *no pl.* Überleben, *das; (of tradition)* Fortbestand, *der; (of building)* Erhaltung, *die;* **fight for ~:** Existenzkampf, *der;* **his ~ as Foreign Minister** *(fig.)* sein politisches Überleben als Außenminister; **the ~ of the fittest** *(Biol.)* [das] Überleben der Stärkeren; b) *(relic)* Überrest, *der*

sur'vival kit n. Notausrüstung, *die*

survive [sə'vaɪv] 1. v. t. überleben; **she ~d her son by 20 years** sie überlebte ihren Sohn um 20 Jahre. 2. v. i. ‹*Person:*› überleben; ‹*Schriften, Gebäude, Traditionen:*› erhalten bleiben; **he'll/you'll** *etc.* **~** *(iron.)* er wird's/du wirst's *usw.* [schon] überleben

survivor [sə'vaɪvə(r)] n. Überlebende, *der/die;* **he's a ~:** er ist nicht unterzukriegen

sus [sʌs] *(Brit. sl.)* 1. n. a) *(suspect)* Verdächtige, *der/die;* b) *(suspicion)* Verdacht, *der;* **the ~ laws** *die Gesetze, nach denen jmd. festgenommen werden darf, wenn er verdächtigt wird, eine strafbare Handlung begehen zu wollen.* 2. v. t., -ss- spitzkriegen *(ugs.)*; **get sb. ~sed** jmdn. durchschauen

~ 'out v. t. *(sl.)* checken *(ugs.)*; spannen *(ugs.)*

susceptibility [səseptɪ'bɪlɪtɪ] n. a) *(being susceptible) (to flattery, persuasion, etc.)* Empfänglichkeit, *die* (to für); *(to illness, injury, etc.)* Anfälligkeit, *die* (to für); **~ to pain** Schmerzempfindlichkeit, *die;* b) *in pl. (feelings)* Feingefühl, *das*

susceptible [sə'septɪbl] *adj.* a) *(sensitive) (to flattery, persuasion, etc.)* empfänglich (to für); *(to illness, injury, etc.)* anfällig (to für); b) *(easily influenced)* empfindsam; beeindruckbar; c) **be ~ of sth.** etw. zulassen; **your work is ~ of improvement** Ihre Arbeit ließe sich verbessern; **~ of proof** beweisbar

suspect 1. [sə'spekt] v. t. a) *(imagine to be likely)* vermuten; **~ the worst** das Schlimmste befürchten; **~ sb. to be sth., ~ that sb. is sth.** glauben *od.* vermuten, daß jmd. etw. ist; **I ~ that he doesn't really want to come** ich vermute, daß er eigentlich gar nicht kommen will; **you, I ~, don't care** dir, habe ich das Gefühl, ist das egal; b) *(mentally accuse)* verdächtigen; **~ sb. of sth./of doing sth.** jmdn. einer Sache verdächtigen/jmdn. verdächtigen, etw. zu tun; **he is ~ed of telling lies** man verdächtigt ihn der Lüge; **~ed of drug-trafficking** des Drogenhandels verdächtig; c) *(mistrust)* bezweifeln ‹*Echtheit*›; **~ sb.'s motives** jmds. Beweggründen mit Argwohn gegenüberstehen. 2. ['sʌspekt] *adj.* fragwürdig; suspekt *(geh.)*; verdächtig ‹*Stoff, Paket, Fahrzeug*›. 3. ['sʌspekt] n. Verdächtige, *der/die;* **political ~s** politisch Verdächtige; **a murder ~:** ein Mordverdächtiger/eine Mordverdächtige

suspected [sə'spektɪd] *adj.* verdächtig; **there is a ~ connection between x and y** man vermutet einen Zusammenhang zwischen x und y; **~ smallpox cases, ~ cases of smallpox** Fälle mit Verdacht auf Pocken

suspend [sə'spend] v. t. a) *(hang up)* [auf]hängen; **be ~ed [from sth.]** [von etw.] [herab]hängen; **be ~ed in mid-air** frei in der Luft schweben; b) *(stop, defer)* suspendieren ‹*Rechte*›; **~ hostilities/the publication of the magazine** Kampfhandlungen/das Erscheinen der Zeitschrift [vorübergehend] einstellen; **~ judgement** sich des Urteils enthalten; **~ the proceedings** die Verhandlungen/das Verfahren aussetzen *(Rechtsw.)*; c) *(remove from post)* ausschließen (from von); sperren ‹*Sportler*›; vom Unterricht ausschließen ‹*Schüler*›; **~ sb. from duty [pending an inquiry]** jmdn. [während einer schwebenden Untersuchung] vom Dienst suspendieren

suspended: ~ ani'mation n. vorübergehender Atemstillstand; **wait in a state of ~ animation** *(fig.)* atemlos warten; **~ particle** n. *(Phys.)* schwebendes Teilchen; **~ 'sentence** n. *(Law)* Strafe mit Bewährung; **he was given a two-year ~ sentence** er erhielt zwei Jahre Haft auf Bewährung *(Rechtsw.)*

suspender belt [sə'spendə belt] n. *(Brit.)* Strumpfbandgürtel, *der*

suspenders [sə'spendəz] n. *pl.* a) *(Brit.) (for stockings)* Strumpfbänder *od.* -halter; *(for socks)* Sockenhalter; b) *(Amer.: for trousers)* Hosenträger

suspense [sə'spens] n. Spannung, *die;* **the ~ is killing me** *(joc.)* ich komme um vor Spannung *(scherzh.)*; ich bin gespannt wie ein Regenschirm *(ugs. scherzh.)*; **keep sb. in ~:** jmdn. auf die Folter spannen

suspension [sə'spenʃn] n. a) *(action of debarring)* Ausschluß, *der; (from office)* Suspendierung, *die; (Sport)* Sperrung, *die;* **be under ~** ‹*Schüler:*› [zeitweilig] vom Unterricht ausgeschlossen sein; ‹*Sportler:*› [zeitweilig] gesperrt sein; b) *(temporary cessation)* Suspendierung, *die; (of publication, train service, hostilities)* [vorübergehende] Einstellung; c) *(hanging)* Aufhängen, *das;* d) *(Chem.)* Suspension, *die;* e) *(Motor Veh.)* Federung, die; *(mounting of wheels)* Radaufhängung, *die;* f) *(Mus.)* Vorhalt, *der*

su'spension bridge n. Hängebrücke, *die*

suspicion [sə'spɪʃn] n. a) *(uneasy feeling)* Mißtrauen, *das* (of gegenüber); *(more specific)* Verdacht, *der; (unconfirmed belief)* Ahnung, *die;* Verdacht, *der;* **have a ~ that ...:** den Verdacht haben, daß ...; **I have my ~s about him** er kommt mir verdächtig vor; ich traue ihm nicht ganz; **view** *or* **regard sb./sth. with ~:** jmdn./etw. mit Mißtrauen begegnen; b) *(suspecting)* Verdacht, *der* (of auf + *Akk.*); **~ is not enough** ein Verdacht genügt nicht; **protected from ~:** gegen Verdächtigungen geschützt; **on ~ of theft/murder** *etc.* wegen Verdachts auf Diebstahl/Mordverdachts *usw.*; **lay oneself**

open to ~: sich verdächtig machen; **be under ~**: verdächtigt werden; **c)** *(trace)* **a ~ of salt** eine Spur Salz

suspicious [səˈspɪʃəs] *adj.* **a)** *(tending to suspect)* mißtrauisch (**of** gegenüber); **be ~ of sb./sth.** jmdm./einer Sache mißtrauen; **b)** *(arousing suspicion)* verdächtig

suspiciously [səˈspɪʃəslɪ] *adv.* **a)** *(as to arouse suspicion)* verdächtig; **look ~ like sth.** verdächtig nach etw. aussehen; **b)** *(warily)* mißtrauisch

suspiciousness [səˈspɪʃəsnɪs] *n., no pl.* Verdächtigkeit, *die; (disposition to suspect)* Argwohn, *der;* Mißtrauen, *das*

sustain [səˈsteɪn] *v. t.* **a)** *(withstand)* widerstehen (+ *Dat.*) ‹*Druck*›; standhalten (+ *Dat.*) ‹*Angriff*›; aushalten ‹*Vergleich*›; tragen ‹*Gewicht*›; **b)** *(support, uphold)* aufrechterhalten; **too little to ~ life** nicht genug zum Leben; **not enough to ~ a family** nicht genug, um eine Familie zu unterhalten; **~ an objection** einem Einwand stattgeben; **c)** *(suffer)* erleiden ‹*Niederlage, Verlust, Verletzung*›; **~ damage** Schaden nehmen; **d)** *(maintain)* bestreiten ‹*Unterhaltung*›; bewahren ‹*Interesse*›; wahren ‹*Ruf*›; [beibe]halten ‹*Geschwindigkeit*›; durchhalten ‹*Rolle*›; **~ a note** *(Mus.)* eine Note aushalten; **~ a task** einer Aufgabe gerecht werden

sustained [səˈsteɪnd] *adj.* **a)** *(prolonged)* länger ...; anhaltend ‹*Beifall*›; ausdauernd ‹*Anstrengung*›; **~ speed** Dauergeschwindigkeit, *die;* **b)** *(Mus.)* ausgehalten

sustaining [səˈsteɪnɪŋ] *adj.* stärkend; nahrhaft ‹*Essen, Mahlzeit*›

sustaining: **~ ˈpedal** *n. (Mus.)* Fortepedal, *das;* **~ ˈprogram** *n. (Amer. Radio and Telev.) nicht von einem Sponsor getragenes Programm*

sustenance [ˈsʌstɪnəns] *n.* **a)** *(nourishment, food)* Nahrung, *die;* **draw** *or* **get one's ~ from sth.** sich von etw. ernähren; **b)** *(nourishing quality)* **there is no ~ in it** es hat keinen Nährwert

suture [ˈsuːtʃə(r)] *(Med.)* **1.** *n. (stitch)* Naht, *die; (thread)* Faden, *der.* **2.** *v. t.* nähen

svelte [svelt] *adj.* grazil; anmutig ‹*Bewegungen*›

SW *abbr.* **a)** [saʊθˈwest] **south-west** SW; **b)** [saʊθˈwestən] **south-western** sw.; **c)** *(Radio)* **short wave** KW

swab [swɒb] **1.** *n.* **a)** *(Med.: absorbent pad)* Tupfer, *der;* **b)** *(Med.: specimen)* Abstrich, *der;* **c)** *(pad or mop for cleaning decks)* Dweil, *der (Seemannsspr.).* **2.** *v. t.,* **-bb- a) ~ [down]** wischen; schwabbern ‹*Deck*› *(Seemannsspr.);* **b)** *(Med.)* betupfen ‹*Wunde*›

Swabia [ˈsweɪbɪə] *pr. n.* Schwaben *(das)*

Swabian [ˈsweɪbɪən] **1.** *adj.* schwäbisch; **sb. is ~**: jmd. ist Schwabe/Schwäbin. **2.** *n.* **a)** *(person)* Schwabe, *der*/Schwäbin, *die;* **b)** *(dialect)* Schwäbisch, *das;* **sb. speaks ~**: jmd. schwäbelt

swaddle [ˈswɒdl] *v. t.* wickeln ‹*Baby*›; **swaddling clothes** *(Bibl.)* Windeln

swag [swæg] *n.* **a)** *(sl.: stolen goods)* Beute, *die;* Sore, *die (Gaunerspr.);* **b)** *(Austral., NZ: bundle)* Bündel, *das*

swagger [ˈswægə(r)] **1.** *v. i.* **a)** *(walk with a ~)* großspurig stolzieren; **b)** *(behave in domineering way)* großspurig auftreten; **c)** *(boast)* angeben *(ugs.);* aufschneiden. **2.** *n. see* **1: a)** großspuriges Stolzieren; **b)** großspuriges Gehabe; **walk with a ~**: arrogant auftreten; **c)** Angeberei, *die (ugs.)*

ˈswagger cane *(Brit.) see* **swagger stick**

swaggering [ˈswægərɪŋ] **1.** *n.* **a)** *(boasting)* Angeberei, *die (ugs.);* **b)** *(manner)* arrogantes *od.* großspuriges Auftreten. **2.** *adj.* stolzierend ‹*Gang*›; großspurig ‹*Gehabe*›

ˈswagger stick *n.* Offiziersstöckchen, *das*

swagman [ˈswægmən] *n., pl.* **swagmen** [ˈswægmən] *(Austral., NZ)* Landstreicher, *der*

Swahili [swɑːˈhiːlɪ, swəˈhiːlɪ] **1.** *adj.* Swahili-; *see also* **English 1. 2.** *n.* **a)** *no pl. (language)* Swahili, *das; see also* **English 2 a; b)** *pl. same (person)* Swahili, *der/die*

swain [sweɪn] *n. (arch./joc.)* **a)** *(peasant)* Bauernbursche, *der;* **b)** *(lover)* Freier, *der*

¹swallow [ˈswɒləʊ] **1.** *v. t.* **a)** schlucken; *(by mistake)* verschlucken ‹*Fischgräte, fig.: Wort, Silbe*›; **~ the bait** *(fig.)* den Köder schlucken *(ugs.);* **b)** *(repress)* hinunterschlucken *(ugs.)* ‹*Stolz, Ärger*›; **~ one's words** [demütig] zurücknehmen, was man gesagt hat; **c)** *(believe)* schlucken *(ugs.),* glauben ‹*Geschichte, Erklärung*›; **I find this hard to ~**: das kann ich kaum glauben; **d)** *(put up with)* schlucken *(ugs.)* ‹*Beleidigung, Unrecht*›. **2.** *v. i.* schlucken. **3.** *n.* Schluck, *der*

~ ˈup *v. t.* **a)** *(make disappear)* verschlucken; schlucken ‹*kleinere Betriebe, Gebiete*›; **I wished the earth would ~ me up** ich wäre am liebsten vor Scham im den Boden versunken; **b)** *(exhaust, consume)* auffressen; verschlingen ‹*große Summen*›

²swallow *n. (Ornith.)* Schwalbe, *die;* **one ~ does not make a summer** *(prov.)* eine Schwalbe macht noch keinen Sommer *(Spr.)*

swallow: **~-dive** *n. (Brit.) Tauchsprung, bei dem die Arme bis kurz vor dem Eintauchen seitlich ausgestreckt werden;* **~-tail** *n.* Schwalbenschwanz, *der*

swam *see* **swim 1, 2**

swamp [swɒmp] **1.** *n.* Sumpf, *der.* **2.** *v. t.* **a)** *(flood)* überschwemmen; **b)** *(overwhelm)* **be ~ed with letters/applications/orders/work** mit Briefen/Bewerbungen/Aufträgen überschwemmt werden/bis über den Hals in Arbeit stecken *(ugs.)*

ˈswampland *n.* Sumpfland, *das*

swampy [ˈswɒmpɪ] *adj.* sumpfig

swan [swɒn] **1.** *n.* Schwan, *der;* **black ~**: Schwarzer Schwan; Trauerschwan, *der.* **2.** *v. i.,* **-nn-** *(sl.)* ziehen; **~ about** *or* **around** herumziehen *(ugs.); (in small area)* rumlaufen *(ugs.);* **~ off** losziehen *(ugs.)*

ˈswan-dive *(Amer.) see* **swallow-dive**

swank [swæŋk] *(coll.)* **1.** *n.* **a)** Angeberei, *die (ugs.);* Angabe, *die (ugs.);* **b)** *(person)* Angeber, *der*/Angeberin, *die.* **2.** *v. i.* angeben *(ugs.)* (**about** mit); **~ around** herumstolzieren *(ugs.)*

swanky [ˈswæŋkɪ] *adj. (coll.)* protzig *(ugs.);* **~ car** Angeberauto, *das*

swan: **~-neck** *n.* Schwanenhals, *der;* **~sdown** *n.* Schwanendaunen *Pl.;* **~-song** *n. (fig.)* Schwanengesang, *der*

swap [swɒp] **1.** *v. t.,* **-pp-** tauschen (**for** gegen); austauschen ‹*Erfahrungen, Erinnerungen*›; **~ jokes** sich *(Dat.)* [gegenseitig] Witze erzählen; **~ places [with sb.]** [mit jmdm.] den Platz *od.* die Plätze tauschen; *(fig.)* [mit jmdm.] tauschen; *see also* **horse 1 a. 2.** *v. i.,* **-pp-** tauschen; **will you ~?** tauschst du? **3.** *n.* Tausch, *der;* **do a ~ [with sb.]** [mit jmdm.] tauschen

sward [swɔːd] *n. (literary)* Rasen, *der;* Rasenfläche, *die*

swarf [swɔːf] *n.* feine Metallspäne

swarm [swɔːm] **1.** *n.* **a)** Schwarm, *der;* **~ [of bees]** Bienenschwarm, *der; (settled in a hive)* Bienenvolk, *das;* **b)** *in pl. (great numbers)* **~s of tourists/children** Scharen von Touristen/Kindern. **2.** *v. i.* **a)** *(move in a ~)* schwärmen; **b)** *(teem)* wimmeln (**with** von); **the shops were ~ing with tourists** in den Geschäften wimmelte es von Touristen

~ up *v. t.* hochklettern

swarthiness [ˈswɔːðɪnɪs] *n., no pl. (complexion)* dunkle Gesichtsfarbe; *(of person)* Dunkelhäutigkeit, *die*

swarthy [ˈswɔːðɪ] *adj.* dunkel ‹*Gesichtsfarbe*›; dunkelhäutig ‹*Person*›

swashbuckler [ˈswɒʃbʌklə(r)] *n.* Draufgänger, *der*

swashbuckling [ˈswɒʃbʌklɪŋ] *adj.* draufgängerisch

swastika [ˈswɒstɪkə] *n. (of Nazis)* Hakenkreuz, *das; (ancient symbol)* Swastika, *die*

swat [swɒt] **1.** *v. t.,* **-tt- a)** *(hit hard)* schlagen; hauen *(ugs.);* **b)** *(crush)* totschlagen ‹*Fliege, Wespe*›. **2.** *n.* **a)** *(slap)* Klaps, *der;* **give a fly a ~, take a ~ at a fly** nach einer Fliege schlagen; **b)** *(fly-swatter)* Klatsche, *die*

swatch [swɒtʃ] *n.* **a)** *(sample)* Muster, *das;* **b)** *(collection of samples)* Musterbuch, *das*

swath [swɔːθ] *see* **swathe 2**

swathe [sweɪð] **1.** *v. t.* [ein]hüllen; **~d in bandages** ganz in Bandagen eingewickelt; **~d in mist** in Nebel gehüllt. **2.** *n.* *(cut by mower)* gemähte Bahn; *(broad strip)* breiter Streifen; *(in forest)* Schneise, *die;* **cut a ~ through the corn/the undergrowth/the forest** eine Bahn durch das Getreide/Unterholz schneiden/eine Schneise durch den Wald schlagen

swatter [ˈswɒtə(r)] *n.* Klatsche, *die*

sway [sweɪ] **1.** *v. i.* [hin und her] schwanken; *(gently)* sich wiegen; **~ towards sth.** *(on one's feet)* einer Sache entgegenschwanken; *(lean down to)* sich einer Sache *(Dat.)* zuneigen. **2.** *v. t.* **a)** wiegen ‹*Kopf, Hüften, Zweig, Wipfel*›; hin und her schwanken lassen ‹*Baum, Mast, Antenne*›; **b)** *(have influence over)* beeinflussen; *(persuade)* überreden; **be ~ed by sth.** sich von etw. beeinflussen lassen; **she will not be ~ed over sanctions** sie bleibt in der Frage der Sanktionen hart. **3.** *n.* Herrschaft, *die;* **have sb. under one's ~, hold ~ over sb.** über jmdn. herrschen

swear [sweə(r)] **1.** *v. t.,* **swore** [swɔː(r)], **sworn** [swɔːn] **a)** schwören ‹*Eid usw.*›; **they swore eternal fidelity** sie schworen sich *(Dat.)* ewige Treue; **I could have sworn [that] it was him** ich hätte schwören können, daß er es war; *see also* **blind 2 b; b)** *(administer oath to)* vereidigen ‹*Zeugen*›; **~ sb. to secrecy** jmdn. auf Geheimhaltung einschwören; *see also* **sworn. 2.** *v. i.,* **swore, sworn a)** *(use ~-words)* fluchen; **b) ~ to sth.** *(be certain of)* etw. beschwören; einen Eid auf etw. *(Akk.)* ablegen; **I wouldn't like to ~ to it** *(coll.)* ich will es nicht beschwören; **c)** *(take oath)* schwören, einen Eid ablegen (**on** auf + *Akk.*). **3.** *n.* Fluch, *der;* **have a ~**: fluchen

~ at *v. t.* beschimpfen

~ by *v. t. (coll.: have confidence in)* schwören auf (+ *Akk.*)

~ ˈin *v. t.* vereidigen ‹*Geschworenen, Zeugen*›

~ ˈout *v. t. (Amer.)* **~ a warrant out against sb.** gegen jmdn. durch eine eidliche [Straf]anzeige einen Haftbefehl erwirken

ˈswear-word *n.* Kraftausdruck, *der;* Fluch, *der;* **use ~s** fluchen

sweat [swet] **1.** *n.* **a)** Schweiß, *der;* **in** *or* **by the ~ of one's brow** im Schweiße seines Angesichtes; **be in a ~ [with fear]** [vor Angst] schwitzen; **be in a ~ to do sth.** *(fig.: be anxious)* danach fiebern, etw. zu tun; **I came** *or* **broke out in a ~**: mir brach der [Angst]schweiß aus; **don't get in such a ~!** reg dich nicht so auf!; **be all of a ~ at the prospect of the exam** beim Gedanken an die Prüfung ins Schwitzen geraten *od.* kommen; **b)** *(spell of ~ing)* **have a good ~**: richtig schwitzen; **c)** *(drudgery)* Plagerei, *die;* Plackerei, *die (ugs.);* **no ~!** *(coll.)* kein Problem! *(ugs.);* **d)** *(drops on surface)* Kondenswasser, *das; (on cheese)* Fetttröpfchen. *See also* **cold sweat. 2.** *v. i.,* **~ed** *or (Amer.)* **~ a)** *(perspire)* schwitzen; **~ like a pig** *(coll.)* schwitzen wie die Sau *(salopp);* **~ with fear** vor Angst schwitzen; **b)** *(fig.: suffer)* **he made me sit outside ~ing** er ließ mich draußen sitzen und schmoren *(ugs.);* **c)** *(drudge)* sich placken *(ugs.);* **we had to ~ to get the job finished** wir mußten uns anstrengen, um mit der Arbeit fertig zu werden; **make sb. ~**

(make work in bad conditions) jmdn. schwitzen *od. (ugs.)* schuften lassen; **d)** *(produce surface moisture)* schwitzen. **3.** *v. t.* **a)** *(employ in bad conditions)* schwitzen *od. (ugs.)* schuften lassen; **b)** ~ **blood** *(fig.)* Blut und Wasser schwitzen *(ugs.)*; **c)** *(emit like ~)* ausschwitzen; **d)** ~ **it out** *(coll.)* durchhalten; ausharren

'sweat-band *n.* Schweißband, *das*

sweated labour [swetɪd 'leɪbə(r)] *n.* unterbezahlte [Schwer]arbeit; *(workers)* unterbezahlte Arbeitskräfte

sweater ['swetə(r)] *n.* Pullover, *der*

sweat: ~-gland *n.* Schweißdrüse, *die*; **~-shirt** *n.* Sweatshirt, *das*; **~-shop** *n.* ausbeuterische [kleine] Klitsche *(ugs.)*

sweaty ['swetɪ] *adj. (moist with sweat)* schweißig; schweißnaß; schwitzend ⟨*Käse*⟩

Swede [swi:d] *n.* Schwede, *der*/Schwedin, *die*

swede *n.* Kohlrübe, *die*

Sweden ['swi:dn] *pr. n.* Schweden *(das)*

Swedish ['swi:dɪʃ] **1.** *adj.* schwedisch; **sb. is ~:** jmd. ist Schwede/Schwedin; *see also* **English 1. 2.** *n.* Schwedisch, *das*; *see also* **English 2 a**

sweep [swi:p] **1.** *v. t.,* **swept** [swept] **a)** fegen *(bes. nordd.)*; kehren *(bes. südd.)*; **~ the board, ~ all before one** *(fig.: win all awards)* auf der ganzen Linie siegen; **b)** *(move with force)* fegen; **the current swept the logs along** die Strömung riß die Hölzer mit; **the wave of protest swept the opposition into office** die Protestwelle katapultierte die Opposition an die Macht; **c)** *(traverse swiftly)* **~ the hillside/plain** ⟨*Wind:*⟩ über die Hügel/Ebene fegen; **~ the country** ⟨*Epidemie, Mode:*⟩ das Land überrollen; ⟨*Feuer:*⟩ durch das Land fegen; **searchlights swept the sky** Suchscheinwerfer huschten über den Himmel; **~ an area with fire** *(Mil.)* ein Gebiet mit Feuer bestreichen; **d)** *(search)* durchsuchen **(for** nach); **~ a channel for mines** eine Fahrrinne nach Minen absuchen. *See also* **carpet 1 a. 2.** *v. i.,* **swept a)** *(clean)* fegen *(bes. nordd.)*; kehren *(bes. südd.)*; **b)** *(go fast, in stately manner)* ⟨*Vogel:*⟩ gleiten; ⟨*Mensch, Auto:*⟩ rauschen; ⟨*Wind usw.:*⟩ fegen; **c)** *(extend)* sich erstrecken; **the road ~s to the left** die Straße macht einen großen Bogen nach links; **his glance swept from left to right** sein Blick glitt von links nach rechts. **3.** *n.* **a)** *(cleaning)* **give sth. a ~:** etw. fegen *(bes. nordd.)*; etw. kehren *(bes. südd.)*; **make a clean ~** *(fig.) (get rid of everything)* gründlich aufräumen; *(win all prizes)* gründlich abräumen *(ugs.)*; **make a clean ~ of the prizes** alle Preise einheimsen *(ugs.)*; **b)** *see* **chimney-sweep; c)** *(coll.) see* **sweepstake; d)** *(motion) (of arm)* ausholende Bewegung; **with an impatient ~ of his hand** mit einer ungeduldigen Handbewegung; **e)** *(stretch)* **a wide/an open ~ of country** ein weiter Landstrich; **f)** *(curve of road, river)* Bogen, *der*; **the wide ~ of the bay** die geschwungene Kurve der Bucht; **g)** *(sortie by aircraft)* Einsatz, *der (Milit.)*

~ a'side *v. t.* **a)** *(dismiss)* beiseite schieben ⟨*Einwand, Zweifel*⟩; überrennen ⟨*gegnerische Mannschaft*⟩; aus dem Weg scheuchen ⟨*Reporter*⟩; **b)** *(push aside)* wegfegen; beiseite fegen

~ a'way *v. t.* fortreißen; *(fig.)* hinwegfegen *(geh.)* ⟨*Traditionen*⟩; *(abolish)* aufräumen mit ⟨*Privilegien, Korruption*⟩

~ 'by *v. i.* vorbeirauschen

~ 'down *v. i.* **a) ~ down on sb./sth.** sich auf jmdn./etw. stürzen; **b) the hills ~ down to the sea** die Berge fallen in sanftem Bogen zum Meer hinab

~ 'in *v. i.* **a)** *(enter majestically)* einziehen; **b)** *(Polit.)* [mit großer Mehrheit] an die Macht kommen

~ 'off 1. *v. i.* abrauschen *(ugs.)*. **2.** *v. t.* fortreißen; *see also* **foot 1 a**

~ 'out 1. *v. t.* ausfegen *(bes. nordd.)*; auskehren *(bes. südd.)*. **2.** *v. i.* abrauschen *(ugs.)*

~ 'up 1. *v. t.* zusammenfegen *(bes. nordd.)*; zusammenkehren *(bes. südd.)*. **2.** *v. i.* angerauscht kommen

sweeper ['swi:pə(r)] *n.* **a) [road] ~** *(person)* Straßenfeger, *der (bes. nordd.)*; Straßenkehrer, *der (bes. südd.)*; *(machine)* Straßenkehrmaschine, *die*; *see also* **carpet-sweeper; mine-sweeper; b)** *(Footb.)* Ausputzer, *der*

sweeping ['swi:pɪŋ] **1.** *adj.* **a)** *(without limitations)* pauschal; **b)** *(far-reaching)* weitreichend ⟨*Einsparung*⟩; umfassend ⟨*Reform*⟩; durchschlagend ⟨*Sieg, Erfolg*⟩; umwälzend ⟨*Veränderung*⟩; **c)** *(moving in a wide curve)* ausholend ⟨*Geste, Bewegung*⟩; schwungvoll ⟨*Knicks, Verbeugung*⟩; schweifend ⟨*Blick*⟩. **2.** *n. in pl.* Kehricht, *der*

sweepingly ['swi:pɪŋlɪ] *adv.* pauschal

sweep: ~-'second hand *n. (Horol.)* Zentralsekundenzeiger, *der*; **~stake** *n.* **a)** *(race, contest)* Sweepstake[rennen], *das*; **b)** *(lottery) Pferdetoto, bei dem sich die Gewinnsumme aus den Einsätzen zusammensetzt*

sweet [swi:t] **1.** *adj.* **a)** *(to taste)* süß; **~ tea** gesüßter Tee; **have a ~ tooth** gern Süßes mögen; **with a ~ tooth like yours ...:** da du so gern *od.* viel Süßes ißt ...; **b)** *(lovely)* süß; reizend ⟨*Wesen, Gesicht, Mädchen, Kleid*⟩; **~ dreams!** träum[e]/träumt süß!; **how ~ of you!** wie nett *od.* lieb von dir!; **keep sb. ~:** jmdn. bei [guter] Laune halten; **he's ~ on her** *(dated coll.)* er hat eine Schwäche für sie; **at one's own ~ will, in one's own ~ way** wie es einem [gerade] paßt; **go one's own ~ way** machen, was einem paßt; **c)** *(fragrant)* süß; frisch ⟨*Atem*⟩; **be ~ with sth.** süß nach etw. duften; **the ~ smell of success** *(fig.)* die Süße des Erfolgs *(geh., scherzh.)*; **d)** *(musical)* süß *(geh.)*; lieblich ⟨*Stimme, Musik, Klang*⟩. *See also* **basil; chestnut 1 a; pepper 1 b; sweet potato; seventeen 1; sixteen 1; violet 1 a. 2.** *n.* **a)** *(Brit.: piece of confectionery)* Bonbon, *das od. der*; *(with chocolate, fudge, etc.)* Süßigkeit, *die*; **b)** *(Brit.: dessert)* Nachtisch, *der*; Dessert, *das*; **for ~:** zum Nachtisch *od.* Dessert; **c)** *in pl. (delights)* Freuden; Wonnen *(geh.)*; **d)** *(darling)* **[my] ~** *(female)* [meine] Liebste; *(male)* [mein] Liebster

sweet: ~-and-'sour *attrib. adj.* süßsauer; **~bread** *n. (Gastr.)* Bries, *das*; **~ brier** *n.* Weinrose, *die*; **~ corn** *n.* Zuckermais, *der*

sweeten ['swi:tn] *v. t.* **a)** *(add sugar etc. to)* süßen; **b)** *(add fragrance to)* süß machen; versüßen; *(remove bad smell of)* reinigen ⟨*Luft, Atem*⟩; **c)** *(make agreeable)* versüßen ⟨*Leben, Abend*⟩; milde stimmen ⟨*Person*⟩; *see also* **pill b**

sweetener ['swi:tnə(r)] *n.* **a)** Süßstoff, *der*; **use honey as a ~:** Honig zum Süßen verwenden; **b)** *(bribe)* kleine Aufmerksamkeit *(iron.)*

'sweetheart *n.* Schatz, *der*; Liebling, *der*; **an old ~:** eine alte Liebe *(ugs.)*; **how long have they been ~s?** wie lange gehen sie schon miteinander? *(ugs.)*

sweetie ['swi:tɪ] *n.* **a)** *(Brit. child lang.) see* **sweet 2 a; b)** *(coll.: darling)* Schatz, *der*; **~ [pie]** *(term of endearment)* Liebling, *der*; Schätzchen, *das (ugs.)*

sweetish ['swi:tɪʃ] *adj.* süßlich

sweetly ['swi:tlɪ] *adv.* lieb; süß ⟨*spielen, singen*⟩; **run ~** ⟨*Motor:*⟩ schön rund laufen

sweet: ~meal *adj.* **~meal biscuits** süße Vollkornkekse; **~meat** *n.* Süßigkeit, *die*

sweetness ['swi:tnɪs] *n., no pl.* **a)** *(in taste)* Süße, *die*; **b)** *(fragrance)* süßer Duft; **c)** *(melodiousness)* Süße, *die (geh.)*; **d) all is ~ and light** es herrscht eitel Freude und Sonnenschein *(meist scherzh.)*

sweet: ~ 'pea *n. (Bot.)* Wicke, *die*; **~ po'tato** *n.* Batate, *die*; Süßkartoffel, *die*; **~-scented** *adj.* süß [duftend]; wohlriechend; **~-shop** *n. (Brit.)* Süßwarengeschäft, *das*; **~-smelling** *adj. see* **~-scented; ~-talk** *(Amer.)* **1.** *n.* Süßholzgeraspel, *das (ugs.)*; **2.** *v. t.* **~-talk sb. [into doing sth.]** jmdn. beschwatzen[, etw. zu tun]; **~-tempered** ['swi:ttempəd] *adj.* sanftmütig; **~ 'william** *n. (Bot.)* Bartnelke, *die*

swell [swel] **1.** *v. t.,* **~ed, swollen** ['swəʊlən] *or* **~ed a)** *(increase in size, height)* anschwellen lassen; aufquellen lassen ⟨*Holz*⟩; **b)** *(increase amount of)* anschwellen lassen; vergrößern; **~ the ranks [of participants]** die Zahl der Teilnehmer vergrößern; **c)** blähen ⟨*Segel*⟩. **2.** *v. i.,* **~ed, swollen** *or* **~ed a)** *(expand)* ⟨*Körperteil:*⟩ anschwellen; ⟨*Segel:*⟩ sich blähen; ⟨*Backen:*⟩ sich aufblähen; ⟨*Material:*⟩ aufquellen; **b)** *(increase in amount)* ⟨*Anzahl:*⟩ zunehmen; ⟨*Gehalt:*⟩ steigen; **c)** *(become louder)* anschwellen (**[in]to** zu); **d)** *(fig.)* ⟨*Herz:*⟩ schwellen *(geh.)*. **3.** *n.* **a)** *(of sea)* Dünung, *die*; **b)** *(Mus.)* Schwellwerk, *das*; **c)** *(dated coll.)* feiner Herr/feine Dame; **the ~s** die feinen Leute; *(smart set)* die Schickeria *(ugs.)*; **d)** *(act, condition)* Schwellen, *das*. **4.** *adj. (coll.)* **a)** *(dated: stylish, socially prominent)* schick; fein; **b)** *(Amer.: excellent)* toll *(ugs.)*

'swell-box *n. (Mus.)* Jalousieschweller, *der*

swelling ['swelɪŋ] **1.** *n.* Schwellung, *die (Med.)*. **2.** *adj.* **a)** *(growing larger, louder)* anschwellend; **b)** *(increasing)* wachsend; steigend ⟨*Flut*⟩; **c)** *(bulging)* gebläht ⟨*Segel*⟩

'swell-organ *n. (Mus.)* Schwellwerk, *das*

swelter ['sweltə(r)] *v. i.* [vor Hitze] [fast] vergehen; **~ in the heat** in der Hitze schmoren *(ugs.)*; **~ing** glühend heiß ⟨*Tag, Wetter*⟩; **~ing heat** Bruthitze, *die*

swept *see* **sweep 1, 2**

swept: ~-back *adj.* **~-back wing** positiv gepfeilter Flügel; **~-back hair** zurückgekämmtes Haar; **~-wing** *adj.* ⟨*Flugzeug*⟩ mit Pfeilflügeln

swerve [swɜ:v] **1.** *v. i. (deviate)* einen Bogen *od. (ugs.)* Schlenker machen; **~ to the right/left** nach rechts/links [aus]schwenken; **~ from its path** ⟨*Fahrzeug:*⟩ ausscheren; **~ in the air** ⟨*Vogel, Ball:*⟩ in der Luft abdrehen; **she never ~d from her duty** sie hat ihre Pflicht immer treu erfüllt. **2.** *n.* **a)** *(divergence from course)* Bogen, *der*; Schlenker, *der (ugs.)*; **b)** *(swerving motion)* **put a ~ on a ball** einem Ball [einen] Effet geben

swift [swɪft] **1.** *adj.* schnell; flink, schnell ⟨*Bewegung*⟩; **~ action** rasches Handeln; **~ retribution** prompte Bestrafung; **have a ~ temper, be ~ to anger** jähzornig sein. **2.** *n. (Ornith.)* Mauersegler, *der*

swiftly ['swɪftlɪ] *adv.* schnell; *(soon)* bald

swiftness ['swɪftnɪs] *n.* Schnelligkeit, *die*; **~ of action** schnelles *od.* rasches Handeln

swig [swɪg] *(coll.)* **1.** *v. t.,* **-gg-** schlucken *(ugs.)*; [herunter]kippen *(ugs.)*. **2.** *v. i.,* **-gg-** [hastig] trinken. **3.** *n.* Schluck, *der*; **have/take a ~ [of beer** *etc.***]** einen tüchtigen Schluck [Bier *usw.*] trinken/nehmen

swill [swɪl] **1.** *v. t.* **a)** *(rinse)* **~ [out]** [aus]spülen; **~ down the floor** den Fußboden abspülen; **b)** *(derog.: drink greedily)* hinunterspülen *(ugs.)*. **2.** *n.* **a)** *(rinsing)* Spülen, *das*; **give sth. a ~ [out]/down** etw. [aus]spülen/abspülen; **b)** *(derog.: drink)* Brühe, *die (ugs. abwertend)*; **c)** *(for pigs)* Schweinefutter, *das*

swim [swɪm] **1.** *v. i.,* **-mm-, swam** [swæm], **swum** [swʌm] **a)** schwimmen; **~ with/against the tide/stream** *(fig.)* mit dem/gegen den Strom schwimmen; **b)** *(fig.: be flooded, overflow)* **~ with** *or* **in sth.** in etw. *(Dat.)* schwimmen; **her eyes swam with tears** ihre Augen schwammen; **the deck was ~ming with water** das Deck stand unter Wasser; **c)** *(appear to whirl)* **~ [before sb.'s eyes]** [vor jmds. Augen] verschwimmen; **d)** *(have dizzy sensation)* **my head was ~ming** mir war schwindelig. *See also* **sink 2 a. 2.** *v. t.,* **-mm-,**

swam, swum schwimmen ⟨*Strecke*⟩; durchschwimmen ⟨*Fluß, See*⟩; ~ **[the] breast-stroke/crawl** brustschwimmen/kraulen. **3.** *n.* **a) have a/go for a** ~: schwimmen/schwimmen gehen; **do you fancy a** ~? möchtest du schwimmen gehen?; **a refreshing** ~: ein erfrischendes Bad; **I like an early morning** ~: ich gehe gern frühmorgens schwimmen; **b) be in the** ~ **[of things]** mitten im Geschehen sein

swimmer ['swɪmə(r)] *n.* Schwimmer, *der*/Schwimmerin, *die;* **[not] be a** ~: [nicht] schwimmen können; **be a good/poor** ~: gut/schlecht schwimmen können

swimming ['swɪmɪŋ] **1.** *n.* Schwimmen, *das;* **like** ~: gern schwimmen. **2.** *attrib. adj.* schwimmend

swimming: ~**-baths** *n. pl.* Schwimmbad, *das;* ~**-costume** *n.* Badeanzug, *der;* ~**-lesson** *n.* Schwimmstunde, *die;* ~**-lessons** Schwimmunterricht, *der*

swimmingly ['swɪmɪŋlɪ] *adv. (coll.)* glänzend; go ~: wie am Schnürchen klappen *(ugs.)*

swimming: ~**-pool** *n.* Schwimmbecken, *das; (in house or garden)* Swimmingpool, *der; (building)* Schwimmbad, *das;* ~**-trunks** *n. pl.* Badehose, *die*

'swim-suit *n.* Badeanzug, *der*

swindle ['swɪndl] **1.** *v. t.* betrügen; ~ **sb. out of sth.** jmdn. um etw. betrügen; *(take by persuasion)* jmdm. etw. abschwindeln. **2.** *n.* Schwindel, *der;* Betrug, *der*

swindler ['swɪndlə(r)] *n.* Schwindler, *der*/Schwindlerin, *die*

swine [swaɪn] *n., pl. same* **a)** *(Amer./formal/Zool.)* Schwein, *das;* **b)** *(derog.: contemptible person)* Schwein, *das (abwertend);* **c)** *(coll.: nasty thing)* harter Brocken *(ugs.);* **be a** ~ **to operate** ⟨*Maschine:*⟩ verteufelt schwer zu bedienen sein *(ugs.);* **a** ~ **of a job** eine verteufelt *(ugs.) od. (salopp)* tierisch schwere Arbeit. *See also* **pearl b**

swine: ~**-fever** *n.* Schweinepest, *die;* ~**-herd** *n.* Schweinehirt, *der*

swing [swɪŋ] **1.** *n.* **a)** *(apparatus)* Schaukel, *die;* **b)** *(spell of* ~*ing)* Schaukeln, *das;* **want/have a** ~: schaukeln wollen/schaukeln; **c)** *(Sport: strike, blow)* Schlag, *der; (Boxing)* Schwinger, *der; (Golf)* Schwung, *der;* **take a** ~ **at sb./sth.** zum Schlag gegen jmdn./auf etw. *(Akk.)* ausholen; **d)** *(of suspended object)* Schwingen, *das;* **in full** ~ *(fig.)* in vollem Gang[e]; **e)** *(steady movement)* Rhythmus, *der;* **the party went with a** ~: auf der Party herrschte eine tolle Stimmung *(ugs.);* **get into/be in the** ~ **of things** *or* **it** richtig reinkommen/richtig drin sein *(ugs.);* **f)** *(Mus.)* Swing, *der;* **g)** *(shift)* Schwankung, *die; (of public opinion)* Wende, *die; (amount of change in votes)* Abwanderung, *die;* **a** ~ **to the Left/Right** ein Linksruck/Rechtsruck *(Politik Jargon). See also* **pendulum; roundabout 1 b. 2.** *v. i.,* **swung** [swʌŋ] **a)** *(turn on axis, sway)* schwingen; *(in wind)* schaukeln; ~ **open** ⟨*Tür:*⟩ aufgehen; **be** ~**ing at anchor** schwojen *(Seemannsspr.);* **b)** *(go in sweeping curve)* schwenken; **the plane swung low over the field** das Flugzeug schwenkte über dem Feld in den Tiefflug; ~ **from sb.'s arm/a tree** an jmds. Arm/einem Baum schwingen *(geh.) od.* baumeln; **c)** *(go with* ~*ing gait)* beschwingt gehen; ~ **into action** *(fig.)* loslegen *(ugs.);* **d)** *(move oneself by* ~*ing)* sich schwingen; ~ **up** sich hinaufschwingen; **the car swung out of the drive** der Wagen schwenkte aus der Einfahrt; **e)** *(sl.: be executed by hanging)* baumeln *(salopp);* **he'll** ~ **for it** dafür wird er baumeln; **f) be** ~**ing** *(sl.: be lively)* auf vollen Touren laufen *(ugs.);* **g)** *(sl.: be promiscuous)* die Abwechslung lieben *(ugs. verhüll.);* ~ **both ways** *(sl.)* es mit Männlein wie Weiblein machen *(ugs. verhüll.).* **3.** *v. t.,* **swung a)** schwingen; *(rock)* schaukeln; ~ **one's legs** mit den Beinen baumeln; die Beine baumeln lassen; ~ **a key on a chain** mit einem Schlüssel an einer Kette schlenkern; ~ **sth. round and round** etw. kreisen *od.* im Kreise wirbeln lassen; **cranes** ~ **cargo on to the ship** Kräne befördern schwingende Lasten auf das Schiff; **b)** *(cause to face in another direction)* schwenken; ~ **sb. round** jmdn. herumwirbeln; **he swung the car off the road/into the road** er schwenkte [mit dem Auto] von der Straße ab/in die Straße ein; **c)** *(have influence on)* umschlagen lassen ⟨*öffentliche Meinung*⟩; ~ **the elections** den Ausgang der Wahlen entscheiden; **what swung it for me ...:** was für mich den Ausschlag gab ...; **d)** *(suspend by its ends)* aufhängen ⟨*Hängematte*⟩; **e)** *(sl.: arrange)* deichseln *(salopp). See also* **cat a**

~ **at** *v. t.* ~ **at sb./sth.** zum Schlag auf jmdn./etw. ausholen

~ **'round** *v. i.* sich schnell umdrehen (**on** nach); *(in surprise)* herumfahren

swing: ~ **bridge** *n.* Drehbrücke, *die;* ~**-'door** *n.* Pendeltür, *die*

swingeing ['swɪndʒɪŋ] *adj. (Brit.)* hart ⟨*Schlag*⟩; *(fig.)* drastisch ⟨*Kürzung, Maßnahme*⟩; scharf ⟨*Attacke*⟩

swinging ['swɪŋɪŋ] *adj.* **a)** schwingend; **b)** *(with strong rhythm)* [stark] rhythmisch; schwungvoll ⟨*Schritt*⟩; **c)** *(sl.: lively)* wild *(ugs.);* swingend *(ugs.)*

'swing-wing *n.* Schwenkflügel, *der*

swipe [swaɪp] *(coll.)* **1.** *v. i.* ~ **at** [wild] schlagen nach; eindreschen auf (+ *Akk.*) *(ugs.).* **2.** *v. t.* **a)** *(hit hard)* knallen *(ugs.);* **b)** *(sl.: steal)* klauen *(ugs.).* **3.** *n.* [wuchtiger] Schlag; **take a wild** ~ **at sth.** wild auf etw. *(Akk.)* losschlagen

swirl [swɜ:l] **1.** *v. i.* wirbeln. **2.** *v. t.* umherwirbeln. **3.** *n.* **a)** *(eddying motion)* **with a** ~ **of the paddle** durch Herumwirbeln des Paddels; **b)** *(spiralling shape)* Spirale, *die*

swish [swɪʃ] **1.** *v. t.* schlagen mit ⟨*Schwanz*⟩; sausen lassen ⟨*Stock*⟩. **2.** *v. i.* zischen; ~ **past** ⟨*Auto:*⟩ vorbeirauschen. **3.** *n.* Zischen, *das.* **4.** *adj. (coll.)* schick *(ugs.)*

Swiss [swɪs] **1.** *adj.* Schweizer; schweizerisch; **sb. is** ~: jmd. ist Schweizer/Schweizerin. **2.** *n.* Schweizer, *der*/Schweizerin, *die;* **the** ~ *pl.* die Schweizer

Swiss: ~ **'chard** *see* **chard;** ~ **'cheese** *n.* Schweizer Käse, *der;* ~ **cheese plant** Fensterblatt, *das;* ~ **'French** *adj.* welschschweizerisch; ~ **'German 1.** *adj.* schweizerdeutsch; **2.** *n.* Schweizerdeutsch, *das;* ~ **'guards** *n. pl. (in Vatican)* Schweizergarde, *die;* ~ **'roll** *n.* Biskuitrolle, *die*

switch [swɪtʃ] **1.** *n.* **a)** *(esp. Electr.)* Schalter, *der;* **b)** *(Amer. Railw.)* Weiche, *die;* **c)** *(change with another)* Wechsel, *der; (change of procedure)* Umstellung, *die* (**from** von, **to** auf + *Akk.*); ~ **of roles** Rollentausch, *der;* **d)** *(flexible shoot, whip)* Gerte, *die;* **e)** *(tress of hair)* Haarteil, *das.* **2.** *v. t.* **a)** *(change)* ~ **sth. [over] to sth.** etw. auf etw. *(Akk.)* umstellen *od. (Electr.)* umschalten; ~ **a player to another position** einen Spieler auf eine andere Position stellen; ~ **sb. to night duty** jmdn. in den Nachtdienst versetzen; ~ **one's vote to another party** seine Stimme einer anderen Partei geben; ~ **the conversation to another topic** das Gespräch auf ein anderes Thema lenken; **b)** *(exchange)* tauschen; **c)** *(Railw.: transfer with* ~*)* [mittels einer Weiche] umleiten; **d)** *(swish)* schlagen mit ⟨*Schwanz*⟩; sausen lassen ⟨*Rohrstock*⟩. **3.** *v. i.* wechseln; ~ **[over] to sth.** auf etw. *(Akk.)* umstellen *od. (Electr.)* umschalten

~ **a'round 1.** *v. t.* umstellen ⟨*Möbel, Dienstplan*⟩. **2.** *v. i.* [die Stellung] wechseln

~ **'off** *v. t. & i.* ausschalten; *(also fig. coll.)* abschalten

~ **'on 1.** *v. t.* einschalten; anschalten; **be** ~**ed on** *(sl.) (high on drugs)* angeturnt sein *(ugs.); (up-to-date)* auf Draht sein *(ugs.);* **be** ~**ed on to jazz/rock** *etc.* auf Jazz/Rock *usw.* stehen *(ugs.).* **2.** *v. i.* sich anschalten

~ **'over 1.** *v. t. see* ~ **2 a. 2.** *v. i. see* ~ **3**

~ **'round** *see* ~ **around**

~ **'through** *v. t.* durchstellen ⟨*Telefongespräch, Anrufer*⟩

switch: ~**back** *n. (Brit.) (road)* [berg]auf und [berg]ab führende Straße; *(roller-coaster)* Achterbahn, *die;* **that road is a real** ~**back:** diese Straße ist ein einziges Rauf und Runter *(ugs.);* ~**-blade** *n.* Springmesser, *das;* ~**board** *n.* **a)** *(Teleph.)* [Telefon]zentrale, *die;* Vermittlung, *die;* ~**board operator** Telefonist, *der*/Telefonistin, *die;* **b)** *(Electr.)* Schalttafel, *die;* ~**-engine** *n. (Amer. Railw.)* Rangierlok[omotive], *die;* ~**gear** *n. (Electr.)* Schaltvorrichtung, *die;* ~**-over** *see* **change-over;** ~**-yard** *n. (Amer.)* Rangierbahnhof, *der*

Switzerland ['swɪtsələnd] *pr. n.* die Schweiz

swivel ['swɪvl] **1.** *n.* Drehgelenk, *das.* **2.** *v. i., (Brit.)* **-ll-** sich drehen. **3.** *v. t., (Brit.)* **-ll-** drehen

'swivel chair *n.* Drehstuhl, *der*

swiz, swizz [swɪz] *n., pl.* **swizzes** *(Brit. sl.)* Beschiß, *der (ugs.);* Schwindel, *der*

'swizzle-stick ['swɪzlstɪk] *n.* Sektquirl, *der*

swollen ['swəʊlən] **1.** *see* **swell 1, 2. 2.** *adj.* geschwollen; angeschwollen ⟨*Fluß*⟩; **eyes** ~ **with weeping** verweinte Augen; **have a** ~ **head** *(fig.)* sehr eingebildet *od.* von sich eingenommen sein

swollen-headed ['swəʊlənhedɪd] *adj.* eingebildet

swoon [swu:n] *(literary)* **1.** *v. i.* **a)** *(faint)* ohnmächtig werden; **b)** *(go into ecstasies)* ~ **over sb./sth.** von jmdm./etw. schwärmen. **2.** *n. (literary)* Ohnmacht, *die*

swoop [swu:p] **1.** *n.* **a)** *(downward plunge)* Sturzflug, *der;* **at a** *or* **one [fell]** ~: auf einen Schlag *(ugs.);* **b)** *(coll.: raid)* Razzia, *die;* **make a** ~ **on a house/an area** eine Razzia in einem Haus/einem Bezirk machen. **2.** *v. i.* *(plunge suddenly)* herabstoßen; *(pounce)* ~ **on sb.** sich auf jmdn. stürzen; *(to attack)* gegen jmdn. einen Schlag führen; **the police** ~**ed on several addresses** die Polizei führte in mehreren Wohnungen Razzien durch; **we'll** ~ **tomorrow** wir schlagen morgen zu

swoosh [swu:ʃ] **1.** *v. i.* rauschen; ~ **by** vorbeirauschen. **2.** *n. (sound)* Rauschen, *das;* **go past with a** ~: vorbeirauschen

swop *see* **swap**

sword [sɔ:d] *n.* Schwert, *das;* **put sb. to the** ~ *(literary)* jmdn. [mit dem Schwert] töten; *see also* **cross 2 a; Damocles**

sword: ~**-dance** *n.* Schwert[er]tanz, *der;* ~**fish** *n.* Schwertfisch, *der;* ~**-play** *n. (Fencing)* [Schwert]fechten, *das;* ~**sman** ['sɔ:dzmən] *n., pl.* ~**smen** ['sɔ:dzmən] [Schwert]fechter, *der;* ~**smanship** ['sɔ:dzmənʃɪp] *n., no pl.* Fechtkunst, *die;* ~**-stick** *n.* Stockdegen, *der;* ~**-swallower** ['sɔ:dswɒləʊə(r)] *n.* Schwertschlucker, *der*

swore *see* **swear 1, 2**

sworn [swɔ:n] **1.** *see* **swear 1, 2. 2.** *attrib. adj.* **a)** *(bound by an oath)* verschworen ⟨*Freund*⟩; ~ **enemy** Todfeind, *der;* **b)** *(certified by oath)* beeidigt; ~ **evidence** Aussage unter Eid; ~ **affidavit/statement** eidesstattliche Versicherung/eidliche Erklärung

swot [swɒt] *(Brit. coll.)* **1.** *n.* Streber, *der*/Streberin, *die (abwertend).* **2.** *v. i.,* **-tt-** büffeln *(ugs.)*

~ **'up** *v. t.* büffeln *(ugs.)*

swotting ['swɒtɪŋ] *n. (Brit. coll.)* Büffelei, *die (ugs.)*

swum *see* **swim 1, 2**

swung *see* **swing 2, 3**

sybarite ['sɪbəraɪt] *n.* Sybarit, *der (geh.)*

sycamore ['sɪkəmɔ:(r)] *n.* Bergahorn, *der; (Amer.: plane-tree)* Platane, *die*

sycophancy ['sɪkəfænsɪ, 'sɪkəfənsɪ] *n.* Kriecherei, *die;* Speichelleckerei, *die*

sycophant ['sɪkəfænt, 'sɪkəfənt] *n.* Kriecher, *der;* Schranze, *die*

syllabic [sɪ'læbɪk] *adj.* **a)** Silben-; **b)** *(Pros.)* silbenzählend

syllable ['sɪləbl] *n. (lit. or fig.)* Silbe, *die;* **she did not utter a ~ of reproach** mit keiner Silbe äußerte sie einen Vorwurf; **in words of one ~** *(fig.)* mit [sehr] einfachen Worten

syllabub ['sɪləbʌb] *n. (Gastr.) aromatisierte Süßspeise aus geschlagener Sahne; (with wine)* Weinschaumcreme, *die*

syllabus ['sɪləbəs] *n., pl.* **~es** *or* **syllabi** ['sɪləbaɪ] Lehrplan, *der; (for exam)* Studienplan, *der*

syllogism ['sɪlədʒɪzm] *n. (Logic)* Syllogismus, *der*

sylph [sɪlf] *n. (Mythol.) (male)* Sylphe, *der; (female; also fig.)* Sylphide, *die*

'sylphlike *adj.* sylphidenhaft *(geh.)*

symbiosis [sɪmbɪ'əʊsɪs], *pl.* **symbioses** [sɪmbɪ'əʊsi:z] *n. (Biol.; also fig.)* Symbiose, *die*

symbiotic [sɪmbɪ'ɒtɪk] *adj.* symbiotisch

symbol ['sɪmbl] *n.* Symbol, *das* **(of** für)

symbolic [sɪm'bɒlɪk], **symbolical** [sɪm'bɒlɪkl] *adj.*, **symbolically** [sɪm'bɒlɪkəlɪ] *adv.* symbolisch

symbolise *see* **symbolize**

symbolism ['sɪmbəlɪzm] *n.* **a)** Symbolik, *die;* **b)** *(Art, Literature)* Symbolismus, *der*

Symbolist ['sɪmbəlɪst] *n.* Symbolist, *der*/Symbolistin, *die; attrib.* symbolistisch

symbolize ['sɪmbəlaɪz] *v. t.* symbolisieren

symmetric [sɪ'metrɪk], **symmetrical** [sɪ'metrɪkl] *adj.*, **symmetrically** [sɪ'metrɪkəlɪ] *adv.* symmetrisch

symmetry ['sɪmɪtrɪ] *n.* Symmetrie, *die*

sympathetic [sɪmpə'θetɪk] *adj.* **a)** *(showing pity)* mitfühlend; *(understanding)* verständnisvoll; **b)** *(favourably inclined)* wohlgesinnt; geneigt ‹*Leser*›; **be ~ to a cause/to new ideas** einer Sache wohlwollend gegenüberstehen/für neue Ideen empfänglich *od.* zugänglich sein; **give sb. a ~ hearing** ein offenes Ohr für jmdn. haben; **he is not at all ~ to this idea** er ist von dieser Idee ganz und gar nicht angetan; **c)** *(to one's taste, likeable)* ansprechend; sympathisch ‹*Person, Persönlichkeit*›; **I find sb./sth. ~:** ich finde jmdn./etw. sympathisch; jmd./etw. ist mir sympathisch; **d)** *(Med.)* sympathetisch ‹*Schmerz, Leiden*›; *(Anat.)* sympathisch ‹*Nervensystem*›; **e)** *(Mus.)* mitschwingend ‹*Saite, Ton*›; **f)** *(Phys.)* **~ vibration** Mitschwingen, *das*

sympathetically [sɪmpə'θetɪkəlɪ] *adv. (with pity)* mitfühlend; *(understandingly)* verständnisvoll; **treat a subject ~:** ein Thema einfühlsam behandeln

sympathetic: ~ 'nerve *n. (Anat.)* Sympathikus, *der;* **~ 'nervous system** *n. (Anat.)* sympathisches *od.* sympathetisches Nervensystem

sympathise, sympathiser *see* **sympathiz-**

sympathize ['sɪmpəθaɪz] *v. i.* **a)** *(feel or express sympathy)* **~ with sb.** mit jmdm. [mit]fühlen *od.* Mitleid haben; *(by speaking)* sein Mitgefühl mit jmdm. äußern; **~ with sb. over the death of a friend** jmds. Trauer beim Tod eines Freundes teilen; **I do ~:** es tut mir wirklich leid; **b) ~ with** *(have understanding for)* Verständnis haben für ‹*jmds. Not, Denkweise usw.*›; *(Polit.: share ideas of)* sympathisieren mit ‹*Partei usw.*›

sympathizer ['sɪmpəθaɪzə(r)] *n.* Sympathisant, *der*/Sympathisantin, *die*

sympathy ['sɪmpəθɪ] *n.* **a)** *(sharing feelings of another)* Mitgefühl, *das;* **in deepest ~:** mit aufrichtigem Beileid; **my sympathies are with you in your sorrow** ich fühle mit Ihnen in Ihrem Schmerz; **b)** *(agreement in opinion or emotion)* Sympathie, *die;* **my sympathies are with Schmidt** ich bin auf Schmidts Seite; **he has radical sympathies/no ~ with the radicals** er sympathisiert/sympathisiert nicht mit den Radikalen; **be in/out of ~ with sth.** mit etw. sympathisieren/nicht sympathisieren; **are you in ~ with what we are trying to do?** stimmst du unseren Zielen zu?; **come out** *or* **strike in ~ with sb.** mit jmdm. in einen Sympathiestreik treten; **vibrate in ~:** mitschwingen

'sympathy strike *n.* Sympathiestreik, *der*

symphonic [sɪm'fɒnɪk] *adj.* sinfonisch; symphonisch

symphony ['sɪmfənɪ] *n. (Mus.)* **a)** Sinfonie, *die;* **b)** *(esp. Amer.) see* **symphony orchestra**

'symphony orchestra *n.* Sinfonieorchester, *das*

symposium [sɪm'pəʊzɪəm] *n., pl.* **symposia** [sɪm'pəʊzɪə] Symposion, *das;* Symposium, *das*

symptom ['sɪmptəm] *n. (Med.; also fig.)* Symptom, *das*

symptomatic [sɪmptə'mætɪk] *adj. (Med.; also fig.)* symptomatisch **(of** für)

synagogue *(Amer.:* **synagog)** ['sɪnəgɒg] *n.* Synagoge, *die*

sync, synch [sɪŋk] *(coll.) n.* **a) in/out of ~:** synchron/nicht synchron; **b)** *(fig. coll.: in tune)* **be in ~/out of ~:** harmonieren/nicht harmonieren **(with** mit); **he is out of ~ with the rest** er hat nicht die gleiche Wellenlänge wie die anderen

synchromesh ['sɪŋkrəmeʃ] *(Motor Veh.) n.* **~ [gearbox]** Synchrongetriebe, *das;* **there is ~ on all gears** alle Gänge sind synchronisiert

synchronic [sɪŋ'krɒnɪk, sɪn'krɒnɪk] *adj. (Ling.)* synchronisch

synchronisation, synchronise *see* **synchroniz-**

synchronization [sɪŋkrənaɪ'zeɪʃn] *n.* Synchronisierung, *die*

synchronize ['sɪŋkrənaɪz] **1.** *v. t.* **a)** synchronisieren ‹*Vorgänge, Maschinen, Bild und Ton*›; **b)** *(set to same time)* gleichstellen ‹*Uhren*›; **we'd better ~ [our] watches** wir sollten Uhrenvergleich machen. **2.** *v. i.* ‹*Bild und Ton:*› synchron sein

synchronized 'swimming *n. (Sport)* Synchronschwimmen, *das*

synchronous ['sɪŋkrənəs] *adj.* synchron; **~ motor** *(Electr.)* Synchronmotor, *der*

syncopate ['sɪŋkəpeɪt] *v. t. (Mus., Ling.)* synkopieren

syncopation [sɪŋkə'peɪʃn] *n. (Mus., Ling.)* Synkopierung, *die*

syncope ['sɪŋkəpɪ] *n. (Ling., Med.)* Synkope, *die*

syndicalism ['sɪndɪkəlɪzm] *n.* Syndikalismus, *der*

syndicate 1. ['sɪndɪkət] *n.* **a)** *(for business, in organized crime)* Syndikat, *das;* **b)** *(in newspapers) Presseagentur, die Beiträge ankauft und an eine od. mehrere Zeitungen vertreibt;* **c) pools/lottery ~:** Tippgemeinschaft, *die.* **2.** ['sɪndɪkeɪt] *v. t.* in mehreren Zeitungen gleichzeitig veröffentlichen ‹*Bericht usw.*›

syndrome ['sɪndrəʊm] *n. (Med.; also fig.)* Syndrom, *das*

synod ['sɪnəd] *n.* Synode, *die*

synonym ['sɪnənɪm] *n.* Synonym, *das*

synonymous [sɪ'nɒnɪməs] *adj.* **a)** *(Ling.)* synonym **(with** mit); **b) ~ with** *(fig.: suggestive of, linked with)* gleichbedeutend mit

synonymy [sɪ'nɒnəmɪ] *n. (Ling.)* Synonymie, *die*

synopsis [sɪ'nɒpsɪs], *n., pl.* **synopses** [sɪ'nɒpsi:z] Inhaltsangabe, *die; (overview)* Abriß, *der*

synoptic [sɪ'nɒptɪk] *adj.* synoptisch

syntactic [sɪn'tæktɪk] *adj.*, **syntactically** [sɪn'tæktɪkəlɪ] *adv. (Ling.)* syntaktisch

syntax ['sɪntæks] *n. (Ling.)* Syntax, *die*

synthesis ['sɪnθɪsɪs] *n., pl.* **syntheses** ['sɪnθɪsi:z] Synthese, *die*

synthesise, synthesiser *see* **synthesiz-**

synthesize ['sɪnθɪsaɪz] *v. t.* **a)** *(form into a whole)* zur Synthese bringen; **b)** *(Chem.)* synthetisieren; **c) ~ speech** eine Kunstsprache schaffen; **~d speech** Kunstsprache, *die*

synthesizer ['sɪnθɪsaɪzə(r)] *n. (Mus.)* Synthesizer, *der*

synthetic [sɪn'θetɪk] **1.** *adj.* **a)** *(man-made)* synthetisch; **~ fibre** Kunstfaser, *die; see also* **resin b; b)** *(sham)* unecht. **2.** *n.* Kunststoff, *der;* **~s** *(Textiles)* Synthetics

synthetically [sɪn'θetɪkəlɪ] *adv.* synthetisch

syphilis ['sɪfɪlɪs] *n. (Med.)* Syphilis, *die*

syphilitic [sɪfɪ'lɪtɪk] *(Med.)* **1.** *n.* Syphilitiker, *der*/Syphilitikerin, *die.* **2.** *adj.* syphilitisch

Syracuse ['saɪrəkju:z] *pr. n.* Syrakus *(das)*

Syria ['sɪrɪə] *pr. n.* Syrien *(das)*

Syrian ['sɪrɪən] **1.** *adj.* syrisch; **sb. is ~:** jmd. ist Syrer/Syrerin. **2.** *n.* Syrer, *der*/Syrerin, *die*

syringa [sɪ'rɪŋgə] *n. (Bot.)* **a)** *(mock orange)* Falscher Jasmin; **b)** *(lilac)* Flieder, *der*

syringe [sɪ'rɪndʒ] **1.** *n.* Spritze, *die; see also* **hypodermic 1. 2.** *v. t.* spritzen; ausspritzen ‹*Ohr*›

syrup ['sɪrəp] *n.* **a)** Sirup, *der;* **cough ~:** Hustensaft, *der;* **b)** *(fig.: sickly sentiment)* süßlicher Kitsch *(abwertend)*

syrupy ['sɪrəpɪ] *adj.* **a)** *(like syrup)* sirupähnlich; **b)** *(fig.: cloyingly sweet)* süßlich

system ['sɪstəm] *n.* **a)** *(lit. or fig.)* System, *das; (of roads, railways also)* Netz, *das;* **root ~** *(Bot.)* Wurzelgeflecht, *das; see also* **'go 4; b)** *(Anat., Zool.: body)* Körper, *der; (part)* **digestive/muscular/nervous/reproductive ~:** Verdauungsapparat, *der*/Muskulatur, *die*/Nervensystem, *das*/Fortpflanzungssystem, *das;* **get sth. out of one's ~** *(fig.)* etw. loswerden; *(by talking)* sich *(Dat.)* etw. von der Seele reden; **c)** *no art. (methodical procedure)* System *o. Art.;* **d)** *(Geol.)* Formation, *die*

systematic [sɪstə'mætɪk] *adj.*, **systematically** [sɪstə'mætɪkəlɪ] *adv.* systematisch

systematisation, systematise *see* **systematiz-**

systematization [sɪstəmətaɪ'zeɪʃn] *n.* Systematisierung, *die*

systematize ['sɪstəmətaɪz] *v. t.* systematisieren **(into** zu)

systemic [sɪ'stemɪk] *adj. (Biol.)* systemisch

systems: ~ analysis *n.* Systemanalyse, *die;* **~ analyst** *n.* Systemanalytiker, *der*/-analytikerin, *die*

systolic [sɪs'tɒlɪk] *adj. (Physiol.)* systolisch

T

T, t [ti:] *n., pl.* **Ts** *or* **T's a)** *(letter* T, t, *das;* **to a T** ganz genau; haargenau; **that's her to a T** das ist sie, wie sie leibt und lebt; **cross the t's** *(fig.)* peinlich genau sein; **b)** *(T-shaped object)* T, *das;* **T-junction** Einmündung, *die (in eine Vorfahrtsstraße);* **T-bone steak** T-bone-Steak, *das;* **T-shirt** T-shirt, *das;* **T-square** *see* **square 1 j**

t. *abbr.* **a) ton[s]** [britische] Tonne[n]; **b) tonne[s]** t

TA *abbr. (Brit.)* **Territorial Army**

ta [tɑː] *int. (Brit. coll.)* danke

¹tab [tæb] **1.** *n.* **a)** *(projecting flap)* Zunge, *die; (label)* Schildchen, *das; (on clothing)* Etikett, *das; (with name)* Namensschild, *das; (on file [card])* Reiter, *der;* **b)** *(Amer. coll.: bill)* Rechnung, *die;* **pick up the ~:** die Zeche bezahlen; **c)** *(Amer. coll.: price)* Preis, *der;* **d) keep ~s** *or* **a ~ on sb./sth.** *(watch)* jmdn./etw. [genau] beobachten; **e)** *(Brit. Mil.: on collar)* Kragenspiegel, *der;* **f)** *(Theatre)* Hängestück, *das;* **g)** *(Aeronaut.)* Trimmruder, *das;* Hilfsruder, *das.* **2.** *v. t.,* **-bb-** *see* **1 a:** mit Zunge/Schildchen/Etikett/Namensschild/Reitern versehen

²tab *see* **tabulator**

Tabasco, (P) [tə'bæskəʊ] *n.* Tabasco, *der;* Tabascosoße, *die*

tabby ['tæbɪ] *n.* **a) ~ [cat]** Tigerkatze, *die;* **b)** *(female cat)* [weibliche] Katze; Kätzin, *die*

tabernacle ['tæbənækl] *n.* **a)** *(Bibl.)* Stiftshütte, *die;* **b)** *(Relig.: meeting-house)* Gotteshaus, *das;* **c)** *(Eccl.: receptacle)* Tabernakel, *der*

table ['teɪbl] **1.** *n.* **a)** Tisch, *der;* **at ~:** bei Tisch; **sit down at ~:** sich zu Tisch setzen; **after two whiskies he was under the ~** *(coll.)* nach zwei Whisky lag er unter dem Tisch *(ugs.);* **drink sb. under the ~:** jmdn. unter den Tisch trinken *(ugs.);* **get sb./get round the ~:** jmdn. an einen Tisch bringen/sich an einen Tisch setzen; **turn the ~s [on sb.]** *(fig.)* [jmdm. gegenüber] den Spieß umdrehen *od.* umkehren; *see also* **²lay 1 e; b)** *(list)* Tabelle, *die;* **~ of contents** Inhaltsverzeichnis, *das;* **~ of logarithms** Logarithmentafel, *die;* **learn one's ~s** das Einmaleins lernen; **say one's nine times ~:** die Neunerreihe aufsagen; **c)** *(company at ~)* Runde, *die;* **d)** *(food provided)* **keep a good/wretched ~:** eine ausgezeichnete/jämmerliche Küche führen. **2.** *v. t.* **a)** *(bring forward)* einbringen, *(ugs.)* auf den Tisch legen ‹*Antrag, Resolution*›; **b)** *(Amer.: shelve)* auf Eis legen *(ugs.)* ‹*Plan usw.*›

tableau ['tæbləʊ] *n., pl.* **~x** ['tæbləʊz] *(lit. or fig.)* Tableau, *das*

'table-cloth *n.* Tischdecke, *die;* Tischtuch, *das*

table d'hôte [tɑːbl 'dəʊt] *n.* Table d'hôte, *die (geh.);* **~ menu** Tageskarte, *die*

table: ~-knife *n.* Messer, *das;* Tischmesser, *das (veralt.);* **~-lamp** *n.* Tischlampe, *die;* **~land** *n. (Geog.)* Tafelland, *das;* **~-leg** *n.* Tischbein, *das;* **~-linen** *n.* Tischwäsche, *die;* **~ manners** *n. pl.* Tischmanieren *Pl.;* **~-mat** *n.* Set, *das;* **T~ 'Mountain** *pr. n.* Tafelberg, *der;* **~-napkin** *n.* Serviette, *die;* **~ salt** *n.* Tafelsalz, *das;* **~spoon** *n.* Servierlöffel, *der;* **~spoonful** *n.* Servierlöffel[voll], *der*

tablet ['tæblɪt] *n.* **a)** *(pill)* Tablette, *die;* **b)** *(piece)* Stück, *das;* **c)** *(stone slab)* Tafel, *die;* **d)** *(for writing on)* [Schreib]tafel, *die; (Amer.: pad)* Notizblock, *der*

table: ~-talk *n., no pl.* Tischgespräch, *das;* **sb.'s ~-talk** jmds. Tischgespräche; **~ tennis** *n. (Sport)* Tischtennis, *das;* **~ tennis bat** Tischtennisschläger, *der;* **~-top 1.** *n.* Tischplatte, *die;* **2.** *adj.* an einer Tischplatte angebracht ‹*Dosenöffner usw.*›; Tisch‹*kühlschrank, -waschmaschine*›; **~ware** *n., no pl.* Geschirr, Besteck und Gläser; **~ wine** *n.* Tischwein, *der*

tabloid ['tæblɔɪd] *n. (kleinformatige, bebilderte)* Boulevardzeitung; **the ~s** *(derog.)* die Boulevardpresse; **~ journalism** Sensationsjournalismus, *der*

taboo, tabu [tə'buː] **1.** *n.* Tabu, *das;* **be under a ~:** tabu sein. **2.** *adj.* tabuisiert; Tabu‹*wort*›; **be ~:** tabu sein. **3.** *v. t.* tabuisieren

tabular ['tæbjʊlə(r)] *adj.* tabellarisch

tabulate ['tæbjʊleɪt] *v. t.* tabellarisch darstellen; tabellarisieren

tabulation [tæbjʊ'leɪʃn] *n.* tabellarische Aufstellung; Tabellarisierung, *die*

tabulator ['tæbjʊleɪtə(r)] *n.* Tabulator, *der*

tachograph ['tækəgrɑːf] *n. (Motor Veh.)* Fahrt[en]schreiber, *der*

tachometer [tə'kɒmɪtə(r)] *n.* Tachometer, *der od. das*

tacit ['tæsɪt] *adj.,* **tacitly** ['tæsɪtlɪ] *adv.* stillschweigend

taciturn ['tæsɪtɜːn] *adj.* schweigsam; wortkarg

taciturnity [tæsɪ'tɜːnɪtɪ] *n., no pl.* Schweigsamkeit, *die;* Wortkargheit, *die*

¹tack [tæk] **1.** *n.* **a)** *(small nail)* kleiner Nagel; **carpet ~:** Teppichnagel, *der;* **shoe ~:** Täcks, *der; see also* **brass tacks; b)** *(temporary stitch)* Heftstich, *der;* **c)** *(Naut.) (direction of vessel; also fig.)* Kurs, *der; (in zigzag)* Kreuzen, *das;* **be on the port/starboard ~:** auf Backbord-/Steuerbordhalsen liegen; **on the right/wrong ~** *(fig.)* auf dem richtigen/falschen Weg *od.* Kurs; **change one's ~, try another ~** *(fig.)* einen anderen Kurs einschlagen. **2.** *v. t.* **a)** *(stitch loosely)* heften; **b)** *(nail)* festnageln. **3.** *v. i. (Naut.)* kreuzen

~ 'down *v. t.* annageln; festnageln

~ 'on *v. t.* anhängen (to an + *Akk.*)

²tack *n. (Horse-riding)* **[riding] ~:** Sattel- und Zaumzeug, *das*

¹tackiness ['tækɪnɪs] *n., no pl.* Klebrigkeit, *die*

²tackiness *n., no pl. (coll. derog.)* **a)** *(tastelessness)* Geschmacklosigkeit, *die;* **b)** *(tattiness)* Schäbigkeit, *die*

tackle ['tækl] **1.** *v. t.* **a)** *(come to grips with)* angehen, in Angriff nehmen ‹*Problem usw.*›; **~ sb. about/on/over sth.** jmdn. auf etw. *(Akk.)* ansprechen; *(ask for sth.)* jmdn. um etw. angehen; **b)** *(Sport)* angreifen ‹*Spieler*›; *(Amer. Footb.; Rugby)* fassen. **2.** *n.* **a)** *(equipment)* Ausrüstung, *die;* **shaving ~:** Rasierzeug, *das; see also* **fishing-tackle; b)** *(Sport)* Angriff, *der; (sliding ~)* Tackling, *das; (Amer. Footb., Rugby)* Fassen und Halten; **c)** *see* **block 1 n**

tackling ['tæklɪŋ] *n. (Sport)* Tackling, *das*

'tack-room *n.* Sattelkammer, *die*

¹tacky ['tækɪ] *adj.* klebrig

²tacky *adj. (coll. derog.)* **a)** *(tasteless)* geschmacklos; **b)** *(tatty)* schäbig

tact [tækt] *n.* Takt, *der;* **he has no ~:** er hat kein Taktgefühl

tactful ['tæktfl] *adj.,* **tactfully** ['tæktfəlɪ] *adv.* taktvoll

tactfulness ['tæktflnɪs] *n., no pl.* Taktgefühl, *das*

tactic ['tæktɪk] *n.* Taktik, *die;* **delaying ~:** Verzögerungstaktik, *die; see also* **tactics**

tactical ['tæktɪkl] *adj.* **a)** taktisch ‹*Fehler, Manöver, Rückzug*›; **~ voting** taktische Stimmabgabe; **b)** *(skilled in tactics)* taktisch klug; **have a good ~ sense** taktisch klug *od.* geschickt sein

tactically ['tæktɪkəlɪ] *adv.* taktisch

tactician [tæk'tɪʃn] *n.* Taktiker, *der*/Taktikerin, *die*

tactics ['tæktɪks] *n. pl.* **a)** *(methods)* Taktik, *die;* **dubious ~:** zweifelhafte Methoden; **b)** *constr. as sing. (Mil.)* Taktik, *die*

tactile ['tæktaɪl] *adj.* **a)** *(using touch)* Tast‹*organ*›; taktil *(Med.);* **b)** *(tangible)* tastbar

tactless ['tæktlɪs] *adj.* taktlos

tactlessly ['tæktlɪslɪ] *adv.* taktlos; *as sentence-modifier* taktloserweise

tactlessness ['tæktlɪsnɪs] *n., no pl.* Taktlosigkeit, *die*

tadpole ['tædpəʊl] *n.* Kaulquappe, *die*

taffeta ['tæfɪtə] *n. (Textiles)* Taft, *der*

taffrail ['tæfreɪl] *n. (Naut.)* Heckreling, *die*

Taffy ['tæfɪ] *n. (coll.: Welshman)* Waliser, *der*

taffy *n. (Amer.)* Karamelbonbon, *das*

¹tag [tæg] **1.** *n.* **a)** *(label)* Schild, *das; (on clothes)* Etikett, *das; (on animal's ear)* Ohrmarke, *die;* **b)** *(loop)* Schlaufe, *die;* **c)** *(metal etc. point at end of lace)* Senkelstift, *der;* **d)** *(stock phrase)* Zitat, *das;* geflügeltes Wort; **e)** *(Amer.: licence-plate)* Nummernschild, *das. See also* **price-tag. 2.** *v. t.,* **-gg-** *(attach)* anhängen (**to** an + *Akk.*); **~ together** aneinanderhängen; zusammenheften ‹*Blätter, Papier*›; *(fig.)* aneinanderreihen. **3.** *v. i.,* **-gg-: ~ behind** [nach]folgen; **~ after sb.** hinter jmdm. hertrotteln *(ugs.)*

~ a'long *v. i.* hinterherlaufen; **do you mind if I ~ along?** darf ich mich anschließen?

~ 'on *v. t.* anhängen (to an + *Akk.*)

²tag *n. (game)* Fangen, *das*

tag: ~-day *(Amer.) see* **flag-day b; ~ 'question** *n. (Ling.)* Frageanhängsel, *das;* **~ wrestling** *n. (Sport)* Ringkampf *zwischen zwei Mannschaften von je zwei Ringern, von denen nur einer im Ring steht und sich von seinem Partner ablösen lassen kann*

tail [teɪl] **1.** *n.* **a)** Schwanz, *der;* **tops and ~s** *(of carrots, turnips)* obere und untere Enden; **b)** *(fig.)* **have sb./sth. on one's ~** *(coll.)* jmdn./etw. auf den Fersen haben *(ugs.);* **be/keep on sb.'s ~** *(coll.)* jmdm. auf den Fersen sein/bleiben *(ugs.);* **with one's ~ between one's legs** mit eingezogenem Schwanz *(ugs.);* **sb. has his ~ up** jmd. ist übermütig; **turn ~ [and run]** Fersengeld geben *(ugs.);* die Flucht ergreifen; **c)** *(of comet)* Schweif, *der;* **d) [shirt-]~:** Hemdzipfel, *der (ugs.);* **e)** *(of man's coat)* Schoß, *der;* **f)** *in pl. (man's evening dress)* Frack, *der;* **g)** *in pl. (on coin)* **~s [it is]** Zahl; *see* **head 1 e; h)** *(Mus.: stem of note)* [Noten]hals, *der;* **i)** *(part of letter below line)* Unterlänge, *die;* **j)** *(sl.: person keeping watch)* Schatten, *der;* **have/put a ~ on sb.** jmdn. beschatten lassen. **2.** *v. t.* **a)** *(remove stalks of)* **top and ~ gooseberries** Stachelbeeren putzen; **b)** *(sl.: follow)* beschatten

~ 'away *see* **~ off**

~ 'back *v. i.* sich stauen. *See also* **tailback**

~ 'off *v. i.* **a)** *(decrease)* zurückgehen; **b)** *(fade into silence)* ersterben *(geh.);* verstummen

tail: ~back *n. (Brit.)* Rückstau, *der;* **~-board** *n.* hintere Bordwand; **~ coat** *n.* Frack, *der;* **~-end** *n. (hindmost end)* Schwanz, *der; (fig.)* Ende, *das;* **come in at the ~-end** erst am Ende hinzustoßen; **~-fin** *n. (Aeronaut.)* Seitenflosse, *die;* **~-gate 1.** *n. (Motor Veh.)* Heckklappe, *die;* **2.** *v. i. (Amer.)* zu dicht auffahren

'tail-lamp *(esp. Amer.) see* **tail-light**

tailless ['teɪllɪs] *adj.* schwanzlos; **the animal was ~:** das Tier hatte keinen Schwanz

'tail-light *n.* Rück- *od.* Schlußlicht, *das*

tailor ['teɪlə(r)] **1.** *n.* Schneider, *der*/Schneiderin, *die; see also* **baker. 2.** *v. t.* **a)** schneidern; **b)** *(fig.)* **~ed to** *or* **for sb./sth.** für jmdn./etw. maßgeschneidert; **~ed to sb.'s needs** auf jmds. Bedürfnisse zugeschnitten

tailored ['teɪləd] *adj.* maßgeschneidert; **~ suit** Maßanzug, *der; (for woman)* Schneiderkostüm, *das*

tailoring ['teɪlərɪŋ] *n., no pl.* Schneiderei, *die;* Schneidern, *das*

'tailor-made *adj. (lit. or fig.)* maßgeschneidert

tailor's: ~ chalk *n.* Schneiderkreide, *die;* **~ 'dummy** *n.* Schneiderpuppe, *die; (fig.)* Geck, *der*/Modepuppe, *die*

tail: ~-piece *n.* **a)** *(appendage)* Anhang, *der;* **b)** *(Mus.: for string-ends)* Saitenhalter, *der;* **c)** *(decoration)* [Schluß]vignette, *die;* **~pipe** *n.* Auspuffendstück, *das;* **~plane** *n. (Aeronaut.)* Höhenleitwerk, *das;* **~-skid** *n. (Aeronaut.)* Sporn, *der;* **~spin** *n.* **a)** *(of aircraft)* Trudeln, *das;* **b)** *(fig.: state of panic)* **send sb./go into a ~spin** jmdn. in Panik versetzen/zu rotieren anfangen *(ugs.);* **~wheel** *n. (Aeronaut.)* Spornrad, *das;* **~ wind** *n.* Rückenwind, *der*

taint [teɪnt] **1.** *n.* Makel, *der;* **hereditary ~:** erbliche Belastung. **2.** *v. t.* verderben; beflecken ‹*Ruf*›; **be ~ed with sth.** mit etw. behaftet sein *(geh.)*

Taiwan [taɪ'wɑːn] *pr. n.* Taiwan *(das)*

Taiwanese [taɪwə'niːz] **1.** *adj.* taiwanesisch. **2.** *n.* Taiwanese, *der*/Taiwanesin, *die*

take [teɪk] **1.** *v. t.*, **took** [tʊk], **taken** ['teɪkn] **a)** *(get hold of, grasp, seize)* nehmen; **~ sb.'s arm** jmds. Arm nehmen; **~ sb. by the hand/arm** jmdn. bei der Hand/am Arm nehmen; **he took me by the arm/elbow and steered me in the direction of the exit** er faßte mich am Arm/Ellbogen und dirigierte mich zum Ausgang; **~ matters into one's own hands** *(fig.)* die Sache selbst in die Hand nehmen; *see also* ^{1}**bit a;** ^{1}**bull 1 a; devil 1 c;** ^{2}**hold 3 a; law d; life a; b)** *(capture)* einnehmen ‹*Stadt, Festung*›; machen ‹*Gefangenen*›; fassen ‹*Banditen*›; *(chess)* schlagen; nehmen; *(Cards)* stechen; *see also* ^{2}**hold 3 a; hostage; possession d; short 2 c; storm 1 d; surprise 1; c)** *(gain, earn)* ‹*Laden*:› einbringen; ‹*Person*:› einnehmen; ‹*Film, Stück*:› einspielen; *(win)* gewinnen ‹*Satz, Spiel, Preis, Titel*›; erzielen ‹*Punkte*›; *(Cards)* machen ‹*Stich*›; **~ a wicket** *(Cricket)* einen Schlagmann zum Ausscheiden bringen; **~ first/second** *etc.* **place** den ersten/zweiten *usw.* Platz belegen; *(fig.)* an erster/zweiter *usw.* Stelle kommen; **~ the biscuit** *(Brit. coll.)* or *(coll.)* **cake** *(fig.)* alle/alles übertreffen; **d)** *(assume possession of)* nehmen; *(~ away with one)* mitnehmen; *(steal)* mitnehmen *(verhüll.)*; *(obtain by purchase)* besorgen ‹*Eintrittskarte, [Logen]platz*›; kaufen, *(by rent)* mieten ‹*Auto, Wohnung, Haus*›; nehmen ‹*Klavier-, Deutsch-, Fahrstunden*›; mitmachen ‹*Tanzkurs*›; *(buy regularly)* nehmen; lesen ‹*Zeitung, Zeitschrift*›; *(subscribe to)* beziehen; *(obtain)* erwerben ‹*akademischen Grad*›; *(form a relationship with)* sich *(Dat.)* nehmen ‹*Frau, Geliebten usw.*›; ins Haus nehmen ‹*zahlende Gäste*›; **that woman took my purse** die Frau hat mir meinen Geldbeutel gestohlen; **he took his degree at Sussex University** er hat sein Examen an der Universität von Sussex gemacht; **~ place** stattfinden; *(spontaneously)* sich ereignen; ‹*Wandlung*:› sich vollziehen; **I'll ~ this handbag/the curry, please** ich nehme diese Handtasche/das Curry; **who has ~n my pencil?** wer hat meinen Bleistift weggenommen?; **~ [private] pupils** [Privat]stunden geben; **he took her as** *or* **for his wife** er nahm sie zur Frau; *see also* **order 1 c, h; possession d; silk 1 a; e)** *(avail oneself of, use)* nehmen; machen ‹*Pause, Ferien, Nickerchen*›; nehmen ‹*Beispiel, Zitat usw.*› **(from** aus); **~ the opportunity to do/of doing sth.** die Gelegenheit dazu benutzen, etw. zu tun; **~ the car/bus into town** mit dem Auto/Bus in die Stadt fahren; **~ two eggs** *etc. (in recipe)* man nehme zwei Eier *usw.*; **~ all the time you want** nimm dir ruhig Zeit; **a story ~n from life** eine Geschichte aus dem Leben; **a quotation ~n from Pope** ein Zitat aus Pope; **[let's] ~ a more recent example/my sister [for example]** nehmen wir ein Beispiel neueren Datums/einmal meine Schwester; **thou shalt not ~ God's name in vain** *(Bibl.)* du sollst den Namen Gott[es] nicht unnütz führen; **do I hear someone taking my name in vain?** *(coll. joc.)* wer lästert denn da gerade über mich?; *see also* **advantage a; advice a; cure 1 c;** ^{1}**leave c; liberty; time 1 b; f)** *(carry, guide, convey)* bringen; **~ sb.'s shoes to the mender['s]/sb.'s coat to the cleaner's** jmds. Schuhe zum Schuster/jmds. Mantel in die Reinigung bringen; **~ a message to sb.** jmdm. eine Nachricht überbringen; **the pipe ~s the water to the tank** das Rohr führt das Wasser zum Tank; **~ sb. to school/hospital** jmdn. zur Schule/ins Krankenhaus bringen; **~ sb. to visit sb.** jmdn. zu Besuch bei jmdm. mitnehmen; **~ sb. to the zoo/cinema/to dinner** mit jmdm. in den Zoo/ins Kino/zum Abendessen gehen; **~ sb. into one's home/house** jmdn. bei sich aufnehmen; **the road ~s you/story ~s us to London** die Straße führt nach/die Erzählung führt uns nach London; **my job has ~n me all over the world** ich bin beruflich in der ganzen Welt gereist; **his ability will ~ him far/to the top** mit seinen Fähigkeiten wird er es weit bringen/wird er ganz nach oben kommen; **~ sb./sth. with one** jmdn./etw. mitnehmen; **~ home** mit nach Hause nehmen; *(earn)* nach Hause bringen ‹*Geld*›; *(accompany)* nach Hause bringen *od.* begleiten; *(to meet one's parents etc.)* mit nach Hause bringen; *see also* **take-home; ~ sb. before sb.** jmdn. jmdm. vorführen; **~ sb. through/over sth.** *(fig.)* mit jmdm. etw. durchgehen; **~ in hand** *(begin)* in Angriff nehmen; *(assume responsibility for)* sich kümmern um; **~ sb. into partnership [with one]/into the business** jmdn. zu seinem Teilhaber machen/in sein Geschäft aufnehmen; **~ an axe to sth.** etw. fällen; *(fig.)* bei etw. den Rotstift ansetzen; **~ a stick** *etc.* **to sb.** den Stock *usw.* bei jmdm. gebrauchen; **~ sth. to pieces** *or* **bits** etw. auseinandernehmen; **you can/can't ~ sb./sth. anywhere** *(fig. coll.)* man kann jmdn./etw. überallhin/nirgendwohin mitnehmen; **you can't ~ it 'with you** *(coll.)* man kann es ja nicht mitnehmen; *see also* **confidence e; court 1 d; head 1 b; g)** *(remove)* nehmen; *(deduct)* abziehen; **~ sth./sb. from sb.** jmdm. etw./jmdn. wegnehmen; **I took the parcel from her** ich nahm ihr das Paket ab; **death has ~n him from us** *(fig.)* der Tod hat ihn uns genommen; **the children were ~n from their parents by the authorities** die Kinder wurden den Eltern von Amts wegen weggenommen; **be ~n from sb.** *(fig.)* jmdm. genommen werden; **~ all the fun/hard work out of sth.** einem alle Freude an etw. *(Dat.)* nehmen/einem die schwere Arbeit bei etw. ersparen; *see also* **life a;** ^{1}**wind 1 a; h)** *(conceive, experience)* **sb. ~s courage from sth.** etw. macht jmdm. Mut; **~ courage!** nur Mut!; **i) be ~n ill** *or (coll.)* **sick** krank werden; **be ~n ill with food poisoning** eine Lebensmittelvergiftung bekommen; **j)** *(make)* machen ‹*Foto, Kopie*›; *(photograph)* aufnehmen; **hate having one's photograph/picture ~n** sich gar nicht gern fotografieren lassen; **the camera ~s good photographs** die Kamera macht gute Bilder *od.* Fotos; **~ sb.'s fingerprints** jmdm. Fingerabdrücke abnehmen; **k)** *(perform, execute)* aufnehmen ‹*Brief, Diktat*›; machen ‹*Prüfung, Sprung, Spaziergang, Reise, Umfrage*›; durchführen ‹*Befragung, Volkszählung*›; ablegen ‹*Gelübde, Eid*›; übernehmen ‹*Rolle, Part*›; treffen ‹*Entscheidung*›; **~ a fall/tumble** stürzen/straucheln; **~ a step forward/backward** einen Schritt vor-/zurücktreten; **~ a turn for the better/worse** eine Wende zum Besseren/Schlechteren nehmen; **~ a scene/movement more slowly** eine Szene/einen Satz langsamer nehmen; *see also* **action a;** ^{2}**bow 3; effect 1 d; vote 1 a; l)** *(negotiate)* nehmen ‹*Zaun, Mauer, Hürde, Kurve, Hindernis*›; **the bus took the corner too fast** der Bus ist zu schnell um die Kurve gefahren; **m)** *(conduct)* halten ‹*Gottesdienst, Andacht, Unterricht*›; **he ~s the older pupils in Latin** er hat die älteren Schüler in Latein; **Ms X ~s us for maths** in Mathe haben wir Frau X; **n)** *(be taught, be examined in)* **~ Latin at school** in der Schule Latein haben; **~ Latin in an exam** in einem Examen in Latein geprüft werden; **~ an examination/a test** eine Prüfung machen; **o)** *(consume)* trinken ‹*Tee, Kaffee, Kognak usw.*›; einnehmen *(geh.)* ‹*Mahlzeit*›; nehmen ‹*Zucker, Milch, Überdosis, Tabletten, Medizin*›; **~ some food** etwas essen; **~ sugar in one's tea** den Tee mit Zucker trinken; **what can I ~ for a cold?** was kann ich gegen eine Erkältung nehmen?; **to be ~n three times a day** dreimal täglich einzunehmen; **not to be ~n [internally]** nicht zur innerlichen Anwendung; *see also* **bite 3 a; drug 1 b; medicine; sip 3; p)** *(occupy)* einnehmen ‹*Sitz im Parlament*›; übernehmen, antreten ‹*Amt*›; **~ sb.'s seat** sich auf jmds. Platz setzen; **is that/this seat ~n?** ist da/hier noch frei?; *see also* **back seat; chair 1 a, b; place 1 f, j; seat 1 b; q)** *(need, require)* brauchen ‹*Platz, Zeit*›; haben ‹*Kleider-, Schuhgröße usw.*›; *(Ling.)* haben ‹*Objekt, Plural-s*›; gebraucht werden mit ‹*Kasus*›; **this verb ~s 'sein'** dieses Verb wird mit „sein" konjugiert; **the wound will ~ some time to heal** es braucht einige Zeit, bis die Wunde geheilt ist; **the ticket-machine ~s 20p and 50p coins** der Fahrkartenautomat nimmt 20-Pence- und 50-Pence-Stücke; **the work is taking too much of my time** die Arbeit kostet mich zuviel Zeit; **as long as it ~s** so lange wie nötig; **sth. ~s an hour/a year/all day** etw. dauert eine Stunde/ein Jahr/einen ganzen Tag; **it ~s an hour** *etc.* **to do sth.** es dauert eine Stunde *usw.*, [um] etw. zu tun; **the meat ~s three hours to cook** das Fleisch braucht drei Stunden, bis es gar ist; **sb. ~s** *or* **it ~s sb. a long time/an hour** *etc.* **to do sth.** jmd. braucht lange/eine Stunde *usw.*, um etw. zu tun; **what took you so long?** was hast du denn so lange gemacht?; **~ a lot of money/£3,000** viel Geld/3 000 Pfund kosten; **~ a lot of work/effort/courage** viel Arbeit/Mühe/Mut kosten; **it took all my strength/determination** ich brauchte all meine Kraft/Entschlossenheit; **it doesn't ~ much to make him happy** es gehört nicht viel dazu, ihn glücklich zu machen; **have [got] what it ~s** das Zeug dazu haben; **he took a lot of/some convincing** er war schwer/nicht so leicht zu überzeugen; **these windows ~ a lot of cleaning** diese Fenster sind schwer zu putzen; **it will ~ [quite] a lot of explaining** es wird schwer zu erklären sein; **that story of his ~s some believing** die Geschichte, die er da erzählt, ist kaum zu glauben; **it ~s an expert to notice the difference** nur ein Fachmann kann den Unterschied feststellen; **it would ~ a saint to get along with him** man müßte ein Heiliger sein, um mit ihm auszukommen; **it ~s a thief to know a thief** nur ein Dieb kennt einen Dieb; **it ~s all sorts to make a world** es gibt solche und solche; *see also* **beating b; time 1 b; r)** *(accommodate, hold)* fassen; *(support)* tragen; **the car will ~ six adults** in dem Auto haben sechs Erwachsene Platz; **that room can't ~ a grand piano** in das Zimmer paßt kein Flügel; **s)** *(ascertain and record)* notieren ‹*Namen, Adresse, Autonummer usw.*›; zu Protokoll nehmen ‹*Hergang eines Unfalls usw.*›; fühlen ‹*Puls*›; messen ‹*Temperatur, Größe usw.*›; **~ sb.'s measurements for a new suit** [bei] jmdm. für einen neuen Anzug Maß nehmen; **~ the minutes of a meeting** bei einer Sitzung [das] Protokoll führen; **~ a reading from the barometer** den Barometerstand ablesen; **t)** *(apprehend, grasp)* **~ sb.'s meaning/drift,** *(arch.)* **~ sb.** verstehen, was jmd. meint; **... if you ~ my meaning ...**, Sie verstehen?; **~ sb.'s point** jmds. Standpunkt verstehen; **~ it [that] ...:** annehmen, [daß] ...; **can I ~ it that ...?** kann ich davon ausgehen, daß ...?; **am I to ~ it that ...?** soll ich das so verstehen, daß ...?; **~ sth. to mean sth.** etw. so verstehen, daß ...; **what do you ~ that to mean/signify?** wie verstehen Sie das/was bedeutet das Ihrer Meinung nach?; **~ sth. as settled/as a compliment/refusal** etw. als erledigt betrachten/als eine Ablehnung/ein Kompliment auffassen; **~ sb./sth. for/to be sth.** jmdn./etw. für etw. halten; **what do you ~ me for?** wofür halten Sie mich?; **I ~ him to be in his fifties** ich schätze ihn zwischen fünfzig und sechzig; **not know how to ~ sb.'s reply** nicht wissen, wie man jmds. Antwort verstehen soll; **~ what sb. says the wrong way** jmdn. falsch verstehen; *see also* **gospel b; grant 1c; literally a; word 1b; u)** *(treat or react to in a specified manner)* aufnehmen; **~ sth. like a man** etw. wie ein Mann nehmen; **~ sth. well/badly/hard** etw. gut/schlecht/nur schwer verkraften; **sb. ~s sth. very badly/hard** etw. trifft jmdn. sehr; **~ sth. calmly** *or* **coolly** etw. gelassen [auf- *od.* hin]nehmen; **~ sth. as read** etw. als bekannt voraussetzen; **you can/may ~ it as read that ...:** du kannst sicher sein, daß ...; **taking it all in all, taking one thing with another** alles in allem; *see also* **amiss 2; easy 2; heart 1b, c; kindly 1c; stride 1a; v)** *(accept)* annehmen; **~ money** *etc.* **[from sb./for sth.]** Geld *usw.* [von jmdm./für etw.] [an]nehmen; **will you ~ £500 for the car?** wollen Sie den Wagen für 500 Pfund verkaufen?; **[you can] ~ it or leave it** entweder du bist damit einverstanden, oder du läßt es bleiben; **I can ~ it or leave it** *(am indifferent)* ich mache mir nicht besonders viel daraus; **~ the hint** den Wink verstehen; **he can never ~ a hint** er hat kein Feingefühl; **I know how to take a hint** ich verstehe schon; **~ sb.'s word for it** sich auf jmdn. *od.* jmds. Wort[e] verlassen; **you can ~ his word for it that ...:** wenn er es sagt, kannst du dich darauf verlassen, daß ...; **you don't have to ~ my word for it** du brauchst es mir nicht zu glauben; **~ things as they come, ~ it as it comes** es nehmen, wie es kommt; *see also* **advice a; chance 1e; consequence a; risk 1a; w)** *(receive, submit to)* einstecken [müssen] ‹*Schlag, Tritt, Stoß*›; *(Boxing)* nehmen [müssen] ‹*Schlag*›; *(endure, tolerate)* aushalten; vertragen ‹*Klima, Alkohol, Kaffee, Knoblauch*›; verwinden ‹*Schock*›; *(put up with)* sich *(Dat.)* gefallen lassen [müssen] ‹*Kritik, Grobheit*›; **~ one's punishment bravely** seine Strafe tapfer ertragen; **the boxer/the car took a lot of punishment** der Boxer mußte viel einstecken/das Auto mußte eine Menge aushalten; **~ no nonsense** sich *(Dat.)* nichts bieten lassen; **~ 'that!** nimm das!; **~ it** *(coll.)* es verkraften; *(referring to criticism, abuse)* damit fertigwerden; **There's a lot of pressure on you. – I can ~ it** Du stehst sehr unter Druck. – Ich werde damit schon fertig; **x)** *(adopt, choose)* ergreifen ‹*Maßnahmen*›; unternehmen ‹*Schritte*›; einschlagen ‹*Weg*›; sich entschließen zu ‹*Schritt, Handlungsweise*›; **~ the wrong road** die falsche Straße nehmen; **~ a firm** *etc.* **stand [with sb./on** *or* **over sth.]** jmdm. gegenüber/hinsichtlich einer Sache nicht nachgeben; **~ the easy way out** die einfachste Lösung wählen; *see also* **resistance a; side 1i; view 1d; y)** *(receive, accommodate)* [an]nehmen ‹*Bewerber, Schüler*›; aufnehmen ‹*Gäste*›; annehmen ‹*Farbe, Glanz*›; **the city ~s its name from its founder** die Stadt ist nach ihrem Gründer benannt; **the rock ~s its colour from the minerals** der Fels hat seine Farbe von den Mineralien; **z)** *(swindle)* **he was taken for £500 by the con-man** *(coll.)* der Schwindler hat ihm 500 Pfund abgeknöpft *(ugs.)*; **aa) be ~n with sb./sth.** von jmdm./etw. angetan sein; **bb)** *(copulate with)* nehmen. **2.** *v. i.*, **took, taken a)** *(be successful, effective)* ‹*Transplantat:*› vom Körper angenommen werden; ‹*Impfung:*› anschlagen; ‹*Pfropfreis:*› anwachsen; ‹*Sämling, Pflanze:*› angehen; ‹*Feuer:*› zu brennen beginnen; ‹*trockenes Holz:*› Feuer fangen; ‹*Farbe:*› aufgenommen werden; ‹*Anstrich, Leim:*› halten; ‹*Fisch:*› [an]beißen; **b)** *(detract)* **~ from sth.** etw. schmälern; **c) ~ ill** *or (coll.)* **sick** krank werden; **d) ~ well/badly** *(Photog.)* sich gut/schlecht fotografieren lassen. **3.** *n.* **a)** *(Telev., Cinemat.)* Einstellung, *die;* Take, *der od. das (fachspr.)*; *see also* **double take; b)** *(takings)* Einnahme, *die;* **our ~ was over £200 for the day** unsere Tageseinnahme betrug über 200 Pfund; **~ [of the loot]** Anteil [an der Beute]; **c)** *(catch of fish)* Fang, *der; (catch of game)* Jagdbeute, *die*

~ a'back *see* **aback**

~ after *v. t.* **a) ~ after sb.** *(resemble)* jmdm. ähnlich sein; *(take as one's example)* es jmdm. gleichtun; **b)** *(Amer.: chase after)* nachsetzen (+ *Dat.*)

~ a'long *v. t.* mitnehmen

~ a'part *see* **apart b**

~ a'round *v. t.* **a)** *(take with one)* überallhin mitnehmen; **b)** *(show around)* herumführen

~ a'side *see* **aside 1**

~ a'way *v. t.* **a)** *(remove)* wegnehmen; *(to a distance)* mitnehmen; **~ sth. away from sb.** jmdm. etw. abnehmen; **~ sb.'s licence/passport away** jmdm. den Führerschein/Paß abnehmen; **what the taxman gives with one hand, he ~s away with the other** was der Fiskus mit der einen Hand gibt, das nimmt er mit der anderen wieder; **to ~ away** ‹*Pizza, Snack usw.*› zum Mitnehmen; **tablets that will ~ away the pain** Tabletten, die einem die Schmerzen nehmen; **~ away sb.'s rights/privileges/freedom/job** jmdm. seine Rechte/Privilegien/die Freiheit/seinen Arbeitsplatz nehmen; **~ away all the flavour of the food** dem Essen jeden Geschmack nehmen; **alcohol ~s away all your worries** Alkohol vertreibt die Sorgen; **it has ~n away all the pleasure in my win** es hat mir die Freude am Sieg verdorben; **no one can ~ that away from you** das kann dir niemand nehmen; **~ sb. away** jmdn. wegbringen; ‹*Polizei:*› jmdn. abführen; **~ him away!** schafft ihn fort!; hinweg mit ihm! *(geh.)*; **~ a child away from its parents/home/from school** ein Kind den Eltern wegnehmen/aus seiner häuslichen Umgebung herausreißen/aus der Schule nehmen; **~ sb. away from his/her work** jmdn. von der Arbeit abhalten; **my job ~s me away from my family/from home a lot** mein Beruf entzieht mich oft der Familie/durch meine Arbeit bin ich oft von zu Hause weg; **death/a cruel fate has ~n our father away from us** der Tod/ein grausames Schicksal hat uns den Vater genommen; **~ sb. away to the cells** jmdn. in seine Zelle bringen; **~ sb. away for a holiday** mit jmdm. in Urlaub fahren; *see also* **breath a; b)** *(Math.: deduct)* abziehen. *See also* **takeaway**

~ a'way from *v. t.* schmälern

~ 'back *v. t.* **a)** *(retract, have back)* zurücknehmen; wieder einstellen ‹*Arbeitnehmer*›; wieder [bei sich] aufnehmen ‹*Ehepartner*›; *(reclaim)* sich *(Dat.)* wiedergeben lassen; **b)** *(return)* zurückbringen; *(~ somewhere again)* wieder bringen ‹*Person*›; *(carry or convey back)* wieder mitnehmen; **that ~s me back [to my childhood]** das weckt bei mir [Kindheits]erinnerungen; **c)** *(Printing)* hochnehmen; raufziehen *(ugs.)*

~ 'down *v. t.* **a)** *(carry or lead down)* hinunterbringen; **this path ~s you down to the harbour** auf diesem Weg kommen Sie zum Hafen [hinunter]; **b)** *(lower or lift down)* abnehmen ‹*Bild, Ankündigung, Weihnachtsschmuck*›; einholen ‹*Fahne*›; umlegen ‹*Mast*›; herunterziehen, herunterlassen ‹*Hose*›; tiefer setzen ‹*Zeile*›; **~ a box down from a shelf** eine Schachtel von einem Regal herunternehmen; **c)** *(dismantle)* abreißen; abbauen ‹*Gerüst, Zelt*›; **d)** *(write down)* aufnehmen ‹*Brief, Personalien*›; aufschreiben ‹*Autonummer*›; mitschreiben ‹*Vortrag*›; **e)** *(humiliate)* ducken; *see also* **peg 1**

~ 'in *v. t.* **a)** *(convey to a place)* hinbringen; *(conduct)* hineinführen ‹*Gast*›; **~ sb. in a cup of tea** jmdm. eine Tasse Tee [hinein]bringen; **~ the car in for a service** das Auto zur Wartung bringen; **~ sb. in [in the car]** jmdn. [mit dem Auto] reinfahren *(ugs.)*; **I took the car in** ich fuhr mit dem Auto rein *(ugs.)*; **the police took him in for questioning** die Polizei nahm ihn zum Verhör mit; **b)** *(bring indoors)* hereinholen; **~ in parcels for sb.** Pakete für jmdn. annehmen; **~ in the washing from the line** die Wäsche von der Leine [ab]nehmen [und hereinholen]; **c)** *(accept for payment)* **~ in washing** für andere Leute waschen; **d)** *(receive, admit)* aufnehmen; *(for payment)* vermieten an (+ *Akk.*); [auf]nehmen ‹*[Kur]gäste*›; **~ in lodgers** ‹*Haus-, Wohnungseigentümer:*› Zimmer vermieten; ‹*Mieter:*› untervermieten; **e)** *(make narrower)* enger machen ‹*Kleidungsstück*›; **f)** *(include, comprise)* einbeziehen; **g)** *(coll.: visit)* mitnehmen *(ugs.)*; **our tour took in most of the main sights** auf unserer Rundfahrt haben wir die wichtigsten Sehenswürdigkeiten besichtigt; **h)** *(understand, grasp)* begreifen; überblicken, erfassen ‹*Lage*›; **I cannot ~ in any more of this lecture** ich kann mich auf diese Vorlesung nicht mehr konzentrieren; **I have won – I can't ~ it in yet** ich habe gewonnen – ich kann es noch gar nicht richtig begreifen; **i)** *(observe)* erfassen; *(watch, listen to)* mitbekommen; **j)** *(deceive)* einwickeln *(salopp)*; **be ~n in [by sb./sth.]** sich [von jmdm./durch etw.] einwickeln lassen *(salopp)*; *see also* **take-in**

~ 'off 1. *v. t.* **a)** abnehmen ‹*Deckel, Hut, Bild, Hörer, Tischtuch, Verband*›; abziehen ‹*Kissenbezug*›; ausziehen ‹*Schuhe, Handschuhe*›; ablegen ‹*Hut, Mantel, Schmuck*›; ‹*Säure:*› wegätzen ‹*Farbe*›; **~ off sb.'s/one's clothes** jmdm./sich die Kleider ausziehen; **~ sth. off the fire** etw. vom Feuer nehmen; **~ a door off the hinges** eine Tür aus den Angeln heben; **~ the cover off a pillow/bed** ein Kissen abziehen/ein Bett abdecken; **~ a parcel off sb.** jmdm. ein Paket abnehmen; **~ your hands off me!** faß mich nicht an!; **~ your feet off the settee!** nimm die Füße vom Sofa!; **~ off one's make-up** sich abschminken; **the heat has ~n the paint off the door** durch die Hitze ist die Farbe von der Tür abgeblättert; **b)** *(transfer from)* übernehmen ‹*Passagiere, Besatzung, Fracht*›; *(withdraw from a programme)* aus dem Programm nehmen; **~ sb. off sth.** jmdn. von etw. holen; *(withdraw from job, assignment, etc.)* jmdm. etw. entziehen; **he was ~n off the case** er wurde von dem Fall abgezogen; **~ sth. off a list/the menu** etw. von einer Liste streichen/von der Speisekarte nehmen; **~ a train/bus off a route** einen Zug/Bus vom Fahrplan streichen; **~ the weight off one's feet** seine Beine ausruhen; **~ years/ten years off sb.** jmdn. um Jahre jünger machen/jmdn. zehn Jahre jünger machen; *see also* **edge 1a; eye 1a; gilt 1a; hat a; mind 1c; smile 1; c)** *(cut off)* abtrennen; *(with saw)* absägen; *(with knife, scissors, etc.)* abschneiden; *(amputate)* abnehmen; **she had an inch ~n off her hair** sie ließ sich *(Dat.)* ihr Haar 2 cm kürzer schneiden; **d)** *(lead, conduct)* **~ sb. off to hospital/prison** jmdn. ins Krankenhaus/Gefängnis bringen; **~ sb. off on a stretcher/by ambulance** jmdn. auf einer Bahre/im Krankenwagen wegbringen; **~ sb. off to Paris** mit jmdm. nach Paris fahren; **I shall ~ my family off on** *or* **for a holiday** ich werde mit meiner Familie wegfahren *od.* in Urlaub fahren; **~ oneself off home/to bed** nach Hause/ins Bett gehen; **e)** *(deduct)* abziehen; **~ sth. off sth.** etw. von etw. abziehen; **~ £10 off the price** den Preis um zehn Pfund reduzieren; **f) ~ off weight/a few pounds** *(lose weight)* abnehmen/einige Pfund abnehmen; **the diet has ~n pounds off my weight** die Diät hat mich um Pfunde leichter gemacht; **g)** *(have free)* ~ **a day** *etc.* **off** sich *(Dat.)* einen Tag *usw.* frei nehmen *(ugs.)*; ~ **time off [work** *or* **from work]** sich *(Dat.)* frei nehmen; **h)** *(mimic)* nachmachen *(ugs.)*. **2.** *v.i.* **a)** *(Aeronaut.)* starten; **b)** *(Sport)* ‹*Springer, Pferd:*› abspringen; **c)** *(coll.: leave quickly)* losrennen; ~ **off after sb./sth.** hinter jmdm./etw. herrennen; **d)** *(become successful)* ‹*Wirtschaft:*› sich [sprunghaft] aufwärts entwickeln; ‹*Verkaufszahlen:*› [sprunghaft] steigen; ‹*Produkt, Kampagne:*› einschlagen; ‹*Person:*› Karriere machen; **his career is taking off** er macht eine steile Karriere. *See also* **take-off**

~ **'on 1.** *v.t.* **a)** *(undertake)* übernehmen; annehmen ‹*Herausforderung, Wette usw.*›; auf sich *(Akk.)* nehmen ‹*Bürde*›; *(accept responsibility for)* sich einlassen auf (+ *Akk.*) ‹*Person*›; sich *(Dat.)* aufbürden *od.* aufladen ‹*Sache*›; **b)** *(enrol, employ)* einstellen; aufnehmen ‹*Schüler, Studenten*›; annehmen ‹*Privatschüler*›; **c)** *(acquire, assume)* annehmen ‹*Farbe, Form, Ausdruck, Ausmaße*›; erhalten ‹*Bedeutung*›; **d)** *(accept as opponent)* sich auf eine Auseinandersetzung einlassen mit; es aufnehmen mit; den Kampf aufnehmen mit ‹*Regierung, Gesetz*›; **I'll** ~ **you on** *(in a contest)* ich nehme es mit dir auf; *(in a bet)* die Wette gilt; **e)** *(take on board)* aufnehmen; **f)** *(transport farther)* weiterbringen. **2.** *v.i.* **a)** *(coll.: get upset)* sich aufregen; **don't** ~ **on so!** reg dich nicht so auf!; hab dich nicht so! *(ugs. abwertend)*; **b)** *(be successful)* einschlagen

~ **'out** *v.t.* **a)** *(remove)* herausnehmen; ziehen ‹*Zahn*›; ~ **sth. out of sth.,** ~ **out sth. from sth.** etw. aus etw. [heraus]nehmen; ~ **out a pizza** *etc.* sich *(Dat.)* eine Pizza *usw.* mitnehmen; **'... to** ~ **out'** „... zum Mitnehmen"; ~ **out a nail from a piece of wood/a splinter from sb.'s finger** einen Nagel aus einem Stück Holz ziehen/jmdm. einen Splitter aus dem Finger ziehen; ~ **a stain/mark out of a dress** einen Fleck aus einem Kleid entfernen; **the strong sun** ~**s all the natural moisture out of your skin** die starke Sonnenbestrahlung entzieht der Haut ihre natürliche Feuchtigkeit; ~ **the colour/vitamins out of sth.** etw. ausbleichen/einer Sache *(Dat.)* die Vitamine entziehen; ~ **sb. out of the courtroom** jmdn. aus dem Gerichtssaal führen; **the train took us out of the city** der Zug brachte uns aus der Stadt [heraus]; ~ **it/a lot out of sb.** *(fig.)* jmdn. mitnehmen/sehr mitnehmen; **b)** *(destroy)* zerstören; *(fig.) (Footb. etc.)* ausschalten; *(kill)* töten; **c)** *(withdraw)* abheben ‹*Geld*›; **d)** *(deduct)* abziehen **(of** von); **e)** *(go out with)* ~ **sb. out** mit jmdm. ausgehen; ~ **sb. out for a walk/drive** mit jmdm. einen Spaziergang/eine Spazierfahrt machen; ~ **sb. out to** *or* **for lunch/dinner** jmdn. zum Mittagessen/Abendessen einladen; ~ **sb. out to the cinema/the theatre/a restaurant** jmdn. ins Kino/Theater/zum Essen einladen; ~ **the dog out [for a walk]** den Hund ausführen; ~ **sb. out of himself/herself** *(fig.)* jmdn. auf andere Gedanken bringen; **f)** *(get issued)* erwerben; erhalten; abschließen ‹*Versicherung*›; ausleihen ‹*Bücher*›; aufgeben ‹*Anzeige*›; ~ **out a subscription to sth.** etw. abonnieren; **g)** ~ **it/sth. out on sb./sth.** seine Wut/etw. an jmdm./etw. auslassen. *See also* **take-out**

~ **'over 1.** *v.t.* **a)** *(assume control of)* übernehmen; ~ **sth. over from sb.** etw. von jmdm. übernehmen; ~ **over the lead** *(Sport)* in Führung gehen; **let sth.** ~ **over one's life** *(fig.)* sein Leben von etw. bestimmen lassen; ~ **sb./sth. over** *(fig.)* von jmdm./etw. Besitz ergreifen; ~ **over the world** die Weltherrschaft an sich reißen; **b)** *(carry or transport over)* ~ **sb./sth. over to sb./sb.'s flat/Guildford** jmdn./etw. zu jmdm./in jmds. Wohnung/nach Guildford bringen *od.* *(ugs.)* rüberbringen; **I'll** ~ **you/it over next time** ich werde dich/es nächstes Mal mitnehmen; **c)** *(Printing)* rübernehmen *(ugs.)*. **2.** *v.i.* übernehmen; ‹*Manager, Firmenleiter:*› die Geschäfte übernehmen; ‹*Regierung, Präsident:*› die Amtsgeschäfte übernehmen; ‹*Junta:*› die Macht übernehmen; ‹*Beifahrer:*› das Steuer übernehmen; **other organizations will** ~ **over [from it] and carry out its functions** andere Organisationen werden seine Funktion übernehmen; **the night nurse** ~**s over at 10 p.m.** um zehn Uhr tritt die Nachtschwester ihren Dienst an. *See also* **take-over**

~ **'round** *v.t.* **a)** *(carry, deliver)* vorbeibringen; **I'll** ~ **you round one day** ich nehme dich einmal mit hin; **b)** *(show around)* [herum]führen; ~ **sb. round the factory** jmdn. durch die Fabrik führen

~ **to** *v.i.* **a)** *(get into habit of)* ~ **to doing sth.** anfangen, etw. zu tun; es sich *(Dat.)* angewöhnen, etw. zu tun; ~ **to drugs/gambling/crime** zu Drogen greifen/dem Spiel/der Kriminalität verfallen; **b)** *(escape to)* sich flüchten in (+ *Akk.*); ~ **to the [life]boats** sich in die Boote retten; *see also* **bed 1a**; **[1]heel 1a**; **c)** *(develop a liking for)* sich hingezogen fühlen zu ‹*Person*›; sich erwärmen für ‹*Sache*›; *(adapt oneself to)* sich gewöhnen an (+ *Akk.*); *see also* **[1]duck 1a**

~ **'up 1.** *v.t.* **a)** *(lift up)* hochheben; *(pick up)* aufheben; aufnehmen ‹*Staub, Partikel, Laub*›; herausnehmen ‹*Pflanzen*›; herausreißen ‹*Schienenstrang, Dielen*›; aufreißen ‹*Straße*›; hochholen, aufnehmen ‹*Masche*›; **he took up his book again** *(started to read again)* er nahm seine Lektüre wieder auf; *see also* **[2]arm 1a; cudgel 1; [1]gauntlet d; glove a**; **b)** *(move up)* weiter nach oben rücken; *(shorten)* kürzer machen; **c)** *(carry or lead up)* ~ **sb./sth. up** jmdn./etw. hinaufbringen **(to** zu); **I'll** ~ **you up one day** ich werde dich einmal mit hinaufnehmen; ~ **sth. up to sb.** jmdm. etw. hinaufbringen; **he took the suitcase up to the top floor with him** er nahm den Koffer mit in den obersten Stock; **d)** *(absorb)* aufnehmen; **e)** *(wind up)* aufwickeln; *see also* **[1]slack 2a**; **f)** *(occupy, engage)* beanspruchen; **I'm sorry to have** ~**n up so much of your time** es tut mir leid, Ihre Zeit so lange in Anspruch genommen zu haben; **most of my time is** ~**n up with ...:** ich verbringe die meiste Zeit mit ...; **be** ~**n up with sth./sb.** von etw./jmdm. in Anspruch genommen sein; **g)** ergreifen ‹*Beruf*›; anfangen ‹*Jogging, Tennis, Schach, Gitarre*›; ~ **up a musical instrument** ein Instrument zu spielen beginnen; ~ **sth. up as a hobby/profession** etw. zu seinem Hobby/Beruf machen; ~ **up German/a hobby** anfangen, Deutsch zu lernen/sich *(Dat.)* ein Hobby zulegen; **h)** *(start, adopt)* aufnehmen ‹*Arbeit, Kampf*›; antreten ‹*Stelle*›; übernehmen ‹*Pflicht, Funktion*›; einnehmen ‹*Haltung, Position*›; eintreten für, sich einsetzen für ‹*Sache*›; ~ **up a/one's position** ‹*Polizeiposten, Politiker:*› Position beziehen; **i)** *(accept)* annehmen; aufnehmen ‹*Idee, Vorschlag, Kredit, Geld*›; kaufen ‹*Aktien*›; ~ **up an option** optieren *(Rechtsw.)*; **j)** *(raise, pursue further)* aufgreifen; ~ **sth. up with sb.** sich in einer Sache an jmdn. wenden; **k)** ~ **sb. up [on sth.]** *(accept)* jmdn. [in bezug auf etw. *(Akk.)*] beim Wort nehmen; *(challenge)* jmdm. [in bezug auf etw. *(Akk.)*] widersprechen; **I might** ~ **you up on that offer/challenge** dein Angebot/deine Herausforderung werde ich vielleicht annehmen; **he took me up on the remark I had made** er hatte gegen meine Bemerkung etwas einzuwenden; **l)** *(join in)* einfallen in (+ *Akk.*) ‹*Ruf*›; sich beteiligen an (+ *Dat.*) ‹*Kampf*›; **m)** *(continue, resume)* [wieder] aufnehmen; weiterführen ‹*Geschichte*›; ~ **up sth. where one/sb. has left off** mit etw. da fortfahren, wo man/jmd. aufgehört hat; **n)** **be [very]** ~**n up with sb./sth.** mit jmdm./etw. [sehr] beschäftigt sein. **2.** *v.i.* **a)** *(coll.: become friendly)* ~ **up with sb.** sich mit jmdm. einlassen; **b)** *(continue)* einsetzen; ~ **up where sb./sth. has left off** da einsetzen, wo jmd./etw. aufgehört hat; **c)** *(wind up)* aufwickeln. *See also* **take-up**

~ **upon** *v.t.* ~ **upon oneself** auf sich *(Akk.)* nehmen ‹*Aufgabe, Pflicht, Verantwortung*›; ~ **upon oneself the right to do sth.** sich *(Dat.)* [einfach] das Recht nehmen, etw. zu tun; ~ **it upon oneself to do sth.** es auf sich *(Akk.)* nehmen, etw. zu tun; *(unwarrantably)* sich *(Dat.)* herausnehmen *(ugs.)*, etw. zu tun

take: ~-away *n.* *(restaurant)* Restaurant mit Straßenverkauf; *(meal)* Essen zum Mitnehmen; *attrib.* ‹*Restaurant*› mit Straßenverkauf; ‹*Essen, Mahlzeit*› zum Mitnehmen; **let's get a Chinese ~-away for our supper** laß uns beim Chinesen was zum Abendessen holen *(ugs.)*; **~-home** *attrib. adj.* **~-home pay/wages** Nettolohn, *der;* **~-in** *n.* *(coll.)* Schwindel, *der (abwertend)*

taken *see* **take 1, 2**

take: ~-off *n.* **a)** *(Sport)* Absprung, *der;* *(board)* [Ab]sprungbalken, *der;* **~-off speed** Geschwindigkeit beim Absprung; **b)** *(Aeronaut.)* Start, *der;* Take-off, *das (fachspr.)*; **be cleared/ready for ~-off** Starterlaubnis haben/startklar sein; **~-off speed** Abhebegeschwindigkeit, *die;* **c)** *(coll.: caricature)* Parodie, *die;* **do a ~-off of sb.** jmdn. parodieren; **d)** *(Econ.)* [rapider] Aufschwung; **~-out** *(Amer.) see* **take-away**; **~-over** *n.* *(Commerc.)* Übernahme, *die;* **~-over bid** Übernahmeangebot, *das*

taker ['teɪkə(r)] *n.* *(of a bet)* Wetter, *der;* *(of shares etc.)* Käufer, *der;* **there were no ~s [for the offer]** niemand hat [das Angebot] angenommen; *(at betting)* keiner nahm die Wette an; **any ~s?** *(at auction)* wer bietet?

'take-up *n.* **a)** *(response)* **a ~ of over 2,000** über 2 000 Interessenten; **~ has been very poor/low** es gab kaum *od.* sehr wenig Interessenten; **b)** *(winding up)* Aufwickeln, *das;* Aufwick[e]lung, *die;* *attrib.* Aufwickel‹*spule, -geschwindigkeit*›

taking ['teɪkɪŋ] *n.* **a)** *in pl.* *(amount taken)* Einnahmen; **b)** *(seizure)* Einnahme, *die;* **c)** **they are yours/his** *etc.* **for the ~:** du kannst/er kann *usw.* sie haben; **victory was his for the ~:** sein Sieg war so gut wie sicher

talc [tælk] *n.* **a)** Talkum, *das;* **b)** *(Min.)* Talk, *der*

talcum ['tælkəm] *n.* **~ [powder]** Talkumpuder, *der;* Talkum, *das;* *(as cosmetic)* Körperpuder, *der*

tale [teɪl] *n.* **a)** *(story)* Erzählung, *die;* Geschichte, *die* **(of** von, **about** über + *Akk.*); **fisherman's ~[s]** Anglerlatein, *das;* **b)** *(piece of gossip)* Geschichte, *die (ugs.)*. *See also* **tell 1b; thereby; wife; woe a**

talent ['tælənt] *n.* **a)** *(ability)* Talent, *das;* **have [great/no** *etc.*] **~ [for sth.]** [viel/kein *usw.*] Talent [zu *od.* für etw.] haben; **have a ~ for music** musikalisches Talent haben; **have a [great] ~ for doing sth.** das Talent haben, etw. zu tun; **b)** *(people with ability)* Talente; Begabungen; **the [local] ~** *(sl.: girls/men)* die interessanten Frauen/*(ugs.)* Typen am Ort; **c)** *(arch.: measure, money)* Talent, *das*

talented ['tæləntɪd] *adj.* talentiert; **this is a ~ essay** dieser Aufsatz zeugt von Talent

talent: ~-scout, ~-spotter *ns.* Talentsucher, *der;* **~-spotting** *n.* Talentsuche, *die*

tale-teller *n.* **a)** *see* **story-teller**; **b)** *(sneak/gossip)* jmd., der andere anschwärzt/schlechtmacht

talisman ['tælɪzmən] *n.* Talisman, *der*

talk [tɔːk] **1.** *n.* **a)** *(discussion)* Gespräch, *das;* **have a ~ [with sb.] [about sth.]** [mit jmdm.] [über etw. *(Akk.)*] reden *od.* sprechen; **have a long ~ on the phone** lange miteinander telefonieren; **I've enjoyed our ~:** es war nett, mit Ihnen zu sprechen; **could I have a ~ with you?** könnte ich Sie einmal sprechen?; **have** *or* **hold ~s [with sb.]** [mit jmdm.] Gespräche führen; **b)** *(speech, lecture)* Vortrag, *der;* **give a ~/a series of ~s [on sth./sb.]** einen Vortrag/eine Vortragsreihe [über etw./jmdn.] halten; **c)** *no pl. (form of communication)* Sprache, *die;* **sailors'/men's ~:** Seemanns-/Männersprache, *die;* **d)** *no pl. (talking)* Gerede, *das (abwertend);* **there's too much ~ [of ...]** es wird zuviel [von ...] geredet; **he is all ~ [and no action]** er redet nur [und tut nichts]; **there is [much/some] ~ of ...:** man hört [häufig/öfter] von ...; **be the ~ of the town/neighbourhood** *etc.* Stadtgespräch/das Thema in der Nachbarschaft *usw.* sein. *See also* **big 1g; small talk. 2.** *v.i.* **a)** *(speak)* sprechen, reden **(with, to mit)**; *(lecture)* sprechen; *(converse)* sich unterhalten; *(have ~s)* Gespräche führen; *(gossip)* reden; **be ~ing in German** deutsch sprechen; **love to hear oneself ~:** sich gern reden hören; **can't** *or* **doesn't she ~!** *(coll.)* die kann vielleicht reden!; **we must ~:** wir müssen miteinander reden; **~ on the phone** telefonieren; **we ~ on the phone every day** wir telefonieren jeden Tag miteinander; **~ to sb. on the phone** mit jmdm. telefonieren; **he sat through the entire meal without ~ing** er hat während des ganzen Essens kein Wort gesagt; **keep sb. ~ing** jmdn. in ein [längeres] Gespräch verwickeln; **she kept me ~ing for an hour** ich mußte mich eine Stunde lang mit ihr unterhalten; **now you're ~ing!** *(coll.)* das hört sich schon besser an; **that's no way to ~/~ to your uncle** das darfst du nicht sagen/so darfst du aber nicht mit deinem Onkel reden!; **don't ~ to 'me like that!** mit mir kannst du so nicht reden!; **who do you think you're ~ing to?** was bildest du dir ein, so mit mir zu sprechen?; **it's easy for you/him** *etc.* **to ~:** du hast/er hat *usw.* gut reden; **look who's ~ing** *(iron.)* das mußt du gerade sagen; **you/he** *etc.* **can** *(iron.) or* **can't ~:** sei du nur ganz still!; **don't ~ daft** *(coll.)* rede doch kein dummes Zeug!; **I'll ~ to that boy when he gets in** *(coll.: scold)* ich werde mal ein ernstes Wort mit dem Jungen reden, wenn er nach Hause kommt; **could I ~ to you for a moment?** könnte ich Sie einen Augenblick sprechen?; **~ to sb. seriously** mit jmdm. ein ernstes Wort reden; **may I ~ with Mr Smith, please?** kann ich bitte Herrn Smith sprechen?; **get ~ing [to sb.]** [mit jmdm.] ins Gespräch kommen; **~ to oneself** mit sich selbst sprechen; Selbstgespräche führen; **ships ~ to each other by radio** Schiffe verständigen sich über Funk; **~ of** *or* **about sb./sth.** über jmdn./etw. reden; **everyone's ~ing about him/his divorce** er/seine Scheidung ist in aller Munde; **everyone is ~ing about his new film** jeder spricht von seinem neuen Film; **~ of** *or* **about doing sth.** davon reden, etw. zu tun; **get oneself ~ed about** sich ins Gespräch bringen; **[not] know what one is ~ing about** [gar nicht] wissen, wovon man redet; **[not] know what sb. is ~ing about** [nicht] wissen, was jmd. meint *od.* wovon jmd. spricht; **~ about trouble** *etc.*! *(coll.)* da erzähl mir noch einer was von Schwierigkeiten *usw.*!; **What are you ~ing about? Of course he's not going to resign** Was redest du da? Natürlich tritt er nicht zurück; **~ing of holidays** *etc.* da wir [gerade] vom Urlaub *usw.* sprechen; apropos Urlaub *usw.*; **b)** *(have power of speech)* sprechen; **animals don't ~:** Tiere können nicht sprechen; **c)** *(betray secrets)* reden; **the prisoner refused to ~:** der Gefangene verweigerte jede Aussage; **make sb. ~:** jmdn. zum Reden bringen; **we have ways of making you ~:** wir werden Sie schon noch zum Reden bringen. *See also* **big 2; hat b; head 1b. 3.** *v.t.* **a)** *(utter, express)* **~ [a load of] nonsense** [eine Menge] Unsinn *od.* *(ugs.)* Stuß reden; **b)** *(discuss)* **~ politics/music** *etc.* über Politik/Musik *usw.* reden; **~ business** geschäftliche Dinge besprechen; *(get down to business)* zur Sache kommen; *see also* **shop 1b; c)** *(use)* sprechen ‹*Sprache, Dialekt usw.*›; **d)** *(bring into certain condition)* **~ oneself hoarse** sich heiser reden; **~ oneself** *or* **one's way out of trouble** sich aus Schwierigkeiten herausreden; **he ~ed himself into/out of the job** er hat im Gespräch so eine gute/schlechte Figur gemacht, daß er die Stelle bekommen/nicht bekommen hat; **~ sb. into/out of sth.** jmdn. zu etw. überreden/jmdm. etw. ausreden; **~ oneself into believing sth.** sich *(Dat.)* etw. einreden. *See also* **donkey**

~ at *v.t.* einreden auf (+ *Akk.*)

~ away 1. *v.i.* sich [angeregt] unterhalten **(to mit). 2.** *v.t.* **a)** verplaudern ‹*Zeit*›; **b) ~ sb.'s fears away** jmdm. seine Angst ausreden

~ 'back *v.i* **a)** *(reply)* antworten; **b)** *(reply defiantly)* widersprechen **(to** *Dat.*)

~ 'down 1. *v.t.* **a)** *(silence)* in Grund und Boden reden; **b)** *(guide)* Landekommandos geben (+ *Dat.*). **2.** *v.i.* **~ down to sb.** von oben herab *od.* herablassend mit jmdm. reden

~ 'out *v.t.* **a)** *(discuss)* ausdiskutieren; **b)** *(Parl.)* **~ out a bill** die Verabschiedung eines Gesetzes verfahrensmäßig blockieren

~ 'over *v.t.* **a) ~ sth. over [with sb.]** etw. [mit jmdm.] besprechen; **b)** *(persuade)* **~ sb. over** jmdn. überreden

~ 'round *v.t.* **a)** *(persuade)* **~ sb. round** jmdn. überreden; **b)** *(skirt)* **~ round sth.** um etw. herumreden *(ugs.)*

~ 'through *v.t.* **~ sb. through sth.** etw. mit jmdm. durchgehen *od.* durchsprechen; **~ sth. through** etw. durchsprechen

~ 'up 1. *v.t.* loben. **2.** *v.i. see* **speak up a**

talkative ['tɔ:kətɪv] *adj.* gesprächig; geschwätzig *(abwertend)*

talkativeness ['tɔ:kətɪvnɪs] *n., no pl.* Gesprächigkeit, *die;* Geschwätzigkeit, *die (abwertend)*

talked-about ['tɔ:ktəbaʊt] *attrib. adj. see* **talked-of**

talked-of ['tɔ:ktɒv] *attrib. adj.* **a much ~ book/play/project** ein vieldiskutiertes Buch/Stück/Projekt; **a much ~ actor/artist** ein Schauspieler/Künstler, der in aller Munde ist

talker ['tɔ:kə(r)] *n.* **a)** Redner, *der*/Rednerin, *die;* **the parrot is an excellent ~:** der Papagei kann ausgezeichnet sprechen; **she is a great ~** *(talks a lot)* sie redet viel; **be a fast ~:** [sehr] schnell sprechen; *(fig. sl.)* verdammt gut reden können *(ugs.);* **b)** *(one who talks but does not act)* Schwätzer, *der*/Schwätzerin, *die;* **he's just a ~:** er redet immer nur

talkie ['tɔ:kɪ] *n. (coll.)* Tonfilm, *der*

talking ['tɔ:kɪŋ] **1.** *n.* Reden, *das;* **there's been so much ~:** es ist so viel geredet worden; **'no ~'** „bitte nicht sprechen"; **do [all] the ~:** das Gespräch dominieren; **let me do the ~:** überlaß lieber mir das Reden. **2.** *adj.* sprechend; **~ doll** Sprechpuppe, *die;* **~ book** Hörbuch, *das;* **~ film** *or* **picture** Tonfilm, *der*

talking: ~ 'heads *n.pl. (Telev. sl. derog.)* Leute, die man nur reden sieht; **~ point** *n.* Gesprächsthema, *das;* **~-shop** *n. (derog.)* Quasselbude, *die (ugs. abwertend);* **~-to** ['tɔ:kɪŋtu:] *n. (coll.)* Standpauke, *die (ugs.);* **give sb. a good ~-to** jmdm. eine ordentliche Standpauke halten *(ugs.)*

'talk-show *n.* Talk-Show, *die*

tall [tɔ:l] **1.** *adj.* **a)** hoch; groß ‹*Person, Tier*›; **grow ~:** groß werden; wachsen; **feel ten feet ~** *(fig.)* riesig stolz sein; **b)** *(coll.: excessive)* **a ~ tale** eine unglaubwürdige Geschichte; **that is a ~ order** das ist ziemlich viel verlangt; *see also* **[1]story a. 2.** *adv.* **stand six feet** *etc.* **~:** 6 Fuß *usw.* groß sein; **stand ~:** aufrecht stehen; *(be proud)* erhobenen Hauptes stehen/gehen *usw. (geh.); see also* **walk 1a**

tall: ~boy *n.* Doppelkommode, *die;* Tallboy, *der;* **~ 'hat** *see* **top hat**

tallish ['tɔ:lɪʃ] *adj.* ziemlich hoch; ziemlich groß ‹*Person*›

tallness ['tɔ:lnɪs] *n., no pl.* Höhe, *die; (of person)* Größe, *die*

tallow ['tæləʊ] *n.* Talg, *der*

'tallow candle *n.* Talgkerze, *die*

tall 'ship *n.* Windjammer, *der*

tally ['tælɪ] **1.** *n.* **a)** *(record)* **sb.'s ~ is 18 goals** jmd. kann 18 Tore für sich verbuchen; **a player with a ~ of 18 goals** ein Spieler, der 18 Tore für sich verbuchen kann; **keep a [daily] ~ of sth.** [täglich] über etw. *(Akk.)* Buch führen; **b)** *(label, ticket)* Schild, *das.* **2.** *v.i.* übereinstimmen

tally-'ho 1. *int.* ≈ horrido. **2.** *n., pl.* **~s** ≈ Horrido, *das*

Talmud ['tælmʊd, 'tælməd] *n.* Talmud, *der*

talon ['tælən] *n.* Klaue, *die;* **~s** *(fig.: long fingernails)* Krallen *(ugs. abwertend)*

tamarind ['tæmərɪnd] *n.* Tamarinde, *die*

tamarisk ['tæmərɪsk] *n. (Bot.)* Tamariske, *die*

tambourine [tæmbə'ri:n] *n. (Mus.)* Tamburin, *das*

tame [teɪm] **1.** *adj.* **a)** zahm; *(joc.)* hauseigen ‹*Anarchist, Genie*›; **grow/become ~:** zahm werden; **b)** *(spiritless)* lahm *(ugs.),* lustlos ‹*Einwilligung, Anerkennung, Kampagne, Versuch*›; zahm *(ugs.)* ‹*Besprechung, Kritik*›; **c)** *(dull)* wenig aufregend; lasch ‹*Stil*›. **2.** *v.t. (lit. or fig.)* zähmen

tameable ['teɪməbl] *adj. (lit. or fig.)* zähmbar; **be [not] ~:** sich [nicht] zähmen lassen

tamely ['teɪmlɪ] *adv.* **a)** *(docilely)* zahm *(ugs.);* **b)** *(fig.: unexcitingly)* lahm *(ugs.);* wenig aufregend

tameness ['teɪmnɪs] *n., no pl.* **a)** *(docility)* Zahmheit, *die;* **b)** *see* **tame 1b:** Lahmheit, *die (ugs.);* Lustlosigkeit, *die;* Zahmheit, *die (ugs.);* **c)** *(dullness)* Langweiligkeit, *die; (of style)* Laschheit, *die*

tamer ['teɪmə(r)] *n.* Dompteur, *der*/Dompteuse, *die;* **a ~ of wild animals** ein Tierbändiger

Tamil ['tæmɪl] **1.** *adj.* tamilisch. **2.** *n.* **a)** *(person)* Tamile, *der*/Tamilin, *die;* **b)** *(language)* Tamil, *das*

tam-o'-shanter [tæmə'ʃæntə(r)] *n.* Tam-o'-Shanter, *der; zur schottischen Tracht gehörende Tellermütze mit Pompon*

tamper ['tæmpə(r)] *v.i.* **~ with** sich *(Dat.)* zu schaffen machen an (+ *Dat.*); *(make unauthorized changes in)* unerlaubte Änderungen vornehmen an (+ *Dat.*) ‹*Schriftstück, Text*›; *(attempt to bribe)* zu bestechen versuchen ‹*Jury, Zeugen*›; *(fig.)* ändern wollen ‹*Regeln, Tradition*›; **the brakes had been ~ed with** jmd. hatte sich an den Bremsen zu schaffen gemacht

'tamper-proof *adj.* einbruchsicher ‹*Schloß*›; verplombt ‹*Gasuhr*›; aufbruchsicher ‹*Münztelefon*›

tampon ['tæmpɒn] *n.* Tampon, *der*

[1]tan [tæn] **1.** *v.t.,* **-nn- a)** gerben; **b)** *(bronze)* ‹*Sonne:*› bräunen; ‹*Person:*› braun werden lassen ‹*Körperteil*›; **the sun had ~ned them dark brown** die Sonne hatte sie dunkelbraun gebrannt; **c)** *(sl.: beat)* das Fell gerben *(salopp)* (+ *Dat.*); *see also* **[2]hide. 2.** *v.i.,* **-nn-** braun werden. **3.** *n.* **a)** *(colour)* Gelbbraun, *das;* **b)** *(sun-~)* Bräune, *die;* **have/get a ~:** braun sein/werden; **c)** *(~ning agent)* Gerbmittel, *das.* **4.** *adj.* gelbbraun

[2]tan *abbr. (Math.)* **tangent** tan

tandem ['tændəm] **1.** *adv.* hintereinander; **be driven ~** ‹*Pferde:*› hintereinander im

Gespann laufen; **drive/ride** ~ ‹*Kutscher, Radfahrer:*› Tandem fahren. **2.** *n.* (*lit. or fig.*) Tandem, *das;* ~ **bicycle** Tandem, *das;* **coupled/harnessed in** ~: hintereinandergekoppelt/-gespannt; **work in** ~ (*fig.*) zusammenarbeiten

tandoori [tænˈdʊərɪ] *n.* (*Gastr.*) Tandoorigericht, *das; attrib.* Tandoori‹*restaurant, -hühnchen*›; ~ **cooking** Tandooriküche, *die*

tang [tæŋ] *n.* **a)** (*taste/smell*) **[sharp]** ~: scharfer Geschmack/Geruch; **[spicy/salty]** ~: würziger/salziger Geschmack/Geruch; **there is a** ~ **of autumn in the air** es riecht nach Herbst; **b)** (*of chisel, knife, sword*) Angel, *die*

tangent [ˈtændʒənt] (*Math.*) **1.** *n.* Tangente, *die;* (*in triangle*) Tangens, *der;* **run/be drawn at a** ~ **to a curve/circle** eine Kurve/einen Kreis in einem Punkt berühren; **go** *or* **fly off at a** ~ (*fig.*) plötzlich vom Thema abschweifen. **2.** *adj.* Tangenten-; ~ **plane** Tangentialebene, *die;* **be** ~ **to** tangieren (*fachspr.*), in einem Punkt berühren ‹*Kurve, Kreis*›

tangential [tænˈdʒenʃl] *adj.* (*Math.*) Tangential-; (*fig.: peripheral*) nebensächlich; nicht zur Sache gehörend ‹*Kommentar, Information*›; **be merely** ~ **to sth.** (*fig.*) etw. nur am Rande berühren

tangerine [tændʒəˈriːn] **1.** *n.* **a)** (*fruit*) ~ **[orange]** Tangerine, *die;* **b)** (*colour*) Orangerot, *das.* **2.** *adj.* orangerot

tangible [ˈtændʒɪbl] *adj.* **a)** (*perceptible by touch*) fühlbar ‹*Schwellung, Verdickung, Verhärtung*›; **b)** (*fig.: real, definite*) greifbar; spürbar, merklich ‹*Unterschied, Verbesserung*›; handfest ‹*Beweis*›; ~ **assets** (*Econ.*) Sachanlagevermögen, *das*

tangibly [ˈtændʒɪblɪ] *adv.* deutlich ‹*sichtbar*›; **be** ~ **different** sich merklich unterscheiden (**from** von); **sth. can be** ~ **proved** es gibt handfeste Beweise für etw.; **you should have been more** ~ **rewarded** man hätte dir eine handfestere Belohnung geben sollen

Tangier[s] [tænˈdʒɪə(z)] *pr. n.* Tanger (*das*)

tangle [ˈtæŋgl] **1.** *n.* Gewirr, *das;* (*in hair*) Verfilzung, *die;* (*fig.: dispute*) Auseinandersetzung, *die;* **be in a** ~: sich verheddert haben (*ugs.*); ‹*Haar:*› sich verfilzt haben; (*fig.*) ‹*Angelegenheiten:*› in Unordnung (*Dat.*) sein; ‹*Person:*› verwirrt sein; **get oneself into a** ~ (*fig.*) sich in eine schwierige Lage bringen. **2.** *v.t.* verheddern (*ugs.*); verfilzen ‹*Haar*›. **3.** *v.i.* sich verheddern (*ugs.*); ‹*Haar:*› sich verfilzen

~ ˈ**up 1.** *v.t.* verheddern (*ugs.*); verfilzen ‹*Haar*›; **become** *or* **get** ~**d up** sich verheddern (*ugs.*); **he's got** ~**d up in a rather unpleasant affair** (*coll.*) er ist in eine ziemlich unangenehme Sache verstrickt; **get** ~**d up with sb.** (*fig.*) sich mit jmdm. einlassen. **2.** *v.i. see* ~ **3**

~ **with** *v.t.* (*coll.*) ~ **with sb.** sich mit jmdm. anlegen

tangled [ˈtæŋgld] *adj.* verheddert (*ugs.*); verfilzt ‹*Haar*›; (*confused, complicated*) verworren; verwickelt ‹*Angelegenheit*›

tango [ˈtæŋgəʊ] **1.** *n., pl.* ~**s** Tango, *der.* **2.** *v.i.* Tango tanzen; **it takes two to** ~ (*fig. coll.*) dazu gehören immer noch zwei

tangy [ˈtæŋɪ] *adj.* scharf; (*spicy*) würzig; (*acid*) bitter; (*salty*) salzig

tank [tæŋk] *n.* **a)** Tank, *der;* (*Railw.: in tender*) Wasserkasten, *der;* (*for fish etc.*) Aquarium, *das;* (*for catching rain-water*) Auffangbecken, *das;* **fill the** ~ (*with petrol*) volltanken; **b)** (*Mil.*) Panzer, *der*

~ ˈ**up 1.** *v.i.* (*get fuel*) auftanken. **2.** *v.t.* auftanken; **get** ~**ed up** (*sl.: drunk*) sich volltanken (*salopp*)

tankard [ˈtæŋkəd] *n.* Krug, *der;* **a** ~ **of beer** *etc.* ein Krug Bier *usw.*

ˈ**tank-car** *n.* (*Railw.*) Kesselwagen, *der*

tanked-up [tæŋkˈtʌp] *adj.* (*sl.*) vollgetankt (*salopp*)

ˈ**tank-engine** *n.* (*Railw.*) Tenderlokomotive, *die*

tanker [ˈtæŋkə(r)] *n.* (*ship*) Tanker, *der;* Tankschiff, *das;* (*aircraft*) Tankflugzeug, *das;* (*vehicle*) Tank[last]wagen, *der*

tank: ~ **top** *n.* ≈ Pullunder, *der;* ~-**trap** *n.* (*Mil.*) Panzersperre, *die;* (*ditch*) Panzergraben, *der;* ~-**waggon** *n.* (*Brit. Railw.*) Kesselwagen, *der*

tanned [tænd] *adj.* **a)** (*treated by tanning*) gegerbt; **b)** (*bronzed*) braungebrannt

tanner [ˈtænə(r)] *n.* (*person*) Gerber, *der* /Gerberin, *die*

tannery [ˈtænərɪ] *n.* Gerberei, *die*

tannic [ˈtænɪk] *adj.* ~ **acid** (*Chem.*) Tannin, *das*

tannin [ˈtænɪn] *n.* (*Chem.*) Tannin, *das*

tanning [ˈtænɪŋ] *n.* **a)** (*of hides*) Gerben, *das;* (*craft also*) Gerberei, *die; attrib.* Gerb-; **b)** (*bronzing*) Bräunung, *die; attrib.* Bräunungs-; **c)** (*sl.: beating*) Abreibung, *die* (*ugs.*); **give sb. a** ~: jmdm. das Fell gerben (*salopp*)

Tannoy, (P) [ˈtænɔɪ] *n.* Lautsprecher, *der;* **over** *or* **on the** ~: über Lautsprecher

tansy [ˈtænzɪ] *n.* (*Bot.*) Rainfarn, *der*

tantalise, tantalising, tantalisingly *see* **tantaliz-**

tantalize [ˈtæntəlaɪz] *v.t.* reizen; (*tease also*) zappeln lassen (*ugs.*); (*with promises*) [falsche] Hoffnungen wecken bei

tantalizing [ˈtæntəlaɪzɪŋ] *adj.* verlockend; **a** ~ **puzzle** ein Rätsel, das einen nicht losläßt

tantalizingly [ˈtæntəlaɪzɪŋlɪ] *adv.* [falsche] Hoffnungen weckend; verlockend ‹*schön, nah, duften, lächeln*›

tantamount [ˈtæntəmaʊnt] *pred. adj.* **be** ~ **to sth.** gleichbedeutend mit etw. sein; einer Sache (*Dat.*) gleichkommen

tantrum [ˈtæntrəm] *n.* Wutanfall, *der;* (*of child*) Trotzanfall, *der;* **be in a** ~: einen Wutanfall/Trotzanfall haben; **get into/ throw a** ~: einen Wutanfall/Trotzanfall bekommen

Tanzania [tænzəˈniːə] *pr. n.* Tansania (*das*)

Tanzanian [tænzəˈniːən] **1.** *adj.* tansanisch; **sb. is** ~: jmd. ist Tansanier/Tansanierin. **2.** *n.* Tansanier, *der*/Tansanierin, *die*

Taoiseach [ˈtiːʃæx] *n.* (*Ir. Parl.*) Premierminister/-ministerin [der Republik Irland]

Taoism [ˈtaʊɪzm] *n.* (*Relig.*) Taoismus, *der*

Taoist [ˈtaʊɪst] (*Relig.*) **1.** *adj.* taoistisch. **2.** *n.* Taoist, *der*/Taoistin, *die*

[1]**tap** [tæp] **1.** *n.* **a)** Hahn, *der;* (*on barrel, cask*) [Zapf]hahn, *der;* **hot/cold[-water]** ~: Warm-/Kaltwasserhahn, *der;* **leave the** ~ **running** den Wasserhahn laufen lassen; **on** ~: vom Faß *nachgestellt;* **be on** ~ (*fig.*) zur Verfügung stehen; **have on** ~ (*fig.*) zur Verfügung haben ‹*Geld, Mittel*›; an der Hand haben ‹*Experten*›; **b)** (*plug*) Zapfen, *der;* Spund, *der;* **c) [telephone]** ~: Telefonüberwachung, *die.* **2.** *v.t.,* **-pp- a)** (*make use of*) erschließen ‹*Reserven, Ressourcen, Bezirk, Markt, Land, Einnahmequelle*›; anzapfen (*fig. ugs.*) ‹*Reserven, Ressourcen*›; ~ **sb. for money/information** jmdn. anzapfen (*ugs.*); ~ **sb. for a few pounds** versuchen, bei jmdm. ein paar Pfund lockerzumachen (*ugs.*); **b)** (*Teleph.: intercept*) abhören; anzapfen (*ugs.*); **c)** (*pierce*) anzapfen ‹*Baum, Faß*›; anstechen ‹*Faß*›; (*draw off*) abzapfen ‹*Bier*›; ~ **a tree for resin** einen Baum zur Harzgewinnung anzapfen; **d)** (*Metalw.*) ein Gewinde schneiden in (+ *Akk.*)

~ ˈ**off** *v.t.* abzapfen (**into** in + *Akk.*)

[2]**tap 1.** *v.t.,* **-pp-** (*strike lightly*) klopfen an (+ *Akk.*); (*on upper surface*) klopfen auf (+ *Akk.*); ~ **one's fingers on the table** (*repeatedly*) mit den Fingern auf den Tisch trommeln; ~ **one's finger against one's forehead** sich (*Dat.*) mit dem Finger an die Stirn tippen; ~ **one's foot** mit dem Fuß auf den Boden klopfen; ~ **one's foot to the music** mit dem Fuß den Takt schlagen; ~ **sb. on the shoulder** jmdm. auf die Schulter klopfen/(*more lightly*) tippen. **2.** *v.i.,* **-pp-:** ~ **at/ on sth.** an etw. (*Akk.*) klopfen; (*on upper surface*) auf etw. (*Akk.*) klopfen. **3.** *n.* (*light blow, rap*) Klopfen, *das;* (*given to naughty child*) Klaps, *der* (*ugs.*); **give a nail a little** ~: leicht auf einen Nagel klopfen; **there was a** ~ **at/on the door** es klopfte an die Tür; **I felt a** ~ **on my shoulder** jemand klopfte/(*more lightly*) tippte mir auf die Schulter; ~**s** (*Amer. Mil.: signal*) Zapfenstreich, *der*

~ **aˈway** *v.i.* ‹*Schreibkraft, Funker am Morsegerät:*› vor sich hin klappern; ~ **away on the table with one's fingers/a ruler** mit den Fingern/einem Lineal auf dem Tisch trommeln

~ ˈ**in** *v.t.* einklopfen ‹*Nagel usw.*›

~ ˈ**out** *v.t.* **a)** (*knock out*) ausklopfen ‹*Pfeife*›; herausklopfen ‹*Nagel, Keil*›; **b)** klopfen ‹*Rhythmus, Takt*›; (*write*) (*in Morse*) morsen ‹*Nachricht*›; (*on typewriter*) tippen (*ugs.*)

tap: ~-**dance 1.** *n.* Step[tanz], *der;* **do a** ~-**dance** steppen. **2.** *v.i.* Step tanzen; steppen; ~-**dancer** *n.* Steptänzer, *der*/-tänzerin, *die;* ~-**dancing** *n.* Steptanz, *der;* Steppen, *das*

tape [teɪp] **1.** *n.* **a)** Band, *das;* **adhesive/ (*coll.*) sticky** ~: Klebstreifen, *der;* Klebeband, *das; see also* **red tape; b)** (*Sport*) Zielband, *das;* **breast the** ~: durchs Ziel gehen; **c)** (*for recording*) [Ton]band, *das* (**of** mit); **[have sth.] on** ~: [etw.] auf Band (*Dat.*) [haben]; **put/record sth. on** ~, **make a** ~ **of sth.** etw. auf Band (*Akk.*) aufnehmen; **blank** ~: unbespieltes Band; **d) [paper]** ~: Papierstreifen, *der;* (*punched with holes*) Lochstreifen, *der;* **come in on the** ~: ‹*Nachricht:*› über Fernschreiber kommen. **2.** *v.t.* **a)** (*record on* ~) [auf Band (*Akk.*)] aufnehmen; ~**d music** Tonbandmusik, *die;* **b)** (*bind with* ~) [mit Klebeband *od.* Klebstreifen] zukleben ‹*Paket*›; kleben ‹*Einband, eingerissene Seite*›; **c) have got sb./sth.** ~**d** (*sl.*) jmdn. durchschaut haben/etw. im Griff *od.* unter Kontrolle haben

~ ˈ**down** *v.t.* [mit Klebeband] festkleben

~ ˈ**on** *v.t.* [mit Klebeband] ankleben

~ ˈ**over** *v.t.* [mit Klebeband] überkleben

~ **toˈgether** *v.t.* [mit Klebeband] zusammenkleben

~ ˈ**up** *v.t.* [mit Klebeband] zukleben; [mit Klebeband] zusammenkleben ‹*zerrissene Seite, zerbrochene Pfeife usw.*›

tape: ~ **cassette** *n.* Tonbandkassette, *die;* ~ **deck** *n.* Tapedeck, *das;* ~-**machine** *n.* Fernschreiber, *der;* ~-**measure** *n.* Bandmaß, *das;* (*for measuring garments etc.*) [Zenti]metermaß, *das;* ~-**player** *n.* Tonband[wiedergabe]gerät, *das*

taper [ˈteɪpə(r)] **1.** *v.t.* sich verjüngen lassen; ~ **[to a point]** spitz zulaufen lassen; **be** ~**ed** sich verjüngen; (*to a point*) spitz zulaufen. **2.** *v.i.* sich verjüngen; ~ **[to a point]** spitz zulaufen. **3.** *n.* **a) [wax]** ~: Wachsstock, *der;* **b)** (*narrowing*) Verjüngung, *die*

~ **away** *see* ~ **off 2**

~ ˈ**off 1.** *v.t.* **a)** *see* ~ **1; b)** (*fig.: decrease gradually*) drosseln ‹*Produktion*›. **2.** *v.i.* **a)** *see* ~ **2; b)** (*fig.: decrease gradually*) zurückgehen

tape: ~-**record** [ˈteɪprɪkɔːd] *v.t.* [auf Tonband (*Akk.*)] aufnehmen *od.* aufzeichnen; ~ **recorder** *n.* Tonbandgerät, *das;* ~ **recording** *n.* Tonbandaufnahme, *die*

tapered [ˈteɪpəd] *adj.* sich verjüngend; (*to a point*) spitz zulaufend; ~ **trousers** unten eng geschnittene Hose

tapering [ˈteɪpərɪŋ] *adj.* sich verjüngend; (*to a point*) spitz zulaufend; **be** ~: sich verjüngen; (*to a point*) spitz zulaufen

ˈ**tape-slide show** *n.* vertonte Diaschau

tapestry [ˈtæpɪstrɪ] *n.* Gobelingewebe, *das;* (*wall-hanging*) Bildteppich, *der;* Tapisserie, *die;* (*fig.*) Darstellung, *die;* **Gobelin** ~: Gobelin[teppich], *der;* **the Bayeux ~:** der Bayeux-Teppich

'tapeworm *n.* Bandwurm, *der*

tapioca [tæpɪ'əʊkə] *n.* Tapioka, *die*

tapir ['teɪpə(r), 'teɪpɪə(r)] *n. (Zool.)* Tapir, *der*

tappet ['tæpɪt] *n. (Mech. Engin.)* Mitnehmer, *der;* **~ rod** Stößel, *der*

tap: ~room *n.* Schankraum, *der;* **~-root** *n. (Bot.)* Pfahlwurzel, *die;* **~-water** *n.* Leitungswasser, *das*

[1]tar [tɑ:(r)] **1.** *n.* Teer, *der;* **high-~/low-~ cigarette** Zigarette mit hohem/niedrigem Teergehalt; *(fig.)* **beat** *or* **knock the ~ out of sb.** *(Amer. coll.)* jmdn. fertigmachen *(salopp);* **spoil the ship for a ha'p'orth of ~:** am falschen Ende sparen. **2.** *v. t.*, **-rr-** teeren; **~red road** Teerstraße, *die;* **~ and feather sb.** jmdn. teeren und federn; **they are ~red with the same brush** *or* **stick** *(fig.)* der eine ist nicht besser als der andere

[2]tar *n.* **[Jack] ~** *(coll.)* Teerjacke, *die (scherzh.)*

tarantella [tærən'telə], **tarantelle** ['tærən'tel] *n. (Mus.)* Tarantella, *die*

tarantula [tə'ræntjʊlə] *n. (Zool.)* Tarantel, *die*

tardily ['tɑ:dɪlɪ] *adv.* **a)** *(slowly)* [zögernd] langsam; **b)** *(late)* spät; *(too late)* zu spät

tardy ['tɑ:dɪ] *adj.* **a)** *(slow)* [zögernd] langsam; **b)** *(late)* spät; *(too late)* zu spät; **be ~** *(Amer.)* mit Verspätung kommen **(for,** to zu); **be ~ in doing sth.** etw. erst spät tun

tare [teə(r)] *n. (Commerc.)* Tara, *die; (of lorry, car)* Leergewicht, *das*

target ['tɑ:gɪt] **1.** *n.* **a)** *(lit. or fig.)* Ziel, *das;* **be the ~ of** *or* **a ~ for his mockery/fury** *(fig.)* die Zielscheibe seines Spottes/Zornes sein; **production/export/savings ~:** Produktions-/Export-/Sparziel, *das;* **fixed/moving/towed ~:** feststehendes Ziel/bewegliches Ziel/Schleppscheibe, *die;* **hit/miss the/one's/its ~:** [das Ziel] treffen/das Ziel verfehlen; **set oneself a ~** *(fig.)* sich *(Dat.)* ein Ziel setzen *od.* stecken; **set oneself a ~ of £5,000** sich *(Dat.)* 5 000 Pfund zum Ziel setzen; **set sb. a ~ of six months** jmdm. eine Frist von sechs Monaten setzen; **reach one's ~** *(fig.)* sein Ziel erreichen; **be on/off** *or* **not on ~** ‹*Geschoß, Schuß:*› treffen/danebengehen; **be on ~** *(fig.)* ‹*Sparer, Sammler:*› auf dem Wege dahin sein[, sein Ziel zu erreichen]; **be on ~ for sth.** *(lit. or fig.)* auf etw. *(Akk.)* zusteuern; **be above/below ~** *(fig.)* das Ziel über-/unterschritten haben; **b)** *(Sport)* Ziel- *od.* Schießscheibe, *die;* **c)** *(Phys.)* Target, *das. See also* **sitting target. 2.** *v. t.* zielen auf ‹*Käufergruppe*›; **~ benefits at those most in need** Unterstützung auf die Bedürftigsten konzentrieren; **independently ~ed warheads** *(Mil.)* unabhängig voneinander lenkbare Einzelsprengköpfe; **be ~ed on sth.** auf etw. *(Akk.)* gerichtet sein; **be ~ed on** *or* **at sth.** *(fig.)* auf etw. *(Akk.)* abzielen

target: ~ date *n.* vorgesehener Termin; **~ figure** *n. (esp. Commerc.)* Ziel, *das;* **~ language** *n.* Zielsprache, *die;* **~ practice** *n., no art.* Schießübungen

tariff ['tærɪf] *n.* **a)** *(tax)* Zoll, *der; (table or scale of customs duties)* Zolltarif, *der;* **[import] ~:** Einfuhr- *od.* Importzoll, *der;* **b)** *(list of charges)* Tarif, *der;* Preisliste, *die;* **railway/postal ~:** Eisenbahn-/Posttarif, *der;* **hotel ~:** Hotelpreise

Tarmac, tarmac ['tɑ:mæk] **1.** *n.* **(P) a)** Makadam, *der (Bauw.);* **b)** *(at airport)* Rollbahn, *die.* **2.** *v. t.*, **-ck-** makadamisieren *(Bauw.)*

tar macadam [tɑ: mə'kædəm] *n.* Makadam, *der (Bauw.)*

tarn [tɑ:n] *n.* [kleiner] Bergsee

tarnish ['tɑ:nɪʃ] **1.** *v. t.* stumpf werden lassen ‹*Metall*›; *(fig.)* beflecken ‹*Ruf, Namen*›. **2.** *v. i.* ‹*Metall:*› stumpf werden, anlaufen. **3.** *n.* **a)** *(action)* Anlaufen, *das;* **b)** *(discolouring film)* Beschlag, *der;* Überzug, *der*

tarnished ['tɑ:nɪʃt] *adj.* stumpf ‹*Metall*›; *(fig.)* befleckt ‹*Ruf, Name, Image*›

tarot ['tærəʊ] *n.* Tarock, *das od. der;* **~ card** Tarockkarte, *die*

tarpaulin [tɑ:'pɔ:lɪn] *n.* Persenning, *die*

tarpon ['tɑ:pən] *n. (Zool.)* Tarpun, *der*

tarragon ['tærəgən] *n. (Bot.)* Estragon, *der*

[1]tarry ['tɑ:rɪ] *adj.* teerig; teerverschmiert ‹*Hand, Kleidung*›; ‹*Strand, Felsen*› voller Teer

[2]tarry ['tærɪ] *v. i. (literary)* verweilen *(geh.); (be slow)* säumen *(geh.);* **~ awhile** ein Weilchen bleiben

[1]tart [tɑ:t] *adj.* herb; sauer ‹*Obst usw.*›; *(fig.)* scharfzüngig

[2]tart *n.* **a)** *(Brit.) (filled pie)* ≈ Obstkuchen, *der; (small pastry)* Obsttörtchen, *das;* **jam ~:** Marmeladentörtchen, *das;* **b)** *(sl.: prostitute)* Nutte, *die (salopp)*

~ 'up *v. t. (Brit. coll.)* **~ oneself up, get ~ed up** *(dress gaudily)* sich auftakeln *(ugs.); (smarten oneself up)* sich feinmachen; **~ a pub/restaurant up** *(fig.)* eine Kneipe/ein Lokal aufmotzen *(ugs.)*

tartan ['tɑ:tən] **1.** *n.* Schotten[stoff], *der; (pattern)* **the Stewart ~:** der Stewart *(Textilw.); das Schottenmuster des Stewart-Clans.* **2.** *adj.* **a)** Schotten‹*rock, -jacke*›; **~ plaid/rug** Tartan, *der;* **b) T~ track (P)** Tartanbahn, *die*

Tartar ['tɑ:tə(r)] **1.** *adj.* tatarisch; Tataren-. **2.** *n.* **a)** *(person)* Tatar, *der*/Tatarin, *die;* **b)** *(language)* Tatarisch, das; **c)** *(violent-tempered person)* Choleriker, *der*/Cholerikerin, *die*

tartar *n.* **a)** *(Chem.)* Tartarus, *der (fachspr.);* Weinstein, *der; see also* **cream of tartar; b)** *(scale on teeth)* Zahnstein, *der*

tartare ['tɑ:tɑ:(r)] *adj.* **~ sauce, sauce ~** *see* **tartar sauce; steak ~** *see* **steak**

tartaric acid [tɑ:tærɪk 'æsɪd] *n. (Chem.)* Weinsäure, *die*

tartar sauce ['tɑ:tɑ:(r)] *n. (Gastr.)* Remoulade[nsoße], *die*

tartly ['tɑ:tlɪ] *adv.* in scharfem Ton ‹*sprechen, antworten*›

tartness ['tɑ:tnɪs] *n., no pl. see* **[1]tart:** Herbheit, *die;* Säure, *die; (fig.)* Scharfzüngigkeit *die*

tarty ['tɑ:tɪ] *adj. (sl.)* nuttig *(ugs. abwertend)*

Tarzan ['tɑ:zən] *n.* Tarzan, *der (fig.)*

task [tɑ:sk] *n.* Aufgabe, *die;* **set sb. the ~ of doing sth.** jmdm. auftragen, etw. zu tun; **set oneself the ~ of doing sth.** es sich *(Dat.)* zur Aufgabe machen, etw. zu tun; **undertake the ~ of doing sth.** sich der Aufgabe *(Dat.)* unterziehen, etw. zu tun; **carry out/perform a ~:** eine Aufgabe erfüllen; **take sb. to ~:** jmdm. eine Lektion erteilen

task: ~ force, ~ group *ns. (sent out)* Sonderkommando, *das; (set up)* Sonderkommission, *die;* **~master** *n.* **a hard ~master** ein strenger Vorgesetzter; *(teacher)* ein strenger Lehrmeister

Tasmania [tæz'meɪnɪə] *pr. n.* Tasmanien *(das)*

Tasmanian [tæz'meɪnɪən] **1.** *adj.* **a)** tasmanisch; **b)** *(Zool.)* **~ devil/wolf** Beutelteufel/-wolf, *der.* **2.** *n.* Tasmanier, *der*/Tasmanierin, *die*

tassel ['tæsl] *n.* Quaste, *die*

taste [teɪst] **1.** *v. t.* **a)** schmecken; *(try a little)* probieren; kosten; **she barely ~d her food** sie hat ihr Essen kaum angerührt; **she hadn't ~d food for two days** sie hatte seit zwei Tagen keinen Bissen gegessen; **b)** *(recognize flavour of)* [heraus]schmecken; **c)** *(fig.: experience)* kosten *(geh.)* ‹*Macht, Freiheit, [Miß]erfolg, Glück, Niederlage*›. **2.** *v. i.* **a)** *(have sense of flavour)* schmecken; **b)** *(have certain flavour)* schmecken **(of** nach); **not ~ of anything** nach nichts schmecken. **3.** *n.* **a)** *(flavour)* Geschmack, *der;* **to ~:** nach Geschmack ‹*verdünnen*›; **this dish has no ~:** dieses Gericht schmeckt nach nichts; **there's a ~ of garlic in sth.** etw. schmeckt nach Knoblauch; **leave a nasty/bad** *etc.* **~ in the mouth** *(lit. or fig.)* einen unangenehmen/üblen *usw.* Nachgeschmack hinterlassen; **b)** *(sense)* **[sense of] ~:** Geschmack[ssinn], *der;* **c)** *(discernment)* Geschmack, *der;* **person of ~:** Person mit Geschmack; **he is a person of ~:** er hat Geschmack; **~ in art/music** Kunst-/Musikgeschmack, *der;* **have good ~ in clothes** sich geschmackvoll kleiden; **it would be bad ~ to do that** es wäre geschmacklos *od.* eine Geschmacklosigkeit, das zu tun; **in good/bad ~:** geschmackvoll/geschmacklos; **in the best/worst of ~:** äußerst geschmackvoll/geschmacklos; **d)** *(sample) (lit. or fig.)* Kostprobe, *die;* **have a ~ of** probieren ‹*Speise, Getränk*›; kennenlernen ‹*Freiheit, jmds. Jähzorn, Arroganz*›; **do you want a ~?** möchtest du mal kosten *od.* probieren?; **first ~ of success/of life in a big city** erstes Erfolgs-/Großstadterlebnis; **give sb. a ~ of sth.** *(lit. or fig.)* jmdm. eine Kostprobe einer Sache *(Gen.)* geben; **give sb. a ~ of the whip** jmdm. die Peitsche zu spüren *od. (geh.)* schmecken geben; **a ~ of things to come** ein Vorgeschmack dessen, was noch kommt; *see also* **medicine; e)** *(liking)* Geschmack, *der* **(in** für); **have a/no ~ for sth.** an etw. *(Dat.)* Geschmack/keinen Geschmack finden; **have expensive ~s in clothes** *etc.* eine Vorliebe für teure Kleidung *usw.* haben; **be/not be to sb.'s ~:** nach jmds./nicht nach jmds. Geschmack sein; **it's a question** *or* **matter of ~:** das ist eine Frage des Geschmacks; das ist Geschmackssache; **each** *or* **everyone to his ~:** jeder nach seinem Geschmack; **~s differ** die Geschmäcker sind verschieden *(ugs. scherzh.);* **there's no accounting for ~:** über Geschmack läßt sich nicht streiten; *see also* **acquire b**

'taste-bud *n. (Anat., Zool.)* Geschmacksknospe, *die*

tasteful ['teɪstfl] *adj.* geschmackvoll; ‹*Person*› mit Geschmack

tastefully ['teɪstfəlɪ] *adv.* geschmackvoll

tasteless ['teɪstlɪs] *adj.* geschmacklos

tastelessly ['teɪstlɪslɪ] *adv.* geschmacklos; *as sentence-modifier* geschmackloserweise

taster ['teɪstə(r)] *n.* Verkoster, *der*/Verkosterin, *die*

tastily ['teɪstɪlɪ] *adv.* lecker

tastiness ['teɪstɪnɪs] *n., no pl.* leckerer Geschmack

tasty ['teɪstɪ] *adj.* lecker; **be a ~ morsel** *(lit. or fig.)* ein Leckerbissen sein

[1]tat [tæt] *n., no pl. (coll.)* Schrott, *der (ugs.)*

[2]tat *see* **[2]tit**

ta-ta [tæ'tɑ:] *int. (child lang.)* ata, ata! *(Kinderspr.); (coll.)* tschüs! *(ugs.)*

tattered ['tætəd] *adj.* zerlumpt ‹*Kleidung, Person*›; zerrissen ‹*Segel*›; zerfleddert ‹*Buch, Zeitschrift*›; *(fig.)* ramponiert *(ugs.)* ‹*Ruf*›

tatters ['tætəz] *n. pl.* Fetzen; **be in ~:** in Fetzen sein; *(fig.)* ‹*Karriere, Leben:*› ruiniert sein; ‹*Argument, Strategie:*› zunichte sein

tattily ['tætɪlɪ] *adv.* schäbig *(abwertend)*

tattiness ['tætɪnɪs] *n., no pl.* Schäbigkeit, *die (abwertend)*

tatting ['tætɪŋ] *n.* Schiffchen- *od.* Okkiarbeit, *die; (lace)* Schiffchen- *od.* Okkispitze, *die*

tattle ['tætl] *v. i.* tratschen *(ugs. abwertend)*

[1]tattoo [tə'tu:] **1.** *v. t.* tätowieren; **~ sth. on sb.'s arm** jmdm. etw. auf den Arm tätowieren. **2.** *n.* Tätowierung, *die*

[2]tattoo *n.* **a)** *(Mil.: signal)* Zapfenstreich, *der;* **beat** *or* **sound the ~:** den Zapfenstreich schlagen/blasen; **b)** *(drumming noise)* Trommeln, *das;* **there was a ~ on the door** jemand trommelte gegen die Tür; **he/his fingers beat a ~ on the table** *(coll.)* er trommelte mit den Fingern auf den Tisch; **c)** *(military show)* **~:** Großer Zapfenstreich

tattooed [tə'tu:d] *adj.* tätowiert

tattooer [tə'tu:ə(r)], **tattooist** [tə'tu:ɪst] *ns.* Tätowierer, *der*/Tätowiererin, *die*

tatty ['tætɪ] *adj. (coll.)* schäbig *(abwertend)*; zerfleddert ⟨*Zeitschrift, Buch*⟩; *(inferior)* mies *(ugs.)* ⟨*Publikation, Firma*⟩; *(threadbare)* billig ⟨*Argument, Ausrede*⟩

taught *see* **teach**

taunt [tɔ:nt] **1.** *v.t.* verspotten (**about** wegen); **~ sb. with being a weakling** jmdn. als Schwächling verspotten. **2.** *n.* spöttische Bemerkung; **the ~ of cowardice** *or* **of being a coward hurt him deeply** daß man ihn als Feigling verspottete, traf ihn tief

taunting ['tɔ:ntɪŋ] **1.** *adj.* spöttisch. **2.** *n.* Spott, *der*

Taurean ['tɔ:rɪən] *n. (Astrol.)* Stier, *der*

Taurus ['tɔ:rəs] *n. (Astrol., Astron.)* der Stier; der Taurus; *see also* **Aries**

taut [tɔ:t] *adj.* **a)** *(tight)* straff ⟨*Seil, Kabel, Saite*⟩; gespannt ⟨*Muskel*⟩; **b)** *(fig.: tense)* angespannt ⟨*Nerven, Ausdruck*⟩; **c)** *(fig.: concise)* kurz ⟨*Geschichte, Erzählung*⟩; knapp ⟨*Stil*⟩

tauten ['tɔ:tn] **1.** *v.t.* straffen. **2.** *v.i.* sich straffen; ⟨*Muskel:*⟩ sich spannen

tautly ['tɔ:tlɪ] *adv.* **a)** *(tightly)* straff; **b)** *(fig.: tensely)* zum Zerreißen; **c)** *(fig.: tersely)* knapp ⟨*geschrieben*⟩; straff ⟨*gebaut*⟩

tautological [tɔ:tə'lɒdʒɪkl], **tautologous** [tɔ:'tɒləgəs] *adjs.* tautologisch; **~ expression/statement** Tautologie, *die;* **it is ~ to talk about ...:** es ist eine Tautologie, von ... zu sprechen

tautology [tɔ:'tɒlədʒɪ] *n.* Tautologie, *die*

tavern ['tævən] *n. (literary)* Schenke, *die*

tawdriness ['tɔ:drɪnɪs] *n., no pl.* Flitter, *der;* **the ~ of sb.'s finery** jmds. Flitterstaat

tawdry ['tɔ:drɪ] *adj.* billig und geschmacklos; *(fig.)* zweifelhaft

tawny ['tɔ:nɪ] *adj.* gelbbraun

tawny 'owl *n. (Ornith.)* Waldkauz, *der*

tax [tæks] **1.** *n.* **a)** Steuer, *die;* **pay 20% in ~ [on sth.]** 20% Steuern [für etw.] zahlen; **a third of my income will go in ~:** ein Drittel meines Einkommens geht an das Finanzamt; **before/after ~:** vor Steuern/nach Abzug der Steuern; **free of ~:** steuerfrei; *(after ~, ~ paid)* nach Abzug der Steuern; netto; **~ paid, net of ~:** nach Abzug der Steuern; netto; **for ~ reasons** aus steuerlichen Gründen; **for ~ purposes** steuerlich gesehen; fürs Finanzamt *(ugs.)*; *see also* **capital gains tax; corporation b; direct tax; income tax; poll-tax; purchase tax; value-added tax; b)** *(fig.: burden)* Belastung, *die* (**on** für). **2.** *v.t.* **a)** *(impose ~ on)* besteuern; *(pay ~ on)* versteuern ⟨*Einkommen*⟩; **~ sb. on his/her income** jmds. Einkommen besteuern; **I am** *or* **my income is ~ed at 30%** ich bezahle 30% Lohnsteuer/Einkommensteuer; **b)** *(make demands on)* strapazieren ⟨*Mittel, Kräfte, Geduld usw.*⟩; **c)** *(accuse)* beschuldigen, bezichtigen (**with** *Gen.*); **~ sb. with doing sth.** jmdn. beschuldigen *od.* bezichtigen, etw. getan zu haben

taxable ['tæksəbl] *adj.* steuerpflichtig

tax: **~ allowance** *n.* Steuerfreibetrag, *der;* **~ assessment** *n.* Steuerbescheid, *der*

taxation [tæk'seɪʃn] *n. (imposition of taxes)* Besteuerung, *die; (taxes payable)* Steuern; **subject to ~:** steuerpflichtig

tax: **~ avoidance** *n.* Steuerminderung, *die;* **~ bill** *n.* Steuerbescheid, *der; (amount)* Steuerschuld, *die;* **~ bracket** *n.* Stufe im Steuertarif; **move into a higher ~ bracket** nach einem höheren Steuersatz besteuert werden; **~-collector** *n.* Finanzbeamte, *der*/-beamtin, *die;* **~-deductible** *adj.* steuerabzugsfähig; [steuerlich] absetzbar; **~ demand** *n.* Steuerforderung, *die;* **~ disc** *n.* Steuerplakette, *die;* **~ dodge** *n.* Steuertrick, *der;* **~-dodger** *n.* Steuerbetrüger, *der*/-betrügerin, *die;* **~ evasion** *n.* Steuerhinterziehung, *die;* **~-exempt** *adj. (Amer.)* steuerbefreit; steuerfrei ⟨*Einkommen*⟩; **~ exile** *n.* **a)** *(person)* Steuerflüchtling, *der;* **b)** *(place)* Steueroase, *die (ugs.)*; **~ form** *n.* Steuerformular, *das;* **~-free 1.** *adj.* steuerfrei; *(after payment of tax)* Netto-; **~-free allowance** Steuerfreibetrag, *der;* **2.** *adv.* steuerfrei; *(after payment of tax)* netto; **~ haven** *n.* Steueroase, *die (ugs.)*; Steuerparadies, *das (ugs.)*

taxi ['tæksɪ] **1.** *n.* Taxi, *das;* **go by ~:** mit dem Taxi fahren. **2.** *v.i.*, **~ing** *or* **taxying** ['tæksɪɪŋ] *(Aeronaut.)* ⟨*Flugzeug:*⟩ rollen; ⟨*Pilot:*⟩ das Flugzeug rollen lassen; **~ to a stop** ⟨*Flugzeug:*⟩ ausrollen. **3.** *v.t.*, **~ing** *or* **taxying** *(Aeronaut.)* rollen lassen

'taxi-cab *see* **taxi 1**

taxidermist ['tæksɪdɜ:mɪst] *n.* Taxidermist, *der*/Taxidermistin, *die;* Präparator, *der*/Präparatorin, *die*

taxidermy ['tæksɪdɜ:mɪ] *n.* Taxidermie, *die*

'taxi-driver *n.* Taxifahrer, *der*/-fahrerin, *die*

taximeter ['tæksɪmi:tə(r)] *n.* Taxameter, *das od. der;* Fahrpreisanzeiger, *der*

taxing ['tæksɪŋ] *adj.* strapaziös, anstrengend ⟨*Arbeit, Rolle, Reise*⟩; schwierig ⟨*Problem*⟩

'tax inspector *n.* Steuerinspektor, *der*/-inspektorin, *die*

taxi: **~-rank** *(Brit.)*, *(Amer.)* **~ stand** *ns.* Taxistand, *der;* **~way** *n.* Rollbahn, *die*

tax: **~man** *n. (coll.)* Finanzbeamte, *der*/-beamtin, *die;* **a letter from the ~man** ein Brief vom Finanzamt; **work for the ~man** [nur noch] fürs Finanzamt arbeiten *(fig.)*; **~ office** *n.* Finanzamt, *das*

taxonomy [tæk'sɒnəmɪ] *n. (Biol.)* Taxonomie, *die*

tax: **~payer** *n.* Steuerzahler, *der*/-zahlerin, *die;* **~paying** *attrib. adj.* Steuern zahlend...; **~ rebate** *n.* Steuererstattung, *die;* **~ relief** *n.* Steuererleichterung, *die;* **get ~ relief on insurance premiums** Versicherungsprämien von der Steuer absetzen; **~ return** *n.* Steuererklärung, *die;* **~ year** *n.* Steuerjahr, *das*

TB *abbr.* **tuberculosis** Tb, *die;* **~ sufferer** Tb-Kranke, *der/die*

T-bone *see* **T b**

te [ti:] *n. (Mus.)* si

tea [ti:] *n.* **a)** Tee, *der;* **mint/fennel ~:** Kräuter-/Fencheltee, *der;* **early morning ~:** *frühmorgens [vor dem Aufstehen] getrunkener Tee;* **[not] be sb.'s cup of ~** *(fig. coll.)* [nicht] jmds. Fall sein *(ugs.)*; **be just** *or* **exactly** *or* **very much sb.'s cup of ~** *(fig. coll.)* genau *od.* ganz jmds. Fall sein *(ugs.)*; **not for all the ~ in China** *(coll.)* nicht um alles in der Welt; **[come to sb. for] ~ and sympathy** *(fig. coll.)* Trost und Rat [bei jmdm. suchen]; **b)** *(meal)* **[high] ~:** Abendessen, *das;* **afternoon ~:** [Nachmittags]tee, *der*

tea: **~-bag** *n.* Teebeutel, *der;* **~-boy** *n.* ≈ Stift, *der (ugs.)*; *jüngerer Mann, der in einer Firma, Behörde o. ä. den Pausentee usw. zubereitet;* **~-break** *n. (Brit.)* Teepause, *die;* **~-caddy** *n.* Teebüchse, *die;* **~cake** *n.* **a)** *(Brit.: sweet bread bun)* ≈ Rosinenbrötchen, *das;* **b)** *(Amer.: sweet cake)* Keks, *der;* **~cakes** Teegebäck, *das*

teach [ti:tʃ] **1.** *v.t.*, **taught** [tɔ:t] unterrichten; *(at university)* lehren; **You can't dance? I'll ~ you** Du kannst nicht tanzen? Ich bringe es dir bei *od.* zeige es dir; **~ music** *etc.* **to sb., ~ sb. music** *etc.* jmdn. in Musik *usw.* unterrichten; jmdm. Musikunterricht *usw.* geben; **~ oneself** es sich *(Dat.)* selbst beibringen; **~ sb./oneself/an animal sth.** jmdm./sich/einem Tier etw. beibringen; **~ sb./oneself/an animal to do sth.** jmdm./sich/einem Tier beibringen, etw. zu tun; *(train)* jmdn./sich/ein Tier dazu erziehen, etw. zu tun; **~ sb. to ride/to play the piano** jmdm. das Reiten/Klavierspielen beibringen; **T~ yourself French/car maintenance** *(book-title)* Französisch zum Selbststudium/Wie warte ich mein Auto selbst?; **this experience has taught me one thing ...:** diese Erfahrung hat mich eins gelehrt ...; **I'll/that'll ~ you** *etc.* **to do that!** *(coll. iron.)* ich werde/das wird dich *usw.* lehren, das zu tun! *(iron.)*; **that'll ~ him/you** *etc.*! *(coll. iron.)* das hat er/hast du *usw.* nun davon! *(iron.)*; **~ sb. how/that ...:** jmdm. beibringen, wie/daß ...; ⟨*Bibel, Erfahrung:*⟩ jmdn. lehren, wie/daß ...; **~ sb. tolerance** *or* **to be tolerant** jmdn. Toleranz lehren; jmdn. lehren, tolerant zu sein; **~ school** *(Amer.)* Lehrer/Lehrerin sein; *see also* **dog 1 a; lesson c. 2.** *v.i.*, **taught** unterrichten; **he wants to/is going to ~:** er will Lehrer werden/wird Lehrer

teachable ['ti:tʃəbl] *adj.* lernfähig ⟨*Kind, Tier*⟩; erlernbar ⟨*Eigenschaft*⟩; **a ~ subject** ein Fach, das man gut lehren kann

teacher ['ti:tʃə(r)] *n.* Lehrer, *der*/Lehrerin, *die;* **she's a university/evening-class ~:** sie lehrt an der Universität/unterrichtet an der Abendschule; **kindergarten ~:** ≈ Vorschullehrer, *der*/-lehrerin, *die;* **geography/music ~:** Geographie-/Musiklehrer, *der*/Geographie-/Musiklehrerin, *die*

teacher: **~-training** *n.* Lehrerausbildung, *die;* **~ training college** *n.* ≈ pädagogische Hochschule

'tea-chest *n.* Teekiste, *die*

'teach-in *n.* Teach-in, *das*

teaching ['ti:tʃɪŋ] *n.* **a)** *(act)* Unterrichten, *das* (**of** von); **the ~ of languages, language ~:** der Sprachunterricht; **I enjoy ~ very much** [das] Unterrichten macht mir großen Spaß; **all the ~ at this school is in French** an der Schule wird nur in französischer Sprache unterrichtet; **b)** *no pl., no art. (profession)* Lehrberuf, *der;* **want to go into** *or* **take up** *or* **do ~:** Lehrer/Lehrerin werden wollen; **c)** *(doctrine)* Lehre, *die*

teaching: **~ aid** *n.* Lehr- *od.* Unterrichtsmittel, *das;* **~ hospital** *n.* Ausbildungskrankenhaus, *das;* **~-machine** *n.* Lernmaschine, *die;* **~ method** *n.* Lehr- *od.* Unterrichtsmethode, *die;* **~ profession** *n.* Lehrberuf, *der;* **~ staff** *n.* Lehrerkollegium, *das*

tea: **~-cloth** *n.* **a)** *(for table)* ≈ Kaffeedecke, *die;* **b)** *(for drying)* Geschirrtuch, *das;* **~-cosy** *n.* Teewärmer, *der;* **~cup** *n.* Teetasse, *die; see also* **storm 1 a; ~cupful** *n.* Tasse, *die;* **a ~cupful of sugar** eine Tasse Zucker; **~ dance** *n.* Tanztee, *der;* **~-garden** *n.* **a)** *(public place)* ≈ Gartencafé, *das;* **b)** *(plantation)* Teeplantage, *die;* **~-house** *n.* Teehaus, *das*

teak [ti:k] *n.* **a)** *(wood)* Teak[holz], *das; attrib.* Teak[holz]⟨*öl, -furnier, -möbel*⟩; **b)** *(tree)* Teakbaum, *der*

'tea-kettle *n.* Teekessel, *der*

teal [ti:l] *n., pl. same (Ornith.)* Krickente, *die*

tea: **~-lady** *n. Frau, die in einer Firma, Behörde o. ä. den Pausentee usw. zubereitet;* **~-leaf** *n.* Teeblatt, *das;* **read the ~-leaves** ≈ aus dem Kaffeesatz lesen

team [ti:m] **1.** *n.* **a)** *(group)* Team, *das; (Sport also)* Mannschaft, *die;* **a football/cricket ~:** eine Fußball-/Kricketmannschaft; **a ~ of scientists** eine Gruppe *od.* ein Team von Wissenschaftlern; **a research ~:** eine Forschungsgruppe; **make a good ~:** ein gutes Team *od.* Gespann sein; **work as a ~:** im Team zusammenarbeiten; **b)** *(draught animals)* Gespann, *das;* **a ~ of oxen/horses** ein Gespann Ochsen/Pferde; **a ~ of four horses** ein Vierergespann [Pferde]. **2.** *v.t. see* **~ up 1. 3.** *v.i. see* **~ up 2**

~ 'up 1. *v.t.* zusammenbringen. **2.** *v.i.* sich zusammentun *(ugs.)*

'tea-maker *n.* Teemaschine, *die*

team: **~ effort** *n.* Team- *od.* Gemeinschaftsarbeit, *die;* **a great ~ effort** eine großartige Gemeinschaftsleistung; **thanks**

to good ~ effort dank guter Teamarbeit; ~ **game** *n.* Mannschaftsspiel, *das;* **~-leader** *n.* Gruppenleiter, *der*/-leiterin, *die;* **~-mate** *n.* Mannschaftskamerad, *der*/-kameradin, *die;* **~-member** *n.* Mitglied des Teams/der Mannschaft/der Gruppe; ~ **'spirit** *n.* Teamgeist, *der; (Sport also)* Mannschaftsgeist, *der*

teamster ['ti:mstə(r)] *n. (Amer.)* Lkw-Fahrer, *der*/-Fahrerin, *die*

'team-work *n.* Teamarbeit, *die;* **by ~:** in Teamarbeit

tea: ~-party *n.* Teegesellschaft, *die;* **~-plantation** *n.* Teeplantage, *die;* **~-planter** *n. (proprietor)* Teeplantagenbesitzer, *der*/-besitzerin, *die; (cultivator)* Teepflanzer, *der*/-pflanzerin, *die;* **~pot** *n.* Teekanne, *die*

¹tear [teə(r)] **1.** *n.* Riß, *der; see also* **wear 1 a. 2.** *v. t.,* **tore** [tɔ:(r)], **torn** [tɔ:n] **a)** *(rip; lit. or fig.)* zerreißen; *(pull apart)* auseinanderreißen; *(damage)* aufreißen; ~ **open** aufreißen ‹*Brief, Schachtel, Paket*›; ~ **one's dress [on a nail]** sich *(Dat.)* das Kleid [an einem Nagel *(Dat.)*] aufreißen; ~ **one's finger-nail** sich *(Dat.)* einen Fingernagel einreißen; ~ **a muscle** sich *(Dat.)* einen Muskelriß zuziehen; **a torn muscle** ein Muskel[faser]riß; ~ **sb.'s heart** *(fig.)* jmdm. das Herz zerreißen *(geh.);* ~ **a hole/gash in sth.** ein Loch/eine klaffende Wunde in etw. *(Akk.)* reißen; ~ **sth. in half** *or* **in two** etw. entzweireißen; ~ **to shreds** *or* **pieces** *(lit.)* zerfetzen; in Stücke reißen ‹*Flagge, Kleidung, Person*›; ~ **to shreds** *(fig.) (destroy)* ruinieren ‹*Ruf, Leumund*›; zerrütten ‹*Nerven*›; zunichte machen ‹*Argument, Alibi*›; auseinandernehmen *(salopp)* ‹*Mannschaft*›; *(criticize)* verreißen *(ugs.);* **a country torn by war** ein durch Krieg zerrissenes Land; **I was torn by** *or* **with grief** mein Herz war von Kummer zerrissen *(geh.);* **be torn between two things/people/between x and y** zwischen zwei Dingen/Personen/x und y hin- und hergerissen sein; **be torn as to what to do** hin- und hergerissen sein [und nicht wissen, was man tun soll]; **that's torn it** *(Brit. fig. coll.)* das hat alles vermasselt *(salopp);* **b)** *(remove with force)* reißen; ~ **sth. out of** *or* **from sb.'s hands/a book** jmdm. etw. aus der Hand reißen/etw. aus einem Buch [heraus]reißen; **the wind tore the cap from his head** der Wind riß ihm die Mütze vom Kopf; ~ **a child from its parents/home** *(fig.)* ein Kind seinen Eltern entreißen/aus seiner vertrauten Umgebung reißen; ~ **oneself from sb./a place** *(fig.)* sich von jmdm./einem Ort losreißen; ~ **one's hair** *(fig.)* sich *(Dat.)* die Haare raufen *(ugs.).* **3.** *v. i.,* **tore, torn a)** *(rip)* [zer]reißen; **it ~s along the perforation** es läßt sich entlang der Perforation abreißen; ~ **in half** *or* **in two** entzweireißen; durchreißen; **b)** *(move hurriedly)* rasen *(ugs.);* ~ **past** vorbeirasen *(ugs.);* ~ **along the street** die Straße hinunterrasen *(ugs.);* ~ **off** losrasen *(ugs.);* **come ~ing out/past** heraus-/vorbeigerast kommen *(ugs.)*

~ **apart** *v. t. (lit. or fig.)* auseinanderreißen; *(coll.: criticize)* zerreißen *(ugs.);* **they tore the place apart** sie haben den Laden auseinandergenommen *(ugs.)*

~ **at** *v. t.* zerren an (+ *Dat.*); ~ **at sb.'s heartstrings** *(fig.)* jmdm. sehr zu Herzen gehen

~ **a'way** *v. t.* wegreißen; abreißen ‹*Tapete, Verpackung*›; ~ **away sb.'s mask** *(fig.)* jmds. Maske herunterreißen; ~ **sb./oneself away [from sb./sth.]** *(fig.)* jmdn./sich [von jmdm./etw.] loseisen *(ugs.);* ~ **oneself away [from a sight/book/game]** *(fig.)* sich [von einem Anblick/Buch/Spiel] losreißen; *see also* **tearaway**

~ **'down** *v. t.* herunterreißen; niederreißen ‹*Zaun, Mauer*›; abreißen ‹*Gebäude*›; *(fig.)* niederreißen ‹*Schranken*›

~ **into** *v. t.* ‹*Geschoß:*› ein Loch reißen in (+ *Akk.*); ‹*Säge:*› sich [hinein]fressen in (+ *Akk.*); ‹*Raubtier:*› zerfleischen; *(fig.: tell off, criticize)* heftig angreifen

~ **'off** *v. t.* abreißen; *see also* **tear-off**

~ **'out** *v. t.* herausreißen; ausreißen ‹*Baum*›; *see also* ~ **2 b**

~ **'up** *v. t.* **a)** *(remove)* aufreißen ‹*Straße, Bürgersteig*›; herausreißen ‹*Zaun, Pflanze*›; ausreißen ‹*Baum*›; **b)** *(destroy)* zerreißen; *(fig.)* für null und nichtig erklären ‹*Vertrag, Abkommen*›

²tear [tɪə(r)] *n.* Träne, *die;* **there were ~s in her eyes** sie hatte *od.* ihr standen Tränen in den Augen; **with ~s in one's eyes** mit Tränen in den Augen; **cry ~s of joy/rage/frustration** Freudentränen/Tränen der Wut/Enttäuschung vergießen; **cry ~s of laughter** Tränen lachen; **burst into ~s** in Tränen ausbrechen; **move sb. to ~s** jmdn. zu Tränen rühren; **bore sb. to ~s** jmdn. zu Tode langweilen; **be in ~s** in Tränen aufgelöst sein; **French/Cooking without ~s** *(book-title)* Französisch/Kochen leicht gemacht; **be wet with ~s** tränennaß sein; *see also* **crocodile tears; dissolve 2 a; reduce 1 b; ¹shed b; vale**

tearaway ['teərəweɪ] **1.** *adj.* rabaukenhaft *(ugs.).* **2.** *n.* Rabauke, *der (ugs.)*

tear [tɪə(r)]: **~-drop** *n.* Träne, *die;* **~-duct** *n. (Anat.)* Tränenkanal, *der*

tearful ['tɪəfl] *adj. (crying)* weinend; *(wet with tears)* tränenüberströmt; *(accompanied by tears)* tränenreich ‹*Versöhnung, Abschied, Anlaß*›; **say a ~ goodbye** sich unter Tränen verabschieden; **she was looking very ~:** sie sah sehr verweint aus; *(about to cry)* sie schien den Tränen nahe

tearfully ['tɪəfəlɪ] *adv.* unter Tränen

tear-gas ['tɪəgæs] *n.* Tränengas, *das*

tearing ['teərɪŋ] *adj.* **a)** reißend ‹*Geräusch*›; **b)** *(coll.: violent)* rasend; **be in a ~ hurry** schrecklich in Eile sein

tear-jerker ['tɪədʒɜ:kə(r)] *n. (coll.)* Schnulze, *die (ugs. abwertend);* **this film is a real ~:** in diesem Film wird kräftig auf die Tränendrüsen gedrückt

tear-off ['teərɒf] *attrib. adj.* ~ **calendar** Abreißkalender, *der;* ~ **slip** Abriß, *der*

tea: ~-room *n.* Teestube, *die;* ≈ Café, *das;* **~-rose** *n.* Teerose, *die*

tear-sheet ['teəʃi:t] *n.* Belegseite, *die*

tear-stained ['tɪəsteɪnd] *adj.* tränenüberströmt ‹*Gesicht*›; ‹*Brief, Buchseite*› mit Tränenspuren

tease [ti:z] **1.** *v. t.* **a)** necken; ~ **sb. [about sth.]** jmdn. [mit etw.] aufziehen *(ugs.);* jmdn. [wegen etw.] verspotten; **he's only teasing you** er macht nur Spaß *(ugs.);* **stop teasing the dog** hör auf, den Hund zu ärgern; ~ **sb. that he has done sth.** jmdn. damit aufziehen *(ugs.),* daß er etw. getan hat; **the children ~d their father for sweets** *or* **to give them sweets** *(Amer.)* die Kinder lagen ihrem Vater damit in den Ohren *(ugs.),* daß er ihnen Süßigkeiten geben sollte; **b)** *(Textiles) (separate fibres of)* krempeln ‹*Flachs, Wolle*›; hecheln ‹*Flachs*›; *(dress with teasels)* [auf]rauhen; **c)** *(Amer. Hairdressing)* toupieren. **2.** *v. i.* seine Späße machen; **I'm only teasing** ich mache nur Spaß. **3.** *n. (coll.)* **he/she is a great ~:** er/sie muß einen immer aufziehen *(ugs.)*

~ **'out** *v. t.* **a)** *(disentangle)* auskämmen; kämmen, krempeln ‹*Wolle, Flachs*›; hecheln ‹*Flachs*›; **b)** *(get out, lit. or fig.)* herausholen; ~ **out the facts** die Tatsachen herausarbeiten

teasel ['ti:zl] *n.* **a)** *(Bot.)* Karde, *die;* **common/fuller's ~:** Wilde Karde/Weberkarde, *die;* **b)** *(Textiles)* Karde, *die*

teaser ['ti:zə(r)] *n.* **a)** *(coll.: puzzle)* **brain-~:** Denk[sport]aufgabe, *die;* **be a [real] ~** *(fig.)* eine harte Nuß sein *(ugs.);* **b)** *(one who teases)* **he/she is a great ~:** er/sie muß einen immer aufziehen *(ugs.)*

tea: ~-service, ~-set *ns.* Tee-Service, *das;* **~-shop** *(Brit.) see* **tea-room**

teasing ['ti:zɪŋ] *adj.* neckend; **he was in a ~ mood** er war in der Stimmung, andere aufzuziehen *(ugs.)*

teasingly ['ti:zɪŋlɪ] *adv.* neckend; **speak ~:** frotzeln; **ask sb. sth. ~:** jmdn. frotzelnd etw. fragen

tea: ~spoon *n.* Teelöffel, *der;* **~spoonful** *n.* Teelöffel, *der;* **a ~spoonful** ein Teelöffel [voll]; **~-strainer** *n.* Teesieb, *das*

teat [ti:t] *n.* **a)** *(nipple)* Zitze, *die;* **b)** *(of rubber or plastic)* Sauger, *der*

tea: ~-table *n.* Teetisch, *der;* **be at the ~-table** beim Tee sitzen; **~-things** *n. pl. (coll.)* Teegeschirr, *das;* **~-time** *n.* Teezeit, *die;* **~-towel** *n.* Geschirrtuch, *das;* **~-tray** *n.* Teebrett, *das;* **~-trolley** *n.* Teewagen, *der;* **~-urn** *n.* Teebehälter, *der;* **~-wagon** *(Amer.) see* **~-trolley**

teazel, teazle ['ti:zl] *see* **teasel**

Tech (Tec) [tek] *n. (coll.)* Fachhochschule, *die;* FH, *die*

technical ['teknɪkl] *adj.* **a)** technisch ‹*Problem, Detail, Daten, Fortschritt*›; *(of particular science, art, etc.)* fachlich; Fach‹*kenntnis, -berater, -sprache, -begriff, -wörterbuch*›; *(of the execution of a work of art)* technisch ‹*Fertigkeit, Schwierigkeit*›; ~ **expertise/expert** Sachkenntnis, *die*/Fachmann, *der;* ~ **college/school** Fachhochschule, *die*/Fachschule, *die;* **[highly] ~ book** [reines] Fachbuch; **the text is very/highly ~:** es ist ein reiner Fachtext; **the text is too ~ for me** der Text ist zu fachsprachlich für mich; **explain sth. without being** *or* **getting too ~:** etw. erklären, ohne sich zu fachsprachlich auszudrücken; ~ **hitch** technisches Problem; ~ **term** Fachbegriff, *der;* Fachausdruck, *der;* Fachterminus, *der;* **for ~ reasons** aus technischen Gründen; **b)** *(strictly interpreted) (Law)* formaljuristisch; ~ **knock-out** *(Boxing)* technischer K.o.

technical 'drawing *n. (Brit.)* technisches Zeichnen

technicality [teknɪ'kælɪtɪ] *n.* **a)** *no pl. (technical quality)* technischer Charakter; *(of book, text, style)* fachsprachlicher Charakter; **b)** *(technical expression)* Fachausdruck, *der;* **c)** *(technical distinction)* technisches Detail; *(technical point)* technische Frage; **legal/financial/military technicalities** rechtliche/finanzielle/militärische [Detail]fragen; **be acquitted on a ~:** auf Grund eines Formfehlers freigesprochen werden

technically ['teknɪkəlɪ] *adv.* **a)** technisch; *(in a particular science, art, etc.)* fachlich; **b)** *(strictly speaking)* im Prinzip; *(Law)* formaljuristisch

technician [tek'nɪʃn] *n.* Techniker, *der*/Technikerin, *die*

Technicolor, *(Amer.* **P)** ['teknɪkʌlə(r)] *n. (Cinemat.)* Technicolor ⓦ, *das*

technique [tek'ni:k] *n.* Technik, *die; (procedure)* Methode, *die*

technocracy [tek'nɒkrəsɪ] *n.* Technokratie, *die*

technocrat ['teknəʊkræt] *n.* Technokrat, *der*/Technokratin, *die*

technocratic [teknəʊ'krætɪk] *adj.* technokratisch

technological [teknə'lɒdʒɪkl] *adj.,* **technologically** [teknə'lɒdʒɪkəlɪ] *adv. see* **technology:** technisch; technologisch

technologist [tek'nɒlədʒɪst] *n.* Technologe, *der*/Technologin, *die;* ‹*Lebensmittel-, Erdöl-*›techniker, *der*/-technikerin, *die*

technology [tek'nɒlədʒɪ] *n.* Technik, *die; (application of science)* Technologie, *die;* **science and ~:** Wissenschaft und Technik; **college of ~:** Fachhochschule für Technik

techy *see* **tetchy**

tectonic [tek'tɒnɪk] *(Geol.)* **1.** *adj.* tektonisch. **2.** *n. in pl.* Tektonik, *die;* **plate ~s** Plattentektonik, *die*

Ted [ted] *n. (Brit. coll.)* Teddy-Boy, *der*

teddy ['tedɪ] *n.* ~ **[bear]** Teddy[bär], *der*

Teddy: ~ **boy** *n. (Brit.)* Teddy-Boy, *der;* ~ **girl** *n. (Brit.)* Teddy-Girl, *das*

Te Deum [ti: 'di:əm, teɪ 'deɪəm] *n. (hymn)* Tedeum, *das*

tedious ['ti:dɪəs] *adj.* langwierig ⟨*Reise, Arbeit*⟩; *(uninteresting)* langweilig

tediously ['ti:dɪəslɪ] *adv.* langatmig ⟨*reden, schreiben*⟩; *(uninterestingly)* langweilig; ~ **familiar** bis zum Überdruß bekannt; ~ **repeat sth.** etw. bis zum Überdruß wiederholen; **a ~ long meeting** eine lange, langweilige Besprechung

tediousness ['ti:dɪəsnɪs] *n., no pl. (of work, journey)* Langwierigkeit, *die; (of book, lecture, wait)* Langweiligkeit, *die*

tedium ['ti:dɪəm] *n. (of journey)* Langwierigkeit, *die; (of waiting)* Langweiligkeit, *die;* **an hour of unrelieved ~:** eine unendlich langweilige Stunde

tee [ti:] **1.** *n.* **a)** *(Golf)* Tee, *das;* **b) to a ~** *(coll.)* = **to a T** *see* **T a. 2.** *v.t. see* ~ **up 1**

~ **'off** *v.i. (Golf)* abschlagen

~ **'up** *(Golf)* **1.** *v.t.* auf das Tee legen; aufteen *(fachspr.)*. **2.** *v.i.* den Ball auf das Tee legen

tee-hee [ti:'hi:] *int.* hihi

teem [ti:m] *v.i.* **a)** *(abound)* wimmeln **(with** von); **b)** *(rain heavily)* ~ **[with rain]** in Strömen regnen

~ **'down** *v.i.* **it/the rain was ~ing down** es regnete in Strömen

teeming ['ti:mɪŋ] *adj.* **a)** *(pouring)* strömend ⟨*Regen*⟩; **b)** *(abundant)* wimmelnd ⟨*Menschenmenge*⟩; *(crowded)* von Menschen wimmelnd ⟨*Straße*⟩

teen [ti:n] *adj.* Teenager-

teenage ['ti:neɪdʒ], **teenaged** ['ti:neɪdʒd] *attrib. adj.* im Teenageralter *nachgestellt*

teenager ['ti:neɪdʒə(r)] *n.* Teenager, *der; (loosely)* Jugendliche, *der/die*

teens [ti:nz] *n. pl.* Teenagerjahre; **be out of/in one's ~:** aus den Teenagerjahren heraussein/in den Teenagerjahren sein; **fashions from tots to ~:** Kinder- und Jugendmoden

teensy-weensy ['ti:nzɪ wi:nzɪ], **teeny** ['ti:nɪ] *adjs. (child lang./coll.)* klitzeklein *(ugs.)*

teeny: ~**-bopper** *n. (coll.) Popfan im Teenageralter;* ~**-weeny** *see* **teeny**

teepee *see* **tepee**

'tee-shirt *n.* T-shirt, *das*

teeter ['ti:tə(r)] *v.i.* **a)** *(waver)* wanken; ~ **on the edge** *or* **brink of sth.** schwankend am Rande einer Sache *(Gen.)* stehen; *(fig.)* am Rande einer Sache *(Gen.)* stehen; **b)** *(Amer.: see-saw)* wippen; *(fig.)* hin- und herschwanken

teeth *pl. of* **tooth**

teethe [ti:ð] *v.i.* zahnen

teething ['ti:ðɪŋ] *n.* Zahnen, *das*

teething: ~**-ring** *n.* Beißring, *der;* ~ **troubles** *n.pl.* Beschwerden während des Zahnens; **have ~ troubles** *(fig.)* ⟨*Person, Vorhaben:*⟩ Anfangsschwierigkeiten haben; ⟨*Maschine usw.:*⟩ Kinderkrankheiten haben

teetotal [ti:'təʊtl] *adj.* abstinent lebend; alkoholfrei ⟨*Restaurant, Hotel, Feier*⟩; **sb. is ~:** jmd. ist Abstinenzler/Abstinenzlerin

teetotaler *(Amer.) see* **teetotaller**

teetotalism [ti:'təʊtəlɪzm] *n.* Abstinenz, *die*

teetotaller [ti:'təʊtələ(r)] *n.* Abstinenzler, *der/*Abstinenzlerin, *die*

Teflon, (P) ['teflɒn] *n.* Teflon ⓌⓏ, *das*

tektite ['tektaɪt] *n. (Min.)* Tektit, *der*

Tel., tel. *abbr.* **telephone** Tel.

telecast ['telɪkɑ:st] **1.** *v.t.,* **telecast** [im Fernsehen] senden. **2.** *n.* Fernsehsendung, *die*

telecommunication [telɪkəmju:nɪ'keɪʃn] *n.* **a)** *(long-distance communication)* Fernmeldeverkehr, *der; attrib.* Fernmelde-; **b)** *in pl. (science)* Fernmelde- *od.* Nachrichtentechnik, *die; attrib.* Fernmelde- *od.* Nachrichten⟨*techniker, -satellit*⟩

telegram ['telɪgræm] *n.* Telegramm, *das;* **by ~:** telegrafisch

telegraph ['telɪgrɑ:f] **1.** *n.* **a)** *(for sending telegrams)* Telegraf, *der; attrib.* Telegrafen-; **ship's ~:** Maschinentelegraf, *der (Technik); see also* **bush telegraph; b)** *(semaphore apparatus)* Semaphor, *der;* **c)** *(Sports, Racing: board)* Anzeigetafel, *die.* **2.** *v.t.* **a)** telegrafieren; telegrafisch anweisen ⟨*Geld*⟩; **b)** *(Boxing coll.)* telegrafieren ⟨*Schlag*⟩. **3.** *v.i.* telegrafieren; ~ **for sb.** jmdn. telegrafisch rufen lassen

telegraphese [telɪgrɑ:'fi:z] *n.* Telegrammstil, *der*

telegraphic [telɪ'græfɪk] *adj.* telegrafisch; Telegramm⟨*adresse, -stil*⟩

telegraphist [tɪ'legrəfɪst] *n.* Telegrafist, *der/*Telegrafistin, *die*

telegraph: ~**-line** *n.* Telegrafenleitung, *die;* ~ **pole,** ~ **post** *ns.* Telegrafenmast, *der;* ~**-wire** *n.* Telegrafendraht, *der*

telegraphy [tɪ'legrəfɪ] *n.* Telegrafie, *die*

telemessage ['telɪmesɪdʒ] *n. (Brit.)* Telegramm, *das*

telemeter ['telɪmi:tə(r), tɪ'lemɪtə(r)] **1.** *n.* Fernmeßgerät, *das.* **2.** *v.i.* Meßwerte telemetrisch übertragen; **~ing device** Fernmeßgerät, *das.* **3.** *v.t.* telemetrisch übertragen

telemetry [tɪ'lemɪtrɪ] *n.* Telemetrie, *die*

teleological [telɪə'lɒdʒɪkl] *adj. (Philos.)* teleologisch

teleology [telɪ'ɒlədʒɪ] *n. (Philos.)* Teleologie, *die*

telepathic [telɪ'pæθɪk] *adj.* telepathisch; **be ~:** telepathische Fähigkeiten haben

telepathically [telɪ'pæθɪkəlɪ] *adv.* telepathisch

telepathy [tɪ'lepəθɪ] *n.* Telepathie, *die;* **by ~:** telepathisch

telephone ['telɪfəʊn] **1.** *n.* Telefon, *das; attrib.* Telefon-; ~ **answering machine** Anrufbeantworter, *der;* **[public] ~:** öffentlicher Fernsprecher *(Amtsspr.);* [öffentliches] Telefon; **answer the ~:** Anrufe entgegennehmen; *(on one occasion)* ans Telefon gehen; *(speak)* sich melden; **by ~:** telefonisch; **over** *or* **on the ~:** am Telefon; **speak** *or* **talk to sb. on the** *or* **by ~:** mit jmdm. telefonieren; **be on the ~** *(be connected to the system)* Telefon haben; *(be speaking)* telefonieren **(to** mit); **it's your sister on the ~:** deine Schwester ist am Apparat; **get on the ~ to sb.** jmdn. anrufen; **get sb. on the ~:** jmdn. telefonisch erreichen; **be wanted on the ~:** am Telefon verlangt werden. **2.** *v.t.* anrufen; telefonisch übermitteln ⟨*Nachricht, Ergebnis usw.*⟩ **(to** *Dat.*); ~ **the office/~ home** im Büro/zu Hause anrufen. **3.** *v.i.* anrufen; ~ **for a taxi/the doctor** nach einem Taxi/dem Arzt telefonieren; ~ **to ask how ...:** telefonisch anfragen, wie ...; **can we ~ from here?** können wir von hier aus telefonieren?

telephone: ~ **book** *n.* Telefonbuch, *das;* ~ **booth,** *(Brit.)* ~**-box** *ns.* Telefonzelle, *die;* ~ **call** *n.* Telefonanruf, *der;* Telefongespräch, *das;* **make a ~ call** ein Telefongespräch führen; **have** *or* **receive a ~ call** einen Anruf erhalten; **there was a ~ call for you** es hat jemand für Sie angerufen; **there was a ~ call for you from your brother** Ihr Bruder hat angerufen; **inland ~ call** Inlandsgespräch, *das;* **international ~ call** Auslandsgespräch, *das;* ~ **directory** *n.* Telefonverzeichnis, *das;* Telefonbuch, *das;* ~ **exchange** *n.* Fernmeldeamt, *das;* ~ **kiosk** *n.* Telefonzelle, *die;* ~ **line** *n.* Telefonleitung, *die;* ~ **message** *n.* telefonische Nachricht; ~ **number** *n.* Telefonnummer, *die;* ~ **operator** *n.* Telefonist, *der/*Telefonistin, *die;* ~ **receiver** *n.* Telefonhörer, *der;* ~ **subscriber** *n.* Fernsprechteilnehmer, *der/*-teilnehmerin, *die*

telephonic [telɪ'fɒnɪk] *adj.* telefonisch

telephonist [tɪ'lefənɪst] *n.* Telefonist, *der/*Telefonistin, *die*

telephony [tɪ'lefənɪ] *n.* Fernsprechwesen, *das*

telephoto [telɪ'fəʊtəʊ] *adj. (Photog.)* telefotografisch; ~ **lens** Teleobjektiv, *das*

teleprinter ['telɪprɪntə(r)] *n.* Fernschreiber, *der;* ~ **network** Fernschreibnetz, *das*

teleprompter, *(Amer.* **P)** ['telɪprɒmptə(r)] *n.* Teleprompter ⓌⓏ, *der*

telescope ['telɪskəʊp] **1.** *n.* Teleskop, *das;* Fernrohr, *das.* **2.** *v.t.* zusammenschieben ⟨*Antenne, Rohr*⟩; ineinanderschieben ⟨*Abschnitte, Waggons*⟩; *(fig.)* komprimieren **(into** zu). **3.** *v.i.* sich zusammenschieben; ⟨*Abschnitte, Waggons:*⟩ sich ineinanderschieben

telescopic [telɪ'skɒpɪk] *adj.* **a)** teleskopisch; ~ **lens** Teleobjektiv, *das;* **b)** *(collapsible)* ausziehbar; Teleskop⟨*antenne, -mast*⟩; ~ **umbrella** Taschenschirm, *der*

Teletex, (P) ['telɪteks] *n.* Teletex, *das*

teletext ['telɪtekst] *n.* Teletext, *der*

telethon ['telɪθɒn] *n.* Marathonsendung, *die (für einen guten Zweck)*

Teletype, (P) ['telɪtaɪp], *(Amer.)* **teletypewriter** [telɪ'taɪpraɪtə(r)] *n.* Fernschreiber, *der*

televise ['telɪvaɪz] *v.t.* im Fernsehen senden *od.* übertragen; **~d football** Fußballübertragungen im Fernsehen

television ['telɪvɪʒn, telɪ'vɪʒn] *n.* **a)** *no pl., no art.* das Fernsehen; **colour/black and white ~:** das Farb-/Schwarzweißfernsehen; **the best-paid jobs are in ~:** die bestbezahlten Stellen gibt es beim Fernsehen; **go into ~:** zum Fernsehen gehen; **we have ten hours of ~ a day** bei uns gibt es täglich 10 Stunden Fernsehprogramm; **make/not make good ~:** sich gut/schlecht für das Fernsehen eignen; **live ~:** Live-Sendungen [im Fernsehen]; **on ~:** im Fernsehen; **what's on ~?** was läuft *od.* gibt's im Fernsehen?; **watch ~:** fernsehen; **b)** *(~ set)* Fernsehapparat, *der;* Fernseher, *der (ugs.);* **portable ~:** tragbares Fernsehgerät; Portable, *der od. das. See also* **closed-circuit; commercial television**

television: ~ **advertising** *n.* Fernsehwerbung, *die;* ~ **aerial** *n.* Fernsehantenne, *die;* ~ **camera** *n.* Fernsehkamera, *die;* ~ **channel** *n.* [Fernseh]kanal, *der;* ~ **coverage** *n.* Fernsehberichterstattung, *die;* **there will be full ~ coverage of sth.** das Fernsehen wird ausführlich über etw. *(Akk.)* berichten; ~ **engineer** *n.* Fernsehtechniker, *der/*-technikerin, *die;* ~ **licence** *n. (Brit.)* Fernsehgenehmigung, *die (die jährlich gegen Zahlen der Gebühren erneuert wird); attrib.* ~ **licence fee** Fernsehgebühren *Pl.;* ~ **personality** *n.* Fernsehgröße, *die (ugs.);* ~ **picture** *n.* Fernsehbild, *das;* ~ **programme** *n.* Fernsehsendung, *die; (sequence)* Fernsehprogramm, *das;* **my favourite ~ programme** meine Lieblingssendung im Fernsehen; ~ **screen** *n.* Bildschirm, *der;* ~ **serial** *n.* Fernsehserie, *die;* ~ **set** *n.* Fernsehgerät, *das;* ~ **studio** *n.* Fernsehstudio, *das;* ~ **transmitter** *n.* Fernsehsender, *der;* ~ **viewer** *n.* Fernsehzuschauer, *der/*-zuschauerin, *die*

Telex, telex ['teleks] **1.** *n.* Telex, *das;* **by ~:** über Telex. **2.** *v.t.* telexen ⟨*Nachricht*⟩; ein Telex schicken (+ *Dat.*) ⟨*Person, Firma*⟩

tell [tel] **1.** *v.t.,* **told** [təʊld] **a)** *(make known)* sagen ⟨*Name, Adresse, Alter*⟩; *(give account of)* erzählen ⟨*Neuigkeit, Sorgen*⟩; anvertrauen ⟨*Geheimnis*⟩; ~ **sb. sth.** *or* **sth. to sb.** jmdm. etw. sagen/erzählen/anvertrauen; **if he asks, ~ him** sag's ihm, wenn er fragt; ~ **sb. the way to the station** jmdm. den Weg zum Bahnhof beschreiben; ~ **sb. the time** jmdm. sagen, wie spät es ist; jmdm. die Uhrzeit sagen; ~ **sb. goodbye/good night** *(Amer.)* jmdm. auf Wiedersehen/gute Nacht sagen; ~ **all** auspacken *(ugs.);* ~ **me another!** *(coll.)* du kannst mir viel erzählen *(ugs.);* ~ **sb. [something] about sb./sth.**

jmdm. [etwas] von jmdm./etw. erzählen; ~ **sb. nothing/all about what happened** jmdm. nichts davon/alles erzählen, was passiert ist; **will you ~ him [that] I will come?** sag ihm bitte, daß ich kommen werde; **they ~ me/us [that] ...** *(according to them)* man sagt, daß ...; **I['ll] ~ you what, ...**: paß mal auf, ...; **I'll ~ you what I'll do** weißt du, was ich machen werde?; ~ **everyone/***(coll.)* **the world [that/how** *etc.*] jedem/*(ugs.)* aller Welt erzählen[, daß/wie *usw.*]; **more than I/words can ~**: mehr, als ich es mit Worten ausdrücken kann/als Worte es ausdrücken können; **I cannot ~ you how ...** *(cannot express how ...)* ich kann dir gar nicht sagen, wie ...; **I couldn't ~ you** *(I don't know)* das kann ich nicht sagen; **I can ~ you, ...** *(I can assure you)* ich kann dir sagen, ...; **..., I can ~ you ...**, das kann ich dir sagen; **you can't ~ me [that] ...** *(it can't be true that ...)* du kannst mir doch nicht erzählen, daß ...; **you can't ~ him anything** *(he won't accept advice)* er läßt sich *(Dat.)* ja nichts sagen; *(he is well-informed)* ihm kannst du nichts erzählen; **words cannot ~ how ..., no words can ~ how ...**: es läßt sich nicht mit Worten ausdrücken, wie ...; **..., let me ~ you** *(let me assure you)* ..., das kann ich dir sagen; **let me ~ you that ...**: ich kann dir versichern, daß ...; **..., I ~ you** *or* **I'm ~ing you ...**, das sage ich dir; **you're ~ing me** *or* **are you ~ing me [that] ...?** du willst mir doch wohl nicht erzählen, daß ...?; **you're ~ing 'me!** *(coll.)* wem sagst du das! *(ugs.)*; **he keeps ~ing me [that] ...**: er erzählt mir ständig, daß ...; **..., or so they keep ~ing us** das erzählen sie uns jedenfalls immer; **I don't need to ~ you [that] ...**: ich brauche dir wohl nicht extra zu sagen, daß ...; **be told sth. by sb.** etw. von jmdm. erfahren; **I was told that ...**: mir wurde gesagt, daß ...; **so I've been told** *(I know that)* [das] habe ich schon gehört; **... or so I've been/I'm told** ..., wie ich gehört habe/höre; **... or so we are told** ..., so heißt es jedenfalls; **but he won't be told** *(won't accept advice)* aber er läßt sich ja nichts sagen; **didn't I ~ you?** *(I told you so)* hab' ich's nicht gleich gesagt?; **no, don't ~ me, let me guess** [nein,] sag's nicht, laß mich raten; **don't ~ me [that] ...** *(expressing incredulity, dismay, etc.)* jetzt sag bloß nicht, [daß] ...; **you aren't trying** *or* **don't mean to ~ me [that] ...?** du wirst doch nicht sagen wollen, daß ...?; **b)** *(relate, lit. or fig.)* erzählen; **has he ever told you the story of how ...**: hat er dir jemals die Geschichte erzählt, wie ...; ~ **one's own story** *or* **tale** *(give one's own account)* selbst erzählen *od.* berichten; **sth. ~s its own story** *or* **tale** *(needs no comment)* etw. spricht für sich selbst; ~ **a different story** *or* **tale** *(reveal the truth)* eine andere Sprache sprechen *(fig.)*; **every picture ~s a story** das spricht Bände; **live** *or* **survive to ~ the tale** überleben; ~ **tales [about sb.]** *(gossip; reveal secret)* [über jmdn.] tratschen *(ugs. abwertend)*; ~ **tales [to sb.]** *(report)* andere/einen anderen [bei jmdm.] anschwärzen; [bei jmdm.] petzen *(Schülerspr. abwertend)*; ~ **tales** *(lie)* Lügengeschichten erzählen; ~ **tales out of school** *(fig.)* aus der Schule plaudern; **dead men ~ no tales** Tote reden nicht; **the blood stains told their own tale** die Blutflecken sprachen für sich; **now it can be told** jetzt kann man es ja erzählen; **c)** *(instruct)* sagen; ~ **sb. [not] to do sth.** jmdm. sagen, daß er etw. [nicht] tun soll; jmdm. sagen, er soll[e] etw. [nicht] tun; **I thought I told you to go to bed** ich habe dir doch gesagt, daß du ins Bett gehen sollst; ~ **sb. what to do** jmdm. sagen, was er tun soll; **no one ~s 'me what to do** ich lasse mir keine Vorschriften machen; **do as** *or* **what I ~ you** tu, was ich dir sage; **I shan't** *or* **won't ~ you again, don't let me have to ~ you again** ich sag's dir nicht noch einmal; **do as you are told** tu, was man dir sagt; **d)** *(determine)* feststellen; *(see, recognize)* erkennen **(by** an + *Dat.*); *(with reference to the future)* [vorher]sagen; ~ **the time [from the sun]** [am Stand der Sonne] erkennen, wie spät es ist; **the child can't ~ the time yet** das Kind kennt die Uhr noch nicht; ~ **the difference [between ...]** den Unterschied [zwischen ...] erkennen *od.* feststellen; **I can't ~ which of the twins ...**: ich kann nicht sagen, welcher der Zwillinge ...; **it's impossible/difficult to ~ [if/what** *etc.*] es ist unmöglich/schwer zu sagen[, ob/was *usw.*]; **it's easy to ~ whether ...**: es läßt sich leicht sagen, ob ...; **you never can ~ how/what** *etc.* man weiß nie, wie/was *usw.*; **how could you ~ he was a policeman?** woran hast du erkannt, daß es ein Polizist war?; **e)** *(distinguish)* unterscheiden; **[not] be able to ~ right from wrong** [nicht] zwischen richtig und falsch unterscheiden können; **f)** *(utter)* sagen; ~ **the truth and shame the devil** die Wahrheit sagen, auch wenn es nicht leichtfällt; *see also* **fib 1; ¹lie 1 a; truth b; g)** *(count)* auszählen ‹*Wählerstimmen*›; **all told** insgesamt. **2.** *v.i.*, **told a)** *(determine)* **how can you ~?** wie kann man das feststellen *od.* wissen?; **it's difficult to ~**: das ist schwer zu sagen; **[it's] hard to ~**: [das ist] schwer zu sagen; **I can ~ he's lying** ich merke ihm an, daß er lügt; **the difference is so slight, even the experts can hardly ~**: der Unterschied ist so gering, daß selbst die Experten ihn kaum erkennen können; **how can one ~?, how can** *or* **do you ~?** woran kann man das erkennen?; **as far as one/I can ~, ...**: wie es aussieht, ...; **you never can ~**: man kann nie wissen; **who can ~?** wer kann das sagen *od.* will das wissen?; **b)** *(give information)* erzählen **(of, about** von); *(give evidence)* ~ **of sth.** von etw. Zeugnis geben *od.* ablegen; **c)** *(reveal secret)* es verraten; **time [alone] will ~**: das wird sich [erst noch] zeigen; **d)** *(produce an effect)* sich auswirken; ‹*Wort, Fausthieb, Schuß:*› sitzen; **quality ~s** *or* **will ~** *(be important)* Qualität ist das, was zählt; **he made every blow ~**: jeder seiner Schläge saß; **make every shot ~**: dafür sorgen, daß jeder Schuß sitzt; ~ **in favour of sb.** *or* **in sb.'s favour** sich zu jmds. Gunsten auswirken; ~ **against sb./sth.** sich nachteilig für jmdn./auf etw. *(Akk.)* auswirken. *See also* **fortune c; marine 2 a; ¹so 2; what 5 a**

~ **a'part** *v.t.* auseinanderhalten

~ **'off** *v.t.* **a)** *(coll.: scold)* ~ **sb. off [for sth.]** jmdn. [für *od.* wegen etw.] ausschimpfen; ‹*Chef:*› jmdn. [für *od.* wegen etw.] rüffeln *(ugs.)*; *see also* **telling-off; b)** *(assign)* ~ **sb. off [for sth.]** jmdn. [zu etw.] abkommandieren

~ **on** *v.t.* **a)** *(affect)* ~ **on sb./sth.** sich bei jmdm. bemerkbar machen/sich [nachteilig] auf etw. *(Akk.)* auswirken; **b)** *(coll.: inform against)* ~ **on sb.** jmdn. verpetzen *(Schülerspr. abwertend)*

~ **upon** *see* ~ **on a**

teller ['telə(r)] *n.* **a)** *(in bank) see* **¹cashier; b)** *(counter of votes)* Stimmenzähler, *der*/-zählerin, *die*

telling ['telɪŋ] **1.** *adj.* *(effective, striking)* schlagend ‹*Argument, Antwort*›; wirkungsvoll ‹*Worte, Phrase, Stil*›; *(revealing)* vielsagend ‹*Lächeln, Blick*›; verräterisch ‹*Röte, Reaktion*›; ~ **blow** *(Boxing)* Wirkungstreffer, *der*; *(fig.)* empfindlicher Schlag; **with ~ effect** mit durchschlagender Wirkung. **2.** *n.* Erzählen, *das*; **he did not need any ~, he needed no ~**: dazu brauchte man ihn nicht lange *od.* eigens aufzufordern; **that would be ~**: damit würde ich ein Geheimnis verraten; **there's no ~ what/how ...**: man weiß nie, was/wie ...; **there's no** *or* **never any ~ with her** bei ihr weiß man nie[, woran man ist]; *see also* **lose 2 a**

tellingly ['telɪŋlɪ] *adv.* wirkungsvoll; **be ~ effective** eine deutlich sichtbare Wirkung zeigen

telling-'off *n.* *(coll.)* Standpauke, *die (ugs.)*; **give sb. a ~**: jmdn. ausschimpfen **(for** wegen); ‹*Chef:*› jmdn. rüffeln *(ugs.)*; **get a ~**: Schimpfe kriegen *(ugs.)*; ‹*Untergebener:*› einen Rüffel kriegen *(ugs.)*

'tell-tale *n.* **a)** Klatschmaul, *das (ugs. abwertend)*; Petze, *die (Schülerspr. abwertend)*; *attrib.* vielsagend ‹*Blick, Lächeln*›; verräterisch ‹*Röte, Fleck, Glanz, Zucken, Zeichen*›; **b)** *(indicator)* Anzeiger, *der*; *(for recording attendance)* Stechuhr, *die*

tellurium [te'ljʊərɪəm] *n.* *(Chem.)* Tellur, *das*

telly ['telɪ] *n.* *(Brit. coll.)* Fernseher, *der (ugs.)*; Glotze, *die (salopp)*; **watch ~**: Fernsehen gucken *(ugs.)*; **what's on [the] ~?** was kommt im Fernsehen?

temerity [tɪ'merɪtɪ] *n.* Kühnheit, *die*; **have the ~ to do sth.** die Stirn haben, etw. zu tun

temp [temp] *(Brit. coll.)* **1.** *n.* Zeitarbeitskraft, *die*; *attrib.* ~ **agency** Zeitarbeitsunternehmen, *das*. **2.** *v.i.* Zeitarbeit machen

temper ['tempə(r)] **1.** *n.* **a)** *(disposition)* Naturell, *das*; **be in a good/bad ~**: gute/schlechte Laune haben; gut/schlecht gelaunt sein; **be in a foul** *or* **filthy ~**: eine miese Laune haben *(ugs.)*; **keep/lose one's ~**: sich beherrschen/die Beherrschung verlieren; **lose one's ~ with sb.** die Beherrschung bei jmdm. verlieren; **control one's ~**: sich beherrschen; **b)** *(anger)* **fit/outburst of ~**: Wutanfall, *der*/-ausbruch, *der*; **have a ~**: jähzornig sein; **be in/get into a ~**: wütend sein/werden **(over** wegen); **be in a terrible ~**: schrecklich wütend sein; **c)** *(degree of hardness of metal)* Härte, *die*. **2.** *v.t.* **a)** *(moderate)* mäßigen; mildern ‹*Trostlosigkeit, Strenge, Kritik*›; ~ **sb.'s enthusiasm/radical views** jmds. Begeisterung dämpfen/Radikalismus mildern; ~ **justice with mercy** bei aller Gerechtigkeit Milde walten lassen *(geh.)*; **b)** *(Metallurgy)* anlassen; **c)** *(Mus.)* temperieren

tempera ['tempərə] *n.* *(Art)* Tempera, *die*

temperament ['temprəmənt] *n.* **a)** *(nature)* Veranlagung, *die*; Natur, *die*; *(disposition)* Temperament, *das*; **have an artistic ~**: künstlerisch veranlagt sein; **b)** *(passionate disposition)* Temperament, *das*

temperamental [temprə'mentl] *adj.* **a)** *(having changeable moods)* launisch *(abwertend)*; launenhaft; **be a bit ~** *(fig. coll.)* ‹*Auto, Maschine:*› seine Mucken haben *(ugs.)*; **b)** *(caused by, relating to temperament)* anlagebedingt; **suffer from a ~ inability to cope with stress** von Natur aus nicht fähig sein, Streß zu bewältigen

temperamentally [temprə'mentəlɪ] *adv.* **a)** *(in a temperamental manner)* launisch *(abwertend)*; **the car tends to behave ~** *(fig. coll.)* das Auto hat gelegentlich seine Mucken *(ugs.)*; **b)** *(by reason of temperament)* der Veranlagung nach

temperance ['tempərəns] *n.* **a)** *(moderation)* Mäßigung, *die*; *(in one's eating, drinking)* Mäßigkeit, *die*; **b)** *(total abstinence)* Abstinenz, *die*

temperate ['tempərət] *adj.* gemäßigt; **be ~ in one's eating/drinking** maßvoll *od.* mäßig im Essen/Trinken sein; ~ **climate** *(Geog.)* gemäßigtes Klima; *see also* **zone 1**

temperature ['temprɪtʃə(r)] *n.* **a)** Temperatur, *die*; **what is the ~?** wieviel Grad sind es?; **the ~ is below/above ...**: die Temperatur liegt unter/über ... *(Dat.)*; **there are no extremes of ~**: es gibt keine extremen Temperaturen; **the ~ rose during the debate** *(fig.)* die Debatte wurde im Verlauf immer hitziger; **at a ~ of 10°** bei einer Temperatur von 10° ‹*kochen*›; auf eine Temperatur von 10° ‹*einstellen*›; **keep the room at a ~ of 10°** die Zimmertemperatur auf 10° *(Dat.)* halten; **at high/low ~s** bei hohen/niedrigen

Temperaturen; **b)** *(Med.)* Temperatur, *die;* **have** *or* **run a ~** *(coll.)* Temperatur *od.* Fieber haben; **have a slight/high ~:** leichtes/hohes Fieber haben; **take sb.'s ~:** jmds. [Körper]temperatur messen; **a cold accompanied by a ~:** eine fiebrige Erkältung; *see also* **run 3 l**

tempered ['tempəd] *adj.* **a)** *(Metallurgy)* vergütet; **b)** *(Mus.)* temperiert

tempest ['tempɪst] *n. (lit. or fig.)* Sturm, *der;* **~ in a teapot** *(Amer.)* Sturm im Wasserglas

tempestuous [tem'pestjʊəs] *adj. (lit. or fig.)* stürmisch; **be in a ~ rage** vor Wut rasen

Templar ['templə(r)] *n. (Hist.)* **[Knight] ~:** Templer, *der;* Tempelritter, *der;* **the [Knights] ~s** der Templerorden

template ['templɪt] *n.* Schablone, *die*

¹temple ['templ] *n.* Tempel, *der; (Amer.: synagogue)* Synagoge, *die*

²temple *n. (Anat.)* Schläfe, *die*

templet *see* **template**

tempo ['tempəʊ] *n., pl.* **~s** *or* **tempi** ['tempi:] **a)** *(fig.: pace)* **the ~ of life in the town** der Rhythmus der Stadt; **the campaign ~ stepped up** der Wahlkampf ging in die heiße Phase über; **b)** *(Mus.: speed)* Tempo, *das*

temporal ['tempərl] *adj.* **a)** *(of this life)* diesseitig *(geh.);* irdisch; *(secular)* weltlich; **~ power** *(Eccl.)* weltliche Macht; **lords ~** *(Brit. Parl.) weltliche Mitglieder des britischen Oberhauses;* **b)** *(of time)* zeitlich; **c)** *(Anat.)* Schläfen-; **d)** *(Ling.)* temporal

temporally ['tempərəlɪ] *adv.* zeitlich

temporarily ['tempərərɪlɪ] *adv.* vorübergehend

temporary ['tempərərɪ] **1.** *adj.* vorübergehend; provisorisch ‹*Gebäude, Büro*›; **~ worker** Aushilfe, *die.* **2.** *n.* Aushilfe, *die;* Aushilfskraft, *die*

temporise, temporiser *see* **temporiz-**

temporize ['tempəraɪz] *v.i.* **a)** *(adopt indecisive policy)* sich nicht festlegen; **b)** *(act so as to gain time)* sich abwartend verhalten; **~ with sb.** jmdn. hinhalten; **c)** *(comply temporarily)* Kompromisse eingehen; sich fügen

temporizer ['tempəraɪzə(r)] *n.* **a)** *(one who compromises)* Kompromißler, *der*/Kompromißlerin, *die (abwertend);* **b)** *(one who acts to gain time)* Hinhaltetaktiker, *der*/-taktikerin, *die*

tempt [tempt] *v.t.* **a)** *(attract)* **~ sb. out/into the town** jmdn. hinauslocken/in die Stadt locken; **~ sb. to do sth.** in jmdm. den Wunsch wecken, etw. zu tun; **b)** *(cause to have strong urge)* **~ sb. to do sth.** jmdn. geneigt machen, etw. zu tun; **be ~ed to do sth.** versucht sein, etw. zu tun; **I'm ~ed to question this** das möchte ich fast bezweifeln; **be ~ed to resign** an Rücktritt denken; **be strongly ~ed to dismiss sb.** sehr versucht sein, jmdn. zu entlassen; **c)** *(entice)* verführen; **be ~ed into doing sth.** sich dazu verleiten lassen, etw. zu tun; **~ sb. away from sth.** jmdn. von etw. weglocken; **don't ~ me!** verleite mich nicht!; **are you sure I can't ~ you to have a whisky?** kann ich dich wirklich nicht zu einem Whisky überreden?; **d)** *(provoke)* herausfordern; **~ fate** *or* **providence** das Schicksal herausfordern

temptation [temp'teɪʃn] *n.* **a)** *no pl. (attracting)* Verlockung, *die; (being attracted)* Versuchung, *die; (enticing)* Verführung, *die* **(into** zu); *(being enticed)* Versuchung, *die (geh.);* **feel a ~ to do sth.** versucht sein, etw. zu tun; **please resist the ~ to make any funny remarks** mach jetzt bitte keine dummen Witze; **give in to [the] ~:** der Versuchung erliegen; **the T~** *(Relig.)* die Versuchung [Jesu]; **b)** *(thing)* Verlockung, *die* (to zu); **special offers are just a ~ to spend money** Sonderangebote verleiten nur dazu, Geld auszugeben; **c) lead us not into ~** *(Bibl.)* führe uns nicht in Versuchung

tempter ['temptə(r)] *n.* Verführer, *der;* **the T~** *(Relig.)* der Versucher

tempting ['temptɪŋ] *adj.* **a)** *(inviting)* verlockend; verführerisch; **b)** *(enticing)* verführerisch

temptingly ['temptɪŋlɪ] *adv.* **a)** *(attractively)* verlockend; verführerisch; **b) leave money lying about ~:** Geld [verführerisch] offen herumliegen lassen

temptress ['temptrɪs] *n.* Verführerin, *die*

ten [ten] **1.** *adj.* zehn; **feel ~ feet tall** *(fig.)* sehr stolz auf sich *(Akk.)* sein; *see also* **eight 1. 2.** *n.* **a)** *(number, symbol)* Zehn, *die;* **b)** *(set of ~)* Zehnerpackung, *die; (of cards)* Zehnerstoß, *der;* **c) bet sb. ~ to one that ...** *(fig.)* jede Wette halten, daß ... *(ugs.). See also* **eight 2 a, c, d**

tenable ['tenəbl] *adj.* **a)** haltbar; *(fig.)* haltbar ‹*Theorie, Annahme*›; vertretbar ‹*Standpunkt*›; **b) ~ for five years** auf fünf Jahre befristet ‹*Arbeitsverhältnis, Stelle*›; **~ at the university of ...:** [anzutreten] an der Universität ...

tenacious [tɪ'neɪʃəs] *adj.* **a)** *(holding fast)* hartnäckig haftend ‹*Dornen, Samen*›; **hold sth. in a ~ grip** etw. hartnäckig *od.* eisern festhalten; **b)** *(resolute)* hartnäckig; **be ~:** sich hartnäckig halten; **be ~ of sth.** hartnäckig an etw. *(Dat.)* festhalten; **c)** *(retentive)* **~ memory** hervorragendes Gedächtnis; **d)** *(strongly cohesive)* fest; **a very ~ link** eine sehr beständige Verbindung

tenaciously [tɪ'neɪʃəslɪ] *adv.* zäh; *(resolutely)* hartnäckig

tenacity [tɪ'næsɪtɪ] *n., no pl.* Hartnäckigkeit, *die; (resoluteness)* Beharrlichkeit, *die;* Hartnäckigkeit, *die;* **~ of life** zäher Lebenswille

tenancy ['tenənsɪ] *n.* **a)** *(of flat, residential building)* Mietverhältnis, *das; (of farm, shop)* Pachtverhältnis, *das;* **have ~ of a flat** eine Wohnung gemietet haben; **~ agreement** Miet-/Pachtvertrag, *der;* **b)** *(period)* Mietdauer, *die;* **c)** *(occupation of post)* Bekleidung, *die;* **~ of the post will be for 10 years** die Stelle ist auf 10 Jahre befristet

tenant ['tenənt] **1.** *n.* **a)** *(of flat, residential building)* Mieter, *der*/Mieterin, *die; (of farm, shop)* Pächter, *der*/Pächterin, *die;* **b)** *(occupant)* Bewohner, *der*/Bewohnerin, *die;* **c)** *(Law) (possessor)* Besitzer, *der*/Besitzerin, *die; (owner)* Eigentümer, *der*/Eigentümerin, *die.* **2.** *v.t.* mieten ‹*Wohnung, Haus usw.*›; pachten ‹*Land, Bauernhof, Geschäft*›

'tenant farmer *n.* Pächter, *der*/Pächterin, *die*

tenantry ['tenəntrɪ] *n.* **a)** *(people)* Mieter; *(of farm, shop)* Pächter; **b)** *(condition)* Mietverhältnis, *das; (of farm, shop)* Pachtverhältnis, *das*

tench [tentʃ] *n., pl. same (Zool.)* Schleie, *die*

¹tend [tend] *v.i.* **a)** *(be moving or directed)* ‹*Strom, Bach:*› fließen **(towards** in Richtung); ‹*Sterne:*› zustreben **(towards** auf + *Akk.*); *(fig.)* sich zubewegen **(towards** auf + *Akk.*); **this ~s to suggest that ...:** dies deutet darauf hin, daß ...; **all opinions ~ to the same conclusion** alle Meinungen führen zur gleichen Schlußfolgerung; **b)** *(be apt or inclined)* **~ to do sth.** dazu neigen *od.* tendieren, etw. zu tun; **~ to sth.** zu etw. neigen; **it ~s to get quite cold there at nights** es wird dort nachts oft sehr kalt; **he ~s to get upset if ...:** er regt sich leicht auf, wenn ...

²tend *v.t.* sich kümmern um; hüten ‹*Schafe*›; bedienen ‹*Maschine*›; **the rice has to be ~ed carefully** der Reis erfordert sorgfältige Pflege

tendency ['tendənsɪ] *n. (inclination)* Tendenz, *die;* **artistic tendencies** künstlerische Neigungen; **have a ~ to do sth.** dazu neigen, etw. zu tun; **there is a ~ for everyone to get complacent** die Leute neigen dazu, selbstzufrieden zu werden

tendentious [ten'denʃəs] *adj.*, **tendentiously** [ten'denʃəslɪ] *adv. (derog.)* tendenziös

tendentiousness [ten'denʃəsnɪs] *n., no pl. (derog.)* tendenziöse Färbung

¹tender ['tendə(r)] *adj.* **a)** *(not tough)* zart; **b)** *(sensitive)* empfindlich; **~ spot** *(fig.)* wunder Punkt; **c)** *(loving)* zärtlich; liebevoll; **~ loving care** liebevolle Zuwendung; **d)** *(requiring careful handling)* heikel; **e)** *(delicate)* zart ‹*Gesundheit, Konstitution*›; **be of ~ age** *or* **years** noch sehr jung sein; **at a ~ age** in jungen Jahren; **at the ~ age of twelve** im zarten Alter von zwölf Jahren. *See also* **mercy 1 b**

²tender *n. (Naut., Railw.)* Tender, *der*

³tender 1. *v.t.* **a)** *(present)* einreichen ‹*Rücktritt*›; anbieten ‹*Rat*›; vorbringen ‹*Entschuldigung*›; **b)** *(offer as payment)* anbieten; **~ a £20 note** mit einer 20-Pfund-Note bezahlen; **please ~ exact fare** bitte den genauen Betrag bereithalten; **the cash register records the amount ~ed** die Registrierkasse zeigt den gezahlten Geldbetrag an. **2.** *v.i.* **~ for sth.** ein Angebot für etw. einreichen. **3.** *n.* **a)** Angebot, *das;* **put in a ~:** ein Angebot einreichen; **put sth. out to ~:** etw. ausschreiben; **b) legal ~:** gesetzliches Zahlungsmittel

tender: ~foot *n., pl.* **~foots** *or* **~feet** Greenhorn, *das; (in Scouts)* Neuling, *der;* **~-hearted** ['tendəhɑ:tɪd] *adj.* weichherzig

tenderize ['tendəraɪz] *v.t. (Cookery)* zart machen; *(by beating)* weich klopfen

tenderizer ['tendəraɪzə(r)] *n. (Cookery)* Fleischklopfer, *der*

'tenderloin *n. (Gastr.)* **a)** *(Brit.)* Lendenstück, *das;* **b)** *(Amer.)* Filet, *das*

tenderly ['tendəlɪ] *adv.* **a)** *(gently)* behutsam ‹*behandeln*›; **b)** *(lovingly)* zärtlich

tenderness ['tendənɪs] *n., no pl.* **a)** *(of meat etc.)* Zartheit, *die;* **b)** *(loving quality)* Zärtlichkeit, *die;* **c)** *(delicacy)* Empfindlichkeit, *die*

tendon ['tendən] *n. (Anat.)* Sehne, *die;* **Achilles ~:** Achillessehne, *die*

tendril ['tendrɪl] *n.* Ranke, *die*

tenement ['tenɪmənt] *n.* **a)** *(Scot.: house containing several dwellings)* Mietshaus, *das;* Mietskaserne, *die (abwertend);* **b)** *(dwelling-place)* Behausung, *die;* **c)** *(Amer.: house containing several apartments)* **~[-house]** Mietshaus, *das;* **d)** *(Law)* Besitz, *der*

Tenerife [tenə'ri:f] *pr. n.* Teneriffa *(das)*

tenet ['tenɪt, 'ti:net] *n.* Grundsatz, *der*

ten: ~fold ['tenfəʊld] *adj., adv.* zehnfach; *see also* **eightfold; ~-gallon 'hat** *n.* Cowboyhut, *der*

tenner ['tenə(r)] *n. (coll.) (Brit.)* Zehnpfundschein, *der;* Zehner, *der (ugs.); (Amer.)* Zehndollarschein, *der;* Zehner, *der (ugs.)*

tennis ['tenɪs] *n., no pl.* Tennis, *das;* **real** *or* **royal** *or (Amer.)* **court ~:** Real *od.* Royal *od.* Court Tennis, *das; see also* **lawn tennis; table tennis**

tennis: ~ 'arm *n. (Med.)* Tennisarm, *der;* **~-ball** *n.* Tennisball, *der;* **~-club** *n.* Tennisverein, *der;* **~-court** *n.* **a)** *(for lawn ~)* Tennisplatz, *der; (for indoor ~)* Tennishalle, *die;* **b)** *(for real ~)* Tennishalle, *die;* Ballhaus, *das (hist.);* **~ 'elbow** *n., no pl., no art. (Med.)* Tennisell[en]bogen, *der;* **~-match** *n.* Tennismatch, *das;* Tennisspiel, *das;* **~-player** *n.* Tennisspieler, *der*/-spielerin, *die;* **~-racket** *n.* Tennisschläger, *der*

tenon ['tenən] *n. (Woodw.)* Zapfen, *der*

'tenon-saw *n. (Woodw.)* Feinsäge, *die;* feste Zapfensäge *(fachspr.)*

tenor ['tenə(r)] *n.* **a)** *(Mus.: voice, singer, part)* Tenor, *der;* **~ voice** Tenorstimme, *die;* **b)** *(prevailing course)* Verlauf, *der;* **the general ~ of his life** seine allgemeine Lebensführung; **c)** *(of argument, speech)* Tenor, *der;* **d)** *(Law) (actual wording)* Wortlaut, *der;* Tenor, *der (fachspr.); (exact copy)* Abschrift, *die;* **e)** *(Mus.: instrument with range like ~)* Tenor, *der;* ~ **saxophone/recorder** Tenorsaxophon, *das*/-blockflöte, *die*

tenpenny ['tenpənɪ] *adj.* für zehn Pence *nachgestellt*

tenpenny 'piece *n. (Brit.)* Zehnpencemünze, *die*

tenpin bowling [tenpɪn 'bəʊlɪŋ] *n.* Bowling, *das*

¹tense [tens] *n. (Ling.)* Zeit, *die;* **in the present/future** *etc.* ~: im Präsens/Futur *usw.*

²tense 1. *adj.* **a)** *(taut; showing nervous tension)* gespannt; **her face was ~ with anxiety** ihr Gesicht war vor Sorge angespannt; **his voice was ~ with emotion** seine Stimme bebte vor Erregung; **a ~ silence** eine [an]gespannte Stille; **b)** *(causing nervous tension)* spannungsgeladen. **2.** *v.i.* **sb. ~s** jmds. Muskeln spannen sich an; **he ~d with fear** er verkrampfte sich vor Angst. **3.** *v.t.* anspannen

~ **'up** *v.i.* ‹*Muskeln:*› sich anspannen; ‹*Person:*› sich verkrampfen

tensely ['tenslɪ] *adv.* **a)** *(tightly)* straff; **b)** *(with nervous tension)* angespannt; ~ **gripping** packend ‹*Geschichte, Film*›

tenseness ['tensnɪs] *n., no pl. (of person)* Anspannung, *die; (of situation etc.)* Angespanntheit, *die*

tensile ['tensaɪl] *adj.* **a)** Zug‹*belastung, -festigkeit*›; **b)** *(capable of being stretched)* zugfest

tension ['tenʃn] **1.** *n.* **a)** *(latent hostility)* Spannung, *die;* ~ **between the police and the people is on the increase** die Spannungen zwischen Polizei und Bevölkerung wachsen; **there is a lot of ~ between them** zwischen ihnen herrscht ein gespanntes Verhältnis; **there is a high level of ~ in that area** die Lage in diesem Gebiet ist sehr angespannt; **racial ~**: Rassenspannungen *Pl.;* **b)** *(mental strain)* Anspannung, *die;* **c)** *no pl. (of violin string, tennis racquet)* Spannung, *die;* **d)** *(stretching; Mech. Engin.)* Spannung, *die;* **e)** *(Knitting)* Festigkeit, *die;* **check the ~**: eine Maschenprobe machen. *See also* **surface tension. 2.** *v.t.* spannen

tent [tent] *n.* Zelt, *das*

tentacle ['tentəkl] *n.* **a)** *(Zool., Bot.)* Tentakel, *der od. das;* **b)** *(fig.)* Fühler, *der; (with sinister connotations)* Fangarm, *der*

tentative ['tentətɪv] *adj.* **a)** *(not definite)* vorläufig; **make a ~ suggestion** einen Vorschlag in den Raum stellen; **say a ~ 'yes'** vorläufig „ja" sagen; **b)** *(hesitant)* zaghaft

tentatively ['tentətɪvlɪ] *adv.* **a)** *(not definitely)* vorläufig; **b)** *(hesitantly)* zaghaft

tenterhooks ['tentəhʊks] *n. pl.* **be on ~**: [wie] auf glühenden Kohlen sitzen; **keep sb. on ~**: jmdn. auf die Folter spannen

tenth [tenθ] **1.** *adj.* zehnt...; *see also* **eighth 1. 2.** *n.* **a)** *(in sequence)* zehnte, *der/die/das; (in rank)* Zehnte, *der/die/das; (fraction)* Zehntel, *das;* **b)** *(day)* **the ~ of May** der zehnte Mai; **the ~ [of the month]** der Zehnte [des Monats]. *See also* **eighth 2**

'tent-peg *n.* Zeltpflock, *der;* Hering, *der*

tenuity [te'nju:ɪtɪ] *see* **tenuousness**

tenuous ['tenjʊəs] *adj.* dünn ‹*Faden*›; zart ‹*Spinnwebe*›; *(fig.)* dünn ‹*Atmosphäre*›; dürftig ‹*Argument*›; unbegründet ‹*Anspruch*›; **there are only ~ connections** es bestehen kaum Verbindungen; **he had but a ~ hold on life** sein Leben hing nur noch an einem seidenen Faden

tenuously ['tenjʊəslɪ] *adv.* dünn; *(fig.)* schwach; [nur] locker ‹*verbunden sein*›; **cling only ~ to life** nur noch einen schwachen Lebenswillen haben

tenuousness ['tenjʊəsnɪs] *n., no pl.* Dünne, *die; (fig.)* Dürftigkeit, *die*

tenure ['tenjə(r)] *n.* **a)** *(right, title)* Besitztitel, *der;* **b)** *(possession)* Besitz, *der;* **his ~ of the house is only for a limited period** er kann nur eine begrenzte Zeit über das Haus verfügen; **c)** *(period)* ~ **[of office]** Amtszeit, *die;* **d)** *(permanent appointment)* Dauerstellung, *die;* **have [security of] ~**: eine Dauerstellung haben

tenuto [tə'nu:təʊ] *adj., adv. (Mus.)* tenuto

tepee ['ti:pi:] *n.* Tipi, *das*

tepid ['tepɪd] *adj.* **a)** lauwarm; **b)** *(fig.)* halbherzig ‹*Interesse, Willkommensgruß*›; verhalten ‹*Lob, Begeisterung*›

tequila [te'ki:lə] *n. (drink)* Tequila, *der*

tercentenary [tɜ:sen'ti:nərɪ, tɜ:sen'tenərɪ] **1.** *adj.* Dreihundertjahr‹*feier, -feierlichkeiten*›. **2.** *n.* Dreihundertjahrfeier, *die*

term [tɜ:m] **1.** *n.* **a)** *(word expressing definite concept)* [Fach]begriff, *der;* **scientific/legal/medical ~**: wissenschaftlicher/juristischer/medizinischer Fachausdruck; **~ of reproach** Vorwurf, *der;* **in ~s of money/politics** unter finanziellem/politischem Aspekt; **in ~s of financial success** vom finanziellen Erfolg her gesehen; **in set ~s** klipp und klar; *see also* **contradiction; b)** *in pl. (conditions)* Bedingungen; **he does everything on his own ~s** er tut alles, wie er es für richtig hält; **~s of surrender** Kapitulationsbedingungen; **~s of contract** Vertragsbedingungen; **accept sb. on his own ~s** jmdn. so akzeptieren, wie er ist; **come to** *or* **make ~s [with sb.]** sich [mit jmdm.] einigen; **come to ~s [with each other]** sich einigen; **come to ~s with sth.** *(be able to accept sth.)* mit etw. zurechtkommen; *(resign oneself to sth.)* sich mit etw. abfinden; **come to ~s with oneself** mit sich selbst ins reine kommen; **~s of reference** *(Brit.)* Aufgabenbereich, *der;* **~s of trade** Austauschverhältnis, *das (Wirtsch.);* **c)** *in pl. (charges)* Konditionen; **their ~s are ...**: sie verlangen ...; **hire-purchase on easy ~s** Ratenkauf zu günstigen Bedingungen; *see also* **inclusive b; d) in the short/long/medium ~**: kurz-/lang-/mittelfristig; **e)** *(Sch.)* Halbjahr, *das; (Univ.: one of two/three/four divisions per year)* Semester, *das*/Trimester, *das*/Quartal, *das;* **during ~**: während des Halbjahres/Semesters *usw.;* **out of ~**: in den Ferien; **end of ~**: Halbjahres-/Semesterende *usw.;* **f)** *(limited period)* Zeitraum, *der; (of insurance policy etc.)* Laufzeit, *die; (period of tenure)* ~ **[of office]** Amtszeit, *die;* **g)** *(completion of pregnancy)* **[full] ~**: normale Schwangerschaftszeit; **h)** *(period of imprisonment)* Haftzeit, *die;* **be put in prison for a long ~**: für eine längere Haftstrafe ins Gefängnis kommen; **i)** *in pl. (mode of expression)* Worte; **praise in the highest ~s** in den höchsten Tönen loben; **talk in vague ~s of sth.** sich in vagen Andeutungen über etw. *(Akk.)* ergehen; **in flattering ~s** mit schmeichelnden Worten; *see also* **uncertain e; j)** *in pl. (relations)* **be on good/poor/friendly ~s with sb.** mit jmdm. auf gutem/schlechtem/freundschaftlichem Fuß stehen; *see also* **equal 1 a; speaking 1 a; k)** *(Logic, Math.)* Term, *der.* **2.** *v.t.* nennen

termagant ['tɜ:məgənt] *n.* Furie, *die*

terminal ['tɜ:mɪnl] **1.** *n.* **a)** *(Electr.)* Anschluß, *der; (of battery)* Pol, *der;* **b)** *(for train or bus)* Bahnhof, *der; (for airline passengers)* Terminal, *der od. das;* **helicopter ~**: Hubschrauberlandeplatz, *der;* **c)** *(Teleph., Computing)* Terminal, *das.* **2.** *adj.* **a)** End‹*bahnhof, -station*›; **b)** *(concluding)* abschließend ‹*Worte*›; End‹*reim, -silbe*›; **the ~ problem** das letzte große Problem; **c)** *(Med.)* unheilbar; **have a ~ illness** unheilbar krank sein; **a ~ case** ein hoffnungsloser Fall; **d)** *(Bot.)* ~ **bud** Terminalknospe, *die;* **e)** *(Zool., Anat.)* End‹*glied, -lappen*›

terminally ['tɜ:mɪnəlɪ] *adv. (Med.)* ~ **ill** unheilbar krank

terminal ve'locity *n. (Phys.)* Grenzgeschwindigkeit, *die*

terminate ['tɜ:mɪneɪt] **1.** *v.t.* **a)** *(bring to an end)* beenden; **the contract was ~d** der Vertrag wurde gelöst; **b)** *(Med.)* unterbrechen ‹*Schwangerschaft*›. **2.** *v.i.* **a)** *(come to an end)* enden; ‹*Vertrag:*› ablaufen; **b)** *(Ling.)* enden; auslauten

termination [tɜ:mɪ'neɪʃn] *n.* **a)** *no pl. (coming to an end)* Ende, *das; (of lease)* Ablauf, *der;* **b)** *no pl. (bringing to an end)* Beendigung, *die; (of a marriage)* Auflösung, *die;* **c)** *(Med.)* Schwangerschaftsabbruch, *der*

terminological [tɜ:mɪnə'lɒdʒɪkl] *adj.* terminologisch; *(of science of terminology)* Terminologie-

terminologically [tɜ:mɪnə'lɒdʒɪkəlɪ] *adv.* terminologisch

terminologist [tɜ:mɪ'nɒlədʒɪst] *n.* Terminologe, *der*/Terminologin, *die*

terminology [tɜ:mɪ'nɒlədʒɪ] *n.* Terminologie, *die*

terminus ['tɜ:mɪnəs] *n., pl.* **~es** *or* **termini** ['tɜ:mɪnaɪ] *(end of route or line)* Ende, *das; (of bus, train, etc.)* Endstation, *die*

termite ['tɜ:maɪt] *n. (Zool.)* Termite, *die*

tern [tɜ:n] *n. (Ornith.)* Seeschwalbe, *die*

ternary ['tɜ:nərɪ] *adj.* ternär

terrace ['terəs, 'terɪs] **1.** *n.* **a)** *(row of houses)* Häuserreihe, *die;* **b)** *(adjacent to house; Agric.: on hillside)* Terrasse, *die;* **c)** *in pl. (Footb.)* Ränge; **d)** *(Geol.)* Terrasse, *die;* Stufe, *die.* **2.** *v.t.* terrassieren

'terraced house, 'terrace-house *ns.* Reihenhaus, *das*

terracotta [terə'kɒtə] *n., no pl., no indef. art.* Terrakotta, *die*

terra firma [terə 'fɜ:mə] *n., no pl., no art.* fester Boden; **be back on ~**: wieder festen Boden unter den Füßen haben

terrain [te'reɪn] *n.* Gelände, *das;* Terrain, *das (bes. Milit.)*

terrapin ['terəpɪn] *n. (Zool.)* Sumpfschildkröte, *die*

terrestrial [tə'restrɪəl, tɪ'restrɪəl] **1.** *adj.* **a)** terrestrisch ‹*Raumschiff, Bevölkerung*›; Erd‹*satellit, -bevölkerung*›; *(mundane)* irdisch; weltlich; **the ~ globe** der Erdball; **a ~ globe** ein Erdglobus; *see also* **magnetism a; b)** *(of the land)* kontinental; terrestrisch *(Geol.);* **c)** *(Biol.)* Land-. **2.** *n.* Erdbewohner, *der*/-bewohnerin, *die*

terrible ['terɪbl] *adj.* **a)** *(coll.: very great or bad)* schrecklich *(ugs.);* fürchterlich *(ugs.);* **I feel ~ about doing it** es tut mir schrecklich leid, es zu tun; **b)** *(coll.: incompetent)* schlecht; **be ~ at maths/tennis/carpentry** in Mathe schlecht sein/schlecht Tennis spielen/ein schlechter Tischler sein; **c)** *(causing terror)* furchtbar. *See also* **enfant terrible**

terribly ['terɪblɪ] *adv.* **a)** *(coll.: very)* unheimlich *(ugs.);* furchtbar *(ugs.);* **b)** *(coll.: appallingly)* furchtbar *(ugs.);* **c)** *(coll.: incompetently)* schlecht; **d)** *(fearfully)* auf erschreckende Weise

terrier ['terɪə(r)] *n.* Terrier, *der*

terrific [tə'rɪfɪk] *adj. (coll.)* **a)** *(great, intense)* irrsinnig *(ugs.);* Wahnsinns- *(ugs.);* unwahrscheinlich *(ugs.);* **b)** *(magnificent)* sagenhaft *(ugs.);* **c)** *(highly expert)* klasse *(ugs.);* toll *(ugs.);* **be ~ at sth.** in etw. *(Dat.)* Spitze sein *(ugs.);* **a ~ singer** ein Spitzensänger/eine Spitzensängerin *(ugs.)*

terrifically [tə'rɪfɪkəlɪ] *adv. (coll.: extremely)* wahnsinnig *(ugs.)*

terrify ['terɪfaɪ] *v.t.* **a)** *(fill with terror)* angst machen (+ *Dat.*); **terrified** verängstigt; **b)** *(coll.: make very anxious)* angst machen (+ *Dat.*); **be terrified that ...**: Angst haben, daß ...; **c)** *(scare)* Angst einjagen (+ *Dat.*); ~ **sb. into doing sth.** jmdm. eine solche Angst einjagen, daß er etw. tut

terrifying ['terɪfaɪɪŋ] *adj.* **a)** *(causing terror)* entsetzlich ‹*Erlebnis, Film, Buch, Theaterstück*›; erschreckend ‹*Klarheit, Gedanke*›; furchterregend ‹*Anblick*›; beängstigend ‹*Geschwindigkeit, Neigungswinkel*›; **b)** *(for-*

midable) furchterregend; beängstigend ⟨*Gelehrsamkeit, Förmlichkeit, Intensität*⟩

terrifyingly ['terɪfaɪɪŋlɪ] *adv.* beängstigend ⟨*dicht, knapp*⟩; entsetzlich ⟨*einsam*⟩

terrine [tə'ri:n] *n.* **a)** *(dish)* Steinguttopf, *der;* **b)** *(Gastr.)* Terrine, *die*

territorial [terɪ'tɔ:rɪəl] **1.** *adj.* **a)** territorial; Gebiets⟨*anspruch, -hoheit usw.*⟩; Hoheits⟨*gewässer, -gebiet usw.*⟩; Gelände⟨*vorteil*⟩; ~ **possessions** Territorialbesitz, *der;* **b)** *(limited to a district)* regional begrenzt ⟨*Maßnahme, Regelung*⟩. **2. T~** *n. (Brit. Mil.)* Landwehrsoldat, *der*

Territorial 'Army *n. (Brit. Mil.)* Landwehr, *die;* Territorialarmee, *die*

territorially [terɪ'tɔ:rɪəlɪ] *adv.* territorial

territorial 'waters *n. pl.* Hoheitsgewässer

territory ['terɪtərɪ] *n.* **a)** *(Polit.)* Staatsgebiet, *das;* Hoheitsgebiet, *das;* **b)** *(fig.: area of knowledge or action)* Gebiet, *das;* **c)** *(of commercial traveller etc.)* Bezirk, *der;* **d)** *(large tract of land)* Region, *die;* Gebiet, *das;* **e)** *(Amer.: land not yet a full State)* Territorium, *das;* **f)** *(Zool.)* Revier, *das;* **g)** *(Sport)* Spielfeldhälfte, *die*

terror ['terə(r)] *n.* **a)** *(extreme fear)* [panische] Angst; **in ~:** in panischer Angst; **reign of ~:** Schreckensherrschaft, *die;* **the [Red] T~, the Reign of T~** *(Hist.)* die Schreckensherrschaft [der Französischen Revolution]; **b)** *(person or thing causing ~)* Schrecken, *der;* **c) [holy] ~** *(troublesome person)* Plage, *die; (formidable person)* Schrecken, *der*

terrorisation, terrorise *see* **terroriz-**

terrorism ['terərɪzm] *n.* Terrorismus, *der; (terrorist acts)* Terror, *der;* **acts of ~:** Terrorakte

terrorist ['terərɪst] *n.* Terrorist, *der*/Terroristin, *die; attrib.* Terror⟨*gruppe, -organisation*⟩

terroristic [terə'rɪstɪk] *adj.* terroristisch

terrorization [terəraɪ'zeɪʃn] *n., no pl.* Terror, *der*

terrorize ['terəraɪz] *v.t.* **a)** *(frighten)* in [Angst und] Schrecken versetzen; **b)** *(coerce by terrorism)* terrorisieren; *(intimidate)* durch Terror[akte] einschüchtern; **~ sb. into submission** jmdn. durch Terror in die Knie zwingen

terror: ~-stricken, ~-struck *adjs.* zu Tode erschrocken

terry ['terɪ] *adj. (Textiles)* **~ towel** Frottier[hand]tuch, *das;* **~ towelling** Frottee, *das od. der*

terse [tɜ:s] *adj.* **a)** *(concise)* kurz und bündig; **b)** *(curt)* knapp

tersely ['tɜ:slɪ] *adv.* **a)** *(concisely)* in kurzen Worten; **b)** *(curtly)* kurz angebunden

terseness ['tɜ:snɪs] *n., no pl.* **a)** *(conciseness)* Bündigkeit, *die;* **b)** *(curtness)* Knappheit, *die*

tertiary ['tɜ:ʃərɪ] *adj.* **a)** *(of third order or rank)* tertiär; **b)** *(next after secondary)* **~ education** der tertiäre Bildungsbereich; **c) T~** *(Geol.)* tertiär

Terylene, (P) ['terɪli:n] *n.* Terylen, *das* Ⓦ

terza rima [teətsə 'ri:mə] *n. (Pros.)* Terzine, *die*

tessellated ['tesəleɪtɪd] *adj.* mosaikartig; tessellarisch

tessellation [tesə'leɪʃn] *n.* mosaikartige Musterung

test [test] **1.** *n.* **a)** *(examination) (Sch.)* Klassenarbeit, *die; (Univ.)* Klausur, *die; (short examination)* Test, *der;* **~ of character** Charakterprüfung, *die;* **put sb./sth. to the ~:** jmdn./etw. erproben; **b)** *(critical inspection, analysis)* Test, *der;* **c)** *(basis for evaluation)* Prüfstein, *der;* **d)** *(Cricket)* Test Match, *das;* **e)** *(ground of admission or rejection)* Aufnahmeprüfung, *die;* **f)** *(Chem.)* Reagens, *das;* **serve as a ~ for starch** zum Nachweis von Stärke dienen. **2.** *v.t.* **a)** *(examine, analyse)* untersuchen ⟨*Wasser, Gehör, Augen*⟩; testen ⟨*Gehör, Augen*⟩; prüfen ⟨*Schüler*⟩; überprüfen ⟨*Hypothese, Aussage, Leitungen*⟩; **~ a pupil on his/her vocabulary** einem Schüler/einer Schülerin die Vokabeln abfragen; **~ the accuracy of a statement** den Wahrheitsgehalt einer Aussage überprüfen; **~ sb. for AIDS** jmdn. auf Aids untersuchen; **~ the reaction of the work-force** sehen, wie die Belegschaft reagiert; **b)** *(try severely)* auf die Probe stellen; **c)** *(Chem.)* analysieren; **~ a substance for sth.** eine Substanz auf etw. *(Akk.)* untersuchen; **send sth. for ~ing** etw. zur Analyse schicken

~ out *v.t.* ausprobieren ⟨*neue Produkte*⟩ **(on an +** *Dat.***)**; erproben ⟨*Theorie, Idee*⟩

testament ['testəmənt] *n.* **a) Old/New T~** *(Bibl.)* Altes/Neues Testament; **b)** *see* ²**will 1b**

testamentary [testə'mentərɪ] *adj.* testamentarisch

testator [te'steɪtə(r)] *n.* Erblasser, *der (Rechtsspr.)*

testatrix [te'steɪtrɪks] *n.* Erblasserin, *die (Rechtsspr.)*

test: ~ ban *n.* Atom[waffen]teststopp, *der;* **~ ban treaty** *n.* [Atom]teststopp-Abkommen, *das;* **~ bed** *n. (Aeronaut.)* Prüfstand, *der;* **~ card** *n. (Telev.)* Testbild, *das;* **~ 'case** *n. (Law)* Musterprozeß, *der;* **~ drive** *n.* Probefahrt, *die;* **~-drive** *v.t.* probefahren

tester ['testə(r)] *n.* Prüfer, *der*/Prüferin, *die; (device)* Prüfgerät, *das; (sample)* Probe, *die*

'test flight *n.* Testflug, *der;* Erprobungsflug, *der;* **first ~:** Jungfernflug, *der*

testicle ['testɪkl] *n. (Anat., Zool.)* Testikel, *der (fachspr.);* Hoden, *der*

testify ['testɪfaɪ] **1.** *v.i.* **a) ~ to sth.** etw. bezeugen; **~ to sb.'s high intelligence** jmdm. große Intelligenz bescheinigen; **this testifies to his skills** das zeugt von seinen Fähigkeiten; **b)** *(Law)* **~ against sb./before sth.** gegen jmdn./vor etw. *(Dat.)* aussagen. **2.** *v.t.* **a)** *(declare)* bestätigen; **b)** *(be evidence of)* beweisen

testily ['testɪlɪ] *adv.* gereizt

testimonial [testɪ'məʊnɪəl] *n.* **a)** *(certificate of character)* Zeugnis, *das; (recommendation)* Referenz, *die;* **b)** *(gift)* Geschenk [als Ausdruck der Wertschätzung]

testimony ['testɪmənɪ] *n.* **a)** *(witness)* Aussage, *die;* **bear ~ to sth., be ~ to** *or* **of sth.** etw. beweisen; von etw. zeugen; **have sb.'s ~ for sth.** jmds. Wort für etw. haben; **~ of his respectability** Zeichen *od.* Beweis seiner Anständigkeit; **b)** *(Law)* [Zeugen]aussage, *die;* **c)** *no pl. (statements)* Angaben

testiness ['testɪnɪs] *n., no pl.* Gereiztheit, *die*

testis ['testɪs] *n., pl.* **testes** ['testi:z] *see* **testicle**

'test match *n. (Sport)* Test Match, *das*

testosterone [te'stɒstərəʊn] *n. (Physiol.)* Testosteron, *das*

test: ~ paper *n.* **a)** *(Educ.)* Übungsarbeit, *die; (Univ.)* Übungsklausur, *die;* **b)** *(Chem.)* Indikatorpapier, *das;* **~-piece** *n.* Pflicht[übung], *die; (Mus.)* Pflichtstück, *das;* **~ pilot** *n. (Aeronaut.)* Testpilot, *der*/-pilotin, *die;* **~-tube** *n. (Chem., Biol.)* Reagenzglas, *das;* **~-tube baby** *(coll.)* Retortenbaby, *das (ugs.)*

testy ['testɪ] *adj.* leicht reizbar ⟨*Person*⟩; gereizt ⟨*Antwort*⟩

tetanus ['tetənəs] *n. (Med.)* Tetanus, *der (fachspr.);* [Wund]starrkrampf, *der*

tetchy ['tetʃɪ] *adj.* leicht reizbar; *(on single occasion)* gereizt

tête-à-tête [teɪtɑ:'teɪt] **1.** *n.* Tête-à-tête, *das (veralt.);* Gespräch unter vier Augen. **2.** *adj.* privat; **~ interview/discussion** Gespräch/Diskussion unter vier Augen; **~ conversation** Zwiegespräch, *das.* **3.** *adv.* unter vier Augen

tether ['teðə(r)] **1.** *n.* **a)** *(chain)* Kette, *die; (rope)* Strick, *der;* **b)** *(fig.: limit)* Grenze, *die;* **give sb. a short ~:** jmdn. an der kurzen Leine halten; **be at the end of one's ~:** am Ende [seiner Kraft] sein. **2.** *v.t.* anbinden **(to** an**)**

tetrahedron [tetrə'hi:drən] *n., pl.* **~s** *or* **tetrahedra** [tetrə'hi:drə] *(Geom.)* Tetraeder, *das*

Teuton ['tju:tən] *n. (Hist.)* Teutone, *der*/Teutonin, *die*

Teutonic [tju:'tɒnɪk] *adj.* **a)** *(Germanic)* germanisch; **b)** *(with Germanic characteristics)* [typisch] deutsch; teutonisch *(abwertend, auch scherzh.);* **c)** *(Hist.: of the Teutons)* teutonisch

Texan ['teksn] **1.** *adj.* texanisch. **2.** *n.* Texaner, *der*/Texanerin, *die*

text [tekst] *n.* **a)** Text, *der;* **they couldn't agree on the ~ of the agreement** sie konnten sich über den Wortlaut des Vertrages nicht einigen; **b)** *(passage of Scripture)* Bibelstelle, *die;* **take as one's ~:** als Predigttext nehmen; predigen über (+ *Akk.*); **c)** *(Amer.: book) see* **textbook; d)** *in pl. (books to be studied)* [Pflicht]lektüre, *die*

'textbook *n. (Educ.)* Lehrbuch, *das; attrib.* **~ case** Paradefall, *der;* **~ landing** Bilderbuchlandung, *die*

textile ['tekstaɪl] **1.** *n.* Stoff, *der;* **~s** Textilien *Pl.* **2.** *adj. (woven)* textil; **~ fabrics** Textilien *Pl.*

textual ['tekstjʊəl] *adj.* textlich

textual 'criticism *n.* Textkritik, *die*

textural ['tekstʃərl] *adj.* strukturell

texture ['tekstʃə(r)] *n.* **a)** Beschaffenheit, *die; (of fabric, material)* Struktur, *die; (of food)* Konsistenz, *die;* **have a smooth ~:** sich glatt anfühlen; **b)** *(of prose, music, etc.)* Textur, *die (geh.);* **c)** *(Art)* materielle Struktur

textured ['tekstʃəd] *adj.* Struktur⟨*garn, -farbe*⟩; **~ vegetable protein** Sojafleisch, *das*

textureless ['tekstʃəlɪs] *adj.* gestaltlos ⟨*Prosa, Gemälde, Darbietung*⟩; formlos ⟨*Masse*⟩

Th. *abbr.* **Thursday** Do.

Thai [taɪ] **1.** *adj.* **a)** *(of Thailand)* thailändisch; **b)** *(Ethnol./Ling.)* Thai-. **2.** *n.* **a)** *pl.* **~s** *or same* Thai, *der/die;* Thailänder, *der*/Thailänderin, *die;* **b)** *(language)* Thai, *das*

Thailand ['taɪlænd] *pr. n.* Thailand *(das)*

Thailander ['taɪlændə(r)] *see* **Thai 2a**

thalamus ['θæləməs] *n. (Anat.)* Thalamus, *der*

thalidomide [θə'lɪdəmaɪd] *n. (Med.)* Contergan, *das* Ⓦ; Thalidomid, *das*

thalidomide: ~ baby, ~ child *ns.* Contergankind, *das (ugs.)*

Thames [temz] *pr. n.* Themse, *die; see also* **father 1g; fire 1a**

than [ðən, *stressed* ðæn] *conj.* **a)** *(in comparison)* als; **I know you better ~ [I do] him** ich kenne dich besser als ihn; **I know you better ~ he [does]** ich kenne dich besser als er; **you are taller ~ he [is]** *or (coll.)* **him** du bist größer als er; *see also* **rather; b)** *(introducing statement of difference)* als; **anywhere else ~ at home** überall außer zu Hause; *see also* **none 1; other 1c, 2b, 3**

thank [θæŋk] *v.t.* **~ sb. [for sth.]** jmdm. [für etw.] danken; sich bei jmdm. [für etw.] bedanken; **I don't know how to ~ you** ich weiß gar nicht, wie ich Ihnen danken soll; **I can't ~ you enough** ich kann Ihnen gar nicht genug danken; **have sb./sth. to ~ for sth.** jmdm./einer Sache etw. zu verdanken haben; **have [only] oneself to ~ for sth.** etw. sich *(Dat.)* selbst zuzuschreiben haben; **he won't ~ you for that/for doing that** *(iron.)* er wird dir dafür nicht gerade dankbar sein/er wird dir nicht gerade dankbar sein, daß du das getan hast; **~ God** *or* **goodness** *or* **heaven[s]** Gott sei Dank; **[I] ~ you** danke; *(slightly formal)* vielen Dank; **no, ~ you** nein, danke; **yes, ~ you** ja, bitte; danke, ja; **doing very nicely, ~ you** es läuft alles prima *(auch iron.)*; **I can do without language like that, ~ you!** *(iron.)* auf diesen Ton kann ich verzichten, vielen Dank!; **~ you very much [indeed]** vielen herzlichen Dank; **I'll stay in London, ~ you** *(iron.)* vielen Dank, ich bleibe lieber in London; **~ing 'you** *(coll.)* danke; **~ you for nothing!** *(iron.)* danke bestens!; **I will ~ you to do as you are told** *(iron.)* ich wäre dir sehr verbunden, wenn du tätest, was man dir sagt; **~ one's [lucky] stars that ...**: dem Himmel danken, daß ...

thankful ['θæŋkfl] *adj.* dankbar; **I am just ~ that it's all over** ich bin nur froh, daß das jetzt alles vorüber ist

thankfully ['θæŋkfəlɪ] *adv.* **a)** *(gratefully)* dankbar; **b)** *(as sentence-modifier: fortunately)* glücklicherweise

thankfulness ['θæŋkflnɪs] *n., no pl.* Dankbarkeit, *die*

thankless ['θæŋklɪs] *adj.* undankbar ‹*Aufgabe, Person*›

thanks [θæŋks] *n. pl.* **a)** *(gratitude)* Dank, *der;* **accept sth. with ~**: etw. dankend annehmen; **smile one's ~**: dankend lächeln; **they gave me little ~** *or (iron.)* **much ~ they gave me for my troubles** sie haben mir meine Mühen kaum gedankt; **that's all the ~ one gets** das ist nun der Dank dafür!; **give ~ [to God]** dem Herrn danken; das Dankgebet sprechen; **~ to** *(with the help of)* dank; *(on account of the bad influence of)* wegen; **~ to you** dank deiner; *(reproachfully)* deinetwegen; **no ~ to you** *(iron.)* dein Verdienst war es nicht; **it is small** *or* **no ~ to him that we won** ihm haben wir es jedenfalls nicht zu verdanken, daß wir gewonnen haben; **~ to his arriving in time** dank seines rechtzeitigen Erscheinens; *see also* **return 2 a; b)** *(as formula expressing gratitude)* danke; **no, ~**: nein, danke; **yes, ~**: ja, bitte; **~ awfully** *or* **a lot** *or* **very much, many ~** *(coll.)* vielen *od.* tausend Dank

thanksgiving ['θæŋksgɪvɪŋ] *n.* **a)** *(expression of gratitude)* Dankbarkeit, *die;* **T~ [Day]** *(Amer.)* [amerikanisches] Erntedankfest; Thanksgiving Day, *der;* **b)** *(Relig.)* Dankgebet, *das*

'**thank-you** *n. (coll.)* Dankeschön, *das;* **a warm** *or* **hearty ~**: ein herzliches Dankeschön; **~ letter** Dankbrief, *der;* **give sb. a ~ present** jmdm. zum Dank etwas schenken

that 1. [ðæt] *adj., pl.* **those** [ðəʊz] **a)** dieser/diese/dieses; **~ son of yours** Ihr/dein Sohn; **b)** *expr. strong feeling* der/die/das; **never will I forget ~ day** den Tag werde ich nie vergessen; **c)** *(coupled or contrasted with 'this')* der/die/das [da]. **2.** *pron., pl.* **those a)** der/die/das; **who is ~ in the garden?** wer ist das [da] im Garten?; **what bird is ~?** was für ein Vogel ist das?; **I know all ~**: ich weiß das alles; **I 'am ~!** das kannst du wohl glauben!; **those below the standard will be rejected** alle, die den Anforderungen nicht genügen, werden abgelehnt; **and [all] ~**: und so weiter; **like ~**: *(of the kind or in the way mentioned, of ~ character)* so; **[just] like ~** *(without effort, thought)* einfach so; **don't be like ~!** sei doch nicht so; **if she 'wants to be like ~**: wenn sie sich so anstellen will; **don't talk like ~**: hör auf, so zu reden; **he is 'like ~**: so ist er eben; **~ is [to say]** *introducing explanation* das heißt; *introducing reservation* das heißt; genauer gesagt; **if they'd have me, ~ is** das heißt, wenn sie mich nehmen; **'~'s more like it** *(of suggestion, news)* das hört sich schon besser an; *(of action, work)* das sieht schon besser aus; **~'s right!** *expr. approval* gut *od.* recht so; *(iron.)* nur so weiter!; *(coll.: expr. assent)* jawohl; **~'s a good boy/girl** das ist lieb [von dir, mein Junge/Mädchen]; *(with request)* sei so lieb *usw.;* **~ will do** das reicht; **sb./sth. is not as ... as all '~** *(coll.)* so ... ist jmd./etw. nun auch wieder nicht; **[so] ~'s '~** *(it's finished)* so, das wär's; *(it's settled)* so ist es nun mal; **you are not going to the party, and ~'s '~!** du gehst nicht zu der Party, und damit Schluß!; *see also* **at d; how 1; it g, j; take 1 w; this 2 e; with g; b)** *(Brit.: person spoken to)* **who is ~?** wer ist da?; *(behind wall etc.)* wer ist denn da?; *(on telephone)* wer ist am Apparat?; **who was ~?** wer war das? **3.** [ðət] *rel. pron., pl. same* der/die/das; **the people ~ you got it from** die Leute, von denen du es bekommen hast; **the box ~ you put the apples in** die Kiste, in die du die Äpfel getan hast; **is he the man ~ you saw last night?** ist das der Mann, den Sie gestern abend gesehen haben?; **everyone ~ I know** jeder, den ich kenne; **this is all [the money] ~ I have** das ist alles [Geld], was ich habe; **they ~ ...**: diejenigen, die *od.* welche ...; **what is it ~ is making you sad?** was stimmt dich so traurig?. **4.** [ðæt] *adv. (coll.)* so; **he may be daft, but he's not [all] '~ daft** er mag ja blöd sein, aber so blöd [ist er] auch wieder nicht; **a nail about ~ long** ein etwa so langer Nagel. **5.** [ðət] *rel. adv.* der/die/das; **at the speed ~ he was going** bei der Geschwindigkeit, die er hatte; **tell the way ~ the accident happened** erzählen, wie der Unfall geschah; **the day ~ I first met her** der Tag, an dem ich sie zum ersten Mal sah. **6.** [ðət, *stressed* ðæt] *conj.* **a)** *introducing statement; expr. result, reason or cause* daß; **b)** *expr. purpose* **[in order] ~**: damit; **he died ~ others might live** er starb, damit andere [weiter]leben konnten; **c)** *expr. wish* **oh ~ I could forget her!** ach, daß ich sie doch vergessen könnte! *See also* **not b; now 2**

thatch [θætʃ] **1.** *n.* **a)** *(of straw)* Strohdach, *das; (of reeds)* Schilf- *od.* Reetdach, *das; (of palm-leaves)* Palmblattdach, *das; (material)* Stroh, *das*/Schilf, *das*/Palmblätter; *(roofing)* Dachbedeckung, *die;* **b)** *(coll.: hair)* Matte, *die (salopp).* **2.** *v. t.* mit Stroh/Schilf/Palmblättern decken

thatched [θætʃt] *adj.* strohgedeckt/schilf- *od.* reetgedeckt; gedeckt ‹*Dach*›; Stroh-/Schilf-/Reet‹*dach*›

thatcher ['θætʃə(r)] *n.* Dachdecker, *der*/-deckerin, *die*

Thatcherism ['θætʃərɪzm] *n. (Polit.)* Thatcherismus, *der*

thaw [θɔː] **1.** *n.* **a)** *(warmth)* Tauwetter, *das;* **b)** *(act of ~ing)* **after the ~**: nachdem es getaut hat/hatte; **c)** *(fig.)* Tauwetter, *das;* Tauwetterperiode, *die.* **2.** *v. i.* **a)** *(melt)* auftauen; **b)** *(become warm enough to melt ice etc.)* tauen; **it looks like ~ing** es sieht nach Tauwetter aus; **c)** *(fig.: become less aloof or hostile)* auftauen; **d)** *(lose numbness)* [wieder] warm werden. **3.** *v. t.* **a)** *(cause to melt)* auftauen; **b)** *(fig.: cause to be less aloof or hostile)* auftauen; entspannen ‹*Atmosphäre*›; **c)** *(cause to lose numbness)* aufwärmen

~ 'out *see* **~ 2, 3**

the [*before vowel* ðɪ, *before consonant* ðə, *when stressed* ðiː] **1.** *def. art.* **a)** der/die/das; **all ~ doors** alle Türen; **play ~ piano** Klavier spielen; **if you want a quick survey, this is ~ book** für einen raschen Überblick ist dies das richtige Buch; **it's** *or* **there's only ~ one** es ist nur dieser/diese/dieses eine; **he lives in ~ district** er wohnt in dieser Gegend; **he was quite ~ philosopher about his misfortune** er trug sein Unglück wie ein Philosoph; **£5 ~ square metre/~ gallon/~ kilogram** 5 Pfund der Quadratmeter/die Gallone/das Kilogramm; **14 miles to ~ gallon** 14 Meilen auf eine Gallone; ≈ 20 l auf 100 km; **a scale of one mile to ~ inch** ein Maßstab von 1:63 360; **none but ~ brave deserves ~ fair** allein dem Tapferen gehört die Schöne; **b)** *(denoting one best known)* **it is '~ restaurant in this town** das ist das Restaurant in dieser Stadt; **red is '~ colour this year** Rot ist in diesem Jahr die Farbe; **she is no relation to '~ Kipling** mit dem Kipling ist sie nicht verwandt; **c)** *with names of diseases* **have got ~ toothache/measles** *(coll.)* Zahnschmerzen/die Masern haben; **d)** *(Brit. coll.: my, our, etc.)* mein/unser *usw.;* **leave ~ wife and ~ dog at home** Frau und Hund zu Hause lassen; **e)** *(Scot., Ir.: with name of clan)* **~ Macnab** das Oberhaupt des Macnab-Clans. **2.** *adv.* **~ more I practise ~ better I play** je mehr ich übe, desto *od.* um so besser spiele ich; **I am not ~ more inclined to help him because he is poor** ich würde ihm genauso gern helfen, wenn er nicht arm wäre; **his car runs ~ faster for having been tuned properly** jetzt, wo es richtig eingestellt ist, fährt sein Auto schneller; **so much ~ worse for sb./sth.** um so schlimmer für jmdn./etw.; *see also* **all 3; more 1 b, 3 h**

theatre (*Amer.:* **theater**) ['θɪətə(r)] *n.* **a)** Theater, *das;* **at the ~**: im Theater; **go to the ~**: ins Theater gehen; **b)** *(lecture ~)* Hörsaal, *der;* **c)** *(Brit. Med.) see* **operating-theatre; d)** *(dramatic art)* **the ~**: das Theater; **go into the ~**: zum Theater gehen *(ugs.);* **e)** *no pl., no art.* **make good ~**: sehr bühnenwirksam sein; sich gut für die Bühne eignen; **f)** *(scene of action)* Schauplatz, *der; (of war)* Kriegsschauplatz, *der*

theatre: ~-goer *n.* Theaterbesucher, *der*/-besucherin, *die;* **~-going 1.** *n., no pl., no indef. art.* Theaterbesuche; **~-going is on the increase** die Zahl der Theaterbesucher steigt; **2.** *adj.* **the ~-going public/type** die Theaterbesucher/der typische Theaterbesucher; **~ sister** *n. (Brit. Med.)* OP-Schwester, *die;* **~ weapon** *n. (Mil.)* Kurzstreckenrakete, *die*

theatrical [θɪ'ætrɪkl] *adj.* **a)** schauspielerisch; **a ~ company** eine Schauspiel- *od.* Theatertruppe; **b)** *(showy)* theatralisch ‹*Benehmen, Verbeugung, Person*›

theatrically [θɪ'ætrɪkəlɪ] *adv.* **a) ~, the play was a disaster** was die Aufführung angeht, war das Stück ein Reinfall; **b)** *(showily)* theatralisch

theatricals [θɪ'ætrɪklz] *n. pl.* **a)** *(dramatic performances)* Theateraufführungen; **private** *or* **amateur ~**: Amateur- *od.* Laientheater, *das;* **b)** *(showy actions)* Theatralik, *die (geh.)*

Thebes [θiːbz] *pr. n. (Greek/Egyptian Ant.)* Theben *(das)*

thee [ðiː] *pron. (arch./poet./dial.)* dich; *(as indirect object)* dir; *(Relig.: God)* Dich/Dir; *see also* **¹her**

theft [θeft] *n.* Diebstahl, *der;* **~ of cars** Autodiebstahl, *der*

their [ðeə(r)] *poss. pron. attrib.* **a)** ihr; *see also* **²her; our a; b)** *(coll.: his or her)* **who has forgotten ~ ticket?** wer hat seine Karte vergessen?

theirs [ðeəz] *poss. pron. pred.* ihrer/ihre/ihres; *see also* **hers; ours**

theism ['θiːɪzm] *n. (Philos.)* Theismus, *der*

theist ['θiːɪst] *n. (Philos.)* Theist, *der*/Theistin, *die*

them [ðəm, *stressed* ðem] *pron.* **a)** sie; *(as indirect object)* ihnen; *see also* **¹her; b)** *(coll.: him/her)* ihn/sie

thematic [θɪ'mætɪk] *adj.* thematisch

thematically [θɪ'mætɪkəlɪ] *adv. (with regard to topic[s]; also Mus.)* thematisch; **arrange ~**: nach Themen ordnen

theme [θiːm] *n.* **a)** *(of speaker, writer, or thinker)* Gegenstand, *der;* Thema, *das;* **b)** *(Mus.)* Thema, *das;* Leitmotiv, *das;* **a ~ from 'My Fair Lady'** eine Melodie aus My Fair Lady; **c)** *(Amer. Educ.)* Aufsatz, *der*

theme: ~ music *n.* Titelmelodie, *die;* **~ park** *n. Freizeitpark, dessen Attraktionen und Einrichtungen auf ein bestimmtes Thema bezogen sind;* **~ song** *n.* **a)** *see* **~ music; b)** *see* **signature tune; ~ tune** *see* **signature tune**

themselves [ðəm'selvz] *pron.* **a)** *emphat.* selbst; **they ~ were astonished** sie waren selbst ganz erstaunt; **the results ~ were ...:**

die Ergebnisse an sich waren ...; b) *refl.* sich ‹*waschen usw.*›; sich selbst ‹*die Schuld geben, regieren*›. *See also* **herself; ourselves**

then [ðen] **1.** *adv.* **a)** *(at that time)* damals; **the ~ existing laws** die damals geltenden *od.* damaligen Gesetze; **~ and there, there and ~:** auf der Stelle; *see also* **now 1 a; b)** *(after that)* dann; **~ [again]** *(and also)* außerdem; **the journey will take a long time, and ~ don't forget that it gets dark early** die Fahrt wird lange dauern, und dann dürft ihr auch nicht vergessen, daß es früh dunkel wird; **but ~** *(after all)* aber schließlich; **c)** *(in that case)* dann; **~ why didn't you say so?** warum hast du dann nichts gesagt?; **hurry up, ~:** dann beeil dich aber; **but ~ again** aber andererseits; **d)** *expr. grudging or impatient concession* dann eben; **well, take it, ~:** dann nimm es eben; **e)** *(accordingly)* [dann] also; **the cause of the accident, ~, seems to be established** die Ursache des Unfalls scheint [dann] also festzustehen. *See also* **²well 1 d, g; what 5 a. 2.** *n.* **before ~:** vorher; davor; **by ~:** bis dahin; **from ~ on** von da an; **till ~:** bis dahin; **oh, we should get there long before ~:** ach, bis dahin sind wir längst dort; **since ~:** seitdem. **3.** *adj.* damalig

thence [ðens] *adv. (arch./literary)* **[from] ~:** von dort; *(for that reason)* von daher

thence: ~'forth, ~'forward *advs. (arch./literary)* **[from] ~forth** *or* **~forward** seit dieser Zeit; von da an

theodolite [θɪ'ɒdəlaɪt] *n. (Surv.)* Theodolit, *der*

theologian [θi:ə'ləʊdʒɪən] *n.* Theologe, *der*/Theologin, *die*

theological [θi:ə'lɒdʒɪkl] *adj.* theologisch; Theologie‹*student, -dozent*›

theology [θɪ'ɒlədʒɪ] *n.* **a)** *no pl., no indef. art.* Theologie, *die;* **b)** *(religious system)* Glaubenslehre, *die*

theorem ['θɪərəm] *n. (Math.)* [Lehr]satz, *der;* Theorem, *das (fachspr.)*

theoretic [θɪə'retɪk], **theoretical** [θɪə'retɪkl] *adj.* theoretisch; **your arguments are only ~:** deine Argumentation ist reine Theorie

theoretically [θi:ə'retɪkəlɪ] *adv.* theoretisch

theoretician [θɪərɪ'tɪʃn] *n.* Theoretiker, *der*/Theoretikerin, *die*

theorise *see* **theorize**

theorist ['θɪərɪst] *n.* Theoretiker, *der*/Theoretikerin, *die*

theorize ['θɪəraɪz] *v. i.* theoretisieren

theory ['θɪərɪ] *n. (also Math.)* Theorie, *die;* **~ of evolution/music** Evolutions-/Musiktheorie, *die;* **in ~:** theoretisch; **it's a ~!** das wäre eine Möglichkeit; **I always go on the ~ that ...:** ich gehe immer davon aus, daß ...; **have a ~ that ...:** die Theorie vertreten, daß ...

theosophic [θi:ə'sɒfɪk], **theosophical** [θi:ə'sɒfɪkl] *adj.* theosophisch

theosophy [θɪ'ɒsəfɪ] *n., no pl., no indef. art.* Theosophie, *die*

therapeutic [θerə'pju:tɪk] *adj.* therapeutisch; *(curative)* therapeutisch wirksam

therapeutically [θerə'pju:tɪkəlɪ] *adv.* therapeutisch

therapeutics [θerə'pju:tɪks] *n., no pl. (Med.)* Therapeutik, *die*

therapist ['θerəpɪst] *n. (Med.)* Therapeut, *der*/Therapeutin, *die*

therapy ['θerəpɪ] *n. (Med., Psych.)* Therapie, *die;* [Heil]behandlung, *die;* **undergo ~:** sich einer Therapie *(Dat.)* unterziehen

there [ðeə(r)] **1.** *adv.* **a)** *(in/at that place)* da; dort; *(fairly close)* da; **sb. has been ~ before** *(fig. coll.)* jmd. weiß Bescheid; **~ or ~a'bouts** so ungefähr; **be down/in/up ~:** da unten/drin/oben sein; **~ goes ...:** da geht/fährt *usw.* ...; **are you ~?** *(on telephone)* sind Sie noch da *od. (ugs.)* dran?; **~ and then = then and ~** *see* **then 1 a;** *see also* **all 3; here 1 a; b)** *(calling attention)* **hello** *or* **hi ~!** hallo!; **you ~!** Sie da!; **move along ~!** weitergehen!; **~'s a good** *etc.* **boy/girl = that's a good** *etc.* **boy/girl** *see* **that 2 a;** *see also* **for 1 h; c)** *(in that respect)* da; **so ~:** und damit basta *(ugs.);* **~ you are wrong** da irrst du dich; **~, it is a loose wire** da haben wir's – ein loser Draht; **~ it is** *(nothing can be done about it)* da kann man nichts machen; **~ you are** *(giving sth.)* [da,] bitte schön; **~ you have it** *(fig.)* da ist der Punkt; *see also* **2 b; rub 3; d)** *(to that place)* dahin, dorthin ‹*gehen, gelangen, fahren, rücken, stellen*›; **we got ~ and back in two hours** wir brauchten für Hin- und Rückweg [nur] zwei Stunden; **down/in/up ~:** dort hinunter/hinein/hinauf; **get ~ first** jmdm./den anderen zuvorkommen; **get ~** *(fig.) (achieve)* es [schon] schaffen; *(understand)* es verstehen; **e)** [ðə(r), *stressed* ðeə(r)] *(as introductory function-word)* da; **was ~ anything in it?** war da irgend etwas drin? *(ugs.);* **~ is enough food** es gibt genug zu essen; **~ are many kinds of ...:** es gibt viele Arten von ...; **~ were four of them** sie waren zu viert; **~ was once an old woman who ...:** es war einmal eine alte Frau, die ...; **~ was no beer left** es gab kein Bier mehr; **~ appears to be some error** da scheint ein Irrtum unterlaufen zu sein; **~'s no time for that now** dafür haben wir/habe ich jetzt keine Zeit; **~ being no further point in waiting, I left** weil es keinen Zweck mehr hatte, noch länger zu warten, ging ich; **... if ever ~ was one ...** wie er/sie/es im Buche steht; **what is ~ for supper?** was gibt's zum Abendessen?; **not a sound was ~ to indicate their presence** kein Laut verriet ihre Anwesenheit; **seldom has ~ been more fuss** selten hat es soviel Aufhebens gegeben; **a fine mess ~ is!** da sieht es vielleicht aus! *(ugs.).* **2.** [ðeə(r)] *int.* **a)** *(to soothe child etc.)* **~, ~:** na, na *(ugs.);* **b)** *expr. triumph or dismay* **~ [you are]!** da, siehst du!; **~, you've dropped it!** da, jetzt hast du es doch fallen lassen!; *see also* **1 c. 3.** *n.* da, dort; **near ~:** da *od.* dort in der Nähe; **the tide comes up to ~:** die Flut kommt bis dahin *od.* da hoch

there: ~abouts ['ðeərəbaʊts] *adv.* **a)** *(near that place)* da [in der Nähe]; **the locals ~abouts** die Leute, die dort wohnen; **b)** *(near that number)* **two litres or ~abouts** zwei Liter [so] ungefähr; *see also* **there 1 a; ~'after** *adv.* danach; **~by** [ðeə'baɪ, 'ðeəbaɪ] *adv.* dadurch; **~by hangs a tale** dazu gibt es noch etwas zu erzählen; **~fore** *adv.* deshalb; also; **~'from** *adv. (arch.)* daraus; **~'in** *adv. (formal)* darin; **~'of** *adv. (formal)* davon; **the island and all the ports ~of** die Insel und alle ihre Häfen; **~'to** *adv. (formal)* dazu; **~u'pon** *adv.* **a)** *(soon after that)* kurz darauf; alsbald *(veralt.);* **b)** *(in consequence of that)* daraufhin; **~'with** *adv. (formal)* damit

therm [θɜ:m] *n. (Brit.)* englische Einheit der Wärmemenge *(ca. 1,055 × 10^8 J)*

thermal ['θɜ:ml] **1.** *adj.* thermisch ‹*Erscheinung, Anforderungen*›; Wärme‹*dämmung, -strahlung*›; **~ underwear** kälteisolierende Unterwäsche. **2.** *n. (Aeronaut.)* Thermik, *die*

thermally ['θɜ:məlɪ] *adv.* thermisch

thermal: ~ 'springs *n. pl.* Thermalquelle, *die;* **~ 'unit** *n. (Phys.)* Wärmeeinheit, *die*

thermionic [θɜ:mɪ'ɒnɪk]: **~ 'tube** *(Amer.),* **~ 'valve** *(Brit.) ns. (Electronics)* Glühkathodenröhre, *die*

thermocouple ['θɜ:mək:ʌpl] *n. (Phys.)* Thermoelement, *das*

thermodynamic [θɜ:mədaɪ'næmɪk] *adj.* thermodynamisch

thermodynamics [θɜ:mədaɪ'næmɪks] *n., no pl. (Phys.)* Thermodynamik, *die*

thermometer [θə'mɒmɪtə(r)] *n.* Thermometer, *das; see also* **clinical a**

thermonuclear [θɜ:məʊ'nju:klɪə(r)] *adj. (Phys.)* thermonuklear ‹*Waffe*›; Kern‹*fusion, -energie*›; Atom‹*krieg, -energie*›

thermoplastic [θɜ:məʊ'plæstɪk] **1.** *adj.* **a)** thermoplastisch; **b) ~ tiles** Kunststofffliesen. **2.** *n.* Thermoplast, *der*

Thermos, thermos, (P) ['θɜ:məs] *n.* **~ [flask/jug/bottle]** Thermosflasche, *die* (Wz)

thermostat ['θɜ:məstæt] *n.* Thermostat, *der*

thermostatic [θɜ:mə'stætɪk] *adj.* Temperatur‹*regler, -schalter*›

thermostatically [θɜ:mə'stætɪklɪ] *adv.* durch ein/das Thermostat ‹*kontrolliert, reguliert*›

thesaurus [θɪ'sɔ:rəs] *n., pl.* **thesauri** [θɪ'sɔ:raɪ] *or* **~es** Thesaurus, *der*

these *pl. of* **this 1, 2**

thesis ['θi:sɪs] *n., pl.* **theses** ['θi:si:z] **a)** *(proposition)* These, *die;* **b)** *(dissertation)* Dissertation, *die,* Doktorarbeit, *die* **(on** über + *Akk.*)

Thespian ['θespɪən] **1.** *adj.* Theater-. **2.** *n.* Schauspieler, *der*/Schauspielerin, *die*

they [ðeɪ] *pron.* **a)** sie; **b)** *(people in general)* man; **c)** *(coll.: he or she)* **everyone thinks ~ know best** jeder denkt, er weiß es am besten; **d)** *(those in authority)* sie; die *(ugs.).* *See also* **their; theirs; them; themselves**

they'd [ðeɪd] **a) = they would; b) = they had**

they'll [ðeɪl] **= they will**

they're [ðeə(r)] **= they are**

they've [ðeɪv] **= they have**

thick [θɪk] **1.** *adj.* **a)** dick; breit, dick ‹*Linie*›; **that's laying it on [a bit] ~** *(fig. coll.)* das ist ja wohl etwas dick aufgetragen *(ugs.);* **isn't she laying it on a bit ~?** *(fig. coll.)* trägt sie da nicht ein bißchen zu dick auf? *(ugs.);* **that's** *or* **it's a bit ~!** *(Brit. fig. coll.)* das ist ein starkes Stück! *(ugs.);* **get the ~ end of the stick** *(fig.)* den schlechteren Teil erwischen; **have a ~ skin** *(fig.)* ein dickes Fell haben *(ugs.);* **a rope two inches ~, a two-inch ~ rope** ein zwei Zoll starkes *od.* dickes Seil; **b)** *(dense)* dicht ‹*Haar, Nebel, Wolken, Gestrüpp usw.*›; dichtgedrängt ‹*Menschenmenge*›; **c)** *(filled)* **~ with** voll von; **air ~ with fog and smoke** von Nebel und Rauch erfüllte Luft; **the air was ~ with rumours** überall gingen Gerüchte um; **the furniture was ~ with dust** auf den Möbeln lag eine dicke Staubschicht; **d)** *(of firm consistency)* steif ‹*Gallerte*›; dickflüssig ‹*Sahne*›; *(containing much solid matter)* dick ‹*Suppe, Schlamm, Brei, Kleister*›; **e)** *(stupid)* dumm; **you're just plain ~:** du bist ganz einfach doof *(salopp);* **[as] ~ as two short planks** *(coll.)* dumm wie Bohnenstroh *(ugs.);* **f)** *(coll.: intimate)* **be very ~ with sb.** mit jmdm. dick befreundet sein *(ugs.);* **be [as] ~ as thieves** dicke Freunde sein *(ugs.);* **g)** tief ‹*Dunkelheit*›; **h)** *(not clear)* trüb ‹*Wetter, Morgen, Fluß*›; **have a ~ head** einen dicken Kopf haben *(ugs.);* **i)** *(Printing)* fett; **j)** *(numerous)* dicht; **they are ~/not exactly ~ on the ground** die gibt es wie Sand am Meer/die sind dünn gesät *(ugs.);* **k)** *(indistinct)* dumpf; **his speech was ~** *(with drink)* er sprach mit schwerer Zunge *(geh.);* **l)** *(marked)* **he has a ~ German accent** er hat einen starken deutschen Akzent. **2.** *n., no pl., no indef. art.* **in the ~ of** mitten in (+ *Dat.*); **in the ~ of it** *or* **things** mitten drin; **in the ~ of the battle** im dichtesten Kampfgetümmel; **she is always in the ~ of things** sie ist bei allem immer voll dabei *(ugs.);* **stay with sb./stick together through ~ and thin** mit jmdm./zusammen durch dick und dünn gehen. **3.** *adv.* **snow was falling ~:** es schneite dicke Flocken; **blows rained on him ~ and fast** die Schläge prasselten nur so auf ihn nieder; **job offers/complaints came in ~ and fast** es kam eine Flut von Stellenangeboten/Beschwerden

thick 'ear *n. (Brit. sl.)* **give sb. a ~:** jmdm. ein paar hinter die Ohren geben *(ugs.)*

T-Z ENGLISH GERMAN

thicken [θɪkn] **1.** *v.t.* dicker machen; eindicken ‹*Sauce*›. **2.** *v.i.* **a)** dicker werden; **sb.'s waist[line] ~s** jmds. Taille wird umfangreicher; **b)** *(become dense)* ‹*Nebel:*› dichter werden; **c)** *(become blurred)* **his speech ~ed** er bekam eine schwere Zunge *(geh.)*; **d)** *(become complex)* **the plot ~s!** die Sache wird kompliziert!; *(iron.)* die Sache wird langsam interessant!

thickening ['θɪknɪŋ] *n. (in food)* Bindemittel, *das; (in dye)* Verdickungsmittel, *das*

thicket ['θɪkɪt] *n.* Dickicht, *das*

thick: ~ 'head *n.* dicker Kopf *(ugs.)*; **~head** *n.* Dummkopf, *der;* **~-'headed** *adj.* dumm

thickly ['θɪklɪ] *adv.* **a)** *(in a thick layer)* dick; **b)** *(densely, abundantly)* dicht; **c)** *(in great numbers)* **hailstones fell ~**: die Hagelkörner prasselten nur so herab; **d)** *(indistinctly)* mit schwerer Zunge *(geh.)*; *(from emotion)* undeutlich ‹*sprechen*›

thickness ['θɪknɪs] *n.* **a)** Dicke, *die;* **be two metres in ~**: zwei Meter dick sein; **a plank whose ~ is two centimetres** ein Brett mit einer Dicke *od.* Stärke von 2 Zentimetern; **~ of paper/card** Papier-/Kartonstärke, *die;* **b)** *no pl. (denseness)* Dichte, die; *(of hair)* Fülle, *die;* **c)** *no pl. (firm consistency) (of jelly)* Steifheit, *die; (of cream)* Dickflüssigkeit, *die; (of soup, mud, porridge, glue)* Dicke, *die;* **d)** *(layer)* Lage, *die;* **e)** *no pl. (stupidity)* Dummheit, *die*

thicko ['θɪkəʊ] *n., pl.* **~s** *(coll.)* Schwachkopf, *der (ugs.)*

thick: ~set *adj.* **a)** *(stocky)* gedrungen; **b)** *(set close together)* dicht nebeneinanderstehend ‹*Bäume, Häuser*›; **~-skinned** *adj. (fig.)* unsensibel; dickfellig *(ugs. abwertend)*

thief [θi:f] *n., pl.* **thieves** [θi:vz] Dieb, *der*/Diebin, *die;* **like** *or* **as a ~ in the night** wie ein Dieb in der Nacht *(geh.)*; *see also* **Latin 2; take 1q; thick 1f**

thieve [θi:v] **1.** *v.i.* stehlen; **he makes a living out of petty thieving** er lebt vom Gelegenheitsdiebstahl. **2.** *v.t.* stehlen

thievish ['θi:vɪʃ] *adj.* diebisch ‹*Wesen, Art*›

thigh [θaɪ] *n.* **a)** *(Anat.)* Oberschenkel, *der;* **b)** *(Zool.)* Schenkel, *der*

thigh: ~-bone *n. (Anat.)* Oberschenkelknochen, *der;* **~-boot** *n.* Kanonenstiefel, *der;* Schaftstiefel, *der*

-thighed [θaɪd] *adj. in comb.* -schenkelig

thimble ['θɪmbl] *n.* Fingerhut, *der*

thimbleful ['θɪmblfʊl] *n.* Fingerhut [voll], *der;* **in ~s** in winzigen Mengen

thin [θɪn] **1.** *adj.* **a)** *(of small thickness or diameter)* dünn; *see also* **ice 1a; wedge 1a;** **b)** *(not fat)* dünn; **a tall, ~ man** ein großer, hagerer Mann; **as ~ as a rake** *or* **lath** spindeldürr; **c)** *(narrow)* schmal ‹*Baumreihe*›; dünn ‹*Linie*›; **d)** *(sparse)* dünn, schütter ‹*Haar*›; fein ‹*Regen, Dunst*›; spärlich ‹*Publikum, Besuch*›; gering ‹*Beteiligung*›; dünn ‹*Luft*›; **the country's population is ~**: das Land ist dünn bevölkert *od.* besiedelt; **he is already ~ on top** *or* **going ~ on top** bei ihm lichtet es sich oben schon; **the attendance at the meeting was ~**: die Versammlung war schwach besucht; **be ~ on the ground** *(fig.)* dünn gesät sein; **vanish** *or* **disappear into ~ air** *(fig.)* sich in Luft auflösen; **it won't appear out of ~ air!** *(fig.)* es fällt nicht einfach vom Himmel!; **produce a delicious meal out of ~ air** *(fig.)* ein köstliches Essen aus dem Nichts zaubern; **e)** *(lacking substance or strength)* dünn ‹*Bier, Blut, Stimme*›; **f)** *(fig.: inadequate)* dürftig; fadenscheinig ‹*Ausrede*›; **sb.'s patience is wearing ~**: jmds. Geduld geht zu Ende; jmdm. reißt allmählich der Geduldsfaden *(ugs.)*; **sb.'s credibility begins to wear ~**: jmd. verliert immer mehr an Glaubwürdigkeit; **g)** *(sl.: wretched)* enttäuschend, unbefriedigend ‹*Zeit*›; **he had a pretty ~ time [of it]** er machte eine ziemlich schlimme Zeit durch; **h)** *(consisting of ~ lines)* fein ‹*Handschrift*›; *(Printing)* mager. *See also* **thick 2. 2.** *adv.* dünn. **3.** *v.t.,* **-nn- a)** *(make less deep or broad)* dünner machen; **b)** *(make less dense, dilute)* verdünnen; **c)** *(reduce in number)* dezimieren; **d)** *(remove young fruit from)* ausbrechen ‹*Reben*›; ausdünnen ‹*Obstbäume*›. **4.** *v.i.,* **-nn-** ‹*Haar, Nebel:*› sich lichten; ‹*Menschenmenge:*› sich zerstreuen; **~ down to a mere trickle** zu einem kleinen Rinnsal werden

~ 'out 1. *v.i.* ‹*Menschenmenge:*› sich verlaufen; ‹*Verkehr:*› abnehmen; ‹*Reihen der Zuschauer:*› sich lichten; ‹*Häuser:*› spärlicher werden. **2.** *v.t. (Hort., Forestry)* vereinzeln, ausdünnen ‹*Pflanzen*›; lichten ‹*Wald*›

thine [ðaɪn] *poss. pron. (arch./poet./dial.)* **a)** *pred.* deiner/deine/dein[e]s; der/die/das deinige *(geh.)*; *see also* **hers; b)** *attrib.* dein

thing [θɪŋ] *n.* **a)** *(inanimate object)* Sache, *die;* Ding, *das;* **what's that ~ in your hand?** was hast du da in der Hand?; **be a rare ~**: etwas Seltenes sein; **books are strange** *or* *(coll.)* **funny ~s, aren't they?** Bücher sind schon etwas Seltsames, nicht wahr?; **neither one ~ nor the other** weder das eine noch das andere; **I haven't a '~ to wear** ich habe nichts zum Anziehen; **you haven't a ~ to worry about** du brauchst dir überhaupt keine Sorgen zu machen; **not a ~**: überhaupt *od.* gar nichts; **b)** *(action)* **that was a foolish/friendly ~ to do** das war eine große Dummheit/das war sehr freundlich; **that was a mean ~ to do to your brother** das war sehr gemein deinem Bruder gegenüber; **it was the right ~ to do** es war das einzig Richtige; **she is expecting to do great ~s** sie hat große Dinge vor; **the only ~ now is to shout for help** es bleibt uns jetzt nichts anderes mehr übrig, als um Hilfe zu rufen; **we can't do a ~ about it** wir können nichts dagegen tun; **do ~s to sb./sth.** *(fig. coll.)* auf jmdn./etw. eine enorme Wirkung haben *(ugs.)*; **she does ~s to me** *(fig. coll.)* sie macht mich total an *(ugs.)*; **c)** *(fact)* [Tat]sache, *die;* **a ~ which is well known to everybody** eine allgemein bekannte Tatsache; **it's a strange ~ that ...**: es ist seltsam, daß ...; **for one ~, you don't have enough money[, for another ~ ...]** zunächst einmal hast du nicht genügend Geld [, außerdem ...]; **and another ~, why were you late this morning?** und noch etwas: Warum bist du heute morgen so spät gekommen?; **the best/worst ~ about the situation/her** das Beste/Schlimmste an der Situation/an ihr; **know/learn a ~ or two about sth./sb.** sich mit etw./jmdm. auskennen/einiges über etw. *(Akk.)* lernen/über jmdn. erfahren; **I'll teach him a ~ or two!** dem werde ich's [mal] zeigen!; **the [only] ~ is that ...**: die Sache ist [nur] die, daß ...; *see also* **another 1a, d, 2c; d)** *(idea)* **say the first ~ that comes into one's head** das sagen, was einem gerade so einfällt; **what a ~ to say!** wie kann man nur so etwas sagen!; **have a ~ about sb./sth.** *(coll.) (be obsessed about)* auf jmdn./etw. abfahren *(salopp)*; *(be prejudiced about)* etwas gegen jmdn./etw. haben; *(be afraid of or repulsed by)* einen Horror vor jmdm./etw. haben *(ugs.)*; **e)** *(task)* **she has a reputation for getting ~s done** sie ist für ihre Tatkraft bekannt; **a big ~ to undertake** ein großes Unterfangen; **f)** *(affair)* Sache, *die;* Angelegenheit, *die;* **make a mess of ~s** alles vermasseln *(salopp)*; **make a [big] ~ of sth.** *(regard as essential)* auf etw. besonderen Wert legen; *(get excited about)* sich über etw. *(Akk.)* aufregen; **you don't have to make such a big ~ of it!** nun mach mal halblang! *(ugs.)*; **it's one ~ after another** es kommt eins zum anderen; **g)** *(circumstance)* **take ~s too seriously** alles zu ernst nehmen; **how are ~s?** wie geht's [dir]?; **it was a terrible ~**: es war furchtbar; **a strange ~ struck me** mir fiel etwas Seltsames auf; **it was a lucky ~ he didn't do that** es war ein Glück, daß er das nicht tat; **as ~s stand [with me]** so wie die Dinge [bei mir] liegen; **one has to accept these ~s** man muß sich eben damit abfinden; **~s don't work out like that** die Realität sieht anders aus; **it's just one of those ~s** *(coll.)* so was kommt schon mal vor *(ugs.)*; *see also* **close 1g; good 1b; h)** *(individual, creature)* Ding, *das;* **she is in hospital, poor ~**: sie ist im Krankenhaus, das arme Ding; **you spiteful ~!** du [gemeines] Biest!; **she's a kind old ~**: sie ist sehr liebenswürdig *od.* *(ugs.)* furchtbar nett; *see also* **old 1c, d; i)** *in pl. (personal belongings, outer clothing)* Sachen; **put one's ~s on** sich *(Dat.)* etwas überziehen; **wash up the dinner ~s** das Geschirr vom Abendessen abwaschen; **j)** *in pl. (matters)* **an expert/authority on ~s historical** ein Fachmann/eine Autorität in geschichtlichen Fragen; **as regards ~s financial I haven't a clue** von finanziellen Dingen habe ich keine Ahnung; **~s feminine** Frauenangelegenheiten; **and ~s** *(coll.)* und so *(ugs.)*; **k)** *(product of work)* Sache, *die;* **the latest ~ in hats** der letzte Schrei in der Hutmode; **a little ~ of mine** etwas von mir; **l)** *(special interest)* **what's your ~?** was machst du gerne?; **do one's own ~** *(coll.)* sich selbst verwirklichen; **we each do our own ~ on holiday** im Urlaub macht jeder von uns, was er will; **m)** *(coll.: sth. remarkable)* **now 'there's a ~!** das ist ja ein Ding! *(ugs.)*; **n)** *in pl. (Law)* Sachen; **~s real** unbewegliche Sachen; Immobilien; **~s personal** bewegliche Sachen; Mobilien *(fachspr.)*; **o) the ~** *(what is proper or needed or important)* das Richtige; **blue jeans are the ~ among teenagers** Bluejeans sind der Hit *(ugs.)* unter den Teenagern; **telling jokes is not the ~ for an occasion such as this one** es ist unpassend, bei einer Gelegenheit wie dieser Witze zu erzählen; **the ~ is to get orders** es geht vor allem darum, Aufträge zu bekommen; **the ~ about him is his complete integrity** sein wesentlicher Vorzug ist seine vollkommene Integrität; **but the ~ is, will she come in fact?** aber die Frage ist, wird sie auch tatsächlich kommen?; **p)** *(sl.: penis)* **his ~**: sein Ding *(ugs.)*. *See also* **first 1, 2a; good 1d; ¹last 1; ¹see 1a; sure 3**

thingamy ['θɪŋəmɪ], **thingumabob** ['θɪŋəməbɒb], **thingumajig** ['θɪŋəmədʒɪg], **thingumbob** ['θɪŋəmbɒb], **thingummy** ['θɪŋəmɪ], **thingy** ['θɪŋɪ] *ns. (coll.)* Dings, *der/die/das (salopp)*; Dingsbums, *der/die/das (ugs.)*; **you know, ~, ...** *(person)* du weißt schon, der/die Dingsda, ...; *(object)* du weißt schon, das Dingsda, ...

think [θɪŋk] **1.** *v.t.,* **thought** [θɔ:t] **a)** *(consider)* meinen; **we ~ [that] he will come** wir denken *od.* glauben, daß er kommt; **we do not ~ it probable** wir halten es nicht für wahrscheinlich; **I ~ it a shame that ...**: ich finde, es ist eine Schande, daß ...; **he ~s himself very fine** er meint, er sei etwas Besonderes; **it is not thought proper** es gilt als unschicklich; **he is thought to be a fraud** man hält ihn für einen Betrüger; **what do you ~?** was meinst du?; **what do you ~ of** *or* **about him/it?** was hältst du von ihm/davon?; **I thought to myself ...**: ich dachte mir [im stillen]; **that's what 'they ~!** das meinen die!; **..., don't you ~?** ..., findest *od.* meinst du nicht auch?; **where do you ~ you are?** was glaubst du eigentlich, wo du bist?; **who does he/she ~ he/she is?** für wen *od.* wofür hält er/sie sich eigentlich?; **you** *or* **one** *or* **anyone would ~ that ...**: man sollte [doch] eigentlich annehmen, daß ...; **I ~ not** ich glaube nicht; **I should '~ so/~ 'not!** *(indignant)* das will ich meinen/das will ich nicht hoffen; **I thought as much** *or* **so** das habe ich mir schon gedacht; **I ~ so** ich glaube schon; **do you really ~ so?** findest du wirklich? **I wouldn't ~ so** das glaube ich kaum; **yes, I ~ so too** ja, das finde ich auch *(ugs.)*; **I should ~ not!** *(no!)* auf keinen Fall; **you are a model of tact, I 'don't ~!** *(coll. iron.)* du bist mir vielleicht ein Ausbund von Taktgefühl! *(iron.)*; **that'll be great fun, I 'don't ~** *(coll. iron.)* das kann ja lustig werden *(ugs. iron.)*; **I'll have made my fortune by then, I 'don't ~** *(coll. iron.)* na klar, bis dahin habe ich mein Glück gemacht *(iron.)*; **to ~ [that] he should treat me like this!** man sollte es nicht für möglich halten, daß er mich so behandelt!; **this animal was thought to be extinct** dieses Tier galt als ausgestorben; **I wouldn't have thought it possible** ich hätte das nicht für möglich gehalten; **b)** *(coll.: remember)* **~ to do sth.** daran denken, etw. zu tun; **c)** *(intend)* **he ~s to deceive us** er will uns täuschen; **we thought to return early** wir hatten vor *od.* gedachten, früh zurückzukehren; **that's what 'they ~!** das meinen die [vielleicht]!; **d)** *(imagine)* sich *(Dat.)* vorstellen. **2.** *v. i.*, **thought a)** [nach]denken; **I ~, therefore I am** ich denke, also bin ich; **we want to make the students ~:** wir möchten die Studenten zum Denken bringen; **animals cannot ~:** Tiere können nicht denken; **I need time to ~:** ich muß es mir erst überlegen; **ability to ~:** Denkfähigkeit, *die;* **I've been ~ing** ich habe nachgedacht; **~ in German** *etc.* deutsch *usw.* denken; **it makes you ~:** es macht *od.* stimmt einen nachdenklich; **just ~!** stell dir das mal vor!; **~ for oneself** sich *(Dat.)* seine eigene Meinung bilden; **~ [to oneself] ...:** sich *(Dat.)* im stillen denken ...; bei sich denken ...; **let me ~:** laß [mich] mal nachdenken *od.* überlegen; **I would ~ again** ich würde mir das noch mal überlegen; **there's still time to ~ again** du kannst/wir können das noch einmal überdenken; **you'd better ~ again!** da hast du dich aber geschnitten! *(ugs.)*; **~ twice** es sich *(Dat.)* zweimal überlegen; **this made her ~ twice** das gab ihr zu denken; *see also* **big 2; b)** *(have intention)* **I ~ I'll try** ich glaube *od.* denke, ich werde es versuchen; **we ~ we'll enter for the regatta** wir haben vor, an der Regatta teilzunehmen. *See also* **aloud; ²fit 1 c. 3.** *n. (coll.)* **have a [good] ~:** es sich *(Dat.)* gut überlegen; **have a ~ about that!** denk mal drüber nach! *(ugs.)*; **you have [got] another ~ coming!** da irrst du dich aber gewaltig!

~ about *v. t.* **a)** *(consider)* nachdenken über (+ *Akk.*); **what are you ~ing about?** woran *od.* was denkst du [gerade]?; **give sb. something to ~ about** jmdm. etwas geben, worüber er/sie nachdenken kann; *(to worry about)* jmdm. zu denken geben; **it doesn't bear ~ing about** man darf gar nicht daran denken; **b)** *(consider practicability of)* sich *(Dat.)* durch den Kopf gehen lassen; sich *(Dat.)* überlegen; **it's worth ~ing about** es ist überlegenswert

~ a'head *v. i.* vorausdenken

~ 'back to *v. t.* sich zurückerinnern an (+ *Akk.*); **I thought back to when it had first begun** ich erinnerte mich daran, wie es anfing

~ of *v. t.* **a)** *(consider)* denken an (+ *Akk.*); **I have many things to ~ of** ich muß an so vieles denken; **... but I can't ~ of everything at once!** ... aber ich habe schließlich auch nur einen Kopf!; **he ~s of everything** er denkt einfach an alles; **he never ~s of anyone but himself** er denkt immer nur an sich; **[just] ~ or to ~ of it!** man stelle sich *(Dat.)* *od.* stell dir das bloß vor!; **[now I] come to ~ of it, ...:** wenn ich es mir recht überlege, ...; **b)** *(be aware of in the mind)* denken an (+ *Akk.*); **we ~ of you a lot** wir denken oft an dich; **c)** *(consider the possibility of)* denken an (+ *Akk.*); **we must be ~ing of going home soon** wir müssen bald ans Nachhausegehen denken; **be ~ing of getting a new car** mit dem Gedanken spielen, sich *(Dat.)* ein neues Auto anzuschaffen; **be ~ing of resigning** sich mit dem Gedanken tragen, zurückzutreten; **not for a minute would she ~ of helping anybody else** ihr würde es nicht im Traum einfallen, anderen zu helfen; **I couldn't ~ of such a thing** *or* **of doing that** das würde mir nicht im Traum einfallen; **I don't know what she was ~ing of!** ich weiß nicht, was sie sich dabei gedacht hat!; **d)** *(choose from what one knows)* **I want you to ~ of a word beginning with B** überlege dir ein Wort, das mit B beginnt; **~ of a number, double it and ...:** denk dir eine Zahl, verdopple sie und ...; **e)** *(have as idea)* **we'll ~ of something** wir werden uns etwas einfallen lassen; **can you ~ of anyone who ...?** fällt dir jemand ein, der ...?; **we're still trying to ~ of a suitable title for the book** wir suchen noch immer einen passenden Titel für das Buch; **he's never yet thought of showing gratitude** bis jetzt ist es ihm noch nie eingefallen, sich dankbar zu zeigen; **I would have telephoned if I had thought of it** ich hätte angerufen, wenn ich daran gedacht hätte; **what 'will they ~ of next?** was werden sie sich *(Dat.)* wohl [sonst] noch alles einfallen lassen?; **f)** *(remember)* sich erinnern an (+ *Akk.*); **I just can't ~ of her name** ich komme einfach nicht auf ihren Namen; **g) ~ little/nothing of sb./sth.** *(consider contemptible)* wenig/nichts von jmdm./etw. halten; **~ little/nothing of doing sth.** *(consider insignificant)* wenig/nichts dabei finden, etw. zu tun; **~ much** *or* **a lot** *or* **well** *or* **highly of sb./sth.** viel von jmdm./etw. halten; **not ~ much of sb./sth.** nicht viel von jmdm./etw. halten. *See also* **better 3 a**

~ 'out *v. t.* **a)** *(consider carefully)* durchdenken ⟨*Plan, Idee*⟩; **~ out what the long-term solution may be** sich *(Dat.)* darüber Gedanken machen, wie eine langfristige Lösung aussehen könnte; **b)** *(devise)* sich *(Dat.)* ausdenken ⟨*Plan, Verfahren*⟩; **the plan had been thought out in a hurry** der Plan entstand unter Zeitdruck

~ 'over *v. t.* sich *(Dat.)* überlegen; überdenken; **~ things over** die Lage überdenken; **I will ~ it over** ich lasse es mir durch den Kopf gehen

~ 'through *v. t.* [gründlich] durchdenken ⟨*Problem, Angelegenheit*⟩

~ 'up *v. t. (coll.)* sich *(Dat.)* ausdenken ⟨*Plan*⟩; **they thought up ideas of their own** sie entwickelten ihre eigenen Ideen

thinkable ['θɪŋkəbl] *adj.* **a)** *(capable of being thought about)* denkbar; **b)** *(conceivably possible)* vorstellbar

thinker ['θɪŋkə(r)] *n.* Denker, *der*/Denkerin, *die*

thinking ['θɪŋkɪŋ] **1.** *n.* **in modern ~ ...:** nach heutiger Auffassung ...; **what is your ~ on this question?** wie ist deine Meinung zu dieser Frage?; **to my [way of] ~:** meiner Meinung nach. **2.** *attrib. adj.* [vernünftig] denkend

'thinking-cap *n.* **put on one's ~:** scharf nachdenken; seinen Geist anstrengen

think: ~-piece *n.* Kommentar, *der;* **~-tank** *n.* **a)** *(organization)* Beraterstab, *der;* **b)** *(Amer. sl.: brain)* [Ge]hirnkasten, *der (salopp scherzh.)*

'thin-lipped *adj.* dünnlippig ⟨*Mund, Person*⟩

thinly ['θɪnlɪ] *adv.* **a)** dünn; **b)** *(sparsely)* spärlich ⟨*bevölkert, bewaldet*⟩; dünn ⟨*besiedelt*⟩; schwach ⟨*besucht*⟩; **c)** *(inadequately)* leicht ⟨*bekleidet*⟩; *(fig.)* dürftig ⟨*verschleiert, verkleidet*⟩

thinner ['θɪnə(r)] **1.** *adj., adv. compar. of* **thin 1, 2. 2.** *n.* **~[s]** Verdünner, *der;* Verdünnungsmittel, *das*

thinness ['θɪnnɪs] *n., no pl.* **a)** *(lack of depth etc.)* Dünne, *die;* geringe Dicke; **b)** *(slimness)* Magerkeit, *die;* **c)** *(sparseness)* Spärlichkeit, *die;* **d)** *(slightness of consistency)* Dünnflüssigkeit, *die;* **e)** *(lack of substance or strength)* Dürftigkeit, *die;* **the ~ of her voice** ihre dünne Stimme; **f)** *(fig.: inadequacy)* Dürftigkeit, *die*

'thin-skinned *adj. (fig.)* empfindlich; dünnhäutig *(geh.)*

third [θɜ:d] **1.** *adj.* dritt...; **the ~ finger** der Ringfinger; **~ largest/highest** *etc.* drittgrößt.../-höchst... *usw.*; **come in/be ~:** dritter/dritte sein/als dritter/dritte ankommen; **every ~ week** jede dritte Woche; **a ~ part** *or* **share** ein Drittel. **2.** *n.* **a)** *(in sequence)* dritte, *der/die/das;* *(in rank)* Dritte, *der/die/das;* *(fraction)* Drittel, *das;* **be the ~ to arrive** als dritter/dritte ankommen; **b)** *(~ form)* dritte [Schul]klasse; Dritte, *die (Schuljargon)*; **c)** *(Motor Veh.)* dritter Gang; **in ~:** im dritten [Gang]; **change into ~:** in den dritten [Gang] schalten; **d)** *(Brit. Univ.)* Drei, *die;* **he has a ~ [in History]** er hat eine Drei [in Geschichte]; **get** *or* **take** *or* **be awarded a ~ in one's finals** sein Examen mit [der Note] Drei bestehen; **e)** *(Mus.)* Terz, *die;* **f)** *(day)* **the ~ of May** der dritte Mai; **the ~ [of the month]** der Dritte [des Monats]. *See also* **eighth 2**

third: ~-best 1. ['--] *adj.* drittbest...; **2.** [-'-] *n., no pl.* Drittbeste, *der/die/das;* **~ 'class** *n.* **a)** *(set ranking after second class)* dritte Kategorie; **b)** *(Transport)* dritte Klasse; **c)** *(Brit. Univ.) see* **third 2 d; ~-class 1.** ['--] *adj.* **a)** drittklassig; **he got a ~-class degree** er hat einen Abschluß mit der Note Drei; **b)** Dritte[r]-Klasse-⟨*Wagen, Reisender, Fahrkarte*⟩; ⟨*Wagen, Fahrkarte*⟩ dritter Klasse; ⟨*Reisender*⟩ der dritten Klasse; **2.** [-'-] *adv.* dritter Klasse ⟨*reisen*⟩; **~ de'gree** *see* **degree i; ~ 'force** *n.* dritte Kraft; **~ form** *see* **form 1 d; ~ 'gear** *n., no pl. (Motor Veh.)* dritter Gang; *see also* **gear 1 a**

thirdly ['θɜ:dlɪ] *adv.* drittens

third: ~ 'man *n. (Cricket)* [weit zurückstehender] Eckmann; **~ 'party** *n.* Dritte, *der/die;* dritte Person; *attrib.* **~-party insurance** Haftpflichtversicherung, *die;* **be covered by ~-party insurance** haftpflichtversichert sein; **take out ~-party insurance** eine Haftpflichtversicherung abschließen; **~ 'person** *n.* **a)** *see* **~ party; b)** *see* **person d; ~ 'rail** *n. (Railw.)* Stromschiene, *die;* **~-rate** *adj.* drittklassig; **~ 'reading** *see* **reading g; T~ 'World** *n.* dritte Welt; **countries of the T~ World, T~ World countries** Länder der dritten Welt

thirst [θɜ:st] **1.** *n.* Durst, *der;* **die of ~:** verdursten; *(fig.: be very thirsty)* vor Durst sterben *(ugs.)*; **~ for knowledge** Wissensdurst, *der;* **~ for revenge/after fame** Rachedurst, *der*/Ruhmsucht, *die;* **~ for news** sehnsüchtiges Warten auf Nachricht. **2.** *v. i.* **~ for revenge/knowledge** nach Rache/Wissen dürsten *(geh.)*

thirstily ['θɜ:stɪlɪ] *adv.* durstig

'thirst-quencher *n.* Durstlöscher, *der*

thirsty ['θɜ:stɪ] *adj.* **a)** durstig; **be ~:** Durst haben; **sb. is ~ for sth.** *(fig.)* jmd. *od.* jmdn. dürstet nach etw. *(dichter.)*; **~ after gain/for knowledge/revenge** *(fig.)* gewinnsüchtig/wißbegierig/rachedurstig *(geh.)*; **b)** *(coll.: causing thirst)* durstig machend; **this is ~ work** diese Arbeit macht durstig

thirteen [θɜ:'ti:n] **1.** *adj.* dreizehn; *see also* **eight 1. 2.** *n.* Dreizehn, *die; see also* **eight 2 a, d; eighteen 2**

thirteenth [θɜ:'ti:nθ] **1.** *adj.* dreizehnt...; *see also* **eighth 1. 2.** *n.* **a)** *(fraction)* Dreizehntel, *das;* **b) Friday the ~:** Freitag, der Dreizehnte. *See also* **eighth 2**

thirtieth ['θɜ:tɪɪθ] **1.** *adj.* dreißigst...; *see also* **eighth 1. 2.** *n. (fraction)* Dreißigstel, *das; see also* **eighth 2**

thirty ['θɜ:tɪ] **1.** *adj.* dreißig; **one-and-~** *(arch.) see* **thirty-one 1;** *see also* **eight 1. 2.** *n.* Dreißig, *die;* **one-and-~** *(arch.) see* **thirty-one 2;** *see also* **eight 2 a; eighty 2**

thirty: **~-'first** *etc. adj.* einunddreißigst... *usw.; see also* **eighth 1**; **~-'one** *etc.* **1.** *adj.* einunddreißig *usw.; see also* **eight 1**; **2.** *n.* Einunddreißig *usw., die; see also* **eight 2 a**; **~-'second-note** *n. (Amer. Mus.)* Zweiunddreißigstel[note], *die*

this [ðɪs] **1.** *adj., pl.* **these** [ði:z] **a)** dieser/diese/dieses; *(with less emphasis)* der/die/das; **at ~ time** zu dieser Zeit; **before ~ time** vorher; zuvor; **these days** heut[zutag]e; **I'll say ~ much/I can tell you ~ much ...:** soviel kann ich sagen/soviel kann ich dir verraten ...; **b)** *(that is the present)* dieser/diese/dieses; **all ~ week** die[se] ganze Woche; **by ~ time** inzwischen; mittlerweile; **c)** *(of today)* **~ morning/evening** *etc.* heute morgen/abend *usw.*; **where are you going to eat ~ lunch-time?** wo wirst du heute zu Mittag essen?; **d)** *(just past)* **these last three weeks** die letzten drei Wochen; **~ day has been a really hard one** der heutige Tag war wirklich anstrengend; **e)** *(to come)* **~ Monday** nächsten Montag; **it will not be wanted these eight months** es wird in den nächsten acht Monaten nicht gebraucht werden; **f)** *(coll.: previously unspecified)* **they dug ~ great big trench** sie hoben einen riesigen Graben aus; **I was in the pub when ~ fellow came up to me** ich war in der Kneipe, als [so] einer *od.* so'n Typ auf mich zukam *(ugs.)*; **g) he's tried ~ drink and that [drink]** *or* **~ and that drink** er hat schon so manchen Drink *od.* schon allerlei Drinks probiert; **I went to ~ doctor and that** ich ging von einem Arzt zum anderen. *See also* **that 1 c**; **world b. 2.** *pron., pl.* **these a) what's ~?** was ist [denn] das?; **what is all ~?:** was soll das alles?; **what flower is ~?:** was ist das für eine Blume?; **fold it like ~!** falte es so!; **I knew all ~ before** ich wußte dies *od.* das alles schon vorher; **~ is not fair!** das ist nicht fair!; **what's all ~ about Jan and Angela separating?** stimmt das, daß Jan und Angela sich trennen wollen?; **what's ~ about holidays?** was war da mit Ferien?; **John, ~ is Mary** John, das ist Mary; *see also* **¹it j**; **b)** *(the present)* **before ~:** bis jetzt; **c)** *(Brit. Teleph.: person speaking)* **~ is Andy [speaking]** hier [spricht *od.* ist] Andy; **d)** *(Amer. Teleph.: person spoken to)* **who did you say ~ was?** wer ist am Apparat?; mit wem spreche ich, bitte?; **e) ~ and that** dies und das; **~, that, and the other** alles mögliche. **3.** *adv. (coll.)* so; **~ much** so viel

thistle ['θɪsl] *n.* Distel, *die*

'thistledown *n.* Distelwolle, *die*; **[as] light as ~:** leicht wie eine Feder

thither ['ðɪðə(r)] *adv. (arch.)* dorthin; *see also* **hither**

tho' *see* **though**

thong [θɒŋ] *n.* [Leder]riemen, *der*

thoracic [θɔ:'ræsɪk] *adj. (Anat.)* Thorax-; Brust〈*höhle, -segment, -wirbel*〉

thorax ['θɔ:ræks] *n., pl.* **thoraces** ['θɔ:rəsi:z] *or* **~es** *(Anat., Zool.)* Thorax, *der*

thorn [θɔ:n] *n.* **a)** *(part of plant)* Dorn, *der*; **be on ~s** *(fig.)* wie auf Nesseln sitzen *(ugs.)*; **b)** *(plant)* Dornenstrauch, *der*; **c) a ~ in the flesh** *or* **side/in sb.'s flesh** *or* **side** ein Pfahl im Fleische/im Fleische für jmdn.

thorn-bush *n.* Dornbusch, *der*

thornless ['θɔ:nlɪs] *adj.* dornenlos

thorny ['θɔ:nɪ] *adj.* **a)** dornig; **b)** *(fig.: difficult)* heikel; dornenreich 〈*Weg*〉

thorough ['θʌrə] *adj.* **a)** gründlich; durchgreifend 〈*Reform*〉; genau 〈*Beschreibung, Anweisung*〉; **b)** *(downright)* ausgemacht 〈*Halunke, Nervensäge*〉; tief 〈*Verachtung*〉. *See also* **³bass 2 c**

thorough: **~bred 1.** *adj.* **a)** reinrassig 〈*Tier*〉; vollblütig 〈*Pferd*〉; **b)** *(fig.)* rassig 〈*Sportwagen*〉; **2.** *n.* **a)** reinrassiges Tier; *(horse)* Rassepferd, *das; (Horse Racing)* Vollblut, *das*; **b)** *(fig.: car)* Klassewagen, *der (ugs.)*; **~fare** *n.* Durchfahrtsstraße, *die*; **'no ~fare'** „Durchfahrt verboten"; *(on foot)* „kein Durchgang"; **~going** *adj.* **a)** *see* **thorough a**; **b)** *(extreme)* radikal 〈*Konservative, Sozialist*〉; ausgemacht 〈*Halunke*〉

thoroughly ['θʌrəlɪ] *adv.* gründlich 〈*untersuchen, prüfen*〉; gehörig 〈*müde, erschöpft*〉; so richtig 〈*genießen*〉; ausgesprochen 〈*langweilig*〉; zutiefst 〈*beschämt*〉; *(completely)* völlig 〈*durchnäßt, verzogen*〉; total 〈*verdorben, verwöhnt*〉; **be ~ fed up with sth.** *(sl.)* von etw. die Nase gestrichen voll haben *(ugs.)*; **be ~ delighted with sth.** sich außerordentlich über etw. *(Akk.)* freuen

thoroughness ['θʌrənɪs] *n., no pl.* Gründlichkeit, *die*

those *see* **that 1, 2**

¹thou [ðaʊ] *pron. (arch./poet./dial.)* du; *(Relig.: God)* Du

²thou [θaʊ] *n., pl. same (coll.)* **a)** *see* **thousand 2 a**; **b)** *(Mech. Engin.)* tausendstel Inch

though [ðəʊ] **1.** *(conj.)* **a)** *(despite the fact that)* obwohl; **late ~ it was** obwohl es so spät war; **the car, ~ powerful, is also economical** der Wagen ist zwar stark, aber [zugleich] auch wirtschaftlich; **b)** *(but nevertheless)* aber; **a slow ~ certain method** eine langsame, aber *od.* wenn auch sichere Methode; **c)** *(even if)* **[even] ~:** auch wenn; **as ~ = as if** *see* **if 1 a**; **d)** *(and yet)* **~ you never know** obwohl man nie weiß; **she read on, ~ not to the very end** sie las weiter, wenn auch nicht bis ganz zum Schluß. **2.** *adv. (coll.)* trotzdem; **I like him ~:** ich mag ihn aber [trotzdem]; **you don't know him, ~:** aber du kennst ihn nicht

thought [θɔ:t] **1.** *see* **think 1, 2. 2.** *n.* **a)** *no pl.* Denken, *das*; **[lost] in ~:** in Gedanken [verloren *od.* versunken]; **quick as ~:** blitzschnell; **Greek/Western ~:** das Denken der Griechen/das westliche Denken; **b)** *no pl., no art. (reflection)* Überlegung, *die*; Nachdenken, *das*; **act without ~:** gedankenlos handeln; **after serious ~:** nach reiflicher Überlegung; **c)** *(consideration)* Rücksicht, *die* **(for** auf + *Akk.*); **he has no ~/is full of ~ for others** er nimmt keine Rücksicht auf andere/ist sehr rücksichtsvoll anderen gegenüber; **give [plenty of] ~ to sth., give sth. [plenty of] ~:** [reiflich] über etw. *(Akk.)* nachdenken; **give no ~ to sth.** an etw. *(Akk.)* nicht denken; **he never gave the matter a moment's ~:** er dachte keinen Augenblick daran; **take ~:** überlegen; **she criticized his lack of ~ for his parents** sie kritisierte, daß er zu wenig an seine Eltern dachte; **built with some ~ for the crew** mit Blick auf die Mannschaft gebaut; **with no ~ for her own safety** ohne an ihre eigene Sicherheit zu denken; **d)** *(idea, conception)* Gedanke, *der*; **I've just had a ~!** mir ist gerade ein [guter] Gedanke gekommen; **it's the ~ that counts** der gute Wille zählt; **his one ~ is how to get rich** er hat nichts anderes im Sinn, als reich zu werden; **he hasn't a ~ in his head** er ist ein Schussel *(ugs.)*; **at the [very] ~ of sth./of doing sth./that ...:** beim [bloßen] Gedanken an etw. *(Akk.)*/daran, etw. zu tun/, daß ...; **that's** *or* **there's a ~!** das ist aber eine [gute] Idee!; **don't give it another ~:** mach dir darüber keine Gedanken; **she is [constantly] in his ~s** er muß ständig an sie denken; *see also* **penny c**; **e)** *in pl. (opinion)* Gedanken; **I'll tell you my ~s on the matter** ich sage dir, wie ich darüber denke; **f)** *(intention)* **have no ~ of doing sth.** überhaupt nicht daran denken, etw. zu tun; **give up all ~[s] of sth./doing sth.** sich *(Dat.)* etw. aus dem Kopf schlagen/es sich *(Dat.)* aus dem Kopf schlagen, etw. zu tun; **have some ~s of doing sth.** sich mit dem Gedanken tragen *od.* mit dem Gedanken spielen, etw. zu tun; **nothing was further from my ~s** nicht im Traum hätte ich daran gedacht; **g)** *(somewhat)* **a ~ arrogant/more considerate** ein wenig arrogant/rücksichtsvoller

thoughtful ['θɔ:tfl] *adj.* **a)** *(meditative)* nachdenklich; **b)** *(considerate)* rücksichtsvoll; *(helpful)* aufmerksam; **c)** *(showing original thought)* gedankenreich; *(well thought out)* [gut] durchdacht; wohlüberlegt 〈*Bemerkung*〉

thoughtfully ['θɔ:tfəlɪ] *adv.* **a)** *(meditatively)* nachdenklich; **b)** *(considerately)* rücksichtsvollerweise; **she ~ provided blankets** sie war so umsichtig, Decken bereitzustellen; **c)** *(in a well-thought-out manner)* **a ~ written article** ein gut durchdachter Artikel

thoughtfulness ['θɔ:tflnɪs] *n., no pl. see* **thoughtful: a)** Nachdenklichkeit, *die*; **b)** Rücksicht, *die* **(for** auf + *Akk.*); **c)** Gedankenreichtum, *der*; Wohlüberlegtheit, *die*

thoughtless ['θɔ:tlɪs] *adj.* **a)** gedankenlos; **~ of the danger, ...:** ohne an die Gefahr zu denken ...; **b)** *(inconsiderate)* rücksichtslos; **c)** *(due to lack of thought)* leichtfertig 〈*Fehler*〉

thoughtlessly ['θɔ:tlɪslɪ] *adv.* gedankenlos; **he ~ gave his son a box of matches** in seiner Gedankenlosigkeit gab er seinem Sohn eine Schachtel Streichhölzer

thoughtlessness ['θɔ:tlɪsnɪs] *n., no pl.* **a)** Gedankenlosigkeit, *die*; **b)** *(lack of consideration)* Rücksichtslosigkeit, *die*

thought: **~ process** *n.* Denkprozeß, *der*; **~-provoking** *adj.* nachdenklich stimmend; **be ~-provoking** nachdenklich stimmen; **~-reader** *n.* Gedankenleser, *der*/-leserin, *die*; **you must be/I'm not a ~-reader** du kannst wohl Gedanken lesen/ich bin doch kein Hellseher; **~-reading** *n.* Gedankenlesen, *das*; **~-transference** *n.* Gedankenübertragung, *die*

thousand ['θaʊznd] **1.** *adj.* **a)** tausend; **a** *or* **one ~:** eintausend; **two/several ~:** zweitausend/mehrere tausend; **one and a half ~:** [ein]tausendfünfhundert; **a** *or* **one ~ and one** [ein]tausend[und]eins; **a** *or* **one ~ and one people** [ein]tausendundeine Person; **a T~ and one Nights** Tausendundeine Nacht; **b) a ~ [and one]** *(fig.: innumerable)* tausend *(ugs.)*; **a ~ thanks** tausend Dank; **a ~ apologies** ich bitte tausendmal um Entschuldigung. *See also* **pity 1 b**; **time 1 f. 2.** *n.* **a)** *(number)* tausend; **a** *or* **one/two ~:** ein-/zweitausend; **a ~ and one** [ein]tausend[und]eins; **a ~-to-one chance** eine Chance von tausend zu eins; **she/this chance is one in a ~** *(fig.)* sie ist einmalig/das ist eine einmalige Chance; **b)** *(symbol)* Tausend, *die*; *(in adding numbers by columns)* Tausender, *der (Math.)*; *(set or group)* Tausend, *das*; **c)** *(indefinite amount)* **~s** Tausende; **they came by the ~** *or* **in their ~s** sie kamen zu Tausenden; **~s and ~s of people** tausend und aber tausend Menschen

'thousandfold 1. *adv.* tausendfach. **2.** *adj.* tausendfach. **3.** *n.* Tausendfache, *das*; *see also* **hundredfold 3**

thousandth ['θaʊzndθ] **1.** *adj.* tausendst...; **a ~ part** ein Tausendstel; *see also* **eighth 1. 2.** *n.* **a)** *(fraction)* Tausendstel, *das*; **b)** *(in sequence)* tausendste, *der/die/das*; *(in rank)* Tausendste, *der/die/das*

thraldom ['θrɔ:ldəm] *n., no pl. (literary)* Sklaverei, *die*

thrall [θrɔ:l] *n. (literary)* **a)** *(slave, lit. or fig.)* Sklave, *der*/Sklavin, *die* **(to, of** *Gen.*); *(serf)* Hörige, *der/die*; **b) have** *or* **hold sb. in ~** *(fig.)* jmdn. in seinen Bann geschlagen haben

thralldom *(Amer.) see* **thraldom**

thrash [θræʃ] **1.** *v. t.* **a)** *(beat)* [ver]prügeln; **~ the life out of sb.** jmdm. die Seele aus dem Leib prügeln *(ugs.)*; **b)** *(defeat)* vernichtend schlagen; **c)** *see* **thresh. 2.** *v. i.* **a) ~ at sth.** auf etw. *(Akk.)* einschlagen; **b)** *(Naut.)* **~ to windward** luvwärts gegen die See knüppeln. **3.** *n. (sl.: party)* große Fete

~ a'bout, ~ a'round *v. i.* sich hin- und herwerfen; ‹*Fisch:*› zappeln
~ 'out *v. t.* ausdiskutieren ‹*Problem, Frage*›; ausarbeiten ‹*Plan*›; ~ **out the whole business** Klarheit in die ganze Sache bringen

thrashing ['θræʃɪŋ] *n.* **a)** *(beating)* Prügel *Pl.;* **give sb. a ~:** jmdm. eine Tracht Prügel verpassen *(ugs.);* **get a ~:** Prügel bekommen; **b)** *(defeat)* Schlappe, *die;* **give sb. a ~:** jmdm. vernichtend schlagen

thread [θred] **1.** *n.* **a)** Faden, *der;* **sb. has not a dry ~ on him** jmd. hat keinen trockenen Faden [mehr] am Leib *(ugs.);* **b)** *(fig.)* **hang by a ~** *(be in a precarious state)* an einem [dünnen *od.* seidenen] Faden hängen; *(depend on sth. still in doubt)* auf Messers Schneide stehen; **lose the ~:** den Faden verlieren; **take** *or* **pick up the ~ of the conversation** den Gesprächsfaden wieder aufnehmen; **gather up the ~s of sth.** etw. erläuternd zusammenfassen; **c)** *(sth. very thin)* **a ~ of light/water** ein feiner Lichtstrahl/ein Rinnsal *(geh.);* **d)** *(Mech. Engin.: of screw)* Gewinde, *das.* **2.** *v. t.* **a)** *(pass ~ through)* einfädeln; auffädeln ‹*Perlen*›; *(make chain of)* aufreihen; **b)** *(place in position)* einfädeln ‹*Film, Tonband*› **(through** in + *Akk.*); **c) ~ one's way through sth.** *(lit. or fig.)* sich durch etw. schlängeln; **d)** *(Mech. Engin.)* mit einem Gewinde versehen

thread: ~bare *adj.* **a)** *(worn)* abgenutzt; abgetragen ‹*Kleidung*›; **b)** *(fig.)* abgedroschen ‹*Argument*› *(ugs.);* **~worm** *n.* *(Zool., Med.)* Fadenwurm, *der*

threat [θret] *n.* **a)** Drohung, *die;* **make a ~ against sb.** jmdm. drohen; **under ~ of** unter Androhung von; **sb./sth. is under ~ of sth.** jmdm./einer Sache droht etw.; **issue ~s to sb.'s life** Morddrohungen gegen jmdn. richten; **b)** *(indication of sth. unpleasant)* **at the slightest ~ of sth.** wenn etw. auch nur ganz entfernt droht; **there is a ~ of rain** es kann Regen geben; **c)** *(danger)* Bedrohung, *die* **(to** für); **a ~ to our liberty** eine Bedrohung unserer Freiheit

threaten ['θretn] *v. t.* **a)** *(use threats towards)* bedrohen; **~ sb. with prosecution/a beating** jmdm. Verfolgung/Schläge androhen; **I am ~ed with a visit from my mother** *(joc.)* mir droht ein Besuch meiner Mutter *(scherzh.);* **b)** *(announce one's intention)* **~ to do sth.** damit drohen, etw. zu tun; **the fire ~ed to engulf the whole village** *(fig.)* das Feuer drohte das ganze Dorf einzuschließen; **~ to commit suicide/to resign** mit Selbstmord/dem Rücktritt drohen; **c)** drohen mit ‹*Gewalt, Repressalien, Rache usw.*›; **the sky ~s rain** am Himmel hängen drohende Regenwolken; **d)** *abs.* **when danger ~s** wenn [eine] Gefahr droht

threatening ['θretnɪŋ] *adj.* drohend; bedrohlich ‹*Gegenwart, Verhalten, Situation*›; **~ letter** Drohbrief, *der*

threateningly ['θretnɪŋlɪ] *adv.* drohend; **~ close** bedrohlich nahe

three [θri:] **1.** *adj.* drei; **~ parts wine and one part ...:** drei Teile Wein und ein Teil ...; **be ~ parts finished** dreiviertel fertig sein; *see also* **cheer 1 a; eight 1; R b. 2.** *n.* **a)** *(number, symbol)* Drei, *die;* **b)** *(set of ~ people)* Dreiergruppe, *die;* **the ~ [of them]** die Drei. *See also* **eight 2 a, c, d**

three: ~-cornered ['θri:kɔ:nəd] *adj.* dreieckig; **~-cornered hat** Dreispitz, *der;* **~-cornered contest** Wettkampf mit drei Teilnehmern; **~-di'mensional** *adj.* dreidimensional; **~fold** *adj., adv.* dreifach; *see also* **eightfold; ~-'four time** *n.* *(Mus.)* Dreivierteltakt, *der;* **~-handed** *adj.* *(Cards)* ‹*Bridge usw.*› zu dritt; **~-lane** *adj.* dreispurig; **~-legged** ['θri:legd, 'θri:legɪd] *adj.* dreibeinig; **~-legged race** *n.* *Wettlauf zwischen Paaren, bei denen jeweils das linke Bein des einen Partners mit dem rechten Bein des anderen zusammengebunden ist;* **~-line 'whip** *see* **whip 1 c; ~pence** ['θrepəns, 'θrɪpəns] *n.* *(Brit. Hist.)* drei Pence; **~penny** ['θrepənɪ, 'θrɪpənɪ] *adj.* *(Brit. Hist.)* Drei-Pence-; *see also* **²bit g; ~-phase** *adj.* Dreiphasen-; dreiphasig; **~-phase current** Dreiphasenstrom, *der;* **~-piece** *adj. see* **piece 1 b; ~-pin** *adj. see* **pin 1 c; ~-ply 1.** *adj.* dreilagig; dreifädig ‹*Wolle*›; **2.** *n.* **a)** *(wool)* dreifädige Wolle; **b)** *(wood)* dreischichtiges [Sperr]holz; **~-point** *attrib. adj.* **~-point landing** *(Aeronaut.)* Dreipunktlandung, *die;* **~-point turn** *(Brit. Motor Veh.) Wendemanöver auf engem Raum, bei dem vorwärts, rückwärts und wieder vorwärts gefahren wird;* **~-quarter 1.** *adj.* dreiviertel; **~-quarter portrait** *(down to hips)* Dreiviertelporträt, *das;* *(of face)* Halbprofilporträt, *das;* **~-quarter length** dreiviertellang; **~-quarter back** *see* **2; 2.** *n.* *(Rugby)* Dreiviertel, *der;* **~-quarters 1.** *n.* **a)** drei Viertel **(of** *Gen.*); **~-quarters of an hour** eine Dreiviertelstunde; **b)** *attrib.* Dreiviertel‹*mehrheit usw.*›; **2.** *adv.* dreiviertel ‹*voll*›; zu drei Vierteln ‹*fertig*›; **~score** *adj.* *(arch.)* sechzig; **~score and ten** siebzig

threesome ['θri:səm] *n.* Dreigespann, *das;* Trio, *das;* **go as a ~:** zu dritt gehen

three: ~-way *adj.* Dreiwege-; **~-way adapter** *(Electr.)* Dreifachstecker, *der;* **~-way intersection** Kreuzung, an der sich drei Straßen treffen; **~-way tie** Unentschieden, bei dem drei Spieler/Mannschaften die gleiche Punktzahl *usw.* haben; **~-way profit split** Dreiteilung des Gewinns; **~-way play-off** Stechen *(Sport)* von drei Teilnehmern; **~-'wheeler** *n.* Dreirad, *das (Kfz-W.)*

thresh [θreʃ] *v. t.* *(Agric.)* dreschen

thresher ['θreʃə(r)] *n.* **a)** *(Agric.)* *(person)* Drescher, *der*/Drescherin, *die;* *(machine)* Dreschmaschine, *die;* **b)** *(Zool.: shark)* Fuchshai, *der;* Drescher, *der*

threshing ['θreʃɪŋ]: **~-floor** *n.* *(Agric.)* Tenne, *die;* **~-machine** *n.* *(Agric.)* Dreschmaschine, *die*

threshold ['θreʃəʊld] *n.* **a)** *(lit. or fig.)* Schwelle, *die;* **be on the ~ of sth.** *(fig.)* an der Schwelle einer Sache *(Gen.)* stehen; **pain ~** *(Physiol., Psych.)* Schmerzschwelle, *die;* **b)** *(Phys.)* Schwellenwert, *der*

threw *see* **throw 1**

thrice [θraɪs] *adv.* *(arch./literary)* dreimal

thrift [θrɪft] *n.* **a)** *no pl.* Sparsamkeit, *die;* **b)** *(Bot.)* Grasnelke, *die*

'thrift account *n.* *(Amer.)* Sparkonto, *das*

thriftily ['θrɪftɪlɪ] *adv.* sparsam

thriftiness ['θrɪftɪnɪs] *n., no pl.* Sparsamkeit, *die*

thrifty ['θrɪftɪ] *adj.* sparsam

thrill [θrɪl] **1.** *v. t.* *(excite)* faszinieren; *(delight)* begeistern; **be ~ed by/with sth.** von etw. fasziniert/begeistert sein; **we were ~ed to have your letter** wir haben uns wahnsinnig über deinen Brief gefreut *(ugs.);* *see also* **²bit a. 2.** *v. i.* **~ with** zittern *od.* *(geh.)* beben vor (+ *Dat.*); **~ to** wie elektrisiert sein bei; **~ with horror** vor Entsetzen schaudern; **~ with excitement** ein Prickeln der Erregung verspüren; **~ at the sight of sth./at sb.'s touch** beim Anblick einer Sache *(Gen.)*/bei jmds. Berührung von einem Schauder überlaufen werden. **3.** *n.* **a)** *(wave of emotion)* Erregung, *die;* **a ~ of joy/pleasure** freudige Erregung; **a ~ of excitement/hate/horror** prickelnde Erregung/ein starkes Haßgefühl/ein Schauder *(geh.)* des Entsetzens; **a ~ of anticipation** prickelnde Vorfreude; **b)** *(exciting experience)* aufregendes Erlebnis; *(titillation)* Nervenkitzel, *der (ugs.);* **sb. gets a ~ out of sth.** etw. erregt jmdn.; **cheap ~s** anspruchsloser Nervenkitzel *(ugs.);* **this film will give you the ~ of a lifetime** dieser Film wird das Aufregendste sein, was du je erlebt hast; **~s and spills** Nervenkitzel, *der*

thriller ['θrɪlə(r)] *n.* Thriller, *der*

thrilling ['θrɪlɪŋ] *adj.* aufregend; spannend ‹*Buch, Film, Theaterstück, Geschichte*›; packend ‹*Ereignis*›; mitreißend ‹*Musik*›; prickelnd ‹*Gefühl*›

thrive [θraɪv] *v. i.* **~d** *or* **throve** [θrəʊv], **~d** *or* **thriven** ['θrɪvn] **a)** *(grow vigorously)* wachsen und gedeihen; **~ on good food/sunlight** bei guter Ernährung/Sonnenschein prächtig gedeihen; **b)** *(prosper)* aufblühen **(on** bei); **business is thriving** das Geschäft floriert; **a thriving businessman** ein erfolgreicher Geschäftsmann; **c)** *(grow rich)* reich werden; **~ on other people's misfortune** sich am Unglück der anderen bereichern

thro' *see* **through**

throat [θrəʊt] *n.* **a)** *(outside and inside of neck)* Hals, *der;* *(esp. inside)* Kehle, *die;* **look down sb.'s ~:** jmdm. in den Hals *od.* Rachen schauen; **pour sth. down one's ~:** etw. hinunterschütten; **cancer of the ~:** Kehlkopfkrebs, *der;* **a [sore] ~:** Halsschmerzen; **cut sb.'s ~:** jmdm. die Kehle durchschneiden; **cut one's own ~** *(fig.)* sich *(Dat.)* ins eigene Fleisch schneiden; **cut one another's ~s** *(fig.)* sich *(Dat.)* gegenseitig das Wasser abgraben; **ram** *or* **cram** *or* **shove** *or* **thrust sth. down sb.'s ~** *(fig.)* jmdm. etw. aufzwingen; **b)** *(of bottle, vase)* Hals, *der;* *(of blast-furnace)* Gicht, *die (Hüttenw.)*

-throated [θrəʊtɪd] *adj. in comb.* -halsig ‹*Mensch, Tier*›; **full-~:** aus vollem Halse

throat: ~ lozenge *n.* Halspastille, *die;* **~ microphone** *n.* Kehlkopfmikrophon, *das*

throaty ['θrəʊtɪ] *adj.* **a)** *(produced in throat)* kehlig; **b)** *(hoarse)* heiser

throb [θrɒb] **1.** *v. i.,* **-bb- a)** *(palpitate, pulsate)* pochen; **his fingers were ~bing [with pain]** er hatte einen pochenden Schmerz in den Fingern; **b)** *(vibrate)* ‹*Motor, Artillerie:*› dröhnen; **the walls seemed to ~:** die Wände schienen zu vibrieren. **2.** *n.* **a)** *(palpitation)* Pochen, *das;* **be ~bing with life** voll von pulsierendem Leben sein; **he felt a sudden ~ of pain** ein plötzlicher Schmerz durchfuhr ihn; **b)** *(vibration)* Dröhnen, *das;* *(loud)* Hämmern, *das*

throes [θrəʊz] *n. pl.* Qual, *die;* **~ of childbirth** Geburtswehen *Pl.;* **death-~:** Todesqual[en] *(geh.);* **be in the ~ of sth.** *(fig.)* mitten in etw. *(Dat.)* stecken *(ugs.)*

thrombosis [θrɒm'bəʊsɪs] *n., pl.* **thromboses** [θrɒm'bəʊsi:z] *(Med.)* Thrombose, *die*

throne [θrəʊn] *n.* Thron, *der;* **succeed to the ~:** die Thronfolge antreten; **on the ~** *(coll. joc.)* auf den Thron *od.* Topf *(ugs. scherzh.)*

'throne-room *n.* Thronsaal, *der*

throng [θrɒŋ] **1.** *n.* [Menschen]menge, *die;* **stand in a ~ around sb.** eine [Menschen]traube um jmdn. bilden; **~s of people** Scharen von Menschen; **join the ~** *(joc.)* sich ins Gewühl stürzen. **2.** *v. i.* strömen **(into** in + *Akk.*); *(press)* sich drängen; **~ round the notice-board** sich um das Schwarze Brett drängen. **3.** *v. t.* sich drängen in (+ *Dat.*)

throttle ['θrɒtl] **1.** *n.* *(Mech. Engin.)* **~[-valve]** Drosselklappe, *die;* **~[-pedal]** *(Motor Veh.)* Gas[pedal], *das;* **~[-lever]** Gashebel, *der;* **at full ~** *(Motor Veh.)* mit Vollgas. **2.** *v. t.* erdrosseln; *(fig.)* ersticken

~ **back, ~ down 1.** *v. t.* drosseln ‹*Motor*›. **2.** *v. i.* den Motor drosseln

through [θru:] **1.** *prep.* **a)** durch; *(fig.)* **search/read ~ sth.** etw. durchsuchen/durchlesen; **wait ~ ten long years** zehn lange Jahre hindurch warten; **live ~ sth.** *(survive)* etw. überleben; *(experience)* etw. erleben; **sit ~ a long sermon** eine lange Predigt hindurch still sitzen bleiben; **b)** *(Amer.: up to and including)* bis [einschließlich]; **c)** *(by reason of)* durch; infolge von ‹*Vernachlässigung, Einflüssen*›; **it was all ~ you that we were late** es war nur deine Schuld, daß wir zu spät gekommen sind; **it all came about ~ his not knowing the way** alles kam so, weil er den Weg nicht wußte; **it happened ~ no fault of yours** es geschah nicht durch deine Schuld; **conceal sth. ~ shame** etw. aus Scham verheimlichen. **2.** *adv.* **a) let sb. ~:** jmdn. durchlassen; **book your tickets ~ to Vienna** löst eure Fahrkarten durchgehend bis Wien; **be a Communist/be wet ~ and ~:** durch und durch Kommunist/naß sein; **be ~ with a piece of work/with sb.** mit einer Arbeit fertig/mit jmdm. fertig *(ugs.)* sein; **we are ~!** *(have succeeded/finished)* wir haben es geschafft!; *(with each other)* wir sind miteinander fertig!; **b)** *(Teleph.)* **be ~:** durch sein *(ugs.);* **be ~ to sb.** mit jmdm. verbunden sein. **3.** *adj.* durchgehend ‹*Zug*›; **~ coach** *or* **carriage** Kurswagen, *der* **(for** nach); **~ traffic** Durchgangsverkehr, *der;* **'no ~ road'** „keine Durchfahrt[sstraße]"

through: ~-composed *adj. (Mus.)* durchkomponiert; **~'out 1.** *prep.* **~out the war/period** den ganzen Krieg/die ganze Zeit hindurch; **spread ~out the country** sich im ganzen Land verbreiten; **2.** *adv. (entirely)* ganz; *(always)* stets; die ganze Zeit [hindurch]; **lined with fur ~out** ganz mit Pelz gefüttert; **repainted ~out** von oben bis unten neu gestrichen; **~put** *n.* Durchsatz, *der (Wirtsch.);* **~way** *n. (Amer.: expressway)* Schnellstraße, *die*

throve *see* **thrive**

throw [θrəʊ] **1.** *v. t.*, **threw** [θru:], **thrown** [θrəʊn] **a)** werfen; **~ sth. to sb.** jmdm. etw. zuwerfen; **~ sth. at sb.** etw. nach jmdm. werfen; **~ me that towel, please** wirf mal bitte das Handtuch rüber *(ugs.);* **the hose ~s a jet of water 50 feet** der Schlauch spritzt das Wasser 50 Fuß weit; **this cannon ~s 50-mm. shells** diese Kanone schießt 50-mm-Geschosse; **~ a punch/punches** zuschlagen; **~ a left/right** eine Linke/Rechte schlagen; **~ oneself on one's knees/to the floor/into a chair** sich auf die Knie/zu Boden/in einen Sessel werfen; **~ oneself down** sich niederwerfen; **~ oneself at sb.** sich auf jmdn. werfen; *(fig.)* sich jmdm. an den Hals werfen *(ugs.);* **~ good money after bad** *(fig.)* [noch mehr] Geld hinauswerfen; *see also* **glass 2; b)** *(fig.)* **~ sb. out of work/into prison** jmdn. entlassen *od. (ugs.)* hinauswerfen/ins Gefängnis werfen *(geh.);* **be ~n upon one's own resources** selbst für sich aufkommen müssen; **~ sb. into confusion** jmdn. durcheinanderbringen; **~ oneself into a task** sich in eine Arbeit *(Akk.)* stürzen; **~ sth. into disarray** *or* **disorder** etw. durcheinanderbringen; *see also* **scent 1 b; c)** *(project, direct)* werfen; **~ an icy look at sb.** jmdm. einen eisigen Blick zuwerfen; *see also* **[1]light 1 h; d)** *(bring to the ground)* zu Boden werfen ‹*Ringer, Gegner*›; *(unseat)* abwerfen ‹*Reiter*›; **e)** *(coll.: disconcert)* ‹*Frage:*› aus der Fassung bringen; **f)** *(cause to change position)* **~ troops into action** Truppen in den Kampf werfen; **~ a switch/lever** einen Schalter/Hebel betätigen; **~ the car into reverse** den Rückwärtsgang einlegen *od. (salopp)* reinhauen; *see also* **open 1 a; g)** *(construct)* **~ a bridge across a river** eine Brücke über einen Fluß schlagen; **h)** *(Textiles)* **~ silk** Seidenfäden drehen; **i)** *(Pottery)* drehen; **j) ~ a fit/tantrum** einen Anfall/Wutanfall bekommen; **k) ~ a party** *(coll.)* eine Party schmeißen *(ugs.);* **l)** *(Amer.: lose intentionally)* absichtlich verlieren ‹*Kampf, Rennen*›; **m)** *(Cards)* ausspielen; *(discard)* abwerfen; **n)** *also abs. (Games)* werfen; **~ [the/a dice]** würfeln. **2.** *n.* **a)** *(act)* Wurf, *der;* **the first ~ went to the champion** *(Wrestling)* der erste Wurf gelang dem Meister; **$5 a ~** *(sl.: each)* $5 das Stück; *see also* **stone 1 a; b)** *(Geol.) (fault)* Verwerfung, *die*

~ a'bout *v. t.* herumwerfen *(ugs.);* **~ one's arms about** mit den Armen fuchteln *(ugs.);* **~ one's money about** *(fig.)* mit Geld um sich werfen; *see also* **weight 1 a**

~ a'round *v. t.* **a)** *see* **~ about; b)** *(surround with)* **~ a cordon around an area** ein Gebiet abriegeln

~ a'way *v. t.* **a)** *(get rid of, waste)* wegwerfen; *(discard)* abwerfen ‹*Spielkarte*›; **~ away money on sth.** Geld für etw. wegwerfen; **~ oneself away on sb.** sich an jmdn. wegwerfen; **b)** *(lose by neglect)* verschenken ‹*Vorteil, Vorsprung, Spiel usw.*›; **c)** *(Theatr.)* beiläufig fallenlassen ‹*Worte*›. *See also* **throw-away**

~ 'back *v. t.* **a)** *(return, repulse)* zurückwerfen; **be ~n back on sth.** *(fig.)* auf etw. *(Akk.)* zurückgreifen müssen; **b)** *(move back rapidly)* zurückschlagen ‹*Bettuch, Vorhang, Teppich*›; zurückwerfen ‹*Kopf*›. *See also* **throw-back**

~ 'down *v. t.* **~ down [on the ground]** auf den Boden werfen; **it's ~ing it down** *(coll.)* es gießt [wie aus Eimern] *(ugs.); see also* **[1]gauntlet d**

~ 'in *v. t.* **a)** *(include as free extra)* [gratis] dazugeben; **with ... ~n in** mit ... als Zugabe; **b)** *(interpose)* einstreuen ‹*Bemerkung*›; **c)** *(Footb., Rugby)* einwerfen; *see also* **throw-in; d)** *(Cricket)* [vom Außenfeld] in das Innenfeld [zurück]werfen; **e) ~ one's hand in** *(Cards)* aussteigen *(ugs.); (fig.: withdraw)* aufgeben. *See also* **lot g; towel 1 a**

~ 'off *v. t.* **a)** *(discard)* ablegen ‹*Maske, Verkleidung*›; von sich werfen ‹*Kleider*›; *(get rid of)* loswerden ‹*Erkältung, lästige Person*›; **b)** *(perform or write casually)* [mühelos] hinwerfen ‹*Rede, Gedicht usw.*›

~ 'on 1. *v. t.* sich werfen in ‹*Kleider*›. **2.** *v. refl.* **~ oneself [up]on sb.** sich auf jmdn. stürzen; **~ oneself [up]on sb.'s mercy** sich jmdm. auf Gnade oder Ungnade ausliefern

~ 'out *v. t.* **a)** *(discard)* wegwerfen; **b)** *(expel)* **~ sb. out [of sth.]** jmdn. [aus etw.] hinauswerfen *(ugs.);* **~ sb. out of work** jmdn. hinauswerfen *(ugs.);* **c)** *(refuse)* verwerfen ‹*Plan usw.*›; **d)** *(put forward tentatively)* in den Raum stellen ‹*Vorschläge*›; **e) ~ out one's chest** die Brust herausdrücken; **f)** *(confuse)* durcheinanderbringen; aus dem Konzept bringen ‹*Sprecher*›; **the mistake threw us out in our calculation/results** der Fehler warf unsere Rechnung um *(ugs.)*/verfälschte unsere Ergebnisse; **g)** *(radiate)* ausstrahlen ‹*Wärme*›. *See also* **throw-out**

~ 'over *v. t.* sitzenlassen *(ugs.)* ‹*Freund[in] usw.*›; den Rücken kehren (+ *Dat.*) ‹*Partei, Bekannten, Familie*›

~ to'gether *v. t.* **a)** *(assemble hastily)* zusammenhauen *(ugs.);* zusammenwerfen ‹*Zutaten, Ideen*›; herzaubern ‹*Essen*›; zusammenschustern *(ugs. abwertend)* ‹*Aufsatz, Artikel*›; zusammenschreiben ‹*Buch, Artikel, Rede*›; **b)** *(bring together)* zusammenwürfeln

~ 'up 1. *v. t.* **a)** *(lift quickly)* hochwerfen ‹*Arme, Hände*›; [plötzlich] hochschieben ‹*Fenster*›; **b)** *(erect quickly)* hochziehen *(salopp)* ‹*Gebäude*›; **c)** *(give up)* hinwerfen *(ugs.)* ‹*Arbeit*›; aufgeben ‹*Versuch*›; abbrechen ‹*Laufbahn, Ausbildung*›; **d)** *(produce)* hervorbringen ‹*Führer, Ideen usw.*›; **e)** *(coll.: vomit)* ausspucken *(ugs.).* **2.** *v. i. (coll.: vomit)* brechen *(ugs.);* **he makes me want to ~ up** ich finde ihn zum Kotzen *(derb)*

throw: ~-away 1. *adj.* **a)** *(disposable)* Wegwerf-; Einweg-; **b)** *(underemphasized)* beiläufig [gesprochen] ‹*Bemerkung*›; **2.** *n.* **a)** *(disposable thing)* Wegwerfartikel, *der; (bottle)* Einwegflasche, *die;* **b)** *(remark)* beiläufige Bemerkung; **~-back** *n.* Rückkehr, *die* **(to** zu); **he/this horse is a ~-back** in ihm/diesem Pferd schlägt altes Blut wieder durch

thrower ['θrəʊə(r)] *n.* Werfer, *der*/Werferin, *die; (Pottery)* Dreher, *der*/Dreherin, *die*

'throw-in *n. (Footb., Rugby)* Einwurf, *der*

thrown *see* **throw 1**

throw: ~-out *n.* **a) have a ~-out** ausmisten *(ugs.);* **b) sb.'s ~-outs** das, was jmd. wegwerfen will; *(clothes)* jmds. abgelegte Kleider; **these are ~-outs** diese sind zum Wegwerfen; **~-rug** *n. (Amer.)* Überwurf, *der*

thru *(Amer.) see* **through**

thrum [θrʌm] **1.** *v. t.*, **-mm-** klimpern auf (+ *Dat.*) ‹*Gitarre usw.*›; trommeln auf (+ *Dat.*) ‹*Tisch usw.*›; **~ a tune** eine Melodie [herunter]klimpern. **2.** *v. i.*, **-mm-** *(on guitar)* klimpern **(on** auf + *Dat.*); *(on flat surface)* trommeln **(on** auf + *Dat.*)

[1]thrush [θrʌʃ] *n. (Ornith.)* Drossel, *die*

[2]thrush *n., no pl., no art. (Med.)* Soor, *der;* Soormykose, *die*

thrust [θrʌst] **1.** *v. t.*, **thrust a)** *(push suddenly)* stoßen; **he ~ his fist into my face** er stieß mir seine Faust ins Gesicht; **~ a letter into sth.** einen Brief in etw. *(Akk.)* stecken; **~ out one's hand** die Hand ausstrecken; **~ a ten-pound note into sb.'s hand** jmdm. eine Zehnpfundnote in die Hand drücken; *(fig.)* **~ aside** beiseite schieben; in den Wind schlagen ‹*Warnungen*›; **~ extra work [up]on sb.** jmdm. zusätzliche Arbeit aufbürden; **~ oneself/one's company upon sb.** sich/seine Gesellschaft jmdm. aufdrängen; **fame was ~ upon her** sie wurde unversehens berühmt; **b) ~ one's way through/into/out of sth.** sich durch/in/aus etw. drängen; **c)** *(pierce)* **~ sb./sth. through** jmdn./etw. durchbohren. **2.** *v. i.*, **thrust a)** *(push)* **~ at sb.** nach jmdm. stoßen; **b)** *(force one's way)* **~ through the crowd/to the front** sich durch die Menge/nach vorn drängen *od.* kämpfen. **3.** *n.* **a)** *(sudden push)* Stoß, *der;* **b)** *(fig.: verbal attack)* Seitenhieb, *der* **(at** auf + *Akk.*); **c)** *(gist)* Stoßrichtung, *die;* **d)** *(Mil.: advance)* Vorstoß, *der;* **e)** *(force) (of jet engine)* Schub, *der; (of arch)* Gewölbeschub, *der*

'thrust-bearing *n. (Mech. Engin.)* Axiallager, *das*

thruster ['θrʌstə(r)] *n. (Astronaut.)* Korrekturtriebwerk, *das*

thrustful ['θrʌstfl] *adj.* energisch

thrusting ['θrʌstɪŋ] *adj.* [energisch und] zielstrebig

thruway *(Amer.) see* **throughway**

thud [θʌd] **1.** *v. i.*, **-dd-** dumpf schlagen; **~ to the floor/ground** dumpf [auf dem Fußboden/Boden] aufschlagen. **2.** *n.* dumpfer Schlag; **fall with a ~ [to the ground]** dumpf [auf dem Boden] aufschlagen; **the ~ of hoofbeats** dröhnender Hufschlag

thug [θʌg] *n.* Schläger, *der;* **football ~s** Fußballrowdys

thuggery ['θʌgərɪ] *n., no pl.* Schlägerunwesen, *das*

thuggish ['θʌgɪʃ] *adj.* aggressiv ‹*Verhalten, Fußballfan*›; **~ lout** Schläger, *der;* **~ youth** jugendlicher Schläger

thumb [θʌm] **1.** *n.* Daumen, *der;* **give sb. the ~s down on a proposal/idea** jmds. Vorschlag/Idee ablehnen; **get the ~s down** ‹*Idee:*› verworfen werden; ‹*Kandidat:*› abgelehnt werden; **give a project the ~s up** für ein Projekt grünes Licht geben; **get the ~s up** ‹*Person, Projekt:*› akzeptiert werden; **have ten ~s, be all ~s** zwei linke Hände haben *(ugs.);* **have sb. under one's ~:** jmdn. unter der Fuchtel haben *(ugs.);* **be under sb.'s ~:** unter jmds. Fuchtel stehen; *see also* **rule 1 a; stick out 2 b. 2.** *v. t.* **a) ~ a lift** einem Autofahrer winken, um sich mitnehmen zu lassen; *(hitch-hike)* per Anhalter fahren; **b)** *(turn over)* [mit dem Daumen] durchblättern ‹*Buch*›; [mit dem Daumen] umblättern ‹*Seiten*›; **well-~ed** abgegriffen ‹*Buch*›; **c) ~ one's nose [at sb.]** [jmdm.] eine lange Nase machen

~ through *v. t.* [mit dem Daumen] durchblättern ‹*Buch*›

thumb: ~-index 1. *n.* Daumenregister, *das;* **2.** *v. t.* mit Daumenregister ausstatten; **~-indexed edition** Ausgabe mit Daumenregister; **~-nail** *n.* Daumennagel, *der;* **~-nail sketch** *(Art)* Miniaturportrait, *das; (fig.: brief description)* kurze Beschreibung; **~-print** *n.* Daumenabdruck, *der;* **~screw** *n. (Hist.)* Daumenschraube, *die;* **~-stall** *n.* Däumling, *der;* **~-sucking** ['θʌmsʌkɪŋ] *n., no pl., no indef. art.* Daumenlutschen, *das;* **~tack** *(Amer.) n.* Reißzwecke, *die*

thump [θʌmp] **1.** *v.t.* **a)** *(strike heavily)* [mit Wucht] schlagen; **I'll ~ you if ...:** ich hau' dir eine, wenn ... *(ugs.);* **they ~ed each other** sie prügelten sich; **~ the door with one's fist** mit der Faust an die Tür hämmern; **b)** *(play on piano etc.)* **~ [out] a tune** eine Melodie hämmern *(ugs.).* **2.** *v.i.* **a)** hämmern **(at, on** gegen); ‹*Herz:*› heftig pochen; **b)** *(move noisily)* **~ around** herumpoltern; **~ down the stairs** die Treppe hinabpoltern. **3.** *n.* **a)** *(blow)* Schlag, *der;* **b)** *(dull sound)* Bums, *der (ugs.);* dumpfer Schlag

thumping ['θʌmpɪŋ] *(coll.)* **1.** *adj. (huge)* gewaltig *(ugs.);* überwältigend ‹*Mehrheit*›; faustdick *(ugs.)* ‹*Lüge*›. **2.** *adv.* **~ great** riesengroß *(ugs.);* **a ~ big majority** eine überwältigende Mehrheit

thunder ['θʌndə(r)] **1.** *n.* **a)** *no pl., no indef. art.* Donner, *der;* **roll/crash of ~:** Donnerrollen, *das*/-schlag, *der;* **b)** *(fig.: censure)* Donnerwetter, *das (ugs.);* **c) steal sb.'s ~** *(fig.)* jmdm. die Schau stehlen *(ugs.).* **2.** *v.i.* **a)** donnern; **b)** *(speak)* **~ against sth.** gegen etw. wettern *(ugs.);* **~ at sb.** jmdn. andonnern *(ugs.).* **3.** *v.t.* [mit Donnerstimme] brüllen; **~ [out] orders at sb.** jmdm. Befehle zubrüllen

thunder: ~bolt *n.* **a)** Blitzschlag [mit Donner]; *(from god)* Blitzstrahl, *der (geh.);* **b)** *(fig.: unexpected event)* **come as something of a ~bolt** wie ein Blitz einschlagen; **~-box** *n. (coll.)* Plumpsklo[sett], *das (ugs.);* **~clap** *n.* **a)** Donnerschlag, *der;* **b)** *(fig.)* **come** *or* **be like a ~clap** wie der Blitz einschlagen; **~-cloud** *n.* Gewitterwolke, *die*

thundering ['θʌndərɪŋ] *(coll.)* **1.** *adj. (huge)* gewaltig *(ugs.)* ‹*Erfolg*›; faustdick *(ugs.)* ‹*Lüge*›; **be in a ~ rage** eine Mordswut haben *(ugs.).* **2.** *adv.* **~ great** gewaltig *(ugs.);* **we had a ~ good time** wir hatten einen unheimlichen Spaß

thunderous ['θʌndərəs] *adj.* donnernd; **in a ~ voice** mit Donnerstimme

thunder: ~-shower *n.* Gewitterschauer, *der;* **~storm** *n.* Gewitter, *das; (very heavy)* Gewittersturm, *der;* **~struck** *adj. (fig.: amazed)* **be ~struck** wie vom Donner gerührt sein

thundery ['θʌndərɪ] *adj.* gewittrig; **it looks ~:** es sieht nach Gewitter aus

Thuringia [θʊə'rɪŋgɪə] *pr. n.* Thüringen *(das)*

Thuringian [θʊə'rɪŋgɪən] **1.** *adj.* thüringisch ‹*Stadt*›; Thüringer ‹*Wald, Dialekt*›. **2.** *n.* Thüringer, *der*/Thüringerin, *die*

Thurs. *abbr.* **Thursday** Do.

Thursday ['θɜːzdeɪ, 'θɜːzdɪ] **1.** *n.* Donnerstag, *der.* **2.** *adv. (coll.)* **she comes ~s** sie kommt donnerstags. *See also* **Friday**

thus [ðʌs] *adv.* **a)** *(in the way indicated)* so; *(thereby)* dadurch; **I picture the process as happening ~ ...:** ich stelle mir den Ablauf folgendermaßen vor: ...; **b)** *(accordingly)* deshalb; daher; **c)** *(to this extent)* **~ much/far** so viel/so weit

thwack [θwæk] *see* **whack 1, 2 a**

thwart [θwɔːt] **1.** *v.t.* durchkreuzen ‹*Pläne, Absichten*›; vereiteln ‹*Versuch*›; **~ sb.** jmdm. einen Strich durch die Rechnung machen; **she was ~ed in her plans** ihre Pläne wurden durchkreuzt. **2.** *n. (Naut.)* Ducht, *die (fachspr.);* Ruderbank, *die*

thy [ðaɪ] *poss. pron. attrib. (arch./poet./dial.)* dein; *see also* [2]**her**

thyme [taɪm] *n. (Bot.)* Thymian, *der;* **wild ~:** Feldthymian, *der;* Quendel, *der*

thymus ['θaɪməs] *n., pl.* **~es** *or* **thymi** ['θaɪmaɪ] **~ [gland]** *(Anat.)* Thymus, *der;* Thymusdrüse, *die*

thyroid ['θaɪrɔɪd] *n.* **~ [gland]** *(Anat., Zool.)* Schilddrüse, *die*

thyself [ðaɪ'self] *pron. (arch./poet./dial.)* **a)** *emphat.* selbst; **b)** *refl.* dich/dir; **know ~!** erkenne dich selbst! *See also* **herself**

ti *see* **te**

tiara [tɪ'ɑːrə] *n.* **a)** *(pope's crown)* Tiara, *die;* **b)** *(jewelled band)* Diadem, *das*

Tibet [tɪ'bet] *pr. n.* Tibet *(das)*

Tibetan [tɪ'betn] **1.** *adj.* tibetisch; **sb. is ~:** jmd. ist Tibeter/Tibeterin. **2.** *n.* **a)** *(person)* Tibeter, *der*/Tibeterin, *die;* **b)** *(language)* Tibetisch, *das*

tibia ['tɪbɪə] *n., pl.* **~e** ['tɪbɪiː] *or* **~s** *(Anat.)* Tibia, *die (fachspr.);* Schienbein, *das*

tic [tɪk] *n.* Tic, *der (Med.);* nervöse Muskelzuckung

tich [tɪtʃ] *see* **titch**

tichy *see* **titchy**

Ticino [tɪ'tʃiːnəʊ] *pr. n.* das Tessin

[1]**tick** [tɪk] **1.** *v.i.* ticken; **what makes sb. ~** *(fig.)* worauf jmd. anspricht. **2.** *v.t.* **a)** mit einem Häkchen versehen; **b)** *see* **~ off a. 3.** *n.* **a)** *(of clock etc.)* Ticken, *das;* **b)** *(Brit. coll.: moment)* Sekunde, *die;* **half a ~!, just a ~!** Momentchen! *(ugs.);* **I'll be with you in a ~** *or* **two ~s** ich komme gleich; **c)** *(mark)* Häkchen, *das;* **put a ~ against your preference** kennzeichnen Sie das, was Sie bevorzugen, mit einem Häkchen

~ a'way *v.i.* [weiter] ticken; **the minutes ~ed away** die Minuten verstrichen

~ 'off *v.t.* **a)** *(cross off)* abhaken; **b)** *(coll.: reprimand)* rüffeln *(ugs.)*

~ 'over *v.i.* **a)** im Leerlauf laufen; **~ over noisily/too slowly/too fast** im Leerlauf [zu] laut/zu langsam/zu schnell drehen; **b)** *(fig.)* **~ over [nicely]** *(progress satisfactorily)* ganz gut laufen *(ugs.);* **keep things ~ing over while I'm away** sieh zu, daß alles gemächlich weiterläuft, während ich weg bin. *See also* **tick-over**

[2]**tick** *n. (Zool.) (arachnid)* Zecke, *die; (insect)* Lausfliege, *die*

[3]**tick** *n. (coll.: credit)* **buy on ~:** auf Pump kaufen *(salopp);* **can I have it on ~?** kann ich das anschreiben lassen?

ticker ['tɪkə(r)] *n.* **a)** *(coll.: watch)* Zwiebel, *die (ugs. scherzh.);* **b)** *(coll.: tape-machine)* Ticker, *der (ugs.);* **c)** *(joc.: heart)* Pumpe, *die (salopp)*

'ticker-tape *n. (Amer.)* [Papier]streifen, *der (aus dem Fernschreiber);* **~ welcome** Konfettiparade, *die*

ticket ['tɪkɪt] **1.** *n.* **a)** Karte, *die; (for concert, theatre, cinema, exhibition)* [Eintritts]karte, *die; (for public transport)* Fahrschein, *der; (of cardboard)* Fahrkarte, *die; (for aeroplane)* Flugschein, *der;* Ticket, *das; (for ship)* Fahrschein, *der;* Ticket, *das; (of lottery, raffle)* Los, *das; (for library)* Ausweis, *der; (for car park)* Parkschein, *der;* **cloakroom/pawn ~:** Garderobenmarke, *die*/Pfandschein, *der;* **entrance by ~ only** Einlaß nur gegen Eintrittskarte; **price ~:** Preisschild, *das;* **[parking]~:** Strafmandat, *das;* Strafzettel, *der (ugs.);* **b)** *(certificate) (Naut.)* Patent, *das; (Aeronaut.)* Pilotenschein, *der;* **c)** *(Amer. Polit.) (list of candidates)* [Wahl]liste, *die;* **run on the Democratic/Republican ~:** für die Demokraten/Republikaner kandidieren; **run on a youth ~** *(fig.)* mit einem auf Jungwähler zugeschnittenen Programm antreten; *see also* **split 3 c; d) be [just] the ~** *(sl.)* genau das Richtige sein. **2.** *v.t.* auszeichnen ‹*Waren*›

ticket: ~-agency *n.* Kartenvorverkaufsstelle, *die;* **~-agent** *n.* Inhaber/Inhaberin einer Kartenvorverkaufsstelle; **~-collector** *n. (on train)* Schaffner, *der*/Schaffnerin, *die; (on station)* Fahrkartenkontrolleur, *der*/-kontrolleurin, *die;* **~-holder** *n.* Besitzer/Besitzerin einer Eintrittskarte; **~-inspector** Fahrkartenkontrolleur, *der*/-kontrolleurin, *die;* **~-office** *n.* Kartenschalter, *der; (for public transport)* Fahrkartenschalter, *der; (for advance booking)* Kartenvorverkaufsstelle, *die*

ticking ['tɪkɪŋ] *n. (Textiles)* Drillich, *der;* Drell, *der (fachspr.)*

ticking-'off *n. (sl.)* Rüffel, *der (ugs.)*

tickle ['tɪkl] **1.** *v.t.* **a)** *(touch lightly)* kitzeln; **~ sb.'s ribs** *(fig.)* jmdn. zum Lachen bringen; *abs.* **don't ~!** kitzle mich nicht!; **you're tickling!** das kitzelt!; **b)** *(amuse)* **be ~d by sth.** sich über etw. *(Akk.)* amüsieren; **be ~d pink about sth.** *(coll.)* sich wahnsinnig über etw. *(Akk.)* freuen *(ugs.);* **~ sb.'s fancy** jmdn. reizen. **2.** *v.i.* kitzeln. **3.** *n.* Kitzeln, *das;* **give sb. a ~:** jmdn. kitzeln

ticklish ['tɪklɪʃ] *adj. (lit. or fig.)* kitzlig

tickly ['tɪklɪ] *adj. (coll.)* kitzlig

tick: ~-over *n. (Motor Veh.)* Leerlauf, *der;* **~-tack-'toe** *(Amer.)* = **noughts and crosses** *see* **nought a; ~-tock** ['tɪktɒk] *n.* **a)** *no pl. (sound)* Ticktack, *das;* **b)** *(child lang.: clock)* Ticktack, *die (Kinderspr.)*

tidal ['taɪdl] *adj.* Gezeiten-; **~ river** Tidefluß, *der;* **~ basin/harbour** Tidebecken, *das*/-hafen, *der (Seemannsspr.);* **~ power-station** Gezeitenkraftwerk, *das*

tidal: ~ flow *n. (Transport)* dem Verkehrsfluß angepaßtes System der Verkehrsführung; **~ wave** *n.* Flutwelle, *die;* **a ~ wave of enthusiasm/protest** *(fig.)* eine gewaltige Welle der Begeisterung/von Protesten

tidbit ['tɪdbɪt] *(Amer.) see* **titbit**

tiddledy-wink ['tɪdldɪwɪŋk] *(Amer.) see* **tiddly-wink**

tiddler ['tɪdlə(r)] *n. (Brit. coll./child lang.)* **a)** *(fish)* Fischchen, *das;* **b)** *(child)* Kleine, *das;* **~s** *(things)* Kleinzeug, *das (ugs. abwertend)*

tiddl[e]y ['tɪdlɪ] *adj. (Brit.)* **a)** *(sl.: slightly drunk)* angesäuselt *(ugs.);* **b) ~ [little]** *(coll.: very small)* klitzeklein *(ugs.)*

tiddly-wink *n.* **a)** *(counter)* farbiges Plättchen; **b) ~s** *sing. (game)* Flohhüpfen, *das*

tide [taɪd] **1.** *n.* **a)** *(rise or fall of sea)* Tide, *die (nordd., bes. Seemannsspr.);* **high ~:** Flut, *die;* **low ~:** Ebbe, *die;* **the ~s** die Gezeiten; **sail on the next ~:** mit der nächsten Flut auslaufen; **cut off/washed up by the ~:** von der Flut abgeschnitten/angeschwemmt; **the ~ is in/out** es ist Flut/Ebbe; **when the ~ is in/out** bei Flut/Ebbe; **the rise and fall of the ~s** Ebbe und Flut; der Tidenhub *(Seemannsspr.); see also* **turn 1 g; b)** *(fig.: trend)* Trend, *der;* **go with/against the ~:** mit dem/gegen den Strom schwimmen; **the ~ of war was turning** das Kriegsglück wendete sich; **rising ~ of opposition** zunehmende Opposition; *see also* **turn 3 c. 2.** *v.t.* **~ sb. over** jmdm. über die Runden helfen *(ugs.);* **I have enough to ~ me over/over the winter** ich habe genug, um mich über Wasser zu halten/um durch *od.* über den Winter zu kommen; **~ sb. over a difficult period** jmdm. über eine schwierige Zeit hinweghelfen

'tide-gate *n. (Naut.)* Fluttor, *das*

tideless ['taɪdlɪs] *adj.* gezeitenlos

tide: ~-mark *n.* **a)** Flutmarke, *die;* **b)** *(Brit. coll.: line on body, bath, etc.)* Schmutzrand, *der;* **~-table** *n. (Naut.)* Gezeitentafel, *die;* **~way** *n. (of river)* Tidefluß, *der; (channel)* Priel, *der; (current)* Gezeitenströmung, *die*

tidily ['taɪdɪlɪ] *adv.* ordentlich; *(clearly)* übersichtlich ‹*präsentieren, gestalten*›

tidiness ['taɪdɪnɪs] *n., no pl.* Ordentlichkeit, *die*

tidings ['taɪdɪŋz] *n. pl. (literary)* Kunde, *die (geh.)*

tidy ['taɪdɪ] **1.** *adj.* **a)** *(neat)* ordentlich; aufgeräumt ‹*Zimmer, Schreibtisch*›; **make oneself/a room ~:** sich zurechtmachen/ein Zimmer aufräumen; **have ~ habits** ein ordentlicher Mensch sein; **b)** *(coll.: considerable)* ordentlich *(ugs.);* **a ~ sum** *or* **penny**

ein hübsches Sümmchen *(ugs.)*. **2.** *n.* *(receptacle)* **kitchen/bathroom/desk ~:** Behälter für Küchen-/Badezimmer-/Schreibtischutensilien; **sink ~:** Einsatzkörbchen für die Spüle. **3.** *v.t.* aufräumen ‹*Zimmer*›; **~ oneself** sich zurechtmachen; **~ one's hair** sich kämmen; *abs.* **be busy ~ing** mit [dem] Aufräumen beschäftigt sein

~ a'way *v.t.* wegräumen

~ 'up 1. *v.i.* aufräumen. **2.** *v.t.* aufräumen; in Ordnung bringen ‹*Text*›

tie [taɪ] **1.** *v.t.*, **tying** ['taɪɪŋ] **a)** binden (**to** an + *Akk.*, **into** zu); **~ the prisoner's legs together** dem Gefangenen die Beine zusammenbinden; **~ an apron round you[r waist]** binde dir eine Schürze um; **can he ~ his own shoes/tie?** kann er sich *(Dat.)* die Schuhe/die Krawatte selbst binden?; **~ a knot** einen Knoten machen; *see also* **hand 1a; b)** *(Sport: gain equal score in)* **~ the match** unentschieden spielen; **they ~d the match at 3 all** es stand unentschieden drei beide; **c)** *(restrict)* binden (**to** an + *Akk.*); **d)** *(Building)* verbinden ‹*Balken*›. **2.** *v.i.*, **tying a)** *(be fastened)* **it won't ~:** es läßt sich nicht binden; **it ~s at the back** es wird hinten gebunden; **where does the sash ~?** wo bindet man die Schärpe?; **b)** *(have equal scores, votes, etc.)* **~ for second place in the competition/election** mit gleicher Punktzahl den zweiten Platz im Wettbewerb/mit gleicher Stimmenzahl den zweiten Platz bei der Wahl erreichen; **~ 6 : 6** mit 6 : 6 ein Unentschieden erreichen. **3.** *n.* **a)** Krawatte, *die; see also* **old 1f; b)** *(cord etc. for fastening)* Band, *das;* **~ fastening** Verschnürung, *die;* **c)** *(fig.)* *(bond)* Band, *das; (restriction)* Bindung, *die;* **~s of friendship/family ~s** Freundschafts-/Familienbande *Pl. (geh.);* **have ~s with a firm** Beziehungen zu einer Firma unterhalten; **find that sth. is a ~:** sich durch etw. gebunden fühlen; **be a ~ for sb.** für jmdn. eine Belastung sein; **d)** *(Building)* Binder, *der;* **e)** *(Amer. Railw.)* Schwelle, *die;* **f)** *(Mus.)* Haltebogen, *der;* **g)** *(equality) (of scores)* Punktgleichheit, *die; (of votes)* Patt, *das;* Stimmengleichheit, *die;* **there was a ~ for third place** zwei Teilnehmer landeten punktgleich auf dem dritten Platz; **end in** *or* **be a ~:** unentschieden *od.* mit einem Unentschieden enden; **h)** *(Sport: match)* Begegnung, *die;* **draw an easy ~:** einen leichten Gegner ziehen; **i)** *(Amer.: shoe)* Schnürschuh, *der*

~ 'back *v.t.* zurückbinden; **~ one's hair back in a pony-tail** sein Haar hinten zu einem Pferdeschwanz zusammenbinden

~ 'down *v.t.* **a)** *(fasten)* festbinden; **b)** *(fig.: restrict)* binden; **there are too many things tying me down here** ich bin hier zu sehr gebunden; **be ~d down by sth.** durch etw. gebunden *od.* eingeschränkt sein; **~ sb. down to conditions/a time/a schedule** jmdn. auf Bedingungen/eine Zeit/einen Zeitplan festlegen

~ 'in 1. *v.i.* **~ in with sth.** zu etw. passen. **2.** *v.t.* **~ sth. in with sth.** etw. mit etw. abstimmen; *see also* **tie-in**

~ 'up *v.t.* **a)** *(bind)* festbinden; festmachen ‹*Boot*›; **~ up a parcel with string** ein Paket verschnüren; **~ sth. up in[to] bundles** etw. zu Bündeln zusammenbinden; **b)** *(complete arrangements for)* abschließen; **~ up a few loose ends** *(fig.)* ein paar letzte Kleinigkeiten erledigen; **c)** *(make unavailable)* fest anlegen ‹*Geld*›; **~ up property** Eigentum einer Verfügungsbeschränkung unterwerfen; **d)** *see* **~ in 2; e)** *(keep busy)* beschäftigen; **I am ~d up this evening** ich habe heute abend zu tun. *See also* **tie-up**

tie: ~-bar *n.* *(Building)* Anker, *der;* **~-beam** *n.* *(Building)* Binderbalken, *der;* **~-break, ~-breaker** *ns.* Tie-Break, *der od. das;* **~-clip** *n.* Krawattenhalter, *der*

tied [taɪd] *adj.* *(Brit.)* **a) ~ cottage** *or* **house** *(of farm-worker)* Wohnhaus für Farmarbeiter; *(of caretaker etc.)* Dienstwohnhaus, *das;* **b) ~ house** *(public house supplying one brewer's beers)* Vertragsgaststätte, *die*

tie: ~-in *n.* *gleichzeitige [Wieder]aufführung eines Films o.ä. mit der [Neu]veröffentlichung des zugrunde liegenden Buches;* **~-on** *adj.* Anhänge-; **~-on label** Anhänger, *der;* **~-pin** *n.* Krawattennadel, *die*

tier [tɪə(r)] *n.* **a)** *(row)* Rang, *der;* **b)** *(unit)* Stufe, *die*

tiered [tɪəd] *adj.* gestuft ‹*Hörsaal, Theater*›; **a three-~ wedding cake** eine dreistöckige Hochzeitstorte; **a three-~ shelf [unit]** ein Regal mit drei Fächern

tie-rod *n.* **a)** *(Motor Veh.)* Spurstange, *die;* **b)** *(Building)* Querlatte, *die*

Tierra del Fuego [tɪerə del 'fweɪgəʊ] *pr. n.* Feuerland *(das)*

tie-up *n.* Verbindung, *die*

tiff [tɪf] *n.* Krach, *der (ugs.);* Streit, *der;* **have a ~ with sb. over sth.** mit jmdm. wegen etw. Krach haben

tiger ['taɪgə(r)] *n.* **a)** *(Zool.)* Tiger, *der;* **American ~** *see* **jaguar; paper ~** *(fig.)* Papiertiger, *der;* **ride a ~** *(fig.)* mit dem Feuer spielen; **b)** *(fierce or energetic person)* Kämpfernatur, *die*

tiger: ~-cat *n.* *(Zool.)* Tigerkatze, *die;* **~-eye** *n.* *(Min.)* Tigerauge, *das;* **~-lily** *n.* *(Bot.)* Tigerlilie, *die;* **~-moth** *n.* *(Zool.)* Bärenspinner, *der;* **~-shark** *n.* *(Zool.)* Tigerhai, *der*

tight [taɪt] **1.** *adj.* **a)** *(firm)* fest; fest angezogen ‹*Schraube, Mutter*›; festsitzend ‹*Korken, Deckel*›; **be very ~:** sehr fest sitzen; **the drawer/window is ~:** die Schublade/das Fenster klemmt; **b)** *(close-fitting)* eng ‹*Kleid, Hose, Schuh usw.*›; **this shoe is rather [too] ~** *or* **a rather ~ fit** dieser Schuh ist etwas zu eng; **c)** *(impermeable)* **~ seal/joint** dichter Verschluß/dichte Fuge; **d)** *(taut)* straff; **a ~ feeling in one's chest** ein Gefühl der Beklemmung *od.* Enge in der Brust; **e)** *(with little space)* knapp; gedrängt ‹*Programm*›; **it is a ~ space** der Platz ist knapp; es ist [zu] wenig Platz; **it is a ~ squeeze with seven people in the car** es ist sehr eng zu siebt im Wagen; **f)** *(strict)* streng ‹*Kontrolle, Disziplin*›; straff ‹*Organisation*›; **g)** *(Econ.)* knapp ‹*Geld*›; angespannt ‹*Markt*›; **h)** *(coll.: stingy)* knauserig *(ugs.);* **i)** *(difficult to negotiate)* **a ~ corner** eine enge Kurve; **be in/get oneself into a ~ corner** *or (coll.)* **spot [over sth.]** *(fig.)* [wegen etw.] in der Klemme sein/in die Klemme geraten *(ugs.);* **j)** *(coll.: drunk)* voll *(salopp);* **get ~:** sich vollaufen lassen *(salopp);* **she got ~ on a couple of drinks** nach ein paar Drinks war sie voll *(salopp);* **k)** *(Sport: evenly contested)* hart umkämpft; knapp ‹*Rennen*›. **2.** *adv.* **a)** *(firmly)* fest; **hold ~!** halt dich fest!; *see also* **sit 1b; sleep 2a; b)** *(so as to leave no space)* [ganz] voll; **a train packed ~ with commuters** ein mit Pendlern vollgestopfter Zug *(ugs.)*. **3.** *n.* *in pl.* **a)** *(Brit.)* **[pair of] ~s** Strumpfhose, *die;* **b)** *(of dancer etc.)* Trikothose, *die*

tighten ['taɪtn] **1.** *v.t.* **a)** [fest] anziehen ‹*Knoten, Schraube, Mutter usw.*›; straffziehen ‹*Seil, Schnur*›; anspannen ‹*Muskeln*›; verstärken ‹*Griff*›; **~ one's belt** *(fig.)* den Gürtel enger schnallen *(ugs.);* **b)** *(make stricter)* verschärfen ‹*Kontrolle, Gesetz, Vorschrift*›. **2.** *v.i.* **a)** sich spannen; ‹*Knoten:*› sich zusammenziehen; **her hands ~ed on the steering-wheel** ihre Hände krampften sich um das Steuer; **b)** *(become stricter)* ‹*Gesetze, Bestimmungen:*› verschärft werden

~ 'up 1. *v.t.* **a)** anziehen; *(retighten)* nachziehen; **b)** *(make stricter)* verschärfen ‹*Gesetze, Bestimmungen, Kontrollen*›; **~ up security** die Sicherheitsmaßnahmen verschärfen. **2.** *v.i.* härter durchgreifen; **~ up on security/drunken driving** die Sicherheitsmaßnahmen verschärfen/bei Trunkenheit am Steuer schärfer durchgreifen

tight: ~-'fisted *adj.* geizig; **a ~-fisted old fellow** ein alter Geizhals; **~-fitting** *adj.* enganliegend ‹*Pullover, Trikot*›; **~-lipped** *adj.* **a)** *(without emotion)* mit zusammengepreßten Lippen *nachgestellt;* **b)** *(silent)* verschwiegen

tightly ['taɪtlɪ] *adv.* **a)** *(firmly)* fest; **fit ~** ‹*Maschinenteil usw.:*› fest sitzen; ‹*Kleidungsstück:*› eng anliegen; **fasten sth. ~:** etw. gut befestigen; **put the cork in ~:** den Korken fest hineindrücken; **b)** *(strictly)* streng; **c)** *(tautly)* straff; **d)** *(closely)* dicht; **~ packed** vollgestopft *(ugs.)* ‹*Zug, Koffer*›; **a ~ organized schedule** ein gedrängtes Programm; **e) ~ fought** *(evenly contested)* hart umkämpft

tightness ['taɪtnɪs] *n., no pl.* **a)** *(lack of leakage)* Dichtheit, *die;* **b)** *(firmness)* Festigkeit, *die;* *(closeness of fit)* enger Sitz; **c)** *(strictness of control or discipline)* Schärfe, *die;* Strenge, *die;* **d)** *(tautness)* Straffheit, *die;* **feel [a] ~ across the chest** ein Gefühl der Beklemmung in der Brust haben; **e)** *(of schedule)* Gedrängtheit, *die;* **f)** *(Econ.: scarcity)* Knappheit, *die; (of market)* Angespanntheit, *die;* **g)** *(of bend in road)* Enge, *die;* **h) ~ with money** Knauserigkeit, *die (ugs.);* **i)** *(Sport: of match)* Ausgeglichenheit, *die*

'tightrope *n.* Drahtseil, *das;* **walk a ~** *(fig.)* einen Balanceakt vollführen

tigress ['taɪgrɪs] *n.* *(Zool.)* Tigerin, *die*

tilde ['tɪldə] *n.* *(Ling.)* Tilde, *die*

tile [taɪl] **1.** *n.* **a)** *(on roof)* Ziegel, *der; (on floor, wall)* Fliese, *die; (on stove; also esp. designer ~)* Kachel, *die;* **spend the night on the ~s** *(fig. sl.)* die ganze Nacht durchsumpfen *(salopp);* **b)** *(Games)* Spielstein, *der*. **2.** *v.t.* [mit Ziegeln] decken ‹*Dach*›; fliesen ‹*Wand, Fußboden, Bad*›; kacheln ‹*Wand, Bad*›; **~d roof** Ziegeldach, *das;* **~d floor** Fliesenboden, *der*

tiler ['taɪlə(r)] *n.* *(of roofs)* Dachdecker, *der*/-deckerin, *die; (of floors, walls)* Fliesenleger, *der*/-legerin, *die*

tiling ['taɪlɪŋ] *n., no pl., no indef. art. see* **tile 1a: a)** *(fixing tiles) (on roof)* [Dach]decken, *das; (on floor)* Fliesen[legen], *das; (on wall)* Kacheln, *das;* Fliesen, *das;* **b)** *(set of tiles)* Ziegel/Kacheln/Fliesen

¹till [tɪl] *v.t.* *(Agric.)* bestellen

²till 1. *prep.* bis; *(followed by article + noun)* bis zu; **not [...] ~:** erst; **from morning ~ evening** von morgens bis abends; *see also* **until 1. 2.** *conj.* bis; *see also* **until 2**

³till *n.* Kasse, *die;* **at the ~:** an der Kasse; **have/put one's hand** *or* **fingers in the ~** *(fig.)* in die Kasse greifen

tillage ['tɪlɪdʒ] *n., no pl. (Agric.)* *(tilling)* Bestellung, *die; (land tilled)* Ackerland, *das*

tiller ['tɪlə(r)] *n.* *(Naut.)* Pinne, *die (Seemannsspr.)*

tilt [tɪlt] **1.** *v.i.* **a)** kippen; **the chair ~s back** die Sessellehne kippt nach hinten; **the board ~ed [up] when he stepped on it** das Brett schnellte hoch, als er darauftrat; **b)** *(Hist.: joust)* tjostieren; **~ at** mit der Lanze angreifen; *(fig.)* anprangern; *see also* **windmill a. 2.** *v.t.* kippen; neigen ‹*Kopf*›. **3.** *n.* **a)** *(sloping position)* Schräglage, *die;* **give sth. a ~:** etw. kippen *od.* schräg stellen; **a 45° ~:** eine Neigung *od.* ein Neigungswinkel von 45°; **b)** *(fig.: attack)* Angriff, *der;* **have** *or* **make a ~ at sb./sth.** jmdn./etw. angreifen *od.* attackieren; **c) [at] full ~:** mit voller Wucht

tilth [tɪlθ] *n.* Ackerkrume, *die;* **rake a seedbed to a good ~:** ein Saatbeet gut [auf]lockern

timber ['tɪmbə(r)] **1.** *n.* **a)** *no pl.* *(wood for building)* [Bau]holz, *das;* **sawn ~:** Schnittholz, *das;* **b)** *(type of wood)* Holzart, *die;* Holz, *das;* **c)** *no pl., no indef. art.* *(trees)*

Wald, *der;* **cut down** *or* **fell ~:** Holz schlagen; **put land under ~:** Land aufforsten *(Forstw.);* **standing ~:** Baumholz, *das (Forstw.);* **d)** *(beam, piece of wood)* Balken, *der; (Naut.)* Spant, *das;* **floor ~s** [Boden]balken; *see also* **²shiver 2. 2.** *int. (Forestry)* Holz

timbered [ˈtɪmbəd] *adj.* **a)** *(wooded)* bewaldet; **b)** *(built of wood)* hölzern; Holz-; *(covered with planks)* holzverkleidet

timber: ~-framed *adj.* Fachwerk⟨bau, -haus⟩; ⟨*Rathaus, Jagdschloß usw.*⟩ in Fachwerkbauweise; **~-framing** *n., no pl., no indef. art. (structure)* Fachwerk, *das; (method)* Fachwerkbauweise, *die*

timbering [ˈtɪmbərɪŋ] *n., no pl., no indef. art.* Balkenwerk, *das; (of timber-framed house)* Fachwerk, *das*

timber: ~-line *n. (Geog.)* Baumgrenze, *die;* **~-yard** *n.* Holzlager, *das*

timbre [ˈtæmbə(r), ˈtæbr] *n. (Mus.)* Timbre, *das*

Timbuctoo [tɪmbʌkˈtuː] *pr. n.* Timbuktu *(das)*

time [taɪm] **1.** *n.* **a)** *no pl., no art.* Zeit, *die;* **the greatest composer of all ~:** der größte Komponist aller Zeiten; **for all ~:** für immer [und ewig]; **past/present/future ~:** Vergangenheit, *die*/Gegenwart, *die*/Zukunft, *die;* **stand the test of ~:** die Zeit überdauern; sich bewähren; **in [the course of] ~, as ~ goes on/went on** mit der Zeit; im Laufe der Zeit; **as old as ~:** uralt; **~ will tell** *or* **show** die Zukunft wird es zeigen; **~ and tide wait for no man** das Rad der Zeit läßt sich nicht anhalten; **at this point** *or* **moment in ~:** zum gegenwärtigen Zeitpunkt; **~ flies** die Zeit vergeht [wie] im Fluge; **how ~ flies!** wie [schnell] die Zeit vergeht!; **work against ~:** unter Zeitdruck arbeiten; **in ~, with ~** *(sooner or later)* mit der Zeit; *see also* **healer; b)** *(interval, available or allotted period)* Zeit, *die;* **in a week's/month's/year's ~:** in einer Woche/in einem Monat/Jahr; **there is ~ for that** dafür ist *od.* haben wir noch Zeit; **it takes me all my ~ to do it** es beansprucht meine ganze Zeit, es zu tun; **it took me all my ~ to persuade him** ich hatte die größte Mühe, ihn zu überreden; **give one's ~ to sth.** einer Sache *(Dat.)* seine Zeit opfern; **waste of ~:** Zeitverschwendung, *die;* **spend [most of one's/a lot of] ~ on sth./[in] doing sth.** [die meiste/viel] Zeit mit etw. zubringen/damit verbringen, etw. zu tun; **I have been waiting for some/a long ~:** ich warte schon seit einiger Zeit/schon lange; **she will be there for [quite] some ~:** sie wird ziemlich lange dort sein; **spend some ~ in a place** sich eine Zeitlang an einem Ort aufhalten; **be pressed for ~:** keine Zeit haben; *(have to finish quickly)* in Zeitnot sein; **pass the ~:** sich *(Dat.)* die Zeit vertreiben; **length of ~:** Zeit[dauer], *die;* **make ~ for sb./sth.** sich *(Dat.)* für jmdn./etw. Zeit nehmen; **a short ~ ago** vor kurzem; **that's a long ~ ago** das ist schon lange her; **in one's own ~:** in seiner Freizeit; *(whenever one wishes)* wann man will; **one's ~ is one's own** man kann über seine Zeit frei verfügen; **take one's ~ [over sth.]** sich *(Dat.)* [für etw.] Zeit lassen; *(be slow)* sich *(Dat.)* Zeit [mit etw.] lassen; **~ is money** *(prov.)* Zeit ist Geld *(Spr.);* **we're out of ~, our ~'s up** unsere Zeit ist um; **on ~** *(Amer.: on hire-purchase)* auf Raten; **in [good] ~** *(not late)* rechtzeitig; **all the** *or* **this ~:** die ganze Zeit; *(without ceasing)* ständig; **all the ~ you're standing there arguing things are only getting worse** während du hier herumstehst und argumentierst, wird alles nur immer schlimmer; **since ~ immemorial** *or* **out of mind** seit undenklichen Zeiten; **in [less than** *or* **next to] 'no ~:** innerhalb kürzester Zeit; im Nu *od.* Handumdrehen; **it was 'no ~ [at all] before she was back** sie war im Nu zurück; **in 'half the ~:** in der Hälfte der Zeit; **'half the ~** *(coll.: as often as not)* die halbe Zeit; **it will take [some] ~:** es wird einige Zeit dauern; **have ~ on one's hands** viel Zeit und Muße haben; *(have nothing to do)* nichts zu tun haben; **have the/no ~:** Zeit/keine Zeit haben; **have no ~ for sb./sth.** für jmdn./etw. ist einem seine Zeit zu schade; **we have no ~ to lose** wir dürfen keine Zeit verlieren; **there is no ~ to lose** *or* **be lost** es ist keine Zeit zu verlieren; **lose no ~ in doing sth.** *(not delay)* etw. unverzüglich tun; **lose no ~ doing sth.** *(not waste ~)* keine Zeit damit vergeuden, etw. zu tun; **do ~** *(sl.)* eine Strafe absitzen *(ugs.);* **he lived out his ~ in peace** er verbrachte den Rest seines Lebens in Ruhe; **in my '~** *(heyday)* zu meiner Zeit *(ugs.); (in the course of my life)* im Laufe meines Lebens; **in 'my ~** *(period at a place)* zu meiner Zeit *(ugs.);* **in my father's ~:** zu [Leb]zeiten meines Vaters; **~ off** *or* **out** freie Zeit; **get/take ~ off** frei bekommen/sich *(Dat.)* frei nehmen *(ugs.);* **take ~ out to look at this properly** nimm dir die Zeit, um dir das richtig anzuschauen; **T~!** *(Boxing)* Stop!; Time!; *(Brit.: in pub)* Feierabend!; **~, [ladies and] gentlemen, please!** wir machen Feierabend, meine [Damen und] Herren!; *see also* **gain 2 a; hand 1 c; serve 1 d; c)** *no pl. (moment or period destined for purpose)* Zeit, *die;* **harvest/Christmas ~:** Ernte-/Weihnachtszeit, *die;* **there is a ~ and place for everything** alles zu seiner Zeit; **now is the ~ to do it** jetzt ist die richtige Zeit, es zu tun; **~ for lunch** Zeit zum Mittagessen; **it is ~ to go** es wird Zeit zu gehen; **it's ~ [about] they were going** es ist [an der] Zeit, daß sie gehen; **his ~ was drawing near** *(~ of death)* seine Zeit nahte *(geh. verhüll.);* **look/get old before one's ~:** vorzeitig altern; **and not before ~:** und es wurde auch Zeit; **when the ~ comes/came** wenn es so weit ist/als es so weit war; **on ~** *(punctually)* pünktlich; **ahead of ~:** zu früh ⟨*ankommen*⟩; vorzeitig ⟨*fertig werden*⟩; **all in good ~:** alles zu seiner Zeit; **you'll find out in good ~:** du wirst es früh genug herausfinden; *see also* **be 2 a; behind 2 e; d)** *in sing. or pl. (circumstances)* Zeit, *die;* **~s are good/bad/have changed** die Zeiten sind gut/schlecht/haben sich verändert; **have a good ~:** Spaß haben *(ugs.);* sich amüsieren; **have quite a ~ [of it]** viel durchmachen; **have a hard ~ [of it]** eine schwere Zeit durchmachen; *see also* **life e; e)** *(associated with events or person[s])* Zeit, *die;* **in ~ of peace/war** in Friedens-/Kriegszeiten; **in Tudor/Napoleon's/ancient ~s** zur Zeit der Tudors/Napoleons/der Antike; **in prehistoric ~s** in vorgeschichtlicher Zeit; **in former/modern ~s** früher/heutzutage; **scientists of the ~:** Wissenschaftler jener Zeit; **the good old ~s** die gute alte Zeit; **Queen Victoria and her ~[s]** Königin Viktoria und ihre Zeit; **~ 'was when ...:** es gab eine Zeit, da ...; **ahead of** *or* **before one's/its ~:** seiner Zeit voraus; **at 'one ~** *(previously)* früher; *see also* **behind 2 c; f)** *(occasion)* Mal, *das;* **this ~:** diesmal; **for the first ~:** zum ersten Mal; **[the] second ~ [a]round** beim zweiten Mal; **next ~ you come** wenn du das nächste Mal kommst; **ten/a hundred/a thousand ~s** zehn-/hundert-/tausendmal; **~s without number** unzählige Male; **I've told you a hundred ~s ...:** ich habe dir schon hundertmal gesagt, ... *(ugs.);* **many ~s** sehr oft; **many's the ~ [that] ..., many a ~ ...:** viele Male ...; **there are/were ~s when ...:** es gibt Zeiten, wenn .../es gab Zeiten, als ...; **at all ~s** jederzeit; **at ~s** gelegentlich; **from ~ to ~:** von Zeit zu Zeit; **at other ~s** sonst; **at all other ~s** zu allen anderen Zeiten; **at one ~ or another** irgendwann einmal; **this is no ~ to do that** es ist jetzt nicht die Zeit, das zu tun; **at a ~ like this/that** unter diesen/solchen Umständen; **at the** *or* **that ~** *(in the past)* damals; **it depends on which doctor is on duty at the ~:** es hängt davon ab, welcher Arzt gerade Bereitschaftsdienst hat; **at one ~, at [one and] the same ~** *(simultaneously)* gleichzeitig; **at the same ~** *(nevertheless)* gleichwohl; **at the best of ~s** im günstigsten Fall; **a 'fine ~** *(iron.)* genau die richtige Zeit *(iron.);* **between ~s** zwischendurch; **~ and [~] again, ~ after ~:** immer [und immer] wieder; **pay sb. £6 a ~:** jmdm. für jedes Mal 6 Pfund zahlen; **oranges cost 16p a ~:** Orangen kosten 16 Pence das Stück; **one at a ~:** einzeln; **one stone at a ~:** jeweils nur ein Stein; **two at a ~:** jeweils zwei; **hand me the cups two at a ~:** reich mir immer zwei Tassen gleichzeitig; **for hours/weeks at a ~:** stundenlang/wochenlang [ohne Unterbrechung]; **at this ~** *(Amer.)* heute; *(at this moment)* jetzt; *see also* **be 2 a; every a; g)** *(point in day etc.)* [Uhr]zeit, *die;* **at the same ~ every morning** jeden Morgen um dieselbe Zeit; **what ~ is it?, what is the ~?** wie spät ist es?; **have you [got] the ~?** kannst du mir sagen, wie spät es ist?; **tell the ~** *(read a clock)* die Uhr lesen; **~ of day** Tageszeit, *die;* **[at this] ~ of [the] year** [um diese] Jahreszeit; **this ~ of the month** diese Zeit im Monat; **at this ~ of [the] night** zu dieser Nachtstunde; **know the ~ of day** *(fig.)* sich auskennen; **not give sb. the ~ of day** jmdm. nicht einmal guten Tag sagen; **pass the ~ of day** *(coll.)* ein paar Worte wechseln; **by this/that ~:** inzwischen; **by the ~ [that] we arrived** bis wir hinkamen; **[by] this ~ tomorrow** morgen um diese Zeit; **keep good ~** ⟨*Uhr:*⟩ genau *od.* richtig gehen; **h)** *(amount)* Zeit, *die;* **make good ~:** gut vorwärtskommen; **get paid ~ and a half** 50 % Zuschlag bekommen; **[your] ~'s up!** deine Zeit ist um *(ugs.) od.* abgelaufen; **i)** *(multiplication)* mal; **three ~s four** drei mal vier; **four ~s the size of/higher than sth.** viermal so groß wie/höher als etw.; **~s sign** Malzeichen, *das;* **magnified six ~s** auf das Sechsfache vergrößert; **j)** *(Mus.) (duration of note)* Zeitdauer, *die; (measure)* Takt, *der;* **in three-four ~:** im Dreivierteltakt; **keep in ~ with the music** den Takt halten; **out of ~/in ~:** aus dem/im Takt; **keep ~ with sth.** bei etw. den Takt [ein]halten; **k)** *(dated: date of childbirth)* **she is near** *or* **nearing her ~:** ihre Zeit rückt näher *(geh. verhüll.).* **2.** *v. t.* **a)** *(do at correct ~)* zeitlich abstimmen; **be well/ill ~d** zur richtigen/falschen Zeit kommen; **b)** *(set to operate at correct ~)* justieren *(Technik);* einstellen; **~ the bomb to explode at 4 p.m.** den Zeitzünder der Bombe auf 16 Uhr einstellen; **c)** *(arrange time of arrival/departure of)* **the bus is ~d to connect with the train** der Bus hat einen direkten Anschluß an den Zug; **be ~d to take 90 minutes** fahrplanmäßig 90 Minuten dauern; **d)** *(measure time taken by)* stoppen; **~ an egg** auf die richtige Kochdauer für ein Ei achten

time: ~-and-'motion *adj.* REFA-⟨*Techniker, Fachmann*⟩; **~-and-motion study** Arbeitsstudie, *die;* **~ bomb** *n. (lit. or fig.)* Zeitbombe, *die;* **~ capsule** *n. Behälter mit Zeitdokumenten, der bei der Grundsteinlegung von [öffentlichen] Bauten eingemauert wird;* **~-check** *n.* Zeitvergleich, *der; (to verify)* Blick auf die Uhr; **~-consuming** *adj.* **a)** *(taking ~)* zeitaufwendig; **b)** *(wasteful of ~)* zeitraubend; **~ exposure** *n. (Photog.)* Zeitaufnahme, *die;* **~ factor** *n., no pl.* Zeitfaktor, *der;* **~-fault** *n. (Show Jumping)* Zeitfehler, *der;* **~-fuse** *n.* Zeitzünder, *der;* **~-honoured** *adj.* altehrwürdig *(geh.);* althergebracht ⟨*Brauch, Vorstellung*⟩; **~keeper** *n.* **a)** *(person)* Zeitnehmer, *der*/-nehmerin, *die;* **b) the watch is a good/bad ~keeper** die Uhr geht genau/nicht genau; **~-keeping** *n.* **a)** *(Sport)* Zeitmessung, *die;* Zeitnahme, *die;* **b)** *(at work)* Einhaltung der Arbeitsstunden; **~-lag** *n.* zeit-

liche Verzögerung; **~-lapse** *attrib. adj. (Photog., Cinemat., Telev.)* Zeitraffer-
timeless ['taɪmlɪs] *adj. (rhet./poet.)* zeitlos
'time-limit *n.* Frist, *die;* **put a ~ on sth.** eine Frist für etw. setzen
timeliness ['taɪmlɪnɪs] *n., no pl.* Rechtzeitigkeit, *die*
'time lock *n.* Zeitschloß, *das*
timely ['taɪmlɪ] *adj.* rechtzeitig; **be ~:** zur rechten Zeit kommen; **a ~ piece of advice** ein [guter] Rat zur rechten Zeit
time: ~-machine *n.* Zeitmaschine, *die;* **~ 'out** *n. (Sport)* Spielunterbrechung, *die; (called by one team)* Auszeit, *die;* **~piece** *n.* Chronometer, *das*
timer ['taɪmə(r)] *n.* **a)** *see* **timekeeper a; b)** *(device)* Kurzzeitmesser, *der; (with switch)* Schaltuhr, *die*
time: ~-scale *n.* Zeitskala, *die;* **~-share 1.** *attrib. adj.* **~-share apartment** *Ferienwohnung, an der man einen Besitzanteil hat, der es einem erlaubt, eine bestimmte Zeit pro Jahr in dieser Wohnung zu verbringen;* **2.** *n. see* **~-sharing b; ~-sharing** *n., no pl., no art.* **a)** *(Computing)* Time-sharing, *das;* **b)** *(joint ownership) Eigentum an einer Ferienwohnung o. ä., das für eine festgelegte Zeit des Jahres gilt;* Time-sharing, *das (Wirtsch.);* **~-sheet** *n.* Stundenzettel, *der;* **~-signal** *n.* Zeitzeichen, *das;* **~-signature** *n. (Mus.)* Taktbezeichnung, *die;* **~-switch** *n.* Zeitschalter, *der;* **~table** *n.* **a)** *(scheme of work)* Zeitplan, *der; (Educ.)* Stundenplan, *der;* **b)** *(Transport)* Fahrplan, *der;* **~-travel** *n.* Reise durch die Zeit; **~ warp** *n.* Verwerfung im Raum-Zeit-Kontinuum; **~-worn** *adj.* abgegriffen ‹*Witz, Klischee*›; verwittert ‹*Gebäude*›; **~-zone** *n.* Zeitzone, *die*
timid ['tɪmɪd] *adj.* **a)** scheu ‹*Tier, Vogel*›; **b)** *(fearful)* ängstlich ‹*Person, Miene, Worte*›; **c)** *(lacking boldness)* zaghaft; *(shy)* schüchtern
timidity [tɪ'mɪdɪtɪ] *n., no pl. see* **timid:** Scheu, *die;* Ängstlichkeit, *die;* Schüchternheit, *die*
timidly ['tɪmɪdlɪ] *adv. see* **timid:** scheu; ängstlich; schüchtern
timing ['taɪmɪŋ] *n., no pl.* **a)** zeitliche Abstimmung; Timing, *das;* **that was perfect ~!** *(as sb. arrives)* du kommst gerade im richtigen Augenblick!; **the ~ of the statement was excellent** der Zeitpunkt für die Erklärung war hervorragend [gewählt]; **b)** *(Theatre)* Timing, *das;* **c)** *(Motor Veh.)* **ignition/valve ~:** Zündeinstellung, *die*/Ventilsteuerzeiten; **adjust the [ignition] ~:** die Zündung einstellen
timorous ['tɪmərəs] *adj.* ängstlich; verängstigt ‹*Tier*›; *(lacking boldness)* zaghaft ‹*Stimme, Auftreten*›
timpani ['tɪmpənɪ:] *n. pl. (Mus.)* Kesselpauken; Timpani *(fachspr.)*
timpanist ['tɪmpənɪst] *n. (Mus.)* Paukist, *der*/Paukistin, *die*
tin [tɪn] **1.** *n.* **a)** *(metal)* Zinn, *das;* **~[-plate]** Weißblech, *das;* **b)** *(Cookery)* **cooking ~s** Back- und Bratformen; **c)** *(Brit.: for preserving)* [Konserven]dose, *die;* **a ~ of peas** eine Dose Erbsen; **d)** *(with separate or hinged lid)* Dose, *die;* **bread ~:** Brotkasten, *der.* **2.** *v. t.*, **-nn-** *(Brit.)* zu Konserven verarbeiten. **3.** *attrib. adj.* Zinn-; *see also* **lid a**
tincture ['tɪŋktʃə(r)] *n.* **a)** *(solution)* Tinktur, *die;* **b)** *(slight flavour)* leichter Geschmack; *(unpleasant)* Beigeschmack, *der; (fig.)* Anflug, *der;* **a ~ of green/red** ein Stich ins Grüne/Rote
tinder ['tɪndə(r)] *n.* Zunder, *der*
'tinder-box *n.* Zunderbüchse, *die (veralt.); (fig.: person)* Hitzkopf, *der; (fig.: thing)* Pulverfaß, *das;* **the old houses are like ~es** die alten Häuser sind wie Zunder
tine [taɪn] *n.* **a)** *(of deer)* Ende, *das (Jägerspr.);* **b)** *(of rake, fork)* Zinke, *die*
tin 'foil *n., no pl.* Stanniol, *das; (aluminium foil)* Alufolie, *die*
ting-a-ling ['tɪŋəlɪŋ] **1.** *n.* Klingeling, *das.* **2.** *adv.* klingeling
tinge [tɪndʒ] **1.** *v. t.*, **~ing** ['tɪndʒɪŋ] tönen; **a white curtain ~d with pink** ein weißer, ins Zartrosa gehender Vorhang; **her black hair was ~d with grey** ihr schwarzes Haar war graumeliert; *(fig.)* **her admiration was ~d with envy** ihre Bewunderung war nicht ganz frei von Neid. **2.** *n.* [leichte] Färbung; *(fig.)* Hauch, *der;* **a ~ of red in the sky** eine leicht rötliche Färbung des Himmels; **white with a ~ of blue** weiß mit einem Stich ins Bläuliche
tingle ['tɪŋgl] **1.** *v. i.* **a)** *(feel sensation)* kribbeln; **b)** *(cause sensation)* **~ in sb.'s ears** jmdm. in den Ohren klingen *od.* tönen. **2.** *n.* Kribbeln, *das;* **feel a ~ of excitement** vor Aufregung ganz kribbelig sein *(ugs.)*
tin: ~ 'god *n.* Götze, *der (geh.);* Abgott, *der;* **~ 'hat** *n. (sl.)* Blechdeckel, *der (salopp);* **~horn** *(Amer.)* **1.** *n.* Angeber, *der (ugs.);* **2.** *adj.* angeberisch *(ugs.)*
tinker ['tɪŋkə(r)] **1.** *n.* Kesselflicker, *der;* **I don't give a ~'s cuss** *(coll.)* es ist mir völlig Wurs[ch]t *(ugs.).* **2.** *v. i.* **~ with sth.** an etw. *(Dat.)* herumbasteln *(ugs.)/(incompetently; also fig.)* herumpfuschen *(ugs.)*
tinkle ['tɪŋkl] **1.** *n.* Klingeln, *das; (of coins)* Klimpern, *das;* **give sb. a ~** *(Brit. coll.: telephone call)* bei jmdm. anklingeln *(ugs.).* **2.** *v. t.* klingeln mit; klimpern mit ‹*Münzen*›. **3.** *v. i.* ‹*Glocke:*› klingeln; ‹*Münzen:*› klimpern; **~ on a piano** auf einem Klavier klimpern
'tin mine *n.* Zinnbergwerk, *das*
tinned [tɪnd] *adj. (Brit.)* Dosen-; **be ~:** aus der Dose sein
tinny ['tɪnɪ] *adj.* **a)** *(metallic)* Metall‹*geschmack*›; blechern ‹*Klang*›; **taste ~:** nach Metall *od. (ugs.)* Büchse schmecken; **b)** *(of inferior quality)* billig; **be ~:** Tinnef sein *(ugs.)*
tin: ~-opener *n. (Brit.)* Dosen-, Büchsenöffner, *der;* **~-pan 'alley** *n.* die Schlagerindustrie; **~ 'plate** *n.* Weißblech, *das;* **~-plate** *v. t.* verzinnen; **~-plating** *n.* Verzinnung, *die;* **~pot** *adj. (derog.)* schäbig; **~pot town** Kaff, *das (ugs.);* **~pot little firm** [kleine] Klitsche *(ugs.);* **~pot dictator** Operettendiktator, *der*
tinsel ['tɪnsl] *n.* **a)** *(thread)* Metallfaden, *der; (for decoration)* Lametta, *das; (strip)* Lahn, *der (Textilw.); (sheet)* Metallfolie, *die;* **b)** *also attrib.* **~ [glamour]** Talmiglanz, *der*
tin: ~smith *n.* Blechschmied, *der;* **~ 'soldier** *n.* Zinnsoldat, *der*
tint [tɪnt] **1.** *n.* Farbton, *der;* **flesh ~s** Fleischtöne; **autumn ~s** herbstliche Farbtöne; **red with a blue ~:** Rot mit einem Stich ins Blaue. **2.** *v. t.* tönen; kolorieren ‹*Zeichnung, Stich*›; **~ with blue** blau tönen/kolorieren
tin: ~ tack *n.* [verzinnter] Drahtstift; **~ 'whistle** *n.* Blechflöte, *die*
tiny ['taɪnɪ] *adj.* winzig; **a ~ bit better** *(coll.)* ein klein wenig besser; **sb.'s ~ mind** *(derog.)* jmds. Spatzenhirn *(salopp)*
[1]tip [tɪp] **1.** *n. (end, point)* Spitze, *die;* **the ~ of his nose/finger/toe** seine Nasen-/Finger-/Zehenspitze; **on the ~s of one's toes** auf Zehenspitzen; **from ~ to toe** vom Scheitel bis zur Sohle; **it is on the ~ of my tongue** es liegt mir auf der Zunge; **a cigarette with a [filter-]~:** eine Zigarette mit Filter. **2.** *v. t.*, **-pp- ~ sth. [with stone/brass]** etw. mit einer [Stein-/Messing]spitze versehen; **~ped cigarette** Filterzigarette, *die*
[2]tip 1. *v. i.*, **-pp-** *(lean, fall)* kippen; **~ over** umkippen; **~ [up]** ‹*Sitz:*› nach oben klappen. **2.** *v. t.*, **-pp- a)** *(make tilt)* kippen; neigen ‹*Kopf*›; **~ one's hat [to sb.]** *(Amer.)* seinen Hut lüften[, um jmdn. zu grüßen]; **~ the balance** *(fig.)* den Ausschlag geben; *see also* **[2]scale 1 b; b)** *(make overturn)* umkippen; *(Brit.: discharge)* kippen; **'no ~ping', 'no rubbish to be ~ped'** „Müll abladen verboten"; **he was ~ped into the ditch** er wurde in den Graben geworfen; **c)** *(mention as likely winner etc.)* voraussagen ‹*Sieger*›; **~ sb. to win** auf jmds. Sieg tippen; **be ~ped for the Presidency/a post** als Favorit für die Präsidentschaftswahlen/einen Posten genannt werden; **d)** *(sl.: give)* geben; **~ sb. the wink** *(fig.)* jmdm. Bescheid sagen; *(~ sb. off)* jmdm. einen Tip geben *(ugs.);* **e)** *(give money to)* **~ sb. [20p]** jmdm. [20 Pence] Trinkgeld geben. **3.** *n.* **a)** *(money)* Trinkgeld, *das;* **as a ~:** als Trinkgeld; **b)** *(special information)* Hinweis, *der;* Tip, *der (ugs.); (advice)* Rat, *der;* **hot ~:** heißer Tip; **give sb. a ~ about doing sth.** jmdm. einen Tip geben, wie man etw. macht; **c)** *(Brit.: place for refuse)* Müllkippe, *die;* **d)** *(derog.: untidy place)* Schweinestall, *der;* **e)** *(Mining)* Halde, *die*
~ 'off *v. t.* **~ sb. off** jmdm. einen Hinweis *od. (ugs.)* Tip geben; **be ~ped off by sb.** einen Hinweis *od. (ugs.)* Tip von jmdm. erhalten; *see also* **tip-off**
~ 'over *v. t. & i.* umkippen
~ 'up *v. t.* hochklappen ‹*Sitz*›
tip: ~-and-'run raid *n.* Blitzangriff [mit anschließendem sofortigem Rückzug]; **~-off** *n.* Hinweis, *der*
tipper ['tɪpə(r)] *n. (Brit. Motor Veh.)* Kipper, *der*
tipple ['tɪpl] **1.** *v. i.* trinken. **2.** *n. (coll.: drink)* **have a ~:** einen trinken *(ugs.);* **what's your ~?** was trinken Sie?
tippler ['tɪplə(r)] *n.* Trinker, *der*/Trinkerin, *die;* **be a ~:** gern einen trinken *(ugs.)*
tipsily ['tɪpsɪlɪ] *adv. (coll.)* angeheitert; beschwipst *(ugs.)*
tipster ['tɪpstə(r)] *n.* Tipgeber, *der*/-geberin, *die*
tipsy ['tɪpsɪ] *adj. (coll.)* angeheitert; beschwipst *(ugs.)*
tip: ~toe 1. *v. i.* auf Zehenspitzen gehen; *(walk quietly)* sich schleichen *od.* stehlen; **2.** *adv.* auf Zehenspitzen; **3.** *n.* **on ~toe[s]** auf Zehenspitzen; **stand on ~toe** sich auf die Zehenspitzen stellen; **be standing on ~toe** auf den Zehenspitzen stehen; **~top** ['tɪptɒp] *(coll.)* **1.** *adj.* ausgezeichnet; tipptopp *(ugs.);* **it was a ~top hotel** das Hotel war tipptopp; **be in ~top condition** in einem Topzustand/‹*Mensch:*› in Topform sein; **2.** *adv.* tipptopp *(ugs.);* ausgezeichnet; **~-up seat** *n.* Klappsitz, *der*
TIR *abbr. (Brit.)* **Transport International Routier** *Internationaler Straßentransport*
tirade [taɪ'reɪd, tɪ'reɪd] *n.* Tirade, *die (geh.);* **a ~ of abuse** eine Schimpfkanonade *(ugs.)*
[1]tire ['taɪə(r)] *(Amer.) see* **tyre**
[2]tire 1. *v. t.* ermüden. **2.** *v. i.* müde werden; ermüden; **~ of sth./doing sth.** einer Sache *(Gen.)* überdrüssig werden/es müde werden *(geh.),* etw. zu tun
~ 'out *v. t.* erschöpfen; **~ oneself out doing sth.** etw. bis zur Erschöpfung tun
tired ['taɪəd] *adj.* **a)** *(weary)* müde; **b)** *(fed up)* **be ~ of sth./doing sth.** etw. satt haben/es satt haben *od. (geh.)* es müde sein, etw. zu tun; **get** *or* **grow ~ of sb./sth.** jmds./einer Sache überdrüssig werden; **c)** *(fig.: hackneyed)* abgegriffen; abgedroschen *(ugs.)*
tiredness ['taɪədnɪs] *n., no pl.* Müdigkeit, *die*
tireless ['taɪəlɪs] *adj.*, **tirelessly** ['taɪəlɪslɪ] *adv.* unermüdlich
tiresome ['taɪəsəm] *adj.* **a)** *(wearisome)* mühsam; **b)** *(annoying)* lästig; **how ~!** so ein Ärger!
tiresomely ['taɪəsəmlɪ] *adv.* **a)** *(wearisomely)* mühsam; **~ lengthy** mühsam und langwierig; **b)** *(annoyingly)* lästigerweise; **~ facetious** auf unangenehme Art albern

tiring ['taɪərɪŋ] *adj.* ermüdend; anstrengend ⟨*Tag, Person*⟩

tiro ['taɪərəʊ] *n., pl.* ~s Anfänger, *der*/Anfängerin, *die*

'tis [tɪz] *(arch./poet.)* = **it is**

tissue ['tɪʃu:, 'tɪsju:] *n.* **a)** *(woven fabric; also Biol.)* Gewebe, *das;* **b)** *(absorbent paper)* **[paper]** ~: Papiertuch, *das; (handkerchief)* Papiertaschentuch, *das;* **c)** *(for wrapping)* ~ **[paper]** Seidenpapier, *das;* **d)** *(fig.: web)* Geflecht, *das;* ~ **of lies** Lügengewebe, *das*

[1]tit [tɪt] *n. (Ornith.)* Meise, *die; see also* **blue tit; great tit**

[2]tit *n.* **it's ~ for tat** wie du mir, so ich dir; **give sb. ~ for tat** es jmdm. mit gleicher Münze heimzahlen

[3]tit *n. (coarse)* **a)** *(nipple)* Zitze, *die (derb);* **b)** *usu. pl. (breast)* Titte, *die (derb)*

[4]tit *n. (sl.: fool)* Trottel, *der (ugs.)*

Titan ['taɪtən] *n. (fig.)* Titan, *der (geh.)*

titanic [taɪ'tænɪk] *adj.* gigantisch

titanium [taɪ'teɪnɪəm, tɪ'teɪnɪəm] *n. (Chem.)* Titan, *das*

titbit ['tɪtbɪt] *n.* **a)** *(food)* Häppchen, *das (ugs.);* **b)** *(piece of news)* Neuigkeit, *die*

titch [tɪtʃ] *n. (coll.)* Knirps, *der (ugs.)*

titchy ['tɪtʃɪ] *adj. (coll.)* klitzeklein *(ugs.)*

tithe [taɪð] *n. (Hist.)* Zehnt[e], *der;* **pay ~s** den Zehnten bezahlen; ~ **barn** Zehntscheuer, *die*

Titian ['tɪʃn] **1.** *pr. n.* Tizian *(der).* **2.** *n.* ~ **[red]** Tizianrot, *das.* **3.** *adj.* ~ **[red]** tizianrot

titillate ['tɪtɪleɪt] *v. t.* erregen; ~ **sb.'s palate** jmds. Gaumen kitzeln

titillation [tɪtɪ'leɪʃn] *n.* Kitzel, *der*

titivate ['tɪtɪveɪt] *v. t. (coll.)* aufmöbeln *(ugs.);* ~ **[oneself]** sich zurechtmachen

title ['taɪtl] *n.* **a)** *(of book etc.)* Titel, *der; (of article, chapter)* Überschrift, *die;* **the flyweight ~** *(Sport)* der Titel im Fliegengewicht; **the ~s** *(Cinemat., Telev.)* der Vorspann; **b)** *(of person)* Titel, *der; (of nobility)* [Adels]titel, *der; (of organization)* Name, *der;* **people with ~s** Adlige; **c)** *(Law: recognized claim)* Rechtsanspruch, *der* (**to** auf + *Akk.*); ~ **[of ownership]** Besitztitel, *der*

titled ['taɪtld] *adj.* adlig

title: ~-deed *n. (Law)* Eigentumsurkunde, *die;* **~-holder** *n. (Sport)* Titelhalter, *der*/-halterin, *die;* **~-page** *n.* Titelseite, *die;* **~-role** *n.* Titelrolle, *die*

'titmouse *n. (Ornith.)* Meise, *die*

titter ['tɪtə(r)] **1.** *v. i.* kichern. **2.** *n.* **~[s]** Kichern, *das*

tittle-tattle ['tɪtltætl] **1.** *n.* Klatsch, *der (ugs. abwertend).* **2.** *v. i.* klatschen *(ugs. abwertend)*

titular ['tɪtjʊlə(r)] *adj.* **a)** *(only in name)* nominell *(geh.)* ⟨*Führer, Staatsoberhaupt*⟩; **b)** *(going with title)* Adels⟨*rang*⟩; mit einem Adelstitel verbunden ⟨*Besitztümer*⟩; **c)** ~ **hero** Titelheld, *der*

tizzy ['tɪzɪ] *n. (sl.)* **be in a/get into a ~:** durchdrehen *(ugs.)* **(over** wegen); **be all of a ~:** ganz aus dem Häuschen sein *(ugs.)*

'T-junction *see* **T b**

TNT *abbr.* **trinitrotoluene** TNT, *das*

to 1. [*before vowel* tʊ, *before consonant* tə, *stressed* tu:] *prep.* **a)** *(in the direction of and reaching)* zu; *(with name of place)* nach; **go to work/to the theatre** zur Arbeit/ins Theater gehen; **to Paris/France** nach Paris/Frankreich; **go from town to town** von Stadt zu Stadt ziehen; **throw the ball to me** wirf mir den Ball zu; **to bed with you!** ins Bett mit dir/euch!; **b)** *(towards a condition or quality)* zu; **appoint sb. to a post** jmdn. auf einen Posten berufen; **be born to a fortune** reich geboren sein; **c)** *(as far as)* bis zu; **from London to Edinburgh** von London [bis] nach Edinburgh; **increase from 10% to 20%** von 10% auf 20% steigen; **from green to violet** von Grün bis Violett; **d)** *(next to, facing)* **with one's back to the wall** mit dem Rücken zur Wand; **e)** *(implying comparison, ratio, etc.)* **[compared] to** verglichen mit; im Vergleich zu; **3 is to 4 as 6 is to 8** 3 verhält sich zu 4 wie 6 zu 8; **it's ten to one he does sth.** die Chancen stehen zehn zu eins, daß er etw. tut; **sing to a guitar** zur Gitarre singen; **f)** *introducing relationship or indirect object* **to sb./sth.** jmdm./einer Sache *(Dat.);* **lend/give/write/explain** *etc.* **sth. to sb.** jmdm. etw. leihen/geben/schreiben/erklären *usw.;* **speak to sb.** mit jmdm. sprechen; **relate to sth.** sich auf etw. *(Akk.)* beziehen; **to me** *(in my opinion)* meiner Meinung nach; **be pleasant to the taste** gut schmecken; **secretary to the Minister** Sekretär des Ministers; **be a good father to one's children** seinen Kindern ein guter Vater sein; **a room to oneself** ein eigenes Zimmer; **get four apples to the pound** vier Äpfel je Pfund bekommen; **there is a moral to this tale** diese Geschichte hat eine Moral; **is there a point to all this?** hat das alles einen Sinn?; **that's all there is to it** mehr ist nicht dazu zu sagen; **what's that to you?** was geht das dich an?; **to repair of rear door** *(in bill or account)* Reparatur [der] Hintertür; **g)** *(until)* bis; **to the end** bis zum Ende; **to this day** bis heute; **five [minutes] to eight** fünf [Minuten] vor acht; **one minute/two minutes to eight** eine Minute/zwei Minuten vor acht; **h)** *with infinitive of a verb* zu; (*expressing purpose, or after* **too**) um [...] zu; **want to know** wissen wollen; **do sth. to annoy sb.** etw. tun, um jmdn. zu ärgern; **too young to marry** zu jung, um zu heiraten; zu jung zum Heiraten; **too hot to drink** zu heiß zum Trinken; **to rebel is pointless** es ist sinnlos zu rebellieren; **he woke to find himself in a strange room** er erwachte und fand sich in einem fremden Zimmer wieder; **those days are gone, never to return** diese Zeit ist vorbei und wird nie wiederkehren *(geh.);* **to be honest/precise, ...:** offen/genau[er] gesagt, ...; **to use a technical term** um einen Fachausdruck zu gebrauchen; **to hear him talk ...:** wenn man ihn reden hört, ...; **i)** *as substitute for infinitive* **he would have phoned but forgot to** er hätte angerufen, aber er vergaß es; **she didn't want to go there, but she had to** sie wollte nicht hingehen, aber sie mußte; **he said he would ring her, but he had no time to** er sagte, er wolle sie anrufen, aber er hatte keine Zeit [dazu]; **you should buy it; you'd be silly not to** du solltest es kaufen; du wärst dumm, wenn du es nicht tätest. **2.** [tu:] *adv.* **a)** *(just not shut)* **be to** ⟨*Tür, Fenster:*⟩ angelehnt sein; **push a door to** eine Tür anlehnen; **b) to and fro** hin und her

toad [təʊd] *n. (Zool.; fig. derog.)* Kröte, *die*

toad: ~flax *n. (Bot.)* Leinkraut, *das;* **~-in-the-hole** *n. (Gastr.) Würstchen, in einen Teig eingebacken;* **~stool** *n.* Giftpilz, *der; (Bot.)* Schirmpilz, *der*

toady ['təʊdɪ] **1.** *n.* Kriecher, *der.* **2.** *v. i.* ~ **[to sb.]** [vor jmdm.] kriechen *(abwertend)*

toast [təʊst] **1.** *n.* **a)** *no pl., no indef. art.* Toast, *der;* **a piece of ~:** eine Scheibe Toast; **cheese/egg on ~:** Toast mit Käse/Ei; **as warm as ~** *(fig.)* schön warm *(ugs.);* **b)** *(call to drink)* Toast, *der;* **drink/propose a ~ to sb./sth.** auf jmdn./etw. trinken/einen Toast auf jmdn./etw. ausbringen; **be the ~ of the town** von der ganzen Stadt gefeiert werden. **2.** *v. t.* **a)** rösten; toasten ⟨*Brot*⟩; **b)** *(fig.: warm)* ~ **one's feet** sich *(Dat.)* die Füße wärmen; ~ **oneself in the sun** in der Sonne rösten *(scherzh.);* **c)** *(drink in honour of)* trinken auf (+ *Akk.*)

toaster ['təʊstə(r)] *n.* Toaster, *der*

'toasting-fork *n.* Gabel zum Rösten vor dem offenen Feuer

toast: ~-master *n. jmd., der bei einem öffentlichen Essen die Toasts ausbringt;* **~-rack** *n.* Toastständer, *der*

tobacco [tə'bækəʊ] *n. pl.* **~s** Tabak, *der*

tobacco: ~ jar *n.* Tabak[s]dose, *die;* ~ **leaf** *n.* Tabakblatt, *das*

tobacconist [tə'bækənɪst] *n.* Tabak[waren]händler, *der*/-händlerin, *die; see also* **baker**

to'bacco-pouch *n.* Tabak[s]beutel, *der*

toboggan [tə'bɒgən] **1.** *n.* Schlitten, *der;* Toboggan, *der.* **2.** *v. i.* Schlitten fahren

toby ['təʊbɪ] *n.* ~ **[jug]** Figurenkrug, *der;* Toby jug, *der*

toccata [tə'kɑ:tə] *n. (Mus.)* Tokkata, *die*

Toc H [tɒk 'eɪtʃ] *n. (Brit.) christlich und sozial orientierte Vereinigung [ehemaliger Armeeangehöriger]*

tod [tɒd] *n. (Brit. sl.)* **on one's ~:** [ganz] allein

today [tə'deɪ] **1.** *n.* heute; **~'s newspaper** die Zeitung von heute; **~'s film industry** die heutige Filmindustrie; **live for ~:** für den Tag leben. **2.** *adv.* heute; **a week/fortnight [from] ~:** heute in einer Woche/in vierzehn Tagen; **a year [ago] ~:** heute vor einem Jahr; **early ~:** heute früh; **later [on] ~:** später [am Tage]; **earlier ~:** heute vor wenigen Stunden

toddle ['tɒdl] *v. i.* **a)** *(with tottering steps)* mit wackligen Schritten gehen; wackeln *(ugs.);* **b)** *(coll.: leave)* ~ **[off]** sich verziehen *(ugs.);* **I must ~ [along** *or* **off] now** ich muß mich jetzt auf die Socken machen *(ugs.);* **c)** *(coll.: go)* ~ **along** *or* **down to the post** zum Postamt wandern *(ugs.)*

toddler ['tɒdlə(r)] *n.* ≈ Kleinkind, *das;* **he is only a ~:** er hat gerade laufen gelernt

toddy ['tɒdɪ] *n.* Toddy, *der;* **rum ~:** ≈ Grog, *der*

to-do [tə'du:] *n.* Getue, *das (ugs.);* **make a great ~ about sth.** viel Theater um etw. machen *(ugs.);* **there was a great ~ when ...:** es gab eine große Aufregung, als ...:

toe [təʊ] **1.** *n.* **a)** *(Anat.)* Zeh, *der;* Zehe, *die;* **be on one's ~s** *(fig.)* auf Zack sein *(ugs.);* **keep sb. on his/her ~s** *(fig.)* jmdn. in Trab halten *(ugs.);* **turn up one's ~s** *(sl. euphem.: die)* ins Gras beißen *(salopp);* **b)** *(of footwear)* Spitze, *die;* **at the ~:** an den Zehen; **the ~s of the boots are reinforced** die Stiefel sind an der Spitze verstärkt; **c)** *(Zool.)* Zeh, *der.* **2.** *v. t.,* **~ing** *(fig.)* ~ **the line** *or (Amer.)* **mark** sich einordnen; **refuse to ~ the line** aus der Reihe tanzen *(ugs.);* ~ **the party line** linientreu sein

'toe-cap *n.* Vorderkappe, *die; (of boot)* Stiefelkappe, *die;* **steel ~:** Stahlkappe, *die*

-toed [təʊd] *adj. in comb.* -zehig

'toe: ~-hold *n.* Tritt, *der; (fig.)* **gain a ~-hold** einen Fuß in die Tür bekommen; **have only a ~-hold in Europe** nur ein kleines Gebiet in Europa haben; *(for sales)* in Europa nur schwach vertreten sein; **~-nail** *n.* Zeh[en]nagel, *der*

toff [tɒf] *n. (Brit. sl. dated)* Lackaffe, *der (ugs. abwertend)*

toffee ['tɒfɪ] *n.* **a)** Karamel, *der;* **b)** *(Brit.: piece)* Toffee, *das;* Sahnebonbon, *das;* **c) sb. can't do sth. for ~** *(fig. sl.)* jmd. kann etw. nicht für fünf Pfennig tun *(ugs.)*

toffee: ~-apple *n.* mit Karamel überzogener Apfel am Stiel; **~-nosed** *adj. (Brit. sl.)* hochnäsig

tog [tɒg] **1.** *n.* **a)** *in pl. (sl.: garments)* Klamotten *(ugs.);* **b)** *(Textiles) Einheit für das Wärmerückhaltevermögen von Textilien.* **2.** *v. t.* **-gg-:** ~ **[oneself] out** *or* **up** sich in Schale werfen *(ugs.);* **they were ~ged out in their Sunday best** sie waren mit ihrem besten Sonntagsstaat ausstaffiert

toga ['təʊgə] *n. (Roman Ant.)* Toga, *die*

together [tə'geðə(r)] *adv.* **a)** *(in or into company)* zusammen; **sit down ~:** sich zusammensetzen; **gather ~:** sich [ver]sammeln; **soloist and orchestra were not ~:** Solist und Orchester spielten nicht im Takt; **taken all ~:** alle zusammengenommen; **~ with** zusammen mit; **b)** *(simultaneously)* gleichzeitig; **all ~ now!** jetzt alle zusammen *od.* im

Chor!; **c)** *(one with another)* miteinander; **put them ~ to compare them** halte sie nebeneinander, um sie zu vergleichen; **d)** *(without interruption)* **for weeks/days/hours ~:** wochen-/tage-/stundenlang; **for three days ~:** drei Tage hintereinander; **e)** *(coll.: organized)* **not ~** chaotisch *(ugs.)* ‹*Person*›

togetherness [tə'geðənɪs] *n., no pl.* Zusammengehörigkeit, *die*

toggle ['tɒgl] *n.* **a)** *(button)* Knebelknopf, *der;* **b)** *(cross-piece)* Knebel, *der*

'toggle-switch *n. (Electr.)* Kippschalter, *der*

Togo ['təʊgəʊ], **Togoland** ['təʊgəʊlænd] *pr. ns.* Togo *(das)*

Togolese [təʊgəʊ'li:z] **1.** *adj.* togolesisch. **2.** *n., pl. same* Togolese, *der*/Togolesin, *die*

toil [tɔɪl] **1.** *v. i.* **a)** *(work laboriously)* schwer arbeiten; sich abarbeiten; **~ at/over sth.** sich mit etw. abplagen/abmühen; **~ through a book** sich mühsam durch ein Buch arbeiten; **~ [away] on sth.** sich mit etw. abmühen; **b)** *(move laboriously)* sich schleppen; **the train ~ed up the incline** der Zug mühte sich die Steigung hinauf; **~ on** sich weiterschleppen. **2.** *n.* [harte] Arbeit; **with much ~:** mit großer Mühe; **the ~s of the day** die Mühen des Tages

toiler ['tɔɪlə(r)] *n. (for peace, justice, etc.)* Kämpfer, *der*/Kämpferin, *die*

toilet ['tɔɪlɪt] *n.* **a)** Toilette, *die;* **down the ~:** in die Toilette; **go to the ~:** auf die Toilette gehen; **be in the ~:** auf der Toilette sein; **on the ~** *(coll.)* auf dem Klo *(ugs.);* **b)** *(washing and dressing)* Toilette, *die;* **be at one's ~** *(dated)* bei der Toilette sein

toilet: ~-bag *n.* Kulturbeutel, *der;* **~-bowl** *n.* Toilettenbecken, *das;* Klosettbecken, *das;* **~-brush** *n.* Klosettbürste, *die;* **~-paper** *n.* Toilettenpapier, *das*

toiletries ['tɔɪlɪtrɪz] *n.pl.* Körperpflegemittel; Toilettenartikel

toilet: ~-roll *n.* Rolle Toilettenpapier; **~-roll holder** *n.* Toilettenpapierhalter, *der;* **~-seat** *n.* Klosettbrille, *die (ugs.);* Toilettensitz, *der;* **~ soap** *n.* Toilettenseife, *die;* **~ tissue** *see* **toilet-paper; ~-training** *n.* Sauberkeitserziehung, *die;* **~ water** *n.* Toilettenwasser, *das;* Eau de Toilette, *das*

toils [tɔɪlz] *n.pl. (literary)* Fangnetz, *das;* Fanggarn, *das (Jägerspr.); (fig.)* Fallstrick, *der*

'toil-worn *adj.* abgearbeitet ‹*Person*›; erschöpft ‹*Reisender*›; abgehärmt ‹*Gesicht*›

toing and froing [tu:ɪŋ ən 'frəʊɪŋ] *n.* Hin und Her, *das*

Tokay [tə'keɪ] *n.* Tokaier, *der;* Tokajer, *der*

token ['təʊkn] **1.** *n.* **a)** *(voucher)* Gutschein, *der; see also* **book token; gift token; record token; b)** *(counter, disc)* Marke, *die;* Jeton, *der;* **c)** *(sign)* Zeichen, *das; (evidence)* Beweis, *der;* **as a** *or* **in ~ of sth.** als Zeichen/zum Beweis einer Sache; **he received a present as a** *or* **in ~ of his 30 years' service with the firm** anläßlich seiner dreißigjährigen Zugehörigkeit zur Firma erhielt er ein Geschenk; **d) by the same** *or* **this ~:** ebenso; **if you don't believe me, then by the same ~ you can't believe him** wenn du mir nicht glaubst, dann heißt das, daß du ihm auch nicht glauben kannst; **his wages are low and, by the same ~, not nearly enough to make him stay in this job** seine Bezahlung ist schlecht und daher natürlich auch nicht ausreichend, ihn in diesem Job zu halten; **e)** *(keepsake)* Abschiedsgeschenk, *das;* Andenken, *das.* **2.** *attrib. adj.* symbolisch ‹*Preis*›; nominal *(Wirtsch.)* ‹*Lohnerhöhung, Miete*›; *(minimal)* geringfügig ‹*Schaden*›; **a ~ woman/black person on the staff** eine Alibifrau/ein Alibischwarzer als Mitarbeiterin/Mitarbeiter; **his offer of help is only a ~ offer** sein Hilfsangebot ist nur ein Proforma-Angebot; **offer** *or* **put up ~ resistance** pro forma Widerstand leisten; **~ strike** Warnstreik, *der*

tokenism ['təʊkənɪzm] *n.* **sth. is just ~:** etw. hat nur Alibifunktion

Tokyo ['təʊkjəʊ] *pr. n.* Tokio *(das)*

told *see* **tell**

tolerable ['tɒlərəbl] *adj.* **a)** *(endurable)* erträglich **(to, for** für); **b)** *(fairly good)* leidlich; annehmbar; **a very ~ lunch** ein sehr ordentliches Mittagessen; **How are things? – Oh, ~:** Wie geht's? – Oh, es geht

tolerably ['tɒlərəblɪ] *adv.* leidlich; annehmbar; einigermaßen ‹*gut, richtig*›

tolerance ['tɒlərəns] *n.* **a)** Toleranz, *die* **(for, towards,** gegen[über]); **have no ~ for sth.** für etw. kein Verständnis haben; etw. nicht tolerieren [können]; **a mother with three children needs a lot of ~:** eine Mutter mit drei Kindern braucht viel Verständnis; **b)** *(Med., Mech. Engin.)* Toleranz, *die*

tolerant ['tɒlərənt] *adj.* **a)** tolerant **(of, towards** gegen[über]); **be ~ of criticism** Kritik vertragen; **b)** *(Med.)* widerstandsfähig

tolerate ['tɒləreɪt] *v. t.* **a)** dulden; tolerieren *(geh.);* **this material will ~ high temperatures/hard wear** dieses Material ist hitzebeständig/strapazierfähig; **b)** *(put up with)* **~ sb./sth.** sich mit jmdm./etw. abfinden; **she ~d his moods** sie ließ seine Launen über sich *(Akk.)* ergehen; **~ one another** sich [gegenseitig] akzeptieren; **how can you ~ this awful man?** wie kannst du diesen schrecklichen Mann ertragen?; **I can't ~ football/fanaticism** ich kann Fußball/Fanatismus nicht ausstehen; **c)** *(sustain)* ertragen ‹*Schmerzen, Hitze, Lärm*›; **d)** *(Med.)* vertragen

toleration [tɒlə'reɪʃn] *n.* Tolerierung, *die (geh.);* **religious/mutual ~:** religiöse/gegenseitige Toleranz

¹toll [təʊl] *n.* **a)** *(tax, duty)* Gebühr, *die; (for road)* [Straßen]gebühr, *die;* Maut, *die (bes. österr.);* **b)** *(damage etc. incurred)* Aufwand, *der;* **take** *or* **exact a /its ~ of sth.** einen Tribut an etw. *(Dat.)* fordern *(fig.);* **the hurricane took ~ of 5,000 lives** der Hurrikan forderte 5 000 Todesopfer; **the revolution took a heavy ~ of human life** die Revolution forderte viele Menschenleben; **time took its ~ of him** er mußte dem Alter Tribut zollen; **c)** *(Amer.: Teleph.)* [Gesprächs]gebühr, *die*

²toll 1. *v. t.* läuten; ‹*Turmuhr:*› schlagen ‹*Stunde*›. **2.** *v. i.* läuten

toll: ~-bar *n. Schlagbaum auf gebührenpflichtigen Straßen oder Brücken;* Mautschranke, *die (bes. österr.);* **~-bridge** *n.* gebührenpflichtige Brücke; Mautbrücke, *die (bes. österr.);* **~ call** *n. (Amer. Teleph.)* gebührenpflichtiges Gespräch; **~-free** *adj., adv. (Amer. Teleph.)* gebührenfrei; **~-gate** *n.* Absperrung vor einer gebührenpflichtigen Straße/Brücke; **~-road** *n.* gebührenpflichtige Straße; Mautstraße, *die (bes. österr.)*

tom [tɒm] *n.* **a) any** *or* **every Tom, Dick, and Harry** Hinz und Kunz *(ugs. abwertend);* **it's me you're talking to, not any Tom, Dick, and Harry** du sprichst mit mir, nicht mit irgend jemandem; **every Tom, Dick, and Harry is talking about it** alle Welt redet davon; **any Tom, Dick, or Harry can open a shop** jeder, der Lust hat, kann einen Laden aufmachen; **b)** *(cat)* Kater, *der. See also* **peeping Tom**

tomahawk ['tɒməhɔ:k] *n.* Tomahawk, *der; see also* **bury b**

tomato [tə'mɑ:təʊ] *n., pl.* **~es** Tomate, *die*

tomato: ~-juice *n.* Tomatensaft, *der;* **~ 'ketchup** *n.* Tomatenketchup, *der od. das;* **~ 'purée** *n.* Tomatenmark, *das;* **~ 'sauce** *n.* **a)** Tomatensoße, *die;* **b)** *see* **~ ketchup; ~ 'soup** *n.* Tomatensuppe, *die*

tomb [tu:m] *n.* **a)** *(grave)* Grab, *das;* **b)** *(monument)* Grabmal, *das;* **c) the ~** *(state of death)* das Grab *(geh.);* der Tod; **his ghost came back from the ~:** sein Geist kehrte aus dem Grab zurück; **[as] silent as the ~:** totenstill; **the village/the house is/seems [as] silent as the ~:** im Dorf/Haus herrscht Totenstille; **d)** *(vault)* Gruft, *die (geh.)*

tombola [tɒm'bəʊlə] *n.* Tombola, *die*

'tomboy *n.* Wildfang, *der*

'tombstone *n.* Grabstein, *der;* Grabmal, *das*

'tom-cat *n.* Kater, *der*

tome [təʊm] *n.* dicker Band; Wälzer, *der (ugs.)*

tom: ~fool *attrib. adj.* blödsinnig; **~'foolery** *n.* Blödsinn, *der (ugs.)*

Tommy ['tɒmɪ] *n. (coll.: British soldier)* Tommy, *der*

tommy: ~-gun *n.* Maschinenpistole, *die;* **~-rot** *n., no pl., no indef. art.* Unfug, *der;* Quatsch, *der (ugs.)*

tomorrow [tə'mɒrəʊ] **1.** *n.* **a)** morgen; **~ morning/afternoon/evening/night** morgen früh *od.* vormittag/nachmittag/abend/nacht; **~ is another day** *(prov.)* morgen ist auch [noch] ein Tag *(Spr.);* **~ never comes** *(prov.)* morgen, morgen, nur nicht heute[, sagen alle faulen Leute] *(Spr.);* **You always say you'll do it some time. But with you, ~ never comes!** Du sagst immer, daß du es einmal tust. Aber bei dir heißt das am Sankt Nimmerleinstag; **~'s edition/newspaper** die morgige Ausgabe/Zeitung; die Ausgabe/Zeitung von morgen; **~'s events will bear me out** morgen wird man sehen, daß ich recht habe; **~ evening's concert** das Konzert morgen abend *od.* am morgigen Abend; **b)** *(the future)* Morgen, *das;* **who knows what ~ will bring?** wer weiß, was die Zukunft bringt?; **like there's no ~** *(coll.)* als gäbe es kein Morgen; als ginge morgen die Welt unter; **the men and women of ~:** die Männer und Frauen von morgen; **~'s world** die Welt von morgen. **2.** *adv.* **a)** morgen; **a week/month [from] ~:** morgen in einer Woche/in einem Monat; **a year [ago] ~:** morgen vor einem Jahr; **[I'll] see you ~!** *(coll.)* bis morgen!; **never put off till ~ what you can do today** *(prov.)* was du heute kannst besorgen, das verschiebe nicht auf morgen *(Spr.);* **the day after ~:** übermorgen; **this time ~:** morgen um diese Zeit; **~ afternoon/morning** morgen nachmittag/früh; **~ evening** *or* **night** morgen abend; **b)** *(in the future)* morgen; **what will the world be like ~?** wie wird die Welt von morgen aussehen?

tom: T~ 'Thumb *n.* **a)** *(Lit.)* Däumling, *der;* **b)** *(diminutive person)* Knirps, *der (ugs.);* **~tit** *n. (Ornith.)* Blaumeise, *die;* **~-tom** *n. (Mus.)* Tomtom, *das*

ton [tʌn] *n.* **a)** Tonne, *die;* **a five-~ lorry** ein Lastwagen von fünf Tonnen [Leergewicht]; ein Fünftonner *(ugs.);* **[long] ~:** Tonne, *die;* 1016,05 kg; **metric ~:** metrische Tonne; **[short] ~:** Tonne, *die;* 907,185 kg; **two ~[s] of coal** zwei Tonnen Kohle; *see also* **brick 1 a; b)** *(Naut.)* Tonne, *die;* **gross ~:** Bruttoregistertonne, *die;* **net** *or* **register ~:** Registertonne, *die;* **c)** *(fig. coll.: a lot)* **it weighs [half] a ~:** es ist zentnerschwer *(fig.);* **I've asked him ~s of times** ich habe ihn x-mal gefragt *(ugs.);* **~s [of food/people/reasons** *etc.***]** haufenweise *(ugs.)* [Essen/Leute/Gründe *usw.*]; **d)** *(Brit. sl.: 100 m.p.h.)* **do a** *or* **the ~:** mit 160 Sachen fahren; **e)** *(Cricket sl.) see* **century b**

tonal ['təʊnl] *adj.* **a)** *(Ling.)* intonatorisch; **~ language** Tonsprache; **~ changes** *or* **variations** Klangvariationen; **b)** tonal *(Musik);* **c)** *(Art)* **~ differences between colours** Unterschiede in den Farbtönen

tonality [tə'nælɪtɪ] *n.* **a)** *(Mus.)* Tonalität, *die;* **b)** *(Art)* Farbwirkung, *die*

tonally ['təʊnəlɪ] *adv. (Mus.)* tonal

tone [təʊn] **1.** *n.* **a)** *(sound)* Klang, *der; (Teleph.)* Ton, *der;* **the clear ~s of the speaker** die klare Stimme des Redners; **the**

[shrill] ~s of her voice ihre [schrille] Stimme; **a high-/low-pitched ~**: ein hoher/tiefer Ton; **b)** *(style of speaking)* Ton, *der;* **don't speak to me in that ~ [of voice]** sprich mit mir nicht in diesem Ton; **in an angry** *etc.* **~, in angry** *etc.* **~s** in ärgerlichem *usw.* Ton; **in a ~ of reproach/anger** *etc.* in vorwurfsvollem/wütendem *usw.* Ton; **c)** *(tint, shade)* [Farb]ton, *der;* **~s of blue** Blautöne; blaue Töne; **grey with a blue ~**: bläulichgrau; **d)** *(style of writing)* [Grund]stimmung, *die; (of letter)* Ton, *der;* **e)** *(Mus.) (note)* Ton, *der; (quality of sound)* Klang, *der; (Brit.: interval)* Intervall, *das;* **whole-~ scale** Ganztonleiter, *die; see also* **fundamental 1 b; f)** *(fig.: character)* Stimmung, *die;* **a ~ of quiet elegance** eine Atmosphäre stiller Eleganz; **the peaceful ~ of the discussions** die friedliche Atmosphäre der Gespräche; **give a serious/flippant ~ to sth.** einer Sache *(Dat.)* eine ernsthafte/frivole Note verleihen; **lower/raise the ~ of sth.** das Niveau einer Sache *(Gen.)* senken/erhöhen; **set the ~**: den Ton angeben; **set the ~ of** *or* **for sth.** für etw. bestimmend sein; **g)** *(Art: general effect of colour)* Farbgebung, *die;* Kolorit, *das;* **h)** *(degree of brightness)* Schattierung, *die;* Nuancierung, *die;* **bright ~**: Helligkeit, *die;* **i)** *(Photog.)* Ton, *der;* **j)** *(accent on syllable)* Betonung, *die;* Akzent, *der; (way of pronouncing)* Ton, *der;* **k)** *(Physiol.: firmness of muscles)* Tonus, *der; (of athlete etc.)* Fitneß, *die;* **keep oneself** *or* **one's body in ~**: sich fit halten. **2.** *v. t.* **a)** *(modify colouring of)* tönen; abtönen ⟨*Farbe*⟩; **~ paint [with] a darker/lighter shade** Farbe abdunkeln/aufhellen; **b)** *(Photog.)* tonen; **~ sth. a reddish-brown** etw. rötlichbraun tonen. **3.** *v. i. see* **~ in**

~ 'down *v. t.* **a)** *(Art)* [ab]dämpfen ⟨*Farbe*⟩; **~ a painting down** die Farben eines Bildes abdämpfen; **b)** *(fig.: soften)* mäßigen ⟨*Sprache*⟩; abschwächen ⟨*Verbalattacke, Forderung*⟩; dämpfen ⟨*Erregung, Begeisterung*⟩; besänftigen ⟨*Wut*⟩

~'in *v. i.* farblich harmonieren

~ 'up 1. *v. t.* **a)** *(Art)* **~ up a picture/colour** die Farben eines Bildes/eine Farbe kräftiger machen; **b)** *(Physiol.)* fit machen; straffen ⟨*Muskeln, Körper*⟩; stärken ⟨*Nerven*⟩. **2.** *v. i.* sich fit machen

tone: ~-arm *n.* Tonarm, *der;* **~ control** *n. (process)* Klangregelung, *die; (device)* Klangregler, *der;* Tonblende, *die;* **~-'deaf** *adj.* ohne musikalisches Gehör *(Musik);* **be ~-deaf** kein musikalisches Gehör haben; **~-deaf people** Leute ohne musikalisches Gehör; **~ language** *n. (Ling.)* Tonsprache, *die*

toneless ['təʊnlɪs] *adj.* **a)** tonlos ⟨*Stimme, Antwort*⟩; **b)** *(Mus.)* monoton; **c)** *(dull)* stumpf ⟨*Farbe*⟩

tone: ~ painting *n. (Mus.)* Tonmalerei, *die;* **~ poem** *n.* **a)** *(Mus.)* Tondichtung, *die;* **b)** *(Art) Gemälde, bei dem die Farbtöne auf poetische Weise harmonisieren*

toner ['təʊnə(r)] *n.* **a)** *(Photog.)* Toner, *der;* **b)** *(cosmetic)* Tönungsmittel, *das*

tongs [tɒŋz] *n. pl.* **[pair of] ~**: Zange, *die; see also* **curling-tongs; fire-tongs; hammer 1 a; sugar-tongs**

tongue [tʌŋ] *n.* **a)** Zunge, *die;* **bite one's ~** *(lit. or fig.)* sich auf die Zunge beißen; **put out your ~, please** strecken Sie [bitte] mal Ihre Zunge heraus!; **put** *or* **stick one's ~ out [at sb.]** [jmdm.] die Zunge herausstrecken; **with one's ~ hanging out** mit [heraus]hängender Zunge; **he came into the pub with his ~ hanging out** *(fig.)* ihm hing die Zunge aus dem Hals, als er in das Gasthaus kam; **he made the remark ~ in cheek** *(fig.)* er meinte die Bemerkung nicht ernst; **hold one's ~** *(fig.)* stillschweigen; **keep a civil ~ in one's head** seine Zunge hüten; *see also* **edge 1 a; b)** *(meat)* Zunge, *die;* **c)** *(manner or power of speech)* **find/lose one's ~**: seine Sprache wiederfinden/die Sprache verlieren; **have you lost your ~?** hat es dir die Sprache verschlagen?; hast du die Sprache verloren?; **get one's ~ round sth.** etw. aussprechen; **the name is difficult to get one's ~ round** bei dem Namen bricht man sich *(Dat.)* die Zunge ab *od.* verrenkt man sich *(Dat.)* die Zunge *(ugs.);* **have a ready/sharp/wicked** *etc.* **~**: eine flinke/scharfe/böse *usw.* Zunge haben; **the hounds gave ~**: die Hunde gaben Hals *(Jägerspr.);* **give ~**: sprechen; **d)** *(language)* Sprache, *die;* Zunge, *die (geh., dichter.);* **gift of ~s** *(Bibl.)* Zungenreden, *das; see also* **confusion a; mother tongue; e)** *(of shoe)* Zunge, *die;* **f)** *(promontory)* **~ [of land]** Landzunge, *die;* **g)** *(of bell)* Klöppel, *der;* **h)** *(of buckle)* Dorn, *der;* **i)** *(Woodw.)* Feder, *die;* **j)** *(pointer of scale etc.)* Zunge, *die;* **k)** *(Mus.)* Zunge, *die;* **l) there were ~s of flame rising from the fire** von der Feuerstelle züngelten Flammen empor. *See also* **cat a; [1]tip 1; [1]wag 2**

tongue: ~-in-'cheek *adj.* nicht ernst gemeint; *(ironical)* ironisch; *see also* **tongue a; ~-lashing** *n.* Rüffel, *der (ugs.);* **give sb. a ~-lashing** jmdm. einen Rüffel geben; jmdn. zusammenstauchen *(ugs.);* **get a ~-lashing [from sb.]** [von jmdm.] einen Rüffel bekommen/zusammengestaucht werden *(ugs.);* **~-tied** *adj.* schüchtern; gehemmt; **the boy sat ~-tied the whole evening** der Junge saß den ganzen Abend da und brachte kein Wort heraus; **be ~-tied [with** *or* **by fear/embarrassment** *etc.*] [vor Angst/Verlegenheit *usw.*] kein Wort herausbringen; **~-twister** *n.* Zungenbrecher, *der (ugs.)*

tonic ['tɒnɪk] **1.** *n.* **a)** *(Med.)* Tonikum, *das;* **it was as good as a ~**: es hat mir/ihm *usw.* richtig gutgetan; **b)** *(fig.: invigorating influence)* Wohltat, *die (geh.);* **the good news/his visit was a welcome ~**: die gute Nachricht/sein Besuch war eine wahre Wohltat; **c)** *(~ water)* Tonic, *das;* **gin** *etc.* **and ~**: Gin *usw.* [mit] Tonic; **d)** *(Mus.)* Tonika, *die.* **2.** *adj.* **a)** *(Med.)* kräftigend; tonisch *(fachspr.); (fig.)* wohltuend ⟨*Wirkung*⟩; **b)** *(Mus.)* tonisch

tonic: ~ 'accent *n. (Phonet.: of word)* Betonung, *die;* **~ sol-'fa** *n. (Mus.)* Tonika-Do-System, *das;* **~ water** *n.* Tonic[wasser], *das*

tonight [tə'naɪt] **1.** *n.* **a)** *(this evening)* heute abend; **~ has been such fun** heute abend war es so lustig; **after ~** nach dem heutigen Abend; **I enjoyed ~**: es war ein schöner Abend; **~'s [news]paper** die heutige Abendzeitung; **~'s performance** die heutige [Abend]vorstellung; **~'s the night!** heute abend ist es soweit!; **~'s weather will be cold** heute abend wird es kalt; **b)** *(this or the coming night)* heute nacht; **~ will be colder** heute nacht wird es kälter werden. **2.** *adv.* **a)** *(this evening)* heute abend; **b)** *(during this or the coming night)* heute nacht; **[I'll] see you ~!** bis heute abend!

tonnage ['tʌnɪdʒ] *n. (Naut.)* **a)** Tonnage, *die;* **b)** *(charge on cargo)* Tonnageabgabe, *die*

tonne ['tʌn] *n.* [metrische] Tonne

tonsil ['tɒnsl] *n. (Anat.)* [Gaumen]mandel, *die;* **have one's ~s out** sich *(Dat.)* die Mandeln herausnehmen lassen

tonsillectomy [tɒnsə'lektəmɪ] *n. (Med.)* Mandeloperation, *die;* Tonsillektomie, *die (fachspr.)*

tonsillitis [tɒnsə'laɪtɪs] *n. (Med.)* Mandelentzündung, *die;* Tonsillitis, *die (fachspr.)*

tonsure ['tɒnʃə(r)] *(Relig.)* **1.** *n.* Tonsur, *die.* **2.** *v. t.* tonsurieren

ton-'up *adj. (sl.)* **~ boys** Motorradrocker; **~ machine** Feuerstuhl, *der (ugs.)*

too [tu:] *adv.* **a)** *(excessively)* zu; **far** *or* **much ~ much** viel zu viel; **~ much** zuviel; **I've had ~ much to eat/drink** ich habe zuviel gegessen/getrunken; **but not ~ much, please** aber bitte nicht allzuviel; **the problem/he was ~ much for her** sie war der Aufgabe/ihm nicht gewachsen; **things are getting ~ much for me** es wird mir allmählich zu viel; es wächst mir allmählich über den Kopf; **this is '~ much!** *(indignantly)* jetzt reicht's!; **she's/that's just '~ much** *(intolerable)* sie ist/das ist zuviel! *(ugs.); (sl.: wonderful)* sie ist/das ist echt spitze *(ugs.);* **~ difficult a task** eine zu schwierige Aufgabe; **none ~** *or* **not any ~ easy** nicht allzu leicht; *(less than one had expected)* gar nicht so leicht; **he is none ~** *or* **not any ~ clever/quick** *etc.* er ist nicht der Schlauste/Schnellste *usw.*; **none ~ soon** keinen Augenblick zu früh; **the holidays can come none ~ soon as far as I am concerned** für mich können die Ferien nicht früh genug kommen; *see also* **all 3; good 1 b, e; many 1 a; much 1 a, 3 d; only 2 d; b)** *(also)* auch; **she can sing, and play the piano, ~**: sie kann singen und auch *od.* außerdem Klavier spielen; **I have been [to Berlin, and] to Cologne, ~**: ich war [in Berlin und] auch *od.* außerdem in Köln; **I, ~, have been to Cologne, 'I have been to Cologne, ~**: ich war auch in Köln; auch ich war in Köln; **c)** *(coll.: very)* besonders; **I'm not feeling ~ good** mir geht es nicht besonders [gut]; **I'm not ~ sure** ich bin mir nicht ganz sicher; **not ~ pleased** nicht gerade erfreut; **you're '~ kind!** zu nett von dir!; **the dessert was '~ delicious** die Nachspeise war zu köstlich; **d)** *(moreover)* **he lost in twenty moves, and to an amateur ~**: er verlor in zwanzig Zügen, und noch dazu gegen einen Amateur; **there was frost last night, and in May/Spain ~!** es hat letzte Nacht gefroren, und das im Mai/in Spanien!

toodle-oo [tu:dl'u:] *int. (Brit. sl.)* tschüs *(ugs.);* ciao *(ugs.)*

took *see* **take 1, 2**

tool [tu:l] **1.** *n.* **a)** Werkzeug, *das; (garden ~)* Gerät, *das;* **set of ~s** Werkzeug, *das; see also* **[3]down 4 d; b)** *(machine)* Werkzeugmaschine, *die;* **electrical ~**: Elektrowerkzeug, *das; see also* **machine tool; c)** *(Mech. Engin.: lathe ~)* Meißel, *der;* **d)** *(fig.: means)* [Hilfs]mittel, *das;* **knowledge is a great ~ in the hands of men** [das] Wissen ist für den Menschen ein großartiges Werkzeug; **pen and paper are the writer's basic ~s** Feder und Papier sind das wichtigste Handwerkszeug des Schriftstellers; **the ~s of the trade** das Handwerkszeug; das Rüstzeug; **e)** *(fig.: person)* Werkzeug, *das;* **a mere ~ [in the hands] of the dictator** ein bloßes Werkzeug des Diktators; **f)** *(sl.: penis)* Apparat, *der (ugs.);* Gerät, *das (salopp).* **2.** *v. t.* **a)** bearbeiten; **b)** *(Bookbinding)* prägen

~ 'up *v. t.* mit Maschinen ausrüsten; **the expense of ~ing-up** die Kosten für die Anschaffung von Maschinen

tool: ~-bag *n.* Werkzeugtasche, *die;* **~-box, ~-case** *ns.* Werkzeugkasten, *der;* **~-chest** *n.* Werkzeugschrank, *der;* **~-holder** *n.* **a)** *(in lathe)* Meißelhalter, *der;* **b)** *(handle)* Werkzeuggriff, *der*

tooling ['tu:lɪŋ] *n.* **a)** *(Building)* [steinmetzmäßige] Bearbeitung; **b)** *(Bookbinding)* Prägen, *das; (thing tooled)* Prägung, *die*

tool: ~-kit *n. (Brit.)* Werkzeugsatz, *der; (more general)* Werkzeug, *das; (for vehicle)* **is there a ~-kit?** gibt es Bordwerkzeug?; **~-maker** *n.* Werkzeugmacher, *der/*-macherin, *die;* **~-pusher** *n.* Bohrtechniker, *der;* **~-set** *n.* Werkzeugsatz, *der;* **~-shed** *n.* Geräteschuppen, *der*

toot [tu:t] **1.** *v. t.* tuten; **the boy ~ed his toy trumpet** der Junge blies in seine Spielzeugtrompete; **the driver ~ed his horn** der Fahrer hupte. **2.** *v. i.* **a)** *(on wind instrument)* blasen; *(on whistle, pipe)* pfeifen; *(on car etc. horn)* hupen; **b)** ⟨*Hupe:*⟩ hupen; ⟨*Lokomotive, Pfeife:*⟩ pfeifen; ⟨*Nebelhorn, Schiff:*⟩

tuten. **3.** *n.* Tuten, *das; (of pipe, whistle)* Pfeifen, *das;* **give a ~ on one's/its horn** ‹*Autofahrer, Auto usw.*:› hupen

tooth [tu:θ] *n., pl.* **teeth** [ti:θ] **a)** Zahn, *der;* **say sth. between one's teeth** etw. mit zusammengebissenen Zähnen hervorstoßen; **draw sb.'s teeth** *(lit.)* jmdm. die Zähne ziehen; *(fig.)* jmdn. kaltstellen; **sth.'s teeth have been drawn** *(fig.)* etw. ist unschädlich gemacht worden; **have a ~ out/filled** sich *(Dat.)* einen Zahn ziehen/füllen lassen; **armed to the teeth** bis an die Zähne bewaffnet; **cast** *or* **fling sth. in sb.'s teeth** *(fig.)* jmdm. etw. [wutentbrannt] unter die Nase reiben *(ugs.)*; **~ and nail** verbissen ‹*kämpfen, bekämpfen*›; **I'm going to fight ~ and nail to keep this house** ich werde dieses Haus mit Zähnen und Klauen verteidigen; **get one's teeth into sth.** *(fig.)* etw. in Angriff nehmen; **sb. would give his back teeth for sth./to do sth.** *(fig.)* jmd. würde alles für etw. geben/alles dafür *od.* darum geben, etw. zu tun; **in the teeth of criticism** ungeachtet der Kritik; **sail in the teeth of the wind** gegen den Wind segeln; **put teeth into a law, give a law some teeth** ein Gesetz zu einem wirksamen Instrument machen; **show one's teeth** ‹*Hund:*› die Zähne fletschen; *(fig.)* die Zähne zeigen *(ugs.)*; *see also* **edge 1 a; false teeth; kick 1 a, 3 a; ¹lie 2; ¹long 1 a; set 1 p; skin 1 a; b)** *(of rake, fork, comb)* Zinke, *die; (of cog-wheel, saw, comb)* Zahn, *der;* **c)** *(liking)* **have a ~ for salad** eine Vorliebe für Salat haben; Salat gern essen; *see also* **sweet 1 a; d)** *(Bot.)* Zahn, *der;* **have teeth** gezähnt sein

tooth: ~ache *n.* Zahnschmerzen *Pl.;* Zahnweh, *das (ugs.)*; **~-brush** *n.* Zahnbürste, *die;* **~-brush moustache** Bürste, *die (fig.)*

toothed [tu:θt] *adj.* **a)** *(Mech. Engin.)* gezähnt; **~ wheel** Zahnrad; **b)** *(Bot.)* gezähnt; **c)** *in comb. (having teeth)* **sharp-~** ‹*Tier*› mit scharfen Zähnen

'tooth-glass *n.* Zahnputzglas, *das*

toothless ['tu:θlɪs] *adj.* zahnlos

tooth: ~-mug *n.* Zahnputzbecher, *der;* **~paste** *n.* Zahnpasta, *die;* **~pick** *n.* Zahnstocher, *der;* **~-powder** *n.* Zahnpulver, *das*

toothsome ['tu:θsəm] *adj.* köstlich

toothy ['tu:θɪ] *adj.* **give sb. a ~ smile** jmdn. mit entblößten Zähnen anlächeln; **he is a bit ~:** er hat ein ziemliches Pferdegebiß *(ugs.)*

toothypeg ['tu:θɪpeg] *n. (child lang.)* Beißerchen, *das*

tootle ['tu:tl] *v. i.* **a)** blasen; dudeln *(ugs. abwertend); (on whistle)* pfeifen; *(on flute)* flöten; **~ on sth.** in etw. *(Akk.)* blasen; **b)** *(coll.: move casually)* zuckeln *(ugs.)*; *(walk casually)* schlendern; *(drive casually)* juckeln *(ugs.)*; **I'm just tootling off to the shops/pub** ich gehe nur eben was einkaufen/ich gehe nur eben in die Kneipe *(ugs.)*

too-too *(coll.)* **1.** ['tu:tu:] *pred. adj. (marvellous)* himmlisch *(ugs.)*; *(la-di-da)* oberfein *(ugs.)*. **2.** [tu:'tu:] *adv.* überaus; über die Maßen *(geh.)*; *(too)* übertrieben

tootsy[-wootsy] ['tʊtsɪ(wʊtsɪ)] *n. (joc./child lang.)* Füßchen, *das*

¹top [tɒp] **1.** *n.* **a)** *(highest part)* Spitze, *die; (of table)* Platte, *die; (of bench seat)* Sitzfläche, *die; (top floor)* oberstes Stockwerk; *(flat roof, roof garden)* Dach, *das; (rim of glass, bottle, etc.)* Rand, *der; (top end)* oberes Ende; *(crest of wave)* Kamm, *der; (of tree)* Spitze, *die;* Wipfel, *der;* **the ~ of his head is smooth and shiny** sein Kopf ist oben glatt und glänzend; **a cake with a cherry on ~:** ein Kuchen mit einer Kirsche [oben]drauf; **at the ~:** oben; **at the ~ of the building/hill/pile/stairs** oben im Gebäude/[oben] auf dem Hügel/[oben] auf dem Stapel/oben an der Treppe; **bake at the ~ of the oven** auf der obersten Schiene des Backofens backen; oben im Backofen backen; **be at/get to** *or* **reach the ~ [of the ladder** *or* **tree]** *(fig.)* auf der obersten Sprosse [der Leiter] stehen/die oberste Sprosse [der Leiter] erreichen *(fig.)*; oben sein/nach oben kommen *(ugs.)*; **be/get on ~ of a situation/subject** eine Situation/eine Materie im Griff haben/in den Griff bekommen; **don't let it get on ~ of you** *(fig.)* laß dich davon nicht unterkriegen! *(ugs.)*; **the driver didn't notice me until he was right on ~ of me** *(fig.)* der Fahrer bemerkte mich erst, als er mich schon fast umgefahren hatte; **he put it on [the] ~ of the pile** er legte es [oben] auf den Stapel; **on ~ of one another** *or* **each other** aufeinander; **live on ~ of each other** übereinander wohnen; *(too close)* sehr beengt leben; **on ~ of sth.** *(fig.: in addition)* zusätzlich zu etw.; **on ~ of everything else** zu alledem noch; **come/be on ~ of sth.** *(be additional)* zu etw. [hinzu]kommen; **on ~ of that, this happens!** *(fig.)* zu allem Überfluß passiert auch noch das!; **on ~ of the world** *(fig.)* überglücklich; **be/go thin on ~:** licht auf dem Kopf sein/werden; **be on ~:** ganz oben sein/liegen; **the English team is on ~:** die englische Mannschaft ist [dem Gegner] überlegen; **come out on ~** *(be successful)* Erfolg haben; *(win)* gewinnen; **get to the ~** *(fig.)* eine Spitzenposition erringen; ganz nach oben kommen *(ugs.)*; **from ~ to toe** von Kopf bis Fuß; **a Tory from ~ to toe** ein Tory vom Scheitel bis zur Sohle; **be over the ~:** übertrieben *od.* überzogen sein; **go over the ~** *(Mil.)* den Graben verlassen; *(fig.) (take decisive step)* eine endgültige Entscheidung treffen; *(be excessive)* über die Stränge schlagen *(ugs.)*; es übertreiben *(ugs.)*; **he searched the house from ~ to bottom** er durchsuchte das Haus von oben bis unten; **take it from the ~** *(coll.)* noch einmal von vorne anfangen; *see also* **head 1 a; b)** *(highest rank)* Spitze, *die;* **the man at the ~:** der [oberste] Chef *od. (ugs.)* Boß; **~ of the table** *(Sport)* Tabellenspitze, *die;* **[at the] ~ of the list of things to do/agenda is ...:** ganz oben auf der Liste der Dinge, die getan werden müssen/auf der Tagesordnung steht ...; **be [at the] ~ of the class** der/die Klassenbeste sein; **go to the ~ of the class!** *(fig. coll.)* alle Achtung!; **~ of the bill** *(Theatre)* Zugpferd, *das;* **be ~ of the charts** *or* **pops** an der Spitze der Hitparade stehen; die Hitparade anführen; *(fig.)* die Nummer eins sein; **c)** *(of vegetable)* Kraut, *das;* **~s of turnips, turnip-~s** das Kraut von Rüben; **d)** *(upper surface)* Oberfläche, *die; (of cupboard, wardrobe, chest)* Oberseite, *die;* **on [the] ~ of sth.** [oben] auf etw. *(position: Dat./direction: Akk.)*; **don't forget to paint along the ~ of the door** vergiß nicht, die Tür von oben zu streichen; **cut off the ~ [of the apple]** oben ein Stück [vom Apfel] abschneiden; **cut the ~ off an egg** ein Ei köpfen; **they climbed to the ~ of the hill/slope** sie kletterten auf den Hügel/den Hang hinauf; **he laid his hand on the ~ of her head** er legte ihr seine Hand auf den Kopf; **e)** *(folding roof)* Verdeck, *das;* **f)** *(upper deck of bus, boat)* Oberdeck, *das;* **g)** *(cap of pen)* [Verschluß]kappe, *die;* **h)** *(cream on milk)* Sahne, *die;* Rahm, *der (regional, bes. südd., österr., schweiz.)*; **i)** *(upper part of page)* oberer Teil; **at the ~ [of the page]** oben [auf der/die Seite]; **be ten lines from the ~:** in der zehnten Zeile [von oben] stehen; **j)** *(upper garment)* Oberteil, *das; (blouse, T-shirt)* Top, *das (Textilw.)*; **k)** *(turn-down of sock)* Umschlag, *der;* **l)** *(head end)* Kopf, *der; (of bed)* Kopfende, *das; (of street)* oberes Ende; *(of beach)* oberer Teil; **m)** *(utmost)* Gipfel, *der;* **shout/talk at the ~ of one's voice** aus vollem Halse schreien/so laut wie möglich sprechen; **n) be the ~s** *(coll.) (the best)* der/die/das Größte sein *(ugs.)*; *(marvellous)* spitze sein *(ugs.)*; **he's ~s at squash** er spielt hervorragend Squash; **the ~ of the morning [to you]!** *(Ir.)* einen wunderschönen guten Morgen!; **o)** *(surface)* Oberfläche, *die;* **p)** *(upper of shoe)* Oberteil, *das;* **q)** *(lid)* Deckel, *der; (of bottle, glass jar, etc.)* Deckel, *der; (stopper)* Stöpsel, *der; (silver foil, crown cork)* Verschluß, *der; see also* **¹blow 2 h; r)** *(Bookbinding)* Kopfschnitt, *der;* **s)** *(upper part of boot)* Stulpe, *die;* **t)** *(Naut.: platform)* Saling, *die (Seemannsspr.)*; **u)** *(Brit. Motor Veh.)* größter Gang *(Kfz-W.)*; **in ~:** im größten Gang. **2.** *adj.* oberst...; höchst... ‹*Ton, Preis*›; **~ end** oberes Ende; **the/a ~ award** die höchste/eine hohe Auszeichnung; **the/a ~ chess-player** der beste Schachspieler/einer der besten Schachspieler *od.* ein Spitzenschachspieler; **~ scientists/actors** *etc.* hochkarätige Wissenschaftler/Schauspieler *usw.*; **~ sportsman/job/politician** Spitzensportler, *der*/Spitzenposition, *die*/Spitzenpolitiker, *der;* **the ~ pupil/school/marks** der beste Schüler/die beste Schule/die besten Noten; **~ score/nation/pop-star** höchste Punktzahl/führende Nation/größter Popstar; **a ~ Conservative** ein Spitzenpolitiker der Konservativen Partei; **~ names in industry** Spitzen der Industrie; **~ manager/management** Topmanager/-management; **a ~ speed of 100 m.p.h.** eine Spitzen- *od.* Höchstgeschwindigkeit von 100 Meilen pro Stunde; **go at ~ speed** mit Spitzen- *od.* Höchstgeschwindigkeit fahren; **the machine was working at ~ speed** die Maschine lief auf Hochtouren; **I was working at ~ speed** ich arbeitete auf Hochtouren; **read sth. at ~ speed** etw. im Schnellverfahren lesen; **be/come ~ [in a subject]** [in einem Fach] der/die Beste sein/werden; **give sth. ~ priority** einer Sache *(Dat.)* höchste Priorität einräumen; **have a record in the ~ ten** eine Platte in den Top-ten haben; **in the ~ left/right corner** in der linken/rechten oberen Ecke; **on the ~ floor** im obersten Stockwerk; **the ~ men in the firm** die Spitze der Firma; **they are the ~ men in the firm** sie stehen an der Spitze der Firma; **the ~ people** *(in society)* die Spitzen der Gesellschaft; *(in a particular field)* die besten Leute; *see also* **form 1 f; gear 1 a. 3.** *v. t.,* **-pp- a)** *(cover)* **the hills were ~ped with** *or* **by snow** die Hügelspitzen waren schneebedeckt; **a church ~ped with** *or* **by a dome** eine mit einer Kuppel gekrönte Kirche; **~ a pudding with cream** Sahne auf einen Pudding geben; **a pudding ~ped with cream** ein Pudding mit Sahne obendrauf; **b)** *(Hort.: cut ~ off)* stutzen ‹*Pflanze*›; kappen ‹*Baum*›; **c)** *(be taller than)* überragen; **he ~s six feet** er ist über sechs Fuß groß; **d)** *(surpass, excel)* übertreffen; **exports have ~ped [the] £40 million [mark/level]** die Exporte haben die [Grenze von] 40 Millionen Pfund überschritten; **the fish ~ped 2 lb.** der Fisch wog über zwei Pfund; **~ an offer** ein Angebot überbieten; **~ that for a score/story!** überbiete diese Punktzahl/erzähl eine bessere Geschichte!; **to ~ it all** [noch] obendrein; **e)** *(head)* anführen; **~ the bill** *(Theatre)* das Zugpferd sein; **f)** *(reach ~ of)* **~ the hill/wave** auf die Spitze des Hügels/den Kamm der Welle gelangen

~ 'off 1. *v. t. (coll.)* beschließen. **2.** *v. i. (coll.)* schließen

~ 'out *v. t. (Building)* richten *(Bauw.)*; **~ping-out ceremony** Richtfest, *das*

~ 'up *(Brit. coll.)* **1.** *v. t.* auffüllen ‹*Batterie, Tank, Flasche, Glas*›; **~ up the petrol/oil/water** Benzin/Öl/Wasser nachfüllen; **can I ~ you up?** darf ich dir/Ihnen nachschenken?; **~ up sb.'s drink** jmdm. nachschenken. **2.** *v. i. (fill one's tank up)* volltanken; *(fill one's glass up)* sich nachschenken; **~ up with petrol/oil/water** den Tank mit Benzin/Öl/Wasser auffüllen. *See also* **top-up**

²top *n. (toy)* Kreisel, *der; see also* **sleep 2 a**
top and 'tail *v. t.* **a)** *(start and end)* einleiten und beschließen ⟨*Vortrag usw.*⟩; **b)** ~ **gooseberries** *etc.* Stachelbeeren *usw.* putzen *(durch Entfernen des Stiels und des abgestorbenen Blütenteils am anderen Ende)*
topaz ['təʊpæz] *n. (Min.)* Topas, *der;* **false ~:** Goldtopas, *der*
top: ~ **'billing** *n. (Theatre) prominentester Platz auf einem Plakat/in einer Werbung;* **he vied with her for the ~ billing** er wetteiferte mit ihr um die Rolle des Stars; **give sb. ~ billing** jmdn. groß herausbringen *(ugs.);* **in this film, Richard Burton shares ~ billing with Elizabeth Taylor** in diesem Film sind Richard Burton und Elizabeth Taylor die großen Stars; **~-boot** *n.* langschäftiger Stulpenstiefel; ~ **'brass** *see* **brass 1 g;** ~ **coat** *n.* **a)** *(overcoat)* Überzieher, *der;* Mantel, *der;* **b)** *(of paint)* Deckanstrich, *der;* ~ **copy** *n.* Original, *das;* ~ **'dog** *n. (fig. sl.)* Boß, *der (ugs.);* **he/the company came out ~ dog [amongst his/its rivals]** er/die Firma setzte sich [gegen die Konkurrenz] durch; ~ **'drawer** *n.* **a)** oberste Schublade; **b)** *(fig.: high social status)* **sb. is not out of the ~ drawer** jmd. gehört nicht gerade zur Crème de la crème; *attrib.* Oberschicht-; **~-dress** *v. t. (Agric.)* oberflächlich düngen ⟨*Land, Acker*⟩; **~-dressing** *n.* **a)** *(Agric.)* Oberflächendüngung, *die; (substance)* Oberflächendünger, *der;* **b)** *(fig.: superficial show)* Kosmetik, *die;* **the whole ceremony is just ~-dressing** die ganze Zeremonie ist nur Fassade
topee *see* **topi**
toper ['təʊpə(r)] *n. (arch./literary)* Zecher, *der*/Zecherin, *die*
top: **~-flight** *attrib. adj.* erstrangig; Spitzen⟨*sportler, -politiker*⟩; ~ **fruit** *n. (Brit. Hort.)* Baumobst, *das;* ~ **'hat** *n.* Zylinder[hut], *der;* **~-heavy** *adj.* oberlastig; kopflastig ⟨*Baum, Pflanze, Bürokratie*⟩; **don't make your load ~-heavy** sorg dafür, daß der Schwerpunkt der Ladung nicht zu hoch liegt; **she is a bit ~-heavy** sie hat einen ganz schönen Vorbau *(ugs. scherzh.);* **~-'hole** *adj. (Brit. dated sl.)* famos *(ugs. veralt.)*
topi ['təʊpɪ] *n. (Anglo-Ind.)* Tropenhelm, *der*
topiary ['təʊpɪərɪ] *n. (Hort.) Kunst des ornamentalen Beschnitts von Bäumen und Sträuchern*
topic ['tɒpɪk] *n.* Thema, *das;* **~ of debate/conversation** Diskussions-/Gesprächsthema, *das*
topical ['tɒpɪkl] *adj.* **a)** aktuell; **b)** *(with regard to topics)* nach Sachgebieten *nachgestellt;* **c)** *(Med.)* lokalisiert
topicality [tɒpɪ'kælɪtɪ] *n., no pl.* Aktualität, *die*
topically ['tɒpɪkəlɪ] *adv.* **a)** mit aktuellem Bezug; **b)** *(with regard to topics)* nach Sachgebieten
'topknot *n.* **a)** *(ribbon)* Haarschleife, *die;* **b)** *(tuft of hair)* Haarknoten, *der*
topless ['tɒplɪs] *adj.* **a) a ~ statue/column** eine Statue/Säule mit fehlendem oberem Teil; **b) a ~ dress/swimsuit** ein busenfreies Kleid/ein Oben-ohne-Badeanzug; **c)** *(barebreasted)* barbusig; ~ **girl/waitress** Oben-ohne-Mädchen, *das*/-Bedienung, *die;* **go/bathe ~:** oben ohne gehen/baden
top: **~-level** *attrib. adj.* Gipfel⟨*treffen, -konferenz*⟩; Spitzen⟨*politiker, -funktionär*⟩; **~-level discussions/negotiations/talks/deals** Diskussionen/Verhandlungen/Gespräche/Vereinbarungen auf höchster Ebene; **~-line** *adj. (Commerc.)* **~-line profit** Bruttogewinn, *der;* **~mast** *n. (Naut.)* Stenge, *die*
topmost ['tɒpməʊst, 'tɒpməst] *adj.* oberst... ⟨*Schicht, Stufe*⟩; höchst... ⟨*Gipfel, Beamte, Note*⟩
top-'notch *adj. (coll.)* phantastisch *(ugs.)*

topographer [tə'pɒgrəfə(r)] *n.* Topograph, *der*/-graphin, *die*
topographic [tɒpə'græfɪk], **topographical** [tɒpə'græfɪkl] *adj.* topographisch
topography [tə'pɒgrəfɪ] *n.* **a)** Topographie, *die;* **b)** *(features)* örtliche *od. (geh.)* topographische Gegebenheiten; Topographie, *die (geh.);* **I'm not acquainted with the ~ of the area/town** *etc.* ich kenne mich in der Gegend/Stadt *usw.* nicht aus
topology [tə'pɒlədʒɪ] *n. (Math.)* Topologie, *die*
topper ['tɒpə(r)] *n. (coll.: hat)* Zylinder, *der;* Angströhre, *die (ugs. scherzh.)*
topping ['tɒpɪŋ] **1.** *n. (Cookery)* Überzug, *der;* **ice-cream with a ~ of whipped cream/of raspberry syrup** Eis mit Sahne/Himbeersirup [obendrauf]; **put on a ~ of cream/chopped nuts** das Ganze mit Sahne überziehen/mit gehackten Nüssen bestreuen; **cover sth. with a ~ of mashed potato/sliced potatoes** etw. mit einer Schicht Kartoffelbrei/Kartoffelscheiben bedecken. **2.** *adj. (Brit. dated sl.: excellent)* famos *(ugs.);* formidabel
topple ['tɒpl] **1.** *v. i.* fallen; **the tower/pile ~d to the ground** der Turm/Stapel fiel um *od.* kippte um; **the tower ~d and fell** der Turm wankte und stürzte um; ~ **[from power]** *(fig.)* stürzen. **2.** *v. t.* stürzen; ~ **a pile/wall [to the ground]** einen Stapel/eine Mauer umstürzen *od.* umwerfen; ~ **sb./a government [from power]** ⟨*Gegner:*⟩ jmdn./eine Regierung stürzen; ⟨*Skandal, Abstimmung:*⟩ jmdn./eine Regierung zu Fall bringen
~ **'down** *v. i.* hinab-/herabfallen; ⟨*Stapel, Turm:*⟩ umstürzen, umfallen
~ **'over 1.** *v. i.* ⟨*Turm, Stapel, Baum, Auto:*⟩ umstürzen, umfallen; ⟨*Vase, Ohnmächtiger:*⟩ umfallen; **he lost his balance on the edge of the cliff and ~d over** er verlor am Rand des Kliffs sein Gleichgewicht und stürzte hinunter. **2.** *v. t.* umstürzen; umwerfen
top: **~-quality** *attr. adj.* [qualitativ] hochwertig; **~-ranking** *attrib. adj.* Spitzen⟨*funktionär, -beamter, -politiker, -sportler, -orchester, -delegierter*⟩; hochrangig ⟨*Offizier*⟩; erstrangig ⟨*Autor, Schauspieler*⟩; führend ⟨*Wissenschaftler*⟩; **~-ranking party member** Mitglied der Parteispitze; **~sail** ['tɒpseɪl, 'tɒpsl] *n. (Naut.) (on square-rigger)* Marssegel, *das; (on schooner)* Toppsegel, *das;* ~ **'secret** *adj.* streng geheim; **~side** *n.* **a)** *(joint of beef)* Oberschale, *die;* **b)** *(Naut.)* obere Bordwand; **~soil** *n. (Agric.)* Mutterboden, *der; (of field)* [Acker]krume, *die;* ~ **spin** *n. (Sport)* Vorwärtsdrall, *der; (tennis, table tennis)* Topspin, *der*
topsy-turvy [tɒpsɪ'tɜ:vɪ] **1.** *adv.* verkehrtrum *(ugs.);* auf dem Kopf *(ugs.)* ⟨*stehen, liegen*⟩; **turn sth. ~** *(lit. or fig.)* etw. auf den Kopf stellen *(ugs.);* **this development turned my plans ~:** diese Entwicklung warf meine Pläne um *od. (ugs.)* über den Haufen. **2.** *adj.* chaotisch; **the room/house was ~:** das ganze Zimmer/Haus war auf den Kopf gestellt; *(fig.)* **a world where things are all ~:** eine Welt, in der alles auf dem Kopf steht; **a ~ way of reasoning** eine verquere Art zu denken; **it's a ~ world** es ist eine verkehrte Welt; **the whole world has turned ~:** die ganze Welt steht kopf *(ugs.)*
top: ~ **'table** *n.* Tisch am Kopf der Tafel; **~-up** *n. (coll.)* Auffüllung, *die;* **sth. needs a ~-up** etw. muß [wieder] aufgefüllt werden; **the oil needs a ~-up** es muß Öl nachgefüllt werden; **give the tank/oil a ~-up** den Tank auffüllen/Öl nachfüllen; **would you like/can I give you a ~-up?** soll/kann ich dir noch mal nachgießen?; **I need a ~-up** ich muß mir noch mal nachgießen/nachgießen lassen
toque [təʊk] *n.* Toque, *die*

tor [tɔ:(r)] *n.* Felsenspitze, *die; (hill)* Hügel, *der*
torch [tɔ:tʃ] *n.* **a) [electric] ~** *(Brit.)* Taschenlampe, *die;* **b)** *(blowlamp) (for welding)* Schweißbrenner, *der; (for soldering)* Lötlampe, *die; (for cutting)* Schneidbrenner, *der;* **c)** *(flaming stick etc.)* Fackel, *die;* **carry a ~ for sb.** *(fig.)* jmdn. verehren; **hand on the ~** *(fig.)* die Fackel weiterreichen *(geh.);* **d)** *(lamp on pole)* Öllampe [an einer Stange]
torch: ~ **battery** *n. (Brit.)* Taschenlampenbatterie, *die;* **~light** *n., no pl., no indef. art.* Licht der/einer Taschenlampe; *(of flaming stick)* Fackelschein, *der;* **by ~light** im Schein einer Taschenlampe/Fackel; **~light procession** Fackelzug, *der;* **a ~light ceremony/parade/tattoo** eine Zeremonie/Parade/ein Zapfenstreich im Fackelschein; ~ **song** *n.* bluesartiger sentimentaler Song von unerwiderter Liebe
tore *see* **'tear 2, 3**
toreador ['tɒrɪədɔ:(r)] *n.* Toreador, *der*
torment 1. ['tɔ:ment] *n.* Qual, *die;* **be in ~:** Qualen ausstehen; **suffer ~s** Qualen erleiden; **be a ~ to sb., be sb.'s ~:** jmdn. quälen *od.* peinigen; **the suspense/uncertainty was a ~:** die Spannung/Ungewißheit war unerträglich. **2.** [tɔ:'ment] *v. t.* **a)** quälen; peinigen; **be ~ed by** *or* **with sth.** von etw. gequält werden; **b)** *(tease, worry)* quälen; **Don't ~ me so! Tell me ...:** Spann mich nicht auf die Folter! Sag mir ...
tormentor [tɔ:'mentə(r)] *n.* Folterer, *der; (fig.)* Peiniger, *der*
torn *see* **'tear 2, 3**
tornado [tɔ:'neɪdəʊ] *n., pl.* **~es** Wirbelsturm, *der; (in North America)* Tornado, *der; (fig.: outburst, volley)* Orkan, *der*
torpedo [tɔ:'pi:dəʊ] **1.** *n., pl.* **~es** Torpedo, *der;* **aerial ~:** Lufttorpedo, *der.* **2.** *v. t. (auch fig.)* torpedieren
torpedo: **~-boat** *n. (Navy)* Torpedoboot, *das;* **~-tube** *n.* Torpedorohr, *das*
torpid ['tɔ:pɪd] *adj.* **a)** träge; träge fließend ⟨*Gewässer*⟩; **b)** *(Zool.)* torpid
torpidity [tɔ:'pɪdɪtɪ], **torpor** ['tɔ:pə(r)] *ns., no pl.* **a)** Trägheit, *die; (of water)* träges Fließen; **b)** *(Zool.)* Torpidität, *die*
torque [tɔ:k] *n. (Mech.)* Drehmoment, *das*
torque: ~ **converter** *n. (Motor Veh.)* Drehmomentwandler, der; ~ **wrench** *n.* Drehmomentschlüssel, *der*
torr [tɔ:(r)] *n., pl. same (Phys.)* Torr, *das*
torrent ['tɒrənt] *n.* **a)** reißender Bach; *(stream having steep course)* Sturzbach, *der;* **mountain ~:** reißender Gebirgsbach; **a brook, sometimes swollen into a ~:** ein Bächlein, das manchmal zu einem reißenden Strom anschwillt; **a ~ of rain** ein Regenguß; **the rain came down in ~s** es regnete in Strömen; **b)** *(fig.: violent flow)* Flut, *die;* Schwall, *der*
torrential [tə'renʃl] *adj.* **a)** reißend ⟨*Gebirgsbach, Fluten*⟩; wolkenbruchartig ⟨*Regen, Schauer*⟩; **the rain was ~:** es regnete in Strömen; **a ~ cloudburst** ein heftiger Wolkenbruch; **b)** *(fig.)* überwältigend; gewaltig; **a ~ flow of words/insults/questions** ein Schwall von Worten/Beleidigungen/Fragen
torrid ['tɒrɪd] *adj.* **a)** *(intensely hot)* glutheiß; **a ~ land** ein [von der Hitze] versengtes Land; **the ~ heat of the desert** die Gluthitze der Wüste; **b)** *(fig.: intense, ardent)* glühend *(geh.);* ⟨*Liebesszene*⟩ voller Leidenschaft
torsion ['tɔ:ʃn] *n.* Verwindung, *die;* Torsion, *die (Physik, Technik);* ~ **bar** Torsionsstab, *der*
torso ['tɔ:səʊ] *n., pl.* **~s a)** *(Art)* Torso, *der;* **b)** *(human trunk)* Rumpf, *der;* **bare ~:** nackter Oberkörper; **c)** *(fig.: incomplete work)* Torso, *der*
tort [tɔ:t] *n. (Law)* [zivilrechtliches] Delikt; unerlaubte Handlung

tortilla [tɔːˈtiːljə] *n.* Tortilla, *die*

tortoise [ˈtɔːtəs] *n.* Schildkröte, *die*

tortoiseshell [ˈtɔːtəsʃel] *n.* Schildpatt, *das; attrib.* Schildpatt-

tortoiseshell: ~ ˈbutterfly *n.* Fuchs, *der;* **~ ˈcat** *n.* Katze mit Schildpattzeichnung

tortuous [ˈtɔːtjʊəs] *adj.* **a)** *(full of twists and turns)* verschlungen ‹*Weg*›; gewunden ‹*Flußlauf*›; **b)** *(fig.: circuitous)* umständlich; verworren ‹*Argumentation, Denken, Sprache*›; **a ~ speaker/writer** ein Redner/Schriftsteller, der viele Worte macht

tortuously [ˈtɔːtjʊəslɪ] *adv.* **a)** *(with twists and turns)* verschlungen; **the road/path/river runs ~ through the fields** die Straße/der Weg/Fluß windet sich *od.* schlängelt sich durch die Felder; **b)** *(fig.: circuitously)* umständlich; **a ~ reasoned argument** ein verworrenes Argument; **a ~ argued case** eine umständliche Argumentation; **a ~ complex legal document** ein verwirrend komplexer juristischer Schriftsatz

tortuousness [ˈtɔːtjʊəsnɪs] *n., no pl.* **a) the ~ of the road/river** die vielen Windungen der Straße/des Flusses; **b)** *(fig.: circuitousness)* Umständlichkeit, *die*

torture [ˈtɔːtʃə(r)] **1.** *n.* **a)** Folter, *die;* **the ~s of the Inquisition** die Folterungen der Inquisition; **the ~ of sb.** jmds. Folterung; **practise ~:** foltern; **instrument of ~:** Folterwerkzeug, *das;* Folterinstrument, *das;* **b)** *(fig.: agony)* Qual, *die;* **it was ~:** es war eine Tortur; **the exam was sheer ~:** das Examen war der reinste Horror *(ugs.) od.* die Hölle; **suffer the ~s of the damned** Höllenqualen erleiden. **2.** *v. t.* foltern; *(fig.)* quälen

ˈtorture-chamber *n.* Folterkammer, *die*

torturer [ˈtɔːtʃərə(r)] *n.* Folterer, *der*/Folterin, *die*

Tory [ˈtɔːrɪ] *(Brit. Polit. coll.)* **1.** *n.* Tory, *der.* **2.** *adj.* Tory-; **he is/they are ~:** er ist ein Tory/sie sind Tories

Toryism [ˈtɔːrɪɪzm] *n., no pl. (Brit. Polit. coll.)* Toryismus, *der*

tosh [tɒʃ] *n. (sl.)* Quark, *der (ugs.)*

toss [tɒs] **1.** *v. t.* **a)** *(throw upwards)* hochwerfen; **~ a ball in one's hand** einen Ball mit der Hand immer wieder hochwerfen und auffangen; **~ a pancake** einen Pfannkuchen [durch Hochwerfen] wenden; **~ sb. in a blanket** jmdn. mit einer Decke in die Höhe schleudern; *see also* **caber; b)** *(throw casually)* werfen; schmeißen *(ugs.);* **~ it over!** *(coll.)* schmeiß es/ihn/sie rüber *(ugs.);* **~ sth. to sb.** jmdm. etw. zuwerfen; **c) ~ a coin** eine Münze werfen; **~ sb. for sth.** mit jmdm. durch Hochwerfen einer Münze um etw. losen; **d) be ~ed by a bull/horse** von einem Stier auf die Hörner genommen werden/von einem Pferd abgeworfen werden; **e)** *(move about)* hin und her werfen; ‹*Baum/Blume*› wiegen ‹*Zweige/Köpfe*›; **f)** *(Cookery: mix gently)* wenden; **~ a salad in oil** einen Salat mit Öl anmachen; **g) ~ one's head** den Kopf zurückwerfen. **2.** *v. i.* **a)** *(be restless in bed)* sich hin und her werfen; **~ and turn** sich [schlaflos] im Bett wälzen; **b)** ‹*Schiff, Boot:*› hin und her geworfen werden; ‹*Halm, Korn, Äste, Blume:*› sich wiegen; ‹*Federbusch, Hutfeder, Locken:*› wippen; ‹*Mähne, Haar*› flattern; **c)** *(toss coin)* eine Münze werfen; **~ for sth.** mit einer Münze um etw. losen. **3.** *n.* **a)** *(of coin)* **~ of a coin** Hochwerfen einer Münze; **the decision depends on the ~ of a coin** die Entscheidung wird durch Hochwerfen einer Münze gefällt; **the game was decided by the ~ of a coin** das Spiel wurde durch Hochwerfen einer Münze entschieden; **argue the ~** *(fig.)* die Entscheidung nicht akzeptieren wollen; **lose/win the ~:** bei der Auslosung verlieren/gewinnen; *(Footb.)* die Seitenwahl verlieren/gewinnen; **b) give a contemptuous/proud ~ of the head** den Kopf verächtlich/stolz in den Nacken werfen; **c)** *(throw)* Wurf, *der;* **give a pancake a ~:** einen Pfannkuchen [durch Hochwerfen] wenden; **d)** *(Brit.: throw from horse)* Abwerfen, *das;* **a bad ~:** ein schlimmer Sturz vom Pferd; **take a ~:** abgeworfen werden

~ about, ~ around 1. *v. i.* **a)** *(be restless in bed)* sich [schlaflos] im Bett wälzen; **b)** *see* **~ 2 b. 2.** *v. t.* **~ sth. around** *or* **about** etw. herumwerfen; etw. *od.* mit etw. rumschmeißen *(ugs.); (fig.)* etw. in die Debatte werfen

~ aˈside *v. t.* **a)** *(throw to one side)* hinwerfen; hinschmeißen *(ugs.);* **the mouldy apples were ~ed aside** die schimmligen Äpfel wurden weggeworfen; **b)** *(fig.: reject, abandon)* beiseite schieben; **~ aside all caution** alle Vorsicht außer acht lassen

~ aˈway *v. t.* wegwerfen; wegschmeißen *(ugs.)*

~ ˈback *v. t.* zurückwerfen ‹*Kopf, Haar*›; runterkippen *(ugs.)* ‹*Getränk*›

~ ˈdown *see* **~ off 1 a**

~ ˈoff 1. *v. t.* **a)** *(drink off)* runterkippen *(ugs.);* **b)** *(produce casually)* hinwerfen; hinhauen *(ugs. abwertend);* fallenlassen ‹*Bemerkung*›; **I just ~ed off the first names that came into my head** ich spuckte einfach die ersten besten Namen aus, die mir einfielen; **c)** *(sl.: masturbate)* **~ sb. off** jmdm. einen runterholen *(salopp).* **2.** *v. i. & refl. (sl.)* sich *(Dat.)* einen runterholen *(salopp)*

~ ˈout *v. t.* **a)** *(throw out)* **~ sb. out** jmdn. rauswerfen *od. (ugs.)* -schmeißen; **~ sth. out** etw. wegwerfen *od. (ugs.)* -schmeißen; **b)** *(fig.: reject)* [kurzerhand] ablehnen

~ ˈup 1. *v. i.* eine Münze werfen; **~ up for sth.** mit einer Münze um etw. losen. **2.** *v. t.* **a)** *(throw)* hochwerfen; in die Luft werfen

ˈtoss-up *n.* **a)** *(tossing of coin)* Hochwerfen einer Münze; **a ~ decides who ...:** wer ..., wird durch Hochwerfen einer Münze entschieden; **have a ~:** eine Münze werfen; **have a ~ for sth.** mit einer Münze um etw. losen; **b)** *(even chance)* **it is a ~ [whether ...]** es ist noch ganz ungewiß[, ob ...]; **They are both very good. It is a ~ between the two** Sie sind beide sehr gut. Man kann nicht sagen, wer besser ist

[1]tot [tɒt] *n. (coll.)* **a)** *(small child)* kleines Kind; Wicht, der *(fam.);* **tiny ~:** kleiner Wicht; **b)** *(dram of liquor)* Gläschen, *das;* **will you have a ~ of rum?** möchtest du ein Gläschen *od.* Schlückchen Rum haben?

[2]tot *v. t. & i.*, **-tt-** *(coll.)* **~ up 1.** *v. t.* zusammenziehen *(ugs.).* **2.** *v. i.* sich summieren; sich [zusammen]läppern *(ugs.);* **that ~s up to £5** das macht zusammen 5 Pfund *(ugs.)*

total [ˈtəʊtl] **1.** *adj.* **a)** *(comprising the whole)* gesamt; Gesamt‹*gewicht, -wert, -bevölkerung usw.*›; **what are your ~ debts?** wieviel Schulden hast du insgesamt?; **a ~ increase of £100** eine Steigerung von insgesamt 100 Pfund; *see also* **sum 1 a; b)** *(absolute)* völlig *nicht präd.;* **~ idiot** *(coll.)* Vollidiot, *der;* **be in ~ ignorance of sth.** von etw. überhaupt *od.* absolut nichts wissen; **a ~ beginner** ein absoluter Anfänger; **~ nonsense** totaler Unsinn; **have ~ contempt/scorn for sth.** etw. zutiefst verachten; **have a ~ lack of interest in sth.** sich für etw. absolut nicht interessieren; **a ~ success/shock** ein voller Erfolg/totaler *od.* absoluter Schock; **his surrender/refusal was ~:** er gab völlig auf/er weigerte sich strikt; **the silence was ~:** es herrschte völlige Stille; *see also* **abstinence a. 2.** *n.* *(number)* Gesamtzahl, *die; (amount)* Gesamtbetrag, *der; (result of addition)* Summe, *die;* **a ~ of 200/£200** *etc.* insgesamt 200/200 Pfund *usw.;* **in ~:** insgesamt; *see also* **grand 1 c; subtotal. 3.** *v. t., (Brit.)* **-ll- a)** *(add up)* addieren, zusammenzählen, zusammenrechnen ‹*Zahlen, Posten, Beträge*›; **b)** *(amount to)* [insgesamt] betragen; **the visitors ~led 131** die Zahl der Besucher betrug [insgesamt] 131; **c)** *(Amer. sl.: wreck)* zusammenfahren *(ugs.)*

~ ˈup 1. *v. t.* addieren; zusammenrechnen/-zählen. **2.** *v. i.* **~ up to sth.** sich auf etw. *(Akk.)* belaufen

total eˈclipse *n. (Astron.)* totale Finsternis

totalitarian [təʊtælɪˈteərɪən] *adj. (Polit.)* totalitär

totalitarianism [təʊtælɪˈteərɪənɪzm] *n. (Polit.)* Totalitarismus, *der*

totality [təˈtælɪtɪ] *n.* **a)** *(completeness)* Gesamtheit, *die; (of person)* Ganzheit, *die;* **b)** *(aggregate)* Gesamtheit, *die;* **the ~ of the debt** die Gesamtschuld; **c)** *(Astron.)* Totalität, *die (fachspr.)*

totalizator [ˈtəʊtəlaɪzeɪtə(r)] *n. (Horse-racing)* **a)** *(device)* Totalisatoranzeigetafel, *die;* **b)** *(system)* Totalisator, *der;* Toto, *das*

totally [ˈtəʊtəlɪ] *adv.* völlig

total: ~ reˈcall *n.* **have [the power of] ~ recall** ein absolutes Erinnerungsvermögen haben; **~ ˈwar** *n.* totaler Krieg

[1]tote [təʊt] *v. t. (coll.)* schleppen; **~ a gun** eine Kanone mit sich rumschleppen *(ugs.)*

[2]tote *n. (Horse-racing sl.)* **a)** *(device)* Totoanzeigetafel, *die;* **b)** *(system)* Toto, *das*

tote: ~ bag *n.* ≈ Reisetasche, *die;* **~ box** *n. (Amer.)* [Transport]kiste, *die*

totem [ˈtəʊtəm] *n.* Totem, *das (Völkerk.)*

totemism [ˈtəʊtəmɪzm] *n.* Totemismus, *der (Völkerk.)*

ˈtotem-pole *n.* Totempfahl, *der (Völkerk.)*

t'other, tother [ˈtʌðə(r)] *adj., pron.* = **the other**

totter [ˈtɒtə(r)] *v. i.* **a)** *(move unsteadily)* wanken; taumeln; *(esp. owing to drunkenness)* torkeln; **the child/blind man went ~ing across the room** das Kind ging mit tapsenden *(ugs.)*/der Blinde ging mit tastenden Schritten durch das Zimmer; **b)** *(be on point of falling)* schwanken; wanken *(geh.);* **make sth. ~:** etw. ins Schwanken bringen; **~ on the brink of collapse/chaos/bankruptcy/ruin** *(fig.)* am Rande des Zusammenbruchs/Chaos/Bankrotts/Ruins stehen

tottery [ˈtɒtərɪ] *adj.* wack[e]lig; **a ~ old man** ein alter Mann mit wackligen *(ugs.) od.* unsicheren Beinen; **have ~ legs** wacklig *(ugs.) od.* unsicher auf den Beinen sein; **feel ~:** sich wacklig *(ugs.) od.* unsicher auf den Beinen fühlen

totting-ˈup [tɒtɪŋˈʌp] *n.* **a)** Zusammenrechnen, *das;* **the ~ of the votes** die Auszählung der Stimmen; **b)** *(Brit. law) Berücksichtigung einschlägiger Vorstrafen, bes. bei der Entscheidung über einen Führerscheinentzug*

toucan [ˈtuːkən] *n. (Ornith.)* Tukan, *der*

touch [tʌtʃ] **1.** *v. t.* **a)** *(lit. or fig.)* berühren; *(inspect by ~ing)* betasten; **~ one's hat [to sb.]** sich *(Dat.)* [jmdm. zum Gruß] an den Hut tippen; **~ the sky** *(fig.)* an den Himmel stoßen; **~ sb. on the shoulder** jmdm. auf die Schulter tippen; *see also* **barge-pole; bottom 1 d; wood b; b)** *(cause contact between, apply)* **~ A to B** B mit A berühren; **~ one's hand to one's hat** mit der Hand an den Hut tippen; **~ a match to sth.** ein [brennendes] Streichholz an etw. *(Akk.)* halten; **he ~ed the wires together** er hielt die Drähte aneinander; **~ glasses** anstoßen; **c)** *(harm, interfere with)* anrühren; **the police can't ~ you [for it]** die Polizei kann dich nicht [dafür] belangen; **He can't ~ you here. You are safe** Hier kann er dir nichts tun *od.* anhaben. Du bist sicher; **d)** *(Mus.)* **~ the keys of a piano/harpsichord** *etc.* in die Tasten eines Klaviers/Spinetts *usw.* greifen; **~ the strings [of a guitar/lute/harp** *etc.***]** in die Saiten [einer Gitarre/Laute/Harfe *usw.*] greifen; **e)** *(fig.: rival)* **~ sth.** an etw. *(Akk.)* heranreichen; **nobody can ~ her for speed/at tennis/as an actress** niemand kann es mit ihr an Schnelligkeit/im Tennis/als Schauspielerin aufnehmen; **That horse is the fastest. There is none to ~ it** Dieses Pferd ist das schnellste. Keines kommt an es heran; **there is nothing to ~ a glass of whisky before**

bed es geht nichts über ein Glas Whisky vor dem Schlafengehen; **f)** *(affect emotionally)* rühren; **it ~ed him to the heart/it ~ed his heart** es rührte ihn ans Herz/es rührte sein Herz; **be ~ed with pity/remorse/sadness** von Mitleid/Reue/Traurigkeit angerührt sein *(geh.)*; **g)** *(concern oneself with)* anrühren; **whatever I ~ – I'm a failure at it** was ich auch anfange, es mißlingt mir alles; **I would not ~ it** ich würde die Finger davon lassen *(ugs.)*; **everything he ~es turns to gold** *(fig.)* er hat bei allem, was er tut, eine glückliche Hand; **I haven't even ~ed the washing up yet** ich habe mit dem Abwasch noch nicht mal angefangen; **h)** *(tinge)* färben; **her hair was chestnut ~ed with blonde streaks** sie hatte kastanienbraunes Haar mit blonden Strähnen; **i) ~ sb. for a loan/£5** *(sl.)* jmdn. anpumpen *(salopp)*/um 5 Pfund anpumpen *od.* anhauen *(salopp)*; **j)** *(Geom.)* berühren; tangieren *(fachspr.)*; **k)** *(reach)* erreichen; **l)** *(anger, wound)* treffen; **~ sb.'s pride/self-esteem** *etc.* jmdn. in seinem Stolz/in seinem Selbstwertgefühl *usw.* treffen; **m)** *(concern)* berühren; **this does not ~ the point at issue** das hat nichts mit unserem Thema zu tun; **n)** *(injure or damage slightly)* schädigen; **~ sb.** jmdm. schaden; **he was hardly ~ed by the fall** bei dem Sturz hatte er kaum etwas abbekommen; **o)** *(have effect on)* angreifen. **2.** *v. i.* sich berühren; ⟨*Grundstücke:*⟩ aneinanderstoßen; **don't ~!** nicht anfassen!; **'please do not ~'** „bitte nicht berühren!". **3.** *n.* **a)** Berührung, *die;* **the rider gave his horse a ~ of the spurs/the whip** der Reiter ließ sein Pferd die Sporen/die Peitsche spüren; **I like the warm ~ of her body** ich spüre gerne ihren warmen Körper [an meiner Haut]; **the surface has a soft/rough/cold/warm** *etc.* **~:** die Oberfläche fühlt sich weich/rauh/kalt/warm *usw.* an; **a ~ of the** *or* **one's hand** eine Berührung mit der Hand; **at a ~:** bei bloßer Berührung; **the machine can be stopped at a ~:** die Maschine läßt sich mit einem Fingerdruck abstellen; **be soft/warm** *etc.* **to the ~:** sich weich/warm *usw.* anfühlen; **b)** *no pl., no art.* *(faculty)* **[sense of] ~:** Tastsinn, *der;* **find out sth. by ~:** etw. ertasten; **c)** *(small amount)* **a ~ of salt/pepper** *etc.* eine Spur Salz/Pfeffer *usw.*; **a ~ of irony/sadness** *etc.* ein Anflug von Ironie/Traurigkeit *usw.*; **have a ~ of rheumatism** ein bißchen Rheuma haben; **have a ~ of genius** etwas Geniales haben; **she has a ~ of style/class [about her]** sie hat irgendwie Stil/Klasse; **the palms give a ~ of class/elegance to the restaurant** die Palmen geben dem Restaurant eine stilvolle/elegante Note; **he has a ~ of grey in his hair** er hat ein paar graue Strähnen im Haar; **a ~** *(slightly)* ein [ganz] kleines bißchen; **a ~ higher/too high** eine Idee höher/zu hoch; **a ~ unrealistic** eine Idee zu unrealistisch; *see also* **sun 1; d)** *(game of tag)* Fangen, *das;* **e)** *(Art: stroke)* Strich, *der;* *(fig.)* Detail, *das;* **to mention it in such a way was a clever/subtle ~:** es auf eine solche Weise zu erwähnen, war ein schlauer/raffinierter Einfall; **the book needs a few more humorous ~es** dem Buch fehlen noch ein paar humorvolle Tupfer; **the realistic ~es in the production of the play** die realistischen Elemente in der Inszenierung des Stücks; **add** *or* **put the final ~es to sth.** etw. *(Dat.)* den letzten Schliff geben; letzte Hand an etw. *(Akk.)* legen; **it was now completed except for a few final ~es** es war nun bis auf einige noch fehlende I-Tüpfelchen fertiggestellt; *see also* **finishing touch; f)** *(manner, style)* *(on keyboard instrument, typewriter)* Anschlag, *der;* *(of writer, sculptor)* Stil, *der;* *(of painter)* Pinselführung, *die;* **have the ~ of genius/the professional ~:** genial/professionell gemacht sein; **show the ~ of a genius/professional** die Handschrift eines Genies/Profis verraten; **the play bore/revealed his ~:** das Stück trug/verriet seine Handschrift; **you need to have the right ~:** man muß das richtige Gespür haben; **he just didn't have the ~:** er hatte einfach nicht genug Talent; **this flat needs a woman's ~:** diese Wohnung braucht die Hand einer Frau; **a personal ~:** eine persönliche *od.* individuelle Note; **lose one's ~:** seinen Schwung verlieren; *(Sport)* seine Form verlieren; **I see you haven't lost your ~!** du bist ja noch ganz der/die Alte! *(ugs.)*; **he's lost his ~:** er war schon mal besser in Form; **I must be losing my ~:** ich bin wohl auf dem absteigenden Ast *(ugs.)*; *see also* **common 1 b; g)** *(communication)* **be in/out of ~ [with sb.]** [mit jmdm.] Kontakt/keinen Kontakt haben; **I shall be in ~ with them** ich werde mit ihnen Kontakt aufnehmen; **they said they would be in ~ with me today** sie haben gesagt, sie würden sich heute bei mir melden; **Goodbye! I'll be in ~:** Auf Wiedersehen! Ich melde mich mal wieder; **they have not been in ~ for a whole week** wir haben/ich habe seit einer ganzen Woche nichts von ihnen gehört; **be in/out of ~ with sth.** über etw. (+ *Akk.*) auf dem laufenden/nicht auf dem laufenden sein; **he is out of** *or* **not in ~ with reality/the real world** er ist wirklichkeitsfremd/weltfremd; **get in ~ [with sb.]** mit jmdm. Kontakt/Verbindung aufnehmen; **get in ~ with us by letter/at this number** schreiben Sie uns/rufen Sie uns unter dieser Nummer an; **she immediately got in ~ with the doctor/police/her lawyer** sie setzte sich sofort mit dem Arzt/der Polizei/ihrem Anwalt in Verbindung; **keep in ~ [with sb.]** [mit jmdm.] in Verbindung *od.* Kontakt bleiben; **keep in ~!** laß von dir hören!; **I've kept in ~ with him since we were children** meine Verbindung mit ihm ist seit unserer Kindheit nie abgerissen; **keep in ~ with sth.** sich über etw. *(Akk.)* auf dem laufenden halten; **lose ~ with sb.** den Kontakt zu jmdm. verlieren; **we have lost ~:** wir haben keinen Kontakt mehr [zueinander]; **lose ~ with sth.** etw. aus den Augen verlieren; **have lost ~ with sth.** über etw. *(Akk.)* nicht mehr auf dem laufenden sein; **put sb. in ~ with sb.** jmdn. mit jmdm. zusammenbringen; **her doctor put her in ~ with a specialist** ihr Arzt hat sie zu einem Spezialisten geschickt; **h)** *(Footb., Rugby: part of field)* Aus, *das;* Mark, *die (Rugby)*; **in ~:** im Aus; **he ran/the ball went into ~:** er rannte/der Ball ging ins Aus; **i)** *(sl.)* **be an easy** *or* **a soft ~** *(be a person who gives money readily)* leicht rumzukriegen sein *(ugs.)*

~ at *v. t.* *(Naut.)* anlegen in (+ *Dat.*)

~ 'down *v. i.* **a)** *(Rugby)* den Ball niederlegen; *(Amer. Footb.)* den Ball hinter die Grundlinie bringen; **b)** ⟨*Flugzeug:*⟩ aufsetzen; *(land)* landen; *see also* **touchdown**

~ 'in *v. t.* *(Art)* hineinmalen; *(fig.)* ausführen ⟨*Details*⟩

~ 'off *v. t.* **a)** *(explode)* zünden ⟨*Bombe, Sprengladung, Feuerwerkskörper*⟩; auslösen ⟨*Explosion, Mine*⟩; **b)** *(fig.: trigger off)* auslösen

~ on *v. t.* **a)** *(treat briefly)* ansprechen; **the book ~es on the subject often** in dem Buch wird das Thema immer wieder gestreift; **b)** *(verge on)* grenzen an (+ *Akk.*)

~ 'up *v. t.* **a)** *(improve)* ausbessern; retuschieren ⟨*Photographie*⟩; auffrischen ⟨*Make-up*⟩; in Ordnung bringen ⟨*Haar*⟩; ausfeilen ⟨*Text*⟩; **b)** *(sl.: fondle)* befummeln *(ugs.)*

~ upon *see* touch on a

touch: ~-and-'go *adj.* prekär ⟨*Situation*⟩; **it is ~-and-go [whether ...]** es steht auf des Messers Schneide[, ob ...]; **~down** *n.* **a)** *(Amer. Footb.)* Touchdown, *der;* **b)** *(Aeronaut.)* Landung, *die*

touché ['tu:ʃeɪ] *int.* *(Fencing)* Treffer!; *(fig.)* eins zu null für dich!

touched [tʌtʃt] *pred. adj.* **a)** *(moved)* gerührt; **b)** *(coll.: mad)* meschugge *(salopp)*

touchiness ['tʌtʃɪnɪs] *n., no pl.* *(irritability, over-sensitiveness)* [Über]empfindlichkeit, *die;* *(precariousness)* Heikelkeit, *die*

touching ['tʌtʃɪŋ] **1.** *adj.* rührend; *(moving)* bewegend; ergreifend. **2.** *prep.* *(arch./literary)* **~ sth.** etw. betreffend

touchingly ['tʌtʃɪŋlɪ] *adv.* rührend; *(movingly)* bewegend; ergreifend; **tell/depict sth. ~:** etw. ergreifend erzählen/schildern

touch: ~-judge *n.* *(Rugby)* Seitenrichter, *der;* **~-line** *n.* *(Footb., Rugby)* Seitenlinie, *die;* Marklinie, *die (Rugby)*; **~-me-not** *n.* *(Bot.)* Rührmichnichtan, *das;* **~-paper** *n.* Zündpapier, *das;* *(on firework)* Papierlunte, *die;* **~stone** *n.* *(fig.)* Prüfstein, *der;* **~-type** *v. i.* blindschreiben; **~-typing** *n.* Blindschreiben, *das;* **~-up paint** *n.* Ausbesserungslack, *der*

touchy ['tʌtʃɪ] *adj.* empfindlich ⟨*Person*⟩; heikel ⟨*Thema, Sache*⟩

tough [tʌf] **1.** *adj.* **a)** fest ⟨*Material, Stoff, Leder, Metall, Werkstoff*⟩; zäh ⟨*Fleisch, fachspr.: Werkstoff, Metall, Kunststoff*⟩; widerstandsfähig ⟨*Straßenbelag, Bodenbelag, Gummi, Glas, Haut*⟩; strapazierfähig ⟨*Kleidung, Stoff, Schuhe, Seil*⟩; **be [as] ~ as leather/old boots** zäh wie Leder/wie eine Schuhsohle sein; *(fig.)* hart im Nehmen sein *(ugs.)*; **b)** *(hardy, unyielding)* zäh ⟨*Person*⟩; **his parents want him to be ~ when he grows up** seine Eltern wollen, daß aus ihm ein harter Mann wird; **~ guy** *(coll.)* knallharter Bursche; **a ~ customer** *(coll.)* ein harter Brocken *(ugs.)*; *(stubborn person)* Dickschädel, *der (ugs.)*; **c)** *(difficult, trying)* schwierig; vertrackt *(ugs.)* ⟨*Problem*⟩; hart ⟨*Kampf, Wettkampf*⟩; strapaziös ⟨*Reise*⟩; schwer ⟨*Zeit*⟩; **we had a ~ time** wir haben viel durchgemacht; **we had a ~ time convincing her** es hat uns viel Mühe gekostet, sie zu überzeugen; **it's a ~ life being a housewife** als Hausfrau hat man es schwer; **things/life can get ~ if you run out of money** wenn man kein Geld mehr hat, kann das Leben sehr schwer werden; **it was ~ going, the going was ~:** es war ein Schlauch *(ugs.)*; **d)** *(severe, harsh)* hart; **get ~** *(coll.)* andere Saiten aufziehen; **a get-~ policy** eine Politik des harten Durchgreifens; **get ~ with sb.** *(coll.)* jmdn. hart anfassen; **e)** *(coll.: unfortunate, hard)* **~ luck** Pech, *das;* **that's ~ [luck]** so'n Pech *(ugs.)* *od.* *(salopp)* Mist!; **be ~ on sb.** hart für jmdn. sein; **f)** *(stiff)* zäh ⟨*Schlamm, Ton, Brei*⟩; **g)** *(Amer.: violent, criminal)* gewalttätig; **a ~ town/neighbourhood** eine Stadt/Gegend, in der das Leben rauh ist. **2.** *n.* Rowdy, *der (abwertend)*

toughen ['tʌfn] **1.** *v. t.* größere Festigkeit geben (+ *Dat.*); zäher machen *(fachspr.)* ⟨*Werkstoff, Metall, Kunststoff*⟩; abhärten, *(geh.)* stählen ⟨*Person, Körper*⟩; verschärfen ⟨*Gesetz, Widerstand*⟩; **his hard life has ~ed him** *(fig.)* sein schweres Leben hat ihn gehärtet *od.* hart gemacht; **he has ~ed his attitude towards law-breakers** er hat gegenüber Gesetzesbrechern eine härtere Haltung eingenommen; **~ one's policy/stand** einen härteren [politischen] Kurs einschlagen/einen härteren Standpunkt einnehmen; **this setback will only ~ my resolve** dieser Rückschlag wird mich in meiner Entschlossenheit nur noch bestärken. **2.** *v. i.* fester werden; ⟨*Werkstoff, Metall, Kunststoff:*⟩ zäher werden *(fachspr.)*; ⟨*Widerstand:*⟩ sich verschärfen; ⟨*Entschlossenheit:*⟩ stärker werden; ⟨*Standpunkt, Position, politischer Kurs:*⟩ sich verhärten

~ 'up 1. *v. t.* abhärten; stählen *(geh.)*; verschärfen ⟨*Gesetz, Verbrechensbekämpfung*⟩; **~ up one's attitude/policy** eine härtere Haltung einnehmen/einen härteren [politischen] Kurs einschlagen. **2.** *v. i.* sich abhärten; sich stählen *(geh.)*; *(fig.)* ⟨*Politik, Ein-*

stellung:) sich verhärten; ⟨*Widerstand:*⟩ sich verschärfen

toughie ['tʌfɪ] *n. (coll.)* **a)** *(problem)* harte Nuß *(ugs.)*; **b)** *(person)* Rabauke, *der (ugs.)*

tough-'minded *adj.* hart

toughness ['tʌfnɪs] *n., no pl.* **a)** *see* **tough 1 a:** Festigkeit, *die;* Zäheit, *die;* Zähigkeit, *die (fachspr.);* Widerstandsfähigkeit, *die;* Strapazierfähigkeit, *die;* **b)** *see* **tough 1 b:** Zähigkeit, *die;* **c)** *(fig.) (of problem, job)* Schwierigkeit, *die; (of fight, contest, law, policy, attitude, penalty, measure)* Härte, *die;* **the ~ of the exercise** die Schwierigkeit der Übung; **the ~ of life as an unmarried mother** die Schwierigkeiten, mit denen eine ledige Mutter zu kämpfen hat; **d)** *(stiffness)* Zäheit, *die;* **e)** *(Amer.: violence)* **the ~ of the mining towns** das rauhe Leben in den Bergarbeiterstädten

toupee, toupet ['tu:peɪ] *n.* Toupet, *das*

tour [tʊə(r)] **1.** *n.* **a)** [Rund]reise, *die;* Tour, *die (ugs.);* **a ~ of** *or* **through Europe** eine Reise durch Europa/eine Europareise; **a world ~/round-the-world ~:** eine Weltreise/Reise um die Welt; **they made a ~ of France** sie machten eine Frankreichreise; **a ~ of the capital cities of Europe/of the overseas branches of the firm** eine Rundreise zu den Hauptstädten Europas/zu den überseeischen Tochtergesellschaften der Firma; **a walking/cycling ~:** eine Wanderung/[Fahr]radtour; **a motoring/bus ~:** eine Auto-/Busreise; **b)** *(Theatre, Sport)* Tournee, *die;* Tour, *die (Jargon);* **a ~ of the provinces, a provincial ~:** eine Tournee/Tour durch die Provinz; **be/go on ~:** auf Tournee/Tour sein/gehen; **he has gone on ~ to Europe** er ist auf [einer] Europatournee; **take a play on ~:** mit einem Stück auf Tournee/Tour gehen; **c)** *(excursion, inspection) (of museum, palace, house)* Besichtigung, *die;* **go on/make/do a ~ of** besichtigen ⟨*Museum, Haus, Schloß usw.*⟩; **a ~ of the countryside/the city/the factory** ein Ausflug in die Umgebung/eine Besichtigungstour durch die Stadt/ein Rundgang durch die Fabrik; **d) ~ [of duty]** Dienstzeit, *die;* **between [sb.'s] ~s [of duty]** bevor jmd. einen neuen Posten antritt/antrat. *See also* **conduct 2 e; grand tour; guided tour; inspection. 2.** *v. i.* **a) ~/go ~ing in** *or* **through a country** eine Reise *od. (ugs.)* Tour durch ein Land machen; **be ~ing in a country** auf einer Reise *od. (ugs.)* Tour durch ein Land sein; **b)** *(Theatre, Sport, exhibition)* eine Tournee *od. (Jargon)* Tour machen; *(be on ~)* auf Tournee *od. (Jargon)* Tour sein; touren *(Jargon); (go on ~)* auf Tournee *od. (Jargon)* Tour gehen. **3.** *v. t.* **a)** besichtigen ⟨*Stadt, Gebäude, Museum*⟩; **~ a country/region** eine Reise *od. (ugs.)* Tour durch ein Land/Gebiet machen; **~ an area on foot/by bicycle** eine Wanderung/Radtour durch eine Gegend machen; **b)** *(Theatre, Sport)* **~ a country/the provinces** eine Tournee *od. (Jargon)* Tour durch das Land/die Provinz machen; **~ India/Europe** eine Indien-/Europatournee *od. (Jargon)* -tour machen

tour de force [tʊədə'fɔ:s] *n., pl.* **~s de force** [tʊədə'fɔ:s] Glanzleistung, *die*

tourer ['tʊərə(r)] *n. (Motor Veh.)* Kabriolimousine, *die*

touring ['tʊərɪŋ]: **~-car** *see* **tourer; ~ company** *n. (Theatre)* Gastspielensemble, *das;* **~ exhibition** *n.* Wanderausstellung, *die;* **~ holiday** *n.* **have a ~ holiday in a country** in den Ferien/im Urlaub durch ein Land fahren/*(on foot)* durch ein Land wandern; **have a ~ holiday** in den Ferien/im Urlaub eine Reise/*(on foot)* Wanderung machen

tourism ['tʊərɪzm] *n., no pl., no indef. art.* **a)** Tourismus, *der;* **~ has increased** der Tourismus hat zugenommen; **b)** *(operation of tours)* Touristik, *die;* **work/be involved in ~:** in der Touristikbranche arbeiten/tätig sein

tourist ['tʊərɪst] **1.** *n.* Tourist, *der*/Touristin, *die.* **2.** *attrib. adj.* Touristen-; **special ~ rates** ermäßigte Preise für Touristen

tourist: ~ agency *n.* Reisebüro, *das;* **~ attraction** *n.* Touristenattraktion, *die;* **~ board** *n. (Brit.)* Amt für Fremdenverkehrswesen; **~ class** *n.* Touristenklasse, *die;* **~ guide** *n.* **a)** *(person)* Touristenführer, *der*/-führerin, *die;* **b)** *(book)* Reiseführer, *der* (to, of von); **~ hotel** *n.* Touristenhotel, *das;* **~ industry** *n.* **a)** *(business)* Tourismusindustrie, *die;* **b)** *(firms)* Touristik[branche], *die;* **~ infor'mation centre, ~ office** *ns.* Fremdenverkehrsbüro, *das;* Touristeninformation, *die (ugs.);* **~ season** *n.* Touristensaison, *die;* **~ trade** *see* **~ industry; ~ trap** *n. (bar, restaurant, etc.)* [auf Touristen spezialisierter] Nepplladen *(ugs.); (town, place)* Ort, an dem Touristen geneppt werden *(ugs.)*

touristy ['tʊərɪstɪ] *adj. (derog.)* auf Tourismus getrimmt *(ugs.);* Touristen⟨*stadt, -nest, -gegend*⟩ *(ugs. abwertend)*

tourmaline ['tʊəməlɪn, 'tʊəməli:n] *n. (Min.)* Turmalin, *der*

tournament ['tʊənəmənt] *n. (Hist.; Sport)* Turnier, *das*

tournedos ['tʊənədəʊ] *n., pl. same (Gastr.)* Tournedos, *das*

tourney ['tʊənɪ] *(Hist.; Sport coll.) see* **tournament**

tourniquet ['tʊənɪkeɪ] *n. (Med.)* Tourniquet, *das*

'tour operator *n.* Reiseveranstalter, *der*/-veranstalterin, *die*

tousle ['taʊzl] *v. t.* zerzausen

tout [taʊt] **1.** *v. i.* **~ [for business/custom/orders]** Kunden anreißen *(ugs.) od.* werben; **~ for customers/buyers** Kunden/Käufer anreißen *(ugs.) od.* werben; **~ for a hotel** für ein Hotel Gäste werben. **2.** *n.* Anreißer, *der*/Anreißerin, *die (ugs.);* Kundenwerber, *der*/-werberin, *die;* **ticket ~:** Kartenschwarzhändler, *der*/-händlerin, *die*

¹tow [təʊ] **1.** *v. t.* schleppen; ziehen ⟨*Anhänger, Wasserskiläufer, Handwagen*⟩; **he ~ed my car to get it started** er hat meinen Wagen angeschleppt; **he ~ed his sister [behind him]** *(fig.)* er zog seine Schwester hinter sich *(Dat.)* her; **~ed load** *(Motor Veh.)* Anhängelast, *die.* **2.** *n.* Schleppen, *das;* **My car's broken down. – Do you want a ~?** Mein Wagen ist stehengeblieben. – Soll ich Sie [ab]schleppen?; **give a boat/car a ~:** ein Boot/einen Wagen schleppen; **give a car a ~ [to get it started]** ein Auto anschleppen; **have sth. in** *or* **on ~:** etw. im Schlepp[tau] haben; **have sb. in ~** *(fig.)* jmdn. im Schlepptau haben *(ugs.);* **take sb. in ~** *(fig.)* jmdn. unter seine Fittiche nehmen; **'on ~'** „wird geschleppt"; **take a boat/car in ~:** ein Boot/einen Wagen in Schlepp nehmen

~ a'way *v. t.* abschleppen

²tow *n. (Textiles)* Hede, *die;* Werg, *das*

toward [tə'wɔ:d], **towards** [tə'wɔ:dz] *prep.* **a)** *(in direction of)* **~ sb./sth.** auf jmdn./etw. zu; **the ship sailed ~ France/the open sea** das Schiff fuhr in Richtung Frankreich/offenes Meer; **~ [the] town** in Richtung [auf die] Stadt; **point ~ the north** nach Norden zeigen; **march ~ the north** nach Norden *od.* in Richtung Norden *od.* in nördlicher Richtung marschieren; **look ~ the sea** in Richtung Meer blicken; **turn ~ sb.** sich zu jmdm. umdrehen; **the village is farther [to the] south, ~ Dover** das Dorf liegt weiter südlich, in Richtung Dover; **point ~ the horizon** zum Horizont deuten; **sit/stand with one's back [turned] ~ sth.** mit dem Rücken zu etw. sitzen/stehen; **turn one's face/back ~ sb./sth.** jmdm./einer Sache das Gesicht/den Rücken zuwenden; **my back was ~ the door** mein Rücken war der Tür zugewandt; **hold out one's hands ~ sb.** jmdm. die Hände entgegenstrecken; **my house faces ~ the park/sea** die Vorderseite meines Hauses liegt zum Park/Meer hin; **the country was drifting ~ war/economic chaos** das Land trieb dem Krieg/wirtschaftlichem Chaos zu; **he was sliding ~ disaster/financial ruin** er schlitterte in das Verderben/in den finanziellen Ruin; **b)** *(in relation to)* gegenüber; **feel sth. ~ sb.** jmdm. gegenüber etw. empfinden; **his attitude ~ death** seine Einstellung zum Tod; **be fair/unfair** *etc.* **~ sb.** jmdm. gegenüber *od.* zu jmdm. fair/unfair *usw.* sein; **his conduct ~ us** sein Verhalten uns gegenüber; **feel angry/sympathetic ~ sb.** böse auf jmdn. sein/Verständnis für jmdn. haben; **c)** *(for)* **a contribution ~ sth.** ein Beitrag zu etw.; **save up ~ a car/one's holidays** auf *od.* für einen Wagen/für seine Ferien sparen; **proposals ~ solving a problem** Vorschläge zur Lösung eines Problems; **work together ~ a solution** gemeinsam auf eine Lösung hinarbeiten; **contribute ~ sth.** zu etw. beitragen; **it is/it brings us a step ~ achieving our aim** es bringt uns einen Schritt näher zum Ziel; **efforts are being made ~ reconciliation** man bemüht sich um Versöhnung; **d)** *(near)* gegen; **~ the end of May/of the year** *etc.* [gegen] Ende Mai/des Jahres; **it is getting ~ midnight/your bedtime** es geht auf Mitternacht zu/es ist bald Schlafenszeit für dich; **~ the end of his life/of the book** gegen Ende seines Lebens/des Buches; **sit ~ the front/back of the bus** vorne/hinten im Bus sitzen; **~ the bottom of the list** ziemlich weit unten auf der Liste

'tow-bar *n. (Motor Veh.)* Anhängerkupplung, *die; (bar fitted between broken-down vehicle and towing vehicle)* Abschleppstange, *die*

towel ['taʊəl] **1.** *n.* **a)** Handtuch, *das;* **throw in the ~** *(Boxing; also fig.)* das Handtuch werfen. **2.** *v. t., (Brit.)* **-ll-** abtrocknen; **~ one's/sb.'s face/arms** *etc.* **[dry]** sich/jmdm. das Gesicht/die Arme *usw.* abtrocknen; **~ oneself** sich abtrocknen

towelling *(Amer.:* **toweling)** ['taʊəlɪŋ] *n., no pl., no indef. art.* Frottierware, *die;* Frottee, *das (ugs.)*

'towel-rail *n.* Handtuchhalter, *der*

tower ['taʊə(r)] **1.** *n.* **a)** Turm, *der; (Aeronaut.)* Tower, *der;* Kontrollturm, *der; see also* **control tower; cooling tower; water-tower; b)** *(fortress)* Festung, *die;* Wehrturm, *der;* **the T~ [of London]** der Tower [von London]; **c) be a ~ of strength [to sb.]** *(fig.)* [jmdm.] ein fester Rückhalt sein; **d)** *see* **tower block.** *See also* **ivory tower. 2.** *v. i.* in die Höhe ragen; aufragen; **~ to [a height of] 200 feet** 200 Fuß hoch aufragen

~ above, ~ over *v. t.* **~ above** *or* **over sb./sth.** *(lit. or fig.)* jmdn./etw. überragen; **she saw the giant ~ing above her** sie sah die ragende Gestalt des Riesen über sich *(Dat.) (geh.);* **the building/mountain ~s above** *or* **over the town/landscape** das Gebäude/der Berg ragt über der Stadt/Landschaft *(geh.)*

tower: ~ block *n.* Hochhaus, *das;* **~ crane** *n.* Turmdrehkran, *der*

towering ['taʊərɪŋ] *attrib. adj.* **a)** hoch aufragend; riesenhaft ⟨*Gestalt*⟩; **~ height** schwindelnde Höhe; **b)** *(fig.)* herausragend ⟨*Leistung, Gestalt*⟩; **c)** *(fig.: violent, intense)* blind ⟨*Wut*⟩; maßlos ⟨*Ehrgeiz, Stolz*⟩; **be in/fly into a ~ passion** *or* **rage** von blinder Wut ergriffen sein/werden

'tow-line *n.* Schleppseil, *das; (Naut.)* Schlepptrosse, *die*

town [taʊn] *n.* **a)** Stadt, *die;* **the ~ of Cambridge** die Stadt Cambridge; **in [the] ~:** in der Stadt; **the ~** *(people)* die Stadt; **be the toast of the ~:** ein gefeierter Star/gefeierte Stars sein; **on the outskirts/in the centre of ~:** in den Randbezirken der Stadt/in der Stadtmitte *od.* Innenstadt; **go [up] to ~:** in die Stadt fahren; **we went [up] to ~ from**

York *(to London)* wir sind von York nach London gefahren; **be in/out of ~:** in der Stadt/nicht in der Stadt sein; **head out of ~:** stadtauswärts fahren/gehen/reiten *usw.*; **he is well known about ~:** er ist stadtbekannt; ihn kennt die ganze Stadt; **it's all over ~ [that ...]** die ganze Stadt redet davon[, daß ...]; **the best coffee/tea/cake** *etc.* **in ~:** der beste Kaffee/Tee/Kuchen *usw.* in der Stadt; **go out/have a night on the ~** *(coll.)* [in die Stadt gehen und] einen draufmachen *(ugs.)*; **go to ~** *(fig. coll.)* in die vollen gehen (on bei) *(ugs.)*; **man about ~:** *Mann, der an allen gesellschaftlichen und kulturellen Ereignissen einer Stadt teilnimmt; see also* **gown b; paint 2a; talk 1d; b)** *(business or shopping centre)* Stadt, *die;* **in ~:** in der Stadt; **go into ~:** in die Stadt gehen/fahren

town: ~ 'centre *n.* Stadtmitte, *die;* Stadtzentrum, *das;* **the ~ centres** die Innenstädte; **Brighton still has an old ~ centre** Brighton hat noch einen alten Stadtkern; **~ 'clerk** *n.* ≈ [Ober]stadtdirektor, *der*/-direktorin, *die;* **~ 'council** *n. (Brit.)* Stadtrat, *der;* **~ 'councillor** *n. (Brit.)* Stadtrat, *der*/-rätin, *die;* **~ 'crier** *n.* städtischer Ausrufer; **~ gas** *n., no pl., no indef. art.* Stadtgas, *das;* **~ 'hall** *n.* Rathaus, *das;* **~ house** *n.* **a)** *(residence in town)* Stadthaus, *das;* **b)** *(terrace-house)* Reihenhaus, *das*

townie ['taʊni:] *n.* Stadtmensch, *der*

town: ~ 'mayor *n. (Brit.)* [Stadt]bürgermeister, *der*/-bürgermeisterin, *die;* **~ 'planner** *n.* Stadtplaner, *der*/-planerin, *die;* **~ 'planning** *n.* Stadtplanung, *die*

townscape ['taʊnskeɪp] *n.* **a)** *(Art, Photog.)* Stadtansicht, *die;* **b)** *(town's appearance)* Stadtbild, *das*

townsfolk ['taʊnzfəʊk] *n. pl.* Städter *Pl.*; **the ~:** *(inhabitants)* die Stadtbevölkerung; *(citizens)* die Bürger [der Stadt]

township ['taʊnʃɪp] *n.* **a)** *(Amer.: division of county)* Township, *die; Verwaltungseinheit unterhalb der County;* **b)** *(Amer. Surv.)* Township, *die; 36 Quadratmeilen großes quadratisches Stück Land;* **c)** *(Austral., NZ) (small town)* Ortschaft, *die;* Siedlung, *die; (site) Areal für eine neue Siedlung;* **d)** *(S. Afr.: non-white urban area)* Township, *die; von Farbigen bewohnte, städtische Siedlung*

town: ~sman ['taʊnzmən] *n., pl.* **~smen** ['taʊnzmən] Stadtbewohner, *der;* Städter, *der; (citizen)* [Stadt]bürger, *der;* **[fellow] ~sman** *(fellow citizen)* Mitbürger, *der;* **~speople** ['taʊnzpi:pl] *see* **townsfolk; ~swoman** ['taʊnzwʊmən] *n.* Stadtbewohnerin, *die;* Städterin, *die; (citizen)* [Stadt-]bürgerin, *die*

tow: ~-path *n.* Leinpfad, *der;* Treidelpfad, *der;* **~-rope** *n.* Abschleppseil, *das;* **~-start** *n. (Motor Veh.)* [Start durch] Anschleppen; **give sb. a ~-start** jmdn. anschleppen; **~truck** *n. (Amer.)* Abschleppwagen, *der*

toxaemia *(Amer.:* **toxemia***)* [tɒk'si:mɪə] *n. (Med.)* **a)** *(blood-poisoning)* Toxämie, *die;* **b)** *(in pregnancy)* Schwangerschaftstoxikose, *die*

toxic ['tɒksɪk] *adj.* **a)** giftig; toxisch *(fachspr.)*; **b)** *(caused by poison)* toxisch *(fachspr.)*; toxigen *(fachspr.)*

toxicity [tɒk'sɪsɪtɪ] *n., no pl.* Giftigkeit, *die;* Toxizität, *die (fachspr.)*

toxicology [tɒksɪ'kɒlədʒɪ] *n.* Toxikologie, *die*

toxin ['tɒksɪn] *n.* Toxin, *das*

toy [tɔɪ] **1.** *n. (lit. or fig.)* Spielzeug, *das;* **~s** Spielzeug, *das;* Spielwaren *Pl. (Wirtsch.)*. **2.** *adj.* **a)** Spielzeug-; **b)** *(Breeding)* Zwerg-. **3.** *v. i.* **~ with the idea of doing sth.** mit dem Gedanken spielen, etw. zu tun; **~ with one's food** mit seinem Essen herumspielen/in seinem Essen herumstochern; **~ with sb.** *(flirt)* mit jmdm. flirten; *(not be serious)* mit jmdm. spielen *od.* sein Spiel treiben

toy: ~-boy *n. (coll.)* Gespiele, *der (scherzh.)*; **~shop** *n.* Spielwarengeschäft, *das;* **~ 'soldier** *n.* Spielzeugsoldat, *der*

¹trace [treɪs] **1.** *v. t.* **a)** *(copy)* durchpausen; abpausen; **~ sth. on to sth.** etw. auf etw. *(Akk.)* pausen; **b)** *(delineate)* zeichnen ⟨*Form, Linie*⟩; malen ⟨*Buchstaben, Wort*⟩; *(fig.)* entwerfen; **she ~d our route on the map with her finger/with a pen** sie zeichnete unsere Route mit dem Finger/Stift auf der Landkarte nach; **c)** *(follow track of)* folgen (+ *Dat.*); verfolgen; **the leak was ~d to an old cast-iron main** man fand das Leck an einer alten gußeisernen Hauptleitung; **~ a river to its source** einen Fluß [bis] zur Quelle zurückverfolgen; **the doctors ~d the infection to some dirty instruments** die Ärzte fanden heraus, daß die Infektion von verunreinigten Instrumenten herrührte; **he had to resign when the leak was ~d to his office** er mußte zurücktreten, als man die undichte Stelle in seiner Behörde ausfindig machte; **the police ~d him to Spain** die Polizei spürte ihn in Spanien auf; **d)** *(observe, find)* finden; **~ a connection** einen Zusammenhang sehen; **e)** *(Archaeol.)* erkennen; **~ Roman roads** den Verlauf von alten Römerstraßen rekonstruieren. **2.** *n.* **a)** *(visible sign)* Spur, *die; (of buildings, road)* [Über]rest, *der;* **there is no ~ of your letter in our records** in unseren Aufzeichnungen findet sich kein Hinweis auf Ihr Schreiben; **I can't find any ~ of him/it** *(cannot locate)* ich kann ihn/es nirgends finden; **lose [all] ~ of sb.** jmdn. [völlig] aus den Augen verlieren; **all ~ of the climbers has been lost** von den Bergsteigern fehlt jede Spur; **sink without ~:** sinken, ohne eine Spur zu hinterlassen; *(fig.)* in der Versenkung verschwinden *(ugs.)*; ⟨*bekannte Persönlichkeit:*⟩ von der Bildfläche verschwinden *(ugs.)*; **b)** *(track left behind)* Spur, *die (of animal also)* Fährte, *die; (of recording instrument)* Kurve, *die;* **c)** *(Electronics)* Spur, *die;* **d)** *(small amount)* Spur, *die;* **a ~ of a smile/of sarcasm** ein Anflug eines Lächelns/von Sarkasmus; **the product contains a ~ of impurity** das Produkt enthält eine winzige Menge an Fremdstoffen

~ 'back *v. t.* zurückverfolgen; **the rumour was ~d back to a journalist** als Quelle des Gerüchts wurde ein Journalist ausfindig gemacht

~ 'out *see* **~ 1b**

~ 'over *see* **~ 1a**

²trace *n. (strap of harness)* Strang, *der; (of horse's headstall)* Zuggurt, *der;* **kick over the ~s** *(fig.)* über die Stränge schlagen *(ugs.)*

traceable ['treɪsəbl] *adj.* **a) sth. is ~ to sth./through sth.** etw. läßt sich bis zu etw./durch etw. hindurch zurückverfolgen; **this effect is ~ to the following cause** diese Wirkung läßt sich auf folgende Ursache zurückführen; **b)** *(discoverable)* auffindbar; **this is a feature ~ in all his novels/paintings** dieses Merkmal läßt sich in allen seinen Romanen/Bildern entdecken

'trace element *n. (Chem.)* Spurenelement, *das*

tracer ['treɪsə(r)] *n.* **a)** *(Mil.)* Leuchtspurgeschoß, *das;* **b)** *(radioactive isotope)* Indikator, *der*

tracery ['treɪsərɪ] *n.* **a)** *(Archit.)* Maßwerk, *das;* **bar ~:** Maßwerk, *das;* **plate ~:** negatives Maßwerk; **b)** *(pattern, network)* Filigranmuster, *das*

trachea [trə'ki:ə] *n., pl.* **~e** [trə'ki:i:] **a)** *(Anat.)* Trachea, *die (fachspr.)*; Luftröhre, *die;* **b)** *(Zool.)* Trachee, *die (Zool.)*

tracheotomy [treɪkɪ'ɒtəmɪ] *n. (Med.)* Luftröhrenschnitt, *der;* Tracheotomie, *die (fachspr.)*

trachoma [trə'kəʊmə] *n. (Med.)* Trachom, *das (Med.)*

tracing ['treɪsɪŋ] *n.* **a)** *(action)* [Durch]pausen, *das;* [Ab]pausen, *das;* **do some ~:** einiges durch- *od.* abpausen; **b)** *(copy)* Pause, *die;* Kopie, *die*

'tracing-paper *n.* Pauspapier, *das*

track [træk] **1.** *n.* **a)** Spur, *die; (of wild animal)* Fährte, *die;* **~s** *(footprints)* [Fuß]spuren; *(of animal also)* Fährte, *die;* **cover one's ~s** *(fig.)* seine Spur verwischen; **be on sb.'s ~:** jmdm. auf der Spur sein; *(fig.: in possession of clue to sb.'s plans)* jmdm. auf die Schliche gekommen sein; **they will be on our ~:** sie kommen uns auf die Spur/*(fig.)* auf die Schliche; **be on the right/wrong ~** *(fig.)* auf der richtigen/falschen Spur sein; **keep ~ of sb./sth.** jmdn./etw. im Auge behalten; **he couldn't keep ~ of her in the crowd** er verlor sie in der Menge aus den Augen; **the police [successfully] kept ~ of him** die Polizei blieb ihm auf der Spur; **they kept ~ of his movements/intentions/plans** sie waren jederzeit über seinen Aufenthaltsort/seine Absichten/Pläne auf dem laufenden; **The situation is very complicated. I can't keep ~ of it** Die Situation ist sehr verworren. Ich habe den Überblick verloren; **without keeping accounts I can't keep ~ of what I spend** wenn ich nicht Buch führe, verliere ich den Überblick über meine Ausgaben; **lose ~ of sb./sth.** jmdn./etw. aus den Augen verlieren; **the police lost ~ of the gang's movements** die Polizei war über den Aufenthaltsort der Bande nicht mehr auf dem laufenden; **he has lost ~ of the situation** er ist über die Situation nicht mehr auf dem laufenden; **she lost ~ of the story** sie hat bei der Geschichte den Überblick verloren; **without keeping accounts you can easily lose ~ of what you spend** wenn man nicht Buch führt, kann man leicht die Übersicht über seine Ausgaben verlieren; **make ~s** *(coll.) (depart)* sich auf die Socken machen *(ugs.)*; *(run off)* türmen *(ugs.)*; **we'd better make ~s for home/the station** *(coll.)* wir sollten uns langsam auf die Socken machen und zusehen, daß wir nach Hause/zum Bahnhof kommen *(ugs.)*; **stop [dead] in one's ~s** *(coll.)* auf der Stelle stehenbleiben; **stop sb. [dead] in his ~s** *(coll.)* jmdn. auf der Stelle stehenbleiben lassen; **b)** *(path)* [unbefestigter] Weg; *(footpath)* Pfad, *der; (fig.)* Weg, *der;* **the road has only a single ~:** die Straße hat nur eine Spur *od.* ist nur einspurig; **they followed in the same ~** *(fig.)* auch sie gingen denselben Weg; *see also* **beaten 2a; c)** *(Sport)* Bahn, *die;* **cycling/greyhound ~:** Radrennbahn, *die*/Windhundrennbahn, *die;* **circuit of the ~:** Bahnrunde, *die;* **d)** *(Railw.)* Gleis, *das;* **thousands of miles of ~:** Tausende von Meilen Gleise; **be born/live across the ~s** *or* **on the wrong side of the ~s** *(Amer. fig. coll.)* auf der Schattenseite geboren sein/leben *(fig.)*; **'keep off the ~'** „Betreten der Gleise verboten"; **single/double ~:** eingleisige/zweigleisige Strecke; **the train left the ~:** der Zug entgleiste; **e)** *(course taken)* Route, *die; (of rocket, satellite, comet, missile, hurricane, etc.)* Bahn, *die;* **f)** *(of tank, tractor, etc.)* Kette, *die;* **g)** *(section of record)* Stück, *das;* Track, *der (Jargon)*; **h)** *see* **sound-track; i)** *(groove on record)* Rille, *die;* **j)** *(section of tape)* Spur, *die;* **two-/four-~ tape recorder** Zwei-/Vierspurtonbandgerät, *das;* **k)** *(Motor Veh.: distance between wheels)* Spur[weite], *die;* **l)** *(Amer. Educ.)* Kurs, *der.* **2.** *v. t.* **a) ~ an animal** die Spur/Fährte eines Tieres verfolgen; **the police ~ed him [to Paris]** die Polizei folgte seiner Spur [bis nach Paris]; **~ a rocket/satellite** die Bahn einer Rakete/eines Satelliten verfolgen; **b)** *(Archaeol.)* rekonstruieren; nachvollziehen ⟨*Entwicklung*⟩; **c)** *(Amer.: leave trail of)* **~ dirt over the floor/~ [up] the floor with dirt** Schmutzspuren auf dem Fußboden hinterlassen

~ 'down *v.t.* aufspüren; ~ **a criminal down to his hide-out** einen Verbrecher in seinem Versteck aufspüren

tracker ['trækə(r)] *n.* **a)** Fährtensucher, *der;* **he is an experienced ~ of animals** er hat viel Erfahrung im Aufspüren von Tieren; **b)** ~ **[dog]** Spürhund, *der*

'**track events** *n. pl. (Athletics)* Laufwettbewerbe

tracking ['trækɪŋ]: ~ **shot** *n. (Cinemat., Telev.)* Fahrt, *die;* ~ **station** *n. (Astronaut.)* Bahnverfolgungsstation, *die*

track-laying *adj.* Raupen-

trackless ['træklɪs] *adj.* **a)** *(without path)* weglos; **b)** *(without footprints etc.)* keinerlei Spuren aufweisend

track: ~ **record** *n. (fig.)* **his ~ record is good, he has a good ~ record** er hat gute Leistungen vorzuweisen; **what's his ~ record?** was hat er vorzuweisen?; **this product has a very good ~ record** dieses Produkt hat sich als sehr erfolgreich erwiesen; ~ **shoe** *n.* Rennschuh, *der;* ~ **suit** *n.* Trainingsanzug, *der;* ~ **system** *n. (Amer. Educ.)* Kurssystem, *das;* ~**way** *n.* **a)** *(beaten path)* [Trampel]pfad, *der;* **b)** *(ancient roadway)* alte Straße

[1]**tract** [trækt] *n.* **a)** *(area)* Gebiet, *das;* **a narrow/vast ~ [of land]** ein schmaler Streifen [Land]/ein riesiges Gebiet; **b)** *(Anat.)* Trakt, *der*

[2]**tract** *n. (pamphlet)* [Flug]schrift, *die;* Traktat, *der (veralt.)*

tractable ['træktəbl] *adj.* fügsam; leicht formbar ‹*Material*›

traction ['trækʃn] *n., no pl., no indef. art.* **a)** *(drawing along)* Traktion, *die (fachspr.);* Ziehen, *das;* **steam/electric ~:** Dampf-/Elektrotraktion, *die;* **b)** *(grip of tyre etc.)* Haftung, *die;* **c)** *(Med.)* Zug, *der;* **in ~:** im Zug- *od.* Streckverband; **d)** *(Amer. Transport)* öffentliche Verkehrsmittel; ~ **company** Verkehrsgesellschaft, *die*

'**traction-engine** *n.* Zugmaschine, *die; (for agricultural use)* Traktor, *der*

tractor ['træktə(r)] *n.* **a)** Traktor, *der;* **b)** *(Motor Veh.) (lorry unit)* Zugwagen, *der;* Zugfahrzeug, *das; (of articulated lorry)* Sattelzugmaschine, *die*

trad [træd] *(Mus. coll.)* **1.** *adj.* traditional *(Jargon);* ~ **jazz** Traditional Jazz, *der.* **2.** *n., no pl., no indef. art.* Traditional, *der (Jargon)*

trade [treɪd] **1.** *n.* **a)** *(line of business)* Gewerbe, *das;* **the wool/furniture/hotel ~:** die Woll-/Möbel-/Hotelbranche; **the retail/wholesale ~:** der Einzel-/Großhandel; **he's a butcher/lawyer/baker** *etc.* **by ~:** er ist von Beruf Metzger/Rechtsanwalt/Bäcker *usw.;* **trick of the ~:** einschlägiger Trick; **know the tricks of the ~:** die einschlägigen Tricks kennen; **do sth. using every trick of the ~:** etw. nach allen Regeln der Kunst tun; *see also* **jack of all trades; b)** *no pl., no indef. art (commerce)* Handel, *der;* **be bad/good for ~:** schlecht/gut fürs Geschäft sein; **do ~ with sb.** mit jmdm. Geschäfte machen; **do ~ with a country** mit einem Land Handel treiben; **domestic** *or* **home ~:** Binnenhandel, *der;* **foreign ~:** Außenhandel, *der; see also* **balance 1 i; board 1 i; free trade; term 1 b; c)** *no pl. (business done)* Geschäft, *das; (between countries)* Handel, *der;* **a large share of the ~ in wool/leather goods/grain** ein großer Anteil am Geschäft mit Wolle/Lederwaren/Getreide; **an increase in ~:** eine Umsatzsteigerung; **do a good/roaring ~ [in sth.]** ein gutes Geschäft/ein Riesengeschäft [mit etw.] machen; **how's ~?** wie gehen die Geschäfte; wie geht das Geschäft?; **d)** *(craft)* Handwerk, *das;* **learn/study for a ~:** einen Handwerksberuf [er]lernen; **e)** *no pl., no indef. art. (persons)* **the ~:** die Branche; **sell to the ~:** an Wiederverkäufer verkaufen; **special discounts for [the] ~:** Sonderrabatte für Wiederverkäufer; **f)** *in pl. (Meteorol.)* Passat, *der;* **g)** *(Amer.: a transaction)* Geschäft, *das; (exchange)* Tausch, *der.* **2.** *v.i.* **a)** *(buy and sell)* Handel treiben; ~ **as a wholesale/retail dealer** ein Großhandels-/Einzelhandelsgeschäft betreiben; **they ~ as Henry Brooks & Co.** sie firmieren als Henry Brooks und Co.; ~ **at a store** *(Amer.)* in einem Geschäft einkaufen; ~ **in sth.** in *od.* mit etw. *(Dat.)* handeln; **we don't ~ with that firm** wir unterhalten zu dieser Firma keine Geschäftsbeziehungen; **b)** *(have an exchange)* tauschen; ~ **with sb. for sth.** jmdm. etw. abhandeln; **c)** *(carry merchandise)* Handelswaren befördern; ~ **to a place** Handelsgüter an einen Ort transportieren. **3.** *v.t.* **a)** tauschen; austauschen ‹*Waren, Grüße, Informationen, Geheimnisse*›; sich *(Dat.)* sagen ‹*Beleidigungen*›; **b)** ~ **sth. for sth.** etw. gegen etw. tauschen; ~ **an old car** *etc.* **for a new one** einen alten Wagen *usw.* für einen neuen in Zahlung geben

~ '**in** *v.t.* in Zahlung geben; einlösen ‹*Gutschein, Kupon usw.*›; *see also* **trade-in**

~ '**off** *v.t. (coll.);* ~ **sth. off for sth.** etw. gegen etw. tauschen; *see also* **trade-off**

~ **on** *v.t. (fig.)* ~ **on sth.** aus etw. Kapital schlagen; sich *(Dat.)* etw. zunutze machen

~ '**up** *v.i.* sich verbessern

~ **upon** *see* ~ **on**

trade: ~ **balance** *n. (Econ.)* Handelsbilanz, *die;* ~ **cycle** *n. (Brit. Econ.)* Konjunkturzyklus, *der;* ~ **deficit** *n. (Econ.)* Handelsbilanzdefizit, *das;* ~ **directory** *n.* Branchenadreßbuch, *das;* ~ '**discount** *n.* Branchenrabatt, *der; (in book ~)* Kollegenrabatt, *der;* ~ **fair** *n.* [Fach]messe, *die;* ~ **gap** *see* ~ **deficit;** ~**-in 1.** *n.* **a)** *(part exchange)* Inzahlungnahme, *die* (**on** *Gen.*); **we offer a ~-in on your old car** wir nehmen Ihren alten Wagen in Zahlung; **can you give me a ~-in on my old car?** nehmen Sie meinen alten Wagen in Zahlung?; **b)** *(item)* **we'll accept your old car as a ~-in** wir nehmen Ihren alten Wagen in Zahlung. **2.** *attrib. adj.* **the ~-in value of your car is low** der Preis, zu dem Ihr Wagen in Zahlung genommen wird, ist niedrig; ~ **journal** *n.* Fachzeitschrift, *die;* ~**-last** *n. (Amer. coll.)* **swap ~-lasts** Komplimente von dritten austauschen; ~ **mark** *n.* **a)** Warenzeichen, *das;* **b)** *(fig.)* **leave one's ~ mark on sth.** einer Sache *(Dat.)* seinen Stempel aufdrücken; **it bore all the ~ marks of this director's style** es trug den Stempel *od.* die Handschrift dieses Regisseurs; **honesty/straightforwardness/stubbornness is her ~ mark** sie zeichnet sich durch Ehrlichkeit/Direktheit/Hartnäckigkeit aus; *see also* **registered;** ~ **name** *n.* **a)** *(name used in the trade)* Fachbezeichnung, *die;* **b)** *(proprietary name)* Markenname, *der;* **c)** *(name of business)* Firmenname, *der;* ~**-off** *n.* Tauschgeschäft, *das; (fig.)* Handel, *der;* ~ **paper** *see* ~ **journal;** ~ **plates** *n. pl. (Motor Veh.)* ≈ rote Kennzeichen; ~ **price** *n.* Einkaufspreis, *der*

trader ['treɪdə(r)] *n.* **a)** Händler, *der*/Händlerin, *die;* **b)** *(Naut.)* Handelsschiff, *das*

'**trade route** *n.* Handelsweg, *der;* Handelsstraße, *die*

tradescantia [trædɪs'kæntɪə] *n. (Bot.)* Tradeskantie, *die*

trade: ~ '**secret** *n.* Geschäftsgeheimnis, *das;* ~**sman** ['treɪdzmən] *n., pl.* ~**smen** ['treɪdzmən] **a)** *(shopkeeper)* [Einzel]händler, *der;* Ladeninhaber, *der;* ~**smen's entrance** Lieferanteneingang, *der;* **b)** *(craftsman)* Handwerker, *der;* ~**speople** ['treɪdzpi:pl] *n. pl.* **a)** *(shopkeepers)* [Einzel]händler; Ladeninhaber; **b)** *(craft workers)* Handwerker; ~**s'** '**union** *see* ~ **union; T~s Union** '**Congress** *pr. n. (Brit.)* Gewerkschaftsbund, *der;* ~ **surplus** *n. (Econ.)* Handelsbilanzüberschuß, *der;* ~ '**union** *n.* Gewerkschaft, *die; attrib.* Gewerkschafts-; ~-'**unionism** *n., no pl.* Gewerkschaftswesen, *das;* ~-'**unionist** *n.* Gewerkschaft[l]er, *der*/Gewerkschaft[l]erin, *die;* ~ **wind** *n. (Meteorol.)* Passatwind, *der*

trading ['treɪdɪŋ] *n.* Handel, *der;* ~ **on the Stock Exchange** das Geschäft an der Börse; **the ~ of pounds for dollars** der Verkauf von Pfund gegen Dollar

trading: ~ **estate** *n. (Brit.)* Gewerbegebiet, *das;* ~ **hours** *n. pl.* Geschäftszeit, *die;* **during/outside ~ hours** während/außerhalb der Geschäftszeit; **'Trading hours: ...'** „Geschäftszeiten: ..."; ~ **partner** *n.* Handelspartner, *der;* ~**-post** *see* [3]**post 1 e;** ~ **stamp** *n.* Rabattmarke, *die*

tradition [trə'dɪʃn] *n.* Tradition, *die; (story)* [mündliche] Überlieferung; **family ~:** Familientradition, *die;* **he is no respecter of ~:** er hält nicht viel von der Tradition; **old universities rich in ~:** alte traditionsreiche Universitäten; **he has no sense of ~** *or* **no feeling for ~:** er hat keinen Sinn für Tradition; **in the best ~[s]** nach bester Tradition; **break with ~:** mit der Tradition brechen; **by ~:** traditionell[erweise]; ~ **has it that ...:** es heißt, daß ...

traditional [trə'dɪʃənl] *adj.* **a)** traditionell; mündlich überliefert ‹*Geschichte*›; herkömmlich ‹*Erziehung, Einrichtung, Methode*›; überkommen ‹*Brauch, Sitte, Werte, Moral*›; **it is ~ to do sth.** es ist Tradition, etw. zu tun; **b)** *(Art, Lit.)* konventionell; **c)** *(Mus.)* traditionell ‹*Jazz*›

traditionalism [trə'dɪʃənəlɪzm] *n., no pl.* Traditionalismus, *der*

traditionalist [trə'dɪʃənəlɪst] *n.* Traditionalist, *der*/Traditionalistin, *die*

traditionally [trə'dɪʃənəlɪ] *adv. (in a traditional manner)* traditionell; *(by tradition)* traditionell[erweise]; ~, **gifts are exchanged at Christmas** an Weihnachten werden traditionell Geschenke ausgetauscht; **the Oxford Union is ~ a good training-ground for politicians** die Oxford Union ist seit je eine gute Schule für künftige Politiker; **a ~ designed exterior** ein traditionelles Exterieur

traduce [trə'dju:s] *v.t. (literary: defame)* verleumden

traducer [trə'dju:sə(r)] *n. (literary)* Verleumder, *der*/Verleumderin, *die*

traffic ['træfɪk] **1.** *n., no pl.* **a)** *no indef. art.* Verkehr, *der;* ~ **is heavy/light** es herrscht starker/geringer Verkehr; ~ **will increase** der Verkehr wird zunehmen; **b)** *(trade)* Handel, *der;* **the ~ in goods/wool/steel between the two countries** der Handelsverkehr mit Gütern/Wolle/Stahl zwischen den beiden Ländern; **there is a brisk ~ in stolen goods/pornography** es wird ein schwunghafter Handel mit Diebesgut/Pornographie getrieben; ~ **in drugs/arms** Drogen-/Waffenhandel, *der;* **c)** *(amount of business)* Verkehr, *der;* ~ **in these goods/in furs/in grain has increased** der Umschlag an diesen Gütern/an Pelzen/Getreide ist gestiegen; **d)** *(Teleph., Radio)* **telephone/radio ~:** Fernsprech-/Funkverkehr, *der.* **2.** *v.i.,* **-ck-** Geschäfte machen; ~ **in sth.** mit etw. handeln *od.* Handel treiben; *(fig.)* mit etw. schachern *(abwertend);* ~ **in drugs** Drogen dealen. **3.** *v.t.,* **-ck-** handeln mit; *(barter, exchange)* Tauschhandel treiben mit

traffic: ~ **calming** *n.* Verkehrsberuhigung, *die;* ~ **circle** *n. (Amer.)* Kreisverkehr, *der;* ~ **cone** *n.* Pylon, *der;* Leitkegel, *der;* ~ **cop** *n. (Amer. coll.)* Verkehrspolizist, *der*/-polizistin, *die;* ~ **hold-up** *see* ~ **jam;** ~ **island** *n.* Verkehrsinsel, *die;* ~ **jam** *n.* [Verkehrs]stau, *der*

trafficker ['træfɪkə(r)] *n.* Händler, *der*/Händlerin, *die;* ~ **in drugs, drug ~:** Drogenhändler, *der*/-händlerin, *die*

traffic: ~ **lights** *n. pl.* [Verkehrs]ampel,

die; ~ **police** *n.* Verkehrspolizei, *die;* ~ **policeman** *n.* Verkehrspolizist, *der;* ~ **sign** *n.* Verkehrszeichen, *das;* ~ **signals** *see* ~ **lights;** ~ **warden** *n. (Brit.)* Hilfspolizist, *der; (woman)* Hilfspolizistin, *die;* Politesse, *die*

tragedian [trəˈdʒiːdɪən] *n.* **a)** *(Lit.)* Tragödiendichter, *der*/-dichterin, *die;* **b)** *(Theatre)* Tragöde, *der*

tragedienne [trədʒiːdɪˈen] *n. fem. (Theatre)* Tragödin, *die*

tragedy [ˈtrædʒɪdɪ] *n.* **a)** *(sad event or fact)* Tragödie, *die; (sad story)* tragische Geschichte; **the** ~ **[of it] is that ...:** das Tragische [daran] ist, daß ...; **b)** *(accident)* Tragödie, *die;* **earthquake ~/bomb ~:** Erdbebenkatastrophe, *die*/blutiger Bombenanschlag; **c)** *(Theatre)* Tragödie, *die;* Trauerspiel, *das*

tragic [ˈtrædʒɪk] *adj.* **a)** tragisch; **a** ~ **waste of talent/money** eine schlimme Vergeudung von Talenten/Geldverschwendung; **b)** *attrib. (Theatre)* tragisch; ~ **actor/actress** Tragöde, *der*/Tragödin, *die;* ~ **irony** tragische Ironie

tragically [ˈtrædʒɪkəlɪ] *adv.* tragisch; **their predictions have been** ~ **fulfilled** ihre Prophezeiungen haben sich auf tragische Weise erfüllt; ~, **she had a fatal accident** tragischerweise erlitt sie einen tödlichen Unfall

tragicomedy [trædʒɪˈkɒmɪdɪ] *n. (Lit.)* Tragikomödie, *die*

trail [treɪl] **1.** *n.* **a)** Spur, *die; (of meteor)* Schweif, *der;* **a** ~ **of blood** eine Blutspur; ~ **of smoke/dust** Rauch-/Staubfahne, *die;* **he left a** ~ **of broken marriages/misery behind him** überall, wo er auftauchte, hinterließ er zerbrochene Ehen/Elend; *see also* **condensation trail; vapour trail; b)** *(Hunting)* Spur, *die;* Fährte, *die;* **be on the** ~ **of an animal** der Fährte eines Tieres folgen; **be off the** ~ *(lit. or fig.)* nicht auf der richtigen Spur *od.* Fährte sein; **be/get on sb.'s** ~ *(lit. or fig.)* jmdm. auf der Spur *od.* Fährte sein/jmdm. auf die Spur *od.* Fährte kommen; **be hard** *or* **hot on the** ~ **of sb.** *(lit. or fig.)* jmdm. dicht auf den Fersen sein *(ugs.);* **he was hot** *or* **hard on the** ~ **of the stolen goods** bei der Suche nach dem Diebesgut hatte er eine heiße Spur [gefunden]; **c)** *(path)* Pfad, *der; (wagon* ~*)* Weg, *der;* **there was no path or** ~ **of any kind** es gab keinerlei Weg oder Pfad; *see also* **²blaze 2; nature trail. 2.** *v. t.* **a)** *(pursue)* verfolgen; *(shadow)* beschatten; ~ **sb./an animal to a place** jmdm./einem Tier bis zu einem Ort folgen; **b)** *(drag)* ~ **sth. [after** *or* **behind one]** etw. hinter sich *(Dat.)* herziehen; ~ **sth. on the ground** etw. über den Boden schleifen lassen; **he ~ed his hand/fingers in the water as the boat went along** er ließ seine Hand/Finger mit dem fahrenden Boot durchs Wasser gleiten; **a train/car went by, ~ing clouds of smoke/dust** ein Zug/Auto fuhr vorbei und zog eine Rauch-/Staubwolke hinter sich *(Dat.)* her; ~ **sb. by 20 points** 20 Punkte hinter jmdm. liegen. **3.** *v. i.* **a)** *(be dragged)* schleifen; **the bird's wing/dog's leg was ~ing** der Flügel des Vogels/das Bein des Hundes schleifte am Boden; **a cloud of dust ~ed behind the car** hinter dem Wagen zog sich eine Staubwolke hin; **b)** *(hang loosely)* herabhängen; ~ **to the ground** auf den Boden hängen; **c)** *(walk wearily etc.)* trotten; *(lag)* hinterhertrotten; **d)** *(Sport: be losing)* zurückliegen; **the runner was ~ing badly** der Läufer lag weit zurück; **be ~ing by two goals to three** mit zwei zu drei Toren im Rückstand sein; **e)** *(creep)* ‹*Pflanze:*› kriechen

~ **aˈway** *see* ~ **off**

~ **beˈhind** *v. i.* hinterhertrödeln *(ugs.); (Sport)* zurückliegen

~ **ˈoff** *v. i.* **a)** *(fade into silence)* **his voice/shout ~ed off into a whisper/into silence** seine Stimme/sein Schreien wurde schwächer, bis er schließlich nur noch flüsterte/bis er schließlich ganz verstummte; **her words/speech ~ed off [into silence]** sie verstummte allmählich; **b)** *(move slowly)* lostrotten; abtrotten

trail: ~ **bike** *n. leichtes, geländegängiges Motorrad;* ≈ Enduro, *das;* **~-blazer** *n. (fig.: pioneer)* Bahnbrecher, *der*/Bahnbrecherin, *die;* Wegbereiter, *der*/Wegbereiterin, *die*

trailer [ˈtreɪlə(r)] *n.* **a)** *(Motor Veh.)* Anhänger, *der; (boat* ~ *also)* Trailer, *der; (Amer.: caravan)* Wohnanhänger, *der;* **b)** *(Cinemat., Telev.)* Trailer, *der;* **c)** *(Bot.)* Ranke, *die*

ˈ**trailing edge** *n.* Hinterkante, *die; (of sail)* Achterliek, *das*

train [treɪn] **1.** *v. t.* **a)** ausbilden **(in** in + *Dat.*); erziehen ‹*Kind*›; abrichten ‹*Hund*›; dressieren ‹*Tier*›; schulen ‹*Geist, Auge, Ohr*›; bilden ‹*Charakter*›; ~ **sb. as a teacher/soldier/engineer** jmdn. zum Lehrer/Soldaten/Ingenieur ausbilden; ~ **sb. for a profession** jmdn. auf einen Beruf vorbereiten *od.* für einen Beruf ausbilden; ~ **sb. for a career as an officer** jmdn. zum Offizier ausbilden; **he/she has been well/badly/fully ~ed** er/sie besitzt eine gute/schlechte/umfassende Ausbildung; **b)** *(Sport)* trainieren; ~ **oneself** trainieren; **c)** *(teach and accustom)* ~ **an animal to do sth./to sth.** einem Tier beibringen, etw. zu tun/etw. beibringen; **the police dog was ~ed to kill** der Polizeihund war zum Töten abgerichtet; ~ **oneself to do sth.** sich dazu erziehen, etw. zu tun; ~ **a child to do sth./to sth.** ein Kind dazu erziehen, etw. zu tun/zu etw. erziehen; ~ **sb. to use a machine** jmdn. in der Bedienung einer Maschine schulen; **you've got him well ~ed** *(joc.)* du hast ihn dir gut erzogen; **d)** *(Hort.)* ziehen; erziehen *(fachspr.);* **the vines are ~ed and supported by poles** die Reben werden an die stützenden Pfosten gezogen *od. (fachspr.)* erzogen; ~ **a plant up/against a wall/trellis** eine Pflanze an einer Mauer/einem Spalier ziehen *od. (fachspr.)* erziehen; **e)** *(aim)* richten **(on auf** + *Akk.*). **2.** *v. i.* **a)** eine Ausbildung machen; **he is ~ing as** *or* **to be a teacher/doctor/engineer** er macht eine Lehrer-/Arzt-/Ingenieursausbildung; **he is ~ing as a soldier** er läßt sich zum Soldaten ausbilden; **he is ~ing for a responsible position** er bereitet sich auf eine verantwortliche Stellung vor; **he is ~ing for a career as an officer/for the ministry/for the law** er macht eine Offiziers-/Priester-/Rechtsanwaltsausbildung; **b)** *(Sport)* trainieren. **3.** *n.* **a)** *(Railw.)* Zug, *der;* **go** *or* **travel by** ~: mit dem Zug *od.* der Bahn fahren; **the 2 o'clock ~:** der Zweiuhrzug; **on the ~:** im Zug; **which is the ~ for Oxford?** welcher Zug fährt nach Oxford?; **b)** *(of skirt etc.)* Schleppe, *die;* **c)** *(Ornith.)* Schwanz, *der;* **d)** *(retinue)* Gefolge, *das;* **the king/minister had brought a** ~ **of advisers/attendants with him** der König/Minister hatte ein großes Gefolge von Beratern/Begleitern mitgebracht; **the long** ~ **of mourners** der lange Trauerzug; **the tornado brought havoc in its ~:** der Tornado hinterließ Verwüstungen; **e)** *(line, series)* Zug, *der;* **a long** ~ **of causes** eine lange Kette von Ursachen; **an unlucky** ~ **of events** eine unglückliche [Aufeinander]folge von Ereignissen; ~ **of thought** Gedankengang, *der;* **be in** ~ *(formal)* im Gange sein; **everything is now in** ~ **for the party/ceremony/election** alle Vorbereitungen für die Party/Feier/Wahl sind jetzt im Gange

~ ˈ**up** *v. t.* heranbilden; **our workers have been ~ed up to a very high standard** unsere Arbeiter sind sehr gut ausgebildet

trainable [ˈtreɪnəbl] *adj.* leicht erziehbar ‹*Kind*›; ausbildungsfähig ‹*Arbeiter*›

train: **~-bearer** *n.* Schleppenträger, *der*/-trägerin, *die;* **~-driver** *n.* Lokomotivführer, *der*/-führerin, *die*

trained [treɪnd] *adj.* ausgebildet ‹*Arbeiter, Lehrer, Arzt, Stimme*›; abgerichtet ‹*Hund*›; dressiert ‹*Tier*›; geschult ‹*Geist, Auge, Ohr*›

trainee [treɪˈniː] *n.* Auszubildende, *der/die; (business management* ~*)* Trainee, *der/die; (in academic, technical professions)* Praktikant, *der*/Praktikantin, *die;* **a ~ manager/nurse/teacher/doctor/cook** *etc.* ein Manager/eine Krankenschwester/ein Lehrer/Arzt/Koch *usw.* in Ausbildung

trainer [ˈtreɪnə(r)] *n.* **a)** *(Sport)* [Konditions]trainer, *der*/-trainerin, *die;* **b)** *(Aeronaut.) (aircraft)* Trainer, *der; (simulator)* Flugsimulator, *der;* **c)** *in pl. see* **training shoes**

train: ~ **fare** *n.* Fahrpreis, *der;* **how much is the** ~ **fare to Oxford?** wieviel kostet die Bahnfahrt nach Oxford?; **we shall reimburse your** ~ **fare** wir erstatten Ihnen die Kosten der Bahnfahrt; **~-ferry** *n.* Eisenbahnfähre, *die*

training [ˈtreɪnɪŋ] *n., no pl.* **a)** Ausbildung, *die;* **b)** *(Sport)* Training, *das;* **be in** ~ *(train)* trainieren; im Training sein; *(be fit)* in [guter] Form sein; **be out of ~:** außer Form sein; **go into ~:** mit dem Training anfangen; **keep in ~:** sich in Form halten; in Form bleiben

training: **~-camp** *n. (Mil.)* Ausbildungslager, *das; (Boxing)* Trainingslager, *das;* ~ **college** *n.* berufsbildende Schule; *(Brit. Hist.)* Lehrerseminar, *das;* **~-course** *n.* Lehrgang, *der;* ~ **film** *n.* Lehrfilm, *der;* **~-ground** *n. (Mil.)* Übungsplatz, *der; (fig.)* Schule, *die;* ~ **scheme** *n.* Ausbildungsprogramm, *das;* **be on a** ~ **scheme** an einem Ausbildungsprogramm teilnehmen; **~-ship** *n. (Naut.)* Schulschiff, *das;* ~ **shoes** *n. pl.* Trainingsschuhe

train: ~ **journey** *n.* Bahnfahrt, *die; (long)* Bahnreise, *die;* **~-load** *n.* **~-loads of coal/livestock/tourists** *etc.* ganze Züge voll Kohle/Vieh/Touristen *usw.;* **football fans arrived in** *or* **by ~-loads** ganze Züge voll Fußballfans kamen; ~ **service** *n.* Zugverbindung, *die;* [Eisen]bahnverbindung, *die; (whole system)* Eisenbahnsystem, *das;* **a better** ~ **service** bessere Zugverbindungen; ~ **set** *n.* [Modell]eisenbahn, *die;* **~sick** *adj.* **a ~sick child/man** ein Kind/Mann, dem vom Zugfahren schlecht geworden ist; **he gets ~sick** ihm wird beim Zugfahren schlecht; **~-spotter** *n. jmd., der als Hobby die Nummern von Lokomotiven aufschreibt;* **~-spotting** *n., no pl., no indef. art.: das Aufschreiben von Lokomotivnummern als Hobby;* ~ **station** *n. (Amer.)* Bahnhof, *der*

traipse [treɪps] *v. i. (coll.)* latschen *(salopp)*

~ **about,** ~ **around** *v. i.* rumlatschen *(salopp)*

trait [treɪ] *n.* Eigenschaft, *die;* ~ **of character** Charaktereigenschaft, *die;* **a marked** ~ **in her character** eine ausgeprägte Charaktereigenschaft bei ihr; **it is a national** ~ **[of the British]** es gehört zum [britischen] Nationalcharakter

traitor [ˈtreɪtə(r)] *n.* Verräter, *der*/Verräterin, *die;* **be a** ~ **to one's country/the king/the cause/one's faith** ein Verräter seines Landes/des Königs/der Sache/seines Glaubens sein; **you are a** ~ **to yourself!** du hast deine eigenen Überzeugungen verraten!; **turn ~:** zum Verräter/zur Verräterin werden

traitorous [ˈtreɪtərəs] *adj.* verräterisch; **a** ~ **man/woman** ein Verräter/eine Verräterin; **such conduct is** ~**!** solches Verhalten ist Verrat!

trajectory [trəˈdʒektərɪ] *n. (Phys.)* [Flug-]bahn, *die*

tra-la [trəˈlɑː] *int.* trallа[la]

tram [træm] *n.* **a)** *(Brit.)* Straßenbahn, *die;* **go by ~:** mit der Straßenbahn fahren; **on the ~:** in der Straßenbahn; **b)** *(Mining)* Hund, *der;* Förderwagen, *der*

tram: **~car** *n.* **a)** *see* **tram a; b)** *(one car)*

Straßenbahnwagen, *der;* ~**lines** *n. pl. (Brit.)* **a)** Straßenbahnschienen; **b)** *(fig.: rigid principles)* starre Vorschriften; **c)** *(Tennis coll.)* Korridor, *der*

trammel ['træml] **1.** *v. t., (Brit.)* **-ll-** einengen. **2.** *n. in pl.* Fesseln; **the ~s of convention** die Fesseln der Konvention

tramp [træmp] **1.** *n.* **a)** *(vagrant)* Landstreicher, *der*/-streicherin, *die; (in city)* Stadtstreicher, *der*/-streicherin, *die;* **b)** *(sound of steps)* Schritte; *(of horses)* Getrappel, *das; (of elephants)* Trampeln, *das;* **the ~ of marching feet** Marschschritte; **c)** *(walk)* [Fuß]marsch, *der;* **d)** *(sl.: dissolute woman)* Flittchen, *das (ugs. abwertend);* Nutte, *die (derb abwertend);* **e)** *(Naut.)* Tramp, *der;* Trampschiff, *das.* **2.** *v. i.* **a)** *(tread heavily)* trampeln; **b)** *(walk)* marschieren. **3.** *v. t.* **a)** **~ one's way** trotten; **b)** *(traverse)* durchwandern; *(with no particular destination)* durchstreifen; **c)** *(tread on)* herumtrampeln auf (+ *Dat.*); **~ the earth** die Erde festtreten

~ 'down *v. t.* niedertrampeln *(ugs.);* **~ sth. down [until it is flat]** etw. festtreten

trample ['træmpl] **1.** *v. t.* zertrampeln; **~ sth. to the ground** etw. zu Boden trampeln; **~ sth. into the ground** etw. in den Boden treten; **he was ~d to death by elephants** er wurde von Elefanten zu Tode getrampelt. **2.** *v. i.* trampeln

~ 'down *v. t.* niedertrampeln

~ on *v. t.* herumtrampeln auf (+ *Dat.*); **~ on sb./sth./sb.'s feelings** *(fig.)* jmdn./etw./jmds. Gefühle mit Füßen treten

trampoline ['træmpəli:n] **1.** *n.* Trampolin, *das.* **2.** *v. i.* Trampolin springen

'tramp steamer *n.* Trampschiff, *das*

tram: ~-ride *n. (Brit.)* Straßenbahnfahrt, *die;* **~road** *n. (Amer.) see* **tramlines a;** **~-route** *n. (Brit.)* Straßenbahnlinie, *die;* **~-stop** *n.* Straßenbahnhaltestelle, *die;* **~-ticket** *n. (Brit.)* Straßenbahnfahrschein, *der od.* -fahrkarte, *die;* **~way** *n. (Brit.) see* **tramlines a**

trance [trɑ:ns] *n.* **a)** Trance, *die; (half-conscious state, hypnotic state, ecstasy, etc.)* tranceartiger Zustand; **be** *or* **lie in a ~:** in Trance/in einem tranceartigen Zustand sein; **fall** *or* **go into a ~:** in Trance/in einen tranceartigen Zustand fallen; **put** *or* **send sb. into a ~:** jmdn. in Trance/in einen tranceartigen Zustand versetzen; **she's been walking about in a ~ all day** sie ist den ganzen Tag wie in Trance herumgelaufen; **b)** *(Med.: catalepsy)* Katalepsie, *die*

tranche [trɑ:nʃ] *n. (Finance)* Tranche, *die*

tranny ['trænɪ] *n. (Brit. sl.)* Transistor, *der (ugs.)*

tranquil ['træŋkwɪl] *adj.* ruhig; friedlich ⟨*Stimmung, Szene*⟩

tranquilize, tranquilizer *(Amer.) see* **tranquillize, tranquillizer**

tranquillise, tranquilliser *see* **tranquillize, tranquillizer**

tranquillity [træŋ'kwɪlɪtɪ] *n.* Ruhe, *die; (of a scene)* Friedlichkeit, *die;* **live in peace and ~:** in Ruhe und Frieden leben

tranquillize ['træŋkwɪlaɪz] *v. t.* beruhigen; **the unruly prisoner was quickly ~d** der aufsässige Gefangene wurde schnell ruhiggestellt

tranquillizer ['træŋkwɪlaɪzə(r)] *n. (Med.)* Tranquilizer, *der;* Beruhigungsmittel, *das;* **~ gun** Betäubungsgewehr, *das*

tranquilly ['træŋkwɪlɪ] *adv.* ruhig; friedlich ⟨*leben*⟩

transact [træn'sækt] *v. t.* **~ business [with sb.]** [mit jmdm.] Geschäfte tätigen *(Kaufmannsspr., Papierdt.);* **the two countries have ~ed business for a long time** die beiden Länder unterhalten seit langem Handelsbeziehungen; **our company ~s business with many foreign firms** unsere Gesellschaft unterhält Geschäftsbeziehungen mit vielen ausländischen Firmen

transaction [træn'sækʃn] *n.* **a)** *(doing of business)* **after the ~ of their business** nachdem sie das Geschäftliche erledigt hatten; **most banks close for the ~ of business at 3 p.m.** die meisten Banken schließen für den Publikumsverkehr um 15 Uhr; **b)** *(piece of business)* Geschäft, *das; (financial)* Transaktion, *die;* **c)** *in pl. (reports of a society)* Sitzungsberichte *Pl.*

transalpine [træns'ælpaɪn] transalpin

transatlantic [trænsət'læntɪk] *adj.* **a)** *(Brit.: American)* transatlantisch; amerikanisch; **b)** *(Amer.: European)* transatlantisch; europäisch; **c)** *(crossing the Atlantic)* transatlantisch; **a ~ voyage** eine Reise über den Atlantik; **he is a regular ~ traveller** er reist regelmäßig über den Atlantik; **~ communications** Verbindungen über den Atlantik

transceiver [træn'si:və(r)] *n. (Radio)* Sende- und Empfangsgerät, *das*

transcend [træn'send] *v. t.* **a)** *(be beyond range of)* übersteigen; hinausgehen über ⟨*Grenzen*⟩; *(Philos.)* transzendieren; **b)** *(surpass)* übertreffen; **~ sb. in beauty** jmdn. an Schönheit übertreffen

transcendence [træn'sendəns], **transcendency** [træn'sendənsɪ] *n., no pl. (Philos., Theol.)* Transzendenz, *die*

transcendent [træn'sendənt] *adj. (Philos., Theol.)* transzendent

transcendental [trænsen'dentl] *adj.* **a)** *(Philos.)* transzendental; **b)** *(Math.)* transzendent

transcendentalism [trænsen'dentəlɪzm] *n. (Philos.)* Transzendentalismus, *der*

Transcendental Medi'tation, *(Amer.: P) n.* Transzendentale Meditation

transcontinental [trænskɒntɪ'nentl] *adj.* transkontinental

transcribe [træn'skraɪb] *v. t.* **a)** *(copy in writing)* abschreiben; aufschreiben ⟨*mündliche Überlieferung*⟩; mitschreiben ⟨*Rede*⟩; protokollieren ⟨*Sitzung, Verhandlung usw.*⟩; **~ a tape/a taped interview** von einem Tonband/von der Tonbandaufzeichnung eines Interviews eine Niederschrift anfertigen; **~ one's rough notes** aus seinen kurzen Notizen eine Reinschrift herstellen; **b)** *(record)* aufzeichnen; **~ a record on to tape/a tape on to a record** eine Schallplatte auf Tonband überspielen/von einem Tonband eine Schallplattenaufnahme machen; **c)** *(Mus.)* transkribieren; **d)** *(transliterate)* transkribieren; umschreiben; **~ some shorthand/sth. from a shorthand version** ein Stenogramm/etw. in Langschrift übertragen

transcript ['trænskrɪpt] *n.* Abschrift, *die; (of trial, interview, speech, conference)* Protokoll, *das; (of tape, taped material)* Niederschrift, *die*

transcription [træn'skrɪpʃn] *n.* **a)** *(transcribing)* Abschrift, *die; (of proceedings, speeches)* Protokollieren, *das; (of rough notes)* Reinschrift, *die; (of spoken text, tapes, etc.)* Niederschrift, *die; (of record on to tape)* Überspielung, *die; (of tape on to a record)* Übertragung, *die; (Mus.)* Transkription, *die; (from shorthand)* Übertragung [in Langschrift]; *(transliteration)* Transkription, *die;* Umschrift, *die;* **b)** *(transcribed material)* Abschrift, *die; (of proceedings, speech)* Protokoll, *das; (of rough notes)* Reinschrift, *die; (of text, tape, etc.)* Niederschrift, *die; (of record)* [Tonband]aufnahme, *die; (Mus.)* Transkription, *die; (from shorthand)* Langschriftfassung, *die; (transliteration)* Transkription, *die;* Umschrift, *die*

transducer [træns'dju:sə(r)] *n. (Electr.)* Wandler, *der*

transept ['trænsept] *n. (Eccl. Archit.)* Querschiff, *das;* **north/south ~:** nördlicher/südlicher Kreuzarm

transfer 1. [træns'fɜ:(r)] *v. t.,* **-rr- a)** *(move)* verlegen (**to** nach); überweisen ⟨*Geld*⟩ (**to** auf + *Akk.*); transferieren ⟨*große Geldsumme*⟩; übertragen ⟨*Befugnis, Macht*⟩ (**to** *Dat.*); **~ a prisoner to a different gaol** einen Gefangenen in ein anderes Gefängnis verlegen *od.* überführen; **~ one's affections to someone new** seine Gunst jemand anderem schenken; **~ one's allegiance [from sb.] to sb.** [von jmdm.] zu jmdm. überwechseln; **b)** übereignen ⟨*Gegenstand, Grundbesitz*⟩ (**to** *Dat.*); **~ sth. into new ownership** etw. einem neuen Besitzer *od.* jemand anderem übereignen; **c)** versetzen ⟨*Arbeiter, Angestellte, Schüler*⟩; *(Football)* transferieren; **d)** übertragen ⟨*Bedeutung, Sinn*⟩; **e)** *(copy)* umdrucken ⟨*Zeichnung*⟩. **2.** *v. i.,* **-rr- a)** *(change to continue journey)* umsteigen; **~ from Heathrow to Gatwick** zum Weiterflug *od.* Umsteigen von Heathrow nach Gatwick fahren; **we had to ~ to a special bus** wir mußten in einen Sonderbus umsteigen; **b)** *(move to another place or group)* wechseln; ⟨*Firma:*⟩ übersiedeln. **3.** ['trænsfɜ:(r)] *n.* **a)** *(moving)* Verlegung, *die; (of powers)* Übertragung, *die* (**to** an + *Akk.*); *(of money)* Überweisung, *die; (of large sums)* Transfer, *der (Wirtsch.);* **b)** *(of employee, pupil)* Versetzung, *die; (of football player)* Transfer, *der;* Wechsel, *der;* **c)** *(Amer.: ticket)* Umsteigefahrkarte, *die;* **d)** *(picture)* Abziehbild, *das;* **e)** *(conveyance of property)* Übertragung, *die;* Übereignung, *die*

transferability [trænsfɜrə'bɪlɪtɪ] *n., no pl.* Übertragbarkeit, *die*

transferable [træns'fɜ:rəbl, 'trænsfərəbl] *adj.* übertragbar; frei transferierbar ⟨*Devisenkonto*⟩

transferable 'vote *n.* übertragbare [Wähler]stimme

'transfer company *n. (Amer.)* Transportunternehmen, *das*

transference ['trænsfərəns] *n.* Übertragung, *die*

'transfer: ~ fee *n. (Footb.)* Ablösesumme, *die;* Transfersumme, *die (fachspr.);* **~ list** *n. (Footb.)* Transferliste, *die*

transfiguration [trænsfɪgə'reɪʃn] *n.* Transfiguration, *die (fachspr.);* Verklärung Christi, *die;* **the T~** *(Relig.)* das Fest der Verklärung

transfigure [træns'fɪgə(r)] *v. t.* verklären

transfix [træns'fɪks] *v. t.* **a)** *(pierce through)* durchbohren; **b)** *(root to the spot)* erstarren lassen, lähmen ⟨*Person*⟩; **be/stand ~ed** wie gelähmt *od.* angewurzelt sein/dastehen

transform 1. [træns'fɔ:m] *v. t.* **a)** verwandeln; **~ heat into energy** Wärme in Energie umwandeln; **the caterpillar is ~ed into a butterfly** die Raupe verwandelt sich zu einem Schmetterling; **I felt ~ed** ich fühlte mich wie umgewandelt; **a new coat of paint would ~ the room** ein neuer Anstrich, und man würde das Zimmer nicht wiedererkennen; **b)** *(Electr.) (in potential)* transformieren; umspannen; *(in type)* umformen. **2.** ['trænsfɔ:m] *n. (Math., Ling.)* Transformation, *die*

transformation [trænsfə'meɪʃn] *n.* **a)** Verwandlung, *die;* **b)** *(Math., Ling.)* Transformation, *die;* **c)** *(Phys.)* Elementumwandlung, *die;* Transmutation, *die; (of heat into energy)* Umwandlung, *die*

transformational [trænsfə'meɪʃənl] *adj. (esp. Ling.)* Transformations-

transformational 'grammar *n. (Ling.)* Transformationsgrammatik, *die*

transfor'mation scene *n. (Theatre)* Verwandlungsszene, *die*

transformer [træns'fɔ:mə(r)] *n. (Electr.)* Transformator, *der*

transfuse [træns'fju:z] *v. t.* **a)** *(Med.)* transfundieren *(fachspr.);* übertragen; **b)** *(permeate, lit. or fig.)* erfüllen; durchdringen

transfusion [træns'fju:ʒn] *n. (Med.)* Transfusion, *die;* Übertragung, *die; see also* **blood transfusion**

transgress [træns'gres] *v. t.* übertreten; *abs.* **he was ~ing** er hat sich einer Übertretung *(Gen.)* schuldig gemacht *(geh.)*

transgression [træns'greʃn] *n.* Übertretung, *die*

transgressor [træns'gresə(r)] *n.* Übertreter, *der*/Übertreterin, *die* (**of** *Gen.*); *(sinner)* Sünder, *der*/Sünderin, *die* (**of** gegen)

transience ['trænziəns], **transiency** ['trænziənsi] *n.* Vergänglichkeit, *die*

transient ['trænziənt] **1.** *adj.* **a)** kurzlebig; vergänglich; **b)** *(Mus.)* durchgehend. **2.** *n.* **a)** *(temporary guest)* Durchreisende, *der/die;* **b)** *(Electr.)* Ausgleichsvorgang, *der*

transistor [træn'sistə(r)] *n.* **a)** ~ **[radio]** Transistor, *der;* Transistorradio, *das;* **b)** *(Electronics)* Transistor, *der*

transistorize [træn'sistəraiz] *v. t.* *(Electronics)* transistorisieren

transit ['trænsit] *n.* **a)** Transit, *der;* **passengers in ~:** Transitreisende; Durchreisende; **be in ~:** auf der Durchreise sein; **b)** *(conveyance)* Transport, *der;* **goods in ~ from London to Hull** Waren auf dem Transport von London nach Hull; **c)** *(Astron.)* Durchgang, *der*

'transit camp *n.* Durchgangslager, *das*

transition [træn'siʒn, træn'ziʃn] *n.* **a)** Übergang, *der; (sudden change)* Wechsel, *der;* **age/period of ~:** Übergangszeit, *die;* **b)** *(Mus.)* Ausweichung, *die;* **c)** *(Art)* Übergang, *der*

transitional [træn'siʒənl, træn'ziʃənl] *adj.* Übergangs-; **be ~ between a and b** den Übergang von a zu b bilden

tran'sition: ~ element *n.* *(Chem.)* Übergangselement, *das;* **~ point** *n.* *(Phys.)* Umwandlungspunkt, *der*

transitive ['trænsitiv] *adj.*, **transitively** ['trænsitivli] *adv.* *(Ling.)* transitiv

'transit lounge *n.* Transithalle, *die;* Transitlounge, *die*

transitoriness ['trænsitərinis] *n.*, *no pl.* Vergänglichkeit, *die; (fleetingness)* Flüchtigkeit, *die*

transitory ['trænsitəri] *adj.* vergänglich; *(fleeting)* flüchtig

transit: ~ passenger *n.* Transitpassagier, *der;* **~ visa** *n.* Transitvisum, *das;* Durchreisevisum, *das*

translatable [træns'leitəbl] *adj.* übersetzbar; **some words are not ~ into other languages** manche Wörter lassen sich nicht in andere Sprachen übersetzen

translate [træns'leit] **1.** *v. t.* **a)** übersetzen; **~ a novel from English into German** einen Roman aus dem Englischen ins Deutsche übersetzen; **~ 'Abgeordneter' as 'Deputy'** „Abgeordneter" mit „Deputy" übersetzen; **b)** *(convert)* **~ a vision into reality/words into action[s]** eine Vision Wirklichkeit werden lassen/Worte in die Tat/in Taten umsetzen; **c)** *(Relig.)* überführen ‹*Reliquien*›; **d)** *(Eccl.)* versetzen ‹*Bischof*›. **2.** *v. i.* sich übersetzen lassen

translation [træns'leiʃn] *n.* **a)** Übersetzung, *die;* **error in ~:** Übersetzungsfehler, *der;* **his works are available in ~:** seine Werke liegen in Übersetzung *od.* übersetzt vor; **read sth. in ~:** etw. in der Übersetzung lesen; **b)** *(conversion)* Umsetzung, *die;* **c)** *(Eccl.)* Translation, *die (fachspr.);* Versetzung, *die*

translator [træns'leitə(r)] *n.* Übersetzer, *der*/Übersetzerin, *die*

transliterate [træns'litəreit] *v. t.* transliterieren (**into** in + *Akk.*)

transliteration [trænslitə'reiʃn] *n.* Transliteration, *die* (**into** in + *Akk.*)

translucency [træns'lu:sənsi] *n.*, *no pl. see* **translucent:** Eigenschaft, durchscheinend zu sein; Durchsichtigkeit, *die*

translucent [træns'lu:sənt] *adj.* **a)** *(partly transparent)* durchscheinend; **b)** *(transparent)* durchsichtig

transmigrate [trænsmai'greit] *v. i.* **a)** *(pass into different body)* übergehen; **b)** *(migrate)* ziehen

transmigration [trænsmai'greiʃn] *n.* **~ [of souls]** Seelenwanderung, *die;* **the ~ of the soul into another body** der Übergang der Seele in einen anderen Körper

transmission [træns'miʃn] *n.* **a)** *(passing on) see* **transmit a:** Übersendung, *die;* Übertragung, *die;* Überlieferung, *die;* [Weiter]vererbung, *die;* **b)** *(Radio, Telev.)* Ausstrahlung, *die; (via satellite also; by wire)* Übertragung, *die;* **c)** *(Motor Veh.) (drive)* Antrieb, *der; (gearbox)* Getriebe, *das;* **manual/automatic ~:** Schalt-/Automatikgetriebe, *das*

transmit [træns'mit] *v. t.*, **-tt-** **a)** *(pass on)* übersenden ‹*Nachricht*›; übertragen ‹*Recht, Krankheit*›; überliefern ‹*Wissen, Kenntnisse*›; *(genetically)* [weiter]vererben ‹*Eigenschaft*›; **b)** durchlassen ‹*Licht*›; übertragen ‹*Druck, Schall*›; leiten ‹*Wärme, Elektrizität*›; **c)** *(Radio, Telev.)* ausstrahlen; *(via satellite also; by wire)* übertragen

transmittal [træns'mitl] *see* **transmission a**

transmitter [træns'mitə(r)] *n.* Sender, *der*

transmogrification [trænsmɒgrifi'keiʃn] *n.* *(joc.)* [wundersame] Verwandlung

transmogrify [træns'mɒgrifai] *v. t.* *(joc.)* auf wundersame Weise verwandeln (**into** in + *Akk.*)

transmutation [trænsmju:'teiʃn] *n.* **a)** Umwandlung, *die* (**into** in + *Akk.*); **b)** *(Phys.)* Transmutation, *die;* Elementumwandlung, *die;* **c)** *(Biol.)* Umbildung, *die*

transmute [træns'mju:t] *v. t.* umwandeln

transnational [træns'næʃənl] *adj.* übernational

transoceanic [trænsəʊʃi'ænik, trænsəʊsi'ænik] *adj.* transozeanisch; überseeisch

transom ['trænsəm] *n.* *(Archit.)* Quersprosse, *die*

transom 'window *n.* Oberlicht, *das*

transparency [træns'pærənsi] *n.* **a)** Durchsichtigkeit, *die; (fig. also)* Durchschaubarkeit, *die;* Fadenscheinigkeit, *die (abwertend);* **b)** *(Photog.)* Transparent, *das; (slide)* Dia, *das*

transparent [træns'pærənt] *adj.* durchsichtig; *(fig.) (obvious)* offenkundig; *(easily understood)* klar

transparently [træns'pærəntli] *adv.* offenkundig; **~ lucid** klar und einleuchtend ‹*Darstellung*›; **~ obvious** ganz offenkundig

transpiration [trænspi'reiʃn] *n.* **a)** *(perspiration)* Schwitzen, *das;* Transpiration, *die (geh.);* **b)** *(Bot.)* Transpiration, *die*

transpire [træn'spaiə(r)] **1.** *v. i.* **a)** *(coll.: happen)* passieren; **b)** *(come to be known)* sich herausstellen; **she had not, it ~d, seen the letter** sie hatte, so stellte sich heraus, den Brief nicht gesehen; **c)** *(Bot.)* transpirieren; **d)** *(be given off as perspiration)* ‹*Feuchtigkeit:*› ausgedünstet werden. **2.** *v. t.* ausdünsten

transplant 1. [træns'plɑ:nt] *v. t.* **a)** *(Med.)* transplantieren *(fachspr.),* verpflanzen ‹*Organ, Gewebe*›; **b)** *(plant in another place)* umpflanzen; **c)** *(fig.: move to another place)* umsiedeln; verlegen ‹*Institution*›. **2.** ['trænsplɑ:nt] *n.* **a)** *(Med.) (operation)* Transplantation, *die (fachspr.);* Verpflanzung, *die; (thing transplanted)* Transplantat, *das (fachspr.);* **b)** *(Hort.)* umgesetzte Pflanze

transplantation [trænsplɑ:n'teiʃn] *n.* *(Med.)* Transplantation, *die (fachspr.);* Verpflanzung, *die*

transport 1. [træn'spɔ:t] *v. t.* **a)** *(convey)* transportieren; befördern; **b)** *(literary: affect with emotion)* anrühren, anwandeln *(geh.);* **~ed with joy** von Freude überkommen; **c)** *(Hist.)* deportieren ‹*Sträfling*›. **2.** ['trænspɔ:t] *n.* **a)** *(conveyance)* Transport, *der;* Beförderung, *die; attrib.* Transport-; Beförderungs-; **b)** *(means of conveyance)* Verkehrsmittel, *das; (for persons also)* Fortbewegungsmittel, *das;* **~ was provided** für die Beförderung wurde gesorgt; **be without ~:** kein [eigenes] Fahrzeug haben; **his only ~ is a battered car** er hat nur ein verbeultes Auto; **Ministry of T~:** Verkehrsministerium, *das;* **the ~ has arrived** der Wagen ist da; **c)** *(vehement emotion)* Ausbruch, *der;* **be in/send sb. into ~s of joy** außer sich vor Freude sein/jmdn. in helles Entzücken versetzen; **d)** *(Mil.)* [Truppen]transporter, *der*

transportable [træn'spɔ:təbl] *adj.* transportabel

transportation [trænspə'teiʃn] *n.* **a)** *(conveying)* Transport, *der;* Beförderung, *die;* **~ by air/sea/road/rail** Luft-/See-/Straßen-/Bahntransport, *der;* **b)** *(Amer.) see* **transport 2b;** **c)** *(Hist.: of convict)* Deportation, *die*

'transport café *n.* *(Brit.)* Fernfahrerlokal, *das*

transporter [træn'spɔ:tə(r)] *n.* *(vehicle)* Transporter, *der*

trans'porter bridge *n.* Schwebefähre, *die (Technik)*

transpose [træns'pəʊz] *v. t.* **a)** *(cause to change places)* vertauschen; **b)** *(change order of)* umstellen; **c)** *(Mus.)* transponieren

transposition [trænspə'ziʃn] *n. see* **transpose:** Vertauschung, *die;* Umstellung, *die;* *(Mus.)* Transposition, *die*

transsexual [træns'seksjʊəl, træns'sekʃʊəl] **1.** *adj.* transsexuell. **2.** *n.* Transsexuelle, *der/die*

trans-ship [træns'ʃip, træn'ʃip] *v. t.*, **-pp-** umladen

trans-shipment [træns'ʃipmənt, træn'ʃipmənt] *n.* Umschlag, *der*

transubstantiate [trænsəb'stænʃieit] *v. t.* *(Theol.)* [ver]wandeln

transubstantiation [trænsəbstænʃi'eiʃn] *n.* *(Theol.)* Transubstantiation, *die;* Wandlung, *die*

transuranic [trænsjʊ'rænik] *adj.* *(Chem.)* transuranisch

transverse ['trænsvɜ:s] *adj.* querliegend; Quer‹*balken, -lage, -streifen, -verstrebung*›; **~ flute** Querflöte, *die;* **~ wave** *(Phys.)* Transversalwelle, *die;* **~ section** Querschnitt, *der*

transversely ['trænsvɜ:sli] *adv.* quer

transvestism [træns'vestizm] *n.* *(Psych.)* Transvestismus, *der*

transvestist [træns'vestist], **transvestite** [træns'vestait] *n.* *(Psych.)* Transvestit, *der*

Transylvania [trænsil'veiniə] *pr. n.* Transsilvanien *(das) (veralt.);* Siebenbürgen *(das)*

trap [træp] **1.** *n.* **a)** *(lit. or fig.)* Falle, *die;* **set a ~ for an animal** eine Falle für ein Tier legen *od.* [auf]stellen; **set a ~ for sb.** *(fig.)* jmdm. eine Falle stellen; **fall into a/sb.'s ~** *(fig.)* in die/jmdm. in die Falle gehen; **b)** *(sl.: mouth)* Klappe, *die (salopp);* Fresse, *die (derb);* **shut your ~!, keep your ~ shut!** halt die Klappe *(salopp) od. (derb)* Fresse!; **c)** *see* **speed trap;** **d)** *(for releasing bird)* Kasten, *der; (for throwing ball etc. into the air)* Wurfmaschine, *die;* **e)** *(section of pipe)* Geruchsverschluß, *der;* Siphon, *der;* **f)** *(carriage) (leichter zweirädriger)* Einspänner; **g)** *(Golf)* Bunker, *der;* **h)** *(Greyhound-racing)* Box, *die;* **i)** *see* **trapdoor;** **j)** *in pl. (coll.: percussion instruments)* Schießbude, *die (ugs.).* **2.** *v. t.*, **-pp-** **a)** *(catch)* [in *od.* mit einer Falle] fangen ‹*Tier*›; *(fig.)* in eine Falle locken ‹*Person*›; **be ~ped** *(fig.)* in eine Falle gehen/in der Falle sitzen; **be ~ped in a cave/by the tide/in the snow** in einer Höhle festsitzen/von der Flut abgeschnitten sein/im Schnee steckengeblieben sein; **she ~ped him into contradicting himself** sie brachte ihn durch eine List dazu, sich zu widersprechen; **b)** *(confine)* einschließen; *(immobilize)* einklemmen ‹*Person, Körperteil*›; **~ one's finger/foot** sich *(Dat.)* den Finger/Fuß einklemmen; **c)** *(entangle)* verstricken; **d)** stoppen ‹*Ball*›

'trapdoor *n.* Falltür, *die*

trapeze [trə'pi:z] *n.* Trapez, *das*

trapezium [trə'pi:zɪəm] *n., pl.* **trapezia** [trə'pi:zɪə] *or* **~s** *(Geom.)* **a)** *(Brit.)* Trapez, *das;* **b)** *(Amer.)* Trapezoid, *das*

trapezoid ['træpɪzɔɪd] *n. (Geom.)* **a)** *(Brit.)* Trapezoid, *das;* **b)** *(Amer.)* Trapez, *das*

trapper ['træpə(r)] *n.* Fallensteller, *der; (in North America)* Trapper, *der*

trappings ['træpɪŋz] *n. pl.* **a)** [äußere] Zeichen; *(of power, high office)* Insignien; **b)** *(ornamental harness)* ≈ Schabracke, *die*

Trappist ['træpɪst] *n.* Trappist, *der; attrib.* Trappisten-

trash [træʃ] **1.** *n., no pl., no indef. art.* **a)** *(rubbish)* Abfall, *der;* **b)** *(badly made thing)* Mist, *der (ugs. abwertend); (bad literature)* Schund, *der (ugs. abwertend);* **be [just] ~:** nichts taugen; **c)** *(nonsensical talk)* Mist, *der (ugs. abwertend);* **what ~ he talks!** was der für 'n Mist redet!; **d)** *(worthless person)* Ratte, *die (derb); (worthless persons)* Gesindel, *das (abwertend);* Pack, *das (abwertend);* **white ~** *(Amer. derog.)* weißes Gesindel *od.* Pack *(abwertend).* **2.** *v. t.* wegwerfen; wegschmeißen *(ugs.)*

'trashcan *n. (Amer.)* Mülltonne, *die*

trashy ['træʃɪ] *adj.* minderwertig; Schund‹*literatur, -roman*›

trattoria [trætə'ri:ə] *n.* Trattoria, *die*

trauma ['trɔ:mə] *n., pl.* **~ta** ['trɔ:mətə] *or* **~s** Trauma, *das (fachspr.); (injury also)* Verletzung, *die; (shock also)* Schock, *der*

traumatic [trɔ:'mætɪk] *adj.* **a)** *(Med.)* traumatisch; **b)** *(coll.: devastating)* furchtbar

travel ['trævl] **1.** *n.* **a)** Reisen, *das; attrib.* Reise-; **be off on one's ~s** verreist sein; **if you see him on your ~s, ...** *(joc.)* wenn er dir über den Weg läuft, ...; **b)** *(range of motion)* Weg, *der;* **there's a lot of ~ on the handbrake** der Handbremshebel hat einen sehr langen Weg. **2.** *v. i., (Brit.)* **-ll- a)** *(make a journey)* reisen; *(go in vehicle)* fahren; **~ a lot** viel reisen; **b)** *(coll.: withstand long journey)* **~ [well]** ‹*Ware:*› lange Transporte vertragen; **~ badly** ‹*Ware:*› lange Transporte nicht vertragen; **c)** *(work as ~ling sales representative)* reisen; Vertreter/Vertreterin sein; **~ in stationery** in Schreibwaren reisen *(Kaufmannsspr.);* **d)** *(move)* sich bewegen; ‹*Blick, Schmerz:*› wandern; ‹*Tier:*› sich fortbewegen; ‹*Licht, Schall:*› sich ausbreiten; **e)** *(coll.: move briskly)* kacheln *(ugs.);* **that car can really ~:** das Auto zieht ganz schön ab *(ugs.);* **we were really ~ling** wir hatten einen ganz schönen Zahn drauf *(ugs.).* **3.** *v. t., (Brit.)* **-ll-** zurücklegen ‹*Strecke, Entfernung*›; bereisen ‹*Bezirk*›; benutzen, passieren ‹*Weg, Straße*›; **we had ~led 10 miles** wir waren 10 Meilen gefahren

~ a'bout, ~ a'round 1. *v. i.* umherreisen. **2.** *v. t.* **~ around the country** durchs Land reisen *od.* fahren

travel: ~ agency *n.* Reisebüro, *das;* **~ agent** *n.* Reisebürokaufmann, *der/*-kauffrau, *die;* **the ~ agent made a mistake** das Reisebüro hat einen Fehler gemacht

travelator ['trævəleɪtə(r)] *n.* Fahr- *od.* Rollsteig, *der*

travel: ~ brochure *n.* Reiseprospekt, *der;* **~ bureau** *n.* Reisebüro, *das*

traveled, traveler, traveling *(Amer.) see* **travell-**

travelled ['trævld] *adj. (Brit.)* **be much ~** ‹*Person:*› weit gereist sein; **be well ~** ‹*Weg, Straße:*› viel befahren sein

traveller ['trævlə(r)] *n. (Brit.)* **a)** Reisende, *der/die;* **be a poor ~:** das Reisen nicht [gut] vertragen; **b)** *(sales representative)* Vertreter, *der/*Vertreterin, *die;* **c)** *in pl. (gypsies etc.)* fahrendes Volk

traveller: ~'s cheque *n.* Reisescheck, *der;* **~'s tale** *n.* phantastischer Reisebericht; **they're just ~'s tales** das sind nur Phantastereien *(abwertend)*

travelling ['trævlɪŋ] *adj. (Brit.)* Wander‹*zirkus, -ausstellung, -bühne*›

travelling: ~-bag *n.* Reisetasche, *die;* **~ clock** *n.* Reisewecker, *der;* **~ 'crane** *n.* Laufkran, *der;* **~ expenses** *n. pl.* Reisekosten *Pl.;* **~ 'fellowship** *n. (Univ.)* ≈ Auslandsstipendium, *das;* **~ rug** *n.* Reisedecke, *die;* **~ 'salesman** *n.* Vertreter, *der;* **~ 'wave** *n. (Phys.)* fortschreitende Welle

travelogue (*Amer.:* **travelog**) ['trævəlɒg] *n.* Reisebericht, *der*

travel: ~-sick *adj.* reisekrank; **~-sickness** *n., no pl.* Reisekrankheit, *die;* **~-sickness pill** *n.* Tablette gegen Reisekrankheit

traverse ['trævəs, trə'vɜ:s] **1.** *v. t.* **a)** überqueren ‹*Gebirge*›; durchqueren ‹*Gebäude, Gebiet*›; **b)** ‹*Kanal, Mauer:*› durchziehen ‹*Gebiet*›; **c)** *(Mountaineering)* traversieren. **2.** *n. (Mountaineering)* Traversierung, *die*

travesty ['trævɪstɪ] **1.** *n.* **a)** *(parody)* Karikatur, *die;* **be a ~ [of justice]** ein Hohn [auf die Gerechtigkeit] sein; **b)** *(Lit.: burlesque)* Travestie, *die (fachspr.).* **2.** *v. t.* ins Lächerliche ziehen

Travolator, (P) ['trævəleɪtə(r)] *see* **travelator**

trawl [trɔ:l] **1.** *v. i.* mit dem Grundnetz fischen. **2.** *n.* **a)** Fischen mit dem Grundnetz; **b) ~[-net]** Grund[schlepp]netz, *das;* **~[-line]** *(Amer.)* Langleine, *die*

trawler ['trɔ:lə(r)] *n. (vessel)* [Fisch]trawler, *der*

trawlerman ['trɔ:ləmən] *n.* ≈ Hochseefischer, *der*

tray [treɪ] *n.* **a)** Tablett, *das;* **baking-~:** Backblech, *das;* **b)** *(for correspondence)* Ablagekorb, *der*

'tray-cloth *n.* Deckchen für ein Tablett

trayful ['treɪfʊl] *n.* Tablett voll

treacherous ['tretʃərəs] *adj.* **a)** treulos ‹*Person*›; heimtückisch ‹*Intrige, Feind*›; **b)** *(deceptive)* tückisch; **the ice looks pretty ~:** das Eis sieht nicht sehr vertrauenerweckend aus

treacherously ['tretʃərəslɪ] *adv.* heimtückisch

treachery ['tretʃərɪ] *n.* Verrat, *der;* **act of ~:** Verrat, *der*

treacle ['tri:kl] *n. (Brit.)* **a)** *(golden syrup)* Sirup, *der;* **b)** *see* **molasses**

treacle 'pudding *n. mit Sirup übergossener Mehlpudding*

treacly ['tri:klɪ] *adj.* sirupartig; *(fig.)* süßlich *(abwertend)*

tread [tred] **1.** *n.* **a)** *(of tyre, shoe, boot, etc.)* Lauffläche, *die;* **2 millimetres of tread on a tyre** 2 Millimeter Profil auf einem Reifen; **b)** *(manner of walking)* Gang, *der; (sound of walking)* Schritt, *der;* **walk with a springy/catlike ~:** einen federnden/katzenhaften Gang haben; **the ~ of feet** Schritte; **c)** *(of staircase)* [Tritt]stufe, *die.* **2.** *v. i.,* **trod** [trɒd], **trodden** ['trɒdn] *or* **trod** treten **(in/on** in/auf + *Akk.*); *(walk)* gehen; **~ carefully** *or* **lightly** *(fig.)* behutsam vorgehen; **~ on sb.'s toes** *(lit. or fig.)* jmdm. auf die Füße treten; **~ on the heels of sb./sth.** *(fig.)* jmdm./einer Sache auf den Fersen sein *(ugs.);* **~ dirt into the carpet/all over the house** Schmutz in den Teppich treten/im ganzen Haus herumtreten; *see also* **foot 1 a. 3.** *v. t.,* **trod, trodden** *or* **trod a)** *(walk on)* treten auf (+ *Akk.*); stampfen ‹*Weintrauben*›; *(fig.)* gehen ‹*Weg*›; **~ the stage** *or* **boards** *(Theatre)* auf der Bühne *od.* auf den Brettern stehen; **be trodden underfoot** mit Füßen getreten werden; **~ water** *(Swimming)* Wasser treten; **b)** *(make by walking or ~ing)* austreten ‹*Weg*›

~ 'down *v. t.* festtreten ‹*Erde*›; *(crush, destroy)* zertreten ‹*Blume, Beet*›

~ 'in *v. t.* festtreten

~ 'out *v. t.* austreten ‹*Feuer, Zigarette*›; stampfen ‹*Weintrauben*›

treadle ['tredl] *n.* Tritt, *der*

'treadmill *n. (lit. or fig.)* Tretmühle, *die*

treason ['tri:zn] *n.* **a) [high] ~:** Hochverrat, *der;* **b)** *(disloyalty)* Verrat, *der*

treasonable ['tri:zənəbl], **treasonous** ['tri:zənəs] *adjs.* verräterisch; **a ~ offence** Verrat

treasure ['treʒə(r)] **1.** *n.* **a)** Schatz, *der;* Kostbarkeit, *die;* **art ~s** Kunstschätze; **b)** *no pl., no indef. art. (riches)* Schätze; **buried ~:** ein vergrabener Schatz; **voyage in quest of ~:** Schatzsuche, *die;* **c)** *(coll.: valued person)* Schatz, *der (ugs.).* **2.** *v. t.* in Ehren halten; die Erinnerung bewahren an (+ *Dat.*); **I'll always ~ this moment/the memory of that day** ich werde diesen Augenblick/Tag niemals vergessen

~ 'up *v. t.* wie einen Schatz hüten

treasure: ~-house *n.* Schatzkammer, *die; (fig.)* [wahre] Fundgrube; **~-hunt** *n.* Schatzsuche, *die*

treasurer ['treʒərə(r)] *n.* **a)** *(of club, society)* Kassenwart, *der/*-wartin, *die; (of club, party)* Schatzmeister, *der/*-meisterin, *die; (of company)* Leiter/Leiterin der Finanzabteilung; **b)** *(local government official)* Leiter/Leiterin der Finanzverwaltung

treasure trove ['treʒə trəʊv] *n.* Schatz, *der; (fig.: valuable source)* [wahre] Fundgrube

treasury ['treʒərɪ] *n.* **a)** *(place where treasure is stored)* Schatzkammer, *die;* **b)** *(fig.)* Fundgrube, *die; (as book-title)* Schatzkästchen, *das;* **c)** *(place where public revenues are kept)* Schatzamt, *das;* **d)** *(government department)* **the T~:** das Finanzministerium; **the First Lord of the T~** *(Brit.)* der Premierminister/die Premierministerin *(als nomineller Leiter/nominelle Leiterin des „treasury")*

treasury: T~ bench *n. (Brit. Parl.)* Regierungsbank, *die;* **~ bill** *n. (Finance)* Schatzwechsel, *der;* **~ tag** *n. kurze Kordel mit Metallstiften an den Enden zum Zusammenhalten von [gelochten] Blättern*

treat [tri:t] **1.** *n.* **a)** [besonderes] Vergnügen; *(sth. to eat)* [besonderer] Leckerbissen; **what a ~ [it is] to do/not to have to do that!** welch ein Genuß *od.* eine Wohltat, das zu tun/nicht tun zu müssen!; **it was a real ~ to have an entire afternoon at home on my own** es war eine richtige Wohltat, einen ganzen Nachmittag zu Hause für mich allein zu haben; **give sb. a ~:** jmdm. eine besondere Freude machen; **have a ~ in store for sb.** noch eine besondere Freude für jmdn. auf Lager haben; **there was a ~ in store for them** auf sie wartete noch eine besondere Freude; **go down a ~** *(coll.)* ‹*Essen, Getränk:*› prima schmecken *(ugs.);* **work a ~** *(coll.)* ‹*Maschine:*› prima arbeiten *(ugs.);* ‹*Plan:*› prima funktionieren *(ugs.);* **b)** *(entertainment) Vergnügen, für dessen Kosten jmd. anderes aufkommt;* **lay on a special ~ for sb.** jmdm. etwas Besonderes bieten; **as a Christmas ~ I shall take my sister to the theatre** als Weihnachtsgeschenk lade ich meine Schwester ins Theater ein; **c)** *(act of ~ing)* Einladung, *die;* **it's my ~:** ich lade dich/euch ein; **stand ~ for sb.** jmdn. einladen. **2.** *v. t.* **a)** *(act towards)* behandeln; **~ sth. as a joke** etw. als Witz nehmen; **~ sth. with contempt** für etw. nur Verachtung haben; **b)** *(Med.)* behandeln; **~ sb. for sth.** jmdn. wegen etw. behandeln; *(before confirmation of diagnosis)* jmdn. auf etw. *(Akk.)* behandeln; **c)** *(apply process to)* behandeln ‹*Material, Stoff, Metall, Leder*›; klären ‹*Abwässer*›; **d)** *(handle in literature etc.)* behandeln; **~ sth. fully** etw. ausführlich behandeln; **e)** *(provide with at own expense)* einladen; **~ sb. to sth.** jmdm. etw. spendieren; **~ oneself to a holiday/a new hat** sich *(Dat.)* Urlaub gönnen/sich *(Dat.)* einen neuen Hut leisten. **3.** *v. i.*

~ **with sb. [for sth.]** mit jmdm. [über etw. *(Akk.)*] verhandeln
treatise ['tri:tɪs, 'tri:tɪz] *n.* Abhandlung, *die*
treatment ['tri:tmənt] *n.* **a)** Behandlung, *die;* **receive rough ~ from sb.** von jmdm. grob behandelt werden; **his ~ of the staff/you** die Art, wie er das Personal/dich behandelt; **her ~ at the hands of her uncle** die Art, wie ihr Onkel sie behandelt/behandelt hat; **give sb. the [full] ~** *(coll.) (treat cruelly/harshly)* jmdn. in die Mangel nehmen *(salopp); (entertain on a lavish scale)* jmdn. verwöhnen; **b)** *(Med.)* Behandlung, *die;* **be having ~ for sth.** wegen etw. in Behandlung sein; **need immediate medical ~:** sofort ärztlich behandelt werden müssen; **c)** *(processing)* Behandlung, *die; (of sewage)* Klärung, *die*
treaty ['tri:tɪ] *n.* **a)** [Staats]vertrag, *der;* **make** *or* **sign a ~:** einen Vertrag schließen; **the ~ of Rome** die Römischen Verträge; **the ~ of Versailles** der Versailler Vertrag; **b)** *see* **private treaty**
treble ['trebl] **1.** *adj.* **a)** dreifach; **~ row** Dreierreihe, *die;* **~ the amount compared to ...:** dreimal so viel wie ...; **sell sth. for ~ the price** etw. dreimal so teuer verkaufen; **b)** *(Brit. Mus.)* **~ voice** Sopranstimme, *die.* **2.** *n.* **a)** *(Brit. Mus.)* **he is a ~/is singing the ~:** er singt Sopran/den Sopran; **b)** *(~ quantity etc.)* Dreifache, *das;* **c)** *(Darts)* dreifach zählender Treffer; **d)** *(Racing)* Dreifachwette, *die.* **3.** *v.t.* verdreifachen; **be ~d** ⟨*Wert einer Aktie usw.:*⟩ sich verdreifachen. **4.** *v.i.* sich verdreifachen
treble: ~ 'chance *n. Art des Fußballtotos mit dreifacher Gewinnchance;* **~ clef** *n. (Mus.)* Violinschlüssel, *der;* **~ re'corder** *n. (Mus.)* Altflöte, *die*
trebly ['treblɪ] *adv.* dreifach; **be ~ fortunate** in dreifacher Hinsicht Glück haben
tree [tri:] *n.* Baum, *der;* **not grow on ~s** *(fig.)* nicht [einfach] vom Himmel fallen; *see also* **Christmas tree; family tree; shoe-tree; [1]top 1a**
tree: ~-creeper *n. (Ornith.)* Baumläufer, *der;* **~-fern** *n. (Bot.)* Baumfarn, *der;* **~-frog** *n.* Laubfrosch, *der;* **~-house** *n.* Baumhaus, *das*
treeless ['tri:lɪs] *adj.* baumlos
tree: ~-line *see* **timber-line; ~-lined** *adj.* von Bäumen gesäumt; **~-ring** *see* **annual 1c; ~-shaded** *adj.* von Bäumen beschattet *(geh.);* **~ surgeon** *n.* Baumchirurg, *der;* **~ surgery** *n.* Baumchirurgie, *die;* **~-top** *n.* [Baum]wipfel, *der;* **~-trunk** *n.* Baumstamm, *der*
trefoil ['trefɔɪl, 'tri:fɔɪl] *n.* **a)** *(clover)* Klee, *der; (plant with similar leaves)* Dreiblatt, *das;* **b)** *(Archit.)* Dreipaß, *der*
trek [trek] **1.** *v.i.,* **-kk-** **a)** ziehen **(across** durch); **b)** *(travel by ox-wagon)* trecken. **2.** *n.* **a)** [schwierige] Reise; **b)** *(journey by ox-wagon, organized migration)* Treck, *der*
trellis ['trelɪs] *n.* Gitter, *das; (for plants)* Spalier, *das;* **~-work** Gitterwerk, *das*
tremble ['trembl] **1.** *v.i.* zittern **(with** *vor + Dat.*); **~ for sb./sth.** *(fig.)* um jmdn./etw. zittern; **I ~ to think what .../at the thought** *(fig.)* mir wird bange, wenn ich daran denke, was .../wenn ich daran denke. **2.** *n.* Zittern, *das;* **be all of a ~** *(coll.)* am ganzen Körper zittern; **there was a ~ in her voice** ihre Stimme zitterte
trembling ['tremblɪŋ] **1.** *adj.* zitternd. **2.** *n.* Zittern, *das*
tremendous [trɪ'mendəs] *adj.* **a)** *(immense)* gewaltig; enorm ⟨*Fähigkeiten*⟩; **b)** *(coll.: wonderful)* großartig
tremendously [trɪ'mendəslɪ] *adv.* wahnsinnig *(ugs.)*
tremolo ['tremələʊ] *n., pl.* **~s** *(Mus.)* **a)** Tremolo, *das;* **b)** *(in organ)* **~ [stop]** Tremulant, *der*
tremor ['tremə(r)] *n.* **a)** Zittern, *das;* **feel a ~ of delight/fear** freudig erregt sein/vor Angst zittern; **there was a ~ of anger in her voice** ihre Stimme zitterte vor Wut; **without a ~:** ohne zu zittern; **b) [earth] ~** *(Geol.)* leichtes Erdbeben
tremulous ['tremjʊləs] *adj.* **a)** *(trembling)* zitternd; **be ~:** zittern; **b)** *(timid)* zaghaft ⟨*Lächeln*⟩; ängstlich ⟨*Person*⟩
tremulously ['tremjʊləslɪ] *adv.* **a)** mit zitternder Stimme ⟨*sprechen*⟩; **b)** *(timidly)* zaghaft
trench [trentʃ] **1.** *n.* Graben, *der; (Geog.)* [Tiefsee]graben, *der; (Mil.)* Schützengraben, *der.* **2.** *v.t. (dig ditch in)* mit einem Graben durchziehen
trenchant ['trentʃənt] *adj.* deutlich, energisch ⟨*Kritik, Sprache*⟩; energisch ⟨*Verteidiger, Kritiker, Politik*⟩; prägnant ⟨*Stil*⟩; scharf ⟨*Verstand*⟩
trenchantly ['trentʃəntlɪ] *adv.* energisch ⟨*verteidigen, argumentieren, unterstützen*⟩
'trench coat *n. (Mil.)* Wettermantel, *der; (coat in this style)* Trenchcoat, *der*
trencherman ['trentʃəmən] *n.* [guter] Esser
trench: ~ mortar *n. (Mil.)* Granatwerfer, *der;* **~ 'warfare** *n.* Grabenkrieg, *der*
trend [trend] **1.** *n.* **a)** Trend, *der;* **population ~s** die Bevölkerungsentwicklung; **upward ~:** steigende Tendenz; **b)** *(fashion)* Mode, *die;* [Mode]trend, *der;* **set the ~:** den Trend bestimmen; **c)** *(line of direction)* Verlauf, *der.* **2.** *v.i.* **a)** *(take a course)* verlaufen; **b)** *(fig.: move)* sich entwickeln; **~ upward** steigen
trendily ['trendɪlɪ] *adv. (Brit. coll.)* modisch
trendiness ['trendɪnɪs] *n., no pl. (Brit. coll.)* modische Art
'trend-setter *n.* Trendsetter, *der*
trendy ['trendɪ] *(Brit. coll.)* **1.** *adj.* modisch; Schickimicki⟨*kneipe, -wohngegend*⟩ *(ugs.);* fortschrittlich-modern ⟨*Geistlicher, Lehrer*⟩. **2.** *n.* Schickimicki, *der (ugs.)*
trepidation [trepɪ'deɪʃn] *n.* Beklommenheit, *die;* **with some ~, not without ~:** ziemlich beklommen; **wait in ~:** voller Beklommenheit warten; **a look of ~:** ein banger Blick
trespass ['trespəs] **1.** *v.i.* **a) ~ on** unerlaubt betreten ⟨*Grundstück*⟩; eingreifen in (+ *Akk.*) ⟨jmds. Rechte⟩; **'no ~ing'** „Betreten verboten!"; **~ on sb.'s preserve** *(fig.)* sich in jmds. Angelegenheiten *(Akk.)* einmischen; **~ on sb.'s time/privacy** *(fig.)* jmds. Zeit über Gebühr in Anspruch nehmen/jmds. Privatsphäre verletzen; **b)** *(literary/arch.: offend)* freveln *(geh. veralt.)* **(against** an + *Dat.*); **as we forgive those who ~ against us** *(Relig.)* wie wir vergeben unseren Schuldigern. **2.** *n.* **a) forgive us our ~es** *(Relig.)* vergib uns unsere Schuld; **b)** *(Law) (on land)* Hausfriedensbruch, *der; (on a person)* ≈ Körperverletzung, *die; (on goods)* ≈ Eigentumsdelikt, *das*
trespasser ['trespəsə(r)] *n.* Unbefugte, *der/die;* **'~s will be prosecuted'** „Betreten verboten, Zuwiderhandlungen werden verfolgt"; **~ on sb.'s land** Person, die unerlaubt jmds. Land betritt
tress [tres] *n. (literary/arch.)* Haarstrang, *der; (curly)* Locke, *die;* **she combed her ~es** sie kämmte ihr [langes] Haar
trestle ['tresl] *n.* **a)** [Auflager]bock, *der;* **b) ~[-table]** Tapeziertisch, *der*
trews [tru:z] *n. pl. (Brit.)* *enganliegende Hose [im Schottenmuster]*
triad ['traɪæd] *n.* **a)** Triade, *die;* Dreiheit, *die;* **b)** *(Mus.)* Dreiklang, *der*
trial ['traɪəl] *n.* **a)** *(Law)* [Gerichts]verfahren, *das;* **be on ~ [for murder]** [wegen Mordes] angeklagt sein; **go on ~ [for one's life]** [wegen eines Verbrechens, auf das die Todesstrafe steht,] vor Gericht gestellt werden; **bring sb. to ~, put sb. on ~:** jmdm. den Prozeß machen **(for** wegen); **the case was brought to ~:** der Fall wurde vor Gericht verhandelt; **b)** *(testing)* Test, *der;* **subject sth. to further ~:** weitere Tests mit etw. durchführen; **be given ~s** getestet werden; **sea ~** *(Naut.)* Probefahrt, *die;* **employ sb. on ~:** jmdn. probeweise einstellen; **be on ~** ⟨*Person:*⟩ in der Probezeit sein; ⟨*Maschine:*⟩ getestet werden; **give sb. a ~:** es mit jmdm. versuchen; **give sth. a ~:** etw. ausprobieren; **[by] ~ and error** [durch] Ausprobieren; **~ of strength** Kraftprobe, *die;* **c)** *(trouble)* Prüfung, *die (geh.);* Problem, *das;* **find sth. a ~:** etw. als lästig empfinden; **be a ~ to sb.** jmdm. zu schaffen machen; **that child is a real ~:** das Kind ist eine richtige Plage; **d)** *(Sport) (competition)* Prüfung, *die; (for selection)* Testspiel, *das. See also* **jury a; tribulation a**
trial: ~ 'balance *n. (Bookk.)* Probebilanz, *die;* **~ match** *see* **trial d; ~ pack** *n.* Probepackung, *die;* **~ 'run** *n.* **a)** *(of car)* Testfahrt, *die; (of machine)* Probelauf, *der;* **b)** *(fig.)* Probelauf, *der;* **have a ~ run of sth., give sth. a ~ run** etw. testen
triangle ['traɪæŋgl] *n.* **a)** Dreieck, *das; see also* **eternal a; b)** *(Mus.)* Triangel, *das od. der*
triangular [traɪ'æŋgjʊlə(r)] *adj.* **a)** dreieckig; dreiseitig ⟨*Pyramide*⟩; **b)** *(between three persons etc.)* Dreier⟨*beziehung, -wettbewerb*⟩
triangulate [traɪ'æŋgjʊleɪt] *v.t. (Surv.)* triangulieren
triangulation [traɪæŋgjʊ'leɪʃn] *n. (Surv.)* Triangulation, *die*
Triassic [traɪ'æsɪk] *(Geol.)* **1.** *adj.* Trias-. **2.** Trias, *die*
tribal ['traɪbl] *adj.* Stammes-
tribalism ['traɪbəlɪzm] *n.* Tribalismus, *der (fachspr.)*
tribalistic [traɪbə'lɪstɪk] *adj.* Stammes-; tribalistisch *(fachspr.)*
tribe [traɪb] *n.* **a)** Stamm, *der;* **b)** *(derog.)* Bande, *die (abwertend);* **c)** *(Biol.)* Tribus, *die;* **d)** *in pl. (joc.: large numbers)* Horde, *die;* **whole ~s of children** ganze Horden von Kindern
tribesman ['traɪbzmən] *n., pl.* **tribesmen** ['traɪbzmən] Stammesangehörige, *der*
tribulation [trɪbjʊ'leɪʃn] *n.* **a)** *(great affliction)* Kummer, *der;* **bring sb. ~:** jmdm. Kummer bereiten; **trials and ~s** Probleme und Sorgen; **b)** *(cause of trouble etc.)* **be a ~ to sb.** jmdm. zur Last fallen
tribunal [traɪ'bju:nl, trɪ'bju:nl] *n.* **a)** Schiedsgericht, *das; (court of justice)* Gericht, *das; see also* **rent tribunal; b)** *(fig.)* Tribunal, *das*
[1]tribune ['trɪbju:n] *n. (platform)* [Redner]tribüne, *die*
[2]tribune *n. (Hist.)* **~ [of the people]** Volkstribun, *der*
tributary ['trɪbjʊtərɪ] **1.** *adj.* **a)** *(paying tribute)* tributpflichtig; **b) ~ river** *(of larger river)* Nebenfluß, *der; (of lake, stream, etc.)* Zufluß, *der.* **2.** *n.* **a)** *(river) (flowing into larger river)* Nebenfluß, *der; (flowing into lake, stream, etc.)* Zufluß, *der;* **b)** *(State)* tributpflichtiger Staat
tribute ['trɪbju:t] *n.* **a)** *(regard)* Tribut, *der* **(to** an + *Akk.*); **pay ~ to sb./sth.** jmdm./einer Sache den schuldigen Tribut zollen *(geh.);* **in silent ~:** in stiller Ehrerbietung; **floral ~s** Blumen [als Zeichen der Anerkennung]; *(to deceased person)* Blumen und Kränze; **as a ~ to his work** zur Würdigung seiner Arbeit; **she is a ~ to her teacher/trainer** sie macht ihrem Lehrer/Trainer alle Ehre; **b)** *(payment)* Tribut, *der*
trice [traɪs] *n.* **in a ~:** im Handumdrehen
tricentenary [traɪsen'ti:nərɪ, traɪsen'tenərɪ] *see* **tercentenary**
trichinosis [trɪkɪ'nəʊsɪs] *n. (Med.)* Trichinose, *die*
trichloride [traɪ'klɔ:raɪd] *n. (Chem.)* Trichlorid, *das*

trick [trɪk] **1.** *n.* **a)** Trick, *der;* **I suspect some ~:** es könnte ein Trick sein; **it was all a ~:** das war [alles] nur Bluff; **it was such a shabby ~ [to play on her]** es war [ihr gegenüber] eine derartige Gemeinheit *od.* dermaßen gemein; **b)** *(feat of skill etc.)* Kunststück, *das;* **try every ~ in the book** es mit allen Tricks probieren; **he never misses a ~** *(fig.)* ihm entgeht nichts; **that should do the ~** *(coll.)* damit dürfte es klappen *(ugs.);* **know a ~ worth two of that** etwas viel Besseres wissen; **c)** *(knack)* **get** *or* **find the ~ [of doing sth.]** den Dreh finden[, wie man etw. tut]; **d) how's ~s?** *(coll.)* was macht die Kunst? *(ugs.);* **e)** *(mannerism)* Eigenart, *die;* **have a ~ of doing sth.** die Eigenart haben, etw. zu tun; **f)** *(prank)* Streich, *der;* **play a ~ on sb.** jmdm. einen Streich spielen; **my hearing-aid is playing ~s on me again** mein Hörgerät spielt mal wieder verrückt *(ugs.);* **be up to one's [old] ~s again** immer noch auf dieselbe Tour reisen *(ugs.);* **be up to sb.'s ~s** wissen, was jmd. im Schilde führt; **~ or treat** Trick-or-Treat, *das (Kinderspiel);* **g)** *(illusion)* **~ of vision/lighting/the light** Augentäuschung, *die;* **h)** *(Cards)* Stich, *der;* **take a ~:** einen Stich machen; **i)** *(prostitute's customer)* Freier, *der.* See also **bag 1 a; trade 1 a. 2.** *v. t.* täuschen; hereinlegen; **~ sb. into doing sth.** jmdn. mit einem Trick *od.* einer List dazu bringen, etw. zu tun; **~ sb. out of/into sth.** jmdm. etw. ablisten. **3.** *adj.* **~ photograph** Trickaufnahme, *die;* **~ photography** Trickfotografie, *die;* **~ question** Fangfrage, *die*

~ 'out, ~ 'up *v. t.* schmücken; **~ oneself out** *or* **up** sich herausputzen **(in** mit**)**

trick 'cyclist *n.* **a)** Kunstradfahrer, *der*/-fahrerin, *die;* **b)** *(joc.: psychiatrist)* Seelendoktor, *der*/-doktorin, *die (ugs. scherzh.)*

trickery ['trɪkərɪ] *n.* [Hinter]list, *die;* **piece of ~:** List, *die;* Trick, *der*

trickiness ['trɪkɪnɪs] *n., no pl.* Verzwicktheit, *die (ugs.)*

trickle ['trɪkl] **1.** *n.* Rinnsal, *das (geh.)* **(of** von**);** **in a ~:** als Rinnsal; **a ~ of rain ran down the window** Regenwasser rann am Fenster hinunter; **there was a ~ of people leaving the room** *(fig.)* einige wenige Menschen verließen nacheinander den Raum; **the ~ of people leaving the hall swelled to a flood** *(fig.)* erst leerte sich die Halle nur langsam, doch dann strömten die Menschen hinaus; **supplies of food have shrunk to a ~** *(fig.)* die Versorgung mit Nahrungsmitteln ist fast versiegt. **2.** *v. i.* rinnen; *(in drops)* tröpfeln; *(fig.)* ⟨*Ball:*⟩ langsam rollen; **~ out** ⟨*Zuschauer:*⟩ nach und nach [hinaus]gehen; **~ through** *or* **out** ⟨*Informationen:*⟩ durchsickern. **3.** *v. t.* tröpfeln

'trickle charger *n. (Electr.)* Erhaltungslader, *der*

trickster ['trɪkstə(r)] *n.* Schwindler, *der*/Schwindlerin, *die*

tricky ['trɪkɪ] *adj.* **a)** *(full of difficulties)* verzwickt *(ugs.);* **it is ~ doing sth.** es ist gar nicht so einfach, etw. zu tun; **b)** *(crafty)* raffiniert; trickreich ⟨*Spieler*⟩

tricolour (*Amer.:* **tricolor**) ['trɪkələ(r), 'traɪkələ(r)] *n.* Trikolore, *die*

tricorn ['traɪkɔ:n] *n., adj.* **~ [hat]** Dreispitz, *der*

tricot ['trɪkəʊ, 'tri:kəʊ] *n.* **a)** *(hand-knitted woollen fabric)* Wollgestrick, *das;* **b)** *(plain-knitted cloth)* Jerseystoff, *der;* **c)** *(ribbed woollen cloth)* Trikot[stoff], *der*

tricycle ['traɪsɪkl] **1.** *n.* Dreirad, *das.* **2.** *v. i.* Dreirad fahren

trident ['traɪdənt] *n.* dreizackiger Fischspeer; *(held by Britannia etc.)* Dreizack, *der*

Tridentine [trɪ'dentaɪn] *adj.* tridentinisch

tried *see* **try 2, 3**

triennial [traɪ'enɪəl] *adj.* **a)** *(lasting three years)* dreijährig; **b)** *(once every three years)* dreijährlich

triennially [traɪ'enɪəlɪ] *adv.* alle drei Jahre

trier [traɪə(r)] *n.* **he's a real ~:** er wirft die Flinte nicht so schnell ins Korn; **but at least he's a ~:** aber er gibt sich *(Dat.)* wenigstens Mühe

Trieste [tri:'est] *pr. n.* Triest *(das)*

trifle ['traɪfl] **1.** *n.* **a)** *(Brit. Gastron.)* Trifle, *das;* **b)** *(thing of slight value)* Kleinigkeit, *die;* **the merest ~:** die geringste Kleinigkeit; **it's only a ~:** es ist nichts Besonderes; **c)** *(small amount of money)* Kleinigkeit, *die;* **it only costs a ~:** es kostet so gut wie nichts; **d) a ~ tired/angry** *etc.* ein bißchen müde/böse *usw.* **2.** *v. i.* tändeln

~ a'way *v. t.* vergeuden

~ with *v. i.* spielen mit ⟨*jmds. Gefühlen*⟩; nicht ernst genug nehmen ⟨*Person*⟩; **he is not a person you can ~ with** er läßt nicht mit sich spaßen

trifling ['traɪflɪŋ] *adj.* unbedeutend ⟨*Angelegenheit, Irrtum*⟩; lächerlich ⟨*Gedanke*⟩; gering ⟨*Gefahr, Wert*⟩; [lächerlich] gering ⟨*Summe*⟩; **~ objects/gifts** Kleinigkeiten

trifocal [traɪ'fəʊkl] *(Optics)* **1.** *adj.* Trifokal-. **2.** *n. in pl.* Trifokalgläser *Pl.*

triforium [traɪ'fɔ:rɪəm] *n., pl.* **triforia** [traɪ'fɔ:rɪə] *(Archit.)* Triforium, *das (fachspr.)*

trigger ['trɪgə(r)] **1.** *n.* **a)** *(of gun)* Abzug, *der;* *(of machine)* Drücker, *der;* **pull the ~:** abdrücken; *(fig.)* den Startschuß geben; **be quick on the ~** *(fig.)* prompt reagieren; **b)** *(that sets off reaction)* Auslöser, *der.* **2.** *v. t.* **~ [off]** auslösen

'trigger-happy *adj.* schießwütig; *(fig.)* kriegslüstern ⟨*General, Politiker*⟩

trigonometric [trɪgənə'metrɪk], **trigonometrical** [trɪgənə'metrɪkl] *adj. (Math.)* trigonometrisch

trigonometry [trɪgə'nɒmɪtrɪ] *n. (Math.)* Trigonometrie, *die*

trike [traɪk] *n.(coll.)* Dreirad, *das*

trilateral [traɪ'lætərl] **1.** *adj.* *(having three sides)* dreiseitig; *(involving three parties also)* trilateral *(geh.).* **2.** *n.* Dreieck, *das*

trilby ['trɪlbɪ] *n. (Brit.)* **~ [hat]** Klapprandhut, *der;* Herrenhut, *der*

trilingual [traɪ'lɪŋgwəl] *adj.* dreisprachig

trill [trɪl] **1.** *n.* **a)** Trillern, *das;* **b)** *(Mus.)* Triller, *der.* **2.** *v. i.* trillern. **3.** *v. t.* rollen ⟨*r*⟩

trillion ['trɪljən] *n.* **a)** *(Brit.)* Trillion, *die;* **b)** *(Amer.: million million)* Billion, *die*

trilobite ['traɪləbaɪt] *n. (Palaeont.)* Trilobit, *der*

trilogy ['trɪlədʒɪ] *n.* Trilogie, *die*

trim [trɪm] **1.** *v. t.,* **-mm-** **a)** schneiden ⟨*Hecke*⟩; [nach]schneiden ⟨*Haar*⟩; beschneiden *(auch fig.)* ⟨*Papier, Hecke, Docht, Budget*⟩; **~ £100 off** *or* **from a budget** ein Budget um 100 Pfund kürzen; **b)** *(ornament)* besetzen **(with** mit**);** **c)** *(adjust balance of)* trimmen ⟨*Boot, Schiff, Flugzeug*⟩; **d)** richtig stellen ⟨*Segel*⟩; **~ one's sails before the wind** *(fig.)* sich nach der Decke strecken. **2.** *adj.* proper; gepflegt ⟨*Garten*⟩; **keep sth. ~:** etw. in Ordnung halten. **3.** *n.* **a)** *(state of adjustment)* Bereitschaft, *die;* **find sth. in [perfect] ~:** etw. in [bester] Ordnung vorfinden; **everything was in good** *or* **proper ~:** alles war in bester Ordnung; **be in fine physical ~:** in guter körperlicher Verfassung sein; **get/be in ~** *(suitably dressed)* sich angemessen anziehen/angemessen angezogen sein; *(healthy)* sich trimmen/in Form *od.* fit sein; **b)** *(proper balance) (of ship)* Trimm, *der; (of aircraft)* [stabile] Fluglage; **be in/out of ~** ⟨*Schiff:*⟩ in/nicht in Trimm sein; ⟨*Flugzeug:*⟩ in stabiler/unstabiler Fluglage sein; **c)** *(cut)* Nachschneiden, *das;* **my hair needs a ~:** ich muß mir die Haare nachschneiden lassen; **give a hedge a ~:** eine Hecke nachschneiden; **just a ~, please** *(said to hairdresser)* nur nachschneiden, bitte; **d)** *(adornment) see* **trimming a; e)** *(of car)* Innenausstattung, *die; (on door panel)* Zierleiste, *die*

~ a'way *v. t. see* **~ off**

~ 'down *v. t. (fig.)* verringern; **her figure needed ~ming down** sie mußte etwas für ihre Figur tun

~ 'off *v. t.* abschneiden; *(fig.)* abnehmen

trimaran ['traɪməræn] *n. (Naut.)* Trimaran, *der*

trimmer ['trɪmə(r)] *n.* Schneider, *der;* **hedge-~:** Heckenschere, *die*

trimming ['trɪmɪŋ] *n.* **a)** *(decorative addition)* Verzierung, *die;* **lace ~s** Spitzenbesatz, *der;* **b)** *in pl. (coll.: accompaniments) (for main dish)* Beilagen; *(extra fittings on car)* Extras; **with all the ~s** mit allem Drum und Dran *(ugs.);* **c)** *in pl. (pieces cut off)* Abfall, *der (vom Zuschneiden); (of meat)* abgeschnittene Stücke

trimness ['trɪmnɪs] *n., no pl.* adrettes Aussehen; **the ~ of her figure** ihre gepflegte Figur

Trinidad ['trɪnɪdæd] *pr. n.* Trinidad *(das)*

Trinidadian [trɪnɪ'dædɪən] **1.** *adj.* trinidadisch; **sb. is ~:** jmd. ist Trinidader/Trinidaderin. **2.** *n.* Trinidader, *der*/Trinidaderin, *die*

Trinity ['trɪnɪtɪ] *n.* **a)** *(Theol.)* **the [Holy] ~:** die [Heilige] Dreifaltigkeit *od.* Dreieinigkeit *od.* Trinität; **b)** *(Eccl.)* **~ [Sunday]** Dreifaltigkeitssonntag, *der*

Trinity 'term *n. (Brit. Univ.)* Sommertrimester, *das*

trinket ['trɪŋkɪt] *n.* **a)** *(piece of jewellery)* kleines, billiges Schmuckstück; *(on bracelet)* Anhänger, *der;* **b)** *(ornament)* Schmuckgegenstand, *der*

trio ['tri:əʊ] *n., pl.* **~s** Trio, *das;* **string/piano ~** *(Mus.)* Streich-/Klaviertrio, *das*

trioxide [traɪ'ɒksaɪd] *n. (Chem.)* Trioxid, *das*

trip [trɪp] **1.** *n.* **a)** *(journey)* Reise, *die;* Trip, *der (ugs.); (shorter)* Ausflug, *der;* Trip, *der (ugs.);* **two ~s were necessary to transport everything** zwei Fahrten waren nötig, um alles zu transportieren; **make a ~ to London** nach London fahren; **b)** *(coll.: visit for stated purpose)* Gang, *der;* **I must make a ~ to the loo** ich muß mal aufs Klo; **make a ~ to the hairdresser's** zum Friseur gehen; **c)** *(coll.: drug-induced hallucinations)* Trip, *der (Jargon);* **[good/bad] ~ on LSD** [guter/schlechter] LSD-Trip. *See also* **round trip. 2.** *v. i.,* **-pp-** **a)** *(stumble)* stolpern **(on** über + *Akk.***);** **b)** *(coll.: hallucinate while on drugs)* **~ [on LSD]** auf einem [LSD-]Trip sein; **c)** *(walk etc. with light steps)* trippeln; **d)** *(fig.: make a mistake)* einen Fehler machen. **3.** *v. t.,* **-pp-** **a)** *(cause to stumble) see* **~ up 2 a; b)** *(release)* lichten ⟨*Anker*⟩; betätigen ⟨*Schalter*⟩; auslösen ⟨*Alarm*⟩

~ over *v. t.* stolpern über (+ *Akk.*)

~ 'up 1. *v. i.* **a)** *(stumble)* stolpern; **b)** *(fig.: make a mistake)* einen Fehler machen. **2.** *v. t.* **a)** *(cause to stumble)* stolpern lassen; **b)** *(cause to make a mistake)* aufs Glatteis führen *(fig.)*

tripartite [traɪ'pɑ:taɪt] *adj.* **a)** *(in three parts)* **~ division** Dreiteilung, *die;* **b)** *(involving three parties)* trilateral *(geh.);* dreiseitig

tripe [traɪp] *n.* **a)** Kaldaunen; *(individual piece)* Kaldaune, *die;* **b)** *(sl.: rubbish)* Quatsch, *der (ugs. abwertend)*

triple ['trɪpl] **1.** *adj.* **a)** *(threefold)* dreifach; **b)** *(three times greater than)* **~ the ...:** der/die/das dreifache ...; **at ~ the speed** mit der dreifachen Geschwindigkeit *od.* dreimal so schnell; **~ the number of machines** dreimal so viele Maschinen. **2.** *n.* Dreifache, *das.* **3.** *v. i.* sich verdreifachen. **4.** *v. t.* verdreifachen

triple: T~ Al'liance *n. (Hist.)* Dreibund, *der;* **~ 'crown** *n.* **a)** *(Sport)* Triple Crown, *die;* dreifacher Triumph; **b)** *(Pope's tiara)* dreifache Krone; Tiara, *die;* **~ jump** *n.* *(Sport)* Dreisprung, *der*

triplet ['trɪplɪt] *n.* **a)** Drilling, *der;* **b)** *(Pros.)* Dreireim, *der;* **c)** *(Mus.)* Triole, *die*

'triple time *n. (Mus.)* Dreiertakt, *der*

Triplex, (P) ['trɪpleks] *n.* ~ **[glass]** Sicherheitsglas, *das; (laminated)* Verbundglas, *das*

triplicate ['trɪplɪkət] **1.** *adj.* dreifach. **2.** *n.* Drittausfertigung, *die;* Triplikat, *das (geh.);* **in ~:** in dreifacher Ausfertigung

triply ['trɪplɪ] *adv.* dreifach

trip 'mileage recorder *n. (Motor Veh.)* Tageskilometerzähler, *der*

tripod ['traɪpɒd] *n.* Dreibein, *das;* [dreibeiniges] Stativ

tripos ['traɪpɒs] *n. (Brit.) Abschlußprüfung für den Honours-Degree an der Universität Cambridge*

tripper ['trɪpə(r)] *n. (Brit.)* Ausflügler, *der/*Ausflüglerin, *die*

triptych ['trɪptɪk] *n. (Art)* Triptychon, *das*

'trip-wire *n.* Stolperdraht, *der*

trisect [traɪ'sekt] *v. t.* dreiteilen

trisyllabic [traɪsɪ'læbɪk] *adj. (Ling.)* dreisilbig

trisyllable [traɪ'sɪləbl] *n. (Ling. Pros.)* dreisilbiges Wort; **be a ~:** dreisilbig sein *od.* drei Silben haben

trite [traɪt] *adj.,* **tritely** ['traɪtlɪ] *adv.* banal

triteness ['traɪtnɪs] *n., no pl.* Banalität, *die*

tritium ['trɪtɪəm] *n. (Chem.)* Tritium, *das*

triumph ['traɪəmf, 'traɪʌmf] **1.** *n.* Triumph, *der* **(over** über + *Akk.*); *(Rom. Ant.: procession also)* Triumphzug, *der;* **in ~:** im Triumph; **an expression of ~:** ein triumphierender Ausdruck. **2.** *v. i.* triumphieren **(over** über + *Akk.*)

triumphal [traɪ'ʌmfl] *adj.* triumphal ‹*Erfolg*›; Triumph‹*bogen, -zug*›

triumphant [traɪ'ʌmfənt] *adj.* **a)** *(victorious)* siegreich; *see also* **church b; b)** *(exulting)* triumphierend ‹*Blick*›; ~ **shouts** Triumphgeschrei, *das;* **the look in her eyes was ~:** sie hatte einen triumphierenden Blick

triumphantly [traɪ'ʌmfəntlɪ] *adv.* triumphierend; **be ~ successful** einen triumphalen Erfolg haben

triumvirate [traɪ'ʌmvərət] *n.* Triumvirat, *das*

trivalent [traɪ'veɪlənt] *adj. (Chem.)* dreiwertig

trivet ['trɪvɪt] *n.* **a)** *(in pressure-cooker)* Dreifuß, *der;* **b)** *(Amer.: used under hot dishes)* [dreifüßiger] Untersetzer

trivia ['trɪvɪə] *n. pl.* Belanglosigkeiten

trivial ['trɪvɪəl] *adj.* **a)** belanglos; trivial *(geh.);* **b)** *(concerned only with ~ things)* oberflächlich ‹*Person*›

triviality [trɪvɪ'ælɪtɪ] *n.* Belanglosigkeit, *die;* Trivialität, *die (geh.)*

trivialize ['trɪvɪəlaɪz] *v. t.* auf eine belanglose Ebene bringen; trivialisieren *(geh.)*

trivially ['trɪvɪəlɪ] *adv.* oberflächlich

trochaic [trə'keɪɪk] *(Pros.) adj.* trochäisch

trochee ['trəʊkiː] *n. (Pros.)* Trochäus, *der*

trod, trodden *see* **tread 2, 3**

troglodyte ['trɒglədaɪt] *n.* **a)** *(cave-dweller)* Höhlenbewohner, *der/*-bewohnerin, *die;* **b)** *(fig.)* Einsiedler, *der/*Einsiedlerin, *die*

troika ['trɔɪkə] *n.* Troika, *die*

Trojan ['trəʊdʒən] **1.** *n.* **a)** *(fig.)* **work like a ~:** arbeiten wie ein Pferd; **b)** *(inhabitant of Troy)* Trojaner, *der/*Trojanerin, *die.* **2.** *adj.* trojanisch; **the T~ War** der Trojanische Krieg

Trojan 'Horse *n.* Trojanisches Pferd *(geh.); (fig. also)* Danaergeschenk, *das (geh.)*

¹troll [trəʊl] **1.** *v. t. (fish)* [mit der Schleppangel] fischen. **2.** *v. i. (fish)* [mit der Schleppangel] fischen **(for** *Akk.*)

²troll *n. (Mythol.)* Troll, *der*

trolley ['trɒlɪ] *n.* **a)** *(Brit.: on rails)* Draisine, *die;* **b)** *(Brit.: for serving food)* Servierwagen, *der;* **c)** *(Brit.)* **[supermarket] ~:** Einkaufswagen, *der;* **d)** *see* **luggage trolley; e)** *(Amer.)* **~[-car]** Straßenbahn, *die;* **f) he's off his ~** *(sl.: insane)* bei ihm ist eine Schraube locker *(salopp)*

'trolley bus *n. (Brit.)* Oberleitungsomnibus, *der*

trollop ['trɒləp] *n.* **a)** *(slut)* Schlampe, *die;* **b)** *(prostitute)* Dirne, *die*

trolly *see* **trolley**

trombone [trɒm'bəʊn, 'trɒmbəʊn] *n.* Posaune, *die*

trombonist [trɒm'bəʊnɪst] *n.* Posaunist, *der/*Posaunistin, *die*

trompe-l'œil [trɒmp'lʌiː] *(Art)* **1.** *n.* Trompe-l'œil, *das od. der.* **2.** *adj.* Trompe-l'œil-

troop [truːp] **1.** *n.* **a)** *in pl.* Truppen; **our best ~s** unsere besten Soldaten; **b)** *(of cavalry)* Schwadron, *die; (artillery and armour)* Batterie, *die;* **c)** *(assembled company)* Schar, *die;* **d)** *(of Scouts)* ≈ Gruppe, *die. See also* **household troops. 2.** *v. i.* strömen; *(in an orderly fashion)* marschieren; **~ in/out** hinein-/hinausströmen. **3.** *v. t.* **~ing the colour[s]** *(Brit.)* Fahnenparade, *die*

'troop-carrier *n.* Truppentransporter, *der*

trooper ['truːpə(r)] *n.* **a)** *(soldier)* einfacher Soldat; **swear like a ~** *(coll.)* wie ein Fuhrmann fluchen *(ugs.);* **b)** *(Amer.: policeman)* Polizist, *der*

'troop-ship *n. (Mil.)* Truppentransporter, *der*

trope [trəʊp] *n. (Rhet.)* Trope, *die (fachspr.)*

trophy ['trəʊfɪ] *n.* **a)** Trophäe, *die;* **b)** *(competition)* **T~:** ≈ Pokal, *der*

tropic ['trɒpɪk] *n.* **the T~s** *(Geog.)* die Tropen; **the ~ of Cancer/Capricorn** *(Astron., Geog.)* der Wendekreis des Krebses/Steinbocks

tropical ['trɒpɪkl] *adj.* tropisch; Tropen‹*krankheit, -kleidung*›

tropical: ~ **'medicine** *n.* Tropenmedizin, *die;* ~ **'rain forest** *n.* tropischer Regenwald

troposphere ['trɒpəsfɪə(r), 'trəʊpəsfɪə(r)] *n.* Troposphäre, *die*

Trot [trɒt] *n. (sl.: Trotskyist)* Trotzkist, *der/*Trotzkistin, *die*

trot 1. *n.* **a)** *(action of trotting)* Trab, *der;* **at a ~:** im Trab; **b)** *(journey on horseback)* Ausritt, *der;* **c)** *(coll.)* **on the ~** *(in succession)* hintereinander; **every weekend for five weeks on the ~:** an fünf Wochenenden hintereinander; **be on the ~:** auf Trab sein *(ugs.);* **keep sb. on the ~** *(continually busy)* jmdn. auf Trab halten *(ugs.);* **d) have the ~s** *(sl.: diarrhoea)* Dünnpfiff haben *(salopp).* **2.** *v. i.,* **-tt- a)** traben; **b)** *(coll.: go)* traben *(ugs.);* **~ along now** geh jetzt. **3.** *v. t.,* **-tt-** traben lassen ‹*Pferd*›

~ 'out *v. t. (fig. coll.)* **a)** *(produce for approval)* vorführen; **b)** *(produce unthinkingly)* kommen mit *(ugs.)*

troth [trəʊθ] *n. (arch.)* **a) in ~, by my ~:** bei meiner Ehre!; **b)** *(faith)* Treue, *die;* **plight one's ~:** das Eheversprechen geben

Trotskyism ['trɒtskɪɪzm] *n.* Trotzkismus, *der*

Trotskyist ['trɒtskɪɪst], **Trotskyite** ['trɒtskɪaɪt] *ns.* Trotzkist, *der/*Trotzkistin, *die*

trotter ['trɒtə(r)] *n.* **a)** Fuß, *der;* **pigs' ~s** *(Cookery)* Schweinsfüße; **b)** *(horse)* Traber, *der*

trotting ['trɒtɪŋ] *n.* Trabrennen, *das*

'trotting race *n.* Trabrennen, *das*

troubadour ['truːbədʊə(r)] *n.* Troubadour, *der*

trouble ['trʌbl] **1.** *n.* **a)** Ärger, *der;* Schwierigkeiten *Pl.;* **have ~ with sb./sth.** mit jmdm./etw. Ärger haben; **all his ~s** alle seine Probleme; **put one's ~s behind one** seine Probleme vergessen; **be out of ~:** aus den Schwierigkeiten heraussein; **keep out of ~:** nicht [wieder] in Schwierigkeiten kommen; **in ~:** in Schwierigkeiten; **be in ~ with the police** Ärger mit der Polizei haben; **are you looking for ~?** du willst wohl Ärger [bekommen]?; **be in serious** *or* **real** *or* **a lot of ~ [over sth.]** [wegen einer Sache] in ernsten *od.* großen Schwierigkeiten sein; **get sb. into ~:** jmdn. in Schwierigkeiten bringen; **get a girl into ~** *(coll.)* einem Mädchen ein Kind machen *(ugs.);* **get into ~ [over sth.]** [wegen einer Sache] in Schwierigkeiten geraten; **get into ~ with the bank/law** Ärger *od.* Schwierigkeiten mit der Bank bekommen/mit dem Gesetz in Konflikt geraten; **there'll be ~ [if ...]** es wird Ärger geben[, wenn ...]; **what's** *or* **what seems to be the ~?** was ist denn?; was ist los? *(ugs.); (doctor's question to patient)* wo fehlt's denn?; **you are asking for ~** *(coll.)* du machst dir nur selber Schwierigkeiten; **that's asking for ~** *(coll.)* das muß ja Ärger geben; **make** *or* **cause ~** *(cause disturbance)* Ärger machen **(about** wegen); *(cause disagreement)* Zwietracht säen; **make ~ for sb.** jmdm. Ärger *od.* Schwierigkeiten machen; **give sb. no ~:** jmdm. keine Schwierigkeiten bereiten *od.* machen; **b)** *(faulty operation)* Probleme; **engine/clutch/brake ~:** Probleme mit dem Motor/der Kupplung/der Bremse; **the engine is giving ~:** mit dem Motor stimmt etwas nicht; **c)** *(disease)* **suffer from heart/liver ~:** Probleme mit dem Herz/der Leber haben; es am Herz/an der Leber haben *(ugs.);* **she's got some ~ with her back** ihr Rücken macht ihr zu schaffen; **d)** *(cause of vexation etc.)* Problem, *das;* **half the ~** *(fig.)* das größte Problem; **your ~ is that ...:** dein Fehler ist, daß ...; **their daughter is such a terrible ~ to them** ihre Tochter macht ihnen solche Sorgen; **e)** *(inconvenience)* Mühe, *die;* **it's more ~ than it's worth** es lohnt sich nicht; **dishwashers are more ~ than they are worth** mit Geschirrspülmaschinen hat man doch nur Ärger; **I don't want to put you to any ~:** ich möchte Ihnen keine Umstände machen; **not worth the ~:** nicht der Mühe wert; **give sb. no ~:** jmdm. keine Mühe machen; **take the ~ to do sth., go to the ~ of doing sth.** sich *(Dat.)* die Mühe machen, etw. zu tun; **go to** *or* **take a lot of/some ~:** sich *(Dat.)* sehr viel/viel Mühe geben; **please don't go to a lot of ~:** bitte machen Sie sich *(Dat.)* nicht allzuviel Umstände; **of course I'll help you – [it's] no ~ at all** natürlich helfe ich dir – das macht keine Umstände *od.* das ist nicht der Rede wert; **nothing was too much ~ for her** nichts war ihr zuviel; **f)** *(source of inconvenience)* **be a ~ [to sb.]** jmdm. zur Last fallen; **he won't be any ~:** er wird [Ihnen] keine Schwierigkeiten machen; **the children are no ~:** die Kinder sind keine Last; **g)** *in sing. or pl. (unrest)* Unruhen; **h) ~ and strife** *(Brit. sl.: wife)* bessere Hälfte *(ugs. scherzh.).* **2.** *v. t.* **a)** *(agitate)* beunruhigen; **don't let it ~ you** mach dir deswegen keine Sorgen; **be ~d about money matters** Geldsorgen haben; **b)** *(inconvenience)* stören; **[I'm] sorry to ~ you** bitte entschuldigen Sie die Störung; **can I ~ you with one more question?** darf ich Ihnen noch eine letzte Frage stellen?; **my back ~s me sometimes** mein Rücken macht mir manchmal zu schaffen; **c)** *(in requests)* **may I ~ you to shut the door?** dürfte ich Sie bitten, die Tür zu schließen?; **may I ~ you to mind your own business?** *(iron.)* kümmern Sie sich gefälligst um Ihre eigenen Angelegenheiten!; **I'll ~ you to wipe your feet** *(iron.)* putz dir gefälligst die Schuhe ab. **3.** *v. i.* **a)** *(be disturbed)* sich *(Dat.)* Sorgen machen **(over** um); **don't ~ about it** mach dir deswegen keine Gedanken; **b)** *(make an effort)* sich bemühen; **don't ~ to explain/to get up/to see me out** du brauchst mir gar nichts zu erklären/bitte bleiben Sie sitzen/Sie brauchen mich nicht hinauszubringen

troubled ['trʌbld] *adj.* **a)** *(worried)* besorgt; **what are you so ~ about?** was macht dir denn solche Sorgen?; **b)** *(restless)* unruhig; schlecht ‹*Traum*›; **c)** *(agitated)* aufgewühlt; unruhig ‹*Zeit*›; bewegt ‹*Geschichte*›; *see also* **pour 1 a**

trouble: ~-free *adj.* problemlos; harmonisch ‹*Ehe*›; **~-maker** *n.* Unruhestifter, *der/*-stifterin, *die;* **~-shooter** *n.: jemand, der Störungen od. Probleme findet und beseitigt;* Troubleshooter, *der; (in disputes)* Vermittler, *der/*Vermittlerin, *die;* **~-shooting** *n.: das Finden und Beseitigen von Störungen od. Problemen; (in disputes)* Vermittlung, *die*

troublesome ['trʌblsəm] *adj.* schwierig; lästig ‹*Krankheit*›

'trouble-spot *n.* **a)** Unruheherd, *der;* **b)** *(in machine)* Schwachstelle, *die*

trough [trɒf] *n.* **a)** Trog, *der;* **a drinking-~:** ein Wassertrog; **b)** *(between waves)* Wellental, *das;* **c)** *(Meteorol.)* Trog, *der;* **a ~ of low pressure** eine Tiefdruckrinne; **d)** *(Econ., on graph)* Talsohle, *die*

trounce [traʊns] *v. t.* **a)** *(defeat)* vernichtend schlagen; **b)** *(beat severely)* durchprügeln *(ugs.)*

troupe [tru:p] *n.* Truppe, *die*

trouper ['tru:pə(r)] *n.* Komödiant, *der/*Komödiantin, *die;* **an old ~** *(fig.)* ein alter Hase; **sb. is a good ~:** jmd. ist ein guter Kollege/eine gute Kollegin

trouser ['traʊzə]: **~-leg** *n.* Hosenbein, *das;* **~ pocket** *n.* Hosentasche, *die;* **~-press** *n.* Bügelpresse, *die;* Hosenbügler, *der*

trousers ['traʊzəz] *n. pl.* **[pair of] ~:** Hose, *die;* Hosen *Pl.;* **catch sb. with his ~ down** *(fig. sl.)* jmdn. unvorbereitet treffen; **wear the ~** *(fig.)* die Hosen anhaben *(ugs.)*

'trouser suit *n. (Brit.)* Hosenanzug, *der*

trousseau ['tru:səʊ] *n., pl.* **~s** *or* **~x** ['tru:səʊz] Aussteuer, *die*

trout [traʊt] *n., pl. same* Forelle, *die*

trout: ~ farm *n.* Forellenzuchtbetrieb, *der;* **~-fishing** *n.* Forellenfang, *der*

trowel ['traʊəl] *n.* **a)** Kelle, *die;* **lay it on with a ~** *(fig.)* [es] dick auftragen *(ugs. abwertend);* **b)** *(Hort.)* Pflanzkelle, *die*

Troy [trɔɪ] *pr. n.* Troja *(das)*

troy *n.* **~ [weight]** Troygewicht, *das*

truancy ['tru:ənsɪ] *n.* [Schule]schwänzen, *das (ugs.);* unentschuldigtes Fernbleiben vom Unterricht; **be expelled for ~:** wegen Schwänzerei der Schule verwiesen werden

truant ['tru:ənt] **1.** *n.* [Schul]schwänzer, *der/*-schwänzerin, *die (ugs.);* **play ~:** [die Schule] schwänzen *(ugs.).* **2.** *adj.* [schule]schwänzend *(ugs.).* **3.** *v. i.* schwänzen *(ugs.);* unentschuldigt fehlen

truce [tru:s] *n.* Waffenstillstand, *der;* **call a ~:** einen Waffenstillstand schließen; *see also* **[1]flag 1**

[1]truck [trʌk] **1.** *n.* **a)** *(road vehicle)* Last[kraft]wagen, *der;* Lkw, *der;* **b)** *(Brit. Railw.: wagon)* offener Güterwagen; **c)** *(porter's barrow)* Gepäckkarren, *der;* **d)** *(Railw.: bogie)* Drehgestell, *das;* **e)** *(wheeled stand)* Hund, *der.* **2.** *v. t.* [per Lastwagen] transportieren. **3.** *v. i. (Amer.)* Lastwagen fahren

[2]truck *n.* **a) have no ~ with sb./sth.** *(fig.)* mit jmdm./etw. nichts zu tun haben; **b)** *(Amer.: produce)* Gemüse, *das;* **~ farm** Gemüsebaubetrieb, *der*

'truck driver *n.* Lastwagenfahrer, *der/*-fahrerin, *die; (long-distance)* Fernfahrer, *der/*-fahrerin, *die*

trucker ['trʌkə(r)] *n. (Amer.)* **a)** *(market gardener)* Gemüsegärtner, *der/*-gärtnerin, *die;* **b)** *see* **truck driver**

trucking ['trʌkɪŋ] *n. (Amer.)* Lkw-Fahren, *das; (as business)* Lkw-Transport, *der*

truckle ['trʌkl] *v. i.* **~ [to sb.]** [jmdm. gegenüber] klein beigeben; *(fawn)* [vor jmdm.] kriechen

'truckle-bed *n.* Rollbett, *das*

'truck-load *n.* Wagenladung, *die;* **sand by the ~:** ganze Wagenladungen Sand

truculence ['trʌkjʊləns], **truculency** ['trʌkjʊlənsɪ] *ns., no pl.* Aufsässigkeit, *die*

truculent ['trʌkjʊlənt] *adj.* aufsässig

truculently ['trʌkjʊləntlɪ] *adv.* aufsässig

trudge [trʌdʒ] **1.** *v. i.* trotten; *(through mud, snow, etc.)* stapfen. **2.** *v. t.* entlangtrotten; *(through mud, snow, etc.)* entlangstapfen. **3.** *n.* [beschwerlicher] Fußmarsch

true [tru:] **1.** *adj.,* **~r** ['tru:ə(r)], **~st** ['tru:ɪst] **a)** *(in accordance with fact)* wahr; wahrheitsgetreu ‹*Bericht, Beschreibung*›; **is it ~ that ...?** stimmt es, daß ...?; **[only] too ~:** nur zu wahr; **that is too good to be ~:** das ist zu schön, um wahr zu sein; **sb. is too good to be ~:** jmd. ist einfach zu gut; **[that's] ~ [enough]** [das] stimmt; **..., it is ~:** ..., das stimmt; **you never spoke a ~r word** da hast du wirklich recht; **he is so rude, it isn't ~** *(coll.)* er ist unglaublich unhöflich; **come ~** ‹*Traum, Wunsch:*› Wirklichkeit werden, wahr werden; ‹*Befürchtung, Prophezeihung:*› sich bewahrheiten; **b)** richtig ‹*Vorteil, Einschätzung*›; *(rightly so called)* eigentlich; **the frog is not a ~ reptile** der Frosch ist kein echtes Reptil; **c)** *(not sham)* wahr; echt, wahr ‹*Freund, Freundschaft, Christ*›; **that's not a ~ antique** das ist keine echte Antiquität; **d)** *(accurately conforming)* getreu ‹*Wiedergabe*›; **be ~ to sth.** einer Sache *(Dat.)* genau entsprechen; **~ to type** typisch; **~ to life** lebensecht; **e)** *(loyal)* treu; **remain ~ to sth.** einer Sache *(Dat.)* treu bleiben; **~ to one's word** *or* **promise** getreu seinem Versprechen; **f)** *(in correct position)* gerade ‹*Pfosten*›; **g)** *(Geog.)* **~ north** geographischer Norden. *See also* **colour 1 e, h; form 1 g. 2.** *n.* **out of [the] ~:** schief ‹*Mauer, Pfosten, Räder*›. **3.** *adv.* **a)** *(truthfully)* aufrichtig ‹*lieben*›; **speak ~:** die Wahrheit sagen; **tell me ~:** sag mir die Wahrheit; **b)** *(accurately)* gerade; genau ‹*zielen*›; **c)** *(without variation)* ohne Veränderung. **4.** *v. t.* **~ [up]** richten; *(alter shape of)* zurichten; *(balance)* auswuchten ‹*Rad*›

true: ~-blue 1. *adj.* in der Wolle gefärbt; **~-blue Tory** Erzkonservative, *der/die;* **2.** *n.* Hundertfünfzigprozentige, *der/die (abwertend);* **~-born** *adj.* echt; rechtmäßig ‹*Erbe*›; **~-life** *adj.* aus dem Leben gegriffen ‹*Geschichte, Drama*›; **this is a ~-life story** diese Geschichte hat das Leben geschrieben; **~-love** *n.* Geliebte, *der/die;* Schatz, *der;* **~-love knot** *n.: komplizierter Schleifenknoten, der das feste Band der Liebe symbolisiert*

trueness ['tru:nɪs] *n., no pl.* **a)** *(loyalty)* Treue, *die;* **b)** *(conformity)* genaue Entsprechung; **~ to life** Lebensechtheit, *die;* **c)** *(correctness)* Paßgenauigkeit, *die; (of wheel)* rundes Laufen

truffle ['trʌfl] *n.* Trüffel, *die od. (ugs.) der*

truism ['tru:ɪzm] *n.* Binsenweisheit, *die*

truly ['tru:lɪ] *adv.* **a)** *(genuinely)* wirklich; **be ~ grateful** wirklich sehr *od.* aufrichtig dankbar sein; **he was first, ~ he was!** er war Erster, ganz bestimmt!; **~, I don't think he will make it** ehrlich gesagt, ich glaube nicht, daß er es schafft; **b)** *(accurately)* zutreffend, richtig ‹*darstellen, sagen*›; **c)** *(faithfully)* treu; *see also* **really; [2]well 2 b; yours c**

[1]trump [trʌmp] **1.** *n. (Cards)* Trumpf, *der;* **play a ~** *(lit. or fig.)* einen Trumpf ausspielen; **turn up ~s** *(Brit. coll.) (turn out better than expected)* doch noch ein voller Erfolg werden; *(do the right thing)* die Situation retten; **as usual Bertha turned up ~s** wie immer hat Bertha wahre Wunder vollbracht; **hold all the ~s** *(fig.)* alle Trümpfe in der Hand haben *od.* halten. **2.** *v. t.* übertrumpfen. **3.** *v. i.* Trumpf spielen

~ up *v. t. (coll.)* konstruieren; **~ed up charge** falsche Beschuldigung

[2]trump *n. (arch./poet.: trumpet)* Trompete, *die; see also* **last trump**

'trump card *n. (lit. or fig.)* Trumpf, *der;* **play one's ~** *(lit. or fig.)* seinen [größten *od.* stärksten] Trumpf ausspielen

trumpery ['trʌmpərɪ] *(dated)* **1.** *n.* **a)** *(worthless articles)* Krimskrams, *der (ugs.);* **b)** *(rubbish)* Unsinn, *der;* **trumperies** Firlefanz, *der;* **c)** *(worthless finery)* Tand, *der (veralt.).* **2.** *adj. (showy but worthless)* billig

trumpet ['trʌmpɪt] **1.** *n. (Mus., Bot.)* Trompete, *die;* **~ blast** Trompetenstoß, *der; see also* **blow 2 d. 2.** *v. t. & i.* trompeten

'trumpet call *n.* Trompetensignal, *das; (fig.)* Aufruf, *der*

trumpeter ['trʌmpɪtə(r)] *n.* Trompeter, *der/*Trompeterin, *die*

truncate [trʌŋ'keɪt] *v. t.* **a)** stutzen ‹*Baum, Spitze*›; **~d cone/pyramid** stumpfer Kegel/stumpfe Pyramide; **b)** *(fig.)* kürzen

truncheon ['trʌntʃn] *n.* Schlagstock, *der*

trundle ['trʌndl] *v. t. & i.* rollen

trunk [trʌŋk] *n.* **a)** *(of elephant etc.)* Rüssel, *der;* **b)** *(large box)* Schrankkoffer, *der;* **c)** *(of tree)* Stamm, *der;* **d)** *(of human or animal body)* Rumpf, *der;* **e)** *(Amer.: of car)* Kofferraum, *der;* **f)** *in pl. (Brit.: shorts)* Unterhose, *die;* **[swimming] ~s** Badehose, *die;* **g)** *(of nerve, artery, etc.)* Stamm, *der*

'trunk-call *n.* Ferngespräch, *das*

trunk: ~-line *n. (Railw.)* Hauptstrecke, *die; (Teleph.)* Fernleitung, *die;* **~-road** *n. (Brit.)* Fernstraße, *die*

truss [trʌs] **1.** *n.* **a)** *(of roof etc.)* Gebälk, *das; (of bridge)* Sprengwerk, *das;* **~ joint** Fachwerkknoten, *der;* **~ post** Hängesäule, *die;* **b)** *(of flowers etc.)* Büschel, *das; (of tomatoes)* Fruchttraube, *die (Landw.);* **c)** *(Med.: belt)* Bruchband, *das;* **d)** *(Brit.: of hay)* Bündel, *das;* Ballen, *der.* **2.** *v. t.* **a)** *(tie up before cooking)* dressieren ‹*Truthahn, Huhn*›; **b) ~ [up]** fesseln

trust [trʌst] **1.** *n.* **a)** *(firm belief)* Vertrauen, *das;* **place** *or* **put one's ~ in sb./sth.** sein Vertrauen auf *od.* in jmdn./etw. setzen; **have [every] ~ in sb./sth.** [volles] Vertrauen zu jmdm./etw. haben; **our ~ is in God** wir vertrauen auf Gott; **I don't have any ~ in him** ich vertraue ihm nicht; ich habe kein Vertrauen zu ihm; **b)** *(reliance)* **take sth. on ~:** etw. einfach glauben; **c)** *(organization managed by trustees)* Treuhandgesellschaft, *die;* **[charitable] ~:** Stiftung, *die;* **d)** *(body of trustees)* Treuhänder *Pl.; (of charitable ~)* [Stiftungs]beirat, *der;* Kuratorium, *das;* **e)** *(organized association of companies)* Trust, *der;* **f)** *(commercial credit)* **on ~:** auf Kredit; **g)** *(responsibility)* **he failed in his ~:** er hat das in ihn gesetzte Vertrauen enttäuscht; **position of ~:** Vertrauensstellung, *die;* **h)** *(obligation)* Verpflichtung, *die;* **public ~:** Verpflichtung der Öffentlichkeit gegenüber; **i)** *(Law)* Treuhand[schaft], *die; (property)* Treugut, *das;* **hold in ~:** treuhänderisch verwalten. *See also* **brains trust; investment a; unit trust. 2.** *v. t.* **a)** *(rely on)* trauen (+ *Dat.*); vertrauen (+ *Dat.*) ‹*Person*›; **not ~ sb. an inch** jmdm. nicht über den Weg trauen; **you can ~ him to do his best** du kannst dich darauf verlassen, daß er sein Bestes tut; **a ~ed servant/friend** ein getreuer Diener/Freund *(geh.);* **he was widely ~ed by them** er genoß *od.* besaß das Vertrauen der meisten von ihnen; **he/what he says is not to be ~ed** er ist nicht vertrauenswürdig/auf das, was er sagt, kann man sich nicht verlassen; **~ sb. with sth.** jmdm. etw. anvertrauen; **~ 'you/'him!** *etc. (coll. iron.)* typisch!; **~ 'him to get it wrong!** er muß natürlich einen Fehler machen!; **b)** *(hope)* hoffen; **I ~ he is not hurt?** er ist doch hoffentlich nicht verletzt?; **c)** *(entrust)* anvertrauen (**to** *Dat.*). **3.** *v. i.* **a) ~ to** sich verlassen auf (+ *Akk.*); **b)** *(believe)* **~ in sb./sth.** auf jmdn./etw. vertrauen

trust: ~-buster *n.: jmd., der [auf der Grundlage der Antitrustgesetze] gegen Trusts vorgeht;* **~ company** *n.* Treuhandgesellschaft, *die;* **~-deed** *n.* Treuhandvertrag, *der*

trustee [trʌ'sti:] *n.* **a)** *(person holding*

property in trust; also fig.) Treuhänder, *der*/Treuhänderin, *die;* **the Public T~** *(Brit.)* der staatliche Vermögensverwalter; **b)** *(one appointed to manage institution)* Verwalter, *der;* Kurator, *der;* **Board of T~s** Vorstand, *der;* Kuratorium, *das;* **c)** *(country supervising territory)* Treuhandmacht, *die*
trusteeship [trʌ'sti:ʃɪp] *n.* **a)** *(office)* Treuhänderschaft, *die;* **b)** *(supervision of trust territory)* Treuhandschaft, *die;* Mandat, *das*
trustful ['trʌstfl] *adj.*, **trustfully** ['trʌstfəlɪ] *adv.* vertrauensvoll
'trust fund *n.* Treuhandvermögen, *das*
trusting ['trʌstɪŋ] *adj.*, **trustingly** ['trʌstɪŋlɪ] *adv.* vertrauensvoll
trustworthiness ['trʌstwɜ:ðɪnɪs] *n., no pl.* Vertrauenswürdigkeit, *die*
trustworthy ['trʌstwɜ:ðɪ] *adj.* vertrauenswürdig
trusty ['trʌstɪ] **1.** *adj. (arch./joc.)* [ge]treu *(dichter.).* **2.** *n.* Kalfaktor, *der*
truth [tru:θ] *n., pl.* ~s [tru:ðz, tru:θs] **a)** *no pl.* Wahrheit, *die;* **the ~ of that is open to question** es ist fraglich, ob das zutrifft; **there is some/not a word of** *or* **no ~ in that** es ist etwas Wahres/kein wahres Wort/nichts Wahres daran; **in ~** *(literary),* **of a ~** *(arch.)* wahrlich *(geh.);* **b)** *(what is true)* Wahrheit, *die; (principle)* Grundsatz, *der;* **tell the [whole] ~:** die [ganze] Wahrheit sagen; **the ~ is that I forgot** um ehrlich zu sein, ich habe es vergessen; **to tell the ~, ~ to tell** ehrlich gesagt. *See also* **moment a; out 1 h**
'truth drug *n.* Wahrheitsdroge, *die*
truthful ['tru:θfl] *adj.* ehrlich; wahrheitsgetreu ‹*Darstellung, Schilderung*›; **be ~ about sth.** die Wahrheit über etw. *(Akk.)* sagen
truthfully ['tru:θfəlɪ] *adv.* ehrlich
truthfulness ['tru:θflnɪs] *n., no pl.* Wahrheitstreue, *die*
try [traɪ] **1.** *n.* **a)** *(attempt)* Versuch, *der;* **have a ~ at sth./doing sth.** etw. versuchen/versuchen, etw. zu tun; **at least he had a good ~:** er hat sich *(Dat.)* wenigstens Mühe gegeben; **give sb./sth. a ~:** jmdm. eine Chance geben/etw. einmal ausprobieren; **I'll give him another ~** *(ask him again for help, a favour, etc.)* ich versuche es noch einmal bei ihm; *(give him another chance)* ich versuche es noch einmal mit ihm; *(on telephone)* ich versuche noch einmal, ihn zu erreichen; **give it a ~:** es versuchen; **b)** *(Rugby)* Versuch, *der;* **score two tries** zwei Versuche erzielen *od.* legen; **c)** *(Amer. Footb.)* Versuch, noch einen Punkt zu erzielen. **2.** *v. t.* **a)** *(attempt, make effort)* versuchen; **it's ~ing to rain** es tröpfelt ein wenig; **the sun is ~ing to come out** *or* **shine** es sieht so aus, als käme die Sonne bald heraus; **do ~ to be on time** bitte versuche, pünktlich zu sein; **it's no use ~ing to do sth.** es hat keinen Zweck zu versuchen, etw. zu tun; **I've given up ~ing to do sth.** ich versuche schon gar nicht mehr, etw. zu tun; **~ one's best** sein Bestes tun; **don't ~ anything!** keine Tricks!; **don't even ~ to excuse yourself** versuche erst gar nicht, dich zu entschuldigen; **b)** *(test usefulness of)* probieren; **if the stain is difficult to remove, ~ soap and water** wenn der Fleck schwer zu entfernen ist, versuche *od.* probiere es doch mal mit Wasser und Seife; **I've tried all the bookshops for this book** ich habe in allen Buchhandlungen versucht, dieses Buch zu bekommen; **you can always ~ the supermarket** du kannst es auf jeden Fall mal im Supermarkt versuchen; **if you can't find it, ~ the top shelf** wenn du es nicht finden kannst, schau mal auf dem obersten Regal nach; **~ one's hand at sth.** sich an etw. *(Dat.)* versuchen; **~ shaking it!** probier es mal mit Schütteln!; **I'll ~ anything once** ich probiere alles einmal aus; **c)** *(test)* auf die Probe stellen ‹*Fähigkeit, Kraft, Mut, Geduld*›; **~ the rope** ausprobieren, ob das Seil auch hält; **~ the door/window [to see if it's locked]** versuchen, die Tür/das Fenster zu öffnen[, um zu sehen, ob sie/es verschlossen ist]; **~ sb. in Sales** jmdn. zur Probe im Verkauf einsetzen; **be tried and found wanting** gewogen und zu leicht befunden werden; **these** *or* **such things are sent to ~ us** das sind die Prüfungen, die uns das Schicksal auferlegt; **d)** *(Law.: take to trial)* **~ a case** einen Fall verhandeln; **~ sb. [for sth.]** jmdn. [wegen einer Sache] vor Gericht stellen; jmdm. [wegen einer Sache] den Prozeß machen; **he was tried for murder** er stand wegen Mordes vor Gericht; **he was tried before a jury** er wurde vor ein Schwurgericht gestellt. *See also* **fall 1 i; ¹size 1 a. 3.** *v. i.* es versuchen; **she wasn't even ~ing** sie hat sich *(Dat.)* überhaupt keine Mühe gegeben *od.* es gar nicht erst versucht; **it was not for want of ~ing** es lag nicht daran, daß er/sie *usw.* sich nicht bemüht hätte; **if at first you don't succeed, ~, ~, ~ again** wenn es dir nicht gleich gelingt, mußt du es immer wieder versuchen; **you can't say I didn't ~:** du kannst nicht sagen, daß ich es nicht versucht hätte; **~ as he might** sosehr er sich auch bemühte; **~ and do sth.** *(coll.)* versuchen, etw. zu tun; **~ hard/harder** sich *(Dat.)* viel/mehr Mühe geben
~ for *v. t.* **a)** *(compete for)* sich bemühen um ‹*Arbeitsstelle, Stipendium*›; kämpfen um ‹*Sieg im Sport*›; **~ for gold** es auf eine Goldmedaille abgesehen haben; **b)** *(seek to reach)* **~ for the summit** den Gipfel in Angriff nehmen; **he had been ~ing so hard for it** er hatte so sehr darum gekämpft
~ 'on *v. t.* **a)** anprobieren ‹*Kleidungsstück*›; **b)** *(Brit. coll.)* **~ it on** provozieren; **don't ~ anything/it on with me** lege dich nicht mit mir an; *see also* **try-on**
~ 'out *v. t.* **~ sth./sb. out** etw. ausprobieren/jmdm. eine Chance geben; **let's ~ him out in Sales** setzen wir ihn doch zur Probe im Verkauf ein; *see also* **try-out**
trying ['traɪɪŋ] *adj.* **a)** *(testing)* schwierig; **b)** *(difficult to endure)* anstrengend; **be ~ for sb./sth.** jmdm./einer Sache sehr zusetzen *(ugs.)*
try: ~-on *n. (coll.)* **a)** *(Brit. joke)* Scherz, *der; (lie)* Lüge, *die;* **it's just a ~-on** *(to discover whether sth. will be tolerated)* er/sie probiert nur aus, wie weit er/sie gehen kann; **b)** *(of clothes)* Anprobe, *die;* **~-out** *n.* Erprobung, *die;* **give sth. a ~-out** etw. ausprobieren; **have a ~-out** ‹*Maschine usw.:*› ausprobiert werden; **would you like [to have] a ~-out?** möchten Sie mal probieren?; *(of vehicle)* möchten Sie eine Probefahrt machen?; **~-sail** ['traɪsl] *n. (Naut.)* Gaffelsegel, *das;* **~-square** *n.* Anschlagwinkel, *der*
tryst [trɪst] *n. (arch./literary)* Stelldichein, *das (veralt.);* **keep/break ~:** zu einem Stelldichein gehen/nicht gehen; **make a ~:** sich zu einem Stelldichein verabreden
tsar [zɑ:(r)] *n. (Hist.)* Zar, *der*
tsarina [zɑ:'ri:nə] *n. (Hist.) (empress)* Zarin, *die; (tsar's wife)* Zariza, *die*
tsarism ['zɑ:rɪzm] *n. (Hist.)* Zarentum, *das;* Zarismus, *der*
tsarist ['zɑ:rɪst] *(Hist.)* **1.** *adj.* zaristisch. **2.** *n.* Zarist, *der*/Zaristin, *die*
tsetse [fly] ['tsetsɪ (flaɪ)] *n.* Tsetsefliege, *die*
T-shirt *n.* T-Shirt, *das*
tsp., *pl.* **tsps** *abbr.* **teaspoon[s]** Teel.
T-square *see* **square j**
TT *abbr.* **a) teetotal; b) Tourist Trophy** *Motorradrennen auf der Insel Man*
TU *abbr.* **Trade Union**
Tu. *abbr.* **Tuesday** Di.
tub [tʌb] *n.* **a)** Kübel, *der;* **b)** *(for ice-cream etc.)* Becher, *der;* **c)** *(Brit. coll.: bath)* Bad, *das;* **d)** *(derog./joc.: boat)* Kahn, *der (ugs.)*
tuba ['tju:bə] *n. (Mus.)* Tuba, *die*
tubbiness ['tʌbɪnɪs] *n.* Rundlichkeit, *die; (of child also)* Pummeligkeit, *die (ugs.)*
tubby ['tʌbɪ] *adj.* rundlich; pummelig *(ugs.),* rundlich ‹*Kind*›
tube [tju:b] *n.* **a)** *(for conveying liquids etc.)* Rohr, *das;* **be down the tube[s]** *(sl.)* am Ende sein *(ugs.);* **he was down the ~[s] to the tune of £270,000** *(sl.)* er saß mit Schulden in Höhe von 270 000 Pfund in der Tinte *(ugs.);* **go down the ~[s]** *(sl.)* den Bach runter gehen *(ugs.);* **b)** *(small cylinder)* Tube, *die; (for sweets, tablets)* Röhrchen, *das;* **c)** *(Anat., Zool.)* Röhre, *die;* **d)** *(cathode-ray ~)* Röhre, *die; (coll.: television)* **watch the ~:** vor der Röhre sitzen *(ugs.);* **be on the ~:** im Fernsehen sein; **e)** *(Amer.: thermionic valve)* Röhre, *die;* **f)** *(Brit. coll.: underground railway)* U-Bahn, *die;* **g)** *see* **inner tube**
tubeless ['tju:blɪs] *adj.* schlauchlos ‹*Reifen*›
tuber ['tju:bə(r)] *n. (Bot.)* Knolle, *die*
tubercle ['tju:bəkl] *n. (Med.)* Tuberkel, *der*
tubercular [tju:'bɜ:kjʊlə(r)] *adj. (Med.)* tuberkulös
tuberculin [tju:'bɜ:kjʊlɪn] *n.* Tuberkulin, *das*
tuberculin-'tested *adj.* tuberkulingetestet
tuberculosis [tju:bɜ:kjʊ'ləʊsɪs] *n., no pl. (Med.)* Tuberkulose, *die;* **pulmonary ~:** Lungentuberkulose, *die*
tuberose ['tju:bərəʊz] *n. (Bot.)* Tuberose, *die*
tube: ~ station *n. (Brit. coll.)* U-Bahnhof, *der;* **~ train** *n. (Brit. coll.)* U-Bahn-Zug, *der*
tubful ['tʌbfʊl] *n.* Kübel [voll], *der;* **a ~ of water** ein Kübel Wasser
tubing ['tju:bɪŋ] *n.* Rohre *Pl.*
'tub-thumper *n.* Demagoge, *der*
tubular ['tju:bjʊlə(r) *adj.* **a)** *(tube-shaped)* rohrförmig; **b)** *(made of ~ pieces)* Stahlrohr‹*möbel, -stuhl*›
tubular 'bells *n. pl.* Glockenspiel, *das*
TUC *abbr. (Brit.)* **Trades Union Congress**
tuck [tʌk] **1.** *v. t.* **a)** stecken; **he ~ed his legs under him** er schlug die Beine unter; **b)** *(put ~s in)* Biesen nähen in (+ *Akk.*). **2.** *n.* **a)** *(in fabric) (for decoration)* Biese, *die; (to shorten or tighten)* Abnäher, *der;* **b)** *no pl., no indef. art. (Brit. Sch. coll.: food)* Erfrischungen [und Süßigkeiten]
~ a'way *v. t.* **a)** wegstecken; **the house is ~ed away behind the trees** das Haus liegt versteckt hinter den Bäumen; **b)** *(coll.: eat)* verputzen *(ugs.);* **she can certainly ~ it away** sie kann ganz schön was verputzen *(ugs.)*
~ 'in 1. *v. t.* hineinstecken; **~ in the blankets** die Decken an den Seiten feststecken; **~ your shirt in!** steck dein Hemd in die Hose! **2.** *v. i. (coll.)* zulangen *(ugs.); see also* **tuck-in**
~ into *v. i. (coll.: eat)* **~ into sth.** sich *(Dat.)* etw. schmecken lassen
~ 'up *v. t.* **a)** hochkrempeln ‹*Ärmel, Hose*›; hochnehmen ‹*Rock*›; **b)** *(cover snugly)* zudecken; **be ~ed up [in bed]** zugedeckt [im Bett] sein
'tuck-box *n. (Brit. Sch.)* Kiste [mit Süßigkeiten *usw.*]
¹tucker ['tʌkə(r)] *n. (Austral. coll.: food)* Futter, *das (ugs.);* **some ~:** etwas zu futtern *(ugs.)*
²tucker *v. t. (Amer.)* **~ [out]** *(coll.)* fix und fertig machen *(ugs.);* **be ~ed [out]** fix und fertig *od.* total groggy sein *(ugs.)*
tuck: ~-in *n. (Brit. coll.)* [reichliches] Essen; **they had a really good ~-in** sie hatten ordentlich was zu futtern *(ugs.);* **~-shop** *n. (Brit. Sch.) Laden für Erfrischungen, Süßigkeiten usw. in einer Schule*
Tudor ['tju:də(r)] *(Brit. Hist.)* **1.** *n.* Tudor, *der/die.* **2.** *attrib. adj.* Tudor-
Tudor: ~ 'rose *n.* Tudorrose, *die;* **~ style** *n.* Tudorstil, *der*
Tue., Tues. *abbrs.* **Tuesday** Di.
Tuesday ['tju:zdeɪ, 'tju:zdɪ] **1.** *n.* Dienstag, *der.* **2.** *adv. (coll.)* **she comes ~s** sie kommt dienstags. *See also* **Friday**

tufa ['tju:fə] *n. (Geol.)* Sinter, *der*
tuff [tʌf] *n. (Geol.)* Tuff, *der*
tuft [tʌft] *n.* Büschel, *das;* ~ **of grass/hair** Gras-/Haarbüschel, *das*
tufted ['tʌftɪd] *adj.* **a)** *(having tufts)* büschelig; ~ **carpet** Tuftingteppich, *der;* **b)** *(with tuft of feathers on head)* Hauben-; ~ **duck** Reiherente, *die;* ~ **puffin** Schopfhund, *der*
tug [tʌg] **1.** *n.* **a)** Ruck, *der;* **he felt a ~ on the fishing-line** er spürte, wie etwas an der Angel zog; **he gave the rope a ~:** er zerrte am Seil; ~ **of love [battle]** *(coll.) Streit bei der Ehescheidung, wem das Kind zugesprochen wird;* ~**-of-war** *(lit. or fig.)* Tauziehen, *das;* **b)** ~ **[boat]** Schlepper, *der;* **c)** *(fig.: emotional pain)* **it was a ~:** es tat weh *(ugs.);* **she felt a big ~ at parting** der Abschied fiel ihr sehr schwer. **2.** *v. t.*, **-gg-** ziehen; schleppen ‹*Boot*›; **be ~ged this way and that** *(fig.)* hin- und hergerissen sein. **3.** *v. i.*, **-gg-** zerren (**at** an + *Dat.*); ~ **at sb.'s heart-strings** *(fig.)* jmdm. das Herz zerreißen
tuition [tju:'ɪʃn] *n.* Unterricht, *der;* **extra ~:** Nachhilfeunterricht, *der;* ~ **fees** *(Sch.)* Schulgeld, *das; (Univ.)* Studiengebühren *Pl.; (for private ~)* Unterrichtshonorar, *das*
tulip ['tju:lɪp] *n.* Tulpe, *die*
'**tulip-tree** *n.* Tulpenbaum, *der*
tulle [tju:l] *n. (Textiles)* Tüll, *der*
tum [tʌm] *n. (joc.)* Bauch, *der*
tumble ['tʌmbl] **1.** *v. i.* **a)** *(fall suddenly)* stürzen; fallen; ~ **off sth.** von etw. fallen; **b)** *(move in headlong fashion)* stürzen; ~ **into/out of sth.** in/aus etw. eilen; ~ **into bed** ins Bett fallen; **c)** ‹*Preise usw.:*› fallen; *(sharply)* stürzen. **2.** *v. t.* **a)** *(fling headlong)* schleudern; **b)** *(rumple)* durcheinanderbringen, zerzausen ‹*Haar*›. **3.** *n.* Sturz, *der;* **she's taken [a bit of] a ~:** sie ist hingefallen
~ **on** *v. t. (chance on)* stolpern über (+ *Akk.*)
~ '**over** *v. i.* hinfallen; ‹*Kartenhaus:*› umfallen
~ **to** *v. t. (Brit. coll.)* durchschauen
tumble: ~**-bug** *n.* Kotkäfer, *der;* ~**down** *adj.* verfallen; ~**-drier** *n.* Wäschetrockner, *der;* ~**dry** *v. t.* im Automaten trocknen
tumbler ['tʌmblə(r)] *n.* **a)** *(glass) (short)* Whiskyglas, *das; (long)* Wasserglas, *das;* **b)** *(in lock)* Zuhaltung, *die;* **c)** *see* **tumble-drier; d)** *(acrobat)* Bodenakrobat, *der*/-akrobatin, *die;* **e)** *(pigeon)* Tümmler, *der*
tumblerful ['tʌmbləfʊl] *n.* Glas[voll], *das;* **a ~ of water** ein Glas Wasser
'**tumbler switch** *n.* Kippschalter, *der*
'**tumble-weed** *n. (Amer.)* Steppenläufer, *der*
tumbrel ['tʌmbrl], **tumbril** ['tʌmbrɪl] *n. (Hist.)* Karren, *der*
tumescence [tjʊ'mesəns] *n.* Schwellung, *die*
tumescent [tju:'mesənt] *adj.* anschwellend; **make ~:** anschwellen lassen
tummy ['tʌmɪ] *n. (child lang./coll.)* Bäuchlein, *das;* **I've got an upset ~:** ich habe mir den Magen verdorben
tummy: ~**-ache** *n. (child lang./coll.)* Bauchweh, *das;* ~**-button** *n. (child lang./coll.)* Bauchnabel, *der;* ~ **upset** *n. (child lang./coll.)* Magenverstimmung, *die*
tumour *(Brit.; Amer.:* **tumor**) ['tju:mə(r)] *n.* Tumor, *der*
tumult ['tju:mʌlt] *n.* **a)** *(commotion, uproar)* Tumult, *der;* **be in ~:** sich in Aufruhr befinden; **b)** *(confused state of mind)* Verwirrung, *die;* **his mind was in a ~:** er war innerlich in Aufruhr
tumultuous [tju:'mʌltjʊəs] *adj.* **a)** stürmisch ‹*Empfang, Beifall*›; **b)** wild ‹*Fluß, Sturm, Leidenschaft*›
tumulus ['tju:mjʊləs] *n., pl.* **tumuli** ['tju:mjʊlaɪ] Tumulus, *der*
tun [tʌn] *n.* Faß, *das*
tuna ['tju:nə] *n., pl. same or* ~**s a)** *(fish)* Thunfisch, *der;* **b)** *(as food)* ~**[-fish]** Thunfisch, *der; attrib.* Thunfisch-
tundra ['tʌndrə] *n. (Geog.)* Tundra, *die*
tune [tju:n] **1.** *n.* **a)** *(melody)* Melodie, *die;* **change one's ~, sing another** *or* **a different ~** *(fig.) (behave differently)* sein Verhalten ändern; *(assume different tone)* einen anderen Ton anschlagen; **call the ~:** den Ton angeben; **b)** *(correct pitch)* **sing in/out of ~:** richtig/falsch singen; **be in/out of ~** ‹*Instrument:*› richtig gestimmt/verstimmt sein; **c)** *(fig.: agreement)* **be in/out of ~ with sth.** mit etw. in Einklang/nicht in Einklang stehen; **he doesn't feel in ~ with their attitudes/ideas** ihre Einstellungen/Vorstellungen sind ihm fremd; **d)** *(amount)* **to the ~ of [£50,000]** sage und schreibe [50 000 Pfund]. **2.** *v. t.* **a)** *(Mus.: put in ~)* stimmen; **b)** *(Radio, Telev.)* einstellen (**to** auf + *Akk.*); **stay ~d!** bleiben Sie auf dieser Welle!; **c)** einstellen ‹*Motor, Vergaser*›; *(for more power)* frisieren ‹*Motor, Auto*›
~ '**in** *v. i. (Radio, Telev.)* ~ **in to a station** einen Sender einstellen; ~ **in at five o'clock to hear the details!** schalten Sie [Ihr Radio/Ihren Fernseher] um fünf Uhr ein, wenn Sie die Einzelheiten hören wollen; ~ **in to** *(fig.)* sich einstellen auf (+ *Akk.*)
~ '**up 1.** *v. i.* [die Instrumente] stimmen. **2.** *v. t.* einstellen
tuneful ['tju:nfl] *adj.*, **tunefully** ['tju:nfəlɪ] *adv.* melodisch
tunefulness ['tju:nflnɪs] *n., no pl.* Melodik, *die*
tuneless ['tju:nlɪs] *adj.*, **tunelessly** ['tju:nlɪslɪ] *adv.* unmelodisch
tunelessness ['tju:nlɪsnɪs] *n., no pl.* Mangel an Melodik
tuner ['tju:nə(r)] *n.* **a)** *(Mus.)* Stimmer, *der*/Stimmerin, *die;* **b)** *(knob etc.)* Einstellknopf, *der;* Tuner, *der (Technik);* **c)** *(radio)* Tuner, *der*
tungsten ['tʌŋstən] *n.* Wolfram, *das*
tunic ['tju:nɪk] *n.* **a)** *(part of uniform) (of soldier, policeman)* Uniformjacke, *die; (of schoolgirl)* Kittel, *der;* **b)** *(Fashion)* Kasack, *der;* **c)** *(body-garment) (in ancient Greece)* Chiton, *der; (in ancient Rome)* Tunika, *die*
tuning ['tju:nɪŋ] *n.* **a)** *(Mus.)* Stimmen, *das;* **b)** *(Radio)* Einstellen, *das;* **c)** *(Motor Veh.)* Einstellen, *das; (to increase power)* Frisieren, *das;* Tuning, *das;* **the engine needs ~:** der Motor muß eingestellt werden
tuning: ~**-fork** *n. (Mus.)* Stimmgabel, *die;* ~**-peg,** ~**-pin** *ns. (Mus.)* Wirbel, *der*
Tunis ['tju:nɪs] *pr. n.* Tunis *(das)*
Tunisia [tju:'nɪzɪə] *pr. n.* Tunesien *(das)*
Tunisian [tju:'nɪzɪən] **1.** *adj.* tunesisch; **sb. is ~:** jmd. ist Tunesier/Tunesierin. **2.** *n.* Tunesier, *der*/Tunesierin, *die*
tunnel ['tʌnl] **1.** *n.* **a)** Tunnel, *der; (dug by animal)* Gang, *der;* **b)** *(Motor Veh.)* **[transmission] ~:** Kardantunnel, *der;* **c) wind ~:** Windkanal, *der.* **2.** *v. i.*, *(Brit.)* **-ll-** einen Tunnel graben; ~ **under sth.** etw. untertunneln; ~ **through sth.** durch etw. *(Akk.)* einen Tunnel graben. **3.** *v. t.*, *(Brit.)* **-ll-** ~ **one's way out** sich *(Dat.)* einen Weg nach draußen graben
'**tunnel vision** *n.* Röhrengesichtsfeld, *das (Med.); (fig.)* enges Blickfeld
tunny ['tʌnɪ] *n. (Zool.)* Thunfisch, *der*
tup [tʌp] *n. (Brit.)* Widder, *der*
tuppence ['tʌpəns] *see* **twopence**
tuppenny ['tʌpənɪ] *see* **twopenny**
turban ['tɜ:bən] *n.* Turban, *der*
turbaned ['tɜ:bənd] *adj.* mit einem Turban [auf dem Kopf] *nachgestellt*
turbid ['tɜ:bɪd] *adj.* **a)** *(muddy)* trüb[e]; dicht ‹*Nebel, Rauchwolke*›; **b)** *(fig.: confused)* wirr
turbidity [tɜ:'bɪdɪtɪ] *n., no pl.* **a)** *(muddiness)* Trübheit, *die;* **b)** *(fig.: confusion)* Verworrenheit, *die*
turbine ['tɜ:baɪn] *n.* Turbine, *die*
turbo ['tɜ:bəʊ] *n. (coll.)* Turbo, *der*
turbo: ~**-charged** *adj.* mit Turbolader *nachgestellt;* ~**-charger** *n.* Turbolader, *der;* ~**-jet** *n.* Turbojet, *der;* ~**-jet engine** *n.* Turboluftstrahltriebwerk, *das;* ~**-prop** *n.* Turbo-Prop-Flugzeug, *das;* ~**-prop engine** Turbo-Prop-Triebwerk, *das*
turbot ['tɜ:bət] *n. (Zool.)* Steinbutt, *der*
turbulence ['tɜ:bjʊləns] *n., no pl.* **a)** *(agitation)* Aufgewühltheit, *die; (fig.)* Aufruhr, *der; (unruliness)* Unruhe, *die;* **b)** *(Phys.)* Turbulenz, *die*
turbulent ['tɜ:bjʊlənt] *adj.* **a)** aufgewühlt ‹*Gedanken, Wellen, Leidenschaften*›; turbulent ‹*Herrschaft, Kindheit*›; ungestüm ‹*Menge*›; aufrührerisch ‹*Stadt, Mob*›; **b)** *(Phys.)* turbulent
turd [tɜ:d] *n. (coarse)* **a)** *(lump of excrement)* Scheißhaufen, *der (derb);* **b)** *(contemptible person)* Scheißkerl, *der (derb)*
tureen [tjʊə'ri:n] *n.* Terrine, *die*
turf [tɜ:f] **1.** *n., pl.* ~**s** *or* **turves** [tɜ:vz] **a)** *no pl. (covering of grass etc.)* Rasen, *der;* **b)** *(cut patch of grass)* [abgestochenes] Rasenstück; Sode, *die (bes. nordd.);* **lay ~:** Fertigrasen verlegen; **c) the ~** *(racecourse)* der Turf *(Pferdesport);* die Rennbahn; *(horse-racing)* der Pferderennsport. **2.** *v. t.* mit Fertigrasen bedecken
~ '**out** *v. t. (sl.)* rausschmeißen *(ugs.);* ~ **sb. out of sth.** jmdn. aus etw. [raus]schmeißen
~ '**over** *v. t.* mit Rasenstücken bedecken
'**turf accountant** *n.* Buchmacher, *der*
turgid ['tɜ:dʒɪd] *adj.* **a)** *(inflated)* [an]geschwollen; **b)** *(fig.)* geschwollen; schwülstig *(abwertend)*
turgidly ['tɜ:dʒɪdlɪ] *adv.* geschwollen *(abwertend)*
Turk [tɜ:k] *n.* Türke, *der*/Türkin, *die*
Turkey ['tɜ:kɪ] *pr. n.* die Türkei
turkey *n.* **a)** *(fowl)* Truthahn, *der*/Truthenne, *die; (esp. as food)* Puter, *der*/Pute, *die;* **b)** *(sl. derog.: stupid person)* Schwachkopf, *der (ugs. abwertend);* **c)** *(Amer. sl.: flop)* Reinfall, *der;* **d) talk ~** *(Amer. coll.)* Tacheles reden *(ugs.)*
turkey: ~ **buzzard** *n.* Truthahngeier, *der;* ~**cock** *n.* Truthahn, *der; (fig.)* Angeber, *der (abwertend);* **red as a ~cock** *(from heat or exertion)* krebsrot; *(with anger or embarrassment)* puterrot; ~ **vulture** *see* ~ **buzzard**
Turkish ['tɜ:kɪʃ] **1.** *adj.* türkisch; **sb. is ~:** jmd. ist Türke/Türkin; *see also* **English 1. 2.** *n.* Türkisch, *das; see also* **English 2 a**
Turkish: ~ '**bath** *n.* türkisches Bad; ~ **delight** *n. mit Puderzucker bestreutes, gelatinehaltiges Konfekt;* Rachatlukum, *das;* Lokum, *das;* ~ '**towel** *n.* Frotteehandtuch, *das*
Turk: ~**'s cap** *n. (Bot.)* Türkenbundlilie, *die;* ~**'s** '**head** *n. (knot)* türkischer Bund
turmeric ['tɜ:mərɪk] *n.* Gelbwurzel, *die; (spice)* Kurkuma, *die*
turmoil ['tɜ:mɔɪl] *n.* Aufruhr, *der;* [wildes] Durcheinander; **everything/her mind was in [a] ~:** es herrschte ein wildes Durcheinander/sie war völlig durcheinander
turn [tɜ:n] **1.** *n.* **a) it is sb.'s ~ to do sth.** jmd. ist an der Reihe, etw. zu tun; **it's your ~ [next]** du bist als nächster/nächste dran *(ugs.) od.* an der Reihe; **wait one's ~:** warten, bis man an der Reihe ist; **your ~ will come** du kommst auch [noch] an die Reihe; **by ~s** abwechselnd; **each of us in ~ had to give his name** wir mußten nacheinander *od.* der Reihe nach unsere Namen nennen; **he gave it to her, and she in ~ passed it on to me** er gab es ihr, und sie wiederum reichte es an mich weiter; **in one's ~:** wiederum; **out of ~** *(before or after one's ~)* außer der Reihe; *(fig.)* an der falschen Stelle ‹*lachen*›; **she tried to throw the dice out of ~:** sie wollte würfeln, obwohl sie nicht an der Reihe war; **excuse me if I'm talking out of ~** *(fig.)* entschuldige, wenn ich etwas Unpassendes sage; **your remark was out of ~** *(fig.)* Ihre

Bemerkung war fehl am Platz; **take a ~ at the wheel** für eine Weile das Steuer übernehmen; **take [it in] ~s** sich abwechseln; **take ~s at doing sth., take it in ~s to do sth.** etw. abwechselnd tun; **she was unhappy and cheerful, in ~s** sie war abwechselnd unglücklich und fröhlich; *see also* **about 1 f, g; serve 1 c; b)** *(rotary motion)* Drehung, *die;* **give the handle a ~:** den Griff [herum]drehen; **have/show a good ~ of speed** schnell sein; **put on a ~ of speed** einen Zahn zulegen *(ugs.);* **[done] to a ~:** genau richtig [zubereitet]; **c)** *(change of direction)* Wende, *die;* **take a ~ to the right/left, do** *or* **make** *or* **take a right/left ~:** nach rechts/links abbiegen; **'no left/right ~'** „links/rechts abbiegen verboten!"; **make a ~ to port/starboard** nach Backbord/Steuerbord abdrehen; **the tide was on the ~:** die Flut/Ebbe setzte gerade ein; **the ~ of the year/century** die Jahres-/Jahrhundertwende; **be on the ~** *(be about to change)* sich [zum Besseren/ Schlechteren] wenden; *(be about to go sour)* ⟨*Milch usw.:*⟩ einen Stich haben *(ugs.);* **a ~ of fortune** eine Schicksalswende; **take a favourable ~** *(fig.)* sich zum Guten wenden; **take a ~ for the better/worse** *see* **take 1 k; d)** *(deflection)* Biegung, *die;* **e)** *(bend)* Kurve, *die; (corner)* Ecke, *die;* **at every ~** *(fig.) (constantly)* ständig; *(wherever one goes)* überall; **f)** *(short performance on stage etc.)* Nummer, *die;* **do one's ~:** auftreten; **g)** *(change of tide)* **~ of the tide** Gezeitenwechsel, *der;* **there will be a ~ of the tide** *(fig.)* das Blatt wird sich wenden; **h)** *(character)* **be of a mechanical/humorous/speculative ~:** technisch begabt sein/von humorvollem Schlag sein/einen Hang zum Spekulativen haben; **a child with a more enquiring ~ of mind than his brother** ein Kind, das eher Fragen stellt als sein Bruder; **those of a democratic ~ of mind** die demokratisch Eingestellten; **i)** *(literary: formation)* Rundung, *die;* **the graceful ~ of her ankle** ihr wohlgeformter Knöchel; **j)** *(form of expression)* **an elegant ~ of speech/phrase** eine elegante Ausdrucksweise; **k)** *(service)* **do sb. a good/bad ~:** jmdm. einen guten/schlechten Dienst erweisen; **do good ~s** Gutes tun; **one good ~ deserves another** *(prov.)* hilfst du mir, so helf ich dir; **l)** *(each round in coil of rope etc.)* Umwick[e]lung, *die;* **m)** *(coll.: fright)* **give sb. quite a ~:** jmdm. einen gehörigen Schrecken einjagen *(ugs.);* **n)** *(coll.: spell of illness etc.)* **have a nasty ~:** einen schlimmen Anfall haben; **I just had a little ~:** ich hatte einen kleinen Schwächeanfall; **o)** *(short walk)* **take a ~:** eine Runde drehen *od.* machen; **p)** *(short ride)* Runde, *die;* **go out for a ~ on one's bicycle** eine Runde mit dem Fahrrad drehen; **q)** *(Mus.)* Doppelschlag, *der;* **r)** *(Brit. St. Exch.: jobber's profit margin)* Gewinnspanne, *die. See also* **about-turn; three-point. 2.** *v. t.* **a)** *(make revolve)* drehen; **~ the tap** am Wasserhahn drehen; **~ the key in the lock** den Schlüssel im Schloß herumdrehen; **he ~ed the wheel sharply [to the right]** er riß das Steuer scharf [nach rechts] herum; **b)** *(reverse)* umdrehen; wenden ⟨*Pfannkuchen, Matratze, Auto, Heu, Teppich*⟩; umgraben ⟨*Erde*⟩; umlegen ⟨*Kragen*⟩; **~ sth. upside-down** *or* **on its head** *(lit. or fig.)* etw. auf den Kopf stellen; **~ a record** eine Platte umdrehen; **~ sth. back to front** die Vorderseite einer Sache nach hinten drehen; **~ the page** umblättern; **c)** *(give new direction to)* drehen, wenden ⟨*Kopf*⟩; **she could still ~ heads** die Leute drehten sich immer noch nach ihr um; **~ a hose/gun on sb./sth.** einen Schlauch/ein Gewehr auf jmdn./etw. richten; **~ one's chair to face the window** seinen Stuhl zum Fenster drehen; **~ one's attention/mind to sth.** sich/seine Gedanken einer Sache *(Dat.)* zuwenden; **~ one's thoughts to a subject** sich [in Gedanken] mit einem Thema beschäftigen; **~ a car into a road** [mit einem Auto] in eine Straße einbiegen; **~ the course of history** dem Gang der Geschichte eine Wende geben; **~ one's eyes on sb.** jmdm. seine Augen zuwenden; **he ~ed his steps homeward** er lenkte seine Schritte heimwärts; **~ the tide [of sth.]** [bei etw.] den Ausschlag geben; **this incident ~ed the tide of opinion in her favour** dieser Vorfall führte einen Meinungsumschwung zu ihren Gunsten herbei; **~ sb. from his purpose** jmdn. von seinem Vorhaben abbringen; **d)** *(send)* **~ sb. loose on sb./sth.** jmdn. auf jmdn./etw. loslassen; **~ sb. from one's door/off one's land** jmdn. von seiner Tür/von seinem Land verjagen; **~ a dog on sb.** einen Hund auf jmdn. hetzen; **e)** *(put)* leeren ⟨*Inhalt eines Koffers, einer Büchse*⟩; stürzen ⟨*Pudding, Kuchen usw.*⟩ **(on to** auf + *Akk.*); **f)** *(cause to become)* verwandeln; **the cigarette smoke has ~ed the walls yellow** der Zigarettenrauch hat die Wände vergilben lassen; **~ the lights low** das Licht dämpfen; **~ a play/ book into a film** ein Theaterstück/Buch verfilmen; **~ water into electricity/a church into a theatre** Wasser in Elektrizität/eine Kirche in ein Theater umwandeln; **the thought ~ed him pale** der Gedanke ließ ihn erbleichen *(geh.);* **g)** *(make sour)* sauer werden lassen ⟨*Milch*⟩; **h)** *(translate)* übertragen **(in** in + *Akk.*); **i) ~ sb.'s stomach** jmdm. den Magen umdrehen; **j)** *(make conceited)* **~ sb.'s head** jmdm. zu Kopf steigen; **~ sb.'s brain** jmds. Sinne *od.* Geist verwirren *(geh.);* **k)** *(shape in lathe)* drechseln ⟨*Holz*⟩; drehen ⟨*Metall, Ton*⟩; **l)** drehen ⟨*Pirouette*⟩; schlagen ⟨*Rad, Purzelbaum*⟩; **m)** *(reach the age of)* **~ 40** 40 [Jahre alt] werden; **she has not ~ed 30 yet** sie ist noch keine 30 [Jahre alt]; **n) it's just ~ed 12 o'clock/quarter past 4** es ist gerade 12 Uhr/viertel nach vier vorbei; **it's not yet ~ed 4 o'clock** es ist noch nicht ganz 4 Uhr; **o)** *(gain)* **~ a penny/profit** einen Gewinn machen; **~ a quick penny** eine schnelle Mark machen *(ugs.);* **p)** wenden ⟨*Kragen, Jacke usw.*⟩; **q)** *(resist and divert)* abprallen lassen; **the bullet was ~ed by the door** die Kugel prallte an der Tür ab; **r)** *(blunt)* stumpf machen; **~ the edge of criticism** *(fig.)* der Kritik die Spitze abbrechen *od.* nehmen; **s)** *(go round)* umrunden ⟨*Kap, Landzunge*⟩; **~ the flank of an army** einer Streitmacht die Flanke aufrollen; **t)** *(give elegant form to)* **he knows how to ~ a compliment** er versteht es, Komplimente zu machen; **~ verses** Verse dichten *od.* schmieden. *See also* **account 3 h; back 1 a; coat 1 a; corner 1 a; deaf 1 b; evidence 1 b; hair a; hand 1 a; honest e; phrase 2 a; table 1 a; tail 1 c; turtle c. 3.** *v. i.* **a)** *(revolve)* sich drehen; ⟨*Wasserhahn, Schlüssel:*⟩ sich drehen lassen; **the earth ~s on its axis** die Erde dreht sich um ihre Achse; **he couldn't get the key to ~:** er konnte den Schlüssel nicht drehen; **b)** *(reverse direction)* ⟨*Person:*⟩ sich herumdrehen; ⟨*Auto:*⟩ wenden; **the car ~ed upside-down** das Auto überschlug sich; **~ back to front** sich von hinten nach vorne drehen; **c)** *(take new direction)* sich wenden; *(turn round)* sich umdrehen; **heads ~ed when she ...:** die Leute sahen *od.* drehten sich nach ihr um, als sie ...; **his thoughts/attention ~ed to her** er wandte ihr seine Gedanken/Aufmerksamkeit zu; **left/right ~!** *(Mil.)* links/rechts um!; **he ~ed to the man standing next to him** er wandte sich dem Mann zu, der neben ihm stand; **~ into a road/away from the river** in eine Straße einbiegen/vom Fluß abbiegen; **~ to the left** nach links abbiegen/⟨*Schiff, Flugzeug:*⟩ abdrehen; **~ up/down a street** in eine Straße einbiegen; **~ towards home** den Heimweg einschlagen; **profits are ~ing upward** die Gewinne steigen; **everywhere the eye ~s ...:** wohin sich das Auge wendet ...; **when the tide ~s** wenn die Ebbe/Flut kommt; *(fig.)* wenn sich das Blatt wendet; **not know where** *or* **which way to ~** *(fig.)* keinen Ausweg [mehr] wissen; **my luck has ~ed** *(fig.)* mein Glück hat sich gewendet; **d)** *(become)* werden; **~ traitor/statesman/Muslim** zum Verräter/zum Staatsmann/Moslem werden; **~ [in]to sth.** zu etw. werden; *(be transformed)* sich in etw. *(Akk.)* verwandeln; **her face ~ed green** sie wurde [ganz] grün im Gesicht; **e)** *(change colour)* ⟨*Laub:*⟩ sich [ver]färben; **f)** *(become sour)* ⟨*Milch:*⟩ sauer werden; **g) my stomach ~s** mir dreht sich der Magen um *(ugs.);* **h)** *(become giddy)* **sb.'s head is ~ing** jmdm. dreht sich alles [im Kopf]. *See also* **¹grave; ¹heel 1 b; toss 2 a; worm 1 a**

~ a'bout 1. *v. i.* sich umdrehen; ⟨*Kompanie:*⟩ kehrtmachen; *(fig.)* eine Kehrtwendung machen. **2.** *v. t.* wenden ⟨*Auto, Boot usw.*⟩. *See also* **turn-about**

~ against *v. t.* **a) ~ against sb.** sich gegen jmdn. wenden; **~ sb. against sb.** jmdn. gegen jmdn. aufbringen; **b) they ~ed his own arguments against him** sie verwendeten seine eigenen Argumente gegen ihn

~ a'round *see* **~ round**

~ a'way 1. *v. i.* sich abwenden; **~ away from sth.** *(fig.)* sich von etw. abwenden. **2.** *v. t.* **a)** *(avert)* abwenden; **b)** *(send away)* wegschicken; *(refuse admittance also)* abweisen

~ 'back 1. *v. i.* **a)** *(retreat, lit. or fig.)* umkehren; kehrtmachen *(ugs.);* **there can be no ~ing back** es gibt kein Zurück *od.* keinen Weg zurück; **b)** *(in book etc.)* zurückgehen. **2.** *v. t.* **a)** *(cause to retreat)* zurückweisen; zurückschlagen ⟨*Feind*⟩; **b)** *(fold back)* zurückschlagen ⟨*Bettdecke, Teppich*⟩; herunterschlagen ⟨*Kragen*⟩; **don't ~ back the corner of the page** bitte mach keine Eselsohren in die Buchseiten *(ugs.)*

~ 'down *v. t.* **a)** *(fold down)* herunterschlagen ⟨*Kragen, Hutkrempe*⟩; umknicken ⟨*Buchseite*⟩; [nach unten] umschlagen ⟨*Laken*⟩; **b)** *(reduce level of)* niedriger stellen ⟨*Heizung, Kochplatte*⟩; dämpfen ⟨*Licht*⟩; herunterdrehen ⟨*Gas, Heizung*⟩; leiser stellen ⟨*Ton, Radio, Fernseher*⟩; **c)** *(reject, refuse)* ablehnen; abweisen ⟨*Bewerber, Kandidaten usw.*⟩. *See also* **turndown**

~ 'in 1. *v. t.* **a)** *(fold inwards)* nach innen drehen; einschlagen ⟨*Stoffkante*⟩; einrollen ⟨*Blatt*⟩; **b)** *(hand in)* abgeben; **c)** *(surrender)* [der Polizei] übergeben; **~ oneself in** sich stellen; **d)** *(register)* hinlegen *(ugs.)*⟨*Auftritt, Leistung*⟩; **e)** *(coll.: give up)* aufstecken *(ugs.)* ⟨*Arbeit*⟩; hinschmeißen *(salopp)* ⟨*Arbeit, Dienstabzeichen*⟩; **f) ~ it in!** *(coll.: stop that)* hör auf damit! **2.** *v. i.* **a)** *(incline inwards)* nach innen gebogen sein; *(narrow)* sich verjüngen; **b)** *(enter)* einbiegen; **c)** *(coll.: go to bed)* in die Falle gehen *(salopp);* **d) ~ in on oneself** sich in sich selbst zurückziehen

~ 'off 1. *v. t.* **a)** abschalten; abstellen ⟨*Wasser, Gas*⟩; zudrehen ⟨*Wasserhahn*⟩; **b)** *(coll.: cause to lose interest)* anwidern; **~ sb. off sth.** jmdm. etw. vermiesen *(ugs.).* **2.** *v. i.* abbiegen. *See also* **turn-off**

~ on 1. *v. t.* **a)** [-'-] anschalten; einlassen ⟨*Badewasser*⟩; aufdrehen ⟨*Wasserhahn, Gas*⟩; *(fig.: start showing)* aufsetzen ⟨*Miene*⟩; **b)** [-'-] *(coll.: cause to take interest)* anmachen *(ugs.);* ⟨*Droge:*⟩ anturnen *(ugs.);* **whatever ~s you on!** jedem das Seine!; *see also* **turn-on; c)** ['--] *(be based on)* ⟨*Argument:*⟩ beruhen auf (+ *Dat.*); ⟨*Gespräch, Diskussion*⟩ sich drehen um *(ugs.);* **d)** ['--] *(become hostile towards)* sich wenden gegen; *(attack)* angreifen; **there's no need to ~ on me like that** du brauchst mich nicht so anzufahren. **2.** [-'-] *v.i. (switch on)* einschalten

~ 'out 1. *v. t.* a) *(expel)* hinauswerfen *(ugs.)*; ~ **sb. out of a room/out into the street** jmdn. aus einem Zimmer weisen *od. (ugs.)* werfen/auf die Straße werfen *od.* setzen; ~ **sb. out of his office** *(temporarily)* jmdn. aus seinem Büro ausquartieren; b) *(switch off)* ausschalten; abdrehen ‹*Gas*›; c) *(incline outwards)* nach außen drehen ‹*Füße, Zehen*›; d) *(equip)* ausstaffieren; e) *(produce)* produzieren; hervorbringen ‹*Fachkräfte, Spezialisten*›; *(in great quantities)* ausstoßen; f) *(Brit.) (empty)* ausräumen; ausschütten ‹*Büchse*›; schütten ‹*Bohnen usw.*›; stürzen ‹*Götterspeise usw.*›; *(clean)* [gründlich] aufräumen; *(get rid of)* wegwerfen; ~ **out one's pockets** seine Taschen umdrehen; ~ **sth. inside out** etw. nach außen stülpen *od.* drehen; g) *(Mil.)* ~ **out [the guard]** [die Wache] antreten lassen; ~ **out the guard!** Wache angetreten! 2. *v. i.* a) *(prove to be)* **sb./sth. ~s out to be sth.** jmd./etw. stellt sich als jmd./etw. heraus *od.* erweist sich als jmd./etw.; **it ~s out that ...:** es stellt sich heraus, daß ...; **as it ~ed out, as things ~ed out** wie sich [nachher] herausstellte; b) *(come to be eventually)* **the day ~ed out wet** der Tag wurde regnerisch; **see how things ~ out** sehen, wie sich die Dinge entwickeln; ~ **out to be sth.** sich zu etw. entwickeln; **everything ~ed out well/all right in the end** alles endete gut; **she didn't ~ out well** aus ihr ist nichts geworden; c) *(end)* **the story ~ed out happily** die Geschichte ging gut aus; **the expedition ~ed out well** die Expedition hatte Erfolg; d) *(appear)* ‹*Menge, Fans usw.:*› erscheinen; **he ~s out every Saturday to watch his team** er kommt jeden Samstag, um seine Mannschaft zu sehen; e) *(coll.: get out of bed)* aus den Federn steigen *(ugs.)*; f) *(coll.: go out of doors)* rausgehen *(ugs.)*; g) *(play)* ~ **out for a team** für eine Mannschaft spielen *od.* antreten; h) *(point outwards)* sich nach außen drehen. *See also* **turn-out**

~ 'over 1. *v. t.* a) *(cause to fall over)* umwerfen; **the car was ~ed over on to its roof** *(by accident)* das Auto überschlug sich und blieb auf dem Dach liegen; b) *(expose the other side of)* umdrehen; umgraben ‹*Erde*›; ~ **a page over** umblättern; ~ **over two pages at once** eine Seite überschlagen; c) drehen ‹*Motor*›; d) ~ **sth. over [in one's mind]** sich *(Dat.)* etw. hin und her überlegen; e) *(hand over)* übergeben (**to** *Dat.*) ‹*Betrieb, Amt*›; f) *(Commerc.)* umschlagen ‹*Waren*›; ~ **over £150,000 a month** einen Umsatz von 150 000 Pfund im Monat haben. 2. *v. i.* a) *(tip over)* umkippen; ‹*Boot:*› kentern, umschlagen; ‹*Auto, Flugzeug:*› sich überschlagen; b) *(from one side to the other)* sich umdrehen; ~ **over on to one's back** sich auf den Rücken drehen; c) ‹*Motor:*› laufen; d) *(feel moved by fear, nausea)* **my stomach ~ed over at the thought of it** beim Gedanken daran drehte sich mir der Magen um *(ugs.)*; e) *(~ a page)* weiterblättern. *See also* **turnover**

~ 'round 1. *v. i.* a) sich umdrehen; ~ **round and go back the same way** umkehren und denselben Weg zurückgehen; **[not] have time to ~ round** *(fig.)* [k]eine Minute Zeit haben; b) *(rotate)* sich drehen; c) ~ **round and do sth.** *(fig.)* plötzlich etw. tun; **they cannot ~ round and blame us** sie können nicht auf einmal uns die Schuld geben; d) *(change for better)* ‹*Geschäfte:*› sich erholen. 2. *v. t.* a) *(unload and reload)* be- und entladen ‹*Frachtschiff*›; abfertigen ‹*Passagierschiff*›; b) *see* ~ **about 2**; c) *(reverse)* umdrehen; auf den Kopf stellen *(ugs.)* ‹*Theorie, Argument*›; ~ **a company round** *(Commerc.)* eine Firma aus der Krise führen. *See also* **turn-round**

~ **to** 1. ['--] *v. t.* a) *(set about)* ~ **to work** an die Arbeit gehen; b) *(go to for help etc.)* ~ **to sb./sth.** sich an jmdn. wenden/etw. zu Hilfe nehmen; ~ **to God** sich Gott zuwenden; ~ **to sb. for money** jmdn. um Geld bitten; ~ **to a book** ein Buch zu Rate ziehen; ~ **to sb. for comfort/help/advice** bei jmdm. Trost/Hilfe/Rat suchen; ~ **to drugs** zu Drogen greifen; ~ **to drink/one's work** *(seeking consolation)* sich in den Alkohol/seine Arbeit flüchten; **make sb. ~ to drink** jmdn. dem Alkohol in die Arme treiben; c) *(go on to consider next)* ~ **to a subject/topic** sich einem Thema zuwenden; *see also* ~ **2 a, c.** 2. [-'-] *v. i.* zugreifen

~ 'up 1. *v. i.* a) *(make one's appearance)* erscheinen; aufkreuzen *(ugs.)*; b) *(happen)* passieren; geschehen; c) *(present itself)* auftauchen; ‹*Gelegenheit:*› sich bieten; ‹*Lösung:*› sich finden; **something is sure to ~ up** irgend etwas wird sich schon finden; d) *(be found)* sich finden. 2. *v. t.* a) *(dig up)* freilegen; *(fig.)* ans Licht bringen; **I ~ed up a lot of interesting information** ich habe viele interessante Informationen aufgetrieben; b) hochschlagen ‹*Kragen, Hutkrempe*›; **her nose is ~ed up** sie hat eine Stupsnase; c) lauter stellen, *(ugs.)* aufdrehen ‹*Ton, Fernseher, Radio*›; aufdrehen ‹*Wasser, Heizung, Gas*›; heller machen ‹*Licht*›; d) *(Brit.: find and refer to)* heranziehen ‹*Artikel, Buch*›; e) ~ **it up!** *(Brit. sl.)* hör auf damit!; *see also* **nose 1 a; toe 1 a**

~ **upon** *see* ~ **on 1 c, d**

turn: ~-about *n. (~ing about)* Wende, *die; (fig.)* Kehrtwendung, *die;* **a welcome ~-about in her fortunes** eine willkommene Wende ihres Geschicks; **~coat** *n.* Abtrünnige, *der/die;* **~-down** *attrib. adj.* **~-down collar** Umlegekragen, *der*

turned-up ['tɜ:ndʌp] *adj.* ~ **nose** Stupsnase, *die (ugs.)*

turner ['tɜ:nə(r)] *n.* Drechsler, *der*/Drechslerin, *die*

turning ['tɜ:nɪŋ] *n.* a) *(off road)* Abzweigung, *die; (fig.)* Kreuzweg, *der (geh.)*; **take the second ~ to the left** die zweite Abzweigung nach links nehmen; b) *(use of lathe)* Drechseln, *das;* c) *in pl. (shavings)* Späne

turning: ~-circle *n. (Motor Veh.)* Wendekreis, *der;* **~-point** *n.* Wendepunkt, *der*

turnip ['tɜ:nɪp] *n.* Kohlrübe, *die;* Steckrübe, *die*

'turnip-top *n.* Rübenblätter *Pl.*

turn: ~key 1. *n. (Hist.)* Kerkermeister, *der.* 2. *adj.* schlüsselfertig; **a ~key contract** ein Vertrag, der schlüsselfertige Lieferung garantiert; **~-off** *n.* a) *(turning)* Abzweigung, *die; (off motorway)* Ausfahrt, *die;* **the Leicester ~-off** die Abzweigung nach Leicester/die Ausfahrt Leicester; b) *(coll.: repellent person or thing)* **be a ~-off** abstoßend sein; **be a ~-off for sb.** jmdn. abstoßen; **~-on** *n. (coll.)* **be a ~-on [for sb.]** [jmdn.] anmachen *(ugs.)*; **~-out** *n.* a) *(~ing out for duty)* Einsatz, *der;* Ausrücken, *das;* b) *(number voting)* **~-out [of voters]** Wahlbeteiligung, *die;* c) *(number assembled)* Beteiligung, *die* (**for** an + *Dat.*); **there was a large ~-out of fans at the airport** eine große Zahl von Fans war zum Flughafen gekommen; d) *see* **output 1 a**; e) *see* **clear-out**; **~over** *n.* a) *(tart etc.)* **apple/apricot ~over** Apfel-/Aprikosentasche, *die;* **meat ~over** Fleischpastete, *die;* b) *(Commerc.) (of business, money)* Umsatz, *der; (of stock)* Umschlag, *der;* c) *(of staff)* Fluktuation, *die; (of patients in hospital)* Zu- und Abgang, *der;* **~pike** *n.* a) *(Brit. Hist.: toll road)* gebührenpflichtige Straße; b) *(Amer.: expressway)* gebührenpflichtige Autobahn; **~-round** *n.* a) *(adoption of new policy)* Kehrtwendung, *die;* b) *(of ship, aircraft, people)* Abfertigung, *die; (of material)* Bearbeitung, *die;* **~stile** *n.* Drehkreuz, *das;* **~table** *n.* a) *(for gramophone record)* Plattenteller, *der;* b) *(for reversing locomotive etc.)* Drehscheibe, *die;* **~-up** *n.* a) *(Brit. Fashion)* Aufschlag, *der;* **with ~-ups** ‹*Hose*› mit Aufschlag; b) *(Brit. coll.: unexpected event)* **a ~-up [for the book]** eine Riesenüberraschung *(ugs.)*

turpentine ['tɜ:pntaɪn] *n.* a) Terpentin, *das;* b) **[oil of] ~:** Terpentin, *das (ugs.)*; Terpentinöl, *das;* ~ **substitute** Terpentinersatz, *der*

turpitude ['tɜ:pɪtju:d] *n.* Verworfenheit, *die (geh.)*

turps [tɜ:ps] *n. (coll.)* Terpentin, *das (ugs.)*

turquoise ['tɜ:kwɔɪz] 1. *n.* a) Türkis, *der;* b) *(colour)* Türkis, *das.* 2. *adj.* a) türkis[farben]; b) ~ **ring** Türkisring, *der*

turquoise: ~ 'blue *n.* Türkisblau, *das;* ~ **'green** *n.* Türkisgrün, *das*

turret ['tʌrɪt] *n.* a) *(Archit.)* Türmchen, *das;* b) *(of tank etc.)* [Geschütz]turm, *der;* c) *(Mech. Engin.)* Revolverkopf, *der*

turreted ['tʌrɪtɪd] *adj.* ‹*Schloß*› mit Mauertürmchen

'turret lathe *n.* Revolverdrehmaschine, *die*

turtle [tɜ:tl] *n.* a) *(marine reptile)* Meeresschildkröte, *die;* b) *(Amer.: freshwater reptile)* Wasserschildkröte, *die;* c) **turn ~** ‹*Schiff, Boot:*› kentern; ‹*Auto:*› sich überschlagen

turtle: ~-dove *n.* Turteltaube, *die;* **~-neck** *n.* Stehbundkragen, *der;* **~-neck pullover** Pullover mit Stehbund

turves *see* **turf 1 b**

Tuscan ['tʌskən] 1. *adj.* a) *(of Tuscany)* toskanisch; b) *(Archit.)* ~ **order** toskanische Ordnung. 2. *n.* a) *(language)* Toskanisch, *das;* b) *(person)* Toskaner, *der*/Toskanerin, *die*

Tuscany ['tʌskənɪ] *pr. n.* Toskana, *die*

tush [tʌʃ] *int. (arch.)* pah

tusk [tʌsk] *n. (of elephant)* Stoßzahn, *der; (of boar, walrus)* Hauer, *der*

tussle ['tʌsl] 1. *n.* Gerangel, *das (ugs.)*; **they had a ~ over the project** *(fig.)* es gab zwischen ihnen ein Gerangel wegen des Projekts. 2. *v. i.* sich balgen; *(fig.)* sich auseinandersetzen (**about** wegen)

tussock ['tʌsək] *n. (clump of grass etc.)* [Gras]büschel, *das*

tut[-tut] [tʌt('tʌt)] 1. *int.* na[, na]. 2. *v. i.*, **-tt-:** ~ **[with disapproval]** [mißbilligend] „Na, na!" sagen

tutelage ['tju:tɪlɪdʒ] *n. (guardianship)* Vormundschaft, *die; (of king etc.)* Schutzherrschaft, *die; (tuition)* Anleitung, *die;* **a child in ~:** ein unter Vormundschaft stehendes Kind; **be under sb.'s ~:** unter jmds. Obhut stehen *(geh.)*

tutelar ['tju:tɪlə(r)], **tutelary** ['tju:tɪlərɪ] *adjs.* a) *(protective)* Schutz‹*göttin, -gottheit, -heiliger*›; b) *(of a guardian)* ~ **authority** Vormundschaft, *die*

tutor ['tju:tə(r)] 1. *n.* a) *(private teacher)* **[private] ~:** [Privat]lehrer, *der*/-lehrerin, *die; (for extra help)* Nachhilfelehrer, *der*/-lehrerin, *die;* **piano ~:** Klavierlehrer, *der*/-lehrerin, *die; (book)* Klavierschule, *die;* b) *(Brit. Univ.)* ≈ Tutor, *der;* c) *(Amer.: college teacher)* Dozent, *der.* 2. *v. t.* a) ~ **sb.** *(teach privately)* jmdm. Privatstunden geben; *(give extra lessons to)* jmdm. Nachhilfestunden geben; ~ **sb. in French/the piano** jmdm. Französisch-/Klavierstunden geben; b) *(arch./literary)* unterweisen *(geh.)*; *(discipline)* erziehen

tutorial [tju:'tɔ:rɪəl] 1. *adj.* Tutoren-. 2. *n. (Brit. Univ.) (for less advanced students)* ≈ Tutorium, *das; (for more advanced students)* ≈ Kolloquium, *das*

tutti-frutti [tʊtɪ'fru:tɪ] *n. (Gastr.)* Tuttifrutti, *das*

tutu ['tu:tu:] *n.* Tutu, *das*

tu-whit tu-whoo [tʊwɪt tʊ'wu:] *int.* [h]uhu

tux [tʌks] *n. (Amer. coll.)*, **tuxedo** [tʌk'si:dəʊ] *n., pl.* **~s** *or* **~es** *(Amer.)* Smoking, *der*

TV [ti:'vi:] *n.* **a)** *(television)* Fernsehen, *das; attrib.* Fernseh⟨*star, -magazin, -programm*⟩; **TV dinner** ≈ Fertigmahlzeit, *die;* **on TV** im Fernsehen; **b)** *(television set)* Fernseher, *der (ugs.)*

twaddle ['twɒdl] *n.* Gewäsch, *das (ugs.);* **talk utter ~:** völligen Blödsinn reden *(ugs.);* **don't talk such ~!** hör auf mit dem Gewäsch!

twain [tweɪn] *(arch./poet.) n.* **cut/split in ~:** entzweischneiden/in zwei Teile teilen; **never the ~ shall meet** die beiden werden nie zueinanderfinden

twang [twæŋ] **1.** *v. i.* ⟨*Bogen:*⟩ mit vibrierendem Ton zurückschnellen; **hear the guitar ~ing away** das Klimpern der Gitarre hören *(ugs.).* **2.** *v. t.* zupfen ⟨*Saite*⟩; **~ a guitar** auf einer Gitarre [herum]klimpern *(ugs.).* **3.** *n.* **a)** *(nasal tone of voice)* **[nasal] ~:** Näseln, *das;* **speak with a ~:** näseln; **b)** *(of bowstring, string of musical instrument)* vibrierender Ton

'twas [twɒz] *(arch./poet.)* = **it was**

twat [twæt, twɒt] *n.* **a)** *(coarse: vagina)* Fotze, *die (vulg.);* **b)** *(derog. sl.: idiot)* Arschloch, *das (derb)*

tweak [twi:k] **1.** *v. t.* **~ sb. in the arm, ~ sb.'s arm** jmdn. in den Arm kneifen; **~ sb.'s ear** jmdn. am Ohr ziehen. **2.** *n.* Kneifen, *das;* **give sb./sth. a ~:** jmdn./etw. kneifen

twee [twi:] *adj.,* **tweer** ['twi:ə(r)], **tweest** ['twi:ɪst] *(Brit. derog.)* geziert ⟨*Wesen, Art, Ausdrucksweise*⟩; kitschig ⟨*Stil, Bild*⟩; Bilderbuch⟨*dorf, -landhaus*⟩; niedlich, putzig ⟨*Kleidung, Dorf*⟩

tweed [twi:d] *n.* **a)** *(fabric)* Tweed, *der; attrib.* Tweed-; **b)** *in pl. (clothes)* Tweedkleidung, *die;* Tweedsachen *(ugs.)*

tweedy ['twi:dɪ] *adj.* **a)** *(coll.: dressed in tweeds)* in Tweed gekleidet; **b)** *(fig.: heartily informal)* burschikos

'tween-deck[s] *n. (Naut.)* Zwischendeck, *das*

tweet [twi:t] **1.** *n.* Zwitschern, *das;* **~, ~!** piep, piep! **2.** *v. i.* zwitschern

tweeter ['twi:tə(r)] *n.* Hochtonlautsprecher, *der*

tweezers ['twi:zəz] *n., pl.* **[pair of] ~:** Pinzette, *die*

twelfth [twelfθ] **1.** *adj.* zwölft...; *see also* **eighth 1. 2.** *n.* **a)** *(fraction)* Zwölftel, *das;* **b)** *(Mus.)* Duodezime, *die; see also* **eighth 2**

Twelfth: ~ Day *n.* Dreikönigstag, *der;* **t~ man** *n. (Cricket)* Ersatzspieler, *der;* **~ Night** *n.* Vorabend des Dreikönigstages

twelve [twelv] **1.** *adj.* zwölf; **~ noon** [zwölf Uhr] Mittag; **~ midnight** [zwölf Uhr] Mitternacht; *see also* **eight 1. 2.** *n. (number, symbol)* Zwölf, *die;* **the T~:** die Zwölf; die zwölf Apostel; *see also* **eight 2 a, d**

twelve: ~month *n. (literary)* **a ~month** zwölf Monate; **~-'note, ~-'tone** *adjs. (Mus.)* Zwölfton-

twentieth ['twentɪɪθ] **1.** *adj.* zwanzigst...; *see also* **eighth 1. 2.** *n. (fraction)* Zwanzigstel, *das; see also* **eighth 2**

twenty ['twentɪ] **1.** *adj.* zwanzig; **one-and-~** *(arch.) see* **twenty-one 1;** *see also* **eight 1. 2.** *n.* Zwanzig, *die;* **one-and-~** *(arch.) see* **twenty-one 2;** *see also* **eight 2 a; eighty 2**

twenty: ~-first *etc. adj.* einundzwanzigst... *usw.; see also* **eighth 1; ~-four-hour** *see* **hour a; ~-one** *etc.* **1.** *adj.* einundzwanzig *usw.; see also* **eight 1; 2.** *n.* Einundzwanzig *usw., die; see also* **eight 2 a**

'twere [twə(r), *stressed* twɜ:(r)] *(arch./poet.)* = **it were** 's wäre

twerp [twɜ:p] *n. (sl.) (male)* Blödmann, *der (derb); (female)* blöde Kuh *(derb)*

twice [twaɪs] *adv.* **a)** *(two times)* zweimal; **she didn't have to be asked ~!** da brauchte man sie nicht zweimal zu fragen!; **~ a year** zweimal im Jahr; **~ weekly** zweimal wöchentlich *nicht attrib.;* **his ~-weekly visit** sein Besuch zweimal in der Woche; **b)** *(doubly)* doppelt; **~ as strong** *etc.* doppelt so stark *usw.;* **he's ~ her age** er ist doppelt so alt wie sie; **have ~ the strength** doppelt so stark sein; **he is ~ the man he was** aus ihm ist ein ganz anderer Mensch geworden; **fly at ~ the speed of sound** mit doppelter Schallgeschwindigkeit fliegen; **sell sth. at ~ the price** *(coll.)* etw. zum doppelten Preis verkaufen; *see also* **think 2 a**

twiddle ['twɪdl] **1.** *v. t.* herumdrehen an (+ *Dat.*) *(ugs.);* zwirbeln ⟨*Schnurrbart*⟩; **~ one's cigar** seine Zigarre [zwischen den Fingern] drehen; **~ one's thumbs** *(lit. or fig.)* Däumchen drehen *(ugs.).* **2.** *v. i.* **~ with sth.** mit etw. spielen; an etw. *(Dat.)* herumfummeln *(ugs.);* **~ one's moustache** seinen Schnurrbart zwirbeln. **3.** *n.* Drehung, *die;* **give sth. a ~:** an etw. *(Dat.)* drehen

[1]twig [twɪg] *n.* **a)** *(small branch)* Zweig, *der;* **b)** *(divining-rod)* Wünschelrute, *die*

[2]twig *(coll.)* **1.** *v. t.* **-gg- a)** *(understand)* kapieren *(ugs.);* **b)** *(notice)* mitkriegen *(ugs.).* **2.** *v. i.* **-gg- a)** *(understand)* es kapieren *(ugs.);* **b)** *(notice)* es mitkriegen *(ugs.)*

twilight ['twaɪlaɪt] *n.* **a)** *(evening light)* Dämmerlicht, *das;* Zwielicht, *das;* **b)** *(period of half-light)* Dämmerung, *die;* **the ~ of the Gods** *(Norse myth.)* die Götterdämmerung; **in the ~ of history** *(fig.)* in grauer Vorzeit; **c)** *(fig.: intermediate state)* Dämmer, *der (dichter.);* **his ~ years** sein Lebensabend

twilight: ~ 'sleep *n. (Med.)* Dämmerschlaf, *der;* **~ zone** *n.* **a)** Niemandsland, *das;* **b)** *(decaying urban area)* heruntergekommene Gegend

twill [twɪl] *n. (Textiles)* **a)** *(weave)* Köperbindung, *die;* **b)** *(fabric)* Köper, *der*

'twill [twɪl] *(arch./poet.)* = **it will**

twin [twɪn] **1.** *attrib. adj.* **a)** Zwillings-; **~ brother/sister** Zwillingsbruder, *der*/-schwester, *die;* **b)** *(forming a pair)* Doppel-; doppelt ⟨*Problem, Verantwortung*⟩; **the ~ threats of war and inflation** die doppelte Bedrohung durch Krieg und Inflation; **c)** *(Bot.)* paarig; **d)** Doppel⟨*vergaser, -propeller, -schraube usw.*⟩. **2.** *n.* **a)** Zwilling, *der;* **his ~:** sein Zwillingsbruder/seine Zwillingsschwester; **b)** *(Astrol.)* **the T~s** die Zwillinge; *see also* **Aries; c)** *(exact counterpart)* Gegenstück, *das;* Pendant, *das.* **3.** *v. t.,* **-nn-** eng verbinden; **Bottrop is ~ned with Blackpool** Bottrop und Blackpool sind Partnerstädte

twin: ~ 'bed *n.* eines von zwei [gleichen] Einzelbetten; **~ beds** zwei Einzelbetten; **~-bedded** *adj.* **a ~-bedded room** ein Zweibettzimmer

twine [twaɪn] **1.** *n.* Bindfaden, *der; (thicker)* Kordel, *die; (for nets)* Garn, *das.* **2.** *v. t.* **a)** *(form by twisting strands together)* [zusammen]drehen; **b)** *(form by interlacing)* winden *(geh.)* ⟨*Kranz, Girlande*⟩; **c)** *(coil)* schlingen; **~ sth. round [and round] sth.** etw. [mehrmals] um etw. schlingen; **~ the flowers round the pole** den Mast mit Blumen umwinden. **3.** *v. i.* sich winden **(about, around** um)

twin-engined ['twɪnendʒɪnd] *adj.* zweimotorig

twinge [twɪndʒ] *n.* Stechen, *das;* **a ~ of toothache/rheumatism** ein stechender Zahnschmerz/ziehender rheumatischer Schmerz; **~s** Wehwehchen *Pl. (ugs.);* **he suffers from ~s in wet weather** bei feuchtem Wetter zwickt und zwackt es ihn überall; **~[s] of remorse/conscience** *(fig.)* Gewissensbisse

twinkle ['twɪŋkl] **1.** *v. i.* **a)** *(sparkle)* ⟨*Sterne, Augen:*⟩ funkeln, blitzen **(with** vor + *Dat.*); **b)** *(move rapidly)* flink trippeln. **2.** *v. t.* **~ one's eyes** mit den Augen funkeln. **3.** *n.* **a)** in **a ~:** im Handumdrehen; **b)** *(sparkle of the eyes)* Funkeln, *das;* **'...', she said with a ~ in her eye** „...", sagte sie augenzwinkernd; **with a mischievous ~:** mit Schalk in den Augen

twinkling ['twɪŋklɪŋ] *n.* **in a ~, in the ~ of an eye** im Handumdrehen

twin: ~set *n. (Brit.)* Twinset, *das;* **~ town** *n. (Brit.)* Partnerstadt, *die;* **~-tub** *n.* halbautomatische Waschmaschine *(mit separater Schleuder)*

twirl [twɜ:l] **1.** *v. t.* **a)** *(spin)* [schnell] drehen; **he ~ed his partner around the dance-floor** er wirbelte seine Partnerin über die Tanzfläche; **b)** *(twiddle)* zwirbeln ⟨*Schnurrbart*⟩; drehen ⟨*Haar*⟩. **2.** *v. i.* wirbeln **(around** über + *Akk.*); **sb. ~s around** jmd. wirbelt herum. **3.** *n.* **a)** *(twirling)* [Herum]wirbeln, *das;* **give one's moustache a ~:** seinen Schnurrbart zwirbeln; **have a ~ on the dance floor** über die Tanzfläche wirbeln; **b)** *(flourish made in writing)* Schnörkel, *der*

twirly ['twɜ:lɪ] *adj.* gewunden; verschnörkelt ⟨*Schrift*⟩

twist [twɪst] **1.** *v. t.* **a)** *(distort)* verdrehen ⟨*Worte, Bedeutung*⟩; **~ out of shape** verbiegen; **~ one's ankle** sich *(Dat.)* den Knöchel verrenken; **her face was ~ed with pain** ihr Gesicht war schmerzverzerrt; **~ sb.'s arm** jmdm. den Arm umdrehen; *(fig.)* jmdm. [die] Daumenschrauben anlegen *(scherzh.);* **I didn't have to ~ his arm** ich brauchte ihn nicht lange zu überreden; **b)** *(wind about one another)* flechten ⟨*Blumen, Haare*⟩ **(into** zu); **c)** *(rotate)* drehen; *(back and forth)* hin und her drehen; *see also* **knife 1; d)** *(interweave)* verweben; **e)** *(give spiral form to)* drehen **(into** zu); **f)** *(Brit. coll.: cheat)* beschummeln *(ugs.);* **~ sb. out of sth.** jmdn. um etw. beschummeln *(ugs.);* **g)** *(wrench)* **~ sth. from sb.'s grasp** jmdm. etw. aus der Hand winden. *See also* **little finger. 2.** *v. i.* **a)** sich winden; **~ and turn** sich drehen und winden; **~ around sth.** sich um etw. winden; **~ from sb.'s grasp** sich aus jmds. Griff winden; **b)** *(take twisted position)* sich winden; **he ~ed round in his chair** er verrenkte sich in seinem Sessel; **c)** *(dance)* twisten. **3.** *n.* **a)** *(thread etc.)* Zwirn, *der;* *(loosely twisted)* Twist, *der;* **b) ~ of lemon/orange** Zitronen-/Orangenscheibe, *die;* **c)** *(twisting)* Drehung, *die;* **give sth. a ~:** an etw. *(Dat.)* drehen; **full of ~s and turns** ⟨*Straße*⟩ voll[er] Biegungen und Kurven; **d)** *(unexpected occurrence)* überraschende Wendung; **~ of fate** Laune des Schicksals; **e)** *(peculiar tendency)* **give a ~ to sth.** etw. verdrehen; **he has an odd ~ to his character** er ist ein bißchen verschroben; **a criminal ~:** eine kriminelle Neigung; **f) round the ~:** = **round the bend** *see* **[1]bend 1 b; g)** *(swindle)* Schwindel, *der (abwertend);* **h)** *(Amer.: change of procedure)* [überraschender] Wandel; **i)** *(dance)* Twist, *der;* **do the ~:** Twist tanzen; twisten

~ 'off 1. *v. t.* abdrehen. **2.** *v. i.* **the cap ~s off** der Verschluß läßt sich abdrehen

~ to'gether *v. t.* zusammendrehen ⟨*Fäden*⟩

twisted ['twɪstɪd] *adj.* verbogen; *(fig.)* verdreht *(ugs. abwertend)* ⟨*Geist*⟩; verquer ⟨*Humor*⟩

twister ['twɪstə(r)] *n.* **a)** Schwindler, *der*/Schwindlerin, *die;* Gauner, *der*/Gaunerin, *die;* **b)** *(Amer.: tornado)* Tornado, *der*

twisty ['twɪstɪ] *adj.* kurvig; kurvenreich

twit [twɪt] **1.** *v. t.,* **-tt-** *see* **taunt 1. 2.** *n. (Brit. sl.)* Trottel, *der (ugs.)*

[1]twitch [twɪtʃ] **1.** *v. t.* **a)** zupfen; **b)** zucken mit ⟨*Nase, Schwanz*⟩; wackeln mit ⟨*Ohr*⟩. **2.** *v. i.* **a)** *(pull sharply)* zupfen **(at** an + *Dat.*); **b)** ⟨*Mund, Lippen, Hand, Nase:*⟩ zucken. **3.** *n.* Zucken, *das*

[2]twitch [grass] *see* **[2]couch**

twitchy ['twɪtʃɪ] *adj. (nervy)* nervös; *(irritable)* reizbar

twitter ['twɪtə(r)] **1.** *n.* **a)** *(coll.: excited state)* **be in a ~, be all of a ~:** [vor Spannung] ganz kribbelig sein *(ugs.);* **b)** *(chirping)* Zwit-

schern, *das;* Gezwitscher, *das.* **2.** *v.i.* zwitschern; ‹*Person:*› schnattern *(ugs.)*
twittish ['twɪtɪʃ] *adj. (Brit. sl.)* trottelhaft *(ugs.)*
'twixt [twɪkst] *prep. (poet./arch.)* zwischen
two [tu:] **1.** *adj.* zwei; **a box/shirt or ~:** ein, zwei Schachteln/Hemden; ein oder zwei Schachteln/Hemden; *see also* **eight 1. 2.** *n. (number, symbol)* Zwei, *die;* **the ~:** die beiden; die zwei; **just the ~ of us** nur wir zwei *od.* beiden; **it's as clear as ~ and ~ make four** es ist so klar, wie zwei mal zwei vier sind *(ugs.)*; **put ~ and ~ together** *(fig.)* zwei und zwei zusammenzählen; **cut/break in ~:** zweiteilen/entzweibrechen; **~ and ~, ~ by ~** *(~ at a time)* [zu] zwei und zwei; zu zweien; **that makes ~ of us** *(coll.)* mir geht's/ging's genauso *(ugs.)*; **~ can play at that game** das kann ich auch. *See also* **cheer 1 a; eight 2 a, c, d; [1]game 1 a; penny c**
two: ~-bit *adj. (Amer.)* **a)** *(costing 25 cents)* 25-Cent-; **b)** *(of poor quality)* mies *(ugs.)*; **~-by-'four 1.** *n. (piece of wood) Holzbalken mit einer Stärke von 2 auf 4 Zoll;* **2.** *adj. (Amer. fig.)* Westentaschen-; **~-dimensional** *adj.* zweidimensional; *(fig.)* oberflächlich; **~-door** *attrib. adj.* zweitürig ‹*Auto*›; **~-edged** *adj. (lit. or fig.)* zweischneidig; **~-faced** *adj. (fig.)* falsch *(abwertend)*; **be ~-faced** ‹*Person:*› zwei Gesichter haben; **~-'fisted** *adj.* **a)** *(Brit.: clumsy)* ungeschickt; **be ~-fisted** zwei linke Hände haben *(ugs.)*; **b)** *(Amer.: vigorous)* kernig; markig
twofold ['tu:fəʊld] *adj., adv.* **a)** zweifach; **be ~:** zweifacher Art *od.* Natur sein; **b)** *(double)* **a ~ increase** ein Anstieg auf das Doppelte; **increase ~:** sich verdoppeln
two: ~-four-time *n. (Mus.)* Zweivierteltakt, *der;* **~-'handed** *adj.* **a)** *(having two hands)* zweihändig; **b)** *(requiring both hands)* beidhändig; **c)** *(requiring two persons)* **~-handed poker** *(Cards)* Zwei-Mann-Poker, *der;* **~-party system** *n.* Zweiparteiensystem, *das;* **~pence** ['tʌpəns] *n. (Brit.)* zwei Pence; *see also* **care 2 c; ~penny** ['tʌpənɪ] *attrib. adj. (Brit.)* Zwei-Pence-; **~penny-halfpenny** [tʌpnɪ'heɪpnɪ] *attrib. adj. (Brit.)* unwichtig; lächerlich; *(of poor quality)* mies *(ugs.)*; **~penny-halfpenny novel** Groschenroman, *der (abwertend)*; **~-piece 1.** *n.* Zweiteiler, *der;* **2.** *adj.* zweiteilig; **~-pin** *see* **pin 1 c; ~-ply** *adj.* zweifädig ‹*Seil, Wolle, Zwirn*›; aus zweifädiger Wolle gewebt ‹*Teppich*›; zweilagig ‹*Holz, Papier*›; **~-seater 1.** [-'--] *n.* Zweisitzer, *der;* **2.** ['---] *attrib. adj.* zweisitzig
twosome ['tu:səm] *n.* **a)** Paar, *das;* **b)** *(Golf)* Zweier, *der*
two: ~-step *n.* Twostep, *der;* **~-storey** *adj.* zweigeschossig; **~-stroke** *adj. (Mech. Engin.)* Zweitakt‹*motor, -verfahren*›; **~-time** *v.t. (sl.)* **~-time sb.** *(be unfaithful)* jmdm. fremdgehen *(ugs.)*; *(cheat)* ein falsches Spiel mit jmdm. treiben; **~-timing** *adj. (sl.)* falsch; **~-tone** *adj.* **a)** *(in colour)* zweifarbig; **a car in ~-tone green** ein Auto in zwei Grüntönen; **b)** *(in sound)* Zweiklang-
'twould [twʊd] *(arch./poet.)* = **it would**
two: ~-up-~-down *n.* kleines [Reihen]haus; **~-way** *adj.* **a)** *(in both directions)* zweibahnig *(Verkehrsw.)*; **'~-way traffic ahead'** „Achtung, Gegenverkehr"; **b)** *(involving an exchange between ~ parties)* gegenseitig; **~-way scholarship programme** akademisches Austauschprogramm; **~-way radio** Funksprechgerät, *das;* **c)** *(Electr.)* **~-way switch** Zweiwege[um]schalter, *der;* **d)** **~-way tap** Zweiwegehahn, *der;* **e)** **~-way mirror** Einwegspiegel, *der;* **~-'wheeler** *n.* Zweirad, *das*
tycoon [taɪ'ku:n] *n.* Magnat, *der;* Tycoon, *der*
tying *see* **tie 1, 2**
tyke [taɪk] *n.* **a)** *(dog)* Köter, *der;* **b)** *(Brit.: churlish person)* Kerl, *der;* **c)** *(Yorkshireman)* **[Yorkshire] ~:** *Mann aus der Grafschaft Yorkshire;* **d)** *(child)* Bengel, *der*
tympani *see* **timpani**
tympanist *see* **timpanist**
type [taɪp] **1.** *n.* **a)** Art, *die; (person)* Typ, *der;* **what ~ of car ...?** was für ein Auto ...?; **her beauty is of another ~:** sie verkörpert einen anderen Typ von Schönheit; **she dislikes men of that ~:** sie mag diesen Typ [von] Mann nicht; **she's not my ~:** sie ist nicht mein Typ; **he's not the ~ to let people down** er ist nicht der Typ, der andere im Stich läßt; **a Burgundy ~ wine** eine Art Burgunder; **he is a different ~ of person** er ist eine andere Art Mensch *od.* ein anderer Typ; **books of this ~:** derartige Bücher; **true to ~:** erwartungsgemäß; **b)** *(coll.: character)* Type, *die (ugs.)*; **c)** *(Printing)* Drucktype, *die;* **be in small/italic ~:** kleingedruckt/kursiv gedruckt sein; **in ~:** druckfertig. **2.** *v.t.* **a)** *(do typing of)* [mit der Maschine] schreiben; tippen *(ugs.)*; **~d letter** maschinegeschriebener Brief; **b)** *(classify)* typisieren. **3.** *v.i.* maschineschreiben
~ 'in *v.t.* eintippen *(ugs.)*; [mit der Schreibmaschine] einfügen
~ 'out *v.t.* [mit der Schreibmaschine] abschreiben; abtippen *(ugs.)*; *(without original copy)* [in die Maschine] schreiben; tippen *(ugs.)*
~ 'up *v.t.* tippen
-type [taɪp] *in comb.* -artig; **ceramic-~ materials** keramikartiges Material; **Cheddar-~ cheese** Käse nach Cheddar-Art
type: ~-cast *v.t.* [auf eine bestimmte Rolle] festlegen; abstempeln; **be ~cast as the devoted wife** auf die Rolle der treuen Ehefrau festgelegt sein; **~-face** *n.* Schriftbild, *das;* **~script 1.** *n.* maschine[n]geschriebene Fassung; Typoskript, *das;* **in ~script** maschine[n]geschrieben; **be still in ~script** erst als Typoskript vorliegen; **2.** *adj. see* **typewritten; ~set** *v.t. (Printing)* setzen; **~setter** *n. (person)* [Schrift]setzer, *der/*-setzerin, *die;* **~setting** *n.* [Schrift]setzen, *das;* **~setting machine** Setzmaschine, *die;* **~-size** *n.* Schriftgrad, *der;* **~-wheel** *see* **daisy-wheel**
'typewriter *n.* Schreibmaschine, *die;* **~ ribbon** Farbband, *das*
'typewritten *adj.* maschine[n]geschrieben; mit der [Schreib]maschine geschrieben
typhoid ['taɪfɔɪd] *n. (Med.)* **~ [fever]** Typhus, *der*
typhoon [taɪ'fu:n] *n.* Taifun, *der*
typhus ['taɪfəs] *n. (Med.)* Fleckfieber, *das*
typical ['tɪpɪkl] *adj.* typisch **(of** für); **that's just ~!** [das ist mal wieder] typisch! *(ugs.)*
typically ['tɪpɪklɪ] *adv.* typischerweise; **~, she turned up late** wie üblich kam sie zu spät
typify ['tɪpɪfaɪ] *v.t.* **a)** *(represent)* [symbolhaft] darstellen; **b)** *(be an example of)* **~ sth.** als typisches Beispiel für etw. dienen
typing ['taɪpɪŋ] *n.* Maschineschreiben, *das;* **his ~ is excellent** er kann sehr gut maschineschreiben; **how is your ~?** kannst du [gut] maschineschreiben?; **can you do this piece of ~ for me?** kannst du das für mich [mit der Maschine] schreiben *od. (ugs.)* tippen?
typing: ~ error *n.* Tippfehler, *der (ugs.)*; **~ pool** *n.* Schreibzentrale, *die*
typist ['taɪpɪst] *n.* Schreibkraft, *die;* **shorthand ~:** Stenotypist, *der/*-typistin, *die;* **she is [not] a good ~:** sie kann [nicht] gut maschineschreiben
typo ['taɪpəʊ] *n., pl.* **~s** *(coll.)* Druckfehler, *der (ugs.)*
typographer [taɪ'pɒgrəfə(r)] *n.* Typograph, *der/*Typographin, *die*
typographic [taɪpə'græfɪk], **typographical** [taɪpə'græfɪkl] *adj.* typographisch; **~ error** Setzfehler, *der*
typography [taɪ'pɒgrəfɪ] *n.* Typographie, *die*
typology [taɪ'pɒlədʒɪ] *n.* Typologie, *die*
tyrannical [tɪ'rænɪkl, taɪ'rænɪkl] *adj.* tyrannisch
tyrannically [tɪ'rænɪkəlɪ, taɪ'rænɪkəlɪ] *adv.* tyrannisch; **behave ~ to sb.** jmdn. tyrannisieren
tyrannize (tyrannise) ['tɪrənaɪz] **1.** *v.i.* als Tyrann herrschen; **~ over sb.** jmdn. tyrannisieren. **2.** *v.t.* ‹*Chef, Vater, Ehemann:*› tyrannisieren; ‹*Herrscher:*› als Tyrann herrschen über (+ *Akk.*)
tyrannous ['tɪrənəs] *adj.* tyrannisch
tyranny ['tɪrənɪ] *n.* Tyrannei, *die*
tyrant ['taɪrənt] *n. (lit. or fig.)* Tyrann, *der*
tyre ['taɪə(r)] *n.* Reifen, *der*
tyre: ~-chain *n.* Schneekette, *die;* **~-gauge** *n.* Reifendruckprüfer, *der;* **~ pressure** *n.* Reifendruck, *der*
tyro *see* **tiro**
Tyrol [tɪ'rəʊl] *pr. n.* Tirol *(das)*
Tyrolean [tɪrə'li:ən] *adj.* Tiroler
tzar *etc. see* **tsar** *etc.*

U

[1]U, u [ju:] *n., pl.* **Us** *or* **U's** U, u, *das*
[2]U *adj. (Brit. coll.)* für die Oberschicht typisch ‹*Benehmen, Ausdruck, Sprache*›; **be U** ‹*Person:*› ein [typischer] Vertreter der Oberschicht sein
[3]U *abbr.* **a)** *(Brit.)* **universal** jugendfrei ‹*Film*›; **b) University** Univ.
UAE *abbr.* **United Arab Emirates** VAE
UB 40 [ju:bi: 'fɔ:tɪ] *n. (Brit.)* **a)** *(card)* Arbeitslosenausweis, *der;* **b)** *(coll.)* Arbeitslose, *der/die*
'U-bend *n.* U-Rohr, *das;* Knie, *das (ugs.)*
ubiquitous [ju:'bɪkwɪtəs] *adj.* allgegenwärtig
'U-boat *n. (Hist.)* [deutsches] U-Boot
udder ['ʌdə(r)] *n.* Euter, *das*
UDI *abbr.* **Unilateral Declaration of Independence** einseitige Unabhängigkeitserklärung
UDR *abbr.* **Ulster Defence Regiment** *nordirische paramilitärische Organisation zur Unterstützung der Britischen Armee*
UEFA [ju:'eɪfə] *abbr.* **Union of European Football Associations** UEFA, *die*
UFO ['ju:fəʊ] *n., pl.* **~s** Ufo, *das*
Uganda [ju:'gændə] *pr. n.* Uganda *(das)*
Ugandan [ju:'gændən] **1.** *adj.* ugandisch; **sb. is ~:** jmd. ist Ugander/Uganderin. **2.** *n.* Ugander, *der/*Uganderin, *die*
ugh [ʌh, ʊh, ɜ:h] *int.* bah
ugli ['ʌglɪ] *n.* **~ [fruit]** Tangelo, *die*
ugliness ['ʌglɪnɪs] *n., no pl.* Häßlichkeit, *die*
ugly ['ʌglɪ] *adj.* **a)** *(in appearance, morally)* häßlich; **~ duckling** *(fig.)* häßliches Entlein *(ugs. scherzh.)*; **as ~ as sin** *(coll.)* potthäßlich *(ugs.)*; häßlich wie die Nacht; **b)** *(nasty)* übel ‹*Wunde, Laune, Szene usw.*›; **~ customer** *(fig. coll.)* unangenehmer Zeitgenosse/unangenehme Zeitgenossin; **have an**

~ **temper** übellaunig sein; **c)** *(stormy)* übel ‹*Wetter, Nacht*›; bedrohlich ‹*Himmel*›
UHF *abbr.* **ultra-high frequency** UHF
UHT *abbr.* **ultra heat treated** ultrahocherhitzt; UHT milk H-Milch, *die*
UK *abbr.* **United Kingdom**
ukase [ju:'keɪz] *n.* Ukas, *der*
Ukraine [ju:'kreɪn] *pr. n.* Ukraine, *die*
Ukrainian [ju:'kreɪnɪən] **1.** *adj.* ukrainisch; **sb. is ~:** jmd. ist Ukrainer/Ukrainerin; *see also* **English 1. 2.** *n.* **a)** *(person)* Ukrainer, *der*/Ukrainerin, *die;* **b)** *(language)* Ukrainisch, *das; see also* **English 2 a**
ukulele [ju:kə'leɪlɪ] *n.* *(Mus.)* Ukulele, *die od. das*
ulcer ['ʌlsə(r)] *n.* Geschwür, *das;* *(fig.)* [Krebs]geschwür, *das (fig.);* **mouth ~[s]** Aphthe, *die (Med.)*
ulcerate ['ʌlsəreɪt] **1.** *v. i.* *(Med.)* ulzerieren *(fachspr.);* geschwürig werden. **2.** *v. t.* ein Geschwür verursachen in (+ *Dat.*); **an ~d stomach** ein geschwüriger Magen
ulceration [ʌlsə'reɪʃn] *n.* **a)** *(process)* Geschwürbildung, *die;* **b)** *(ulcers)* Geschwüre
ulcerous ['ʌlsərəs] *adj.* *(Med.)* geschwürig; *(fig.)* **racism is an ~ growth in society** der Rassismus ist ein Geschwür am Leibe der Gesellschaft
ulna ['ʌlnə] *n., pl.* **ulnae** ['ʌlni:] *(Anat.)* Elle, *die*
Ulster ['ʌlstə(r)] *pr. n.* Ulster *(das)*
ulster *n.* *(coat)* Ulster, *der*
Ulster: ~man ['ʌlstəmən] *n., pl.* **~men** ['ʌlstəmən] *(inhabitant)* Bewohner von Ulster; *(native)* [geborener] Nordire; **~woman** *n.* *(inhabitant)* Bewohnerin von Ulster; *(native)* [geborene] Nordirin
ult. [ʌlt] *abbr.* *(Commerc.)* **ultimo**
ulterior [ʌl'tɪərɪə(r)] *adj.* hintergründig; geheim; **~ motive/thought** Hintergedanke, *der*
ultimate ['ʌltɪmət] **1.** *attrib. adj.* **a)** *(final)* letzt...; *(eventual)* endgültig ‹*Sieg*›; letztendlich ‹*Rettung*›; größt... ‹*Opfer*›; **~ result/goal/decision** Endergebnis, *das*/Endziel, *das*/endgültige Entscheidung; **in the ~ analysis** letzten Endes; **he exercises ~ jurisdiction/authority** er hat die höchste richterliche Gewalt/Autorität inne; **the ~ deterrent** das äußerste Abschreckungsmittel; **b)** *(fundamental)* tiefst... ‹*Grundlage, Wahrheit*›; **~ principles** Grundprinzipien; **the ~ particles of matter** die elementaren Teilchen der Materie; **the ~ origin** der eigentliche Ursprung; **c)** *(maximum)* maximal; **~ speed** Höchstgeschwindigkeit, *die;* **d)** *(best/greatest conceivable)* **the ~ washing machine** die Waschmaschine in Perfektion; **this is the ~ luxury** das ist der Gipfel an Luxus. **2.** *n.* **the ~** *(maximum)* das absolute Maximum; *(minimum)* das absolute Minimum; **the ~ in comfort/luxury/style/fashion** der Gipfel an Bequemlichkeit/Luxus/das Exzellenteste an Stil/in der Mode
ultimately ['ʌltɪmətlɪ] *adv.* **a)** *(in the end)* schließlich; **b)** *(in the last analysis)* letzten Endes; *(basically)* im Grunde [genommen]
ultimatum [ʌltɪ'meɪtəm] *n., pl.* **~s** *or* **ultimata** [ʌltɪ'meɪtə] Ultimatum, *das;* **give sb. an ~:** jmdm. ein Ultimatum stellen
ultimo ['ʌltɪməʊ] *adj.* *(Commerc.)* des vergangenen Monats
ultra ['ʌltrə] **1.** *n.* Ultra, *der (Politikjargon).* **2.** *adj.* extremistisch
ultra- ['ʌltrə] *pref.* ultra‹*konservativ, -modern*›; hyper‹*modern, -modisch*›
ultrama'rine *n.* Ultramarin, *das*
ultra'sonic *adj.* Ultraschall-
ultra'sonically *adv.* mit Ultraschall
ultra'sonics *n., no pl.* **a)** *see* **ultrasound; b)** *(science)* Lehre vom Ultraschall
ultra'sound *n., no pl.* Ultraschall, *der*
ultra'violet *adj.* *(Phys.)* ultraviolett ‹*Strahlen, Licht*›; *(using ~ radiation)* UV-‹*Lampe, Filter*›; **~ treatment** UV-Bestrahlung, *die*
ululate ['ju:ljʊleɪt] *v. i.* *(literary)* heulen; *(with grief)* wehklagen *(geh.)*
Ulysses ['ju:lɪsi:z, ju:'lɪsi:z] *pr. n.* Odysseus *(der)*
um [m, əm, ʌm] **1.** *int.* äh[m]. **2.** [ʌm] *v. i.,* **-mm-** *(coll.)* **~ and ah** herumdrucksen *(ugs.)*
umbel ['ʌmbl] *n.* *(Bot.)* Dolde, *die*
umber ['ʌmbə(r)] *n.* **[raw/burnt] ~:** [ungebrannte/gebrannte] Umbra
umbilical cord [ʌm'bɪlɪkl kɔ:d] *n.* Nabelschnur, *die*
umbra ['ʌmbrə] *n., pl.* **~e** ['ʌmbri:] *or* **~s** *(Astron.)* **a)** *(in eclipse)* Kernschatten, *der;* **b)** *(in sunspot)* Umbra, *die*
umbrage ['ʌmbrɪdʒ] *n., no pl., no indef. art.* **take ~ [at** *or* **over sth.]** [an etw. (+ *Dat.*)] Anstoß nehmen
umbrella [ʌm'brelə] *n.* **a)** [Regen]schirm, *der;* **telescopic ~:** Taschenschirm, *der;* **put up an ~:** einen Schirm aufspannen; **b)** *(fig.: protection)* Schutz, *der;* *(Mil.)* *(barrage)* Sperrfeuer, *das; (air cover)* Jagdschutz, *der;* **the ~ of the Welfare State** das soziale Netz des Wohlfahrtsstaates; **c)** *(fig.: unifying agency)* **the company X comes under the ~ of company Y** die Firma X ist eine Tochtergesellschaft der Firma Y; **an ~ organization/group** eine Dachorganisation/eine übergeordnete Gruppe
um'brella-stand *n.* Schirmständer, *der*
umlaut ['ʊmlaʊt] *n.* **a)** *(vowel change)* Umlaut, *der;* **b)** *(mark)* Umlautzeichen, *das*
umpire ['ʌmpaɪə(r)] **1.** *n.* Schiedsrichter, *der*/-richterin, *die.* **2.** *v. i.* schiedsrichtern; Schiedsrichter/-richterin sein. **3.** *v. t.* schiedsrichtern bei ‹*Spiel, Wettkampf*›; pfeifen ‹*Fußballspiel usw.*›
umpteen [ʌmp'ti:n] *adj.* *(coll.)* zig *(ugs.);* x *(ugs.)*
umpteenth [ʌmp'ti:nθ] *adj.* *(coll.)* zigst... *(ugs.);* **for the ~ time** zum zigsten *od.* x-ten Mal *(ugs.)*
UN *abbr.* **United Nations** UN[O], *die*
'un [ən] *pron.* *(coll.)* **a)** *(person)* Typ, *der;* **he's a tough/bad ~:** er ist ein zäher/übler Bursche *(ugs.);* **b)** *(thing)* **a big ~:** ein großer/eine große/ein großes; **big ~s and little ~s** Große und Kleine; *see also* **wrong 'un**
unabashed [ʌnə'bæʃt] *adj.* ungeniert; *(without shame)* schamlos; *(undaunted)* unerschrocken ‹*Kämpfer*›
unabated [ʌnə'beɪtɪd] *adj.* unvermindert
unable [ʌn'eɪbl] *pred. adj.* **be ~ to do sth.** nicht in der Lage sein, etw. zu tun; etw. nicht tun können; **he wanted to attend but was ~ to** er wollte kommen, aber er war dazu nicht in der Lage
unabridged [ʌnə'brɪdʒd] *adj.* ungekürzt
unaccented [ʌnək'sentɪd] *adj.* unbetont
unacceptable [ʌnək'septəbl] *adj.* unannehmbar; **[be] not ~:** durchaus akzeptabel [sein]; **the ~ face of capitalism** die Kehrseite des Kapitalismus
unaccommodating [ʌnə'kɒmədeɪtɪŋ] *adj.* ungefällig; *(inflexible)* unnachgiebig
unaccompanied [ʌnə'kʌmpənɪd] *adj.* ohne Begleitung ‹*reisen, singen*›; unbegleitet ‹*Gepäck, Chor*›; *(on aircraft etc.)* **~ minor** alleinreisendes Kind; **~ by sth.** nicht begleitet von etw.; **pieces for ~ horn/violin** Solostücke für Horn/Violine
unaccountable [ʌnə'kaʊntəbl] *adj.* unerklärlich
unaccountably [ʌnə'kaʊntəblɪ] *adv.* unerklärlicherweise; *(with adj.)* unerklärlich
unaccounted [ʌnə'kaʊntɪd] *adj.* **~ for** unauffindbar; **several passengers are still ~ for** einige Passagiere werden noch vermißt; **the discrepancy remains ~ for** die Diskrepanz läßt sich nicht erklären
unaccustomed [ʌnə'kʌstəmd] *adj.* ungewohnt; **be ~ to sth.** etw. *(Akk.)* nicht gewöhnt sein; **~ as I am to public speaking ...:** obwohl ich kein Redner bin ...
unacquainted [ʌnə'kweɪntɪd] *adj.* **be [completely] ~ with sth.** mit etw. [überhaupt] nicht vertraut sein
unadopted [ʌnə'dɒptɪd] *adj.* *(Brit.)* von der Gemeinde nicht unterhalten ‹*Straße*›
unadorned [ʌnə'dɔ:nd] *adj.* schmucklos; ungeschminkt ‹*Wahrheit*›; schlicht ‹*Stil*›
unadulterated [ʌnə'dʌltəreɪtɪd] *adj.* **a)** *(pure)* unverfälscht; rein ‹*Wasser, Wein*›; **b)** *(utter)* völlig; **~ rubbish** absoluter Quatsch
unadventurous [ʌnəd'ventʃərəs] *adj.* bieder ‹*Person*›; ereignislos ‹*Leben*›; *(lacking ideas)* einfallslos ‹*Inszenierung, Buch usw.*›; **he is an ~ cook** er macht beim Kochen keine Experimente
unaffected [ʌnə'fektɪd] *adj.* **a)** *(not affected)* unberührt; *(Med.)* nicht angegriffen ‹*Organ*›; **the area was ~ by the strike** die Gegend war vom Streik nicht betroffen; **she seems to have been ~ by the experience** diese Erfahrung scheint keine Wirkung auf sie gehabt zu haben; **b)** *(natural)* natürlich; ungekünstelt; **~ astonishment** blankes Staunen
unaffectedly [ʌnə'fektɪdlɪ] *adv.* natürlich; ungekünstelt
unafraid [ʌnə'freɪd] *adj.* **be ~ [of sb./sth.]** keine Angst [vor jmdm./etw.] haben
unaided [ʌn'eɪdɪd] *adj.* ohne fremde Hilfe; **by one's own ~ efforts** ohne jede fremde Hilfe; **walk ~:** ohne Hilfe gehen
unalike [ʌnə'laɪk] *pred. adj.* unähnlich; **they are so ~:** sie sind sich *(Dat.)* so unähnlich
unalloyed [ʌn'ælɔɪd, ʌnə'lɔɪd] *adj.* nicht legiert ‹*Metall*›; *(fig.)* rein; ungetrübt ‹*Freude, Glück*›
unalterable [ʌn'ɔ:ltərəbl, ʌn'ɒltərəbl] *adj.* unabänderlich ‹*Gesetz, Schicksal*›; unverrückbar ‹*Entschluß*›
unaltered [ʌn'ɔ:ltəd, ʌn'ɒltəd] *adj.* unverändert
unambiguous [ʌnæm'bɪgjʊəs] *adj.* unzweideutig
unambitious [ʌnæm'bɪʃəs] *adj.* ‹*Person*› ohne Ergeiz; anspruchslos ‹*Buch*›; **be ~/a bit ~:** keinen/wenig Ehrgeiz haben
un-American [ʌnə'merɪkn] *adj.* **a)** *(not typically American)* unamerikanisch; **b)** *(contrary to US interests)* antiamerikanisch; **~ activities** unamerikanische Umtriebe
unanimity [ju:nə'nɪmɪtɪ] *n., no pl.* Einmütigkeit, *die;* **be in perfect ~ over sth.** in etw. *(Dat.)* völlig übereinstimmen
unanimous [ju:'nænɪməs] *adj.* einstimmig; **be ~ in doing sth.** etw. einmütig tun; **be ~ in rejecting** *or* **in their** *etc.* **rejection of sth.** etw. einmütig ablehnen; **the meeting was ~ as to ...:** die Versammlung war einer Meinung über ...
unanimously [ju:'nænɪməslɪ] *adv.* einstimmig
unannounced [ʌnə'naʊnst] *adj.* unangemeldet
unanswerable [ʌn'ɑ:nsərəbl] *adj.* unbeantwortbar ‹*Frage*›; unlösbar ‹*Rätsel, Problem*›; unwiderlegbar ‹*Argument*›
unanswered [ʌn'ɑ:nsəd] *adj.* unbeantwortet; **go ~, be left ~:** unbeantwortet bleiben
unapologetic [ʌnəpɒlə'dʒetɪk] *adj.* **he was quite ~ about it** er machte keinerlei Anstalten, sich zu entschuldigen
unappealing [ʌnə'pi:lɪŋ] *adj.* unansehnlich ‹*Person*›; nicht verlockend ‹*Aussicht*›
unappetizing [ʌn'æpɪtaɪzɪŋ] *adj.* unappetitlich; unerfreulich ‹*Zukunft, Aussicht*›
unappreciative [ʌnə'pri:ʃɪətɪv, ʌnə'pri:sɪətɪv] *adj.* undankbar; **be ~ of sth.** etw. nicht zu würdigen wissen
unapproachable [ʌnə'prəʊtʃəbl] *adj.* unzugänglich
unarguable [ʌn'ɑ:gjʊəbl] *adj.* unhaltbar
unarm [ʌn'ɑ:m] *see* **disarm 1**
unarmed [ʌn'ɑ:md] *adj.* unbewaffnet; **~ combat** Kampf ohne Waffen
unartistic [ʌnɑ:'tɪstɪk] *adj.* unkünstlerisch; **be ~:** keinen Sinn für Kunst haben

unashamed [ʌnəˈʃeɪmd] *adj.* schamlos; *(not embarrassed)* ungeniert; unverhohlen ⟨*Individualist*⟩; **naked and ~**: nackt und ungeniert
unashamedly [ʌnəˈʃeɪmɪdlɪ] *adv.* ungeniert; unverhohlen ⟨*individualistisch*⟩
unasked [ʌnˈɑːskt] *adj.* **a)** *(uninvited)* ungebeten; **b)** *(not asked for)* **~ [for]** ungefragt
unassailable [ʌnəˈseɪləbl] *adj.* **a)** *(not open to assault)* uneinnehmbar; **an ~ lead** ein nicht aufzuholender Vorsprung; **b)** *(irrefutable)* unwiderlegbar
unassisted [ʌnəˈsɪstɪd] *see* **unaided**
unassuming [ʌnəˈsjuːmɪŋ] *adj.* bescheiden; unprätentiös *(geh.)*
unattached [ʌnəˈtætʃt] *adj.* **a)** *(not fixed)* nicht befestigt; **b)** *(without a partner)* ungebunden
unattainable [ʌnəˈteɪnəbl] *adj.* unerreichbar
unattempted [ʌnəˈtemptɪd] *adj.* **the climb remains ~**: die Ersteigung ist noch nicht versucht worden
unattended [ʌnəˈtendɪd] *adj.* **a) ~ to** *(not dealt with)* unerledigt, unbearbeitet ⟨*Post, Angelegenheit*⟩; nicht bedient ⟨*Kunde*⟩; nicht behandelt ⟨*Patient, Wunde*⟩; **leave a customer/patient ~ to** einen Kunden nicht bedienen/einen Patienten nicht behandeln; **he left the faults ~ to** er hat sich um die Fehler nicht gekümmert; **b)** *(not supervised)* unbeaufsichtigt ⟨*Kind*⟩; unbewacht ⟨*Parkplatz, Gepäck*⟩; **leave a patient ~**: einen Patienten allein lassen; **travel ~**: ohne Begleitung reisen
unattractive [ʌnəˈtræktɪv] *adj.* unattraktiv; unschön ⟨*Ort, Merkmal*⟩; wenig verlockend ⟨*Angebot, Vorschlag*⟩; **not ~**: nicht ohne Reiz
unauthorized [ʌnˈɔːθəraɪzd] *adj.* unbefugt; nicht autorisiert ⟨*Biographie*⟩; nicht genehmigt ⟨*Demonstration*⟩; **no entry for ~ persons** Zutritt für Unbefugte verboten
unavailable [ʌnəˈveɪləbl] *adj.* nicht erhältlich ⟨*Ware*⟩; **be ~ for comment** zu einer Stellungnahme nicht zur Verfügung stehen; **the manager is ~**: der Manager ist nicht zu sprechen
unavailing [ʌnəˈveɪlɪŋ] *adj.* vergeblich
unavoidable [ʌnəˈvɔɪdəbl] *adj.* unvermeidlich; **~ delays** unvermeidbare Verzögerungen
unavoidably [ʌnəˈvɔɪdəblɪ] *adv.* **we were ~ delayed** unsere Verspätung ließ sich nicht vermeiden; **he has been ~ detained** er konnte nicht verhindern, daß er aufgehalten wurde
unaware [ʌnəˈweə(r)] *adj.* **be ~ of sth.** sich *(Dat.)* einer Sache *(Gen.)* nicht bewußt sein; **he was not ~ of this fact** diese Tatsache war ihm durchaus bekannt
unawares [ʌnəˈweəz] *adv.* unerwartet; **come upon sb./catch sb. ~**: jmdn. überraschen; **take sb. ~**: für jmdn. unerwartet kommen
unbalanced [ʌnˈbælənst] *adj.* **a)** unausgewogen; **b)** *(mentally ~)* unausgeglichen
unbar [ʌnˈbɑː(r)] *v. t.*, **-rr-** entriegeln
unbearable [ʌnˈbeərəbl] *adj.*, **unbearably** [ʌnˈbeərəblɪ] *adv.* unerträglich
unbeatable [ʌnˈbiːtəbl] *adj.* unschlagbar *(ugs.)*
unbeaten [ʌnˈbiːtn] *adj.* **a)** *(not defeated)* ungeschlagen; **they lost their ~ record** ihre Siegesserie endete; **b)** *(not surpassed)* unerreicht; **this record is still ~**: dieser Rekord ist immer noch ungebrochen
unbecoming [ʌnbɪˈkʌmɪŋ] *adj.* **a)** *(improper)* unschicklich *(geh.)*; **conduct ~ to a soldier** ein für einen Soldaten ungebührliches Verhalten; **b)** *(not attractive)* unvorteilhaft ⟨*Kleidung, Frisur*⟩; unschön ⟨*Nase*⟩
unbeknown [ʌnbɪˈnəʊn] *adj.* *(coll.)* **~ to me/her/her boss** ohne mein/ihr Wissen/ohne Wissen ihres Chefs
unbelievable [ʌnbɪˈliːvəbl] *adj.* **a)** *(hardly believable)* unglaublich; **b)** *(tremendous)* unwahrscheinlich ⟨*Hunger, Durst*⟩
unbelievably [ʌnbɪˈliːvəblɪ] *adv.* **a)** *as intensifier* unglaublich ⟨*dumm, dick, jung usw.*⟩; **b)** *as sentence-modifier (not believably)* **~, the rider managed to stay on the horse** es war kaum zu glauben, aber der Reiter konnte sich auf dem Pferd halten
unbeliever [ʌnbɪˈliːvə(r)] *n.* Ungläubige, *der/die*
unbelieving [ʌnbɪˈliːvɪŋ] *adj.* ungläubig
unbend [ʌnˈbend] **1.** *v. t.*, **unbent** [ʌnˈbent] geradebiegen ⟨*Draht, Metall, Stoßstange*⟩; auseinanderbiegen ⟨*Büroklammer*⟩; **~ one's body *or* oneself** sich aufrichten. **2.** *v. i.*, **unbent a)** *(sit/stand up)* sich aufrichten; **b)** *(become affable)* aus sich *(Dat.)* herausgehen
unbending [ʌnˈbendɪŋ] *adj.* *(inflexible)* unbeugsam
unbiased, unbiassed [ʌnˈbaɪəst] *adj.* unvoreingenommen
unbidden [ʌnˈbɪdn] *adj.* unaufgefordert; *(uninvited)* ungebeten
unbind [ʌnˈbaɪnd] *v. t.*, *forms as* **bind 1** losbinden ⟨*Mensch, Tier*⟩; lösen ⟨*Haare*⟩
unbirthday [ʌnˈbɜːθdeɪ] *adj.* *(Brit. coll.)* **~ present** Geschenk ohne besonderen Anlaß
unbleached [ʌnˈbliːtʃt] *adj.* ungebleicht
unblemished [ʌnˈblemɪʃt] *adj.* makellos ⟨*Haut, Lack, Ruf*⟩; unbefleckt *(geh.)* ⟨*Ehre*⟩
unblinking [ʌnˈblɪŋkɪŋ] *adj.* unverwandt ⟨*Blick*⟩; unbewegt ⟨*Haltung, Miene*⟩
unblock [ʌnˈblɒk] *v. t.* frei machen *od.* bekommen; **remain ~ed** frei bleiben
unblushing [ʌnˈblʌʃɪŋ] *adj.* *(fig.)* schamlos
unbolt [ʌnˈbəʊlt] *v. t.* aufriegeln
unborn [ʌnˈbɔːn, *attrib.* ˈʌnbɔːn] *adj.* ungeboren; **generations [yet] ~**: künftige Generationen
unbosom [ʌnˈbʊzəm] *v. refl.* **~ oneself [to sb.]** [jmdm.] sein Herz ausschütten
unbound [ʌnˈbaʊnd] *adj.* **a)** *(not tied)* offen ⟨*Haar*⟩; **Prometheus ~**: der entfesselte Prometheus; **b)** ungebunden ⟨*Buch*⟩
unbounded [ʌnˈbaʊndɪd] *adj.* **a)** *(unchecked)* uneingeschränkt ⟨*Freiheit*⟩; unkontrolliert ⟨*Gefühl*⟩; **b)** *(unlimited)* grenzenlos
unbowed [ʌnˈbaʊd] *adj.* ungebeugt; **bloody but ~**: angeschlagen, aber unbesiegt
unbreakable [ʌnˈbreɪkəbl] *adj.* unzerbrechlich
unbridled [ʌnˈbraɪdld] *adj.* *(fig.)* ungezügelt ⟨*Machtstreben*⟩; bodenlos *(ugs.)* ⟨*Unverschämtheit*⟩; grenzenlos ⟨*Enthusiasmus*⟩
un-British [ʌnˈbrɪtɪʃ] *adj.* unbritisch
unbroken [ʌnˈbrəʊkn] *adj.* **a)** *(undamaged)* heil; unbeschädigt; **b)** *(not interrupted)* ununterbrochen; **~ sleep/peace/silence** ungestörter Schlaf/Friede/durch nichts unterbrochene Stille; **have a night's ~ sleep** die Nacht durchschlafen; **c)** *(not surpassed)* ungebrochen ⟨*Rekord*⟩; **d)** *(Equit.)* nicht zugeritten ⟨*Pferd*⟩
unbuckle [ʌnˈbʌkl] *v. t.* aufschnallen
unbuilt [ʌnˈbɪlt] *adj.* ungebaut; **~ on** *(not occupied by a building)* unbebaut
unburden [ʌnˈbɜːdn] *v. t.* *(literary)* befreien ⟨*Gewissen*⟩; **~ oneself/one's heart [to sb.]** [jmdm.] sein Herz ausschütten; **~ oneself of sth.** sich von etw. befreien; **to her he could ~ himself of all his anxieties** ihr konnte er alle seine Ängste anvertrauen
unbusinesslike [ʌnˈbɪznɪslaɪk] *adj.* **he is ~, he has an ~ approach** er geht nicht wie ein Geschäftsmann an die Dinge heran
unbutton [ʌnˈbʌtn] *v. t.* aufknöpfen
unbuttoned [ʌnˈbʌtnd] *adj.* *(lit. or fig.)* aufgeknöpft; offen
uncalled-for [ʌnˈkɔːldfɔː(r)] *adj.* unangebracht
uncannily [ʌnˈkænɪlɪ] *adv.* unheimlich
uncanny [ʌnˈkænɪ] *adj.* **a)** *(seemingly supernatural)* unheimlich; **b)** *(mysterious)* verblüffend
uncap [ʌnˈkæp] *v. t.*, **-pp-** öffnen ⟨*Flasche*⟩
uncared-for [ʌnˈkeədfɔː(r)] *adj.* vernachlässigt
uncaring [ʌnˈkeərɪŋ] *adj.* gleichgültig
uncarpeted [ʌnˈkɑːpɪtɪd] *adj.* teppichlos
unceasing [ʌnˈsiːsɪŋ] *adj.* unaufhörlich; **the rain was ~**: es regnete ununterbrochen
unceasingly [ʌnˈsiːsɪŋlɪ] *adv.* ununterbrochen
uncensored [ʌnˈsensəd] *adj.* unzensiert
unceremonious [ʌnserɪˈməʊnɪəs] *adj.* **a)** *(informal)* formlos; **b)** *(abrupt)* brüsk
unceremoniously [ʌnserɪˈməʊnɪəslɪ] *adv.* ohne Umschweife
uncertain [ʌnˈsɜːtn, ʌnˈsɜːtɪn] *adj.* **a)** *(not sure)* **be ~ [whether ...]** sich *(Dat.)* nicht sicher sein[, ob ...]; **I am ~ of his loyalty** ich bin mir seiner Treue nicht sicher; **b)** *(not clear)* ungewiß ⟨*Ergebnis, Zukunft, Schicksal*⟩; **of ~ age/origin** unbestimmten Alters/unbestimmter Herkunft; **a play of ~ authorship** ein Stück, dessen Verfasser nicht [sicher] bekannt ist; **it is still ~ whether ...**: es ist noch ungewiß, ob ...; **it is ~ who was the inventor** der Erfinder ist nicht [genau] bekannt; **c)** *(unsteady)* unsicher ⟨*Schritte*⟩; **d)** *(changeable)* unbeständig ⟨*Charakter, Wetter*⟩; unstet ⟨*Dasein*⟩; wechselnd ⟨*Gesundheitszustand*⟩; flackernd ⟨*Schein*⟩; **e)** *(ambiguous)* vage; **in no ~ terms** ganz eindeutig
uncertainly [ʌnˈsɜːtnlɪ, ʌnˈsɜːtɪnlɪ] *adv.* **a)** *(without definite aim)* ziellos; **b)** *(without confidence)* unsicher
uncertainty [ʌnˈsɜːtntɪ, ʌnˈsɜːtɪntɪ] *n.* **a)** *no pl. (doubtfulness)* Ungewißheit, *die*; **there is some ~ about it** es ist etwas ungewiß; **any ~ about it was dispelled** jeder Zweifel darüber wurde ausgeräumt; **b)** *(doubtful point)* Unklarheit, *die;* **c)** *no pl. (hesitation)* Unsicherheit, *die;* **the ~ of his touch** seine unsichere Hand
unˈcertainty principle *n.* *(Phys.)* Unschärferelation, *die*
unchallenged [ʌnˈtʃælɪndʒd] *adj.* unangefochten; **go ~** ⟨*Autorität, Position:*⟩ nicht in Frage gestellt werden; **let a statement go ~**: eine Behauptung unwidersprochen lassen
unchangeable [ʌnˈtʃeɪnʒəbl] *adj.* unabänderlich
unchanged [ʌnˈtʃeɪndʒd] *adj.* unverändert
unchanging [ʌnˈtʃeɪndʒɪŋ] *adj.* unveränderlich; **~ monotony** gleichförmige Eintönigkeit
uncharacteristic [ʌnkærɪktəˈrɪstɪk] *adj.* uncharakteristisch **(of** für); ungewohnt ⟨*Grobheit, Schärfe*⟩
uncharged [ʌnˈtʃɑːdʒd] *adj.* ungeladen
uncharitable [ʌnˈtʃærɪtəbl] *adj.*, **uncharitably** [ʌnˈtʃærɪtəblɪ] *adv.* lieblos
uncharted [ʌnˈtʃɑːtɪd] *adj.* auf keiner Landkarte verzeichnet; unerforscht ⟨*Wildnis*⟩; unbekannt ⟨*Insel, Gewässer*⟩; *(fig.)* **the ~ regions of the psyche** die unerforschten Bereiche der Psyche
unchecked [ʌnˈtʃekt] *adj.* **a)** *(not examined)* ungeprüft; **b)** *(unrestrained)* ungehindert; nicht eingedämmt ⟨*Epidemie, Inflation*⟩; **sth. goes ~**: gegen etw. wird nichts getan
unchivalrous [ʌnˈʃɪvlrəs] *adj.* unritterlich
unchristian [ʌnˈkrɪstjən] *adj.* unchristlich
uncivil [ʌnˈsɪvɪl, ʌnˈsɪvl] *adj.* unhöflich
uncivilized [ʌnˈsɪvɪlaɪzd] *adj.* unzivilisiert; primitiv ⟨*Zustände*⟩; **an ~ hour** eine unchristliche Tageszeit *(ugs. scherzh.)*
unclaimed [ʌnˈkleɪmd] *adj.* herrenlos; nicht abgeholt ⟨*Brief, Preis*⟩; **the money is still ~**: bis jetzt hat niemand Anspruch auf das Geld erhoben
unclassified [ʌnˈklæsɪfaɪd] *adj.* nicht klassifiziert; *(not subject to security classification)* nicht geheim
uncle [ˈʌŋkl] *n.* **a)** Onkel, *der;* **b)** *(sl.: pawn-*

broker) Pfandleiher, *der;* **c) cry ~** *(Amer. coll.: surrender)* sich geschlagen geben
unclean [ʌn'kli:n] *adj.* unrein
Uncle: ~ **'Sam** *n. (coll.)* Uncle Sam *(der);* ~ **'Tom** *n. (Amer.) den Weißen gegenüber gefügiger Schwarzer in den USA*
unclothed [ʌn'kləʊðd] *adj.* unbekleidet
unclouded [ʌn'klaʊdɪd] *adj.* wolkenlos; *(fig.)* ~ **mind/happiness** klarer Verstand/ungetrübtes Glück
uncluttered [ʌn'klʌtəd] *adj.* ordentlich
uncoil [ʌn'kɔɪl] **1.** *v. t.* abwickeln. **2.** *v. refl.* sich abwickeln; ‹*Schlange:*› sich strecken
uncoloured (*Amer.:* **uncolored**) [ʌn'kʌləd] *adj. (lit. or fig.)* ungefärbt; ~ **by prejudice** von keinem Vorurteil gefärbt
uncomfortable [ʌn'kʌmfətəbl] *adj.* **a)** *(causing physical discomfort)* unbequem; **b)** *(feeling discomfort)* **be ~:** sich unbehaglich fühlen; **the heat made me ~:** durch die Hitze fühlte ich mich unbehaglich; **c)** *(uneasy, disconcerting)* unangenehm; peinlich ‹*Stille*›; **his gaze made me ~:** sein Blick war mir unangenehm; **if you feel ~ about it** wenn es dir unangenehm ist; **sb. has an ~ awareness of sth.** jmd. ist sich *(Dat.)* einer Sache *(Gen.)* peinlich bewußt
uncomfortably [ʌn'kʌmfətəblɪ] *adv.* **a)** *(with physical discomfort)* unbequem; ~ **oppressive** unangenehm [und] drückend; **b)** *(uneasily)* unbehaglich; **be** *or* **feel ~ aware of sth.** sich *(Dat.)* einer Sache *(Gen.)* peinlich bewußt sein
uncommitted [ʌnkə'mɪtɪd] *adj.* unbeteiligt
uncommon [ʌn'kɒmən] *adj.* ungewöhnlich; **it is not ~ for him to be found there** es ist [ganz und gar] nicht ungewöhnlich, daß man ihn dort findet
uncommonly [ʌn'kɒmənlɪ] *adv.* ungewöhnlich
uncommunicative [ʌnkə'mju:nɪkətɪv] *adj.* verschlossen
uncomplaining [ʌnkəm'pleɪnɪŋ] *adj.*, **uncomplainingly** [ʌnkəm'pleɪnɪŋlɪ] *adv.* klaglos
uncompleted [ʌnkəm'pli:tɪd] *adj.* unvollendet
uncomplicated [ʌn'kɒmplɪkeɪtɪd] *adj.* unkompliziert
uncomplimentary [ʌnkɒmplɪ'mentərɪ] *adj.* wenig schmeichelhaft; **be ~ about sb./sth.** sich nicht sehr schmeichelhaft über jmdn./etw. äußern
uncomprehending [ʌnkɒmprɪ'hendɪŋ] *adj.* verständnislos
uncompromising [ʌn'kɒmprəmaɪzɪŋ] *adj.*, **uncompromisingly** [ʌn'kɒmprəmaɪzɪŋlɪ] *adv.* kompromißlos
unconcealed [ʌnkən'si:ld] *adj.* unverhohlen
unconcern [ʌnkən'sɜ:n] *n., no pl.* Gleichgültigkeit, *die*
unconcerned [ʌnkən'sɜ:nd] *adj.* gleichgültig; *(free from anxiety)* unbekümmert; **sb. is ~ about sb./sth.** jmdm. ist jmd./etw. gleichgültig; **she seemed ~ as to the outcome** das Ergebnis schien ihr gleichgültig zu sein; **he is ~ with** *or* **about style** er kümmert sich nicht um Stil
unconcernedly [ʌnkən'sɜ:nɪdlɪ] *adv.* gleichgültig; *(free from anxiety)* unbekümmert
unconditional [ʌnkən'dɪʃənl] *adj.* bedingungslos ‹*Kapitulation*›; kategorisch ‹*Ablehnung*›; ‹*Versprechen*› ohne Vorbehalte
unconditionally [ʌnkən'dɪʃənəlɪ] *adv.* bedingungslos; kategorisch ‹*ablehnen*›; ohne Vorbehalte ‹*versprechen*›
unconfirmed [ʌnkən'fɜ:md] *adj.* unbestätigt
uncongenial [ʌnkən'dʒi:nɪəl] *adj.* unsympathisch ‹*Person*›; **I find him/the work ~:** er ist mir unsympathisch/die Arbeit sagt mir nicht zu *od.* liegt mir nicht; **an ~ atmosphere** ein unangenehmes Klima
unconnected [ʌnkə'nektɪd] *adj.* **a)** nicht verbunden; ~ **with any party** nicht parteigebunden; **b)** *(disjointed, isolated)* zusammenhanglos
unconquerable [ʌn'kɒŋkərəbl] *adj.* unbezwingbar; unerschütterlich ‹*Entschlossenheit*›
unconquered [ʌn'kɒŋkəd] *adj.* nicht erobert
unconscionable [ʌn'kɒnʃənəbl] *adj.* übertrieben lang ‹*Zeit*›; übertrieben hoch ‹*Betrag*›
unconscionably [ʌn'kɒnʃənəblɪ] *adv.* übertrieben
unconscious [ʌn'kɒnʃəs] **1.** *adj.* **a)** *(Med.: senseless)* bewußtlos; **b)** *(unaware)* **be ~ of sth.** sich einer Sache *(Gen.)* nicht bewußt sein; **I was ~ of what was going on around me** ich war mir nicht bewußt *od.* wußte nicht, was um mich herum vorging; **she was ~ of the tragedy** sie wußte nichts von der Tragödie; **he was ~ of the change in her** er merkte *od.* bemerkte nicht, daß sie sich verändert hatte; **c)** *(not intended; Psych.)* unbewußt; unfreiwillig ‹*Komik*›; **an ~ act** eine unbewußt begangene Tat. **2.** *n.* Unbewußte, *das*
unconsciously [ʌn'kɒnʃəslɪ] *adv.* unbewußt; **~, he was falling under her spell** ohne es zu merken, verfiel er ihrem Zauber
unconsciousness [ʌn'kɒnʃəsnɪs] *n., no pl.* **a)** *(loss of consciousness)* Bewußtlosigkeit, *die;* **b)** *(unawareness)* fehlende Bewußtheit
unconsidered [ʌnkən'sɪdəd] *adj.* **a)** *(disregarded)* unbedeutend; **b)** *(not based on consideration)* unüberlegt, vorschnell ‹*Bemerkung*›
unconstitutional [ʌnkɒnstɪ'tju:ʃənl] *adj.*, **unconstitutionally** [ʌnkɒnstɪ'tju:ʃənəlɪ] *adv. (in State)* verfassungswidrig; *(in other organization)* satzungswidrig
unconstrained [ʌnkən'streɪnd] *adj.* ungezwungen
uncontaminated [ʌnkən'tæmɪneɪtɪd] *adj.* unverschmutzt, nicht verseucht **(with** von); *(fig.)* unverdorben **(with** durch)
uncontested [ʌnkən'testɪd] *adj.* unangefochten; **go ~:** nicht angefochten werden; **it was an ~ election** bei der Wahl gab es keinen Gegenkandidaten
uncontrollable [ʌnkən'trəʊləbl] *adj.* unkontrollierbar; **become ~:** außer Kontrolle geraten; **the child is ~:** das Kind ist nicht zu bändigen
uncontrollably [ʌnkən'trəʊləblɪ] *adv.* unkontrollierbar; unbeherrscht ‹*lachen*›; hemmungslos ‹*weinen usw.*›
uncontrolled [ʌnkən'trəʊld] *adj.* unkontrolliert; **leave ~:** nicht kontrollieren; ~ **dogs/children** herrenlose Hunde/unbeaufsichtigte Kinder
uncontroversial [ʌnkɒntrə'vɜ:ʃl] *adj.* nicht kontrovers; **be ~:** keinerlei Widerspruch hervorrufen; **he is an ~ figure** er gibt keinen Anlaß zu Kontroversen
unconventional [ʌnkən'venʃənl] *adj.*, **unconventionally** [ʌnkən'venʃənəlɪ] *adv.* unkonventionell
unconverted [ʌnkən'vɜ:tɪd] *adj.* **a)** *(not rebuilt)* nicht umgebaut; **b)** *(Relig.)* nicht konvertiert; **he is** *or* **remains ~ [to sth.]** er läßt sich nicht [zu etw.] bekehren
unconvinced [ʌnkən'vɪnst] *adj.* nicht überzeugt; **remain ~:** sich nicht überzeugen lassen; **his arguments left her ~:** seine Argumente überzeugten sie nicht
unconvincing [ʌnkən'vɪnsɪŋ] *adj.* nicht überzeugend
unconvincingly [ʌnkən'vɪnsɪŋlɪ] *adv.* nicht überzeugend; **he argues very ~:** seine Argumente überzeugen ganz und gar nicht
uncooked [ʌn'kʊkt] *adj.* roh; **the cake was still ~ in the centre** der Kuchen war in der Mitte noch nicht durchgebacken
uncooperative [ʌnkəʊ'ɒpərətɪv] *adj.* unkooperativ; wenig entgegenkommend; *(unhelpful)* wenig hilfsbereit; **a bit less ~:** ein bißchen hilfsbereiter
uncoordinated [ʌnkəʊ'ɔ:dɪneɪtɪd] *adj.* unkoordiniert; **very ~:** überhaupt nicht koordiniert
uncork [ʌn'kɔ:k] *v. t.* entkorken
uncorroborated [ʌnkə'rɒbəreɪtɪd] *adj.* unbestätigt
uncountable [ʌn'kaʊntəbl] *adj. (Ling.)* unzählbar
uncounted [ʌn'kaʊntɪd] *adj.* nicht gezählt
uncouple [ʌn'kʌpl] *v. t.* abkoppeln ‹*Hunde, Waggon, Lokomotive*›
uncouth [ʌn'ku:θ] *adj.* **a)** *(lacking refinement)* ungeschliffen; ungehobelt ‹*Person, Benehmen*›; grob ‹*Bemerkung, Sprache*›; **b)** *(boorish)* unkultiviert; flegelhaft *(abwertend)*
uncouthness [ʌn'ku:θnɪs] *n., no pl.* **a)** *(lack of refinement)* Ungeschliffenheit, *die; (of remark, language)* Grobheit, *die;* **b)** *(boorishness)* Unkultiviertheit, *die;* Flegelhaftigkeit, *die (abwertend)*
uncover [ʌn'kʌvə(r)] *v. t.* **a)** *(remove cover from)* aufdecken; freilegen ‹*Wunde, Begrabenes*›; ~ **one's head** die Kopfbedeckung abnehmen; **b)** *(disclose)* aufdecken ‹*Skandal, Verschwörung, Wahrheit*›
uncovered [ʌn'kʌvəd] *adj.* unbedeckt; **[with head] ~:** ohne Kopfbedeckung
uncritical [ʌn'krɪtɪkl] *adj.* unkritisch; **be ~ of sth.** etw. nicht kritisieren
uncritically [ʌn'krɪtɪkəlɪ] *adv.* unkritisch
uncross [ʌn'krɒs] *v. t.* ~ **one's legs** seine Beine wieder nebeneinanderstellen/nebeneinanderlegen
uncrossed [ʌn'krɒst] *adj. (Brit.)* **an ~ cheque/postal order** ein Barscheck/Postbarscheck
uncrowded [ʌn'kraʊdɪd] *adj.* nicht überlaufen
uncrowned [ʌn'kraʊnd] *adj. (lit. or fig.)* ungekrönt
UNCTAD ['ʌŋktæd] *abbr.* **United Nations Conference on Trade and Development** Welthandels- und Entwicklungskonferenz [der Vereinten Nationen]
unction ['ʌŋkʃn] *see* **extreme 1 d**
unctuous ['ʌŋktjʊəs] *adj.* salbungsvoll; ölig
uncultivated [ʌn'kʌltɪveɪtɪd] *adj.* **a)** *(Agric.)* nicht bestellt; **b)** unkultiviert
uncultured [ʌn'kʌltʃəd] *adj.* unkultiviert
uncured [ʌn'kjʊəd] *adj.* **a)** *(not made healthy)* ungeheilt; **b)** *(not prepared for keeping)* ungepökelt ‹*Fleisch*›; ungeräuchert ‹*Fisch*›; nicht getrocknet ‹*Häute, Tabak*›
uncurl [ʌn'kɜ:l] **1.** *v. t.* auseinanderrollen. **2.** *v. refl.* sich strecken. **3.** *v. i.* sich auseinanderrollen
uncurtained [ʌn'kɜ:tənd] *adj.* vorhanglos; **be ~:** keine Vorhänge haben
uncut [ʌn'kʌt] *adj.* **a)** *(not cut)* nicht geschnitten ‹*Gras, Haare usw.*›; nicht gemäht ‹*Rasen*›; **b)** *(with pages not trimmed)* unbeschnitten ‹*Buch*›; *(not slit open)* nicht aufgeschnitten ‹*Seiten*›; **c)** *(not shaped by cutting)* ungeschliffen ‹*Edelstein*›; **d)** *(not shortened)* ungekürzt ‹*Buch, Film*›
undamaged [ʌn'dæmɪdʒd] *adj.* unbeschädigt
undated [ʌn'deɪtɪd] *adj.* undatiert
undaunted [ʌn'dɔ:ntɪd] *adj.* unverzagt; ~ **by threats** durch Drohungen nicht eingeschüchtert
undecided [ʌndɪ'saɪdɪd] *adj.* **a)** *(not settled)* nicht entschieden; **b)** *(hesitant)* unentschlossen; **be ~ whether to do sth.** sich *(Dat.)* noch unschlüssig sein, ob man etw. tun soll
undecipherable [ʌndɪ'saɪfərəbl] *adj.* **be ~:** sich nicht entziffern lassen
undeclared [ʌndɪ'kleəd] *adj.* **a)** nicht erklärt ‹*Krieg*›; **b)** nicht deklariert ‹*zollpflich-*

tige Waren⟩; ~ **income** *(for tax)* nicht angegebenes Einkommen

undefeated [ʌndɪ'fi:tɪd] *adj.* ungeschlagen ⟨*Mannschaft*⟩; unbesiegt ⟨*Heer*⟩

undefended [ʌndɪ'fendɪd] *adj.* **a)** unverteidigt; *(not protected)* ungeschützt; **b)** *(Law)* unverteidigt; **be** ~: keinen Verteidiger haben; **the case was** ~: der Fall wurde ohne Verteidigung verhandelt

undefiled [ʌndɪ'faɪld] *adj.* unverdorben; *(not desecrated)* unbefleckt

undefined [ʌndɪ'faɪnd] *adj.* nicht definiert; *(indefinite)* unbestimmt

undelivered [ʌndɪ'lɪvəd] *adj.* nicht zugestellt ⟨*Postsendung*⟩; nicht überbracht ⟨*Botschaft, Nachricht*⟩; *(on letter)* **if** ~: wenn unzustellbar

undemanding [ʌndɪ'mɑ:ndɪŋ] *adj.* anspruchslos

undemocratic [ʌndemə'krætɪk] *adj.* undemokratisch

undemonstrative [ʌndɪ'mɒnstrətɪv] *adj.* zurückhaltend

undeniable [ʌndɪ'naɪəbl] *adj.* unbestreitbar; **it is ~ that ...**: es ist nicht zu leugnen, daß ...; **produce ~ evidence** Beweise vorlegen, deren Echtheit nicht bezweifelt werden kann

undeniably [ʌndɪ'naɪəblɪ] *adv.* unbestreitbar

undependable [ʌndɪ'pendəbl] *adj.* unzuverlässig

under ['ʌndə(r)] **1.** *prep.* **a)** *(underneath, below) (indicating position)* unter (+ *Dat.*); *(indicating motion)* unter (+ *Akk.*); **from ~ the table/bed** unter dem Tisch/Bett hervor; **b)** *(undergoing)* ~ **treatment** in Behandlung; ~ **repair** in Reparatur; ~ **construction** im Bau; **be ~ investigation** untersucht werden; **fields ~ cultivation** bebaute Felder; ~ **threat of extinction** vom Aussterben bedroht; ~ **sentence of death** zum Tode verurteilt; *see also* **discussion b; influence 1; pain; c)** *(in conditions of)* bei ⟨*Streß, hohen Temperaturen usw.*⟩; **d)** *(subject to)* unter (+ *Dat.*); **bring a country ~ one's rule** ein Land unter seine Herrschaft bringen; ~ **the doctor, ~ doctor's orders** in ärztlicher Behandlung; *see also* **delusion; illusion b; impression g; misapprehension; e)** *(in accordance with)* ~ **the circumstances** unter den gegebenen *od.* diesen Umständen; ~ **the terms of the will/contract/agreement** nach den Bestimmungen des Testaments/Vertrags/Abkommens; **f)** *(with the use of)* unter (+ *Dat.*); ~ **an assumed name** *or* **alias/a pen-name** unter falschem Namen/unter einem Pseudonym; **g)** *(less than)* unter (+ *Dat.*); *(esp. with time, amount)* weniger als; **no one ~ a bishop** niemand unter Bischofsrang; **the mile was run in ~ four minutes** die Meile wurde in weniger als *od.* unter vier Minuten gelaufen; **for ~ five pounds** für weniger als fünf Pfund; *see also* **age 1a; h)** *(at foot of)* ~ **the hill/walls** am Fuße des Berges/der Mauern; **i)** *(Naut.: in the lee of)* **close ~ the island** im Schutze der nahen Insel; **j)** *(planted with)* **field ~ corn/rice/beans** mit Getreide/Reis/Bohnen bestandenes Feld. **2.** *adv.* **a)** *(in or to a lower or subordinate position)* darunter; **stay** ~ (~ *water)* unter Wasser bleiben; *see also* **go under; b)** *(in/into a state of unconsciousness)* **be ~/put sb. ~**: in Narkose liegen/jmdn. in Narkose versetzen

under: ~a'chieve *v. i.* unter dem erreichbaren Leistungsniveau bleiben; **~achiever** [ʌndərə'tʃi:və(r)] *n.* Schüler/Schülerin mit enttäuschenden Leistungen; **be an ~achiever** *see* **~achieve; ~'act** *v. t. & i.* unterspielen ⟨*Theaterjargon*⟩; **~arm 1.** *adj.* **a)** *(Tennis, Cricket, etc.)* ⟨*Aufschlag, Wurf*⟩ von unten; **b)** *(in armpit)* Achsel⟨*haare, -schweiß*⟩; **2.** *adv.* von unten ⟨*aufschlagen, werfen*⟩; **~belly** *n.* *(Zool.)* Bauch, *der; (of aircraft)* Unterseite, *die;* **[soft] ~belly** *(fig.)* verwundbare Stelle; **~body** *n.* Unterseite, *die;* **~brush** *n.* *(Amer.)* Unterholz, *das;* **~carriage** *n.* Fahrwerk, *das;* **~'charge** *v. t.* **~charge sb. [by several pounds]** jmdm. [einige Pfund] zuwenig berechnen; **~clothes** *n. pl.,* **~clothing** *see* **~wear; ~coat** *n.* **a)** *(layer of paint)* Grundierung, *die;* **b)** *(paint)* Grundierfarbe, *die;* **c)** *(of animal)* Unterhaar, *das;* **~'cooked** *adj.* zu kurz gekocht/gebraten; noch nicht gar; **~cover** *adj. (disguised)* getarnt; *(secret)* verdeckt; *(engaged in international spying)* geheim[dienstlich]; **~cover agent** Untergrund-/Geheimagent, *der;* **~croft** *n. (Eccl.)* Krypta, *die;* **~current** *n.* Unterströmung, *die; (fig.: underlying feeling)* Unterton, *der;* **he sensed an ~current of resentment** er spürte eine unterschwelligen Groll; **~'cut** *v. t.,* **undercut** unterbieten; **~de'veloped** *adj.* unterentwickelt; **~de'velopment** *n., no pl.* Unterentwicklung, *die;* **~dog** *n.* **a)** *(in fight, match)* Unterlegene, *der/die;* **b)** *(fig.: disadvantaged person)* Benachteiligte, *der/die;* **the ~dogs of society** die sozial Unterprivilegierten; **~'done** *adj.* halbgar; **I don't like my steak ~done** ich habe mein Steak gern gut durchgebraten; **~'emphasis** *n.* zu schwache Betonung; **there is an ~emphasis on it** es kommt nicht deutlich genug zum Ausdruck; **~'emphasize** *v. t.* zuwenig betonen; **~em'ployed** *adj.* unterbeschäftigt; **~em'ployment** *n.* Unterbeschäftigung, *die;* **~estimate 1.** [ʌndər'estɪmeɪt] *v. t.* unterschätzen; **2.** [ʌndər'estɪmət] *n.* Unterschätzung, *die;* **that figure is a considerable ~estimate** diese Zahl ist viel zu niedrig geschätzt; **~ex'pose** *v. t. (Photog.)* unterbelichten; **~ex'posure** *n. (Photog.)* Unterbelichtung, *die;* **~'fed** *adj.* unterernährt; **~felt** *n.* Filzunterlage, *die;* **~-'fives** *n. pl.* Kinder unter fünf Jahren; **~'floor heating** *n.* [Fuß]bodenheizung, *die;* **~'foot** *adv.* am Boden; **it's rough/muddy ~foot** der Boden ist uneben/matschig; **be trodden/trampled ~foot** mit Füßen getreten/zertrampelt werden; *(fig.: be maltreated)* wie der letzte Dreck behandelt werden *(salopp);* **~garment** *n.* Wäschestück, *das;* **~garments** Unterwäsche, *die;* **~'go** *v. t., forms as* [1]**go 1** durchmachen ⟨*schlimme Zeiten*⟩; ertragen ⟨*Demütigung*⟩; **~go treatment/an operation** sich einer Behandlung/Operation unterziehen; **~go a change** sich verändern; **~go repairs** repariert werden; **~grad** [ʌndə'græd] *coll.),* **~'graduate** *ns.* **~graduate [student]** Student/Studentin vor der ersten Prüfung; **~graduate course** Lehrveranstaltung für Studenten vor der ersten Prüfung; **~ground 1.** [--'-] *adv.* **a)** *(beneath surface of ground)* unter der Erde; *(Mining)* unter Tage; **an explosion ~ground** eine unterirdische Explosion; **b)** *(fig.) (in hiding)* im Untergrund; *(into hiding)* in den Untergrund; **go ~ground** untertauchen; in den Untergrund gehen; **2.** ['---] *adj.* **a)** unterirdisch ⟨*Höhle, See*⟩; **~ground railway** Untergrundbahn, *die;* **~ground car-park** Tiefgarage, *die;* **b)** *(fig.: secret)* **~ground activity** Tätigkeit im Untergrund; **~ground organization/movement/press** Untergrundorganisation/-bewegung/-presse; **3.** *n.* **a)** *(railway)* U-Bahn, *die;* **b)** *(clandestine movement)* Untergrund, *der;* Untergrundbewegung, *die;* **~growth** *n.* Unterholz, *das;* **~hand, ~handed 1.** *adjs.* **a)** *(secret)* heimlich; **b)** *(crafty)* hinterhältig; **2.** *advs.* heimlich; **~hung** *adj.* vorgeschoben ⟨*Unterkiefer*⟩; **~in'sured** *adj.* unterversichert; [1]**~'lay** *see* **~lie;** [2]**~lay 1.** [--'-] *v. t., forms as* [2]**lay 2** unterlegen; **2.** ['---] *n.* Unterlage, *die;* **~'lie** *v. t., forms as* [2]**lie 2 a)** *(lie under)* **~lie sth.** unter etw. *(Dat.)* liegen; **b)** *(fig.: be [at] the basis of)* **~lie sth.** einer Sache *(Dat.)* zugrundeliegen; **~lying cause of sth.** eigentliche Ursache für etw.; **~line 1.** [--'-] *v. t. (lit. or fig.)* unterstreichen; **2.** ['---] *n.* Unterstreichung, *die*

underling ['ʌndəlɪŋ] *n. (derog.)* Untergebene, *der/die*

under: ~'lining *n.* Unterstreichung, *die;* **there is too much ~lining** es ist zuviel unterstrichen; **~'lying** *see* **~lie; ~'manned** *adj.* [personell] unterbesetzt; **~manned industries** Industriezweige, in denen Arbeitskräftemangel herrscht; **~'manning** *n.* [personelle] Unterbesetzung; **~'mentioned** *adj.* *(Brit.)* untengenannt; untenerwähnt; **~'mine** *v. t.* **a)** unterhöhlen; ⟨*Wasser:*⟩ unterspülen; **b)** *(fig.) (weaken)* untergraben; erschüttern ⟨*Vertrauen*⟩; unterminieren ⟨*Autorität*⟩; schwächen ⟨*Gesundheit*⟩

underneath [ʌndə'ni:θ] **1.** *prep. (indicating position)* unter (+ *Dat.*); *(indicating motion)* unter (+ *Akk.*); **from ~ the bed** unter dem Bett hervor. **2.** *adv.* darunter. **3.** *n.* Unterseite, *die*

under: ~'nourished *adj.* unterernährt; **~'paid** *adj.* unterbezahlt; **~pants** *n. pl.* Unterhose, *die;* Unterhosen *Pl.;* **~-part** *n.* Unterseite, *die;* **~pass** *n.* Unterführung, *die;* **~'pay** *v. t., forms as* **pay 2** unterbezahlen; **~'payment** *n.* Unterbezahlung, *die;* **~'pin** *v. t.* [ab]stützen; *(fig.)* untermauern; **~pin a social system** die Grundlage eines gesellschaftlichen Systems bilden; **~'play** *v. t.* **a)** *(Theatre)* zurückhaltend spielen ⟨*Rolle, Szene*⟩; **b)** *(play down)* herunterspielen; **~'privileged** *adj.* unterprivilegiert; **~pro'duction** *n., no pl., no indef. art.* Unterproduktion, *die;* **~'rate** *v. t.* unterschätzen; **be ~rated** [allgemein] unterschätzt werden; **~ripe** *adj.* nicht ausgereift; **~'score** *see* **~line 1; ~score** *see* **~line 2; ~sea** *attrib. adj.* Unterwasser-; **~seal 1.** *v. t.* mit [einem] Unterbodenschutz versehen; **be ~sealed** Unterbodenschutz haben; **2.** *n.* Unterbodenschutz, *der;* **~secretary** *n.* **a)** *(esp. Amer.: assistant to secretary)* Unterstaatssekretär, *der;* **b)** *(Brit.)* **[Parliamentary] U~secretary** [Parlamentarischer] Staatssekretär; **~'sell** *v. t., forms as* **sell 1: a)** *(sell at lower price than)* [im Preis] unterbieten; **b)** *(present inadequately)* nicht genug anpreisen; **~selling actually boosted her business** ihre verhaltene Werbestrategie hat eher zur Geschäftsbelebung geführt; **~-'sexed** *adj.* sexuell lustlos; **~shirt** *n. (Amer.)* Unterhemd, *das;* **~'shoot** *v. t., forms as* **shot 1, 2: ~shoot the runway** vor der Landebahn aufsetzen; **~shorts** *n. pl. (Amer.)* Unterhose, *die;* **~shot** *see* **~hung; ~-side** *n.* Unterseite, *die;* **~signed** *adj. (esp. Law)* **the ~signed** der/die Unterzeichnete/*(pl.)* die Unterzeichneten *(Papierdt.);* **~sized** *adj.* unter Normalgröße *nachgestellt;* [ziemlich] klein geraten ⟨*Mensch, Tier*⟩; **~skirt** *n.* Unterrock, *der;* **~slung** *adj. (Motor Veh.)* [tiefer als die Achsen] hängend ⟨*Fahrgestell, Rahmen*⟩; **~'spend 1.** *v. t., forms as* **spend: ~spend a budget/an allowance** ein Budget unterschreiten/eine Zuwendung nicht ganz ausgeben; **2.** *v. i., forms as* **spend: ~spend by £500,000** das Budget um 500 000 Pfund unterschreiten; **~spend on sth.** zu wenig für etw. ausgeben; *(save)* an etw. *(Dat.)* sparen; **~'staffed** *adj.* unterbesetzt; **be ~staffed** an Personalmangel leiden

understand [ʌndə'stænd] **1.** *v. t.,* **understood** [ʌndə'stʊd] **a)** verstehen; **~ sth. by sth.** etw. unter etw. *(Dat.)* verstehen; **~ mathematics** mathematisches Verständnis haben; **~ carpentry** sich auf das Schreinern verstehen; **I cannot ~ his doing it** ich kann nicht verstehen *od.* begreife nicht, warum er es tut; **is that understood?** ist das klar?; **make oneself understood** sich verständlich machen; **b)** *(have heard)* gehört haben; **I ~ that**

you wish to leave us wie ich höre, wollen Sie uns verlassen; **I ~ him to be a distant relation** ich glaube, er ist ein entfernter Verwandter; **c)** *(take as implied)* **~ sth. from sb.'s words** etw. aus jmds. Worten entnehmen; **I understood [that] we were to be paid expenses** ich dachte, daß wir Spesen bekommen sollten; **it was understood that ...:** es wurde allgemein angenommen, daß ...; **do I ~ that ...?** gehe ich recht in der Annahme, daß ...?; **am I to ~ that you refuse my offer?** wollen Sie damit sagen, daß Sie mein Angebot ablehnen?; **it was understood between them that ...:** es herrschte [stillschweigendes] Einverständnis zwischen ihnen, daß ...; **d)** *(supply mentally)* hinzudenken; **be understood** *(Gram.)* ausgelassen werden; **he is seething ('with rage' understood)** er kocht (gemeint ist „vor Wut"). *See also* **give 1e; make 1f. 2.** *v. i.*, **understood a)** *(have understanding)* verstehen; **~ about sth.** etwas von etw. verstehen; **he doesn't ~ about it [being my job]** er sieht es nicht ein[, daß es meine Aufgabe ist]; **now I ~!** jetzt begreife ich es!; **I quite ~:** ich verstehe schon; **b)** *(gather, hear)* **if I ~ correctly** wenn ich mich nicht irre; **your offer is, I ~, still open** Ihr Angebot ist, so nehme ich an, noch offen; **he is, I ~, no longer here** er ist, wie ich höre, nicht mehr hier

understandable [ʌndəˈstændəbl] *adj.* verständlich

understandably [ʌndəˈstændəblɪ] *adv.* verständlicherweise

understanding [ʌndəˈstændɪŋ] **1.** *adj. (able to sympathize)* verständnisvoll; **you could be a bit more ~:** du könntest etwas mehr Verständnis zeigen. **2.** *n.* **a)** *(agreement)* Verständigung, *die;* **reach an ~ with sb.** sich mit jmdm. verständigen; **the good ~ between them** das gute Einverständnis zwischen ihnen; **have a secret ~ with sb.** eine geheime Vereinbarung mit jmdm. haben; **on the ~ that ...:** unter der Voraussetzung, daß ...; **on the clear** *or* **distinct ~ that ...** *(condition)* unter der ausdrücklichen Bedingung, daß ...; **there has never been much ~ between them** sie haben sich nie besonders gut vertragen; **b)** *(intelligence)* Verstand, *der;* **c)** *(insight, comprehension)* Verständnis, *das* **(of, for** für); **a person of great ~:** ein sehr verständnisvoller Mensch; **beyond ~:** unbegreiflich; **my ~ of the matter is that she has won** so wie ich es verstehe, hat sie gewonnen

understandingly [ʌndəˈstændɪŋlɪ] *adv.* verständnisvoll

under: ~state *v. t.* **a)** herunterspielen; **~state the case** untertreiben; **b)** *(represent inadequately)* zu gering veranschlagen; **~ˈstatement** *n. (avoidance of emphasis)* Untertreibung, *die;* Understatement, *das;* **~steer** *(Motor Veh.)* **1.** [--ˈ-] *v. i.* untersteuern; **2.** [ˈ---] *n.* Untersteuern, *das;* **~ˈstocked** *adj.* unterversorgt; **the shops were ~stocked** die Läden hatten zu wenig Ware *od.* Vorräte [auf Lager]; **~ˈstood** *see* **understand; ~study 1.** *n.* Ersatzspieler, *der*/-spielerin, *die;* zweite Besetzung; **2.** *v. t.* **~study sb.** jmds. Rolle als Ersatzspieler/-spielerin einstudieren; **~-subˈscribed** *adj. (St. Exch.)* unterzeichnet; **~-surface** *n.* Unterseite, *die;* **~ˈtake** *v. t., forms as* **take 1: a)** *(set about)* unternehmen; **~take a task** eine Aufgabe übernehmen; **~take to do sth.** sich verpflichten, etw. zu tun; **b)** *(guarantee)* **~take sth./that ...:** sich für etw. verbürgen/sich dafür verbürgen, daß ...; **~taker** *n.* Leichenbestatter, *der*/-bestatterin, *die;* **[firm of] ~takers** Bestattungsunternehmen, *das;* **~taking** *n.* **a)** *no pl. (taking on) (of task)* Übernehmen, *das; (of journey etc.)* Unternehmen, *das;* **b)** *(task)* Aufgabe, *die;* **a dangerous ~taking** ein gefährliches Unterfangen; **c)** *(business)* Unternehmen, *das;* Betrieb, *der;* **d)** *(pledge)* Versprechen, *das;* **give an ~taking that .../to do sth.** zusichern, daß .../sich verpflichten, etw. zu tun; **I'll need an ~taking from you that ...:** du mußt mir [fest] versprechen, daß ...; **~tone** *n.* **a)** *(low voice)* **in ~tones** *or* **an ~tone** in gedämpftem Ton; **b)** *(undercurrent)* **~tone of criticism** kritischer Unterton; **c)** *(subdued colour)* Tönung, *die;* **~tow** *n.* Unterströmung, *die;* **~-ˈused** *adj.* nicht voll genutzt; **~valuˈation** *n.* Unterbewertung, *die;* **~ˈvalue** *v. t.* unterbewerten; **~vest** *n.* Unterhemd, *das;* **~water 1.** [ˈ----] *attrib. adj.* Unterwasser-; **2.** [--ˈ--] *adv.* unter Wasser; **~wear** *n., no pl., no indef. art.* Unterwäsche, *die;* **~ˈweight** *adj.* untergewichtig; **be ~weight** Untergewicht haben; **~whelm** [ʌndəˈwelm] *v. t. (joc.)* nicht gerade überwältigen *(spött.);* **~world** *n. (lit. or fig.)* Unterwelt, *die;* **~ˈwrite** *v. t., forms as* **write 1: a)** *(accept liability for)* [als Versicherer] unterzeichnen; **~write a risk** ein Risiko versichern; **~write a share issue** die Übernahme von unverkauften Aktien garantieren; **b)** *(finance)* finanzieren; **~writer** *n. (of insurance policy)* Versicherer, *der; (of stock issue)* Garant, *der*/Garantin, *die*

undeserved [ʌndɪˈzɜːvd] *adj.* unverdient

undeservedly [ʌndɪˈzɜːvɪdlɪ] *adv.* unverdientermaßen

undeserving [ʌndɪˈzɜːvɪŋ] *adj.* unwürdig **(of** *Gen.***)**; **not ~ of attention** schon beachtenswert

undesigned [ʌndɪˈzaɪnd] *adj.* ungeplant

undesirability [ʌndɪzaɪərəˈbɪlɪtɪ] *n., no pl.* Unerwünschtheit, *die*

undesirable [ʌndɪˈzaɪərəbl] **1.** *adj.* unerwünscht; **it is ~ that ...:** es ist nicht wünschenswert, daß ... **2.** *n.* unerwünschte Person

undesirably [ʌndɪˈzaɪərəblɪ] *adv.* unerwünscht

undesired [ʌndɪˈzaɪəd] *adj.* unerwünscht

undetectable [ʌndɪˈtektəbl] *adj.* nicht nachweisbar

undetected [ʌndɪˈtektɪd] *adj.* unentdeckt; **go** *or* **pass ~:** unentdeckt bleiben

undeterred [ʌndɪˈtɜːd] *adj.* nicht entmutigt **(by** durch**)**; **remain ~:** sich nicht abschrecken lassen; **continue ~:** unbeirrt weitermachen

undeveloped [ʌndɪˈveləpt] *adj.* **a)** *(immature)* nicht voll ausgebildet; **b)** *(Photog.)* nicht entwickelt; **c)** *(not built on)* nicht bebaut

undiagnosed [ʌndaɪəgˈnəʊzd] *adj.* nicht diagnostiziert; **die of an ~ brain tumor** an einem nicht erkannten Gehirntumor sterben

undid *see* **undo**

undies [ˈʌndɪz] *n. pl. (coll.)* Unterwäsche, *die*

undifferentiated [ʌndɪfəˈrenʃɪeɪtɪd] *adj.* undifferenziert

undigested [ʌndɪˈdʒestɪd, ʌndaɪˈdʒestɪd] *adj. (lit. or fig.)* unverdaut

undignified [ʌnˈdɪgnɪfaɪd] *adj.* würdelos; **consider it ~ to do sth.** es für unter seiner Würde halten, etw. zu tun

undiluted [ʌndaɪˈljuːtɪd] *adj.* unverdünnt; **~ pleasure/nonsense** ungetrübte Freude/barer Unsinn

undiminished [ʌndɪˈmɪnɪʃt] *adj.* unvermindert; **her enthusiasm remained ~:** ihre Begeisterung ließ nicht nach

undimmed [ʌnˈdɪmd] *adj.* nicht gedämpft; ungetrübt ⟨*Augenlicht*⟩

undipped [ʌnˈdɪpt] *adj.* nicht abgeblendet

undischarged [ʌndɪsˈtʃɑːdʒd] *adj.* **a)** *(Finance)* unbeglichen ⟨*Schuld*⟩; nicht entlastet ⟨*Schuldner*⟩; **b)** *(not unloaded)* nicht entladen; **c)** *(not fired off)* nicht abgeschossen

undisciplined [ʌnˈdɪsɪplɪnd] *adj.* undiszipliniert

undisclosed [ʌndɪsˈkləʊzd] *adj.* geheim; **an ~ sum** ein nicht genannter Betrag

undiscoverable [ʌndɪˈskʌvərəbl] *adj.* nicht feststellbar

undiscovered [ʌndɪˈskʌvəd] *adj.* unentdeckt

undiscriminating [ʌndɪˈskrɪmɪneɪtɪŋ] *adj.* unkritisch; *(undemanding)* anspruchslos

undisguised [ʌndɪsˈgaɪzd] *adj.* unverhohlen

undismayed [ʌndɪsˈmeɪd] *see* **undeterred**

undisputed [ʌndɪˈspjuːtɪd] *adj.* unbestritten ⟨*Fertigkeit, Kompetenz*⟩; unangefochten ⟨*Führer, Autorität*⟩

undistinguished [ʌndɪˈstɪŋgwɪʃt] *adj.* mittelmäßig; *(ordinary)* gewöhnlich

undisturbed [ʌndɪˈstɜːbd] *adj.* **a)** *(untouched)* unberührt; **b)** *(not interrupted)* ungestört; **c)** *(not worried)* ungerührt

undivided [ʌndɪˈvaɪdɪd] *adj.* ungeteilt ⟨*Sympathie, Aufmerksamkeit*⟩; geschlossen ⟨*Front*⟩; uneingeschränkt ⟨*Loyalität*⟩

undo [ʌnˈduː] **1.** *v. t.*, **undoes** [ʌnˈdʌz], **undoing** [ʌnˈduːɪŋ], **undid** [ʌnˈdɪd], **undone** [ʌnˈdʌn] **a)** *(unfasten)* aufmachen; **b)** *(cancel)* ungeschehen machen; **his successor undid all his work** sein Nachfolger machte sein ganzes Werk zunichte. **2.** *v. i., forms as* **1** ⟨*dress etc.:*⟩ **~ at the back** hinten aufgemacht werden

undoing [ʌnˈduːɪŋ] *n., no pl., no indef. art.* **be sb.'s ~:** jmds. Verderben sein

undone [ʌnˈdʌn] *adj.* **a)** *(not accomplished)* unerledigt; **leave the work** *or* **job ~:** die Arbeit liegen lassen; **b)** *(not fastened)* offen; **he went out with his shoe-laces ~:** er ging mit offenen Schnürsenkeln aus dem Haus

undoubted [ʌnˈdaʊtɪd] *adj.* unzweifelhaft

undoubtedly [ʌnˈdaʊtɪdlɪ] *adv.* zweifellos

undraw [ʌnˈdrɔː] *v. t., forms as* **draw 1** aufziehen ⟨*Vorhang*⟩

undreamed-of [ʌnˈdriːmdɒv], **undreamt-of** [ʌnˈdremtɒv] *adjs. (unheard of)* unerhört; *(unimaginable)* unvorstellbar; ungeahnt ⟨*Reichtum*⟩; **such a thing was ~:** an so etwas hätte man nicht im Traum gedacht

undress [ʌnˈdres] **1.** *v. t.* ausziehen; entkleiden *(geh.)*; **get ~ed** sich ausziehen; **can he ~ himself?** kann er sich selbst ausziehen? **2.** *v. i.* sich ausziehen. **3.** *n.* **a) ~ [uniform]** Freizeitkleidung, *die; (Mil.)* Ausgehuniform, *die;* **b)** *no pl., no art.* **in a state of ~:** halbbekleidet

undressed [ʌnˈdrest] *adj.* **a)** *(not clothed)* unbekleidet; *(no longer clothed)* ausgezogen; *(not yet clothed)* nicht angezogen; **b)** *(unfinished)* unbearbeitet ⟨*Stein, Holz*⟩; ungegerbt ⟨*Leder, Haut*⟩; **c)** *(not bandaged etc.)* nicht verbunden; **leave a wound ~:** eine Wunde nicht verbinden

undrinkable [ʌnˈdrɪŋkəbl] *adj.* nicht trinkbar; ungenießbar

undue [ʌnˈdjuː] *attrib. adj.* übertrieben; übermäßig; unangemessen hoch ⟨*Gewinn*⟩; unberechtigt ⟨*Optimismus*⟩; **~ influence** *(Law)* ungebührliche Beeinflussung; **attract ~ attention** zuviel Aufmerksamkeit auf sich *(Akk.)* lenken; **there is no ~ hurry** es hat keine besondere Eile

undulate [ˈʌndjʊleɪt] *v. i.* **a)** *(move with wavelike motion)* wallen *(geh.)*; **b)** *(have wavelike form)* wogen *(geh.)*; **the hills ~ southwards** die Hügel erstrecken sich in sanften Wellen nach Süden

undulating [ˈʌndjʊleɪtɪŋ] *adj.* Wellen⟨*linie, -bewegung*⟩; **~ country/hills** sanfte Hügellandschaft; **~ road** auf- und abführende Straße

undulation [ʌndjʊˈleɪʃn] *n.* **a)** *(wavy motion)* Wellenbewegung, *die;* **b)** *(wavy line)* Wellenlinie, *die*

unduly [ʌnˈdjuːlɪ] *adv.* übermäßig; übertrieben ⟨*ängstlich*⟩; unangemessen ⟨*hoch*⟩; **not ~ worried** nicht besonders beunruhigt; **in an ~ hurried manner** in unangebrachter Eile

undying [ʌn'daɪɪŋ] *adj.* ewig; unsterblich ⟨*Ruhm*⟩; unversöhnlich ⟨*Haß*⟩
unearned [ʌn'ɜ:nd] *adj.* unverdient; ~ **income** Kapitalertrag, *der*
unearth [ʌn'ɜ:θ] *v. t.* **a)** *(dig up)* ausgraben; **b)** *(fig.: discover)* aufdecken; zutage fördern
unearthly [ʌn'ɜ:θlɪ] *adj.* **a)** *(mysterious)* unheimlich; **b)** *(coll.: terrible)* ~ **din** Höllenlärm, *der (ugs.)*; **at an ~ hour** in aller Herrgottsfrühe
unease [ʌn'i:z] *see* **uneasiness**
uneasily [ʌn'i:zɪlɪ] *adv.* **a)** *(anxiously)* mit Unbehagen; **b)** *(with embarrassment)* **be ~ aware of sth.** sich *(Dat.)* einer Sache *(Gen.)* peinlich bewußt sein; **c)** *(restlessly)* unruhig ⟨*schlafen, sitzen*⟩
uneasiness [ʌn'i:zɪnɪs] *n., no pl.* **a)** *(anxiety)* [ängstliches] Unbehagen; **b)** *(restlessness)* Unruhe, *die*
uneasy [ʌn'i:zɪ] *adj.* **a)** *(anxious)* besorgt; **be ~ about sth.** sich wegen etw. Sorgen machen; **he felt ~:** ihm war unbehaglich zumute; **b)** *(restless)* unruhig ⟨*Schlaf*⟩; **c)** *(disturbing)* quälend ⟨*Zweifel, Verdacht*⟩; ~ **conscience** schlechtes Gewissen
uneatable [ʌn'i:təbl] *adj.* ungenießbar
uneaten [ʌn'i:tn] *adj.* ungegessen
uneconomic [ʌni:kə'nɒmɪk, ʌnekə'nɒmɪk] *adj.* unrentabel; **the mine is ~ to run** das Bergwerk ist unwirtschaftlich
uneconomical [ʌni:kə'nɒmɪkl, ʌnekə'nɒmɪkl] *adj.* verschwenderisch ⟨*Person*⟩; ~ **[to run]** unwirtschaftlich
uneconomically [ʌni:kə'nɒmɪkəlɪ, ʌnekə'nɒmɪkəlɪ] *adv.* verschwenderisch; unwirtschaftlich
unedifying [ʌn'edɪfaɪɪŋ] *adj.* **a)** *(uninformative)* unergiebig; **b)** *(not uplifting)* unerquicklich *(geh.)*; unerfreulich
unedited [ʌn'edɪtɪd] *adj.* unredigiert
uneducated [ʌn'edjʊkeɪtɪd] *adj.* ungebildet
unemotional [ʌnɪ'məʊʃənl] *adj.* emotionslos; nüchtern
unemphatic [ʌnɪm'fætɪk] *adj.* ausdruckslos
unemployable [ʌnɪm'plɔɪəbl] *adj.* als Arbeitskraft ungeeignet; **his behaviour makes him ~:** er kann wegen seines Verhaltens nirgends eingestellt werden
unemployed [ʌnɪm'plɔɪd] **1.** *adj.* **a)** *(out of work)* arbeitslos; **b)** *(with nothing to do)* beschäftigungslos. **2.** *n. pl.* **the ~:** die Arbeitslosen
unemployment [ʌnɪm'plɔɪmənt] *n., no pl., no indef. art.* Arbeitslosigkeit, *die*; *(number unemployed)* Arbeitslosenzahl, *die*
unemployment: ~ benefit *n.* Arbeitslosengeld, *das*; ~ **figures** *n. pl.* Arbeitslosenzahl, *die*
unencumbered [ʌnɪn'kʌmbəd] *adj.* **a)** *(unburdened)* unbelastet; **travel ~ by baggage** ohne viel Gepäck reisen; **b)** *(free from mortgage etc.)* lastenfrei
unending [ʌn'endɪŋ] *adj.* endlos; ewig ⟨*Fortschritt*⟩; **her ordeal seemed ~:** ihre Qualen schienen nie enden zu wollen
unendingly [ʌn'endɪŋlɪ] *adv.* endlos
unendurable [ʌnɪn'djʊərəbl] *adj.* unerträglich
unenforceable [ʌnɪn'fɔ:səbl] *adj.* nicht durchsetzbar
un-English [ʌn'ɪŋglɪʃ] *adj.* unenglisch
unenlightened [ʌnɪn'laɪtnd] *adj.* unaufgeklärt ⟨*Zeit*⟩; rückständig ⟨*Land, Volk*⟩; **leave sb. ~:** jmdn. im dunkeln lassen
unenterprising [ʌn'entəpraɪzɪŋ] *adj.* wenig unternehmungslustig; **an ~ person** eine Person ohne Unternehmungsgeist
unenthusiastic [ʌnɪnθju:zɪ'æstɪk, ʌnɪnθu:zɪ'æstɪk] *adj.* wenig begeistert (**about** von); distanziert ⟨*Buchkritik*⟩
unenviable [ʌn'envɪəbl] *adj.* wenig beneidenswert
unequal [ʌn'i:kwl] *adj.* **a)** *(not equal)* unterschiedlich; ungleich ⟨*Kampf*⟩; **b)** *(inadequate)* **be ~ or show oneself ~ to sth.** einer Sache *(Dat.)* nicht gewachsen sein; **be ~ to the strain** ⟨*Material:*⟩ die Belastung nicht aushalten; **c)** *(of varying quality)* ungleichmäßig
unequalled (*Amer.:* **unequaled**) [ʌn'i:kwld] *adj.* unerreicht; unübertroffen; *(in negative sense)* beispiellos ⟨*Dummheit*⟩; ~ **for beauty** von unvergleichlicher Schönheit
unequally [ʌn'i:kwəlɪ] *adj.* ungleichmäßig
unequivocal [ʌnɪ'kwɪvəkl] *adj.*, **unequivocally** [ʌnɪ'kwɪvəkəlɪ] *adv.* eindeutig
unerring [ʌn'ɜ:rɪŋ] *adj.* untrüglich ⟨*Instinkt, Geschmack*⟩; unbedingt ⟨*Treffsicherheit*⟩; mathematisch ⟨*Genauigkeit*⟩; unfehlbar ⟨*Instinkt*⟩; unerschütterlich ⟨*Zielstrebigkeit*⟩
unerringly [ʌn'ɜ:rɪŋlɪ] *adv.* mit untrüglicher Sicherheit
UNESCO [ju:'neskəʊ] *abbr.* **United Nations Educational, Scientific and Cultural Organization** UNESCO, *die*
unessential [ʌnɪ'senʃl] *see* **inessential**
unethical [ʌn'eθɪkl] *adj.*, **unethically** [ʌn'eθɪkəlɪ] *adv.* unmoralisch
uneven [ʌn'i:vn] *adj.* **a)** *(not smooth)* uneben; **b)** *(not uniform)* ungleichmäßig; unregelmäßig ⟨*Pulsschlag*⟩; unausgeglichen ⟨*Temperament*⟩; **an ~ performance** ein Auftritt mit Höhen und Tiefen; **c)** *(odd)* ungerade ⟨*Zahl*⟩
unevenly [ʌn'i:vnlɪ] *adv.* ungleichmäßig
unevenness [ʌn'i:vnnɪs] *n.* **a)** *(roughness)* Unebenheit, *die*; **b)** *(irregularity)* Ungleichmäßigkeit, *die*; *(of pulse)* Unregelmäßigkeit, *die*; *(of temperament)* Unausgeglichenheit, *die*; **the ~ of the essays** das unterschiedliche Niveau der Aufsätze
uneventful [ʌnɪ'ventfl] *adj.* **a)** *(quiet)* ereignislos; ruhig ⟨*Leben*⟩; **b)** *(normal)* ⟨*Fahrt, Landung*⟩ ohne Zwischenfälle; **be ~** ⟨*Fahrt usw.:*⟩ ohne Zwischenfälle verlaufen
uneventfully [ʌnɪ'ventfəlɪ] *adv.* ohne Zwischenfälle
unexampled [ʌnɪg'zɑ:mpld] *adj.* beispiellos
unexceptionable [ʌnɪk'sepʃənəbl] *adj.* untadelig ⟨*Charakter*⟩; fehlerlos ⟨*Arbeit*⟩
unexceptional [ʌnɪk'sepʃənl] *adj.* alltäglich; *(average)* durchschnittlich
unexciting [ʌnɪk'saɪtɪŋ] *adj.* wenig aufregend; *(boring)* langweilig
unexpected [ʌnɪk'spektɪd] *adj.* unerwartet; **this news was entirely ~:** diese Nachricht kam völlig unerwartet
unexpectedly [ʌnɪk'spektɪdlɪ] *adv.* unerwartet
unexpired [ʌnɪk'spaɪəd] *adj.* noch gültig; noch nicht abgelaufen ⟨*Mandat*⟩
unexplainable [ʌnɪk'spleɪnəbl] *adj.* unerklärlich
unexplained [ʌnɪk'spleɪnd] *adj.* ungeklärt; unentschuldigt ⟨*Abwesenheit*⟩
unexploded [ʌnɪk'spləʊdɪd] *adj.* nicht explodiert *od.* detoniert
unexplored [ʌnɪk'splɔ:d] *adj.* unerforscht
unexposed [ʌnɪk'spəʊzd] *adj.* **a)** *(not brought to light)* unaufgeklärt; nicht entlarvt ⟨*Verbrecher*⟩; **b)** *(Photog.)* unbelichtet
unexpressed [ʌnɪk'sprest] *adj.* unausgesprochen
unexpressive [ʌnɪk'spresɪv] *adj.* ausdruckslos
unexpurgated [ʌn'ekspəgeɪtɪd] *adj.* unzensiert
unfading [ʌn'feɪdɪŋ] *adj.* unvergänglich
unfailing [ʌn'feɪlɪŋ] *adj.* unerschöpflich; nie versagend ⟨*gute Laune*⟩; unfehlbar ⟨*Heilmittel*⟩; **with ~ regularity** *(iron.)* mit schöner Regelmäßigkeit
unfailingly [ʌn'feɪlɪŋlɪ] *adv.* stets
unfair [ʌn'feə(r)] *adj.* unfair; ungerecht, unfair ⟨*Kritik, Urteil*⟩; unlauter ⟨*Wettbewerb*⟩; ungerecht ⟨*Strafe*⟩; **an ~ share** ein ungerechtfertigt hoher Anteil; **be ~ to sb.** jmdm. gegenüber ungerecht sein
unfairly [ʌn'feəlɪ] *adv.* **a)** *(unjustly)* ungerecht; unfair ⟨*spielen*⟩; **b)** *(unreasonably)* zu Unrecht
unfairness [ʌn'feənɪs] *n., no pl.* Ungerechtigkeit, *die*; *(Sport)* Unfairneß, *die*
unfaithful [ʌn'feɪθfl] *adj.* untreu; ungenau ⟨*Übersetzung*⟩; ~ **to sb./sth.** jmdm./einer Sache untreu
unfaithfulness [ʌn'feɪθflnɪs] *n., no pl.* Untreue, *die*
unfaltering [ʌn'fɔ:ltərɪŋ] *adj.* unbeirrbar ⟨*Glaube, Sicherheit*⟩; fest ⟨*Stimme, Schritt*⟩
unfamiliar [ʌnfə'mɪljə(r)] *adj.* **a)** *(strange)* unbekannt; fremd ⟨*Stadt*⟩; ungewohnt ⟨*Arbeit, Tätigkeit*⟩; **b)** *(not well acquainted)* nicht vertraut; **be ~ with sth.** sich mit etw. nicht auskennen; **workers ~ with this type of machine** Arbeiter, die sich mit diesem Maschinentyp nicht [gut] auskennen; **he is not ~ with German** die deutsche Sprache ist ihm einigermaßen vertraut
unfamiliarity [ʌnfəmɪlɪ'ærɪtɪ] *n., no pl.* **a)** *(strangeness)* Fremdheit, *die*; *(of activity)* Ungewohntheit, *die*; **b)** ~ **with sth.** *(poor knowledge of)* Unvertrautheit mit etw.; **his ~ with computers** seine fehlende Erfahrung mit Computern
unfashionable [ʌn'fæʃənəbl] *adj.* unmodern ⟨*Kleidung*⟩; nicht eben schick ⟨*Wohngegend*⟩; **become ~:** aus der Mode kommen; **a view now ~:** eine jetzt überholte Ansicht
unfasten [ʌn'fɑ:sn] **1.** *v. t.* **a)** öffnen; **b)** *(detach)* lösen. **2.** *v. i.* ~ **at the back** hinten geöffnet werden
unfastened [ʌn'fɑ:snd] *adj.* nicht verschlossen ⟨*Tür*⟩; offen ⟨*Verschluß, Knöpfe*⟩
unfathomable [ʌn'fæðəməbl] *adj.* **a)** *(incomprehensible)* unergründlich; **b)** *(immeasurable)* unermeßlich
unfathomed [ʌn'fæðəmd] *adj.* unergründet
unfavourable (*Amer.:* **unfavorable**) [ʌn'feɪvərəbl] *adj.* **a)** *(negative)* ungünstig; unfreundlich ⟨*Kommentar, Reaktion*⟩; negativ ⟨*Kritik, Antwort*⟩; **my suggestion got an ~ response** die Reaktion auf meinen Vorschlag war ablehnend; **be ~ to a proposal** einen Vorschlag ablehnen; **b)** *(tending to make difficult)* ungünstig (**to, for** für); widrig ⟨*Wind*⟩; **an atmosphere ~ to calm discussion** eine Atmosphäre, die einer ruhigen Diskussion abträglich ist; **a climate ~ to growth** ein wachstumsfeindliches Klima
unfavourably (*Amer.:* **unfavorably**) [ʌn'feɪvərəblɪ] *adv.* ungünstig; **be ~ disposed towards sb./sth.** jmdm./etw. gegenüber ablehnend eingestellt sein; **react ~ to a suggestion** auf einen Vorschlag ablehnend reagieren
unfeeling [ʌn'fi:lɪŋ] *adj.* *(unsympathetic)* gefühllos
unfeelingly [ʌn'fi:lɪŋlɪ] *adv.* herzlos
unfeigned [ʌn'feɪnd] *adj.* aufrichtig; unverhohlen
unfenced [ʌn'fenst] *adj.* nicht eingezäunt
unfettered [ʌn'fetəd] *adj.* ungehindert; ~ **by scruples** frei von Skrupeln
unfilled [ʌn'fɪld] *adj.* frei, offen ⟨*Stelle*⟩; *(empty)* leer
unfinished [ʌn'fɪnɪʃt] *adj.* **a)** *(not completed)* unvollendet ⟨*Gedicht, Werk*⟩; unerledigt ⟨*Arbeit, Geschäft*⟩; **the U~ [Symphony]** die Unvollendete; **b)** *(in rough state)* unbearbeitet
unfit [ʌn'fɪt] **1.** *adj.* **a)** *(unsuitable)* ungeeignet; ~ **for human consumption** zum Verzehr nicht geeignet; ~ **for vehicles** nicht befahrbar; **b)** *(not physically fit)* nicht fit; **she hates to be ~:** sie will unbedingt fit sein; ~ **for military service** [wehrdienst]untauglich. **2.** *v. t.*, **-tt-** untauglich machen; *see also* **unfitted**

unfitness [ʌn'fɪtnɪs] *n., no pl.* **a)** *(unsuitability)* fehlende Eignung; **b)** *(poor physical condition)* **[state of]** ~: schlechte körperliche Verfassung
unfitted [ʌn'fɪtɪd] *adj. (unsuited)* ungeeignet
unflagging [ʌn'flægɪŋ] *adj.* unermüdlich
unflappable [ʌn'flæpəbl] *adj. (coll.)* unerschütterlich; **an ~ person** jemand, der sich durch nichts aus der Ruhe bringen läßt
unflattering [ʌn'flætərɪŋ] *adj.* wenig schmeichelhaft; unvorteilhaft ⟨*Kleid, Licht*⟩; **very ~**: gar nicht schmeichelhaft
unfledged [ʌn'fledʒd] *adj.* **a)** *(unfeathered)* [noch] ungefiedert; **b)** *(fig.: inexperienced)* unerfahren
unflinching [ʌn'flɪntʃɪŋ] *adj.* unerschrocken; unbeirrbar ⟨*Entschlossenheit*⟩; **remain ~**: nicht zurückweichen
unfold [ʌn'fəʊld] **1.** *v. t.* **a)** *(open folds of)* entfalten; ausbreiten ⟨*Zeitung, Landkarte*⟩; **~ one's arms** die Arme ausstrecken; **b)** *(fig.: reveal)* **~ sth. to sb.** jmdm. etw. darlegen. **2.** *v. i.* **a)** *(open out)* ⟨*Knospe:*⟩ sich öffnen; ⟨*Flügel:*⟩ sich entfalten; **the landscape ~ed before us** *(fig.)* die Landschaft breitete sich vor unseren Augen aus; **b)** *(develop)* sich entwickeln; ⟨*Geheimnis:*⟩ sich aufklären; **as the story ~ed** im weiteren Verlauf der Geschichte
unforeseeable [ʌnfɔ:'si:əbl] *adj.* unvorhersehbar; **be ~**: nicht vorauszusehen sein
unforeseen [ʌnfɔ:'si:n] *adj.* unvorhergesehen
unforgettable [ʌnfə'getəbl] *adj.* unvergeßlich
unforgivable [ʌnfə'gɪvəbl] *adj.* unverzeihlich
unforgiving [ʌnfə'gɪvɪŋ] *adj.* nachtragend
unformed [ʌn'fɔ:md] *adj.* unausgereift
unforthcoming [ʌnfɔ:θ'kʌmɪŋ] *adj.* zugeknöpft (**about** hinsichtlich)
unfortified [ʌn'fɔ:tɪfaɪd] *adj.* **a)** *(without fortification)* unbefestigt; **b)** *(not enriched)* nicht gespritet ⟨*Wein*⟩
unfortunate [ʌn'fɔ:tʃʊnət, ʌn'fɔ:tʃənət] **1.** *adj.* **a)** *(unlucky)* unglücklich; *(unfavourable)* ungünstig ⟨*Tag, Zeit*⟩; **the poor ~ woman** die arme bedauernswerte Frau; **be ~ [enough] to do sth.** das Pech haben, etw. zu tun; **b)** *(regrettable)* bedauerlich. **2.** *n.* Unglückliche, *der/die*
unfortunately [ʌn'fɔ:tʃʊnətlɪ, ʌn'fɔ:tʃənətlɪ] *adv.* leider
unfounded [ʌn'faʊndɪd] *adj. (fig.)* unbegründet; **the rumours are totally ~**: die Gerüchte entbehren jeder Grundlage
unfreeze [ʌn'fri:z] *v. t. & i.,* **unfroze** [ʌn'frəʊz], **unfrozen** [ʌn'frəʊzn] auftauen
unfrequented [ʌnfrɪ'kwentɪd] *adj.* menschenleer; einsam
unfriendly [ʌn'frendlɪ] *adj.* unfreundlich; negativ ⟨*Kritik*⟩; feindlich ⟨*Staat*⟩; **the bull looked ~ to him** der Stier schien ihm feindselig [zu sein]
unfrock [ʌn'frɒk] *v. t.* **~ sb.** jmdn. des [Priester]amtes entheben
unfruitful [ʌn'fru:tfl] *adj.* **a)** *(sterile)* unfruchtbar; **b)** *(unprofitable)* fruchtlos
unfulfilled [ʌnfʊl'fɪld] *adj.* **a)** unerfüllt ⟨*Person*⟩; **b)** *(not carried out)* unerledigt
unfunny [ʌn'fʌnɪ] *adj.* **[distinctly/decidedly] ~**: [ganz und gar] nicht witzig *od.* komisch
unfurl [ʌn'fɜ:l] **1.** *v. t.* aufrollen; losmachen ⟨*Segel*⟩. **2.** *v. i.* sich aufrollen
unfurnished [ʌn'fɜ:nɪʃt] *adj.* unmöbliert
ungainly [ʌn'geɪnlɪ] *adj.* unbeholfen; ungelenk
ungallant [ʌn'gælənt] *adj.* unliebenswürdig; ungalant
ungenerous [ʌn'dʒenərəs] *adj.* **a)** *(petty)* kleinlich; **b)** *(mean)* wenig großzügig
ungentlemanly [ʌn'dʒentlmənlɪ] *adj.* unfein; *(impolite)* unhöflich; **it is ~**: es gehört sich nicht für einen Gentleman
unget-at-able [ʌnget'ætəbl] *adj.* unerreichbar; unzugänglich ⟨*Fonds*⟩
unglazed [ʌn'gleɪzd] *adj.* **a)** nicht glasiert ⟨*Keramik*⟩; **b)** nicht verglast ⟨*Fenster*⟩
ungodliness [ʌn'gɒdlɪnɪs] *n., no pl.* Gottlosigkeit, *die*
ungodly [ʌn'gɒdlɪ] *adj.* **a)** *(impious)* gottlos; **b)** *(coll.: outrageous)* unchristlich *(ugs.)*
ungovernable [ʌn'gʌvənəbl] *adj.* unkontrollierbar; unregierbar ⟨*Volk*⟩
ungracious [ʌn'greɪʃəs] *adj.* unhöflich; *(tactless)* taktlos
ungraciously [ʌn'greɪʃəslɪ] *adv.* unhöflich; *(tactlessly)* taktlos
ungrammatical [ʌngrə'mætɪkl] *adj.,* **ungrammatically** [ʌngrə'mætɪkəlɪ] *adv.* ungrammatisch
ungrateful [ʌn'greɪtfl] *adj.* undankbar
ungrounded [ʌn'graundɪd] *adj.* **a)** *see* **unfounded; b)** *(Amer. Electr.)* ohne Erdung
ungrudging [ʌn'grʌdʒɪŋ] *adj.* bereitwillig; *(generous)* großzügig; herzlich ⟨*Gastfreundschaft*⟩; neidlos ⟨*Bewunderung*⟩
unguarded [ʌn'gɑ:dɪd] *adj.* **a)** *(not guarded)* unbewacht; **b)** *(incautious)* unvorsichtig; **in an ~ moment he gave away some vital information** als er einen Moment nicht aufpaßte, verriet er einige wichtige Informationen
unguardedly [ʌn'gɑ:dɪdlɪ] *adv.* unvorsichtig
ungulate ['ʌŋgjʊlət] *n. (Zool.)* Huftier, *das*
unhampered [ʌn'hæmpəd] *adj.* unbehindert; **~ by conscience** nicht von Gewissensbissen geplagt
unhappily [ʌn'hæpɪlɪ] *adv.* **a)** *(unfortunately)* unglücklicherweise; leider; **b)** *(without happiness)* unglücklich
unhappiness [ʌn'hæpɪnɪs] *n., no pl.* Bekümmertheit, *die;* **despite his ~ about the consequences** obwohl er Bedenken über die Folgen hatte; **she spent ten years of ~ with him** sie verbrachte zehn unglückliche Jahre mit ihm; **he has been the cause of much ~ to her** er hat ihr viel Kummer gemacht
unhappy [ʌn'hæpɪ] *adj.* **a)** *(sad, causing misfortune)* unglücklich; *(not content)* unzufrieden (**about** mit); **be** *or* **feel ~ about doing sth.** Bedenken haben, etw. zu tun; **b)** *(unfortunate)* unglückselig ⟨*Zeit, Zufall*⟩; unglücklich ⟨*Zusammenstellung, Wahl*⟩
unharmed [ʌn'hɑ:md] *adj.* unbeschädigt; *(uninjured)* unverletzt
unharness [ʌn'hɑ:nɪs] *v. t.* abschirren
unhealthily [ʌn'helθɪlɪ] *adv.* krankhaft; ungesund ⟨*leben*⟩
unhealthiness [ʌn'helθɪnɪs] *n., no pl.* Krankhaftigkeit, *die; (of place, habit)* Gesundheitsschädlichkeit, *die*
unhealthy [ʌn'helθɪ] *adj.* **a)** *(not in good health, harmful to health)* ungesund; **b)** *(unwholesome)* ungesund, krankhaft ⟨*Gier*⟩; schädlich ⟨*Einfluß*⟩; schlecht ⟨*Angewohnheit*⟩; **c)** *(coll.: risky)* gefährlich
unheard [ʌn'hɜ:d] *adj.* **a)** **~-of** *(unknown)* [gänzlich] unbekannt; *(unprecedented)* beispiellos; *(outrageous)* unerhört; **that's ~ of** das ist noch nie dagewesen; **this was an ~-of achievement fifty years ago** vor fünfzig Jahren war eine solche Leistung unvorstellbar; **b)** *(not heard)* **go ~**: ungehört bleiben
unheeded [ʌn'hi:dɪd] *adj.* unbeachtet; **go ~**: nicht beachtet werden; ⟨*Gebet, Wunsch:*⟩ nicht erhört werden
unheedful [ʌn'hi:dfʊl] *adj.* **~ of** ungeachtet (+ *Gen.*)
unhelpful [ʌn'helpfl] *adj.* wenig hilfsbereit ⟨*Person*⟩; ⟨*Bemerkung, Kritik*⟩ die einem nicht weiterhilft
unhelpfully [ʌn'helpfəlɪ] *adv.* wenig hilfsbereit
unhesitating [ʌn'hezɪteɪtɪŋ] *adj.* unverzüglich; **she was ~ in her support for him** sie zögerte keinen Augenblick, ihn zu unterstützen
unhesitatingly [ʌn'hezɪteɪtɪŋlɪ] *adv.* ohne zu zögern
unhinged [ʌn'hɪndʒd] *adj.* **his/her mind is ~**: er/sie hat den Verstand verloren
unhitch [ʌn'hɪtʃ] *v. t.* losmachen; ausspannen ⟨*Pferd*⟩; abkoppeln ⟨*Anhänger*⟩
unholy [ʌn'həʊlɪ] *adj.* **a)** *(wicked)* unheilig ⟨*Allianz*⟩; **b)** *(coll.: dreadful)* fürchterlich *(ugs.)* ⟨*Krawall, Durcheinander*⟩
unhook [ʌn'hʊk] *v. t.* **a)** *(detach from hook)* vom Haken nehmen; **b)** *(unfasten by releasing hook)* aufhaken ⟨*Kleid*⟩; loshaken ⟨*Tor*⟩
unhoped-for [ʌn'həʊptfɔ:(r)] *adj.* unverhofft
unhurried [ʌn'hʌrɪd] *adj.,* **unhurriedly** [ʌn'hʌrɪdlɪ] *adv.* gemächlich
unhurt [ʌn'hɜ:t] *adj.* unverletzt
unhygienic [ʌnhaɪ'dʒi:nɪk] *adj.* unhygienisch
UNICEF ['ju:nɪsef] *abbr.* **United Nations Children's Fund** UNICEF, *die*
unicorn ['ju:nɪkɔ:n] *n. (Mythol.)* Einhorn, *das*
unicycle ['ju:nɪsaɪkl] *n.* Einrad, *das*
unidentified [ʌnaɪ'dentɪfaɪd] *adj.* nicht identifiziert; **~ flying object** unbekanntes Flugobjekt
unidiomatic [ʌnɪdɪə'mætɪk] *adj.,* **unidiomatically** [ʌnɪdɪə'mætɪkəlɪ] *adv.* nicht idiomatisch
unification [ju:nɪfɪ'keɪʃn] *n.* Einigung, *die; (of system)* Vereinheitlichung, *die*
uniform ['ju:nɪfɔ:m] **1.** *adj. (the same for all)* einheitlich; *(unvarying)* gleichbleibend ⟨*Strömung, Temperatur, Qualität*⟩; gleichmäßig ⟨*Tempo*⟩; **be of ~ shape/size/appearance, be ~ in shape/size/appearance** die gleiche Form/Größe/das gleiche Aussehen haben; **~ rows of houses** gleichförmige Häuserzeilen. **2.** *n.* Uniform, *die;* **in/out of ~**: in/ohne Uniform; **be in/out of ~**: Uniform/keine Uniform tragen
uniformed ['ju:nɪfɔ:md] *adj.* uniformiert
uniformity [ju:nɪ'fɔ:mɪtɪ] *n.* Einheitlichkeit, *die; (constant nature)* Gleichmäßigkeit, *die;* **impose ~ of belief on ...**: jmdm. einen einheitlichen Glauben auferlegen (+ *Dat.*)
uniformly ['ju:nɪfɔ:mlɪ] *adv.* **a)** *(unvaryingly)* einheitlich; **b)** *(equally)* gleichmäßig
unify ['ju:nɪfaɪ] *v. t.* einigen ⟨*Volk, Land*⟩; vereinheitlichen ⟨*System, Wirtschaft*⟩
unilateral [ju:nɪ'lætərl] *adj.* einseitig
unilateralist [ju:nɪ'lætərəlɪst] *n.* Befürworter der einseitigen Abrüstung
unilaterally [ju:nɪ'lætərəlɪ] *adv.* einseitig
unimaginable [ʌnɪ'mædʒɪnəbl] *adj.* unvorstellbar
unimaginative [ʌnɪ'mædʒɪnətɪv] *adj.,* **unimaginatively** [ʌnɪ'mædʒɪnətɪvlɪ] *adv.* phantasielos
unimpaired [ʌnɪm'peəd] *adj.* unbeeinträchtigt; **he emerged from the trial with ~ prestige** er überstand den Prozeß ohne Prestigeverlust
unimpeachable [ʌnɪm'pi:tʃəbl] *adj.* **a)** *(blameless)* unanfechtbar; untadelig ⟨*Ruf*⟩; **b)** *(beyond question)* unbezweifelbar; absolut zuverlässig ⟨*Quelle*⟩
unimpeded [ʌnɪm'pi:dɪd] *adj.* ungehindert
unimportance [ʌnɪm'pɔ:təns] *n., no pl.* Unwichtigkeit, *die;* Bedeutungslosigkeit, *die*
unimportant [ʌnɪm'pɔ:tənt] *adj.* unwichtig; bedeutungslos
unimpressed [ʌnɪm'prest] *adj.* nicht beeindruckt
unimpressive [ʌnɪm'presɪv] *adj.* nicht eindrucksvoll; unscheinbar ⟨*Gebäude*⟩; *(unconvincing)* nicht überzeugend
uninfluenced [ʌn'ɪnflʊənst] *adj.* unbeeinflußt
uninformative [ʌnɪn'fɔ:mətɪv] *adj.* inhaltslos ⟨*Text*⟩; **he is ~ about his plans** er verrät nichts über seine Pläne
uninformed [ʌnɪn'fɔ:md] *adj.* **a)** *(not in-*

formed) uninformiert; **be [entirely] ~ about the development** [überhaupt] nichts von der Entwicklung wissen; **b)** *(based on ignorance)* auf Unkenntnis beruhend ‹*Urteil, Ansicht*›; **~ guess** reine Vermutung

uninhabitable [ʌnɪn'hæbɪtəbl] *adj.* unbewohnbar

uninhabited [ʌnɪn'hæbɪtɪd] *adj.* unbewohnt

uninhibited [ʌnɪn'hɪbɪtɪd] *adj.* ungehemmt; ohne Hemmungen *nachgestellt*

uninitiated [ʌnɪ'nɪʃɪeɪtɪd] *adj.* uneingeweiht; **~ in the mysteries** nicht in die Geheimnisse eingeweiht; **the ~**: Außenstehende

uninjured [ʌn'ɪndʒəd] *adj.* unverletzt

uninspired [ʌnɪn'spaɪəd] *adj.* einfallslos; **I am/feel ~**: mir fehlt die Inspiration

uninspiring [ʌnɪn'spaɪərɪŋ] *adj.* langweilig

uninsured [ʌnɪn'ʃʊəd] *adj.* nicht versichert

unintelligent [ʌnɪn'telɪdʒənt] *adj.* nicht intelligent; **pretty ~**: ziemlich dumm

unintelligible [ʌnɪn'telɪdʒɪbl] *adj.* unverständlich

unintended [ʌnɪn'tendɪd] *adj.* unbeabsichtigt

unintentional [ʌnɪn'tenʃənl] *adj.*, **unintentionally** [ʌnɪn'tenʃənəlɪ] *adv.* unabsichtlich; *(Law)* nicht vorsätzlich

uninterested [ʌn'ɪntrestɪd, ʌn'ɪntrɪstɪd] *adj.* desinteressiert (**in** an + *Dat.*)

uninteresting [ʌn'ɪntrestɪŋ, ʌn'ɪntrɪstɪŋ] *adj.* uninteressant

uninterrupted [ʌnɪntə'rʌptɪd] *adj.* **a)** *(continuous)* ununterbrochen; nicht unterbrochen; **b)** *(not disturbed)* ungestört

uninvited [ʌnɪn'vaɪtɪd] *adj.* ungeladen

uninviting [ʌnɪn'vaɪtɪŋ] *adj.* wenig verlockend; wenig einladend ‹*Ort, Wetter*›

uninvolved [ʌnɪn'vɒlvd] *adj.* unbeteiligt (**in** an + *Dat.*); **be** *or* **remain ~**: sich nicht beteiligen

union ['ju:nɪən, 'ju:njən] *n.* **a)** *(trade ~)* Gewerkschaft, *die;* **b)** *(political unit)* Union, *die;* **'State of the U~' message** *(Amer. Polit.)* Regierungserklärung zur Lage der Nation; **c) [Students'] U~**: Studentenvereinigung, *die;* **d)** *(marriage)* eheliche Verbindung; **e)** *(concord)* Einigkeit, *die;* **they lived together in perfect ~**: sie lebten einträchtig zusammen; **f)** *(uniting)* Vereinigung, *die*

unionism ['ju:nɪənɪzm, 'ju:njənɪzm] *n.* **a)** *(of trade unions)* Gewerkschaftswesen, *das;* **b)** *(Brit. Polit.)* unionistische Bestrebungen; *Befürwortung der parlamentarischen Einheit von Großbritannien und Nordirland*

unionist ['ju:nɪənɪst, 'ju:njənɪst] *n.* **a)** *(member of trade union)* Gewerkschafter, *der*/Gewerkschafterin, *die; (advocate of trade unions)* Gewerkschaftsanhänger, *der*/-anhängerin, *die;* **b)** U~ *(Polit.)* Unionist, *der*/Unionistin, *die*

unionize (unionise) ['ju:nɪənaɪz, 'ju:njənaɪz] *v. t.* **~ a company** in einer Firma eine Gewerkschaftsorganisation aufbauen; **~d labour** gewerkschaftlich organisierte Arbeitskräfte

Union: ~ **'Jack** *n. (Brit.)* Union Jack, *der;* ~ **of Soviet Socialist Republics** *pr. n. (Hist.)* Union der Sozialistischen Sowjetrepubliken; **u~ suit** *n. (Amer.)* Hemdhose, *die (veralt.);* Leibchenhose, *die (landsch.)*

unique [ju:'ni:k] *adj.* **a)** *(unparalleled)* einzigartig; *(not repeated)* einmalig ‹*Gelegenheit, Angebot*›; **this vase is ~**: diese Vase ist ein Einzelstück; **this problem is ~ to our society** dieses Problem gibt es nur in unserer Gesellschaft; **these animals are ~ to Australia** diese Tiere kommen nur in Australien vor; **b)** *(coll.: remarkable)* einmalig

uniquely [ju:'ni:klɪ] *adv.* **a)** *(exclusively)* einzig und allein; **that distinction is ~ his** die Auszeichnung besitzt nur *od.* allein er; **b)** *(to a unique degree)* einzigartig; einmalig ‹*talentiert, begabt*›

uniqueness [ju:'ni:knɪs] *n., no pl.* Einzigartigkeit, *die*

unisex ['ju:nɪseks] *adj.* Unisex‹*mantel, -kleidung*›; **~ hairdresser** Damen-und-Herren-Frisör

unison ['ju:nɪsən] **1.** *n.* **a)** *(Mus.)* Unisono, *das;* **in ~**: unisono; einstimmig; **act in ~** *(fig.)* vereint handeln; **act in ~ with sb.** in Übereinstimmung mit jmdm. handeln; **b)** *(concord)* Einmütigkeit, *die.* **2.** *adj. (Mus.)* unisono gesungen/gespielt

unit ['ju:nɪt] *n.* **a)** *(element, group, regarded as complete; also Mil.)* Einheit, *die; (in complex mechanism)* Element, *das;* **x-ray ~**: Röntgenabteilung, *die;* **armoured ~** *(Mil.)* Panzereinheit, *die;* **motor ~** *(Railw.)* Triebwagen, *der;* **b)** *(in adding numbers by columns)* Einer, *der (Math.);* **the ~s column** die Einerspalte; **c)** *(quantity chosen as standard)* [Maß]einheit, *die; (of gas, electricity)* Einheit, *die;* **~ of length/monetary ~**: Längen-/Währungseinheit, *die;* **d)** *(piece of furniture)* Element, *das;* **kitchen ~**: Küchenelement, *das;* **wall ~**: Wandschrank, *der;* **e)** *(esp. electrical device)* Gerät, *das;* **f)** *(building)* **shop ~**: Ladenlokal, *das;* **residential ~**: Wohneinheit, *die;* **factory ~**: Fabrikgebäude, *das;* **g)** *(Brit. Finance)* Anteil[sschein] [an einem Investmentfonds]

Unitarian [ju:nɪ'teərɪən] *(Relig.)* **1.** *n.* Unitarier, *der*/Unitarierin, *die.* **2.** *adj.* unitarisch

unitary ['ju:nɪtərɪ] *adj.* einheitlich

unite [ju:'naɪt] **1.** *v. t.* vereinigen; verbinden ‹*Einzelteile*›; einen, einigen ‹*Partei, Mitglieder*›. **2.** *v.i.* **a)** *(join together)* sich vereinigen; ‹*Elemente:*› sich verbinden; ‹*gebrochene Knochen:*› zusammenwachsen; **b)** *(join forces)* sich vereinigen; *(form merger)* sich zusammenschließen; **~ in doing sth.** etw. vereint *od.* gemeinsam tun

united [ju:'naɪtɪd] *adj.* **a)** *(harmonious)* einig; **a ~ front** eine geschlossene Front; **~ we stand, divided we fall** gemeinsam siegen wir, getrennt fallen wir; **b)** *(combined)* vereint *(geh.);* gemeinsam; **their ~ efforts found the solution** ihre gemeinsamen Anstrengungen führten zur Lösung

United: ~ **Arab 'Emirates** *pr. n. pl.* Vereinigte Arabische Emirate; ~ **'Kingdom** *pr. n.* Vereinigtes Königreich [Großbritannien und Nordirland]; ~ **'Nations** *pr. n. sing.* Vereinte Nationen *Pl.;* ~ **Re'formed Church** *n.* Vereinigte Reformierte Kirche; ~ **'States** *see* **state 1 e**; ~ **States of A'merica** *n. sing.* Vereinigte Staaten von Amerika

unit: ~ **'furniture** *n.* Anbaumöbel *Pl.;* ~ **'price** *n. (Commerc.)* Stückpreis, *der;* ~ **'trust** *n. (Brit. Finance)* ≈ Investmentfonds, *der*

unity ['ju:nɪtɪ] *n.* **a)** *(state of being united)* Einheit, *die; (of work of art, idea)* [innere] Geschlossenheit; **their ~ of purpose** die Gemeinsamkeit ihres Wollens; **the dramatic unities** die drei Einheiten ‹*Literaturw.*›; **b)** *(Math.)* Einselement, *das;* **c)** *(harmony)* Eintracht, *die*

universal [ju:nɪ'vɜ:sl] *adj.* **a)** *(prevailing everywhere)* allgemein; allgemeingültig ‹*Regel, Wahrheit*›; **less ~**: weniger häufig *od.* verbreitet; **there was ~ terror** überall herrschte große Angst; **become ~**: sich allgemein verbreiten; **b)** *(involving or versed in all fields of knowledge)* universal ‹*Bildung, Wissen*›; universell begabt ‹*Person*›; **~ genius** Universalgenie, *das;* **c)** *(common to all members of a class)* universell; **d)** *(meeting varied requirements)* Universal-; **~ remedy** Universalmittel, *das*

universality [ju:nɪvɜ:'sælɪtɪ] *n., no pl.* **a)** *(universal prevalence)* allgemeine Verbreitung; **b)** *(universal comprehensiveness)* Universalität, *die*

universal: ~ **'joint** *n.* Kardangelenk, *das;* ~ **'language** *n.* Universalsprache, *die*

universally [ju:nɪ'vɜ:səlɪ] *adv.* allgemein; **~ opposed to these politics/hostile to foreigners** diese Politik einmütig ablehnen/ausnahmslos fremdenfeindlich sein

universe ['ju:nɪvɜ:s] *n.* **a)** Universum, *das; (world; fig.: mankind)* Welt, *die;* **b)** *see* **cosmos b**

university [ju:nɪ'vɜ:sɪtɪ] *n.* Universität, *die; attrib.* Universitäts-; **go to ~**: auf die *od.* zur Universität gehen; **at ~**: an der Universität

unjust [ʌn'dʒʌst] *adj.* ungerecht (**to** *Dat.* + gegenüber); **it would be ~ not to refer to X** es ist ein Gebot der Fairneß, X zu zitieren

unjustifiable [ʌn'dʒʌstɪfaɪəbl] *adj.* ungerechtfertigt; **be ~**: nicht zu rechtfertigen sein

unjustifiably [ʌn'dʒʌstɪfaɪəblɪ] *adv.* ungerechtfertigterweise

unjustified [ʌn'dʒʌstɪfaɪd] *adj.* ungerechtfertigt; **you are entirely ~ in thinking ...**: du glaubst ganz zu Unrecht, ...

unjustly [ʌn'dʒʌstlɪ] ungerechterweise; zu Unrecht

unkempt [ʌn'kempt] *adj.* **a)** *(dishevelled)* ungekämmt ‹*Haare*›; **b)** *(untidy)* ungepflegt

unkind [ʌn'kaɪnd] *adj.* unfreundlich; **be ~ to sb./animals** jmdn./Tiere schlecht behandeln

unkindly [ʌn'kaɪndlɪ] *adv.* unfreundlich; **fate treated her ~**: das Schicksal meinte es nicht gut mit ihr

unkindness [ʌn'kaɪndnɪs] *n.* Unfreundlichkeit, *die*

unknot [ʌn'nɒt] *v. t.*, **-tt-** entknoten

unknowing [ʌn'nəʊɪŋ] *see* **unwitting**

unknowingly [ʌn'nəʊɪŋlɪ] *see* **unwittingly**

unknown [ʌn'nəʊn] **1.** *adj.* unbekannt; **an ~ number of people died in the accident** die Zahl der Todesopfer bei dem Unfall ist nicht bekannt; **sb./sth. is ~ to sb.** jmd./etw. ist jmdm. nicht bekannt; **a drug ~ to us** ein uns unbekanntes Heilmittel; **it is ~/not ~ for him to do such a thing** es ist nie vorgekommen/ist schon vorgekommen, daß er so etwas getan hat; **~ territory** *(lit. or fig.)* unbekanntes Terrain; **the U~ Soldier** *or* **Warrior** der Unbekannte Soldat; **murder by person** *or* **persons ~**: Mord durch unbekannten Täter; **~ strengths/reserves** *(unsuspected)* ungeahnte Kräfte/Reserven; *see also* **country a; quantity e. 2.** *adv.* **~ to sb.** ohne daß jmd. davon weiß/wußte. **3.** *n.* **a) the ~**: das Unbekannte; **fear of the ~**: Angst vor dem Unbekannten; **journey/voyage into the ~** *(lit. or fig.)* Reise in unbekannte Regionen; **b)** *(person)* **an ~**: ein Unbekannter/eine Unbekannte; **c)** *(Math.: quantity)* Unbekannte, *die;* **an equation with two ~s** eine Gleichung mit zwei Unbekannten; **d)** *(factor)* unbekannte Größe

unlabelled (*Amer.:* **unlabeled**) [ʌn'leɪbld] *adj.* ‹*Flasche, Behälter*› ohne Etikett *od.* Beschriftung; ‹*Gepäck, Koffer, Paket*› ohne Aufkleber/Anhänger; unbeschriftet ‹*Dokument, Aktenordner, Tonband*›

unlace [ʌn'leɪs] *v. t.* aufschnüren

unladen [ʌn'leɪdn] *adj.* **~ weight** Leergewicht, *das*

unladylike [ʌn'leɪdɪlaɪk] *adj.* nicht sehr damenhaft; **very ~**: gar nicht damenhaft

unlatch [ʌn'lætʃ] **1.** *v. t.* aufklinken. **2.** *v. i.* sich aufklinken lassen

unlawful [ʌn'lɔ:fl] *adj.* ungesetzlich; gesetzwidrig; **~ possession of firearms/drugs** illegaler Waffen-/Drogenbesitz; **~ assembly** verbotene Versammlung

unlawfully [ʌn'lɔ:fəlɪ] *adv.* gesetzwidrig

unleaded [ʌn'ledɪd] *adj.* bleifrei ‹*Benzin*›

unlearn [ʌn'lɜ:n] *v. t., forms as* **learn 1** vergessen ‹*Idee, Kenntnisse*›; ablegen ‹*Gewohnheit*›

unleash [ʌn'li:ʃ] *v. t.* von der Leine lassen ‹*Hund*›; *(fig.)* freien Lauf lassen (+ *Dat.*) ‹*Gefühlen, Leidenschaften, Kräften*›; entfesseln ⟨*Sturm der Entrüstung*⟩; ~ **sth. [up]on sb.** an jmdm. etw. auslassen; ~ **violence/[a] war on a country** Gewalt/Krieg über ein Land bringen

unleavened [ʌn'levnd] *adj.* ohne Treibmittel *nachgestellt;* ungesäuert ⟨*Brot*⟩

unless ['ʌn'les, ən'les] *conj.* es sei denn; wenn ... nicht; **I shall not do it ~ I am paid for it** ich werde es nur tun, wenn ich dafür bezahlt werde; **I shall expect you tomorrow ~ I hear from you/hear to the contrary** falls *od.* sofern ich nichts von dir/nichts Gegenteiliges höre, erwarte ich dich morgen; **I might go, but not ~ I'm asked to** vielleicht gehe ich, aber nur, wenn man mich darum bittet; ~ **I'm [very much] mistaken** wenn ich mich nicht [sehr] irre *od.* täusche; ~ **he comes soon, I shall leave** wenn er nicht bald kommt, dann gehe ich; ~ **otherwise indicated** *or* **stated** wenn nicht anders angegeben

unlettered [ʌn'letəd] *adj.* **a)** *(illiterate)* analphabetisch; **b)** *(uneducated)* ungebildet

unliberated [ʌn'lɪbəreɪtɪd] *adj.* nicht emanzipiert ⟨*Frau*⟩; unfrei ⟨*Massen, Land*⟩

unlicensed [ʌn'laɪsənst] *adj.* ⟨*Händler, Makler, Buchmacher*⟩ ohne Konzession; ⟨*Pilot*⟩ ohne Lizenz; nicht angemeldet ⟨*Hund, Radio, Fernsehgerät, Auto*⟩; ~ **premises** Gaststättenbetrieb ohne [Schank]konzession

unlighted [ʌn'laɪtɪd] *see* **unlit**

unlike [ʌn'laɪk] **1.** *adj.* nicht ähnlich; unähnlich; *(unequal)* ~ **signs** *(Math.)* ungleiche Vorzeichen; ~ **poles** *(Phys.)* ungleiche Pole; **they are ~:** sie sind sich *(Dat.)* nicht ähnlich. **2.** *prep.* **be ~ sb./sth.** jmdm./einer Sache nicht ähnlich sein; **those people are ~ us** diese Leute sind nicht wie wir; **be not ~ sb./sth.** jmdm./etw. nicht unähnlich sein *od.* ganz ähnlich sein; **his new novel is ~ his previous ones** sein neuer Roman ist anders als seine früheren; **sth. is ~ sb.** *(not characteristic of)* etw. sieht jmdm. gar nicht ähnlich *(ugs.)*; etw. ist für jmdn. nicht typisch; **it is ~ him to be late** es sieht ihm gar nicht ähnlich *(ugs.) od.* es ist sonst nicht seine Art, zu spät zu kommen; ~ **her brother, she likes walking** im Gegensatz zu ihrem Bruder geht sie gern spazieren; **she sings quite ~ other singers** sie singt ganz anders als andere Sängerinnen

unlikelihood [ʌn'laɪklɪhʊd] *n., no pl.* Unwahrscheinlichkeit, *die;* **despite the ~ of the player's being fit** obwohl der Spieler wahrscheinlich nicht fit sein wird

unlikely [ʌn'laɪklɪ] *adj.* **a)** unwahrscheinlich; unglaubwürdig ⟨*Geschichte, Erklärung*⟩; **be ~ to do sth.** etw. wahrscheinlich nicht tun; **in the ~ event that ...:** sollte der unwahrscheinliche Fall eintreten, daß ...; **he's ~ to be chosen for the part/post** er wird die Rolle/Stelle kaum bekommen; **it is not ~ that ...:** es ist durchaus wahrscheinlich, daß ...; **b)** *(unsuitable)* **an ~ candidate/man for the job** ein Bewerber, der für den Posten kaum geeignet sein dürfte; **she looked in every likely and ~ place to find her key** sie suchte an allen möglichen und unmöglichen Stellen ihren Schlüssel

unlimited [ʌn'lɪmɪtɪd] *adj.* unbegrenzt; grenzenlos, unendlich ⟨*Himmel, Meer, Geduld*⟩; ~ **drinks** eine unbegrenzte Zahl von Getränken; ~ **liability** *(Commerc.)* unbeschränkte Haftung; ~ **company** *(Commerc.)* Gesellschaft mit unbeschränkter Haftung; ~ **mileage** unbegrenzte Meilenzahl

[1]**unlined** [ʌn'laɪnd] *adj. (without lining)* ungefüttert ⟨*Kleidung, Briefumschlag*⟩

[2]**unlined** *adj. (without lines)* unliniert ⟨*Papier*⟩

unlisted [ʌn'lɪstɪd] *adj.* nicht eingetragen; ~ **stock/securities** *(Finance)* nicht notierte Wertpapiere; ~ **[telephone] number** Geheimnummer, *die*

unlit [ʌn'lɪt] *adj.* unbeleuchtet ⟨*Straße, Korridor, Zimmer*⟩; nicht angezündet ⟨*Lampe, Kamin, Kerze*⟩

unload [ʌn'ləʊd] **1.** *v. t.* **a)** entladen ⟨*Lastwagen, Waggon*⟩; löschen ⟨*Schiff, Schiffsladung*⟩; ausladen ⟨*Gepäck*⟩; ~ **a donkey** einem Esel die Last abnehmen; **the bus/ship ~ed its passengers** die Fahrgäste stiegen aus dem Bus/Schiff; **b)** *(dispose of; Commerc.: sell off, dump)* abstoßen ⟨*Aktien, Wertpapiere*⟩; ~ **goods on the market** Waren auf den Markt werfen; ~ **sb./sth. on [to] sb.** *(fig.)* jmdn./etw. bei jmdm. abladen ⟨*Kinder, Hund, Probleme, Sorgen*⟩; ~ **one's job/responsibility on[to] sb. else** seine Aufgabe/Verantwortung auf jmd. anders *(Akk.)* abwälzen; **c)** entladen ⟨*Gewehr, Pistole*⟩; ~ **[the film from] a camera** den Film aus einer Kamera nehmen. **2.** *v. i.* ⟨*Schiff:*⟩ gelöscht werden; ⟨*Lastwagen:*⟩ entladen werden; **start ~ing** mit dem Entladen anfangen

unloaded [ʌn'ləʊdɪd] *adj.* **a)** nicht beladen ⟨*Schiff, Lastwagen, Waggon*⟩; **b)** nicht geladen ⟨*Gewehr, Pistole*⟩

unlock [ʌn'lɒk] *v. t.* **a)** aufschließen; lösen ⟨*Rad, Taste*⟩; **~ed** unverschlossen ⟨*Tür, Tor*⟩; **leave the door ~ed when you go out** schließ die Tür nicht ab, wenn du gehst; **the gate was left ~ed** das Tor war nicht abgeschlossen; *(fig.)* ~ **a secret/puzzle** ein Geheimnis/Rätsel entschlüsseln; **this book has ~ed the world of literature for him** dieses Buch hat ihm die Welt der Literatur erschlossen; **b)** *(fig.: release)* lösen ⟨*Hand, Umarmung*⟩

unlooked-for [ʌn'lʊktfɔ:(r)] *adj.* unerwartet; **a virtue perhaps ~ in him** eine Tugend, die man bei ihm vielleicht nicht erwartet hätte

unloose [ʌn'lu:s] *see* **loose 2**

unlovable [ʌn'lʌvəbl] *adj.* wenig liebenswert

unloved [ʌn'lʌvd] *adj.* ungeliebt

unlovely [ʌn'lʌvlɪ] *adj.* unschön ⟨*Anblick, Gegenstand, Haus*⟩; reizlos ⟨*Person, Gesicht, Stadt*⟩; *(in character)* nicht sehr sympathisch ⟨*Person*⟩

unluckily [ʌn'lʌkɪlɪ] *adv.* unglücklich; *as sentence-modifier* unglücklicherweise: ~ **for him/her** *etc.* zu seinem/ihrem *usw.* Pech

unlucky [ʌn'lʌkɪ] *adj.* **a)** unglücklich; *(not successful)* glücklos; **be [very/really] ~:** [großes/wirkliches] Pech haben; **lucky at cards, ~ in love** Glück im Spiel, Pech in der Liebe; **b)** *(bringing bad luck)* **an ~ date/number** ein Unglückstag/eine Unglückszahl; **an ~ sign/omen** ein schlechtes Zeichen/Omen; **be born under an ~ star** unter keinem glücklichen Stern geboren sein; **be ~:** Unglück bringen; **it was ~ [for him] that he couldn't come** es war Pech [für ihn], daß er nicht kommen konnte

unmade [ʌn'meɪd] *adj.* ungemacht ⟨*Bett*⟩; unbefestigt ⟨*Straße*⟩

unmade-up [ʌnmeɪd'ʌp] *adj.* ungeschminkt ⟨*Gesicht, Person*⟩

unmake [ʌn'meɪk] *v. t.,* **unmade** [ʌn'meɪd] rückgängig machen ⟨*Vereinbarung, Entscheidung*⟩; fallenlassen ⟨*Plan*⟩; ruinieren ⟨*Laufbahn*⟩

unman [ʌn'mæn] *v. t.,* **-nn- a)** ~ **sb.** *(deprive of strength)* jmdm. die Kraft nehmen; *(deprive of courage)* jmdn. verzagen lassen; **~ned by grief** von Kummer geschwächt; **b)** *(emasculate, castrate)* entmannen

unmanageable [ʌn'mænɪdʒəbl] *adj.* **a)** *(difficult to control)* widerspenstig ⟨*Kind, Pferd, Haare*⟩; unkontrollierbar ⟨*Situation*⟩; **the car/boat became ~:** der Wagen/das Boot war nicht mehr zu kontrollieren; **b)** *(unwieldy)* sperrig; unhandlich ⟨*Buch*⟩

unmanly [ʌn'mænlɪ] *adj.* unmännlich

unmanned [ʌn'mænd] *adj.* unbemannt ⟨*Leuchtturm, Raumschiff, Bahnübergang*⟩; *(with nobody in attendance)* nicht besetzt ⟨*Schalter, Rezeption*⟩; unbewacht ⟨*Posten, Eingang*⟩

unmannerly [ʌn'mænəlɪ] *adj.* unmanierlich ⟨*Person, Benehmen*⟩; ungehörig ⟨*Benehmen*⟩; **it is ~ to do that** es gehört sich nicht, das zu tun

unmarked [ʌn'mɑ:kt] *adj.* **a)** *(without markings)* ⟨*Schachtel, Kiste*⟩ ohne Aufschrift; nicht gezeichnet ⟨*Wäschestück*⟩; anonym ⟨*Grab*⟩; **an ~ police car** ein Zivilfahrzeug der Polizei; **b)** *(not spoilt by marks)* fleckenlos ⟨*Fußboden, Oberfläche*⟩; makellos ⟨*Haut, Pfirsich, Apfel*⟩; unbeschädigt ⟨*Teller, Buch*⟩; **after ten rounds, the boxer was still ~:** nach zehn Runden war der Boxer immer noch nicht gezeichnet; **his face was ~ by the accident** sein Gesicht zeigte keine Spuren des Unfalls; **c)** *(not corrected)* unkorrigiert ⟨*Klassenarbeit*⟩; **d)** *(not noticed)* unbemerkt; **e)** *(Sport)* ungedeckt ⟨*Spieler*⟩; **f)** *(Ling.)* nicht markiert ⟨*Form*⟩

unmarketable [ʌn'mɑ:kɪtəbl] *adj.* unverkäuflich

unmarriageable [ʌn'mærɪdʒəbl] *adj.* **be ~:** nicht zu verheiraten sein

unmarried [ʌn'mærɪd] *adj.* unverheiratet; ledig; ~ **mother/couple** ledige Mutter/unverheiratetes Paar

unmask [ʌn'mɑ:sk] *v. t.* ~ **sb.** jmdm. die Maske entreißen; *(fig.)* jmdn. entlarven (**as** als); ~ **a plot/sb.'s intentions** *etc.* eine Verschwörung/jmds. Absichten *usw.* aufdecken

unmasking [ʌn'mɑ:skɪŋ] *n.* Entlarvung, *die*

unmatched [ʌn'mætʃt] *adj.* **be ~ [for sth.]** [in etw. *(Dat.)*] unübertroffen sein

unmentionable [ʌn'menʃənəbl] *adj.* unaussprechlich ⟨*Sünde, Verbrechen*⟩; **an ~ topic/subject** ein Thema, über das man nicht spricht

unmerciful [ʌn'mɜ:sɪfl] *adj.* erbarmungslos; unbarmherzig

unmercifully [ʌn'mɜ:sɪfəlɪ] *adv.* erbarmungslos; unbarmherzig; **treat sb. ~:** jmdn. unbarmherzig behandeln

unmerited [ʌn'merɪtɪd] *adj.* unverdient

unmetalled [ʌn'metld] *adj. (Brit.)* unbefestigt ⟨*Straße*⟩

unmethodical [ʌnmɪ'θɒdɪkl] *adj.* unmethodisch

unmindful [ʌn'maɪndfl] *adj.* **be ~ of sth.** etw. nicht beachten

unmistakable [ʌnmɪ'steɪkəbl] *adj.* deutlich; unmißverständlich ⟨*Drohung, Befehl*⟩; klar ⟨*Beweis*⟩; unverwechselbar ⟨*Handschrift, Stimme, Silhouette*⟩; **an ~ sign of sth.** ein sicheres Zeichen für etw.; **there was ~ fear/relief in his voice** in seiner Stimme schwang deutlich Furcht/Erleichterung mit

unmistakably [ʌnmɪ'steɪkəblɪ] *adv.* unverkennbar

unmitigated [ʌn'mɪtɪgeɪtɪd] *adj.* vollkommen ⟨*Unsinn, Schwachkopf*⟩; einzig ⟨*Übel, Lüge*⟩; **an ~ scoundrel** ein Erzschurke; **be an ~ disaster** *(coll.)* eine einzige Katastrophe sein *(ugs.)*

unmixed [ʌn'mɪkst] *adj.* unvermischt; *(fig.)* ungetrübt ⟨*Freude, Vergnügen*⟩; **his joy was not ~ with sadness** in seine Freude mischte sich Traurigkeit

unmolested [ʌnmə'lestɪd] *adj.* unbelästigt

unmoor [ʌn'mʊə(r), ʌn'mɔ:(r)] *v. t. & i.* [bei einem Boot] die Leinen losmachen. **2.** *v. i.* die Leinen losmachen

unmotivated [ʌn'məʊtɪveɪtɪd] *adj.* unmotiviert

unmounted [ʌn'maʊntɪd] *adj.* nicht gefaßt ⟨*Edelstein*⟩; nicht aufgezogen ⟨*Bild*⟩

unmourned [ʌn'mɔ:nd] *adj.* unbeweint

unmoved [ʌn'mu:vd] *adj.* unbewegt; ungerührt; **be/remain ~ by sb.'s pleas** sich von jmds. Bitten nicht rühren *od.* erweichen lassen; **he was ~ by the accusations** er ließ sich von den Anschuldigungen nicht aus der Ruhe bringen; **remain ~ by an argument**

von einem Argument nicht beeindruckt sein

unmusical [ʌnˈmjuːzɪkl] *adj.* unmelodisch 〈*Gesang, Stimme*〉; unmusikalisch 〈*Person*〉

unnameable [ʌnˈneɪməbl] *adj.* unbestimmt 〈*Angst*〉; unsagbar 〈*Qual*〉

unnamed [ʌnˈneɪmd] *adj.* **a)** *(unidentified)* [namentlich] nicht genannt 〈*Ort, Person, Medizin*〉; ungenannt 〈*Wohltäter*〉; **b)** *(having no name)* namenlos 〈*Findling*〉; **an ~ island/lake/mountain** eine Insel/ein See/Berg ohne Namen; **a species so far ~**: eine Art, die bisher noch keinen Namen hat

unnatural [ʌnˈnætʃrəl] *adj.* **a)** unnatürlich; *(abnormal)* nicht normal; *(perverted)* widernatürlich; *(uncaring)* herzlos 〈*Mutter, Kind usw.*〉; **not ~**: ganz natürlich; **a mother who is cruel to her children is ~**: eine Mutter, die grausam zu ihren Kindern ist, ist widernatürlich *od.* *(ugs.)* nicht normal; **b)** *(affected)* unnatürlich; gekünstelt

unnaturally [ʌnˈnætʃrəlɪ] *adv.* **a)** unnatürlich; **not ~**: natürlich; wie man sich denken kann; **he expected, not ~, that his father would help him** natürlich rechnete er damit, daß sein Vater ihm helfen werde; **b)** *(affectedly)* unnatürlich; gekünstelt

unnavigable [ʌnˈnævɪgəbl] *adj.* nicht schiffbar 〈*Fluß*〉

unnecessarily [ʌnˈnesɪsərɪlɪ] *adv.* **a)** unnötig[erweise] 〈*sich ärgern, sich aufregen, sich sorgen*〉; **spend money/time ~**: unnötig Geld/Zeit aufwenden; **b)** *(excessively)* unnötig 〈*streng, kompliziert*〉; **be ~ high/long** höher/länger als nötig sein

unnecessary [ʌnˈnesəsərɪ] *adj.* unnötig; **it is ~ for sb. to do sth.** es ist unnötig *od.* es muß nicht sein, daß jmd. etw. tut; **no, thank you, that's quite ~**: danke, das ist gar nicht nötig

unneighbourly [ʌnˈneɪbəlɪ] *adj.* nicht gutnachbarlich; **they are ~**: sie sind schlechte Nachbarn

unnerve [ʌnˈnɜːv] *v. t.* entnerven

unnerving [ʌnˈnɜːvɪŋ] *adj.* entnervend; zermürbend 〈*Warten*〉; nervenaufreibend 〈*Erlebnis*〉; **be [too] ~**: [zuviel] Nerven kosten; **an ~ reaction/incident** eine Reaktion, die/ein Vorfall, der an die Nerven geht/ging

unnoticed [ʌnˈnəʊtɪst] *adj.* unbemerkt; **~ by her, he came in** er trat ein, ohne daß sie es bemerkte; **pass** *or* **go ~**: unbemerkt bleiben

unnumbered [ʌnˈnʌmbəd] *adj.* *(without numbers)* nicht numeriert; unpaginiert 〈*Buchseite*〉; 〈*Haus*〉 ohne Hausnummer

UNO [ˈjuːnəʊ] *abbr.* **United Nations Organization** UNO, *die*

unobjectionable [ʌnəbˈdʒekʃənəbl] *adj.* gefällig; **sth./sb. is ~**: gegen etw./jmdn. gibt es nichts einzuwenden

unobservant [ʌnəbˈzɜːvənt] *adj.* unaufmerksam; **be an ~ person** ein schlechter Beobachter sein

unobserved [ʌnəbˈzɜːvd] *adj.* unbeobachtet

unobstructed [ʌnəbˈstrʌktɪd] *adj.* frei 〈*Weg, Rohr, Ausgang*〉; ungehindert 〈*Vormarsch, Durchfahrt*〉

unobtainable [ʌnəbˈteɪnəbl] *adj.* nicht erhältlich; **number ~** *(Teleph.)* kein Anschluß unter dieser Nummer; **the 'number ~' tone** der Ton für eine Nummer ohne Anschluß

unobtrusive [ʌnəbˈtruːsɪv] *adj.* unaufdringlich 〈*Geste, Bemerkung, Muster, Farbe*〉; unauffällig 〈*Riß, Bewegung*〉; **make oneself ~**: sich unauffällig verhalten

unobtrusively [ʌnəbˈtruːsɪvlɪ] *adv.* unaufdringlich; unauffällig 〈*hinausschleichen, verschwinden*〉

unoccupied [ʌnˈɒkjʊpaɪd] *adj.* **a)** *(empty)* unbesetzt; nicht belegt 〈*Bett*〉; unbewohnt 〈*Haus, Wohnung, Raum*〉; **b)** *(not busy)* unbeschäftigt; **~ moments** freie Augenblicke

unoffending [ʌnəˈfendɪŋ] *adj.* harmlos; *(innocent)* unschuldig

unofficial [ʌnəˈfɪʃl] *adj.* inoffiziell; **an ~ strike** ein wilder Streik; **take ~ action** einen wilden Streik durchführen

unofficially [ʌnəˈfɪʃəlɪ] *adv.* inoffiziell

unopened [ʌnˈəʊpnd] *adj.* ungeöffnet; noch nicht aufgegangen 〈*Knospe, Blüte*〉

unopposed [ʌnəˈpəʊzd] *adj.* unangefochten 〈*Kandidat, Wahlsieger*〉; ungehindert 〈*Vormarsch*〉; **the bill was given an ~ second reading** *(Parl.)* der Gesetzentwurf wurde bei der zweiten Lesung ohne Abstimmung angenommen

unorganized [ʌnˈɔːgənaɪzd] *adj.* **a)** *(untidy)* unsystematisch 〈*Arbeitsweise*〉; konfus 〈*Essay, Person*〉; ungeordnet 〈*Struktur, Leben*〉; **b)** *(not belonging to a union)* nicht [gewerkschaftlich] organisiert

unoriginal [ʌnəˈrɪdʒɪnl] *adj.* unoriginell

unoriginality [ʌnərɪdʒɪˈnælɪtɪ] *n., no pl.* fehlende Originalität

unorthodox [ʌnˈɔːθədɒks] *adj.* unorthodox *(geh.)*

unostentatious [ʌnɒstenˈteɪʃəs] *adj.* schlicht; unprätentiös *(geh.)*

unpack [ʌnˈpæk] *v. t. & i.* auspacken; **do one's ~ing** auspacken

unpaid [ʌnˈpeɪd] *adj.* **a)** *(not yet paid)* unbezahlt; nicht bezahlt; **~ for** nicht bezahlt; **the workmen/troops have been ~ for months** die Arbeiter/Truppen haben monatelang keinen Lohn/Sold erhalten; **b)** *(not providing or receiving a salary)* unbezahlt 〈*Arbeit, Stelle, Freiwilliger usw.*〉; *(honorary)* ehrenamtlich; **~ leave** unbezahlter Urlaub

unpalatable [ʌnˈpælətəbl] *adj.* ungenießbar; *(fig.)* unverdaulich 〈*Tatsache, Wahrheit*〉

unparalleled [ʌnˈpærəleld] *adj.* beispiellos; unvergleichlich 〈*Schönheit*〉

unpardonable [ʌnˈpɑːdənəbl] unverzeihlich; **~ sin** *(Relig.; also fig.)* Todsünde, *die*

unparliamentary [ʌnpɑːləˈmentərɪ] *adj.* gegen die parlamentarischen Regeln verstoßend; **~ expression** der Würde des Parlaments nicht angemessene Redeweise

unpatriotic [ʌnpætrɪˈɒtɪk, ʌnpeɪtrɪˈɒtɪk] *adj.* unpatriotisch

unpaved [ʌnˈpeɪvd] *adj.* ungepflastert

unpeeled [ʌnˈpiːld] *adj.* ungeschält

unpeg [ʌnˈpeg] *v. t.*, **-gg-** abnehmen 〈*Wäsche*〉; **~ a tent** bei einem Zelt die Pflöcke herausziehen

unperceptive [ʌnpəˈseptɪv] *adj.* unaufmerksam; nicht sehr tiefgründig 〈*Bemerkung*〉

unperfumed [ʌnˈpɜːfjuːmd] *adj.* unparfümiert

unperson [ˈʌnpɜːsn] *n.* Unperson, *die*

unperturbed [ʌnpəˈtɜːbd] *adj.* **he was ~ by the prospect of ...**: die Aussicht auf ... beunruhigte ihn nicht; **remain ~**: sich nicht aus der Ruhe bringen lassen; **they were ~ by my presence** sie ließen sich durch meine Gegenwart nicht stören; **the minister seemed ~ by the developments** der Minister schien von den Entwicklungen unbeeindruckt

unpick [ʌnˈpɪk] *v. t.* auftrennen

unpin [ʌnˈpɪn] *v. t.*, **-nn-** abnehmen 〈*Zettel, Brosche*〉; **~ sb.'s/one's hair** jmdm./sich die Nadeln aus dem Haar nehmen; **~ the seam** die Nadeln aus dem Saum nehmen

unplaced [ʌnˈpleɪst] *adj.* *(Sport)* unplaziert

unplanned [ʌnˈplænd] *adj.* nicht geplant; ungeplant

unplayable [ʌnˈpleɪəbl] *adj.* **a)** *(Sport)* unbespielbar 〈*Spielfeld*〉; unspielbar 〈*Ball*〉; unerreichbar 〈*Aufschlag, Return*〉; **b)** *(Music)* unspielbar; **c)** *(too damaged to be played)* nicht abspielbar 〈*Schallplatte, Tonband*〉

unpleasant [ʌnˈplezənt] *adj.* unangenehm; unfreundlich 〈*Bemerkung*〉; böse 〈*Lächeln*〉; **she can be really ~**: sie kann sehr unangenehm werden; **be ~ with sb.** zu jmdm. unfreundlich sein

unpleasantly [ʌnˈplezəntlɪ] *adv.* unangenehm; böse 〈*lächeln*〉; unfreundlich 〈*antworten*〉

unpleasantness [ʌnˈplezəntnɪs] *n.* **a)** *no pl.* *(unpleasant nature)* Unerfreulichkeit, *die;* *(of person)* Unfreundlichkeit, *die;* **the ~ of a taste/smell** das Unangenehme an einem Geschmack/Geruch; **the ~ of the weather/one's neighbour** das unangenehme Wetter/die Unfreundlichkeit seines Nachbarn; **b)** *(bad feeling, quarrel)* Verstimmung, *die;* **there has been a lot of ~ between them** zwischen ihnen ist viel Unerfreuliches geschehen *od.* gewesen

unpleasing [ʌnˈpliːzɪŋ] *adj.* unschön; **not ~ to the eye** ganz angenehm anzusehen

unplug [ʌnˈplʌg] *v. t.*, **-gg- a)** *(Electr.: disconnect)* **~ a radio/a television set** den Stecker eines Radio-/Fernsehgeräts herausziehen; **always ~ electrical appliances at night** bei Elektrogeräten nachts stets den Stecker aus der Steckdose ziehen; **b)** *(take plug out of)* **~ sth.** den Stöpsel aus etw. ziehen

unplumbed [ʌnˈplʌmd] *adj.* nicht ausgelotet 〈*Gewässer*〉; *(fig.)* [noch] unergründet 〈*Geheimnis, Möglichkeiten*〉; **~ depths [of the sea/** *(fig.)* **of the human mind]** nicht ausgelotete Tiefen [des Meeres/*(fig. geh.)* des menschlichen Geistes]

unpolished [ʌnˈpɒlɪʃt] *adj.* unpoliert 〈*Holz, Marmor, Schuhe, Reis*〉; *(fig.)* ungeschliffen 〈*Person, Manieren, Sprache*〉

unpolluted [ʌnpəˈluːtɪd] sauber 〈*Wasser, Fluß, Umwelt*〉

unpopular [ʌnˈpɒpjʊlə(r)] *adj.* unbeliebt 〈*Lehrer, Regierung usw.*〉; unpopulär 〈*Maßnahme, Politik*〉; **be ~ with sb.** *(not liked)* 〈*Person:*〉 bei jmdm. unbeliebt sein; 〈*Maßnahme, Steuern:*〉 bei jmdm. unpopulär sein; *(out of favour)* **I'm rather ~ with my wife at the moment** meine Frau ist auf mich zur Zeit ziemlich schlecht zu sprechen; **if I don't finish it today, I shall be very ~ with my boss** wenn ich heute damit nicht fertig werde, mache ich mich bei meinem Chef ziemlich unbeliebt

unpopularity [ʌnpɒpjʊˈlærɪtɪ] *n., no pl. see* **unpopular:** Unbeliebtheit, *die* **(with** bei); Unpopularität, *die* **(with** bei)

unposted [ʌnˈpəʊstɪd] *adj.* nicht aufgegeben *od.* abgeschickt

unpractical [ʌnˈpræktɪkl] *adj.* unpraktisch

unpractised (*Amer.:* **unpracticed**) [ʌnˈpræktɪst] *adj.* **a)** *(not skilled)* ungeübt; **be ~ in sth./in doing sth.** in etw. *(Dat.)* ungeübt sein/darin ungeübt sein, etw. zu tun; **b)** *(not put into practice)* nicht ausgeübt 〈*Handwerk*〉; ungenutzt 〈*Fähigkeit*〉

unprecedented [ʌnˈpresɪdentɪd] *adj.* beispiellos; [noch] nie dagewesen; **it is ~ for the Queen to comment publicly** es ist [vorher] noch nie dagewesen, daß die Königin öffentlich Stellung genommen hat

unprecedentedly [ʌnˈpresɪdentɪdlɪ] *adv.* unerhört; außergewöhnlich

unpredictable [ʌnprɪˈdɪktəbl] *adj.* unberechenbar 〈*Person, Charakter, Wetter*〉; **the outcome of the election is quite ~**: das Wahlergebnis läßt sich kaum voraussagen

unprejudiced [ʌnˈpredʒʊdɪst] *adj.* unvoreingenommen

unpremeditated [ʌnprɪˈmedɪteɪtɪd] *adj.* nicht vorsätzlich 〈*Verbrechen*〉; nicht geplant 〈*Angriff, Tat*〉

unprepared [ʌnprɪˈpeəd] *adj.* **a)** *(not yet prepared)* nicht vorbereitet 〈*Zimmer, Mahlzeit*〉; **be [not] ~ for sth.** auf etw. *(Akk.)* [nicht] unvorbereitet sein; **b)** *(improvised)* Stegreif〈*rede, -erklärung*〉

unpreparedness [ʌnprɪˈpeərɪdnɪs] *n., no pl. see* **unreadiness**

unprepossessing [ʌnpriːpəˈzesɪŋ] *adj.* wenig attraktiv; unansehnlich; wenig einnehmend 〈*Aussehen, Person*〉

unpresentable [ʌnprɪˈzentəbl] *adj.* **sb. is ~:** mit jmdm. kann man sich nicht sehen lassen; **your clothes are ~:** in deinen Sachen kannst du dich nicht sehen lassen

unpretentious [ʌnprɪˈtenʃəs] *adj.* unprätentiös *(geh.)*; einfach ⟨*Wein, Mahlzeit, Stil, Haus*⟩; bescheiden ⟨*Benehmen, Person*⟩

unpriced [ʌnˈpraɪst] *adj.* ohne Preisangabe *nachgestellt*

unprincipled [ʌnˈprɪnsɪpld] *adj.* skrupellos; **be ~:** keine Prinzipien haben

unprintable [ʌnˈprɪntəbl] *adj. (lit. or fig.)* nicht druckreif

unproductive [ʌnprəˈdʌktɪv] *adj.* unfruchtbar ⟨*Boden, Gegend*⟩; fruchtlos ⟨*Diskussion, Anstrengung, Nachforschung*⟩; unproduktiv ⟨*Zeit, Arbeit, Kapital*⟩

unprofessional [ʌnprəˈfeʃənl] *adj.* **a)** *(contrary to standards)* standeswidrig; **b)** *(amateurish)* unfachmännisch; stümperhaft

unprofitable [ʌnˈprɒfɪtəbl] *adj.* unrentabel ⟨*Zeche, Investition, Geschäft*⟩; wenig einträglich ⟨*Arbeit*⟩; *(fig.)* fruchtlos

unpromising [ʌnˈprɒmɪsɪŋ] *adj.* nicht sehr vielversprechend

unprompted [ʌnˈprɒmptɪd] *adj.* spontan

unpronounceable [ʌnprəˈnaʊnsəbl] *adj.* unaussprechbar

unpropitious [ʌnprəˈpɪʃəs] *adj.* ungünstig

unprotected [ʌnprəˈtektɪd] *adj.* ungeschützt (**against** vor + *Dat.*, gegen); nicht geschützt ⟨*Art, Tier*⟩; **an ~ machine** eine Maschine ohne Schutzvorrichtung[en]; **hands ~ by gloves** Hände, die nicht durch Handschuhe geschützt sind; **employees/buildings ~ by legislation** Angestellte ohne gesetzlichen Schutz/Gebäude, die nicht unter Denkmalschutz stehen; **~ sex** ungeschützter Geschlechtsverkehr

unproved [ʌnˈpruːvd], **unproven** [ʌnˈpruːvn] *adj.* **a)** *(not proved)* unbewiesen; **b)** *(untested)* ungeprüft; **his courage/ability is still ~:** sein Mut/seine Fähigkeit ist noch nicht auf die Probe gestellt worden; **he is ~ as an administrator** er hat seine Fähigkeiten als Verwalter noch nicht unter Beweis gestellt

unprovided [ʌnprəˈvaɪdɪd] *pred. adj.* **a) ~ for** unversorgt ⟨*Witwe, Kind usw.*⟩; nicht vorgesehen ⟨*Ereignis*⟩; **b) ~ with sth.** mit etw. nicht versehen

unprovoked [ʌnprəˈvəʊkt] *adj.* grundlos; **do sth. ~:** etw. ohne [äußere] Veranlassung tun

unpublished [ʌnˈpʌblɪʃt] *adj.* unveröffentlicht

unpunctual [ʌnˈpʌŋktjʊəl] *adj.* unpünktlich

unpunished [ʌnˈpʌnɪʃt] *adj.* ungesühnt ⟨*Verbrechen*⟩; unbestraft ⟨*Verbrecher*⟩; **go ~:** ohne Strafe bleiben; ⟨*Verbrecher:*⟩ straffrei ausgehen

unpurified [ʌnˈpjʊərɪfaɪd] *adj.* ungereinigt; nicht gereinigt; *(fig.)* ungeläutert

unputdownable [ʌnpʊtˈdaʊnəbl] *adj. (coll.)* **an ~ book** ein Buch, das man nicht aus der Hand legt; **this novel is ~:** diesen Roman legt man nicht aus der Hand

unqualified [ʌnˈkwɒlɪfaɪd] *adj.* **a)** *(lacking qualifications)* unqualifiziert; ⟨*Arzt*⟩ ohne Abschluß; **be ~ for sth.** für etw. nicht qualifiziert sein; **be ~ to do sth.** nicht dafür qualifiziert sein, etw. zu tun; **he is ~ to be president** er ist für das Amt des Präsidenten nicht qualifiziert; **b)** *(absolute)* uneingeschränkt ⟨*Zustimmung*⟩; rein ⟨*Freude, Vergnügen*⟩; voll ⟨*Erfolg*⟩; **c)** *(Ling.: not qualified)* nicht [näher] bestimmt

unquenchable [ʌnˈkwentʃəbl] *adj.* unlöschbar ⟨*Durst*⟩; unstillbar ⟨*Verlangen*⟩

unquestionable [ʌnˈkwestʃənəbl] *adj.* unbezweifelbar ⟨*Tatsache, Beweis*⟩; unbestreitbar ⟨*Recht, Fähigkeiten, Ehrlichkeit*⟩; unanfechtbar ⟨*Autorität*⟩; **an ~ decision/ruling/judgement** eine Entscheidung/Verfügung, die/ein Urteil, das nicht angefochten werden kann

unquestionably [ʌnˈkwestʃənəblɪ] *adv.* zweifellos; ohne Frage

unquestioned [ʌnˈkwestʃənd] *adj.* unangefochten ⟨*Fähigkeit, Macht, Autorität, Recht*⟩; unbestritten ⟨*Talent*⟩; **his ability/loyalty is ~:** seine Fähigkeit/Loyalität steht außer Frage

unquestioning [ʌnˈkwestʃənɪŋ] *adj.*, **unquestioningly** [ʌnˈkwestʃənɪŋlɪ] *adv.* bedingungslos; blind

unquiet [ʌnˈkwaɪət] *adj.* unruhig

unquotable [ʌnˈkwəʊtəbl] *adj.* nicht zitierfähig

unquote [ʌnˈkwəʊt] *v. i.* **..., quote, ..., ~:** ..., Zitat, ..., Ende des Zitats

unquoted [ʌnˈkwəʊtɪd] *adj. (Commerc.)* unnotiert

unravel [ʌnˈrævl] **1.** *v. t. (Brit.)* **-ll-** entwirren; *(undo)* aufziehen; *(fig.)* **~ a mystery/the truth/a plot** ein Geheimnis enträtseln/die Wahrheit aufdecken/ein Komplott aufdecken. **2.** *v. i. (Brit.)* **-ll-** aufgehen; sich aufziehen

unread [ʌnˈred] *adj.* ungelesen

unreadable [ʌnˈriːdəbl] *adj.* **a)** *(illegible)* unleserlich; *(fig.: unfathomable)* unergründlich; **b)** *(too difficult, boring, etc.)* unlesbar

unreadiness [ʌnˈredɪnɪs] *n., no pl.* **[state of] ~:** mangelnde Vorbereitung; **~ to do sth.** mangelnde Bereitschaft, etwas zu tun

unready [ʌnˈredɪ] *adj.* nicht bereit; **the country is ~ for war** das Land ist für einen Krieg nicht gerüstet; **he is ~ for that position** er ist noch nicht so weit, daß er diese Position übernehmen könnte

unreal [ʌnˈrɪəl] *adj.* unwirklich

unrealistic [ʌnrɪəˈlɪstɪk] *adj.* unrealistisch

unreality [ʌnrɪˈælɪtɪ] *n., no pl.* Unwirklichkeit, *die*

unrealizable [ʌnˈrɪəlaɪzəbl] *adj.* unrealisierbar; nicht verwirklichbar

unrealized [ʌnˈrɪəlaɪzd] *adj.* **a)** *(not achieved)* unerfüllt ⟨*Hoffnung, Ehrgeiz*⟩; nicht erreicht ⟨*Ziel*⟩; nicht verwirklicht ⟨*Plan*⟩; ungenutzt ⟨*Potential, Fähigkeiten*⟩; **~ assets/profits** *(Commerc.)* nicht realisierte Vermögenswerte/Gewinne; **b)** *(not recognized or known)* ungeahnt ⟨*Mut, Kraft*⟩; unentdeckt ⟨*Talent*⟩

unreasonable [ʌnˈriːzənəbl] *adj.* unvernünftig; übertrieben ⟨*Ansprüche, Forderung*⟩; übertrieben [hoch] ⟨*Preis, Kosten*⟩; **I am not an ~ man, but ...:** ich erwarte nun wirklich nicht viel, aber ...; **spend an ~ length of time on sth.** sich übertrieben lange mit etw. beschäftigen; **arrive at an ~ hour** zu einer unmöglichen Uhrzeit ankommen; **I'm only asking you to spare me half an hour of your time – is that [so] ~?** ich bitte dich nur um eine halbe Stunde; das ist doch nicht zu viel verlangt, oder?

unreasonableness [ʌnˈriːzənəblnɪs] *n., no pl.* Unvernünftigkeit, *die;* **the ~ of these prices/costs** die übertriebene Höhe dieser Preise/Kosten

unreasonably [ʌnˈriːzənəblɪ] *adv.* unvernünftig ⟨*sich benehmen*⟩; *(excessively)* übertrieben; **this – not ~ – he refused to do** das lehnte er – nicht ohne Berechtigung – ab

unreasoning [ʌnˈriːzənɪŋ] *adj.* irrational; blind ⟨*Haß, Wut, Eifersucht, Fanatiker*⟩

unreceptive [ʌnrɪˈseptɪv] *adj.* unempfänglich (**to, for** für)

unrecognizable [ʌnˈrekəgnaɪzəbl] *adj.* **be [absolutely** *or* **quite] ~:** [überhaupt] nicht wiederzuerkennen sein; **the disguise/beard made him ~:** mit der Verkleidung/dem Bart war er nicht wiederzuerkennen

unrecognized [ʌnˈrekəgnaɪzd] *adj.* **a)** *(not identified)* unerkannt; **be ~ by sb.** von jmdm. nicht erkannt werden; **b)** *(not officially recognized)* nicht anerkannt; **c)** *(not appreciated)* nicht [gebührend] gewürdigt ⟨*Talent, Genie*⟩; nicht [genügend] beachtet ⟨*Gefahr, Tatsache*⟩

unrecorded [ʌnrɪˈkɔːdɪd] *adj.* **a)** *(not documented)* nicht [dokumentarisch] belegt; **b)** *(not recorded)* nicht aufgezeichnet; unbespielt, leer ⟨*Tonband, Kassette*⟩

unreel [ʌnˈriːl] **1.** *v.t.* abwickeln; abspulen ⟨*Film, Tonband*⟩. **2.** *v.i.* sich abwickeln; sich abspulen

unrefined [ʌnrɪˈfaɪnd] *adj.* **a)** *(not refined)* nicht raffiniert; ungebleicht *(Mehl)*; **b)** *(fig.)* unkultiviert, ungeschliffen ⟨*Geschmack, Manieren, Person, Sprache*⟩

unreflecting [ʌnrɪˈflektɪŋ] *adj.* gedankenlos

unregenerate [ʌnrɪˈdʒenərət] *adj.* *(unrepentant, obstinate)* uneinsichtig; *(wicked)* sündig ⟨*Lebenswandel*⟩

unregistered [ʌnˈredʒɪstəd] *adj.* nicht eingetragen; nicht approbiert ⟨*Arzt*⟩; nicht zugelassen ⟨*Rechtsanwalt, Buchmacher, Krankenschwester, Fahrzeug*⟩; nicht eingeschrieben ⟨*Postsendung*⟩; nicht [gesetzlich] geschützt ⟨*Warenzeichen*⟩

unregulated [ʌnˈregjʊleɪtɪd] *adj.* unkontrolliert

unrehearsed [ʌnrɪˈhɜːst] *adj.* **a)** *(performed without rehearsal)* [vorher] nicht geprobt; **perform a play ~:** ein Stück ohne vorherige Probe[n] spielen; **b)** *(not planned)* nicht vorgesehen; **c)** *(spontaneous)* spontan

unrelated [ʌnrɪˈleɪtɪd] *adj.* unzusammenhängend; **be ~** *(not connected)* nicht miteinander zusammenhängen; *(not related by family)* nicht [miteinander] verwandt sein; **be ~ to sth.** mit etw. in keinem Zusammenhang stehen; mit etw. nichts zu tun haben

unrelenting [ʌnrɪˈlentɪŋ] *adj.* unvermindert, nicht nachlassend ⟨*Hitze, Kälte, Regen*⟩; unerbittlich ⟨*Kampf, Opposition, Verfolgung, Haß*⟩; unnachgiebig ⟨*Entschlossenheit, Ehrgeiz*⟩; unvermindert ⟨*Kraft, Stärke*⟩; hartnäckig ⟨*Kämpfer*⟩; **the heat/pressure/pace is ~:** die Hitze/der Druck/die Geschwindigkeit läßt nicht nach; **be ~ in one's determination to do sth.** unnachgiebig entschlossen sein, etw. zu tun; **be ~ in one's battle** *or* **fight against sth.** etw. unnachgiebig bekämpfen; **remain ~:** unnachgiebig *od.* unerbittlich bleiben

unreliability [ʌnrɪlaɪəˈbɪlɪtɪ] *n., no pl.* Unzuverlässigkeit, *die*

unreliable [ʌnrɪˈlaɪəbl] *adj.* unzuverlässig

unrelieved [ʌnrɪˈliːvd] *adj.* unvermindert ⟨*Schmerz, Armut, Anstrengung*⟩; unaufhörlich ⟨*Regen, Lärm*⟩; tödlich ⟨*Langeweile, Eintönigkeit*⟩; **~ by sth.** nicht durch etw. gemildert; **a forbidding landscape, ~ by vegetation of any kind** eine Landschaft, deren Ödheit auch nicht das kleinste Pflänzchen belebt; **a gloomy film, ~ by even the slightest touch of humour** ein Film, dessen Düsterkeit durch kein Fünkchen von Humor aufgehellt wird

unremarkable [ʌnrɪˈmɑːkəbl] *adj.* nicht weiter bemerkenswert; unauffällig ⟨*Person, Lebensweise*⟩; **totally/pretty ~:** absolut nicht/kaum bemerkenswert

unremitting [ʌnrɪˈmɪtɪŋ] *adj.* nicht nachlassend; unermüdlich ⟨*Anstrengung, Versuche, Sorge*⟩; beharrlich ⟨*Kampf*⟩; **he was ~ in his efforts to help them** er bemühte sich unermüdlich, ihnen zu helfen

unremittingly [ʌnrɪˈmɪtɪŋlɪ] *adv.* unermüdlich ⟨*kämpfen, arbeiten, sich bemühen*⟩; unnachgiebig ⟨*Widerstand leisten*⟩

unremunerative [ʌnrɪˈmjuːnərətɪv] *adj.* wenig einträglich *od. (geh.)* lukrativ

unrepeatable [ʌnrɪˈpiːtəbl] *adj.* **a)** *(unique)* einzigartig; einmalig ⟨*Angebot, Preis*⟩; **b)** *(not fit to be repeated)* **sth. is ~:** etw. ist nicht zitierfähig; **an ~ remark/story/joke** eine Bemerkung/Geschichte, die/ein Witz, der nicht salonfähig ist

unrepentant [ʌnrɪˈpentənt] *adj.* **a)** *(impenitent)* reuelos ⟨*Sünder*⟩; **die ~:** sterben, ohne bereut zu haben; **be ~:** keine Reue zeigen; **be ~ about sth.** etw. nicht bereuen; **b)** *(unreformed, obstinate)* halsstarrig; stur

unreported [ʌnrɪˈpɔ:tɪd] *adj.* nicht angezeigt ⟨*Verbrechen*⟩; ⟨*Fall, Versuch*⟩ über den nicht berichtet wurde; **it went ~:** darüber wurde nicht berichtet

unrepresentative [ʌnreprɪˈzentətɪv] *adj.* nicht repräsentativ (**of** für); *(Polit.)* nicht demokratisch gewählt ⟨*Regierung, Führer*⟩; **be ~ of sth.** etw. nicht repräsentieren

unrepresented [ʌnreprɪˈzentɪd] *adj.* nicht vertreten

unrequited [ʌnrɪˈkwaɪtɪd] *adj.* unerwidert

unreserved [ʌnrɪˈzɜ:vd] *adj.* **a)** *(not booked)* nicht reserviert; **b)** *(full, without any reservations)* uneingeschränkt ⟨*Zustimmung, Aufnahme, Entschuldigung usw.*⟩; **he was ~ in his praise** er geizte nicht mit Lob; **c)** *(free from reserve)* offen ⟨*Person, Wesensart*⟩

unreservedly [ʌnrɪˈzɜ:vɪdlɪ] *adv.* **a)** *(fully, without any reservations)* uneingeschränkt; **he ~ withdrew the allegation** er nahm die Anschuldigung in vollem Umfang zurück; **b)** *(frankly, openly)* offen

unresolved [ʌnrɪˈzɒlvd] *adj.* **a)** *(not solved)* ungelöst; nicht gelöst; **b)** *(undecided)* **be ~:** sich [noch] nicht entschieden haben; **c)** *(Mus.)* nicht aufgelöst

unresponsive [ʌnrɪˈspɒnsɪv] *adj.* **be ~:** nicht reagieren (**to** auf + *Akk.*); **an ~ audience** ein teilnahmsloses Publikum

unrest [ʌnˈrest] *n.* Unruhen *Pl.*; **there is widespread ~ among the population** ein großer Teil der Bevölkerung ist unzufrieden

unrestrained [ʌnrɪˈstreɪnd] *adj.* uneingeschränkt ⟨*Freude, Begeisterung, Wachstum, Überfluß*⟩; unbeherrscht ⟨*Gefühlsäußerung, Wut, Gewalt*⟩; unkontrolliert ⟨*Entwicklung, Wachstum*⟩; ungeniert ⟨*Sprache, Benehmen*⟩

unrestricted [ʌnrɪˈstrɪktɪd] *adj.* unbeschränkt; uneingeschränkt; frei ⟨*Sicht*⟩; **have ~ use of sth.** etw. uneingeschränkt nutzen [dürfen]

unrevealed [ʌnrɪˈvi:ld] *adj.* verborgen

unrewarded [ʌnrɪˈwɔ:dɪd] *adj.* **go ~:** keine Belohnung bekommen; ⟨*Tat, Mühe:*⟩ nicht belohnt werden

unrewarding [ʌnrɪˈwɔ:dɪŋ] *adj.* unbefriedigend; undankbar ⟨*Aufgabe*⟩; **financially ~:** wenig einträglich *od. (geh.)* lukrativ

unrighteous [ʌnˈraɪtʃəs] *adj.* **a)** *(wicked)* schlecht; **b)** *(unjust)* ungerecht

unripe [ʌnˈraɪp] *adj.* unreif

unrivalled (*Amer.:* **unrivaled**) [ʌnˈraɪvld] *adj.* unvergleichlich; beispiellos; unübertroffen ⟨*Ruf, Luxus, Erfahrung, Könnerschaft*⟩; **our goods are ~ in** *or* **for quality** unsere Waren sind in ihrer Qualität konkurrenzlos *od.* unerreicht; **a landscape ~ for beauty** *or* **of ~ beauty** eine Landschaft von unvergleichlicher Schönheit

unroadworthy [ʌnˈrəʊdwɜ:ðɪ] *adj.* nicht verkehrssicher

unroll [ʌnˈrəʊl] **1.** *v. t.* aufrollen. **2.** *v. i.* sich aufrollen; *(fig.)* ⟨*Geschichte, Handlung:*⟩ sich entrollen; **he watched the landscape ~ before his eyes** er betrachtete die Landschaft, die sich vor seinen Augen auftat

unromantic [ʌnrəˈmæntɪk] *adj.* unromantisch

unruffled [ʌnˈrʌfld] *adj.* ruhig; glatt ⟨*Gewässer, Haar, Feder*⟩; **listen with ~ calm/composure** mit unerschütterlicher Ruhe/ruhiger Gefaßtheit zuhören; **he was/remained ~ by all the fuss/criticism** er ließ sich von der ganzen Aufregung/Kritik nicht aus der Ruhe bringen

unruled [ʌnˈru:ld] unliniert ⟨*Papier*⟩

unruliness [ʌnˈru:lɪnɪs] *n.* Ungebärdigkeit, *die*

unruly [ʌnˈru:lɪ] *adj.* ungebärdig ⟨*Person, Benehmen*⟩; widerspenstig ⟨*Haar, Person, Benehmen*⟩

unsaddle [ʌnˈsædl] *v. t.* **a)** absatteln ⟨*Pferd usw.*⟩; **b)** abwerfen ⟨*Reiter*⟩

unsafe [ʌnˈseɪf] *adj.* **a)** nicht sicher ⟨*Leiter, Konstruktion*⟩; baufällig ⟨*Gebäude*⟩; nicht verkehrssicher ⟨*Fahrzeug*⟩; gefährlich ⟨*Maschine, Leitungen, Spielzeug*⟩; **the food is ~ to eat** das Essen ist ungenießbar; **he looked ~ on top of the ladder** es sah gefährlich aus, wie er oben auf der Leiter stand; **feel ~:** sich unsicher fühlen; **it is ~ to do that** es ist gefährlich, das zu tun; **b)** *(untenable)* unhaltbar ⟨*Annahme, Urteil usw.*⟩; **the conviction was ~:** die Verurteilung war juristisch nicht haltbar

unsaid [ʌnˈsed] *adj.* ungesagt; unausgesprochen; **leave sth. ~:** etw. ungesagt lassen; **some things are better left ~:** manche Dinge bleiben besser ungesagt

unsaleable [ʌnˈseɪləbl] *adj.* unverkäuflich

unsalted [ʌnˈsɔ:ltɪd, ʌnˈsɒltɪd] *adj.* ungesalzen

unsanitary [ʌnˈsænɪtərɪ] *adj.* unhygienisch

unsatisfactorily [ʌnsætɪsˈfæktərɪlɪ] *adv.* unbefriedigend; **perform one's tasks ~:** unbefriedigende Leistungen erbringen; **end ~:** zu einem unbefriedigenden Abschluß kommen

unsatisfactory [ʌnsætɪsˈfæktərɪ] *adj.* unbefriedigend; nicht befriedigend; schlecht ⟨*Service, Hotel*⟩; mangelhaft ⟨*schulische Leistung*⟩

unsatisfied [ʌnˈsætɪsfaɪd] *adj.* unzufrieden; unerfüllt ⟨*Wunsch, Bedürfnis*⟩; nicht befriedigt ⟨*Wunsch, Bedürfnis, Neugier, Nachfrage*⟩; nicht gestillt ⟨*Hunger, Neugier, Appetit*⟩; unbeglichen ⟨*Schuld*⟩; **sexually ~:** sexuell nicht befriedigt; **leave sb. ~:** jmdn. nicht befriedigen

unsatisfying [ʌnˈsætɪsfaɪɪŋ] *adj.* unbefriedigend; nicht sättigend ⟨*Mahlzeit*⟩

unsaturated [ʌnˈsætʃəreɪtɪd, ʌnˈsætjʊreɪtɪd] *adj.* ungesättigt

unsavoury (*Amer.:* **unsavory**) [ʌnˈseɪvərɪ] *adj.* unangenehm ⟨*Geruch, Geschmack, Mahlzeit*⟩; zwielichtig ⟨*Charakter, Person*⟩; zweifelhaft ⟨*Ruf, Geschäfte, Angelegenheit*⟩; unerfreulich ⟨*Einzelheiten*⟩

unscalable [ʌnˈskeɪləbl] *adj.* unbezwinglich ⟨*Berg, Höhe*⟩

unscaled [ʌnˈskeɪld] *adj.* [noch] nicht bezwungen ⟨*Berg, Höhe*⟩

unscathed [ʌnˈskeɪðd] *adj.* unversehrt ⟨*Person*⟩; unbeschädigt ⟨*Sache*⟩; *(fig.)* **he emerged from the scandal ~/with his reputation ~:** er überlebte den Skandal ohne einen Flecken auf seiner Weste *(ugs.)*/ohne daß sein Ruf Schaden genommen hätte

unscented [ʌnˈsentɪd] *adj.* nicht parfümiert ⟨*Seife, Shampoo*⟩

unscheduled [ʌnˈʃedju:ld] *adj.* außerplanmäßig

unscholarly [ʌnˈskɒləlɪ] *adj.* unwissenschaftlich ⟨*Buch, Methode*⟩; **be ~** ⟨*Person:*⟩ kein Gelehrter sein

unschooled [ʌnˈsku:ld] *adj.* *(without education)* ungebildet; *(without training)* ungeschult

unscientific [ʌnsaɪənˈtɪfɪk] *adj.* unwissenschaftlich ⟨*Methode, Buch, Ansatz usw.*⟩; **be ~** ⟨*Person:*⟩ kein Wissenschaftler sein

unscientifically [ʌnsaɪənˈtɪfɪkəlɪ] *adv.* unwissenschaftlich

unscramble [ʌnˈskræmbl] *v. t.* *(lit. or fig.)* entwirren; *(Teleph.: decode)* entschlüsseln

unscratched [ʌnˈskrætʃt] *adj.* *(unhurt)* unverletzt

unscrew [ʌnˈskru:] **1.** *v. t.* ab- *od.* losschrauben ⟨*Regal, Deckel usw.*⟩; herausdrehen ⟨*Schraube*⟩. **2.** *v. i.* ⟨*Brett, Verschluß:*⟩ sich abschrauben lassen; ⟨*Schraube:*⟩ sich lösen *od.* abschrauben lassen; **come ~ed** sich lösen

unscripted [ʌnˈskrɪptɪd] *adj.* frei vorgetragen ⟨*Rede*⟩; nicht von einem Skript abgelesen ⟨*Interview, Rundfunksendung*⟩; **an ~ play** ein Stegreifstück

unscrupulous [ʌnˈskru:pjʊləs] *adj.* skrupellos; **be ~ about money** in Geldangelegenheiten skrupellos sein

unscrupulously [ʌnˈskru:pjʊləslɪ] *adv.* skrupellos

unscrupulousness [ʌnˈskru:pjʊləsnɪs] *n., no pl.* Skrupellosigkeit, *die*

unseal [ʌnˈsi:l] *v. t.* *(break seal of)* entsiegeln; *(open)* öffnen ⟨*Brief, Paket, Behälter*⟩

unsealed [ʌnˈsi:ld] *adj.* offen; unverschlossen; *(without a seal)* nicht versiegelt

unseasonable [ʌnˈsi:zənəbl] *adj.* nicht der Jahreszeit entsprechend ⟨*Wetter, Hitze, Schnee*⟩; **the weather is ~:** das Wetter entspricht nicht der Jahreszeit

unseasonably [ʌnˈsi:zənəblɪ] *adv.* [für die Jahreszeit] ungewöhnlich ⟨*kalt, warm*⟩

unseasoned [ʌnˈsi:znd] *adj.* **a)** *(not flavoured)* ungewürzt; **b)** *(not matured)* nicht abgelagert ⟨*Holz*⟩; unerfahren ⟨*Soldat*⟩

unseat [ʌnˈsi:t] *adj.* **a)** *(remove from office)* abwählen; **b)** *(throw)* aus dem Sattel werfen; ⟨*Pferd:*⟩ abwerfen

unseaworthy [ʌnˈsi:wɜ:ðɪ] *adj.* nicht seetüchtig

unsecured [ʌnsɪˈkjʊəd] *adj.* **a)** *(not fixed)* nicht gesichert; **b)** *(Finance: without security)* ohne Sicherheit[en] *nachgestellt*

unseeded [ʌnˈsi:dɪd] *adj.* *(Tennis)* nicht gesetzt

unseeing [ʌnˈsi:ɪŋ] *adj.* blind; leer ⟨*Blick, Auge*⟩

unseemly [ʌnˈsi:mlɪ] *adj.* unschicklich; ungehörig ⟨*Benehmen*⟩; ungebührlich ⟨*Eile, Benehmen*⟩

unseen [ʌnˈsi:n] **1.** *adj.* **a)** *(not seen)* ungesehen; unbekannt ⟨*Text*⟩; **~ translation** *(Brit. Sch., Univ.)* Übersetzung eines unbekannten Textes *(aus einer Fremdsprache)*; **b)** *(invisible)* unsichtbar. **2.** *n.* *(Brit. Sch., Univ.)* **Latin/French ~:** Übersetzung eines unbekannten Textes aus dem Lateinischen/Französischen

unselfconscious [ʌnselfˈkɒnʃəs] *adj.*, **unselfconsciously** [ʌnselfˈkɒnʃəslɪ] *adv.* unbefangen

unselfconsciousness [ʌnselfˈkɒnʃəsnɪs] *n.* Unbefangenheit, *die*

unselfish [ʌnˈselfɪʃ] *adj.*, **unselfishly** [ʌnˈselfɪʃlɪ] *adv.* selbstlos

unselfishness [ʌnˈselfɪʃnɪs] *n., no pl.* Selbstlosigkeit, *die*

unsentimental [ʌnsentɪˈmentl] *adj.* unsentimental ⟨*Person*⟩; **be totally ~ about sth.** einer Sache *(Dat.)* gegenüber keinerlei sentimentale Gefühle haben

unserviceable [ʌnˈsɜ:vɪsəbl] *adj.* unbrauchbar

unsettle [ʌnˈsetl] *v. t.* durcheinanderbringen; verwirren ⟨*menschlichen Geist*⟩; stören ⟨*Friede*⟩; verstören ⟨*Kind, Tier*⟩; erschüttern ⟨*Stabilität, emotionales Gleichgewicht*⟩; aus dem Gleichgewicht bringen ⟨*Wirtschaft, Markt*⟩

unsettled [ʌnˈsetld] *adj.* **a)** *(changeable)* wechselhaft; *(fig.)* unstet *(geh.)*, ruhelos ⟨*Leben*⟩; unsicher ⟨*Zukunft*⟩; **b)** *(upset)* verstimmt ⟨*Magen*⟩; gestört ⟨*Verdauung*⟩; unruhig ⟨*Zeit, Land*⟩; instabil *(geh.)* ⟨*Wirtschaft, Markt*⟩; **be/feel ~:** aus dem [gewohnten] Gleis sein; **c)** *(open to further discussion)* ungeklärt ⟨*Angelegenheit, Frage*⟩; **d)** *(unpaid)* unbezahlt

unsettling [ʌnˈsetlɪŋ] *adj.* störend ⟨*Vorfall, Einfluß*⟩; beunruhigend ⟨*Nachricht*⟩; unruhig ⟨*Zeit*⟩; *(Finance)* destabilisierend ⟨*Einfluß*⟩; **have an unsettling effect on sb.** jmdn. aus dem Gleichgewicht bringen; **this constant travelling is ~:** dieses ständige Reisen bringt einen aus dem Gleis

unshaded [ʌnˈʃeɪdɪd] *adj.* schattenlos; nackt ⟨*Glühbirne, Licht*⟩; **the ~ areas of the**

design die nicht schattierten Teile der Zeichnung
unshak[e]able [ʌn'ʃeɪkəbl] *adj.* unerschütterlich
unshaken [ʌn'ʃeɪkn] *adj.* **be ~**: nicht erschüttert sein
unshaven [ʌn'ʃeɪvn] *adj.* unrasiert; **go ~**: sich nicht rasieren
unsheathe [ʌn'ʃi:ð] *v.t.* aus der Scheide ziehen
unshed [ʌn'ʃed] *adj.* ungeweint ⟨*Tränen*⟩
unshockable [ʌn'ʃɒkəbl] *adj.* **be ~**: durch nichts zu erschüttern sein
unshrinkable [ʌn'ʃrɪŋkəbl] *adj.* *(Textiles)* nicht einlaufend; schrumpffrei; **be ~**: nicht einlaufen
unsighted [ʌn'saɪtɪd] *adj.* **be ~**: in der *od.* seiner Sicht behindert sein
unsightliness [ʌn'saɪtlɪnɪs] *n., no pl.* Häßlichkeit, *die*
unsightly [ʌn'saɪtlɪ] *adj.* unschön
unsigned [ʌn'saɪnd] *adj.* nicht unterzeichnet ⟨*Brief, Dokument*⟩; unsigniert ⟨*Gemälde*⟩
unsinkable [ʌn'sɪŋkəbl] *adj.* unsinkbar
unsized [ʌn'saɪzd] *adj.* **~ paper/textiles** ungeleimtes Papier/ungeschlichtete Textilien
unskilful [ʌn'skɪlfl] *adj.* ungeschickt; **be ~ in sth.** bei etw. ungeschickt vorgehen
unskilled [ʌn'skɪld] *adj.* **a)** *(lacking skills)* ungeschickt; stümperhaft; **b)** *(without special training)* ungelernt ⟨*Arbeiter*⟩; **~ in sth.** in etw. *(Dat.)* unerfahren; **c)** *(done without skill)* schlecht; stümperhaft; **d)** keine besonderen Fertigkeiten erfordernd ⟨*Arbeit*⟩; **~ jobs** Stellen für ungelernte Arbeiter; Hilfsarbeiterstellen; **the work is ~**: die Arbeit erfordert keine besonderen Fertigkeiten
unskillful *(Amer.) see* **unskilful**
unslept-in [ʌn'sleptɪn] *adj.* **the bed was ~**: in dem Bett hatte niemand geschlafen
unsmiling [ʌn'smaɪlɪŋ] *adj.* ernst
unsmoked [ʌn'sməʊkt] *adj.* ungeräuchert
unsnarl [ʌn'snɑ:l] *v.t.* entwirren
unsociability [ʌnsəʊʃə'bɪlɪtɪ] *n.* Ungeselligkeit, *die*
unsociable [ʌn'səʊʃəbl] *adj.* ungesellig
unsocial [ʌn'səʊʃl] *adj.* ungesellig; **at this ~ hour** *(joc.)* zu dieser unchristlichen Tageszeit; **work ~ hours** nachts/sonn- und feiertags arbeiten
unsold [ʌn'səʊld] *adj.* unverkauft
unsolicited [ʌnsə'lɪsɪtɪd] *adj.* nicht angefordert *od.* erbeten; nicht bestellt ⟨*Waren*⟩; unverlangt eingesandt ⟨*Manuskript*⟩; **~ mail** Wurfsendungen
unsolved [ʌn'sɒlvd] *adj.* ungelöst; unaufgeklärt ⟨*Verbrechen*⟩
unsophisticated [ʌnsə'fɪstɪkeɪtɪd] *adj.* schlicht, einfach ⟨*Person, Geschmack, Vergnügen, Spiel*⟩; unkompliziert ⟨*Maschine, Küche, Methode*⟩; einfach ⟨*Wein*⟩; **~ food** Hausmannskost, *die*
unsound [ʌn'saʊnd] *adj.* **a)** *(diseased)* nicht gesund; krank; **his health is ~**: seine Gesundheit ist angeschlagen *od.* angegriffen; **b)** *(defective)* baufällig ⟨*Gebäude*⟩; morsch ⟨*Holz*⟩; brüchig ⟨*Mauerwerk*⟩; **structurally ~**: baufällig; **c)** *(ill-founded)* wenig stichhaltig; anfechtbar ⟨*Gesetz*⟩; nicht vertretbar ⟨*Ansichten, Methoden*⟩; **d)** *(unreliable)* unzuverlässig; **the firm is financially ~**: die Firma steht finanziell auf schwachen Füßen; **e) of ~ mind** unzurechnungsfähig; **he killed her while of ~ mind** als er sie tötete, war er nicht zurechnungsfähig
unsoundness [ʌn'saʊndnɪs] *n., no pl. (of health)* Schwäche, *die; (of structure)* Baufälligkeit, *die; (of theory, argument, decision)* Zweifelhaftigkeit, *die;* **~ of mind** Unzurechnungsfähigkeit, *die*
unsparing [ʌn'speərɪŋ] *adj.* **a)** *(lavish)* großzügig; **work with ~ energy** mit voller Kraft arbeiten; **give sb. one's ~ help/support** jmdm. seine volle Hilfe/Unterstützung geben; **be ~ of** *or* **in sth.** mit etw. nicht geizen; **be ~ in one's efforts** keine Mühe scheuen; **b)** *(merciless)* schonungslos
unsparingly [ʌn'speərɪŋlɪ] *adj.* **a)** großzügig; **b)** *(mercilessly)* schonungslos
unspeakable [ʌn'spi:kəbl] *adj.* unbeschreiblich; *(indescribably bad)* unsäglich
unspeakably [ʌn'spi:kəblɪ] *adv.* unbeschreiblich; unsäglich ⟨*häßlich*⟩
unspecified [ʌn'spesɪfaɪd] *adj.* nicht näher bezeichnet; nicht genannt ⟨*Anzahl, Summe*⟩; **the job was for an ~ length of time** die Stelle war nicht befristet
unspectacular [ʌnspek'tækjʊlə(r)] *adj.* wenig eindrucksvoll
unspent [ʌn'spent] *adj.* nicht ausgegeben ⟨*Geld*⟩; **I still had 30 pence ~ in my pocket** ich hatte noch 30 Pence in der Tasche
unspoiled [ʌn'spɔɪld], **unspoilt** [ʌn'spɔɪlt] *adj.* unverdorben; unberührt ⟨*Dorf, Landschaft*⟩; genießbar ⟨*Lebensmittel*⟩
unspoken [ʌn'spəʊkn] *adj.* ungesagt; *(tacit)* unausgesprochen; stillschweigend ⟨*Übereinkunft*⟩; **be left ~**: ungesagt bleiben
unsporting [ʌn'spɔ:tɪŋ], **unsportsmanlike** [ʌn'spɔ:tsmənlaɪk] *adjs.* unsportlich
unstable [ʌn'steɪbl] *adj.* **a)** nicht stabil; instabil *(geh.)*; labil ⟨*Wirtschaft, Beziehungen, Verhältnisse*⟩; **the country is ~**: die Lage im Land ist nicht stabil *od.* ist unsicher; **[mentally/emotionally] ~**: [psychisch] labil; **b)** *(Phys.)* instabil; *see also* **equilibrium**
unstamped [ʌn'stæmpt] *adj.* ungestempelt; *(unfranked)* unfrankiert
unstated [ʌn'steɪtɪd] *adj.* nicht genannt
unstatesmanlike [ʌn'steɪtsmənlaɪk] *adj.* wenig staatsmännisch
unsteadily [ʌn'stedɪlɪ] *adv.* unsicher ⟨*gehen*⟩; unregelmäßig ⟨*schlagen, brennen*⟩
unsteadiness [ʌn'stedɪnɪs] *n., no pl. see* **unsteady**: Unsicherheit, *die;* Instabilität, *die;* Wechselhaftigkeit, *die;* Ungleichmäßigkeit, *die;* Wackeligkeit, *die*
unsteady [ʌn'stedɪ] *adj.* unsicher; instabil ⟨*Wirtschaft, Markt*⟩; wechselhaft ⟨*Entwicklung*⟩; ungleichmäßig ⟨*Flamme, Rhythmus*⟩; wackelig ⟨*Leiter, Stuhl, Tisch, Konstruktion*⟩; **be ~ on one's feet** unsicher auf den Beinen sein
unstick [ʌn'stɪk] *v.t.*, **unstuck** [ʌn'stʌk] [ab]lösen; *see also* **unstuck**
unstinting [ʌn'stɪntɪŋ] *adj.* großzügig; **be ~ in sth.** mit etw. nicht geizen; **be ~ in one's efforts** keine Mühe scheuen
unstitch [ʌn'stɪtʃ] *v.t.* auftrennen ⟨*Naht, Saum*⟩; **the seam has come ~ed** der Saum ist aufgegangen
unstoppable [ʌn'stɒpəbl] *adj.* unhaltbar ⟨*Schuß aufs Fußballtor*⟩; unerreichbar ⟨*Aufschlag*⟩; *(fig.)* unaufhaltsam; **she is ~**: sie ist nicht aufzuhalten
unstrap [ʌn'stræp] *v.t.* aufschnallen
unstreamed [ʌn'stri:md] *adj.* *(Sch.)* nicht in Parallelzüge *od.* leistungshomogene Gruppen eingeteilt
unstressed [ʌn'strest] *adj.* **a)** *(not subjected to stress)* nicht belastet; **b)** *(Phonet.)* unbetont
unstructured [ʌn'strʌktʃəd] unstrukturiert
unstrung [ʌn'strʌŋ] *adj.* **a) come ~** ⟨*Perlen usw.:*⟩ von der Schnur fallen; **b)** entnervt ⟨*Person*⟩; zerrüttet ⟨*Nerven*⟩
unstuck [ʌn'stʌk] *adj.* **come ~**: sich lösen; ⟨*Briefumschlag:*⟩ aufgehen; *(fig. coll.: come to grief, fail)* ⟨*Person:*⟩ baden gehen *(ugs.)* (over mit); ⟨*Projekt, Plan, Theorie, Geschäft:*⟩ in die Binsen gehen *(ugs.)*
unstudied [ʌn'stʌdɪd] *adj.* ungekünstelt
unsubsidized [ʌn'sʌbsɪdaɪzd] *adj.* nicht subventioniert
unsubstantial [ʌnsəb'stænʃl] *adj.* **a)** immateriell; *(ghostly)* körperlos ⟨*Wesen*⟩; leicht ⟨*Konstruktion*⟩; **b)** *(inadequate)* wenig nahrhaft ⟨*Essen*⟩
unsubstantiated [ʌnsəb'stænʃɪeɪtɪd] *adj.* unhaltbar; unbegründet
unsubtle [ʌn'sʌtl] *adj.* plump
unsuccessful [ʌnsək'sesfl] *adj.* erfolglos; **be ~**: keinen Erfolg haben; **the operation was ~**: die Operation hatte keinen Erfolg *od.* mißlang; **be ~ in an examination/competition** eine Prüfung nicht bestehen/in einem Wettbewerb unterliegen *od.* keinen Erfolg haben; **he has been ~ in his attempt to find a job** es ist ihm nicht gelungen, eine Stelle zu finden
unsuccessfully [ʌnsək'sesfəlɪ] *adv.* erfolglos; vergebens ⟨*versuchen*⟩
unsuitability [ʌnsu:tə'bɪlɪtɪ, ʌnsju:tə'bɪlɪtɪ] *n., no pl.* Ungeeignetsein, *das; (for job)* mangelnde Eignung
unsuitable [ʌn'su:təbl, ʌn'sju:təbl] *adj.* ungeeignet; **~ clothes** *(for weather, activity)* unzweckmäßige Kleider; *(for occasion, age)* unpassende Kleider; **be ~ for sb./sth.** für jmdn./etw. ungeeignet sein; **this sort of behaviour is ~ for a teacher** ein solches Verhalten gehört sich nicht für einen Lehrer
unsuitably [ʌn'su:təblɪ, ʌn'sju:təblɪ] *adv.* unpassend; **she dresses ~ for her age/figure** sie kleidet sich unpassend für ihr Alter/unvorteilhaft für ihre Figur; **be ~ dressed for a hike** für eine Wanderung unzweckmäßig gekleidet sein
unsuited [ʌn'su:tɪd, ʌn'sju:tɪd] *adj.* ungeeignet; **be ~ for** *or* **to sb./sth.** für jmdn./etw. ungeeignet sein; ⟨*Verhalten, Sprache:*⟩ für jmdn./etw. unpassend sein; **John and Mary are ~ to each other** John und Mary passen nicht zusammen; **he is ~ to be a teacher** er eignet sich nicht zum Lehrer
unsullied [ʌn'sʌlɪd] *adj.* *(literary)* unbefleckt; unberührt ⟨*Schnee*⟩; makellos ⟨*Glanz, Ruf*⟩
unsung [ʌn'sʌŋ] *adj.* unbesungen ⟨*Held, Tat*⟩
unsupported [ʌnsə'pɔ:tɪd] *adj.* **a)** nicht abgestützt; **if left ~, the branches will break** wenn man die Äste nicht [ab]stützt, brechen sie; **the old man walked ~**: der alte Mann ging ohne fremde Hilfe; **b)** *(Mil.)* ohne Unterstützung *nachgestellt; (without cover)* ungedeckt; **an ~ unit** eine ohne Unterstützung operierende Einheit; **c)** *(fig.)* durch nichts gestützt ⟨*Anschuldigung, Forderung, Theorie*⟩; **~ by sb./sth.** nicht gestützt durch jmdn./etw.; **a project ~ by funds** ein finanziell nicht gefördertes Projekt; **we do not accept cheques ~ by cheque cards** wir akzeptieren keine Schecks ohne Scheckkarte
unsure [ʌn'ʃʊə(r)] *adj.* unsicher; **be ~ about sb./sth.** sich *(Dat.)* über jmdn./etw. nicht im klaren sein; **be ~ whether to do sth.** sich *(Dat.)* nicht sicher sein, ob man etw. tun soll; **be ~ of sb./sth.** sich *(Dat.)* jmds./einer Sache nicht sicher sein; **be ~ of a date/of one's facts** ein Datum nicht genau wissen/seine Fakten nicht genau kennen; **be ~ of oneself** unsicher sein
unsurpassable [ʌnsə'pɑ:səbl] *adj.* unübertrefflich; *(unique)* einzigartig
unsurpassed [ʌnsə'pɑ:st] *adj.* unübertroffen; **a landscape ~ in beauty** eine Landschaft von unübertroffener Schönheit; **a novel ~ for suspense** ein Roman von unübertroffener Spannung; **his speeches were ~ for wit** seine Reden waren von unübertroffenem Witz
unsurprising [ʌnsə'praɪzɪŋ] *adj.* wenig überraschend
unsurprisingly [ʌnsə'praɪzɪŋlɪ] *adv.* wie zu erwarten war
unsuspected [ʌnsə'spektɪd] *adj.* **a)** *(not known about)* ungeahnt ⟨*Talent, Kräfte, Stärke, Tiefe, Charme*⟩; unvermutet ⟨*Defekt, Leck, Ergebnis, Folge*⟩; **he showed an ~ streak of ruthlessness** er zeigte sich überraschend rücksichtslos; **b)** *(not under suspicion)* **be ~**: nicht verdächtigt werden; nicht

unter Verdacht stehen; ~ **by anyone** ohne verdächtigt zu werden

unsuspecting [ʌnsə'spektɪŋ] *adj.*, **unsuspectingly** [ʌnsə'spektɪŋlɪ] *adv.* nichtsahnend

unsweetened [ʌn'swi:tnd] *adj.* ungesüßt

unswerving [ʌn'swɜ:vɪŋ] *adj.* **a)** *(not turning aside)* schnurgerade; **follow an ~ course** *(fig.)* seinen Weg unbeirrt fortsetzen; **b)** *(steady, constant)* unerschütterlich ‹*Glaube, Treue*›; unbeirrbar ‹*Entschlossenheit, Zuneigung*›; **be ~ in sth.** an etw. *(Dat.)* unbeirrbar *od.* unerschütterlich festhalten

unswervingly [ʌn'swɜ:vɪŋlɪ] *adv.* unerschütterlich ‹*treu*›; unbeirrbar ‹*unterstützen, festhalten, folgen*›

unsymmetrical [ʌnsɪ'metrɪkl] *adj.* unsymmetrisch

unsympathetic [ʌnsɪmpə'θetɪk] *adj.* **a)** wenig mitfühlend; **be ~:** kein Mitgefühl zeigen; **be ~ to sth./not ~ to sth.** kein Verständnis/durchaus Verständnis für etw. haben; **b)** *(unlikeable)* unsympathisch

unsympathetically [ʌnsɪmpə'θetɪkəlɪ] *adv.* ohne Mitgefühl

unsystematic [ʌnsɪstə'mætɪk] *adj.*, **unsystematically** [ʌnsɪstə'mætɪkəlɪ] *adv.* unsystematisch

untainted [ʌn'teɪntɪd] *adj.* unverdorben ‹*Lebensmittel*›; makellos ‹*Ruf*›

untalented [ʌn'tæləntɪd] *adj.* untalentiert

untameable [ʌn'teɪməbl] *adj.* unzähmbar; *(fig.)* unbezähmbar; unbezwinglich ‹*Wildnis*›

untamed [ʌn'teɪmd] *adj.* *(lit. or fig.)* ungezähmt; wild

untangle [ʌn'tæŋgl] *v.t.* entwirren; *(fig.)* entwirren ‹*Geschichte, Situation, Handlung*›; in Ordnung bringen ‹*Finanzen, Angelegenheit*›

untapped [ʌn'tæpt] *adj.* nicht angezapft; *(fig.: not used)* ungenutzt ‹*Talent*›; nicht angebrochen ‹*Vorräte*›; unerschlossen ‹*Bodenschätze, Markt*›

untarnished [ʌn'tɑ:nɪʃt] *adj.* *(lit. or fig.)* makellos; rein; nicht angelaufen ‹*Silber*›; **his name is ~ by corruption** sein Name ist nicht durch Korruption befleckt *(geh.)*

untasted [ʌn'teɪstɪd] *adj.* unberührt; **leave one's food ~:** sein Essen nicht anrühren; *(fig.)* **~ pleasures/delights** nie genossene *od.* gekostete Vergnügen/Freuden

untaught [ʌn'tɔ:t] *adj.* **a)** *(not instructed)* **be [completely] ~ in sth.** in etw. *(Dat.)* [überhaupt] nicht ausgebildet sein; **b)** *(not acquired by teaching)* natürlich ‹*Begabung*›; angeboren ‹*Fähigkeit*›

untaxed [ʌn'tækst] *adj.* unversteuert ‹*Einkommen, Waren*›; **an ~ car** ein Auto, für das die [Kraftfahrzeug]steuer nicht bezahlt ist

unteachable [ʌn'ti:tʃəbl] *adj.* nicht bildungsfähig ‹*Person, Kind*›; nicht lehrbar ‹*Fach, Fertigkeit*›

untenable [ʌn'tenəbl] *adj.* unhaltbar

untenanted [ʌn'tenəntɪd] *adj.* unbewohnt; leerstehend

untended [ʌn'tendɪd] *adj.* ungepflegt ‹*Garten*›

untested [ʌn'testɪd] *adj.* nicht erprobt; **a drug ~ on humans** ein an Menschen [noch] nicht erprobtes Medikament

unthankful [ʌn'θæŋkfl] *adj.* undankbar

unthinkable [ʌn'θɪŋkəbl] **1.** *adj.* unvorstellbar. **2.** *n.* **the ~:** das Unvorstellbare

unthinkably [ʌn'θɪŋkəblɪ] *adv.* unvorstellbar

unthinking [ʌn'θɪŋkɪŋ] *adj.*, **unthinkingly** [ʌn'θɪŋkɪŋlɪ] *adv.* gedankenlos; **~, I took the key** ganz in Gedanken, nahm ich den Schlüssel

unthought [ʌn'θɔ:t] *adj.* **~ of** undenkbar; **hitherto ~-of disadvantages/objections** Nachteile/Einwände, an die bisher noch niemand gedacht hat/hatte

unthread [ʌn'θred] *v.t.* vom Faden abziehen ‹*Perlen*›

untidily [ʌn'taɪdɪlɪ] *adv.* unordentlich

untidiness [ʌn'taɪdɪnɪs] *n., no pl. see* **untidy:** Ungepflegtheit, *die;* Unaufgeräumtheit, *die;* Unordentlichkeit, *die;* Unsauberkeit, *die*

untidy [ʌn'taɪdɪ] *adj.* ungepflegt ‹*Äußeres, Person, Garten*›; unaufgeräumt ‹*Bücher, Spielzeug, Zimmer*›; unordentlich, unsauber ‹*Manuskript*›

untie [ʌn'taɪ] *v.t.*, **untying** [ʌn'taɪɪŋ] aufknüpfen, aufknoten ‹*Faden, Seil, Paket*›; aufbinden ‹*Knoten, Schnürsenkel*›; losbinden ‹*Pferd, Boot, Seil vom Pfosten*›; **~ sb./sb.'s hands** jmdn./jmds. Hände von den Fesseln befreien

untied [ʌn'taɪd] *adj.* offen ‹*Schnürsenkel*›; ungebunden ‹*Krawatte*›; **leave sth. ~:** etw. nicht zusammenbinden; **come ~:** sich lösen; ‹*Schnürsenkel:*› aufgehen

until [ən'tɪl] **1.** *prep.* bis; *(followed by article + noun)* bis zu; **~ [the] evening/night/the end** bis zum Abend/bis in die Nacht/bis zum Ende; **~ his death/retirement** bis zu seinem Tod/seiner Pensionierung; **~ next week** bis nächste Woche; **~ then** *or* **that time** bis dahin *od.* dann; **~ soon after sth.** bis kurz nach etw.; **not ~:** erst; **not ~ Christmas/the summer/his birthday/this morning** erst an Weihnachten/im Sommer/an seinem Geburtstag/heute morgen; **yes, but not ~ [then]** ja, aber nicht vorher. **2.** *conj.* bis; **~ you find the key, we shall not be able to get in** solange du den Schlüssel nicht findest, kommen wir nicht hinein; **I am not coming ~ I am asked** ich komme erst, wenn man mich einlädt; solange man mich nicht einlädt, komme ich nicht; **I did not know ~ you told me** ich wußte das nicht, bis du es mir gesagt hast; **not ~ I saw him ...:** erst, als ich ihn sah, ...

untimely [ʌn'taɪmlɪ] **1.** *adj.* **a)** *(inopportune)* ungelegen; *(inappropriate)* unpassend; **be ~:** ungelegen kommen/unpassend sein; **an ~ frost** ein nicht der Jahreszeit entsprechender Frost; **an ~ measure/action** eine zur Unzeit getroffene Maßnahme; **his joke was ~:** er machte seinen Witz im unpassenden Moment; **not ~:** zur rechten Zeit; **b)** *(premature)* vorzeitig; allzu früh ‹*Tod*›; **he came to an ~ end** er starb allzu früh. **2.** *adv.* *(inopportunely)* unpassend; *(prematurely)* allzu früh

untiring [ʌn'taɪərɪŋ] *adj.* unermüdlich; **be ~ in one's efforts for sb./to do sth.** sich unermüdlich für jmdn. einsetzen/sich unermüdlich bemühen, etw. zu tun

untiringly [ʌn'taɪərɪŋlɪ] *adv.* unermüdlich

unto ['ʌntʊ, 'ʌntə] *prep.* *(arch./literary)* **a)** *see* **to 1; b)** *(Bibl.)* **come ~ me** kommet zu mir *(bibl.)*; **~ us a child is born** uns ist ein Kind geboren; **~ this day** bis zum heutigen Tage; **faithful ~ death** getreu bis in den Tod

untold [ʌn'təʊld] *adj.* **a)** *(immeasurable)* unbeschreiblich; unsagbar ‹*Elend*›; unermeßlich ‹*Reichtümer, Anzahl*›; **b)** *(countless)* unzählig; **c)** *(not related)* nicht erzählt

untouchable [ʌn'tʌtʃəbl] **1.** *adj.* **a)** *(beyond reach)* unberührbar; **sth. is ~:** etw. kann nicht berührt werden; ; **b)** *(above criticism/reproach)* unantastbar. **2.** *n.* Unberührbare, *der/die*

untouched [ʌn'tʌtʃt] *adj.* **a)** *(not handled, untasted)* unberührt; **leave sth. ~:** etw. nicht anrühren; **'~ by human hand'** *(on packaged food)* ≈ „hygienisch verpackt"; **a cup of tea still ~:** eine noch unberührte Tasse Tee; **b)** *(not changed)* unverändert; **c)** *(not affected)* unberührt; **be ~ by sth.** von etw. unberührt bleiben; **they had left her jewellery ~:** sie hatten ihren Schmuck nicht angerührt; **a town ~ by the war/a people ~ by the pressures of modern times** eine vom Krieg verschont gebliebene Stadt/ein Volk, das von den Zwängen der heutigen Zeit unberührt geblieben ist; **she remained ~ by his tears** seine Tränen ließen sie kalt; **d)** *(unequalled)* unerreicht

untoward [ʌntə'wɔ:d, ʌn'təʊəd] *adj.* **a)** *(unfavourable)* ungünstig; unglücklich ‹*Unfall*›; **in case something ~ were to happen** falls Schwierigkeiten auftauchen/ein Unglück geschieht; **nothing ~ happened** es gab keine Schwierigkeiten/es passierte kein Unheil; **b)** *(unseemly)* ungehörig

untraceable [ʌn'treɪsəbl] *adj.* unauffindbar; **be ~:** nicht aufzuspüren sein

untraced [ʌn'treɪst] *adj.* noch nicht gefunden

untrained [ʌn'treɪnd] *adj.* unausgebildet; ungelernt ‹*Arbeitskräfte*›; nicht dressiert ‹*Tier*›; **to the ~ eye/ear** dem ungeschulten Auge/Ohr; **be ~ in sth.** in etw. *(Dat.)* ungeübt sein

untrammelled *(Amer.:* **untrammeled)** [ʌn'træmld] *adj.* *(fig.)* unbeschränkt ‹*Freiheit*›; **young people ~ by tradition/convention** junge Leute, die sich von Traditionen/Konventionen nicht einengen lassen

untranslatable [ʌntræns'leɪtəbl] *adj.* unübersetzbar

untravelled *(Amer.:* **untraveled)** [ʌn'trævld] *adj.* der/die nicht weit herumgekommen ist; kaum befahren ‹*Straße*›

untreated [ʌn'tri:tɪd] *adj.* unbehandelt

untried [ʌn'traɪd] *adj.* **a)** *(not tested)* unerprobt; **a new treatment, ~ on humans** eine neue, an Menschen noch nicht erprobte Behandlung; **leave nothing ~:** nichts unversucht lassen; **b)** *(Law)* nicht vor Gericht gestellt ‹*Person*›; nicht verhandelt ‹*Fall*›

untrodden [ʌn'trɒdn] *adj.* unberührt ‹*Schnee*›; verlassen ‹*Weg*›

untroubled [ʌn'trʌbld] *adj.* ungestört ‹*Schlaf, Ruhe*›; sorglos ‹*Gesicht, Geist*›; ruhig ‹*Wasser*›; sorgenfrei ‹*Zeit, Leben*›; **he seemed ~ by the news** die Nachricht schien ihn nicht zu beunruhigen; **we were ~ by doubts/worries** auf uns lasteten keine Zweifel/Sorgen

untrue [ʌn'tru:] *adj.* **a)** *(false)* unwahr; **that's ~:** das ist nicht wahr; **b)** *(unfaithful)* **~ to sb./sth.** jmdm./etw. untreu; **c)** ungenau ‹*Ergebnis, Meßgerät*›

untrustworthy [ʌn'trʌstwɜ:ðɪ] *adj.* unzuverlässig

untruth [ʌn'tru:θ] *n., pl.* **~s** [ʌn'tru:ðz, ʌn'tru:θs] Unwahrheit, *die*

untruthful [ʌn'tru:θfl] *adj.* verlogen *(abwertend)*; **an ~ story** eine Lügengeschichte *(abwertend)*; **I am not being ~:** ich lüge nicht

untruthfully [ʌn'tru:θfəlɪ] *adv.* nicht der Wahrheit entsprechend ‹*antworten, etw. sagen*›

untruthfulness [ʌn'tru:θflnɪs] *n., no pl.* *(of story)* Unwahrheit, *die;* *(of person)* Verlogenheit, *die (abwertend)*

untuneful [ʌn'tju:nfl] *adj.* unmelodisch

unturned [ʌn'tɜ:nd] *adj. see* **stone 1 a**

untutored [ʌn'tju:təd] *adj.* ungeschult

untypical [ʌn'tɪpɪkl] *adj.* untypisch **(of** für)

unusable [ʌn'ju:zəbl] *adj.* unbrauchbar

[1]**unused** [ʌn'ju:zd] *adj.* *(new, fresh)* unbenutzt; *(not utilized)* ungenutzt; ungestempelt ‹*Briefmarke*›; **he still had three days ~ leave** er hatte noch drei Tage Urlaub gut

[2]**unused** [ʌn'ju:st] *adj.* *(unaccustomed)* **be ~ to sth./to doing sth.** etw. *(Akk.)* nicht gewohnt sein/nicht gewohnt sein, etw. zu tun; **we are not ~ to sudden crises** plötzliche Krisen sind für uns nichts Ungewohntes

unusual [ʌn'ju:ʒʊəl] *adj.* ungewöhnlich; *(exceptional)* außergewöhnlich; **an ~ number of ...:** eine ungewöhnlich große Zahl von ...; **it is ~ for him to do that** er tut das gewöhnlich nicht; **it is not ~ for her to do that** es ist durchaus nicht ungewöhnlich, daß sie das tut

unusually [ʌn'ju:ʒʊəlɪ] *adv.* ungewöhnlich;

as sentence-modifier ~ **[for him], he was late** er kam zu spät, was für ihn ganz ungewöhnlich ist

unusualness [ʌn'ju:ʒʊəlnɪs] *n., no pl.* Ungewöhnlichkeit, *die*

unutterable [ʌn'ʌtərəbl] *adj.*, **unutterably** [ʌn'ʌtərəblɪ] *adv.* unsäglich

unvarnished [ʌn'vɑ:nɪʃt] *adj.* unlackiert ‹*Holz*›; unglasiert ‹*Keramik*›; *(fig.)* ungeschminkt ‹*Wahrheit*›

unvarying [ʌn'veərɪɪŋ] *adj.* gleichbleibend

unveil [ʌn'veɪl] *v. t.* **a)** entschleiern ‹*Gesicht*›; enthüllen ‹*Statue, Gedenktafel*›; *(fig.: introduce publicly)* vorstellen ‹*neues Auto, Produkt, Modell*›; **b)** *(reveal)* veröffentlichen, *(geh.)* enthüllen ‹*Plan, Projekt*›

unveiling [ʌn'veɪlɪŋ] *n.* Enthüllung, *die; (fig.)* Vorstellung, *die;* **the ~ ceremony** die [feierliche] Enthüllung

unventilated [ʌn'ventɪleɪtɪd] *adj.* ungelüftet; *(having no permanent ventilation system)* unbelüftet

unverifiable [ʌn'verɪfaɪəbl] *adj.* nicht nachprüfbar ‹*Tatsache*›

unverified [ʌn'verɪfaɪd] *adj.* nicht nachgeprüft

unversed [ʌn'vɜ:st] *adj.* nicht bewandert (**in** in + *Dat.*)

unvoiced [ʌn'vɔɪst] *adj.* **a)** unausgesprochen ‹*Ansichten, Gefühle, Zweifel*›; **b)** *(Phonet.)* stimmlos

unwaged [ʌn'weɪdʒd] *adj.* arbeitslos

unwanted [ʌn'wɒntɪd] *adj.* unerwünscht; **one's ~ clothes/books** die Kleider/Bücher, die man nicht mehr [haben] will

unwarily [ʌn'weərɪlɪ] *adv.* unvorsichtig

unwarrantable [ʌn'wɒrəntəbl] *adj.* nicht zu rechtfertigend *nicht präd.*; ungerechtfertigt

unwarrantably [ʌn'wɒrəntəblɪ] *adv.* **be ~ severe with sb.** so streng mit jmdm. sein, daß es nicht zu rechtfertigen ist

unwarranted [ʌn'wɒrəntɪd] *adj.* ungerechtfertigt

unwary [ʌn'weərɪ] *adj.* unvorsichtig; unüberlegt ‹*Tat, Schritt*›

unwashed [ʌn'wɒʃt] *adj.* ungewaschen ‹*Person, Kleidung*›; ungespült ‹*Geschirr*›; **the great ~** *(derog.)* der Pöbel

unwavering [ʌn'weɪvərɪŋ] *adj.* gleichmäßig ‹*Flamme, Licht*›; fest ‹*Blick*›; *(fig.: firm, resolute)* unerschütterlich

unwearable [ʌn'weərəbl] *adj.* **sth. is ~:** etw. kann man nicht anziehen *od.* tragen

unwelcome [ʌn'welkəm] *adj.* unwillkommen; ungebeten ‹*Besucher*›; unerwünscht ‹*Anwesenheit*›

unwell [ʌn'wel] *adj.* unwohl; **look ~:** nicht wohl *od.* gut aussehen; **he feels ~** *(feels poorly)* er fühlt sich nicht wohl; *(feels sick)* ihm ist [es] schlecht *od.* übel; **she is ~:** es geht ihr nicht gut

unwholesome [ʌn'həʊlsəm] *adj. (lit. or fig.)* ungesund

unwieldiness [ʌn'wi:ldɪnɪs] *n., no pl. (of tool, weapon)* Unhandlichkeit, *die; (of box, shape, parcel)* Sperrigkeit, *die; (fig.: complexity)* Kompliziertheit, *die*

unwieldy [ʌn'wi:ldɪ] *adj.* unhandlich ‹*Werkzeug, Waffe*›; sperrig ‹*Karton, Form, Paket*›; *(fig.)* kompliziert ‹*Name, Titel, Organisation usw.*›

unwilling [ʌn'wɪlɪŋ] *adj.* widerwillig ‹*Partner, Unterstützung, Zustimmung*›; unfreiwillig ‹*Helfer*›; **an achievement that commands our ~ admiration/respect** eine Leistung, die wir wider Willen bewundern/respektieren müssen; **be ~ to do sth.** etw. nicht tun wollen; **we are not ~ but unable to help** wir wollen durchaus helfen, können [es] aber nicht; **be ~ for sb. to do sth.** *or* **that sb. should do sth.** nicht wollen, daß jmd. etw. tut; **be ~ for sth. to be done** *or* **that sth. should be done** nicht wollen, daß etw. getan wird

unwillingly [ʌn'wɪlɪŋlɪ] *adv.* widerwillig

unwillingness [ʌn'wɪlɪŋnɪs] *n., no pl.* Widerwille, *der;* **~ to help/listen** mangelnde Bereitschaft zu helfen/zuzuhören

unwind [ʌn'waɪnd] **1.** *v. t.,* **unwound** [ʌn'waʊnd] abwickeln; abspulen ‹*Film*›; **the girl unwound her arms from around his neck** das Mädchen löste seine Arme von seinem Hals. **2.** *v. i.,* **unwound a)** *(unreel)* sich abwickeln; **b)** *(fig.: unfold)* sich entwickeln; **c)** *(coll.: relax)* sich entspannen

unwise [ʌn'waɪz] *adj.* unklug; **if you are ~ enough to ignore my advice** wenn du so unklug bist, meinen Rat nicht anzunehmen

unwisely [ʌn'waɪzlɪ] *adv.* unklug; *as sentence-modifier* unklugerweise

unwitting [ʌn'wɪtɪŋ] *adj.* ahnungslos ‹*Opfer*›; unwissentlich ‹*Komplize, Urheber*›; *(unintentional)* unbeabsichtigt ‹*Fehler, Handlung*›; ungewollt ‹*Beleidigung*›

unwittingly [ʌn'wɪtɪŋlɪ] *adv.* unwissentlich; unabsichtlich ‹*beleidigen*›

unwonted [ʌn'wəʊntɪd] *adj.* ungewohnt

unworkable [ʌn'wɜ:kəbl] *adj.* unbrauchbar ‹*Material*›; nicht abbaubar ‹*Flöz*›; *(fig.: impracticable)* unbrauchbar ‹*System*›; undurchführbar ‹*Plan, Projekt*›

unworkmanlike [ʌn'wɜ:kmənlaɪk] *adj.* nicht fachmännisch

unworldly [ʌn'wɜ:ldlɪ] *adj.* weltabgewandt; *(naïve, not worldly-wise)* weltfremd

unworn [ʌn'wɔ:n] *adj.* **a)** *(new)* ungetragen ‹*Kleidung*›; **b)** *(not damaged)* nicht abgetreten ‹*Teppich, Treppe*›; nicht abgetragen ‹*Kleidungsstück*›; nicht abgenutzt ‹*Maschinenteil*›; nicht abgefahren ‹*Reifen*›; **completely ~:** überhaupt nicht abgetreten/abgetragen/abgenutzt/abgefahren

unworried [ʌn'wʌrɪd] *adj.* unbekümmert; **she was completely ~ by it** sie machte sich *(Dat.)* keine Sorgen darum

unworthily [ʌn'wɜ:ðɪlɪ] *adv.* unwürdig

unworthiness [ʌn'wɜ:ðɪnɪs] *n., no pl.* Unwürdigkeit, *die*

unworthy [ʌn'wɜ:ðɪ] *adj.* unwürdig; **receive ~ treatment** in einer Weise behandelt werden, die man nicht verdient hat; **be [not] ~ of sth.** einer Sache nicht [un]würdig sein; **an incident ~ of notice/of sb.'s attention** ein Vorfall, der keine Beachtung/der jmds. Beachtung nicht verdient; **be ~ of sb./sth.** ‹*Verhalten, Einstellung usw.:*› einer Person/Sache *(Gen.)* unwürdig sein

unwrap [ʌn'ræp] *v. t.,* **-pp-** auswickeln; abwickeln ‹*Bandage*›

unwritten [ʌn'rɪtn] *adj.* ungeschrieben; nicht schriftlich festgehalten ‹*Märchen, Lied, Vertrag, Verfassung*›; unbeschrieben ‹*Papier, Seite*›

unyielding [ʌn'ji:ldɪŋ] *adj.* hart; *(fig.)* unnachgiebig; unerschütterlich ‹*Mut*›; unbeirrbar ‹*Entschlossenheit*›; unerbittlich ‹*Widerstand*›

unyoke [ʌn'jəʊk] *v. t.* aus dem Joch nehmen; ausspannen ‹*Zugtier, Wagen, Pflug*›

unzip [ʌn'zɪp] **1.** *v. t.,* **-pp-** öffnen ‹*Reißverschluß*›; **~ a dress/bag** *etc.* den Reißverschluß eines Kleides/einer Tasche *usw.* öffnen; **can you ~ me, please?** kannst du mir bitte den Reißverschluß öffnen *od. (ugs.)* aufmachen?; **her dress had come ~ped** der Reißverschluß ihres Kleides war aufgegangen. **2.** *v. i,* **-pp-: the dress ~s at the back** das Kleid hat hinten einen Reißverschluß; **this bag/dress won't ~:** der Reißverschluß dieser Tasche/dieses Kleides geht nicht auf *(ugs.)*

up [ʌp] **1.** *adv.* **a)** *(to higher place)* nach oben; *(in lift)* aufwärts; **[right] up to sth.** *(lit. or fig.)* [ganz] bis zu etw. hinauf; **the bird flew up to the roof** der Vogel flog aufs Dach [hinauf]; **up into the air** in die Luft [hinauf] ...; **climb up on sth./climb up to the top of sth.** auf etw. *(Akk.)* [hinauf]steigen/bis zur Spitze einer Sache hinaufsteigen; **the lift went up to the top of the building** der Lift fuhr bis zur obersten Etage des Gebäudes; **the way up [to sth.]** der Weg hinauf [zu etw.]; **on the way up** *(lit. or fig.)* auf dem Weg nach oben; **up here/there** hier herauf/dort hinauf; **high/higher up** hoch/höher hinauf; **farther up** weiter hinauf; **half-way/a long/little way up** den halben Weg/ein weites/kurzes Stück hinauf; **up and up** immer höher; **up and away** auf und davon; **come on up!** komm [hier/weiter] herauf!; **up it** *etc.* **comes/goes** herauf kommt/hinauf geht es *usw.*; **up you go!** rauf mit dir! *(ugs.); see also* **hand 1 a; b)** *(to upstairs)* rauf *(bes. ugs.);* herauf/hinauf *(bes. schriftsprachlich);* nach oben; **c)** *(to place regarded as higher)* rauf *(bes. ugs.);* herauf/hinauf *(bes. schriftsprachlich);* **go up to the shops/the end of the road** zu den Geschäften/zum Ende der Straße gehen; **d)** *(to place regarded as more important)* **go up to Leeds from the country** vom Land in die Stadt Leeds *od.* nach Leeds fahren; **e)** *(northwards)* rauf *(bes. ugs.);* herauf/hinauf *(bes. schriftsprachlich);* **come up from London to Edinburgh** von London nach Edinburgh [he]raufkommen; **f)** *(Brit.: to capital)* rein *(bes. ugs.);* herein/hinein *(bes. schriftsprachlich);* **go up to town** *or* **London** nach London gehen/fahren; **get up to London from Reading** von Reading nach London [he]reinfahren; **g)** *(Brit.: to university)* **up to university/Oxford** auf die Universität/nach Oxford; **h)** *(Naut.: with rudder to leeward)* in Luv; **put the helm up** das Ruder in Luv legen; **i)** *(in higher place)* oben; **up here/there** hier/da oben; **[right] up at sth.** [ganz] oben auf/an etw. *(Dat.);* **high up** hoch oben; **he is something high up in the Army** *(fig.)* er ist ein hohes *od.* großes Tier in der Armee *(ugs.);* **an order from high up** *(fig.)* ein Befehl von ganz oben *(ugs.);* **higher up in the mountains** weiter oben in den Bergen; **the picture should be higher up** das Bild müßte höher hängen; **farther up** weiter oben; **half-way/a long/little way up** auf halbem Weg nach oben/ein gutes/kurzes Stück weiter oben; **10 metres up** 10 Meter hoch; **live four floors** *or* **storeys up** im vierten Stockwerk wohnen; **his flat is on the next floor up** seine Wohnung ist ein Stockwerk höher; **j)** *(erect)* hoch; **keep your head up** halte den Kopf hoch; *see also* **chin; k)** *(out of bed)* **be up** aufsein; **up and about** auf den Beinen; **l)** *(in place regarded as higher; upstairs)* oben; **m)** *(in place regarded as more important; Brit.: in capital)* **up in town** *or* **London/Leeds** in London/Leeds; **n)** *(in north)* **up [north]** oben [im Norden] *(ugs.);* **o)** *(Brit.: at univeristy)* **up at university/Oxford** an der Universität/in Oxford; **p)** *(in price, value, amount)* **prices have gone/are up** die Preise sind gestiegen; **butter is up [by ...]** Butter ist [...] teurer; **the dollar is/these shares are up** der Dollar ist/diese Aktien sind im Wert gestiegen; *(at high level)* **the temperature was up in the thirties** die Temperatur lag über dreißig Grad; **q)** *(including higher limit)* **up to** bis ... hinauf; **up to midday/up to £2** bis zum Mittag/bis zu 2 Pfund; **r)** *(in position of gain)* **we're £300 up on last year** wir liegen 300 Pfund über dem letzten Jahr; **the takings were £500 up on the previous month** die Einnahmen lagen 500 Pfund über denen des Vormonats; **s)** *(ahead)* **be three points/games/goals up** *(Sport)* mit drei Punkten/Spielen/Toren vorn liegen; **be three points up on sb.** drei Punkte vor jmdm. sein *od.* liegen; **t)** *(as far as)* **up to sth.** bis zu etw.; **she is up to Chapter 3** sie ist bis zum dritten Kapitel gekommen *od.* ist beim dritten Kapitel; **where are you/have you got up to [now]?** *(in book)* wie weit bist du?/wie weit bist du jetzt gekommen?; **up to here/there** bis hier[hin]/bis dorthin; **I've had it up to here** *(coll.)* mir steht es bis hier [hin] *(ugs.)*; **up to now/then/ that time/last week** bis jetzt/damals/zu jener Zeit/zur letzten Woche; *see also* **¹ear a; eye 1a; neck 1a; point 1e; u) up to** *(comparable with)* **be up to expectation[s]** den Erwartungen entsprechen; **his last opera is not up to the others he has written** seine neueste Oper reicht an seine früheren nicht heran; **v) up to** *(capable of)* **[not] be/feel up to sth.** einer Sache *(Dat.)* [nicht] gewachsen sein/ sich einer Sache *(Dat.)* [nicht] gewachsen fühlen; **[not] be/feel up to doing sth.** [nicht] in der Lage sein/sich nicht in der Lage fühlen, etw. zu tun; **are you sure you're up to it?** meinst du wirklich, daß du das schaffst?; **not be up to much** nicht viel taugen; **my cooking isn't up to much** ich koche nicht besonders gut; **be up to sb.'s dodges/fiddles** jmds. Schliche kennen; **he is up to all the dodges** er ist mit allen Wassern gewaschen *(ugs.)*; **w) up to** *(derog.: doing)* **be up to sth.** etw. anstellen *(ugs.)*; **what is he up to?** was hat er [bloß] vor?; **what do you think you're up to?** was fällt Ihnen [denn *od.* eigentlich] ein?; **I'm sure he's up to something** er führt sicher etwas im Schilde; **I wonder what he's up to with it** ich frage mich, was er damit vorhat; **x) up to** *(incumbent on)* **it is [not] up to sb. to do sth.** es ist [nicht] jmds. Sache, etw. zu tun; **it is up to us to help them** es ist unsere Pflicht, ihnen zu helfen; **now it's up to him to do something** nun liegt es bei *od.* an ihm, etwas zu tun; **it's not up to me to say** das kann ich nicht sagen; **the decision/ choice is [not] up to me** die Entscheidung/ Wahl hängt [nicht] von mir ab; **it's/that's up to you** *(is for you to decide)* es/das hängt von dir ab; *(concerns only you)* es/das ist deine Sache; **y)** *(close)* **up against sb./sth.** an jmdm./etw. ⟨*lehnen*⟩; an jmdn./etw. ⟨*stellen*⟩; **sit up against the wall** mit dem Rücken zur *od.* an der Wand sitzen; **up near/by sth.** direkt neben etw.; **z)** *(confronted by)* **be up against a problem/difficulty** *etc. (coll.)* vor einem Problem/einer Schwierigkeit *usw.* stehen; **find oneself up against the law/the authorities** mit dem Gesetz/mit den Behörden in Konflikt kommen; **be up against a tough opponent** es mit einem harten Gegner zu tun haben; **they don't realize what sort of competition they will be up against** sie wissen nicht, mit welcher Art von Konkurrenz sie es zu tun haben werden; **be up against it** in großen Schwierigkeiten stecken; *see also* **come up i; aa) up and down** *(upwards and downwards)* hinauf und hinunter; *(to and fro)* auf und ab; **the children are jumping up and down on the settee** die Kinder springen auf dem Sofa herum; **be up and down** *(coll.: variable)* Hochs und Tiefs haben; **How are you? – Oh, up and down** Wie geht es Ihnen? – Ach, mal so, mal so *(ugs.)*; *see also* **up-and-down; bb)** *(facing upwards)* **'this side/way up'** *(on box etc.)* „[hier] oben"; **turn sth. this/the other side/way up** diese/ die andere Seite einer Sache nach oben drehen; **the right/wrong way up** richtig/verkehrt *od.* falsch herum; **which way up is the painting supposed to be?** was soll auf dem Bild oben [und unten] sein?; wie herum ist das Bild denn richtig? *(ugs.)*; **cc)** *(finished, at an end)* abgelaufen; **time is up** die Zeit ist abgelaufen; **it is all up with him** mit ihm ist es vorbei *od.* aus *(ugs.)*; *see also* **¹game 1b. 2.** *prep.* **a)** *(upwards along)* rauf *(bes. ugs.)*; herauf/hinauf *(bes. schriftsprachlich)*; **walk up sth.** etw. hinaufgehen; **higher up the valley** weiter oben im Tal; **up hill and down dale** bergauf und bergab; **curse sb. up hill and down dale** jmdn. in Grund und Boden verfluchen; **b)** *(upwards through)* **force a liquid up a pipe** eine Flüssigkeit durch eine Röhre nach oben pressen; **c)** *(upwards over)* **up sth.** etw. *(Akk.)* hinauf; **ivy grew up the wall** Efeu wuchs die Mauer hinauf; **mud was splattered up the back of his coat** sein Mantel war den ganzen Rücken hinauf mit Schlamm bespritzt; **d)** *(along)* **go up the road/corridor/track** die Straße/den Korridor/den Weg hinauf- *od.* entlanggehen; **come up the street** die Straße herauf- *od.* entlangkommen; **turn up a side-street** in eine Seitenstraße einbiegen; **I'm going up the pub** *(Brit. coll.)* ich gehe in die Kneipe; **walk up and down the platform** auf dem Bahnsteig auf und ab gehen; **up and down the land** landauf, landab; **e)** *(at or in higher position in or on)* [weiter] oben; **further up the ladder/coast** weiter oben auf der Leiter/an der Küste; **a house up the mountain** ein Haus oben am Berg; **live/sail up the river** flußaufwärts wohnen/segeln; **f) up yours/ up them!** *(sl.)* du kannst/die können mich [mal]! *(salopp)*; **g)** *(from bottom to top along)* **up the side of a house** an der Seite eines Hauses hinauf. *See also* **country b; creek d; gum-tree; ¹pole a; sleeve a; spout 1a; stage 1a. 3.** *adj.* **a)** *(directed upwards)* aufwärts führend ⟨*Rohr, Kabel*⟩; ⟨*Rolltreppe*⟩ nach oben; nach oben gerichtet ⟨*Kolbenhub*⟩; **up train/line/journey** *(Railw.)* Zug/Gleis/ Fahrt Richtung Stadt; **b)** *(well informed)* **be up in a subject/on the news** in einem Fach auf der Höhe [der Zeit] sein/über alle Neuigkeiten Bescheid wissen *od.* gut informiert sein; **c) up for** *(in line for)*: **be up for a post/for promotion** Kandidat/Kandidatin für eine Stelle/Beförderung sein; **d)** *(coll.: ready)* **tea['s]/grub['s] up!** Tee/Essen ist fertig!; **e)** *(coll.: amiss)* **what's up?** was ist los? *(ugs.)*; **what's up with him** *etc.***?** was ist los mit ihm *usw.*? *(ugs.)*; **something is up** irgendwas ist los *(ugs.)*. **4.** *n. in pl.* **the ups and downs** *(lit. or fig.)* das Auf und Ab; *(fig.)* die Höhen und Tiefen; **life is full of ups und downs** das Leben ist ein dauerndes Auf und Ab; **we've had our ups und downs** wir haben Höhen und Tiefen durchlebt. **5.** *v. i.*, **-pp-** *(coll.)* **up and leave/resign** einfach abhauen *(ugs.)*/kündigen; **he ups and says ...:** da sagt er doch [ur]plötzlich ... **6.** *v. t.*, **-pp-** *(coll.)* *(increase)* erhöhen; *(raise up)* heben

'up-and-coming *adj. (coll.)* aufstrebend

up-and-'down *attrib. adj.* **~ movement/ motion** Aufundabbewegung, *die*; **an ~ life/~ years** *(fig.)* ein Leben/Jahre mit Höhen und Tiefen; **an ~ sort of a year** ein bewegtes Jahr

up-and-'over door *n.* Kipptür, *die*

'up-and-up *n. (coll.)* **be on the ~:** auf dem aufsteigenden Ast sein *(ugs.)*

'upbeat 1. *n. (Mus.)* Auftakt, *der*. **2.** *adj. (coll.) (optimistic)* optimistisch; *(cheerful)* fröhlich; **~ news/export figures** zuversichtlich stimmende Neuigkeiten/Exportraten

up'braid *v. t.* **~ sb. with sth./for [doing] sth.** jmdm. wegen etw. Vorwürfe machen/ jmdm. vorwerfen, daß er etw. getan hat

upbringing ['ʌpbrɪŋɪŋ] *n.* Erziehung, *die*

'up-country *adj.* **a) an ~ town/region/dialect** eine Stadt/ein Gebiet im Landesinneren/ein Dialekt, wie er im Landesinneren gesprochen wird; **b)** *(countrified, unsophisticated)* **a little ~ town/place** ein kleiner Flecken/kleines Fleckchen auf dem Land; **plain ~ folk/people** einfache Leute vom flachen Land

'up current *n. (in air)* Aufwind, *der*

update 1. [ʌp'deɪt] *v. t. (bring up to date)* aktualisieren; auf den neuesten *od.* aktuellen Stand bringen; *(modernize)* modernisieren; **an ~d version/edition** eine aktualisierte Fassung/Ausgabe. **2.** ['ʌpdeɪt] *n.* Lagebericht, *der* **(on zu)**; *(~d version)* Neuausgabe, *die*

'up draught *n.* [Luft]zug von unten

up-'end 1. *v. t. (lit. or fig.)* auf den Kopf stellen; *(knock down)* zu Boden schlagen ⟨*Gegner*⟩. **2.** *v. i.* ⟨*Schiff:*⟩ sich mit dem Heck nach oben stellen [und sinken]

'upfield *adv. (Sport)* in Richtung des gegnerischen Tores

up 'front *adv. (coll.)* **a)** *(at the front)* vorne; **b)** *(as down payment)* im voraus

'up grade *n. (Amer.)* Steigung, *die*; **be on the ~** *(fig.)* ⟨*Wirtschaft:*⟩ im Aufschwung sein; **he was on the ~:** es ging bergauf mit ihm

upgrade [ʌp'greɪd] *v. t.* **a)** *(raise)* befördern ⟨*Beschäftigte*⟩; aufwerten ⟨*Stellung*⟩; **~ fees/salaries/payments in line with inflation** Gebühren/Gehälter/Zahlungen entsprechend der Inflationsrate erhöhen; **b)** *(improve)* verbessern; **the stadium will be ~d to Olympic standards** das Stadion wird den olympischen Normen entsprechend ausgebaut

upheaval [ʌp'hi:vl] *n.* Aufruhr, *der*; *(commotion, disturbance)* Durcheinander, *das*; **the ~ of moving house** das Durcheinander eines Umzugs; **an emotional ~:** ein Aufruhr der Gefühle; **social/political ~:** soziale/ politische Umwälzung

up'hill 1. *adj.* bergauf führend ⟨*Weg, Pfad*⟩; ⟨*Fahrt, Reise*⟩ bergauf; *(fig.)* **an ~ task/ struggle** eine mühselige Aufgabe/ein harter Kampf. **2.** *adv.* bergauf; **it's ~ all the way** es geht immer bergauf; **our task will be ~ all the way** *(fig.)* unsere Aufgabe wird bis zum Schluß mühselig sein

up'hold *v. t.*, **upheld** [ʌp'held] **a)** *(support)* unterstützen; hochhalten, wahren ⟨*Tradition, Ehre*⟩; schützen ⟨*Verfassung*⟩; **b)** *(confirm)* aufrechterhalten ⟨*Forderung, Einwand*⟩; einhalten ⟨*Vertrag*⟩; bestätigen ⟨*Urteil*⟩; anerkennen ⟨*Einwand, Beschwerde*⟩

up'holder *n.* Wahrer, *der*/Wahrerin, *die*

upholster [ʌp'həʊlstə(r)] *v. t.* polstern; **~ sth. in** *or* **with sth.** etw. in etw. *(Dat.)* *od.* mit etw. polstern; *see also* **well-upholstered**

upholsterer [ʌp'həʊlstərə(r)] *n.* Polsterer, *der*/Polsterin, *die*

upholstery [ʌp'həʊlstərɪ] *n.* **a)** *(craft)* Polster[er]handwerk, *das*; *attrib.* Polster-; **b)** *(padding)* Polsterung, *die*; *(cover also)* Bezug, *der*; *attrib.* Polster-; **~ fabric** Polster- *od.* Möbelstoff, *der*

'upkeep *n.* Unterhalt, *der*

upland ['ʌplənd] **1.** *n. in pl.* Hochland, *das*. **2.** *adj.* Hochland-

uplift 1. [-'-] *v. t.* aufrichten ⟨*Volk, Seele, Geist*⟩; erheben *(geh.)* ⟨*Hand, Kopf, Stimme*⟩; **parts of the earth's crust were ~ed** Teile der Erdkruste hoben sich; **be/feel ~ed by sth.** *(fig.)* durch etw. erhoben *od.* erbaut werden/sich durch etw. erhoben *od.* erbaut fühlen; **voices ~ed in song/praise** zum Gesang/Lobpreis erhobene Stimmen. **2.** ['--] *n.* Erhebung, *die*; Erbauung, *die*; **spiritual ~:** geistige Erhebung

up'lifting *adj. (fig.)* erhebend

'up-market *adj.* exklusiv ⟨*Waren, Hotel, Geschäft*⟩; Luxus⟨*güter, -hotel, -restaurant*⟩; anspruchsvoll ⟨*Kunde*⟩; gehoben ⟨*Geschmack*⟩; **an ~ magazine** eine Zeitschrift für den anspruchsvollen Konsumenten; **go ~:** exklusiver [und teurer] werden

upon [ə'pɒn] *prep.* **a)** *(indicating direction)* auf (+ *Akk.*); *(indicating position)* auf (+ *Dat.*); **b)** *see* **on 1a, b, g; a house ~ the river bank** ein Haus am Flußufer

upper ['ʌpə(r)] **1.** *compar. adj.* **a)** ober... ⟨*Nil, Themse usw., Atmosphäre*⟩; Ober⟨*grenze, -lippe, -arm usw., -schlesien, -österreich usw., -kreide, -devon usw.*⟩; *(Mus.)* hoch ⟨*Tonlage, Noten*⟩; **~ circle** *(Theatre)* oberer Rang; **the temperatures will be in the ~ twenties** die Temperaturen werden über fünfundzwanzig Grad liegen; **have/get/gain the ~ hand [of sb./sth.]** die Oberhand [über jmdn./etw.] haben/erhalten/gewinnen; *see also* **jaw 1a; lip a; b)** *(in rank)* ober...; **the ~ ranks/echelons of the civil service/Army** die oberen *od.* höheren Ränge des Beamtentums/der Armee; **~ class[es]** Oberschicht, *die*; **~**

middle class obere Mittelschicht; **the ~ crust** *(coll.)* die oberen Zehntausend. **2.** *n.* **a)** *(of footwear)* Oberteil, *das;* **'leather ~s'** „Obermaterial Leder"; **be [down] on one's ~s** *(coll.)* auf dem trockenen sitzen *(ugs.);* **b)** *(sl.: drug)* Aufputschmittel, *das;* Speed, *das (Jargon)*

upper: ~ case 1. *n.* Großbuchstaben; **in ~ case** in Großbuchstaben; **2.** *adj.* groß ‹*Buchstabe*›; **U~ Chamber** *n. (Parl.)* Oberhaus, *das;* **~-class** *adj.* Oberschicht-; **~-class people/family/accent** Leute/Familie aus der Oberschicht/Akzent der Oberschicht; **be very ~-class** ‹*Person:*› ein typischer Vertreter der Oberschicht sein; ‹*Akzent, Herkunft:*› typisch für die Oberschicht sein; **~-crust** *adj. (coll.)* **~-crust accent/family** Akzent/Familie der oberen Zehntausend; **be very ~-crust** ‹*Person:*› ein typischer Vertreter der oberen Zehntausend sein; **~-cut** *n. (Boxing)* Uppercut, *der;* Aufwärtshaken, *der;* **~ 'deck** *n. (of ship, bus)* Oberdeck, *das;* **U~ House** *n.* Oberhaus, *das;* **~most 1.** *adj.* oberst...; **~most aim/desire** höchstes Ziel/größter Wunsch; **the questions that are ~most on the agenda** die Fragen, die auf der Tagesordnung ganz oben stehen; **be ~most in sb.'s mind** jmdn. am meisten beschäftigen; **2.** *adv.* ganz oben; obenauf; **face ~most** mit dem Gesicht nach oben; **come ~most** *(fig.)* an erster Stelle stehen; **U~ 'Rhine** *pr. n.* Hochrhein [und Oberrhein]

uppish ['ʌpɪʃ] *adj. (coll.)* hochnäsig *(ugs.);* **be/get ~ about sth./with sb.** über etw. *(Akk.)* die Nase rümpfen/jmdn. von oben herab behandeln

uppishness ['ʌpɪʃnɪs] *n., no pl. (coll.)* Hochnäsigkeit, *die (ugs.)*

uppity ['ʌpɪtɪ] *adj. (coll.)* hochnäsig *(ugs.);* **get ~:** sich aufblasen *(ugs.)*

upright ['ʌpraɪt] **1.** *adj.* **a)** aufrecht; steil ‹*Schrift*›; **a chair with an ~ back** ein Stuhl mit einem geraden Rücken[teil]; **~ piano** Klavier, *das;* **~ freezer** Tiefkühlschrank, *der;* **~ vacuum cleaner** ≈ Handstaubsauger, *der;* **set/stand/hold sth. ~:** etw. aufrecht hinstellen/halten; **stand ~:** aufrecht stehen; **sit ~:** aufrecht sitzen; **hold oneself ~:** sich geradehalten; **please make sure that your seat is in the ~ position** bitte stellen Sie Ihre Rückenlehnen senkrecht; *see also* **¹bolt 4; b)** *(fig.: honourable)* aufrecht; **be ~ in sth.** rechtschaffen in etw. *(Dat.)* sein. **2.** *n.* **a)** *(of frame)* seitliche Leiste; *(of ladder)* Holm, *der; (of scaffolding etc.)* [aufrechter] Stützpfeiler; *(Footb.)* Pfosten, *der;* **b)** *(piano)* Klavier, *das*

uprightly ['ʌpraɪtlɪ] *adv.* aufrecht; *(fig.)* aufrecht; rechtschaffen

uprightness ['ʌpraɪtnɪs] *n., no pl.* **a)** aufrechte Stellung; *(of plant)* aufrechter Wuchs; **b)** *(fig.)* Aufrichtigkeit, *die;* Rechtschaffenheit, *die*

'uprising *n.* Aufstand, *der*

up-river *see* **upstream**

'uproar *n.* Aufruhr, *der;* Tumult, *der;* **be in [an] ~:** in Aufruhr sein

uproarious [ʌp'rɔ:rɪəs] *adj.* lärmend ‹*Menge*›; überwältigend ‹*Begrüßung, Stimmung*›; zum Schreien komisch *(ugs.)* ‹*Witz, Anblick, Komödie*›; schallend ‹*Gelächter*›

uproariously [ʌp'rɔ:rɪəslɪ] *adv.* lärmend; schallend ‹*lachen*›; **be ~ funny** zum Totlachen sein *(ugs.)*

up'root *v. t.* [her]ausreißen; ‹*Sturm:*› entwurzeln; *(fig.: eradicate)* ausmerzen ‹*Übel*›; **~ sb.** jmdn. aus der gewohnten Umgebung herausreißen; **people were ~ed by the war** die Menschen wurden durch den Krieg entwurzelt

upsadaisy ['ʌpsədeɪzɪ] *int.* hoppla

upset 1. [ʌp'set] *v. t.,* **-tt-, upset a)** *(overturn)* umkippen; *(accidentally)* umstoßen ‹*Tasse, Vase, Milch usw.*›; **~ sth. over sth.** etw. über etw. *(Akk.)* kippen; **b)** *(distress)* erschüttern; mitnehmen *(ugs.); (disturb the composure or temper of)* aus der Fassung bringen; *(shock, make angry, excite)* aufregen; **it ~s the children to hear their parents quarrelling** es belastet die Kinder, wenn sie ihre Eltern streiten hören; **the smallest thing ~s her** jede Kleinigkeit regt sie auf; **don't let it ~ you** nimm es nicht so schwer; **~ oneself** sich aufregen; **c)** *(make ill)* **sth. ~s sb.** etw. bekommt jmdm. nicht; **sth. ~s sb.'s stomach/digestion** etw. schlägt jmdm. auf den Magen/die Verdauung; **d)** *(disorganize)* stören; durcheinanderbringen ‹*Plan, Berechnung, Arrangement*›; *(defeat)* ausschalten; **this incident has seriously ~ our chances** dieser Vorfall hat unsere Chancen erheblich vermindert. **2.** *v. i.,* **-tt-, upset** umkippen. **3.** *adj.* **a)** *(overturned)* umgekippt; **b)** *(distressed)* bestürzt; *(agitated)* aufgeregt; *(unhappy)* unglücklich; *(put out)* aufgebracht; verärgert; *(offended)* gekränkt; **be ~ [about sth.]** *(be distressed)* [über etw. *(Akk.)*] bestürzt sein; *(be angry)* sich [über etw. *(Akk.)*] ärgern; **we were very ~ to hear of his illness** die Nachricht von seiner Krankheit ist uns sehr nahegegangen *od.* hat uns sehr bestürzt; **when they get back they'll be very/so ~ to have missed you** wenn sie zurückkommen, wird es ihnen sehr leid tun, dich verpaßt zu haben; **get ~ [about/over sth.]** sich [über etw. *(Akk.)*] aufregen; **there's no point in getting ~ about it** es hat keinen Sinn, sich darüber aufzuregen; **c)** ['--] *(disordered)* **an ~ stomach** ein verdorbener Magen; **have an ~ stomach** sich *(Dat.)* den Magen verdorben haben; **d)** *(disorganized)* gestört ‹*Routine, Mechanismus, System*›; durcheinandergebracht ‹*Plan, Berechnung, Mechanismus, System*›. **4.** ['ʌpset] *n.* **a)** *(overturning)* Umkippen, *das;* **b)** *(agitation)* Aufregung, *die; (shock)* Schock, *der; (annoyance)* Verärgerung, *die;* **sth. is a great ~ for** *or* **to sb.** etw. nimmt jmdn. sehr mit *(ugs.) od.* geht jmdm. sehr nahe; **emotional ~:** seelischer Schock; **have an ~:** einiges durchmachen [müssen]; **c)** *(slight quarrel)* Mißstimmung, *die;* **d)** *(slight illness)* Unpäßlichkeit, *die;* **digestive/stomach ~:** Verdauungsstörung, *die*/Magenverstimmung, *die;* **e)** *(disturbance)* Zwischenfall, *der; (confusion, upheaval)* Aufruhr, *der;* Durcheinander, *das;* **an ~ in his plans/calculations/routine** eine Störung seiner Pläne/Berechnungen/Routine; **f)** *(surprising result)* Überraschung, *die;* **a by-election ~:** eine Überraschung bei der Nachwahl

up'setting *adj.* erschütternd; *(sad)* traurig; bestürzend; schlimm ‹*Zeit*›; *(annoying)* ärgerlich; **being mugged/sacked was a very ~ experience for her** ausgeraubt/entlassen zu werden, war ein Erlebnis, das sie ganz schön mitgenommen hat *(ugs.);* **my mother found the obscene language ~:** meine Mutter fand die obszöne Sprache anstößig; **she missed her train, and what was even more ~, she was late for the opera** sie verpaßte ihren Zug, aber noch ärgerlicher für sie war es, daß sie dadurch zu spät in die Oper kam; **it was/I found it ~ that X was promoted instead of me** ich ärgerte mich, daß X an meiner Stelle befördert wurde; **the constant changes have been rather ~ for the children** die laufenden Veränderungen haben die Kinder ziemlich aus dem Gleis gebracht; **these pictures are ~ to a child** diese Bilder sind für ein Kind [zu] erschütternd

'upshot *n.* Ergebnis, *das;* **what will be the ~ of it [all]?** was wird bei der [ganzen] Sache herauskommen? *(ugs.);* **he hummed and hawed a bit and, well, the ~ of the matter/of it [all] was that ...:** er druckste ein bißchen herum, aber schließlich [und endlich] kam heraus *od.* stellte sich heraus, daß ...; **in the ~:** letztendlich

upside 'down 1. *adv.* verkehrt herum; **turn sth. ~** *(lit. or fig.)* etw. auf den Kopf stellen; **the plane flew ~:** das Flugzeug flog auf dem Kopf *(ugs.).* **2.** *adj.* auf dem Kopf stehend ‹*Bild*›; **be ~:** auf dem Kopf stehen; **the car came to rest ~:** der Wagen blieb auf dem Dach liegen; **the acrobat hung ~:** der Akrobat hing mit dem Kopf nach unten *od.* kopfüber; *(fig.)* **the whole world seems to be ~:** die ganze Welt scheint Kopfzustehen; **an upside-down world/view of the situation/logic** eine verkehrte Welt/Sicht der Dinge/Logik

up'stage 1. *adv. (Theatre)* im Hintergrund [der Bühne]; **move ~:** sich zum Hintergrund der Bühne bewegen. **2.** *adj. (Theatre)* **an ~ door/entrance** eine Hintertür/ein Hintereingang zur Bühne. **3.** *v. t. (Theatre)* **~ sb.** jmdn. zwingen, sich vom Publikum abzuwenden; *(fig. coll.)* jmdm. die Schau stehlen *(ugs.)*

upstairs 1. [-'-] *adv.* nach oben ‹*gehen, kommen*›; oben ‹*sein, wohnen*›; *see also* **kick 3a. 2.** ['--] *adj.* im Obergeschoß *nachgestellt.* **3.** [-'-] *n.* Obergeschoß, *das*

up'standing *adj.* **a)** *(strong and healthy)* stattlich; **fine ~ children** nette, gesunde und kräftige Kinder; **b)** *(honest)* aufrichtig; aufrecht; **c) be ~** *(stand up)* sich erheben

'upstart 1. *n.* Emporkömmling, *der.* **2.** *adj.* **an ~ landowner** ein emporgekommener Grundbesitzer; **~ ideas/pretensions** Ideen/Angeberei eines Emporkömmlings/von Emporkömmlingen

'upstate *(Amer.)* **1.** *adj.* **~ New York** nördlicher Teil des Staates New York; **an ~ town** eine Stadt im nördlichen Teil des Staates. **2.** *adv.* **live ~:** im nördlichen Teil des Staates leben; **go/travel ~:** in den nördlichen Teil des Staates fahren/reisen

upstream 1. [-'-] *adv.* flußaufwärts. **2.** ['--] *adj.* flußaufwärts gelegen ‹*Ort*›

'up-stroke *n.* **a)** *(in writing)* Aufstrich, *der;* **b)** *(Mech.: of piston)* Aufwärtshub, *der*

'upsurge *n.* Aufwallen, *das (geh.);* **she felt an ~ of tenderness** sie fühlte Zärtlichkeit in sich *(Dat.)* aufwallen

'upswept *adj.* hochgekämmt ‹*Haar*›; hochgezogen ‹*Linie, Auspuffrohr*›

'upswing *n. (of pendulum, arms)* Aufwärtsschwung, *der; (fig., esp. Commerc.)* Aufschwung, *der*

upsy-daisy ['ʌpsɪdeɪzɪ] *int.* hoppla

'uptake *n.* **be quick/slow on** *or* **in the ~** *(coll.)* schnell begreifen/schwer von Begriff sein *(ugs.)*

uptight [ʌp'taɪt, 'ʌptaɪt] *adj. (coll.)* **a)** *(tense)* nervös **(about** wegen); *(touchy, angry)* sauer *(ugs.)* **(about** wegen); **make sb. ~:** jmdm. auf die Nerven gehen *od.* fallen *(ugs.);* **b)** *(Amer.: rigidly conventional)* **[very] ~:** stockkonservativ *(ugs.)*

'uptime *n. (Computing)* Betriebszeit, *die*

up to 'date *pred. adj.* **be/keep [very] ~:** auf dem [aller]neusten Stand sein/bleiben; [ganz] up to date sein/bleiben; **keep/bring sth. ~:** etw. auf dem neusten Stand halten/auf den neusten Stand bringen; **bring sb. ~ with all the news** jmdn. auf den neusten Stand der Informationen bringen

up-to-'date *attrib. adj. (current)* aktuell; *(modern)* modern; aktuell ‹*Mode*›

up-to-the-'minute *adj.* hochaktuell

'upturn *n.* Aufschwung, *der* **(in** *Gen.*); **an ~ in prices** ein Anstieg der Preise

'upturned *adj.* **a)** *(upside-down)* umgedreht; **b)** *(turned upwards)* hochgeschlagen ‹*Rand, Krempe*›; nach oben gerichtet ‹*Gesicht, Auge*›; **~ nose** Stupsnase, *die*

upward ['ʌpwəd] **1.** *adj.* nach oben *nachgestellt;* nach oben gerichtet; **~ movement/trend** *(lit. or fig.)* Aufwärtsbewegung, *die*/-trend, *der;* **~ gradient** *or* **slope** Steigung, *die;* **move in an ~ direction** sich aufwärts *od.* nach oben bewegen; **~ mobility**

(in social status) sozialer Aufstieg. **2.** *adv.* aufwärts ‹*sich bewegen*›; nach oben ‹*sehen, gehen*›; *see also* **face up[ward]**

upwardly ['ʌpwədlɪ] *adv.* aufwärts; nach oben; ~ **mobile** *(in social status)* sozial aufsteigend ‹*Person*›; **be ~ mobile** sozial aufsteigen

upwards ['ʌpwədz] *adv.* **a)** *see* **upward 2; b)** ~ **of** mehr als; über; **they cost £200 and ~:** sie kosten 200 Pfund und darüber

upwind 1. *adv.* [ʌp'wɪnd] gegen den Wind. **2.** ['ʌpwɪnd] *adj.* **approach from the ~ side** sich mit dem Wind im Rücken nähern

Urals ['jʊərlz] *pr. n. pl.* Ural, *der*

uranium [jʊə'reɪnɪəm] *n. (Chem.)* Uran, *das*

Uranus ['jʊərənəs, jʊə'reɪnəs] *pr. n. (Astron.)* Uranus, *der*

urban ['ɜ:bn] *adj.* städtisch; Stadt‹*gebiet, -bevölkerung, -planung, -sanierung, -guerilla*›; ~ **life** Leben in der Stadt; ~ **sociology** Stadtsoziologie, *die;* ~ **decay** Verslumung, *die;* ~ **district** *(Brit. Hist.) Gruppe von Städten, die von einem gewählten Rat verwaltet wurde;* ~ **sprawl** unkontrollierte Ausdehnung städtischer Randgebiete; *see also* **renewal b**

urbane [ɜ:'beɪn] *adj.*, **urbanely** [ɜ:'beɪnlɪ] *adv.* weltmännisch

urbanise *see* **urbanize**

urbanity [ɜ:'bænɪtɪ] *n.* Urbanität, *die;* **urbanities** weltmännische Umgangsform[en]

urbanize ['ɜ:bənaɪz] *v.t.* urbanisieren ‹*Land*›; verstädtern [lassen] ‹*Landbevölkerung*›; **become ~d** verstädtern

urchin ['ɜ:tʃɪn] *n.* **a)** *(child)* Range, *die; (boy)* Strolch, *der; see also* **street urchin; b)** *see* **sea-urchin**

Urdu ['ʊədu:, 'ɜ:du:] *n.* **1.** *adj.* Urdu-; *see also* **English 1. 2.** Urdu, *das; see also* **English 2 a**

urea [jʊə'rɪə, 'jʊərɪə] *n. (Chem.)* Harnstoff, *der*

ureter [jʊə'ri:tə] *n. (Anat.)* Harnleiter, *der;* Ureter, *der (fachspr.)*

urethra [jʊə'ri:θrə] *n., pl.* **~e** [jʊə'ri:θri:] *or* **~s** *(Anat.)* Harnröhre, *die;* Urethra, *die (fachspr.)*

urge [ɜ:dʒ] **1.** *v.t.* **a)** ~ **sb. to do sth.** jmdn. drängen, etw. zu tun; ~ **sb. to sth.** jmdn. zu etw. drängen; **we ~d him to reconsider** wir rieten ihm dringend, es sich *(Dat.)* noch einmal zu überlegen; ~ **sth. [on *or* upon sb.]** [jmdn.] zu etw. drängen; ~ **caution/vigilance/patience [on *or* upon sb.]** [jmdn.] zur Vorsicht/Wachsamkeit/Geduld mahnen; ~ **on *or* upon sb. the need for sth./for doing sth.** jmdm. die Notwendigkeit einer Sache/die Notwendigkeit, etw. zu tun, ans Herz legen; **the leaders ~ acceptance of the offer** die Führer dringen auf Annahme des Angebotes; ~ **that sth. [should] be done** darauf dringen, daß etw. getan wird; **b)** *(drive on)* [an]treiben; ~ **forward/onward** vorwärts treiben; *(fig.)* treiben; **c)** *(put forward)* vorbringen; ~ **sb.'s youth/inexperience/the difficulty of sth.** jmds. Jugend/Unerfahrenheit/die Schwierigkeit einer Sache zu bedenken geben; ~ **sth. on sb.** jmdm. etw. eindringlich nahelegen. **2.** *n.* Trieb, *der;* **have/feel an/the ~ to do sth.** den Drang verspüren, etw. zu tun; **resist the ~ to do sth.** dem [inneren] Drang widerstehen, etw. zu tun

~ **'on** *v.t.* antreiben; *(hasten)* vorantreiben; *(encourage)* anfeuern; **~d on by hunger/ambition** vom Hunger/Ehrgeiz getrieben

urgency ['ɜ:dʒənsɪ] *n., no pl.* Dringlichkeit, *die; (earnestness)* Eindringlichkeit, *die;* **there is no ~:** es eilt nicht *od.* ist nicht dringend; **be of the utmost ~:** äußerst dringend sein; **a matter of great ~:** eine sehr dringende Angelegenheit

urgent ['ɜ:dʒənt] *adj.* **a)** *(pressing)* dringend; *(to be dealt with immediately)* eilig; **be in ~ need of sth.** etw. dringend brauchen; **give ~ consideration to sth.** etw. vordringlich in Betracht ziehen; **matters/problems of an ~ nature** dringende Angelegenheiten/drängende Probleme; **on ~ business** in dringenden Geschäften; **at sb.'s ~ request** auf jmds. Drängen; **it is ~:** es eilt; **it is ~ that sb. should do sth. *or* does sth.** jmd. muß dringend etw. tun; **if it's ~, call a doctor** in dringenden Fällen den Arzt rufen; **b)** *(earnest and persistent)* eindringlich; **be ~ in one's demand/plea for sth.** etw. dringend fordern/eindringlich um etw. bitten

urgently ['ɜ:dʒəntlɪ] *adv.* **a)** *(pressingly)* dringend; *(without delay)* eilig; **he had to leave ~ for London on business** er mußte in dringenden Geschäften nach London abreisen; **b)** *(earnestly)* eindringlich

uric ['jʊərɪk] *adj.* ~ **acid** *(Chem.)* Harnsäure, *die*

urinal [jʊə'raɪnl, 'jʊərɪnl] *n. (fitting)* Urinal, *das;* **[public] ~:** [öffentliche] Herrentoilette; Pissoir, *das*

urinary ['jʊərɪnərɪ] *adj.* Harn-; ~ **diseases** Erkrankungen der Harnwege

urinate ['jʊərɪneɪt] *v.t.* urinieren

urination [jʊərɪ'neɪʃn] *n.* Urinieren, *das*

urine ['jʊərɪn] *n.* Urin, *der;* Harn, *der; attrib.* Urin-; Harn-

urn [ɜ:n] *n.* **a) tea/coffee ~:** Tee-/Kaffeemaschine, *die;* **b)** *(vessel)* Urne, *die*

urogenital [jʊərə'dʒenɪtl] *adj. (Anat., Med.)* urogenital; ~ **disease/infection** Erkrankung/Infektion des Urogenitaltraktes

urologist [jʊər'ɒlədʒɪst] *n.* Urologe, *der*/Urologin, *die*

urology [jʊə'rɒlədʒɪ] *n.* Urologie, *die*

Ursa ['ɜ:sə] *pr. n. (Astron.)* ~ **Major/Minor** Großer/Kleiner Bär

Uruguay ['jʊərəgwaɪ] *pr. n.* Uruguay *(das)*

Uruguayan [jʊərə'gwaɪən] **1.** *adj.* uruguayisch; **sb. is ~:** jmd. ist Uruguayer/Uruguayerin. **2.** *n.* Uruguayer, *der*/Uruguayerin, *die*

US *abbr.* **United States** USA; *attrib.* US-

us [əs, *stressed* ʌs] *pron.* **a)** uns; **it's us** wir sind's *(ugs.)*; **one of us** einer von uns; **b)** *(sl.: me)* **give us a clue/kiss!** gib mir 'nen Tip/Kuß! *(ugs.)*

u/s *abbr.* **unserviceable** unbrauchbar

USA *abbr.* **United States of America** USA; *attrib.* der USA *nachgestellt*

usable ['ju:zəbl] *adj.* brauchbar; gebräuchlich ‹*Wort*›; **this nail is no longer ~:** dieser Nagel ist nicht mehr zu gebrauchen

USAF *abbr.* **United States Air Force** Luftwaffe der Vereinigten Staaten

usage ['ju:zɪdʒ, 'ju:sɪdʒ] *n.* **a)** Brauch, *der;* Gepflogenheit, *die (geh.)*; **~s and customs** Sitten und Gebräuche; **commercial ~:** Handelsbrauch, *der;* **sanctified by ~:** durch Herkommen Recht geworden; **a custom sanctified by ~:** eine Sitte, die zum Gewohnheitsrecht geworden ist; **be in common ~:** allgemein gebräuchlich sein; **b)** *(Ling.: use of language)* Sprachgebrauch, *der;* ~ **[of a word]** Verwendung [eines Wortes]; **in American** *etc.* **~:** im amerikanischen *usw.* Sprachgebrauch; **in common ~:** im allgemeinen Sprachgebrauch; allgemein gebräuchlich ‹*Wort usw.*›; **c)** *(treatment)* Behandlung, *die;* **have rough ~:** schlecht behandelt werden

usance ['ju:zəns] *n. (Commerc.)* Zahlungsfrist für ausländische Wechsel

use 1. [ju:s] *n.* **a)** Gebrauch, *der; (of dictionary, calculator, room)* Benutzung, *die; (of word, expression; of pesticide, garlic)* Verwendung, *die; (of name, title)* Führung, *die; (of alcohol, drugs)* Konsum, *der;* **the ~ of brutal means/methods/of trickery** die Anwendung brutaler Mittel/Methoden/von Tricks; **the ~ of troops/tear-gas/arms/violence** der Einsatz von Truppen/Tränengas/der Waffengebrauch/die Gewaltanwendung; **achieve sth. by the ~ of deception** etw. durch Täuschung erreichen; **constant/rough ~:** dauernder Gebrauch/schlechte Behandlung; **[not] be in ~:** [nicht] in Gebrauch sein; **be no longer in ~:** nicht mehr verwendet werden; **be in daily** *etc.* **~:** täglich *usw.* in Gebrauch *od.* Benutzung sein; **the word is [not] in everyday ~:** das Wort ist [nicht] allgemein gebräuchlich; **bring into ~:** in Gebrauch nehmen; **come into ~:** in Gebrauch kommen; **[be] out of ~:** außer Betrieb [sein]; **go/fall/pass/drop out of ~:** außer Gebrauch kommen; **instructions/directions for ~:** Gebrauchsanweisung, *die;* **ready for [immediate] ~:** [sofort] gebrauchsfertig; **instruments for ~ by doctors/dentists** Instrumente für den ärztlichen/zahnärztlichen Bedarf; **batteries for ~ in *or* with watches** Batterien [speziell] für Armbanduhren; **a course for ~ in schools** ein Kurs für die Schule *od.* zur Verwendung im Schulunterricht; **for the ~ of sb.** für jmdn.; **for personal/private ~:** für den persönlichen Gebrauch/den Privatgebrauch; **these computers are intended for home/office ~:** diese Computer sind Homecomputer/sind für den Einsatz im Büro gedacht; **for external ~ only** nur zur äußerlichen Anwendung; **for ~ in an emergency/only in case of fire** für den Notfall/nur bei Feuer zu benutzen; **with ~:** durch den Gebrauch; **with constant ~:** durch dauernden Gebrauch; **with careful** *etc.* **~:** bei sorgsamer *usw.* Behandlung; **make ~ of sb./sth.** jmdn./etw. gebrauchen/*(exploit)* ausnutzen; **a good cook will make ~ of any left-overs** ein guter Koch/eine gute Köchin verwendet alle Reste; **make ~ of one's connections/friendship with sb.** von seinen Verbindungen/seiner Freundschaft zu jmdm. Gebrauch machen; **make the best ~ of sth./it** das Beste aus etw./daraus machen; **make good ~ of, turn *or* put to good ~:** gut nutzen ‹*Zeit, Talent, Geld*›; **put sth. to ~:** etw. verwenden; **put sth. to effective ~:** etw. wirkungsvoll einsetzen; **b)** *(utility, usefulness)* Nutzen, *der;* **these tools/clothes will be of ~ to sb.** dieses Werkzeug wird/diese Kleider werden für jmdn. von Nutzen sein; **is it of [any] ~?** ist das [irgendwie] zu gebrauchen *od.* von Nutzen?; **these addresses might be of ~ to you** diese Adressen könnten für dich von Nutzen sein *od.* kannst du vielleicht gebrauchen; **be of ~ to the enemy/police** für den Feind/die Polizei von Nutzen sein; **can I be of any ~ to you?** kann ich dir irgendwie helfen?; **it is of [great] ~ for this work** man kann es für diese Arbeit [sehr gut] brauchen; **I did not find the book of any practical ~:** das Buch hatte für mich keinen praktischen Nutzen; **be [of] no ~ [to sb.]** [jmdm.] nichts nützen; **I wouldn't be [of] any ~ to you** ich könnte dir kein bißchen helfen; **he is [of] no ~ in a crisis/as a manager** er ist in einer Krise/als Manager zu nichts nütze *od. (ugs.)* nicht zu gebrauchen; **it's no ~ [doing that]** es hat keinen Zweck *od.* Sinn[, das zu tun]; **it wouldn't be any ~:** es hätte [überhaupt] keinen Sinn *od.* Zweck; **I have an umbrella at home. – That's no/not much ~ [to us] now** Ich habe einen Schirm zu Hause. – Das nützt [uns] jetzt nichts/nicht viel; **you're/that's a fat lot of ~** *(coll. iron.)* du bist ja eine schöne Hilfe/davon haben wir aber was *(ugs. iron.)*; **what's the ~ of that/of doing that?** was nützt das/was nützt es, das zu tun?; **what's the ~?** was nützt es?; **oh well, what's the ~!** ach, was soll's schon! *(ugs.)*; **c)** *(purpose)* Verwendung, *die;* Verwendungszweck, *der;* **a tool with many ~s** ein vielfältig zu verwendendes Werkzeug; **have its/one's ~s** seinen Nutzen haben; **have/find a ~ for sth./sb.** für etw./jmdn. Verwendung haben/finden; **have no/not much ~ for sth./sb.** etw./jmdn. nicht/kaum brauchen; *(fig.: dislike)* nichts/nicht viel für etw./jmdn. übrig haben; **have no further ~ for sb./sth.** für jmdn. keine

Verwendung mehr haben/etw. nicht mehr brauchen; **put sth. to a good/a new ~:** etw. sinnvoll/auf neu[artig]e Weise verwenden; **d)** *(right or power of using)* **have the ~ of sth.** etw. benutzen können; **[have the] ~ of kitchen and bathroom** Küchen- und Badbenutzung [haben]; **can I have the ~ of your car while you are away?** kann ich deinen Wagen benutzen, während du weg bist?; **let sb. have** *or* **allow sb.** *or* **give sb. the ~ of sth.** jmdn. etw. benutzen lassen; **he has [the] full/only restricted ~ of his arm** er kann seinen Arm uneingeschränkt/nur eingeschränkt benutzen; **he has lost the ~ of an arm/eye** er kann einen Arm nicht mehr benutzen/er kann auf einem Auge nichts mehr sehen; **e)** *(custom, familiarity)* **~s and customs** Sitten und Gebräuche; **long ~ has reconciled me to it** die Gewohnheit hat mich damit versöhnt; **f)** *(Eccl.: ritual)* Ritual, *das;* **g)** *(Law)* Nießbrauch, *der.* **2.** [ju:z] *v. t.* **a)** benutzen; nutzen ‹*Gelegenheit*›; anwenden ‹*Gewalt*›; einsetzen ‹*Tränengas, Wasserwerfer*›; in Anspruch nehmen ‹*Firma, Agentur, Agenten, Dienstleistung*›; nutzen ‹*Zeit, Gelegenheit, Talent, Erfahrung*›; führen ‹*Namen, Titel*›; **do you know how to ~ this tool?** kannst du mit diesem Werkzeug umgehen?; **the swindler/actor ~s the name John Smith** der Betrüger/Schauspieler nennt sich John Smith; **anything you say may be ~d in evidence** was Sie sagen, kann vor Gericht verwendet werden; **~ sb.'s name [as a reference]** sich [als Empfehlung] auf jmdn. berufen; **I could ~ the money/a drink/the door could ~ a coat of paint** *(coll.)* ich könnte das Geld brauchen/einen Drink vertragen *(ugs.)*/die Tür könnte einen Anstrich brauchen *od. (ugs.)* vertragen; **~ one's money [to do sth.]** sein Geld verwenden[, um etw. zu tun]; **the money is there to be ~d** das Geld ist da, um ausgegeben zu werden; **~ one's time to do sth.** seine Zeit dazu nutzen, etw. zu tun; **b)** *(consume as material)* verwenden; **~ gas/oil for heating** mit Gas/Öl heizen; **the camera ~s 35 mm film** für die Kamera braucht man einen 35-mm-Film; **'~ sparingly'** „sparsam verwenden!"; **c)** *(finish consuming)* verbrauchen; **she has ~d the last of the milk** sie hat den letzten Rest Milch aufgebraucht; **d)** *(take habitually)* **~ drugs/heroin** *etc.* Drogen/Heroin *usw.* nehmen; **~ alcohol** Alkohol trinken *od.* konsumieren; **e)** *(employ in speaking or writing)* benutzen; gebrauchen; verwenden; **~ strong language** Kraftausdrücke gebrauchen; **f)** *(exercise, apply)* Gebrauch machen von ‹*Autorität, Einfluß, Können, Urteilsvermögen, Menschenverstand*›; **~ diplomacy/tact [in one's dealings** *etc.* **with sb.]** [bei jmdm.] diplomatisch vorgehen/[zu jmdm.] taktvoll sein; **~ care** vorsichtig sein; **~ care in doing sth.** etw. vorsichtig tun; **he ~d all his strength** er wandte seine ganze Kraft auf; **~ a method/system/tactics** eine Methode anwenden/nach einem [bestimmten] System/einer [bestimmten] Taktik vorgehen; **~ other/stronger methods/tactics** andere/härtere Methoden/eine andere/härtere Taktik anwenden; **~ every means at one's disposal to do sth.** mit allen einem zur Verfügung stehenden Mitteln versuchen, etw. zu tun; **g)** *(take advantage of)* **~ sb.** jmdn. ausnutzen; **don't let them ~ you** laß dich nicht [von ihnen] ausnutzen; **h)** *(treat)* behandeln; **~ sb./sth. well/badly** jmdn./etw. gut/schlecht behandeln; **i) ~d to** ['ju:st tə] *(formerly)* **I ~d to live in London/work in a factory** früher habe ich in London gelebt/in einer Fabrik gearbeitet; **he ~d to be very shy** er war früher sehr schüchtern; **before I started taking these vitamins, I ~d to be tired all the time** bevor ich anfing, diese Vitamine zu nehmen, war ich immer müde; **my mother always ~d to say ...:** meine Mutter hat immer gesagt *od.* pflegte zu sagen ...; **life ~d to be much more leisurely [than it is now]** früher war das Leben viel beschaulicher [als heute]; **this ~d to be my room** das war [früher] mein Zimmer; **it ~d to be thought ...:** früher glaubte man ...; **things aren't what they ~d to be** es ist nichts mehr so wie früher; **he smokes much more than he ~d to** er raucht viel mehr als früher; **there ~d to be ...:** es gab früher/früher gab es ...; **I ~d not** *or* **I did not ~** *or (coll.)* **I didn't ~** *or (coll.)* **I ~[d]n't to smoke** früher habe ich nicht geraucht; **didn't he ~ to work here?** *(coll.)* hat er nicht früher hier gearbeitet?; **~[d]n't there to be a shop here?** *(dated coll.)* war hier nicht früher ein Laden?; **Does he smoke? He ~d not to** *or (coll.)* **He didn't ~ to** Raucht er? Früher hat er das nicht getan; **there never ~d to be all this violence** diese ganze Gewalttätigkeit gab es früher nicht

~ 'up *v. t.* aufbrauchen; verwenden ‹*[Essens]reste*›; verbrauchen, erschöpfen ‹*Kraft, Geld, Energie*›; **~ up a dozen eggs** ein Dutzend Eier verbrauchen

used 1. *adj.* **a)** [ju:zd] *(no longer new)* gebraucht; benutzt ‹*Handtuch, Teller*›; gestempelt ‹*Briefmarke*›; **~ car** Gebrauchtwagen, *der;* **~-car salesman** Gebrauchtwagenhändler, *der;* **b)** [ju:st] *(accustomed)* **~ to sth.** [an] etw. *(Akk.)* gewöhnt; etw. gewohnt; **be/get ~ to sb./sth.** [an] jmdn./etw. gewöhnt sein/sich an jmdn./etw. gewöhnen; **I'm not ~ to this kind of treatment** *or* **to being treated in this way** ich bin eine solche Behandlung nicht gewohnt; ich bin es nicht gewohnt, so behandelt zu werden; **you'll soon be ~ to it** du wirst dich bald *od.* schnell daran gewöhnen; **[not] be ~ to sb. doing sth./to having sb. do sth.** [es] [nicht] gewohnt sein, daß jmd. etw. tut; **she was ~ to getting up early** sie war daran gewöhnt, früh aufzustehen; **she is not ~ to drinking alcohol** sie ist es nicht gewöhnt, Alkohol zu trinken. **2.** [ju:st] *see* **use 2 i**

useful ['ju:sfl] *adj.* **a)** nützlich; praktisch ‹*Werkzeug, Gerät, Auto*›; brauchbar ‹*Rat, Idee, Wörterbuch*›; hilfreich ‹*Gespräch, Rat, Idee, Wörterbuch*›; **~ life** *(of machine etc.)* Lebensdauer, *die;* **~ load** Nutzlast, *die;* **he is a ~ person to know** es ist nützlich, ihn zu kennen; **English is the most ~ language** mit Englisch kommt man am weitesten; **this is ~ to know** das ist gut zu wissen; **this would be ~ to have** es wäre gut *od.* nützlich, wenn man das hätte; **be ~ to sb.** jmdm. *od.* für jmdn. nützlich sein; jmdm. nützen; **the guide was most ~ for finding our way about** der Führer hat uns sehr geholfen, uns zurechtzufinden; **the chest would be very ~ for storing my books** die Truhe würde sich sehr gut zum Lagern meiner Bücher eignen; **it would be ~ to have a tap in the garden** es wäre praktisch, wenn im Garten ein Wasserhahn wäre; **sb. finds sth. ~:** etw. nützt jmdm.; **those screws will come in ~ for my woodwork** diese Schrauben werde ich noch gut zum Schreinern brauchen können; **make oneself ~:** sich nützlich machen; **serve no ~ purpose** zu nichts nütze sein; **b)** *(coll.: worthwhile)* ordentlich *(ugs.);* ansehnlich ‹*Betrag, Stück, Arbeit*›; beachtlich ‹*Vorsprung*›; wertvoll ‹*Mitglied einer Mannschaft*›

usefully ['ju:sfəlɪ] *adv.* **a course one might ~ follow** ein Kurs, den zu verfolgen nützlich sein könnte; **a book you could ~ read** ein Buch, von dessen Lektüre du profitieren könntest; **is there anything we can ~ do?** können wir uns irgendwie nützlich machen?; **~ spend an evening doing sth.** einen Abend sinnvoll damit verbringen, etw. zu tun; **everybody should be ~ employed [in some work]** jeder sollte eine nützliche Beschäftigung haben

usefulness ['ju:sflnɪs] *n., no pl.* Nützlichkeit, *die;* Brauchbarkeit, *die;* **limit the ~ of sth.** den Nutzen einer Sache einschränken; **have outlived one's/its ~:** zu nichts mehr nütze *od.* zu gebrauchen sein

useless ['ju:slɪs] *adj.* unbrauchbar ‹*Werkzeug, Gerät, Rat, Vorschlag, Idee, Material*›; nutzlos ‹*Wissen, Information, Fakten, Protest, Anstrengung, Kampf*›; vergeblich ‹*Anstrengung, Maßnahme, Kampf, Klage*›; zwecklos ‹*Widerstand, Protest, Argumentieren*›; **be ~ to sb.** jmdm. nichts nützen; **credit cards are ~ there** Kreditkarten nützen einem dort nichts; **be ~ at sth.** zu etw. nicht zu gebrauchen sein; **oh, you're ~!** du bist doch zu nichts zu gebrauchen! *(ugs.);* **feel ~:** sich nutzlos fühlen; **it's ~ to do that** *or* **doing that** es hat keinen Zweck *od.* Sinn, das zu tun; **he's worse than ~:** er ist zu gar nichts nütze

uselessly ['ju:slɪslɪ] *adv.* unnütz, sinnlos ‹*verschwenden, aufwenden*›; vergeblich ‹*kämpfen, protestieren*›; **throw away one's life ~:** sein Leben sinnlos wegwerfen

uselessness ['ju:slɪsnɪs] *n., no pl. (of tool, device, advice, information, suggestion, material)* Unbrauchbarkeit, *die; (of protest, effort, struggle)* Vergeblichkeit, *die; (of action, measure, war)* Sinnlosigkeit, *die; (of resistance)* Zwecklosigkeit, *die*

user ['ju:zə(r)] *n.* Benutzer, *der*/Benutzerin, *die; (of drugs, alcohol)* Konsument, *der*/Konsumentin, *die; (of coal, electricity, gas)* Verbraucher, *der*/Verbraucherin, *die; (of telephone)* Kunde, *der*/Kundin, *die*

'user-friendly *adj.* benutzerfreundlich; **explain sth. in ~ terms** etw. allgemeinverständlich erklären

usher ['ʌʃə(r)] **1.** *n. (in court)* Gerichtsdiener, *der; (at cinema, theatre, church)* Platzanweiser, *der*/-anweiserin, *die.* **2.** *v. t.* führen; geleiten *(geh.);* **~ sb. into sb.'s presence** jmdn. vor jmdn. führen *od. (geh.)* geleiten; **~ sb. to his seat** jmdn. an seinen Platz führen

~ 'in *v. t.* **~ sb. in** jmdn. hineinführen *od. (geh.)* -geleiten; **~ sth. in** *(fig.)* etw. einläuten

~ 'out *v. t.* hinausführen *od. (geh.)* -geleiten

usherette [ʌʃə'ret] *n.* Platzanweiserin, *die*

USN *abbr.* **United States Navy** Marine der Vereinigten Staaten

USS *abbr.* **United States Ship** *Schiff aus den Vereinigten Staaten*

USSR *abbr. (Hist.)* **Union of Soviet Socialist Republics** UdSSR, *die; attrib.* der UdSSR *nachgestellt*

usual ['ju:ʒʊəl] *adj.* üblich; **be ~ for sb.** bei jmdm. üblich sein; **it is ~ for sb. to do sth.** es ist üblich, daß jmd. etw. tut; **[no] better/bigger/more** *etc.* **than ~:** [nicht] besser/größer/mehr *usw.* als gewöhnlich *od.* üblich; **as [is] ~,** *(coll.)* **as per ~:** wie üblich; **as is ~ in such cases** wie in solchen Fällen üblich; **the/your ~, sir?** wie immer, der Herr? *(ugs.); see also* **business b**

usually ['ju:ʒʊəlɪ] *adv.* gewöhnlich; normalerweise; **more than ~ tired** *etc.* noch müder *usw.* als üblich; ganz ungewöhnlich müde *usw.;* **this time we were more than ~ careful** diesmal waren wir noch vorsichtiger als sonst

usufruct ['ju:zjʊfrʌkt] *n. (Law)* Nutznießung, *die*

usurer ['ju:ʒərə(r)] *n.* Wucherer, *der*/Wucherin, *die*

usurp [ju:'zɜ:p] *v. t.* sich *(Dat.)* widerrechtlich aneignen ‹*Titel, Recht, Position*›; usurpieren *(geh.)* ‹*Macht, Thron*›; **~ the leading role in the enterprise** die wichtigste Rolle im Unternehmen an sich *(Akk.)* reißen; **the man who had ~d his place in his wife's affections** der Mann, der jetzt im Herzen seiner Frau seinen Platz erobert hatte

usurpation [ju:zə'peɪʃn] *n. (of right, title,*

position, authority) widerrechtliche Aneignung; *(of power, the throne)* Usurpation, *die (geh.)*

usurper [ju:'zɜ:pə(r)] *n.* Usurpator, *der (geh.)*

usury ['ju:ʒərɪ] *n.* Wucher, *der;* **practise ~:** Wucher treiben

utensil [ju:'tensɪl] *n.* Utensil, *das;* **writing ~s** Schreibutensilien

uterine ['ju:təraɪn, 'ju:tərɪn] *adj. (Anat., Med.)* Gebärmutter-; uterin *(fachspr.)*

uterus ['ju:tərəs] *n., pl.* **uteri** ['ju:təraɪ] *(Anat.)* Gebärmutter, *die;* Uterus, *der (fachspr.)*

utilisable, utilisation, utilise *see* **utiliz-**

utilitarian [ju:tɪlɪ'teərɪən] **1.** *adj.* **a)** *(functional)* funktionell; utilitär ‹*Ziele*›; **b)** *(Philos.)* utilitaristisch. **2.** *n. (Philos.)* Utilitarist, *der;* Utilitarier, *der*

utilitarianism [ju:tɪlɪ'teərɪənɪzm] *n. (Philos.)* Utilitarismus, *der*

utility [ju:'tɪlɪtɪ] **1.** *n.* **a)** Nutzen, *der;* **of great ~:** sehr nutzbringend; von großem Nutzen; **total/marginal ~** *(Econ.)* Gesamt-/Grenznutzen, *der;* **b)** *see* **public utility. 2.** *adj.* Vielzweck-; *(functional)* funktionell; **~ goods/furniture** Gebrauchsgüter/-möbel

utility: ~ man *n. (Amer.)* **a)** *(Theatre)* Chargenspieler, *der*/-spielerin, *die;* **b)** *(Sport)* vielseitig einsetzbarer Spieler; **c)** *(odd-job man)* Mädchen für alles *(ugs.)*; **~ program** *n. (Computing)* Dienstprogramm, *das;* **~ room** *n. Raum, in den [größere] Haushaltsgeräte (z. B. Waschmaschine) installiert sind;* **~ routine** *n. (Computing) see* **~ program**

utilizable ['ju:tɪlaɪzəbl] *adj.* nutzbar

utilization [ju:tɪlaɪ'zeɪʃn] *n.* Nutzung, *die*

utilize ['ju:tɪlaɪz] *v. t.* nutzen

utmost ['ʌtməʊst] **1.** *adj.* äußerst...; tiefst... ‹*Verachtung*›; höchst... ‹*Verehrung, Gefahr*›; größt... ‹*Höflichkeit, Eleganz, Einfachheit, Geschwindigkeit*›; **of [the] ~ importance** von äußerster Wichtigkeit; **with the ~ caution** mit größter *od.* äußerster Vorsicht; **with the ~ ease/care/reluctance** mit größter Leichtigkeit/äußerster Sorgfalt/größter Zurückhaltung; **to the ~ degree** bis zum äußersten. **2.** *n.* Äußerste, *das;* **do** *or* **try one's ~ to do sth.** mit allen Mitteln versuchen, etw. zu tun; **to the ~:** bis zum Äußersten; **to the ~ of one's ability/strength** so gut man eben kann/mit aller Kraft; **try sb.'s patience to the ~:** jmds. Geduld auf das äußerste strapazieren

Utopia [ju:'təʊpɪə] *n. (place)* Utopia *(das)*; *(impractical scheme)* Utopie, *die*

Utopian [ju:'təʊpɪən] **1.** *adj.* utopisch. **2.** *n.* Utopist, *der*/Utopistin, *die*

¹utter ['ʌtə(r)] *attrib. adj.* vollkommen, völlig ‹*Chaos, Verwirrung, Fehlschlag, Ablehnung, Friede, Einsamkeit, Unsinn*›; ungeheuer ‹*Elend, Dummheit, Freude, Glück, Schönheit*›; größt... ‹*Freude, Vergnügen*›; **be in ~ despair/misery** völlig verzweifelt/niedergeschlagen sein; **be an ~ mystery** völlig rätselhaft sein; **be an ~ stranger to sb.** jmdm. völlig fremd sein; **~ fool** Vollidiot, *der (ugs.)*

²utter ['ʌtə(r)] *v. t.* **a)** von sich geben ‹*Schrei, Seufzer, Ächzen*›; **b)** *(say)* sagen ‹*Wahrheit, Wort*›; schwören ‹*Eid*›; äußern ‹*Drohung*›; zum Ausdruck bringen ‹*Gefühle*›; **the last words he ~ed** die letzten Worte, die er sprach; **she never ~ed a sound** sie gab keinen Ton von sich; **this word/her name must not be ~ed in his presence** dieses Wort/ihr Name darf in seiner Gegenwart nicht gesagt *od.* ausgesprochen werden; **c) ~ a libel** *(Law)* eine Verleumdung verbreiten

utterance ['ʌtərəns] *n.* **a) ~ of a sigh/groan** ein Seufzen/Stöhnen; **give ~ to sth.** etw. zum Ausdruck bringen; einer Sache Ausdruck verleihen; **b)** *(spoken words)* Worte *Pl.; (Ling.)* [sprachliche] Äußerung; *(sentence)* Satz, *der;* **c)** *(power of speech)* Sprache, *die*

utterly ['ʌtəlɪ] *adv.* völlig; vollkommen; restlos ‹*elend, deprimiert*›; absolut ‹*entzückend, bezaubernd*›; hinreißend ‹*schön*›; äußerst ‹*dumm, lächerlich*›; aus tiefster Seele ‹*verabscheuen, ablehnen, bereuen*›

uttermost ['ʌtəməʊst] **a)** *see* **utmost 1, 2; b)** *(most distant)* entferntest...; **to the ~ ends of the earth** bis ans äußerste Ende der Welt

'U-turn *n.* Wende [um 180°]; **the driver/car made a ~:** der Fahrer/Wagen wendete; **'No ~s'** „Wenden verboten"; **make a ~ [on sth.]** *(fig.)* eine Kehrtwendung [bei etw.] vollziehen *od.* machen

UV *abbr.* **ultraviolet** UV

uvula ['ju:vjʊlə] *n., pl.* **~e** ['ju:vjʊli:] *(Anat.)* Zäpfchen, *das;* Uvula, *die (fachspr.)*

uvular ['ju:vjʊlə(r)] *adj. (Anat., Ling.)* uvular; **the ~ 'r'** das Zäpfchen-R

V

¹V, ¹v [vi:] *n., pl.* **Vs** *or* **V's a)** *(letter)* V, v, *das;* **b)** *(Roman numeral)* V; **c)** *(V-shaped thing)* V, *das;* **d) V1/V2** *(Hist.)* V1/V2, *die. See also* **V-neck; V-necked; V-sign**

²V, ²v *abbr.* **volt[s]** V

v. *abbr.* **a)** ['vɜ:səs, vi:] **versus** gg.; **b) very; c) verse**

vac [væk] *n. (Brit. Univ. coll.)* Semesterferien *Pl.;* **the long ~:** die Sommersemesterferien

vacancy ['veɪkənsɪ] *n.* **a)** *(job)* freie Stelle; **fill a ~:** eine [freie] Stelle besetzen; **have a ~ [on one's staff]** eine freie Stelle *od.* Stelle frei haben; **'vacancies'** *(notice outside factory)* „Stellen frei"; *(in newspaper)* „Stellenangebote"; **b)** *(unoccupied room)* freies Zimmer; **have a ~:** ein Zimmer frei haben; **'vacancies'** „Zimmer frei"; **'no vacancies'** „belegt"; **c)** *no pl. (of look, mind, etc.)* Leere, *die*

vacant ['veɪkənt] *adj.* **a)** *(not occupied)* frei; **'~'** *(on door of toilet)* „frei"; **'situations ~'** „Stellenangebote"; **a house with ~ possession** ein bezugsfertiges Haus; **b)** *(mentally inactive)* leer

vacantly ['veɪkəntlɪ] *adv.* leer; **stare/gaze ~ at sb./into space** jmdn. mit leerem Blick anstarren/abwesend ins Leere starren

vacate [və'keɪt] *v. t.* räumen ‹*Gebäude, Büro, Wohnung*›; aufgeben ‹*Stelle, Amt*›; niederlegen ‹*Amt*›

vacation [və'keɪʃn] **1.** *n.* **a)** *(Brit. Law, Univ.: recess)* Ferien *Pl.;* **b)** *(Amer.) see* **holiday 1 b; c)** *(vacating) (of a room, building)* Räumung, *die; (of a post)* Aufgeben, *das; (of an office)* Niederlegen, *das.* **2.** *v. i. (Amer.)* **~ [at/in a place]** [an einem Ort] Urlaub machen

vacationer [və'keɪʃənə(r)], **vacationist** [və'keɪʃənɪst] *ns. (Amer.)* Urlauber, *der*/Urlauberin, *die*

vaccinate ['væksɪneɪt] *v. t. (Med.)* impfen

vaccination [væksɪ'neɪʃn] *n. (Med.)* Impfung, *die; attrib.* Impf-; **have a ~:** geimpft werden

vaccine ['væksi:n, 'væksɪn] *n.* Impfstoff, *der*

vacillate ['væsɪleɪt] *v. i. (lit. or fig.)* schwanken; **~ about doing sth.** schwanken, ob man etw. tun soll oder nicht; **~ on sth.** bezüglich einer Sache schwanken

vacillating ['væsɪleɪtɪŋ] *adj.* schwankend

vacillation [væsɪ'leɪʃn] *n.* Schwanken, *das*

vacua *pl. of* **vacuum 1 a**

vacuity [və'kju:ɪtɪ] *n.* Leere, *die; (of book, play)* Geistlosigkeit, *die*

vacuous ['vækjʊəs] *adj.* leer; geistlos, nichtssagend ‹*Buch, Theaterstück, Bemerkung*›

vacuously ['vækjʊəslɪ] *adv.* leer

vacuum ['vækjʊəm] **1.** *n.* **a)** *pl.* **vacua** ['vækjʊə] *or* **~s** *(Phys.; also fig.)* Vakuum, *das;* **perfect/partial ~:** ideales Vakuum/Unterdruck, *der; (fig.)* **her death has left a ~ in our lives** ihr Tod hat in unserem Leben eine Lücke hinterlassen; **live in a ~** *(lit. or fig.)* im luftleeren Raum leben; **b)** *pl.* **~s** *(coll.: ~ cleaner)* Sauger, *der (ugs.).* **2.** *v. t.& i.* [staub]saugen

vacuum: ~ bottle *(Amer.) see* **~ flask; ~ brake** *n. (Railw.)* Unterdruckbremse, *die;* **~-clean** *v. t. & i.* [staub]saugen; **~ cleaner** *n.* Staubsauger, *der;* **~ flask** *n. (Brit.)* Thermosflasche, *die;* **~-gauge** *n. (Physics)* Vakuummeter, *das;* **~-packed** *adj.* vakuumverpackt; **~ pump** *n.* Vakuumpumpe, *die;* **~ tube** *n. (Electronics)* Vakuumröhre, *die;* Elektronenröhre, *die*

vade-mecum [veɪdɪ'mi:kəm, vɑ:dɪ'meɪkəm] *n.* Vademekum, *das (geh.)*

vagabond ['vægəbɒnd] **1.** *n.* Landstreicher, *der*/Landstreicherin, *die (oft abwertend);* Vagabund, *der*/Vagabundin, *die (veralt.).* **2.** *adj.* umherziehend, vagabundierend ‹*Mensch, Stamm*›; **~ life** Vagabundenleben, *das*

vagaries ['veɪgərɪz] *n. pl. (lit. or fig.)* Launen *Pl.;* **the ~ of life/politics** die Wechselfälle des Lebens/der Politik

vagina [və'dʒaɪnə] *n., pl.* **~e** [və'dʒaɪni:] *or* **~s** *(Anat.)* Scheide, *die;* Vagina, *die (fachspr.)*

vaginal [və'dʒaɪnl] *adj.* Scheiden-; vaginal *(fachspr.)*

vagrancy ['veɪgrənsɪ] *n., no indef. art., no pl.* Landstreicherei, *die; (in cities)* Stadtstreicherei, *die*

vagrant ['veɪgrənt] **1.** *adj.* vagabundierend; **~ life** Vagabundenleben, *das.* **2.** *n.* Landstreicher, *der*/Landstreicherin, *die (oft abwertend); (in cities)* Stadtstreicher, *der*/Stadtstreicherin, *die*

vague [veɪg] *adj.* vage; verschwommen, undeutlich ‹*Form, Umriß*›; undefinierbar ‹*Farbe*›; *(absent-minded)* geistesabwesend; *(inattentive)* unkonzentriert; **describe sth. in ~ terms** etw. vage beschreiben; **not have the ~st idea** *or* **notion** nicht die blasseste *od.* leiseste Ahnung haben; **be ~ about sth.** etw. nur vag[e] andeuten; *(in understanding)* nur eine vage Vorstellung von etw. haben

vaguely ['veɪglɪ] *adv.* vage; ungefähr ‹*wissen*›; entfernt ‹*bekannt sein, erinnern an*›; schwach ‹*sich erinnern*›; **he was ~ alarmed/sad/disappointed** er war irgendwie beunruhigt/traurig/enttäuscht; **look/taste ~ like sth.** entfernt aussehen/schmecken wie etw.; **understand sth. ~:** etw. in etwa verstehen; **she looked at me ~** *(uncertainly)* sie sah mich unsicher an; *(absent-mindedly)* sie sah mich zerstreut an

vagueness ['veɪgnɪs] *n., no pl.* Vagheit, *die; (of outline, shape)* Verschwommenheit, *die; (of policy)* Unbestimmtheit, *die; (absent-mindedness)* Zerstreutheit, *die; (uncertainty)* Unsicherheit, *die*

vain [veɪn] *adj.* **a)** *(conceited)* eitel; **be ~ about sth.** sich *(Dat.)* auf etw. *(Akk.)* viel einbilden; **b)** *(useless)* leer ‹*Drohung, Versprechen, Worte, Reden*›; eitel *(geh.)*

⟨*Triumph, Vergnügungen*⟩; vergeblich ⟨*Hoffnung, Erwartung, Versuch*⟩; **in ~**: vergeblich; vergebens; *see also* **take 1 e**
vainglorious [veɪn'glɔ:rɪəs] *adj.* *(formal/literary)* prahlerisch ⟨*Reden, Angebereien*⟩; dünkelhaft ⟨*Person, Auftreten*⟩
vainly ['veɪnlɪ] *adv.* **a)** *(uselessly)* vergebens; vergeblich; **b)** *(in a conceited way)* eitel; angeberisch
Valais ['væleɪ] *pr. n.* Wallis, *das*
valance ['væləns] *n.* Volant, *der*
vale [veɪl] *n.* *(arch./poet.)* Tal, *das;* **this ~ of tears** *(fig.)* dies Jammertal
valediction [vælɪ'dɪkʃn] *n.* *(act)* Abschied, *der;* *(words)* Abschiedsgruß, *der*
valedictory [vælɪ'dɪktərɪ] *adj.* Abschieds-; **~ remarks** Bemerkungen zum Abschied; **~ speech/address** *(Amer.)* Abschiedsrede/-ansprache, *die*
valence ['veɪləns] *(esp. Amer.)*, **valency** ['veɪlənsɪ] *ns.* *(Chem., Phys.)* *(unit)* Wertigkeit, *die;* Valenz, *die (fachspr.);* **~ bond** kovalente Bindung
valentine ['væləntaɪn] *n.* **a)** *jmd., dem man am Valentinstag einen Gruß schickt;* **b) ~ [card]** Grußkarte zum Valentinstag; **c) St. V~'s Day** Valentinstag, *der*
valerian [və'lɪərɪən] *n.* *(Bot., Pharm.)* Baldrian, *der*
valet ['vælɪt, 'væleɪ] *n.* **a)** Kammerdiener, *der;* **b)** *(hotel employee) für den Reinigungsservice zuständiger Hotelangestellter;* **~ service** Reinigungs[- und Reparatur]service
'valet parking *n.* Parkservice, *der*
valetudinarian [vælɪtju:dɪ'neərɪən] **1.** *adj.* **a)** *(sickly)* kränkelnd; **b)** *(anxious about health)* hypochondrisch. **2.** *n.* **a)** *(sickly person)* kränklicher Mensch; **b)** *(hypochondriac)* Hypochonder, *der*
Valhalla [væl'hælə] *n.* *(Mythol.)* Walhall[a], *das*
valiant ['væljənt] *adj.* tapfer; kühn *(geh.);* **he made a ~ effort to disguise his disappointment** er versuchte tapfer, seine Enttäuschung zu verbergen; **it was a ~ try/effort** es war ein tapferer Versuch
valiantly ['væljəntlɪ] *adv.* tapfer; kühn *(geh.)*
valid ['vælɪd] *adj.* **a)** *(legally acceptable)* gültig; berechtigt ⟨*Anspruch*⟩; *(having legal force)* rechtskräftig; bindend ⟨*Vertrag*⟩; **b)** *(justifiable)* stichhaltig ⟨*Argument, Einwand, Theorie*⟩; triftig ⟨*Grund*⟩; zuverlässig ⟨*Methode*⟩; begründet ⟨*Entschuldigung, Einwand*⟩
validate ['vælɪdeɪt] *v.t.* rechtskräftig machen ⟨*Anspruch, Vertrag, Testament*⟩; bestätigen, beweisen ⟨*Hypothese, Theorie*⟩; für gültig erklären ⟨*Wahl*⟩
validation [vælɪ'deɪʃn] *n.* *(of claim, contract, etc.)* Gültigkeitserklärung, *die;* *(of theory, hypothesis)* Bestätigung, *die*
validity [və'lɪdɪtɪ] *n., no pl.* **a)** *(of ticket, document)* Gültigkeit, *die;* *(of claim, contract, marriage, etc.)* Rechtsgültigkeit, *die;* **~ check** *(Computing)* Gültigkeitskontrolle, *die;* **b)** *(of argument, excuse, objection, theory)* Stichhaltigkeit, *die;* *(of reason)* Triftigkeit, *die;* *(of method)* Zuverlässigkeit, *die*
validly ['vælɪdlɪ] *adv.* *(lawfully)* rechtsgültig; *(properly)* überzeugend; mit [vollem] Recht ⟨*beanspruchen, geltend machen*⟩
valise [və'li:z] *n.* *(esp. Amer.)* Reisetasche, *die*
Valkyrie [væl'kɪərɪ, 'vælkɪrɪ] *n.* *(Mythol.)* Walküre, *die*
valley ['vælɪ] *n.* **a)** *(lit. or fig.)* Tal, *das;* **~ bottom** Talsohle, *die;* **b)** *(of roof)* [Dach]kehle, *die;* **U-shaped/V-shaped ~**: Trogtal, *das*/Kerbtal, *das (Geog.);* *see also* **hanging valley; rift valley; river valley**
valor *(Amer.)* *see* **valour**
valorous ['vælərəs] *adj.* *(literary)* tapfer
valour ['vælə(r)] *n.* Tapferkeit, *die;* **fight with ~**: tapfer kämpfen; *see also* **discretion a**
valuable ['væljʊəbl] **1.** *adj.* wertvoll; **be ~ to sb.** für jmdn. wertvoll sein. **2.** *n., in pl.* Wertgegenstände; Wertsachen
valuation [væljʊ'eɪʃn] *n.* Schätzung, *die;* **make/get a ~ of sth.** etw. schätzen/etw. schätzen lassen; **what is the ~?** wie hoch ist der Schätzwert?; **set a high/low** *etc.* **~ on sth.** den Schätzwert für etw. hoch/niedrig *usw.* ansetzen; **accept sb. at his/her own ~**: jmds. Selbsteinschätzung teilen *od.* akzeptieren
value ['vælju:] **1.** *n.* **a)** Wert, *der;* **be of great/little/some/no ~ [to sb.]** [für jmdn.] von großem/geringem/einigem/keinerlei Nutzen sein; **they are taught too few things of real ~ for their future** man lehrt sie zu wenig, was ihnen in der Zukunft wirklich nützen wird; **information that is of great ~ to scientists** Informationen, die für Wissenschaftler überaus wertvoll *od.* von großem Wert sind; **this drug has been of some ~ in the treatment of cancer** dieses Medikament hat sich bei der Behandlung von Krebskranken als bedingt wirksam erwiesen; **be of [no] practical ~ to sb.** für jmdn. von [keinerlei] praktischem Nutzen sein; **set** *or* **put a high/low ~ on sth.** etw. hoch/niedrig einschätzen; **attach great ~ to sth.** einer Sache *(Dat.)* große Wichtigkeit beimessen; **b)** *(monetary worth)* Wert, *der;* **it has a ~ of one pound** es ist ein Pfund wert; **what would be the ~ of it?** was ist es wohl wert?; **know the ~ of sth.** wissen, was etw. wert ist; **sth./nothing of ~**: etw./nichts Wertvolles; **an object of ~**: ein Wertgegenstand; **items of great/little/no ~**: sehr wertvolle/nicht sonderlich wertvolle/wertlose Gegenstände; **be of great/little/no** *etc.* **~**: viel/wenig/nichts *usw.* wert sein; **increase** *or* **go up in ~**: an Wert gewinnen; wertvoller werden; **decline** *or* **decrease** *or* **fall** *or* **go down in ~**: an Wert verlieren; **an increase/decrease in ~**: ein Wertzuwachs/-verlust; **put a ~ on sth.** den Wert einer Sache schätzen; **sth. to the ~ of ...**: etw. im Werte von ...; **c)** *(equivalent)* Wert, *der;* **he offered less than the ~ of the house** er bot weniger, als das Haus wert war; **be good/poor etc. ~ [for money]** seinen Preis wert/nicht wert sein; **customers want [good] ~ for money** Kunden wollen für ihr Geld auch etwas bekommen; **£5 for a tiny steak – do you call that good ~?** 5 Pfund für ein winziges Steak – nennen Sie das reell?; **this handbook is excellent/very good ~ at £10** dieses Handbuch ist die 10 Pfund, die es kostet, unbedingt wert; **get [good]/poor ~ [for money]** etwas/nicht viel für sein Geld bekommen; **give sb. poor ~ for money** jmdm. für sein Geld nicht viel bieten; **d)** *in pl.* *(principles)* Werte; Wertvorstellungen; **e)** *(rank, significance)* Wert, *der;* **[time] ~** *(Mus.)* Zeitwert, *der;* **~ of a colour, colour ~**: Farbwert, *der;* **f)** *(numerical quantity)* *(Math.)* [Zahlen]wert, *der;* *(Phys.)* Größe, *die;* **give x** *or* **let x have the ~ 3** x sei 3. **2.** *v.t.* **a)** *(appreciate)* schätzen; **his work has been ~d highly by experts** seine Arbeit hat bei Experten hohe Anerkennung gefunden; **if you ~ your life** wenn dir dein Leben lieb ist; **b)** *(put price on)* schätzen, taxieren **(at** auf + *Akk.*)
value added 'tax *n.* *(Brit.)* Mehrwertsteuer, *die*
valued ['vælju:d] *adj.* geschätzt ⟨*Freund, Kollege, Kunde*⟩; wertvoll ⟨*Rat, Hilfe*⟩; **thank you for your ~ order** *(Commerc. dated)* wir bedanken uns für Ihren geschätzten Auftrag *(veralt.)*
'value-judgement *n.* Werturteil, *das*
valueless ['væljʊlɪs] *adj.* wertlos
valuer ['væljʊə(r)] *n.* Schätzer, *der;* Taxator, *der*
valve [vælv] *n.* **a)** Ventil, *das;* *see also* **safety-valve; b)** *(Anat., Zool.)* Klappe, *die;* **c)** *(Brit.: thermionic ~)* Röhre, *die*
vamoose [və'mu:s] *v.i.* *(Amer. sl.)* verduften *(ugs.)*
[1]**vamp** [væmp] **1.** *n.* *(of shoe)* Oberleder, *das.* **2.** *v.t.* *(Mus.)* improvisieren ⟨*Begleitung*⟩; improvisierend begleiten ⟨*Melodie*⟩. **3.** *v.i.* *(Mus.)* improvisierend begleiten
~ 'up *v.t.* *(put together)* zusammenschustern *(ugs. abwertend);* *(renovate)* aufmöbeln *(ugs.)*
[2]**vamp** *n.* *(woman)* Vamp, *der*
vampire ['væmpaɪə(r)] *n.* Vampir, *der*
'vampire bat *n.* *(Zool.)* Vampir, *der*
[1]**van** [væn] *n.* **a) [delivery] ~**: Lieferwagen, *der;* **baker's/laundry ~**: Bäckerauto, *das*/Wäschereiauto, *das (ugs.);* **b)** *(Brit. Railw.)* [geschlossener] Wagen; **c)** *(Brit.: caravan)* **[camping] ~**: Wohnwagen, *der*
[2]**van** *n.* *(foremost part)* Vorhut, *die;* *(fig.: leaders of movement, opinion)* Vorkämpfer *Pl.;* **be in the ~ of a movement/the attack** zu den Vorkämpfern einer Bewegung gehören/den Angriff anführen
[3]**van** *n.* *(Tennis)* Vorteil, *der*
vanadium [və'neɪdɪəm] *n.* *(Chem.)* Vanadium, *das*
vandal ['vændl] *n.* **a)** Rowdy, *der;* **~-proof** unzerstörbar; **b)** *(Hist.)* **V~**: Wandale, *der;* Vandale, *der*
vandalise *see* **vandalize**
vandalism ['vændəlɪzm] *n.* Wandalismus, *der;* Vandalismus, *der;* **act of ~** *(destruction)* [mutwillige] Zerstörung; *(damaging)* [mutwillige] Beschädigung; **to demolish this beautiful old building would be an act of ~**: dieses schöne alte Gebäude abzureißen wäre Wandalismus
vandalize ['vændəlaɪz] *v.t.* *(destroy)* [mutwillig] zerstören; *(damage)* [mutwillig] beschädigen
Vandyke [væn'daɪk]: **~ beard** *n.* Henriquatre, *der;* **~ brown** *n.* Van-Dyck-Braun, *das*
vane [veɪn] *n.* **a)** *(weathercock)* *(in shape of arrow)* Wetterfahne, *die;* *(in shape of cock)* Wetterhahn, *der;* **b)** *(blade)* Blatt, *das;* *(of windmill)* Flügel, *der;* *(of watermill, turbine)* Schaufel, *die*
vanguard ['vængɑ:d] *n.* **a)** *(Mil., Navy)* Vorhut, *die;* **b)** *(fig.: leaders)* Vorreiter; *(of literary, artistic, etc. movement)* Avantgarde, *die;* **in the ~ of [public] opinion** der öffentlichen Meinung stets um eine Nasenlänge voraus; **be in the ~ of progress/a movement** an der Spitze des Fortschritts/einer Bewegung stehen
vanilla [və'nɪlə] **1.** *n.* **a)** Vanille, *die;* **b)** *see* **vanilla-pod. 2.** *adj.* Vanille-
va'nilla-pod *n.* *(Bot.)* Vanilleschote, *die*
vanish ['vænɪʃ] *v.i.* **a)** *(disappear; coll.: leave quickly)* verschwinden; **~ from sight [behind sth.]** [hinter etw. *(Dat.)*] verschwinden; **~ into the distance** in der Ferne verschwinden; **the smile ~ed from his face** das Lächeln verschwand aus seinem Gesicht; **~ off the face of the earth** von der Erde verschwinden; *see also* **thin 1 d; b)** *(cease to exist)* ⟨*Gebäude:*⟩ verschwinden; ⟨*Sitte, Tradition:*⟩ untergehen; ⟨*Art, Gattung:*⟩ aussterben; ⟨*Zweifel, Bedenken:*⟩ sich auflösen; ⟨*Angst:*⟩ sich legen; ⟨*Hoffnung, Chancen:*⟩ schwinden; **c)** *(Math.)* Null werden
vanishing ['vænɪʃɪŋ]: **~ act** *see* **~ trick; ~-cream** *n.* Feuchtigkeitscreme, *die;* Vanishing-Creme, *die (fachspr.);* **~-point** *n.* *(Art, Math.)* Fluchtpunkt, *der;* *(fig.)* Nullpunkt, *der;* **dwindle to ~-point** auf den Nullpunkt zurückgehen; **~ trick** *n.* Zaubertrick *(bei dem etwas verschwindet);* **do** *or* **perform a ~ trick with sth.** etw. wegzaubern *od.* verschwinden lassen; **he did his [usual] ~ trick** *(fig. coll.)* er verdrückte sich [wie üblich] *(ugs.)*
vanity ['vænɪtɪ] *n.* **a)** *(pride, conceit)* Eitelkeit, *die;* **b)** *(worthlessness)* Nichtigkeit, *die;*

Eitelkeit, *die (geh.)*; *(of efforts, hopes, dreams)* Vergeblichkeit, *die*; **all is ~**: alles ist eitel *(geh.)*; **c)** *(worthless thing)* **these things are vanities** das ist alles bloß Tand *(geh.)*; **d)** *(Amer.: dressing-table)* Frisierkommode, *die*

vanity: ~ **bag** *n.* Kosmetiktäschchen, *das*; ~ **case** *n.* Kosmetikkoffer, *der*; **V~ 'Fair** *n.* Jahrmarkt der Eitelkeiten

vanquish ['væŋkwɪʃ] *v. t. (literary)* bezwingen

vantage ['vɑ:ntɪdʒ] *n.* **a)** *(position of superiority)* Vorteil, *der*; **b)** *see* **advantage c**

vantage: ~**-ground** *n. (Mil.)* günstige [Ausgangs]position; ~**-point** *n.* Aussichtspunkt, *der*; *(fig.)* **his ~-point as director** der Überblick, den er als Direktor hat/hatte

vapid ['væpɪd] *adj.* schal ‹*Geschmack, Vergnügen*›; leer ‹*Gerede, Umgangsformen*›; geistlos ‹*Gerede, Vortrag, Bemerkung, Ergüsse*›; unverbindlich ‹*Lächeln*›; nichtssagend ‹*Erscheinung, Person*›

vapidity [və'pɪdɪtɪ] *n.* Schalheit, *die*; *(of conversation, remark, book, speech, etc.)* Geistlosigkeit, *die*; **the ~ of his smile/expression** sein unverbindliches Lächeln/sein nichtssagender Gesichtsausdruck

vapor *(Amer.) see* **vapour**

vaporize (vaporise) ['veɪpəraɪz] *v. t. & i.* verdampfen

vaporizer ['veɪpəraɪzə(r)] *n.* **a)** Verdampfer, *der*; **b)** *(atomizer)* Zerstäuber, *der*

vapour ['veɪpə(r)] *n. (Brit.)* **a)** Dampf, *der*; *(mist)* Dunst, *der*; **~s** *(rising from the ground)* Schwaden; *(arch.: melancholy)* Schwermut, *die*; **b)** *(Phys.)* Dampf, *der*; **turn into [a] ~**: zu Dampf werden; **c)** *(Med.: inhalant)* Dampf, *der*

vapour: ~ **bath** *n. (Med.)* Dampfbad, *das*; ~ **trail** *n. (Aeronaut.)* Kondensstreifen, *der*

variability [veərɪə'bɪlɪtɪ] *n.* **a)** *(ability to be altered)* Variabilität, *die*; **b)** *(inconsistency, changeability)* Unbeständigkeit, *die*; *(of health, balance)* Labilität, *die*

variable ['veərɪəbl] **1.** *adj.* **a)** *(alterable)* veränderbar; **be ~**: verändert werden können; ‹*Gerät*:› eingestellt werden können; **b)** *(inconsistent, changeable)* unbeständig ‹*Wetter, Wind, Strömung, Stimmung, Leistung*›; wechselhaft ‹*Wetter, Launen, Schicksal, Qualität, Erfolg*›; labil ‹*Gesundheit, Gleichgewicht*›; schwankend ‹*Kosten*›; **How's your health? – Oh, ~**: Wie geht's gesundheitlich? – Mal so, mal so; **with ~ success** mit wechselndem Erfolg; **c)** *(Astron., Math.)* veränderlich; variabel. **2.** *n.* **a)** *(Math.)* Variable, *die*; Veränderliche, *die*; **b)** *(Astron.)* Veränderliche, *der*; **c)** *(fig.: varying factor)* veränderliche Größe; Variable, *die*

'variable star *n. (Astron.)* Veränderliche, *der*

variably ['veərɪəblɪ] *adv.* variabel; beliebig, stufenlos ‹*anpaßbar, einstellbar*›; unterschiedlich ‹*stark*›

variance ['veərɪəns] *n.* **a)** Uneinigkeit, *die*; *(between philosophies, ideologies)* Nichtübereinstimmung, *die*; **be at ~**: [sich *(Dat.)*] uneinig sein (**on** über + *Akk.*); ‹*Theorien, Meinungen, Philosophien usw.*:› nicht übereinstimmen; **be at ~ with sb./sth.** [sich *(Dat.)*] mit jmdm. uneinig sein/mit etw. nicht übereinstimmen; **this development has set the team at ~**: diese Entwicklung hat zu Meinungsverschiedenheiten im Team geführt; **b)** *(Statistics)* Varianz, *die*

variant ['veərɪənt] **1.** *attrib. adj.* verschieden; **three ~ spellings/readings** drei [verschiedene] Schreibweisen/Lesarten; ~ **type** *(Biol.)* Variante, *die.* **2.** *n.* Variante, *die*

variation [veərɪ'eɪʃn] *n.* **a)** *(varying)* Veränderung, *die*; *(in style, diet, routine, programme)* Abwechslung, *die*; *(difference)* Unterschied, *der*; **be subject to ~** ‹*Preise*:› Schwankungen unterworfen sein; ‹*Regeln*:› Änderungen unterworfen sein; **~s in weather conditions** unbeständiges Wetter; **no ~ of the rules is allowed** die Regeln dürfen nicht geändert werden; ~ **in price/colour** Preis-/Farbunterschied, *der*; **the ~s of light and shade** der Wechsel von Licht und Schatten; **~s from earlier editions** Unterschiede im Vergleich zu früheren Ausgaben; **b)** *(variant)* Variante, *die* (**of, on** *Gen.*); **c)** *(Mus.)* Variation, *die*; **~s on a theme** Variationen über ein Thema; **d)** *(Biol., Ballet, Math.)* Variation, *die*

variational [veərɪ'eɪʃənl] *attrib. adj. (Mus., Math.)* Variations-

varicoloured (*Brit.*; *Amer.*: **varicolored**) ['veərɪkʌləd] *adj.* bunt

varicose vein [værɪkəʊs 'veɪn] *n. (Med.)* Krampfader, *die*

varied ['veərɪd] *adj. (differing)* unterschiedlich; vielfältig ‹*Freuden*›; *(marked by variation)* abwechslungsreich ‹*Land, Diät, Leben*›; vielseitig ‹*Arbeit, Stil, Sammlung*›; vielgestaltig ‹*Landschaft*›; bunt ‹*Mischung*›; buntgemischt ‹*Gruppe*›

variegate ['veərɪgeɪt] *v. t.* [farblich] auflockern

variegated ['veərɪgeɪtɪd] *adj. (Bot.)* mehrfarbig; panaschiert ‹*grüne Blätter*›

variegation [veərɪ'geɪʃn] *n.* **a)** Buntheit, *die*; **b)** *(Bot.)* Mehrfarbigkeit, *die*; *(on green leaves)* Panaschierung, *die*

variety [və'raɪətɪ] *n.* **a)** *(diversity)* Vielfältigkeit, *die*; *(in style, diet, routine, programme)* Abwechslung, *die*; **add** *or* **give ~ to sth.** etw. abwechslungsreicher gestalten; **for the sake of ~**: zur Abwechslung; **~ is the spice of life** *(prov.)* Abwechslung macht Freude; **b)** *(assortment)* Auswahl, *die* (**of** an + *Dat.*, von); **in a ~ of sizes/ways** in verschiedenen Größen/auf verschiedene Art; **for a ~ of reasons** aus verschiedenen Gründen; **a wide ~ of birds/flowers** viele verschiedene Vogelarten/Blumen; **c)** *(Theatre)* Varieté, *das*; *(Telev.) (varietéähnliche)* Shows; **d)** *(form)* Art, *die*; *(of fruit, vegetable, cigarette)* Sorte, *die*; **rare varieties of butterflies** seltene Exemplare von Schmetterlingen; **e)** *(Biol.) (subspecies)* Unterart, *die*; Varietät, *die (fachspr.)*; *(cultivated)* Züchtung, *die*; Rasse, *die*

variety: ~ **act** *n.* Varietényummer, *die*; ~ **artist** *n. (Theatre)* Varietékünstler, *der*/-künstlerin, *die*; *(Telev.)* Showstar, *der*; ~ **entertainment** *see* ~ **show**; ~ **meat** *n. (Amer.)* Innereien [und eßbare Schlachtabfälle]; ~ **show** *n.* **a)** *(Theatre)* Varieté, *das*; *(single performance)* Varietévorstellung, *die*; **b)** *(Telev.) (varietéähnliche)* Show; ~ **store** *n. (Amer.)* Kramladen, *der*; ~ **theatre** *n.* Varieté[theater], *das*

variola [və'raɪələ] *n. (Med.)* Pocken *Pl.*

various ['veərɪəs] *adj.* **a)** *pred. (different)* verschieden; unterschiedlich; *(manifold)* vielfältig; **the causes of this are many and ~**: es gibt hierfür viele verschiedene Ursachen; **b)** *attrib. (several)* verschiedene; **at ~ times** mehrere Male

variously ['veərɪəslɪ] *adv.* unterschiedlich; **she has been ~ described as a liar and a paragon of virtue** sie ist mal als Lügnerin, mal als Muster an Tugend beschrieben worden

varlet ['vɑ:lɪt] *n. (Hist.: page)* Bursche, *der*; *(arch./joc.: rascal)* Schurke, *der (abwertend)*

varmint ['vɑ:mɪnt] *n. (Amer./dial.) (animal)* Biest, *das (ugs.)*; *(person)* Halunke, *der*; *(child)* Racker, *der (fam.)*

varnish ['vɑ:nɪʃ] **1.** *n.* **a)** Lack, *der*; *(transparent)* Lasur, *die*; **clear ~**: Klarlack, *der*; *see also* **nail varnish**; **b)** *(Art)* Firnis, *der*; **c)** *(Ceramics)* Glasur, *die*; **d)** *(glossiness, lit. or fig.)* Glanz, *der*; **high ~**: Hochglanz, *der.* **2.** *v. t.* **a)** lackieren; *(with transparent ~)* lasieren; **b)** *(Art)* firnissen; **c)** *(Ceramics)* glasieren; **d)** *(fig.: gloss over)* beschönigen; übertünchen ‹*Fehler, Verbrechen, Laster*›

varsity ['vɑ:sɪtɪ] *n. (Brit. Univ. coll.)* Uni, *die (ugs.)*

vary ['veərɪ] **1.** *v. t.* verändern; ändern ‹*Bestimmungen, Programm, Methode, Verhalten, Stil, Route, Kurs*›; abwandeln ‹*Rezept, Muster*›; *(add variety to)* abwechslungsreicher gestalten; ~ **one's diet** sich abwechslungsreich ernähren; ~ **one's tone to suit the situation** seinen Ton der Situation anpassen. **2.** *v. i.* **a)** *(become different)* sich ändern; ‹*Preis, Nachfrage, Qualität, Temperatur*:› schwanken; *(be different)* unterschiedlich sein; *(between extremes)* wechseln; *(deviate)* abweichen; **Are you busy? – Oh, it varies** Hast du viel zu tun? – Ach, ganz unterschiedlich; ~ **between A and B** *or* **from A to B** zwischen A *(Dat.)* und B *(Dat.)* schwanken; ~ **in weight/size/shape/colour** *etc.* im Gewicht/in der Größe/Form/Farbe variieren (**from ... to ...**: zwischen ... + *Dat.* und ... + *Dat.*); **these items ~ in size/price** diese Artikel gibt es in verschiedenen Größen/Preislagen; **they ~ in their opinions/in character** sie haben unterschiedliche Meinungen/sind charakterlich verschieden; **the two books ~ on this matter** dieser Sachverhalt wird in den beiden Büchern unterschiedlich beurteilt; **opinions ~ on this point** die Meinungen gehen in diesem Punkt auseinander; **b)** ~ **[directly]/inversely as sth.** sich direkt proportional/umgekehrt proportional zu etw. ändern

varying ['veərɪɪŋ] *attrib. adj.* wechselnd; wechselhaft, veränderlich ‹*Wetter*›; *(different)* unterschiedlich; **in ~ colours** in verschiedenen Farben; **continually ~ prices** ständig schwankende Preise; **at ~ prices** zu unterschiedlichen Preisen

vascular ['væskjʊlə(r)] *adj. (Anat., Bot.)* vaskulär; *(Anat., Med.)* Gefäß-; ~ **plant** Gefäßpflanze, *die*

vase [vɑ:z] *n.* Vase, *die*

vasectomize [və'sektəmaɪz] *v. t. (Med.)* [durch Vasektomie] sterilisieren

vasectomy [və'sektəmɪ] *n. (Med.)* Vasektomie, *die*

Vaseline, (P) ['væsəli:n] *n., no pl., no indef. art.* Vaseline, *die*

vassal ['væsl] *n.* **a)** *(Hist.)* Vasall, *der*/Vasallin, *die*; **b)** *(rhet.: slave)* Knecht, *der*/Magd, *die (fig.)*

vast [vɑ:st] *adj.* **a)** *(huge)* riesig; weit ‹*Fläche, Meer, Kontinent, Welt[raum]*›; gewaltig ‹*Wolken[massen]*›; umfangreich ‹*Sammlung*›; **b)** *(coll.: great)* enorm; Riesen‹*menge, -summe, -fehler*›; unermeßlich ‹*Reichtümer*›; überwältigend ‹*Mehrheit*›; **a ~ amount of time/money/a ~ number of things** enorm viel Zeit/viel Geld/viele Dinge; **~ sums of money** enorm hohe Summen; **to a ~ extent** größtenteils; **he has done a ~ amount of work in this field** er hat auf diesem Gebiet enorm viel geleistet

vastly ['vɑ:stlɪ] *adv. (coll.)* enorm; weitaus ‹*besser*›; weit ‹*überlegen, unterlegen*›; überaus, äußerst ‹*wichtig, dankbar*›; in hohem Maße ‹*beeinflussen*›; gewaltig ‹*sich verbessern, irren, überschätzen, unterschätzen*›; köstlich ‹*sich amüsieren*›; **in a ~ different sense** in einem völlig anderen Sinn

vastness ['vɑ:stnɪs] *n., no pl.* **a)** *(hugeness)* [immense *od.* ungeheure] Weite; *(of building, crowd, army)* [immense *od.* ungeheure] Größe; *(of collection etc.)* [riesiger] Umfang; **b)** *(greatness)* [immenses] Ausmaß; *(of knowledge)* [immenser] Umfang

VAT [vi:eɪ'ti:, væt] *abbr.* **value added tax** MwSt.

vat [væt] *n.* Bottich, *der*; *(in paper-making)* Bütte, *die*

Vatican ['vætɪkən] *pr. n.* Vatikan, *der*

Vatican: ~ **'City** *pr. n.* Vatikanstadt, *die*; ~ **'Council** *n. (Hist.)* Vatikanisches Konzil

Vaud [vəʊ] *pr. n.* Waadt, *die*

vaudeville ['vɔ:dəvɪl, 'vəʊdəvɪl] *n. (Theatre,*

Mus.) Varieté, *das;* **appear in ~:** im Varieté auftreten; **a ~ show** eine Varietévorstellung
¹vault [vɔ:lt, vɒlt] **1.** *n.* **a)** *(Archit.)* Gewölbe, *das;* **the ~ of heaven** *(poet.)* das Himmelsgewölbe *(dichter.);* **b)** *(cellar)* [Gewölbe]keller, *der; see also* **wine-vault; c)** *(in bank)* Tresorraum, *der;* **d)** *(tomb)* Gruft, *die.* **2.** *v. t.* *(Archit.)* wölben
²vault 1. *v. i.* *(leap)* sich schwingen; *(Gymnastics)* springen. **2.** *v. t.* sich schwingen über (+ *Akk.*); *(Gymnastics)* springen über (+ *Akk.*). **3.** *n.* Sprung, *der;* **straddle/squat/side ~:** Grätsche, *die*/Hocke, *die*/Flanke, *die*
vaulted ['vɔ:ltɪd, 'vɒltɪd] *adj.* *(Archit.)* gewölbt
vaulting ['vɔ:ltɪŋ, 'vɒltɪŋ] *n.* *(Archit.)* Wölbung, *die*
'vaulting-horse *n.* *(Gymnastics)* [Sprung]pferd, *das*
vaunt [vɔ:nt] *(literary) v. t.* sich brüsten mit; **~ that ...:** sich [damit] brüsten, daß ...; **~ sth. as sth.** etw. als etw. preisen; **much ~ed** vielgepriesen *od.* -gerühmt
VC *abbr.* **Victoria Cross**
VD [vi:'di:] *n.* Geschlechtskrankheit, *die;* **get** *or* **catch ~:** sich *(Dat.)* eine Geschlechtskrankheit zuziehen
VDU *abbr.* **visual display unit**
've [v] *(coll.)* = **have**
veal [vi:l] *n., no pl.* Kalb[fleisch], *das; attrib.* Kalbs-; **roast ~:** Kalbsbraten, *der*
veal 'cutlet *n.* Kalbsschnitzel, *das*
vector ['vektə(r)] *n.* *(Math., Aeronaut., Biol.)* Vektor, *der*
vectorial [vek'tɔ:rɪəl] *adj.* *(Math.)* vektoriell
Veda ['veɪdə, 'vi:də] *n.* *(Hindu Relig.)* Weda, *der*
VE day [vi:'i: deɪ] *n.* der 8. Mai 1945; der Tag des Sieges [im 2. Weltkrieg]
¹veer [vɪə(r)] **1.** *v. i.* **a)** ⟨*Wind:*⟩ [sich] im Uhrzeigersinn drehen; ⟨*Schiff, Flugzeug:*⟩ abdrehen; ⟨*Auto:*⟩ ausscheren; **~ to the north** ⟨*Wind:*⟩ auf Nord drehen; ⟨*Schiff:*⟩ nach Norden drehen; **~ off course/off the road** *(unintentionally)* vom Kurs/von der Straße abkommen; *(intentionally)* vom Kurs abdrehen/von der Straße abbiegen; **the driver had to ~ to avoid the sheep** der Fahrer mußte das Steuer herumreißen, um dem Schaf auszuweichen; **~ out of control** außer Kontrolle geraten und ins Schleudern kommen; **go ~ing along the road** in Schlangenlinien die Straße entlangfahren; **~ gently/sharply to the right** ⟨*Straße:*⟩ eine leichte/scharfe Rechtskurve machen; **b)** *(fig.: change)* schwanken **(from ... to ...:** zwischen ... + *Dat.* und ... + *Dat.*); **~ from one extreme to the other** ⟨*Person:*⟩ von einem Extrem ins andere fallen; ⟨*Stimmung:*⟩ von einem Extrem ins andere umschlagen; **~ to the left** *(in politics)* auf Linkskurs umschwenken. **2.** *v. t.* **a) ~ the car to the left/right** den Wagen nach links/rechts herumreißen; **b)** *(fig.)* abbringen. **3.** *n.* Ausscheren, *das;* **the driver struggled to control the ~:** der Fahrer versuchte, den Wagen noch abzufangen
~ a'way, ~ 'off *v. i.* **a)** ⟨*Schiff, Flugzeug:*⟩ abdrehen; ⟨*Auto:*⟩ ausscheren; ⟨*Fahrer, Straße:*⟩ abbiegen; **b)** *(fig.: change)* **~ away** *or* **off from sth.** von etw. abkommen
~ 'round 1. *v. i.* drehen; *(through 180°)* wenden; **skid and ~ [right] round** ins Schleudern geraten und sich um die eigene Achse drehen. **2.** *v. t.* wenden
²veer *v. i.* *(Naut.)* **~ and haul** fieren und holen
veg [vedʒ] *n., pl. same (coll.)* Gemüse, *das;* **meat and two ~:** Fleisch mit Kartoffeln und Gemüse
vegan ['vi:gən] **1.** *n.* Veganer, *der*/Veganerin, *die;* strenger Vegetarier/strenge Vegetarierin. **2.** *adj.* vegan; streng vegetarisch
vegetable ['vedʒɪtəbl] **1.** *n.* **a)** Gemüse, *das;* **spring/summer/winter ~:** Frühjahrs-/Sommer-/Wintergemüse, *das;* **fresh ~s** frisches Gemüse; **green ~s** Grüngemüse, *das;* **do you want ~s/a ~ with your steak?** hätten Sie gern Gemüse/eine Portion Gemüse zu Ihrem Steak?; **meat and two ~s** Fleisch mit Kartoffeln und Gemüse; *see also* **kingdom d; b)** *(fig.)* **become/be a ~** *(as result of injury or illness)* nur noch [dahin]vegetieren; **you're just a ~/you'll turn into a ~** *(as result of dull routine, lack of ambition, etc.)* du vegetierst nur so vor dich hin/bald wirst du nur noch vor dich hin vegetieren. **2.** *adj.* Gemüse⟨*suppe, -extrakt*⟩; **~ butter** Pflanzenbutter, *die;* **~ matter** pflanzliche Stoffe
vegetable: ~ dish *n.* **a)** *(food)* Gemüsegericht, *das;* **b)** *(bowl)* Gemüseschüssel, *die;* **~ dye** *n.* Pflanzenfarbe, *die;* **~ garden** *n.* Gemüsegarten, *der;* **~ knife** *n.* Küchenmesser, *das;* **~ 'marrow** *see* **marrow a; ~ oil** *n.* *(Cookery)* Pflanzenöl, *das*
vegetarian [vedʒɪ'teərɪən] **1.** *n.* Vegetarier, *der*/Vegetarierin, *die.* **2.** *adj.* vegetarisch; **sb. is ~:** jmd. ist Vegetarier/Vegetarierin
vegetarianism [vedʒɪ'teərɪənɪzm] *n., no pl., no indef. art.* Vegetarismus, *der*
vegetate ['vedʒɪteɪt] *v. i.* **a)** *(Bot.)* wachsen [und gedeihen]; **b)** *(fig.)* *(as result of injury or illness)* nur noch [dahin]vegetieren; *(as result of dull routine, lack of ambition, etc.)* vor sich *(Akk.)* hin vegetieren
vegetation [vedʒɪ'teɪʃn] *n., no pl.* **a)** *(plants)* Vegetation, *die;* **b)** *(fig.)* *(as result of injury or illness)* Dahinvegetieren, *das;* *(as result of dull routine, lack of ambition, etc.)* Stumpfsinnigkeit, *die*
vegetative ['vedʒɪtətɪv] *adj.* *(Biol., Bot.)* vegetativ
vehemence ['vi:əməns] *n., no pl.* Heftigkeit, *die;* Vehemenz, *die;* **with ~:** heftig; vehement *(geh.)*
vehement ['vi:əmənt] *adj.* heftig; vehement; leidenschaftlich ⟨*Gefühle, Rede*⟩; stark ⟨*Wunsch, Abneigung*⟩; hitzig ⟨*Debatte*⟩
vehemently ['vi:əməntlɪ] *adv.* heftig; vehement; **hate each other ~:** einander bis aufs Blut hassen; **dislike each other ~:** eine heftige Abneigung gegeneinander empfinden
vehicle ['vi:ɪkl] *n.* **a)** Fahrzeug, *das;* **b)** *(fig.: medium)* Vehikel, *das;* **the pulpit as a ~ for propaganda** die Kanzel als Bühne für Propaganda; **this newspaper is their ~:** diese Zeitung ist ihr Sprachrohr; **c)** *(Art)* Bindemittel, *das;* **d)** *(Pharm.)* Vehiculum, *das;* Konstituens, *das*
vehicular [vɪ'hɪkjʊlə(r)] *adj.* Fahrzeug-
veil [veɪl] **1.** *n.* **a)** Schleier, *der;* **take the ~** *(Relig.)* den Schleier nehmen *(geh.);* **b)** *(Jewish Relig. Hist.)* [Tempel]vorhang, *der;* **beyond the ~** *(fig.)* im Jenseits; **c)** *(fig.: obscuring medium)* Schleier, *der;* **~ of mist/clouds** Dunst-/Wolkenschleier, *der;* **under the ~ of patriotism** unter dem Deckmantel des Patriotismus; **draw a ~ over sth.** den Mantel des Schweigens über etw. *(Akk.)* breiten. **2.** *v. t.* **a)** verschleiern; **b)** *(fig.: cover)* verhüllen; *(conceal)* verbergen ⟨*Gefühle, Motive*⟩ **(with, in** hinter + *Dat.*); verschleiern ⟨*Fakten, Wahrheit, Bedeutung*⟩; **~ sth. in secrecy** *or* **mystery** etw. mit dem Schleier des Geheimnisses umgeben
veiled [veɪld] *adj.* **a)** verschleiert; **b)** *(fig.: covert)* versteckt ⟨*Groll, Drohung*⟩; verhüllt ⟨*Anspielung*⟩
vein [veɪn] *n.* **a)** Vene, *die;* *(in popular use: any blood-vessel)* Ader, *die;* **b)** *(Geol., Mining, Zool.)* Ader, *die;* **c)** *(Bot.)* Blattrippe, *die;* Ader, *die;* **d)** *(streak)* Ader, *die;* **~s** *(in wood, marble)* Maserung, *die;* **e)** *(fig.: character, tendency)* Zug, *der;* *(of truth)* Spur, *die;* *(of superstition, aggression)* Anflug, *der;* **a ~ of melancholy/humour** ein melancholischer/humorvoller Zug; **have a poetic ~:** eine dichterische Ader haben; **f)** *(fig.)* *(mood)* Stimmung, *die;* *(style)* Art, *die;* **be in a happy/sad ~:** frohgelaunt/traurig gestimmt sein; **be in the [right] ~ [for sth./for doing sth.]** in der [richtigen] Stimmung sein [zu etw./, etw. zu tun]; **in a similar ~:** vergleichbarer Art
veined [veɪnd] *adj.* geädert; gemasert ⟨*Holz*⟩; **red marble ~ with white** roter Marmor, weißgeädert
velar ['vi:lə(r)] *adj.* *(Phonet.)* velar
Velcro, (P) ['velkrəʊ] *n., no pl., no indef. art.* Klettverschluß, *der* ⓌⓏ
veld, veldt [velt] *n.* *(S. Afr.)* Steppe, *die*
vellum ['veləm] *n.* **a)** *(parchment)* Pergament, *das;* *(manuscript also)* Pergamenthandschrift, *die;* **b)** *(writing-paper)* Velin[papier], *das*
velocity [vɪ'lɒsɪtɪ] *n.* Geschwindigkeit, *die;* **at** *or* **with a ~ of ...:** mit einer Geschwindigkeit von ...; **~ of the wind, wind ~:** Windgeschwindigkeit, *die;* **~ of light** *(Phys.)* Lichtgeschwindigkeit, *die*
velour[s] [və'lʊə(r)] *n.* *(Textiles)* Velours, *der*
velum ['vi:ləm] *n., pl.* **vela** ['vi:lə] *(Bot., Zool.)* Velum, *das;* *(Anat.)* Velum, *das;* Gaumensegel, *das*
velvet ['velvɪt] **1.** *n.* **a)** Samt, *der;* **[as] smooth as ~:** weich wie Samt; samtweich; **b)** *(Zool.)* Bast, *der.* **2.** *adj.* aus Samt *nachgestellt;* Samt-; *(soft as ~)* samten; samtweich; **he operates with an iron hand in a ~ glove** er gibt sich entgegenkommend, in der Sache aber bleibt er unnachgiebig
velveteen [velvɪ'ti:n] **1.** *n.* *(Textiles)* Baumwollsamt, *der;* Velveton, *der (fachspr.).* **2.** *adj.* aus Baumwollsamt *nachgestellt;* Velveton-
velvety ['velvɪtɪ] *adj.* *(having the feel of velvet)* samtig; samtweich; *(characteristic of velvet; also fig.)* samtig; samten; **smooth** *or* **soft and ~:** weich und samten
Ven. *abbr.* **Venerable** Hochw.
venal ['vi:nl] *adj.* käuflich, korrupt ⟨*Person*⟩; korrupt ⟨*Verhalten, Praktiken*⟩; eigennützig ⟨*Interessen, Motive, Dienste*⟩
venality [vi:'nælɪtɪ] *n., no pl. see* **venal:** Käuflichkeit, *die;* Korruptheit, *die;* Eigennützigkeit, *die*
vend [vend] *v. t.* **a)** *(Law)* veräußern; *(as a business)* Handel treiben mit; **b)** *(offer for sale)* verkaufen
vendee [ven'di:] *n.* *(Law)* Käufer, *der*/Käuferin, *die*
vender ['vendə(r)] *n.* Verkäufer, *der*/Verkäuferin, *die;* **street ~:** Straßenhändler, *der*/-händlerin, *die;* **newspaper ~:** Zeitungsverkäufer, *der*/-verkäuferin, *die*
vendetta [ven'detə] *n.* **a)** Hetzkampagne, *die;* *(feud)* Fehde, *die;* **conduct a ~ against sb./sth.** eine Hetzkampagne gegen jmdn./etw. führen; **b)** *(killings)* Blutrache, *die;* *(in Italy also)* Vendetta, *die*
'vending-machine *n.* [Verkaufs]automat, *der*
vendor ['vendə(r), 'vendɔ:(r)] *n.* **a)** *(esp. Law)* Verkäufer, *der*/Verkäuferin, *die;* **street ~:** Straßenhändler, *der*/-händlerin, *die;* **newspaper ~:** Zeitungsverkäufer, *der*/-verkäuferin, *die;* **b)** *see* **vending-machine**
veneer [vɪ'nɪə(r)] **1.** *n.* **a)** *(thin covering of wood)* Furnier, *das;* *(layer in plywood)* Furnierblatt, *das;* **b)** *(fig.: disguise)* Tünche, *die;* **beneath a ~ of respectability/civilization** hinter einer Fassade der Wohlanständigkeit/der Zivilisiertheit; **have only a ~ of education** sich *(Dat.)* nur den Anschein von Bildung geben; **it's just a ~:** es ist nur schöner Schein. **2.** *v. t.* furnieren
venerable ['venərəbl] *adj.* **a)** ehrwürdig; heilig ⟨*Reliquien*⟩; **b)** *(Eccl.)* **the V~ A. W. Morgan** Hochwürden A. W. Morgan
venerate ['venəreɪt] *v. t.* verehren; hochachten; ehren ⟨*Eltern, Wort Gottes*⟩; in Ehren halten ⟨*jmds. Andenken, Traditionen, heilige Orte*⟩

veneration [venəˈreɪʃn] *n.* **a)** *(reverence)* Ehrfurcht, *die* (of, for vor + *Dat.*); **in ~ of** zu Ehren (+ *Gen.*); **hold sb./sth. in ~:** jmdn./etw. verehren; **hold sb.'s memory in ~:** jmds. Andenken in Ehren halten; **b)** *(venerating, being venerated)* Verehrung, *die* (of für); **the community's ~ of its traditions** der tiefe Respekt, den die Gemeinde für ihre Traditionen empfindet/empfand

venereal [vɪˈnɪərɪəl] *adj. (Med.)* venerisch; **~ clinic** Klinik für Geschlechtskrankheiten; **~ virus** Virus, das eine venerische Krankheit hervorruft

veˈnereal disease *n. (Med.)* Geschlechtskrankheit, *die;* venerische Krankheit *(fachspr.)*

Venetian [vɪˈni:ʃn] **1.** *adj.* venezianisch; **sb. is ~:** jmd. ist Venezianer/Venezianerin; **~ glass** Muranoglas, *das.* **2.** *n.* **a)** *(person)* Venezianer, *der*/Venezianerin, *die;* **b)** *(dialect)* Venezianisch, *das;* venezianischer Dialekt

venetian ˈblind *n.* Jalousie, *die*

Venezuela [venɪˈzweɪlə] *pr. n.* Venezuela *(das)*

Venezuelan [venɪˈzweɪlən] **1.** *adj.* venezolanisch; **sb. is ~:** jmd. ist Venezolaner/Venezolanerin. **2.** *n.* Venezolaner, *der*/Venezolanerin, *die*

vengeance [ˈvendʒəns] *n.* **a)** Rache, *die;* Vergeltung, *die;* **he wrought a cruel ~ on his enemies** er übte grausame Rache an seinen Feinden; **take ~ [up]on sb. [for sth.]** sich an jmdm. [für etw.] rächen; **b) with a ~** *(coll.)* gewaltig *(ugs.);* **go to work with a ~** *(coll.)* sich tüchtig ins Zeug legen *(ugs.)*

vengeful [ˈvendʒfl] *adj.* rachedurstig *(geh.);* rachsüchtig *(geh.)*

venial [ˈvi:nɪəl] *adj.* **a)** *(pardonable)* verzeihlich; entschuldbar; leichter ‹*Vergehen*›; **b)** *(Theol.)* läßlich ‹*Sünde*›

veniality [vi:nɪˈælɪtɪ] *n., no pl.* **a)** Entschuldbarkeit, *die;* **b)** *(Theol.)* Läßlichkeit, *die*

Venice [ˈvenɪs] *pr. n.* Venedig *(das)*

venison [ˈvenɪsn, ˈvenɪzn] *n., no pl.* Hirsch[fleisch], *das; (of roe)* Reh[fleisch], *das;* **roast ~:** Hirsch-/Rehbraten, *der;* **~ steak** Hirsch-/Rehsteak, *das*

venom [ˈvenəm] *n.* **a)** *(Zool.)* Gift, *das;* **b)** *(fig.)* Boshaftigkeit, *die;* Gehässigkeit, *die;* **unleash one's ~ on sb.** jmdn. angiften *(ugs.);* **the ~ of her hatred** ihr giftiger Haß; **say sth. with great** *or* **real ~:** etw. sehr giftig sagen; **there was much ~ in his criticism** seine Kritik war wirklich giftig

venomous [ˈvenəməs] *adj.* **a)** *(Zool.)* giftig; Gift‹*schlange, -stachel*›; **b)** *(fig.)* giftig *(ugs.);* boshaft

venomously [ˈvenəməslɪ] *adv. (fig.)* giftig *(ugs.);* boshaft

venous [ˈvi:nəs] *adj.* **a)** *(Anat., Zool.)* venös; **b)** *(Bot.)* geädert

[1]vent [vent] **1.** *n.* **a)** *(for gas, liquid to escape)* Öffnung, *die;* **b)** *(of gun, cannon, etc.)* Zündloch, *das;* Zündkanal, *der;* **c)** *(in barrel)* Spundloch, *das;* **d)** *(Mus.)* Griffloch, *das;* **e)** *(flue)* [Rauch]abzug, *der;* **f)** *(Geol.)* [Vulkan]schlot, *der;* **g)** *(fig.: for emotions)* Ventil, *das (fig.);* **give ~ to** Luft machen (+ *Dat.*) ‹*Ärger, Wut*›; freien Lauf lassen (+ *Dat.*) ‹*Gefühlen*›; Ausdruck verleihen (+ *Dat.*) ‹*Freude*›; **h)** *(Zool.)* Kloake, *die.* **2.** *v. t. (fig.)* freien Lauf lassen (+ *Dat.*) ‹*Kummer, Schmerz*›; Luft machen (+ *Dat.*) ‹*Ärger, Wut*›; **~ one's anger on sb.** seinen Ärger an jmdm. auslassen *od.* abreagieren; *see also* **spleen b**

[2]vent *n. (in garment)* Schlitz, *der;* **a jacket with a ~:** ein Jackett mit Rückenschlitz

vent-hole *see* **[1]vent 1 a**

ventilate [ˈventɪleɪt] *v. t.* **a)** lüften; *(by permanent installation)* belüften; **b)** *(fig.) (submit to public consideration)* [offen] erörtern; *(voice)* kundtun, äußern ‹*Meinung*›; vorbringen ‹*Beschwerden*›; **c)** *(Physiol.)* mit Sauerstoff versorgen

ventilation [ventɪˈleɪʃn] *n.* **a)** *no pl.* Belüftung, *die;* **the rooms need regular ~:** die Zimmer müssen regelmäßig gelüftet werden; **this room has inadequate ~:** dieses Zimmer ist unzureichend *od.* schlecht belüftet; **b)** *no pl. (installation)* Lüftung, *die;* **c)** *(fig.) (open discussion)* [offene] Erörterung; Aussprache, *die* (of über + *Akk.*); *(voicing) (of opinion)* Äußerung, *die; (of grievances)* Vorbringen, *das;* **d)** *no pl., no art. (Physiol.)* Sauerstoffzufuhr, *die*

ventiˈlation shaft *n. (Mining)* Wetterschacht, *der*

ventilator [ˈventɪleɪtə(r)] *n.* **a)** Lüftung[svorrichtung], *die; (fan)* Ventilator, *der;* **b)** *(Med.)* Beatmungsgerät, *das;* **be put on a ~:** an ein Beatmungsgerät angeschlossen werden

ventral [ˈventrl] *adj.* **a)** *(Anat., Zool.)* ventral *(fachspr.);* Bauch-; **b)** *(Bot.)* ventral

ventricle [ˈventrɪkl] *n. (Anat.)* Ventrikel, *der*

ventriloquism [venˈtrɪləkwɪzm] *n., no pl.* Bauchreden, *das*

ventriloquist [venˈtrɪləkwɪst] *n.* Bauchredner, *der*/-rednerin, *die*

venture [ˈventʃə(r)] **1.** *n.* **a)** Unternehmung, *die;* **their ~ into space/the unknown** ihre Reise in den Weltraum/ins Unbekannte; **a new ~ in sth.** ein neuer Vorstoß in etw. *(Dat.);* **her latest ~ is surfing** neuerdings hat sie sich aufs Surfen verlegt *(ugs.);* **sth. is quite a** *or* **some ~:** etw. ist ein gewagtes *od.* mutiges Unterfangen; **I can't lose much by the ~:** ich kann bei dem Versuch nicht viel verlieren; **b)** *(Commerc.)* Unternehmung, *die;* **a successful ~:** ein erfolgreiches Geschäft; **a new publishing ~:** ein neues verlegerisches Vorhaben *od.* Projekt; **join a ~:** sich einem Unternehmen anschließen; *see also* **joint 2 a. 2.** *v. i.* **a)** *(dare)* wagen; **if I might ~ to suggest ...:** wenn Sie [mir] gestatten, möchte ich vorschlagen ...; **may I ~ to ask ...:** darf ich mir erlauben, zu fragen ...; **I would even ~ to say ...:** ich würde sogar so weit gehen, zu sagen ...; **b)** *(dare to go)* sich wagen; **dare to ~:** sich wagen; **~ further into the cave** sich weiter *od.* tiefer in die Höhle vorwagen; **~ [away] from home** sich von zu Hause fort wagen; **~ abroad/into society** sich ins Ausland/in Gesellschaft wagen; **~ out of doors** sich vor die Tür wagen; **~ into a new area of research** *(fig.)* sich auf ein neues Forschungsgebiet vorwagen; **he would never ~ too far** *(fig.)* er würde sich nie zu weit vorwagen. **3.** *v. t.* **a)** wagen ‹*Bitte, Bemerkung, Blick, Vermutung*›; zu äußern wagen ‹*Ansicht*›; sich *(Dat.)* erlauben ‹*Frage, Scherz, Bemerkung*›; **~ an explanation for sth.** etw. zu erklären versuchen; **if I might ~ a suggestion** wenn ich mir einen Vorschlag erlauben darf; **'How about ...?', he ~d** „Wie wär's mit ...?" schlug er vor; **b)** *(risk, stake)* aufs Spiel setzen ‹*Leben, Ruf, Vermögen, Glück*›; setzen ‹*Wettsumme*› (on auf + *Akk.*); **~ money in** *or* **on sth.** Geld in etw. *(Akk.)* stecken; *see also* **nothing 1 a**

~ ˈforth *(literary) see* **~ out**

~ on *v. t.* sich einlassen auf (+ *Akk.*); sich wagen an (+ *Akk.*) ‹*Aufgabe*›; sich wagen auf (+ *Akk.*) ‹*Reise*›

~ ˈout *v. i.* sich hinauswagen; **~ out on to the sea** sich auf das Meer hinauswagen

~ upon *see* **~ on**

venturer [ˈventʃərə(r)] *n.* **a)** *(Commerc. Hist.)* Unternehmer, *der*/Unternehmerin, *die;* **b)** *(adventurer)* Abenteurer, *der*/Abenteu[r]erin, *die*

ˈVenture Scout *n. (Brit.)* ≈ Rover, *der; Pfadfinder im Alter von 16 bis 20 Jahren*

venturesome [ˈventʃəsəm] *adj.* wagemutig ‹*Person, Tat*›; *(hazardous)* abenteuerlich ‹*Unternehmen, Reise*›

venue [ˈvenju:] *n. (Sport)* [Austragungs]ort, *der; (Mus., Theatre)* [Veranstaltungs]ort, *der; (meeting-place)* Treffpunkt, *der*

Venus [ˈvi:nəs] *pr. n.* **a)** *(Astron.)* Venus, *die;* **b)** *(Roman Mythol.)* Venus *(die)*

Venusian [vɪˈnju:zɪən] **1.** *adj. (Astron.)* Venus-. **2.** *n.* Venusbewohner, der/-bewohnerin, *die*

Venus['s] ˈfly-trap *n. (Bot.)* Venusfliegenfalle, *die*

veracious [vəˈreɪʃəs] *adj.* **a)** aufrichtig ‹*Person*›; **assume sb. to be ~:** davon ausgehen, daß jmd. die Wahrheit sagt; **b)** *(true)* wahr; wahrheitsgetreu ‹*Schilderung, Bericht*›

veraciously [vəˈreɪʃəslɪ] *adv.* wahrheitsgemäß ‹*darstellen*›; **speak ~:** die Wahrheit sprechen

veracity [vəˈræsɪtɪ] *n., no pl.* **a)** *(of person)* Aufrichtigkeit, *die;* **b)** *(of statement etc.)* Wahrheitstreue, *die;* **have ~:** wahrheitsgetreu sein

veranda[h] [vəˈrændə] *n.* Veranda, *die*

verb [vɜ:b] *n. (Ling.)* Verb, *das;* Verbum, *das (fachspr.)*

verbal [ˈvɜ:bl] *adj.* **a)** *(relating to words)* sprachlich; **~ memory** Gedächtnis für Worte *od.* Sprache; **his skills are ~:** seine Fähigkeiten liegen auf sprachlichem Gebiet; **the distinction is purely ~:** der Unterschied besteht nur in der Wortwahl; **b)** *(oral)* mündlich; verbal, mündlich ‹*Bekenntnis, Anerkennung, Protest*›; **c)** *(Ling.)* verbal; **a ~ group** eine Verb[al]gruppe

verbalize (verbalise) [ˈvɜ:bəlaɪz] *v. t.* **a)** *(express)* in Worte fassen, *(geh.)* verbalisieren ‹*Gefühle*›; **b)** *(Ling.: make into verb)* verbalisieren

verbally [ˈvɜ:bəlɪ] *adv.* **a)** *(regarding words)* sprachlich; mit Worten, verbal ‹*beschrieben*›; **b)** *(orally)* mündlich; verbal, mündlich ‹*protestieren*›; **c)** *(Ling.)* verbal

verbal ˈnoun *n. (Ling.)* Verbalsubstantiv, *das*

verbatim [vɜˈbeɪtɪm] **1.** *adv.* im Wortlaut ‹*veröffentlichen*›; [wort]wörtlich ‹*sagen, abschreiben, zitieren*›. **2.** *adj.* wortgetreu; [wort]wörtlich

verbena [vəˈbi:nə] *n. (Bot.)* **a)** Eisenkraut, *das;* Verbene, *die (fachspr.);* **b) [lemon] ~:** Zitronenstrauch, *der*

verbiage [ˈvɜ:bɪɪdʒ] *n., no pl., no indef. art.* **a)** *(wordiness)* Geschwätzigkeit, *die;* **b)** *(words)* Geschwätz, *das*

verbose [vəˈbəʊs] *adj.* geschwätzig; weitschweifig ‹*Roman, Vortrag, Autor*›; langatmig ‹*Rede, Redner, Stil*›; **he is too ~:** er macht zu viele Worte

verbosely [vəˈbəʊslɪ] *adv.* weitschweifig; langatmig

verboseness [vəˈbəʊsnɪs], **verbosity** [vəˈbɒsɪtɪ] *ns.* **a)** *(wordiness)* Weitschweifigkeit, die; Langatmigkeit, *die;* **b)** *(words)* Geschwafel, *das*

verdant [ˈvɜ:dənt] *adj. (literary)* [saft]grün

verdict [ˈvɜ:dɪkt] *n.* **a)** *(Law)* Urteil, *das;* [Urteils]spruch, *der;* **open ~:** *Feststellung eines gewaltsamen Todes ohne Nennung der Ursache (bei einer gerichtlichen Untersuchung);* **~ of guilty/not guilty** Schuld-/Freispruch, *der;* **reach a ~:** zu einem Urteil kommen; *see also* **bring in d; return 2 h; b)** *(judgement)* Urteil, *das* (on über + *Akk.*); *(decision)* Entscheidung, *die;* **the ~ of the electors** die Entscheidung der Wähler; **what's your ~ on the affair/novel?** wie beurteilst du die Sache/wie ist dein Urteil über den Roman?; **give** *or* **pass a/one's ~ [on sb./sth.]** ein/sein Urteil [über jmdn./etw.] abgeben

verdigris [ˈvɜ:dɪgrɪs] *n.* **a)** *(Chem.)* Grünspan, *der;* **b)** *(rust on metal)* Patina, *die*

verdure [ˈvɜ:djə(r)] *n. (literary)* **a)** *(greenness)* Grün, *das;* **b)** *(green vegetation)* [dichtes] Grün

[1]verge [vɜ:dʒ] *n.* **a)** *(grass edging)* Rasensaum, *der; (on road)* Bankette, *die;* **'keep off the ~'** „Bankette nicht befahrbar"; *see also* **soft verge; b)** *(brink, border, lit. or fig.)*

Rand, *der; (fig.: point at which something begins)* Schwelle, *die;* **be on the ~ of economic collapse/of war/of death** am Rand des wirtschaftlichen Zusammenbruchs/an der Schwelle des Krieges/Todes stehen; **be on the ~ of despair/tears/a breakthrough/a breakdown** der Verzweiflung/den Tränen/dem Durchbruch/einem Nervenzusammenbruch nahe sein; **be on the ~ of doing sth.** kurz davor stehen, etw. zu tun; **bring sb./sth. to the ~ of sth.** jmdn./etw. an den Rand von etw. bringen

²**verge** *v.i.* ‹*Hügel, Land:*› abfallen; **~ to[wards] sth.** *(fig.)* einer Sache *(Dat.)* zustreben; **~ towards old age** langsam alt werden

~ on *v.t.* [an]grenzen an (+ *Akk.*); **be verging on 70** an die 70 sein; **an estate verging on four acres** *(fig.)* ein Grundstück von fast vier Morgen [Größe]; **be verging on tears/madness** den Tränen/dem Wahnsinn nahe sein; **blue verging on grey** *(fig.)* ein Blau, das schon fast grau wirkt; **be verging on bankruptcy** vor dem Bankrott stehen

verger ['vɜːdʒə(r)] *n. (Eccl.)* Küster, *der*

Vergil *see* **Virgil**

verifiable ['verɪfaɪəbl] *adj.* nachprüfbar; **this is an easily ~ statement** diese Behauptung läßt sich leicht nachprüfen

verification [verɪfɪ'keɪʃn] *n.* **a)** *(check)* Überprüfung, *die;* **~ of the accounts** Prüfung der Bücher; **be open to ~:** sich überprüfen lassen; **b)** *(confirmation)* Nachweis, *der;* **I'll need some ~ of your identity** ich brauche dann noch einen Ausweis von Ihnen; **c)** *(bearing out)* Bestätigung, *die;* **a ~ of their prediction** ein Beweis für die Richtigkeit ihrer Prognose

verify ['verɪfaɪ] *v.t.* **a)** *(check)* überprüfen; prüfen ‹*Bücher*›; **ring sb. up to ~ the news** jmdn. anrufen, um sich *(Dat.)* die [Richtigkeit der] Nachricht bestätigen zu lassen; **b)** *(confirm)* bestätigen ‹*Vermutung, Diagnose*›; bekräftigen ‹*Anspruch, Forderung*›; nachweisen ‹*Identität*›; **c)** *(bear out)* bestätigen; beweisen ‹*Theorie*›

verily ['verɪlɪ] *adv. (arch.)* wahrlich *(veralt.);* **no** *or* **nay, ~:** nein, fürwahr *(veralt.)*

verisimilitude [verɪsɪ'mɪlɪtjuːd] *n., no pl.* Wahrheitsgehalt, *der; (in work of art)* Realistik, *die;* **sth. is designed to add** *or* **give ~ to a story** etw. soll eine Geschichte realistischer erscheinen lassen

veritable ['verɪtəbl] *adj. (literary)* richtig; wahr, richtig ‹*Engel, Genie*›; wahr ‹*Wunder*›

veritably ['verɪtəblɪ] *adv. (literary)* wirklich [und wahrhaftig]; **it was ~ miraculous** es war ein wahres Wunder; **a ~ suicidal thing to do** der reinste Selbstmord *(ugs.);* **the place ~ swam with wine** der Wein floß buchstäblich in Strömen

verity ['verɪtɪ] *n. (literary)* Wahrheit, *die*

vermicelli [vɜːmɪ'selɪ, vɜːmɪ'tʃelɪ] *n. (Gastr.)* Vermicelli; Fadennudeln

vermicide ['vɜːmɪsaɪd] *n. (Med.)* Wurmmittel, *das*

vermiform ['vɜːmɪfɔːm] *adj.* wurmförmig; *see also* **appendix b**

vermifuge ['vɜːmɪfjuːdʒ] *(Med.) n.* Wurmmittel, *das*

vermilion [və'mɪljən] **1.** *n. (substance)* Zinnober, *der; (colour)* Zinnoberrot, *das.* **2.** *adj.* zinnoberrot

vermin ['vɜːmɪn] *n., no pl., no indef. art.* Ungeziefer, *das; (fig. derog.)* Pack, *das (abwertend);* Abschaum, *der (abwertend)*

verminous ['vɜːmɪnəs] *adj.* ungezieferverseucht; voller Ungeziefer *nachgestellt; (fig. derog.)* übel

vermouth ['vɜːməθ, və'muːθ] *n.* Wermut-[wein], *der*

vernacular [və'nækjʊlə(r)] **1.** *adj.* **a)** *(native)* landessprachlich; ‹*Predigt, Zeitung*› in der Landessprache; *(not learned or technical)* volkstümlich; *(in dialect)* mundartlich; **~ language** Landessprache, *die*/Volkssprache, *die*/Mundart, *die;* **the ~ dialect** der regionale Dialekt; **b) ~ architecture** volkstümliche Baukunst. **2.** *n.* **a)** *(native language)* Landessprache, *die; (dialect)* Dialekt, *der;* **b)** *(jargon)* Sprache, *die; (of a profession or group)* Jargon, *der;* **scientific/legal ~:** Wissenschafts-/Juristenjargon, *der;* **thieves' ~:** Gaunersprache, *die;* **~ of youth** Jugendsprache, *die;* **c)** *(homely speech)* Umgangssprache, *die;* **if you'll excuse the ~** *(joc.)* wenn ich das mal so sagen darf

vernal ['vɜːnl] *adj.* Frühlings-; *see also* **equinox a**

vernier ['vɜːnɪə(r)] *n. (Mech. Engin.)* Nonius, *der*

veronica [və'rɒnɪkə] *n. (Bot.)* Ehrenpreis, *das od. der*

verruca [ve'ruːkə] *n., pl.* **~e** [ve'ruːsiː] *or* **~s** *(Med.)* Warze, *die;* Verruca, *die (fachspr.)*

versatile ['vɜːsətaɪl] *adj.* vielseitig; *(mentally)* flexibel; *(having many uses)* vielseitig verwendbar

versatility [vɜːsə'tɪlɪtɪ] *n., no pl.* Vielseitigkeit, *die; (mental)* Flexibilität, *die; (variety of uses)* vielseitige Verwendbarkeit

verse [vɜːs] *n.* **a)** *(line)* Vers, *der;* **b)** *(stanza)* Strophe, *die;* **of** *or* **in** *or* **with five ~s** fünfstrophig; **c)** *no pl., no indef. art. (poetry)* Lyrik, *die;* **write some ~:** einige Verse schreiben; **piece of ~:** Gedicht, *das;* **written in ~:** in Versform; **put sth. into ~:** etw. in Verse fassen; **d)** *(in Bible)* Vers, *der; see also* **blank verse; chapter a**

versed [vɜːst] *adj.* **be [well] ~ in sth.** sich in etw. *(Dat.)* [gut] auskennen; **he's [well] ~ in such matters** er ist in diesen Dingen [sehr] versiert

verse: ~ drama *n. (Lit.)* Versdrama, *das;* **~ translation** *n. (Lit.)* Übertragung in Versform

versification [vɜːsɪfɪ'keɪʃn] *n.* **a)** *(composing of verse)* Versedichten, *das; (derog.)* Verseschmieden, *das;* **b)** *(metrical form)* Versbau, *der;* **c)** *(poetical version)* Versfassung, *die*

versifier ['vɜːsɪfaɪə(r)] *n.* Versdichter, *der*/-dichterin, *die; (derog.)* Versemacher, *der*/-macherin, *die*

versify ['vɜːsɪfaɪ] **1.** *v.t.* in Verse fassen. **2.** *v.i.* Gedichte schreiben; *(derog.)* Verse schmieden

version ['vɜːʃn] *n.* Version, *die; (in another language)* Übersetzung, *die; (in another form also)* Fassung, *die; (of vehicle, machine, tool)* Modell, *das; see also* **authorize b; revise 1 a**

verso ['vɜːsəʊ] *n., pl.* **~s a)** *(Printing, Bibliog.) (left-hand page)* linke Seite; *(back of leaf)* Verso, *das (fachspr.);* Rückseite, *die;* **b)** *(Num.)* Revers, *der (fachspr.);* Rückseite, *die*

versus ['vɜːsəs] *prep.* gegen

vert [vɜːt] *(Her.)* **1.** *n.* Grün, *das.* **2.** *adj.* grün

vertebra ['vɜːtɪbrə] *n., pl.* **~e** ['vɜːtɪbriː] *(Anat.)* Wirbel, *der;* **~e** *(backbone)* Wirbelsäule, *die*

vertebral ['vɜːtɪbrəl] *adj. (Anat.)* vertebral *(fachspr.);* Wirbel-; **~ column/muscles** Wirbelsäule, *die*/Rückenmuskulatur, *die*

vertebrate ['vɜːtɪbrət, 'vɜːtɪbreɪt] *(Zool.)* **1.** *adj.* Wirbel‹*tier*›; Wirbeltier‹*skelett, -fossilien, -zoologie*›; ‹*Stamm*› der Wirbeltiere. **2.** *n.* Wirbeltier, *das*

vertex ['vɜːteks] *n., pl.* **vertices** ['vɜːtɪsiːz] *or* **~es a)** *(highest point)* Gipfel, *der; (of tower, turret)* Spitze, *die; (Archit.: of dome, arch)* Scheitel[punkt], *der;* **b)** *(Geom.) (of curve, surface, angle)* Scheitel[punkt], *der; (of triangle, polygon)* Eckpunkt, *der*

vertical ['vɜːtɪkl] **1.** *adj.* **a)** senkrecht; senkrecht aufragend *od.* abfallend ‹*Klippe*›; **be ~:** senkrecht stehen; **b)** *(esp. Econ., Sociol.: combining levels, stages, etc.)* vertikal; *see also* **integration d. 2.** *n.* senkrechte *od.* vertikale Linie; **be out of [the] ~:** nicht im *od.* außer Lot sein

vertically ['vɜːtɪkəlɪ] *adv.* **a)** senkrecht; vertikal; **b)** *(esp. Econ., Sociol.: so as to combine levels, stages, etc.)* vertikal

vertical: ~ 'plane *n. (Geom.)* Vertikalebene, *die;* **~ 'take-off** *n. (Aeronaut.)* Senkrechtstart, *der;* **~ 'take-off aircraft** *n. (Aeronaut.)* Senkrechtstarter, *der*

vertices *pl. of* **vertex**

vertiginous [və'tɪdʒɪnəs] *adj.* schwindelerregend ‹*Höhe, Abgrund usw.*›

vertigo ['vɜːtɪgəʊ] *n., pl.* **~s** Schwindel, *der;* Vertigo, *die (Med.);* **give sb. ~:** jmdn. schwindelig machen; **she got ~:** ihr wurde schwindelig; **attack of ~:** Schwindelanfall, *der*

vervain ['vɜːveɪn] *n. (Bot.)* Eisenkraut, *das*

verve [vɜːv] *n.* Schwung, *der; (of artist, orchestra's playing, sports team's play)* Temperament, *das; (of music, sb.'s writing)* Ausdruckskraft, die **(of, in** *Gen.***)**

very ['verɪ] **1.** *attrib. adj.* **a)** *(precise, exact)* genau; **you must do it this ~ day** du mußt es noch heute tun; **on the ~ day when ...:** genau am [selben] Tag, an dem ...; **you're the ~ person I wanted to see** genau dich wollte ich sehen; **at the ~ moment when ...:** im selben Augenblick, als ...; **just this ~ moment ...:** gerade eben ...; **in the ~ centre** genau in der Mitte; **the ~ opposite** genau das Gegenteil; **the ~ thing** genau das Richtige; **the ~ stones cry out** das schreit ja zum Himmel; **b)** *(extreme)* **at the ~ back/front** ganz hinten/vorn; **at the ~ edge of the cliff** ganz am Rand der Klippe; **at the ~ end/beginning** ganz am Ende/Anfang; **from the ~ outset** *or* **beginning** von Anfang an; **go to the ~ end of the street** ganz bis ans Ende der Straße gehen; **climb to the ~ top of the hill** bis auf den Gipfel des Berges steigen; **a ~ little more** ein ganz kleines bißchen mehr; **only a ~ little** nur ein ganz kleines bißchen; **c)** *(mere)* bloß ‹*Gedanke*›; **at the ~ thought** allein schon beim Gedanken; **the ~ fact of his presence** allein schon seine Anwesenheit; **the ~ mention** allein schon die Erwähnung; **d)** *(absolute)* absolut ‹*Minimum, Maximum*›; **do one's ~ best** *or* **utmost** sein menschenmöglichstes tun; **the ~ most I can offer is ...:** ich kann allerhöchstens ... anbieten; **it's the ~ least** das ist das Allermindeste; **£50 at the ~ most** allerhöchstens 50 Pfund; **they should at the ~ least consider the proposal** sie sollten das Angebot zumindest einmal in Erwägung ziehen; **be the ~ first to arrive** als allererster ankommen; **for the ~ last time** zum allerletzten Mal; **e)** *(used as emphatic or intensive)* **his ~ mother** seine eigene Mutter; **before their ~ eyes** vor ihren Augen; **be caught in the ~ act** auf frischer Tat ertappt werden; **be the ~ picture of health** wie die Gesundheit in Person aussehen; **under sb.'s ~ nose** *(fig. coll.)* direkt vor jmds. Augen *(Dat.);* **f)** *(arch.: real)* wahr ‹*Grund, Seelenfriede, Seele*›; richtig ‹*Teufel*›; rein ‹*Wahnsinn*›. **2.** *adv.* **a)** *(extremely)* sehr; **it's ~ near** es ist ganz in der Nähe; **in the ~ near future** in allernächster Zukunft; **it's ~ possible that ...:** es ist sehr gut möglich, daß ...; **~ probably** höchstwahrscheinlich; **she's ~/so ~ thin** sie ist sehr dünn/so dünn; **how ~ rude [of him]!** das ist aber unhöflich [von ihm]!; **[yes,] ~ much [so]** [ja,] sehr; **~ much prettier/better** [sehr] viel hübscher/besser; **not ~ much** nicht sehr; **~ little** [nur] sehr wenig ‹*verstehen, essen*›; **there's ~ little reason to do it** es spricht kaum etwas dafür, es zu tun; **thank you [~,] ~ much** [vielen,] vielen Dank; **[yes,] thank you ~ much** o ja, sehr gern; **no, thank you ~ much** nein, danke vielmals; **you are [~,] ~ kind** *(thank-*

ing) das ist [wirklich] sehr freundlich von Ihnen; **not ~ big** *(not extremely big)* nicht sehr groß; *(not at all big)* nicht gerade groß; *see also* **reverend 1; ¹so1 a, 2; b)** *(absolutely)* aller⟨*best..., -letzt..., -leichtest...*⟩; **at the ~ latest** allerspätestens; **the ~ last thing I expected** das, womit ich am allerwenigsten gerechnet hatte; **keep sth. for one's ~ own** etw. für sich ganz allein behalten; **have sth. of one's ~ own** etw. haben, das einem ganz allein gehört; **c)** *(precisely)* **the ~ same one** genau der-/die-/dasselbe; **that is the ~ word he used** das ist genau das Wort, das er gebrauchte; **meet the ~ next day** sich gleich am nächsten Tag treffen; **in his ~ next sentence/breath** schon im nächsten Satz/Atemzug; **d) ~ good** *(accepting)* sehr wohl; *(agreeing)* sehr schön; **~ well** *expr. reluctant consent* also gut; na schön; **that's all ~ well, but ...**: das ist ja alles schön und gut, aber ...

very high 'frequency *n. (Radio)* Ultrakurzwelle, *die*

Very light ['verı laıt, 'vıərı laıt] *n. (Mil.)* Leuchtkugel, *die*

vesicle ['vesıkl] *n.* **a)** *(Anat., Geol.)* Blase, *die;* **b)** *(Zool., Bot., Med.)* Bläschen, *das*

vespers ['vespəz] *n., constr. as sing. or pl. (Eccl.)* Vesper, *die*

vessel ['vesl] *n.* **a)** *(receptacle; also Anat., Bot.)* Gefäß, *das;* **[drinking-]~**: Trinkgefäß, *das; see also* **blood-vessel; b)** *(Naut.)* Schiff, *das;* **c)** *(Bibl./joc.: person)* Typ, *der;* **weak ~**: unsicherer Kantonist/unsichere Kantonistin *(ugs.);* **the weaker ~**: das schwache Geschlecht *(ugs.); (Bibl.)* das schwächere Gefäß

vest [vest] **1.** *n.* **a)** *(Brit.: undergarment)* Unterhemd, *das; (woman's)* Hemd, *das;* **b)** *(Amer.: waistcoat)* Weste, *die.* **2.** *v. t.* **~ sb. with sth., ~ sth. in sb.** jmdm. etw. verleihen; **be ~ed with the power to do sth.** berechtigt sein, etw. zu tun; **~ sb. with [rights in] sth.** jmdm. Ansprüche auf etw. *(Akk.)* einräumen; **be ~ed in sb.** jmdm. übertragen sein; **by the authority ~ed in me** kraft der mir verliehenen Vollmacht; *see also* **vested. 3.** *v. i.* **~ in sb.** jmdm. übertragen werden

vestal ['vestl] *(Roman Mythol.)* **1.** *adj.* vestalisch ⟨*Gesetz, Gelübde*⟩; ⟨*Schrein, Feuer*⟩ der Vesta. **2.** *n. see* **vestal virgin**

vestal 'virgin *n.* Vestalin, *die*

vested ['vestıd] *adj.* **~ interest/right** wohlerworbener Anspruch; *(established by law)* gesetzlicher Anspruch; **~ interests** *(groups of persons)* Interessengruppen; **have a ~ interest in sth.** *(fig.)* ein persönliches Interesse an etw. *(Dat.)* haben

vestibule ['vestıbju:l] *n.* **a)** *(indoors)* [Eingangs]halle, *die;* **b)** *(external porch)* Vorhalle, *die;* **c)** *(Amer. Railw.)* Vorraum, *der;* **d)** *(Anat.)* Innenohrvorhof, *der;* Vestibulum, *das (fachspr.)*

vestige ['vestıdʒ] *n.* **a)** Spur, *die;* **not the slightest** *or* **least ~** *or* **not a single ~ [of sth. remains]** nicht das geringste *od.* nicht die Spur [ist von etw. übrig]; **not a ~ of truth/honour** kein Fünkchen Wahrheit/Ehre; **b)** *(Biol.)* Rudiment, *das*

vestigial [ve'stıdʒıəl] *adj.* rudimentär *(geh.; fachspr.);* spärlich ⟨*Überreste*⟩; verkümmert ⟨*Tradition, Brauch*⟩

vestment ['vestmənt] *n.* [Priester]gewand, *das; (worn on special occasions)* Ornat, *das*

'vest-pocket *attr. adj. (Amer.)* Taschen-; im [Westen]taschenformat *nachgestellt; (fig.: very small)* Miniatur⟨*modell, -ausgabe, -version*⟩

vestry ['vestrı] *n. (Eccl.)* Sakristei, *die*

Vesuvius [vı'su:vıəs] *pr. n.* der Vesuv

¹vet [vet] **1.** *n.* Tierarzt, *der/*-ärztin, *die.* **2.** *v. t.*, **-tt-** überprüfen; **~ an article for errors** einen Artikel auf Fehler [hin] durchsehen

²vet *(Amer. coll.) see* **veteran 1**

vetch [vetʃ] *n. (Bot.)* Wicke, *die*

veteran ['vetərən] **1.** *n.* Veteran, *der/*Veteranin, *die;* **V~s' Day** *amerikanischer Gedenktag anläßlich des Waffenstillstandes 1918 u. 1945.* **2.** *attrib. adj.* altgedient ⟨*Offizier, Politiker, Schauspieler*⟩

veteran 'car *n. (Brit.)* Veteran, *der*

veterinarian [vetərı'neərıən] *(Amer.) see* **veterinary surgeon**

veterinary ['vetərınərı] *attrib. adj.* tiermedizinisch; veterinär; **~ science/medicine** Veterinär- *od.* Tiermedizin, *die;* **~ practice** Tierarztpraxis, *die;* **course of ~ training** Ausbildung zum Tierarzt; **~ college** Institut für Tiermedizin

veterinary 'surgeon *n. (Brit.)* Tierarzt, *der/*-ärztin, *die*

veto ['vi:təʊ] **1.** *n., pl.* **~es a) [power** *or* **right of] ~**: Veto[recht], *das; see also* **pocket veto; b)** *(rejection, prohibition)* Veto, *das* **(on** gegen, **from** von seiten); **has there been a ~ of the bill?** hat jemand sein Veto gegen den Gesetzentwurf eingelegt?; **put a** *or* **one's ~ on sth.** sein Veto gegen etw. erheben *od.* einlegen. **2.** *v. t.* sein Veto einlegen gegen

vex [veks] *v. t.* [ver]ärgern; *(cause to worry)* beunruhigen; *(dissatisfy, disappoint)* bekümmern; **[be enough to] ~ a saint** den bravsten Menschen in Harnisch bringen; **be ~ed about** *or* **at sth.** sich über etw. *(Akk.)* ärgern; **be ~ed that ...**: sich darüber ärgern, daß ...; **I am ~ed that ...**: es ärgert mich, daß ...; **be ~ed with sb.** sich über jmdn. ärgern

vexation [vek'seıʃn] *n.* **a)** *(act of harassing)* Belästigung, *die;* **take pleasure in the ~ of sb.** sich *(Dat.)* ein Vergnügen daraus machen, jmdn. zu ärgern; **b)** *(state of irritation)* Verärgerung, *die* **(with, at** über + *Akk.*); *(state of worry)* Beunruhigung, *die; (dissatisfaction, disappointment)* Kummer, *der;* **suffer [much] ~**: [viel] Ärger/Kummer haben; **cause sb. ~** *(irritate)* jmdm. Ärger bereiten; *(worry)* jmdn. in Unruhe versetzen; *(disappoint)* jmdm. Kummer machen; **have the ~ of seeing sth. happen** verärgert/bekümmert mit ansehen müssen, wie etw. geschieht; **c)** *(annoying thing)* Ärgernis, *das* **(to, for** für); **constant ~s from sb.** ständige Belästigungen durch jmdn.; **d)** *(Law)* Schikane, *die*

vexatious [vek'seıʃəs] *adj.* **a)** ärgerlich; unausstehlich ⟨*Person*⟩; **it is ~ that .../to ...**: es ist ärgerlich, daß .../zu ...; **b)** *(Law)* schikanös

vexatiously [vek'seıʃəslı] *adv.* **a)** ungehörig ⟨*sich benehmen, sich verhalten*⟩; **he said, rather ~, that ...**: sehr zu meinem Ärger/Kummer sagte er, daß ...; **~ complicated** lästig und kompliziert; **b)** *(Law)* aus Schikane; schikanös ⟨*sich verhalten*⟩

vexed [vekst] *adj.* **a)** *(annoyed)* verärgert **(by** über + *Akk.*); *(distressed)* bekümmert **(by** über + *Akk.*); **b) ~ question** vieldiskutierte Frage

vexing ['veksıŋ] *adj.* lästig ⟨*Angelegenheit, Problem, Sorgen*⟩; ärgerlich ⟨*Zwickmühle*⟩

VFR *abbr. (Aeronaut.)* **visual flight rules** Sichtflugregeln

VG *abbr.* **very good**

VHF *abbr.* **very high frequency** UKW

via ['vaıə] *prep.* über (+ *Akk.*) ⟨*Ort, Sender, Telefon*⟩; auf (+ *Dat.*) ⟨*Weg*⟩; durch ⟨*Eingang, Schornstein, Person*⟩; per ⟨*Post*⟩

viability [vaıə'bılıtı] *n., no pl.* **a)** *(of foetus, animal, plant)* Lebensfähigkeit, *die; (of seed)* Keimfähigkeit, *die;* **b)** *(fig.) (of state, company)* Lebensfähigkeit, *die; (feasibility)* Realisierbarkeit, *die*

viable ['vaıəbl] *adj.* **a)** *(capable of maintaining life)* lebensfähig; keimfähig; **be more ~ than ...**: besser überleben als ...; **b)** *(fig.)* lebensfähig ⟨*Staat, Firma*⟩; *(feasible)* realisierbar

viaduct ['vaıədʌkt] *n.* Viadukt, *das od. der*

viands ['vaıəndz] *n. pl. (formal)* Eßwaren *Pl.; (for journey)* Wegzehrung, *die (geh.)*

vibes [vaıbz] *n. pl. (coll.)* **a)** *(Mus.)* Vibraphon, *das;* **b)** *(vibrations)* Schwingungen; Vibrations *(salopp);* **I get good ~ from him** er törnt *od.* macht mich an *(ugs.);* **give sb. bad ~**: jmdn. abtörnen *(ugs.);* **feel those ~, man!** das törnt echt an! *(ugs.)*

vibrant ['vaıbrənt] *adj.* **a)** *(vibrating)* vibrierend; schwingend, vibrierend ⟨*Saite, Draht*⟩; **b)** *(thrilling)* pulsierend ⟨*Leben*⟩; schwungvoll ⟨*Vorstellung*⟩; lebensprühend ⟨*Atmosphäre*⟩; dynamisch ⟨*Kraft*⟩; lebhaft ⟨*Farbe, Rot*⟩; **be ~ with activity/life** vor Aktivitäten/Leben *(Dat.)* sprühen; **a painting ~ with colour** ein farbenprächtiges Gemälde; **c)** *(resonant)* volltönend ⟨*Stimme*⟩; voll ⟨*Ton*⟩

vibraphone ['vaıbrəfəʊn] *n. (Mus.)* Vibraphon, *das*

vibrate [vaı'breıt] **1.** *v. i.* **a)** vibrieren; *(under strong impact)* beben; **b)** *(resound)* [nach]klingen; **the sound of the anvil ~d in the streets** das Klingen des Ambosses hallte durch die Straßen; **c)** *(Phys.)* schwingen; ⟨*Glocke:*⟩ vibrieren; **d)** *(thrill)* ⟨*Stadt, Party, Aufsatz:*⟩ sprühen **(with** vor + *Dat.*); ⟨*Stimme, Körper:*⟩ vibrieren **(with** vor + *Dat.*). **2.** *v. t.* vibrieren lassen; zum Schwingen bringen ⟨*Saite*⟩

vibration [vaı'breıʃn] *n.* **a)** *(vibrating)* Vibrationen; *(visible)* Vibrieren, *das; (under strong impact)* Beben, *das;* **send ~s** *or* **a ~ through sth.** ⟨*Erdstoß:*⟩ etw. erzittern lassen; **b)** *(Phys.)* Schwingung, *die;* **c)** *in pl. (fig.)* **get some ~s** etwas spüren; **his presence gives me bad ~s** in seiner Gegenwart fühle ich mich [irgendwie] unwohl; **I get good ~s from this place/music** dieser Ort/diese Musik hat eine wohltuende Ausstrahlung

vibrational [vaı'breıʃənl] *adj. (Phys.)* Schwingungs-

vibrato [vı'brɑ:təʊ] *n., pl.* **~s** *(Mus.)* Vibrato, *das*

vibrator [vaı'breıtə(r)] *n.* **a)** Vibrator, *der;* **b)** *(Electr.)* Zerhacker, *der*

viburnum [vaı'bɜ:nəm] *n. (Bot.)* Schneeball, *der*

vicar ['vıkə(r)] *n.* Pfarrer, *der;* **lay ~**: *Laie, der Teile der Liturgie singt*

vicarage ['vıkərıdʒ] *n.* Pfarrhaus, *das*

vicar apos'tolic *n. (RC Ch.)* Apostolischer Vikar

vicarious [vı'keərıəs] *adj.* **a)** *(delegated)* Stellvertreter-; **his authority** *or* **power is ~**: er hat Stellvertreterbefugnisse; **b)** *(done for another)* stellvertretend; **perform ~ work/tasks** Arbeit/Aufgaben stellvertretend erledigen; **~ suffering[s]** *(Theol.)* stellvertretendes Leiden; **c)** *(experienced through another)* nachempfunden ⟨*Freude, Erregung usw.*⟩; **~ [sexual] satisfaction** Ersatzbefriedigung, *die;* **take a ~ delight in sb.'s success** sich mit jmdm. *od.* für jmdn. über dessen Erfolg *(Akk.)* freuen

vicariously [vı'keərıəslı] *adv.* **a)** *(as a substitute for another)* stellvertretend; **b)** *(by means of a substitute)* indirekt

vicariousness [vı'keərıəsnıs] *n., no pl.* stellvertretender Charakter; **the ~ of this experience** die Mittelbarkeit dieses Erlebnisses

¹vice [vaıs] *n.* **a)** Laster, *das;* **a life/den of ~**: ein Lasterleben/eine Lasterhöhle; **b)** *(defect)* Fehler, *der;* **he has no redeeming ~**: er hat aber auch gar kein[e] Laster

²vice *n. (Brit.: tool)* Schraubstock, *der*

³vice *n. (coll.: deputy)* Vize, *der (ugs.)*

vice- *pref.* Vize-

vice: ~-'admiral *n. (Navy)* Vizeadmiral, *der;* **~-'chairman** *n.* stellvertretender Vorsitzender; **~-'chairmanship** *n.* Amt des/der stellvertretenden Vorsitzenden; **~-'chancellor** *n. (Univ.)* Vizekanzler, *der/*Vizekanzlerin, *die*

'vicelike *adj.* eisern ⟨*Griff*⟩; fest ⟨*Umklammerung, Schwitzkasten*⟩

vice: ~-'**presidency** *n.* Amt des Vizepräsidenten/der Vizepräsidentin; ~-'**president** *n.* Vizepräsident, *der/*-präsidentin, *die;* ~-'**principal** *n. (Educ.)* stellvertretender Leiter/stellvertretende Leiterin; ~'**regal** *adj.* eines/des Vizekönigs *nachgestellt*
viceroy ['vaɪsrɔɪ] *n.* Vizekönig, *der*
viceroyship ['vaɪsrɔɪʃɪp] *n.* Amt eines Vizekönigs
'**vice squad** *n. (Police)* Sittenpolizei, *die*
vice versa [vaɪsɪ 'vɜ:sə] *adv.* umgekehrt
vicinity [vɪ'sɪnɪtɪ] *n.* **a)** *(neighbourhood)* Umgebung, *die;* **from London or its** ~: aus London und Umgebung; **in our** ~: nicht weit von uns [entfernt]; **in the immediate** ~: ganz in der Nähe; **in the** ~ **[of a place]** in der Nähe [eines Ortes]; **in the** ~ **of 50** *(fig.)* so um die 50; **b)** *no pl. (nearness)* Nähe, *die;* **in close** ~ **to the church** ganz in der Nähe der Kirche
vicious ['vɪʃəs] *adj.* **a)** *(malicious, spiteful)* böse; boshaft ‹*Äußerung*›; böswillig ‹*Versuch, Kritik*›; bösartig ‹*Äußerung, Tier*›; **b)** *(depraved)* übel ‹*Benehmen, Charakter*›; *(addicted to vice)* verdorben; *(wicked)* skrupellos ‹*Tyrann, Verbrecher*›; schlecht ‹*Person, Menschheit*›; **c)** *(violent, severe)* brutal; unerträglich ‹*Wetter, Schmerz*›
vicious 'circle *n.* Teufelskreis, *der*
viciously ['vɪʃəslɪ] *adv.* **a)** *(maliciously, spitefully)* boshaft; auf gehässige Weise ‹*kritisieren*›; **b)** *(violently, severely)* brutal
viciousness ['vɪʃəsnɪs] *n., no pl.* **a)** *(maliciousness, spitefulness)* Boshaftigkeit, *die; (of animal)* Bösartigkeit, *die;* **b)** *(depravity)* Lasterhaftigkeit, *die; (of tyrant, criminal, government)* Skrupellosigkeit, *die;* **c)** *(violence, severity)* Brutalität, *die; (of weather, pain)* Unerträglichkeit, *die*
vicious 'spiral *n.* Teufelskreis, *der;* **the** ~ **of wage increases and price rises** die Lohn-Preis-Spirale
vicissitude [vɪ'sɪsɪtju:d] *n.* steter Wandel; ~**s** *(fickleness)* Unbeständigkeit, *die;* **the** ~**s of life** die Wechselfälle des Lebens
victim ['vɪktɪm] *n.* **a)** Opfer, *das; (of sarcasm, abuse)* Zielscheibe, *die (fig.);* **be the** ~ **of sb.'s anger/envy/policy** unter jmds. Zorn/Neid/Politik *(Dat.)* zu leiden haben; **be one's own** ~: das Opfer seiner selbst sein; **be a** ~ **of fortune** dem Schicksal ausgeliefert sein; **fall [a]** ~ **to sth.** das Opfer einer Sache *(Gen.)* werden; **fall** ~ **to the plague/to drought/famine** der Pest/Trockenheit/Hungersnot *(Dat.)* zum Opfer fallen; **fall a** ~ **to love/sb.'s charms** sein Herz verlieren/jmds. Charme *(Dat.)* erliegen; **b)** *(dupe)* Opfer, *das;* **I refuse to be made his** ~: ich lasse mich von ihm nicht täuschen; **c)** *(Relig.)* Opfer, *das; (animal)* Opfertier, *das;* **human sacrificial** ~**s** Menschenopfer
victimisation, victimise *see* **victimiz-**
victimization [vɪktɪmaɪ'zeɪʃn] *n.* Schikanierung, *die; (selective punishment)* gezielte Bestrafung
victimize ['vɪktɪmaɪz] *v. t.* **a)** *(make a victim)* schikanieren; **be** ~**d [by sb.]** unter jmdm. zu leiden haben; **b)** *(punish selectively)* gezielt bestrafen
victor ['vɪktə(r)] *n.* Sieger, *der/*Siegerin, *die*
Victoria [vɪk'tɔ:rɪə] *pr. n.* **a)** *(Hist., as name of ruler etc.)* Viktoria *(die);* **b)** *(Geog.)* Victoria *(das)*
victoria *n.* ~ **[plum]** Königin-Viktoria-Pflaume, *die*
Victoria: ~ '**Cross** *n. (Brit.)* Viktoriakreuz, *das;* ~ '**Falls** *n. pl.* Victoriafälle *Pl.*
Victorian [vɪk'tɔ:rɪən] **1.** *adj.* viktorianisch. **2.** *n.* Viktorianer, *der/*Viktorianerin, *die*
Victoriana [vɪktɔ:rɪ'ɑ:nə] *n. pl.* viktorianische Antiquitäten
victorious [vɪk'tɔ:rɪəs] *adj.* **a)** siegreich; **be** ~ **over sb./sth.** über jmdn./etw. siegreich bleiben; **be** ~ **in one's struggle** aus seinem Kampf siegreich hervorgehen; **b)** *(marked by victory)* erfolgreich ‹*Verteidigung, Kreuzzug*›; siegreich ‹*Feldzug, Eroberung, Angriff*›; triumphierend ‹*Gruß, Lächeln*›; ~ **procession** Triumphzug, *der*
victoriously [vɪk'tɔ:rɪəslɪ] *adv.* erfolgreich; siegreich ‹*kämpfen, zurückkehren*›; triumphierend ‹*rufen, lächeln, marschieren*›
victory ['vɪktərɪ] *n.* Sieg, *der* **(over** über + *Akk.*); *attrib.* Sieges-; **achieve** ~: den Sieg erringen; **be sure of** ~: der sichere Sieger sein; **lead one's troops to** ~: seine Truppen zum Sieg führen; ~ **will be ours** der Sieg wird unser sein; **gain** *or* **win a** ~ **over sb./sth.** einen Sieg über jmdn./etw. erringen; *see also* **moral victory; Pyrrhic**
victual ['vɪtl] *(formal)* **1.** *n. in pl.* Eßwaren *Pl.; (of fort, ship, for journey)* Proviant, *der.* **2.** *v. t., (Brit.)* **-ll-** verproviantieren
victualler ['vɪtələ(r)] *n.* **licensed** ~ *(Brit.)* Gastwirt, *der/*-wirtin, *die*
vide ['vaɪdɪ, 'vɪdeɪ, 'vi:deɪ] *v. t. imper.* siehe
video ['vɪdɪəʊ] **1.** *adj.* Video‹*recorder, -kassette, -kopf*›. **2.** *n., pl.* ~**s a)** *(~ recorder)* Videorecorder, *der; (~ film, ~tape, ~ recording)* Video, *das (ugs.);* **have sth. on** ~: etw. auf Video haben *(ugs.);* **b)** *(visual element of TV broadcasts)* Bild, *das.* **3.** *v. t. see* **videotape 2**
video: ~ **camera** *n.* Videokamera, *die;* ~ **cas'sette** *n.* Videokassette, *die;* ~ **cas'sette recorder** *n.* Videokassettenrecorder *der;* ~ **disc** *n.* Bild- *od.* Videoplatte, *die;* ~ **film** *n.* Videofilm, *der;* ~ **frequency** *n.* Videofrequenz, *die;* ~ **game** *n.* Videospiel, *das;* ~**gram** ['vɪdɪəʊgræm] *n. bespielte Videokassette od. -platte, die keine private Kopie und kein Fernsehmitschnitt ist;* ~ '**nasty** *n.* Horrorvideo, *das;* ~**phone** *n.* Bildtelefon, *das;* ~ **recorder** *n.* Videorecorder, *der;* ~ **recording** *n.* Videoaufnahme, *die;* ~ **signal** *n.* Videosignal, *das;* ~**tape 1.** *n.* Videoband, *das;* **2.** *v. t.* [auf Videoband *(Akk.)*] aufnehmen; ~ **telephone** *n.* Bildtelefon, *das;* ~**tex** ['vɪdɪəʊteks], ~**text** *n.* Bildschirmtext, *der; (teletext)* Videotext, *der*
vie [vaɪ] *v. i.,* **vying** ['vaɪɪŋ] ~ **[with sb.] for sth.** [mit jmdm.] um etw. wetteifern; ~ **with sb. in sth.** jmdn. mit etw. zu übertreffen suchen
Vienna [vɪ'enə] **1.** *pr. n.* Wien *(das).* **2.** *attrib. adj.* Wiener
Viennese [vɪə'ni:z] **1.** *adj.* Wiener; **sb. is** ~: jmd. ist Wiener/Wienerin. **2.** *n., pl. same* Wiener, *der/*Wienerin, *die*
Vietnam [vɪet'næm] *pr. n.* **a)** Vietnam *(das);* **b)** ~ **[War]** Vietnamkrieg, *der*
Vietnamese [vɪetnə'mi:z] **1.** *adj.* vietnamesisch. **2.** *n., pl. same* **a)** *(person)* Vietnamese, *der/*Vietnamesin, *die;* **b)** *(language)* Vietnamesisch, *das*
view [vju:] **1.** *n.* **a)** *(range of vision)* Sicht, *die;* **get a good** ~ **of sth.** etw. gut sehen können; **have** *or* **get one's first** ~ **of sth.** etw. zum ersten Mal zu sehen bekommen; **have a clear/distant** ~ **of sth.** etw. deutlich/in der Ferne sehen können; **be out of/in** ~: nicht zu sehen/zu sehen sein; **come into** ~: in Sicht kommen; **be lost to** ~: nicht mehr zu sehen sein; **disappear from** ~: verschwinden; **leave the back exposed to [the]** ~: ‹*Kleid:*› den Rücken freilassen; **our hotel has a good** ~ **of the sea** von unserem Hotel aus kann man das Meer gut sehen; **in full** ~ **of everyone in the street** vor den Augen aller Passanten; *see also* **'full 1 d; 'hide 1 c; b)** *(what is seen)* Aussicht, *die;* **the** ~**s from here** die Aussicht von hier; **a house with fine** ~**s** ein Haus mit schöner Aussicht; **a room with a** ~: ein Zimmer mit Aussicht; **just for the** ~**/views** nur um die Aussicht zu genießen; **c)** *(picture)* Ansicht, *die;* **photographic** ~: Foto, *das;* **take a** ~ **of sth.** ein Bild von etw. machen; **d)** *(opinion)* Ansicht, *die;* **what is your** ~ *or* **are your** ~**s on this?** was meinst du dazu?; **what is your** ~ **of him?** was hältst du von ihm?; **be grateful for sb.'s** ~ **of** *or* ~**s on sth.** jmdm. für eine Stellungnahme zu etw. dankbar sein; **don't you have any** ~**[s] about it?** hast du keine Meinung dazu?; **the** ~**s of the public** die öffentliche Meinung; **the general/majority** ~ **is that ...:** die Allgemeinheit/Mehrheit ist der Ansicht, daß ...; **take a favourable** ~ **of sth.** etw. billigen; **have** *or* **hold** ~**s about** *or* **on sth.** eine Meinung über etw. *(Akk.)* haben; **hold** *or* **take the** ~ **that ...:** der Ansicht sein, daß ...; **in my** ~: meiner Ansicht nach; **in sb.'s** ~: nach jmds. Ansicht; **I take a different** ~: ich bin anderer Ansicht; **take a critical/grave/optimistic** ~ **of sth.** etw. kritisch/ernst/optimistisch beurteilen; *see also* **dim 1 e; 'long 1 a; poor 1 i; e) be on** ~ ‹*Waren, Haus:*› besichtigt werden können; ‹*Bauplan:*› [zur Einsicht] ausliegen; **have sth. in** ~ *(fig.)* etw. im Auge haben; **in** ~ **of sth.** *(fig.)* angesichts einer Sache; **keep sth. in** ~ *(fig.)* etw. im Auge behalten; **with a** ~ **to** *or* **with a** *or* **the** ~ **of doing sth.** in der Absicht, etw. zu tun; **with a** ~ **to sth.** *(fig.)* mit etw. im Auge; **with this in** ~: in Anbetracht dessen; *see also* **point 1 k; f)** *(survey)* Betrachtung, *die; (of house, site)* Besichtigung, *die;* **on taking a closer** ~: bei näherer Betrachtung; **if we take a broad** *or* **general** ~ **of the problem** bei allgemeiner Betrachtung des Problems; **give a** ~ **of sth.** ‹*Buch:*› einen Überblick über etw. *(Akk.)* geben; *see also* **private view[ing]. 2.** *v. t.* **a)** *(look at)* sich *(Dat.)* ansehen; **b)** *(consider)* betrachten; beurteilen ‹*Situation, Problem*›; ~**ed in this light ...:** so gesehen ...; ~**ed ethically** aus ethischer Sicht; **I** ~ **the matter differently** ich sehe das anders; **c)** *(inspect)* besichtigen; **ask to** ~ **sth.** darum bitten, etw. besichtigen zu dürfen. **3.** *v. i. (Telev.)* fernsehen
viewdata ['vju:deɪtə] *n. (Teleph.)* Bildschirmtextsystem, *das*
viewer ['vju:ə(r)] *n.* **a)** *(Telev.)* [Fernseh]zuschauer, *der/*-zuschauerin, *die;* **b)** *(Photog.) (for cine film)* Filmbetrachter, *der; (for slides)* Diabetrachter, *der*
'**viewfinder** *n. (Photog.)* Sucher, *der*
viewing ['vju:ɪŋ] *n.* **a)** *(Telev.)* Fernsehen, *das;* ~ **has decreased** der Fernsehkonsum ist zurückgegangen; ~ **figures** Einschaltquoten; **at peak** ~ **time** zur besten Sendezeit; **b)** *(of house, at auction, etc.)* Besichtigung, *die; see also* **private view[ing]**
viewpoint ['vju:pɔɪnt] *n.* Standpunkt, *der;* Sehweise, *die;* **from a general/the political/the social** ~ **...:** allgemein/politisch/gesellschaftlich gesehen *od.* betrachtet, ...; **seen from that** ~ **...:** so gesehen *od.* betrachtet, ...; **see sth. from sb.'s** ~: etw. aus jmds. Sicht sehen
vigil ['vɪdʒɪl] *n.* **a)** Wachen, *das;* **nocturnal** ~: Nachtwache, *die;* **keep** ~ **[over sb.]** [bei jmdm.] wachen; **b)** *(Relig.)* Vigil, *die*
vigilance ['vɪdʒɪləns] *n., no pl.* Wachsamkeit, *die;* **exercise** ~ **lest sb. escape** wachsam sein, damit jmd. nicht entkommt; **escape sb.'s** ~: jmds. Wachsamkeit *(Dat.)* entgehen; jmdm. entgehen
'**vigilance committee** *n. (Amer.)* Bürgerwehr, *die*
vigilant ['vɪdʒɪlənt] *adj.* wachsam; **be** ~ **for sth.** auf etw. *(Akk.)* achten
vigilante [vɪdʒɪ'læntɪ] *n.* Mitglied einer/der Bürgerwehr; ~ **group** Bürgerwehr, *die*
vigilantly ['vɪdʒɪləntlɪ] *adv.* wachsam
vignette [vi:'njet] *n.* **a)** *(Lit.)* Skizze, *die;* **b)** *(Art, Photog.)* vignettiertes Bild
vigor *(Amer.) see* **vigour**
vigorous ['vɪgərəs] *adj.* kraftvoll; kräftig ‹*Person, Tier, Stoß, Pflanze, Wachstum, Trieb*›; robust ‹*Gesundheit*›; leidenschaftlich ‹*Debattierer, Debatte, Verteidigung, Befürworter*›; heftig ‹*Nicken, Attacke, Kritik, Protest*›; intensiv ‹*Gymnastik, Denksport*›; energisch ‹*Versuch, Anstrengung, Leugnen,*

Maßnahme⟩; schwungvoll ⟨*Rede*⟩; **be too ~ for sb.** ⟨*Gymnastik:*⟩ zu anstrengend für jmdn. sein

vigorously ['vɪɡərəslɪ] *adv.* heftig; leidenschaftlich ⟨*musizieren, reden, schreiben*⟩; intensiv ⟨*Gymnastik treiben*⟩; energisch ⟨*versuchen, beginnen*⟩; kräftig ⟨*schrubben, reiben, ziehen, drücken, wachsen*⟩

vigour ['vɪɡə(r)] *n. (Brit.)* **a)** *(of person, animal, sexuality)* Vitalität, *die; (of limbs, body)* Kraft, *die; (of health)* Robustheit, *die; (of debate, argument, struggle, protest, denial, attack, criticism)* Heftigkeit, *die; (of performance, speech)* Schwung, *der; (of words, style, mind, intellect)* Lebendigkeit, *die;* **with ~:** schwungvoll ⟨*musizieren, reden, singen, schauspielern*⟩; kräftig ⟨*reiben, schrubben, drücken, ziehen*⟩; **b)** *(Bot.)* Wuchskraft, *die*

Viking ['vaɪkɪŋ] *n. (Hist.)* Wikinger, *der*/Wikingerin, *die; attrib.* Wikinger-

vile [vaɪl] *adj.* **a)** *(base)* verwerflich *(geh.)*; abscheulich ⟨*Sünde, Charakter, Verbrechen*⟩; gemein ⟨*Verleumdung*⟩; vulgär ⟨*Sprache*⟩; *(repulsive)* widerwärtig; **don't be so ~!** sei nicht so gemein!; **be ~ to sb.** gemein zu jmdm. sein; **b)** *(coll.: very unpleasant)* scheußlich *(ugs.)*

vilely ['vaɪllɪ] *adv.* **a)** in verwerflicher Weise *(geh.)*; **act/behave ~:** abscheulich handeln/gemein sein; **speak ~ of sb.** abscheuliche Dinge über jmdn. sagen; **b)** *(coll.: very unpleasantly)* scheußlich *(ugs.)*

vileness ['vaɪlnɪs] *n., no pl. see* **vile: a)** Verwerflichkeit, *die (geh.)*; Abscheulichkeit, *die;* Gemeinheit, *die;* Vulgarität, *die;* Widerwärtigkeit, *die;* **b)** Scheußlichkeit, *die (ugs.)*

vilification [vɪlɪfɪ'keɪʃn] *n.* Verunglimpfung, *die (geh.)*

vilify ['vɪlɪfaɪ] *v. t.* verunglimpfen *(geh.)*

villa ['vɪlə] *n.* **a)** *(holiday house)* **[holiday] ~:** Ferienhaus, *das;* **b)** *(country house)* **[country] ~:** Landhaus, *das;* **c)** *(Brit.: suburban house) besseres Einfamilienhaus*

village ['vɪlɪdʒ] *n.* Dorf, *das; attrib.* Dorf⟨*leben, -kneipe usw.*⟩

village: ~ 'green *n.* Dorfwiese, *die;* **~ 'idiot** *n.* Dorftrottel, *der*

villager ['vɪlɪdʒə(r)] *n.* Dorfbewohner, *der*/-bewohnerin, *die*

villain ['vɪlən] *n.* **a)** *(scoundrel)* Verbrecher, *der; (arch. derog.)* Schurke, *der;* **b) ~ [of the piece]** *(Theatre; also fig.)* Bösewicht, *der;* **c)** *(coll.: rascal)* [kleiner] Halunke *(scherzh.)*

villainous ['vɪlənəs] *adj.* **a)** gemein; abscheulich; **b)** *(coll.: very bad)* scheußlich *(ugs.)*

villainously ['vɪlənəslɪ] *adv.* gemein; abscheulich; in gemeiner *od.* abscheulicher Weise ⟨*morden, Verrat üben, sich verschwören*⟩

villainy ['vɪlənɪ] *n.* Gemeinheit, *die;* Abscheulichkeit, *die;* **forsake ~:** aller Gemeinheit abschwören

villein ['vɪlɪn] *n. (Hist.)* Leibeigene, *der/die*

vim [vɪm] *n., no pl. (coll.)* Schwung, *der;* **put some [more] ~ into it!** leg dich mal ein bißchen [mehr] ins Zeug! *(ugs.)*

vinaigrette [vɪnɪ'ɡret] *n.* **a)** *(smelling-bottle)* Riechfläschchen, *das;* **b) ~ [sauce]** *(Cookery)* Vinaigrette, *die*

vindicate ['vɪndɪkeɪt] *v. t.* **a)** *(justify, establish)* verteidigen, rechtfertigen ⟨*Person, Meinung, Handeln, Verhalten, Anspruch, Politik*⟩; retten ⟨*Ruf, Ehre, Stellung*⟩; beweisen ⟨*Mut, Ehrlichkeit, Integrität, Behauptung*⟩; *(confirm)* bestätigen ⟨*Recht, Meinung, Urteil, Theorie*⟩; **b)** *(exonerate)* rehabilitieren

vindication [vɪndɪ'keɪʃn] *n. see* **vindicate: a)** Verteidigung, *die;* Rechtfertigung, *die;* Beweis, *der* **(of** für); Bestätigung, *die;* **be a ~ of sth.** etw. rechtfertigen/verteidigen/beweisen/bestätigen; **in ~ of his claim/conduct** *etc.* zur Rechtfertigung seines Anspruchs/Benehmens *usw.;* **b)** Rehabilitierung, *die;* **be a full ~ of sb.** jmdn. vollständig rehabilitieren

vindictive [vɪn'dɪktɪv] *adj.* nachtragend ⟨*Person*⟩; unversöhnlich ⟨*Stimmung*⟩; **~ act/move/attack** Racheakt, *der (geh.)*; **feel ~ or be in a ~ mood [towards sb.]** Rachegefühle [gegenüber jmdm.] hegen; **make sb. [feel] ~:** Rachegefühle bei jmdm. wecken; **be purely ~** ⟨*Tat:*⟩ ein reiner Racheakt sein

vindictively [vɪn'dɪktɪvlɪ] *adv.* aus Rache; **act or behave ~ [towards sb.]** sich nachtragend [gegenüber jmdm.] verhalten

vindictiveness [vɪn'dɪktɪvnɪs] *n., no pl.* Rachsucht, *die (geh.)*; **the ~ of sb.'s nature/mood** jmds. nachtragendes Wesen/jmds. Rachsucht; **feel ~ towards sb.** Rachegefühle gegen jmdn. hegen; **an attitude of ~:** eine nachtragende Haltung

vine [vaɪn] *n.* **a)** Weinrebe, *die;* **b)** *(stem of trailer or climber)* Ranke, *die;* **c)** *(Amer.: trailing or climbing plant)* Rankengewächs, *das*

vinegar ['vɪnɪɡə(r)] *n.* Essig, *der;* **[as] sour as ~:** sehr sauer; *(fig.)* säuerlich ⟨*Miene, Lächeln*⟩; sauertöpfisch *(ugs.)* ⟨*Person*⟩

vinegary ['vɪnɪɡərɪ] *adj.* sauer; *(fig.)* säuerlich; **have a ~ taste** wie Essig schmecken

'vine-leaf *n.* [Wein]rebenblatt, *das;* **stuffed vine-leaves** *(Gastr.)* gefüllte Weinblätter

vineyard ['vɪnjɑːd, 'vɪnjəd] *n.* Weinberg, *der*

vintage ['vɪntɪdʒ] **1.** *n.* **a)** *(season's wine)* Jahrgang, *der; (season's grapes)* Traubenernte, *die;* **last/this year's ~:** der letzte/dieser Jahrgang; **the 1981 ~/a 1983 ~:** der 81er/ein 83er; **b)** *(fig.: particular period)* Jahrgang, *der; (of car, machine)* Baujahr, *das;* **a car of rather ancient ~/1955 ~:** ein Auto ziemlich alten Datums/Baujahr 1955; **music of '60s/1940s ~:** Musik aus den 60ern/40er Jahren; **of modern ~:** neueren Datums; **c)** *(grape-harvest; season)* Weinlese, *die;* **d)** *(quality wine)* erlesener Wein. **2.** *adj.* erlesen ⟨*Wein, Sekt, Whisky*⟩; herrlich ⟨*Komödie, Melodie*⟩; brillant ⟨*Leistung, Interpretation*⟩; *(old-fashioned)* alt ⟨*Modell*⟩; altmodisch ⟨*Stil*⟩; **this year has been a ~ year for port** dieses Jahr war ein gutes Jahr für Portwein; **this play is ~ Pinter** dies ist eines der typischsten und besten Pinter-Stücke

vintage 'car *n. (Brit.)* [zwischen 1917 und 1930 gebauter] Oldtimer

vintner ['vɪntnə(r)] *n.* Weinhändler, *der*/-händlerin, *die*

vinyl ['vaɪnɪl] *n.* **a)** Vinyl, *das;* **b)** *(polyvinyl chloride)* PVC, *das*

viol ['vaɪəl] *n. (Mus.)* Viola, *die*

¹viola [vɪ'əʊlə] *n. (Mus.)* Bratsche, *die;* **~-player** Bratschist, *der*/Bratschistin, *die*

²viola ['vaɪələ] *n. (Bot.)* **a)** Veilchen, *das;* **b)** *(hybrid)* Stiefmütterchen, *das*

viola da gamba [vɪəʊlə də 'ɡæmbə] *n. (Mus.)* Gambe, *die*

violate ['vaɪəleɪt] *v. t.* **a)** verletzen; brechen ⟨*Vertrag, Versprechen, Gesetz*⟩; verstoßen gegen ⟨*Regel, Vorschrift, Prinzipien, Bestimmungen*⟩; verletzen ⟨*Vorschrift*⟩; stören ⟨*Ruhe, Frieden*⟩; verschandeln ⟨*Wälder, Landschaft*⟩; **b)** *(profane)* schänden; entheiligen ⟨*Sabbat*⟩; **c)** *(rape)* vergewaltigen; schänden *(veralt.)*

violation [vaɪə'leɪʃn] *n. see* **violate: a)** Verletzung, *die;* Bruch, *der;* Verstoß, *der* **(of** gegen); Störung, *die;* Verschandelung, *die;* **traffic ~:** Verkehrsdelikt, *das;* **be/act in ~ of** verletzen/brechen/verstoßen gegen; **do sth. in ~ of one's promise/oath** etw. entgegen seinem Versprechen/Eid tun; **they tested nuclear weapons in ~ of the treaty** sie testeten Atomwaffen, obwohl sie damit gegen den Vertrag verstießen; **b)** Schändung, *die;* Entheiligung, *die;* **c)** Vergewaltigung, *die;* Schändung, *die (veralt.)*

violence ['vaɪələns] *n., no pl.* **a)** *(intensity, force)* Heftigkeit, *die; (of blow, waterfall)* Wucht, *die; (of temper)* Ungestüm, *das; (of contrast)* Kraßheit, *die;* **b)** *(brutality)* Gewalt, *die; (at public event)* Gewalttätigkeiten; **psychological ~:** seelische Grausamkeit; **by or with ~:** mit Gewalt; **a man of ~:** ein Mann der Gewalt; **resort to or use ~:** Gewalt anwenden; **commit ~:** Gewalttaten verüben; **do ~ to sth.** *(fig.)* einer Sache *(Dat.)* Gewalt antun; **c)** *(Law)* Gewalt, *die;* **threaten sb. with ~:** jmdm. Gewalt androhen; **threat of ~:** Gewaltandrohung, *die;* **act/crime of ~:** Gewalttat, *die*/Gewaltverbrechen, *das;* **robbery with ~:** [bewaffneter] Raubüberfall

violent ['vaɪələnt] *adj.* gewalttätig; heftig ⟨*Schlag, Attacke, Leidenschaft, Auseinandersetzung, Erschütterung, Reaktion, Schmerzen, Wind*⟩; wuchtig ⟨*Schlag, Stoß*⟩; schwer ⟨*Schock*⟩; krass ⟨*Gegensatz, Kontrast*⟩; grell ⟨*Farbe*⟩; knall⟨*rot, -grün usw.*⟩; Gewalt⟨*verbrecher, -tat*⟩; gnadenlos ⟨*Hitze*⟩; **don't be so ~:** sei nicht so aggressiv; **he has a ~ temper, his character or temper is ~:** er neigt zum Jähzorn; **by ~ means** gewaltsam ⟨*öffnen*⟩; unter Gewaltanwendung ⟨*jmdn. überreden*⟩; **~ death** gewaltsamer *od.* unnatürlicher Tod

violently ['vaɪələntlɪ] *adv. (by means of violence)* brutal; *(with great vigour, intensity)* heftig; *(to a high degree)* völlig ⟨*verstört*⟩; äußerst ⟨*schmerzhaft, verstört, aufgeregt*⟩; absolut ⟨*gegensätzlich*⟩; **live/die ~:** ein gewalttätiges Leben führen/eines gewaltsamen Todes sterben; **discourage sb. from acting/behaving ~:** jmdn. von Gewalttätigkeiten abhalten; **I dislike him ~:** er ist mir äußerst zuwider; **I was ~ ill** ich mußte mich heftig übergeben; **contrast ~:** in eklatantem Widerspruch stehen **(with** zu); **the colours clash ~:** die Farben passen überhaupt nicht zusammen

violet ['vaɪələt] **1.** *n.* **a)** Veilchen, *das;* **sweet ~:** Märzveilchen, *das;* Wohlriechendes Veilchen *(Bot.)*; **shrinking ~** *(fig.)* schüchternes Pflänzchen *(ugs.)*; **don't be such a shrinking ~:** sei kein Angsthase; **b)** *(colour)* Violett, *das;* **dressed in ~:** violett gekleidet. **2.** *adj.* violett

violin [vaɪə'lɪn] *n. (Mus.)* Violine, *die*

violin: ~ case *n.* Geigenkasten, *der;* **~ concerto** *n.* Violinkonzert, *das*

violinist [vaɪə'lɪnɪst] *n. (Mus.)* Geiger, *der*/Geigerin, *die*

violin: ~-maker *n.* Geigenbauer, *der*/-bauerin, *die;* **~-player** *n.* Geiger, *der*/Geigerin, *die;* **~ sonata** *n.* Violinsonate, *die;* **~-teacher** *n.* Geigenlehrer, *der*/-lehrerin, *die*

violoncello [vaɪələn'tʃeləʊ] *n., pl.* **~s** *(Mus. formal)* Violoncello, *das*

VIP [viːaɪ'piː] *n.* Prominente, *der/die;* **the ~s** die Prominenz

viper ['vaɪpə(r)] *n.* **a)** *(Zool.)* Viper, *die;* **common ~:** Kreuzotter, *die;* **b)** *(fig.)* Schlange, *die (abwertend)*; **nourish or nurse a ~ in one's bosom** eine Schlange am Busen nähren *(geh.)*

viperish ['vaɪpərɪʃ] *adj. (fig.)* giftig ⟨*Blick*⟩; scharf ⟨*Zunge*⟩; gehässig ⟨*Mundwerk, Ausdrucksweise*⟩; niederträchtig ⟨*Angriff, Charakter*⟩; Schmäh⟨*rede, -wort*⟩

VIP: ~ lounge *n.* VIP-Halle, *die;* **~ treatment** *n.* Vorzugsbehandlung, *die;* **give sb. ~ treatment** jmdn. mit allen Ehren behandeln

virago [vɪ'rɑːɡəʊ] *n., pl.* **~s** zänkisches Weib *(abwertend)*

viral ['vaɪərl] *adj. (Med.)* Virus-

Virgil ['vɜːdʒɪl] *pr. n.* Vergil *(der)*

virgin ['vɜːdʒɪn] **1.** *n.* **a)** Jungfrau, *die;* **she/he is still a ~:** sie ist noch Jungfrau/er ist noch unschuldig; **b) the [Blessed] V~ [Mary]** *(Relig.)* die [Heilige] Jungfrau [Maria]; **c)**

(Astrol.) **the V~:** die Jungfrau; *see also* **archer b. 2.** *adj.* **a)** *(chaste)* jungfräulich; **b)** *(untouched, unspoiled)* unberührt ‹*Land, Wälder*›; jungfräulich ‹*Schnee*›; makellos ‹*Weiß*›; **~ soil** *(esp. fig.)* unberührter Boden
virginal ['vɜːdʒɪnl] **1.** *adj.* jungfräulich. **2.** *n. in pl. (Mus. Hist.)* Spinett, *das*
virgin 'birth *n.* **a)** *(Biol.)* Jungfernzeugung, *die;* **b)** *(Relig.)* jungfräuliche Geburt
Virginia [vəˈdʒɪnɪə] **1.** *pr. n.* Virginia *(das).* **2.** *n.* **~ [tobacco]** Virginia[tabak], *der;* **~ cigarettes** Virginiazigaretten
Virginia 'creeper *n. (Bot.)* Wilder Wein
Virginian [vəˈdʒɪnɪən] **1.** *adj.* virginisch; Virginier-. **2.** *n.* Virginier, *der*/Virginierin, *die*
Virgin 'Islands *pr. n. pl.* Jungferninseln *Pl.*
virginity [vəˈdʒɪnɪtɪ] *n.* Unschuld, *die; (of girl also)* Jungfräulichkeit, *die*
Virgo ['vɜːgəʊ] *n., pl.* **~s** *(Astrol., Astron.)* die Jungfrau; die Virgo; *see also* **Aries**
Virgoan ['vɜːgəʊən] *n. (Astrol.)* Jungfrau, *die*
virile ['vɪraɪl] *adj.* **a)** *(masculine)* männlich; maskulin *(geh.);* **b)** *(sexually potent)* viril; **c)** *(fig.: forceful, vigorous)* kraftvoll
virility [vɪˈrɪlɪtɪ] *n.* **a)** Männlichkeit, *die;* **b)** *(sexual potency)* Virilität, *die;* Manneskraft, *die;* **c)** *(fig.)* kraftvoller Schwung
virologist [vaɪəˈrɒlədʒɪst] *n.* Virologe, *der*/Virologin, *die*
virology [vaɪəˈrɒlədʒɪ] *n.* Virologie, *die*
virtual ['vɜːtjʊəl] *adj.* **a) a ~ ...:** so gut wie ein/eine ...; praktisch ein/eine ... *(ugs.);* **he is the ~ head of the business** er ist quasi der Chef des Geschäfts *(ugs.);* **the whole day was a ~ disaster** der ganze Tag war geradezu eine Katastrophe; **the traffic came to a ~ standstill** der Verkehr kam praktisch zum Stillstand *(ugs.);* **b)** *(Optics, Mech.)* virtuell ‹*Bild, Verrückung*›
virtually ['vɜːtjʊəlɪ] *adv.* so gut wie; praktisch *(ugs.)*
virtual 'reality *n. (Computing)* virtuelle Realität
virtue ['vɜːtjuː] *n.* **a)** *(moral excellence)* Tugend, *die; (chastity)* Tugendhaftigkeit, *die;* **~ is its own reward** *(prov.)* die Tugend trägt ihren Lohn in sich selbst; *see also* **easy 1 c; b)** *(advantage)* Vorteil, *der;* Vorzug, *der;* **what is the ~ in that?** welchen Vorteil hat das?; **there's no ~ in doing that** es bringt keinen Vorteil, das zu tun; **c) by ~ of** auf Grund, aufgrund (+ *Gen.*). *See also* **necessity a**
virtuosity [vɜːtjʊˈɒsɪtɪ] *n., no pl.* Virtuosität, *die;* **perform with ~:** virtuos spielen
virtuoso [vɜːtjʊˈəʊzəʊ] *n., pl.* **virtuosi** [vɜːtjʊˈəʊziː] *or* **~s** Virtuose, *der*/Virtuosin, *die; attrib.* virtuos ‹*Spiel, Aufführung*›; **a ~ performer** ein Virtuose/eine Virtuosin
virtuous ['vɜːtjʊəs] *adj.* **a)** *(possessing moral rectitude)* rechtschaffen ‹*Person*›; brav ‹*Kind*›; tugendhaft ‹*Leben*›; **if you're feeling ~ you can ...** *(iron.)* wenn du etwas Gutes tun willst, kannst du ...; **that was ~ of you** *(iron.)* das war wirklich löblich *(iron.);* **b)** *(chaste)* keusch
virtuously ['vɜːtjʊəslɪ] *adv.* löblicherweise; **live ~:** ein rechtschaffenes Leben führen; **we ~ went to bed at ten** *(joc.)* wir sind brav um zehn ins Bett gegangen
virtuousness ['vɜːtjʊəsnɪs] *n., no pl. (of person)* Rechtschaffenheit, *die; (of action, life)* Tugendhaftigkeit, *die*
virulence ['vɪrʊləns, 'vɪrjʊləns] *n., no pl.* **a)** *(Med.)* Virulenz, *die; (of poison)* starke Wirkung; **b)** *(fig.: malignancy)* Bosheit, *die*
virulent ['vɪrʊlənt, 'vɪrjʊlənt] *adj.* **a)** *(Med.)* virulent; starkwirkend ‹*Gift*›; **b)** *(fig.: malignant)* heftig; scharf ‹*Angriff*›
virulently ['vɪrʊləntlɪ, 'vɪrjʊləntlɪ] *adv.* heftig; scharf ‹*kritisieren, angreifen*›; **be ~ anticommunist** ein erbitterter Gegner/eine erbitterte Gegnerin des Kommunismus sein
virus ['vaɪərəs] *n.* Virus, *das;* **a ~ infection** eine Virusinfektion
visa ['viːzə] *n.* Visum, *das*
visage ['vɪzɪdʒ] *n. (literary)* Antlitz, *das (geh.); (ugly)* Fratze, *die*
vis-à-vis [viːzɑːˈviː] **1.** *prep.* **a)** *(facing)* gegenüber; **b)** *(compared with)* im Vergleich zu. **2.** *adv.* **stand ~:** sich *(Dat.)* gegenüberstehen. **3.** *n., pl. same* **a)** *(person facing another)* Gegenüber, *das;* Vis-à-Vis, *das (veralt.);* **b)** *(Amer.: social partner)* Partner, *der*/Partnerin, *die*
viscera ['vɪsərə] *n. pl. (Anat.)* Eingeweide
visceral ['vɪsərl] *adj. (Anat.)* Eingeweide-
viscid ['vɪsɪd] *adj.* dickflüssig; sämig
viscose ['vɪskəʊz, 'vɪskəʊs] *n.* Viskose, *die*
viscosity [vɪsˈkɒsɪtɪ] *n.* **a)** *no pl. (quality)* Dickflüssigkeit, *die;* **b)** *(Phys.: of oil etc.)* Viskosität, *die*
viscount ['vaɪkaʊnt] *n.* Viscount, *der*
viscountcy ['vaɪkaʊntsɪ] *n.* Viscountwürde, *die*
viscountess ['vaɪkaʊntɪs] *n.* Viscountess, *die*
viscous ['vɪskəs] *adj.* dickflüssig; *(Phys.)* viskos
vise *(Amer.) see* **²vice**
visibility [vɪzɪˈbɪlɪtɪ] *n., no pl.* **a)** *(being visible)* Sichtbarkeit, *die;* **b)** *(range of vision)* Sicht, *die; (Meteorol.)* Sichtweite, *die;* **reduce ~ to ten metres** die Sichtweite auf zehn Meter verringern
visible ['vɪzɪbl] *adj.* **a)** *(also Econ.)* sichtbar; **be ~ to the naked eye** mit bloßem Auge erkennbar sein; **~ to observers in X** für Beobachter in X zu sehen; **highly ~** *(fig.)* unübersehbar; **b)** *(apparent)* erkennbar; **with ~ impatience** mit sichtlicher Ungeduld
visibly ['vɪzɪblɪ] *adv.* sichtlich
Visigoth ['vɪzɪgɒθ] *n. (Hist.)* Westgote, *der*/Westgotin, *die*
vision ['vɪʒn] *n.* **a)** *(sight)* Sehkraft, *die;* **[range of] ~:** Sichtweite, *die;* **[field of] ~:** Sehfeld, *das; see also* **¹line 1 c; b)** *(dream)* Vision, *die;* Gesicht, *das (geh.); (person seen in dream)* Phantom, *das;* **a ~ in white** *(fig.)* ein Traum in Weiß; **be a [real] ~:** traumhaft schön sein; **c)** *usu. pl. (imaginings)* Phantasien; Phantasiebilder; **have ~s of sth.** von etw. phantasieren; *(more specific)* sich *(Dat.)* etw. ausmalen; **have ~s of having to do sth.** kommen sehen, daß man etw. tun muß; **d)** *(insight, foresight)* Weitblick, *der;* **a man/woman of ~:** ein Mann/eine Frau mit Weitblick; **e)** *(Telev.)* Bild, *das;* **in sound and ~:** in Ton und Bild; **the programme will continue in ~ only until sound is restored** wegen vorübergehenden Tonausfalls z. Z. nur Bildempfang
visionary ['vɪʒənərɪ] **1.** *adj.* **a)** *(imaginative)* phantasievoll; *(fanciful)* phantastisch; **b)** *(imagined)* eingebildet; imaginär *(geh.);* **c)** *(seeing visions)* visionär; **~ power** visionäre *od.* hellseherische Kraft. **2.** *n.* Visionär, *der*/Visionärin, *die;* Hellseher, *der*/Hellseherin, *die (auch fig.)*
visit ['vɪzɪt] **1.** *v. t.* **a)** besuchen; aufsuchen ‹*Arzt*›; **~ the sick** Krankenbesuche machen; **b)** *(dated: afflict)* heimsuchen; **be ~ed with sth.** von etw. heimgesucht werden; **c)** *(Bibl.: inflict punishment for)* **~ the iniquity of the fathers upon the children** der Väter Missetat an den Kindern heimsuchen. **2.** *v. i.* **a)** einen Besuch/Besuche machen; **be ~ing in a town** als Besucher in einer Stadt sein; **I'm only ~ing** ich bin nur zu Besuch; **spend the afternoon ~ing** nachmittags Besuche machen; **~ at a hotel** *(Amer.)* in einem Hotel absteigen; **be ~ing with sb.** *(Amer.)* bei jmdm. zu Besuch sein; **b)** *(Amer.: chat)* plaudern. **3.** *n.* **a)** Besuch, *der;* **pay** *or* **make a ~ to sb.** jmdm. einen Besuch abstatten; **pay a ~** *(coll.: go to the toilet)* aufs Klo gehen *(ugs.);* **she was in London on a ~ to some friends** sie war in London bei Freunden zu Besuch; **have** *or* **receive a ~ [from sb.]** [von jmdm.] besucht werden; **we shall be honoured to receive a ~ from you** es wird uns *(Dat.)* eine Ehre sein, Sie als Besucher zu empfangen; **we had a ~ from the police** wir hatten Besuch von der Polizei; **a ~ to a** *or* **the theatre/a museum** ein Theater-/Museumsbesuch; **a ~ to the British Museum** ein Besuch des Britischen Museums; **a ~ to Rome/the USA** ein Besuch *od.* Aufenthalt in Rom/in den USA; **I'm going on a two-day ~ to Athens** ich fahre für zwei Tage nach Athen; **a ~ to the dentist['s]** ein Besuch beim Zahnarzt; **a home ~ by the doctor [to sb.]** ein Hausbesuch des Arztes [bei jmdm.]; **b)** *(Amer.: chat)* Plauderei, *die*
visitation [vɪzɪˈteɪʃn] *n.* **a)** *(official inspection by bishop etc.)* Visitation, *die;* **a ~ of the sick** eine Krankenvisitation; **b)** *(coll. joc.: protracted visit)* Heimsuchung, *die (ugs. scherzh.);* **we had a ~ from the director today** der Direktor hat uns heute heimgesucht *(ugs. scherzh.);* **c)** *(dated: punishment)* Heimsuchung, *die;* **a ~ of the plague** *(arch.)* eine Heimsuchung durch die Pest
visiting ['vɪzɪtɪŋ] *n.* Besuche *Pl.;* Besuchsdienst, *der;* **she does prison ~:** sie macht Gefängnisbesuche
visiting: ~-card *n.* Visitenkarte, *die (auch fig.);* **~ hours** *n. pl.* Besuchszeiten; **what are the ~ hours in this hospital?** wann ist in diesem Krankenhaus Besuchszeit?; **~ pro'fessor** *n.* Gastprofessor, *der*/-professorin, *die;* **~ team** *n. (Sport)* Gastmannschaft, *die*
visitor ['vɪzɪtə(r)] *n.* **a)** Besucher, *der*/Besucherin, *die; (to hotel, beach, etc.)* Gast, *der;* **have ~s/a ~:** Besuch haben; **we've got a ~ staying for a fortnight** wir haben für vierzehn Tage Besuch *od.* einen Gast; **the ~s** *(Sport)* die Gäste; *see also* **prison visitor; b)** *(Ornith.)* Zugvogel, *der;* **summer ~s** Sommergäste
'visitors' book *n.* Gästebuch, *das;* **sign the ~:** sich ins Gästebuch eintragen
visor ['vaɪzə(r)] *n.* **a)** *(of helmet)* Visier, *das;* **b)** *(eye-shade, peak of cap)* Schirm, *der;* **c)** *(Motor Veh.)* **[sun] ~:** Blendschirm, *der*
vista ['vɪstə] *n.* **a)** *(view)* [Aus]blick, *der* (of auf + *Akk.*); *(long, narrow view)* Perspektive, *die;* **b)** *(fig.)* **open up new ~s** neue Perspektiven eröffnen
Vistula ['vɪstjʊlə] *pr. n.* Weichsel, *die*
visual ['vɪzjʊəl, 'vɪʒjʊəl] *adj.* **a)** *(related to vision)* Seh‹*nerv, -organ*›; **~ sense** Gesichtssinn, *der;* **b)** *(attained by sight)* visuell; optisch ‹*Eindruck, Darstellung*›; bildlich ‹*Vorstellungsvermögen*›; **the ~ arts** die bildenden und darstellenden Künste; **a ~ landing** eine Sichtlandung; **~ display** *(Computing)* Sichtanzeige, *die*
visual: ~ aids *n. pl.* Anschauungsmaterial, *das;* **~ dis'play unit** *n.* Bildschirmgerät, *das*
visualisation, visualise *see* **visualiz-**
visualization [vɪzjʊəlaɪˈzeɪʃn, vɪʒjʊəlaɪˈzeɪʃn] *n.* *(making visual)* Veranschaulichung, *die; (imagining)* Sichvorstellen, *das*
visualize ['vɪzjʊəlaɪz, 'vɪʒjʊəlaɪz] *v. t.* **a)** *(imagine)* sich *(Dat.)* vorstellen; **I can't ~ myself in retirement** ich als Rentner, das kann ich mir nicht vorstellen; **b)** *(envisage, foresee)* voraussehen; **I do not ~ many changes** ich rechne nicht mit großen Veränderungen
visually ['vɪzjʊəlɪ, 'vɪʒjʊəlɪ] *adv.* **a)** *(with regard to vision)* optisch; bildnerisch ‹*begabt*›; **b)** *(by visual means)* bildlich; **record sth. ~:** etw. in Bildern festhalten
vital ['vaɪtl] **1.** *adj.* **a)** *(essential to life)* lebenswichtig; **~ functions** Vitalfunktionen; **b)** *(essential)* unbedingt notwendig; *(crucial)* entscheidend, ausschlaggebend ‹*Frage, Entschluß*› (to für); **it is of ~ importance** *or* **~ that you ...:** es ist von entscheidender Bedeutung, daß Sie ...; **is it ~ for**

you to go? müssen Sie unbedingt gehen?; **your co-operation is ~ to** *or* **for the success of the plan** Ihre Mitarbeit ist unerläßlich für den Erfolg des Plans; **c)** *(full of life)* lebendig, kraftvoll ‹*Stil*›; vital ‹*Person*›. **2.** *n. pl. see* **vital parts**

vitality [vaɪˈtælɪtɪ] *n., no pl.* **a)** *(ability to sustain life)* Lebenskraft, *die;* **b)** *(liveliness)* Vitalität, *die; (of prose, style, language)* Lebendigkeit, *die; (energy)* Energie, *die;* **c)** *(fig.: of institution, organization, etc.)* Dauerhaftigkeit, *die*

vitally [ˈvaɪtəlɪ] *adv.* vital; **~ important** von allergrößter Wichtigkeit; *(crucial)* von entscheidender Bedeutung

vital ˈparts *n. pl.* **the ~** *(dated or joc.)* die lebenswichtigen Organe; *(genitals)* die edlen Teile *(scherzh.)*

vital staˈtistics *n.pl.* **a)** *(data)* Bevölkerungsstatistik, *die;* **b)** *(coll.: woman's body measurements)* Maße; **her ~ are 34–26–34** sie hat die Maße 34/26/34

vitamin [ˈvɪtəmɪn, ˈvaɪtəmɪn] *n.* Vitamin, *das;* **~ C** Vitamin C

vitamin: ~ deficiency *n.* Vitaminmangel, *der;* **~ pill** *n.* Vitamintablette, *die*

vitiate [ˈvɪʃɪeɪt] *v. t.* **a)** *(impair quality of, corrupt)* beeinträchtigen; **b)** *(invalidate)* zunichte machen; hinfällig machen ‹*Vereinbarung, Vertrag*›

viticulture [ˈvɪtɪkʌltʃə(r)] *n.* Weinbau, *der*

vitreous [ˈvɪtrɪəs] *adj.* **a)** *(glasslike)* glasartig; **~ china** Halbporzellan, *das;* **~ enamel** Glasemail, *das;* **b)** *(Anat.)* **~ body** *or* **humour** Glaskörper, *der*

vitrification [vɪtrɪfɪˈkeɪʃn] *n.* Fritten, *das*

vitrify [ˈvɪtrɪfaɪ] *v. t. & i.* fritten

vitriol [ˈvɪtrɪəl] *n.* **a)** *(Chem.)* Vitriol, *das;* **b)** *(fig.: virulence)* ätzende Schärfe

vitriolic [vɪtrɪˈɒlɪk] *adj.* ätzend; giftig ‹*Bemerkung*›; geharnischt ‹*Attacke, Rede*›

vituperate [vɪˈtjuːpəreɪt, vaɪˈtjuːpəreɪt] *v. i. (literary)* wettern (**against** gegen)

vituperation [vɪtjuːpəˈreɪʃn, vaɪtjuːpəˈreɪʃn] *n. (literary)* Schmähungen *Pl. (geh.)*

vituperative [vɪˈtjuːpərətɪv, vaɪˈtjuːpərətɪv] *adj. (literary)* schmähend; **~ language** *or* **speech** Schmähreden; **~ attack on sb.** Schmährede/*(written)* Schmähschrift gegen jmdn.

viva [ˈvaɪvə] *(Brit. Univ. coll.)* **1.** *n.* Mündliche, *das (ugs.).* **2.** *v. t.* mündlich prüfen

vivacious [vɪˈveɪʃəs] *adj.* lebhaft; lebendig ‹*Stil*›; munter ‹*Lachen, Lächeln*›; bunt ‹*Kleider*›

vivaciously [vɪˈveɪʃəslɪ] *adv.* lebhaft; munter ‹*lächeln, lachen*›; bunt ‹*angezogen*›; lebendig ‹*schreiben*›

vivacity [vɪˈvæsɪtɪ] *n., no pl.* Lebhaftigkeit, *die; (of smile, laugh)* Munterkeit, *die; (of style)* Lebendigkeit, *die*

vivarium [vaɪˈveərɪəm] *n., pl.* **vivaria** [vaɪˈveərɪə] Vivarium, *das*

viva voce [vaɪvə ˈvəʊtsɪ, vaɪvə ˈvəʊsɪ] *(Univ.)* **1.** *adv., adj.* mündlich. **2.** *n.* mündliche Prüfung; *(doctoral)* Rigorosum, *das*

vivid [ˈvɪvɪd] *adj.* **a)** *(bright)* strahlend ‹*Helligkeit*›; hell ‹*Blitz*›; lebhaft ‹*Farbe*›; **b)** *(animated)* lebhaft ‹*Person*›; **c)** *(clear, lifelike)* lebendig ‹*Schilderung, Romanfigur*›; lebhaft ‹*Phantasie, Erinnerung*›; **d)** *(intense)* heftig ‹*Schmerz*›; kraftvoll ‹*Töne*›

vividly [ˈvɪvɪdlɪ] *adv.* **a)** *(brightly)* hell; **a ~ coloured dress** ein Kleid in lebhaften Farben; **b)** *(clearly)* lebendig ‹*beschreiben*›; **remember sth. ~:** sich lebhaft an etw. *(Akk.)* erinnern

vividness [ˈvɪvɪdnɪs] *n., no pl.* **a)** *(brightness)* Helligkeit, *die;* **b)** *(liveliness, realism)* Lebhaftigkeit, *die; (of description)* Lebendigkeit, *die*

viviparous [vɪˈvɪpərəs, vaɪˈvɪpərəs] *adj. (Zool.)* vivipar *(fachspr.);* lebendgebärend

vivisect [ˈvɪvɪsekt] *v. t.* vivisezieren *(fachspr.)*

vivisection [vɪvɪˈsekʃn] *n.* Vivisektion, *die (fachspr.)*

vivisectionist [vɪvɪˈsekʃənɪst] *n.: jmd., der Vivisektionen durchführt/befürwortet*

vixen [ˈvɪksn] *n.* **a)** *(Zool.)* Füchsin, *die;* **b)** *(fig.: woman)* Drachen, *der (ugs.)*

viz [vɪz] *adv.* d. h.

vizier [vɪˈzɪə(r), ˈvɪzɪə(r)] *n.* Wesir, *der*

vizor *see* **visor**

ˈV-neck *n.* V-Ausschnitt, *der*

ˈV-necked *adj.* ‹*Pullover, Kleid*› mit V-Ausschnitt

vocabulary [vəˈkæbjʊlərɪ] *n.* **a)** *(list)* Vokabelverzeichnis, *das;* **learn ~:** Vokabeln lernen; **~ test** Vokabeltest, *der;* **b)** *(language of particular field)* Vokabular, *das;* **c)** *(range of language)* Wortschatz, *der*

vocal [ˈvəʊkl] **1.** *adj.* **a)** *(concerned with voice)* stimmlich; **a ~ organ** ein Stimmorgan; **b)** *(expressing oneself freely)* gesprächig; lautstark ‹*Minderheit, Gruppe, Protest*›; **he was very ~ about his rights** er sprach sehr viel von seinen Rechten. **2.** *n. (Mus.)* Vokalpartie, *die;* Vocal, *das (fachspr.)*

ˈvocal cords *n.pl.* Stimmbänder

vocalic [vəˈkælɪk] *(Phonet.) adj.* vokalreich

vocalise *see* **vocalize**

vocalist [ˈvəʊkəlɪst] *n.* Sänger, *der*/Sängerin, *die (bei einer Band od. Combo)*

vocalize [ˈvəʊkəlaɪz] *v.t. & i.* vokalisieren

vocal: ~ music *n.* Vokalmusik, *die;* **~ score** *n. (Mus.)* Vokalpartitur, *die*

vocation [vəˈkeɪʃn] *n.* **a)** *(call to career; also Relig.)* Berufung, *die;* **he felt no ~ for the ministry** er fühlte sich nicht zum Geistlichen berufen; **teaching is a ~ as well as a profession** Lehrer sein ist Berufung und Beruf zugleich; **b)** *(special aptitude)* Begabung, *die* (**for** für); **c)** *(profession)* Beruf, *der*

vocational [vəˈkeɪʃənl] *adj.* berufsbezogen

vocational: ~ college *n.* Berufsschule, *die;* **~ guidance** *n.* Berufsberatung, *die;* **~ training** *n.* berufliche Bildung

vocative [ˈvɒkətɪv] *(Ling.)* **1.** *adj.* Vokativ-; **~ case** Vokativ, *der.* **2.** *n.* Vokativ, *der*

vociferate [vəˈsɪfəreɪt] **1.** *v. i.* wettern; zetern. **2.** *v. t.* herausschreien ‹*Flüche usw.*›

vociferation [vəsɪfəˈreɪʃn] *n.* Gezeter, *das; (of opinions etc.)* Herausschreien, *das*

vociferous [vəˈsɪfərəs] *adj.* *(noisy)* laut; krakeelend *(ugs.)* ‹*Zwischenrufer usw.*›; *(insistent)* lautstark ‹*Forderung, Protest*›

vociferously [vəˈsɪfərəslɪ] *adv.* laut; lautstark ‹*protestieren usw.*›

vociferousness [vəˈsɪfərəsnɪs] *n., no pl.* Lautstärke, *die*

vodka [ˈvɒdkə] *n.* Wodka, *der*

vogue [vəʊg] *n.* Mode, *die;* **the ~ for large hats** die Mode mit den großen Hüten; **there is a ~ for holidays on canal boats** Urlaub auf Kanalbooten ist große Mode; **be in/come into ~:** in Mode sein/kommen; **go out of ~:** aus der Mode kommen; **have** *or* **enjoy a ~:** ‹*Künstler usw.:*› gerade sehr populär sein

ˈvogue-word *n.* Modewort, *das*

voice [vɔɪs] **1.** *n.* **a)** *(lit. or fig.)* Stimme, *die;* **in a firm/loud ~:** mit fester/lauter Stimme; **like the sound of one's own ~:** sich selbst gerne reden hören; **lose one's ~:** die Stimme verlieren; **be in [good]/bad ~:** [gut]/nicht [gut] bei Stimme sein; **make one's ~ heard** sich verständlich machen; *(fig.)* sich *(Dat.)* Gehör verschaffen; **b)** *(expression)* **give ~ to sth.** einer Sache *(Dat.)* Ausdruck geben; **c)** *(expressed opinion)* Stimme, *die;* **with one ~:** einstimmig; **lend one's ~ to sth.** in etw. *(Akk.)* einstimmen; **have a/no ~ in the matter** ein/kein Mitspracherecht bei der Angelegenheit haben; **d)** *(Mus.)* Stimme, *die;* **[singing] ~:** Singstimme, *die;* **study ~:** Gesang studieren; **setting for five ~s** fünfstimmige Vertonung; **e)** *(Phonet.)* stimmhafter Laut; **f)** *(Ling.)* Genus verbi, *das;* **the active/passive ~:** das Aktiv/Passiv. **2.** *v. t.* **a)** *(express)* zum Ausdruck bringen ‹*Meinung*›; **b)** *esp. in p.p. (Phonet.)* stimmhaft aussprechen; **a ~d consonant** ein stimmhafter Konsonant

ˈvoice-box *n.* Kehlkopf, *der*

voiceless [ˈvɔɪslɪs] *adj.* **a)** stumm; sprachlos *(geh.);* **b)** *(Phonet.)* stimmlos

voice: ~-over *n.* Begleitkommentar, *der;* **~-print** *n.* Sonogramm, *das;* **~ teacher** *n.* Gesang[s]lehrer, *der*/-lehrerin, *die;* **~ vote** *n. (Amer.)* Abstimmung durch Zuruf

void [vɔɪd] **1.** *adj.* **a)** *(empty)* leer; öd [und leer] ‹*Gelände*›; **b)** *(invalid)* ungültig; **his efforts were rendered ~:** seine Bemühungen wurden zunichte gemacht; *see also* **null; c)** *(Cards)* **my hand was ~ in hearts** ich hatte kein Herz auf der Hand; **d)** *(lacking)* **~ of** ohne [jeden/jedes/jede]; **a proposal wholly ~ of sense** ein Vorschlag ohne jeden Sinn. **2.** *n.* **a)** *(empty space)* Nichts, *das;* **the vast desert ~s** die endlose Öde der Wüste; **b)** *(fig.)* **nobody can fill the ~ left by his death** keiner kann die große Lücke füllen, die sein Tod hinterlassen hat; **there was an aching ~ in her heart** sie spürte im Innern ein schmerzliches Gefühl der Leere; **c)** *(Cards)* **have a ~ in spades** kein Pik haben. **3.** *v. t.* **a)** *(render invalid)* auflösen ‹*Vertrag*›; ablösen ‹*Rente*›; *(Law)* für ungültig erklären ‹*Vertrag, Vereinbarung*›; **b)** *(empty)* entleeren ‹*Blase, Darm*›

voile [vɔɪl, vwɑːl] *n. (Textiles)* Voile, *der*

vol. *abbr.* **volume** Bd.

volatile [ˈvɒlətaɪl] *adj.* **a)** *(Chem.)* flüchtig; volatil *(fachspr.);* **~ oil** *see* **ethereal oil; b)** *(fig.) (lively)* impulsiv; *(changeable)* unbeständig ‹*Mensch, Laune*›; *(likely to erupt)* explosiv ‹*Temperament*›; brisant ‹*Lage*›

volatilise *see* **volatilize**

volatility [vɒləˈtɪlɪtɪ] *n., no pl.* **a)** *(Chem.)* Flüchtigkeit, *die;* Volatilität, *die (fachspr.);* **b)** *(fig.) see* **volatile b:** Impulsivität, *die;* Unbeständigkeit, *die;* Explosivität, *die;* Brisanz, *die*

volatilize [vəˈlætɪlaɪz] **1.** *v. t. (Chem.)* verflüchtigen. **2.** *v. i.* sich verflüchtigen

vol-au-vent [ˈvɒləʊvɑ̃] *n. (Gastr.)* Pastete, *die;* **chicken ~:** Königinpastete, *die*

volcanic [vɒlˈkænɪk] *adj.* **a)** vulkanisch; **~ eruption** Vulkanausbruch, *der;* **~ in origin** vulkanischen Ursprungs; **b)** *(fig.: violent)* leidenschaftlich

volcano [vɒlˈkeɪnəʊ] *n., pl.* **~es** Vulkan, *der*

vole [vəʊl] *n.* Wühlmaus, *die;* **field ~:** Feldmaus, *die;* **American ~:** Neuweltmaus, *die; see also* **water-vole**

Volga [ˈvɒlgə] *pr. n.* Wolga, *die*

volition [vəˈlɪʃn] *n.* Wille, *der;* **of one's own ~:** aus eigenem Willen; freiwillig

volley [ˈvɒlɪ] **1.** *n.* **a)** *(discharge of missiles)* Salve, *die;* **a ~ of stones/arrows** ein Hagel von Steinen/Pfeilen; ein Stein-/Pfeilhagel; **b)** *(fig.)* **a ~ of oaths/curses** eine Schimpfkanonade; **direct a ~ of questions at sb.** jmdn. mit Fragen bombardieren; **c)** *(Tennis)* Volley, *der; (Football)* Volleyschuß, *der;* **half-~:** Halfvolley, *der.* **2.** *v. t. (Tennis, Football)* vollieren

ˈvolleyball *n.* Volleyball, *der*

vols. *abbr.* **volumes** Bde.

volt [vəʊlt] *n. (Electr.)* Volt, *das*

voltage [ˈvəʊltɪdʒ] *n. (Electr.)* Spannung, *die;* **high/low ~:** Hoch-/Niederspannung, *die;* **what's the ~ here?** was für eine Netzspannung hat man hier?

ˈvoltage regulator *n. (Electr.)* Spannungsregler, *der*

volte-face [vɒltˈfæs] *n. (fig.)* Kehrtwendung, *die*

voltmeter [ˈvəʊltmiːtə(r)] *n. (Electr.)* Voltmeter, *das;* Spannungsmesser, *der*

volubility [vɒljʊˈbɪlɪtɪ] *n., no pl.* Redseligkeit, *die (abwertend); (of speech)* Wortreichtum, *der*

voluble [ˈvɒljʊbl] *adj.* redselig *(abwertend);*

wortreich ⟨*Rede*⟩; **be ~ in sb.'s defence** jmdn. wortreich verteidigen

volubly ['vɒljʊblɪ] *adv.* wortreich

volume ['vɒlju:m] *n.* **a)** *(book, set of periodicals)* Band, *der;* **a two-~ edition** eine zweibändige Ausgabe; *(on periodical)* **V~ II no. 3** Jahrgang II, Nr. 3; *see also* **speak 2 c; b)** *(loudness)* Lautstärke, *die; (of voice)* Volumen, *das;* **turn the ~ up/down** das Radio *usw.* lauter/leiser stellen; **~ of sound** Klangfülle, *die;* **c)** *(amount of space)* Rauminhalt, *der;* Volumen, *das; (amount of substance)* Teil, *der;* **two ~s of hydrogen to one of oxygen** zwei Teile Wasserstoff auf einen Teil Sauerstoff; **d)** *(amount, quantity) (of sales etc.)* Volumen, *das;* **~ of traffic/passenger travel** Verkehrs-/Passagieraufkommen, *das;* **he produced a considerable ~ of church music** er hat ein umfangreiches kirchenmusikalisches Werk geschaffen; **e)** *in pl. (mass)* **~s of black smoke** schwarze Rauchschwaden; **I've got ~s of work to do** ich habe ungeheuer viel Arbeit

volume: ~ control *n.* Lautstärkeregelung, *die; (device)* Lautstärkeregler, *der;* **~ production** *n.* Serienproduktion, *die;* **~ sales** *n. pl.* verkaufte Stückzahl

voluminous [və'lju:mɪnəs, və'lu:mɪnəs] *adj.* **a)** *(great in quantity)* voluminös *(geh.);* sehr umfangreich; *(prolific)* sehr produktiv ⟨*Autor*⟩; **b)** *(bulky, loose)* weit ⟨*Kleider*⟩; voluminös *(geh.)* ⟨*Tasche usw.*⟩; voluminös *(scherzh.),* beleibt ⟨*Person*⟩; **~ garment** wallendes Gewand

voluntarily ['vɒləntərɪlɪ] *adv.* freiwillig

voluntary ['vɒləntərɪ] **1.** *adj.* **a)** freiwillig; **~ army** Freiwilligenarmee, *die;* **~ organizations** Freiwilligenverbände; **V~ Service Overseas** *(Brit.)* Freiwilliger Entwicklungsdienst; **b)** *(controlled by will)* willkürlich ⟨*Muskeln, Bewegungen*⟩. **2.** *n. (Mus.)* Voluntary, *das*

volunteer [vɒlən'tɪə(r)] **1.** *n.* Freiwillige, *der/die;* **any ~s?** Freiwillige vor!; **as a ~:** als Freiwilliger/Freiwillige; *attrib.* **~ army/force** Freiwilligenheer, *das*/Freiwilligenverband, *der.* **2.** *v. t. (offer)* anbieten ⟨*Hilfe, Dienste*⟩; zur Verfügung stellen ⟨*Spende*⟩; herausrücken mit *(ugs.)* ⟨*Informationen, Neuigkeiten*⟩; **~ advice** unerbetene Ratschläge erteilen. **3.** *v. i.* sich [freiwillig] melden; **~ to do** *or* **for the shopping** sich zum Einkaufen bereiterklären

voluptuary [və'lʌptjʊərɪ] *n.* Genußmensch, *der;* Hedonist, *der*/Hedonistin, *die (geh.)*

voluptuous [və'lʌptjʊəs] *adj.* **a)** *(sexually alluring)* üppig ⟨*Figur, Kurven, Blondine*⟩; aufreizend ⟨*Bewegungen*⟩; sinnlich ⟨*Mund*⟩; **b)** *(concerned with pleasures)* ausschweifend; sinnlich, erregend ⟨*Gefühl*⟩

voluptuously [və'lʌptjʊəslɪ] *adv.* üppig ⟨*geformt*⟩; sinnlich ⟨*küssen*⟩; aufreizend ⟨*sich bewegen*⟩

voluptuousness [və'lʌptjʊəsnɪs] *n. (sexual allure)* Üppigkeit, *die; (of movements, mouth)* Sinnlichkeit, *die*

volute [və'lju:t] *n. (Archit.)* Volute, *die*

vomit ['vɒmɪt] **1.** *v. t.* **a)** erbrechen; **b)** *(fig.: send out)* **~ [out]** [aus]speien ⟨*Rauch, Asche, Lava*⟩. **2.** *v. i.* sich übergeben; [sich] erbrechen. **3.** *n.* Erbrochene, *das*

voodoo ['vu:du:] *n.* **a)** *(witchcraft)* Wodu, *der;* **b)** *(spell)* Woduzauber, *der*

voracious [və'reɪʃəs] *adj.* **a)** *(ravenous)* gefräßig ⟨*Person, Tier*⟩; unbändig ⟨*Appetit*⟩; **b)** *(fig.: insatiable)* unersättlich ⟨*Lust, Leser*⟩

voraciously [və'reɪʃəslɪ] *adv. (lit. or fig.)* gierig ⟨*verschlingen, lesen*⟩; **be ~ hungry** einen unbändigen Hunger haben

voracity [və'ræsɪtɪ] *n., no pl.* Gefräßigkeit, *die; (fig.: insatiability)* Gier, *die*

vortex ['vɔ:teks] *n., pl.* **vortices** ['vɔ:tɪsi:z] *or* **~es** *(whirlpool, whirlwind)* Wirbel, *der; (eddying current; also fig.: whirl)* Strudel, *der*

Vosges [vəʊʒ] *pr. n. pl.* Vogesen *Pl.*

votary ['vəʊtərɪ] *n.* **a)** *(Relig.)* Gottesdiener, *der*/-dienerin, *die;* **b)** *(literary: ardent follower)* Anhänger, *der*/-hängerin, *die*

vote [vəʊt] **1.** *n.* **a)** *(individual ~)* Stimme, *die;* **a majority of ~s** eine Stimmenmehrheit; **my ~ goes to X, X has my ~** *(fig. coll.)* ich stimme *od.* bin für X; **b)** *(act of voting)* Abstimmung, *die;* **take a ~ on sth.** über etw. *(Akk.)* abstimmen; *see also* **[1]put 1 e; c)** *(right to ~)* **have/be given** *or* **get the ~:** das Stimmrecht haben/bekommen; **d)** *(collective)* Stimmen; *(result)* Abstimmungsergebnis, *das;* **the ~ in favour of capital punishment** die Stimmenzahl für die Todesstrafe; **the Irish/Black/Labour/Conservative ~:** die Stimmen der Iren/Schwarzen/Labourpartei/Konservativen; **e)** *(expression of opinion)* Votum, *das;* **give sb. a ~ of confidence/no confidence** jmdm. sein Vertrauen/Mißtrauen aussprechen; **~ of confidence/no confidence** Vertrauens-/Mißtrauensvotum, *das;* **propose a ~ of thanks** eine Dankadresse halten; **f)** *(Brit. Parl.: money granted)* Etat, *der.* **2.** *v. i.* abstimmen; *(in election)* wählen; **~ for/against** stimmen für/gegen; **~ for Smith** wählen Sie Smith; **~ on a motion** über einen Antrag abstimmen; **~ to do sth.** beschließen, etw. zu tun; **~ by acclamation/ballot/[a] show of hands** durch Akklamation/mit Stimmzetteln/durch Handzeichen abstimmen; **~ with one's feet** *(fig.)* mit den Füßen abstimmen; **~ Conservative/Labour** *etc.* die Konservativen/Labour *usw.* wählen. **3.** *v. t.* **a)** *(elect)* **~ sb. Chairman/President** *etc.* jmdn. zum Vorsitzenden/Präsidenten *usw.* wählen; **~ sb. on to a committee** jmdn. in einen Ausschuß wählen; *(approve)* **~ a sum of money for sth.** einen Betrag für etw. bewilligen; **b)** *(coll.: pronounce)* bezeichnen; **~ sth. a success/failure** etw. als Erfolg/Mißerfolg bezeichnen; **c)** *(coll.: suggest)* vorschlagen; **I ~ [that] we go home** ich schlage vor *od.* bin dafür, daß wir nach Hause gehen

~ 'down *v. t.* niederstimmen

~ 'in *v. t.* wählen ⟨*Partei, Regierung*⟩

~ 'out *v. t.* abwählen

~ 'through *v. t.* stimmen für ⟨*Gesetz*⟩

'vote-catching *n.* Stimmenfang, *der;* **~ concessions** Zugeständnisse im Hinblick auf die Wahl

voter ['vəʊtə(r)] *n.* Wähler, *der*/Wählerin, *die;* **the turn-out of ~s** die Wahlbeteiligung

voting ['vəʊtɪŋ] *n.* Abstimmen, *das; (in election)* Wählen, *das;* **the ~ was 220 for, 165 against** das Ergebnis der Abstimmung war 220 [Stimmen] dafür, 165 dagegen

voting: ~ paper *n.* Stimmzettel, *der;* **~ system** *n.* Wahlsystem, *das*

votive ['vəʊtɪv] *adj.* Votiv⟨*bild, -kerze*⟩

vouch [vaʊtʃ] **1.** *v. t.* **~ that ...:** sich dafür verbürgen, daß ... **2.** *v. i.* **~ for sb./sth.** sich für jmdn./etw. verbürgen

voucher ['vaʊtʃə(r)] *n.* **a)** Gutschein, *der;* Voucher, *der (Tourismus);* **b)** *(proof of payment)* Beleg, *der*

vouchsafe [vaʊtʃ'seɪf] *v. t. (dated, formal)* gewähren; zu geben geruhen *(geh.)* ⟨*Auskünfte*⟩; **~ to do sth.** geruhen, etw. zu tun *(geh.)*

vow [vaʊ] **1.** *n.* Gelöbnis, *das; (Relig.)* Gelübde, *das;* **make** *or* **take a ~ of loyalty to sb.** jmdm. gegenüber ein Treuegelöbnis ablegen; **lovers' ~s** Treueschwüre; **be under a ~:** an ein Gelübde gebunden sein; **be under a ~ of silence** zu schweigen gelobt haben; *(Relig.)* ein Schweigegelübde abgelegt haben. **2.** *v. t.* **~ sth./to do sth.** etw. geloben/geloben, etw. zu tun; **~ to take revenge on sb.** jmdm. Rache schwören

vowel ['vaʊəl] *n.* Vokal, *der;* Selbstlaut, *der;* **~ sound** Vokallaut, *der*

vox populi [vɒks 'pɒpjʊli:] *n.* Vox populi, *die (geh.);* Stimme des Volkes

voyage ['vɔɪɪdʒ] **1.** *n.* Reise, *die; (sea ~)* Seereise, *die;* **outward/homeward ~, ~ out/home** Hin-/Rückreise, *die;* **a ~ to the moon** ein Mondflug; **he was on a ~ of discovery** *(lit. or fig.)* er war auf einer Entdeckungsreise. **2.** *v. i. (literary)* reisen. **3.** *v. t.* bereisen; befahren ⟨*Meere*⟩

voyager ['vɔɪɪdʒə(r)] *n. (literary)* Reisende, *der/die; (sea ~)* Seereisende, *der/die*

voyeur [vwɑ:'jɜ:(r)] *n.* **a)** *(sexual)* Voyeur, *der;* **b)** *(prying observer)* Gaffer, *der (ugs.)*

voyeurism [vwɑ:'jɜ:rɪzm] *n., no pl.* Voyeurismus, *der;* Voyeurtum, *das*

VP *abbr.* **Vice-President** VP

vroom [vru:m, vrʊm] *int.* brumm

vs *abbr.* **versus** gg.

'V-shaped *adj.* V-förmig

'V-sign *n.* **a)** *(sign for victory)* Siegeszeichen, *das;* **b)** *(gesture of abuse, contempt) Zeichen, das „Du kannst mich mal!" signalisiert*

VSO *abbr.* **Voluntary Service Overseas**

VTO[L] ['vi:tɒl] *abbr. (Aeronaut.)* **vertical take-off [and landing]** Senkrechtstart [und -landung]

vulcanise *see* **vulcanize**

vulcanite ['vʌlkənaɪt] *n.* Hartgummi, *der;* Ebonit, *der (fachspr.)*

vulcanize ['vʌlkənaɪz] *v. t.* vulkanisieren

vulgar ['vʌlgə(r)] *adj.* **a)** vulgär; ordinär ⟨*Person, Benehmen, Witz, Film*⟩; geschmacklos ⟨*Kleidung*⟩; **b) the ~ tongue** *(dated)* die Volkssprache; **c)** *(Math.)* **~ fraction** gemeiner Bruch

vulgarise *see* **vulgarize**

vulgarism ['vʌlgərɪzm] *n. (Ling.)* Vulgarismus, *der*

vulgarity [vʌl'gærɪtɪ] *n., no pl.* Vulgarität, *die; (of clothing)* Geschmacklosigkeit, *die;* **her ~ puts me off** ihre ordinäre *od.* gewöhnliche Art stößt mich ab

vulgarize ['vʌlgəraɪz] *v. t.* vulgarisieren; verderben ⟨*Charakter, Person*⟩

vulgarly ['vʌlgəlɪ] *adv.* vulgär; ordinär; geschmacklos ⟨*sich kleiden*⟩

Vulgate ['vʌlgeɪt, 'vʌlgət] *n. (Bibl.)* Vulgata, *die*

vulnerability [vʌlnərə'bɪlɪtɪ] *n., no pl.* **a)** Angreifbarkeit, *die; (to criticism, temptation)* Anfälligkeit, *die* **(to** für); **b)** *(to injury)* Empfindlichkeit, *die* **(to** gegen); Schutzlosigkeit, *die; (emotional)* Verletzlichkeit, *die*

vulnerable ['vʌlnərəbl] *adj.* **a)** *(exposed to danger)* angreifbar; **a ~ spot/point** ein schwacher Punkt; **be ~ to sth.** für etw. anfällig sein; **be ~ to attack/in a ~ position** leicht angreifbar sein; **be economically ~:** wirtschaftlich in einer prekären Lage sein; **~ to criticism** leicht zu kritisieren; *(easily hurt)* leicht durch Kritik verletzt; **b)** *(susceptible to injury)* empfindlich **(to** gegen); *(without protection)* schutzlos; **~ to infection** anfällig für Infektionen; **look young and ~:** jung und schutzlos aussehen; **emotionally ~:** verletzlich

vulture ['vʌltʃə(r)] *n. (lit. or fig.)* Geier, *der*

vulva ['vʌlvə] *n. (Anat.)* Vulva, *die*

vying *see* **vie**

W

W, w ['dʌblju:] *n., pl.* Ws *or* W's W, w, *das*

W. *abbr.* a) watt[s] W; b) west W.; c) western w.

w. *abbr.* with m.

WAAF *abbr. (Brit. Hist.)* a) Women's Auxiliary Air Force; b) [wæf] *Mitglied der Women's Auxiliary Air Force*

WAC *abbr. (Amer.)* a) Women's Army Corps; b) [wæk] *Mitglied des Women's Army Corps*

wacky ['wækɪ] *adj. (sl.)* bekloppt *(salopp);* verrückt *(ugs.)* ‹Komödie›

wad [wɒd] 1. *n.* a) *(material)* Knäuel, *das; (smaller)* Pfropfen, *der;* a ~ of cotton wool ein Wattebausch; b) *(of papers)* Bündel, *das;* ~s of money bündelweise Geld; he earns ~s of money *(fig.)* er verdient jede Menge Geld. 2. *v. t.,* -dd- a) *(form into ~)* zusammenknüllen; b) *(line)* füttern ‹Kleidungsstück›; *(stuff)* ausstopfen ‹Zwischenräume›; c) *(protect with cotton wool)* wattieren

wadding ['wɒdɪŋ] *n. (lining)* Futter, *das; (for packing)* Füllmaterial, *das;* Füllsel *Pl.;* cotton ~: Wattierung, *die*

waddle ['wɒdl] 1. *v. i.* watscheln. 2. *n.* watschelnder Gang

wade [weɪd] 1. *v. i.* waten; *(in snow, sand)* stapfen. 2. *v. t.* durchwaten, waten durch ‹Fluß, Bach›

~ **'in** *v. i. (fig. coll.)* [gleich] losgehen; *(tackle task)* sich hineinknien *(ugs.)*

~ **into** *v. t. (fig. coll.)* losgehen auf (+ *Akk.*); ~ into the meal reinhauen *(ugs.)*

~ **through** *v. t.* a) waten durch; stapfen durch ‹Schnee, Unkraut›; b) *(fig. coll.)* durchackern *(ugs.)* ‹Manuskript, Buch›

wader ['weɪdə(r)] *n.* a) *(Ornith.)* Watvogel, *der;* b) *in pl. (boots)* Watstiefel

wadi ['wɒdɪ, 'wɑ:dɪ] *n. (Geog.)* Wadi, *das*

wading bird ['weɪdɪŋ bɜ:d] *see* wader a

wafer ['weɪfə(r)] *n.* a) Waffel, *die; (very thin)* Oblate, *die;* b) *(Eccl.)* Hostie, *die;* c) *(Electronics)* Wafer, *der*

'wafer-thin *adj.* hauchdünn

[1]waffle ['wɒfl] *n. (Gastr.)* Waffel, *die*

[2]waffle *(Brit. coll.: talk)* 1. *v. i.* schwafeln *(ugs. abwertend);* faseln *(ugs. abwertend).* 2. *n.* Geschwafel, *das (ugs. abwertend);* Faselei, *die (ugs. abwertend)*

'waffle-iron *n.* Waffeleisen, *das*

waft [wɒft, wɑ:ft] 1. *v. t.* wehen. 2. *v. i.* ‹Geruch, Duft:› ziehen, *(with perceptible air-movement)* wehen. 3. *n.* Hauch, *der*

[1]wag [wæg] 1. *v. t.,* -gg- ‹Hund:› wedeln mit ‹Schwanz›; ‹Vogel:› wippen mit ‹Schwanz›; ‹Person:› schütteln ‹Kopf›; it was a case of the tail ~ging the dog *(fig.)* da hat der Schwanz mit dem Hund gewedelt *(ugs.);* ~ one's finger at sb. jmdm. mit dem Finger drohen. 2. *v. i.,* -gg- ‹Schwanz:› wedeln/*(of bird)* wippen; her tongue never stops ~ging ihre Zunge steht niemals still; set people's tongues ~ging den Leuten etwas zu reden geben. 3. *n. (of dog's tail)* Wedeln, *das* (of mit); *(of bird's tail)* Wippen, *das* (of mit); *(of person's head)* Schütteln, *das* (of *Gen.*); with a ~ of its tail/his head mit einem Schwanzwedeln/Kopfschütteln

[2]wag *n. (facetious person)* Witzbold, *der (ugs.)*

wage [weɪdʒ] 1. *n. in sing. or pl.* Lohn, *der;* sb.'s weekly ~[s] jmds. Wochenlohn; a job at a reasonable ~/with reasonable ~s eine anständig bezahlte Arbeit; ~s of sin *(fig.)* Lohn der Sünde; der Sünde Lohn *(veralt.).* 2. *v. t.* führen ‹Krieg, Feldzug›; ~ war on or against crime *(fig.)* gegen das Verbrechen zu Felde ziehen

wage: ~-**claim** *n.* Lohnforderung, *die;* ~-**earner** *n.* Lohnempfänger, *der/*-empfängerin, *die;* be the ~-earner of the family der Ernährer/die Ernährerin der Familie sein; ~ **freeze** *n.* Lohnstopp, *der;* ~ **increase** *n.* Lohnerhöhung, *die;* ~ **packet** *n.* Lohntüte, *die;* the size of his ~ packet wieviel er in der Lohntüte hat

wager ['weɪdʒə(r)] *(dated, formal)* 1. *n.* Wette, *die;* a ~ of £50 eine Wette um 50 Pfund. 2. *v. t.* wetten; *(on a horse)* setzen; ~ one's life/one's whole fortune on sth. seinen Kopf/sein ganzes Vermögen auf etw. *(Akk.)* verwetten; I ~ you £10 that ...: ich wette mit dir um 10 Pfund, daß ... 3. *v. i.* wetten; he's there by now, I'll ~: ich möchte wetten, daß er inzwischen da ist

wage: ~ **scale** *n.* Tarif, *der;* Lohnskala, *die;* ~ **slave** *n.* Lohnsklave, *der*

waggish ['wægɪʃ] *adj.* witzig ‹Bemerkung›; be in a ~ mood zu Scherzen aufgelegt sein

waggle ['wægl] *(coll.)* 1. *v. t.* ~ its tail ‹Hund:› mit dem Schwanz wedeln; ‹Vogel:› mit dem Schwanz wippen; ~ a loose tooth an einem lockeren Zahn wackeln. 2. *v. i.* hin und her schlagen; the dog's tail ~d der Hund wedelte mit dem Schwanz. 3. *n.* Hin- und Herschlagen, *das; (of tail)* Wedeln, *das*

waggon *etc. (Brit.) see* wagon *etc.*

Wagnerian [vɑ:g'nɪərɪən] 1. *n.* Wagnerianer, *der/*Wagnerianerin, *die.* 2. *adj.* wagnerianisch; *(of Wagner)* Wagner[i]sch; ~ singer Wagnersänger, *der/*-sängerin, *die*

wagon ['wægən] *n.* a) *(horse-drawn)* Wagen, *der;* covered ~: Planwagen, *der;* hitch one's ~ to a star *(fig.)* sich *(Dat.)* ein hohes Ziel setzen; b) *(Amer.: motor vehicle)* Wagen, *der;* c) [water-]~: Wasserwagen, *der;* d) go/be on the ~ *(go/be teetotal)* keinen Tropfen mehr/keinen Tropfen anrühren; e) *(trolley)* Wagen, *der;* f) *(Brit. Railw.)* Wagen, *der;* Waggon, *der (volkst.)*

wagoner ['wægənə(r)] *n.* Fuhrmann, *der*

'wagonload *n.* [Wagen]ladung, *die*

'wagtail *n. (Ornith.)* Bachstelze, *die*

waif [weɪf] *n.* Heimatlose, *der/die; (child)* verlassenes Kind; *(animal)* herrenloses Tier; ~s and strays *(children)* obdachlose Kinder; *(animals)* streunende Tiere

wail [weɪl] 1. *v. i.* a) *(lament)* klagen *(geh.)* (for um); jammern *(ugs.)* (for um); ‹Kind:› heulen; stop ~ing! hör auf zu jammern!; b) *(fig.)* ‹Wind, Sirene:› heulen. 2. *n.* a) *(cry)* klagender Schrei; ~s Geheul, *das; (esp. fig.: complaints)* Gejammer, *das;* ~s of protest Protestgeschrei, *das;* a ~ of pain ein Schmerzensschrei; b) *(fig.: of wind etc.)* Heulen, *das;* Geheul, *das*

Wailing 'Wall *n.* Klagemauer, *die*

wainscot ['weɪnskət], **wainscoting** ['weɪnskətɪŋ] *ns.* Täfelung, *die*

waist [weɪst] *n.* a) *(part of body or garment)* Taille, *die;* tight round the ~: eng in der Taille; *see also* [1]strip 1 a; b) *(Amer.) (blouse)* Bluse, *die; (bodice)* Mieder, *das;* c) *(narrow part)* Einbuchtung, *die; (of violin)* Mittelbügel, *der; (Naut.: of ship)* Mittelschiff, *das*

'waistband *n.* Gürtelbund, *der; (of trousers)* [Hosen]bund, *der; (of skirt)* [Rock]bund, *der*

waistcoat ['weɪskəʊt, 'weɪstkəʊt] *n. (Brit.)* Weste, *die*

'waist-deep 1. *adj.* bis zur Taille reichend; be ~: einem bis zur Taille reichen. 2. *adv.* bis zur Taille

waisted ['weɪstɪd] *adj.* tailliert ‹Kleidungsstück›

waist: ~-'**high** *see* waist-deep; ~**line** *n.* Taille, *die;* be bad for the ~line schlecht für die schlanke Linie sein

wait [weɪt] 1. *v. i.* a) warten; ~ [for] an hour eine Stunde warten; ~ a moment Moment mal; keep sb. ~ing, make sb. ~: jmdn. warten lassen; how long have you been ~ing? wie lange wartest du schon?; ~ to see sth. happen darauf warten, daß etw. passiert; 'repairs [done]/keys cut while you ~' „Reparatur-/Schlüsselschnelldienst"; she ~ed to see what would happen if ...: sie wollte abwarten, was passiert, wenn ...; sth. is still ~ing to be done etw. muß noch gemacht werden; ~ and see abwarten[, was passiert]; [just] ~ and see! warte doch ab!; sth. can/can't *or* won't ~: etw. kann/kann nicht warten; this bill can't ~: diese Rechnung muß sofort bezahlt werden; I can't ~ to do sth. *(am eager)* ich kann es kaum erwarten, etw. zu tun; I can hardly ~ *(lit. or iron.)* ich kann es kaum erwarten; I can't ~ *(for lavatory)* es ist dringend; [just] you ~! warte mal ab!; *(as threat)* warte nur!; b) ~ at *or (Amer.)* on table servieren; ‹Ober:› kellnern *(ugs.).* 2. *v. t.* a) *(await)* warten auf (+ *Akk.*); ~ one's chance/opportunity auf eine [günstige] Gelegenheit warten; ~ one's turn warten, bis man dran ist *od.* drankommt; ~ sb.'s convenience warten, bis es jmdm. paßt; b) *(delay)* ~ lunch/supper [for sb.] mit dem Mittag-/Abendessen [auf jmdn.] warten. 3. *n.* a) *(act, time)* after a long/short ~: nach langer/kurzer Wartezeit; there is quite a ~ for appointments auf einen Termin muß man ziemlich lange warten; have a long/short ~ for sth. lange/nicht lange auf etw. *(Akk.)* warten müssen; b) *(watching for enemy)* lie in ~: im Hinterhalt liegen; lie in ~ for sb./sth. jmdm./einer Sache auflauern; c) *in pl. (Brit.: carol-singers)* Sternsinger

~ **a'bout,** ~ **a'round** *v. i.* herumstehen

~ **be'hind** *v. i.* noch hier-/dableiben; ~ behind for sb. auf jmdn. warten

~ **for** *v. t.* warten auf (+ *Akk.*); ~ for the rain to stop warten, bis der Regen aufhört; we'll ~ for a fine day wir warten einen schönen Tag ab; I can hardly ~ for the day when ...: ich kann den Tag kaum erwarten, an dem ...; it was worth ~ing for es hat sich gelohnt, darauf zu warten; ~ for it! warte/wartet!; *(to create suspense before saying something surprising)* warte ab!

~ **'in** *v. i.* zu Hause warten (for auf + *Akk.*)

~ **on** *v. t.* a) *(serve)* bedienen; b) *(await)* warten auf (+ *Akk.*)

~ **'out** *v. t.* ~ out a storm *etc.* warten, bis ein Sturm *usw.* vorüber *od.* vorbei ist

~ **'up** *v. i.* aufbleiben (for wegen)

waiter ['weɪtə(r)] *n.* Kellner, *der;* ~! Herr Ober!

waiting ['weɪtɪŋ] *n.* a) Warten, *das;* 'no ~' „Halteverbot"; b) *no pl., no art. (working as waiter)* Servieren, *das;* Kellnern, *das (ugs.)*

waiting: ~ **game** *n.* Hinhaltetaktik, *die;* play a ~ game erst einmal abwarten; sich erst einmal bedeckt halten *(ugs.);* ~-**list** *n.* Warteliste, *die;* a five-year ~-list eine Wartezeit von fünf Jahren; ~-**room** *n.* Wartezimmer, *das; (at railway or bus station)* Warteraum, *der; (larger)* Wartesaal, *der*

waitress ['weɪtrɪs] *n.* Serviererin, *die;* Kellnerin, *die (veralt.);* ~! Fräulein! *(veralt.);* there is ~ service in the ground-floor restaurant das Restaurant im Erdgeschoß ist mit Bedienung

waive [weɪv] *v. t.* verzichten auf (+ *Akk.*); nicht vollstrecken ‹Strafe›; nicht anwenden ‹Regel›

waiver ['weɪvə(r)] *n. (Law)* Verzicht, *der* (of auf + *Akk.*)

[1]wake [weɪk] 1. *v. i.,* woke [wəʊk] *or (arch.)* ~d, woken ['wəʊkn] *or (arch.)* ~d a) *(cease sleeping)* aufwachen; *(fig.)* ‹Natur, Ge-

fühle:⟩ erwachen; **we woke to a bright, cold morning** der Morgen war klar und frisch, als wir aufwachten; **I woke to the sound of soft music** beim Aufwachen hörte ich leise Musik; **b)** ~ **to sth.** *(fig.: realize)* etw. erkennen; sich *(Dat.)* einer Sache *(Gen.)* bewußt werden. **2.** *v. t.* **woke** *or (arch.)* **~d, woken** *or (arch.)* **~d a)** wecken; *(fig.)* erwecken *(geh.)* ⟨*die Natur, Erinnerungen*⟩; wecken ⟨*Erinnerungen*⟩; **be quiet, you'll ~ your baby brother** sei still, sonst wacht dein Brüderchen auf!; ~ **the dead** die Toten erwecken *(geh.) od.* aufwecken; ~ **the country to the danger of war** *(fig.)* dem Land die Kriegsgefahr bewußt machen; **b)** *(cause)* hervorrufen ⟨*Echo*⟩. **3.** *n.* **a)** *(Ir.: watch by corpse)* Totenwache, *die;* **b)** *usu. pl. (N. Engl.)* **~s week, the ~s** ≈ Kirmes, *die*

~ **'up 1.** *v. i. (lit. or fig.)* aufwachen; ~ **up!** wach auf!; *(fig.: pay attention)* paß besser auf!; ~ **up to sth.** *(fig.: realize)* etw. erkennen; sich *(Dat.)* einer Sache *(Gen.)* bewußt werden. **2.** *v. t.* **a)** *(rouse from sleep)* wecken; **b)** *(fig.: enliven)* wachrütteln; Leben bringen in (+ *Akk.*) ⟨*Stadt*⟩; **you need to ~ your ideas up a bit** du müßtest dich ein bißchen zusammenreißen

²wake *n.* **a)** *(water)* Kielwasser, *das;* **b)** *(air)* Turbulenz, *die;* **c)** *(fig.)* **in the ~ of sth./sb.** im Gefolge von etw./in jmds. Gefolge; **follow in the ~ of sb./sth.** jmdm./einer Sache folgen; **bring sth. in its ~:** etw. zur Folge haben; **leave a cloud of dust/trail of destruction in its ~:** eine Staubwolke/eine Spur der Verwüstung hinterlassen

wakeful ['weɪkfl] *adj.* **a)** *(sleepless)* schlaflos ⟨*Nacht*⟩; **a ~ child** ein Kind, das schlecht schläft; **b)** *(vigilant)* wachsam

wakefulness ['weɪkflnɪs] *n., no pl.* **a)** *(sleeplessness)* Schlaflosigkeit, *die;* **b)** *(vigilance)* Wachsamkeit, *die*

waken ['weɪkn] **1.** *v. t.* **a)** wecken; **b)** *(fig.: arouse)* wecken ⟨*Interesse, Gefühl*⟩; erregen ⟨*Zorn*⟩. **2.** *v. i. see* **¹wake 1**

waking ['weɪkɪŋ] *adj.* **in one's ~ hours** den ganzen Tag; von früh bis spät; **spend all one's ~ hours [on] doing sth.** etw. von früh bis spät tun; ~ **dream** Wachtraum, *der*

Wales [weɪlz] *pr. n.* Wales *(das); see also* **prince b**

walk [wɔ:k] **1.** *v. i.* **a)** laufen; *(as opposed to running)* gehen; *(as opposed to driving)* zu Fuß gehen; **you can ~ there in five minutes** es sind nur 5 Minuten zu Fuß bis dorthin; **'~'/'don't ~'** *(Amer.: at pedestrian lights)* „gehen"/„warten"; ~ **on crutches/with a stick** an Krücken/am Stock gehen; **learn to ~:** laufen lernen; **can the child ~ yet?** kann das Kind schon laufen?; **be ~ing on air** *(fig.)* sich wie im siebten Himmel fühlen; ~ **tall** *(fig.)* erhobenen Hauptes gehen *(fig.)*; **b)** *(exercise)* gehen; marschieren *(ugs.)*; **c)** *(appear)* ⟨*Geist:*⟩ erscheinen; **d)** *(go with slow gait)* ⟨*Pferd:*⟩ gehen; **e)** *(Cricket coll.)* rausgehen; **f)** *(coll.: go missing)* Beine bekommen *(fig. ugs.)*. **2.** *v. t.* **a)** entlanggehen; ablaufen ⟨*Strecke, Weg*⟩; durchwandern ⟨*Gebiet*⟩; ~ **the course** *(Sport)* die Strecke abgehen; ⟨*Reiter:*⟩ den Parcours abgehen; ~ **the** *or* **his beat** ⟨*Polizist:*⟩ seine Runde gehen; ~ **the streets** durch die Straßen gehen/*(aimlessly)* laufen; *(as prostitute)* auf den Strich gehen *(ugs.)*; ~ **the boards** *(be actor)* auf den Brettern stehen; ~ **it** *(coll.)* zu Fuß gehen; laufen *(ugs.)*; **he ~ed it** *(fig. coll.: won easily)* es war ein Spaziergang für ihn; *see also* **plank 1 a; b)** *(cause to ~; lead)* führen; ausführen ⟨*Hund*⟩; ~ **sb. round the room** jmdn. im Zimmer herumführen; ~ **sb. off his/her feet** jmdn. [bis zur Erschöpfung] durch die Gegend schleifen *(ugs.)*; **c)** *(accompany)* bringen; **he ~ed his girl-friend home** er brachte seine Freundin nach Hause; **d)** *(push)* schieben ⟨*Fahrrad, Motorrad*⟩. **3.** *n.* **a)** Spaziergang, *der;* **go [out] for** *or* **take** *or* **have a ~:** einen Spaziergang machen; **take sb./the dog for a ~:** jmdn./den Hund spazierenführen; **a ten-mile ~:** eine Wanderung von zehn Meilen; *(distance)* **ten minutes' ~ from here** zehn Minuten zu Fuß von hier; *see also* **space walk; b)** *(gait)* Gang, *der; (characteristic)* normale Gangart; **I know her by her ~:** ich erkenne sie am Gang; **c)** *(walking speed)* Schrittempo, *das;* **his horse/she slowed to a ~:** sein Pferd ging nur noch im Schritt/sie verfiel in ein normales Schrittempo; **d)** *(Sport: race)* Wettbewerb im Gehen; **the 10,000 metres ~:** das 10 000-m-Gehen; **e)** *(path, route)* [Spazier]weg, *der;* **a milkman's/postman's ~:** die Tour eines Milchmanns/Briefträgers; **f) people from all ~s of life** Leute aus den verschiedensten gesellschaftlichen Gruppierungen

~ **a'bout** *v. i.* herumlaufen; in der Gegend herumlaufen *(ugs.); see also* **walkabout**

~ **a'way** *v. i.* **a)** weggehen; **she was lucky to ~ away from the accident** sie hatte großes Glück, den Unfallort unverletzt verlassen zu können; **b)** *(fig.)* ~ **away from the opposition** *or* **competition** *(coll.: defeat)* der Konkurrenz weglaufen; **he tried to ~ away from the problem** *(ignore it)* er versuchte, dem Problem aus dem Weg zu gehen; ~ **away with sth.** *(coll.) (win easily)* etw. spielend leicht gewinnen; *(steal)* sich mit etw. davonmachen *(ugs.)*; ~ **away with all the prizes** alle Preise einheimsen *(ugs.)*

~ **'in** *v. i.* **a)** *(enter)* hereinkommen/hineingehen; reinkommen/-gehen *(ugs.)*; **'please ~ in'** „[bitte] eintreten, ohne zu klopfen"; **b)** *(enter without permission)* hinein-/hereinspazieren; ~ **in on sb./sth.** bei jmdm./etw. hereinplatzen *(ugs.)*

~ **into** *v. t.* **a)** *(enter)* betreten; treten in (+ *Akk.*) ⟨*Pfütze*⟩; *(without permission)* eindringen in (+ *Akk.*) ⟨*Haus*⟩; **b)** *(hit by accident)* laufen gegen ⟨*Pfosten, Laternenpfahl*⟩; ~ **into sb.** mit jmdm. zusammenstoßen; ~ **into a trap** *(lit. or fig.)* in eine Falle gehen; **the boxer ~ed straight into a right hook** der Boxer lief voll in den rechten Haken [hinein]; **you ~ed straight into that one!** da hast du dich aber reinlegen lassen!; **c)** *(coll.: come easily into)* **she ~ed into the top job** ihr ist der Topjob einfach zugefallen

~ **'off 1.** *v. i.* **a)** *(leave)* weggehen; verschwinden; **he has ~ed off with another woman** er ist mit einer anderen Frau durchgebrannt *(ugs.)*; **b)** ~ **off with sth.** *(coll.)* sich mit etw. davonmachen *(ugs.)*; ~ **off with all the prizes** alle Preise einheimsen *(ugs.)*; **he ~ed off with the fight** er hat den Kampf lässig gewonnen. **2.** *v. t.* **I'll have to ~ off some of this fat** ich muß mehr laufen, um ein paar Pfunde loszuwerden *(ugs.)*; ~ **off a hangover** einen Spaziergang machen, um seinen Kater loszuwerden

~ **'on** *v. i.* **a)** *(go further)* weitergehen; ~ **on!** *(to horse)* hü!; **b)** *(go on stage)* auf die Bühne kommen; ~ **on as the policeman or the butler** Statistenrollen wie den Polizisten oder Butler spielen

~ **'out** *v. i.* **a)** *(leave)* hinausgehen; rausgehen *(ugs.)*; **b)** *(Mil.: leave barracks)* ausgehen; **c)** *(leave in protest)* aus Protest den Saal verlassen; *(leave organization)* austreten; **d)** *(go on strike)* in den Streik *od.* Ausstand treten; **e)** *(Brit. dated: be courting)* miteinander gehen *(ugs.)*; ~ **out with sb.** mit jmdm. gehen *(ugs.). See also* **walk-out**

~ **'out of** *v. t.* **a)** *(leave)* gehen aus; **b)** *(leave in protest)* verlassen ⟨*Saal, Versammlung*⟩

~ **'out on** *v. t. (coll.)* verlassen; sitzenlassen *(ugs.)* ⟨*Frau, Mann*⟩; hinschmeißen *(ugs.)* ⟨*Job*⟩

~ **'over** *v. t.* ~ **[all] over sb.** jmdn. fertigmachen *(ugs.); see also* **walk-over**

~ **'up** *v. i.* **a)** *(approach)* sich nähern; ~ **up to sb.** zu jmdm. hingehen; **he ~ed up to me** er kam zu mir [heran]; ~ **up to the door** zur Tür gehen; ~ **up! ~ up!** *(said by showman)* immer hereinspaziert!; **b)** *(ascend)* hochlaufen; nach oben laufen; *see also* **walk-up**

'walkabout *n.* **a)** *(through crowds)* Bad in der Menge *(scherzh.)*; **go on a ~:** sich unters Volk mischen; **b)** *(Austral.: in bush)* Buschwanderung, *die*

walker ['wɔ:kə(r)] *n.* **a)** Spaziergänger, *der*/-gängerin, *die; (in race)* Geher, *der*/Geherin, *die; (rambler, hiker)* Wanderer, *der*/Wanderin, *die;* **sb. is a good ~:** jmd. ist gut zu Fuß; **b)** *(frame)* Laufgestell, *das; (baby-~)* Laufstuhl, *der*

walkies ['wɔ:kɪz] *n. pl. (coll.)* **go ~:** Gassi gehen *(ugs.)*; **~!** *(said to dog)* komm Gassi! *(ugs.)*

walkie-talkie [wɔ:kɪ'tɔ:kɪ] *n.* Walkie-talkie, *das*

walking ['wɔ:kɪŋ] **1.** *attrib. adj.* **a ~ dictionary/encyclopaedia** *(joc.)* ein wandelndes Wörterbuch/Konversationslexikon; **the ~ wounded** die gehfähigen Verwundeten; *see also* **disaster area. 2.** *n., no pl., no art.* [Spazieren]gehen, *das;* Laufen, *das;* **you ought to do more ~:** Sie sollten mehr zu Fuß gehen *od.* spazierengehen; *attrib.* **at ~ pace** im Schrittempo; **be within ~ distance** zu Fuß zu erreichen sein; **we are within ~ distance [of it]** wir können es zu Fuß erreichen

walking: ~ holiday *n.* Wanderurlaub, *der;* **~ shoe** *n.* Wanderschuh, *der;* **~-stick** *n.* Spazierstock, *der;* **she cannot manage now without a ~-stick** sie kommt nicht mehr ohne Stock aus; **~-tour** *n.* Wanderung, *die*

Walkman, (P) ['wɔ:kmən] *n., pl.* **Walkmans** Walkman, *der*

walk: ~-on part *n. (Theatre)* Statistenrolle, *die;* **~-out** *n.* Arbeitsniederlegung, *die;* **~-over** *n. (fig.: easy victory)* Spaziergang, *der (ugs.)*; **~-up** *n. (Amer.)* Haus ohne Aufzug; **~way** *n.* Fußweg, *der; (over machinery etc.)* Laufsteg, *der*

wall [wɔ:l] **1.** *n.* **a)** *(of building, part of structure)* Wand, *die; (external, also free-standing)* Mauer, *die;* **town/garden ~:** Stadt-/Gartenmauer, *die;* **the south ~ of the house** die Südwand des Hauses; **a concrete ~:** eine Betonwand/-mauer; **the Great W~ of China** die Chinesische Mauer; **the Berlin W~** *(Hist.)* die [Berliner] Mauer; **b)** *(internal)* Wand, *die;* **be hanging on the ~:** an der Wand hängen; **hang a picture on the ~:** ein Bild an die Wand hängen; **within these four ~s** *(fig.)* innerhalb dieser vier Wände; **I'm tired of [staring at] my own four ~s** mir fällt die Decke auf den Kopf *(ugs.)*; **~s have ears** die Wände haben Ohren; **drive** *or* **send sb. up the ~** *(fig. coll.)* jmdn. auf die Palme bringen *(ugs.)*; **go up the ~** *(fig. coll.)* die Wände hochgehen *(ugs.)*; **go to the ~** *(fig.)* an die Wand gedrückt werden; *see also* **back 1 a; c)** *(Mount., Min.)* Wand, *die; (fig.)* Mauer, *die;* **a ~ of water/fire** eine Wasser-/Feuerwand; **the North W~ of the Eiger** die Eigernordwand; **a ~ of silence/prejudice** *(fig.)* eine Mauer des Schweigens/von Vorurteilen; **d)** *(esp. Footb.: protective row)* Mauer, *die;* **a ~ of troops/policemen/tanks** eine Mauer von Soldaten/Polizisten/Panzern; **e)** *(Anat., Zool., Bot.: outer layer)* Wand, *die;* **abdominal ~:** Bauchwand, *die.* **2.** *v. t.* **[be] ~ed** von einer Mauer/Mauern umgeben [sein]; **X is a ~ed city/town** X hat eine Stadtmauer

~ **'in** *v. t.* mit einer Mauer umgeben; *(fig.)* umzingeln

~ **'off** *v. t.* abteilen

~ **'up** *v. t.* zumauern; einmauern ⟨*Person*⟩

wallaby ['wɒləbɪ] *n. (Zool.)* Wallaby, *das*

wallah ['wɒlə] *n. (dated sl.)* **television/advertising ~:** Fernseh-/Werbefritze, *der (ugs.)*

wall: ~ bars *n. pl.* Sprossenwand, *die;*

~-**board** *n.* Wandfaserplatte, *die;* ~**chart** *n.* Schautafel, *die;* ~-**covering** *n.* (*~paper*) Tapete, *die;* (*~-hanging*) Wandbehang, *der;* ~-**cupboard** *n.* Hängeschrank, *der*

wallet ['wɒlɪt] *n.* Brieftasche, *die;* (*for cheque card etc.*) Etui, *das*

wall: ~**flower** *n.* **a)** (*Bot.*) Goldlack, *der;* **b)** (*coll.: person*) Mauerblümchen, *das* (*ugs.*); ~-**hanging** *n.* Wandbehang, *der;* ~-**light** *n.* Wandlampe, *die;* ~ **map** *n.* Wandkarte, *die*

Wallonia [wɒ'ləʊnɪə] *pr. n.* Wallonien (*das*)

Walloon [wɒ'lu:n] **1.** *n.* **a)** (*person*) Wallone, *der*/Wallonin, *die;* **b)** (*dialect*) Wallonisch, *das; see also* **English 2 a. 2.** *adj.* wallonisch; *see also* **English 1**

wallop ['wɒləp] (*coll.*) **1.** *v. t.* (*hit*) schlagen; (*with repeated blows*) [ver]prügeln; **he ~ed him one over the head** (*sl.*) er hat ihm eins übergebraten (*salopp*). **2.** *n.* Schlag, *der;* **give sb./sth. a ~:** auf jmdn./etw. draufhauen (*ugs.*); **he fell down with a ~:** er fiel mit einem Plumps hin

walloping ['wɒləpɪŋ] (*coll.*) **1.** *n.* **a)** (*thrashing*) **a ~:** eine Tracht Prügel (*ugs.*); **b)** (*defeat*) **get a ~:** eins übergebraten kriegen (*salopp*). **2.** *adj.* gepfeffert (*ugs.*) ‹*Niederlage, Rechnung*›; faustdick (*ugs.*) ‹*Lüge*›

wallow ['wɒləʊ] **1.** *v. i.* **a)** (*roll around*) sich wälzen; ‹*Schiff:*› schlingern; (*in mud also*) sich suhlen; **b)** (*fig.: take delight*) schwelgen (**in** in + *Dat.*); **be ~ing in money** (*coll.*) im Geld schwimmen (*ugs.*); **~ in luxury** im Luxus baden *od.* schwelgen. **2.** *n.* **a)** (*mudbath*) Schlammbad, *das;* **like a good ~ in the mud** sich gern im Schlamm wälzen *od.* suhlen; **b)** (*fig.: indulgence*) **he likes to have a good ~ [in sentiment]** er schwelgt gern in Gefühlen

wall: ~-**painting** *n.* Wandgemälde, *das;* ~**paper 1.** *n.* Tapete, *die;* **2.** *v. t.* tapezieren; ~ **socket** *n.* (*Electr.*) Wandsteckdose, *die;* **W~ Street** *n.* [die] Wall Street; die Wallstreet; ~-**to**-~ *adj.* (*covering floor*) ~-**to**-~ **carpeting** Teppichboden, *der;* ~-**unit** *n.* Hängeelement, *das*

wally ['wɒlɪ] *n.* (*Brit. sl.*) Blödmann, *der* (*salopp*)

walnut ['wɔ:lnʌt] *n.* **a)** (*nut*) Walnuß, *die;* **b)** (*tree*) [Wal]nußbaum, *der;* **c)** (*wood*) Nußbaumholz, *das*

walrus ['wɔ:lrəs, 'wɒlrəs] *n.* Walroß, *das;* ~ **moustache** Walroßbart, *der* (*ugs.*)

Walter Mitty [wɒltə 'mɪtɪ] *see* **Mitty**

waltz [wɔ:lts, wɔ:ls, wɒlts, wɒls] **1.** *n.* Walzer, *der;* **can you dance the ~?** können Sie Walzer tanzen? **2.** *v. i.* Walzer tanzen; **~ round the room** durchs Zimmer tanzen

~ '**in** *v. i* (*fig. coll.*) angetanzt kommen (*ugs.*)

~ '**off**, ~ '**out** *v. i.* (*fig. coll.*) abtanzen (*ugs.*)

wan [wɒn] *adj.* fahl (*geh.*); bleich; **~ smile** mattes Lächeln

wand [wɒnd] *n.* Stab, *der;* (*magician's ~*) Zauberstab, *der*

wander ['wɒndə(r)] **1.** *v. i.* **a)** (*go aimlessly*) umherirren; (*walk slowly*) bummeln; **she ~ed over to me** sie kam zu mir herüber; **I must be ~ing** (*coll.*) ich muß mich auf die Socken machen (*ugs.*); **b)** (*stray*) ‹*Katze:*› streunen; ‹*Schafe:*› sich verlaufen; **~ from the trail** vom Weg abkommen; **~ from the path of righteousness, ~ from the straight and narrow** (*fig.*) vom Pfad der Tugend abkommen; **the car ~s badly** der Wagen hält schlecht Spur; **c)** (*fig.: stray from subject*) abschweifen; **his thoughts ~ed back to his childhood** seine Gedanken schweiften zurück in die Kindheit. **2.** *v. t.* wandern durch; **~ the world** durch die Welt ziehen. **3.** *n.* (*coll.: walk*) Spaziergang, *der;* **let's go for a ~:** komm, laufen wir ein bißchen rum (*ugs.*); **I'll go for** *or* **take a ~ round** *or* **through the town** ich werd' mal einen Bummel durch die Stadt machen

~ **a'bout** *v. i.* sich herumtreiben

~ **a'long** *v. i.* dahintrotten; ‹*Fahrzeug:*› dahinzockeln (*ugs.*)

~ '**in** *v. i.* hineinspazieren; (*towards speaker*) hereinspaziert kommen

~ '**off** *v. i.* **a)** (*stray*) weggehen; ‹*Kind:*› sich selbständig machen (*scherzh.*); **b)** (*coll.: go away*) sich davonmachen (*ugs.*)

wanderer ['wɒndərə(r)] *n.* Streuner, *der*/Streunerin, *die;* (*traveller*) Wandervogel, *der* (*veralt. scherzh.*)

wandering ['wɒndərɪŋ] **1.** *adj.* **a)** (*nomadic*) Wander‹*stamm, -volk*›; ~ **minstrel** (*Hist.*) fahrender Spielmann; **b)** (*meandering*) sich windend ‹*Strom*›; (*fig.: disjointed*) weitschweifig ‹*Rede*›; wirr ‹*Gedanken*›; (*joc.*) vorwitzig (*scherzh.*) ‹*Hände*›. **2.** *n. in pl.* **a)** (*travels*) Wanderschaft, *die;* **in** *or* **on his ~s** auf seiner Wanderschaft; **b)** (*straying*) **the ~s of his mind/thoughts** sein wirres Denken/seine wirren Gedanken

Wandering 'Jew *n.* **the ~:** der Ewige Jude; (*fig.*) **a ~:** ein Ahasver (*geh.*)

wanderlust ['wɒndəlʌst] *n.* Reiselust, *die;* (*related to distant places*) Fernweh, *das*

wane [weɪn] **1.** *v. i.* ‹*Mond:*› abnehmen; ‹*Kraft, Einfluß, Macht:*› schwinden, abnehmen; ‹*Ruf, Ruhm:*› verblassen; **the light is waning** es wird langsam dunkler. **2.** *n.* **be on the ~** ‹*Mond:*› abnehmen; (*fig.*) schwinden; dahinschwinden (*geh.*)

wangle ['wæŋgl] (*coll.*) **1.** *v. t.* (*get by devious means*) organisieren (*ugs.*) ‹*Karte, Einladung*›; **~ sth. out of sb.** jmdm. etw. abluchsen (*ugs.*); **can you ~ it for me?** kannst du das für mich deichseln? (*ugs.*). **2.** *n.* Kniff, *der;* **by a ~:** durch Schiebung (*ugs.*)

wank [wæŋk] (*Brit. coarse*) **1.** *v. t.* wichsen (*derb*). **2.** *v. t.* **~ sb. off** jmdm. einen abwichsen (*vulg.*). **3.** *n.* **have a ~:** sich (*Dat.*) einen abwichsen (*derb*)

wanker ['wæŋkə(r)] *n.* (*Brit. coarse*) Wichser, *der* (*derb*)

wanly ['wɒnlɪ] *adv.* schwach ‹*beleuchtet*›; matt ‹*lächeln*›

wanna ['wɒnə] (*coll.*) = **want to; want a**

want [wɒnt] **1.** *v. t.* **a)** (*desire*) wollen; **I ~ my mummy** ich will zu meiner Mama; **I ~ it done by tonight** ich will, daß es bis heute abend fertig wird; **I don't ~ there to be any misunderstanding** ich will *od.* möchte nicht, daß da ein Mißverständnis aufkommt; **I don't ~ you to get the idea that I am stingy** ich möchte nicht, daß Sie den Eindruck gewinnen, ich sei geizig; **b)** (*require, need*) brauchen; **'W~ed – cook for small family'** „Koch/Köchin für kleine Familie gesucht"; **you're ~ed on the phone** du wirst am Telefon verlangt; **feel ~ed** das Gefühl haben, gebraucht zu werden; **what you ~ is a good holiday** Sie brauchen mal richtigen Urlaub; **the windows ~ painting** die Fenster müßten gestrichen werden; **what that naughty girl ~s is a good wallop** was dem frechen Gör fehlt, ist eine anständige Tracht Prügel (*ugs.*); **you ~ to be [more] careful** (*ought to be*) du solltest vorsichtig[er] sein; **you ~ to see a solicitor about that** Sie müßten sich in der Sache an einen Anwalt wenden; **c) ~ed [by the police]** [polizeilich] gesucht (**for** wegen); **he is a ~ed man** er wird [polizeilich] gesucht; **d)** (*lack*) **sb./sth. ~s sth.** jmdm./einer Sache fehlt es an etw. (*Dat.*); **all the soup ~s is some salt** der Suppe fehlt nur noch ein bißchen Salz. **2.** *n.* **a)** *no pl.* (*lack*) Mangel, *der* (**of** an + *Dat.*); **there is no ~ of ...:** es fehlt nicht an ... (*Dat.*); **for ~ of sth.** aus Mangel an etw. (*Dat.*); **for ~ of a better word** in Ermangelung eines besseren Ausdrucks; **he took the flat for ~ of anything better** er nahm die Wohnung, weil er nichts Besseres finden konnte; **b)** *no pl.* (*need*) Not, *die;* **suffer ~:** Not leiden; **be in ~ of sth.** (*dated, literary*) einer Sache (*Gen.*) bedürfen (*geh.*); **c)** (*desire*) Bedürfnis, *das;* **we can supply all your ~s** wir können alles liefern, was Sie brauchen; **~ ad** (*Amer.*) Kaufgesuch, *das.* **3.** *v. i.* **a)** (*arch.: be in ~*) Not leiden; **b)** (*esp. Amer. coll.*) **~ in/out** rein-/rauswollen

~ **for** *v. t.* (*dated*) **sb. ~s for nothing** *or* **doesn't ~ for anything** jmdm. fehlt es an nichts; **~ for money** an Geldmangel (*Dat.*) leiden

wanting ['wɒntɪŋ] *adj.* **be ~:** fehlen; **sb./sth. is ~ in sth.** jmdm./einer Sache fehlt es an etw. (*Dat.*); **be found ~:** für unzureichend befunden werden

wanton ['wɒntən] **1.** *adj.* **a)** (*dated: licentious*) lüstern; wollüstig ‹*Person, Gedanken, Benehmen*›; **b)** (*wilful*) mutwillig ‹*Beschädigung, Grausamkeit, Verschwendung*›; leichtfertig ‹*Vernachlässigung*›; **c)** (*luxuriant, wild*) üppig ‹*Wachstum, Vielfalt*›; **d)** (*capricious*) übermütig; mutwillig (*veralt.*). **2.** *n.* (*dated*) (*woman*) Kokotte, *die* (*veralt.*); (*man*) Lüstling, *der* (*veralt.*)

wantonly ['wɒntənlɪ] *adv.* **a)** (*dated: licentiously*) lüstern; wollüstig; **b)** (*wilfully*) mutwillig; leichtfertig ‹*vernachlässigen*›

wantonness ['wɒntənnɪs] *n., no pl.* **a)** (*dated: licentiousness*) Lüsternheit, *die;* **b)** (*wilfulness*) Mutwilligkeit, *die*

war [wɔ:(r)] *n.* **a)** Krieg, *der;* **between the ~s** zwischen den Weltkriegen; **declare ~:** den Krieg erklären (**on** *Dat.*); **an act of ~:** ein kriegerischer Akt; **a ~ of conquest/aggression** ein Eroberungs-/Angriffskrieg; **be at ~:** sich im Krieg befinden; **make ~:** Krieg führen (**on** gegen); **go to ~:** in den Krieg ziehen (**against** gegen); **carry the ~ into the enemy's camp** (*fig.*) den Spieß umdrehen; **look as though one/it has been in the ~s** ziemlich mitgenommen aussehen; **b)** (*science*) Kriegführung, *die;* **the art of ~:** die Kriegskunst; **laws of ~:** Kriegsrecht, *das;* **rights of ~:** Kriegsrechte; **c)** (*fig.: conflict*) Krieg, *der;* **price ~:** Preiskrieg, *der;* **~ of nerves** Nervenkrieg, *der;* **~ of words** Wortgefecht, *das;* **d)** (*fig.: fight, campaign*) Kampf, *der* (**on, against** gegen); **declare ~ on poverty** der Armut den Kampf ansagen

'**war baby** *n.* [Nach]kriegskind, *das*

warble ['wɔ:bl] *v. t. & i.* trällern

warbler ['wɔ:blə(r)] *n.* (*Ornith.*) Grasmücke, *die*

war: ~ **bride** *n.* Kriegsbraut, *die;* ~ **correspondent** *n.* Kriegsberichterstatter, *der*/-berichterstatterin, *die;* ~ **crime** *n.* Kriegsverbrechen, *das;* ~ **criminal** *n.* Kriegsverbrecher, *der*/-verbrecherin, *die;* ~-**cry** *n.* **a)** (*battle-cry*) Kriegsruf, *der;* **b)** (*slogan*) Schlachtruf, *der*

ward [wɔ:d] *n.* **a)** (*in hospital*) Station, *die;* (*single room*) Krankensaal, *der;* **geriatric/maternity ~:** geriatrische Abteilung/Entbindungsstation, *die;* **she's in W~ 3** sie liegt auf Station 3; **b)** (*minor*) Mündel, *das od. die;* **~ [of court]** (*Law*) Mündel [unter Amtsvormundschaft]; **c)** (*electoral division*) Wahlbezirk, *der;* **d)** (*Hist.: bailey*) [Burg-]hof, *der*

~ '**off** *v. t.* **a)** (*prevent*) abwehren; schützen vor (+ *Dat.*) ‹*Erkältung, Depressionen*›; abwenden ‹*Gefahr*›; **b)** (*keep at distance*) sich (*Dat.*) vom Leibe halten ‹*Verehrer*›

war: ~ **damage** *n.* Kriegsschäden *Pl.;* ~-**dance** *n.* Kriegstanz, *der*

warden ['wɔ:dn] *n.* **a)** (*president, governor*) Direktor, *der*/Direktorin, *die;* (*of college, school*) Rektor, *der*/Rektorin, *die;* (*of hostel, sheltered housing*) Heimleiter, *der*/-leiterin, *die;* (*of youth hostel*) Herbergsvater, *der*/-mutter, *die;* **b)** (*supervisor*) Aufseher, *der*/Aufseherin, *die;* **[air-raid] ~:** Luftschutzwart, *der; see also* **churchwarden**

warder ['wɔ:də(r)] *n.* (*Brit.*) Wärter, *der;* Aufseher, *der*

wardress ['wɔ:drɪs] *n.* Wärterin, *die;* Aufseherin, *die*

wardrobe ['wɔːdrəʊb] *n.* **a)** *(piece of furniture)* Kleiderschrank, *der;* **folding ~:** Kleidersack, *der;* **b)** *(stock of clothes)* Garderobe, *die; (in theatre)* Kostüme *Pl.*

wardrobe: ~ master/mistress *ns. (Theatre)* Gewandmeister, *der*/-meisterin, *die;* **~ trunk** *n.* Schrankkoffer, *der*

'wardroom *n. (Navy)* Offiziersmesse, *die*

-wards [wədz] *adv. suff.* -wärts

wardship ['wɔːdʃɪp] *n.* Vormundschaft, *die*

'ward sister *n.* Stationsschwester, *die*

ware [weə(r)] *n.* **a)** *(pottery)* Steinzeug, *das;* **Delft ~:** Delfter Keramik; **b)** *in pl. (goods)* Ware, *die*

warehouse 1. ['weəhaʊs] *n. (repository)* Lagerhaus, *das; (part of building)* Lager, *das; (Brit.: retail or wholesale store)* Großmarkt, *der.* **2.** ['weəhaʊs, 'weəhaʊz] *v. t.* einlagern ‹*Möbel*›

warehouseman ['weəhaʊsmən] *n., pl.* **warehousemen** ['weəhaʊsmən] Lagerist, *der*

warfare ['wɔːfeə(r)] *n. (lit. or fig.)* Krieg, *der;* **in modern ~:** in der modernen Kriegführung; **economic ~:** Wirtschaftskrieg, *der; see also* **open 1 h**

war: ~-game *n.* Kriegsspiel, *das;* **~-gaming** *n. (Mil.)* Sandkastenspiele *Pl.; (as hobby) das Nachstellen historischer Schlachten mit Spielzeugsoldaten;* **~-god** *n.* Kriegsgott, *der;* **~ grave** *n.* Kriegs- *od.* Soldatengrab, *das;* **~head** *n.* Sprengkopf, *der;* **~-horse** *n. (Hist., fig.)* Schlachtroß, *das*

warily ['weərɪlɪ] *adv.* vorsichtig; *(suspiciously)* mißtrauisch; **tread ~** *(lit. or fig.)* vorsichtig sein

wariness ['weərɪnɪs] *n., no pl.* Vorsicht, *die* **(of** vor + *Dat.*); **~ of strangers** Mißtrauen gegen Fremde

'warlike *adj.* **a)** *(bellicose)* kriegerisch; **b)** *(military)* Kriegs‹*vorbereitungen, -gerät*›

war-lord *n.* Kriegsherr, *der*

warm [wɔːm] **1.** *adj.* **a)** warm; **come inside and get ~:** komm rein und wärm dich auf; **I am very ~ from running** mir ist sehr warm vom Rennen; **it's ~ work** bei der Arbeit kommt man ins Schwitzen; **keep sb.'s food ~:** jmdm. das Essen warm halten; **keep a seat/job ~ for sb.** *(fig.)* jmdm. einen Platz/eine Stellung freihalten; **b)** *(enthusiastic)* herzlich ‹*Grüße, Dank*›; eng ‹*Freundschaft*›; lebhaft ‹*Interesse*›; begeistert ‹*Unterstützung, Applaus*›; *see also* **reception a; welcome 2 b; c)** *(cordial, sympathetic)* warm ‹*Herz, Wesen, Gefühl*›; herzlich ‹*Lächeln*›; echt empfunden ‹*Hochachtung*›; **the thought of her kindness gives me a ~ feeling** wenn ich an ihre Güte denke, wird mir warm ums Herz; **d)** *(passionate)* heiß ‹*Temperament, Küsse*›; **e)** *(animated)* hitzig; heftig ‹*Entrüstung*›; **f)** *(unpleasant)* ungemütlich; **he left when things began to get too ~ for him** er ging, als ihm die Sache zu ungemütlich wurde; **g)** *(recent)* heiß ‹*Spur*›; **h)** *(in games: close)* **you're getting ~!** warm! **2.** *v. t.* wärmen; warm machen ‹*Flüssigkeit*›; **~ one's hands** sich *(Dat.)* die Hände wärmen; **the thought [of ...] ~ed [the cockles of] his heart** bei dem Gedanken [an ... *(Akk.)*] wurde ihm warm ums Herz. **3.** *v. i.* **a) ~ to sb./sth.** *(come to like)* sich für jmdn./etw. erwärmen; **my heart ~ed to her** sie wurde mir sympathischer; **the speaker ~ed to his subject** der Redner steigerte sich in sein Thema hinein; **b)** *(get ~er)* warm werden. **4.** *n.* **a)** *(~ing)* **give the food a ~:** das Essen aufwärmen; **have a ~ by the fire** sich am Kamin/Ofen *usw.* aufwärmen; **b)** *(warmth)* **the ~:** die Wärme

~ 'up 1. *v. i.* **a)** *(get ~)* warm werden; ‹*Motor:*› warmlaufen; **b)** *(prepare)* ‹*Sportler:*› sich aufwärmen; **c)** *(fig.: become animated)* warm werden; ‹*Party:*› in Schwung kommen; ‹*Publikum:*› in Stimmung kommen. **2.** *v. t.* aufwärmen ‹*Speisen*›; erwärmen ‹*Raum, Zimmer*›; warmlaufen lassen ‹*Motor*›; *(fig.)* in Stimmung bringen ‹*Publikum*›. *See also* **warm-up**

warm-blooded ['wɔːmblʌdɪd] *adj.* **a)** warmblütig ‹*Tier*›; **~-blooded animals** Warmblüter; **b)** *(fig.: passionate)* heißblütig; temperamentvoll

warmed-over ['wɔːmdəʊvə(r)] *(Amer.),* **warmed-up** ['wɔːmdʌp] *adjs.* aufgewärmt

'war memorial *n.* Kriegerdenkmal, *das*

'warm-hearted *adj.* herzlich; warmherzig ‹*Person*›

'warming-pan *n.* Wärmepfanne, *die*

warmish ['wɔːmɪʃ] *adj.* lau[warm]; warm ‹*Wetter*›

warmly ['wɔːmlɪ] *adv.* **a)** *(to maintain warmth)* warm; **b)** *(enthusiastically)* herzlich ‹*willkommen heißen, gratulieren, begrüßen, grüßen, danken*›; wärmstens ‹*empfehlen*›; begeistert ‹*sprechen von, applaudieren*›; **c)** *(animatedly)* hitzig

warmonger ['wɔːmʌŋgə(r)] *n.* Kriegshetzer, *der*/-hetzerin, *die*

warmongering ['wɔːmʌŋgərɪŋ] *n.* Kriegshetze, *die*

warmth [wɔːmθ] *n.* **a)** *(state of being warm; also of colour)* Wärme, *die;* **b)** *(enthusiasm, affection, cordiality)* Herzlichkeit, *die;* Wärme, *die;* **the ~ of her temperament** ihr ungestümes Temperament; **c)** *(animation)* Hitzigkeit, *die; (indignation)* Schärfe, *die;* **in the ~ of the debate** in der Hitze des Gefechts *(fig.)*

'warm-up *n.* **have a ~** *(lit., Sport)* sich aufwärmen; **give a meal a ~:** ein Essen aufwärmen; **~ [lap]** *(Motor Racing)* Aufwärmrunde, *die*

warn [wɔːn] *v. t.* **a)** *(inform, give notice)* warnen **(against, of, about** vor + *Dat.*); **~ sb. that ...:** jmdn. darauf hinweisen, daß ...; **you can't say I didn't ~ you** Sie können nicht behaupten, ich hätte Sie nicht gewarnt; **you have been ~ed!** ich habe/wir haben dich gewarnt!; **~ sb. not to do sth.** jmdn. davor warnen, etw. zu tun; **you might have ~ed us you were going to be late** du hättest uns wissen lassen können, daß du später kommen würdest; **b)** *(admonish)* ermahnen; *(officially)* abmahnen

~ 'off *v. t.* **a)** warnen; **~ sb. off doing sth.** jmdn. davor warnen, etw. zu tun; **b)** *(Racing)* Platzverbot erteilen (+ *Dat.*)

warning ['wɔːnɪŋ] **1.** *n.* **a)** *(advance notice)* Vorwarnung, *die;* **he gave me no ~ of his intentions** er hat mir seine Absichten nicht angekündigt; **we had no ~ of their arrival** sie kamen ohne Vorwarnung; **give sb. plenty of/a few days' ~:** jmdm. rechtzeitig/ein paar Tage vorher Bescheid sagen; **b)** *(lesson)* Lehre, *die;* **let that be a ~ to you** laß dir/laßt euch das eine Warnung sein; **c)** *(caution)* Verwarnung, *die; (less official)* Warnung, *die.* **2.** *attrib. adj.* Warn‹*schild, -zeichen, -signal usw.*›; **~ light/shot** Warnleuchte, *die*/-schuß, *der;* **~ notice** Warnung, *die;* **a ~ look/gesture** ein warnender Blick/eine warnende Geste

'War Office *n. (Brit. Hist.)* Kriegsministerium, *das*

warp [wɔːp] **1.** *v. i. (become bent)* sich verbiegen; ‹*Holz, Schallplatte:*› sich verziehen. **2.** *v. t.* **a)** *(cause to become bent)* verbiegen; **the sun had ~ed the boards** durch die Sonne hatten sich die Bretter verzogen; **b)** *(fig.: pervert)* verformen; verbiegen; **~ed** getrübt ‹*Urteilsvermögen*›; pervertiert ‹*Denken, Gehirn*›; **a ~ed sense of humour** ein abartiger Humor. **3.** *n.* **a)** *(Weaving)* Kettfaden, *der;* Kette, *die (fachspr.);* **b)** *(bent state)* Werfen, *das (fachspr.); (bend in a board etc.)* verzogene Stelle; **there is a ~ in the record** die Platte hat sich verzogen; **c)** *(fig.: perversion)* Perversion, *die; see also* **time warp**

war: ~-paint *n. (also fig. coll. joc.)* Kriegsbemalung, *die;* **~-path** *n.* Kriegspfad, *der;* **be on the ~-path** auf dem Kriegspfad sein; *(fig.)* in Rage sein; **~-plane** *n.* Kampfflugzeug, *das;* **~ poet** *n.* Kriegslyriker, *der*

warrant ['wɒrənt] **1.** *n.* **a)** *(written order) (for sb.'s arrest)* Haftbefehl, *der;* **[search-]~:** Durchsuchungsbefehl, *der;* **b)** *(authority)* Befugnis, *die; (justification)* Rechtfertigung, *die;* **c)** *(dividend voucher)* Dividendenschein, *der;* **d)** *(Law)* Vollmacht, *die;* **~ of attorney** anwaltliche Vollmacht. **2.** *v. t.* **a)** *(justify)* rechtfertigen; **her small income does not ~ such expenditure** ihr geringes Einkommen erlaubt ihr solche Ausgaben nicht; **b)** *(guarantee)* garantieren; garantieren für ‹*Produkt, Artikel*›; **we ~ [you] the diamond is genuine** wir garantieren [Ihnen], daß der Diamant echt ist; **you'll like it, I** *or* **I'll ~ you** es wird dir gefallen, das garantiere ich dir

warrantable ['wɒrəntəbl] *adj.* vertretbar; **be ~:** zu rechtfertigen sein

'warrant-officer *n.* Warrant Officer, *der; Dienstgrad zwischen Oberstabsfeldwebel/Oberstabsbootsmann und Leutnant/Leutnant z. S.*

warranty ['wɒrəntɪ] *n.* **a)** *(Law)* Garantie, *die;* **it is still under ~:** es steht noch unter *od.* darauf steht noch Garantie; *see also* **guarantee 2 a; b)** *(justification)* Rechtfertigung, *die*

warren ['wɒrn] *n.* **a)** *see* **rabbit-warren; b)** *(fig.: densely populated area)* Ameisenhaufen, *der (fig.); (maze)* Labyrinth, *das*

warring ['wɔːrɪŋ] *adj.* kriegführend; *(fig.)* sich bekämpfend *nicht präd.*

warrior ['wɒrɪə(r)] *n.* **a)** *(esp. literary)* Krieger, *der (geh.);* **b)** *attrib. (martial)* kriegerisch; **a ~ nation/race** ein Kriegervolk

Warsaw ['wɔːsɔː] **1.** *pr. n.* Warschau *(das).* **2.** *attrib. adj.* Warschauer; **~ Pact** *(Hist.)* Warschauer Pakt

'warship *n.* Kriegsschiff, *das*

wart [wɔːt] *n.* Warze, *die;* **~s and all** *(fig.)* schonungslos; ungeschminkt [bis ins kleinste Detail]

'wart-hog *n.* Warzenschwein, *das*

war: ~time *n.* **a)** Kriegszeit, *die;* **in** *or* **during ~time** während des Krieges; im Krieg; **b)** *attrib.* Kriegs‹*rationierung, -evakuierung usw.*›; **~time England** [das] England während des Krieges; **a ~time love affair** eine Kriegsliebe; **~-weary** *adj.* kriegsmüde; **~-widow** *n.* Kriegswitwe, *die;* Kriegerwitwe, *die (geh. veralt.)*

wary ['weərɪ] *adj.* vorsichtig; *(suspicious)* mißtrauisch **(of** gegenüber); **be ~ of** *or* **about doing sth.** sich davor hüten, etw. zu tun; **be ~ of sb./sth.** sich vor jmdm./etw. in acht nehmen; **keep a ~ eye on sb.** jmdn. genau beobachten

'war-zone *n.* Kriegsgebiet, *das*

was *see* **be**

wash [wɒʃ] **1.** *v. t.* **a)** waschen; **~ oneself/one's hands** *(also euphem.)***/face/hair** sich waschen/sich *(Dat.)* die Hände *(auch verhüll.)*/das Gesicht/die Haare waschen; **~ the clothes** Wäsche waschen; **~ the dishes** abwaschen; [Geschirr] spülen; **~ the floor** den Fußboden aufwischen *od.* feucht wischen; **~ one's hands of sb./sth.** mit jmdm./etw. nichts mehr zu tun haben wollen; **I don't wish to have anything more to do with the whole business. I ~ my hands of it** Ich will mit der ganzen Geschichte nichts mehr zu tun haben. Für mich ist die Sache erledigt; **b)** *(remove)* waschen ‹*Fleck*› **(out of** aus); abwaschen ‹*Schmutz*› **(off** von); **c)** *(by licking)* putzen; **the cat ~ed its face** die Katze putzte sich; **the cat ~ed its fur** die Katze putzte sich *(Dat.)* das Fell; **d)** *(carry along)* spülen; **be ~ed overboard/ashore** über Bord/an Land gespült werden; **be ~ed downstream** von der Strömung mitgerissen werden; **e)** ‹*Wellen, Meer:*› bespülen ‹*Klippen, Ufer*›. *See also* **linen 1 b. 2.** *v. i.* **a)** sich waschen; **b)** *(clean clothes)* waschen; **c)** ⟨*Stoff, Kleidungsstück, Handtuch:*⟩ sich waschen lassen; **that won't ~** *(fig. coll.)* das zieht nicht *(ugs.)*; **an interesting theory, but it won't ~:** eine interessante Theorie, aber sie läßt sich nicht halten; **d)** *(sweep)* ⟨*Brandung, Wellen:*⟩ spülen; **~ over/against sth.** etw. überspülen/gegen etw. spülen. **3.** *n.* **a) give sb./sth. a [good] ~:** jmdn./etw. [gründlich] waschen; **the baby/car needs a ~** *or (coll.)* **could do with a ~:** das Kind/Auto müßte mal gewaschen werden; **I must have a ~ before lunch** ich muß mich vor dem Essen noch waschen; **b)** *(laundering)* Wäsche, *die;* **it is in the ~:** es ist in der Wäsche; **it'll all come out in the ~** *(fig. coll.)* das wird sich alles klären; **the week's ~:** die Wäsche von einer Woche; **c)** *(of ship, aircraft, etc.)* Sog, *der;* **d)** *(lotion)* Waschlotion, *die;* **a ~ for disinfecting the mouth** ein desinfizierendes Mundwasser; *see also* **eyewash; mouthwash; e)** *(pig food)* Schweinefutter, *das*

~ a'way *v. t.* **a)** wegspülen; hinwegspülen *(geh.)*; **b) ~ a stain/the mud away** einen Fleck/den Schmutz auswaschen

~ 'down *v. t.* **a)** *(clean dirt from) (with a hose)* abspritzen ⟨*Auto, Deck, Hof*⟩; *(with soap and water)* abwaschen; aufwaschen ⟨*Fußboden*⟩; **b)** *(help to go down)* runterspülen *(ugs.)*; **we lunched on beef ~ed down with beer** wir aßen Roastbeef und tranken Bier dazu

~ 'off 1. *v. t.* **~ sth. off** etw. abwaschen. **2.** *v. i.* abgehen; *(from fabric etc.)* herausgehen

~ 'out *v. t.* **a)** *(clean)* auswaschen ⟨*Kleidungsstück*⟩; ausscheuern ⟨*Topf*⟩; ausspülen ⟨*Mund*⟩; **~ dirt/marks out of clothes** Schmutz/Flecken aus Kleidern [her]auswaschen; **b)** *(stop; prevent from taking place)* ins Wasser fallen lassen ⟨*Sportveranstaltung*⟩; **several matches have been ~ed out** mehrere Spiele sind ins Wasser gefallen; **c)** *(damage)* unterspülen ⟨*Brückenpfeiler, Straße*⟩. *See also* **washed-out; wash-out**

~ 'over *v. t.* **a)** *(fig. coll.: not affect)* **~ over sb.** ⟨*Streit, Lärm, Unruhe usw.:*⟩ jmdn. gar nicht berühren; **she just sat back and let everything/the criticism ~ over her** sie saß einfach da und ließ alles/die Kritik an sich *(Dat.)* ablaufen *(ugs.)*; **b)** *(sweep over)* spülen über (+ *Akk.*)

~ 'up 1. *v. t.* **a)** *(Brit.: clean)* **~ the dishes up** das Geschirr abwaschen *od.* spülen; **b)** *(carry to shore)* anspülen ⟨*Leiche, Strandgut, Wrackteile usw.*⟩. **2.** *v. i.* **a)** abwaschen; spülen; **who's going to help me ~ up?** wer hilft mir beim Abwaschen *od.* Spülen?; **b)** *(Amer.)* sich *(Dat.)* [Gesicht und Hände] waschen. *See also* **washed-up; washing-up**

washable ['wɒʃəbl] *adj.* waschbar ⟨*Stoff*⟩; abwaschbar ⟨*Tapete, Farbe*⟩

wash: ~-and-'wear *adj.* bügelfrei; **~-basin** *n.* Waschbecken, *das;* **~board** *n.* Waschbrett, *das;* **~-bowl** *see* **~-basin; ~-cloth** *n.* **a)** *(Brit.: dishcloth)* Abwaschlappen, *der;* Spültuch, *das;* **b)** *(Amer.: facecloth)* Waschlappen, *der;* **~-day** *n.* Waschtag, *der*

washed-'out *adj.* **a)** *attrib. (faded by washing)* verwaschen ⟨*Farbe, Kleidungsstück*⟩; **b)** *(fig.: exhausted)* abgespannt; mitgenommen; **I was** *or* **felt limp and ~:** ich fühlte mich schlapp und ausgelaugt

washed-'up *adj. (sl.)* kaputt *(ugs.)*

washer ['wɒʃə(r)] *n. (Mech. Engin.)* Unterlegscheibe, *die; (of tap)* Dichtungsring, *der;* Dichtungsscheibe, *die*

'washerwoman *n.* Waschfrau, *die*

'wash-hand basin Handwaschbecken, *das*

washing ['wɒʃɪŋ] *n., no pl., no indef. art.* **a)** *(clothes to be washed)* Wäsche, *die;* **take in ~:** Wäsche ins Haus nehmen; [zu Hause] für Kunden waschen; **b)** *(cleansing)* Waschen, *das;* **do the ~:** waschen; **children often don't like ~:** Kinder waschen sich oft nicht gerne; **the car needs a good ~:** der Wagen muß mal wieder gründlich gewaschen werden

washing: ~-day *n.* Waschtag, *der;* **~-machine** *n.* Waschmaschine, *die;* **~-powder** *n.* Waschpulver, *das;* **~-soda** *n.* Bleichsoda, *das (veralt.)*; Natriumkarbonat, *das;* **~-'up** *n. (Brit.)* Abwasch, *der;* **do the ~-up** den Abwasch machen; abwaschen; **there was ~-up everywhere** überall stand schmutziges Geschirr herum; **the ~-up took him hours** er brauchte Stunden für den Abwasch; **~-'up liquid** *n.* Spülmittel, *das;* **~-'up machine** *see* **dishwasher a**

wash: ~-leather *n.* Fensterleder, *das;* **~-out** *n.* **a)** *(sl.: failure)* Pleite, *die (ugs.)*; Reinfall, *der (ugs.)*; **b)** *(sl.: useless person)* Niete, *die (salopp abwertend)*; **c)** *(breach in road etc.)* Unterspülung, *die;* **~-room** *n. (Amer.)* WC, *das;* Waschraum, *der (verhüll.)*; **~-stand** *n.* Waschtisch, *der;* **~-tub** *n.* Waschbottich, *der;* Waschzuber, *der;* **~-woman** *(Amer.) see* **washerwoman**

washy ['wɒʃɪ] *adj.* **a)** *(too watery)* wäßrig, dünn ⟨*Tee, Suppe*⟩; **b)** *(faded-looking)* verwaschen ⟨*Farbe*⟩; **c)** *(feeble)* verschwommen ⟨*Ansichten, Meinungen*⟩; schwach, *(ugs.)* saft- und kraftlos ⟨*Inszenierung, Übersetzung*⟩

wasn't ['wɒznt] *(coll.)* = **was not;** *see* **be**

Wasp [wɒsp] *n. (Amer. derog.)* Angehöriger des weißen amerikanischen Bürgertums *(angelsächsischer Herkunft und protestantischer Konfession)*

wasp *n.* Wespe, *die*

waspish ['wɒspɪʃ] *adj.*, **waspishly** ['wɒspɪʃlɪ] *adv.* bissig

waspishness ['wɒspɪʃnɪs] *n., no pl.* Bissigkeit, *die*

'wasp-waist *n.* Wespentaille, *die*

wassail ['wɒseɪl, 'wɒsl] *(arch.)* **1.** *n.* **a)** *(festivity)* Trinkgelage, *das;* **b)** *(liquor)* Wein/Bier, *mit verschiedenen Zutaten gewürzt.* **2.** *v. i.* zechen

wastage ['weɪstɪdʒ] *n.* **a)** *(loss by wear etc.)* Schwund, *der;* **b) [natural] ~** *(Admin.)* ≈ natürliche Fluktuation

waste [weɪst] **1.** *n.* **a)** *(useless remains)* Abfall, *der;* **disposal of ~:** Abfallbeseitigung, *die;* **kitchen ~, ~ from the kitchen** Küchenabfälle *Pl.*; **b)** *(extravagant use)* Verschwendung, *die;* Vergeudung, *die;* **it's a ~ of time/money/energy** das ist Zeit-/Geld-/Energieverschwendung; **it would be a ~ of effort** das wäre vergeudete Mühe; **it's a ~ of your time and mine** wir verschwenden beide nur unsere Zeit; **go** *or* **run to ~:** vergeudet werden; **c)** *see* **waste-pipe; d)** *(desert)* Wüste, *die. See also* **cotton waste. 2.** *v. t.* **a)** *(squander)* verschwenden; vergeuden (**on** auf + *Akk.*, an + *Akk.*); **he is ~d on an audience like that** für ein solches Publikum ist er zu schade; **all his efforts were ~d** all seine Mühe war umsonst; **don't ~ my time!** stehlen Sie mir nicht die Zeit!; **you didn't ~ much time, did you?** da hast du aber keine Zeit verloren!; **~ one's life** sein Leben vergeuden; **you're wasting your breath** *or* **words!** deine Worte kannst du dir sparen!; **~ not, want not** *(prov.)* spare in der Zeit, so hast du in der Not *(Spr.)*; **b) be ~d** *(reduced)* ⟨*Vorräte, Bevölkerung:*⟩ abnehmen, schrumpfen; **c)** *(cause to shrink)* aufzehren ⟨*Kräfte*⟩; auszehren ⟨*Körper*⟩; **a ~d arm** ein geschrumpfter Arm; **d)** *(ravage)* verwüsten ⟨*Land*⟩; **e)** *(treat as ~ paper)* makulieren; **f)** *(sl.: murder)* umlegen *(salopp)*. **3.** *v. i.* dahinschwinden; *(gradually)* im Schwinden begriffen sein. **4.** *adj.* **a)** *(not wanted)* **~ material** Abfall, *der;* **~ food** Essensreste *Pl.*; **~ product** Abfallprodukt, *das;* **~ water** Abwasser, *das;* **b)** *(uncultivated)* brach; brachliegend *nicht präd.*; **lie ~:** brachliegen; **c) lay sth. ~, lay ~ sth.** etw. verwüsten

~ a'way *v. i.* immer mehr abmagern

waste: ~-basket *see* **waste-paper basket; ~ disposal** *n.* Abfallbeseitigung, *die;* Entsorgung, *die (Amtsspr.)*; **~-di'sposal unit** *n.* Müllzerkleinerer, *der*

wasteful ['weɪstfl] *adj.* **a)** *(extravagant)* verschwenderisch; **too much ~ expenditure** zuviel Geldverschwendung; **b)** *(causing waste)* unwirtschaftlich; **be ~ of sth.** etw. vergeuden

wastefully ['weɪstfəlɪ] *adv.* verschwenderisch; **sth. is ~ thrown away** etw. wird verschwenderischerweise weggeworfen; **he's ~ extravagant with money** er geht mit dem Geld außerordentlich verschwenderisch um

wastefulness ['weɪstflnɪs] *n., no pl.* **a)** *(extravagance)* Verschwendung, *die; (character trait)* Verschwendungssucht, *die;* **~ in the use of public funds** Verschwendung öffentlicher Gelder; **b)** *(of manufacturing process)* Unwirtschaftlichkeit, *die*

waste: ~land *n. (not cultivated)* Ödland, *das; (not built on)* unbebautes Land; *(fig.)* Einöde, *die;* **~ 'paper** *n.* Papierabfall, *der;* **~-'paper basket** *n.* Papierkorb, *der;* **~-pipe** *n.* Abflußrohr, *das;* **~-processor** *n.* Müllzerkleinerer, *der*

waster ['weɪstə(r)] *n.* Verschwender, *der/*Verschwenderin, *die*

wasting ['weɪstɪŋ] *adj.* **a)** *(diminishing)* schwindend; von Schwund befallen ⟨*Muskel*⟩; **b)** *(reducing vitality, robustness)* **a ~ disease** eine Krankheit, bei der der Patient mehr und mehr verfällt

wastrel ['weɪstrl] *n.* **a)** *(good-for-nothing)* Nichtsnutz, *der;* **b)** *(wasteful person)* Verschwender, *der/*Verschwenderin, *die*

watch [wɒtʃ] **1.** *n.* **a) [wrist-/pocket-]~:** [Armband-/Taschen]uhr, *die;* **b)** *(constant attention)* Wache, *die;* **keep ~:** Wache halten; **keep [a] ~ for sb./sth.** auf jmdn./etw. achten *od.* aufpassen; **keep a [good** *or* **close] ~ on sb./sth.** [gut] auf jmdn./etw. aufpassen; **keep [a] ~ for enemy aircraft** nach feindlichen Flugzeugen Ausschau halten; **keep a close ~ on the time** genau auf die Zeit achten; **they kept a ~ on all his activities** sie überwachten alle seine Aktivitäten; **the police were on the ~ for car thieves** die Polizei hielt nach Autodieben Ausschau; **c)** *(Naut.)* Wache, *die;* **starboard/port ~:** Steuerbord-/Backbordwache, *die;* **the officer of the ~:** der wachhabende Offizier; *see also* **dog-watch; set 1 m; d)** *(Hist.: street-guard)* Wache, *die; (one person)* Wachmann, *der;* **e)** *(period of wakefulness at night)* Nachtwache, *die;* **in the ~es of the night** beim nächtlichen Wachen *(geh.)*. **2.** *v. i.* **a)** *(wait)* **~ for sb./sth.** auf jmdn./etw. warten; **~ for signs of improvement** nach Anzeichen einer Verbesserung Ausschau halten; **b)** *(keep watch)* Wache stehen. **3.** *v. t.* **a)** *(observe)* sich *(Dat.)* ansehen ⟨*Sportveranstaltung, Fernsehsendung*⟩; **~ [the] television** *or* **TV** fernsehen; Fernsehen gucken *(ugs.)*; **~ sth. [on television** *or* **TV]** sich *(Dat.)* etw. [im Fernsehen] ansehen; **~ sb. do** *or* **doing sth.** zusehen, wie jmd. etw. tut; **he just ~ed her drown** er sah einfach zu, wie sie ertrank; **we are being ~ed** wir werden beobachtet; **she had him ~ed** sie ließ ihn beobachten; **the police were ~ing the house** die Polizei beobachtete das Haus; **I want all of you to ~ this closely** ich möchte, daß ihr euch *(Dat.)* dies alle genau anseht; **I shall ~ your career with interest** ich werde Ihre Karriere mit Interesse verfolgen; **~ one's weight** auf sein Gewicht achten; **~ sheep/goats** *etc.* Schafe/Ziegen *usw.* hüten; **just ~ me!** *(coll.)* paß/paßt mal auf! *(ugs.)*; **~ this space** *(fig.)* man darf gespannt sein; das wird sich zeigen; **a ~ed pot never boils** *(prov.)* wenn man auf etwas wartet, kommt es einem wie eine Ewigkeit vor; *see also* **clock 1 a; b)** *(be careful of, look after)* achten auf (+ *Akk.*); **~ your man-**

ners! *(coll.)* benimm dich!; ~ **your language!** *(coll.)* drück dich bitte etwas gepflegter *od.* nicht so ordinär aus!; ~ **him, he's an awkward customer** *(coll.)* paß/paßt auf, er ist mit Vorsicht zu genießen *(ugs.)*; ~ **how you go/drive** paß auf!/fahr vorsichtig!; ~ **it** *or* **oneself** sich vorsehen; **[just]** ~ **it [or you'll be in trouble]!** paß bloß auf[, sonst gibt's Ärger]! *(ugs.)*; *see also* **step 1 a; c)** *(look out for)* warten auf (+ *Akk.*); ~ **one's chance** die Gelegenheit abwarten
~ **'out** *v. i.* **a)** *(be careful)* sich vorsehen; aufpassen; ~ **out! There's a car coming!** Vorsicht! Da kommt ein Auto!; **b)** *(look out)* ~ **out for sb./sth.** auf jmdn./etw. achten; *(wait)* auf jmdn./etw. warten
~ **'over** *v. t.* sich kümmern um; in Obhut nehmen ⟨*Wertgegenstand*⟩; ⟨*Gott, Schutzengel:*⟩ wachen über (+ *Akk.*); **she ~ed over the children as they played in the garden** sie paßte auf die Kinder auf, die im Garten spielten
watch: ~-case *n.* Uhrgehäuse, *das;* **~-chain** *n.* Uhrkette, *die;* **~-dog** *n.* Wachhund, *der; (fig.)* Wächter, *der;* Aufpasser, *der (ugs.)*; **the ~-dog function of the press** *(fig.)* das Wächteramt der Presse
watcher ['wɒtʃə(r)] *n.* Beobachter, *der*/Beobachterin, *die;* **sky-~s** Sterngucker, *der;* **television-~s** Fernsehzuschauer; **royalty-~s** Leute, die das Leben der königlichen Familie genau verfolgen
watchful ['wɒtʃfl] *adj.* wachsam; **be ~ for** *or* **against sth.** vor etw. *(Dat.)* auf der Hut sein; **keep ~ guard** wachen; **spend a ~ night** eine Nacht durchwachen; **keep a ~ eye on sb./sth.** ein wachsames Auge auf jmdn./etw. haben
watchfully ['wɒtʃfəlɪ] *adv.* wachsam
watchfulness ['wɒtʃflnɪs] *n., no pl.* Wachsamkeit, *die*
'watch-glass *n.* Uhrglas, *das*
watching brief ['wɒtʃɪŋ bri:f] *n.* Kontrollfunktion, *die;* **keep** *or* **hold a ~:** Stallwache halten
watch: ~maker *n.* Uhrmacher, *der*/Uhrmacherin, *die;* **~man** ['wɒtʃmən] *n., pl.* **~men** ['wɒtʃmən] Wachmann, *der;* **~-strap** *n.* [Uhr]armband, *das;* **~-tower** *n.* Wachturm, *der;* **~word** *n.* Parole, *die*
water ['wɔ:tə(r)] **1.** *n.* **a)** Wasser, *das;* **this fruit is 80 per cent ~:** diese Frucht besteht zu 80 Prozent aus Wasser; **be under ~** ⟨*Straße, Sportplatz usw.:*⟩ unter Wasser stehen; **the island across** *or* **over the ~:** die Insel drüben; **the upper ~s of a river** der Oberlauf eines Flusses; **send/carry sth. by ~:** etw. auf dem Wasserweg versenden/befördern; **be in deep ~[s]** *(fig.)* in großen Schwierigkeiten sein; **get [oneself] into deep ~** *(fig.)* sich in große Schwierigkeiten bringen; **make ~** *(urinate)* Wasser lassen; *(Naut.: leak)* Wasser machen; **on the ~** *(in boat etc.)* auf dem Wasser; **pour** *or* **throw cold ~ on sth.** *(fig.)* einer Sache *(Dat.)* einen Dämpfer aufsetzen; ~ **under the bridge** *or* **over the dam** *(fig.)* Schnee von gestern *(fig.)*; **a lot of ~ has flowed under the bridge since then** seitdem ist schon viel Wasser den Rhein hinabgeflossen; *see also* **high water; ²hold 1 f; low water; spend a; b)** *in pl. (part of the sea etc.)* Gewässer *Pl.*; **cross the ~s** übers Meer fahren; **cast one's bread upon the ~s** mit offenen Händen geben; **c)** *in pl. (mineral ~ at spa etc.)* Heilquelle, *die;* Brunnen, *der;* **take** *or* **drink the ~s** eine Brunnenkur machen; **d)** *(brilliance of gem)* Wasser, *das;* **of the first ~** *(lit. or fig.)* reinsten Wassers; **a fool of the first ~:** ein Narr erster Güte *(iron.)*; **a genius of the first ~:** ein Genie ersten Ranges. **2.** *v. t.* **a)** bewässern ⟨*Land*⟩; wässern ⟨*Pflanzen*⟩; ~ **the flowers** die Blumen [be]gießen; **tears ~ed the ground** Tränen benetzen den Boden; **b)** *(adulterate)* verwässern ⟨*Wein, Bier usw.*⟩; **c)** ⟨*Fluß:*⟩ bewässern ⟨*Land*⟩; **d)** *(give drink of ~ to)* tränken ⟨*Tier, Vieh*⟩. **3.** *v. i.* **a)** ⟨*Augen:*⟩ tränen; **her eyes were ~ing from the smoke** von dem Rauch tränten ihr die Augen; **b)** *(run with saliva)* **my mouth was ~ing as ...:** mir lief das Wasser im Munde zusammen, als ...; **the very thought of it** *or* **just to think of it made my mouth ~:** allein bei dem Gedanken lief mir das Wasser im Munde zusammen; *see also* **mouth-watering; c)** *(take in supply of ~)* Wasser aufnehmen; **d)** *(go to drink)* ⟨*Tier:*⟩ saufen; **lions ~ing at dusk** Löwen in der Dämmerung an der Tränke
~ **'down** *v. t. (lit. or fig.)* verwässern
water: ~-bed *n.* Wasserbett, *das;* **~-bird** *n.* Wasservogel, *der;* **~-biscuit** *n.* Cracker, *der;* Kräcker, *der;* **~-boatman** *n.* *(Zool.)* Rückenschwimmer, *der;* **~-borne** *adj.* **a)** *(transported)* auf dem Wasserweg befördert ⟨*Güter*⟩; **~-borne traffic** Verkehr zu Wasser; **b)** *(transmitted)* durch [Trink]wasser übertragen ⟨*Infektion*⟩; **c)** *(afloat)* flott ⟨*Schiff, Boot*⟩; **~-bottle** *n.* Wasserflasche, *die;* **~-buffalo** *n.* Wasserbüffel, *der;* ~ **bus** *n.* Fahrgastschiff, *das;* Linienschiff, *das;* **~-butt** *n.* Regentonne, *die;* **~-cannon** *n.* Wasserwerfer, *der;* **W~-carrier** *n. (Astrol.)* Wassermann, *der;* *see also* **archer b; ~-cart** *n.* Wasserkarren, *der; (for sprinkling roads)* Sprengwagen, *der;* **~-closet** *n.* Toilette, *die;* WC, *das;* Wasserklosett, *das (veralt.)*; **~-colour** *n.* **a)** *(paint)* Wasserfarbe, *die;* **b)** *(picture)* Aquarell, *das;* **c)** *no pl., no indef. art. (Art)* Aquarellmalerei, *die;* **~-colourist** *n.* Aquarellmaler, *der*/-malerin, *die;* **~-cooled** *adj.* wassergekühlt ⟨*Motor usw.*⟩; **~-cooler** *n.* Kühltank, *der;* **~course** *n. (stream etc.)* Wasserlauf, *der; (bed)* Flußbett, *das;* **~cress** *n.* Brunnenkresse, *die;* **~-diviner** *n.* [Wünschel]rutengänger, *der*/-gängerin, *die*
watered ['wɔ:təd] *adj.* ~ **silk** Moiré, *der*
water: ~fall *n.* Wasserfall, *der;* **~-fowl** *n.* Wasservogel, *der; (collectively)* Wassergeflügel, *das;* **~front** *n.* Ufer, *das;* **down on the ~front** unten am Wasser; **a ~front location/restaurant** eine Gegend/ein Restaurant am Wasser; **W~gate** *n. (fig.)* Watergate, *das;* **~-glass** *n. (Chem.)* Wasserglas, *das;* **~-heater** *n.* Heißwassergerät, *das;* **~-hole** *n.* Wasserloch, *das;* **~-ice** *n.* ≈ Sorbet, *das;* ≈ Fruchteis, *das*
wateriness ['wɔ:tərɪnɪs] *n., no pl.* Wäßrigkeit, *die;* Wässerigkeit, *die*
watering ['wɔ:tərɪŋ] *n.* Bewässerung, *die; (of flowers, house-plants)* Gießen, *das;* **give the plants a thorough ~:** die Pflanzen gut wässern *od.* gießen
watering: ~-can *n.* Gießkanne, *die;* **~-hole** *n.* **a)** *see* **water-hole; b)** *(sl.: bar)* Pinte, *die (salopp)*; Destille, *die (salopp)*; **~-place** *n.* **a)** *(for animals)* Wasserstelle, *die;* Tränke, *die;* **b)** *(seaside resort)* Seebad, *das; (spa)* Kurbad, *das*
water: ~-jacket *n.* Kühl[wasser]mantel, *der;* **~-jump** *n.* Wassergraben, *der*
waterless ['wɔ:təlɪs] *adj.* wasserlos
water: ~-level *n.* **a)** *(in reservoir etc.)* Wasserstand, *der;* Pegelstand, *der;* **b)** *(below which ground is saturated)* Grundwasserspiegel, *der;* **c)** *(to determine horizontal)* Wasserwaage, *die;* **~-lily** *n.* Seerose, *die;* **~-line** *n. (Naut.)* Wasserlinie, *die;* **~logged** ['wɔ:təlɒgd] *adj.* vollgesogen ⟨*Holz*⟩; ⟨*Boot*⟩ voll Wasser; naß, feucht ⟨*Boden*⟩; aufgeweicht ⟨*Sportplatz*⟩; **a ~logged ship** ein Schiff, das voll Wasser gelaufen ist
Waterloo [wɔ:tə'lu:] *n.* **the Battle of ~:** die Schlacht bei Belle-Alliance *od.* Waterloo; **meet one's ~:** sein Waterloo erleben
water: ~-main *n.* Hauptwasserleitung, *die;* **a burst ~-main** ein Wasserrohrbruch; **~man** ['wɔ:təmən] *n., pl.* **~men** ['wɔ:təmən] *(plying for hire)* Fährmann, *der; (oarsman)* Ruderer, *der;* **~mark 1.** *n.* Wasserzeichen, *das;* **2.** *v. t.* mit Wasserzeichen versehen; **~marked paper** Papier mit Wasserzeichen; **~-meadow** *n.* Feuchtwiese, *die;* **~-melon** *n.* Wassermelone, *die;* ~ **meter** *n.* Wasseruhr, *die;* **~-mill** *n.* Wassermühle, *die;* **~-pipe** *n.* **a)** Wasserrohr, *das;* **b)** *(hookah)* Wasserpfeife, *die;* **~-pistol** *n.* Wasserpistole, *die;* ~ **polo** *n.* Wasserball, *der;* Wasserballspiel, *das;* **~-polo ball** Wasserball, *der;* **~-power** *n.* Wasserkraft, *die;* **~proof 1.** *adj.* wasserdicht; wasserfest ⟨*Farbe*⟩; **2.** *n.* Regenhaut, *die; (raincoat)* Regenmantel, *der;* **3.** *v. t.* wasserdicht machen; imprägnieren ⟨*Stoff*⟩; wetterfest machen ⟨*Holzzaun, Gartenmöbel*⟩; **~-rat** *n.* Wasserratte, *die;* **~-rate** *n.* Wassergeld, *das;* **the ~-rates** die Wassergebühren; **~-repellent** *adj.* wasserabstoßend; **~-resistant** *adj.* wasserundurchlässig; wasserfest ⟨*Farbe*⟩; **~shed** *n.* **a)** *(fig.: turning-point)* Wendepunkt, *der;* **b)** *(Geog.)* Wasserscheide, *die;* **~side** *n.* Ufer, *das; attrib.* **a ~side restaurant** ein Restaurant am Wasser; **~-ski 1.** *n.* Wasserski, *der;* **2.** *v. i.* Wasserski laufen; **~-skiing** *n., no pl., no art.* Wasserskilaufen, *das;* **~-softener** *n.* Wasserenthärter, *der;* **~-soluble** *adj.* wasserlöslich; **~spout** *n.* **a)** *(Meteorol.)* Wasserhose, *die;* **b)** *(pipe)* Abfluß, *der;* **~-supply** *n.* **a)** *no pl., no indef. art. (providing)* Wasserversorgung, *die;* **b)** *(stored drinking ~)* Trinkwasser, *das; (amount)* [Trink]wasservorrat, *der;* **~-table** *n.* Grundwasserspiegel, *der;* ~ **tap** *n.* Wasserhahn, *der;* **~tight** *adj. (lit. or fig.)* wasserdicht; **~tight compartment** wasserdichte Abteilung; **you can't treat these topics as if they were a series of ~tight compartments** man kann diese Dinge nicht völlig isoliert voneinander betrachten; ~ **torture** *n.* Wasserfolter, *die;* **~-tower** *n.* Wasserturm, *der;* ~ **vapour** *n.* Wasserdampf, *der;* **~-vole** *n.* Schermaus, *die;* **~-wagon** *see* **wagon c; ~way** *n.* Wasserstraße, *die;* **inland ~ways** Binnenwasserstraßen; **~-weed** *n., no pl., no indef. art.* Wasserpflanzen *Pl.*; **~-wheel** *n.* Wasserrad, *das; (used to raise ~)* Schöpfrad, *das;* **~-wings** *n. pl.* Schwimmflügel; **~works** *n.* **a)** *sing., pl. same (system)* Wasserversorgungssystem, *das; (establishment)* Wasserwerk, *das;* **b)** *pl. (sl.: tears)* **turn on the ~works** losheulen *(ugs.)*; **c)** *pl. (coll.: urinary system)* Blase, *die;* **he's got something wrong with his ~works** er hat was an der Blase *(ugs.)*
watery ['wɔ:tərɪ] *adj.* wäßrig, wässerig ⟨*Essen, Suppe*⟩; feucht ⟨*Augen*⟩; dünn ⟨*Getränk*⟩; *(fig.: insipid)* [saft- und] kraftlos ⟨*Stil*⟩; müde, matt ⟨*Lächeln*⟩; *(fig.: pale)* matt ⟨*Farbton*⟩; fahl ⟨*Mond, Himmel*⟩; **a ~ grave** ein feuchtes *od.* nasses Grab
watt [wɒt] *n. (Electr., Phys.)* Watt, *das;* **how many ~s is this bulb?** wieviel Watt hat diese Birne?
wattage ['wɒtɪdʒ] *n. (Electr.)* Wattzahl, *die;* **what ~ is this bulb?** wieviel Watt hat diese Birne?
'watt-hour *n. (Electr.)* Wattstunde, *die*
¹wattle ['wɒtl] *n.* **a)** *(material)* Flechtwerk, *das;* **a ~ fence** ein Flechtzaun; ~ **and daub** Lehmflechtwerk, *das;* **b)** *in sing. or pl. (twigs)* Geflecht, *das;* Flechtwerk, *das;* **c)** *(Bot.)* Gerberakazie, *die*
²wattle *n. (Ornith.)* Kehllappen, *der*
wave [weɪv] **1.** *n.* **a)** *(lit. or fig.)* Welle, *die;* Woge, *die (geh.)*; *(in hair, Phys.)* Welle, *die;* **rule the ~s** die Meere beherrschen; **his hair has a natural ~ in it** sein Haar ist von Natur aus wellig; **a ~ of enthusiasm/prosperity/pain** eine Welle der Begeisterung/des Wohlstands/des Schmerzes; **a ~ of depression overtook him** er versank in tiefe Depression; **~s of immigrants** Einwanderungswel-

len; ~s of attackers Angriffswellen; *see also* **cold wave; heat wave; permanent wave; b)** *(gesture)* **give sb. a ~:** jmdm. zuwinken; **with a ~ of one's hand** mit einem Winken. **2.** *v.i.* **a)** ⟨*Fahne, Flagge, Wimpel:*⟩ wehen; ⟨*Baum, Gras, Korn:*⟩ sich wiegen; ⟨*Kornfeld:*⟩ wogen; **b)** *(gesture with hand)* winken; **~ at** *or* **to sb.** jmdm. winken. **3.** *v.t.* **a)** schwenken; *(brandish)* schwingen ⟨*Schwert, Säbel*⟩; **~ one's hand at** *or* **to sb.** jmdm. winken; **~ one's handkerchief [in the air]** mit dem Taschentuch winken; **they ~d their arms in exultation** sie ruderten vor Begeisterung mit den Armen; **she ~d her umbrella angrily at him** sie drohte ihm wütend mit dem Regenschirm; **stop waving that rifle/those scissors around** hör auf, mit dem Gewehr/der Schere herumzufuchteln *(ugs.)*; **~ sb. on/over** jmdn. weiter-/herüberwinken; **~ sb. to do sth.** jmdm. durch Winken zu verstehen geben, daß er etw. tun soll; **~ goodbye to sb.** jmdm. zum Abschied zuwinken; **she ~d acknowledgement to him** sie winkte ihm zu, um [ihm] zu danken; **b)** *(make wavy)* wellen

~ a'side *v.t.* **a)** *(refuse to accept)* abtun ⟨*Zweifel, Einwand*⟩; **he refused the dish, waving it aside** er wollte das Essen nicht und winkte ab; **b)** *(signal to move aside)* **I tried to speak but she ~d me aside** ich wollte reden, aber sie winkte ab

~ a'way *v.t.* wegwinken

~ 'down *v.t.* [durch Winken] anhalten

~ 'off *v.t.* **~ sb. off** jmdm. nachwinken

wave: ~band *n.* Wellenbereich, *der;* **~ equation** *n. (Phys.)* Wellengleichung, *die;* **~-form** *n.* Wellenform, *die;* **~-front** *n.* Wellenfront, *die;* **~length** *n. (Radio, Telev., Phys.; also fig.)* Wellenlänge, *die;* **be on sb.'s ~length** *(fig.)* die gleiche Wellenlänge wie jmd. haben; **be on the same ~length [as sb.]** *(fig.)* die gleiche Wellenlänge [wie jmd.] haben; **~ power** *n.* Wellenkraft, *die*

waver ['weɪvə(r)] *v.i.* **a)** *(begin to give way)* wanken; **start** *or* **begin to ~:** ins Wanken geraten; **b)** *(be irresolute)* schwanken **(between** zwischen + *Dat.*); **c)** *(flicker)* ⟨*Kerze, Licht:*⟩ flackern; ⟨*Schatten:*⟩ tanzen; **d)** *(tremble)* ⟨*Stimme, Ton:*⟩ zittern

waverer ['weɪvərə(r)] *n.* Zauderer, *der*/ Zauderin, *die*

wavering ['weɪvərɪŋ] *adj.* **a)** wankend ⟨*Mut, Entschlossenheit*⟩; schwankend ⟨*Unterstützung*⟩; **b)** *(flickering)* flackernd ⟨*Kerze, Licht*⟩; tanzend ⟨*Schatten*⟩; zitternd ⟨*Stimme, Ton*⟩

wavy ['weɪvɪ] *adj.* **a)** *(undulating)* wellig; wogend ⟨*Gras*⟩; **b)** *(forming wave-like curves)* geschlängelt; **~ line** Schlangenlinie, *die;* **~ pattern** Wellenmuster, *das*

¹wax [wæks] **1.** *n.* **a)** Wachs, *das;* **be [like] ~ in sb.'s hands** [wie] Wachs in jmds. Händen sein; **b)** *(in ear)* Schmalz, *das;* **c)** *see* **sealing-wax.** *See also* **paraffin wax. 2.** *adj.* Wachs-. **3.** *v.t.* wachsen; wichsen ⟨*Schnurrbart*⟩

²wax *v.i.* **a)** *(increase)* ⟨*Mond:*⟩ zunehmen; **~ and wane** *(fig.)* zu- und abnehmen; **the political parties may ~ and wane, but he ...:** die politischen Parteien mögen gewinnen und verlieren, er aber ...; **b)** *(become)* werden; **~ enthusiastic about sth.** über etw. *(Akk.)* ins Schwärmen geraten; **she ~ed indignant about the rudeness of the officials** sie empörte sich [immer mehr] über die Unhöflichkeit der Beamten

wax 'crayon *n.* Wachsmalstift, *der*

waxed [wækst] *adj.* gewachst; gewichst ⟨*Schnurrbart*⟩; **~ paper** Wachspapier, *das*

waxen ['wæksn] *adj.* **a)** *(pale, smooth)* wächsern ⟨*Blässe, Haut*⟩; **b)** *(arch.: made of wax)* wächsern; wächsen *(dichter. veralt.)*

waxing ['wæksɪŋ] **1.** *adj. (increasing)* zunehmend; wachsend ⟨*Begeisterung, Unmut*⟩. **2.** *n., no pl. (increase)* Zunehmen, *das; (of enthusiasm, indignation)* Zunahme, *die;* [An]wachsen, *das*

wax: ~work *n.* Wachsfigur, *die;* **~works** *n. sing., pl. same* Wachsfigurenkabinett, *das*

waxy ['wæksɪ] *adj.* **a)** *(easily moulded)* wachsweich; weich wie Wachs *nicht attr.;* **b)** *(pale, smooth)* wächsern ⟨*Blässe, Glanz, Haut*⟩

way [weɪ] **1.** *n.* **a)** *(road etc., lit. or fig.)* Weg, *der;* **across** *or* **over the ~:** gegenüber; **go the ~ of all good things** den Weg alles Irdischen gehen; **the Way of the Cross** der Kreuzweg; *see also* **flesh 1c; b)** *(route)* Weg, *der;* **ask the** *or* **one's ~:** nach dem Weg fragen; **ask the ~ to ...:** fragen *od.* sich erkundigen, wo es nach ... geht; **pick one's ~:** sich *(Dat.)* einen Weg suchen; **he picked his ~ through the mud** er bahnte sich mühsam einen Weg durch den Schlamm; **show sb. the way** jmdn. den Weg zeigen; **show the ~** *(fig.)* den Weg weisen; **lead the ~:** vorausgehen; *(fig.: show how to do sth.)* es vormachen; **point the ~ to a new solution to the problem** den Weg zu einer neuen Lösung des Problems aufzeigen; **find the** *or* **one's ~ in/out** den Eingang/Ausgang finden; **find a ~ out** *(fig.)* einen Ausweg finden; **I'll take the letter to the post office – it's on my ~:** ich bringe den Brief zur Post – sie liegt auf meinem Weg; **how did your cigarettes find their way into my coat-pocket?** wie kommen deine Zigaretten in meine Manteltasche?; **'W~ In/ Out'** „Ein-/Ausgang"; **go to Italy by ~ of Switzerland** über die Schweiz nach Italien fahren; **there's no ~ out** *(fig.)* es gibt keinen Ausweg; **the ~ back/down/up** der Weg zurück/nach unten/nach oben; **go one's ~:** weggehen; seiner Wege gehen *(veralt.)*; **go one's own ~/their separate ~s** *(fig.)* eigene/ getrennte Wege gehen; **be going sb.'s ~** *(coll.)* denselben Weg wie jmd. haben; **things are really going my ~ at the moment** *(fig.)* im Moment läuft [bei mir] alles so, wie ich es mir vorgestellt habe; **things could have gone the other ~:** es hätte auch anders ausgehen können; **money came his ~:** er kam zu Geld; **many offers came his ~:** er kriegte viele Angebote; **he worked at any job that came his ~:** er arbeitete in jedem Job, den er kriegen konnte; **I wish some better luck would come my ~:** ich wünschte mir, etwas mehr Glück zu haben; **I feel as though nothing nice has come my ~ for ages** mir ist, als hätte ich schon ewig nichts Schönes mehr erlebt; **when a girl like that comes your ~:** wenn dir so ein Mädchen begegnet *od. (ugs.)* über den Weg läuft; **be [a bit] out of sb.'s ~:** ein [kleiner] Umweg [für jmdn.] sein; **go out of one's ~ to collect sth. for sb.** einen Umweg machen, um etw. für jmdn. abzuholen; **go out of one's ~ to be helpful** sich *(Dat.)* besondere Mühe geben, hilfsbereit zu sein; **out of the ~:** abgelegen; **nothing out of the ~** *(fig.)* nichts Un- *od.* Außergewöhnliches; *see also* **find 1i; go 1b, p, q; go down b; keep out of b; lose 1c; out-of-the-way; take 1t; way-out; c)** *(method)* Art und Weise, *die;* **there is a right ~ and a wrong ~ of doing it** es gibt einen richtigen und einen falschen Weg, es zu tun; **that is not the ~ to do it** so macht man das nicht; **do it this ~:** mach es so; **do it my ~:** mach es wie ich; **I did it my ~:** ich habe es auf meine Art gemacht; **it's awful the ~ he swears** es ist fürchterlich, wie er flucht; **I don't like the ~ she smiles** mir gefällt ihr Lächeln nicht; **I don't like the ~ it gets dark so early** mir gefällt nicht, daß es schon so früh dunkel wird; **I object to** *or* **don't like the ~ he looks at me** ich mag nicht, wie er mich ansieht; **that's no ~ to speak to a lady** so spricht man nicht mit einer Dame; **it was his ~ of working** das war seine Art zu arbeiten; **he has a strange ~ of talking** er hat eine seltsame Sprechweise *od.* Art zu sprechen; **from** *or* **by the ~ [that] she looked at me, I knew that there was something wrong** an ihrem Blick konnte ich erkennen, daß etwas nicht stimmte; **she has a strange ~ of behaving** sie hat ein merkwürdiges Benehmen; **what a ~ to behave!** wie kann man sich nur so benehmen!; **she has a very original ~ of saying/seeing things** sie hat eine sehr originelle Art, etwas zu sagen/die Dinge zu sehen; **find a** *or* **some ~ of doing sth.** einen Weg finden, etw. zu tun; **find a ~:** einen Weg finden; **there are no two ~s about it** da gibt es gar keinen Zweifel; **Are you going to give me that money? – No ~!** *(coll.)* Gibst du mir das Geld? – Nichts da! *(ugs.)*; **there was no ~ he would change his stand** er würde auf gar keinen Fall seinen Standpunkt ändern; **no ~ is he coming with us** es kommt überhaupt nicht in Frage, daß er mit uns kommt; **one ~ or another** irgendwie; **~s and means [to do sth.** *or* **of doing sth.]** Mittel und Wege, etw. zu tun; **be built** *or* **made that ~** *(fig. coll.)* so gestrickt sein *(fig. ugs.)*; **be that ~** *(coll.)* so sein; **better that ~:** besser so; **either ~:** so oder so; **that ~, we can ...:** auf die Weise können wir ...; *see also* **hard 1b; mend 1b; d)** *(desired course of action)* Wille, *der;* **get** *or* **have one's [own] ~, have it one's [own] ~:** seinen Willen kriegen; **all right, have it your own ~[, then]!** na gut *od.* schön, du sollst deinen Willen haben!; **e)** *in sing. or (Amer. coll.) pl. (distance between two points)* Stück, *das;* **a little ~:** ein kleines Stück[chen]; *(fig.)* ein klein[es] bißchen; **it's a long ~ off** *or* **a long ~ from here** es ist ein ganzes Stück von hier aus; es ist weit weg von hier; **the summer holidays are only a little ~ away** bis zu den Sommerferien ist es nicht mehr lange; **we went a little/a long/ some ~ with him** wir sind ein kleines/ganzes/ziemliches Stück mit ihm gegangen/ gefahren *usw.*; **there's [still] some ~ to go yet** es ist noch ein ganzes Stück; *(fig.)* es dauert noch ein Weilchen; **I went a little/a long/ some ~ to meet him** ich bin ihm ein kleines/ ganzes/ziemliches Stück entgegengegangen/-gefahren *usw.*, um mich mit ihm zu treffen; *(fig.)* ich bin ihm etwas/sehr/ziemlich entgegengekommen; **it is still a long ~ off perfection** *or* **from being perfect** es ist noch weit davon entfernt, vollkommen zu sein; **India is a long ~ away** *or* **off** Indien ist weit weg; **by a long ~** *(fig.)* bei weitem; **your work isn't good enough yet – not by a long ~:** Ihre Arbeit ist noch nicht gut genug – bei weitem nicht; **have gone/come a long ~** *(fig.)* es weit gebracht haben; **go a long ~ toward sth./doing sth.** viel zu etw. beitragen/viel dazu beitragen, etw. zu tun; **a little kindness/politeness goes a long ~:** ein bißchen Freundlichkeit/Höflichkeit ist viel wert *od.* hilft viel; **all the ~:** den ganzen Weg; **go all the ~ [with sb.]** *(fig.)* [jmdm.] in jeder Hinsicht zustimmen; *(sl.: have full sexual intercourse)* es [mit jmdm.] richtig machen *(salopp)*; **f)** *(room for progress)* Weg, *der;* **block the ~:** den Weg versperren; **his ~ to promotion was blocked by a jealous rival** seine Karriere wurde durch einen neidischen Rivalen versperrt; **leave the ~ open for sth.** *(fig.)* etw. möglich machen; **clear the ~ [for sth.]** *(lit. or fig.)* [einer Sache *(Dat.)*] den Weg freimachen; **be in sb.'s** *or* **the ~:** [jmdm.] im Weg sein; **you are in my ~:** du bist [mir] im Wege; **get in sb.'s ~** *(lit. or fig.)* jmdm. im Wege stehen; **put difficulties/obstacles in sb.'s ~** *(fig.)* jmdm. Schwierigkeiten bereiten/Hindernisse in den Weg legen; **make ~ for sth.** für etw. Platz schaffen *od. (fig.)* machen; **make ~ for sb.** für jmdn. Platz machen; **make ~ for the Mayor!** Platz für den Bürgermeister!; **make ~!** Platz da!; **[get] out of the/my ~!**

[geh] aus dem Weg!; **move one's car out of the ~:** seinen Wagen aus dem Weg fahren; **can you get your books out of the ~?** kannst du deine Bücher woanders hinlegen?; **I must put that pile of old newspapers out of the ~:** ich muß den Stapel alte Zeitungen wegräumen; **please get the children out of the ~ while I do this painting** bitte sorge dafür, daß die Kinder nicht im Weg sind, während ich hier streiche; **get sth. out of the ~** *(settle sth.)* etw. erledigen; **let's get the awkward questions out of the ~ first** wir wollen erst einmal die schwierigen Fragen hinter uns bringen; **he'll be out of the ~ for a very long time** *(in prison)* er ist für lange Zeit aus dem Verkehr gezogen; **he wanted this troublesome rival out of the ~ [for good]** er wollte diesen lästigen Rivalen [für immer] aus dem Weg haben; *see also* **¹bar 2c; give way; keep out of b; ¹see 1a; stand 1h; g)** *(journey)* **on his ~ to the office/London** auf dem Weg ins Büro/nach London; **on the ~ out to Singapore** auf dem Hinweg/der Hinfahrt/dem Hinflug nach Singapur; **on the ~ back from Nigeria** auf dem Rückweg/der Rückfahrt/dem Rückflug von Nigeria; **she is just on the** *or* **her ~ in/out** sie kommt/geht gerade; **be on the ~ in** *(fig. coll.)* ‹*Mode, Popstar usw.:*› im Kommen sein *(ugs.)*; **be on the ~ out** *(fig. coll.) (be losing popularity)* passé sein *(ugs.)*; *(be reaching end of life)* ‹*Hund, Auto, Person:*› es nicht mehr lange machen *(ugs.)*; **we stopped on the ~ to have lunch** wir hielten unterwegs zum Mittagessen an; **on her ~ home** auf dem Nachhauseweg; **they're on their ~:** sie sind unterwegs; **on the ~ there** auf dem Hinweg; **be well on the ~ to becoming an alcoholic/a top-class player** auf dem besten Weg sein, Alkoholiker/ein Spitzenspieler zu werden; **the book is well on the** *or* **its ~ to completion** das Buch nähert sich dem Abschluß; **be on the ~** *(coll.)* ‹*Kind:*› unterwegs sein *(ugs.)*; **[be] on your ~!** nun geh schon!; **by the ~:** übrigens; **I saw your mother, by the ~:** übrigens, ich habe deine Mutter getroffen; **all this is by the ~:** das alles nur nebenbei; **h)** *(specific direction)* Richtung, *die;* **she went this/that/the other ~:** sie ist in diese/die/die andere Richtung gegangen; **look this ~, please** sieh/seht bitte hierher!; **he wouldn't look my ~:** er hat nicht zu mir herübergesehen; **which ~ is he looking/going?** in welche Richtung *od.* wohin sieht/geht er?; **I will call next time I'm [down] your ~:** wenn ich das nächste Mal in deiner Gegend bin, komme ich [bei dir] vorbei; **she lives Brighton ~** *(coll.)* sie wohnt in der Gegend von Brighton; **out Hendon ~** *(coll.)* draußen bei Hendon; **look the other ~** *(lit. or fig.)* weggucken; **the other ~ about** *or* **round** andersherum; **this/which ~ round** so/wie herum; **stand sth. the right/wrong ~ up** etw. richtig/falsch herum stellen; **turn sth. the right ~ round** etw. richtig herum drehen; **'this ~ up'** „hier oben"; *see also* **look 1a; wrong 1c; i)** *(advance)* Weg, *der;* **fight/push** *etc.* **one's ~ through** sich durchkämpfen/-drängen; **be under ~** ‹*Person:*› aufgebrochen sein; ‹*Fahrzeug:*› abgefahren sein; *(fig.: be in progress)* ‹*Besprechung, Verhandlung, Tagung:*› im Gange sein; **get sth. under ~** *(fig.)* etw. in Gang bringen; **get under ~:** wegkommen; **make one's ~ to Oxford/the station** nach Oxford/zum Bahnhof gehen/fahren; **Do you need a lift? – No, I'll make my own ~:** Soll ich dich mitnehmen? – Nein, ich komme alleine; **make one's [own] ~ in the world** seinen Weg gehen *(fig.)*; **make** *or* **pay its ~:** ohne Verlust arbeiten; **pay one's ~:** für sich selbst aufkommen; **j)** *(respect)* Hinsicht, *die;* **in [exactly] the same ~:** [ganz] genauso; **in some ~s** in gewisser Hinsicht; **in one ~:** auf eine Art; **not in any ~:** in keiner Weise; **in every ~:** in jeder Hinsicht; **in a ~:** auf eine Art; **in more ~s than one** auf mehr als eine Art; **in no ~:** auf keinen Fall; durchaus nicht; **one ~ and** *or* **or another** irgendwie; **k)** *(state)* Verfassung, *die;* **in a bad ~:** schlecht; **they are in a very bad ~:** es geht ihnen sehr schlecht; **the ~ things are, we shall never manage to get out of debt** so, wie die Dinge liegen, werden wir nie schuldenfrei sein; **we are all in the same ~ here** wir sind hier alle in der gleichen Lage *od.* Situation; **and she stayed that ~:** und das ist sie auch geblieben; **either ~:** so oder so; **in a small ~:** in bescheidenem Rahmen; **by ~ of** *(as a kind of)* als; *(for the purpose of)* um ... zu; **by ~ of illustration/greeting/apology/introduction** zur Illustration / Begrüßung / Entschuldigung/Einführung; **by ~ of business** geschäftlich; **he is by ~ of being a humorist** er ist eine Art von Humorist; **offer something in the ~ of a concession** eine Art Konzession anbieten; *see also* **family a; l)** *(custom)* Art, *die;* **get into/out of the ~ of doing sth.** sich *(Dat.)* etw. an-/abgewöhnen; **he has a ~ of leaving his bills unpaid** es ist so seine Art, seine Rechnungen nicht zu bezahlen; **these bright ideas have a ~ of turning out badly** solche brillanten Ideen haben es an sich *(Dat.)*, zu nichts Gutem zu führen; **in its ~:** auf seine/ihre Art; **~ of life** Lebensstil, *der;* **change one's ~s** sich ändern; **~ of thinking** Denkungsart, *die;* **to my ~ of thinking** meiner Meinung nach; **that's just the ~ of the world** das ist ganz natürlich; **that's the ~ it goes** so ist es nun mal; **m)** *(normal course of events)* **be the ~:** so *od.* üblich sein; **that is always the ~:** das ist immer so; **n)** *(ability to charm sb. or attain one's object)* **he has a ~ with him** er hat so eine Art; **she has a ~ with children/animals** sie kann mit Kindern/Tieren gut umgehen; **o)** *(specific manner)* Eigenart, *die;* **I soon got into his ~s** ich hatte mich bald an seine Art gewöhnt; **fall into bad ~s** schlechte [An]gewohnheiten annehmen; **I soon got into the ~ of it** *or* **of things** ich hatte mich bald daran gewöhnt; **it's only his ~:** das ist so seine Art; **p)** *(sphere)* Gebiet, *das;* **he is in the grocery ~:** er ist in der Lebensmittelbranche; **a few things in the stationery ~:** ein paar Büroartikel; **q)** *(ordinary course)* Rahmen, *der;* **in the ~ of business** geschäftlich; **in the ordinary ~ [of things] there would be no problem** normalerweise gäbe es keine Schwierigkeiten; **r)** *(movement of ship etc.)* Fahrt, *die;* **gather ~:** Fahrt aufnehmen; **lose ~:** die Fahrt verlangsamen; **the vessel has ~ on [her]** das Schiff macht Fahrt; **s)** *in pl. (parts)* Teile *Pl.;* **split sth. [in] three ~s** etw. in drei Teile teilen; **t)** *in pl. (down which ship is launched)* Helling, *die;* **u)** *as name of road* Weg, *der.* **2.** *adv.* weit; **~ off/ahead/above** weit weg von/weit voraus/weit über; **~ back** *(coll.)* vor langer Zeit; **~ back in the early fifties/before the war** vor langer Zeit, Anfang der fünfziger Jahre/vor dem Krieg; **~ up in the clouds** hoch oben in den Wolken; **he was ~ out with his guess, his guess was ~ out** er lag mit seiner Schätzung gewaltig daneben; **~ down south/in the valley** tief [unten] im Süden/Tal

way: ~-bill *n.* Frachtbrief, *der;* **~farer** ['weɪfeərə(r)] *n.* Wandersmann, *der (geh. veralt.)*; **~faring** ['weɪfeərɪŋ] *adj.* **a ~-faring man/woman** ein Wandersmann/eine Wanderin; **~'lay** *v.t., forms as* **²lay 1: a)** *(ambush)* überfallen; **b)** *(stop for conversation)* abfangen; **~mark** *n.* Wegmarke, *die;* Wegzeichen, *das;* **~-'out** *adj. (coll.)* verrückt *(ugs.)*; irre *(salopp)*; **~side** *n.* Wegrand, *der;* **fall by the ~side** *(fig.)* auf der Strecke bleiben *(ugs.)*; **~side flowers/inns** Blumen/Gasthöfe am Wegrand; **~station** *n. (Amer. Railw.)* Haltepunkt, *der*

wayward ['weɪwəd] *adj.* eigenwillig; ungezügelt ‹*Talent, Macht*›

waywardly ['weɪwədlɪ] *adv.* eigenwillig; unberechenbar ‹*sich verändern*›

waywardness ['weɪwədnɪs] *n., no pl.* Eigenwilligkeit, *die*

WC *abbr.* **water-closet** WC, *das*

we [wɪ, *stressed* wiː] *pl. pron.* wir; **how are we feeling today?** *(coll.)* wie geht's uns denn heute? *(ugs.)*; **the royal 'we'** der Pluralis majestatis; *see also* **our; ours; ourselves; us**

weak [wiːk] *adj.* **a)** *(lit. or fig.)* schwach; matt ‹*Lächeln*›; schwach ausgeprägt ‹*Kinn*›; jämmerlich ‹*Kapitulation*›; *(easily led)* labil ‹*Charakter, Person*›; **go/feel ~ at the knees** weiche Knie kriegen/haben; **the ~er sex** das schwache Geschlecht; **~ with hunger/excitement** schwach vor Hunger/Aufregung; **~ eyes** *or* **sight** schlechte Augen; **a ~ stomach** ein empfindlicher Magen; **have a ~ chest** schwach auf der Brust sein; **be ~ in the head** schwachsinnig sein; **his French/maths is rather ~, he's rather ~ in French/maths** in Französisch/Mathematik ist er ziemlich schwach; **a ~ hand** *(Cards)* ein schlechtes Blatt; **in a ~ moment** in einem schwachen Moment; **sb.'s ~ side** *or* **point** jmds. schwache Seite *od.* schwacher Punkt *od.* Schwachpunkt; **his logic is a bit ~:** seine Logik steht auf ziemlich schwachen Füßen; **he has only a ~ case** seine Sache steht auf schwachen Füßen; *see also* **vessel c; b)** *(watery)* schwach ‹*Kaffee, Tee*›; wäßrig, wässerig ‹*Suppe*›; dünn ‹*Bier, Suppe, Kaffee, Tee*›; **c)** *(Ling.)* schwach ‹*Konjugation, Deklination, Verb*›; unbetont ‹*Endung, Vokal, Silbe*›

weaken ['wiːkn] **1.** *v.t.* schwächen; beeinträchtigen ‹*Augen*›; entkräften, schwächen ‹*Argument*›; lockern ‹*Griff*›; **be ~ed by stress/too much work** durch Streß/zuviel Arbeit angegriffen werden; **the foundations of the house had been ~ed by the earthquake** durch das Erdbeben waren die Fundamente des Hauses in Mitleidenschaft gezogen worden. **2.** *v.i.* ‹*Kraft, Entschlossenheit:*› nachlassen; **the patient was visibly ~ing** der Patient wurde sichtlich schwächer; **the pound ~ed against the dollar** das Pfund wurde gegenüber dem Dollar schwächer; **~ in one's resolve** in seinem Vorsatz schwankend werden; **his hold on power was ~ing** er hielt die Macht nicht mehr so fest in der Hand

weak-kneed ['wiːkniːd] *adj.* **a) be ~:** weiche Knie haben **(with** vor + *Dat.***)**; **b)** *(fig.)* feige

weakling ['wiːklɪŋ] *n.* Schwächling, *der*

weakly ['wiːklɪ] **1.** *adv.* schwach; matt ‹*lächeln*›; **be ~ indulgent** schwach und nachgiebig sein. **2.** *adj.* schwächlich

'weak-minded *adj.* **a)** *(lacking strength of purpose)* entschlußlos; unentschlossen; **b)** *(mentally deficient)* schwachsinnig

weakness ['wiːknɪs] *n.* Schwäche, *die; (in argument, defence)* schwacher Punkt; **the ~ of her character** ihre Charakterschwäche; **I have a ~ for sweet things** ich habe eine Schwäche für Süßigkeiten

weak-willed *adj.* willensschwach

¹weal [wiːl] *n. (literary: welfare)* Wohl, *das;* **for the public** *or* **general ~:** zum Wohle der Allgemeinheit; **~ and woe, ~ or woe** Wohl und Weh[e] *(geh.)*

²weal *n. (ridge on flesh)* Striemen, *der*

wealth [welθ] *n., no pl.* **a)** *(abundance)* Fülle, *die;* **a great ~ of detail** große Detailfülle; **~ of words** Wortreichtum, *der;* **b)** *(riches, being rich)* Reichtum, *der*

'wealth tax *n.* Vermögenssteuer, *die*

wealthy ['welθɪ] **1.** *adj.* reich. **2.** *n.pl.* **the ~:** die Reichen

wean [wiːn] *v.t.* abstillen; entwöhnen ‹*Tier*›; **~ sb. [away] from sth.** *(fig.)* jmdm. etw. abgewöhnen

weapon ['wepən] *n. (lit. or fig.)* Waffe, *die;* **use sth. as a ~:** etw. als Waffe benutzen
weaponry ['wepənrı] *n.* Waffen *Pl.*
wear [weə(r)] **1.** *n., no pl., no indef. art.* **a)** *(rubbing)* **~ [and tear]** Verschleiß, *der;* Abnutzung, *die;* **show signs of ~:** Verschleiß- *od.* Abnutzungserscheinungen aufweisen; **the ~ and tear on sb.'s nerves** *(fig.)* jmds. Nervenverschleiß; **the worse for ~:** abgetragen ⟨*Kleider*⟩; abgelaufen ⟨*Schuhe*⟩; abgenutzt ⟨*Teppich, Sessel, Möbel*⟩; **feel the worse for ~:** sich angeschlagen fühlen *(ugs.);* **b)** *(clothes, use of clothes)* Kleidung, *die;* **clothes for everyday ~:** Alltagskleidung, *die;* **a jacket for casual ~:** ein Freizeit- *od. (veralt.)* Sportsakko; **children's/ladies' ~:** Kinder-/Damen[be]kleidung, *die;* **c)** *(capacity for enduring rubbing)* **there is a great deal of/no ~ [left] in it** es/das *usw.* hat noch eine große Lebensdauer/keine große Lebensdauer mehr; **there's a great** *or* **good deal of ~ still in those shoes** die Schuhe halten noch lange. **2.** *v. t.,* **wore** [wɔ:(r)], **worn** [wɔ:n] **a)** tragen ⟨*Kleidung, Schmuck, Bart, Brille, Perücke, Abzeichen*⟩; **I haven't a thing to ~:** ich habe überhaupt nichts anzuziehen; **what on earth am I going to ~ tonight?** was soll ich heute abend bloß anziehen?; **what size shoes do you ~?** welche Schuhgröße haben Sie?; **~ the crown** *(fig.)* die Krone tragen; **~ one's hair long** lange Haare tragen; **always ~ a smile** immer lächeln; **~ a joyful smile** glücklich lächeln; **~ a frown** ein finsteres Gesicht machen; **~ a sour look** eine saure Miene aufsetzen; **~ one's years well** sich gut gehalten haben; *see also* **heart 1b; trousers; b)** abtragen ⟨*Kleidungsstück*⟩; abtreten, abnutzen ⟨*Teppich*⟩; **be worn [smooth]** ⟨*Stufen:*⟩ ausgetreten sein; ⟨*Gestein:*⟩ ausgewaschen sein; ⟨*Gesicht:*⟩ abgehärmt sein; **the old coat was badly worn** der alte Mantel war ganz abgewetzt; **a [badly] worn tyre** ein [stark] abgefahrener Reifen; **he had worn his trousers into holes** seine Hose hatte überall Löcher; **c)** *(make by rubbing)* scheuern; **the water had worn a channel in the rock** das Wasser hatte sich durch den Felsen gefressen; **d)** *(exhaust)* erschöpfen; **e)** *(coll.: accept)* **I won't ~ that!** das nehme ich dir/ihm *usw.* nicht ab! *(ugs.).* **3.** *v. i.,* **wore, worn a)** ⟨*Kante, Saum, Kleider:*⟩ sich durchscheuern; ⟨*Absätze, Schuhsohlen:*⟩ sich ablaufen; ⟨*Teppich:*⟩ sich abnutzen; **~ thin** *(fig.)* ⟨*Idealismus:*⟩ sich langsam legen, nachlassen; ⟨*Freundschaft, Stil:*⟩ verflachen, oberflächlicher werden; ⟨*Witz, Ausrede:*⟩ schon reichlich alt sein; **my patience is ~ing thin** meine Geduld geht allmählich zur Neige *od.* ist langsam erschöpft; **b)** *(endure rubbing)* ⟨*Material, Stoff:*⟩ halten; *(fig.)* sich halten; **~ well/badly** sich gut/schlecht tragen
~ a'way 1. *v. t.* abschleifen ⟨*Kanten, Grate*⟩; **be worn away** ⟨*Stufen:*⟩ ausgetreten werden; ⟨*Inschrift:*⟩ verwittern; **she has been worn away to a shadow** sie ist zu einem Schatten ihrer selbst geworden. **2.** *v. i.* sich abnutzen; ⟨*Gestein:*⟩ verwittern; ⟨*Schuhabsätze:*⟩ sich ablaufen; *(fig.: weaken, lessen)* dahinschwinden
~ 'down 1. *v. t.* **a) be worn down** ⟨*Stufen:*⟩ ausgetreten werden; ⟨*Absätze:*⟩ sich ablaufen; ⟨*Reifen:*⟩ sich abfahren; ⟨*Berge:*⟩ abgetragen werden; **b)** *(fig.)* **~ down sb.'s resistance/defence/opposition** jmds. Widerstand/Verteidigung/Opposition zermürben; **having to do this for hours at a stretch can ~ one down** es kann einen fertigmachen *(ugs.),* wenn man das stundenlang ununterbrochen tun muß. **2.** *v. i.* ⟨*Absätze:*⟩ sich ablaufen; ⟨*Reifen:*⟩ sich abfahren; **the stick/tooth had worn down to a stump** der Stock/Zahn war nur noch ein Stummel
~ 'off 1. *v. i.* ⟨*Auflage, Schicht:*⟩ abgehen; ⟨*Muster:*⟩ sich verlieren; *(fig.: pass away gradually)* sich legen; ⟨*Wirkung, Schmerz:*⟩ nachlassen; **the sheen had long since worn off the material** der Stoff hatte schon lange seinen Glanz verloren. **2.** *v. t.* **be worn off** ⟨*Auflage, Schicht:*⟩ abgehen
~ 'on *v. i.* ⟨*Nachmittag, Winter usw.:*⟩ voranschreiten; **as the day/evening wore on** im Laufe des Tages/Abends
~ 'out 1. *v. t.* **a)** *(make useless)* aufbrauchen; ablaufen ⟨*Schuhe*⟩; auftragen ⟨*Kleidungsstück*⟩; **b)** *(fig.: exhaust)* kaputtmachen *(ugs.);* **his patience was worn out** seine Geduld war erschöpft; **~ oneself out** sich kaputtmachen *(ugs.);* **be worn out** kaputt sein *(ugs.).* **2.** *v. i.* *(become unusable)* kaputtgehen; **his patience finally wore out** seine Geduld war schließlich erschöpft
~ 'through 1. *v. i.* sich durchscheuern; **my trousers have worn through at the knee** meine Hose ist an den Knien durchgescheuert. **2.** *v. t.* durchscheuern
wearable ['weərəbl] *adj.* **sth. that is still/not ~:** etw., das man noch/nicht anziehen kann
wearer ['weərə(r)] *n.* Träger, *der*/Trägerin, *die*
wearily ['wıərılı] *adv.* müde
weariness ['wıərınıs] *n., no pl.* **a)** *(tiredness)* Erschöpfung, *die;* **b)** *(boredom)* Überdruß, *der* **(with** an + *Dat.*)
wearing ['weərıŋ] *adj.* **a)** *(tiring)* ermüdend; **b)** *(boring)* langweilig; ermüdend
'wearing apparel *n. (formal)* Bekleidung, *die*
wearisome ['wıərısəm] *adj.*, **wearisomely** ['wıərısəmlı] *adv. (lit. or fig.)* ermüdend
weary ['wıərı] **1.** *adj.* **a)** *(tired)* müde; **~ to death** sterbensmüde *(geh.);* **b)** *(bored, impatient)* **be ~ of sth.** einer Sache *(Gen.)* überdrüssig sein; etw. satt haben *(ugs.);* **c)** *(tiring)* ermüdend. **2.** *v. t.* **be wearied by sth.** durch etw. erschöpft sein; **a ~ing day** ein anstrengender Tag; **all this bickering was beginning to ~ me** allmählich hatte ich das ganze Gezänk satt *(ugs.).* **3.** *v. i.* **~ of sth./sb.** einer Sache/jmds. überdrüssig werden
weasel ['wi:zl] **1.** *n.* Wiesel, *das.* **2.** *v. i.* *(Amer.)* **a)** *(quibble)* drumherumreden *(ugs.);* **b)** *(default)* sich herauslavieren *(ugs.);* **~ on an obligation** sich aus einer Verpflichtung herausstehlen
weasel: ~-faced *adj.* **be ~-faced** ≈ ein Rattengesicht haben; **a ~-faced little man** ≈ ein kleiner Mann mit einem Rattengesicht; **~ word** *n.* vager *od.* unscharfer Begriff
weather ['weðə(r)] **1.** *n.* Wetter, *das;* **what's the ~ like?** wie ist das Wetter?; **the ~ has turned cooler** es ist kühler geworden; **he goes out in all ~s** er geht bei jedem Wetter hinaus; **he is feeling under the ~** *(fig.)* er ist [zur Zeit] nicht ganz auf dem Posten; **make heavy ~ of sth.** *(fig.)* sich mit etw. schwertun. **2.** *attrib. adj.* **a) keep a** *or* **one's ~ eye open [for sth.]** Ausschau [nach etw. *(Dat.)*] halten; **keep a ~ eye on sth.** ein wachsames Auge auf etw. *(Akk.)* haben; **b)** *(Naut.)* luvseitig; **the ~ side** die Luvseite; *see also* **gauge 1c. 3.** *v. t.* **a)** *(expose to open air)* auswittern ⟨*Kalk, Holz*⟩; **b) be ~ed** ⟨*Gesicht:*⟩ wettergegerbt sein; **c)** *(wear away)* verwittern lassen ⟨*Gestein*⟩; **rocks ~ed by wind and water** Felsen, die durch Wind und Wasser verwittert sind; **d)** *(come safely through)* abwettern ⟨*Sturm*⟩; *(fig.)* durchstehen ⟨*schwere Zeit*⟩. **4.** *v. i.* **a)** *(be discoloured)* ⟨*Holz, Farbe:*⟩ verblassen; *(wear away)* **~ [away]** ⟨*Gestein:*⟩ verwittern; **b)** *(survive exposure)* wetterfest sein; **a paint that ~s very well** eine sehr wetterfeste Farbe
weather: ~-beaten *adj.* wettergegerbt ⟨*Gesicht, Haut*⟩; verwittert ⟨*Felsen, Gebäude*⟩; **~-board** *n.* Wetterbrett, *das;* **~-boarding** *n., no pl., no indef. art.*, **~-boards** *n. pl.* Schindeln *Pl.;* **~-chart** *n.* Wetterkarte, *die;* **~cock** *n.* Wetterhahn, *der;* **~ conditions** *n. pl.* Witterungsverhältnisse; **what are the ~ conditions at the moment?** wie ist das Wetter im Augenblick?; **~ forecast** *n.* Wettervorhersage, *die*
weathering ['weðərıŋ] *n., no pl., no indef. art.* Verwitterung, *die*
weather: ~man *n.* Meteorologe, *der;* **~-map** *n.* Wetterkarte, *die;* **~proof 1.** *adj.* wetterfest; **2.** *v. t.* wetterfest machen; **~-report** *n.* Wetterbericht, *der;* **~ satellite** *n.* Wettersatellit, *der;* **~ ship** *n.* Wetterschiff, *das;* **~-station** *n.* Wetterwarte, *die;* **~-strip** *n.* Dichtungsstreifen, *der;* **~-vane** *n.* Wetterfahne, *die;* **~-wise** *adj.* **be ~-wise** die Wetterregeln kennen; *(fig.)* die Wetterzeichen am Horizont erkennen
¹weave [wi:v] **1.** *n. (Textiles)* Bindung, *die.* **2.** *v. t.,* **wove** [wəʊv], **woven** ['wəʊvn] **a)** *(intertwine)* weben ⟨*[Baum]wolle, Garn, Fäden*⟩; **~ sth. into sth.** etw. zu etw. verweben; **~ threads together** Fäden miteinander verweben; **~ flowers into wreaths** aus Blumen Kränze flechten; **b)** *(make by weaving)* weben ⟨*Textilien*⟩; flechten ⟨*Girlande, Korb, Kranz*⟩; **c)** *(fig.)* einflechten ⟨*Nebenhandlung, Thema usw.*⟩ **(into** in + *Akk.*); **d)** *(fig.: contrive)* ausspinnen ⟨*Geschichte*⟩; **~ a story around an idea** eine Idee zu einer Geschichte ausspinnen. **3.** *v. i.,* **wove, woven** *(make fabric by weaving)* weben
²weave *v. i.* **a)** *(move repeatedly from side to side)* torkeln; **b)** *(take devious course)* sich schlängeln; **~ between the obstacles** sich zwischen den Hindernissen hindurchschlängeln; **c) get weaving** *(sl.)* hinmachen *(ugs.);* **get weaving!** mach/macht schon *(ugs.) od.* hin!
weaver ['wi:və(r)] *n.* **a)** Weber, *der*/Weberin, *die;* **b)** *(Ornith.) see* **weaver-bird**
'weaver-bird *n.* Webervogel, *der*
weaving ['wi:vıŋ] *n.* Weben, *das;* **an intricate piece of ~:** eine feine Webarbeit
web [web] *n.* **a)** Netz, *das;* **spider's ~:** Spinnennetz, *das;* **b)** *(woven fabric)* Gewebe, *das; (fig.)* Gespinst, *das;* **a ~ of lies/intrigue** ein Gespinst von Lügen/Intrigen; **c)** *(membrane)* Interdigitalhaut, *die (Anat.); (of duck, goose, etc.)* Schwimmhaut, *die;* **d)** *(gossamer etc.)* Gespinst, *das;* **e)** *(vane of feather)* Federfahne, *die;* **f)** *(endless wire mesh)* Drahtgeweberolle, *die; (paper-roll)* Papierbahn, *die*
webbed [webd] *adj.* **~ feet/toes** Schwimmfüße
webbing ['webıŋ] *n.* Gurtstoff, *der*
web: ~-foot *n.* Schwimmfuß, *der;* Ruderfuß, *der (Zool.);* **~-footed** *adj.* schwimmfüßig; **~-'offset** *n. (Printing)* Rollenoffset[druck], *der;* **~-toe** *see* **~-foot; ~-toed** *see* **~-footed**
wed [wed] **1.** *v. t.,* **-dd- a)** *(rhet.: marry)* heiraten; ehelichen *(veralt., scherzh.); (perform wedding ceremony for)* trauen ⟨*Brautpaar*⟩; **b)** *(fig.: unite)* vereinen **(to** mit). **2.** *v. i.* *(rhet.)* heiraten; sich vermählen *(geh.). See also* **newly-wed**
we'd [wıd, *stressed* wi:d] **a) = we had; b) = we would**
Wed. *abbr.* **Wednesday** Mi.
wedded ['wedıd] *adj.* **a)** *(married)* angetraut; **a ~ couple** ein getrautes Paar; *see also* **wife; b)** *(of marriage)* **~ life** Eheleben, *das;* **~ love** eheliche Liebe; Gattenliebe, *die (geh.);* **~ bliss** Eheglück, *das;* **c)** *(fig.: devoted)* **be ~ to an idea/a dogma/a party** sich einer Idee/einem Dogma/einer Partei verschrieben haben; **be ~ to the view that ...:** immer noch davon überzeugt sein, daß ...; **he's ~ to his work** er ist mit seiner Arbeit verheiratet; **d)** *(fig.: united)* vereint **(to** mit)
wedding ['wedıŋ] *n.* Hochzeit, *die;* **have a registry office/a church ~:** sich standesamtlich/kirchlich trauen lassen; standesamt-

lich/kirchlich heiraten; *see also* **diamond wedding; golden wedding; ruby wedding; shotgun; silver wedding**

wedding: ~ anniversary *n.* Hochzeitstag, *der;* **~ breakfast** *n.* Hochzeitsessen, *das;* **~-cake** *n.* Hochzeitskuchen, *der;* **~-day** *n.* Hochzeitstag, *der;* **~-dress** *n.* Brautkleid, *das;* Hochzeitskleid, *das;* **~ march** *n. (Mus.)* Hochzeitsmarsch, *der;* **~-night** *n.* Hochzeitsnacht, *die;* **~ present** *n.* Hochzeitsgeschenk, *das;* **~-ring** *n.* Ehering, *der;* Trauring, *der*

wedge [wedʒ] **1.** *n.* **a)** Keil, *der;* **it's the thin end of the ~** *(fig.)* so fängt es immer an; **be careful that it isn't the thin end of the ~** *(fig.)* paß auf, daß das nicht ausufert *od.* überhand nimmt!; **these disturbances proved to be just the thin end of the ~:** diese Unruhen erwiesen sich bloß als der Anfang; **b) a ~ of cake** ein Stück Torte; **a ~ of cheese** eine Ecke Käse; **the seats were arranged in ~s** die Sitzreihen waren keilförmig angeordnet; **c)** *(heel)* Keilabsatz, *der;* **d)** *(shoe)* Schuh mit Keilabsatz; **e)** *(Golf)* Keil, *der.* **2.** *v. t.* **a)** *(fasten)* verkeilen; **~ a door/window open** eine Tür/ein Fenster festklemmen, damit sie/es offen bleibt; **b)** *(pack tightly)* verkeilen; **there were five of them ~d together in the back of the car** sie saßen zu fünft eingezwängt *od.* zusammengepfercht hinten im Wagen; **the book had got ~d in behind the cupboard** das Buch war hinter dem Schrank eingeklemmt

'wedge-shaped *adj.* keilförmig

Wedgwood ['wedʒwʊd] *n.* **a)** *(pottery)* Wedgwood, *das;* **b)** *no pl. (colour)* Wedgwoodblau, *das*

wedlock ['wedlɒk] *n. (literary)* Ehe, *die;* Ehebund, *der (geh.);* **born in/out of ~:** ehelich/unehelich geboren

Wednesday ['wenzdeɪ, 'wenzdɪ] **1.** *n.* Mittwoch, *der; see also* **Ash Wednesday. 2.** *adv. (coll.)* **she comes ~s** sie kommt mittwochs. *See also* **Friday**

¹wee [wi:] *adj.* **a)** *(child lang./Scot.)* klein; lütt *(nordd.);* **b)** *(coll.: extremely small)* **a ~ bit** ein ganz klein bißchen *(ugs.)*

²wee *see* **wee-wee**

weed [wi:d] **1.** *n.* **a)** Unkraut, *das;* **~s** Unkräuter; Unkraut, *das;* **it's only a ~:** das ist bloß Unkraut; **a garden overgrown with ~s** ein von Unkraut überwucherter Garten; **b)** *(coll./arch.: tobacco)* **the ~:** das Kraut *(ugs.);* **c)** *(sl.: marijuana)* Stoff, *der (salopp);* **the ~:** Stoff *(salopp);* **d)** *(weakly person)* Kümmerling, *der (abwertend). See also* **weeds. 2.** *v. t.* jäten. **3.** *v. i.* [Unkraut] jäten

~ 'out *v. t. (fig.)* aussieben

weeding ['wi:dɪŋ] *n., no pl., no indef. art.* [Unkraut]jäten, *das;* **do the/some ~:** Unkraut jäten

'weed-killer *n.* Unkrautvertilgungsmittel, *das*

weeds [wi:dz] *n. pl.* **widow's ~:** Trauer- *od.* Witwenkleidung, *die*

weedy ['wi:dɪ] *adj.* **a)** von Unkraut überwachsen; **b)** *(coll.: scrawny)* spillerig *(ugs.);* schmächtig

week [wi:k] *n.* Woche, *die;* **what day of the ~ is it today?** was für ein Wochentag ist heute?; **can you come to see us for a ~?** kannst du [für] eine Woche zu uns kommen?; **he was away for a ~:** er war [für] eine Woche weg; **I haven't seen you for ~s** ich habe dich seit Wochen nicht gesehen; **~s ago** vor Wochen; **it will be finished in a ~:** es ist in einer Woche fertig; **three times a ~:** dreimal die *od.* in der Woche; **£40 a** *or* **per ~:** 40 Pfund die *od.* in der *od.* pro Woche; **a ~'s leave/rest** eine Woche Urlaub/Pause; **the other ~:** vor ein paar *od.* zwei, drei Wochen; **for several ~s** mehrere Wochen lang; wochenlang; **come every ~:** jede Woche kommen; **once a ~** *or* **every ~:** einmal die Woche *od.* in der Woche; einmal wöchentlich; **~ in ~ out** Woche für Woche; **in a ~['s time]** in einer Woche; **in two ~s[' time]** in zwei Wochen; in vierzehn Tagen; **take a ~'s holiday** [sich *(Dat.)*] eine Woche Urlaub nehmen; **from ~ to ~, ~ by ~:** Woche für *od.* um Woche; **a three-~ period** ein Zeitraum von drei Wochen; **at six-~ intervals** in sechswöchigem Abstand; **a two-~ visit** ein zweiwöchiger Besuch; **a six-~[s]-old baby** ein sechs Wochen altes *od.* sechswöchiges Baby; **a ~ [from] today/from** *or* **on Monday, today/Monday ~:** heute/Montag in einer Woche; **a ~ ago today/Sunday** heute/Sonntag vor einer Woche; **tomorrow ~:** morgen in einer Woche; **in** *or* **during the ~:** während der Woche; **42-hour/five-day ~:** 42-Stunden-Woche, *die*/Fünftagewoche, *die; see also* **knock 1 c; next 1 b, 3 b**

week: ~day *n.* Werktag, *der;* Wochentag, *der;* **on ~days** werktags; wochentags; *attrib.* **~day opening times** Öffnungszeiten an Werktagen; **~day timetable** Werktagsfahrplan, *der;* **~end** [-'-, '--] *n.* Wochenende, *das;* **at the ~end** am Wochenende; **at** *or* *(Amer.)* **on ~ends** an Wochenenden; **a long ~end** ein verlängertes Wochenende; **go/be away for the ~end** übers Wochenende wegfahren/weg sein; **~-long** *adj.* einwöchig

weekly ['wi:klɪ] **1.** *adj.* wöchentlich; **~ wages** Wochenlohn, *der;* **a ~ season-ticket/magazine** eine Wochenkarte/Wochenzeitschrift; **on a ~ basis** wöchentlich; **at ~ intervals** wöchentlich; einmal pro Woche; **three-~:** dreiwöchentlich; **at three-~ intervals** in dreiwöchigen Abständen. **2.** *adv.* wöchentlich; einmal die Woche *od.* in der Woche. **3.** *n. (newspaper)* Wochenzeitung, *die; (magazine)* Wochenzeitschrift, *die*

weekly re'turn *n.* **~ [ticket]** Wochenrückfahrkarte, *die*

'week-night *n.* **on a ~:** abends an einem Werktag; **on ~s** werktags abends

weeny ['wi:nɪ] *adj. (child lang./coll.)* klitzeklein *(ugs.)*

weeny-bopper *n. (coll.) acht- bis zwölfjähriger [weiblicher] Popfan*

weep [wi:p] **1.** *v. i.,* **wept** [wept] **a)** weinen; **~ with** *or* **for joy/rage** vor Freude/Zorn weinen; **~ for sb./sth.** um jmdn./etw. weinen; **the child was ~ing for his mother** das Kind weinte nach seiner Mutter; **it makes you want to ~:** man könnte weinen; **b)** ‹*Wunde:*› nässen. **2.** *v. t.,* **wept a)** weinen ‹*Tränen*›; **b)** *(lament over)* beweinen; **c) ~ one's eyes** *or* **heart out** sich *(Dat.)* die Augen aus dem Kopf weinen; **d)** *(exude)* absondern ‹*Eiter*›. **3.** *n.* **have a ~:** sich ausweinen; **I had a little ~:** ich habe geweint

weepie ['wi:pɪ] *n. (coll.)* Schmachtfetzen, *der (salopp)*

weeping 'willow *n.* Trauerweide, *die*

weepy ['wi:pɪ] **1.** *adj.* weinerlich. **2.** *n. see* **weepie**

weevil ['wi:vɪl] *n.* Rüsselkäfer, *der*

'wee-wee *(coll.)* **1.** *n.* Pipi, *das (ugs.);* **do a ~:** Pipi machen. **2.** *v. i.* Pipi machen *(ugs.)*

weft [weft] *n.* **a)** *(set of threads)* Schuß, *der;* **b)** *(yarn)* Schußfaden, *der*

weigh [weɪ] **1.** *v. t.* **a)** *(find weight of)* wiegen; **the shop assistant was ~ing the fruit for her** die Verkäuferin wog ihr das Obst ab; **b)** *(estimate value of)* abwägen; **~ sb. and find him/her wanting** jmdn. wiegen und zu leicht befinden; **c)** *(consider)* abwägen; **~ in one's mind whether ...:** sich *(Dat.)* überlegen, ob ...; **~ the consequences of one's actions** sich *(Dat.)* die Folgen seines Handelns klarmachen; **~ the fact that ...:** die Tatsache berücksichtigen, daß ...; **~ one's words** seine Worte abwägen; **d)** *(balance in one's hand)* wiegen; **e)** *(have the weight of)* wiegen; **it ~s very little** es wiegt sehr wenig; **a steak ~ing two pounds** ein zwei Pfund schweres Steak. *See also* **anchor 1; ton c. 2.** *v. i.* **a) ~ [very] heavy/light** [sehr] viel/wenig wiegen; **b)** *(be important)* **~ with sb.** bei jmdm. Gewicht haben; **~ in sb.'s favour** für jmdn. sprechen. **3.** *n.* **under ~ = under way** *see* **way 1 i**

~ a'gainst *v. t. (fig.)* sprechen gegen; **~ heavily against sb.** sehr *od.* stark gegen jmdn. sprechen

~ 'down *v. t.* **a)** *(cause to sag)* **fruit ~ed down the branches of the tree** die Äste des Baumes bogen sich unter der Last der Früchte; **be ~ed down by packages** mit Paketen schwer beladen sein; **b)** *(cause to be anxious or depressed)* niederdrücken; **~ed down with cares** bedrückt von Sorgen; **~ed down with sorrow** gramgebeugt

~ 'in *v. i.* **a)** *(Sport)* sich wiegen lassen; **~ in at 200 kg** 200 kg auf die Waage bringen; *see also* **weigh-in; b)** *(coll.: lend one's support)* sich einschalten

~ on *v. t.* lasten auf (+ *Dat.*); **~ [heavily] on sb.'s mind** jmdm. [schwer] auf der Seele liegen

~ 'out *v. t.* abwiegen

~ 'up *v. t.* abwägen; sich *(Dat.)* eine Meinung bilden über (+ *Akk.*) ‹*Person*›

~ upon *see* **~ on**

weigh: ~bridge *n.* Brückenwaage, *die;* **~-in** *n. (Sport)* Wiegen, *das;* **at the ~-in** beim Wiegen

'weighing-machine *n.* Waage, *die*

weight [weɪt] **1.** *n.* **a)** *(heaviness)* Gewicht, *das;* **she is twice your ~:** sie wiegt doppelt soviel wie du; **what is your ~?** wieviel wiegen Sie?; **be under/over ~:** zuwenig/zuviel wiegen; Unter-/Übergewicht haben; **throw one's ~ about** *or* **around** *(fig. coll.)* sich wichtig machen; *see also* **gold 1 a; b)** *(scale of heaviness)* Gewicht, *das;* **~s and measures** Maße und Gewichte; **avoirdupois/troy ~:** Avoirdupois-/Troygewicht, *das;* **c)** *(heavy body)* Gewicht, *das;* **lift ~s** Lasten heben; **d)** *(piece of metal used in weighing)* Gewicht, *das;* **e)** *(Athletics)* Kugel, *die;* **f)** *(load to be supported)* Gewicht, *das;* **g)** *(surface density of cloth etc.)* Qualität, *die;* **h)** *(fig.: heavy burden)* Last, *die;* **it would be a ~ off my mind if ...:** mir würde ein Stein vom Herzen fallen, wenn ...; **i)** *(importance)* Gewicht, *das;* **men of ~:** Leute von Gewicht; bedeutende Leute; **give due ~ to sth.** einer Sache *(Dat.)* die nötige Beachtung schenken; **carry ~:** ins Gewicht fallen; **his opinion carries no ~ with me** seine Meinung ist für mich unbedeutend; **j)** *(preponderance)* Übergewicht, *das;* **the ~ of evidence is against him** praktisch alle Beweise sprechen gegen ihn; **~ of numbers** zahlenmäßiges Übergewicht. *See also* **atomic weight; dead weight; pull 1 g. 2.** *v. t.* **a)** *(add ~ to)* beschweren; **circumstances are rather ~ed in his favour/against him** *(fig.)* er wird durch die Umstände ziemlich begünstigt/benachteiligt; **b)** *(hold with ~)* **~ [down]** beschweren; *(fig.)* belasten; **c)** *(Statistics)* gewichten

weighting ['weɪtɪŋ] *n. (Admin.)* Zulage, *die;* **London ~:** Ortszulage für London

weightless ['weɪtlɪs] *adj.* schwerelos

weightlessness ['weɪtlɪsnɪs] *n.* Schwerelosigkeit, *die*

weight: ~-lifter *n.* Gewichtheber, *der*/-heberin, *die;* **~-lifting** *n., no pl., no indef. art.* Gewichtheben, *das;* **~-watcher** *n.* Schlankheitsbewußte, *der/die*

weighty ['weɪtɪ] *adj.* **a)** *(heavy)* schwer; **b)** *(important)* gewichtig

weir [wɪə(r)] *n.* Wehr, *das*

weird [wɪəd] *adj.* **a)** *(coll.: odd)* bizarr; verrückt *(ugs.);* **b)** *(uncanny)* unheimlich; phantastisch ‹*Geschichte*›

weirdie ['wɪədɪ] *n. (coll.)* Freak, *der (ugs.)*

weirdly ['wɪədlɪ] *adv. see* **weird:** bizarr; verrückt *(ugs.);* unheimlich

weirdness ['wɪədnɪs] *n., no pl.* **a)** *(coll.: oddness)* Verrücktheit, *die (ugs.);* **b)** *(uncanniness)* Unheimlichkeit, *die*

weirdo ['wɪədəʊ] *n., pl.* ~**s** *see* **weirdie**

welcome ['welkəm] **1.** *int.* willkommen; ~ **home/to England!** willkommen zu Hause/in England!; ~ **aboard!** willkommen an Bord! **2.** *n.* **a)** Willkommen, *das;* **a gesture of** ~: eine Willkommensgeste; **outstay** *or* **overstay one's** ~: zu lange bleiben; **bid sb.** ~: jmdn. willkommen heißen; **give sb. a warm** ~: jmdn. herzlich willkommen heißen; **b)** *(reception)* Empfang, *der;* **give a proposal a warm** ~: einen Vorschlag zustimmend aufnehmen; **the committee gave her proposals a rather cool** ~: das Gremium nahm ihre Vorschläge ziemlich kühl auf; **give sb. a warm** ~ *(iron.)* jmdn. gebührend empfangen *(iron.);* **we got a really hot** ~ **from the enemy artillery** *(iron.)* die feindliche Artillerie bereitete uns einen recht heißen Empfang *(iron.);* **receive a rather cool** ~: ziemlich kühl empfangen werden. **3.** *v. t.* **a)** *(greet with pleasure)* begrüßen; willkommen heißen *(geh.);* ~ **sb. with open arms** jmdn. mit offenen Armen begrüßen *od.* willkommen heißen; **b)** *(receive)* empfangen. **4.** *adj.* **a)** willkommen; gefällig ⟨*Anblick*⟩; **make sb. [feel]** ~: jmdm. das Gefühl geben *od.* vermitteln, willkommen zu sein; **b)** *pred.* **you are** ~ **to take it** du kannst es gern nehmen; **you may have it and** ~: du kannst es gerne haben; **no one's ever managed to do it, but you're** ~ **to have a go** bis jetzt hat es noch keiner geschafft, aber Sie können es ja gern mal versuchen; **you are** ~ *(it was no trouble to me)* gern geschehen!; keine Ursache!; **if you want to stay here for the night you are more than** ~: wenn Sie die Nacht über hier bleiben möchten, sind Sie herzlich willkommen

welcoming ['welkəmɪŋ] *adj.* einladend; **a** ~ **cup of tea awaited us** zur Begrüßung erwartete uns eine Tasse Tee; **the crowd burst into** ~ **applause** die Menge klatschte zur Begrüßung

weld [weld] **1.** *v. t.* **a)** *(unite)* verschweißen; *(repair, make, or attach by* ~*ing)* schweißen (**[on]to** an + *Akk.*); ~ **two pipes together** zwei Rohre zusammenschweißen; **b)** *(fig.: unite closely)* zusammenschweißen (**into** zu); ~ **two elements together** zwei Elemente zusammenschweißen. **2.** *n.* Schweißnaht, *die*

welder ['weldə(r)] *n.* **a)** *(person)* Schweißer, *der*/Schweißerin, *die;* **b)** *(machine)* Schweißgerät, *das*

welding ['weldɪŋ] *n., no pl., no indef. art.* Schweißen, *das*

welfare ['welfeə(r)] *n.* **a)** *(health and prosperity)* Wohl, *das;* **b)** *(social work; payments etc.)* Sozialhilfe, *die;* Wohlfahrt, *die (veralt.); the* ~ **people** die Leute vom Sozialamt *od. (veralt.)* von der Wohlfahrt; **be on** ~ *(Amer.)* Sozialhilfe bekommen

welfare: W~ **'State** *n.* Wohlfahrtsstaat, *der;* ~ **work** *n.* Sozialarbeit, *die;* **do** ~ **work** in der Sozialarbeit *od. (veralt.)* bei der Wohlfahrt tätig sein; ~ **worker** *n.* Sozialarbeiter, *der*/-arbeiterin, *die*

welkin ['welkɪn] *n. (poet./literary)* Firmament, *das (dichter.)*

[1]**well** [wel] **1.** *n.* **a)** *(water* ~*, mineral spring)* Brunnen, *der;* **b)** *see* **oil well; c)** *(Brit.: of lawcourt) Teil des Gerichtssaals, der für die Anwälte bestimmt ist;* **d)** *(Archit.)* Schacht, *der; (of staircase)* Treppenloch, *das;* **e)** *(fig.: source)* Quell, *der (dichter.). See also* **artesian. 2.** *v.i. (literary)* sich ergießen

~ **'up** *v.i.* ⟨*Tränen, Wasserstrahl:*⟩ aufsteigen; ⟨*Gefühle, Scham, Zorn:*⟩ aufwallen *(geh.)*

[2]**well 1.** *int.* **a)** *expr. astonishment* mein Gott; meine Güte; nanu; ~, ~! sieh mal einer an!; *see also* **never c; b)** *expr. relief* mein Gott; **c)** *expr. concession* na ja; ~ **then, let's say no more about it** schon gut, reden wir nicht mehr davon; **d)** *expr. resumption* nun; ~ **[then], who was it?** nun, wer war's?; **e)** *expr. qualified recognition of point* ~**[, but] ...:** na ja, aber ...; ja schon, aber ...; **f)** *expr. resignation* **[oh]** ~: nun denn; **ah** ~: na ja; **g)** *expr. expectation* ~ **[then]?** na? **2.** *adv.*, **better** ['betə(r)], **best** [best] **a)** *(satisfactorily)* gut; **the business is doing** ~: das Geschäft geht gut; **do** ~ **for oneself** Erfolg haben; **do** ~ **out of sth.** mit etw. ein gutes Geschäft machen; **the patient is doing** ~: dem Patienten geht es gut; **a** ~ **situated house** ein günstig gelegenes Haus; **you did** ~ **to come** gut, daß du gekommen bist; ~ **begun is half done** *(prov.)* ein guter Anfang ist schon die halbe Arbeit; **didn't he do** ~**!** hat er sich nicht gut geschlagen?; **you would do** ~ **to ...:** Sie täten gut daran, zu ...; **come off** ~: gut abschneiden; **you're** ~ **out of it** es ist gut, daß du damit nichts mehr zu tun hast; **we're** ~ **rid of them** wir sind froh, daß wir sie los sind; *see also* [1]**do 2d; b)** *(thoroughly)* gründlich ⟨*trocknen, polieren, schütteln*⟩; tüchtig ⟨*verprügeln*⟩; genau ⟨*beobachten*⟩; gewissenhaft ⟨*urteilen*⟩; **be** ~ **able to do sth.** durchaus *od.* sehr wohl in der Lage sein, etw. zu tun; **sb. is** ~ **aware that ...:** jmdm. ist sehr wohl bewußt, daß ...; **I'm** ~ **aware of what has been going on** mir ist sehr wohl klar *od.* bewußt, was sich abgespielt hat; **let** *or* **leave** ~ **alone** sich zufrieden geben; **the translator could not leave** ~ **alone** der Übersetzer hat nur verschlimmbessert; **be** ~ **worth it/a visit/the effort** es/einen Besuch/die Mühe durchaus wert sein; **he** ~ **deserved the honour** er hat die Ehre allemal verdient; **be** ~ **pleased** sehr erfreut sein; **she was not so** ~ **pleased** sie war nicht sonderlich erfreut; ~ **out of sight** *(very far off)* völlig außer Sichtweite (**of** *Gen.*); **make sure you keep the child** ~ **out of sight** sorg auf jeden Fall dafür, daß keiner das Kind sieht; ~ **past the minimum age** längst über dem Mindestalter; **we arrived** ~ **before the performance began** wir kamen eine ganze Zeit vor Beginn der Vorstellung; **be** ~ **in with sb.** bei jmdm. gut angeschrieben sein; ~ **and truly** vollkommen; **I know only too** ~ **how/what etc. ...:** ich weiß nur zu gut, wie/was *usw.* ...; **c)** *(considerably)* weit; **he is** ~ **up in the list** er steht ziemlich weit oben auf der Liste; **she is** ~ **on in years** sie ist nicht mehr die Jüngste; **it was** ~ **on into the afternoon** es war schon spät am Nachmittag; **he is** ~ **past** *or* **over retiring age** er hat schon längst das Rentenalter erreicht; **he is** ~ **past** *or* **over forty** er ist weit über vierzig; **be** ~ **away** *(lit. or fig.)* einen guten Vorsprung haben; *(coll.: be drunk)* ziemlich benebelt sein *(ugs.);* **d)** *(approvingly, kindly)* gut, anständig ⟨*jmdn. behandeln*⟩; **like sb.** ~ **[enough]** jmdn. [sehr] gut leiden können; **think** ~ **of sb./sth.** eine gute Meinung von jmdm./etw. haben; **speak** ~ **of sb./sth.** sich positiv über jmdn./etw. äußern; **wish sb.** ~: jmdm. alles Gute wünschen; **stand** ~ **with sb.** [sich] gut mit jmdm. stehen; **e)** *(in all likelihood)* sehr wohl; **f)** *(easily)* ohne weiteres; **you cannot very** ~ **refuse their help** du kannst ihre Hilfe nicht ohne weiteres *od.* nicht gut ausschlagen; **g) as** ~ *(in addition)* auch; ebenfalls; *(as much, not less truly)* genauso; ebenso; *(with equal reason)* genausogut; ebensogut; *(advisable)* ratsam; *(equally well)* genauso gut; **Coming for a drink? – I might as** ~: Kommst du mit, einen trinken? – Warum nicht?; **you might as** ~ **go** du kannst ruhig gehen; **that is [just] as** ~ *(not regrettable)* um so besser; **it was just as** ~ **that I had ...:** zum Glück hatte ich ...; **as** ~ **as** *(in addition to):* **A as** ~ **as B:** B und auch [noch] A; **she can sing** ~ **as dance** sie kann singen und auch tanzen; **as** ~ **as helping** *or (coll.)* **help me, she continued her own work** sie half mir und machte dabei noch mit ihrer eigenen Arbeit weiter. *See also* **best 2; better 2;** [1]**do 1u;** [2]**live 1a; may a; pretty 2; speak 1a. 3.** *adj.* **a)** *(in good health)* gesund; **How are you feeling now? – Quite** ~**, thank you** Wie fühlen Sie sich jetzt? – Ganz gut, danke; **look** ~: gut *od.* gesund aussehen; **I am perfectly** ~: ich fühle mich bestens; **get** ~ **soon!** gute Besserung!; **he hasn't been very** ~ **lately** es geht ihm in letzter Zeit nicht sehr gut; **feel** ~: sich wohl fühlen; **she wanted to come, but she isn't** ~ **enough** sie wollte kommen, aber es geht ihr nicht so gut; **make sb.** ~: jmdn. gesund machen; **b)** *pred. (satisfactory)* **I am very** ~ **where I am** ich bin hier sehr zufrieden; **all's** ~: es ist alles in Ordnung; **all's** ~ **that ends** ~ *(prov.)* Ende gut, alles gut; **all is not** ~ **with sb./sth.** mit jmdm./etw. ist etwas nicht in Ordnung; **[that's all]** ~ **and good** [das ist alles] gut und schön; **all being** ~: wenn alles gutgeht; **c)** *pred. (advisable)* ratsam. *See also* **all 2d; very 2d**

we'll [wɪl, *stressed* wi:l] = **we will**

well: ~**-advised** *see* **advised;** ~**-aimed** *adj.* gezielt ⟨*Schuß, Tritt, Stoß, Schlag*⟩; ~**-appointed** *adj.* gut ausgestattet; ~**-balanced** *adj.* **a)** *(sensible)* ausgeglichen ⟨*Person*⟩; ausgewogen ⟨*Plan*⟩; **b)** *(equally matched)* harmonisch ⟨*Paar*⟩; gleich stark ⟨*Mannschaften*⟩; ~**-behaved** *adj. see* **behave 1a;** ~**-being** *n.* Wohl, *das;* **she felt a sense of** ~**-being** sie fühlte sich wohl; ~**-bred** *adj.* **a)** *(having good manners)* anständig; **b)** *(of good stock)* ⟨*Schwein, Pferd*⟩ aus guter Zucht; ~**-built** *adj.* ⟨*Person*⟩ mit guter Figur; **be** ~**-built** eine gute Figur haben; ~**-chosen** *adj.* wohlgesetzt ⟨*Worte*⟩; wohlüberlegt ⟨*Bemerkungen*⟩; **a few** ~**-chosen words** ein paar wohlüberlegte Worte; *(reprimand)* ein paar warme Worte *(iron.);* ~**-conducted** *adj.* gut geleitet *od.* organisiert; ~**-connected** *adj.* ⟨*Person*⟩ mit guten Beziehungen; ~**-defined** *adj.* klar definiert; ~**-deserved** *adj.* wohlverdient ⟨*Lob, Ruhe*⟩; verdient ⟨*Belohnung, Prügel*⟩; ~**-disposed** *see* **disposed;** ~ **done** *adj. (Cookery)* durchgebraten; durch *nicht attr.;* **order a steak** ~ **done** ein durchgebratenes Steak bestellen; ~**-dressed** *adj.* gutgekleidet *präd. getrennt geschrieben;* ~**-earned** *adj.* wohlverdient; ~**-educated** *adj.* gebildet ⟨*Person, Benehmen*⟩; ~**-equipped** *adj.* gut ausgestattet ⟨*Büro, Studio, Krankenwagen*⟩; gut ausgerüstet ⟨*Polizei, Armee, Expedition, Flugzeug*⟩; ~**-established** *adj.* bewährt; ~**-fed** *adj.* wohlgenährt; ~**-founded** *adj.* [wohl] fundiert; ~**-groomed** *adj.* gepflegt; ~ **'grounded** *adj.* **a)** *(trained)* **be** ~ **grounded in a subject** gute Grundkenntnisse in einem Fach haben; **b)** *see* ~**-founded;** ~**-heeled** *adj. (coll.)* gutbetucht *(ugs.) präd. getrennt geschrieben*

wellies ['welɪz] *n. pl. (Brit. coll.)* Gummistiefel

'well-informed *adj.* **a) she is one of the most** ~ **people I have ever met** von allen, die ich kenne, weiß sie am besten Bescheid; **b)** *(having access to reliable information)* gutunterrichtet *präd. getrennt geschrieben*

wellington ['welɪŋtən] *n.* ~ **[boot]** Gummistiefel, *der*

well: ~**-intentioned** ['welɪntenʃənd] *adj.* gutgemeint *präd. getrennt geschrieben;* ~**-judged** *adj.* gut gezielt; ~**-kept** *adj.* gepflegt; in gutem Zustand *nachgestellt;* wohlgehütet ⟨*Geheimnis*⟩; ~**-knit** *adj.* gut gebaut ⟨*Körper, Figur, Sportler*⟩; ~**-known** *adj.* **a)** *(known to many)* bekannt; **b)** *(known thoroughly)* vertraut; ~**-loved** *adj.* beliebt; ~ **made** *adj.* **a)** *(skilfully manufactured)* gut [gearbeitet]; **b)** *(having good build)* gut gebaut; ~**-mannered** *adj. see* **mannered b;** ~**marked** *adj.* gut gekennzeichnet ⟨*Strecke, Wanderung*⟩; ~**-matched** *adj.* einander ebenbürtig ⟨*Gegner, Mannschaften*⟩; **they are a** ~**-matched couple** sie passen gut zueinander; ~-**meaning** *adj.* wohlmeinend; **be ~-meaning** es gut meinen; ~-**meant** *adj.* gutgemeint; ~**nigh** *adv. (rhet.)* nahezu; ~ **off** *adj.* **a)** *(rich)* wohlhabend; **sb. is ~ off** jmdm. geht es [finanziell] gut; **b) be ~ off for sth.** *(provided with)* mit etw. gut versorgt sein; **c)** *(favourably situated)* **she is perfectly ~ off** es geht ihr ausgezeichnet; ~ **oiled** *adj. (fig. sl.: drunk)* abgefüllt *(salopp);* ~ **paid** *adj.* gutbezahlt *präd. getrennt geschrieben;* **he's ~ paid enough** er kriegt genug bezahlt; ~-**preserved** *adj.* gut erhalten ⟨*Holz, Mumie, (scherzh.) Achtzigjährige usw.*⟩; ~-**read** ['welred] *adj.* belesen; ~-**rounded** *adj.* **a)** *(complete and symmetrical)* abgerundet; **b)** *(complete and ~ expressed)* ausgewogen; ~-**spent** *adj.* sinnvoll verbracht ⟨*Zeit*⟩; vernünftig ausgegeben ⟨*Geld*⟩; ~-**spoken** *adj.* sprachlich gewandt; mit angenehmer Sprachweise *nachgestellt;* ~-**stocked** *adj.* gut gefüllt ⟨*Kühlschrank, Vorratskammer, Hausbar*⟩; ~-**thought-out** *adj.* gut durchdacht; ~-**thumbed** *adj.* zerlesen ⟨*Buch*⟩; ~-**timed** *adj.* zeitlich gut gewählt; ~-**to-do** *adj.* wohlhabend; ~-**tried** *adj.* bewährt; ~-**trodden** *adj. (lit. or fig.)* ausgetreten; ~-**turned** *adj.* wohlgesetzt; ~-**upholstered** *adj. (fig. joc.)* gut gepolstert; ~-**wisher** *n.* Sympathisant, *der*/Sympathisantin, *die;* **cards and gifts from ~-wishers** Kartengrüße und Geschenke; ~-**worn** *adj.* abgetragen ⟨*Kleidungsstück*⟩; abgenutzt ⟨*Teppich*⟩; abgegriffen ⟨*Einband, Buch, Zeitschrift*⟩; ausgetreten ⟨*Pfad*⟩; abgedroschen ⟨*Redensart, Ausdruck*⟩

Welsh [welʃ] **1.** *adj.* walisisch; **sb. is ~:** jmd. ist Waliser/Waliserin; *see also* **corgi; English 1. 2.** *n.* **a)** *(language)* Walisisch, *das; see also* **English 2 a; b)** *pl.* **the ~:** die Waliser

welsh *v. i. (leave without paying)* sich davonmachen, ohne zu bezahlen; sich auf französisch verabschieden *(ugs.)*

~ **on** *v. t. (coll.)* ~ **on sb./sth.** jmdn. sitzen lassen/sich um etw. herumdrücken *(ugs.)*

Welsh: ~**man** ['welʃmən] *n., pl.* ~**men** ['welʃmən] Waliser, *der;* ~ '**rabbit,** ~ '**rarebit** *ns.* Käsetoast, *der;* ~**woman** *n.* Waliserin, *die*

welt [welt] *n.* **a)** *(of shoe)* Rahmen, *der;* **b)** *(heavy blow)* Hieb, *der;* **c)** *(trimming)* Bündchen, *das;* **d)** *see* [2]**weal**

Weltanschauung [veltan'ʃaʊʊŋ] *n.* **a)** *(philosophy of life)* Weltanschauung, *die;* **b)** *(conception of the world)* Weltbild, *das*

welter ['weltə(r)] **1.** *v. i.* sich wälzen. **2.** *n.* Chaos, *das;* **a ~ of foam** eine schäumende Flut; **a ~ of emotions** ein Sturm von Gefühlen

'**welterweight** *n. (Boxing etc.)* Weltergewicht, *das; (person also)* Weltergewichtler, *der*

Wenceslas ['wensɪsləs] *pr. n. (Hist.)* Wenzel *(der)*

wench [wentʃ] *n. (arch./joc.)* Mädel, *das; (arch.: maid-servant)* Magd, *die (veralt.)*

Wend [wend] *n.* Wende, *der*/Wendin, *die*

wend *v.t. (literary/arch.)* ~ **one's way homewards** sich auf den Heimweg machen; **they ~ed their way back towards the village** sie machten sich auf den Weg zurück ins Dorf

Wendy house ['wendɪ haʊs] *n.* Spielhaus, *das*

went *see* [1]**go 1, 2**

wept *see* **weep 1, 2**

were *see* **be**

we're [wɪə(r)] = **we are**

weren't *(coll.)* = **were not;** *see* **be**

werewolf ['wɪəwʊlf, 'weəwʊlf] *n., pl.* **werewolves** ['wɪəwʊlvz, 'weəwʊlvz], **werwolf** ['wɜ:wʊlf] *n., pl.* **werwolves** ['wɜ:wʊlvz] *(Mythol.)* Werwolf, *der*

west [west] **1.** *n.* **a)** Westen, *der;* **the ~:** West *(Met., Seew.); (Amer.: western part of US)* der Westen; **in/to[wards]/from the ~:** im/nach *od. (geh.)* gen/von Westen; **to the ~ of** westlich von; westlich (+ *Gen.*); **b)** *(European civilization)* Westen, *der;* Abendland, *das;* **c)** *(Cards)* West. *See also* **east 1; Far West; Middle West; Wild West. 2.** *adj.* westlich; West⟨*küste, -wind, -grenze, -tor*⟩. **3.** *adv.* westwärts; nach Westen; ~ **of** westlich von; westlich (+ *Gen.*); **go ~** *(fig. sl.: be killed or wrecked or lost)* hopsgehen *(salopp);* ~ **by north/south** *see* [1]**by 1 d;** *see also* **east 3**

West: ~ '**Africa** *pr. n.* Westafrika *(das);* ~ '**Bank** *pr. n.* **the ~ Bank** *(of the Jordan)* das Wesjordanland; ~ **Ber'lin** *pr. n. (Hist.)* West-Berlin *(das);* Berlin (West) *(Amtsspr.);* **w~bound** *adj.* ⟨*Zug usw.*⟩ in Richtung Westen; ~ **Country** *n. (Brit.)* Westengland, *das;* ~ '**End** *n. (Brit.)* Westend, *das;* **the ~ End theatres** die Theater des Londoner Westends

westering ['westərɪŋ] *attrib. adj.* im Westen stehend

westerly ['westəlɪ] **1.** *adj.* **a)** *(in position or direction)* westlich; **in a ~ direction** nach Westen; **b)** *(from the west)* ⟨*Wind*⟩ aus westlichen Richtungen; **the wind was ~:** der Wind kam aus Westen. **2.** *adv.* **a)** *(in position)* westlich; *(in direction)* nach West[en]; **b)** *(from the west)* aus *od.* von West[en]. **3.** *n.* West[wind], *der*

western ['westən] **1.** *adj.* westlich; West⟨*grenze, -hälfte, -seite, -fenster, -wind*⟩; ~ **Germany** Westdeutschland, *das; see also* **bloc; Middle Western. 2.** *n.* Western, *der*

westerner ['westənə(r)] *n.* Abendländer, *der*/Abendländerin, *die*

Western: ~ '**Europe** *pr. n.* Westeuropa *(das);* ~ **Euro'pean 1.** *adj.* westeuropäisch; **2.** *n.* Westeuropäer, *der*/-europäerin, *die*

westernization [westənaɪ'zeɪʃn] *n.* Verwestlichung, *die*

westernize ['westənaɪz] *v. t.* verwestlichen

westernmost ['westənməʊst] *adj.* westlichst...

West: ~ '**German** *(Hist.)* **1.** *adj.* westdeutsch; **2.** *n.* Westdeutsche, *der/die;* ~ '**Germany** *pr. n. (Hist.)* Westdeutschland *(das);* ~ '**Indian 1.** *adj.* westindisch; **2.** *n.* Westinder, *der*/-inderin, *die;* ~ '**Indies** *see* **Indies b**

Westminster ['westmɪnstə(r)] *n. (Brit.: Parliament)* Westminster *(das);* London *(das) (ugs.)*

west: ~-**north-'**~ **1.** *n.* Westnordwest[en], *der;* **2.** *adj.* westnordwestlich; **3.** *adv.* nach Westnordwest[en]; **W~ of 'England** *pr. n.* Westengland *(das)*

Westphalia [west'feɪlɪə] *pr. n.* Westfalen *(das)*

Westphalian [west'feɪlɪən] **1.** *adj.* westfälisch. **2.** *n.* Westfale, *der*/Westfalin, *die*

West: ~ **Side** *n. (Amer.)* West Side, *die;* **w~-south-'**~ **1.** *n.* Westsüdwest[en], *der;* **2.** *adj.* westsüdwestlich; **3.** *adv.* nach Westsüdwest[en]

westward ['westwəd] **1.** *adj.* nach Westen gerichtet; *(situated towards the west)* westlich; **in a ~ direction** nach Westen; [in] Richtung Westen. **2.** *adv.* westwärts; **they are ~ bound** sie fahren nach *od.* [in] Richtung Westen. **3.** *n.* Westen, *der*

westwards ['westwədz] *see* **westward 2**

wet [wet] **1.** *adj.* **a)** naß; ~ **with tears** tränenfeucht; ~ **behind the ears** *(fig.)* feucht hinter den Ohren *(ugs.);* ~ **to the skin,** ~ **through** naß bis auf die Haut; **b)** *(rainy)* regnerisch; feucht ⟨*Klima*⟩; **c)** *(recently applied)* frisch ⟨*Farbe*⟩; '~ **paint'** „frisch gestrichen"; **d)** *(sl.: feeble)* schlapp *(ugs.);* schlappschwänzig *(salopp);* **e)** *(Brit. Polit. coll.)* pflaumenweich *(ugs. abwertend);* schlappschwänzig *(salopp abwertend). See also* **blanket 1 a;** [1]**rag a. 2.** *v. t.,* **-tt-, wet** *or* **wetted a)** befeuchten; *see also* **whistle 3 c; b)** *(urinate on)* ~ **one's bed/pants** das Bett/sich *(Dat.)* die Hosen naß machen. **3.** *n.* **a)** *(moisture)* Feuchtigkeit, *die;* **b)** *(rainy weather)* Regenwetter, *das; (rainy conditions)* Nässe, *die;* **c)** *(sl.: feeble person)* Flasche, *die (salopp abwertend);* **d)** *(Brit. Polit. coll.)* Schlappschwanz, *der (salopp abwertend)*

wet: ~**back** *n. (Amer. coll.)* illegaler mexikanischer Einwanderer; ~ '**dream** *n.* feuchter Traum

wether ['weðə(r)] *n. (Zool.)* Hammel, *der*

wet: ~**lands** *n. pl.* Feuchtgebiete; ~ **look** *n.* Hochglanz, *der; (of hair)* Wet-Look, *der*

wetness ['wetnɪs] *n., no pl.* **a)** *(being wet)* Nässe, *die;* **a patch of ~:** ein nasser Fleck; **b)** *(being rainy)* Feuchtigkeit, *die*

wet: ~-**nurse 1.** *n.* Amme, *die;* **2.** *v. t. (fig. derog.)* bemuttern; ~ **suit** *n.* Tauchanzug, *der*

wetting ['wetɪŋ] *n.* **get a ~:** naß werden; **give sb. a ~:** jmdn. naß machen

'**wetting agent** *n.* Netzmittel, *das*

we've [wɪv, *stressed* wi:v] = **we have**

WFTU *abbr.* **World Federation of Trade Unions** WGB

whack [wæk] **1.** *v. t. (coll.: strike heavily)* hauen *(ugs.).* **2.** *n.* **a)** *(coll.: heavy blow)* Schlag, *der;* **give sb. a ~ on the bottom** jmdm. eins auf den Hintern geben *(ugs.);* **b)** *(sl.: share)* Anteil, *der;* **c)** *(coll.: attempt)* **have a ~ at sth./at doing sth.** etw. probieren/probieren, etw. zu tun; **d) out of ~** *(Amer.)* aus dem Leim *(ugs.);* **e) top ~** *(coll.)* Spitzentarif, *der*

whacked [wækt] *adj. (Brit. coll.: tired out)* erledigt *(ugs.);* kaputt *(ugs.)*

whacking ['wækɪŋ] **1.** *adj. (sl.)* satt *(salopp).* **2.** *adv. (sl.)* wahnsinnig *(salopp);* ~ **great lies** faustdicke Lügen. **3.** *n. (coll.)* Tracht Prügel, *die*

whacko ['wækəʊ] *int. (Brit. dated sl.)* juchhe; juchhu

whale [weɪl] *n., pl.* ~**s** *or same* **a)** *(Zool.)* Wal, *der;* Walfisch, *der (volkst.);* **right ~:** Glattwal, *der;* **b)** *no pl. (coll.)* **we had a ~ of a [good] time** wir haben uns bombig *(ugs.) od.* toll *(ugs.)* amüsiert; **it made a ~ of a difference** es machte ungeheuer viel aus *(ugs.)*

'**whalebone** *n.* Fischbein, *das*

whaler ['weɪlə(r)] *n.* Walfänger, *der*

whaling ['weɪlɪŋ] *n., no pl., no indef. art.* Walfang, *der; attrib.* Walfang-

wham [wæm] **1.** *int.* wumm. **2.** *n.* Knall, *der.* **3.** *v. t.,* **-mm-:** ~ **sb.** jmdm. einen Schlag versetzen. **4.** *v. i.,* **-mm-** knallen

wharf [wɔ:f] *n., pl.* **wharves** [wɔ:vz] *or* ~**s** Kai, *der;* Kaje, *die (nordd.)*

what [wɒt] **1.** *interrog. adj.* **a)** *asking for selection* welch...; ~ **book did you choose?** welches Buch hast du ausgesucht?; **b)** *asking for statement of amount* wieviel; *with pl. n.* wie viele; ~ **men/money has he?** wie viele Leute/wieviel Geld hat er?; **I know ~ time it starts** ich weiß, um wieviel Uhr es anfängt; ~ **more can I do/say?** was kann ich sonst noch tun/sagen?; ~ **more do you want?** was willst du [noch] mehr?; **c)** *asking for statement of kind* was für; ~ **kind of man is he?** was für ein Mensch ist er?; ~ **good** *or* **use is it?** wozu soll das gut sein? *See also* **price 1 d. 2.** *excl. adj.* **a)** *(how great)* was für; ~ **a fool you are!** was für ein Dummkopf du doch bist!; ~ **impudence** *or* **cheek/luck!** was für eine Unverschämtheit *od.* Frechheit/was für ein Glück!; **b)** *before adj. and n. (to what extent)* was für. **3.** *rel. adj.* **we can dispose of ~ difficulties there are remaining** wir können die verbleibenden Schwierigkeiten ausräumen; **lend me ~ money you can** leih mir soviel Geld, wie du kannst; **I will give you ~ help I can** ich werde dir helfen, so gut ich kann. **4.** *adv.* **a)** *(to what extent)* ~ **do I care?** was kümmert's mich?; ~ **does it matter?** was macht's?; **b)** ~ **with ...:** wenn man an ... denkt; ~ **with**

changing jobs and moving house I haven't had time to do any studying da ich eine neue Stellung angetreten habe und umgezogen bin, hatte ich keine Zeit zum Lernen; ~ **with one thing and another** wie das so ist *od.* geht. **5.** *interrog. pron.* **a)** *(~ thing)* was; ~ **is your name?** wie heißt du/heißen Sie?; ~ **about ...?** *(is there any news of ...?, ~ will become of ...?)* was ist mit ...?; ~ **about a game of chess?** wie wär's mit einer Partie Schach?; ~ **to do?** was tun?; **~-d'you-[ma-]call-him/-her/-it, ~'s-his/-her/-its-name** wie heißt er/sie/es noch; ~ **for?** wozu?; ~ **do you want the money for?** wozu *od.* wofür willst du das Geld?; **and/or ~ 'have you** und/oder was sonst noch [alles]; ~ **if ...?** was ist, wenn ...?; ~ **is he?** was ist er für einer?; ~ **is it** *etc.* **like?** wie ist es *usw.*?; **I've lost a pen here somewhere – Well, ~ is it like?** Ich habe hier irgendwo einen Stift verloren. – Was ist es denn für einer?; ~ **next?** *(fig.)* sonst noch was?; ~ **not** wer weiß was alles; ~ **'of him/her?** was ist mit ihm/ihr?; ~ **'of it?** was ist dabei?; was soll [schon] dabeisein?; ~ **do you say** *or (Amer.)* ~ **say we have a rest?** was hältst du davon, wenn wir mal Pause machen?; wie wär's mit einer Pause?; ~ **will people say?** was werden die Leute sagen?; **all she ever thinks about is ~ people will say** sie denkt immer nur daran, was die Leute sagen; **[I'll] tell you ~:** weißt du, was; paß mal auf; **[and] ~ then?** [na] und?; **or ~?** oder was?; **so ~?** na und?; **b)** *asking for confirmation* ~? wie?; was? *(ugs.)*; **you did ~?** was hast du gemacht?; **nice day, ~?** *(Brit. coll.)* schöner Tag, was? *(ugs.)*; **c)** *in rhet. questions equivalent to neg. statement* ~ **is the use in trying/the point of going on?** wozu [groß] versuchen/weitermachen? *See also* **give 2 c; know 1 c. 6.** *rel. pron.* **a)** *(that which)* was; **do ~ I tell you** tu, was ich dir sage; ~ **little I know/remember** das bißchen, das ich weiß/an das ich mich erinnere; **this is ~ I mean: ...:** ich meine Folgendes: ...; **give me ~ you can** gib mir, soviel du kannst; **I disagree with ~ you are saying** ich stimme dem nicht zu, was du sagst; **tell sb. ~ to do** *or* ~ **he can do with sth.** *(coll. iron.)* jmdm. sagen, wo er sich *(Dat.)* etw. hinstecken kann *(salopp)*; ~ **is more** außerdem; zusätzlich; **the weather being ~ it is ...:** so, wie es mit dem Wetter aussieht, ...; **for ~ it is** in seiner Art; **b)** *(uneducated: who, which)* wo *(salopp)*; **it's the poor ~ gets the blame** die Armen müssen immer alles ausbaden. *See also* **but 1 b; come m. 7.** *excl. pron.* was; ~ **she must have suffered!** wie sie gelitten haben muß!

whate'er [wɒt'eə(r)] *(poet.)*, **whatever** [wɒt'evə(r)] **1.** *adj.* **a)** *rel. adj.* ~ **measures we take** welche Maßnahmen wir auch immer ergreifen; ~ **materials you will need** alle Materialien, die du vielleicht brauchst; **b)** *(notwithstanding which)* was für ... auch immer; ~ **problems you encounter** auf welche Probleme Sie auch stoßen [mögen]; **c)** *(at all)* überhaupt; **I can't see anyone ~:** ich kann überhaupt niemanden sehen. **2.** *pron.* **a)** *rel. pron.* was für ... [auch immer]; ~ **you do to complain, they will still take no notice** man kann sich beschweren, wie man will, sie beachten es doch nicht; **do ~ you like** mach, was du willst; **b)** *(notwithstanding anything)* was auch [immer]; ~ **happens, ...:** was auch geschieht, ...; **c) or ~:** oder was auch immer; oder sonst was *(ugs.)*; **d)** *(coll.)* = **what ever** *see* **ever e**

'whatnot *n.* **a)** *(coll.: indefinite thing)* Dingsbums, *das (ugs.)*; **b)** *(stand with shelves)* Etagere, *die*

whatsit ['wɒtsɪt] *n. (coll.) (thing)* Dingsbums, *das (ugs.)*; *(person)* Dingsda, *der (ugs.)*

whatsoe'er [wɒtsəʊ'eə(r)] *(poet.)*, **whatsoever** [wɒtsəʊ'evə(r)] *see* **whatever**

wheat [wi:t] *n., no pl., no indef. art.* Weizen, *der*; **sort out** *or* **separate the ~ from the chaff** *(fig.)* die Spreu vom Weizen trennen

'wheat-belt *n. (Geog.)* Weizengürtel, *der*

wheaten ['wi:tn] *adj.* Weizen-

wheat: ~ germ *see* **germ; ~-meal** *n. (Brit.)* Weizen[vollkorn]mehl, *das*

whee [wi:] *int.* juchhe

wheedle ['wi:dl] *v. t.* **a)** *(coax)* ~ **sb.** jmdm. gut zureden; ~ **sb. into doing sth.** jmdm. so lange gut zureden, bis er etw. tut; **b)** *(get by cajoling)* sich *(Dat.)* verschaffen; ~ **sth. out of sb.** jmdm. etw. abschwatzen *(ugs.)*

wheel [wi:l] **1.** *n.* **a)** Rad, *das*; *(of roller-skate)* Rolle, *die*; **[potter's] ~:** Töpferscheibe, *die*; **[roulette] ~:** Roulett, *das*; **reinvent the ~** *(fig.)* sich mit Problemen aufhalten, die längst gelöst sind; **get oneself some ~s** *(coll.)* sich *(Dat.)* einen fahrbaren Untersatz zulegen *(ugs.)*; **put** *or* **set the ~s in motion** *(fig.)* die Sache in Gang setzen; **the ~s of bureaucracy turn slowly** *(fig.)* die Mühlen der Bürokratie mahlen langsam; **there are ~s within ~s** *(fig.)* es spielen Dinge eine Rolle, von denen man gar nichts ahnt; **break sb. on the ~** *(Hist.)* jmdn. rädern; *see also* **butterfly a; oil 2 a; shoulder 1 a; 'spoke a; b)** *(for steering) (Motor Veh.)* Lenkrad, *das*; *(Naut.)* Steuerrad, *das*; **at** *or* **behind the ~** *(of car)* am *od.* hinterm Steuer; *(of ship; also fig.)* am Ruder; **c)** *(movement in a circle)* Kreisbewegung, *die*; **the ~[s] of the vultures** das Kreisen der Geier; **d)** *(Mil.: drill movement)* Schwenkung, *die*; **left/right ~:** Links-/Rechtsschwenkung, *die.* **2.** *v. t.* **a)** *(turn round)* wenden; **b)** *(Mil.)* schwenken lassen; **c)** *(push)* schieben; ~ **oneself** *(in a wheelchair)* fahren. **3.** *v. i.* **a)** *(turn round)* kehrtmachen; **b)** *(circle)* kreisen; **c)** *(Mil.)* schwenken; **left/right ~!** links/rechts schwenkt!

~ **a'bout, ~ a'round 1.** *v. t.* herumdrehen; wenden ⟨*Pferd*⟩. **2.** *v. i.* kehrtmachen; *(face the other way)* sich umdrehen; *(fig.)* kreisen; ⟨*Tänzer:*⟩ sich im Kreise drehen

~ **'in** *v. t.* hinein-/hereinschieben

~ **'out** *v. t.* hinaus-/herausschieben; ~ **sb. out** *(fig. derog.)* jmdn. vorführen

~ **'round** *see* ~ **about**

wheel: ~ and 'deal *v. i.* mauscheln; **~barrow** *n.* Schubkarre, *die*; Schubkarren, *der*; **~barrow race** *n.* Schubkarrenrennen, *das*; **~base** *n. (Motor Veh., Railw.)* Radstand, *der*; **~-brace** *n.* Radschlüssel, *der*; *(cross-shaped)* Kreuzschlüssel, *der*; **~chair** *n.* Rollstuhl, *der*; **~-clamp** *n.* Parkkralle, *die*

wheeled [wi:ld] *adj.* mit Rädern *nachgestellt*; ⟨*Möbel, Kulisse usw.*⟩ auf *od.* mit Rollen; ~ **vehicle** Räderfahrzeug, *das*

-wheeled *adj. in comb.* ⟨*vier-, sechs-, acht*⟩räd[e]rig

wheeler-dealer [wi:lə'di:lə(r)] *n.* Mauschler, *der*/Mauschlerin, *die*; *(financial)* Geschäftemacher, *der*/-macherin, *die*

'wheel-house *n. (Naut.)* Steuerhaus, *das*

wheelie ['wi:lɪ] *n. (sl.) Fahren auf dem Hinterrad*; Wheelie, *das*; **do a ~/do ~s** auf dem Hinterrad fahren; ein Wheelie/Wheelies fahren

wheeling ['wi:lɪŋ] *n., no pl., no indef. art.* Kreisen, *das*

wheeling and 'dealing *n.* Mauschelei, *die*; *(shady deals)* undurchsichtige Geschäfte; **there is a lot of ~ going on** es wird eifrig gemauschelt

wheel: ~ of 'fortune *n.* Glücksrad, *das*; **~ of 'life** *n. (Buddhism)* Rad des Lebens *od.* Werdens; **~-spin** *n. (Motor Veh., Railw.)* Durchdrehen der Räder; **because of ~-spin** wegen durchdrehender Räder; **~wright** ['wi:lraɪt] *n.* Stellmacher, *der*

wheeze [wi:z] **1.** *v. i.* schnaufen; keuchen. **2.** *n.* **a)** Schnaufen, *das*; Keuchen, *das*; **give a [loud] ~:** [laut] schnaufen *od.* keuchen; **b)** *(sl.) (trick)* Trick, *der*; *(plan)* Idee, *die*; **think up a ~:** einen Dreh finden *(ugs.)*; **a good ~ for making money** eine gute Masche, zu Geld zu kommen

~ **'out** *v. t.* keuchen

wheezy ['wi:zɪ] *adj. (coll.)* pfeifend, keuchend ⟨*Atem, Stimme*⟩; asthmatisch ⟨*Husten*⟩; schnaufend ⟨*Orgel*⟩; **be ~** ⟨*Atem:*⟩ pfeifend gehen, pfeifen; ⟨*Person:*⟩ pfeifend atmen

whelk [welk] *n. (Zool.)* Wellhornschnecke, *die*

whelp [welp] **1.** *n.* Welpe, *der.* **2.** *v. i. (also derog.)* werfen

when [wen] **1.** *adv.* **a)** *(at what time)* wann; **say ~** *(coll.: pouring drink)* sag halt; **that was ~ I intervened** das war der Moment, wo ich eingriff; **the best part of the film was ~ the car exploded** das Beste in dem Film war die Szene, als das Auto explodierte; **b)** *(at which)* **the time ~ ...:** die Zeit, zu der *od. (ugs.)* wo/*(with past tense)* als ...; **the day ~ ...:** der Tag, an dem *od. (ugs.)* wo/*(with past tense)* als ...; **do you remember [the time] ~ we ...:** erinnerst du dich daran, wie wir ... **2.** *conj.* **a)** *(at the time that)* als; *(with present or future tense)* wenn; ~ **[I was] young** als ich jung war; in meiner Jugend; ~ **in doubt** im Zweifelsfall; *(with gerund)* ~ **cleaning the gun** beim Putzen des Gewehrs; ~ **speaking French** wenn ich/sie *usw.* Französisch spreche/spricht *usw.*; **b)** *(whereas)* **why do you go abroad ~ it's cheaper here?** warum fährst du ins Ausland, wo es doch hier billiger ist?; **I received only £5 ~ I should have got £10** ich bekam nur 5 Pfund, hätte aber 10 Pfund bekommen sollen; **c)** *(considering that)* wenn; **how can I finish it ~ you won't help?** wie soll ich es fertigmachen, wenn du nicht hilfst?; **d)** *(and at that moment)* als. **3.** *pron.* **by/till ~ ...?**; bis wann ...?; **from/since ~ ...?** ab/seit wann ...?; ~ **are we invited for?** für wann sind wir eingeladen?; **but that was yesterday, since ~ things have changed** aber das war gestern, und inzwischen hat sich manches geändert. **4.** *n.* Wann, *das*; *see also* **where 4**

whence [wens] *(arch./literary)* **1.** *adv.* woher; ~ **did you learn this news?** wo[her] hast du das erfahren?; **the village ~ comes the famous cheese** das Dorf, aus dem der berühmte Käse kommt; **the source ~ these evils spring** die Quelle dieser Übel; **these are the facts, ~ we can conclude that ...:** das sind die Tatsachen, aus denen wir schließen können, daß ...; ~ **my doubts about his abilities** daher meine Zweifel über seine Fähigkeiten. **2.** *conj. (to the place from which)* dorthin, woher; **he returned it ~ it came** er brachte es dorthin zurück, wo es herkam. **3.** *pron.* **from ~** *see* **1**

whene'er [wen'eə(r)] *(poet.)*, **whenever** [wen'evə(r)] **1.** *adv.* **a)** wann immer; **or ~** oder wann immer; **b)** *(coll.)* = **when ever** *see* **ever e. 2.** *conj.* jedesmal wenn

whensoe'er [wensəʊ'eə(r)] *(poet.)*, **whensoever** [wensəʊ'evə(r)] *adv.* wann auch immer

where [weə(r)] **1.** *adv.* **a)** *(in or at what place)* wo; ~ **shall we sit?** wo wollen wir sitzen *od.* uns hinsetzen?; wohin wollen wir uns setzen?; ~ **was I?** *(fig.)* wo war ich stehengeblieben?; ~ **did Orwell say/write that?** wo *od.* an welcher Stelle sagt/schreibt Orwell das?; ~ **is the harm in it/the sense of it?** *(rhet.)* was macht das schon/welchen *od.* was für einen Sinn hat das?; **this is ~ I was born** hier bin ich geboren; **b)** *(from what place)* woher; ~ **did you get that information?** wo hast du das erfahren?; **c)** *(to what place, to which)* wohin; **she's going ~ she's wanted** sie geht dahin, wo sie gebraucht wird; ~ **shall I put it?** wohin soll ich es legen?; wo soll ich es hinlegen?; **the town ~ they were going** die Stadt, wohin sie fuhren;

~ **do we go from here?** *(fig.)* was tun wir jetzt *od.* als nächstes?; **I know ~ I'm going** *(fig.)* ich weiß, was ich erreichen will; **d)** *(in what respect)* inwiefern; **I don't know ~ they differ/I've gone wrong** ich weiß nicht, worin sie sich unterscheiden/wo ich den Fehler gemacht habe; **~ he is weakest is in maths** am schwächsten ist er in Mathematik; **that is ~ you are wrong** in diesem Punkt irrst du dich; **e)** *(in which)* wo; **in the box ~ I keep my tools** in der Kiste, worin *od.* in der ich mein Werkzeug habe; **f)** *(in what situation)* wo; **~ will/would they be if ...?** was wird/würde aus ihnen, wenn ...?; **~ would I be without you?** was täte ich ohne dich?; **~ will it all end?** wo wird das noch enden? **2.** *conj.* wo; **~ uncertain, leave blank** bei Unsicherheit [bitte] freilassen; **delete ~ inapplicable** Nichtzutreffendes [bitte] streichen. **3.** *pron.* **near/not far from ~ it happened** nahe der Stelle/nicht weit von der *od.* unweit der Stelle, wo es passiert ist; **from ~ I'm standing** von meinem Standort [aus]; **they continued from ~ they left off** sie machten da weiter, wo sie aufgehört hatten; **to Oxford, from ~ we took a train to London** nach Oxford, wo wir den Zug nach London nahmen; **within ten metres of ~ we stood** keine zehn Meter von der Stelle, wo wir standen; **we drove out to ~ the air was fresh and clean** wir fuhren dorthin, wo die Luft frisch und sauber war; **~ [...] from?** woher [...]?; von wo [...]?; **~ do/have you come from?** woher kommst du?; wo kommst du her?; **he is never sure ~ his next meal is coming from** er weiß nie, woher er seine nächste Mahlzeit kriegt; **~ [...] to?** wohin [...]?; **~ are you going to?** wohin gehst du?; wo gehst du hin?; **~ have you got to [in the book]?** wie weit bist du [in dem Buch]? **4.** *n.* Wo, *das;* **I can't recall the ~ and when [of it]** ich weiß nicht mehr, wo und wann [es war]

whereabouts 1. [weərə'baʊts] *adv. (in what place)* wo; *(to what place)* wohin. **2.** [weərə'baʊts] *pron.* **~ are you from?** woher kommst du? **3.** ['weərəbaʊts] *n., constr. as sing. or pl. (of thing)* Verbleib, *der; (of person)* Aufenthalt[sort], *der;* **her/its present ~ is** *or* **are unknown** wo sie sich zur Zeit aufhält/wo es sich zur Zeit befindet, ist unbekannt

where: ~'as *conj.* **a)** während; **he is very quiet, ~ as she is an extrovert** er ist sehr ruhig, sie dagegen ist eher extravertiert; **b)** *(Law: considering that)* in Anbetracht dessen, daß; da; **~'by** *adv.* **a)** *(by which)* mit dem/der/denen; mit dessen/deren Hilfe; **b)** *(dated/literary: by what means?)* wie; **~ by shall I know this?** woran erkenne ich das?

where'er [weər'eə(r)] *(poet.) see* **wherever**

wherefore ['weəfɔ:(r)] **1.** *adv. (arch./literary)* weshalb. **2.** *n.* **the whys and ~s** *see* **why 3**

where: ~'in *adv. (formal)* **a)** *(in which)* worin; in dem/der/denen; **b)** *(in what respect)* inwiefern; worin ‹*sich unterscheiden, sich finden*›; womit ‹*dienen*›; **~'of** *adv. (formal) (of which)* von dem/der/denen; woraus ‹*gemacht sein*›; **the house ~ he is the owner** das Haus, dessen Eigentümer er ist

wheresoe'er [weəsəʊ'eə(r)] *(poet.),*

wheresoever [weəsəʊ'evə(r)] *adv., conj.* wo auch immer

whereupon [weərə'pɒn] *adv.* worauf

wherever [weər'evə(r)] **1.** *adv.* **a)** *(in whatever place)* wo immer; **sit ~ you like** setz dich, wohin du magst; **I'll find him, ~ he lives** ich werde ihn finden, wo er auch wohnt *od.* wohnen mag; **or ~:** oder wo immer; oder sonstwo *(ugs.);* **b)** *(to whatever place)* wohin immer; **I shall go ~ I like** ich gehe, wohin ich will; **I shall go ~ there is work** ich gehe dahin, wo es Arbeit gibt; **or ~:** oder wohin immer; oder sonstwohin *(ugs.);* **c)** *(coll.)* = **where ever** *see* **ever e. 2.** *conj.* **a)** *(in every place that)* überall [da], wo; **~ security is involved** wann immer es um die Sicherheit geht; **do it ~ possible** tun Sie es, wo *od.* wenn [irgend] möglich; **b)** *(to every place that)* wohin auch; **~ he went** wohin er auch ging; wo er auch hinging. **3.** *pron.* wo ... auch; **~ you're going to** wo du auch hingehst; wohin du auch gehst; **~ it/he comes from** wo es/er auch herkommt; woher es/er auch kommt; **carry on reading from ~ you've got to** lies da weiter, bis wohin du gekommen bist

wherewithal ['weəwɪðɔ:l] *n. (coll.)* **the ~:** das nötige Kleingeld *(ugs.)*

wherry ['werɪ] *n.* **a)** *(rowing-boat)* [Ruder]kahn, *der;* **b)** *(Brit.: barge)* [Last]kahn, *der*

whet [wet] *v. t.,* **-tt- a)** *(sharpen)* wetzen; **b)** *(fig.: stimulate)* anregen ‹*Appetit*›; erregen ‹*Interesse*›; reizen ‹*Neugier*›

whether ['weðə(r)] *conj.* ob; **I don't know ~ to go [or not]** ich weiß nicht, ob ich gehen soll [oder nicht]; **the question [of] ~ to do it [or not]** die Frage, ob man es tun soll [oder nicht]; **~ you like it or not, I'm going** ob es dir paßt oder nicht, ich gehe; *see also* **doubt 1 a, 3; no 2 c**

'whetstone *n. (lit. or fig.)* Wetzstein, *der*

whew [hwju:] *int. expr. surprise* oh; *expr. consternation etc.* puh; *expr. relief* ah

whey [weɪ] *n., no pl., no indef. art.* Molke, *die*

which [wɪtʃ] **1.** *adj.* **a)** *interrog.* welch...; **~ one** welcher/welche/welches; **~ ones** welche; **~ one of you did it?** wer von euch hat es getan?; **~ way** *(how)* wie; *(in ~ direction)* wohin; **b)** *rel.* welch... *(geh.);* **I told him to go to the doctor, ~ advice he took** ich habe ihm geraten, zum Arzt zu gehen, was er auch getan hat; **he usually comes at one o'clock, at ~ time I'm having lunch/by ~ time I've finished** er kommt immer um ein Uhr; dann esse ich gerade zu Mittag/bis dahin bin ich schon fertig; **a 5 × 4 camera (~ size I prefer)** eine 5 × 4-Kamera (das Format, das ich vorziehe). **2.** *pron.* **a)** *interrog.* welcher/welche/welches; **~ of you?** wer von euch?; **~ is ~?** welcher/welche/welches ist welcher/welche/welches?; **I can't tell ~ is ~:** ich kann sie nicht auseinanderhalten *od.* unterscheiden; **b)** *rel.* der/die/das; welcher/welche/welches *(veralt.); referring to a clause* was; **of ~:** dessen/deren; **everything ~ I predicted** alles, was ich vorausgesagt habe; **the crime of ~ you accuse him** das Verbrechen, dessen Sie ihn anklagen; **the house of ~ I am speaking** das Haus, von dem *od.* wovon ich rede; **the bed on ~ she lay** das Bett, auf dem *od.* worauf sie lag; **he grinned, from ~ I gathered he wasn't serious** er grinste, woraus ich schloß, daß es nicht sein Ernst war; **the shop opposite/near ~ we parked** der Laden, gegenüber dem/in dessen Nähe wir parkten; **I have received your kind gift, for ~ many thanks** ich habe dein nettes Geschenk bekommen. Vielen Dank dafür; **I intervened, after ~ they calmed down** ich griff ein, worauf[hin] sie sich beruhigten; **Our Father, ~ art in Heaven** *(Rel.)* Vater unser, der du bist im Himmel

whichever [wɪtʃ'evə(r)] **1.** *adj.* **a)** *(any ... that)* der *od.* derjenige, der/die *od.* diejenige, die/das *od.* dasjenige, das/die *od.* diejenigen, die; **go ~ way you want** es ist egal, welchen Weg du nimmst; **take ~ apple/apples you wish** nimm den Apfel, den du willst/die Äpfel, die du willst; **..., ~ period is the longer ...** , je nachdem, welches der längere Zeitraum ist; **b)** *(no matter which/who/whom)* welcher/welche/welches ... auch; **~ way you go** welchen Weg du auch nimmst; **c)** *(coll.)* = **which ever** *see* **ever e. 2.** *pron.* **a)** *(any one[s] that)* der *od.* derjenige, der/die *od.* diejenige, die/das *od.* dasjenige, das/die *od.* diejenigen, die; **~ of you/the children wins will get a prize** wer von euch gewinnt/das Kind, das gewinnt, bekommt einen Preis; **a list of ~ of the children want to come** eine Liste aller Kinder, die kommen wollen; **at a walk, trot, or gallop, ~ you please** gehend, im Trab oder im Galopp, [ganz] wie du magst; **to dinner – or supper, ~ it ought to be called** zum Diner – oder Abendessen, wie immer man es nennen soll; **b)** *(no matter which one[s])* welcher/welche/welches ... auch; **~ of them comes/come** wer von ihnen auch kommt; **c)** *(coll.)* = **which ever** *see* **ever e**

whichsoever [wɪtʃsəʊ'evə(r)] *(arch.) see* **whichever 1 a, b, 2 a, b**

whiff [wɪf] *n.* **a)** *(smell)* [leichter] Geruch; *(puff, breath)* Hauch, *der;* **~s of smoke** Rauchwölkchen; **a ~ of honeysuckle** ein leichter Geißblattduft; **the ~ from his smelly feet** der Geruch seiner Schweißfüße; **give her another ~ of chloroform** gib ihr noch mal etwas Chloroform; **catch a ~ of sth.** den Geruch von etw. wahrnehmen; **b)** *(fig.: trace)* Hauch, *der;* **the faintest ~ of sentiment** der leiseste Anflug von Sentimentalität

Whig [wɪg] *(Hist.)* **1.** *n.* Whig, *der.* **2.** *attrib. adj.* Whig-

while [waɪl] **1.** *n.* Weile, *die;* **quite a** *or* **quite some ~, a good ~:** eine ganze Weile; ziemlich lange; **it takes a ~:** es dauert eine Weile *od.* Zeitlang; **[for] a ~:** eine Weile; **where have you been all the** *or* **this ~?** wo warst du die ganze Zeit?; **[only] a little** *or* **short ~ ago** [erst] kürzlich *od.* vor kurzem; **all the ~ we were there** die ganze Zeit, als wir da waren; **a long ~:** lange; **a long ~ ago** *or* **back** vor langer Zeit; **between ~s** zwischendurch; **for a little** *or* **short ~:** eine kleine Weile; **stay a little ~ [longer]** bleib noch ein Weilchen; **I haven't seen him for a long ~:** ich habe ihn lange nicht [mehr] gesehen; **in a little** *or* **short ~:** gleich; **in a long ~:** lange; seit langem; **be worth [sb.'s] ~:** sich [für jmdn.] lohnen; **make sth. worth sb.'s ~:** jmdn. für etw. entsprechend belohnen; **I'll make it worth your ~:** es soll dein Schaden nicht sein; **once in a ~:** von Zeit zu Zeit [mal]; hin und wieder [mal]; **he read the newspaper smoking a cigar the ~:** er las die Zeitung und rauchte dabei eine Zigarre. **2.** *conj.* **a)** während; *(as long as)* solange; **~ in London he took piano lessons** als er in London war, nahm er Klavierstunden; **don't smoke ~ in bed** rauchen Sie nicht im Bett; **could you get me a paper as well ~ you are about it?** könntest du mir auch eine Zeitung mitbringen, wenn du schon dabei bist?; **b)** *(although)* obgleich; **c)** *(whereas)* während. **3.** *v. t.* **~ away the time** sich *(Dat.)* die Zeit vertreiben **(by, with** mit); **~ away the evening/an hour** sich *(Dat.)* den Abend über/eine Stunde lang die Zeit vertreiben

whilst [waɪlst] *(Brit.) see* **while 2**

whim [wɪm] *n. (mood)* Laune, *die; (idea)* Spleen, *der;* **he acts as the ~ takes him** er handelt je nach Laune

whimper ['wɪmpə(r)] **1.** *n.* **~[s]** Wimmern, *das; (of dog etc.)* Winseln, *das;* **with a ~:** wimmernd/winselnd; **he gave a ~ of pain** er wimmerte vor Schmerz; **not with a bang but a ~** *(fig.)* sang- und klanglos. **2.** *v. i.* wimmern; ‹*Hund:*› winseln. **3.** *v. t.* in weinerlichem Ton vorbringen ‹*Klage*›; **'...', he ~ed** „...", wimmerte er

whimsical ['wɪmzɪkl] *adj.* **a)** *(frivolous)* launenhaft; *(odd, fanciful)* spleenig; *(tinged with humour)* launig; humorig; *(teasing)* neckisch ‹*Blick, Lächeln*›; **b)** *(odd-looking)* kurios; ulkig *(ugs.)*

whimsicality [wɪmzɪ'kælɪtɪ] *n., no pl. see* **whimsical: a)** Launenhaftigkeit, *die;* Spleenigkeit, *die;* Launigkeit, *die;* Humorigkeit, *die;* **b)** Kuriosität, *die;* Ulkigkeit, *die (ugs.)*

whimsically ['wɪmzɪkəlɪ] *adv.* launenhaft; *(teasingly)* neckisch ‹*ansehen, lächeln*›; **he said ~ that ...:** er machte die launige Bemerkung, daß ...
whimsy ['wɪmzɪ] *n.* **a)** *no pl. see* **whimsicality a; b)** *(idea)* Spleen, *der*
whine [waɪn] **1.** *v.i.* **a)** *(make moaning sound)* heulen; ‹*Hund:*› jaulen; ‹*Baby:*› quengeln *(ugs.)*; **~ for mercy/alms** um Gnade/Almosen winseln *(abwertend)*; **b)** *(complain)* jammern; **he's been whining to the boss about it** er hat dem Chef darüber etwas vorgejammert. **2.** *n.* **a)** *(sound)* Heulen, *das; (esp. of dog)* Jaulen, *das;* **the ~ in his voice** der winselnde Ton in seiner Stimme; **the baby's ~s** das Gequengel des Babys *(ugs.)*; **b)** *(complaint)* ~[s] Gejammer, *das*
whiner ['waɪnə(r)] *n.* Jammerer, *der;* **be a ~:** immer was zu jammern haben
whinge [wɪndʒ] *v.i.*, **~ing** *(coll.) see* **whine 1 b, 2 b**
whinny ['wɪnɪ] **1.** *v.i.* wiehern. **2.** *n.* Wiehern, *das;* **whinnies** Gewieher, *das*
whip [wɪp] **1.** *n.* **a)** Peitsche, *die;* **use one's ~ on** *or* **take one's ~ to sb./a horse** jmdm./einem Pferd die Peitsche geben; *see also* **crack 1 a, 3 c; b)** *(Brit. Parl.: official)* Einpeitscher, *der*/Einpeitscherin, *die (Jargon)*; **chief ~:** Haupteinpeitscher, *der*/-einpeitscherin, *die (Jargon);* Fraktionsgeschäftsführer, *der*/-führerin, *die (Amtsspr.)*; **c)** *(Brit. Parl.: notice)* **[three-line] ~:** *[verbindliche] Aufforderung zur Teilnahme an einer Plenarsitzung [wegen einer wichtigen Abstimmung];* **issue a three-line ~:** Fraktionszwang verhängen; **take/be deprived of/resign the ~:** in die Fraktion eintreten/aus der Fraktion ausgeschlossen werden/aus der Fraktion austreten; **d)** *(Hunting: whipper-in)* Pikör, *der;* **e)** *(Cookery)* Schaumspeise, *die.* **2.** *v.t.*, **-pp- a)** *(lash)* peitschen; **the rider ~ped his horse** der Reiter gab seinem Pferd die Peitsche; **he was ~ped in public** er wurde öffentlich ausgepeitscht; **the rain ~ped the window-panes** der Regen peitschte [gegen] die Fensterscheiben; **b)** *(Cookery)* schlagen; **~ sth. until stiff/to a froth** etw. steif/schaumig schlagen; **c)** *(move quickly)* reißen ‹*Gegenstand*›; **she ~ped it out of my hand** sie riß es mir aus der Hand; **he quickly ~ped it out of sight** er ließ es schnell verschwinden; **~ sth. from one's pocket** etw. blitzschnell aus der Tasche ziehen; **~ sb. into hospital** jmdn. schleunigst ins Krankenhaus bringen; **she was ~ped through customs** sie wurde am Zoll blitzschnell abgefertigt; **d)** *(sl.: defeat)* auseinandernehmen *(salopp bes. Sport)*; **e)** *(sl.: steal)* klauen *(ugs.)*; **f)** *(bind)* umwickeln; [be]takeln *(Seemannsspr.)*; *(Sewing: overcast)* umnähen; **g)** *(fig.: reprove, criticize)* **~ sb./sth.** jmdm. die Leviten lesen/etw. geißeln; **h) ~ a top** kreiseln; einen Kreisel treiben. **3.** *v.i.*, **-pp- a)** *(move quickly)* flitzen *(ugs.)*; **he ~ped down the stairs** er sauste *od.* flitzte die Treppe hinunter; **~ through a book in no time** ein Buch in Null Komma nichts durchlesen *(ugs.)*; **b)** *(lash)* peitschen
~ a'way *v.t.* wegreißen **(from** *Dat.***)**
~ 'back *v.i.* **a)** *(spring back)* zurückschnellen; **b)** *(return quickly)* zurückflitzen *(ugs.)*
~ 'in 1. *v.i.* reinwitschen *(ugs.)*; **the wind came ~ping in** der Wind kam reingefegt *(ugs.)*. **2.** *v.t. (Hunting)* [mit der Peitsche] wieder zur Meute treiben ‹*Hunde*›
~ 'off *v.t.* **a)** *(snatch off)* herunterreißen; ‹*Wind:*› herunterfegen; **~ one's clothes off** seine Kleider von sich werfen; **~ off one's hat** [sich *(Dat.)*] den Hut vom Kopf reißen; **~ sb. off to hospital/France** jmdn. schleunigst ins Krankenhaus/nach Frankreich bringen; **b)** *(Hunting)* [mit der Peitsche] zurücktreiben ‹*Hunde*›
~ 'on *v.t.* **a)** *(put on quickly)* draufwerfen; **~ one's coat/clothes on** sich in seinen Mantel/seine Kleider werfen; **~ one's hat on** schnell seinen Hut aufsetzen; **b)** *(urge on)* mit der Peitsche antreiben; *(fig.)* antreiben; anspornen
~ 'out 1. *v.t.* [blitzschnell] herausziehen; **~ sb.'s appendix/tonsils out** jmds. Blinddarm/Mandeln schleunigst herausnehmen. **2.** *v.i.* rauswitschen *(ugs.)*
~ 'round *v.i.* **a)** *(turn quickly)* herumschnellen; **b)** *(go quickly)* **~ round to see sb.** *or* **to sb.'s place** schnell bei jmdm. vorbeischauen; **I'm just ~ping round to my neighbour's/to the shops** ich gehe nur schnell zum Nachbarn/einkaufen; *see also* **whip-round**
~ 'up *v.t.* **a)** *(snatch up)* [blitz]schnell aufheben; **b)** *(Cookery)* [kräftig] schlagen; **c)** *(arouse)* aufpeitschen ‹*Wellen*›; *(fig.)* anheizen *(ugs.)*, anfachen *(geh.)* ‹*Emotionen, Interesse*›; schüren ‹*Haß, Unzufriedenheit*›; **he knows how to ~ up enthusiasm in his pupils** er versteht es, seine Schüler zu begeistern; **~ up trouble/a riot** die Leute zu Unruhen/zum Aufruhr aufstacheln; **d)** *(coll.: make quickly)* schnell hinzaubern ‹*Gericht, Essen*›
whip: ~cord *n.* **a)** *(cord)* Peitschenschnur, *die;* **b)** *(fabric)* Whipcord, *der;* **~ hand** *n.* **have** *or* **hold the ~ hand [of** *or* **over sb.]** *(fig.)* die Oberhand [über jmdn.] haben; **~lash** *n.* **a)** Peitschenriemen, *der;* **b)** *(Med.)* **~lash [injury]** Peitschenschlagverletzung, *die;* Schleudertrauma, *das*
whipped 'cream *n.* Schlagsahne, *die*
whipper-in [wɪpər'ɪn] *(Hunting)* Pikör, *der*
whipper-snapper ['wɪpəsnæpə(r)] *n.* *(dated)* [junger] Dachs; *(cheeky)* Frechdachs, *der*
whippet ['wɪpɪt] *n.* Whippet, *der*
whipping ['wɪpɪŋ] *n.* **a)** *(flogging)* Schlagen [mit der Peitsche]; *(as form of punishment)* Prügelstrafe, *die; (flagellation)* Geißelung, *die;* **give sb. a ~:** jmdn. auspeitschen; *(with stick etc.)* jmdm. eine Tracht Prügel verpassen *(ugs.)*; *(sl.: defeat)* jmdm. eins überbraten *(salopp)*; **get** *or* **take** *or* **be given a ~:** ausgepeitscht werden; *(sl.: be defeated)* eins übergebraten kriegen *(salopp)*; **b)** *(cord)* Umwicklung, *die;* Takling, *der (Seemannsspr.)*
whipping: ~-boy *n. (Hist.; also fig.)* Prügelknabe, *der;* **~-cream** *n.* [flüssige] Schlagsahne; **~-top** *n.* [Treib]kreisel, *der*
whippoorwill ['wɪpʊəwɪl] *n. (Ornith.)* Whip-Poor-Will, *der*
whippy ['wɪpɪ] *adj.* biegsam; elastisch
whip: ~-round *n. (Brit. coll.)* Sammlung, *die;* **have** *or* **hold a ~-round [for sb./sth.]** [für jmdn./etw.] den Hut herumgehen lassen *(ugs.)*; **~-saw** *v.t. (Amer. fig.) beim Poker betrügen, indem man zusammen mit dem Partner den Einsatz erhöht;* **~stock** *n.* Peitschenstiel, *der*
whir [wɜ:(r)] **1.** *v.i.*, **-rr-** *see* **whirr 1. 2.** *n. see* **whirr 2**
whirl [wɜ:l] **1.** *v.t.* **a)** *(rotate)* [im Kreis] herumwirbeln; **b)** *(fling)* schleudern; *(with circling motion)* wirbeln ‹*Blätter, Schneeflocken usw.*›; **c)** *(convey rapidly)* in Windeseile fahren; **the train ~ed us to our destination** der Zug brachte uns in Windeseile ans Ziel. **2.** *v.i.* **a)** *(rotate)* wirbeln; **the ice-skaters ~ed at a tremendous speed** die Eisläufer wirbelten in ungeheurer Geschwindigkeit [im Kreis herum]; **~ing dervish** tanzender Derwisch; **b)** *(move swiftly)* sausen; *(with circling motion)* wirbeln; **I could see the leaves ~ing in the wind** ich sah, wie die Blätter vom Wind herumgewirbelt wurden; **c)** *(fig.: reel)* **everything/the room ~ed about me** mir drehte sich alles/das Zimmer drehte sich vor meinen Augen; **the excitements of the city made her head ~:** von den aufregenden Eindrücken der Stadt wirbelte ihr der Kopf. **3.** *n.* **a)** Wirbeln, *das;* **the wind threw up a ~ of leaves/sand** der Wind wirbelte Blätter/Sand auf; **she was** *or* **her thoughts were** *or* **her head was in a ~** *(fig.)* ihr schwirrte der Kopf; **b)** *(bustle)* Trubel, *der;* **her dull life suddenly became a ~ of activity** ihr eintöniges Leben war plötzlich voller Trubel und Betriebsamkeit; **the social ~:** der Trubel des gesellschaftlichen Lebens; **c)** *(coll.: attempt)* **give sb./sth. a ~:** jmdn./etw. mal probieren
~ a'bout 1. *v.t.* herumwirbeln. **2.** *v.i.* herumwirbeln; ‹*Vögel:*› sich tummeln
~ a'long 1. *v.t.* ‹*Fluß:*› mitreißen; **~ sb. along** mit jmdm. dahinsausen. **2.** *v.i.* dahinsausen
~ a'round *see* **~ about**
~ a'way, ~'off 1. *v.t.* in Windeseile wegfahren; **~ sb. off** *or* **away somewhere** jmdn. in Windeseile irgendwohin bringen. **2.** *v.i.* lossausen
~ 'round 1. *v.t.* [im Kreis] herumwirbeln. **2.** *v.i.* [im Kreis] herumwirbeln; ‹*Rad, Rotor, Strudel:*› wirbeln; **the leaf ~ed round as it fell** das Blatt drehte sich im Fall in einem Wirbel
~ 'up *v.t.* aufwirbeln; hochwirbeln
whirligig ['wɜ:lɪgɪg] *n.* **a)** *(top)* Kreisel, *der; (toy windmill)* Windrädchen, *das;* **b)** *(Zool.)* Taumelkäfer, *der;* Kreiselkäfer, *der*
whirl: ~pool *n.* Strudel, *der; (bathing pool)* Whirlpool, *der;* **~wind** *n.* **a)** Wirbelwind, *der; (stronger)* Wirbelsturm, *der;* **sow the wind and reap the ~wind** *(prov.)* Wind säen und Sturm ernten; **b)** *(fig.: tumult)* Wirbel, *der;* Trubel, *der;* **I've been caught up all week in a ~wind of activity** für mich war die ganze Woche über ständig Trubel; **~wind romance** heftige Romanze
whirlybird ['wɜ:lɪbɜ:d] *n. (sl.: helicopter)* Hubschrauber, *der*
whirr [wɜ:(r)] **1.** *v.i.* surren; ‹*Heuschrecke, Grille usw.:*› zirpen; ‹*Flügel eines Vogels, Propeller:*› schwirren. **2.** *n. see* **1:** Surren, *das;* Zirpen, *das;* Schwirren, *das*
whisk [wɪsk] **1.** *n.* **a)** Wedel, *der;* **b)** *(Cookery)* Schneebesen, *der; (part of mixer)* Rührbesen, *der;* **c)** *(movement)* wischende Bewegung; **a few ~s of the broom** ein paar Besenstriche *od.* Striche mit dem Besen; **the horse gave a ~ of its tail** das Pferd schlug mit dem Schwanz. **2.** *v.t.* **a)** *(Cookery)* [mit dem Schnee-/Rührbesen] schlagen; **b)** *(convey rapidly)* in Windeseile bringen; **the taxi will ~ you to town in no time** das Taxi bringt dich im Nu in die Stadt; **c)** *(flip)* schlagen mit ‹*Schwanz*›. **3.** *v.i.* sausen; schießen *(ugs.)*
~ a'way *v.t.* **a)** *(flap away)* wegscheuchen; **b)** *(remove suddenly)* **~ sth. away [from sb.]** [jmdm.] etw. [plötzlich] wegreißen; **c)** *(convey rapidly)* in Windeseile wegbringen; **~ sb. away to the station** jmdn. in Windeseile zum Bahnhof bringen
~ 'off *v.t.* **a)** *(flap off) see* **~ away a; b)** *(remove suddenly)* [plötzlich] wegreißen; **~ one's coat off** seinen Mantel von sich werfen; **~ off one's hat** rasch den Hut abnehmen; **c)** *see* **~ away c**
~ 'up *see* **~ 2 a**
whisker ['wɪskə(r)] *n.* **a)** *in pl. (hair on man's cheek)* Backenbart, *der;* **b)** *(Zool.) (of cat, mouse, rat)* Schnurrhaar, *das; (of walrus)* Bartborste, *die;* **a walrus's ~s** der Bart eines Walrosses; *see also* **cat's whiskers; c)** *(fig. coll.: small distance)* **be within a ~ of sth./doing sth.** kurz vor etw. *(Dat.)* stehen/kurz davorstehen, etw. zu tun; **win by a ~:** ganz knapp gewinnen
whiskered ['wɪskəd] *adj.* backenbärtig; ‹*Tier*› mit Schnurrhaaren
whiskery ['wɪskərɪ] *adj.* backenbärtig; **be ~:** einen [mächtigen] Backenbart haben
whiskey *(Amer., Ir.)*, **whisky** ['wɪskɪ] *n.* Whisky, *der; (Irish or American ~)* Whiskey, *der*

whisper ['wɪspə(r)] **1.** *v. i.* **a)** flüstern; **~ to sb.** jmdm. etwas zuflüstern; **~ to me so that no one else will hear** flüster es mir ins Ohr, damit es niemand [anders] hört; **~ to each other** miteinander flüstern; **b)** *(speak secretly)* tuscheln; **~ against sb.** über jmdn. tuscheln; **c)** *(rustle)* [leise] rauschen; säuseln *(geh.)*; flüstern *(poet.)*. **2.** *v. t.* **a)** flüstern; **~ sth. to sb./in sb.'s ear** jmdm. etw. zuflüstern/ins Ohr flüstern; **~ it to me so that no one else will hear** flüster es mir ins Ohr, damit es niemand [anders] hört; **~ sb. to do sth./that ...:** jmdm. zuflüstern, er solle etw. tun/daß ...; **b)** *(rumour)* [hinter vorgehaltener Hand] erzählen; **the story is being ~ed about the village that ...:** im Dorf macht die Geschichte die Runde, daß ...; **it is ~ed that ...:** man munkelt, daß ... *(ugs.)*. **3.** *n.* **a)** *(whispered speech)* Flüstern, *das;* **in a ~, in ~s** im Flüsterton; **b)** *(whispered remark)* **their ~s** ihr Geflüster; *see also* **stage whisper; c)** *(rumour)* Gerücht, *das;* **there were ~s that ...:** es gab Gerüchte, daß ...; man munkelte, daß ... *(ugs.)*; **d)** *(rustle)* [leises] Rauschen; Säuseln, *das (geh.)*; Flüstern, *das (poet.)*

whispering: ~ campaign *n.* Verleumdungskampagne, *die;* **~-gallery** *n.* Flüstergalerie, *die*

whist [wɪst] *n. (Cards)* Whist, *das; see also* **drive 1 k**

whistle ['wɪsl] **1.** *v.i.* pfeifen; **~ at a girl** hinter einem Mädchen herpfeifen; **the spectators ~d at the referee** die Zuschauer pfiffen den Schiedsrichter aus; **he ~d loudly when he heard how valuable it was** er ließ ein lautes Pfeifen vernehmen, als er hörte, wie wertvoll es war; **~ to sb.** jmdm. pfeifen; **~ for sth.** nach etw. pfeifen; **the policeman ~d for help/reinforcement** der Polizist pfiff, um Hilfe/Verstärkung herbeizurufen; **the referee ~d for half-time** der Schiedsrichter pfiff Halbzeit; **~ in the dark** *(fig.)* seine Angst verdrängen; **you can ~ for it!** *(fig. coll.)* da kannst du lange warten! **2.** *v. t.* **a)** pfeifen; **b)** *(summon)* her[bei]pfeifen; **he ~d his dog and it came running** er pfiff seinem Hund, und er kam angelaufen. **3.** *n.* **a)** *(sound)* Pfiff, *der; (whistling)* Pfeifen, *das;* **the joyful ~s of the birds** das fröhliche Zwitschern der Vögel *od.* Vogelgezwitscher; **give a [brief] ~:** [kurz] pfeifen; **he gave a ~ of surprise** er ließ ein überraschtes Pfeifen vernehmen; **b)** *(instrument)* Pfeife, *die;* **penny** *or* **tin ~:** Blechflöte, *die;* **the referee blew his ~:** der Schiedsrichter pfiff; **[as] clean/clear as a ~** *(fig.)* blitzsauber/absolut frei; **get away [as] clean as a ~:** ganz unbehelligt davonkommen; **blow the ~ on sb./sth.** *(fig.)* jmdn./etw. auffliegen lassen *(ugs.)*; **c)** *(coll.: throat)* **wet one's ~** *(coll.)* sich *(Dat.)* die Kehle anfeuchten *(ugs.)*

~ 'back *v.t.* zurückpfeifen

~ 'up *v. t.* [he]ranpfeifen

whistle: ~-blower *n. (fig.) jmd., der etw. auffliegen läßt;* **~-stop** *n. (Amer.)* **a)** *(Railw.) (small town)* kleines Nest *(ugs.) (an einer Bahnlinie); (station)* Bedarfshaltepunkt, *der;* **b)** *(Polit.) kurzer Auftritt eines Politikers während einer Wahlkampfreise; (rapid visit)* Stippvisite, *die;* **~-stop tour/campaign** Reise mit vielen Kurzaufenthalten/Wahlkampf[reise] mit vielen kurzen Auftritten *od.* Terminen

whistling: ~-buoy *n. (Naut.)* Heulboje, *die;* **~ 'kettle** *n.* Pfeifkessel, *der*

whit [wɪt] *n., no pl., no def. art. (arch./literary)* **no ~, not a ~:** kein bißchen; **it matters not a ~:** es macht überhaupt nichts; **not a ~ of sense** nicht ein Funke [von] Verstand

white [waɪt] **1.** *adj.* **a)** weiß; **[as] ~ as snow** schneeweiß; **he prefers his coffee ~** *(Brit.)* er trinkt seinen Kaffee am liebsten mit Milch; **b)** *(pale)* weiß; *(through illness)* blaß; bleich; *(through fear or rage)* bleich; weiß; **[as] ~ as chalk** *or* **a sheet** kreidebleich; **go** *or* **turn ~:** weiß *od.* bleich werden; erbleichen *(geh.)*; **he was ~ with rage** er war weiß *od.* bleich vor Wut; *see also* **bleed 2 a; c) ~r than ~** *(fig.: morally pure)* engelrein *(geh.)*; **d)** *(light-skinned)* weiß; **~ people** Weiße *Pl.;* **~ oppression** Unterdrückung durch die Weißen. **2.** *n.* **a)** *(colour)* Weiß, *das;* **b)** *(of egg)* Eiweiß, *das;* **c)** *(of eye)* Weiße, *das;* **the ~s of their eyes** das Weiße in ihren Augen; **d) W~** *(person)* Weiße, *der/die;* **e)** *(~ clothes)* **dressed in ~:** weiß gekleidet; **~s** weißer Dreß; *(laundry)* Weißwäsche, *die;* **f)** *(Printing)* Zwischenraum, *der;* **g)** *(butterfly)* Weißling, *der;* **h)** *(Snooker)* weiße Kugel

white: ~ 'ant *n.* Termite, *die;* **~bait** *n., pl. same: junger Hering/junge Sprotte o. ä.;* **~beam** *n. (Bot.)* Mehlbeere, *die;* **~ 'bread** *n.* Weißbrot, *das;* **~ cell** *n. (Anat., Zool.)* weißes Blutkörperchen; **~ 'Christmas** *n.* weiße Weihnachten; **~ 'coffee** *n. (Brit.)* Kaffee mit Milch; **~-'collar** *adj.* **~-collar worker** Angestellte, *der/die;* **~-collar union** Angestelltengewerkschaft, *die;* **~ corpuscle** *see* **~ cell; ~ 'currant** *n.* weiße Johannisbeere; **~ 'dwarf** *n. (Astron.)* weißer Zwerg; **~ 'elephant** *see* **elephant; ~-faced** *adj.* [kreide]bleich; **~ fish** *n.* **a)** *(light-coloured fish) [Speise]fisch mit weißlicher od. silbriger Färbung;* Weißfisch, *der;* **b)** *(lake-fish)* Weißfisch, *der;* Renke, *die;* **~ 'flag** *n.* weiße Fahne; **W~ 'Friar** *n.* Karmeliter, *der;* **~ 'frost** *n.* Reif, *der;* **~ 'gold** *n.* Weißgold, *das;* **~ goods** *n. pl. (Commerc.)* **a)** *(fabrics)* Weißwaren *Pl.;* **b)** *(appliances)* weiße Ware; **W~hall** *pr. n. (Brit. Polit.: Government)* Whitehall *(das);* **~ heat** *n.* **a)** *(Phys.)* Weißglut, *die;* **to a ~ heat** bis zum Weißglühen; **at [a] ~ heat** in weißglühendem Zustand; **b)** *(fig.)* Glut, *die;* **work at ~ heat** auf Hochtouren arbeiten; **~ 'hope** *n.* Hoffnungsträger, *der*/Hoffnungsträgerin, *die;* **~ 'horse** *n.* **a)** Schimmel, *der;* **b)** *in pl. (on waves)* Schaumkronen; **~-'hot** *adj.* **a)** *(Phys.)* weißglühend; **b)** *(fig.)* glühend; **W~ House** *pr. n. (Amer. Polit.)* **the W~ House** das Weiße Haus; **~ 'knight** *n. (fig.)* Retter in der Not; **~ 'lead** *n.* Bleiweiß, *das;* **~ 'lie** *see* **'lie 1 a; ~ 'light** *n. (Phys.)* weißes Licht; **~ 'line** *n. (in middle of road)* Mittellinie, *die; (at side of road)* Randlinie, *die;* **~-lipped** ['waɪtlɪpt] *adj.* mit kreidebleichen Lippen *nachgestellt;* **~ 'magic** *n.* weiße Magie; **~ man** *n. (Anthrop.)* Weiße, *der;* **the ~ man** *(~ people)* der weiße Mann; **~ 'meat** *n.* weißes Fleisch [und Geflügel]; **~ 'metal** *n.* Weißmetall, *das;* **W~ 'Monk** *n.* Zisterzienser, *der*

whiten ['waɪtn] **1.** *v. t.* weiß machen; weißen ⟨*Wand, Schuhe*⟩. **2.** *v. i.* **a)** *(become white)* weiß werden; **b)** *(turn pale)* [kreide]weiß werden

whitener ['waɪtənə(r)] *n. (for shoes)* Schuhweiß, *das; (bleaching agent)* Bleichmittel, *das; (for coffee)* Kaffeeweißer, *der*

whiteness ['waɪtnɪs] *n., no pl.* **a)** Weiß, *das;* **b)** *(paleness)* Blässe, *die*

white: ~ 'night *n.* schlaflose Nacht; **~ 'noise** *n. (Phys.)* weißes Rauschen; **~-out** *n. (Meteorol.)* Whiteout, *der;* **W~ 'Paper** *n. (Brit.) öffentliches Diskussionspapier über Vorhaben der Regierung;* **W~ 'Russia** *pr. n.* Weißrußland *(das);* **W~ 'Russian 1.** *adj.* weißrussisch; **sb. is W~ Russian** jmd. ist Weißrusse/-russin; **2.** *n.* Weißrusse, *der*/-russin, *die;* **~ 'sale** *n. (Commerc.)* ≈ Weiße Woche/Wochen; Weißwarenausverkauf, *der;* **~ 'sauce** *n.* weiße *od.* helle Soße; **W~ 'Sea** *pr. n.* Weiße Meer, *das;* **~ 'slave** *n.* weiße Sklavin; *Opfer des Mädchenhandels;* **~ slave trade** *or* **traffic** Mädchenhandel, *der;* **~ 'spirit** *n. (Chem.)* Terpentin[öl]ersatz, *der;* **~ 'stick** *n.* Blindenstock, *der;* **~ 'sugar** *n.* weißer Zucker; **~ su'premacy** *n.* Überlegenheit der weißen Rasse; **~thorn** *n. (Bot.)* Weißdorn, *der;* **~-throat** *n. (Ornith.)* **a)** *(warbler)* Grasmücke, *die;* **b)** *(Amer.: sparrow)* Weißkehlammerfink, *der;* **~ 'tie** *n.* **a)** *(bow-tie)* weiße Fliege *od.* Schleife(, *die zum Cutaway getragen wird*); **b)** *(evening dress)* Frack, *der;* **is it dinner jacket or ~ tie?** soll man im Smoking oder im Frack erscheinen?; **~ 'trash** *see* **trash 1 d; ~-wall 'tyre** *n.* Weißwandreifen, *der;* **~wash 1.** *n.* **a)** [weiße] Tünche; *(fig.)* Schönfärberei, *die;* **the report is a ~wash of the Government** der Bericht versucht, die Regierung reinzuwaschen; **b)** *(defeat)* Zu-Null-Niederlage, *die;* **2.** *v. t.* **a)** [weiß] tünchen; **the report ~washes the Government** *(fig.)* der Bericht zielt darauf ab, die Regierung reinzuwaschen; **be ~washed** *(Finance)* [als Gemeinschuldner] entlastet werden; **b)** *(defeat)* zu Null schlagen; **~ 'water** *n. (foamy)* weiß schäumendes Wasser; *(shallow)* Flachwasser, *das;* **~-water canoeing** Wildwassersport, *der;* **~ 'wedding** *n.* Hochzeit in Weiß; **have a ~ wedding** in Weiß heiraten; **~ 'whale** *n. (Zool.)* Weißwal, *der;* **~ 'wine** *n.* Weißwein, *der;* **~ woman** *n. (Anthrop.)* Weiße, *die;* **~wood** *n.* Weißholz, *das*

Whitey ['waɪtɪ] *n. (coll. derog.)* weißes Schwein *(derb)*

whither ['wɪðə(r)] *(arch./rhet.)* **1.** *adv.* wohin; **~ democracy/Ulster?** *(fig. rhet.)* wohin *od. (geh.)* quo vadis, Demokratie/Ulster?; **the town ~ he was sent** die Stadt, in die er geschickt wurde. **2.** *conj.* dorthin *od.* dahin, wohin; *(to wherever)* wohin auch; **I shall go ~ she goes** ich werde gehen, wo immer sie hingeht

whiting ['waɪtɪŋ] *n., pl. same (Zool.)* Wittling, *der*

whitish ['waɪtɪʃ] *adj.* weißlich

Whit Monday [wɪt 'mʌndeɪ, wɪt 'mʌndɪ] *n.* Pfingstmontag, *der*

Whitsun ['wɪtsn] *n.* Pfingsten, *das od. Pl.;* **at ~:** zu *od.* an Pfingsten; **next/last ~:** nächste/letzte Pfingsten

Whitsunday, Whit Sunday [wɪt'sʌndeɪ, wɪt'sʌndɪ] *n.* Pfingstsonntag, *der*

Whitsuntide ['wɪtsntaɪd] *n.* Pfingstzeit, *die*

whittle ['wɪtl] **1.** *v. t.* schnitzen an (+ *Dat.*); **~ a stick to a point** einen Stock anspitzen. **2.** *v. i.* **~ at sth.** an etw. *(Dat.)* [herum]schnitzen

~ a'way, ~ 'down *v. t. (fig.)* **a)** *(completely)* auffressen ⟨*Gewinn, Geldmittel usw.*⟩; **~ away sb.'s rights/power** jmdm. nach und nach alle Rechte/alle Macht nehmen; **b)** *(partly)* allmählich reduzieren ⟨*Anzahl, Team, Gewinn, Verlust*⟩; verkürzen ⟨*Liste*⟩

Whit [wɪt]: **~ week** *n.* Pfingstwoche, *die;* **~ week'end** *n.* Pfingstwochenende, *das*

whiz, whizz [wɪz] **1.** *v. i.,* **-zz-** zischen; **we could hear the arrows/shells whizzing above our heads** wir hörten das Zischen der über uns hinwegfliegenden Pfeile/Granaten. **2.** *n.* Zischen, *das;* **with a ~:** zischend

~ 'past *v. i.* vorbeizischen; ⟨*Vogel:*⟩ vorbeischießen

'whiz[z]-kid *n. (coll.)* Senkrechtstarter, *der;* **he is a financial ~:** er macht eine steile Karriere als Finanzmann; **a mathematical ~:** ein mathematisches Wunderkind *(ugs. scherzh.)*

WHO *abbr.* **World Health Organization** WHO, *die*

who [hʊ, *stressed* hu:] *pron.* **a)** *interrog.* wer; *(coll.: whom)* wen; *(coll.: to whom)* wem; **~ are you talking about?** *(coll.)* von wem *od.* über wen sprichst du?; **~ did you give it to?** *(coll.)* wem hast du es gegeben?; **it was John – ~ else?** es war John – wer [denn] sonst?; **it was Mr ~?** es war Herr wie?; **I don't know ~'s ~ in the firm yet** ich kenne die Leute in der Firma noch nicht richtig; **he knows ~'s ~ in the publishing world** er weiß, wer in der Verlagsbranche welche Rolle spielt; **~ am I to object/argue** *etc.*? wie könnte ich Einwände erheben/etwas dagegen sagen *usw.*?; **~ would have thought it?** *(rhet.)* wer hätte das gedacht!; **b)** *rel.* der/die/das; *pl.* die; *(coll.: whom)* den/die/das; *(coll.: to whom)* dem/der/denen; **any person/he/those ~ ...:** wer ...; **they ~ ...:** diejenigen, die *od.* welche ...; **everybody ~ ...:** jeder, der ...; **I/you ~ ...:** ich, der ich/du, der du ...; **the man ~ I met last week/~ you were speaking to** *(coll.)* der Mann, den ich letzte Woche getroffen habe/mit dem du gesprochen hast; **c)** *(arch.: whoever)* wer

whoa [wəʊ] *int.* brr

who'd [hʊd, *stressed* hu:d] **a)** = **who had; b)** = **who would**

whodun[n]it [hu:'dʌnɪt] *n. (coll.)* Krimi, *der (ugs.)*

whoe'er [hu:'eə(r)] *(poet.),* **whoever** [hu:'evə(r)] *pron.* **a)** wer [immer]; **~ comes will be welcome** jeder, der kommt, ist willkommen; **marry/give it to ~ you like** heirate, wen/gib es, wem du willst; **b)** *(no matter who)* wer ... auch; **~ you may be** wer Sie auch sind; **~ you saw, it was not John** wen du auch gesehen hast, es war nicht John; **c)** *(coll.)* = **who ever** *see* **ever e**

whole [həʊl] **1.** *adj.* **a)** ganz; **give me your ~ attention, please** ich bitte um Ihre ganze Aufmerksamkeit; **that's the ~ point [of the exercise]** das ist der ganze Zweck der Übung *(ugs.)*; **the ~ lot [of them]** [sie] alle; **a ~ lot of people** eine ganze Menge Leute; *see also* **hog 1 a; b)** *(intact)* ganz; **roast sth. ~:** etw. im ganzen braten; **c)** *(undiminished)* ganz; **three ~ hours** drei volle Stunden. **2.** *n.* **a) the ~:** das Ganze; **the ~ of my money/the village/London** mein ganzes *od.* gesamtes Geld/das ganze Dorf/ganz London; **he spent the ~ of that year/of Easter abroad** er war jenes Jahr/zu Ostern die ganze Zeit im Ausland; **the ~ of Shakespeare** *or* **of Shakespeare's works** Shakespeares gesamte Werke; **until he had completed the ~ of it** bis er es ganz fertig hatte; **b)** *(total of parts)* Ganze, *das;* **as a ~:** als Ganzes; **sell sth. as a ~:** etw. im ganzen verkaufen; **on the ~:** im großen und ganzen; **on the ~ I am against it** alles in allem bin ich dagegen

whole: ~ 'cloth *n.* Tuchbahn, *die;* **[made up] out of ~ cloth** *(Amer. fig.)* von vorne bis hinten erfunden; **~food** *n.* Vollwertkost, *die;* **~-hearted** [həʊl'hɑ:tɪd] *adj.* herzlich ⟨*Dank, Dankbarkeit, Glückwünsche*⟩; tiefempfunden ⟨*Dankbarkeit, Reue*⟩; rückhaltlos ⟨*Unterstützung, Hingabe, Ergebenheit*⟩; leidenschaftlich ⟨*Anhänger, Verfechter usw.*⟩; **with ~-hearted devotion/dedication** mit äußerster Hingabe; **~-heartedly** [həʊl'hɑ:tɪdlɪ] *adv.* von ganzem Herzen ⟨*gratulieren, danken, zustimmen*⟩; rückhaltlos ⟨*unterstützen*⟩; **~ 'holiday** *n.* ganzer freier Tag; **~-length** *see* **full-length; ~ 'life insurance** *n.* Todesfallversicherung, *die;* **~ meal** *n.* Vollkornmehl, *das;* **~meal** *adj.* Vollkorn-; **~ 'milk** *n.* Vollmilch, *die*

wholeness ['həʊlnɪs] *n., no pl.* Ganzheit, *die; (completeness)* Vollständigkeit, *die*

whole: ~ note *n. (Amer. Mus.)* ganze Note; **~ 'number** *n. (Math.)* ganze Zahl; **~sale 1.** *adj.* **a)** *(Commerc.)* Großhandels-; **~sale dealer** *or* **merchant** Großhändler, *der/*-händlerin, *die;* **~sale grocer** Lebensmittelgroßhändler, *der/*-großhändlerin, *die;* **the ~sale trade** der Großhandel; **our business is ~sale only** wir sind ein reines Großhandelsgeschäft; **these prices are ~sale** das sind Großhandelspreise; **b)** *(fig.: on a large scale)* massenhaft; Massen-; **in a ~sale way** massenweise; **c)** *(fig.: indiscriminate)* pauschal; **2.** *adv.* **a)** *(Commerc.)* en gros ⟨*[ein]kaufen, verkaufen*⟩; im Großhandel ⟨*[ein]kaufen*⟩; *(at wholesale price)* zum Einkaufs- *od.* Großhandelspreis; **b)** *(fig.: on a large scale)* massenweise; **c)** *(fig.: indiscriminately)* pauschal; **he punished them ~sale** er bestrafte sie samt und sonders; **3.** *n. (Commerc.)* Großhandel, *der;* **4.** *v. t. (Commerc.)* en gros *od.* als Großhändler/-händlerin verkaufen

wholesaler ['həʊlseɪlə(r)] *n. (Commerc.)* Grossist, *der/*Grossistin, *die (fachspr.);* Großhändler, *der/*-händlerin, *die*

wholesome ['həʊlsəm] *adj.* gesund; bekömmlich ⟨*Essen, Getränk*⟩; erbaulich ⟨*Lektüre, Thema, Anblick*⟩; positiv ⟨*Einfluß*⟩

wholesomely ['həʊlsəmlɪ] *adv.* **~ cooked food** auf gesunde Art zubereitetes Essen

wholesomeness ['həʊlsəmnɪs] *n., no pl.* Bekömmlichkeit, *die; (fig.: of reading, subject, etc.)* Erbaulichkeit, *die*

whole: ~-time *see* **full-time; ~ tone** *n. (Mus.)* Ganzton, *der;* **~ 'wheat** *n.* Vollweizen, *der*

who'll [hʊl, *stressed* hu:l] = **who will**

wholly ['həʊllɪ] *adv.* völlig; durch und durch ⟨*böse*⟩; **a ~ bad example** ein in jeder Hinsicht schlechtes Beispiel

'wholly-owned *adj. (Commerc.)* **~ subsidiary** hundertprozentige Tochter

whom [hu:m] *pron.* **a)** *interrog.* wen; *as indirect object* wem; **to ~/of ~ did you speak?** mit wem/von wem haben Sie gesprochen?; **b)** *rel.* den/die/das; *pl.* die; *as indirect object* dem/der/dem; *pl.* denen; **the children, the mother of ~ ...:** die Kinder, deren Mutter ...; **five children, all of ~ are coming** fünf Kinder, die alle mitkommen; **ten candidates, only the best of ~ ...:** zehn Kandidaten, von denen nur die besten ...; **c)** *(arch.: whomever)* wen/wem

whomever [hu:m'evə(r)], **whomsoever** [hu:msəʊ'evə(r)] *pron.* **a)** wen [immer]; *as indirect object* wem [immer]; **b)** *(no matter whom)* wen ... auch; *as indirect object* wem ... auch

whoop [wu:p] **1.** *v. i.* [aufgeregt] schreien; *(with joy, excitement)* juchzen *(ugs.);* jauchzen. **2.** *v. t.* **~ it up** *(coll.)* die Sau rauslassen *(salopp); (Amer.: stir up enthusiasm)* Stimmung machen. **3.** *n.* [aufgeregter] Schrei; *(of joy, excitement)* Juchzer, *der (ugs.);* Jauchzer, *der;* **with loud ~s** mit lautem Geschrei; **~ of joy** Freudenschrei, *der*

whoopee 1. [wʊ'pi:] *int.* juhu. **2.** ['wʊpi:] *n.* **make ~** *(coll.)* die Sau rauslassen *(ugs.)*

whooping ['hu:pɪŋ]: **~ cough** *n. (Med.)* Keuchhusten, *der;* **~ swan** *n. (Ornith.)* Singschwan, *der*

whoops [wʊps] *int.* hoppla

whoosh [wʊʃ] **1.** *v. i.* brausen; ⟨*Rakete, Geschoß:*⟩ zischen; **a train ~ed past** ein Zug brauste vorbei. **2.** *n.* Brausen, *das; (of rocket, projectile)* Zischen, *das;* **with a [loud] ~:** [laut] brausend/zischend

whop [wɒp] *v. t.,* **-pp-** *(sl.)* vermöbeln *(salopp); (fig.: defeat)* bügeln *(salopp)*

whopper ['wɒpə(r)] *n. (coll.)* **a)** Riese, *der;* **a ~ of a marrow/fish** ein Riesending von einem Kürbis/Fisch *(ugs.);* **b)** *(lie)* faustdicke Lüge; **tell a ~:** faustdick lügen

whopping ['wɒpɪŋ] *(coll.)* **1.** *adj.* riesig; Riesen- *(ugs.);* gepfeffert *(ugs.)* ⟨*Rechnung*⟩; faustdick ⟨*Lüge*⟩. **2.** *adv.* **~ big** *or* **great** *see* **1**

whore [hɔ:(r)] *(derog.)* **1.** *n.* **a)** *(prostitute)* Hure, *die;* **b)** *(loose woman)* Flittchen, *das.* **2.** *v. i.* **~ [around]** [herum]huren

'whore-house *n. (derog.)* Hurenhaus, *das (abwertend)*

whorl [wɔ:l] *n.* **a)** *(Bot.)* Wirtel, *der;* Quirl, *der;* **b)** *(circle in fingerprint)* Wirbel, *der;* **c)** *(turn of spiral)* Windung, *die*

whortleberry ['wɜ:tlbərɪ] *see* **bilberry**

who's [hu:z] **a)** = **who is; b)** = **who has**

whose [hu:z] *pron.* **a)** *interrog.* wessen; **b)** *rel.* dessen/deren/dessen; *pl.* deren; **the people ~ house this is** die Leute, denen dieses Haus gehört

whosesoever [hu:zsəʊ'evə(r)], **whosever** [hu:z'evə(r)] *pron.* wessen ... auch; **~ it is, ...:** wem er/sie/es auch gehört, ...

whosoe'er [hu:səʊ'eə(r)] *(poet.),* **whosoever** [hu:səʊ'evə(r)] wer auch immer

Who's Who [hu:z 'hu:] *n.* biographisches Lexikon; Who's who, *das*

who've [hʊv, *stressed* hu:v] *(coll.)* = **who have**

why [waɪ] **1.** *adv.* **a)** *(for what reason)* warum; *(for what purpose)* wozu; **~ is that?** warum das?; **and this/that is ~ I believe ...:** und darum glaube ich ...; **~ not buy it, if you like it?** kauf es dir doch, wenn es dir gefällt; **~ do we need another car?** wozu brauchen wir noch ein Auto?; **b)** *(on account of which)* **the reason ~ he did it** der Grund, aus dem *od.* warum er es tat; **I can see no reason ~ not** ich wüßte nicht, warum nicht. **2.** *int.* **~, certainly/of course!** aber sicher!; **~, if it isn't Jack!** na, das ist doch Jack!; aber das ist ja Jack!; **What should I do? – W~, pay up** Was soll ich machen? – Na *od.* Nun, zahlen!; **~, yes, I think so** jaja, ich glaube schon. **3.** *n.* **the ~s and wherefores** das Warum und Weshalb

WI *abbr.* **a) West Indies; b)** *(Brit.)* **Women's Institute**

wick [wɪk] *n.* Docht, *der;* **get on sb.'s ~** *(fig. sl.)* jmdm. auf den Keks gehen *(salopp)*

wicked ['wɪkɪd] **1.** *adj.* **a)** *(evil)* böse; schlecht ⟨*Charakter, Person, Welt*⟩; niederträchtig ⟨*Gedanken, Plan, Verhalten*⟩; schändlich ⟨*Gesetz, Buch*⟩; **the ~ villain** der Schurke; der Bösewicht *(veralt.);* **it was ~ of you to torment the poor cat** es war gemein von dir, die arme Katze zu quälen; **torture is ~:** die Folter ist etwas Böses; **b)** *(vicious)* boshaft ⟨*Zunge*⟩; übel ⟨*Schlag, Wetter, Wind, Frost, Geruch*⟩; **have a ~ temper** furchtbar jähzornig sein; **c)** *(coll.: scandalous)* himmelschreiend; sündhaft *(ugs.)* ⟨*Preis*⟩; **it's ~ how he's been treated** wie man ihn behandelt hat, das schreit zum Himmel; **it's a ~ shame** es ist eine wahre Schande; **d)** *(mischievous)* schalkhaft *(geh.);* **a ~ little fellow** ein kleiner Schlingel *(scherzh.);* **there was a ~ gleam in his eye** ihm sah der Schalk aus den Augen; **suddenly a ~ idea came to him** plötzlich fiel ihm etwas ganz Tückisches ein. **2.** *n. pl.* **the ~:** die Bösen

wickedly ['wɪkɪdlɪ] *adv.* **a)** *(evilly)* niederträchtig; *as sentence-modifier* niederträchtigerweise; **~ acquired gains** auf niederträchtige Weise erzielte Gewinne; **b)** *(viciously)* fürchterlich ⟨*kalt, schmerzend*⟩; **~ accurate** ätzend ⟨*Satire, Kritik, Karikatur*⟩; **c)** *(coll.: scandalously)* himmelschreiend; sündhaft *(ugs.)*⟨*teuer*⟩; **d)** *(mischievously)* schalkhaft; **a ~ playful look** ein verschmitzter Blick

wickedness ['wɪkɪdnɪs] *n.* **a)** *no pl. see* **wicked a:** Bosheit, *die;* Schlechtigkeit, *die;* Niederträchtigkeit, *die;* Schändlichkeit, *die;* **b)** *(evil act)* Niederträchtigkeit, *die;* **the greatest ~ that anyone can commit** die schlimmste Bosheit, die ein Mensch begehen kann; **c)** *no pl. (viciousness)* Boshaftigkeit, *die;* **d)** *no pl. (coll.: scandalousness)* Schändlichkeit, *die;* **the ~ of this waste** so eine himmelschreiende Verschwendung; **the ~ of the prices** die sündhaft hohen Preise; **e)** *no pl. (mischievousness)* Schalkhaftigkeit, *die;* **the ~ in her sense of humour** das Schalkhafte an ihrer Art Humor

wicker ['wɪkə(r)] *n.* Korbgeflecht, *das; attrib.* Korb⟨*waren, -möbel, -stuhl*⟩; geflochten ⟨*Korb, Matte*⟩; **~ fence** Flechtzaun, *der*

'wickerwork *n.* **a)** *(material)* Korbgeflecht, *das;* **b)** *(articles)* Korbwaren

wicket ['wɪkɪt] *n.* **a)** *(Cricket) (stumps)* Tor, *das;* Wicket, *das; (part of innings)* Spielabschnitt, *der mit dem Ausscheiden eines*

Schlagmannes endet; (central area of pitch) Wurfbahn, *die;* **another ~ has fallen** *or* **is down** noch ein Schlagmann ist aus; **at the ~:** [als Schlagmann] auf dem Spielfeld; **keep ~:** als Torwächter spielen; **lose one's ~** ⟨*Schlagmann:*⟩ ausscheiden; **they lost four ~s** vier Schlagmänner ihrer Mannschaft sind ausgeschieden; **take a ~:** einen Schlagmann zum Ausscheiden bringen; **third** *etc.* **~:** *Spielabschnitt zwischen zweitem und drittem usw. Schlagmannwechsel;* **win by two ~s** mit acht ausgeschiedenen Schlagmännern gewinnen; *see also* **sticky wicket; b)** *(gate)* Tor, *das;* **c)** *(Amer.: window-like opening)* Fenster, *das;* **d)** *(Amer.: croquet hoop)* Tor, *das*

wicket: ~-gate *n.* Tor, *das;* **~-keeper** *n. (Cricket)* Torwächter, *der*/-wächterin, *die;* Wicketkeeper, *der*

widdle ['wɪdl] *(coll./child lang.) see* **pee**

wide [waɪd] **1.** *adj.* **a)** *(broad)* breit; groß ⟨*Unterschied, Abstand, Winkel, Loch*⟩; weit ⟨*Kleidung*⟩; **allow** *or* **leave a ~ margin** *(fig.)* viel Spielraum lassen; **three feet ~:** drei Fuß breit; **b)** *(extensive)* weit; umfassend ⟨*Lektüre, Wissen, Kenntnisse*⟩; weitreichend ⟨*Einfluß*⟩; vielseitig ⟨*Interessen*⟩; groß ⟨*Vielfalt, Bekanntheit, Berühmtheit*⟩; reichhaltig ⟨*Auswahl, Sortiment*⟩; breit ⟨*Publizität*⟩; weitverzweigt ⟨*Netz*⟩; **have ~ appeal** weite Kreise ansprechen; **it has now achieved ~ acceptance** es wird jetzt weithin akzeptiert; **a species of ~ distribution** eine weitverbreitete Art; **the ~ world** die weite Welt; **I'll search the ~ world over** ich werde auf der ganzen weiten Welt suchen; **c)** *(liberal)* großzügig; **d)** *(fully open)* weit geöffnet; **e)** *(off target)* **be ~ of sth.** etw. verfehlen; **be ~ of the mark** *(fig.)* ⟨*Annahme, Bemerkung:*⟩ nicht zutreffen; **you're ~ of the mark** *(fig.)* du liegst falsch *(ugs.); see also* **berth 1a; f)** *(Brit. sl.)* **~ boy** gerissener Kerl *(ugs.).* **2.** *adv.* **a)** *(fully)* weit; **open ~!** ganz [weit] aufmachen!; **~ awake** hellwach; *(fig. coll.)* gewitzt; **I'm ~ awake to your tricks** ich durchschaue deine Tricks; *see also* **wide open; b)** *(off target)* **shoot ~:** danebenschießen; **fall ~ of the target, go ~:** das Ziel verfehlen; **aim ~/~ of sth.** daneben/neben etw. *(Akk.)* zielen; **c)** *(widely)* weit; *see also* **far 1d. 3.** *n.* **a)** *(Cricket)* Weitball, *der;* **b) dead to the ~:** fix und fertig *(ugs.)*

-wide *in comb.* **city-/county-~:** in der ganzen Stadt/Grafschaft *nachgestellt;* **Europe-~:** europaweit; *see also* **countrywide; world-wide** *etc.*

wide: ~-angle 'lens *n. (Photog.)* Weitwinkelobjektiv, *das;* **~-eyed** *adj. (surprised)* mit großen Augen *nachgestellt;* **gaze with ~-eyed innocence** mit großen, unschuldigen [Kinder]augen gucken

widely ['waɪdlɪ] *adv.* **a)** *(over a wide area)* weit ⟨*verbreitet, gestreut*⟩; locker, in großen Abständen ⟨*verteilt*⟩; **a ~ distributed species** eine weitverbreitete Art; **he has travelled ~ in Europe** er ist in Europa viel gereist; **advertise a product ~:** für ein Produkt in großem Stil werben; **a ~ travelled man** ein weitgereister Mann; **a ~ read man** ein [sehr] belesener Mann; **b)** *(by many people)* weithin ⟨*bekannt, akzeptiert*⟩; **a ~ held view** eine weitverbreitete Ansicht; **it is ~ rumoured that ...:** allgemein wird gemunkelt *(ugs.),* daß ...; **it is not ~ understood why ...:** es wird vielfach nicht verstanden *od.* viele verstehen nicht, warum ...; **c)** *(in a wide sense)* im weiten Sinne ⟨*gebraucht*⟩; weit ⟨*interpretiert*⟩; **d)** *(greatly)* stark, erheblich ⟨*sich unterscheiden*⟩; sehr ⟨*verschieden, unterschiedlich*⟩

widen ['waɪdn] **1.** *v.t.* verbreitern; *(fig.)* erweitern; vergrößern ⟨*Unterschied, Gegensatz*⟩; **let's ~ our campaign to include young people** wir wollen unsere Kampagne auch auf die jungen Leute ausdehnen. **2.** *v.i.* sich verbreitern; breiter werden; *(fig.)* sich erweitern; ⟨*Interessen:*⟩ vielfältiger werden; ⟨*Unterschied, Gegensatz:*⟩ größer werden; **the valley ~s into a plain** das Tal erweitert sich zu einer Ebene

~ 'out *v.i.* sich verbreitern; breiter werden; **~ out into sth.** sich zu etw. erweitern

wide: ~-open *attrib. adj.,* **~ 'open** *pred. adj.* weit aufstehend *od.* geöffnet ⟨*Fenster, Tür*⟩; weit aufgerissen ⟨*Mund, Augen*⟩; weit ⟨*Landschaft, Fläche*⟩; **the ~-open spaces of North America** die Weite der nordamerikanischen Landschaft; **be ~ open** ⟨*Fenster, Tür:*⟩ weit offenstehen; ⟨*Mund, Augen:*⟩ weit aufgerissen sein; **be ~ open to attack/criticism/immoral influences** Angriffen/der Kritik/moralisch verderblichen Einflüssen ausgesetzt sein; **be ~ open to exploitation** der Ausbeutung schutzlos preisgegeben sein; **lay** *or* **leave oneself/sb. ~ open to sth.** sich/jmdn. einer Sache *(Dat.)* schutzlos preisgeben; **the contest is still ~ open** der Wettbewerb *od.* der Ausgang des Wettbewerbs ist noch völlig offen; **a ~-open town** *(Amer.)* eine Stadt, in der jeder macht, was er will; **~-ranging** ['waɪdreɪndʒɪŋ] *adj.* weitgehend ⟨*Maßnahme, Veränderung*⟩; weitreichend ⟨*Auswirkungen*⟩; ausführlich ⟨*Diskussion, Gespräch*⟩; universal ⟨*Geist*⟩; **~ 'screen** *n. (Cinemat.)* Breitwand, *die;* **~spread** *adj.* weitverbreitet *präd. getrennt geschr.* ⟨*Art, Ansicht*⟩; groß ⟨*Nachfrage, Beliebtheit*⟩; von vielen geteilt ⟨*Sympathie*⟩; **become ~spread** sich [weit] ausbreiten; **there was a ~spread demand for reform** Reformen wurden allgemein *od.* allerseits gefordert

widgeon ['wɪdʒən] *n. (Ornith.)* Pfeifente, *die*

widow ['wɪdəʊ] **1.** *n.* **a)** Witwe, *die;* **be left/made a ~:** zur Witwe werden; **golf ~** *(joc.)* Golfwitwe, *die; see also* **black widow; grass widow; b)** *(Cards)* zusätzliches Blatt; **c)** *(Printing)* Hurenkind, *das.* **2.** *v.t.* zur Witwe machen ⟨*Frau*⟩; zum Witwer machen ⟨*Mann*⟩; **be ~ed** zur Witwe/zum Witwer werden **(by** durch)

widowed ['wɪdəʊd] *adj.* verwitwet

widower ['wɪdəʊə(r)] *n.* Witwer, *der*

widowhood ['wɪdəʊhʊd] *n.* Witwenschaft, *die;* **[the state of] ~:** der Witwenstand; **during her ~:** als sie Witwe war

widow's: ~ 'peak *n. in der Stirnmitte spitz zulaufender Haaransatz;* **~ 'pension** *n.* Witwenrente, *die;* **~ 'weeds** *see* **weeds**

width [wɪdθ] *n.* **a)** *(measurement)* Breite, *die; (of garment)* Weite, *die;* **what is the ~ of ...?** wie breit/weit ist ...?; **be half a metre in ~:** einen halben Meter breit/weit sein; **b)** *(large scope)* großer Umfang; *(of definition)* Weite, *die; (of interests)* Vielseitigkeit, *die;* **c)** *(piece of material)* Bahn, *die*

widthways ['wɪdθweɪz], **widthwise** ['wɪdθwaɪz] *adv.* in der Breite; **insert the card ~ into the machine** die Karte quer in den Automaten stecken

wield [wi:ld] *v.t. (literary)* führen *(geh.); (fig.)* ausüben ⟨*Macht, Einfluß usw.*⟩; **~ a stick/sword** einen Stock/ein Schwert schwingen

wiener ['vi:nə(r)] *n. (Amer.)* Würstchen, *das*

wife [waɪf] *n., pl.* **wives** [waɪvz] Frau, *die;* **give my regards to your** *or (coll.)* **the ~:** grüßen Sie Ihre Frau *od. (geh.)* Gattin von mir; **make sb. one's ~:** jmdn. zur Frau nehmen; **lawful wedded ~** *(Eccl.)* rechtmäßig angetraute Frau; **old wives' tale** Ammenmärchen, *das*

wife-swapping ['waɪfswɒpɪŋ] *n. (coll.)* Partnertausch, *der*

wig [wɪg] *n.* Perücke, *die*

wigging ['wɪgɪŋ] *n.* Rüffel, *der (ugs.)*

wiggle ['wɪgl] *(coll.)* **1.** *v.t.* hin und her bewegen; **~ one's ears/bottom** mit den Ohren/dem Hintern wackeln *(ugs.).* **2.** *v.i.* wackeln; *(move)* sich schlängeln; **make one's ears ~:** mit den Ohren wackeln; **~ into sth.** sich in etw. *(Akk.)* zwängen; **~ out of sth.** sich aus etw. winden/*(fig.)* herauswinden. **3.** *n.* Wackeln, *das;* **get a ~ on** *(Amer. sl.)* sich ranhalten *(ugs.)*

wiggly ['wɪglɪ] *adj.* schlangenlinienförmig ⟨*Naht, Saum*⟩; Schlangenlinien⟨*muster, -form*⟩; **~ line** Schlangenlinie, *die*

wigwam ['wɪgwæm] *n.* Wigwam, *der*

wild [waɪld] **1.** *adj.* **a)** *(undomesticated)* wildlebend ⟨*Tier*⟩; *(uncultivated)* wildwachsend ⟨*Pflanze*⟩; **an animal in its ~ state** ein Tier in freier Wildbahn *od.* in Freiheit; **grow ~:** wild wachsen; **~ beast** wildes Tier; **b)** *(rough)* unzivilisiert; *(bleak)* wild ⟨*Landschaft, Gegend*⟩; **c)** *(unrestrained)* wild; ungezügelt; wild, wüst ⟨*Bursche, Unordnung, Durcheinander*⟩; wütend ⟨*Mob*⟩; **he was a little ~:** er führte ein etwas ungestümes Leben; **~ and woolly** *(coll.)* wüst ⟨*Aussehen, Kerl*⟩; verrückt ⟨*Ideen*⟩; **run ~** ⟨*Pferd, Hund:*⟩ frei herumlaufen; ⟨*Kind:*⟩ herumtoben; ⟨*Pflanzen:*⟩ wuchern; *(derog.)* ⟨*Hund:*⟩ herumstreunen; **let one's imagination run ~:** seiner Phantasie freien Lauf lassen; **d)** *(stormy)* stürmisch; tobend ⟨*Wellen*⟩; **e)** *(excited)* rasend ⟨*Wut, Zorn, Eifersucht, Beifall*⟩; unbändig ⟨*Freude, Wut, Zorn, Schmerz*⟩; wild ⟨*Erregung, Zorn, Geschrei*⟩; erregt ⟨*Diskussion*⟩; panisch ⟨*Angst*⟩; irr ⟨*Blick*⟩; **be/become ~ [with sth.]** [vor etw. *(Dat.)*] außer sich *(Dat.)* sein/außer sich *(Akk.)* geraten; **send** *or* **drive sb. ~:** jmdn. rasend vor Erregung machen; **f)** *(coll.: very keen)* **be ~ about sb./sth.** wild auf jmdn./etw. sein; **be ~ to do sth.** wild darauf sein, etw. zu tun; **I'm not ~ about it** ich bin nicht wild darauf *(ugs.);* **g)** *(coll.: angry)* wütend; **be ~ with** *or* **at sb.** eine Wut auf jmdn. haben; **make** *or* **drive sb. ~:** jmdn. in Rage bringen *(ugs.);* **I was ~ when I heard ...:** ich sah rot *(ugs.) od.* wurde wild *(ugs.),* als ich hörte, ...; **h)** *(reckless)* ungezielt ⟨*Schuß, Schlag*⟩; unbedacht ⟨*Verhalten, Versprechen, Gerede*⟩; aus der Luft gegriffen ⟨*Anschuldigungen, Behauptungen*⟩; abwegig ⟨*Geschichte*⟩; maßlos ⟨*Übertreibung*⟩; irrwitzig ⟨*Plan, Idee, Versuch, Hoffnung*⟩; **he made a ~ guess** er hat aufs Geratewohl *od. (ugs.)* ins Blaue hinein geschätzt; *see also* **dream 1c. 2.** *n.* **the ~[s]** die Wildnis; **see an animal in the ~:** ein Tier in freier Wildbahn sehen; **in the ~s** *(coll.)* in der Pampa *(ugs.);* **[out] in the ~s of Yorkshire** *(coll.)* im tiefsten Yorkshire *(ugs.);* **the call of the ~:** der Ruf der Wildnis. **3.** *adv.* wild; **shoot ~** *(randomly)* wild in die Gegend ballern *(ugs.)*

wild: ~ 'boar *n. (Zool.)* Wildschwein, *das;* **~ card** *n.* **a)** *(Cards)* wilde Karte; **b)** *(Tennis)* Wild card *(ugs.);* **~ 'cat** *n. (Zool.)* Wildkatze, *die;* **~cat** *attrib. adj.* fragwürdig; **~cat strike** wilder Streik; **~cat well** Aufschlußbohrung, *die;* Wildcatbohrung, *die*

wilderness ['wɪldənɪs] *n.* Wildnis, *die; (desert)* Wüste, *die;* **cry in the ~** *(fig.)* tauben Ohren predigen; **a voice [crying] in the ~** *(fig.)* ein Rufer in der Wüste; **be in the ~** *(Polit.)* alle Bedeutung verloren haben

wild: ~-eyed *adj.* mit irrem Blick *nachgestellt;* **~fire** *n. (Mil. Hist.)* griechisches Feuer; *see also* **spread 2a; ~fowl** *n., pl. same* Federwild, *das; (Cookery)* Wildgeflügel, *das;* **~-'goose chase** *n. (fig.: hopeless quest)* aussichtslose Suche; **send sb. on a ~-goose chase** jmdn. einem Phantom nachjagen lassen; **~ 'horse** *n.* Wildpferd, *das;* **~ horses would not drag it from me** *(fig.)* eher beiße ich mir die Zunge ab[, als daß ich es erzähle]; **~ horses would not make me leave here** keine zehn Pferde kriegen mich von hier weg *(ugs.);* **~life** *n. no pl., no indef. art.* die Tier- und Pflanzenwelt; die Natur;

~**life park/reserve/sanctuary** Naturpark, *der*/-reservat, *das*/-schutzgebiet, *das*

wildly ['waɪldlɪ] *adv.* **a)** *(unrestrainedly)* wild; **run ~ all over the house** ‹*Kinder:*› wie wild im ganzen Haus herumtoben; **b)** *(stormily)* wild; **the wind blew ~:** der Wind blies heftig; **c)** *(excitedly)* rasend ‹*eifersüchtig*›; unbändig ‹*verliebt, sich freuen, sich verlieben*›; wild ‹*schreien, applaudieren*›; erregt ‹*diskutieren*›; **I'm not ~ interested in it** *(iron.)* ich interessiere mich nicht übermäßig dafür; **be ~ excited about sth.** über etw. *(Akk.)* ganz aus dem Häuschen sein *(ugs.)*; **he looked ~ about him** er blickte irr um sich; **d)** *(recklessly)* aufs Geratewohl; maßlos ‹*übertreiben*›; wirr ‹*daherreden, denken*›; **hit out ~:** [wie] wild um sich schlagen; **~ inaccurate** völlig ungenau

'wild man *n.* **a)** *(Anthrop.)* Wilde, *der;* **b)** *(Polit.)* Scharfmacher, *der*

wildness ['waɪldnɪs] *n., no pl.* **a)** *(bleakness)* Wildheit, *die;* **b)** *(lack of restraint)* Wildheit, *die;* **I was frightened by the ~ of the mob** der wütende Mob machte mir angst; **after the ~ of his youth** nach seiner wilden *od.* stürmischen Jugend; **c)** *(storminess)* **the ~ of the weather/sea** das stürmische Wetter/die stürmische See; **the ~ of the waves/storm** die Gewalt der Wellen/des Sturms; **d)** *(excitement)* **the ~ of her joy** die Unbändigkeit, mit der sie sich freute; **the ~ of her jealousy** ihre rasende Eifersucht; **the ~ of their cheers/applause** die Begeisterung, mit der sie jubelten/applaudierten; **e)** *(of blow, shot)* Ungezieltheit, *die; (of promise, words)* Unbedachtheit, *die; (of scheme, attempt, idea, hope, quest)* Irrwitzigkeit, *die;* **f)** *(distractedness)* **the ~ of his look/eyes** sein irrer Blick; **there was a dangerous ~ in his eyes** seine Augen hatten etwas gefährlich Irres

wild: ~ **'oat** *see* **oat b**; ~ **'rice** *n. (Bot.)* Wasserreis, *der;* ~ **'silk** *n.* Wildseide, *die;* ~ **'thyme** *see* **thyme**; **W~ 'West** *pr. n.* Wilder Westen

wile [waɪl] *n.* List, *die;* Schlich, *der*

wilful ['wɪlfl] *adj.* **a)** *(deliberate)* vorsätzlich; bewußt ‹*Täuschung*›; **b)** *(obstinate)* starrsinnig

wilfully ['wɪlfəlɪ] *adv.* **a)** *(deliberately)* vorsätzlich; bewußt ‹*täuschen*›; **b)** *(obstinately)* starrsinnig

wilfulness ['wɪlflnɪs] *n., no pl.* **a)** *(deliberateness)* Vorsätzlichkeit, *die;* **b)** *(obstinacy)* Starrsinnigkeit, *die;* **out of ~:** aus Starrsinn

wiliness ['waɪlɪnɪs] *n., no pl. see* **wily**: Gewieftheit, *die;* Raffiniertheit, *die;* **the ~ of a fox** die Schläue eines Fuchses

¹will [wɪl] **1.** *v.t., only in pres.* **will,** *neg. (coll.)* **won't** [wəʊnt], *past* **would** [wʊd], *neg. (coll.)* **wouldn't** ['wʊdnt] **a)** *(consent to)* wollen; **They won't help me. W~/Would you?** Sie wollen mir nicht helfen. Bist du bereit?; **you ~ help her, won't you?** du hilfst ihr doch *od.* du wirst ihr doch helfen, nicht wahr?; **the car won't start** das Auto will nicht anspringen *od.* springt nicht an; **if you ~:** wenn Sie wollen; *(in request)* bitte; **~/would you pass the salt, please?** gibst du bitte mal das Salz rüber?/würdest du bitte mal das Salz rübergeben?; **~/would you come in?** kommen Sie doch herein; **now just listen, ~ you!** jetzt hör/hört gefälligst zu!; **~ you be quiet!** willst du/wollt ihr wohl ruhig sein!; **well, if you '~ go rock-climbing, ...:** bitte, wenn du unbedingt klettern gehen mußt, ...; **b)** *(be accustomed to)* pflegen; **the car ~ occasionally break down** das Auto hat ab und zu mal eine Panne; **he ~ sit there hour after hour** er pflegt dort stundenlang zu sitzen; *(emphatic)* **children '~ make a noise** Kinder machen [eben] Lärm; **..., as young people '~: ...,** wie alle jungen Leute [es tun]; **he '~ insist on doing it** er besteht unbedingt darauf, es zu tun; **it 'would have to rain** natürlich mußte es regnen; **c)** *(wish)* wollen; **~ you have some more cake?** möchtest *od.* willst du noch etwas Kuchen?; **it shall be as you ~:** ganz wie Sie wünschen *(geh.) od.* wollen; **do as/what you ~:** mach, was du willst; **call it what [ever] you ~:** nenn es, wie du willst; **would to God that ...:** wollte Gott, daß ...; **d)** *(be able to)* **the box ~ hold 5 lb. of tea** in die Kiste gehen 5 Pfund Tee; **the theatre ~ seat 800** das Theater hat 800 Sitzplätze. **2.** *v. aux., forms as* **1: a)** *expr. simple future* werden; **this time tomorrow he ~ be in Oxford** morgen um diese Zeit ist er in Oxford; **tomorrow he ~ have been here a month** morgen ist er einen Monat hier; **one more cherry, and I ~ have eaten a pound** noch eine Kirsche und ich habe ein Pfund gegessen; **if today is Monday, tomorrow ~ be Tuesday** wenn heute Montag ist, ist morgen Dienstag; **b)** *expr. intention* **I promise I won't do it again** ich verspreche, ich mach's nicht noch mal; **You won't do that, ~ you? – Oh yes, I ~!** Du machst es doch nicht, oder? – Doch[, ich mach's]!; **~ do** *(coll.)* wird gemacht; mach ich *(ugs.)*; **c)** *in conditional clause* **if he tried, he would succeed** wenn er es versuchen würde, würde er es erreichen; **he would like/would have liked to see her** er würde sie gerne sehen/er hätte sie gerne gesehen; **d)** *(request)* **~ you please tidy up** würdest du bitte aufräumen?

²will 1. *n.* **a)** *(faculty)* Wille, *der;* **freedom of the ~:** Willensfreiheit, *die;* **have a ~ of one's own** [s]einen eigenen Willen haben; **an iron ~, a ~ of iron** ein eiserner Wille; **strength of ~:** Willensstärke, *die;* **b)** *(Law: testament)* Testament, *das;* **under his father's ~:** auf Grund des Testaments seines Vaters; *see also* **remember d; c)** *(desire)* **at ~:** nach Belieben; **~ to live** Lebenswille, *der;* **you must have the ~ to win** du mußt gewinnen wollen; **~ to** *or* **for peace** Friedenswille, *der;* Wille zum Frieden; **he has the power to do it, but lacks the ~:** er könnte es zwar, aber er will es nicht; **against one's/sb.'s ~:** gegen seinen/jmds. Willen; **of one's own [free] ~:** aus freien Stücken; **clash of ~s** ≈ Kollision der Interessen; **do sth. with a ~:** etw. mit großem Eifer *od.* Elan tun; **where there's a ~ there's a way** *(prov.)* wo ein Wille ist, ist auch ein Weg; **Thy ~ be done** *(Bibl.)* Dein Wille geschehe; *see also* **free will; d)** *(disposition)* **with the best ~ in the world** bei allem Wohlwollen; *in neg. clause* beim besten Willen; *see also* **good will; ill will. 2.** *v.t.* **a)** *(intend)* wollen; **God has ~ed it so** Gott hat es so gewollt; **b)** *(compel by ~)* durch Willenskraft erzwingen; **~ oneself to do sth.** sich zwingen, etw. zu tun; **~ sb. to do sth.** ‹*Hypnotiseur, Therapeut:*› jmdm. suggerieren, etw. zu tun; **~ sb. to win** jmds. Sieg mit aller Kraft herbeiwünschen. **3.** *v.i.* wollen; **if God so ~s, God ~ing** so Gott will

-willed [wɪld] *adj. in comb.* **strong-/weak-~:** willensstark/-schwach; **be iron-~:** einen eisernen Willen haben

willful *etc. (Amer.) see* **wilful** *etc.*

William ['wɪljəm] *pr. n. (Hist., as name of ruler etc.)* Wilhelm *(der)*

willies ['wɪlɪz] *n. pl. (sl.)* **sb. gets the ~:** jmdm. wird ganz anders *(ugs.)*; **it gives me the ~:** dabei wird mir ganz anders *(ugs.)*

willing ['wɪlɪŋ] **1.** *adj.* **a)** *(ready)* willig; **ready and ~:** bereit; **be ~ to do sth.** bereit sein, etw. zu tun; **I'm ~ to believe you're right** ich will gerne glauben, daß du recht hast; **she'd be more ~ to do it/to help if ...:** sie wäre eher dazu bereit/eher bereit zu helfen, wenn ...; **he was ~ to be converted** er ließ sich bereitwillig bekehren; **if my daughter is ~, then you may marry her** wenn meine Tochter es will, dürfen Sie sie heiraten; **b)** *attrib. (readily offered)* willig; **she gave ~ assistance/help** sie half bereitwillig; **lend a ~ hand** bereitwillig helfen. **2.** *n.* **show ~:** guten Willen zeigen

willingly ['wɪlɪŋlɪ] *adv.* **a)** *(with pleasure)* gern[e]; **their ~ offered services** ihre bereitwillig angebotenen Dienste; **b)** *(voluntarily)* freiwillig; **they did not come ~:** sie kamen nur widerstrebend

willingness ['wɪlɪŋnɪs] *n., no pl.* Bereitschaft, *die;* **eager ~:** Beflissenheit, *die;* **he always shows a ~ to help** er ist immer bereit zu helfen

will-o'-the-wisp [wɪləðə'wɪsp] *n.* **a)** Irrlicht, *das;* **b)** *(fig.)* Schimäre, *die*

willow ['wɪləʊ] *n.* Weide, *die*

willow: ~**-herb** *n. (Bot.)* Weidenröschen, *das;* ~**-pattern** *n.* Weidenmuster, *das;* ~**-warbler** *n. (Ornith.)* Laubsänger, *der*

willowy ['wɪləʊɪ] *adj.* gertenschlank

'will-power *n.* Willenskraft, *die;* **her ~ has cracked** ihr Wille ist gebrochen

willy ['wɪlɪ] *n. (sl./child lang.)* Pimmel, *der (salopp, fam.)*

willy-nilly [wɪlɪ'nɪlɪ] *adv.* wohl oder übel ‹*etw. tun müssen*›; **it will happen ~:** es wird so oder so passieren

wilt [wɪlt] **1.** *v.i.* **a)** *(Bot.: wither)* welk werden; welken; **b)** *(fig.: lose vigour)* ‹*Person:*› schlapp werden, *(ugs.)* abschlaffen; ‹*Interesse, Begeisterung:*› abflauen; ‹*Hoffnung, Energie, Kraft*› dahinschwinden. **2.** *v.t.* *(Bot.)* welken lassen; **the drought has ~ed the plants** durch die Trockenheit sind die Pflanzen welk geworden

Wilton ['wɪltən] *n.* Wiltonteppich, *der*

wily ['waɪlɪ] *adj.* listig; gewieft ‹*Person*›; raffiniert ‹*Trick, Argumentation, Plan usw.*›

wimp [wɪmp] *n. (coll. derog.)* Schlappschwanz, *der (ugs.)*

wimpish [wɪmpɪʃ] *adj. (coll. derog.)* lahmarschig *(derb)*

win [wɪn] **1.** *v.t.,* **-nn-, won** [wʌn] **a)** gewinnen; bekommen ‹*Stipendium, Auftrag, Vertrag, Recht*›; ernten ‹*Beifall, Dank*›; **~ the long jump** im Weitsprung gewinnen; **~ an argument/debate** aus einem Streit/einer Debatte als Sieger hervorgehen; **~ promotion** befördert werden; **~ sb. sth.** jmdm. etw. einbringen; **~ sb. sb.'s friendship** jmdm. jmds. Freundschaft gewinnen; **her sad story won his sympathy** ihre traurige Geschichte fand sein Mitgefühl; **~ a reputation [for oneself]** sich *(Dat.)* einen Ruf erwerben *od.* einen Namen machen; **~ sth. from** *or* **off sb.** jmdm. etw. abnehmen; **you can't ~ them all** *(coll.)*, **you ~ some, you lose some** *(coll.)* man kann nicht immer Glück haben; *see also* **spur 1 a; toss 3 a; b)** *(sl.: steal)* organisieren *(ugs.)*; **c) ~ one's way to the top** *(fig.)* sich an die Spitze hocharbeiten; **~ one's way to a scholarship** sich *(Dat.)* ein Stipendium verdienen; **~ oneself a place in the history books** sich *(Dat.)* einen Platz in den Geschichtsbüchern sichern; **~ one's way into sb.'s heart/affections** jmds. Herz/Zuneigung gewinnen; **d)** *(Mining)* gewinnen. **2.** *v.i.,* **-nn-, won a)** gewinnen; *(in battle)* siegen; **you ~** *(have defeated me)* du hast gewonnen *(ugs.)*; **those who ~:** die Gewinner/Sieger; **~ or lose** wie es auch ausgeht/ausgehen würde; **you can't ~** *(lit. or fig.) (coll.)* da hat man keine Chance *(ugs.)*; *(you can't satisfy everyone)* man kann es nicht allen recht machen; *see also* **canter 1; hand 1 g; head 1 a; b) ~ clear/free** sich befreien. **3.** *n.* Sieg, *der;* **have a ~:** gewinnen

~ **'back** *v.t.* zurückgewinnen

~ **'out** *v.i. (coll.)* ~ **out [over sb./sth.]** sich [gegen jmdn./etw.] durchsetzen

~ **'over,** ~ **'round** *v.t.* bekehren; *(to one's side)* auf seine Seite bringen; *(convince)* überzeugen; **~ sb. over** *or* **round to a plan/to a faith/to one's point of view** jmdn. für einen Plan gewinnen/zu einem Glauben bekehren/zu seiner Ansicht bekehren *od.* von seiner Ansicht überzeugen

~ **'through** *v.i.* Erfolg haben; **~ through to the next round** die nächste Runde erreichen

wince [wɪns] **1.** *v. i.* zusammenzucken (**at** bei); **she did not ~ when the dentist started drilling** sie verzog keine Miene, als der Zahnarzt anfing zu bohren; **he ~d under the pain/the insult** der Schmerz/die Beleidigung ließ ihn zusammenzucken. **2.** *n.* Zusammenzucken, *das;* **give a ~ [of pain]** [vor Schmerz] zusammenzucken; **without a ~:** ohne eine Miene zu verziehen; ohne mit der Wimper zu zucken

winceyette [wɪnsɪ'et] *n. (Brit. Textiles)* Flanell, *der*

winch [wɪntʃ] **1.** *n.* **a)** *(crank)* Kurbel, *die;* **b)** *(Brit. Fishing)* Rolle, *die;* Haspel, *die;* **c)** *(windlass)* Winde, *die.* **2.** *v. t.* winden; mit einer Winde ziehen; **~ up** hochwinden

¹wind [wɪnd] **1.** *n.* **a)** Wind, *der;* **before the ~** *(Naut.)* vor dem Wind; **be in the ~** *(fig.)* in der Luft liegen; **down the ~:** mit dem Wind; in der Richtung des Windes; **see how** *or* **which way the ~ blows** *or* **lies** *(fig.)* sehen, woher der Wind weht; **into the ~** *(Naut.)* in den Wind; **off the ~** *(Naut.)* aus dem Wind; **like the ~:** wie der Wind ‹*laufen, fahren usw.*›; **sail close to** *or* **near the ~:** hart am Wind segeln; *(fig.)* sich hart an der Grenze des Erlaubten bewegen; **sail too close to** *or* **near the ~** *(fig.)* den Bogen überspannen; **take the ~ out of sb.'s sails** *(fig.)* jmdm. den Wind aus den Segeln nehmen; **throw sb.'s advice to the ~s** jmds. Rat in den Wind schlagen; **throw caution/discretion/one's principles to the ~s** alle Vorsicht/alle Diskretion/seine Grundsätze über Bord werfen; **to the [four] ~s** in alle [vier] Winde; **the ~[s] of change** ein frischer Wind *(fig.); see also* **whirlwind a; b)** *no pl. (Mus.) (stream of air) (in organ)* Wind, *der; (in other instruments)* Luftstrom, *der; (instruments)* Bläser; **c)** *no pl. (blast of air)* Luftstrom, *der; (of missile)* Druckwelle, *die;* **d)** *(Hunting)* Witterung, *die;* **get ~ of sth.** *(fig.)* Wind von etw. bekommen; **e)** *no pl., no indef. art. (flatulence)* Blähungen; **break ~:** eine Blähung abgehen lassen; **get/have the ~ up** *(sl.)* Manschetten *(ugs.) od.* Schiß *(salopp)* kriegen/haben; **put the ~ up sb.** *(sl.)* jmdm. Schiß machen *(salopp);* **f)** *(breath)* **lose/have lost one's ~:** außer Atem kommen/sein; **recover** *or* **get one's ~:** wieder zu Atem kommen; **you need a lot of ~ to run such a long distance** der Atem darf einem nicht so schnell ausgehen, wenn man so eine lange Strecke laufen will; **get one's second ~** *(lit. or fig.)* sich wieder steigern; **pause to get one's second ~** *(fig.)* eine Pause machen, um einen neuen Anlauf zu nehmen; **g)** *no pl., no art. (empty words)* [leeres] Geschwätz. **2.** *v. t.* **a)** *(make breathless)* außer Atem bringen; **the blow ~ed him** der Schlag nahm ihm den Atem; **be ~ed** außer Atem sein; **he was ~ed by the blow to his stomach** nach dem Schlag in die Magengrube schnappte er nach Luft; **b)** *(burp)* ein Bäuerchen machen lassen *(fam.)* ‹*Baby*›

²wind [waɪnd] **1.** *v. i.,* **wound** [waʊnd] **a)** *(curve)* sich winden; *(move)* sich schlängeln; **the road wound through/among the hills** die Straße wand *od.* schlängelte sich zwischen den Hügeln hindurch; **b)** *(coil)* sich wickeln. **2.** *v. t.,* **wound a)** *(coil)* wikkeln; *(on to reel)* spulen; **~ wool into a ball** Wolle zu einem Knäuel aufwickeln; **~ sth. off sth./on [to] sth.** etw. von etw. [ab]wickeln/auf etw. *(Akk.)* [auf]wickeln; **~ sb. round one's finger** jmdn. um den Finger wickeln *(ugs.);* **b)** *(with key etc.)* aufziehen ‹*Uhr*›; **c) ~ one's/its way** sich winden; sich schlängeln; **a road ~ing its way among the mountains** eine Straße, die sich zwischen den Bergen hindurchwindet *od.* -schlängelt; **d)** *(coil into ball)* zu einem Knäuel/zu Knäueln aufwickeln; **e)** *(surround)* wickeln; *(cover with coil)* umwickeln; bewickeln ‹*Spule*›; **he wound the injured arm in a piece of cloth** er umwickelte den verletzten Arm mit einem Tuch; **f)** *(winch)* winden; **~ sth. with a winch** etw. mit einer Winde ziehen. **3.** *n.* **a)** *(curve)* Windung, *die;* **b)** *(turn)* Umdrehung, *die;* **give sth. a ~:** etw. aufziehen; **give the clock one more ~:** die Uhr noch [um] eine Umdrehung weiter aufziehen

~ 'back *v. t. & i.* zurückspulen

~ 'down 1. *v. t.* **a)** *(lower)* mit einer Winde herunter-/hinunterlassen; herunterdrehen ‹*Autofenster*›; **b)** *(fig.: reduce gradually)* einschränken; drosseln ‹*Produktion*›; *(and cease)* allmählich einstellen; auslaufen lassen ‹*Produktion*›. **2.** *v. i. (lose momentum)* ablaufen; *(fig.)* ‹*Produktion:*› zurückgehen; *(cease)* auslaufen

~ 'forward *see* **~ on**

~ 'in *v. t.* einrollen ‹*Angelschnur*›; einholen ‹*Fisch, Tau*›; *(on to sth.)* aufwickeln

~ 'on *v. t. & i.* weiterspulen

~ 'up 1. *v. t.* **a)** *(raise)* hochwinden; *(winch up)* [mit einer Winde] hochziehen; hochdrehen ‹*Autofenster*›; **b)** *(coil)* aufwickeln; **c)** *(with key etc.)* aufziehen ‹*Uhr*›; **d)** *(make tense)* aufregen; erregen; **get wound up** sich aufregen; sich erregen; **she was wound up to a fury** sie kochte vor Wut; **e)** *(coll.: annoy deliberately)* auf die Palme bringen *(ugs.);* **f)** *(conclude)* beschließen ‹*Debatte, Rede*›; **g)** *(Finance, Law)* auflösen; einstellen ‹*Aktivitäten*›; **~ up one's affairs** seine Angelegenheiten in Ordnung bringen. **2.** *v. i.* **a)** *(conclude)* schließen; **he wound up for the Government** er sprach als letzter Redner aus dem Regierungslager; **..., he said, ~ing up: ...** sagte er abschließend; **~ up with ice-cream** mit Eis abschließen; **b)** *(Commerc.)* ‹*Firma:*› aufgelöst werden; **c)** *(coll.: end up)* **~ up in prison/hospital** [zum Schluß] im Gefängnis/Krankenhaus landen *(ugs.);* **~ up with a broken leg** sich *(Dat.)* am Ende noch ein gebrochenes Bein einhandeln. *See also* **wind-up**

wind [wɪnd]: **~bag** *n. (derog.)* Schwätzer, *der*/Schwätzerin, *die;* **~ band** *n. (Mus.)* Blaskapelle, *die; (section of orchestra)* Bläsergruppe, *die;* **~-blown** *adj.* vom Wind zerzaust ‹*Haar*›; **~-break** *n.* Windschutz, *der;* **~breaker** *(Amer.),* **~-cheater** *(Brit.) ns.* Windjacke, *die;* **~-chest** *n. (Mus.)* Windlade, *die;* **~-chill** *n. (Meteorol.)* **~-chill [factor** *or* **index]** Wind-chill-Index, *der;* **~-cone** *see* **wind-sock**

winded ['wɪndɪd] *adj.* nach Luft schnappend *nicht präd.;* **be ~:** außer Atem sein

winder ['waɪndə(r)] *n. (of watch)* Krone, *die; (of clock, toy)* Aufziehschraube, *die; (key)* Schlüssel, *der*

wind [wɪnd]: **~fall** *n.* **a)** Stück Fallobst; *(apple)* Fallapfel, *der;* **~s** Fallobst, *das;* **b)** *(fig.)* warmer Regen *(ugs.);* **repeated ~falls** ein warmer Regen nach dem anderen; **~ farm** *n.* Windpark, *der;* Windfarm, *die;* **~-flower** *n. (Bot.)* Windröschen, *das;* **~-force** *n. (Meteorol.)* Windstärke, *die;* **~-gauge** *n. (Meteorol.)* Windmesser, *der;* **~hover** *n. (Ornith.)* Rüttelfalke, *der*

winding ['waɪndɪŋ] **1.** *attrib. adj.* gewunden; **the ~ procession** der sich dahinschlängelnde Zug. **2.** *n.* **a)** *in pl. (of road, river)* Windungen; **b)** *(Electr.)* Wicklung, *die*

winding: ~ sheet *n.* Leichentuch, *das;* **~ 'staircase** *n.* Wendeltreppe, *die*

wind [wɪnd]: **~ instrument** *n. (Mus.)* Blasinstrument, *das;* **~-jammer** ['wɪnddʒæmə(r)] *n. (Naut.)* Windjammer, *der*

windlass ['wɪndləs] *n.* Winde, *die*

windless ['wɪndlɪs] *adj.* windstill

windmill ['wɪndmɪl] *n.* **a)** Windmühle, *die; (to drive generator, water pump, etc.)* Windrad, *das;* **tilt at** *or* **fight ~s** *(fig.)* gegen Windmühlen kämpfen; **b)** *(toy)* Windrädchen, *das*

window ['wɪndəʊ] *n.* **a)** Fenster, *das;* **break a ~:** eine Fensterscheibe zerbrechen; ‹*Einbrecher:*› eine Fensterscheibe einschlagen; **go out of the ~** *(fig. coll.)* den Bach runtergehen *(ugs.);* **b)** *(fig.: means of observation)* **a ~ on the West/world** ein Fenster zum Westen/zur Welt; **a ~ on life** ein Spiegel des Lebens; **c)** *(for display of goods)* [Schau]fenster, *das;* **d)** *(for issue of tickets etc.)* Schalter, *der;* **e)** *(Astronaut.: time when launch is possible)* Startfenster, *das;* **f)** *(Computing)* Fenster, *das*

window: ~-box *n.* Blumenkasten, *der;* **~-cleaner** *n.* Fensterputzer, *der*/-putzerin, *die;* **~-cleaning** *n.* Fensterputzen, *das;* **~ display** *n.* Schaufensterauslage, *die;* **~-dresser** *n.* Schaufensterdekorateur, *der*/-dekorateurin, *die;* **~-dressing** *n.* Schaufensterdekoration, *die; (fig.)* Schönfärberei, *die;* **~ envelope** *n.* Fenster[brief]umschlag, *der;* **~-frame** *n.* Fensterrahmen, *der;* **~-ledge** *n. (inside)* Fensterbank, *die; (outside)* Fenstersims, *der od. das;* **~-pane** *n.* Fensterscheibe, *die;* **~-seat** *n. (in building)* Fensterbank, *die; (in train etc.)* Fensterplatz, *der;* **~-shopper** *n.* Schaufensterbummler, *der*/-bummlerin, *die;* **~-shopping** *n.* Schaufensterbummeln, *das;* **go ~-shopping** einen Schaufensterbummel machen; **~-sill** *see* **~-ledge**

wind [wɪnd]: **~pipe** *n. (Anat.)* Luftröhre, *die;* **~ power** *n.* Windkraft, *die;* **~ proof** *adj.* windabweisend; **~proof jacket** Windjacke, *die;* **~ pump** *n.* Windpumpe, *die;* **~-rose** *n. (Meteorol.)* Windrose, *die;* **~screen,** *(Amer.)* **~shield** *ns. (Motor Veh.)* Windschutzscheibe, *die;* **~screen/shield-wiper** Scheibenwischer, *der;* **~-sleeve, ~-sock** *ns. (Aeronaut.)* Windsack, *der;* **~surfer** *n.* Windsurfer, *der;* **~surfing** *n. (Sport)* Windsurfen, *das;* **~-swept** *adj.* windgepeitscht; vom Wind zerzaust ‹*Person, Haare*›; **the ~-swept lake** der vom Wind bewegte See; **~-tunnel** *n. (Aeronaut.)* Windkanal, *der*

wind-up ['waɪndʌp] *n.* **a)** *(end)* [Ab]schluß, *der;* **b)** *(sl.: attempt to annoy)* **is this a ~?** willst du mich auf die Palme bringen? *(ugs.)*

windward ['wɪndwəd] **1.** *adj.* **~ side** Windseite, *die;* Luvseite, *die (bes. Seemannsspr.);* **in a ~ direction** gegen den Wind; luvwärts *(Seemannsspr.);* **W~ Islands** *pr. n. pl.* Inseln über dem Winde. **2.** *adv.* gegen den Wind. **3.** *n.* Windseite, *die;* Luv, *die (Seemannsspr.);* **sail to ~:** gegen den Wind segeln; **get to ~ of sth.** auf die Windseite einer Sache *(Gen.)* gehen/fahren *usw.*

windy ['wɪndɪ] *adj.* **a)** windig ‹*Tag, Ort, Wetter*›; **b)** *(wordy, empty)* phrasenhaft; Phrasen dreschend *(abwertend)* ‹*Person*›; **he is ~ and ineffectual** er drischt nur Phrasen und tut nichts; **c)** *(sl.: frightened)* **be/get ~:** Manschetten *(ugs.) od. (salopp)* Schiß haben/kriegen

wine [waɪn] *n.* **a)** Wein, *der;* **~, women, and song** Wein, Weib und Gesang; **put new ~ in old bottles** *(fig.)* neuen Wein in alte Schläuche füllen; *see also* **spirit 1 k; b)** *(colour)* Weinrot, *das*

wine: ~ and 'dine *v. t.* in großem Stil *od. (ugs.)* groß bewirten; **be ~d and dined at sb.'s expense** auf jmds. Kosten schlemmen; **~-bar** *n.* Weinstube, *die;* **~bottle** *n.* Weinflasche, *die;* **~-cellar** *n.* [Wein]keller, *der;* **~-cooler** *n.* Weinkühler, *der;* **~glass** *n.* Weinglas, *das;* **~-grower** *n.* Winzer, *der;* **~-growing 1.** *n.* Weinbau, *der;* **2.** *adj.* **~-growing area** Weingegend, *die;* **~-list** *n.* Weinkarte, *die;* **~-making** *n. Herstellung von Wein zu Hause in kleineren Mengen;* **~-merchant** *n.* Weinhändler, *der*/-händlerin, *die;* **~-merchants** *(business)* Weinhandlung, *die;* **~-'red** *adj.* weinrot

winery ['waɪnərɪ] *n.* Weinkellerei, *die*

wine: ~-**taster** *n.* Weinverkoster, *der/* -verkosterin, *die;* ~-**tasting** ['waɪnteɪstɪŋ] *n.* Weinprobe, *die;* ~-**vault** *n.* Weinkeller, *der;* ~-'**vinegar** *n.* Weinessig, *der;* ~-**waiter** *n.* Weinkellner, *der*

wing [wɪŋ] **1.** *n.* **a)** *(Ornith., Archit., Sport)* Flügel, *der;* **take** ~: auffliegen; **on the** ~: im Fluge; **spread** *or* **stretch one's** ~**s** *(fig.)* sich auf eigene Füße stellen; **take sb. under one's** ~: jmdn. unter seine Fittiche nehmen; **lend sb.** ~**s/lend** ~**s to sb.'s feet** jmdn./jmds. Schritte beflügeln; **b)** *(Aeronaut.)* [Trag]flügel, *der;* Tragfläche, *die;* ~**s** *(badge)* Pilotenabzeichen, *das;* Fliegerabzeichen, *das;* **get/have [got] one's** ~**s** seinen Pilotenschein kriegen/haben; **c)** *in pl. (Theatre)* Kulissen; **wait in the** ~**s** *(fig.)* auf seine Chance warten; **d)** *(Brit. Motor Veh.)* Kotflügel, *der;* **e)** *(Air Force)* Geschwader, *das.* **2.** *v. t.* **a)** *(wound)* am Flügel treffen, *(Jägerspr.)* flügeln ‹*Vogel*›; am Arm treffen ‹*Person*›; **b)** *(fig.: speed)* beflügeln *(geh.);* **c)** *(fly)* ~ **one's way** fliegen. **3.** *v. i.* fliegen

wing: ~-**case** *n. (Zool.)* Deckflügel, *der;* ~-**chair** *n.* Ohrensessel, *der;* ~-'**collar** *n.* Ecken- *od.* Klappenkragen, *der;* ~ **commander** *n. (Brit. Air Force)* Geschwaderkommandeur, *der*

wingding ['wɪŋdɪŋ] *n. (Amer. sl.)* **a)** *(party)* Sause, *die (salopp);* **b)** *(seizure)* [simulierter] Krampfanfall; **throw a** ~: einen Krampfanfall simulieren

winged [wɪŋd] *adj.* **a)** *(having wings)* geflügelt; **b)** *(wounded)* flügellahm geschossen; geflügelt *(Jägerspr.)*

-**winged** *adj. in comb.* mit ... Flügeln *nachgestellt;* **white-/black-/short-/long-**~: weiß-/schwarz-/kurz-/langflügelig

winger ['wɪŋə(r)] *n. (Sport)* Außenstürmer, *der/*-stürmerin, *die;* Flügel, *der*

wing: ~-**mirror** *n. (Brit. Motor Veh.)* Außenspiegel, *der;* ~-**nut** *n.* Flügelmutter, *die;* ~-**span,** ~-**spread** *ns.* [Flügel]spannweite, *die;* ~-**tip** *n.* Flügelspitze, *die*

wink [wɪŋk] **1.** *v. i.* **a)** *(blink)* blinzeln; *(as signal)* zwinkern; ~ **at sb.** jmdm. zuzwinkern; **be as easy as** ~**ing** kinderleicht *od.* ein Kinderspiel sein; **do sth. as easy as** ~**ing** *(coll.)* etw. mit Leichtigkeit tun; **b)** *(twinkle, flash)* blinken; **c)** ~ **at sth.** *(fig.: ignore)* über etw. *(Akk.)* hinwegsehen. **2.** *v. t.* **a)** ~ **one's eye/eyes** blinzeln; *(as signal)* zwinkern; ~ **one's eye at sb.** jmdm. zuzwinkern; **b)** *(flash)* blinken ‹*Signal, Nachricht usw.*›. **3.** *n.* **a)** Blinzeln, *das; (signal)* Zwinkern, *das;* **give sb. a [secret/sly/knowing** *etc.***]** ~: jmdm. [heimlich/verschmitzt/wissend *usw.*] zuzwinkern; *see also* ²**tip 2 d; b) not get a** ~ **of sleep, not sleep a** ~: kein Auge zutun; *see also* **forty 1**

winker ['wɪŋkə(r)] *n. (Motor Veh.)* Blinker, *der*

winkle ['wɪŋkl] **1.** *n.* Strandschnecke, *die.* **2.** *v. t.* ~ **out** herausholen, *(ugs.)* rauspfriemeln ‹*Gegenstand, Substanz*›; herausholen ‹*Person, Tier*›; ~ **sth. out of sb.** *(fig.)* etw. aus jmdm. rauskriegen *(ugs.)*

'**winkle-picker** *n. (sl.) spitzer Schuh*

winner ['wɪnə(r)] *n.* **a)** Sieger, *der/*Siegerin, *die; (of competition or prize)* Gewinner, *der/*Gewinnerin, *die; (winning shot)* Siegestreffer, *der; (winning goal)* Siegestor, *das;* **who is the** ~ **in this deal?** wer profitiert bei diesem Geschäft mehr?; **b)** *(successful thing)* Erfolg, *der; (successful play, product)* Renner, *der (ugs.);* Hit, *der (ugs.);* **you're on [to] a** ~ **with this idea/book** *(coll.)* diese Idee/dieses Buch wird garantiert ein Renner *od.* Hit *(ugs.)*

winning ['wɪnɪŋ] *adj.* **a)** *attrib.* siegreich; ~ **team** siegreiche Mannschaft; Siegermannschaft, *die;* **the** ~ **captain** der Kapitän der Siegermannschaft; **b)** *attrib. (bringing victory)* den Sieg bringend; ~ **number** Gewinnzahl, *die;* **the** ~ **entry** die preisgekrönte Einsendung; **c)** *(charming)* einnehmend; gewinnend ‹*Lächeln*›

winningly ['wɪnɪŋlɪ] *adv.* einnehmend; gewinnend ‹*lächeln*›

'**winning-post** *n. (Sport)* Zielpfosten, *der*

winnings ['wɪnɪŋz] *n. pl.* Gewinn, *der*

winnow ['wɪnəʊ] *v. t. (Agric.)* worfeln; *(fig.)* scheiden; trennen

~ '**out** *v. t. (Agric.)* ausscheiden ‹*Spreu*›

wino ['waɪnəʊ] *n., pl.* ~**s** *(sl.)* Wermutpenner, *der/*-pennerin, *die (salopp)*

winsome ['wɪnsəm] *adj.* einnehmend; gewinnend ‹*Lächeln*›; **a** ~ **couple** ein reizendes Paar; **look** ~: reizend aussehen

winter ['wɪntə(r)] **1.** *n.* Winter, *der;* **in [the]** ~: im Winter; **last/next** ~: letzten/nächsten Winter; **the** ~ **of 1947–8** *or* **of 1947** der Winter 1947–48 *od.* [des Jahres] 1947; ~**'s day** Wintertag, *der.* **2.** *attrib. adj.* Winter-. **3.** *v. i.* den Winter verbringen; ‹*Truppe, Tier:*› überwintern

winter: ~ **garden** *n.* Wintergarten, *der;* ~**green** *n. (Bot.) (Pyrola)* Wintergrün, *das; (Gaultheria)* Gaultheria, *die*

winterize (winterise) ['wɪntəraɪz] *v. t.* winterfest machen

winter: ~ '**jasmine** *see* **jasmin[e]; W**~ **O'lympics** *see* **Olympics;** ~ '**quarters** *n. pl. (Mil.)* Winterquartier, *das;* Winterlager, *das;* ~ '**sleep** *n.* Winterschlaf, *der;* ~ '**solstice** *see* **solstice a;** ~ '**sport** *n.* **a)** *usu. in pl.* Wintersport, *der;* **b)** *(particular sport)* Wintersportart, *die;* ~-**time** *n.* Winter[s]zeit, *die;* **in [the]** ~-**time** im Winter; ~-**weight** *adj. (Textiles)* Winter-; **the coat is** ~-**weight** dies ist ein Wintermantel

wintry ['wɪntrɪ] *adj.* **a)** winterlich; rauh ‹*Klima*›; kalt ‹*Wind*›; ~ **shower** Schneegestöber, *das;* **cold and** ~: winterlich kalt; **b)** *(fig.)* frostig ‹*Lächeln*›

wipe [waɪp] **1.** *v. t.* **a)** abwischen; [auf]wischen ‹*Fußboden*›; *(dry)* abtrocknen; ~ **one's mouth** sich *(Dat.)* den Mund abwischen; ~ **one's brow/eyes/nose** sich *(Dat.)* die Stirn wischen/die Tränen abwischen/die Nase abwischen; ~ **one's feet/shoes** [sich *(Dat.)*] die Füße/Schuhe abtreten; ~ **sb./sth. clean/dry** jmdn./etw. abwischen/abtrocknen; *see also* **floor 1 a; b)** *(get rid of)* [ab]wischen; löschen ‹*Bandaufnahme*›; ~ **one's/sb.'s tears/the tears from one's/sb.'s eyes** sich/jmdm. die Tränen abwischen/aus den Augen wischen; ~ **sb./sth. off the face of the earth** jmdn./etw. vollständig *od.* restlos austilgen; ~ **that smile off your face!** hör auf, so unverschämt zu grinsen!; **I'll soon** ~ **the smile off your face** dir wird das Grinsen gleich vergehen; *see also* **map 1 b. 2.** *n.* **a)** Wisch, *der (ugs.);* **give sth. a** ~: etw. abwischen; *(dry sth.)* etw. abtrocknen; **this glass/your face needs a** ~: dieses Glas/dein Gesicht müßte einmal abgewischt werden; **b)** *(tissue)* Reinigungstuch, *das (aus Papier)*

~ **a'way** *v. t.* wegwischen; ~ **away a tear/one's tears** sich *(Dat.)* eine Träne/die Tränen abwischen

~ '**down** *v. t.* abwischen; *(dry)* abtrocknen

~ '**off** *v. t.* **a)** *(remove)* wegwischen; löschen ‹*Bandaufnahme*›; **b)** *(pay off)* zurückzahlen ‹*Schulden*›; ablösen ‹*Hypothek*›

~ '**out** *v. t.* **a)** *(clean)* auswischen; **b)** *(remove)* wegwischen; *(erase)* auslöschen; **c)** *(cancel)* tilgen; zunichte machen ‹*Vorteil, Gewinn usw.*›; **d)** *(destroy, abolish)* ausrotten ‹*Rasse, Tierart, Feinde*›; ersticken ‹*Widerstand*›; ausmerzen ‹*Seuche, Korruption, Terrorismus*›; **e)** *(coll.: murder)* aus dem Weg räumen

~ '**over** *v. t.* wischen über (+ *Akk.*)

~ '**up 1.** *v. t.* **a)** aufwischen; **b)** *(dry)* abtrocknen. **2.** *v. i.* abtrocknen

wiper ['waɪpə(r)] *n.* **a)** *(Motor Veh.)* Wischer, *der;* **b)** *(Electr.)* Kontaktarm, *der*

'**wiper blade** *n. (Motor Veh.)* Wischerblatt, *das*

wire ['waɪə(r)] **1.** *n.* **a)** Draht, *der;* **pull** ~**s** *(fig.)* = **pull strings** *see* **string 1 a; b)** *(barrier)* Drahtverhau, *der od. das; (fence)* Drahtzaun, *der; see also* **mesh 1 b; c)** *(Electr., Teleph.)* Leitung, *die;* **a piece** *or* **length of** ~: ein Stück [Leitungs]draht; **telephone/telegraph** ~: Telefon-/Telegrafenleitung, *die;* **the** ~**s were humming** die Drähte summten; **get one's** *or* **the** ~**s crossed** *(fig.)* auf der Leitung stehen *(ugs.); see also* **live wire; d)** *(coll.: telegram)* Telegramm, *das.* **2.** *v. t.* **a)** *(fasten with* ~*)* mit Draht zusammenbinden; *(stiffen with* ~*)* mit Draht versteifen; ~ **sth. together** etw. mit Draht verbinden; **b)** *(Electr.)* ~ **sth. to sth.** etw. an etw. *(Akk.)* anschließen; ~ **a house** *(lay wiring circuits)* in einem Haus die Stromleitungen legen; **is the house** ~**d for a telephone?** hat das Haus einen Telefonanschluß?; ~ **a studio for sound** in einem Studio Tonleitungen [ver]legen; **c)** *(coll.: telegraph)* ~ **sb.** jmdm. *od.* an jmdn. telegrafieren; ~ **money** Geld telegrafisch überweisen. **3.** *v. i. (coll.)* telegrafieren; **she** ~**d for him to come** sie telegrafierte ihm, er solle kommen

~ '**up** *v. t. (Electr.)* anschließen **(to** an + *Akk.***)**

wire: ~ '**brush** *n.* Drahtbürste, *die;* ~-**cutters** *n. pl.* Drahtschneider, *der;* ~ **gauge** *n.* **a)** *(instrument)* Drahtlehre, *die;* **b)** *(series of sizes) Standardsstärken für Drähte/Bleche;* ~-**haired** *adj. (Zool.)* drahthaarig; Drahthaar‹*terrier, -fox*›

wireless ['waɪəlɪs] **1.** *adj. (Brit.) see* **radio 2 a. 2.** *n.* **a)** *(Brit.)* Radio, *das;* **b)** *(telegraphy)* Funk, *der;* **by** ~: über Funk *(Akk.)*

wireless: ~ **set** *n. (Brit. dated)* Radioapparat, *der (veralt.);* ~ **te'legraphy** *n.* drahtlose Telegrafie

wire: ~ '**netting** *see* **netting b;** ~ '**rope** *n.* Drahtseil, *das;* ~-**strippers** *n. pl.* Abisolierzange, *die;* ~-**tapping** *see* **phone-tapping;** ~ '**wheel** *n. (Motor Veh.)* [Draht]speichenrad, *das;* ~ '**wool** *n.* Stahlwolle, *die;* ~-**worm** *n. (Zool.)* Drahtwurm, *der*

wiring ['waɪərɪŋ] *n., no pl., no indef. art. (Electr.)* [elektrische] Leitungen

'**wiring diagram** *n. (Electr.)* Schaltplan, *der;* Schaltbild, *das*

wiry ['waɪərɪ] *adj.* drahtig; drahtartig ‹*Stengel*›

wisdom ['wɪzdəm] *n., no pl.* **a)** Weisheit, *die;* **worldly** ~: Weltklugheit, *die;* **b)** *(prudence)* Klugheit, *die;* **where is the** ~ **of such a move/in doing that?** was für einen Sinn hat solch ein Schritt/hat es, das zu tun?; **her words are always full of** ~: was sie sagt, ist immer sehr klug; **words of** ~: weise Worte; *(advice)* weise Ratschläge

'**wisdom tooth** *n.* Weisheitszahn, *der*

¹**wise** [waɪz] *adj.* **a)** weise; vernünftig ‹*Meinung*›; **be** ~ **after the event** so tun, als hätte man es immer schon gewußt; **b)** *(prudent)* klug ‹*Vorgehensweise*›; vernünftig ‹*Lebensweise, Praktik*›; **the** ~ **thing to do would be to ...:** am klügsten wäre es, ... zu ...; **you'd be** ~ **to ignore it** du tätest gut daran, es zu ignorieren; **c)** *(informed)* **be none the** *or* **no/not much** ~**r** kein bißchen *od.* nicht/nicht viel klüger als vorher sein; **without anyone's being [any] the** ~**r** ohne daß es jemand merkt; **d)** *(coll.: aware)* **be** ~ **to sb./sth.** jmdn./etw. kennen; **be** ~ **to what's going on** wissen, was läuft *(ugs.);* **she was** ~ **to the fact that ...:** ihr war klar, daß ...; **get** ~ **to sb./sb.'s tricks** jmdm. auf die Schliche kommen; **get** ~ **to sth.** etw. spitzkriegen *(ugs.);* **get** ~ **to sb.'s plans** dahinterkommen *(ugs.),* was jmd. vorhat; **put sb.** ~: jmdm. die Augen öffnen; **put sb.** ~ **to sth.** jmdn. über etw. *(Akk.)* aufklären; **put sb.** ~ **to sb.** jmdm., was jmdn. betrifft, die Augen öffnen

~ '**up** *(Amer. sl.)* **1.** *v. t.* ~ **sb. up [to sth.]** jmdn. [über etw.] aufklären; **I'd like to** ~ **you up to him** ich möchte dir über ihn die

Augen öffnen. **2.** *v. i.* ~ **up to sth.** sich *(Dat.)* über etw. klarwerden; ~ **up to sb./sb.'s tricks** jmdm. auf die Schliche kommen

²wise *n. (arch.: manner)* Weise, *die*

-wise *adv. in comb.* **a)** *(in the direction of)* **length~**: der Länge nach; **clock~**: im Uhrzeigersinn; **b)** *(coll.: as regards)* -mäßig; was ... betrifft; **weather~**: wettermäßig; was das Wetter betrifft; **health~**: in puncto Gesundheit; gesundheitlich

wise: ~**acre** *n.* Klugschwätzer, *der*/-schwätzerin, *die (ugs. abwertend)*; ~**crack** *(coll.)* **1.** *n.* witzige Bemerkung; **make a ~crack** witzeln **(about** über + *Akk.*); **2.** *v. i.* witzeln; ~ **guy** *n. (coll.)* Klugscheißer, *der (salopp abwertend)*

wisely ['waɪzlɪ] *adv.* **a)** weise; **live ~**: das Leben eines Weisen führen; **b)** *(prudently)* klug; *as sentence-modifier* klugerweise

wise 'man *n.* Weise, *der; (arch.: magician)* Magier, *der;* **the Three W~ Men** *(Bibl.)* die drei Weisen [aus dem Morgenland]

wish [wɪʃ] **1.** *v. t.* **a)** *(desire, hope)* wünschen; **I ~ I was** *or* **were rich** ich wollte *od. (geh.)* wünschte, ich wäre reich; **I do ~ he would come** wenn er nur kommen würde; **I ~ you would shut up** es wäre mir lieb, wenn du den Mund hieltest; **it is to be ~ed that ...** *(formal)* es ist zu hoffen *od.* man muß hoffen, daß ...; **'~ you were here'** *(on postcard)* „schade, daß du nicht hier bist"; **b)** *with inf. (want)* wünschen *(geh.)*; **do you really ~ me to go?** ist es wirklich dein Wunsch *od.* möchtest du wirklich, daß ich gehe?; **I ~ to go** ich möchte *od.* will gehen; **I ~ you to stay** ich möchte *od.* will, daß du bleibst; **I ~ it [to be] done** ich wünsche *(geh.) od.* möchte *od.* will, daß es getan wird; **c)** *(say that one hopes sb. will have sth.)* wünschen; ~ **sb. luck/success** *etc.* jmdm. Glück/Erfolg *usw.* wünschen; ~ **sb. good morning/a happy birthday** jmdm. guten Morgen sagen/zum Geburtstag gratulieren; ~ **sb. ill/well** jmdm. [etwas] Schlechtes/alles Gute wünschen; **I ~ him no harm** ich wünsche ihm nichts Schlechtes; **d)** *(coll.: foist)* ~ **sb./sth. on sb.** *(coll.)* jmdm. jmdn./etw. aufhalsen *(ugs.)*. **2.** *v.i.* wünschen; **come on, ~!** nun, wünsch dir was!; ~ **for sth.** sich *(Dat.)* etw. wünschen; **or is that too much to ~ for?** *(iron.)* oder is das [vielleicht] zuviel verlangt?; **what more could one ~ for?** was will man mehr?; **they have everything they could possibly ~ for** sie haben alles, was sie sich *(Dat.)* nur wünschen können; **she ~ed for something to happen** sie wünschte, daß etwas passierte. **3.** *n.* **a)** Wunsch, *der;* **her ~ is that ...**: es ist ihr Wunsch *od.* sie wünscht, daß ...; **I have no [great/particular] ~ to go** ich habe keine [große/besondere] Lust zu gehen; **I have no ~ for fame/anything** mir ist an Ruhm *(Dat.)* nicht gelegen/ich habe keine Wünsche; **make a ~**: sich *(Dat.)* etwas wünschen; **the ~ is father to the thought** *(prov.)* der Wunsch ist der Vater des Gedankens; **your ~ is my command** *(joc.)* dein Wunsch ist mir Befehl *(scherzh.)*; **send sb. one's best ~es for a speedy recovery** jmdm. die besten Wünsche für eine schnelle Genesung schicken; **she sends you her good/best ~es** sie läßt dich herzlich grüßen; **with best/[all] good ~es, with every good ~**: mit den besten/allen guten Wünschen **(on,** for zu); **b)** *(thing desired)* **get** *or* **have one's ~**: seinen Wunsch erfüllt bekommen; **at last he has [got] his ~**: endlich ist sein Wunsch in Erfüllung gegangen

~ **a'way** *v. t.* wegwünschen

'wishbone *n. (Ornith.)* Gabelbein, *das*

wishful ['wɪʃfl] *adj.* sehnsuchtsvoll *(geh.)* ‹*Blick, Verlangen*›; ~ **thinking** Wunschdenken, *das*

'wish-fulfilment *n. (Psych.)* Wunscherfüllung, *die*

'wishing-well *n.* Wunschbrunnen, *der*

wishy-washy ['wɪʃɪwɒʃɪ] *adj.* labberig *(ugs.)*; *(fig.)* lasch

wisp [wɪsp] *n. (of straw)* Büschel, *das;* ~ **of hair** Haarsträhne, *die;* ~ **of cloud/smoke** Wolkenfetzen, *der*/Rauchfahne, *die;* **she is just a ~ of a girl** sie ist nur ein Strich

wispy ['wɪspɪ] *adj.* dünn ‹*Gras, Haar*›; schmächtig ‹*Person, Figur*›; ~ **clouds/smoke** Wolkenfetzen/Rauchfähnchen

wistaria [wɪ'steərɪə], **wisteria** [wɪ'stɪərɪə] *n. (Bot.)* Glyzine, *die;* Glyzinie, *die*

wistful ['wɪstfl] *adj.* wehmütig; melancholisch ‹*Person, Typ*›; traurig ‹*Augen*›

wistfully ['wɪstfəlɪ] *adv.* wehmütig

wistfulness ['wɪstflnɪs] *n., no pl.* Wehmütigkeit, *die;* Wehmut, *die (geh.)*; *(of eyes)* Traurigkeit, *die;* **a look/an expression full of ~**: ein wehmutsvoller Blick/Ausdruck *(geh.)*

¹wit [wɪt] *n.* **a)** *(humour)* Witz, *der;* **have a ready ~**: schlagfertig sein; **b)** *(intelligence)* Geist, *der;* **battle of ~s** intellektueller Schlagabtausch; **be at one's ~'s** *or* **~s' end** sich *(Dat.)* keinen Rat mehr wissen; **he was at his ~'s** *or* **~s' end to know what to do next** er wußte nicht mehr weiter; **collect** *or* **gather one's ~s** zu sich kommen; **drive sb. out of his/her ~s** jmdn. um den Verstand bringen; **frighten** *or* **scare sb. out of his/her ~s** jmdm. Todesangst einjagen; **be frightened** *or* **scared out of one's ~s** Todesangst haben; **have/keep one's ~s about one** auf Draht sein *(ugs.)*/nicht den Kopf verlieren; **live by one's ~s** sich irgendwie durchschlagen *od.* durchs Leben schlagen; **c)** *(person)* geistreicher Mensch

²wit *v.i.* **to ~**: nämlich

witch [wɪtʃ] *n. (lit. or fig.)* Hexe, *die; see also* **sabbath c**

witch: ~**craft** *n., no pl.* Hexerei, *die;* ~**-doctor** *n.* Medizinmann, *der;* ~**-hazel** *see* **wych-hazel**; ~**-hunt** *n. (lit. or fig.)* Hexenjagd, *die* **(for** auf + *Akk.*)

witching ['wɪtʃɪŋ] *adj.* **the ~ hour** die Geisterstunde

with [wɪð] *prep.* **a)** mit; **put sth. ~ sth.** etw. zu etw. stellen/legen; **have no pen to write ~**: nichts zum Schreiben haben; **I'll be ~ you in a minute** ich komme gleich; **a frontier ~ a country** eine Grenze zu einem Land; **be ~ it** *(coll.)* up to date sein; **not be ~ sb.** *(coll.: fail to understand)* jmdm. nicht folgen können; **I'm not ~ you** *(coll.)* ich komme nicht mit; **he that is not ~ me is against me** wer nicht mit mir ist, der ist wider mich *(bibl.)*; **be one ~ sb./sth.** mit jmdm./etw. eins sein; **b)** *(in the care or possession of)* bei; **I have no money ~ me** ich habe kein Geld dabei *od.* bei mir; **c)** *(owing to)* vor (+ *Dat.*); **tremble ~ fear** vor Angst zittern; **d)** *(displaying)* mit; ~ **courage** mutig; **handle ~ care** vorsichtig behandeln; **e)** *(while having)* bei; **sleep ~ the window open** bei offenem Fenster schlafen; **speak ~ one's mouth full** mit vollem Mund sprechen; **f)** *(in regard to)* **be patient ~ sb.** mit jmdm. geduldig sein; **have influence ~ sb.** auf jmdn. Einfluß haben; **what do you want ~ me?** was wollen Sie von mir?; **how are things ~ you?** wie geht es dir?; **what can he want ~ it?** was mag er damit vorhaben?; **g)** *(at the same time as, in the same way as)* mit; ~ **that** damit; **h)** *(employed by)* bei; **i)** *(despite)* trotz; *see also* **²will 1 d**

withal [wɪ'ðɔ:l] *(arch.) adv.* obendrein

with'draw 1. *v.t., forms as* **draw: a)** *(pull back, retract)* zurückziehen; **b)** *(remove)* nehmen *(fig.)* **(from** aus); abziehen ‹*Truppen*› **(from** aus); ~ **sth. from circulation/an account** etw. aus dem Verkehr ziehen/von einem Konto abheben. **2.** *v.i., forms as* **draw 1, 2** sich zurückziehen

withdrawal [wɪð'drɔ:əl] *n.* **a)** Zurücknahme, *die;* **b)** *(removal) (of privilege)* Entzug, *der; (of troops)* Abzug, *der; (of money)* Abhebung, *die;* **make a ~ from the bank** Geld von der Bank abheben; **c)** *(from drugs)* Entzug, *der;* ~ **symptoms** Entzugserscheinungen

with'drawal slip *n.* Auszahlungsschein, *der*

with'drawn *adj. (unsociable)* verschlossen

withe [wɪθ, wɪð, waɪð] *n.* Weidenrute, *die*

wither ['wɪðə(r)] **1.** *v. t.* **a)** *(shrivel)* verdorren lassen; **the plants had been ~ed by the heat** die Pflanzen waren durch die Hitze verdorrt; **age cannot ~ her** *(literary)* ihre Schönheit welkt nicht mit dem Alter; **b)** *(overwhelm with scorn)* mit Verachtung strafen. **2.** *v. i.* [ver]welken

~ **a'way** *v. i. (lit. or fig.)* dahinwelken *(geh.)*

~ **'up** *see* ~ **2**

withered ['wɪðəd] *adj.* verwelkt ‹*Gras, Pflanze*›; verkrüppelt ‹*Gliedmaße*›

withering ['wɪðərɪŋ] *adj.* vernichtend ‹*Blick, Bemerkung*›; sengend ‹*Hitze*›

witheringly ['wɪðərɪŋlɪ] *adv.* voller Verachtung

withers ['wɪðəz] *n. pl.* Widerrist, *der*

with'hold *v.t., forms as* **²hold: a)** *(refuse to grant)* verweigern; versagen *(geh.)*; **b)** *(hold back)* verschweigen ‹*Wahrheit*›; ~ **sth. from sb.** jmdm. etw. vorenthalten

with'holding tax *n. (Amer.)* Abzug[s]steuer, *die*

within [wɪ'ðɪn] **1.** *prep.* **a)** *(on the inside of)* innerhalb; ~ **myself/yourself** *etc.* in meinem/deinem *usw.* Inneren; ~ **doors** drinnen; im Haus; **her heart sank ~ her** *(literary)* aller Mut verließ sie; *see also* **wheel 1 a**; **b)** *(not beyond)* im Rahmen (+ *Gen.*); ~ **the meaning of the Act** *etc.* im Sinne des Gesetzes *usw.*; **stay/be ~ the law** den Boden des Gesetzes nicht verlassen; ~ **oneself** ohne sich zu verausgaben; *see also* **¹bound 1 a; means b; reason 1 b; c)** *(not farther off than)* ~ **eight miles of sth.** acht Meilen im Umkreis von etw.; **we were ~ eight miles of our destination when ...**: wir waren kaum noch acht Meilen von unserem Ziel entfernt, als ...; *see also* **sight 1 f; d)** *(subject to)* innerhalb; **work ~ certain conditions** unter bestimmten Bedingungen arbeiten; **e)** *(in a time no longer than)* innerhalb; binnen; ~ **an/the hour** innerhalb einer Stunde. **2.** *adv. (arch./literary)* **a)** *(inside)* innen; **b)** *(in spirit)* im Innern

without [wɪ'ðaʊt] **1.** *prep.* **a)** ohne; ~ **doing sth.** ohne etw. zu tun; **can you do it ~ his knowing?** kannst du das machen, ohne daß er davon weiß?; ~ **end** ohne Ende; **b)** *(arch.: outside)* außerhalb. **2.** *adv. (arch./literary)* **a)** *(outside)* außen; **b)** *(in outward appearance)* nach außen hin. **3.** *conj. (arch./coll.)* **you're not coming in here ~ you've been invited** du kommst hier nicht herein, ohne daß du eingeladen wärest *(geh.)*

with'stand *v. t.,* **withstood** [wɪθ'stʊd] standhalten (+ *Dat.*); aushalten ‹*Beanspruchung, hohe Temperaturen*›

withy ['wɪðɪ] *see* **withe**

witless ['wɪtlɪs] *adj.* **a)** *(foolish)* töricht; **b)** *(insane)* geistesgestört; **c)** *(dull-witted)* beschränkt *(abwertend)*

witness ['wɪtnɪs] **1.** *n.* **a)** Zeuge, *der*/Zeugin, *die* **(of, to** *Gen.*); **be a ~ against oneself** gegen sich selbst zeugen; **as God is my ~** *(fig.)* Gott ist mein Zeuge! *(geh.)*; **b)** *see* **eyewitness; c)** *no pl. (evidence)* Zeugnis, *das (geh.)*; **bear ~ to** *or* **of sth.** ‹*Person:*› etw. bezeugen; *(fig.)* von etw. zeugen; **d)** *no pl. (confirmation)* **in ~ of sth.** zum Zeugnis *(geh.)* einer Sache; **call sb. to ~**: jmdn. zum Zeugen aufrufen; **e)** *no pl. (proof)* ~ **to** *or* **of sth.** Zeugnis für etw. *(geh.)*. **2.** *v. t.* **a)** *(see)* ~ **sth.** Zeuge/Zeugin einer Sache *(Gen.)* sein; **sth. is ~ed by sb.** jmd. ist Zeuge/Zeugin einer Sache *(Gen.)*; ~ **scenes of brutality** brutale Szenen mitansehen müssen; **they have**

~**ed many changes** sie haben viele Veränderungen erlebt; **b)** *(attest genuineness of)* bestätigen ‹*Unterschrift, Echtheit eines Dokuments*›; *see also* **hand 1 l. 3.** *v. i.* ~ **against/to sth.** Zeugnis gegen/für etw. ablegen *(geh.)*; **[as]** ~ **...:** wie ... bezeugt
witness: ~-**box** *(Brit.)*, ~-**stand** *(Amer.)* *ns.* Zeugenstand, *der*
witter ['wɪtə(r)] *v. i. (Brit. coll.)* ~ **[on]** quatschen *(ugs. abwertend)*
witticism ['wɪtɪsɪzm] *n.* Witzelei, *die*
wittily ['wɪtɪlɪ] *adv.* geistreich
wittiness ['wɪtɪnɪs] *n., no pl.* Witz, *der*
witting ['wɪtɪŋ] *adj.* bewußt
wittingly ['wɪtɪŋlɪ] *adv.* wissentlich
witty ['wɪtɪ] *adj.* **a)** witzig; **b)** *(possessing wit)* geistreich ‹*Person*›
wives *pl. of* **wife**
wizard ['wɪzəd] **1.** *n.* **a)** *(sorcerer)* Zauberer, *der;* **b)** *(very skilled person)* Genie, *das* **(at** in + *Dat.*); **she's a** ~ **with a computer** sie vollbringt wahre Wunder mit einem Computer. **2.** *adj. (dated sl.)* zauberhaft
wizardry ['wɪzədrɪ] *n.* **a)** *(sorcery)* Zauberei, *die;* **b)** *(seemingly magical technique)* Zauberkunst, *die (meist Pl.)*; **footballing** ~: [Fuß]ballartistik, *die*
wizened ['wɪzənd] *adj.* runz[e]lig
wk. *abbr.* **week** Wo.
WNW [westnɔ:θ'west] *abbr.* **west-north-west** WNW
woad [wəʊd] *n.* Färberwaid, *der*
wobble ['wɒbl] **1.** *v. i.* **a)** *(rock)* wackeln; ‹*Kompaßnadel:*› zittern; **I was wobbling like a jelly** ich zitterte wie Espenlaub; **b)** *(go unsteadily)* wackeln *(ugs.)*; **c)** *(fig.: waver)* schwanken; **d)** *(quaver)* vibrieren; ‹*Stimme:*› zittern. **2.** *n.* **a)** *(unequal motion)* Flattern, *das (ugs.)*; **walk with a** ~: schwankend gehen; **the front wheel has developed a** ~: das Vorderrad eiert *(ugs.)*; **b)** *(change of direction, piece of vacillation)* Schwankung, *die;* **c)** *(quaver)* Vibrieren, *das; (in voice)* Zittern, *das*
wobbly ['wɒblɪ] *adj.* wack[e]lig; zitt[e]rig ‹*Schrift, Hand, Stimme*›; zitternd ‹*Pudding*›; holp[e]rig ‹*Fahrt*›; eiernd *(ugs.)* ‹*Rad*›
Woden ['wəʊdn] *pr. n. (Mythol.)* Wotan *(der)*
wodge [wɒdʒ] *n. (Brit. coll.)* **a** ~ **of press cuttings** ein Packen Zeitungsausschnitte; **a great** ~ **of cake/butter** ein mächtiges Stück Kuchen/Butter
woe [wəʊ] *n. (arch./literary/joc.)* **a)** *(distress)* Jammer, *der;* **a scene of** ~ **greeted her** ein jammervoller Anblick bot sich ihr; **a tale of** ~: eine jammervolle Geschichte; ~ **is me!** weh[e] mir!; ~ **betide you!** wehe dir!; **b)** *in pl. (troubles)* Jammer, *der;* **pour out one's** ~**s [to sb.]** [jmdm.] sein Leid klagen
woebegone ['wəʊbɪgɒn] *adj.* jammervoll
woeful ['wəʊfl] *adj.* **a)** *(deplorable)* beklagenswert; **b)** *(distressed)* jammervoll
woefully ['wəʊfəlɪ] *adv.* **a)** *(deplorably)* beklagenswert; **b)** *(in a distressed manner)* jammervoll
wog [wɒg] *n. (sl. derog.)* Kanake, *der (ugs. abwertend)*
wok [wɒk] *n. (Cookery)* Wok, *der*
woke, woken *see* **'wake 1, 2**
wold [wəʊld] *n. (Geog.)* Hochebene, *die;* **the Yorkshire W**~**s** die York Wolds
wolf [wʊlf] **1.** *n., pl.* **wolves** [wʊlvz] **a)** *(Zool.)* Wolf, *der;* **cry** ~ **[too often]** *(fig.)* [zu oft] Zetermordio schreien *(ugs.)*; **keep the** ~ **from the door** *(fig.)* den größten Hunger stillen; **be a** ~ **in sheep's clothing** *(fig.)* ein Wolf im Schafspelz sein; **throw sb. to the wolves** *(fig.)* jmdn. fallenlassen; **b)** *(coll.: sexually aggressive man)* Aufreißer, *der (salopp)*; *see also* **lone wolf. 2.** *v. t.* ~ **[down]** verschlingen
wolf: ~-**cub** *n.* **a)** *(Zool.)* Wolfsjunge, *das;* **b)** *(Brit. Hist.: Cub Scout)* Wölfling, *der;* ~**hound** *n.* Wolfshund, *der (volkst.)*
wolfish ['wʊlfɪʃ] *adj.* wölfisch; **a** ~ **hunger/appetite** ein Wolfshunger *(ugs.)*
'wolf-pack *n. (Navy, Air Force)* in Rudeltaktik operierende Einheit
wolfsbane ['wʊlfsbeɪn] *n. (Bot.)* Eisenhut, *der*
'wolf-whistle 1. *n.* anerkennender Pfiff. **2.** *v. i.* anerkennend pfeifen
wolverine (wolverene) ['wʊlvəri:n] *n. (Zool.)* Vielfraß, *der*
wolves *pl. of* **wolf 1**
woman ['wʊmən] *n., pl.* **women** ['wɪmɪn] **a)** Frau, *die;* **women and children first** Frauen und Kinder zuerst; **shut up,** ~**!** *(derog.)* halt's Maul, Alte! *(derb)*; **a** ~**'s work is never done** eine Frau hat immer etwas zu tun; **that's** ~**'s work** das ist Frauenarbeit; **women's page** Frauenseite, *die;* **women's [toilet]** Damen[toilette], *die;* **the shop sells women's clothing** in dem Geschäft wird Damenkleidung verkauft; **he wears women's clothing** er trägt Frauenkleider; **the other** ~: die Geliebte; ~ **of the streets** Straßenmädchen, *das; see also* **honest d; house 1 a; little 1 a; old woman; past 2 b; world a; b)** *attrib. (female)* weiblich; ~ **friend** Freundin, *die;* ~ **doctor** Ärztin, *die;* **a** ~ **driver** eine Frau am Steuer; **c)** *no pl.* **[the]** ~ *(an average* ~*)* die Frau; **d)** *(coll.: char*~*)* Putzfrau, *die;* **e)** *(arch.: female attendant)* Zofe, *die;* **f)** *(feminine emotions)* **the** ~ **in her** die Frau in ihr
'woman-hater *n.* Frauenhasser, *der;* Weiberfeind, *der*
womanhood ['wʊmənhʊd] *n., no pl.* Weiblichkeit, *die;* **reach** ~: zur Frau werden
womanise, womaniser *see* **womanize, womanizer**
womanish ['wʊmənɪʃ] *adj. (derog.)* weibisch *(abwertend)*
womanize ['wʊmənaɪz] *v. i.* den Frauen nachstellen; **with all his womanizing** mit all seiner Schürzenjägerei *(ugs.)*
womanizer ['wʊmənaɪzə(r)] *n.* Schürzenjäger, *der*
woman: ~**kind** *n., no pl., no indef. art.* das weibliche Geschlecht; **the whole of** ~**kind** alle Frauen; ~**like** *adj.* fraulich
womanliness ['wʊmənlɪnɪs] *n., no pl.* Fraulichkeit, *die*
womanly ['wʊmənlɪ] *adj.* fraulich; weiblich
woman's rights *see* **women's rights**
womb [wu:m] *n.* **a)** *(Anat.)* Gebärmutter, *die;* **the child in the** ~: das Kind im Mutterleib; **in her** ~: in ihrem Leib *(geh.)*; *see also* **fruit 1 d; b)** *(fig.: place of development)* Schoß, *der (geh. fig.)*
wombat ['wɒmbæt] *n. (Zool.)* Wombat, *der*
women *pl. of* **woman**
Women: w~**folk** *n. pl.* Frauen; Frauensleute, *Pl. (veralt.)*; **w**~**kind** *see* **womankind;** ~**'s 'Institute** *n. (Brit.) britischer Frauenverband;* ~**'s 'Lib** *(coll.) see* ~**'s Liberation;** ~**'s Libber** [wɪmɪnz 'lɪbə(r)] *n. (coll.)* Emanze, *die (ugs. abwertend)*; Frauenrechtlerin, *die;* ~**'s Libe'ration** *n.* die Frauenbewegung; **w**~**'s 'rights** *n. pl.* die Rechte der Frau
won *see* **win 1, 2**
wonder ['wʌndə(r)] **1.** *n.* **a)** *(extraordinary thing)* Wunder, *das;* **do** *or* **work** ~**s** Wunder tun *od.* wirken; *(fig.)* Wunder wirken; ~**s will never cease** *(iron.)* Wunder über Wunder!; **small** *or* **what** *or* **[it is] no** ~ **[that] ...:** [es ist] kein Wunder, daß ...; **the** ~ **is, ...:** das Erstaunliche ist, ...; **b)** *(marvellously successful person)* Wunderkind, *das; (marvellously successful thing)* Wunderding, *das;* **boy/girl** ~: Wunderkind, *das;* **the seven** ~**s of the world** die Sieben Weltwunder; **c)** *no pl. (feeling)* Staunen, *das;* **a feeling of** ~: ein Staunen; **be lost in** ~: in Staunen versunken sein; **look at sb. in open-mouthed** ~: jmdn. mit offenem Mund anstaunen; *see also* **nine 1. 2.** *adj.* Wunder-. **3.** *v. i.* sich wundern; staunen (**at** über + *Akk.*); **that's not to be** ~**ed at** darüber braucht man sich nicht zu wundern; **I shouldn't** ~ **[if ...]** *(coll.)* es würde mich nicht wundern[, wenn ...]; **Why do you ask? – Oh, I was just** ~**ing** Warum fragst du? – Ach, nur so; **I** ~ *expr. agreement with another's doubts* das frage ich mich auch; *expr. disagreement with another's assertion* es sollte mich wundern; **I don't think we'll see him again. – I** ~: Den sehen wir nie wieder. – Da wäre ich nicht so sicher. **4.** *v. t.* **a)** sich fragen; **I** ~ **what the time is** wieviel Uhr mag es wohl sein?; **I was** ~**ing what to do** ich habe mir überlegt, was ich tun soll; **I** ~ **whether I might open the window** dürfte ich vielleicht das Fenster öffnen?; **she** ~**ed if ...** *(enquired)* sie fragte, ob ...; **I** ~ **if you'd mind if ...?** würde es Ihnen etwas ausmachen, wenn ...?; **b)** *(be surprised to find)* ~ **[that] ...:** sich wundern, daß ...
wonderful ['wʌndəfl] *adj.* wunderbar; wundervoll
wonderfully ['wʌndəfəlɪ] *adv.* wunderbar; ~ **beautiful** wunderschön; ~ **charming** einfach bezaubernd
wondering ['wʌndərɪŋ] *adj.*, **wonderingly** ['wʌndərɪŋlɪ] *adv.* staunend
'wonderland *n.* **a)** *(wonderful place)* Paradies, *das;* **b)** *(fairyland)* Wunderland, *das*
wonderment ['wʌndəmənt] *n., no pl.* Verwunderung, *die;* **say sth. in** ~: etw. voll Verwunderung sagen; **in** ~ **at** voll Verwunderung über (+ *Akk.*); **her mouth was open in** ~: ihr stand vor Staunen der Mund offen
'wonder-worker *n.* Wundertäter, *der/*-täterin, *die*
wondrous ['wʌndrəs] *adj.*, **wondrously** ['wʌndrəslɪ] *adv. (poet.)* wundersam *(geh.)*
wonky ['wɒŋkɪ] *adj. (Brit. sl.)* wack[e]lig; *(crooked)* schief; **a bit** ~ **[on one's legs]** etwas wack[e]lig [auf den Beinen] *(ugs.)*
wont [wəʊnt] **1.** *pred. adj. (arch./literary)* gewohnt; **as he was** ~ **to say** wie er zu sagen pflegte. **2.** *n. (literary)* Gepflogenheit, *die (geh.)*; **as was her** ~: wie sie zu tun pflegte
won't [wəʊnt] *(coll.)* = **will not;** *see* **'will**
wonted ['wəʊntɪd] *attrib. adj. (literary)* gewohnt; **with one's** ~ **courtesy** mit gewohnter Höflichkeit
woo [wu:] *v. t.* **a)** *(literary: court)* ~ **sb.** um jmdn. werben *(geh.)*; **b)** *(seek to win)* umwerben ‹*Kunden, Wähler*›; ~ **away** abwerben ‹*Arbeitskräfte*›; **c)** *(coax)* umwerben
wood [wʊd] *n.* **a)** *in sing. or pl. (area with trees)* Wald, *der;* **sb. cannot see the** ~ **for the trees** *(fig.)* jmd. sieht den Wald vor [lauter] Bäumen nicht *(scherzh.)*; **be out of the** ~ *(Brit.) or (Amer.)* ~**s** *(fig.)* über den Berg sein *(ugs.)*; **b)** *(substance, material)* Holz, *das;* **touch** ~ *(Brit.)*, **knock [on]** ~ *(Amer.)* unberufen!; **you'd better touch** ~ **when you say that** wenn du das sagst, klopfst du besser dreimal auf Holz; **c)** *(cask for beer, wine, etc.)* **from the** ~: vom Faß; **matured in the** ~: in Holzfässern gereift; **d)** *(Bowls)* Kugel, *die;* **e)** *(Golf)* Holzschläger, *der;* Holz, *das*
wood: ~ **anemone** *n. (Bot.)* Buschwindröschen, *das;* Anemone, *die;* ~**bind** ['wʊdbaɪnd], ~**bine** ['wʊdbaɪn] *n. (Bot.)* **a)** *(wild honeysuckle)* Waldgeißblatt, *das;* **b)** *(Amer.: Virginia creeper)* Jungfernrebe, *die;* ~ **carving** *n. (craft, object)* Holzschnitzerei, *die;* ~**chuck** *n. (Zool.)* Waldmurmeltier, *das;* ~**cock** *n., pl. same (Ornith.)* Waldschnepfe, *die;* ~**craft** *n., no pl.* **a)** *(knowledge of forest conditions)* Kenntnis des Waldes; **b)** *(skill in* ~ *work)* Holzschnitzerei, *die;* ~**cut** *n. (Art)* Holzschnitt, *der;* ~**cutter** *n.* **a)** Holzfäller, *der;* **b)** *(Art)* Holzschnitzer, *der*
wooded ['wʊdɪd] *adj.* bewaldet
wooden ['wʊdn] *adj.* **a)** hölzern ‹*Brücke, Spielzeug*›; Holz‹*haus, -brücke, -bein, -griff, -spielzeug*›; **b)** *(fig.: stiff)* hölzern

wooden: ~head *n. (derog.)* Holzkopf, *der (salopp abwertend);* **~headed** *adj. (derog.)* dumm; **~ 'horse** *n. (fig.)* Trojanisches Pferd

woodenly ['wʊdnlɪ] *adv.* ausdruckslos ⟨*blicken, starren*⟩; tonlos ⟨*sagen*⟩

woodenness ['wʊdnnɪs] *n., no pl.* Hölzernheit, *die*

wooden 'spoon *see* **'spoon 1 a**

wood: ~ hyacinth *see* **hyacinth a; ~land** ['wʊdlənd] *n.* Waldland, *das;* Wald, *der; attrib.* Wald-; **~-louse** *n. (Zool.)* Kellerassel, *die;* **~man** ['wʊdmən] *n., pl.* **~men** ['wʊdmən] Waldarbeiter, *der;* **~pecker** *n.* Specht, *der;* **~-pigeon** *n.* Ringeltaube, *die;* **~pile** *n.* Holzstapel, *der;* Holzstoß, *der; see also* **nigger; ~-pulp** *n.* Holzschliff, *der;* **~ruff** *n. (Bot.)* **[sweet] ~ruff** Waldmeister, *der;* **~-screw** *n.* Holzschraube, *die;* **~-shed** *n.* Holzschuppen, *der;* **~ sorrel** *n. (Bot.)* Waldsauerklee, *der*

woodsy ['wʊdzɪ] *adj. (Amer.)* waldig

wood: ~-wind *n. (Mus.)* Holzblasinstrument, *das;* **the ~-wind [section]** die Holzbläser; **~-wind instrument** Holzblasinstrument, *das;* **~work** *n., no pl.* **a)** *(making things out of ~)* Arbeiten mit Holz; **~work and metalwork** *(Sch.)* Werkunterricht, *der;* **b)** *(things made of ~)* Holzarbeit[en]; **crawl out of the ~work** *(coll.)* [aus dem Nichts] auftauchen *(ugs.);* **~worm** *n., no pl., no art.* Holzwurm; **it's got ~worm** da ist der Holzwurm drin *(ugs.)*

woody ['wʊdɪ] *adj.* **a)** *(well-wooded)* waldreich; **b)** *(consisting of wood)* holzig ⟨*Pflanze[nteil], Wurzel*⟩; Holz⟨*stamm*⟩; **c)** *(resembling wood)* holzig; *see also* **nightshade**

wooer ['wu:ə(r)] *n.* Verehrer, *der (veralt.)*

¹woof [wu:f] *see* **weft**

²woof [wʊf] **1.** *n.* [dumpfes] Bellen; **at the sound of the dog's ~:** als der Hund aufbellte; **give a short ~:** kurz aufbellen; **~ ~! went the dog** wau, wau! bellte der Hund. **2.** *v. i.* [dumpf] bellen; **~ at sb.** jmdn. anbellen

woofer ['wʊfə(r)] *n.* Baß[lautsprecher], *der*

wool [wʊl] *n.* **a)** Wolle, *die; attrib.* Woll-; **pull the ~ over sb.'s eyes** jmdm. etwas vormachen *(ugs.);* **b)** *(garments)* Wolle, *die. See also* **cotton wool; dye 2; glass wool; steel wool; wire wool**

woolen *(Amer.) see* **woollen**

'wool-gathering 1. *n., no pl.* Hirngespinste *(abwertend).* **2.** *adj.* zerstreut; **she's ~ again** sie träumt schon wieder

woollen ['wʊlən] **1.** *adj.* wollen; **~ goods** Wollwaren, *Pl.* **2.** *n.* **a)** *in pl. (garments)* Wollsachen *Pl.;* **b)** *(fabric)* Wollgewebe, *das;* Wollstoff, *der*

woolliness ['wʊlɪnɪs] *n., no pl.* Verschwommenheit, *die*

woolly ['wʊlɪ] **1.** *adj.* **a)** wollig; Woll⟨*pullover, -mütze*⟩; **b)** *(confused)* verschwommen; **c)** *(indistinct)* unklar; undeutlich ⟨*Klang, Geräusch*⟩. *See also* **wild 1 c. 2.** *n. (coll.)* **a)** *(Brit.: knitted garment)* **[winter] woollies** [Winter]wollsachen *Pl. (ugs.);* **a ~:** ein Wollpullover/eine Wolljacke; **b)** *in pl. (Amer.: undergarments)* wollene Unterwäsche

wool: ~-pack *n.* Schäfchenwolken *Pl.;* **W~sack** *n. (Brit. Parl.) großes, mit Wolle gefülltes Sitzkissen des Lord Chancellors im britischen Oberhaus*

woozy ['wu:zɪ] *adj. (coll.)* **a)** *(dizzy)* duselig *(ugs.);* **b)** *(slightly drunk)* angeduselt *(salopp)*

wop [wɒp] *n. (sl. derog.)* Spaghettifresser, *der (salopp abwertend)*

Worcester[shire] sauce [wʊstə(ʃɪə) 'sɔ:s, wʊstə(ʃə) 'sɔ:s] *n.* Worcestersoße, *die*

word [wɜ:d] **1.** *n.* **a)** Wort, *das;* **have no ~s for sth.** für etw. keine Worte finden; **be beyond ~s** sich mit Worten nicht ausdrücken lassen; **~s cannot describe it** mit Worten läßt sich das nicht beschreiben; **in a** *or* **one ~** *(fig.)* mit einem Wort; **[not] in so many ~s** [nicht] ausdrücklich; **in other ~s** mit anderen Worten; **not a ~ of sth.** kein Wort von etw.; **bad luck/drunk is not the ~ for it** Pech/betrunken ist gar kein Ausdruck dafür *(ugs.);* **that's not the ~ I would have used** das ist gar kein Ausdruck *(ugs.);* **put sth. into ~s** etw. in Worte fassen; **'rude' would be a better ~ for it** „unverschämt" wäre ein treffenderes Wort dafür ; **~ for ~:** Wort für Wort; **without a** *or* **one/another ~:** ohne ein/ein weiteres Wort; **too funny** *etc.* **for ~s** unsagbar komisch *usw.;* **the written ~:** das geschriebene Wort; *see also* **fail 2 e; play 1 b, 2 a; b)** *(thing said)* Wort, *das;* **hard ~s** harte Worte; **exchange** *or* **have ~s** einen Wortwechsel haben; **a man of few ~s** ein Mann von wenig Worten; **have a ~ [with sb.] about sth.** [mit jmdm.] über etw. *(Akk.)* sprechen; **could I have a ~ [with you]?** kann ich dich mal sprechen?; **have ~s with sb.** sich mit jmdm. streiten; **say a few ~s** ein paar Worte sprechen; **suit the action to the ~:** seinen Worten Taten folgen lassen; **it's his ~ against mine** sein Wort steht gegen meins; **take sb. at his/her ~:** jmdn. beim Wort nehmen; **~ of command/advice** Kommando, *das*/Rat, *der;* **don't say** *or* **breathe a ~ to anyone** sag niemandem auch nur ein Sterbenswort; **at a ~ of command** auf Befehl; **the W~ [of God]** *(Bible)* das Wort [Gottes]; **in the ~s of Shakespeare ...:** mit Shakespeares Worten: ...; **put in a good ~ for sb. [with sb.]** [bei jmdm.] ein [gutes] Wort für jmdn. einlegen; **never have a good ~ to say about anybody** nie etwas Gutes über andere zu sagen haben; **never say a bad ~ about anybody** nie etwas Schlechtes über andere sagen; **[it's] all ~s** [das sind] nichts als leere Worte; **c)** *(promise)* Wort, *das;* **doubt sb.'s ~:** jmds. Wort in Zweifel ziehen; **give [sb.] one's ~:** jmdm. sein Wort geben; **keep/break one's ~:** sein Wort halten/brechen; **I give you my ~ for it** ich gebe Ihnen mein Wort darauf; **upon my ~** *(dated)* auf mein Wort; **upon my ~!** *(dated)* meiner Treu! *(veralt.);* **my ~!** meine Güte!; **my** *etc.* **~ of honour** mein *usw.* Ehrenwort; **a man of his ~:** ein Mann von Wort; **be as good as/better than one's ~:** sein Wort halten/mehr als halten; **sb.'s ~ is [as good as] his/her bond** man kann auf jmds. Wort *(Akk.)* bauen; *see also* **take 1 v; d)** *no pl. (speaking)* Wort, *das;* **by ~ of mouth** durch mündliche Mitteilung; **e)** *in pl. (text of song, spoken by actor)* Text, *der;* **f)** *no pl., no indef. art. (news)* Nachricht, *die;* **~ had just reached them** die Nachricht hatte sie gerade erreicht; **~ has it** *or* **the ~ is [that] ...:** es geht das Gerücht, daß ...; **~ went round that ...:** es ging das Gerücht, daß ...; **send/leave ~ that/of when ...:** Nachricht geben/eine Nachricht hinterlassen, daß/wenn ...; **is there any ~ from her?** hat sie schon von sich hören lassen?; **g)** *(command)* Kommando, *das;* **just say the ~:** sag nur ein Wort; **at the ~ 'run', you run!** bei dem Wort „rennen" rennst du!; **h)** *(password)* Parole, *die (Milit.);* **give the ~:** die Parole sagen; *see also* **sharp 1 f; i)** *(Computing)* Wort, *das.* **2.** *v. t.* formulieren

wordage ['wɜ:dɪdʒ] *n.* die Anzahl der Wörter

word: ~ associaton *n.* assoziative Verknüpfung von Wörtern; **~-blind** *adj. (Med.)* wortblind; **~-break** *n.* Trennung, *die;* **~-deaf** *adj.* worttaub *(Med.);* **~-division** *n.* Silbentrennung, *die;* **~-formation** *n. (Ling.)* Wortbildung, *die;* **~-game** *n.* Buchstabenspiel, *das*

wordiness ['wɜ:dɪnɪs] *n., no pl.* Weitschweifigkeit, *die*

wording ['wɜ:dɪŋ] *n.* Formulierung, *die;* Wortwahl, *die;* **the exact ~ of the contract** der genaue Wortlaut des Vertrages

wordless ['wɜ:dlɪs] *adj.* **a)** *(not expressed in words)* wortlos; stumm ⟨*Schmerz, Trauer*⟩; **b)** *(not accompanied by words)* ohne Worte *nachgestellt*

word: ~ list *n.* Wortliste, *die;* **~ order** *n. (Ling.)* Wortstellung, *die;* **~-'perfect** *adj.* **be ~-perfect** seinen Text beherrschen; ⟨*Rede:*⟩ perfekt vorgetragen sein; **~-picture** *n.* anschauliche Schilderung; Wortgemälde, *das;* **~-play** *n., no pl., no indef. art.* Wortspiel, *das;* **~ processing** *n.* Textverarbeitung, *die;* **~ processor** *n.* Textverarbeitungssystem, *das*

wordy ['wɜ:dɪ] *adj.* weitschweifig

wore *see* **wear 2, 3**

work [wɜ:k] **1.** *n.* **a)** *no pl., no indef. art.* Arbeit, *die;* **at ~** *(engaged in ~ing)* bei der Arbeit; *(fig.: operating)* am Werk (*see also* **e**); **be at ~ on sth.** an etw. *(Dat.)* arbeiten; *(fig.)* auf etw. *(Akk.)* wirken; **set to ~** ⟨*Person:*⟩ sich an die Arbeit machen; **set sb. to ~:** jmdn. an die Arbeit schicken; **get to ~ on sb./sth.** jmdn. bearbeiten *(ugs.)*/mit [der Arbeit an] etw. *(Dat.)* anfangen; **all ~ and no play** immer nur arbeiten; **have one's ~ cut out** viel zu tun haben; sich ranhalten müssen *(ugs.);* **the ~ of a moment** *etc.* das Werk eines Augenblicks *usw.;* **that's too much like hard ~:** das könnte ja in Arbeit ausarten; **make light ~ of sth.** mit etw. leicht fertig werden; *see also* **day a; short 1 a; thirsty b; b)** *(thing made or achieved)* Werk, *das;* **a good day's ~:** eine gute Tagesleistung; **do a good day's ~:** ein tüchtiges Stück Arbeit hinter sich bringen; **is that all your own ~?** hast du das alles selbst gemacht?; **~ of art** Kunstwerk, *das; see also* **good 1 g; c)** *(book, piece of music)* Werk, *das;* **a ~ of reference/literature/art** ein Nachschlagewerk/literarisches Werk/Kunstwerk; **d)** *in pl. (all compositions of author or composer)* Werke; **e)** *(employment)* Arbeit, *die,* **out of ~:** arbeitslos; ohne Arbeit; **be in ~:** eine Stelle haben; **go out to ~:** arbeiten gehen; **put people out of ~:** Leute um ihren Arbeitsplatz bringen; **at ~** *(place of employment)* auf der Arbeit; **from ~:** von der Arbeit; **the conditions at ~:** die Arbeitsbedingungen; **f)** *in pl., usu. constr. as sing. (factory)* Werk, *das;* **g)** *in pl. (Mil.)* Werke; Befestigungen; **h)** *in pl. (operations of building etc.)* Arbeiten; *see also* **clerk c; public works; i)** *in pl. (machine's operative parts)* Werk, *das;* **j)** *in pl. (sl.: all that can be included)* **the [whole/full] ~s** der ganze Kram *(ugs.);* **give sb. the ~s** *(fig.) (give sb. the best possible treatment)* jmdn. richtig verwöhnen *(ugs.); (tell sb. everything)* jmdm. alles erzählen; *(give sb. the worst possible treatment)* jmdn. fertigmachen *(salopp);* **k)** *no pl. (ornamentation)* Verzierung, *die; (ornamented or ornamental article[s])* Arbeit, *die;* **l)** *no pl., no indef. art. (knitting, needlework)* Handarbeit, *die;* **m)** *(Phys.)* Arbeit, *die. See also* **nasty 1 a; piece 1 d. 2.** *v. i.,* **~ed** *or (arch./literary)* **wrought** [rɔ:t] **a)** arbeiten; **be ~ing all morning over a hot oven** den ganzen Morgen am Herd stehen *(ugs.);* **~ with sb.** mit jmdm. zusammenarbeiten; **~ to rule** Dienst nach Vorschrift machen; **~ for a cause** *etc.* für eine Sache *usw.* arbeiten; **~ against sth.** *(impede)* einer Sache *(Dat.)* entgegenstehen; *see also* **work-to-rule; b)** *(function effectively, have intended effect)* funktionieren; ⟨*Charme:*⟩ wirken (**on** auf + *Akk.*); **make the washing-machine/television ~:** die Waschmaschine/den Fernsehapparat in Ordnung bringen; **make a relationship/an arrangement ~:** dafür sorgen, daß eine Beziehung klappt *(ugs.)*/eine Regelung funktioniert; **it doesn't ~ like that** *(fig.)* so geht das nicht; **c)** ⟨*Rad, Getriebe, Kette:*⟩ laufen; **d)** *(be craftsman)* **~ in a material** mit *od. (fachspr.)* in einem Material arbeiten; **e)** ⟨*Faktoren, Einflüsse:*⟩ wirken (on auf + *Akk.*); ~ **to do sth.** darauf hinwirken, etw. zu tun; ~ **against** arbeiten gegen; *see also* ~ **on**; **f)** *(make its/one's way)* sich schieben; ~ **loose** sich lockern; ~ **round** ⟨*Kleidung:*⟩ herumrutschen; ⟨*Wind:*⟩ sich drehen; **be ~ing upstream** ⟨*Angler:*⟩ sich stromaufwärts arbeiten; ~ **round to a question** *(fig.)* sich zu einer Frage vorarbeiten; **start at the end and ~ back** fang hinten an, und arbeite dich nach vorne; **g)** *(be agitated)* ⟨*Gesichtszüge:*⟩ arbeiten; **h)** *(Naut.: sail)* sich arbeiten; **i)** *(ferment, lit. or fig.)* arbeiten. **3.** *v. t.*, **~ed** *or (arch./literary)* **wrought: a)** *(operate)* bedienen ⟨*Maschine*⟩; fahren ⟨*Schiff*⟩; betätigen ⟨*Bremse*⟩; **a pump that is ~ed by hand/by a wind-wheel** eine Pumpe, die von Hand betätigt/von einem Windrad angetrieben wird; **~ed by electricity** elektrisch betrieben; *see also* **oracle d; b)** *(get labour from)* arbeiten lassen; ~ **horses/oxen to death** Pferde/Ochsen zu Tode schinden; **he ~s his employees hard** er nimmt seine Angestellten hart heran; *see also* **bone 1 a; death a; c)** *(get material from)* ausbeuten ⟨*Steinbruch, Grube*⟩; **d)** *(operate in or on)* ⟨*Vertreter:*⟩ bereisen; **beggars ~ing the main street** Bettler, die auf der Hauptstraße arbeiten/arbeiteten; **e)** *(control)* steuern; **f)** *(effect)* bewirken ⟨*Änderung*⟩; wirken ⟨*Wunder*⟩; ~ **one's mischief** Unheil anrichten; ~ **one's will [upon sb./sth.]** Einfluß [auf jmdn./etw.] ausüben; **I'll ~ it if I can** *(sl.)* ich werde das schon irgendwie deichseln *(ugs.)*; ~ **it** *or* **things so that ...** *(sl.)* es deichseln, daß ... *(ugs.)*; **g)** *(cause to go gradually)* führen; ~ **a key/rod into sth.** einen Schlüssel/eine Stange [vorsichtig] in etw. *(Akk.)* einführen; ~ **one's way up/into sth.** sich hocharbeiten/in etw. *(Akk.)* hineinarbeiten; **h)** *(get gradually)* bringen; ~ **oneself out of sth./into a position** sich von etw. befreien/sich in eine Position hocharbeiten; **i)** *(knead, stir)* ~ **sth. into sth.** etw. zu etw. verarbeiten; *(mix in)* etw. unter etw. *(Akk.)* rühren; **j)** *(gradually excite)* ~ **oneself into a state/a rage** sich aufregen/in einen Wutanfall hineinsteigern; ~ **sb. into a state** jmdn. aufregen; **k)** *(make by needlework etc.)* arbeiten; aufsticken ⟨*Muster*⟩ (on auf + *Akk.*); **l)** *(purchase, obtain with labour)* abarbeiten; *(fig.)* ~ **one's keep** für sein Geld etwas leisten; **she ~ed her way through college** sie hat sich *(Dat.)* ihr Studium selbst verdient; **he ~ed his way up from office boy to company chairman** er hat sich vom Bürogehilfen zum Generaldirektor hochgearbeitet; *see also* **passage f; m)** *(Math.)* lösen ⟨*Rechenaufgabe, Problem*⟩

~ **a'way** *v. i.* ~ **away [at sth.]** [an etw. *(Dat.)*] arbeiten

~ **'in** *v. t. (include)* hineinbringen; *(mix in)* hineinrühren; *(rub in)* einreiben; *see also* **work-in**

~ **'off** *v. t.* **a)** *(get rid of)* loswerden; abreagieren ⟨*Wut*⟩; ~ **sth. off on sb./sth.** etw. an jmdm./etw. auslassen; ~ **off some excess energy** überschüssige Energie loswerden; **b)** *(pay off)* abtragen ⟨*Schuld*⟩

~ **on 1.** ['--] *v. t.* **a)** *(expend effort on)* ~ **on sth.** an etw. *(Dat.)* arbeiten; **b)** *(use as basis)* ~ **on sth.** von etw. ausgehen; **c)** *(try to persuade)* ~ **on sb.** jmdn. bearbeiten *(ugs.)*. **2.** [-'-] *v. i.* weiterarbeiten

~ **'out 1.** *v. t.* **a)** *(find by calculation)* ausrechnen; **b)** *(solve)* lösen ⟨*Problem, Rechenaufgabe*⟩; **c)** *(resolve)* ~ **things out with sb./for oneself** die Angelegenheit mit jmdm./sich selbst ausmachen; **things ~ themselves out** es erledigt sich alles von selbst; **d)** *(devise)* ausarbeiten ⟨*Plan, Strategie*⟩; **e)** *(make out)* herausfinden; *(understand)* verstehen; **I can't ~ him out** ich werde aus ihm nicht klug; **f)** *(Mining: exhaust)* ausbeuten. **2.** *v. i.* **a)** *(be calculated)* **sth. ~s out at £250/[an increase of] 22%** etw. ergibt 250 Pfund/bedeutet [eine Steigerung von] 22%; **it will ~ out more expensive to buy the car on h.p.** es wird mehr kosten, das Auto auf Kredit zu kaufen; **b)** *(give definite result)* ⟨*Gleichung, Rechnung:*⟩ aufgehen; **c)** *(have result)* laufen; **things ~ed out [well] in the end** es ist schließlich doch alles gutgegangen; **things didn't ~ out the way we planned** es kam ganz anders, als wir geplant hatten; **how are the new arrangements ~ing out?** wie klappt es mit der neuen Regelung? *(ugs.)*; **d)** *(train)* trainieren; *see also* **work-out**

~ **'over** *v. t.* **a)** *(examine thoroughly)* durcharbeiten; **b)** *(coll.: beat up)* in die Mache nehmen *(salopp)*

~ **through** *v. t.* durcharbeiten

~ **towards** *v. t. (lit. or fig.)* hinarbeiten auf (+ *Akk.*)

~ **'up 1.** *v. t.* **a)** *(develop)* verarbeiten (into zu); *(create)* erarbeiten; **b)** *(excite by degrees)* aufpeitschen ⟨*Menge*⟩; **get ~ed up** sich aufregen; ~ **oneself up into a rage/fury** sich in einen Wutanfall/in Raserei hineinsteigern; **c)** *(acquire familiarity with)* ~ **up one's French/maths/history** seine Französisch-/Mathematik-/Geschichtskenntnisse vertiefen; **d)** *(mix)* verarbeiten (into zu). **2.** *v. i.* **a)** *(advance gradually)* ~ **up to sth.** ⟨*Musik:*⟩ sich zu etw. steigern; ⟨*Geschichte, Film:*⟩ auf etw. *(Akk.)* zusteuern; **I'll have to ~ up to it** ich muß darauf hinarbeiten; **b)** ⟨*Rock usw.:*⟩ sich hochschieben

workable ['wɜːkəbl] *adj.* **a)** *(capable of being worked)* bebaubar ⟨*Land*⟩; abbauwürdig ⟨*Mine*⟩; **be ~** ⟨*Mörtel:*⟩ sich verarbeiten lassen; ⟨*Stahl:*⟩ sich bearbeiten lassen; ⟨*Mine:*⟩ sich ausbeuten lassen; **b)** *(feasible)* durchführbar

workaday ['wɜːkədeɪ] *adj.* alltäglich

workaholic [wɜːkə'hɒlɪk] *n. (coll.)* arbeitswütiger Mensch; Workaholic, *der (Psych.)*; *attrib.* arbeitswütig

work: ~-bag *n.* [Hand]arbeitsbeutel, *der;* **~-basket** *n.* Handarbeitskorb, *der;* **~-bench** *n.* Werkbank, *die; (of tailor, glazier)* Arbeitstisch, *der;* **~-box** *n.* Nähkasten, *der;* **~-camp** *n.: Lager freiwilliger Helfer; (labour camp)* Arbeitslager, *das;* **~day** *n.* Werktag, *der*

worker ['wɜːkə(r)] *n.* **a)** Arbeiter, *der*/Arbeiterin, *die;* **he is not one of the world's ~s** *(coll.)* er hat die Arbeit nicht gerade erfunden *(ugs.)*; ~ **of miracles** Wundertäter, *der;* **b)** *(Zool.)* Arbeiterin, *die*

worker: ~ **bee** *n. (Zool.)* Arbeiterbiene, *die;* ~ **'priest** *n. (Eccl.)* Arbeiterpriester, *der*

work: ~ **ethic** *n., no pl.* Arbeitsethos, *das;* ~ **experience** *n.* Arbeitserfahrung, *die;* **~-force** *n.* Belegschaft, *die;* **~-horse** *n. (lit. or fig.)* Arbeitspferd, *das;* **~house** *n. (Brit. Hist., Amer.)* Arbeitshaus, *das;* **~-in** *n.* Betriebsbesetzung, *die (mit Weiterführung der Arbeit bei drohender Aussperrung)*

working ['wɜːkɪŋ] **1.** *n.* **a)** Arbeiten, *das;* **forbid sb.'s ~:** verbieten, daß jmd. arbeitet; **b)** *(way sth. works)* Arbeitsweise, *die;* **I cannot follow the ~s of his mind** ich kann seinen Gedankengängen nicht folgen; **the ~s of fate** die Wege des Schicksals; **c)** *(Mining)* Stollen, *der.* **2.** *adj.* **a)** handlungsfähig ⟨*Mehrheit*⟩; ⟨*Entwurf, Vereinbarung*⟩ als Ausgangspunkt; **b)** *(in employment)* arbeitend; werktätig; ~ **man** *(labourer)* Arbeiter, *der*

working: ~ **'breakfast** *n.* Arbeitsfrühstück, *das;* ~ **'capital** *n. (Commerc.)* Betriebskapital, *das;* ~ **'class** *n.* Arbeiterklasse, *die;* **~-class** *adj.* der Arbeiterklasse *nachgestellt;* **sb. is ~-class** jmd. gehört zur Arbeiterklasse; ~ **clothes** *n. pl.* Arbeitskleidung, *die;* ~ **'day** *n.* **a)** *(portion of the day)* Arbeitstag, *der;* **b)** *(day when work is done) see* **workday;** ~ **'drawing** *n.* Konstruktionszeichnung, *die; (for building)* Bauplan, *der;* ~ **girl** *n.* berufstätige junge Frau; **she's a ~ girl** *(coll. euphem.)* sie ist im horizontalen Gewerbe tätig *(ugs. scherzh.)*; ~ **'hours** *n. pl.* Arbeitszeit, *die;* ~ **hy'pothesis** *n.* Arbeitshypothese, *die;* ~ **'knowledge** *n.* ausreichende Kenntnisse (of in + *Dat.*); **sb. with a ~ knowledge of these machines** jmd., der im Umgang mit diesen Maschinen erfahren ist; ~ **'lunch** *n.* Arbeitsessen, *das;* ~ **'model** *n.* funktionsfähiges Modell; ~ **'mother** *n.* berufstätige Mutter; ~ **'order** *n.* betriebsfähiger Zustand; **be in good ~ order** betriebsbereit sein; **~-'out** *n.* **a)** *(calculation of results)* Berechnung, *die;* **b)** *(elaboration of details)* Ausarbeitung, *die;* **~-'over** *n. (sl.)* Abreibung, *die (ugs.)*; ~ **party** *n. (Brit.)* Arbeitsgruppe, *die;* ~ **'title** *n.* Arbeitstitel, *der;* ~ **'week** *n.* Arbeitswoche, *die;* **a 35-hour ~ week** eine 35-Stunden-Woche; ~ **'wife** *n.* berufstätige Ehefrau; ~ **'woman** *n.* berufstätige Frau

work: ~-load *n.* Arbeitslast, *die;* **increase sb.'s ~-load** jmds. Arbeitspensum erhöhen; **~man** ['wɜːkmən] *n., pl.* **~men** ['wɜːkmən] Arbeiter, *der;* **council ~man** städtischer Arbeiter; **a bad ~man quarrels with** *or* **blames his tools** *(prov.)* ein schlechter Handwerker schimpft über sein Werkzeug; **~manlike** ['wɜːkmənlaɪk] *adj.* fachmännisch; **do a ~manlike job** fachmännisch arbeiten; **~manship** ['wɜːkmənʃɪp] *n., no pl.* **a)** *(person's skill)* handwerkliches Können; **b)** *(quality of execution)* Kunstfertigkeit, *die;* **c)** *no indef. art. (thing made)* Werk, *das;* **~mate** *n. (Brit.)* Arbeitskollege, *der*/-kollegin, *die;* **~-out** *n.* [Fitneß]training, *das;* **have a good ~-out** hart trainieren; **go for a ~-out** zum [Fitneß]training gehen; **~-people** *n. pl.* Arbeiter; ~ **permit** *n.* Arbeitserlaubnis, *die;* **~piece** *n.* Werkstück, *das;* **~-place** *n.* Arbeitsplatz, *der;* **~-room** *n.* Arbeitsraum, *der;* **~-sharing** *n.* Job-sharing, *das;* **~sheet** *n.* **a)** *(recording ~ done etc.)* Arbeitszettel, *der;* **b)** *(for student)* Formular mit Prüfungsfragen; **~shop** *n.* **a)** *(place) (room)* Werkstatt, *die; (building)* Werk, *das;* **b)** *(meeting)* Workshop, *der;* Arbeitstreffen, *das;* **drama ~shop** Theaterworkshop, *der;* **~-shy** *adj.* arbeitsscheu; **~-space** *n.* Arbeitsraum, *der;* **~-station** *n.* **a)** *(in manufacturing)* Fertigungsstation, *die;* **b)** *(Computing)* graphischer Arbeitsplatz; ≈ Terminal, *das;* ~ **study** *n.* Arbeitsstudien; *(case)* Arbeitsstudie, *die;* ~ **surface** *see* **~top;** **~-table** *n.* Arbeitstisch, *der;* **~top** *n.* Arbeitsplatte, *die;* **~-to-'rule** *n.* Dienst nach Vorschrift

world [wɜːld] *n.* **a)** Welt, *die; attrib.* Welt-; **the ~'s worst novel** der schlechteste Roman der Welt; **the biggest aspidistra in the ~:** die größte Schusterpalme der Welt; **go/sail round the ~:** eine Weltreise machen/die Welt umsegeln; **money makes the ~ go round** Geld regiert die Welt; **that's what/it's love that makes the ~ go round** darum/um die Liebe dreht sich letztlich alles; **it's the same the ~ over** es ist doch überall das gleiche; **the eyes of the ~ are on them** die Welt blickt auf sie; **all the ~** *or* **the whole ~ knows** alle Welt *(ugs.)* weiß; **[all] the ~ over, all over the ~:** in *od.* auf der ganzen Welt; **it's the same the whole ~ over** es ist überall das gleiche; **people from all over the ~ wrote to him** er bekam Post aus aller Welt; **give sth. to the ~:** etw. der Welt übergeben *(fig.)*; **lead the ~ [in sth.]** [in etw. *(Dat.)*] führend in der Welt sein; **the Old/New W~:** die Alte/Neue Welt; **the Roman ~:** die römische Welt; **she had the ~ at her feet** die ganze Welt lag ihr zu Füßen; **who/what in the ~ was it?** wer/was in aller Welt war es? *(ugs.)*; **how in the ~ was it that ...?** wie in aller Welt *(ugs.)* war es möglich, daß ...?; **nothing in**

the ~ **would persuade me** um nichts in der Welt ließe ich mich überreden; **not for anything in the ~:** um nichts in der Welt; **look for all the ~ as if ...:** geradezu aussehen, als ob ...; **in a ~ of one's own** in einer anderen Welt *(fig.)*; **the external ~:** die Außenwelt *od.* äußere Welt; **the ~ of dreams** die Welt der Träume; **not do sth. for the** *or* **to gain the whole ~:** etw. um alles in der Welt nicht tun; **be all the ~ to sb.** jmdm. das Wichtigste/Liebste auf der Welt sein; **think the ~ of sb.** große Stücke auf jmdn. halten *(ugs.)*; **I would give the ~ to know why ...:** ich gäbe alles darum, zu wissen, warum ...; **~ politics** Weltpolitik, *die;* **all alone in the ~:** ganz allein auf der Welt; **the Napoleons of this ~:** die Napoleons dieser Erde; **sb. is not long for this ~:** jmds. Tage sind gezählt; **out of this ~** *(fig. coll.)* phantastisch *(ugs.)*; **the other** *or* **next ~, the ~ to come** das Jenseits; die zukünftige Welt; **bring into the ~** *(possess at one's birth)* in die Welt bringen; *(deliver at birth)* auf die Welt holen; *(beget)* in die Welt setzen *(ugs.)*; *(give birth to)* zur Welt bringen; **come into the ~:** auf die Welt kommen; **the best of all possible ~s** die beste aller Welten; **get the best of both ~s** am meisten profitieren; **the ~'s end, the end of the ~:** das Ende der Welt; **it's not the end of the ~** *(iron.)* davon geht die Welt nicht unter *(ugs.)*; **~ without end** in alle Ewigkeit; **know/have seen a lot of the ~:** die Welt kennen/viel von der Welt gesehen haben; **see the ~:** die Welt kennenlernen; **a man/woman of the ~:** ein Mann/eine Frau mit Welterfahrung; **think that all's right with the ~:** glauben, daß die Welt in Ordnung ist; **take the ~ as it is** *or* **as one finds it** alles nehmen, wie es kommt; **what 'is the ~ coming to?** wo soll das noch hinführen? *(ugs.)*; **how goes the ~ with you?** wie geht's[, wie steht's]?; **all the ~ and his wife** alle Welt *(ugs.)*; **go up/come down in the ~:** [gesellschaftlich] aufsteigen/absteigen; *see also* **oyster; b)** *(domain)* **the literary/scientific/ancient/sporting/animal ~:** die literarische/wissenschaftliche/antike Welt *(geh.)*/die Welt *(geh.)* des Sports/die Tierwelt; **the ~ of letters/art/sport** die Welt *(geh.)* der Literatur/Kunst/des Sports; **c)** *(vast amount)* **a ~ of meaning/trouble** eine unendliche Bedeutungsfülle/Fülle von Schwierigkeiten; **it will do him a** *or* **the ~ of good** es wird ihm unendlich guttun; **a ~ of difference** ein weltweiter Unterschied; **a ~ away from sth.** Welten von etw. entfernt; **they are ~s apart in their views** ihre Ansichten sind Welten voneinander entfernt

world: W~ 'Bank *n.* Weltbank, *die;* **~-beater** *n.* **be a ~-beater** zur Spitzenklasse gehören; **~ 'champion** *n.* Weltmeister, *der*/-meisterin, *die;* **W~ 'Cup** *n. (Sport)* Worldcup, *der;* **~-famous** *adj.* weltberühmt; **~ 'language** *n.* Weltsprache, *die*

worldliness ['wɜ:ldlɪnɪs] *n., no pl.* Weltlichkeit, *die*

worldly ['wɜ:ldlɪ] *adj.* weltlich; weltlich eingestellt ⟨*Person*⟩

worldly: ~ 'goods *n. pl.* weltliche Güter; **~ 'wisdom** *n.* Weltklugheit, *die;* **~ 'wise** *adj.* weltklug

world: ~ 'power *n.* Weltmacht, *die;* **~ 'record** *n.* Weltrekord, *der;* **~-record holder** Weltrekordhalter, *der*/-halterin, *die;* **W~ Series** *n. (Amer. Sport) Baseball-Ausscheidungen zwischen den Gewinnern der bedeutendsten Ligen der USA;* **~-shaking** *adj.* welterschütternd; **~-view** *n.* Weltsicht, *die;* **~ 'war** *n.* Weltkrieg, *der;* **the First/Second W~ War, W~ War I/II** der erste/zweite Weltkrieg; der 1./2. Weltkrieg; **~-weary** *adj.* lebensüberdrüssig; **~-wide 1.** ['--] *adj.* weltweit *nicht präd.*; **2.** [-'-] *adv.* weltweit

worm [wɜ:m] **1.** *n.* **a)** Wurm, *der;* **[even] a ~ will turn** *(prov.)* auch der Wurm krümmt sich, wenn er getreten wird *(Spr.)*; **b)** *in pl. (intestinal parasites)* Würmer; **c)** *(fig.: contemptible person)* Wurm, *der;* **feel like a ~:** sich *(Dat.)* klein und häßlich vorkommen; **he's a real ~:** er ist ein richtiger Widerling. **2.** *v. t.* **a) he ~ed his hand into his trouser pocket** er zwängte seine Hand in die Hosentasche; **~ one's way through sth.** sich durch etw. winden *(geh.) od.* zwängen; **~ oneself** *or* **one's way into sth.** *(fig.)* sich in etw. *(Akk.)* hineindrängen; **~ oneself into sb.'s favour** sich in jmds. Gunst *(Akk.)* schleichen; **b)** *(draw by crafty persistence)* **~ sth. out of sb.** etw. aus jmdm. herausbringen *(ugs.)*; **c)** *(rid of ~s)* entwurmen. **3.** *v.i.* sich winden

worm: ~-cast *n.* Kothäufchen des Regenwurms; **~-eaten** *adj.* wurmstichig; *(fig.)* vom Zahn der Zeit angenagt; **~-gear** *n.* Schneckengetriebe, *das (Technik)*; **~-hole** *n.* Wurmloch, *das;* **~-powder** *n.* Wurmpulver, *das;* **~'s-eye-'view** *n.* Froschperspektive, *die (auch fig.)*

'wormwood *n.* Wermut, *der*

wormy ['wɜ:mɪ] *adj.* wurmig ⟨*Apfel*⟩; von Würmern befallen ⟨*Tier*⟩; wurmreich ⟨*Boden, Erde*⟩

worn *see* **wear 2, 3**

'worn-out *attrib. adj.* abgetragen ⟨*Kleidungsstück*⟩; abgenutzt ⟨*Teppich*⟩; abgedroschen ⟨*Redensart, Ausdruck*⟩; erschöpft, *(ugs.)* erledigt ⟨*Person*⟩

worried ['wʌrɪd] *adj.* besorgt; **give sb. a ~ look** jmdn. besorgt ansehen; **you had me ~:** ich habe mir [deinetwegen] Sorgen gemacht; **don't look so ~!** schau nicht so bekümmert drein!; **~ sick** krank vor Sorge; **be much** *or* **very ~:** sich *(Dat.)* große Sorgen machen

worrier ['wʌrɪə(r)] *n.* **be too much of a ~:** sich *(Dat.)* immer [zuviel] Sorgen machen; **he's a [real] ~:** er macht sich *(Dat.)* um alles Sorgen

worrisome ['wʌrɪsəm] *adj.* besorgniserregend

worry ['wʌrɪ] **1.** *v. t.* **a)** beunruhigen; **it worries me to death to think that ...:** ich sorge mich zu Tode, wenn ich [daran] denke, daß ...; **~ oneself [about sth.]** sich *(Dat.)* um etw. Sorgen machen; **~ oneself sick [about sb./sth.]** krank vor Sorge [um jmdn./etw.] werden; **b)** *(bother)* stören; **c) ~ a bone** ⟨*Hund usw.:*⟩ an einem Knochen [herum]nagen; **d)** *(attack)* ⟨*Hund usw.:*⟩ reißen ⟨*Schaf*⟩. **2.** *v. i.* sich *(Dat.)* Sorgen machen; sich sorgen; **~ about sth.** sich *(Dat.)* um etw. Sorgen machen; **don't ~ about it** mach dir deswegen keine Sorgen!; **'I should ~** *(coll. iron.)* was kümmert mich das?; **not to ~** *(coll.)* kein Problem *(ugs.)*. **3.** *n.* Sorge, *die;* **sth. is the least of sb.'s worries** etw. ist jmds. geringste Sorge; **it must be a great ~ to you** es muß dir große Sorgen bereiten

'worry beads *n. pl. Perlenschnur zur Beschäftigung für nervöse Hände*

worrying ['wʌrɪɪŋ] **1.** *adj.* **a)** *(causing worry)* beunruhigend; **sth. is very ~ for sb.** etw. macht jmdm. große Sorgen; **b)** *(full of worry)* sorgenvoll ⟨*Zeit, Woche usw.*⟩; **it is a ~ time for her** sie hat zur Zeit große Sorgen. **2.** *n.* **~ only makes everything worse** sich *(Dat.)* Sorgen zu machen macht alles nur noch schlimmer

worse [wɜ:s] **1.** *adj. compar. of* **bad 1** schlechter; schlimmer ⟨*Schmerz, Krankheit, Benehmen*⟩; **things could not/could be ~:** es kann nicht mehr schlimmer kommen/es könnte schlimmer sein; **the food is bad, and the service ~:** das Essen ist schlecht und die Bedienung noch schlechter; **his manners are ~ than a pig's** er benimmt sich schlimmer als ein Schwein; **he's getting ~:** mit ihm wird es schlimmer; *(his health)* ihm geht es schlechter; **be ~ than useless** ⟨*Sache:*⟩ mehr als unbrauchbar sein; ⟨*Person:*⟩ ein hoffnungsloser Fall sein; **be [none] the ~ for sth.** ⟨*Sache:*⟩ in [k]einem schlechteren Zustand wegen etw. sein; **sb. is [none] the ~ for sth.** jmdm. geht es wegen etw. [nicht] schlechter; **~ and ~:** immer schlechter/schlimmer; **to make matters ~, ...:** zu allem Übel ...; **it could have been ~:** es hätte schlimmer sein *od.* kommen können; **~ luck!** so ein Pech!; *see also* **drink 1 d; liquor a; wear 1 a. 2.** *adv. compar. of* **badly** schlechter; schlimmer, schlechter ⟨*sich benehmen*⟩; **~ and ~:** immer schlechter/schlimmer; *see also* **better 3 a; off 1 i. 3.** *n.* Schlimmeres; **she might do ~ than settle for that job** es wäre bestimmt kein Fehler, wenn sie sich für die Stelle entschiede; **go from bad to ~:** immer schlimmer werden; **or ~:** oder noch Schlimmeres; **~ still** schlimmer noch; **a change for the ~:** eine Wende zum Schlechteren; **take a turn for the ~:** sich verschlechtern; ⟨*Krankheit:*⟩ sich verschlimmern; **nobody will think any the ~ of you** niemand wird deswegen schlechter von dir denken; **there is ~ to come** es kommt noch schlimmer; *see also* **worst 3**

worsen ['wɜ:sn] **1.** *v. t.* verschlechtern; verschlimmern ⟨*Knappheit*⟩. **2.** *v. i.* sich verschlechtern; ⟨*Hungersnot, Sturm, Problem:*⟩ sich verschlimmern; **she ~ed in the night** ihr Zustand hat sich über Nacht verschlimmert

worship ['wɜ:ʃɪp] **1.** *v. t., (Brit.)* **-pp- a)** verehren ⟨*Gott, Götter, Kaiser*⟩; anbeten ⟨*Gott, Götter*⟩; **b)** *(idolize)* abgöttisch verehren; **he ~s the ground she walks on** er küßt den Boden unter ihren Füßen. **2.** *v. i., (Brit.)* **-pp- a)** am Gottesdienst teilnehmen; **b)** *(be full of adoration)* tiefe Verehrung empfinden. **3.** *n.* **a)** Anbetung, *die;* *(service)* Gottesdienst, *der;* **public ~:** [öffentlicher] Gottesdienst; **dedicated as a place of ~:** dem Gottesdienst geweiht; **gather for ~:** sich zum Gottesdienst versammeln; **freedom of ~:** Glaubensfreiheit, *die;* **b)** *(adoration)* Verehrung, *die;* **an object of ~:** ein Gegenstand der Verehrung; **the ~ of wealth/intellect** die Anbetung des Wohlstands/Intellekts; **c)** *(form of address)* **Your/His W~:** *Anrede für Richter, Bürgermeister;* ≈ Euer/seine Ehren

worshiper *(Amer.) see* **worshipper**

worshipful ['wɜ:ʃɪpfl] *adj. (Brit.) Titulierung von Friedensrichtern, Zünften, Freimaurerlogen usw.*

worshipper ['wɜ:ʃɪpə(r)] *n.* **a)** *(in church etc.)* Gottesdienstbesucher, *der*/-besucherin, *die;* **b)** *(of deity)* Anbeter, *der*/Anbeterin, *die;* **c)** *(of person, money, etc.)* Verehrer, *der*/Verehrerin, *die;* **be a ~ of sth.** etw. anbeten *(fig.)*

worst [wɜ:st] **1.** *adj. superl. of* **bad 1: a)** *see* **worse 1:** schlechtest.../schlimmst...; **be ~:** am schlechtesten/schlimmsten sein; **the ~ thing about it was ...:** das Schlimmste daran war ...; **the ~ thing you could do** das Schlechteste, was du machen könntest; **b)** *(least efficient, of poorest quality)* schlechtest... **2.** *adv. superl. of* **badly** am schlimmsten; am schlechtesten ⟨*gekleidet*⟩. **3.** *n.* **a) [the] ~:** der/die/das Schlimmste; **you saw him at his ~:** du hast ihn in seinem schlimmsten Zustand erlebt; **prepare for the ~:** sich auf das Schlimmste gefaßt machen; **at ~, at the [very] ~:** schlimmstenfalls; im [aller]schlimmsten Fall[e]; **get** *or* **have the ~ of it** *(be defeated)* [vernichtend] geschlagen werden; *(suffer the most)* am meisten zu leiden haben; **if the ~** *or* **it comes to the ~** *(Brit.)*, **if worse comes to ~** *(Amer.)* wenn es zum Schlimmsten kommt; **do your ~:** mach, was du willst!; **let him do his ~:** er soll machen, was er will; **b)** *(what is of poorest quality)* Schlechteste, *der/die/das.* **4.** *v. t.* [vernichtend] schlagen; **be ~ed in argument** sich geschlagen geben müssen

worsted ['wʊstɪd] *n. (Textiles)* Kammgarn, *das*
wort [wɜːt] *n.* [Bier]würze, *die*
worth [wɜːθ] **1.** *adj.* **a)** *(of value equivalent to)* wert; **it's ~/not ~ £80** es ist 80 Pfund wert/80 Pfund ist es nicht wert; **it is not ~ much** *or* **a lot [to sb.]** es ist [jmdm.] nicht viel wert; **be ~ the money** das Geld wert sein; **not ~ a penny** keinen Pfennig wert *(ugs.)*; **it's ~ a lot to me that ...:** es bedeutet mir viel, daß ...; **he's ~ the lot of you put together** er ist soviel wert wie ihr alle zusammen; **for what it is ~:** was immer auch davon zu halten ist; *see also* **gold 1 a; b)** *(worthy of)* **is it ~ hearing/the effort?** ist es hörenswert/der Mühe wert?; **is it ~ doing?** lohnt es sich?; **if it's ~ doing, it's ~ doing well** wenn schon, denn schon; **it isn't ~ it** es lohnt sich nicht; **an experience ~ having** eine lohnenswerte Erfahrung; **it's ~ a try** es ist einen Versuch wert; **it would be [well] ~ it** *(coll.)* es würde sich [sehr] lohnen; **be well ~ sth.** durchaus *od.* sehr wohl etw. wert sein; **you can have my opinion for what it's ~:** ich kann dir sagen, was meine bescheidene Meinung ist; **it's more than my job's ~:** es könnte mich meine Stelle kosten; **c) be ~ sth.** *(possess)* etw. wert sein *(ugs.)*; **run/cycle for all one is ~** *(coll.)* rennen/fahren, was man kann. *See also* **salt 1 a; while 1. 2.** *n.* **a)** *(equivalent of money etc. in commodity)* **ten pounds' ~ of petrol** Benzin für zehn Pfund; *(more formal)* Benzin im Wert von zehn Pfund; **b)** *(value, excellence)* Wert, *der;* **of great/little/no ~:** von hohem/geringem Wert/ohne Wert. *See also* **money's-worth; pennyworth**
worthily ['wɜːðɪlɪ] *adv.* ehrenhaft; zu Recht ‹*verdienen*›
worthiness ['wɜːðɪnɪs] *n., no pl.* Ehrenhaftigkeit, *die; (of cause, charity)* Wert, *der*
worthless ['wɜːθlɪs] *adj.* **a)** *(valueless)* wertlos; **b)** *(despicable)* nichtswürdig
'**worthwhile** *attrib. adj.* lohnend; *see also* **while 1**
worthy ['wɜːðɪ] **1.** *adj.* **a)** *(adequate, estimable)* würdig; verdienstvoll ‹*Tat*›; angemessen ‹*Belohnung*›; **~ of the occasion** dem Anlaß angemessen; **b)** *(deserving)* würdig; verdienstvoll ‹*Sache, Organisation*›; **be ~ of the name** den Namen verdienen; **~ of note/mention** erwähnenswert; **is he ~ of her?** ist er ihrer würdig? **2.** *n.* **a)** *(person of distinction)* Würdenträger, *der;* **b) local worthies** *(joc.)* örtliche Honoratioren
wotcher ['wɒtʃə(r)] *int. (Brit. sl.)* hallo *(ugs.)*
would *see* **[1]will**
would-be ['wʊdbiː] *attrib. adj.* **a ~ philosopher** ein Möchtegernphilosoph; **a ~ aggressor** ein möglicher Aggressor
wouldn't ['wʊdnt] *(coll.)* = **would not;** *see* **[1]will**
[1]wound [wuːnd] **1.** *n. (lit. or fig.)* Wunde, *die;* **a war ~:** eine Kriegsverletzung; **receive a ~ in the chest/leg** an der Brust/am Bein verwundet werden; **a knife-~ across the palm** eine Schnittwunde quer über die Handfläche; **this was a great ~ to her pride** *(fig.)* das verletzte ihren Stolz zutiefst. **2.** *v. t.* verwunden; *(fig.)* verletzen; **be ~ed in the thigh/arm** am Oberschenkel/Arm verwundet werden
[2]wound *see* **[2]wind 1, 2**
wove, woven *see* **[1]weave 2, 3**
[1]wow [waʊ] **1.** *int.* hoi. **2.** *n. (sl.)* **be a ~:** eine Wucht sein *(salopp)*. **3.** *v. t. (sl.)* umhauen *(ugs.)*
[2]wow *n. (Electronics)* Jaulen, *das (fig.)*
WP *abbr.* **word processor**
w. p. b. *abbr.* **waste-paper basket**
WPC *abbr.* **woman police constable** Wachtmeisterin, *die*
w. p. m. *abbr.* **words per minute** WpM
wraith [reɪθ] *n.* Gespenst, *das*
'**wraithlike** *adj.* gespenstisch
wrangle ['ræŋgl] **1.** *v. i.* [sich] streiten. **2.** *n.* Streit, *der;* **what are those two having such a ~ about?** worüber streiten die beiden sich denn so?
wrap [ræp] **1.** *v. t.,* **-pp- a)** einwickeln; *(fig.)* hüllen; **~ped** abgepackt ‹*Brot usw.*›; **~ sth. in paper/cotton wool** etw. in Papier/Watte [ein]wickeln; **~ sth. [a]round sth.** *(lit. or fig.)* etw. um etw. wickeln; **~ one's arms around sb.** die Arme um jmdn. schlingen; **b)** *(arrange)* schlingen ‹*Schal, Handtuch usw.*› **(about, round** um); **she ~ped her motor cycle round a tree** *(coll.)* sie hat ihr Motorrad um einen Baum gewickelt *(ugs.)*. **2.** *n.* Umschlag[e]tuch, *das;* **take the ~s off sth.** *(fig.)* etw. der Öffentlichkeit vorstellen; **under ~s** *(fig.)* unter Verschluß; **keep sth. under ~s** etw. geheimhalten
~ 'up 1. *v. t.* **a)** *see* **wrap 1; wrapped up; b)** *(fig.: conclude)* abschließen; **that just about ~s it up for today** damit sind wir für heute fertig. **2.** *v. i.* **a)** *(put on warm clothing)* sich warm einpacken *(ugs.)*; **mind you ~ up well** du mußt dich gut einpacken *(ugs.)*; **b)** *(sl.: be quiet)* den Rand halten *(salopp)*
'**wraparound 1.** *adj.* **a)** Wickel‹*kleid, -rock*›; **b)** Panorama‹*windschutzscheibe, -sonnenbrille*›. **2.** *n.* Wickelrock, *der*
wrapped up [ræpt 'ʌp] *adj.* **be ~ in one's work** in seine Arbeit völlig versunken sein; **she is very ~ in her family** sie geht ganz in ihrer Familie auf; **be too ~ in one's problems** zu sehr mit seinen [eigenen] Problemen beschäftigt sein; **a country whose prosperity is ~ in its shipping** ein Land, dessen Reichtum eng mit seiner Schiffahrt verknüpft ist
wrapper ['ræpə(r)] *n.* **a)** *(around newspaper etc.)* Streifband, *das (Postw.)*; **b)** *(around sweet etc.)* **sweet-/toffee-~[s]** Bonbonpapier, *das;* **c)** *(of book) see* **jacket c**
wrapping ['ræpɪŋ] *n.* Verpackung, *die;* **~s** Verpackung, *die; (fig.)* Hülle, *die (dichter.)*
'**wrapping-paper** *n. (strong paper)* Packpapier, *das; (decorative paper)* Geschenkpapier, *das*
wrasse [ræs] *n. (Zool.)* Lippfisch, *der*
wrath [rɒθ] *n. (poet./rhet.)* Zorn, *der*
wrathful ['rɒθfl] *adj. (poet./rhet.)* zornig
wreak [riːk] *v. t.* **a)** *(inflict)* **~ vengeance on sb.** an jmdm. Rache nehmen; **b)** *(vent)* auslassen ‹*Wut, Ärger*› **(on** an + *Dat.*); **c)** *(cause)* anrichten ‹*Verwüstung, Unheil*›
wreath [riːθ] *n., pl.* **wreaths** [riːðz, riːθs] Kranz, *der;* **a ~ of smoke** ein Ring aus Rauch
wreathe [riːð] **1.** *v. t.* **a)** *(encircle)* umkränzen; **her face was ~d in smiles** ein Lächeln umspielte ihre Lippen; **b)** *(form into wreath)* zu einem Kranz flechten *od. (geh.)* winden; **c)** *(make by interweaving)* flechten; winden *(geh.)*. **2.** *v.i.* sich winden; ‹*Rauch:*› sich ringeln *od.* kräuseln **(from** aus)
wreck [rek] **1.** *n.* **a)** *(destruction)* Schiffbruch, *der; (fig.)* Zerstörung, *die;* **b)** *(ship)* Wrack, *das;* **c)** *(broken remains, lit. or fig.)* Wrack, *das;* **she was a physical/mental ~:** sie war körperlich/geistig ein Wrack; **I feel/you look a ~** *(coll.)* ich fühle mich kaputt *(ugs.)*/du siehst kaputt aus *(ugs.)*. **2.** *v. t.* **a)** *(destroy)* ruinieren; zu Schrott fahren ‹*Auto*›; **be ~ed** *(shipwrecked)* ‹*Schiff, Person:*› Schiffbruch erleiden; **a ~ed ship/aircraft** ein wrackes *od. (fachspr.)* havariertes Schiff/Flugzeug; **b)** *(fig.: ruin)* zerstören; ruinieren ‹*Gesundheit, Urlaub*›; verderben ‹*Party, Urlaub*›; zunichte machen ‹*Hoffnung, Plan*›; zerrütten ‹*Ehe*›
wreckage ['rekɪdʒ] *n.* Wrackteile; *(fig.)* Trümmer *Pl.*
wrecker ['rekə(r)] *n.* **a)** *(who disrupts deliberately)* Umstürzler, *der*/Umstürzlerin, *die;* **b)** *(who brings about shipwreck for profit)* Strandräuber, *der;* **c)** *(employed in demolition)* Abwracker, *der;* **d)** *(who recovers wrecked ships)* Bergungsarbeiter, *der;* **e)** *(Amer.: breakdown vehicle)* Bergungsfahrzeug, *das;* Abschleppfahrzeug, *das;* **f)** *(Amer.: train)* Hilfszug, *der*
'**wrecking bar** *n.* Brechstange, *die*
Wren [ren] *n. (Brit.)* *Angehörige des weiblichen Marinedienstes;* **join the ~s** in den weiblichen Marinedienst eintreten
wren *n.* Zaunkönig, *der*
wrench [rentʃ] **1.** *n.* **a)** *(tool)* verstellbarer Schraubenschlüssel; **pipe ~:** Rohrzange, *die;* **screw ~:** Franzose, *der;* **b)** *(Amer.) see* **spanner; c)** *(violent twist)* Verrenkung, *die;* **give one's ankle/shoulder a ~:** sich *(Dat.)* den Knöchel/die Schulter verrenken; **give a ~ at the door-handle** an der Türklinke reißen; **d)** *(fig.)* **be a great ~ [for sb.]** sehr schmerzhaft für jmdn. sein; **what a ~ it must have been for her** wie schmerzlich muß es für sie gewesen sein. **2.** *v. t.* **a)** *(tug violently)* reißen; **~ at sth.** an etw. *(Dat.)* reißen; **~ sth. round/off/open** etw. herum-/ab-/aufreißen; **~ sth. from sb.** jmdm. etw. entreißen; **b)** *(injure by twisting)* **~ one's ankle** *etc.* sich *(Dat.)* den Knöchel *usw.* verrenken
wrest [rest] *v. t.* **~ sth. from sb./sb.'s grasp** *(lit. or fig.)* jmdm./jmds. Griff etw. entreißen *od. (geh.)* entwinden; **~ a confession from sb.** jmdm. ein Geständnis abnötigen *(geh.)*; **~ sth. from sth.** einer Sache *(Dat.)* etw. abringen
wrestle ['resl] **1.** *n.* **a)** *(hard struggle)* Ringen, *das;* **b)** *(wrestling-match)* Ringkampf, *der;* **have a ~:** einen Ringkampf austragen. **2.** *v. i.* **a)** ringen; **b)** *(fig.: grapple)* sich abmühen; **~ with one's conscience** mit seinem Gewissen ringen; **~ with the controls of the aircraft** mit der Steuerung des Flugzeugs kämpfen. **3.** *v. t.* **~ sth. from sth.** etw. mühsam von etw. entfernen
wrestler ['reslə(r)] *n.* Ringer, *der*/Ringerin, *die*
wrestling ['reslɪŋ] *n., no pl., no indef. art.* Ringen, *das;* **~-match** Ringkampf, *der*
wretch [retʃ] *n.* Kreatur, *die; (joc.: child)* Gör, *das*
wretched ['retʃɪd] *adj.* **a)** *(miserable)* unglücklich; **feel ~ about sb./sth.** *(be embarrassed)* über jmdn./etw. todunglücklich sein; **feel ~** *(be very unwell)* sich elend fühlen; **b)** *(coll.: damned)* elend *(abwertend)*; **I wish he would control that ~ dog of his!** wenn er nur besser auf seinen elenden Köter aufpassen würde!; **c)** *(very bad)* erbärmlich; miserabel ‹*Wetter*›; **she's had a bout of ~ health** es ging ihr gesundheitlich sehr schlecht; **d)** *(causing discomfort)* schrecklich ‹*Reise, Erfahrung, Zeit*›
wretchedly ['retʃɪdlɪ] *adv.* **a)** *(in misery)* jämmerlich ‹*weinen*›; jammervoll ‹*anblicken*›; **b)** *(very badly)* erbärmlich
wretchedness ['retʃɪdnɪs] *n., no pl.* **a)** *(misery)* Elend, *das;* **b)** *(badness)* Erbärmlichkeit, *die*
wrick *see* **[2]rick**
wriggle ['rɪgl] **1.** *v. i.* **a)** zappeln; **~ [about] on one's chair** auf dem Stuhl herumrutschen *(ugs.)*; **b)** *(make one's/its way by wriggling)* sich winden; **a worm ~d across the lawn** ein Wurm schlängelte sich über den Rasen; **~ free of the ropes** sich aus den Stricken winden; **~ out of a difficulty** *etc.* *(fig.)* sich aus einer schwierigen Situation *usw.* herauswinden. **2.** *v. t.* **a) ~ one's way** *(lit. or fig.)* sich schlängeln; **~ one's way out of a difficulty** *etc.* sich aus einer schwierigen Situation *usw.* herauswinden; **b)** *(move)* **~ one's hips** die Hüften kreisen lassen. **3.** *n.* Windung, *die*
wriggly ['rɪglɪ] *adj.* sich windend ‹*Wurm, Aal*›; zappelnd ‹*Fisch, Kind*›
wring [rɪŋ] *v. t.,* **wrung** [rʌŋ] **a)** wringen; **~ out** auswringen; **~ the water out of the towels** das Wasser aus den Handtüchern

wringen; **b)** *(squeeze forcibly)* ~ **sb.'s hand** jmdm. fest die Hand drücken; *(twist forcibly)* ~ **one's hands** die Hände ringen *(geh.)*; ~ **the neck of an animal** einem Tier den Hals umdrehen; **I could have wrung his neck** *(fig.)* ich hätte ihm den Hals umdrehen können; **c)** *(extract)* wringen; ~ **sth. from** *or* **out of sb.** *(fig.)* jmdm. etw. abpressen; **d)** *(distress)* ~ **the heart** einem das Herz abdrücken

wringer ['rɪŋə(r)] *n.* Wringmaschine, *die*

wringing wet [rɪŋɪŋ 'wet] *adj.* tropfnaß; **our clothes were** ~: unsere Kleider waren zum Auswringen

wrinkle ['rɪŋkl] **1.** *n.* Falte, *die; (in paper)* Knick, *der.* **2.** *v. t.* falten; in Falten legen ⟨*Stirn*⟩; kräuseln ⟨*Nase*⟩. **3.** *v. i.* sich in Falten legen

wrinkled ['rɪŋkld] *adj.* runz[e]lig; ~ **with age** runzlig vom Alter

wrinkly ['rɪŋklɪ] **1.** *adj.* runz[e]lig. **2.** *n. (sl.)* Grufti, *der (ugs.)*

wrist [rɪst] *n.* Handgelenk, *das;* **slash one's** ~**s** sich *(Dat.)* die Pulsadern aufschneiden; **the glove was too tight at the** ~: der Handschuh war zu eng am Handgelenk

wrist: ~**band** *n.* **a)** *(cuff)* Manschette, *die;* **b)** *see* **sweat-band;** ~**-watch** *n.* Armbanduhr, *die*

¹writ [rɪt] *n. (Law)* **a)** Verfügung, *die;* **serve a** ~ **on sb.** jmdm. eine Verfügung zustellen; **sb.'s** ~ **runs in ...** *(fig.)* jmds. Macht reicht bis nach ...; **b)** *(Crown document) königlicher Erlaß, mit dem ein Peer ins Parlament gerufen wird/mit dem Parlamentswahlen ausgerufen werden;* **c)** *(Relig.)* **Holy W**~: die Heilige Schrift

²writ *see* **write 2 a**

write [raɪt] **1.** *v. i.,* **wrote** [rəʊt], **written** ['rɪtn] schreiben; ~ **to sb./a firm** jmdm./an eine Firma schreiben; ~ **for a fresh supply** schriftlich eine neue Lieferung anfordern; **she** ~**s for a living** sie ist Schriftstellerin; *see also* **home. 2.** *v. t.,* **wrote, written: a)** schreiben; ausschreiben ⟨*Scheck*⟩; **the written language** die Schriftsprache; ~ **it, don't print it** schreibe es nicht in Druckschrift, sondern in Schreibschrift; **written applications** schriftliche Anträge; **the paper had been written all over** das Papier war ganz vollgeschrieben; **it is written that ...:** es steht geschrieben, daß ...; **be written into the contract** [ausdrücklich] im Vertrag stehen; ~ **sb. into/out of a serial** für jmdn. eine Rolle in einer Serie schreiben/jmdm. einen Abgang aus einer Serie verschaffen; **writ large** *(fig.)* im Großformat *(fig.)*; **b)** *(Amer./Commerc./coll.:* ~ *letter to)* anschreiben; **c)** *in pass. (fig.: be apparent)* **sb. has sth. written in his face** jmdm. steht etw. im Gesicht geschrieben; **guilt was written all over her face** die Schuld stand ihr ins Gesicht geschrieben; **she had 'career woman' written all over her** man sah ihr die Karrierefrau schon von weitem an; **d)** *(Computing)* schreiben; ~ **in** *or* **into** *or* **on** *or* **to a disc** auf eine Diskette schreiben; **e)** *see* **underwrite**

~ **a'way** *v. i.* ~ **away for sth.** etw. [schriftlich] anfordern

~ **'back** *v. i.* zurückschreiben

~ **'down** *v. t.* **a)** *(record)* aufschreiben; **b)** *(Commerc.: reduce nominal value of)* abschreiben *(Wirtsch.)*

~ **'in 1.** *v. i.* hinschreiben *(ugs.)*; *(include)* hineinschreiben; ~ **in for sth.** etw. [schriftlich] anfordern; ~ **in to sb.** an jmdn. schreiben. **2.** *v. t. (Amer. Polit.)* eintragen; *see also* **write-in**

~ **'off 1.** *v. t.* **a)** *(compose with ease)* herunterschreiben *(ugs.)*; **b)** *(cancel)* abschreiben ⟨*Schulden, Verlust*⟩; *(fig.)* ~ **sb. off** [**as a failure** *etc.*] jmdn. [als Versager] abschreiben *(ugs.)*; **c)** *(destroy)* zu Schrott fahren. **2.** *v. i. see* ~ **away.** *See also* **write-off**

~ **'out** *v. t.* **a)** ausschreiben ⟨*Scheck*⟩; schreiben ⟨*Rezept*⟩; **b)** *(~ in final form)* ausarbeiten; *(~ in full)* ausschreiben; **c)** *(from serial)* verschwinden lassen

~ **'up** *v. t.* **a)** *(praise)* eine gute Kritik schreiben über (+ *Akk.*); **b)** *(~ account of)* einen Bericht schreiben über (+ *Akk.*); *(~ in full)* aufarbeiten; **c)** *(bring up to date)* auf den neuesten Stand bringen. *See also* **write-up**

write: ~**-in** *n. (Amer.) Kandidat, der nicht auf dem offiziellen Stimmzettel steht, sondern vom Wähler selbst eingetragen wird;* **he received 10,000** ~**-in votes** sein Name wurde auf zehntausend Stimmzettel geschrieben; ~**-off** *n. (person)* Versager, *der*/Versagerin, *die; (event)* Reinfall, *der; (vehicle)* Totalschaden, *der*

writer ['raɪtə(r)] *n.* **a)** *(author)* Schriftsteller, *der*/Schriftstellerin, *die; (of letter, article)* Schreiber, *der*/Schreiberin, *die;* Verfasser, *der*/Verfasserin, *die; (of lyrics, advertisements)* Texter, *der*/Texterin, *die; (of music)* Komponist, *der*/Komponistin, *die;* **be a** ~: Schriftsteller/Schriftstellerin sein; **the present** ~: der Autor/die Autorin des vorliegenden Textes; **a** ~ **of historical fiction** ein Verfasser/eine Verfasserin historischer Romane; **b) be a good/bad** ~ *(as to handwriting)* eine gute/schlechte Schrift haben

writer's 'cramp *n. (Med.)* Schreibkrampf, *der*

'write-up *n.* Bericht, *der; (by critic)* Kritik, *die;* **get a good** ~: gut besprochen werden

writhe [raɪð] *v. i. (lit. or fig.)* sich winden; **he/it makes me** ~ *(with embarrassment)* er/es bringt mich in ziemliche Verlegenheit; *(with disgust)* er/es ist mir zuwider

writing ['raɪtɪŋ] *n.* **a)** Schreiben, *das;* **at the time of** ~: als dies geschrieben wurde; **put sth. in** ~: etw. schriftlich machen *(ugs.)*; *see also* **commit d; b)** *(handwriting)* Schrift, *die;* **c)** *(composing)* Schreiben, *das;* **creative-**~ **course** Kurs für kreatives Schreiben; **earn sth. from one's** ~: mit Schreiben etw. verdienen; **this poem is a lovely piece of** ~: dieses Gedicht ist herrlich geschrieben; **d)** *(something written)* Schrift, *die;* **the** ~**s of Plato** die Platonischen Schriften; **the** ~ **on the wall** *(fig.)* das Menetekel an der Wand; **she's seen the** ~ **on the wall** sie hat die Zeichen erkannt; **the** ~ **is on the wall for this department** diese Abteilung hat keine Zukunft

writing: ~**-case** *n.* Schreibmappe, *die;* ~**-desk** *n.* Schreibpult, *das;* Sekretär, *der;* ~**-pad** *n.* Schreibblock, *der;* ~**-paper** *n.* Schreibpapier, *das;* Briefpapier, *das*

written *see* **write**

wrong [rɒŋ] **1.** *adj.* **a)** *(morally bad)* unrecht *(geh.)*; *(unfair)* ungerecht; **you were** ~ **to be so angry** es war nicht richtig von dir, so ärgerlich zu sein; **what's** ~ **with sth./that?** was ist gegen etw./dagegen einzuwenden?; **what's** ~ **with having a drink?** warum sollte man nicht mal ein Glas trinken?; **b)** *(mistaken)* falsch; **be** ~ ⟨*Person:*⟩ sich irren; **I was** ~ **about you** ich habe mich in dir geirrt; **the clock is** ~: die Uhr geht falsch; **the clock is** ~ **by ten minutes** die Uhr geht 10 Minuten vor/nach; **how** ~ **can you be** *or* **get!** wie man sich irren kann!; **c)** *(not suitable)* falsch; **give the** ~ **answer** eine falsche Antwort geben; **that was the** ~ **move to make** das war genau das Falsche; **say/do the** ~ **thing** das Falsche sagen/tun; **you've come to the** ~ **person** Sie sind bei mir an der falschen Adresse; **be the** ~ **person for the job** für die Stelle ungeeignet sein; **take the** ~ **turning** falsch abbiegen; **get hold of the** ~ **end of the stick** *(fig.)* alles völlig falsch verstehen; [**the**] ~ **way round** verkehrt herum; *see also* **go down b; number 1 a; d)** *(out of order)* nicht in Ordnung; **there's something** ~ **here/with him** hier/mit ihm stimmt etwas nicht; **there's nothing** ~: es ist alles in Ordnung; **what's** ~**?** ist etwas nicht in Ordnung? *See also* **wrong side. 2.** *adv.* falsch; **get it** ~: es falsch *od.* verkehrt machen; *(misunderstand)* sich irren; **I got the answer** ~ **again** meine Antwort war wieder falsch; **get sb.** ~: jmdn. falsch verstehen; **go** ~ *(take* ~ *path)* sich verlaufen; *(fig.)* ⟨*Person:*⟩ vom rechten Weg abkommen *(fig. geh.)*; ⟨*Maschine, Mechanismus:*⟩ kaputtgehen *(ugs.)*; ⟨*Angelegenheit:*⟩ danebengehen *(ugs.)*; **you can't go** ~ **if you study engineering** wenn du auf die Ingenieurschule gehst, kannst du gar nichts verkehrt machen; **the television/dishwasher has gone** ~: der Fernseher/die Spülmaschine ist kaputt *(ugs.)*. **3.** *n.* **a)** *(what is morally bad)* Unrecht, *das;* **know the difference between right and** ~: zwischen Recht und Unrecht unterscheiden können; **two** ~**s don't make a right** das gibt nur ein Unrecht mehr; **do** ~: unrecht tun; **she can do no** ~: sie kann überhaupt nichts Unrechtes tun; **be in the** ~: im Unrecht sein; **put sb. in the** ~: jmdn. ins Unrecht setzen; **b)** *(injustice)* Unrecht, *das* (**towards** gegenüber); **suffer a** ~**/many** ~**s** Unrecht/viel Unrecht erleiden; **do** ~ **to sb., do sb. a** ~: jmdm. ein Unrecht zufügen; **do sb.** ~: jmdm. unrecht tun. **4.** *v. t.* ~ **sb.** *(treat unjustly)* jmdn. ungerecht behandeln; *(mistakenly discredit)* jmdm. unrecht tun

wrong: ~**doer** *n.* Übeltäter, *der*/-täterin, *die;* Missetäter, *der*/-täterin, *die (geh.)*; ~**doing** *n.* **a)** *no pl., no indef. art.* Missetaten *(geh.)*; **b)** *(instance)* Missetat, *die (geh.)*; ~**-'foot** *v. t.* **a)** *(Sport)* ~**-foot sb.** jmdn. auf dem falschen Fuß erwischen *(Sportjargon)*; **b)** *(fig. coll.)* unvorbereitet treffen; **he was** ~**-footed by that** darauf war er überhaupt nicht vorbereitet

wrongful ['rɒŋfl] *adj.* **a)** *(unfair)* unrecht *(geh.)*; **b)** *(unlawful)* rechtswidrig

wrongfully ['rɒŋfəlɪ] *adv.* **a)** *(unfairly)* unrecht *(geh.)*⟨*handeln*⟩; zu Unrecht ⟨*beschuldigen*⟩; **b)** *(unlawfully)* rechtswidrig

'wrong-headed *adj.* starrköpfig *(abwertend)* (**about** in + *Dat.*)

wrongly ['rɒŋlɪ] *adv.* **a)** *(inappropriately, incorrectly)* falsch; **b)** *(mistakenly)* zu Unrecht; **I believed,** ~, **that ...:** ich habe fälschlicherweise geglaubt, daß ...; **c)** *see* **wrongfully a**

wrongness ['rɒŋnɪs] *n., no pl.* **a)** *(moral* ~*)* Unrecht, *das;* **b)** *(inappropriateness, mistakenness)* Unrichtigkeit, *die*

wrong: ~ **side** *n.* **a)** *(of fabric)* linke Seite; [**the**] ~ **side out/up** verkehrt herum; **b) be on the** ~ **side of thirty** die dreißig überschritten haben; **get on the** ~ **side of sb./the law** *(fig.)* jmdn. falsch anfassen/mit dem Gesetz in Konflikt geraten; *see also* **bed 1 a; blanket 1 a;** ~ **'un** *n. (coll.: person)* falscher Fuffziger *(salopp)*

wrote *see* **write**

wrought *see* **work 2**

wrought 'iron *n.* Schmiedeeisen, *das; attrib.* schmiedeeisern ⟨*Tor, Zaun*⟩

wrung *see* **wring**

WRVS *abbr. (Brit.)* **Women's Royal Voluntary Service** *britischer Hilfsdienst für Menschen in Not*

wry [raɪ] *adj.,* ~**er** *or* **wrier** ['raɪə(r)], ~**est** *or* **wriest** ['raɪɪst] ironisch ⟨*Blick*⟩; fein ⟨*Humor, Witz*⟩; **a** ~ **smile** ein schiefes Lächeln; **make** *or* **pull a** ~ **face** das Gesicht verziehen

wryly ['raɪlɪ] *adv.* ironisch ⟨*blicken, sagen*⟩; schief ⟨*lächeln*⟩

WSW [westsaʊθ'west] *abbr.* **west-south-west** WSW

wt. *abbr.* **weight** Gew.

WW *abbr. (Amer.)* **World War** WK

wych-hazel ['wɪtʃheɪzl] *n.* **a)** *(shrub)* Virginische Zaubernuß; **b)** *(lotion)* Hamameliswasser, *das*

X

¹X, x [eks] *n., pl.* **Xs** *or* **X's** ['eksɪz] **a)** *(letter)* X, x, *das;* **b)** *(Math.)* x; **c)** *(unknown person or number)* **Mr X** Herr X; **x tons of cement** soundso viel Tonnen Zement; **x number of ...** *(coll.)* x ... *(ugs.);* **d)** *(Roman numeral)* X; **e)** *(cross-shaped symbol)* Kreuz, *das;* **x marks the spot** die Stelle ist durch ein Kreuz markiert

²X *symb. (Brit. Hist.)* nicht jugendfrei

xenon ['zenɒn] *n. (Chem.)* Xenon, *das*

xenophobe ['zenəfəʊb] *n.* Fremdenfeindliche, *der/die;* Xenophobe, *der/die*

xenophobia [zenə'fəʊbɪə] *n.* Fremdenfeindlichkeit, *die;* Xenophobie, *die*

xerography [zɪə'rɒgrəfɪ, ze'rɒgrəfɪ] *n.* Xerographie, *die (Druckw.)*

Xerox, (P), xerox ['zɪərɒks, 'zerɒks] **1.** *n.* **a)** *(process)* Xerographie, *die (Druckw.);* **b)** *(copy)* Xerokopie, *die.* **2. xerox** *v. t.* xerokopieren

Xmas ['krɪsməs, 'eksməs] *n. (coll.)* Weihnachten, *das*

X-rated ['eksreɪtɪd] *adj. (Brit. Hist.)* nicht jugendfrei ‹*Film*›

'X-ray 1. *n.* **a)** *in pl.* Röntgenstrahlen *Pl.;* X-Strahlen *Pl.;* **b)** *(picture)* Röntgenaufnahme, *die;* **c)** *attrib.* Röntgen-. **2.** *v. t.* röntgen; durchleuchten ‹*Gepäck*›

xylophone ['zaɪləfəʊn] *n. (Mus.)* Xylophon, *das*

Y

¹Y, y [waɪ] *n., pl.* **Ys** *or* **Y's a)** *(letter)* Y, y, *das;* **b)** *(Math.)* y

²Y *abbr.* **a)** *(Amer.)* **YMCA/YWCA** CVJM/CVJF; **b) yen**

y. *abbr.* **year[s]** J.

yacht [jɒt] **1.** *n.* **a)** *(for racing)* Segelboot, *das;* Segeljacht, *die;* **b)** *(for pleasure travel etc.)* Jacht, *die.* **2.** *v. i.* segeln

'yacht-club *n.* Jachtklub, *der*

yachting ['jɒtɪŋ] *n., no pl., no art.* Segeln, *das; attrib.* Segel-

yachtsman ['jɒtsmən] *n., pl.* **yachtsmen** ['jɒtsmən] Segler, *der*

yack [jæk], **yackety-yack** [jækətɪ'jæk] *(sl. derog.)* **1.** *n.* Gequassel, *das (ugs. abwertend).* **2.** *v. i.* quasseln *(ugs. abwertend)*

yah [jɑ:] *int.* **~ [boo sucks]** bäh

yahoo [jə'hu:] *n.* Untier, *das (fig.)*

yak [jæk] *n. (Zool.)* Jak, *der*

Yale, (P) [jeɪl]: **~ key** *n.* Yaleschlüssel, *der* Ⓦ *(Technik);* ≈ Sicherheitsschlüssel, *der;* **~ lock** *n.* Yaleschloß, *das* Ⓦ *(Technik);* ≈ [Zylinder]sicherheitsschloß, *das*

Yalta ['jæltə] *pr. n.* Jalta *(das)*

yam [jæm] *n.* **a)** *(plant, tuber)* Jamswurzel, *die;* **b)** *(Amer.) see* **sweet potato**

yammer ['jæmə(r)] *(coll./dial.)* **1.** *v. i.* maulen *(ugs.);* **he's always ~ing on about sth.** dauernd muß er über etw. *(Akk.)* maulen. **2.** *n.* Gemaule, *das (ugs. abwertend)*

yang [jæŋ] *n., no pl., no indef. art. (Chinese Philos.)* Yang, *das*

Yank [jæŋk] **1.** *n.* **a)** *(Brit. coll.: American)* Yankee, *der;* Ami, *der (ugs.);* **b)** *(Amer.: inhabitant of New England or northern States)* Yankee, *der.* **2.** *adj.* **a)** *(Brit. coll.: American)* Ami- *(ugs.);* **b)** *(Amer.: of New England or northern States)* Yankee-

yank *(coll.)* **1.** *v. t.* reißen an (+ *Dat.*); **~ sth. off/out** etw. ab-/ausreißen. **2.** *n.* Reißen, *das;* **give a ~ at sth.** an etw. *(Dat.)* reißen; **give the rope a good ~:** kräftig am Seil ziehen

Yankee ['jæŋkɪ] *see* **Yank**

yap [jæp] **1.** *v. i.,* **-pp- a)** *(bark shrilly)* kläffen; **b)** *(coll.: talk)* quatschen *(salopp abwertend); (complainingly)* lamentieren *(ugs. abwertend).* **2.** *n.* Kläffen, *das;* **give a ~:** kläffen

yarborough ['jɑ:bərə] *n. (Cards) Blatt (bei Whist und Bridge), bei dem keine Karte höher als 9 ist*

¹yard [jɑ:d] *n.* **a)** Yard, *das;* **by the ~:** ≈ meterweise; *(fig.)* am laufenden Band *(ugs.);* **sell books by the ~** *(fig.)* Bücher meterweise verkaufen; **have a face a ~ long** ein Gesicht wie drei Tage Regenwetter machen; **b)** *in pl. (coll.: great amount)* **have/get** *etc.* **~s of sth.** etw. massenweise haben/bekommen *usw.;* **~s of toilet-paper** meterweise Toilettenpapier; **c)** *(Naut.)* Rah[e], *die;* **d) ~ of ale** *(Brit.)* [Stangen]glas, *das;* Stange, *die (bes. westd.);* **e)** *see* **square 2 b; f)** *see* **cubic b**

²yard *n.* **a)** *(attached to building)* Hof, *der;* **in the ~:** auf dem Hof; **b)** *(for manufacture)* Werkstatt, *die; (for storage)* Lager, *das; (ship~)* Werft, *die;* **builder's ~:** Bauhof, *der;* **c)** *(Amer.: garden)* Garten, *der;* **d) the Y~** *(Brit. coll.) see* **Scotland Yard.** *See also* **back yard; goods yard**

yard: ~-arm *n. (Naut.)* Rahnock, *das od. die;* **~stick** *n.* **a)** Meßstab, *der;* Maßstab, *der (veralt.);* **b)** *(fig.: standard)* Maßstab, *der*

yarn [jɑ:n] **1.** *n.* **a)** *(thread)* Garn, *das;* **b)** *(coll.: story)* Geschichte, *die; (of sailor)* [Seemanns]garn, *das;* **have a ~ with sb.** *(chat)* mit jmdm. plauschen *(bes. südd.) od.* klönen *(nordd.); see also* **spin 1 a. 2.** *v. i. (coll.)* Geschichten erzählen; ‹*Seemann:*› [s]ein Garn spinnen

yarrow ['jærəʊ] *n. (Bot.)* Schafgarbe, *die*

yashmak ['jæʃmæk] *n.* Jaschmak, *der*

yaw [jɔ:] *(Naut., Aeronaut.)* **1.** *v. i.* gieren. **2.** *n.* Gieren, *das*

yawl [jɔ:l] *n. (Naut.)* Yawl, *die;* Heckmaster, *der*

yawn [jɔ:n] **1.** *n.* **a)** Gähnen, *das;* **give a [long] ~:** [herzhaft] gähnen; **there were a few ~s** es wurde ein paarmal gegähnt; **b) be a ~** *(sl.: be boring)* zum Gähnen langweilig sein. **2.** *v. i.* **a)** gähnen; **~ with exhaustion** vor Müdigkeit gähnen; **b)** *(fig.)* ‹*Abgrund, Kluft, Spalte:*› gähnen *(geh.)*

yawning ['jɔ:nɪŋ] *adj.* gähnend *(auch fig. geh.)*

yawp [jɔ:p] *(Amer.)* **1.** *v. i.* **a)** *(squawk)* kreischen; **b)** *(talk foolishly)* faseln *(ugs. abwertend).* **2.** *n.* **a)** *(squawk)* Gekreisch[e], *das;* **b)** *(foolish talk)* Gefasel, *das (ugs. abwertend)*

yaws [jɔ:z] *n. sing. (Med.)* Himbeerpocken *Pl.;* Frambösie, *die (fachspr.)*

yd[s]. *abbr.* **yard[s]** Yd[s].

¹ye [ji:] *pron. (arch./poet./dial./joc.)* Ihr *(veralt.); (as direct or indirect object)* Euch *(veralt.)*

²ye *adj. (pseudo-arch.)* = **the**

yea [jeɪ] *(arch.)* **1.** *adv.* ja. **2.** *n.* Ja, *das* **~s and nays** Ja- und Neinstimmen; **~ and nay** Ja und Nein

yeah [jeə] *adv. (coll.)* ja; **[oh] ~?** [ach] ja?

year [jɪə(r)] *n.* **a)** Jahr, *das;* **solar ~:** Sonnenjahr, *das;* **sidereal ~:** siderisches Jahr; Sternjahr, *das;* **she gets £10,000 a ~:** sie verdient 10 000 Pfund im Jahr; **~ in ~ out** jahrein, jahraus; **~ after ~:** Jahr für *od.* um Jahr; **all [the] ~ round** das ganze Jahr hindurch; **in a ~['s time]** in einem Jahr; **once a ~, once every ~:** einmal im Jahr; **Christian** *or* **Church** *or* **ecclesiastical ~** *(Eccl.)* Kirchenjahr, *das;* liturgisches Jahr *(kath. Kirche);* **a ten-~-old** ein Zehnjähriger/eine Zehnjährige; **a ten-~[s]-old child/animal/thing** ein zehn Jahre altes Kind/Tier/Ding; **in her thirtieth ~:** in ihrem 30. Lebensjahr; **financial** *or* **fiscal** *or* **tax ~:** Finanz- *od.* Rechnungsjahr, *das;* **calendar** *or* **civil ~:** Kalenderjahr, *das;* **school ~:** Schuljahr, *das;* **for a ~ and a day** ein Jahr und einen Tag [lang]; **a ~ [from] today** *etc.* heute *usw.* in einem Jahr; **a ~ [ago] today** *etc.* heute *usw.* vor einem Jahr; **... of the ~** *(best)* ... des Jahres; *see also* **¹by 1 m; dot 1 c; from b; grace 1 e; leap year; lord 1 b; sabbatical 1; b)** *(group of students)* Jahrgang, *der;* **first-~ student** Student/Studentin im ersten Jahr; **c)** *in pl. (age)* **he doesn't look his ~s** man sieht ihm seine Jahre nicht an; **be old for** *or* **beyond one's ~s** *(unexpectedly mature)* für sein Alter schon sehr reif sein; *(looking older than one is)* älter wirken, als man ist; **be young for one's ~s** jünger wirken, als man ist; **be getting on/be well on in ~s** in die Jahre kommen/in vorgerücktem Alter sein *(geh.);* **d)** *in pl. (very long time)* Jahre; **she looks ~s older** sie sieht um Jahre älter aus; **sth. has put ~s on sb.** etw. hat jmdn. um Jahre altern lassen; **take ~s off sb./sb.'s life** jmdn. um Jahre jünger/älter machen

'year-book *n.* Jahrbuch, *das*

yearling ['jɪəlɪŋ] **1.** *n. (Zool., Agric.)* Jährling, *der.* **2.** *adj. (a year old)* einjährig

'year-long *adj. (lasting a year)* einjährig; *(lasting the whole year)* ganzjährig

yearly ['jɪəlɪ] **1.** *adj.* **a)** *(annual)* jährlich; **ten-~:** zehnjährig; **at twice-~ intervals** zweimal im Jahr; **b)** *(lasting a year)* Einjahres- ‹*vertrag, -abonnement*›. **2.** *adv.* jährlich

yearn [jɜ:n] *v. i.* **~ for** *or* **after sth./for sb./to do sth.** sich nach etw./jmdm. sehnen/sich danach sehnen, etw. zu tun

yearning ['jɜ:nɪŋ] **1.** *n.* Sehnsucht, *die.* **2.** *adj.* sehnsüchtig ‹*Blick, Liebe*›; sehnlich ‹*Wunsch, Gebet*›

'year-round *adj.* ganzjährig

yeast [ji:st] *n.* Hefe, *die*

yeast: ~ cake *n.* **a)** *(mass of ~)* Hefewürfel, *der;* **b)** *(cake made with ~)* Hefekuchen, *der;* **~ pastry** *n.* Hefeteig, *der*

yeasty ['ji:stɪ] *adj.* hefig

yell [jel] **1.** *n.* **a)** gellender Schrei; **let out a ~:** einen Schrei ausstoßen; **when supper's ready, I'll give you a ~** *(coll.)* wenn das Abendessen fertig ist, rufe ich dich; **b)** *(Amer.: students' cry)* Anfeuerungsruf, *der.* **2.** *v. i.* [gellend] schreien; **~ with rage/laughter** wütend schreien/vor Lachen brüllen; **~ at each other** einander anschreien. **3.** *v. t.* [gellend] schreien

yellow ['jeləʊ] **1.** *adj.* **a)** gelb; flachsblond ‹*Haar*›; golden ‹*Getreide*›; vergilbt ‹*Papier*›; **b)** *(fig. coll.: cowardly)* feige; **have got/show a ~ streak** feige *od.* ein Feigling sein. *See also* **¹flag 1. 2.** *n.* **a)** *(colour)* Gelb, *das;* **b)** *(pigment)* Gelbton, *der;* **c)** *(~ clothes)* **dressed in ~:** gelb gekleidet; **d)** *(Snooker)* gelbe Kugel; **e)** *(butterfly)* Gelbling, *der; (brimstone)* Zitronenfalter, *der;*

clouded ~: Postillon, *der.* **3.** *v. t. & i.* vergilben

yellow: ~-belly *n. (sl. derog.)* Feigling, *der (ugs.);* ~ **'fever** *n. (Med.)* Gelbfieber, *das;* **~hammer** *n. (Ornith.)* Goldammer, *die*

yellowish ['jeləʊɪʃ] *adj.* gelblich

yellow 'line *n. (Brit.)* gelbe [Markierungs]linie; **I'm on double ~s** ich stehe im Parkverbot

yellowness ['jeləʊnɪs] *n., no pl.* gelbe Farbe

yellow 'pages, (P) *n. pl.* gelbe Seiten; Branchenverzeichnis, *das*

yelp [jelp] **1.** *v.i.* aufheulen *(ugs.);* ⟨*Hund:*⟩ jaulen. **2.** *n.* Heulen, *das; (of dog)* Jaulen, *das;* **the child/dog gave a ~:** das Kind heulte auf/der Hund jaulte

yelping ['jelpɪŋ] *n.* Geheule, *das (ugs.); (of dog)* Gejaule, *das*

Yemen ['jemən] *pr. n.* **[the] ~:** [der] Jemen

Yemeni ['jemənɪ] **1.** *adj.* jemenitisch. **2.** *n.* Jemenit, *der*/Jemenitin, *die*

Yemenite ['jemənaɪt] *n. see* **Yemeni 2**

¹yen [jen] *n., pl. same (Japanese currency)* Yen, *der*

²yen *n. (coll.: longing)* Drang, *der* **(for** nach); **sb. has a ~ to do sth.** es drängt jmdn. danach, etw. zu tun

yeoman ['jəʊmən] *n., pl.* **yeomen** ['jəʊmən] **a)** *(with small estate)* Kleinbauer, *der;* **b)** *(Hist.: freeholder)* Freisasse, *der;* **c)** *(Brit. Mil. Hist.)* Angehöriger der Yeomanry; **d)** ~ **[of signals]** *(Brit. Navy)* Signalmaat, *der;* **e)** *(Amer. Navy) Marineunteroffizier, der mit Verwaltungsarbeiten betraut ist*

Yeoman of the 'Guard *n. (Brit. Mil.)* königlicher Leibgardist; *(in popular use: warder in Tower of London)* Wärter im Tower von London

yeomanry ['jəʊmənrɪ] *n., no pl.* Yeomanry, *die (hist.); berittene Freiwilligentruppe*

'yeoman['s] service *n.* **give sb. ~:** jmdm. gute Dienste tun; **do ~:** gute Dienste leisten

yep [jep] *int. (Amer. coll.)* ja

yes [jes] **1.** *adv.* ja; *(in contradiction)* doch; **~, sir** jawohl!; **I didn't do it! – Oh ~ you did!** Ich war es nicht! – Doch warst du es!; **~?** *(indeed?)* ach ja?; *(what do you want?)* ja?; *(to customer)* ja, bitte?; **say '~':** ja sagen; **say ~ to a proposal** einem Vorschlag zustimmen; **she'll say ~ to anything** sie sagt zu allem ja und amen; **~ and no** ja und nein; jein *(scherzh.); see also* **¹oh. 2.** *n., pl.* **~es** Ja, *das*

'yes-man *n. (coll. derog.)* Jasager, *der (abwertend)*

yesterday ['jestədeɪ, 'jestədɪ] **1.** *n.* **a)** gestern; **the day before ~:** vorgestern; **~'s paper** die gestrige Zeitung; die Zeitung von gestern; **~ morning/afternoon/evening/night** gestern vormittag/nachmittag/abend/nacht; **a week [from] ~:** gestern in einer Woche; **a year [ago] ~:** gestern vor einem Jahr; **~ evening's concert** das Konzert gestern abend *od.* am gestrigen Abend; **b)** *(recent time)* **of ~:** von gestern; **all our ~s** unsere Vergangenheit; **be ~'s men** passé sein. **2.** *adv.* **a)** gestern; **the day before ~:** vorgestern; **~ morning/afternoon/evening/night** gestern vormittag/nachmittag/abend/nacht; **b)** *(in the recent past)* gestern; *see also* **born 1**

yet [jet] **1.** *adv.* **a)** *(still)* noch; **have ~ to reach sth.** etw. erst noch erreichen müssen; **have a few days free ~:** noch ein paar Tage frei haben; **much ~ remains to be done** noch bleibt viel zu tun; *see also* **as 4; b)** *(hitherto)* bisher; **the play is his best ~:** das Stück ist sein bisher bestes; **c)** *neg. or interrog. (so soon as now/then)* **not [just] ~:** [jetzt] noch nicht; **never ~:** noch nie; **need you go just ~?** mußt du [jetzt] schon gehen?; **is he dead ~?** ist er schon gestorben?; **you haven't seen anything** *or (coll.)* **ain't seen nothing ~:** das ist noch gar nichts; **d)** *(before all is over)* doch noch; **he could win ~:** er könnte noch gewinnen; **e)** *with compar. (even)* noch; **f)** *(nevertheless)* doch; **g)** *(again)* noch; **~ again** *or* **once more** noch einmal; **nor ~:** noch [...] jemals; **she has never voted for that party, nor ~ intends to** sie hat nie für diese Partei gestimmt, und sie hat es auch nicht vor. **2.** *conj.* doch; **a faint ~ unmistakable smell** ein schwacher, aber unverkennbarer Geruch

yeti ['jetɪ] *n.* Yeti, *der;* Schneemensch, *der*

yew [ju:] *n.* **a)** *(tree)* Eibe, *die;* **b)** *(wood)* Eibenholz, *das*

'yew-tree *see* **yew a**

'Y-fronts, (P) *n. pl. Herrenunterhose mit y-förmiger Vorderseite*

YHA *abbr. (Brit.)* **Youth Hostels Association** Jugendherbergsverband, *der*

Yid [jɪd] *n. (sl. derog.)* Itzig, *der (ugs. abwertend)*

Yiddish ['jɪdɪʃ] **1.** *adj.* jiddisch; *see also* **English 1. 2.** *n.* Jiddisch, *das; see also* **English 2 a**

yield [ji:ld] **1.** *v. t.* **a)** *(give)* bringen; hervorbringen ⟨*Ernte*⟩; tragen ⟨*Obst*⟩; abwerfen ⟨*Gewinn*⟩; ergeben ⟨*Resultat, Informationen*⟩; **b)** *(surrender)* übergeben ⟨*Festung*⟩; lassen ⟨*Vortritt*⟩; abtreten ⟨*Besitz*⟩ **(to** an + *Akk.*); ~ **the point** [in diesem Punkt] nachgeben; **~ a point to sb.** jmdm. in einem Punkt nachgeben; **~ ground to the enemy** vor dem Feind zurückweichen; **~ right of way** Vorfahrt gewähren. **2.** *v. i.* **a)** *(surrender)* sich unterwerfen; **~ to threats/temptation** Drohungen *(Dat.)* nachgeben/der Versuchung *(Dat.)* erliegen; **~ to persuasion/sb.'s entreaties** sich überreden lassen/jmds. Bitten *(Dat.)* nachgeben; **the girl had ~ed to the wily seducer** das Mädchen war dem raffinierten Verführer erlegen; **b)** *(be or feel inferior)* **~ to none in sth.** niemandem in etw. *(Dat.)* nachstehen; **c)** *(give right of way)* Vorfahrt gewähren; **d)** *(Amer.: allow another the right to speak)* **~ to sb.** jmdm. das Wort überlassen. **3.** *n.* **a)** Ertrag, *der;* **b)** *(revenue from tax etc.)* Aufkommen, *das;* **c)** *(return on investment)* Zins[ertrag], *der;* **a 10% ~:** 10% Zinsen; **the ~ on this bond** die Zinsen für dieses Wertpapier

~ 'up *v. t.* **a)** *(surrender)* übergeben ⟨*Stadt, Festung*⟩; ausliefern ⟨*Gefangenen, sich selbst*⟩; **b)** *(reveal)* enthüllen ⟨*Geheimnis*⟩; hervorbringen ⟨*Reichtum, Ertrag, Ernte*⟩

'yield point *n. (Phys.)* Fließgrenze, *die*

yin [jɪn] *n., no pl., no indef. art. (Chinese Philos.)* Yin, *das*

yip [jɪp] *(Amer.)* **1.** *v. i.,* **-pp-** *see* **yelp 1. 2.** *n. see* **yelp 2**

yippee ['jɪpi:] *int.* hurra

YMCA *abbr.* **Young Men's Christian Association** CVJM

yob [jɒb] *n. (Brit. sl.)* Rowdy, *der (abwertend)*

yobbish ['jɒbɪʃ] *adj. (Brit. sl.)* rowdyhaft

yobbo ['jɒbəʊ] *n., pl.* **~s** *see* **yob**

yodel ['jəʊdl] **1.** *v. i. & t., (Brit.)* **-ll-** jodeln. **2.** *n.* Jodeln, *das*

Yoga ['jəʊgə] *n.* Joga, *der od. das*

yoghurt ['jɒgət] *n.* Joghurt, *der od. das*

yogi ['jəʊgɪ] *n. (Hindu Philos.)* Yogi[n], *der;* Jogi[n], *der*

yogurt *see* **yoghurt**

yo-heave-ho ['jəʊhi:vhəʊ] = **heave ho** *see* **heave 2 b**

yo[-ho]-ho [jəʊ(həʊ)'həʊ] *int.* **a)** *(to attract attention)* he *(ugs.);* **b)** = **heave ho** *see* **heave 2 b**

yoke [jəʊk] **1.** *n.* **a)** *(for animal)* Joch, *das;* **b)** *(for person)* [Trag]joch, *das;* **c)** *(of garment)* Sattel, *der (Textilw.);* **d)** *(fig.: bond, oppressive control)* Joch, *das (geh.);* **e)** *(pair of oxen etc.)* Joch, *das.* **2.** *v. t.* **a)** ins Joch spannen ⟨*Tier*⟩; **~ an animal to sth.** ein Tier vor etw. *(Akk.)* spannen; **b)** *(fig.: couple)* verbinden

yokel ['jəʊkl] *n. (derog.)* [Bauern]tölpel, *der*

yolk [jəʊk] *n.* Dotter, *der;* Eigelb, *das*

'yolk-sac *n. (Zool.)* Dottersack, *der*

Yom Kippur [jɒm 'kɪpə(r)] = **Day of Atonement** *see* **atonement b**

yomp [jɒmp] *(sl.) v.i. & t.* stapfen

yon [jɒn] *(arch./poet./dial.)* **1.** *adj.* **~ mountain/field** jener Berg/jenes Feld dort *(geh.).* **2.** *adv.* dort drüben; *see also* **hither**

yonder ['jɒndə(r)] *(literary)* **1.** *adj.* **~ tree/peasant** jener Baum/Bauer dort *(geh.).* **2.** *adv.* dort drüben

yoo-hoo ['ju:hu:] *int.* juhu

yore [jɔ:(r)] *n. (literary)* **of ~:** von früher [her] ⟨*kennen*⟩; **customs of ~:** Bräuche von einst; **in days of ~:** in früheren Tagen

yorker ['jɔ:kə(r)] *n. (Cricket) Ball, der so geworfen wird, daß er direkt vor dem Schlagmann auftrifft*

Yorkist ['jɔ:kɪst] *(Hist.)* **1.** *adj.* zum Hause York gehörig; des Hauses York *nachgestellt.* **2.** *n.* Mitglied/Anhänger des Hauses York

Yorkshire ['jɔ:kʃɪə(r), 'jɔ:kʃə(r)]: **~man** ['jɔ:kʃɪəmən, jɔ:kʃəmən] *n., pl.* **~men** ['jɔ:kʃɪəmən, jɔ:kʃəmən] Mann aus Yorkshire; **~ 'pudding** *n. (Gastr.)* Yorkshirepudding, *der;* **~ 'terrier** *n.* Yorkshireterrier, *der;* **~ tyke** *see* **tyke c; ~woman** *n.* Frau aus Yorkshire

you [jʊ, *stressed* 'ju:] *pron.* **a)** *sing./pl.* du/ihr; *as polite address sing. or pl.* Sie; *as direct object* dich/euch/Sie; *as indirect object* dir/euch/Ihnen; *refl.* dich/dir/euch/sich; **it was ~:** du warst/ihr wart/Sie waren es; **~'re another** *(coll.)* du bist selber einer/eine/eins *(ugs.);* **~-know-what/-who** du weißt/ihr wißt/Sie wissen schon, was/wer/wen/wem; **that hat is not quite ~:** dieser Hut paßt nicht ganz zu dir/Ihnen; **b)** *(one)* man; **smoking is bad for you** Rauchen ist ungesund. *See also* **¹he; ¹her; your; yours; yourself; yourselves**

'you-all *pron. (Amer. coll.)* ihr/Sie [alle]

you'd [jʊd, *stressed* ju:d] **a)** = **you had; b)** = **you would**

you'll [jʊl, *stressed* ju:l] **a)** = **you will; b)** = **you shall**

young [jʌŋ] **1.** *adj.,* **~er** ['jʌŋgə(r)], **~est** ['jʌŋgɪst] **a)** *(lit. or fig.)* jung; neu, jung ⟨*Wein*⟩; **a very ~ child** ein ganz kleines Kind; **the ~ boys** die [kleinen] Jungen; **~ at heart** im Herzen jung geblieben; **sb. is not getting any ~er** jmd. wird auch nicht jünger; **you ~ rascal** du [kleiner] Racker *(fam.);* **you're only ~ once** man ist nur einmal jung; **she's a ~ sixty** sie ist eine jung gebliebene Sechzigerin; **the night is still ~:** die Nacht ist jung; **~ Jones** der junge Jones *(ugs.);* **at a ~ age** in jungen Jahren; **he's not as ~ as he used to be** er ist nicht mehr der Jüngste; **b)** *in compar. (of two namesakes)* jünger; *(Scot.: heir)* Erbe, *der;* **Teniers the Y~er** Teniers der Jüngere; **c)** *(characteristic of youth)* jugendlich; **~ love/fashion** junge Liebe/Mode; **d)** *(Polit.)* **Y~ Conservatives/Liberals** *etc.* Junge Konservative/Liberale *usw. See also* **hopeful 2; married 2; shoulder 1 b; year c. 2.** *n. pl. (of animals)* Junge; *(of humans)* Kinder; **with ~:** trächtig; **the ~** *(~ people)* die jungen Leute; **~ and old** jung und alt

young: ~ 'blood *see* **blood 1 c; ~ day[s]** *n. [pl.]* Jugendjahre *Pl.;* **in my ~ days** in meiner Jugend[zeit]; **~ 'family** *n.* junge Familie; **have a ~ family** kleine Kinder haben; **~ 'fogey** *n. junger angepaßter und erzkonservativer Mann*

youngish ['jʌŋgɪʃ] *adj.* ziemlich jung

young: ~ 'lady *n.* **a)** junge Dame; **b)** *(girl-friend)* Freundin, *die;* **~ 'man** *n.* **a)** junger Mann; **b)** *(boy-friend)* Freund, *der;* **Y~ Pretender** *see* **pretender**

youngster ['jʌŋstə(r)] *n.* **a)** *(child)* Kleine, *der/die/das;* **b)** *(young person)* Jugendliche, *der/die;* **you're just a ~ compared with me** im

Vergleich zu mir bist du noch jung; **come on, you ~s!** kommt, ihr jungen Hüpfer! *(ugs.)*

young: ~ thing *n.* junges Ding *(ugs.)*; **~ 'un** *n. (coll.)* **he's only a ~ 'un** er ist noch jung; **all the ~ 'uns** das ganze junge Gemüse *(ugs.)*; **~ 'woman** *n.* **a)** junge Frau; **b)** *(girl-friend)* Freundin, *die*

your [jə(r), *stressed* jʊə(r), jɔː(r)] *poss. pron. attrib.* **a)** *(of you, sing./pl.)* dein/euer; *in polite address* Ihr; **~ average TV viewer** *(coll.)* der durchschnittliche Fernsehzuschauer; **b)** *(one's)* **it's bad for ~ health/eyesight** es ist schlecht für die Gesundheit/Augen. *See also* **^{2}her; our a**

you're [jə(r), *stressed* jʊə(r), jɔː(r)] = **you are**

yours [jʊəz, jɔːz] *poss. pron. pred.* **a)** *(to or of you, sing.)* deiner/deine/dein[e]s; *(to or of you, pl.)* eurer/eure/eures; *in polite address* Ihrer/Ihre/Ihr[e]s; **you and ~:** du und die Deinen/das Deine; **what's ~?** *(coll.)* was nimmst du/nehmen Sie?; *see also* **hers; ours; b)** *(your letter)* Ihr Brief; *(Commerc.)* Ihr Schreiben; **c)** *(ending letter)* **~ [obediently]** Ihr [sehr ergebener *(geh.)*]; **~ truly** in alter Verbundenheit Dein/Deine; *(in business letter)* mit freundlichen Grüßen; *(joc.: I)* meine Wenigkeit *(scherzh.)*; *see also* **ever a; faithfully; sincerely c; up 2 f**

yourself [jə'self, jʊə'self, jɔː'self] *pron.* **a)** *emphat.* selbst; **for ~:** für dich/Sie selbst; **you must do sth. for ~:** du mußt selbst etw. tun; **how's ~?** *(sl.)* wie geht's? *(ugs.)*; *(as reply)* und selbst? *(ugs.)*; **relax and be ~:** entspann dich und gib dich ganz natürlich; **b)** *refl.* dich/dir/sich. *See also* **herself; myself**

yourselves [jə'selvz, jʊə'selvz, jɔː'selvz] *pron.* **a)** *emphat.* selbst; **for ~:** für euch/Sie selbst; **b)** *refl.* euch/sich. *See also* **herself; ourselves**

youth [juːθ] *n.* **a)** *no pl., no art.* Jugend, *die*; **she has kept her ~:** sie hat sich *(Dat.)* ihr jugendliches Aussehen bewahrt; **b)** *pl.* **~s** [juːðz] *(young man)* Jugendliche, *der*; **c)** *constr. as pl. (young people)* Jugend, *die*; **d)** *no pl., no art. (fig.: early stage of development etc.)* Anfangsstadium, *das*; **in its [early] ~:** in den [ersten] Anfängen

youth: ~ centre *n.* Jugendzentrum, *das*; **~ club** *n.* Jugendklub, *der*; **~ 'custody** *n. (Brit.)* Jugendstrafe, *die*; **~ 'custody centre** *n. (Brit.)* Jugendstrafanstalt, *die*

youthful ['juːθfl] *adj.* jugendlich

youthfulness ['juːθflnɪs] *n., no pl.* **a)** *(being young)* Jugend, *die*; **b)** *(having freshness of youth)* Jugendlichkeit, *die*

youth: ~ hostel *n.* Jugendherberge, *die*; **~ hosteller** *n.* Herbergsgast, *der*

you've [jʊv, *stressed* juːv] = **you have**

yowl [jaʊl] **1.** *n.* **~[s]** Jaulen, *das*; *(of cat)* Maunzen, *das*; *(of wolf)* Heulen, *das*; **give a ~:** jaulen/maunzen/heulen. **2.** *v.i.* jaulen; ‹*Katze:*› maunzen; ‹*Wolf:*› heulen

Yo-Yo, (P) ['jəʊjəʊ] *n., pl.* **~s** Jo-Jo, *das*

yr. *abbr.* **a)** year[s] J.; **b)** your

yrs. *abbr.* **a)** years J.; **b)** yours

'Y-shaped *adj.* Y-förmig

yucca ['jʌkə] *n. (Bot.)* Yucca, *die*; Palmlilie, *die*

yuck *see* **yuk**

yucky *see* **yukky**

Yugoslav ['juːgəslɑːv] *see* **Yugoslavian**

Yugoslavia [juːgə'slɑːvɪə] *pr. n. (Hist.)* Jugoslawien *(das)*

Yugoslavian [juːgə'slɑːvɪən] **1.** *adj.* **a)** *(Hist.)* jugoslawisch; **sb. is ~:** jmd. ist Jugoslawe/Jugoslawin; **b)** *(Ling.)* *see* **Serbo-Croat 2. 2.** *n.* **a)** *(Hist.: person)* Jugoslawe, *der*/Jugoslawin, *die*; **b)** *(Ling.)* *see* **Serbo-Croat 1**

yuk [jʌk] *int. (sl.)* bäh; äks

yukky ['jʌkɪ] *adj. (sl.)* eklig

yule [juːl] *see* **yule-tide**

yule: ~-log *n.* Weihnachtsblock, *der* *(Volksk.)*; *(in Scandinavia)* Julblock, *der* *(Volksk.)*; **~-tide** *n. (arch.)* Weihnachtszeit, *die*

yummy ['jʌmɪ] *(coll.)* **1.** *adj.* lecker. **2.** *int. (child lang.)* lecker, lecker; *(not referring to food)* au fein

yum-yum [jʌm'jʌm] *int.* lecker, lecker

yuppie ['jʌpɪ] *n. (coll.)* Yuppie, *der*

YWCA *abbr.* **Young Women's Christian Association** CVJF

Z

Z, z [zed] *n., pl.* **Zs** *or* **Z's a)** *(letter)* Z, z, *das*; **b)** *(Math.)* z

zabaglione [zɑbɑ'ljəʊneɪ] *n. (Gastr.)* Zabaglione, *die*; Zabaione, *die*

Zaire [zɑː'ɪə(r)] *pr. n.* Zaire *(das)*

Zambezi [zæm'biːzɪ] *pr. n.* Sambesi, *der*

Zambia ['zæmbɪə] *pr. n.* Sambia *(das)*

Zambian ['zæmbɪən] **1.** *adj.* sambisch. **2.** *n.* Sambier, *der*/Sambierin, *die*

zany ['zeɪnɪ] *adj.* irre komisch *(ugs.)*; Wahnsinns‹*humor, -komiker*›

Zanzibar [zænzɪ'bɑ(r)] *pr. n.* Sansibar *(das)*

Zanzibari [zænzɪ'bɑːrɪ] **1.** *adj.* sansibarisch. **2.** *n.* Sansibarer, *der*/Sansibarerin, *die*

zap [zæp] *(sl.)* **1.** *int.* zack. **2.** *v.t.,* **-pp- a) ~ sb. [one]** jmdm. eine knallen *(ugs.)*; **b)** *(do away with, kill)* erledigen *(salopp)*

zeal [ziːl] *n., no pl.* **a)** *(fervour)* Eifer, *der*; **b)** *(hearty endeavour)* Hingabe, *die*

zealot ['zelət] *n.* **a)** *(zealous person)* Besessene, *der/die*; **b)** *(fanatic)* Eiferer, *der*/Eiferin, *die*; Zelot, *der*/Zelotin, *die (geh.)*

zealous ['zeləs] *adj.* **a)** *(fervent)* glühend *(geh.)* ‹*Verehrer*›; begeistert ‹*Fan*›; **b)** *(eager)* eifrig

zealously ['zeləslɪ] *adv.* **a)** *(fervently)* mit glühendem Eifer *(geh.)*; begeistert ‹*anfeuern*›; **b)** *(eagerly)* eifrig ‹*suchen, arbeiten*›

zebra ['zebrə, 'ziːbrə] *n.* Zebra, *das*

zebra: ~ 'crossing *n. (Brit.)* Zebrastreifen, *der*; **~ finch** *(Ornith.) n.* Zebrafink, *der*

zebu ['ziːbjuː] *n. (Zool.)* Zebu, *der od. das*

zed [zed] *(Brit.)*, **zee** [ziː] *(Amer.) ns.* Zett, *das*

Zen [zen] *n., no pl., no art. (Relig.)* Zen, *das*

zenith ['zenɪθ] *n. (lit. or fig.)* Zenit, *der*

zephyr ['zefə(r)] *n. (literary)* Zephir, *der (dichter. veralt.)*

Zeppelin ['zepəlɪn] *n.* Zeppelin, *der*

zero ['zɪərəʊ] **1.** *n., pl.* **~s a)** *(nought)* Null, *die*; **b)** *(fig.: nil)* null; **her chances are ~:** ihre Aussichten sind gleich Null *(ugs.)*; **c)** *(starting point of scale; of temperature)* Null, *die*; **in ~ gravity** im Zustand der Schwerelosigkeit; **absolute ~** *(Phys.)* absoluter Nullpunkt; **d) ~ [hour]** die Stunde X. *See also* **ground zero. 2.** *v.i.* **~ in on sth.** *(take aim at sth.)* sich auf etw. *(Akk.)* einschießen; *(focus one's attention on sth.)* sich auf etw. *(Akk.)* konzentrieren

zero: ~ option *n. (Polit.)* Nullösung, *die*; **~-'rated** *adj.* **~-rated goods** nicht mehrwertsteuerpflichtige Güter

zest [zest] *n.* **a)** *(lit. or fig.)* Würze, *die*; **add a ~ to the dish** das Gericht würzig machen; **add ~ and life to sth.** etw. beleben; **b)** *(gusto)* Begeisterung, *die*; **~ for living** Lebenslust, *die*; **c)** *(peel)* Schale, *die*

zestful ['zestfl] *adj.* freudig; ‹*Person*› voller Begeisterung

zeugma ['zjuːgmə] *n. (Ling., Lit.)* Zeugma, *das (Sprachw.)*

Zeus [zjuːs] *pr. n. (Greek Mythol.)* Zeus *(der)*

zigzag ['zɪgzæg] **1.** *adj.* zickzackförmig; Zickzack‹*muster, -anordnung*›; **~ line** Zickzacklinie, *die*; **steer a ~ course** im Zickzack fahren/laufen *usw.* **2.** *adv.* zickzack. **3.** *n.* Zickzacklinie, *die.* **4.** *v.i.,* **-gg-** im Zickzack verlaufen/‹*Person:*› laufen

zilch [zɪltʃ] *n., no pl., no art. (Amer. sl.)* rein *od.* reineweg gar nichts *(ugs.)*; **be ~:** gleich Null sein *(ugs.)*

zillion ['zɪljən] *n. (coll.)* **a ~ mosquitoes** Myriaden von Stechmücken; **~s of dollars** zig *(ugs.)* Millionen Dollar

Zimbabwe [zɪm'bɑːbwɪ] *pr. n.* Simbabwe *(das)*

Zimbabwean [zɪm'bɑːbwɪən] **1.** *adj.* simbabwisch. **2.** *n.* Simbabwer, *der*/Simbabwerin, *die*

zinc [zɪŋk] *n.* Zink, *das*

zing [zɪŋ] *(coll.)* **1.** *n.* Schwung, *der.* **2.** *v.i.* ‹*Geschoß:*› sirren

zinnia ['zɪnɪə] *n. (Bot.)* Zinnie, *die*

Zion ['zaɪən] *n., no pl.* Zion, *das*

Zionism ['zaɪənɪzm] *n., no pl.* Zionismus, *der*

Zionist ['zaɪənɪst] *n.* Zionist, *der*/Zionistin, *die*

zip [zɪp] **1.** *n.* **a)** Reißverschluß, *der*; **b)** *(fig.: energy, vigour)* Schwung, *der*; **c)** *(sound)* Zischen, *das.* **2.** *v.t.,* **-pp- a)** *(close)* **~ [up] sth.** den Reißverschluß an etw. *(Dat.)* zuziehen; **I put on the jacket and ~ped it up** ich zog die Jacke an und machte den Reißverschluß zu; **~ sb. up** jmdm. den Reißverschluß zumachen; **b) ~ [up]** *(enclose)* [durch Schließen des Reißverschlusses] einpacken *(ugs.)*; **he was ~ped [up] into his sleeping-bag** er wurde in seinen Schlafsack gepackt *(ugs.)*. **3.** *v.i.,* **-pp- a)** *(fasten)* **~ [up]** mit Reißverschluß geschlossen werden; **the dress ~s up [at the back/side]** das Kleid hat [hinten/seitlich] einen Reißverschluß; **the lining ~s in easily** das [Ausreiß]futter läßt sich leicht einziehen; **it won't ~ up** der Reißverschluß läßt sich nicht zuziehen; **b)** *(move fast)* sausen

'zip-bag *n.* Tasche mit Reißverschluß

'Zip code *n. (Amer.)* Postleitzahl, *die*

zip: ~-fastener *see* **zip 1 a**; **~ gun** *n. (Amer.)* selbstgebastelte Pistole

zipper ['zɪpə(r)] *n.* *see* **zip 1 a**

zippy ['zɪpɪ] *adj. (coll.)* spritzig

zirconium [zɜː'kəʊnɪəm] *n. (Chem.)* Zirkonium, *das*; Zirconium, *das (fachspr.)*

zit [zɪt] *n. (Amer. sl.)* Pickel, *der*

zither ['zɪðə(r)] *n. (Mus.)* Zither, *die*

zodiac ['zəʊdɪæk] *n. (Astron.)* Tierkreis, *der*; Zodiakus, *der (fachspr.)*; **sign of the ~** *(Astrol.)* Tierkreiszeichen, *das*; Sternzeichen, *das*

zodiacal [zə'daɪəkl] *adj. (Astron., Astrol.)* Tierkreis-; zodiakal *(fachspr.)*

zodiacal 'light *n. (Astron.)* Zodiakallicht, *das*

zombie (*Amer.:* **zombi**) ['zɒmbɪ] *n. (lit. or fig.)* Zombie, *der*

zonal ['zəʊnl] *adj.* zonal; **~ tariff** Zonentarif, *der*

zone [zəʊn] **1.** *n.* Zone, *die*; **[time] ~:** Zeitzone, *die*; **Temperate Z~:** gemäßigte Zone. **2.** *v.t.* [in Zonen] einteilen

zoning ['zəʊnɪŋ] *n.* Zoneneinteilung, *die*

zonked [zɒŋkt] *adj. (sl.)* **be ~** *(by drugs)* stoned sein *(Drogenjargon)*; *(by alcohol)* zusein *(salopp)*; *(be tired)* erschlagen sein *(ugs.)*

zoo [zu:] *n.* Zoo, *der*
'zoo-keeper *n.* Zoowärter, *der/*-wärterin, *die*
zoological [zu:ə'lɒdʒɪkl] *adj.* zoologisch
zoological 'garden[s] *n.* zoologischer Garten
zoologist [zu:'ɒlədʒɪst] *n.* Zoologe, *der*/Zoologin, *die*
zoology [zu:'ɒlədʒɪ] *n.* Zoologie, *die*
zoom [zu:m] **1.** *v.i.* **a)** *(move quickly)* rauschen; **we ~ed along on our bicycles** wir sausten auf unseren Fahrrädern daher; **~ through a script** ein Manuskript überfliegen; **b)** *(Aeronaut.)* das Flugzeug steil hochziehen; **c)** *(Photog.)* ‹*Kamera, Objektiv:*› die Brennweite stufenlos verändern; ‹*Bild:*› herangeholt werden. **2.** *n. see* **zoom lens**
~ 'in *v.i.* **a)** *(Cinemat., Telev.)* zoomen *(fachspr.);* nahe heranfahren; **~ in on sth.** auf etw. *(Akk.)* zoomen *(fachspr.);* etw. nahe heranholen; **b) ~ in on sth.** *(fig.)* sich auf etw. *(Akk.)* konzentrieren
'zoom lens *n. (Photog.)* Zoomobjektiv, *das;* Gummilinse, *die (ugs.)*
Zoroastrianism [zɒrəʊ'æstrɪənɪzm] *n. (Relig.)* Zoroastrismus, *der*
zucchini [zʊ'ki:nɪ] *n., pl. same or* **~s** *(esp. Amer.)* Zucchino, *der*
zugzwang ['tsu:ktsvɑ:ŋ] *n. (Chess)* Zugzwang, *der*
Zulu ['zu:lu:] **1.** *n.* **a)** *(person)* Zulu, *der/die;* **b)** *(language)* Zulu, *das.* **2.** *adj.* Zulu-
Zurich ['zjʊərɪk] **1.** *pr. n.* Zürich *(das).* **2.** *attrib. adj.* **a)** *(of canton)* des Kantons Zürich *nachgestellt;* **b)** *(of city)* Züricher; Zürcher *(schweiz.)*
zygomatic bone [zaɪgə'mætɪk bəʊn] *n. (Anat.)* Jochbein, *das*
zygote ['zaɪgəʊt] *n. (Biol.)* Zygote, *die*

The Revision of German Orthography
die neue Regelung der Rechtschreibung

In July 1996, after much debate, wide-ranging changes to the spelling of German were agreed and ratified by the governments of Germany, Austria, and Switzerland. The following list, whilst not all-encompassing, details those changes which may be of interest to the user of this dictionary. It is worth noting that although these reforms are valid immediately, they will not be expected to be reflected in all written texts until 2005. Until that date, both old and new spellings will be acceptable.

The following list contains words which are not included in the A–Z text of this dictionary. Nonetheless, it is the editors' view that the learner of German will gain a better overview of the systematic changes involved by studying a more comprehensive list of words affected by the reforms.

The following summary lists the most important changes:

1. The ß character
The ß character, which is generally replaced in Switzerland by a double s, will be retained in Germany and Austria, but will only be written after a long vowel (as in Fuß, Füße) and after a diphthong (as in Strauß, Sträuße).

Fluß, Baß, keß, läßt, Nußknacker become in future: *Fluss, Bass, kess, lässt, Nussknacker*

2. Nominalized adjectives
Nominalized adjectives will be written with a capital even in set phrases.

sein Schäfchen ins trockene bringen, im trüben fischen, im allgemeinen become in future: *sein Schäfchen ins Trockene bringen, im Trüben fischen, im Allgemeinen*

3. Words from the same word family
In certain cases the spelling of words belonging to the same family will be made uniform.

numerieren, überschwenglich become in future: *nummerieren* (like Nummer), *überschwänglich* (being related to Überschwang)

4. The same consonant repeated three times
When the same consonant repeated three times occurs in compounds, all three will be written even when a vowel follows.

Brennessel, Schiffahrt become in future: *Brennnessel, Schifffahrt* (exceptions are dennoch, Drittel, Mittag)

5. Verb, adjective and participle compounds
Verb, adjective and participle compounds will be written more frequently than previously in two words.

spazierengehen, radfahren, ernstgemeint, erdölexportierend become in future: *spazieren gehen, Rad fahren, ernst gemeint, Erdöl exportierend*

6. Compounds containing numbers in figures
Compounds containing numbers in figures will in future be written with a hyphen.

24karätig, 8pfünder become in future: *24-karätig, 8-Pfünder*

7. The division of words containing *st*
The *st* will be treated like a normal combination of consonants and no longer be indivisible.

Ha-stig, Ki-ste become in future: *has-tig, Kis-te*

8. The division of words containing *ck*
The combination *ck* will not be divided and will go on to the next line.

Bäk-ker, schik-ken become in future: *Bä-cker, schi-cken*

9. The division of foreign words
Compound foreign words which are hardly recognized as such today may be divided by syllables, without regard to their original components.

He-li-ko-pter (from the Greek helix and pteron) may also become in future: *He-li-kop-ter*

10. The comma before *und*
Where two complete clauses are connected by *und* a comma will not be obligatory.

Karl war in Schwierigkeiten, und niemand konnte ihm helfen. may also become in future: *Karl war in Schwierigkeiten und niemand konnte ihm helfen.*

11. The comma with infinitives and participles
Even longer clauses containing an infinitive or participle will not have to be divided off with a comma.

Er begann sofort, das neue Buch zu lesen. Ungläubig den Kopf schüttelnd, verließ er das Zimmer. may also become in future: *Er begann sofort das neue Buch zu lesen. Ungläubig den Kopf schüttelnd verließ er das Zimmer.*

An asterisk * denotes new spelling variants which are to be regarded as preferred forms

A

OLD	NEW
[gestern, heute, morgen] abend	[gestern, heute, morgen] Abend
aberhundert	*also:* Aberhundert
Aberhunderte	*also:* aberhunderte
abertausend	*also:* Abertausend
Abertausende	*also:* abertausende
Abfluß	Abfluss
abgeblaßt	abgeblasst
Abguß	Abguss
Ablaß	Ablass
Abriß	Abriss
Abschluß	Abschluss
Abschuß	Abschuss
absein	ab sein
Abszeß	Abszess
abwärtsgehen	abwärts gehen
in acht nehmen	in Acht nehmen
außer acht lassen	außer Acht lassen
8achser	8-Achser
der/die achte, den/die ich sehe	der/die Achte, den/die ich sehe
jeder/jede achte kommt mit	jeder/jede Achte kommt mit
achtgeben	Acht geben
achthaben	Acht haben
8jährig	8-jährig
der/die 8jährige	der/die 8-Jährige
8mal	8-mal
achtmillionenmal	acht Millionen Mal
8tonner	8-Tonner
achtunggebietend	Achtung gebietend
über Achtzig	über achtzig
Mitte [der] Achtzig	Mitte [der] achtzig
in die Achtzig kommen	in die achtzig kommen
die achtziger Jahre	*also:* die Achtzigerjahre*
die Achtzigerjahre	*also:* die achtziger Jahre
ackerbautreibende Völker	Ackerbau treibende Völker
Action-painting	Actionpainting *also:* Action-Painting
ade sagen	*also:* Ade sagen*
Aderlaß	Aderlass
Adhäsionsverschluß	Adhäsionsverschluss
Adreßbuch	Adressbuch
afro-amerikanisch	afroamerikanisch
afro-asiatisch	afroasiatisch
Afro-Look	Afrolook
After-shave	Aftershave
ich habe ähnliches erlebt	ich habe Ähnliches erlebt
und/oder ähnliches (u. ä./o. ä.)	und/oder Ähnliches (u. Ä./o. Ä.)
Alkoholmißbrauch	Alkoholmissbrauch
alleinerziehend	allein erziehend
alleinseligmachend	allein selig machend
alleinstehend	allein stehend
es ist das allerbeste, daß …	es ist das Allerbeste, dass …
im allgemeinen	im Allgemeinen
allgemeingültig	allgemein gültig
allgemeinverständlich	allgemein verständlich
allzubald	allzu bald
allzufrüh	allzu früh
allzugern	allzu gern
allzulange	allzu lange
allzuoft	allzu oft
allzusehr	allzu sehr
allzuviel	allzu viel
allzuweit	allzu weit
Alma mater	Alma Mater
Alpdruck	*also:* Albdruck
Alptraum	*also:* Albtraum
als daß	als dass
aus alt mach neu	aus Alt mach Neu
für alt und jung	für Alt und Jung
er ist immer der alte geblieben	er ist immer der Alte geblieben
alles beim alten lassen	alles beim Alten lassen
Alter ego	Alter Ego
altwienerisch	alt-wienerisch
Amboß	Amboss
Anbiß	Anbiss
andersdenkend	anders denkend
andersgeartet	anders geartet
anderslautend	anders lautend
aneinanderfügen	aneinander fügen
aneinandergeraten	aneinander geraten
aneinandergrenzen	aneinander grenzen
aneinanderlegen	aneinander legen
aneinanderreihen	aneinander reihen
angepaßt	angepasst
Angepaßtheit	Angepasstheit
Anglo-Amerikaner	Angloamerikaner
jmdm. angst machen	jmdm. Angst machen
anheimfallen	anheim fallen
anheimstellen	anheim stellen
Anlaß	Anlass
anläßlich	anlässlich
Anriß	Anriss
Anschiß	Anschiss
Anschluß	Anschluss
ansein	an sein
der Archimedische Punkt	der archimedische Punkt
im argen liegen	im Argen liegen
bei arm und reich	bei Arm und Reich
Armee-Einheit	*also:* Armeeeinheit
Aschantinuß	Aschantinuss
As	Ass
aufeinanderbeißen	aufeinander beißen
aufeinanderfolgen	aufeinander folgen
aufeinandertreffen	aufeinander treffen
aufgepaßt!	aufgepasst!
aufgerauht	aufgeraut
Aufguß	Aufguss
Auflösungsprozeß	Auflösungsprozess
aufrauhen	aufrauen
Aufriß	Aufriss
Aufschluß	Aufschluss
aufschlußreich	aufschlussreich
ein aufsehenerregendes Ereignis	ein Aufsehen erregendes Ereignis
aufsein	auf sein
auf seiten	aufseiten *also:* auf Seiten
der aufsichtführende Lehrer	der Aufsicht führende Lehrer
aufwärtsgehen	aufwärts gehen
aufwendig	*also:* aufwändig
auseinanderbiegen	auseinander biegen
auseinanderfallen	auseinander fallen
auseinandergehen	auseinander gehen
auseinanderhalten	auseinander halten
auseinanderleben	auseinander leben
auseinanderreißen	auseinander reißen
auseinandersetzen	auseinander setzen
Ausfluß	Ausfluss
Ausguß	Ausguss
Ausschluß	Ausschluss
Ausschuß	Ausschuss
aussein	aus sein
aufs äußerste gespannt	*also:* aufs Äußerste gespannt
außerstande	*also:* außer Stande

B

OLD	NEW
Bajonettverschluß	Bajonettverschluss

OLD	NEW
Ballettänzerin	Balletttänzerin *also:* Ballett-Tänzerin
Ballokal	Balllokal *also:* Ball-Lokal
Bänderriß	Bänderriss
jmdm. [angst und] bange machen	jmdm. [Angst und] Bange machen
bankrott gehen	Bankrott gehen
Baroneß	Baroness
baselstädtisch	basel-städtisch
baß erstaunt	bass erstaunt
Baß	Bass
Baßgeige	Bassgeige
Baßsänger	Basssänger *also:* Bass-Sänger
Baukostenzuschuß	Baukostenzuschuss
beeinflußbar	beeinflussbar
Beeinflußbarkeit	Beeinflussbarkeit
beeinflußt	beeinflusst
befaßt	befasst
Begrüßungskuß	Begrüßungskuss
behende	behände
Behendigkeit	Behändigkeit
beieinanderhaben	beieinander haben
beieinandersein	beieinander sein
beieinandersitzen	beieinander sitzen
beieinanderstehen	beieinander stehen
beifallheischend	Beifall heischend
beisammensein	beisammen sein
Beischluß	Beischluss
belemmert	belämmert
jeder beliebige	jeder Beliebige
Beschiß	Beschiss
Beschluß	Beschluss
beschlußfähig	beschlussfähig
Beschlußfassung	Beschlussfassung
Beschuß	Beschuss
ich will im besonderen erwähnen …	ich will im Besonderen erwähnen …
bessergehen	besser gehen
es ist das beste, wenn …	es ist das Beste, wenn …
aufs beste geregelt sein	*also:* aufs Beste geregelt sein
zum besten geben	zum Besten geben
zum besten haben/halten	zum Besten haben/halten
das erste beste	das erste Beste
bestehenbleiben	bestehen bleiben
Bestelliste	Bestellliste *also:* Bestell-Liste
bestgehaßt	bestgehasst
bestußt	bestusst
Betelnuß	Betelnuss
um ein beträchtliches höher	um ein Beträchtliches höher
in betreff	in Betreff
betreßt	betresst
Bettuch [*zu: Bett*]	Betttuch *also:* Bett-Tuch
bevorschußt	bevorschusst
bewußt	bewusst
bewußtlos	bewusstlos
Bewußtlosigkeit	Bewusstlosigkeit
Bewußtsein	Bewusstsein
in bezug auf	in Bezug auf
bezuschußt	bezuschusst
Bibliographie	*also:* Bibliografie
Bierfaß	Bierfass
die Bismarckschen Sozialgesetze	die bismarckschen Sozialgesetze *also:* die Bismarck'schen Sozialgesetze
Biß	Biss
bißchen	bisschen
du sollst bitte sagen	*also:* du sollst Bitte sagen*
es ist bitter kalt	es ist bitterkalt

OLD	NEW
Bittag	Bitttag *also:* Bitt-Tag
Blackout	*also:* Black-out*
blankpoliert	blank poliert
blaß	blass
Bläßhuhn/Bleßhuhn	Blässhuhn/Blesshuhn
bläßlich	blässlich
blaßrosa	blassrosa
Blattschuß	Blattschuss
der blaue Planet [*die Erde*]	der Blaue Planet
blaugestreift	blau gestreift
bläulichgrün	bläulich grün
bleibenlassen	bleiben lassen
blendendweiß	blendend weiß
blondgefärbt	blond gefärbt
Bluterguß	Bluterguss
Bonbonniere	*also:* Bonboniere
Börsentip	Börsentipp
im bösen wie im guten	im Bösen wie im Guten
Boß	Boss
Bouclé	*also:* Buklee
braungebrannt	braun gebrannt
bräunlichgelb	bräunlich gelb
des langen und breiten	des Langen und Breiten
breitgefächert	breit gefächert
Brennessel	Brennnessel *also:* Brenn-Nessel
Bruderkuß	Bruderkuss
Brummbaß	Brummbass
brütendheiß	brütend heiß
buntgefiedert	bunt gefiedert
buntschillernd	bunt schillernd
Büroschluß	Büroschluss
Butterfaß	Butterfass

C

OLD	NEW
Cashewnuß	Cashewnuss
Centre Court	Centrecourt *also:* Centre-Court
Chansonnier	*also:* Chansonier
Choreographie	*also:* Choreografie
Cleverneß	Cleverness
Comeback	*also:* Come-back*
Common sense	Commonsense *also:* Common Sense
Corned beef	Cornedbeef *also:* Corned Beef
Corpus delicti	Corpus Delicti
Countdown	*also:* Count-down*

D

OLD	NEW
dabeisein	dabei sein
Dachgeschoß	Dachgeschoss [*in Austria still written with ß*]
dahinterklemmen	dahinter klemmen
dahinterkommen	dahinter kommen
Dampfschiffahrt	Dampfschifffahrt
Danaidenfaß	Danaidenfass
darauffolgend	darauf folgend
Darmverschluß	Darmverschluss
darüberstehen	darüber stehen
dasein	da sein
daß	dass
daß-Satz	dass-Satz *also:* Dasssatz
datenverarbeitend	Daten verarbeitend
Dein [*in letters*]	dein
mein und dein verwechseln	Mein und Dein verwechseln
die Deinen	*also:* die deinen
die Deinigen	*also:* die deinigen
Dekolleté	*also:* Dekolletee
Delikateßgurke	Delikatessgurke

OLD	NEW
Delikateßsenf	Delikatesssenf
	also: Delikatess-Senf
Delphin	*also:* Delfin
Denkprozeß	Denkprozess
wir haben derartiges nicht bemerkt	wir haben Derartiges nicht bemerkt
dessenungeachtet	dessen ungeachtet
des weiteren	des Weiteren
auf deutsch	auf Deutsch
deutschsprechend	Deutsch sprechend
das d'Hondtsche System	das d'hondtsche System
	also: das d'Hondt'sche System
diät leben	Diät leben
Dich [*in letters*]	dich
dichtbehaart	dicht behaart
dichtgedrängt	dicht gedrängt
Differential	*also:* Differenzial*
Diktaphon	*also:* Diktafon
Dir [*in letters*]	dir
Doppelpaß	Doppelpass
dortbleiben	dort bleiben
dortzulande	*also:* dort zu Lande
draufsein	drauf sein
Dreß	Dress
etwas aufs dringendste fordern	*also:* etwas aufs Dringendste fordern
drinsein	drin sein
jeder dritte, der mitwollte	jeder Dritte, der mitwollte
zum dritten	zum Dritten
die dritte Welt	die Dritte Welt
drückendheiß	drückend heiß
Du [*in letters*]	du
auf du und du stehen	auf Du und Du stehen
im dunkeln tappen	im Dunkeln tappen
im dunkeln bleiben	im Dunkeln bleiben
dünnbesiedelt	dünn besiedelt
Dünnschiß	Dünnschiss
durcheinanderbringen	durcheinander bringen
durcheinandergeraten	durcheinander geraten
durcheinanderlaufen	durcheinander laufen
Durchfluß	Durchfluss
Durchlaß	Durchlass
durchnumerieren	durchnummerieren
Durchschuß	Durchschuss
durchsein	durch sein
dußlig	dusslig
Dußligkeit	Dussligkeit
Dutzende Reklamationen	*also:* dutzende Reklamationen
Dutzende von Reklamationen	*also:* dutzende von Reklamationen

E

OLD	NEW
ebensogut	ebenso gut
ebensosehr	ebenso sehr
ebensoviel	ebenso viel
ebensowenig	ebenso wenig
an Eides Statt	an Eides statt
sein eigen nennen	sein Eigen nennen
sich zu eigen machen	sich zu Eigen machen
einbleuen	einbläuen
aufs eindringlichste warnen	*also:* aufs Eindringlichste warnen
das einfachste ist, wenn …	das Einfachste ist, wenn …
Einfluß	Einfluss
einflußreich	einflussreich
aufs eingehendste untersuchen	*also:* aufs Eingehendste untersuchen
einiggehen	einig gehen
Einlaß	Einlass
einläßlich	einlässlich
Einriß	Einriss
Einschluß	Einschluss
Einschuß	Einschuss

OLD	NEW
Einschußstelle	Einschussstelle
	also: Einschuss-Stelle
Einsendeschluß	Einsendeschluss
einwärtsgebogen	einwärts gebogen
der/die/das einzelne kann …	der/die/das Einzelne kann …
jeder einzelne von uns	jeder Einzelne von uns
bis ins einzelne geregelt	bis ins Einzelne geregelt
ins einzelne gehend	ins Einzelne gehend
einzelnstehend	einzeln stehend
der/die/das einzige wäre …	der/die/das Einzige wäre …
kein einziger war gekommen	kein Einziger war gekommen
er als einziger/sie als einzige hatte …	er als Einziger/sie als Einzige hatte …
das einzigartige ist, daß …	das Einzigartige ist, dass …
Eisenguß	Eisenguss
die eisenverarbeitende Industrie	die Eisen verarbeitende Industrie
eisigkalt	eisig kalt
eislaufen	Eis laufen
Eisschnellauf	Eisschnelllauf
Eisschnelläufer	Eisschnellläufer
energiebewußt	energiebewusst
aufs engste verflochten	*also:* aufs Engste verflochten
engbefreundet	eng befreundet
engbedruckt	eng bedruckt
Engpaß	Engpass
nicht im entferntesten beabsichtigen	*also:* nicht im Entferntesten beabsichtigen
auf das entschiedenste zurückweisen	*also:* auf das Entschiedenste zurückweisen
Entschluß	Entschluss
ein Entweder-Oder gibt es hier nicht	ein Entweder-oder gibt es hier nicht
Entwicklungsprozeß	Entwicklungsprozess
erblaßt	erblasst
Erdgeschoß	Erdgeschoss [*in Austria still written with* ß]
Erdnuß	Erdnuss
die erdölexportierenden Länder	die Erdöl exportierenden Länder
erfaßbar	erfassbar
erfaßt	erfasst
Erguß	Erguss
erholungsuchende Großstädter	Erholung suchende Großstädter
Erlaß	Erlass
ermeßbar	ermessbar
ernstgemeint	ernst gemeint
ernstzunehmend	ernst zu nehmend
erpreßbar	erpressbar
nicht den erstbesten nehmen	nicht den Erstbesten nehmen
der erste, der gekommen ist	der Erste, der gekommen ist
das reicht fürs erste	das reicht fürs Erste
zum ersten, zum zweiten, zum dritten	zum Ersten, zum Zweiten, zum Dritten
die Erste Hilfe	die erste Hilfe
das erstemal	das erste Mal
zum erstenmal	zum ersten Mal
Erstkläßler	Erstklässler
die Erstplazierten	die Erstplatzierten
eßbar	essbar
Eßbesteck	Essbesteck
Eßecke	Essecke
essentiell	*also:* essenziell*
Eßlöffel	Esslöffel
eßlöffelweise	esslöffelweise
Eßtisch	Esstisch
etlichemal	etliche Mal
Euch [*in letters*]	euch
Euer [*in letters*]	euer
die Euren	*also:* die euren
die Eurigen	*also:* die eurigen
Existentialismus	*also:* Existenzialismus*
existentialistisch	*also:* existenzialistisch*
existentiell	*also:* existenziell*
Exportüberschuß	Exportüberschuss

OLD	NEW
Exposé	*also:* Exposee
expreß	express
Expreßreinigung	Expressreinigung
Expreßzug	Expresszug
Exzeß	Exzess

F

OLD	NEW
Fabrikationsprozeß	Fabrikationsprozess
fahrenlassen	fahren lassen
Fairneß	Fairness
Fair play	Fairplay
	also: Fair Play
fallenlassen	fallen lassen
Fallinie	Falllinie
	also: Fall-Linie
Fallout	*also:* Fall-out*
Familienanschluß	Familienanschluss
Fangschuß	Fangschuss
Faß	Fass
faßbar	fassbar
Faßbier	Fassbier
Fäßchen	Fässchen
faßlich	fasslich
du faßt	du fasst
Fast food	Fastfood
	also: Fast Food
Faxanschluß	Faxanschluss
Feedback	*also:* Feed-back*
Fehlpaß	Fehlpass
Fehlschuß	Fehlschuss
jmdm. feind sein	jmdm. Feind sein
feingemahlen	fein gemahlen
fernliegen	fern liegen
fertigbringen	fertig bringen
fertigstellen	fertig stellen
Fertigungsprozeß	Fertigungsprozess
festangestellt	fest angestellt
festumrissen	fest umrissen
festverwurzelt	fest verwurzelt
fettgedruckt	fett gedruckt
feuerspeiende Drachen	Feuer speiende Drachen
die fischverarbeitende Industrie	die Fisch verarbeitende Industrie
Fitneß	Fitness
Flachschuß	Flachschuss
fleischfressende Pflanzen	Fleisch fressende Pflanzen
Flohbiß	Flohbiss
das Bier floß in Strömen	das Bier floss in Strömen
flötengehen	flöten gehen
Fluß	Fluss
flußabwärts	flussabwärts
flußaufwärts	flussaufwärts
Flußbett	Flussbett
Flüßchen	Flüsschen
Flußdiagramm	Flussdiagramm
flüssigmachen	flüssig machen
Flußsand	Flusssand
	also: Fluss-Sand
Flußschiffahrt	Flussschifffahrt
	also: Fluss-Schifffahrt
Flußspat	Flussspat
	also: Fluss-Spat
die Haare fönen	die Haare föhnen
folgendes ist zu beachten	Folgendes ist zu beachten
wie im folgenden erläutert	wie im Folgenden erläutert
Fraktionsausschuß	Fraktionsausschuss
Fraktionsbeschluß	Fraktionsbeschluss
Free climbing	Freeclimbing
	also: Free Climbing
Free Jazz	*also:* Freejazz
Freßgier	Fressgier
Freßpaket	Fresspaket
Freßsack	Fresssack
	also: Fress-Sack
Friedensschluß	Friedensschluss
frischgebacken	frisch gebacken
fritieren	frittieren
frohgelaunt	froh gelaunt
frühverstorben	früh verstorben
Full-time-Job	Fulltimejob
	also: Full-Time-Job
Fünfpaß	Fünfpass
funkensprühend	Funken sprühend
Funkmeßtechnik	Funkmesstechnik
fürbaß	fürbass
fürliebnehmen	fürlieb nehmen
Fußballänderspiel	Fußballländerspiel
	also: Fußball-Länderspiel

G

OLD	NEW
Gangsterboß	Gangsterboss
im ganzen gesehen	im Ganzen gesehen
im großen und ganzen	im Großen und Ganzen
Gärungsprozeß	Gärungsprozess
Gäßchen	Gässchen
gefangenhalten	gefangen halten
gefangennehmen	gefangen nehmen
gefaßt	gefasst
gefirnißt	gefirnisst
es ist das gegebene, schnell zu handeln	es ist das Gegebene, schnell zu handeln
gegeneinanderprallen	gegeneinander prallen
gegeneinanderstoßen	gegeneinander stoßen
von allen gehaßt	von allen gehasst
geheimhalten	geheim halten
gehenlassen	gehen lassen
Gelaß	Gelass
gutgelaunt	gut gelaunt
gelblichgrün	gelblich grün
Gemse	Gämse
wir haben gemußt	wir haben gemusst
die Wunde hat genäßt	die Wunde hat genässt
aufs genaueste festgelegt	*also:* aufs Genaueste festgelegt
genaugenommen	genau genommen
genausogut	genauso gut
genausowenig	genauso wenig
Generalbaß	Generalbass
sie genoß den Sonnenschein	sie genoss den Sonnenschein
Genuß	Genuss
genüßlich	genüsslich
Genußmittel	Genussmittel
genußsüchtig	genusssüchtig
Geographie	*also:* Geografie
es hat gut gepaßt	es hat gut gepasst
wir haben gepraßt	wir haben geprasst
frisch gepreßter Saft	frisch gepresster Saft
geradehalten	gerade halten
geradesitzen	gerade sitzen
geradestellen	gerade stellen
Gerichtsbeschluß	Gerichtsbeschluss
um ein geringes weniger	um ein Geringes weniger
es geht ihn nicht das geringste an	es geht ihn nicht das Geringste an
nicht im geringsten stören	nicht im Geringsten stören
geringachten	gering achten
geringschätzen	gering schätzen
Geruchsverschluß	Geruchsverschluss
Geschäftsschluß	Geschäftsschluss
er wurde geschaßt	er wurde geschasst
Geschichtsbewußtsein	Geschichtsbewusstsein
Geschirreiniger	Geschirrreiniger
	also: Geschirr-Reiniger
Geschoß	Geschoss [*in Austria still written with* ß]
gestern abend/morgen/nacht	gestern Abend/Morgen/Nacht
alle waren gestreßt	alle waren gestresst
getrenntlebend	getrennt lebend
Gewinnummer	Gewinnnummer
	also: Gewinn-Nummer

OLD	NEW
gewiß	gewiss
Gewissensbiß	Gewissensbiss
Gewißheit	Gewissheit
gewißlich	gewisslich
ich habe es gewußt	ich habe es gewusst
Ginkgo	*also:* Ginko
Glacéhandschuh	*also:* Glaceehandschuh
glänzendschwarz	glänzend schwarz
glattgehen	glatt gehen
glatthobeln	glatt hobeln
glattschleifen	glatt schleifen
glattstreichen	glatt streichen
das gleiche tun	das Gleiche tun
aufs gleiche hinauskommen	aufs Gleiche hinauskommen
gleich und gleich gesellt sich gern	Geich und Gleich gesellt sich gern
gleichlautend	gleich lautend
Gleisanschluß	Gleisanschluss
Glimmstengel	Glimmstängel
glühendheiß	glühend heiß
Gnadenerlaß	Gnadenerlass
die Goetheschen Dramen	die goetheschen Dramen
	also: die Goethe'schen Dramen
Graphit	*also:* Grafit
Graphologie	*also:* Grafologie
gräßlich	grässlich
graugestreift	grau gestreift
grellbeleuchtet	grell beleuchtet
Grenzfluß	Grenzfluss
Greuel	Gräuel
greulich	gräulich
griffest	grifffest
jmdn. aufs gröbste beleidigen	*also:* jmdn. aufs Gröbste beleidigen
grobgemahlen	grob gemahlen
ein Programm für groß und klein	ein Programm für Groß und Klein
im großen und ganzen	im Großen und Ganzen
das größte wäre, wenn …	das Größte wäre, wenn …
Großschiffahrtsweg	Großschifffahrtsweg
groß schreiben [*mit großem Anfangsbuchstaben*]	großschreiben
grünlichgelb	grünlich gelb
Guß	Guss
Gußeisen	Gusseisen
gußeisern	gusseisern
guten Tag sagen	*also:* Guten Tag sagen*
es im guten versuchen	es im Guten versuchen
gutaussehend	gut aussehend
gutbezahlt	gut bezahlt
gutgehen	gut gehen
gutgehend	gut gehend
gutgelaunt	gut gelaunt
gutgemeint	gut gemeint
guttun	gut tun
gutunterrichtet	gut unterrichtet

H

OLD	NEW
haftenbleiben	haften bleiben
haltmachen	Halt machen
Hämorrhoide	*also:* Hämorride
händchenhaltend	Händchen haltend
handeltreibend	Handel treibend
Handkuß	Handkuss
Handout	*also:* Hand-out*
hängenbleiben	hängen bleiben
hängenlassen	hängen lassen
Happy-End	Happyend
	also: Happy End
Haraß	Harass
Hard cover	Hardcover
	also: Hard Cover
Hard-cover-Einband	Hardcovereinband
	*also:*Hard-Cover-Einband

OLD	NEW
hartgekocht	hart gekocht
Haselnuß	Haselnuss
Haselnußstrauch	Haselnussstrauch
	also: Haselnuss-Strauch
Haß	Hass
haßerfüllt	hasserfüllt
häßlich	hässlich
Häßlichkeit	Hässlichkeit
Haßliebe	Hassliebe
du haßt	du hasst
Hauptschulabschluß	Hauptschulabschluss
nach Hause	*in Austria and Switzerland*
	also: nachhause
zu Hause	*in Austria and Switzerland*
	also: zuhause
haushalten	*also:* Haus halten
Haushaltsausschuß	Haushaltsausschuss
Hawaii-Insel	*also:* Hawaiiinsel
heiligsprechen	heilig sprechen
Heilungsprozeß	Heilungsprozess
heimlichtun	heimlich tun
heißbegehrt	heiß begehrt
heißgeliebt	heiß geliebt
heißumkämpft	heiß umkämpft
helleuchtend	hell leuchtend
hellicht	helllicht
hellila	helllila
hellodernd	hell lodernd
heransein	heran sein
heraussein	heraus sein
herbstlichgelb	herbstlich gelb
Heringsfaß	Heringsfass
hersein	her sein
herumsein	herum sein
heruntersein	herunter sein
Herzas	Herzass
jmdn. auf das herzlichste begrüßen	*also:* jmdn. auf das Herzlichste begrüßen
heute abend/mittag/nacht	heute Abend/Mittag/Nacht
Hexenschuß	Hexenschuss
hierbleiben	hier bleiben
hierlassen	hierlassen
hiersein	hier sein
hierzulande	*also:* hier zu Lande
High-Fidelity	Highfidelity
	also: High Fidelity
High-Society	Highsociety
	also: High Society
hilfesuchend	Hilfe suchend
hinaussein	hinaus sein
es wurde etwas hineingeheimnißt	es wurde etwas hineingeheimnisst
hinsein	hin sein
hintereinanderfahren	hintereinander fahren
hintereinandergehen	hintereinander gehen
hintereinanderschalten	hintereinander schalten
hinterhersein	hinterher sein
hinübersein	hinüber sein
er hißt die Flagge	er hisst die Flagge
Hochgenuß	Hochgenuss
Hochschulabschluß	Hochschulabschluss
aufs höchste erfreut sein	*also:* aufs Höchste erfreut sein
hofhalten	Hof halten
die Hohe Schule	die hohe Schule
hohnlachen	*also:* Hohn lachen
das holzverarbeitende Gewerbe	das Holz verarbeitende Gewerbe
Hosteß	Hostess
Hot dog	Hotdog
	also: Hot Dog
ein paar hundert	*also:* ein paar Hundert
viele Hunderte	*also:* viele hunderte
Hunderte von Zuschauern	*also:* hunderte von Zuschauern
Hungers sterben	*also:* hungers sterben
hurra schreien	*also:* Hurra schreien*

I

OLD	NEW
auch Ihr seid herzlich eingeladen [*in letters*]	auch ihr seid herzlich eingeladen
im allgemeinen	im Allgemeinen
im besonderen	im Besonderen
Imbiß	Imbiss
Imbißstand	Imbissstand *also:* Imbiss-Stand
im einzelnen	im Einzelnen
im nachhinein	im Nachhinein
Impfpaß	Impfpass
imstande	*also:* im Stande
im übrigen	im Übrigen
im voraus	im Voraus
im vorhinein	im Vorhinein
in betreff	in Betreff
in bezug auf	in Bezug auf
Indizes	*also:* Indices
Indizienprozeß	Indizienprozess
ineinanderfließen	ineinander fließen
ineinandergreifen	ineinander greifen
inessentiell	*also:* inessenziell*
Informationsfluß	Informationsfluss
in Frage stellen	*also:* infrage stellen
in Frage kommen	*also:* infrage kommen
innesein	inne sein
insektenfressende Pflanzen	Insekten fressende Pflanzen
instand halten	*also:* in Stand halten
instand setzen	*also:* in Stand setzen
I-Punkt	i-Punkt
irgend etwas	irgendetwas
irgend jemand	irgendjemand
I-Tüpfelchen	i-Tüpfelchen

J

OLD	NEW
ja sagen	*also:* Ja sagen*
Jagdschloß	Jagdschloss
Jäheit	Jähheit
Jahresabschluß	Jahresabschluss
2jährig, 3jährig, 4jährig …	2-jährig, 3-jährig, 4-jährig …
ein 2jähriger, 3jähriger, 4jähriger kann das noch nicht verstehen	ein 2-Jähriger, 3-Jähriger, 4-Jähriger kann das noch nicht verstehen
Jaß	Jass
du jaßt	du jasst
Jauchefaß	Jauchefass
jedesmal	jedes Mal
Job-sharing	Jobsharing
Joghurt	*also:* Jogurt
Joint-venture	Jointventure *also:* Joint Venture
Judaskuß	Judaskuss
Julierpaß	Julierpass
Jumbo-Jet	Jumbojet
für jung und alt	für Jung und Alt

K

OLD	NEW
Kabelanschluß	Kabelanschluss
Kabinettsbeschluß	Kabinettsbeschluss
Kaffee-Ernte	*also:* Kaffeeernte
Kaffee-Ersatz	*also:* Kaffeeersatz
Kalligraphie	*also:* Kalligrafie
kalorienbewußt	kalorienbewusst
kaltlächelnd	kalt lächelnd
Kameraverschluß	Kameraverschluss
Kammacher	Kammmacher *also:* Kamm-Macher
Kämmaschine	Kämmmaschine *also:* Kämm-Maschine
Kammuschel	Kammmuschel *also:* Kamm-Muschel
Känguruh	Känguru
Kanonenschuß	Kanonenschuss
Kapselriß	Kapselriss
Karamel	Karamell
karamelisieren	karamellisieren
2karäter, 3karäter, 4karäter …	2-Karäter, 3-Karäter, 4-Karäter…
2karätig, 3karätig, 4karätig …	2-karätig, 3-karätig, 4-karätig …
Karoas	Karoass
Kartographie	*also:* Kartografie
Kaßler	Kassler
Katarrh	*also:* Katarr
kegelschieben	Kegel schieben
Kellergeschoß	Kellergeschoss [*in Austria still written with* ß]
kennenlernen	kennen lernen
Kennummer	Kennnummer *also:* Kenn-Nummer
die Keplerschen Gesetze	die keplerschen Gesetze *also:* die Kepler'schen Gesetze
keß	kess
Keßheit	Kessheit
Ketchup	*also:* Ketschup*
Kickdown	*also:* Kick-down*
Kick-off	*also:* Kickoff
an Kindes Statt	an Kindes statt
Kindesmißhandlung	Kindesmisshandlung
Kißchen	Kisschen
sich über etwas im klaren sein	sich über etwas im Klaren sein
klardenkend	klar denkend
klarsehen	klar sehen
klarwerden	klar werden
Klassenbewußtsein	Klassenbewusstsein
Klassenhaß	Klassenhass
klatschnaß	klatschnass
Klausenpaß	Klausenpass
klebenbleiben	kleben bleiben
Klee-Einsaat	*also:* Kleeeinsaat
Klee-Ernte	*also:* Kleeernte
bis ins kleinste geregelt	bis ins Kleinste geregelt
ein Staat im kleinen	ein Staat im Kleinen
ein Programm für groß und klein	ein Programm für Groß und Klein
kleingedruckt	klein gedruckt
kleinschneiden	klein schneiden
klein schreiben [*mit kleinem Anfangsbuchstaben*]	kleinschreiben
Klemmappe	Klemmmappe *also:* Klemm-Mappe
Klettverschluß	Klettverschluss
klitschnaß	klitschnass
es wäre das klügste, wenn …	es wäre das Klügste, wenn …
knapphalten	knapp halten
Knockout	*also:* Knock-out*
kochendheiß	kochend heiß
kohleführende Flöze	Kohle führende Flöze
Kolanuß	Kolanuss
Kollektivbewußtsein	Kollektivbewusstsein
Kolophonium	*also:* Kolofonium
Koloß	Koloss
Kombinationsschloß	Kombinationsschloss
Kommiß	Kommiss
Kommißbrot	Kommissbrot
Kommißstiefel	Kommissstiefel *also:* Kommiss-Stiefel
Kommuniqué	*also:* Kommunikee
Kompaß	Kompass
kompreß	kompress
Kompromiß	Kompromiss
kompromißbereit	kompromissbereit
kompromißlos	kompromisslos
Kompromißlösung	Kompromisslösung
Komteß	Komtess
Konferenzbeschluß	Konferenzbeschluss
Kongreß	Kongress
Kongreßhalle	Kongresshalle

OLD	NEW
Kongreßsaal	Kongresssaal
	also: Kongress-Saal
Kongreßstadt	Kongressstadt
	also: Kongress-Stadt
Königsschloß	Königsschloss
Kontrabaß	Kontrabass
Kontrollampe	Kontrolllampe
	also: Kontroll-Lampe
Kontrolliste	Kontrollliste
	also: Kontroll-Liste
Kopfnuß	Kopfnuss
Kopfschuß	Kopfschuss
kopfstehen	Kopf stehen
Koppelschloß	Koppelschloss
krank schreiben	krankschreiben
kraß	krass
Kraßheit	Krassheit
krebserregende Substanzen	Krebs erregende Substanzen
Kreiselkompaß	Kreiselkompass
Kreppapier	Krepppapier
	also: Krepp-Papier
Kreuzas	Kreuzass
die kriegführenden Parteien	die Krieg führenden Parteien
Kriminalprozeß	Kriminalprozess
Kristallüster	Kristalllüster
	also: Kristall-Lüster
kroß	kross
krummnehmen	krumm nehmen
KSZE-Schlußakte	KSZE-Schlussakte
Kunststoffolie	Kunststofffolie
	also: Kunststoff-Folie
Küraß	Kürass
den kürzeren ziehen	den Kürzeren ziehen
kürzertreten	kürzer treten
kurzgebraten	kurz gebraten
kurzhalten	kurz halten
Kurzpaß	Kurzpass
Kurzschluß	Kurzschluss
kurztreten	kurz treten
Kuß	Kuss
Küßchen	Küsschen
kußecht	kussecht
Kußhand	Kusshand
du/er/sie küßt	du/er/sie/küsst
Küstenschiffahrt	Küstenschifffahrt
Kwaß	Kwass

L

OLD	NEW
Ladenschluß	Ladenschluss
die La-Fontaineschen Fabeln	die la-fontaineschen Fabeln
	also: die la-Fontaine'schen Fabeln
Lamé	*also:* Lamee
Lamellenverschluß	Lamellenverschluss
etwas des langen und breiten erklären	etwas des Langen und Breiten erklären
langgestreckt	lang gestreckt
länglichrund	länglich rund
langstengelig	langstängelig
langziehen	lang ziehen
Lapsus linguae	Lapsus Linguae
läßlich	lässlich
du läßt	du lässt
zu Lasten	*also:* zulasten
Lattenschuß	Lattenschuss
laubtragende Bäume	Laub tragende Bäume
auf dem laufenden sein	auf dem Laufenden sein
laufenlassen	laufen lassen
Laufpaß	Laufpass
Layout	*also:* Lay-out*
Lebensgenuß	Lebensgenuss
Leberabszeß	Leberabszess
die lederverarbeitende Industrie	die Leder verarbeitende Industrie
leerstehend	leer stehend
leichenblaß	leichenblass
es ist mir ein leichtes, das zu tun	es ist mir ein Leichtes, das zu tun
leichtentzündlich	leicht entzündlich
leichtfallen	leicht fallen
leichtmachen	leicht machen
leichtnehmen	leicht nehmen
leichtverderblich	leicht verderblich
leichtverständlich	leicht verständlich
jmdm. leid tun	jmdm. Leid tun
Lenkradschloß	Lenkradschloss
Lernprozeß	Lernprozess
der letzte, der gekommen ist	der Letzte, der gekommen ist
als letzter fertig sein	als Letzter fertig sein
das letzte, was sie tun würde	das Letzte, was sie tun würde
bis ins letzte geklärt	bis ins Letzte geklärt
letzteres trifft zu	Letzteres trifft zu
zum letztenmal	zum letzten Mal
leuchtendblau	leuchtend blau
Lichtmeß	Lichtmess
es wäre uns das liebste, wenn …	es wäre uns das Liebste, wenn …
liebenlernen	lieben lernen
liebgewinnen	lieb gewinnen
liebhaben	lieb haben
liegenbleiben	liegen bleiben
liegenlassen	liegen lassen
Live-Mitschnitt	*also:* Livemitschnitt
Lizentiat	*also:* Lizenziat*
Lorbaß	Lorbass
Löß	*also:* Löss [*when pronounced with a short* ö]
Lößboden	*also:* Lössboden [*when pronounced with a short* ö]
Lößschicht	*also:* Lössschicht oder Löss-Schicht [*when pronounced with a short* ö]
Lötschenpaß	Lötschenpass
Love-Story	*also:* Lovestory
Luftschiffahrt	Luftschifffahrt
Luftschloß	Luftschloss

M

OLD	NEW
Magistratsbeschluß	Magistratsbeschluss
2mal, 3mal, 4mal …	2-mal, 3-mal, 4-mal …
Malaise	*also:* Maläse
Marschkompaß	Marschkompass
maschineschreiben	Maschine schreiben
maßhalten	Maß halten
Matrizes	*also:* Matrices
Maulkorberlaß	Maulkorberlass
Megaphon	*also:* Megafon
Mehrheitsbeschluß	Mehrheitsbeschluss
Meldeschluß	Meldeschluss
Meniskusriß	Meniskusriss
wir haben das menschenmögliche getan	wir haben das Menschenmögliche getan
Mesner	*also:* Messner
Meßband	Messband
meßbar	messbar
Meßbecher	Messbecher
Meßbuch	Messbuch
Meßdaten	Messdaten
Meßdiener	Messdiener
Meßfühler	Messfühler
Meßgewand	Messgewand
Meßinstrument	Messinstrument
Meßopfer	Messopfer
Meßstab	Messstab
	also: Mess-Stab
Meßtischblatt	Messtischblatt
Metallguß	Metallguss
Metallegierung	Metalllegierung
	also: Metall-Legierung

OLD	NEW
die metallverarbeitende Industrie	die Metall verarbeitende Industrie
Midlife-crisis	Midlifecrisis
	also: Midlife-Crisis
Milchgebiß	Milchgebiss
millionenmal	Millionen Mal
Milzriß	Milzriss
nicht im mindesten	*also:* nicht im Mindesten
mißachten	missachten
Mißbildung	Missbildung
mißbilligen	missbilligen
Mißbrauch	Missbrauch
Mißerfolg	Misserfolg
Mißernte	Missernte
mißfallen	missfallen
Mißfallenskundgebung	Missfallenskundgebung
Mißgeburt	Missgeburt
Mißgeschick	Missgeschick
mißglücken	missglücken
Mißgunst	Missgunst
mißgünstig	missgünstig
Mißklang	Missklang
Mißkredit	Misskredit
mißlich	misslich
mißlingen	misslingen
mißmutig	missmutig
mißraten	missraten
Mißstand	Missstand
Mißtrauen	Misstrauen
mißtrauisch	misstrauisch
Mißverständnis	Missverständnis
Mißwirtschaft	Misswirtschaft
mit Hilfe	*also:* mithilfe
[gestern, heute, morgen] mittag	[gestern, heute, morgen] Mittag
Mixed Pickles	*also:* Mixedpickles*
modebewußt	modebewusst
wir sprachen über alles mögliche	wir sprachen über alles Mögliche
sein möglichstes tun	sein Möglichstes tun
3monatig, 4monatig, 5monatig …	3-monatig, 4-monatig, 5-monatig …
3monatlich, 4monatlich, 5monatlich …	3-monatlich, 4-monatlich, 5-monatlich …
Monographie	*also:* Monografie
Mop	Mopp
Mordprozeß	Mordprozess
morgen abend, mittag, nacht	morgen Abend, Mittag, Nacht
[gestern, heute] morgen	[gestern, heute] Morgen
Moto-Cross	*also:* Motocross
Mückenschiß	Mückenschiss
Mulläppchen	Mullläppchen
	also: Mull-Läppchen
Multiple-choice-Verfahren	Multiplechoiceverfahren
	also: Multiple-Choice-Verfahren
Muskatnuß	Muskatnuss
Muskelriß	Muskelriss
ich muß	ich muss
du mußt	du musst
ich müßte	ich müsste
du müßtest	du müsstest
Mußheirat	Mussheirat
müßiggehen	müßig gehen
Musterprozeß	Musterprozess
Myrrhe	*also:* Myrre

N

OLD	NEW
nachfolgendes gilt auch …	Nachfolgendes gilt auch …
nach Hause	*in Austria and Switzerland*
	also: nachhause
im nachhinein	im Nachhinein
Nachlaß	Nachlass
Nachlaßverwalter	Nachlassverwalter
[gestern, heute, morgen] nachmittag	[gestern, heute, morgen] Nachmittag
Nachschuß	Nachschuss
der nächste, bitte!	der Nächste, bitte!
als nächstes wollen wir …	als Nächstes wollen wir …
im nachstehenden heißt es …	im Nachstehenden heißt es …
[gestern, heute, morgen] nacht	[gestern, heute, morgen] Nacht
nahebringen	nahe bringen
nahelegen	nahe legen
naheliegen	nahe liegen
naheliegend	nahe liegend
etwas des näheren erläutern	etwas des Näheren erläutern
näherliegen	näher liegen
nahestehen	nahe stehen
nahestehend	nahe stehend
Narziß	Narziss
Narzißmus	Narzissmus
narzißtisch	narzisstisch
naß	nass
naßforsch	nassforsch
naßgeschwitzt	nass geschwitzt
naßkalt	nasskalt
Naßrasur	Nassrasur
Naßschnee	Nassschnee
	also: Nass-Schnee
nationalbewußt	nationalbewusst
Nationaldreß	Nationaldress
Nebelschlußleuchte	Nebelschlussleuchte
Nebenanschluß	Nebenanschluss
nebeneinandersitzen	nebeneinander sitzen
nebeneinanderstehen	nebeneinander stehen
nebeneinanderstellen	nebeneinander stellen
Nebenfluß	Nebenfluss
im nebenstehenden wird gezeigt …	im Nebenstehenden wird gezeigt …
Necessaire	*also:* Nessessär
Negligé	*also:* Negligee
nein sagen	*also:* Nein sagen*
Netzanschluß	Netzanschluss
es aufs neue versuchen	es aufs Neue versuchen
auf ein neues!	auf ein Neues!
neueröffnet	neu eröffnet
New Yorker	*also:* New-Yorker
nichtrostend	*also:* nicht rostend
Nichtseßhafte	Nichtsesshafte
nichtssagend	nichts sagend
No-future-Generation	No-Future-Generation
die notleidende Bevölkerung	die Not leidende Bevölkerung
in Null Komma nichts	in null Komma nichts
das Thermometer steht auf Null	das Thermometer steht auf null
Nullage	Nulllage
	also: Null-Lage
Nulleiter	Nullleiter
	also: Null-Leiter
Nullösung	Nulllösung
	also: Null-Lösung
numerieren	nummerieren
Numerierung	Nummerierung
Nuß	Nuss
Nüßchen	Nüsschen
Nußknacker	Nussknacker
Nußschale	Nussschale
	also: Nuss-Schale
Nußschinken	Nussschinken
	also: Nuss-Schinken
Nußschokolade	Nussschokolade
	also: Nuss-Schokolade
Nußstrudel	Nussstrudel
	also: Nuss-Strudel
Nußtorte	Nusstorte

O

OLD	NEW
O-beinig	*also:* o-beinig
obenerwähnt	oben erwähnt

OLD	NEW
obenstehend	oben stehend
Obergeschoß	Obergeschoss [*in Austria still written with* ß]
offenbleiben	offen bleiben
offenlassen	offen lassen
offenstehen	offen stehen
O-förmig	*also:* o-förmig
des öfteren	des öfteren
ölmeßstab	ölmessstab
Ordonnanz	*also:* Ordonanz
Orthographie	*also:* Orthografie

P

OLD	NEW
Panther	*also:* Panter
die papierverarbeitende Industrie	die Papier verarbeitende Industrie
Pappmaché	*also:* Pappmaschee
parallellaufend	parallel laufend
parallelschalten	parallel schalten
Paranuß	Paranuss
Parlamentsbeschluß	Parlamentsbeschluss
Parnaß	Parnass
Parteikongreß	Parteikongress
Parteitagsbeschluß	Parteitagsbeschluss
Paß	Pass
Paßbild	Passbild
passé	*also:* passee
Paßform	Passform
Paßgang	Passgang
paßgerecht	passgerecht
Paßkontrolle	Passkontrolle
Paßstelle	Passstelle
	also: Pass-Stelle
Paßstraße	Passstraße
	also: Pass-Straße
Paßwort	Passwort
Patentverschluß	Patentverschluss
patschnaß	patschnass
Perkussionsschloß	Perkussionsschloss
Personenschiffahrt	Personenschifffahrt
Petitionsausschuß	Petitionsausschuss
Pfeffernuß	Pfeffernuss
Pferdegebiß	Pferdegebiss
pflichtbewußt	pflichtbewusst
Pflichtbewußtsein	Pflichtbewusstsein
Pfostenschuß	Pfostenschuss
Pikas	Pikass
Pimpernuß	Pimpernuss
er pißt	er pisst
Pistolenschuß	Pistolenschuss
pitschnaß	pitschnass
Platitüde	Plattitüde
	also: Platitude
Playback	*also:* Play-back*
plazieren	platzieren
pleite gehen	Pleite gehen
polyphon	*also:* polyfon
Pornographie	*also:* Pornografie
Portemonnaie	*also:* Portmonee
Potemkinsche Dörfer	potemkinsche Dörfer
	also: Potemkin'sche Dörfer
potentiell	*also:* potenziell*
potthäßlich	potthässlich
Poussierstengel	Poussierstängel
präferentiell	*also:* präferenziell*
er praßt	er prasst
preisbewußt	preisbewusst
Preisnachlaß	Preisnachlass
Preßform	Pressform
Preßluftbohrer	Pressluftbohrer
Preßsack	Presssack
	also: Press-Sack
Preßschlag	Pressschlag
	also: Press-Schlag
Preßspan	Pressspan
	also: Press-Span
du preßt	du presst
Preßwehe	Presswehe
Prinzeßbohne	Prinzessbohne
privatversichert	privat versichert
probefahren	Probe fahren
Problembewußtsein	Problembewusstsein
Produktionsprozeß	Produktionsprozess
Profeß	Profess
Programmusik	Programmmusik
	also: Programm-Musik
Progreß	Progress
Prozeß	Prozess
Prozeßkosten	Prozesskosten
Prozeßbevollmächtigte	Prozessbevollmächtigte
prozeßführend	prozessführend
Prozeßkosten	Prozesskosten
Prozeßrechner	Prozessrechner
pudelnaß	pudelnass
Pulverfaß	Pulverfass
pußlig	pusslig

Q

OLD	NEW
Quadrophonie	*also:* Quadrofonie
qualitätsbewußt	qualitätsbewusst
Quartalsabschluß	Quartalsabschluss
Quellfluß	Quellfluss
Quentchen	Quäntchen
Querpaß	Querpass
Quickstep	Quickstepp

R

OLD	NEW
radfahren	Rad fahren
Radikalenerlaß	Radikalenerlass
radschlagen	Rad schlagen
Rammaschine	Rammmaschine
	also: Ramm-Maschine
zu Rande kommen	*also:* zurande kommen
Rassenhaß	Rassenhass
ich raßle mit den Ketten	ich rassle mit den Ketten
zu Rate ziehen	*also:* zurate ziehen
Räterußland	Räterussland
Ratsbeschluß	Ratsbeschluss
Ratschluß	Ratschluss
Rauchfaß	Rauchfass
rauh	rau
rauhbeinig	raubeinig
Rauhfasertapete	Raufasertapete
Rauhfrost	Raufrost
Rauhhaardackel	Rauhaardackel
Rauhnächte	Raunächte
Rauhputz	Rauputz
Rauhreif	Raureif
Rausschmiß	Rausschmiss
recht haben	Recht haben
recht behalten	Recht behalten
recht bekommen	Recht bekommen
jmdm. recht geben	jmdm. Recht geben
Rechtens sein	rechtens sein
Rechtsbewußtsein	Rechtsbewusstsein
Redaktionsschluß	Redaktionsschluss
Regenguß	Regenguss
regennaß	regennass
Regreß	Regress
Regreßanspruch	Regressanspruch
Regreßpflicht	Regresspflicht
regreßpflichtig	regresspflichtig
reichgeschmückt	reich geschmückt
reichverziert	reich verziert
Reifungsprozeß	Reifungsprozess
Reisepaß	Reisepass
Reißverschluß	Reißverschluss

OLD	NEW
Reißverschlußsystem	Reißverschlusssystem
	also: Reißverschluss-System
Reschenpaß	Reschenpass
Rettungsschuß	Rettungsschuss
Rezeß	Rezess
Rhein-Main-Donau-Großschiffahrtsweg	Rhein-Main-Donau-Großschifffahrtsweg
das ist genau das richtige für mich	das ist genau das Richtige für mich
mit etwas richtigliegen	mit etwas richtig liegen
richtigstellen	richtig stellen
Riß	Riss
rißfest	rissfest
Roheit	Rohheit
Rolladen	Rollladen
	also: Roll-Laden
Rommé	*also:* Rommee
rosigweiß	rosig weiß
Roß	Ross
Roßbreiten	Rossbreiten
Roßhaarmatratze	Rosshaarmatratze
Roßkastanie	Rosskastanie
Roßkur	Rosskur
Rößl	Rössl
Roßtäuscherei	Rosstäuscherei
de rote Planet [*Mars*]	der Rote Planet
rotgestreift	rot gestreift
rotglühend	rot glühend
rötlichbraun	rötlich braun
die Rubensschen Gemälde	die rubensschen Gemälde
	also: die Rubens'schen Gemälde
Rückfluß	Rückfluss
Rückpaß	Rückpass
Rückschluß	Rückschluss
rückwärtsgewandt	rückwärts gewandt
Ruhegenuß	Ruhegenuss
ruhenlassen	ruhen lassen
ruhigstellen	ruhig stellen
Runderlaß	Runderlass
Rußland	Russland

S

OLD	NEW
Säbelraßler	Säbelrassler
Saisonnier	*also:* Saisonier
Saisonschluß	Saisonschluss
Salutschuß	Salutschuss
Salzfaß	Salzfass
Samenerguß	Samenerguss
Sammelanschluß	Sammelanschluss
Sankt Gallener	*also:* Sankt-Gallener
sanktgallisch	sankt-gallisch
Sanmarinese	San-Marinese
sanmarinesisch	san-marinesisch
sauberhalten	sauber halten
saubermachen	sauber machen
sausenlassen	sausen lassen
Saxophon	*also:* Saxofon
sein Schäfchen ins trockene bringen	sein Schäfchen ins Trockene bringen
Schalenguß	Schalenguss
Schallehre	Schalllehre
	also: Schall-Lehre
Schalloch	Schallloch
	also: Schall-Loch
Schalterschluß	Schalterschluss
etwas auf das schärfste verurteilen	*also:* etwas auf das Schärfste verurteilen
er schaßte ihn	er schasste ihn
ein schattenspendender Baum	ein Schatten spendender Baum
schätzenlernen	schätzen lernen
Schauprozeß	Schauprozess
Scheidungsprozeß	Scheidungsprozess
schießenlassen	schießen lassen

OLD	NEW
Schiffahrt	Schifffahrt
	also: Schiff-Fahrt
Schippenas	Schippenass
Schiß	Schiss
Schlachtroß	Schlachtross
Schlagfluß	Schlagfluss
Schlammasse	Schlammmasse
	also: Schlamm-Masse
schlechtgehen	schlecht gehen
schlechtgelaunt	schlecht gelaunt
das schlimmste ist, daß …	das Schlimmste ist, dass …
sie haben ihn auf das schlimmste getäuscht	*also:* sie haben ihn auf das Schlimmste getäuscht
er schliß Federn	er schliss Federn
Schlitzverschluß	Schlitzverschluss
Schloß	Schloss
Schlößchen	Schlösschen
Schloßherr	Schlossherr
Schloßpark	Schlosspark
Schluß	Schluss
Schlußbemerkung	Schlussbemerkung
schlußendlich	schlussendlich
schlußfolgern	schlussfolgern
Schlußfolgerung	Schlussfolgerung
Schlußlicht	Schlusslicht
Schlußpfiff	Schlusspfiff
Schlußpunkt	Schlusspunkt
Schlußsatz	Schlusssatz
	also: Schluss-Satz
Schlußspurt	Schlussspurt
	also: Schluss-Spurt
Schlußstrich	Schlussstrich
	also: Schluss-Strich
Schlußverkauf	Schlussverkauf
Schlußwort	Schlusswort
Schmerfluß	Schmerfluss
sie schmiß mit Steinen	sie schmiss mit Steinen
Schmiß	Schmiss
Schmuckblattelegramm	Schmuckblatttelegramm
	also: Schmuckblatt-Telegramm
schmutziggrau	schmutzig grau
Schnappschloß	Schnappschloss
Schnappschuß	Schnappschuss
Schnee-Eifel	*also:* Schneeeifel
Schnee-Eule	*also:* Schneeeule
Schneewächte	Schneewechte
Schnellimbiß	Schnellimbiss
Schnelläufer	Schnellläufer
	also: Schnell-Läufer
schnellebig	schnelllebig
Schnellebigkeit	Schnelllebigkeit
Schnellschuß	Schnellschuss
Schnepper	*also:* Schnäpper
schneppern	*also:* schnäppern
schneuzen	schnäuzen
Schokoladenguß	Schokoladenguss
aufs schönste übereinstimmen	*also:* aufs Schönste übereinstimmen
er schoß	er schoss
Schoß [einer Pflanze]	Schoss
Schräglaufend	schräg laufend
Schraubverschluß	Schraubverschluss
schreckensblaß	schreckensblass
Schreckschußpistole	Schreckschusspistole
Schrittempo	Schritttempo
	also: Schritt-Tempo
Schrotschuß	Schrotschuss
Schulabschluß	Schulabschluss
an etwas schuld haben	an etwas Schuld haben
sich etwas zuschulden kommen lassen	*also:* sich etwas zu Schulden kommen lassen
schuldbewußt	schuldbewusst
Schuldenerlaß	Schuldenerlass
Schulschluß	Schulschluss
Schulstreß	Schulstress

OLD	NEW
Schulterschluß	Schulterschluss
Schuß	Schuss
schußbereit	schussbereit
schußfest	schussfest
schußlig	schusslig
Schußlinie	Schusslinie
Schußschwäche	Schussschwäche
	also: Schuss-Schwäche
Schußwaffe	Schusswaffe
Schußwechsel	Schusswechsel
schwachbetont	schwach betont
schwachbevölkert	schwach bevölkert
aus schwarz weiß machen	aus Schwarz Weiß machen
Schwarze Magie	schwarze Magie
schwarzgefärbt	schwarz gefärbt
schwarzrotgolden	*also:* schwarz-rot-golden
schwerfallen	schwer fallen
schwernehmen	schwer nehmen
schwertun	schwer tun
schwerverständlich	schwer verständlich
Schwimmeister	Schwimmmeister
	also: Schwimm-Meister
Science-fiction	Sciencefiction
	also: Science-Fiction
Sechspaß	Sechspass
See-Elefant	*also:* Seeelefant
jedem das Seine	*also:* jedem das seine
das Seine beitragen	*also:* das seine beitragen
die Seinen	*also:* die seinen
die Seinigen	*also:* die seinigen
seinlassen	sein lassen
Seismograph	*also:* Seismograf
auf seiten	aufseiten
	also: auf Seiten
von seiten	vonseiten
	also: von Seiten
selbständig	*also:* selbstständig
Selbständigkeit	*also:* Selbstständigkeit
selbstbewußt	selbstbewusst
Selbstbewußtsein	Selbstbewusstsein
selbsternannt	selbst ernannt
selbstgebacken	selbst gebacken
selbstgemacht	selbst gemacht
selbstgestrickt	selbst gestrickt
Selbstschuß	Selbstschuss
selbstverdient	selbst verdient
seligpreisen	selig preisen
seligsprechen	selig sprechen
Senatsbeschluß	Senatsbeschluss
Sendeschluß	Sendeschluss
Sendungsbewußtsein	Sendungsbewusstsein
Sensationsprozeß	Sensationsprozess
Séparée	*also:* Separee
sequentiell	*also:* sequenziell*
seßhaft	sesshaft
Seßhaftigkeit	Sesshaftigkeit
S-förming	*also:* s-förmig
die Shakespeareschen Sonette	die shakespeareschen Sonette
	also: die Shakespeare'schen Sonette
Short story	Shortstory
	also: Short Story
Showbusineß	Showbusiness
Showdown	*also:* Show-down*
Shrimp	*also:* Schrimp
auf Nummer Sicher gehen	*also:* auf Nummer sicher gehen
das sicherste ist, wenn …	das Sicherste ist, wenn …
Sicherheitsschloß	Sicherheitsschloss
Sicherheitsverschluß	Sicherheitsverschluss
siedendheiß	siedend heiß
siegesbewußt	siegesbewusst
siegesgewiß	siegesgewiss
Simplonpaß	Simplonpass
die Singende Säge	die singende Säge
Siphonverschluß	Siphonverschluss

OLD	NEW
sitzenbleiben	sitzen bleiben
sitzenlassen	sitzen lassen
Skipaß	Skipass
Small talk	Smalltalk
	also: Small Talk
so daß	sodass
	also: so dass
Sommerschlußverkauf	Sommerschlussverkauf
alles sonstige besprechen wir morgen	alles Sonstige besprechen wir morgen
Soufflé	*also:* Soufflee
soviel du willst	so viel du willst
soviel wie	so viel wie
noch einmal soviel	noch einmal so viel
es ist soweit	es ist so weit
soweit wie möglich	so weit wie möglich
ich kann das sowenig wie du	ich kann das so wenig wie du
Sowjetrußland	Sowjetrussland
hier gilt kein Sowohl-Als-auch	hier gilt kein Sowohl-als-auch
Spaghetti	*also:* Spagetti
Spantenriß	Spantenriss
spazierenfahren	spazieren fahren
spazierengehen	spazieren gehen
Speichelfluß	Speichelfluss
Sperrad	Sperrrad
	also: Sperr-Rad
Sperriegel	Sperrriegel
	also: Sperr-Riegel
Spliß	Spliss
du splißt	du splisst
eine sporenbildende Pflanze	eine Sporen bildende Pflanze
Sportdreß	Sportdress
Sprenggeschoß	Sprenggeschoss [*in Austria still written with* ß]
Spritzguß	Spritzguss
es sproß neues Grün	es spross neues Grün
Sproß	Spross
Sproßachse	Sprossachse
Sprößchen	Sprösschen
Sprößling	Sprössling
staatenbildende Insekten	Staaten bildende Insekten
Stahlroß	Stahlross
Stallaterne	Stalllaterne
	also: Stall-Laterne
Stammutter	Stammmutter
	also: Stamm-Mutter
standesbewußt	standesbewusst
Standesbewußtsein	Standesbewusstsein
Startschuß	Startschuss
steckenbleiben	stecken bleiben
steckenlassen	stecken lassen
Steckschloß	Steckschloss
Steckschuß	Steckschuss
stehenbleiben	stehen bleiben
stehenlassen	stehen lassen
Stehimbiß	Stehimbiss
Steilpaß	Steilpass
Stemmeißel	Stemmmeißel
	also: Stemm-Meißel
Stendelwurz	Ständelwurz
Stengel	Stängel
Step	Stepp
Steptanz	Stepptanz
Stereophonie	*also:* Stereofonie
Steuererlaß	Steuererlass
Steuermeßbetrag	Steuermessbetrag
Stewardeß	Stewardess
stiftengehen	stiften gehen
etwas im stillen vorbereiten	etwas im Stillen vorbereiten
Stilleben	Stillleben
	also: Still-Leben
stillegen	stilllegen
Stillegung	Stilllegung
Stoffarbe	Stofffarbe
	also: Stoff-Farbe

OLD	NEW
Stoffetzen	Stofffetzen *also:* Stoff-Fetzen
Stoffülle	Stofffülle *also:* Stoff-Fülle
Stop	Stopp
Straferlaß	Straferlass
Strafprozeß	Strafprozess
Strafprozeßordnung	Strafprozessordnung
Straß	Strass
Streifschuß	Streifschuss
Streitroß	Streitross
strenggenommen	streng genommen
strengnehmen	streng nehmen
aufs strengste unterschieden	*also:* aufs Strengste unterschieden
Streß	Stress
der Lärm streßt	der Lärm stresst
Streßsituation	Stresssituation *also:* Stress-Situation
2stündig, 3stündig, 4stündig …	2-stündig, 3-stündig, 4-stündig …
2stündlich, 3stündlich, 4stündlich …	2-stündlich, 3-stündlich, 4-stündlich …
Stuß	Stuss
substantiell	*also:* substanziell*
Sustenpaß	Sustenpass

T

OLD	NEW
Tablettenmißbrauch	Tablettenmissbrauch
tabula rasa machen	Tabula rasa machen
zutage treten	*also:* zu Tage treten
2tägig, 3tägig, 4tägig …	2-tägig, 3-tägig, 4-tägig …
Tankschloß	Tankschloss
Tarifabschluß	Tarifabschluss
Täßchen	Tässchen
ein paar tausend	*also:* ein paar Tausend
Tausende von Zuschauern	*also:* tausende von Zuschauern
T-bone-Steak	T-Bone-Steak
Tee-Ei	*also:* Teeei
Tee-Ernte	*also:* Teeernte
Teerfaß	Teerfass
Telephon	Telefon
Telephonanschluß	Telefonanschluss
Thunfisch	*also:* Tunfisch
Tie-Break	*also:* Tiebreak
aufs tiefste gekränkt	*also:* aufs Tiefste gekränkt
tiefbewegt	tief bewegt
tiefempfunden	tief empfunden
tiefverschneit	tief verschneit
Tintenfaß	Tintenfass
Tip	Tipp
todblaß	todblass
Todesschuß	Todesschuss
Tolpatsch	Tollpatsch
tolpatschig	tollpatschig
Tomatenketchup	*also:* Tomatenketschup
Topographie	*also:* Topografie
Torschlußpanik	Torschlusspanik
Torschuß	Torschuss
totenblaß	totenblass
totgeboren	tot geboren
traditionsbewußt	traditionsbewusst
Tränenfluß	Tränenfluss
tränennaß	tränennass
Traß	Trass
Trekking	*also:* Trecking
treuergeben	treu ergeben
triefnaß	triefnass
auf dem trockenen sitzen	auf dem Trockenen sitzen
sein Schäfchen ins trockene bringen	sein Schäfchen ins Trockene bringen
tropfnaß	tropfnass
Troß	Tross
im trüben fischen	im Trüben fischen

OLD	NEW
Truchseß	Truchsess
Trugschluß	Trugschluss
Trumpfas	Trumpfass
Tuffelsen	Tufffelsen *also:* Tuff-Felsen
Türschloß	Türschloss

U

OLD	NEW
übelgelaunt	übel gelaunt
übelnehmen	übel nehmen
übelriechend	übel riechend
Überbiß	Überbiss
Überdruß	Überdruss
übereinanderlegen	übereinander legen
übereinanderliegen	übereinander liegen
übereinanderwerfen	übereinander werfen
Überfluß	Überfluss
Überflußgesellschaft	Überflussgesellschaft
Überguß	Überguss
überhandnehmen	überhand nehmen
übermorgen abend, nachmittag	übermorgen Abend, Nachmittag
Überschuß	Überschuss
überschwenglich	überschwänglich
überwächtet	überwechtet
ein übriges tun	ein Übriges tun
im übrigen wissen wir doch alle …	im Übrigen wissen wir doch alle …
alles übrige später	alles Übrige später
die übrigen kommen nach	die Übrigen kommen nach
übrigbehalten	übrig behalten
übrigbleiben	übrig bleiben
übriglassen	übrig lassen
U-förmig	*also:* u-förmig
Ultima ratio	Ultima Ratio
Umdenkprozeß	Umdenkprozess
die Liste umfaßt alles Wichtige	die Liste umfasst alles Wichtige
Umriß	Umriss
Umrißzeichnung	Umrisszeichnung
Umschichtungsprozeß	Umschichtungsprozess
Umschluß	Umschluss
umsein	um sein
um so [mehr, größer, weniger …]	umso [mehr, größer, weniger …]
Umstellungsprozeß	Umstellungsprozess
Umwandlungsprozeß	Umwandlungsprozess
Umwelteinfluß	Umwelteinfluss
sich ins unabsehbare ausweiten	sich ins Unabsehbare ausweiten
unangepaßt	unangepasst
Unangepaßtheit	Unangepasstheit
unbeeinflußbar	unbeeinflussbar
unbeeinflußt	unbeeinflusst
Anzeige gegen Unbekannt	Anzeige gegen unbekannt
unbewußt	unbewusst
und ähnliches (u. ä.)	und Ähnliches (u. Ä.)
unendlichemal	unendliche Mal
unerläßlich	unerlässlich
unermeßlich	unermesslich
Unfairneß	Unfairness
unfaßbar	unfassbar
unfaßlich	unfasslich
ungewiß	ungewiss
Ungewißheit	Ungewissheit
unigefärbt	uni gefärbt
im unklaren bleiben	im Unklaren bleiben
im unklaren lassen	im Unklaren lassen
unmißverständlich	unmissverständlich
unpäßlich	unpässlich
Unpäßlichkeit	Unpässlichkeit
unplaziert	unplatziert
unrecht haben	Unrecht haben
unrecht behalten	Unrecht behalten
unrecht bekommen	Unrecht bekommen
Unrechtsbewußtsein	Unrechtsbewusstsein
unselbständig	*also:* unselbstständig

OLD	NEW
Unselbständigkeit	*also:* Unselbstständigkeit
die Unseren	*also:* die unseren
die Unsrigen	*also:* die unsrigen
untenerwähnt	unten erwähnt
untenstehend	unten stehend
unterbewußt	unterbewusst
Unterbewußtsein	Unterbewusstsein
unterderhand	unter der Hand
untereinanderstehen	untereinander stehen
Untergeschoß	Untergeschoss [*in Austria still written with* ß]
ohne Unterlaß	ohne Unterlass
Untersuchungsausschuß	Untersuchungsausschuss
unvergeßlich	unvergesslich
unerläßlich	unerlässlich
unzähligemal	unzählige Mal

V

OLD	NEW
va banque spielen	*also:* Vabanque spielen
Varieté	*also:* Varietee
veranlaßt	veranlasst
verantwortungsbewußt	verantwortungsbewusst
Verantwortungsbewußtsein	Verantwortungsbewusstsein
Verbiß	Verbiss
verblaßt	verblasst
verbleuen	verbläuen
im verborgenen blühen	im Verborgenen blühen
das verdroß uns	das verdross uns
Verdruß	Verdruss
du verfaßt	du verfasst
vergeßlich	vergesslich
Vergeßlichkeit	Vergesslichkeit
Vergißmeinnicht	Vergissmeinnicht
du vergißt	du vergisst
verhaßt	verhasst
auf jmdn. ist Verlaß	auf jmdn. ist Verlass
verläßlich	verlässlich
Verläßlichkeit	Verlässlichkeit
verlorengehen	verloren gehen
vermißt	vermisst
Vermißtenanzeige	Vermisstenanzeige
er hat den Zug verpaßt	er hat den Zug verpasst
das Geld wurde verpraßt	das Geld wurde verprasst
Verriß	Verriss
verschiedenes war noch unklar	Verschiedenes war noch unklar
verschiedenemal	verschiedene Mal
Verschiß	Verschiss
Verschluß	Verschluss
Verschlußkappe	Verschlusskappe
Verschlußsache	Verschlusssache *also:* Verschluss-Sache
verselbständigen	*also:* verselbstständigen
Versorgungsengpaß	Versorgungsengpass
Vertragsabschluß	Vertragsabschluss
Vertragsschluß	Vertragsschluss
V-förmig	*also:* v-förmig
Vibraphon	*also:* Vibrafon
viel zuviel	viel zu viel
viel zuwenig	viel zu wenig
vielbefahren	viel befahren
vielgelesen	viel gelesen
Vierpaß	Vierpass
aus dem vollen schöpfen	aus dem Vollen schöpfen
voneinandergehen	voneinander gehen
von seiten	vonseiten *also:* von Seiten
vorangehendes gilt auch …	Vorangehendes gilt auch …
im vorangehenden heißt es …	im Vorangehenden heißt es …
im voraus	im Voraus
vorgefaßt	vorgefasst
vorgestern abend, mittag, morgen	vorgestern Abend, Mittag, Morgen
Vorhängeschloß	Vorhängeschloss
vorhergehendes gilt auch …	Vorhergehendes gilt auch …
im vorhergehenden heißt es …	im Vorhergehenden heißt es …
im vorhinein	im Vorhinein
das vorige gilt auch …	das Vorige gilt auch …
im vorigen heißt es …	im Vorigen heißt es …
Vorlegeschloß	Vorlegeschloss
vorliebnehmen	vorlieb nehmen
[gestern, heute, morgen] vormittag	[gestern, heute, morgen] Vormittag
Vorschlußrunde	Vorschlussrunde
Vorschuß	Vorschuss
Vorschußlorbeeren	Vorschusslorbeeren
vorstehendes gilt auch …	Vorstehendes gilt auch …
im vorstehenden heißt es …	im Vorstehenden heißt es …
vorwärtsgehen	vorwärts gehen
vorwärtskommen	vorwärts kommen

W

OLD	NEW
ein wachestehender Soldat	ein Wache stehender Soldat
Wachsabguß	Wachsabguss
Wächte	Wechte
Waggon	*also:* Wagon
Wahlausschuß	Wahlausschuss
Walkie-talkie	Walkie-Talkie
Walnuß	Walnuss
Walroß	Walross
Wandlungsprozeß	Wandlungsprozess
Warnschuß	Warnschuss
Wasserschloß	Wasserschloss
wäßrig	wässrig
Wehrpaß	Wehrpass
weichgekocht	weich gekocht
Weinfaß	Weinfass
aus schwarz weiß machen	aus Schwarz Weiß machen
weißgekleidet	weiß gekleidet
Weißrußland	Weißrussland
des weiteren wurde gesagt …	des Weiteren wurde gesagt …
weitgereist	weit gereist
weitreichend	weit reichend
weitverbreitet	weit verbreitet
Werkstattage	Werkstatttage *also:* Werkstatt-Tage
Werkstofforschung	Werkstoffforschung *also:* Werkstoff-Forschung
es besteht im wesentlichen aus …	es besteht im Wesentlichen aus …
Wetteufel	Wettteufel *also:* Wett-Teufel
Wetturnen	Wettturnen *also:* Wett-Turnen
widereinanderstoßen	widereinander stoßen
wieviel	wie viel
Winterschlußverkauf	Winterschlussverkauf
Wißbegierde	Wissbegierde
wißbegierig	wissbegierig
ihr wißt	ihr wisst
du wußtest	du wusstest
wir wüßten gern …	wir wüssten gern …
Witterungseinfluß	Witterungseinfluss
Wollappen	Wolllappen *also:* Woll-Lappen
Wollaus	Wolllaus *also:* Woll-Laus
als ob er wunder was getan hätte	als ob er Wunder was getan hätte
sich wundliegen	sich wund liegen
Wurfgeschoß	Wurfgeschoss [*in Austria still written with* ß]

X, Y

OLD	NEW
X-beinig	*also:* x-beinig
X-förmig	*also:* x-förmig
zum x-tenmal	zum x-ten Mal

Z

OLD	NEW
Zäheit	Zähheit
Zahlenschloß	Zahlenschloss
Zäpfchen-R	*also:* Zäpfchen-r

OLD	NEW
Zaubernuß	Zaubernuss
Zechenstillegung	Zechenstilllegung
Zeilengußmaschine	Zeilengussmaschine
2zeilig, 3zeilig, 4zeilig ...	2-zeilig, 3-zeilig, 4-zeilig ...
eine Zeitlang	eine Zeit lang
zur Zeit [*derzeit*]	zurzeit
Zellehre	Zelllehre *also:* Zell-Lehre
Zellstoffabrik	Zellstofffabrik *also:* Zellstoff-Fabrik
Zersetzungsprozeß	Zersetzungsprozess
zielbewußt	zielbewusst
Zierat	Zierrat
zigtausend	*also:* Zigtausend
zigtausende	*also:* zigtausende
Zippverschluß	Zippverschluss
Zirkelschluß	Zirkelschluss
Zivilprozeß	Zivilprozess
Zivilprozeßordnung	Zivilprozessordnung
Zoo-Orchester	*also:* Zooorchester
sich zu eigen machen	sich zu Eigen machen
zueinanderfinden	zueinander finden
Zufluß	Zufluss
sich zufriedengeben	sich zufrieden geben
zufriedenlassen	zufrieden lassen
zufriedenstellen	zufrieden stellen
zugrunde gehen	*also:* zu Grunde gehen
zugrunde legen	*also:* zu Grunde legen
zugrunde liegen	*also:* zu Grunde liegen
zugrundeliegend	zugrunde liegend *also:* zu Grunde liegend
zugrunde richten	*also:* zu Grunde richten
zugunsten	*also:* zu Gunsten
Zu Hause	*in Austria and Switzerland also:* zuhause
bei uns zulande	bei uns zu Lande
zulasten	*also:* zu Lasten
jmdm. etwas zuleide tun	*also:* jmdm. etwas zu Leide tun
zumute sein	*also:* zu Mute sein
Zündschloß	Zündschloss
Zungenkuß	Zungenkuss
Zungen-R	*also:* Zungen-r
sich etwas zunutze machen	*also:* sich etwas zu Nutze machen
jmdm. zupaß kommen	jmdm. zupass kommen
zugepreßt	zugepresst
zu Rande kommen	*also:* zurande kommen
jmdn. zu Rate ziehen	*also:* jmdn. zurate ziehen
sie hat zurückgemußt	sie hat zurückgemusst
zur Zeit [*derzeit*]	zurzeit
Zusammenfluß	Zusammenfluss
zusammengefaßt	zusammengefasst
zusammengepaßt	zusammengepasst
zusammengepreßt	zusammengepresst
Zusammenschluß	Zusammenschluss
zusammensein	zusammen sein
zuschanden werden	*also:* zu Schanden werden
sich etwas zuschulden kommen lassen	*also:* sich etwas zu schulden kommen lassen
Zuschuß	Zuschuss
Zuschußbetrieb	Zuschussbetrieb
zusein	zu sein
zustande bringen	*also:* zu Stande bringen
zustande kommen	*also:* zu Stande kommen
zutage födern	*also:* zu Tage fördern
zutage treten	*also:* zu Tage treten
zuungunsten	*also:* zu Ungunsten
zuviel	zu viel
Zuwege bringen	*also:* zu Wege bringen
zuwenig	zu wenig
die zwanziger Jahre	*also:* die Zwanzigerjahre*
die Zwanzigerjahre	*also:* die zwanziger Jahre
das Zweite Gesicht	das zweite Gesicht
er hat wie kein zweiter gearbeitet	er hat wie kein Zweiter gearbeitet
jeder zweite war krank	jeder Zweite war krank
Zweitkläßler	Zweitklässler
Zwischengeschoß	Zwischengeschoss [*in Austria still written with* ß]

Kleine Formenlehre des Englischen

Das Verb

Die Stammformen

Die regelmäßigen Verben bilden das Präteritum und das gleichlautende 2. Partizip mit Hilfe der Endung *-ed:*

call – called – called

Hierbei sind die folgenden Besonderheiten zu beachten:

Ein auslautender Konsonant wird häufig verdoppelt, und *-c* wird zu *-ck-:*

dub – dubbed
pod – podded
hug – hugged
focus – focused *od.* focussed
panic – panicked

Ein auslautendes *-e* fällt aus:

love – loved
tie – tied
dye – dyed
guarantee – guaranteed

Ein auslautendes, auf einen Konsonanten folgendes *-y* wird zu *-i-:*

worry – worried
satisfy – satisfied

Die Stammformen der unregelmäßigen Verben sind im englisch-deutschen Wörterverzeichnis bei dem jeweiligen Stichwort angegeben (vgl. S. 16). Außerdem sind sie in der Liste auf S. 1655 f. verzeichnet. (Zu den Hilfsverben und den Modalverben s. u., S. 1652 f.)

Das Präsens

Die 3. Person Singular Präsens der Vollverben (außer *have* und *be*) wird durch die Endung *-s,* nach *s, sh, ch, x, o* zu *-es* erweitert, gebildet:

read – reads
see – sees
miss – misses
fish – fishes
reach – reaches
mix – mixes
echo – echoes
do – does

Hierbei wird ein auslautendes, auf einen Konsonanten folgendes *-y* zu *-ie-:*

cry – cries
worry – worries

Alle übrigen finiten Präsensformen haben keine Personalendungen. Sie lauten wie der Infinitiv.

Das Präteritum

Das Präteritum hat keine Personalendungen und lautet (außer im Falle von *be*) in allen Personen gleich.

Das Futur

Das Futur wird gewöhnlich aus *will,* in der 1. Person Singular und Plural auch aus *shall* und dem Infinitiv gebildet:

you/he/she/it/they will win
I/we will *oder* shall win

Das Konditional Präsens

Das Konditional Präsens wird gewöhnlich aus *would,* in der 1. Person Singular und Plural auch aus *should* und dem Infinitiv gebildet:

you/he/she/it/they would win
I/we would *oder* should win

Das Perfekt

Das Perfekt wird aus dem Präsens von *have* und dem 2. Partizip gebildet:

I have seen/gone/been *usw.*

Das Plusquamperfekt

Das Plusquamperfekt wird aus dem Präteritum von *have* und dem 2. Partizip gebildet:

I had seen/gone/been *usw.*

Das Futur II

Das Futur II wird aus dem Futur I von *have* und dem 2. Partizip gebildet:

I will/shall havc seen/gone/been *usw.*

Das Konditional Perfekt

Das Konditional Perfekt wird aus dem Konditional Präsens von *have* und dem 2. Partizip gebildet:

I would/should have seen/gone/been *usw.*

Das Passiv

Das Passiv wird aus den Formen des Hilfsverbs *be* und dem 2. Partizip gebildet:

I am/was/have been *usw.* stopped

Die Verlaufsform

Neben den vom Deutschen her vertrauten einfachen Verbformen gibt es im Englischen die sogenannte Verlaufsform (continuous tenses). Diese wird aus den Formen von *be* und dem 1. Partizip (s. S. 1652) gebildet:

I am/you were/they had been *usw.* reading

Die Verlaufsform wird vor allem verwendet, um auszudrücken, daß ein Vorgang noch nicht beendet ist bzw. ein Zustand noch andauert:

They were having supper.
The old house is still standing there.

Die Verlaufsform des Präsens kann daneben aber auch in futurischem Sinne, etwa zum Ausdruck einer Absicht verwendet werden:

I'm travelling to London next week.

Die *going to*-Form
Zum Ausdruck des Zukünftigen hat das Englische neben der mit *will/shall* gebildeten Futurform noch eine weitere Form. Sie ist zusammengesetzt aus der Verlaufsform von *go* und dem Infinitiv mit *to* des betreffenden Verbs.
Durch diese *going to*-Form wird, wenn sie im Präsens steht, ausgedrückt, daß etwas geschehen wird, weil es geplant oder beabsichtigt ist, oder daß etwas mit großer Gewißheit geschehen wird:

I'm going to stay with friends.
I'm not going to accept that.
It's going to rain.

Durch die *going to*-Form im Präteritum kann ausgedrückt werden, daß etwas geplant oder beabsichtigt war, jedoch nicht geschehen ist:

I was going to phone you yesterday, but I forgot.

Mit dem Hilfsverb *do* gebildete Verbformen
In Fragesätzen, die nicht ein Fragewort als Subjekt haben, und in mit *not* verneinten Sätzen werden die einfachen Präsens- und Präteritumformen der Vollverben mit dem Hilfsverb *do* gebildet:

Does he like it? – He does not like it.
aber: Who likes it? – No one likes it.

Dies gilt außer im verneinten Imperativ nicht für das Kopulaverb *be:*

Is he a doctor? – No, he is not a doctor.
aber: Do not be so noisy.

Das Vollverb *have* kommt in Verneinung und Frage mit und ohne *do* vor:

Do they have a car? – No, they do not have a car.
Have you any idea? – No, I haven't a clue.

Ebenfalls mit *do* gebildet werden emphatische Formen in nicht verneinten Aussage- und Aufforderungssätzen:

But I 'did see him.
'Do listen to me.
'Do be quiet.

Die *ing*-Form
Die mit der Endung *-ing* gebildete Verbform ist je nach Gebrauch entweder 1. Partizip oder Gerundium. Ein auslautender Konsonant wird häufig verdoppelt; *-c* wird zu *-ck-:*

dub – dubbing
pod – podding
hug – hugging
focus – focusing *od.* focussing
panic – panicking

Ein auf einen Konsonanten folgendes auslautendes *-e* fällt aus:

live – living

Ein auslautendes *-ie* wird zu *-y-:*

die – dying

Die Formen der Hilfsverben *have, be, do*
(In Klammern sind – soweit vorhanden – jeweils die zugehörigen Kurzformen und die Kurzformen der verneinten Formen angegeben.)

have

Präsens:	3. Person Singular	has ('s; hasn't)
	alle übrigen Personen	have ('ve; haven't)
Präteritum:	alle Personen	had ('d; hadn't)

(Das 2. Partizip *had* spielt nur beim Vollverb *have* eine Rolle.)

be

Präsens:	1. Person Singular	am ('m; *nur in Fragesätzen:* aren't)
	3. Person Singular	is ('s; isn't)
	alle übrigen Personen	are ('re; aren't)
Präteritum:	1. und 3. Person Singular	was (wasn't)
	alle übrigen Personen	were (weren't)
2. Partizip:		been

do

Präsens:	3. Person Singular	does (doesn't)
	alle übrigen Personen	do (don't)
Präteritum:	alle Personen	did (didn't)

(Das 2. Partizip *done* spielt nur beim Vollverb *do* eine Rolle.)

Die Formen der Modalverben *can, may, must, shall, will*
Diese Verben, von denen *shall* und *will* auch als nicht modale Hilfsverben verwendet werden (vgl. **Futur** und **Konditional**), haben keine infiniten, sondern nur die folgenden, jeweils in allen Personen gleichlautenden, finiten Formen:

Vollform	Kurzform	Kurzform verneint
Präsens		
can; *verneint:* cannot		can't
may		mayn't
must		mustn't
shall	'll	shan't
will	'll	won't
Präteritum		
could		couldn't
might		mightn't
must		mustn't
should	'd	shouldn't
would	'd	wouldn't

Für die fehlenden Formen werden, je nach Bedeutung, verschiedene Ersatzformen verwendet: so z. B. für die fehlenden Formen von *can* im Sinne von „fähig sein zu" die entsprechenden Formen der Fügung *be able to* (z. B. *I shall be able to come*).

Das Substantiv

Das Genus

Im Englischen ist, anders als im Deutschen, das Genus der Substantive praktisch nur für den richtigen Gebrauch des Personal- und des Possessivpronomens von Bedeutung.
Es stimmt in der Regel mit dem natürlichen Geschlecht überein; Substantive, die männliche Personen bezeichnen, sind Maskulina, solche, die weibliche Personen bezeichnen, sind Feminina, alle übrigen sind in der Regel Neutra.
Zu beachten sind jedoch die folgenden Besonderheiten:
Substantive, die Personen beiderlei Geschlechts bezeichnen können (z. B. *friend, teacher*) sind je nach vorliegender Bedeutung Maskulina oder Feminina.
Substantive wie *child* und *baby* sowie Substantive, die Tiere beiderlei Geschlechts bezeichnen können (z. B. *elephant, cat*) sind je nach vorliegender Bedeutung Maskulina oder Feminina. Wenn das Geschlecht jedoch dem Sprecher unbekannt ist, dann werden sie als Neutra behandelt.
Geschlechtsspezifische Tierbezeichnungen haben dagegen meist das dem natürlichen Geschlecht entsprechende Genus (z. B. *tom-cat, lioness, ewe, he-goat, she-bear*).
Bezeichnungen für Schiffe (z. B. *ship, boat, steamer*), Schiffsnamen, manchmal auch Bezeichnungen für andere Fahrzeuge (z. B. *car, train, aeroplane*) sowie, besonders in literarischem Stil, Länder- und Städtenamen (z. B. *Britain, Europe, Paris*) können als Feminina verwendet werden.
Fluß- und Bergnamen, das Substantiv *sun* sowie bestimmte Abstrakta (z. B. *death, love*) werden in literarischem Stil oft als Maskulina verwendet.
Die Substantive *moon, earth, sea* und bestimmte Abstrakta (z. B. *fortune, nature, liberty*) können in poetischem Stil als Feminina verwendet werden.

Der Plural

Der Plural der Substantive wird in der Regel durch Anhängen der Endung *-s*, nach *s, sh, ch, x, z* und in einigen Fällen nach *o* zu *-es* erweitert, gebildet:

cat – cats
bus – buses
bush – bushes
beach – beaches
box – boxes
fez – fezes
Negro – Negroes
aber: dynamo – dynamos

Hierbei sind die folgenden Besonderheiten zu beachten:
Ein auslautendes, auf einen Konsonanten folgendes *-y* wird in der Regel zu *-ie-:*

lady – ladies
fly – flies

Einige auf *-f* oder *-fe* endende Substantive lauten im Plural auf *-ves:*

leaf – leaves
life – lives

Einige Substantive haben eine unregelmäßige, manche auch eine mit dem Singular übereinstimmende Pluralform (z. B. *man – men, child – children, sheep – sheep*). Solche Pluralformen wie auch diejenigen auf *-ves* sind im englisch-deutschen Wörterverzeichnis jeweils beim entsprechenden Stichwort angeführt.

Der Genitiv

Der Genitiv Singular aller Substantive und der Genitiv Plural der Substantive mit unregelmäßigem (nicht auf *-s* lautendem) Plural wird durch Anhängen von *'s* gebildet:

man's
men's
James's

Ebenso bei nicht auf *-s* endenden pluralischen Substantiven:

people – people's

Der Genitiv Plural der Substantive, die im Plural die Endung *-s* bzw. *-es* haben, wird durch einen hinter dem Plural *-s* stehenden Apostroph gekennzeichnet:

fathers'
Joneses'

Der Genitiv Singular eines auf *-s* ausgehenden Eigennamens wird oft nur durch einen Apostroph gekennzeichnet:

Dickens' *neben* Dickens's
James' *neben* James's

Griechische und lateinische Eigennamen auf *-s* haben im Genitiv stets nur einen Apostroph:

Socrates'
Augustus'

Dies gilt auch für auf *-s* endende Substantive in Verbindung mit *for ... sake:*

for goodness' sake

Die Steigerung der Adjektive und Adverbien

Einsilbige Adjektive werden – mit Ausnahme solcher, die aus Partizipien entstanden sind (z. B. *pleased*) und soweit sie keine unregelmäßigen Steigerungsformen haben (s. u.) – stets mit Hilfe der

Suffixe *-er* (für den Komparativ) und *-est* (für den Superlativ) gesteigert:

clean – cleaner – cleanest
short – shorter – shortest

Ein auslautendes *-b, -d, -g, -m, -n, -p* oder *-t* nach kurzem Vokal wird verdoppelt:

big – bigger – biggest
hot – hotter – hottest

Ein auslautendes *-e* fällt aus:

large – larger – largest
wide – wider – widest
free – freer – freest

Ein auf einen Konsonanten folgendes auslautendes *-y* wird meist zu *-i-*:

dry – drier – driest
aber: shy – shyer *oder* shier – shyest *oder* shiest

Von den zweisilbigen Adjektiven werden solche auf *-y*, solche mit Endbetonung und einige weitere ebenfalls meist auf diese Art gesteigert, wobei ein auf einen Konsonanten folgendes auslautendes *-y zu -i-* wird und ein auslautendes *-e* ausfällt:

narrow – narrower – narrowest
easy – easier – easiest
polite – politer – politest

Alle zweisilbigen Adjektive können aber auch durch ein vorangestelltes *more* (für den Komparativ) bzw. *most* (für den Superlativ) gesteigert werden.
Stets mit *more* und *most* werden alle übrigen Adjektive (insbesondere auch diejenigen, die aus Partizipien entstanden sind, wie z. B. *bored, lasting, delighted*) gesteigert.
Von Adjektiven abgeleitete Adverbien auf *-ly* werden mit vorangestelltem *more* und *most* gesteigert:

carefully – more/most carefully
easily – more/most easily

Die übrigen Adverbien werden soweit sie keine unregelmäßigen Steigerungsformen haben (wie z. B. *much, well*) mit Hilfe der Suffixe *-er* und *-est* gesteigert:

fast – faster – fastest
soon – sooner – soonest
hard – harder – hardest

Hierbei gelten auch die oben für die mit *-er* und *-est* steigernden Adjektive genannten, den Stammauslaut betreffenden Besonderheiten.

Einige wenige Adjektive und Adverbien haben unregelmäßige Steigerungsformen.
Diese sind im englisch-deutschen Wörterverzeichnis sowohl beim zugehörigen Positiv als auch an ihrer alphabetischen Stelle angeführt.

Pronomen

In der folgenden Übersicht sind die Formen der wichtigsten Pronomen aufgeführt.

Personalpronomen

	Subjektsform	Objektsform
1. Pers. Sing.	I	me
2. Pers. Sing.	you	you
3. Pers. Sing.	he/she/it	him/her/it
1. Pers. Pl.	we	us
2. Pers. Pl.	you	you
3. Pers. Pl.	they	them

Reflexivpronomen

	Sing.	Pl.
1. Pers.	myself	ourselves
2. Pers.	yourself	yourselves
3. Pers.	himself/ herself/itself	themselves

Possessivpronomen

attributiv gebraucht:

	Sing.	Pl.
1. Pers.	my	our
2. Pers.	your	your
3. Pers.	his/her/its	their

alleinstehend gebraucht:

	Sing.	Pl.
1. Pers.	mine	ours
2. Pers.	yours	yours
3. Pers.	his/hers/–	theirs

Demonstrativpronomen
Die Demonstrativpronomen *this* und *that* haben außer diesen Singularformen nur noch je eine weitere Form: *these* (Plural zu *this*) und *those* (Plural zu *that*).

Relativpronomen

who
Subjektsform Sing. u. Pl.: who
Objektsform Sing. u. Pl.: whom, who
Genitiv Sing. u. Pl.: whose

which
(keine weiteren Formen)

that
(keine weiteren Formen)

Interrogativpronomen

who
Subjektsform: who
Objektsform: whom, who
Genitiv: whose

which
(keine weiteren Formen)

what
(keine weiteren Formen)

Englische unregelmäßige Verben

Die im englisch-deutschen Wörterverzeichnis mit einer hochgestellten Ziffer versehenen unregelmäßigen Verben haben diese Ziffer auch in dieser Liste. Ein Sternchen (*) weist darauf hin, daß die korrekte Form von der jeweiligen Bedeutung abhängt.

Infinitive *Infinitiv*	Past Tense *Präteritum*	Past Participle *2. Partizip*
abide	abided, abode	abided, abode
arise	arose	arisen
awake	awoke	awoken
be	was *sing.*, were *pl.*	been
bear	bore	borne
beat	beat	beaten
beget	begot, *(arch.)* begat	begotten
begin	began	begun
behold	beheld	beheld
bend	bent	bent
beseech	besought, beseeched	besought, beseeched
bet	bet, betted	bet, betted
bid	*bade, bid	*bidden, bid
bind	bound	bound
bite	bit	bitten
bleed	bled	bled
bless	blessed	blessed, blest
blow	blew	*blown, blowed
break	broke	broken
breed	bred	bred
bring	brought	brought
broadcast	broadcast, broadcasted	broadcast, broadcasted
build	built	built
burn	burnt, burned	burnt, burned
burst	burst	burst
bust	bust, busted	bust, busted
buy	bought	bought
cast	cast	cast
catch	caught	caught
chide	chided, chid	chided, chid, chidden
choose	chose	chosen
[1]cleave	cleaved, clove, cleft	cleaved, cloven, cleft
cling	clung	clung
come	came	come
cost	*cost, costed	*cost, costed
countersink	countersunk	countersunk
creep	crept	crept
cut	cut	cut
deal	dealt	dealt
dig	dug	dug
dive	dived, *(Amer.)* dove	dived
[1]do	did	done
draw	drew	drawn
dream	dreamt, dreamed	dreamt, dreamed
drink	drank	drunk
drive	drove	driven
dwell	dwelt	dwelt
eat	ate	eaten
fall	fell	fallen
feed	fed	fed
feel	felt	felt
fight	fought	fought
find	found	found
flee	fled	fled

Infinitive *Infinitiv*	Past Tense *Präteritum*	Past Participle *2. Partizip*
fling	flung	flung
floodlight	floodlit	floodlit
fly	flew	flown
forbear	forbore	forborne
forbid	forbade, forbad	forbidden
forecast	forecast, forecasted	forecast, forecasted
foretell	foretold	foretold
forget	forgot	forgotten
forgive	forgave	forgiven
forsake	forsook	forsaken
freeze	froze	frozen
gainsay	gainsaid	gainsaid
get	got	got, *(Amer.)* gotten
gird	girded, girt	girded, girt
give	gave	given
go	went	gone
grind	ground	ground
grow	grew	grown
hamstring	hamstringed, hamstrung	hamstringed, hamstrung
hang	*hung, hanged	*hung, hanged
have	had	had
hear	heard	heard
heave	*heaved, hove	*heaved, hove
hew	hewed	hewed, hewn
hide	hid	hidden
hit	hit	hit
hold	held	held
hurt	hurt	hurt
inlay	inlaid	inlaid
input	input, inputted	input, inputted
inset	inset, insetted	inset, insetted
interweave	interwove	interwoven
keep	kept	kept
ken	kenned, kent	kenned
kneel	knelt, *(esp. Amer.)* kneeled	knelt, *(esp. Amer.)* kneeled
knit	knitted, knit	knitted, knit
know	knew	known
lay	laid	laid
lead	led	led
lean	leaned, *(Brit.)* leant	leaned, *(Brit.)* leant
leap	leapt, leaped	leapt, leaped
learn	learnt, learned	learnt, learned
leave	left	left
lend	lent	lent
let	let	let
[2]lie	lay	lain
light	lighted, lit	lighted, lit
lose	lost	lost
make	made	made
mean	meant	meant
meet	met	met
mow	mowed	mown, mowed
output	output, outputted	output, outputted
outshine	outshone	outshone
overhang	overhung	overhung
pay	paid	paid

Infinitive *Infinitiv*	Past Tense *Präteritum*	Past Participle *2. Partizip*
plead	pleaded, *(esp. Amer., Scot., literary)* pled	pleaded, *(esp. Amer., Scot., literary)* pled
prove	proved	proved, *(esp. Amer., Scot., literary)* proven
put	put	put
quit	quitted, *(Amer.)* quit	quitted, *(Amer.)* quit
read [ri:d]	read [red]	read [red]
reeve	rove, reeved	rove, reeved
rend	rent	rent
rid	rid	rid
ride	rode	ridden
[2]ring	rang	rung
rise	rose	risen
run	ran	run
saw	sawed	sawn, sawed
say	said	said
see	saw	seen
seek	sought	sought
sell	sold	sold
send	sent	sent
set	set	set
sew	sewed	sewn, sewed
shake	shook	shaken
shear	sheared	shorn, sheared
shed	shed	shed
shine	*shone, shined	*shone, shined
shit	shitted, shit, shat	shitted, shit, shat
shoe	shod	shod
shoot	shot	shot
show	showed	shown, showed
shrink	shrank, shrunk	shrunk
shrive	shrove	shriven
shut	shut	shut
sing	sang	sung
sink	sank, sunk	sunk
sit	sat	sat
slay	slew	slain
sleep	slept	slept
slide	slid	slid
sling	slung	slung
slink	slunk	slunk
slit	slit	slit
smell	smelt, smelled	smelt, smelled
smite	smote	smitten
sow	sowed	sown, sowed
speak	spoke	spoken
speed	*sped, speeded	*sped, speeded
spell	spelled, *(Brit.)* spelt	spelled, *(Brit.)* spelt

Infinitive *Infinitiv*	Past Tense *Präteritum*	Past Participle *2. Partizip*
spend	spent	spent
spill	spilt, spilled	spilt, spilled
spin	spun	spun
spit	spat, spit	spat, spit
split	split	split
spoil	spoilt, spoiled	spoilt, spoiled
spread	spread	spread
spring	sprang	sprung
stand	stood	stood
stave	*staved, stove	*staved, stove
steal	stole	stolen
stick	stuck	stuck
sting	stung	stung
stink	stank, stunk	stunk
strew	strewed	strewed, strewn
stride	strode	stridden
strike	struck	struck, stricken
string	strung	strung
strive	strove	striven
sublet	sublet	sublet
swear	swore	sworn
sweep	swept	swept
swell	swelled	swollen, swelled
swim	swam	swum
swing	swung	swung
take	took	taken
teach	taught	taught
tear	tore	torn
tell	told	told
think	thought	thought
thrive	thrived, throve	thrived, thriven
throw	threw	thrown
thrust	thrust	thrust
tread	trod	trodden, trod
unbend	unbent	unbent
understand	understood	understood
undo	undid	undone
unsay	unsaid	unsaid
wake	woke, *(arch.)* waked	woken, *(arch.)* waked
wear	wore	worn
[1]weave	wove	woven
weep	wept	wept
wet	wet, wetted	wet, wetted
win	won	won
[2]wind [waɪnd]	wound [waʊnd]	wound [waʊnd]
work	worked, *(arch., literary)* wrought	worked, *(arch., literary)* wrought
wring	wrung	wrung
write	wrote	written

Die Zeichensetzung im Englischen

Apostroph

a) Der Apostroph steht als Auslassungszeichen:

I'm (= I am) they'd (= they had/would)
he's (= he is/has) the summer of '68 (= 1968)
thro' (= through)

Gelegentlich wird er – jedoch unnötigerweise – auch bei einigen Kurzformen wie *bus, cello, flu, phone, plane* gesetzt (*'bus* usw.).

b) Der Apostroph steht zur Kennzeichnung des Genitivs. Näheres hierzu findet sich unter „Kleine Formenlehre des Englischen" auf S. 1653.

c) Manchmal steht der Apostroph mit einem s zur Bildung des Plurals von Buchstaben, Zahlen oder Abkürzungen, z. B.:

pronounce the r's more clearly;
during the 1960's; all the MP's

Doppelpunkt

a) Der Doppelpunkt steht zur Markierung des Beginns einer Aufzählung nach einem Gattungsnamen oder einem die Aufzählung ankündigenden Ausdruck wie z. B. *as follows, in the following manner:*

His library consists of two books: the Bible and Shakespeare.
Proceed as follows: switch on the computer, insert a disk, and press any key.

b) Der Doppelpunkt steht vor Sätzen oder Ausdrücken, die den vorausgehenden Satz erläutern oder erklären:

The garden had been neglected for a long time: it was overgrown and full of weeds.

(Statt des Doppelpunkts kann hier auch ein Punkt, jedoch kein Komma stehen.)

Komma

a) Das Komma steht zwischen Adjektiven, die ein Substantiv in gleicher Weise attribuieren:

a cautious, eloquent man

Wenn mehrere Adjektive ein Substantiv in unterschiedlicher Weise attribuieren oder wenn ein Adjektiv das andere attribuiert, steht dagegen kein Komma:

a distinguished foreign author; a bright red tie

b) Das Komma steht zwischen den Gliedern einer Aufzählung. Wenn vorletztes und letztes Aufzählungsglied durch eine Konjunktion verbunden sind, steht das Komma vor dieser Konjunktion:

potatoes, peas, and carrots; potatoes, peas, or carrots; potatoes, peas, etc.; red, white, and blue

c) Das Komma steht zwischen nebengeordneten Hauptsätzen, die nicht durch ein anderes Satzzeichen voneinander getrennt sind:

Cars turn here, and coaches go straight on.

Es steht jedoch nicht, wenn es sich um eng zusammengehörige Sätze handelt:

Do as I tell you and you'll never regret it.

d) Das Komma steht vor und hinter aus einem oder mehreren Wörtern bestehenden Einschüben sowie vor und hinter Zwischensätzen:

I am sure, however, that it will not happen.
Fred, who is bald, complained of the cold.

Es steht jedoch nicht vor und hinter notwendigen Relativsätzen:

Men who are bald should wear hats.

e) Das Komma steht nach am Satzanfang stehenden Infinitiv- und Partizipalgruppen und gleichwertigen verblosen Teilen:

To be sure of arriving on time, she left an hour early.
Worn out by their journey, the children soon fell asleep.

f) Das Komma steht zwischen einer adverbialen Bestimmung und dem übrigen Satz sowie zwischen Haupt- und Nebensatz, wenn ohne Komma ein Mißverständnis möglich wäre:

In the valley below, the villages looked very small.
He did not go to church, because he was playing golf.
In 1980, 2000 seemed a long time off.

g) Das Komma steht nach Wörtern, die eine direkte Rede einleiten:

They answered, 'Here we are'.

h) Das Komma steht in Briefen nach der Anrede (*Dear Sir, Dear John* usw.) und nach der Grußformel (*Yours sincerely* usw.)
Nicht notwendig ist ein Komma zwischen Monat und Jahr in Datumsangaben (z. B. *in December 1989*) oder zwischen Hausnummer und Straßenname in Adressen (z. B. *12 Acacia Avenue*).

Semikolon

Das Semikolon steht zwischen Teilsätzen oder Satzstücken, wo ein Komma eine zu schwache, ein Punkt jedoch eine zu starke Zäsur bedeuten würde. D. h., es steht typischerweise zwischen Sätzen, die inhaltlich etwa gleiches Gewicht und grammatisch eine ähnliche Struktur haben:

To err is human; to forgive, divine.

Punkt

a) Der Punkt steht am Satzende, sofern kein Frage- oder Ausrufezeichen steht; das folgende Wort beginnt in der Regel mit einem Großbuchstaben.

b) Der Punkt steht nach Abkürzungen. Wenn ein Abkürzungspunkt ans Satzende zu stehen kommt, dient er gleichzeitig als Schlußpunkt:

She also kept dogs, cats, birds, etc.
aber: She also kept pets (dogs, cats, birds, etc.).

c) Wenn ein Satz mit einer Anführung schließt, die ihrerseits mit einem Punkt, Fragezeichen oder Ausrufezeichen endet, entfällt der Schlußpunkt:

He cried, 'Be off!' But the child would not move.

Wenn die Anführung jedoch kurz ist und der übrige Satz deutlich größeres Gewicht hat, steht der Punkt außerhalb der Anführungszeichen:

Over the entrance to the temple at Delphi were written the words 'Know thyself'.

Anführungszeichen

a) Anführungszeichen haben gewöhnlich die Form '...' („halbe Anführungszeichen"); Anführungszeichen der Form "..." stehen bei einer Anführung innerhalb einer Anführung; bei einer Anführung innerhalb einer angeführten Anführung stehen wiederum halbe Anführungszeichen:

'I said, "He used the word 'murder' although no-one had told him how Smith died".'

b) Schließende Anführungszeichen stehen vor allen weiteren Satzzeichen, es sei denn, diese sind Bestandteil der Anführung:

Did Nelson really say, 'Kiss me, Hardy'?
aber: Then she asked, 'What is your name?'.

Das Komma am Schluß einer Anführung, auf die Ausdrücke wie *he said* folgen, ersetzt den Schlußpunkt des angeführten Satzes und steht innerhalb der Anführungszeichen:

'That is nonsense,' he said.

Die Kommas, durch die *he said* usw. eingeschlossen wird, wenn es die Anführung unterbricht, stehen gewöhnlich außerhalb der Anführungszeichen:

'That', he said, 'is nonsense.'

Das erste Komma steht jedoch innerhalb der Anführungszeichen, wenn es auch ohne die Unterbrechung stehen müßte:

'That, my dear fellow,' he said, 'is nonsense.'

Outline of German grammatical forms

The following outline is intended to be used in conjunction with the grammatical information included in the Dictionary, which it complements and explains. It does not attempt to cover all forms.

Verbs

General notes

a) Verbs with prefixes, such as *ab-*, *auf-*, *er-*, *mit-*, and *zer-*, are conjugated like the corresponding simple verbs, e.g. *absagen* like *sagen*, but see the section on past participles below.

b) *ß* is used, and not *ss*,

before a consonant;
at the end of a word;
between two vowels, the first of which is long:

hissen	schmeißen
gehißt	ich schmiß
	sie schmissen

c) To discover the stem of a verb, take away the *-en* (or just the *-n* if the penultimate letter ist not *-e-*) from the end of the infinitive (the form given as a headword in the German-English section of the Dictionary):

machen	handeln
mach-	handel-

Regular verbs

Participles

Present
Add *-d* to the infinitive:

lachen
lachend

Past
Add *ge-* and *-t* to the stem:

machen
gemacht

If the stem ends with *-d, -t*, or a consonant + *m* or *n*, add *ge-* and *-et* to the stem:

reden	trocknen
geredet	getrocknet

If the infinitive ends with *-ieren* or *-eien*, add *-t* to the stem:

diskutieren	prophezeien
diskutiert	prophezeit

Verbs with a separable prefix (marked with | in the German-English section of the Dictionary) that is not followed by another prefix add *-ge-* between the prefix and the stem and *-[e]t* to the end of the stem:

an|klagen	zu|leiten
angeklagt	zugeleitet

Verbs with

a) any of the inseparable prefixes *be-, em-, ent-, er-, ge-, ver-*, and *zer-*

b) an inseparable prefix (marked by · in the German-English section of the Dictionary)

c) a separable prefix (marked by | in the German-English section of the Dictionary) that is followed by an inseparable prefix

add *-[e]t* to the stem:

a)	beneiden	gehören
	beneidet	gehört
b)	durch·leuchten	über·blicken
	durchleuchtet	überblickt
c)	zu|bereiten	aus|erwählen
	zubereitet	auserwählt

Active

a) Indicative

Present

	machen
ich	mache
du	machst
er/sie/es	macht
wir	machen
ihr	macht
sie/Sie	machen

If the stem ends with *-l* or *-r*, the 1st person singular may omit the preceding *-e-:*

lächeln
ich lächele *or* lächle

If the stem ends with *-s, -ß, x*, or *-z*, the 2nd person singular adds only *-t:*

rasen	boxen
du rast	du boxt

If the stem ends with *-d, -t*, or a consonant + *m* or *n*, the 2nd person singular adds *-est*, and the 2nd person plural adds *-et:*

	reden
du	redest
ihr	redet

Preterite (or past or imperfect)

	machen
ich	machte
du	machtest
er/sie/es	machte
wir	machten
ihr	machtet
sie/Sie	machten

If the stem ends with *-d, -t*, or a consonant + *m* or *n*, add *-e-* to the stem first:

	reden
ich	redete
du	redetest
er/sie/es	redete
wir	redeten
ihr	redetet
sie/Sie	redeten

Future
Present indicative of *werden* + infinitive:

reden
ich werde reden *etc.*

Perfect
Present indicative of *sein* or *haben* + past participle:

reisen	machen
ich bin gereist *etc.*	ich habe gemacht *etc.*

Verbs which take *sein* are labelled accordingly in the German-English section of the Dictionary.

Pluperfect
Preterite indicative of *sein* or *haben* (see note at **Perfect**) + past participle:

reisen	machen
ich war gereist *etc.*	ich hatte gemacht *etc.*

Future perfect
Future indicative of *sein* or *haben* (see note at **Perfect**) + past participle:

reisen	machen
ich werde gereist	ich werde gemacht
sein *etc.*	haben *etc.*

b) Subjunctive

Present

	machen
ich	mache
du	machest
er/sie/es	mache
wir	machen
ihr	machet
sie/Sie	machen

If the stem ends with *-l* or *-r*, the preceding *-e-* may be omitted:

lächeln
ich lächele *or* lächle *etc.*

Preterite
Identical with preterite indicative.

c) Conditional

Present
Preterite subjunctive of *werden* + infinitive:

ich würde reden *etc.*

Perfect
Preterite subjunctive of *sein* or *haben* + past participle:

reisen	machen
ich wäre gereist *etc.*	ich hätte gemacht *etc.*

or present conditional of *sein* or *haben* + past participle:

reisen	machen
ich würde gereist	ich würde gemacht
sein *etc.*	haben *etc.*

Verbs which take *sein* are labelled accordingly in the German-English section of the Dictionary.

d) Imperative

2nd person singular	red[e]!
2nd person plural	redet!
2nd person (polite)	reden Sie!

Passive

General note
Passive tenses are formed from the corresponding active tense of *werden* + past participle.

a) Infinitives

Present	geliebt [zu] werden
Perfect	geliebt worden [zu] sein

b) Indicative

Present	ich werde geliebt *etc.*
Preterite	ich wurde geliebt *etc.*
Future	ich werde geliebt werden *etc.*
Perfect	ich bin geliebt worden *etc.*
Pluperfect	ich war geliebt worden *etc.*
Future perfect	ich werde geliebt worden sein *etc.*

c) Subjunctive

Present	ich werde*) geliebt *etc.*
Preterite	ich würde geliebt *etc.*
Future	ich werde*) geliebt werden *etc.*
Perfect	ich sei geliebt worden *etc.*
Pluperfect	ich wäre geliebt worden *etc.*
Future perfect	ich werde*) geliebt worden sein *etc.*

*) NB du werdest ...; er/sie/es werde ...

d) Conditional

Present	ich würde geliebt [werden]
Perfect	ich wäre geliebt worden

e) Imperative

2nd person singular	sei *or* werde gegrüßt!
2nd person plural	seid *or* werdet gegrüßt!
2nd person (polite)	seien *or* werden Sie gegrüßt!

Irregular verbs

These are conjugated as regular verbs except for the forms given in the table (pp. 1665–1667) and the preterite indicative:

a) Preterite indicative

If the form given in the table ends with *-te*, the tense is conjugated as for a regular verb; otherwise as follows:

	singen
ich	sang
du	sangst
er/sie/es	sang
wir	sangen
ihr	sangt
sie/Sie	sangen

If the form given ends with *-s* or *-ß*, the 2nd person singular adds only *-t:*

blasen	gießen
blies	goß
du bliest	du goßt

b) Compound tenses of modal verbs

The past participle forms shown in the table are not used with an infinitive, but only where the verb functions as a full verb (usually with a direct object or an indication of direction):

Er hat es gedurft. Ich habe damals kein Englisch gekonnt. Sie hat nach Frankfurt gemußt.

Where the verb is used with an infinitive, i. e. modally, the infinitive form is used instead:

Sie hat kommen müssen. Wir hatten zusehen dürfen.

Nouns

Singular

The first or only ending given in the entry for a noun in the German-English section of the Dictionary is the genitive singular. Shown here are examples of each, together with the corresponding other cases.

	Stadt ... ~ ...	**Manna** ... ~[s] ...	**Feuer** ... ~s ...	**Buch** ... ~[e]s ...
Nom.	die Stadt	das Manna	das Feuer	das Buch
Acc.	die Stadt	das Manna	das Feuer	das Buch
Gen.	der Stadt	des Manna[s]	des Feuers	des Buch[e]s
Dat.	der Stadt	dem Manna	dem Feuer	dem Buch[e]

	Löwe ... ~n ...	**Name** ... ~ns ...	**Bär** ... ~en ...	**Herz** ... ~ens ...
Nom.	der Löwe	der Name	der Bär	das Herz
Acc.	den Löwen	den Namen	den Bären	das Herz
Gen.	des Löwen	des Namens	des Bären	des Herzens
Dat.	dem Löwen	dem Namen	dem Bären	dem Herzen

Plural

The second ending (if any) given in the entry for a noun in the German-English section of the Dictionary is used for each plural case, except that, if it does not end with *-n* or *-s*, the dative plural adds *-n:*

	Fahrer ... ~s, ~	**Frau** ... ~, ~en	**Streik** ... ~[e]s, ~s
Nom.	die Fahrer	die Frauen	die Streiks
Acc.	die Fahrer	die Frauen	die Streiks
Gen.	der Fahrer	der Frauen	der Streiks
Dat.	den Fahrern	den Frauen	den Streiks

	Nacht ... ~, Nächte	**Brettel** ... ~s, ~[n]	**Bild** ... ~[e]s, ~er
Nom.	die Nächte	die Brettel[n]	die Bilder
Acc.	die Nächte	die Brettel[n]	die Bilder
Gen.	der Nächte	der Brettel[n]	der Bilder
Dat.	den Nächten	den Bretteln	den Bildern

The genitive singular or the plural form is given in full in the German-English section of the Dictionary if it involves changes to the stem:

Faß ... Fasses, Fässer

Adjectival declension

If a noun entry gives no endings but instead states *'adj. Dekl.'*, noun and adjective endings are as follows:

	Masc.	Fem.	Neut.	Pl. (all genders)
	¹Alte der; *adj. Dekl.*	**²Alte die;** *adj. Dekl.*	**³Alte das;** *adj. Dekl.*	**⁴Alte** *Pl.; adj. Dekl.*
Nom.	der gute Alte	die gute Alte	das gute Alte	die guten Alten
Acc.	den guten Alten	die gute Alte	das gute Alte	die guten Alten
Gen.	des guten Alten	der guten Alten	des guten Alten	der guten Alten
Dat.	dem guten Alten	der guten Alten	dem guten Alten	den guten Alten
Nom.	ein guter Alter	eine gute Alte	ein gutes Altes	gute Alte
Acc.	einen guten Alten	eine gute Alte	ein gutes Altes	gute Alte
Gen.	eines guten Alten	einer guten Alten	eines guten Alten	guter Alter
Dat.	einem guten Alten	einer guten Alten	einem guten Alten	guten Alten

Endings for personal names

The genitive singular ending of personal names is *-s*, or, if the name ends with *-s, -ß, -x*, or *-z*, it is simply an apostrophe or sometimes *-ens:*

Barbaras Buch   Hans' Auto *or* Hansens Auto

If a title (other than *Herr*) or more than one name is given, only the last element has an ending:

Frau Brauns Hut
König Ottokars Glück und Ende
eine Symphonie Ludwig van Beethovens

Following words in apposition are declined as well as the name:

Nom.	Wilhelm der Erste	Heinrich der Vogler
Acc.	Wilhelm den Ersten	Heinrich den Vogler
Gen.	Wilhelms des Ersten	Heinrichs des Voglers
Dat.	Wilhelm dem Ersten	Heinrich dem Vogler

When used as names, the words for family members take *-s* in the genitive singular:

Vaters/Mutters Aktentasche

The genitive singular of a name does not take an ending if preceded by an article or other inflected word other than *Herrn:*

eine Ausgabe des „Grünen Heinrich"
but: Herrn Dr. Baiers Praxis

Surnames often have an *-s* in the plural, especially when denoting a family:

[die] Remanns wohnen nebenan

If the name ends with *-s*, *-ß*, *-x*, or *-z*, the ending is *-ens:*

[die] Schwarzens

Adjectives and adverbs

Article and adjective endings

a) Weak declension

The qualifying words *der/die/das, dieser/diese/dieses, jener/jene/jenes, all..., welch..., solch..., beide, sämtliche,* etc. and any following adjectives are declined as follows:

	Masc.	Fem.	Neut.	Pl. (all genders)
Nom.	der gute Tag	die gute Frau	das gute Buch	die guten Dinge
Acc.	den guten Tag	die gute Frau	das gute Buch	die guten Dinge
Gen.	des guten Tag[e]s	der guten Frau	des guten Buch[e]s	der guten Dinge
Dat.	dem guten Tag[e]	der guten Frau	dem guten Buch[e]	den guten Dingen

b) Mixed declension

The qualifying words *ein* and *kein,* possessive adjectives, and any following adjectives are declined as follows:

Nom.	ein guter Tag	eine gute Frau	ein gutes Buch	keine guten Bücher
Acc.	einen guten Tag	eine gute Frau	ein gutes Buch	keine guten Bücher
Gen.	eines guten Tag[e]s	einer guten Frau	eines guten Buch[e]s	keiner guten Bücher
Dat.	einem guten Tag[e]	einer guten Frau	einem guten Buch[e]	keinen guten Büchern

c) Strong declension

Adjectives are declined as follows when preceded either by no qualifying word or by an indeclinable one, e.g. *viel, mehr, wenig, weniger, manch, solch,* or *welch,* or by *dessen, deren, ander..., einig..., etlich..., folgend,* or *mehrer...:*

Nom.	guter Wein	gute Milch	gutes Bier	gute Dinge
Acc.	guten Wein	gute Milch	gutes Bier	gute Dinge
Gen.	guten Wein[e]s	guter Milch	guten Biers	guter Dinge
Dat.	gutem Wein[e]	guter Milch	gutem Bier[e]	guten Dingen

d) Exceptions

Plural adjectives preceded by numerals follow the strong declension in formal language but the mixed declension in colloquial language.

Adjectives which are marked *'indekl. Adj.'* or which end with *-er* and are derived from place names do not inflect at all:

klasse	Berliner
ein klasse Wagen	die Berliner Philharmoniker

Adjectives which end with *-el* drop the *-e-* when inflected and in their comparative forms:

übel
ein übler Mensch

and adjectives which end with *-en* and *-er* sometimes drop the *-e-:*

trocken	finster
trock[e]nes Holz	die finst[e]re Nacht

but *clever* does not:

clever
ein cleverer Trick

and the *-e-* is always dropped in:

integer	makaber
eine integre Persönlichkeit	eine makabre Geschichte

and when *-er* is preceded by *-au-* or *-eu-:*

teuer	sauer
ein teures Haus	saure Gurken

Adjectives which end with a vowel, other than those marked *'indekl. Adj.'*, drop the vowel:

müde
die müden Arbeiter

The adjective *hoch* drops its *-c-* when inflected:

eine hohe Stirn

Comparison of adjectives and adverbs

The regular endings are *-er, -st...:*

positive	schön
comparative	schöner
superlative attributive adjective	schönst...
superlative predicative adjective	am schönsten
superlative adverb	am schönsten

Irregular forms are given in the German-English section of the Dictionary:

arm ... ärmer ... ärmst...

See also above for adjectives ending with *-el, -en,* and *-er.*

If an adjective or adverb ends with *-d, -t, -sch, -s, -ß, -x, -z,* a long vowel, or a diphthong and has only one syllable or is stressed on its last syllable, the superlative ending is *-est...:*

laut	zäh	genau
lautest...	zähest...	genauest...

Pronouns

Personal pronouns

Nom.	Acc.	Gen.	Dat.
ich	mich	meiner	mir
du	dich	deiner	dir
er	ihn	seiner	ihm
sie	sie	ihrer	ihr
es	es	seiner	ihm
wir	uns	unser	uns
ihr	euch	euer	euch
sie	sie	ihrer	ihnen
Sie	Sie	Ihrer	Ihnen

Reflexive and reciprocal pronouns are the same as personal pronouns, except that the accusative and dative forms of *er, sie, es, sie,* and *Sie* are *sich.*

Possessive pronouns *(mein, dein, sein, ihr, unser, euer,* and *Ihr)*

	Masc.	Fem.	Neut.	Pl. (all genders)
Nom.	mein	meine	mein	meine
Acc.	meinen	meine	mein	meine
Gen.	meines	meiner	meines	meiner
Dat.	meinem	meiner	meinem	meinen

euer is usually contracted in all inflected forms, e.g. *eure.*

When used other than attributively, i.e. as independent pronouns, these forms differ:

Nom. masc.:	meiner *etc.*, uns[e]rer, eurer
Nom. and acc. neut.:	mein[e]s *etc.*, uns[e]res, eures

Demonstrative pronouns (*dieser, jener, der, derjenige,* and *derselbe*)

dieser and *jener:*

	Masc.	Fem.	Neut.	Pl. (all genders)
Nom.	dieser	diese	dieses	diese
Acc.	diesen	diese	dieses	diese
Gen.	dieses	dieser	dieses	dieser
Dat.	diesem	dieser	diesem	diesen

der is the same as when a definite article, except for:

	Masc.	Fem.	Neut.	Pl. (all genders)
Gen.	dessen	deren	dessen	derer *or* deren
Dat.				denen

derjenige and *derselbe* are declined as if two separate words:

	Masc.	Fem.	Neut.	Pl. (all genders)
Nom.	derjenige	diejenige	dasjenige	diejenigen
Acc.	denjenigen	diejenige	dasjenige	diejenigen
Gen.	desjenigen	derjenigen	desjenigen	derjenigen
Dat.	demjenigen	derjenigen	demjenigen	denjenigen

Relative pronouns

	Masc.	Fem.	Neut.	Pl. (all genders)
Nom.	der *or* welcher	die *or* welche	das *or* welches	die *or* welche
Acc.	den *or* welchen	die *or* welche	das *or* welches	die *or* welche
Gen.	dessen	deren	dessen	deren
Dat.	dem *or* welchem	der *or* welcher	dem *or* welchem	denen *or* welchen

Interrogative pronouns

welch follows the strong adjective declension (see p. 1662). The declensions of *was* and *wer* are given at their entries in the Dictionary.

Indefinite pronouns

etwas, was, and *nichts* are invariable. Other indefinite pronouns are declined as follows:

Nom.	man	jemand	niemand
Acc.	einen	jemand[en]	niemand[en]
Gen.	eines	jemandes	niemandes
Dat.	einem	jemand[em]	niemand[em]

German irregular verbs

Irregular and partly irregular verbs are listed alphabetically by infinitive. 1st, 2nd, and 3rd person present and imperative forms are given after the infinitive, and preterite subjunctive forms after the preterite indicative, where they take an umlaut, change *e* to *i*, etc.
Verbs with a raised number in the German-English section of the Dictionary have the same number in this list.

Compound verbs (including verbs with prefixes) are only given if a) they do not take the same forms as the corresponding simple verb, e.g. *befehlen*, or b) there is no corresponding simple verb, e.g. *bewegen*.

An asterisk (*) indicates a verb which is also conjugated regularly.

Infinitive *Infinitiv*	Preterite *Präteritum*	Past Participle *2. Partizip*
[1]backen (du bäckst, er bäckt; *auch:* du backst, er backt)	backte, *älter:* buk (büke)	gebacken
befehlen (du befiehlst, er befiehlt; befiehl!)	befahl (beföhle, befähle)	befohlen
beginnen	begann (begänne, *seltener:* begönne)	begonnen
beißen	biß	gebissen
bergen (du birgst, er birgt; birg!)	barg (bärge)	geborgen
bersten (du birst, er birst; birst!)	barst (bärste)	geborsten
[2]bewegen	bewog (bewöge)	bewogen
biegen	bog (böge)	gebogen
bieten	bot (böte)	geboten
binden	band (bände)	gebunden
bitten	bat (bäte)	gebeten
blasen (du bläst, er bläst)	blies	geblasen
bleiben	blieb	geblieben
bleichen*	blich	geblichen
braten (du brätst, er brät)	briet	gebraten
brechen (du brichst, er bricht; brich!)	brach (bräche)	gebrochen
brennen	brannte (brennte)	gebrannt
bringen	brachte (brächte)	gebracht
denken	dachte (dächte)	gedacht
dingen*	dang (dänge)	gedungen
dreschen (du drischst, er drischt; drisch!)	drosch (drösche)	gedroschen
dringen	drang (dränge)	gedrungen
dünken* (es dünkt *auch:* deucht)	deuchte	gedeucht
dürfen (ich darf, du darfst, er darf)	durfte (dürfte)	gedurft
empfehlen (du empfiehlst, er empfiehlt, empfiehl!)	empfahl (empföhle, *seltener:* empfähle)	empfohlen
erlöschen (du erlischst, er erlischt, erlisch!)	erlosch (erlösche)	erloschen
erschallen	erscholl (erschölle)	erschollen
[1, 3]erschrecken (du erschrickst, er erschrickt, erschrick!)	erschrak (erschräke)	erschrocken
essen (du ißt, er ißt, iß!)	aß (äße)	gegessen
fahren (du fährst, er fährt)	fuhr (führe)	gefahren
fallen (du fällst, er fällt)	fiel	gefallen
fangen (du fängst, er fängt)	fing	gefangen
fechten (du fichtst, er ficht; ficht!)	focht (föchte)	gefochten
finden	fand (fände)	gefunden
flechten (du flichtst, er flicht; flicht!)	flocht (flöchte)	geflochten
fliegen	flog (flöge)	geflogen
fliehen	floh (flöhe)	geflohen

Infinitive *Infinitiv*	Preterite *Präteritum*	Past Participle *2. Partizip*
fließen	floß (flösse)	geflossen
fressen (du frißt, er frißt, friß!)	fraß (fräße)	gefressen
frieren	fror (fröre)	gefroren
gären*	gor (göre)	gegoren
gebären (*geh.:* du gebierst, sie gebiert; gebier!)	gebar (gebäre)	geboren
geben (du gibst, er gibt; gib!)	gab (gäbe)	gegeben
gedeihen	gedieh	gediehen
gehen	ging	gegangen
gelingen	gelang (gelänge)	gelungen
gelten (du giltst, er gilt; gilt!)	galt (gölte, gälte)	gegolten
genesen	genas (genäse)	genesen
genießen	genoß (genösse)	genossen
geschehen (es geschieht)	geschah (geschähe)	geschehen
gewinnen	gewann (gewönne, gewänne)	gewonnen
gießen	goß (gösse)	gegossen
gleichen	glich	geglichen
gleiten	glitt	geglitten
glimmen	glomm (glömme)	geglommen
graben (du gräbst, er gräbt)	grub (grübe)	gegraben
greifen	griff	gegriffen
haben (du hast, er hat)	hatte (hätte)	gehabt
halten (du hältst, er hält)	hielt	gehalten
[1]hängen	hing	gehangen
hauen	hieb	gehauen
heben	hob (höbe)	gehoben
heißen	hieß	geheißen
helfen (du hilfst, er hilft; hilf!)	half (hülfe, *selten:* hälfe)	geholfen
kennen	kannte (kennte)	gekannt
kiesen*	kor (köre)	gekoren
klimmen*	klomm (klömme)	geklommen
klingen	klang (klänge)	geklungen
kneifen	kniff	gekniffen
kommen	kam (käme)	gekommen
können (ich kann, du kannst, er kann)	konnte (könnte)	gekonnt
kreischen*	krisch	gekrischen
kriechen	kroch (kröche)	gekrochen
küren*	kor (köre)	gekoren
[1]laden (du lädst, er lädt)	lud (lüde)	geladen
[2]laden (du lädst, er lädt; *veralt., landsch.:* du ladest, er ladet)	lud (lüde)	geladen
lassen (du läßt, er läßt)	ließ	gelassen
laufen (du läufst, er läuft)	lief	gelaufen
leiden	litt	gelitten
leihen	lieh	geliehen
[1,2]lesen (du liest, er liest; lies!)	las (läse)	gelesen
liegen	lag (läge)	gelegen
lügen	log (löge)	gelogen
mahlen	mahlte	gemahlen
meiden	mied	gemieden

Infinitive *Infinitiv*	Preterite *Präteritum*	Past Participle *2. Partizip*
melken* (du milkst, er milkt; milk!; du melkst, er melkt; melke!)	molk (mölke)	gemolken
messen (du mißt, er mißt; miß!)	maß (mäße)	gemessen
mißlingen	mißlang (mißlänge)	mißlungen
mögen (ich mag, du magst, er mag)	mochte (möchte)	gemocht
müssen (ich muß, du mußt, er muß)	mußte (müßte)	gemußt
nehmen (du nimmst, er nimmt; nimm!)	nahm (nähme)	genommen
nennen	nannte (nennte)	genannt
pfeifen	pfiff	gepfiffen
pflegen*	pflog (pflöge)	gepflogen
preisen	pries	gepriesen
[1]quellen (du quillst, er quillt; quill!)	quoll (quölle)	gequollen
raten (du rätst, er rät)	riet	geraten
reiben	rieb	gerieben
reißen	riß	gerissen
reiten	ritt	geritten
rennen	rannte (rennte)	gerannt
riechen	roch (röche)	gerochen
ringen	rang (ränge)	gerungen
rinnen	rann (ränne, *seltener:* rönne)	geronnen
rufen	rief	gerufen
salzen*	salzte	gesalzen
saufen (du säufst, er säuft)	soff (söffe)	gesoffen
saugen*	sog (söge)	gesogen
schaffen*	schuf (schüfe)	geschaffen
schallen*	scholl (schölle)	geschallt
scheiden	schied	geschieden
scheinen	schien	geschienen
scheißen	schiß	geschissen
schelten (du schiltst, er schilt; schilt!)	schalt (schölte)	gescholten
[1]scheren	schor (schöre)	geschoren
schieben	schob (schöbe)	geschoben
schießen	schoß (schösse)	geschossen
schinden	schindete	geschunden
schlafen (du schläfst, er schläft)	schlief	geschlafen
schlagen (du schlägst, er schlägt)	schlug (schlüge)	geschlagen
schleichen	schlich	geschlichen
[1]schleifen	schliff	geschliffen
schleißen*	schliß	geschlissen
schließen	schloß (schlösse)	geschlossen
schlingen	schlang (schlänge)	geschlungen
schmeißen	schmiß	geschmissen
schmelzen (du schmilzt, er schmilzt; schmilz!)	schmolz	geschmolzen
schnauben*	schnob (schnöbe)	geschnoben
schneiden	schnitt	geschnitten
schrecken* (du schrickst, er schrickt; schrick!)	schrak (schräke)	geschreckt

Infinitive *Infinitiv*	Preterite *Präteritum*	Past Participle *2. Partizip*
schreiben	schrieb	geschrieben
schreien	schrie	geschrie[e]n
schreiten	schritt	geschritten
schweigen	schwieg	geschwiegen
[1]schwellen (du schwillst, er schwillt; schwill!)	schwoll (schwölle)	geschwollen
schwimmen	schwamm (schwömme, *seltener:* schwämme)	geschwommen
schwinden	schwand (schwände)	geschwunden
schwingen	schwang (schwänge)	geschwungen
schwören	schwor (schwüre)	geschworen
sehen (du siehst, er sieht; sieh[e]!)	sah (sähe)	gesehen
sein (ich bin, du bist, er ist, wir sind, ihr seid, sie sind; sei!)	war (wäre)	gewesen
senden*	sandte (sendete)	gesandt
sieden*	sott (sötte)	gesotten
singen	sang (sänge)	gesungen
sinken	sank (sänke)	gesunken
sinnen	sann (sänne, *veralt.:* sönne)	gesonnen
sitzen	saß (säße)	gesessen
sollen (ich soll, du sollst, er soll)	sollte	gesollt
spalten*	spaltete	gespalten
speien	spie	gespie[e]n
spinnen	spann (spönne, spänne)	gesponnen
spleißen*	spliß	gesplissen
sprechen (du sprichst, er spricht; sprich!)	sprach (spräche)	gesprochen
sprießen	sproß (sprösse)	gesprossen
springen	sprang	gesprungen
stechen (du stichst, er sticht; stich!)	stach (stäche)	gestochen
stecken*	stak (stäke)	gesteckt
stehen	stand (stünde, *auch:* stände)	gestanden
stehlen (du stiehlst, er stiehlt; stiehl!)	stahl (stähle, *seltener:* stöhle)	gestohlen
steigen	stieg	gestiegen
sterben (du stirbst, er stirbt; stirb!)	starb (stürbe)	gestorben
stieben	stob (stöbe)	gestoben
stinken	stank (stänke)	gestunken
stoßen (du stößt, er stößt)	stieß	gestoßen
streichen	strich	gestrichen
streiten	stritt	gestritten
tragen (du trägst, er trägt)	trug (trüge)	getragen
treffen (du triffst; er trifft; triff!)	traf (träfe)	getroffen
treiben	trieb	getrieben
treten (du trittst, er tritt; tritt!)	trat (träte)	getreten
triefen*	troff (tröffe)	getroffen
trinken	trank (tränke)	getrunken
trügen	trog (tröge)	getrogen
tun	tat (täte)	getan
verderben (du verdirbst, er verdirbt; verdirb!)	verdarb (verdürbe)	verdorben
verdrießen	verdroß (verdrösse)	verdrossen
vergessen (du vergißt, er vergißt, vergiß!)	vergaß (vergäße)	vergessen
verlieren	verlor (verlöre)	verloren
verlöschen (du verlischst, er verlischt; verlisch!)	verlosch (verlösche)	verloschen
[1]wachsen (du wächst, er wächst)	wuchs (wüchse)	gewachsen
wägen	wog (wöge)	gewogen
waschen (du wäschst, er wäscht)	wusch (wüsche)	gewaschen
weben*	wob (wöbe)	gewoben
weichen	wich	gewichen
weisen	wies	gewiesen
wenden*	wandte (wendete)	gewandt
werben (du wirbst, er wirbt; wirb!)	warb (würbe)	geworben
werden (du wirst, er wird; werde!)	wurde, *dichter.:* ward (würde)	geworden; *als Hilfsv.:* worden
werfen (du wirfst, er wirft; wirf!)	warf (würfe)	geworfen
[1]wiegen	wog (wöge)	gewogen
[1]winden	wand (wände)	gewunden
wissen (ich weiß, du weißt, er weiß)	wußte (wüßte)	gewußt
wollen (ich will, du willst, er will)	wollte	gewollt
wringen	wrang (wränge)	gewrungen
zeihen	zieh	geziehen
ziehen	zog (zöge)	gezogen
zwingen	zwang (zwänge)	gezwungen

Key points of German orthography and punctuation

Use of capital and small initial letters

The use of capital and small initial letters in German is governed by the following guidelines.

a) The first word of a sentence has a capital initial letter.

b) All true nouns have capital initial letters:

Himmel, Kindheit, Reichtum, Verständnis

c) All types of word have capital initial letters when they are used as nouns:

das Gute, der Abgeordnete, allerlei Schönes, etwas Wichtiges, die Deinigen, ein Achtel, das Auf und Nieder, das Entweder-Oder, das Lesen, das Zustandekommen, das In-den-Tag-hineinleben

d) In correspondence, pronouns of address have capital initial letters. The polite form *Sie* and the accompanying possessive pronoun *Ihr* always have capital initials, but the reflexive pronoun *sich* always has a small initial:

Liebe Tante,
heute möchte ich *Dir* herzlich für *Dein* Weihnachtsgeschenk danken ...
Würden *Sie* mir bitte *Ihr* Programmheft leihen?
Setzen *Sie sich*.

e) Words which are derived from geographical names and which end in *-er* have capital initial letters:

die Schweizer Industrie, eine Kölner Firma

f) Adjectives ending in *-isch* which are derived from geographical names have small initials unless they form a part of proper name:

chinesische Seide, westfälischer Schinken
but: Holsteinische Schweiz

g) When nouns function other than as nouns they have small initial letters:

anfangs, abends, sonntags, ein bißchen, schuld sein, es tut mir leid

One word or two?

The continuing development of the conventions governing spelling and punctuation in German means that it is impossible to say for certain when words are written together (as one word) and when separately (as two words). The following examples are designed to serve as a general guide only. In cases of doubt write as two words.

a) Words are written together if they combine to form a new meaning:

Du sollst dich nicht so gehenlassen.
Er wird mir die Summe gutschreiben.

Words are written separately if they retain their original meanings:

Du mußt den Teig jetzt gehen lassen.
Der Schüler kann gut schreiben.

b) Compounds formed with a noun are written as one word if the noun no longer embodies a separate concept:

wetterleuchten, kopfstehen, infolge, zugunsten

Words are written separately if the noun retains its independent meaning:

Sorge tragen, Posten stehen, unter Bezugnahme auf, in Frage kommen

The continuing development of the language means that some words are found in both forms:

Dank sagen *and* danksagen, auf Grund *and* aufgrund

The comma

The role of the comma is to divide the sentence and indicate the pauses occurring in speech.

a) In lists, the comma is placed between words of the same type or between similar groups of words if they are not linked by *und* or *oder:*

Feuer, Wasser, Luft und Erde.
Wir gingen bei gutem, warmem Wetter spazieren.
Das Autorennen findet am Montag, den 5. Mai statt.
(Here, the comma divides two statements of time; compare b.)

b) The comma separates following qualifying phrases from the rest of the sentence:

In Frankfurt, der bekannten Handelsstadt, befindet sich ein großes Messegelände.
Das Schiff kommt wöchentlich einmal, und zwar sonntags.
Das Autorennen findet am Montag, dem 5. Mai, statt.
(Here, an embedded phrase is enclosed by commas; compare a.)

c) An infinitive phrase is usually divided from the rest of the sentence by a comma; *zu* + infinitive alone is not divided off.

Wir hatten keine Gelegenheit, uns zu sehen.
but: Wir hatten keine Gelegenheit zu baden.

d) The comma separates main clauses. However the comma is not used between main clauses linked by *und* or *oder* if one part of the sentence is common to both clauses:

Ich kam, ich sah, ich siegte.
Wir trinken noch ein Bier, und dann gehe ich nach Hause.
but: Sie bestiegen den Wagen und fuhren davon. (*Sie* is common to both clauses)
Er geht ins Kino und sein Bruder ins Konzert. (*geht* is common to both clauses)

e) The comma separates the subordinate clause from the main clause:

Daß du zuverlässig bist, freut mich.
Alle Kinder, die fleißig sind, erhalten ein Buch.

Syllable division in German

Polysyllabic words are divided in accordance with the phonetic syllables which can be identified by pronouncing the word slowly:

Freun-de, Män-ner, for-dern, wei-ter, Or-gel, kal-kig, Bes-se-rung, Bal-kon, Fis-kus, Ho-tel, Pla-net, Kon-ti-nent, Fas-zi-kel, Re-mi-nis-zenz, El-lip-se, Ber-lin, El-ba, Tür-kei

In such cases, a single consonant goes on to the following line; if there is a series of consonants, the last of these goes on to the following line:

tre-ten, nä-hen, Ru-der, rei-ßen, bo-xen, Ko-kon, Kre-ta, Chi-na, An-ker, Fin-ger, war-ten, Fül-lun-gen, Rit-ter, Was-ser, Knos-pen, kämp-fen, Ach-sel, steck-ten, Kat-zen, Städ-ter, Drechs-ler, dunk-le, gest-rig, an-de-re, neh-men, Ar-sen, Hip-pie, Kas-ko, Pek-tin, Un-garn, Hes-sen, At-lan-tik (For exceptions see below.)

Suffixes which begin with a vowel take the preceding consonant when divided:

Freun-din, Bäcke-rei, Lüf-tung

A single vowel is never left on its own:

Ader, eben, Odem
(*not:* A-der, e-ben, O-dem)

The consonant groups *ch* and *sch* – as well as *ph, rh, sh,* and *th* in foreign words – represent single sounds and are not divided:

Bü-cher, Fla-sche, Ma-chete, Pro-phet, Myr-rhe, Ca-shew-nuß, ka-tho-lisch

The following groups of letters are not usually divided in foreign words:

bl, pl, fl, gl, cl, kl, phl; br, pr, dr, tr, fr, vr, gr, cr, kr, phr, str, thr; chth, gn, kn
Pu-bli-kum, Di-plom, Souf-flé, Re-gle-ment, Bou-clé, Zy-klus, Pam-phlet, Fe-bru-ar, Le-pra, Hy-drant, neu-tral, Chif-fre, Li-vree, ne-grid, Sa-kra-ment, In-du-strie, Ar-thri-tis; Ma-gnet, py-knisch

If *ss* is used to stand for *ß* (e.g. on a typewriter without *ß*), it is treated as a single sound, like *ß*, and is not divided:

Grü-sse (*for:* Grü-ße), hei-ssen (*for:* hei-ßen)

ck becomes *k-k* when divided. The division of *ck* in names should be avoided if possible:

Zuk-ker, bak-ken;
(only if absolutely necessary:) Bek-ker, Zwik-kau

If *ck* occurs after a consonant in names or their derivatives, *ck* is regarded as a single consonant and is placed on the following line:

Sen-ckenberg, Fran-cke, bismar-ckisch

st is not divided:

la-sten, We-sten, sech-ste, brem-ste, Dien-stes, Aku-stik, Hy-sterie

An exception to this rule is the division of the components of a compound:

Diens-tag, Haus-tier

Vowel combinations may only be divided if they consist of two or more sounds and there is a distinct syllabic break between them:

Befrei-ung, bö-ig, europä-isch, Muse-um, kre-ie-ren

More closely associated vowels should stay together if possible:

Natio-nen, natio-nal, Flui-dum, asia-tisch, Idea-list, Sexua-lität, poe-tisch, böi-ge, europäi-sche, einei-ige

Words are not divided before the 'lengthening' letters *e* and *i:*

Wie-se
Coes-feld (*pronounced:* kos...)

The following words may not be divided:

Feen, knien, [auf] Knien, Seen

Compound words and words with a prefix are divided in accordance with their constituent word elements:

Diens-tag, war-um, dar-auf, dar-in

The same applies to foreign words:

Atmo-sphäre, Mikro-skop, Inter-esse, Syn-onym, At-traktion, De-szen-denz, in-szenieren

Some foreign words, however, are divided according to phonetic syllables, as the constituent elements of a foreign word are not always generally known:

Epi-sode (*instead of:* Epis-ode)
ab-strakt (*instead of:* abs-trakt)

Compound geographical names are only divided in accordance with their constituent word elements if these can be identified. Otherwise, they are divided in accordance with phonetic syllables:

Main-au, Schwarz-ach

but: Norder-ney, *not:* Nordern-ey (ey = Insel).

If one of three identical consonants has been omitted at the junction of a compound word, the 'missing' consonant is reintroduced when the word is divided:

Schiff-fahrt, Brenn-nessel

but: den-noch, Mit-tag

Word divisions which obey the rules but disrupt the flow of reading should be avoided:

Spar-gelder, *not:* Spargel-der
be-inhalten, *not:* bein-halten

If foreign words, or groups of foreign words or phrases, occur in a German text, word division should be in accordance with the German rules:

a po-ste-rio-ri, Co-ming man, Swin-ging London

Practical guide to writing letters in German

A. The envelope

German conventions for addressing the envelope are different from English in several respects. Firstly, *Herrn* (accusative after a suppressed *an*), *Frau, Fräulein,* and most titles are written above the name, but *Dr.* and *Dipl.-Ing.* go with the name. Then the house number follows the name of the road or street, while the postcode *(Postleitzahl)* precedes the name of the town. On letters from outside the country the *Postleitzahl* may be preceded by D for Germany, A for Austria, and CH for Switzerland.

Herrn
Hans Bauer
Fritz-Busch-Str. 48

A-4976 Eichelbach
Austria

Fräulein
Elisabeth Maybach
Alslebenplatz 12

D-90328 Nürnberg
Germany

Frau Professor
Erika Engelsbach
Niederhornweg 62

CH-8461 Trüllikon
Switzerland

Note that in typed addresses there should be a one-line space before the name of the town.
The address (especially for firms) may simply be a P.O. Box no. *(Postfach).*

Helling Verlag
Postfach 10 08 96

D-69112 Heidelberg

Bundesministerium für
Arbeit und Sozialordnung
Postfach 500

D-53107 Bonn

The title *Frau* is now very widely used for all women over school age, whether they are married or not.

Formulierungshilfen beim Schreiben englischer Briefe

A. Der Umschlag

Im englischsprachigen Raum gelten für die Form der Anschrift die folgenden Hinweise. Der Titel des Adressaten (*Mr, Dr, Professor, Major, Rev.* usw.) steht auf derselben Zeile wie der Name. Die Hausnummer steht vor dem Straßennamen. In Großbritannien steht die Postleitzahl *(postcode)* nach der Grafschaft bzw. Stadt. Großstädte benötigen keine zusätzliche Angabe der Grafschaft; das gleiche gilt für Städte, die einer Grafschaft ihren Namen geben, z. B. York, Cambridge, Oxford. Die britische Post zieht es vor, wenn die Postleitzahl alleine auf der letzten Zeile steht. Der erste Buchstabe bzw. die ersten Buchstaben weisen auf die nächstgelegene größere Stadt hin (CV = Coventry, B = Birmingham, AB = Aberdeen usw.). Bei den Londoner Postleitzahlen aber gibt der erste Teil die alte Bezirksnummer wieder, wobei SE20 für South East 20 steht.

[Mr] James Bainbridge
bzw.
James Bainbridge Esq.
5 Avon Crescent
Kenilworth
Warwickshire
CV8 2PQ

Mrs W. Stockton
Homelea
25 Endersby Avenue
Kings Norton
Birmingham
B38 8CJ

Dr W. F. Butler
Cruck Cottage
Curry Mallet
Taunton
Somerset
TA3 6SP

Ms Laura Stevens
Flat 2
Beverley House
Abbey Road
London
SE20 7NP

Miss A. Gordon
Kirkbrae
10 Strathmore Road
Cults
Aberdeen
AB1 9TJ

Sir Alan and Lady Weston
Aberdare House
Llanyre
Llandrindod Wells
Powys
LD1 6DX

Bei Männern entfällt oft der Titel *Mr;* der Titel *Esq.,* der statt dessen nachgestellt werden kann, ist etwas altmodisch und wird meist in Geschäftsbriefen verwendet. Der Titel *Ms* kann für (meist jüngere) verheiratete und unverheiratete Frauen stehen; er wird heute *Mrs* bzw. *Miss* oft vorgezogen und entspricht ungefähr dem heutigen Gebrauch von *Frau* im deutschsprachigen Raum.
Die Bezeichnung *Esq.* kennt man in den USA nicht, alle anderen Titel werden ähnlich wie in Großbritannien verwendet. Man sieht manchmal die Bezeichnung *Jr.* (= *Junior*) hinter dem Familiennamen, wenn Vater und Sohn den gleichen Vornamen haben.

The *Postleitzahlen* in Germany were changed to 5-digit codes in 1993. This became necessary as there were about 800 duplicate postcodes in existence as a result of reunification.
The first two digits of the new *Postleitzahlen* refer to one of 83 postal regions, e.g. 04 means the Leipzig region, and the last three digits describe the town and area. This means that larger towns and cities now have multiple postcodes.

To send a letter poste restante (to await collection at a post office), mark it *postlagernd* or, for the main post office in a large town, *hauptpostlagernd*. If the addressee is staying with someone, add *bei* or *c/o* plus the host's surname:

Mr John Peacock postlagernd CH-4984 Eiderswyl Switzerland	Miss Jane Summers bei Wolf Immermannstr. 12 D-63755 Großostheim Germany

In a letter to a firm, *Firma* can be placed before the company name, or *Herren* (= Messrs) if the name consists of two or more surnames and the firm is quite small:

Firma Willi Müller	Herren Fieselbach & Grünspan

For larger firms, *Firma* is not used, and the name of any department follows the name of the firm:

Haverkamp & Co. Direktion	Müller-Versand KG Verkaufsabteilung
E-Werke Oberroden Kundendienst	Wilhelmshavener Abendblatt Redaktion

When writing to a particular person within a firm, give the name prefaced by *z. H.* (*zu Händen*, 'for the attention of'). Again, this follows the name of the firm or organization:

Haverkamp & Co. Versandabteilung z. H. Herrn Nesseldorn	Witsch-Werke GmbH Finanzdirektion z. H. Frau Inge Weiß

Variations on this are the abbreviations *i. H. (im Hause), i. Fa. (in Firma),* and *c/o (care of)*. These are placed on confidential letters and precede the name of the firm; *i. H.* is for employees, *i. Fa.* for proprietors or partners, and *c/o* for anyone, including non-employees.

Fräulein Inge Weiß i. H. Witsch-Werke GmbH	Herrn F. Nesseldorn i. Fa. Haverkamp & Co.

Die amerikanische Postleitzahl *(zip code)* steht an letzter Stelle nach dem Staat (heute meist auf zwei Buchstaben abgekürzt). Sie besteht aus einer Folge von fünf Ziffern:

Robert Hale Jr. 1496 Pacific Boulevard Monterey CA 93940	Wm. F. Harris P.O. Box 731 Milville NJ 08332

(CA = California, NJ = New Jersey)

Bei Sendungen an ein Postfach schreibt man *P.O. Box* und die Nummer des Postfachs unter den Namen des Adressaten (Bsp. s. o.)

Postlagernde Sendungen werden mit *Poste restante* bezeichnet und können nur an Hauptpostämter geschickt werden:

Mr Bruce Nichol
Poste restante
Blandford
Dorset

Möchte man jemanden über die Adresse seiner Gastgeber oder Vermieter oder z. B. einer Zeitung erreichen, setzt man *c/o* (= *care of*) vor deren Namen:

Miss Angela Dickens
c/o Hope
12 Helvellyn Road
London
W11 2LY

Schreibt man an eine bestimmte Person in einer Firma oder Organisation, steht der Name des Adressaten vor dem der Firma oder Organisation:

Mrs A. J. Prestwick
Plunkett & Rose Ltd.
Westway Trading Estate
Sevenoaks
Kent
TN15 7PL

In diesem letzten Fall kann man auch schreiben:

Plunkett & Rose Ltd.
For the attention of *od.* FAO *od.* Attn. Mrs A. J. Prestwick,

aber diese Formulierung steht auch öfter oben auf dem Brief selbst.

Wenn man eine Firma anschreibt, deren Name aus mehreren Familiennamen oder aus einem Familiennamen und dem Zusatz *& Co.* besteht, wird oft *Messrs.* vorangestellt:

Messrs. Buckland, Forsyth, & Hardy

Messrs. Bray & Co.

On personal letters, the sender's address should be given on the back of the envelope, preceded by *Absender* or *Abs.*; on business letters it is instead often found in the bottom left-hand corner of the front of the envelope.

Finally, with letters posted in German-speaking countries, the particular kind of delivery required should be written immediately above the address with a gap in between, i.e.

Einschreiben ('Registered')
Eilzustellung ('Express')
Mit Luftpost ('Air Mail')
Wenn unzustellbar, zurück [an (den) Absender]
('If undelivered return to sender')
Drucksache ('Printed matter')
Drucksache zu ermäßigter Gebühr
('Printed matter at reduced rate')
Päckchen ('Small packet')

Examples:

Einschreiben	Mit Luftpost
Herrn Rechtsanwalt Dr. Erwin Hassler Finkstr. 45 50939 Köln	Mr James Forbes 1420 Green Street Encino CA 91316 USA

Schreibt man an eine bestimmte Abteilung in einer Firma oder an den Inhaber einer bestimmten Position, dessen Namen man nicht kennt, steht die Abteilung bzw. die Bezeichnung der Position vor dem Firmennamen:

Sales Department Wayne Pharmaceuticals Inc. 1100 North Street Harrisburg PA 17105	The Manager Barclays Bank 20 Eastgate York YO2 4BQ

In den USA ist es üblich, unter dem Namen des Inhabers einer leitenden Position diese Position anzugeben:

John C. Wagner President Bix Corporation	Paul S. Jackson Export Manager Scanways Furniture Co.

Der Absender steht, wenn er überhaupt angegeben wird, meist auf der Rückseite des Umschlags. Angaben über die Art der Postsendung können in der linken oberen Ecke des Umschlags gemacht werden:

Registered („Einschreiben")
Express („Eilzustellung")
First [Class] *(Brit.)**
Air Mail („Mit Luftpost")
Printed matter („Drucksache")
Small packet („Päckchen")

* Angabe nicht erforderlich; in Großbritannien werden Postsendungen, die nicht „First Class" frankiert sind, „Second Class", also langsamer, befördert.

B. Layout

1. Informal letters

Because German speakers write their address on the back of the envelope, they usually feel no need to include it at the top of the letter as well. They just put the name of the place and the date:

```
                                        Rastatt, 7.4.19..

Lieber Richard,

hoffentlich bist Du gut nach Hause gekommen. Wir ha-
ben uns sehr über Deinen Besuch gefreut.

Beim Aufräumen in Deinem Zimmer, das heißt Rainers
Zimmer, habe ich ein Paar schwarze Turnschuhe gefun-
den, die wohl Dir gehören. Schreib mir, ob Du sie
dringend brauchst, dann schicke ich sie Dir. Sonst
kann Rainer sie im Sommer mitbringen, wenn er zu Euch
fährt.
Ich hoffe, es geht Euch allen gut.

Herzliche Grüße

Uschi
```

Note that in letters *Du, Ihr,* and their derivatives are all written with capitals (including the possessives *Dein* and *Euer*).

B. Gestaltung

1. Privatbriefe

Die Adresse des Absenders steht oben rechts, darunter das Datum, meist in Ziffern, mit Angabe des Wochentags; wenn der Monatsname ausgeschrieben wird, entfällt oft die Angabe des Wochentags:

```
                         24 Copthall Avenue
                         West Drayton
                         Middlesex
                         UB7 2FL
                         24/9/90
                   oder: (Monday) 24th September 1990

Dear Beate,

     I do hope you had a good trip back home. We all
enjoyed having you here very much.
     When I was clearing up in your room (that is,
Ellen's room), I found a pair of brown sandals under
the bed which must be yours. Let me know if you need
them badly, and I'll post them. Otherwise Ellen can
bring them with her when she comes to see you in the
summer.
     Hoping you are all well,

                              Love,

                              Brenda
```

2. Business letters

There are very precise rules for the layout of business letters, laid down as a standard in DIN 5008 of the Deutsches Institut für Normung e. V. The following is a brief summary.
The whole letter is aligned on the left-hand margin without indentation except for quoted matter.
The addressee's address appears in the top left-hand corner in the same form as on the envelope. References and dates of previous correspondence follow, plus the date of the present letter, then after a one-line space the *Betreff* or heading giving the subject of the letter, and after a two-line space the greeting (see below for forms of address).
Paragraphs, quoted items, the form of greeting at the end, and any list of enclosures are all separated by a one-line space. Quotations are indented ten spaces. The list of enclosures *(Anlagen)* and/or indications for distribution come directly below the signature.
When the letter is signed by someone else in the absence of the writer, the abbreviation *i. V. (in Vertretung)* precedes the name.
If the letter goes to a second page, the page is numbered and the addressee's name and the date are repeated.

2. Geschäftsbriefe

Unter dem meist gedruckten Briefkopf stehen am linken Rand die Bezugszeichen *(Our ref. ... Your ref. ...)* und am rechten Rand das Datum. Wenn die Adresse des Absenders nicht schon im Briefkopf enthalten ist, steht sie rechts oben mit dem Datum darunter. In Großbritannien steht der Tag üblicherweise vor dem Monat (heute meist ohne *st, rd* oder *th*), in den USA nach dem Monat (stets ohne *st, rd* oder *th*). Danach folgt die Adresse des Empfängers in der gleichen Form wie auf dem Umschlag. Besondere Anmerkungen wie *Confidential, Personal, For the attention of* ... usw. folgen meist nach der Adresse.
Nach drei Leerzeilen folgt die Anrede; danach kann im britischen Gebrauch ein Komma, in den USA ein Doppelpunkt stehen. Der Betreff wird zwei Leerzeilen unter der Anrede zentriert und unterstrichen. Zwischen den einzelnen Absätzen stehen zwei Leerzeilen. Die erste Zeile des Absatzes wird manchmal noch eingerückt.
Am Ende des Briefes steht nach zwei oder drei Leerzeilen in der rechten Seitenhälfte die Grußformel mit der Unterschrift (s. C). Darunter werden Name und Position des Unterzeichnenden angegeben; falls der Brief im Auftrag unterschrieben wird, steht *p.p.* vor dem Namen.
Links unten folgen gegebenenfalls die Abkürzungen *Encl.* = *Enclosure[s]* (Anlage[n]) bzw. *c.c.* = *carbon copy [to]* (Verteiler).
Ist der Brief länger als eine Seite, schreibt man oben auf das Fortsetzungsblatt links den Empfänger, in der Mitte die Seitenzahl und rechts das Datum.

C. Beginnings and Endings

All the greetings in this section can be followed either by an exclamation mark, in which case the next line starts with a capital, or by a comma, in which case it starts with a small letter.

1. Informal – to someone you know well

Lieber Hans
Liebe Karen
Liebe Meyers *od.* Liebe Familie Meyer
Liebe Hilde, lieber Erwin
between young people:
Hallo Tom
Hallo Erika
standard ending:
Herzliche Grüße [Dein/Deine] ...
more affectionate:
Viele liebe Grüße
to close friends and relations:
Alles Liebe
more informal:
Bis bald
Tschüs

C. Anrede und Grußformel

1. Informelle Privatbriefe an enge Freunde und Verwandte

Dear Charles/Mary,
Dear Ian and Bridget,
an eine Familie:
Dear All,
unter jungen Leuten:
Hi Tim!
liebevoll:
Dearest *or* My dearest [James/Helena],
[My] Darling [Joan/Michael],

ungezwungen:
Yours,
Yours ever,
With [lots of] love from
Love,
liebevoller:
With all my/our love [as always],

2. More formal – in a personal letter to someone you do not know, or do not know well

Lieber Herr Engel
Liebe Frau Schulz
Liebe Frau Ellermann, lieber Herr Ellermann

Mit herzlichen Grüßen
Mit freundlichen Grüßen

3. In a formal business letter

Sehr geehrter Herr Engel
Sehr geehrte Frau Schulz
If the person has a title, omit the name:
Sehr geehrter Herr Direktor
Sehr geehrte Frau Studienrätin
Sehr geehrter Herr General
If there is a title in the address and not a name, give the same here:
Sehr geehrter Herr Bürgermeister
Sehr geehrter Herr Chefredakteur
If the letter is addressed to a firm or organization:
Sehr geehrte Damen und Herren
Sehr geehrte Herren
(The second form, which used to be standard, should only be used where it is known that only males are being addressed.)

Mit freundlichen Grüßen
more formal:
Mit freundlichen/besten Empfehlungen
very formal:
Hochachtungsvoll

2. Formellere Privatbriefe

Dear Mr Aitchison,
Dear Mrs Gold,
Dear Miss Wilding,
Dear Mr and Mrs Smith,
Dear Sir Roger,
Dear Lady Wicksteed,
[With best wishes/kind regards,]
Yours sincerely,/Sincerely,
Yours [very] truly, *(esp. Amer.)*
Sincerely,/Cordially yours, *(Amer.)*

3. Geschäftsbriefe

wenn der Name des Adressaten bekannt ist:
Dear Mr Saunders/Mrs Wilton/Miss Roberts *usw.*,
Yours sincerely *(Brit.)*
Sincerely/Very truly yours, *(Amer.)*
wenn der Name des Adressaten nicht bekannt ist:
Dear Sir,
Dear Madam,
Dear Sir *or* Madam,
Yours faithfully, *(Brit.)*
Yours very truly, *(Amer.)*
wenn eine Firma angeschrieben wird:
Dear Sirs, *(Brit.)*
Gentlemen: *(Amer.)*
Yours faithfully, *(Brit.)*
Yours very truly, *(Amer.)*

D. Some useful letters

1. Booking a hotel

Dorking, 5. Mai 19..

Hotel Bayrischer Hof
Stresemannplatz 4

D-87561 Oberstdorf

Sehr geehrte Damen und Herren,

auf unserer Reise durch Deutschland möchten wir drei Tage in Oberstdorf verbringen/in Oberstdorf Übernachten, und zwar vom 10. bis 13. August./am 10. August. Wir benötigen zwei Doppelzimmer/ein Doppelzimmer (mit Bad/Dusche) und ein Einzelzimmer.

Bitte bestätigen Sie unsere Buchung und teilen Sie uns den Preis für Zimmer mit Frühstück/Halbpension/Vollpension mit. Falls Sie uns zur angegebenen Zeit nicht unterbringen können, wären wir für die Empfehlung eines anderen Hotels in der Nähe sehr dankbar.

Ich möchte noch erwähnen, daß sich mein Sohn ausschließlich vegetarisch ernährt. Bietet Ihr Hotel vegetarische Gerichte an?

Mit freundlichen Grüßen

Robert Paterson

D. Musterbriefe

1. Hotelbuchung

Bertholdstr. 46
D-42103 Wuppertal
Germany

7 April 19..

Weston Manor Hotel
Weston Road
Bath
Avon
BA2 4LD
England

Dear Sirs,

In the course of our tour of the West Country this summer we want to spend three days in Bath, from the 10th to the 13th August./spend the night of the 10th August in Bath. We will require two double rooms/one double room (with bath/shower) and a single room.

Please confirm our booking and let us know what you charge for bed and breakfast/half-board/fullboard. Should you not have the required accommodation at this time we would be grateful if you could recommend another hotel in the vicinity.

I should also mention that our son is a vegetarian. Are you able to offer vegetarian dishes?

Yours faithfully,

Hans Knauer

2. Booking a camp-site

Oxford, 19. April 19..

Campingplatz
"Schöne Aussicht"

D-53518 Adenau

Sehr geehrte Damen und Herren,

bitte reservieren Sie uns einen Zeltplatz/einen Platz für einen Wohnwagen für den 20. August. Wir sind zwei Personen/vier Personen mit Auto.

Teilen Sie mir bitte mit, wie ich den Campingplatz von der Autobahn aus erreichen kann und ob er in unmittelbarer Nähe des Flusses/Dorfs liegt.

Für Ihre Bemühungen möchte ich mich im voraus bedanken.

Mit freundlichen Grüßen

Richard Clarke

2. Buchung eines Campingplatzes

The Manager
South Beach Campsite and
Caravan Park
Sheringham
Norfolk
NR26 8MY
England

Am Graben 26
D-32257 Bünde
Germany

24 May 19..

Dear Sir,

I would like to book a site for a tent/for a caravan for the week of August 20th./for a week from August 20th to 26th inclusive. There are two of us/four of us plus a car.

Please let us know how to find the camp-site coming from Norwich, and whether it is right on the beach./within easy reach of the town.

Thanking you in advance for your trouble,

Yours faithfully,

Robert Schmidt

3. Cancelling a booking

Stockton-on-Tees, 6.7.19..

Frau
Therese Birkenmeyer
Gasthof "Zum Schwarzen Adler"

D-97980 Bad Mergentheim

Sehr geehrte Frau Birkenmeyer,

leider muß ich die für die Woche ab 20. Juli reservierten Zimmer/das für die Zeit vom 20. bis 24. Juli reservierte Zimmer abbestellen. Durch den überraschenden Tod meines Vaters/Da mein Mann ins Krankenhaus mußte, können wir die geplante Reise nicht antreten./müssen wir auf unseren Urlaub verzichten.

Ich bedaure sehr, daß ich so kurzfristig absagen muß./ich Sie nicht früher darüber informieren/davon in Kenntnis setzen konnte.

Mit freundlichen Grüßen

Joan Mason (Mrs)

3. Abbestellung

Mrs. J. Warrington
Lakeview
Wetherby Drive
Windermere
Cumbria
LA23 2BD
England

Westhorner Str. 15
D-06108 Halle/Saale
Germany

6 July 19..

Dear Mrs Warrington,

Unfortunately I have to cancel our reservation/booking for the week of July 20th./for the period from July 20th to 24th. Owing to my father's sudden death/Since my husband has had to go into hospital, we have had to abandon our holiday plans.

I very much regret having to cancel the booking at such short notice./that I could not inform you earlier of this change of plan.

Yours sincerely,

Elke Nordrup

4. Making complaints

a) Restaurant

Invergordon, 7. Juli 19..

Gaststätte "Zum Löwen"
Hauptstr. 149

D-72250 Freudenstadt

Sehr geehrte (Damen und) Herren,

vor zwei Tagen habe ich mit meiner Frau in Ihrer Gaststätte gegessen. Kurz darauf/nach ca. einer Stunde wurde meiner Frau übel. Da der herbeigerufene Arzt feststellte, daß es sich um eine Lebensmittelvergiftung handelt, rief ich sofort in Ihrem Restaurant an. Man teilte mir mit, daß Sie hierfür keine Verantwortung übernehmen.

Diese Erklärung kann ich nicht akzeptieren./Ich finde Ihren Standpunkt unvertretbar. Sollten Sie Ihre Einstellung zu meiner Beschwerde nicht ändern, sehe ich mich gezwungen, Klage gegen Sie zu erheben./die Angelegenheit meinem Rechtsanwalt zu übergeben./Ihren Fachverband über diesen Vorfall zu informieren.

Hochachtungsvoll

Raymond Morris

4. Beschwerden

a) Restaurant

The Manager
Four Seasons Restaurant
27 High Street
Irvine
Ayrshire
KA12 OXY
Scotland

Brunnengasse 7
D-04105 Leipzig
Germany

14 April 19..

Dear Sir,

Two days ago I had a meal in your restaurant with my husband. Shortly after/About an hour later my husband was taken ill. Since the doctor whom we consulted confirmed that it was a case of food-poisoning, I immediately telephoned your restaurant, only to be told that you could not accept any responsibility for this.

I find this attitude/your viewpoint quite unacceptable, and if you insist on adhering to it, I shall have no alternative but to/I shall be forced to take legal action./put the matter in the hands of my solicitor./inform your professional association of the matter.

Yours faithfully,

Ilse Schmidt

b) Shop

Invergordon, 23. Dezember 19..

Schäfer & Cie.
Kaiserstr. 12

D-22358 Hamburg

Sehr geehrte (Damen und) Herren,

vor zwei Tagen habe ich in Ihrem Geschäft eine Armbanduhr gekauft. Am nächsten Morgen/über Nacht blieb die Uhr stehen. Nachdem ich es erfolglos mit einer neuen Batterie versucht hatte, rief ich sofort in Ihrem Geschäft an. Man teilte mir mit, daß Sie hierfür keine Haftung/Garantie übernehmen, weil ich die Uhr geöffnet habe.

Diese Erklärung kann ich nicht akzeptieren./Ich finde Ihren Standpunkt unvertretbar. Sollten Sie Ihre Einstellung zu meiner Beschwerde nicht ändern, sehe ich mich gezwungen, Klage gegen Sie zu erheben./die Angelegenheit meinem Rechtsanwalt zu übergeben./Ihren Fachverband über diesen Vorfall zu informieren.

Hochachtungsvoll

Raymond Morris

b) Geschäft

The Manager
J. Carson & Co.
Eastwood Shopping Centre
Bournemouth
Hants
BH1 3TH
England

Brunnengasse 7
D-04105 Leipzig
Germany

22 July 19..

Dear Sir,

Two days ago I bought a watch in your shop, but by the next morning it had stopped. I tried fitting a new battery, but this made no difference, so I immediately rang up your shop. I was told that you could not accept any liability/that the guarantee was invalidated because I had opened the watch.

I find this attitude/your viewpoint quite unacceptable, and if you insist on adhering to it, I shall have no alternative but to/I shall be forced to take legal action./put the matter in the hands of my solicitor./inform your trade association of the matter.

Yours faithfully,

Ilse Schmidt

5. Applying for a job

a) Exploratory letter

Rosalind Whitehead

10 Whitehaven Crescent
Brighton
Sussex
BN2 7DW
9. März 19..

Schwan-Verlag
Personalabteilung
Friedensallee 66

D-70193 Stuttgart

Sehr geehrte Damen und Herren,

ich möchte mich erkundigen, ob in Ihrem Hause eine Stelle als Fremdsprachensekretärin oder in der Redaktion frei ist.

Ich beabsichtige, zwei bis drei Jahre in Deutschland zu bleiben (evtl. länger, wenn ich eine interessante Arbeitsstelle finde)./Im Juni werde ich mit meinem Mann nach Deutschland übersiedeln/wird mein Mann nach Deutschland versetzt. Mein Mann übernimmt eine Position in der Automobilbranche, und ich möchte gerne in meinem Beruf weiterarbeiten.

Wie Sie aus dem beigefügten Lebenslauf ersehen/dem beigefügten Lebenslauf entnehmen können, habe ich zweieinhalb Jahre in Deutschland als Fremdsprachensekretärin gearbeitet. Nach meiner Rückkehr nach England war ich zunächst als Sekretärin tätig; seit September 19.. arbeite ich als Verlagsassistentin. Ich bin die Betriebsamkeit eines ausgelasteten Büros und das korrekte Arbeiten unter Zeitdruck gewohnt und verstehe es, Termine einzuhalten, ohne daß die Qualität der Arbeit dabei leidet.

Falls Sie eine für mich geeignete Stelle frei haben, würde ich mich freuen, wenn Sie mir Gelegenheit zu einer persönlichen Vorstellung geben könnten. Der früheste Einstellungstermin wäre der 1. Mai./Ich könnte frühestens im Mai anfangen, da ich meine gegenwärtige Arbeit Ende April aufgebe.

Ihre Antwort erwarte ich mit Interesse.

Mit freundlichen Grüßen

Rosalind Whitehead

Anlagen

5. Bewerbung

a) Anfrage wegen einer Stelle

Personnel Manager
Falcon Press International
Willow House
Henry Street
London
WC2E 6BY
England

Volkerstr. 10
D-10787 Berlin
Germany

15 March 19..

Dear Sir or Madam,

I would be grateful if you could let me know whether you have any vacancies for bilingual secretaries or for editorial staff.

I intend to come to England for two or three years, possibly longer if I find an interesting job./In June I am moving to England with my husband who is taking on an important position in the motor industry, and I want to continue my own career in publishing.

As you can see from the enclosed CV I have already worked in England for two and a half years as a bilingual secretary. After returning to Germany I first continued working as a bilingual secretary, and then in September 19.. became an editorial assistant. I am used to the often hectic conditions of a busy office, maintaining accuracy while working under pressure, and keeping to deadlines without allowing quality to suffer.

Should you have a suitable vacancy, I would be glad of the opportunity to present myself for interview. The earliest I could start/make myself available would be 1 May./I could not start before May because I am giving up my present job at the end of April.

I look forward to hearing from you.

Yours faithfully,

Ulrike Schwarz

Encl.

b) Curriculum vitae

Rosalind Whitehead

Lebenslauf

Persönliche Daten

Geboren:	10. Mai 19.. in Derby
Familienstand:	verheiratet (mit Raymond Whitehead, Journalist)
(Eltern:	John Redmond, Arzt Janet Redmond, Lehrerin)

Schulbildung

19.. - 19..	Grundschule in Derby
19.. - 19..	Kegworth Grammar School for Girls (Mädchengymnasium)

Studium

19.. - 19..	University of Sussex: Deutsch, Französisch
19.. - 19..	City of London Polytechnic: Kurs für Übersetzer (Deutsch, Französisch, Italienisch)

Prüfungen

Juni 19..	O-Levels/GCSE in 9 Fächern
Juni 19..	A-Levels in Englisch (B), Französisch (B) und Deutsch (A) A/AS
Juni 19..	BA (Upper Second), Deutsch und Französisch
Juni 19..	Diplom für Übersetzer: Deutsch, Französisch und Italienisch

Berufspraxis

1.9.19.. - 31.3.19..	Fremdsprachensekretärin, Gruber Import und Export GmbH, Sindelfingen
1.5.19.. - heute	zunächst Sekretärin, später Verlagsassistentin, Cornhill Press, Avebury Road, Brighton

Sprachen

Englisch (Muttersprache), Deutsch (fließend in Wort und Schrift), Französisch (sehr gut), Italienisch (gut)

Sonstige Fähigkeiten

Textverarbeitung, Stenografie (Englisch und Deutsch), Führerschein

Brighton, 6.3.19..

b) Lebenslauf

CURRICULUM VITAE

Personal Details

Name:	Ulrike Schwarz
Address:	Volkerstr. 10, D-10787 Berlin
Telephone:	(030) 25 46 07 56
Date of birth:	4 December 19..
Marital Status:	Married

Career History

Education

19..-19..	Primary school in Recklinghausen
19..-19..	Humboldt-Gymnasium, Essen
19..	Abitur (approx. A Level) in 4 subjects (English, French, Physics, History)
19..-19..	University of Münster
19..	Staatsexamen (approx. B.A.) in English and French
April-July 19..	Volkshochschule Essen: courses in typing, word processing, shorthand in German and English

Employment

Sept. 19.. to date	Editorial assistant, Wanner-Verlag Deutzer Str. 90, D-10754 Berlin (cookery and home economics books)
Mar. 19..- Sept. 19..	Bilingual secretary to Foreign Rights Manager, Wanner-Verlag
Oct. 19..- Mar. 19..	Bilingual secretary, Wisehart & Goldschmidt, International Jewellery Dealers, Hatton Garden, London
19..-19..	Various holiday jobs, one with a travel agent, another as an au pair in Scotland

Further skills and interests

Languages: German (mother tongue), English (fluent spoken and written), French (very good)

Clean full driving licence

Cookery, interior decoration

Referees

Professional:

Dr. Manfred Hartmann Wanner-Verlag Deutzer Str. 90 D-10754 Berlin	Mr Bernard Goldschmidt Wisehart and Goldschmidt 45 Hatton Garden London EC1 2DW

Personal:

Walter Eberling Underbergstr. 45 D-45282 Essen	Mrs A. Waters 10 Wesley Avenue Barnes London SW13 8BJ

c) Reply to an advertisement

Cambridge, 6.9.19..

Hanslick & Wagner KG
z. H. Herrn Fritz Müller
Industrieweg 6

D-70173 Stuttgart

Sehr geehrter Herr Müller,

ich möchte mich um die in der 'Frankfurter Allgemeinen Zeitung' vom 4.9. ausgeschriebene Stelle als Systemanalytiker bewerben.

Ich arbeite zur Zeit als Systemanalytiker/Ich arbeite zur Zeit in einer ähnlichen Funktion in einer amerikanischen Computerfirma, die eine Zweigniederlassung hier in Cambridge hat. Die Arbeit hat mir von Anfang an zugesagt/Die Arbeit ist interessant und vielseitig, aber das Projekt, an dem ich arbeite, wird in zwei Monaten fertiggestellt sein/die Zweigniederlassung wird aufgelöst, und ich suche eine ähnliche Stelle, am liebsten in Deutschland. Meine Mutter ist deutscher Abstammung, daher spreche ich fließend deutsch./Ich verfüge über gute Deutschkenntnisse, da meine Mutter deutscher Abstammung ist und ich schon oft in Deutschland war.

c) Bewerbung auf eine Stellenanzeige

Raimundweg 24
D-81677 München
Germany

Ms Barbara Sanderson
Personnel Department
Anglia Computer Systems Ltd.
Woolstone Business Park
Milton Keynes
MK15 OBW
England

17 February 19..

Dear Ms Sanderson,

With reference to the advertisement in yesterday's Guardian/in the Guardian of 16 February, I would like to apply for the post of Systems Analyst.

I am working at the moment as a systems analyst/in a similar position for an American computer firm which has a branch office here in Munich. I have always enjoyed the work/found the work interesting and varied, but the project I am working on comes to an end in two months/the branch office here is being closed, so I am looking for a similar post, preferably in England. My mother is English (by birth) so I speak fluent English./I have a good command of English because my mother is English and I have spent a considerable amount of time in England.

Der als Anlage beigefügte Lebenslauf (und die Zeugnisabschriften) gibt (geben) Auskunft über meinen beruflichen Werdegang. Für weitere Auskünfte stehe ich Ihnen gerne zur Verfügung.

Der früheste Eintrittstermin wäre der 2. Januar, aber ich könnte jederzeit zu einer persönlichen Vorstellung nach Wolfenbüttel kommen. Ihre Antwort erwarte ich mit Interesse./Ihrer Antwort sehe ich mit Interesse entgegen.

Mit freundlichen Grüßen

Alan Davies

Anlagen
Lebenslauf
2 Zeugnisabschriften

The enclosed CV gives details of my career to date. I shall be happy to provide any further information that may be required.

The earliest date on which I could start work would be 2 April but I could come to Milton Keynes for an interview/make myself available for an interview at any time.

I look forward to hearing from you.

Yours sincerely,

Franz Enkenmeyer

6. Asking for a reference

Sehr geehrter Herr Frank,

ich habe mich bei der Firma Schwabe & Co. als Übersetzer beworben und möchte Sie bitten, mir bei Bedarf eine Referenz auszustellen./möchte Ihren Namen als Referenz angeben.

Mit freundlichen Grüßen

William Grant

6. Bitte um Referenz

Dear Mr Wiseman,

I have applied for a position as a translator with the North Sea Oil Corporation and would be very grateful if you could supply them with a reference should this be required./I would like to give your name as a referee.

Yours sincerely,

Karen Pichler

7. Giving a reference

Sehr geehrte Damen und Herren,

mit Ihrem Brief/Schreiben vom 27.8. baten Sie um Auskunft über Herrn William Grant.

Ich kenne Herrn Grant seit fünf Jahren./Herr Grant ist seit fünf Jahren/war fünf Jahre bei uns als Übersetzer tätig. Er ist ein Mann von einwandfreiem Charakter und sehr zuverlässig. Seine Arbeit erledigt er gewissenhaft und termingerecht. Herr Grant wird von seinen Kollegen geschätzt und ist wegen seiner freundlichen und ungezwungenen Art/trotz seines stillen und etwas zurückhaltenden Wesens allgemein beliebt.

Meiner Ansicht nach ist er für die bei Ihnen zu besetzende Stelle (gut) geeignet.

Mit freundlichen Grüßen

Gustav Frank

7. Ausstellung einer Referenz

Dear Mrs Selhurst,

In your letter of 27 August you ask me for my opinion of Karen Pichler's suitability for the post you are offering.

I have known Ms Pichler for five years./Ms Pichler has been working here/worked here for five years as a translator. She is a thoroughly honest and dependable person who works conscientiously and keeps to deadlines. She enjoys the respect of her colleagues and is well liked for her friendly and easy-going manner./ in spite of her quiet and rather retiring nature.

In my opinion she is well suited for the post of translator./for the position mentioned.

Yours sincerely,

David Wiseman

E. Useful phrases according to function

1. Saying thank you

For a letter

personal letter: Vielen *od.* Herzlichen Dank für Deinen Brief / für Deine freundlichen Zeilen.
fairly formal letter: Ich bedanke mich für Ihren Brief.
formal business letter: Wir bestätigen dankend den Eingang *od.* Empfang Ihres Schreibens [vom 5. 9. 89].

E. Formulierungshilfen für verschiedene Situationen

1. Dank

Für einen Brief

persönlicher Brief: Many thanks / Thanks for your letter.
Thank you for your letter.
Geschäftsbrief: We thank you for your letter of 6 September 1989.
formeller Geschäftsbrief: We acknowledge with thanks your letter of the 6. 9. 1989.

For an invitation

Herzlichen Dank für die Einladung [zum Abendessen / zu Deiner Party]. Ich werde bestimmt kommen und freue mich schon sehr darauf. / Leider kann ich nicht kommen, weil ...

Ich bedanke mich für Ihre freundliche Einladung [zum Abendessen / zum Empfang / zur Hochzeit Ihrer Tochter], die ich gerne annehme / die ich leider nicht annehmen kann[, da ich schon anderweitig verpflichtet bin] *(formell)*.

Für eine Einladung

Many thanks for the invitation [to dinner / to your party]. I'd love to come and I'm really looking forward to it. / Unfortunately I can't come because ... *(coll.)*

Richard Edwards has [great] pleasure in accepting / [greatly] regrets he is unable to accept Susan Stewart's kind invitation to dinner / the kind invitation of the Cultural Attaché to a reception / Mr and Mrs David Banks' kind invitation to the wedding of their daughter *(formal)*.
oder:
Richard Edwards thanks ... for his/her/their kind invitation to ..., which he has pleasure in accepting / which he regrets he is unable to accept [due to a previous engagement] *(formal)*.

For a gift

Vielen / Herzlichen / Tausend Dank für das reizende Geschenk / für die schönen Blumen. Das war doch wirklich nicht nötig. / Es war sehr lieb / sehr nett von Dir. Du hast meinen Geschmack genau getroffen. / Es ist genau das, was ich wollte.

Für ein Geschenk

Thank you very much / *(coll.)* Many thanks / Thank you [ever *(coll.)*] so much for the delightful present / for the lovely flowers.
You really shouldn't have [bothered] *(coll.)*. / It was really sweet / kind of you. It's just what I wanted.

For help / donations

Ich bin Ihnen sehr dankbar für die viele Mühe, die Sie sich [meinetwegen] gemacht haben / daß Sie sich [meinetwegen] soviel Mühe gemacht haben.

Ich kann Dir gar nicht sagen, wie dankbar Erich und ich Dir sind, daß Du uns so hilfreich zur Seite gestanden hast.

Haben Sie herzlichsten Dank für Ihre wertvolle Hilfe. / Ich möchte Ihnen unseren herzlichsten Dank für Ihre wertvolle Hilfe aussprechen.

Ich möchte Ihnen im Namen der Abteilung / meiner Kollegen unseren aufrichtigen Dank für Ihre großzügige Spende ausdrücken *(formell)*.

Für Hilfeleistungen / Spenden

I am most grateful for / I greatly appreciate all the trouble you have taken [on my behalf].

Jim and I cannot thank you enough for helping us out.

Please accept / May I offer you our warmest thanks for your valuable assistance *(formal)*.

I would like to offer you on behalf of the department / my colleagues our most sincere *or* grateful thanks for your generous donation *(formal)*.

2. Greetings

On a postcard

Schöne / Viele / Herzliche Grüße aus Freiburg / Spanien
Es grüßen recht herzlich Stephan und Inge

For a birthday

Herzliche Grüße / Herzlichen Glückwunsch / Alles Gute zum Geburtstag

For Christmas [and the New Year]

Frohe *od.* Fröhliche Weihnachten / Ein gesegnetes *od.* frohes Weihnachtsfest [und viel Glück im neuen Jahr / und die besten Wünsche zum neuen Jahr / und einen guten Rutsch ins neue Jahr]

2. Grüße

Auf einer Postkarte

Greetings / Best wishes from the Outer Hebrides
Wish you were here!
All best wishes [from] Helen and Norman

Zum Geburtstag

Many happy returns [of the day]
Happy Birthday
All good *or* best wishes for your birthday

Zu Weihnachten [und zum neuen Jahr]

[Best wishes for] a Merry *or* Happy Christmas and a Prosperous New Year
Christmas Greetings

For Easter

Frohe *od.* Fröhliche Ostern / Ein frohes Osterfest

Zu Ostern

[Best wishes for a] Happy Easter

For a wedding

Dem glücklichen Paar viel Freude am Hochzeitstag [und viel Glück im künftigen gemeinsamen Leben]

Zu einer Hochzeit

Every good wish to the happy couple / to the bride and bridegroom on their wedding day [and in the years to come]

For an exam

Viel Erfolg bei der bevorstehenden Prüfung
Alles Gute zum Abitur

Zu einer Prüfung

Every success in your [forthcoming] exams.
All good wishes for your A-levels / GCSEs

For a house move

Viel Glück im neuen Heim

Zum Umzug

Every happiness in your new home

For an illness

Gute Besserung!

Bei einem Krankheitsfall

Get well soon!
All best wishes for a speedy recovery

3. Congratulations

Herzlichen Glückwunsch / Herzliche Glückwünsche / Ich gratuliere / Wir gratulieren [herzlichst] zum neuen Baby / zur bestandenen Prüfung / zum neuen Job / zur Beförderung / zur Verlobung.

Ich habe mich sehr über Deinen Erfolg bei der Prüfung gefreut. Das hast Du gut gemacht!

Ich habe / Wir haben mit großer Freude von Deiner / Eurer bevorstehenden Vermählung gehört. Herzlichen Glückwunsch und alles Gute für die Zukunft!

3. Gratulation

Congratulations / Many congratulations / I/We congratulate you [most sincerely] on the [arrival of the] new baby / on passing the exam / on the new job / on your promotion / on your engagement.

I was delighted to hear of your success in the exam. Well done!

I/We have just heard the wonderful news of your forthcoming marriage and offer you my/our sincerest *or* heartiest congratulations and best wishes for your future happiness.

4. Apologizing, expressing regret

Es tut mir aufrichtig leid / Ich bedaure sehr, daß ich Ihnen soviel Kummer bereitet habe.

Ich muß mich bei Ihnen entschuldigen, daß ich Sie fälschlicherweise beschuldigt habe.

Ich nehme alles zurück und bitte vielmals / tausendmal um Entschuldigung.

Nimm es mir nicht übel, daß ich nicht früher geschrieben habe. / Es tut mir leid, daß Du so lange auf ein Lebenszeichen von mir warten mußtest.

Ich muß mich für die so späte Beantwortung Ihres Briefes entschuldigen / muß mich entschuldigen, daß diese Geburtstagswünsche so verspätet eintreffen.

Ich bitte [vielmals] um Entschuldigung / muß Sie für meinen Fehler um Verzeihung bitten.

Bitte entschuldigen Sie mein Versehen.

Verzeih! Es war alles nur ein dummes Mißverständnis.

4. Entschuldigung, Bedauern

I am really *or* genuinely sorry / I greatly *or* very much regret that I have caused you so much trouble.

I owe you an apology / Please accept my humble apology for the wrongful accusation.

I take back all that I said and apologize unreservedly.

Sorry not to have written earlier. / *(joc.)* I'm sorry you've had to wait such a long time for any sign of life.

I must apologize for the delay in replying to your letter / for being so late with these birthday wishes.

I beg you to / I must ask you to forgive / excuse my mistake *(formal)*.

Please excuse my oversight.

Sorry! It was all a stupid misunderstanding.

Zu unserem Bedauern müssen wir Ihnen mitteilen, daß wir diesen Artikel nicht mehr führen *(formell)*.

We regret to have to inform you / To our regret we must inform you that we no longer stock this item *(formal)*.

Leider können wir diesen Posten nicht einzeln liefern.

Unfortunately we cannot supply this part separately.

5. Cancelling a visit

Leider wird aus meinem geplanten Besuch zu Weihnachten nichts werden. / Leider kann ich Deine / Eure Einladung nicht annehmen, da etwas dazwischengekommen ist. Meine Mutter ist schwer krank. / Ich habe mir das Bein gebrochen. / Ich muß wegen dringender Geschäfte verreisen. Kannst Du mich auch bei Deiner Schwester entschuldigen? Es tut mir sehr leid / Ich finde es wirklich schade, daß wir uns nicht sehen werden.

5. Absagen

Unfortunately / *(coll.)* I'm afraid I can't come to see you as arranged at Christmas / we can't accept your invitation for the 9th owing to unforeseen circumstances. My mother is seriously ill. / I have broken my leg. / I have to go away on urgent business. Please tell your sister from me how sorry I am / *(formal)* convey my apologies to your sister. It is a great disappointment to me. / I shall really miss seeing you.

6. Expressing sympathy

Du Arme / Armer! Es tut mir wirklich leid, daß Du diese Operation vor Dir hast.

Inge erzählte mir von Deinem Unfall. Du tust mir wirklich leid. / Du hast mein volles Mitgefühl, daß Du so etwas durchmachen mußtest. / Ich kann es Dir nachfühlen, was Du durchgemacht hast, und hoffe, daß es Dir bald wieder besser geht.

6. Teilnahme

You poor thing! I am sorry to hear that you have to have this operation *(coll.)*.

Francis told me of your accident. I feel really sorry for you / I feel for you / I sympathize with you having to go through such an experience, and I hope you will soon be on the mend.

7. Condolences

Zutiefst erschüttert lasen / hörten wir vom Tode Ihres / Deines Mannes.

Ich möchte Ihnen unser aufrichtiges Beileid zu Ihrem schweren Verlust ausdrücken. / Bitte nehmen Sie mein tiefempfundenes Mitgefühl zu diesem schweren Verlust entgegen. / Ich möchte Ihnen meine herzliche Anteilnahme zu diesem schweren Verlust aussprechen. / Wir möchten Dir unsere tiefe Anteilnahme *od.* unser aufrichtiges Beileid ausdrücken.

Wir sind alle in Gedanken bei Dir. Laß es uns bitte wissen, wenn wir Dir irgendwie behilflich sein können.

7. Kondolenz

I was/We were deeply saddened / It was a great shock to read/hear of the death of your husband.

I would like to assure you of our deepest sympathy in your tragic loss *(formal)*. / You have all my/our sympathy in this great loss. / I/We would like to say how sorry I am/we are. / I/We would like to express my/our sincere condolences *(formal)*.

I am/We are all thinking of you at this time / You are very much in my/our thoughts. Please let me know if there is anything I/we can do.

8. Invitations

Möchtest Du und Georg / Möchtet Ihr beide am 14. zu uns zum Abendessen kommen? Wir haben unsere neuen Nachbarn eingeladen, und ich dachte, Ihr würdet sie auch gerne kennenlernen.

Es würde uns sehr freuen, wenn Sie und Ihre Frau am 14. um 20 Uhr zu uns zum Abendessen kommen könnten. Außer Ihnen haben wir unsere neuen Nachbarn, Herrn und Frau Meyer, eingeladen.

8. Einladungen

I wonder if you and Betty could make it / Would you and Betty be free for dinner on the 14th? We are having our new neighbours, the Wilsons, round, and I'm sure you'd like to meet them *(coll.)*.

We would be very pleased if you and your wife could come to dinner/join us for dinner on the evening of the 14th. We have also invited our new neighbours, Bill and Angela Wilson.

Invitations to a party are usually by word of mouth; there is no set form for written invitations.

Please come to Jennifer's 40th birthday party from 8 o'clock on 23rd September at 12 Parkhurst Gardens, SW4.
Buffet and disco RSVP 081–323 1279

Invitations to a wedding are usually only to the reception, and are preceded or accompanied by a wedding announcement, which occasionally is an invitation as well:

Irene Brinkmann Stefan Hopf

Wir heiraten am Samstag, dem 20. April 19.., um 14 Uhr in der Pfarrkirche Landsberg.

[Zu dieser Feier laden wir Euch herzlich ein.]

Goethestraße 12 Ulrichsweg 4
Landsberg Altötting

more formal style:

Dr. Heinrich und Frau Gertrud Brinkmann geben die bevorstehende Vermählung ihrer Tochter Irene mit Stefan Hopf bekannt.

Die Trauung findet am Samstag, dem 20. April 19.., um 14 Uhr in der Pfarrkirche Landsberg statt.

formell, auf einer Karte:

David Bruce
at Home
Sunday December 5th at 12.00 noon

RSVP Wine and cheese

Bei einer Hochzeit wird gewöhnlich zur Trauungszeremonie und zu einem anschließenden Empfang eingeladen. Freunde können auch eine „Evening Invitation" erhalten, die sich nur auf eine Party nach dem Empfang bezieht.

formell, in gedruckter Form:

Mr and Mrs James Merriweather request the pleasure of your company at the wedding of their daughter Jane to Timothy Wade at St. Swithin's Church, Compton Abbas, on Saturday June 25th 19.. at 3 p.m. [and afterwards at the Golden Cross Hotel]
RSVP

Es wäre wirklich sehr schön, wenn Du im September mit uns nach Italien kommen könntest. / Wir planen für den September eine Italienreise und dachten uns, Du möchtest vielleicht mit uns kommen.

It would be wonderful if you could come with us / join us on our trip to Scotland in September. / We are going to Scotland in September and wonder if you would be interested in coming along.

Wäre es vielleicht möglich, daß Du zu Ostern zu uns kommst? Hans besucht zu der Zeit einen Kurs, Du könntest also in seinem Zimmer schlafen.

Is there any chance that you could come and stay with us at Easter? Edward will be away on a course so you could have his room.

9. Requests

9. Bitten

Könntest Du mich bitte am Donnerstag anrufen? / *(formeller:)* Wäre es Ihnen möglich, mich Donnerstag anzurufen?

Please could you give me a ring on Thursday / Would you be so good *or* kind as to telephone me on Thursday?

Ich wäre Ihnen für die Zusendung eines Musters dankbar.

I would be grateful if you could send me a sample.

Ich wäre Ihnen dankbar, wenn Sie mir in dieser Situation behilflich sein könnten.

I would be grateful for *or* would appreciate your help in this matter.

Ich möchte Sie bitten, das schriftlich zu bestätigen.

Would you please confirm this in writing? / Would you mind confirming this in writing?

Wäre es Ihnen vielleicht möglich, den Empfang für uns zu organisieren?

Could you possibly / Would it be possible for you to organize the reception for us?

Wir bitten um postwendende Bezahlung *od.* Begleichung der Rechnung.

I must ask you to let us have / *(höfliche Forderung:)* Kindly let us have your payment by return of post.

Requesting information

Um Auskunft

Könnten Sie mir bitte die Preise Ihrer Elektroherde mitteilen / Auskunft über Ihre Elektroherde geben?

Please could you tell me / let me know the prices / send me details of your range of electric cookers.

Ich möchte nicht neugierig sein, aber ich würde gern wissen, wo Sie dieses Kleid gekauft haben.

I don't wish to seem inquisitive, but I'd love to know where you bought that dress.

Ich wäre Ihnen dankbar, wenn Sie mir mitteilen könnten, wo ich Ersatzteile bekommen kann.

I would be very grateful for any information you can give me on the availability of spare parts.

Bitte teilen Sie uns unbedingt Ihre neue Anschrift mit *(formell)*. / Vergiß nicht, uns Deine neue Adresse zu schreiben.

Do not forget to inform us of *(formal)* / let us know your new address.

Requesting clarification

Um Klarstellung/Erklärung

Wir bitten um eine Erklärung für Ihre Abreise. / Könnten Sie uns bitte den Grund Ihrer Abreise angeben? / Bitte erklären Sie uns, warum Sie [überraschend] abgereist sind.

Please could you give the reason for your departure / explain the reason for your departure *or* why you have left.

Ich wäre Ihnen dankbar, wenn Sie mir den zweiten Absatz Ihres Briefes genauer erklärten.

I would be grateful if you could clarify the second paragraph in your letter.

Bitte teilen Sie uns mit, warum Sie die Waren nicht mehr annehmen wollen.

May I ask you why you no longer want the goods?

10. Explaining

10. Erklärung, Begründung

Bitte berücksichtigen Sie, daß ich keine Gelegenheit hatte, die Rede vorzubereiten.

You must understand / You will appreciate that I have had no time to prepare a speech.

Er hat wegen fehlender Aufstiegsmöglichkeiten gekündigt. / Er hat gekündigt, weil es für ihn keine Aufstiegsmöglichkeiten gab.

The reason why he left *(coll.)* / The reason for his departure was the lack of prospects. / He left because of *or* on account of the lack of prospects / because there were no prospects of promotion.

Aufgrund seiner Einstellung mir gegenüber werde ich ihn in Zukunft nicht mehr beschäftigen.

In view of *or* In the light of *or* Given his uncooperative attitude I am not giving him any more work.

Die verspätete Lieferung ergab sich aus Gründen, auf die wir keinen Einfluß hatten.

The delay in delivery is due to circumstances beyond our control.

11. Advice, suggestions

11. Ratschläge, Vorschläge

Ich finde, Du solltest es [lieber] Deinem Vater überlassen.

I think you should *or* ought to let your father do it.

[Wenn ich Dir einen Rat geben darf –] frag doch Herrn Klee.

[If I may make a suggestion –] why don't you ask Mrs Potterton?

Ich schlage vor, wir fahren mit dem Zug. / Darf ich vorschlagen, mit dem Zug zu fahren?

I suggest we take the train. / Might I suggest we take the train?

Ich würde Dir raten, nicht hinzugehen.

My advice would be / I would advise you not to go.

Ich würde vorschlagen, sie alle auf einmal einzuladen. / Wenn Du mich fragst – ich würde sie alle auf einmal einladen.

My idea would be to invite them all at once. / If you ask me *or* ask my opinion *or* want my advice, I would invite them all at once.

An Deiner Stelle würde ich das Geld annehmen.

If I were you I would just take the money.

Wenn ich die Möglichkeit hätte, würde ich nicht zögern.

[If I were] given the chance, I wouldn't hesitate.

Vor allen Dingen nimm Dir warme Kleidung mit. / Nimm Dir auf alle Fälle warme Kleidung mit.

Be sure to take / Whatever you do, take thick clothes with you.

Geben Sie ihm das Geld unter keinen Umständen.

Under no circumstances let him have the money.

Sieh zu *od.* Achte darauf, daß Du genug zu Essen im Haus hast.

Make sure you have enough food in the house.

Ich würde Ihnen raten / Es wäre [vielleicht] ratsam *od.* gut, es Ihrer Frau zu sagen.

It might be / would be a good idea/wise/advisable/ as well to tell your wife about it.

Es ist immer gut, ein paar Sicherungen in Reserve zu haben.

It is always a good idea / wise / advisable / as well to have spare fuses handy.

Es ist oft von Vorteil / Es hat seine Vorteile / Vieles spricht dafür, die Sache selbst zu erledigen.

There is something / a lot to be said for doing the job oneself.

Du solltest Dir mal überlegen, ob Du Dein Kind nicht zu Hause bekommen möchtest.

You should consider [the possibility of] having the baby at home.

Und wenn ich Dir das Geld leihen würde?

What if *or* Suppose I were to lend you the money?

Vielleicht hättest Du Lust, Deinen Onkel zu besuchen / *(ugs.)* Wie wär's mit einem Besuch bei Deinem Onkel, während Du hier bist?

You might like / care to visit your uncle / *(coll.)* How about going to see your uncle while you are here?

12. Instructions, need, compulsion

12. Anweisung, Bedürfnis, Zwang

Die Stange mit beiden Händen anfassen und fest drücken.

[You should] place both hands on the bar and push hard.

Das Papier wird wie folgt in die Maschine eingeführt / ist wie folgt in die Maschine einzuführen.

The paper is inserted in the machine as follows: ...

Sehen Sie bitte zu, daß Sie bis 7 Uhr hier sind.

Please *or* Kindly ensure that / see to it that you are here by 7 a.m.

Sie müssen / sollen sich bei Ankunft beim diensthabenden Feldwebel melden. / Sie melden sich bei Ankunft beim diensthabenden Feldwebel.

You must / You are to / You will report to the duty sergeant on arrival.

Du hast zu tun, was ich sage, da gibt's nichts!

You have [got] to do as I say, there are no two ways about it.

Für den Posten müssen Sie eine Lehrerausbildung haben / ist eine Lehrerausbildung Voraussetzung.

You have to have *or* You need a teaching qualification in order to be considered / A teaching qualification is a requirement for this post.

Es ist [absolut] notwendig / unbedingt angeraten / Pflicht *od.* Vorschrift, Schutzkleidung zu tragen.

It is essential / necessary / indispensable / obligatory *or* compulsory to wear protective clothing.

Alle sind verpflichtet, die Erklärung zu unterschreiben.

Everyone is obliged / required to sign this declaration.

Er wurde von den Einbrechern gezwungen, den Safe zu öffnen.

He was forced by the thieves to open the safe.

Muß ich wirklich jetzt kommen? / Ich muß doch nicht etwa jetzt kommen?

Do I really / Surely I don't have to come now?

Sie dürfen keinesfalls Alkohol zu sich nehmen, nachdem Sie diese Pillen genommen haben.

Under no circumstances *or* On no account must you drink alcohol after taking these pills.

13. Approval / disapproval

13. Billigung / Mißbilligung

Ich mag das / mag das nicht *od.* Es gefällt mir / gefällt mir nicht, wie er mich ansieht.

I like / don't like *or* object to the way he looks at me.

Ich liebe / hasse diese Musik *od.* kann diese Musik nicht ausstehen.

I love / hate *or (coll.)* can't stand this music.

Das ist genau das, was ich will. / Genau das will ich nicht.

This is just what I want / what I don't want.

Ich bin von Jazz begeistert *od.* bin ein [begeisterter] Jazzfan. / Ich habe für Jazz nichts übrig.

I am keen on jazz *or* a jazz enthusiast *or* a jazz fan. / I dislike jazz.

Ich stimme diesem Programm völlig / keineswegs zu *od.* bin mit diesem Programm völlig / gar nicht einverstanden.

I approve of *or* endorse *or* am in favour of this policy. / I disapprove of *or* am against *or* opposed to this policy.

Sie unterstützt *od.* befürwortet diesen Plan / ist gegen diesen Plan.

She supports *or* backs this plan. / She opposes this plan.

Er ist ein Befürworter / Gegner von Tierversuchen *od.* ist für / gegen Tierversuche.

He is a supporter / opponent of animal experiments.

Ich bewundere ihn *od.* schätze ihn sehr *od.* habe eine hohe Meinung von ihm / schätze ihn wenig *od.* habe eine schlechte Meinung von ihm.

I admire *or* have a high regard for *or* a high opinion of him. / I have little regard for *or* a low opinion of him.

Sie stehen Ihrer Bewerbung wohlwollend / ablehnend gegenüber.

They view your application favourably / unfavourably *or* take a favourable / unfavourable view of your application.

14. Permitting / forbidding

14. Erlaubnis / Verbot

Du darfst es ihm sagen / darfst es ihm nicht sagen.

You may tell him [if you wish] / may not *or* must not tell him.

Es ist uns erlaubt / nicht erlaubt, die Gefangenen zu besuchen.

We are allowed *or* permitted / not allowed *or* permitted to visit the prisoners.

Rauchen ist hier gestattet / verboten *od.* nicht gestattet.

Smoking is allowed *or* permitted / forbidden *or* prohibited in here.

Ich habe nichts dagegen, wenn Sie sich den Tag freinehmen wollen. / Ich muß Ihnen verbieten, weiteren Urlaub zu nehmen. / Ich bin nicht damit einverstanden, daß Sie weiteren Urlaub nehmen.

I have no objection to *or* nothing against your taking the day off. / I [expressly] forbid you to take / I cannot agree to your taking any more time off work.

15. Desires, intentions

15. Wünsche, Absichten

Was willst Du werden, wenn Du groß bist?

What do you want to be when you grow up?

Ich möchte gern Pilot werden, aber das geht aus gesundheitlichen Gründen nicht.

I would like to be a pilot, but my health is not good enough.

Ich will / möchte gern nach Italien fahren.

I want to go / I would like to go to Italy.

Mich zieht es an den Nil. / Mein großer Wunsch ist es, eine Reise auf dem Nil zu machen.

I have a great desire / longing to take a trip on the Nile.

Du kannst gehen, wenn Du willst.

You can go if you wish *or* want.

Sie hat es sich in den Kopf gesetzt / Ihr größter Wunsch ist, Archäologie zu studieren.

She has set her heart on studying *or* wants above all else to study archaeology.

Ich habe es mir zum Ziel gesetzt, ihn unter allen Umständen zu einem Geständnis zu bewegen.

I mean *or* intend *or* propose to make him confess, come what may.

Bitte teilen Sie mir mit, was Sie vorhaben / teilen Sie mir Ihre Pläne mit.

Please let me know your intentions / what your plans are *or* what you have in mind.

Glaubst Du, sie hat ihn wirklich bewußt ermuntert? – Ja, sie wollte ihn eindeutig [dazu] anstiften.

Do you think she really intended *or* meant to encourage him? – Yes, she had every intention of leading him on.

Mein Ziel ist es / Es ist meine Absicht / Ich habe vor, die beiden Firmen zu fusionieren.

My intention *or* What I have in mind is to / I am planning to merge the two companies.

Sein Ziel ist es / Er plant, hier eine Fabrik zu bauen.

His aim *or* object is to build a factory here.

Mir kommt es allein darauf an, daß es die Arbeiter besser haben.

My sole aim *or* purpose is to better the workers' lot.

Ich habe keineswegs vor / die Absicht, Sie zu entlassen.

I have no intention of dismissing you.

16. Opinions

Ich halte sie für / Meiner Meinung nach ist sie / Ich finde, sie ist die größte Blues-Sängerin.

Meiner Ansicht *od.* Meinung nach / So wie ich es sehe, sind neue Gesetze keine Lösung.

Ich finde / Ich habe den Eindruck, daß junge Leute heute allgemein höflicher sind.

Ich habe das Gefühl, man will uns den Vertrag aufzwingen.

Meine Meinung ist / Ich bin der Meinung, daß Frauen noch immer benachteiligt sind.

Wie ich über die Sache denke, ist Dir offensichtlich nicht wichtig.

Mit seiner Reaktion auf den Vorschlag hatte niemand gerechnet.

Wie er es sieht, liegt die Zukunft der Firma in der Lebensmittelherstellung.

Was ist Ihre Meinung dazu? / Wie sehen Sie die Sache?

Ich teile Ihre Meinung *od.* Ansicht. / Ich bin ganz Ihrer Meinung.

Wir sind uns völlig / teilweise / im großen und ganzen einig. / Wir sind einer Meinung.

Das Ergebnis seiner Ermittlungen stimmt nicht mit Ihren Aussagen überein / untermauert Ihre Aussagen nicht.

Ich bin völlig anderer Meinung / kann Ihrer Meinung nicht zustimmen *od.* beipflichten / kann Ihre Ansicht nicht teilen.

Einigen wir uns [doch] darauf, daß wir in diesem Punkt verschiedener Meinung sind!

16. Meinungen

I think she is / In my opinion she is / I believe her to be the greatest living blues singer.

To my mind / In my opinion / As I see it, further legislation is not the answer.

[Personally] I find *or* reckon/have the impression that young people are generally politer nowadays.

I feel we are being pushed into accepting the deal.

My view [of the matter] / My opinion is that women are still underprivileged.

My feelings / thoughts on the matter are evidently of no importance to you.

His reaction to the proposal was quite unexpected.

He sees the future of the company as lying in food manufacturing.

What is your opinion on this / your view of the matter?

I share your opinion *or* point of view. / I agree entirely with what you say.

We are in complete / partial / broad agreement / thinking on the same lines.

The results of the investigation do not agree with *or* are not consistent with / do not bear out *or* corroborate your claims.

I completely disagree *or* cannot agree at all with your view / with what you say. / I cannot accept your view / what you say.

We must agree to differ on this.

17. Right / wrong

Ich sehe es jetzt ein, Du hattest recht und ich unrecht.

Sie haben diese Behauptung mit Recht angezweifelt – sie stimmt tatsächlich nicht.

Es war nicht richtig, daß sie ihn entlassen haben. / Sie hätten ihn nicht entlassen sollen.

Seine Position anzufechten war falsch, obgleich es zu der Zeit richtig erschien.

Du hast recht / unrecht, daß ... *od.* Deine Annahme, daß ..., ist richtig / falsch.

Diese Behauptung steht im krassen Widerspruch zu den Tatsachen, soweit sie uns bekannt sind.

17. Richtig / falsch

I see now you were right and I was wrong.

You were quite right to query this assertion – it is indeed incorrect.

They were wrong *or* It was wrong of them to dismiss him. / They should not have dismissed him.

Challenging his position was the wrong thing to do, even though it seemed the right thing at the time.

You are correct / wrong in your assumption that ... *or* Your assumption that ... is correct / wrong.

To say this is flying in the face of the facts *or* contrary to the facts as we know them.

18. Doubt / certainty

Ich bin nicht sicher / Ich weiß es nicht [genau] / Ich kann es nicht mit Sicherheit sagen, ob er kommen wird.

Er weiß noch immer nicht / ist noch immer unentschieden, welche Schritte er unternehmen soll. / Er fragt sich noch immer, was er machen soll.

Es bestehen immer noch Zweifel, ob der Plan auch ausgeführt werden kann / ob das Projekt eine Zukunft hat.

Es ist zweifelhaft / fraglich / [sehr] die Frage, ob wir dadurch etwas gewinnen können.

Ich habe meine Zweifel [an seinen Fähigkeiten].

Man kann kaum erwarten, daß er solchen Bedingungen zustimmt, aber man weiß ja nie.

Ich bin [ganz *od.* absolut] sicher *od.* [fest] davon überzeugt, daß sie es getan hat.

Wir sind ganz zuversichtlich *od.* voller Zuversicht, daß wir gewinnen werden.

Es besteht kein Zweifel / Es steht außer Zweifel / Es ist unbestreitbar *od.* nicht zu leugnen, daß sie die beste Chefin ist, die wir je hatten.

Niemand kann abstreiten *od.* leugnen, daß er viel Erfahrung auf diesem Gebiet hat.

Es wird bestimmt einige Zeit Unruhe geben.

18. Zweifel / Sicherheit

I'm not sure *or* certain / I don't know [for sure] / I cannot say with any certainty whether he will come.

He is still uncertain *or* undecided as to what action to take. / He is still wondering what to do.

There is still considerable doubt about *or* as to the feasibility of the plan / surrounding the future of the project.

It is a matter for debate *or* debatable / doubtful whether we will gain anything by this.

I have my doubts [about his competence].

One can hardly expect him to agree to such terms, but you never know.

I'm [quite *or* absolutely] certain *or* sure / positive *or* convinced that she did it.

We are [quietly] confident that we will win.

There can be no doubt *or* question / It is beyond doubt *or* question *or* dispute / It is indisputable *or* undeniable that she is the best boss we have had.

Nobody can deny that he has great experience in this field.

There is bound to be a period of unrest.

19. Expressions of feeling

Amazement

Ich war erstaunt darüber / Mit Erstaunen hörte ich, daß Du Innsbruck verlassen hast.

Zu meinem Erstaunen *od.* Zu meiner großen Überraschung stimmte sie ohne Widerrede zu.

Er war wie vom Blitz getroffen / wie vom Donner gerührt, als er merkte, daß sein Freund ihn betrogen hatte.

Ich war fassungslos / erschüttert, als ich es erfuhr.

Die Nachricht war ein Schock für uns / war ein Blitz aus heiterem Himmel / kam völlig unerwartet.

Der Bau dieses Schiffes war eine enorme / erstaunliche Leistung für die damalige Zeit.

Die Kombination von gelbem Hemd und rosaroten Hosen war schon etwas schockierend.

Disappointment

Das Scheitern des Projekts war eine bittere Enttäuschung / ein harter Schlag für ihn / bedeutete einen schweren Rückschlag für ihn.

Seine Hoffnungen wurden zunichte [gemacht], als man seine Bitte ablehnte.

19. Gefühlsäußerungen

Erstaunen

I was surprised / *(stronger)* amazed *or* astonished to hear that you had left Glasgow.

To my surprise / *(stronger)* amazement *or* astonishment she agreed without a murmur.

He was thunderstruck *or* flabbergasted *or* dumbfounded when he discovered his best friend had tricked him.

I was stunned / *(stronger)* shattered by the news.

The news was quite a shock / a bombshell / a bolt from the blue / took us all by surprise.

The building of this ship was a staggering *or* an astounding achievement for its time.

The combination of a yellow shirt and pink trousers was rather startling.

Enttäuschung

The failure of the project was a bitter disappointment / a heavy blow / a serious setback for him.

His hopes were dashed when his request was refused.

Wir waren bitter enttäuscht *od.* bestürzt / [sehr] ernüchtert.

We were bitterly disappointed *or* sick with disappointment / dismayed / [completely] disenchanted.

Ich fühlte mich im Stich gelassen / betrogen, als er sein Versprechen nicht hielt.

I felt [badly] let down / betrayed when he went back on his promise.

Unser Jahresgewinn entsprach nicht den Erwartungen *od.* war nicht so hoch wie erwartet.

Our annual profits have not come up to *or* have fallen short of expectations.

Sie sahen alle niedergeschlagen / deprimiert / niedergeschmettert aus.

They all looked dejected / crestfallen / *(coll.)* down in the dumps after their defeat.

Alle unsere Bemühungen, die Umweltverschmutzung zu bekämpfen, wurden zunichte gemacht.

All our attempts to combat environmental pollution have been frustrated.

Hope

Hoffnung

Diese neuen Entwicklungen erfüllen uns mit Hoffnung / geben uns Hoffnung / sind vielversprechend / verheißen Gutes für die Zukunft.

These new developments inspire hope / are raising our hopes / are very promising *or* encouraging / augur well [for the future].

Ich setze große Hoffnungen / Erwartungen / Ich setze meine Hoffnungen auf diesen jungen Mann.

I have high hopes *or* expectations of / am pinning my hopes on this young man.

Alle Anzeichen sind positiv / vielversprechend.

All the signs are favourable *or* propitious *or* auspicious.

Es besteht wenigstens ein Hoffnungsschimmer.

There is at last a ray of hope *or* a break in the clouds.

Wir können nicht viel tun, wir können nur das beste hoffen / wir müssen eben optimistisch sein.

There is little we can do, so we must simply hope for the best / look on the bright side.

Fear

Angst

Ich habe große Angst davor, eine Rede halten zu müssen.

I am terrified of *or* dread having to give a speech.

Sie hatte Angst um ihr Leben / fürchtete, daß sie den Verstand verlöre.

She feared for her life / sanity.

Ich habe im Dunkeln Angst, deshalb gruselte es mir in dem Kerker der alten Burg.

I'm afraid of the dark, so the dungeon in that old castle really gave me the creeps *(coll.)*.

Normalerweise ist sie nicht ängstlich, aber diese Bombendrohungen haben aus ihr ein Nervenbündel gemacht / haben sie ganz nervös gemacht.

She doesn't normally get scared easily, but these bomb threats have turned her into a bundle of nerves / made her very jittery *or* jumpy *or* nervy.

Es gibt keinen Grund zur Besorgnis / Du brauchst dich nicht aufzuregen.

There's no cause for concern / no need to get worked up *or (coll.)* get into a flap.

Sie befürchten / haben Angst / zittern und beben, daß sie ihr ganzes Geld verlieren könnten.

They are apprehensive / worried / anxious that they might lose all their money.

Hoffentlich verlieren sie nicht die Nerven und ziehen sich von dem Geschäft zurück.

I hope they don't get cold feet *(coll.) or* lose their nerve and pull out of the deal.

Meine Befürchtungen erwiesen sich als grundlos. / Ich habe mir unnötig Sorgen gemacht.

My fears / apprehensions turned out to be groundless. / I needn't have worried.

Du brauchst nichts zu fürchten, solange Du ihm gegenüber völlig ehrlich bist.

You've nothing to worry about as long as you're perfectly honest with him.

Weights and Measures / Maße und Gewichte

Metric / Metrisch		GB & US
Weight / Gewichte		
10 milligrams (mg.) *10 Milligramm (mg)*	= 1 centigram (cg.) = *1 Zentigramm (cg)*	= 0.154 grain
100 centigrams *100 Zentigramm*	= 1 gram (g.) = *1 Gramm (g)*	= 15.43 grains
1,000 grams *1 000 Gramm*	= 1 kilogram (kg.) = *1 Kilogramm (kg)*	= 2.205 pounds
1,000 kilograms *1 000 Kilogramm*	= 1 tonne (t.) = *1 Tonne (t)*	= 19.684 hundredweight
Length / Längenmaße		
10 millimetres (mm.) *10 Millimeter (mm)*	= 1 centimetre (cm.) = *1 Zentimeter (cm)*	= 0.394 inch
100 centimetres *100 Zentimeter*	= 1 metre (m.) = *1 Meter (m)*	= 39.4 inches / 1.094 yards
1,000 metres *1 000 Meter*	= 1 kilometre (km.) = *1 Kilometer (km)*	= 0.6214 mile ≈ $^5/_8$ mile
Surface / Flächenmaße		
100 square metres (sq. m.) *100 Quadratmeter (m^2)*	= 1 are = *1 Ar (a)*	= 0.025 acre
100 ares *100 Ar*	= 1 hectare (ha.) = *1 Hektar (ha)*	= 2.471 acres
100 hectares *100 Hektar*	= 1 square kilometre (sq. km.) = *1 Quadratkilometer (km^2)*	= 0.386 square mile
Cubic measure / Raummaße		
1 cubic centimetre (cc) *1 Kubikzentimeter (cm^3)*		= 0.06 cubic inches
1,000,000 cubic centimetres *1 000 000 Kubikzentimeter*	= 1 cubic metre (cu. m.) = *1 Kubikmeter (m^3)*	= 35.714 cubic feet / 1.307 cubic yards
Capacity / Hohlmaße		
10 millilitres (ml.) *10 Milliliter (ml)*	= 1 centilitre (cl.) = *1 Zentiliter (cl)*	
10 centilitres *10 Zentiliter*	= 1 decilitre (dl.) = *1 Deziliter (dl)*	
10 decilitres *10 Deziliter*	= 1 litre (l.) = *1 Liter (l)*	= 1.76 pints (2.1 US pints) / 0.22 gallons (0.264 US gallons)

GB & US		Metric / Metrisch

Weight / Gewichte

	1 grain (gr.)	= 0.065 g
437½ grains	= 1 ounce (oz.)	= 28.35 g
16 drams	= 1 ounce	= 28.35 g
16 ounces	= 1 pound (lb.)	= 0.454 kg
14 pounds	= 1 stone (st.)	= 6.35 kg
2 stone	= 1 quarter	= 12.7 kg
4 quarters	= 1 hundredweight (cwt.)	= 50.8 kg
112 pounds	= 1 hundredweight	= 50.8 kg
100 pounds	= 1 short hundredweight	= 45.4 kg
20 hundredweight	= 1 ton	= 1,016.05 kg
2,000 pounds	= 1 short ton	= 0.907 t
2,240 pounds	= 1 long ton	= 1.016 t

Length / Längenmaße

	1 inch (in.)	= 25.4 mm
12 inches	= 1 foot (ft.)	= 30.48 cm
3 feet	= 1 yard (yd.)	= 0.914 m
5½ yards	= 1 rod, pole, or perch	= 5.029 m
22 yards	= 1 chain	= 20.12 m
220 yards	= 1 furlong	= 201.17 m
8 furlongs	= 1 mile	= 1.609 km
1,760 yards	= 1 mile	= 1.609 km
3 miles	= 1 league	= 4.828 km

Surface / Flächenmaße

	1 square inch	= 6.452 cm^2
144 square inches	= 1 square foot	= 929.03 cm^2
9 square feet	= 1 square yard	= 0.836 m^2
484 square yards	= 1 square chain	= 404.68 m^2
4,840 square yards	= 1 acre	= 0.405 ha
40 square rods	= 1 rood	= 10.1171 a
4 roods	= 1 acre	= 0.405 ha
640 acres	= 1 square mile	= 2.59 km^2 / 259 ha

Cubic measure / Raummaße

	1 cubic inch	= 16.4 cm^3
1,728 cubic inches	= 1 cubic foot	= 0.028 m^3
27 cubic feet	= 1 cubic yard	= 0.764 m^3

Capacity / Hohlmaße

4 gills	= 1 pint (pt.) (1.201 US pints)	= 0.568 l
2 pints	= 1 quart (qt.) (1.201 US quarts)	= 1.136 l
4 quarts	= 1 gallon (gal.) (1.201 US gallons)	= 4.546 l

Temperature Conversion / Temperaturumrechnung

	Fahrenheit (°F)	Celsius (°C)	
Boiling point	212	100	Siedepunkt
	194	90	
	176	80	
	158	70	
	140	60	
	122	50	
	104	40	
Body temperature	98.4	37	Körpertemperatur
	86	30	
	68	20	
	50	10	
Freezing point	32	0	Gefrierpunkt
	14	– 10	
	0	– 17,8	
Absolute Zero	– 459.67	– 273,15	Absoluter Nullpunkt

Conversion / Umrechnung

°F → °C: $(°F - 32) \times \frac{5}{9} = °C$ °C → °F: $°C \times \frac{9}{5} + 32 = °F$

Numbers / Zahlen

Cardinal numbers	*Kardinalzahlen*	Ordinal numbers	*Ordinalzahlen*
1 one	*1 eins, ein...*	1st first	*1. erst...*
2 two	*2 zwei*	2nd second	*2. zweit...*
3 three	*3 drei*	3rd third	*3. dritt...*
4 four	*4 vier*	4th fourth	*4. viert...*
5 five	*5 fünf*	5th fifth	*5. fünft...*
6 six	*6 sechs*	6th sixth	*6. sechst...*
7 seven	*7 sieben*	7th seventh	*7. siebt..., siebent...*
8 eight	*8 acht*	8th eighth	*8. acht...*
9 nine	*9 neun*	9th ninth	*9. neunt...*
10 ten	*10 zehn*	10th tenth	*10. zehnt...*
11 eleven	*11 elf*	11th eleventh	*11. elft...*
12 twelve	*12 zwölf*	12th twelfth	*12. zwölft...*
13 thirteen	*13 dreizehn*	13th thirteenth	*13. dreizehnt...*
14 fourteen	*14 vierzehn*	14th fourteenth	*14. vierzehnt...*
15 fifteen	*15 fünfzehn*	15th fifteenth	*15. fünfzehnt...*
16 sixteen	*16 sechzehn*	16th sixteenth	*16. sechzehnt...*
17 seventeen	*17 siebzehn*	17th seventeenth	*17. siebzehnt...*
18 eighteen	*18 achtzehn*	18th eighteenth	*18. achtzehnt...*
19 nineteen	*19 neunzehn*	19th nineteenth	*19. neunzehnt...*
20 twenty	*20 zwanzig*	20th twentieth	*20. zwanzigst...*
21 twenty-one	*21 einundzwanzig*	21st twenty-first	*21. einundzwanzigst...*
22 twenty-two	*22 zweiundzwanzig*	22nd twenty-second	*22. zweiundzwanzigst...*
23 twenty-three	*23 dreiundzwanzig*	23rd twenty-third	*23. dreiundzwanzigst...*
30 thirty	*30 dreißig*	30th thirtieth	*30. dreißigst...*
40 forty	*40 vierzig*	40th fortieth	*40. vierzigst...*
50 fifty	*50 fünfzig*	50th fiftieth	*50. fünfzigst...*
60 sixty	*60 sechzig*	60th sixtieth	*60. sechzigst...*
70 seventy	*70 siebzig*	70th seventieth	*70. siebzigst...*

Cardinal numbers	*Kardinalzahlen*	Ordinal numbers	*Ordinalzahlen*
80 eighty	*80 achtzig*	80th eightieth	*80. achtzigst...*
90 ninety	*90 neunzig*	90th ninetieth	*90. neunzigst...*
100 one hundred	*100 [ein]hundert*	100th [one] hundredth	*100. [ein]hundertst...*
101 one hundred and one	*101 [ein]hundert[und]-eins*	101st [one]hundred and first	*101. [ein]hundert[und]-erst...*
555 five hundred and fifty-five	*555 fünfhundert[und]-fünfundfünfzig*	555th five hundred and fifty-fifth	*555. fünfhundert[und]-fünfundfünfzigst...*
1,000 one thousand	*1 000 [ein]tausend*	1,000th [one] thousandth	*1 000. [ein]tausendst...*
1,001 one thousand and one	*1 001 [ein]tausend-[und]eins*	1,001st one thousand and first	*1 001. [ein]tausend-[und]erst...*
1,347 one thousand, three hundred and forty-seven	*1 347 [ein]tausenddrei-hundert[und]sieben-undvierzig*	1,347th one thousand, three hundred and forty-seventh	*1 347. [ein]tausenddrei-hundert[und]sieben-undvierzigst...*
10,000 ten thousand	*10 000 zehntausend*	10,000th ten thousandth	*10 000. zehntausendst...*
13,438 thirteen thousand, four hundred and thirty-eight	*13 438 dreizehntausend-vierhundert[und]acht-unddreißig*	13,438th thirteen thousand, four hundred and thirty-eighth	*13 438. dreizehntau-sendvierhundert[und]-achtunddreißigst...*
100,000 one hundred thousand	*100 000 [ein]hundert-tausend*	100,000th [one]hundred thousandth	*100 000. [ein]hundert-tausendst...*
1,000,000 one million	*1 000 000 eine Million*	1,000,000th [one] millionth	*1 000 000. millionst...*
2,000,000 two million	*2 000 000 zwei Millio-nen*	2,000,000th two millionth	*2 000 000. zweimil-lionst...*
3,536,000 three million, five hundred and thirty-six thousand	*3 536 000 drei Millionen fünfhundertsechsund-dreißigtausend*	3,536,000th three million, five hundred and thirty-six thousandth	*3 536 000. drei Millionen fünfhundertsechsund-dreißigtausendst...*
1,000,000,000 one thousand million *(Brit.)*; one billion *(Amer.)*	*1 000 000 000 eine Mil-liarde*	1,000,000,000th [one] thousand millionth *(Brit.)*; one billionth *(Amer.)*	*1 000 000 000. mil-liardst...*
2,000,000,000 two thousand million *(Brit.)*; two billion *(Amer.)*	*2 000 000 000 zwei Mil-liarden*	2,000,000,000th two thousand millionth *(Brit.)*; two billionth *(Amer.)*	*2 000 000 000. zweimil-liardst...*
3,436,538,825 three thousand, four hundred and thirty-six million, five hundred and thirty-eight thousand, eight hundred and twenty-five *(Brit.)*; three billion, four hundred and thirty-six million, five hundred and thirty-eight thousand, eight hundred and twenty-five *(Amer.)*	*3 436 538 825 drei Mil-liarden vierhundert-sechsunddreißig Mil-lionen fünfhundert-achtunddreißigtau-sendachthundertfünf-undzwanzig*	3,436,538,825th three thousand, four hundred and thirty-six million, five hundred and thirty-eight thousand, eight hundred and twenty-fifth *(Brit.)*; three billion, four hundred and thirty-six million, five hundred and thirty-eight thousand, eight hundred and twenty-fifth *(Amer.)*	*3 436 538 825. drei Mil-liarden vierhundert-sechsunddreißig Mil-lionen fünfhundert-achtunddreißigtau-sendachthundertfünf-undzwanzigst...*

Vulgar fractions and mixed numbers
Brüche (gemeine Brüche) und gemischte Zahlen

in figures *in Zahlen*	in words	*in Worten*	in figures *in Zahlen*	in words	*in Worten*
$\frac{1}{2}$	a/one half	*ein halb*	$\frac{3}{2}$	three over two	*drei halbe*
$\frac{1}{3}$	a/one third	*ein drittel*	$\frac{11}{10}$	eleven-tenths	*elf zehntel*
$\frac{1}{4}$	a/one quarter	*ein viertel*	$\frac{3}{3}$	three-thirds	*drei drittel*
$\frac{1}{10}$	a/one tenth	*ein zehntel*	$\frac{5}{7}$	five-sevenths	*fünf siebtel/ siebentel*
$\frac{2}{3}$	two-thirds	*zwei drittel*	$\frac{m}{n}$	m over n	*m n-tel*
$\frac{5}{8}$	five-eighths	*fünf achtel*	$\frac{x}{6}$	x over six	*x sechstel*
$\frac{1}{100}$	a/one hundredth	*ein hundertstel*	$1\frac{1}{2}$	one and a half	*ein[und]einhalb*
$\frac{1}{1}$	one over one	*ein eintel*	$2\frac{1}{4}$	two and a quarter	*zwei[und]einvier-tel*
$\frac{4}{1}$	four over one	*vier eintel*	$5\frac{3}{10}$	five and three-tenths	*fünf[und]drei-zehntel*

Decimal numbers / Dezimalzahlen

written as	*geschrieben*	spoken as	*gesprochen*
0.1	*0,1*	nought point one	*null Komma eins*
0.015	*0,015*	nought point nought one five	*null Komma null eins fünf*
1.43	*1,43*	one point four three	*eins Komma vier drei*
11.70	*11,70*	eleven point seven o [əʊ]	*elf Komma sieben null*

Money / Geldbeträge

written as *geschrieben*	spoken as	*gesprochen*
1 DM 1,00 DM 1,– DM	one mark	*eine Mark*
90 Pf 0,90 DM –,90 DM	ninety pfennigs	*neunzig Pfennig[e]*
1,90 DM	one mark ninety pfennigs one mark ninety one ninety	*eine Mark und neunzig Pfennig[e]* *eine Mark [und] neunzig* *eins neunzig*

written as *geschrieben*	spoken as	*gesprochen*
1 000 DM 1 000,00 DM 1 000,– DM 1.000 DM 1.000,00 DM	one *or* a thousand marks	*[ein]tausend Mark*
100,90 DM	one *or* a hundred marks [and] ninety pfennigs	*[ein]hundert Mark und neunzig Pfennig[e]* *hundert Mark neunzig*
149,90 DM	one *or* a hundred and forty-nine marks [and] ninety pfennigs one *or* a hundred and forty-nine ninety	*[ein]hundertneunundvierzig Mark und neunzig Pfennig[e]* *[ein]hundertneunundvierzig Mark neunzig* *hundertneunundvierzig neunzig*
1 500 DM 1 500,00 DM 1 500,– DM 1.500 DM 1.500,00 DM	one thousand, five hundred marks fifteen hundred marks	*[ein]tausendfünfhundert Mark* *fünfzehnhundert Mark* *eins fünf*
3 500 DM	three thousand, five hundred marks three and a half thousand (marks)	*dreitausendfünfhundert Mark* *drei fünf* *dreieinhalbtausend [Mark]*
1p	one penny/one p	*ein Penny*
2p	two pence/two p	*zwei Pence*
50p	fifty pence/fifty p	*fünfzig Pence*
£1 1 pound	one *or* a pound	*ein Pfund*
£1.50	one pound fifty pence *or* p one pound fifty	*ein Pfund fünfzig Pence* *ein Pfund fünfzig*
1.50	one fifty	*eins fünfzig*
£8.34	eight pounds thirty-four pence *or* p eight pounds thirty-four	*acht Pfund vierunddreißig Pence* *acht Pfund vierunddreißig*
8.34	eight thirty-four	*acht vierunddreißig*
£250.95	two hundred and fifty pounds, ninety-five [pence *or* p]	*zweihundertfünfzig Pfund [und] fünfundneunzig [Pence]*
£1,273.40	one thousand, two hundred and seventy-three pounds, forty [pence *or* p] twelve hundred and seventy-three pounds, forty [pence *or* p]	*[ein]tausendzweihundertdreiundsiebzig Pfund [und] vierzig [Pence]* *zwölfhundertdreiundsiebzig Pfund [und] vierzig [Pence]*

Phonetic symbols used in transcriptions of English words / Die für das Englische verwendeten Zeichen der Lautschrift

ɑ:	bah	bɑ:
ɑ̃	ensemble	ɑ̃'sɑ̃mbl
æ	fat	fæt
æ̃	lingerie	'læ̃ʒərɪ
aɪ	fine	faɪn
aʊ	now	naʊ
b	bat	bæt
d	dog	dɒg
dʒ	jam	dʒæm
e	met	met
eɪ	fate	feɪt
eə	fairy	'feərɪ
əʊ	goat	gəʊt
ə	ago	ə'gəʊ
ɜ:	fur	fɜ:(r)
f	fat	fæt
g	good	gʊd
h	hat	hæt
ɪ	bit, lately	bɪt, 'leɪtlɪ
ɪə	nearly	'nɪəlɪ
i:	meet	mi:t
j	yet	jet
k	kit	kɪt
l	lot	lɒt
m	mat	mæt
n	not	nɒt
ŋ	sing	sɪŋ
ɒ	got	gɒt
ɔ:	paw	pɔ:
ɔ̃	fait accompli	feɪt æ'kɔ̃pli:
ɔɪ	boil	bɔɪl
p	pet	pet
r	rat	ræt
s	sip	sɪp
ʃ	ship	ʃɪp
t	tip	tɪp
tʃ	chin	tʃɪn
θ	thin	θɪn
ð	the	ðə
u:	boot	bu:t
ʊ	book	bʊk
ʊə	tourist	'tʊərɪst
ʌ	dug	dʌg
v	van	væn
w	win	wɪn
x	loch	lɒx
z	zip	zɪp
ʒ	vision	'vɪʒn

: Length sign, indicating that the preceding vowel is long, e.g. boot [bu:t]. / Längezeichen, bezeichnet Länge des unmittelbar davor stehenden Vokals, z. B. boot [bu:t].

' Stress mark, immediately preceding a stressed syllable, e.g. ago [ə'gəʊ]. / Betonung, steht unmittelbar vor einer betonten Silbe, z. B. ago [ə'gəʊ].

(r) An 'r' in parentheses is pronounced only when immediately followed by a vowel sound, e.g. pare [peə(r)]; pare away [peər ə'weɪ]. / Ein „r" in runden Klammern wird nur gesprochen, wenn im Textzusammenhang ein Vokal unmittelbar folgt, z. B. pare [peə(r)]; pare away [peər ə'weɪ].

Time of day / Uhrzeit

	written as *geschrieben*	spoken as *gesprochen*
	7.40, 7.40 a.m. / 0740, 07.40	twenty to eight, seven forty [a.m.] / [o] seven forty
	7.40, 7.40 p.m. / 1940, 19.40	twenty to eight, seven forty [p.m.] / nineteen forty
	[0]7.40 Uhr	*zehn [Minuten] nach halb acht, zwanzig [Minuten] vor acht, sieben Uhr vierzig*
	19.40 Uhr	*neunzehn Uhr vierzig*
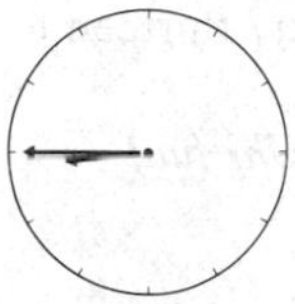	8.45, 8.45 a.m. / 0845, 08.45	[a] quarter to nine, eight forty-five [a.m.] / [o] eight forty-five
	8.45, 8.45 p.m. / 2045, 20.45	[a] quarter to nine, eight forty-five [p.m.] / twenty forty-five
	[0]8.45 Uhr	*Viertel vor neun, (landsch.:) dreiviertel neun, fünfzehn Minuten vor neun, acht Uhr fünfundvierzig*
	20.45 Uhr	*zwanzig Uhr fünfundvierzig*
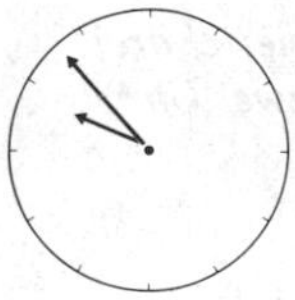	9.53, 9.53 a.m. / 0953, 09.53	seven minutes to ten, nine fifty-three [a.m.] / [o] nine fifty-three
	9.53, 9.53 p.m. / 2153, 21.53	seven minutes to ten, nine fifty-three [p.m.] / twenty-one fifty-three
	[0]9.53 Uhr	*sieben [Minuten] vor zehn, neun Uhr dreiundfünfzig*
	21.53 Uhr	*einundzwanzig Uhr dreiundfünfzig*
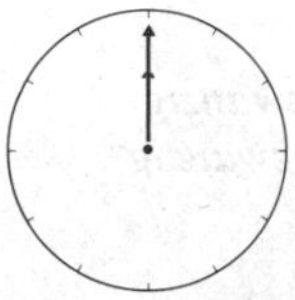	12.00, 12.00 midnight / 0000, 00.00, 2400, 24.00	twelve o'clock, twelve [midnight], midnight / o o double o, twenty-four hundred hours (note: 00.00 indicates the beginning of a day 24.00 indicates the end of a day)
	12.00, 12.00 noon / 1200, 12.00	twelve o'clock, twelve [noon], noon / twelve hundred hours
	0 Uhr, 24 Uhr / [0]0.00 Uhr, 24.00 Uhr	*null Uhr, vierundzwanzig Uhr*
	12 Uhr / 12.00 Uhr	*zwölf Uhr*
		(Anm.: 0 Uhr bezeichnet den Beginn, 24 Uhr das Ende eines Tages.)
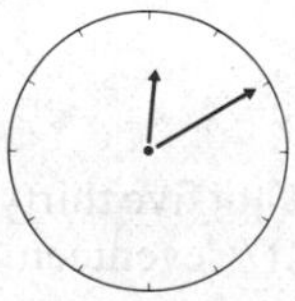	12.10, 12.10 a.m. / 0010, 00.10	ten past twelve, twelve ten [a.m.], ten past midnight / o o ten
	12.10, 12.10 p.m. / 1210, 12.10	ten past twelve, twelve ten [p.m.] / twelve ten
	[0]0.10 Uhr	*zehn [Minuten] nach zwölf, null Uhr zehn*
	12.10 Uhr	*zwölf Uhr zehn*

Time of day / Uhrzeit

	written as *geschrieben*	spoken as *gesprochen*
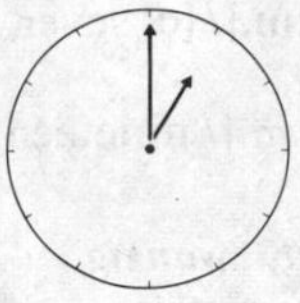	1.00, 1.00 a.m. / 0100, 01.00	one o'clock, one [a.m.] / [o (əʊ)] one hundred hours
	1.00, 1.00 p.m. / 1300, 13.00	one o'clock, one [p.m.] / thirteen hundred hours
	1 Uhr / [0]1.00 Uhr	*eins, ein Uhr*
	13 Uhr / 13.00 Uhr	*dreizehn Uhr*
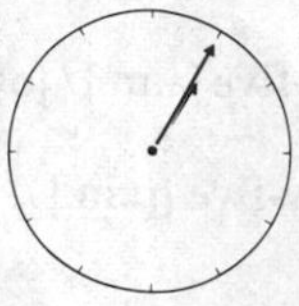	1.05, 1.05 a.m. / 0105, 01.05	five past one, one o five [a.m.] / [o] one o five
	1.05, 1.05 p.m. / 1305, 13.05	five past one, one o five [p.m.] / thirteen o five
	[0]1.05 Uhr	*fünf [Minuten] nach eins, ein Uhr fünf*
	13.05 Uhr	*dreizehn Uhr fünf*
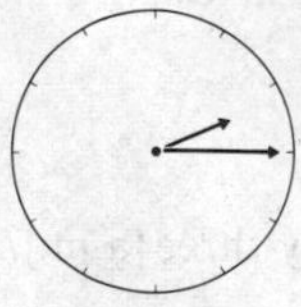	2.15, 2.15 a.m. / 0215, 02.15	two fifteen [a.m.], [a] quarter past two / [o] two fifteen
	2.15, 2.15 p.m. / 1415, 14.15	two fifteen [p.m.], [a] quarter past two / fourteen fifteen
	[0]2.15 Uhr	*Viertel nach zwei, (landsch.:) viertel drei, fünfzehn Minuten nach zwei, zwei Uhr fünfzehn*
	14.15 Uhr	*vierzehn Uhr fünfzehn*
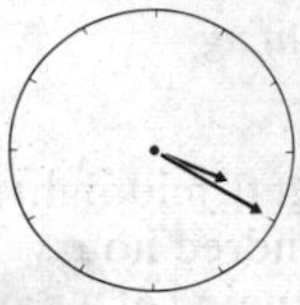	3.20, 3.20 a.m. / 0320, 03.20	three twenty [a.m.], twenty past three / [o] three twenty
	3.20, 3.20 p.m. / 1520, 15.20	three twenty [p.m.], twenty past three / fifteen twenty
	[0]3.20 Uhr	*zehn [Minuten] vor halb vier, zwanzig [Minuten] nach drei, drei Uhr zwanzig*
	15.20 Uhr	*fünfzehn Uhr zwanzig*
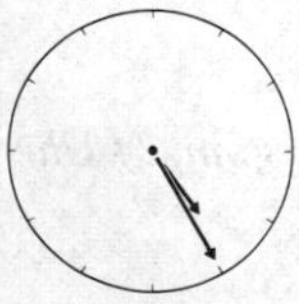	4.25, 4.25 a.m. / 0425, 04.25	twenty-five past four, four twenty-five [a.m.] / [o] four twenty-five
	4.25, 4.25 p.m. / 1625, 16.25	twenty-five past four, four twenty-five [p.m.] / sixteen twenty-five
	[0]4.25 Uhr	*fünf [Minuten] vor halb fünf, vier Uhr fünfundzwanzig*
	16.25 Uhr	*sechzehn Uhr fünfundzwanzig*
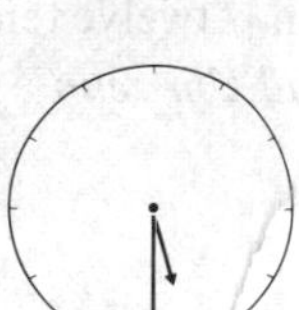	5.30, 5.30 a.m. / 0530, 05.30	half past five, five thirty [a.m.] / [o] five thirty
	5.30, 5.30 p.m. / 1730, 17.30	half past five, five thirty [p.m.] / seventeen thirty
	[0]5.30 Uhr	*halb sechs, fünf Uhr dreißig*
	17.30 Uhr	*siebzehn Uhr dreißig*
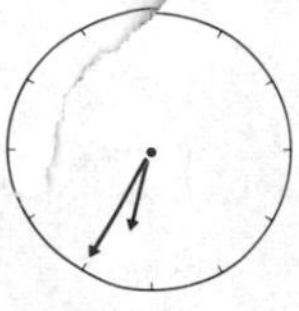	6.35, 6.35 a.m. / 0635, 06.35	twenty-five to seven, six thirty-five [a.m.] / [o] six thirty-five
	6.35, 6.35 p.m. / 1835, 18.35	twenty-five to seven, six thirty-five [p.m.] / eighteen thirty-five
	[0]6.35 Uhr	*fünf [Minuten] nach halb sieben, sechs Uhr fünfunddreißig*
	18.35 Uhr	*achtzehn Uhr fünfunddreißig*